Baker Book House has undertaken the reprinting of this major reference work in order to make it once more available to seminaries, universities, colleges, libraries, and students of the Bible and religion everywhere. The twelve-volume set reappears in its original size and format, uniformly bound in sturdy buckram binding. The set is priced at $12.95 per volume on a subscription basis, and is being reprinted at the rate of four volumes per year. This makes the purchase of this valuable set easy for any serious student of religion. Single volumes may be purchased at $14.95 per volume.

Publishing Schedule

Vol. I – A-B, September 1968
Vol. II – C-D, December 1968
Vol. III – E-G, March 1969
Vol. IV – H-J, June 1969
Vol. V – K-Mc, September 1969
Vol. VI – Me-Nev, December 1969
Vol. VII – New-Pes, March 1970
Vol. VIII – Pet-Re, June 1970
Vol. IX – Rh-St, September 1970
Vol. X – Su-Z, December 1970
Vol. XI – Supplement A-Cn, March 1971
Vol. XII – Supplement Co-Z, June 1971

CYCLOPÆDIA

OF

BIBLICAL,

THEOLOGICAL, AND ECCLESIASTICAL

LITERATURE.

PREPARED BY

THE REV. JOHN M'CLINTOCK, D.D.,

AND

JAMES STRONG, S.T.D.

VOL. XII.

SUPPLEMENT.—CO–Z.

WITH ADDENDA—A-Z.

BAKER BOOK HOUSE
Grand Rapids, Michigan

Reprinted 1970 by
Baker Book House Company

Standard Book Number: 8010-5877-5

Library of Congress Catalog Card Number: 68-56007

Printed in the United States of America

LIST OF WOOD-CUTS IN VOL. XII.

SUPPLEMENT

TO THE

CYCLOPÆDIA

OF

BIBLICAL, THEOLOGICAL, AND ECCLESIASTICAL LITERATURE.

Co.

Coales, Thomas Thompson, an English Congregational minister, was born at Aldwinkle, Northamptonshire, in 1784 or 1785. He studied at Cheshunt College, and labored successively at Ashbourne, Birmingham, Thrapston, Ebley, Gower, Hereford, Sleaford, St. Ives, Middleton, Kidderminster, Alfriston, Farringdon, and East Grinstead. In 1850 he returned to Ashbourne, where he remained till his death, Oct. 26, 1853. See (Lond.) *Cong. Year-book*, 1855, p. 209.

Coan, George Whitefield, D.D., a Presbyterian minister, was born at Bergen, Genesee Co., N. Y., Dec. 30, 1817. He graduated from Williams College in 1846, and from the Union Theological Seminary in 1849; was licensed to preach, and ordained June 6 of the same year. He selected Persia as the field of his labors, and in October he sailed for Ooroomiah, where he continued the labors of Perkins, Grant, Stoddard, Fisk, and Rice. After thirteen years of labor there his health failed, and he was compelled to return to America, but, two years later, having recruited his strength, he again sought his mission field, in 1864. Ten years of faithful toil again broke his health, and once more he sought its restoration in his native clime. Dr. Coan's heart was still with his brethren, and he availed himself of every opportunity to present the claims of Persia to the various Presbyterian churches in this country. He died at Wooster, O., Dec. 21, 1879. See *N. Y. Observer*, Jan. 1, 1880. (W. P. S.)

Coan, Leander Samuel, a Congregational minister, was born in Exeter, Me., Nov. 17, 1837. He attended the Exeter and Garland high-schools, and graduated from Bangor Theological Seminary in 1862. He was acting pastor in Amherst and Aurora, from May, 1862, to June, 1863, when he was ordained as pastor of that parish. In May, 1864, he was dismissed to enter the army. From August, 1865, to September, 1867, he was acting pastor in Boothbay; from November, 1867, to November, 1870, preached in Brownville, and the following year in Somerset, Mass. From 1872 to 1874 he was city missionary in Fall River; from December, 1875, to June, 1879, he preached in Alton, N. H. When the Constitutional Convention of New Hampshire convened in 1877, he was elected its chaplain. He died Sept. 24, 1879. See *Cong. Year-book*, 1880, p. 16.

Coanes, John, an English Congregational minister, was born at Mile End, London, in 1777. He became a member of the Church in early life, entered Homerton College before he was twenty, and settled as a minister at Walworth, where he labored ten years. He afterwards labored successively at Morley, near Leeds, Reeth, in Yorkshire, Aylesbury, Folkestone, in Kent, Wycliffe Chapel, London, and Watford, Herts, where he remained five years, then resigned the active ministry, and retired to Hunton Bridge, near Watford. Here he taught a day-school, and preached occasionally for two years. His last days were spent at Bexley Heath, where he died, Nov. 6, 1862. Mr. Coanes was noted for his blameless life and faithful exhibition of evangelical truth. See (Lond.) *Cong. Year-book*, 1863, p. 216.

Coarb (Cowarb, or Comharba; in Latin, *corba; meaning conterraneus*, or, *of the same region*) is the title in the Celtic-Irish and Scottish churches of the abbatial successor of the original founder of a monastery. So an abbot of Hy would be called the coarb of Columba; of Armagh, the coarb of Patrick, etc. The common use of the word dates from late in the 8th century, when such abbacies had become hereditary in many cases, and not only so, but had passed into the hands, in some instances, of laymen, while a prior discharged the spiritual office. Later the coarb became to a monastery what the *herenach* or *airchinneach* (i. e. lay advocate) was to any church, monastic or not. A female coarb occurs once or twice (Reeves, *ad Adamn. Vita St. Columbœ*, add. notes, p. 404). Coarbs that were still clergy became styled in Ireland, later, plebani=rural deans, or archpresbyters, or chorepiscopoi (in the later sense of the word), i. e. the head of a "plebs ecclesiastica," viz. of clergy who served chapels under him as rector. See Reeves, *Coltorio Visitation*, p. 4 n., 145, 209; Robertson, *Early Scotl.* i, 330.

Coat, The Holy. Its miracles are commemorated on Oct. 1 in the *Georgian Calendar*. See Holy Coat of Treves.

Coate, Michael, a Methodist Episcopal minister, was born at Burlington, N. J., in 1767. He was converted in 1794; served the Church as an exhorter and local preacher, and in 1795 became a member of the New York Conference. He died a member of the Philadelphia Conference, Aug. 1, 1814. Mr. Coate was remarkably meek and devout, lively and zealous, practical and exemplary. See *Minutes of Annual Conferences*, 1815, p. 255; Sprague, *Annals of the Amer. Pulpit*, vii, 253.

Coate, Samuel, a Methodist Episcopal minister, entered the New York Conference in 1794, and after travelling Flanders Circuit, N. J., and Albany Circuit, N. Y., went in 1806 to Canada as a co-laborer with Dunham, Coleman, and Wooster. In 1806 he was stationed at Montreal. His later history is unrecorded. See Stevens, *Hist. of the M. E. Church*, iii, 195, 476; iv, 274; Sprague, *Annals of the Amer. Pulpit*, vii, 255, 256.

Coates, Alexander, an English Wesleyan preacher, a native of North Britain, was converted young; began his ministry in 1741, and died at Newcastle-upon-Tyne, Oct. 6, 1765. He was the oldest preacher in the connection. His abilities were extraordinary; he was very popular, and his conversation wonderfully pleasant and instructive. See Atmore, *Meth. Memorial*, s. v.; Myles, *Chronol. Hist. of the Methodists* (4th ed.), p. 168; Stevens, *Hist. of Methodism*, i, 420; Wesley, *Journals*, Oct. 7, 1765.

Coates, John, an English Wesleyan minister, was born at Iron-Acton, Gloucestershire, in 1783. He was received into the sacred office in 1806, toiled with unwearied assiduity for forty-four years, and died, Feb. 8, 1860. "His success may be traced in the circuits he travelled." See *Minutes of the British Conference*, 1860, p. 404.

Coates, Richard, an English Methodist preacher, began to travel in connection with the Wesleyan Conference in 1764, being appointed to the Staffordshire Circuit. The severity of the winter and his excessive labors brought on a disorder of which he died, at Wednesbury, Staffordshire, in 1765, aged twenty-eight. He was a lively, pious, zealous, and useful young man. See Atmore, *Meth. Memorial*, s. v.

Coatlantanna, in Mexican mythology, was the *Flora* of the Mexicans, in whose honor great floral festivals were held.

Coats, Calvin S., a Methodist Episcopal minister, was born in Orangeville, Wyoming Co., N. Y., May 15, 1809. He experienced conversion at the age of sixteen; spent some time as an exhorter and local preacher, and in 1831 entered the Genesee Conference, wherein he labored with marked zeal and fidelity until failing health, in 1868, caused him to become a superannuate, which relation he held to the close of his life, Feb. 11, 1875. Mr. Coats was remarkable for the activity of his intellect, the strength of his convictions, and his restless zeal in Christian work. See *Minutes of Annual Conferences*, 1875, p. 119.

Coatts, William (1), a Scotch clergyman, held a bursary of theology at the Glasgow University in 1702; was licensed to preach in 1714; called to the living at Dalmellington in 1717, and ordained; resigned in August, 1755, and died Feb. 6, 1757. See *Fasti Eccles. Scoticanæ*, ii, 109, 110.

Coatts, William (2), a Scotch clergyman, took his degree at Glasgow University in 1725; was licensed to preach in 1726; became tutor in the family of Dunlop; was presented to the living at Kilmaurs in 1735, but was opposed and hindered by heritors and parishioners for a long time; was ordained in May, 1739, and died May 2, 1777. See *Fasti Eccles. Scoticanæ*, ii, 180.

Coaxtitli, in Mexican mythology, was a rude deity, apparently the god of the fruit-bearing earth. He is represented as a sitting, long-haired man, with closed eyes, grasping something in his clumsy hands, perhaps a loaf of bread. The strange decoration of his head seems to chararacterize him as a priest; at least, the latter carried something similar, as we know from designs and busts.

Figure of Coaxtitli.

Cob, Thomas, an English martyr, suffered death by burning, in Suffolk, Aug. 12, 1555, for his confession of Christ. See Fox, *Acts and Monuments*, vii, 382.

Cobain, Edward, an Irish Wesleyan minister, was converted in youth, commenced preaching on the Newry mission in 1810, and died Aug. 16, 1856. His long labors were blessed with many gracious revivals. See *Minutes of the British Conference*, 1857.

Cobăli (Κόβαλοι, *rogues*), in Greek mythology (similar to the German *Koboldęn*, i. e. "goblins"), were small, tantalizing spirits, which played all manner of possible tricks. They were worshipped by the ancient Sarmatians, viz. the Borussi, Samogitæ, Lithuanians, Livonians, etc. These spirits, they believed, dwelt in the most secret parts of their houses. The people presented to them the daintiest meats.

Cobard, Jacques, a French martyr, was a schoolmaster in the city of Saint-Mihiel, in Lorraine, who maintained against three priests that the sacrament of baptism and of the Lord's Supper did not avail unless received with faith. For this, and also for his confession, which he, being in prison, sent of his own accord by his mother to the judge, he was burned, most quietly suffering, in 1545, in Lorraine. See Fox, *Acts and Monuments*, iv, 401.

Cobarrubias, Alonzo de, an eminent Spanish architect, flourished about 1450. He first introduced Roman architecture into Spain; erecting, among other works, the magnificent cathedral of Toledo, and, at Valentia, the monastery and temple of the order of San Girolamo.

Cobb, Alden, a Free-will Baptist minister, was born in New York, in March, 1802. He was converted in 1833, and soon afterwards was publicly set apart to the ministry. His labors were chiefly in the state of New York, especially at Dansville, Middlesex, North Potter, Sparta, Italy, Scottsburg, and Jerusalem. He died in Middlesex, Aug. 10, 1868. See *Free-will Baptist Register*, 1870, p. 75, 76. (J. C. S.)

Cobb, Allen H., a Methodist Episcopal minister, was born at Barnstable, Mass., Nov. 21, 1780. He joined the Church in early life, and in 1802 was admitted into the Maine Conference, in which he served faithfully until poverty compelled him in 1809 to locate, when he retired to New Gloucester, and nine years later moved to Durham, where he died, Sept. 15, 1856. Mr. Cobb represented Durham nine years in the legislature, was two years a senator from Cumberland, and two years a member of the executive council. He was emphatically the friend of the poor, the widow, and the orphan. See *Minutes of Annual Conferences*, 1857, p. 286.

Cobb, Alvan, a Congregational minister, was born about 1788, his ancestors being early settlers in Plymouth, Mass. He graduated from Brown University in 1813, and was installed pastor of the West Church in Taunton in 1815, where he continued for nearly forty-six years. At his house was formed the Doctrinal Tract and Book Society, since enlarged into the Congregational Board of Publication, of which he was director until his death at Taunton, April 2, 1861. Mr. Cobb instructed several young men in theology, published several *Sermons, Doctrinal Tract, No.* 23, besides thirty periodical articles. In theology he was an Emmonsite. See *Cong. Quarterly*, 1861, p. 308.

Cobb, Archibald Parritt, a Presbyterian minister, was born at Parsippany, Morris Co., N. J., Nov. 9, 1821. He prepared for college at home, entered the sophomore class at Princeton, from which he graduated in 1850; then from the Princeton Theological Seminary in 1853, remaining there one year longer as tutor. He was licensed to preach in Montclair, April 20, 1853, and was ordained April 19, 1854, when he became a stated supply in the Witherspoon (colored) Presbyterian Church at Princeton. The following year he was installed pastor of the South Street Presbyterian Church, Philadelphia, where he remained six years, and was then called to the pastorate of the Tennent Church, Freehold, N. J., where he remained until the close of his life, Feb. 2, 1881. See *Necrol. Report of Princeton Theol. Sem.* 1881, p. 70. (W. P. S.)

Cobb, Asahel, a Congregational minister, was born at Abington, Mass., May 8, 1793. After pursuing a preparatory course of study in Litchfield, Conn., he graduated from Hamilton College in 1823, and from Andover Theological Seminary in 1826. On Dec. 12 of that year he was ordained assistant pastor at Mattapoisett, Mass., from which he was dismissed in 1830. The following year he was installed at Sandwich, where he served eleven years. From 1844 to 1848 he was acting pastor at North Falmouth, the succeeding year at West Yarmouth, and in 1854 at Little Compton, R. I. For about eleven years he was pastor of First Church, New Bedford, but was not regularly dismissed until 1870. He resided thereafter, without charge, at Sandwich, Mass., and died there, May 2, 1876. He served two terms in the Massachusetts Legislature—the first in 1843 and 1844, and the second in 1852 and 1853. See *Cong. Quarterly*, 1877, p. 413.

Cobb, Edward, held for many years the stations successively of elder and minister in the Society of Friends (Orthodox), and died in Portland, Me., Nov. 3, 1832, aged fifty-seven years. See *The Friend*, vi, 56.

Cobb, Frank Woodbury, a Congregational minister, was born at Durham, Me., Nov. 20, 1851. After preliminary study at the Lewiston High School, he graduated from Bates College in 1873, and five years afterwards from Yale Divinity School (?). He was ordained pastor of the Church at Three Rivers, in Palmer, Mass., Feb. 12, 1879, and died there, Sept. 4, 1880. See *Cong. Year-book*, 1881, p. 20.

Cobb, Henry K., a Methodist Episcopal minister, was born at Randolph, Orange Co., Vt., May 7, 1827. He received an early Unitarian training, was converted when about fifteen, lapsed into sin, and several years later was reclaimed by the Methodists. In 1853 he was admitted into the Vermont Conference; in 1869 was transferred to the West Wisconsin Conference, to fill a difficult appointment in the city of Madison, and labored there until his sudden death, Nov. 25, the same year. Mr. Cobb was an effective speaker, a beloved pastor, an ardent friend. See *Minutes of Annual Conferences*, 1870, p. 251.

Cobb, James E., a minister of the Methodist Episcopal Church South, entered the Arkansas Conference in 1848, was agent of the American Bible Society in 1850, editor of the *Memphis Christian Advocate* from 1852 to 1855; transferred to St. Louis Conference in 1856; to the Washita Conference in 1857; appointed to Columbus African Mission in 1858; president and agent of Arkadelphia Female College in 1862; agent for Trans-Mississippi Army Tract Society in 1864, and afterwards served on charges in the Little Rock Conference until 1870, when he was transferred to the Louisiana Conference, and appointed president of Homer College, which position he filled four consecutive years. The remainder of his life was spent as presiding elder. He died April 28, 1879, about fifty-five years old. Mr. Cobb was intensely earnest as a preacher, and deeply pious in his daily life. See *Minutes of Annual Conferences of the M. E. Church South*, 1879, p. 37.

Cobb, John, a Scotch clergyman, took his degree from the University of St. Andrews in 1682, became a helper in the parish of Birsay and Harray, and was transferred to Kirkwall in 1689, being the last minister appointed before Episcopacy was abolished. He was promoted to Stronsay and Eday in 1696, transferred to St. Andrews and Deerness in 1700, and died before January, 1719, aged about fifty-seven years. See *Fasti Eccles. Scoticanæ*, iii, 378, 386, 393, 408.

Cobb, Nathaniel, a Congregational minister, son of Rev. Oliver Cobb, was born at Rochester, Mass., March 9, 1800. He graduated from Brown University in 1821, and from Andover Theological Seminary in 1825. The following year he served as a home missionary in Harwich. Having been ordained at Dartmouth, Oct. 31, 1827, as an evangelist, he labored as acting pastor in Nantucket for two years, and then (1829–30) in Bloomfield and Huntsburg, O. In October of the latter year he was installed pastor in Hampden and Kirtland. From Kirtland he was dismissed in 1833, and from Hampden in 1834. Meanwhile he was serving as acting pastor (1832–33) in Mesopotamia, and from 1833 to 1835 in Bristol and Parkman; also, during the same time, was acting pastor in Southington. From 1835 to 1837 he labored in the Presbyterian Church at Clear Creek; the three years following he preached at Mount Eaton, and from 1841 to 1845 at Salem. Twice he was engaged as a Bible agent and colporteur, viz., in 1840 and 1841, and from 1845 to 1849. The year succeeding the last date he was city missionary in New Bedford, Mass.; in 1851 he was acting pastor in North Falmouth, and in 1852 and 1853 in Chilmark. Subsequently he resided, without charge, in Kingston, and died at Taunton, Nov. 15, 1878. See *Cong. Year-book*, 1879, p. 39.

Cobb, William Alexander McKendree, a minister of the Methodist Episcopal Church South, son of Rev. Jesse B. Cobb, was born in Granville County, N. C., Sept. 2, 1817. He became religious very early, studied earnestly, began preaching in 1838, and in 1839 entered the Tennessee Conference, in which he travelled a few months, and was transferred to the Arkansas Conference. In 1849 he was transferred to the Indian Mission Conference, and served the Creeks and Cherokees until 1854, when ill-health obliged him to retire from active service. In 1861 he undertook the presidency of the Female College in Cross County, Ark., where he did excellent service till the institution was broken up by the war in 1864. In 1866 he entered the White River Conference, and labored zealously until his decease, Jan. 2, 1873. Mr. Cobb excelled in all ministerial duties. See *Minutes of Annual Conferences of the M. E. Church South*, 1873, p. 885.

Cobb, William Newell, a Methodist Episcopal minister, was born at McLean, Tompkins Co., N. Y., July 15, 1818. He received an excellent common-school education; at the age of eighteen engaged in civil-engineering, which he followed six years; experienced religion during the time; served two years as class-leader; in 1842 entered the Genesee Conference; was transferred to the Oneida Conference the following year, and died Aug. 3, 1878. Mr. Cobb's labors were highly acceptable. In the pulpit he was always practical, logical, and eminently edifying. In daily life he was judicious, solicitous, energetic, and faithful. See *Minutes of Annual Conferences*, 1879, p. 67.

Cobban, Robert, a Methodist Episcopal minister, was born in Aberdeen, Scotland, Sept. 10, 1824. He emigrated with his parents to Canada when seven years old, experienced conversion at the age of sixteen, and joined the Wesleyan Methodists, who soon after licensed him to preach. He removed to Fond du Lac County, Wis., in 1851, and in the same year entered the Wisconsin Conference. Failing health obliged him to locate in 1859, and he retired to his farm in Chippewa County. In 1860 he re-entered the effective service in the Northwest Wisconsin Conference, and after two years' labor was put upon the supernumerary list, in which relation he served on circuits until 1867, when he again entered the effective ranks, and continued zealous and faithful until his death, Jan. 4, 1870. Mr. Cobban was prompt in every duty as a minister, and highly esteemed by all who knew him. See *Minutes of Annual Conferences*, 1870, p. 251.

Cobbe, Charles, an Irish prelate, was born at Winchester, England, where he received the rudiments of his education. He then went to Trinity College, Oxford, but took his degree of D.D. in the University of Dublin, March 9, 1735. His first ecclesiastical preferment was to the rectory of Skreen, in the diocese of Meath. He was afterwards appointed dean of Ardagh, whence he was promoted to the see of Killala and Achonry, May 30, 1720. In 1726 he was translated to the see of Dromore, and from that, March, 1731, to Kildare, with which latter dignity he held the deanery of Christ Church, Dublin, and the preceptory of Tully, in the county of Kildare. On July 19, 1734, he was sworn privy-councillor, and was finally translated to the see of Dublin, March 4, 1742. He was one of the spiritual lords who desired leave of absence from the trial of lord Netterville by protestation in 1743; and also one of the council who subscribed the proclamation of February, 1744. In 1745, on the breaking-out of the rebellion in Scotland, he sent a letter to his clergy to remind them of the excellence of the Protestant faith, and to entreat them to be steadfast in the profession of it. In 1759 archbishop Cobbe was very active in procuring the investment of the charitable donations of Andrew and the Rev. William Wilson, in the county of Westmeath, for the purpose of building a hospital for aged Protestants. He died at St. Sepulchre's, April 12, 1765. See D'Alton, *Memoirs of the Archbishops of Dublin*, p. 339.

Cobbin, Ingram, an English Congregational minister, was born in London in December, 1777. He entered Hoxton College in 1798, and was ordained pastor at South Molton in 1802. His health being very uncertain, he changed location frequently, soon leaving South Moulton for Banbury, and thence removing to Holloway. After preaching awhile at Putney, and then at Crediton, he became assistant secretary to the British and Foreign Bible Society, and two years later attempted the pastorate at Worcester, but broke down in his first sermon. A similar attempt was made subsequently at Lymington, and with a like result. In 1819 he interested himself, with other ministers and gentlemen, in the formation of the Home Missionary Society, and became its first secretary. His health continuing feeble, he relinquished public life in 1828, and died at Camberwell, March 10, 1851. Mr. Cobbin published, among other works, *Evangelical Synopsis: — Bible Remembrancer: —* and various *Commentaries.* See (Lond.) *Cong. Year-book*, 1851, p. 212.

Cobden, Edward, D.D., an English divine and chaplain in ordinary to George II, was educated at Trinity College, Oxford, and King's College, Cambridge, where he took his master's degree in 1713. Early in life he was chaplain to bishop Gibson, to whom he was indebted for preferment to the united rectories of St. Austin and St. Faith, in London, with that of Acton, in Middlesex, a prebend in St. Paul's, another at Lincoln, and the archdeaconry of London. Dr. Cobden collected his whole works in 1757, under the title of *Discourses and Essays.* Another noted work was *Concio ad Clerum, XI Cal. Maii* (1752). He died April 22, 1764. See Chalmers, *Biog. Dict.* s. v.; Allibone, *Dict. of Brit. and Amer. Authors*, s. v.

Coberley, William, an English martyr, was a native of the county of Wiltshire, and a farmer by occupation. He openly asserted that the bishop of Rome was Antichrist, and God's enemy. He was examined and condemned to be burned, March 25, 1556. See Fox, *Acts and Monuments*, viii, 102.

Cobhran, an Irish saint, is said by St. Ængus to have been the son of Neuain, or Euain, and of Mineloth, sister of St. Columba; but as there are in the calendars a Cobhran of Cluain, or Cluain-Euach, commemorated July 9, and Cobhran of Cluain-Cuallacta, commemorated Aug. 2, it is difficult to decide which dedication belongs to the nephew and disciple of St. Columba.

Cobia, Daniel, a Protestant Episcopal minister, was born at Charleston, S. C., Sept. 13, 1811. On leaving school he entered Charleston College, from which he graduated in 1829. In 1830 he entered the General Theological Seminary in New York city, from which he duly graduated. In 1833 he was ordained deacon, and immediately took charge of St. Stephen's Chapel, Charleston, especially interesting himself in Sunday-school work. Three churches in his native city having invited him to become pastor, he accepted the invitation from St. Philip's, beginning his ministry there in September, 1834. He was ordained priest Sept. 13, 1835. After spending a short time at Wilmington, N. C., and at St. Mary's, Ga., for the benefit of his health, he sailed for the island of St. Thomas, and, a few days after, for the island of St. Croix, where his health improved somewhat; but he soon began rapidly to decline, and died in Charleston, S. C., Feb. 8, 1837. Mr. Cobia was a remarkably eloquent preacher, and his chief characteristic was his religious zeal. One volume of his sermons was issued after his death. See Sprague, *Annals of the Amer. Pulpit*, v, 719.

Cobleigh, Nelson Ebenezer, D.D., LL.D., a Methodist Episcopal minister, was born at Littleton, N. H., Nov. 24, 1814. He studied in the common school at Newbury, Vt., and worked his way through Wesleyan University, Conn., graduating in 1843. In 1844 he entered the New England Conference, and, in 1853, accepted the chair of ancient languages in McKendree College, Ill. The following year he was elected to the same position in Lawrence University, Wis., and in 1857 was recalled to McKendree College, as president. In 1863 he became editor of *Zion's Herald*, Boston. Overwork and the rigorous climate obliged him to retire from all active labor in 1867, and he sought the milder climate of East Tennessee, where he was soon elected to the presidency of Wesleyan University, at Athens, Tenn. In 1872 he was elected editor of the *Methodist Advocate*, Atlanta, Georgia, in which capacity he labored with marked zeal and ability to the close of his life, Feb. 1, 1874. Dr. Cobleigh was in the truest and highest sense a great and good man. He was intellectually earnest, deeply and uniformly pious, thoroughly devoted to his work, a cheerful, energetic laborer; had few equals as an educator; was pathetic, logical, and powerful as a preacher; as a writer, clear, pure, and graceful. See *Minutes of Annual Conferences*, 1874, p. 131; Simpson, *Cyclop. of Methodism*, s. v.

Coblentz, Council of (*Concilium Confluentinum*), a provincial synod, was held in 922 by order of the two kings, Charles the Simple, of France, and Henry, of Germany. Eight bishops were present, Hermann, archbishop of Cologne, presiding, who drew up eight canons, of which no more than five have come down to us. The only one of any importance is the sixth, which directs that all monks shall submit in everything to the jurisdiction and control of the bishop of the diocese; also marriages between relations, as far as the sixth degree, are forbidden. See Labbe, *Concil.* ix, 579; Landon, *Manual of Councils*, s. v.

Cobo, Bernabé de, a Spanish Jesuit, was born at Lopera, in the province of Jaen, in 1582. He was missionary to Mexico and Peru for fifty years, and, on all his journeys, studied with ardor natural history, and particularly botany. He died at Lima, Sept. 9, 1657, leaving works in MS., which were brought to Spain and placed in the library of Seville; they consist of ten volumes, including a history of the Indians. See Hoefer, *Nouv. Biog. Générale*, s. v.

Cobo, Juan, a Spanish Dominican, was born at Alcazar de Consuegra, near Toledo. He became a monk at Ocaña, and engaged first in teaching in different convents of his order, and afterwards attached himself to foreign missions. Cobo sailed for Mexico in May, 1586, where, in a short time, he became very famous as a preacher, but was soon afterwards sent to the Philippine Isles. Cobo arrived at Manilla in June, 1588, and, in order to instruct the Chinese resident there, studied that language. In 1592 he was appointed to the chair of theology at Manilla, but was soon after sent to the emperor of Japan, on an embassy of alliance, which he accomplished successfully. On his return, in November, 1592, the vessel was cast upon the coast of Formosa, and all the passengers were massacred by the inhabitants. Cobo composed several works for the use of missionaries, especially on the Chinese language, for which see Hoefer, *Nouv. Biog. Générale*, s. v.; *Biog. Universelle*, s. v.

Cobthach, an early Irish Christian, the son of Brendan, and brother of St. Baithen, St. Columba's successor at Iona, is mentioned among the companions of St. Columba in crossing from Ireland to Iona. Camerarius, without authority, places him in the calendar on Aug. 7.—Smith, *Dict. of Christ. Biog.* s. v.

Coburn, David Nichols, a Congregational minister, was born at Thompson, Conn., Sept. 11, 1808. He received his preparatory education at Monson Academy, Mass., and graduated at Amherst College in 1838, and from the theological institute at Hartford in 1841. He was ordained at Ware, Mass., Sept. 21, 1842, where he remained until April 17, 1845. From thence he removed to Monson, where he remained without charge until his death, Dec. 7, 1877. Mr. Coburn published *A Historical Discourse*, delivered at Ware, May 9, 1851, on the centenary of the first Church there. See *Hist. Cat. of the Theol. Inst. of Conn.* 1881, p. 30. (W. P. S.)

Coburn, Jesse, a Baptist minister, was born at Fitzwilliam, N. H., in 1787, and removed with his parents to Braintree, Vt., in 1797. He was converted at the age of thirteen; was subsequently ordained in Cornish, N. H., and for several years labored in churches in that state and Vermont until in 1818 he moved to Hanover, N. H., and took charge of the Church in that town, preaching much, also, in all the region round about. He died Dec. 22, 1833. (J. C. S.)

Coburn, John R., a minister of the Methodist Episcopal Church South, was born in Charleston County, S. C., Sept. 18, 1799. He was converted in 1827, joined the South Carolina Conference in 1828, and continued in the regular work of the ministry until 1877, when he was placed on the superannuated list. During the greater part of this time he was a missionary to the blacks on the Atlantic coast. He died in Florence, S. C., Sept. 29, 1880. Mr. Coburn was faithful, self-sacrificing, zealous, and abundantly successful. See *Minutes of Annual Conferences of the M. E. Church South,* 1880, p. 213.

Cob-wall is a wall built of unburnt clay, mixed with straw. This material is still used in some parts of the country for cottages and outbuildings, and was formerly employed for houses of a better description: it is supposed also to be the material of which the domestic edifices of the ancients, including even the Greeks and Romans in their most civilized period, were chiefly built.

Cocagne, Jean Baptiste, a Methodist Episcopal minister, was born at Rosières, France, Oct. 1, 1821. He received a careful Roman Catholic training; emigrated with his parents to Cape Vincent, Jefferson Co., N. Y., in 1831, and was there apprenticed to a Protestant family, in which he experienced religion. After uniting with the Methodists, receiving license to exhort, and supporting himself during a four-year course at Gouverneur and Fairfield seminaries, he entered the Black River Conference in 1846. In 1851 he had charge of the French mission in New York city; in 1852 was transferred to the Michigan Conference to take charge of the French mission in Detroit, and in 1856 received a retransfer to the Black River Conference. He sailed Nov. 1, 1856, for a visit to his native land, in the steamer *Lyonnaise*, which was wrecked on the following Sabbath night, and he was drowned. Mr. Cocagne was kind, frank, generous, and ardent. See *Minutes of Annual Conferences*, 1857, p. 365; Simpson, *Cyclop. of Methodism*, s. v.

Cocca (**Coga, Choca,** or **Cuach**), of Cill-Choca, a female Irish saint, commemorated Jan. 8 and June 6, is supposed to be the same as elsewhere called *Ercuat* (q. v.) or *Erguat*, the cook and embroideress or robemaker of St. Columba, *Cocca* being a form of "Coqua," a *cook* (Todd and Reeves, *Mart. Doneg.* p. 379; O'Hanlon, *Irish Saints*, i, 13[illegible]).

Coccius (or **Coccyus**, i. e. **Köchlin**), **Hulderic**, a German theologian, was born at Freiburg in 1525. He studied at Basle, and became preacher in 1564, professor of exegesis of the New Test. in 1569, and doctor of theology. He died in 1585, leaving, *Index et Præfatio in Opera D. Gregorii Pontificis* (Basle, 1551):—*Jo. Lud. Opera* (ibid. 1555). See Hoefer, *Nouv. Biog. Générale*, s. v.

Coccius, Jodocus (1), a canon of Jülich, who was born of Lutheran parentage, and died about 1618, is the author of *Thesaurus Catholicus* (Cologne, 1599, fol.; 1619, 2 vols.). See Hartzheim, *Bibl. Colon.* p. 210; Räss, *Convertiten*, viii, 500; Streber, in Wetzer u. Welte's *Kirchen-Lexikon*, s. v. (B. P.)

Coccius, Jodocus (or **Jos**) (2), a German Jesuit, born in 1581 at Trier, was for some time professor of theology and first chancellor of the theological academy at Molsheim, in Alsatia, and died Oct. 25, 1622, at Ruffach. He wrote, among other works, *Parallelon Biblicum* (Molsheim, 1618):—*Theses Theologicæ* (ibid. 1619):—*De Arcano Scripturæ Sensu* (ibid. 1620):—*De Antichristo* (ibid. 1621):—*S. Missæ Sacrificium ab Hæreticorum Injuriis Vindicatum* (ibid. 1622). See Streber, in Wetzer u. Welte's *Kirchen-Lexikon*, s. v.; Hoefer, *Nouv. Biog. Générale*, s. v.

Coccopani, Giovanni, an Italian painter and architect, was born at Florence in 1582, and executed a number of pictures for the churches of Lombardy. In 1622 he was invited to Vienna, where he was employed by the emperor in the wars as state engineer. He was appointed professor of mathematics at Florence on the death of Castelli, and was afterwards invited to Rome to fill the chair in the academy of that city, but he refused to quit Florence. He died there in 1649. See Spooner, *Biog. Hist. of the Fine Arts*, s. v.; Hoefer, *Nouv. Biog. Générale*, s. v.

Cocha, of Ros-bennachair (County Clare), an Irish saint, is commemorated June 29. In the *Life of St. Ciaran*, of Saighir, there is an account of the many services St. Ciaran did to St. Cocha, and of their lasting friendship. She was St. Ciaran's nurse, and through him her monastery at Rosbanagher was founded in the 6th century (Todd and Reeves, *Mart. Doneg.* p. 183, 379; Lanigan, *Eccl. Hist. of Ireland*, i, 405).

Cochelet, Anastase, a French Carmelite, was born at Mézières in 1551. He was a noted preacher, and for a time had to retire to Antwerp. He returned in 1617, and died at Rheims in 1624, leaving a number of works against the Reformers, for which see Hoefer, *Nouv. Biog. Générale*, s. v.

Cochin, Charles Nicolas (1), a French designer and engraver, was born in Paris in 1688, and studied painting until he was nineteen, when he devoted himself to engraving. The following are some of his principal plates: *The Meeting of Jacob and Esau; Jacob and Laban; Jacob Pursued by Laban; Rebekah with the Servant of Abraham; The Trinity and the Assumption; The Lame Man Cured.* He died in 1754. See Spooner, *Biog. Hist. of the Fine Arts*, s. v.; Hoefer, *Nouv. Biog. Générale*, s. v.

Cochin, Charles Nicolas (2), son of the foregoing, an eminent French designer and engraver, was born in Paris in 1715, and was instructed by his father. He wrote several books relating to the arts, which were highly valued. He died April 29, 1790. The following are some of his plates: *The Infant Jesus Holding a Cross; The Virgin; The Crucifixion.* See Chalmers, *Biog. Dict.* s. v.; Spooner, *Biog. Hist. of the Fine Arts*, s. v.; *Biog. Universelle*, s. v.

Cochin, Jacques Denis, a French theologian and philanthropist, was born in Paris, Jan. 1, 1726. He was made pastor of St. Jacques-du-Haut-Pas in 1756, and became famous by his zeal and charity. In 1780 he conceived the idea of founding a hospital for the poor in the faubourg St. Jacques, himself subscribing 37,000 francs for that purpose, and, with the liberality of others, the building was finished in July, 1782. Abbé Cochin died June 3, 1783, at Paris, leaving several devotional works, for which see Hoefer, *Nouv. Biog. Générale*, s. v.

Cochin, Jean Denis Marie, a French philanthropist, was born in 1789. He occupied several civil offices, but is best known as the founder of the asylum homes of Paris, and by his efforts to improve and extend public primary instruction. He died in 1841, leaving some works on these benevolent subjects. See Hoefer, *Nouv. Biog. Générale*, s. v.

Cochin, Nicolas (or **Natalis**), a French designer and engraver, was born at Troyes, in Champagne, about 1619. He settled at Paris, where he engraved a great number of plates, among them, *Melchizedek and Abraham; Abraham Sending away Hagar; The Children of Israel Crossing the Red Sea; St. John Preaching in the Wilderness; The Repose in Egypt; The Conversion of St. Paul; The Adoration of the Magi; Pharaoh and his Host Swallowed up in the Red Sea.* He died in 1695. See Spooner, *Biog. Hist. of the Fine Arts*, s. v.; Hoefer, *Nouv. Biog. Générale*, s. v.

Cochlear. See SPOON.

Cochran, Hugh, a Scotch clergyman, chaplain to Sir Alexander Maxwell's family, was licensed to preach in 1715; presented to the living at Kilmaurs in 1722, ordained in 1723, and died April 9, 1733, aged forty-eight years. See *Fasti Eccles. Scoticanæ*, ii, 179.

Cochran, Isaac C., a Methodist Episcopal minister, was born in Vermont about 1821. He joined the Presbyterians in early life; removed to Michigan at the age of seventeen; spent several years successfully as a school-teacher; became principal of Clarkston Academy in 1853; joined the Methodists, and in 1861 entered the Detroit Conference. During 1865 and 1866 he was supernumerary, and principal of Owosso Union School. He died in the midst of his ministerial labors at Utica, Mich., Oct. 25, 1867. Mr. Cochran had a cultured mind and heart. See *Minutes of Annual Conferences*, 1868, p. 174.

Cochran, John (1), a Scotch clergyman, took his degree at Edinburgh University in 1646; was admitted to the living at Strathblane in 1650, and ordained; took the side of the Resolutioners in 1651; submitted to episcopacy in 1662, and resigned in July, 1690. See *Fasti Eccles. Scoticanæ*, ii, 372.

Cochran, John (2), a Scotch clergyman, was called to the living at Symington in 1712, and ordained. He died before April 25, 1722. See *Fasti Eccles. Scoticanæ*, ii, 145.

Cochran, Joseph Gallup, a Presbyterian minister, was born at Springville, N. Y., Feb. 5, 1817. He graduated from Amherst College in 1842, and from Union Theological Seminary in 1847; was ordained June 10 of the same year, and commissioned by the Presbyterian Board as a missionary to Seir, Persia, where for eight years he labored earnestly. In 1865 he returned to the United States, and in 1867 again sought, with renewed zeal, his foreign field, where, after four years more of faithful service, he died at Ooroomiah, Persia, Nov. 2, 1871. See *The Presbyterian*, Feb. 17, 1872. (W. P. S.)

Cochran, Samuel, a Methodist Episcopal minister, was born in Halifax, Vt., Aug. 31, 1778. He was converted in 1800; labored some time as exhorter and local preacher, and in 1804 entered the New York Conference, wherein he served the Church faithfully thirty-eight years. He died in the spring of 1845. Mr. Cochran was energetic, devoted, and successful in his ministry, and kind in all his social relations. See *Minutes of Annual Conferences*, 1846, p. 31.

Cochrane, John, a Scotch clergyman, was licensed to preach in 1811; became assistant minister at Lilliesleaf, and afterwards minister to the Presbyterian congregation at Falstone, and then that at North Shields; was presented to the living at Hawick in 1823, and died Sept. 12, 1832, aged forty-two years. See *Fasti Eccles. Scoticanæ*, i, 499.

Cochrane, Sylvester, a Congregational minister, was born at Antrim, N. H., May 8, 1796. He graduated from Dartmouth College in 1823, and was ordained at Poultney, Vt., in 1827, where he labored six years with great success. In 1837 he removed to Michigan, and preached in Vermontville and Howell, and for the Presbyterian Church in Northville. He died March 14, 1860, at Northville. Mr. Cochrane was an able and faithful minister, and an advocate of all moral reforms. See *Cong. Quarterly*, 1860, p. 344.

Cochrane, William, a Scotch clergyman, took his degree at Edinburgh University in 1639; was licensed to preach, and became a helper to Mr. Naine at Dysart in 1651; was elected schoolmaster of that parish, admitted to the living there in 1657, conforming to episcopacy, and was instituted in 1666. There is no further record of him. See *Fasti Eccles. Scoticanæ*, iii, 410.

Cock, *in Christian Art.* Representations of this bird frequently occur on tombs, from the earliest period. When not associated with the figure of St. Peter, it appears to be a symbol of the resurrection, our Lord being supposed by the early Church to have broken from the grave at the early cock-crowing. A peculiar awe seems always to have attached to that hour, at which all wandering spirits have, through the Middle Ages, been supposed to vanish from the earth. *Hamlet* and the ancient ballad called *The Wife of Usher's Well* occur to us as salient examples of a universal superstition. Prudentius's hymn *Ad Galli Cantum* (*Cathem.* i, 16) adopts the idea of the cock-crowing as a call to the general judgment. See Aringhi, ii, 328, 329 (in a complete list of animal symbols).

Fighting-cocks seem to symbolize the combat with secular or sensual temptations. The practice of training them for combat has probably always existed in the East, and certainly was in favor at Athens (comp. Aristoph. *Av.*; 1 Cor. ix, 27). See Bottari, iii, 137.

Fighting-cocks. (From an antique cup.)

Two cocks accompany the Good Shepherd in Bottari, plate clxxii (from the tympanum of an arch in the cemetery of St. Agnes).

Cock, Alexander, a Scotch clergyman, was licensed to preach in 1777; presented to the living at Cruden in 1778, and ordained. He died July 10, 1837, aged eighty-one years. See *Fasti Eccles. Scoticanæ*, iii, 606.

Cock, James, a Scotch clergyman, was called to the living at Keithhall and Kinkell in 1738, and died Feb. 17, 1776, aged seventy-seven years, leaving two sons in the ministry, Alexander at Cruden, and William at Rathen. See *Fasti Eccles. Scoticanæ*, iii, 585.

Cock (or **Kock**), **Jerome**, a Flemish painter and engraver, was born at Antwerp in 1510. He applied himself chiefly to engraving. The following are some of his principal plates: *Moses with the Tables of the Law; Daniel in the Lions' Den; Samson and Delilah;* a set of eight female figures, *Jael, Ruth, Abigail, Judith, Esther, Susanna,* the *Virgin Mary* and *Mary Magdalene; The Resurrection; The Last Judgment; The Temptation of St. Anthony.* He died in 1570. See Hoefer, *Nouv. Biog. Générale,* s. v.; Spooner, *Biog. Hist. of the Fine Arts,* s. v.

Cock, William, a Scotch clergyman, took his degree at King's College, Aberdeen, in 1776; was licensed to preach in 1782; presented to the living at Culsalmond in 1794, and ordained in 1795; transferred to Rathen in 1801, and died July 1, 1848, aged ninety-one years. See *Fasti Eccles. Scoticanæ,* iii, 579, 639.

Cockayn, George, an English Independent minister, was descended from an ancient family in Derbyshire. He is said to have been educated at Cambridge, and in the time of the civil wars held the living of St. Pancras, Soper Lane, London. He was a celebrated preacher, and in November, 1648, preached the fast-day sermon before the House of Commons. He became chaplain to one of Oliver Cromwell's lords, and in 1657 published a funeral sermon with the title *Divine Astrology.* He was ejected from his living in 1660, when he founded the Church at Hare Court, London, and was the first preacher there. He had distinguished citizens in his Church, yet he suffered much persecution from the royalists. He was a man of ability and learning, took part in compiling an English-Greek Lexicon, in 1658, and died in 1689. See Wilson, *Dissenting Churches,* iii, 279.

Cockburn, Henry, a Scotch clergyman, took his degree at the University of St. Andrews in 1613; and was presented to the living at Channelkirk in 1625. He was a member of the General Assembly in 1638, but was suspended by that of 1648, and deposed in 1650 for praying in public for the army in England under the duke of Hamilton. He afterwards suffered great misery and privation, but was restored to the ministry in 1659, and had an act of parliament in his favor in 1661. He was employed at Earlston for fifteen months, and returned to Channelkirk in 1662. See *Fasti Eccles. Scoticanæ,* i, 521, 522, 523.

Cockburn, John, D.D., a Scotch clergyman, nephew to the bishop of Aberdeen, where he was educated, was called to the living at Udny in 1676; transferred to the living at Old Deer in 1681; scrupled at taking the test imposed by parliament, but did so in 1682, and was transferred to Ormiston in 1683. He was the first who projected a periodical account of literature in Scotland, and secured a license to print the monthly transactions and account of books out of the *Universal Bibliotheke,* which was recalled in 1688, and he was forbidden to print any more. He was deprived by the privy council in 1689, for not praying for the king and queen, and other acts of disloyalty. In 1698 he was appointed by the bishop of London as minister of the Episcopal congregation at Amsterdam, and in 1709 was promoted to the rectory of Northall, Middlesex, where he died Nov. 20, 1729. His son Patrick was an English vicar. His publications were, *Jacob's Vow* (1686):—*Bibliotheca Universalis* (1688):—*Eight Sermons on Several Occasions* (1691):—*Inquiry into the Nature, Necessity, and Evidence of the Christian Faith* (1696, 1697):—*Fifteen Sermons on Various Subjects* (1697):—*Bourignonianism Detected* (1698):—*Right Notions of God and Religion* (1708):—*Answer to Queries Concerning Important Points in Religion* (1717):—*History and Examination of Duels* (1720):—*Specimen of Remarks Concerning Affairs and Persons in Scotland* (1724). See *Fasti Eccles. Scoticanæ,* i, 301; iii, 617, 620; Allibone, *Dict. of Brit. and Amer. Authors,* s. v.

Cockburn, Patrick (1), a Scotch clergyman, was educated at St. Andrews; entered into holy orders when young; went to Paris and taught Oriental languages in the university there, with approbation; but embracing the Protestant faith, returned to Scotland, and was appointed, in 1562, the first Protestant minister at Haddington. He had to supply certain kirks monthly, and was chaplain of Trinity Aisle in 1563. Complaints were made that he neither attended provincial nor general assemblies. He died in 1568. His publications were, *Oratio de Utilitate et Excellentia Verbi Dei* (Paris, 1551):—*De Vulgari Sacræ Scripturæ Phrasi* (ibid. 1552):—*In Orationem Dominicampia Meditatio* (1555):—*In Symbolum Apostolicum Comment.* (Lond. 1561). See *Fasti Eccles. Scoticanæ,* i, 311; Hoefer, *Nouv. Biog. Générale,* s. v.; Chalmers, *Biog. Dict.* s. v.

Cockburn, Patrick (2), an English clergyman, husband of the noted writer Catharine Cockburn, was born about 1678, and was many years vicar of Long-Horseley, Northumberland. He died in 1749. He wrote, *Penitential Office* (1721):—*Praying for Superiors,* etc. (1728, 1739):—*An Inquiry into the Truth and Certainty of the Mosaic Deluge* (1750). See Allibone, *Dict. of Brit. and Amer. Authors,* s. v.

Cockburn, Robert, a Scotch clergyman, was promoted to the see of Ross in 1508, and was still bishop there in 1515. He died in 1521. See Keith, *Scottish Bishops,* p. 190.

Cockburne, James, a Scotch clergyman, took his degree at Edinburgh University in 1653; was licensed to preach in 1662; presented to the living of Abbey St. Bathans in 1664, and ordained; ten years later was censured for immorality, and transferred to Pencaitland in 1674. Under accusation of scandal he resigned in 1684, and died in April, 1687. See *Fasti Eccles. Scoticanæ,* i, 348, 406.

Cockburne, John, a Scotch clergyman, took his degree at the University of St. Andrews in 1612; was presented to the living at Humbie in 1617; instituted in 1618, and resigned before Aug. 23, 1648, owing to age and infirmity. See *Fasti Eccles. Scoticanæ,* i, 337.

Cockburne, Samuel, a Scotch clergyman, took his degree at Edinburgh University in 1600; was appointed to the living at Kirkmichael, Banffshire, in 1601, having also Inveraven in charge; was transferred to Minto in 1609, and died before Aug. 5, 1624. See *Fasti Eccles. Scoticanæ,* i, 506; iii, 237.

Cockburne, William, a Scotch clergyman, took his degree at the University of St. Andrews in 1627; became chaplain to John, earl of Cassillis, and was admitted to the living at Kirkmichael in 1638. In 1651 he did not take part with either Resolutioners or Protesters, but was confined to his parish in 1662 for nonconformity, and died in August, 1677, aged about seventy years. See *Fasti Eccles. Scoticanæ,* ii, 119.

Cocke, Stephen F., a Presbyterian minister, was born in Virginia. He was a student in Union Seminary, Virginia, and then spent part of a year in Princeton Seminary. He was ordained by the Presbytery of West Hanover in 1836 as pastor at Bethany, Va.; stated supply at Fincastle in 1837; pastor at same place from 1839 to 1844; pastor at Little Rock, Ark., in 1846; stated supply at Victoria, Texas, from 1846 to 1849; home missionary at Port Lavacca from 1849 to 1852; served in some agency in Indianola from 1852 to 1856, and died in the latter year. See *Gen. Cat. of Princeton Theol. Sem.* 1881, p. 81.

Cocker, Thomas, an English Congregational minister, was born at Ashton-under-Lyne, April 9, 1840. He early became a member of the Congregational Church and a village preacher, and was educated for the ministry in an academy and in Lancashire Independent College, where he studied from 1860 to 1865. In the latter year he became pastor of Copeland Street Chapel, Stoke-upon-Trent, in which relation he continued during the remainder of his life. He was two years secretary to the North Staffordshire Congregational Union, and was also its president. He was accidentally killed, Feb. 1, 1881. See (Lond.) *Cong. Year-book*, 1882, p. 289.

Cockerton, Thomas, an English Baptist minister, was born at Soham, Cambridgeshire, July 26, 1839. He was converted under the preaching of Rev. C. H. Spurgeon, in whose "Pastor's College" he pursued his studies. He was settled at Thorpe-le-Soken, Essex, three or four years; was then for over two years at Castle Donnington; afterwards removed to Daventry, but, after laboring a short time, ruptured a blood-vessel, and died in his native place, June 4, 1868. See (Lond.) *Baptist Hand-book*, 1869, p. 137, 138. (J. C. S.)

Cockin, John, an English Congregational minister, was born at Thornton, near Bradford, in 1783. In youth he was remarkable for his studious habits. When about eleven years old he was led to Christ by reading Doddridge's *Rise and Progress of Religion in the Soul*, and some years afterwards was admitted to Church fellowship at Queen Street, Sheffield, where he was apprenticed to a bookseller. In 1804 he entered the Independent Academy, Idle, and at the close of his course settled at the Lane Chapel, Holmfirth, near Huddersfield, where he remained forty-three years, during which period he was kept from his work only one Sunday by illness. The last twelve years of his life were spent almost in seclusion at Halifax, where he died, Oct. 17, 1861. Both in the pulpit and on the platform Mr. Cockin was effective and popular. In conversation he excelled. He had a great ascendency over others, and possessed a strong character. He wrote and published a *Life* of his father, the Rev. Joseph Cockin, *Sketches after Reading*, and one or two controversial pamphlets on Calvinism. See (Lond.) *Cong. Year-book*, 1862, p. 226.

Cockin, Joseph, an English Congregational minister, was born at Frizinghall, near Bradford, March 12, 1852. He conceived a desire to become a missionary in early childhood, and from that time read and studied with this end in view. He was educated at Cheshunt College by the London Missionary Society, for service in the foreign field; was ordained at Salem Chapel, Bradford, March 12, 1877, and sailed on the 29th for his station at Hope Fountain, Central Africa. He entered heartily upon his work, but his robust constitution yielded to the deadly climate, and he died Feb. 3, 1880. See (Lond.) *Cong. Year-book*, 1881, p. 363.

Cocking, Samuel, a Wesleyan Methodist missionary, sent out by the British Conference, died at Bangalore, a few months after landing in India, April 30, 1861. He was a pious, humble, diligent young man. See *Minutes of the British Conference*, 1861, p. 27.

Cocking, Thomas, an English Wesleyan minister, entered the sacred work in 1819, and for more than half a century was a practical, earnest preacher, greatly beloved. He died at Alford, Oct. 6, 1870, in his eighty-first year. Mr. Cocking wrote, *A Sketch of Wesleyan Methodism, with its History in the Grantham Circuit* (1836, 12mo):—*Sabbath Desecration* (London, 1847, 2d ed. 12mo), an excellent practical tractate. See *Minutes of the British Conference*, 1871, p. 13.

Cocks, John, an English Baptist minister, was born at Great Farrington, Devon, Oct. 12, 1783. He was a dissipated youth; came to London in early life; met with religious companions; was converted under the ministry of Dr. Jenkins; joined the Church at Orange Street, and began to preach. In 1817 he became pastor of a Church at Calstock, but went to Crediton, Devon, in 1821, and became a successful home missionary. In 1826 he removed to Minehead; in 1833 to Highbridge, and in 1834 became pastor of the Church at Twerton, Bath. In 1841 he was called to Amersham, Bucks, where he remained till his death, Dec. 12, 1850.

Cocks, William Francis, an English Wesleyan missionary, was born in the parish of St. Agnes, Cornwall. He was converted at fifteen; began to preach at nineteen; entered the conference at twenty-four, and was appointed to the mission work. After two years and a half spent in study at Richmond he was sent to the St. Vincent District, West Indies. He died in July, 1881, in the thirty-first year of his age. See *Minutes of the British Conference*, 1882, p. 43.

Cocq, Florent de, a Flemish theologian of the Premonstrant Order, lived in the latter half of the 17th century, and wrote, *Principia Totius Theologiæ Moralis et Speculativæ* (1683):—*Conversio Vera et Apostolica* (Liege, 1685):—*De Jure et Justitia*. See Hoefer, *Nouv. Biog. Générale*, s. v.

Cocquault, Pierre, a French historian, a native of Reims, was canon of the Church of that place, and died in 1645, leaving, *Mémoires pour Servir à l'Histoire Ecclésiastique de Reims*, preserved in MS. at the library of Reims:—*Mémoires pour la Révendication des Églises des Pays-Bas*, in MS. (ibid.):—*Table Chronologique de l'Histoire de Reims* (ibid. 1650). See Hoefer, *Nouv. Biog. Générale*, s. v.

Cocquelin, Nicolas, a French poet and theologian, was born at Corberie, near Lassay, district of Orne, in 1640. He was chancellor of the Church, and of the University of Paris, and sought to prevent the revocation of the edict of Nantes. He died at Paris in 1693, leaving *Interpretation des Psaumes et des Cantiques* (Paris, 1686; Bordeaux, 1731; Limoges, s. a.):—*Le Manuel d'Épictète* (Paris, 1688), mostly in verse:—*Traité de ce qui est dû aux Puissances* (ibid. 1690). See Hoefer, *Nouv. Biog. Générale*, s. v.

Cocȳtus, in Greek mythology, was the name of the muddy stream which Charon crossed in carrying the souls of the dead to the kingdom of shades. It is a tributary of the Acheron.

Coda, Bartolommeo (surnamed *Ariminense*), an eminent Italian painter, son and pupil of the following, was born in Ferrara, and lived till 1558. His chief painting is a *Virgin between Sts. Roche and Sebastian*, in the Church of San Rocco at Pesaro. See Hoefer, *Nouv. Biog. Générale*, s. v.

Coda (or **Codi**), **Benedetto**, a Ferrarese painter, was born about 1460, and studied under Giovanni Bellini. He is said to have painted several pictures for the churches at Rimini. The principal are *The Marriage of the Virgin*, in the cupola of the cathedral, and his picture of *The Rosary*, in the Church of the Dominicans. He died about 1520. See Spooner, *Biog. Hist. of the Fine Arts*, s. v.; Hoefer, *Nouv. Biog. Générale*, s. v.

Coddæus, Gulielmus (*Willem van der Codde*), a Dutch Orientalist, born at Leyden in 1575, was appointed in 1601 to the chair of Hebrew in his native city, but deprived in 1619 for refusing to subscribe to the statutes of the synod of Dort, and died about 1630. His principal works are, *Notæ ad Grammaticam Hebræam* (Leyden, 1612):—*Hoseas Propheta cum Commentariis*, etc. (ibid. 1621):—*Fragmenta Comœdiarum Aristophanis* (ibid. 1625). See Hoefer, *Nouv. Biog. Générale*, s. v.; Jöcher, *Allgemeines Gelehrten-Lexikon*, s. v.

Coddæus, Petrus (*Pieer van der Codde*), a Dutch theologian of the order of the Oratory, was born at Amsterdam in 1648. In 1683 he was made pastor at Utrecht, and in 1688 titular archbishop of Sebaste, and apostolic vicar of the united provinces. Being accused of holding the principles of Jansenism, he went to Rome in 1700, in order to justify himself, but in 1704 his doctrine was condemned by a decree of the Inquisition, and he was deprived of the spiritual administration of the Catholics of Holland. He died at Utrecht, Dec. 18, 1710, leaving *Declarationes super Pluribus Interrogationibus*, etc. (Rome, 1701). See Hoefer, *Nouv. Biog. Générale*, s. v.; Jöcher, *Allgemeines Gelehrten-Lexikon*, s. v.

Coddiāni was, according to Epiphanius (*Hær.* xxvi, p. 85), a nickname given to an impure sect of

Gnostic heretics. He explains the word as "plattermen," deriving it from a Syriac word, *codda* (Aram. קִידָ), a platter or dish; and says they got the name because, on account of their "pollution," no one could eat with them, and it was necessary that their food should be given to them separately.

Codding, Ichabod, a Congregational minister and lecturer, was born at Bristol, N. Y., in 1811. He early manifested the eloquence and zeal for reform which characterized his whole life, becoming a popular speaker on temperance at the age of seventeen. At twenty he entered Canandaigua Academy, and prepared for college, teaching in the English department at the same time. In 1834 he entered Middlebury College, and began a fervid attack upon slavery, which resulted in his leaving the college. For the next five years he traversed the New England States and New York, as the agent of the American Anti-slavery Society, and though persecuted and often seriously injured by mobs, never lost his self-command, nor displayed a violent or vindictive spirit. In 1842 Mr. Codding went West, and having entered the Congregational ministry, spent the remainder of his life as pastor successively at Princeton, Lockport, Joliet, Baraboo, Wis., and Bloomington, Ill., lecturing meantime in almost all parts of Illinois against slavery. He died in Baraboo, Wis., June 17, 1866. See *Appleton's Annual Cyclop.* 1866, p. 567.

Coddington, Eli H., a Methodist Episcopal minister, was born in Champaign County, Ill., July 1, 1837. He removed with his parents to Henry County, Ia., in his boyhood; was converted in his nineteenth year; soon after entered the Iowa Wesleyan University, and in 1861 enlisted in the Fourteenth Iowa Infantry. He lost his left arm at the battle of Fort Donelson; was discharged, and on returning home re-entered college, but soon rejoined the army as captain of Company H, Forty-fifth Iowa Infantry. After serving his full term he again resumed his college course; graduated with credit in June, 1866; was admitted into the Iowa Conference in the following September, and in 1873 closed his effective services and entered upon the superannuated relation, which he sustained to the close of his life, July 30, 1877. Mr. Coddington was intensely patriotic, studious, and devout. See *Minutes of Annual Conferences*, 1877, p. 85.

Codex. For the important Biblical MSS., see each under its specific name; as Amiatine; Angelic; Argenteus, etc.

Codington, George Spencer, a Congregational minister, was born at Seneca Falls, N. Y., April 8, 1838. After having studied at the Syracuse High School, he went to sea, returning in 1860, after three years' absence. In 1861 and 1862 he was a student in Michigan University. During the three years following he served in the army, and then entered the Commercial College in Indianapolis. In 1870 he graduated from the Chicago Theological Seminary, and was ordained an evangelist July 1 of that year at Lacon, Ill., where he was acting pastor till 1871. In 1872 he removed to Dakota, there organized churches at Dell Rapids and Medway, in charge of which he remained until death, at Ann Arbor, Mich., Sept. 19, 1878. He was a representative in Dakota legislature in 1876. See *Cong. Year-book*, 1879, p. 40.

Codomann, Lorenz, a German Protestant chronologist, was born at Flotz, Sept. 15, 1529. He was successively co-rector at Amberg, rector at Hof, pastor at Eger, and superintendent at Germersheim and at Bayreuth, where he died, April 2, 1590. His principal works are, *Supputatio Præteritorum Annorum Mundi* (Leipsic, 1572):—*Annales Sacræ Scripturæ* (Wittenberg, 1581). See Hoefer, *Nouv. Biog. Générale*, s. v.; Jöcher, *Allgemeines Gelehrten-Lexikon*, s. v.

Codratus. See Quadratus.

Codurc, Philippe, a French theologian, was a native of Annonay. Having been minister at Nismes, he renounced Protestantism, and became a Catholic. He was versed in the Oriental languages. He died in 1660. His principal works are, *Commentarii in Jobum*, explanatory of every Heb. term from the Rabbins (Paris, 1651):—*Traduction des Livres de Job et Solomon*, with notes (ibid. 1647, 1657). See Hoefer, *Nouv. Biog. Générale*, s. v.

Coduri (*Abûl Hosein*), Ahmed, a learned Mussulman doctor, of the sect of Abu Hanefi, was born at Nissabur in 367 of the Hegira. He held the office of *réis* of the Hanefi sect in Irak, and died in 428 of the same æra (A.D. 1037). Among his works the most celebrated is a *Treatise on Dogmas of Hanefi*, founder of the sect which bore his name. See D'Herbelot, *Bibliothèque Orientale*, s. v.

Coe, Harvey, a Presbyterian minister, was born at Granville, Mass., Oct. 6, 1785. He was converted in 1804; graduated at Williams College in 1811; was licensed to preach in 1812, and settled in what was then called the Connecticut Western Reserve, O. He joined Portage Presbytery in 1833, and was appointed agent of the American Board of Commissioners for Foreign Missions. He died March 9, 1860. He entered the ministry with patriotic zeal, and the blessing of the Lord crowned his labors. See Wilson, *Presb. Hist. Almanac*, 1861, p. 158.

Coe, James R., a Protestant Episcopal clergyman, was rector, in 1854, at Bethlehem, Conn.; in 1857, of St. James's Church, Winsted; in 1860, of St. John the Evangelist's Church, Stockport, N. Y., where he remained until 1865. He then removed to Oakfield, as principal of Carey College Seminary, and became rector of St. Michael's Church, in connection with which he performed missionary work until his death, March 16, 1874, at the age of fifty-six years. See *Prot. Episc. Almanac*, 1875, p. 144.

Coe, Jonas, D.D., a Presbyterian minister, was born March 20, 1759. He was educated at Rutgers College, New Brunswick, N. J.; studied theology privately; was taken under the care of the New York Presbytery in 1790, and was licensed to preach in 1791. In 1792 he accepted a call to the united congregations of Troy and Lansingburg, where he labored effectually for eleven years, and afterwards at Troy alone, until his death in 1842. He was a faithful pastor and an able minister. See Sprague, *Annals of the Amer. Pulpit*, iii, 576.

Coe, Jonathan, an Episcopal minister, was born at Winsted, Conn., and graduated at Wesleyan University in 1839. He pursued his theological studies under the tuition of Rev. Dr. Jarvis, of Middletown, was ordained in 1843, and in that and the following year had charge of parishes in Bethlehem and Northfield. From 1847 to 1852 he was rector of the parish in Winsted; from 1852 to 1866, of parishes in Athens and Coxsackie, N. Y. He died April 25, 1866. See *Wesleyan University Alumni Record*, p. 33; *Amer. Quar. Church Rev.* July, 1866, p. 311. (J. C. S.)

Coe, Noah, a Congregational and Presbyterian minister, was born at Durham, Conn., May 24, 1786. He graduated at Yale College in 1808; pursued his theological studies in part at Andover in 1809 and 1810; was ordained July 3, 1811, and preached in Chester, N. Y., for two years. In 1814 he was installed over the Presbyterian Church in New Hartford, where he remained until 1835. In 1836 he commenced preaching in the Second Congregational Church in Greenwich, Conn., where he was installed May 23, 1837. He was dismissed May 20, 1845, and was not again a settled pastor, though he preached and labored almost continuously until he was over seventy. From 1848 to 1854 he was engaged as a city missionary in New York city, and in Williamsburg, L. I. He then removed to New Haven, Conn. From November, 1854, to February, 1856, he served as stated supply of the Congregational Church in Northfield, Conn., and for the succeeding year supplied the Congregational Church at New Preston Hill. He died at Hartford, May 9, 1871. He was vigilant and diligent in his parish, instructive and faithful in the pulpit. See *Obituary Record of Yale College*, 1871; *Presbyterianism in Central N. Y.* p. 216.

Coe, Philemon Elmer, a Protestant Episcopal minister, was born in New York city, June 20, 1815. He graduated at the College of New Jersey in 1834, spent two years thereafter in Princeton Theological Seminary, and graduated at the Union Theological Seminary in 1839. He was ordained to the ministry in the Protestant Episcopal Church, June 30, 1843; became rector at Hammondsport, N. Y., in 1844, and was home missionary at Medina and Royalton, from 1845 to 1850. His next engagements were as home missionary at Stafford, rector at Plainfield and Scotch Plains (1851-59), and at Westfield, N. J., where he died, Dec. 20, 1873. (W. P. S.)

Coe, Samuel Goodrich, a Congregational minister, son of Rev. Noah Coe, was born at New Hartford, Oneida Co., N. Y., Oct. 22, 1819. He graduated at Yale College in 1838, and immediately entered the Yale Law School. In 1840 he established himself in the practice of the law at Berlin, Conn., but soon after entered the Yale Divinity School, and graduated in 1843. He was ordained over the Church at Middlebury, Vt., July 14, 1844, and remained there until compelled to leave by failing health, in November, 1850. Dec. 13 of the same year he was installed pastor of the First Church, Danbury, Conn. Here his strength again gave way, in 1864, and he resigned, and did not again accept a permanent pastorate. He resided four years at Ridgefield, and supplied the Church there until 1868. A period of illness followed this service, but in 1869 he so far improved in health as to preach for six months in the Second Presbyterian Church in Cleveland, O. He died at New Haven, Conn., Dec. 7, 1869. Mr. Coe was master of a vigorous style, and was a very impressive preacher. See *Cong. Quarterly*, 1870, p. 302.

Coeddi. See CAETI.

Coëffeteau, Guillaume, a French theologian, was born at St. Calais, Sarthe, in 1589. Having completed his theological studies and been ordained priest, he became rector of Bagnolet, near Paris. He declined to be coadjutor of the bishop of Marseilles, his brother, and contented himself with a pension of two thousand livres. In 1623 he resigned at Bagnolet, in order to retire to the college of Bayeux, where he composed the greater part of his works. He died at Paris at the Dominican house, Rue Sainte-Honoré, in 1660, leaving an edition of the poem of Simon Nanquier, with notes: —*De Lubrico Temporis Curriculo* (Paris, 1616):—*Compendiosa Formandæ Orationis Concionisque Ratio* (ibid. 1643). His posthumous works were published by his nephew, James Hallier, under the title, *Florilegium*, etc. (ibid. 1667). See Hoefer, *Nouv. Biog. Générale*, s. v.

Coëffeteau, Nicolas, a celebrated French theologian and preacher, was born at St. Calais, a little village near Le Mains, in 1574. At the age of fourteen he entered the Dominican order, in the city of Mans. Later, being sent to Paris, he completed his studies with honor at the convent of St. Jacques, and entered upon a course of philosophy with brilliant success. Henry IV chose him, in 1602, as his ordinary preacher; his brotherhood, after having appointed him definitor of the congregation of France, elected him by acclamation prior of the convent of St. Jacques, and although he was unable to fulfil the required conditions, he was allowed, through the interposition of Henry IV, to assume the position. In 1606 he was appointed vicar-general of the congregation of France. His writings against Peter Du Moulin, James I, king of England, and Duplessis Mornay, added to his celebrity. In 1617 he was made bishop of Dardania, *in partibus infidelium*, and as suffragan of the bishop of Mentz, he went to govern this diocese, where Calvinism was rapidly gaining ground. In return for this service he was appointed, in 1621, bishop of Marseilles, but his failing health did not permit him to assume this position. Abbé de Marolles, in his *Mémoires*, gives an account of the death of Coëffeteau, which occurred at Paris, April 21, 1623. From a large number of works we mention the following: *L'Hydre Abattue par l'Hercule Chrétien* (Paris, 1603):—*Examen du Livre de la Confession de Foi Publie sous le Nom du Roy de la Grande-Bretagne* (ibid. 1604): —*La Défense de la Sainte-Eucharistie* (ibid. 1606):—*Le Montagne Sainte de la Tribulation* (ibid. eod.):—*Premier Essai des Questions Théologiques*, etc. (ibid. 1607), which the Sorbonne prohibited him from completing:—*Le Sacrifice de l'Église Catholique* (ibid. 1608):—*Tableau des Passions Humaines* (ibid. 1615, 1621, 1623; translated into English, under the title, *Picture of Human Passions*, Lond. 1621):—*Tableau de la Pénitence de la Madeleine* (Paris, 1620):—*Tableau de l'Innocence* (ibid. 1621):—*La Marguerite Chrétienne* (ibid. 1627):—a collection of theological works, entitled *Œuvres du R. P. Coëffeteau, Contenant un Nouveau Traité des Noms de l'Eucharistie*, etc. (ibid. 1622). See Hoefer, *Nouv. Biog. Générale*, s. v.; *Biog. Universelle*, s. v.; Jöcher, *Allgemeines Gelehrten-Lexikon*, s. v.

Coelchus. See COLGA.

Cœlestiāni. See CŒLESTINE; PELAGIUS.

Cœlestinus, a French theologian of the Capuchin order, was born about 1596 at Mont de Marsan, and died at Toulouse in 1659. His principal works are, *Synopsis Prosopochronica Historiæ Ecclesiasticæ* (Toulouse, 1644): —*Prosopochronica S. Scripturæ* (Paris, 1648):—*Clavis David, sive Arcana Scripturæ S.* (Bordeaux, 1650):—*Speculum sine Macula* (ibid. 1651). See Hoefer, *Nouv. Biog. Générale*, s. v.

Cœllacus. See CEOLLACH.

Coëllo, Alonso Sanchez, an eminent Portuguese painter, was born in 1515, and resided chiefly in Spain. He painted a number of works for the churches of Madrid. His master-piece is in San Geronimo, representing *The Martyrdom of St. Sebastian*, with the figures of Christ and the Virgin. He died in 1590. See Spooner, *Biog. Hist. of the Fine Arts*, s. v.; Hoefer, *Nouv. Biog. Générale*, s. v.

Coëllo, Gaspar, a Portuguese missionary of the Jesuit order, was born at Oporto in 1531. He preached the Gospel upon the coast of Malabar for eighteen years, and went to Japan in 1571, where he became noted for the zeal with which he labored for the conversion of the idolaters. In 1581 he became vice-provincial of the mission, and died at Conzuca, in Japan, May 7, 1590. His letters have been published in the *Relations du Japon* (1575, 1582, 1588). See *Biog. Universelle*, s. v.; Hoefer, *Nouv. Biog. Générale*, s. v.

Coemaca (or **Coemoca**). See CAEMHOG.

Coeman. See CAEMHAN.

Coemgen (**Caoimhghen**, or **Kevin**), abbot of Glendalough, commemorated June 3, was born possibly in A.D. 498. In Celtic his name signifies "fair-begotten," and he belongs to the second order of Irish saints. He was early made a priest. Having fled to Glendalough, through fear of being elected abbot, he founded a monastery there in A.D. 549. He died in A.D. 618 (Lanigan, *Ecclesiastical History of Ireland*, ii, 43 sq.; Butler, *Lives of the Saints*, vi, 69, 70.

Coëmptio (*mutual purchase*) was one of the methods of contracting marriages among the ancient Romans, in which the parties solemnly bound themselves to each other by giving and receiving a piece of money. See MARRIAGE.

Coen, JOHN, a Methodist Episcopal minister, was born Jan. 19, 1827. He joined the Church in 1846, was licensed to preach in 1848, and in 1850 was received into the Pittsburgh Conference, wherein he labored with acceptability and success until his death, Feb. 14, 1861. Mr. Coen was pleasant and companionable, consistent and uniform in his daily life; clear, logical, and convincing as a preacher, and abundantly successful as a pastor. See *Minutes of Annual Conferences*, 1861, p. 34.

Coena. See ETHELGERT.

Cœna DOMINI. See MAUNDY-THURSDAY.

Cœna PURA. See GOOD-FRIDAY.

Cœnae. See AGAPAE.

Coenburga (or **Quoenburga**) is the name of two early English saints:

1. A daughter of Heriburg, being abbess of Watton, York, and a nun in that house, was cured of an infirmity by John, bishop of York, about A.D. 686 (Bede, *H. E.* v, 3).

2. An abbess, associated with the abbess Cuenburga and others in a proposal for mutual intercessory prayer (Haddan and Stubbs, *Councils*, iii, 342). See CUENBURH.

Coenferth, one of two presbyters from the diocese of Worcester, attesting an act of the Council of Clovesho, Oct. 12, 803 (Haddan and Stubbs, *Councils*, iii, 546).

Coengils. See CENGILLE.

Coengilsus. See CENGILLUS.

Cœnobium (*κοινόβιον*, from *κοινός*, *common*, and *βίος*, *life*) is equivalent to *monastery* in the *later* sense of that word. Cassian says "monasterium" may be the dwelling of a single monk, "cœnobium" must be of several; the former word expresses only the place, the latter the manner of living (*Coll.* xviii, 10). The neglect of this distinction has led to much inaccuracy in attempting to fix the date of the first "cœnobia" or communities of monks under one roof and under one government. Thus Helyot ascribes their origin to Antony, the famous anchorite of the Thebaid in the 3d century (*Ordres Relig. Diss. Prelim.* § 5). But the counter opinion, which ascribes it to Pachomius of Tabenna a century later, is more probable; for it seems to have been the want of some fixed rule to control the irregularities arising from the vast number of eremitæ, with their cells either entirely isolated from one another or merely grouped together casually, which gave the first occasion to "cœnobia." In fact, the growth of cœnobitism seems to have been very gradual. Large numbers of ascetics were collected near the Mons Nitrius [see CELLITÆ], and doubtless elsewhere also, long before Pachomius had founded his cœnobium. But the interval is considerable between this very imperfect organization of monks thus herding lawlessly together and the symmetrical arrangement of the Benedictine system. Very probably the earliest cœnobia were of women; for, though the word "virgins," in the account of Antony having his sister in the charge of devout women, is by no means conclusive, the female eremites would naturally be the first to feel the need of combination for mutual help and security.

The origin of the cœnobitic life is traced back to the time before the Christian æra. Something similar is seen in the pages of Plato (*Legg.* 780, 1), and the Pythagoreans are described by Aulus Gellius as living together and having a community of goods (*Noctes Atticœ*, i, 9).

Opinions have been divided among the admirers of asceticism as to the comparative merits of the solitary life and the cœnobitic. Cassian (*Coll.* xix, 3) looks up to the life of perfect solitude as the pinnacle of holiness, for which the cœnobitic life is only a preparatory discipline. Theophylact (*St. Narc.* iv, 20) interprets "those who bear fruit an hundred-fold" in the parable as virgins and eremites. Basil (*Reg.* c. 1), on the contrary, and the sagacious Benedict (*Reg.* c. 1), prefer the life of the cœnobite as safer, more edifying, less alloyed by the taint of selfishness. Even Jerome (*Epp. ad Rustic.* 125; *Ad Heliod.* 14), his monastic fervor notwithstanding, prefers life in the community to life in utter solitude, though at first he seems to have been a zealous upholder of the contrary opinion. Doubtless experience had impressed on him the perils of solitude. Legislators found it expedient to curb the rage for eremitism. Justinian ordered monks to stay within the "cœnobia." Similarly Charlemagne discouraged hermits, while protecting cœnobitic monks, and the seventh council of Toledo censured roving and solitary monks. Even in the East the same distrust prevailed of persons undertaking more than they could bear. Thus the council in Trullo enjoined a sojourn of some time in a cœnobium as the preliminary to life in the desert. Benedict aptly illustrates the difference, from his point of view, between these two forms of asceticism. The solitary, he says, leaves the line of battle to fight in single combat. See MONASTICISM.

"Cœnobium" is used sometimes in mediæval writers for the "basilica," or church of the monastery. "Cloister" and "convent" are frequently used for "cœnobium." See also ASCETICISM; BENEDICTINE RULE; MONASTERY.

Cœnred, king of the Mercians, succeeded his uncle, Ethelred, on the resignation of the latter in 704. In 709 he followed the example of his uncle, resigned his crown, and went to Rome in company with Offa, king of the East-Saxons, where he remained for the rest of his life. In Rome, Constantine being pope then, Coenred was shorn and made a monk "ad limina apostolorum," continuing to his last hours in prayers, fastings, and alms-deeds (Bede, *H. E.* v, 19). Coenred was the fifth of the Anglo-Saxon kings who abdicated on religious grounds, following Ethelred.

Coens, HENRICUS, a minister of the Reformed (Dutch) Church, sailed from Holland Oct. 7, 1725. He served at Aquackanonck (now Passaic), N. J., Second River (now Belleville), Pompton (now Pompton Plains); at Ponds from 1730, and died Feb. 14, 1735. He wrote to Holland a detailed account of the troubles between the churches of Second River and Aquackanonck. See Corwin, *Manual of the Ref. Church in America*, 3d ed. p. 213.

Cœnuald (**Coenwald**, or **Kenwald**), a monk, was sent by archbishop Theodore to Rome, bearing written charges against Wilfred before pope Agatho. Malmesbury represents him as supporting the charges in harsh and bitter terms.

Cœnwalch (or **Cœnuualh**) was the eleventh bishop of London. His episcopate falls between 789, when Eadgar was bishop, and 796, when Eadbald, his successor, died. His name is attached to a questionable or spurious charter of Offa, dated 793.

Coëtivy, ALAIN DE, a French prelate, was born in Brittany, Nov. 8, 1407. He was successively bishop of Dol, of Carnouailles, and of Avignon, and was regarded as one of the most virtuous ecclesiastics of his time. He was made cardinal in 1448, performed many important missions, and died at Rome, July 22, 1474. See Hoefer, *Nouv. Biog. Générale*, s. v.

Coëtlogon, FRANÇOIS DE, coadjutor of the bishop of Quimper in 1666, afterwards titulary bishop in 1668, was born in Brittany, France, June 3, 1631. He founded in his diocese a large seminary, as well as a house of retreat, and participated in the labors of the assembly of bishops in July, 1699—the assembly which condemned the *Maximes des Saints* of Fénelon. He died at Quimper, Nov. 6, 1706, leaving *Réflexions, Sentences, et Maximes tirées des Œuvres de Saint François-de-Sales* (Paris, 1698). See Hoefer, *Nouv. Biog. Générale*, s. v.

Coëtlosquet, JEAN GILES DE, a French prelate, was born at Saint-Pol-de-Léon, Sept. 15, 1700. He was chancellor of Bourges, and became bishop of Limoges in 1739; was preceptor of the duke of Berry, then of Louis XVI and his brothers, which functions, according to custom, admitted him into the French Academy in 1761. He died in Paris, March 21, 1784. See Hoefer, *Nouv. Biog. Générale*, s. v.

Cœtus (a *coming together*, or *assembly*) is the name of an ecclesiastical association or assembly in the Reformed (Dutch) Church in America. It was organized in 1747, being designed to supply the want of a classis or synod in this country, and was composed of ministers and elders who were in favor of the independence of the Church. Its powers were too limited to enable it to accomplish all that was hoped from its organization. For a full account, see REFORMED CHURCH IN AMERICA. A similar body also existed in the GERMAN REFORMED CHURCH IN AMERICA (q. v.). (W. J. R. T.)

Cœur, PIERRE LOUIS, a French prelate, was born at Tarare (Rhône), March 14, 1805. In 1820 he became a Carthusian monk, and spent several years in the study of theology. In 1824 he was made professor at the seminary of L'Argentière, and afterwards in the seminary of Saint-Irène, where he wrote an *Essai sur l'Indifference en Matière Religieuse*. He became subdeacon in 1825, deacon in 1826, and priest in 1829. In 1827 he went to Paris to attend the Sorbonne and the Collége de France. He next devoted himself to preaching for several years, with marked success, and obtained a membership in the academy at Clermont-Ferrand. In 1834 he was canon of Nantes, in 1838 of Bordeaux; in 1839 he was appointed vicar-general of Arras, and in 1841 titulary canon of the metropolis. He afterwards taught sacred eloquence with great success. He was appointed to the episcopal see of Troyes Oct. 16, 1848, and consecrated Feb. 25, 1849. He died Oct. 16, 1860. He was a collaborator on the *Revue Religieuse et Édifiante*. See Hoefer, *Nouv. Biog. Générale*, s. v.

Coffen, an early Welsh saint, was patron of Llangofen, in Monmouthshire, and of St. Goven Chapel, in Pembrokeshire (Rees, *Welsh Saints*, p. 307).

Coffin. The following additional particulars are from Walcott, *Sac. Archæol.* s. v.:

"The early Christians adopted the custom of the heathens in using coffins. Stone coffins were ordered for the interment of monks, by abbot Warin, of St. Alban's, 1183–95; they had hitherto been buried under the green turf. In the 10th and following two centuries a low coped coffin of stone, with a hollow for the body, and a circular cavity for the head, was in use; one palm deep in St. Anselm's time. The boat shape is the most ancient, the ridge being next in point of age. St. Richard of Chichester, in the 13th century, was buried in a wooden coffin. Those of the Templars, in the Temple Church, London, are of lead, decorated with ornaments of elaborate design in low relief. An old legend represents St. Cuthbert, in his stone coffin, floating down the Tweed."

Ancient Stone Coffins.

Coffin, Charles (1), a French hymnist, was born Oct. 4, 1676, at Buzancy. He studied at Beauvais and at Plessis. In 1718 he succeeded the celebrated historian, M. Rollin, as rector of the Paris University, which position he held until his death in 1749. At the instance of Monsieur de Vintimille, archbishop of Paris, he composed the hymns for the new Paris breviary. To grace of rhythm they join the most touching simplicity and tenderness. His works were published in 2 vols., Paris, 1755. Several of his hymns were also translated into English by Mason Neale and John Chandler. A number of these translations are also found in *Lyra Messianica*, p. 16, 36, 41, 160, 164, 169, 181, 264, 372. See Miller, *Singers and Songs of the Church*, p. 142; Lichtenberger, *Encyclop. des Sciences Religieuses*, s. v. (B. P.)

Coffin, Charles (2), D.D., a Presbyterian minister, was born at Newburyport, Mass., Aug. 15, 1775; graduated at Harvard College in 1793; studied theology privately, and was licensed by Essex Middle Association, May 14, 1799. He spent several years raising the endowment for Greenville College, Tenn., of which he became vice-president, and in 1810 president. In 1827 he became president of East Tennessee University at Knoxville, and remained there until 1833. He died June 3, 1853. See Sprague, *Annals of the Amer. Pulpit*, iv, 246.

Coffin, Charles B., a Protestant Episcopal clergyman, was inducted into the ministerial office in 1868. In 1870 he was assistant minister of St. Luke's Church, New York city, which relation he sustained until 1873. In the following year he became rector of Trinity Church, Haverstraw, N. Y. He died July 9, 1875, aged forty-six years. See *Prot. Episc. Almanac*, 1876, p. 149.

Coffin, Nehemiah Cogswell, a Presbyterian minister, was born in New Hampshire in 1816. He graduated from Dartmouth College in 1836; studied theology for one year (1839) in Andover Theological Seminary, and graduated from Lane Theological Seminary in 1841. He was ordained Sept. 10, 1843; was stated supply at Fearing, O., from 1842 to 1845; at Bethel and Bremen, in 1845 and 1846; at Hebron, from 1846 to 1851; teacher at Granville Female College, in 1851 and 1852; stated supply at Piqua, from 1852 to 1860; was without charge at Sandusky, in 1860 and 1861, and at Marblehead, from 1861 until his death there, Jan. 9, 1868. See *Trien. Cat. of Andover Theol. Sem.* 1870, p. 140.

Coffin, Stephen, a Free-will Baptist minister, was born at Alton, N. H., March 8, 1792, the youngest of fourteen children. He was converted at the age of twenty-one, and in 1839 became a member of the Church in Wolfborough. In the winter of 1841 he was ordained, and afterwards labored as an evangelist, spending most of the autumns and winters in preaching to destitute churches, and holding protracted meetings for nearly a year in Wisconsin and Illinois. He died in Dover, N. H., March 4, 1867. See *Free-will Baptist Register*, 1868, p. 88. (J. C. S.)

Coffing, JACKSON GREEN, a Congregational minister, was born at Redstone, Pa., Sept. 21, 1824. He graduated at Marietta College in 1853; was a student at Union Theological Seminary from 1853 to 1856; then a resident licentiate in 1856 and 1857; was ordained Nov. 9, 1856; was a foreign missionary at Aintab, Western Asia, from 1857 to 1861; also at Hajin and Adana, in 1861 and 1862, and was assassinated at Alexandretta, March 26, 1862. See *Gen. Cat. of Union Theol. Sem.* 1876, p. 77.

Coggeshall, FREEBORN, a Protestant Episcopal

clergyman, was born at Newport, R. I., Dec. 31, 1845. When he was a child his parents removed to Providence, and he fitted for college in the high-school of that city. He graduated with the highest honors of his class at Brown University in 1867. He immediately entered the General Theological Seminary in New York, where he was a student for three years, with the exception of six months, which were spent in travel in the old world. He was ordained a deacon June 12, 1871, and commenced a mission at Elmwood, near Providence. He was ordained presbyter Dec. 22 of the same year, and for about a year was assistant rector of the "House of Prayer" in Newark, N. J. He was assistant rector of the Church of the Advent in Boston, from the fall of 1872 until June, 1874, when he resigned his office and went abroad, intending to spend three or four years in theological and literary study at the University of Oxford. While engaged in his studies he performed ministerial duties in Oxford and the neighboring villages. Two years were devoted to most congenial work, and he had made his arrangements to return to his native country, when he died at Oxford, Oct. 6, 1876. See *Brown University Necrology*, 1877. (J. C. S.)

Coggeshalle, Ralph de, a learned English Cistercian and historian, is chiefly known by his *Chronicle of the Holy Land*, which is valuable because he was an eye-witness of the facts related. He was at Jerusalem, and was wounded there during the siege of that city by Saladin. He died about 1228. See Chalmers, *Biog. Dict.* s. v.; Allibone, *Dict. of Brit. and Amer. Authors*, s. v.

Coggin, David, a Congregational minister, was born in Massachusetts in 1817; graduated from Dartmouth College in 1836, and from Andover Theological Seminary in 1841; was ordained May 11, 1842; was pastor at Westhampton, Mass., and remained there until his death, April 28, 1852. See *Trien. Cat. of Andover Theol. Sem.* 1870, p. 145.

Coggin, Jacob, a Congregational minister, was born at Woburn, Mass., Sept. 5, 1782. He graduated from Harvard College in 1803; studied theology with his pastor, Rev. Jonas Chickering, and was ordained in Tewksbury, Oct. 22, 1806. Here he was sole pastor for more than forty years. Twice he represented Tewksbury in the legislature; was chosen, in 1852, a presidential elector, and in 1853 was a delegate to the convention for revising the constitution of the state. Governor Clifford appointed him one of the inspectors of the state's alms-house, upon the establishment of that institution, and he was chaplain of it till his decease, Dec. 12, 1854. See *Necrology of Harvard College*, p. 41. (J. C. S.)

Coghill, Donald R. M., an English Wesleyan minister, was born in Glasgow, Scotland, where he was converted at the age of fifteen, and was educated at the university there. He was received by the conference in 1834, and sent to Hexham, next to Aberdeen, and finally to Wigton. In 1840 bodily affliction compelled him to give up the active work. He died April 9, 1842. See *Minutes of the British Conference*, 1842.

Cogitōsus, a monk of Kildare, is commemorated on April 18, in the *Mart. Tallaght*, where he is called "the wise." There is great diversity in the dates of his life, as given by different writers, but Lanigan and Petrie prove incontestably that Cogitosus must have written previously to A.D. 831, when Kildare was first plundered, and must have flourished at latest in the beginning of the 9th century (Lanigan, *Eccles. Hist. of Ireland*, i, 379 sq.).

Cogler, Nerignandus, a German poet of the Benedictine order, who lived in the early part of the 17th century, wrote *Stillæ Poeticæ et Profanæ* (Augsburg, 1730). See Hoefer, *Nouv. Biog. Générale*, s. v.

Cognac, Councils of (*Concilium Copriniacense* or *Campaniacum*), were French provincial synods as follows:

I. Held on the Monday after the octave of Easter, 1238, by Gérard de Malemort, archbishop of Bordeaux, together with his suffragans. Thirty-eight canons, or articles of regulation, were published, among which we find some that show what great abuses had then crept into the monastic system.

9. Orders that each bishop shall take care that sentences of excommunication pronounced by a brother bishop be enforced within his own diocese.

12 and 13. Forbid priests and monks to act as advocates in any cause, save that of their own churches or of the poor.

18. Fines those who continue forty days in a state of excommunication.

19. Directs that not only those persons who maltreat a clergyman shall be excluded from holding any ecclesiastical office or preferment, but their descendants also to the third generation.

20. Forbids abbots to give money to their monks in lieu of board, lodging, and clothing; also to take any entrance-fee from new-comers. Orders that, if the revenues of the house are too small for the maintenance of a large number of monks, the number shall be reduced.

22. Forbids monks to leave their walls without leave, and to eat abroad.

25. Orders that if either monk or canon shall be found to possess any property, he shall be deprived of church burial.

29. Forbids them to eat their meals with lay persons.

30. Forbids their living alone in priories, etc.

See Labbe, *Concil.* xi, 556.

II. Held in 1255, by the same archbishop, in which thirty-nine canons were published. The first seventeen are but a repetition of those of the Council of Cognac in 1238.

19. Relates to fasting and abstinence.

20. Prohibits, under pain of excommunication, to eat flesh in Lent, especially on the first Sunday.

21. Contains a list of festivals to be observed throughout the year.

22. Declares that there are but ten prefaces.

23. Forbids the laity to enter the choir during service.

24. Directs that women about the time of their confinement shall confess and communicate.

26. Excommunicates those who attend fairs and markets on Sundays or festival days.

38. Forbids the married clergy to exercise any ecclesiastical jurisdiction.

39. Forbids to bury any corpse within the church, except that of the founder, the patron, or the chaplain.

See Labbe, *Concil.* xi, 746.

III. Held in 1260, by Pierre de Roncevaux, archbishop of Bordeaux. Nineteen statutes were made.

1. Forbids night-service or vigils either in the church or church-yard, on account of the disorders committed by the people who attended.

2. Forbids an ancient custom of dancing within the church on the day of the festival of the Holy Innocents, and choosing a mock bishop.

5. Forbids a priest to marry parties belonging to another parish without the license of the chaplain or prior belonging to that parish.

7. Forbids, under anathema, cock-fighting, then much practiced in schools.

15 and 16. Forbid extra-parochial burial without the curate's permission. One object of this canon was to prevent the ecclesiastical burial of excommunicated persons.

See Labbe, *Concil.* xi, 799.

IV. Held in 1262, by the archbishop of Bordeaux. Seven statutes were published.

1. Lays under an interdict those places in which ecclesiastical persons or property were forcibly detained.

5. Enjoins the clergy to say the office within churches with closed doors in places under interdict, and forbids any of the parishioners attending.

Another council was held by the same archbishop in the following year; the place is uncertain. Seven articles were agreed upon, of which the second declares that a person under sentence of excommunication for twelve months shall be looked upon as a heretic. See Labbe, *Concil.* xi, 820-822.

Cognatius. See Cagnazzo.

Cognatus (or Cousin), Johannes, a Flemish historian and theologian, lived in the early part of the 17th century; was canon of the cathedral of Tournay, and wrote, *De Fundamentis Religionis* (Douay, 1597):—

De Prosperitate ex Exitio Salomonis (ibid. 1599):—*Histoire de Tournai* (in French, ibid. 1619, 2 vols.):—*Historia Sanctorum* (ibid. 1621). See Hoefer, *Nouv. Biog. Générale*, s. v.

Cogshall, ISRAEL, a Methodist Episcopal minister, was born near Schenectady, N. Y., Sept. 22, 1820. He was converted at the age of nineteen; soon afterwards received license to exhort; removed to Michigan, where he was licensed to preach, and, after spending some time teaching school and preaching, was admitted into the Michigan Conference in 1843. At the opening of the Rebellion, he was appointed chaplain of the 19th regiment of Michigan Volunteers; on his return from the army served two years as agent of Albion College, and then again entered the regular itinerant ranks, in which he remained faithful until his death, April 7, 1879. Mr. Cogshall was thoroughly devoted to all the interests of the Church. He was a man of decided opinions and strong convictions, kind, sympathetic, active, studious, and successful. See *Minutes of Annual Conferences*, 1879, p. 65.

Cogswell, James, D.D., a Congregational minister, was born at Saybrook, Conn., Jan. 6, 1720. He graduated at Yale College in 1742, and was ordained in 1744 over the Church in Canterbury, where he labored twenty-seven years. His next charge was Scotland, from 1772 to 1804. He died at the house of his son, Dr. Mason Fitch Cogswell, in Hartford, Jan. 2, 1807. He was "learned, social, benevolent, submissive." He published six *Sermons*. See *Cong. Quarterly*, 1859, p. 353.

Cogswell, Jonathan, D.D., a Presbyterian minister, was born at Rowley, Mass., Sept. 2, 1782. He was converted when seventeen years of age, was educated at Harvard College, ordained in 1810, and stationed at Saco, where he labored with great success for eighteen years. In 1829 he was called to New Britain, Conn., where he labored faithfully for five years. In 1834 he was elected professor of ecclesiastical history in the theological seminary at East Windsor. He retired from public life on account of failing health, in 1844, and resided at New Brunswick, N. J., until his death, Aug. 1, 1864. See Wilson, *Presb. Hist. Almanac*, 1865, p. 85.

Cohana Forseh, in Lamaism, is an idol of the Tartars and Kalmucks, which seems to bear a resemblance to Siva, of India—at least, he is the destroyer. In one of his eight hands he holds a human head by the hair, and a skeleton head in another; out of the fire which surrounds him there is a skull visible. A broad chain of similar ornaments hangs below the breast and thigh. His three eyes see the present, the future, and the past; his eight hands are armed with all sorts of instruments of torture for his victims. At his feet there is a woman, whose head he seems to be about to cut off. He lives entirely in flames, and in these he kills every one who approaches him; therefore Cohana Forseh is the most terrific idol in the entire Tartar circle of deities.

Figure of Cohana Forseh.

Cohen, Abraham BEN-SABATA, a Jewish scholar, was born at Zante in 1670. He died in 1729. He composed a *Paraphrase of the Psalms* in Hebrew verse, published at Venice in 1719. See Hoefer, *Nouv. Biog. Générale*, s. v.; Fürst, *Bibl. Jud.* s. v. Zanti.

Cohen, Moses, a French rabbi of the 3d century, was born at Lunel, in Languedoc. He combated the principles of the famous Maimonides, and gained the esteem of his co-religionists by various works which have not been published. See Hoefer, *Nouv. Biog. Générale*, s. v.

Cohon, ANTHYME DENIS, a French prelate, was born at Craon, in Anjou, in 1594. He was sent to his uncle, canon of the cathedral of Mans, to commence his studies, and thus had no difficulty in gaining admittance to the college of Angers. He hesitated for a time between oratory and law, but finally chose the former. On the resignation of his uncle he became canon of Mans, and later bishop of Nismes. His conduct during the pestilence of 1640 was worthy of much praise. In 1641 he assisted at the assembly of Nantes. On the death of cardinal Richelieu, who had been his patron and protector, he attached himself to cardinal Mazarin. But the Protestants and even the Catholics became his enemies, and Mazarin was obliged to remove him, and he accordingly sent him to the see of Dol. Cohon soon after abdicated in favor of Robert Cupif. After spending two years at the priory of St. Lonan, Cohon returned to the court, and rendered valuable service to Mazarin. At the consecration of Louis XIV he occupied the pulpit of the church at Rheims, and pronounced a discourse. Having already received the abbey of Flaran, after the consecration the young king also gave to him the abbey of Le Tronchet. His recall to the bishopric of Nismes only surrounded him again with trouble and difficulties, and he died there Nov. 7, 1670, leaving, *Lettre a M. le Cardinal de Lyon*, found in MS. in the national library:—*Lettre Contenant la Cabale Secrète avec Mazarin* (Paris, 1649):—*A qui Aime la Vérité* (anonymous):—*Ordonnances Synodales du Diocèse de Nismes* (1670). See Hoefer, *Nouv. Biog. Générale*, s. v.; *Biog. Universelle*, s. v.

Coifi was the chief of the heathen priests of Ædwin, king of Northumbria, in A.D. 627. He advised his master to accept Christianity at the preaching of Paulinus, and he himself desecrated the temple at Goodmanham, where he had so often officiated (Bede, *H. E.* ii, 13).

Coimbra, Bernardo de, a Portuguese Benedictine of the convent of Alcobaça, an encyclopædist of the middle ages, of whom little is known. His book, still in MS., contains, *De Cœlo et Terra, de Luce, Aquis, Sole, Luna et Stellis, de Picibus et Avibus; de Paradiso de Formatione Primi Hominis; de Adam, Eva et Serpente, de Sex Diebus et Septimana; de Adam, Eva et Filiis Eorum; de Enos, Enoch et Noe; de Arca et Diluvio; de Corvo et Columba; de Iride; de Vinea Noe et Inebriatione Ejus;* and in the fourth part, *de Corporali et Spirituali Fornicationi; de Lapsu Cujusdam Virginis; de Violatore Virginis*, etc. See Hoefer, *Nouv. Biog. Générale*, s. v.

Coimbra, Manoel de (1), a Portuguese theologian, born at Obidos, Brazil, was an indefatigable translator, and died in the 17th century, at the age of eighty years, leaving a large number of works, among which we cite, *Banquete da Alma* (1687):—*Practica dos Exercicios Spirituaes de Santo Ignacio* (Lisbon, 1687):—*Astro Vespertino de S. Lucar Theresa de Jesus* (1689):—*Relaçam do Sumptuoso Apparato na Canonisação de Cinco Santos: S. Laurenço Justiniano, S. João Capistrano, S. João de Sahagun, S. João de Deos e S. Paschoal Baylon* (ibid. 1691).

Coimbra, Manoel de (2), a Portuguese theologian, was born in the 17th century, in Coimbra, and belonged to a noble family. He entered the order of St. Francis, and became guardian of the convent of San Francisco de Covilhão in 1695; and occupied the same position at Coimbra about 1706. He became definitor of his order in the chapter of 1709, and died in 1727, leaving, *Epitome Historial da Vida e Virtudes e Portentos do Invicto e Glorioso Padre S. João Capistrano*, etc. (Lisbon, 1692).

Coinchenn (or **Conchenn**) was the name of two Irish virgin saints in the 7th and 8th centuries:

1. COINCHENN OF CAEL-ACHADH is commemorated Aug. 20. Her monastery was probably at Killeigh, King's County, and she died about A.D. 743, according to the Irish annals (Colgan, *Acta Sanctorum*, p. 607).

2. COINCHENN, THE DEVOUT, flourished, according to Colgan, in Ulster, in the beginning of the 7th century. She became abbess of Cill-Sleibhe, and died in 654. She is commemorated on March 13 (Lanigan, *Eccl. Hist. of Ireland*, iii, 38 sq.; O'Donovan, *Four Masters*, i, 168 n., 267).

Coiner, ERASMUS T., a Methodist Episcopal minister, was born in Ross County, O., Feb. 2, 1832. He removed, at the age of sixteen, with his parents to Des Moines County, Ia.; experienced religion in 1852; entered Mount Pleasant Collegiate Institute the same year; graduated at Iowa Wesleyan University in 1857; received license to exhort the same year, and entered the Iowa Conference. In 1861 he enlisted in the Fourth Iowa Cavalry, and was made first lieutenant of company D, in which capacity he proved himself a good soldier and officer, as well as an exemplary Christian. He died at Jacksonport, Arkansas, June 28, 1863. See *Minutes of Annual Conferences*, 1863, p. 156.

Coiningen, in the Irish martyrologies, is called the pupil of St. Mac Tail, bishop of Cill-Cuilinn, who died about A.D. 548, and is said to have been denounced by the clergy of Leinster on her account. She is identified with "St. *Cuach* of Cill-Fionmaighe" in the County Wicklow, and is commemorated April 29.

Coinsi, GAUTIER DE, a French ecclesiastic and poet, was born at Amiens in 1177. He was successively prior of the abbey of Vic-sur-Aisne, and of that of St. Médard of Soissons. He died in 1236, leaving in manuscript a French translation in verse of the *Miracles de Notre-Dame*, written originally in Latin by Hugh Farsi, Herman, Guibert of Nogent, etc. Several copies of this MS. are found in the imperial library of Paris. Some of the accounts of Coinsi were published by Legrand d'Aussi in his *Recueil des Fabliaux*. See Hoefer, *Nouv. Biog. Générale*, s. v.; *Biog. Universelle*, s. v.

Cointa. See QUINTA.

Coinualch (Coinwalch, or **Cenwalh)**, king of Wessex, succeeded his father Cynegils in 643, being still a heathen. In 645, having been driven from his country by Penda, king of Mercia, he took refuge with Anna, king of the East-Angles, at whose court he was converted to Christianity, and baptized by Felix, the bishop of the East-Angles. After three years of exile he returned and introduced Christianity into his dominions. The West-Saxon kingdom was greatly developed during his reign. He is the traditional founder of the see and cathedral of Winchester (Bede, *H. E.* iii, 7; iv, 12). He died in 672.

Coislin, Henri Charles DE CAMBOUT, *duke of*, a French prelate, nephew of the following, was born at Paris, Sept. 15, 1664. He became successively prince-bishop of Metz, first almoner of the king, and member of the French Academy. Like his uncle, he displayed remarkable charity towards his diocesans; but he had a controversy with Rome, particularly on the bull *Unigenitus*. He bequeathed to the abbey of St. Germain the celebrated library inherited by him from chancellor Seguier. Montfauçon gave a catalogue of the Greek manuscripts of the large collection, to a great extent destroyed by a fire in 1793, the remains of which have been collected in the national library. Coislin died in 1732, having published a *Choix des Statuts Synodaux* of his predecessors in 1699:—*Rituel* (1713). See Hoefer, *Nouv. Biog. Générale*, s. v.; *Biog. Universelle*, s. v.

Coislin, Pierre de CAMBOUT DE, a French prelate, was born at Paris in 1636. He became bishop of Orleans, first almoner of the king, then grand almoner of France, and cardinal. He was held in high veneration for his benevolence, and the wise manner in which he accomplished the duties of his office, and for the aid which he rendered the Calvinists in allaying the persecution directed against them by the government after the revocation of the edict of Nantes. He died Feb. 5, 1706. See Hoefer, *Nouv. Biog. Générale*, s. v.; *Biog. Universelle*, s. v.

Coit, Gurdon Saltonstall, D.D., a Protestant Episcopal minister, was born in Connecticut in 1809. He graduated at Yale College in 1828; studied theology in Andover Theological Seminary one year; was ordained deacon Aug. 8, 1830, and presbyter at St. John's Church, Bridgeport, Conn., in 1863; was rector of Christ Church, West Haven, in 1864 and 1865; of St. Michael's Church, Naugatuck, in 1866. After this time he preached occasionally, and died at Southport, Nov. 10, 1869. See *Trien. Cat. of Andover Theol. Sem.* 1870, p. 97.

Coit, John Calkins, a Presbyterian minister, was born at New London, Conn., in 1799. For a time he studied and practiced law, and was president of a bank in Cheraw, S. C. He was finally ordained and installed pastor of an old-school Presbyterian Church in Cheraw. His ecclesiastical and political sentiments were of a very decided character. During the last few years of his life he was without pastoral charge, and, for the improvement of his health, resided in Wisconsin, North Carolina, and South Carolina successively. He died in Cheraw, Feb. 6, 1863. See *Obituary Record of Yale College*, 1864.

Coit, John Summerfield, a Methodist Episcopal minister, was born in New Jersey in 1828. He received a careful religious training; was apprenticed to a carpenter in Newark at the age of seventeen; experienced religion about this time; served the Church as class-leader, exhorter, and local preacher; spent a year and a half in hard study at Pennington Seminary; and in 1853 was admitted into the New Jersey Conference. In 1867 he was transferred to the Des Moines Conference, and in it served zealously until his death, Jan. 7, 1868. Mr. Coit was emphatically a good man, and an humble, devoted, and useful preacher. He was ever ready and courageous. His preaching was sound, practical, and earnest. See *Minutes of Annual Conferences*, 1868, p. 283.

Coit, Joseph, a Congregational minister, was born at New London, Conn., April 4, 1673. He graduated at Harvard College in 1697, and was settled for several years on the Quinebaug, being ordained in 1705 and dismissed in 1748. His territory included what is now Plainfield and Canterbury. He died July 1, 1750, universally lamented. See *Cong. Quarterly*, 1860, p. 289.

Coit, Joseph Howland, D.D., a Protestant Episcopal clergyman, was born in New York city, Nov. 3, 1802. He graduated from Columbia College in 1820; studied two years thereafter in Princeton Theological Seminary; was ordained deacon in 1825; spent nearly the whole of his ministerial life, after 1832, as rector of Trinity Church, Plattsburgh, N. Y., and died there, Oct. 1, 1866. See *Prot. Episc. Almanac*, 1867, p. 101; *Gen. Cat. of Princeton Theol. Sem.* 1882, p. 39.

Coit, J. Townsend, a Presbyterian minister, was born at Buffalo, N. Y., May 8, 1824. He graduated at Yale College in 1844; during his college course was converted; entered the theological seminary at Andover, Mass., in 1845; after completing his studies, sailed for Europe in 1849, and remained there two years. In 1851 he was licensed by the Niagara Presbytery; in 1854, accepted a call from the Church at Albion, N. Y., where he labored for five years; in 1860, accepted a call from the Church of St. Peter's, in Rochester, and died Jan. 23, 1863. See Wilson, *Presb. Hist. Almanac*, 1864, p. 105.

Cok, James, a Scotch clergyman, was admitted the first Protestant minister at Ladykirk in 1585, and was before the assembly in 1597 "for tryal of the ministers of Orkney." There is no further record of him. See *Fasti Eccles. Scoticanæ*, iii, 412.

Cok, Thomas, a Scotch clergyman, took his degree at Edinburgh University in 1612; was admitted to the living of Cross and Burness before July, 1624, the first minister after the parish was formed; transferred to Ladykirk in 1635, and died Jan. 28, 1646, aged about fifty-four years. See *Fasti Eccles. Scoticanæ*, iii, 409, 412.

Cokburne, James, a Scotch clergyman, was presented by the king to the parsonage and vicarage of Ayr in 1573, with the gift of the emolument of Kilmoir in 1576; had a presentation to the living at Muckhart in 1585, and was deposed for non-residence in 1591. See *Fasti Eccles. Scoticanæ*, ii, 776.

Coker, George W., a Baptist minister, was born in Macon County, Tenn., June 11, 1818. He united with the Church in 1837, and soon after was licensed to preach. In March, 1841, he moved to Wayne County, south-east Missouri, where he was ordained in April, 1843. He next took up his residence in Bollinger County, where he lived about twenty years, and during that time had the pastoral care of several churches, itinerating much in that region, and acting as missionary of the Cape Girardeau Association. He moved to Carlyle, Ill., in 1864, where he gathered a church, of which he was pastor, and subsequently had charge of one or two other churches. He died May 25, 1874. See Borum, *Sketches of Tennessee Ministers*, 150-152. (J. C. S.)

Cola, Gennaro di, an old Neapolitan painter, was born in 1320, and studied under Maestro Simone. The principal works of this artist are the altar-piece in Santa Maria, Naples, representing the *Virgin and Dead Christ*, with angels holding the instruments of the passion; *A Magdalene* in the chapel of the same church; *The Nativity* and *The Annunciation*, in the tribune of San Giovanni. He died in 1370. See Spooner, *Biog. Hist. of the Fine Arts*, s. v.; Hoefer, *Nouv. Biog. Générale*, s. v.

Colachus. See Cellach.

Colan, Wilson, a Free-will Baptist minister, was born at Newmarket, N. H., in 1775. In early life he removed to Berwick, Me., and in 1800 removed to Waterville, where he became a Christian, and united with the Church. Subsequently he was ordained. In 1812 he removed to Fairfield, a few miles from Waterville, where he had purchased a farm. He preached on the Sabbath, and attended the meetings of his denomination, quarterly and yearly. Thus he spent fifteen years, and then devoted himself wholly to ministerial work, travelling among the poor churches, seldom receiving anything for his services, but rather contributing from his own resources to help his needy brethren. He died at Fairfield, Aug. 1, 1846. See *Free-will Baptist Register*, 1848, p. 79, 80. (J. C. S.)

Colangelo, Francesco, an Italian theologian and scholar, was born at Naples, Nov. 25, 1769. In 1783 he entered the congregation of the Oratory of Italy, in which he occupied high positions, and in 1820 was raised to the episcopal see of Castellamare. In 1825 he was appointed president of the Council of Public Instruction in the kingdom of Naples. He died Jan. 15, 1836, leaving, *Opuscoli Scientifici di Filalete:—Raccolta di Opere Appartenenti Alla Storia Letteraria:—Il Galileo Proposto Alla Gioventù:—Vita del Pontano:—Vita di Antonio Beccadelli, detto il Panarmita:—Vita di Gio. Battista della Porta:—Vita de San Nazzaro:—La Irreligiosa Libertà di Pensare:—Apologia della Religione Cristiana:—Istoria de' Filosofi e Matematici Napolitani:—Omelia di S. Gio. Crisostomo Intitolata che Cristo sia Dio*, translated from the Greek, with notes. See Hoefer, *Nouv. Biog. Générale*, s. v.

Colas, Jean François (also called *de Guyenne*), a French scholar, was born at Orleans in 1702. He entered the Jesuit order, but withdrew on account of his health, and became successively canon of Saint-Pierre-Empont and of the royal church of Saint-Aignan. He died Nov. 3, 1772, leaving, *Oraison Funèbre de Louis d'Orléans* (Orleans, 1752):—*Discours sur la Pucelle d'Orléans* (ibid. 1760):—*Le Manuel du Cultivateur dans le Vignoble d'Orléans* (ibid. 1770). See Hoefer, *Nouv. Biog. Générale*, s. v.

Colb, Andrew, a Scotch clergyman, was the first Protestant minister to the parish of Redgorton, appointed in 1574, having Luncarty in charge; was presented to the vicarage in 1577, and continued in 1591. See *Fasti Eccles. Scoticanæ*, ii, 655.

Colbenschlag (or **Colbenius**), Stephen, a German engraver, was born at Salzburg in 1591. He visited Italy early, and afterwards Rome, where he resided chiefly, and engraved several plates after the Italian masters, among which are, *The Descent from the Cross; The Adoration of the Shepherds*. He died in 1683. See Spooner, *Biog. Hist. of the Fine Arts*, s. v.

Colberg, Ehregott Daniel, a Lutheran theologian of Germany, was born at Colberg, in Pomerania, Jan. 26, 1659. He studied at the different universities, was for a time professor of ethics and history at Greifswald, afterwards pastor and member of consistory at Wismar, where he died, Oct. 30, 1698. He wrote, *De Tolerantia Diversarum Religionum in Politia:—De Origine et Progressu Hæresium et Errorum in Ecclesia;—De Sapienta Veterum Hebræorum:—Platonisch-hermetisches Christenthum*. See Jöcher, *Allgemeines Gelehrten-Lexikon*, s. v.; Winer, *Handbuch der theol. Lit.* i, 501. (B. P.)

Colberg, Johann, father of the preceding, died doctor and professor of theology at Greifswald, Sept. 19, 1687, leaving, *De Syncretismo:—De Libris Symbolicis:—De Verbo Dei*. See Witte, *Diarium Biographicum;* Jöcher, *Allgemeines Gelehrten-Lexikon*, s. v. (B. P.)

Colbert, Michel, a French ascetic theologian, was born about 1633. He entered the order of Præmonstrants, and became abbot-general in 1670. He died at Paris, March 29, 1702, leaving *Lettres d'un Abbé à ses Religieux* (Paris):—*Lettres de Consolation*, addressed to his sister on the loss of her husband. See Hoefer, *Nouv. Biog. Générale*, s. v.; *Biog. Universelle*, s. v.

Colbert de Seignelay, a French prelate and statesman, was born in 1736 at Castle Hill, in Scotland, the original seat of the Colbert family. Being sent while young to France, he embraced the ecclesiastical calling, shortly after obtained the abbeys of Val-Richer and Sorèze, and became vicar-general of Toulouse at the age of twenty-six. He was appointed, in 1781, bishop of Rode, and held various important positions in the ecclesiastical affairs of his time. Colbert joined great knowledge with sincere piety and pure morals. He died about 1808. See Hoefer, *Nouv. Biog. Générale*, s. v.

Colburn, Hanford, a Methodist Episcopal minister, was received into the Oneida Conference at its organization in 1832, ordained deacon, and sent to Danby Station, which then had only three members, without church, parsonage, or salary, but before a year closed he had a great revival. Subsequently he served Newark, Owego, and Binghamton. He was then made financial agent of Cazenovia Seminary, and in 1840 elected to the principalship of that institution. Being driven by sickness in his family to enter the mercantile business, he located at Elmira; also practiced medicine, which he had studied in his youth, at Albion. At the time of his death, in 1881, he was a member of the Central New York Conference. Mr. Colburn was a wise counsellor, a faithful friend, and a man of God. See *Minutes of Annual Conferences*, 1881, p. 330.

Colburn, Jonas, a Congregational minister, was born at Dracut, Mass., Oct. 25, 1789. He studied at Phillips Academy, Andover, graduated at Middlebury College in 1817, and at Andover Theological Seminary in 1820; travelled a year in western New York as a missionary, and then returned and preached for a short time in several villages in New England, when he was ordained, in 1824, over the Church in Leverett, Mass. His other charges were Stoneham, Mass., and Wells, Me., whence he was dismissed in 1844; and did not again take a settled charge, but preached in various villages according to opportunity. He died in Chicopee, Mass., Nov. 19, 1862. See *Cong. Quarterly*, 1862, p. 191.

Colburn, Moses McLellan, a Congregational minister, was born at Fair Haven, Vt., Sept. 17, 1819. He studied at Burr Seminary, Manchester, and graduated from the University of Vermont in 1844; then taught in Montpelier two years, and graduated from Andover Theological Seminary in 1850. The next year he was ordained pastor of Pacific Church, New Bedford, Mass.; in 1852 was installed at South Dedham (now Norwood), where he remained until 1866; in that year became acting pastor at Waukegan, Ill.; and after a four years' service assumed the same relation to the Church at St. Joseph, Mich., where he remained until his death, Jan. 26, 1876. Mr. Colburn was a conscientious student and an instructive preacher. See *Cong. Quarterly*, 1877, p. 413, 431.

Colburn, Samuel S., a minister in the Methodist Episcopal Church South, was born in Greene County, Tenn., May 1, 1807. He removed to Lafayette County, Mo., in 1831, was converted in 1832, licensed to preach in 1833, and in 1835 entered the Missouri Conference, laboring therein continuously until 1859, when he became superannuated; but still continued to preach, as health permitted, until his death, Aug. 26, 1875. Mr. Colburn was a man of thorough consecration, untiring energy, and living piety. See *Minutes of Annual Conferences of the M. E. Church South*, 1875, p. 235; Simpson, *Cyclop. of Methodism*, s. v.

Colburn, Samuel W., a Congregational minister, was born in Lebanon, N. H., about 1785. He graduated from Dartmouth College in 1808, was ordained at West Taunton, Mass., Aug 29, 1809, and remained there until Dec. 9, 1812. For some months he performed missionary labor in the state of Rhode Island. His health having been restored, he became pastor of the Third Church in East Abington, Mass., Oct. 13, 1813, and remained until Feb. 5, 1830. His subsequent pastorates, which were not of long duration, were at Newark, N. J., West Attleboro, and Sandwich, Mass., and Little Campton, R. I. He died in New York city, Dec. 19, 1854. See *Memorials of R. I. Congregational Ministers.* (J. C. S.)

Colburn, Zerah, for several years an itinerant minister of the Methodist Church, was born at Cabot, Vt., Sept. 1, 1804. He was remarkably precocious, and so noted, as a child, for talent in computation that his father exhibited him in different cities in America and in Europe. Zerah spent three years in the Westminster school in London. On the death of his father in London, in 1824, he returned to the United States, and became a member of the Congregational Church in Burlington, Vt., but not long afterwards joined the Methodists. Mr. Colburn is said to have displayed no uncommon ability as a preacher, and to have lost his peculiar mathematical power. He died at Norwich, Vt., March 2, 1839. (J. C. S.)

Colby, Gardner, a distinguished Baptist layman and philanthropist, was born at Bowdoinham, Me., Sept. 3, 1810. When but twenty years of age he opened a store in Boston, and steadily rose in mercantile success, carrying on for many years the manufacture of woollen goods, in connection with Hon. J. Wiley Edmunds, and during the late civil war becoming a large government contractor for the army. In 1870 he was interested in the building of the Wisconsin Central Railroad, and in securing the government appropriation of lands along its line. Early in his business life he formed the habit of cheerful giving; for years was a trustee and treasurer of the Newton Theological Institution; and gave liberally to Brown University, of which he was a trustee for nearly a quarter of a century. The cause of missions, both home and foreign, found in him an efficient helper. In 1867 the name of Waterville College was changed to that of Colby University, in testimony of the appreciation of the corporation of a gift of $50,000 made to the institution by Mr. Colby. He died at his residence in Newton Centre, April 2, 1879. See *The Boston Advertiser*, May, 3, 1879; *The Watchman*, April 10, 1879; Cathcart, *Baptist Encyclop.* s. v. (J. C. S.)

Colby, John, a Baptist minister, was born in Sandwich, N. H., Dec. 9, 1787, but at fifteen years of age moved to what is now Sutton, Vt. He made a profession of his faith by baptism Dec. 8, 1805, about four years after was licensed to preach, was ordained Nov. 30, 1809, and spent nearly the whole of 1811 in New Hampshire as an itinerant. His work was greatly blessed, revivals of religion everywhere following his labors, especially in Montville, Me., where many were converted. Mr. Colby continued his itinerant work for the next year or two, visiting many sections of New England, and preaching with great zeal and unction. On his way south for the benefit of his health, he died at Norfolk, Va., Dec. 23, 1818. See Barrett, *Memoirs of Eminent Ministers*, p. 55-63. (J. C. S.)

Colclazer, Thomas, a Methodist Episcopal minister, was born in Georgetown, D. C., April 5, 1811. He was converted in Ohio in 1830, and in 1851 entered the North Indiana Conference, in which he labored with zeal and fidelity until his death, Sept. 26, 1865. Mr. Colclazer was a plain, earnest man, a good preacher, and a faithful Christian. See *Minutes of Annual Conferences*, 1866, p. 69.

Colcu. See Colga.

Colczawa, Charles, a Bohemian scholar of the Jesuit order, who lived in the early half of the 18th century, wrote, *Exercitationes Dramaticæ* (Prague, 1703, 3 vols.):—*Progymnasmata in Triplici Genere Chriarum* (ibid. 1708). See Hoefer, *Nouv. Biog. Générale*, s. v.

Colden is the family name of several Scotch clergymen, of whom we notice the following:

1. Alexander, took his degree at the University of Edinburgh in 1675; became minister to the Presbyterian congregation at Enniscorthy, Ireland; was called to the living at Bonkle, Scotland, in 1690; was a member of the General Assembly the same year, and also in 1692; was transferred to Dunse in 1693, and promoted to Oxnam in 1700. He scrupled to take the oath of abjuration, but did so in 1719. He died June 29, 1738, aged eighty-three years. Mr. Colden wrote the preface to Boston's *Crook in the Lot*, and was a true friend of that author, and a minister of true piety, learning, wisdom, and diligence. See *Fasti Eccles. Scoticanæ*, i, 404-408, 510, 511.

2. George, took his degree at the University of St. Andrews in 1627, was presented to the living at Kinross in 1641, and died while attending a meeting of the synod at St. Andrews, April 5, 1665, aged sixty years. See *Fasti Eccles. Scoticanæ*, ii, 596.

3. JAMES, son of the minister at Oxnam, was licensed to preach in 1722; presented to the living at Whitsome in 1723, and ordained; and died Sept. 20, 1754, aged fifty-eight years. See *Fasti Eccles. Scoticanæ*, i, 451.

4. JOHN, second Protestant minister at Borthwick in 1586; was transferred to Newlands, but was refused in 1592; resigned in 1594, and was admitted to Kinross. He, with two others, was appointed to sharply rebuke the earl and countess of Morton for entertaining in their house the earl of Huntly and others. He was a member of the assembly in 1602, and was one of forty-two who signed a protest to parliament in 1606 against the introduction of episcopacy. He opposed the archbishop taking the moderator's chair at the synod in 1607, for which he was censured and restricted to his parish. He died before Oct. 6, 1640. His son George succeeded to the benefice. See *Fasti Eccles. Scoticanæ*, i, 252, 266; ii, 596.

5. ROBERT, took his degree at the University of St. Andrews in 1626; was first a minister in Ireland, but was driven off by the cruelty of the rebels, and a collection was made for him in the kirk at Dunfermline in March, 1643. He was appointed minister at Bonkle, Scotland, in 1650, and died after March 29, 1664. See *Fasti Eccles. Scoticanæ*, i, 408.

6. THOMAS, took his degree at the University of St. Andrews in 1657, was appointed to the living at Dalmeny in 1664, transferred to Carsphairn in 1669, and continued in March, 1672. See *Fasti Eccles. Scoticanæ*, i, 181, 705.

Colding, PAUL JANUS, a Danish scholar, who lived in the early half of the 17th century, and preached at Winding, in the isle of Zealand, wrote *Etymologicum Latinum, cum Interpretatione Donica* (Rostock, 1622). See Hoefer, *Nouv. Biog. Générale*, s. v.

Cole, Albert (1), a Congregational minister, was born at Saco, Me., Feb. 19, 1809. He graduated from Bowdoin College in 1834; studied at the Theological Institute of Connecticut, and completed his course at Bangor, Me., in 1837; was ordained at Blue Hills, Oct. 24, the same year, and, after a successful pastorate, was dismissed Aug. 23, 1843. He died at his native place, March 23, 1845. See *Hist. Cat. of Theological Institute of Connecticut*, p. 15. (J. C. S.)

Cole, Albert (2), a Congregational minister, was born at Cornish, Me., July 15, 1818. He studied at Limerick Academy, and graduated from Bangor Theological Seminary in 1846; was ordained pastor of the Church in Winslow March 24, 1847, and dismissed Dec. 31, 1850. About three years he was acting pastor in Sanford, and held the same position in Limerick from 1853 until December, 1855, when he was installed pastor. Although he resigned this parish in March, 1857, he was not dismissed until March, 1860. He was acting pastor in Cornish from 1858 until his death, Jan. 29, 1881. See *Cong. Year-book*, 1882, p. 25.

Cole, Baxter, an English Independent minister, studied under Dr. Marryat in London. He was first a teacher at Peckham, then morning preacher at Ropemaker's Walk, Moorfields. In 1765 he removed to Wymondham, Norfolk; but in 1766 returned to London, and devoted himself to literary pursuits, for which his learning, piety, diligence, and sound judgment qualified him. He was actively employed in publishing Dr. Lardner's works; in 1793 in editing the *Protestant Dissenters' Magazine*, and several other publications. He died in Essex (his native place), Oct. 13, 1794, aged about seventy years. See Wilson, *Dissenting Churches*, ii, 554.

Cole, Benjamin (1), a Baptist minister, was born in Maine about 1760, and was licensed by the Lewiston Conference (so called), and ordained an evangelist in 1801. In 1802 he was chosen pastor of the Church in Lewiston, and continued in this relation nearly forty years, with the exception of a few short intervals, when he was engaged in missionary labors in destitute sections of the state of Maine. He died in September, 1839. See Millett, *History of Baptists in Maine*, p. 440. (J. C. S.)

Cole, Benjamin (2), a Canadian Methodist minister, was born in Quebec in 1825. He was converted in 1849, entered the Wesleyan ministry in 1855, retired in 1870, and died at Abbotsford, Aug. 2, 1870. He was generous, cheerful, social, an enthusiastic musician, a true friend, and deeply pious. See Carroll, *Case and his Contemporaries* (Toronto), 1867, v, 250.

Cole, Charles, an English Baptist minister, was born at Wellow, Somerset, May 20, 1733. He was brought up in the Church of England, converted in 1753 under a Baptist minister, baptized in 1756; began to preach in May, 1758, at Whitchurch, and for fifty-four years continued to minister there and in some villages around; his church increasing fourfold. He died Dec. 3, 1813. Mr. Cole published some hymns in 1789 with the title *A Threefold Alphabet of New Hymns*. See Gadsby, *Hymn-writers*, p. 39.

Cole, Clifford, a Free-will Baptist minister, was born at Stark, N. H., Feb. 19, 1813. He was converted at the age of fifteen, and united with the Methodist Episcopal Church, of which his parents were members, but subsequently joined a Free-will Baptist Church. He was licensed to preach in 1842; ordained Jan. 13, 1845, and became pastor of the Stark and Milan Church, where, for twenty years, he continued to be loved and respected in the community and blessed in his labors. He died June 10, 1882. See *Morning Star*, July 12, 1882. (J. C. S.)

Cole, Erastus, a Presbyterian minister, was born at Colesville, N. Y., Aug. 13, 1796. He was educated in Oneida Academy, and began his ministerial labors in Colesville. In 1839 he removed to Litchfield, O., where he was pastor for two years; then to Huron, in 1841, where he remained for six years. He died Oct. 18, 1862. Mr. Cole was regarded by his associates as an able, evangelical, and earnest preacher of the Gospel. See Wilson, *Presb. Hist. Almanac*, 1863, p. 290.

Cole, George (1), an English Baptist minister, was born at Bodiest, Northamptonshire, Jan. 13, 1798. He was converted at the age of fifteen, joined the Wesleyans, and became a local preacher. In 1823 he united with a Baptist church in Kimbolton. He studied under his pastor, and in 1826 was ordained in Lynn, Norfolk; in 1828 became pastor in Kenilworth, in 1831 in Leamington, and in 1838 removed to Evesham, Worcestershire. In 1842 he accepted a call to the Church Street Church, Blackfriars, London. His next pastorate was in Exeter, and his last in Naunton, Gloucestershire, where he died, Dec. 31, 1857. See (Lond.) *Baptist Hand-book*, 1858, p. 48. (J. C. S.)

Cole, George (2), a Baptist educator and editor, was born at Sterling, Conn., June 22, 1808, and graduated from Brown University in 1834. From that year to 1837 he was professor of mathematics in Granville College (now Denison University), O. In 1838 he became editor of what is now *The Journal and Messenger* at Cincinnati, which office he held for nine years. For several years he was engaged in secular business, being, for a part of the time, one of the editors of the *Cincinnati Gazette*. In 1856 he returned to his old position as editor of *The Journal and Messenger*, and remained in this position until 1864. He died in Dayton, Ky., July 14, 1868. See Cathcart, *Baptist Encyclop.* p. 245. (J. C. S.)

Cole, George Washington, a Protestant Episcopal minister, was born at Saco, Me., Jan. 5, 1805, and graduated from Bowdoin College in 1830. After teaching in Germantown, Pa., for a year, he pursued a course of theological study in the General Theological Seminary of New York. For two years thereafter he was a professor in Bristol College, Pa.; was next rector of a parish in Westchester for a year; of a parish in Tecumseh, Mich., four years; and had entered upon his ministerial duties in Kalamazoo, when he died, in 1840. See *Hist. of Bowdoin College*, p. 408. (J. C. S.)

Cole, Isaac D., a minister of the Reformed (Dutch) Church, was born at Spring Valley, N. Y., Jan. 25, 1799. His early life was passed in the Collegiate Church of New York city, under the instructions of Drs. J. H. Livingston, J. N. Abeel, and G. A. Kuypers; and from 1807 to the date of his conversion, in 1818, under the ministry of Christian Bork. Owing to repeated attacks of blindness, brought on by excessive study, his attempts to enter college were defeated. In 1826 he became a successful teacher in New York city. The difficulty with his eyes having passed away, he graduated from New Brunswick Seminary in 1829; was licensed by the Classis of New York, Aug. 4 of that year; and ordained by the Classis of Paramus, May 24, 1831. He was assistant pastor at Tappan from November, 1829, to May 24, 1831; colleague at Tappan until Dec. 12, 1832; Second Church, Totowa, till Dec. 16, 1833; Tappan again, to Feb. 9, 1864; and afterwards remained without a charge, but occasionally supplied the Presbyterian Church at New Hempstead, N. Y., till Aug. 30, 1878, when he died. He was a plain, strong, clear, honest, earnest, loving man and preacher. See Corwin, *Manual of the Ref. Church in America* (3d ed.), p. 213.

Cole, James, an English Baptist minister, was born in 1776, converted in early life, and became pastor of an Independent Church in Bury St. Edmunds. In 1801 he was baptized by immersion, and became, in 1806, the pastor of the Baptist Church in the same place in which he began his ministerial work. Here he remained until 1817, and then removed to Otley, where, for more than sixteen years, he labored with much acceptance and success. He died May 26, 1837. See (Lond.) *Baptist Hand-book*, 1838, p. 22. (J. C. S.)

Cole, Jirah D., D.D., a Baptist minister, was born at Catskill, N. Y., Jan. 14, 1802. He was converted under the ministry of Dr. Howard Malcom, then a youthful pastor in Hudson; was baptized in Catskill, March 4, 1821. He pursued his literary and theological studies at Hamilton, graduating in 1826. After supplying the Church in Greenville for a short time, he was ordained, Sept. 12, 1827, and was pastor in Ogden until Nov. 21, 1831; for three years at Fredonia; then supplied the Second Church, Rochester, several months; supplied the Church at Parma Corners for a time, and for two years and a half preached at Fabius. After this he became the soliciting agent of the Missionary Union, one year in New York and another in Ohio, Indiana, Illinois, and Missouri. The two following years he was pastor in Ithaca, N. Y.; then agent of the American Baptist Home Society for Maine, New Hampshire, and Vermont; for five years (1843-48) pastor at Whitesborough, N. Y., and meanwhile acted as corresponding secretary of the New York Baptist Convention. From 1848 to 1850 he was pastor at Nunda. In 1850 he received an appointment to the north-western agency of the Missionary Union, and had his headquarters at Chicago. This position he held for seven and a half years; then became pastor in Delavan, Ill., and in 1860 in Barry. His other pastorates were in Galva, Cordova, Atlanta, Lockport, and Rosetta, Ill., and Valparaiso, Ind. He died in Chicago, March 27, 1883. During this long period of service he performed a large amount of work as an author and compiler. He was one of the editorial committee appointed to prepare the memorial volume of the first half century of Madison University, and was also the author of a *History of the Rock Island Association.* As the appointed historian of the Baptists of Illinois, he left, at his decease, a work in MSS., which is represented as being one of great value. See the *Chicago Standard*, April 5, 1883; Cathcart, *Bapt. Encyclop.* p. 246. (J. C. S.)

Cole, Joseph, an English Wesleyan minister, commenced his ministry in 1780; retired in 1815, residing at Carmarthen, and died Jan. 8, 1826, aged seventy-eight. He had peculiar tact in rebuking sin with effect, yet without giving offence. See *Minutes of the British Conference*, 1826.

Cole, Leroy, a Methodist Episcopal minister, was born in Essex County, Va., June 5, 1749. He was converted in 1777; the same year was licensed to preach, and admitted into the travelling connection. He began his ministry in North Carolina; preached regularly until long after the Revolution; served the Church some years as a local preacher, and spent his latter life as a superannuate of the Kentucky Conference, dying triumphantly, Feb. 6, 1830. See *Minutes of Annual Conferences*, 1831, p. 115.

Cole, Nathaniel, a Baptist minister, was born at Swansea, Mass., July 14, 1780. In his youth he removed to Otsego County, N. Y., where he was employed partly as a mechanic, and partly in teaching. In 1806 he settled as a merchant in Southfield, Madison Co., where he was also a magistrate, and then county judge. In 1812 he represented the town in the New York Assembly. In 1816 he was baptized by Rev. Nathaniel Moore, and united with the Church in Fenner. With but limited preparation for the Christian ministry, he was ordained April 8, 1818, continued to preach for nine years, and died July 4, 1827. Mr. Cole was a peacemaker, yet firm, bold, decided, quick, ready, and communicative. See Haynes, *Bapt. Cyclop.* i, 181. (J. C. S.)

Cole, Robert W., a minister in the Methodist Episcopal Church South, was born in East Tennessee in 1818. He received an early religious education; became eminently pious in youth, and at the age of eighteen entered the Tennessee Conference. In 1841 he was transferred to the Memphis Conference; spent 1843 and 1844 very usefully as a local preacher; re-entered the effective ranks in 1845, and was appointed to the Belmont Circuit, where he died, Oct. 8, 1846. Mr. Cole was extremely modest and retiring, and never appeared to be conscious of his intellectual powers. He was sound in judgment and doctrine, and eminently equipped with all the Christian graces. See *Minutes of Annual Conferences of the M. E. Church South*, 1846, p. 78.

Cole, Samuel (1), a Congregational minister, was born at Mexico, N. Y., Jan. 18, 1807. He received his preparatory education at Oneida Institute and at Oberlin, and graduated from Oberlin Theological Seminary in 1838. In 1839 he was ordained an evangelist at Oberlin, and labored as such for some years. He was acting pastor at West Tisbury, Mass., from 1851 to 1855; at Weymouth, O., from 1855 to 1861; West Gloucester, Mass., from 1861 to 1867; at Saybrook, O., from 1867 to 1871; at Randolph, from 1872 to 1876. From thence he removed to Kingsville, where he remained without charge until his death, March 15, 1877. (W. P. S.)

Cole, Samuel (2), a Baptist minister, was born in Massachusetts in 1823. He graduated from Waterville College in 1850, and from the theological seminary in Rochester in 1852. He had a vigorous intellect, and took high rank as a scholar. His ordination took place in Belfast, Me., July 27, 1853. During his short pastorate he gave himself to the work with an intensity of devotion rarely excelled. "Humble, studious, and spiritual, success attended his efforts, and a brilliant future opened before him." Prostrated by disease brought on by overwork, he went to his father's house in Beverly, Mass., and died there, Nov. 11, 1854. See *Watchman and Reflector*, Dec. 21, 1854. (J. C. S.)

Cole, Thomas (1), an English divine, was born in 1726. He was educated at Queen's College, Cambridge, where he took the degree of LL.B. in 1751. At the time of his death, June 6, 1796, he was vicar of Dulverton. He was the author of, *The Arbour, or, The Rural*

Philosopher (1756, 4to):—*Discourses on Luxury, Infidelity, and Enthusiasm* (1760, 12mo):—*The Life of Hubert*, a narrative, descriptive, and didactic poem (1795, 8vo). See *The* (Lond.) *Annual Register*, 1796, p. 62.

Cole, Thomas (2), a celebrated painter, was born at Bolton-le-Moors, Lancashire, England, Feb. 1, 1801. His parents, who had previously lived in America, returned in 1819, and settled in Philadelphia, where young Cole applied himself to wood-engraving and music. In 1820 he began portrait-painting in Steubenville, O., and afterwards took up historical painting. In 1825 he removed to New York city, and laid the foundation of his fame by painting scenes among the Catskills. His finest pictures are the four called *The Voyage of Life*, which have been engraved. He died at Catskill, N. Y., Feb. 11, 1847. A *Memoir* of him has been written by Rev. L. L. Noble (N. Y. 1855).

Cole, Thomas (3), a Presbyterian minister, was born in Delaware. He spent over two years (1824, 1825) in Princeton Theological Seminary, and was then ordained by the Presbytery of Gallipolis, O. He was in 1830 and 1831 stated supply for a church in New Richmond; labored as missionary in Ohio in 1832 and 1833; was pastor in Augusta, Ky., in 1836, for a Congregational Church; agent for the American Bible Society, St. Louis, Mo., from 1855 until his death, July 18, 1870. See *Gen. Cat. of Princeton Theol. Sem.* 1881, p. 49.

Cole, William, an English clergyman and an eminent antiquary, was born at Little Abington, Cambridgeshire, Aug. 3, 1714. He was educated at Saffron-Walden, Eton, and Clare Hall, Cambridge, where he was admitted to one of Freeman's scholarships in April, 1734. During 1736 and 1737 he travelled in Flanders and Portugal. In 1739 he was made commissioner of peace in the county of Cambridge. He was ordained deacon in 1744, and was for some time curate to Dr. Oakes, rector of Wethersfield, in Suffolk. He was admitted to priest's orders in 1745, and elected a fellow of the Society of Antiquaries in 1747. He went to France in 1768, after having been rector for some years of Bletchley, in Buckinghamshire, which place he resigned March 20, 1767. He then removed to Waterbeche, and from thence to Milton, near Cambridge, where he died, Dec. 16, 1782. Among his works are Grose's *Antiquities*:—Bentham's *Ely*:—*Life of Cardinal Pole*:—*Collection of Poems*, and some *Sermons*, which he left to Cambridge University. See Chalmers, *Biog. Dict.* s. v.; Allibone, *Dict. of Brit. and Amer. Authors*, s. v.

Cole, William J., a Methodist Episcopal minister, was born about 1843. He began preaching at the age of eighteen, under the direction of the Canadian Wesleyan Conference; removed to Charleston, S. C., in 1865; immediately connected himself with the South Carolina Mission Conference, and in its active ranks died, July 13, 1867. Mr. Cole possessed uncommon mental power, a remarkable winsomeness of manner, a prepossessing personal appearance, and an energy and perseverance that knew no hinderance. See *Minutes of Annual Conferences*, 1868, p. 11.

Colebrooke, Thomas, a famous Sanscrit scholar, was born in London, England, in 1765. In 1782 he went to India, where he devoted himself to the study of Sanscrit. After an absence of thirty years he returned to London, and died there in 1837. He was one of the first scholars who made Europe acquainted with the religion, legislation, history, and science of the Hindûs. His essays, published in the *Transactions of the Asiatic Society* at Calcutta and London, were reprinted in 1837, under the title of *Miscellaneous Essays*. His paper on the philosophy of the Hindûs was translated into French by Pauthier. See Lichtenberger, *Encyclop. des Sciences Religieuses*, s. v. (B. P.)

Colefax, William, an English Congregational minister, was born near Nantwich in 1792. He was left an orphan in early childhood; converted in his twentieth year; received his ministerial training at Idle Academy, and was ordained pastor in 1821 at Hexham. In 1833 he removed to Pudsey, Yorkshire, where he continued till 1846, when he resigned the ministry. He died March 6, 1872. See (Lond.) *Cong. Year-book*, 1873, p. 321.

Coleman, Andrew (1), an extraordinary young Irish Methodist preacher, was born in Coleraine, County Antrim. At the age of seventeen he had mastered the usual studies of a college curriculum. He was converted under the ministry of Thomas Barber, a Wesleyan evangelist; in 1785 was recommended to the Dublin Conference, and sent to the Sligo Circuit. After a few months' exhausting labor he returned to Coleraine, and died, June 18, 1786, aged eighteen years. Coleman's was a lovely character—humble, modest, affectionate, and thoroughly consecrated. He had a brilliant mind and a wonderful memory. See Etheridge, *Life of Dr. Adam Clarke*, p. 51; Clarke, *Miscellaneous Works* (edited by Everett), xii, 348: Everett, *Wesleyan Centenary Takings*, i, 229.

Coleman, Andrew (2), a Methodist Episcopal minister, was born in West Virginia, April 5, 1790. He entered the Pittsburgh Conference in 1825; in 1842 was transferred to the Rock River Conference; in 1844 became a member of the Iowa Conference, and in 1856 of the Upper Iowa Conference. The following were his appointments: Dubuque, Rock Island, Burlington, Burlington District, De Moines District, Pittsburgh Circuit, Iowa City District, Pioneer Circuit, Lisbon, De Witt, Cedar Rapids, Rockdale, La Motte, Iowa City Circuit, De Witt Circuit. In 1872 he became superannuated, and resided at Oskaloosa, Ia., where he died, May 4, 1881. Mr. Coleman was an eminently godly man, of catholic spirit and ardent zeal. See *Minutes of Annual Conferences*, 1881, p. 321.

Coleman, Henry, an English Congregational minister, was born at Harrold, Bedfordshire, March 11, 1809. He was educated at Newport-Pagnell College, and settled at Wickhambrook, in Suffolk, in 1838. Here he labored with eminent success until the beginning of 1864, when he removed to Halesworth, and thence, in 1868, to Penryn, Cornwall, where he continued ten years. He retired finally from active service in August, 1879, and died at Southampton, Aug. 11, 1882. See (Lond.) *Cong. Year-book*, 1883, p. 271.

Coleman, Isaiah B., a Free-will Baptist minister, was born March 7, 1809. He was licensed to preach May 10, 1834; ordained in March, 1835, and served as pastor of the Church in West Stephentown, N. Y., about forty years. He assisted in the organization of several churches of his denomination, and was ever ready to respond to calls upon his services as a minister of the Gospel. He died March 14, 1883. See *The Morning Star*, April 4, 1883. (J. C. S.)

Coleman, James, a Methodist Episcopal minister, was born in Black River Township, N. J., Oct. 30, 1766, of Presbyterian parents, who removed west of the Alleghanies in 1777, and settled on the Monongahela river. About the close of the Revolution he was converted, licensed to exhort, and in 1791 entered the itinerant ranks, and was appointed to Ohio Circuit. Subsequently he served several years as a missionary in Upper Canada, where he endured dreadful privations, and exhibited wonderful zeal and fidelity. His latter years were spent as a superannuate in the New York Conference. He died at his residence in Ridgefield, Conn., Feb. 5, 1842. Mr. Coleman was a man of very limited intellectual culture, but of many Christian graces. His great faith, singleness of heart, and marvellous unction in prayer made him powerful in the extension of Christ's kingdom. See *Minutes of Annual Conferences*, 1842, p. 309.

Coleman, James A., a Methodist Episcopal minister, was born at Baltimore, Md. He was converted at the age of fourteen, licensed to exhort two years later, two later to preach, and at the age of nineteen was employed as junior preacher on Castle Fin Circuit, Baltimore Conference. In 1851 he became a member of the conference, was sent as junior preacher to Shrewsbury Circuit, and afterwards in turn to Westminster, Liberty, and Hampstead, Md.; was appointed to Alleghany Circuit in 1855; afterwards served Bedford Circuit, Cassville, and Birmingham Circuit, Pa.; became chaplain in the United States navy on board a receiving-ship in the harbor of Brooklyn, N. Y., and thirteen months later removed to Philadelphia, Pa., where he remained a superannuate, until his death, March 30, 1879. Mr. Coleman was affable, earnest, affectionate, and pre-eminently successful. See *Minutes of Annual Conferences*, 1880, p. 23.

Coleman, John, a Protestant Episcopal minister, was a native of Bath Parish, Dinwiddie Co., Va. He was educated and prepared for the ministry principally by the Rev. Devereux Jarratt; but the war of the Revolution prevented his obtaining orders in England. In 1780 he became a Methodist local preacher, but left that Church in 1784. In 1787 he was admitted to holy orders, and became minister of St. John's and St. James's parishes, in Baltimore County, Md. For four years (1799-1803) he was rector of St. Thomas's Parish, in the same county, and then returned to that of St. James. He died in Baltimore County, Jan. 21, 1816, aged fifty-eight years. Mr. Jarratt committed to Mr. Coleman the publication of his *Autobiography*. For seventeen years the latter was a member of the Standing Committee, and five times was a delegate to the General Convention. In 1804 he was named as a candidate for the suffragan episcopate of Maryland, but failing health prevented his election. See Sprague, *Annals of the Amer. Pulpit*, v, 220.

Coleman, Lyman, D.D., an eminent Presbyterian or Congregational divine and educator, was born at Middlefield, Mass., June 14, 1796. He graduated at Yale College in 1817, and for three succeeding years was principal of the Latin Grammar School in Hartford, Conn.; next a tutor in Yale College for four years, during which time he studied theology. From 1828 to 1835 he was pastor of the Congregational Church at Belchertown, Mass. After this he taught, first at the Burr and Burton Seminary in Vermont, next for seven years as principal of the English department of Phillips Academy, Andover. He then made a visit to Germany, and spent seven months in study with Neander, the eminent historian, which resulted in the preparation of his learned work, *Primitive Christianity*. On his return he was made professor of German in Princeton College. He continued there and at Amherst and Philadelphia the next fourteen years, having also a connection with various other institutions. In 1856 he revisited Europe, and extended his travels to the Holy Land, the Desert, and Egypt. In 1861 he succeeded Dr. Cattell in the chair of ancient languages in Lafayette College, but after 1862 devoted himself solely to Latin. For many years he continued his lectures to the students on Biblical and physical geography. He was also professor of Hebrew, conducting classes in that study for fifteen years. He died at Easton, Pa., May 16, 1882. Eminent in solid abilities, in accurate scholarship, in stores of accumulated learning, in extended usefulness, Dr. Coleman was no less eminent in the graces of the Spirit. His principal published works are, *The Antiquities of the Christian Church:—The Apostolical and Primitive Church:—Historical Geography of the Bible:—Ancient Christianity Exemplified:—Historical Text-book and Atlas of Biblical Geography:—A Manual on Prelacy and Ritualism;* all of which have been republished in England. See *The Presbyterian*, March 25, 1882; Allibone, *Dict. of Brit. and Amer. Authors*, s. v.; Kellogg, *Commemorative Sermon* (Easton, 1882). (W. P. S.)

Coleman, Reuben, a Methodist Episcopal minister, entered the travelling ministry in connection with the Texas Conference, in 1870, and labored faithfully until his decease, Dec. 3, 1875. Mr. Coleman was a man of commanding presence, irreproachable character, and of earnestness and effectiveness in the ministry. See *Minutes of Annual Conferences*, 1876, p. 8.

Coleman, Seymour, a Methodist Episcopal minister, was born in Litchfield County, Conn., Dec. 23, 1794, of devout Huguenot parents. About 1812 he removed with them to Fulton County, N. Y., where he engaged in school-teaching from the age of eighteen to thirty-one, meanwhile zealously continuing his study of books and men. He was also, during this time, admitted to the bar of Fulton County; but soon after gave up his profession, began preaching, and in 1828 entered the New York Conference. In 1832, on the formation of the Troy Conference, he became a member of it. His appointments extended through all the districts of that large conference. He died at his post, Jan. 23, 1877. Mr. Coleman was endowed with a forcible intellect, and natural heroism. His religious experience was rich, and his daily life unsullied. See *Minutes of Annual Conferences*, 1877, p. 67.

Coleman, Thomas (1), a Puritan divine, was born at Oxford, England, in 1598. He was vicar of Blyton, and subsequently rector of St. Peter's, Cornhill, London, and died in 1647. He published sermons and theological treatises (1643-46). See Allibone, *Dict. of Brit. and Amer. Authors*, s. v.

Coleman, Thomas (2), an English Congregational minister, was born at Kettering in 1798, and was studiously and religiously inclined from childhood. He was refused admission to Hoxton Academy on account of the loss of one of his eyes, yet he persevered in the work of self-improvement. In 1822 he became pastor of the Independent Church at Wollaston, Northamptonshire, and in 1831 at Ashley and Wilbarston. Failure of health in 1867 compelled him to resign. Subsequently he became totally blind, yet, from the tenacity of his memory and his disciplined habits of thought, he continued to preach almost to the end of his life, frequently conducting the whole service himself. He died at Market Harborough, Dec. 30, 1872. Mr. Coleman is spoken of as being "a strenuous student." His historical acquirements, especially, were very considerable. He published, *Memorials of the Independent Churches in Northamptonshire:—The Two Thousand Confessors of 1662:—The English Confessors after the Reformation to the Days of the Commonwealth;* also other works, chiefly expository, as well as contributing many articles to denominational periodicals. See (Lond.) *Cong. Year-book*, 1874, p. 318.

Coleman, Thomas Clarke, a minister of the Methodist Episcopal Church South, was born in Jefferson County, Ga., Feb. 8, 1794. He was left an orphan when but a few months old; was converted about 1810; licensed to exhort in 1826, to preach in 1832, and in 1838 entered the Georgia Conference. For about twenty years he labored on circuits, and in mission fields in Georgia and Florida. Failure of health then obliged him to retire from all stated services, and he spent the following years in great bodily suffering. He died July 25, 1875. Mr. Coleman had scarcely any early educational advantages. His wife taught him to read. His mental habits were fixed before he entered the ministry, and he never acquired the capacity for sermonizing; yet he was a preacher of rare success through the power of his exhortations and prayers. He was all aflame with zeal and devotion. His life was exemplary, full of pathos, sympathy, and deep devotion. See *Minutes of Annual Conferences of the M. E. Church South*, 1875, p. 173.

Coleman, William (1), an English Baptist minister, was born in 1776. His first settlement in the ministry was at Lessness Heath, Kent, where he was ordained in 1809. Here he remained from 1809 to 1823, and then removed to Colnbrook, Bucks, where he was pastor from 1823 to 1845. In 1846 he accepted a call to the Church at Bexley Heath, Kent, where he died, Oct. 4, 1848. See (Lond.) *Baptist Hand-book*, 1849, p. 41. (J. C. S.)

Coleman, William (2), a Canadian Methodist minister, was a Cornishman. He was converted at nineteen; emigrated to Canada in 1831; was a lay evangelist for six years; entered the ministry in 1837, retired in 1872, and died at his home at Scarborough, Ont., May 27, 1879, aged seventy-one years. Mr. Coleman was a man of thorough consecration and of strong and constant piety. See *Minutes of the Toronto Conference*, 1879, p. 15.

Coleman, William A., a Baptist minister, was born of Episcopal parentage, near St. John, N. B., November, 1816. He united with the Baptist Church at Portland, Dec. 25, 1840; was ordained at North Esk in 1845; labored in several fields, baptized one thousand and fifty persons, and died at Sackville, March 7, 1877. He was characterized by executive ability, judgment, dignity, calmness, and humility. See *Minutes of Baptist Convention of N. S.*, etc., 1877; Bill, *Fifty Years with the Baptists*, p. 537.

Colendal, Heinrich, a German theologian of the Jesuit order, was born at Cologne, April 15, 1672. He was successively missionary, professor of theology at Osnabruck, royal chaplain at Dresden, preacher and rector at Cologne. He died Jan. 23, 1729. His principal works are, *Confabulatio Catholicum inter et Lutheranum* (Cologne, 1710):—*Osnabrugensis Rusticus Edoctus* (ibid. eod.):—*Nullitas Sacerdotii Lutheranorum* (ibid. 1713). See Hoefer, *Nouv. Biog. Générale*, s. v.

Coleoni, Celestini, an Italian historian and theologian of the Capuchin order, a native of Bergamo, lived in the early half of the 17th century. His principal works are, *Istoria Quadripartita di Bergamo* (Bergamo and Brescia, 1617, 1619, 3 vols.):—*Vita S. Patritii*, etc. (Brescia, 1617):—*De Matrimonio Gratæ Virginis* (ibid. 1719):—*Vita Firmi et Rustici* (ibid. 1618). See Hoefer, *Nouv. Biog. Générale*, s. v.

Colenso, John William, D.D., an Anglican prelate, was born at St. Austell, Cornwall, Jan. 24, 1814. He took all but the highest mathematical honors at Cambridge in 1836; was successively a master at Harrow (1838), a resident fellow and private tutor at St. John's College, Cambridge (1842), rector of Forncett St. Mary, near Norwich (1846), and was consecrated bishop of Natal on the creation of that see in 1853. Great excitement was caused by his publication of *St. Paul's Epistle to the Romans, newly Translated* (1861), in which he denied the doctrine of eternal punishment. But a still greater agitation was caused by his *Pentateuch and Book of Joshua Critically Examined* (in seven parts, 1862–79), in which he questioned the authenticity of the Pentateuch. This called forth innumerable replies and criticisms, and even severe Church discipline. The bishop of Capetown, who, by the various letters patent, was metropolitan of the Church of England in South Africa, summoned the bishop of Natal to his tribunal on a charge of heresy, and deposed him from office. The judicial committee of the privy council set aside, on constitutional grounds, the sentence of deposition. The trustees of the Colonial Church Bishoprics' Fund nevertheless withheld bishop Colenso's salary, and he sued for it before lord Romilly, master of the rolls. That judge declared that heresy would be a justification for withholding the salary, and that, if the charge were preferred, it would be his duty to try it in accordance with the law of the Church of England. But the charge was not preferred, and, of course, the Capetown deposition could not be held a justification. Thus the bishop of Natal continued to enjoy his salary and the property of his see, and with a good conscience, for it was the opinion of his friends that a charge of heresy could not have been maintained against him under the standards of the Church of England. He died at Natal, June 20, 1883. Besides a series of mathematics for schools, and some minor works, bishop Colenso published, *Lectures on the Pentateuch and the Moabite Stone* (1873):—the *New Bible Commentary Critically Examined* (1871–74). He also translated the New Test. and part of the Old Test. into the Zulu language, and published a Zulu grammar with dictionary. (B. P.)

Coler, Jakob, a Lutheran theologian of Germany, was born at Grätz, in Voightland, in 1537. He studied at Frankfort-on-the-Oder, was in 1564 pastor at Lauban, in Upper Lusatia, and in 1573 at Neukirch, where he held a colloquy with L. Crentzheim and M. Flacius, concerning original sin. In 1575 he was made doctor of theology and professor of Hebrew at Frankfort; in 1577 he was called to Berlin as member of consistory; became in 1600 superintendent of the Güstrow district in the duchy of Mecklenburg, and died March 7, 1612. He assisted Hutter in the edition of his famous Hebrew Bible, and wrote, *De Immortalitate Animæ:—De Exorcismo:—De Libero Arbitrio*. See Köller, *Wolaviographia*; Jöcher, *Allgemeines Gelehrten-Lexikon*, s. v. (B. P.)

Coler, Johann Christoph, a German Protestant theologian and bibliographer, was born Sept. 7, 1691, at Alten-Gottern, near Langensalza. He studied at Wittenberg, and was made adjunct to the philosophical faculty in 1716. In 1720 he became pastor at Brücken, but four years later went to Weimar, as teacher at the gymnasium. In 1725 he was appointed pastor of St. James's, in 1731 court preacher, and died at Weimar, March 7, 1736. His principal works are some academical dissertations: *De Ephræmo et Joanne Damasceno* (Wittenberg, 1714):—*Historia Gothofr. Arnoldi* (ibid. 1718):—*Acta Litteraria Academiæ Wittebergensis* (ibid. 1719):—*Bibliotheke Theologische* (Leips. 1724–36):—*Anthologia, seu Epistolæ Varii Argumenti* (ibid. 1725):—*Acta Historico-ecclesiastica*, an ecclesiastical gazette, written in German (Weimar, 1734). See Hoefer, *Nouv. Biog. Générale*, s. v.

Coler, Johann Jakob, a German theologian, was born at Zurich in the 16th century. He was one of the pupils of Theodore Beza, and wrote *An Anima Rationalis sit ex Traduce* (Zurich, 1586). The success of this little treatise was very great, and Rodolphe Goclenius printed it a second time in his collection of writings upon the origin and nature of the soul, *De Hominis Perfectione* (Marburg, 1694). We are also indebted to Coler for *Præfatio in Epistolas Hutteni*, with a collection of letters from Hutten (Nuremberg, 1604). See Hoefer, *Nouv. Biog. Générale*, s. v.

Coleridge, John, an English clergyman, father of the poet, was vicar of Ottery St. Mary, in Devonshire, and died about 1781. He published *A Critical Latin Grammar:—Miscellaneous Dissertations Arising from the 17th and 18th Chapters of the Book of Judges* (1768). He is said to have been a man of learning and research. See Allibone, *Dict. of Brit. and Amer. Authors*, s. v.

Coleridge, William Hart, a bishop of the Church of England, was appointed to the see of Barbadoes at its erection in 1824, and resigned the bishopric in 1841. Upon the establishment of St. Augustine's College, Canterbury, he was chosen its first warden, possessing eminent talent for the education of missionaries. He died at Ottery St. Mary, Devonshire, Dec. 21, 1849, in the sixtieth year of his age. His scholarship was unquestionable. See *Amer. Quar. Church Rev.* 1850, p. 160.

Coles, John, an English Baptist minister, was born at Luton, Bedfordshire, in 1782. He was ordained Nov. 5, 1813, pastor at Poplar, Middlesex, and remained there until 1818. His next settlement was at Workingham, Berkshire, where he remained from 1819 to 1839. Besides performing his home duties, he labored extensively in the neighboring villages. On completing his term of service, he retired from ministerial labor. He died in London, Jan. 9, 1842. See (Lond.) *Baptist Hand-book*, 1842, p. 24. (J. C. S.)

Coles, Thomas, an English Baptist minister, was born in the parish of Hawling, Gloucestershire, Aug. 31, 1779. Soon after joining the Church of which the Rev. Benjamin Beddome was the pastor, he entered the college at Bristol, where he studied for a time, and then became a student in Marischal College, Aberdeen, where he graduated A.M. In Scotland, he devoted himself with great zeal to the spiritual welfare of the young. He was ordained at Bourton, Nov. 17, 1801, where he remained during his entire ministerial life, nearly thirty-nine years, "highly esteemed by his brethren, and very useful in the public denominational institutions of the county." He died Sept. 23, 1840. See *Report of English Baptist Unions*, 1841, p. 33. (J. C. S.)

Colette, *Saint*, a French nun and reformer, whose family name was *Boilet*, was born at Corbie, in Picardy, Jan. 13, 1380. From infancy she was remarkable for her piety. After having lived successively at the house of the Beguines, the sisters of the third order of St. Francis, then in a hermitage, she entered the order of the nuns of St. Clare, and conceived the thought of working a reform. Benedict XIII, Pedro de Luna, the acknowledged pope at Avignon, approved her design, and invested her with the necessary power to accomplish it. She failed in France, but succeeded in Savoy, Burgundy, the Netherlands, and Spain. She died at Ghent, March 6, 1446, and her canonization was pronounced March 3, 1807, by Pius VII. See Hoefer, *Nouv. Biog. Générale*, s. v.

Coletti (or **Coleti**), **Giovanni Domenico**, an Italian scholar of the Jesuit order, brother of Niccolo, was born in 1727. He was for ten years missionary to Mexico. On his return to Italy he resided at the College of Bagnacavallo, and retired to his family after the suppression of his order. He died at Venice in 1799. His principal works are, *Vida de S. Juan Apostoli* (Lima, 1761):—*Dizionario Storico-Geografico dell' America Meridionale* (Venice, 1771):—*Notize Istoriche della Chiesa di San Pietro in Sylvis di Bagnacavallo* (ibid. 1774):—*Memorie Istoriche Intorno al Cav. Cesare Ercolani* (ibid. 1776):—*Luciferi Episcopi Calaritani Vita, cum Notis, Operibus Præfixa* (ibid. 1778):—*Hispellates Inscriptiones Emendatæ* (ibid. 1780):—*De Nova Ovarii Voce et Officio* (ibid. 1781):—*Notæ et Siglæ quæ in Nummis et Lapidibus apud Romanos Obtinebant Explicatæ* (ibid. 1785):—*Lettera Sopra l'Iscrizione Pemmoniana dell' Altare di San Martino di Cividale Friuli* (ibid. 1789):—*Triclinium Opiterginum* (ibid. 1794), also a large number of MSS., preserved by his family. See Hoefer, *Nouv. Biog. Générale*, s. v.

Coletti (or **Coleti**), **Jacopo** (or **Giacomo**), an Italian scholar of the Jesuit order, lived at the close of the 18th century. On the suppression of the Jesuits, he returned to his family and devoted himself to study and ecclesiastical labors. His principal works are, *Dissertazione Sugli Antichi Pedagogii* (Venice, 1780, inserted in the *Opusculi Ferraresi*):—*De Situ Stridonis, Urbis Natalis S. Hieronymi* (ibid. 1784). Coletti also worked on a continuation of the *Illyricum Sacrum* of Daniele Farlati, and the publication of the work of Lucifero, bishop of Cagliari, by his brother Giovanni Domenico. See Hoefer, *Nouv. Biog. Générale*, s. v.

Coletti (or **Coleti**), **Niccolo**, a learned Italian ecclesiastic, was born at Venice in 1680. He resigned the direction of a library and printing establishment which he had formed at Paris, in order to devote himself entirely to the study of history and ecclesiastical antiquities. Coletti died in 1765. He published a new edition of the *Italia Sacra* of Ughelli, purged of several errors, and continued it from 1648, where the author had left it, down to the 18th century. This edition, commenced in 1717, was completed in 1733, ten vols., in fol. Coletti likewise worked on a new edition of the *Collection des Conciles* of Labbe, which he enriched with notes and valuable additions. He also wrote, *Series Episcoporum Cremonensium Aucta* (Milan, 1749):—*Monumenta Ecclesiæ Venetæ S. Moïsis* (1758). See Hoefer, *Nouv. Biog. Générale*, s. v.

Coley, Charles H., a Protestant Episcopal clergyman, resided, in 1857, in Madison, Ga., while yet a deacon, and subsequently, in 1859, became rector in that place of the Church of the Advent. In 1861 he was assistant minister of Christ Church, Savannah, a position in which he remained until 1868, when he became rector of the Church of the Redeemer, Shelbyville, Tenn.; in 1870 was rector of St. Mark's Church, Brunswick, Ga.; in 1872 officiated in Christ Church, Savannah; and in 1873 became rector of Trinity Church, Demopolis, Ala. He died March 26, 1874, aged forty-three years. See *Prot. Episc. Almanac*, 1875, p. 144.

Coley, James M., a Baptist minister, was born at Cazenovia, N. Y., in 1806. He pursued his studies in the literary and theological institution at Hamilton, where he graduated in 1828. Subsequently he spent one year (1833–34) at the Newton Theological Institution, and was ordained at Charlemont, Mass. For two years he was pastor at Beverly, which place he left in February, 1836. His other settlements were in Binghamton and Carmel, N. Y., Norwich, Conn., Albany and Waverly, N. Y. His labors at Albany were especially blessed. On giving up the pastoral office he removed to Auburn, Ill. A few years after, he went to California for his health, and died at San José, Jan. 8, 1883. He was an able preacher, of commanding presence, and an uncommonly impressive delivery. See *The Watchman*, March 29, 1883. (J. C. S.)

Coley, Samuel, a Wesleyan minister, was born at Birmingham, England, Feb. 17, 1825. He was converted when about six years of age, joined the Wesleyans at twelve, began to preach at sixteen, and after a three years' residence at the theological school at Richmond, received an appointment to the Hastings Circuit in 1847. He filled some of the most important stations of the Church. In 1873 he was appointed theological tutor at Headingly. He resigned this position in 1880, and in August of the same year settled at Warwick, and died Oct. 30 following. "As a preacher he stood in the first rank of the most popular men of the day." His theological lectures "were models of clearness in the exposition of truth." He published comparatively little. His *Life of Thomas Collins* is one of the best of Christian biographies. See *Minutes of the British Conference*, 1881, p. 20.

Colfridus. See CEOLFRID.

Colga (or **Colchu**; Irish, *Coelchu*), is the name of several early Irish saints:

1. COLGA, "*the Wise*," lector of Clonmacnoise, was a man of eminent piety and learning, and acquired the name of chief scribe or master of all the Scots. He was appointed to preside over the great school of Clonmacnoise; was a special friend and correspondent of Alcuin, at Charlemagne's court, and composed the *Scopa Devotionis*, or *Besom of Devotion*, a collection of most ardent prayers in the form of litanies, and full of the warmest devotion to God. He died about A.D. 796, and is commemorated on Feb. 20 (Lanigan, *Eccl. Hist. of Ireland*, iii, 228 sq.; Todd and Reeves, *Mart. Doneg.* p. 55).

2. COLGUS, or COLGANUS, was of the powerful family of the Hy-Fiachrach, in Connaught. He is chiefly known in connection with St. Columba. He flourished about A.D. 580, and probably died in his native land, according to St. Columba's promise (Lanigan, *Eccl. Hist. of Ireland*, ii, 328).

3. COLGIUS, or COLCIUS, son of Cellach, was another

disciple and associate of St. Columba. According to the Irish annals he died about A.D. 622 (Lanigan, *Eccl. Hist. of Ireland*, ii, 328; Colgan, *Acta Sanctorum*, p. 381, 382.

4. COLGA, abbot of Lusk, in Leinster, flourished about A.D. 694, and was one of the chief prelates who attended the synod at Armagh, convened by Flann Febhla and St. Adamnan about A.D. 697 (Lanigan, *Eccl. Hist. of Ireland*, iii, 140).

5. COLGA, or CAOLCHU, of Lui-Airthir, is commemorated Sept. 24 (Todd and Reeves, *Mart. Doneg.* p. 257).

Colgan, THOMAS, a missionary of the Church of England, came to America in 1726 to take charge of the Church in Rye, N. Y., under the direction of the Society for the Propagation of the Gospel in Foreign Parts; but afterwards became assistant to the Rev. William Vesey, rector of Trinity Church, New York city, and remained in that position until 1732, when he became minister of the Church in Jamaica, L. I. He died there in 1755. See Sprague, *Annals of the Amer. Pulpit*, v, 16.

Colhard, CHRISTIAN, a German poet and theologian, who lived in the early part of the 18th century, wrote, *Ara Eucharistica* (Frankfort, 1704, 1728):—*Epistolæ Familiares Carmine Elegiaco* (Berlin, about 1720):—*Epistolographia Metrica* (ibid. 1724). See Hoefer, *Nouv. Biog. Générale*, s. v.

Coli, GIOVANNI, an Italian painter, was born at Lucca in 1634, and studied under Pietro da Cortona. Some of his works are in the churches of Rome. The most celebrated were the frescos in the tribune of the Church of San Martino, in Lucca. The whole cloister of the monastery of the Carmelites was painted by him. He died in 1681. See Spooner, *Biog. Hist. of the Fine Arts*, s. v.; Hoefer, *Nouv. Biog. Générale*, s. v.

Colidi. See CULDEES.

Coligny (or **Coligne**), ODET DE, a French prelate, son of marshal de Châtillon and Louise de Montmorenci, was born July 10, 1517. When hardly sixteen years of age he was appointed one of the cardinals who were to elect the pope. He went to Rome to take his place in the consistory, and assisted in the election of Paul III, who made him archbishop of Toulouse in 1534, and relieved him from the obligation of residing at Rome. He was raised to the episcopal see of Beauvais in 1535, and took a great interest not only in the affairs of his country, but also promoted arts and sciences. In 1550 he was called to Rome to assist in the election of pope Julius III. In 1554 he gave to his diocese the *Constitutions Synodales*, which were intended to suppress certain abuses. The firm attitude of the Parisian parliament against the house of Guise, in 1558, which sought to bring France under the yoke of the inquisition, delivered Coligny from a snare, since he was designed to be one of the three inquisitor-generals. Without pronouncing himself openly for the new faith, to which his brothers already adhered, he put himself politically on their side and against the Guises, assisted at the assembly held in Fontainebleau in 1560, and finally broke with the Church of Rome in 1561 by celebrating at Beauvais the Lord's Supper in accordance with the Protestant rite. A tumult which soon broke out endangered his life. He gave up his ecclesiastical dignities, and assumed the title of count of Beauvais. During the first religious war he accompanied his brothers and Condé to Orleans, and after the peace of Amboise he returned to the court of France. In the meantime he had been reported to the inquisition at Rome as a heretic, and on his refusal to appear before the tribunal, the pope hurled at him a bull of excommunication, March 31, 1563. He was henceforth called by his family name, *Châtillon*, although he himself retained his title of cardinal Coligny. In 1568 he negotiated the peace which followed the siege of Chartres. The violation of the peace by Catharine de' Medici necessitated the retreat of Condé and Coligny to La Rochelle. Châtillon's life, as well as that of Condé, being endangered, he succeeded in sailing to England, where he hoped to serve the cause of his brothers and of liberty. He publicly married Elizabeth de Hauteville. Queen Elizabeth treated him with due respect, and his influence often neutralized the measures of the French ambassador, Lamothe-Fénélon. After the peace of 1570, the latter changed his attitude towards the cardinal, and even entered into direct relations with him in the hope of securing his co-operation. Châtillon, upon an invitation of Gaspard de Coligny to return to France, made his preparations for the journey, but died Feb. 14, 1571, under suspicion of being poisoned, which a post-mortem examination justified. He was buried at Canterbury. In Odet de Coligny the French Protestants lost one of their firmest supporters. See De Bouchet, *Pr. de Christ. de la Maison de Coligny*, p. 347–442; Brantôme, *Homines Illust.* s. v., "Le Cardinal de Châtillon;" Dupont-White, *La Ligne à Beauvais; Corresp. Diplom. de Lamothe-Fénélon*, i, p. 16 sq.; ii, p. 49 sq.; iii, p. 17 sq.; iv, p. 12 sq.; Delaborde, in Lichtenberger's *Encyclop. des Sciences Religieuses*, s. v. (B. P.)

Colla. See EOLLA.

Collace is the family name of several Scotch clergymen:

1. ANDREW, took his degree at King's College, Aberdeen, in 1611; was presented to the living at Gariock in 1615, transferred to Ecclesgreig in 1619, to Dundee in 1635; deposed in 1639 for drunkenness, sacrilege, and disobedience to the General Assembly; was settled at Dunse in 1663, and died Sept. 13, 1664, aged about seventy-three years. See *Fasti Eccles. Scoticanæ*, i, 404; iii, 689, 863, 870.

2. DAVID, was appointed to the living at Drainie in 1633, and ordained, and died June 3, 1681. See *Fasti Eccles. Scoticanæ*, iii, 161.

3. FRANCIS, took his degree at Edinburgh University in 1610; was presented to the vicarage of Channelkirk in 1614, and admitted to the living in 1615; signed the protestation for the liberties of the kirk in 1617; was transferred to Gordon in 1625, and died in 1647, aged about fifty-seven years. See *Fasti Eccles. Scoticanæ*, i, 521, 525.

4. JOHN, was appointed to the living at Fettercairn in 1580; had Newdosk under his care in 1585, and died March 16, 1587. See *Fasti Eccles. Scoticanæ*, iii, 866.

Collaceroni, AGOSTINO, an Italian painter, was a native of Bologna, and studied under Padre Pozzi. He was an eminent perspective artist, and was much employed in adorning the churches at Rome, Bologna, and other cities. He flourished about 1700.

Collado, DIEGO, a Spanish Dominican, was born at Mezzadas, in Estremadura. He assumed the habit of his order at Salamanca in 1600. After having taught belles-lettres, he embarked for Japan in 1619, and, in spite of persecution, preached the Gospel for several years. In 1625 his superiors sent him to Rome to solicit of the pope more extended powers. While in Europe he published several works, the material for which he had collected in his travels. Urban VIII having at length delivered a brief favorable to the wishes of the missionaries, Collado went to Spain in 1632, obtained of the king letters-patent for the foundation of a convent of his order in the Philippine Islands, and embarked again in 1635. Arriving there, he met with much opposition from the governor, but nevertheless succeeded in carrying out his project. Being recalled to Spain in 1638, he embarked, but the ship was wrecked, and he perished. His works are, *Ars Grammatica Linguæ Japonicæ* (Rome, 1631):—*Dictionarium sive Thesauri Linguæ Japonicæ* (ibid.; compendium, 1632):—*Historia Ecclesiastica de las Successas de la Christiandad de Japon* (Madrid, 1632):—*Modus Confitendi et Examenandi Pœnitentem Japonensem*, etc. (Rome, 1631):—

Dictionarium Linguæ Sinensis (still unpublished). See Hoefer, *Nouv. Biog. Générale*, s. v.; Chalmers, *Biog. Dict.* s. v.

Colladon, Nicolas, a Swiss Protestant theologian of French origin, lived in the latter part of the 16th century. He left Bourges, where he was minister, retired to Geneva, and became, in 1564, rector of the academy of that place. Two years later he succeeded Calvin as professor of theology. The boldness of his preaching brought him into difficulty with the sovereign council of Geneva, and he retired to Lausanne, where he taught belles-lettres. He translated into French Beza's work, *De Hæreticis Gladio Puniendis* (1560); and wrote *Methodus Facillima ad Explicationem Apocalypseos Johannis* (Morges, 1591):—*Jesus Nazarenus, ex Matthæo, chap. ii, v.* 32 (Lausanne, 1586). See Hoefer, *Nouv. Biog. Générale*, s. v.; *Biog. Universelle*, s. v.

Collaert, Adrian, a Flemish designer and engraver, was born at Antwerp about 1520, studied in his native city, and died there in 1567. The following are his principal works: *The Last Judgment; The Israelitish Women Celebrating the Destruction of the Egyptian Host in the Red Sea; The Calling of St. Andrew to the Apostleship.* See Spooner, *Biog. Hist. of the Fine Arts*, s. v.; Hoefer, *Nouv. Biog. Générale*, s. v.; Chalmers, *Biog. Dict.* s. v.

Collaert, Hans, a Flemish engraver, son and scholar of Adrian, was born at Antwerp about 1540. He visited Rome for improvement, afterwards returning to Flanders, where he executed a number of plates dated from 1555 to 1622. The following are the principal: *St. John Preaching in the Wilderness; Moses Striking the Rock;* and the subjects from the lives of Christ and the Virgin. See Spooner, *Biog. Hist. of the Fine Arts*, s. v.; Hoefer, *Nouv. Biog. Générale*, s. v.

Collar. The neck-cloth worn by the clergy does not date earlier than the beginning of the 18th century. The ruff of the time of Elizabeth fell into desuetude before the falling collars of the time of James and Charles I.

Collas, a learned French missionary and astronomer, of the Jesuit order, was born at Thionville about 1731. He taught mathematics at the University of Lorraine, and in 1767 went to Pekin, where he acted as mathematician to the emperor of China. He died Jan. 22, 1781, leaving several very important sketches, inserted in a collection of the *Mémoires* upon the Chinese, viz.: *État des Reparations et Additions Faites à l'Observatoire Vâti depuis Longtemps dans le Maison des Missionnaires Français à Pekin*, and others. See Hoefer, *Nouv. Biog. Générale*, s. v.; *Biog. Universelle*, s. v.

Collatines. See Oblates.

Collatio is a term for the reading from the lives or *collationes* of the fathers, which St. Benedict (*Regula*, c. 42) instituted in his monasteries before compline. Such compilations as the *collationes* of John Cassian were read. Ardo Smaragdus, however, says that this service was called *collatio* because the monks questioned each other on the portions to be read. The Benedictine practice is to hold this service in the church, and this is probably in accordance with the founder's intention, for he evidently contemplated the collation being held in the same place as compline (Ducange, s. v.).

Collation is (1) the free assignment of a vacant canonry or benefice; (2) reading of devout books from the pulpit by the reader of the week, followed by an exposition from the superior in chapter; (3) a sermon after a funeral; (4) a lecture on the catechism established in 1622; (5) the monastic supper. During the first four centuries there was but one full meal taken daily by monastics, and that was supper (*cœna*). When the mid-day meal was adopted, a slender repast of bread, wine, and dry fruit, not worthy of the name of supper, was taken after vespers, during the reading, or "collation," of the Scripture or fathers—and so the name was given to the meal, and adopted by laymen and priests. The *jentaculum*, or breakfast, consisted of a basin of soup.

Collatius, Petrus Apollonius, an Italian priest and poet, a native of Novarra, lived at the close of the 15th century. He wrote, *De Eversione urbis Jerusalem Carmen Heroïcum* (Milan, 1481; republished under the title *Apollonius, de Excidio Hierosolymitano*, Paris, 1540; Antwerp, 1586), a poem on the destruction of Jerusalem under Vespasian:—*Heroicum Carmen de Duello Davidis et Goliæ, Elegiæ et Epigrammata* (ibid. 1692; republished several times). See Hoefer, *Nouv. Biog. Générale*, s. v.

Colle, Raffaellino dal, an Italian painter, was born at Colle, near Borgo San Sepolcro, in Tuscany, about 1490, and was a pupil of Raphael. Later in life Colle resided at Borgo San Sepolcro, where he kept a school of design. He died at Rome in 1530. His works are to be found at Urbino, at Perugia, at Pesaro, and at Gubbio. The best are, *The Resurrection*, and an *Assumption*, in the churches at Borgo San Sepolcro. See *Encyclop. Brit.* (9th ed.) s. v.; Hoefer, *Nouv. Biog. Générale*, s. v.; Rose, *Biog. Dict.* s. v.; Graves's ed. of Bryan's *Dict. of Painters*, s. v.

Collect is (1) a church appointed as the starting-point and place of assembly of a procession going to a station, as, for instance, the collect was at Santa Sabina, on the Aventine, when the station was fixed at the basilica of St. Paul; (2) a prayer so called, because collected into one form out of many petitions, or from the people being joined in as one, or because offered for the whole collective Church, or a particular Church. Most collects end "through Jesus Christ," because the Father bestows his gifts through the mediation of Christ only. The five parts of a collect are the *invocation;* the *reason* on which the petition is founded; the *petition* itself; the *benefit* hoped for; and *ascription* of praise, or mention of the Lord Jesus, or both. The collects in the mass were composed by pope Gelasius. At St. Alban's, in the 12th century, they were limited to seven. The collects were included in the Collectarium, and the collects at the end of the communion service, matins, and even-song, etc., fulfil the definition of micrologus, as the concluding prayer in an office, in which the priest gathers up and collects all the prayers of the people, to offer them to God. Out of the eighty-three used in the English Church, fifty-nine are traceable to the 6th century.

Collecta. See Cornelia.

Collecta, in liturgical phraseology, is (1) the collecting of alms or contributions of the faithful. From Leo the Great we learn that such a collection was sometimes made on a Sunday, sometimes on Monday or Tuesday, for the benefit and sustenance of the poor. These collections seem to have been distinct from oblations. (2) The gathering together of the people for divine service. Jerome (*Epist.* 27) states that the sound of *Alleluia* called monks to say their offices (*ad collectam*). Pachomius (*Regula*, c. 17) speaks of the *collecta* in which oblation was made; he also distinguishes between the *collecta domus*, the service held in the several houses of a monastery, and the *collecta major*, at which the whole body of monks was brought together to say their offices. In this rule, collecta has very probably the same sense as *Collatio*. (3) A society or brotherhood. So in the 15th canon of the first council of Nantes (Hincmar, *Capitula ad Presbyt.* c. 14).

Collectarium is a book of collects or short prayers, anciently called a "coucher." The latter word appears to be thus derived: collectarium, collectier, colctier, coulctier, couctier, couchier, coucher. The term "coucher" is frequently found in English mediæval MSS., and occasionally in church inventories and churchwardens' accounts.

Collectio is a name, in the Gallican missals, for

certain forms of prayer and praise. The principal of these are the *Collectio post Nomina*, which follows the recitation of the names on the diptychs; the *Collectio ad Pacem*, which accompanies the giving of the kiss of peace; the *Collectio post Sanctus*, which immediately follows the "Holy, Holy, Holy," and the *Collectio post Eucharistiam*, after communion.

Colledge, Thomas, an English Congregational minister, was born at Wirksworth, July 6, 1804, of pious parents. He joined the Church at the age of seventeen, and at twenty-three began preaching. In 1832 he entered Rotherham College, and at the close of his course became pastor at Reeth, Yorkshire. Thence he removed to Riddings, where he died, Aug. 23, 1875. See (Lond.) *Congregational Year-book*, 1876, p. 323.

College of Augurs was the institution of soothsayers among the ancient Romans. See Augur.

Colleges of Piety were associations for the study of the Bible and the promotion of personal piety among certain of the Lutherans in the 17th century. See Pietism.

Collegia de Propaganda Fide. See Collegia Pontifica; Propaganda.

Collegium Dendrophorium (*the College of the Dendrophori*, from δένδρον, *a tree*, and φέρω, *to carry*), were a class of heathen (probably priests) whose duty it was to carry branches of trees in processions in honor of the gods.

Collen, a Welsh saint of the 7th century, was patron of Llangollen, in Denbighshire, and is commemorated on May 20 (Rees, *Welsh Saints*, p. 302).

Colleoni, Girolamo, an Italian painter, was born at Bergamo about 1495. His paintings in the Church of San Antonio dell' Ospitale, at Bergamo, were destroyed by fire. There is one in San Erasmo, near Bergamo, which represents *The Virgin and Infant, with Magdalene and Saints*, and is one of his most esteemed works. See Spooner, *Biog. Hist. of the Fine Arts*, s. v.; Rose, *Gen. Biog. Dict.* s. v.

Colleschi, Francesco, a learned Italian theologian, who died in 1746, wrote, *Dissertazione della Letteratura de' Sacerdoti Antichi*, in the *Raccolta Caloger.* vol. xxxiv:—*Dissertazione della Religione degli Indiani*. See Hoefer, *Nouv. Biog. Générale*, s. v.

Collet, Pierre, a French theologian and doctor of divinity, was born at Terney, near Montoire (Loir-et-Cher), Sept. 6, 1693. From his youth he was employed at the house of the brothers of Saint-Lazare, and taught theology in several houses of his order. He was afterwards principal of the Collége des Bons-Enfants in Paris, and died there Oct. 16, 1770. He wrote a large number of works, among them, *De Quinque Jansenii Propositionibus* (Paris, 1730):—*Traité des Dispenses en Général* (ibid. 1742, 1746, 1752, 1758, 1759, 1777, 1788, 1828; Avignon, 1829):—*Institutiones Theologiæ* (Paris, 1744, 1756):—*Institutiones Theologiæ Moralis* (ibid. 1758, which is the fifth edition, the dates of the others being unknown):—*Institutiones Theologiæ Scholasticæ* (Lyons, 1765, 1767, 1768; Paris, 1775):—*Vie de Saint-Vincent-de-Paul* (Nancy, 1748; Paris, 1818, with some writings from St. Vincent de Paul):—*Lettre d'un Théologien au R. P. A. de G.* (Antony of Gasquet) (Brussels, 1763):—*Traité des Devoirs de la Vie Religieuse* (Lyons, 1765; Paris, 1773):—*L'Écolier Chrétien* (ibid. 1769):—*Le Dévotion au Sacré Cœur de Jésus* (ibid. 1770):—*Traité des Exorcismes de l'Église* (ibid. eod.):—*Instructions sur les Devoirs des Gens de la Compagne* (ibid. eod.). See Hoefer, *Nouv. Biog. Générale*, s. v.; Chalmers, *Biog. Dict.* s. v.

Collett, Thomas, an English Congregational minister, was born at Lostwithiel, Cornwall, Feb. 8, 1797. He joined the Church in early manhood; received his ministerial training at Hackney Academy; began his ministry at Witney, Oxfordshire; and finally settled at Dawlish, on the south coast of Devon, in 1824. In June, 1866, Mr. Collett resigned his pulpit, but continued to reside among the scenes of his lifelong labors, beloved by all who knew him, until his death, June 10, 1869. See (Lond.) *Cong. Year-book*, 1870, p. 281.

Colley, Benjamin, an English Wesleyan minister, was born at Tollerton, near Easingwold, Yorkshire. He united with the Methodists in 1761; and, having received Episcopal ordination, was in that year invited by Wesley to officiate in the Methodist chapels in London, which he did. In 1762 he was "carried away by the enthusiasm of George Bell and Thomas Maxfield." He was soon restored, however, by John Manners; and in July, 1763, was engaged in the work at Newcastle-upon-Tyne. Thereafter, until his death in 1767, he was a faithful and godly worker. Although he deeply regretted his slip, he was ever after subject to strong temptations; and, as Wesley (who believed his backsliding cost him his life) says, "he went heavily all his days." See Atmore, *Meth. Memorial*, s. v.; Wesley, *Journal*, Nov. 8, 1767.

Colley, Thomas, an English minister of the Society of Friends, was born at Smeaton, near Pontefract, Yorkshire, in 1742. He was brought up in the Established Church; religiously awakened before he reached his majority, and joined the Methodists, among whom he was zealous, active, and much esteemed. About 1764 he united with the Friends, and in 1768 began his ministry. In 1779, in company with Philip Madin, of Sheffield, he visited the West India islands, and performed considerable Christian labor there. Some years after he travelled extensively in North America. Subsequently he itinerated much in his native land, and was very useful in his vocation. He died in Sheffield, June 12, 1812. See *Piety Promoted*, iv, 29, 33. (J. C. S.)

Colli, Antonio, an Italian painter of the Roman school, flourished about 1700, and studied under Andrea Pozzi. He painted the great altar in the Church of San Pantaleo. See Spooner, *Biog. Hist. of the Fine Arts*, s. v.

Collie, William, a Scotch clergyman, took his degree at King's College, Aberdeen, in 1718; became schoolmaster at Drainie in 1732, and assistant minister at Duffus; was presented to the living at Drainie in 1741, and ordained. He died April 29, 1768, aged about seventy years. See *Fasti Eccles. Scoticanæ*, i, 161.

Collier, Arthur, an English metaphysician and divine, was born at the rectory of Langford Magna, near Sarum, Oct. 12, 1680, and was educated at Salisbury Grammar School and Pembroke College, Oxford. In 1704 he was presented to the benefice of Langford Magna, where he continued until his death, in 1732. In religion he was an Arian, and also a High Churchman, on grounds which his associates could not understand. The following are some of his works: *Treatise on the Logos*, in seven sermons (1732):—*New Inquiry after Truth*, on the non-existence of an external world:—*Specimen of True Philosophy*. See *Encycl. Brit.* 9th ed. s. v.; Hoefer, *Nouv. Biog. Générale*, s. v.

Collier, Ephraim Robins, a Baptist minister, who died in 1840, graduated at Harvard College in 1826, and had rare classical tastes and excellent scholarship. See Sprague, *Annals of the Amer. Pulpit*, vi, 378.

Collier, Ezra W., a (Dutch) Reformed minister, was born at Plymouth, Mass., about 1832. He graduated at Rutgers College in 1849, and at New Brunswick Theological Seminary in 1854. He was noted in his student life for close application, literary culture, and scholarly enthusiasm. His first settlement was with Manhattan Reformed Church, New York city (1854–56). For the next ten years he was pastor in Freehold, N. J.

His health being greatly impaired he removed to Coxsackie, N. Y.; but after a year was obliged to relinquish all active duties. He lingered in great feebleness until his death in 1869. He was one of the most brilliant and devoted of the younger ministers of his Church, and heroic in the utterance of his views, a true scholar, and a Christian gentleman. His studies took a wide range —beyond mere professional requirements. In 1865 he edited a volume of posthumous *Sermons* by his brother, Rev. Joseph A. Collier, to which he prefixed an interesting biographical sketch. (W. J. R. T.)

Collier, Francis, an English Wesleyan minister, was converted at the age of twenty under the preaching of John Nelson; commenced his ministry at Derby in 1796; travelled twenty-three circuits, becoming a supernumerary in 1837 at Taunton, and died June 25, 1851, aged eighty-two. He was an able preacher, and stood high in the connection. See *Minutes of the British Conference*, 1851.

Collier, F. G., an English Congregational minister, was born at Hartlepool, Feb. 6, 1847. He was educated at the Lancashire Independent College, and ordained at Wigan in 1871. He accepted the pastorate of New Chapel, Horwich, which, after four years, he was forced to resign on account of failing health. He died at West Kirby, Cheshire, March 30, 1881. See (Lond.) *Cong. Year-book*, 1883, p. 273.

Collier, Joseph, an English Wesleyan minister, was born at Stockport, Oct. 31, 1770. He was converted at the age of fourteen; admitted into the ministry in 1795; was prostrated on the Bradford Circuit, but still labored; became a supernumerary in 1811, first residing in Bury, subsequently in Exeter and at Kingsdown, Bristol; resumed his ministry at Haverford-West in 1813, and travelled several circuits. His last was Nottingham, where he died, May 27, 1842. See *Minutes of the British Conference*, 1842; *Wesl. Meth. Mag.* 1850, p. 337 sq.

Collier, John (1), a Scotch clergyman, took his degree at the University of St. Andrews in 1650; was presented to the living at Firth and Stenness in 1662; transferred to Carrington in 1663; deprived for refusing the test in 1681; and died in Edinburgh Nov. 13, 1691, aged about sixty-two years. See *Fasti Eccles. Scoticanæ*, i, 270; iii, 396.

Collier, John (2), an English Wesleyan Methodist minister, was born at Little Houghton, Northamptonshire, in 1803. He united with the Church in 1821; was received by the Conference for the ministry in 1829; toiled for thirty-five years on some of the most laborious circuits; became a supernumerary in 1864; and died at Torquay, Feb. 27, 1870. Mr. Collier was instrumental in saving many souls, and was earnest, faithful, and amiable. See *Minutes of the British Conference*, 1870, p. 26.

Collier, Richard, a Lutheran minister, was a native of Dundalk, Ireland. Arriving in America in his youth, he settled in Easton, Pa., and for many years was engaged in teaching. In 1833 he was licensed by the New York Synod; in 1834 was ordained pastor at Spruce Run, N. J., and served there twenty-seven years. He died in New York city, Jan. 1, 1861. See *Lutheran Observer*, Jan. 18, 1861.

Collier, Thomas, an English Baptist minister, was born about 1600. For some time he preached with great success in the island of Guernsey, although his enemies spoke in bitter terms of him. In 1645 Mr. Collier, in order to vindicate himself, published *Certain Queries or Points, now in Controversy, Examined*, in which he maintained, like Roger Williams, that magistrates have no power whatever to establish Church government, or to compel any persons to observe the government of Christ. He was the author of several other works of a controversial character. See Haynes, *Baptist Cyclop.* i, 178. (J. C. S.)

Collier, William, an English divine, was born in 1742. He was for many years a tutor in Trinity College, Cambridge; rector of Orwell, Cambridgeshire; and Hebrew professor from 1771 to 1790. He died Aug. 4, 1803, at which time he was senior fellow of Trinity College. Mr. Collier published, by subscription, *Poems on Several Occasions, with Translations from Authors in Different Languages, Dedicated to Prince William of Gloucester* (1800, 2 vols. 12mo). See *The* (Lond.) *Annual Register*, 1803, p. 516; Allibone, *Dict. of Brit. and Amer. Authors*, s. v.

Colliette, Louis Paul, a French antiquarian of the middle of the 18th century, was curate of Gricourt, near St. Quentin, and wrote, *La Vie de St. Quentin* (St. Quentin, 1767):—*Mémoires Ecclésiastiques* (Cambray, 1771–72, 3 vols.). See Hoefer, *Nouv. Biog. Générale*, s. v.; *Biog. Universelle*, s. v.

Colliflower, William F., a minister of the (German) Reformed Church, was born in Washington County, Md., Feb. 14, 1814. He received his education in the Reformed High School and Theological Seminary at York, Pa.; was licensed to preach by the Classis of Maryland in 1836; soon afterwards entered upon the ministerial work in Virginia, being ordained and installed as pastor of the Mill Creek charge. He labored successively in Virginia, Maryland, and Pennsylvania, and died in Frederick, Md., April 30, 1882. Mr. Colliflower was a man of fair talents, great energy, and sincere piety; popular and successful as a preacher. (D. Y. H.)

Collin, Friedrich Eberhard, a Lutheran theologian of Germany, was born at Worms, Dec. 25, 1684. In 1709 he was appointed preacher at Dertingen; in 1724 was called as deacon to Zeulenroda, and in 1725 to Lobenstein, where he died, June 15, 1727. He wrote, *Eigentliche Gestalt eines Christen* (Giessen, 1711):—*Das Werk des Glaubens in Kraft* (Wertheim, 1719):—*Grosser Ernst des Wahren Christenthums* (Halle, eod.):—*Warnung Christi vor den Falschen Propheten* (Frankfort, 1723):—*Gemeinschaft der Schmach Christi* (ibid. 1724):—*Kampf und Sieg der Ersten Blutzeugen Christi nebst Seinem Leben* (Berlin, 1744). See *Nachrichten von Rechtschaffenen Predigern* (Halle, 1775), vol. i; Jöcher, *Allgemeines Gelehrten-Lexikon*, s. v. (B. P.)

Collin, Jean, a French theologian of the Jesuit order, was born at St. Junien, and lived about the middle of the 17th century. He was almoner to the king, and preached with success at Val-de-Grace, and in the principal cities of the kingdom. He published, among other works, *Le Prélat de Saint-Grégoire* (Paris, 1640):—*Histoire Sacrée des Principaux Saints du Diocèse de Limoges* (Limoges, 1672). He left also a large number of MSS., a catalogue of which was published by abbé Nadaud. See Hoefer, *Nouv. Biog. Générale*, s. v.

Collin, Nicholas, D.D., a Swedish missionary, was born in 1745. He received a classical education in his native country, and intended to join the army, but as he grew to manhood his attention was turned towards the ministry. He arrived, May 12, 1770, in the Delaware river, as a sort of assistant at large to the rectors of the Swedish churches in New Jersey and Pennsylvania. He is claimed as a minister of the Protestant Episcopal Church, because the parishes with which he was connected as a missionary all united with that body; but he was ordained in Sweden, and to the Swedish Church he always considered himself as owing allegiance. His assistant ministers were always of the Episcopal Church, and he used its liturgy. In consequence of the recall of Rev. John Weisell to Sweden, Dr. Collin was appointed rector in his stead in 1773 at Raccoon, Pa., and Penn's Neck, N. J., and remained there until July, 1786, his residence being at Swedesborough. In 1778 he urged his own recall upon the archbishop of Upsal, Sweden, but the king desired that the Swedish missionaries should remain in America until the result of the war should be known; so that it was not until 1783 that he received permission to sail for Sweden. In that year, however, he did not consider it wise to leave his field of labor, and at his suggestion he was permitted to remain, and to assume charge of the churches of Wicaco (now a part of the city of Philadelphia), Kingsessing, and Upper Merion. In July, 1786, he removed from Swedesborough to Philadelphia. During seven years of his residence at the former place he was provost (or superintendent) over all the Swedish churches in Pennsylvania. He died in Philadelphia, in October, 1831. Dr. Collin was a man of considerable learning, being acquainted with at least twelve languages. For many years he was a member of the American Philosophical Society. The only work which he left is a MS. translation of Acrelius's *History of New Sweden*, undertaken in 1799 at the request of the Historical Society of New York. See Sprague, *Annals of the Amer. Pulpit*, v, 277.

Collin, Nicolas, a French theologian, was born about the commencement of the 18th century. He was canon-regular of the strict Observatists of the Premonstrant order, and prior of Rengeval. He died at Nancy in 1788, leaving *Observations Critiques sur le Traité des Dispenses* (Nancy, 1765; Paris, 1770):—*Du Signe de la Croix* (Paris, 1775):—*De l'Eau Bénite* (ibid. 1776):—*Du Pain Bénit*, etc. (ibid. 1777):—*Des Processions de l'Église Catholique* (ibid. 1779):—*Du Respect aux Églises* (ibid. 1781). See Hoefer, *Nouv. Biog. Générale*, s. v.

Collin, Richard, a German designer and engraver, was born at Luxemburg in 1626. He visited Rome while young, and studied under Sandrart; but afterwards returned to Antwerp and Brussels, where he was appointed engraver to the king of Spain. The following are some of his principal works: *Esther before Ahasuerus; Christ Bearing his Cross; St. Arnold.*

Collīna, one of the inferior rural deities, supposed by the Romans to reign over the hills.

Collina, Abondio, a learned Italian Camaldule, was born at Bologna in 1691. For ten years he was professor of geography and nautical science at the Institute of Sciences, and of geometry at the university of his native city. He died in December, 1753, leaving *Antiche Relazioni dell' Indie e della China* (Bologna, 1749):—a translation of a part of *Voyages de Deux Arabes*, published in French by abbé Renaudot. Collina wrote numerous poems and dissertations. See Hoefer, *Nouv. Biog. Générale*, s. v.

Collina, Bonifacio, an Italian scholar of the order of Camaldules, brother of Abondio, was born at Bologna in 1689. He taught philosophy at the university of his native city, and died in 1770. He published a large part of his writings under the title, *Opere Diverse* (Bologna, 1774), in which we find academical memoirs, tragedies, and scraps of prose upon religious subjects. He also wrote several *Lives* of the Camaldule saints. See Hoefer, *Nouv. Biog. Générale*, s. v.

Collings, John, D.D., an eminent English nonconformist divine, and voluminous writer, was born at Boxstead, in Essex, in 1623; educated at Emmanuel College, Cambridge; and died at Norwich, Jan. 17, 1690. He wrote many books of controversy and practical divinity, the most singular of which is his *Weaver's Pocketbook*. In Poole's *Annotations on the Bible*, Collings wrote those on the last six chapters of Isaiah, the whole of Jeremiah, Lamentations, the four Evangelists, the epistles to the Corinthians, Galatians, Timothy, Philemon, and the Revelations. See Chalmers, *Biog. Dict.* s. v.; Allibone, *Dict. of Brit. and Amer. Authors*, s. v.

Collings, William, an English Baptist minister, was born in Walworth, Aug. 8, 1814. He was baptized March 2, 1836, and began at once to preach. In 1842 he commenced his pastorate at Kingston-on-Thames, and remained until 1856, when he accepted a call to the Church in Gloucester, and was successful in bringing it up from a depressed state to one of strength and prosperity. He died Sept. 10, 1869. See (Lond.) *Baptist Hand-book*, 1870, p. 190, 191. (J. C. S.)

Collington, John, an English clerical writer of the last part of the 16th and the first part of the 17th centuries, was a native of Somersetshire; educated at Lincoln College, Oxford; made priest on the Continent; returned to England, and was cast into the Tower of London; condemned, afterwards reprieved, set free, and sent out of the country. He returned, and for thirty years zealously advanced his own (Roman Catholic) religion. Though in restraint, he was alive in 1611, and an old man. See Fuller, *Worthies of England* (ed. Nuttall), iii, 106.

Collins, an English martyr, was a prominent lawyer in London, burned at Smithfield in 1538, for rebuking the priest. See Fox, *Acts and Monuments*, v, 251.

Collins, Abel, a minister of the Society of Friends, died at North Stonington, Conn., Sept. 17, 1834, aged sixty-four years. See *The Friend*, viii, 20.

Collins, Augustus Baldwin, a Congregational minister, son of general Augustus Collins, was born at Guilford, Conn., May 24, 1789. He studied at Yale College, but did not complete his course. Rev. Drs. Andrew Yates and T. M. Cooley were his tutors in theology. In 1817 he was acting pastor at Montgomery, Mass., and in the following year was ordained pastor at Andover, Conn., from which charge he was dismissed in 1827. In the beginning of 1828 he was installed as minister at Preston, where he served until 1847, when he became acting pastor at West Stafford. He was regularly installed there May 10, 1848, and left April 19, 1852. About two months after he entered upon his duties as acting pastor at Barkhamsted. In 1858 he held the same position at Wolcott, also at Long Ridge, in Stamford. After 1852 he resided at Norwalk, without charge. He died there, March 16, 1876. See *Cong. Quarterly*, 1877, p. 413.

Collins, Barnabas V., a minister of the Reformed (Dutch) Church, graduated from Lafayette College, Easton, Pa., and in 1842 from the theological seminary at New Brunswick, N. J. He was licensed by the Classis of New York the same year; served the Church at West Farms, N. Y., until 1845; Ponds, Bergen Co., N. J., until 1867, and thereafter was without a charge till his death, in 1877. See Corwin, *Manual of the Ref. Church in America*, 3d ed. p. 218.

Collins, Benjamin, a Methodist Episcopal minister, was born in Sussex County, N. J., in 1785. In 1819 he joined the Philadelphia Conference, in which he remained energetic and faithful until his death, in August, 1831. See *Minutes of Annual Conferences*, 1833, p. 162.

Collins, Britton Estol, a Presbyterian minister, was born in Philadelphia, Pa., Feb. 2, 1801. He entered Princeton Seminary in 1824, and remained two years; was licensed by the Presbytery of Philadelphia in April, 1828; received under the care of the Huntingdon Presbytery, April 8, 1830, and ordained as an evangelist June 16 following. His first pastoral charge was at Millerstown, then in the bounds of Huntingdon Presbytery, he being installed there in October, 1832. He resigned his charge in 1839, and in October of same year was called to Shirleysburgh. This call he did not accept, but agreed to act as stated supply, in which relation he continued till October, 1853, when he retired. During the remaining years of his life, so long as he was able to preach, he spent his time in missionary labor in different parts of the presbytery—chiefly in the churches of Moshannon, Unity, and Mapleton, successively. The last of these owes its existence largely to his liberality and indefatigable labors. He died April 12, 1876. Mr. Collins was a man of humble and undoubted piety; of great simplicity of character; a diligent, faithful, and self-denying pastor; universally respected and loved. See *Necrol. Report of Princeton Theol. Sem.* 1877, p. 22.

Collins, Charles, D.D., a minister in the Methodist Episcopal Church South, was born in North Yarmouth, Me., April 17, 1813. He received an elementary education at Portland, and the Maine Wesleyan Institute; after several years of school-teaching entered Wesleyan University, Middletown, Conn., and before he was twenty-five years of age graduated, taking the first honors, and was elected as the first president of Emory and Henry College, near Abingdon, Va. During the years of his student life he had embraced religion, and dedicated all his energies to it and education, and having united with the Holston Conference, labored abundantly and effectively in the pulpit during his service in Emory and Henry College. His controversial papers against Romanism, in 1844, exhibit his talent and ability in polemic theology; as do also his tracts, published in 1848, entitled *Methodism and Calvinism Compared.* He was also at this time editor of the *Southern Repertory and College Review*, and was a regular contributor to the *Ladies' Repository*, and various church papers and periodicals. In 1852 he was elected president of Dickinson College, and filled that position eight years, during which time he declined the presidency of Centenary College, La., and of Central College, Mo.; the chancellorship of the University of Missouri, of Michigan, and of Southern University, Greensborough, Ala. In 1860 he was transferred to the Memphis Conference, and took charge of the State Female College at Memphis, Tenn., becoming sole proprietor of the buildings and grounds, and placing it under the patronage of the Memphis Conference. In the service of that college he closed his life and labors, July 10, 1875. Dr. Collins was amiable, grave, sympathetic, studious, learned; a popular, able writer; an humble, earnest preacher, and an exemplary Christian. See *Minutes of Annual Conferences of the M. E. Church South*, 1875, p. 210; Simpson, *Cyclop. of Methodism*, s. v.

Collins, Daniel, a Presbyterian minister, was a native of Guilford, Conn.; graduated from Yale College in 1760; studied theology under the Rev. Dr. Bellamy; was ordained pastor in Lanesborough, April 17, 1764, and died Aug. 26, 1822, aged eighty-three. See Sprague, *Annals of the Amer. Pulpit*, iii, 498.

Collins, Elisha, a Baptist minister, was born in Halifax County, Va., Oct. 20, 1788. He was converted in 1815; was baptized April 23, 1823; licensed Dec. 6, the same year; studied with Rev. Abner W. Clifton, and was ordained Nov. 5, 1825. His first pastorate was with the Salem Church, near the Prince Edward County line. He became one of the earliest advocates of temperance in the country. In 1835 he removed to Tennessee, where, for a time, he found himself in an uncongenial atmosphere. A large majority of Baptists were opposed to missions, and forbade his preaching in their houses. Gradually the opposition gave way, and he became at different times pastor of the McLemoresville, Bible Union, Lexington, and other churches. He died near Lexington, in September, 1854. See Borum, *Sketches of Tenn. Ministers*, p. 131-134. (J. C. S.)

Collins, Elizabeth, a minister of the Society of Friends, was born Jan. 4, 1755, in Upper Evesham, N. J. In 1779 she was appointed a minister, and travelled through many of the states, doing efficient work for the Master. The most striking characteristic in her life was her intense interest in and concern for the poor. She died Feb. 1, 1831. See *Annual Monitor*, 1834, p. 99.

Collins, George D., a Methodist Episcopal minister, was born at Medford, N. J., July 9, 1845. He was converted in 1865; studied two and a half years in Pennington Seminary; served one year as assistant on Columbus Circuit, and in 1872 was admitted into the New Jersey Conference, and stationed at Dennisville. He served in 1873 and 1874 at Groveville, where one hundred and fifty were added to the Church; from 1875 to 1877 at Union Street Church, Trenton, where two hundred were converted; in 1878 at Washington, South River, where he had some success, and was returned in 1879. He labored until April 20 of that year, when he was prostrated with fever, then attacked with hemorrhage of the lungs, and died Aug. 3 following. Mr. Collins was pre-eminently a man of one work, giving all his time and energies to the ministry. See *Minutes of Annual Conferences*, 1880, p. 91.

Collins, Hiram B., a Methodist Episcopal minister, was born at Vincennes, Ind., May 4, 1829. He was left fatherless in childhood; received a careful religious training; spent some years as a teacher; was received by the Methodist Episcopal Church by letter from the Presbyterian Church in 1858; was given license to exhort the same year, and in the following was admitted into the South-eastern Indiana Conference, wherein he served with zeal and fidelity until his death, Sept. 4, 1864. Mr. Collins brought into the ministry a well-developed intellect, refined taste, superior literary attainments, an energetic character, and a heart in living sympathy with the interests of humanity and religion. He was a sound theologian, an excellent preacher, and a faithful and successful pastor. See *Minutes of Annual Conferences*, 1864, p. 162.

Collins, Isaac, a Methodist Episcopal minister, was born in Baltimore County, Md., June 11, 1789. He was converted in 1810; served in the war of 1812 under general Harrison, being known as a praying soldier; received license to preach in 1819, and in 1823 was admitted into the Baltimore Conference. He became supernumerary in 1859, and superannuated in 1862, and died May 25, 1870. Mr. Collins was a plain, earnest, able, useful preacher. See *Minutes of Annual Conferences*, 1871, p. 19.

Collins, Isaac Foster, a Methodist Episcopal minister, was born at Wolcott, Wayne Co., N. Y., Aug. 24, 1819. He was converted in 1838, removed to Arkansas in 1840, and in the following year entered the Arkansas Conference, and was appointed to teach and preach among the Cherokee Indians. In 1843 he was sent to the Lower Cherokee mission; in 1844 was set off with the Indian Mission Conference, and in 1845 was sent among the Choctaw Indians, to teach in Morris Seminary. In 1846 he located and went to Michigan; began regular work the next year in the Michigan Conference; in 1853 returned to the Arkansas Conference, and was appointed among the Cherokees; in 1854 was transferred to the Missouri Conference, and employed on the Omaha mission. On the formation of the Kansas and Nebraska Conference, in 1856, he became one of its members, and, on its division, he fell within the bounds of the Kansas Conference, and died a member of its active ranks, April 26, 1862. Mr. Collins was decidedly a true friend, an honest man, an exemplary Christian, and a thorough, uncompromising Methodist preacher. He was dignified in appearance, humble in spirit, and very neat in person. See *Minutes of Annual Conferences*, 1863, p. 22.

Collins, Isaac Wright, a Presbyterian minister, was born in Crawford County, Pa., Aug. 25, 1833. He was educated at Westminster College, New Wilmington, and studied theology in the Allegheny Seminary. He was licensed to preach by Lakes Presbytery in 1862, and became pastor successively at Neshannock and West Salem, Wis. He died May 20, 1865. He was an earnest, pious, and zealous laborer in the Master's vineyard. See Wilson, *Presb. Hist. Almanac*, 1866, p. 259.

Collins, James, an English Methodist minister, was born in Devon, England, Feb. 20, 1841. He was converted in early life. While yet young he removed to Canada, and settled in the Pickering mission, where he became a local preacher among the Bible Christians, and was recommended to the conference of 1867. He labored on the Hampton, Cobourg, Hungerford, Wiarton, Lindsay, Fenelon, and Berrytown stations. He died March 6, 1875. He was a diligent student, an earnest preacher, a man of unquestioned piety, and a successful minister of the gospel. See *Minutes of the Conference*, 1875.

Collins, John (1), a Scotch clergyman, was licensed to preach in 1631; presented to the living at Campsie in 1639; after long opposition, was ordained in 1641, and was murdered about Martinmas, 1648. See *Fasti Eccles. Scoticanæ*, ii, 63.

Collins, John (2), an English Independent minister, came over to America with his father in his youth; in 1649 was a fellow of Harvard College, Cambridge, Mass., and returned to England when Oliver Cromwell was lord protector. He became chaplain to general Monk. He was silenced but not ejected in 1662, and became pastor at Lime-street Independent Church, London. He was one of the first six persons chosen to deliver the Merchants' Lecture at Pinner's Hall in 1672. He died in London, Dec. 3, 1687. He was a minister of uncommon ability, and an eloquent preacher, so that few persons went from his preaching unaffected. See Wilson, *Dissenting Churches*, i, 225–229.

Collins, John (3), an English Independent minister, son of the foregoing, was born in London about 1673. He studied at the University of Utrecht; returning to England, was ordained co-pastor at Lime Street, with the Rev. Robert Bragge, in 1698, and was chosen one of the Merchants' lecturers. In 1702 he assisted at the ordination, in Mark Lane, of Dr. Isaac Watts. He was a good preacher, a friend of Matthew Henry, who informs us that he fell dead suddenly at his study door, March 19, 1714. See Wilson, *Dissenting Churches*, i, 240, 241.

Collins, John (4), a minister of the Society of Friends, was born at Charlestown, R. I., Dec. 12, 1716, his father being also a minister in the same denomination. He became an eminent preacher among the Friends, and for many years sat at the head of the New England Yearly Meeting. He had a thorough acquaintance with the disciplinary affairs of the society, and "was much engaged, and took much pains, in endeavoring to have the Africans or negroes freed from slavery, and often testified against that wicked practice." He died at Stonington, Conn., Oct. 1, 1778. See *R. I. Biographical Cyclop.* p. 100. (J. C. S.)

Collins, John (5), a Methodist Episcopal minister, was born in Sussex County, Del., in April, 1764. He grew up to be a man of great bodily strength, and fierce and revengeful passions; but married a woman of remarkable amiableness, and shortly afterwards was converted. He immediately began exhorting and preaching, and in 1803 entered the Philadelphia Conference, wherein he labored without intermission until within a few weeks of his death, which occurred March 30, 1827. Mr. Collins had some very objectionable qualities in his character, still he labored with untiring zeal and did much good. See *Minutes of Annual Conferences*, 1827, p. 542; *Methodist Magazine*, x, 289.

Collins, John (6), a Presbyterian minister, was born in Somerset County, Md., Feb. 16, 1769. He was licensed by the Presbytery of Lewes in 1791. After graduating at Princeton College, he assumed the presidency of Washington Academy, in his native county. In 1797 he purchased an estate in New Castle County, Del., whither he removed, and became and continued to be pastor of the Presbyterian Church in St. George's until his death, April 12, 1804. See Alexander, *Princeton College in the 18th Century.*

Collins, Joseph Lansfield, an English Congregational minister, was born at Stowmarket, Suffolk, in 1843. He was converted and joined the Church in his youth, and in 1863 entered Cheshunt College, where he spent three years. He was two years in the pastorate at Ipswich, and in January, 1869, accepted a call to the Church at Finchingfield, where he remained until his death, March 31, 1881. See (Lond.) *Cong. Year-book*, 1882, p. 290.

Collins, J. B., a Free-will Baptist minister, was born in 1821; converted in 1839, and united with the Church in Morristown, Vt. Four years after, he commenced his ministerial labors, removed to Clinton County, N. Y., in 1845, and shortly after settled in Franklin, where he was ordained. After several years he removed to St. Lawrence County, and labored in that section and in Jefferson County until 1877. He preached successively in Morristown, Depauville, Philadelphia, Keeseville, and other places. In 1877 he took charge of the Church in Dickinson Centre; in 1880 he became pastor of the Church in Underhill Centre, Vt., and preached a part of the time at East Cambridge. He died in March, 1883. See *Morning Star*, July 25, 1883. (J. C. S.)

Collins, Levi, a Presbyterian minister, was born at Somers, Conn., Feb. 12, 1777. After receiving a careful academic education, he graduated at Yale College in 1802. He was ordained by the Holland Association in 1832. On account of ill-health he did not take a pastoral charge, but spent most of his time in teaching. He was principal of Monroe Academy, Mass., for eight years, and died at Belvidere, Ill., Dec. 10, 1859. See Wilson, *Presb. Hist. Almanac*, 1861, p. 159.

Collins, Nathaniel (1), a Congregational minister, graduated at Harvard College in 1660, was ordained at Middletown, Conn., Nov. 4, 1668, and died Dec. 28, 1684. See Sprague, *Annals of the Amer. Pulpit*, i, 183.

Collins, Nathaniel (2), a Congregational minister, graduated at Harvard College in 1697, was ordained at Enfield, Conn., the same year, and died in 1756, aged seventy-nine years. See Sprague, *Annals of the Amer. Pulpit*, i, 183.

Collins, Nicholas, an English Methodist preacher, was born at St. Breward, Cornwall, Dec. 28, 1806. He was converted at twenty; joined the Bible Christians; was a useful local preacher several years; entered the ministry in 1833, and for six years did good work among the people. In 1839 his health failed, and he died at Limehead, July 7, 1841.

Collins, Robert H., a Methodist Episcopal minister, was born in Kent County, Del., May 12, 1833. He was converted near Memphis, Mo., in 1858; licensed to preach in 1859, entered the Des Moines Conference in 1863, and was afterwards transferred to the Missouri Conference. His health failing in 1874, obliged him to become a superannuate, and he died Jan. 26, 1875. Mr. Collins was a consistent Christian gentleman, an unusually good preacher, and an excellent pastor. See *Minutes of Annual Conferences*, 1875, p. 46.

Collins, Robert S., a minister in the Methodist Episcopal Church South, son of Rev. McKissey Collins, was born in Greenville District, S. C., Aug. 11, 1811. He removed to western Tennessee in 1823, where he experienced religion in 1829; received license to preach in 1831, and in 1833 was admitted into the Tennessee Conference. In 1834 he was transferred to the Mississippi Conference; in 1839, located; in 1840 re-entered the conference, and died June 9, 1848. As a man, Mr. Collins was high-minded and honorable; as a Christian, eminently meek and gentle; as a preacher, systematic, able, impressive, popular, and useful; and in his domestic relations exemplary. See *Minutes of Annual Conferences of the M. E. Church South*, 1848, p. 183.

Collins, Samuel (1), a scholar of the 17th century, was the son of Baldwin Collins, who was born at Coventry, a pious preacher, very bountiful to the poor, and whom queen Elizabeth constantly called father Collins. Samuel was born and educated at Eton; became fellow of King's College, Cambridge; afterwards provost and regius professor there, being a man of admirable wit and memory, and the most fluent Latinist of the age. He retained his professorship throughout his life, read his lectures twice a week for forty years, declined the bishopric of Bristol, and died in 1651. See Fuller. *Worthies of England* (ed. Nuttall), i, 209.

Collins, Samuel (2), a Congregational minister, was born at Columbia, Conn., in 1747. He graduated at Dartmouth College in 1775; was ordained pastor in Sandown, N. H., in 1780; in 1788 was installed pastor of the Presbyterian Church in Hanover Centre, and in 1795 removed to Craftsbury, Vt., where he was pastor of the Congregational Church until 1804. He died Jan. 7, 1807. See *Cong. Quarterly*, 1864, p. 157.

Collins, Samuel (3), an English Baptist minister, was born at Culworth, Northamptonshire, Dec. 22, 1798. He was received into the Church at the age of twenty, and manifested a desire to preach; in 1826 went to supply the pulpit at Grundesburgh, and after preaching one year was chosen pastor of the society, in which relation he continued for nearly fifty years. He took an active part in the organization of the Suffolk County Home Mission in 1831, and was its secretary for more than forty years. He originated, in 1833, the *Gospel Herald*, a low-priced Baptist magazine, and edited it for twenty-five years. He was unable to preach during the last three years of his life, and died June 17, 1881. See (Lond.) *Baptist Hand-book*, 1882, p. 298.

Collins, William (1), an English Baptist minister, studied under the famous Dr. Busby at Westminster School; travelled on the continent for increased knowledge; had valuable offers in the Church of England, but accepted a joint pastorate with Dr. N. Cox at the Baptist Church (now New Broadstreet), London, in 1675. He was also distinguished as a physician, and signed the Baptist Confession of Faith drawn up and issued in 1688. He occupied a prominent and useful position in London, and died Oct. 30, 1702. See Wilson, *Dissenting Churches*, ii, 181–185.

Collins, William (2), an English painter of very considerable merit, was born in London in 1788. In 1821 he was elected a royal academician; in 1837 visited Italy, and in 1840 produced *Our Saviour in the Temple*. Some of his paintings have been sold at a very high price. He died in London, in February, 1847. See Spooner, *Biog. Hist. of the Fine Arts*, s. v.; Hoefer, *Nouv. Biog. Générale*, s. v.

Collins, William F., a Methodist Episcopal minister, was born at Northumberland, Saratoga Co., N. Y., Aug. 16, 1811. In 1834 he entered the New York Conference, and for thirty-six years, without interruption, ardently pursued his sacred calling, turning many to righteousness. He died March 21, 1870. Mr. Collins was a man of more than ordinary intellect, a very practical, spiritual preacher, and an indefatigable pastor. See *Minutes of Annual Conferences*, 1870, p. 105.

Collinson, Septimus, D.D., an English divine, was born about 1739. He took his degree of M.A. in 1767; in 1796 became provost of Queen's College, Oxford; and in 1798 was elected Margaret professor of divinity there. In his office of professor he labored with unexampled efficiency and zeal. The lectures on the *Thirty-nine Articles*, which he delivered in that capacity, evinced deep research, sound judgment, and great moderation. Dr. Collinson was a liberal benefactor to all public institutions of acknowledged utility. He died in 1827. See (Lond.) *Christian Remembrancer*, February, 1827, p. 128.

Collinsworth, John, a Methodist Episcopal minister, was born in Virginia, Feb. 22, 1786. He embraced religion in his thirteenth year, and in 1807 was admitted into the South Carolina Conference. In 1816 he located, on account of ill-health; re-entered the effective ranks in 1827, and died at his post, Sept. 4, 1834. Mr. Collinsworth was laborious and useful. See *Minutes of Annual Conferences*, 1835, p. 345; Sprague, *Annals of the Amer. Pulpit*, vii, 443.

Collios (or **Colius**), Francesco, an Italian theologian, was born near Milan towards the close of the 16th century. He was grand penitentiary of the diocese, and died at Milan in 1640, leaving *De Sanguine Christi Libri Quinque* (Milan, 1617):—*An Christus Oblatum sibi in Circumcisione Præputium Rursus in Resurrectionem Acceperit*:—*De Animabus Paganorum Libri Octo* (ibid. 1622, 1623.) See Hoefer, *Nouv. Biog. Générale*, s. v.

Collison, George, an English Independent minister and educator, was born in Beverley, Yorkshire, Jan. 6, 1772. He received a superior education for that period, and when about seventeen years of age was articled to a solicitor. In 1792, having experienced religion, he entered Hoxton College, in 1797 became assistant-tutor in that institution, and on Sept. 14 of the same year was ordained pastor of the Independent Church at Walthamstow, which office he held jointly with his tutorship. In 1801 he relinquished his engagements at Hoxton, and in 1803 became tutor in the Hackney Theological Seminary, which was just then founded. He resigned his pastorate at Walthamstow in 1837, but held his office in Hackney until his death, Feb. 6, 1847. Mr. Collison was a man of great purity of character, a sound divine, and eminently catholic in spirit. He was one of the founders of the London Missionary and Religious Tract societies, and an ardent supporter of all similar institutions. See (Lond.) *Evangelical Magazine*, 1847, p. 137; 1848, p. 1.

Collison, John Wesley, an Irish Wesleyan minister, was born near Armagh, March 11, 1853. He was converted at the age of seventeen, joined the Methodist Society, and became a prayer leader, tract distributer, and a local preacher. After passing through the usual course of study he was duly admitted to the ministry. He died at Clontarf, near Dublin, July 27, 1880. His life was short, but eminently successful as a preacher of Christ and winner of souls. See *Minutes of the British Conference*, 1881, p. 54.

Cölln, Wilhelm von (or *William of Cologne*), a celebrated old German painter, was born at Herle, near Cologne, and was settled as early as 1370 at the latter place. His principal works are the picture of the tomb of Cerno von Falkenstein, in St. Castor's Church at Coblentz, painted in 1388; the large altarpiece of the Church of St. Clara at Cologne, in twenty-six parts, representing the *Life and Passion of Christ*, which is now in the cathedral. He has a *Crucifixion* and an *Infant Jesus* in the Wallraf Museum at Cologne.

Collobium. See Colobium.

Collocatio designates a custom among the ancient Greeks and Romans of laying out the corpse of a dead person on a bed or couch, and placing it outside the house (afterwards at the threshold), to give ocular proof that the person was really dead, or, perhaps, that the death had not been by violence. A honey-cake was laid beside the corpse as a gift to Cerberus, and painted earthen vessels were arranged beside the bed, and buried with the corpse. The ceremony lasted two days.

Collombet, François Zénon, a French Catholic writer, was born at Sièges (Jura), March 28, 1808. In 1827, wishing to embrace the ecclesiastical calling, he was sent to the Seminary of St. Irænæus at Lyons; but his progress in theology not being great, he renounced the project of entering orders. Having formed an intimate friendship with one of his co-disciples, M. Gregoire, he prepared, in connection with him, various works. He died at Lyons, Oct. 16, 1853, leaving numerous translations and other productions, for which see Hoefer, *Nouv. Biog. Générale*, s. v.

Collop-Monday is a name for the Monday after Quinquagesima Sunday; so called because on that day the faithful began to leave off the use of flesh-meat—"collop" being a name descriptive of a piece of meat or flesh.

Collord, Isaac, a Methodist Episcopal minister, was born in New York city, June 25, 1794. He labored at sailmaking in his youth, became a member of the John Street Methodist Church in 1810, removed to Cincinnati in 1811, and with his father engaged in the tanning business; served in the war of 1812, received license to preach in 1818, and in 1819 entered the Ohio Conference. In 1848 he became superannuated, which relation he sustained until his death, March 8, 1875. Mr. Collard lived an eventful, zealous, faithful life. He was eminently genial and companionable. See *Minutes of Annual Conferences*, 1875, p. 222.

Collow, John, a Scotch clergyman, was called to the living at Penpont in 1736, and died Jan. 12, 1766. See *Fasti Eccles. Scoticanæ*, i, 669.

Colluthians were an heretical sect of the 4th century, founded by Colluthus (q. v.), a presbyter of Alexandria. His tenets resembled those of the Manichæans (q. v.), holding that God did not create the wicked, and that he was not the author of the evils that befall men. Colluthus was deposed by the Council of Alexandria (324), and died before 340, after which the sect rapidly disappeared.

Collūthus is the name of several persons in the early Church:

1. A martyr under Maximian in the Thebaid, commemorated on May 19.

2. A presbyter and founder of a sect at Alexandria early in the 4th century. He assumed to exercise episcopal functions, but the Council of Alexandria, under Hosius (A.D. 324), decided that he was only a presbyter, and consequently Ischyras and others ordained by him were to be accounted mere laymen (Athanas. *Apol. Contr. Arian.* 12, 75-77, 80, 106, 152). Colluthus was regarded as a schismatic rather than a heretic. Epiphanius mentions in general terms (*Hær.* 69, 728) that Colluthus taught some perverse things, and founded a sect, which was soon dispersed (Tillemont, vi, 231).

3. A monophysite, extracts from whose writings were read at the Lateran Council, A.D. 649.

Collyer, Isaac J. P., a Methodist Episcopal minister, was born in Seekonk, Mass., May 19, 1814. He was converted and licensed to exhort in his youth, and in 1844 entered the New England Conference, in which he labored until his death, May 7, 1872. Mr. Collyer was remarkable for his noble, manly form and bearing; the strength, independence, quickness, penetration, and earnestness of his mind; his strong imagination, practical good sense, and ardent piety. See *Minutes of Annual Conferences*, 1873, p. 53.

Collyer, William, an English Baptist minister, was born at Ivinghoe, Bucks, in 1793. About the year 1814 he gave his heart to God, but was not baptized until Aug. 29, 1822, and was received into the Church Oct. 6, following. In 1824 he began to assist his own pastor in the Ivinghoe Church, and at the death of the latter took the oversight of the flock. About 1831 he was urged to accept ordination as regular pastor, which at first he declined, but on Easter Tuesday, April 1, 1834, he was ordained pastor of the Particular Baptist Church at Ivinghoe. His labors were eminently successful for many years. He died June 9, 1879. See (Lond.) *Baptist Hand-book*, 1880, p. 291.

Collyer, William Bengg, D.D., LL.D., F.S.A., an English dissenting minister, was born at Blackheath Hill, near London, April 14, 1782. He studied at Homerton College under Dr. J. Pye Smith, and became pastor of a dissenting church at Peckham, now a suburb of London, before he was twenty years of age, which post he occupied with great honor and usefulness to the end of his life. At his ordination in 1801 the church numbered only one hundred and ten members, but it soon increased in membership, and in 1818 Hanover Church was built; for about twelve years he was pastor of Salter's Hall Chapel, which afterwards became a Baptist Church. For half a century Dr. Collyer was the most popular dissenting minister in London, attracting large audiences to his church. He died in London, Jan. 9, 1854. His lectures were published at intervals, from 1809 to 1823, and embraced *Scripture Prophecy, Facts, Miracles, Parables, Doctrines, Duties, Comparisons.* In 1812 he printed a collection of hymns for the use of his congregation, nine hundred and seventy-nine in all, fifty-seven of which were his own. In 1837 he published *Services Suited to the Marriage Service*, to which were attached eighty-nine hymns by himself. See *New York Observer*, June 10, 1880; *Cong. Year-book*, 1855, p. 210. (W. P. S.)

Collyrĭdes were a species of cakes of kneaded dough, which were anciently offered to the gods as sacred gifts, from the notion, entertained by the heathens of all ages, that the gods delighted in the same things that were pleasing to men. See Collyridians.

Collyva is an oblation used in the Greek Church in commemoration of the resurrection of the dead. It consists of cakes made principally of boiled wheat and currants, the surface of the top being ornamented with the edible grains of the pomegranate, almonds, etc., and is presented on a plate before the chancel of the church. They are brought on certain days by the friends of hose who have died within a year or two. The friends claim that the soul of the deceased comes down during the service and eats a grain or two of the wheat.

Colma (or **Columba**), an Irish virgin-saint of Leitir, and her sisters, were pupils or foster-children of St. Comgall of Bangor. She is commemorated Jan. 22 (O'Hanlon, *Irish Saints*, i, 401, 402).

Colman is a very common name in Irish hagiology. In the table of the *Mart. Doneg.* are given 97 Colmans, and in the index 113. Colgan enumerated more than 130; and Usher says there are upwards of 230. We notice here only those best known. They all seem to have flourished about the 6th or 7th century.

1. The son of Comgellain, was a man deeply versed in legal and ecclesiastical learning, and a great friend of St. Columba. He died in the year of the eclipses, A.D. 625 (Lanigan, *Eccl. Hist. of Ireland*, ii, 238).

2. Son of Daire, bishop of Doire-mor, is commemorated May 20 and July 31. He was a friend and neighbor of St. Pulcherius. Colman must have flourished in the beginning of the 7th century (Colgan, *Acta Sanctorum*, p. 169; c. 2, 173, 593; c. 22; Lanigan, *Eccl. Hist. of Ireland*, i, 401, 402; ii, 210 sq.).

3. Son of Duach, of Cill-mac-Duach, commemorated Feb. 3, was a man of great virtue and miracles. He followed Christ from his youth, and at length retired to a hermit-cell, near the place where afterwards the Church of Kilmacduagh was built. The day of his commemoration there is Oct. 27 (Colgan, *Acta Sanctorum*, 245 sq.; Lanigan, *Eccl. Hist. of Ireland*, ii, 341 sq.; *Dublin Penny Journal*, i, 200).

4. Son of Eochaidh, is commemorated Jan. 1. There are several other Colmans in the calendars having this patronymic, two being celebrated on Sept. 6, and a fourth on Oct. 27. The present Colman is first mentioned as driving St. Columba for a whole day in a cart without a linchpin, and is said to have been the founder of the monastery which in the native dialect is called Snamluthair. He must have been a young man in the days of St. Columba (O'Hanlon, *Irish Saints*, i, 26).

5. Son of Fintan, is commemorated Dec. 14 in *Mart. Doneg.*, but others call him son of Finnbar, and about A.D. 703 the Irish annals give the obit of Colman, son of Finnbar, abbot of Lismore (Colgan, *Acta Sanctorum*, p. 793). See No. 25.

6. Son of Lenin, of Cluain-uamha (Cloyne), commemorated Nov. 24, is regarded by Lanigan among the saints of the second order in Ireland, and believed to have flourished in the 6th century. He was brother of St. Brigida (q. v.), daughter of Lenin, and was one of the saints belonging to the family of St. Foilan. He seems at first to have been a poet attached to the court of Ædh Caemh, king of Cashel, about the middle of the 6th century, and after his conversion to have attended St. Jarlath's school at Clonfois, where he was next in order of sanctity to St. Brendan of Clonfert. He died about A.D. 604. His character as a poet appears in the very elegant metrical *Life of St. Senan*, which he composed, and of which we have now but a fragment; the substance of it is incorporated into Colgan's second *Life of St. Senan* (*Acta Sanctorum*, p. 104, c. 2, 533; c. 22, 539; Lanigan, *Eccl. Hist. of Ireland*, ii, 41 sq., 212 sq.; Todd, *St. Patrick*, p. 208; Ware, *Irish Antiq.* p. 144).

7. Son of Lugaidh, priest of Cluain Bruchais, is commemorated July 12. He was a grandson of Laeghaire, king of Ireland, and is given among those of that race who embraced the faith (Colgan, *Acta Sanctorum*, iii, c. 3). He lived not later than the middle of the 6th century.

8. Son of Murchu, has had attributed to him and his two brothers (Colman, the oldest, being a bishop, and the others priests) the authorship of a hymn in praise of Michael the archangel; it is given in the *Book of Hymns*, and edited by Dr. Todd. He seems to have belonged to Connaught, and for a time, at least, was engaged in missionary labors on the Continent before becoming abbot of Moville, where he died, A.D. 735 (Todd, *Book of Hymns*, Fasc. ii, 165 sq.).

9. Son of Roi, of Reachrainn, is commemorated June 16. His mother, Eithne, was the mother also of many other saints, such as St. Columba, St. Maedoc of Ferns, and St. Comgan of Glen-Uissen. He is also called Colman the Deacon, and received from St. Columba the church which that saint had built at Reachrainn (Todd and Reeves, *Mart. Doneg.* p. 171; Reeves, *Adamnan*, pp. lxx, 164; and *Eccl. Antiq.* p. 292).

10. Son of Ronan, is commemorated March 30. Colgan places him among the disciples of St. Columba.

11. Son of Tighernach, is commemorated Jan. 3. He is classed among the disciples and relatives of St. Columba. He was the brother of St. Begbile, St. Conandil, and St. Cuan Caein (Todd and Reeves, *Mart. Doneg.* p. 15; O'Hanlon, *Irish Saints*, i, 195).

12. Son of Ua Laoighse, is commemorated May 15. He was a bishop at Tulach-mic-Comghaill. He was a contemporary of St. Columba, and is twice mentioned in the life of that saint. St. Colman died probably some time between the death of St. Fintan and St. Columba (Lanigan, *Eccl. Hist. of Ireland*, ii, 177, 229 sq.).

13. Surnamed *Mac-Ui-Tealduibh*, is commemorated Feb. 8 and Dec. 12. This is *Columbanus*, one of the bishops to whom pope John IV, A.D. 640 (while yet but pope-elect), addressed the well-known letter urging the Scots to observe the true Easter, and avoid the Pelagian heresy (Bede, *Eccl. Hist.* ii, c. 19). He was bishop of Clonard, and according to the Irish annals died about A.D. 654 (Lanigan, *Eccl. Hist. of Ireland*, ii, 412; Reeves, *Eccl. Antiq.* p. 149 n.).

14. Of Ardbo, is commemorated Feb. 21. He was the son of Aedh, and descended from Colla Uais, monarch of Ireland in the beginning of the 4th century. His church was on the margin of Loch Eachach, in the north-east of Ireland (Todd and Reeves, *Mart. Doneg.* p. 55).

15. Abbot of Cam-Achadh (where he is commemorated March 31), and of Cammus (commemorated Oct. 30). See No. 24.

16. Of Cill-mic-Eoghain, is commemorated Oct 1. This saint was surnamed *Cille*. He was the son of Eugenius, son of Murdoch, and descended from the family of the Oirghialli (Oriel) in Ulster (Todd and Reeves, *Mart. Doneg.* p. 265; Colgan, *Acta Sanctorum*, p. 713, c. 4).

17. Of Cill-Ruaidh, is commemorated Oct. 16. He is only mentioned in connection with St. Ailbhe, who died, according to Irish annals, after the beginning of the 6th century.

18. Of Cluain-Erard (Clonard, in Meath), is commemorated Feb. 9. Among the saints, prelates, and illustrious men in the school and church of Clonard, Colgan (*Acta Sanctorum*, p, 406, c. 5) cites from the *Four Masters*, A.D. 700, the death in that year of Colman-ua-heirc, abbot of Clonard. He must not be confounded with No. 13.

19. Of Comhraire, at Uisneach, is commemorated Sept. 25. *Mart. Doneg.* (by Todd and Reeves, p. 259) says Bronach, daughter of Milinc, son of Buan, with whom Patrick was in bondage, was his mother.

20. Of Druim-mor (Dromore), is commemorated June 6 and 7. This saint is likewise known as *Colmoc*, probably, too, as *Calmaig*. In the Irish martyrologies he is usually called *Mocholmog*, bishop of Dromore. The dates of his birth and death are unknown, but he evidently flourished in the very beginning of the 6th century, and is not to be confounded with Colman Ela, who flourished half a century later. About 500, he founded the noble monastery of Dromore. He compiled, like others of his time, a rule for his monks. He was buried in Dromore. As Colmac, Colmoc, and Calmaig, he appears to have several dedications in Scotland. In the Scotch calendars his feast is June 6, and in the Irish, June 7 (Todd and Reeves, *Mart. Doneg.* p. 149; Lanigan, *Eccl. Hist. of Ireland*, i, 424, 431 sq.; Todd, *Book of Hymns*, Fasc. i, 100 sq.; and *St. Patrick*, p. 131).

21. Of Glendalough, was the son of Uithecar. His festival is Dec. 12. He died A.D. 660, and was contemporary with several other Colmans in the third class of Irish saints (Lanigan, *Eccl. Hist. of Ireland*, iii, 4; Forbes, *Kal. of Scott. Saints*, p. 304).

22. Of Glem-Delmhaic, is commemorated Nov. 12. The history of this Colman is very obscure, but his memory is preserved in the dedication at Clara or Claragh, in Kilkenny.

23. Of Lindisfarne and Inis-bo-finn, being connected with two countries, has a double commemoration, in Scotland on Feb. 18, and in Ireland on Aug. 8. He was consecrated, A.D. 661, as bishop Finan's successor in the see of Lindisfarne. He attended the council of Whitby in 664 on the Easter controversy, where he represented the Scottish party, and was defeated. See WILFRID. Accompanied by all his Scottish or Irish monks, and about thirty of the English, St. Colman returned to his parent monastery of Hy. Soon after, A.D. 668, he sailed to the west of Ireland, and dwelt on the island called Inishbofin. Owing to a dispute between his disciples, he built another monastery at Mayo, where he placed his English monks, while he and the others remained at Inishbofin, where he died Aug. 8, A.D. 676, and where the ruins of his church are still to be seen in the town-land of Knock (Bede, *Eccl. Hist.* iii, c. 25; iv, c. 4; Lanigan, *Eccl. Hist. of Ireland*, iii, 59 sq.; Neander, *Gen. Church Hist.* [Edinb. 1849] v, 28 sq.; Forbes, *Kal. of Scott. Saints*, p. 303, 304).

24. Of Linn-Uachaille, or Lann, is commemorated March 30. Colgan (*Acta Sanctorum*, p. 792, 793), who has collected all the scattered notices regarding this saint, says that his mother was Lassara, and he was a native of Ulster. He had two or three churches, in which he is commemorated as above, and also Oct. 30. He died March 30, A.D. 699, according to the *Four Masters*. This saint is often called *Mocholmoc* (Lanigan, *Eccl. Hist. of Ireland*, iii, 146; Todd and Reeves, *Mart. Doneg.* p. 91, 289; O'Donovan, *Four Masters*, i, 300 n.).

25. Otherwise called *Mocholmog*, of Lismore, is commemorated Jan. 21. His father was Finbarr. Colman flourished in the reign of Cennfaeladh, king of Ireland, who died A.D. 769. After the death of St. Jarula or

Hierlog, Jan. 16, A.D. 699, Colman succeeded him as bishop and abbot of Lismore, whither scholars were attracted from all quarters. Colman died Jan. 22, A.D. 703 (Colgan, *Acta Sanctorum*, p. 154, 155; Lanigan, *Eccl. Hist. of Ireland*, iii, 145–147; O'Hanlon, *Irish Saints*, i, 397 sq.).

26. Also called *Alainn*, is commemorated Dec. 14. His identity is uncertain.

27. Otherwise known as *Dubhchuilenn*, of Duŋ in the Renna, and of many other places, is commemorated Nov. 24. He flourished A.D. 570, and was contemporary with saints Kevin, Mobhi, Clairenech, Colman of Doiremor, Colman Ela, etc. He must be distinguished from Colman of Cloyne, whose festival is on the same day (Colgan, *Acta Sanctorum*, p. 193, col. 1).

28. Surnamed *Eala*, *Ela*, or *Colmanellus*, is commemorated Sept. 26. He was the son of Beognai. By his mother, Mór, he was a nephew of St. Columba. He was born in Glennaichle, now Glenelly, A.D. 555. He founded the monastery at Lann-Eala, in Ferceall (now Lynally). He probably died A.D. 611 (O'Donovan, *Four Masters*, i, 235; Lanigan, *Eccl. Hist. of Ireland*, ii, 304 sq.). Many places in Ayrshire and Argyleshire were dedicated to his memory (Forbes, *Kal. of Scott. Saints*, p. 305).

29. Otherwise named *Finn*, is commemorated April 4. In the days when it was customary to join companions under one leader for Christian teaching and practice, we find Colman Finn in the litany of St. Aengus (Colgan, *Acta Sanctorum*, p. 436 n[2]; Reeves, *Adamnan*, p. 300). He died A.D. 771, according to the *Four Masters*, who call him "Colum Finn the anchoret."

30. Also called *Imramha*, of Fathan Beg, in Inis Eoghain, is commemorated July 8. Among the abbots and saints of the Church of Fahan, where Colgan says there was at one time a noble monastery, and now there is only a parish church, there is cited, without date, "S. Colmanus cogn. Imromha, etc." He is placed in the list before St. Murus or Mura, who must have died sometime before A.D. 658, as that is the date given for the death of Cellach, St. Mura's successor (Lanigan, *Eccl. Hist. of Ireland*, ii, 37, 38).

31. Surnamed *Itadach*, or "The Thirsty," is commemorated March 5. His name does not appear in the calendars, yet his faithfulness is duly chronicled in the *Life of St. Patrick*, by Evinus and Jocelyne. In his strict observance of the rule of fasting he would not quench his thirst in the harvest-field, and died in consequence at Trian Conchobuir about A.D. 445 (Lanigan, *Eccl. Hist. of Ireland*, i, 319).

32. Also called *Mór*, son of Luachan, is commemorated June 17.

33. Surnamed *Muiliun*, "of the Mill," is commemorated Jan. 1. He is said to have been of Doire Chaochain (now Derrykeighan). In St. Aengus's tract on the *Mothers of the Irish Saints*, his mother is given as Bronach, the daughter of Milchu, son of Buan, with whom St. Patrick was in captivity. This Bronach is also given as the mother of St. Mochaoi, or Caelan, who died A.D. 497, and others, which is the only clue we have to the period when he lived (Todd and Reeves, *Mart. Doneg.* p. 3; O'Hanlon, *Irish Saints*, i, 18).

34. Surnamed *Priscus*, A.D. 800, is not to be found in the calendars, but Hector Boethuis gives a Colmanus Priscus, who, with St. Medan, St. Modan, and St. Euchinus, was preacher among the Picts and Scots (*Scotor. Hist.* lib. viii, fol. 151 a, ed. 1575). He was patron saint of the Church of Llangolman and of Capel Colman, in Pembrokeshire (Rees, *Welsh Saints*, p. 190).

35. Also called *Stellain*, of Tir-da-Glas (now Terryglass, in Tipperary), is commemorated May 26. Little appears to be known regarding him. He died A.D. 624 (Colgan, *Acta Sanctorum*, p. 247 n[2]; Lanigan, *Eccl. Hist. of Ireland*, ii, 24).

36. Otherwise named *Ua Cluasaigh*. This Colman is of unknown parentage. He was *Fer-Leghinn*, or lecturer in the theological school at Cork, and is best known as the tutor or master of St. Cumin Foda of Clonfert. He wrote a panegyric on his pupil. It is quoted by the *Four Masters* at A.D. 661. He composed a hymn, intended as a protection against the plague; it is given, with translation and notes, in the *Book of Hymns* edited by Dr. Todd. He died during a pestilence in Ireland, about A.D. 661 or 662 (Todd, *Book of Hymns*, Fasc. i, 86, 93; ii, 121 sq.; O'Donovan, *Four Masters*, i, 271, 272).

37. Also styled *Ua Fiachrach*, of Senbotha (now Templeshambo, in Wexford), is commemorated Oct. 27. He was the son of Eochaidh Brec, and was related to Niall of the Nine Hostages. This Colman was a contemporary of St. Colman Macduach, and of St. Maidoc of Ferus, who flourished in the beginning of the 7th century. His monastery was situated at the foot of Mount Leinster. The year of his death is unknown (Lanigan, *Eccl. Hist. of Ireland*, iii, 2, 5; Todd and Reeves, *Mart. Doneg.* p. 287).

38. Also designated as *Ua Eirc*, was abbot of Clonard, and died A.D. 700. His chief feast was Dec. 5, but he appears to have been also commemorated Feb. 9 (Colgan, *Acta Sanctorum*, p. 406, c. 5; Todd and Reeves, *Mart. Doneg.* p. 327). See No. 18.

39. Likewise styled *Ua Liathain*, "doctor," A.D. 725, is commemorated July 25. Colgan calls him bishop of Lismore and a famous doctor, and says he died about A.D. 725, which is the year given in the *Four Masters* as the date when "S. Colman O'Liadain, a select doctor, died."

40. Of Uamhach (Huamacensis), scribe of Armagh, died in 725, and is commemorated Nov. 24 (Todd and Reeves, *Mart. Doneg.* p. 317).

41. Commemorated Oct. 1, is supposed to be Colman of Cill-mic-Eoghain, who is of the race of Colla-da-Chrioch. See No. 16. Colgan numbers among the saints of the family of Oirghialli (Oriel), and race of Colla-da-Chrioch, St. Colman, surnamed *Kille*, son of Eoghain, etc., and gives his feast as Oct. 1.

Colman, Ebenezer, a Congregational minister, was born at Ashby, Mass. In 1815 he graduated from Brown University; subsequently studied theology at Rindge, N. H., under the tutorship of Rev. Seth Payson, and after three years was ordained pastor at Tiverton, R. I. His fields of labor comprised much of Rhode Island and New Hampshire until 1842, when he removed to western New York, where he remained until 1855. The last three years of his ministry were spent with the Church at Lamoille, Ill. He resided in Detroit, Mich., during the last year of his life, and died there, June 15, 1859, aged sixty-nine years. His preaching is said to have been solemn and convincing. See *Cong. Quarterly*, 1860, p. 84.

Colman, Henry, a Unitarian minister, was born in Boston, Mass., Sept. 12, 1785, and graduated at Dartmouth College in 1805. He was ordained, and installed minister of the Second Congregational Church in Hingham in 1807, where he remained until 1820. From 1825 to 1831 he officiated as pastor of a new Unitarian society in Salem, and afterwards moved to Deerfield, where he devoted himself to farming. He was appointed agricultural commissioner of the state of Massachusetts, and after passing considerable time in making a tour of inspection in that state, and in preparing several reports, spent six years (1842–48) in Europe. The results of his observations during this time were published on his return. In 1849 he revisited Europe in the hope of benefiting his health, but died in London soon after his arrival, Aug. 14, 1849. He published a great number of single *Sermons*. See Sprague, *Annals of the Amer. Pulpit*, viii, 213.

Colman, James, a Baptist missionary, was born in Boston, Mass., Feb. 19, 1794. He was ordained there Sept. 10, 1817, having received his appointment as a missionary the May previous. He arrived at Calcutta April 15, 1818. After remaining for a time in Rangoon, he removed to Chittagong, and thence to Cox's Bazaar, Nov. 12, 1821. He died of jungle fever, July 4, 1822. Mr. Colman was a young man of sincere piety, and consecrated to his work. (J. C. S.)

Colman, Robert, an English Wesleyan minister, was born at Holt, Norfolk, in 1805. He united with the Church in London in his sixteenth year; entered the ministry in 1829; retired from the active work in 1867; resided first at Hardway, Gosport; went to St. Helen's in October, 1871, and died there, Nov. 17 ensuing. He clearly explained and earnestly enforced the doctrines and duties of Christianity. See *Minutes of the British Conference*, 1872, p. 17.

Colmar, Johann, a Lutheran theologian, was born at Nuremberg, June 19, 1684. He studied at Altdorf, where, in 1709, he became magister, on presenting his *De Stoicorum et Peripateticorum Circa Gradum Necessitatis Honorum Externorum ad Summam Beatitudinem Disceptatione*. Having completed his studies at Jena, he was appointed, in 1715, inspector of the alumni at Altdorf. In 1719 he was called to his native place as rector of the hospital-school, and died April 2, 1737. He wrote, *Antihenoticon seu de Causa Negati Lutheranos Inter et Calvinianos Unionis Successus Disquisitio Methodo Mathematica Instituta* (1714):—*Disp. de Summa Judæorum Astorgia, ad Mich. ii*, 5 (1716):—*De Affectuum Caussis* (1719). See Wills, *Nürnberger Gelehrten-Lexikon;* Jöcher, *Allgemeines Gelehrten-Lexikon*, s. v. (B. P.)

Colmar, John, an English Wesleyan missionary, was sent to the West Indies in 1816, where he labored until his sudden death, on the island of Tortola, Sept. 15, 1818. Colmar was a young man of genuine piety. See *Minutes of the British Conference*, 1819.

Colmar, Joseph Ludwig, a Roman Catholic theologian of Germany, was born at Strasburg, June 22, 1760. Having received holy orders, he was appointed professor at the royal college of his native place. In 1802 he was made bishop of Mayence, and died Dec. 15, 1818. Besides sermons and pastoral letters, he published *Sententiæ S. Ignatii pro Quolibet die Mensis Distributæ* (Mayence, 1809–12). See Döring, *Die Gelehrten Theologen Deutschlands*, i, 261 sq.; Winer, *Handbuch der theol. Lit.* ii, 113, 147. (B. P.)

Colmenares, Diego de, a Spanish historian, was born at Segovia in 1586. He entered the priestly order while very young, and was for a long time rector of the Church of St. John of Segovia. At the age of thirty-four he resolved to write the history of his native city, and spent fourteen years in collecting the necessary information. At last, in 1634, he published his book, the first of the kind written in Spain. It was entitled *Historia de la Insigne Ciudad de Sigovia y Compendio de las Historias de Castilla* (Segovia, 1634). He died in 1651. See Hoefer, *Nouv. Biog. Générale*, s. v.

Colmus, an early Scotch saint, is said by Camerarius and Dempster to have been a bishop of the Orkney islands, and is commemorated on March 9 and June 6. But the name probably belongs to two or more individuals, and may be the same as the *Colmach, Colman*, and *Colme* of the Scotch calendars, and of the litany of Dunkeld (Forbes, *Kal. of Scottish Saints*, p. 305, 306).

Colobium (κολόβιον) was a tunic with very short sleeves only, and fitting closely about the arm. The tradition was that Sylvester, bishop of Rome, ordered that *deacons* should wear dalmatics in offices of holy ministry, in place of the colobia, which had previously been in use. From this circumstance of the colobium being regarded as the special vestment of a deacon, it is sometimes called *lebiton* (i. e. *leviton*) or *lebitonarium*, a word which reappears in ecclesiastical Greek of the 5th and later centuries (λεβιτών). The monastic colobium in Palestine, if not elsewhere, had upon it a purple "sign," probably a cross, used, perhaps, as a mark of service under Christ. Examples of the Greek colobium may be seen in the ancient mosaics of the 4th century, in the church of St. George at Thessalonica.

Cologna, Abraham da, an Italian rabbi, was born at Mantua in 1755. Having devoted himself from youth to the study of Jewish theology and philosophy, he was made a member of the College of the *Dotti* at Mantua, and in 1806 was called to Paris as ecclesiastical member of the body of distinguished Israelites assembled by Napoleon. In 1808 he was appointed one of the three grand rabbis of the central consistory; in 1812 its president, and in 1826 left Paris to assume the office of first rabbi at Trieste. He died there in 1832. Cologna was one of the principal collaborators of the *Israélite Français*, a periodical, published for some time at Paris. He also left a pamphlet upon the work of M. Bail, *Les Juifs au Dix-Neuvième Siècle*, and another on the same work, addressed to Sylvester of Sacy. See Hoefer, *Nouv. Biog. Générale*, s. v.

Cologne, Councils of (*Concilium Coloniense* or *Agrippinense*), were provincial synods as follows:

I. Said to have been held A.D. 346, to condemn Euphratas, bishop of Cologne (for denying our Lord's divinity), who was, however, at Sardica as an orthodox bishop the year after (*Pagi ad an.* 346, n. 6; Mansi, *Concil.* ii, 1371–1378). Baronius and Cave think the council spurious. Sirmond supposes that Euphratas recanted; others that he was acquitted; others that there were two successive bishops of Cologne so named.

II. Another council is reported to have been held in 782, under Charlemagne, but this was apparently a political council; nothing is known of it ecclesiastically (Labbe and Cossart, *Concil.* vi, 1827, from Eginhard).

III. Held April 1, 887. In it the ancient canons were confirmed, and censures pronounced against those who pillaged the property of the Church, oppressed the poor, and married within the forbidden limits. See Labbe, *Concil.* xi, 396.

IV. Held March 12, 1260, by Conrad, archbishop of Cologne. In it were drawn up fourteen canons of discipline for the clergy, and eighteen for monks. Among the former:

1. Is directed against those of the clergy who kept mistresses: forbids them to be present at the marriage of their children, or to leave them anything by will.
3. Declares that all clergy should know how to read, and to chant the praises of God, and orders such as cannot do so to provide a deputy.
7. Orders that in churches belonging to canons, if there be no dormitory, one shall forthwith be built, and that the said canons shall occupy it, that they may always be ready to assist at matins: also forbids them to eat or sleep out of the confines of their church, i. e. the dormitory.

See Labbe, *Concil.* xi, 784.

V. Held in 1266, by Engilbert, archbishop of Cologne. Fifty-four canons were drawn up, which are chiefly against the plunderers of the Church, and those who killed, injured, and defrauded ecclesiastics. The last orders that the names of sacrilegious persons shall be kept in a book, and constantly read out. See Labbe, *Concil.* xi, 835.

VI. Held in 1280, by Sifridus (Sifroi), archbishop of Cologne. Eighteen canons were drawn up.

1. Relates to the life and conversation of the clergy, and forbids them to play at games of chance; directs them to say daily the office of the Blessed Virgin.
3. Relates to the state, etc., of the religious, and forbids monks or nuns to have any sort of property.
7. Treats at length of the sacrament of the altar, and directs that before celebrating the communion the priests shall have said matins and prime, and have confessed, if they have the opportunity.
8. Treats of the sacrament of penance.
9. Of orders.
10. Of matrimony.

See Labbe, *Concil.* xi, 1107.

VII. Held about the year 1300, by Wichbold, archbishop of Cologne; twenty-two canons were published.

2. Orders deans to deliver in writing a list of all non-resident incumbents in their deaneries.
15. Orders all priests in the diocese to excite their parishioners to contribute towards the fabric of the cathedral of Cologne.
17. Orders that the clerks appointed to ring the bells shall not be illiterate persons, but, if occasion require, able to assist the priest at the altar.

See Labbe, *Concil.* xi, 1439.

VIII. Held March 9, 1310, by Henry, archbishop of Cologne, and three bishops; twenty-nine canons were published.

11. Directs that the epistles and gospels shall be read only by persons in holy orders.
16. Directs that those persons whose office it is to ring the church bells shall know how to read, in order that they may be able to make the responses; and also that they shall wear the alb during divine service.
17. Directs that the rural deans shall provide that all their churches be furnished with proper ornaments.
21. Forbids to pronounce a curse against any person in the church, or to sing the *Media Vita* against any one, without the bishop's leave.
23. Directs that in future the year shall commence at the festival of Christmas, according to the use of the Roman Church.

Others forbid parishioners to receive the holy communion, at Easter, at the hands of any but their own curates; order nuns to keep close to their cloisters, and monks to observe strictly the rule of poverty.

See Labbe, *Concil.* xi, 1517.

IX. Held in 1423, by Thierry, archbishop of Cologne; eleven canons were decreed.

Among other things, it was ordered that clergymen convicted of incontinence should be deposed, if, after due warning, they did not amend their scandalous life; that priests alone shall be named to preach indulgence and to collect alms; that canons and other clerks refrain from talking during divine service, under penalty of losing allowance.

The ninth canon is directed against the doctrines of Wycliffe and John Huss.

See Labbe, *Concil.* xii, 360.

X. Held in 1452, by cardinal Cusa, legate *à latere* for Germany.

Here it was decreed that a provincial council should be held at Cologne every three years, so that a synod should occur annually in one of the three dioceses; that all Jews, of both sexes, should have their dress marked with a circle, in order to distinguish them; that the clergy should keep their hair cut short; also, that processions with the holy sacrament should not be permitted to take place too frequently, and then that all should be done with extreme reverence.

See Labbe, *Concil.* xiii, 1378.

XI. Held in 1536, by Hermann, archbishop of Cologne, assisted by his suffragans, and several others. The acts of this council are divided into fourteen articles, each article containing several decrees relating to the discipline of the church.

Art. I. Consists of thirty-six canons, and treats of the duties of bishops, especially in ordaining and visiting. Among other things: 4. Buying and selling of benefices, and worldly motives in giving them, are denounced as detestable; also, 32. Pluralities are condemned, and those who have the pope's license for a plurality of benefices are bidden to inquire of their consciences whether they have God's license also.

Art. II. Relates to the offices of the Church, etc., and contains thirty-two canons. Bishops are exhorted to reform their breviaries where they are defective, and to purge out all false or doubtful legends, which have been inserted (*nescimus qua incuria*) instead of passages from Holy Scripture; directions are given that the breviary be recited with reverence and attention, and that the mass be celebrated with proper devotion. 15. Defines the proper use of organs, which, it states, are intended to excite devotion, and not profane emotions of joy. With regard to the morals and conduct of the clergy, it states (22) that pride, luxury, and avarice are the principal causes of their evil reputation; and (in 23, 24, 25) that they ought to abstain from great feasts and good living, and from drunkenness and other like vices.

Arts. III, IV, and V relate to cathedral and other churches, and those who serve them, to the mendicant friars, etc., and contain in all fifty-seven canons. Canons are ordered to live canonically, as their name imports, to remember the original intention of their institution, which was, that they should dwell together, etc.; if they fail on any occasion to be present at mass after the epistle, or at the hours after the first psalm, they shall be deprived of their allowance. Non-residence is forbidden. Persons having cure of souls are exhorted to be careful to exhibit a pattern to their flocks.

Art. VI. Relates to the preaching of the word of God, and contains twenty-seven canons; states that the preacher ought constantly to read in and meditate upon the Holy Scriptures; to accommodate his discourse to the understanding of his hearers; to avoid profane eloquence and worldly declamation, and everything tending to the ridiculous; shows how the clergy are to instruct the people upon controverted subjects, and to repress vice. Canon 26. Directs that the decalogue and creed shall be plainly recited immediately after the sermon.

Art. VII. Relates to the sacraments of the Church, and contains fifty-two canons. It reckons seven sacraments; directs that the clergy should instruct the people that the visible part of a sacrament is but the sensible sign of the effect produced upon the soul; it treats of each of the seven sacraments in detail. Among other things, it declares that, in order to be admitted to the communion, it is necessary to have a pure conscience, a heart truly penitent, and a lively faith, to realize the truth of Christ's body offered and his blood poured forth in that sacrament. With regard to the communion in both kinds, canon 15 directs the priest to teach those of his parishioners who are hurt at the denial of the cup, that the layman, who receives the bread only, receives as fully and completely both the body and the blood of our Lord as the priest does, who receives in both kinds; that the Church, out of reverence to the sacrament, and for the salvation of the faithful, hath thought proper so to order it, and that, consequently, the laity, being assured that they do receive both the body and blood of Christ, should submit to its judgment.

Art. VIII. Containing seven canons, is upon the subject of the maintenance of the clergy; it forbids any fee for the administration of the sacraments or for burials; it also enjoins the restoration of tithes by those laymen who had usurped them.

Art. IX. Containing twenty-one canons, speaks of the usages and customs of the Church; directs that fasting, being an ordinance of the Church, may not be neglected, and declares that to eat sumptuous breakfasts on days appointed to be observed with fasting, is not obedience to the spirit of the Church's injunction; it also explains the appointment of Rogation days, and declares that Sunday is to be observed and kept holy; that on that day it is the duty of the faithful to hear mass and the sermon, and to sing the psalms and hymns; forbids fairs to be held on that day, and the frequenting of taverns.

Art. X. Contains nineteen canons, and relates to monastic discipline.

Art. XI. Contains eight canons, relating to almshouses, hospitals, and similar establishments; states that it is the bishop's duty to look after the repair of those which have fallen into decay, and to provide for the spiritual care of those persons who dwell in them.

Art. XII. Contains nine canons, relating to schools, libraries, etc.

Art. XIII. Relates to contests about ecclesiastical jurisdiction, etc., and contains four canons.

Art. XIV. Relates to episcopal and other visitations, and contains twenty-four canons.

See Labbe, *Concil.* xiv, 484.

XII. Held in 1549, by Adolphus, archbishop. Several statutes were made for the reformation of the Church; the six principal methods recommended are the following:

1. It was ordered that the education of the young should be confided to those persons only whose purity of faith and life was known, and who had undergone an examination by the ordinary, or by persons approved by him. That no suspected or heretical works should be allowed in colleges or universities.
2. It is declared that the examination of candidates for orders, and of persons to be instituted to benefices, belongs to the bishop alone, or to persons authorized by him; and that those who desire to be ordained shall give public notice of the same.
3. The clergy are ordered to inflict the penalty enjoined by the canons upon those whose sins have deserved it, and not to remit it for money. Pluralities are forbidden.
4. The end of episcopal visitations is declared to be the correction of vice, and the restoration of purity of life and discipline. Bishops are exhorted to take but few followers with them in their visitations, to avoid burdening their clergy.
5. The necessity of holding ecclesiastical synods is shown, in order to preserve the faith and discipline of the Church in their integrity, and to maintain purity of morals, to insure the reformation of abuses.
6. Treats of the re-establishment of ecclesiastical discipline.

These statutes were approved by the emperor's letters-patent. See Labbe, *Concil.* xiv, 627.—Landon, *Man. of Councils*, s. v.

Cologne, DANIEL and WILLIAM OF. See CÖLLN.

Colomb, JEAN, a learned French theologian, was born at Limoges, Nov. 12, 1688. He entered the Benedictine order in 1707, and died in 1773. Having become collaborator of Rivet, he continued, after the death of that scholar, the *Histoire Littéraire de la France.* He also wrote *Histoire de l'Abbaye de Saint-Vincent du Mans* (still in MS.). See Hoefer, *Nouv. Biog. Générale*, s. v.

Colomba, *Saint* (1), a Christian virgin, called the first martyr of Celtic Gaul, suffered at Sens under Marcus Aurelius, according to one authority, but according to other and more probable accounts, under the emperor Aurelian, about 273. In the 7th century she was an object of great veneration at Paris, and Dagobert caused a magnificent shrine to be placed in the Benedictine church at Sens, in honor of her. This was destroyed when the church was pillaged by the Calvinists. She is commemorated as St. *Columba* on Dec. 31. See Hoefer, *Nouv. Biog. Générale*, s. v.

Colomba, *Saint* (2), a Spanish martyr, was born at Cordova. While very young she was placed under the care of her sister. Elizabeth, in the monastery of Tabennæ. Being driven from this place, together with the other nuns, by the Moors, she took refuge at Cordova, and, when arraigned, boldly declared herself a Christian, and was beheaded Oct. 17, 853. Her body, which was thrown into the Guadalquivir, was recovered by the Christians and interred in the Church of St. Eulalia at Cordova. An order of St. Columba was founded in 1379 by John I, but it did not survive its founder. See Hoefer, *Nouv. Biog. Générale*, s. v.

Colomban. See COLUMBANUS.

Colombano, ANTONIO MARIA, an Italian painter, a native of Correggio, flourished from 1596 to 1616. There are fifteen pictures mentioned as executed by this artist, representing subjects from the life of the Virgin and the infancy of Christ.

Colombel, NICOLAS, a French painter, was born at Sotteville, near Rouen, in 1646, studied under Lesueur, and subsequently visited Rome for improvement. He was elected professor of the Royal Academy of Paris in 1705. Among his best productions, at Versailles, are *Moses Saved by Pharaoh's Daughter* and *Moses Defending the Daughters of Jethro.* He died at Paris in 1717. See Spooner, *Biographical History of the Fine Arts*, s. v.; Hoefer, *Nouv. Biog. Générale*, s. v.

Colombière, CLAUDE DE LA, a French Jesuit, was born at Saint-Symphorien, near Lyons, in 1641. He was two years court-preacher to the duke of York, afterwards James II of England, but was eventually banished, and retired to Parai, in Burgundy, where he died, Feb. 15, 1682. He was a famous preacher, and became noted for his "devotion to the Sacred Heart of Jesus," a sentiment which the notorious Marie Alacoque carried to the extreme of fanaticism. His *Sermons* were published (Lyons, 1757, 6 vols.), also a few treatises on practical religion.

Colombini, Giovanni, a painter of the Venetian school, was born at Trevigi about 1700, and studied under Sebastiano Ricci. His chief works are in the convent of the Dominicans at Trevigi.

Colombini, *San* **Giovanni**, a noted Italian ecclesiastic, was a member of a distinguished family in Sienna, and a magistrate there. It is said that one day, being obliged to wait for his repast, his wife gave him as a means of diversion the *Lives of the Saints* to read. This so impressed him that he resigned his civil office, proceeded to distribute a great part of his goods to the poor, turned his house into a hospital, and collected a number of disciples, who received from the people the name *Jesuates*, because they often spoke the name of Jesus in a loud voice. Urban V approved this novel institution, under the order of St. Augustine. These Jesuates were originally laymen, and applied themselves to the preparation of medicaments, but in 1606 they received permission to take sacred orders. They were suppressed in 1669 by Clement IX. Colombini died July 31, 1367. See Hoefer, *Nouv. Biog. Générale*, s. v.

Colomiès (Lat. *Colomesius*), PAUL, a learned French Protestant, was born at La Rochelle, Dec. 2, 1638. He studied philosophy and theology at Saumur, learned Hebrew under the celebrated Cappel, allied himself at Paris with Isaac Vossius, and accompanied him to Holland. In 1681 he went to England, and became librarian to Sancroft, archbishop of Canterbury; lost this place in consequence of the disgrace of his protector, and died of chagrin at London, Jan. 13, 1692. He wrote, *Gallia Orientalis* (Hague, 1665):—*Exhortation de Tertullien aux Martyrs* (ibid. 1673):—*Rome Protestante* (Lond. 1675):—*Theologorum Presbyterianorum Icones* (1682):—*Parallèle de la Pratique de l'Église Ancienne et de Celle des Protestants de France* (eod.):—*Bibliothèque Choisie* (La Rochelle, eod.; Amsterdam, 1699):—*Ad Gulielmi Cave Chartophylacem Ecclesiasticum Paralipomena: Accedit de Scriptis Photii Dissertatio, et Passio S. Victoris Massiliensis* (Lond. 1686, 1689; Leips. 1687):—*Lettre a M. Justel*, etc. (Lond. 1686). John Albert Fabricius published the greater part of the works of Colomiès in a volume entitled *Colomesii Opera, Theologi, Critici, et Historici Argumenti, Junctim Edita* (Hamb. 1709). Colomiès was also the editor of the following: *S. Clementis Epistolæ duæ ad Corinthios, Interpretibus Patricio Junio, Gottifredo Wendelino, et Joh. Bap. Cotelerio* (Vienna, 1682), and others. See *Biog. Universelle*, s. v.

Colomme, JEAN BAPTISTE SÉBASTIEN, a French theologian, was born at Pau, April 12, 1712. He was superior of the Barnabites, and died at Paris in 1788, leaving *Dictionnaire Portatif de l'Écriture Sainte* (Paris, 1775; first published under the title *Notice sur l'Écriture Sainte*, ibid. 1773):—*Manuel des Religieuses* (ibid. 1779):—*Éternité Malheureuse* (transl. from the Latin of Drexelius, ibid. 1788). He also wrote a translation of the *Opuscula* of Thomas à Kempis (ibid. 1785), and an enlarged edition of the same, entitled *Vie Chrétienne, ou Principes de la Sagesse* (1774; Avignon, 1779). See Hoefer, *Nouv. Biog. Générale*, s. v.

Colon, BERNARD, a learned French theologian of the Benedictine order, who died in 1709, wrote *Traité des Vers Latins* (Paris, 1664), and several memorial sermons. See Hoefer, *Nouv. Biog. Générale*, s. v.

Colonātus. In the *Mart. Doneg.* (by Todd and Reeves, p. 191) there are two entries at July 8, but Dr. Todd shows that they both belong to the same persons, namely, to St. Cilian (q. v.) and his companions, who evangelized Würzburg, and suffered there. Colonatus is said to have been honored in the Enzie, Banffshire (Forbes, *Kal. of Scott. Saints*, p. 306). See COLMAN.

Colonia, André de, a French theologian of the Minorite order, who was born at Aix, in Provence, in 1617, and died at Marseilles in 1688, wrote some theological and other works, for which see Hoefer, *Nouv. Biog. Générale*, s. v.

Colonia, Dominique de, a French scholar and antiquarian, was born at Aix, in Provence, Aug. 25, 1660. He became a Jesuit, and resided at Lyons for fifty-nine years, where he taught successively the lower studies, rhetoric, and elementary theology. He died at Lyons, Sept. 12, 1741, leaving many works, among which we cite *Antiquités de la Ville de Lyon:—Pratique de Piété* (Paris, 1717):—*La Religion Chrétienne Autorisée par le Témoignage des Anciens Païens* (ibid.

1718; ibid. and Besançon, 1826):—*Bibliothèque Jansén-iste* (ibid. 1722, 1731, and elsewhere under different titles). In the *Journal de Trévoux* various memoirs by Colonia are found. See Hoefer, *Nouv. Biog. Générale*, s. v.; *Biog. Universelle*, s. v.

Colonĭca. See MACARIUS.

Colonna, Ascanio, an Italian prelate, was born about 1560; was made cardinal in 1586, afterwards viceroy of Aragon, and died at Rome, May 17, 1608, leaving *De Monarchia Siciliæ*, which is a critique upon the treatise of Baronius, *Monarchia Siciliana*, and is found, with the response of Baronius, in the *Thesaurus Antiquitatum Siciliæ* of Grævius. See Hoefer, *Nouv. Biog. Générale*, s. v.

Colonna, Egidio. See ÆGIDIUS.

Colonna, Francesco, an Italian scholar, was born at Venice about 1449. While young he entered the Dominican order, was professor of grammar and belles-lettres in the convent of that order at Treviso in 1467, and in 1473 was made doctor of theology at Padua. He died in 1527, leaving a very singular work, a kind of allegorical romance, entitled *Hypnerotomachia Poliphili*, intended to show that human passions are but dreams (originally published at Venice in 1499; an inferior edition, ibid. 1545; transl. into French, Paris, 1546, also 1554, 1561; improved version, by Vernille, ibid. 1600; literal translation by Le Grand, ibid. 1804; Parma, 1811; English transl. Lond. 1592, not complete). See Hoefer, *Nouv. Biog. Générale*, s. v.

Colonna, Giacomo (1), an Italian prelate, was made cardinal by Nicholas III, and afterwards chief counsellor of the papal court, while his relatives were loaded with similar honors by Nicholas IV. But Boniface VIII stripped the Colonna family of their privileges, and Giacomo retired to France. He is believed to have taken part in the conspiracy of Sciarra Colonna, in concert with Nogaret, against the pope. The dignity of cardinal was restored to him by Clement V, Dec. 17, 1305, and the bull against the Colonnas was recalled at the intercession of Philip the Fair. Giacomo died in 1318. See Hoefer, *Nouv. Biog. Générale*, s. v.

Colonna, Giacomo (2), an Italian prelate, lived in the early part of the 14th century. Pope John XXII appointed him bishop of Lombez in return for the courage he manifested in publishing at Rome the excommunication pronounced against Louis of Bavaria. As a protector of Petrarch, Colonna contributed much to bring about the coronation of that poet at Rome in 1341, and Petrarch addressed to him a *canzone*. See Hoefer, *Nouv. Biog. Générale*, s. v.

Colonna, Giovanni, an Italian prelate, was made cardinal by pope Honorius in 1216, and was present as legate at the taking of Damietta by St. Louis. Falling into the hands of the Saracens he was condemned to be sawn asunder, but his courage won the admiration of his captors, and he was set at liberty. He founded the hospital of the Lateran at Rome, and died there in 1255, leaving *Historia Sacra*, which is in MS., besides some *Letters on the Holy Land*, to be found in Ughelli. See Hoefer, *Nouv. Biog. Générale*, s. v.

Colonna, Giovanni Paolo, one of the greatest Italian musical composers, was born in 1640. He received his education at Rome, where Carissimi, Benevoli, and others were his teachers. He then made Bologna his residence, where he soon became the head of the musical school, and died Nov. 28, 1695. His compositions are for the most part of a religious character. The most important he issued in twelve collections, published at Bologna. The first appeared as Op. 1, under the title *Salmi Brevi a 8 Voci* (1681), and the last as Op. 12, under the title *Psalmi ad Vesperas* (1694). See *Biog. Universelle*, s. v. (B. P.)

Colonna, Pompeo, an Italian prelate, was at first bishop of Rieti. Turbulent and passionate, he gave himself up to his fondness for arms, and took an active part in all the revolutions of the Roman court, but was nevertheless a patron of literature. He had the legateship of the March of Ancona, the bishopric of Aversa, the archbishopric of Montereale, and was viceroy of Naples. He died at Naples, June 28, 1532, leaving *De Laudibus Mulierum*, a poem, in MS. See Hoefer, *Nouv. Biog. Générale*, s. v.

Colorbasians. See COLARBASUS.

Colorites were a congregation of Augustinian monks, founded in the 16th century by Bernard of Rogliano, in Calabria. The name is said to have been derived from Colorito, a hill in the district of Naples, on which there is a church dedicated to the Virgin Mary. The order was not fully established until 1591, and a few years later they avowed submission to the general of the Augustinians. Their habit consisted of a dark-colored gown and a mantle that reached only to the knees.

Colors, ECCLESIASTICAL. The following details are from Walcott, *Sac. Archæol.* s. v.:

"In some foreign churches the dignity of feasts was attempted to be shown by a graduated scale of colors. A curious analogy has been traced between the three common chord notes, the third, fifth, and eighth, and the three primary colors of the solar ray; also of the seven notes of the major diatonic scale and the colors of the solar spectrum, so that various instruments have been ingeniously represented as colors—the oboe as yellow, the flute white, the trumpet scarlet, etc.

"Jerome mentions that one dress was worn in sacred ministrations, and another in ordinary life; and pope Stephen III enjoined the ecclesiastical vestments to be used only in church. Possibly about the 6th century the fashion of vestments became fixed. Salvian, Paulinus of Nola, and pope Celestine, in 428, allude to the adoption of a distinct dress by priests. In France it was the practice in the 5th century; and the monks, by the adoption of a habit, promoted the movement. At Constantinople, in the 4th century, the Catholics wore black, and the Novatians white, out of doors. Chrysostom celebrated in white, which he mentions as the church-dress. In the early times of the church white was used, certainly in the 4th century, as appears from the writings of Jerome, Gregory of Tours, Isidore of Seville, and Fortunatus. Anastatius speaks of it in the lives of Popes Leo III and IV, Gregory IV, and Sergius II; and in the mosaics at St. Paul's-Without, at Rome, white robes, sometimes adorned with bands of violet or gold, appear, as worn by the early popes. From the 9th century red, blue, and green were gradually permitted in vestments, but prescript colors were not generally adopted until the 11th or 12th century, white being retained for the amice, alb, surplice, and the cope and chasuble on feasts of the Nativity, Epiphany, All-Saints, and St. John the Baptist. They are first mentioned by the author of the 'Treatise on Divine Offices' about the 11th century, and afterwards, in the 13th century, by Durandus, bishop of Mende, and Innocent III. The Greeks, about the same period, adopted these colors, reserving red, however, for fast-days and memorials of saints. The Greek Church requires white at Christmas, Epiphany, and Easter; blue or violet in Passion Week, in Advent, Lent, and at burials; and white and green at Pentecost. No doubt the common color for altar-cloths—which is red, and the ordinary color of the Salisbury rite—was observed in England, owing to the Sarum use being prescribed for the whole southern province in 1541. The national custom differed greatly from the Roman, as in the use of red instead of violet on Sundays in Lent, and from Septuagesima to Easter, on Ash-Wednesday, Maunday-Thursday, Good-Friday, and the Great Saturday, or Easter eve, on Sunday in Trinity, and in processions; while gold color was used instead of white on confessors' days.

"Festivals were usually distinguished by *white*, as emblematical of the purity of the life of saints, although sometimes by red, as symbolical of the heroism of the death of martyrs. Catechumens wore white robes during the octave after their baptism. The pope wears white; and on great days the bishop's chair was draped in white to represent divine truth. The dead were wrapped in white, in memory of our Lord's winding-sheet. *Violet*, mentioned by Durandus, in addition to white, red, black, and green, was used on common days, and in Advent, Lent, and on vigils, as the penitential color nearest to black. Violet, worn on Embers and vigils, being a mixture of black for sorrow and red for love, betokens penitence, grief for sins, inspired by the love of Christ. Our Lord wears violet sometimes, as a type of the Man of Sorrows. Nuns wore violet: so did Benedictine abbots until recent times, and penitents in primitive times. Violet was the color of the parchment used for church books in the time of Jerome, and at a later date. Violet typified truth, deep love, and humility. *Jacinth* represents Christian prudence; *purple* royalty and justice. At burials, masses for the dead, and on Good-Friday, *black* is worn. By the Salisbury use, *crocus* or *saffron*, gold color, is prescribed on feasts of the confessors, as emblematical of the preciousness of their faith; but at Laon on Good-Friday, in allusion to the envy of the Jews. Pale yellow, as in the dress of Judas, signifies deceit. *Red*, by the Salisbury use, was enjoined on Ash-Wednesday, Sundays in Lent, and the three latter days of Holy Week, as the symbol of sin (Isaiah i, 18); as the sign of majesty and might on Sundays (Isaiah lxiii, 1); and of blood, in the commemoration of the passion, death, and burial of our crucified Lord; and so on Good-Friday at Bourges, Sens, Mans, and by the Ambrosian rite. The latter requires it also on Corpus Christi, as the great mystery of Christ's love, and, like the Church of Lyons, on the Circumcision, in memory of the first shedding of his blood, and the first act of his love; whereas the Roman use employs white on the former day, in allusion to the mystery of faith; red on Pentecost personifies the divine love of the Holy Spirit; and in funeral services of the Greeks, and the ancient rites of France, and by the pope on Good-Friday, as showing that love is the cause of their sorrow. Red is the ordinary color of the Salisbury and Ambrosian rites, as green is of the Roman. Red was used in Lent, being the vigil of the Passion, from Septuagesima to Easter eve, at Bourges, Nevers, Sens, and Mans. Black chasubles with red orphreys were used from Passion-Sunday to Easter at Paris, and at funerals in parts of Germany and Flanders. Red and white were the Dominical colors in England. Martyrs were buried in a scarlet colobium or dalmatic, the symbol of charity and blood-shedding. *Blue* (*indicum, blodium*) was worn on the Continent, like violet, on All-Saints' Day, in Advent, and on Septuagesima, and on feasts of St. Mary, as in England, in Spain, and Naples. It was probably used at Salisbury on ferials in Advent. Our Lord and the Virgin Mary wear red and blue. Blue, the color of heaven, was the emblem of piety, sincerity, godliness, contemplation, expectation, love of heavenly things."

Colossæ. We give a few additional particulars of this place from Kitto's *Pict. Bible*, note to Col. iv.:

"Though a town of considerable note, it was by no means the principal one of Phrygia; for when that great province was ultimately divided into Phrygia Pacatiana and Phrygia Salutaris, it ranked but as the sixth city of the former division. The town was seated on an eminence to the south of the Meander, at a place where the river Lycus began to run under ground, as it did for five furlongs, after which it again rose and flowed into the Meander. This valuable indication of the site of Colossæ, furnished by Herodotus (l. vii, c. 30), establishes the truth of the received conclusion, that the ancient city is represented by the modern village of *Khonas*. The approach to Khonas, as well as the village itself, is beautiful, abounding in tall trees, from which vines of most luxuriant growth are suspended. In the immediate neighborhood of the village are several vestiges of an ancient city, consisting of arches, vaults, squared stones, while the ground is strewed with broken pottery, which so generally and so remarkably indicates the sites of ancient towns in the East. That these ruins are all that now remain of Colossæ there seems no just reason to doubt."

The town now contains about four thousand inhabitants, and has a khan. The ruins, which lie three miles north of the town, are of the Roman period, but they contain no inscriptions. See Murray, *Hand-book for Asia Minor*, p. 326.

Colossiānus. See FIRMUS.

Coloumelle, LANDULFE DE, a French chronicler, was canon of Chartres after his uncle Ralph, about 1330. He wrote a chronicle from the foundation of the world down to his own time, entitled, *Breviaire Historial;* twice published in full in Latin (Poitiers, 1479; Paris, eod.). Labbe printed some fragments in the first volume of his *Library of Manuscripts*, among others, the eulogies on Philip the Fair, king of France, and his two sons, Louis the Stubborn and Philip the Long. See Hoefer, *Nouv. Biog. Générale*, s. v.

Colpias (*Wind*) was, in Phœnician mythology, the primæval deity of the wind, who, with his wife Baan, or night, begot Æon and Protogonus, the first mortal men.

Colquhoun, James, a Scotch clergyman, took his degree at Glasgow University in 1635; was called to the living at Whithorn in 1664; transferred to Penninghham in 1665. Having persecuted some of his parishioners, he was ousted by them in 1689, when he went to Ireland, got a benefice there, and died at an advanced age. See *Fasti Eccles. Scoticanæ*, i, 743, 748.

Colquhoun, John (1), a Scotch clergyman, received a bursary of theology at the Glasgow University in 1735; was licensed to preach in 1739; presented by the king to the living at Baldernock in 1745, and ordained; and died July 21, 1772. He published a sermon in 1766, *The Apostles the Light of the World.* See *Fasti Eccles. Scoticanæ*, ii, 343.

View of Khonas, thought to be the modern representative of Colossæ.

Colquhoun, John (2), D.D., a Scotch clergyman, was born at Luss in January, 1748; educated at the universities of Glasgow and Edinburgh; licensed to preach in 1780; called to the living of St. John's, Edinburgh, in 1781, and died Nov. 27, 1827. He was never absent from his charge excepting on sacramental occasions; his duties were discharged with zeal, and his life was one of sincerity and simplicity. He wrote, *A Treatise on Spiritual Comfort* (1815):—*On the Law and Gospel* (1816):—*On the Covenant of Grace* (1818):—*Catechism for Directing Young Communicants* (1821):—*On the Covenant of Works* (eod.):—*View of Saving Faith* (1824):—*Collection of the Promises of Scripture* (1825):—*View of Evangelical Repentance* (eod.):—*Sermons on Doctrinal Subjects* (posthumous, 1836). See *Fasti Eccles. Scoticanæ*, i, 109.

Colquhoun, Malcolm, a Scotch clergyman, was licensed to preach in 1794; appointed minister at the Gaelic chapel, Dundee, in 1796, and ordained; and died March 19, 1819, aged sixty-one years. See *Fasti Eccles. Scoticanæ*, iii, 700.

Colquhoun, Robert, a Scotch prelate, was made bishop of Argyle in 1473, and was so in 1495. See Keith, *Scottish Bishops*, p. 288.

Colson, Ebenezer, a Methodist Episcopal minister, was born at Plainfield, Mass., about 1805. He was converted at the age of fifteen, and at twenty-four entered the Oneida Conference. In 1844 he joined the Genesee Conference, in which he labored as health would permit, until his death, Dec. 16, 1864. Mr. Colson was a true man, deeply pious and faithful. See *Minutes of Annual Conferences*, 1864, p. 134.

Colston, Edward, an English philanthropist, was born at Bristol, Nov. 2, 1630. Having amassed a fortune in Spanish trade, he spent nearly all of it in establishing charitable institutions, such as schools and hospitals, in Bristol and other cities of England. He died Oct. 11, 1721.

Colston, William Hungerford, D.D., a Church-of-England divine, was born in 1774. He graduated at St. Mary's Hall, Oxford, in 1796; was for fifty-seven years rector of West Lydford, and for the same period an active magistrate and a deputy-lieutenant of Somersetshire, and also rector of Clapton. He died at Bath, Oct. 8, 1856. See Hardwick, *Annual Biography*, 1856, p. 230.

Colt, Adam, A.M., a Scotch clergyman, regent in the Edinburgh University, was admitted to the living at Borthwick in 1595; presented to the new erection in 1596; transferred to Inveresk in 1597; was one of the royal commissioners, and nominated a minister for Edinburgh; was at the general assemblies of 1601 and 1602; in 1606 was selected as one of eight, for a conference at London previous to the establishment of episcopacy; detained in London ten months, then returned, and confined within his parish; resigned the charge in 1641, and died soon after his last sermon, March 24, 1643, "having much reputation for learning, wisdom, and piety; for grace and gifts, faithfulness and success." See *Fasti Eccles. Scoticanæ*, i, 266, 285, 286.

Colt, John, a Scotch clergyman, was licensed to preach in 1635; admitted to the living at Langnewton in 1642; conformed to episcopacy, and continued in February, 1665. See *Fasti Eccles. Scoticanæ*, i, 486.

Colt, Milton, a Methodist Episcopal minister, was born in Oswego County, N. Y., in 1810. He received an early religious education; was converted in his twentieth year; licensed to preach in 1830, and in 1833 entered the Pittsburgh Conference. He ended his short but highly successful career Jan. 1, 1836. Mr. Colt was remarkable for his energy and piety. See *Minutes of Annual Conferences*, 1837, p. 484.

Colt, Oliver (1), A.M., a Scotch clergyman, Regent of Humanity in the Edinburgh University, was appointed to the living at Holyrood House, Edinburgh, in 1611; transferred to Foulden in 1614; presented to the vicarage of Lammerton in 1616, and died before 1630. See *Fasti Eccles. Scoticanæ*, i, 88, 438.

Colt, Oliver (2), a Scotch clergyman, took his degree at Edinburgh University in 1621; was licensed to preach in 1627; appointed helper to his father at the living of Inveresk in 1632, and ordained; was a member of the General Assembly in 1638; presented to the living in 1641, in succession to his father; had protection from earl Montrose during the war in 1645, and took shelter in Dundee from the invading army of England in 1651. He died Dec. 30, 1679, aged eighty-one years. He was a man of marked diligence, piety, persuasiveness, and integrity. See *Fasti Eccles. Scoticanæ*, i, 286.

Coltart, James, a Scotch clergyman, tutor in the family of colonel McLean, was licensed to preach in 1810; presented to the living at Fintry in 1822, and ordained; and died June 11, 1840. See *Fasti Eccles. Scoticanæ*, ii, 355.

Coltellini, Michele, a Ferrarese painter, flourished about 1517. His principal works are at Ferrara: in San Andrea, *The Virgin and Infant*, with saints; in the sacristy of the Augustines, a picture of *St. Monica*, with four saints of that order; and in Santa Maria, *St. Francis Receiving the Stigmata.*

Colton, Asa Smith, a Protestant Episcopal minister, was born at Champion, Jefferson Co., N. Y., Oct. 26, 1804. He received his preparatory education at Guilford, and graduated at Hamilton College in 1827. He then taught one year at Freehold, N. J.; entered Princeton Theological Seminary in November, 1828, where he remained nearly two years; then studied one year with the Rev. Thomas H. Skinner, D.D., in Philadelphia; was licensed by the Presbytery of Philadelphia, Oct. 30, 1830, and taught three years in Philadelphia. Having united with the Protestant Episcopal Church, he was admitted to deacon's orders, Aug. 4, 1833, and ordained a presbyter, Aug. 27, 1839. He taught in Morristown, N. J., from 1834 to 1836; preached and taught in Bordentown, from 1837 to 1839; was missionary in Bucks County, Pa., in 1839 and 1840; taught privately at Gulf Mills, Montgomery Co., from 1840 to 1842; was rector of St. Andrew's Church, West Vincent, and St. Mark's, Honeybrook, both in Chester Co., from 1842 to 1845; of Christ Church, Towanda, from 1845 to 1847; at Pike, from 1847 to 1849; of St. Peter's Church, Montgomery Co., St. Paul's, Point of Rocks, and minister of Zion's Parish, Urbana, Ind., from 1849 to 1854; taught and supplied several vacant parishes at Wilmington, Del., from 1854 to 1859; and afterwards resided at Princeton, N. J., preaching occasionally until his death, Aug. 19, 1881. See *Necrol. Report of Princeton Theol. Sem.* 1882, p. 22.

Colton, Benjamin, a Congregational minister, was born at Long Meadow, Mass. He graduated at Yale College in 1710; was ordained pastor of the Church at West Hartford, Feb. 24, 1713, and died March 1, 1749. See Sprague, *Annals of the Amer. Pulpit*, i, 180.

Colton, Caleb C., an English clergyman, was educated at Eton, and King's College, Cambridge, and became vicar of Kew and Petersham. A passion for gaming so embarrassed him financially that he was compelled to abscond to America in 1828, to avoid his creditors. He next took up his residence at Paris, where he is said to have been very successful at play, clearing £25,000 in less than two years. The dread of an impending surgical operation unbalanced his mind, and he blew out his brains at Fontainebleau in 1832. He published, *Narrative of the Sampford Ghost* (1810):—*Hypocrisy, a Satirical Poem* (1812):—*Napoleon, a Poem* (eod.):—*Lines on the Conflagration of Moscow* (1816):—*Lacon, or Many Things in Few Words* (1820). See Allibone, *Dict. of Brit. and Amer. Authors*, s. v.

Colton, George, a Congregational minister, son of Rev. Benjamin Colton, of West Hartford, graduated at Yale College in 1756; was ordained at Bolton, Nov. 9, 1763, and died in 1812. See Sprague, *Annals of the Amer. Pulpit*, i, 180.

Colton, Henry Martyn, a Congregational minister, was born at Royalton, N. Y. He graduated at Yale College, and remained one year after graduation, pursuing a select course in philosophy and languages. The next three years were spent in the Yale Divinity School, and in November, 1852, he was ordained pastor of the First Congregational Church in Woodstock, Conn. In January, 1855, he removed to East Avon, and supplied the pulpit of the Congregational Church until April, 1857. In this year Mr. Colton established a classical school in Middletown, which continued for eleven years. In September, 1858, he opened the "Yale School for Boys," in New York city, and conducted it till the time of his death, June 2, 1872. See *Obituary Record of Yale College*, 1872.

Colton, John, an English divine of the 14th century, was born at Terrington, Norfolk, and became chaplain to William Bateman, bishop of Norwich, and the first master (by appointment of the founder) of Gonville Hall, Cambridge. Leland says he was a man "plus quam mediocriter doctus et bonus," for which qualities it is presumed Henry IV promoted him to be bishop of Armagh and primate of Ireland (or, as Fuller says, correcting Pits, this was done by Richard II). He was employed at the court of Rome in the schism between pope Urban VI and Clement VII, which occasioned the writing of his learned treatise, *De Causa Schismatis*, and another book as a sequel, *De Remedius Ejusdem.* He is supposed to have resigned his archbishopric before his death, which occurred in 1404. See Warens, *De Scriptoribus Hibernicis*, p. 129; Fuller, *Worthies of England* (ed. Nuttall), ii, 459.

Colton, Richard Francis, a Protestant Episcopal clergyman, became assistant minister of the Church of the Atonement, in Philadelphia, in 1866; the following year was instructor in Hebrew in the Divinity School of that city; in 1870, retaining his place in the Divinity School, he assumed the rectorship of the Church of Our Saviour, Jenkintown, in which offices he remained until his death, in July, 1880. See Whittaker, *Church Almanac and Directory*, 1881, p. 172.

Colton, Simeon, D.D., a Congregational minister, was born at Long Meadow, Mass., about 1786. He graduated from Yale College in 1806, was ordained at Palmer, June 19, 1811, and dismissed Nov. 13, 1821. For a time he was engaged in teaching at Munson, also in North Carolina, and subsequently became president of a college in one of the south-western states. See *Hampden Pulpit*, p. 97. (J. C. S.)

Colton, Walter, a Congregational minister, was born at Rutland, Vt., May 9, 1797. He graduated from Yale College in 1822, and from Andover Theological Seminary in 1825; was ordained June 5, 1827; was professor of moral philosophy and Biblical literature at the Military Academy, Middletown, Conn., from 1825 to 1830; and editor of the *American Spectator*, Washington, D. C., in 1830 and 1831. In the latter year he was appointed chaplain of the navy, and ordered to the Mediterranean; while there gathered the materials for his *Ship and Shore in Madeira, Lisbon, and the Mediterranean* (New York, 1835); in 1835 was assigned to the naval station at Charlestown, Mass.; in 1837 edited the *Colonization Herald*, and in 1838 the *North American*, Philadelphia; in 1845 was ordered to the Pacific coast, and July 28, 1846, was appointed alcalde of Monterey, in California, by the American military authorities; established the first newspaper (*Alta California*), and built the first schoolhouse in California. Having returned to Philadelphia in 1849, he died there Jan. 22, 1851. His *Deck and Port*, and *Three Years in California*, were published in 1850, and a volume of *Literary Remains* in 1851. See *Gen. Cat. of Andover Theol. Sem.* 1870, p. 64; Allibone, *Dict. of Brit. and Amer. Authors*, s. v.

Coltrin, Cyrus, a Free-will Baptist minister, was born at Lenox, Madison Co., N. Y., Dec. 10, 1813. He went to Illinois about 1848, having been previously ordained, and labored within the bounds of the Fox and Rock River Quarterly Meetings. In 1869 he removed to Iowa. Broken in health by hardships as an evangelist in a new and sparsely settled country, he died at Waltham, Tama Co., Sept. 13, 1872. See *Morning Star*, July 8, 1874. (J. C. S.)

Coltrin, Nathaniel Potter, a Congregational minister, was born at Steubenville, O., Feb. 17, 1820. He graduated from Wabash College in 1845; was a member of Lane Theological Seminary one year, in the class of 1849; was ordained (by the Illinois, now the Quincy, Association) at Mendon, Ill., Oct. 13, 1850; was acting pastor at Jacksonville, until April, 1851; at Chandlerville, and Round Prairie (now Plymouth), from 1851 to 1857; at Griggsville, from 1857 to 1861; for a short time chaplain in the army, after which he preached a year at Litchfield, having no church; from December, 1862, to May, 1864, was acting pastor at Wythe; chaplain of the 33d Regiment until December, 1865; during 1866 was without charge; and finally acting pastor at Sandoval and Clement until his death at Centralia, Dec. 26, 1877. (W. P. S.)

Colum. See STRAINER.

Colum (or **Colam**), is the primary form of the name which becomes also *Columbus, Columba*, and, as a diminutive, *Colman, Colmoc, Columban*, and with the prefixes *da* and *mo* becomes *Dacholmoc* and *Mocholmoc*, or *Mocholmog.* See COLMAN. It appears as the proper name of Irish saints, but more or less interchangeable with the other forms.

1. Son of Aedh of Cuil-Damhain, or Cuil-Brinin, is commemorated Nov. 8 and Dec. 11.

2. Of Tirdaglas, is commemorated Dec. 13. He is often called son of Crimthainn, or of Ui Crimthainn, so that the abbots of Tirdaglas were styled the coarbs of Colum Mac-Crimthainn. He was a pupil of St. Finian at Clonard. About A.D. 548, he founded the celebrated monastery of Tirdaglas. He died, with many other saints, of the great epidemic, about A.D. 552 (Reeves, *Adamnan*, p. 186, 332; Lanigan, *Eccl. Hist. of Ireland*, ii, 71; Butler, *Lives of the Saints*, xii, 259).

3. Cruimthir (priest) Colum, of Domhuach-mor Maighe Imchlair, is commemorated June 4 in the *Mart. Doneg.* On this day Colgan places the Columbanus or Columba, presbyter of Kill-Ernain (in Meath, or Limerick), who is said to have been one of those who met St. Patrick as he returned from Rome, and received from him the skin to form the book-satchel, which remained in the Church of Kill-Ernain.

4. A priest of Enach, is commemorated Sept. 22. Colgan places him among the disciples of St. Columba, but this is denied by Lanigan (*Eccl. Hist. of Ireland*, ii, 141, 407).

5. Of Inis-Cealtra, is often mentioned in Irish history, but the details of his life are lost. He had his monastery on one of the islands in Lough Derg, now included in the parish of Innishcaltra, and called the island of seven churches. He died of the great epidemic A.D. 548, and is to be distinguished from St. Caimin (commemorated March 24) of the same place (O'Donovan, *Four Masters*, i, 187).

6. Of Ros-Glanda, is commemorated Sept. 6. See COLMAN (4) son of Eochaidh.

7. Gobha (the Smith), is commemorated June 7. Colgan identifies Columbus Coilriginus (whose soul Columbus in Hy is said to have seen carried by the angels to the heavenly joys for his abundant alms to the poor) with this Colum or Columbus the Smith. See Smith, *Dict. of Christ. Biog.* s. v.

Columba (*a dove*) is a vessel shaped like a dove. Anciently the sacrament was reserved within a vessel of precious metal made in the form of a dove, which was suspended before the high-altar by a chain from the roof of the church. To this chain was hung a co-

Columba Suspended from the Roof.

rona-like dish, basin, or disk, enclosed by other chains, on which the dove itself was placed. This vessel opened on the back; while in the body of it was formed a receptacle for the host. The custom of reserving the sacrament in such a vessel was originally common to East and West. Perpetuus, bishop of Tours, A.D. 474, left in his will a silver dove to Amalarius, a priest. It is recorded of Basil the Great that he reserved the Lord's body in a dove made of gold. The smaller example, illustrated by the engravings here given, is from the celebrated French collection of M. le Comte de Bastard. The "peristerium," however, occurs in several old English inventories of Church *ornamenta*. See DOVES.

Columba on a Basin.

The Dove Opened.

Figures of doves, as appropriate ecclesiastical symbols, were likewise suspended over English baptisteries, and are sometimes found carved on the canopies of fonts. As symbolic representations of the Holy Spirit, they are likewise carved over altars; and sometimes, as on the brass corona at Thame Church, Oxfordshire, they symbolize the light and glory of God. Examples of this custom are found in illuminated MSS., and such vessels exist in several foreign sacristies, though their use has lately given place to the ordinary tabernacle. See TABERNACLE.

Columba is the name of several early saints besides the bishop of Iona and the virgin martyr. See also COLOMBA.

1. Said to have flourished about A.D. 640, is often given as the first bishop of Dunkeld, and the educator of St. Cuthbert and St. Brigida (Lanigan, *Eccl. Hist. of Ireland*, ii, 165). Dr. Reeves, however (*Adamnan*, p. 6 n., 296-298), says that the only Columba connected with Dunkeld is St. Columba of Iona, whose relics were deposited there, and who was honored as the patron saint on June 9 (Grub, *Eccl. Hist. of Scotland*, i, 129 sq.).

2. Another Columba was the son of the regulus or lord of Appleby, Congere, Troclyngham, and Malemath, all situated in England, who is said to have been raised from the dead, and baptized by St. Blane (q. v.). He is buried at Dunblane, Perthshire (Forbes, *Kal. of Scot. Saints*, p. 307).

Columbānus (or **Colomban**), *Saint*, was a French poet, and abbot of Trudo (St. Trond). He died about the middle of the 9th century. Among the works of Rabanus Maurus is a poem or dirge on the death of Charlemagne, written by a certain Colomban, who is supposed to have been the abbot of St. Trond. To him is also attributed the poem entitled *De Origine atque Primordiis Gentis Francorum* (*Stirpis Carolinæ*). It was written about the year 840, and dedicated to Charles the Bald, and published with the notes of Thomas Aquinas (Paris, 1644). See *Histoire Littéraire de la France*, iv, 422, and ix; Migne, *Patrol. Lat.* cvi, p. 1257.

Columbarium (so called from its resemblance to a dove-cote) was a Roman vault with recesses for the funereal ashes. It is an utterly untenable view, that this distinctively pagan arrangement, essentially belonging to the practice of burning the dead, which was held by the Christians in such abhorrence, is ever found within the limits of, or in close connection with, a Christian catacomb. The misconception has arisen from the fact that the Christian excavators in carrying forward their subterranean galleries not unfrequently came into contact with the walls of a heathen columbarium. As soon as this unintentional interference with the sanctity of the tomb was discovered, the *fossores* proceeded to repair their error. The gallery was abruptly closed, and a wall was built at its end to shut it off from the columbarium. Padre Marchi (*Monum. Primit.* p. 61) describes his discovery of a gallery in the catacombs of St. Agnes closed in this way with a ruined wall, on the other side of which was a plundered columbarium. This is probably the true explanation of the fact that a passage has been found connecting a large heathen tomb full of columbaria, on the Via Appia, near the Porta San Sebastiano, with a catacomb. See Röstell, *Beschreib. d. Rom*, p. 389; Raoul-Rochette, *Tableau des Catacombes*, p. 283.

Columbi, Dominique, a French historian and Jacobin monk, who died Oct. 6, 1696, wrote *Histoire de Sainte-Madeleine* (Aix, 1688). See Hoefer, *Nouv. Biog. Générale*, s. v.

Columbi, Jean, a French theologian and historian of the Jesuit order, was born in 1592 at Manosque, in Provence. He was successively, in the College of Lyons, professor of rhetoric, of philosophy, of theology, and of Holy Scriptures, and died at Lyons, Dec. 11, 1679, leaving, *De Rebus Gestis Episcoporum Valentinorum et Diensium* (Lyons, 1638):—*Quod Joannes Montlucius non Fuerit Hæreticus* (1640):—*De Rebus Gestis Episcoporum Vivarensium* (1651):—*De Rebus Gestis Episcoporum Vasionensium* (1656):—*Commentaria in Sacram Scripturam* (Lyons, 1656, vol. i):—*De Rebus Gestis Episcoporum Listariensium* (1663). See Hoefer, *Nouv. Biog. Générale*, s. v.

Columbus, Jonas, a Swedish Protestant theologian, became pastor of Dalecarlia, made a great effort to impress with dignity the acts of worship in that province, and especially the music in the churches. He died in 1669, leaving some poems.

His son Samuel died July 8, 1679. He was also a poet, and a collection of his works was published by J. Renstierna in 1687. See Hoefer, *Nouv. Biog. Générale*, s. v.

Columcille. See Columba, *Saint*.

Colvener, George, a Flemish theologian, was born at Louvain in 1564. He was provost of the college and chancellor of the University of Douay, and died in 1649, leaving, *Joh. Niederi Formicarium*, with notes (Douay, 1602):—*Chronicon Cameracense et Atrabatense* of Balderic (ibid. 1615):—*Miraculorum et Exemplorum Memorabilium Libri duo*, of Thomas de Cantipré, with the life of the author (ibid. 1627):—*Kalendarium S. V. Mariæ Novissimum* (ibid. 1638). See Hoefer, *Nouv. Biog. Générale*, s. v.

Colver, Nathaniel, D.D., a Baptist minister, was born at Orwell, Vt., May 10, 1794. He had limited facilities for obtaining an early education, but his natural endowments were such that he took an honorable position among the ministers of his denomination. He served as a soldier in the war of 1812, and for some time followed the business of tanning. After he was settled in life, his thoughts were turned towards the ministry. For several years he preached in Vermont and New York, until, in 1836, he was called to the pastoral charge at Union Village, N. Y., where he remained seven years. During this period he made for himself a high reputation, both as a preacher and an eloquent pleader for temperance and anti-slavery. In 1843 he was invited as pastor to Tremont Temple, Boston. For thirteen years he prosecuted his work with eminent success, adding constantly to his reputation as a pulpit orator and a platform speaker. Leaving Boston, he went to the West, spending a year in Detroit, then a year or two in Cincinnati, and finally taking up his residence in Chicago, where—with the exception of a short time when he had charge of the "Colver Institute," an institution at Richmond, Va., where he devoted himself to the work of preparing colored students for the ministry—he spent the remainder of his life. He died at Chicago, Dec. 25, 1870. More than sixteen hundred converts were baptized by him. (J. C. S.)

Colvill (Colville, or Colwil) is the name of a number of Scotch clergymen:

1. Alexander (1), was born in 1620, near St. Andrews; became rector of the University of Edinburgh, and died there in 1676, leaving, among other works of controversy, *Hudibras Écossais*, a poem in the style of Butler, directed against the Presbyterians. See Hoefer, *Nouv. Biog. Générale*, s. v.

2. Alexander (2), was licensed to preach in 1755; called to the living at Gask in 1763; transferred to Ormiston in 1765, and died Nov. 3, 1813. He published *An Account of the Parish*. See *Fasti Eccles. Scoticanæ*, i, 303; ii, 765.

3. George, D.D., studied theology in the Edinburgh University; was licensed to preach in 1821; presented to the living at Kilwinning in 1824, and ordained; transferred to Beith in 1831, and died May 13, 1852. His son George was minister at Canonbie. See *Fasti Eccles. Scoticanæ*, ii, 161, 183.

4. Henry, was presented to the parsonage and vicarage of Mukhart in 1577, and to the living at Orphir in 1580, and continued in 1595. He was "hunted to a savage death on the Noup of Nesting," July 9, 1596, and Gilbert Pacok was beheaded at the market cross, Edinburgh, for his part of the murder. See *Fasti Eccles. Scoticanæ*, iii, 399.

5. John (1), took his degree at the University of St. Andrews about 1561; was presented to the chantry of Glasgow in 1567, and remained the minister at Kilbride when it was separated in 1569. He was accused of neglect and non-residence in 1575; deserted his charge in 1578, but on examination before the synod was acquitted. He was appointed master of requests the same year; was ambassador to queen Elizabeth in 1582; was found guilty of treason in 1584, and imprisoned in Edinburgh; afterwards restored, and named one of the lords of session in 1587, but resigned within a month. Disappointed, he joined the earl of Bothwell in his seditious practices, was driven from the kingdom, became a papist, wrote bitterly against Protestant principles, and died at Paris in November, 1605, in great want and misery. His several published works were chiefly in defence of his own erratic conduct. See *Fasti Eccles. Scoticanæ*, ii, 288.

6. John (2), took his degree at the University of St. Andrews in 1635; was admitted to the living at Kirknewton in 1648, and died in February, 1663, aged about forty-eight years. See *Fasti Eccles. Scoticanæ*, i, 142.

7. John (3), A.M., was regent in the old college, St. Andrews, presented to the living at Mid-Calder in 1663, and died in 1671, aged about forty-one years. See *Fasti Eccles. Scoticanæ*, i, 175.

8. Patrick, took his degree at Edinburgh University in 1629; was appointed to the living at Beith in 1645, and ordained; was a member of the General Assembly in 1648; was appointed, in 1654, one of those for authorizing admissions to the ministry; elected moderator of the synod in 1661, which was the last meeting they held previous to the re-establishment of the presbytery after the Revolution. He was a very learned and good man, and died in May, 1662, aged about fifty-three years. See *Fasti Eccles. Scoticanæ*, ii, 159.

9. Robert (1), became minister at Culross in 1593; was one of the forty who, in 1606, consulted about holding the assembly at Aberdeen against the king's authority; signed, with forty-one others, a protest to parliament against the introduction of Episcopacy, and was one of the fifty-five who petitioned parliament in behalf of the liberties of the Kirk in 1617. He continued in 1629 with an assistant, and died in 1630. See *Fasti Eccles. Scoticanæ*, ii, 584.

10. Robert (2), took his degree at Edinburgh University in 1682; was appointed to the living at Barra in 1694; transferred to Glenluce in 1698; resigned in July, 1714, and retired to Stranraer, where he died, June 6, 1729, aged seventy years. See *Fasti Eccles. Scoticanæ*, i, 334, 766.

11. Robert (3), took his degree at Edinburgh University in 1691; became schoolmaster at Jedburgh, and was licensed to preach there in 1695; admitted to the living at Annan in 1696, and ordained; transferred to Yetholm in 1699, and died before March 2, 1731, aged about sixty years. See *Fasti Eccles. Scoticanæ*, i, 477, 613.

12. ROBERT (4), was licensed to preach in 1758; presented to the second charge at Dysart the same year, and ordained. A libel was charged against him, to part of which he confessed, and for which he was suspended in 1784, but allowed an assistant. He died Jan. 23, 1788. He published, *Britain*, a poem (1757):—*Caledonian Heroine*, a poem (1771):—*Atalanta*, a poem (1777):—*The Downfall of the Papal Confederacy* (1788):—*Poetical Works* (1789, 2 vols.):—*Savannah*, a poem (1793):—*To the Memory of the Hon. William Leslie*, a poem:—*Extracts from Synod Sermon*, etc. See *Fasti Eccles. Scoticanæ*, ii, 538.

13. WILLIAM (1), brother of lord Colvill, took his degree at the University of St. Andrews in 1617; was elected minister of Cramond in 1635; changed to the second charge at Greyfriars in 1638; was a member of the General Assembly the same year; promoted to Trinity College Church, Edinburgh, in 1639; the same year sent by the Covenanters to the king of France to solicit his aid against the despotic actions of Charles I. He and his papers were seized in England, and he was imprisoned, till released in 1640 by the Scottish army. When the Tron Church was made a new parish, in 1641, he was appointed the first incumbent. In 1645 he obtained protection from the marquis of Montrose, for which he was suspected of treason, in 1648 suspended, and deposed in 1649. In 1652 he was made a prisoner, but was restored to the ministry in 1654; appointed to the Collegiate Church at Perth in 1655; refused a bishopric, and was promoted to the principalship of Edinburgh University in 1662. See *Fasti Eccles. Scoticanæ*, i, 31, 55, 133; ii, 615.

14. WILLIAM (2), took his degree at Edinburgh University; was licensed to preach in 1821; presented to the living at Eaglesham in 1829, and ordained. He died March 12, 1859, aged fifty-nine years. See *Fasti Eccles. Scoticanæ*, ii, 66.

Colvin, ROBERT, D.D., a Scotch clergyman, a native of Sanquhar, was tutor in the family of Hope Johnston; was licensed to preach in 1805; presented to the living at Johnston in 1808, and ordained in 1809. He died Sept. 4, 1851, aged seventy-two years. He left two sons, Walter, minister of Cramond, and Robert Francis, minister of Kirkpatrick-Juxta. See *Fasti Eccles. Scoticanæ*, i, 651.

Colvius, Andrew, a Protestant divine, was born at Dort in 1594. He became minister of several Walloon churches, and at length of that in Dort; and in 1620 went to Venice as chaplain to Paul Sarpi, whose work on the Inquisition he translated into Latin (Rotterdam, 1651). He died in 1671. He was an industrious writer in some branches of science, philosophy, and poetry, and published, in 1655, a *Catalogus Musæi Andreæ Colvii*.

Colvius, Nicholas, son of the foregoing, was born in 1634, became co-pastor at Dort in 1655, afterwards pastor at Amsterdam, and died in 1717.

Colwell, Charles, an English Methodist preacher, was a native of Cornwall. He entered the English Wesleyan ministry in 1810, became a supernumerary at Falmouth in 1837, removed to Helstone, Cornwall, in 1838, and died June 20, 1860, in the seventy-eighth year of his age. See *Minutes of the British Conference*, 1860.

Colwell, John W., a Free-will Baptist minister, was born about 1810. He was ordained at Rochester, Mass., Sept. 3, 1841, and was pastor there four years; at Charlestown and Richmond, R. I., in 1846. During the next five years he organized a Church at Cranston. He died April 26, 1852, on board the steamer off the coast of Mexico, near Acapulco. See *Free-will Baptist Register*, 1853, p. 87.

Colymbion (κολύμβιον) is a vessel used for containing holy water (q. v.) at the entrance of a church. A representation of such a vessel is found in one of the mosaics of the Church of San Vitale at Ravenna, and is here engraved. It is noteworthy that the aspergillum which hangs from the arch above the basin is in shape not unlike those of modern times (Neale, *Eastern Church*, introduction, p. 215).

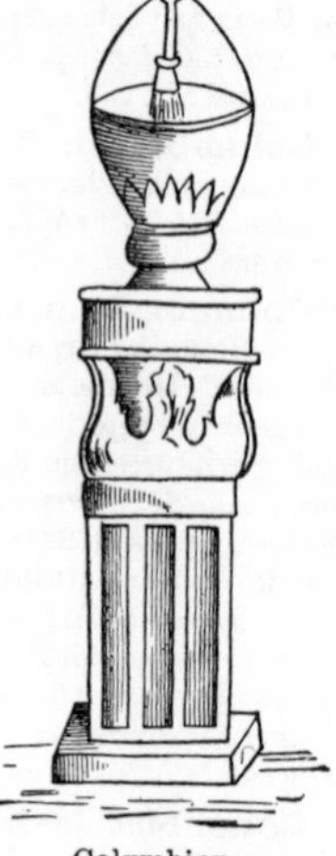

Colymbion.

Colyns, DAVID, a Dutch painter, was born at Amsterdam about 1650. There are two very highly esteemed pictures by him, at Amsterdam, representing the *Israelites Fed with Manna*, and *Moses Striking the Rock*. See Spooner, *Biog. Hist. of the Fine Arts*, s. v.

Comaigh (Lat. *Comagia*), a virgin, is commemorated as an Irish saint May 27. She was the daughter of Eochaidh. Her mother was Aiglema. She had a monastery at Suamhluthair, and also her brother, Colman (q. v.) (Reeves, *Adamnan*, p. 172 sq.).

Coman (or **Comman**), son of Ernan, is commemorated as an Irish saint March 18. He was a brother of Cumin Finn, abbot of Hy. He went to Hy as a monk, and was alive in the time of St. Adamnan. His church is Kilchoman, in the Rinns of Islay. The date of his death is unknown.

Comande, FRANCESCO, a Sicilian painter, was born at Messina about 1580, studied under Deodato Guinaccia, and painted in conjunction with his brother, Giovanni Simone. His best pictures are, *The Martyrdom of St. Bartholomew*, in the church of that saint at Messina, and *The Adoration of the Magi*, in the monastery of Basico. See Spooner, *Biog. History of the Fine Arts*, s. v.; Hoefer, *Nouv. Biog. Générale*, s. v.

Comasius was a *rhetor* in the 5th century, who turned monk, and still continued in the monastery collecting "the rubbish" of classical Greek literature, for which he is severely rebuked by Nilus (*Epist.* ii, 73, p. 153; ii, 257, p. 251).

Comb, ECCLESIASTICAL. A comb of ivory or precious metal, with which the first tonsure was made and the hair was arranged in the sacristy, was one of the *ornamenta* found in ancient sacristies for the practical use of the clergy. Each cleric had his own. The comb was usually buried with the priest on his decease. St. Cuthbert's, of ivory, found in his tomb when opened, remains in the library of Durham Cathedral, and St. Loup's, of the 12th century, at Sens. The latter is jewelled and has symbolical animals. See IVORIES.

Comb, GEORGE, an English Baptist minister, was born at Edinburgh, Feb. 12, 1782. At the age of twenty-six he was converted, and united with the Church at Guildford. He studied for the ministry, in due time took charge of a new Church at Horsell Common, and in 1823 accepted a call to Oxford Street, London, where he remained until his death, Feb. 20, 1841. See (Lond.) *Baptist Hand-book*, 1841, p. 37. (J. C. S.)

Combadaxus, a deity of the eastern Asiatics, was a bonze, or Indian priest, while living.

Combalot, Théodore, a famous Roman Catholic preacher of France, was born at Châtenay, in the Isère Department, Aug. 21, 1798. At the age of twenty-three he received holy orders, and pope Gregory XVI, before whom he once preached, appointed him apostolic vicar. For a number of years he acted as vicar-general of Rouen, Arras, and Montpellier, and died suddenly at Paris, March 19, 1873. He wrote, *Eléments de Philosophie Catholique* (Paris, 1833):—*La Connaissance de Jésus-Christ* (1841; 4th ed. 1852):—*Mémoire Adressé aux Évêques de France*, etc. (1844), for which he was imprisoned for thirty days:—*Conférences sur les Grandeurs de la Sainte-Vierge* (1845):—*Lettre à M. Guizot*, etc. (1858). See Lichtenberger, *Encyclop. des Sciences Religieuses*, s. v.; Vapereau, *Dict. des Contemporains*, s. v. (B. P.)

Combé, Marie Magdaleine *de Cyz de*, a Dutch nun, was born at Leyden in 1656. She was brought up in the Calvinistic belief, and at the age of nineteen married a wealthy gentleman of Holland, Adrian de Combé, from whom she soon afterwards separated. She went to France, joined the Catholics, and by the aid of the abbot, La Bermondieu, rector of St. Sulpicius, obtained a pension of two hundred pounds. In 1686 she formed a religious community called *Le Bon Pasteur*, which the king took under his protection. The order spread through the province, and was confirmed by letters-patent in 1698, after the death of its founder, which occurred at Paris, June 16, 1692. Boileau published a *Vie de Madame Combé* (Paris, 1700, 1732). See Hoefer, *Nouv. Biog. Générale*, s. v.; *Biog. Universelle*, s. v.

Comber, Thomas (1), D.D., an English divine, uncle of the dean of Durham, was born in Sussex, Jan. 1, 1575, and educated at Trinity College, Cambridge, where he became a fellow, October, 1597. He was preferred to the deanery of Carlisle in August, 1630, and made master of Trinity College in October, 1631. In 1642 he was imprisoned, plundered, and deprived of all his preferments. He died at Cambridge, in February, 1653.

Comber, Thomas (2), an English clergyman, great-grandson of the dean of Durham, was rector of Oswaldkirk, Yorkshire. He published, *Memoir of the Life and Writings of Dean Comber* (1779):—*Sermons* (1807):—*History of the Massacre of St. Bartholomew* (1810):—*Adultery Analyzed* (eod.):—*A Scourge for Adulterers, Duellists, Gamesters, and Self-murderers* (anon., eod.). See Allibone, *Dict. of Brit. and Amer. Authors*, s. v.

Combes, Andrew J., a Methodist Episcopal minister, was born in Indiana, Nov. 12, 1845. He lived successively in Illinois, Iowa, and Nebraska; was converted in 1865, licensed to preach in 1872, and in 1875 entered the Nebraska Conference, wherein he labored heroically until his death, in 1878. See *Minutes of Annual Conferences*, 1878, p. 61.

Combes, Francisco, a Spanish Jesuit and traveller, was born at Saragossa in 1613. He was sent to the Philippine Islands to propagate the Catholic faith. On his way to Rome to represent his province, he died at Acapulco, in 1663, leaving, in Spanish, a *History of the Islands of Mindanao* (Madrid, 1667). See Hoefer, *Nouv. Biog. Générale*, s. v.

Combet, Claude, a French Dominican, was born at Lyons in 1614. He was bachelor of the University of Paris, and became a famous preacher. He died at Lyons in 1689, leaving, *Oraison Funèbre de Louis XIII* (Lyons, 1643):—*Oraison Funèbre de la Reine Anne d'Autriche* (Vannes, 1666). See Hoefer, *Nouv. Biog. Générale*, s. v.

Combonus, Hieronymus, an Italian Hebraist, lived in the early part of the 17th century. He belonged to the order of Observantists, and was professor of Hebrew at Bergamo. He wrote, *Compendium in quo Quidquid ad Hebraicam Linguam Legendam Pertinet Continetur* (Bergamo, 1616). See Hoefer, *Nouv. Biog. Générale*, s. v.

Comdhan. See Comgan; Congan.

Come, *Saint*. See Cosmas.

Comegern was eighth bishop of Llandaff, contemporary with Ywyr, king of Gwynedd (Stubbs, *Register*, p. 156).

Comeiras, Victor *Delpuech de*, a French ecclesiastic and geographer, was born at St. Hippolyte-du-Gard, Sept. 11, 1733. He was abbot of Sylvanès, and vicar-general of Beauvais, but was deprived of his position at the Revolution, and died at Paris, March 29, 1805. He wrote vols. xxii-xxxii of *L'Abrégé de l'Histoire Générale des Voyages* (Paris, 1780-1801; vols. i-xx were published by La Harpe):—*La Voix du Sage* (ibid. 1799):—*Histoire de l'Astronomie*, transl. from Bailly (ibid. 1806). Other writings remain in MS. See Hoefer, *Nouv. Biog. Générale*, s. v.; *Biog. Universelle*, s. v.

Comès. See Lectionary.

Comestor (or *le Mangeur*, i. e. *devourer* of books), Pierre, a French theologian, was born at Troyes. He was successively canon and dean of Troyes, then, in 1164, chancellor of the Church of Paris and master of the school of philosophy. He gave up his benefices in order to become canon-regular of St. Victor at Paris. At his death, which occurred in that city Oct. 21, 1198 (others say 1178 or 1185), he left all his goods to the poor. He wrote, among other works, *Scholastica Historia super Novum Testamentum* (written before 1176, and published at Reutling, 1471; Utrecht, 1473; Strasburg, 1483, 1502; Basle, 1486; Paris, 1513; Haguenau, 1519; Lyons, 1526; Venice, 1728; transl. into French in 1494 by Guyart des Moulins, under the title: *La Bible Historie;* Paris, without date, with engravings):—*Catena Temporum* (transl. into Gothic-French by Jehan de Rely, under the title, *Mer des Histoires;* Paris, 1488):—*Sermones*, under the name of *Pierre de Blois* (Mayence, 1600, 1605; Lyons, 1677, and often since). See Hoefer, *Nouv. Biog. Générale*, s. v.; *Biog. Universelle*, s. v.

Comfort, David, a Presbyterian minister, a graduate of Princeton, was licensed to preach by the Presbytery of New Brunswick in 1798, and soon after became pastor of the Presbyterian Church at Kingston, N. J., where he labored during a long life. From 1816 till his death, in 1853, he was a trustee of Princeton College. Mr. Comfort was honored and beloved by all. See Alexander, *Princeton College in the 18th Century.*

Comfort, David D., a minister of the Methodist Episcopal Church South, was received on trial in the North Mississippi Conference in 1880, and died in September, 1882. See *Minutes of Annual Conferences of the M. E. Church South*, 1882, p. 104.

Comfort, Silas, D.D., a Methodist Episcopal minister, was born at Deer Park, Orange Co., N. Y., May 18, 1803. He was converted at the age of nine, became a class-leader at eighteen, a travelling preacher at twenty, and in 1827 entered the Genesee Conference. Then began in earnest his student life, studying on horseback, by torchlight, amid the confusion of families, always rising at four o'clock. Thus the dead languages, science, general literature, Biblical criticism, and systematic theology were thoroughly explored by him. During his forty-five years in the ministry he served sixteen years as presiding elder, wrote several valuable volumes, and contributed largely to the first periodicals of the Church. In 1835 he was transferred to the Missouri Conference, returned to the Oneida Conference seven years later, and in it labored until his sudden death, Jan. 10, 1868. See *Minutes of Annual Conferences*, 1868, p. 105; Simpson, *Cyclop. of Methodism*, s. v.

Comfort, William C., a Methodist Episcopal minister, received an early religious training, was converted at the age of twenty, and, after exercising his talents as a local preacher a short time, was admitted into the Michigan Conference, wherein he labored many years faithfully until his death, June 15, 1862. Mr. Comfort was a man of decided opinions and uncompromising integrity. See *Minutes of Annual Conferences*, 1862, p. 206.

Comfortable Words, THE. A modern feature in the existing Anglican form for the celebration of the holy communion, first introduced in the second prayer-book of Edward VI., A.D. 1552, consisting of four texts of Scripture, which the priest is directed to address to the people. These words follow the absolution, and precede the preface.

Comforted, THE, one of the two classes (the *consolati* or comforted, and the *fœderati* or confederated) into which the Manichæan congregations were anciently divided. See MANICHÆISM. The Albigenses (q. v.) classified their people in precisely the same way, and the *comforted* led a life of celibacy and strict austerity.

Comgall (or **Congall**) is the name of several early Irish saints:

1. An abbot of Bangor, commemorated May 10. He was one of the most prominent leaders of monasticism in Ireland, and is said to have had three thousand monks under him at one time in various affiliated houses. His parents were Setna or Sedna, and Brig or Briga, and he was born about A.D. 517. After teaching for some years, he founded, in 558, his great monastery at Bangor, County Down, Ireland, to which multitudes flocked. Comgall drew up for it and kindred institutions a rule which was one of the most famous in Ireland. His most noted disciples at Bangor were Cormac, son of Diarmaid and king of South Leinster, and St. Columbanus (q. v.). While on a visit to Scotland, he founded a monastery in Heth. Comgall died at Bangor on May 10, 602, and was buried there. In 824 the Danes plundered the city and abbey, and, breaking open his shrine, scattered the contents to the four winds (see Reeves, *Eccl. Hist.* p. 93-95, 152-154, and *Adamnan*, p. 213, 317; Ussher, *Eccl. Antiq.* c. 17, in *Works*, vi, 473 sq.). Comgall is commemorated in the Scotch calendars, but Camerarius places him on Jan. 2, and suggests a Scotch Bangor. See Lanigan, *Eccl. Hist. of Ireland*, ii, c. 10; Todd and Reeves, *Mart. Doneg.* p. 123; Butler, *Lives of the Saints*, v, 195 sq.; Forbes, *Kal. of Scott. Saints*, p. 108-110.

2. Son of Eochaidh, commemorated Sept. 4. His monastery was at Both-conais, in Inis-Eoghan. He is said to have received this monastery from St. Cianan of Duleek. He belongs to the 8th century (Todd and Reeves, *Mart. Doneg.* p. 237; Lanigan, *Eccl. Hist. of Ireland*, i, 345; iii, 162).

3. Of Gobhal-linin, commemorated July 28. His monastery was at what is now Galloon. On July 27, Butler (*Lives of the Saints*, vii, 425) gives a short memoir of St. Congall, abbot of Jabhualhini.

Comgan (**Comdhan**, or **Comman**) is the name of two early Irish saints:

1. Of Cluain-Connaidh, commemorated Oct. 13. There is a St. *Comganus* named among the relatives of St. Columba, who is supposed to be the same as this Comgan. See CONGAN.

2. Of Glenn-Uissen, commemorated Feb. 27. He was the son of Diarmaid, and his mother was Ethne. He founded a monastery in his native province at Ceauw-indis, and succeeded St. Diarmaid in the government of the monastery at Glenn-Uissen. He died about A.D. 569, it is supposed (Lanigan, *Ecclesiastical History of Ireland*, ii, 76 sq.; Reeves, *Adamnan*, lxx, note).

Comi, GIROLAMO, a painter of Modena, flourished about 1550. He painted sacred subjects, and was much employed by the churches in ornamental work. One of his pictures in San Michele at Bosco is dated 1563. See Spooner, *Biog. Hist. of the Fine Arts*, s. v.; Hoefer, *Nouv. Biog. Générale*, s. v.

Comiers, CLAUDE, a learned French mathematician, was born at Embrun. He was canon there, provost of the chapter of Ternant, doctor of theology, and apostolic prothonotary; also professor of mathematics at Paris, and was considered an able physician and chemist. He had contributed to the *Journal des Savants* from 1676 to 1678, and had invented several curious machines. Having become blind in 1690, he entered the hospital of Quinze-Vingts, where he took the title of *aveugle royal* because he had a pension from the king. He died at Paris in October, 1693, leaving *La Nouvelle Science de la Nature des Comètes* (Lyons, 1665):—*Instruction pour Reunir les Églises Prétendues Reformées à l'Église Romaine* (Paris, 1678):—*Traité des Langues et Écritures* (in the *Mercure* of Sept., Oct. 1684, and Feb. 1685):—*Traité des Prophéties* (ibid. of Aug., Sept., Dec. 1689, and Sept. 1690):—*Lettre à une Dame Nouvellement Convertie à la Religion Catholique* (ibid. of Dec. 1691), and many other pieces. See Hoefer, *Nouv. Biog. Générale*, s. v.; *Biog. Universelle*, s. v.

Comin (or **Cumin**). See COMYN.

Comingo, HENRY G., D.D., a Presbyterian minister, was born at Harrodsburg, Ky., Feb. 2, 1809. He was carefully reared by Christian parents; graduated from Centre College, Danville, in 1832; studied two years (1833-34) in Princeton Theological Seminary; was licensed in 1836 by the New Brunswick Presbytery, and became pastor, May 24, 1837, in Steubenville, O., where he labored until the close of his life, Dec. 1, 1861. He was a living Christian and an earnest minister of the gospel. See Wilson, *Presb. Hist. Almanac*, 1863, p. 155.

Comingoe, BRUIN ROMCAS, a German Reformed minister, was a native of Germany. He was pastor at Lunenburg, Nova Scotia, for forty-nine years, from 1770. Old age and ill-health caused him to resign in 1819. He returned to Germany soon after, and nothing more was heard of him. See Harbaugh, *Fathers of the Germ. Ref. Church*, ii, 159.

Comitibus, BLASEUS DE, an Italian theologian, was born at Milan. He was a Minorite, and for fifteen years regent of the order at Prague; then director of the grand seminary, and theologian to the archbishop. He died at Prague in 1685, leaving *De Deo Trino et Uno* (Prague, 1682):—*De Intellectu, Scientia, Providentia, Prædestinatione et Reprobatione* (ibid.):—*De Creatione, Statu Innocentiæ, Angelis*, etc. (ibid. 1688). See Hoefer, *Nouv. Biog. Générale*, s. v.

Comitin, JEAN BAPTISTE, a French theologian of the Jesuit order, who lived in the latter part of the 17th century, wrote *Défense de l'Honneur des Saints* (Dijon, 1657):—*Initium Sapientiæ et Finis, Timor et Amor Dei* (Châlons, 1662, 1672):—*Selectæ de Fide Controversiæ* (about 1666). See Hoefer, *Nouv. Biog. Générale*, s. v.

Comitolo, Neapolio, an Italian prelate, was born at Perugia in 1544, of the family of the counts of Colle-Mezzo. He at first followed the profession of law, but afterwards obtained an abbey, and became auditor of the Rota; was appointed bishop of Perugia in 1591, founded a college and several religious societies, and died there, Aug. 24, 1624, leaving, in Latin, a *History of the Bishops of Perugia*, a collection of the decisions of the tribunal of the Rota, and some liturgical works. See Hoefer, *Nouv. Biog. Générale*, s. v.

Comitolo, Paolo, an Italian theologian of the same family as the foregoing, was born at Perugia in 1545. He was not more than fourteen years of age when he became a Jesuit, and later one of the best casuists of that society. He taught successively rhetoric, the Sacred Scriptures, and moral theology. He died at

Perugia, Feb. 18, 1626. His principal works are *Catena Illustrium Authorum in Librum Job* (transl. from the Greek, Lyons, 1586; Venice, 1587):—*Consilia seu Responsa Moralia* (Lyons, 1609):—*Doctrina de Contractu Universo* (ibid. 1615). See Hoefer, *Nouv. Biog. Générale*, s. v.

Comman is a not uncommon name among the Irish saints, and is often exchanged with *Colman, Comgan, Coeman.*

1. *Mac Va Theimhue*, commemorated Feb. 27. Colgan (*Acta Sanctorum*, p. 417) distinguishes "St. Comgan Hua-Teanne" from St. Comgan of Glenn-uissen, who is commemorated on the same day, and gives from the Irish *Annals* the date of the former's death as A.D. 663. O'Donovan thinks he was the brother of Muirchu Maccuthennuis, who wrote a life of St. Patrick from the dictation of Aidus, bishop of Sletty, and if so he may have been the son of Cogitosus (q. v.).

2. Of Roscommon (Ross-Commain), commemorated Dec. 26. It is thought he died A.D. 742. He is said to have been of the race of Irial, son of Conall Cearnach. He wrote a monastic rule, and in the *Annals*, about the year 790, there is mention made of the promulgation of "the law of St. Coman" thoughout the three divisions of Connaught (O'Donovan, *Four Masters*, i, 343, 349, 395; Todd and Reeves, *Mart. Doneg.* p. 349; Lanigan, *Ecclesiastical History of Ireland*, ii, 225; iii, 177).

Commandery (*commenda*, a benefice), or **Preceptory** (*præceptio*, a first share), is a cell of the Templars and Hospitallers for collecting demesne-rents, and a home for veteran members of those orders. The president paid himself first his own pension, and then accounted for the residue. These houses remain at Swingfield, Cliburn, and Worcester.

Commātrēs is a term sometimes used in ancient writers to denote sponsors in baptism.

Commemoration, in its liturgical use, designates:

1. The recitation of the names of those for whom intercession is made in the mass. See DIPTYCH.

2. The introduction of the names of certain saints or events in the divine office. Such commemorations are generally of the cross, of the Virgin Mary, of St. Peter and St. Paul, and for peace.

3. According to the rubrics of the Roman breviary, when a greater festival falls on the day of a "simple" festival, the latter is "commemorated" by the introduction of certain portions of its proper service into that of the greater festival.

4. In the Church of England "commemoration" takes place when two festivals concur, and the office for the greater is used, while the collect only of the lesser is said; or when a festival coincides with a greater Sunday; or a festival of the second class falls on a greater week-day, and the same rule is observed. In Lent, Advent, on ember-days, and greater ferials, a special collect is used.

Commemoration-day, in the University of Oxford, is an annual solemnity in remembrance of the founders and benefactors of the university, when speeches are made, prize compositions recited, and honorary degrees conferred upon distinguished persons. In colleges a form of prayer, prescribed in queen Elizabeth's reign, is used during term, in pious memory of founders and benefactors. The proper Psalms are cxlv, cxlvi, cxlvii; the lesson, Ecclesiasticus xliv. The suffrage is:

"The just shall be had in everlasting remembrance;
He shall not be afraid of evil tidings.
The souls of the righteous are in the hand of God;
Neither doth any torment touch them."

Then follows a collect. At Oxford the commemoration by the university is also called *encænia.*

Commemoration of the Departed is the solemn remembrance of the faithful in Christ who have passed from hence with the sign of faith, and now rest in the sleep of peace. A prayer substantially containing such a commemoration is found in every ancient liturgy. Prayer for the dead has been pronounced legal by the highest ecclesiastical court in England, but is a relic of Romanism.

Commenda. See DIOCESE; MONASTERY.

Commendatio (παράθεσις), i. e. *collect.* (1) In the third Council of Carthage it is provided that if a *commendatio* of the dead takes place in the afternoon, it must consist of prayers only, without the celebration of mass. In the African code, the set forms to be ordinarily used in churches seem to be summed up under the heads *preces, præfationes, commendationes, manus impositiones.*

(2) But the word παράθεσις is also used to designate the prayers made in the congregation on behalf of the catechumens. Alexius Aristenus (quoted by Suicer, s. v.) explains it, when designating a part of divine service, as "the prayers over the catechumens, whereby we commend them to the Lord."

Commendation is (1) the act of commending; a favorable representation in words; (2) the act of commending the dying to the mercy and favor of God.

Commendatory is one having the grant of a benefice in trust for life, and enjoying the revenues.

Commendatory Letters. The earliest trace of the practice connected with these words is to be found in 2 Cor. iii, 1. St. Paul, it would seem, had been taunted by rivals, who came with letters of commendation (ἐπιστολαὶ συστατικαί) from the Church of Jerusalem with the absence of such credentials in his own case, with his attempts to make up for the omission by reiterated self-commendation. The passage shows the practice was already common, and, of course, necessary. Letters of this kind may have been in previous use among the Jews, and thus helped to maintain their unity as a people through all the lands of the dispersion. Other instances of it in the apostolic ages are to be found in the letter given to Apollos by the disciples at Ephesus (Acts xviii, 27), in the mention of Zenas and Apollos in the Epistle to Titus (iii, 13). The letter to Philemon, though more distinctly personal, has somewhat of the same character. The practice became universal, and it may be said, without exaggeration, that no single practice of the early Christian Church tended so much as this to impress on it the stamp of unity and organization. The bishop of any congregation, in any part of the empire, might commend a traveller, layman, or cleric to the good offices of another. The precautions against imposture might sometimes, as in the instance of Peregrinus, told by Lucian—perhaps also in that of the "false brethren" of Gal. ii, 4—be insufficient, but, as a rule, it did its work, and served as a bond of union between all Christian churches.

Those outside the Church's pale, however arrogant might be their claims, could boast of no such proof of their oneness. They were cut off from what was in the most literal sense of the term the "communion of saints." It was the crowning argument of Augustine and Optatus against the Donatists that their letters would not be received in any churches but their own; that they were therefore a sect with no claim to catholicity, no element of permanence. When Paul of Samosata was deposed by the so-called second council of Antioch, the bishops who passed sentence on him wrote to Dionysius of Rome and Maximus of Alexandria, requesting them not to address their letters to him, but to Domnus, whom they had appointed in his place. The letter of Cyprian on the election of Cornelius and that to Stephen are examples of the same kind. The most remarkable testimony, however, to the extent and the usefulness of the practice is found in the wish of

Julian to reorganize heathen society on the same plan, and to provide, in this way, shelter and food for any non-Christian traveller who might be journeying to a strange city (Sozomen, *H. E.* v, 16).

As the Church became wealthier and more worldly, the restrictive side of the practice became the more prominent; it was then what the passport system has been in the intercourse of modern Europe, a check on the free movement of clergy, or monks, or laymen. Thus it was made penal (and the penalty was excommunication) for any one to receive either cleric or layman who came to a city not his own without these letters. Those who brought them were even then subject to a scrutiny, with the alternative of being received into full fellowship if it were satisfactory, or, if it were otherwise, of having to be content with some immediate relief. So the Council of Elvira seeks to maintain the episcopal prerogative in this matter, and will not allow *literae confessoriae* (letters certifying that the bearer was one who had suffered in persecution) to take the place of the regular commendatory letters. It would appear that the abuse had spread so far that the "confessor's" passport was handed from one to another without even the insertion of the name, as a check payable to bearer. The Council of Chalcedon renewed the prohibition of the apostolic canon against allowing any strange cleric, even as reader, to officiate in another city without the "commendatory letters" from his own bishop. That of Antioch (A.D. 341) makes special restrictions in regard to the various kinds of letters. That of Arles places those who have received commendatory letters under the surveillance of the bishop of the city to which they go, with the provision that they are to be excommunicated if they begin "to act contrary to discipline," and extends the precaution to political offences, or to the introduction of a democratic element into the government of the Church. The system spread its ramifications over all provinces. It was impossible for the presbyter who had incurred the displeasure of his bishop to find employment in any other diocese. Without any formal denunciation the absence of the commendatory letter made him a marked man. The unity of the Church became a terrible reality to him.

It will have been noticed that other terms appear as applied to these letters, and it may be well to register the use and significance of each.

1. The old term was still retained, as in the Council of Chalcedon, where the prominent purpose was to commend the bearer of the letter, whether cleric or layman, to the favor and good offices of another bishop.

2. The same letters were also known as "canonical" "in accordance with the *rule* of the Church." This is the word used in the letter from the synod of Antioch, by the councils of Antioch and Laodicea. The Latin equivalent seems to have been the *literæ formatæ*, i. e. drawn up after a known and prescribed form, so as to be a safeguard against imposture. It was stated at the Council of Chalcedon by Atticus, bishop of Constantinople, that it was agreed by the bishops at the councils of Nicæa that every such letter should be marked with certain letters, in honor of the three Persons of the Trinity. In the West the signature or seal of the bishop was probably the guarantee of genuineness. The first mention of the use of a seal-ring occurs, it is believed, in Augustine.

3. From the use of the letters as admitting clergy or laymen to communion they were known as *communicatoriæ* in Latin, and by a Greek equivalent.

4. The *literæ pacificæ* appear to commend the bearer for eleemosynary aid. They are to be given to the poor and those who need help, clerics or laymen; especially, according to the Greek canonists, to those who had suffered oppression at the hands of civil magistrates. The word is used also by the Council of Antioch, as applied to letters which might be given by presbyters as well as bishops.

5. There were "letters dimissory," like those of modern times. The word is of later use than the others, and occurs first in the council in Trullo, in a context which justifies the distinction drawn, that it was used in reference to a permanent settlement of the bearer, "commendatory," when the sojourn in another diocese was only temporary.

Commendatory Prayer is a name given to the thanksgiving offered by the bishop in the early Church near the close of the morning service. It is called *εὐχαριστία ὀρθρινὴ* (morning thanksgiving), and is in these words: "O God, the God of spirits and of all flesh, with whom no one can compare, whom no one can approach, that givest the sun to govern the day, and the moon and the stars to govern the night; look down now upon us with the eyes of thy favor, and receive our morning thanksgivings, and have mercy upon us. For we have not spread forth our hands to any strange god; for there is not any new god among us, but thou, our eternal and immortal God, who hast given us our being through Christ, and our well-being through him also. Vouchsafe by him to bring us to everlasting life; with whom unto thee be glory, honor, and adoration, in the Holy Ghost, world without end. Amen." — Bingham, *Antiq.* bk. xiii, ch. x, § vii.

Commentaries, Biblical. We supplement our article on this subject, in vol. ii, by a notice of the principal expository works that have appeared later.

Lange's *Bibelwerk*, as translated and augmented by the various (chiefly American) scholars, under the general supervision of Dr. Schaff, covers the entire Bible, including the Apocrypha, in twenty-five large octavo volumes, and is the most complete thesaurus of exegetical, critical, doctrinal, and practical comment extant. The additions by the American editors have greatly enhanced its value.

Keil and Delitzsch on the entire Old Test. (transl. in Clark's *Foreign Theological Library*, Edinb. 25 vols. 8vo) is, on the whole, the best simply *exegetical* commentary for scholars. The authors have shrunk from no difficulty, but have met every question in a careful, evangelical, and earnest spirit; and have brought to their task the ripest fruits of learning. Their readers, of course, will not agree with them on every point, but they will have reason to weigh well their judgment and their arguments. There is promise of a continuation of the work into the New Test. Delitzsch has published notes on Hebrews (transl. likewise by the Messrs. Clark), and Keil has begun his comments on the Gospels. For the present, however, their work must be supplemented by

Meyer on the New Test. (likewise in an English dress, by the Messrs. Clark of Edinb., 20 vols. 8vo, not embracing Rev.). This is perhaps, on the whole, the best exegetical manual for scholars on the New Test., being accurate, moderately rationalistic, and sufficiently copious for most purposes.

The Bible Commentary, or, as it is generally designated, *The Speaker's Commentary* (republished by the Scribners, N. Y. 10 vols. 8vo), is peculiarly available for both scholars and ordinary readers, as it embraces a large amount of valuable exposition in a comparatively small compass. It is especially good on archæological questions; is eminently conservative, and particularly commendable for its brief but excellent introductions to the several books.

Wordsworth (*The Holy Bible, with Notes*, together with his *Greek Testament, with Notes*, covering, together, the entire canonical Scriptures [Lond. 1856-64, and several later editions, 10 vols. imperial 4to]) is throughout sound and judicious; suggestive but not exhaustive; scholarly rather than profound.

The Pulpit Commentary, by a number of English scholars (similar in this respect to *The Bible Commentary* above, but more practical and copious), of which about thirty volumes, octavo, have already appeared, and which is intended to cover the whole Bible, has many excellent features, happily combining sound learning and practical piety. It is adapted to general readers.

The Cambridge Bible is a series of small volumes for popular use (especially schools), and yet containing the results of the latest criticisms and researches, prepared by various English divines, and edited by dean Perowne, a large portion of which has already been issued.

Whedon's *Commentary* is intended for English readers, especially Sunday-school teachers, and is admirably pithy and suggestive. The New-Test. part (N. Y. and Lond. 5 vols. 12mo) has lately been completed by Dr. Whedon himself, and the Old Test. has been intrusted to various scholars, who have already issued three volumes in similar style, and are expected to finish the work in five volumes more.

Jamieson, Fausset, and Brown have combined in a practical commentary on the entire Scriptures, which has been published in several forms in Scotland, and reprinted in Philadelphia in one thick volume. The annotations are brief, but spiritual, and well adapted to ordinary readers.

Cowles has prepared a very judicious series of notes on all the Biblical books (N. Y. 16 vols. 12mo), for pastors, teachers, and general readers.

Stier's *Words of the Lord Jesus*, together with his *Words of the Angels*, covers many very important passages of the New Test., and is an almost unique specimen of exhaustive comment in the most evangelical and practical spirit. The whole has been republished by Tibbals & Son, New York, in three compact octavo volumes, with valuable improvements from Clark's translation out of the original German.

Ellicott's *Commentary for English Readers* (of which the New-Test. portion, prepared by various eminent British clergymen, has appeared in London in three super-royal octavo volumes; and of which the Old Test. is in course of publication on a similar plan) is delightfully fresh and instructive.

Dr. Schaff is also editing an elegantly illustrated commentary on the New Test., prepared by able American scholars, several volumes of which have already appeared, giving the results of criticism and explorations in a popular form.

The issue of the Anglo-American Revised New Test., recently followed by the revised version of the Old Test., has given a powerful stimulus to Bible study, and the International Sunday-school Series of lessons has wonderfully aided in the same direction, especially the comments thereon abundantly issued in books and periodicals.

Among recent expositions on particular books of the Bible, available in an English dress for scholars, we notice as specially valuable, Ellicott's admirable notes on the Pastoral Epistles of Paul (reprinted in 2 vols. 8vo, at Andover); Murphy, on Genesis, Exodus, Leviticus, and the Psalms (reprinted, ibid.); Godet, on Luke, John, and Romans (transl. in Clark's *Foreign Evangelical Library*, Edinb.); Luthardt, on John's Gospel (ibid.); Haupt, on 1 John (ibid.); Philippi, on Romans (ibid.); Gloag, on the Acts (ibid.); Glasgow, on Revelations (ibid.); Lightfoot, on the Pauline Epistles (Galatians, Philippians, Colossians, and Philemon, already issued by Macmillan, Lond.); Eadie, on Galatians, Ephesians, Colossians, and Thessalonians (Lond. and Edinb., in part reprinted by Carter, N. Y.); Hodge, on Romans (new ed. Phila. 1871), Corinthians, and Ephesians; Turner, on Romans, Galatians, Ephesians, and Hebrews (N. Y. 1852–56); Demarest, on Peter (ibid. 1851–62); Hackett, on the Acts (new ed. Bost. 1858); Perowne, on the Psalms (new ed. Lond. 1870); Gardner, on Jude (Bost. 1856); Moore, on Haggai, Zechariah, and Malachi (N. Y. eod.); Wright, on Ecclesiastes (Lond. 1883).

An excellent and discriminating review of exegetical writers, in past and recent times, may be found in Terry's *Biblical Hermeneutics* (N. Y. 1883), p. 603–738.

Commentators, ANCIENT. See INTERPRETATION, BIBLICAL.

Commerce, CHRISTIAN VIEWS OF. It would be difficult to find in the Bible a passage that disparages trade, whether with or without a handicraft. In the Old Testament as the calling of Bezaleel and Aholiab puts the highest honor on the skill of the artisan, so the ordinary processes of trade are no less sanctified by connecting them with God and his law (Lev. xix, 35, 36; Deut. xxv, 13–15; Prov. xl, 1; xvi, 10, 23; xxxi, 24; Micah. vi, 11). Nor is it amiss to observe that the Jewish custom, still prevalent, of bringing up every boy, without exception, to a business, trade, or handicraft, appears to be immemorial, and may serve to explain both the calling by our Lord of fishermen as apostles, and his own training as a carpenter (Mark vi, 3), as well as the tent-making of Paul, Aquila, and Priscilla (Acts xviii, 3). No incompatibility, therefore, between the exercise of a trade and the Christian calling, whether among the laity or the clergy, can be coeval with the Church, and all legislation to this effect must belong to what may be termed the secondary, not the primary, æra of its development. The places in which the gospel seems to have preferably taken root were busy commercial cities, such as Antioch, Corinth, Ephesus. The age in which Christianity forced itself on the notice of the pagan world, and was honored with imperial persecution, the time of Nero, was also one of great commercial activity. Under the later emperors trade was looked upon as an occupation of inferior dignity. A constitution of Theodosius and Valentinian (A.D. 436) required all bankers, jewellers, dealers in silver or clothing, apothecaries, and other traffickers to be removed from provincial offices, "in order that every place of honor and official service (militia) should be cleared of the like contagion." Traders generally, except the metropolitan bankers, were again excluded from the *militia* by a constitution of Justin. Soldiers, conversely, were, by a constitution of Leo (A.D. 458), forbidden to trade; and a constitution of Honorius and Theodosius forbade men of noble birth, conspicuous dignity, or hereditary wealth, to exercise a trade. The exercise of the smaller trades and handicrafts often differed little from slavery. A constitution of the emperor Constantine (A.D. 329) speaks of freedmen—artificers belonging to the state—and desires them to be brought back, if enticed out of the city where they reside. The bakers seem to have been in an almost lower condition still, since their status is expressly treated as servile. Curiously enough, the swineherds of the capitals, as carrying on a labor for the benefit of the Roman people, were specially exempted from all sordid duties. Ironworkers were to be marked in the arm, and formed also a hereditary caste, the admission to which was regulated with especial care. In the interior of the empire trade was not only restricted by monopolies which under Justinian were carried to a cruel height, but by the reservation of various articles for imperial use, as gold and silver tissue or embroidery, and the dye of the "holy murex." Buying and selling seems to have been in a great measure carried on at fairs and in markets. Fairs were often held on saints' days, though St. Basil condemns the practice; thus, there was a fair in Lucania on the birthday of St. Cyprian; a thirty days' fair free of toll in Edessa at the feast of St. Thomas the Apostle, etc. Notwithstanding the low estimation in which trade was held it seems clear that, until Justinian's time, at least, it was not held civilly incompatible with the clerical office. Hippolytus (3d century) shows us the future pope Calixtus, set up by Carpophorus as a banker, holding his bank in the "Piscina Publica," and receiving deposits from widows and brethren. A law of Constantine and Julian, indeed (A.D. 357), sought to compel trader clerics, among others, to devote their gains to charitable uses. The next passage indicates a custom still more strange to us: that of workshops, and even taverns, being kept for the benefit of the Church. Other enactments indicate to us the extent of the trade which was carried on in the eastern capital on this behalf, and the singular character of a portion of it. In consideration of the cathedral undertaking what in modern French parlance would be termed the "Pompes Funèbres," Constantine granted to it nine hundred and eighty workshops, of the various trades of the city, to be held free of all tax; Anastasius added one hundred and fifty more. The guilds of the city complained that the number of tax-free establishments was ruining them. It is clear that in the 6th century a very considerable amount of trade, including the liquor traffic, was carried on on behalf of the Church and its charitable establishments in the capital of the eastern empire. If we turn from the Roman to the barbarian world, the codes of the latter till the time of Charlemagne scarcely contain an allusion to trade.

One form of trade was always forbidden by the Church—that of earning a livelihood by usury. See USURY. In other respects it was long before trade was deemed by the Church itself incompatible with clerical functions, though the fathers might inveigh against it as a form of worldliness. The growth of some general feeling on the subject is, however, to be traced in the Council of Elvira (A.D. 305), which forbids bishops, priests, and deacons to depart from their places for the sake of trade, or to go round the provinces seeking lucrative markets. To obtain their livelihood they may, indeed, send a son, a freedman, an agent, or any one else; and if they wish to trade let them do so within the province. The main object clearly was to preserve to their flocks the benefits of their ministrations, not to put dishonor on trading itself. A collection of decrees of very doubtful authority, attributed to the Nicene council, contains among its "statutes for priests," a provision that the priest shall not be a barber, a surgeon, or a worker in iron, the two former prohibitions turning, probably, on blood-letting in its most literal form, the latter on the providing instruments for bloodshed.

The fourth Council of Carthage (A.D. 397) forbids clerics to go to markets, except to buy, under pain of degradation, but at the same time enacts that "a cleric, however learned in the word of God, shall seek his livelihood by means of a handicraft;" that "a cleric shall provide for himself food and clothing by a handicraft or by agriculture, without detriment to his office;" and that "all clerics who have strength to work shall learn both handicrafts and letters." These enactments indicate that, at all events in this quarter of the Church, a distinction was made between trade and handicrafts, and that the exercise of the former by clerics was restrained, while the latter was enjoined.

By the time of the Council of Chalcedon (A.D. 451) the line between "secular" and "religious" employments appears to have become much more sharply marked. The 3d canon speaks of clerics who for filthy lucre carry on secular business, and forbids them to do so—a prohibition which would seem to include every form of trade, but which cannot have been so considered, since the Council of Chalcedon is expressly named as one of the four to whose canons force of law is given by Justinian's code (A.D. 533), which expressly recognises both clerical trading and trading on behalf of the Church.

In the West, however, the feeling against clerical trading became continually stronger; a letter of pope Gelasius I. (A.D. 492–496) to the bishops of Lucania speaks of his having heard from Picenum that very many clerics there are occupied with dishonorable business and filthy lucre, and enjoins them to abstain from unworthy gain, and from every device or desire of business of any kind, or else from the fulfilment of clerical functions. The Council of Tarragona (A.D. 516) enacts that "whosoever will be in the clergy, let him not be careful to buy too cheap or sell too dear, or let him be removed from the clergy." A further provision implies a prohibition both of trade and of usury. The third Council of Orleans (A.D. 538) in like manner forbids clerics from the rank of deacons upwards to carry on business like public traders, or to carry on a forbidden business under another's name. In spite of these enactments, we find in the letters of Gregory the Great (A.D. 590–603) mention made of a ship-building bishop in Campania.

The capitularies of Charlemagne (mostly, if not always, invested with the sanction of the Church) deal repeatedly with the subject of trade. The ecclesiastical capitulary of 789 enacts that measures and weights be equal and just, "whether in cities or whether in monasteries, whether for giving or whether for receiving." The Frankfort Capitulary of 794 is one of several which attempt to fix the prices of victuals. The pitch of actual cruelty is reached in the "Capitula de Judæis," where every Jew is forbidden to have money in his house, to sell wine, victuals, or any other thing, under pain of confiscation of all his goods, and imprisonment, till he come into the imperial presence. The utter absence of all notion of a possible right to freedom in trading is well expressed in one of the Capitula published A.D. 803: "That no man presume to sell or buy or measure otherwise than as the lord emperor has commanded."

Markets are not to be held on the Lord's day (various councils of the 9th century), except where they have been held of old and lawfully. Forestalling for covetousness' sake is forbidden (Capitulary of Aix-la-Chapelle of 809). The Council of Friuli (A.D. 791) even forbade generally the carrying on of secular business to an immoderate extent.

Presbyters were by one capitulary forbidden to trade, or gather riches in any wise by filthy lucre (A.D. 806). On the other hand the Council of Mayence (A.D. 813) more guardedly forbids clerics and monks to have unjust weights or measures, or to carry on an unjust trade; "nevertheless a just trade is not to be forbidden, on account of divers necessities; for we read that the holy apostles traded," the rule of St. Benedict being referred to as a further authority. Trade was, however, forbidden to penitents, "because it is difficult that between the dealing of seller and buyer sin should not intervene."

The exact meaning of some of the later texts above referred to is rendered somewhat doubtful through the gradual narrowing of the term *negotium* and its derivatives, from the sense of business in its widest meaning to the specific one of trade. They show, however, that while the vocations of the early apostles were still remembered, and the rule of St. Benedict had raised the dignity of labor itself, the growing Judaistic distinction between "secular" and "religious" acts and matters, so foreign to the true spirit of Christianity, had by the 9th century begun to render the very idea of trade incompatible with the clerical calling, not so much, as in early times, by reason of its distracting the minister from his sacred functions, as on account of a supposed inherent dishonor attached to it. A comparison with civil legislation shows that the distinction is in itself a result of the secularizing of the Church. The ultra-refined officialism of the later Roman empire, which made the sovereign the only source of honor, and excluded the independent trader (one specially rich class excepted) even from the merely civil *militia*, on the one hand —the rude savagery of the barbarian on the other, which looked upon war and warlike sports as the only employments worthy of a man, and almost utterly ignored in legislation the very existence of the trader—must both, whatever phenomena to the contrary may present themselves in Justinian's code, have reacted profoundly upon the spirit of the Church. The service of God, which soon claimed the title of a *militia*, must have the exclusiveness of one, whether the term were used in the Roman official sense or in the warlike barbarian one; whatever was incompatible with the dignity of the functionary of an earthly sovereign, of the soldier of an earthly chief, must be incompatible also with that of a minister of God, a soldier in his host. At the same time, the influence of this distinction had not gone so far as to exclude the whole realm of trade from Church solicitude, and it is remarkable to observe in the canons of French councils of the beginning of the 9th century similar enactments against dishonesty in trade to those of the Pentateuch. See COVETOUSNESS; DEBTOR.

Commineréll, JOHANN PAUL, a German theologian, was born at Heilbronn, July 29, 1720. He studied at Tübingen, where he took his degrees in 1739; then travelled through Germany, England, and Holland. On his return he performed various ecclesiastical functions, especially at Carlsruhe. He died at Göppingen in 1774, leaving, *Heilige Kanzel Reden über dans erste Buch Mose* (Carlsruhe, 1783):—*Acht Predigten über den Propheten Iesaiam*. See Hoefer, *Nouv. Biog. Générale*, s. v.

Comministri are the presbyters in the early Christian Church who assisted in the administration of the sacraments. Subsequently they regularly administered the ordinances themselves. See PRESBYTER.

Commistio (or **Commixtio**). In the Roman missal, after the breaking of the host (see FRACTION), the priest places a particle in the chalice, saying to himself, "May this commixtion and consecration of the body and blood of our Lord Jesus Christ avail to us who receive it unto life eternal." This practice appears to be an ancient one, and to be considered as a kind of consecration (q. v.). It is found in the liturgy of St. James, where the priest, after breaking the bread, places the portion which he holds in his right hand in the chalice, saying, "The union of the all-holy body and precious blood of our Lord and God and Saviour Jesus Christ." The fourth Council of Toledo (A.D. 633), canon 18, orders the commixtion to take place between the Lord's Prayer and the benediction. Cranmer explained the ceremony as signifying the joining together of Christ's body and blood at the resurrection, which before were severed at the time of his passion.

Common House (or **Parlor**) in a monastery is the calefactory; a common room, with a fire in winter, for the monks.

Common of Saints is a festal service in honor of a particular kind or class of saints, e. g. a martyr, a virgin, or confessor; suitable, consequently, for any festival commemorating one of the class in which the name of the saint commemorated is introduced in the collect and at the other appointed places.

Commoner, at Oxford, a student who is not dependent on the foundation for support, but who pays for his own board or *commons*, together with all other collegiate charges.

Commotiæ, in Roman mythology, were nymphs of the Cutilian lake, in the country of the Sabines, where there was a floating island.

Communar was (1) the bursar in a cathedral, who distributed the commons or general capitulary fund, and paid stipends; (2) an officer, called the master of the common house, who provided a fire in the calefactory and certain luxuries on festivals.

Communicāles is a term used to designate the vessels used in holy communion, which on certain days were carried in procession at Rome.

Communio, in liturgical use, is (1) an anthem in the Roman and cognate missals, said by the celebrant after he has taken the ablutions. It is so called because it was originally appointed to be sung during the communion of the people, and was sung antiphonally after each verse of a psalm, which was continued till the priest gave the signal for the *Gloria*, when the communion of the people was ended. Afterwards the *Communio* was looked upon more as an act of thanksgiving to be said *after* the communion. It varies with the day. (2) An anthem in the Mozarabic missal sung by the *choir* after the communion has taken place. There are only two forms: one used in Lent, the other during the rest of the year.—Smith, *Dict. of Christ. Antiq.* s. v.

Communio Præsanctificatōrum, the reception on Good Friday by the priest of the reserved sacrament in the Roman Church, as follows: The celebrant places it on the paten, and then on the corporal. In the meantime the deacon puts wine and the sub-deacon water into the chalice, which, however, are neither blessed nor consecrated on this day. The celebrant next places the chalice on the altar, the deacon covering it with the pall. The celebrant then incenses the offerings and altar, washes his hands, and recites the *Orate Fratres* and *Pater Noster*. Then all kneel to worship the sacrament, which the celebrant, without any prayer, divides into three parts, placing one in the chalice. He then communicates himself of both sacrament and chalice (with the particle), and proceeds to receive the ablutions in the ordinary way. See PRÆSANCTIFICATIO.

Communion OF CHILDREN. See INFANT COMMUNION.

COMMUNION, CLERICAL, a term employed by the early Christian writers in opposition to lay communion (q. v.), to denote the full exercise of all the duties of the clerical office. It is also called *ecclesiastical communion*.

COMMUNION, ECCLESIASTICAL. See COMMUNION, CLERICAL.

COMMUNION, FREE (or OPEN), is a term used in opposition to *Close Communion*, to denote the admission of all believers to the Lord's table. See COMMUNION.

COMMUNION, HOLY. We excerpt the following particulars concerning the celebration of this rite in primitive times from Walcott, *Sac. Archæol.* s. v.:

"In early times, after the benediction by the bishop, which followed the Lord's Prayer, the deacon called the people to communion, saying 'Attend;' and then the celebrant said, 'Holy [things] for holy [persons];' to which the answer was, 'One holy, one Lord Jesus Christ, to the glory of God the Father, blessed forever, amen;' followed by the *Gloria in Excelsis*. The eucharistic bread was broken before the ministration, and in the Greek Church immediately after the consecration. The Latins divided each bread into three, the Greeks into four segments. The latter used two fractions; one before consecration, into three parts, at the words 'He brake it;' and the second, properly so called, when each part was subdivided, before the Lord's Prayer and after the reading of the diptychs. The Mozarabic rite prescribes nine parts to be made, in allusion to the nine mysteries of the life of Christ, the conception, nativity, circumcision, transfiguration, passion, death, resurrection, glory, and kingdom. The fraction was succeeded by the mixture mentioned by the fourth Council of Toledo and that of Orange in 441. After the call 'Holy for the holy,' the congregation communicated, the bishop, priests, clergy, ascetics, women, deaconesses, virgins, widows, children, and then the rest present. The distribution was made by deacons, but in later times the priest ministered the bread, and the deacon the chalice. Deacons sometimes administered the bread, with the restriction that they were not to do so to priests or to the people without the order of a priest. In Spain priests and deacons communicated at the altar, minor clerks within the choir, and the people at the chancel. The Greeks also allowed only the former within the sanctuary. Persons in the East received either prostrate, kneeling, or standing, bowing the head at the ministration. In the West priests alone received in the latter posture. The words of ministration were at first 'The body of Christ, and the blood of Christ;' to which the faithful replied, 'Amen.' In the time of Gregory the Great they were expanded thus, 'The body of our Lord Jesus Christ preserve thy soul;' and in the age of Charlemagne, 'The body of our Lord Jesus Christ preserve thee to everlasting life.' Men received in the hollow of the right hand, bare, crossed over the left, throne-like, as Cyril of Jerusalem says; and women in a linen cloth, called the dominical, from which they raised the element to their lips. The chalice was administered by the deacon, who held it by its two handles, and at length the calamus was used by the people."

COMMUNION, INFANT. See INFANT COMMUNION.

COMMUNION, STRICT, is the same as *Close Communion*. See COMMUNION.

COMMUNION OF THE SICK. Although the church is the proper place for a celebration, yet, in cases of necessity, the holy communion was administered, in ancient times, in crypts, at the tombs of martyrs, in a prison, on the celebrant's breast, in the deacon's hands, in a tent, a hut, a house, in the fields, at sea, by a bedside—anywhere, except in the burial-places of the heathen. See VIATICUM.

COMMUNION OF STRANGERS (*communio peregrina*). Strangers and travellers, in the early ages of the Christian Church, were required to have testimonials of their regular standing in the Church, in order to be admitted to the privileges of communion. Otherwise they were treated as members under censure, although they were permitted to receive support from the funds of the Church when necessary. Clergymen under censure were treated in the same way. Then they could neither officiate nor be present at the celebration of the Lord's supper until they had given the required satisfaction. See Gardner, *Faiths of the World*, s. v. See COMMENDATORY LETTERS.

Communion-books. See LITURGICAL BOOKS.

Communion-cloth is a long cloth of white linen spread over the altar-rails at the time of communion, held at each end by an acolyte, and supported by each of the faithful who come to communicate, so that no irreverence, by accident or otherwise, may occur to the sacrament.

Communions is a name given to Psa. xxiii, xxxiv, xlii, cxviii, or cxlv, sung during the administration in the Greek Church; and mentioned by Jerome, Cyril of Jerusalem, the apostolical constitutions, and early liturgies.

Community OF GOODS. See COMMUNISM; MONASTICISM.

Comnat (**Comnatan**, or **Connat**), an Irish saint, commemorated January 1, appears among the prelates of Kildare on this day; but of her abbacy we know nothing beyond its close. She died abbess of Kildare in A.D. 590 (Todd and Reeves, *Mart. Doneg.* p. 5; O'Hanlon, *Irish Saints*, i, 24, 25).

Comnena, Anna, was a Byzantine princess, the daughter of the emperor Alexius Comnenus, illustrious by her birth, and by the circumstances of her life, but more illustrious by her accomplishments, and by the important historical work which she transmitted to posterity. Whether her subject, her opportunities, her talents, her rank, her associations, or her disappointed ambition be considered, her quaint production is calculated to excite and to reward the liveliest interest. The time in which she lived and wrote, the memorable transactions which she witnessed and in which she often participated, the notable personages with whom she came in contact, the troubles, perils, and perplexities by which she was surrounded, the grand and startling events which she recorded, combine to give a peculiar fascination to her Memoirs. In a dark and dreary age, but one of varied and heroic adventure, in the desperate struggle of a great but declining empire, she related, for the instruction of other times, the strange vicissitudes of fortune—the hopes, the alarms, and the efforts of the wild period, when the East, the West, and the North, the exhausted culture of the old, and the rude chivalry of the new civilization were intermingled with the fierce fury of Tartar and Saracenic violence. That she lived in the days of the emperor Henry IV, the countess Matilda, Godfrey de Bouillon, and Kilidje Arslan, is evidence of the eventful character of the time. That she beheld the passage of the first crusaders, and was, in all probability, acquainted with Peter the Hermit, Bohemond, Tancred, and the other leaders, gives assurance of the highest interest in her reminiscences. That she was brought up in the Byzantine court, familiar with its delusive splendors, its secrets, its vices, its intrigues, and its hazards; that she was herself designated for the imperial crown, may not attest the accuracy or the profundity of her narrative, but certainly confer upon it a breathing charm and a personal reality which may atone for grievous defects. The inflation of her language, the affectations of her learning, the extravagance of her statements, the moral distempers which warp her judgment, may detract seriously from the trustworthiness of her record, and have been amply and too exclusively presented. Serious as are these drawbacks, they do not prevent her biography of her father from being the most attractive in the long list of the Byzantine historians, and also the most instructive.

1. *Life.*—Anna Comnena was the eldest child of the emperor Alexius Comnenus, by his second wife, the empress Irene Ducœnsa. She was born at Constantinople, on Sunday, Dec. 1, 1083, the day of her father's return from his repulse of Bohemond at Iarissa. She was *Porphyrogenita*—born in the Purple Palace—and, a few days after her birth, was proclaimed cæsarissa and heiress of the empire, and was betrothed to the boy Constantine, son of the former emperor, Michael Ducas, and the nominal colleague of her father on the imperial throne. She was at once recognised as the image of her father (*Alexiad*, vi, 8). By this betrothal the Comnenian dynasty assumed some pretensions to be the restoration of the sovereign house of Ducas. The young prince was retained, with his mother, in honorable confinement, and soon died, but not before Durazzo, as is often stated. Anna had three brothers and three sisters. Among the former was Ugly John Kalo-Joannes, about four years younger than herself, who succeeded their father on the throne, and was never forgiven for this intrusion. Her uncles, her aunts, and her cousins, her brothers-in-law, sisters-in-law, nephews and nieces, outrun convenient enumeration. Are they not commemorated by Du Cange, in his serviceable *Familiæ Byzantinæ?* "Her mother, Irene, was the grandniece of the emperor, Constantine Ducas, and her father was the nephew of Isaac, the first emperor of the line of the Comneni." She was thus of imperial blood on both sides. The time of her death has not been determined. As she began her history after the death of her husband, wrote under the reign of her nephew, Manuel, and was still writing after thirty years of surveillance, she may be presumed to have lived to a very advanced age. She grew up in the court in close attendance on her mother, and in more intimate and kindly association with her parents than is usual in sovereign households. In her father's frequent absences on military expeditions, she was more a companion of her mother than a child in the family. On more peaceful removals from Constantinople the empress and the cæsarissa accompanied the emperor. This affectionate intimacy developed from very early years the inquisitive spirit, the mental powers, and the political aptitudes of the young girl, and afforded her the best opportunities for a present and minute knowledge of the prominent persons and important occurrences of the times. The drama proceeded immediately before her eyes. She was unquestionably precocious. She was provided with the best instructors and with the best means of instruction. She had great zeal for learning, quick apprehension, and high capacity. She became a prodigy of erudition in the estimation of her contemporaries, and not merely within the circle of the court. It is certainly a mistake to regard the end

of the 11th and the beginning of the 12th century as an uncultivated period. The name of the empress Eudocia Macrembolissa; the abilities of Michael Psellus, and of John Italus, the precursor and Byzantine counterpart of Abelard; the number, rank, and enthusiasm of their disciples; the historical productions of the highest dignitaries of the state, disprove any such hasty conclusions. The Ducases, and particularly the emperor Michael and his brothers, were noted for their literary zeal (*Alexiad*, v, 8). Tastes may be corrupt, pursuits mistaken, modes of thought distorted, but these aberrations do not preclude diligence of culture. Rhetoric and logic and philosophy, the inflated style of zealots for Attic polish, the arid and tangled ingenuity of the schoolmen, the sophistry of the new Platonists or new Pythagoreans, and of later unnamed sects, were the objects of admiration; but these objects were seriously prosecuted. The imperial Anna was among the most eager and successful of such students. She boasts of having mastered both the Aristotelian and the Platonic philosophy. She expresses decided opinions upon the merits and demerits of John the Italian. She displays in her writings an ample if indiscriminate acquaintance with the classics of ancient Greece. Such studies, however, furnished only the skeleton and vesture of her inquiries. Their substance was very different. The actual range of solid information exhibited in the work of her later life, the patient industry with which she sought, and the quick judgment with which she estimated the most important matters of daily concern, may be recognised under all the extravagant finery with which they were disguised. Her acquaintance with the scholars of the day, her court life, her intercourse with her parents, her familiarity with the statesmen and chief actors of the bustling period in which she lived, furnished her with constant and valued opportunities for the most abundant knowledge, and for the quickest appreciation of what transpired around her. Nor were the habitual dangers by which she was encompassed and which threatened the station and the lives of herself, her family, and her multitudinous relations, without influence in sharpening all her faculties and enlarging her range of reflection. It is necessary to reason back from the characteristics of her subsequent life, and of her Memoirs, to her original predispositions. Grapes are not gathered from a bramble bush.

With remarkable aptitudes, with favoring appliances, with exciting and invigorating experiences, Anna grew up to womanhood, and, if the testimony of herself may be accepted, crowned her intellectual accomplishments with rare beauty and feminine grace. The Comneni were long eminent for talent, and were even more distinguished for their personal appearance. Anna partook of both kinds of endowment. There is every reason to conclude that she was entitled to be regarded as singularly handsome. Such charms as she possessed may have been masculine, like her mind and temperament. This may be an entirely erroneous inference. The illuminated miniature of the celebrated countess Matilda, her contemporary, which adorns the coeval MS. of Donizo, represents a small figure with almost infantile features. Whatever may have been the style of Anna's beauty, in this remarkable historian were united the highest rank, fortune, family, energy, decision, personal appearance, intellect, and learning—a marvellous combination in a princess of the Byzantine empire.

As the young Ducas had disappointed Anna's matrimonial expectations by an early death, her father, for some unascertained reason, bestowed her hand upon Nicephorus Bryennius, the eldest son (Zonar. xviii, 22; Du Cange says grandson) of that Bryennius who had pretended to the empire, but had been defeated, captured, and blinded by Alexius. He was probably much older than herself. She expressed a most devoted attachment to his memory in her lonely and desolate widowhood, though she had not restrained the bitterness of her tongue during their married life (Nicet. Chon. i, 3). Of the course and character of their wedded career we have no information beyond the widow's indistinct regrets. Her husband was a man of education and ability. He was much employed in the incessant military transactions of the times. His death was attributed to poison, administered by direction of his wife's able but unscrupulous nephew, Andronicus. His literary culture is shown by the very interesting history of the Comneni, which was interrupted by his death, and which furnished the example and the stimulus for its continuation by his learned relict (*Alexiad*, *Præf.* iii). He brought his Memoirs down only to the accession of Alexius. His bereaved spouse records for us the whole reign of her father.

Anna Comnena was married, probably, about the time of Peter the Hermit's passage through Constantinople, on his return from the Holy Land and its desecrated sanctities. It was about two years after her marriage that the turbulent, rapacious, arrogant hosts of the Crusaders swarmed round Constantinople, plundering and devastating the famished provinces through which they pursued their lingering and disorderly way. The years that followed were filled with multifarious adventures, with diversified hazards, with wars, with conspiracies, and with romantic tales of heroic achievements and selfish audacity.

The troubled career and the difficult reign of Alexius Comnenus at length drew to a close. His waning life and his days of suffering were curiously watched by the wife of his bosom and the daughter of his heart. His sick-bed was besieged by them, and his palace guarded by their orders, in order to determine the succession according to their wishes. John, the heir and successor, was excluded from his father's presence. Conspiracy was active within and without the city, to secure the imperial crown for Anna and her husband. It is unfortunate that the MS. of the closing chapters of Anna's work is so mutilated as to leave the account of the death-bed scenes unintelligible. The other authorities assert that the sinking emperor was importuned by wife and daughter to declare the latter heiress to the throne. He died without gratifying this desire; and his affectionate wife addressed words of savage contumely to his departing spirit.

Though the desires of the empress and the princess were thus frustrated, the hopes which had been so long entertained, and the aims so long contemplated, were not renounced. The palace was held under guard. Ugly John, the son and brother, was neither informed of the death, nor invited to the presence of the dead emperor. The partisans of the faction were prepared for the seizure of the throne. Their retainers were assembled, military support was organized, and Nicephorus Bryennius was urged to prompt action, and to make himself master of the city and empire. A masculine energy and daring were exhibited by the empress and cæsarissa, which would have been notable in a conquering usurper—*Dux fœmina facti*.

The calm resolution and promptitude of John Comnenus, and the irresolution or conscientiousness of Nicephorus Bryennius, defeated these bold and well-matured schemes. Bryennius refused to perform the part assigned to him—whether unwilling to uphold disloyal practices, or warned by the failure and fate of his father or grandfather, or by mingled motives. His wife ascribed his reluctance or delay to faintness of heart, and expressed her scorn in terms of contempt stronger and coarser than the language of Lady Macbeth.

John secured the throne without serious commotion. His mother and sister were pardoned and put under slight and honorable restraint. Nicephorus Bryennius seems to have been unharmed and uncensured. Even the princely fortunes and the wide domains of his rivals were left untouched by the successful emperor. The representations of his follower, his friend, and his able minister, the Turk, John Axuch, who had been captured by the Crusaders at Nice, dissuaded him from his first purpose of confiscating the possessions of the near relatives who had conspired against him.

Anna was soured for life by her defeat, and poured her long lamentations throughout her history (especially *Alexiad*, xiv, 7). The long-deferred hope, the design nursed in silent anxiety during weary years, were altogether frustrated. The unsisterly dislike of the sovereign was intensified. The wrong that had been prevented seemed an injury received. After the death of her husband, and probably under the reign of her nephew, Manuel, Anna appears to have been compelled to retire, or to seek refuge in a nunnery. There she fanned the ancient flames, cherished the old passions, and relieved her anguish by mingling angry regrets with all her reminiscences—

"In seas of flame her plunging soul is drown'd,
While altars blaze, and angels tremble round."

The date of Anna Comnena's death is wholly unknown. Nothing is recorded of her after the decease of her husband, except what is contained in the venomous moanings of her work and in some very brief notices. One son survived her, Alexius, who took his grandfather's family name, Comnenus (Nicet. Chon. ii, 7), and was captured in the Capitanata by the Normans, against whom he commanded. Her memory has been more effectually preserved by the memorial of her father, which she is supposed to have completed about thirty years after his death. It is only stated by her that she was writing at that time (*Alexiad*, xiv, 7).

2. *The Alexiad.*—The fame of Anna Comnena has been perpetuated by a single literary monument. This is beyond question the most entertaining and instructive of the Byzantine histories, after those of Procopius and Agathias. Nevertheless, the work has been too little esteemed. It has been oftener cited with a sneer than read with fairness and intelligence. Much of the depreciation and neglect must be ascribed to her own extravagant rhetoric, and to unmeasured admiration of her father, equally in his failures and in his achievements. More may, undoubtedly, be attributed to the contempt with which Gibbon has spoken of the history and its author. The supercilious censure of the great historian has repressed curiosity, and prevented considerate judgment, while it has often discouraged examination. It is forgotten that this *Alexiad* is a sort of prose epic, according to the false taste of the age, as the *Philippeid* of Gulielmus Brito, and the *Gesta Friderici* of Gunther Tigurinus, were verse histories of their respective heroes. Yet, whatever censures may be justly passed upon the work, our acquaintance with a most eventful period would be both meagre and distorted without the aid of Anna's discredited labors. A clearer and juster apprehension of some of the most surprising and complex changes in the current of human affairs than has yet been attained may be expected from a cooler, kindlier, and more dispassionate study of her remarkable contribution to the varying story of the Byzantine empire.

The interruption of the history of the Comneni, by the death of Nicephorus Bryennius, induced his disconsolate widow, in her enforced seclusion, to take up the broken thread of the narrative, and to continue it to her father's decease. She had her own abundant recollections of incidents and scenes at which she had been present, of counsels and projects of which she had been cognizant, of conspiracies in which her own fate had been involved. She was familiar with the secrets of the palace, with her husband's labors, with the materials he had gathered, and with the notes which he had prepared. Not content with these sources of knowledge, she diligently pursued, in every quarter, information regarding past events; sought out those who had participated in the grave transactions of the times, or possessed the most thorough acquaintance with them. The zeal for the fulness of historical truth is asserted by herself, but it is also attested by the abundance, the variety, and the minuteness of the knowledge displayed throughout her work. The statements may often be prejudiced, the sentiments affected, the exaggerations frequent, the expression turgid, the rhetorical decorations inappropriate and excessive—but these were the defects of the age. They do not destroy the high qualifications which they conceal by their gaudy splendor. Making due allowance for the grave blemishes which have too much engrossed the attention of critics, the substance that remains is of the highest interest and of the greatest value. The undue depreciations of Anna's *Gesta* has had a very injurious effect on the estimation of that memorable age, when the seeds of growth and the tares of decay were so widely scattered. It has certainly occasioned such a discoloration of the pictures of the crusades as has led to erroneous conceptions of their origin and conduct. Yet Anna, who has been so injudiciously slighted, was their earliest historian, witnessed their passage, was cognizant of their inception and progress, and was personally acquainted with the chiefs of the first, and, probably, with the sovereigns of the second crusade. Much discernment and more than ordinary skill may be required to detect the true lineaments of the personages and the scenes, under the glaring pigments and prodigal daubing of the pictures; but they may be detected, and their detection will reward the labor expended upon the task. But the first crusade constitutes only a small, though a very prominent, part of the narrative. The career of the emperor Alexius forms the subject of the *Alexiad;* and in his troubled and constantly imperilled reign there occurred many other greater dangers, and more arduous problems for statesmanship. It is only necessary to mention some of these to show the multitudinous topics of interest recorded by Anna: the war with Robert Guiscard, and the later war with Bohemond; the wars with the Turks, Romans, Hungarians, Slavonians; the revolts and the conspiracies; the heresies of John Italus, of the Paulicians, and of the Bogomilians; the reconstitution of the army, by which a precedent was furnished for the Ottoman Janizaries; the military stratagems and devices; the ambitious schemes of Norman auxiliaries; the reorganization of the state; the debasement of the coinage; the restoration of the finances; the provision for the poor, the great orphan asylum and the poorhouse; the plagues and famines and physical disturbances; the ceremonies, the occupations, and the amusements of the court. These and numerous other subjects, exhibiting the civil and social aspects of the fainting and beleaguered empire, receive their fullest exposition in the *Alexiad* of Anna Comnena. Later chroniclers contented themselves with copying and abridging her relations, and did credit to themselves and justice to their original by repeating her praises. It belonged to a later age to see only the blemishes, and to remain totally blind to the merits of her work.

3. *Literature.*—Anna Comnena, *Alexias* (ed. Bonn. 1839-76); Du Cange, *Familiæ Augustæ Byzantinæ*, apud. *Script. Rer. Byz.* vol. xxi. (Venet. 1729); Bayle, *Dict. Hist. Crit.*, tit. *Anna Comnena;* Füssli, *Dissertatio de Annæ Alexiade* (Tigur, 1766); Wilken, *Rer. a Comn. Gestar.* l. iv. (Heidelb. 1811); Nikolai, *Gesch. des Byzant. Lit.*, apud. Ersch u. Grüber. *Enkyklopädie;* Calliades, *Anna Comnena* (Constantin. 1879); Krug, *Chronologie des Byzantiner.* (G. F. H.)

Comodi (or **Commodo**), ANDREA, a reputable Florentine painter, was born in 1560, and was the friend and scholar of Cigoli. His principal works are in Rome, among which are the following: *The Baptism of Christ*, in San Giovanni in Fonte; *Christ Bearing the Cross*, in the tribune of San Vitale; and the principal altar-piece in San Carlo a Catinari, representing the titular saint kneeling. He died at Florence in 1638. See Spooner, *Biog. Hist. of the Fine Arts*, s. v.; Hoefer, *Nouv. Biog. Générale*, s. v.

Comp, Jacob S., a Methodist Episcopal minister, was born in Markleville, Pa., June 24, 1845. He experienced religion at the age of fourteen, received license to preach in 1867; graduated from Dickinson Seminary in June, 1869, entered the Central Pennsylvania Conference, and travelled the remainder of that year and all the next on Watsontown Circuit. In 1872 failing health obliged him to retire from the active ranks, and he returned to the home of his childhood, where he died, Nov. 16, 1876. See *Minutes of Annual Conferences*, 1877, p. 26.

Compagnoni, Camillo, an Italian preacher, brother of the bishop of Osimo, was born in 1698, entered the Jesuit order, and distinguished himself by his knowledge and talent as a preacher. He died in 1777. See Hoefer, *Nouv. Biog. Générale*, s. v.

Compagnoni, Pietro, an Italian ecclesiastic, was born at San Lorenzo, near Lugo, March 28, 1802. He received his education first under his uncle; afterwards studied belles-lettres, philosophy, and theology under the famous professor Tommaso Ancarini, who died at Rome in 1830, vicar-general of the Dominicans. Compagnoni, at the age of eighteen, aided by Giovanni Nuvoli, published *Salmi Penitenziali Davide* (Lugo, 1821). After ordination he was made professor of rhetoric and geography in the Lyceum at Lugo, at the same time officiating as preacher. He died Sept. 13, 1833, leaving some minor pieces, for which see *Biog. Universelle*, s. v.

Compagnoni, Pompeo, an Italian prelate and writer, was born at Macerata, March 11, 1693. He studied first in his own town, and in 1712 at Rome, under Gravina. Having entered holy orders, he became archdeacon of Macerata, and auditor to cardinal Francesco Barberini. He was made bishop of Osimo and Cingoli, Oct. 2, 1740, and died July 25, 1774, leaving, besides some minor pieces, a *Memorie della Chiesa d' Osimo* (Rome, 1782, 5 vols. 4to). See Hoefer, *Nouv. Biog. Générale*, s. v.

Compan, *Abbé*, a French scholar, was born at Arles about 1730. He studied jurisprudence and theology in his native country, and was made advocate to the parliament of Paris. Later he entered upon the ecclesiastical calling, and was one of the clergy of Saint André des Arts. He wrote, *L'Esprit de la Religion Chrétienne* (Paris, 1763):—*Le Temple de la Piété, et Œuvres Diverses* (ibid. 1765, 1769):—*Nouvelle Méthode Géographique* (ibid. 1770). See Hoefer, *Nouv. Biog. Générale*, s. v.

Compand (**Compan**, or **Compano**), Jean, a French priest and religious writer, was born at Dalon, in the diocese of Pamiers, in 1771. He was a pupil at the seminary of Cahors, in charge of the priests of Saint-Lazare, having entered that celebrated order; and after having taught philosophy in several seminaries of the province, he was called to the same position in the seminary of Saint-Firmin, at Paris. Later he was almoner of the Hôtel des Invalides, and eventually superior of the seminary at Toulouse. The Revolution forced him to seek an asylum, first at Barcelona, and then at Rome. After twelve years of exile he returned to the capital of Languedoc, where he accepted a chair of theology, and occupied it until 1830. He died Feb. 7, 1835, leaving *Traité des Dispenses de Collet* (with notes, corrections, additions, and explanations):—*Histoire de la Vie de Jésus-Christ* (composed at the request of madame Louise, daughter of Louis XV). See Hoefer, *Nouv. Biog. Générale*, s. v.

Compass, Worship of the. The Chinese were accustomed to pay divine honors to the compass by burning little odoriferous balls, and offering meats and sacrifices to it. They threw gilded paper punctually twice a day into the sea to attract its favor and win it to be propitious. See Gardner, *Faiths of the World*, s. v.

Compassivity is a term used by Romanist writers to express the feelings of a saint on beholding in a vision the sufferings whereby his soul is transpierced with the sword of a *compassive* pain, thus literally enduring the passion of Christ.

Compătres and **Commātres**. See Sponsors.

Compendiense, Concilium. See Compiegne.

Compere, Lee, a Baptist minister, was born in England in 1789. Soon after entering the ministry he went as a missionary to Jamaica, but ill-health obliged him to return after one year. In 1817 he came to America, and for some time labored in South Carolina, having charge for six years of the mission among the Creek Indians. The transfer of the tribe west of the Mississippi broke up the mission. He followed the tide of emigration, until finally he settled in Yazoo County, Miss., where he labored with considerable success for several years. He lived for a time in Arkansas, then removed to Texas, and died there in 1871. See Cathcart, *Baptist Encyclop.* p. 258. (J. C. S.)

Competentes (i. e. *seekers* of the grace of Christ) was an advanced class of candidates for baptism, who had received adequate instruction. They acquired this name on Palm-Sunday, when the Creed was delivered to them; on the second Sunday following the Lord's Prayer was explained in their hearing.

Compiègne, Councils of (*Concilium Compendiense*), were provincial synods, as follows:

I. Held in 756. At this council, Pepin, king of France, several bishops and lords, together with the legates of pope Stephen, were present. An organ sent by the eastern emperor to Pepin was received. Eighteen canons were published, chiefly relating to questions about marriages:

1. Orders the separation of parties marrying within the third degree.
3. Declares that a wife taking the veil without her husband's consent must be given up to him, if he requires it.
5. Allows a free man who marries a slave under the idea that she was free to put her away and to marry again; also allows the same to a free woman.
9. Declares baptism administered by an unbaptized priest, in the name of the blessed Trinity, valid.

See Labbe, *Concil.* vi, 1694.

II. Held Aug. 5, 1235, concerning certain articles which, according to the archbishop of Rheims, violated the liberties of the Church. The archbishop and six of his suffragans proceeded to St. Denis, in order to make a second monition to the king, which step induced the lords to prefer a complaint by letter to the pope against the bishops and clergy; this letter is dated September, 1235. The king (St. Louis), by an ordinance, declared that his own vassals and those of the lords were not bound, in civil matters, to answer any charge in the ecclesiastical courts; and that if the ecclesiastical judge should proceed to excommunicate any one in such a case, he should be compelled to remove the excommunication by the seizure of his temporalities. The pope exhorted St. Louis to revoke this ordinance, declaring, among other things, that God had confided to the pope both the temporal and spiritual government of the world. However, the letter seems to have had little effect upon the king, who refused to revoke the edict. See Labbe, *Concil.* xi, 503.

III. Held in 1277, by Peter, archbishop of Rheims, with eight of his suffragans. They made a decree relating to the insubordinate conduct of the chapters of the cathedral churches of the province, who pretended, among other things, to a right to put a stop to divine service, and to lay the city under an interdict, for the sake of protecting their own immunities. See Labbe, *Concil.* x, 1031.

IV. Held Jan. 4, 1304, by Robert de Courtenay, archbishop of Rheims, assisted by eight bishops, and the deputies of three absent. They made five decrees:

2. Forbids the levying imposts upon the clergy under false pretences.

5. Restricts the dinner of the clergy of the province to two dishes over and above the pottage or soup, except they have some great person at the table.

See Labbe, *Concil.* xi, 1492; Landon, *Man. of Councils*, s. v.

Besides the foregoing, which were the most important councils held at Compiègne, there are notices of others at the same place, of which we present an account from Richard et Giraud, *Bibliothèque Sacrée*, vii, 425:

I. Held in 758, at which Tassillon, duke of Bavaria, pledged fealty to king Pepin (Mansi, i, 607).
II. In 833, at which Louis le Débonnaire was subjected to penance (Labbe, vii; Hardouin, iv).
III. In 871, at which Hincmar, archbishop of Rheims, excommunicated the followers of Carloman, who had revolted against Charles the Bald (Mansi, i, 1013).
IV. In 877, against idolatry.
V. In 1085, by Renaud, archbishop of Rheims, in favor of certain French abbeys (Labbe, x; Hardouin, vi).
VI. In 1256 (*Gallia Christ.* iii, 89).
VII. In 1270, by Jean de Courtenay, archbishop of Rheims, against encroachments upon Church property (Labbe, xi; Hardouin, vii).
VIII. In 1301, at which seven canons were passed, concerning ecclesiastical jurisdiction (Labbe, xi, 2; Hardouin, vii).
IX. In 1329, by Guillaume de Brie, archbishop of Rheims, at which seven canons were enacted, the third relating to clerical jurisdiction.

Compitalia, among the pagan Romans, was a festival celebrated, especially at cross-roads, with plays and banquetings, in honor of the Lares. At the same time, as an atonement to the female dæmon, Mania, honey-cakes and onions were offered. All families of Rome at this festival hung on the outside of their houses as many woollen balls as they had slaves, and as many woollen dolls as there were free people in the house, in order that Mania might take these instead of the slaves. It is stated that, originally, at this festival children were sacrificed, which abomination the consul Brutus ended by instituting the above-mentioned substitute.

Compostella, Councils of (*Concilium ad Sanctum Jacobum*), were provincial synods:

I. Held May 6, 900, upon occasion of the dedication of the Church of St. James. Seventeen bishops were present, together with king Alfonso, his family, and many others. See Labbe, *Concil.* ix, 482.

II. Held in 1056, by Cresconius, archdeacon of Compostella. Among other things, it was decreed that all bishops and priests should say mass daily, and that the clergy should wear hair shirts on days of fasting and penitence. See Labbe, *Concil.* ix, 1087.

Comprising Arch is an architectural term for the large exterior arch of a window, which encloses the subordinate lights and tracery.

Compromise, Election by, is one of the modes of electing the pope. When the cardinals fail to agree upon any one candidate, they sometimes refer the matter to a committee of their own number by way of compromise, binding themselves to nominate as pope the person on whom the arbiters shall fix. See Pope.

Compte, Nicolas de, a French monk, who died at Paris in 1689, is the author of several geographical works, and a *History of the Jews.*

Compton, Robert, an English Baptist minister, was born at Withybrook, Warwickshire, Feb. 21, 1780. He was converted before arriving at eighteen years of age, and united with the Church at Hinckley, Leicestershire. He soon began, as a licentiate, to preach in the neighboring villages. In 1816 he removed to Isleham, Cambridgeshire, and was ordained pastor of the Church there, Oct. 29, 1817. In 1831 his health began to fail, and he died Aug. 8, 1834. See (Lond.) *Baptist Magazine*, 1835, p. 189-191. (J. C. S.)

Compton, Samuel, an English Congregational minister, was born at Gargrave, near Skipton, March 11, 1803. In 1822 he went to Rochdale, joined the Church, and began to assist in conducting cottage-services. He moved to Bury in 1831, to Radcliffe in 1838, to Bradford, Yorkshire, in 1850, and in 1855 to Settle, where he was ordained, having previously labored as home missionary. After twelve years' work at Settle, Mr. Compton retired to Radcliffe, where he died, July 1, 1870. See (Lond.) *Cong. Year-book*, 1871, p. 309.

Compton, William, a minister of the Methodist Episcopal Church South, was born in London, and emigrated to America in early life with his parents. In 1809 he entered the Virginia Conference, and subsequently became a member of the North Carolina Conference, in each of which he labored, as health would permit, to the close of his life, in November, 1847. Mr. Compton was methodical in his work, eminently a Bible student, an excellent preacher, and highly esteemed. See *Minutes of Annual Conferences of the M. E. Church South*, 1847, p. 130.

Compton, William F., a minister of the Methodist Episcopal Church South, was born in Morgan County, Ala., in 1837. He removed to Texas in 1855, united with the Church South, and in 1870 joined the East Texas Conference. In 1874 he was transferred to the North-west Texas Conference, and labored therein till his sudden death in 1878 or 1879. See *Minutes of Annual Conferences of the M. E. Church South*, 1879, p. 78.

Compŭtus. See Calendar.

Comstock, Elkanah, a Baptist minister, was born at New London, Conn., and commenced preaching in 1800. His first settlement was in Albany County, N. Y. Subsequently he went to Cayuga County. The New York Baptist Convention appointed him one of its missionaries to Michigan, and he removed to Pontiac in 1824. Having rare gifts for this position, he "made full proof" of his ministry. In 1834 he returned to visit his native place, somewhat broken in health, and died there at the age of sixty-three. See Cathcart, *Baptist Encyclop.* p. 258. (J. C. S.)

Comstock, Oliver C., a Baptist minister, was born in Oswego County, N. Y., in 1784. He received an academic education, and commenced a course of study with a view to entering the Christian ministry. Subsequently he abandoned his theological studies and turned his attention to medicine, and, in due time, was licensed, and practiced his profession at Trumansburg, N. Y. For two years (1810-12) he was a member of the State House of Representatives, and afterwards was elected a representative from the state of New York to Congress, and was twice re-elected, his whole term of service reaching from May 24, 1813, to March 3, 1819. He retired from the practice of medicine, having decided to return to the vocation of his early choice, and was ordained as a Baptist clergyman. For a time he acted as chaplain of the House of Representatives at Washington. His death occurred at Marshall, Mich., Jan. 11, 1860. See Poore, *Congressional Directory*, p. 342. (J. C. S.)

Comstock, Thomas, a Methodist Episcopal minister, was born in Wayne County, O., March 2, 1829. He was converted in 1841, and in 1854 licensed to preach, and received into the North Indiana Conference. In 1858 he was elected professor in Fort Wayne College. After labonrig in that capacity two years, he again held regular appointments until 1864, when he once more occupied, for a year, a professorship in the same college, then resumed his place in the active ministry, and continued until his death, June 17, 1872. Mr. Comstock was a man of rare culture, a practical, earnest preacher, an extraordinary pastor, and a Christian of deep and uniform piety. See *Minutes of Annual Conferences*, 1873, p. 59.

Comstock, William, a Methodist Episcopal minister, brother of the foregoing, was born in Wayne County, O., May 2, 1832. He removed with his parents to Indiana, and settled on Eel River; was converted in 1843; studied for the ministry, and was admitted into the North Indiana Conference in 1866. In 1871 his health failed, and he died Dec. 11, 1875. Mr. Comstock was a man of great faith and Christian activity. See *Minutes of Annual Conferences*, 1876, p. 37.

Comus, god of nocturnal revels and festivals, was a Grecian deity, represented as a young man crowned with roses or myrtle, holding in one hand a golden cup, and in the other a platter of fruit.

Comyn (**Comin**, or **Cumin**), JOHN, an Irish prelate, was a native of England, and a monk of the Benedictine abbey of Evesham. His education was superior. Sept. 6, 1181, he was elected to the see of Dublin, and was subsequently ordained a priest, at Velletri; March 21, 1182, he was there consecrated archbishop by pope Lucius III. In September, 1184, he was sent to Ireland by the king to prepare for the reception of prince John, earl of Moreton. In 1185 he was one of the English nobles who received John and his train on their arrival at Waterford, and in the same year he obtained from the boy prince, during his sojourn in Ireland, a grant of the bishopric of Glendalough, with all its churches, lands, tithes, etc. In 1186 Comyn held a provincial synod in Dublin, in the Church of the Holy Trinity. He assisted at the coronation of king Richard I, Sept. 3, 1189, and was the witness to that monarch's letters-patent for surrendering to William, king of Scotland, the castles of Rockbork and Berwick. In 1190 this prelate erected a church, dedicated to St. Patrick, in the southern part of Dublin. At the same time he repaired and partly enlarged the choir of the cathedral of Christ Church, and founded and endowed the nunnery of Grace Dieu in Dublin. He died Oct. 25, 1212. See D'Alton, *Memoirs of the Abps. of Dublin*, p. 68.

Conaid, an early British saint, was a companion of St. Sampson. He is called by the French *St. Mein*, and is probably the same as *Mevennius*. He is said to have died A.D. 590, and was commemorated June 15 (Cressy, *Church History of Britain*, lib. xi, c. 28).

Conain. See CONAMHAIL.

Conaing. See CONANG.

Conall, *Saint*. In the *Mart. Doneg.* there are seven Conalls, and Colgan says there are nine or ten in the Irish martyrologies:

1. Son of Aedh, is commemorated April 2. He succeeded St. Cairpre as bishop of Coleraine, having before been abbot of the monastery of Cluain-dallain (Todd and Reeves, *Mart. Doneg.* p. 93; Reeves, *Eccl. Ant.* p. 114 n.).

2. Abbot of Inis-Caeil, is commemorated May 22. Colgan calls him the son of Mannis Cœlius, son of Caitherius. A panegyric written upon him by St. Dallan Forgaill, the poet, enables us to fix his date as prior to A.D. 594. He is said to have brought over from Rome, though probably not promulgated for more than a century after his death, a curious law-tract or rule, still extant, entitled the *Cain Domnaigh*, for the observance of Sunday as a day totally free from labor, with certain unavoidable exceptions (O'Curry, *Lect. Anc. Ireland*, ii, 32, 33; Butler, *Lives of the Saints*, v, 345, 346).

3. A bishop, commemorated March 18. At this date Colgan gives a memoir of St. Conall, founder of the Church of Kilconnell. He was made bishop by St. Patrick. Together with St. Etchen, he ordained, unknown to that official, some persons who were unfit for the episcopate, and was severely rebuked for it by his superior. Lanigan (*Eccl. Hist. of Ireland*, i, 429) doubts the connection with St. Patrick.

4. There is a St. Conall or Connell in Scotland, who gives his name to Kirkconnell, but whom it seems impossible to identify (Forbes, *Kal. of Scot. Saints*, p. 311).

Conamhail (or **Conain**), an early Irish and Scottish saint, son of Failbhe, and abbot of Hy, is commemorated Sept. 11. He was the first abbot of Hy, or Iona, that was not of the race of the founder, and was the last under whom the native usage regarding Easter prevailed. He succeeded St. Adamnan, A.D. 704, and died A.D. 710 (Lanigan, *Ecclesiastical History of Ireland*, iii, 150, 153; Grub, *Ecclesiastical History of Scotland*, i, 113, 114; O'Donovan, *Four Masters*, i, 309).

Conan was fifth of the metropolitan bishops of London in the British period (Stubbs, *Register*, p. 152).

Conan was also a common Irish name, and assumed several forms, as *Cona*, *Conna*, *Connan*, and with the affectionate or honorary prefixes *Do* or *Da*, and *Mo*, *Dachonna*, *Mochonna*, etc. It is given to several early Irish saints:

1. Commemorated Jan. 13. In the Irish calendars, on this day, there are *Mochonna*, bishop of Leamhchoill, and *Mochonna* of Inis-Patraig. The second is likely to have lived on the island of Inis-Patrick (Lanigan, *Eccl. Hist. of Ireland*, i, 303–307; O'Hanlon, *Irish Saints*, i, 191, 195, 447; Todd and Reeves, *Mart. Doneg.* p. 15).

2. *Dil*, of Eas-ruaidh, commemorated March 8. He was the son of Tighernach, and nearly related to St. Columba. He is called also *Conna*, *Connan*, *Conda*, *Mochonda*, and came to be generally and affectionately known as *Conan-dil*, "Connanus dilectus." He had three brothers, saints Begbile, Colman, and Cuan-Caoin. He flourished about the end of the 6th century, and ruled over a monastery, probably of his own foundation, at Cnodain, on the Erne. He probably was also a bishop, and is numbered among the disciples of St. Columba (Lanigan, *Eccl. Hist. of Ireland*, ii, 222, 226; Kelly, *Cal. of Irish Saints*, p. 89).

3. Bishop of Sodor or Man, is commemorated Jan. 26. From the Scotch hagiographies we learn that St. Conan was bishop in Man, or ancient Ebona, in the beginning of the 7th century, and his influence extended through the Hebrides and great part of Scotland. He died about A.D. 648, and is honored in the Hebrides, Perthshire, and Forfarshire (O'Hanlon, *Irish Saints*, i, 446–449; Butler, *Lives of the Saints*, i, 377, 378; Forbes, *Kal. of Scot. Saints*, p. 307, 308).

4. Of Aeg, commemorated Jan. 12. O'Hanlon suggests that St. Conan of Aeg, or Egg, may have given his name to the neighboring island of Canna, among the Hebrides, but beyond the mention of the name and dedication in the calendars there is nothing known of this saint (Reeves, *Adamnan*, p. 308; O'Hanlon, *Irish Saints*, i, 180, 181).—Smith, *Dict. of Christ. Biog.* s. v.

Conang (or **Conaing**), an early Irish saint, son of Lucunan, is commemorated Sept. 23. This person is identified with *Conaingus O'Daithil*, coarb of St. Ailbhe of Emly, and called archbishop in *The Life of Mochæmocus*. If this be so, he died in A.D. 661 (Lanigan, *Eccl. Hist. of Ireland*, iii, 34, 35).

Conant, Daniel M., a Methodist Episcopal minister, was born in Herkimer County, N. Y., Feb. 19, 1786. He joined the Church at the age of eighteen; removed to Ohio in 1819; began preaching there in 1820, amid the hardships of a wilderness life, and in 1835 was admitted into the Ohio Conference. He became superannuated in 1871, but continued to preach until his decease, Dec. 27, 1873. Mr. Conant was a man of good natural abilities, well versed in Methodism, of genuine cheerful temperament, and untarnished life. See *Minutes of Annual Conferences*, 1874, p. 109.

Conant, Gaius, a Congregational minister, was born at Bridgewater, Mass., Sept. 6, 1776, and graduated from Brown University in 1800. He pursued his theological studies in part with Rev. Dr. Fobes of Raynham, but becoming dissatisfied with his Arminian views, placed himself under the tuition of Rev. Dr. Emmons of Franklin. He was ordained Feb. 17, 1808, pastor of the Congregational Church in Paxton; was installed, in April, 1834, over the Second Congregational Church in Plymouth; remained seven years, and then returned to his old home in Paxton, where he died, Feb. 6, 1862. See *Hist. of Mendon Association*, p. 279, 309. (J. C. S.)

Conant, John, D.D., a learned English divine, was born Oct. 18, 1608, at Yealmpton, in Devonshire. He was educated in private schools and at Exeter College, in Oxford, where he was chosen a fellow in 1633, soon after became an eminent tutor, and June 7, 1649, was unanimously chosen rector by his fellows. In 1652 he received priest's orders at Salisbury, and in December, 1654, became divinity professor of the University of Oxford. In October, 1657, he was made vice-chancellor of the university, and held that dignity until Aug. 5, 1660; was deprived of his rectory of Exeter College, Sept. 1, 1662; in 1670 was invited to St. Mary, Aldermanbury, in London, but declined. In 1676 he became archdeaçon of Norwich, and in December, 1681, prebendary in the cathedral of Worcester. He died March 12, 1693. Dr. Conant understood thoroughly the Oriental languages, and was well versed in the Syriac. There have been six volumes of his *Sermons* published (Oxf. 1693-1722). See Chalmers, *Biog. Dict.* s. v.; Allibone, *Dict. of Brit. and Amer. Authors*, s. v.

Conant, Liba, a Congregational minister, was born at Bridgewater, Mass., March 6, 1797. He studied in his native town, graduated from Brown University in 1819, pursued his theological studies with Rev. Holland Weeks, of Abington, and became pastor at Northfield, N. H., where he remained fourteen years. His subsequent pastorates were in Hebron, for nine years, Canaan, Groton, and Oxford, all in New Hampshire. He spent the closing years of his life in Bristol, where he died, April 3, 1881. See *Necrology of Brown University*, 1880-81. (J. C. S.)

Conant, Robert Taft, a Presbyterian minister, was born at Barre, Mass., Sept. 1, 1810. He joined the Congregational Church in 1826; graduated at Amherst College in 1836, and at Auburn Theological Seminary in 1841; commenced preaching at Clintonville, N.Y., in 1840, and was ordained there Nov. 4, 1841; removed to St. Lawrence County in 1849, and united with the old Ogdensburg Presbytery in 1850; preached at Oswegatchie, Morristown, Antwerp, Evanston, and Heuvelton. From 1865, he became a teacher in a classical school at Ogdensburg, also preaching occasionally. He died there, Jan. 28, 1879. Mr. Conant was a profound scholar, and an ardent advocate of temperance. He published only some *Sermons* and articles in periodicals. (W. P. S.)

Conant, Sylvanus, a Unitarian minister, was born at Bridgewater, Mass., in 1722, and graduated at Harvard College in 1740. He was ordained at Middleborough, March 28, 1745, and remained there until his death, Dec. 8, 1777. He was a man of good talents, of deep piety, and of great circumspection in his personal and official deportment. See *Hist. of First Church in Middleborough*, p. 31, 32; Sprague, *Annals of the Amer. Pulpit*, viii, 292. (J. C. S.)

Conant, William, a Congregational minister, was born at Bridgewater, Mass.; graduated at Yale College in 1770; was ordained pastor of the Church in Lyme, N. H., Dec. 22, 1773, and died March 8, 1810, aged sixty-seven years. See Sprague, *Annals of the Amer. Pulpit*, ii, 265.

Conant, William M., a Methodist Episcopal minister, was born at Aurora, O., Sept. 16, 1824. He was converted under the ministry of his father, Rev. D. M. Conant, in early youth; studied at Norwalk Seminary and Ohio Wesleyan University, and in 1849 entered the North Ohio Conference. He died in the midst of his labors, Dec. 28, 1871. Mr. Conant was deeply pious, prudent, attractive, loving, exemplary, and eminently conscientious. See *Minutes of Annual Conferences*, 1872, p. 72.

Conantius, a Spanish prelate of the 7th century, was bishop of Palentia (Palencia, in Old Castile) from the reign of the Visigothic king Gundemar, A.D. 610, to that of Sisenaud, in 636. He subscribed the decrees of the fourth, fifth, and sixth councils of Toledo. He was dignified, eloquent, and devoted, and was acquainted with ecclesiastical music, composing many new melodies. He was the author of a book of discourses on the Psalms (Cave, *Hist. of Lit.* i, 582; Migne, *Patrol.* xcvi, 203).

Conānus. See CUMANUS.

Conca, SEBASTIANO, an Italian painter, was born at Gaeta in 1676, and studied in the school of Solimena. His abilities soon became known, and procured him the patronage of cardinal Ottoboni, who rewarded him liberally for a picture of *Herod and the Wise Men*. He was employed to decorate the Church of St. Clement. His principal works at Rome are *Jeremiah*, in St. John Lateran, and *The Assumption*, in San Martino; at Loretto, *San Niccolo*; at Ancona, *San Saverio*; and at Foligno, *San Agostino*. He died in 1764. See Hoefer, *Nouv. Biog. Générale*, s. v.; Spooner, *Biog. Hist. of the Fine Arts*, s. v.

Concanen, RICHARD LUKE, a Roman Catholic bishop, was a native of Ireland, but at an early age was sent to receive the white habit in Lorraine, at the convent of the Holy Cross, belonging to the Irish Dominicans, from which, at the expiration of his novitiate, he was removed to Santa Maria Sopia Minerva, Rome. He acquired distinction during his course of study, and, at its termination, he was selected to be professor of St. Clement's, the college of the Irish Dominicans in the same city. He also, for several years, filled a chair in the school founded at the Minerva in connection with the celebrated library instituted and endowed by the munificence of the illustrious cardinal Casanate, one of the qualifications of which was a doctorship acquired by teaching the course of St. Thomas Aquinas. While residing at the Minerva, Dr. Concanen became agent to archbishop Troy of Dublin, and such was the esteem in which he was held in the Propaganda, that he influenced every ecclesiastical appointment made for Ireland and the British colonies. Dr. Concanen was also well known in Rome as a preacher in the Italian language—a rare thing for a foreigner to attempt. He had long taken an interest in the American missions, and it was through his advice that the first convent of the Dominicans was founded in Kentucky in 1805. On account of his health, Concanen declined the see of Kilmacduagh, Ireland, but was persuaded to accept the bishopric of the newly formed see of New York, to which he was consecrated in Rome, April 24, 1808. After a residence of forty years in Rome, he went to Naples, intending to take passage for the United States. French authorities, then in possession of that port, detained him prisoner as a British subject. These disappointments and hardships, with age (he was now nearly seventy), proved too much, and he died—not without suspicion of poison—at the convent of St. Dominic, Naples, June 10, 1810. Concanen bore with him the pallium for archbishop Carroll, and bulls of institution for three new bishops. It was not until 1816 that a successor to Concanen was appointed, when John Connolly became the first resident bishop of New York. His library and a legacy of $20,000 Dr. Concanen bequeathed to the Dominican convent of St. Rose, Ky. See De Courcy and Shea, *Hist. of the Cath. Church in the U. S.* p. 90, 353-357; Bayley, *Hist. of the Cath. Church in N. Y.* (1853), p. 53; Brady, *The Episcopal Succession*, ii, 168.

Conceiçam, Agostinho da, a Portuguese theologian of the Franciscan order, was a native of Lamego. He engaged as a sailor and started for Brazil, was shipwrecked, and finally, arriving at his destination, entered upon a religious career, and founded a convent of his order in the city of Cabo Frio, where he died in 1693. He wrote many *Sermons.* See Hoefer, *Nouv. Biog. Générale,* s. v.

Conceiçam (or **Barbosa da Costa**), **Antonio da,** a Portuguese theologian of the Franciscan order, was born at Porto, June 7, 1657. He entered the order in 1673 and distinguished himself by his talent as a preacher. He died April 20, 1713, leaving *Clamores Evangelici* (Lisbon, 1698). See Hoefer, *Nouv. Biog. Générale,* s. v.

Conceiçam, Appolinario da, an ecclesiastical writer of Portugal, was born at Lisbon, July 25, 1692. He was but thirteen years of age when he went to Brazil, joined the Franciscans as a lay brother, Sept. 3, 1711, and was finally taken into the employ of the general of the order. He was appointed chronicler of the Franciscans in 1740, and died, probably at Rio de Janeiro, about 1750, leaving a large number of works, especially, *Pequenos na Terra Grandes no ceo Memorias Historicas dos Religiosos da Ordem Serafica,* etc. (Lisbon, 1732–38):—*Claustro Franciscano Erecto no Dominio da Coroa Portugueza,* etc. (ibid. 1740). See Hoefer, *Nouv. Biog. Générale,* s. v.

Conceiçam, Duarté, a Portuguese theologian, was born at Villavicosa, Oct. 13, 1539. He entered the priesthood in 1614, took charge of several ecclesiastical establishments, and performed various functions. He died Sept. 26, 1662, leaving *Collecçao de Estatutos Estabelicidos em Diversos Capitulos Antecedentes* (1646). See Hoefer, *Nouv. Biog. Générale,* s. v.

Conceiçao, Antonio da, a Portuguese ecclesiastic and theologian, was born at Pombal, May 12, 1522. He was secular canon of St. John the Evangelist, and gained the reputation of a saint. He died May 12, 1601, leaving *E Quatorze Cartas Espirituaes,* published in his *Vie,* by Luiz de Mertola. See Hoefer, *Nouv. Biog. Générale,* s. v.

Conception, The Miraculous. See Mariolatry.

Conception, Antonio de la (called *da Siena*), a Portuguese biographer and theologian, was born at Guimaraes, Portugal. The name of his family was *La Conception.* He completed his studies at Lisbon and Coimbra, went to the Netherlands, and was made doctor at Louvain. He afterwards went to Brittany, where he remained some time with don Antonio, who assumed the title of king of Portugal. Antonio da Siena afterwards went to Rome. He died in 1586, having published notes upon the *Summa* of St. Thomas, and some other works, such as the *Annals* and the *Bibliotheca* of the authors of his order who wrote upon morality and spirituality (Paris, 1647). See Hoefer, *Nouv. Biog. Générale,* s. v.

Conceptione (or **Concezione**), Maria Crucifixa, an Italian nun, was born in Sicily in 1645. She entered the Benedictine convent of St. Rosaire at Palma, took the vows in 1662, and died in 1699, leaving, *Della Orribile Brutezza dell' Anima d'un Sacerdote,* etc. (Rome, 1672; Palermo, 1675, without the name of the author, and in 1695 with her name):—*Scielta di Lettera Spirituali* (Girgenti, 1704); and various other writings which are found in her *Life,* by Jerome Turanus. See Hoefer, *Nouv. Biog. Générale,* s. v.

Conchenn. See Coinchenn.

Concilia Martўrum is a term sometimes applied to the Roman catacombs. See Arenaria.

Concina, Daniele, an Italian theologian, was born at Friuli in 1686. He entered the Dominican order March 16, 1708; distinguished himself by his preaching talent, and received proofs of the esteem of popes Clement XII and Benedict XIV. He died at Venice, Feb. 21, 1756, leaving numerous works, among which we notice, *Animadversiones Critico-Morales in Menda Pontasiana* (Augsburg, 1733):—*Commentarius Historico-Apologeticus,* etc. (Venice, 1736):—*Epistolæ Theologico-Morales* (ibid. 1744):—*In Rescriptum Bened. XIV, Pont. Max.* (ibid. 1745):—*Usura Contractus Trini Dissertationibus Historico-Theologicis Demonstrata,* etc. (ibid.):—*Theologia Christiana Dogmatico-Moralis* (Rome and Venice, 1749); this work is very highly esteemed:—*De Sacramentali Absolutione* (Rome, 1755). See Hoefer, *Nouv. Biog. Générale,* s. v.

Concina, Nicolo, an Italian philosopher, brother of the foregoing, took the habit of a Dominican, was professor of theology and philosophy, and in 1732 taught metaphysics at Padua. In 1748 his health obliged him to retire to Venice, where he died in 1763, leaving *Oratio in Gymnasio Palavino* (Venice, 1732):—*Synopsis Tertiæ Partis Metaphysicæ* (without date):—*Juris Naturalis et Gentium Doctrina Metaphysice Asserta* (Venice, 1736). See Hoefer, *Nouv. Biog. Générale,* s. v.

Conciolo, an Italian painter of the 13th century. At Subiaco is a picture on panel by him, representing the consecration of a church, inscribed "Conciolus Pinxit, 1219." See Spooner, *Biog. Hist. of the Fine Arts,* s. v.; Hoefer, *Nouv. Biog. Générale,* s. v.

Conclamatio was the cry of lamentation which the ancient Romans made over their dead. As soon as the eyes were closed in death, the relatives of the deceased who happened to be present called upon him by name several times at intervals, repeating *ave,* hail, or *vale,* farewell. Hence when any affair was desperate, the phrase was frequently used in reference to this practice, *conclamatum est,* i. e. "all is over." See Mourning.

Conclavists are the attendants on cardinals when met in conclave for the election of a pope. There are usually two to each cardinal, one of them being an ecclesiastic. If the cardinals be princes, or old or infirm, they are sometimes allowed three. They are shut up as strictly as the cardinals themselves, and though the situation of a conclavist is far from being comfortable, it is much coveted. He must be immured in a little corner of his master's cell, and do every menial office for him. A conclavist may assign the pensions which he has out of benefices for a particular sum, which is determined by the order which the pope-elect grants to him who makes the assignment. The office also gives a man the privilege of being a citizen in any town within the ecclesiastical jurisdiction; besides which, he receives a sum of money from the pope after his election. Each conclavist, before entering upon his office, takes an oath that he will not reveal the secrets of the conclave. Conclavists are sometimes the hired tools of foreign governments to procure the election of a particular individual to the papal chair. See Pope.

Concomitance, in ecclesiastical phrase, is the Romish doctrine that under the form of bread the blood of Christ is also received, although the chalice is not partaken.

Concord, *Saint,* a priest and martyr, lived about 170. He was son of Gordianus, a Roman priest of great piety. The persecution of Christians under Marcus Aurelius obliged him to withdraw into retirement. The report of miracles which he accomplished soon made him known. Torquatus, governor of Spoleto, made strenuous efforts to cause him to abjure the Christian faith, but Concord remained resolute. After cruelly torturing him, he threw him into a dungeon. Three days later he was offered the choice of worshipping an idol or giving up his life. Scorning the idol, one of the soldiers cut off his head. He is honored on Jan. 1, and the anniversary of his removal is celebrated July 4. The Spanish clergy claim to have the remains of this saint in a monastery of Gerona, Catalonia. See Hoefer, *Nouv. Biog. Générale*, s. v.

Concordance. We add the following:

I. Hebrew Concordances.—*A Concordance of the Hebrew and Chaldee Scriptures* (London, 1876, an excellent work):—*An English, Hebrew, and Chaldee Lexicon and Concordance for the more Correct Understanding of the English Translation of the Old Testament, by Reference to the Original Hebrew* (ibid. 1866):—*Concordantiæ Nominum Propriorum, quæ in Libris Sacris Continentur, a G. Brecher Inchoata, Finita, Demum a Filio* (Brecher, Frankfort, 1876, on the proper names, but deficient).

II. Greek Concordances *on the New Testament.*—Ταμιεῖον τῆς καινῆς διαθήκης ἐγχειρίδιον, by Schmoller (Stuttgard, 1868):—*A Critical Greek and English Concordance to the New Testament*, by Hudson, revised and completed by Abbott (Boston, 1870).

III. English Concordances.—*The Twofold Concordance to the Words and Subjects of the Holy Bible, Including a Concise Dictionary, a Chronological Arrangement of the Sacred Narrative, and other Tables Designed to Facilitate the Consultation and Study of the Sacred Scriptures* (Edinburgh, 1858):—*Dictionary and Concordance of Scripture Proper Names*, by Henderson (ibid. 1869):—*An Analytical Concordance to the Holy Scriptures; or, The Bible Presented under Distinct and Classified Heads or Topics*, by Eadie (reprinted, New York, 1877):—*An Analytical Concordance to the Bible on an Entirely New Plan. Containing every Word Alphabetically Arranged under its Hebrew or Greek Original, with the Literal Meaning and Pronunciation. Exhibiting about* 311,000 *References, Marking* 30,000 *Readings in the New Testament, with the Latest Information on Biblical Geography and Antiquities*, etc., by Young (Edinburgh, 1880), answering a similar purpose with that of the *Englishman's Hebrew and Greek Concordances.* There have also been issued several concordances to the Revised New Testament. (B. P.)

Concordia, in Roman mythology, was the goddess of union. She had a number of temples at Rome: one on the Capitoline Hill, rebuilt after having been burned to the ground under Constantine and Maxentius, the ruins of which are still shown. Another temple was built in consequence of a vow which L. Manlius had made in Gaul. A third was dedicated by Cn. Flavius, an ædile, during the Samnite war. Concordia appears on coins as a matron, sometimes standing and sometimes sitting, bearing in her left arm a cornucopia, sometimes an olive branch or a shell. Clasped hands are also her symbol.

Concordia, nurse of St. Hippolytus, and a martyr at Rome, is commemorated Aug. 13, in Usuard's *Martyrology.*

Concordius is the name of several early Christians. See also Cordius.

1. A deacon of the Church of Arles, who was present at the election of Hilary to the see of Rome, A.D. 461.

2. A presbyter and martyr at Spoleto, under Antoninus, is commemorated Jan. 1, in Usuard's *Martyrology.* See Concord, St.

3. A bishop of Arles (A.D. 374, circ. 409), canonized as a saint, was one of the twenty-two or thirty bishops present at the first council of Valence (A.D. 374). One of the decrees of this council was that those ecclesiastics who, in order to get rid of the burdens of office, accused themselves of mortal sin, should be taken at their word. Under this canon came Acceptus, bishop of Fregus, whom Concordius defended in the council (Tillemont, *Hist. Eccl.* viii, 551-553).

Concurrence of Holidays. Festivals are said to "concur" when one feast is succeeded by another feast, so that the second even-song of the former concurs with the first even-song of the latter.

Conda. See Conna.

Condé, Nicolas, a theologian of Lorraine, was born at Clermont, in Argonne, in 1609. He became a Jesuit May 2, 1622, and taught rhetoric from 1632 to 1636, and afterwards philosophy until 1639. He was also distinguished as a preacher. He died Oct. 5, 1654, leaving *Oraison Funèbre de Louis XIII* (Dijon, 1643):—*L'Année Chrétienne dans son Parfait Accomplissement* (Paris, 1649):—*Vie da Charles de Lorraine* (ibid. 1652). See Hoefer, *Nouv. Biog. Générale*, s. v.

Condĕdus, *Saint*, a presbyter and recluse (also called *Condelus, Condedes*, and *Candidus*), was a native of Great Britain, but migrated into Gaul in the time of Theodoric, son of Clovis, about A.D. 511. After leading a solitary life for a short time near Fontana Walarici (St. Valery-en-caux, or St. Valery-sur-Somme), and visiting St. Lambert and brothers of the monastery of Fontenelle, he took up his abode upon the island of Belcinaca, in the Seine. Here Condedus built two churches, and he himself was buried in one, but his body subsequently was removed to the monastery of Fontenelle, A.D. 1027. Condedus is commemorated Oct. 21. The date of his death is uncertain (Le Cointe, *Ann. Eccl. Franc.* ii, 58, 316; Migne, *Encyclop. Theol.* xl, 645).

Conder, George William, an English Congregational minister, was born at Hitchin, Nov. 30, 1821. He was educated at the grammar school in his native town; entered business in London; joined the Church in early manhood; received his theological training at Highbury College, and began his ministry in 1845 as co-pastor at High Wycombe. Afterwards he labored successively two years at Ryde, fifteen years at Leeds, six years at Manchester, and finally four years at Forest Hill, a London suburb, where he died, Nov. 8, 1874. Mr. Conder exerted a powerful influence as pastor, open-air preacher, and lecturer; was a public-spirited townsman, an earnest advocate of education, and a nervous and pithy writer of some charming articles for the young. He was also the composer of a few notable hymns. See (Lond.) *Cong. Year-book*, 1875, p. 317; (Lond.) *Evang. Mag.* 1875, p. 95.

Conder, John (1), an English Independent, was chosen assistant to John Nesbitt, in 1710, as pastor at Hare Court, London, and continued there till his death, March 3, 1746. He attended the Salter's Hall Synod in 1719, and sided with both the signers and non-signers, which created considerable mirth. See Wilson, *Dissenting Churches*, iii, 287.

Conder, John (2), D.D., an English Independent minister, was born at Wimpole, in Cambridgeshire, in 1714; educated in London; was ordained at Cambridge in September, 1739; and chosen theological tutor at the Mile End College in 1754, when the institution was opened in that locality. In 1759 he became one of the preachers of the Merchants' Lecture, and in 1760 assistant preacher at the Pavement, near Moorfields, where he continued until his death in 1781. He published the *Sermons* of the Rev. Samuel Hayward of Silver Street about 1760. See Rose, *Gen. Biog. Dict.* s. v.; Wilson, *Dissenting Churches*, ii, 85, 531; iii, 111.

Condict (or **Condit**), **Aaron**, a Presbyterian minister, was born at Orange, N. J., Aug. 6, 1765. He graduated from Princeton in 1788; was licensed to preach by the New York Presbytery in 1790, and soon after accepted a call to Stillwater, N. Y. In 1796 he was installed pastor at Hanover, N. J., where he labored for thirty-five years. He died in April, 1852. His ministerial labors were crowned with great success. See Sprague, *Annals of the Amer. Pulpit*, iv, 39.

Condict, Edward William, a Presbyterian minister, was born at Morristown, N. J., Jan. 17, 1833. He graduated from the College of New Jersey in 1853, and from Princeton Theological Seminary in 1855; was licensed by the Presbytery of Passaic, April 14 of the same year; in October following joined the Presbytery of Lewes, and became a missionary within its bounds. He died at Morristown, Nov. 28, 1858. See Wilson, *Presb. Hist. Almanac*, 1860, p. 69; *Gen. Cat. of Princeton Theol. Sem.* 1881, p. 199.

Condict, Joseph D., a Presbyterian minister, graduated at the College of New Jersey in 1826; was settled as the sixth pastor at Easthampton, L. I., in 1830; dismissed in 1835; installed pastor of the Congregational Church at South Hadley, Mass., in July of the same year; and died in September, 1847. He possessed extraordinary talents, and was distinguished, through his whole ministry, for his zealous and successful labors. See Sprague, *Annals of the Amer. Pulpit*, iv, 39.

Condie, THOMAS, a Scotch clergyman, was licensed to preach in 1741; called to the living at Dairsie in 1747; and died June 28, 1767. See *Fasti Eccles. Scoticanæ*, ii, 487.

Condit, Ira, a Presbyterian minister, was born at Morristown, N. J., March 6, 1772. He graduated at Cannonsburg, Pa., in 1808; studied theology under private instructors, teaching school in the meantime, and was licensed by the Presbytery of Ohio, Oct. 17, 1811. The first year of his labor was spent as a missionary. In 1812 he went to Sandy Creek, and after preaching for some time in various churches, accepted calls from the congregations of Fairfield and Big Sugar Creek. His ordination took place Nov. 8, 1814. In 1827 he accepted a call from Georgetown, O.; was afterwards installed over the congregation of Amity; in 1829 accepted a call from Cool Spring for one third of his time; and in this united charge—Fairfield, Georgetown, Cool Spring—labored till his death in 1836. See *Hist. of the Presbytery of Erie.*

Condit, John Howel, a Presbyterian minister, was born in New Jersey in 1806. He graduated at the College of New Jersey in 1831, and at the Princeton Theological Seminary in 1835. He was ordained evangelist, by the Presbytery of New Jersey, Oct. 5, 1836; preached as a stated supply at Bethesda, Ky., from 1837 to 1839; was pastor at Washington, in the same state, from 1840 to 1868; and died at Ashland, Aug. 1, 1869, See *Gen. Cat. of Princeton Theol. Sem.* 1881, p. 87.

Condit, Jonathan Bailey, D.D., a Presbyterian minister, son of the Rev. Aaron Condit, was born at Hanover, N. J., Dec. 16, 1808. He graduated from Princeton College in 1827, and spent the next year in the Theological Seminary. He was licensed by the Presbytery of Newark, at Orange, N. J., in 1830; was ordained in July, 1831, by a Congregational Council, as pastor at Long Meadow, Mass., where he remained four years and six months. From September, 1835, until May, 1838, he held the position of professor of rhetoric in Amherst College. In June, 1838, was installed pastor of the Second Congregational Church of Portland, Me., with which he remained until December, 1845. In February, 1846, he became pastor of the Second Presbyterian Church, Newark, N. J.; resigned, on account of ill-health, April 15, 1851; from October of that year to June, 1855, was professor of sacred rhetoric and pastoral theology in Lane Theological Seminary; and thereafter, until January, 1874, professor in Auburn Theological Seminary. In 1861 he was elected moderator of the General Assembly (new school). He died at Auburn, N. Y., Jan. 1, 1876. Dr. Condit was a man of the loveliest type of Christian character, reminding one of the apostle John by his sweetness, gentleness, and serenity of spirit. He was eminently courteous and judicious. As a preacher, he was tender, sympathetic, and solemn. As a professor, he was able, instructive, conservative, and safe in his teachings. See *Necrol. Report of Princeton Theol. Sem.* 1876, p. 17. (W. P. S.)

Condĭtor, in Roman mythology, was a god of the fields, and presided over the gathering of the fruits. He was represented with flowing robes, and had some fruits in his arms. In his hand he bore a sickle.

Conditorium, a burial-place among the ancient Greeks and Romans, in which dead bodies were deposited entire, as distinguished from those sepulchres which contained only the bones and ashes. The word *conditorium* is also used to denote the coffin in which a dead body was placed when consigned to the tomb.

Condlaedh. See CONLAED.

Condo, ELI E., a Methodist Episcopal minister, was born July 12, 1846, in East Germantown, Ind. He was converted in 1863, entered the ministry in 1866, was ordained deacon in 1868, and elder in 1871. In 1873 and 1874 he edited the *Carthage Advance*, Mo. He joined the St. Louis Conference in 1878, his previous labors having been in connection with the Evangelical Association. He perished in the tornado which swept over Marshfield, Mo., April 18, 1880. Mr. Condo was a man of fine ability, scholarly attainments, unblemished character, and a good preacher. See *Minutes of Annual Conferences*, 1881, p. 95; *Evangelical Messenger*, May 25, 1880.

Condorcet, JACQUES MARIE DE *Caritat de*, a French prelate, was born at the Château of Condorcet, near Nyons, in Dauphiné, in 1703. He at first inclined towards a military life, but afterwards entered upon an ecclesiastical career, and became grand-vicar of his uncle, Yse de Saléon, bishop of Rodez. In 1741 Condorcet was appointed bishop of Gap, in 1754 of Auxerre, and in 1761 of Lisieux. He was a confessed enemy of the Jansenists, had some lively contests with the clergy, and by his violence even occasioned some disorders in the bishopric of Lisieux. He died Sept. 21, 1783, leaving various writings against the Jansenists. See Hoefer, *Nouv. Biog. Générale*, s. v.

Condren, CHARLES DE, a French theologian, was born at Vaubuin, near Soissons, in 1588. His family at first chose for him a military life, but his great wish was to enter upon an ecclesiastical calling; and in 1616 he was made doctor of the Sorbonne. From that time he renounced the world, consecrated himself to works of charity, and at length, in 1617, entered the society formed by cardinal Bérulle, who appointed him, in 1622, superior of the house of St. Magloire, and chose him as his director. Having become confessor of Gaston, duke of Orleans, he showed great skill in very difficult negotiations. After the death of Bérulle, in 1629, he was unanimously elected general of the oratorio. He refused the archbishoprics of Rheims and of Lyons, as well as the cardinal's hat. He died Jan. 7, 1641, leaving *Discours et Lettres* (Paris, 1643, 1648):—*Idée du Sacerdoce et Sacrifice de Jésus-Christ* (ibid. 1677). See Hoefer, *Nouv. Biog. Génerale*, s. v.; *Biog. Universelle*, s. v.

Conduct (*Conductitius*, a stipendiary) is a term for a chaplain without endowment.

Condy, JEREMY, a Baptist minister, graduated at Harvard College in 1726. After preaching a few years he went to England, and remained till 1738, when he came back at the call of the First Baptist Church in Boston. He was an Arminian, and this caused his removal from the pastorate. He died in 1768, leaving two *Sermons*. See Sprague, *Annals of the Amer. Pulpit*, vi, 37.

Cone, Jonathan, a Congregational minister, was born in Connecticut. He graduated from Yale College in 1808; studied theology at Andover Theological Seminary over a year; was ordained May 22, 1811; and acted as pastor at Bristol, Conn., until 1828, and at Durham, N. Y., from 1830 to 1848. He resided thereafter, without a charge, in New Haven, Conn., until his death, Jan. 4, 1850. See *Trien. Cat. of Andover Theol. Sem.* 1870, p. 20.

Cone, Salmon, a Congregational minister, was born in Bolton, Conn. He graduated from Yale College in 1789; was ordained pastor of the First Church in Colchester, Feb. 29, 1792; and remained there until Aug. 11, 1830. For some time thereafter he preached as a stated supply in the neighboring parish of Goshen. He died March 24, 1834. See Sprague, *Annals of the Amer. Pulpit*, ii, 204.

Cone, William H. C., a minister of the Methodist Episcopal Church South, was born in Greene County, Ga. He began preaching in 1849, and for twelve years was a faithful and laborious member of the Georgia Conference. He died in 1862. Mr. Cone was a remarkably sweet singer, and an earnest preacher. See *Minutes of Annual Conferences of the M. E. Church South*, 1862, p. 401.

Conecte (or **Connecte**), THOMAS, a Carmelite monk, was born at Rennes in the 14th century. He acquired in his native place a great reputation as a preacher, and attracted crowds of hearers in Flanders and various parts of France. He finally passed into Italy, everywhere preaching a reformation among the clergy, but was finally burned at the stake, in Rome, in 1434. See Hoefer, *Nouv. Biog. Générale*, s. v.

Conegliano. See CIMA.

Conei (or **Cowne**; in Lat. *Conæus*), GEORGE, a Scotch theologian, who, while very young, left his native country and went to Modena, then to Rome. Pope Urban VIII sent him as nuncio to the queen of England, Henrietta Maria. He died at Rome, Jan. 10, 1640, leaving *Life of Mary Stuart* (Rome, 1624):—*De Institutione Principis*:—*De Duplici Statu Religionis apud Scotos* (ibid. 1628):—*Proofs of the Catholic Faith*, in three books, with a *Hymn to the Virgin* (Bologna, 1631). See Hoefer, *Nouv. Biog. Générale*, s. v.

Conestaggio, GERONIMO FRANCHI DE, a Genoese historian, was first secretary to cardinal Sforza, next chaplain to Philip III, and eventually bishop of Nardo, and archbishop of Capua. He died in 1635, leaving *Dell' Unione del Regno di Portogello olla Corona di Castiglia* (Genoa, 1585; transl. into French by Th. Nardin, Besançon, 1596; into Latin, Frankfort, 1602; into Spanish, by L. de Bania, Barcelona, 1610):—*Historie delle Guerre delle Germania Inferiore* (Venice, 1614; Holland, 1634):—also *An Expedition against Tunis*, various Italian poems, and the *Life of Sforza, Count of Santa Flore*. See Hoefer, *Nouv. Biog. Générale*, s. v.

Coney, Jeremiah Boice, a Presbyterian minister, was born at Cambridge, N. Y., Dec. 7, 1810. After spending more than two years in Princeton Theological Seminary, he was stated supply at Upper Freehold, N. J., in 1841; was ordained by the Presbytery of Albany, Oct. 4, 1842; pastor at Hamilton Union Church, Guilderland, N. Y., in 1843; pastor thereafter at Princeton, until his death, May 16, 1848. See *Gen. Cat. of Princeton Theol. Sem.* 1881, p. 118.

Coney, Thomas, D.D., an English clergyman, was born about 1676, became prebendary of Wells in 1716, and died April 6, 1752. He published several volumes of sermons, and *Sick Bed* (1747). See Le Neve, *Fasti*; Allibone, *Dict. of Brit. and Amer. Authors*, s. v.

Confalonieri, GIOVANNI AUGUSTINO, an Italian religious author, was born at Milan in 1571. He entered the Jesuit order, was employed in the German missions, and distinguished himself by his learning and talent in controversy. He died April 10, 1639, leaving various works in Latin and Italian, such as *Vita Beatæ Mariæ Virginis* (Dillingen, 1612; Milan, 1620):—*Del Verbo di Dio Umanato* (Milan, 1624):—*Miscellanea Varia* (ibid. 1623):—also a number of MSS. See Hoefer, *Nouv. Biog. Générale*, s. v.

Confarreatio was one of the modes of solemnizing marriage among the ancient Romans. The parties were joined in marriage by the Pontifex Maximus, or *Flamen Dialis*, in presence of at least ten witnesses, by a set form of words, and by tasting a cake made of salt, water, and flour, called *far* or *panis farreus*, which was offered with a sheep in sacrifice to the gods. A marriage effected in this way brought the woman into the possession or power of her husband by the sacred laws. She thus became partner of all his substance and sacred rites, those of the *penates* as well as of the *lares*. If he died intestate and without children she inherited his whole fortune. If he died leaving children, she shared equally with them. If she committed any fault, the husband judged of it along with her relations, and punished her at pleasure. The children of this kind of marriage were called *patrimi* and *matrimi*. From these were chosen the *flamina* of Jupiter and the vestal virgins. See MARRIAGE.

Confederated. See COMFORTED.

Confederated Monasteries are those united in prayer for the dead members, mutual hospitality, and admission to chapter. Westminster was confederated with Bury, Worcester, Malmesbury, St. Albans, Winchester, York, Colchester, Wenlock, Reading, Bermondsey, Tavistock, Tewkesbury, Rochester, Ramsey, Hulme, Canterbury, Shrewsbury, Cirencester, Malvern, Hurley, and Fécamp.

Conference, Lay Electoral, IN THE METHODIST EPISCOPAL CHURCH, is a body consisting of one lay member from each charge within the bounds of an Annual Conference, appointed by the Quarterly Conference, and meeting on the third day of the session of the Annual Conference preceding the General Conference, to elect two lay representatives to the latter body. The latter lay delegates must be at least twenty-five years of age, and church-members for five consecutive years previous to election. See LAY REPRESENTATION.

Conferentie (from Lat. *confero*, to bring together, to unite) is the name of a party in the Reformed (Dutch) Church in America, which was opposed to the *Cœtus*, or party of independence. Its members insisted upon the maintenance of organic ecclesiastical relations with the mother church in Holland, and the education and ordination of ministers in that country. Zeal for a learned ministry and attachment to the Church of Holland led these educated clergy and their adherents into measures which produced the most bitter animosities and lamentable divisions, and which rent the Church in twain, until unity was restored in 1771, through the agency of Dr. Livingston. See REFORMED CHURCH IN AMERICA. (W. J. R. T.)

Confessio was originally the place where a saint or martyr who had "witnessed a good confession" for Christ was buried, and hence the altar raised over his grave, and subsequently the chapel erected on the hallowed spot. From its subterranean position such an altar was known as *descensus*. Of these underground "confessiones" we have many examples in Rome, above all, in the Basilica of St. Peter's. Not unfrequently they were merely imitative, as in the crypts of early churches in England. The term was also used for the altar in the upper church, placed immediately above that built over the martyr's grave, sometimes covered with silver plates, and its canopy.

This memorial to a saint was a tomb beneath an altar containing a window, called the jugulum, or cataract, through which the pilgrim let down a cloth (called the pall, brandeum, sudary, or sanctuary) to touch the body below. It was surrounded by a screen of perforated marble, or a rail of bronze, and was often closed in with pillars, covered with metal plates, and illuminated by lights and candelabra. The theory was, that every church was erected over a catacomb: and where it was impossible to have a real confessio, relics were enclosed within an altar, which was erected on an elevated platform, and called the confessio. The true confessio was the germ of the crypt; in Old St. Peter's it formed a subterranean Chapel of St. Peter. At the beginning of the 13th century the steps to it were removed, and the entrance closed. The altar built over the actual grave was the lower confessio;

the upper confessio was the larger altar of marble erected above it, in the church itself, as at Santa Prisca, San Silvestro, San Martino, and San Lorenzo in Rome.

Concilia martyrum is applied to the burial-places of the martyrs in the catacombs. Jerome uses a similar expression, in speaking of the graves the young Nepotian had been in the habit of decorating with flowers.

Memoriæ martyrum is a term of constant occurrence in early Christian writings for the memorial chapel of a saint or martyr, also called *cella*. The church of St. Euphemia, where she lay buried, in which the Council of Chalcedon was held, is styled in the acts of that council *martyrium;* and also that erected by Constantine over our Lord's sepulchre on Calvary. The word *tropæa* is used for the tombs of Peter and Paul in the Roman cemeteries. See CELLA MEMORIÆ.

Confession is (1) general—made by a congregation; (2) auricular—private, to the priest's ear.

Public confession of sins prevailed in the 4th century, and lasted longer in the West than in the East. Private confession is supposed to have been first appointed during the Decian persecution, from 249 to 251; but public confession in the East was first given up at Constantinople, owing to a scandal in 390. Theodulph, bishop of Orleans (835), ordered confession to be made once a year; and the rule was made absolute by the Council of Lateran (1215). It was usual to confess on the first Sunday in Lent. Tertullian, Origen, and St. Cyril are supposed to allude to private confession.

CONFESSION, LITURGICAL, is the acknowledgment of sins made publicly in certain services of the Church.

I. *The Confession Preceding the Celebration of the Eucharist.*—It has been supposed by some that the Christian presbyters borrowed the custom of confessing sin before the eucharistic celebration from the Jewish priests, who, before sacrificing, confessed their sin in such terms as these: "Verily, O Lord, I have sinned, I have done amiss, and dealt wickedly; I repent and am ashamed of my doings, nor will I ever return unto them." Whether the precedent of the Jewish sacrificing priest were followed or not, no doubt the same feeling which prompted the use of the 26th Psalm in the early part of the liturgy caused also the use of a public general confession by the priest and ministers before the altar.

In many Greek liturgies some acknowledgment of sin and unworthiness forms part of the prothesis, said in the sacristy before entering the sanctuary: in the liturgy of St. James, for instance, the priest adopts the words of the publican, "God be merciful to me a sinner," and of the prodigal, "I have sinned against Heaven and in thy sight." The words of the prodigal are also adopted at greater length in the opening of the Mozarabic liturgy.

For the West, many forms of the liturgical confession of the priest about to celebrate have been preserved. These, it is asserted, were formerly used before the offertory, with which the *Missa Fidelium* began; but in some missals they are directed to be said immediately before the Introit, while the *Gloria in Excelsis* and the Gradual are chanted by the choir. But the ancient formularies of the Roman Church contain no trace of a confession in a set form to be made publicly at the beginning of mass. They only testify that the celebrant, after paying his devotions before the altar in a low voice, with bowed head besought God's pardon for his own sins. The very diversity of the form and manner in saying the confession in different churches shows that no form was prescribed by any central authority, but that the several churches followed independent usages.

The usual place for the liturgical confession before mass is the lowest step of the altar; but there was anciently considerable diversity of practice; for the confession was sometimes made (as in the East) in the sacristy, sometimes by the side of the altar, sometimes in the middle of the presbytery. A peculiar custom, probably derived from ancient times, was long maintained in the Church of St. Martin at Tours, that the celebrant should make his confession at the tomb of that saint.

II. *In the Matin Office.*—Something of the nature of confession of sin appears to have formed part of the matin office from very early times. This custom is thought by some to have been inherited from the synagogue, which has, in the ancient "Eighteen Prayers," the form, "Have mercy upon us, O our Father, for we have transgressed; pardon us, for we have sinned. Look, we beseech thee, on our afflictions; heal, O Lord, our infirmities." Very similarly, the Greek matin office has, "O most Holy Trinity, have mercy on us; purify us from our iniquities, and pardon our sins. Look down upon us, O Holy One; heal our infirmities."

In the 4th century the early matin office of many Eastern churches began with a confession; for St. Basil describes the early matins of the Church of Neo-Cæsarea in the following manner: "The people at early dawn seek the house of prayer, and, after confession, made with sighing and tears to God, rising at length from their prayer, pass to the chanting of the Psalms."

In the Western matin office the confession is made in the form called *Confiteor* (q. v.), from its first word.

III. Confession of past sins formed also one of the preliminaries of baptism, as we learn from Tertullian (*de Baptismo*, c. 20). See BAPTISM.

IV. In all liturgies of the Alexandrian family, and in many other Oriental liturgies, there is found, immediately before communion, a confession, or declaration of faith by the recipient, that the bread and wine are now really and truly the body and blood of Christ. In the Coptic of Basil, the priest, holding the elements, says: "The Holy Body and precious, pure, true Blood of Jesus Christ the Son of our God. *Amen.* This is in very truth the Body and Blood of Emmanuel our God. *Amen.*"

CONFESSION, PSALM OF, is a name applied in the early Christian Church to Psalm li, as being peculiarly appropriate to the case of one confessing his sins.

Confessional. A stone chair found in the catacombs has been presumed to have been thus used. A small recess at the foot of the dormitory stairs of St. Albans, and a stone chair with two armed warders, in the south-arm area of the transept at Gloucester, and two wooden structures at Bishop's Cannings and Tavistock, are said to have served as confessionals. The usual place was a seat in the chancel, in the face of day, and open to all passers-by; the modern closed boxes are of recent introduction. In 1378, women were confessed without the chancel veil, and in an open place, that they might be seen, though not heard, by the people. Men confessed at Easter, Pentecost, and Christmas. Bedyll, writing to Cromwell, recommended the walling up of "the places where the friars heard outward confessions of all comers at certain times of the year." Probably these apertures were in friary churches, in the form of low side windows. One of the 14th or 15th century remains at Nuremberg. It consists of several canopied compartments; the central was occupied by the priest, and the lateral portions by penitents, who entered by the outermost doors. An open metal screen fills the apertures only half-way up. In England confession was ordinarily made openly in the chancel, the priest sitting in the stall on the north-east side, and the penitent kneeling before him. Roger Van der Weyde, who died 1464, painted a confessional chair as standing on the north side of the nave, next the stairs to the chancel, and outside the rood-screen. In Flemish churches, and St. Helen's, Bishopsgate, orifices in the wall served as confessionals.

Confessor. (1) The name of a singer in the councils of Carthage and Toledo in 400, when anthems were forbidden to be sung by nuns and widows, except in the presence of a bishop. Confession of God's name (Psalm cvi, 1) is synonymous with its praise. (2) Saints not actually martyred, who by a good life have witnessed for Christ. Their names were first inserted in the diptychs in the 4th century.

CONFESSOR OF THE HOUSEHOLD was the sub-dean or one of the priests in ordinary of the chapel royal, who read daily prayers to the household, visited the sick, and prepared persons for holy communion. The dean of the royal chapel, Stirling, who was always bishop of Glasgow or Dunblane, was the Scottish king's confessor, and the bishop of Chichester was confessor to the king of England. At St. Paul's cardinals acted as confessors. The confessor of the papal household was a Servite. See PENITENTIARY.

Confirmation OF A BISHOP. On the death, removal, or resignation of a bishop in the Church of England, the dean and chapter of the cathedral which is situated within the vacant diocese make application for the royal license to elect a successor. The crown then issues the license and the bishop is elected, whereupon the crown issues letters-patent to the archbishop of the province, requiring him to proceed with the confirmation and consecration. On the day being fixed for the confirmation, notice is publicly given, and all who object to the election of the party proposed are invited to appear. One or more persons delegated by the dean and chapter present the bishop-elect to the archbishop, or to his representative, the vicar-general. Proof is now given of the election of the bishop, and of the royal assent; after which the bishop takes the usual oaths touching allegiance, supremacy, simony, and obedience to the archbishop. Then follows "The definitive sentence, or the act of confirmation, by which are committed to the bishop elected the care, government, and administration of the spiritual affairs of said bishopric, and he is thus decreed to be installed and enthroned." See BISHOP.

Confiteor is the form of general confession of sins made in the offices of the Church, so called from its first word. This is prescribed:

1. At the beginning of the mass, when the priest says it standing at the steps of the altar, "bowing very low."
2. At the administration of the holy communion at other times.
3. At the administration of extreme unction.
4. Previous to the absolution "in articulo mortis."
5. In the daily office at compline; and at prime, when the office is not double.

Sacramental confession is also directed to begin with the opening words of the "Confiteor." It is prefaced by the versicle "Deus in adjutorium," etc., and is said alternately by the priest and congregation, who each respond with a prayer for the forgiveness of the other; in addition to which the priest pronounces a short formula of absolution over the people. There have been various forms in former ages, but since the publication of the missal of Pius V there has been complete uniformity in this respect throughout the Roman Church. See CONFESSION.

Conforte, DAVID, a Jewish rabbi, was born at Salonica in 1619. In 1644 he went to Palestine, and died there in 1671. He is the author of a chronological work, entitled קוֹרֵא הַדּוֹרוֹת, which treats of the Jewish literati in Turkey, Africa, Italy, etc. (Venice, 1746). It has been edited, with a corrected text, valuable notes, and indices, by David Cassel (Berlin, 1846). See Fürst, *Bibl. Jud.* i, 186; De' Rossi, *Dizionario Storico* (Germ. transl.), p. 86, but more especially Cassel's introduction to his edition of the work. (B. P.)

Confractorium is an anthem in the Ambrosian missal at the breaking of the host. It usually has some reference to the gospel of the day.

Congal (or **Congall**), an early Irish saint, is commemorated Jan. 2. Some say he lived about A.D. 590. He must not be confounded with St. Comgall, abbot of Bangor, in Ireland (Forbes, *Kal. of Scot. Saints*, p. 233, 310).

Congan (**Comdhan**, or **Comgan**) (1), an early Irish saint, is commemorated Oct. 13. He was brother to St. Kentigern and uncle to St. Fillan. He succeeded his father, Cellach Cualann, king of Leinster, A.D. 715. But, leaving his kingdom in company with St. Kentigern and her three sons, he went to Lochelch, where they lived a severe life. He died at a great age, and was buried in Iona. The date of his death is unknown. He has given his name to many places in the islands and west of Scotland (Forbes, *Kalendar of Scottish Saints*, p. 310; Reeves, *Adamnan*, p. 384, 419).

Congan (2), a religious writer, lived in 1120. He entered the order of the Cistercians, and became an abbot in Surrey, England. He composed a *Life of Saint Malachi*, which St. Bernard afterwards wrote at his request. The preface of St. Bernard commenced thus: *Tu mihi, abbas Congane, injungis*, etc. See Hoefer, *Nouv. Biog. Générale*, s. v.

Congdon, Benjamin, a Baptist minister, was born at Pomfret, Conn., in 1803. He united with the Church in his native town, and having prepared himself for the ministry at the New Hampton Theological Institution, was ordained in 1837 pastor of the Second Church in Sanbornton, N. H., where he remained until 1843. He then returned to Connecticut, and finished his ministry in his native town. He died June 28, 1846. Mr. Congdon was a man of an excellent spirit, and much devoted to his work. (J. C. S.)

Congdon, James, a minister and elder connected with the Oswego (N. Y.) Monthly Meeting of the Society of Friends, died there Sept. 24, 1834, aged seventy-five years. See *The Friend*, viii, 132.

Congdon, Sylvester L., a Methodist Episcopal minister, was born at Rhinebeck, N. Y., Jan. 26, 1826. He was converted at the age of seventeen, and in 1847 admitted into the Genesee Conference. He continued faithful and laborious during life, and died May 27, 1868. Mr. Congdon was endowed with a clear and comprehensive mind, marked conscientiousness, an ardent, genial temperament, and a deep spiritual nature. See *Minutes of Annual Conferences*, 1868, p. 154.

Congio, CAMILLO, a Roman designer and engraver, was born about 1604. The following are some of his principal plates: *The Annunciation; The Adoration of the Magi; The Creation of Angels; An Assembly of Saints.*

Congnet, LOUIS HENRI, a French educator, was born at Soissons, Dec. 6, 1795, and died there July 5, 1870. He was canon of the cathedral of Soissons, a member of the Asiatic Society of Paris, and of the Historical Institute of France. He was the inventor of a new method for teaching the Greek language, to which he gave the name *l'Enseignement Positif.* He wrote, *Grammaire de la Langua Grècque* (Soissons, 1840):—*Le Pieux Helléniste*, etc. (in Greek and Latin, Paris, 1845), and several other works. See Hoefer, *Nouv. Biog. Générale*, s. v.

Congregation is the ancient name for a chapter, used by St. Benedict. It designates some religious orders, and in the University of Oxford the assembly of all regent graduates, mainly for the purpose of granting degrees.

CONGREGATION ON THE MORALS OF BISHOPS is a committee of three cardinals, two bishops, four prelates, and a secretary (the pope's auditor), instituted by Innocent XI, to see that churchmen who are raised to the episcopal, or any other, dignity in the Church, should be men of virtuous and regular lives. See CONGREGATION.

Congregational Methodist Church, The, was organized in Monroe County, Ga., May 8, 1852, by the union of three local preachers and eight laymen, all members of the Methodist Episcopal Church, South. Their chief dissatisfaction was with the itinerant ministry and the episcopal polity. They were soon joined by others from the same region, and within a year about a dozen societies were formed in that state. A convention was held at Mount Zion, early in 1855, at which there were present delegates from Georgia, Alabama, and Mississippi, and a complete organization was effected by the ratification of a book of discipline, which had been early put forth by the leaders of the enterprise, and by the adoption of a formal constitution, as follows:

(1) *Church Conferences.*—Composed of all the local church members, who, by a majority vote, elect church officers; namely: an elder or pastor, class-leader, deacon or steward, and clerk. This conference is held monthly; the elder or pastor presides, or, in his absence, a chairman *pro tem.* is elected. Reception or dismissal of members is by majority vote of the members present.

(2) *District Conferences.*—Meet semi-annually, composed of delegates from the local churches, in the ratio of one delegate for every twenty members.

(3) *State Conferences.*—Composed of delegates from the district conferences, meet annually, electing their own officers. They review the acts of the district conferences, change or form new districts, determine all questions of doctrine or discipline, and supply destitute sections of states beyond the districts.

(4) *General Conference.*—Meeting quadrennially, and composed of delegates elected to the state conferences. This makes general rules and regulations for the whole Church, subject to certain restrictions.

The system of government is not purely Congregational. The itinerancy is not observed, and ministers and laymen have equal rights in all the conferences. In doctrine this body does not differ from other Methodists.

In 1872, an official organ, called *The Congregational Methodist*, was established at Opelika, Ala., which has lately been edited by L. T. Jones. In 1888 many of the churches and ministers joined other congregational bodies. In 1893 there were 9 conferences, 214 societies, and 8765 members, chiefly in Alabama. There are also two conferences of colored members, presided over by the presidents of the white conferences, with 9 societies and 319 members. Besides these is a branch called "The New Congregational Methodists," organized in Ware County, Ga., in 1881, and now having 24 societies and 1059 members, chiefly in Georgia.

Other Congregational Methodists, generally called Independents, exist in Maryland, Tennessee, and the District of Columbia, without any Conference connection, having 15 societies and 2569 members in 1893.

Sporadic secessions from Methodist bodies at various times have elsewhere assumed congregational forms, but have soon disbanded or joined other bodies.

Congus (Lat. *Congussius*), bishop and scribe of Armagh, succeeded Suibhne A.D. 730, and held the see for twenty years (Ware, *Irish Bishops*, p. 4; O'Donovan, *Four Masters*, i, 331, 352 n[x], 353).

Coniac, a French Benedictine of the society of St. Maur, was born at Rennes in 1731, and died in Paris in 1802. He commenced the *Collection des Conciles de France* (completed by Labat, Paris, 1785), and published, in connection with J. P. Deforis, the *Collection des Œuvres de Bossuet* (Paris, 1772–1790). See Hoefer, *Nouv. Biog. Générale*, s. v.

Conibear, William, a minister of the Bible Christians, was born at Hiscott, Devonshire, England, in August, 1799. He was converted in 1818, and in 1825 entered the ministry, and was appointed to the Chatham circuit. For twenty-nine years he labored on circuits and stations, making full proof of his ministry. In 1854, becoming very deaf, he took a superannuated relation. He died at Ilfracombe, Sept. 30, 1873. See *Minutes of the Conference*, 1874.

Coninanus, an early Irish saint, who died Dec. 9, A.D. 710, is said to have been abbot of Hy, and preceptor to king Ferquhard's sons (Reeves, *Adamnan*, p. 378, 404).

Coninck, Gilles de, a Flemish theologian, was born at Bailleul in 1571. He was a disciple of Lessius, entered the society of the Jesuits, and taught scholasticism for several years at Louvain, where he died in June, 1633. His principal works are, *In Universam Doctrinam D. Thomæ* (Antwerp, 1616, 1619; Rouen, 1630):—*De Mortalitate, Natura et Effectibus Actuum Supernaturalium; et de Fide, Spe, Charitate* (Antwerp, 1623):—*De Deo Trino et Incarnato* (ibid. 1645). See Hoefer, *Nouv. Biog. Générale*, s. v.

Coningham, John, an English Presbyterian minister, was born about 1670; educated at Edinburgh University, where he took his degree, and settled first at Penrith, Cumberland. In 1700 he removed to Manchester, to assist John Chorlton with his large congregation, and to train students for the ministry. He had much success till prosecuted for keeping a dissenting academy. In 1712 he became pastor at Haberdashers' Hall, London, and was both popular and useful till his premature death, Sept. 1, 1716. See Wilson, *Dissenting Churches*, iii, 133–136.

Conington, John, an English theologian of the 14th century, early took the Franciscan habit, and became general of the order. He defended the papacy against William of Occam. He died at Cambridge in 1330, leaving *Sermones Solemnes in Quadragesimam Gregorii*:—*De Magistro Sententiarum*:—*De Christo Domino*, etc. See Hoefer. *Nouv. Biog. Générale*, s. v.

Conisălus (*cloud of dust*), in Greek mythology, was a dæmon attendant on Priapus (q. v.).

Conklin, Benjamin, a Congregational minister, was settled Nov. 23, 1763, over a Church in Leicester, Mass. He resigned June 30, 1794, and died Jan. 30, 1798. Mr. Conklin was a laborious minister. He was pleasing and interesting, without being brilliant; useful and instructive, without being great. See Alexander, *Princeton College in the 18th Century.*

Conklin, Robert Harvey, a Congregational minister, was born at Claverack, N. Y., April 22, 1808. He was converted at Camden, studied with Rev. Henry Smith of that place, and Rev. Sylvester Eaton, was ordained in 1831 as an evangelist, and labored in that capacity in New York, Springfield, Mass., Providence, R. I., and Ashtabula, O. He died at Cleveland, Dec. 15, 1865. As a preacher, Mr. Conklin was argumentative and earnest, personally amiable and kind, and on all the moral questions of the day his position was that of a radical reformer. See *Cong. Quarterly*, 1866, p. 300.

Conla. See Connla.

Conlaedh (Condlaedh, Con-laidh, or **Conlian)**, an Irish saint, is commemorated May 3. When St. Brigida founded her monastery at Kildare, she chose the learned and pious Conlaedh to be her bishop, but in submission to the monastic authority. He was also St. Brigida's chief artist, artificer, or brazier, for the working in all kinds of metals, and making chalices, patens, bells, shrines, etc. He was devoured by wild dogs or wolves as he was on his way to Rome, A.D. 520 (Todd and Reeves, *Mart. Doneg.* p. 119; Lanigan, *Eccl. Hist. of Ireland*, i, 409, 450; Forbes, *Kal. of Scot. Saints*, p. 311; Todd, *St. Patrick*, p. 19–27.

Conley, Andrew, a minister in the Methodist Episcopal Church South, was born in Williamson County, Tenn., in 1818. He was converted in early life, and in 1845 was admitted into the Tennessee Conference. He located in the fourth year of his ministry. In 1870 he removed to Arkansas, served as supply, and in 1872 entered the White River Conference, wherein he labored until his death, April 19, 1875. See *Minutes of Annual Conferences of the M. E. Church South*, 1875, p. 250.

Conlin, Albert Johann, a German writer, was pastor of Monning, in Bavaria, at the close of the 17th century. He left a voluminous work on religion and morality, in German (Augsburg, 1708). See Hoefer, *Nouv. Biog. Générale*, s. v.

Conmach. See Connmach; Connachtach.

Conn, Hugh, a Presbyterian minister, was born at Macgilligan, Ireland, in 1685. He studied at the school in Faughanvale, and afterwards at the University of Glasgow. A Presbyterian congregation having, through London merchants, who carried on a trade with the Patapsco river, Md., secured him as their minister, he was accordingly sent over, ordained, and installed October, 1715. After two years' service he obtained leave from the presbytery to resign his pastoral charge, on account of his want of success and the paucity of his flock. He received a call from Pomonkey, in the New Castle Presbytery, which he accepted, and was installed. He died almost instantly, June 28, 1752, while preaching at the funeral of a person who had died suddenly. (W. P. S.)

Conna (Conda or **Dachonna)**, an early Irish saint, abbot of Daire-Dachonna, in Ulster, is commemorated April 12. Owing to there being so many saints of this name, it is impossible to keep the lines of identification clear (*Mart. Doneg.* p. 71, 127).

Connachtach (or **Conmach**), an early Irish saint, is commemorated May 10. He was the eighteenth abbot of Hy or Iona, and presided A.D. 801-2. In the *Annals* he is called "choice scribe" (Reeves, *Adamnan*, p. 388; Lanigan, *Eccl. Hist. of Ireland*, iii, 252).

Connell. See **Conall.**

Connell, David, a Scotch clergyman, son of Matthew, took his degree at Glasgow University in 1727; was licensed to preach in 1736, became assistant to his father at Kilbride, and in January, 1744, minister at Blantyre. He died June 15, 1790, aged eighty-three years. See *Fasti Eccles. Scoticanæ*, ii, 290, 291.

Connell, James, a Scotch clergyman, was licensed to preach in 1746; called to the living at Sorn in 1752, and ordained. He died July 14, 1789, aged sixty-seven years. He was eminent for his exemplary discharge of the pastoral, domestic, and social duties. See *Fasti Eccles. Scoticanæ*, ii, 140.

Connell, John Martin, a Presbyterian minister, was born in Philadelphia, Pa., Oct. 22, 1819. He graduated at the University of Pennsylvania in 1838; was licensed by the Presbytery of New Castle, April 14, 1842; was stated supply in Delaware County; at Bladensburg and New Windsor, Md.; at Wilmington, Del., and was killed at Burlington, N. J., Aug. 29, 1855. See *Gen. Cat. of Princeton Theol. Sem.* 1881, p. 122.

Connell, Matthew, a Scotch clergyman, studied theology at Glasgow University; was licensed to preach in 1702; called to the living at Blantyre in 1703; ordained in 1704; transferred to Kilbride in 1720, and died Oct. 1, 1743, aged sixty-five years. He was very useful among his people. See *Fasti Eccles. Scoticanæ*, ii, 140, 290.

Connelly, Henry, a Presbyterian minister, was born at Greensburg, Pa., Nov. 5, 1798. He graduated at Washington College in 1824; was a student in the Associate Reformed Seminary, Allegheny, and part of a year (1830) in Princeton Theological Seminary. He was ordained an evangelist by the Associate Reformed Presbytery of New York, Sept. 21, 1832; became pastor at Bloomingburgh, N. Y., in 1833; principal of the academy, Newburgh, in 1848; agent of the New York Colonization Society; principal of an academy at Goshen in 1867, and died at Newburgh, Aug. 5, 1868. See *Gen. Cat. of Princeton Theol. Sem.* 1881, p. 75.

Connelly, William, a Methodist Episcopal minister, was born in Talbot County, Md., in 1793 or 1794. He labored some time as exhorter and local preacher, and in 1829 entered the Philadelphia Conference, in which he continued diligent until his death, Aug. 8, 1844. As a minister, Mr. Connelly was plain, practical, and powerful; as a friend, warm and generous; a buoyant, happy companion, an exemplary citizen. See *Minutes of Annual Conferences*, 1845, p. 596.

Conner, Aaron, a Methodist Episcopal minister, was born in Peru, May 22, 1822. He removed to Akron, O., with his parents, at the age of seven; was converted at sixteen; went to South Bend, Ind., in 1853, where shortly afterwards he was licensed to preach, and in 1860 was admitted into the North-west Indiana Conference. In 1872 he became superannuated, removed to California, spent five years as agent of the California Bible Society, and died Sept. 28, 1878. See *Minutes of Annual Conferences*, 1879, p. 23.

Conner, Champ C., D.D., a Baptist minister, was born in Culpepper County, Va., March 13, 1811. He united with the Church Sept. 14, 1828, and soon after began to preach; moved to West Tennessee in 1835, and was one of the pioneer Baptist preachers in that section of the state. For a term of years he was president of the Baptist Female College at Hernando, Miss. He died at Indian Mound, Lauderdale Co., Tenn., Feb. 14, 1875, being at the time pastor of four churches. He was a strict Baptist in faith and practice, yet, while he was bold and fearless in the advocacy of the doctrines he held, he was always courteous and respectful to those who differed from him. See Cathcart, *Baptist Encyclop.* p. 269. (J. C. S.)

Conner, Charles W., a Methodist Episcopal minister, was born in Franklin County, O., Oct. 6, 1839. He was converted when a boy; served three years in the Union army; spent two years in study at Abingdon College, and in 1868 entered the Illinois Conference. Having taken a superannuated relation, he removed to Louisiana, Mo., in 1873, engaged in business, and thus continued until his decease, Jan. 27, 1876. As a preacher, Mr. Conner was always interesting and earnest, and, as a citizen, he had a large place in the hearts of the people. See *Minutes of Annual Conferences*, 1876, p. 144.

Conner, George J., a Methodist Episcopal minister, was born at Frederick, Md., April 9, 1829. He was converted at the age of fourteen, and was soon instrumental in leading his Roman Catholic father and Lutheran mother and his sisters to Christ. He graduated at Dickinson College, led a class of students while there, and acted as Sunday-school superintendent; studied medicine also, receiving the degree of M.D., as well as a diploma from the Dental College of Baltimore; and, after serving as principal of the Cassville Seminary eighteen months, became a member of the East Baltimore Conference. In 1859 he joined the Virginia Conference of the Church South, and at the beginning of the Rebellion removed to Parkersburgh, West Va., where he opened a successful seminary for young ladies. Subsequently he re-entered the ministry of the Church South, and in Ashland, Ky., conducted an academy for some time. In 1871 he was admitted into the Cincinnati Conference of the Northern Church. Disease obliged him to retire from regular work in 1872, and he died April 1, 1873. Mr. Conner was a methodical sermonizer; possessed a pleasant, well-trained voice; was a cultured man, a devoted friend, and naturally retiring in disposition. See *Minutes of Annual Conferences*, 1872, p. 79.

Conner, James, a Methodist Episcopal minister, was born in Buckingham County, Va. He was two and a half years in the work; a pious, solid, intelligent man. In the midst of a blameless, useful career he died, in 1789 or 1790. See *Minutes of Annual Conferences*, 1790, p. 37.

Conner, Joseph, a Methodist Episcopal minister,

was born at Rensselaerville, N. Y., July 5, 1810. He was converted in 1831, licensed to exhort in 1837, and in 1840 entered the Troy Conference, wherein he labored zealously until attacked by consumption, which soon terminated in his death, Dec. 27, 1861. Mr. Conner was an excellent minister, modest, devoted, and greatly beloved; powerful in exhortation, mighty in prayer, and sympathizing and faithful in friendship. See *Minutes of Annual Conferences*, 1862, p. 100.

Conner, William, a Presbyterian minister, was born in Allegheny County, Pa., May 17, 1799. He was converted early in life, and from 1820 until 1830 was engaged in business. At thirty years of age he entered Jefferson College, Pa., where he pursued his studies with more than ordinary diligence. He was licensed by the Monongahela Presbytery in 1837, and stationed at Unity, Westmoreland Co., Pa. In 1850 he accepted a call to Bethel; and in 1858 an invitation to Blairsville. He died Sept. 28, 1863. See Wilson, *Presb. Hist. Almanac*, 1864, p. 348.

Connla (or **Conla**) is found twice in the Irish calendars, first as a son of Leinni, bishop, at May 10, and next as a bishop of Rusgach (perhaps Russagh, Westmeath) at Dec. 30. But the most famous person bearing the name was a renowned worker in brass, who lived in the 5th century or early in the 6th (Petrie, *Round Towers*, p. 202, 203).

Connmach (or **Conmach**), an early Irish prelate, succeeded Cudiniscus as bishop of Armagh some time after A.D. 790 (*Four Masters*). He died suddenly in 807, and the *Psalter of Cashel* gives him a rule of fourteen years. Under his influence St. Fothad the Canonist drew up the remonstrance which procured for the clergy of Ireland the right of exemption from military service (Lanigan, *Ecclesiastical History of Ireland*, iii, 233, 244, 252; *Primitive Church History of Ireland*, ii, 1106).

Of Connmach of Ath-blair, commemorated as an Irish saint on July 9, we have no account.

Connolly, John, an eminent Roman Catholic prelate, was born on the banks of the Boyne, near Navan, Ireland, in 1750, and was educated in Belgium. At an early age he proceeded to Rome, and there spent most of his life in the convents of his order, that of St. Dominic. He was for many years agent in that city of the Irish bishops, and filled various chairs as professor. He was selected by the cardinal-bishop of Albano as the examiner of candidates for the priesthood. In these duties he displayed great ability and virtue, and is remembered by his pupils as a man of gentleness of character. In 1814 he was appointed to succeed Concanen as the second bishop of New York, and was consecrated Nov. 6 of that year. His diocese comprised the state of New York and part of New Jersey, in which were thirteen thousand Catholics, three Jesuit fathers, and one secular priest. After a faithful episcopate, Connolly died in New York, Feb. 6, 1825, and was succeeded by Dubois. See De Courcy and Shea, *Hist. of the Cath. Church in the U. S.* p. 375-388.

Connolly, Thomas Louis, D.D., a Roman Catholic dignitary, was born at Cork, Ireland. He joined the Capuchins, and in his eighteenth year went to Rome to prepare himself for holy orders, remaining there six years. He was ordained in Lyons in 1838. Returning to Ireland the following year, he labored in Dublin for three years. In 1842 he accompanied archbishop Walsh to Halifax, N. S., as secretary. In 1845 he was appointed vicar-general of that diocese. In 1851 Pius IX appointed him bishop of St. John, N. B., as successor of bishop Dollard. After administering this diocese for seven years, Dr. Connolly was, on the death of archbishop Walsh, in 1859, transferred to the archiepiscopal see of Halifax, N. S., which he filled for seventeen years. He was admirably fitted for this position. Of an imposing presence, he possessed a powerful eloquence, great energy, sincere and unaffected piety, and magnanimous and broad views. He became loved for innumerable acts of kindness to the poor and unfortunate, and his death, on July 27, 1876, in his sixty-third year, was regretted by all denominations. He was succeeded by Dr. Hannan, who died in 1882. See (N. Y.) *Cath. Almanac*, 1877, p. 73.

Connor. See O'CONNOR.

Connor, James R., a minister of the Methodist Episcopal Church South, was converted in early life, and joined the Church in 1846, in Randolph County, Ala. In 1848 he received license to preach, and in February, 1850, entered the Florida Conference, and was appointed to Hillsborough Mission, where he labored until his death, Dec. 17 of the same year. Mr. Connor was a young man of great promise, able, devout, fervent. See *Minutes of Annual Conferences of the M. E. Church South*, 1850, p. 316.

Connor, Wilson, a Baptist minister, was born in Marlborough District, S. C., July 7, 1768. In his early manhood he was a Methodist preacher, but was baptized at Cheraw, and ordained as a Baptist in Effingham County, Ga., in 1803. Having fallen into a backslidden state, he retired from the active duties of the ministry for a long time. For eighteen years he was justice of the inferior court in Montgomery County, and also a member of the legislature. He was at last brought back to his religious experience, and once more became a preacher of the Gospel. In his latter days his ministry was signally blessed. He was also an earnest advocate of temperance and other good causes. As an evangelist he made the whole state of Georgia his mission field, travelling more than thirty-five thousand miles in thirteen years. For some time he held official connection with the Georgia Baptist Convention as its missionary. He was also actively engaged, for a time, as the financial agent of Mercer University, in collecting funds for that institution. Having preached a most solemn discourse in Telfair County, in the summer of 1844, he sat down and expired instantly. His personal appearance and address were striking. His voice is said to have been extraordinary, resembling the rumbling of distant thunder. See Haynes, *Bapt. Cyclop.* i, 167. (J. C. S.)

Cono (or **Conon**), JOHANN, a German theologian, was born at Nuremberg in 1463. He entered the Dominican order, and went to Padua to study Greek under Marcus Musurus. Erasmus spoke in eulogistic terms of this monk in several of his works. Cono died at Basle, Feb. 21, 1513. In 1512 he published in Greek some treatises of the different fathers of the Church, and the *Institutes* of Justinian, with numerous annotations. See Hoefer, *Nouv. Biog. Générale*, s. v.; Jöcher, *Allgemeines Gelehrten-Lexikon*, s. v.

Conoc. See CANOC.

Conodhar (or **Conodran**), of Fobhar, commemorated as an early Irish saint Nov. 3, seems to have been a person of note, as his death is entered in most of the Irish annals; but of his parentage or life at Fobhar we have no trace. He died A.D. 707 (Todd and Reeves, *Mart. Doneg.* p. 296; Colgan, *Acta Sanctorum*, 145, c. 3).

Conon is the name of several early Christians. See also CONAN.

1. A martyr at Iconium, under Aurelian, is commemorated May 29 in Usuard's Martyrology, and March 5 in the Byzantine.—Smith, *Dict. of Christ. Antiq.* s. v.

2. A martyr under Decius, in Pamphylia, commemorated March 6. He is said in one account to have been a gardener of Nazareth, and a poor, simple, hospitable man. When told the præfect wanted him, he said, "What can he want me for, especially as I am a Christian." When bidden to sacrifice, he groaned, and wished the præfect could renounce idols and come to Christ. His ankles were pierced, and nails were driven through them, and in that state he was made to run before a chariot till he died. Another story was afterwards told of him, or perhaps of another man of the same name, in Isauria, to suit the taste of a later age. He was baptized by the chief captain Michael. He used to make the devils guard his folds, and then shut them up in casks. He taught the people to say, "There is one God, even Conon's." When he was tortured there was a rescue, and he survived two years, and died in peace (*Menolog. Basil.*).

3. Bishop of Edessa, who, in the year 313, laid the foundations of a church in that city, which was completed by his successor, Saades, and enlarged by Aitallaha (Herzog, *Real-Encyklop.* iii, 646).

4. Bishop of Apamea, who, in the Isaurian rebellion in the reign of Anastasius, A.D. 497, "left his throne, and was converted from a priest to a soldier and a general." Conon became a leader of the rebels, and was killed while besieging the town of Claudiopolis, A.D. 498.

5. Bishop of Tarsus (flourished about 601), a disciple of Joannes Philoponus, whose cause he defended in conjunction with Eugenius against the Eutychians, Paul and Stephen, before John, the patriarch of Constantinople. The acts of this disputation existed in the time of Photius, and were read by him. Conon subsequently disagreed with Philoponus as to the perfect equality of the three natures in the Trinity, and, separating from him, founded a new church, of which he acted as bishop. His quarrel with Philoponus led to his anathematization of his former teacher, and the publication of an *Oratio Invectiva*, directed against the views of Philoponus, as to the resurrection of the flesh, which Photius records having read. Photius speaks of Conon and his followers under the name of Tritheists. See CONONITES.

6. Abbot of Lérins, who lived about A.D. 600. Pope Gregory wrote a letter to him on the government of his monastery, commending Conon for his vigor, ability and excellence (Le Cointe, *Ann. Eccl. Franc.* ii, 478).

Conondrius is supposed to have been bishop of Man, consecrated by St. Patrick, A.D. 447 (Stubbs, *Register*, p. 154).

Conov, PETER, a Lutheran theologian of Germany, was born Feb. 8, 1580, at Prenzlow. In 1602 he was preacher at Karnow; in 1605 he was called to Berlin as archdeacon of St. Mary's, and in 1611 to Alt-Brandenburg, where he died, Aug. 18, 1642. He wrote, *Repetitio Sanæ Doctrinæ de vera ac Reali Corporis Præsentia in S. Cœna* (Wittenberg, 1613):—*Antiparathesis Orthodoxiæ Lutheranæ et Heterodoxiæ Calvinianæ* (ibid. 1615), etc. See Jöcher, *Allgemeines Gelehrten-Lexikon*, s. v.; Hoefer, *Nouv. Biog. Génèrale*, s. v. (B. P.)

Conoway, JOHN O., a Methodist Episcopal minister, was born in Baltimore County, Md., in 1810. He was converted at twenty; received into the Ohio Conference in 1835; labored at St. Mary's, Risdon, Finley, Bucyrus, Clarksfield, and Quincy, and died Dec. 8, 1841. See *Minutes of Annual Conferences*, 1843, p. 453.

Conrach (or **Conry**), an early Irish saint, is commemorated Feb. 23. On this day the calendars give *Cruimther Connrach.* Colgan says this is the brother of St. Aidan. His mother is said to have been Sinecha, sister of St. Columba, and he was buried at Durrow (Reeves, *Adamnan*, p. 247, 277).

Conrad, *Saint*, a German prelate, was son of Henry, count of Altdorf, and was educated by Noting, bishop of Constance, who brought him through the various clerical degrees and placed him in charge of his church. The chapter chose him for provost. Noting having died in 934, the people and the clergy of Constance elected Conrad bishop. He fulfilled with zeal his episcopal functions, and founded three churches and a hospital. Three times, according to Udalric, he made a pilgrimage to the Holy Land, returning with the gift of prophecy and miracles. He foretold to St. Gebhard who would be his successor. Conrad died Nov. 26, 976. Pope Calixtus II canonized him at the Council of Lateran, held in 1123. His anniversary is Nov. 26. An account of his miracles is given in the *Chronique de Constance.* A history of his life is given by Ulric or Udalric, one of his successors, as related by Surius. See Hoefer, *Nouv. Biog. Générale*, s. v.; *Biog. Universelle*, s. v.

Conrad OF ASTI, a theologian of Piedmont, entered the Dominican order, of which he became general in 1462, in place of Martial Auribelli, whom Pope Pius II deposed. Paul II having in his turn deposed Conrad, Auribelli was restored to his position. Conrad died at Asti in 1470. His works were, *Commentaria in jus Canonicum:—Summa Casuum Conscientiæ:—Opus Præclarum et Laboriosum quo Dicta B. Thomæ de Aquino per Materias Ordinavit:—Epistola Encyclica in Universum Ordinem*, etc. See Hoefer, *Nouv. Biog. Générale*, s. v.; Jöcher, *Allgemeines Gelehrten-Lexikon*, s. v.

Conrad OF AUSTRIA (or WALDHAUSEN). See WALDHAUSEN, CONRAD.

Conrad OF BEFORT, a German theologian and philosopher of the Capuchin order, who died at Muhlberg, Aug. 12, 1720, wrote *Problemata Philosophica* (Cologne, 1720). See Hoefer, *Nouv. Biog. Générale*, s. v.

Conrad OF BRAUNWEILER, a German biographer, lived about 1090. He belonged to the Benedictine order, and wrote, *Vita Miraculaque Sancti Wolphelmi, Abbatis Bruwilerensis*, which he dedicated to Everhard, abbot of Braunweiler, and to Hermann, abbot of St. Pantaleon of Cologne. See Hoefer, *Nouv. Biog. Générale*, s. v.; Jöcher, *Allgemeines Gelehrten-Lexikon*, s. v.

Conrad OF COLOGNE. See CONRAD OF HIRSCHAU; also CONRAD OF HOCHSTADT.

Conrad OF CONSTANCE. See CONRAD, ST.

Conrad, abbot OF EVERBACH (or ESTERBACH), a German ecclesiastic, was born about 1140, and died in 1226. He left a biography of the principal Cistercian and Clairvaux monks, entitled, *Exordium Magnum Ordinis Cisterciensis.* This contains some historical information worthy of interest, but in the main is a very dry compilation. See Hoefer, *Nouv. Biog. Générale*, s. v.; Jöcher, *Allgemeines Gelehrten-Lexikon*, s. v.

Conrad OF FÜRSTENBERG, a German prelate, was son of Egon or Eginon, count of Urach and of Fürstenberg. After being dean of St. Lambert, at Liege, he became a monk of the Cistercian order, and then abbot of Villers, Brabant. In 1214 he was elected abbot of Clairvaux, and in 1217 head of the general order. In 1219 pope Honorius III appointed him cardinal and bishop of Oporto, and two years after sent him to France to preach against the Albigenses. Conrad afterwards returned to Germany, and published ordinances for the reform of the manners of the clergy. At the death of Honorius III he refused to be a candidate for the papacy, and thus aided the election of Gregory IX, who sent him to preach a crusade against the Mussulmans, and to lead it to the Holy Land. Conrad died during the expedition, Sept. 30, 1227, leaving, *Constitutiones in Germania pro Cleri Reformatione*, published in the *Annales* of Bzovius:—*De Erroribus Albigensium.* See Hoefer, *Nouv. Biog. Générale*, s. v.; Jöcher, *Allgemeines Gelehrten-Lexikon*, s. v.

Conrad OF GEISENFELD, a native of that city, was a Bavarian theologian, who pursued his studies and took his degrees at Vienna. In 1433 he entered the Benedictine order at Melk, in Austria, became prior in 1434, and resigned his functions in 1435. Nevertheless he had charge of reforming several houses of his order. For this purpose he was sent to Augsburg, Etthal, and Tegernsee. He was authorized to remain in this last-named place, where he died, in May, 1460. He left several MS. works on theology, such as *Commentarii Interlineares in Epistolam Sancti Pauli ad Galatas et ad Titum.* See Hoefer, *Nouv. Biog. Générale*, s. v.

Conrad (or **Conrard**) OF HALBERSTADT (called *The Elder*), a German theologian, lived in 1321. He was a Dominican, and definitor of the province of Saxony. He added the indeclinable particles to the Concordance of the Holy Scriptures which Hugh of St. Cher had made; also wrote, *Lectura in Jobum:—Summa Studentium:—Responsorium, seu Tractatus Musæ Philosophicæ:—Sermones de Tempore et de Sanctis*, etc. See Hoefer, *Nouv. Biog. Générale*, s. v.; Jöcher, *Allgemeines Gelehrten-Lexikon*, s. v.

Conrad OF HERESBACH, a learned German theologian, was born at Heresbach, in the duchy of Cleves, Aug. 2, 1496. He studied at Cologne, and in 1522 visited the universities of France and Italy. He was the teacher and counsellor of prince William of Cleves, and died at Wesel, Oct. 14, 1576. He wrote *Psalmorum Explicatio* (Basle, 1578), and several educational works, for which see Hoefer, *Nouv. Biog. Générale*, s. v.; *Biog. Universelle*, s. v.

Conrad OF HIRSCHAU, or OF COLOGNE, a learned German, lived about 1140. He was a Benedictine at the monastery of Hirschau, in the diocese of Cologne. He was a philosopher, rhetorician, poet, and musician, and wrote, *De Musica et Differentia Tonorum*, and other works. See Hoefer, *Nouv. Biog. Générale*, s. v.; Jöcher, *Allgemeines Gelehrten-Lexikon*, s. v.

Conrad OF HOCHSTADT (or OF HOHENSTEDEN), archbishop of Cologne, was son of Lothaire, count of Hochstadt, and was elected in 1238 to succeed the archbishop Henry of Molenarck. After a turbulent administration, he died, Sept. 28, 1261. See Hoefer, *Nouv. Biog. Générale*, s. v.; *Biog. Universelle*, s. v.

Conrad OF LICHTENAU (or *Urspergensis*), known as the *Priest of Ursperg*, a German chronicler, was at first canon at Constance, then took vows at the monastery of Ursperg, of the order of Premonstrants, where he became priest in 1216, and died in 1240 or 1241. He composed a work called, *Life of the Saints*, in twelve books, of which no trace remains. He also wrote, *Chronicon Universale*, commencing with Belus, king of Assyria, and continuing down to 1229. This work was published first by Conrad Pentinger, at Augsburg, in 1515. A second edition, dedicated to the duke of Bavaria, entitled *Prolegomena*, extending down to the time of Charles V, was prepared by Melanchthon, at Strasburg, in 1537; a third edition, by Paul Pierna, published in 1569, bore the name of the author, which the previous editions omitted; and a fourth edition was published, at Strasburg, by Lazarus Zeltner, in 1609. The chronicle of Conrad of Ursperg contains valuable matter upon the history of Germany, and especially as to the contest which was carried on between the emperors and popes in the time in which the author lived. See Hoefer, *Nouv. Biog. Générale*, s. v.; Jöcher, *Allgemeines Gelehrten-Lexikon*, s. v.; *Biog. Universelle*, s. v.

Conrad OF LÖWENBERG (or *Leontorius*), a German scholar, was born at Löwenberg, Suabia, in 1460. He was a Benedictine of the Cistercian order, of the abbey of Mülbrun, Würtemberg, and became secretary to the general of his order in 1490. He died at Engenthal, (Arcta Vallis), near Basle, about 1520. He published, *Textus Biblicus, cum Glossa Ordinaria*, etc. (Nuremberg, 1496; Engenthal, 1499; Basle, 1498–1502; Arcta Vallis, 1506–1508; Lyons, 1520, 1528):—*Postillæ Hugonis de Sancto Caro* (Basle, 1504):—*Opera Sancti Ambrosii* (ibid. 1506):—*Aurelii Augustini Hipponensis Episcopi, ad Marcellinum, de Civitate Dei, contra Paganos, Libri xvii*. See Hoefer, *Nouv. Biog. Générale*, s. v.; *Biog. Universelle*, s. v.

Conrad (by some incorrectly called *Clandarus*), bishop OF LUBECK in 1183, went to Palestine in 1189, became bishop of Hildesheim in 1196, and of Würzburg in 1198. See Jöcher, *Allgemeines Gelehrten-Lexikon*, s. v.

Conrad, cardinal-archbishop OF MENTZ, was son of Otho IV, count of Wittelsbach, and was made archbishop in 1160, at the wish of the emperor Frederick I. In 1162 he made a pilgrimage to the shrine of St. Jago of Compostella. In 1165 Frederick, having convoked the diet of Würzburg in order to acknowledge the antipope, Conrad retired to Tours with the rightful pontiff, Alexander III. Frederick then placed Christian of Buche in the archiepiscopal see of Mentz, and the pope named Conrad cardinal-priest and bishop of Sabina. But he did not resign the archbishopric of Mentz until 1177, after peace was made between the emperor and the pope; in indemnification he was named archbishop of Salzburg. Christian of Buche having died in 1183, Conrad returned to Mentz. The following year he wished to seize that which had belonged, in Thuringia and Hesse, to the lost house of Franconia; but he found an adversary in the landgrave, Louis III. The result was a war of pillage and devastation, lasting for several years. In 1189 Conrad aided Henry VI, prince of Germany, in vanquishing Henry the Lion, duke of Saxony. In January, 1197, the emperor, being unable to go to the Holy Land, as he was urged by the pope, put in his place the warlike archbishop, at the head of a large army. Conrad, with the title of legate, made it one of his tasks on the route to bring back to the Romish Church Livon, king of Armenia, and to reconcile him with Bohemond III, prince of Antioch. We are ignorant of his exploits in Palestine. He returned to Europe and landed in Apulia, July 15, 1199, rendered an account of his mission to pope Innocent III, then went to Mentz, and thence to Thuringia. He desired the same year to hold a diet at Boppard, in order to establish peace between the two competitors for the empire; but Otho refused to grant it. He then went to Hungary, and reconciled the king, Emeric, with Andrew, his brother; and succeeded, in 1200, at the assembly of Andernach, in pacifying the quarrels of the princes of the Rhine. In the same year he died. It was perhaps he who wrote the *Chronicon Rerum Moguntinarum*, giving an account of German events from 1140 to 1152 (published in Helverich's *Hist. German.*, Frankf. 1550.) See Hoefer, *Nouv. Biog. Générale*, s. v.

Conrad OF NUREMBERG, a learned German Benedictine, studied, probably, at Vienna; entered at Gottwig, in 1423, the Benedictine order; later returned to Melk; and in 1426 became abbot of the monastery of Obernburg. His knowledge was varied, embracing mathematics, theology, and music. He died at Obernburg, May 16, 1441, leaving *Reductio Gradualis in Introitibus, Antiphonis, Kyrie Eleëson*, etc.:—*Tractatus utrum Omnia quæ Continet Regularis Institutio sunt Præcepta?* etc.:—*De Phlebotomia, ejus Causis, usu et Effectibus:—De Positione seu Applicatione Ventosarum:—Tractatus Nomina Morborum Exhibens*. These works remain in MS. See Hoefer, *Nouv. Biog. Générale*, s. v.

Conrad OF SCHEUERN (or *Seiren*), in Bavaria, called *The Philosopher*, a German chronicler, lived in the early part of the 13th century. He was a Benedictine, and became prior of his monastery. He wrote, *Chronicon Schirense*, that is, the chronicle of the abbey of Scheuern, from 1196 to 1226, published at Ingolstadt in 1623, and Strasburg in 1716. He wrote more than fifty volumes upon other matters. Aventin says that the works of Conrad, of which he gives a list, aided him greatly in completing his *Annales*. See Hoefer, *Nouv. Biog. Générale*, s. v.; *Biog. Universelle*, s. v.; Jöcher, *Allgemeines Gelehrten-Lexikon*, s. v.

Conrad OF URSPERG. See CONRAD OF LICHTENAU.

Conrad, bishop OF UTRECHT, was born in Suabia. He was at first chamberlain to the archbishop of Cologne; then had charge of the education of prince Henry, afterwards Henry IV, emperor of Germany. After the death of William de Pont, in 1075, Conrad was chosen his successor. He accomplished the construction of the fort of Ysselmonde, opposite Rotterdam. Robert the Frison, count of Flanders, restrained by this fortress, contested its possession with Conrad, who was conquered and taken prisoner, and obliged to yield to Robert a part of Holland as well as the isle of Ysselmonde. The emperor, Henry IV, made amends to the prelate by the gift of the county of Stavoren, on Oct. 30, 1077, and on Feb. 7, 1086, of those of Ostergo and Westergo. Conrad warmly espoused the cause of Henry IV when Gregory VII wished to depose him. He was the architect and designer, as well as the founder, of the college of Notre-Dame at Utrecht. Conrad was assassinated in his palace at Utrecht, April 14, 1099. He wrote, *Pro Imperatore contra Papam*, published in the *Apologia pro Henrico IV* (Hanau, 1611). This discourse, the style of which is concise and smooth, was delivered by Conrad at the assembly of Gerstungen in 1085. See Hoefer, *Nouv. Biog. Générale*, s. v.; *Biog. Universelle*, s. v.; Jöcher, *Allgemeines Gelehrten-Lexikon*, s. v.

Conrad OF WAISSENAU, a German theologian, having lived for some time at the court of the emperor Henry V, entered the order of Premonstrants; and was successively abbot of Waissenau, in Suabia, of Valsery, near Soissons, then general of his order. He was deposed from this office and became abbot of Cuissy, near Laon, where he died in 1241. See Hoefer, *Nouv. Biog. Générale*, s. v.

Conrad, Frederick William, a Methodist Episcopal minister, was a member of the North-western German Conference, and died in the twenty-sixth year of his age, and ninth of his itinerant ministry, at Columbus, Wis., April 16, 1864. See *Minutes of Annual Conferences*, 1864, p. 140.

Conrad, George W., a Methodist Episcopal minister, was born in Franklin County, Ind., Dec. 15, 1836. He joined the Church when fifteen years of age; was educated in Brookville College, where he afterwards became a teacher; removed to Iowa in 1856; received license to preach the same year; in 1857 was admitted to the Iowa Conference; became a supernumerary in 1859; and died April 27, 1860. See *Minutes of Annual Conferences*, 1860, p. 224.

Conrad, Louis L., a Presbyterian minister, was born in Prussia, June 24, 1817. His parents emigrated to the United States in 1829, and settled near Columbia, Pa. He was educated in Lafayette College, Easton, and Hampden-Sidney College, Va. About 1847 he completed his studies, was licensed by the Allegheny Presbytery, and preached at Lawrenceville, Pa. He was settled at Manchester in 1852, where he remained till his death, in 1867. See Wilson, *Presb. Hist. Almanac*, 1868, p. 79.

Conrad (or **Conrard**), **Olivier**, a French poet, a native of Gatinais, lived in 1546. He completed his studies at Paris, and took the habit of a Cordelier at Meung. He distinguished himself by his Latin verses; and so well did he imitate Faustus Andrelinus, that he was surnamed *Faustulus*. He wrote, *Poësies Latines* (Paris, 1530):—*Le Miroir des Pécheurs*:—*La Vie, Faits et Louanges de Saint-Paul* (ibid. 1546). See Hoefer, *Nouv. Biog. Générale*, s. v.; *Biog. Universelle*, s. v.

Conrad, P., a Baptist minister, was born in Wyoming County, N. Y. He pursued his studies at the Hamilton Institution, and in 1842 was sent by the American Baptist Home Mission Society to Wisconsin. His pastorates were at Milwaukee, Geneva, Prairie-du-Lac, and two or three other places. He performed a large amount of work as an itinerant, so that there is hardly a town in the state in which he did not sow the Gospel seed. He was for many years the "Missionary Apostle" of Wisconsin. For a short time Mr. Conrad acted as the financial agent of the American Bible Union in that state; but the work in which he most delighted was missionary work. Having gone to Santa Barbara, Cal., to recruit his health, he died there, Nov. 1, 1875. See Cathcart, *Baptist Encyclop.* p. 270. (J. C. S.)

Conradi, Ernest, a German physician and theologian, was born at Hamburg, March 2, 1677. He studied at Wittenberg, was pastor of the Church of St. George at Bremen, where his father was a merchant, and died there, April 21, 1715, leaving some dissertations, among which we mention, *De Surdorum Enunciationibus* (1698, 1701):—*Finitor Physicus, Scientiæ Naturalis Limites et Confixa Dirigens* (Wittenberg, 1703). See Hoefer, *Nouv. Biog. Générale*, s. v.

Conradi, Ignatius Norbert, a Hungarian theologian and poet, of the order of Pietists, was born at Pesth in 1718. After a journey to Italy he became professor of philosophy at the Academy of the nobility in Vienna; later he was professor of theology at Waitzen and Wesprim; he also filled important offices in his order. He died Aug. 20, 1785, leaving, *De Jani Pannonii Vita et Scriptis Commentarii* (Buda, 1754):—*Eduardi Corsini Dissertationes Agonisticæ* (Leipsic, eod.):—*Paulinianarum Orationum Volumen Secundum* (Buda, eod.). An edition of the *Odes Epigrammes*, and other poems of Conradi, were published by Zimanyi (Pesth, 1792). See Hoefer, *Nouv. Biog. Générale*, s. v.

Conradin OF BORNADA (called *The Happy*), an Italian Dominican, was born near Brescia in 1392. His family being noble and rich, allowed him to pursue his studies at Padua, where, in 1413, he assumed the habit of the Dominicans. He devoted himself to preaching, for which he showed a remarkable talent. The pestilence having broken out at Bologna, Conradin went to its relief. This city was at that time at war with the pope. Conradin, failing in bringing the citizens into submission, published an interdict which the pope had pronounced against them. He was then treated as an enemy, thrown into prison and allowed little food, but his life was wonderfully spared, and, a treaty being concluded, he was set at liberty. Conradin performed with ardor all his tasks, and, the pest again raging, he devoted himself to the sick until he himself fell a victim and died, Nov. 1, 1429. See Hoefer, *Nouv. Biog. Générale*, s. v.

Conradin OF SUABIA. See KONRADIN.

Conran, JOHN, an Irish minister of the Society of Friends, was born in Dublin in 1739. He was brought up in the Established Church, and received a good education, his father being a man of means. He was placed as an apprentice to learn the linen trade at Lisburn. For a time he was inclined to be somewhat dissipated, but when, at the age of thirty-three, he was brought under the ministry of Robert Willis, of America, then on a religious visit to Ireland, the result was his conversion and uniting with the Friends. In 1780 he began, in a quiet way, to speak in public, and was recognized as a minister. At that time there was prevailing a spirit of unbelief in the north of Ireland. Socinianism was spreading. John Conran contended valiantly for what he believed was "the faith once delivered unto the saints." His ministerial work, for many years, was carried on chiefly in Ireland. When nearly eighty years of age he united in a religious visit to all the families of Friends in Dublin, in which he was greatly blessed. His death, which was sudden, took place at the house of a friend, with whom he resided, at Moyallen, June 14. 1827. See *Piety Promoted*, iv, 298-303. (J. C. S.)

Conran. See CAEMHAN.

Conrard. See CONRAD, OLIVIER.

Conrintinus. See CHORENTINUS.

Conrood, STEPHEN, a Baptist minister, was born in Shelby County, Ky., Feb. 4, 1798. He united with the Church in 1812, was licensed to preach in 1828, and ordained a few years later. In 1829 he settled in Greene County, Ill., and for forty years was pastor of a single church at Bethlehem, near Greenfield. During this time he baptized a large number of converts. Although he was very conservative in his ideas, and did not favor some of the movements of the modern Church, he was nevertheless an earnest man of God, and a successful preacher. He died in 1873. See *Minutes of Illinois Anniversaries*, 1873, p. 8. (J. C. S.)

Conry (Lat. *Conrius*), Florence, an Irish theologian, was born in Connaught in 1560. He was a Franciscan, became provincial of his order in Ireland, and was appointed archbishop of Tuam by Clement VIII, who ordered aid to be given by all means to the Spanish forces sent to the relief of the Irish Catholics, against queen Elizabeth. Don Juan d'Aguilla commanded the Spaniards, but the earl of Tyrone having been defeated at Kinsale, Conry was banished, escaped to Belgium, and thence passed on to Spain. He founded a convent of Irish Observantists at Louvain, under the title of St. Anthony of Padua. Conry died at Madrid, Nov. 18, 1629, leaving, *De Sancti Augustini Sensu Circa Beatæ Mariæ Conceptionem* (Antwerp, 1619):—*De Statu Parvulorum sine Baptismo, Juxta Sensum Beati Augustini* (Louvain, 1624, 1635; Rouen, 1643):—*Mirror of Christian Life*, in Irish (Louvain, 1626):—*Compendium Doctrinæ Sancti Augustini Circa Gratiam* (Paris, 1634, 1646):—*Peregrinus Jerichontinus, hoc est de Natura Humana*, etc. (ibid. 1641, 1644):—*De Flagellis Justorum, Juxta Mentem Sancti Augustini* (ibid. 1644):—*Tractatus de Gratia Christi* (ibid. 1646):—*Epistola Diffusa, contra eos qui Assensum Præbuerunt in Parlamento Hiberniæ Proscribendis Bonis*, etc. (given by Philip O'Sullivan, in his *Hist. of Ireland*, vol. iv, book xii). See Hoefer, *Nouv. Biog. Générale*, s. v.

Conscience signifies knowledge in conjunction; that is, in conjunction with the fact to which it is a witness, as the eye is to the action done before it; or, as South observes, it is *a double or joint knowledge*, namely, one of a divine law or rule, and the other of a man's own action. It may be defined to be the judgment which a man passes on the morality of his actions, as to their purity or turpitude; or the secret testimony of the soul, whereby it approves things that are good, and condemns those that are evil. Some object to its being called an act, habit, or faculty. An act, say they, would be represented as an agent, whereas conscience is a testimony. To say it is a habit, is to speak of it as a disposition acting, which is scarcely more accurate than ascribing one act to another; and, besides, it would be strange language to say that conscience itself is a habit. Against defining it by the name of a power or faculty it is objected, that it occasions a false notion of it, as a distinct power from reason.

I. *The moral ground of conscience.* We must distinguish between a rule that of itself and immediately binds the conscience, and a rule that is occasionally of use to direct and satisfy the conscience.

1. The will of God is the only rule immediately binding the conscience. No one has authority over the conscience but God. All penal laws, therefore, in matters of mere conscience, or things that do not evidently affect the civil state, are certainly unlawful.

2. The commands of superiors, not only natural parents, but civil, as magistrates or masters, and every man's private engagements, are rules of conscience in things indifferent.

3. The examples of wise and good men may become rules of conscience; but here it must be observed, that no example or judgment is of any authority against law: where the law is doubtful, and even where there is no doubt, the side of example cannot be taken till inquiry has been first made concerning what the law directs.

II. Conscience has been divided into the following kinds:

1. *Natural*, or that common principle which instructs men of all countries and religions in the duties to which they are all alike obliged. There seems to be something of this in the minds of all men. Even in the darkest regions of the earth, and among the rudest tribes of men, a distinction has ever been made between just and unjust, a duty and a crime.

2. A *right* conscience is that which decides aright, or according to the only rule of rectitude, the law of God. This is also called a *well-informed conscience*, which in all its decisions proceeds upon the most evident principles of truth.

3. A *probable* conscience is that which, in cases that admit of the brightest and fullest light, contents itself with bare probabilities. The consciences of many are of no higher character; and though we must not say a man cannot be saved with such a conscience, yet such a conscience is not so perfect as it might be.

4. An *ignorant* conscience is that which may declare right, but, as it were, by chance, and without any just ground to build on.

5. An *erroneous* conscience is a conscience mistaken in its decisions about the nature of actions.

6. A *doubting* conscience is a conscience unresolved about the nature of actions, on account of the equal or nearly equal probabilities which appear for and against each side of the question.

7. Of an *evil* conscience there are several kinds. Conscience, in regard to actions in general, is evil when it has lost more or less the sense it ought to have of the natural distinctions of moral good and evil: this is a polluted or defiled conscience. Conscience is evil in itself when it gives either none or a false testimony as to past actions; when, reflecting upon wickedness, it feels no pain, it is evil, and said to be seared or hardened (1 Tim. iv, 2). It is also evil when, during the commission of sin, it lies quiet. In regard to future actions, conscience is evil if it does not start at the proposal of sin, or connives at the commission of it.

III. For the right management of conscience, we should, 1. Endeavor to obtain acquaintance with the law of God, and with our own tempers and lives, and frequently compare them together. 2. Furnish conscience with general principles of the most extensive nature and strongest influence; such as the supreme love of God; love to our neighbors as ourselves; and that the care of our souls is of the greatest importance. 3. Preserve the purity and sensibility of conscience. 4. Maintain the freedom of conscience, particularly against interest, passion, temper, example, and the authority of great names. 5. We should accustom ourselves to cool reflection on our past actions. See Moral Sense.

Consciousness is the perception of what passes in a man's own mind. We must not confound the terms *consciousness* and *conscience;* for though the *Latin* be ignorant of any such distinction, including both in the word *conscientia*, yet there is a great deal of difference between them in our language. Consciousness is confined to the actions of the mind, being nothing else than that knowledge of itself which is inseparable from every thought and voluntary motion of the soul. Conscience extends to all human actions, bodily as well as mental. Consciousness is the knowledge of the existence; conscience, of the moral nature of actions. Consciousness is a province of metaphysics; conscience, of morality.

Consecration of the Elements of the Communion. See Eucharist.

CONSECRATION, Eucharistic (*Consecratio, Sanctificatio*). For the distinction between consecration and benediction, see Benediction. The general consideration of the doctrine of eucharistic consecration belongs to theology, and the question is considered here only in its relation to the liturgy.

1. The principal formulæ of consecration are given under Canon of the Liturgy. The most noteworthy difference between the forms of consecration used in the Eastern and Western churches consists in this, that in the Eastern Church the Holy Spirit is invoked, after

the recitation of the words of institution, to descend upon the elements, and make them the body and blood of Christ (see EPICLESIS); and this invocation is commonly thought to imply that consecration would be imperfect without it. In the Western Church the invocation of the Holy Spirit at this part of the liturgy is generally wanting, and the whole consecrating virtue is attributed by Western ritualists to the recitation of the words of institution, accompanied by the fitting gestures. It would seem from the Mozarabic liturgy, however, that such an invocation is an ancient rite which the Latin Church has lost, not an innovation of the Orientals (Neale, *Eastern Church*, introd. p. 492 sq.).

2. In the *Ordo Romanus*, iii, c. 16, the following rubrical directions are given: "After the pope has communicated of the cup, which is held by the archdeacon, the latter pours a portion of the remaining wine into the larger chalice from which the people are to communicate; for wine not consecrated but mingled with the Lord's blood is completely sanctified." The reason of this custom probably was that in a very large congregation it was difficult to consecrate exactly the quantity of wine required. A small portion was, therefore, consecrated in the first instance, and amplified according to the number of communicants by pouring in fresh wine. The whole of the wine in the cup was held to be completely consecrated by mingling with that which had been originally consecrated. The same practice is enjoined in a number of other documents.

3. The placing of a particle of the consecrated bread in the chalice is sometimes called "consecration." See COMMISTIO.

4. On certain days it is an ancient custom not to consecrate the sacred elements. See PRÆSANCTIFIED, LITURGY OF.

Consecration Cross. According to the directions of the ancient Western Pontificals, twelve crosses should either be sculptured or painted in different parts of a new church. Generally, they are found inside; but sometimes (as at Uffington Church, in Berkshire) outside the sacred edifice. Occasionally a recessed stone quatrefoil is charged with a floriated brass cross; but ordinarily consecration crosses are painted either on the walls or pillars. An example of a painted cross may be found under the word BRANCH; another specimen of a consecration cross sculptured within a circle is given from the old cathedral church of Brechin, in

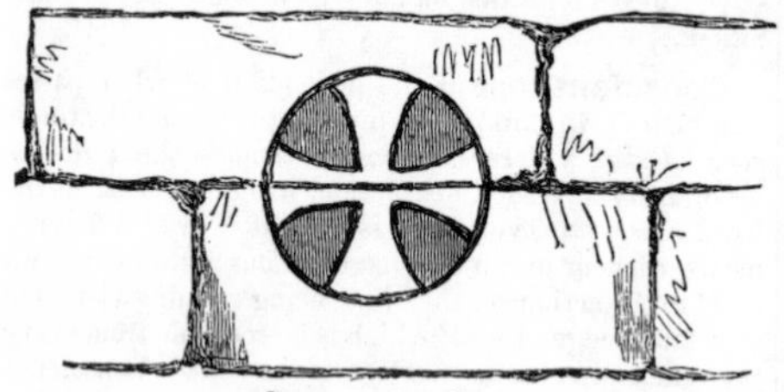

Consecration Cross.

Scotland. In the act of consecrating a church, a Catholic bishop anoints the twelve crosses with holy chrism, "in the name of the Blessed Trinity, to the honor of God and of the glorious Virgin Mary and of all saints," and specially of the saint whose name the church is to bear. Then the crosses are incensed. A branch for a taper is usually placed opposite each consecration cross, and the taper is lighted during the service of consecration; as also, in some places, on the anniversary of that ceremony.

Consensus SENDOMIRIENSIS. See SANDOMIR.

Consent to Marriage. The marriage-law of all countries turns upon one or other of two principles. Either marriage is viewed as a union between persons, or as the disposal of a property. In the former case, the consent of the parties themselves is the main element in it; in the latter, that of some other person or persons. Still, in legislations founded upon the former principle, the element of consent by others comes in as a salutary check upon rash self-disposal by the young; in those founded upon the latter, the recognition of a right of self-sale in the adult may equally check the too authoritative interference of others.

The Jewish law is in its inception essentially personal. Christ needed but to refer to the first history in the Jewish Scriptures in order to bring out the full spirituality of the marriage relation (Matt. xix, 4; Mark x, 6). In Genesis, the woman is at once brought before us as the one "helpmeet" for the man. God simply *brings* the woman to the man, who at once recognises her as bone of his bones, and flesh of his flesh (ii, 20, 22, 23). As the history proceeds, however, other elements develop themselves. Slavery makes its appearance, and the slave-owner is exhibited as giving the slave in marriage (xvi, 3; xxx, 4).

Throughout the patriarchal history (Gen. xxiv, xxix, xxxiv; Exod. ii, 21), under the law (Exod. xxi, 4, 7, 8; xxii, 17; Deut. xxii, 16), in the time of the judges (Josh. xv, 16, 17; Judg. i, 12; xv, 1, 2; xxi, 1, 7, 8; Ruth iv, 10), under the monarchy (1 Sam. xvii, 25; xviii, 19, 21, 27; 2 Sam. xiii, 13; 1 Kings ii, 17), after the captivity (Nehem. xiii, 25), in our Lord's time (Matt. xxiv, 38; Luke xvii, 27), and in the apostolic Church (1 Cor. vii, 38), the right of the father to give his daughter in marriage, of the king to give one who was under his control, is either assumed or asserted.

Among the Jews the power of self-disposal in marriage was singularly wide for either sex, the man being held of full age, and capable of marrying at his will, on the last day of his fifteenth year, the woman in the second half of her twelfth; while, if betrothed under that age by their fathers, girls could repudiate the engagement at ten. Yet the forms used in Jewish practice belong to the material, and not to the spiritual, view of marriage. The prominence given to the *Arrha* (q. v.) or earnest, and the necessity for its being presented to the woman herself either in money or money's worth, show clearly that the grand spirituality of marriage had been lost sight of, that it had come to be viewed essentially as an act of wife-buying; and yet the fact that the woman, from earliest puberty, was reckoned as having the sole right of self-sale, preserved an amount of freedom in the contract. See BETROTHAL.

The Roman law starts from the material view to grow more and more into the spiritual one. Originally the father's "power," scarcely to be distinguished from absolute ownership, overshadows all the domestic relations, extending equally to the wife and to the children of both sexes. Eventually, so far as marriage is concerned, the "power" resolves itself simply into a right of consent. Consent is made the very essence of marriage. The validity of marriages contracted by mere consent was admitted in a constitution of Theodosius and Valentinian, A.D. 449. This consent, moreover, must be at once that of the parties themselves, and of those in whose "power" they are. The Roman law, indeed, never recognised such a thing as the marriage of slaves, and the unions between them, which might be permitted and even respected by their masters, were of no more legal value than the coupling of domestic animals, although they might be recognised by the superior morality of the Church. Where, indeed, a master gave away, or allowed another to give away, his slave girl in marriage to a freeman, or constituted a *dos* upon her, Justinian ruled that this should amount to an enfranchisement. But this of itself shows that marriage and slavery were held to be incompatible. See CONTRACT.

Substantially the Church did little else than follow the municipal law on the subject of consent, eventually adopting the Roman civil law as the basis of her own. If we except a canon of doubtful authority attributed either to the fourth or fifth council of Arles (A.D. 524

or 554), and enacting that widows, before professing continence, may marry whom they will, that virgins may do the same, and that none shall be forced to accept a husband against the will of their parents, the earliest Church enactments seem to belong to the British Isles. An Irish synod of uncertain date, presided over by St. Patrick, speaks thus: "What the father wills, that let the girl do, for the head of the woman is the man; but the will of the girl is to be inquired of the father." The so-called *Excerpta* of Egbert, archbishop of York, in the 8th century, read: "Parents ought to give women to be united to men in marriage, unless the woman absolutely refuse, in which case she may enter a convent;" not a very wide stretch of female freedom. Further on, the husband whose wife has deserted him, and refused for five years to make peace with him, is allowed to marry another woman, "with the bishop's consent."

The council of Friuli (A.D. 791) forbade the marriage of infants, requiring parity of age and mutual consent. The Carlovingian capitularies, which have a sort of mixed clerical and civil authority, enact among other things that none shall marry a widow "without the consent of her priest." It is, however, also enacted that women are not to be compelled to marry, under penalty of treble ban and public penance; or, in default of means, of prison or banishment. Lastly, the edict of Charlemagne, in 814, required inquiry to be made, among other things, as to men who had wives "against the will of their parents." See MARRIAGE.

Consentes, in Roman mythology, were the twelve Etruscan deities who formed the council of Jupiter. They are not all known, but include Juno, Minerva, Summanus, Vulcan, Saturn, Mars; possibly also Vertumnus, Janus, Neptune, Nortia. It was a later error to confound them with the twelve great Grecian deities, Juno, Vesta, Minerva, Ceres, Diana, Venus, Mars, Mercury, Jove, Neptune, Vulcan, and Apollo.

Consentius, a lay theologian of the time of Augustine, lived probably in the Balearic islands, and wrote to submit some of his treatises to Augustine's judgment (August. *Ep.* 119 [221]; ii, 449, ed. Migne).

Consessus CLERI is a name given by Cyprian to the altar-part of the ancient Christian churches, within the rails, where none but the clergy were allowed to enter. See BEMA.

CONSESSUS PRESBYTERIŌRUM are the seats of the presbyters, in the ancient Christian churches, which were ranged in a semicircle on either side of the bishop.

Consignatio ABLUTŌRUM is an ancient Latin term for confirmation of the baptized.

Consignatorium. As the act of blessing by the use of the sign of the cross, e. g. in confirmation, is termed *consignare*, hence the word *consignatorium* is occasionally used to designate the place set apart for that rite. Bishop John of Naples (about 616) is said to have erected a beautiful building, called *consignatorium ablutōrum*, so arranged that the newly baptized should pass in on one side, be presented to the bishop, who sat in the midst, and then pass out by the other side.

Consistentes (*bystanders*, συνεισταμένοι) were an order of penitents in the early Church, who derived their name from being allowed to remain and hear the prayers of the Church after the catechumens and other penitents were dismissed, but were not allowed to make their oblations nor partake of the eucharist. They remained in this class two years. See PENITENTS.

Consistories is a term sometimes applied to certain civil courts of judicature among the ancient Jews, commonly known as the *Small Sanhedrim*. See SANHEDRIM.

Consistory, in the Anglican Church, is the diocesan court of a bishop, in which are tried causes of *voluntary* jurisdiction, that is, affecting visitations, licenses, institutions, and sequestrations; and *contentious* or judicial, touching probate of wills and hearing of cases to be decided, the former by a vicar-general, the latter by an official, but now by the chancellor of the diocese. Criminal clerks were committed to the bishop's prison by this court.

Consolāti is a name applied among the *Cathari* (q. v.), in the 12th century, to those who had received the *consolamentum*. See COMFORTED.

Consortia, *Saint*, was a virgin of Clugny, the daughter of Eucherius (q. v.) and Galla, and is said to have declined an offer of marriage and afterwards built a church. She lived about the end of the 6th century, and is commemorated June 22. Her legend is given at length in Bollandus, *Acta Sanctorum*, June, iv, 250.

Constabile (Lat. *Constabilis*), PAOLO, an Italian theologian of the Dominican order, was born at Ferrara about 1509. Gregory XIII appointed him inquisitor of Ferrara and master of the sacred palace. He was also elected general of his order, and died at Venice, Sept. 17, 1582, leaving *De Causis in Sancto Officio Cognoscendis*. See Hoefer, *Nouv. Biog. Générale*, s. v.; Jöcher, *Allgemeines Gelehrten-Lexikon*, s. v.

Constable, John, a Scotch clergyman, took his degree at the University of St. Andrews in 1674; was presented to the living at Kingoldrum in 1684, and ordained. He died in February, 1703, aged about forty-nine years. See *Fasti Eccles. Scoticanæ*, iii, 753.

Constable, Thomas, D.D., a Scotch clergyman, took his degree at the University of St. Andrews in 1772; was licensed to preach in 1783; presented to the living at Liff in 1785, and ordained. He died April 17, 1817, aged sixty-one years. See *Fasti Eccles. Scoticanæ*, iii, 711.

Constable, William (1), a Scotch clergyman, was licensed to preach in 1785; presented to the living at St. Martin's, Perth, in 1802, and ordained. He died Oct. 6, 1836, in his eightieth year. See *Fasti Eccles. Scoticanæ*, ii, 663.

Constable, William (2), an English Wesleyan minister, was born at St. Albans. He was converted in early life, and began to preach in connection with the conference in 1806, his first station being St. Kitts, W. I. From 1807 he preached in England and Scotland. From 1810 to 1814, "being in doubt with regard to his station in the Church," he retired from the ministry. He finally removed to the Isle of Man, where he died, Oct. 10, 1845. See *Minutes of the British Conference*, 1846, p. 297.

Constance, COUNCIL OF. We give additional particulars of this important synod, from Landon, *Manual of Councils*, s. v.:

> The council was opened on the 5th November, 1414, with solemn prayer, and the *first session* was held on the 16th, in which pope John presided, and delivered an address, exhorting all present to give themselves entirely to the business of the council. After this the bull of convocation was read, and the officers of the council were appointed, viz. ten notaries, one guardian of the council, the auditors of the rota, four advocates, two promoters, four officers to superintend all matters relating to arrangement and ceremony. Lastly, the canon of the eleventh Council of Toledo, held in 675, was read, which relates to the gravity and decorum to be observed in such assemblies.
>
> In the interval between the first and second session, John Huss, who, upon the strength of the emperor's safe-conduct, had ventured to Constance, was treacherously seized and thrown into prison by order of pope John XXIII, and his trial commenced. His accusers, who are said to have been also his personal enemies, drew up a catalogue of his imputed errors, which they presented to the pope and to the council. Among other things, they charged him with having taught publicly that the laity had a right to the communion in both kinds; that in the holy sacrament of the altar the substance of the bread remains unchanged after consecration; that priests living in mortal sin cannot administer the sacraments; that, on the contrary, any other person, being in a state of grace, can do so; that by "the Church" is not to be understood either the pope or the clergy; that the Church cannot possess any

temporalities, and that the laity have a right to deprive her of them.

In this interval, moreover, vast numbers of temporal and spiritual dignitaries arrived; among others, the well-known Peter Daillé, cardinal of Cambray; also the emperor Sigismund, who, on Christmas day, assisted at mass in the habit of a deacon, and chanted the gospel. In the month of February the deputies of Gregory and Benedict arrived, and now several congregations were held, and steps taken to persuade John to abdicate, on account of his notoriously immoral conduct. It was resolved to take the opinion of the various nations composing the council, and for that purpose it was divided into four classes, according to their nations, viz. 1, Italy; 2, France; 3, Germany; 4, England. From each class a certain number of deputies were elected, having at their head a president, who was changed every month. The deputies of each nation then met separately to deliberate upon such measures as they considered best to propose to the council, and when any one class of deputies had agreed upon a measure, it was carried to the general assembly of the four nations; and if the measure, upon consideration, was approved, it was signed and sealed, to be presented at the next session, in order to receive the sanction of the whole council.

In one of these congregations a list of heavy accusations against pope John XXIII was presented, and, in consequence, deputies were sent to him to engage him to resign the pontificate. He, in answer, promised to do so, if his two competitors would, on their part, engage to do the same. Nevertheless, he put off from day to day making any clear and formal act of cession; and during that time the deputies of the University of Paris arrived, with Gerson, their chancellor.

In the *second session* (March 22, 1415) John made a formal declaration, accompanied with an oath, to the effect that he would abdicate, if by that means the schism could be healed. But when, in a subsequent congregation, they proceeded to deliberate about a new election to the pontificate, John, disguised in a postilion's dress, secretly escaped from the city to the castle of Schaffhausen. The council proceeded, nevertheless, to labor to effect the union of the Church, and Gerson made a long discourse tending to establish the superiority of the council over the pope. This discourse was the origin of the question, which was then very warmly agitated, viz. whether the authority of an œcumenical council is greater than that of a pope or not?

In the *third session* (March 25) the cardinal of Florence read a declaration made in the name of the council, by which it is declared, first, that the council is lawfully assembled; secondly, that the flight of the pope cannot dissolve it, and that it shall not separate, nor be transferred to another place, until the union of the Church shall have been effected, and the Church reformed as to faith and morals; thirdly, that John XXIII shall not withdraw his officers from Constance without the approval and consent of the council, nor shall the prelates leave the council without just cause.

The emperor Sigismund was himself present in the *fourth session* (March 30), in which the cardinal of Florence read the five articles upon which the fathers of the council had agreed. The most worthy of note is the decree which declares that the aforesaid Council of Constance having been lawfully assembled in the name of the Holy Spirit, and forming an œcumenical council of the whole Church militant, has received its authority immediately from our Lord Jesus Christ; a power which every person whatsoever, of whatever state or dignity he may be, even the pope himself, must obey in all matters relating to the faith, the extirpation of schism, and the reformation of the Church in its head and in its members. It was also decreed that the pope should not transfer the council to any other place, and declared null and void all processes and censures directed by the pope against those attending the council.

In the *fifth session* (April 6) the articles which had been read in the last were a second time read and unanimously approved. The departure of John was declared to be unlawful, and that he would justly subject himself to corporal punishment and imprisonment should he refuse to return. The emperor was charged to arrest all persons endeavoring to quit Constance in disguise. Also the decree of the Council of Rome against the writings of Wycliffe was confirmed.

The emperor was present in the *sixth session* (April 16), in which pope John XXIII was summoned to present himself at the council, or to issue a bull, declaring that he had vacated the pontificate. A citation was also issued against Jerome of Prague. It is, however, easy to see, by the answer of the latter to the deputies, that his design was only to amuse the council, and thenceforward the fathers resolved to proceed against him as against a notorious heretic and schismatic.

Letters from the University of Paris to its deputies in the council, and others to the emperor, were read, in which both of the parties are exhorted to proceed firmly with the matter of the union, notwithstanding the pope's absence.

In the interval between the sixth and seventh sessions disputes arose among the theologians as to the form in which the decree condemning the doctrines of Wycliffe should be drawn up; some wishing that this condemnation should be made in the name of the pope, with consent of the council, while others insisted upon the omission of the pope's name altogether. Daillé was of the latter opinion, and he composed a treatise in support of his views: he maintained that the position of his adversaries was heretical, viz. that the council had no authority in itself, except through the pope, its head; for in that case, he urged, the Council of Pisa would have possessed no authority, not having been assembled by any pope; and if so, then the election of John himself would be invalid, since he succeeded Alexander V, who had been elected by the Council of Pisa. In the second place, he maintained that this very Council of Pisa was superior to the pope, from the fact that already two popes had been deposed by it; and that any other œcumenical council would possess the same power (Gerson, *Op.* ii, 950).

In the *seventh session* (May 2) John was cited to appear in person with his adherents within nine days, in order to justify himself with respect to the charges of heresy, schism, simony, and various other enormous crimes brought against him; in case of refusal, they declared that they would proceed against him. It may be observed that John, after many removals, had at this time settled at Brisac.

In this session the affair of Jerome of Prague was again discussed.

In the *eighth session* (May 4) the condemnation of Wycliffe's errors was proceeded with. The errors imputed to him were contained in forty-five articles or propositions. He is said in the first three to deny the doctrine of transubstantiation and a real corporal presence. In 4, to assert that a bishop or priest, in mortal sin, cannot perform the proper functions of his office. 6. That God is obliged to obey the devil. 8. That a bad pope has no power over the Church. 13. That they who hinder preaching will be held excommunicated by Christ in the last day. 16. That the temporal powers may, at will, take away the property of the Church. 18. That tithes are merely charitable offerings, which may be denied to the bad ministers. 27. That all things happen by an absolute necessity. 28. That confirmation, ordination, and consecration of places have been reserved to the pope and to bishops solely for the sake of gain. 29. That universities, schools, etc., are mere vanities, which help the devil as much as they do the Church. 34. That all of the order of mendicants are heretics. 35. That no one entering into any order of religion can keep the divine precept, and therefore cannot attain to the kingdom of heaven. 37. That the Church of Rome is the synagogue of Satan. 38. That the decretals are apocryphal, and the clergy who study them fools. 39. That the emperor and secular princes who endowed the Church were seduced by the devil. 41. That it is not necessary to salvation to believe that the Roman Church is supreme among all other churches. 42. That it is folly to put faith in the indulgences of popes and bishops. 44. That Augustine, Benedict, and Bernard are damned, unless they repented of having had property, and of having entered the religious state. 45. That all religions indifferently have been introduced by the devil. All of these forty-five articles, together with all the books written by him, were condemned, and his bones ordered to be dug up, and cast out of consecrated ground.

In the interval between sessions eight and nine, John XXIII was arrested at Fribourg.

In the *ninth session* (May 13) a proposition was received from the pope, offering to send three cardinals to the council to answer the charges brought against him; but the council rejected the offer. Two cardinals and five prelates were nominated to summon the pope thrice at the door of the church, and, as he did not appear, an act declaring this citation was drawn up.

After this session the depositions of witnesses against John were taken; among the ten who came forward were bishops, abbots, and doctors.

On the following day, in the *tenth session* (May 14), the commissioners made their report of the depositions against the pope. After this, having been again cited thrice without appearing, the council proceeded to declare John XXIII convicted of the charges brought against him; viz. of having brought scandal upon the Church by his corrupt life, and of having publicly been guilty of simony, and as such, suspended from the exercise of any of the functions of the papal office, and from every administration, temporal or spiritual, with a prohibition, at the same time, to every Christian, of whatever rank or condition, against obeying him thenceforth directly or indirectly, under penalty of being punished as an abettor of schism. The accusations were contained under seventy heads, all well proved; but fifty only were read in the council (in the following session), relating chiefly to his simony, his worldly life, his vexatious conduct, his false oaths, etc.; other things which decency required to be passed over in silence were suppressed. Sentence of suspension having been thus pronounced, messengers were sent to him to notify to him what the council had decreed. He did not in any way deny the justice of his sentence, and recognised the council as holy and infallible, and at the same time delivered up the seal, ring, and book of supplications, which they demanded of him, begging the council to take measures for his subsistence and honor.

In the *eleventh session* (May 25) the various heads of the accusation against John XXIII were read. Jerome of Prague, who had endeavored to escape, was arrested, and thrown into prison.

In the *twelfth session* (May 29) the sentence of deposition against John XXIII having been read, and unanimously approved, was definitively passed; at the same time, all the three competitors for the papacy were declared incapable of being elected again.

In the *thirteenth session* (June 15) a decree was made, in reply to a petition presented by the Hussites, upon the subject of the communion in both kinds, to this effect, that although Jesus Christ instituted the holy sacrament of the eucharist after supper, under the two kinds of bread and wine, nevertheless, the use sanctioned by the Church is not to celebrate that sacrament after supper, nor even to permit the faithful to receive it otherwise than fasting, except in cases of sickness or other necessity; and that, secondly, although in the primitive Church this sacrament was received by the faithful in both kinds, yet, in after ages, the laity had been permitted to receive in one kind only, viz. the bread, and for this reason, because it ought to be most surely believed that the whole body and the whole blood of Jesus Christ is truly contained under the species of bread; that, therefore, the custom introduced by the Church must be regarded as a law, which may not be rejected or altered at the will of individuals, without the sanction of the Church; and that to maintain that this custom is sacrilegious or unlawful is an error, such that the obstinate perseverance in it deserves to be punished as heresy, and even with the secular arm, if necessary.

In the *fourteenth session* (July 4) several decrees were read: the first of which forbade to proceed to the election of a new pope, without the consent of the council; also the abdication of Gregory XII was received, being made in his name by Charles de Malatesta and cardinal Dominic. Pedro de Luna was called upon to do the same; but he steadily refused to the day of his death, which happened in 1424.

In the *fifteenth session* (July 6) the trial of Huss, who was brought before the council, was terminated. The promoters of the council demanded that the articles preached and taught by John Huss, in Bohemia and elsewhere, being heretical, seditious, deceitful, and offensive to pious ears, should be condemned by the council, and that the books from which they were extracted should be burned. Huss not being willing to retract, was condemned to be degraded and given over to the secular arm, and in the end was cruelly burned alive, on the 6th of July, 1415.

In the same session, the opinion of John Petit, a doctor of Paris, was condemned as heretical, scandalous, and seditious; he maintained that any individual had a right to take away the life of a tyrant, and that the deed was even meritorious; no sentence, however, was passed upon the author of this opinion, who was protected by the duke of Burgundy and other powerful friends.

In the *sixteenth* and *seventeenth sessions* (July 11, 15) preparations were made for the departure of king Sigismund, who proposed to go in person to the king of Aragon, to induce him to renounce the cause of Pedro de Luna.

In the *eighteenth session* (Aug. 17) various decrees were made, one declaring the same credit and obedience to be due towards the bulls of the council as to those of the holy see.

In the *nineteenth session* (Sept. 23) Jerome of Prague, terrified by the horrible end of Huss, was induced to make a recantation of the errors imputed to him. A declaration was also made, in which it was stated that, notwithstanding the safe-conduct of kings, inquisition might always be made into the conduct of heretics.

In the *twentieth session* (Nov. 21) the differences between the bishop of Trent and duke Frederick of Austria were discussed. The twelve chapters of Narbonne, agreed upon between king Sigismund and the deputies of the council and the deputies of Benedict, were approved.

After the session, an assembly was held to consider the reformation of the Church, and the repression of simony.

Also, in the interval between the twentieth and twenty-first sessions, several congregations were held. In one, the affair of John Petit was further discussed; in another, Jerome of Prague, whose retractation was suspected, being brought forward, boldly declared that he had not sincerely retracted, spoke of Huss as a saint, and proclaimed his entire adherence to his doctrine, and to that of Wycliffe.

In the *twenty-first session* (May 30, 1416) Jerome was again brought before the council, and revoking his forced retractation, spoke boldly in favor of his original opinions; sentence was then passed upon him, he was declared to be a relapsed heretic, was excommunicated and anathematized, and, lastly, was handed over to the secular arm, and burned.

Measures were taken in the *twenty-second session* (Oct. 15) to unite the Aragonese to the council, they having acknowledged Benedict XIII.

In the *twenty-third session* (Nov. 5) the proceedings against Benedict XIII (Pedro de Luna) commenced, and he was definitively condemned in the thirty-seventh, when he was deposed, and declared to be a perjurer, and to have brought scandal upon the whole Church, etc.; and, as such, the council degraded and deposed him, deprived him of all his dignities and offices, forbidding him thenceforward to consider himself as pope, and all Christian people to obey him, under pain of being dealt with as abettors of schism and heresy.

In the *thirty-eighth session* (July 28, 1417), the decree of the council, annulling all sentences and censures uttered by Benedict XIII against the ambassadors or allies of the king of Castile, was read.

In the *thirty-ninth session* (Oct. 9) the question of Church reform was entered upon, and several decrees made, one of which declares the necessity of frequently holding councils, in order to check the progress of heresy and schism; and directs that another œcumenical council shall be held five years after the dissolution of the present; a third, seven years after the second; and after that, one every ten years, in a place appointed by the pope at the close of each council, with the approbation and consent of the council; in case of war or pestilence, the pope, with the concurrence of the cardinals, to have power to appoint any other place, and to hasten, but not to retard, the time for assembling. Another decree provides for cases of schism, and orders that, when there shall be two claimants of the papal chair, a council shall be held in the very next year, and that both claimants shall suspend every administration until the council shall have commenced its sittings. The third decree relates to the profession of faith which the newly elected pope was to make in the presence of his electors; in it eight œcumenical councils are recognised, besides the general councils of Lateran, Lyons, and Vienne. A fourth decree is directed against the translation of bishops.

In the *fortieth session* (Oct. 30) a decree containing eighteen well-matured articles of reformation was proposed. It was there provided that the new pope, whom they were about speedily to elect, should labor to reform the Church, in its head and in its members, as well as the court of Rome, in concert with the council, or the national deputies. Its principal articles relate to the annates, the reserves of the apostolic see, the collations to benefices, and the expectatives; what causes may or may not be carried to Rome; in what cases it is lawful to depose a pope, and how it can be done; to the extirpation of simony, to dispensations, to indulgences, and to tithes.

The article upon the annates or first-fruits was very warmly discussed by the cardinals and national deputies, but the latter finally declared that it was necessary to suppress them altogether, and chiefly for this reason, that whereas they had originally been but a voluntary offering to the Roman see, they had subsequently been made, under pretext of custom, an obligatory payment. In fact, we find no mention of annates before the time of Clement V, who for three years imposed them upon England, but was opposed by the parliament. Boniface IX was the first who pretended to claim them as a right attached to the dignity of sovereign pontiff. Moreover, the taxing of benefices was pronounced a simoniacal exaction.

In the *forty-first session* (Nov. 8) it was decreed, that, for this time alone, six prelates of different nations should be chosen within the space of ten days, in order to proceed to the election of the pope with the college of cardinals. Accordingly the electors held a conclave, and on November 11 after, cardinal Colonna was elected pope, and took the style of Martin V. After his coronation, the national deputies having required of him that he would labor to effect a reformation of the Church, he renewed his promise to do so.

In the *forty-second session* (Dec. 28) the new pope presided, and the emperor was present. A bull was read, releasing the emperor from the custody of Balthasar, and ordering him to be delivered over to the pope. The national deputies presented to the pope a memorial on the subject of reform. Martin, troubled by their importunity, gave in a scheme of reformation, based upon the eighteen articles proposed in session forty.

Between this and the forty-third session the pope issued a bull confirming the acts, etc., of the Council of Constance. In the edition of Haguenau, A.D. 1500, this bull is regarded as the act of the council itself, whereas in other editions it appears to be the pope who approves and confirms the council. However this may be, the first article of this bull is worthy of remark, for in it Martin desires that any one suspected in the faith shall swear that he receives all the œcumenical councils, and especially that of Constance; which proves that the pope considered this council lawful and œcumenical, and as he desired that all the acts of this council should be received by all persons, he thereby approves that passed in the fifth session, which declares the superiority of the council to the pope.

In the *forty-third session* (March 21, 1418) decrees were published restraining the abuse of exemptions and dispensations, and condemning simony. The canons relating to modesty of dress in ecclesiastics were renewed, but no other objects of reform were proposed besides those contained in the decree of the fortieth session, and of them six only were drawn up in this forty-third session. The reformation of the college of cardinals and of the court of Rome, which had been decreed by the council, was passed over without notice.

In the *forty-fourth session* (April 19) the pope, in order to satisfy the decree made in the thirty-ninth session, appointed Pavia for the meeting of the next council.

On April 22, 1418, the *last session* was held. After the celebration of high mass, the pope read a discourse to the council, which being ended, one of the cardinals, by order of the pope and council, dismissed the assembly with the words, "Go in peace." This council lasted three years and a half.

See Labbe, *Concil.* xii, 1-294.

Besides this most celebrated council, there are notices of other synods held at Constance, of which we give a brief account from Richard et Giraud, *Bibliothèque Sacrée*, viii, 118:

I. Held in 1044, at which Henry IV of Germany proclaimed a general peace (Labbe, ix; Hardouin, vi).

II. Convened in 1094, by Gebhard of Hirschau, bishop of Constance and legate of pope Urban II, on points of Church discipline, especially the incontinence of priests, simony, and fasting (Labbe, x; Hardouin, vi).

Constans. See CONSTANTINE; CONSTANTINUS.

Constans is a supposed bishop of Winchester, A.D. 293, according to Rudborne (Stubbs, *Register*, p. 153).

Constans, an Irish *saint*, was a priest and anchorite of Eo-inis, in Lough Erne, and is commemorated Nov. 14.

Constant (DE REBECQUE), **David**, a Swiss philosopher, was born at Geneva, March 16, 1638. He pursued his studies in Germany, Holland, and France, under Maresius, Cocceius, Amyraut, and other reformed scholars, with whom he allied himself in friendship. On his return to Lausanne, in 1658, he consecrated himself to the Church, and was appointed pastor at Coppet in 1664. In 1674 he became principal of the college of Lausanne, in 1684 professor of Greek, and in 1703 professor of theology. He died there, Feb. 17, 1733, leaving *Traité de la Providence* (Leyden, 1679):—*Florus, cum Notis Philologicis et Historicis* (Geneva, 1684):—*Erasmi Colloquia, cum Notis* (ibid.):—*Systema Ethico Theologicum* (Lausanne, 1689):—*Transitus per Mare Rubrum* (Geneva, 1690):—*Dissertationes de Uxore Lothi, Rubo Mosis et Serpente Aeneo* (Lausanne, 1693):—*Dissertatio de Zelo.* See Hoefer, *Nouv. Biog. Générale*, s. v.; Jöcher, *Allgemeines Gelehrten-Lexikon*, s. v.

Constant, Philippe. See CONTANT.

Constantia, sister of the emperor Constantine the Great, and wife of the emperor Licinius, was the patroness of Eusebius of Cæsarea and of Arius. She is said to have imbibed the views of the latter—at least, through her influence the emperor Constantine was led to invite Arius to his court, where he soon established an exclusive influence (Robertson, *Hist. of the Christ. Church*, bk. ii, chap. i; Ceillier, iii, 250, 417).

Constantia, *Saint*, a martyr at Nuceria, under Nero, is commemorated Sept. 19 in Usuard's *Martyrology.*

Constantiānus, *Saint*, abbot and recluse, was born in Auvergne in the beginning of the 6th century, and died A.D. 570. He is commemorated Dec. 1 (Le Cointe, *Ann. Eccl. Fran.* i, 398, 863).

Constantin, BONIFACE, a French theologian, belonging to the Jesuit order, was born at Magni (near Geneva) in 1590, was professor of rhetoric and philosophy at Lyons, and died at Vienne, Dauphiné, Nov. 8, 1651. He wrote, *Vie de Cl. de Granger Évêque et Prince de Genève* (Lyons, 1640):—*Historiæ Sanctorum Angelorum Epitome* (ibid. 1652), a singular work upon the history of angels. He also wrote some other works on theology. See Hoefer, *Nouv. Biog. Générale*, s. v.; Jöcher, *Allgemeines Gelehrten-Lexikon*, s. v.

Constantine (or **Constantius**), *Saint*, is represented as a bishop, whose deposition occurred at Gap, in France. He is commemorated April 12 (*Gallia Christiana*, i, 454). See also CONSTANTINUS.

Constantine OF CONSTANTINOPLE, deacon and chartophylax of the metropolitan Church of Constantinople, lived before the 8th century. There is a MS. in the library of the Escurial, a Greek discourse upon the holy martyrs, entitled *Oratio Encomiastica in Omnes Sanctos Martyres.* This discourse is often cited in the *Acta* of the second Council of Nice, which proves that Constantine lived before the holding of this council, or before the 8th century. See Hoefer, *Nouv. Biog. Générale*, s. v.; Smith, *Dict. of Gr. and Rom. Biog.* s. v.

Constantino, MANOEL, a Portuguese scholar, was born at Funchal, Madeira. He became established at Rome, and taught philosophy there. Later he was appointed clerk of the sacred college and professor of theology in the Roman gymnasium. He had acquired a rare facility for writing Latin, without, however, neglecting the study of history, to which he devoted himself closely. He died at Rome in 1614. He wrote, *Insulæ Materiæ Historia*, connected with *Orationes Duæ Habitæ Coram Clemente VIII et Gregorio XIII* (Rome, 1599):—*Historia de Origine atque Vita Regum Lusitaniæ* (ibid. 1601):—*Carmina Varia* (ibid.). These poems were published separately at different dates. He also published at Rome a remarkable work on the origin and history of the kings of Portugal. See Hoefer, *Nouv. Biog. Générale*, s. v.

Constantinople, COUNCILS OF (*Concilium Constantinopolitanum*). The large number of these, and the great importance of several of them, justify a fuller treatment, which we give from Landon, *Man. of Councils*, s. v., and Smith, *Dict. of Christ. Antiq.* s. v.

I. Held A.D. 336, by the Eusebians, under Eusebius of Nicomedia, at which Athanasius was exiled to Treves, Marcellus of Ancyra, with several other bishops, deposed, and Arius ordered to be received into communion by the Alexandrian Church. According to Ruffinus (*Hist.* i, 12) it was convened by order of the emperor, viz. Constantine the Great; and according to Eusebius, the historian (*Contra Marcell.* i, 4), it was exclusively gathered together from the neighborhood of the capital. It seems to have met in February, and not separated till the end of July. See Mansi, *Concil.* ii, 1167-1170.

II. Held A.D. 339 or 340, by order of the emperor Constantius II, to depose Paul, the newly elected bishop there, whose orthodoxy displeased him, and translate Eusebius, his favorite, from Nicomedia to the imperial see. See Mansi, *Concil.* ii, 1275.

III. Held A.D. 360, composed of deputies from the Council of Seleucia, just ended, with some bishops summoned from Bithynia to meet them, about fifty in all. Most of the former were partisans of the metropolitan of Cæsarea, whose name was Acacius, and semi-Arians. A creed was published by them, being the ninth, says Socrates, that had come out since that of Nicæa. It was, in fact, what had been rehearsed at Rimini, with the further declaration that neither substance nor hypostasis were permissible terms in speaking of God. The Son was pronounced to be like the Father, according to the Scriptures, and Aetius, who maintained the contrary opinion, was condemned. A synodical epistle to George, bishop of Alexandria, whose presbyter he was, conveyed the sentence passed upon him and his followers. Several bishops were deposed at the same time, among them Cyril of Jerusalem—all for various causes. Ten bishops, who declined subscribing to these depositions, were to consider themselves deposed till they subscribed. Ulphilas, bishop of the Goths, who had hitherto professed the Nicene faith, was one of those present, and joined in their creed. See Mansi, *Concil.* iii, 325.

IV. Held A.D. 362 or 360, in which sixty-two bishops excommunicated and deposed Macedonius, bishop of Constantinople, for his errors in faith concerning the Holy Spirit. See Mosheim, *Eccl. Hist.* cent. iv, pt. ii. ch. v.

V. The second general council, met in May, A.D. 381, to reassemble the following year, for reasons explained by the bishops in their synodical letter. Owing to this circumstance, and to the fact that its acts have been lost, its proceedings are not easy to unravel. Socrates begins his account of it (*Hist.* v, 8) by saying that the Emperor Theodosius convened a council of bishops of the same faith as himself, in order that the creed settled at Nicæa might prevail, and a bishop be appointed to the see of Constantinople. That the bishops met at his bidding is testified by themselves in their short address to him subsequently, to confirm what they had decreed. Whether they reassembled at his bidding we are not told. Of their number there has never been any dispute, this council having, in fact, gone by the name of that of "the one hundred and fifty fathers" ever since. There were thirty-six bishops of the Macedonian party likewise invited, but they quitted Constantinople in a body when they found that it was the faith of the Nicene fathers to which they would be called upon to subscribe. Of those present, Timothy, bishop of Alexandria, Meletius of Antioch, who presided at first, Cyril of Jerusalem, with the two Gregories, of Nazianzum and Nyssa, were the most considerable, Nectarius and Flavian being added to their number before they separated. The names of all who subscribed have been preserved (Dionys. Exig. ap Justell. *Bibl. Jur. Canon.* ii, 502).

The first question considered was that relating to the Church of Constantinople, and it was declared that Maximus, called the Cynic, had not been lawfully made bishop; that his ordination, and all that he had since done in his pretended character of bishop, was null and void, and that, in fine, he was a usurper of the see of Constantinople. Then they proceeded to elect to the see Gregory Nazianzen, and eventually, notwithstanding his entreaties and tears, obliged him to accept the office. During these proceedings Meletius died, and Gregory of Nazianzum succeeded him as president of the council. He endeavored with all his powers to induce them to leave Paulinus in the see of Antioch, with the view of appeasing the divisions of that Church; but his efforts were ineffectual. The bishops of Macedonia and of Egypt (who had now arrived) vehemently opposed his designs, objecting also to his election, upon the ground that, being already bishop of another see, he ought not to have been translated to that of Constantinople. In consequence of this, Gregory formed the resolution to entreat the fathers to permit him to resign the see of Constantinople, which he in the end did, and Nectarius was elected in his room. During this interval Timothy, bishop of Alexandria, presided over the council; but Nectarius, immediately after his election, took that office upon himself. Now, Nectarius had been a priest in the latter city, but so far from having passed through the inferior degrees, as the canons direct, he had not been even baptized.

Seven canons and a creed appear to have been submitted to the emperor by the assembled fathers for confirmation, at the close of their labors. Whether any canons have been lost seems to admit of some doubt. Socrates speaks of the establishment of patriarchs as one of the things done by this council; and the Arabic paraphrase, under a separate heading, "concerning the order of the prelates, and their rank and place," explains this as follows: "Honor besides, and the primacy, was granted in this council to the bishop of Rome, and he was made first, the bishop of Constantinople second, the bishop of Alexandria third, the bishop of Antioch fourth, and the bishop of Jerusalem fifth"—which is the more remarkable as neither it nor Socrates omits the canon ordaining special prerogatives for new Rome. It is one difficulty connected with these canons, that in all probability they were not all passed at the same council.

1. Confirms the faith of the council of Nicæa, and anathematizes ("extrema execratione ac detestatione") all who deny it, especially the Arians, Eunomians, Eudoxians, Sabellians, Apollinarians, and others.
2. Forbids bishops to go beyond their borders, and to trouble other dioceses. Orders that the bishop of Alexandria shall have the sole administration of Egypt, and that the privileges given to the Church of Antioch by the Nicene canons shall be preserved. Orders that the affairs of the Asian, Pontic, and Thracian dioceses shall be severally administered by their respective bishops, and that the synod of each province shall administer the affairs of the province, according to the canon of Nicæa.
3. By this canon the primacy of honor is given to the bishop of Constantinople after the bishop of Rome, on account, as it states, of the former being "the new Rome."
4. Declares the nullity of the consecration and of the episcopal acts of Maximus.
5. As regards the books of the Western Church, we have also received those in Antioch, who confess one and the same divinity in the three persons of the Holy Trinity.
6. Lays down a rule for ecclesiastical judgments, and permits all persons whatever to bring an accusation against a bishop or any other ecclesiastic on account of any private injury or wrong said to have been received; but in Church matters it directs that no accusation shall be received coming from heretics or schismatics, or from persons excommunicated or deposed, or accused of any crime, before they shall have justified themselves.
7. Gives direction as to the manner in which heretics ought to be received into the Church; Arians, Macedonians, Sabbatians, Novatians, Quartodecimani, and Apollinarians were simply to be required to renounce their errors in writing, to anathematize all heresies, and to be anointed with the holy chrism on the forehead, eyes, nose, mouth, and ears, that they might receive the Holy Spirit. Others, such as the Eunomians (who baptized with one immersion), Montanists, Sabellians, etc., were to be received as heathens, i. e. to be catechised, exorcised, and baptized.

See Labbe, *Concil.* ii, 911.

Of the heretics named in canon 1 the Semi-Arians engaged most attention by far here, from the further error into which they had fallen of late respecting the divinity of the Holy Ghost. All that was ruled by this council on doctrine was directed against them exclusively.

By the word "diocese," in canon 2, is meant a tract embracing several provinces.

Most probably, the third canon, ordaining that in future the see of Constantinople should take honorary precedence next after Rome, was intended to prevent the bishops of Antioch and Alexandria from ever attempting to take such liberties with it again.

Dionysius Exiguus ends his canons of this council with the fourth. Traces of a new series appear with the fifth. It runs as follows: "Concerning the tome of the Westerns, we, too, have received those who professed their belief, at Antioch, in one Godhead of the Father, Son, and Holy Ghost." What was this tome of the Westerns? Some think it was the synodical epistle received from pope Damasus by the Easterns at their second meeting, A.D. 382, to which they wrote their own in reply. Others, with better reason, hold that it was a synodical letter of pope Damasus, addressed to the synod of Antioch A.D. 378 or 379. A third view is, that it was another of his to Paulinus of Antioch some years before. Athanasius sent a letter, in the name of his synod at Alexandria, A.D. 362, to the Church of Antioch, which he calls "a tome" himself, to which Paulinus is expressly said to have subscribed, and in which the indivisibility of the Holy Ghost from the substance both of the Father and the Son is as distinctly set forth as it ever was afterwards. Through Eusebius of Vercelli, to whom it was addressed, and by whom it was in due time subscribed, it would find its way into the West and to Rome, as the rallying-point of the orthodox, and a bond of union, under existing circumstances, between the sees of Alexandria, Antioch, and Rome, whose acceptance of its doctrine can scarce have become known to each other before Macedonius, the ex-patriarch of Constantinople, commenced assailing the divinity of the third person in the Godhead. On this, it would immediately give rise to, and be the foundation of, a series of "tomes" or epistles of the same kind between them, in which Constantinople, being in Arian hands, would take no part, nor Alexandria much, owing to the banishment of its orthodox prelate, Peter, from A.D. 373 to 378, under Valens. Meletius had also been driven from Antioch a year earlier; but his orthodox rival, Paulinus, was allowed to remain; and this would account for the correspondence that went on between him and pope Damasus uninterruptedly while Meletius was away, and of which the prominent topic was the divinity of the Holy Ghost. Now, the synods of Antioch and Rome are confusedly given about this time, yet several were probably held at each place. One thing may well be thought to have been agreed upon at the first synod of Antioch, and possibly Rome too, which was afterwards confirmed in the second, and is evidently referred to by the Constantinopolitan fathers in their synodical letter, namely, the creed, in its enlarged form. Admit this form to have been agreed upon at the synod of Antioch, in conjunction, or not, with that of Rome, A.D. 372, and the use of it in the year following by Epiphanius, bishop of Salamis in Cyprus, as the authorized creed of the Church, is explained; nor is there any reason why Gregory Nyssen, if he composed it at all—as stated by Nicephorus alone—should not have composed it there. But Valens coming to Antioch in April, to persecute the orthodox, the probability would be that this synod was hastily broken up, and remained in abeyance till A.D. 378 or 379, when its proceedings were resumed under Meletius, and confirmed by one hundred and sixty-three bishops, and with its proceedings this creed. All, at the same time, then and there subscribed to the Western tome or letter of pope Damasus. Hence, both the language of the fifth Constantinopolitan canon above mentioned, and of the fathers who framed it, in their synodical letter, where they say that "this, their faith, which they had professed there summarily, might be learned more fully by their Western brethren, on their being so good as to refer to 'the tome' that emanated from the synod of Antioch, and that set forth by the œcumenical council of Constantinople the year before, in which documents they had professed their faith at greater length." Now, what they had set forth themselves was their adherence to the Nicene faith and reprobation of the heresies enumerated in their first canon; what they had received from Antioch and accepted must have been the creed which has since gone by their name, but was certainly not their composition; and whatever else was confirmed there, A.D. 378, including the Western tome. The letter of pope Damasus to Paulinus was written A.D. 372, when there was nobody left at Antioch but Paulinus to write to. The letter addressed in his own name and that of the ninety-three bishops with him, "to the Catholic bishops of the East," was "the tome" received by the synod at Antioch A.D. 378-9; to which they replied the same year. Both letters being on the same subject—as were the synods of 372 and 378-9—it was easy to confuse them.

We now come to the synodical letter of the reassembled Council of Constantinople, A.D. 382, and their proceedings generally. Most of the bishops who had met at Constantinople, A.D. 381, returned thither the following summer. One of their number, Ascholius, bishop of Thessalonica, and Epiphanius and Jerome with him, had gone meanwhile to Rome. Being at Constantinople, they received a synodical letter from the West, inviting them to Rome, where a large gathering was in contemplation. This letter having been lost, we can only guess at its contents from what they say in reply to it, coupled with their fifth canon, which was evidently framed in consequence. The affairs of the East being in imminent peril and confusion, they beg to be excused from going away so far from their sees. The most they could do would be to send deputies into the West. Cyriacus, Eusebius, and Priscianus are named, to explain their proceedings, which they then epitomize, commencing with what has been anticipated above about their faith, and ending with the statement that Nectarius and Flavianus had been appointed canonically to their respective sees, while Cyril was recognised by them as bishop of Jerusalem for the same reason. Thus this letter explains the framing of their fifth canon, and attests its date. The same date is assigned to canon 6, restricting the manner of instituting proceedings against bishops, and reprobating appeals to the secular power. But canon 7, prescribing the distinctions to be observed in admitting heretics into communion, is shown not to belong to this council at all. It is almost identical with the ninety-fifth Trullan canon. Of the creed, little more need be added. It was in existence A.D. 373, having probably been framed at Antioch, in conformity with the synodical letter of Athanasius, A.D. 372, where it was doubtless confirmed A.D. 378-9, and received more probably by the fifth canon of this council A.D. 382, than promulgated separately by the council of the year preceding. Possibly this may have been the creed called by Cassian, as late as A.D. 430, "peculiarly the creed of the city and Church of Antioch." From the portion of it given by him it is as likely to have been this as that of A.D. 363, or any other between them. That there is a family likeness between it and the creed of the Church of Jerusalem, commented on by Cyril, will be seen on comparing them. On this hypothesis alone we can understand why no notice should have been taken of it at the Council of Ephesus, A.D. 431, and in the African code, namely, because it had originated with a provincial, and only been as yet received by a general council. It was promulgated as identical with that of Nicæa for the first time by the fathers of the fourth council.

The dogmatic professions of the council of 381 were confirmed by Theodosius in a constitution dated July 30 of the same year, and addressed to Antonius, proconsul of Asia, by which the churches are ordered to be handed over to the bishops in communion with Nectarius and others who composed it, the Eunomians, Arians, and others having been deprived of their churches by a constitution issued ten days earlier. It was also received by pope Damasus, and has been regarded in the West ever since, so far, as œcumenical. Its first four canons, in the same way, have always been admitted into Western collections. But what passed at the supplemental council of 382 never seems to have been confirmed or received equally. It was in declining to come to this last council that Gregory Nazianzen said, in his epistle to Procopius, "that he had come to the resolution of avoiding every meeting of bishops, for he had never seen any synod end well, or assuage rather than aggravate disorders." His celebrated oration, known as his "farewell" to the council of 381, is inspired by a very different spirit.

See Mansi, *Concil.* iii, 583.

VI. Held A.D. 382, in order to appease the divisions of Antioch, to which see Flavianus had been nominated in the preceding council, during the lifetime of the actual bishop, Paulinus. Most of the bishops who were present at that council also attended here. Nothing certain is known of the proceedings, except that the election of Flavianus was confirmed, and a letter to the Western Church written, to excuse the Orientals from attending the council at Rome held at the same time. A declaration of faith was added on the subject of the Blessed Trinity as well as of the Incarnation. This council further declared that Nectarius had been duly elected to the see of Constantinople, according to the Nicene canons, and it also recognised the election of Flavianus to Antioch. See Labbe, *Concil.* ii, 1014.

VII. There was a meeting of bishops held at Constantinople, by command of Theodosius, A.D. 383, under Nectarius, to devise remedies for the confusion created by so many sees passing out of the hands of the heterodox into those of the orthodox party. The Arian, Eunomian, and Macedonian bishops were required to attend there with confessions of their faith, which the emperor, after examining carefully, rejected in favor of Nicæa. The Novatians alone, receiving this, were placed by him upon equal terms with the orthodox. It is said to have been on this occasion that Amphilochius, bishop of Iconium, on entering the palace, made the usual obeisance to Theodosius, but took no notice of Arcadius, his son, standing at his side (Socrates, *Hist.* v, 10).

VIII. Held A.D. 394, Sept. 29, on occasion of the dedication of the church of the Apostles Peter and Paul, built by Ruffinus, præfect of the Prætorium. The dispute concerning the bishopric of Bostra was brought before this council. Nectarius of Constantinople presided, in the presence of Theophilus of Alexandria, Flavianus of Antioch, Gregory of Nyssa, Palladius of Cæsarea in Cappadocia, and many other bishops of note. It was determined, that although three bishops are sufficient to consecrate, a larger number is required in order to depose. See Labbe, *Concil.* ii, 1151.

IX. Held A.D. 399, attended by twenty-two bishops under Chrysostom, to inquire into seven capital charges brought against Antoninus, bishop of Ephesus. As he died before the witnesses could be examined, Chrysostom, at the request of the Ephesian clergy, went over thither, and, at the head of seventy bishops, appointed Heraclides, a deacon, in his place, and deposed six bishops who had been ordained by Antoninus. Their proceedings contain a reference to the canons of the African Church. Strictly speaking, this last was a synod of Ephesus. See Mansi, *Concil.* iii, 991.

X. Held A.D. 403, by forty or sixty bishops, in support of Chrysostom, unjustly deposed by the pseudo council, "ad Quercum," because of his non-appearance there. Although Arcadius had weakly confirmed this deposition, and banished him into Bithynia, his exile lasted but for *one day*, for the empress Eudoxia, frightened by a terrible earthquake which happened at the time, sent after him to recall him, and he re-entered Constantinople in triumph. See Labbe, *Concil.* ii, 1331.

XI. Held in the same year. After the restoration of Chrysostom to his bishopric, he ordered those priests and bishops who, upon his condemnation, had intruded into the sees and benefices of his followers, to be deposed, and the rightful pastors to be restored; he then demanded of the emperor that his own cause should be considered in a lawful synod. Sixty bishops assembled, who came to the same conclusion with the last council, viz. that Chrysostom had been unlawfully deposed in the council "ad Quercum," and that he should retain the bishopric. See Socrates, *Hist.* viii, 19.

XII. Held A.D. 404, to sit in judgment on Chrysostom, who had been recalled from exile by the emperor and retaken possession of his see, from which he had been deposed by the synod "ad Quercum." Theophilus of Alexandria was not present on this occasion, having had to fly Constantinople on the return of his rival. Still, he was not unrepresented; and Chrysostom had by this time provoked another enemy in the empress Eudoxia, whose statue he had denounced, from the games and revels permitted to be held round it, in offensive proximity to his church. At this synod he seems to have given attendance when the question of his former deposition was argued. Thirty-six bishops had condemned him; but sixty-five bishops, he rejoined, had, by communicating with him, voted in his favor. It is not implied in these words that a synod was actually sitting in his favor now, any more than during the synod "ad Quercum," the deputies from which found him surrounded, but not synodically, by forty bishops, in his own palace. The fourth or twelfth canon of the Council of Antioch was alleged by his opponents: his defence was that it was framed by the Arians. As quoted by his opponents, it was differently worded from what either the fourth or twelfth are now; possibly there may have been an Arian version of these canons, against which his objection held good. The synod, however, decided against him, and his banishment to Comana, on the Black Sea, says Socrates—to Cucusus, in Armenia, say others—followed, where he died.

XIII. Held A.D.426, on the last day of February, when Sisinnius was consecrated bishop there, in the room of Atticus. Afterwards, the errors of the Massalians, or Euchites, were condemned, at the instance of the bishops of Iconium and Sida. A severe sentence was passed on any charged with holding them after this denunciation. See Mansi, *Concil.* iv, 543.

XIV. Held A.D. 428, on the death of Sisinnius, when the well-known Nestorius was consecrated. See Mansi, *Concil.* iv, 543.

XV. Held A.D. 431, Oct. 25, four months after Nestorius had been deposed, to consecrate Maximian in his place. This done, Maximian presided, and joined in a synodical letter, enclosing that of the Council of Ephesus, with its first six canons, as they are called, to the bishops of ancient Epirus, whom attempts had been made to detach from orthodoxy. Letters were written likewise by him and by the emperor to pope Celestine, Cyril, and other bishops, to acquaint them with his elevation, at which all expressed themselves well pleased. Another synod appears to have been held by him the year following, for restoring peace between his own church and that of Antioch. See Mansi, *Concil.* v, 257-292, 1045-1050.

XVI. Held A.D. 443, probably to consider the case of Athanasius, bishop of Perrhe, on the Euphrates, afterwards deposed at Antioch under Domnus. See Mansi, *Concil.* vi, 463.

XVII. Held A.D. 448, Nov. 8, under Flavian, to inquire into a dispute between Florentius, metropolitan of Sardis, and two of his suffragans; but while sitting, it was called upon by Eusebius, bishop of Dorylæum, one of its members, who had, as a layman, denounced Nestorius, to summon Eutyches, archimandrite of a convent of three hundred monks, and as resolute an opponent of Nestorius as himself, on a charge that he felt obliged to press against him. The charge was that he recognised but one nature in Christ. Messengers were despatched to invite Eutyches to peruse what Eusebius had alleged against him. A reply was brought subsequently from Eutyches, that he refused to quit his monastery. A second and third citation followed in succession. Then he promised attendance within a week. At last he appeared, made profession of his faith, and was condemned — thirty-two bishops and twenty-three archimandrites subscribing to his deposition from the priesthood and monastic dignity. The proceedings occupied altogether seven sessions, the last of which was held Nov. 22. Its acts were recited in a subsequent council of the year following at Constantinople; at Ephesus, also, the year following, under Dioscorus; and again, in the first session of the Council of Chalcedon. See Mansi, *Concil.* vi, 495, 649; Labbe, *Concil.* iii, 1466.

XVIII. Held A.D. 449, April 8, of thirty bishops under Thalassius, archbishop of Cæsarea in Cappadocia, by order of the emperor, to re-consider the sentence passed on Eutyches by the council under Flavian, on a representation from the former that its acts had been falsified. This, however, was proved untrue. Another session was held April 27, on a second petition from Eutyches, to have the statement of the official or silentiary, who had accompanied him to the council under Flavian, taken down. This officer declared to having seen the instrument containing his deposition before the session was held at which it was resolved on. The acts of this council are likewise preserved in the first session of that of Chalcedon. See Mansi, *Concil.* vi, 503, 753.

XIX. Held A.D. 450, at which Anatolius was ordained bishop; and at which, some months afterwards, at the head of his suffragans and clergy, he made profession of his faith and subscribed to the celebrated letter of Leo to his predecessor Flavian, in the presence of four legates from Rome, charged to obtain proofs of his orthodoxy. See Mansi, *Concil.* vi, 509. All the bishops, abbots, priests, and deacons at the time in Constantinople were present. Nestorius and Eutyches, together with their dogmas, were anathematized. The pope's legates returned thanks to God that all the Church was thus unanimous in the true faith. Several of the bishops who had yielded to the violence of Dioscorus in the Latrocinium were present in this assembly, and having testified their sorrow for what they had done, desired to condemn the act with its authors, in order to be received back into the communion of the Church; they were subsequently received into communion, and restored to the government of their respective churches. See Labbe, *Concil.* iii, 1475.

XX. Held A.D. 457, under Anatolius, by order of the emperor Leo, whom he had just crowned, to take cognizance of the petitions that had arrived from Alexandria for and against Timothy Ælurus, who had been installed bishop there by the opponents of the Council of Chalcedon, and to consider what could be done to restore peace. The council anathematized Ælurus and his party. See Mansi, *Concil.* vii, 521, 869.

XXI. Held A.D. 459, under Gennadius. Eighty-one bishops subscribed to its synodical letter, still extant, in which the second canon of the Council of Chalcedon is cited with approval against some simoniacal ordinations recently brought to light to Galatia. See Mansi, *Concil.* vii, 911.

XXII. Held A.D. 478, under Acacius, in which Peter, bishop of Antioch, surnamed the Fuller, Paul of Ephesus, and John of Apamea, were condemned; and a letter addressed to Simplicus, bishop of Rome, to acquaint him with, and request him to concur in, their condemnation. A letter was addressed at the same time by Acacius to Peter the Fuller himself, rebuking him for having introduced the clause "Who was crucified for us" into the Trisagion, or hymn to the Trinity. This letter has been printed as issued from a synod five years later, when, in fact, there was no such synod. See Mansi, *Concil.* vii, 1017 sq.

XXIII. Held A.D. 492, under Euphemius, in favor of the Council of Chalcedon; but as he declined removing the name of his predecessor, Acacius, from the sacred diptychs, he was not recognised as bishop by popes Felix and Gelasius, to whom he transmitted its acts, though his orthodoxy was allowed. See Mansi, *Concil.* vii, 1175.

XXIV. Held A.D. 496, by order of the emperor Anastasius I, in which the Henoticon of Zeno was confirmed, Euphemius, bishop of Constantinople, deposed, and Macedonius, the second of that name who had presided there, substituted for him. See Mansi, *Concil.* viii, 186.

XXV. Held A.D. 498, by order of the emperor Anastasius I, in which Flavian, the second bishop of Antioch of that name, and Philoxenus of Hierapolis, took the lead: condemning the Council of Chalcedon and all who opposed the Monophysite doctrine, or would not accept the interpolated clause "Who was crucified for us," in the Trisagion. But it seems probable that this council took place a year later, and that another had met a year earlier, under Macedonius, less hostile to the Council of Chalcedon than this, and of which this was the reaction. See Mansi, *Concil.* viii, 197.

XXVI. Held A.D. 518, July 20, by order of the emperor Justin, at which the names of the councils of Nicæa, Constantinople, Ephesus, and Chalcedon; of Leo of Rome, with Euphemius and Macedonius of Constantinople, were restored in the sacred diptychs; and Severus and all other opponents of the fourth council anathematized. Count Gratus was despatched to Rome by the emperor with letters from himself and the patriarch to pope Hormisdas, hoping that peace might under these circumstances be restored between them. The Easterns had to anathematize Acacius of Constantinople by name, and to erase his and the names of all others, Euphemius and Macedonius included, who had not erased his previously, from the sacred diptychs, before the pope would readmit them to his communion. See Mansi, *Concil.* viii, 435 sq.; Labbe, *Concil.* iv, 1586.

XXVII. Held A.D. 531, under Epiphanius, who was then patriarch, to inquire into the consecration of Stephen, metropolitan of Larissa, within the diocese of Thrace, which had been made without consulting him. Stephen, having been deposed by him on these grounds, appealed to Rome; but the acts of the synod held there to consider his appeal are defective, so that it is not known with what success. See Mansi, *Concil.* viii, 739.

XXVIII. Held A.D. 533, between the Catholics and followers of Severus; the latter were silenced, and many of them returned into the Church. See Labbe, *Concil.* iv, 1763.

XXIX. Held A.D. 536. According to some, three synods were held in Constantinople this year: (1) In which pope Agapetus presided and deposed Anthymus, patriarch of Constantinople; but this the emperor Justinian had already done, besides confirming the election of Mennas in his stead, at the instance of the clergy and people of the city. Agapetus, who had come thither on a mission from Theodatus, king of the Goths, having previously refused his communion, had unquestionably procured his ejection; and he afterwards consecrated Mennas, at the request of the emperor. (2) In which a number of Eastern bishops met to draw up a petition to the pope, requesting him to call upon Anthymus, subsequently to his deposition, but previously to his going back to Trebizond, from which he had been translated, for a retractation of his denial of two natures in Christ; but this can hardly be called a council; and the death of the pope stopped any definitive action on his part. (3) Under Mennas, after the death of the pope, consisting of five actions, the first of which took place May 2, Mennas presiding, and having on his right, among others, five Italian bishops, who had come to Constantinople from the late pope. The first thing brought before the council was a petition from various monastic bodies in Constantinople, Antioch, Jerusalem, and Mount Sinai, to the emperor, begging that the sentence, stayed only by the death of the pope, against Anthymus, might be carried out; a general account of what had passed between them and the pope followed; their petition to him was produced by the Italian bishops present and recited; after it another petition to him from some Eastern bishops on the same subject; and his own letter to Peter, bishop of Jerusalem, in reply. Desirous of following out his decision, the council sent deputies to acquaint Anthymus with its proceedings, and bid him appear there within three days. The second and third actions passed in sending him similar summonses, but, as he could not be found, his condemnation and deposition were at length decreed in the fourth action by the council and its president, and signed by seventy-two bishops or their representatives, and two deacons of the Roman Church. At the fifth and last action a number of documents were recited, mainly referring to Peter, bishop of Apamea, Severus, and other Monophysites. All these having been read, an anathema was passed upon Peter, Severus, and Zoaras, one of their followers, by the council now sitting, and then by Mennas, its president; according to the order observed in the fourth action in passing sentence upon Anthymus. Eighty-eight bishops or their representatives, and two deacons of the Roman Church, as before, subscribed on this occasion. A constitution of the emperor addressed to Mennas confirmed their sentence. See Mansi, *Concil.* viii, 869 sq.; Labbe, *Concil.* v, 1 sq.

XXX. Held A.D. 538 (541, or 543), under Mennas, by order of the emperor Justinian, in support of his edict against the errors of Origen, denounced to him in a petition from four monks of Jerusalem, placed in his hands by Pelagius, a Roman envoy, whom he had sent thither on a different errand, with the express object of injuring Theodore, bishop of Cæsarea, in Cappadocia, surnamed Ascidas, who defended Origen. His edict is in the form of a book against Origen, and addressed to Mennas. It was communicated to the other patriarchs and to pope Vigilius. The council backed it by fifteen anathemas against Origen and his errors, usually placed at the end of the acts of the fifth general council, with which this council came to be subsequently confused, in consequence of their respective acts having formed one volume. See Mansi, *Concil.* ix, 487 sq.

XXXI. Held A.D. 546, under Mennas, to assent to the first edict, now lost, of the emperor Justinian against the three chapters the year before. Some authors pass over this council, and substitute for it another, supposed to have been held by pope Vigilius the year following, after his arrival in February (A.D. 547), at which it was decided to refer passing sentence upon the three chapters to the meeting of the general council about to take place. See Mansi, *Concil.* ix, 125; Labbe, *Concil.* v, 390.

XXXII. Held A.D. 553, the fifth general council, by order of the emperor Justinian, with Eutychius, patriarch of Constantinople, for president; pope Vigilius being on the spot all the time, but declining to attend: indeed, he was not even represented there. The council opened on May 4, in the cathedral. In the first and second sessions, which were styled conferences, Eutychius, the patriarch of Constantinople, Apollinaris of Alexandria, and Domnus of Antioch were present, together with three bishops, deputies of Eustachius, the patriarch of Jerusalem; there were in all one hundred and sixty-five bishops, among whom were five Africans, the only bishops who attended from the West. The following is a summary of its causes and proceedings, with their results:

As far back as his election, A.D. 537, Vigilius had been secretly pledged to the empress Theodora, who favored the Monophysite party, to assent to the condemnation of the three chapters; and this step had been pressed upon the emperor all the more warmly since then, in consequence of the condemnation of the Origenists in a council under Mennas the year following. Theodore, bishop of Cæsarea, a devoted Origenist, and friend of the empress, pointed it out, in fact, as a means of bringing back a large section of the Monophysites to the Church. Their opposition to the fourth general council, he averred, lay in the countenance supposed to be given by it to these writings: 1. The works of Theodore, bishop of Mopsuestia; 2. The letter of Ibas, bishop of Edessa, to Maris; and 3, what Theodoret, bishop of Cyrrhus, had published against Cyril—the third, however, he forbore to name—all held to be tainted with Nestorianism. By condemning them, he seems to have expected that the authority of the council that had treated their authors so favorably would be undermined. Justinian, acting on his advice, had already condemned them twice (A.D. 545 and 551), and the first time had been followed by Vigilius, whose *Judgment*, published at Constantinople, A.D. 548, is quoted in part by the emperor in his address to this council on its assembling. But Vigilius had (A.D. 547) declared against coming to any decision on the subject till it had been discussed in a general council; and to this he went back on ascertaining what indignation his *Judgment* had caused in Africa and in the West, and excommunicated Mennas and Theodore for having gone further. Accordingly, the emperor decided on summoning this council to examine and pronounce upon them; and Eutychius, the Constantinopolitan patriarch, addressed a letter to Vigilius, which was read out at its first session, May 5, requesting him to come and preside over its deliberations. Vigilius assented to their joint examination by himself and the council, but was silent about his attendance. Three patriarchs and a number of bishops accosted him personally, with no better success.

At the *second* session or *collation*, a second interview with him was reported, in which he definitively declined attending; and even on a message from the emperor he would not undertake to do more than examine the chapters by himself, and transmit his opinion on them, not to the council, but to him. Some bishops of Africa and Illyria excused themselves to the deputation sent to invite their attendance.

At the *third collation* the fathers commenced the real business for which they had been convened. They pledged themselves to the exact doctrine and discipline laid down in the four general councils, each and all, preceding their own; one and the same confession of faith had sufficed for them in spite of all the heresies they had met to condemn, and should suffice now. All things in harmony with it should be received; and all things at variance with it rejected. Having thus pledged themselves to the fourth council among the rest, the fathers proceeded to the examination of the three chapters in their *fourth collation*. This was on May 12. Extracts having accordingly been read out from various works of Theodore, both he and they were judged worthy of condemnation.

The next day, or the *fifth collation*, passages for or against Theodore, Cyril, and others, were produced and weighed; and authorities, particularly Augustine, cited in favor of condemning heretics, although dead. At the close of the sitting, extracts from the writings of Theodoret, against Cyril, were recited; on which the fathers remarked that the fourth council had acted wisely in not receiving him till he had anathematized Nestorius.

The *sixth collation* took place May 19. During the interval Vigilius issued his *Constitutum*, dated May 14, in the form of a synodical letter addressed to the emperor, answering and condemning a number of the positions of Theodore, but pleading for Theodoret and Ibas, as having been acquitted by the fourth council. However, the council at its *sixth collation* found the letter of Ibas in question contrary to the Chalcedonian definition, and anathematized it accordingly; but its author escaped.

At the *seventh collation*, May 26 or 30, a communication was read from the emperor in deprecation of the *Constitutum*, addressed to him by the pope, May 14, and on which there had been a good many messages between them, in vain, since. No less than six documents were recited, proving that Vigilius had expressly condemned the three chapters as many times; the last of them, a deposition signed by Theodore, bishop of Cæsarea, and a lay dignitary, to the effect that Vigilius had sworn to the emperor in their presence to do all he could for the condemnation of the three chapters, and never say a word in their favor. Next, an inquiry, by order of the emperor, respecting a picture or statue of Theodoret, said to have been carried about at Cyrrhus in procession, was reported. Lastly, the imperial mandate, which ordained that the name of Vigilius should be removed from the sacred diptychs for his tergiversations on the subject of the three chapters. Unity with the apostolic see would not, he adds, be thereby dissolved, inasmuch as neither Vigilius nor any other individual could, by his own change for the worse, mar the peace of the Church. To all this the council agreed.

Finally, reviewing at its *eighth collation*, June 2, in a singularly well-written compendium, all that it had done previously, and vindicating the course about to be pursued, the council formally condemned the three chapters, and with them the author of the first of them—Theodore—promulgating its definitive sentence in fourteen anathemas, almost identical with those of the emperor, and in which the heresies and heresiarchs thus condemned are specified; Origen among the number, in the eleventh, though not in the corresponding one of the emperor. He had been previously condemned in the council under Mennas A.D. 538, as we have seen. Of these anathemas the Greek version is still extant: of almost every other record of its proceedings the Latin version alone remains. Vigilius, after taking some time to consider, announced his assent to them in two formal documents: the first a decretal epistle, dated Dec. 8 of the same year, and addressed to the Constantinopolitan patriarch, in which, as he says, after the manner of Augustine, he retracts all that he had ever written differently; and the second, another *Constitutum* of great length, dated Feb. 23 of the year following, but without any heading or subscription in its present form. He died on his way home, and Pelagius, the Roman envoy who had been instrumental in condemning Origen, had thus, on becoming pope, to vindicate the condemnation of the three chapters by this council, in the West, where they had been defended all but unanimously, and were upheld obstinately by more than three parts of Italy still. The second Pelagius, twenty-five years later, in his third letter to the bishops of Istria, said to have been written by Gregory the Great, then his deacon, apologized for the conduct of his predecessors and his own therein, by referring to the occasion on which Peter was reproved by Paul (Gal. ii, 11). Gregory, when pope, settled the matter by affirming that he venerated the fifth council equally with the four preceding.

No canons seem to have been passed by this council: many points connected with it are still doubtful; and the documents published as belonging to it greatly need rearranging.

See Mansi, *Concil.* ix, 151-651; Labbe, *Concil.* v, 411, sq.

XXXIII. Held A.D. 565, at which the emperor Justinian endeavored to get the errors of Julian of Halicarnassus, a well-known Monophysite, who maintained the incorruptibility of the body of Christ antecedently to his resurrection, approved, by banishing those who opposed them. See Mansi, *Concil.* ix, 765.

XXXIV. Held A.D. 587, at which a foul charge brought against Gregory, patriarch of Antioch, by a banker of his diocese, was examined. He was honorably acquitted and his accuser punished. This may have been the synod summoned as a general one by the Constantinopolitan patriarch John, in virtue of his assumed title of œcumenical patriarch, and for which he was so severely taken to task by pope Pelagius II; but for this no direct proof is adduced. This is referred to in a letter of Gregory the Great to that patriarch, and a further letter of his some time later, when Cyriacus was patriarch, whose plan of holding another synod for the same purpose he would seem to have anticipated. Mansi conceives this synod to have been held A.D. 598 (*Concil.* ix, 481).

XXXV. Held A.D. 626, under Sergius, to consider the question raised by Paul, a Monophysite of Phasis, in Lazica, and Cyrus, its metropolitan—afterwards translated to Alexandria—before the emperor Heraclius, whether one or two wills and operations were to be ascribed to Christ. Sergius pronounced in favor of one operation and one will; thereby founding the heresy called Monothelism. The question may have originated with Athanasius, patriarch of the Jacobites in Syria, on his promotion to the see of Antioch by Heraclius four years later. See Mansi, *Concil.* x, 585.

XXXVI. Held A.D. 639, under Sergius, and continued—unless there were two distinct councils this year—under Pyrrhus, his successor, at which the exposition of faith by the emperor Heraclius, favorable to Monothelism, was confirmed. Parts of its acts, with the "exposition" in full, were recited in the third sitting of the Lateran, under Martin I, A.D. 649. See Mansi, *Concil.* x, 673.

XXXVII. Held A.D. 665, by order of the emperor Constans II, at which Maximus, the great opponent of the Monothelites, was condemned. See Mansi, *Concil.* xi, 73.

XXXVIII. Held A.D. 666, under Peter, patriarch of Constantinople, and attended by Macedonius of Antioch and the vicar of the patriarch of Alexandria, at which Maximus was condemned a second time, with his disciples. See Mansi, *Concil.* xi, 73.

XXXIX. The sixth general council, held in the banqueting-hall of the palace, called *Trullus* from its domed roof, and lasting from Nov. 7, A.D. 680, to Sept. 16 of the ensuing year. It was convened by the emperor Constantine Pogonatus, in consequence of a request made to him by the patriarchs of Constantinople to permit their removing from the sacred diptychs the name of pope Vitalian, lately deceased, while they were for retaining that of Honorius. In short, they wished to commemorate none of the popes after Honorius till some disputes that had arisen between their own sees and his had been settled, and some newly-coined words explained. Donus dying before this letter could reach Rome, it was complied with at once by his successor, Agatho, who sent three bishops, on behalf of his synod, and two presbyters, and one deacon named John—who subsequently became pope as John V—in his own name, to Constantinople, "to bring about the union of the holy churches of God." On hearing from the "œcumenical pope," as he styles him, to that effect, the emperor issued his summons to George, patriarch of Constantinople—whom he styles œcumenical patriarch—and through him to the patriarch of Antioch, to get ready to come to the council with their respective bishops and metropolitans. Mansuetus, metropolitan of Milan, who had formed part of the Roman synod under Agatho, sent a synodical letter and profession of faith on behalf of his own synod, and Theodore, bishop or archbishop of Ravenna, who had formed part of the same synod, a presbyter, to represent him personally. The number of bishops actually present, it is said, was two hundred and eighty-nine, though the extant subscriptions are under one hundred and eighty. Thirteen officers of the court were there likewise, by command of the emperor, who attended in person, and were ranged round him—on his left were the representatives of the pope and his synod, of the archbishop of Ravenna, and of the patriarch of Jerusalem, then Basil, bishop of Gortyna, in Crete, and the remaining bishops "subject to Rome"—his right being occupied by the patriarchs of Constantinople and Antioch, a presbyter representing the patriarch of Alexandria, the bishop of Ephesus, and "the remaining bishops subject to Constantinople." The business of the council was concluded in eighteen actions or sessions, as follows:

1 (Nov. 7, 680). The legates of Agatho having complained of the novel teaching of four patriarchs of Constantinople, and two other primates, that had for forty-six years or more troubled the whole Church, in attributing one will and operation to the Incarnate Word, Macarius, patriarch of Antioch, and two suffragans of the see of Constantinople favorable to this dogma, briefly replied that they had put out no new terms, but only believed and taught what they had received from general councils and from the holy fathers on the point in question, particularly the patriarchs of Constantinople and Alexandria, named by their opponents, and Honorius, formerly pope of elder Rome. Whereupon the chartophylax, or keeper of the archives of the great Church, was ordered by the emperor to fetch the books of the œcumenical councils from the library of the patriarch. As nothing was said of the acts of the first and second councils on this occasion, we must infer they had been lost previously. The chartophylax was told to produce what he had brought; and immediately two volumes of the acts of the third council were recited by Stephen, a presbyter of Antioch in waiting on Macarius, who forthwith contended that some of Cyril's expressions were favorable to him.

2 (Nov. 10). Two volumes of the acts of the fourth council were read, when the legates of Agatho pointed out that two operations were attributed to Christ by pope Leo.

3 (Nov. 13). Two volumes of the acts of the fifth council were read, when the legates protested that two letters of pope Vigilius, contained in the second volume, had been interpolated, and that a discourse attributed in the first to Mennas, patriarch of Constantinople, was spurious. This last having been proved on the spot from internal evidence, its recital was stopped, the emperor directing further inquiry to be made respecting the letters of the pope.

4 (Nov. 15). Two letters from Agatho were recited—one to the emperor, in his own name, the other to the council, in his own name and that of a synod of one hundred and twenty-five bishops, assembled under him at Rome, previously to the departure of his legates. The burden of both is the same, namely, that what had been defined as of faith by the five general councils preceding it was the summit of his ambition to keep inviolate. Several passages in the Latin version of these letters, on the prerogatives of the Church of Rome, are not found in the Greek. Either, therefore, they have been interpolated in the one, or suppressed in the other.

5 (Dec. 10). Two papers were exhibited by Macarius, and recited, of which the first was headed, "Testimonies from the holy fathers confirmatory of there being one will in Christ, which is also that of the Father and the Holy Ghost."

6 (Feb. 12, 681). A third paper from Macarius, to the same effect as the other two, having been read, the sealing of all three was commanded by the emperor, and intrusted to his own officials and those belonging to the sees of Rome and Constantinople. On the legates affirming that the quotations contained in them had not been fairly made, authentic copies of the works cited were ordered to be brought from the patriarchal library to compare with them.

7 (Feb. 13). A paper headed "Testimonies from the holy fathers demonstrating two wills and operations in Christ" was produced by the legates, and read. Appended to it were passages from the writings of heretics, in which but one will and operation was taught. This paper also was ordered to be sealed, by the emperor.

8 (March 7). The passages adduced by Agatho from the fathers, and by his synod, in favor of two wills and operations, having been examined and confirmed, were pronounced conclusive by all present except Macarius; and the petition to have the name of Vitalian erased from the diptychs was withdrawn by George, the existing patriarch of Constantinople, amid great applause. Macarius being then called upon to make his profession, proved himself a Monothelite; and was convicted of having quoted unfairly from the fathers in his papers, to support his views.

9 (March 8). Examination of the papers of Macarius having been completed, he and his presbyter Stephen were formally deposed as heretics by the council.

10 (March 18). The paper exhibited by the legates was taken in hand; and after a most interesting comparison between it and the authentic works in the patriarchal library, was declared thoroughly correct in its citations; a profession of faith was received from the bishop of Nicomedia and some others, in which Monothelism was abjured.

11 (March 20). A long and remarkable profession of faith, contained in a synodical letter of Sophronius, late patriarch of Jerusalem, and the first to oppose Monothelism, was recited; and after it, at the request of the legates, some more writings of Macarius, since come to hand, that proved full of heresy.

12 (March 22). Several more documents belonging to Macarius having been received from the emperor through one of his officers, which he professed not to have read himself, some were looked through and pronounced irrelevant, but three letters were recited at length, two from Sergius, patriarch of Constantinople, and one from pope Honorius in reply to one of these. Search in the patriarchal archives and proper investigation placed the genuineness of all three beyond doubt. A suggestion brought from the emperor, that Macarius should be restored in the event of his recanting, was peremptorily declined by the council.

13 (March 28). Both the letters of Sergius before mentioned and that of Honorius to him were declared heterodox; and he and his successors, Pyrrhus, Peter, and Paul, Cyrus of Alexandria, and Theodore, bishop of Pharan—on all of whom Agatho had passed sentence previously—with Honorius, whom Agatho had passed over, were definitively cast out of the Church—the only sentence of the kind ever decreed against any pope. Finally, search having been made for all other works of the same kind in the archives, all that could be found were brought out and recited. A large number were pronounced heretical, and burned as such. Letters of Thomas, John, and Constantine, patriarchs of Constantinople, were read likewise, but their orthodoxy was allowed.

14 (April 1). Returning to the letters of pope Vigilius that had been called in question, it was ascertained by careful inquiry that each of the volumes of the fifth council had been tampered with; in one case by inserting the paper attributed to Mennas, in the other by interpolating the letters of Vigilius, in support of heresy. The council ordered both falsifications to be cancelled, besides anathematizing them and their authors. A sermon of Athanasius was produced by the bishop of Cyprus, in which the doctrine of two wills in Christ was clearly laid down. At this sitting Theophanes, the new patriarch of Antioch, is first named among those present.

15 (April 26). Polychronius, a presbyter, undertaking to raise a dead man to life in support of his heretical views, and failing, was condemned as an impostor, and deposed.

16 (Aug. 9). Constantine, another presbyter, affecting to have devised some formula calculated to reconcile Monothelism with orthodoxy, was proved in agreement with Macarius, and similarly condemned. In conclusion, all who had been condemned were anathematized, one after the other, by name, amid cheers for the orthodox.

17 (Sept. 11). The previous acts of the council were read over, and its definition of faith published for the first time.

18 (Sept. 16). The definition having been once more published, was signed by all present, and received the assent of the emperor on the spot, amid the usual acclamations and reprobations. It consisted of three parts: *a*. An introduction, proclaiming entire agreement on the part of the council with the five previous councils, and acceptance of the two creeds promulgated by them as one. *b*. Recital of the two creeds of Nicæa and Constantinople in their pristine forms. *c*. Its own definition, enumerating all previously condemned for Monothelism once more by name, and mentioning with approbation the declaration of pope Agatho and his synod against them, and in favor of the true doctrine, which it proceeded to unfold by course: then reiterating the decree passed by previous councils against the framers and upholders of a faith or creed other than the two forms already specified; and including finally in the same condemnation the inventors and disseminators of any novel terms subversive of its own rulings.

Proceedings terminated in a remarkable address to the emperor on behalf of all present, which was read out, showing that the doctrine of the Trinity had been defined by the first two councils, and that of the Incarnation by the next four, of which this was the last; and a still more remarkable request was appended to it—that he would forward the definition, signed by himself, to the five patriarchal sees of Rome, Constantinople, Alexandria, Antioch, and Jerusalem; which we are told expressly was done. In conclusion, a letter was despatched to the pope in the name of the council, informing him that he would receive a copy of its acts through his legates, and begging that he would confirm them in his reply. The emperor, on his part, exhorted all to receive them, in a special edict; and, as he had promised, addressed a letter in his own name to the Roman synod, dated Dec. 23, A.D. 681 (Agatho dying, according to Cave, Dec. 1), and another to Leo II, soon after his accession, the year following, bespeaking their acceptance. This the new pope granted without hesitation in the fullest manner, even to the condemnation of Honorius as having betrayed the faith; all which he repeated to the bishops of Spain, in sending them a Latin translation of the acts of this council.

It is admitted on all hands that no canons were passed. Several anecdotes of this council found their way into the West. Bede tells us, for instance, that such was the honor accorded there to the legates of Agatho that one of them, the bishop of Oporto, celebrated the eucharist in Latin on Low Sunday, in the Church of St. Sophia, before the emperor and patriarch. Cardinal Humbert asserts it was then explained to the emperor that unleavened bread was enjoined by the Latin rite. But the two striking incidents of this council were: 1. The arrangement of the "bishops subject to Rome," and those "subject to Constantinople" on opposite sides; and, 2. The anathemas passed on pope and patriarch alike.

See Mansi, *Concil.* xi, 189 sq.; Labbe, *Concil.* vi, 587 sq.

XL. Held A.D. 691, in or not earlier than September. The fathers composing it, in their address to the emperor Justinian II, say that they had met at his bidding to pass some canons which had long been needed, owing to the omission of the fifth and sixth councils, contrary to the precedent of the four first, to pass any, whence this council has been commonly styled the *quini-sext*, or a supplement to both. It is, indeed, best known as the *Trullan*, from the hall of the palace in which it was held, although the sixth council had met there also. The number of bishops subscribing to its canons is two hundred and thirteen, of whom forty-three had been present at the sixth council, and at their head, instead of after them, as at the sixth council, the emperor, who signs, however, differently from the rest, as merely accepting and assenting to what had been defined by them. A blank is left immediately after his name for that of the pope, showing clearly that the pope was not represented there; and blanks are subsequently left for the bishops of Thessalonica, Heraclea, Sardinia, Ravenna, and Corinth, who might, had they been present, have been supposed to be acting for him. Basil, indeed, bishop of Gortyna, in Crete, is set down as subscribing on behalf of the whole synod of the Roman Church; but then he is similarly set down among the subscriptions to the sixth council, not having been one of the three deputies sent thither from Rome, and afterwards, in the letter addressed to Agatho by the council, only signing for himself and his own synod. Hence there seems little ground for supposing him to have represented Rome there in any sense. Anastasius, in his life of Sergius I, who was then pope, says that the legates of the apostolic see were present, and deluded into subscribing; but there is nothing in the subscriptions to confirm this, and of the acts nothing further has been preserved. Great controversy prevails as to the extent to which this council has been received in the West: œcumenical it has never been accounted there, in spite of its own claim to be so; and when its canons were sent in six tomes to Sergius, himself a native of Antioch, for subscription, he said he would die sooner than assent to the erroneous innovations which they contained. John VII, the next pope but one, was requested by the emperor to confirm all that he could, and reject the rest; but he sent back the tomes untouched. Constantine is supposed to be the first pope to confirm any of them; but this is inferred solely from the honorable reception given to him at Constantinople by Justinian. Adrian I, in his epistle to Tarasius, read out at the seventh council, is explicit enough: "I, too, receive the same six holy councils, with all the rules constitutionally and divinely promulgated by them; among which is contained" what turns out to be the eighty-second of these canons, for he quotes it at full length. The first canon of the seventh council, confirmed by him, is substantially to the same effect. But the exact truth is probably told by Anastasius, the librarian. "At the seventh council," he says, "the principal see so far admits the rules said by the Greeks to have been framed at the sixth council, as to reject in the same breath whichever of them should prove to be opposed to former canons, or the decrees of its own holy pontiffs, or to good manners." All of them, indeed, he contends had been unknown to the Latins entirely till then, never having been translated; neither were they to be found even in the archives of the other patriarchal sees where Greek was spoken, none of whose occupants had been present to concur or assist in their promulgation. This shows how little he liked these canons himself, nor can it be denied that some of them were dictated by a spirit hostile to the West.

1. The council declared its adherence to the apostolic faith, as defined by the first six œcumenical councils, and condemned those persons and errors which in them had been condemned.

2. The canons which they received and confirmed were set forth, viz. the eighty-five canons attributed to the apostles, those of Nicæa, Ancyra, Neo-Cæsarea, Gangra, Antioch, Laodicea, and those of the œcumenical councils of Constantinople, Ephesus, and Chalcedon, also those of the councils of Sardica and Carthage, and those of Constantinople, under Nectarius and Theophilus; further, they approved the canonical epistles of Dionysius of Alexandria, of Athanasius, Basil of Cæsarea, Gregory of Nyssa, Gregory the Divine, Amphilochius of Iconium, of Timothy, Theophilus, and Cyril of Alexandria, of Gennadius, and, lastly, a canon of Cyprian.

3. Enacts that all priests and deacons who, being married to a second wife, refuse to repent, shall be deposed; that those whose second wives are dead, or who have repented, and live in continence, shall be forbidden to serve at the altar, and to exercise any priestly function in future, but shall retain their rank; that those who have married widows, or who have married after ordination, shall be suspended for a short time, and then restored, but shall never be promoted to a higher order.

7. Restrains the arrogance of deacons; forbids them to take precedence of priests.

9. Forbids clerks to keep taverns.

11. Forbids familiarity with Jews.

13. Allows (notwithstanding the decrees of the Roman Church to the contrary) that married men, when raised to holy orders, should keep their wives and cohabit with them, excepting on those days on which they are to celebrate the holy communion; and declares that no person otherwise fit and desirous for ordination shall be refused on account of his being married, and that no promise shall be extorted from him at the time of ordination, to abstain from his wife, lest God's holy institution of matrimony be thereby dishonored; orders further, that they who shall dare to deprive any priest, deacon, or subdeacon of this privilege, shall be deposed, and that, also, any priest or deacon separating from his wife on pretence of piety, shall, if he persist, be deposed.

14. Enacts that men be not ordained priests before they are thirty years of age, or deacons before twenty-five. Deaconesses to be forty.

15. Sub-deacons to be twenty.

17. Forbids clerks to go from one church to another.

19. Orders those who preside over churches to teach the people at least every Sunday; forbids them to explain Scripture otherwise than the lights of the Church and the doctors have done in their writings.

21. Orders that deposed clerks, who remain impenitent, shall be stripped of every outward mark of their clerical state, and be regarded as men of the world; those who are penitent are permitted to retain the tonsure.

22. Against simony.

23. Forbids to require any fee for administering the holy communion.

24. Forbids all in the sacerdotal order to be present at plays, and orders such as have been invited to a wedding to rise and depart before any thing ridiculous is introduced.

32. Declares that in some parts of Armenia water was not mixed with the wine used at the altar; condemns the novel practice; sets forth the foundation for the catholic use, and orders that every bishop and priest who refuses to mix water with the wine, "according to the order handed down to us by the apostles," shall be deposed.

36. Decrees that the see of Constantinople, according

to the canons of Constantinople and Chalcedon, shall have equal privileges with the throne of old Rome.

40, 41. Of those who shall be admitted into the monastic state.

42. Of hermits.

48. Orders that the wife of one who has been raised to the episcopate, having first separated from her husband of her own free-will, shall be kept, at the bishop's expense, in a monastery far from him, or shall be promoted to the deaconate.

53. Forbids a man to marry her to whose children by a deceased husband he has become godfather.

55. Forbids any to fast on Saturdays and Sundays, even during Lent.

56. Forbids to eat eggs or cheese in Lent.

57. Forbids to offer milk and honey at the altar.

58. Forbids a lay person to administer to himself the holy mysteries, when there is a bishop, priest, or deacon present; offenders to be separated for a week, "that they may be thereby taught not to be wiser than they ought to be."

64. Forbids lay persons to teach, and bids them rather learn of others who have received the grace to teach.

66. Orders all the faithful, for seven days after Easter, to occupy themselves at church in psalms and hymns and spiritual songs.

67. Forbids to eat the blood of any animal; offenders, if clerks, to be deposed.

68. Forbids injury to any of the books of the Old and New Testament.

69. Forbids lay persons to enter the altar-rails.

72. Forbids marriage with heretics.

73. Forbids the use of the cross lying upon the ground, lest by treading on it men should dishonor it.

74. Forbids to celebrate the Agapæ in churches.

75. Relates to the manner of singing psalms to be observed.

83. Forbids to administer the holy eucharist to dead bodies.

84. Orders the baptism of those of whose baptism there exists any doubt.

88. Forbids to take any beast into a church, unless in case of great need a traveller be compelled to do so.

89. Orders the faithful to observe Good Friday with fasting and prayer, and compunction of heart, until the middle of the night of the great Sabbath.

90. Forbids to kneel at church from Saturday night to Sunday night.

111. Of penance and absolution.

This council receives all the apostolical canons, eighty-five in number, though at that time but fifty were received in the Roman Church, but rejects the apostolical constitutions as having been interpolated, and containing many spurious things. Accordingly, the code of the Eastern Church was authoritatively settled, apart, of course, from the one hundred and two canons now added to it, which were formally received themselves, as we have seen, by the second council of Nicæa, and reckoned ever afterwards as the canons of the sixth council. Their general character is thoroughly Oriental, but without disparagement to their practical value. See Mansi, *Concil.* xi, 921 sq.; xii, 47 sq.; Labbe, *Concil.* vi, 1124 sq.

XLI. Held A.D. 712, in the short reign of Philippicus or Bardanes, and under the Monothelite patriarch of his appointment, John VI; at which the sixth council was repudiated and condemned. The copy of its acts belonging to the palace was likewise burned by his order, as we learn from the deacon who transcribed them, and the picture of it that hung there removed. On the death of the tyrant, indeed, John addressed a letter to pope Constantine, to apologize for what had been done; but its tone is not assuring. He testifies, however, to the authentic tomes of the sixth council being safe still in his archives. See Mansi, *Concil.* xii, 187 sq.

XLII. Held A.D. 715, Aug. 11, at which the translation of Germanus from the see of Cyzicus to that of Constantinople was authorized. He had been a party to the Monothelite synod under John three years before; but immediately after his translation he held a synod—most probably in 714, of which this was a continuation—in which he condemned Monothelism. See Mansi, *Concil.* xii, 255 sq.; Labbe, *Concil.* vi, 1451.

XLIII. Held A.D. 730, or, rather, a meeting in the imperial palace, at which the emperor Leo III, better known as the Isaurian, called upon Germanus, the aged patriarch, to declare for the demolition of images, which he had just ordered himself in a second edict against them. The patriarch replied by resigning. See Mansi, *Concil.* xii, 269 sq.; Labbe, *Concil.* vi, 1461.

XLIV. Held A.D. 754, from Feb. 10 to Aug. 8, by order of the emperor Constantine Copronymus, and styling itself œcumenical, or the seventh council, though its claim to both titles has since been set aside in favor of the second council of Nicæa, in which its decrees were reversed. There is no record of its acts extant but what is to be found in the sixth session of that council, where they were cited only to be condemned. As many as three hundred and thirty-eight bishops attended it, but the chief see represented there was that of Ephesus. Their proceedings are given in six tomes, as follows:

1. They deduce the origin of all creature-worship from the devil, to abolish which God sent his Son in the flesh.

2. Christianity being established, the devil, they say, was determined to bring about a combination between it and idolatry; but the emperors had opposed his designs. Already six councils had met, and the present one, following in their steps, declared all pictorial representations unlawful, and subversive of the faith which they professed.

3. Two natures being united in Christ, no one picture or statue could represent Christ as he is; besides, his only proper representation is in the eucharistic sacrifice, of his own institution.

4. There was no prayer in use for consecrating images, nor were representations of the saints to be tolerated any more than of Christ, for Holy Scripture was distinctly against both.

5. The fathers, beginning with Epiphanius, having been cited at some length to the same purpose, the council decreed unanimously that all likenesses, of whatsoever color and material, were to be taken away, and utterly disused in Christian churches.

6. All clergy setting up or exhibiting reverence to images in church or at home were to be deposed; monks and laymen anathematized. Vessels and vestments belonging to the sanctuary were never to be turned to any purpose in connection with images. A series of anathemas was directed against all who upheld them in any sense, or contravened the decrees of this council. Germanus, the late patriarch of Constantinople, George of Cyprus, and John of Damascus, or Mansur, as he was called by the Saracens, were specially denounced as image-worshippers. The usual acclamations to the emperor followed. Before the council separated, Constantine, the new patriarch, was presented to it and approved.

See Mansi, *Concil.* xii, 575; xiii, 203 sq.; Labbe, *Concil.* vi, 1661 sq.

XLV. Held A.D. 786, Aug. 2, by the Iconodulists, but broken up by the violence of the opposite party. See Ignatius of Constantinople, *Vita Tarasii.*

XLVI. Held A.D. 815, by the Iconoclasts, under the emperor Leo; the abbots of Constantinople excused themselves from attending, and the monks deputed to bear to the council their reasons for so doing were driven from the assembly; also, those of the bishops who differed in opinion from the dominant party were trampled upon and maltreated. The council condemned the acts of the second council of Nicæa, A.D. 787, and decreed that all paintings in churches should be defaced everywhere, the sacred vessels destroyed, as well as all Church ornaments. This council has never been recognized by the Western Church. See Labbe, *Concil.* vii, 1299.

XLVII. Held A.D. 842, by the emperor Michael and Theodora, his mother. This council confirmed the second council of Nicæa, anathematized the Iconoclasts, restored images to the churches, deposed the patriarch John, and elected Methodius in his stead. In memory of this council the Greek Church still keeps the second Sunday in Lent (the day on which it was held) holy, as the festival of orthodoxy. See Labbe, *Concil.* vii, 178.2

XLVIII. Held A.D. 858, by the bishops of the province of Constantinople, first, on account of the banishment of Ignatius, the patriarch of Constantinople, by the emperor Bardas, to whom he had justly refused communion after having charitably warned him of the scandal occasioned by his irregular life. They deposed Photius, who had been intruded into the see, with anathema, as well against himself as against all who should dare to acknowledge him to be patriarch. This Photius was one of the most learned and able men of his age; but, led astray by his boundless ambition, by his artifices he procured his election to the patriarchate, although a layman, and was consecrated by Gregory Asbesta, the deposed bishop of Syracuse, Dec. 25, 857.

Forty days after his consecration he held a council, in which sentence of deposition and anathema was pronounced against Ignatius and his followers; and in 861 he convoked another council, at which three hundred and eighteen bishops (including the pope's legates) attended, together with the emperor Michael and a large number of lords and people. To this council Ignatius, having been cited, refused to come, protesting against its irregularity, but some days afterwards he was seized and forcibly brought before it. After a sort of mock trial, he was condemned, and sentence of deposition passed upon him; he was then imprisoned, and subjected to great cruelties. The pope, it should be added, had been deceived into sending legates to this council, and the latter, when at Constantinople, by threats were forced to yield an assent to its proceedings. Ignatius subsequently, in order to deliver himself from the cruelties which he endured, signed (or rather was *forced* to sign) a confession declaring that he had been unlawfully elevated to the see; after this he was delivered from prison, and escaped from Constantinople. Photius then wrote an artful letter to pope Nicholas, to induce him to recognise his elevation to the patriarchate, which he, however, refused to do, and held a council at Rome (863), in which Zachens, one of the legates who attended the pseudo-council of 861, was excommunicated, the other remanded, and Photius himself condemned and deposed. Upon this the latter, in 866, called together another assembly, wherein the emperors Michael and Basil presided, together with the legates of the three great Eastern sees; and this, after hearing witnesses against Nicholas, the pope, pronounced sentence of deposition and excommunication against him. Twenty-one bishops signed this sentence, and about one thousand false signatures were said to have been added. After so bold a step it was impossible to keep up appearances with Rome any longer, and Photius wrote a circular letter to the Oriental bishops, in which he dared to charge with error the whole West. Among other accusations, he charged the Latin Church with adding the word "Filioque" to the original creed. See Labbe, *Concil.* viii, 651, 695, 735.

XLIX. Held A.D. 867. In this council Photius was deposed and driven into banishment, Ignatius, by a decree of the emperor Basil, having been restored to the see.

L. Sometimes called the eighth general council, held A.D. 869, by the emperor Basil, and attended by about one hundred Eastern bishops, and by three legates from pope Adrian II.

The council was opened (Oct. 5) in the Church of St. Sophia. The pope's legates, who had been received by the emperor with the most marked attention and honor, had the first seats assigned to them; the legates of the patriarchs of Antioch and Jerusalem were also present. The first bishops who entered the council-chamber were the twelve who had suffered persecution from Photius in the cause of Ignatius; then the pope's letters to the emperor and to the patriarch were read, also the form of reconciliation which the Roman legates had brought with them.

In the *second session* (Oct. 7) the bishops, priests, deacons, and sub-deacons who had yielded to Photius appeared and testified their repentance, urging, at the same time, in excuse, the evils that they had been made to suffer.

In the *third* and *fourth sessions* (Oct. 11 and 13) Theophilus and Zachary were questioned. The legates from Antioch declared that Photius had never been acknowledged by the Church of Antioch. Also, a letter from the pope to the emperor Michael was read.

Fifth session (Oct. 20). Photius himself was brought before the council and questioned. Being required to submit to the council and to Ignatius, in order to be received into lay communion, he refused to give a definite answer, and was withdrawn.

In the *sixth session* (Oct. 25) the emperor Basil was present, and occupied the chief place. Several bishops who had taken part with Photius were introduced, and exhorted to renounce their schism; they, however, continued firm in their fidelity to him, and Zachary, bishop of Chalcedon, in a long oration, defended Photius from the charges brought against him. The emperor himself, at some length, endeavored to persuade them to renounce Photius and to submit to Ignatius, but they resolutely refused. Ten days were granted them in which to consider the matter.

In the *seventh session* (Oct. 29), Photius again appeared, and with him Gregory of Syracuse; an admonition to himself and his partisans was read, exhorting them, under pain of anathema, to submit to the council. Photius merely answered that he had nothing to say in reply to calumnies, whereupon the legates directed the sentence of excommunication against Photius and Gregory to be read.

In the *eighth session* (Nov. 5) the acts of the council against Ignatius, and several of the books written by Photius, were burned; anathema was pronounced against the Iconoclasts, and finally, the sentence of anathema against Photius was repeated.

In the *ninth session* (Feb. 12, 870), false witnesses whom the emperor Michael, at the instigation of Photius, had brought forward to give evidence against Ignatius, were put to penance. In this session the emperor was not present, but the legate of the patriarch of Alexandria attended.

In the *tenth and last session* (Feb. 28) the emperor Basil attended, with his son Constantine, twenty patricians, the three ambassadors of Louis, emperor of Italy and France, and those of Michael, king of Bulgaria; also a hundred bishops were present. They acknowledged seven preceding œcumenical councils, and declared this to be the eighth. The condemnation pronounced by the popes Nicholas and Adrian against Photius was confirmed.

Twenty-seven canons which had been drawn up in the previous sessions were read; they were chiefly directed against Photius:

3. Enjoins the worship of the sacred image of our Lord equally with the books of the holy Gospels (*æquo honore cum libro S. E.*); also orders the worship of the cross and of images of saints.

7. Forbids persons laboring under anathema to paint the holy images.

11. Anathematizes all who believed with Photius that the body contains two souls.

12. Forbids princes to meddle in the election of bishops.

13. Orders that the higher ranks in each Church shall be filled by the ecclesiastics of that Church, and not by strangers.

16. Reprobates the sacrilegious use made of the holy vestments and garments by the emperor Michael, who employed them in profane shows and games.

21. Enjoins reverence to all the patriarchs, especially to the pope, and declares that even in an œcumenical synod, any matter of complaint or doubt involving the Roman Church should be treated with suitable reverence, without presuming to pass any sentence against the supreme pontiffs of old Rome.

Further, a definition of faith was published in the name of the council, with anathema against all heretics, especially naming Monothelites and Iconoclasts.

The acts of this council were subscribed, in the first place, by the three legates of the pope (the emperor, through humility, refusing to sign first), then by the patriarch Ignatius, and after him by Joseph, legate of Alexandria, Thomas, archbishop of Tyre, who represented the vacant see of Antioch, and the legate of Jerusalem, then by the emperor and his two sons, Constantine and Leo, and, lastly, by one hundred and one bishops.

This council has not the slightest claim to be considered œcumenical; it was, indeed, annulled in the following council, and has always been rejected by the Eastern Church. See Labbe, *Concil.* viii, 962.

LI. Sometimes styled the ninth general, was held A.D. 879, by the emperor Basil, upon the restoration of Photius to the patriarchate of Constantinople, vacated by the death of Ignatius. The legates of pope John VIII and of all the Eastern patriarchs attended, with not less than three hundred and eighty bishops.

In the *first session* Photius presided; the legate of John, cardinal Peter, declared the pope's willingness to recognise Photius as his brother, and produced the presents which he had brought for the latter from Rome. Much was said by Zacharias, bishop of Chalcedon, and others, in praise of Photius, which was greatly applauded by the assembly.

In the *second session* (Nov. 16) the letter of the pope to the emperor, translated into Greek, was read, those parts which were unfavorable to Photius having been altered. The council received the pope's letter relating to union with the latter, but rejected that which claimed Bulgaria as belonging to the Roman obedience. The letter of the pope to Photius was then read, that part, however, being suppressed which declared that Photius ought to have consulted him before returning to the see of Constantinople, and to have asked pardon in full council. The bishops declared that no force or violence had been used by Photius, in order to procure his re-establishment in the see, and that all had been done quietly and in order; afterwards, he himself spoke, declaring that he had been elevated to the patriarchate against his own will, to which the whole council assented. This done, the letters of the eastern patriarchs to the emperor and to Photius were read, being all highly favorable to the latter, acknowledging him to be the lawful patriarch of Constantinople, and inveighing against the synod of 869.

In the *third session* (Nov. 18) the letter of John VIII to the Church of Constantinople was first read, then the acts of all previous councils condemning Photius were annulled, the council declaring, "We reject and anathematize that pretended council (the preceding) in uniting ourselves to the patriarch Photius."

In the *fourth session* (Christmas Eve) the letter of the patriarch of Antioch to Photius was read; it was approved by the council, which declared that the eastern sees had all along recognised Photius. Afterwards, the articles of union were discussed; they were five: 1. Respecting Bulgaria, concerning which nothing was determined; 2. Relating to the consecration of laymen to the see of Constantinople; 3. Forbidding the election of any person to the patriarchate of Constantinople from another Church; 4. Condemning all the councils held against Photius; 5. Excommunicating all who refused to communicate with Photius. The last four were unanimously approved.

In the *fifth session* (Jan. 26, 880) the second council of Nicæa was approved, and received as œcumenical. After the publication of certain canons, the bishops present proceeded to subscribe the acts of the council, the Roman legates being the first, who declared that they acknowledged Photius to be the legitimate patriarch, that they rejected the council of Constantinople in 869, against him, and that if any schismatics should still separate themselves from Photius, their lawful pastor, they ought to be excluded from communion, until they should return to obedience.

The *sixth session* was held (March 10) in the palace, the emperor Basil being present. Here it was agreed to follow the decisions of the seven œcumenical councils in drawing up a profession of faith; thereby, in fact, condemning the addition of the "Filioque."

In the *seventh and last session*, held on Sunday, March 13, in the church, the definition of faith, agreed to in the former session, was read and subscribed, after which the council was dissolved.

The acts of this council were subscribed by the emperor. It was rejected by the Western Church. John VIII very shortly after sent Marinus, his legate, to Constantinople, to revoke his consent to its proceedings, and to declare his concurrence in the sentence of excommunication previously passed against Photius. It does not seem to have been universally received in the East. See Labbe, *Concil.* ix, 324-329.

LII. Held A.D. 1054, by the patriarch Michael Cærularius. In this council the great schism between the Greek and Roman churches was (as it were) consummated. Cærularius had previously written a letter in his own name and that of Leo, archbishop of Acrida, to John, bishop of Trani, in Apulia, in which he publicly accused the Latin Church of error. Among other things laid to their charge was the use of unleavened bread in the holy communion; single immersion in holy baptism; the use of signs by bishops, etc. To this letter Leo IX returned an angry answer, and held a council at Rome, in which the Greek churches were excommunicated. The emperor, however, was anxious to appease matters, and, by his order, Leo sent three legates to Constantinople, Humbert, Peter, archbishop of Amalfi, and Frederick, chancellor of the Church of Rome (afterwards Stephen IX), who by their own conduct fully seconded the arrogance of the pope, and, in 1054, in the church of St. Sophia, solemnly excommunicated Michael Cærularius and Leo of Acrida, with all their adherents; and, leaving a written document to this effect upon the altar, departed, shaking off the dust from their feet. Upon this, Michael called together this council, in which he excommunicated the three legates, with all those who adhered to their views. The jealousy with which the bishops of Rome regarded the claim of the patriarchs of Constantinople to the supremacy over the churches of their own obedience was the true cause of this rupture.

LIII. A council was held by Nicholas III, the patriarch, about the year 1084, in which the decree made in the Council of Constantinople, A.D. 842, in favor of the use of images, was confirmed. Simeon, patriarch of Jerusalem, twenty-three archbishops and bishops, together with many heads of monasteries, were present. The case of Leo, archbishop of Chalcedon, was discussed, and his opinion unanimously condemned, which was to the effect that an *absolute* worship, and not merely *relative*, was due to the holy images. Leo himself submitted to the decision of the council, retracted, and was admitted to communion.

LIV. Held A.D.1118, under John IX, in which the sect of the Bogomili was condemned, and its leader Basilius anathematized and sentenced to be burned. This sect took its rise in Bulgaria. Like the Massalians, in earlier times, they attributed an excessive importance to prayer, and walked about perpetually muttering prayer to themselves; the Lord's prayer they repeated seven times every day, and five times in the night, many of them very much more frequently. From this habit of much praying they derived the name of Bogomili, which, in the Sclavonic language, means, "God have mercy upon us." In their heretical notions they resembled the Manichæans and Paulicians, which last sect arose about the same time. They affected an appearance of extreme sanctity, and wore the monkish dress. Their leader Basilius, a physician, had twelve principal followers whom he designated his apostles, and also some women, who went about spreading the poison of his doctrine everywhere. Basilius, when before the council, refused to deny his doctrine, and declared that he was willing to endure any torment, and death itself. One peculiar notion of this sect was, that no torment could affect them, and that the angels would deliver them even from the fire. Basilius himself was burned in this year. Several of his followers, when seized, retracted; others, among whom were some of those whom he called his apostles, were kept in prison and died there. Several councils were held upon this subject.

LV. Held A.D. 1143, Aug. 20, by the patriarch Michael Oxytes, in which the consecration of two bishops, Clemens and Leontius, performed by the metropolitan alone, was declared to be null and void. They were further condemned as favorers of the sect of the Bogomili. See Leo Allat. *Constit.* l, t. 11, cap. 12, p. 671.

LVI. Held about A.D. 1143. Nyphon, a monk (who had been sentenced in a previous council to be imprisoned until further evidence could be procured against him), was condemned for blasphemy; among other things, for saying, "anathema to the God of the Hebrews." He was put into prison, and remained there during the patriarchate of Michael. See Leo Allat. *Constit.* p. 681; Mansi, *Concil.* xviii; Baronius, *Annal.* A.D. 1143.

LVII. Held A.D. 1156, under the patriarch Lucas Chrysoberges; in which the errors of Soterichus Pantengenus, the patriarch-elect of Antioch, and of some others, were condemned. They asserted that the sacrifice upon the cross was offered to the Father and to the Holy Spirit alone, and not to the Word, the Son of God. The origin of this error seems to have been the fear of admitting the Nestorian doctrine of two persons in Jesus Christ. In a subsequent sitting Soterichus confessed his error, but was judged unworthy of the priesthood.

LVIII. Held A.D. 1261, by the emperor Michael Paleologus, to deliberate upon the recall of Arsenius I, the patriarch, who had withdrawn from Constantinople. The circumstances of the case were as follows: Arsenius (Antorianus) was a monk of Mount Athos, who had been raised to the office of patriarch of Constantinople by the emperor, Theodorus Lascaris II, in 1257. Upon the death of the latter, Michael Paleologus was, in the absence of Arsenius, appointed regent, and shortly after having been associated in the imperial dignity with the young emperor John, Arsenius was obliged, against his own wishes, to crown him; this, however, he did only upon condition that John should hold the first rank. Subsequently, seeing that this condition was not fulfilled, and that Michael was going on in an ill course, he withdrew from his see; to which Michael immediately appointed Nicephorus of Ephesus, in 1260, who died within a few months, when Michael convoked this council to consider about the expediency of recalling Arsenius. After some debate, in the course of which some of the bishops present maintained that Arsenius had not lawfully and canonically vacated the see, and others that he had sufficiently signified his abdication by his words and actions, it was resolved to send a deputation from the council to Arsenius to entreat him to return, which he subsequently did, the emperor promising to forget all that had passed.

LIX. Held A.D. 1266, by the same Michael Paleologus, in which the patriarch Arsenius was deposed and banished. Arsenius, after his recall in 1261, had given offence to the emperor by refusing to acknowledge the consecration of Nicephorus to the patriarchate during his absence; and subsequently learning that Michael had cruelly put out the eyes of the young emperor John, he had boldly excommunicated him; and, upon his continuing obstinate, he had, in a council held three years afterwards, entirely cut him off from the Church. Upon this Michael grievously persecuted him; and upon a false charge of having administered the holy communion to a Turkish prince, he was in this synod excommunicated, deposed, and banished, and Joseph set up in his place. This caused a schism among the Greeks of Constantinople, most of them refusing to acknowledge Joseph. Arsenius died in banishment in 1273.

LX. Held about A.D. 1277, in which John Veccus, or Boccus, who succeeded Joseph I in the patriarchate, made profession of the faith as held by the Church of Rome, and excommunicated those of the Greeks who refused to return into union with that Church. A long synodal letter was written to the pope, humbly deploring the division of the two churches, acknowledging the primacy of Rome, and confessing the Latin faith. This, however, was not done without great opposition; and a new schism arose. See Labbe, *Concil.* xi, 1032–1037.

LXI. Held A.D. 1280, May 3, by the same patriarch, John Veccus, at which eight metropolitans and eight archbishops were present. A passage was read from the writings of Gregory of Nyssa (beginning with these words, "Cum adduceret magnus Moyses"), in which the following words occur: "Spiritus vero Sanctus et a Patre dicitur et ex Filio esse affirmatur." The word "ex," it appeared, had been wilfully erased, and thus the sense of the passage was altered, which otherwise would have assisted towards the re-establishment of union between the churches, since it tended to prove that the Holy Spirit proceeds from the Son as well as from the Father. The zeal of Veccus for a reunion with Rome, and in favor of the Latin faith, brought upon him the ill-will of the Greeks. See Labbe, *Concil.* xi, 1125.

LXII. Held A.D. 1283, in which the patriarch Veccus was condemned; and at a council held the following year, in the palace of Blacquernæ, the celebrated treaty of union agreed upon at the Council of Lyons in 1274, and publicly ratified by Veccus, was annulled, and Veccus himself exiled.

LXIII. Held A.D. 1341, under John XIV, patriarch, who presided, the emperor, Andronicus III, being present. To this council Gregory Palamas, the chief of the Quietists or Hesycastæ, of Mount Athos, was cited to answer the accusation of Barlaam, a Calabrian monk (afterwards bishop of Gieræcé, in Calabria). These Quietists believed that by intense and constant contemplation it was possible to arrive at a tranquillity of mind entirely free from perturbation; and, accordingly, they used to sit in one fixed posture, gazing at the pit of their stomach (hence the title Umbilicani, given them by Barlaam), and pretended that, when so occupied, they could see a divine light beaming forth from the soul, and that this light was the glory of God and the same that illuminated Christ during the transfiguration. The event of the council, however, was that Gregory triumphed, and Barlaam was condemned, and made to ask pardon for his hasty accusation. He subsequently returned to Italy. See Labbe, *Concil.* xi, 1872.

Five other councils were held upon this same subject within the nine following years.

LXIV. A council was held about A.D. 1345, at which the two legates from Rome—Francis, archbishop of Bosphorus, and Richard, bishop of Chersonesus, an Englishman—were present. Their object was to enter into a negotiation for a union of the two churches. As neither the patriarch, John XIV, nor his bishops were capable of managing the business, Nicephorus Gregorius, a learned layman, was called in, by whose advice they avoided all discussion with the legates, and the matter fell to the ground.

LXV. Held about A.D. 1450, upon the subject of the union of the Greek and Latin churches, agreed upon at Florence in 1439. Gregory III, patriarch of Constantinople, was deposed, on account of the consent which he had given, as he allowed, willingly, to that union, and Athanasius elected to his place. This was done in the first session. In the second the unfair means used by the Latins at Florence, in order to effect the union, were dilated on. In the third the question of the procession of the Holy Spirit was argued, and the Latin doctrine on that subject endeavored to be refuted. In the fourth they discussed the following subjects:

1. The authority claimed by the pope over the Oriental and all other churches.
2. The fire of purgatory.
3. The fruition of the saints.
4. The words of consecration.

In all of these they differed from the view taken by the Roman Church. They then added twenty-five articles of complaint against the Latin Church:

1. That they did not paint the images like the archetype.
2. That they adapted secular tunes to ecclesiastical psalmody.
3. That they permitted men and women to sit together in their churches.
4. That they forbade marriage to the clergy.
5. That they did not pray towards the East.
6. That they used unleavened bread in the holy sacrifice.
7. That they asserted whatever is in God to be substance.
8. That the pope had that cross depicted upon his feet which Christ carried on his shoulder.
9. That they allowed the bed-ridden (*cubantem*) to participate in the holy mysteries, and that not with sufficient reverence.
10. That they accepted money from harlots.
11. That they fasted on Saturdays.
12. That they, contrary to the decree of the seventh synod, made paintings to represent the Father.
13. That in crossing themselves they began on the left.
14. That the pope usurped a secular authority.
15. That the pope, for money, absolved Christians from the obligation to fast.
16. That, contrary to holy Scripture, they permitted parents to make their eldest sons sole heirs.
17. That they gave to the image of Christ and to the cross the worship of Latria, which is due only to the Word.
18. That they adored images.
19. That they permitted priests, in a state of fornication, to celebrate mass.
20. That they did not at once anoint the heads of the baptized.
21. That they did not pray *standing* on Saturdays and Sundays.
22. That they ate of things suffocated.
23. That they punished with *temporal fires* those who erred in the faith.
24. That they did not enjoin those who had done any injury to any one to seek forgiveness of him.

The synod, which was numerously attended, ended with the fifth session. See Labbe, *Concil.* xiii, 1365.

LXVI. Held A.D. 1593. A great synod, in which Jeremiah II, patriarch of Constantinople, and Meletius of Alexandria presided. All things relating to the foundation of the new patriarchate of Moscow were confirmed in this council. Up to the end of the 16th century Kieff, which was then the metropolis of Russia, was under the jurisdiction of the patriarch of Constantinople; but about that time Jeremiah II, being at Moscow, the monks of that city earnestly besought him that the people and empire of Moscow might be subjected to an archbishop, *αὐτοκέφαλος*, "qui sui juris esset;" subject, that is, to no superior. This petition the patriarch at once, of his own accord, granted, and confirmed his promise by an oath, at the same time giving a deed drawn up in the Sclavonic tongue, by which the new patriarchate of Moscow was erected; which deed was subscribed by all the priests and monks who were present with him. Having executed this deed, Jeremiah convoked a synod on Jan. 26, 1589, in the imperial city of Moscow, composed of all the bishops and abbots of the empire; in which, the liturgy having been first said in the presence of the emperor, his wife, and the whole senate, Job, archbishop of Rostof, was elected, and declared the first primate and patriarch of the empire of Moscow. Upon the return of Jeremiah to Constantinople, a numerous council of bishops was assembled in the month of February, 1593, by which the erection of the new patriarchate of Moscow was confirmed; and it was declared to be just and right that the state of Moscow, strictly orthodox, etc., should receive ecclesiastical honors in accordance with the spirit of the twenty-eighth canon of Chalcedon, and for other sufficient reasons there stated. Then it was settled and decreed that the Church of Moscow should be thenceforward a patriarchate; that all Russia, with its tributaries northwards, should be subject to it in all matters ecclesiastical; and that the patriarch of Moscow should rank next after the patriarch of Jerusalem, and take precedence of all metropolitans, archbishops, and bishops throughout the whole Catholic and Orthodox Church of Christ. It was further decreed that the election of the patriarch of Moscow should be confirmed by the patriarch of Constantinople, to whom a fixed tribute should be paid. Job, archbishop of Rostof, was then consecrated primate of the empire of Moscow, and patriarch.

LXVII. Held A.D. 1638, Sept. 24, by Cyril of Berœa, patriarch of Constantinople, for the purpose of anathematizing the memory of Cyril Lucar, his predecessor, who died about three months previously, and who was accused of holding many of the peculiar tenets of Calvin. It was decreed that Cyril Lucar should be publicly denounced, and delivered over to an anathema, as well as all those who received his vain dogmas. Thirteen anathemas were then published against him, of which the following is a summary:

1. To Cyril, surnamed Lucar, who has falsely asserted that the whole Eastern Church is of the same belief as Calvin, anathema.
2. To Cyril, who teaches and believes that the holy Church of Christ can lie, anathema.
3. To Cyril, who teaches and believes that God has chosen some to glory before the foundation of the world, and predestinated them without works, and has reprobated others without cause, and that the works of none are sufficient to demand a reward before the tribunal of Christ, anathema.
4. To Cyril, who teaches and believes that the saints are not our mediators and intercessors with God, anathema.
5. To Cyril, who teaches and believes that man is not endued with free will, but that every man has the power of sinning, but not of doing good, anathema.
6. To Cyril, who teaches and believes that there are not seven sacraments, but that only two, i. e. baptism and the eucharist, were handed down to us by Christ in his gospel, anathema.
7. To Cyril, who teaches and believes that the bread offered at the altar, and also the wine, is not changed by the blessing of the priest, and the descent of the Holy Ghost, into the real body and blood of Christ, anathema.
8. To Cyril, who teaches and believes that they who have fallen asleep in piety and good works are not assisted by the alms of their relations and the prayers of the Church, anathema.
9. To Cyril, a new Iconoclast, and the worst of all, anathema.

The 10th and 11th are merely an amplification of the 9th, and the 12th and 13th a recapitulation and enforcement of the whole.

The acts of the council are signed by three patriarchs, viz. Cyril of Constantinople, Metrophanes of Alexandria, and Theophanes of Jerusalem; also by twenty-four archbishops and bishops, and by twenty-one dignitaries of the great Church of Constantinople. See Neale, *Hist. of the Oriental Church.*

LXVIII. Held A.D. 1641, by Parthenius; eight prelates and four dignitaries of the Church attended. The teaching of Cyril Lucar was again condemned, and the use of the word *μετουσίωσις* authorized to express the change in the elements after consecration; but this was not done without opposition, as it was a term unknown to the fathers, and the offspring of Latin scholasticism. See Neale, *Hist. of the Oriental Church.*

LXIX (Council of Jassy), A.D. 1642. Held at Jassy, in Moldavia, but commonly named the synod of Constantinople. Parthenius, the œcumenical patriarch, presided; and the acts of the council (which are incorporated with and authenticated by those of the Council of Bethlehem, A.D. 1672) are signed by twenty-three archbishops and bishops, among whom was Peter Mogilas, archbishop of Kieff, the author of the *Confessio Orthodoxæ Ecclesiæ Catholicæ et Orientalis*, which, as revised by Meletius Syriga, was formally approved. Most of the signatures, however, appear to have been added subsequently, the number of prelates actually present being small.

The decrees of this synod are contained in seventeen chapters, and the condemnation of Cyril Lucar is more fully expressed than it had been in the synod of 1638. All the chapters of Cyril, except the seventh on the incarnation, are condemned. See Neale, *Hist. of the Oriental Church;* Labbe, *Concil.* xv, 1713.

LXX. Held A.D. 1718, April 12; the patriarch, Jeremiah of Constantinople, Samuel of Alexandria, and Chrysanthus of Jerusalem being present, with the clergy of the Church of Constantinople. In this council the twelve proposals of the Scotch and English nonjuring bishops upon the subject of a union between the Greek Church and the nonjuring British churches was considered. The circumstances which led to this scheme were as follows: In 1716 Arsenius, metropolitan of the Thebaid, in Egypt, was in London, and the Scotch bishop, Campbell, forming an acquaintance with him, was led to mention the subject of a union to him. Arsenius entered warmly into the matter, and undertook to forward to the Orientals any proposals upon the subject which the British bishops might agree upon. In consequence twelve proposals were drawn up, which were translated into Greek by bishop Spinkes, and to them was added a declaration expressing wherein they agreed and disagreed with the Oriental Church. The five points of disagreement were as follows:

1. That they denied to the canons of œcumenical councils the same authority with holy Scripture.
2. That they could not pay any kind of worship to the Blessed Virgin.
3. That they could not pray to saints or angels.
4. That they could give no religious veneration to images.
5. That they could not worship the host in the eucharistic sacrifice.

In 1721 "The answer of the orthodox in the East to the proposals sent from Britain for a union and agreement with the Oriental Church" was transmitted through Arsenius, who was then at Moscow. This answer was the synodical judgment agreed upon in this council; it was contained in a long paper, in Greek, accepting the twelve proposals and the articles of agreement, under certain explanations, but warmly defending the Greek Church on the subject of the five articles of disagreement, and insisting upon an entire conformity in each of these particulars. At the same time they forwarded the two declarations of their Church drawn up in the synod of Constantinople (or Bethlehem), under Doritheus, in 1672, and in that under Callinicus, in 1791. See Skinner, *Eccles. Hist. of Scotland*, ii, 634.

LXXI. Held A.D. 1723, in September, upon the same subject as the preceding—Jeremiah of Constantinople, Athanasius of Antioch, Chrysanthus of Jerusalem, Callinicus of Heraclea, Auxentius of Cyzicum, Paisius of Nicomedia, Gerasimus of Nicæa, Parthenius of Chalcedon, Ignatius of Thessalonica, Arsenius of Prusa, Theoctistus of Polypolis, and Callinicus of Varna being present. Upon the receipt of the synodical judgment of the last council, the English bishops, in a synod held at London, in May, 1722, drew up a reply defending their former position by appropriate passages from Holy Scripture and from the fathers, and concluding with the following proposal:

"If our liberty, therefore, is left us in the instances above mentioned; if the Oriental patriarchs and bishops will authentically declare us not obliged to the invocation of saints and angels, the worship of images and the adoration of the host; if they please publicly and authoritatively, by an instrument under their hands, to pronounce us perfectly disengaged in these particulars, both at home and abroad, in their churches and in our own: these relaxing concessions allowed, we hope, may answer the overtures on both sides, and conciliate a union."

In the present council this second communication of the British bishops was considered, and a final answer drawn up and forwarded, telling the Anglican prelates that they had nothing to say different from their former reply; and, far from acceding to any compromise, they boldly declare that

"These doctrines have been long since examined, and rightly and religiously defined and settled by the holy and œcumenical synods, so that it is neither lawful to add anything to them, nor to take anything from them; therefore, they who are disposed to agree with us in the divine doctrines of the orthodox faith must necessarily follow and submit to what has been defined and determined by the ancient fathers and by the holy and œcumenical synods, from the time of the apostles and their holy successors, the fathers of our Church, to this time; we say they must submit to them with sincerity and obedience, and without any scruple or dispute, and this is a sufficient answer to what you have written."

To this epistle they added the confession of faith agreed upon in the synod of Bethlehem, in 1672. See Skinner, *Eccles. Hist. of Scotland*, ii, 637.

In addition to the foregoing, Richard et Giraud (*Bibliothèque Sacrée*, viii, 158 sq.) give several less important councils held at Constantinople, as follows:

I. In 351, against Athanasius.
II. In 438, in favor of the Catholic faith.
III. In 439, on the pretended primacy of the Church at Antioch.
IV. In 451, on the conversion of the Eutychians.
V. In 497, in which Macedonius condemned the defenders of the Council of Chalcedon.
VI. In 520, by Epiphanius, patriarch of Constantinople, concerning his ordination. The council wrote a letter to pope Hormisdas on the subject.
VII. In 560, a synod of Eutychians, followers of Julian of Halicarnassus.
VIII. In 806, by order of Nicephorus, successor to Constantine VII, in which Joseph Œconomos of Constantinople was restored, whom the patriarch Tarasius had degraded for having crowned Theodora, concubine of Constantine.
IX. In 808, in which Constantine's marriage with Theodora was ratified, and several eminent persons were exiled.
X. In 814, by Nicephorus, patriarch of Constantinople, with sixty-six bishops. Antonius, an iconoclastic bishop of Pamphylia, was excommunicated. Mansi places three councils in this year (*Concil.* i, 807).
XI. In 821, in which the Catholic bishops refused to unite in council with heretics, as the emperor Michael II had proposed.
XII. In 832, against image worship.
XIII. In 854, in which Gregory, bishop of Syracuse, was deposed by Ignatius of Constantinople. Mansi assigns this to the year 847 or 848 (*Concil.* i, 930).
XIV. In 856, during the absence of the patriarch Ignatius, in which the adherents of Gregory of Syracuse were condemned (Mansi, i, 947).
XV. In 901, in which Nicholas the Mystic, patriarch of Constantinople, condemned the marriage of the emperor Leo with his fourth wife (Labbe, ix).
XVI. In 944, to depose Trypho, whom Constantine VIII had intruded into the patriarchate of Constantinople until his own son, Theophylact, should be of sufficient age for the office (Labbe, ix; Hardouin, vi).
XVII. In 963, to absolve the emperor Nicephoras Phocas from the ban which the patriarch Polyeuctes had imposed upon him for having two wives; the emperor taking oath of his innocence.
XVIII. In 969 a celebrated dispute was held at Constantinople between the Catholics and the Jacobites, by order of the emperor Nicephorus (Renaudot, *Liturgies Orientales*, ii, 489; Assemani, *Bibliothèque Orientale*, ii, 133; Mansi, *Concil.* supplement, i, 1159).
XIX. In 975, when the patriarch Basil, convicted of crime, was deposed, and Antonius Studites put into his place (Baronius, *Annales*, s. an.).
XX. In 1026, when the patriarch Alexis excommunicated the seditious (Mansi, *Concil.* append. i, 74).
XXI. In 1027, when the same patriarch condemned the sale or transfer of monasteries.
XXII. In 1028, when the same patriarch made certain rules concerning bishops.
XXIII. In 1052, when the patriarch Michael Cærularius defended the marriage of relatives in the seventh degree.
XXIV. In 1066, when the patriarch John Xiphilin declared that there was no difference between marriage and regular betrothal as to the impediments between the parents.
XXV. In 1067, on the same subject.
XXVI. In 1081, when the marriage of two cousins, one of them to a mother, and the other to a daughter, was annulled.
XXVII. In the same year, when the emperor Alexis Comnenus was forbidden to dismember episcopates.
XXVIII. In 1166, when Demetrius Lampenus and others were exiled for having falsely accused the Germans of heresy respecting the divine nature. Marriage was also allowed to the seventh degree of relationship inclusively (Mansi, ii).
XXIX. In 1168, when the Greek Church was entirely separated from the Roman.
XXX. In 1285, on a passage in bk. i, cap. v, of John of Damascus's book on the orthodox faith (Hardouin, vii).
XXXI. In 1297, concerning the anathema hurled by the patriarch Athanasius against the emperor (Mansi, iii).
XXXII. In 1299, in which the marriage of prince Alexis was judged valid, although contracted against the consent of his uncle the emperor.
XXXIII. In 1443, when the patriarch Metrophanes, who had been very zealous for the union of the Greek and Anglican churches, was deposed (Ælatius, *De Concensione*, iii).
XXXIV. In 1565, when the patriarch Joshaphat was deposed for simony.

Constantinus is the name of several early saints and prelates besides those given below and under CONSTANTINE:

1. Bishop in the Romagna in the 4th century, addressed by Ambrose, A.D. 379 (Epistles in Migne, *Patrol. Lat.* xvi, p. 878, 1245; Ceillier, v, 480).

2. Bishop of Laodicea, originally a *magister militum*, consecrated in 510 bishop of Laodicea. He was a leading Monophysite, and as such was deposed by Justin I in the year 518. He is commemorated by the Jacobites on June 26 (Assemani, *Bibl. Orient.* ii, 327; Le Quien, *Oriens Christianus*).

3. Abbot of Monte Cassino after the death of St. Benedict. He ruled the monastery from A.D. 543 to cir. 560. He was one of the four whom St. Gregory consulted as witnesses to the life and works of their founder (Ceillier, xi, 634).

4. *Saint*, is said in the breviary of Aberdeen to have been the son of Paternus, king of Cornwall. He went as a missionary to Scotland, where he was martyred in Cantire, about the end of the 6th century (Forbes, *Kal. of Scot. Saints*, p. 311-314; Butler, *Lives of the Saints*, iii, 148, 149; Lanigan, *Eccl. Hist. of Ireland*, i, 486; ii, 165).

5. Surnamed, or perhaps christened, *Silvanus*, the founder of the Paulicians, was born in Armenia in the latter half of the 7th century. By order of the emperor Constantinus Pogonatus, he was stoned to death. See PAULICIANS.

6. Bishop of Nacolia, in Phrygia, about A.D. 727, the principal supporter, among other bishops, of the emperor Leo III, the Isaurian, in his polemic against images.

7. Constantinus and Peregrinus, *Saints*, were two bishops whose relics were found in the church at Gemirge, in Normandy, but it is not known when or where they lived. They are commemorated in that church June 15.

Constantinus, an Italian martyr, was a citizen of Rome, and for the defence of the Gospel being condemned to be burned, was put in a dung-cart; who, thereat rejoicing, said that he was reputed here as excrements of this world, but yet his death was a sweet odor unto God. This occurred at Rome in 1542. See Fox, *Acts and Monuments*, iv, 398.

Constantinus (or **Constantius**) OF ANTIOCH, a Greek theologian, was priest of the metropolitan church of Antioch, and destined to succeed Flavian, bishop of that place. Porphyry, who desired to obtain this episcopal see, by intrigue at the court of Constantinople obtained of Arcadius an order of exile against Constantinus, who, by the aid of his friends, escaped to Cyprus, where he appears to have passed the remainder of his days. He died about 410 of the Christian æra. He placed in order the thirty-four *Homilies* of John Chrysostom, upon the epistle to the Hebrews. Among the letters of Chrysostom there are two addressed to Constantinus, and he appears to be the author of two other letters attributed generally to Chrysostom. See Hoefer, *Nouv. Biog. Générale*, s. v.

Constantinus LICHUDES, a Greek theologian, was at first protovestiary, and was appointed patriarch of Constantinople in 1058. We have from him two synodal decrees, one upon a culpable slave, the other upon a priest arrested for murder. These two decrees are found, with a Latin translation, in the *Jus Græco-romanum* of Leunclavius. See Hoefer, *Nouv. Biog. Générale*, s. v.

Constantinus MELITENIOTA, a Greek theologian, lived about 1276. A partisan of the union of the Greek and Latin churches, he was exiled to Bithynia, where he died. He wrote the two following treatises: *De Ecclesiastica Unione Latinorum et Græcorum:—De Processione Spiritus Sancti.* These were published, with a Latin translation, in the *Græcia Orthodoxa* of Leo Allatius. See Hoefer, *Nouv. Biog. Générale*, s. v.

Constantinus TIBERIUS, antipope, did not await the death of Paul I in order to obtain the papal power. He was elected in 767 by the influence of his brother Toto, or Teuto, duke of Nepi, who installed him by force of arms. Constantinus was a layman. He assumed the deaconry, disdained the priesthood, and was ordained bishop by George, bishop of Preneste, and afterwards consecrated pope by the same George, assisted by Eustrasius, bishop of Albano, and by Citonatus, bishop of Oporto. A little later, another intruder, Philip, priest of St. Vito, and cardinal-priest, proclaimed himself. He excited a sedition in which Toto was killed. Constantinus took refuge with his other brother Passicus, in the oratorio of St. Cæsarius. He was pursued, dragged from his retreat, and imprisoned in the monastery of Cella Nova, where he was cruelly treated. Stephen IV was named and acknowledged sovereign pontiff, Aug. 5, 768. In April, 769, a council was convoked in St. John of Lateran, which decided that one could not be raised to the papacy who had not been ordained deacon and priest. The election of Constantinus was thus annulled, and he was condemned to pass the remainder of his days in a monastery. During his usurpation he had created eight bishops, eight priests, and four deacons, who could not be confirmed. The letters of the antipope were published by the Jesuit Gretser (Ingolstadt, 1613), and by Duchesne, in his *Collection des Historiens de France.* See Hoefer, *Nouv. Biog. Générale*, s. v.

Constantinus I was 38th patriarch of Constantinople, and succeeded John V, A.D. 674. He died A.D. 677, and was followed by Theodore I (Theophanes, *Chronog.* p. 295).

Constantinus II was 47th patriarch of Constantinople, A.D. 745, according to Theophanes (*Chronog.* p. 660). He had previously been a monk and bishop of Syllium. In A.D. 764, owing to the emperor Constantine Copronymus's ill-will, he was exiled, and in 767 was deposed by Nicetas, who afterwards succeeded him. After enduring horrible cruelties from his enemies, he was beheaded in the year 776 (Niceph. Constantin. *Breviarium*, p. 48). See Smith, *Dict. of Christ. Biog.* s. v.

Constantius, *Saint* (1), a martyr, was born at Perugia. His upright character gained for him the appointment of bishop of his native city. Some years afterwards he was arrested, conducted to Assisi, and beheaded near Ypsello or Foligno. According to the *Bibliothèque Sacrée* the life of this saint, as published by the Bollandists, is not trustworthy. It is certain that the worship of St. Constantius is very ancient, and that there is a church near Perugia which bears his name, also a district of Foligno which is called the country of St. Constantius. He is honored Jan. 29. See Hoefer, *Nouv. Biog. Générale*, s. v.

Constantius, *Saint* (2), lived about 550. He was sacristan of San Stefano, near Ancona. His poverty was great and his humility profound. He is honored Sept. 23. See Hoefer, *Nouv. Biog. Générale*, s. v.

Constantius is likewise the name of a number of early Christian bishops or other notable ecclesiastics. See also CONSTANTINE; CONSTANTINUS.

1. Bishop of Faenza, in the Romagna, A.D. 313, present at the Council of Rome concerning Cæcilian.

2. Bishop of Siscia (in Pannonia, now Sissek, on the Save), attended the Council of Aquileia, A.D. 381.

3. Bishop of Arausio (Orange), was present at the same council.

4 and **5.** Two presbyters of Antioch in the time of Chrysostom.

6. A Manichæan at Rome, in Augustine's time.

7. Bishop of Uzès (Ucetia) in Gaul, A.D. 419.

8. Also called CONSTANTINUS, deacon and secretary of Eutyches, present at the Council of Constantinople, A.D. 448.

9. A bishop sent by Hilary of Arles, in the 5th century, along with bishop Nectarius, to Leo of Rome, on a question of jurisdiction.

10. A priest of Lyons, in the latter half of the 5th century, of noble extraction and literary character, the friend of Sidonius, who gives us our only knowledge of him and his brave exploits when Clermont was besieged by the Visigoths (*Epist.* i, 1; iii, 2; vii, 18; ix, 16).

11. A bishop directed by Avitus (bishop of Vienne, in France, A.D. 497–517) not to refuse communion to trivial offenders.

12. A monk of the abbey of Classis, who failed to be appointed abbot there in the time of Gregory the Great.

13. Bishop of Albi, at the Council of Rheims, A.D. 625, and living in 647. He wrote a joint letter with Dado Desiderius of Cahors (Migne, *Patrol.* lxxxvii, 217).

14. Also called CONSTANTINUS, presbyter of Apamea, in Syria, who explained his peculiar views on Christology at the third Council of Constantinople, A.D. 680, but was excommunicated therefor. See Smith, *Dict. of Christ. Biog.* s. v.

Consuetudinary, in ecclesiastical usage, is a term for (1) the *ritual* or book of constitutions for ceremonials and official duties; (2) a *custumal* or rental of estates.

Consulter WITH FAMILIAR SPIRITS. See NECROMANCER.

Consus (is thought to be derived from *conditus.*

"hidden," or from *consulo*, "to advise") was an ancient Roman god, probably to be referred to the worship of the deities in the infernal regions. When the Roman state was threatened with destruction, because of a scarcity of women, Romulus decided on the rape of the Sabine girls. He pretended to have found hidden in the earth an altar of an unknown god, in whose honor plays were to be celebrated, and for this purpose all neighboring nations were invited. In memory of the success of the scheme there was a yearly festival held, called *Consualia*, at the celebration of which an altar was dug from the earth and plays were performed.

Contacium (*κοντάκιον*) is a name given in the ritual of the Greek Church to a short hymn, and also to the volume containing special liturgies.

Contancin, CYRIQUE, a French Jesuit missionary, was born at Bourges in 1670. In 1700 he was sent to the Chinese missions, and did not return to France until 1731, when he was brought back by some affairs connected with his order. Being appointed superior-general in China, he went to Port Louis, where he took ship Nov. 16, 1733, but died at sea a few days afterwards. His long sojourn in Asia afforded him opportunity for collecting curious documents, and these were published in the *Lettres Édifiantes.* See Hoefer, *Nouv. Biog. Générale,* s. v.

Contant (or **Constant** DE LA MOLLETTE), **Philippe du,** a French theologian, was born at Saint-André, Dauphiné, Aug. 29, 1737. He completed his studies at the Sorbonne, and received the degree of doctor in 1765, preparing a thesis in six languages upon the Holy Scripture, which was published at Paris the same year. He was afterwards vicar-general of Vienne. He was beheaded in 1793. He wrote, *La Genèse Expliquée* (Paris, 1773):—*Essai sur l'Écriture Sainte* (ibid. 1775; this work is preceded by a plate containing several Oriental alphabets):—*Nouvelle Méthode pour Entrer dans le Vrai sens de l'Écriture Sainte* (ibid. 1777):—*L'Exode Expliqué* (ibid. 1780):—*Les Psaumes Expliqués* (ibid. 1781):—*Traité sur la Poésie et la Musique des Hébreux* (ibid. eod.):—*Le Lévitique Expliqué* (ibid. 1785):—*Nouvelle Bible Polyglotte* (very rare). See Hoefer, *Nouv. Biog. Générale,* s. v.

Contant, Pierre, an eminent French architect, was born in 1698 at Ivry-sur-Seine, and studied under Watteau. He erected the convent of Panthemont and the church de la Madeleine, in Paris, and also designed the beautiful church of St. Waast, at Arras. He died at Paris in 1777. See Spooner, *Biog. Hist. of the Fine Arts,* s. v.; Hoefer, *Nouv. Biog. Générale,* s. v.

Contarini, Camillo, an Italian scholar, was born at Venice, Jan. 3, 1644. He completed his studies at the Clementine College in Rome, returned to his native city in 1663, and entered upon public employments with zeal and wisdom. Later he became member of the grand council, and there distinguished himself by his eloquence. He married Maria Donato in 1679, but after her death, in 1698, he took, March 30, 1710, the ecclesiastical habit, and went to Rome, where he presented to Clement XI the first volume of his historical works. He died at Venice, Aug. 17, 1722, leaving *L'Inganno Riconosciuto* (Venice, 1666):—*L'Arbace,* a musical tragedy (ibid. 1667):—*La Genealogia de Domini* (Amsterdam, 1693):—*Istoria della Guerra di Leopoldi I, Imperatore, Contra il Turco, dell' Anno* 1683:—*Il Traditore Tradito,* a tragedy (Venice, 1714):—*Annali delle Guerre per la Monarchia delle Spagne* (ibid. 1720–1722). See Hoefer, *Nouv. Biog. Générale,* s. v.

Contarini, Giovanni, an eminent Venetian painter, was born in 1549, and applied himself at an early age to the study of the works of Titian. He travelled in Germany, where he met with great encouragement from the princes and nobility, especially at the court of the emperor Rudolph II. In the church Della Croce, at Venice, is a picture by this artist of *The Crucifixion,* and in San Francesco is *The Resurrection.* His principal work, however, now in the Louvre, represents the *Virgin and Infant Enthroned, with St. Mark and St. Sebastian.* He died in 1605. See Spooner, *Biog. Hist. of the Fine Arts,* s. v.; Hoefer, *Nouv. Biog. Générale,* s. v.

Contarizo, LUIGI, an Italian theologian, who lived in the early half of the 17th century, wrote *Il Vago e Dilettevole Giardino* (Vicenza, 1602). See Hoefer, *Nouv. Biog. Générale,* s. v.

Conte, Guido del, an artist, so called, whose real name was *Fassi,* a native of Carpi, was born in 1584. He was the inventor of a kind of work called by the Italians scagliola or mischio. From him this method rapidly spread throughout all Italy. Some of his scholars far surpassed him in the execution of altars for churches. He died in 1649. See Spooner, *Biog. Hist. of the Fine Arts,* s. v.

Conte, Jacopino del, a Florentine painter, was born in 1510, and studied under Andrea del Sarto. His principal pictures in Rome are, *St. John Preaching* and *The Descent from the Cross,* in San Giovanni Decollato; *The Dead Christ* and *St. Francis Receiving the Stigmata,* at the Cappuccini á Monte Cavallo. He died at Rome in 1598. See Spooner, *Biog. Hist. of the Fine Arts,* s. v.; Hoefer, *Nouv. Biog. Générale,* s. v.

Contee, BENJAMIN, D.D., a Protestant Episcopal minister, was born at Benfield, Charles Co., Md., in 1755. When the war of the Revolution broke out he entered the American army, and held a commission in 1776. After independence was declared he visited France, Spain, and England. He was a scholarly man, very courteous in his manner. In 1789 he was elected a representative to the first Congress under the new constitution. Though not a public debater, he was profound in investigation and wise in counsel. Washington was his personal friend. Returning from Congress, his father established him as a merchant in Nottingham, Md.; but he was unsuccessful, and returned to Blenheim, where he had been married. Subsequently he became a planter. He accepted the appointment of chief judge of the testamentary court of Charles County, which he held during his life. In May, 1802, the parish of William and Mary, in Charles County, of which he had been vestryman, solicited him to enter holy orders and become their pastor, to which he consented. In June, 1803, he obtained deacon's orders, and in 1805 was placed on the standing committee, and became the official visitor of his own and the adjoining county, a position which he held ever after. The adjoining parish, Trinity, invited him to its pulpits about this time, and he continued to preach there during the following five years, although one church was twelve and the other twenty miles distant from his home. Bishop Claggett's health failing, Dr. Contee became, in August, 1811, rector of St. Paul's parish, a part of the bishop's charge, and in this pastorate he continued for three years. During this time he had five places of worship to supply, the most distant being forty miles away. In 1812 he came very near being elected assistant to the bishop. In 1813 he began to curtail his field of labor, giving up Trinity Church and St. Paul's. William and Mary, the parish in which he resided, was held by him until the date of his death, Jan. 23, 1816. His character was distinguished by self-denial, great zeal, and devotion. See Sprague, *Annals of the Amer. Pulpit,* v, 487.

Contelorio, FELICE, an Italian theologian, was born at Spoleto in 1590. He was doctor of theology and keeper of the Vatican library, and died at Rome, Sept. 28, 1652. He wrote various religious treatises, for which see Hoefer, *Nouv. Biog. Générale,* s. v.; Jöcher, *Allgemeines Gelehrten-Lexikon,* s. v.

Contenson, VINCENT, a French theologian, was

born at Altivillare, in the diocese of Condom, about 1640. He took the Dominican habit at Toulouse, Feb. 2, 1657, and taught philosophy at Albi, then theology at Toulouse. He was very learned, and occupied the chair of eloquence. He died at Creil, Dec. 26, 1674, leaving, *Theologia Mentis et Cordis* (Lyons, 1675, 1681, 1687). See Hoefer, *Nouv. Biog. Générale*, s. v.; Wetzer u. Welte, *Kirchen-Lexikon*, s. v.

Contextus (Contestus, Contestius, or **Contessus)**, *Saint*, an early Christian prelate, is said to have been born near Bayeux, in Gaul, and to have been pious from early youth. He preached so zealously against the prevalent vices as to be subject not only to popular dislike, but to Satanic temptations; but persevered, and in advanced age was made bishop of Bayeux, A.D. cir. 480–513. He is famed for his virtues and good deeds, and his body was translated to Fiscannum (Fécamp). His festival is on Jan. 19.

Conthigirnus. See KENTIGERN.

Continency is that moral virtue by which we restrain concupiscence. There is this distinction between chastity and continence: chastity requires no effort, because it may result from constitution; whereas continency appears to be the consequence of a victory gained over ourselves. The term is usually applied to men, as chastity is to women. See CHASTITY.

Contingent, happening without a foreknown cause, commonly called accidental. An event not come to pass is said to be contingent, which either may or may not be; what is already done is said to have been contingent, if it might or might not have been. What is contingent or casual to us is not so with God. As effects stand related to a second cause, they are oftentimes contingent; but as they stand related to the first cause, they are acts of God's counsel, and directed by his wisdom. See NECESSITY; WILL.

Contobabditæ were a section of the *Agnoëtæ* (q. v.).

Contra votum is a formula of regret in early Christian epitaphs, adopted from paganism after the 8th century, especially in Northern Italy.

Contra-remonstrants. See REMONSTRANTS.

Contract of Marriage may be considered in two senses:

I. *Agreement for Marriage in the Abstract.* The law of the Church on this point is, as on many other points, compounded of the Jewish and Roman laws, under the influence of New-Testament teaching. It is derived mainly from the latter system of legislation, especially in regard to the marriage of the laity; from the former mainly, in regard to that of the clergy. The validity of the marriage-contract generally depends on two points:

1. Strictly speaking, the inherent capacity of the parties for marriage turns only upon three particulars:

(*a*) *Sufficient Age.* On this it may be observed that the old Roman, like the old Jewish law, attached the capacity for marriage by age to the physical fact of puberty; and the same principle is practically followed in all systems of legislation which take notice of age at all in this matter, although it is generally found convenient in the long run to fix an age of legal puberty, without reference to the specific fact. Thus, in the *Digest*, it is provided that the marriage contract is only valid on the part of the wife when she has completed her twelfth year, even though she be already married and living with her husband. Justinian himself, in his *Institutes*, professes to have fixed, on grounds of decency, the age of puberty for the male at fourteen; both which periods have very generally been adopted in modern legislation.

The earlier Roman legislation seems to have fixed an age beyond which a woman could not marry, since we find Justinian abolishing all prohibitions of the earlier Roman law against marriages between men and women above sixty and fifty. Nothing of this kind is to be found in later systems of legislation, although disparity of age in marriage has sometimes been sought to be suppressed.

Physical incapacity in persons of full age has never been held to produce actual inability to enter into the marriage contract, but simply to render the marriage voidable when the fact is ascertained. Nor is the fact one of importance in reference to the marriage relation, except where divorce is put under restrictions. See IMPOTENCY.

(*b*) *Defect of Reason* acts inversely to defect of age. Thus, madness was fatal to the validity of the contract, but did not dissolve it when afterwards supervening.

(*c*) *The Freedom of Will* of the parties, on the other hand, can only be testified by their consent to the marriage (see CONSENT); but it may also be indirectly secured, by limitations of a protective character placed on the exercise of the capacity to contract marriage. According to the jurists of the *Digest*, a man might marry a woman by letters or by proxy if she were brought to his house, but this privilege did not belong to the woman.

There was one large class of persons in whom there was held to be no freedom of will, and, consequently, no capacity to contract marriage. Marriage is simply impossible where the persons of slaves of both sexes are subject, absolutely without limit, to the lusts, natural or unnatural, of a master. The slave, his master's thing, can have no will but his master's; in respect of the civil law, properly so called, i. e. the law made for citizens, he does not exist; his condition is almost equivalent to death itself. Thus the Roman law has never mentioned connections between slaves. Connections between slaves and serfs are indeed mentioned, but without the name of marriage, and only to determine the condition of the offspring, which is fixed by that of the mother. *Rustici*, a class of peasants who seem to have been of higher status than the "serfs," could contract marriage among themselves.

The recognition of slaves' marriages originated, not in the Roman law, but unquestionably in the Jewish law. Although only "Hebrew" servants are mentioned in the passage of Exodus on this subject (xxi, 3, 4, 5, 6), it is clear that the Pentateuch recognised the marriage of persons in a servile condition. With the sweeping away by the Christian dispensation of all distinction between Jew and Gentile it is but natural to suppose that the right of marriage would be extended from the Hebrew slave to the whole slave class. Such right, indeed, was not absolute, as will have been observed, but flowed from the master's will, and was subject to his rights. The master *gave* a wife to his slave; the wife and her children remained his, even when the slave himself obtained his freedom. As respects the marriage of slaves, it appears clearly to have been recognised both by the State and the Church in the reign of Charlemagne.

2. The *Extrinsic Conditions* of the capacity for marriage were very various. Some are purely or mainly moral ones; the leading one of this class, that of the amount of consanguinity which the law of different nations has held to be a bar to the validity of the nuptial contract, will be found treated of under the heads of AFFINITY; COUSINS-GERMAN. Another—singular, because exactly opposite feelings on the subject have prevailed in different countries—is to be found in the prohibition by the later Roman law of marriages between ravishers and their victims, under severe penalties, both for the parties themselves, and the parents who consented to it (Justinian, *Cod.* b. ix, t. xiii, § 1, *Nov.* 143, 150).

Another limitation on the marriage contract, which must be considered rather of a political nature, and which prevails more or less still in the military code of almost every modern nation, was that on the marriage of soldiers. Under the early Roman polity, marriage was absolutely forbidden to soldiers; but the emperor

Claudius allowed them the right, and it seems certain that there were married soldiers under Galba and Domitian. Severus seems, however, to have been the first to allow soldiers to live with their wives. Philip I and II, on the other hand, seem to have restricted soldiers to a first marriage. Under Justinian's Code, the marriage of soldiers and other persons in the *militia* was made free, without solemnities of any sort, so long as the wife was free-born. There having been no regular armies among the barbarian races, nothing answering to the prohibition is to be found in their codes.

There were also restrictions on marriage which must be considered protective in their character, and intended to secure real freedom, as well as the wisdom of choice. To these, in the highest view of the subject, belong those which turn upon the consent of parents (see CONSENT); although this restriction seems generally to have had its historic origin in a much lower sphere of feeling—that of the social dependence and slavery, or quasi-slavery, of children to their parents. Next come the interdictions placed by the Roman law on the marriage of guardians or curators, or their issue, with their female wards.

Lastly come the interdictions on the marriage of officials within their jurisdictions, which are analogous in principle to those on the marriage of guardians with their wards. No official could marry (though he might betroth to himself) a wife born or domiciled within the province in which he held office, unless he had been betrothed to her before; and if he betrothed a woman, she could, after his giving up office, terminate the engagement, on returning the earnest-money; but he could give his daughters in marriage within the province. The marriage of an official contracted against this interdiction seems to have been considered absolutely void.

Among the specially religious restrictions placed on the marriage contract in the early ages of the Church, the one which would first claim our attention is that on the marriage of Christians with Gentiles, or eventually also with Jews and heretics.

That marriage generally was a civil contract, subject to the laws of the state, seems to have been the received doctrine of the early Church; while at the same time it claimed also power to regulate it in the spirit of the Gospel, as is shown, for instance, in the strictness of our Lord and his apostles against divorce, although freely allowed both by the Jewish and the Roman law. Hence pagan betrothals and marriages were, as Selden observes, held valid by the Christians (*Uxor Ebraica*, bk. ii, c. 24).

The next religious restriction of marriage is that connected with the monkish profession, which must be distinguished from the early vow of virginity in the female sex, and from the institution of the Church virgins. The vow of virginity, which for many centuries now has been considered an essential prerequisite of the monastic profession, was not so by any means in the early heroic days of monachism (q. v.).

The prohibition against the marriage of monks and religious women by degrees found its way into the civil law of several of the barbarian kingdoms besides France. Among the laws of king Luitprand of Lombardy, A.D. 721, or later, we find one of this kind as to women, in which their position when they have assumed the religious habit is assimilated to that of girls betrothed under the civil law, whose marriage entails a penalty of five hundred *solidi*. The Visigothic code inflicts "on incestuous marriages and adulteries, or on sacred virgins and widows and penitents, defiled with lay vesture or marriage," the penalties of exile, separation, and forfeiture of property. By the time of the Carlovingians, the civil and ecclesiastical law almost wholly coalesce. In the 6th book of the Capitularies we find one almost in the same terms with the Visigothic law above quoted, declaring that marriage with a virgin devoted to God, a person under the religious habit, or professing the continence of widowhood, is not a true marriage, and requiring the parties to be separated by either the priest or the judge, without even any accusation being lodged with him, the penalty being still perpetual exile. In the East, on the contrary, about the end of the 8th century, it is noted as one of the features of Constantine Copronymus's tyranny, that he compelled monks to marry.

In respect of the marriage of the clergy, however, the restraint which occupies most space in the Church legislation of the period which concerns us, is that on digamous or quasi-digamous marriages, which will be considered under the head of DIGAMY. Meanwhile, however, there was growing up a feeling against all marriage of the clergy while in orders, tending to their absolute celibacy. The notices which occur of other restraints upon clerical marriages are comparatively few and unimportant. See CELIBACY.

II. We have now to say a few words on the contract of marriage, in the sense in which the expression is still used in France (marriage settlement), of the written evidence of the contract itself as between the parties.

The marriage contract among the Romans was habitually certified in writing on waxen tablets, which, however, might also be used after marriage, e. g. on the birth of a child. "Nuptial tablets" were signed both by the parties and by witnesses, and the breaking of them was held to be at least a symbol of the dissolution of marriage, if it had not the actual effect of dissolving it. By a constitution of the emperor Probus, the drawing up of such "tablets" was enacted not to be necessary to establish the validity of the marriage or the father's power over his offspring. They were perhaps not necessarily, though usually, identical with the "dotal tablets," "dotal instruments," or "dotal documents," specifically so called, but must have been comprised with them at least under the general terms "instruments" or "documents;" as to which it is provided, by a constitution of Diocletian and Maximin, that where there is no marriage, "instruments" made to prove marriage are invalid; but that where there are none, a marriage lawfully contracted is not void; nor could the want of signature to such by the father invalidate his consent. Nuptial instruments were by Justinian made necessary in the case of the marriage of stage-players. Under the 74th Novel, indeed, all persons exercising honorable offices, businesses, and professions, short of the highest functions in the state, were required, if they wished to marry without nuptial instruments, to appear in some "house of prayer and declare their intentions before the 'Defender of the Church,'" who, in the presence of three or four of the clerks of the Church, was to draw up an attestation of the marriage, with names and dates, and this was then to be subscribed by the parties, the "Defender," and the three others, or as many more as the parties wished, and if not required by them, to be laid up, so signed, in the archives of the church, i. e. where the holy vases were kept; and without this the parties were not held to have come together "with nuptial will." But this was only necessary where there was no document fixing a *dos* or anti-nuptial donation; nor was it required as to agriculturists, persons of mean condition, or common soldiers. It will be obvious that we have in the above the original of our marriage certificates. See DOWRY; MARRIAGE.

Contredit, ANDRÉ, a French poet and musician, lived about 1290. He was an ecclesiastic, and left *Neuf Chansons Notées* (MS. in the National Library of Paris, No. 7222, containing eight volumes). See Hoefer, *Nouv. Biog. Générale*, s. v.

Contrite literally signifies *beaten* or *bruised*, as with hard blows, or a heavy burden; and so, in Scripture language, imports one whose heart is broken and wounded for sin, in opposition to the heart of stone (Isa. lxvi, 2; Psa. li, 17; lvii, 15). The evidences of a broken and contrite spirit are: (1) Deep conviction of the evil of sin; (2) humiliation under a sense of it (Job xliii, 5, 6); (3) pungent sorrow for it (Zech. xii, 10); (4) ingenuous confession of it (1 John, i, 9); (5) prayer for deliverance from it (Psa. li, 10; Luke xviii, 13); (6) susceptibility of good impressions (Ezek. xi, 19).

Controversy, Religious, is good or evil, according to the principles which it upholds, the purpose in which it originates, the object to which it is applied, and the temper with which it is conducted. If it spring from a mere spirit of contention, from desire of victory, not love of truth, or from stubbornness, that will not be brought into captivity to the obedience of Christ, Christianity will not acknowledge it for her own. If it be employed on questions unbefitting human disputation; questions inaccessible to our finite understandings, unnecessary or unimportant in their issue, and only tending to perpetuate strife, or to unsettle the minds of men, then it is also unworthy of the Christian character. Nor is it void of offence when, however sound its principles, however important its subject, however irrefragable its argument, it is made the vehicle of personal malignity; when it is carried on with a spirit that rends asunder the social ties, and exasperates, instead of endeavoring to soften, the irritable feelings, which, even in its mildest aspect, it is but too apt to excite.

But those evil consequences, which flow from the abuse of controversy, and from causes by no means necessarily connected with religious discussion, ought not to deter us from its proper use, when truth requires its aid. Controversy is worse than useless if it have no better end in view than a display of mental superiority, or the self-gratification which, to minds of a certain cast, it appears to afford. For as, in secular disputes, it is the legitimate end of warfare to produce peace, so, in religious polemics, the attainment of unanimity ought to be the main object. War is waged because peace cannot be obtained without it. Religious controversy is maintained because agreement in the truth is not otherwise to be effected. When this necessity is laid upon us, we do but acquit ourselves of an indispensable duty in defending the charge committed to our care by the use of those weapons with which the armory of the divine Word supplies us. See Van Mildert, *Bampton Lectures.*

Contumeliōsus, a bishop of Riez, in Gaul, A.D. 524. He was addressed by Avitus, bishop of Vienne, concerning a work sent him by the latter. He was a learned man, but of doubtful private morality, and about 534, at the instance of Cæsarius, bishop of Arles, pope John II forbade his exercising episcopal functions. Contumeliosus appealed to pope Agapetus, but the case seems not to have been further determined.

Contumely and **Impudence**, two vices, were adored by the Athenians under the figure of partridges, from a supposed analogy of nature.

Conture, Guillaume, a French architect, was born at Rouen in 1732, and visited Italy early, where he made great improvement. He restored the Church de la Madeleine, and died in 1799.

Contzen, Adam, a Jesuit and controversialist of Belgium, was born in 1573 at Montjoie, in the Jülich territory. In 1595 he joined his order at Treves, was in 1606 appointed a professor of philosophy at Würzburg, and in 1610 professor of theology at the academy in Mayence. He wrote, against the Heidelberg professor Pareus, *Defensio Libri de Gratia Primi Hominis* (Magdeburg, 1613), and *Crudelitas et Idolum Calvinistarum Revelatum* (ibid. 1614). When Pareus tried to harmonize the differences between Lutherans and Calvinists, and to array both parties against Rome, Contzen published *De Unione et Synodo Generali Evangelicorum* (ibid. 1615), and *De Pace Germaniæ Libri Duo* (ibid. 1616). When the first centenary of the Reformation was celebrated, he published *Jubilum Jubilorum* (ibid. 1618). At Munich, where he was called in 1623, he wrote, *In Quatuor Evang.*, a commentary (Cologne, 1626):—*In Epistol. ad Romanos* (ibid. 1629):—*In Epistol. ad Corinthios et ad Galatas* (ibid. 1631). He died May 20, 1635. See K. Brischar, *P. Adam Contzen* (Würzburg, 1829); Streber, in Wetzer u. Welte's *Kirchen-Lexikon*, s. v.; Hoefer, *Nouv. Biog. Générale*, s. v. (B. P.)

Conuualh (or **Conwalh**). See Coinwalch.

Conuulfus (or **Conwulfus**). See Cynewulf.

Convallus (or **Conwall**) is the name of several early Scotch saints:

1. Said by some to have been an abbot in Scotland, and confessor of king Comanus, and to have died in A.D. 527; but according to others an abbot of Iona, who introduced "gang-days" (Rogation-days) into Scotland. His day of commemoration is Oct. 13 or 15. See Forbes, *Kal. of Scottish Saints*, p. 164, 214, 241, 315.

2. A confessor, commemorated May 18 or Sept. 28, probably the Convallus who was a favorite pupil of Kentigern at Glasgow, described as the son of an Irish prince, and as dying in A.D. 612. See Forbes, *Kal. of Scot. Saints*, p. 315.

3. A monk, commemorated Sept. 14, who was brought up in the monastery of Crosraguel in Carrick, and therefore not earlier than the 13th century. See Camerarius, *De Scot. Fort.* p. 173.

Convention, General, is an assembly of clerical and lay deputies belonging to the Protestant Episcopal Church (q. v.) of America.

Converse, Amasa, D.D., a Presbyterian minister, was born at Lyme, N. H., Aug. 21, 1795. He graduated from Dartmouth College in 1822; studied theology at Princeton Theological Seminary for one year; was ordained evangelist by the Presbytery of Hanover, May 5, 1826; was missionary in Virginia during 1826 and 1827; editor of the *Visitor and Telegraph*, Richmond, thereafter until 1839; of the *Christian Observer*, Philadelphia, Pa., until 1861; then went back to Richmond, and was employed there until 1869; and at Louisville, Ky., until his death, Dec. 9, 1872. See *Gen. Cat. of Princeton Theol. Sem.* 1881, p. 44.

Converse, Augustus L., a Protestant Episcopal clergyman of the diocese of South Carolina, was for a number of years rector of the church in Stateburgh, near which place he died, March 21, 1860, aged sixty-two years. See *Prot. Episc. Almanac*, 1861, p. 98.

Converse, John Kendrick, a Presbyterian and Congregational minister, was born at Lyme, N. H., June 15, 1801. His preliminary education was acquired at Thetford Academy. In 1827 he graduated from Dartmouth College, and during the two years following was a teacher and editor in Richmond, Va. Soon after his graduation from Princeton Theological Seminary he was ordained pastor, Aug. 9, 1832, at Burlington, Vt., where he continued to minister for twelve years; and then, for more than twenty-five years was principal of the Burlington Female Seminary. For a long time he was secretary of the Vermont Colonization Society, and was also general agent of the American Colonization Society. He died at Burlington, Oct. 3, 1880. See *Cong. Year-book*, 1881, p. 20; *Necrol. Report of Princeton Theol. Sem.* 1881.

Conversi is a Latin term for lay brothers of a monastery, as having forsaken the world.

Convert is a person who is converted. In a monastic sense, converts are lay friars, or brothers admitted for the service of the house, without orders, and not allowed to sing in the choir.

Conviction, in general, is the assurance of the truth of any proposition. In a religious sense, it is the first degree of repentance, and implies an affecting sense that we are guilty before God; that we can do nothing of ourselves to gain his forfeited favor; that we deserve and are exposed to the wrath of God; that sin is very odious and hateful, yea, the greatest of evils.

There is a *natural* and just conviction which arises from natural conscience, fear of punishment, moral suasion, or alarming providences, but which is not of a permanent nature. *Saving* conviction is a work of the Holy Spirit, as the cause; though the conscience, the law, the gospel, or affliction, may be the means (John xvi, 8, 9).

Convictions of sin differ very much in their degree and pungency, in different persons. It has been observed that those who suffer the most agonizing sensations are such as never before enjoyed the external call of the gospel, or were favored with the tuition of religious parents, but have neglected or notoriously abused the means of grace. To these, conviction is often sudden, and produces that horror and shame which are not soon overcome; whereas those who have sat under the gospel from their infancy have not often such alarming convictions, because they have already some notion of these things, and have much acquaintance with the gospel, which administers to a believing heart immediate comfort. As it is not, therefore, the constant method of the Spirit to convince in one way, it is improper for any to distress themselves because they are not, or have not been, tormented almost to despair: they should be rather thankful that the Spirit of God has dealt tenderly with them, and opened to them the genuine source of consolation in Christ. It is necessary, however, to observe that, in order to repentance and conversion to God, there must be real and lasting conviction, which, though it may not be the same in degree, is the same in nature.

Evangelical conviction differs from legal conviction thus: *legal* arises from a consideration of the divine law, God's justice, power, or omniscience; *evangelical*, from God's goodness and holiness as seen in the cross of Christ, and from a disaffection to sin; legal conviction still conceives there is something remaining good; but evangelical is sensible there is no good at all; legal wishes freedom from pain; evangelical from sin; legal hardens the heart; evangelical softens it; legal is only temporary; evangelical lasting.

Convocation, *in the University of Oxford*, consists of all persons admitted to regency, who have their names on their college books, and have paid all their fees. This assembly gives assent to statutes passed in congregation, confirms leases of lands, makes petitions to Parliament, elects burgesses, and confers honorary degrees, or those given by degree or by diploma.

Conwell, Henry, a Roman Catholic prelate, was born in Ireland, made bishop of Philadelphia, Pa., in 1820, and died in that city, April 21, 1842. See De Courcy and Shea, *Hist. of the Catholic Church in the U. S.* p. 125.

Conwell, W. T., a minister of the Methodist Episcopal Church South, was born near Hazel Green, Morgan Co., Ky., Feb. 19, 1849. He removed to Missouri in 1870, was converted in 1874, and the same year joined the Missouri Conference. He died at Savannah, Mo., May 23, 1881. See *Minutes of Annual Conferences of the M. E. Church South*, 1881, p. 318.

Conybeare, John Josias, A.M., an English divine, was born in 1779. He was elected professor of Anglo-Saxon in Oxford University in 1808, and professor of poetry in 1812. He delivered the Bampton lectures for 1824, on the *Interpretation of Scripture;* and in 1826 was published his *Illustrations of Anglo-Saxon Poetry*, edited by W. D. Conybeare. This work has done much to promote the study of Anglo-Saxon literature. Large portions of the *Song of the Traveller* and *Beowulf* will be found in the volume. Mr. Conybeare was a contributor to the *British Bibliographer*. He died in 1824. See (Lond.) *Christian Remembrancer*, July, 1824, p. 439; Allibone, *Dict. of Brit. and Amer. Authors*, s. v.; *Biog. Universelle*, s. v.

Conyers, Josiah B., a Baptist minister and physician, was born in Bath County, Ky., March 4, 1812. He graduated as M.D. from Transylvania University, and for seven years practiced his profession at Quincy, Ill. He united with the Baptist Church in 1844. Several years afterwards he gave up a lucrative practice, and was ordained a minister at St. Mary's, O., where, and at Delphos and Zanesville, he preached for six years. Although somewhat advanced in life, he became a student in the theological department of Madison University, N. Y., and studied one year at Princeton. In January, 1863, he entered upon the duties of his pastorate in Oneida, Ill. Subsequently he was pastor of the Church at Berwick. He died Aug. 6, 1870, near Tabo, Lafayette Co., Mo. See *Minutes of Ill. Anniversaries*, 1870, p. 11. (J. C. S.)

Conynghame, Daniel, a Scotch clergyman, took his degree at Glasgow University in 1586; was appointed to the living at Kilmalcolm in 1588; was a member of the Court of High Commission in 1619, continued in 1628, but resided at Lochwinnoch in 1646. See *Fasti Eccles. Scoticanæ*, ii, 249.

Conynghame, Hugh, a Scotch clergyman, took his degree at Glasgow University in 1634, became minister of the Presbyterian congregation at Ray, Ireland, but was compelled by persecution to leave that island; was called to the living at Mearns in 1649; became a temporary supply at Erskine in 1641, and continued in January, 1654. . See *Fasti Eccles. Scoticanæ*, ii, 227, 245.

Conzié, François de, a French prelate, brother of the following, was born at Poncin, in Bugey, March 18, 1736. He was first grand-vicar, then bishop of St. Omer, and, in 1774, became archbishop of Tours. As deputy of the clergy to the states-general of 1789, he protested against the reunion of the three orders, resigned in 1791, and went to Aix-la-Chapelle. He afterwards wrote against the civil constitution of the clergy, and published, in June, 1791, a mandate which was condemned, in July of the same year, by the tribunal of Tours, to be torn and burned by the hand of the executioner. He retired to Holland, and died at Amsterdam in 1795. See Hoefer, *Nouv. Biog. Générale*, s. v.; *Biog. Universelle*, s. v.

Conzié, Louis François Marc Hilaire de, a French prelate, was born at Poncin, in Bugey, Jan. 13, 1732. He served first as an officer of dragoons, but was soon made bishop of Arras. He proved himself one of the most violent adversaries of the Revolution. He refused to sit at the states-general, and in a riot came near losing his life in return for his devotion. An indictment being decreed in 1792, he took refuge in England and attached himself to the count of Artois. He exercised great influence in private, and directed the affairs of the royalist party. He became the centre of the intercourse and intrigue which fed the civil war in France. For many years his name was found in nearly all the projects of political insurrections. He is especially memorable as one of the directors of the plot of the *machine infernale*, Dec. 24, 1800. He died in London in December, 1804. See Hoefer, *Nouv. Biog. Générale*, s. v.; *Biog. Universelle*, s. v.

Coo, Roger, an English martyr, was a native of Melford, in Suffolk. He was brought before the bishop, examined, and condemned to be burned, on account of his belief in the true God and his abhorrence of the worship of idols. The sentence was executed at Yoxford, Suffolk, in 1555. See Fox, *Acts and Monuments*, vii, 381.

Cook, Albert A., a Methodist Episcopal minister, was born at Warehouse Point, Conn., Sept. 24, 1817. He early gave proof of a noble character by caring for the family on the death of his father; joined the Church at the age of eighteen, and, after several years of study and teaching, united with the New England Conference in 1842, and began his pastoral life at Feeding Hills, Mass. He continued his ministry at Shelburne Falls, Chester Village (now Huntington), North Brookfield, Princeton, Oxford, and in 1851 at Milford (all in Massachusetts), where he died, Feb. 4, 1880. Mr. Cook spent his latter years as a dentist; was a member of the General Court of Massachusetts in 1850, 1855, and 1864; and served once in the Senate and twice in the House. He was a Christian gentleman, of fine presence and great urbanity; a natural, excellent preacher and expositor; was benevolent, and everywhere highly esteemed. See *Minutes of Annual Conferences*, 1880, p. 66.

Cook, Alexander (1), a Presbyterian minister, was born at St. Monance, near Glasgow, Scotland, Feb. 4, 1760. He received a moderate English education at Glasgow, and learned the trade of a silversmith. He was at Berwick-on-Tweed in 1778, and emigrated to America in 1783; in 1797 was living in Pennsylvania; in 1802 was licensed, and went as a missionary to the Indians, but remained only a short time. In 1803 he was received into the Presbytery of Erie, and accepted calls from the congregations of Slippery Rock and New Castle, where he continued until 1809. In 1810 he was dismissed from the Presbytery of Erie, and connected himself with that of Hartford. About this time he took a commission to labor in South Carolina and Georgia as a missionary. He was also stated supply at Poland, O., from 1812 to 1814. In 1815 he was received into the Presbytery of Ohio, and installed pastor of the Church of Bethany, which relation was dissolved in 1820. In 1821 he was received by the Presbytery of Allegheny, and in the same year installed as pastor of the churches of Ebenezer and Bear Creek. In 1827 he was received into the Presbytery of Steubenville, and for a year supplied the churches of Annapolis and Bloomfield, O. In 1828 he left his home to organize a Church in a Scotch settlement in Ohio. While on this trip he died, Nov. 30, 1828. See *Hist. of the Presbytery of Erie.*

Cook, Alexander (2), a Methodist Episcopal minister, was born in Keskasbig, County Donegal, Ireland, May 5, 1842. He joined the Wesleyans early in life; received a good common English education, and studied two years in the Wesleyan Institute; taught school four years; emigrated to America in 1865, and in 1866 entered the Central Ohio Conference, wherein he served the Church until his death, early in 1870. See *Minutes of Annual Conferences*, 1870, p. 196.

Cook, Archibald, a Scotch clergyman, was licensed to preach in 1822; appointed to the North Church, Inverness, in 1837, after he had spent some years as missionary at Berriedale; joined the Free Secession in 1843, and became minister of the Free Church, Daviot, in 1844. He died May 6, 1865, aged seventy-four years. See *Fasti Eccles. Scoticanæ*, iii, 259.

Cook, Chauncey, a Congregational minister, was born at Wallingford, Conn., March 9, 1778. He graduated from Middlebury College in 1808, studied theology with Dr. Asa Burton, was ordained in 1809, and labored as an evangelist in Vermont and New York. In 1811 he became pastor of the Church in Adams, N. Y., and his successive charges were as follows: Lima, Pittsford, Chili, Greece, Ira, Aurora (Presbyterian Church), all in New York state; Hennepin, Aurora, and Bristol, in Illinois. He died at Ottawa, Ill., March 21, 1860. Mr. Cook's ministry was blessed with many revivals. "He was a progressive man to the last." See *Cong. Quarterly*, 1860, p. 344.

Cook, Cornelius, a Methodist Episcopal minister, was a native of Great Britain, where he was converted, and then called to preach in America. He labored three years in the ministry (in East Jersey, 1787; Dutchess, 1788; Schenectady, 1789), and died in August, 1789. See *Minutes of Annual Conference*, 1790, p. 36.

Cook, Edward, an English Wesleyan missionary, was born at Long Whatton, Leicestershire, Nov. 4, 1806. He was converted in 1828, ordained in London for the missionary work in 1831, and on Jan. 14, 1832, sailed with Rev. Messrs. Edwards and Satchel in the *Caledonia*, for the Cape of Good Hope. His field was the Great Namaqua land. His work was interesting, successful, pursued with great love and enthusiasm, often amid dangers. His health finally giving way under his toils, he commenced a journey to Cape Town, but before he reached the station of his wished-for rest he died, on the banks of the Great Orange River, March 7, 1843. His remains were carried back over fifty miles to Nisbet Bath, and interred in the land of his labor. Besides establishing a church of more than four hundred members, and schools of more than one thousand children at Nisbet Bath, he made frequent journeys to the Damaras and more distant tribes. See *Minutes of the British Conference*, 1843; John Cook, *The Life of Edward Cook* (Liverpool, 1849, 12mo); *Christian Watchman Magazine* (Cape Town), March, 1843.

Cook, Edwin R. T., an Episcopal clergyman, was born in 1825. At the time of his death, July 25, 1865, he was rector of Wainwright Memorial Church, in New York city. Mr. Cook was an able, devoted, and eminently successful pastor. See *Appleton's Annual Cyclop.* 1865, p. 644.

Cook, Elijah, a Free-will Baptist minister, was born in the state of New York in 1793. He removed to the West in 1835, and was a preacher in Michigan. His ordination took place in 1845, and for nearly thirty years after he was engaged in his Master's work. He died at Cook's Prairie, Mich., Jan. 31, 1872. See *Free-will Baptist Register*, 1873, p. 83. (J. C. S.)

Cook, Émile F., a French Methodist preacher, son of Rev. Charles Cook, was born at Niort, June 15, 1829. The happy influence of his godly parents was shown by his conversion at the age of nine years. His mind was drawn to the ministry, and he pursued his classical studies in France and Switzerland; and, to qualify himself for preaching, entered the Wesleyan Theological College at Richmond, England, where, for three years, he manifested the aptitude for pastoral work which ever afterwards characterized his life and labors. He entered the itinerant ministry in France in 1854, when that country was made an independent conference, and labored successfully at Nismes, Nyons, Lausanne, and other important circuits. He was stationed in Paris during the siege, and heroically opened his house as a hospital, and had it filled with the sick and wounded, whom he gathered in person from the battlefield, and his devoted labors were greatly appreciated by both the conference and the citizens. The conference elected him president in 1872, and kept him in the office two years, as a mark of the confidence and affection of his brethren. At the close of his presidential duties he came to America to attend the meeting of the Evangelical Alliance, and afterwards spent some time in pleading in Methodist churches for aid to his native land. He started for home in the steamer *Ville-du-Havre*, but was shipwrecked soon after leaving America. He was picked up, as by a miracle, with barely life left; resumed his journey in the steamer *Loch Earn*, and was again wrecked. Was again rescued, but with little hope of rallying, yet he strove hard to lead the dying to the Saviour. He at length reached England, got home greatly exhausted, and was sent to the south of France; but nature was worn out, yet his mind was calm and serene, and his strong faith remained unshaken. He died Jan. 9, 1874.

Cook, Finlay, a Scotch clergyman, was born at Arran in 1778. He became a catechist at Glasgow; was licensed to preach in 1816; ordained and sent as missionary to Halkirk, Watten, and Reay, and afterwards to Inverness; presented to the living at Cross in 1829; transferred to East Church, Inverness, in 1833, and thence to Reay in 1835; joined the Free Secession in 1843; and died June 12, 1858. He was remarkable for integrity and uprightness, faithful in reproving sin and error. His son, Alexander, was a minister in the Free Church. See *Fasti Eccles. Scoticanæ*, iii, 147, 259, 368.

Cook, George, D.D., a Scottish theologian, was born at St. Andrews between 1780 and 1795. He was pastor of Laurencekirk, and died in 1845. He wrote a *History of the Reformation in Scotland* (Edinb. 1811, 1819, 3 vols.):—a *History of the Church of Scotland* (Lond. 1815, 3 vols.):—*Reality of Christ's Resurrection* (1808), and some minor pieces.

Cook, Henry David, a Scotch clergyman, son of the professor of moral philosophy in St. Andrews, was born Feb. 24, 1791. He took his degree at the University of St. Andrews; was licensed to preach in 1813, and presented to the living at Kilmany in 1815. He died Sept. 19, 1857. He was well acquainted with the history of the Church, and with all its schisms and controversies. See *Fasti Eccles. Scoticanæ*, ii, 499.

Cook, Henry Preston, a Methodist Episcopal minister, was born in Hancock County, Ga., Dec. 8, 1800. He received a careful religious training, experienced conversion in 1817, and in 1820 united with the Mississippi Conference, wherein he labored with zeal and fidelity until his death, in 1826. See *Minutes of Annual Conferences*, 1826, p. 506; *Methodist Magazine*, ix, 359.

Cook, Isaac M., a Presbyterian minister, was born in Pennsylvania. He graduated from Jefferson College in 1841, attended Princeton Theological Seminary for about one year (1842), was ordained by the Presbytery of Beaver, Dec. 17, 1845, and was pastor at Bridgewater, Pa., until his death, in January, 1854. See *Gen. Cat. of Princeton Theol. Sem.* 1881, p. 136.

Cook, Israel B., a Methodist Episcopal minister, was born in 1789. His name first appears in 1813, in connection with Lycoming Circuit of the Genesee Conference. In 1822 he became superannuated, but subsequently was readmitted into the East Baltimore Conference. He died March 7, 1868. See *Minutes of Annual Conferences*, 1868, p. 29

Cook, I. Russell, a Free-will Baptist minister, was born at Acton, Me., in 1821. He removed to Manchester, N. H., where he was converted in 1847, and ordained in 1852. His pastorates were in various places in Maine and New Hampshire, including Gilmanton, where he was pastor for four years, and Buxton, Me., for five years. He died in Rochester, N. H., July 1, 1862. See *Free-will Baptist Register*, 1863, p. 92. (J. C. S.)

Cook, John (1), a Scotch clergyman, took his degree at the University of St. Andrews in 1648; was presented to the living at Eccles in 1663; deprived in 1689 for not praying for the king and queen, and other acts of disloyalty. He died in 1691, aged about sixty-three years. See *Fasti Eccles. Scoticanæ*, i, 412.

Cook, John (2), a Scotch clergyman, was licensed to preach in 1732; called to the living at Abercrombie in 1734, and ordained. He died June 24, 1751. His son John became professor of moral philosophy at St. Andrews. See *Fasti Eccles. Scoticanæ*, ii, p. 403.

Cook, John (3), a Scotch clergyman, was born Nov. 24, 1771. He took his degree at the University of St. Andrews in 1788; was licensed to preach in 1792; appointed minister at Kilmany in 1793, and ordained; appointed professor of Hebrew at St. Mary's College, St. Andrews, and resigned in 1802. He died Nov. 28, 1824. See *Fasti Eccles. Scoticanæ*, ii, 499.

Cook, John (4), an early Wesleyan missionary, was sent to the island of Dominica, W. I., in 1794. On his arrival at Tortola he was seized with putrid fever, and in five days died, "in the prime of his life and the triumph of faith," in 1795 (according to Hill). See Atmore, *Meth. Memorial*, s. v.

Cook, John (5), D.D., a Scotch clergyman, son of the divinity professor at St. Andrews, graduated at that university in 1823. He was factor to St. Mary's College in 1824, licensed to preach in 1828, presented to the living at Laurencekirk in 1829, and ordained; transferred to St. Leonard's, St. Andrews, in 1845; appointed convener of committee on education in 1849, of that for schoolmasters in 1850, and also of three other committees; was moderator of the General Assembly in 1859, assessor to the university court, elected professor of divinity and ecclesiastical history in 1860, and one of the deans of the chapel in 1863. He died April 17, 1869, aged sixty-one years. Dr. Cook published works on *Church Patronage*, *Church Defence*, *Relief of the Poor*, *School Statistics*, a *Catechism*, and a few single *Sermons*. A handsome painted window, placed by his parishioners in the college church, St. Andrews, is one token of the high esteem in which he was held. He had scholarly ability, refined taste, exact and active business habits, affability, and courtesy. See *Fasti Eccles. Scoticanæ*, iii, 879.

Cook, John C., a Methodist Episcopal minister, was born about 1837. He was educated at Dickinson College, where he was converted at the age of nineteen, and in 1860 entered the East Baltimore Conference, wherein he labored with earnest devotion until his death, April 22, 1862. Mr. Cook was a man of great promise, meek and lowly in heart, earnest, faithful. See *Minutes of Annual Conferences*, 1863, p. 10.

Cook, John Lovejoy, a Methodist Episcopal minister, was born in Edinburg, Saratoga Co., N. Y., Jan. 7, 1819, of devout Christian parents. He spent his youth amid the quiet and peace of farm life, where he laid the foundation of his blameless, industrious, Christian character. He was employed in his young manhood by his brother as a manufacturer in Massachusetts and Rhode Island, at which time he was converted, became a class-leader, and received license to preach, and in 1846 was admitted into the Troy Conference. His last eight years were given to the pastorate of the Congregational Church at North Pownall, Vt., where he died May 15, 1878. See *Minutes of Annual Conferences*, 1879, p. 43.

Cook, Joseph, a Baptist minister, was born in Bath, England. He was licensed to preach in 1776. He had previously served as associate pastor at Margate, on the Isle of Thanet, at Dover, Deal, and Folkestone. He then came to America, and was first pastor of a church in Eutaw Springs, S. C., but was obliged to leave during the Revolutionary War. When he returned he found his Church almost extinct, but through his efforts it grew in numbers, spirituality, and influence. He died Sept. 26, 1790. See Sprague, *Annals of the Amer. Pulpit*, vi, 186.

Cook, Joseph B., a Baptist minister, was born in South Carolina about 1776. He was converted at the age of fifteen, and graduated from Brown University in 1797; pursued his theological studies with Rev. Dr. Furman; was ordained as an evangelist, and successively became pastor of the Eutaw, the Beaufort, and the Mount Pisgah churches. He died at his residence in Sumter District, S. C., Aug. 24, 1833. See *Watchman and Reflector*, Sept. 13, 1833. (J. C. S.)

Cook, Nehemiah Baldwin, a Congregational minister, was born at Hampton, N. Y., Sept. 20, 1793. He graduated from Andover Theological Seminary in 1821; in 1823 was appointed a home missionary in Wayne County, Pa., served one year, and was ordained Aug. 31, 1825; from that time till 1833 he was acting pastor of the Presbyterian churches in Babylon and Fresh Pond, L. I., and during the three succeeding years at Riverhead and Southhold. He was installed pastor in Stonington, Conn., March 7, 1838, from which he was dismissed in May, 1859. From June, 1864, to October, 1867, he was acting pastor in Ledyard, and subsequently resided there without charge until his death, Nov. 17, 1879. He published two *Funeral Sermons.* See *Cong. Year-book*, 1880, p. 16.

Cook, Pardon, a Methodist Episcopal minister, was admitted into the Pittsburgh Conference in 1827, preached for thirty-four years, was a superannuate for nineteen years, and died at Marietta, O., in May, 1880, in his eighty-third year. He was pure-minded, cheerful, sweet-spirited, and beloved. See *Minutes of Annual Conferences*, 1880, p. 243.

Cook, Phineas, a Methodist Episcopal minister, was born at Greenfield, Mass., March 10, 1784. He experienced religion in 1800; and in 1803 entered the New York Conference, in which he was an effective preacher for forty years. He spent his latter years as a superannuate, and died May 26, 1861. Mr. Cook was of a warm and lively temperament, open-hearted and frank. See *Minutes of Annual Conferences*, 1862, p. 80.

Cook, Richard, a Methodist Episcopal minister, was born about 1818. He was converted when quite young; joined the Oneida Conference in 1844; continued effective until 1860, when he took a supernumerary relation, on account of ill-health; served as presiding elder in 1861 and 1862; and spent his last fifteen years in New Hartford. He died in September, 1876. Mr. Cook was a fearless advocate of all reforms, and an exemplary Christian. See *Minutes of Annual Conferences*, 1876, p. 137.

Cook, Robert, a Scotch clergyman, took his degree at Marischal College, Aberdeen, in 1813; was presented to the living at Clatt in 1820, and ordained; transferred to Ceres in 1844, and died at Monimail, Dec. 20, 1851, aged fifty-eight years. His publications are, *Sermon on the Abundant Harvest, with Metrical Paraphrases* (1831):—*The Catechist's Poetical Manual* (1834):—*The Young Communicant's Manual* (1849):—*Account of the Parish.* See *Fasti Eccles. Scoticanæ*, iii, 554.

Cook, Samuel, a Baptist minister, was born at Eastham, Mass., in 1791. When he was young his parents removed to Maine. In 1815 he was baptized, and united with the Baptist Church in Clinton. He completed a literary and theological course in 1821 at Waterville College. Soon after, he was ordained pastor of the Church in Effingham, N. H. The subsequent pastorates of Mr. Cook were at Brentwood, Hampton Falls, Hopkinton, Meredith and Dunbarton, all in New Hampshire. He acted, for some years, as the agent of the New Hampshire Baptist Convention, and, for eight years, was the chaplain of the state prison at Concord. He died Feb. 15, 1872. See *Obit. Record of Colby University, Supplement No.* 1, p. 5. (J. C. S.)

Cook, Thomas F, a minister of the Methodist Episcopal Church South, son of Rev. Valentine Cook, was a native of Kentucky. He professed religion in boyhood, labored a number of years acceptably as local preacher, and in 1848 entered the Mississippi Conference. In 1865 he was transferred to the Rio Grande Conference. He died of yellow fever, July 24, 1867. Mr. Cook was a meek, spiritual Christian, a faithful, laborious pastor, and a successful preacher. See *Minutes of Annual Conferences of the M. E. Church South*, 1867, p. 190.

Cook, Walter, a Scotch clergyman, took his degree at the University of Edinburgh in 1709; was licensed to preach in 1722; appointed to the living at Cummertrees in 1728, and ordained. He died April 21, 1759, aged seventy-six years. See *Fasti Eccles. Scoticanæ*, i, 615.

Cook, W. B., a Universalist minister, was born at Marcellus, Onondaga Co., N. Y., Dec. 8, 1810. He entered the ministry in 1843, was ordained in 1846, and labored at the following places: Mottville, Alexander, Lockport, Gaines, Churchville, Newburgh, and Aurora, all in New York; went to Michigan in 1866, and there continued until his decease at Muskegon, June 5, 1871. Mr. Cook was a humble, faithful, diligent preacher. See *Universalist Register*, 1872, p. 144.

Cook, William W., a minister of the Methodist Episcopal Church South, was born at Princeton, Ky., May 2, 1818. He was converted in youth, licensed to preach in 1846, and joined the Louisville Conference in 1854. From 1861 to 1864 he was superannuated. Entering the effective ministry again he labored faithfully until compelled by poor health to take a superannuated relation once more, in which he remained until his death, Oct. 22, 1879. Though his early education was limited, Mr. Cook possessed good natural endowments, and by diligent study became a clear theologian and successful preacher. He was a kind, true man, and an efficient pastor. See *Minutes of Annual Conferences of the M. E. Church South*, 1880, p. 164.

Cooke, Albert, A.B., an English Congregational minister, was born at Uttoxeter, Staffordshire, about 1842. He was educated at Alleyne's Grammar-school and at Lancashire Independent College. On leaving college, in June, 1866, he became pastor of the Church at Newport, Shropshire. In June, 1869, he accepted the pastorate at Acock's Green, Birmingham. In 1874 he resigned this charge to take a school at Frome, in the hope that a more southern climate might repair his shattered health. He died July 30, 1879. See (Lond.) *Cong. Year-book*, 1880, p. 315.

Cooke, Amos Starr, a Congregational missionary, was born at Danbury, Conn., in 1810, and graduated from Yale College in 1834. He went to the Sandwich Islands in the employ of the American Board of Foreign Missions, arriving there in April, 1837. Soon after his arrival he took charge of the education of the higher classes of that country, and remained at the head of the royal school for twelve years. He died at Honolulu, March 20, 1871.

Cooke, Charles, D.D., a Methodist Episcopal minister, was born of Protestant Episcopal parentage in St. Mary's County, Md., Sept. 3, 1799. He experienced religion in 1815, while attending school at the academy in Georgetown, D. C.; soon displayed marked talent as leader of a young people's prayer-meeting; was licensed to preach, and in 1820 entered the Baltimore Conference. In 1824 he became a member of the Pittsburgh Conference; in 1840 was made editor of the *Pittsburgh Christian Advocate*, and subsequently transferred to the Philadelphia Conference. He became superannuated in 1872, and died Aug. 24, 1875. Dr. Cooke was quiet and unobtrusive, firm and true, an exemplary Christian gentleman. See *Minutes of Annual Conferences*, 1876, p. 51; Simpson, *Cyclop. of Methodism*, s. v.

Cooke, Corbett, an English Wesleyan minister, was born at Felmingham, Norfolk, Dec. 2, 1787. He commenced his ministry in 1809; was chairman of a district for twenty-seven years; retired to Guernsey after a ministry of half a century, where, blind but happy, he performed various pastoral duties until his death, May 16, 1866. Mr. Cooke was an argumentative and practical preacher, and his manner was simple and dignified, earnest and persuasive. He wrote *Strictures on a Pamphlet, entitled An Attempt to Show that Election is Beneficial to Many and Injurious to None*:—*The History of Apostolical Succession* (new ed. Lond. 1840, 12mo):—*The Opinions of Rev. John Wesley in Reference to the Relation of Methodism to the Established Church* (Exeter, 1844, 12mo):—*A Plain Statement of Facts* (ibid. 1835, 12mo):—*Church Membership;* Serm. on Acts ii, 47 (Lond. 1862, 12mo). See *A Memorial Volume of the Rev. Corbett Cooke* (Lond. 1868, 8vo); *Minutes of the British Conference*, 1866, p. 31; Stevenson, *Wesleyan Hymn-book and its Associations* (Lond. 1870), p. 367; Osborne, *Meth. Bibliography*, p. 87; *Meth. Magazine* (Lond. 1866), p. 941.

Cooke, Edward, LL.B., an English divine, was rector of Haversham, Bucks. He was an able scholar, and particularly well-versed in whatever related to history, antiquities, and jurisprudence. Besides the *History of Whaddon Chase*, the publication of which was interrupted only by his death, he had made ample collections towards a history of Buckinghamshire, which would probably, had his life been spared, have been completed in a few years. He died Feb. 27, 1824. See (Lond.) *Annual Register*, 1824, p. 214.

Cooke (or **Coke**), **George**, D.D., an English prelate of the 17th century, brother to sir John Cooke, secretary of state, was born at Trusley, Derbyshire, of an ancient and honorable family. He was educated at Pembroke Hall, Cambridge, beneficed at Bigrave, Hertfordshire, made bishop successively of Bristol (1633) and Hereford (1636), and died in 1650. Bishop Cooke was a meek, grave, and quiet man, much beloved of such as were subjected to him, and was in the same condemnation with the rest of his brethren for subscribing the protest in parliament in preservation of their privileges. The times broke the body of his estate so that he had to be relieved by his rich relatives. See Fuller, *Worthies of England* (ed. Nuttall), i, 371.

Cooke, Henry, D.D., LL.D., an Irish Presbyterian divine, was born at Grillagh, County Londonderry, in 1788. He studied at Glasgow University, and settled in 1808 at Dunean, County Antrim, and in 1811 at Donegon, in the same county. In 1817 he attended the medical classes in Trinity College, Dublin, and in 1818 removed as pastor to Killyleagh, County Down, where he engaged in a controversy with a Unitarian minister. In 1824 he was chosen moderator of the synod of Ulster, and three years later carried on a discussion on Arianism with Henry Montgomery. In 1829 he became pastor at Belfast, a position which he retained until his death, Dec. 13, 1868. During this period he was engaged in politico-ecclesiastic discussions, was three times moderator of the General Assembly, and at the close was professor of sacred rhetoric, in the New Presbyterian College of Belfast. Some of his polemical writings have been published. His *Life* was written by J. L. Porter (London, 1871; Belfast, 1875).

Cooke, James, an English Wesleyan minister, was born at Gloucester in 1800. He was early converted, entered the ministry in 1822, and died Jan. 22, 1854. Kind and sympathetic, constant as a friend, his views of Christianity were lofty and comprehensive, his perceptions quick, and his judgments discriminating. See *Minutes of the British Conference*, 1854.

Cooke, James W., a Protestant Episcopal clergyman, was born at Providence, R. I., March 5, 1810. He graduated from Brown University, was minister at Lonsdale, R. I., and then assistant to the late Dr. Milnor of New York city, after which he became rector of St. Michael's, Bristol, R. I. He made a voyage to Aspinwall to examine that place and Panama with a view to missionary operations, but was compelled to return on account of broken health. He died in New York, April 12, 1853, being at the time secretary and general agent of the foreign department of the Protestant Episcopal Missionary Board. Mr. Cooke was an ardent and efficient man. See *Amer. Quar. Church Rev.* 1853, p. 302.

Cooke, John (1), an English clergyman of the latter part of the 18th century, rector of Wentnor, Shropshire, published a *Sermon* (1773):—and *The Preacher's Assistant* (Oxford, 1783, 2 vols.). This work contained an account of various preachers and sermons since the Restoration, and is considered valuable as a list of sermons from which the preacher might select for his library. See Allibone, *Dict. of Brit. and Amer. Authors*, s. v.

Cooke, John (2), an English Congregational minister, was born at Atherstone, Warwickshire, March 25, 1799. He early became a Christian, entered Blackburn Academy in 1821, and was ordained in 1825 to the pastorate at Uttoxeter, where he labored forty years, and where, after a few years' retirement from the sacred office, he died, Feb. 11, 1871. Mr. Cooke was a master of one subject, human nature. See (Lond.) *Cong. Yearbook*, 1872, p. 309.

Cook(e), Joseph, an English Wesleyan preacher, became prominent as an advocate of certain theological tenets, which resulted in his exclusion from that body. He had travelled without objection from 1795. While on the Rochdale Circuit, 1803–5, he began to state the doctrines of justification and the witness of the Spirit differently from the received view. According to Myles, he hardly implied experimental religion, but a firm belief in what the Scriptures declare on these subjects. Promising not to promulgate his opinions, he was removed to the Sunderland Circuit. His friends in Rochdale, not so discreet as their late pastor, published his two sermons on the above subjects without his knowledge. This, of course, led to his arraignment before the conference, and, although treating him with respect and tenderness on account of the esteem in which he was held, they excluded him from their number in 1806, Cooke refusing to renounce his opinions. He then went to Rochdale, where he became the minister of a part of his former Wesleyan society. He published a defense of his doctrines, which was answered by Dr. Coke (q. v.) and Edward Hare (q. v.). Hare's treatise on justification has become a classic. Cooke died in 1811. "The breach which he made is not yet healed in the town of Rochdale" (Myles, 1813). See Myles, *Chronol. Hist. of the Methodists*, s. a. 1806; Smith, *Hist. of Wesleyan Methodism*, ii, 430, 432.

Cooke, Nathaniel Bowen, a Baptist minister, was born at Cambridgeport, Mass., Feb. 26, 1816. He graduated from Brown University in 1840, and passed the next three years as teacher of a select school in Bristol, R. I. He then spent a brief time in the Theological Institution in Newton Centre, Mass., and in 1844 began the study of medicine, attending a course of lectures at the medical school of Harvard University. On receiving his degree he began the practice of his profession, but subsequently returned to school teaching in Webster, Mass., and in Bristol, R. I. In 1862 he was ordained at Greenville, in the town of Leicester, Mass., and in 1869 settled in Lonsdale, R. I., where he died, April 14, 1871. See *Obituary Record of Yale College*, 1870–80; *Necrol. of Brown University*, 1871.

Cooke, Patrick (1), a Scotch clergyman, took his degree at the University of St. Andrews in 1627; was licensed to preach in 1630; admitted to the living at Stenton in 1631, and died Dec. 31, 1635, aged about thirty-nine years. See *Fasti Eccles. Scoticanæ*, i, 383.

Cooke, Patrick (2), a Scotch clergyman, son of the foregoing, was born July 21, 1626; called to the living at Prestonpans in 1653, and ordained in 1654; selected in 1670 as one of the "bishop's evangelists" for enlightening the Presbyterians of the West, and died in August, 1672. See *Fasti Eccles. Scoticanæ*, i, 351.

Cooke, Samuel (1), a minister of the Congregational Church, was born at Hadley, Mass., in 1708. He graduated from Harvard College in 1735; was ordained pastor of the Church in West Cambridge, Sept. 12, 1739, and died June 4, 1783. See Sprague, *Annals of the Amer. Pulpit*, ii, 73.

Cooke, Samuel (2), D.D., a missionary of the Church of England, was educated at the University of Cambridge, and, having been admitted to holy orders, was sent to America, probably as early as 1749, under the auspices of the Society for the Propagation of the Gospel in Foreign Parts, his destination being Monmouth County, N. J. In 1765 he ministered to three churches, located at Shrewsbury, Freehold, and Middletown, but subsequently abandoned Freehold. In

1774 he went to England, but it does not appear that he returned after this to the United States, although he was still in the employ of the missionary society. In 1785 he was at Frederickton, N. B., where he remained until the close of his life. In 1790 he was commissary to the bishop of Nova Scotia. After a period of vacation, on account of ill-health, he resumed his ministerial duties in June, 1791. While crossing the St. John's river, on his return home with his son, the canoe was upset and both were drowned, May 23, 1795. See Sprague, *Annals of the Amer. Pulpit*, v, 224.

Cooke, Theodore, a Congregational minister, was born at Northampton, Mass., Oct. 27, 1815. In 1842 he graduated from Williams College, and in 1845 from Yale Divinity School. After preaching in various places for a time, he was ordained June 10, 1847, and until 1852 was pastor in Stowe, Mass. In 1854 he went to Menasha, Wis., as a home missionary, and remained until 1857, when he returned to New England, taking charge of the Church in Woonsocket, R. I., and preached there nine years. His health failing, in 1867, he returned to Stowe to reside upon his farm, and died Aug. 27, 1871. For a short time he was editor of the *Worcester Gazette.* See *Cong. Quarterly*, 1872, p. 437.

Cooke, William, a Congregational minister, was born at Hadley, Mass. He graduated from Harvard College in 1716; was ordained at Sudbury, March 20, 1723, and died Nov. 12, 1760, aged sixty-four years. See Sprague, *Annals of the Amer. Pulpit*, i, 386.

Cookman, Alfred, A.M., a Methodist Episcopal minister, son of the renowned George G. Cookman, was born at Columbia, Pa., Jan. 4, 1828. He was early consecrated to the ministry by his pious mother; experienced religion while attending the grammar school of Dickinson College; was a diligent and earnest student; received license to preach in 1846, and in 1848 entered the Philadelphia Conference, in which he filled prominent appointments, as also he did successively in the Pittsburgh, Wilmington, New York, and Newark conferences. He died Nov. 13, 1871. Mr. Cookman inherited a measure of his father's ardent temperament, magnetic power, and earnest religious feeling. He everywhere won many to Christ. See *Minutes of Annual Conferences*, 1872, p. 35; Simpson, *Cyclop. of Methodism*, s. v.

Cookson, John, an English Baptist minister, was born in Leeds in 1800. He was converted at the age of thirteen, and early in life became a local preacher. He came to the United States, and prosecuted his theological studies under the Rev. Dr. Sharp of Boston, his maternal uncle. In 1824 he was ordained in Malden, Mass., and subsequently was pastor in South Reading, now Wakefield, and in some other places of the vicinity. In 1862, being somewhat broken in health, he returned to England, and after a time was so far recovered as to be able to take charge of the Church in St. Benedict's Square, London, where he remained till his death in April, 1873. See (Lond.) *Baptist Hand-book*, 1874, p. 265. (J. C. S.)

Cool, Peter, a Flemish engraver, flourished about 1690. He executed a number of plates, among which is one after Martin de Vos, representing *Christ Bearing the Cross*, with St. Veronica and other figures.

Cooley, Eli Field, a Presbyterian minister, was born at Sunderland, Mass., Oct. 13, 1781. He received careful training from his parents, and was educated in the Academy at Hartford, Conn., whither his parents had removed. In 1606 he graduated from the College of New Jersey; in October, 1809, was licensed by the New Brunswick Presbytery; in 1811 was installed at Cherry Valley, N. Y., where he labored until 1819, and then accepted a call from the Presbyterian Church at Middletown Point, N. J.; in 1823 accepted a call to the First Presbyterian Church in Trenton, where he labored till 1857. He died April 22, 1860. See Wilson, *Presb. Hist. Almanac*, 1861, p. 82.

Cooley, Henry Edwards, a Congregational minister, was born at Norwich, Conn., April 5, 1838. He received his preparatory education at Phillips Academy, Andover, graduated from Yale College in 1863, and from Yale Divinity School in 1866; was ordained at the First Church, Plymouth, Aug. 7 of that year, and remained there until March 31, 1869; was acting pastor at the First Church, Winsted, the next year, and the year following at South Weymouth, Mass. He was pastor at Littleton from May 9, 1872, until Oct. 29, 1874, and at Leominster from Nov. 10, 1874, until his death, Feb. 17, 1877. (W. P. S.)

Cooley, Timothy Mather, D.D., a Congregational minister, was born at East Granville, Mass., March 13, 1772. He graduated at Yale College, delivering his oration in Hebrew, and became pastor, at the age of twenty-three, of the Church in his native village, where he continued until 1854, with only an absence of four months on home missionary work. Soon after his settlement he opened a classical school in his own house, and continued it during most of his life. For fifty-seven years he was an active and influential member of the board of trustees of Westfield Academy, and for forty-seven years held the same relation to Williams College. He died at East Granville, Dec. 14, 1859. Dr. Cooley was one of the lights of the New England pulpit. Several of his sermons and addresses have been printed. The number of his publications, including his journal articles, is not far from sixty. He assisted in preparing a collection of the memoirs of all the members of the class of 1792, and in 1850 he presented the volume in MS. to the library of Yale College. See *Obituary Record of Yale College*, 1860; *Cong. Quarterly*, 1860, p. 272.

Cooley, William J., a minister of the Methodist Episcopal Church South, was born Oct. 18, 1818. He was converted in 1840 or 1841; received license to preach, and was admitted into the Tennessee Conference in 1844, in which he labored as his health permitted until 1856, when he became superannuated. He died Dec. 11, 1859. Mr. Cooley was intellectual, and labored with a fair degree of acceptability and success. See *Minutes of Annual Conferences of the M. E. Church South*, 1860, p. 212.

Coolhaas, Gaspard, a Protestant German theologian, was born at Cologne in 1536. After serving several churches he was appointed to Leyden in 1575; presided at the inauguration of the university of that place, and there taught theology until the arrival of William Fougereau, titulary professor. Coolhaas had several discussions with his colleagues; he maintained against Peter Cornelissen that the intervention of the civil magistrate was necessary in the election of elders and deacons. Brandt says that this was the beginning of the dissensions concerning the authority of the civil government in ecclesiastical matters. Coolhaas did not approve the dogma of absolute predestination. In 1578 the synod of Middleburg condemned his writings, but he appealed to the states-general of Holland, who confirmed the synodal sentence, and prohibited him from exercising his ministerial functions. The burgomaster of Leyden sustained Coolhaas in his heterodoxy, and, in spite of a new excommunication of the synod of Harlem, continued to pay him his allowance. After about two years he withdrew. He died in that city in 1615, leaving a large number of works, polemical or apologetic of his opinions, which are now of small account. See Hoefer, *Nouv. Biog. Générale*, s. v.; *Biog. Universelle*, s. v.

Coolhaas, Willem, a Dutch theologian of the family of Gaspard, was born at Deventer, Nov. 11, 1709. He completed his studies at Utrecht, where he received the degree of doctor, after having sustained a thesis upon the sentiment of the mottos πίστις, πιστός, and πιστεύειν. He was appointed minister to Langerak; then, in 1753, professor of languages and Oriental antiquities at Amsterdam, but in 1755 was called to the pastoral functions of the same city. Here he died, in 1772, leaving, *Analogia Temporum et Modorum Hebrææ Linguæ:—Observationes Philologico-Exegeticæ in Quinque Mosis Libros:—De Interrogationibus in Sacro Codice Hebræo*, and two volumes of *Sermons* in Dutch. See Hoefer, *Nouv. Biog. Générale*, s. v.; *Biog. Universelle*, s. v.

Coombe, Thomas, D.D., a minister of the Church of England, was born in Philadelphia about 1746, and graduated from the college there in 1766. He was chosen, Nov. 30, 1772, assistant minister of Christ Church and St. Peter's, in that city. On account of having exhibited a disposition inimical to the American cause, he was imprisoned in September, 1777. Although an appeal was made in his behalf, the executive council of Philadelphia determined to send him from the country. In July, 1778, he went to England and did not again return to America. For some time he was chaplain to lord Carlisle, in Ireland, by whom he was presented with a parish. He was a prebendary of Canterbury, and one of the forty-eight chaplains to the king. He wrote some poems. See Sprague, *Annals of the Amer. Pulpit*, v, 280.

Coombes, William James, an English Congregational minister, was born in 1844. He was apprenticed to a printer at Hertford, in his boyhood; experienced religion at the age of eighteen, and soon distinguished himself for piety, intelligence, and Christian usefulness. In 1866 he entered Cheshunt College, and in 1869 began his ministry at St. Ives, Cornwall. Here he labored beyond his strength, and in 1871, being obliged to quit his charge, sailed to Australia, was much invigorated by the voyage, and soon after his arrival accepted the pastorate at Hawthorn, where he died, Aug. 2, 1873. See (Lond.) *Cong. Year-book*, 1874, p. 319.

Coombs, Abner, a Free-will Baptist minister, was born at Brunswick, Me., Dec. 1, 1794. He was converted at the age of twenty-two, licensed by the Sebec Quarterly Meeting Jan. 9, 1830, and ordained Sept. 22 of the same year. The following churches were organized by him: Foxcroft, Sangerfeld, Kilmarnock, Corinth, Dover, and Hopkinton, all in his native state. He also visited the province of New Brunswick. In September, 1842, he went to Wisconsin, and, for seven years, was pastor of the Honey Creek Church. He performed pastoral work in several other churches in that state, residing in Rochester, Racine Co., where he died, March 15, 1880. See *Morning Star*, May 5, 1880. (J. C. S.)

Coombs, Benjamin, an English Baptist minister, was converted in 1800, at the age of fourteen. He studied at Stepney College for four years, and then became, for a time, a supply at East Dereham, Norfolk. Subsequently he preached for another Church in the same county, and afterwards for a Church in Herefordshire. His longest settlement was in Bridport, in Dorsetshire, where he died, Feb. 4, 1850. Mr. Coombs was a contributor to the pages of his denominational periodicals, "his attainments as a scholar being of no mean order." See (Lond.) *Baptist Magazine*, p. 302, 303. (J. C. S.)

Coon (or **McCoon**), Abram, a Seventh-day Baptist minister, was born at Hopkinton, R. I., in 1763. In 1786 he professed faith in Christ, and was ordained as a minister Aug. 26, 1798. He died in Hopkinton, Sept. 28, 1813. He was an eloquent speaker, sound in doctrine, wise in council, kind and faithful, and as such won and held a high place in public esteem.

His brother Asa, and his nephew William, were also ministers among the Seventh-day Baptists.

Also, his son Daniel was a Sabbatarian minister, born in Hopkinton, Jan. 9, 1792. He was licensed to preach March 22, 1818, ordained April 4, 1819, became pastor in Brookfield, N. Y., and performed some missionary work. In 1836 he returned to Hopkinton, and took charge of the Church of which his father had been pastor. He died May 21, 1858. He was a man of fine presence, and of a genial, sympathetic nature. He spoke with ease, fluency, and vehemence, and was fervent and impassioned in prayer. See *R. I. Biographical Cyclop.* p. 164, 240. (J. C. S.)

Coons, Andrew Nelson, a Methodist Episcopal minister, was born March 20, 1825, of Lutheran parents. In early manhood he was converted, joined the Church, and served efficiently as a local preacher; in 1862 entered the Erie Conference; in 1865 became superannuated, removed to Illinois, worked a short time as an evangelist, and finally went to Oak Ridge, Mo., where he died, May 31, 1866. Mr. Coons was a man of rare talent and culture, and possessed deep piety. See *Minutes of Annual Conferences*, 1866, p. 123.

Cooper, Abraham, an English Wesleyan missionary, was sent to the island of Tobago, W. I., in August, 1835. After two years and three months labor, he returned to England, a victim of consumption, and died at the house of his brother-in-law, in Oldland-Common, near Bristol, June 8, 1838, aged twenty-nine years. "His valuable life was too short." See *Minutes of the British Conference*, 1838.

Cooper, Alexander (1), a Scotch clergyman, took his degree at the University of St. Andrews in 1645; was admitted to the living at Sorbie before 1665; continued in 1671; transferred to Selkirk about 1677, and continued in 1682. See *Fasti Eccles. Scoticanæ*, i, 540, 745.

Cooper, Alexander (2), a Scotch clergyman, was licensed to preach in 1690; appointed to the living at North Uist in 1692, and ordained; submitted to the Presbyterian Church government in June, 1699; and was drowned in August, 1706. See *Fasti Eccles. Scoticanæ*, iii, 135.

Cooper, Alexander (3), a Scotch clergyman, took his degree at Edinburgh University in 1692; refused a call to Durrisdeer in 1697; accepted a call to Traquair in 1698, and was ordained in 1699; in 1711 he had an assistant, and died Aug. 11, 1754. He published *An Essay upon the Chronology of the World* (Edinb. 1722). See *Fasti Eccles. Scoticanæ*, i, 257.

Cooper, Benjamin, a Methodist Episcopal minister, was born in Perry County, O., June 3, 1802. He received a careful religious training; was a bright example of early piety; acquired a good English education; loved the society of the aged and upright from his youth; was very retiring and modest; and in 1827 was admitted into the Ohio Conference, wherein he labored faithfully until his superannuation in 1836. He died May 13, 1846. Mr. Cooper possessed a sound mind, respectable preaching talents, and a sweet spirit. See *Minutes of Annual Conferences*, 1846, p. 74.

Cooper, David (1), M.D., a Scotch clergyman, was licensed to preach at Rotterdam; appointed to the living at Auchinleck in 1732, and ordained; and died July 9, 1751. He published two single *Sermons*. See *Fasti Eccles. Scoticanæ*, ii, 97.

Cooper, David (2), a Baptist minister, was a pioneer of his denomination in south-west Mississippi. He was both physician and preacher in the region where he went in 1802. His labors extended throughout that section of the state, and also into eastern Louisiana. Being an educated man, he exerted his influence in establishing and maintaining institutions of learning. He assisted in the formation of the Mississippi Baptist Association, of which, for several years, he was the moderator. His "circular letters," published in the minutes of the association, are timely and valuable documents. He died in 1830. See Cathcart, *Baptist Encyclop.* p. 274. (J. C. S.)

Cooper, Ebenezer, a Presbyterian minister, was born in South Carolina in 1795. After receiving a careful academical education, he entered the South Carolina College; studied theology in the seminary of the Reformed Presbyterian Church at Philadelphia; was licensed to preach by the Philadelphia Presbytery in 1827, and was pastor, for several years, of Hephzibah Church, in West Tennessee. He died at Cedarville, O., Nov. 13, 1858. See Wilson, *Presb. Hist. Almanac*, 1860, p. 170.

Cooper, Edward, an English clergyman, became rector of Yoxhall in 1809, and died in 1833. He published, *Practical and Familiar Sermons* (7 vols. 12mo): —*The Crisis; Prophecy and Signs of the Times* (1825). See Allibone, *Dict. of Brit. and Amer. Authors*, s. v.

Cooper, Elijah, an English Methodist minister, was born at Norton-in-Hales, Aug. 6, 1828. He lost his parents in youth; was removed to Tunstall, where he attended the Primitive Methodist Sunday-school; became a teacher; was early converted, being always serious; and was accepted as a local preacher, winning many souls to Christ. He began to itinerate in 1854, and for twenty-three years preached faithfully and lovingly in the Tunstall district, his earnest appeals being very successful. In 1878 he settled at Shrewsbury as a supernumerary, working till his death, May 17, 1882.

Cooper, Elizabeth, an English martyr, was a native of Norwich, and dwelt in Lynn. She was at one time made to recant her religion, but being much troubled she entered a popish church while they were having service, and openly revoked her recantation. She was taken immediately and burned, dying happy amid the flames, in 1557. See Fox, *Acts and Monuments*, viii, 380.

Cooper, Eugene Becklard, a Universalist minister, was born at Russell, N. Y., May 6, 1852. He received an early Methodist training, and became an exhorter; but soon after embraced Universalism; graduated from the theological school at Canton in 1876, and took charge of the Universalist society in Mexico, Oswego Co. One year later he removed to Dexter, where he performed but one Sunday's service, when he was taken sick and suddenly died, Sept. 24, 1877. Mr. Cooper was industrious, modest, true to his convictions, amiable, and faithful; an able and acceptable preacher. See *Universalist Register*, 1878, p. 94.

Cooper, Ezekiel F., a Methodist Episcopal minister, was born in Kent County, Del., May 18, 1830. He received a careful moral training; was thoughtful and upright from childhood; was converted at the age of thirteen; received license to preach in 1854, and in 1855 entered the Philadelphia Conference. His health declining, he became a superannuate in 1861, and died June 28, 1862. Mr. Cooper's early disadvantages for acquiring an education were overcome by his natural thirst for knowledge. His prominent mental trait was his power of investigating, analyzing, and reasoning. His sermons were short, concise, clear, instructive, systematic, and uttered with much fervor. See *Minutes of Annual Conferences*, 1863, p. 47.

Cooper, George A. C., a Protestant Episcopal clergyman of the diocese of North Carolina, after his ordination became a teacher, in 1877, in St. Augustine Normal School, Raleigh, N. C., and continued to hold that position until his death in October, 1879. See *Prot. Episc. Almanac*, 1880, p. 170.

Cooper, James (1), a Scotch clergyman, was licensed to preach in 1663; admitted to the living at Wigton before 1664; transferred to Mochrum in 1667, and thence to Humbie in 1681; deprived in 1695 for non-jurancy; instituted to the curacy of Holy Island the same year, and died in 1701. See *Fasti Eccles. Scoticanæ*, i, 337, 730, 740.

Cooper, James (2), an English Congregational minister, was born at Walsall, Jan. 1, 1782, of pious parents. He removed with them to Birmingham, became a Christian in early life, and after suitable trial was employed in preaching in the surrounding villages. In 1803 he was sent to Rotherham College, and on completing his course settled at Wirksworth, Derbyshire, where he labored but one year, then removed to West Bromwich, where he was ordained, and preached twenty years. After this his course was very checkered; having preached at various places, he finally retired to Norwich, where he died, May 27, 1863. Mr. Cooper wrote a book on *Death Personification*. See (Lond.) *Cong. Year-book*, 1864, p. 202.

Cooper, James Ransom, an English Congregational minister, was born at Gosport, Jan. 3, 1792. He received a religious training, joined the Church at the age of seventeen, and soon after removed to London. He obtained his ministerial education at Gosport Academy, and was ordained at Emsworth, Hants, in 1819; removed thence in 1839, and became pastor successively at Pontypool, Wincanton, Old Gravel Lane, London, and finally at Seaford, Sussex. He died Aug. 17, 1867. See (Lond.) *Cong. Year-book*, 1868, p. 264.

Cooper, John (1), D.D., a Scotch clergyman, was licensed to preach in 1742; ordained in 1752 as missionary at Fort William; presented to the living at Glass in 1756, and died Dec. 20, 1795, aged seventy-eight years. See *Fasti Eccles. Scoticanæ*, iii, 199.

Cooper, John (2), a Methodist Episcopal minister, fifteen years in the itinerancy, was modest, blameless, subject to much dejection and sorrow, often in want, and died in great peace in 1789. See *Minutes of Annual Conferences*, 1789, p. 33.

Cooper, John (3), an English Baptist minister, was born at Evesham, Worcestershire, in 1821. When he was about fourteen years of age he joined the Wesleyans, and subsequently became a local preacher, but when about twenty-two joined the Baptists. For two years he remained at home, devoting himself to theological studies, and preaching in the villages. In 1844 he entered Horton College, and in 1849 settled at Ross, in Herefordshire, where he remained about two years, and then removed to Newark-on-Trent, commencing his pastorate in that place in December, 1851. He died Feb. 28, 1853. See (Lond.) *Baptist Handbook*, 1854, p. 46. (J. C. S.)

Cooper, John (4), a Scotch clergyman, studied at Edinburgh University; was licensed to preach in 1824; became assistant minister at Clackmannan, and afterwards at Arbroath; was appointed minister at Pittenweem in 1833; admitted in 1834, and died March 26, 1854, aged fifty-two years. See *Fasti Eccles. Scoticanæ*, ii, 457.

Cooper, John (5), a Methodist Episcopal minister, was born in England. He emigrated to Woodstock, Conn., in early manhood, for the purpose of engaging in a special branch of woollen manufacture; was there converted in 1842; began earnest Christian work at once; was licensed to preach in 1843, and admitted into the Providence Conference, wherein he labored with zeal and fidelity to the close of his life, Oct. 18, 1878. Mr. Cooper possessed a clear and vigorous intellect, and a glowing Christian experience. See *Minutes of Annual Conferences*, 1879, p. 79.

Cooper, John (6), an English Baptist minister, was called to preach at the age of twenty-four by the Church at Rattlesden, Suffolk, and at once employed in the chapels and villages around. The following year he was unanimously chosen to the pastorate of the Church at Wattisham, where he labored faithfully for more than forty-nine years, retiring in September, 1879. For the last fifteen years of his life he was secretary of the Suffolk and Norfolk Association. He was also co-secretary with Samuel Collins (q. v.) of the Home Mission, and an able editor of the *Gospel Herald*. He died

Feb. 22, 1880, in the seventy-sixth year of his age. See (Lond.) *Baptist Hand-book*, 1882, p. 300.

Cooper, John H., a minister of the Methodist Episcopal Church South, was a member of the Memphis Conference seven or eight years, and died in 1862 or 1863. He was gentle in spirit, an able preacher, and a faithful pastor. See *Minutes of Annual Conferences of the M. E. Church South*, 1863, p. 434.

Cooper, Joseph (1), an English nonconformist divine, was born in 1635, and died in 1699. He published, *Eight Sermons on* 1 *Pet. v*, 15 (1663):—*Domus Mosaicæ Clavis* (1673). See Allibone, *Dict. of Brit. and Amer. Authors*, s. v.

Cooper, Joseph (2), an English Baptist minister, was born at Rotherhithe, Surrey, in 1800, and was converted when somewhat mature in years. His first ministerial services were at Orpington and Oxford. In 1835 he was instrumental in forming a church in Garden Row, London Road, which called him to be its pastor, and he remained there till his death, Feb. 17, 1862. See (Lond.) *Baptist Hand-book*, 1863, p. 113. (J. C. S.)

Cooper, Joseph Calvin, a Congregational minister, was born at Plymouth, Mass., May 10, 1820. In early life he rejected the Bible. At the age of seventeen he became a sailor, and led a seafaring life about eight years. After he had settled at Denmark, Ia., he was converted. In 1848 he was engaged as a colporteur of the American Tract Society, and became specially successful in combatting infidelity for two years in southern Iowa. After this he studied theology at home, and commenced preaching in the church at Denmark, while the pastor was absent on vacation. In October, 1852, he was licensed by the Denmark Association, and was ordained May 1, 1853. His roving sailor habits followed him through life, and he went from place to place, especially in southern Iowa, and was always acceptable as a preacher. He labored, in 1856, in Fairfield, and an addition of twenty-five was made to the Church; was settled for some years in Hillsboro', and also preached for a time at Salem, but the most of his ministerial career was spent as an evangelist. He died at Cincinnati, Ia., Aug. 23, 1872. See *Cong. Quarterly*, 1874, p. 315.

Cooper, J., an English Baptist minister, was born at Bath, Oct. 24, 1793. He united with the Church at the age of seventeen, and soon after began to preach in the villages around his native city. He was ordained, April 8, 1819, pastor of a church at Amersham, and remained there until June, 1823, when he resigned; but immediately another church was formed in Amersham, and he became its pastor. His labors were greatly blessed during the seventeen years of his pastorate. In 1840 he removed to Leighton-Buzzard, his ministry here lasting seven years. He next went to Soham, then to Aberdare, and finally returned to Amersham, where he died, Nov. 23, 1871. See (Lond.) *Baptist Hand-book*, 1873, p. 253. (J. C. S.)

Cooper, Myles, D.D., an English clergyman, was born in 1735, and educated at the University of Oxford, taking the degree of A.M. in 1760. He arrived in New York in the fall of 1762, and was at once appointed professor of moral philosophy in King's College, in that city. The following year, upon the resignation of Dr. Johnson, the president of the college, he was elected to fill his place. His administration, supported as he was by able assistants, was very successful. When the war of the Revolution commenced, the affairs of the college became embarrassed. Dr. Cooper was a loyalist, and he found his position so unpleasant that, in 1775, he resigned, returned to England, and became one of the ministers of an Episcopal Church in Edinburgh, in which city he died, May 1, 1785. He was the author of several literary works. See Allen, *Amer. Biog.* s. v.; Sabine, *Loyalists of the Amer. Revolution*, i, 335. (J. C. S.)

Cooper, Peter (1), LL.D., a notable American citizen and philanthropist, was born in the city of New York, Feb. 12, 1791. His early education was confined to one year's schooling. He learned the trade of a hatter with his father, continued at this employment until he was seventeen years of age, and then found a position in a grocery store at twenty-five dollars a year. When he was of age he went to Hempstead, L. I., and worked in a woollen factory, then returned to New York and opened a grocery store. After this he changed his business five times, and finally commenced the manufacture of glue and isinglass, and exerted himself in the development of iron, and railroad and telegraph interests. Ultimately he employed in his various business engagements upwards of two hundred and fifty hands, not one of whom ever went unpaid. In all the panics and business failures in New York his finances were firm, and his wealth increased with his years, which may be attributed to his engaging in no hazardous speculations. When a young man, he conceived the idea of establishing an industrial school of science and art for indigent young men who were obliged to depend upon their own resources, and he established the Cooper Union in New York city, open for instruction in all branches of science and art. He resolved, wisely, to be the executor of his own estate, and see the fruits of his liberality. Yearly three thousand students receive gratuitous education in its halls. He contributed to the building and endowment of the institute nearly one million dollars. He died April 4, 1883, wealthy and honored. See *N. Y. Observer*, April 12, 1883; Drake, *Dict. of Amer. Biog.* s. v.; *Men of the Time*, s. v.; *Autobiography* (N. Y. 1877). (W. P. S.)

Cooper, Peter (2), an English Wesleyan minister, was born at St. Neots, Huntingdonshire, in 1804. He was converted when nineteen years of age, entered the ministry in 1830, retired from active work in 1864, and died at Blackheath, April 20, 1878. His insight into character and his broad common-sense gave him power in dealing with the problems of life. He was a plain, practical preacher; his style was quaint, sometimes epigrammatic; his piety was cheerful and lowly. See *Minutes of the British Conference*, 1878, p. 38.

Cooper, Preston, a minister of the Methodist Episcopal Church South, was born in Warren County, Tenn., Dec. 29, 1806. He was converted in 1827, and in 1828 united with the Mississippi Conference. His health failing, obliged him to become a superannuate in 1857, and he died in July, 1858. Mr. Cooper was a man of extraordinary mental ability, and a laborious student; a courageous preacher, and an energetic pastor. See *Minutes of Annual Conferences of the M. E. Church South*, 1858, p. 36.

Cooper, Richard (1), an English Wesleyan minister, was born at Woodend, Staffordshire, in 1782. He was converted at the age of twenty, entered the ministry in 1814, travelled eighteen circuits, became a supernumerary in 1846 at Windsor, and died Nov. 30, 1848. He was a faithful and godly minister. See *Minutes of the British Conference*, 1849.

Cooper, Richard (2), an English Methodist preacher, son of the foregoing, was received by the British Wesleyan Conference in 1857, sailed for West Africa, labored with success for a short time, and died at St. Mary's, on the Gambia, Aug. 13, 1859, in his twenty-sixth year. See *Minutes of the British Conference*, 1860.

Cooper, Robert (1), a Scotch clergyman, son of the minister at Mochrum, took his degree at Edinburgh University in 1744; was licensed to preach in 1749; appointed minister at Girthon, and ordained; and died Nov. 7, 1776, aged fifty-one years. He was a useful pastor, a worthy man, and a good Christian, having extensive knowledge in several branches of philosophy. See *Fasti Eccles. Scoticanæ*, i, 714.

Cooper, Robert (2), D.D., a Presbyterian minister, was born in the north of Ireland about 1732. He removed to America with his mother in 1741; graduated at New Jersey College in 1763; studied theology privately, and was licensed by the Presbytery of Carlisle, Feb. 22, 1765. In the same year he received a call from the Presbyterian Church at Middle Spring, Cumberland County, Pa., where he labored with great zeal and effect for thirty-one years. He died April 5, 1805. See Sprague, *Annals of the Amer. Pulpit*, iii, 270.

Cooper, Robert (3), a missionary of the Church of England, was a native of Wales. He was sent to South Carolina in 1758, and became rector of Prince William parish. The following year he was chosen assistant minister of St. Philip's Church, Charleston. St. Michael's Church was opened in February, 1761, and from that year until June, 1776, he was its rector. His parishioners declared the pulpit vacant because he espoused the royal cause. Afterwards he went to England and received a pension of one hundred pounds yearly in consideration of his sacrifices for the king. Soon after he was appointed joint curate and joint lecturer at St. Andrew's, Holborn, and evening lecturer at St. Michael's, Cornhill, of which he afterwards became rector. He died in England about 1812, more than eighty years of age. See Sprague, *Annals of the Amer. Pulpit*, v, 171.

Cooper, Samuel (1), D.D., an English divine of the latter part of the last century, rector of Morley and Yelverton, Norfolk, published *Sermons* (1776-90). See Allibone, *Dict. of Brit. and Amer. Authors*, s. v.

Cooper, Samuel (2), D.D., an English divine, was minister of Great Yarmouth, and died in 1800. He published, *Definitions and Axioms Relative to Charity, Charitable Institutions, and the Poor Laws* (1764):—*Sermons* (1782-90):—*Letters to Dr. Priestley* (1800). See Allibone, *Dict. of Brit. and Amer. Authors*, s. v.

Cooper, Samuel (3), an English Baptist minister, was born in 1766, baptized Dec. 16, 1787, and united with the First Church in Birmingham. He was ordained Jan. 18, 1807, and first became pastor at Romsey, Hampshire, having for a few years served the Church in Wallingford as an assistant. Subsequently he settled at Cholsey, where he died, March 7, 1839. See (Lond.) *Baptist Hand-book*, 1839, p. 24. (J. C. S.)

Cooper, Samuel Milroy, a Presbyterian minister, was born in the Kishacoquillas Valley, Pa., in 1814. He graduated at Jefferson College, Cannonsburg, in 1836; studied one year (1837) at Princeton Theological Seminary; was licensed to preach by the Huntingdon Presbytery, April 16, 1840, and ordained Oct. 15 following, as pastor at Lick Run Mills, Centre Co., Pa., and continued to preach there until the spring of 1852. He was also at this time in charge of a female seminary at Jacksonville, and continued in this position for about a year and a half after his pastoral relation closed with the Lick Run Church, when he received a call to Clearfield, and there spent two years. After a trip to Florida for his health, he became stated supply at Little Valley, Pa., but soon returned to the female seminary, the buildings of which belonged to him. His health shortly failed altogether, and he died at East Kishacoquillas, Aug. 16, 1860. See *Hist. of Presbyterianism in Huntingdon*, 1874; *Gen. Cat. of Princeton Theol. Sem.* 1881, p. 114.

Cooper, Solomon, a Methodist Episcopal minister, was born at Easton, Talbot Co., Md., in 1824. He was converted when quite young; removed to Towanda, Pa., in 1844; there joined the Wesleyan Methodists; served faithfully as an exhorter and local preacher several years; and in 1869 was admitted into the Delaware Conference of the Methodist Episcopal Church, and labored in it with great acceptability until his death, Dec. 26, 1877. See *Minutes of Annual Conferences*, 1878, p. 6.

Cooper, Sylvester W., a Methodist Episcopal minister, was born at Troy, N. Y., Oct. 31, 1839. He received a careful religious training; was converted in 1857, and in 1861 entered the Troy Conference, wherein he served the Church with marked zeal and devotedness until his decease, Nov. 23, 1864. Though young, Mr. Cooper was an excellent preacher, a devoted Christian, and a successful pastor. See *Minutes of Annual Conferences*, 1865, p. 76.

Cooper (or **Couper**), **Thomas** (1), D.D., a learned English prelate, was born at Oxford about 1517. He was educated in the school adjoining Magdalen College, of which he became a fellow in 1540. In 1546 he applied himself to the study of physic, and practiced some time in Oxford, being secretly inclined to the Protestant religion; but resumed his study of divinity, in March, 1567, and soon after became dean of Christ-church. In 1569 he was made dean of Gloucester, and in 1570 bishop of Lincoln. In July, 1572, he preached a sermon at St. Paul's Cross, in vindication of the Church of England and its liturgy, which did him much credit. In 1584 he was translated to the bishopric of Winchester, where he died April 29, 1594. His writings were numerous, among them are, *Cooper's Chronicle* (1559):—*Thesaurus Linguæ Romanæ et Britannicæ*, and *Dictionarium Historicum et Poeticum* (1565, fol.). See Chalmers, *Biog. Dict.* s. v.; Allibone, *Dict. of Brit. and Amer. Authors*, s. v.

Cooper, Thomas (2), an English Wesleyan minister, was born at Staincross, near Wakefield, in 1760. At an early period in his life, his parents, who were members of the Established Church, were converted under Methodist preaching. In 1779, Thomas, after prolonged and severe struggles, was himself converted, and on the invitation of Wesley attended the Kingswood School for fifteen months. He travelled twenty-three circuits, and in 1821 settled in Liverpool, where he died after long and complicated affliction, Oct. 1, 1832. "He was a man of sound sense, and of more than ordinary ministerial talent; so that his labors were not only acceptable, but popular and useful." He was a good historian and grammarian, somewhat taciturn, and occasionally sarcastic. See *Wesl. Meth. Mag.* 1835, p. 1, 81; *Minutes of the British Conferences*, 1833; *Wesleyan Takings*, i, 331.

Cooper, Thomas W., a minister of the Methodist Episcopal Church South, was born Jan. 28, 1818. He embraced religion in his sixteenth year; was a pupil in the Manual Labor School near Covington, Ga., in 1837–38; was then licensed to preach, and received into the Georgia Conference. He afterwards became a member of the Florida Conference, and in it did faithful work until his decease, Feb. 24, 1860. Mr. Cooper was a very eloquent declaimer, a successful revivalist, and zealous in all his work. See *Minutes of Annual Conferences of the M. E. Church South*, 1860, p. 269.

Cooper, William (1), a Scotch clergyman, was tutor to Alexander, lord Garliss; called to the living at Mochrum in 1701, and died June 1, 1747. See *Fasti Eccles. Scoticanæ*, i, 740.

Cooper, William (2), D.D., was admitted archdeacon of York, Jan. 21, 1777, and prebendary of Southwell the 25th of the same month. He published *Discourses* (1795, 2 vols.). See Allibone, *Dict. of Brit. and Amer. Authors*, s. v.

Cooper, William (3), an English Congregational minister, was born in Warwickshire, Aug. 28, 1776. He delivered his first sermon Feb. 1, 1795, and a few months later became the most popular preacher of his day. Multitudes pressed to hear him at Spa Fields and Tottenham-Court-Road chapels, as well as in the Tabernacle. He discoursed to the Jews in Zion Chapel, London, Aug. 28, 1796, on his twentieth birthday. The throng was so great that thousands could not gain entrance, and while he was speaking inside four other ministers preached outside. He undertook a tour through various parts of Ulster, Ireland, in the summer of 1799, addressing thousands, and also made a second tour the following summer. He was then called to the pastorate of the Plunket Street Congregational Church, Dublin, and entered upon his labors in April, 1802, where he continued till March, 1828, when he was forced to retire from public effort. He died Jan. 22, 1848. See (Lond.) *Cong. Year-book*, 1848, p. 217.

Cooper, William (4), a Methodist Episcopal minister, was born in Beaver County, Pa., March 25, 1814. He experienced religion in 1836; was licensed to preach in 1837, and in 1840 entered the Pittsburgh Conference, wherein he labored faithfully until the close of 1867. The last year of his life was spent in the service of the Western Seamen's Friend Society, as an agent. He died in 1868 or 1869. Mr. Cooper was of a sober, retiring disposition, a faithful minister, an excellent pastor, and an exemplary Christian. See *Minutes of Annual Conferences*, 1869, p. 45.

Cooper, William Hawes, an English Congregational minister, was born in the city of Bath in 1798. He studied at Trinity College, Dublin, and entered Hoxton Academy to prepare for the ministry in 1816. In 1819 he commenced his labors in a temporary place in Dublin, and soon succeeded in building up a new Congregational Church in that city. He was for some years the resident tutor of the theological seminary of the Irish Evangelical Society, and the secretary of the Congregational Union in Ireland. He endured many and sore trials; was in labors most abundant; refused offers of augmented income to allure him from his chosen duties. He was a warm and generous friend, an affectionate parent, an able tutor and preacher, but troubled occasionally with an infirmity of temper. He died at Manor Street, Dublin, March 1, 1847.

Cooper, William H., D.D., a Presbyterian minister, was born at Pittstown, N. Y., June 27, 1808. He studied for a time under Rev. C. Bogardus, and finished his preparatory course at the New Brunswick Classical School. He graduated from Rutgers College, N. J., in 1830, and entered the theological seminary there, where he remained two years. He was ordained by the Presbytery of Onondaga, and installed pastor of the Church of Wampsville, N. Y., Nov. 23, 1833. After ministering to this church twenty-four years, he was called to the pastorate of the United Presbyterian churches of Belleport and South Haven, Suffolk Co., N. Y., where he was installed Sept. 23, 1856. He died at Parsippany, N. J., Feb. 24, 1880. Dr. Cooper was eminently a preacher and a pastor; a faithful member of the presbytery and synod, and several times represented his presbytery in the general assembly. See *N. Y. Observer*, March 11, 1880. (W. P. S.)

Cooper, W. B., a Baptist minister, was born in Abbeville District, S. C., in 1807. He received a good early education under the direction of his father, a man of rare culture and intellect, and graduated from Columbian College in 1837. He was ordained in Augusta, Ga., in 1838, and in 1839 or 1840 went to Florida, taking up his residence at Madison Court-House. For a period of about thirty-eight years he labored chiefly in Middle Florida, sometimes itinerating in Georgia. He accomplished much for his denomination, which frequently called him to preside at conventional and associational meetings. He died in 1878. See Cathcart, *Baptist Encyclop.* p. 277. (J. C. S.)

Coore, Richard, D.D., an English divine, who died in 1687, published *Practical Exposition of the More Difficult Texts that are Contained in the Holy Bible* (1683), in the preface of which he says, "The dreams in Daniel, and the visions of all the prophets, and the two mystical books of the Canticles and the Revelation are all clearly opened." See Allibone, *Dict. of Brit. and Amer. Authors*, s. v.

Coots, Charles, a Scotch clergyman, held a bursary of theology at Glasgow University in 1698; was licensed to preach in 1702; called to the living at Govan in 1711; ordained in 1712; was chaplain in the royal army at Sterling in 1715, and died Dec. 31, 1745. See *Fasti Eccles. Scoticanæ*, ii, 69.

Cop (Lat. *Copius*), Balthazar, a German poet and philosopher, lived in the latter half of the 16th century. He taught at the gymnasium of Lemgo, embraced the doctrines of the reformed religion, went to the Palatinate, and became superintendent at Neustadt. He wrote, *De Christi Præsentia in sua Ecclesia* (1565):—*Erklärung der Epistel an die Galater* (1587):—*Elegiæ*:—*Epigrammata*. See Hoefer, *Nouv. Biog. Générale*, s. v.

Cope (from *cop*, a covering, or *caput*, the head, over which it was thrown, or *capere*, from taking in the whole body). We give additional particulars concerning this clerical garment from Walcott, *Sac. Archæol.* s. v.:

"There were several kinds of this cloak-like vestment:

"1. *The Processional or Ceremonial Cope*, called the *Pluviale*, worn out of doors, whence its name—a protection from rain in processions. It appears to have been modelled by pope Stephen, in 256, on the Roman *lacerna*, a large, square-hooded cloak, fastened with a brooch upon the breast, and worn by soldiers and civilians in the last age of the Republic, and it resembled the Greek *mandyas* or *chlamys*, a habit of smaller dimensions than the *pallium*. The *lacerna* was usually sad-colored, purple or red. The open part of the cope denoted that eternal life was offered to the minister of holy deportment; and the entire habit was an imitation of the purple robe of mockery, or *sakkos*, which our Lord was compelled to wear. It was also often called the *byrrhus*. The cope was originally a great cloak, worn in processions principally, which in time was gradually enriched with embroidery and gems, so that in the 13th century it had become one of the most magnificent vestments in use, and was known as 'precious.' It frequently had superb orphreys and a hood splendidly worked with figures of saints and other patterns. In pre-Norman times there were, in England, tassels and movable hoods of thin beaten gold and silver, such as William's stole at Ely. Some examples had fringes of bells, like one at Canterbury, which had a little chime of one hundred and forty, in 1108, and others sent by William I to Clugny, or presented by Lanfranc, Ernulph, and Conrad to their minster. One is still preserved at Aix-la-Chapelle, having silver bells round the hem, said to have been given by pope Leo III at the coronation of Charlemagne. There are three copes of the 14th century at Durham, one of which is of crimson silk, with the beheadal of Goliath; two at Langharne; one of green velvet, of the 14th century, at Ely; two at Carlisle of the 15th and 16th centuries; one of crimson velvet, with crowns and stars of Bethlehem, at Chipping-Campden; some of the date of James II, at Westminster; several of the 14th century at Spires; one of the 15th century, found at Waterford Cathedral, at Oscott; some of the 17th century at Riseholme, worn by the bishops of Lincoln at coronations; and others at Wardour Castle, Weston Underwood, and Stonyhurst; some traditionally being said to have been brought from Westminster. The silken copes were distributed in choir by the precentor to the various members, upon great festivals; at other times they were carefully folded and put away in triangular cope-chests. Every canon, at his installation, presented one of these precious or processional copes to the fabric; and every abbot or bishop gave a cope of profession, on his appointment, to Canterbury Cathedral. In England, at the Reformation, the precious

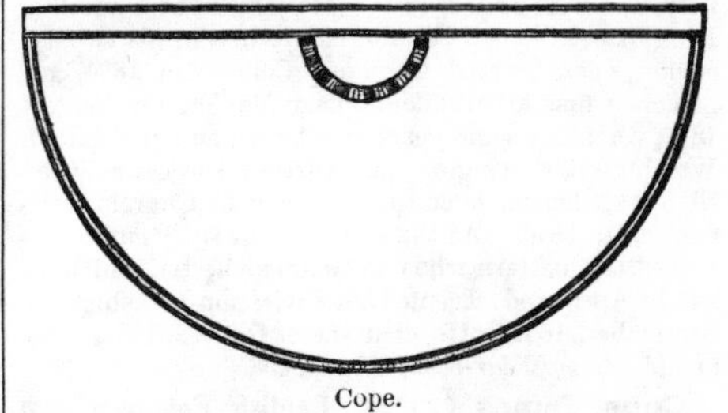

Cope.

copes were, unhappily, too often desecrated to garnish beds as coverlets. Bishop Cosin wore a cope of white satin. Portions of copes are still, in several English churches, used as altar or pulpit cloths.

"2. *The Canonical or Choral Cope* was a large, full, flowing cloak of black woollen stuff, worn by canons and vicars in cathedrals. It is mentioned at Chichester, in the 12th century, as without corsets and open. It opened downwards from the breast, and was sewed up as far as the throat, round which was a hood. In the 15th century, the almuce was sewn on to the cope like a hood, except when it was carried across the shoulders, or thrown over the left arm.

"3. *The Close or Sleeveless Cope*, an ample hood lined with fur, did not open in front, whence its name. The hood was of ermine, like that of the proctors at Oxford. It is seen depicted on the famous wall-painting of Chichester Cathedral—bishop Sherborne being habited in it. In the 13th century all clerks were required to wear close copes in synods, and in the presence of prelates and parochial clergy in their parish; they were to be laid aside on journeys. Black canons, Benedictines, and nuns were to use black, and not colored copes, and faced only with black or white fur of lambs, cats, or foxes. They were forbidden caps by H. Walter's canons in 1200. In 1195 priests were forbidden to wear sleeved copes. In 1222 monks and canons were proscribed burnet or irregular cloth, or girdles of silk, or gold embroidery in their habit, and the nuns were to use no veil of silk. At the close of the 12th century dignitaries were allowed the use of sleeved copes; but in 1222 it was found necessary to forbid the gay colors of red and green adopted for copes. The monk retained the sombre hue of black. At Cambridge doctors of divinity still wear, on formal occasions, a cope of scarlet cloth with ermine bands in front. By the Laudian statutes of Oxford on formal occasions, they are required to wear either the close or open cope; and bachelors of arts, when reading in the Bodleian library, were enjoined to be attired in 'their habit or cope, cowl, and cap.'

"The *Cappa Magna*, worn in processions and during certain functions in Italy at this day, corresponds to the English close cope. It is a large violet-colored habit, with a train and an ermine cape when worn by bishops, but only furred when canons use it."

Cope, Alan, an English Roman Catholic, who died about 1580, published *Historiæ Evangelicæ Veritas* (Lond. 1572):—and, under his own name, the Latin work of Nic. Harpesfield, entitled *Dialogi sex Contra Summi Pontificatus Monasticæ Vitæ*, etc. (Antw. 1566). See Allibone, *Dict. of Brit. and Amer. Authors*, s. v.

Cope, David, a minister of the Society of Orthodox Friends, was born at East Bradford, Chester Co., Pa., Jan. 24, 1787. His first appearance as a minister occurred in his own monthly meeting, when he was about twenty-four years old, but he was not fully approved as such until 1814, four years thereafter. His ministerial labors were mostly within the limits of Philadelphia, but in 1852 he visited the subordinate meetings of Ohio. He died Sept. 24, 1864. See *Memorials, etc., for Pennsylvania*, 1879, p. 479.

Cope, Edward, a Presbyterian minister, was born at Lisbon, N. Y., May 25, 1806. He joined the Church in 1827, studied two years (1833 and 1834) at Centre College, one year in the Western Theological Seminary; graduated from the Auburn Theological Seminary in 1836; was ordained as a missionary to India, and, after a service of ten years, returned on account of ill-health; preached at Norwich, N. Y., and the vicinity, from 1854, and died at Gilbertsville, May 10, 1884. See *Presbyterianism in Central N. Y.* p. 503; *Gen. Cat. of Auburn Theol. Sem.* 1883, p. 46, 289. (W. P. S.)

Cope, James (1), an English Congregational minister, was born Jan. 8, 1800. He joined the Church at King Street Chapel, Birmingham, when in his twenty-second year, entered Cheshunt College in 1824, and preached first at Middleton, near Manchester, Sept. 2, 1827, where for some years he labored, and at Sleaford, Warrington, Farrington, and Alfriston successively, until his settlement over the Independent Church, Newmarket, in 1840. At the end of about six years he removed to Chatteris, then to Godmanchester, which he left in April, and accepted an invitation to Ashford in September, 1851. He died there, Oct. 12, 1852. See (Lond.) *Cong. Year-book*, 1853, p. 208.

Cope, James (2), an English Congregational minister, was born in London, Sept. 16, 1781. He was brought up by a pious mother, converted in early life, and educated at Hoxton Academy; was ordained at Weytown, near Bridport, in 1815; retired from the pastorate in 1823; accepted a call to St. Austell in 1828, and resigned in 1848. He died while on a visit to Plymouth, May 28, 1863. Mr. Cope generally supported himself by keeping a boarding-school. See (Lond.) *Cong. Year-book*, 1864, p. 204.

Cope, Richard, LL.D., F.A.S., a distinguished English Congregational minister, was born in London, near the spot where the Craven Chapel now stands, Aug. 23, 1776. Becoming a junior clerk in St. Albans Street, he was made chaplain of the lady of the house. He was next engaged with Kenneth Mackenzie, of Loch Torridge, Rosshire, Jan. 21, 1793, and while there employed his vacant hours in studying theology, On Dec. 9, 1795, he became the clerk of Edward Leigh, Esq., of Tooke's Court, but his desire for the ministry reviving, he entered Old College, Hoxton, March 5, 1798, and there continued until his removal to Lancaster, June 28, 1800. At the last-named place he conducted a boarding and day school with extraordinary success, preached in sixteen villages, enlarged the chapel four times, and saw numbers added to the Church. He removed to Dublin as professor or tutor in New College, Manor Street, Aug. 1, 1820, but resigned after two years. He then travelled through the north of Ireland on behalf of the Irish Evangelical and London Missionary societies. On Sept. 30, 1822, he became pastor of Salem Chapel, Wakefield, where he was very successful, and removed, April 8, 1836, to Penryn, where the house soon became crowded. In 1840 he erected a chapel at Poliphant, near Launceston, and another at Mylor Bridge, near Penryn, where he preached every Sunday afternoon. His labors for fifty-six years were abundant. During that time he preached three times on Sundays and several times through the week. He died Oct. 26, 1856. See (Lond.) *Cong. Year-book*, 1857, p. 172.

Cope, Samuel, a minister of the Society of Orthodox Friends, was born at East Bradford, Chester Co., Pa., Feb. 28, 1789. His mother, Jane Cope, was a minister for more than fifty years, and died March 28, 1834, aged seventy-three years. When thirty-nine years old Samuel became an elder, and in 1835 was duly acknowledged as a minister. He visited several yearly meetings in the United States. He died Nov. 11, 1871. See *Memorials for Pennsylvania*, 1879, p. 495; *The Friend*, vii, 208.

Cope-chest is a deep and broad wooden chest, semicircular in shape, for containing copes unfolded—an ordinary piece of furniture in the sacristies of our largest and most important churches in past years. Examples are to be seen, among other places, at Wells Cathedral, at Salisbury Cathedral, at York Minster, at Lockinge, Berkshire, and at Brampton, Northamptonshire. See CHESTS.

Copeland, Adoniram Judson, a Congregational minister, was born at Brewer, Me., in March, 1814. He graduated from Bowdoin College in 1840, and from the Bangor Theological Seminary in 1843. After preaching for a time in Maine he removed to Illinois, and accepted a call to the pastorate of the Church at Como, in that state. He died in 1855. See *Hist. of Bowdoin College*, p. 541. (J. C. S.)

Copeland, David, D.D., a Methodist Episcopal minister and educator, was born in Braintree, Vt., Dec. 21, 1832. He graduated from the Wesleyan University in 1855, joined the Genesee Conference in 1858, and was the same year appointed principal of the Springville (N. Y.) Academy. In 1865 he was transferred to the Cincinnati Conference, and became president of the Hillsborough (O.) Female College. In 1872 he was elected principal of the Wyoming Seminary, and in 1873 was transferred to the Wyoming Conference. He died in Royalton, Vt., Dec. 6, 1882. See *Minutes of Annual Conferences*, 1883, p. 88.

Copeland, Edmund, a Methodist Episcopal minister, was born in Braintree, Vt., July 3, 1811. He was converted in 1825, licensed in 1829, and joined the New Hampshire Conference in 1833. In 1834 he was ordained deacon, and in 1836 elder. He was a successful preacher and pastor, and filled several of the best appointments in the conference. In 1852 that body sent him as a delegate to the General Conference. When on Middlesex and Montpelier Circuit he was prostrated by excessive labors, from which he never recovered. He died at Barre, April 16, 1881. Mr. Copeland was modest, retiring, prudent, thoughtful, and devoted. See *Minutes of Annual Conferences*, 1881, p. 94.

Copeland, George W. Doane, a minister of the Protestant Episcopal Church, was born in Boston, Mass., Feb. 22, 1833. In 1860 he graduated from the German Theological Seminary, and was ordained deacon in that year, and priest in 1863. His ministerial life was spent in connection with St. Luke's Church, New York city, though his labors were frequently interrupted by bodily suffering. He died in Boston, May 21, 1864. His character was distinguished by marked piety. See *American Quarterly Church Review*, April, 1865, p. 139.

Copeland, Henry, a minister of the Methodist Episcopal Church South, was admitted into the Memphis Conference in 1846, located in 1850, removed to Vicksburg, and in 1856 entered the Mississippi Conference, wherein he labored until he became superannuated, in 1868. Not long afterwards he removed to British Honduras, and from that time to the close of his life labored constantly and successfully as a missionary there. He died July 24, 1879, aged about sixty years. He was a substantial Christian, faithful minister, and a devoted father and friend. See *Minutes of Annual Conferences of the M. E. Church South*, 1879, p. 49.

Copeland, James, a Methodist Episcopal minister, was born in Reynolds County, Mo., Aug. 21, 1836. He experienced religion, joined the Church South, was licensed to preach, and admitted into the St. Louis Conference in 1853. Being anti-slavery in sentiment, he removed to Illinois at the beginning of the Rebellion, and was admitted into the Southern Illinois Conference. Failing health obliged him to become a superannuate in 1871, which relation he sustained until his death, Oct. 12, 1872. Mr. Copeland was a man of strong convictions, and a plain, practical, earnest, faithful minister. See *Minutes of Annual Conferences*, 1873, p. 137.

Copeland, John (1), an English minister of the Society of Friends, was born at Holderness, Yorkshire, and is referred to as having been "well educated." In 1657 he went to America with Christopher Holder and other Friends, his "companions in tribulation." Returning to his native land, he passed through the vicissitudes which fell to the lot of the Quakers of his age. In 1687 he came again to America. After enduring much persecution, he died, Jan. 9, 1718, at a good old age. See Bowden, *Hist. of Friends in America*, i, 137. (J. C. S.)

Copeland, John (2), a Methodist Episcopal minister, was born in Vermont in 1801. He was converted in 1821, began preaching in 1822, and joined the Genesee Conference in 1823. His first appointment was Eden Circuit, south of Buffalo, and embraced thirty appointments to be filled every four weeks. He became one of the leading men of his conference, eminently useful to the Church. As a presiding elder he was abundant in labors and wise in administration. He was superannuated during the last years of his life, and died at Lima, N. Y., Oct. 7, 1880. See *Minutes of Annual Conferences*, 1881, p. 327.

Copeland, William, an Irish Wesleyan minister, was converted at the age of seventeen. He commenced his labors in 1806, and retired, on account of ill-health, in 1819, settling at Waterford, where he died, Sept. 22, 1822, aged forty-one. He was a man of superior attainments and excellence. See *Minutes of the British Conference*, 1823.

Copeland, William Ransom, a Methodist Episcopal minister, was born in Jackson County, O., Feb. 14, 1835. He united with the Church in 1853, was licensed to exhort in 1856, to preach in 1857, and in the same year entered the Ohio Conference. He died May 4, 1870. Mr. Copeland was a good preacher, a laborious, faithful, and successful pastor. See *Minutes of Annual Conferences*, 1871, p. 249.

Copenhagen, Council of (*Concilium Hafniense*). The place in which this council was held is not altogether certain; it was assembled by Peter Lukins, archbishop of Lund, in 1425. His suffragans, and some other bishops, abbots, etc., were present. A synodal letter was drawn up for the re-establishment of discipline, and the reformation of morals among both clergy and laity. These rules forbid luxury, drunkenness, frequenting wine-shops, carrying arms, having concubines, etc. All troublers of State or Church were excommunicated; nuns were forbidden to leave their convent without permission, and bishops to ordain any one belonging to another diocese without the consent of the bishop of that diocese. See Labbe, *Concil.* xii, 380.—Landon, *Man. of Councils*, s. v.

Copia, in Roman mythology, was the goddess of wealth, an allegorical figure, personifying plenty. See Abundantia; Amalthea.

Copinists were a sect of Universalists (q. v.) who denied the resurrection of the body.

Copland is the family name of several Scotch clergymen:

1. George, was licensed to preach in 1722; called to the living at Birsay and Harray in 1730, and ordained. He died Aug. 9, 1735. See *Fasti Eccles. Scoticanæ*, iii, 393, 394.

2. Patrick (1), was licensed to preach in 1671, and appointed to the living at Cushnie in 1672. He died in 1710. See *Fasti Eccles. Scoticanæ*, iii, 562.

3. Patrick (2), was licensed to preach in 1704; called to the living at Tough in 1706, and ordained. He died Sept. 22, 1745, leaving a son, Dr. Samuel, minister of Fintray. See *Fasti Eccles. Scoticanæ*, iii, 566.

4. Robert, was ordained in 1814 as missionary at Euzie, and presented to the living at Durris in 1823. He died July 3, 1860, aged eighty years. See *Fasti Eccles. Scoticanæ*, iii, 499.

5. Samuel, D.D., took his first degree at King's College, Aberdeen, in 1733; was licensed to preach in 1739; called to the living at Fintray in 1745, and ordained. He died Feb. 19, 1795, aged eighty years. He published, *An Essay on the Christian Character* (1785). See *Fasti Eccles. Scoticanæ*, iii, 503.

6. Thomas, took his degree at the University of St. Andrews in 1603; was appointed in 1615 to the living at Redkirk (Renpatrick), and transferred to Temple in 1620. He died in August, 1631, aged about forty-nine years. See *Fasti Eccles. Scoticanæ*, i, 307, 619.

7. William, was born at Tough in 1709; took his degree at King's College, Aberdeen, in 1731; was licensed to preach in 1740, ordained as a minister at large in 1753, and presented to the living at Forres in 1763. He died May 8, 1772. See *Fasti Eccles. Scoticanæ*, iii, 573.

Copley, William, an English Baptist minister, was born at Bradford, Yorkshire, in 1796. He was converted under the ministry of Rev. Dr. Steadman, at an early age; pursued the usual course of study at the academy in his native place, and was for a short time pastor in Haslingden, Lancashire. In 1821 he removed to Watford, Herts, where he remained till 1825, and then went to Oxford to become co-pastor with Rev. James Hereton, the relation continuing till 1839, when he went to Eythorne, Kent. He remained here until 1846, at which time he became pastor at Blakeney,

Gloucestershire, where he died, April 19, 1857. See (Lond.) *Baptist Hand-book*, 1858, p. 48. (J. C. S.)

Copp, John B., a Free-will Baptist minister, was born at Lebanon, Me., March, 1811; his father, also, being a minister. He united with the Church at an early age. About 1833 he removed to Detroit, in the same state, where he was licensed to preach; and in 1835 was ordained. While teaching in the winter of 1836, in Corinna, a powerful revival commenced in his school and spread in different directions. In 1838 he went to St. Albans, where he resided nine years, preaching mostly in that place and in the adjoining towns. In July, 1847, he went to Ashtabula County, O. A part of his time was devoted to preaching in Geneva, Austinburg, Trumbull, and other places. In 1853 he removed to Flushing, Mich., where he died, Nov. 10, 1855. See *Free-will Baptist Register*, 1857, p. 86. (J. C. S.)

Coppa, Stefano, an Italian engraver, practiced the art at Rome about 1775. He engraved a number of plates, among which is a print of *The Ascension.*

Coppenstein, Johann Andreas, a German Jesuit, who became a famous preacher at Coblentz in 1614, pastor of St. Peter's, at Heidelberg, in 1629, and died there, March 3, 1638, is the author of *Excalvinizatio Catechismi Calvino-Heidelbergensis:—Castigatio Apologiæ Calvino-catecheticæ et Apologistæ Amstelrodamensis:—Controversiarum Luthero-Calvinista Quadriceps:—Luthero-Calvinismi Antichristus, Genealogia et Anti-papista Mendax:—Calvinisticæ fidei Speculum:—Luthero-Calvinismi Infidelitas de Christo et Antichristo.* Most of his writings were published under the title, *J. A. Coppensteinii Controversiæ inter Catholicos et Hæreticos* (1643). See Jöcher, *Allgemeines Gelehrten-Lexikon*, s. v. (B. P.)

Coppi, Jacopo, an Italian painter, was born at Peretola, near Florence, in 1523. There is a fine picture by him, of *The Crucifixion*, in the Church of San Salvatore, at Bologna. He died in 1591.

Coppin, Jean, a French voyager, was born about 1615, and became a cavalry captain in the war between France and Austria. He embarked in 1638 for Egypt, where he spent two years. On the second voyage he visited Tunis and Syria, and was appointed consul at Damietta in 1644. After a sojourn of three years in the East, he returned to Europe with the project of a crusade, in which he vainly attempted to interest the pope. He then addressed the public in a book, entitled *Bouclier de l'Europe* (Puy, 1686; Lyons, 1720). He died about 1690. See Hoefer, *Nouv. Biog. Générale*, s. v.; *Biog. Universelle*, s. v.

Coppola, Giovanni Carlo, an Italian prelate and poet of the first half of the 17th century, was a native of Gallipoli, and became bishop of Muro in 1643. He lived five years on intimate terms with Campanella, and wrote some poems, for which see Hoefer, *Nouv. Biog. Générale*, s. v.

Coptic Monk.

Coptic Monks are the monks of Egypt living in the seven regular convents of that country, two of which are situated in the eastern desert near the Red Sea, four in the Natron Valley, and one at Jebel Koskun, in Upper Egypt. There are also several secondary monasteries, in which the priests are seculars, and into which women are admitted. The Coptic monks practice great austerities, living in deserts, sleeping in their clothes on the ground, and every evening prostrating themselves one hundred and fifty times with their face and breast on the earth. They spring from the lowest class of the people, and live on alms. A period of severe probation is required of all persons applying for admission into the monastic order. Besides making a vow of celibacy, they must perform, in some sequestered convent in the desert, such menial services as fetching wood and water, sweeping the rooms, or waiting upon the monks. See *Histoire du Clergé* (Amst. 1716), i, 93 sq. See Copts.

Coq (Lat. *Coquæus*), Léonard, a French Augustinian monk, was a native of Orleans. He acted as professor of theology and ancient languages at Paris, Florence, and Rome; was confessor to the grand-duchess Christina of Florence; and died Nov. 27, 1615, leaving, among other writings, *Augustini de Civitate Dei cum Commentariis:—Examen Præfationis Monitoriæ Jacobi I Magnæ Britanniæ:—Anti-Mornæus*, etc. See Jöcher, *Allgemeines Gelehrten-Lexikon*, s. v. (B. P.)

Coquelin, François, a French monk of the order of St. Bernard, was born at Salins, and lived in the 17th century. He wrote, *Compendium Vitæ et Miraculorum Sancti Claudii* (Rome, 1652). See Hoefer, *Nouv. Biog. Générale*, s. v.

Coquelin, Jérôme, a French historian, was born at Besançon, July 21, 1690. He entered the Benedictine order, and was the last abbot of Faverney. He died Sept. 1, 1771, leaving in MS. some works relating to the history of Franche Comté. See Hoefer, *Nouv. Biog. Générale*, s. v.; *Biog. Universelle*, s. v.

Coquelin, Nicolas. See Cocquelin.

Coquerel, Athanase Josué, D.D., son of the following, was born at Amsterdam, June 16, 1820. He studied at Geneva, and was ordained in 1843 by his father, at Nismes. On account of his advanced liberal theological views, he had to resign his office, in 1862, and became the head and leader of liberal Protestantism in France. He died at Fismes, July 25, 1875. He was one of the founders of the Societé de l'Histoire du Protestantisme Français, in the year 1852. He also published a volume of unedited letters of Voltaire, on Tolerance, in 1863, and wrote, *Jean Calas et sa Famille* (Fismes, 1857; 2d ed. 1870). He left an unfinished work, *L'Histoire de l'Église Réformée de Paris.* See Lichtenberger, *Encyclop. des Sciences Religieuses*, s. v. (B. P.)

Coquerel, Athanase Laurent Charles, a French Protestant divine, and president of the Presbyterian Council of Paris, was born in that city, Aug. 27, 1795. He pursued his theological studies at Geneva and Montauban, and in 1816 was ordained pastor. During the following twelve years he resided in Holland, and preached with acceptance before Calvinistic congregations at Amsterdam, Leyden, and Utrecht. In 1830 he was called to Paris, and there spent the rest of his life. The first year he was there he established a periodical, entitled *Le Protestant*, which was continued till December, 1833, when he was chosen a member of the consistory. In January, 1834, the first number of the *Libre Examen* appeared, under the joint editorship of Coquerel and Artaud, and was carried on until July, 1836. He rapidly acquired the reputation of a great pulpit orator, and the liberal views which he announced with fearless freedom brought him more and more into antagonism with the rigid Calvinists. He was chosen a member of the Legion of Honor, at Paris, in 1835. After the revolution of February, 1848, Coquerel was elected a member of the National Assembly; and after the *coup d'état* of Dec. 2, 1851, he confined himself to the duties of his pastorate, which he had not ceased to discharge. He died at Paris, Jan. 10, 1868. A large number of his *Sermons* were published, in eight volumes, between 1819 and 1852. Other works by him are, *L'Orthodoxie Moderne*, a reply to Strauss's *Life of Jesus* (Paris, 1841; transl. into Dutch and English):—

Le Christianisme Expérimental, a christology (ibid. 1858; transl. into German by H. Althaus, Hanover, 1859, 2 vols.):—*Histoire Sainte* (1839):—*Projet de Discipline pour les Églises Réformées de France* (ibid. 1861):—*Biographie Sacrée* (1825–26), etc. See Lichtenberger, *Encyclop. des Sciences Religieuses*, s. v.; Zuchold, *Bibl. Theol.* i, 243; *Encyclop. Brit.* 9th ed. s. v.

Coquerel, Charles Augustin, brother of the preceding, was born in Paris, April 17, 1797. He studied theology at Montauban, but after his return to Paris he also studied medicine and other sciences. He was one of the founders of the *Archives du Christianisme* and of the *Annales Protestantes* in 1819, and in 1825 of the *Revue Protestante*. He also published *Histoire des Églises du Désert* (Paris, 1841; Germ. transl. by Schilling, Stuttgart, 1846). He died Feb. 1, 1851. See Lichtenberger, *Encyclop. des Sciences Religieuses*, s. v.; Zuchold, *Bibl. Theol.* i, 243. (B. P.)

Coracion was chief of the Millenarians of Arsinoë, in Egypt, about the middle of the 3d century. He was converted from his chiliastic views by Dionysius, the patriarch of Alexandria (Euseb. *Hist. Eccl.* vii, 24).

Coral, Pierre, a French chronicler of the 13th century, abbot of St. Martin of Toulouse, wrote a chronicle of this monastery. Coral left this abbey in 1276, in order to enter another, and his chronicle does not extend beyond this term. See Hoefer, *Nouv. Biog. Générale*, s. v.

Coras (Lat. *Corasius*), Jacques de, a French Protestant theologian and poet, was born at Toulouse in 1630. He was a pastor in Guienne, and fulfilled several other religious functions. He died in 1677, leaving several poems on Old-Test. characters, for which see Hoefer, *Nouv. Biog. Générale*, s. v.

Corbanus. See Cerban.

Corbeil (Lat. *Corbelius*), Pierre de, a French theologian of the 13th century, was at first canon and doctor at Paris, then bishop of Cambray, and finally archbishop of Sens in 1200. While he taught theology at Paris he had for pupil Innocent III, who, on rising to the papacy, favored his former master, and confided to him important missions. Rigord, Alberic, Vincent of Beauvais, Trithemius, and Henry de Gand all eulogize Corbeil. He died June 3, 1222. Only fragments of his synodal ordinances remain. At the National Library of Paris there is a MS. entitled *Petri de Corbellio Satyra Adversus eos qui Uxares Ducunt*, which is perhaps his. He also wrote some Scriptural comments, still in MS. See Hoefer, *Nouv. Biog. Générale*, s. v.; Jöcher, *Allgemeines Gelehrten-Lexikon*, s. v.

Corbelin, Pierre, a French theologian, was born in Maine about 1480. He taught belles-lettres at the College of Navarre, as John of Launoy attests. Du Verdier includes among his works, *De Divino Missæ Sacrificio:—De Hæreticorum Confutatis Opinionibus* (Toulouse, 1523):—*Petri Corbelini Cenomanensis Adagiales Flosculi* (Paris, 1520). See Hoefer, *Nouv. Biog. Générale*, s. v.

Corbet, John (1), a Scotch clergyman, took his degree at Glasgow University in 1623; became schoolmaster at Renfrew; was appointed minister at Bonhill in 1637; declined the authority of the general assembly in 1638; was deposed in April, 1639, and fled to Ireland, where he played a deceitful part, for which he was "hewed in pieces by two swine-herds in the arms of his wife," in 1641, aged about thirty-eight years. See *Fasti Eccles. Scoticanæ*, ii, 346.

Corbet, John (2), an English nonconformist divine, was born at Gloucester in 1620. He was educated at a grammar school there, and graduated at Oxford in 1639. He preached successively at Gloucester and Chichester, and became rector at Bramshot, in Hampshire, but was ejected in 1662, and afterwards lived privately in London, where he died Dec. 26, 1680. He published an account of the siege of Gloucester, besides several tracts, for which see Chalmers, *Biog. Dict.* s. v.; Allibone, *Dict. of Brit. and Amer. Authors*, s. v.

Corbet, Richard, D.D., an English prelate and poet, was born at Ewell, in Surrey, in 1582, and was educated at Westminster School and Christ Church, Oxford, where, in 1605, he entered into holy orders. In 1618 he went to France, and wrote his *Epistle to Sir Thomas Aylesbury*, and his *Journey to France*, one of his popular poems. King James I made him one of his chaplains in ordinary, and in 1620 advanced him to the deanship of Christ Church. At this time he was vicar of Cassington, near Woodstock, in Oxfordshire. He was promoted to the see of Oxford Sept. 24, 1628, and April 7, 1632, was translated to that of Norwich. He died July 28, 1635. His poems, after passing through three editions, were carefully revised and published by his biographer, Mr. Gilchrist. See Chalmers, *Biog. Dict.* s. v.; Allibone, *Dict. of Brit. and Amer. Authors*, s. v.

Corbett, James, an English Wesleyan missionary, was sent to the West Indies in 1833. He died after a short illness at Spanish Town, Jamaica, June 9, 1835. He was an amiable young man of promising talents. See *Minutes of the British Conferences*, 1835.

Corbett, Thomas, an English Wesleyan preacher, was born in Leicestershire. He began his labors in 1774, and died in 1789. He was a plain, pious, honest man, and though with but ordinary gifts, was generally acceptable. See Atmore, *Meth. Memorial*, s. v.

Corbichon (or **Corbechon**), Jean, a French writer, lived about 1350. He was an Augustinian monk, chaplain of king Charles V, and made himself known by a translation of a Latin treatise, entitled *De Proprietatibus Rerum*. This work, reviewed and corrected by another monk of the order, named Pierre Ferget, was published under the title, *Le Grand Propriétaire* (Lyons, 1482, 1485, 1491, 1500; Paris, 1510; Rouen, 1556). See Hoefer, *Nouv. Biog. Générale*, s. v.; *Biog. Universelle*, s. v.

Corbicus. See Manes.

Corbin, Ira Hamline, a Methodist Episcopal minister, was born in Russia, Herkimer Co., N. Y., Sept. 1, 1812. He was converted at eighteen; licensed to preach at twenty-three, and in 1840 entered the Black River Conference, wherein he labored faithfully until his death, Dec. 11, 1856. See *Minutes of Annual Conferences*, 1857, p. 365.

Corbitt, John A., a minister of the Methodist Episcopal Church South, was born in Tipton County, Tenn., Dec. 28, 1836. He was converted at twenty-one; licensed to preach in 1872, and joined the White River Conference in 1876, when he was ordained deacon. In 1877 he was transferred to the Memphis Conference. He died Jan. 2, 1880, having been for a year a superannuate. He was a faithful preacher, and a close student. See *Minutes of Annual Conferences of the M. E. Church South*, 1880, p. 167.

Corbley, John, a Baptist minister, was born in England in 1733. He came to America and took up his residence in Virginia, where he gave himself to the work of the ministry. In 1768 he was forced to leave the state, on account of the persecutions which were inflicted upon the Baptists. He went to South-western Pennsylvania, and assisted in establishing churches in that region. The Goshen Church in Green County called him to be its pastor in 1775. While here his wife and five children were killed by the Indians. After a life of great usefulness he died in 1803. See Cathcart, *Baptist Encyclop.* p. 277. (J. C. S.)

Corbmac (or **Cormac**) is the name of some forty-eight early Irish saints, of which we here present the best authenticated:

1. Priest in Achadh-finnich, commemorated May 11, according to the *Mart. Doneg.* (Todd and Reeves, p. 125). Colgan mentions a king by this name, son of Diarmaid, who turned monk in his old age, and likewise gives two Cormacs, priests, venerated on the above day (*Acta Sanctorum*, p. 360, *a*).

2. Of Armagh, venerated Feb. 17, seems to have been born near Mt. Usneach, and was baptized by St. Patrick. His father is said to have been Enna (Ennius or Enda), and he was coarb or abbot of Armagh, A.D. 482–497.

3. Of Trim (then Ath-truim), likewise venerated Feb. 17, seems to have been descended from the same family as the preceding, his mother being Funecta (Fuineacht), his brothers also bishops of adjoining sees, and his father's name Colman. He died A.D. 742.

4. Called *Ua Liathain*, abbot of Dermagh (now Durrow), and venerated June 21, was the son of Dima, and is surnamed "Corbmac the Navigator," from his voyages in the Northern Ocean. He afterwards founded a monastery in his own country, but there is no clue to his exact date.

Another anchorite of the same name is assigned to A.D. 865, but is otherwise unknown.

5. Of Munster, commemorated Dec. 14 (some erroneously March 26), was the son of Eugenius, and had several brothers who were saints. He retired to one place of solitude after another, and finally settled in a monastery at Mayo, on the Moy, probably about the middle of the 6th century.

Corbold, Alfred, an English missionary to India, was born at Ipswich, May 7, 1821. Having studied at Bedford, and subsequently at Colton End, he was accepted by the London Missionary Society and appointed to the Guzerat Mission. He was ordained Aug. 7, 1850, at Bunyan Meeting, Bedford; sailed in company with his wife for India, and arrived at his destination in January. From the beginning of 1856 the entire charge of the mission rested on Mr. Corbold. Early in 1860 the mission was transferred to the Irish Presbyterian Missionary Society; and he and his wife, having suffered in health, returned to England. Having been appointed to join the Madras Mission, he again sailed with Mrs. Corbold, arriving in Madras Jan. 31, 1862. There he took charge of the Tamil congregation, at Pursewakum, and three out-stations; while his wife took the superintendence of the native female boarding-school, and three vernacular day-schools for girls. But health again failing them, they returned to England in 1870. Three years later they resumed their labors in Madras. In 1875, illness rendering it necessary for Mr. Corbold to visit England, he returned home with his wife. It soon became evident that the faithful missionary's career was at an end. He died Sept. 28, 1877. See (Lond.) *Evangelical Magazine*, Nov. 1877, p. 688.

Corbyn, A. D., a minister of the Protestant Episcopal Church, was born in Woodstock, Conn., in 1810. He graduated at Yale in 1838; and being admitted to orders, served twelve years in Missouri, and removed to the diocese of Mississippi in 1852, to take charge of St. Paul's Church, Columbus. He was next called to the rectorship of the College of St. Andrew, in 1853, and subsequently to the charge of St. Andrew's Church, in Jackson, where he faithfully served until his death, Oct. 18, 1855. See *Amer. Quar. Church Rev.* 1856, p. 638.

Corbyn, Candia, a Welsh minister of the Society of Friends, was born at Pontypool, Monmouthshire, about 1671. Through the ministry of Thomas Wilson she was brought to the knowledge of the truth in the eighteenth year of her age, and a few years after received "a call to the ministry," in the exercise of which "she was sound and clear." Through a long life she manifested the power of her religion. She died in Worcester, April 28, 1767. See *Piety Promoted*, ii, 423. (J. C. S.)

Corcan (**Curcnaeus**, or **Corcunutan**) is the name of three Irish saints, two of them commemorated Jan. 7, and one Sept. 30; but their identification is very uncertain.

Corcaria (or **Corcair**). See Curcach.

Corcodēmus (**Corcodomus**, **Cocordanus**, **Curcudemus**, etc.), *Saint*, was ordained deacon of Auxerre by pope Sixtus II, and preached in France in the 3d century. He died after the martyrdom of St. Peregrinus, and his relics were translated to the basilica of St. Amatos. He is commemorated May 4. See Bolland, *Acta Sanctorum*, May, i, 452.

Cord, Investiture with the, is a name applied to the ceremony of introducing the young Brahmin into the sacred caste at the age of seven or nine years. Before this time he is regarded as no better than a Sudra; he has no privilege, no rank. By the laws of Menu, a Brahmin is to be distinguished from individuals of the secular classes by a cord (*paita*), which is worn hanging from the left shoulder, and resting on the right side below the loins. It consists of three thick twists of cotton, each formed of numerous smaller threads. These three separate twists, which on marriage are increased to three times three, are considered as emblematical of the three persons in the Hindû Trinity—Brahma, Vishnu, and Siva. The cotton from which the cord is made must be picked from the plant by the hands of Brahmins only, and the thread must be spun and twisted by persons of the same caste. When the cord has been properly manufactured, the father of the young candidate endeavors to ascertain, by the rules of astrology, the month, the week, the day, the hour, the minute which will be most favorable for his son's investiture with the cord. The ceremony and the entertainment last four days, and at the close of each the guests receive numerous presents. For a description of the ceremony see Dubois, *The Hindoos.* See Brahmins; Indian Caste.

Cord, John, a Methodist Episcopal minister, was born in Harford County, Md. He was converted in 1806; officiated some time as exhorter and local preacher, and in 1811 entered the Illinois Conference. A severe loss by fire necessitated his location for a few years, with the exception of which he labored faithfully and successfully until 1826, when failing health obliged him to become a superannuate. He died full of hope, March 23, 1827. See *Minutes of Annual Conferences*, 1828, p. 573.

Cordemoy, Géraud de, a French historian and philosopher, who died Oct. 8, 1684, was a native of Paris. He first practiced law, but soon abandoned his profession, and betook himself to the study of philosophy, especially that of Des Cartes. Bishop Bossuet introduced him to the French court, and he was appointed lector to the dauphin. In the year 1675 he was elected a member of the French Academy. He wrote, *Histoire de France* (from the beginning of the monarchy to the year 987, 2 vols.):—*Six Discours sur la Distinction de l'Âme et du Corps:—Lettre à un Savant Religieux de la Compagnie de Jésus pour Défende le Système de Descartes:—Traités de Métaphysique:—Traité de l'Infaillibilité de l'Église.* See Winer, *Handbuch der theol. Lit.* i, 404; Jöcher, *Allgemeines Gelehrten-Lexikon*, s. v.; Hoefer, *Nouv. Biog. Générale*, s. v.; *Biog. Universelle*, s. v. (B. P.)

Cordemoy, Louis Géraud de, a French theologian, son of the foregoing, was born at Paris, Dec. 7, 1651. He took holy orders, was made doctor of theology, and applied himself to the conversion of the Protestants. After having aided the missions of Saintonge, he was appointed, in 1679, abbot of Fenières, of the order of Cistercians, in the diocese of Clermont, in Auvergne. He died in Paris, Feb. 7, 1722, leaving a number of religious letters and treatises, for which see Hoefer, *Nouv. Biog. Générale*, s. v.; *Biog. Universelle*, s. v.

Corder (Lat. *Corderius*), Balthasar, a Belgian theologian, was born at Antwerp in 1592. He entered the Jesuit order in 1612, and taught theology at Vienna. He was learned in Greek. He died at Rome, June 24, 1650, leaving *Catena LXV Græcorum Pa-*

trum in S. Lucam (Antwerp, 1628):—*Joannis Philoponi in cap. I Genes. de Mundi Creatione Libri IV* (Vienna, 1631):—*Expositio Græcorum Patrum in Psalmos, Digesta in Catenam* (Antwerp, 1643):—*Job Elucidatus* (ibid. 1646):—*Symbola Græcorum Patrum in Evangelium Matthæi* (Toulouse, 1646, 1647):—*S. Cyrilli, Alexandrini Archiepiscopi, Homiliæ XIX in Jeremiam Prophetam, Hactenus Ineditæ* (Antwerp, 1648). See Hoefer, *Nouv. Biog. Générale*, s. v.; Jöcher, *Allgemeines Gelehrten-Lexikon*, s. v. (B. P.)

Cordes, EUTYCHE DE, a Belgian theologian, was born about 1520 at Antwerp. He entered the Benedictine order, in the monastery of St. Justin of Padua, of the congregation of Monte Cassino, was elected abbot of San Fortunato, near Bassano, and was invested with this title when he assisted, Feb. 26, 1562, at the eighteenth session of the Council of Trent, being one of the theologians chosen to arrange the catalogue of suspicious or pernicious books. After the close of the council he returned to the abbey of St. Justin, where he died in September, 1582. He left in MS., *Commentarius in Omnes Epistolas Pauli*:—*Commentarius in Symbolum Apostolorum*:—*Dictionarium Biblicum*. See Hoefer, *Nouv. Biog. Générale*, s. v.; *Biog. Universelle*, s. v.

Cordicôles (from *cor*, the heart, and *colo*, to worship) were a sect of Roman Catholic devotees which arose in France about the middle of the 18th century, professing to worship the sacred heart of Jesus and the heart of the Virgin Mary. See SACRED HEART.

Cordier, a French Jesuit of the 18th century, was chancellor of the University of Pont-à-Mousson, and wrote *Éclaircissements sur la Prédestination* (Pont-à-Mousson, 1746). See Hoefer, *Nouv. Biog. Générale*, s. v.

Cordier, Claude Simon, a French ecclesiastic, canon of Orleans, was born at Orleans in 1704, and died at the same place, Nov. 17, 1772, leaving *La Vie de Sainte-Frémiot de Chantal* (Orleans, 1768, 1772). See Hoefer, *Nouv. Biog. Générale*, s. v.; *Biog. Universelle*, s. v.

Cordier, François, a French monk of the Oratory, who died in 1693, wrote *Vie d'Anne des Anges* (Paris, 1694). See Hoefer, *Nouv. Biog. Générale*, s. v.; *Biog. Universelle*, s. v.

Cordier, Jean, a French Jesuit, taught rhetoric, philosophy, and theology at Rheims; was afterwards rector of the college at Chalons, and died at Dijon, Nov. 22, 1673, in his seventy-fifth year, leaving a work entitled *Familia Sancta*. See Jöcher, *Allgemeines Gelehrten-Lexikon*, s. v.

Cordier, Mathurin, a distinguished French priest, was born in 1479, taught languages at several places in France, and finally in Geneva, where he died in 1564, leaving some grammatical treatises, for which see *Biog. Universelle*, s. v.; Hoefer, *Nouv. Biog. Générale*, s. v.; Jöcher, *Allgemeines Gelehrten-Lexikon*, s. v.; Lichtenberger, *Encyclop. des Sciences Religieuses*, s. v.

Cordiner, JAMES, a Scotch clergyman, took his degree at King's College, Aberdeen, in 1808; became schoolmaster at Gartly in 1825; was licensed as an assistant preacher for nine years; presented to the living at Forgue in 1834, and died March 4, 1849, aged sixty-three years. See *Fasti Eccles. Scoticanæ*, iii, 656.

Cordley, CHRISTOPHER MINTA, a Congregational minister, was born at Oxford, England, in 1821. He emigrated to the United States when twelve years old; graduated at the Western Reserve College, Ohio, with the highest honors, in 1844, and at Andover Theological Seminary in 1847; was ordained two years after in Hopkinton, N. H., and served successively at West Randolph, Mass., in 1852, West Brookfield in 1858, and Lawrence in 1862, where he died, June 26, 1866. Mr. Cordley was a man of great mental acuteness and originality, an earnest and critical student, a powerful and pungent preacher, and one who deeply sympathized with the people at large. See *Cong. Quarterly*, 1867, p. 374.

Cordon, JAMES R., a Methodist Episcopal minister, was born in England, March 7, 1835. He was converted in Detroit, Mich., in 1858, and in the same year entered the Detroit Conference, in which he labored for eighteen years with general acceptability and usefulness. He died April 18, 1876. Wherever Mr. Cordon was known, he was regarded as a devout, earnest, and successful minister; especially in the Sunday-school was he greatly beloved. See *Minutes of Annual Conferences*, 1876, p. 100.

Cordona, JUAN BAUTISTA, a Spanish prelate, who lived in the latter half of the 16th century, wrote, *De Distychis* (Tarragona, 1587):—*De Bibliotheca Regia S. Laurentii in Hispania*. See Hoefer, *Nouv. Biog. Générale*, s. v.

Cordova, COUNCIL OF (*Concilium Cordubense*). Two of these provincial synods are mentioned:

I. Held A.D. 347 or 348, by Osius, bishop of Cordova, which reaffirmed the action of the Council of Sardica (Labbe, ii; Hardouin, i).

II. Held A.D. 852, by order of Abderahman, the Moslem king, who caused the metropolitans of the different provinces to assemble. In this council voluntary martyrdom was condemned. This was not a legitimate synod. Eulogius speaks of it as a pseudo-council, not gathered together lawfully in the Holy Spirit, but collected by the advice of the infidels, and by order of a king, the impious enemy of the Christians. See Labbe, *Concil.* viii, 76; Landon, *Manual of Councils*, s. v

Cordova, Alfonso de, a Spanish theologian, was born at Salamanca in the latter half of the 15th century. He studied medicine at Paris, was first to introduce the doctrine of nominalism into the University of Salamanca, and died in 1542, leaving *Principia Dialectices in Terminos Suppositiones Consequentias* (Salamanca, 1519). See Hoefer, *Nouv. Biog. Générale*, s. v.

Cordova (or **Corduba**), **Antonio de**, a Spanish casuist, lived in the latter half of the 16th century. He belonged to the order of Minorites, and remained for a long time in a convent at Alcala de Henares. He wrote, *Annotationes in Dominicum Cotum* (Alcala, 1553):—*Expositio Regulæ Fratrum Minorum* (Louvain, 1554):—*Commentaria in Quatuor Libris Magistri Sententiarum* (Alcala, 1569):—*Tratado de Casos de Consciencia* (Toledo, 1575):—*Quæstionarium Theologicum* (ibid. 1578):—*Additiones in Compendium Privilegiorum Fratrum Minorum Alphonsi de Casarubios* (Naples, 1595). See Hoefer, *Nouv. Biog. Générale*, s. v.

Cordova, Antonio Fernandez de, a Spanish Jesuit, who died at Grenada in 1634, wrote *Instruccion de Confessores* (Grenada, 1621). See Hoefer, *Nouv. Biog. Générale*, s. v.

Cordova, Fernando de, a Spanish scholar, was born in 1422. He distinguished himself by the extent of his knowledge in theology, philosophy, medicine, mathematics, music, and in the languages, as Greek, Hebrew, Arabic, and Chaldee, and was also familiar with astrology, as well as acquainted with the works of the scholastics, philosophers, and physicians of Europe and the East. He had served with distinction against the Moors, under the colors of the king of Castile, John II, went to Paris, but his great wisdom caused him to be regarded as a sorcerer, and he repaired to Rome, where he found favor with popes Sixtus IV and Alexander VI. He died near the close of the 15th century, having composed a number of works, the more remarkable of which is an introduction to the treatise of Albert the Great, *De Animalibus*; this was published at Rome for the first time in 1478. Among his productions remaining in MS. we cite a commentary upon the *Almagesta* of Ptolemy. See Hoefer, *Nouv. Biog. Générale*, s. v.

Cordovero, MOSES. See MOSES CORDOVERO.

Corella, JAIME DE, a Spanish theologian, was born in 1657. He entered the Capuchin order, was minister of Charles II, king of Spain, and died in 1699, leaving,

Methodus qua Piissime Fiat Exercitium Viæ Sacræ (St. Sebastian, 1689):—*Clavis Cœli* (1694):—*Practica de el Confessionare* (Pampeluna, 1742):—*Summa de la Theologia Moral* (Madrid, 1707). See Hoefer, *Nouv. Biog. Générale*, s. v.

Coren, JACQUES, a French theologian of the order of St. Francis, who lived in the early half of the 17th century, wrote, *Clypeus Patientiæ* (Lyons, 1622):—*Observationes in Evangelia* (ibid. 1627):—*Civitas Avenionensis Pestilentia Laborans* (Avignon, 1630). See Hoefer, *Nouv. Biog. Générale*, s. v.

Corentīnus, *Saint*, born in Brittany, is said to have been consecrated bishop of Cornwall (some say of Quimper, in Brittany) by St. Martin of Tours, and therefore in the 4th century. His day is May 1 (others give Sept. 5 or Dec. 12). See CHORENTINUS.

Corentius. See CARENTIUS; CHORENTIUS.

Corenzio, BELISARIO, a Greek painter, was born in 1558. At the age of twenty-two he went to Venice and entered the school of Tintoretto. One of his best productions is *The Miracle of the Loaves and Fishes*, in the refectory of the Benedictines, which he finished in forty days. He painted many admirable works for the churches of Naples. Some of his principal pictures are, *The Virgin Crowned by the Trinity; The Visitation; The Presentation in the Temple; Life of the Virgin.* He died in 1643. See Spooner, *Biog. Hist. of the Fine Arts*, s. v.; Chalmers, *Biog. Dict.* s. v.

Coret, Jacques, a Belgian theologian, was born about the middle of the 17th century. He entered the Jesuit order, and became celebrated by his virtue and zeal for souls. It is said that so many wished to confess to him that he absolved them *en masse*, not being able to take them singly. He died at Liege, Dec. 16, 1721, leaving several mystic works, under the titles of, *Journal des Anges:—Maison de l'Éternité:—Le Cinquième Ange de l'Apocalypse;* and a historic work, entitled *Vie d'Anne de Beauvais* (Lisle, 1667). See Hoefer, *Nouv. Biog. Générale*, s. v.

Coret, Pierre, a Belgian theologian, was born at Ath, in Hainault, about the middle of the 16th century. He was at first curate of St. Crespin, and afterwards canon of the cathedral of Tournay, in 1574, where he died in 1602, leaving, *Defensio Veritatis* (Antwerp, 1591); which is a refutation of the *Discours Politiques et Militaires* of Lanone:—*Anti-Politicus* (Douay, 1599), a work especially directed against the *République* of Dodin. See Hoefer, *Nouv. Biog. Générale*, s. v.; *Biog. Universelle*, s. v.

Coret-y-Peris, CRISTOVAL, a Spanish theologian and grammarian, was priest of Alboraya, in the kingdom of Valencia, and taught Latin and eloquence at the episcopal school of Valencia. He died about 1760, leaving, *Explicacion de la Syntaxis de Torrella* (Valencia, 1712):—*Noches i Dias Feriadas* (ibid. 1750). See Hoefer, *Nouv. Biog. Générale*, s. v.; *Biog. Universelle*, s. v.

Corey, Abel Moses, a Methodist Episcopal minister, was born near Fostoria, O., July 23, 1833. He experienced religion at the age of eighteen; acquired a good academic education; began preaching in 1860, and in the following year entered the Central Ohio Conference. After laboring in obscure places several years, he was elected state senator, in which capacity he served with much credit four years. In 1871 he again entered the effective itinerant ranks, and continued with marked zeal and success until his death, Oct. 4, 1875. Mr. Corey was clear in thought, apt in expression, generous in sympathy, self-sacrificing in labor, and strong in friendship. See *Minutes of Annual Conferences*, 1876, p. 105.

Corey, David, a Methodist Episcopal minister, was born in 1797. He was converted in 1814; soon after began preaching in northern Vermont; located, and engaged in farming; moved to central New York, joined the Oneida Conference, and, after three years' labor, went west and entered the Illinois Conference. He became a superannuate, and died Aug. 23, 1844. See *Minutes of Annual Conferences*, 1845, p. 585.

Corey, John Edwin, a Congregational minister, was born at Mansfield, Mass., July 29, 1825. He graduated at Amherst College in 1850; was ordained in 1853; labored as an evangelist for a short time in northern Ohio; preached in Massachusetts in the following places: Freetown, Chesterfield, Yarmouth, and North Wrentham, at which latter place he died, Nov. 30, 1865. Mr. Corey was an indefatigable student, and a clear and logical thinker. At the time of his death he had nearly ready for the press a *Manual of Congregational Polity and Principles.* See *Cong. Quarterly*, 1867, p. 201.

Corgen, PIERRE, a French theologian who lived in the early half of the 18th century, belonged to the diocese of Quimper, was doctor of theology, and wrote, *La Dispute Entre le Pape, Saint-Étienne et Saint-Cyprien* (Paris, 1725):—*Dissertation sur le Concile de Rimini* (ibid. 1372):—*Mémoire Touchant les Juges de la Foi* (ibid. 1736):—*Sur le Monothélisme et sur le Sixième Concile Général* (ibid. 1741):—*Défense des Droits des Évêques dans l'Église.* See Hoefer, *Nouv. Biog. Générale*, s. v.

Corinth. The following additional particulars concerning this once famous city are taken from Kitto, *Pict. Bible*, note on 1 Cor. i, 1:

"This great and wealthy city was the metropolis of Achaia, and situated upon the isthmus of the same name, which joins the Peloponnesus to the continent. Its position was highly favorable for that commerce which ultimately rendered it one of the most luxurious cities of the world. For, having two ports, one of which was open to the eastern and the other to the western navigator, while its geographical situation placed it, as it were, in the centre of the civilized world, it became the point where the merchants from every quarter of the globe met and exchanged their treasures. It was also celebrated for the Isthmian Games, to which the apostle makes some striking and remarkably appropriate allusions in his Epistles to the Corinthians. Nor should it be unnoticed that in the centre of the city there stood a famous temple of Venus, in which a thousand priestesses of the goddess ministered to licentiousness, under the guise of religion. From such various causes Corinth had an influx of foreigners of all descriptions, who carried the productions and the vices of all nations into a city in which the merchant, the warrior, and the seaman could have them for money. Devoted to traffic, and to the enjoyment of the wealth which that traffic secured, the Corinthians were exempt from the influence of that thirst for conquest and military glory by which their neighbors were actuated; hence they were seldom engaged in any war except for the defence of their country, or in behalf of the liberties of Greece; yet this city furnished many brave and experienced commanders to other Grecian states, among whom it was common to prefer a Corinthian general to one of their own state. As might be expected, Corinth was not remarkably distinguished for philosophy or science; but its wealth attracted to it the arts, which assisted to enrich and aggrandize it, till it became one of the very finest cities in all Greece. The Corinthian order of architecture took its name from that rich and flowery style which prevailed in its sumptuous edifices, its temples, palaces, theatres, and porticoes. [Yet it is noteworthy that no specimen of this style of architecture has been found there.]

"Corinth still exists as an inhabited town, under the same name *Korinthos.* It is a long, straggling place, which is well-paved, and can boast of a few tolerably good buildings, with a castle of some strength, which under the Turkish rule was kept in a good state of defence. There are still considerable ruins, to attest the ancient consequence of the city, and the taste and elegance of its public buildings. The extensive view from the summit of the high mountain which commands the town, and which was the Acropolis (Acro-Corinth) of the ancient city, is pronounced by travellers to be one of the finest in the world." (See cut on opposite page.)

Corio, HAYMO, an Italian theologian and moralist, a native of Milan, became famous as a preacher, and was appointed consulter to the inquisition by Clement IX. Several times he was offered a bishopric, but declined. He died Sept. 17, 1679, leaving, *Epitome Decretorum Conciliorum S. Mediolanensis Ecclesiæ* (Milan, 1640):—*Manuale Regularis Disciplinæ* (ibid. 1659):—*Concordantiæ Morales in Exodum* (ibid. 1655):—

Remains of a large Temple on the site of Corinth. (Many of the columns have fallen since this view was taken.)

Promptuarium Episcoporum (ibid. 1668):—*Concordantiæ Morales in Genesin* (ibid. 1671):—*In Leviticum* (ibid. 1677):—*In Deuteronomium* (ibid. 1681):—*Vitæ Sanctorum Haymonis et Vermundi de Coriis* (ibid.). See Hoefer, *Nouv. Biog. Générale*, s. v.

Coriolano, Bartolommeo, a Bolognese engraver, second son of Cristoforo, was born in 1599, and was instructed by his father and in the academy of the Caracci. The following are his principal plates: *St. Jerome in Meditation Before a Crucifix; Herodias with the Head of the Baptist; The Virgin, with the Infant Sleeping.* He died in 1676. See Spooner, *Biog. Hist. of the Fine Arts*, s. v.; Hoefer, *Nouv. Biog. Générale*, s. v.

Coriolano, Giovanni Battista, a Bolognese painter and engraver, elder brother of Bartolommeo, was born in 1589, and studied under Gio. Lodovico Valesio. He was employed somewhat upon the churches of Bologna. In the Nunziata is an altar-piece by this master, representing *St. John, St. James*, and *St. Bernard.* He did not attain much distinction. He died in 1649. See Spooner, *Biog. Hist. of the Fine Arts*, s. v.; Hoefer, *Nouv. Biog. Générale*, s. v.

Coriolis, Gaspard Honoré de, a French theologian, was born at Aix about 1735. He became senior clerk at the parliament of Provence, canon of Notre Dame, and vicar-general of Mende. He died at Paris, May 14, 1824, leaving, *Traité de l'Administration du Comté de Provence* (Aix, 1788):—*Exercices de Piété* (Paris, 1816):—*Des Chapitres et des Dignitaires* (ibid. 1822). He also left several MSS., especially *Abrégé de l'Histoire Ecclésiastique.* See Hoefer, *Nouv. Biog. Générale*, s. v.

Corker, James, an English theologian of the Benedictine order, who lived in the second half of the 17th century, wrote, *The Roman Catholic Principles* (Lond. 1680):—*Stafford's Memoirs* (ibid. 1682). See Hoefer, *Nouv. Biog. Générale*, s. v.

Corlett, John, an English Methodist minister, was born on the Isle of Man. He was converted in early life, offered himself to the conference in 1824, and, after a brief appointment to Kendal, entered upon mission work in Newfoundland, where he labored with indefatigable zeal and much success until 1830. He was then sent as chairman to the Bahama District, and there, as also in Barbadoes, Demerara, and Antigua, continued his toil with unabated devotedness until 1860, when he was welcomed back to Jamaica. He still labored abundantly in powerful preaching, in prayer, in erection of chapels, and the introduction of the Gospel into neglected localities, becoming a supernumerary after fifty years' missionary toil. He died Aug. 6, 1877. See *Minutes of the British Conference*, 1878, p. 53.

Corley, Robert J., a minister of the Methodist Episcopal Church South, was born at Marianna, Fla., in 1840. He served in the Confederate army during the war, and entered the Georgia Conference in 1865; became superannuated in 1880, and returned to his birthplace, where he died, March 17, 1881. See *Minutes of Annual Conferences of the M. E. Church South*, 1881, p. 360.

Cormac. See Corbmac.

Cormack, John, D.D., a Scotch clergyman, was brought up as a blacksmith. He gained a prize at Edinburgh University for the best essay, and took his degree there in 1803; was licensed to preach in 1804, and ordained assistant at Stow in 1807. He died Dec. 20, 1840, aged sixty-four years. He published, *A Sermon at the Opening of the Synod* (1810):—*Pastoral Hints to his Parishioners* (1823):—*Inquiry into the Doctrine of Original Sin* (1824):—*On Voluntary Church Association:—Illustrations of Faith* (1839):—*Memoir of the Rev. William Stark:*—besides many contributions to the *Edinburgh Christian Instructor.* He also translated from the French Fénélon's *Lives of the Ancient Philosophers* (1803, 2 vols.), and *The Church of Rome Examined*, by Dr. C. Malan. Dr. Cormack was an ardent student, a faithful minister, and a judicious friend. His fervent piety was enlivened by a natural turn for racy humor. He formed an association for the improvement of servants in his parish. See *Fasti Eccles. Scoticanæ*, i, 534.

Cormacus, a Scotch prelate, was probably bishop of Mortlach, translated to the see of Dunkeld, and is also spoken of as bishop of Aberdeen. He died in 1177. See Keith, *Scottish Bishops*, p. 75.

Corman is thought by some to be the austere cleric (called by others *Paulesius*) who, about A.D. 635, endeavored to convert the Northumbrians. He is commemorated as a bishop and apostle of Anglia, March 12 or 20.

Cormick, Daniel, a Scotch clergyman, was licensed to preach in 1838; appointed to the living at the South Church, Forfar, in 1839, and ordained; joined the Free Secession in 1843. He died May 23, 1848. See *Fasti Eccles. Scoticanæ*, iii, 778.

Corn, Allowance of, was a provision for the maintenance of the clergy, connected with the early stages of the recognition of Christianity by the empire. Constantine, in his zeal for his new creed, ordered the magistrates of each province to supply an annual amount of corn (ἐτήσια σιτηρέσια), not only to the clergy, but to the widows and virgins of the Church (Theodoret, i, 11). When Julian succeeded, he transferred the grant to the ministers of the heathen cultus, which he revived (Sozom. v, 5; Philostorg. vii, 4). Jovian restored it, but on the lower scale of one third of the amount fixed under Constantine. The payment continued, and was declared permanent by Justinian (*De SS. Eccles.* cod. i, tit. 2).

CORN, Ears of, *in Christian Art*, is not so frequent an emblem as might be supposed. See Loaves. The thought seems to have gone always to the bread of life with sacramental allusion. The corn and reaper are represented in a compartment of a vault in the catacomb of Pontianus. Again, the harvest corn is opposed to the vine and cornucopia of fruit (Catacomb of Callixtus).

The more evidently religious use of the ears of corn is in various representations of the fall of man. On the sarcophagus of Junius Bassus (probably A.D. 358) Adam and Eve are carved—the former bearing the corn, in token of his labor on the earth, and the latter a lamb, indicating woman's work, spinning. In a bass-relief from the catacomb of St. Agnes there are two human forms, apparently both male, standing before a sitting figure, supposed to represent the First Person of the Trinity. This may represent the offering of Cain and Abel; at all events, the corn-ears and lamb are either received or presented by the standing figures. As these figures are of no more than mature (even of youthful) appearance, the Second Person may be supposed to be intended by them.

Cornac, Jean, a French preacher, abbot of Villelvin, was a man of high standing with his ecclesiastical superiors, and became intimate counsellor of the duke of Mayenne. He died in 1614. Historians do not mention him, and his works are unpublished. The National Library has four large volumes of his *Sermons*. He was learned in ecclesiastical history. See Hoefer, *Nouv. Biog. Générale*, s. v.

Cornæus, Melchior, a German Jesuit, was born at Brilon, in Westphalia, in 1598. He was professor of philosophy at Toulouse, afterwards of theology at Mayence and Würzburg, and died March 13, 1665. He wrote, *Miracula Ecclesiæ Catholicæ Defensa:—Manes Lutheri et Calvini Judicati:—Ens Rationis Luthero-Calvinicum:—Curriculum Philosophiæ Peripateticæ:—Murus Papyrachus Purgatorii*, etc. See Witte, *Diarium Biographicum*; Alegambe, *Bibliotheca Scriptorum Societatis Jesu*; Jöcher, *Allgemeines Gelehrten-Lexikon*, s. v. (B. P.)

Cornara, Carlo, an Italian painter, was born at Milan in 1605. He painted some works for the churches at Milan, one of the best of which is an altar-piece for the Church of St. Benedict, in Pavia. He died in 1673. See Spooner, *Biog. Hist. of the Fine Arts*, s. v.; Hoefer, *Nouv. Biog. Générale*, s. v.

Cornara, Flaminio. See Cornelius.

Corneille, Jean Baptiste, a French painter and engraver, brother of Michel the Younger, was born at Paris in 1646. He was instructed by his father, visited Rome, where he studied several years, and on his return to Paris was received into the Royal Academy in 1676. He died in 1695. Some of his works are, *St. Peter Delivered from Prison; Christ Appearing to St. John; The Baptist in the Wilderness; Christ and the Samaritan Woman; St. Francis.* See Spooner, *Biog. Hist. of the Fine Arts*, s. v.; Hoefer, *Nouv. Biog. Générale*, s. v.

Corneille, Michel, *the Elder*, a French painter, was born at Orleans in 1603, and studied under Simon Vouet. He executed twelve large pictures for the churches, and was one of the twelve original members of the Royal Academy at Paris. Some of his works are, *The Holy Family, with St. Elizabeth; The Murder of the Innocents; Christ Appearing to Magdalene*, and *The Virgin Suckling the Infant Jesus.* He died at Paris in 1664. See Hoefer, *Nouv. Biog. Générale*, s. v.; Spooner, *Biog. Hist. of the Fine Arts*, s. v.; Chalmers, *Biog. Dict.* s. v.

Corneille, Michel, *the Younger*, a French painter and engraver, son of the foregoing, was born at Paris in 1642. He studied at Rome, and soon after his return to Paris was received into the Academy, painting for his reception-piece *The Calling of Peter and Andrew to the Apostleship.* He engraved a great number of plates, among which are the following: *God Appearing to Abraham; Abraham Setting out with his Son Isaac for the Sacrifice; The Conception of the Virgin; The Baptist Preaching in the Desert; Abraham Sending away Hagar; Christ and the Virgin Appearing to St. Francis; Jacob Wrestling with the Angel.* He died in 1708. See Hoefer, *Nouv. Biog. Générale*, s. v.; Spooner, *Biog. Hist. of the Fine Arts*, s. v.

Cornejo, Damiano, a Spanish theologian, who lived in the latter half of the 17th century, wrote *Chronica Seraphica*, etc. (Madrid, 1682–1698). See Hoefer, *Nouv. Biog. Générale*, s. v.

Cornejo (*de Pedrosa*), **Pedro**, a Carmelite of Salamanca, who died March 31, 1618, was one of the most famous interpreters of the philosophy of Thomas of Aquinas, which he taught at the university of his native place. After his death some of his lectures were published, under the title *Theologia Scholastica et Moralis*, etc. (Bamberg, 1671), preceded by a biographical sketch written by Sanchez d'Avila, bishop of Piacenza. See Hurter, in Wetzer u. Welte's *Kirchen-Lexikon*, s. v. (B. P.)

Cornelians was a name given to the ancient orthodox Christians by the Novatian party, because they held communion with Cornelius, bishop of Rome, rather than with his antagonist. See Novatians.

Cornelison, John, a minister of the Reformed (Dutch) Church, was born at Nyack, N. Y., in 1769. He studied under H. Meyer and J. H. Livingston, and was licensed by the synod of the Reformed Dutch Church in 1791. His first work was as missionary to the northern and western states (1791–93). From 1793 to 1806 he was pastor at Bergen avenue, Jersey City, and at English Neighborhood, Bergen Co., N. J. In 1794 he visited the settlements on the Delaware and Susquehanna rivers (Hanover), and was at Bergen avenue again from 1806 to 1828, when he died. Mr. Cornelison had a noble zeal for the glory of God, and an anxiety for the souls of men. He took great interest in the colored people, many of whom were slaves, and opened a special service for them in his own house. He formed them into classes, teaching them to read, and filling their minds with Gospel truth. See Corwin, *Manual of the Reformed Church in America*, 3d ed. p. 222.

Cornelisz (or **Cornelissen**), Jakob, a Dutch painter, was born at Oost Zanen, in Holland, about 1470. There is a picture by him, of *The Circumcision*, in the old church at Haarlem, painted in 1517, much praised; and a *Descent from the Cross*, at Alkmaar. He died at Amsterdam in 1570.

Cornelius, *Saint.* (1) The centurion, is commemorated as bishop of Cæsarea, on Feb. 2 or Dec. 10; (2) pope, is commemorated as a martyr under Decius, on Sept. 14.

Cornelius is the name of several other early Christian notables:

1. The fourth patriarch of Antioch, A.D. 129-143.

2. Head of the monastery called Mochanseos (Jerome, *Op.* ii, 86, ed. Vall.).

3. A converted Manichæan mentioned by Augustine (*Epist.* 259 [126]; ii, 1073).

4. A monk and bishop of Forum Cornelii, in the 5th century, of noted virtue, the teacher of Chrysologus (Migne, *Patrol. Lat.* liii, 31).

Cornelius (or **Cornara**), **Flaminius**, senator of Venice, where he was born in 1692, and died in 1778, is the author of, *Monumenta Ecclesiæ Venetæ* (1750, 15 vols.):—*Creta Sacra* (1755, 2 vols.):—*Ecclesia Torcellana* (1756, 3 vols.):—*Chiese e Monasteri di Venezia e di Torcello* (Padua, 1758). See Winer, *Handbuch der theol. Lit.* i, 870; Jöcher, *Allgemeines Gelehrten-Lexikon*, s. v. (B. P.)

Cornelius, Samuel (1), D.D., a Baptist minister, was born at Devonport, England, in 1794, and came to the United States with his parents when he was a child. Early in life he joined the Church, in Philadelphia, of which Rev. Dr. William Staughton was the pastor. His first settlement in the ministry was in Norfolk, Va., where he remained from 1817 to 1824, and then took charge of the Church in Alexandria, sustaining this relation thirteen years. He was next pastor of the Church in Mount Holly, N. J., eleven years, a part of this time acting as agent of the Colonization Society. For several years he preached in different places in Michigan, his last pastorate being at Ann Arbor. In all good causes in which his denomination was concerned, Dr. Cornelius took an abiding interest. He died in 1870. See Cathcart, *Baptist Encyclop.* p. 279. (J. C. S.)

Cornelius, Samuel (2), a Protestant Episcopal clergyman, was born at Baltimore in 1827. He was at first a minister of the Methodist Episcopal Church, but in 1867 connected himself with the Protestant Episcopal, officiating at first in Severn Parish, Md. In 1870 he was rector of St. Paul's Church, in Calvert County; in 1878 he removed to Baltimore. He died in October, 1879. See *Prot. Episc. Almanac*, 1880, p. 170.

Cornelius, Thomas, a Methodist Episcopal minister, was born at Baltimore, Md., Nov. 12, 1823, of devout Methodist parents. He experienced conversion in his eleventh year, and in 1845 was admitted into the Baltimore Conference. In 1848 an attack of hemorrhage of the throat obliged him to desist from all active service. He, however, recovered, and in 1850 did regular work, until his sudden death, Oct. 8, 1851. Mr. Cornelius was a young man of great promise, intelligent, dignified, and becoming, and highly exemplary in his daily life. See *Minutes of Annual Conferences*, 1852, p. 12.

Cornelius, William Huff, a Methodist Episcopal minister, was born in Clark County, Ind., April 4, 1819. He removed with his parents in early life to Kentucky, where he was converted, joined the Church, and was licensed to preach in 1846. He was received on trial in the Indiana Conference in 1849, and subsequently served the following charges: Fredericksburg, Hellowville, Leesville, Springville, Bloomfield, Sullivan, Mount Vernon, Cannelton, Corydon, Paoli, Ellettsville, Putnamville, Gosport, Linton, Harrodsburg, Graysville, Bruceville, and Hymera. He was superannuated in 1880, and removed to his farm near Linton, where he died, July 31, 1882. See *Minutes of Annual Conferences*, 1882, p. 308.

Cornell, Frederick Frelinghuysen, D.D., a minister of the Reformed (Dutch) Church, son of Rev. John Cornell, was born at Allentown, N. J., Nov. 16, 1804. He graduated from the College of New Jersey in 1825, and was licensed by the presbytery of Newtown, L. I., in 1829. He was professor of languages in the College of Mississippi, Natchez, in 1828; missionary at Stuyvesant, N. Y., three months in 1829; at Columbiaville, in 1830; Marshallsville, N. J., 1831, 1832; Montville, 1833-35; New York city, Manhattan Church, 1836-56; Pluckemin (Presbyterian), N. J., 1857-64. He was thereafter without a charge till his death, Aug. 7, 1875. See Corwin, *Manual of the Ref. Church in America*, 3d ed. p. 222.

Cornell, John, a minister of the Reformed (Dutch) Church, was born at Northampton, Pa., in 1774. He pursued his classical studies at the Log College, Pa., completing them with Dr. Wilson, in New York city; prosecuted his theological studies under Dr. J. H. Livingston, and was licensed by the classis of New York in 1798. He became pastor of the Presbyterian churches of Allentown and Nottingham, Pa., in 1800, and served them for twenty years. His health becoming impaired, he removed to Somerville, N. J., where he acted as principal of the academy from 1821 to 1828. He removed, in the latter year, to Millstone, and died there in 1835. As an instructor, he was noted for great thoroughness and ability. As a preacher, he was clear, discriminating, and marked by sound judgment; his sermons were instructive, methodical, and impressive. See Corwin, *Manual of the Ref. Church in America*, 3d ed. p. 223.

Cornell, Joseph, a Baptist minister, was born at Swansea, Mass., Feb. 11, 1747. He began preaching in 1780, was pastor at Manchester, and at Galway, N. Y.; travelled under the Massachusetts Missionary Society in New York and Upper Canada, and died July 26, 1826. See Sprague, *Annals of the Amer. Pulpit*, vi, 269.

Cornell, William, D.D., a minister of the Reformed (Dutch) Church, was born in Seneca County, N. Y., in 1834. He graduated from Rutgers College in 1859, and from the New Brunswick Seminary in 1862; was licensed by the classis of Geneva the same year, and became pastor at Minisink, Sussex Co., N. J.; teacher at Freehold, in 1863; pastor at Woodstown Presbyterian Church, in 1864; teacher at Somerville, in 1868, and died there Sept. 11, 1876. See Corwin, *Manual of the Ref. Church in America*, 3d ed. p. 224.

Cornell, William Augustus, a minister of the Reformed (Dutch) Church, graduated from Rutgers College in 1841, from the New Brunswick Seminary in 1844; and was licensed by the classis of New Brunswick the same year. He served the Church at Athens, Greene Co., N. Y., until 1848; Blooming Grove, Rensselaer Co., until 1852, and died in August, 1876. See Corwin, *Manual of the Ref. Church in America*, 3d ed. p. 224.

Corneo, Giambattista, an Italian theologian, was born at Milan in 1607. He was apostolic prothonotary and archivist to the archbishop of Milan, and died in 1690, leaving, *De Sancto Blasio Sebaste, in Armenia* (Milan, 1645):—*De Sancto Manricillo* (ibid. 1646):—*Il Sacro Chialdo* (ibid. 1647):—*Vita del B. Gio. Angelo Parro* (ibid. 1649):—*Origine dell' Instituzione dell' Orazione delle XL Ore* (ibid. eod.). Corneo also left thirty-two volumes of MS. upon other ecclesiastical matters. See Hoefer, *Nouv. Biog. Générale*, s. v.

Corner-stone is the first stone of a church, properly laid on the north-east side, as determined by the orientation of the sun on the day of the feast, or patron saint. At Beaulieu only one stone was found on the ground, and it was in this position; that of Avranches, the solitary relic of a cathedral, is still pointed out. In modern churches the most prominent or convenient corner is selected, and the corner-stone is a square block of suitable size, laid at the angle of the topmost course of the foundation. It is customary to hollow it out in a box-like manner, and to deposit within it memorial papers, etc.

Cornet, Nicolas, a French theologian, was born at Amiens in 1592. He was educated in his native city at a Jesuit school, made doctor of theology at Paris in 1626, and afterwards became grand-master of the College of Navarre, and syndic of the faculty of theology. He refused to be the confessor of Richelieu, but corrected the *Méthodes de Controverse* of that minister, and, it is said, composed the preface. He denounced to the faculty of theology seven propositions, five of which were afterwards condemned at Rome as extracts from the *Augustinus* of Jansenius. This orthodox zeal exposed Cornet to the attacks of the writers of Port Royal. He died at Paris, April 12, 1663. See Hoefer, *Nouv. Biog. Générale*, s. v.; *Biog. Universelle*, s. v.

Corney, George, an English Congregational minister, was born at Keymer, Sussex, in 1794. He was converted when about eleven years old, educated for the ministry at Hackney, became pastor first at Cratfield and Newmarket, and eventually at Barking, where he labored twenty-four years, and died April 28, 1862. Mr. Corney was an earnest and conscientious preacher. See (Lond.) *Cong. Year-book*, 1863, p. 218.

Cornford, Samuel, an English Baptist minister, was born in 1792. He united originally with the Church in Maidstone, for several years was pastor of the Independent Church at Marden, but returned to Maidstone, where he was for a time pastor of the Third Baptist Church, and then of the Fourth Baptist Church. He died Dec. 24, 1837. See (Lond.) *Baptist Hand-book*, 1838, p. 25. (J. C. S.)

Cornforth, Columbus, a Baptist minister, was born in Maine in 1833. He was converted at the age of eighteen, received his collegiate education at Union College, Schenectady, N. Y., and his theological at the Rochester Seminary. He was ordained at Smithport, Pa. During the late civil war he was, for a time, a member of the 42d Pennsylvania Regular Volunteers, and was severely wounded and taken prisoner at the battle of Fredericksburg. Subsequently he served as chaplain of the 150th Pennsylvania Volunteers till the close of the war, and then became inspector and examiner of the Soldiers' Orphan School of Pennyslvania. In 1879 he removed to Kansas, and died at Clyde, in that state, Feb. 10, 1883. See *The Chicago Standard*, March 1, 1883. (J. C. S.)

Cornforth, David, an English Wesleyan minister, was born at Brompton, Yorkshire, Oct. 30, 1786. He was converted at the age of sixteen, entered the ministry in 1814, and died Oct. 3, 1855. He used to preach in barns, private houses, and in the open air. See *Minutes of the British Conference*, 1856.

Cornice. We add the following particulars from Parker, *Gloss. of Architect.* s. v.:

"In Classic architecture each of the orders has its peculiar cornice.

"In the *Norman* style of architecture, a plain face of parapet, slightly projecting from the wall, is frequently used as a cornice, and a row of blocks is often placed under it, sometimes plain, sometimes moulded or carved into heads and other ornaments, when it is called a *corbel-*

Norman Corbel-table, St. Peter's, Oxford.

table. These blocks very commonly have a range of small arches over them. A small plain string is also sometimes used as a cornice.

"In the *Early English* style, the corbel-table continued in use as a cornice, but it is generally more ornamented than in the Norman, and the arches are commonly trefoils, and well moulded; the blocks, also, are more delicately carved, either with a head or some other ornament characteristic of the style, and if there are no arches above them they often support a suite of horizontal mouldings; sometimes there is a range of horizontal mouldings

Early English Cornice, Stanwick, North Hants.

above the arches of the corbel-table, and sometimes the cornice consists of mouldings only, without any corbel-table. The hollow mouldings of the cornice are generally plain, seldom containing flowers or carvings, except the toothed ornament.

"In the *Decorated* style, the cornice is usually very regular; and though in some large buildings it has several mouldings, it principally consists of a slope above, and a deep-sunk hollow, with an astragal under it: in these hollows flowers at regular distances are often placed, and in some large buildings, and in towers, etc., there are fre-

Decorated Cornice, Irchester, c. 1350.

quently heads, and the cornice almost filled with them; other varieties of cornice may also be occasionally met with in this style.

"In the *Perpendicular* style, the cornice is often composed of several small mouldings, sometimes divided by one or two considerable hollows, not very deep: in plain buildings the cornice-mouldings of the preceding style are much adhered to; but it is more often ornamented in the hollow with flowers, etc., and sometimes with figures and

Perpendicular Cornice, Ensham, c. 1450.

grotesque animals. In the latter end of this style, something very analogous to an ornamented frieze is perceived, of which the canopies to the niches in various works are examples: and the angels so profusely introduced in the late rich work are a sort of cornice ornament."

Cornides, Daniel von, a Hungarian historian, was born in 1732 at Szent-Miklos, in the Liptau province. He studied philosophy and theology at Erlangen, and was appointed teacher at the Reformed College in Klausenburg. He accompanied count Teleki on his travels through Italy, Germany, and France, and the count's son to Göttingen. In 1784 he was appointed librarian at the Pesth University, and died Oct. 4, 1787, leaving, *Regum Hungariae, qui Saeculo XI. Regnavere, Genealogia* (Presburg, 1778):—*Bibliotheca Hungarica* (Pesth, 1791):—*Commentatio de Religione Veterum Hungarorum* (Vienna, 1791). (B. P.)

Corning, William H., a Presbyterian minister, was born in Hartford, Conn., in 1822. He was educated in his native place, at Trinity College, was licensed by the Hartford Congregational Association in 1846, and made pastor of the Congregational Church at Clinton, Mass. In 1858 he took charge of the Presbyterian Church at Whitehall, N. Y., where he remained until his death, Oct. 8, 1862. See Wilson, *Presb. Almanac*, 1863, p. 291.

Cornish, Andrew H., a Protestant Episcopal clergyman, was a graduate of the General Theological Seminary, and rector of St. Paul's Church, Pendleton, S. C., for about a quarter of a century. He died May 24, 1875, aged sixty-two years. See *Prot. Episc. Almanac*, 1876, p. 149.

Cornish, George, a minister of the Society of Friends, was born at Redruth, Cornwall, Dec. 24, 1801. He was a coppersmith by trade. As a minister, he did not exercise his gifts beyond his own society. He died Jan. 29, 1877. See *Annual Monitor*, 1878, p. 48.

Cornish, John, an English Presbyterian minister, was born in 1687; was chosen assistant to Joshua Bayes, at the Leather Lane meeting, early in the century, and continued to minister there with acceptance and success till his death, Nov. 28, 1727. He was pious, serious, wise, prudent, and useful. See Wilson, *Dissenting Churches*, iv. 399.

Cornish, John Cory, an English Methodist preacher, was born at Bridgerule, Devon, in 1819. He was converted in his youth, during a revival among the Bible Christians; became a class-leader and a local preacher, and entered the ministry in 1839. He died at Bridgerule, March 17, 1845. His zeal for God knew no limit except that of his strength.

Cornish, John Hamilton, a Protestant Episcopal clergyman, was born in 1815; ordained in 1842; and from 1848 to 1868 was rector of St. Thaddeus's Church, Aiken, S. C. In 1870, though still residing in Aiken, he performed missionary service at Kaolin, and continued to do so until 1875, when he was employed as a missionary at Barnwell and John's Island, in the same state. From 1875 he preached at Barnwell, Toogoodoo, and Pinewood until his death, which occurred in Charleston, May 24, 1878. See *Prot. Episc. Almanac*, 1879, p. 168.

Cornish, Joseph D., a Free-will Baptist minister, was born in Duchess County, N. Y., March 26, 1764. He was converted in 1817, and moved, in 1826, into Chautauqua County, where, in 1827, he was baptized, and united with the Free-will Baptists. In 1830 he commenced preaching, and was ordained in 1836. He died at Sherman, Chautauqua Co., Nov. 17, 1854. He was a good minister, and universally beloved. See *Free-will Baptist Register*, 1856, p. 9. (J. C. S.)

Cornish, Samuel E., a colored Presbyterian minister, was born in New York in 1793. He was licensed by the Presbytery of Philadelphia, Oct. 31, 1819, and in 1823 was called to the First African Church of Philadelphia, where he preached for some years. From 1845 to 1847 he served as a missionary to the colored people of New York city, and during this time organized Emmanuel Church. In 1855 he joined the Nassau Presbytery of Brooklyn, L. I., where he labored till his death, in 1858. See Wilson, *Presb. Hist. Almanac*, 1860, p. 69.

Cornon, JEAN, a French martyr, was a husbandman of Mascon, and unlettered, but one to whom God gave such wisdom that his judges were amazed, when he was condemned by their sentence to be burned for listening to the reading of the Scripture, in 1535. See Fox, *Acts and Monuments*, iv. 397.

Cornu EPISTŎLÆ is the epistle horn of a Christian altar, i. e. the right-hand corner; so reckoned when the looker faces the western side or front of the altar.

CORNU EVANGELII is the gospel horn of a Christian altar, i. e. the left-hand corner, the looker facing the western side or front of the altar.

Cornūtus, a presbyter of Iconium, who boldly confessed himself a Christian, and was beheaded Sept. 12 (his festival day), apparently under Decius.

Cornwall, Alexander, a Scotch clergyman, son of Robert, minister at Linlithgow, was licensed to preach in 1622; ordained minister at Muiravonside in 1627, and presented to the living there in 1633. He was in necessitous circumstances in 1639; suspended in 1640 for using insulting language; and resigned in 1641. He had pecuniary aid from the Kirk-Session in 1646 and 1649; became a schoolmaster and precentor in 1650; in 1652 was charged with marrying and baptizing irregularly, for which he was excommunicated. He was living in poor circumstances in 1659. See *Fasti Eccles. Scoticanæ*, i, 194.

Cornwall, John, a Scotch clergyman, was presented by the king to the living at Linlithgow in 1626, and died in April, 1646. See *Fasti Eccles. Scoticanæ*, i, 159.

Cornwall, Nathaniel Ellsworth, D.D., a Protestant Episcopal clergyman, was born at Granby, Conn., Feb. 6, 1812. He graduated from Trinity College, Hartford, in 1831, and from the General Theological Seminary in 1834. From that year to 1853 he was rector of Trinity Church, in Southport; until 1855 of St. Andrew's Church, Pittsburgh, Pa.; in 1859 of Christ Church, Pelham, N. Y., where he remained until 1862, when he removed to New York city, as rector of the Free Church of St. Matthias. He died there, Aug. 28, 1879. See *Prot. Episc. Almanac*, 1880, p. 170.

Cornwall, Robert, a Scotch clergyman, took his degree at Glasgow University in 1583; was appointed to the living at Ecclesmachan in 1588; transferred to the second charge at Linlithgow in 1597; presented to the living in 1599; transferred to the first charge in the same place in 1608, and died June 5, 1626, aged about sixty-three years. He was a member of the assembly in 1590, 1602, and 1608; and was nominated constant moderator of the presbytery in 1606. See *Fasti Eccles. Scoticanæ*, i, 159, 162, 184.

Cornwall, William, an Irish Wesleyan minister, was converted at an early age, under the ministry of Gideon Ouseley. Being a good Celtic scholar, he was appointed a missionary to the Irish, chiefly in his own province of Connaught. After undergoing numerous privations and hardships, which induced premature decline, he became a supernumerary in 1848, and died May 11, 1860. See *Minutes of the British Conference*, 1860.

Cornwallis, Frederick, an English prelate, son of the first Lord Cornwallis, was appointed canon of Windsor, May 21, 1746; installed a prebendary of Lincoln, April 11, 1747; consecrated bishop of Coventry and Lichfield, Feb. 19, 1750, and appointed prebendary of London, Nov. 8, 1760, and dean of London, Nov. 14, 1766. He was enthroned archbishop of Canterbury, Oct. 6, 1768, and died March 19, 1783. He published several *Sermons*. See Le Neve, *Fasti;* Allibone, *Dict. of Brit. and Amer. Authors*, s. v.

Cornwallis, James, an English prelate, was born in 1743. He received the early part of his education at Eton, whence he removed to Merton College, of which he became a fellow. He was appointed chaplain to the marquis of Townshend, when that nobleman was lord-lieutenant of Ireland, and on his return therefrom was made a prebendary of Westminster in 1770, and presented to the valuable rectories of Wrotham, in Kent, and of Newington, in Oxfordshire. In 1775 he was installed dean of Canterbury, and in 1781 consecrated bishop of Lichfield and Coventry. In 1791 he succeeded to the deanery of Windsor and Wolverhampton, which, in 1794, he exchanged for that of Durham. On the death of his nephew, marquis Cornwallis, without male issue, Aug. 16, 1823, the dignities of earl Cornwallis and viscount Brome devolved upon him. He died in 1824. He published *Sermons* (1777, 1782, 1811). See *The* (Lond.) *Annual Register*, 1824, ii, 205; Allibone, *Dict. of Brit. and Amer. Authors*, s. v.

Cornwell, Francis, an English Baptist minister, lived in the time of Charles I. He was educated at Emmanuel College, Cambridge; was an object of persecution at the hands of archbishop Laud, because he objected to the surplice, kneeling at the Lord's Supper, and making the sign of the cross in baptism. He became an avowed Baptist about 1644, and published, not long after, a work in defence of his principles, entitled, *The Vindication of the Royal Commission of King Jesus*, which "created much excitement and some wrath." He gathered a company of Christians whose faith was in harmony with his own, and became their pastor. Neal speaks of him as "one of the most learned divines that espoused the cause of the Baptists." See Cathcart, *Baptist Encyclop.* p. 280. (J. C. S.)

Cornwell, Waite, a Presbyterian minister, went to Yale College from Middletown, and graduated in 1782. He preached occasionally, but never had charge of a parish. He moved, late in life, to some part of the state of Ohio, where he died in March, 1816. See *Old Redstone.*

Cornwell, W. E., a German Reformed minister, was born in Philadelphia, Dec. 8, 1807. In early life he was a Presbyterian. In 1836 he became a licensed minister in the German Reformed Church, and took charge of a congregation in Montgomery County, Pa. Later, he was pastor at Böhms (in Whitpaine), Pleasantville, and Whitemarsh. In 1850 he left the German Church and was immersed by Rev. Mr. Smith. From 1853 to 1857 he was pastor of the Baptist churches at Norristown, Pa., and Bridgeton, N. J., and later at Princeton. He died March 29, 1858. See Harbaugh, *Fathers of the Germ. Ref. Church*, iii, 488.

Cornyn, John Kinkead, a Presbyterian minister, was born at Carlisle, Pa., Aug. 16, 1815. He graduated at Jefferson College in 1842, and was a student in the Western Theological Institute for three years. He was licensed by the Presbytery of Allegheny, April 3, 1845, and for two years supplied various churches in his presbytery. In 1847 he entered the Presbytery of Erie, where he preached to the congregations of Sturgeonville, Girard, and Harbor Creek. From 1850 he preached in several places, especially at Troy, Pa., but failing health soon obliged him to retire from the active duties of the ministry. He died Dec. 22, 1853. During his period of ill-health he published a work called *Dick Wilson, or, the Rumseller's Victim.* See *Hist. of the Presbytery of Erie.*

Corōna, a martyr in Syria, with Victor (q. v.), under Antoninus, is commemorated May 14.

Corōna Clericālis is a name given to the *tonsure* (q. v.) of the clergy in the ancient Church.

CORONA Lucis (*crown of light*). Crowns of candles or tapers, or, as they were often called, *phari*, in distinction from *canthari*, or oil-lamps, were at an early date suspended in the choir; they were circles, covered with tapers or lamps, hung by chains or ropes from the vault. We extract the following account of them from Walcott, *Sac. Archæol.* s. v.:

"At Tours a standing lamp, with three tapers, is a lingering relic of the custom in France, where glass lustres are now common, but the hanging crown has been revived in England. At Aix-la-Chapelle there is an octagonal crown of the latter part of the 12th century, which was the gift of the emperor Frederick Barbarossa; it is made of bronze gilt, and enamelled, and supports small circular and square towers, which serve as lanterns, sixteen in number; between them are courses of tapers tripled, making in all forty-eight lights. It appears to descend from the dome, as from the vault of heaven, over the tomb of Charlemagne. Another crown of great beauty, the gift of bishop Odo, brother of William of Normandy, adorned the choir of Bayeux, until its destruction in 1562. The earliest on record is that given by pope Leo, which was made of silver, and had twelve towers and thirty-six lamps. Another, of cruciform shape, given by pope Adrian, was hung before the presbytery of St. Peter's at Rome, and lighted with one thousand three hundred and seventy candles. Constantine gave a pharus of gold to burn before St. Peter's tomb; and Leo III added a lustre of porphyry, hung by chains of gold, to burn before the confessio of the apostles. Sixtus III gave a silver pharus to St. Mary Major; Hilary presented ten to St. John Lateran; and Walafrid Strabo mentions one hanging by a cord before the altar at St. Gall. At Durham, in the 12th century, we read that in honor of St. Cuthbert lights were arranged like a crown round the altar, on the candelabrum, and lighted on greater festivals. This is the earliest instance in England. Crowns had little bells, called clamacteria, pendent from them. The corona, the luminous crown or circlet of lights, whether a single hoop or a tier of many, is the most beautiful of all modes of lighting—hanging and flashing like a cloud of fire before the sanctuary in some grand cathedrals, such as those suspended in the midst of the choir of St. Remi at Rheims, Clugny, Toul, and Bayeux, and representing the heavenly Jerusalem, with its gates and towers and angelic warders. The crown of Hildesheim, of the 13th century, is of large dimensions, and is enriched with statues; thirty-six oil-lamps burn upon the double gateway towers; seventy-two wax tapers, arranged in threes, blaze on the intermediate battlements. When these hundred and eight lights, like diamonds of living fire, are seen from a distance, they fuse into a disk-like glory, or a sun. In the Greek churches of the present day there is often a wooden cross, hung with ostrich eggs, suspended from the dome, which, almost in mockery of ancient splendor, is furnished with lights upon festivals. Formerly hanging phari burned before the altar; a lustre of seven branches in the centre of the church, and twelve lights on the sides of the chancel-screens. The lights arranged along the rood-beam were only another form of the crown, in a right line instead of a curve. Three or seven lights typified the divine graces, and twelve the Glorious Company of the Apostles. At the Temple Church (Bristol) there is a beautiful crown, with twelve branches; on the top is the Blessed Mother and the Holy Child, and under them are St. Michael and the dragon. A luminous cross of copper, with intersecting arms, and oil-lamps hanging by chains, of the 13th century, is suspended under the dome of St. Mark's (Venice), and is lighted on great festivals. A perpendicular crown, formerly at Valle Crucis Abbey, and now at Llanarmon, has a figure of the Blessed Virgin, canopied, and four tiers of branches for lights."

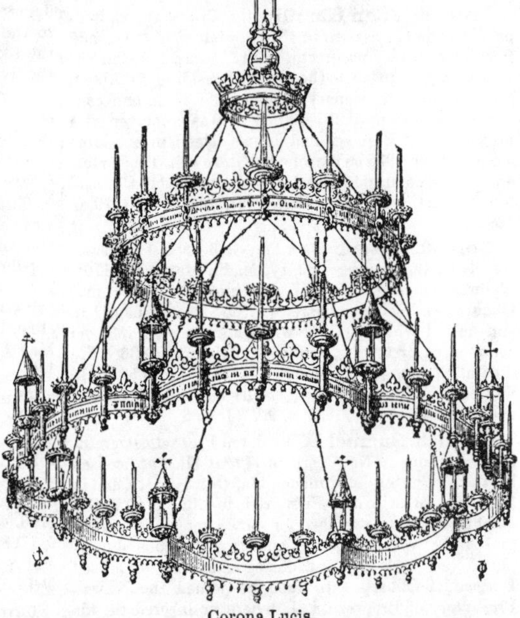
Corona Lucis.

CORONA Nuptiālis is the nuptial crown, i. e., the wreath or ornament placed on the head of the bride in the Western, as well as on the head of the bridegroom in the Eastern Church, at the time of marriage.

CORONA Votīva. In the early ages of Christianity it was by no means unusual for sovereigns and other royal personages to dedicate their crowns to the use of the Church. The gifts thus devoted were known as *Donaria*, and were suspended by chains attached to their upper rim, above an altar or shrine, or in some conspicuous part of the church. Other chains were attached to the lower rim, supporting a lamp, from which usually depended a jewelled cross. The crowned cross thus suspended above the altar was felt to be an appropriate symbol of the triumphs of Christianity, and its use became almost universal.

Pensile Crown. (From the "Palliotto," San Ambrogio, Milan.)

The custom for sovereigns to dedicate their actual crowns to the Church's use led to the construction of imitative crowns, formed for votive purposes alone. Of this usage we find repeated notices in ancient chronicles and documents. They are usually described as having

Pensile Crowns. (From bass-relief, Cathedral of Monza.)

been suspended over the altar, and very frequently mention is made of jewelled crosses appended to them.

The convenience of the form of these donative crowns for the suspension of lamps doubtless gave rise to the custom of constructing large chandeliers after the same model. In these pensile luminaries the shape and character of the royal circle were preserved, but frequently in much larger proportions.

Pensile Crown. (From Mosaic in San Apollinare Nuovo, Ravenna.)

The name *pharus*, though sometimes used for a *corona*, was more properly a standing candelabrum supporting lamps or candles, which, from their number of spreading branches, were sometimes called *arbores*, trees.

Corona, Leonardo DA MURANO, an Italian painter, was born at Murano in 1561, and gained much by the study of the works of Titian and Tintoretto. In the Church of San Fantino is his master-piece, representing *The Crucifixion.* He died at Venice in 1605. See Hoefer, *Nouv. Biog. Générale*, s. v.; Spooner, *Biog. Hist. of the Fine Arts*, s. v.

Corona, Matthias, a Dutch theologian of the order of Carmelites, who lived in the latter half of the 17th century, wrote, *Potestas Infallibilis Petri et Successorum Romanorum Pontificum* (Liege, 1668):—*De Dignitate et Potestate Spirituali Episcoporum* (ibid. 1671). See Hoefer, *Nouv. Biog. Générale*, s. v.

Corona, Tobias, an Italian theologian, originator of the "Milanese" monks, entered into orders in 1583, was confessor of cardinal Justiniani, and general of the community to which he belonged. He was sent to France and to Savoy by pope Gregory XV, and died at Naples in 1627, leaving *I Sagri Tempii*, etc. (Rome, 1625). See Hoefer, *Nouv. Biog. Générale*, s. v.

Coronach was a lamentation at funerals, formerly universal throughout Scotland and Ireland, and still very common in parts of those countries. Combined cries of lamentation were intermingled with expostulations and reproaches bestowed upon the deceased for leaving the world, and the wailing was continued by a train of females which followed the corpse to the burial. The ὀλολυγή of the Greeks and *ululatus* of the Latins designated similar practices among the classical nations; and the resemblance of these words to the common Celtic cries on funeral occasions, *uloghone* and *hullulu*, indicates an etymological affinity. See MOURN.

Coronāti Dies. See FESTIVAL.

Coronāti Quatuor, LEGEND AND FESTIVAL OF, is the title given to four martyrs, Severus, Severianus, Carpophorus, and Victorinus, who suffered martyrdom at Rome in the reign of Diocletian. The tradition respecting them is to the effect that they refused to sacrifice to idols, and were then, at the command of the emperor, beaten to death before the statue of Æsculapius, with scourges loaded with lead. The bodies having lain where they died for five days, were then deposited by pious Christians in a sandpit on the Via Lavicana, three miles from the city, near the bodies of five who had suffered martyrdom on the same day two years before, Claudius, Nicostratus, Symphonianus, Castorius, and Simplicius. See, e. g. the Martyrology of Ado, Nov. 8 (Migne, *Patrol.* cxxiii, 392), who gives the legend more fully than others.

It is stated by Anastasius Bibliothecarius (*ibid.* cxxviii, 699), that pope Honorius I (died A.D. 638) built a church in Rome in their honor. To this church the remains of the martyrs were subsequently transferred by pope Leo IV (died A.D. 855), who had been its officiating priest, and who, finding it in a very ruinous condition on his ascension to the pontificate, restored it with much splendor, and bestowed upon it many gifts. This church was situated on the ridge of the Cœlian Hill, between the Coliseum and the Lateran; and on its site the present church of the Santi Quattro Incoronati was built by pope Pascal II.

As to the appointment of the festival of these martyrs on Nov. 8, which is said to be due to pope Melchiades (died A.D. 314), a curious difficulty has arisen. Thus, in the notice of the festival in the editions of the Gregorian Sacramentary (for the words would appear to be wanting in MS. authority), the remark is made that, it being found impossible to ascertain the natal day of the four martyrs, it was appointed that in their church the natal day of the five other saints, near to whose bodies they had been buried, should be celebrated, that both might have their memory recorded together (*Patrol.* lxxviii, 147).

Coronation of kings and emperors, the most august ceremony of Christian national life, affords a striking example of the manner in which Christianity breathed a new spirit into already existing ceremonies, and elevated them to a higher and purer atmosphere. Under her inspiration a new life animated the old form: heathen accessories gradually dropped off; fresh and appropriate observances were developed; and the whole ceremonial assumed a character in harmony with the changed faith of those who were its subjects. It has been remarked by Dean Stanley (*Memorials of Westminster Abbey*, p. 42) that the rite of coronation, at least in early Christian times, represents two opposite aspects of European monarchy. It was (1) a symbol of the ancient usage of the choice of the leaders by popular election, and of the emperor by the Imperial Guard, derived from the practice of the Gallic and Teutonic nations; and (2) a solemn consecration of the new sovereign to his office by unction with holy oil, and the placing of a crown or diadem on his head by one of the chief ministers of religion, after the example of the ancient Jewish Church. In modern times, the custom has been kept up of calling upon a high ecclesiastical functionary to take a prominent part in this act of public inauguration of a sovereign, in all the countries of Europe where monarchy prevails. See CROWN.

Early Christian Diadem.

CORONATION OF THE VIRGIN is a ceremony performed annually at Rome, in which the pope takes a conspicuous part. An image of the Virgin Mary is arrayed in velvet or satin, adorned with silver and gold, and trimmed with the most costly lace. It is gorgeously decked with necklaces and earrings, and bracelets of precious stones. At the appointed time this figure is placed on an altar, in a church hung round with tapestry and brilliantly lighted. In the presence of immense crowds a service is performed, after which the priests approach the image and crown it. In the course of these ceremonies the priests burn incense before the figure, bow down before it, and mutter prayers to the Virgin. In many respects these ceremonies resemble those followed by the ancient Romans in crowning the statues of their heathen gods. See Seymour, *Pilgrimage to Rome.*

Coronel, Gregor Nuñez, a Portuguese priest who lived in the 16th century, was preacher to the duke of Savoy. Clement VIII, whose confessor he was, appointed him first secretary and consulter of the *Congregatio de Auxiliis*. His treatise against Molina is preserved in MS. in the *Angelica*. He died at Rome in 1620, leaving, *De Vera Christi Ecclesia* (Rome, 1594):—*De Optimo Republicæ Statu* (ibid. 1597):—*Apologeticum de Traditionibus Apostolicis* (ibid. eod.). See Ossinger, *Bibl. Aug.* p. 636; Lanteri, *Sæc. Sex*, ii, 280; Schmalfus, *Hist. Relig. et Eccles. Christ.* v, 244 (giving the substance of Coronel's treatise against Molina); Keller, in Wetzer u. Welte's *Kirchen-Lexikon*, s. v. (B. P.)

Coronel, Paolo, a Spanish convert from Judaism, was born at Segovia in 1480. After his baptism, in 1492, he studied theology, and was appointed professor at the University of Salamanca, where he died, Sept. 30, 1534. He was a celebrated Talmudist, and deeply versed in Hebrew, Greek, Latin, and the Oriental languages. He contributed to the famous *Complutensian Polyglot*. See Fürst, *Bibl. Jud.* i, 189; Wolf, *Bibl. Hebr.* i, 965; Jöcher, *Allgemeines Gelehrten-Lexikon*, s. v.; Lindo, *Hist. of the Jews in Spain*, p. 358. (B. P.)

Coronet. This ornament first appears in the effigy of John of Eltham, who died in 1332. The addition of a marquis's coronet to an archiepiscopal mitre does not date back before the time of Sheldon. Edmundson speaks of it as a novelty. It has since then been drawn as a ducal coronet. The bishops of Durham, who took their title by the grace of God or by divine providence (in distinction from other bishops, who are styled, by divine permission), while still palatine, until 1833, used the coronet by right, or in lieu of it a plume of feathers.

Coronidian Maidens, in Greek mythology, were Metioche and Menippe, the daughters of Orion, both endowed by Minerva with wisdom and rare beauty. When their father had been killed by Diana, a pestilence broke out. The oracle, on being consulted, declared that, in order to atone to the subterranean deities, two maidens must be sacrificed. Then Metioche and Menippe offered themselves as victims, but Pluto changed them into two comets. A temple of the Coronidian Maidens was built by the Æolians.

Corophites is the same as *Agonistici* (q. v.).

Corporal is a word used in the *Sacramentaries* by Gregory the Great, Isidore of Seville, and in the capitulars of the Frankish kings in 800, meaning a fine linen, or canvas, cloth of pure white, according to the Council of Rheims, on which the sacred elements are consecrated, and hence called the corporal, in allusion to the body of Christ, of which bread is the sacrament. Isidore of Pelusium called it the *eileton*, the wrapping-cloth; and Isidore of Damascus speaks of it as the winding-sheet. The centre, on which the chalice and paten stood, were quite plain, the ends alone being of silk, or worked with gold or silver. It was ordered to be used by pope Sixtus I in 125, and Sylvester I, cir. 314, directed it to be of linen and not of stuff, as before. It was also known as the *pall-veil*, or *sindon*, and represented the fine linen in which Joseph of Arimathæa wrapped the Lord's body in the garden tomb. The altar, by canon law, had two palls, and one corporal of plain linen cloth. The removal of the cloth from the consecrated elements typified the manifestation of the mysteries of the Old Test. by the death of Jesus. The earliest corporals covered the entire altar, and hung down at each side; two deacons were required to spread them. See ALTAR-CLOTH; ANTIMENSIUM.

Corporal Acts OF MERCY is an ecclesiastical phrase for (1) feeding the hungry; (2) giving drink to the thirsty; (3) clothing the naked; (4) harboring the stranger; (5) visiting the sick; (6) ministering to prisoners; (7) burying the dead (Matt. xxv, 35; Tobit i, 17).

Corporal Punishment subsisted during the first five centuries of the Christian æra under its most usual forms, as a social degradation, but the liability to it was afterwards greatly extended.

I. *Civil.*—The equality before the law which might have been reached through the extension of Roman citizenship had been by no means attained, but the character of that prerogative itself had become debased, and the exemption from corporal punishment, which still fluttered, like a last rag of the *toga*, on the shoulders of the civic officers, had already been blown off for some. There were decurions who had been flogged, and decurions who could be flogged. Exemption was, indeed, growing to be a privilege attached to the mere possession of wealth. Thus delation, if proved false, or where the delator did not persevere, should he be of mean fortune, which he did not care to lose, was to be punished with the sharpest flogging.

Among the offences which entailed corporal punishment, besides the one already mentioned, may be named false witness. The use of it multiplied, indeed, as the character of the people became lowered, and the Novels are comparatively full of it. The eighth enacts flogging and torture against the taking of money by judges; the one hundred and twenty-third punishes with "bodily torments" those persons, especially stage-players and harlots, who should assume the monastic dress or imitate or make a mock of Church usages; the one hundred and thirty-fourth enacts corporal punishment against those who detained debtors' children as responsible for their father's debt, or who abetted illegal divorces, and requires the adulterous wife to be scourged to the quick. On the other hand, a husband chastising his wife, otherwise than for conduct for which he might lawfully divorce her, was by the one hundred and seventeenth Novel made liable to pay to her, during coverture, the amount of one third of the ante-nuptial gift. The last chapter of the one hundred and thirty-fourth Novel, indeed, professes to inculcate moderation in punishment, and enacts that from henceforth there shall be no other penal mutilation than the cutting off of one hand, and that thieves shall only be flogged. Already, under Constantine, it had been enacted (A.D. 315) that branding should not be in the face, as disfiguring "the heavenly beauty," a law in which the influence of Christian feeling upon the first Christian emperor is strikingly displayed.

Passing from the legislation of the East to that of the West, we find on the whole a very similar course of things. Among the ancient Germans, according to the account of Tacitus, corporal punishment was rare. He notes as a singularity that, in war, none but the priest was allowed to punish, bind, or even strike a soldier. A husband might, indeed, flog his adulterous wife naked through the streets; but otherwise even slaves were rarely beaten.

Among the Anglo-Saxons corporal punishment seems in general to have been confined to slaves, as an alternative for compensation, wherewith the slave "redeemed" or "paid the price of his skin," as it is expressed; e. g. for sacrificing to devils (A.D. 691–725), for working on Sundays (A.D. 688–728). In certain cases of theft the accuser himself was allowed to flog the culprit. A foreigner or stranger wandering out of the way through the woods, who neither shouted nor blew the horn, was to be deemed a thief, and to be flogged or redeem himself.

Capital punishment is again prominent in the Capitularies. The first Capitulary of Carloman (A.D. 742), imposes two years' imprisonment on a fornicating priest, after he has been scourged to the quick. The Capitulary of Metz, 755, following a synod held at the same place, enacts that for incest a slave or freedman shall be beaten with many stripes, as also any "minor" cleric guilty of the like offence. The same enactment, confined to the case of marrying a cousin, and in slightly different language, occurs elsewhere in the general collection. A savage one on conspiracies (A.D. 805) is added to the Salic law, enacting that where conspiracies have been made with an oath—the principal suffering death—the accessories are to flog each other and cut each other's noses off; even if no mischief shall have been done, to shave and flog each other. For conspiracies without an oath, the slave only was to be flogged, the freeman clearing himself by oath or compounding. The same law occurs in the General Capitularies. Another law enacts public flagellation and decalvation for the slave marrying within the seventh degree of consanguinity, and there is also embodied much of the rigorous Visigothic Code as towards the Jews, who are to be decalvated and receive one hundred lashes publicly if they marry within the prohibited degrees. The Visigothic provision against marrying without priestly benedictions, or exceeding in any wise the laws as to dowry, is by this extended to Jews as well as Christians.

II. *Ecclesiastical.*—Here, indeed, we find at first a much higher standard than that of the civil law. Among the persons whose offerings the Apostolic Constitutions require to be rejected are such as "use their slaves wickedly, with stripes or hunger, or hard service." Soon, however, a harsher law must have prevailed. The Council of Elvira (A.D. 305), enacted that if a mistress, inflamed by jealousy, should so flog her handmaid that she should die within three days, she is only to be admitted to communion after seven years' penance (unless in case of dangerous illness), if the act were done wilfully, or after fine, if death were not intended—a provision which speaks volumes indeed of the bitterness of Spanish slavery at this period, but which nevertheless shows the Church taking cognizance of the slave-owner's excesses, and endeavoring to moderate them by its discipline, at least in the case of women. On the other hand, the right of personal chastisement was often arrogated by the clergy themselves, since the Apostolic Canons enact that a bishop, priest, or deacon, striking the faithful who have sinned, or the unfaithful who have done wrong, seeking thereby to make himself feared, is to be deposed, and Augustine clearly testifies to the fact of corporal punishment being judicially inflicted by bishops, in a letter to the præfect Marcellus, in which, while exhorting him not to be too severe in punishing the Donatists, he praises him at the same time for having drawn out the confession of crimes so great by whipping with rods, inasmuch as this "mode of coercion is wont to be applied by the masters of liberal arts, by parents themselves, and often even by bishops in their judgments."

Corporal punishment seems, moreover, to have formed from an early period, if not from the first, a part of the monastic discipline. The rule of Pachomius, translated into Latin by Jerome, imposes the penalty of thirty-nine lashes, to be inflicted before the gates of the monastery (besides fasting), after three warnings, on a monk who persists in the "most evil custom" of talking, as well as for theft. Cassian (end of 4th or beginning of 5th century) places flogging on the same line with expulsion as a punishment for the graver offences against monastic discipline (some of which, indeed, may appear to us very slight), as "open reproaches, manifest acts of contempt, swelling words of contradiction, a free and unrestrained gait, familiarity with women, anger, fightings, rivalries, quarrels, the presumption to do some special work, the contagion of money-loving, the affecting and possessing of things superfluous, which other brethren have not, extraordinary and furtive reflections, and the like." In the rule of Benedict (A.D. 528) corporal punishment seems implied: "If a brother for any, the slightest, cause is corrected in any way by the abbot or any prior, or if he lightly feel that the mind of any prior is wroth or moved against him, however moderately, without delay let him lie prostrate on the earth at his feet, doing satisfaction until that emotion be healed. But if any scorn to do this, let him be either subjected to corporal punishment, or, if contumacious, expelled from the monastery." Here, it will be seen, corporal punishment is viewed as a lighter penalty than expulsion.

In the letters of Gregory the Great, 590–603, the right of inflicting, or at least ordering, personal chastisement is evidently assumed to belong to the clergy. In a letter to Pantaleo the Notary, on the subject of a deacon's daughter who had been seduced by a bishop's nephew, he required either that the offender should marry her, executing the due nuptial instruments, or be "corporally chastised" and put in penance in a monastery, and the pope renews this injunction in a letter to the uncle, bishop Felix, himself. Bishop Andreas of Tarentum, who had had a woman on the roll of the Church cruelly whipped with rods, against the order of the priesthood, so that she died after eight months, was nevertheless only punished by this really great pope with two months' suspension from saying mass. Sometimes, indeed, corporal punishment was inflicted actually in the church, as we see in another letter of the same pope to the bishop of Constantinople, complaining that an Isaurian monk and priest had been thus beaten with rods, "a new and unheard-of mode of preaching." But the same Gregory deemed it fitting that slaves guilty of idolatry, or following sorcerers, should be chastised with stripes and tortures for their amendment. Elsewhere the flogging of penitent thieves seems to be implied.

Towards the end of the same century, the sixteenth

Council of Toledo (A.D. 693), enacted that one hundred lashes and shameful *decalvatio* should be the punishment of unnatural offences. With this and a few other exceptions, however, the enactments of the Church as to corporal punishment chiefly refers to clerics or monks. The Council of Vannes, in 465, had indeed already enacted that a cleric proved to have been drunk should either be kept thirty days out of communion, or subjected to corporal punishment. The first Council of Orleans, in 511, had enacted that if the relict of a priest or deacon were to marry again, she and her husband were, after "castigation," to be separated, or excommunicated if they persisted in living together. Towards the end of the 7th century, the Council of Autun (about 670) enacted that any monk who went against its decrees should either be beaten with rods, or suspended for three years from communion. In the next century, Gregory III (731-741), in his excerpt from the Fathers and the Canons, assigns stripes as the punishment for thefts of holy things. The Synod of Metz, 753, in a canon already quoted in part above as a capitulary, enacted that a slave or freedman without money, committing incest with a consecrated woman, a gossip, a cousin, was to be beaten with many stripes, and that clerics committing the like offence, if minor ones, were to be beaten or imprisoned.

Corporax Cups are vessels of precious metal, suspended by a chain under a canopy, and used for the reservation of the eucharist for the sick. They sometimes took the form of a tiara of crowns, in allusion to Rev. xix, 12, and were covered often by a thin veil of silk or muslin, called the "kerchief of cobweb lawn." At Durham it was of very fine lawn, embroidered with gold and red silk, and finished with four knobs and tassels. That used by St. Cuthbert formed the banner carried to victory at the Red Hills.

Corpreus. See CAIRPRE.

Corpus Christi (French, *Fête Dieu*), the *Feast of the Body of Christ*, kept on the Thursday after Trinity Sunday (or the octave of Pentecost), was instituted in 1264, by pope Urban IV, for a procession bearing the eucharist, with an office and prose composed by Aquinas; the office is also attributed to Robert, bishop of Liege, in 1249. Colleges at Oxford and Cambridge bear this dedication. It afterwards became the chief occasion on which the mysteries were acted by the clergy, and the miracle-plays by guilds. The mother churches began the procession on this day, and subordinate churches on or within the octave. It was an immemorial custom in Spain for the priests to carry the tabernacle upon these occasions raised upon their shoulders. In England, on Corpus-Christi day, they carried the silver pyx under a canopy of silk and cloth-of-gold, borne by four men, preceded by a pageant—Ursula and her maidens, St. George with spear and dragon, the devil's house, St. Christopher bearing the Infant, St. Sebastian pierced with arrows, St. Catharine with sword and wheel, St. Barbara with the chalice and cakes, followed by banners, crosses, candlesticks, reliquaries, cups, and images, which the priests lifted on high, while before them went many sacring bells and musicians, St. John pointing to the Lamb, upon which two, clad as angels, cast sweet-smelling flowers. The highway was strewn with boughs, every wall and window was decorated with branches. In villages the husbandmen went among the cornfields with crosses and banners; and the priest, carrying the blessed bread in a bag round his neck, read the gospel at certain stations, as an amulet against the wind, rain, and foul blasts.

Corradi, Domenico (called *Ghirlandajo*), an eminent Italian painter, was born at Florence in 1451, and was instructed in the school of Alessio Baldovinetti. Two of his best pictures are, *The Resurrection*, and *The Calling of St. Peter and St. Andrew to the Apostleship*. There are many of his works in the churches of Rome, Florence, Pisa, and Rimini. He died in 1495. See Spooner, *Biog. Hist. of the Fine Arts*, s. v.; Rose, *Gen. Biog. Dict.* s. v.

Corradi, Ridolfi (also called *Ghirlandajo*), an Italian painter, son of Domenico, was born at Florence in 1485. He studied under Fra Bartolommeo di S. Marco, and made such rapid advance that he was intrusted by Raphael to finish a picture, begun by him, of the *Virgin and Infant*, for one of the Sienese churches. Several of his first productions are in the churches at Florence, viz., Santi Girolamo and Jacopo. He died in 1560. See Rose, *Gen. Biog. Dict.* s. v.; Spooner, *Biog. Hist. of the Fine Arts*, s. v.

Corradini, PIETRO MARCELLINO, a learned Italian antiquary and prelate, was born at Sezza, June 2, 1658. He became an eminent lawyer, and was afterwards canon of St. John Lateran, and finally cardinal in 1712. He was employed in several diplomatic embassies, and died at Rome, Feb. 8, 1743. He wrote several works on ecclesiastical jurisprudence and history, for which see Hoefer, *Nouv. Biog. Générale*, s. v.; Jöcher, *Allgemeines Gelehrten-Lexikon*, s. v.

Corrado, Carlo, an Italian painter, was born at Naples in 1693, and studied under Solimena. He painted a number of altar-pieces for the churches at Rome, and also a large fresco painting in the ceiling of the Church of Buono Fratelli, which represented *Christ Glorified, and Surrounded by his Saints*. He died in Italy in 1768. See Spooner, *Biog. Hist. of the Fine Arts*, s. v.; Hoefer, *Nouv. Biog. Générale*, s. v.

Corrado, Pirro (Lat. *Pyrrhus Corradus*), an Italian theologian, born in the diocese of Rossano, Calabria, lived in the 17th century. He was prothonotary apostolical, canon of the metropolitan church of Naples, and minister-general of the inquisition at Rome. He wrote, *Praxis Beneficiaria* (Naples, 1656):—*Praxis Dispensationum Apostolicarum* (Cologne, 1672, 1678, 1716; Venice, 1735). See Hoefer, *Nouv. Biog. Générale*, s. v.

Corrado, Quinto Mario, a learned Italian, was born at Oria, Otranto, in 1508. He studied at Bologna under Romulo Amaseo; entered holy orders, and opened a school in his native place. He spent some years at Rome as secretary of cardinals Alexander and Badia. He afterwards taught belles-lettres at Naples and Salerno, and died in his native country in 1575, leaving several educational and other works, for which see Hoefer, *Nouv. Biog. Générale*, s. v.; Jöcher, *Allgemeines Gelehrten-Lexikon*, s. v.

Corranus (or **De Corro**), ANTONIUS, an Italian Protestant divine, was born at Seville, Spain, in 1527, and educated for the Roman Church, but went to England in 1570, and was admitted to the Anglican Church. In 1571 he was made reader in the Temple, London, and afterwards at St. Mary's and Hart Hall, Oxford, and finally prebendary in St. Paul's. He died in London in March, 1591, leaving several Latin works on language and practical religion, including notes on Canticles and Ecclesiastes.

Corraro (Lat. *Corrarius*), **Antonio**, an Italian prelate, was born at Venice in 1359. He was one of the institutors of the society of St. George *in Alga*, and was appointed bishop of Ostia, and afterwards cardinal, by pope Gregory XII, his uncle. After having performed the functions of legate in France and Germany, he passed the last years of his life in a monastery. He died at Padua, Jan. 19, 1445, leaving some works on festivals and casuistry, which have perished.

Another Antonio Corraro, a Benedictine of Venice, who died the same year, had been bishop of Brescia and Ceneda. See *Biog. Universelle*, s. v.; Hoefer, *Nouv. Biog. Générale*, s. v.

Corraro, Gregorio, an Italian writer and ecclesiastic, was born at Venice in 1411; became prothonotary apostolic at Rome, and in 1464 patriarch of Venice. He died at Verona the same year, leaving several works of an ethical rather than strictly religious character, for which see Hoefer, *Nouv. Biog. Générale*, s. v.; *Biog. Universelle*, s. v.

Correa, Diego, a Spanish painter, flourished about 1550. At Piacenza, in the convent of San Vincente, are two pictures by him, representing subjects from the *Life of the Virgin*, and in the Madrid Museum are several pictures representing *The Passion*.

Correa, Manoel (1), a Portuguese Jesuit, was born in 1636 in St. Paul de Loanda, in the African colony of Angola. He went to Lisbon and entered the Jesuit order May 31, 1651; afterwards taught at the University of Evora, received the degree of doctor in 1685, and became rector of the University of Coimbra. Being called to Rome, he was there promoted to the dignity of provincial, appointed assistant of P. Tyrso Gonzales, and died in 1708, leaving *Idea Consilarii* (Rome, 1712). See Hoefer, *Nouv. Biog. Générale*, s. v.

Correa, Manoel (2), a Portuguese Jesuit, was born in 1712. He entered upon the life of a monk in 1729, went to Brazil, taught at Bahia and at Pernambuco, but was arrested in 1758, for an attack upon Joseph I, and sent to Rome, where he died in 1789. His life, written in Latin, contains interesting particulars upon the religious institution to which he belonged. See Hoefer, *Nouv. Biog. Générale*, s. v.

Correa, Pelagio (or **Payo**) **Perez**, surnamed *the Portuguese Joshua*, was born in the early part of the 13th century, according to some historians, at Evora, according to others, at Santarem. He entered the new order of St. James, and was soon regarded as one of the most formidable adversaries of the powerful Mussulmans in the Peninsula. In 1242 he was elected grand master of the order, and at this time the Spanish chroniclers give to his history a truly legendary character. In 1248 he aided in the conquest of Seville by Ferdinand III of Castile. When Alfonso III was securely fixed upon the throne of Portugal, he called to his aid Correa, for the purpose of pushing his conquests. Correa died in 1275. See Hoefer, *Nouv. Biog. Générale*, s. v.; *Biog. Universelle*, s. v.

Correggio. See Allegri, Antonio.

Correspondences is the name applied to one of the principal doctrines which Swedenborg (q. v.) believed himself specially commissioned to promulgate. He taught that there are certain links of harmony and correspondence between the seen and the unseen worlds, so that every object ought to suggest to the mind of man its own appropriate divine truth. The fundamental idea of his system was that matter and spirit are associated together and connected by an eternal law, and all analogies were converted in his mind into predetermined correspondences. See Vaughan, *Hours with the Mystics*.

Corrie, Daniel, a bishop of the Church of England, was born about 1777. Having been nominated a chaplain on the Bengal Establishment, he proceeded to India towards the close of 1806. His first station up the country was at Chunar, where he was soon able to speak to the natives in Hindostanee, of which he had acquired the rudiments on his voyage out. Benares had also the benefit of his visits and ministrations. By the assistance of friends he raised a small church at Secrole, soon after another at Benares, and in 1818 the beautiful church at Chunar, together with a small chapel at Buxar, to the poor invalids and native Christians of which place he extended his labors of love. In 1810 he was removed to Cawnpore to labor with his friend, Henry Martyn, and continued there about a year, until obliged, by illness, to proceed to Calcutta. At the close of 1812 he removed to Agra, and two years later returned to England for the benefit of his health, and while there was much engaged in preaching for the Church Missionary Society in behalf of India. On resuming his missionary labors at Benares he devoted much of his care to establishing schools for the native Hindûs and Mohammedans. In 1819 he became presidency chaplain, and in 1823 archdeacon of Calcutta; but this appointment did not prevent him from working for the native congregations, besides translating Sellon's *Abridgment of Scripture*, the Prayer-book, and many of the homilies, into Hindostanee. He likewise drew up *Outlines of Ancient History*, in English, for the benefit of the native youth. In 1834, after a sojourn of nearly twenty-eight years in India, archdeacon Corrie was called to England to be consecrated bishop of Madras. He returned at once to India, but died Feb. 5, 1837. Bishop Corrie was a man in whose character the Christian graces were beautifully developed. See (Lond.) *Christian Remembrancer*, July, 1837, p. 442.

Corrington, Elijah, a Methodist Episcopal minister, was born in Harrison County, Ky., Jan. 28, 1797. He embraced religion in 1827, was licensed to preach in 1828, removed to Jacksonville, Ill., in 1830, and in 1836 entered the Illinois Conference. With but one year's exception as a superannuate, he labored zealously and successfully until his second superannuation, in 1863. He died late in 1863 or in 1864. See *Minutes of Annual Conferences*, 1864, p. 191.

Corrington, James B., D.D., a Methodist Episcopal minister, was born in Kentucky, Oct. 24, 1801. He was converted in 1828, licensed to preach soon after, in 1830 went to Illinois, and in 1838 joined the Illinois Conference. He located in 1842, but in 1847 was readmitted into the same conference. In 1849 he was appointed presiding elder of the Sparta District, subsequently filling that position on different districts with great acceptability and usefulness. He was a model presiding elder, possessing great executive ability, and being peculiarly adapted to that work. In 1872 he became superannuated, and continued in that relation until his death, Nov. 15, 1880. Dr. Corrington was a delegate to each session of the General Conference from 1852 until 1868. He was a man of marked ability, eminently popular among the masses. His sermons were clear, eloquent, full of pathos and power. See *Minutes of Annual Conferences*, 1881, p. 323.

Corrington, William H., a Methodist Episcopal minister, was born of godly parents in Kentucky in 1826. He removed to Greene County, Ill., at the age of four, with his parents; experienced religion while a student at McKendree College, where he graduated in 1849; for some time afterwards was tutor in that institution, and its financial agent; labored as a teacher in Chester, Mount Carmel, Rockford, and elsewhere, with marked success; became president of Southern Illinois Female Seminary, and in 1861 entered the Southern Illinois Conference. After two years in the ministry he again resumed the presidency of the college. He subsequently re-entered the regular work, and afterwards became presiding elder, which position he resigned but a few weeks before his death, June 6, 1872. Mr. Corrington was a man of sound sense and excellent judgment. His words were few, but plain and practical. His career was an undoubted success. See *Minutes of Annual Conferences*, 1872, p. 136.

Corrody is (1) a payment, in kind or money, made by a monastery to the nominee of a benefactor, who had the right of appointing often an indefinite number of such persons; (2) an allowance by a monastery to servants or outside persons.

Corsawr, John, a Scotch clergyman, took his degree at the University of St. Andrews in 1661, had a unanimous call by the parishioners to the living at South Leith in 1664, and was transferred to Dalgety in 1669. He died May 20, 1680, aged thirty-seven years. See *Fasti Eccles. Scoticanæ*, i, 105; ii, 589.

Corse is a plaited or woven silk ribbon, used as an ornament of vestments.

Corse, Alexander, a Scotch clergyman, was licensed to preach in 1733; called to the living at Abernyte in 1739, and ordained. He died Jan. 26, 1754. See *Fasti Eccles. Scoticanæ*, iii, 702.

Corse, David (1), a Scotch clergyman, was appointed minister at the second charge, Aberdeen, in 1704, and transferred to the first charge in 1705. He died before Oct. 23, 1712. See *Fasti Eccles. Scoticanæ*, iii, 485, 487.

Corse, David (2), a Scotch clergyman, took his degree at King's College, Aberdeen, in 1726; was assistant minister at Dunnottar, and appointed to that living in 1734; ordained in 1735. He died in February, 1736, aged thirty years. See *Fasti Eccles. Scoticanæ*, iii, 862.

Corse, Hugh, a Scotch clergyman, studied at Glasgow University; was licensed to preach in 1701; appointed to the living at Bower the same year, and ordained. He died July 6, 1738, aged sixty-two years. See *Fasti Eccles. Scoticanæ*, iii, 357.

Corse, John, D.D., a Scotch clergyman, was licensed to preach in 1737; appointed to Gorbals Chapel of Ease, Glasgow, in 1739; called to Tron Church as assistant minister in 1743, and ordained. He died Feb. 5, 1782, aged sixty-seven years. See *Fasti Eccles. Scoticanæ*, ii, 12.

Corser, Enoch, a Congregational minister, was born at Boscawen, N. H., Jan. 2, 1787. He attended the academy in Salisbury, and in 1811 graduated from Middlebury College. For three years he taught school in Danvers, Mass.; commenced the study of divinity in May, 1814, with the Rev. Dr. Harris, of Dunbarton, and was licensed in 1815 by the Hopkinton Association. After preaching in Middleton, Mass., and Colebrook, N. H., he was invited to Loudon, where he was ordained as pastor, March 17, 1817. His labors here were attended with great success, and ended Dec. 13, 1837. At Sanbornton Bridge he preached for nearly six years, and in May, 1843, began service as stated supply to the Church at Plymouth. He held the same relation to the Church in Epping for three years, from May, 1845, after which he removed to Boscawen. During the two years following he supplied, for short periods, the churches in Fisherville, Henniker, and Warner. At this time he was compelled to relinquish ministerial labors for several years, on account of an attack of palsy; but in August, 1857, he began service at Loudon, which continued until his death, June 17, 1868. See *Cong. Quarterly*, 1869, p. 285.

Corsĭcus, a presbyter, is honored June 30 as a Christian martyr in Africa.

Corsini, Andrea, an Italian ecclesiastic, was born at Florence, Nov. 30, 1302. He entered the order of Carmelites in 1319, was ordained priest in 1328, and became distinguished by his sermons, and still more by the sanctity of his life. According to the *Bibliothèque Sacrée*, he was made bishop of Fiesole in 1359 or 1360, in spite of his efforts to avoid it, and his life was one of deep humility. He was sent as legate to Bologna by pope Urban V, and appeased the seditions which disturbed that city. He died Jan. 6, 1373, and is commemorated on Feb. 4. Urban VIII canonized him. See Hoefer, *Nouv. Biog. Générale*, s. v.

Corsini, Lorenzo. See Clement XII.

Corsinus. See Corvinus.

Corsned (from *kur*, trial, and *snæd*, a slice) was an ordeal among the Saxons, mentioned as early as 1015, consisted of eating barley-bread and cheese, over which prayers had been said by the priest. The eater, if guilty, was expected to be choked by the morsel. It is supposed that this ceremony was invented in the early ages of Christianity from a presumptuous use of the consecrated elements, and that the Saxon corsned was actually the sacramental bread. The custom long since fell into disuse, though traces of it still exist in certain phrases of abjuration in use among certain classes, such as "I will take the sacrament upon it," "May this morsel be my last." See Ordeal.

Corso, Giovanni Vincente, a Neapolitan painter, was born about 1490. He studied under Giovanni Antonio Amato, and afterwards entered the school of Pierino del Vaga, at Rome. Most of his works in the churches at Naples have been retouched. The best preserved are an admirable picture of *Christ Bearing his Cross*, with many figures, in San Domenico, and *The Adoration of the Magi*, in San Lorenzo. He died at Rome in 1545. See Spooner, *Biographical History of the Fine Arts*, s. v.; Bryan, *Dict. of Painters and Engravers* (ed. Graves), s. v.

Corso, Niccolo, a Genoese painter, flourished about 1503. His works are chiefly in the cloister and refectory of the monastery of the Olivetani at Quarto, near Genoa. The most esteemed is a picture from the life of St. Benedict.

Corson, Charles Wesley, a Methodist Episcopal minister, was born at Beesley's Point, Cape May Co., N. J., Sept. 19, 1838. He was converted in 1852, and in 1872 joined the Genesee Conference, being ordained deacon the same year, and elder two years after. He served successfully Chili, Walworth, and Penfield (all in New York). In 1880 he was appointed to Prattsburg, where he died, Jan. 26, 1881. He was a man of sympathetic nature and true piety, arduous and faithful in his labors. See *Minutes of Annual Conferences*, 1881, p. 328.

Corson, Robert, a Canadian Methodist minister, was born at Clinton, Ont., Sept. 12, 1793. In the war of 1812 he served at the battles of Stony Creek, Queenston Heights, and Lundy's Lane. He was converted in 1817, sent out to preach in 1822, ordained in 1825, became superannuated in 1858, still continued abundant in labors, and died at Cainsville, Ont., Oct. 8, 1878. Mr. Corson had poor fare, poor pay, but tireless energy. He would preach forty sermons a month. He smiled at toil, hardship, and danger. His love of preaching was marvellous; it was a passion, an enthusiasm, an inspiration. See *Minutes of London* (Ont.) *Conference*, 1879, p. 25.

Cort, Cornelius (in Italy, *Cornelio Fiamingo*), an eminent Dutch engraver, was born at Hoorn in 1533 or 1536, and was probably instructed by Jerome Cock. He afterwards established a famous school at Rome, where he died in 1578. The following are some of his numerous prints from different masters: *Adam and Eve, with the Serpent; The Resurrection; The Descent of the Holy Ghost; Christ Walking on the Water; Christ Crowned with Thorns; St. John the Baptist; The Adoration of the Magi; The Entombing of Christ; The Creation of Adam and Eve; Moses and Aaron Before Pharaoh; The Nativity; The Holy Family; The Resurrection of Lazarus; The Death of the Virgin; Christ on the Mount of Olives.* See Spooner, *Biog. Hist. of the Fine Arts*, s. v.; Chalmers, *Biog. Dict.* s. v.; Bryan, *Dict. of Painters and Engravers*, s. v.

Cortasse, Pierre Joseph, a French theologian, was born at Apt, May 21, 1681. He entered the Jesuit order; taught grammar, rhetoric, philosophy, positive theology, and Hebrew in the colleges of his order; and for fourteen years devoted himself to preaching. He died at Lyons, March 24, 1740, leaving, *Traité des Noms Divins Traduit du Grec de Saint-Denis l'Aréopagite* (Lyons, 1739). See Hoefer, *Nouv. Biog. Générale*, s. v.

Corte, Cesare, an Italian painter, the son and scholar of Valerio, was born at Genoa in 1550. His best historical works are in that city. In San Pietro is his picture of *St. Peter at the Feet of the Virgin.* In San Francesco is an altar-piece, representing *Mary*

Magdalene; and in Santa Maria del Carmina are two pictures by him, of *St. Simeon* and *St. Francis.* He died in 1613. See Spooner, *Biog. Hist. of the Fine Arts,* s. v.; Bryan, *Dict. of Painters and Engravers,* s. v.

Corte, Juan de la, a Spanish painter, was born at Madrid in 1597, studied in the school of Velasquez, and was distinguished for his small pictures of sacred subjects. He died at Madrid in 1660. See Hoefer, *Nouv. Biog. Générale,* s. v.; Spooner, *Biog. Hist. of the Fine Arts,* s. v.

Cortese (or **Cortesi**; Fr. *Courtois*), **Giacomo** (or **Jacopo,** called *Il Borgognone*), a Jesuit and painter, was born at St. Hippolyte, in Franche-Comté, in 1621. At the age of fifteen he visited Milan, and afterwards Rome, where he painted a picture of *Magdalene at the Feet of Christ,* in the church of Santa Marta; and, in Il Gesu, *The Adoration of the Magi* and *The Murder of the Innocents.* He died at Rome in 1676. See Chalmers, *Biog. Dict.* s. v.; Spooner, *Biog. Hist. of the Fine Arts,* s. v.; Bryan, *Dict. of Painters and Engravers,* s. v.

Cortese, Guglielmo (likewise called *Il Borgognone*), a painter, brother of the foregoing, was born at St. Hippolyte, in 1628, and was instructed, while young, in the school of Pietro da Cortona, at Rome. His best works are in that city. They are, *The Crucifixion, Joshua's Battle,* a *Madonna, with several Saints.* He died at Rome in 1679. See Spooner, *Biog. Hist. of the Fine Arts,* s. v.; Bryan, *Dict. of Painters and Engravers,* s. v.

Cortesi (or **Cortezi**), Paolo, an Italian theologian, was born at San Geminiano, Tuscany, in 1465. He entered orders, and applied himself to the study of Latin literature. He was apostolic secretary under Alexander VI and Pius III, prothonotary, and finally bishop of Urbino. He died in 1510, leaving, *De Hominibus Doctis Dialogus* (published by Alexander Politi, more than two centuries after the death of Cortesi; Florence, 1734):—*In Quatuor Libros Sententiarum P. Lombardi Commentarii* (Rome, 1503; Paris, 1513; Basle, 1540):—*De Cardinalitu* (1510). See Hoefer, *Nouv. Biog. Générale,* s. v.; Chalmers, *Biog. Dict.* s. v.

Cortois (*de Pressigny*), Gabriel, a French prelate, was born at Dijon, Dec. 11, 1745. After having charge of the abbey of St. Jacques, in 1780, in the diocese of Béziers, he was appointed, in 1785, to the bishopric of St. Malo, and consecrated Jan. 15, 1786. During the Revolution he spent most of his time in Switzerland. On the return of the Bourbons he was appointed member of a commission of bishops and ecclesiastics to examine the wants of the Church, and was sent to Rome as ambassador. In 1816, he was made peer of France, and the following year archbishop of Besançon, but did not take possession until Oct. 31, 1819. He died May 2, 1822. See Hoefer, *Nouv. Biog. Générale,* s. v.

Corvaria (**Corbario,** or **Corvara**), Pietro di. See Nicholas V.

Corvi, Domenico, an Italian painter, was born at Viterbo in 1623, and studied under Mancini. He was one of the most eminent modern Roman masters, and his best works are his night-pieces, as his *Nativity,* in the Church of the Assumption. He died at Rome in 1703. See Hoefer, *Nouv. Biog. Générale,* s. v.; Spooner, *Biog. Hist. of the Fine Arts,* s. v.

Corvinus (or **Corsinus,** properly **Rabe**), Johannes Arnoldus, a Dutch jurist and theologian, devoted himself to preaching in 1606, and embraced the doctrine of the Remonstrants, for which he was deprived of his office as preacher, and, in 1622, obliged to seek an asylum in Schleswig. In 1623 he went to France, sojourned at Paris, Rouen, and Orleans, and was made doctor of law. In 1625 he returned to Amsterdam, and became professor of canon law. He is often confounded with his son, Corvinus of Beldern, who embraced Catholicism. The subject of this sketch died in 1650, leaving *Defensio Sententiæ Jac. Arminii,* etc. (Leyden, 1613):—*Censura Anatomes Arminianismi P. Molinæi* (Frankfort-on-the-Main, 1622), etc. See Hoefer, *Nouv. Biog. Générale,* s. v.; *Biog. Universelle,* s. v.

Corwin, Franklin D., a Methodist Episcopal minister, was born at Jefferson, Chemung Co., N. Y., Oct. 9, 1838. He received an early religious training; was passionately fond of books and study from childhood; entered Rock River Seminary, Ill., in 1857, with the intention of preparing for the law, but, experiencing conversion, repaired to the Garrett Biblical Institute, remained about two years, and then, in 1861, entered the Rock River Conference, in which he labored with much energy and acceptability until his decease, June 24, 1865. As a preacher, Mr. Corwin was studious and careful in preparation, earnest, attractive, and convincing in his delivery; as a pastor, mild, social, and winning. See *Minutes of Annual Conferences,* 1865, p. 225.

Corwin, James, a Methodist Episcopal minister, was born in Pendleton District, S. C., in 1811. After seventeen years of effective service in Indiana, he emigrated to California in 1849, became a member of the first conference in the state, and travelled very extensively between Siskiyou and San Diego. He died Dec. 1, 1876. Mr. Corwin was remarkable in his exemplary life, energy, and devotedness in self-culture and service for the Church, and in his success. See *Minutes of American Conferences,* 1877, p. 100.

Corwin, Jason, a Baptist minister, was born at Franklin, Conn., in February, 1792, of Presbyterian parents. He removed to Cazenovia, N. Y., where he was baptized by elder John Peck, and soon after licensed to preach. He studied at the Theological Institute in Hamilton, was ordained at Woodstock, and in a few months became pastor of the church in Deposit, Delaware Co. Here he remained three years; was then pastor in Penfield, Monroe Co., five years, Webster two years, Binghamton two years, and then removed to Great Bend, Pa. His other pastorates were in Earlville, Bridgewater, Augusta, Clinton, all in N. Y. In 1848 he received an appointment from the American Baptist Home Mission Society, and labored in Illinois four or five years. Subsequently he was an agent of the American Bible Union. He died at Washington, Tazewell Co., Ill., May 15, 1860. See *Minutes of Illinois Anniversaries,* 1860, p. 8, 9. (J. C. S.)

Corwin, Richard, a Methodist Episcopal minister, was born in Mason County, Ky., Aug. 29, 1789. He was piously trained, joined the Church in 1809, entered the ministry in 1817, travelled in Kentucky, was presiding elder for ten years, agent for American Colonization Society in 1834, and died while elder of Louisville District, in 1843. He was consistent, grave, intelligent, and spiritual. See *Minutes of Annual Conferences,* 1843–44, p. 454.

Cory, Andrew, an English Bible Christian preacher, was born at Moorwinstow, Cornwall. He was converted in 1816, became a class-leader and local preacher, entered the ministry in 1818, and travelled the best circuits for fifteen years; was superintendent of circuits and districts several years, treasurer of the Missionary Society, and once president of conference. He was drowned in September, 1833, at St. Neots, Cornwall.

Coryate, George, an English clergyman and Latin poet, was born in the parish of St. Thomas, Salisbury, and was educated at Winchester School and New College, Oxford, where, in 1562, he was admitted a perpetual fellow. In June, 1570, he became rector of Odcombe, and in 1594 was appointed prebendary in the cathedral of York. He died at Odcombe, March 4, 1606, leaving *Poemata Varia Latina* (London, 1611, 4to), and *Descriptio Angliæ, Scotiæ, et Hiberniæ.* See Chalmers, *Biog. Dict.* s. v.; Allibone, *Dict. of Brit. and Amer. Authors,* s. v.

Corybantes, in Greek mythology, were priests

of Rhea or Cybele, who danced, with shrieks and convulsive movements, to express their sorrow at the death of Atys, who loved Cybele. They are often confounded with the *Curetes* or *Cabiri* and the Idæan *Dactyles*.

Cosack, Johann Carl, a Lutheran theologian of Germany, was born Sept. 27, 1813, at Marienwerder, and died Oct. 30, 1868, while professor of theology at Königsberg. He wrote, *Ueber die Taufe der unehelichen Kinder* (Königsberg, 1858):—*Paulus Speratus Leben und Lieder* (Braunschweig, 1861). See Zuchold, *Bibl. Theol.* i, 246. (B. P.)

Cosattini, Giuseppe, an Italian ecclesiastic, canon of Aquileja, was a native of Udine (Friuli), where he flourished from 1672 to 1734. He is particularly noted for his picture of *St. Philip at the Altar*, painted for the congregation of Udine. See Spooner, *Biog. Hist. of the Fine Arts*, s. v.; Hoefer, *Nouv. Biog. Générale*, s. v.

Cosby, Jouett Vernon, a Presbyterian minister, was born July 8, 1816, at Staunton, Va. He was prepared for college at his native place; graduated from Hampden-Sidney College in 1836; taught school three years, then entered the theological seminary at Prince Edward, Va., where he spent two years, but graduated from Princeton Theological Seminary in 1843. He was licensed to preach by East Hanover Presbytery, May 3, 1843; was ordained as an evangelist by the same presbytery at Mount Carmel, Va., Sept. 23 of the same year, and assigned to Southampton as his field of labor, but afterwards supplied the church at Smithfield for two or three years. He commenced labor at Bardstown, Ky., in 1847, and also took charge of the Bardstown Academy. His relation as pastor was dissolved in 1860, and then he supplied the churches of Midway and Clear Creek, and was principal of Rose Hill Female Academy, at Woodford, but in 1864 he returned to Bardstown, and resumed the care of the church as stated supply, and the charge of the academy, where he continued till his death, Nov. 14, 1877. Mr. Cosby was a highly cultivated scholar, a devoted and successful teacher. See *Necrol. Report of Princeton Theol. Sem.* 1878, p. 51.

Cosby, Minor M., a Methodist Episcopal minister, embraced religion when about twenty-one, and two years later entered the Kentucky Conference. He gave full proof of his calling during the four years of his ministry, and died Sept. 5, 1835. Mr. Cosby was a young man of good understanding, great industry, and exemplary life. See *Minutes of Annual Conferences*, 1836, p. 405.

Coscia, Lelipo, a Neapolitan prelate, brother of Niccolo, was born at Benevento, and lived at Rome in 1731. He was, like his brother, an attendant of Benedict XIII, and became private chamberlain and vicar-general. April 8, 1725, he was consecrated bishop of Targo by the pope, who, in April, 1729, appointed him his auditor. After the death of Benedict XIII, Coscia was included in the disgrace of his brother, and shared a similar fate, being deprived of his honors and condemned to suffer imprisonment. Nothing is known of the closing years of his life. See Hoefer, *Nouv. Biog. Générale*, s. v.

Coscia, Niccolo, a Neapolitan prelate, was born at Benevento, Jan. 25, 1682. He was at first domestic and intimate confidant of cardinal Orsini, archbishop of Benevento, who, having become pope under the name of Benedict XIII, made him, in June, 1724, secretary of memorials, with an abbey of a thousand pounds' revenue; consecrated him titular archbishop of Trajanopolis on July 2; declared him assistant bishop of the throne, Aug. 15, and made him cardinal, under the title of *Santa Maria in Dominica* (called the *Novicella*), Sept. 15. Aug. 2, 1725, Coscia was appointed to various other ecclesiastical privileges. Sept. 5, Benedict XIII declared him successor to the archbishopric of Benevento. On the 13th of the same month Coscia received the title of protector-commander of the order of St. John of Jerusalem, with provision for six thousand pounds of revenue. In December he was made protector of the order of Conventual Minors, and, Feb. 10, 1726, of the brotherhood of writers and copyists, and finally, on June 12, præfect of the congregation of the state of Avignon. The bestowal of so much honor brought upon him general hatred. He was from time to time robbed of his honors, and suffered great persecution, especially at the hand of Clement XII. After suffering ten years' imprisonment, he returned to Naples, where he died in 1755. See Hoefer, *Nouv. Biog. Générale*, s. v.; *Biog. Universelle*, s. v.

Coscinomancy, in Grecian superstition, was fortune-telling by means of a sieve. When, for example, a thief was to be detected, the sieve was suspended by a thread in the air, and a number of suspected persons named, the gods being invoked in the meantime. At whosesoever name the sieve moved, he was held to be the thief. See Divination.

Cosens, Peter, a Scotch clergyman, a native of Forfarshire, was licensed to preach in 1806; presented to the living at Torryburn in 1808; ordained in 1809; transferred to Lauder in 1811, and died Aug. 20, 1845, aged sixty-three years, leaving a son, Alexander, minister of Broughton. See *Fasti Eccles. Scoticanæ*, i, 521; ii, 605.

Cosimo, Pietro di, a Florentine historical and portrait painter, was born in 1441, and studied under Cosimo Roselli. He went to Rome and assisted in painting a chapel for the pope, which gave such proofs of his skill that he was much patronized by the nobility, and established a school. He died in 1521.

Cosin, Richard, LL.D., an English divine, and civil and canon lawyer, was dean of the arches, and chancellor of the diocese of Worcester from 1579 until 1598. His works include *An Answer to a Libel, entitled, An Abstract of Certain Acts of Parliament* (1584):—*Conspiracie for Pretended Reformation, viz. Presbyterial Discipline by Hacket, Coppinger, and Arthington* (1592):—*Apologie for Sundrie Proceedings by Jurisdiction Ecclesiasticall* (1594):—*Ecclesiæ Anglicanæ Politria in Tabulas Digesta* (1604); and other works. See Fuller, *Worthies of England;* Allibone, *Dict. of Brit. and Amer. Authors*, s. v.

Cosin, Robert, an English martyr, was a godly man, and did much good by reading the Scriptures to those who could not read. For dissuading his neighbors from image-worship he was condemned and burned at Buckingham in 1533. See Fox, *Acts and Monuments*, iv, 214.

Cosmas (Cosmus, or **Cosmo)**, *Saint*. The following is the full legend of this saint, as given by Mrs. Jamieson, *Legends of the Saints*, p. 433.

> Cosmas and Damian were two brothers, Arabians by birth, but they dwelt in Ægæ, a city of Cilicia. Their father having died while they were yet children, their pious mother, Theodora, brought them up with all diligence, and in the practice of every Christian virtue. Their charity was such that they not only lived in the greatest abstinence, distributing their goods to the infirm and poor, but they studied medicine and surgery, that they might be able to prescribe for the sick, and relieve the sufferings of the wounded and infirm; and the blessing of God being on all their endeavors, they became the most learned and the most perfect physicians that the world had ever seen. They ministered to all who applied to them, whether rich or poor. Even to suffering animals they did not deny their aid, and they constantly refused all payment or recompense, exercising their art only for charity, and for the love of God; and thus they spent their days. At length those wicked emperors, Diocletian and Maximian, came to the throne, in whose time so many saints perished. Among them were the physicians, Cosmas and Damian, who, professing themselves Christians, were seized by Lycias, the proconsul of Arabia, and cast into prison. And first they were thrown into the sea, but an angel saved them; and then into the fire, but the fire refused to consume them; and then they were bound on two crosses and stoned, but of the stones flung at them none reached them, but fell on those who threw

Sts. Cosmas and Damian (after Bicci di Lorenzo, A.D. 1418).

them, and many were killed. So the proconsul, believing that they were enchanters, commanded that they should be beheaded, which was done.

The Greek Church, however, celebrates three pairs of these brothers as saints: (1) July 1, in the time of Carinus; (2) Oct. 27, Arabs, with their brothers Anthimus, Leontius, and Euprepius, martyred under Diocletian; (3) Nov. 1, sons of Theodotus. It is probable that all these are but variations or imitations of one legend.

Cosmas of Alexandria, a deacon. Maximus, abbot of Chrysopolis (A.D. 662), mentions, in a letter to a nobleman named Petrus, a treatise on the union and distinction of two natures in Jesus Christ, which he had addressed to Cosmas. Cosmas had been attracted by Severian opinions, but had returned to the Catholic Church. In a second letter to Cosmas, Maximus professes his sorrow at the calumnies spread abroad against Gregory, præfect of Africa (Migne, *Patrol. Græc.* xci; Maximus, § 307–309, 313, 334; Ceillier, xi, 768, 769).

Cosmas of Jerusalem (surnamed *the Hagiopolite*, also *the Melodist*), who held the second place among Greek ecclesiastical poets, was born at Jerusalem. Being left an orphan at an early age, he was adopted by the father of John of Damascus, and the two foster-brothers were bound together by a friendship which lasted through life. They excited each other to hymnology, and assisted, corrected, and polished each other's compositions. Cosmas, like his friend, became a monk of St. Sabas, and against his will was consecrated bishop of Majuma, near Gaza, in A.D. 743, by John, patriarch of Jerusalem, the same who ordained John of Damascus priest. After administering his diocese with great holiness, he died of old age, about 760, and is commemorated by the Eastern Church Oct. 14.

"Where perfect sweetness dwells, is Cosmas gone;
But his sweet lays to cheer the Church live on,"

says the verse prefixed to his life. His compositions are numerous; the best seem to be his canons on Gregory Nazianzen and the Purification. To him a considerable part of the Octoechus is owing. "He is the most learned of the Greek Church poets, and his fondness for types, boldness in their application, and love of aggregating them, make him the Oriental Adam of St. Victor. It is owing partly to a compressed fulness of meaning, very uncommon in the Greek poets of the Church, partly to the unusual harshness and contraction of his phrases, that he is the hardest of ecclesiastical bards to comprehend" (Neale). The following hymns have been translated into English by Neale:

Χριστὸς γεννᾶται, δοξάσατε (Christmas).
"Christ is born! Tell forth his fame!"

Τῷ πρὸ τῶν αἰώνων.
"Him, of the Father's very Essence."

Ῥάβδος ἐκ τῆς ῥίζης.
"Rod of the Root of Jesse."

Θεὸς ὢν εἰρήνης.
"Father of Peace, and God of Consolation!"

Σπλάγχνων Ἰωνᾶν.
"As Jonah, issuing from his three days' tomb."

Οἱ παῖδες εὐσεβείᾳ.
"The Holy Children boldly stand."

Θαύματος ὑπερφυοῦς ἡ δροσοβόλος.
"The dewy freshness that the furnace flings."

Μυστήριον ξένον.
"O wond'rous mystery, full of passing grace!"

Χορὸς Ἰσραήλ (Transfiguration).
"The choirs of ransomed Israel."

A Latin translation is given in *Bibl. Patrol.* ed. Colon. vii, 536 sq. His hymns were first printed by Aldus (Venice, 1501), and they are to be found in La Bigne, *Bibl. Patrol.* xii, 727 sq.; Migne, *Patrol.* xcviii, and Daniel, *Thesaurus Hymnologicus*, iii, 55. According to Allatius (*De Georgiis*, p. 418) they have been expounded by Joannes Zonaras, Theodorus Prodromus, George of Corinth, and others. See Suidas, s. v. Ιωανν. Δαμασκ.; Joann. Hieros. in *Vita Joann. Damasc.* ed. Oudin, i, 1785; Gallandi, xiii, p. viii; Miræus, *Auctar. de Script. Eccl.;* Vossius, *De Poet. Græc.* c. 9; Saxius in *Onom. Lit.* ii, 85; Fabricius, *Bibl. Græc.* vi, 41; Le Quien, *Vit. Joann. Damasc.* p. 20; Jöcher, *Allgemeines Gelehrten-Lexikon*, s. v.; Smith and Wace, *Dict. of Christ. Biog.* s. v.; Neale, *Hymns of the Eastern Church*, p. 127 sq.; Rambach, *Anthologie Christlicher Gesänge*, i, 136 sq.; Jacobi, *Zur Geschichte des Griechischen Kirchenliedes*, in Brieger's *Zeitschrift für Kirchengeschichte* (Gotha, 1881), v, 210 sq. (B. P.)

Cosmas of Prague, the first Bohemian historian, was born in 1045. In 1086 he was made canon of the Prague chapter; in 1099 he received holy orders, and he died Oct. 21, 1125. When already advanced in years he set himself to write a history of Bohemia. He completed the *Chronica Boemorum* between 1119 and 1125. The first book reaches from the earliest times to the year 1038; the second to 1092; the third to 1125. The *Chronica* was published by Freher in *Script. rerum Bohemicarum* (Hanover, 1602, 1607, 1620); Menke, *Script. rerum Germanicarum* (Leipsic, 1728); Pelzl et Dobrowsky, *Script. rerum Bohemicarum* (Prague, 1783); Köpke in *Monum. Germ.;* Migne, *Patrol. Lat.* clxvi; Emler et Tomek, *Fontes rerum Bohemicarum* (ibid. 1874), ii, 1 sq. It was continued by some anonymous writers, under the title *Continuatores Cosmæ.* See Borowy in Wetzer u. Welte's *Kirchen-Lexikon*, s. v. (B. P.)

Cosmas (usually styled "the Elder") was a monk of St. Saba. After a youth devoted to the study of the liberal arts, philosophy, and theology, when already a presbyter, he was captured and enslaved by the Saracens in a journey from Italy to Damascus, but was redeemed by the father of Joannes Damascenus, who intrusted to his care the education of his son, with his companion

Cosmas (the Younger, "Cosmas of Jerusalem"). After he had completed the instruction of his pupils he retired to the monastery of St. Saba, where he remained till his death, cir. A.D. 750 (Joann. Hierosol. in *Vita Joann. Damasc.;* Moschus, *Prat. Spirit.* c. 40). The greater part of the hymns that pass under the name of Cosmas the Melodist are attributed to him, but in the confusion that exists between the elder and younger Cosmas, it is impossible to assign them to their respective authors with any accuracy.

Cosmas, bishop OF SCYTHOPOLIS, and metropolitan, succeeded Olympius in 466. He was a native of Cappadocia, but, with his two brothers, Chrysippus and Gabriel, was brought up in Syria under the famous abbot St. Euthymius, who on their first application for admission to his monastery rejected them on account of their youth, but afterwards, being warned in a dream, admitted them. Cosmas was ordained deacon by Juvenal of Jerusalem about the time of the Council of Ephesus, and afterwards raised by him to the presbyterate. He was ordained bishop of Scythopolis by Anastasius, Juvenal's successor; held the see for thirty years, and died in 496. The third brother, Gabriel, was ordained priest, and was twenty-four years abbot of the monastery of St. Stephen. He founded a small monastery in honor of the Ascension, in a valley of Olivet, and died at the age of eighty years (Cyrill. Scythop. *Vit. S. Euthem.* 40, 54, etc.; Le Quien, *Oriens Christianus*). See CHRYSIPPUS.

Cosmas OF THEBES was a deacon, deposed A.D. 592 by his bishop, Adrian, for malversation of the goods of the Church. Cosmas and another deposed deacon accused Adrian, by way of revenge, to the emperor Maurice. Maurice, according to the canons, sent the case to John, bishop of Larissa, Adrian's metropolitan, who condemned him. Adrian appealed to Maurice, and was acquitted. The case finally came before Gregory the Great (Gregory, *Epp.* iii, 7; in Migne, *Patrol. Lat.* lxxvii, 609, § 629; Ceillier, xi, 490).

Cosmati, a family of Greek artists, who flourished at Rome as early as the 12th century. They particularly excelled in mosaic paintings. Among them, ADEODATO DI COSIMO COSMATI was the most distinguished, and he was employed in the church of Santa Maria Maggiore in 1290. Several of his name also exercised their talents in the cathedral of Orvieto.

Cosmo, *Saint*. See COSMAS.

Cosmocrător (*κοσμοκράτωρ, governor of the world*), in the system of Valentinus, is an appellation given to the devil, who was represented as having his dwelling in this world, while the Demiurgus, whose creature he was, dwelt in the lowest of the regions above the world (Irenæus, i, 5, p. 26). The name Cosmocrator we may believe to have been derived from Ephes. vi, 12, reference also being had to John xii, 31, whose phrase, "prince of this world," occurs instead of Cosmocrator in the parallel passage of Hippolytus (p. 192). Harvey (*ad Iren.*) gives proof that in the rabbinical dæmonology this Greek word was written in Hebrew characters, and thence infers that the Gnostic application of this word was derived from a Jewish use of it. On the other hand, Massuet (p. xliii) refers to an employment of the word by the later Platonists, to denote the rulers of the seven planetary orbs. But its occurrence in the Epistle to the Ephesians renders any other explanation unnecessary.

In the system of Marcion (Irenæus, i, 27, p. 106), into which the name Cosmocrator probably passed from the Valentinian, it was applied to the God who made the world.

Cosmology, ANCIENT. A remarkable paper on this subject has been published by president Warren (in the *Boston University Year-book*, 1882, p. 17 sq.), in which he maintains a new theory of the Homeric cosmology, and he further asserts that "the Egyptians, Accadians, Assyrians, Babylonians, Phœnicians, Hebrews, Greeks, Iranians, Indo-Aryans, Chinese, Japanese—in fine, all the most ancient historic peoples—possessed in their earliest traceable periods a cosmology essentially identical, and one of a far more advanced type than has been attributed to them." We cite the most essential paragraphs of his paper:

"In ancient thought the grand divisions of the world are four, to wit: The abode of the gods, the abode of living men, the abode of the dead, and, finally, the abode of dæmons. To locate these in correct mutual relations, one must begin by representing to himself the earth as a sphere or spheroid, and as situated within, and concentric with, the starry sphere, *each having its axis perpendicular, and its north pole at the top.* The pole-star is thus in the true zenith, and the heavenly heights centring about it are the abode of the supreme god or gods. According to the same conception, the upper or northern hemisphere of the earth is the proper home of living men; the under or southern hemisphere of the earth, the abode of disembodied spirits and rulers of the dead; and, finally, the undermost region of all, that centring around the southern pole of the heavens, the lowest hell. The two hemispheres of the earth were furthermore conceived of as separated from each other by an equatorial ocean or oceanic current.

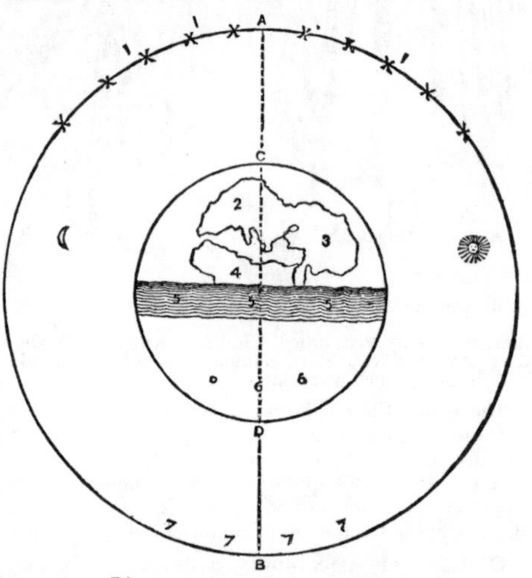

Diagram of Ancient Cosmology.

"To illustrate this conception of the world, let the two circles of the diagram represent respectively the earth-sphere and the outermost of the revolving starry spheres. A is the north pole of the heavens, so placed as to be in the zenith. B is the south pole of the heavens, in the nadir. The line A B is the axis of the apparent revolution of the starry heavens in a perpendicular position. C is the north pole of the earth; D, its south pole; the line C D, the axis of the earth in perpendicular position, and coincident with the corresponding portion of the axis of the starry heavens. The space 1 1 1 1 is the abode of the supreme god or gods; 2, Europe; 3, Asia; 4, Libya, or the known portion of Africa; 5 5 5, the ocean, or 'ocean stream;' 6 6 6, the abode of disembodied spirits and rulers of the dead; 7 7 7 7, the lowest hell.

"The difficulties hitherto experienced in representing in a satisfactory manner the Ygdrasil of Norse mythology, the cosmical 'fig-tree' of the Vedas, the 'winged oak' of Pherecydes, etc., quite disappear when once, with understanding of the supposed true position of the universe in space, the centre line of the trunk of the tree is made coincident with the axis of the starry heavens.

"In any chart or picture of the ancient Iranian cosmology, constructed according to this key, the Iranian Olympus, *Harô berezaiti*, will join the solid earth to heaven, while underneath, the mount of dæmons, dread Arezûra, will penetrate the nether darkness of the lowest hell. In Egyptian and Hindû cosmology the same opposed circumpolar projections of the earth are clearly traceable. To *Harô berezaiti* (Alborz) corresponds Mount Sar of ancient Egyptian mythology, the Kharsak Kurra of the Accadians, the Har Moed of Babylonia (Isa. xiv, 13, 14), the Sumeru of the Hindûs and Buddhists, the Asgard of the Northmen, the Pearl Mountain of the Chinese.

"In like manner, the comparative study of the myths

of the ocean and of the under-worlds of ancient peoples leaves no room for doubt that these, too, were originally adjusted to a geocentric conception of the universe, and to an earth which was figured as a globe. With such a key the most perplexing cosmological problems, such as the origin of the strange concentric *dwîpas* of the Puranas, the origin and significance of the Sabean myth of Ur, the son of Rouhaïa, and many others, receive at once a plain and satisfactory solution.

"Even the *Kojiki*, the most ancient of the sacred books of Japan, should have taught us to credit the early nations of the world with better knowledge of the earth than we have done; for in its beautiful cosmogony the earth revolves, and Izanagi's spear is only its upright axis."

These views Dr. Warren applies, by way of illustration and confirmation, to the famous problem of the *pillars of Atlas*, which classic mythology represents as supporting the universe.

"They are simply the upright axes of earth and heaven. Viewed in their relation to earth and heaven respectively, they are two; but viewed in reference to the universe as an undivided whole, they are one and the same. Being coincident, they are truly one, and yet they are ideally separable. Hence singular or plural designations are equally correct and equally fitting. Transpiercing the globe at the very 'navel or centre of the sea,' Atlas's pillar penetrates far deeper than any recess of the waters' bed, and he may well be said to 'know the depths of the whole sea.' Or this statement may have reference to that primordial sea in which his pillar was standing when the geogonic and cosmogonic process began. In this sense how appropriate and significant would it have been if applied to Izanagi!

"Atlas's pillar, then, is the axis of the world. It is the same pillar apostrophized in the Egyptian document known as the great Harris Magic Papyrus, in these unmistakable words: 'O long column, which commences in the upper and in the lower heavens!' It is, with scarce a doubt, what the same ancient people in their Book of the Dead so happily styled 'the spine of the earth.' It is the Rig-Veda's *vieltragende Achse des unaufhaltsam sich drehenden, nie alternden, nie morschwerdenden, durch den Lauf der Zeiten nicht abgenutzten Weltrads, auf welchem* ALLE WESEN STEHEN. It is the umbrella-staff of Burmese cosmology, the churning-stick of India's gods and dæmons. It is the trunk of every cosmical tree. It is the Tái Kih of the Chinese universe; the tortoise-piercing (earth-piercing) arrow of the Mongolian heaven-god; the spear of Izanagi. It is the cord which the ancient Vedic bard saw stretched from one side of the universe to the other. Is it not the Psalmist's 'line' of the heavens which 'is gone out through' the very 'earth' and on 'to the end of the world'? It is the Irminsul of the Germans, as expressly recognized by Grimm. It is the tower of Kronos. It is the Talmudic pillar which connects the Paradise celestial and the Paradise terrestrial.

"The studies already completed render it certain that every existing systematic exposition of classic mythology is to be supplanted. Equally interesting is the question of the adaptation of this reconstruction of ancient cosmology to throw light on early Hebrew conceptions of the world and of Sheol."

Such a radical reconstruction of ancient cosmology, however, requires further exposition and corroboration in detail before the learned world can be expected to adopt it generally. The Hebrew notions especially, which are developed to a considerable degree in the Bible, should be subjected to a rigid and critical comparison. This task we may hope that the author of the scheme will perform in due time. See PARADISE.

Cosnac, DANIEL DE, a French prelate, was born at the chateau of Cosnac, in Limousin, about 1630. Being destined from his birth for the ecclesiastical calling, he first pursued his studies at Brives and at Périgueux, and went, in 1644, to take the degree of master of arts at the College of Navarre. He received the degree of bachelor of divinity at the University of Paris in 1648, and his licensure two years later. Being admitted, through the kindness of the duke of Bouillon, to the house of the prince of Conti, young as he was, he realized the advantage thus acquired, proving himself a man of uprightness and integrity. He appeared several times in assemblies of the clergy, took part in the grave question of the right of enjoying the revenues of vacant bishoprics, which threatened to make a schism, and was one of the French prelates who aided most in achieving the liberty of the Gallican Church. He had charge of examining the briefs of Innocent XI, and his report is worthy of being read. In 1687 Cosnac was called to the archbishopric of Aix, but, owing to the troubles between France and Rome, he did not take the oath until June 11, 1695. In 1701, the king gave to him the abbey of St. Riquiers of Évreux, and appointed him commander of the order of the Holy Spirit. He died at Aix, Jan. 18, 1708, leaving some *Mémoires* in MS., which were published in 1852 by count Julius de Cosnac. See Hoefer, *Nouv. Biog. Générale*, s. v.; *Biog. Universelle*, s. v.

Cospéan (or **Cospeau**), PHILIPPE DE, a Flemish theologian, was born in Hainault in 1568. He first studied under Justus Lipsius, and then went to Paris. His poverty and his desire for knowledge were so great that, in order to complete his studies, he accepted the position of valet to the abbot of Espernon, afterwards cardinal de la Valette. In 1604 Cospéan received the degree of doctor from the Sorbonne, was appointed bishop of Aire in 1607, and promoted to the bishopric of Nantes, March 17, 1622. He had at his accession a very lively dispute with his chapter, relative to the emoluments during the vacancy. Cospéan declared himself favorable to the Oratorians in their quarrel with the Carmelites. He was charged, in 1627, by cardinal Richelieu, with preparing Francis of Montmorency for death. In 1636 he was transferred to the bishopric of Lisieux. He died at the chateau of Loges, near Lisieux, in 1646, leaving, *Oraison Funèbre, aux Obsèques de Henri le Grand* (Paris, 1610):—*Remontrance du Clergé de France au Roi*:—*Pro Patre Berullio Epistola Apologetica* (Paris, 1622). See Hoefer, *Nouv. Biog. Générale*, s. v.; *Biog. Universelle*, s. v.

Cossa, FRANCESCO, an Italian painter, was a native of Ferrara. He executed some works at Bologna, which are, *Madonnas, with Saints and Angels*. One of them, in the institute, is dated 1474. See Hoefer, *Nouv. Biog. Générale*, s. v.; Spooner, *Biog. Hist. of the Fine Arts*, s. v.

Cossale (or **Cozzale**), ORAZIO, an Italian painter, flourished about 1600. His chief works are, *The Adoration of the Magi*, in the church Della Grazie, at Brescia; and *The Presentation in the Temple*, in Le Miracoli. Cossale was accidentally killed by his son, about 1610. See Hoefer, *Nouv. Biog. Générale*, s. v.; Spooner, *Biog. Hist. of the Fine Arts*, s. v.

Cossart, Gabriel, a French Jesuit, was born at Pontoise in 1615. In 1633 he joined his order, was for some time professor at Paris, and died Sept. 18, 1674. He is the author of *Parthenii Patriarchæ Constantinopolitani Decretum Synodale* (in Greek and Latin, Paris, 1643). He continued and completed the famous collection of councils commenced by abbé Labbé, which he published in 17 vols. folio, with the title, *Conciliorum Collectio Maxima ad Regiam Editionem Exacta, Studio Philippi Labbe et Gabrielis Cossartii e Societate Jesu* (Parisiis, 1671, 1672). See Kobler, in Wetzer u. Welte's *Kirchen-Lexikon*, s. v.; *Biog. Universelle*, s. v.; Hoefer, *Nouv. Biog. Générale*, s. v. (B. P.)

Cossart, Laurent Joseph, a French ecclesiastic, was born Aug. 10, 1753, at Cauchy-la-Tour, near Lillers. After having been master of theology at the grand seminary of St. Nicholas du Chardonnet, he was appointed superior of the seminary of St. Marcellus. From this he passed to the diocese of Boulogne, when he was made rector of Wimille. Cossart fell into official difficulties, and was obliged to retire to the Netherlands, where he found his bishop, who had already preceded him. The invasion of the Netherlands by the French again driving them forth, Cossart went to Düsseldorf. He died in 1830. While at Düsseldorf he published the *Miroir du Clergé*, a new edition of which appeared at Lyons and Paris in 1824. He also wrote, *Cours de Prônes* (1816), in collaboration with other ecclesiasts:—*Science Pratique du Catéchiste* (1838, 1839). See Hoefer, *Nouv. Biog. Générale*, s. v.

Cossiers, (or **Cotsiers**), JAN, a reputable Flemish

historical painter, was born at Antwerp in 1603, and studied under Cornelis de Vos. He executed a number of works for the churches in Flanders, the principal of which are *The Nativity*, at Brussels, in the church of the Jesuits; *The Martyrdom of St. Ursula*, at the Beguinage; *The Presentation*, and a grand picture of *The Crucifixion*, in a church at Mechlin. He was appointed director of the academy at Antwerp in 1639, and died in 1652. See Spooner, *Biog. Hist. of the Fine Arts*, s. v.; Hoefer, *Nouv. Biog. Générale*, s. v.

Cossin, Louis, a French engraver, was born at Troyes about 1633, and died at Paris in 1682. The following are some of his principal plates: *The Virgin Mary; St. John the Evangelist Suspended over a Caldron of Boiling Oil; The Stoning of St. Paul at Lystra.* See Spooner, *Biog. Hist. of the Fine Arts*, s. v.; Hoefer, *Nouv. Biog. Générale*, s. v.

Cossins, George Horwood, an English Congregational minister, was born in the parish of Martock, Somerset, in 1799. He was converted in early life; prepared for the ministry by self-culture and the assistance of his pastor; began preaching at Somerton, and afterwards held the pastorate at Bower Hinton, Martock, for thirty-six years, where he died, Jan. 19, 1878. Mr. Cossins wrote *The Life of Rev. Christopher Hull*, who was the founder of the church at Bower Hinton; and compiled the hymn-book used by his congregation for many years. See (Lond.) *Cong. Year-book*, 1879, p. 308.

Costa, Andrea da, a Portuguese theologian and musician, was born in the early part of the 17th century at Lisbon, and took the habit of the order of the Holy Trinity of that city, Aug. 3, 1650. He devoted himself exclusively to musical composition and the study of the harp, and was harpist to the chapel of Alfonso VI and of Pedro II. He died suddenly, July 6, 1685; but left a large number of works in the musical library of the kings of Portugal, especially *Masses* and *Da Paixao da Dominga de Palmas*, etc. See Hoefer, *Nouv. Biog. Générale*, s. v.

Costa, Cesare, an Italian ecclesiastic of the latter part of the 16th century, was born at Macerata. He taught canon law at Rome, and became successively referendary apostolic and archbishop of Capua. He was sent to Venice as papal nuncio, and died at Naples, Feb. 12, 1602, leaving several works, among which was one of considerable repute, entitled *Variarum Abiguitatum Juris lib. iii* (Venice, 1588; also in Otto's *Thesaur. Juris* [Utrecht, 1733], vol. iv). See Hoefer, *Nouv. Biog. Générale*, s. v.

Costa, Jorge da, a Portuguese prelate, was born in 1406 at Alpedrinha, a village of the diocese of La Guarda; was educated at Lisbon, became a professor there, and a dean of the cathedral; eventually bishop of Evora, archbishop of Lisbon, and cardinal in 1476. He removed to Rome in 1487, and died there, Sept. 19, 1508.

Costa, Lorenzo (*the Elder*), an Italian painter, was born at Ferrara about 1450. He was instructed in the school of Francesco Francia, and then went to Bologna. His first work there was *The Martyrdom of St. Sebastian*, in the church of San Petronio. He also painted an altar-piece, which was considered very fine. He particularly excelled in his countenances of men, as may be seen from those of *The Apostles* at San Petronio, and from his *St. Jerome*. He died about 1530. See Hoefer, *Nouv. Biog. Générale*, s. v.; Spooner, *Biog. Hist. of the Fine Arts*, s. v.

Costa, Manoel da. See Acosta, Emmanuel.

Costadau, Alphonse, a French writer, was born at Alans (Venaissin). At the age of sixteen he became a Dominican monk of the congregation of the Holy Sacrament, and afterwards professor of philosophy and theology. He died at Lyons in 1726, leaving several works on witchcraft, etc., for which see Hoefer, *Nouv. Biog. Générale*, s. v.

Costadoni, Giovanni Domenico (called *Anselm*), an Italian theologian and antiquary, was born at Venice in 1714. He entered the monastery of St. Michael at Murano in 1720, and died at Venice, Jan. 23, 1785. His principal works were upon Christian antiquities and the history of religious orders. Costadoni labored with P. Mittarelli in editing the *Annales Camaldulenses.* See Hoefer, *Nouv. Biog. Générale*, s. v.; *Biog. Universelle*, s. v.

Costaguti, Vincente, an Italian ecclesiastic and musician, was born at Genoa in 1613. He was prothonotary to Urban VIII, secretary of the apostolic court of justice, and in 1643 was made cardinal-deacon under the title of *Santa Maria in Porticu.* He died in 1660, leaving *Discorso alle Musica* (Genoa, 1640):—*Applausi Poetici alte Glorie della Signora Leonora Baroni* (Rome, 1639). See Hoefer, *Nouv. Biog. Générale*, s. v.

Costanzi, Carlo, a very eminent Italian engraver on precious stones, son of Giovanni Costanzi, was born at Naples in 1703. He executed a large number of admirable works, among them a copy of the *Medusa* of Solon. He brought the art to such a high degree of perfection that he gained a knighthood from the king of Portugal. See Spooner, *Biog. Hist. of the Fine Arts*, s. v.; Hoefer, *Nouv. Biog. Générale*, s. v.; *Biog. Universelle*, s. v.

Costard, George, a learned clergyman of the Church of England, was born at Shrewsbury about 1710, and graduated A.M. at Wadham College, Oxford, in 1733. He became a tutor and fellow of his college, and afterwards vicar of Whitchurch, in Dorsetshire. His extensive learning recommended him to the notice of lord-chancellor Northington, who presented him to the vicarage of Twickenham, in Middlesex, in 1764, in which charge he continued until his death, Jan. 10, 1782. Among his publications were, *Observations Tending to Illustrate the Book of Job* (1714), also *Dissertationes Critico-Sacræ* (Oxford, 1752). See Chalmers, *Biog. Dict.* s. v.; Allibone, *Dict. of Brit. and Amer. Authors*, s. v.

Coste, Hilarion de, a French mission friar, was born in Paris, Sept. 6, 1595, of a noble family, originally from Dauphiné, and died in the same city, Aug. 22, 1661, leaving several pious works full of curious particulars, but destitute of critical accuracy, for which see *Biog. Universelle*, s. v.; Chalmers, *Biog. Dict.* s. v.

Coster, François, a Belgian theologian, was born at Mechlin in 1531. In 1551 he was received into the Jesuit ranks by Ignatius Loyola himself. In 1555 he received the degree of doctor of theology at Cologne, and there taught belles-lettres, philosophy, and theology. He was afterwards charged with the mission of propagating Jesuitism in the Low Countries and the Rhenish provinces. He zealously combated the Protestants, and thus obtained the name of *Malleus Hæreticorum.* He died at Brussels, Dec. 6, 1619, leaving *Responsio ad Andream Calliam Calvinistam* (Cologne, 1586):—*Enchiridion Controversiarum* (in Latin and Flemish, ibid. 1600):—*Epistola ad Franciscum Gomarum, contra Anti-Costerum* (ibid.):—*Epistola ad Gasp. Grevinchovium* (ibid.):—*Institutionum Christianarum libri iv* (Antwerp and Cologne, 1604):—*Demonstratio Veteris Orthodoxæ Fidei*, etc. (Cologne, 1607):—*Responsio ad Lucam Osiandrum*, etc. (ibid. 1608), and several other works of controversy or religion, in both Latin and Flemish. See Hoefer, *Nouv. Biog. Générale*, s. v.; Wetzer u. Welte, *Kirchen-Lexikon*, s. v.

Coster, Jean (called *Columba*, from his gentleness), a Belgian commentator, was born at Louvain in 1515. He was prior of the canons-regular of St. Martin in that city, and died there, March 9, 1559, leaving editions and annotations of various Church fathers, for which see Hoefer, *Nouv. Biog. Générale*, s. v.; Jöcher, *Allgemeines Gelehrten-Lexikon*, s. v.

Coster, Johannes, a Flemish theologian, was born at Alost, became master of arts in 1561, and afterwards curate of Oudenarde, where he died, June 10, 1580, leaving a history of the Catholics in heretical cities, under the title, *De Exitu Ægypti et Fuga Babylonis* (Douay, 1580). See Hoefer, *Nouv. Biog. Générale*, s. v.; Jöcher, *Allgemeines Gelehrten-Lexikon*, s. v.

Costerdine, ROBERT, an English Wesleyan minister, was born at Flixton, near Manchester, in October, 1726. He was converted under John Nelson; was a local preacher five years, and in 1764 was appointed to the Epworth Circuit. He was persecuted much, but his sermons had mighty effect. He also labored at Keighley, Sheffield, Manchester, Macclesfield, Wednesbury, etc. He died March 16, 1812. He was a man of patience and self-sacrifice. See *Wesl. Meth. Magazine*, 1814, p. 161.

Costere is a mediæval term for the side-hangings which, suspended on rods, anciently enclosed the altar, or, stretched upon frames, *stood at either end*, to protect the lighted tapers from draughts.

Coston, ZARA HALE, a Methodist Episcopal minister, was born at Litchfield, Herkimer Co., N. Y., Aug. 6, 1793. He experienced conversion at the age of seventeen; was licensed to preach in 1820, and admitted into the Ohio Conference. In 1829 he was transferred to the Pittsburgh Conference, and in it served the Church as health permitted, until 1858, when he became superannuated, and continued to sustain that relation to the close of his life, June 3, 1874. Mr. Coston was amiable, a universal favorite, generous to a fault, and a preacher of ordinary abilities. See *Minutes of Annual Conferences*, 1875, p. 35; Simpson, *Cyclop. of Methodism*, s. v.

Cot (or **Cotus**), *Saint*, an early martyr, was a friend of St. Priscus, and when the latter was beheaded, by order of the emperor Aurelian, Cot seized the head and ran into the forest. Being pursued by the Roman soldiers, he was overtaken and beheaded, in 273. It is said that his body was preserved in the Church of St. Priscus, from which place John Baillet, bishop of Auxerre, exhumed it, Nov. 19, 1480, and exposed it for public veneration. According to the *Bibliothèque Sacrée*, little is known definitely of this man, yet his remains may be seen at Notre Dame, and his festival is celebrated with that of St. Priscus, May 26. See Hoefer, *Nouv. Biog. Générale*, s. v.

Cotbat is the discourse with which the imaums among the Saracens were wont to commence the public prayers on Friday. It consisted of expressions of praise to God and to Mohammed, and was first introduced by the Prophet. In ancient times the caliph, dressed in white, used to pronounce the cotbat in person, a ceremony which was considered a mark of sovereignty. It generally concluded with a prayer for the caliph.

Cote, C. H. O., M.D., a Canadian Baptist minister, was born in Montreal in 1808. He received a collegiate education, studied medicine, and entered on the practice of his profession at L'Acadie in 1831, but in 1833 removed to Napierville. He was a member of the legislative assembly of Lower Canada in 1836, but eventually being one of the leaders in the insurrection of 1837 and 1838, went into exile, and for several years resided in the United States. He had been brought up in the Romish Church, but was converted in June, 1841. He then began to preach, spending two years at Chazy, where a number of French Canadians had settled. As the result of his labors, about fifty converts were made from Romanism. He removed, in the fall of 1843, to St. Pie, and, amid much opposition, went forward in his work, in which he met with the most encouraging success. A Church was formed in that place, of which he was ordained the pastor Aug. 28, 1844. When he left there in 1848, upwards of two hundred persons had been converted. Dr. Cote spent some time in the United States, raising funds for the Grand Ligne Mission, and then returned to the field of his labors, taking charge of the mission station at St. Mary's. Here a Church was about to be formed, made up of converts from Romanism, of which he was to be the pastor, but while attending the annual meeting of the Lamoille Baptist Association at Hinesburg, Sept. 18, 1850, he was seized with illness, and died Oct. 4 following. The only publications of special interest which were the product of his pen were a translation into French of Pengilly's *Scripture Guide on Baptism*, issued by the American Baptist Publication Society, and some other small works for the instruction and benefit of his fellow-countrymen. See *English Baptist Magazine*, 1851, p. 1. (J. C. S.)

Cotelle (*de la Blandinière*), PIERRE JACQUES, a French theologian, was born at Laval about 1709. He was at first rector of Soulaines, in Anjou, next vicar-general of Blois, and superior of the priests of Mt. Valerien. He added ten volumes to the *Conférences Ecclésiastiques du Diocèse d'Angers* of Bobin, in return for which the assembly of the clergy voted him an annual pension of one hundred pistoles. Moultrot has reproduced it in his *Défense du Second Ordre*. Cotelle died in 1795. See Hoefer, *Nouv. Biog. Générale*, s. v.

Cotereau (or **Cottereau**), CLAUDE, a French ecclesiastic, was born at Tours in the 16th century. He entered holy orders, and became canon of Notre Dame at Paris, where he died about 1560. He was learned in philology and canon law, and left several minor treatises, for which see *Biog. Universelle*, s. v.

Coterée, JEAN, a French preacher, was born at Rheims, and lived in 1593. He received the degree of doctor of divinity from the Sorbonne, taught at Douay, and became canon of Tournay. He wrote seven volumes of French sermons, which were published from 1573 to 1593. See Hoefer, *Nouv. Biog. Générale*, s. v.

Cotes, ROGER, a celebrated English divine, mathematician, philosopher, and astronomer, was born July 10, 1682, at Burbage, in Leicestershire, and educated at Leicester School, St. Paul's School, London, and Trinity College, Cambridge, where he took his degrees, and was chosen a fellow in 1705. In January, 1706, he was appointed professor of astronomy and experimental philosophy, took orders in 1713, and the same year published at Cambridge the second edition of sir Isaac Newton's *Mathematica Principia*. He left at his death some admirable tracts. He died June 5, 1716. See Chalmers, *Biog. Dict.* s. v.; Allibone, *Dict. of Brit. and Amer. Authors*, s. v.

Cothman, JOHANN, a German Protestant theologian, was born at Herford, Westphalia, in 1595, studied at Giessen and Rostock, was doctor and professor of theology at Wittenberg, and died at Rostock in 1650, leaving *Dissertatio de Præsentia Corporis et Sanguinis Christi in Sacrosancta Eucharistia:—Destructio Fundamenti Papatus, contra Schillerum:—De Conjugio Comprivignorum*. See Hoefer, *Nouv. Biog. Générale*, s. v.; Jöcher, *Allgemeines Gelehrten-Lexikon*, s. v.

Cothurno, BARTOLOMMEO DEL, an Italian prelate and theologian, was born in the suburbs of Genoa, of a noble and wealthy family, which he abandoned in order to become a Franciscan. His merit raised him to the archbishopric of Genoa. Pope Urban VI appointed him, Sept. 16, 1378, cardinal-priest, with the title of *Santo Lorenzo in Damaso*. Some years after, Urban, then at war with the king of Naples, Charles Durazzo, feared a conspiracy among the cardinals who surrounded him, and at the denunciation of Prignani, his nephew, Jan. 11, 1385, caused Cothurno to be arrested at Lucera, together with five other princes of the Church, and after cruelly torturing him, threw him into the sea, where he was drowned, in December, 1385. Cothurno wrote, *Postilla Sermonum Sacrorum:—Com-*

mentaria Sopra Canticum Canticarum: — and some other religious works. See Hoefer, *Nouv. Biog. Générale*, s. v.; Jöcher, *Allgemeines Gelehrten-Lexikon*, s. v.

Cotignola, Francesco da (called *Marchesi* or *Zanganelli*), an Italian painter, who resided chiefly at Parma, flourished about 1518, and studied under Rondinello. He painted a number of historical works for the churches, the best of which are *The Raising of Lazarus*, at Parma, and *The Baptism of Christ*, at Faenza. See Hoefer, *Nouv. Biog. Générale*, s. v.; Spooner, *Biog. Hist. of the Fine Arts*, s. v.

Cotignon, Michel, a French theologian, who lived in the latter half of the 17th century, was chief priest of Nevers, and wrote *Catalogue Historial des Évêques de Nevers* (Paris, 1616). See Hoefer, *Nouv. Biog. Générale*, s. v.

Cotin, Charles, a French preacher and writer, also counsellor and almoner of the king, was born in Paris in 1604. Being appointed in 1650 to the canonship of Bayeux, he took possession, but resigned it the following year. On May 3, 1655, he was made a member of the French Academy, and, although ridiculed by Boileau and Molière, was admitted to the best literary society of the day. He died in January, 1682. Some of his works are, *Méditations sur les Leçons de Ténèbres*, etc. (Paris, 1634):—*La Vraie Philosophie des Principes du Monde* (ibid. 1646):—*Traité de l'Âme Immortelle* (1655):—*Poésies Chrétiennes* (1657):—*La Pastorale Sacrée* (first in prose, then in verse; one of his most important works):—*Œuvres Mêlées* (1659). See Hoefer, *Nouv. Biog. Générale*, s. v.; Chalmers, *Biog. Dict.* s. v.

Cotolendi, Ignace, a French missionary and theologian, was born at Brignoles, March 24, 1630. He completed his studies at the college of the Jesuits at Aix, received the degree of doctor at Rome, returned to Aix, where he took the ecclesiastical habit, and was appointed rector of Sainte-Marguerite. He left this post in order to devote himself to missions, and on his return to Rome was appointed by pope Alexander VII preacher in the suburbs of Paris and, among other places, at Dreux. He became titular bishop of Metellopolis, and *ad interim* filled the episcopal see of Chartres. He then received letters giving him the authority of apostolic-vicar for the mission of Nankin, Northern China, Corea, and Tartary. He returned to Marseilles with three priests who were to be his companions; visited Malta, Alexandretta, Aleppo, and arrived at Mazulipatam; travelled through various parts of India, and introduced himself as a physician. This gained for him confidence, which aided him in his work as missionary, and he made numerous proselytes. But fatigue and change of climate were too much for his health, and he died at Palacol (East Indies), Aug. 10, 1662. His body was carried to Goa, where a monument was erected to his memory. He wrote, *Vie de Saint-Gaëtan:*—also additions to the *Chroniques* of Gautier, and several religious works. See Hoefer, *Nouv. Biog. Générale*, s. v.

Cotron, Victor, a French Benedictine of the congregation of St. Maur, was born at Rheims in 1614. His diligence as a student reflected honor upon his order, and he wrote the history of several abbeys, especially those of St. Germain of Auxerre, and St. Benedict-on-the-Loire, which remain in MS. He died March 10, 1674, at the abbey of St. Riquier, of which he was prior. See Hoefer, *Nouv. Biog. Générale*, s. v.

Cotta was an Italian tunicle of linen reaching to the knees. Ducange says it was a closed circular surplice.

Cotta, an abbot, attested a charter of Suaebraed, king of the East-Saxons, June 13, A.D. 704.

Cotta, Johann Friedrich, a German theologian, was born at Tübingen, May 12, 1701. He studied in his native city; went to Jena, where he was added to the faculty of philosophy in 1728; travelled through Germany, Holland, England, and France; on his return to Germany in 1734 was appointed titular professor of philosophy at Tübingen; in 1735 taught theology at Göttingen as fellow, and was titular professor of the Oriental languages; in 1739 returned to Tübingen, in order to teach theology, poetry, and philosophy; afterwards occupied other high positions as instructor; and died Dec. 31, 1779. His principal works are, *Themata Miscellanea* (Tübingen, 1718):—*Allerneueste Historie der theologischen Gelehrsamkeit* (ibid. 1722):—*De Origine Masoræ* (ibid. 1726):—*De Probabilismo Morali* (Jena, 1728):—*Traité de la Probabilité* (Rheims or Amsterdam, 1732):—*De Fallibili Pontificis Romani Auctoritate* (Leyden, eod.):—*Flavii Josephi sämmtliche Werke* (Tübingen, 1735):—*De Situ Inaugurationis apud Hebræos* (ibid. 1737):—*Ecclesiæ Romanæ de Attritione et Contritione Contentio* (ibid. 1739):—*De Constitutionibus Apostolicis* (ibid. 1746):—*De Cultu Adorationis* (ibid. 1755):—*De Jure Docendi in Conventibus Sacris* (ibid. 1756):—*De Constitutione Theologiæ* (ibid. 1759):—*De Variis Theologiæ Speciebus* (ibid. eod.):—*De Religione in Genere ac Speciatim Naturali* (ibid. 1761):—*De Religione Gentili* (ibid. eod.):—*De Religione Revelata* (ibid. eod.):—*De Religione Mahommedica* (ibid. eod.):—*De Vita Æterna* (ibid. 1770). See Hoefer, *Nouv. Biog. Générale*, s. v.; Döring, *Die gelehrten Theologen Deutschlands*, s. v.

Cotte, Robert de, an eminent French architect, was born in Paris in 1657. He was appointed director of the Royal Academy of Architecture, and was vice-president of the Academy of Painting and Sculpture. He was greatly esteemed by Louis XIV, who made him a knight of the order of St. Michael. He died in 1735. See Hoefer, *Nouv. Biog. Générale*, s. v.; Spooner, *Biog. Hist. of the Fine Arts*, s. v.

Cotten, James L., D.D., a minister of the Methodist Episcopal Church South, was born in Edgecombe County, N. C., June 1, 1817. He was remarkable in early life for his purity of character, tender sensibilities, and ardent feelings; developed rapidly in mental culture, and became a complete English scholar; experienced religion in his young manhood, and in 1845 entered the Alabama Conference; passed up through all the grades of circuit rider, station preacher, and presiding elder, until his death, in 1872 or 1873. Dr. Cotten possessed a powerful and well-cultured intellect, an imperial imagination, an unquenchable zeal, and an amiable disposition. See *Minutes of Annual Conferences of the M. E. Church South*, 1873, p. 827.

Cotter, Robert N., a minister of the Methodist Episcopal Church South, was born in Hall County, Ga., April 11, 1826. He joined the Church in his seventeenth year, received a very limited education, was several years class-leader and exhorter, and finally, in 1854, entered the Georgia Conference. He continued his ministerial labors until his death, May 6, 1863. Mr. Cotter was a simple, earnest preacher. See *Minutes of Annual Conferences of the M. E. Church South*, 1863, p. 454.

Cottereau, Claude. See Cotereau.

Cottereau (*de Coudray*), **Jean Baptiste Armand**, a French theologian, was born at Tours, Jan. 25, 1697. He was curate of Donne-Marie-en-Montois, president of the ecclesiastical conferences, and a member of the academy of Villefranche. He died in 1770, leaving a few fugitive pieces, for which see Hoefer, *Nouv. Biog. Générale*, s. v.

Cotterel, Alexis François, a French ecclesiastic, doctor of the Sorbonne, curate of Saint-Laurent of Paris, and royal censor, died at Paris, Feb. 5, 1775, leaving some discourses and dissertations, for which see Hoefer, *Nouv. Biog. Générale*, s. v.

Cottĭdes (or **Quottidius**), a deacon and martyr in Cappadocia, is commemorated Sept. 6.

Cotting, John Ruggles, M.D., LL.D., an American Congregational minister and physicist, was born in Acton, Mass., in 1784. He was educated at Harvard and the medical school of Dartmouth College; was ordained about 1810; became very noted for his manufacture of chemical compounds used in the war of 1812 by a company in Boston; was made professor of natural sciences in Amherst College at the close of the war, preaching meantime in the vicinity; subsequently became professor of chemistry in the Berkshire Medical Institute; in 1835 removed to Augusta, Ga.; entered upon a geological and agricultural survey, at first of Burke and Richland counties, then of the entire state; and finally retired to Milledgeville, where he spent his latter years, and died, Oct. 13, 1867. Dr. Cotting prepared text-books of ability and popularity on both chemistry and geology. See *Appleton's Annual Cyclop.* 1867, p. 580.

Cottingham, Lewis Nicholas, a reputable English architect, was born in 1787, in Suffolk. He went to London, and was employed by a skilful architect and surveyor. He commenced his professional career in 1814. In 1822 he received his first public appointment as architect and surveyor to the Cook's Company; in 1825 was appointed architect of the cathedral at Rochester; in 1829 was the successful competitor for the restoration of the interior of the chapel of Magdalen College, Oxford; and in 1833 was intrusted with the restoration of St. Alban's abbey church. He was afterwards employed in the restoration of a number of churches and cathedrals in England and Ireland. He died about 1847.

Cotton, Bartholomew of, a monk of Norwich, England, wrote: *Annales Ecclesiæ Norwicensis,* 1042–1295, *et Historia de Episcopis Norw., ad an.* 1299:—*Accedeunt Continuatio Historiæ ad an.* 1446, *et Successio Episcoporum et Priorum.* See Wharton, *Anglia Sacra;* Allibone, *Dictionary of Brit. and Amer. Authors,* s. v.

Cotton, Henry, an English prelate of the first part of the 17th century, was born at Warblington, Hampshire, being a son of sir Richard Cotton, privy-councillor to Edward VI. He was educated at Magdalen College, Oxford, and was preferred by Queen Elizabeth (his godmother) bishop of Salisbury, Nov. 12, 1598, at the same time that William Cotton, of another family, was made bishop of Exeter, the queen merrily saying that "she hoped that now she had well cottoned the west." He died May 7, 1615. See Fuller, *Worthies of England* (ed. Nuttall), ii, 11.

Cotton, John (1), a Congregational minister, was born in Boston, March 13, 1640. He was pastor at Plymouth, Mass., from June 30, 1669, to Oct. 5, 1697; at Martha's Vineyard from 1664 to 1667; and at Charleston, S. C., from 1698 until his death, Sept. 18, 1699. He rendered great assistance to Thomas Mayhew, at Martha's Vineyard; frequently preached to the Indians at Plymouth, and revised and corrected Eliot's *Indian Bible,* printed at Cambridge in 1685. See Drake, *Amer. Biog.* s. v.; Allibone, *Dict. of Brit. and Amer. Authors,* s. v.

Cotton, John (2), a Congregational minister, was born about 1693. He was pastor at Newton, Mass., and died in 1757. He published several *Sermons.* See Allibone, *Dict. of Brit. and Amer. Authors,* s. v.

Cotton, John (3), a Congregational minister, was born about 1712, and was first pastor at Halifax, Mass. He died in 1789. He published two *Sermons* (1757). See Allibone, *Dict. of Brit. and Amer. Authors,* s. v.

Cotton, John Wallace, an English Wesleyan minister, was born in London, May 30, 1801. He was converted in early youth, joined the Wesleyans, became a local preacher, and an active worker in the City-road Circuit. At the request of Richard Watson, he offered himself to the Church for its ministry in 1827. He labored faithfully in his appointments, and was a painstaking and earnest preacher. In 1863 he retired to Lewisham, where he died, May 9, 1881. See *Minutes of the Brit. Conferences,* 1881, p. 43.

Cotton, Joseph, an English Baptist minister, was born at Derby, Feb. 24, 1810, and attended the preaching of the Rev. J. G. Pike, under whom he was converted and baptized. He studied for the ministry under the Rev. Thomas Stevenson, at Loughborough. He was successively pastor at Isleham, Barton, Holbeach, and Woodhouse Eaves, and in each place his earnest efforts to do good were greatly blessed. He died Nov. 19, 1868.

Cotton, Josiah, a Congregational minister, was a son of Rev. Roland Cotton, of Sandwich, Mass., and great-grandson of Rev. John Cotton, of Boston. He graduated from Harvard College in 1722; was ordained at Providence, R. I., Oct. 23, 1728; installed at Woburn, July 15, 1747; at Sardown, Nov. 28, 1759, and died May 27, 1780, aged seventy-eight years. See Sprague, *Annals of the Amer. Pulpit,* i, 301.

Cotton (or **Coton**), **Pierre,** a French theologian, was born at Neronde, in Forez, in 1564. He studied in Paris and Bourges, went to Turin, and there joined the Jesuit order, against the wishes of his father. After staying some time at Milan, Rome, and other cities of Italy, he went to France, where he preached with success, was received at the court, and gained the confidence of Henry IV, whom he accompanied in his travels as confessor. Cotton refused the archbishopric of Arles and the cardinalate. At the time of the murder of Henry by Ravaillac, May 14, 1610, Cotton attempted to defend his order from the accusations made against them, by a work entitled *Lettre Déclaratoire de la Doctrine des Pères Jésuites* (Paris, 1610). When Albert of Luynes became strongly influential with Louis, Cotton retired from the court, and went to visit the house of the novices of his order at Lyons, where he remained for some time, and finally devoted himself to missionary work in the south of France and in Italy. At length he went to Paris, where he preached before the king. He died in that city, March 19, 1626. Besides the above, Cotton wrote: *Institution Catholique,* in opposition to Calvin's *Institutions:—Genève Plagiaire,* against the Geneva Bible translation (Paris, 1618), which called forth a rejoinder by B. Turretin:—*Défense de la Fidelité des Traductions de la Bible Faites à Genève* (Geneva, 1619):—*Sermon aux les Principales et Plus Difficiles Matières de la Foi* (Paris). See Hoefer, *Nouv. Biog. Générale,* s. v.

Cotton, Stephen, an English martyr, was one of six who were burned at Brentford, seven miles from London, July 14, 1558, for faithful adherence to Christ and his cause. See Fox, *Acts and Monuments,* viii, 479.

Cotton, Thomas, an English Presbyterian, born at Workby, near Rotherham, in 1653, was educated by four eminent tutors, and took his degree at Edinburgh University in 1677. Owing to the persecutions prevailing, Sunday service was long held in his father's house. He then travelled for three years with a gentleman on the Continent. On his return to London he was for a time a tutor, and chaplain to Lady Russell. He had a church in St. Giles parish for some years, but it suffered severely in the Sacheverel riots, in 1709, and he had to flee for safety. He was one of the non-subscribing members at the Salters' Hall synod, 1719. He died at Hampstead, in 1730, much loved and esteemed. He published one *Sermon* (1702). See Wilson, *Dissenting Churches,* iv, 376.

Cotton, Ward, a Congregational minister, was born at Plymouth, Mass. He graduated from Harvard College in 1793; was ordained pastor of the church in Boylston, June 7, 1797; dismissed June 22, 1825, and died in 1843. See Sprague, *Annals of the Amer. Pulpit,* i, 574.

Cotton, William, D.D., an English prelate of the

first part of the 17th century, was born in London, educated at Queen's College, Cambridge, preferred by Elizabeth to be archdeacon of Lewes and canon residentiary of St. Paul's, and consecrated bishop of Exeter Nov. 12, 1598. He is credited by Fuller with having plucked up the seeds of nonconformity sowed in his diocese by Snape, of Jersey. He died of apoplexy, in 1621. He was father of Edward Cotton, D.D. See Fuller, *Worthies of England* (ed. Nuttall), ii, 358.

Cottret, Pierre Marie, a French prelate, was born at Argenteuil, near Paris, May 8, 1768. Having completed his classical studies at Sainte-Barbe, he entered the seminary of St. Louis of Paris, at the close of 1785. In April, 1791, he was called to the priesthood, privately ordained by the bishop of Oléron, and allowed to depart in disguise. He went to Ghent, where he remained as chaplain of the cathedral until June, 1794. Then, after taking refuge for some time in several cities of Germany, he resided at Fritzlau, and thence went to Arolsen as private tutor. After a prolonged sojourn at Frankfort-on-the-Main, he returned to France in October, 1800. In 1802 he was appointed to the chapel of Sannois, in the valley of Montmorency; in 1806 rector of Boissy-Sainte-Léger, and the year following returned to Paris. He now became connected with the *Gazette de France* and the *Journal de l'Empire*. He was appointed adjunct professor of the faculty of theology in 1809, honorary canon of Notre-Dame of Paris, and vice-promoter-general of the diocese, in 1811; was invested with a canonship in 1812; later was placed at the head of the small seminary of Paris. In 1823 he accompanied cardinal Clermont-Tonnerre to Rome. Leo XII appointed him titular bishop of Carystus, and canon of the first order of the chapter of St. Denis. He retired to the diocese of Versailles, and was thence appointed to the see of Beauvais, Dec. 27, 1837. He died at Beauvais, Nov. 13, 1841. Besides his work for the *Gazette de France* and the *Biographie Universelle* of the Michaud brothers, Cottret wrote, from 1822 to 1827, a number of articles upon literary and religious matters in the *Tablettes du Clergé*, and the *Union Ecclésiastique* published several letters of this prelate. He also wrote: *Considérations sur l'État actuel de la Religion Catholique en France et sur les Moyens de la Rétablir* (Paris, 1815) :—*Discours sur la Religion Considérée comme une Nécessité de la Société* (1823):—also an edition of the *Déclaration du Clergé de France de* 1682 (Paris, 1811). See Hoefer, *Nouv. Biog. Générale*, s. v.

Coturius, Julius Cæsar, a German theologian of the Jesuit order, who lived near the latter half of the 17th century, wrote, *Epitome Controversiarum* (Munich, 1643):—*An Quivis in sua Fide Salvari Possit* (Meissen, 1645). See Hoefer, *Nouv. Biog. Générale*, s. v.

Cotys (or **Cotytto**), in Greek mythology, was a Thracian goddess, whose worship, like that of Cybele, was held with noise and tumult, and led finally to licentiousness. In later times she was also honored in Corinth, Athens, and Sicily.

Couard, Christian Ludwig, a Lutheran theologian of Germany, was born at Berlin, April 11, 1793, became doctor of theology and pastor of St. Georges, in the same city, and died there, Dec. 23, 1865. He published, *Predigten über gewöhnliche Perikopen und Freie Texte* (Berlin, 1824; 3d ed. 1851):—*Der verlorene Sohn*, (ibid. 1831):—*Predigten über die Bekehrung des Apostels Paulus* (ibid. 1833):—*Simon Petrus, der Apostel des Herrn* (ibid. 1836, 2 vols.):—*Sammlung von Casualreden aus früherer und neuester Zeit* (Potsdam, 1856, 1858, 2 vols.):—*Evangelische Zeugnisse in Predigten* (ibid. 1855-60, 3 vols.). See Winer, *Handbuch der theol. Lit.* ii, 27, 101, 120, 121, 146; Zuchold, *Bibl. Theol.* i, 247. (B. P.)

Couch, Ezekiel, a minister of the Methodist Episcopal Church South, was born in Pendleton District, S. C., Nov. 1, 1805. He was converted in 1824; licensed to preach in 1836; joined the Memphis Conference in 1840; was ordained deacon in 1841, and elder in 1843. In 1847 he was transferred to the Indian Mission Conference; from 1855 to 1857 was superintendent of the Colbert Institute in the Chickasaw Nation; in 1857 was transferred to the East Texas Conference; in 1864 was a supernumerary, but was made effective the following year; from 1866 to 1871 was superannuated; again made effective in 1872, but at the end of the year was obliged again to take a superannuated relation, in which he continued until his death in 1880. He was a consecrated, zealous, and faithful minister, kind and cordial. See *Minutes of Annual Conferences of the M. E. Church South*, 1880, p. 203.

Couché, Marc, a French theologian, was born at Besançon. He entered the Benedictine order of St. Vanne at Luxeuil, June 10, 1683, then taught theology, and became prior of Mont-Roland. He died about 1751, leaving, *Préceptes d'une Religieuse*:—*Commentaria Theologica in Summam Divi Thomæ*:—*Defensio Decretorum Pontificiorum circa Regulas Morum*:—*Philosophiæ cum Theologia Christiana Connexio*:—*Ad Prolegomena Sanctæ Scripturæ Brevis Manuductio*:—*Apologie des Principaux Points de la Doctrine de Saint-Thomas*:—*Le Vrai Centon Théologique Opposé au Faux*:—*L'Art de Vivre Heureux dans une Communauté Religieuse*, and some treatises upon questions of the time, remaining in MS. See Hoefer, *Nouv. Biog. Générale*, s. v.

Coucher is a name for (1) a register or account book; (2) a church book couched, or lying, on the chancel desk. See Collectarium.

Coucy, Jean Charles, *comte de*, a French theologian and prelate, was born at the castle of Escordal (Rethelois), Sept. 23, 1745. He was successively vicar-general of Rheims, canon of that city (1773), almoner of the queen (1776), abbot of Iny (1777), and bishop of La Rochelle (Jan. 3, 1790). Under the Revolution he retired to Spain, but on the return of the Bourbons he was made archbishop of Rheims (1817), where he died, March 10, 1824. He wrote a *Protestation Addressée a Pie VII* (1802). See Hoefer, *Nouv. Biog. Générale*, s. v.

Coucy, Robert de, a French architect, who died at Rheims about 1300, had chief charge of the rebuilding of the cathedral of that city, which had been destroyed by fire in 1210. In 1297 he completed the ornamentation of the Church of St. Nicaise. See Spooner, *Biog. Hist. of the Fine Arts*, s. v; Hoefer, *Nouv. Biog. Générale*, s. v.

Coudon, Joseph, A.M., a minister of the Protestant Episcopal Church, was a native of Annapolis, Md. He became lay reader in North Elk Parish in 1782, having previously been principal of the Free School in Kent County, which, in 1783, became Washington College. As a lay member of the convention of the diocese he was prominent in organizing the Protestant Episcopal Church, after the Revolution. In 1787 he was ordained deacon, at the age of forty-five, became rector of North Elk Parish, and died there in April, 1792. See Sprague, *Annals of the Amer. Pulpit*, v, 312.

Coudrette, Christophe, a learned French publicist, was born at Paris in 1701, became a priest in 1725, and joined the Jesuits. He was, however, an opponent of the bull *Unigenitus*, and being persecuted by the clerical party, was imprisoned in 1735 at Vincennes, and again in 1738, in the Bastile. Being noted for his opposition to the Jesuits, he was appointed in 1762 to examine their institutions and affairs. He died at Paris, Aug. 4, 1774, leaving, among other works, *Dissertation sur les Bulles Contre Baïus* (Utrecht, 1737, 2 vols.):—*Histoire Générale de la Compagnie de Jésus* (Amsterdam, 1761-67, 6 vols.). See Jöcher, *Allgemeines Gelehrten-Lexikon*, s. v.; *Nouv. Diction. Historique*; Winer, *Handbuch der theol. Lit.* i, 649, 722; *Biog. Universelle*, s. v.; Hoefer, *Nouv. Biog. Générale*, s. v. (B. P.)

Couet (Lat. *Covetus*), JACQUES, a French Reformed theologian, was born at Paris in 1546. Being an adherent of the Reformed Church, he had to leave his country, and on his way to Basle in 1577 held a controversy with Faustus Socinus, against whom he wrote his *De Satisfactione Christi*. In 1588 he was appointed pastor of the French Church at Basle, where he died, Jan. 18, 1608. Besides the work already mentioned, he wrote, *Réponse à Ceux qui Croient Présence du Corps de Christ dans la Cêne* (1588):—*Réponses Chrétiennes à Lescalle* (1593):—*Apologia de Justificatione* (1594):—*Traité de la Prédestination* (1599):—*Conférence Faite à Nancy* (1600):—*Traité du Christianisme* (1602). See Haag, *France Protestante; Bulletin du Protestantisme Français*, xii, 265 sq.; xvi, 353 sq.; *Chrétien Evangélique*, 1868, p. 135–140; Jöcher, *Allgemeines Gelehrten-Lexikon*, s. v.; Lichtenberger, *Encyclop. des Sciences Religieuses*, s. v. (B. P.)

Coughen, JOHN, an English theologian, became a Quaker on hearing an eloquent young woman of that denomination, and afterwards defended their doctrines. He died of the plague in London in 1665. See Hoefer, *Nouv. Biog. Générale*, s. v.

Coughlan, LAWRENCE, an early Methodist preacher, was a native of Ireland, one of the first-fruits of Methodism in that country. He was received on trial by Wesley in 1755, and labored successfully for ten years, when in consequence of having been ordained in 1764 by Erasmus, a Greek bishop, he withdrew from the itinerancy, Charles Wesley taking deep umbrage at such a proceeding. In 1765 he sailed as a missionary to Newfoundland, a year before Philip Embury arrived in New York, and labored there with zeal and success under the auspices of the Society for the Propagation of the Gospel in Foreign Parts, having received reordination from the bishop of London, but still as a Methodist. He formed classes, the first before the close of 1765, and the earliest Methodist society on the west of the Atlantic. On his return, in 1773, to London, Coughlan was minister of the Cumberland Street Chapel, but applied to Wesley for a circuit. While in conversation with the latter in his study, he was seized with paralysis, and died a few days after. Wesley refers to his death in a letter written to John Stretton, of Harbor-Grace, Newfoundland, dated Feb. 25, 1785 (*Meth. Mag.* 1824, p. 307). Coughlan published, in 1776, a book entitled, *Brief Account of the Work of God in Newfoundland*. See Atmore, *Meth. Memorial*, s. v.; Stevens, *Hist. of Methodism*, ii, 329; Myles, *Chron. Hist. of the Methodists*, 1785, p. 169; *Arminian* (*Wesl. Meth.*) *Mag.* 1785, p. 490; Wilson, *Newfoundland and its Missionaries*, p. 123, 134, 141; Smith, *Hist. of Meth. in Eastern British America* (Halifax, 1877, 12mo), p. 41–58; Wesley, *Journal*, Aug. 1768, iii, 324; also *Reports of Society for the Propagation of the Gospel in Foreign Parts*, 1767 sq.

Couillon (Lat. *Covillonus*), JEAN, a Jesuit of Lille, and professor of philosophy and theology at Coimbra, Rome, and Ingolstadt, who died at Rome Aug. 17, 1581, is the author of *Assertiones in Epistolam Primam Pauli ad Corinthios:—Conclusiones ex hac Epistola Deductæ:—Quæstiones in Psalmos*. See Alegambe, *Bibliotheca Scriptorum Societatis Jesu;* Jöcher, *Allgemeines Gelehrten-Lexikon*, s. v. (B. P.)

Coulan, ANTOINE, a French theologian, was born at Alais, Languedoc, Oct. 10, 1667. He was minister of a French Church in London, where he died, Sept. 23, 1694, leaving, *Examen de l'Histoire Critique du Nouveau Testament* (in two parts, Amsterdam, 1696):—*La Défense des Réfugiés* (Deventer, 1691). See Hoefer, *Nouv. Biog. Générale*, s. v.

Coull, ALEXANDER, a Scotch clergyman, was licensed to preach in 1749; presented to the living at Edenkeillie in 1753, ordained in 1754, and died July 10, 1790. See *Fasti Eccles. Scoticanæ*, iii, 184.

Coulling, JAMES D., a minister of the Methodist Episcopal Church South, was born at Richmond, Va., May 20, 1812. He was converted in his eighteenth year; soon became an earnest Christian worker as Sabbath-school teacher and class-leader; began preaching in 1835; and in the following year entered the Virginia Conference, wherein he labored with zeal and faithfulness until his death, Nov. 28, 1866. Honest conscientiousness and earnest fidelity were the prominent features of his character. See *Minutes of Annual Conferences of the M. E. Church South*, 1866, p. 8.

Coulon, CLAUDE ANTOINE, a French preacher and theologian, was born at Salins in 1745. He became a priest, went to Paris, and was chosen grand-vicar by the bishop of Sistéron. He retired during the Revolution, but returned with the Bourbons, and died at Paris, March 10, 1820, leaving *Exhortation à la Persévérance dans la Foi* (Paris, 1792):—*Paraphrase du Psaume*, "*Exaudiat te Dominus*" (Lond. 1799), and some minor *Letters* and *Addresses*. See Hoefer, *Nouv. Biog. Générale*, s. v.

Coulson, David, an English minister of the Society of Friends, was born at Nottingham, April 9, 1713. He was converted in his twenty-sixth year. Some time before this he had become blind; but, nevertheless, about his thirty-third year he visited and preached in all the counties of England except Kent and Sussex. He never met with any fall or accident to lay him up one day in all his travels. He died Dec. 9, 1765. See *Piety Promoted*, ii, 414. (J. C. S.)

Coulson, George J. A., a preacher and novelist, was born in the South in 1819, but came North at the commencement of the late civil war. For a long time he occupied a position at the head of one of the departments in A. T. Stewart's store. Latterly he had been an expert accountant and commercial referee. For many years he was a contributor to religious papers, being an influential member of the Presbyterian Church South, and a diligent theological student. For several months previous to his death he preached in the New East Side Chapel, Paterson, N. J. He died there suddenly, Oct. 27, 1882. Mr. Coulson was the author of *The Lacy Diamond:—The Odd Trump:—Harwood:—Flesh and Spirit:—The Ghost of Redbrook*, and other novels. (W. P. S.)

Coulston, THOMAS, a Scotch clergyman, a native of Dunfermline, was licensed to preach in 1795; presented to the living at Pennycuik in 1798; ordained in 1799; and died March 13, 1829, aged sixty-five years. See *Fasti Eccles. Scoticanæ*, i, 306.

Coultas, Joseph, an English Methodist preacher, grandson of the following, was born at York, June 14, 1821. He was brought up a Wesleyan; toiled successfully in the Sunday-school for some years; became a local preacher at twenty; joined the New Connection in 1850; entered the ministry in 1858; and travelled for twenty-one years in thirteen circuits. In 1875 he was attacked with cerebral disease, of which he died at Sheffield, Nov. 30, 1878. He was a student, a plain preacher, gentle, thoughtful, trustful, and tranquil. See *Minutes of the Conference*.

Coultas, William, an English Wesleyan minister, was born at Seamer, Yorkshire, Aug. 22, 1783. He united with the Church in 1801, was received into the ministry in 1810, and sent to Nevis, W. I., where he labored for six years amid much persecution from the planters. He returned to England in 1817; spent the rest of his life in the ministry in his native land; retired to Southport in 1850; and died Aug. 19, 1866. Mr. Coultas had a resolute will, strong passions, controlled by grace; his manner was rugged, his heart honest, and his life-long fidelity to Christ might well throw into the background his eccentricities. He wrote a *Memoir* of his daughter, Eliza (12mo). See *Minutes of the British Conference*, 1867, p. 10; *Wesl. Meth. Magazine*, 1868, p. 961.

Coulter, David, D.D., a Presbyterian minister,

was born Nov. 8, 1808, near Georgetown, Sussex Co., Del. He early experienced conversion, and united with the Church when about seventeen years of age. After obtaining a good English education in the common schools of his neighborhood, he went to Easton, Pa., and was prepared for college in the Manual Labor School, taught by the Rev. George Junkin, D.D. He graduated from Lafayette College in 1838, and from Princeton Theological Seminary in 1841; was licensed to preach by Newton Presbytery, April 28, the same year; soon after went to Missouri, where, for about two years, he preached at Auxvasse. He was ordained by Missouri Presbytery, July 5, 1843, pastor of the Rocheport and Fayette churches, where he labored zealously and usefully until Aug. 18, 1848; next acted as stated supply at Round Prairie and Millersburg, and pastor of the latter Church from December 10, 1853, to April 3, 1856; and of Hopewell Church, in Lafayette Presbytery, from April 22, 1856, to April 20, 1867, at the same time serving Prairie Church. After preaching at Columbia, Mo., a little over a year, he served the churches of Liberty and Bethel from 1868 to 1874. He was now quite infirm, and at length entirely unable to read; but he tried to preach even to the last. He died at Liberty, Aug. 20, 1878. See *Necrol. Report of Princeton Theol. Sem.* 1879, p. 42.

Coulter, John (1), D.D., a Scotch clergyman, was licensed to preach in 1761; became assistant minister at Kilwinning; was presented to the living at Kirkmaiden in 1763; ordained in 1764; transferred to Stranraer in 1772; and died Feb. 16, 1814, aged eighty-three years. See *Fasti Eccles. Scoticanæ*, i, 752, 762.

Coulter, John (2), a Presbyterian minister, was born near Sunbury, Pa., June 26, 1784. He entered Jefferson College, Canonnsburg, in 1813; studied theology with Dr. McMillan; was licensed by the Ohio Presbytery; and in 1823 became pastor at Muddy Creek, Butler Co., Pa., where he remained for twenty-seven years. He was installed pastor at Sunbury in his seventy-eighth year, and died in Butler County, Dec. 6, 1867. See Wilson, *Presb. Hist. Almanac*, 1868, p. 81.

Coulthurst, Henry William, D.D., an English divine, was born in Barbadoes in 1753. He was educated in England, first at Hipperholme, and afterwards at St. John's College, Cambridge; graduating in 1775, and soon after obtained one of Dr. Smith's prizes for his proficiency in mathematics and natural philosophy. In 1777 he obtained a prize for a dissertation in Latin prose. He was afterwards elected a fellow of Sydney College, held the office of moderator in the years 1784 and 1785, and in the latter part of his residence in the university was tutor of his college. In December, 1790, he became vicar of Halifax. He died suddenly, Dec. 11, 1817. Dr. Coulthurst was a benevolent man, a pious Christian, a zealous minister. See (Lond.) *Christian Observer*, 1817, appendix, p. 869.

Counter-remonstrance of Calvinists *to the States-General.* See Remonstrance.

Coupar, William, a Scotch prelate, was born in 1566 at Edinburgh, and took the degree of master of arts at St. Andrews in 1582. He was licensed to preach in 1586, and entered into the ministry at Bothkennar, Stirling, in the same year. In 1592 he was removed to the town of Perth. He was promoted to the see of Galloway July 31, 1614, where he remained until his death, Feb. 15, 1619. See Keith, *Scottish Bishops*, p. 280.

Coupé (or **Couppé**), Daniel, a Protestant theologian, who lived in the early part of the 17th century, wrote, *Traité des Miracles, contre Bellarmin* (Rotterdam, 1645). See Hoefer, *Nouv. Biog. Générale*, s. v.

Couper is the family name of several Scotch clergymen:

1. James, D.D., was licensed to preach in 1780; presented to the living at Baldernock in 1782; ordained in 1783; elected professor of practical astronomy in Glasgow University; resumed his charge in 1803; and died in January, 1836, aged eighty-three years. See *Fasti Eccles. Scoticanæ*, ii, 344.

2. John (1), son of the minister at Kinfauns, was appointed to the second charge at Brechin in 1724, and ordained; transferred to the first charge in 1731; retired from public duty in 1746, having his charge supplied till 1764 by unordained assistants; and died Jan. 21, 1774, aged seventy-seven years. See *Fasti Eccles. Scoticanæ*, iii, 845.

3. John (2), was licensed to preach in 1737; called to the living at Lochwinnoch in 1750, and ordained. He died Dec. 19, 1787, aged eighty years. He was an excellent scholar, of irreproachable character, and the only minister of his parish of the moderate party in Church politics. See *Fasti Eccles. Scoticanæ*, ii, 225.

4. Matthew, studied at the Glasgow University; held a bursary in theology there in 1676; became a schoolmaster at Mauchline, and afterwards at Ochiltree; was called to the living at Lilliesleaf in 1691; transferred to Ochiltree in 1695, thence to Kinfauns in 1700; and died Feb. 13, 1712, aged sixty years. See *Fasti Eccles. Scoticanæ*, i, 554; ii, 134, 646.

5. Patrick, was born at Scone in 1660; took his degree at the University of St. Andrews in 1678; in 1679 was taken prisoner at Perth as a rebel; imprisoned and fined five or six times for nonconformity and attending field preaching; fled to Scotland; preached at Amsterdam in 1684; after several years of foreign travel, peril, and shipwreck, returned to Scotland; was appointed minister at St. Ninian's, Stirling, in 1688; was member of the assemblies of 1690 and 1692; accepted the living at Pittenweem in 1692, although much opposed; and died June 14, 1740. He was a small, thin, spare man, generous and kind; and was the first to propose a fund for ministers' widows, in 1716. He published, *On Public Oaths* (1704):—*Jacobite Loyalty* (1724):—*a Sermon* (1725). See *Fasti Eccles. Scoticanæ*, ii, 456, 710.

6. Robert (1), took his degree at the University of St. Andrews in 1622; was called to the living at Temple in 1632; and died in 1655. See *Fasti Eccles. Scoticanæ*, i, 307.

7. Robert (2), was born at Clary; presented to the living at Kirkmaiden, as assistant and successor, in 1800; was only three times in the pulpit, for he died at Clary, July 30, 1801, aged twenty-two years. See *Fasti Eccles. Scoticanæ*, i, 762.

8. Simon, took his degree at Edinburgh University in 1667; was appointed to the living at Kirkcudbright in 1678; transferred to the Second Church, Dunfermline, in 1682, and to the First Church in 1686; was charged in 1689 with not praying for the king and queen, and other acts of disloyalty, but was acquitted; was deposed in 1693 for contumacy and contempt of the authority of the Presbytery, and ordered to leave the Church in 1696. He died at Edinburgh, Sept. 20, 1710, aged about sixty-four years. He published, *An Impartial Inquiry into the Order and Government in the Church* (Edinb. 1704). See *Fasti Eccles. Scoticanæ*, i, 689; ii, 568-571.

9. Thomas, took his degree at the University of Edinburgh in 1625; was licensed to preach in 1627; admitted to the living at Saline in 1634; transferred to Menmuir in 1639; thence to Montrose, in 1642; and died in 1661, aged about fifty-six years. See *Fasti Eccles. Scoticanæ*, ii, 602; iii, 841, 844.

Couplet, Philippe, a Belgian missionary, was born at Malines about 1628. He entered the Jesuit order, and in 1659 departed for the mission-field of China. He returned to Europe in 1680, and in 1692 started to return to China, but was overtaken by a violent tempest, and perished. He wrote, *Confucius Sinarum Philosophus* (Paris, 1687), containing a summary of the theology, history, and customs of the Chinese, with a translation of three works of Confucius; *Ta-Hio* (grand science), *Chong-Yung* (the just man), *Lun-Yu* (the book of sentences), a life of Confucius, and the Chinese annals back to 2952 B.C. Couplet also wrote, *Catalogus PP. Societatis Jesu*, etc. (Paris, 1686):—*Historia Candidæ Hiu* (translated into French, Paris, 1688; also in Spanish, at Madrid, and in Flemish, at Antwerp). See Hoefer, *Nouv. Biog. Générale*, s. v.; *Biog. Universelle*, s. v.

Courage is that quality of the mind that enables men to encounter difficulties and dangers. *Natural* courage is that which arises chiefly from constitution; *moral* or *spiritual* is that which is produced from principle, or a sense of duty. Courage and fortitude are often used as synonymous, but they may be distinguished thus: fortitude is firmness of mind that supports pain; courage is active fortitude, that meets dangers, and attempts to repel them. See FORTITUDE. Courage, says Addison, that grows from constitution, very often forsakes a man when he has occasion for it; and when it is only a kind of instinct in the soul, it breaks out on all occasions, without judgment or discretion; but that courage which arises from a sense of duty, and from a fear of offending Him that made us, always acts in a uniform manner, and according to the dictates of right reason.

Courbeville, JOSEPH FRANÇOIS DE, a French Jesuit, who lived in 1740, wrote a large number of works on practical piety, for which see Hoefer, *Nouv. Biog. Générale*, s. v.

Courcelles, Étienne de. See CURCELLÆUS.

Courcelles, Thomas de, a French theologian, was born in 1400, of a noble family of Picardy, and studied at the University of Paris. In 1431 he was canon of Amiens, of Laon, of Therouanne, and *bachelier formé* of theology, and already a very eminent preacher. He was successively sent to councils or congresses at Basle, Bourges, Prague, Rome, and Mantua. In 1440 he refused the cardinalate offered to him by the antipope, Felix V. He was one of the most able defenders of the liberties of the Gallican Church. In 1447, and years following, he was part of the embassy which determined the fate of the pontifical schism. Having become doctor of theology, he was, in 1450, appointed rector of St. Andrew's, Paris, afterwards canon, penitentiary, and dean of the cathedral. In 1461 he pronounced the funeral oration of Charles VII. Being proviseur of the Sorbonne, he was the same year delegated by the pope, with the bishop of Paris, to proceed to the reformation of the order of Fontevrault. Thomas de Courcelles is especially noticeable in history by the part, although secondary, which he played in the condemnation of Joan of Arc. He died Oct. 23, 1469. See Hoefer, *Nouv. Biog. Générale*, s. v.; *Biog. Universelle*, s. v.

Courier, ECCLESIASTICAL. See CURSOR.

Couronne, MATHIEU DE, a French theologian, who lived in the middle of the 17th century, wrote, *Traité de l'Infaillibilité du Pape* (Liege, 1668):—*De la Puissance Temporelle et Spirituelle des Evêques* (ibid. 1671, 1673):—*Des Missions Apostoliques* (ibid. 1675). See Hoefer, *Nouv. Biog. Générale*, s. v.

Court OF HIGH COMMISSION. See HIGH COMMISSION, COURT OF.

COURT, SPIRITUAL, in English ecclesiastical usage, is one for the administration of ecclesiastical justice. Until the time of William the Conqueror the court for the consideration of ecclesiastical and temporal matters was one and the same; but at that period a separation took place. There are six such courts:

1. The *Archdeacon's Court*, which is the lowest, and is held where the archdeacon, either by prescription or composition, has jurisdiction in spiritual or ecclesiastical causes within his archdeaconry. The judge of this court is called the official of the archdeaconry.

2. The *Consistory Courts* of the archbishops and bishops of every diocese are held in their cathedral churches, for trial of all ecclesiastical causes within the diocese. The bishop's chancellor or commissary is the judge.

3. The *Prerogative Court* is held at Doctors' Commons, in London, in which all testaments and last wills are proved, and administrations upon the estates of intestates granted, where the party dies beyond seas or within his province, leaving *bona notabilia*.

4. The *Arches Court* (so called because anciently held in the arched church of St. Mary, in Cheapside, London) is that which has jurisdiction upon appeal in all ecclesiastical causes, except such as belong to the Prerogative Court. The judge is the official principal of the archbishop. See ARCHES, COURT OF.

5. The *Court of Peculiars*, of the archbishop of Canterbury, is subservient to, and in connection with, that of the Arches.

6. The *Court of Delegates* is so called because the judges are delegated and set in virtue of the king's commission, under the great seal, *pro hac vice*, upon appeals to the king on ecclesiastical matters.

These courts proceed according to the civil and canon laws, by citation, libel, or articles, answer upon oath, proofs by witnesses and presumptions, definitive sentence without a jury, and by excommunication for contempt of sentence. In times of intolerance many acts of the most cruel enormity were committed in these courts.

Court, Pierre, a French theologian, was born at Provins in 1665. He took the Benedictine habit in the congregation of St. Vanne, June 1, 1685, became prior of Airy, and died in 1730, leaving *Vie de M. d'Aligre* (Paris, 1712):—*Abrégé du Commentaire de Calmet* (7 or 8 vols.):—*Paraphrases sur le Cantique des Cantiques et sur la Prose des Morts "Dies Iræ"*:—*Recueil de Sequences, Proses Anciennes ou Cantiques*:—*Concordia Discordantium Theologorum*, etc.:—*Histoire de l'Abbaye de Saint-Vanne de Verdun*, and other pieces. See Hoefer, *Nouv. Biog. Générale*, s. v.

Court, Robert, a Scotch clergyman, was born at Muthill, April 18, 1790; licensed to preach in 1815; became assistant minister at Yester, and afterwards at Cranston; ordained in 1831 minister to the Presbyterian Congregation at Maryport; presented to the living at Heriot in 1834; joined the Free Secession in 1843; became minister of the Free Church at Pathhead the same year, and resigned in 1866. See *Fasti Eccles. Scoticanæ*, i, 284.

Courte-cuisse, JEAN DE (Lat. *Johannes de Brevicoxa*, also *de Curtacoxa*, or *de Cortohosa*), a French prelate and theologian, was born at Hallaines, in the Passais (Maine), about 1350. He was educated at the College of Navarre, in Paris, made doctor in 1388, chancellor of the university in 1418, bishop of Paris in 1420, and died at Geneva in 1425. Living at a time when the question of papal schism was rife, he wrote several controversial tracts and sermons, for which see Hoefer, *Nouv. Biog. Générale*, s. v.

Courtenay, Henry Reginald, D.D., an English prelate, was educated at Christ Church, Oxford; became chaplain to the king, prebendary of Exeter in 1772, rector of St. George's, Hanover Square, in 1774, of Lee (in Kent), in 1775, and prebendary of St. Andrew, in the cathedral of Rochester, in 1783. He was consecrated bishop of Bristol, May 11, 1794, and translated to the see of Exeter in 1797. He died June 9, 1803. He published a *Fast Sermon* (1795):—and a *Charge* (1796). See Le Neve, *Fasti*; Allibone, *Dict. of Brit. and Amer. Authors*, s. v.; (Lond.) *Annual Register*, 1803, p. 510.

Courtenay, John, a Scotch clergyman, was licensed to preach in 1635; and presented to the living at Bolton in 1640. He deserted his charge at Whitsunday, 1661, and went to Ireland. See *Fasti Eccles. Scoticanæ*, i, 322.

Courtenay (or **Courtnay**), **William**, an English prelate, was born in the parish of St. Martin's, a suburb of the city of Exeter, about 1342, and was educated in his father's house until he was sent to the University of Oxford. In 1367, after having completed his collegiate course, he was elected chancellor of the university. In 1369 his friends succeeded in obtaining for him the bishopric of Hereford, and his consecration appears to have taken place March 17. He was enthroned Sept. 5, 1370, and translated to the see of Canterbury in 1375. He labored for the improvement of the church edifices, and gave liberal sums himself for that object. He died July 31, 1396. See Hook, *Lives of the Archbishops of Canterbury*, iv, 316 sq.

Courtenay, William A., an English Congregational minister, was born at Falmouth, Dec. 24, 1826. He united with the Church at an early age; entered Hackney College in 1849, and began his ministry at Kelvedon, Essex, in 1852. He afterwards labored successively at North Walsham, Norfolk; at Mile End; at Wardour-street Chapel, Soho; and at the Royal Amphitheatre, Holborn. He died June 9, 1873. See (Lond) *Cong. Year-book*, 1874, p. 320.

Courtice, WILLIAM, an English Methodist preacher, was born at North Devon in 1796. He led a wicked life in his youth; heard Mr. O'Bryan preach in 1815; gave his heart to God and his service to the Bible Christians; entered the ministry in 1820, as a supply for James Thorne, and for more than forty years was one of the most able and successful ministers in the connection, filling some of the highest offices. In 1862 he became a supernumerary, and died suddenly at Devonport, Jan. 2, 1866. See *Minutes of the Conference*, 1866.

Courtie, DAVID, a Scotch clergyman, took his degree at Edinburgh University in 1601; was presented by the king to the living at Stitchel in 1613, and died April 29, 1655, aged eighty-three years. See *Fasti Eccles. Scoticanæ*, i, 474.

Courties, JOHN, an English Wesleyan missionary, was sent to Sierra Leone in 1826. After successfully completing his term of service, he sailed for his native country, but died on the passage, in 1829. See *Minutes of the British Conference*, 1829.

Courtney, Ezra, a Baptist pioneer preacher, was born in Pennsylvania in 1771. He began to preach in the eastern part of the state in 1804, and, after itinerating some years, he became, in 1814, a resident in East Feliciana Parish, La. He died in 1855. He was an efficient and popular preacher, and was often elected moderator of the Mississippi Association, and other bodies of which he was a member. See Cathcart, *Baptist Encyclop.* p. 282. (J. C. S.)

Courtney, John, a Baptist minister, was born in King and Queen County, Va., about 1744. He began his ministry at Richmond, and served the Church over forty years. He died Dec. 18, 1824. See Sprague, *Annals of the Amer. Pulpit*, vi, 291; *Lives of Virginia Baptist Ministers*, p. 99.

Courtney, Peter, LL.D., an English prelate of the 15th century, was born at Powderham, Devonshire. He was preferred dean of Windsor in 1476, bishop of Exeter in 1478, translated to Winchester in 1487, and died Sept. 22, 1492. See Fuller, *Worthies of England* (ed. Nuttall), i, 407; Le Neve, *Fasti.*

Courtney, Richard, an English prelate, a relative of William Courtenay, archbishop of Canterbury, was a man of good lineage and no less learning. He was preferred precentor at Chichester in 1400, dean of St. Asaph in 1402, prebend of York in 1403, dean of Wells in 1410, chancellor of Oxford in 1411, bishop of Norwich in 1413, and died at the siege of Harfleur, Normandy, in the second year of his consecration, and was buried in Westminster. See Fuller, *Worthies of England* (ed. Nuttall), i, 405; Le Neve, *Fasti.*

Courtney, Thomas, a Scotch clergyman, took his degree at Edinburgh University in 1636; was admitted to the living at Merton in 1640; was minister at Kirk-Andrews, in England, in 1661; returned to Scotland in 1663, and was elected one of the ministers at Edinburgh the same year, but did not accept. He is recorded as having possession of the Kirk lands of Home in 1668. See *Fasti Eccles. Scoticanæ*, i, 530.

Courtot, JEAN, a French theologian, was born at Arnay-le-Duc. He entered the congregation of the Oratory in 1632, and was distinguished for ill-will towards the Jesuits. Bourgoing, general of the Oratorians, banished him to Joyeuse, and he was finally excluded from the Oratory in 1652. He died in 1665, leaving, *Manuale Catholicorum* (Paris, 1651), under the name of *Alytophile;* republished, with numerous additions (ibid. 1663); condemned in 1664 and burned:—and several controversial pieces, mostly under the pseudonym of *Jean Cordier.* See Hoefer, *Nouv. Biog. Générale*, s. v.

Courts, CHURCH, among the Presbyterians, are those ecclesiastical associations of ministers and elders, consisting of sessions, presbyteries, synods, and the general assembly, which in Scotland are considered as forming the perfection of Church government and discipline. Each subordinate court takes cognizance of ecclesiastical matters within its own bounds; and from each there is an appeal to that which is above it in order, till the matter is carried before the general assembly, which is the supreme court, and the decision of which is final.

COURTS OF LAW, HEBREW. See JUDICIAL PROCEDURE.

Cousin (Lat. *Cognatus*), **Gilbert**, a French theological author, was born at Nozeroy, Franche-Comté, Jan. 21, 1506. He studied jurisprudence at Dôle in 1526, but soon afterwards devoted himself to the ecclesiastical calling. In 1530 he became copyist to Erasmus, who regarded him as a companion in labor, and aided him in studying Greek, Latin, and belles-lettres. In 1535 Cousin was appointed canon of St. Anthony of Nozeroy, and at the same time devoted himself to teaching. In 1558 he went to Italy with Claude La Baume, archbishop of Besançon, and remained for some time at Padua. On his return to France, Cousin embraced Protestant sentiments. Pope Pius V ordered his arrest for heresy, July 8, 1567. He was taken to the ecclesiastical prison, and died in the same year. His numerous works have been collected and published. A complete catalogue may be seen in Nicéron. See Hoefer, *Nouv. Biog. Générale*, s. v.; *Biog. Universelle*, s. v.

Cousin, Jean (1), a French painter, was born at Soucy, near Sens, about 1501, and was the founder of a French school. He died about 1590. His principal historical work, representing *The Last Judgment*, was formerly in the monastery of the Minim at Vincennes, the windows of which were also painted by him. The best of his works are on glass, in the Church of St. Gervais at Paris. They represent *Christ with the Woman of Samaria, Christ Curing the Paralytic*, and the *Martyrdom of St. Lawrence.* See Hoefer, *Nouv. Biog. Générale*, s. v.; Spooner, *Biog. Hist. of the Fine Arts*, s. v.

Cousin (Lat. *Cognatus*), **Jean** (2), a Belgian religious historian, was born at Tournay, where he was afterwards canon, and where he died in 1621. He wrote, *De Fundamentis Religionis*, containing the following discourses: *De Naturali Dei Cognitione; De Immortalitate Animæ; De Justitia Dei* (Douay, 1597):—*De Prosperitate et Exitio Solomonis* (ibid. 1599):—*Histoire de Tournay* (ibid. 1619, 1620):—*Histoire des Saints de Tournay* (ibid. 1621). See Hoefer, *Nouv. Biog. Générale*, s. v.; *Biog. Universelle*, s. v.

Cousin, Louis, a French writer, was born at Paris, Aug. 12, 1627. He became bachelor of theology at Paris, advocate in 1646, and president of one of the lower courts in October, 1659. He was made member of the French Academy June 15, 1697, chosen royal censor, and charged with the compilation of the *Journal des Savants* from 1687 to 1702. He studied Hebrew at the age of seventy, in order to understand more fully the sacred Scriptures. Nicéron says that he was a man of high integrity, of an admirable spirit of justness, correct judgment, easy and agreeable in conversation. He died Feb. 26, 1707. He devoted his spare time to the translation of works of the ancient ecclesiastical historians, and published several volumes, for which see Hoefer, *Nouv. Biog. Générale*, s. v.; *Biog. Universelle*, s. v.

Cousin, Michael, an English Wesleyan minister, was born at Haworth, Yorkshire, March 20, 1782. He united with the Church in 1802, was appointed to a circuit in 1804, became a supernumerary in Halifax in 1846, and died Nov. 6, 1852. With a vigorous frame, he gave himself with devout ardor to his work, and success resulted from his labors. See *Minutes of the British Conference*, 1853.

Cousins, Marriage of. The course of Church practice on this subject appears to have been this: the traditional Roman prejudice against cousins' marriages, although quite uncountenanced by the Jewish law or practice, commended itself instinctively to the ascetic tendencies of the Western fathers, and through them took root among the Western clergy generally, embodying itself, indeed, temporarily, towards the end of the 4th century, in a general civil law for the Roman empire. But while this law was abrogated in the beginning of the 5th century, and in the East such unions remained perfectly lawful both in the Church and in the State throughout nearly the whole of the period which occupies us, never being condemned by any œcumenical council till that of Constantinople towards the end of the 7th century, in the West the clergy adhered to the harsher view; popes and local synods sought to enforce it; wherever clerical influence could be brought to bear on the barbaric legislators it became apparent; till at last, under the Carlovingian princes, it established itself as a law alike of the State and of the Church. But the history of this restraint upon marriage is that of all others not derived from Scripture itself. Originating probably, all of them, in a sincere though mistaken asceticism, they were soon discovered to furnish an almost inexhaustible mine for the supply of the Church's coffers, through the grant of dispensations, prosecutions in the Church courts, compromises. The baleful alliance between Carlovingian usurpation and Romish priestcraft, in exchange for the subserviency of the clergy to the ambition and the vices of the earlier despots, delivered over the social morality of the people to them, it may be said, as a prey, and the savageness of Carlovingian civil legislation was placed at the service of the newfangled Church discipline of the West. See Affinity; Marriage.

Cousins, James, an English Baptist minister, was born at Freystrope, near Haverford-West, in 1788. He was converted at the age of seventeen, studied at Bristol College, and in 1818 became pastor at Kingstanley, Gloucestershire, where he had great success. He retired in 1843, but continued to preach in various places in the neighborhood until his death, Feb. 17, 1862. See (Lond.) *Baptist Hand-book*, 1863, p. 113. (J. C. S.)

Cousins, Jonathan, an English Wesleyan minister, commenced his itinerancy in 1780, and died at Diss, near Norwich (where he also began his ministry), Oct. 31, 1805, aged forty-nine. He was a man of mild temper and much esteemed by his people. See *Minutes of the British Conference*, 1806.

Coussard, Claude, a French theologian, of the 16th century, wrote *Valdensium ac Quorumdam Aliorum Errores* (Paris, 1548; also in French, by Cappell, Sedan, 1618). See Hoefer, *Nouv. Biog. Générale*, s. v.

Coustant, Pierre, a learned French Benedictine of the order of St. Maur, was born at Compiègne, April 30, 1654, and died at Paris, Oct. 18, 1721, while dean of the abbey of St. Germain-des-Près, leaving several editions of the works of Church fathers and others, for which see Chalmers, *Biog. Dict.* s. v.; Hoefer, *Nouv. Biog. Générale*, s. v.; Wetzer u. Welte, *Kirchen-Lexikon*, s. v.; *Biog. Universelle*, s. v.

Coustou, Guillaume, *the Elder*, a reputable French sculptor, the brother of Nicolas, was born at Lyons in 1678, studied under Coysevox, and soon gained the prize of the Academy. His reputation rapidly increased. Some of his works are, *Christ in the Midst of the Doctors*, at Versailles, and some *Portraits*. He died at Paris, Feb. 22, 1746. See Hoefer, *Nouv. Biog. Générale*, s. v.; Spooner, *Biog. Hist. of the Fine Arts*, s. v.

Coustou, Guillaume, *the Younger*, a French sculptor, son and scholar of the foregoing, was born at Paris in 1716. Having carried off the grand prize of the Academy, he went to Italy with the royal pension. In 1742 he was elected an academician, in 1746 was appointed professor of sculpture, and the king named him keeper of the sculptures in the Louvre. He died at Paris, July 13, 1777. See Hoefer, *Nouv. Biog. Générale*, s. v.; Spooner, *Biog. Hist. of the Fine Arts*, s. v.

Coustou, Nicolas, an ingenious French sculptor, was born at Lyons, Jan. 9, 1658. He studied at Paris under his uncle, Coysevox, and carried off the grand prize of the Royal Academy at the age of twenty-three; then he went to Rome and studied the works of Michael Angelo. In 1693 he was received into the Academy at Paris. The following are some of his works: *The Descent from the Cross*, and the statue of *St. Denis*, in the Church of Notre Dame. He died at Paris, Feb. 1, 1733. See Hoefer, *Nouv. Biog. Générale*, s. v.; Spooner, *Biog. Hist. of the Fine Arts*, s. v.

Cousturier. See Couturier.

Coutinho, Luis, a Portuguese prelate, was born near the close of the 14th century. He was made bishop of Viseu about 1440, and sent by Alfonso V as ambassador to Rome, where he assisted in the election of the antipope Felix V. Under the influence of this illegitimate authority he was made cardinal in 1443. He became bishop of Coimbra, and accompanied the daughter of king Edward when she went to Germany to marry the emperor Frederick III. Having been promoted to the archbishopric of Lisbon in 1452, but not sharing the favor of Alfonso, he retired from court, and withdrew into the solitude of Cintra to seek relief from leprosy, with which, it is said, he was attacked. He died at Cintra in April, 1453, and was interred in the cemetery of the lepers, where a splendid monument was erected to his memory. See Hoefer, *Nouv. Biog. Générale*, s. v.

Couto (Lat. *Coutus*), Sebastião do, a Portuguese theologian, was born about 1567. He belonged to a noble family, and was originally from Olivença. He joined the Jesuits on Dec. 8, 1582. Shortly afterwards he was called successively to the chairs of philosophy at Coimbra and Evora, and was made doctor of theology on June 24, 1596. He was one of the most learned men of his time. He died near Evora, Nov. 20, 1639, leaving, *Commentaria in Dialecticam Aristotelis*:—*Epigrammata in Mortem Francisci de Mendoça* (published in the *Veridarium* of Mendoça, Lyons, 1649). In the library of Evora may be found a collection of theological matter dictated by him in his lectures. See Hoefer, *Nouv. Biog. Générale*, s. v.; Jöcher, *Allgemeines Gelehrten-Lexikon*, s. v.

Couttis (or **Coutts**), Alexander, a Scotch clergyman, took his degree at King's College, Aberdeen, in 1670; was licensed to preach in 1675; presented to the living at Strickathrow in 1677, and ordained. He died April 11, 1695, aged forty-eight years. See *Fasti Eccles. Scoticanæ*, iii, 850.

Coutts (or **Couttis**), Robert, a Scotch clergyman, was born at Largo; studied at St. Andrews and

Edinburgh universities; was licensed to preach in 1796; became assistant in mathematics at St. Andrews; and was presented to the living at the second charge, Brechin, in 1798. He died June 18, 1803, aged thirty-one years. He had a singularly pious and vigorous mind. See *Fasti Eccles. Scoticanæ*, iii, 816, 817.

Couturier, Jacob, a French theologian, was born at Minot, near La Montagne (Burgundy). He was curate of Salives, near Dijon, in the time of the Revolution; was elected deputy to the states-general by the bailiwick of La Montagne, and made himself noticeable by his opposition to the reformers. He refused to take the ecclesiastical oath to the new constitution, and went into exile; but returned to France some time before the 18th Brumaire, and assumed the direction of his parish. He died at Salives, Burgundy, in 1805, leaving *Histoire de l'Ancien Testament* (Dijon, 1825). See Hoefer, *Nouv. Biog. Générale*, s. v.; *Biog. Universelle*, s. v.

Couturier, Jean, a French theologian, brother of Jacob, was born at Minot, near La Montagne, Burgundy, in 1730. He completed his studies at Langres, entered the Jesuit order, and taught rhetoric successively at Langres, Verdun, Pont-à-Mousson, and Nancy. At the time of the suppression of the Jesuits he was appointed curate at Léry. In 1791 he refused to take the oath of allegiance to the new constitution, and was incarcerated soon after, but, being liberated in 1795, he resumed his functions, and, in spite of legal remonstrance, continued them until his death, at Léry, March 22, 1799. He wrote, *Catéchisme Dogmatique et Moral* (Dijon, 1821, 1832):—*La Bonne Journée* (ibid. 1822, 1825; Coutances, 1827):—*Abrégé de la Doctrine Chrétienne* (Dijon, 1822, 1823):—*L'Histoire de Tobie* (ibid. 1823):—and a large number of *Controversies, Meditations, Sermons*, etc., remaining in MS. See Hoefer, *Nouv. Biog. Générale*, s. v.; *Biog. Universelle*, s. v.

Couturier, Nicolas Jérome, a French ecclesiastic, was born in the diocese of Rouen, June 2, 1712. He became preacher to the king, canon of St. Quentin, and died at Paris in 1778, leaving several *Funeral Sermons*.

Couturier (or **Cousturier**), **Pierre** (Lat. *Petrus Sutor*), a French theologian, was born at Chemeré-le-Roy, a village of Laval, in the latter part of the 15th century. Having received the degree of doctor at the Sorbonne, he taught philosophy in the College of St. Barbe. He afterwards became a cenobite, and entered the Carthusian order. In 1519 he was made governor of the Carthusians of Paris. In 1534 he went to another monastery, near Troyes, as prior. He employed his leisure in writing books against the Protestants. He died June 18, 1537, leaving, *De Vita Carthusiana* (Paris, 1522; Louvain, 1572; Cologne, 1609):—*De Triplici Annæ Connubio* (Paris, 1523):—*De Translatione Bibliæ* (ibid. 1525). In reply to Erasmus he wrote *Antapologia* (ibid. 1526):—*Apologeticum* (ibid. eod.):—*Apologia* (ibid. 1531):—*De Potestate Ecclesiæ* (ibid. 1534, 1546). See Hoefer, *Nouv. Biog. Générale*, s. v.

Couvay, Jean, a reputable French engraver, was born at Arles about 1622. The following are his principal works: *The Virgin and Infant; St. John in the Desert; The Magdalene; The Martyrdom of St. Bartholomew.* See Hoefer, *Nouv. Biog. Générale*, s. v.; Spooner, *Biog. Hist. of the Fine Arts*, s. v.

Couvoyon, *Saint*, a Breton abbot, was born at Combsac in 788, being the son of a gentleman named *Conon*. He entered the priesthood, became archdeacon of Vannes, and soon after retired to a solitude in Redon, where he built a monastery under the Benedictine rule, with the aid of Ratwil, lord of the region. In 848 he obtained a decision of pope Leo IV on a question of simony, and thereupon prosecuted four of the neighboring prelates, who were deposed. In 865 he took refuge from the invasion of the Normans with the prince of Bretagne, who built for him a monastery at Plélan, afterwards called that of St. Maxentius. He died there in 868, and his remains were transferred in the 10th century to Redon. His festival is on Dec. 28. See Hoefer, *Nouv. Biog. Générale*, s. v.

Covarrubias (or **Covarruvias**) *y Leyva*, Diego (surnamed *The Spanish Bartole*), a Spanish lawyer and prelate, was born at Toledo, July 25, 1512. He studied under Nicolas Cleynants, Fernando Nuñea, and Azpilcueta, and taught canon law at Salamanca. In 1538 he became professor at Oviedo, later judge at Burgos, and counsellor at Grenada. In 1549 he was nominated archbishop of San Domingo; in 1560 bishop of Ciudad Rodrigo; in 1565 bishop of Segovia, and later of Cuenca. He was engaged in several ecclesiastical reforms and offices, and died at Madrid, Sept. 27, 1577, leaving a number of historical and archæological works, for which see Hoefer, *Nouv. Biog. Générale*, s. v.; *Biog. Universelle*, s. v.

Covel, Samuel, a Methodist Episcopal minister, son of Rev. James Covel, Sr., was converted when a young man, and in 1821 entered the New York Conference. In 1852, on account of ill-health, he became superannuated, and continued to hold that relation to the close of his life, early in 1860. Mr. Covel was a deeply pious man, an ordinary preacher, but had few superiors in ardor or faithfulness in the ministry, or success in revivals. See *Minutes of Annual Conferences*, 1861, p. 91.

Covel, William, an English theologian of the former part of the 17th century, wrote several minor works on ecclesiastical polity, for which see Hoefer, *Nouv. Biog. Générale*, s. v.; Allibone, *Dict. of Brit. and Amer. Authors*, s. v.

Covell, Alanson L., a Baptist minister, was born at Pittstown, N. Y., Jan. 20, 1804. He became pastor of a church in Addison, Vt., and subsequently at Whitesborough, N. Y., also of the First Baptist Church in Albany. He died Sept. 20, 1837. He took a prominent part in the organization of the American and Foreign Bible Society while pastor in Albany. See Sprague, *Annals of the Amer. Pulpit*, vi, 313.

Covell, Joseph Smith, a minister of the Episcopal Church, was born in Killingly, Conn., June 4, 1797. He spent the first eighteen years of his life on his father's farm; fitted for college in part at Woodstock, and graduated from Brown University in 1822. He afterwards took charge of a private school in Newport, R. I., and began his theological studies under the tuition of Rev. Dr. Austin, but, later, connected himself with the Episcopal Church, and in August, 1824, was ordained deacon and became minister of a mission church in St. Albans, Vt. The climate proving to be too rigorous, he removed to Baltimore, where he was ordained a presbyter, in May, 1825, and took charge of a mission station at Princess Anne, on the eastern shore of Maryland. Subsequently he returned to New England, and in October, 1828, was called to the rectorship of St. Paul's Church, Brookfield, Conn., where he remained nine years, and then took charge of Trinity Church, Bristol, for ten years. He afterwards was rector of churches in Essex, Bethlehem, etc., until 1863, when he was called to the rectorship of St. Paul's Church, Huntington. He resigned in July, 1876, and removed to Bridgeport, where he died, March 16, 1880. See *Brown University Necrology*, 1879-1880; Whittaker, *Almanac and Directory*, 1881. (J. C. S.)

Covell, Lemuel, a Baptist minister, was born in the state of New York about the middle of the last century. He was licensed by the Church in Providence, Saratoga Co. Although at first poor and illiterate, so remarkable were his natural abilities that he became one of the most eminent preachers in his denomination. He was blessed with a voice of singular charm, and his address was manly and engaging. He regarded it as his mission to travel extensively among the churches of New York and New England. Not long before his death the Church in Cheshire, Mass., of which Rev. John Leland had been the pastor, called him to be his successor. He accepted their call on condition that he be allowed, a part of the time, to travel, and preach in destitute regions, under the patronage and direction of the Baptist Missionary Society of Boston. While thus engaged, in Upper Canada, he died after a short illness, in October, 1806. See Benedict, *Hist. of the Baptists*, ii, 289. (J. C. S.)

Covenanting, PERSONAL, is a modern term for a solemn transaction by which many pious and devoted Christians have dedicated themselves to the service of God. Such bonds or covenants, written and subscribed with their own hands, have been found among their papers after their death, and it cannot be denied that most of them are exceedingly edifying; but instances have also been known of persons abusing this custom for purposes of superstition and self-righteousness, and of some who have gone as far as to write and sign such a document with their own blood.

Coventry, George, an English Baptist minister, was settled at the Duke Street Church, London, in February, 1731. There was a large tomb in the graveyard belonging to the Coventry family, but it was destroyed when the chapel was pulled down, and the records of the family lost. See Wilson, *Dissenting Churches*, iv, 181.

Coventry, Robert, a Scotch clergyman, was licensed to preach in 1725; called to the living at Kilspindie in 1727, and ordained; and died Feb. 19, 1761. See *Fasti Eccles. Scoticanæ*, ii, 644.

Covetousness. The works of the earliest Christian authorities are full of warnings against the different forms of this vice. The oblations of the covetous were not to be received. Gregory Thaumaturgus, archbishop of Neo-Cæsarea (about A.D. 262) declares that it is impossible to set forth in a single letter all the sacred writings which proclaim not robbery alone to be a fearful crime, but all covetousness, all grasping at others' goods for filthy lucre. Others of the fathers in like manner vigorously denounced the existence of the vice among the clergy.

Gregory of Nyssa observes that the fathers have affixed no punishment to this sin, which he assimilates to adultery; though it be very common in the Church, none inquires of those who are brought to be ordained if they be polluted with it. It is true, a decree from Gratian, ascribed to pope Julius I, A.D. 337-352, denounces as filthy lucre the buying in time of harvest or of vintage, not of necessity but of greed, victuals or wine, in order to sell at a higher price; and the 17th canon of the Council of Nicæa (A.D. 325) is directed against the love of filthy lucre and usury, enacting deposition as the punishment for the cleric. But here, as in a parallel canon of the synod of Seleucia, A.D. 410, it is perhaps to be inferred that the vice was chiefly, if not solely, aimed at under the concrete form of usury (q. v.). That covetousness was as rife in the monastery as in the world may be inferred from Cassian.

The very doubtful "Sanctions and Decrees of the Nicene fathers," apparently of Greek origin, require priests not to be given to heaping up riches, lest they should prefer them to the ministry, and if they do accumulate wealth, to do so moderately. The 3d Council of Orleans, A.D. 538, forbids clerics, from the diaconate upwards, to carry on business as public traders for the greed of filthy lucre, or to do so in another's name. As the time wears on, covetousness seems often to be confounded with avarice, and to be legislated against under that name. See BRIBERY; COMMERCE; USURY. For rapacity in exacting fees, see SPORTULÆ.

Covingtrie, THOMAS, a Scotch clergyman, was baptized June 15, 1685; took his degree at Edinburgh University in 1705; studied divinity at Glasgow; was licensed to preach in 1711; called to the living at Cross and Burness the same year, and ordained; and died Sept. 2, 1744, aged sixty years. See *Fasti Eccles. Scoticanæ*, iii, 410.

Cowan, Andrew, a Scotch clergyman, was licensed to preach in 1719; became missionary in the parish of Westray; was presented to the living in 1734; ordained in 1735; and died July 28, 1760. See *Fasti Eccles. Scoticanæ*, iii, 419.

Cowan, Charles, a Scotch clergyman, studied at the University of St. Andrews; was licensed to preach in 1817; appointed to the living at Fetlar and North Yell in 1822, and ordained. He died Oct. 9, 1829, aged thirty-three years. See *Fasti Eccles. Scoticanæ*, iii, 437.

Cowan, Francis, a Scotch clergyman, was licensed to preach in 1758; presented to the living at Gladsmuir in 1759, and ordained; and died Oct. 28, 1789. See *Fasti Eccles. Scoticanæ*, i, 336.

Cowan, John Fleming, a Presbyterian minister, was born at Parkesburg, Pa., May 6, 1801. He graduated from Jefferson College in 1825, and in 1828 from Princeton Theological Seminary. He was licensed to preach in 1829, and ordained April 4, 1830, with a view to missionary work in Missouri, where he labored for thirty-three years. His first field was Apple Creek, Cape Girardeau Co. After this he was pastor of the Potosi Church in Washington Co. (1836-1852). He then visited and labored in various parts of the state, and died at Carondelet, Sept. 29, 1862. Mr. Cowan was in the fullest sense an evangelist. He acted as agent for the Board of Domestic Missions for three years, and served for a while as chaplain of the hospital at Carondelet. His preaching was practical and instructive. (W. P. S.)

Cowbridge, an English martyr, was burned at Oxford in 1538, for his public communication of the Scriptures. See Fox, *Acts and Monuments*, v, 251.

Cowden, JAMES, a Methodist Episcopal minister, was born in May, 1836. He received an early religious training; experienced conversion in 1853, and in 1855 entered the Rock River Conference. In 1858 he removed to Minnesota for the improvement of his health, but continued effective, and six years later returned and united with the Central Illinois Conference, wherein he served zealously to the close of his life, March 22, 1871. See *Minutes of Annual Conferences*, 1871, p. 195.

Cowdy, SAMUEL, an Irish Methodist preacher, was born in 1799 in County Down. He gave his heart to God, and his life to Methodism at an early age; entered the itinerant ministry in 1832, and for a quarter of a century preached the gospel with soul-converting power on many Irish circuits. In 1860 he became a supernumerary, but labored as he had strength until his death, June 3, 1880, at Portadown.

Cowell, David, a Presbyterian minister, was born at Wrentham, Mass., in 1704. He graduated from Harvard College in 1732. Having studied theology and received license to preach, he went as a supply to Trenton, N. J., in 1735, and in April, 1736, became pastor. At the division of the Presbyterian Church in 1741, Mr. Cowell remained with the old side. On the union of the two synods he joined the New Brunswick Presbytery, and continued in relation with it until his death, Dec. 1, 1760. See Sprague, *Annals of the Amer. Pulpit*, iii, 66.

Cowell, D. B., a Free-will Baptist minister, was born at West Lebanon, Me., Dec. 20, 1806. He received his early education in the academy at Limerick, and at Wolfsborough, N. H.; spent his early manhood in teaching and in mercantile pursuits, several years being passed in Great Falls, where his trade became extensive. At this period of his life he was a Universalist, and subsequently an avowed infidel. In 1833 he was converted, and soon after became a class-leader in the Church at Great Falls. In 1837 he was ordained, and for seven years travelled almost constantly as an itinerant. In

1848 he gave the start to a movement which resulted in the establishment of the West Lebanon Academy. His last fields of labor were with the Walnut Grove Church, N. H., more than a year, and with the churches in Gorham and Standish, Me. Feeble health prevented his preaching much for some time before his death, which occurred April 16, 1884. See *The Morning Star*, June 4, 1884. (J. C. S.)

Cowell, Edward, an English Congregational minister, was born at Ewood Bridge, near Blackburn, Feb. 7, 1830. He became an efficient local preacher among the Wesleyans, but afterwards joined the Congregationalists. In 1862 he supplied the pulpit of Providence Independent Chapel, Marsden, and the following year became its pastor, being ordained Sept. 29. He accepted an invitation to Bretherton in September, 1874, where he labored happily and successfully for five years. He died Feb. 9, 1880. See (Lond.) *Cong. Year-book*, 1881, p. 365.

Cowie, WILLIAM, a Scotch clergyman, a native of Banffshire, took his degree at King's College, Aberdeen, in 1806; was appointed schoolmaster at Mortlach in 1811; licensed to preach in 1812; presented to the living at Cabrach in 1817, and ordained; transferred to Cairnie in 1826; and died June 1, 1866, aged eighty years. See *Fasti Eccles. Scoticanæ*, iii, 196, 551.

Cowing, CHARLES, a Methodist Episcopal minister, was born at Lyman, N. H., Nov. 19, 1796. He was converted in 1818; licensed to exhort in 1824, to preach in 1827, and in 1828 entered the New England Conference, wherein he remained effective, with but a three years' intermission as superannuate, until 1852, when he again became superannuated, and thus continued until his death, in May, 1869. See *Minutes of Annual Conferences*, 1870, p. 111.

Cowl. Benedict ordered the "cuculla," or hood, to be shaggy for winter, and for summer of lighter texture; and a "scapulare" to be worn instead out of doors, as more suitable for field-work, being open at the sides. The "cuculla" protected the head and shoulders, and, as being worn by infants and peasants, was said to symbolize humility; or, by another account, it was to keep the eyes from glancing right or left. It was part of the dress of nuns, as well as of monks, and was worn by the monks of Tabenna at the mass. It seems in their case to have been longer than a hood or cape. Indeed, "cuculla" is often taken as equivalent to "casula," a covering of the whole person; in later writers it means, not the hood only, but the monastic robe, hood and all. These same Pachomiani, or monks of Tabenna, like the Carthusians, drew their hoods forward at meal-times, so as to hide their faces from one another. The "cappa" (probably akin to our "cape") in Italy seems to correspond with the Gallic "cuculla," and both were nearly identical, it is thought, with the "melotes," or sheepskin of the earliest ascetics.

Cowle, JOHN, a minister of the Methodist Episcopal Church South, was born in Huntingdonshire, England, in January, 1815. He went with his parents to Vanderburgh County, Ind., in 1822; removed to Arkansas in 1838; and in 1841 entered the Arkansas Conference. From 1868, he was a superannuate to the close of his life, June 6, 1870. During his entire ministry Mr. Cowle acquitted himself with honor. He was a close student and a laborious minister. See *Minutes of Annual Conferences of the M. E. Church South*, 1870, p. 496.

Cowles, Chauncey Demming, a Congregational minister, was born at Farmington, Conn., June 27, 1812. He graduated from Yale College in 1834; studied theology at Yale Divinity School for two years (1838–40), and was ordained, June 10, 1841, pastor of the Congregational Church in Plainville, where he continued for two years. He then retired from the ministry and removed to Buffalo, N. Y., where he engaged in manufacturing until 1853. He died at his native place, Jan. 12, 1881. See *Obituary Record of Yale College*, 1188.

Cowles, George, a Congregational minister, was born in Connecticut in 1798. He graduated from Yale College in 1821, and from Andover Theological Seminary in 1824; was ordained Jan. 18, 1826, and became pastor at South Danvers (now Peabody), Mass., in 1827. He was lost at sea, near Cape Hatteras, in the wreck of the *Home*, Oct. 9, 1839. See *Trien. Cat. of Andover Theol. Sem.* 1870, p. 57.

Cowles, Henry, D.D., a Congregational minister, was born at Norfolk, Conn., April 24, 1803. He pursued his preparatory studies under Rev. Ralph Emerson, of Norfolk; graduated from Yale College in 1826, and spent two years in Yale Divinity School; was ordained an evangelist, July 1, 1828, at Hartford; for two years was acting pastor at Ashtabula and Sandusky, O., and then served in that relation at Austinburg, to July 29, 1831, when he was installed pastor there, remaining until November, 1835. From that time to 1838 he was professor of Greek and Latin in Oberlin College, O.; the next ten years professor of ecclesiastical history, church polity, and Old Testament language and literature; from 1848 to 1862 editor of the *Oberlin Evangelist;* and subsequently was engaged in literary labor at the same place. From 1851 he was trustee of the college. He died in Janesville, Wis., Sept. 6, 1881. Dr. Cowles was the author of the following publications: *The Holiness of Christians in the Present Life* (1841):—*Gospel Manna for Christian Pilgrims* (1847):—*Commentaries on the Scriptures*, in 16 vols., covering the whole Bible, as follows: *The Minor Prophets* (1867):—*Ezekiel and Daniel* (1869):—*Isaiah* (eod.):—*Jeremiah* (eod.):—*Proverbs, Ecclesiastes, and Song of Solomon* (1870):—*Revelation* (1871):—*Psalms* (1872):—*Pentateuch* (1874):—*Hebrew History from the Death of Moses to the Close of Scripture Narrative* (1875)—*Gospel and Epistles of John* (1876):—*Job* (1877):—*Hebrews* (1878):—*The Shorter Epistles* (1879):—*The Longer Epistles* (1880):—*Luke's Gospel and Acts* (1881):—*Matthew and Mark* (eod.). The profits arising from the sale of these commentaries he gave to the missionary cause. Dr. Cowles also edited a volume of Mr. Finney's *Sermons*, in 1876, entitled *Gospel Themes*, and published a volume entitled *Sin and Suffering in the Universe*. See *Cong. Year-book*, 1882, p. 26; *Obituary Record of Yale College*, 1882.

Cowles, Henry Brown, a minister of the Methodist Episcopal Church South, was born in Fauquier County, Va., Nov. 2, 1803. He experienced conversion in 1818; was licensed to exhort in 1830, and in 1831 connected himself with the Virginia Conference, in which he filled the most prominent stations, to the close of his life, Nov. 28, 1874. Mr. Cowles, became, in 1854, the financial agent of Randolph-Macon College, and raised for the institution an endowment of $100,000. He had a strongly marked character; was noted for his caution and prudence, his sincerity and courage; was a keen judge of character, and a skilful manager of men; was punctual, industrious, and painstaking. See *Minutes of Annual Conferences of the M. E. Church South*, 1875, p. 141; Simpson, *Cyclop. of Methodism*, s. v.

Cowles, Orson, a Congregational minister, was born at East Hartland, Conn., Jan. 14, 1801. He studied at Yale College, and in the theological department, not graduating, however. He was ordained pastor of the Church in North Woodstock in 1832; taught in North Haven two years, and was district secretary of the American Board from 1840 to 1860. He died at North Haven, Dec. 23, 1860. See *Cong. Quarterly*, 1861, p. 211.

Cowles, R. J., a Free-will Baptist minister, was born in Belchertown, Mass., July 10, 1796. He was converted in 1811, and united with the Congregational

Church in his native town. At the age of nineteen he removed to Genesee County, N. Y., and took up his residence in what is now South Byron. In 1823 he removed to Brokenstraw, Pa., and a year later to Sugar Grove. Here he opened a Sabbath-school, and began to preach, receiving a license, in 1832, from the Presbytery of Pennsylvania. In 1839 he united with a Free-will Baptist Church at Wrightsville, and was ordained at Sugar Hill, Feb. 29, 1842. He continued to preach for many years, and died March 29, 1874. See *The Morning Star*, July 22, 1874. (J. C. S.)

Cowmeadow, JOHN, an English Methodist preacher, was received by the British Conference in 1783. In much weakness of body he labored faithfully until his death, in 1786. Wesley, in his *Journal*, speaks of him as a martyr to long and loud preaching; but says, "He had the ornament of a meek and quiet spirit, and was of exemplary behavior." See Atmore, *Meth. Memorial*, s. v.

Cownley, JOSEPH, an early English Methodist preacher, was born at Leominster, Herefordshire, June 26, 1723. Under Wesley's preaching, Cownley was converted at Bath, whither his business as travelling secretary to a magistrate sometimes called him. He was admitted to the itinerancy by Wesley, in Bristol, in 1746. He preached in Staffordshire, confronting the mobs, in Cornwall, Newcastle-upon-Tyne (1747), Ireland (at the peril of his life), and in various parts of England. In spite of a severe fever in 1755, he labored in Newcastle, Edinburgh, and Glasgow. He died at Newcastle, Oct. 8, 1792. Unusually sensitive to discord, Cownley, from his sympathy with the popular movement, was involved in the great agitation of 1792, which resulted in the formation of the Methodist New Connection. He was a life-long friend of the Wesleys and Whitefield. Cownley was a thorough theologian, having read, it is said, nearly every theological work in the language. His mind was capable of abstruse investigation, and Wesley called him withal "one of the best preachers in England." He loved to carry the gospel to the retreats of wretchedness. See *Minutes of the British Conference*, 1793; Jackson, *Early Meth. Preachers*, ii, 1-47 (by John Saulter, 1794); Stevens, *Hist. of Methodism*, iii, 39, 91-93; Smith, *Hist. of Methodism*, ii, 42-44; Atmore, *Meth. Memorial*, p. 90 sq.; Crowther, *Portraiture of Methodism* (Lond. 1814, 2d ed.), p. 346-350.

Cowper, Charles Philip, a Methodist Episcopal minister, was born at Baden, Germany, April 8, 1851. He emigrated to New York city with his parents when four years of age; experienced conversion in 1864; assisted in establishing the first mission for colored people, under the auspices of the Methodist Episcopal Church, in New York city; gave himself to that work with remarkable zeal and self-denial; studied three years at the Wesleyan Academy, Wilbraham, Mass., preaching nearly every Sunday; and in 1873 entered the New York East Conference, wherein he labored with abundant success till his death, July 11, 1875. Mr. Cowper was a young man of considerable promise, sweet in spirit, unassuming in manner, and irreproachable in conduct. His mind was strong, and his will consecrated. See *Minutes of Annual Conferences*, 1876, p. 61.

Cowper, John, a Scotch clergyman, brother of the bishop of Galloway, was a supply at the High Kirk, Edinburgh, in 1586, and became afterwards minister. He refused to pray for queen Mary in the terms of the king's command, for which he was imprisoned in the castle of Blackness; the city paid his expenses, obtained his release, and he was transferred to the Collegiate Church, Glasgow, in 1587, having charge of the eastern district and parish. He was a member of the assemblies of 1593 and 1596, and was appointed to visit that at Lothian in 1602. In 1595 his life was threatened by two men, but the chief offender begged pardon on his knees before the presbytery. He died Dec. 25, 1603. See *Fasti Eccles. Scoticanæ*, i, 7; ii, 7.

Cowper, Spencer, D.D., an English clergyman, second son of lord-chancellor William Cowper, was born in London in 1713. He was educated at Exeter College, Oxford, and became rector of Fordwich, prebendary of Canterbury in 1742, and dean of Durham in 1746. He died March 25, 1774. He published some single *Sermons and Discourses*, and a *Dissertation on the Distinct Powers of Reason and Revelation* (1773). See Allibone, *Dict of Brit. and Amer. Authors*, s. v.; Chalmers, *Gen. Biog. Dict.* s. v.

Cowper, William, an eminent English poet, grand-nephew of lord-chancellor Cowper, grandson of a judge in the court of common pleas, and son of John Cowper, rector of Great Berkhamstead, in Hertfordshire, was born there, Nov. 26, 1731. He appears from his infancy to have been delicate in mind and body, and, after having spent two years of misery in a country school, was placed at Westminster School, where he remained till he was eighteen years old. He was then articled to a solicitor in London, called to the bar in 1754, and resided in the Middle Temple for eleven years, neglecting law, contributing a few papers to *The Connoisseur*, and gradually exhausting his little patrimony. In 1763 one of his powerful kinsmen appointed him to two clerkships in the House of Lords. Doubts of his competency, and the fear of appearing in public assemblies, developed the tendency to insanity which lurked within him. He made several attempts to destroy himself; and was consigned for eighteen months to a lunatic asylum at St. Albans. On his release in 1765, subsisting on the remnant of his property, with assistance from relatives, he took up his residence at Huntingdon, and became a boarder in the house of Mr. Unwin, a clergyman. That gentleman dying two years afterwards, the widow and Cowper removed to Olney, in Buckinghamshire. John Newton was curate of the place; and his religious views accorded with those which had been adopted by the poet, although the association rather increased than lessened the morbid tendencies of the latter. In 1776 appeared the *Olney Hymns*, of which some of the best were furnished by Cowper; but it was only about the time of their publication that the unhappy poet was freed from a second confinement, which had lasted for nearly four years. He had still earlier tried his hand at poetry, having translated an elegy of Tibullus at the age of fourteen, and at eighteen he wrote some beautiful verses *On Finding the Heel of a Shoe*; but diffidence repressed his talents until he had passed his fortieth year. Mrs. Unwin, anxious to engage his mind safely, now urged him to prosecute verse-making. *The Progress of Error* was written; *Truth*, *Table-Talk*, and *Expostulation* followed it; and these with other poems made up a volume which was published in 1782, receiving the approbation of Johnson and other critics, but meeting little attention from the public. The poet's fame, however, was decisively established by his next volume, which, appearing in 1785, contained *The Task* and other poems. The publication of this work, indeed, was an æra in the history of English poetry. It was the point of transition from the eighteenth century to the nineteenth. Natural language was substituted for artificial; themes of universal interest were handled, instead of such as told only on a few cultivated minds; even the seriousness and solemnity of the leading tone had a striking attraction, while it was relieved both by strains of pathos and touches of satiric humor. More novel and original than anything else were those minute and faithful delineations of external scenery, to which no parallel had been seen since Thomson's *Seasons*. Perhaps, also, the didactic form of Cowper's poems, giving them an equivocal character which hovers continually between poetry and argumentation, was an additional recommendation to readers who had long been unaccustomed to the finer and higher kinds of poetical invention. *John Gilpin* is a specimen of his humorous genius, the subject of which is said to have been suggested to him by Lady Austen, one of his literary friends. Cowper now spent six years on his translation of Homer, which appeared in 1791. The neglect which it has experienced is certainly undeserved, at least by his *Odyssey*. His mental alienation, which had repeatedly threatened him with a return, overcame him completely in 1794; and the last six years of his life produced hardly any literary fruits except the pathetic *Castaway*. The death of his friend Mrs. Unwin, in 1796, threw him into a gloom which was hardly ever again dispelled, and he died at Dereham, April 25, 1800. Cowper's chief characteristics are simplicity, individuality, transparency of ideas, bold originality, singular purity, and experimental Christian piety. All his poems bear marks of his mature authorship, his accurate rather than extensive scholarship, and his unwearied desire to benefit mankind. His Christian life, though oppressed by disease, was true, useful, and lovely; and even while suffering under the deranged idea that he was an exception to God's general plan of grace, it is delightful to perceive that it had no tendency to lead him aside from the path of rectitude, or to relax in the least his efforts to maintain the life of religion in his soul. His poems remain a treasure of deep Christian pathos and earnest, pensive thought, and many of them have been incorporated into nearly every collection of religious hymns. Cowper's works were first collected by his friend Hayley (1803-4, with a *Life*); but the best edition is that of Southey (1833-37, also with a *Life*, the most carefully written, and with additional *Letters*, in *Bohn's Standard Library*, 1853). For a copious view of the literature, see Allibone, *Dict. of Brit. and Amer. Authors*, s. v.

Cow-worship. The Egyptian goddesses Athor and Isis, represented as having the head of a cow; Astarte, the Syrian goddess, as wearing the horns of a cow; and the Grecian Juno as having a cow's eyes. Venus is sometimes figured as a cow giving milk to her calf. Io changed into a cow is an emblem of the earth. The cow of Minos, which on each day was white, red, and black, seems to represent the three different aspects which the earth presents in the bright blaze of noon, in the purple tinge of evening or morning, and in the dark shades of night. In the fables of Brahminism, the earth takes the form of a cow named Kamadhuka, which gives its worshippers all they desire. Among the Adighe, a race of Circassians, a cow is offered in sacrifice to *Achin*, the god of horned cattle. According to the cosmogony of the Scandinavian Edda, before the heavens and the earth were created, the cow Audumla was produced in the place where the southern fires of Muspelheim melted the ice of Niflheim. This cow denotes the cosmogonic earth. Among the Hindûs the cow is held in the greatest veneration, particularly the species called the Brahmin or sacred cow, and by many families a cow is kept for the mere purpose of worshipping it. See APIS; MOSCHOLATRY.

Cox, Alfred, an English Baptist minister, was converted in early life; baptized at seventeen at the Counterslip chapel, Bristol, and began to preach in the villages around. He was an agent for the Baptist Home Missionary Society twenty-two years; was pastor at Dunchurch seven years, and was a consistent and devoted minister. He died at Cradley, June 9, 1870.

Cox, Daniel, a Methodist Episcopal minister, was born at Barnard, Vt., in August, 1801. He professed conversion in early manhood, received license to exhort in 1828, and in 1829 entered the East Maine Conference. Failing health in 1838 obliged him to become a superannuate, which relation he sustained to the close of his life, Dec. 28, 1875. See *Minutes of Annual Conferences*, 1876, p. 90.

Cox, Francis Augustus, D.D., LL.D., a distinguished English Baptist minister, was born at Leighton Buzzard, Bedfordshire, in 1783. He was brought up religiously, baptized by his grandfather, entered Bristol College at eighteen, under Dr. Ryland, and graduated at Edinburgh University. In 1804 he was ordained pastor of the Church at Clipston, Northampton, by Sutcliffe, Fuller, and Robert Hall, and the Church prospered so much a new large chapel had to be built. He next succeeded Robert Hall at Cambridge. In 1811 he became pastor of the Church at Shore Place, Hackney, where also his success was such that in 1812 a new chapel was built in Mare Street. Being settled in London, he took an active part in establishing and conducting the *Baptist Magazine*, and was connected with numerous philanthropic institutions. He died at Clapton, London, Sept. 5, 1853. Dr. Cox was the author of some valuable works, including an account of his visit to America. See Cathcart, *Baptist Encyclop.* p. 284.

Cox, Gershom Flagg, A.M., a Methodist Episcopal minister, twin brother of Melville B. Cox, was born at Hallowell, Me., Nov. 9, 1799. He joined the Church at the age of eighteen; was soon licensed to preach, and gave great promise of usefulness; spent several years in Belfast in business, and in 1830 joined the Maine Conference, in which, and in the New England Conference, he labored with but few intermissions as a supernumerary, for more than thirty years. In 1864 he became superannuated, which relation he sustained until his decease in Salem, Nov. 16, 1879. Mr. Cox was a plain, earnest, instructive, Biblical preacher. In his prime he was one of the mighty preachers in New England Methodism, filling with great acceptability her chief pulpits. He was a superior pastor, spiritually minded, conscientious, and prayerful; a man of broad self-culture; was a ready and clear writer, for many years editing *The Maine Wesleyan Journal;* and in addition to numerous contributions to the *Quarterly Review* he was the author of the memoir of Melville B. Cox. See *Minutes of Annual Conferences*, 1880, p. 65.

Cox, G. Davenport, a Baptist minister, was born at Cornwallis, N. S. He was ordained at Clementsvale, Jan. 4, 1865, labored there for several years, then became pastor at Hillsburg, where his fervent labors broke down his constitution, and he died March 25, 1879. His zeal was unflagging, his love for his flock intense. See *Baptist Year-book for the Maritime Provinces*, 1879; Bill, *Fifty Years with the Baptists*, p. 554.

Cox, James, a Wesleyan Methodist missionary, was a native of Bermuda. In 1823 he received his first appointment to his native islands, and in the following year was sent to the West Indies, where he was stationed at St. Kitt's, Antigua, Dominica, Tortola, and Jamaica. Having a strong constitution, he undertook labors to which few men would have been equal. He died at Morant Bay, Jamaica, May 30, 1859. See *Minutes of the British Conference*, 1859.

Cox, John (1), an English Baptist minister, was born in 1746. He commenced ministerial labors in the connection of the countess of Huntington, but afterwards joined a Baptist Church, and for forty-two years was pastor at Horsington, Somerset, where he continued to preach until his death, Jan. 9, 1827. See *New Baptist Miscellany*, 1827, p. 124. (J. C. S.)

Cox, John (2), an English Baptist minister, was born at Lambourn, Berkshire, May 5, 1802. He was converted early in life, entered the ministry soon after he was twenty-one years of age, and during his long career was pastor successively of churches in Reading, Woolwich, and Ipswich, in all of which places he was held in deservedly high esteem as a godly, faithful, and laborious minister of the gospel. He spent his last years in occasional preaching, chiefly in a small chapel near his residence at Foots Cray, in Kent. He died March 17, 1878. He wrote books, pamphlets, and articles for the press in great numbers. See (Lond.) *Baptist Hand-book*, 1880, p. 293.

Cox, John Goodwin, an English Wesleyan minister, grandson of Rev. John Goodwin, one of Wesley's preachers, was born at Bilston, Staffordshire, Oct. 31, 1815. He was pious from his youth; entered the ministry in 1836; died in London, April 1, 1878, and was buried at Wrexham, where he had settled as a supernumerary during the previous year. He was a man of sterling intellect and high moral worth; was well read in philosophy, history, and elegant literature; his sermons were clear, elaborate, sententious, forcible. See *Minutes of the British Conference*, 1878, p. 36.

Cox, John Hayter, an English Congregational minister, was born at Portsea, March 26, 1768, and received his ministerial education at Gosport Academy. In 1789 he began to preach at Fareham, Hampshire, and labored there eighteen years. In 1809 he became pastor at St. Albans, and after five years went to Hadleigh, in Suffolk, where he was installed Oct. 26, 1814. In 1829 he removed to Uley, Gloucestershire, but relinquished this charge, and at the same time the ministry, in 1839, and retired to Kingston, Surrey. He died Jan. 5, 1848. He published, *A Harmony of Scripture*, some anonymous pamphlets, and a *Sermon*. See (Lond.) *Cong. Year-book*, 1848, p. 219.

Cox, Luther J., the bard of the Methodist Protestant Church, was born in Maryland, Dec. 27, 1791. He was licensed to preach in the Methodist Episcopal Church in 1819, but afterwards left it; and was among the first to organize and set in operation the Methodist Protestant Church, in which he acted as a zealous, unstationed minister until 1869, and then was received as a supernumerary member in the Maryland Annual Conference. He died July 26, 1870. With an ardent and devotional temperament he possessed a genius and talent for poetry. He is the author of several popular hymns, especially "An alien from God and a stranger to grace." See Cobhouer, *Founders of the Meth. Prot. Church*, p. 213.

Cox, Margaret, a minister of the Society of Friends, was born in 1814. She labored "with much earnestness and love, yet with becoming modesty. In many instances she was enabled to make full proof of her ministry." She died near Lawrence, Kan., Nov. 12, 1878. See *Friends' Review*, xxxii, 197. (J. C. S.)

Cox, Michael, an Irish prelate, was bishop of Ossory in 1743, and became archbishop of Cashel in 1754. He published a *Sermon* (Dublin, 1748). See Allibone, *Dict. of Brit. and Amer. Authors*, s. v.

Cox, Nehemiah, D.D., an English Particular Baptist, was born at Bedford, being a member of John Bunyan's Church there. He was well educated, and "a very excellent, learned, and judicious divine." He was ordained in October, 1671; in 1673 preached for some time at Hitchin; then at Cranfield; and in 1675 went to London, and was ordained joint pastor of the Church at Petty France, where he continued till the Revolution in 1688. He is said to have been a good Greek and Hebrew scholar, and to have been imprisoned in early life for preaching. He published two *Sermons*, one on the Covenants, against Mr. Whiston; the other an ordination sermon. He died in 1688. See Wilson, *Dissenting Churches*, ii, 185.

Cox, Philip, a Methodist Episcopal minister, was born at Frome, Somersetshire, England. He joined the Wesleyans when about eighteen; and, having emigrated to America, labored in the itinerancy about sixteen years, travelling extensively through the United States. He died Sept. 8, 1793. Mr. Cox was a man of small stature, great spirit, quick apprehension, and sound judgment. See *Minutes of Annual Conferences*, 1794, p. 54.

Cox, Richard, a minister of the Protestant Episcopal Church, was born in New York city in 1808. He was designed for mercantile life, but, comparatively late, entered the ministry, graduating from Columbia College in 1833. Having finished the course at the General Theological Seminary, he was ordained deacon in 1836; was missionary pioneer at Vicksburg, Miss.; rector for several years of St. John's Church, Troy, N. Y.; then of St. Paul's Parish, Woodbury, Conn.; a year or two after became rector of Zion Church, New York city, retaining this position for thirteen years; afterwards was rector of St. John's, Santa Cruz, W. I.; and a short time before his death returned to New York city, where he died, Dec. 16, 1860. See *Amer. Quar. Church Review*, 1861, p. 186.

Cox, Samuel Hanson, D.D., LL.D., an eminent Presbyterian divine, was born at Rahway, N. J., Aug. 25, 1793. His father, who died in 1801, was at that time engaged in a mercantile enterprise in New York city. He was descended from a family which in the 17th century had settled on the eastern shore of Maryland, and was connected for several generations with the Society of Friends. He was educated at Weston, Pa., also received private instruction in Philadelphia, and was a law student in Newark, N. J. In the war of 1812 he served in a volunteer company of riflemen. He studied theology in Philadelphia under Dr. Wilson, was ordained in 1817, and soon after accepted the pastorate of Mendham, Morris Co., N. J. In 1821 he removed to New York city as pastor of the Presbyterian Church in Spring Street, and went from thence to Laight Street, on St. John's Park, in 1825. His congregation here was largely composed of the leading merchants of the city. During the prevalence of the cholera he remained at his post until stricken down by the disease.

Dr. Cox took a leading part in the foundation of the University of the City of New York, and in the literary conventions which were called to aid in its organization. He was appointed to open the instructions of the university with the late Dr. McIlvaine, afterwards bishop of Ohio, and delivered one of the two memorable courses of lectures in the winter of 1831–32, his department being that of moral philosophy.

In impaired health, Dr. Cox visited Europe in 1833, where a speech which he delivered at that time, at the anniversary of the British and Foreign Bible Society in London, gained him great distinction and opened the way to high honors and attentions.

He was elected professor of pastoral theology in the Theological Seminary at Auburn in 1834, and accepted the position; but in 1837 he became pastor of the first Presbyterian congregation in Brooklyn, L. I., where he built a new church in Henry Street. For a long time, both in Brooklyn and New York, he maintained a position of great eminence with unvarying popularity.

In 1845, Dr. Cox attended in London the Evangelical Alliance, of which he was a leading member, and on his return was exposed to peril of shipwreck on the coast of Ireland, when the steamer *Great Britain* was stranded in the bay of Dundrum. In 1852, his health declining, he visited Nassau; but with so little good effect that, against the remonstrances of his people and the most liberal proposals on their part, he resigned his charge and retired to a pleasant property which they enabled him to purchase at Owego, Tioga Co., N. Y. He considered his career as a pastor at an end, but frequently delivered lectures and sermons in New York for several years subsequently.

Dr. Cox for many years was professor of ecclesiastical history in the Union Theological Seminary of New York, and also presided for a time over the Female College at Le Roy. For the last twelve years of his life he lived in great retirement in Westchester County. He died there, Oct. 2, 1880.

The anti-slavery sentiment predominant in England made a great impression on Dr. Cox during his visit there, and although he publicly defended his country while abroad, he soon after his return preached a celebrated sermon against slavery, which, although moderate in tone, drew upon him, as a conspicuous person, a great share of the violence with which the anti-slavery agitators were then visited. He was never identified, however, with their extreme measures, and afterwards took a leading conservative position on all questions connected with the South, which for a long time agitated the Presbyterian Church. In other questions which for a time divided that denomination, his theological standing was with the new school, of which he was a prominent champion; in the order and discipline of his Church, however, he maintained the highest and most thorough old-school position, so far as conformity to the standard is concerned. Although much criticised for personal eccentricities, and especially for a pompous Latinity of style, Dr. Cox has been generally recognised as a man of high character and commanding talents, of great boldness in expressing his strong convictions, and of singular power and magnetism as an orator. As a consistent Christian, his great purity and marked simplicity of character secured to him, through a long and useful life, the uniform respect of his fellow-men.

Dr. Cox wrote largely for the press. Among his publications were, *Quakerism not Christianity* (N. Y. 1833, 8vo):—*Interviews, Memorable and Useful* (N. Y. 1853, 12mo), etc. See *N. Y. Tribune*, Oct. 4, 1880; *N. Y. Observer*, Oct. 7, 1880; Allibone, *Dict. of Brit. and Amer. Authors*, s. v.

Cox, Samuel J., a Methodist Episcopal minister, was born in Monmouth County, N. J., Nov. 2, 1789. He joined the Church in 1809, was licensed to preach in 1812, and not long after admitted on trial in the Philadelphia Conference. He filled successively the following appointments: Sussex Circuit; Snow Hill; Kensington, Phila.; Wilmington, Del.; Union Charge, Phila.; and Salem, N. J. In 1821 he located and removed to Zanesville, O., where he remained until his death, Aug. 23, 1870. Mr. Cox was editor of the *Muskingum Messenger* from 1823 to 1835, and filled various civil offices with eminent ability. (W. P. S.)

Cox, Thomas L., a Methodist Episcopal minister, was born in Washington County, Ky., Jan. 15, 1809; experienced religion at the age of ten; joined the Tennessee Conference when twenty-five, and was immediately transferred to the Alabama Conference, wherein he served the Church with zeal and fidelity until his death, Jan. 18, 1836. See *Minutes of Annual Conferences*, 1836, p. 487.

Cox, William (1), an English Wesleyan minister entered the ministry in 1789, preached for seventeen years, and died at Swansea, Oct. 15, 1809. His life and ministry displayed the attractive charms of genuine Christianity. See *Minutes of the British Conference*, 1810.

Cox, William (2), an English Congregational minister, was born in Warminster in 1813. Removing to Bristol in 1840, he joined the Church in Newfoundland Street Chapel, in that city, the same year. He zealously employed himself in efforts to do good, and having entered the ministry, was sent to Fovant by the Wilts Association, in connection with the Home Missionary Society in London, in 1849, and labored there till 1852, when he was ordained. Failing health compelled him to relinquish his charge in April, 1853, and on May 14 of that year he died. See (Lond.) *Cong. Year-book*, 1854, p. 221.

Coxcie (or **Coxis**), Michael, a reputable Flemish painter, was born at Mechlin in 1497, and was a scholar of Van Orley; afterwards went to Rome, where he applied himself to the study of Raphael. On his return to Flanders he painted many works for the churches, the best of which are at Brussels. *The Last Supper*, in St. Gudule; and *The Death of the Virgin*, in Notre Dame. He died at Antwerp in 1592. See Chalmers, *Biog. Dict.* s. v.; Hoefer, *Nouv. Biog. Générale*, s. v.; Spooner, *Biog. Hist. of the Fine Arts*, s. v.

Coxcox is the name given in Mexican mythology to the patriarch who, together with his wife, Xochiquetzal, escaped the deluge by constructing a boat of cypress wood. This legend is evidently a tradition from the history of Noah. See Deluge.

Coxe, Henry Octavius, a minister of the Church of England, was born in 1811, and educated at Westminster and at Worcester College, Oxford, graduating in 1833. He entered at once upon work in the MS. department at the library of the British Museum, and continued there till 1838, when he became one of the sub-librarians of the Bodleian library. He succeeded the late Dr. Bandinel as head librarian in 1860. On the part of the government Mr. Coxe was sent out to inspect the libraries in the monasteries of the Levant. He was an authority on the date and character of MSS., and he detected one of the forgeries palmed by M. Simonides upon the learned. He died July 10, 1881, at Oxford. Mr. Coxe was the editor and author of many works; the most important of all his labors being the new *Catalogue of the Bodleian Library*. He was curate in a London district while working at the museum; and he was in charge of Wytham, near Oxford, as curate or rector, for twenty-five years, until his death. He was Oxford select preacher in 1842, and Whitehall preacher in 1868; also an honorary fellow of Worcester and Corpus Christi colleges, and chaplain of the latter. (B. P.)

Coxe, Richard Charles, an eminent English divine, was born in 1800. He graduated at Worcester College, Oxford, in 1821, was ordained deacon in 1823, and priest in 1824; in 1841 became vicar of Newcastle-upon-Tyne; in 1843 honorary canon of Durham, and one of the select preachers before the University of Oxford; in 1853 archdeacon of Lindisfarne, with the vicarage of Englingham annexed; and in 1857 canon of Durham. He died at Englingham, Aug. 25, 1865. Archdeacon Coxe was the author of several valuable theological works, a number of sermons, and a few volumes of poems of a high order of merit. See *Appleton's Annual Cyclopædia*, 1865, p. 674.

Coxe, William (1), an English author and divine, was born in Dover Street, Piccadilly, London, March 7, 1747. He was educated at Eton, and at King's College, Cambridge. In 1768 he was chosen a fellow of the latter; and during his residence at the university distinguished himself by his classical attainments, twice gaining the bachelor's prize for the best Latin dissertation. He was ordained, and appointed curate of Denham in 1771; rector of Bemerton in 1788; canon-residentiary of Salisbury in 1803; and archdeacon of Wilts in 1805, which office he held till his death, June 8, 1828. Mr. Coxe, as tutor to the sons of several noblemen, spent, at various times, many years on the Continent, where he neglected no opportunity of collecting information about the countries which he visited. The result appeared in many volumes of travels and history, all of which are characterized by close observation, care, and research. Archdeacon Coxe published, also, several large topographical works, besides some of a religious character. A set of his historical works and travels is published in twenty-four volumes, imperial quarto. See *The* (Lond.) *Annual Register*, 1828, p. 237; Hart, *Manual of Eng. Literature;* Allibone, *Dict. of Brit. and Amer. Authors*, s. v.

Coxe, William (2), a Presbyterian minister, was born in Pennsylvania. He was a student in Jefferson College, and graduated at Princeton Theological Seminary in 1828. He was ordained an evangelist by the Presbytery of New Brunswick, Oct. 8 of the same year; was missionary to New Orleans, La., in 1829; stated supply at Apple Creek, O., from 1832 to 1836; at Lancaster in 1837; pastor there from 1838 to 1849; and thereafter at Piqua until his death, in 1856. See *Gen. Cat. of Princeton Theol. Sem.* 1881, p. 53.

Coxhead, Benjamin, an English Baptist minister, was born June 9, 1772, and baptized at Carter Lane, London, May 27, 1794. He pursued his theological studies at the academy in Bristol; and was ordained at Wild Street Church, London, Oct. 30, 1800, remaining there until 1807, when he removed to Truro, where, for the most of the time, he continued until 1820. For two or three years he was out of the pastorate, in consequence of ill-health. In April, 1824, he accepted a call to Winchester, and was pastor in that city seven years, from 1824 to 1831. He continued to reside in Winchester for five years, preaching when he could, and then removed to Newbury, where, without charge, he preached frequently, until laid aside by the infirmities of age. He died Nov. 12, 1851. See (Lond.) *Baptist Hand-book*, 1852, p. 46. (J. C. S.)

Coxida, ÉLIE DE, a French religious writer, was born near Furnes about 1140. In 1189 he became abbot of the monastery of Dunes (Cistercian), where he acquired extensive celebrity for his knowledge and virtue. He died in 1203, leaving only two *Sermons*, which have been published by Visch in the *Bibliotheca Scriptorum Ordinis Cisterciensis*. See Hoefer, *Nouv. Biog. Générale*, s. v.

Coxis. See COXCIE.

Coxow, THOMAS T., an English Methodist preacher, was born at Hull in 1812. In early life he was converted, and joined the New Connection Methodists. In 1834 he began to itinerate in their ministry, and for nearly ten years preached with acceptance in nine circuits, when, at Halifax, ill-health suspended his labors in 1843, and he retired to Hull, where he died, Aug. 17 of the same year. See *Minutes of the British Conference*.

Coyaco, COUNCIL OF (*Concilium Coyacense*), was held in 1050, at Coyaco, or Coyace, in the diocese of Orvietta, Spain, by Ferdinand I of Castile. Nine bishops attended, and thirteen decrees were published, relating partly to the Church and partly to the state.

2. Orders, under anathema, that all abbots and abbesses shall govern their houses according to the rule of St. Isidore or St. Benedict, and shall submit in all things to their bishop.

3. Orders that churches and the clergy shall be under the control of their bishop, and not under that of any lay person; that suitable vessels and ornaments be provided; that no chalice of wood or earthenware shall be allowed; that the altar shall be made entirely of stone, and shall be consecrated by the bishop. It also directs that in every church the proper priestly vestments shall be provided, viz. the surplice, amice, alb, cinctorium, belt, stole, maniple, and chasuble: also the vestments of the deacon, viz. amice, alb, and stole. Also it orders, that under the chalice shall be placed a paten, and over it a corporal of linen. The host to be made of fine flour, without any admixture; the wine and water to be pure, so that, in the wine and host and water, the sacred Trinity may be signified. That the vestments of priests ministering in the church shall reach to their feet. That they shall have no women in their houses except a mother, or aunt, or sister, or woman of approved character, who shall always be dressed entirely in black; and that they shall teach infants the Creed and Lord's Prayer.

5. Enjoins that archdeacons shall present for ordination only such clerks as shall know the whole psalter, with the hymns and canticles, epistles, gospels, and prayers.

6. Orders all Christian persons to go to church on Saturday evenings, and on Sunday to be present at the matins, mass, and at all the hours; to do no work, nor travel on that day, unless for the purposes of devotion, visiting the sick, burying the dead, executing a secret order of the king, or of defence against the Saracens. Those who break this canon are, according to their rank, either to be deprived of communion for a year, or to receive one hundred lashes.

11. Commands fasting on Friday.

12. Forbids the forcible seizure of those who have taken refuge in a church, or within thirty-one paces of it.

There appears to be some difference in the copies of these canons. See Labbe, *Concil.* ix, 1063.—Landon, *Man. of Councils*, s. v.; Richard et Giraud, *Bibliothèque Sacrée*, s. v.

Coyle, JOHN, a Scotch Congregational minister, was born at Montrose, July 26, 1842. He was converted in his eighteenth year; joined the Wesleyans at first, but soon after became a Congregationalist; received his ministerial education largely under private instructors; and was ordained at Forfar, April 26, 1866, where he labored with great ability, zeal, and devotedness until his death, July 1, 1868. See (Lond.) *Cong. Year-book*, 1869, p. 241.

Coypel, Antoine, a French painter, son and scholar of Noel, was born in Paris in 1661. He went to Rome when quite young, and studied the works of Raphael, Michael Angelo, and the Caracci. At the age of fifteen he returned to Paris with a very superficial knowledge of his profession. He was only nineteen when he painted his *Assumption*, for the Church of Notre Dame, and at twenty he was elected a royal academician. He was appointed painter to the king in 1715. His principal works are at Paris. They are *Christ Curing the Blind*, at the Carthusian convent; *Christ among the Doctors;* and *The Assumption*, in the Church of Notre Dame. He died in 1722. See Hoefer, *Nouv. Biog. Générale*, s. v.; Spooner, *Biog. Hist. of the Fine Arts*, s. v.

Coypel, Noel (surnamed *Le Poussin*), an eminent French painter, was born in Paris in 1628. He studied first under Poncet, and at the age of fourteen entered the school of Quillerier, where he made such rapid progress that his merit procured his election to the Academy in 1659, his reception-picture being *Cain Slaying Abel.* His celebrated *Martyrdom of St. James* was painted for the Church of Notre Dame about this time. He was appointed by the king director of the French Academy at Rome, where he went in 1672. His best productions after this were *The Virgin Caressing the Infant* and *The Holy Family*. He died in 1707. See Spooner, *Biog. Hist. of the Fine Arts*, s. v.; Hoefer, *Nouv. Biog. Générale*, s. v.

Coypel, Noel Nicolas, a French painter, was born in 1692, and was a son of Noel by a second marriage. He received his first instruction from his father, after which he studied in the Academy of Paris, and in 1728 was elected a member of that institution. His best works are the ceiling of the chapel of the Virgin in the Church of St. Saviour, and the altar-piece in the same chapel, representing *The Assumption*. He died in 1735. See Hoefer, *Nouv. Biog. Générale*, s. v.; Spooner, *Biog. Hist. of the Fine Arts*, s. v.

Coysevox, ANTOINE, an eminent French sculptor, was born at Lyons in 1640. Before he was seventeen he distinguished himself by a statue of the *Virgin*, and immediately went to Paris, where he studied under Lerambert and other masters. He produced some fine works, among which were the tomb of cardinal Mazarin, and the monument of Charles le Brun, in the Church of St. Nicolas. He died at Paris, Oct. 10, 1720. See Hoefer, *Nouv. Biog. Générale*, s. v.; Spooner, *Biog. Hist. of the Fine Arts*, s. v.

Cozad, JACOB, a Methodist Episcopal minister, was born July 2, 1819. He experienced religion in early life, received license to exhort in 1841, and in 1842 entered the Indiana Conference. In it he labored faithfully to the close of his life, April 13, 1863. See *Minutes of Annual Conferences*, 1863, p. 212.

Cozza, Carlo, an Italian painter, son and scholar of Giovanni Battista, was born at Ferrara about 1700. He painted several pictures for the churches of his native city, among which are *The Annunciation*, in the Chiesa Nuova; *St. Antonio*, in Santa Lucia; and *St. Francesco da Paolo*, in San Matteo. He died at Ferrara in 1769.

Cozza, Francesco, an Italian painter, was born at Istilo, in Calabria, in 1605, and studied at Rome under Domenichino. One of his best works was at Rome, and represented the *Vergine del Riscatto*, in the Church of Santa Francesca Romana. He died at Rome in 1682. See Hoefer, *Nouvelle Biographie Générale*, s. v.; Spooner, *Biographical History of the Fine Arts*, s. v.

Cozza, Giovanni Battista, an Italian painter, was born at Milan in 1676, and settled at Ferrara while very young, where he executed many works for the churches. The principal are, *The Conception*, in the cathedral; *The Holy Family*, in the Church of Ognissanti; *The Assumption*, in San Guglielmo; and *The Annunciation*, in Santa Lucia. He died at Ferrara in 1742. See Spooner, *Biog. Hist. of the Fine Arts*, s. v.; Hoefer, *Nouv. Biog. Générale*, s. v.

Cozza, Lorenzo, an Italian theologian, was born near Bolsena, March 31, 1654. He entered the order of the Observantists, and after having been successively professor of theology and vice-commissary of his order, was elected its minister-general, May 15, 1723. In December, 1726, Benedict XIII created him cardinal, and he was afterwards promoted to several other ecclesiastical offices. He died at Rome, Jan. 18, 1729, leaving various historical and archæological works in Latin, for which see Hoefer, *Nouv. Biog. Générale*, s. v.; Wetzer u. Welte, *Kirchen-Lexikon*, s. v.

Cozzando, Leonardo, an Italian biographer, was born at Rovato, near Brescia, in 1620. At the age of twelve he entered the order of Servites, and while young taught philosophy at Verona and Vienna. He afterwards became professor of theology, and regent of the College of St. Alexander of Brescia. At the age of twenty-five he was elected member of the Academy of the Erranti. He died Feb. 7, 1702, leaving, *Corsi di Penna* (Brescia, 1645):—*Ristretto dei Prelati della sua Religione* (ibid. 1673):—*Vite del P. Paolo Cigone e del P. Ottavio Pantagolo:—De Magisterio Antiquarum Philosopharum* (Cologne, 1682; Geneva, 1684):—*Libraria Bresciana* (Brescia, 1694); this work contains the lives of five hundred and thirty authors:—*Vago e Curioso Ristretto Profano e Sagro dell' Historia Bresciana* (ibid. eod.). See Hoefer, *Nouv. Biog. Générale*, s. v.

Cozzens, Samuel Woodward, D.D., a Congregational minister, was born in Mayfield, N. Y., Oct. 25, 1801. He graduated from Middlebury College in 1828, and from Andover Theological Seminary in 1831; was ordained at Marblehead, Mass.; became colleague of Rev. Samuel Dana in 1832; in 1837 pastor at Milton; and in 1847 acting pastor of the Second Church, Milton, remaining there until 1851. The Kingsborough (N. Y.) Presbyterian Church was the next in which he labored in the same capacity; and in 1853 he was installed in the Presbyterian Church at Mount Vernon, from which he was dismissed in 1859. During the next nine years he was acting pastor at Weybridge, Vt.; then, in the same relation, he served the Church at South Plymouth, Mass., from 1868 to 1872. He died in Medfield, Aug. 7, 1875. See *Cong. Quarterly*, 1876, p. 422.

Crabb, John M., a Presbyterian minister, was born in Garrard County, Ky., in 1804. He was educated in the Miami University, Oxford, O., and studied theology in the Western Seminary at Allegheny, Pa. In 1838 he was licensed to preach, and engaged at Eaton and Alexandria; subsequently he was pastor of Lima, West Bethesda, and Union churches, in Ohio. He died March 17, 1859. He was a devoted laborer and one of the pioneers of the Church. See Wilson, *Presb. Hist. Almanac*, 1860, p. 69.

Crabbe, George, an English poet and divine, was born at Aldborough, Suffolk, Dec. 24, 1754. When fourteen years of age, being tolerably grounded in mathematics and classics, he was apprenticed to a surgeon near Bury St. Edmunds, but had no liking for the profession, and ultimately proceeded to London to make a trial of literature. For a time he was very unfortunate. At last, when threatened with arrest for debt, he made his case known to Edmund Burke, who received him in a very kindly manner, brought him into his family, introduced him to Fox, Reynolds, Johnson, and other distinguished men, and gave him his criticism and advice concerning the poem of *The Library*, which was published in 1781 (2d ed. 1783), and was favorably noticed. By the assistance of Burke he was enabled to prepare himself for admission to holy orders. In 1782 he was ordained curate of his native place, and shortly after appointed chaplain to the duke of Rutland, at Belvoir Castle. In 1785 he was presented to two small livings in Dorsetshire, in 1789 exchanged them for others in the vale of Belvoir, and in 1813 was preferred to the rectory of Trowbridge, which he held until his death, Feb. 8, 1832. Mr. Crabbe, in addition to the work above mentioned, published, *The Village* (1783):—*The Newspaper* (1785):—*The Parish Register* (1807):—*The Borough* (1810):—*Tales in Verse* (1812):—*Tales of the Hall* (1819). See *The North American Review*, 1834, p. 135; Hoefer, *Nouv. Biog. Générale*, s. v.; Rose, *Gen. Biog. Dict.* s. v.; Allibone, *Dict. of Brit. and Amer. Authors*, s. v.

Crabeth, Dirk and Wouter, two brothers, were very eminent Dutch painters on glass, born at Gouda, in Holland, and flourished about 1560. They executed many works of great merit, especially the magnificent windows of the great church at Gouda, on which are represented, *The Nativity*, *Christ Driving the Money-changers from the Temple*, *The Death of Holofernes*, and *The Profanation of the Temple by Heliodorus*. See Hoefer, *Nouv. Biog. Générale*, s. v.; Spooner, *Biog. Hist. of the Fine Arts*, s. v.

Crabtree, Abraham, an English Wesleyan minister, was born at Heptonstall, near Halifax, in 1785. He entered the ministry in 1811, and died on the Pateley-Bridge Circuit, June 15, 1851. See *Minutes of the British Conference*, 1851.

Crabtree, William, an English Baptist minister, was born near Heptonstall, Yorkshire, March 20, 1806. He was baptized June 14, 1827, studied under the Rev. R. Ingham; after a year's service in Duffield, Derbyshire, was assistant minister, for a time, with Rev. J. Taylor, at Hinckley, Leicestershire, and then removed to Lineholm, in Yorkshire, where he died, May 9, 1854. See (Lond.) *Baptist Hand-book*, 1855, p. 47. (J. C. S.)

Cradock, John, D.D., an Irish prelate, born at Wolverham, and educated at Cambridge, became rector of St. Paul's, Covent Garden, and subsequently chaplain to the duke of Bedford. He accompanied that nobleman to Ireland in 1757, was soon after elected to the see of Kilmore, and on Dec. 4 of the same year was consecrated. In 1772 he was translated to the see of Dublin. In 1773 he was one of the eighteen peers who protested against the passing of a bill for securing the repayment of money lent by Papists to Protestants on mortgages of land. He died Dec. 11, 1778. See D'Alton, *Memoirs of the Abps. of Dublin*, p. 344.

Cradock, Thomas, a missionary of the Church of England, was born at Wolverham, Bedfordshire, in 1718, and was educated at Cambridge. An attachment having sprung up between a sister of the duchess of Bedford and Thomas, he was persuaded by her friends to migrate to Maryland, where it is believed that he arrived in 1742. In October of that year the General Assembly passed an act for the erection of a chapel about twelve miles from Baltimore, to be called St. Thomas's. In 1745 it was made an independent parish. Mr. Cradock became its minister the same year, also keeping a school for several years. Between 1750 and 1753 he preached a sermon which made considerable impression, urging the necessity of electing a bishop in the colony. In 1753 he published a version of the Psalms in heroic verse. About 1763 Mr. Cradock became physically paralyzed, but retained his mental vigor, and continued to fulfil his Sabbath appointments until his death, May 7, 1770. He was a man of varied learning, an intense student, and a preacher of considerable power. See Sprague, *Annals of the Amer. Pulpit*, v, 111.

Cradock, Zachary, D.D., an English clergyman, was born in 1633, and educated at Queen's College, Cambridge. Some years after he was made canon residentiary of Chichester, and elected fellow of Eton College in 1672. In 1680 he was chosen provost of Eton. He died Oct. 16, 1695. Dr. Cradock is known to the world by the high character given him by his contemporaries, and by two fine sermons; viz., one on *Providence*, the other *On the Great End and Design of Christianity*. See Chalmers, *Biog. Dict.* s. v.; Allibone, *Dict. of Brit. and Amer. Authors*, s. v.

Crafts, ELIPHALET PORTER, a Unitarian minister, was born at North Bridgewater (now Brockton), Mass., Nov. 23, 1800. He was fitted for college by his father, who was a clergyman (a graduate of Harvard College in 1785), and graduated from Brown University in 1821. After being engaged for some time in teaching and occasional preaching, he was ordained in November, 1828, and settled in East Bridgewater, where he remained nearly eight years. In 1839 he became pastor in Sandwich, and continued until 1854. After this he resided in East Lexington, teaching, and preaching in vacant pulpits, as he had opportunity. Next, he was minister at Eastport, Me., from 1866 to 1876, and in the latter year removed to Waltham, Mass., where he died, Jan. 16, 1880. See *Brown University Necrology*, 1879-80. (J. C. S.)

Cragg, GEORGE, an English Congregational minister, was born in January, 1793. He joined the Church in early manhood, was ordained at Boroughbridge about 1827, labored there about seventeen years with great success, accepted a call to Leyburn, Yorkshire, where he preached fourteen years, and then removed to Harrowgate, where he died, Dec. 1, 1873. See (Lond.) *Cong. Year-book*, 1875, p. 319.

Craghead. See CRAIGHEAD.

Cragie (or **Craigie**), JOHN, is the name of two Scotch clergymen.

1. Took his degree at the University of St. Andrews in 1697; was licensed to preach in 1702; called to the living at Abercrombie in 1704, and ordained. He died before March 14, 1733, aged about fifty-six years. See *Fasti Eccles. Scoticanæ*, ii, 403.

2. Took his degree at Marischal College, Aberdeen, in 1761; was licensed to preach in 1767; appointed to the living at St. Fergus in 1773, and ordained; transferred to Old Deer in 1798, and died Oct. 9, 1821, aged eighty years. See *Fasti Eccles. Scoticanæ*, iii, 621, 640.

Craig, the name of a number of Scotch clergymen.

1. ALEXANDER (1), took his degree at the University of St. Andrews in 1636; was admitted to the living at Pettinain in 1641, and died in April, 1642, aged about twenty-six years. See *Fasti Eccles. Scoticanæ*, ii, 331.

2. ALEXANDER (2), took his degree at the University of Aberdeen in 1669; was licensed to preach in 1676; appointed to the living at Unst in 1688; deserted his charge about 1697; resided at Fraserburgh in 1702; intruded there in 1708, and was accused of intrusion in 1716. See *Fasti Eccles. Scoticanæ*, iii, 372, 441.

3. ARCHIBALD, took his degree at Edinburgh University in 1810; was licensed to preach in 1812; ordained as assistant in the living at Bedrule in 1832, and in that year published *Introduction to Greek Accentuation*. See *Fasti Eccles. Scoticanæ*, i, 488.

4. GEORGE (1), D.D., was licensed to preach in 1799; presented to the living at Kinross in 1803, and ordained in 1804; assumed the name of *Buchanan* in 1806, and died April 18, 1842. He published *An Account of the Parish*. See *Fasti Eccles. Scoticanæ*, ii, 598.

5. GEORGE (2), was licensed to preach in 1832; appointed to the living at Sprouston in 1834, and ordained in 1835; joined the Free Secession in 1843, and died Feb. 10, 1866. He published *A Sermon at the Opening of the Parish Church* (1838):—*An Account of the Auchterarder Case* (1839):—*A Memoir of Rev. John Sym*, his predecessor. See *Fasti Eccles. Scoticanæ*, i, 473.

6. HUGH, a Covenanter of Edinburgh, studied at Glasgow University in 1667; was for some years a merchant-burgess; was called to the living at Galashiels in 1692, and ordained. He died before April, 1714. See *Fasti Eccles. Scoticanæ*, i, 550.

7. JAMES (1), took his degree at Glasgow University in 1652; was called to the living at Killearn in 1658, and ordained; conformed to Episcopacy; was accused before the privy council of several charges of disloyalty, and acquitted; other charges being brought against him in 1690, he was ousted by the rabble. See *Fasti Eccles. Scoticanæ*, ii, 356.

8. JAMES (2), took his degree at Edinburgh University in 1655; was appointed to the living at Hoddam in 1661, and ordained; transferred to Selkirk in 1666, and to Tranent in 1676; was deprived for refusing the test in 1681; elected by a unanimous vote of the kirk-session, heritors, magistrates, and deacons, to the second charge, Canongate, Edinburgh, in 1687; obliged to remove to an old chapel near the Watergate in 1691; received into communion, and transferred to Duddingston in 1694. He died May 31, 1704, aged about seventy-two years. See *Fasti Eccles. Scoticanæ*, i, 89; iii, 360, 540, 620.

9. JAMES (3), was born at Thornton-loch, in August, 1669; took his degree at Edinburgh University in 1694; was called to the living at Bathans (Yester), in 1701, and ordained; rebuked in 1702 for riding on the Sabbath while preaching in the North; transferred to Dunbar in 1718; promoted to the Old Church, Edinburgh, in 1721, and died Jan. 31, 1731. He published *Poems on Divine Subjects* (Edinburgh, 1727):—*Sermons* (ibid. 1732-1738, 3 vols.). See *Fasti Eccles. Scoticanæ*, i, 15, 364, 369.

10. JAMES (4), a native of Innerwick, was elected doctor in Heriot's Hospital, Edinburgh, in 1739; licensed to preach in 1742; appointed to the living at Currie in 1752, and ordained; became presbytery clerk in 1753, and died June 24, 1792, aged seventy-two years. See *Fasti Eccles. Scoticanæ*, i, 146.

11. JAMES (5), A.M., was licensed to preach in 1795; presented to the living at Dalserf in 1805, and ordained; retired to England with the sanction of the presbytery, and died there, Nov. 9, 1845. See *Fasti Eccles. Scoticanæ*, ii, 281.

12. JOHN, was licensed to preach in 1760; appointed minister at Kirkpatrick-Fleming in 1764; transferred to Ruthwell in 1783, and died Dec. 16, 1798, aged sixty-one years. See *Fasti Eccles. Scoticanæ*, i, 622, 626.

13. ROBERT, A.M., was licensed to preach in 1824; appointed to Stanley chapel in 1826; presented to the living at New Cumnock in 1829, and ordained; transferred to Rothesay in 1835, when Gaelic was no longer required; joined the Free Secession in 1843, and died May 26, 1860, aged sixty-eight years. He published, *Theocracy* (1848):—*The Man Christ Jesus* (1855). See *Fasti Eccles. Scoticanæ*, ii, 105; iii, 30, 31.

14. THOMAS (1), took his degree at the University of St. Andrews in 1603, was licensed to preach in 1611; appointed to the living at New Spynie in 1624, and died in 1639, aged about fifty-six years. See *Fasti Eccles. Scoticanæ*, iii, 171.

15. THOMAS (2). took his degree at Glasgow University in 1617; was licensed to preach in 1620; admitted to the living at Largo before 1631, and continued in 1637, but was deposed in 1640. See *Fasti Eccles. Scoticanæ*, ii, 252.

16. THOMAS (3), took his degree at King's College, Aberdeen, in 1656; became schoolmaster of Dyke; was licensed to preach in 1659; presented to the living at St. Andrew's-Lhanbryd in 1663, and ordained; deprived in 1690 for nonjurancy, and died before 1719. See *Fasti Eccles. Scoticanæ*, iii, 165.

17. THOMAS (4), was licensed to preach in 1743; presented to the living at Guthrie in 1753; ordained in 1754, and died April 16, 1797. See *Fasti Eccles. Scoticanæ*, iii, 796.

18. WILLIAM, D.D., was born in Glasgow in February, 1709; took his degree at the university there; was licensed to preach in 1734; called to the living at

Cambusnethan in 1737, and ordained. He preached the principles of virtue and morality more frequently than his hearers had been accustomed to, so they opposed him; he was transferred to the West Church, Glasgow, in 1738; removed with his congregation to the new Church of St. Andrew in 1761, and died Jan. 13, 1784. Habitually pious, he arrested the attention without alarming the imagination, and touched the heart without rousing the passions. He published, *The Reverence which is Due to the Name of God* (1761):—*The Character and Obligations of a Minister of the Gospel* (1764):—*An Essay on the Life of Jesus Christ* (1767):—*Twenty Discourses on Various Subjects* (Lond. 1775; 2d ed., with *Life*, 1808, 2 vols.). See *Fasti Eccles. Scoticanæ*, ii, 24, 275; Chalmers, *Biog. Dict.* s. v.; Allibone, *Dict. of Brit. and Amer. Authors*, s. v.

Craig, Edward, an English divine, graduated at St. Edmund's Hall, Oxford, and was curate at Glentworth and Saxvy; successively at Watton and Clapham; St. James's, Edinburgh; Staines, Burton-Latimer, and, lastly, perpetual curate of St. James's, Pentonville: in all which places he was eminently useful. He died in 1850. Among his writings are, *Patriarchal Piety* (1826):—*Sermons* (1828). See (Lond.) *Christian Guardian*, April, 1850, p. 199; Allibone, *Dict. of Brit. and Amer. Authors*, s. v.

Craig, Elijah, a Baptist minister, was born in Virginia about 1740, and converted at the age of twenty-four. In 1765 he began to hold religious services in his own tobacco-house, and continued to preach as opportunity presented. He was once imprisoned for so doing, but nevertheless continued his labors. In 1786 he removed to Kentucky, where he died in 1808. See *Lives of Virginia Baptist Ministers*, p. 71-73. (J. C. S.)

Craig, John (1), a Baptist minister, was born in Dublin, Ireland. He came to Maryland, joined the Methodists, served on the British side in the war of independence, went to Nova Scotia in 1784, travelled through the province as a preacher; was ordained pastor of a Baptist Church at Ragged Island; removed to Connecticut in 1732, and remained there two years. He then returned to Nova Scotia, where he died, Dec. 13, 1737, in his eighty-eighth year. See Bill, *Hist. of Baptists in the Maritime Provinces*, p. 232.

Craig, John (2), a pioneer Presbyterian minister, was born in Ireland, Sept. 21, 1710, but was educated in America. He was licensed by the Donegal Presbytery in 1738, sent to Deer Creek, Md., and in 1739 to Opequhon Irish Tract, and other places in western Virginia. In 1740 he was ordained pastor at Shenandoah and South River, resigned in 1754, and died April 21, 1774. He was a man mighty in the Scriptures, in perils often, in labors abundant. (W. P. S.)

Craig, John Liggett, a Presbyterian minister, was born at Allegheny, Pa., Dec. 7, 1828. He graduated at Duquesne College, Pittsburgh, in 1846; studied theology in the Associate Reformed Seminary, Allegheny; was licensed by Monongahela Associate Reformed Presbytery in 1850, and in 1854 accepted a call to the Reformed Presbyterian Church at Princeton, Ind. In 1864 he was appointed chaplain of the 17th regiment Indiana Veterans. He died in July, 1866. See Wilson, *Presb. Hist. Almanac*, 1866, p. 260.

Craig, J. N., D.D., a Presbyterian minister, born in 1814, was licensed to preach by New Brunswick Presbytery, in 1836; pastor at Rogersville and New Providence, Tenn.; afterwards twenty-two years in Columbus, Miss., and six years in St. Louis, Mo.; professor of moral science in the University of Mississippi until 1880. He was moderator of the General Assembly in 1863. He died May 15, 1882. He was a man of superior intelligence and strong character. See *Christian Observer*, May 24, 1882.

Craig, Lewis, a Baptist minister, was born in Orange County, Va., about 1737, and converted in 1765. Being arrested June 4, 1768, while engaged in public worship, and thrown into jail at Fredericksburg, he preached to crowds of people through the prison bars. In 1770 he became pastor of the Upper Spottsylvania Church. In 1771 he was again imprisoned three months. After preaching in several places in Kentucky, he was pastor of South Elkhorn Church about nine years. In 1792 he moved to Bracken County, Ky., in which he organized several churches. He died suddenly about 1828. See Cathcart, *Baptist Encyclop.* p. 285. (J. C. S.)

Craig, Thomas, an English Congregational minister, was born in Edinburgh in 1780. He was converted in early life; received his ministerial training at Homerton College; and was ordained in 1802 at Bocking, where he labored until his death, June 21, 1865. See (Lond.) *Cong. Year-book*, 1866, p. 243.

Craig, Wheelock, a Congregational minister, was born at Augusta, Me., in July, 1824. He graduated at Bowdoin College in 1843, in 1847 at the Bangor Theological Seminary, and for several years was engaged in teaching. In 1849 he was ordained in New Castle, and the next year accepted a call to the Trinitarian Church in New Bedford, Mass. In May, 1868, he went abroad for his health, but died at Neufchatel, Switzerland, in November following. See *Hist. of Bowdoin College*, p. 577, 578. (J. C. S.)

Craighead, Alexander, a Presbyterian minister, was born in Pennsylvania. He was licensed by Donegal Presbytery in 1734, and sent to Middle Octorara and "over the river." He was ordained Nov. 18, 1735, but disputes arising from a difference of views, he was suspended. He joined Newcastle Presbytery in 1754; met with Hanover Presbytery in 1757, and was sent to Rocky River, in North Carolina, and to other vacancies. He died in March, 1766. See Webster, *Hist. of the Presb. Church in America*, 1857.

Craighead, John, a Presbyterian minister, a graduate of Princeton College, received ordination from Donegal Presbytery about 1767, and was pastor at Rocky Spring, Pa., until 1798. He died April 20, 1799. See Alexander, *Princeton College in the 18th Century*.

Craighead, Robert, Sr., a Scotch clergyman, took his degree at the University of St. Andrews in 1653; was ordained over the Presbyterian congregation at Castle Finn, County Donegal, Ireland, before 1661; went to Glasgow in June, 1689; had a call to fill vacancies in the city of Glasgow; returned to Ireland in 1690, and was admitted to Derry; went back to Glasgow in 1698; settled at his former charge about 1700, and died there in September, 1711, aged about seventy-eight years. He published *An Answer to a Discourse on the Inventions of Men in Worship* (1694):—*Advice to Communicants* (1695):—*Advice for Assurance of Salvation* (1702):—*Answer to the Bishop of Derry's Second Admonition* (1697):—*Warning and Advice to the Christian* (1701):—*Walking with God* (1712). See *Fasti Eccles. Scoticanæ*, ii, 16, 18.

Craighead, Robert, *Jr.*, an Irish Presbyterian minister, was born at Castle Finn, County Donegal, in 1684. He took his degree of A.M. at the University of Glasgow in 1702, studied divinity at Edinburgh and Leyden, and in 1709 was ordained colleague to Mr. Iredell, in Capel Street, or Mary's Abbey, Dublin, where he died, July 30, 1738. Both he and his father were brilliant and effective workers on behalf of the Irish Presbyterians. See Reid, *Hist. of the Presb. Church in Ireland*.

Craighead, Thomas, a Presbyterian minister, was a native of Scotland. He is said to have studied medicine as well as divinity, and, after being settled in Ireland for ten or twelve years, went, in 1715, to New England, and was employed in the ministry at Freetown, near Fall River, Mass., until 1723. In 1724 he was received by New Castle Presbytery, and became pastor at White Clay, Pa. In 1733 he was installed at Pequea, but was dismissed in 1736, and became a supply at Hanover Paxton, and Conedogwinnit. He was installed at Hopewell in 1738, and in April, 1739, he dropped dead in the pulpit. See Webster, *Hist. of the Presb. Church in America*, 1857.

Craighead, Thomas B., a Presbyterian minister, was ordained by the Presbytery of Orange in 1780. For a few months he preached at Sugar Creek, his native place, and then removed to Tennessee, where he was brought to trial before the presbytery for holding certain Pelagian views; and the controversy which arose lasted for many years. Mr. Craighead was one of the founders of Davidson Academy (afterwards Nashville University), and became its first president, which position he held for over two years. His publications are, *A Sermon on Regeneration:—Letters to Rev. J. P. Campbell:—The Philosophy of the Human Mind* (1833): —*The Powers and Susceptibilities of the Human Mind* (1834, 12mo):—*A Defence of the Elkhorn Association* (1822). Mr. Craighead excelled as an extemporaneous orator, but not as a writer. See Alexander, *Princeton College in the* 18th *Century*.

Craigie. See CRAGIE.

Craik, ALEXANDER, D.D., a Scotch clergyman, was licensed to preach in 1798; became rector at the Dundee Academy in 1809; was presented to the living at Liberton in 1813, and died at Edinburgh, Oct. 19, 1856, aged eighty-three years. He published, *A Letter to Mr. John Brown* (1820):—*A Sermon in the Scottish Pulpit:—An Account of the Parish.* See *Fasti Eccles. Scoticanæ*, i, 226, 227.

Crail, ADAM, a Scotch prelate, was promoted to the see of Aberdeen about 1207, and died in 1227. See Keith, *Scottish Bishops*, p. 106.

Crain, Eli B., a minister of the Methodist Episcopal Church South, was born in Boyle County, Ky., March 24, 1807. He was converted about 1826, in 1833 entered the Kentucky Conference, and, with the exception of three years, labored in the effective ranks until 1853. He died Jan. 10, 1867. See *Minutes of Annual Conferences of the M. E. Church South*, 1867 p. 161.

Crain, Francis M., a minister of the Methodist Episcopal Church South, was born in Autauga County, Ala., June 18, 1828, professed religion in 1847, in 1852 was licensed to preach and admitted into the Alabama Conference, and died April 19, 1859. See *Minutes of Annual Conferences of the M. E. Church South*, 1859, p. 160.

Crallo, a Welsh *saint* of the 6th century, was patron of Llangrallo, otherwise Coychurch, in Glamorganshire (Rees, *Welsh Saints*, p. 222).

Cram, JACOB, a Congregational minister, was born at Hampton Falls, N. H., Oct. 12, 1762, and graduated at Dartmouth College in 1782. He was ordained at Hopkinton, N. H., Jan. 25, 1789, and dismissed Jan. 5, 1792. He labored as a missionary among the Stockbridge Indians in western New York, until May, 1801, and then settled, without charge, in Exeter, N. H., where he died, Dec. 21, 1833. See *Hist. of the Mendon Association*, p. 223. (J. C. S.)

Cramb, A. B., a Baptist minister, was born in Weare, N. H., July 2, 1827. He removed to Illinois in 1840; settled in Woodford County, near Metamora; pursued his studies at Shurtleff College; was licensed to preach in 1848, and ordained Oct. 13, 1849, his principal pastorates being at Metamora, Ill., and St. Cloud, Minn. He died Feb. 19, 1857. See Cathcart, *Baptist Encyclop.* p. 286. (J. C. S.)

Crambeth, MATTHEW DE, a Scotch prelate, was bishop of the see of Dunkeld in 1289, and died in 1312. See Keith, *Scottish Bishops*, p. 81.

Cramer, Andreas, a Lutheran theologian of Germany, was born in 1582 at Heimersleben, near Magdeburg. He studied at Helmstädt, was in 1607 rector at Quedlinburg, and in 1615 pastor of St. John's at Magdeburg. During the thirty years' war he had to leave that place, and was appointed in 1631 superintendent at Mühlhausen, where he died in 1640. His writings, which are of a controversial character, are given in Jöcher, *Allgemeines Gelehrten-Lexikon*, s. v. (B. P.)

Cramer, Daniel, a Lutheran theologian of Germany, was born at Reetz, in the Neumark, Jan. 20, 1568, and died Oct. 5, 1637, at Stettin, being doctor and professor of theology, pastor of St. Mary's, and member of consistory. He wrote, *Sana Doctrina de Prædestinatione:—Schola Prophetica:—Arbor Hæreticæ Consanguinitatis:—Methodus Tractandi Textum Scripturæ Sacræ:—Isagoge ad Libros Propheticos et Apostolicos:—Disp. Theol. de Descensu Christi ad Inferos, de Regno Christi, de Quæstione: an Hæretico sit Fides Servanda:—De Distinguendo Decalogo quoad Præceptorum Numerum*, and others. See Jöcher, *Allgemeines Gelehrten-Lexikon*, s. v.; Winer, *Handbuch der theol. Lit.* i, 721, 764, 807; Hoefer, *Nouv. Biog. Générale*, s. v. (B. P.)

Cramer, Heinrich Matthias August, a Protestant theologian of Germany, was born Aug. 10, 1745. He studied at Halle, was in 1775 appointed pastor of St. Wipert's at Quedlinburg, and died April 12, 1801. He translated R. Simon's *Histoire Critique* into German, with valuable additions (Halle, 1776–1780), and wrote, *Briefe über Inquisitionsgericht und Ketzerverfolzung* (Leipsic, 1785, 2 vols.):—*Lebensgeschichte Jesu von Nazareth* (ibid. 1787). See Döring, *Die gelehrten Theologen Deutschlands*, i, 280 sq.; Winer, *Handbuch der theol. Lit.* i, 9, 74, 765; ii, 257, 394. (B. P.)

Cramer, Jean Jacob, a Swiss Protestant theologian, was born at Ellg, near Zurich, Jan. 24, 1673. After having travelled in Germany, France, Holland, and England, he was successively professor of Hebrew at Zurich and of theology at Herborn. He died at Zurich, Feb. 9, 1702, leaving, *Theologia Israelis* (Frankfort, 1705):—*Commentarius Posthumus in Codicem Succah* (Utrecht, 1720):—some dissertations, the most interesting of which are published under the title, *De Ara Exteriore Templi Secundi* (1697). See Hoefer, *Nouv. Biog. Générale*, s. v.; Jöcher, *Allgemeines Gelehrten-Lexikon*, s. v.

Cramer, Jean Rudolph, a learned Protestant divine of Switzerland, was born at Ellg, in the canton of Zurich, Feb. 14, 1678, and was instructed in the classics by his father. He studied medicine at first, but turned his attention to divinity in 1693, and was admitted into the ministry in 1699. In 1701 he went to Leyden, and in 1702 published his *Seven Dissertations on the Hilcoth Biccurim.* He was chosen Hebrew professor at Zurich on Sept. 18 of the same year. In 1705 he was appointed to teach sacred and profane history, and in 1725 was made professor of theology. He died July 14, 1737. His works are very numerous. Among them are *Constitutiones de Primitivis R. Mosis F. Maimonis:—Decas Thesium Theologicarum* (1704, 4to):—*De Summa Prædicationis Apostolicæ* (1725, 4to). See Chalmers, *Biog. Dict.* s. v.; Jöcher, *Allgemeines Gelehrten-Lexikon*, s. v.

Cramer, Johann Daniel, a Reformed theologian of Germany, was born at Hanau, May 5, 1672. In 1693 he was professor of philosophy and philology, and in 1709 was made doctor of theology on presenting a dissertation, *Disp. de Gratiæ Divinæ Progressu ad Posteros Credentium.* He died at Zerbst, Oct. 23, 1715. See Jöcher, *Allgemeines Gelehrten-Lexikon*, s. v. (B. P.)

Cramer, Johann Friedrich Heinrich, a Lutheran theologian of Germany, was born at Dahlen, Sept. 2, 1754. After being deacon at the Kreuz Kirche in Dresden, he was in 1815 appointed pastor there, and died Sept. 4, 1820. He published, *Kurze Erklärungen und Beobachtungen über Abschnitte der heil. Schrift* (Leipsic, 1811):—*Predigten über die Evangelien u. Epi-*

steln (Zittau, 1818, 1820, 1826, 2 vols.):—*Geschichte des Christenthums und der Kirche*:—*Ueber die Nachahmung Jesu* (Dresden, 1791; 5th ed. 1808):—*Beicht-und Communionbuch* (ibid. 1794; 15th ed. 1828). See Winer, *Handbuch der theol. Lit.* ii, 127, 134, 316, 361, 366. (B. P.)

Cramer, Johann Jacob, a Lutheran theologian of Germany, was born at Leipsic, March 11, 1658. He studied at his native place and at Wittenberg, was preacher at St. Thomas's and afterwards pastor of St. John's, at Leipsic, and died Jan. 11, 1702. He wrote, *De Promissionibus Vitæ Æternæ in Vet. Testamento*:—*De Syllogismo Christi in Joh. viii, 47*:—*De Vocatione Messiæ ad Sacerdotium*:—*Theologia Israelis* (published after his death, Frankfort, 1705):—*De Scholarum Perpetuo in Ecclesia Dei Usu* (Herborn, 1710). See Jöcher, *Allgemeines Gelehrten-Lexikon*, s. v.; Fürst, *Bibl. Jud.* i, 190. (B. P.)

Cramer, John Anthony, an English philologist of German extraction, was born in 1793 at Mitloedi, in the canton of Glarus, studied in England, and was in 1822 preacher at Binsey, in Oxfordshire. In 1831 he was made principal at New Inn Hall, Oxford, was in 1842 professor of history at Oxford University, and died at Brighton, Aug. 24, 1848. He is best known as the author of *Anecdota Græca Codicum Manuscriptorum Bibliothecæ Oxoniensis* (Oxford, 1834-37, 4 vols.):—*Anecdota Græca e Codicibus Manuscriptis Bibliothecæ Regiæ Parisiensis* (ibid. 1839-41, 4 vols.):—*Catenæ Græcorum Patrum in Novum Testamentum* (ibid. eod. 7 vols.):—*Study of Modern History* (ibid. 1843). See Hoefer, *Nouv. Biog. Générale*, s. v. (B. P.)

Cramer, John Kearsley, a Presbyterian minister, was born at Williamsport, Md., Sept. 24, 1824. He graduated from Jefferson College in 1848, and studied theology part of a year in Princeton Theological Seminary. He was stated supply at Charlotte Court-house, Va., in 1852 and 1853; also at Washington, D. C., in 1854 and 1855; ordained by the Presbytery of Carlisle, April 13, 1859; pastor at Williamsport and Welsh Run, Md., from 1859 to 1861; stated supply at Havre de Grace in 1861, and pastor from 1863 to 1866; pastor-elect at Churchville from 1866 to 1868, and died at Cumberland, Dec. 19, 1869. See *Gen. Cat. of Princeton Theol. Sem.* 1881, p. 173.

Cramer, Ludwig Dankegott, a Protestant theologian of Germany, was born April 19, 1791, at Baumersroda, near Freiburg. He studied at Wittenberg, and in 1812 commenced his lectures on moral philosophy there. In 1817 he was called to Rostock as professor of theology, but in the following year went to Leipsic as successor of Keil, and died Jan. 8, 1824. He wrote, *Doctrina Judæorum de Præexistentia Animarum* (Wittenberg, 1810):—*Ueber den Mysticismus in der Philosophie* (ibid. 1811):—*Systematische Darstellung der Moral der Apokryphen des Alten Testaments* (Leipsic, 1814):—*De Sacra Librorum V. T. Auctoritate* (ibid. 1819):—*Progr. de Bibliologia in Sacris N. T. Libris Proposita* (ibid. 1822, 1823):—*Vorlesungen über die christl. Dogmatik* (ed. by Näbe, ibid. 1829). See Döring, *Die gelehrten Theologen Deutschlands*, i, 283; Winer, *Handbuch der theol. Lit.* i, 239, 294, 302, 310, 430; ii, 200; Zuchold, *Bibl. Theol.* i, 248. (B. P.)

Cramer, Matthias, a German controversialist, was born at Aix-la-Chapelle, and died Nov. 12, 1557. He published, *Catholica ac Orthodoxa Religio* (Colon. 1542):—*De Catholicæ Fidei Regula Assertio* (1556). See Hartzheim, *Bibl. Colon.* p. 243; Streber, in Wetzer u. Welte's *Kirchen-Lexikon*, s. v. (B. P.)

Cramond, James, a Scotch clergyman, took his degree at King's College, Aberdeen, in 1644; was licensed to preach in 1646; went to England as preacher to a regiment, for which he was debarred the privileges of a minister; but on his repentance the assembly readmitted him in 1650, and he was called to the living at Fearn in 1653. He died in 1690, aged about sixty-six years. See *Fasti Eccles. Scoticanæ*, iii, 831.

Cramond, Robert, D.D., a Scotch clergyman, took his degree at Marischal College, Aberdeen, in 1764; was ordained minister of the Presbyterian Congregation at Etal in 1775, and admitted to the living at Yarrow in 1776. He died Feb. 14, 1791, aged fifty years. See *Fasti Eccles. Scoticanæ*, i, 564.

Cramp, John Mockett, D.D., an eminent Baptist educator and author, was born at St. Peter's, Isle of Thanet, England, July 25, 1791, and educated at Stepney College. He was successively pastor at Southwark, London, in 1818; St. Peter's, Isle of Thanet, from 1827 to 1842 (part of the time assisting his father, Rev. Thomas Cramp), and Hastings in 1842. In 1844 he assumed the presidency of an unsuccessful Baptist College in Montreal, Canada, which he held until 1849. He was editor, in that city, of *The Register* from 1844 to 1849, of *The Colonial Protestant* (with Rev. W. Taylor, D.D.) in 1848 and 1849, and of *The Pilot* from 1849 to 1851. In 1857 he became president of Acadia College, Wolfville, N. S., and the remainder of his busy life he devoted to furthering the cause of Baptist education and religion in the maritime provinces. Until he resigned his position in 1869, his influence was pre-eminent in all questions of denominational and educational politics. He found his college weak and poor; he left it on a firm foundation, with an able staff of instructors, and a good attendance of students. The home and foreign mission enterprise and the temperance movement shared his earnest support. He died at his home in Wolfville, Dec. 7, 1881. Dr. Cramp was an eminent linguist and historian, a celebrated theologian, and as a patristic scholar and in Church history had few equals in the dominion. His works are, *A Text-book of Popery; or, A History of the Council of Trent* (Lond. 1831; enlarg. ed. Lond. and N. Y. 1851, 8vo), a one-sided commentary on the history and decrees of the council, from the standpoint of a narrow and violent Protestantism; a valuable work, however, containing vast information:—*The Reformation in Europe* (Lond. 1844, 18mo):—*Lectures for the Times* (ibid. eod.):—*Introductory Theological Address* (Halifax, N. S., 1851):—*Portraiture from Life, by a Bereaved Husband* (ibid. 1862):—*The Great Ejectment of* 1862 (ibid. eod.):—*Catechism of Christian Baptism* (ibid. and Phila. 1865, 18mo), an able presentation, answered by Rev. D. D. Currie:—*History of the Baptists from the Apostolic Times to the Close of the* 18*th Century* (Lond. 1868, 8vo, which has been translated into German), a work whose value is lessened by its dogmatic spirit:—*Paul and Christ* (ibid. and Halifax, 1873), a delightful and finely written book:—*The Lamb of God* (Edinb. 1874). His *Memoirs* of Madame Feller and of Dr. Cote are records of certain mission and educational work in the province of Quebec. See *The Wesleyan*, Feb. 3, 1882; Morgan, *Biblioth. Canadensis*, s. v.

Cramp, Stephen T., a Methodist Episcopal minister, was born at Sandhurst, Kent, England, May 21, 1842. He was converted in 1859, emigrated to the United States, entered the Wyoming Conference in 1864, and in it labored zealously until his decease, Jan. 19, 1870. He was fervent in spirit, and untiring in energy. See *Minutes of Annual Conferences*, 1870, p. 131.

Cramp, Thomas, an English Baptist minister, was born at St. Peter's, Isle of Thanet, in 1769. He was converted at the age of eighteen, and joined the Church at Shallows, near his birthplace; very soon commenced the work of the ministry, and took charge of the Church in his native place, St. Peter's, and died Nov. 17, 1851. See (Lond.) *Baptist Handbook*, 1852, p. 46. (J. C. S.)

Cramp-rings are rings of precious metal, supposed to prevent cramp. They are attributed by Hospinian to the claim of Westminster Abbey to the possession of the ring given by St. John, in the guise of a pilgrim, to

Edward the Confessor. On Good Fridays the kings of England used to bless finger-rings for this superstitious purpose.

Crampton, Ralph S., a Presbyterian minister, was born at Madison, Conn., Oct. 23, 1799. He studied theology in the seminary at Bangor, Me., was licensed by a Congregational association in 1827, and about 1837 joined the Detroit Presbytery. He was secretary of the American and Foreign Christian Union, agent for the New York Temperance Society for three years, and for the same length of time secretary of the Illinois State Temperance Society. He died in Rochester, N. Y., March 25, 1864. See Wilson, *Presb. Hist. Almanac*, 1866, p. 212.

Cranach (or **Kranach**), Lucas van, an old German painter and eminent engraver, was born at Cranach, in the province of Bamberg, in 1472. At an early period in life he entered into the service of the electoral house of Saxony, with one of the princes of which he made a pilgrimage to the Holy Land in 1493, and with another shared five years' imprisonment, after the fatal battle of Mühlberg. He died at Weimar, Oct. 16, 1553. The following are some of his principal works: *Adam and Eve in Paradise; St. John Preaching in the Wilderness; The Passion of Our Saviour*, in fourteen prints; *The Twelve Apostles; St. Christopher Carrying the Infant Jesus*. See Hoefer, *Nouv. Biog. Générale*, s. v.; Spooner, *Biog. Hist. of the Fine Arts*, s. v.

Crandal (or **Crandall**), **Joseph**, a Baptist minister, was born at Friertown, R. I., in 1771. In 1774 his parents removed to Chester, N. S. He was converted at the age of twenty-two, ordained, in 1799, pastor at Sackville, N. B., and did the work of an evangelist all through the region in which he lived. In 1825 he itinerated in Prince Edward's Island. He died Feb. 20, 1858. See Cathcart, *Baptist Encyclop.* p. 286; Bill, *Funeral Sermon.* (J. C. S.)

Crandal, William Alfred, a Baptist minister, was born in Westmoreland County, N. B. He was ordained at Amherst in 1858: labored in Restigouche County as home missionary; became pastor at Norton, and at Elgin; preached at Lutes Mount, Moncton, and other localities under direction of the Home Mission Board, and died Dec. 17, 1875. See *Baptist Year-book of N. S., N. B., and P. E. I.*, 1876, p. 35.

Crandall, Andrew Jackson, a Methodist Episcopal minister, was born at Germantown, Chenango Co., N. Y., in 1813. He experienced conversion at thirteen; studied about three years at Cazenovia Seminary, and in 1834 connected himself with the Oneida Conference. In 1848 he was transferred to the Missouri Conference, in which he labored with zeal, fidelity, and marked success until his death in August, 1849. Mr. Crandall published two or three *Addresses*. See *Minutes of Annual Conferences*, 1850, p. 510; Sprague, *Annals of the Amer. Pulpit*, vii, 803.

Crandall, Peter, a Baptist minister, probably a brother of Joseph Crandal, was born in Rhode Island in 1770. When he was five years of age his father removed to Chester, N. S. He commenced preaching in 1800; travelled extensively and successfully; was pastor at Digby for twenty-nine years, and died April 2, 1838. See Bill, *Hist. of Baptists in the Maritime Provinces*, p. 229.

Crandall, Phineas, a Methodist Episcopal minister, was born at Montville, Conn., Sept. 12, 1793. He was converted when about twenty years of age; licensed to exhort in 1817; to preach in 1818; in 1820 joined the New England Conference; in 1854 became a supernumerary; in 1856 a superannuate, and died Nov. 5, 1878. See *Minutes of Annual Conferences*, 1879, p. 51.

Crandall, Smith, a Methodist Episcopal minister, was a member of the Georgia Conference, and died in 1840, in Cherokee County, Ga. See *Minutes of Annual Conferences*, 1842, p. 302.

Crandall, Timothy, a Free-will Baptist minister, was born in 1790. He was converted at the age of seventeen; united with the Society of Friends, and for twenty-one years was an acceptable minister in that denomination. In 1843 he joined a Free-will Baptist Church; made himself highly useful as a preacher, especially in Otselic, N. Y., and died in Smyrna, May 15, 1853. See *Free-will Baptist Register*, 1855, p. 85. (J. C. S.)

Crandon, Philip, a Methodist Episcopal minister, was born at Rochester, Mass., Jan. 4, 1810. He experienced religion in 1823; was licensed to preach in 1834, and in 1835 entered the New England Conference. He died at his post in 1875 or 1876. See *Minutes of Annual Conferences*, 1876, p. 74.

Crane, Caleb, a Methodist Episcopal minister, was born in Tennessee about 1801, of pious parents. He was converted when about seventeen, and in 1822 was admitted into the Kentucky Conference. About 1832 he removed to Cape Girardeau County, Mo., and in 1849 entered the Missouri Conference. He died Nov. 22, 1851. See *Minutes of Annual Conferences*, 1852, p. 131.

Crane, Daniel, a Presbyterian minister, was born at Bloomfield, N. J., April 13, 1780. He graduated at Nassau Hall (College of New Jersey) in 1799; was licensed by the Morris County Presbytery in 1803, and preached at Chester. In 1808 he accepted a call to Fishkill, N. Y., and in 1820 took charge of a Congregational Church in Waterbury, Conn. In 1825 he returned to Fishkill, taught school for two years, and then accepted a call to the Presbyterian Church in Chester, N. J. He died at Cornwall, N. Y., in April, 1861. See Wilson, *Presb. Hist. Almanac*, 1862, p. 179.

Crane, D. M., a Baptist minister, was born at Brookline, Vt., Feb. 25, 1812. He joined the Baptist Church at the age of sixteen, and three years afterwards was licensed to preach. He studied at Shelburne Falls and Middleborough, Mass., took a partial course at Brown University, was ordained in June, 1837, at Brookline, Vt., remaining one year; afterwards was pastor at Grafton for four years, and at North Springfield three years. His subsequent pastorates were at Northampton, three years; Union Baptist Church, Boston, twelve; North Dorchester, Mass., six; Woonsocket, R. I., two, and for brief periods in three or four other places; his last being at Northampton. He died at West Acton, Sept. 4, 1879. See *The Watchman*, Oct. 30, 1879. (J. C. S.)

Crane, Eber, a Baptist minister, was born in Killingworth, Conn., May 3, 1808. When he was eight years old his parents removed to Marietta, O. At the age of seventeen he united with the Church, and for a time studied at South Reading, now Wakefield, and in Newton Theological Institution. He was ordained at Amesbury, Mass., Sept. 30, 1832; became a missionary in the West; subsequently was pastor at Akron, McConnelsville, Garrettsville, and for short periods at other points in Ohio. In August, 1853, he took up his residence in Mount Pleasant, Ia., and for many years devoted himself to the service of feeble churches in the neighborhood in which he lived. He died early in April, 1884. See *Chicago Standard*, April 17, 1884. (J. C. S.)

Crane, Elias Winans, a Presbyterian minister, was born at Elizabeth, N. J., March 18, 1796. He graduated from the College of New Jersey in 1814, and spent the next two years in teaching. He then studied theology at Princeton for one year; became stated supply in Morristown for one year; was ordained by the Presbytery of New Jersey, Jan. 5, 1820; was pastor at Springfield, N. J., till 1826, and thereafter at Jamaica, L. I., until his death, Nov. 10, 1840. See *Gen. Cat. of Princeton Theol. Sem.* 1881, p. 24.

Crane, Elijah, a Methodist Episcopal minister, was born at Bethel, Vt., about 1800. He was converted in 1816; received license to exhort in 1818; to preach in 1821, and in 1822 entered the New York Conference. In 1833 he was transferred to the Ohio Conference, became a member of the Michigan Conference on its formation, and labored faithfully until 1859, when his health failed. He died April 23, 1868. See *Minutes of Annual Conferences*, 1868, p. 193.

Crane, James Burnet, a Congregational minister, was born at Middletown, Conn., Jan. 26, 1819. He studied law, and was for a time in business; in 1850 and 1851 he studied in the theological seminary at Princeton, N. J., and was ordained and installed colleague pastor over the First Congregational Church in Middletown, Jan. 11, 1854. He resigned this charge April 15, 1856; entered the United States army as hospital chaplain in April, 1863, and remained until the close of the war. He died in Elizabeth, N. J., Sept. 30, 1868. See *Obituary Record of Yale College*, 1869.

Crane, James Lyon, a Congregational minister, was born at Leesville, O., Feb. 25, 1822. He received his preparatory education at Cleveland Heights Academy, and until 1864 was a farmer and manufacturer in Berea and Oberlin. He was ordained as an evangelist at Morenci, Mich., Nov. 22, 1865; was acting pastor there until 1867; at Adams from 1867 to 1872; at Bedford from 1873 to 1876; at Michigan Centre and Napoleon from 1876 until his death, Aug. 15, 1877.

Crane, James Lyons, a Methodist Episcopal minister, was born at Mount Eaton, Wayne Co., O., Aug. 30, 1823. He was converted in 1840; removed to Illinois in 1842; attended a seminary at Paris about three years, in 1846 received license to preach, and joined the Illinois Conference. After holding many of the most important appointments, in 1861 he became chaplain of the 21st Regiment of Illinois Volunteers, of which U. S. Grant was colonel. He died of paralysis, July 29, 1879. As a preacher Mr. Crane was original and bold; a man of marked individuality, and thoroughly evangelical. See *Minutes of Annual Conferences*, 1879, p. 41.

Crane, John, a Methodist Episcopal minister, was born near Nashville, Tenn., in 1787. He joined the Church at the age of twelve; at twenty entered the Western Conference, and continued to labor until near the close of his life, Feb. 14, 1813. See *Minutes of Annual Conferences*, 1813, p. 220.

Crane, John R., D.D., a Congregational minister, was born at Newark, N. J., April 16, 1787. He graduated from Princeton College in 1805; studied law in Newark for over two years; but in the winter of 1807 was converted, and soon afterwards entered the Andover Theological Seminary. Being licensed in 1812 by the Presbytery of New Jersey, he preached in Danbury, Conn.; and afterwards in the Northern Liberties, Philadelphia; but was twice temporarily laid aside by lung disease. Nov. 4, 1818, he was ordained pastor of the First Congregational Church, Middletown, Conn., where he served until his death, Aug. 17, 1853. See Sprague, *Annals of the Amer. Pulpit*, ii, 562.

Crane, Jonathan, D.D., a Congregational minister, was born at Schenectady, N. Y., March 27, 1814. He graduated from Union College in 1832, and from Auburn Theological Seminary in 1835. He was ordained at Attleborough, Mass., Oct. 20, 1836; remained there until June 12, 1854; was then installed over the Twentieth Street Congregational Church, New York city; from 1858 to 1859 was acting pastor at Attleborough, and for some months in Waltham, Mass., and Patchogue, N. Y.; Oct. 18, 1860, was installed over the Church at Middletown, N. Y.; resigned in 1868; was acting pastor at St. Joseph, Mo., until 1869; thence he removed to Kalamazoo, Mich., and supplied neighboring churches until 1875; Marshall and Mattawan, 1870 to 1873; Plainville Presbyterian Church, 1874; in 1875 returned to his pastorate in Middletown, and remained until his death, Dec. 25, 1877. He published, *Memorial of Mrs. Hannah Sanford:—Memorial of Jonathan Crane*, his father. (W. P. S.)

Crane, Jonathan Townley, D.D., a Methodist Episcopal minister, was born near Elizabeth, N. J., June 19, 1819, of Presbyterian parentage. He received an early, careful religious training; was left an orphan at the age of thirteen; experienced religion at eighteen; graduated at Princeton College in 1843; was licensed to preach the next spring, and employed by the presiding elder on Parsippany Circuit; and in 1845 entered the New Jersey Conference. His fields of labor were: in 1845, six months on Asbury Circuit, and six at Quarantine and Port Richmond; 1846, Hope; 1847, Belvidere; 1848 to May, 1849, Orange; from June, 1849, to 1857, principal of Pennington Seminary; 1858 and 1859, Trinity Church, Jersey City; 1860 and 1861, Haverstraw; 1862 and 1863, Central Church, Newark; 1864 to 1866, Morristown; 1867, Hackettstown; 1868 to 1871, Newark District; 1872 to 1875, Elizabeth District; 1876 and 1877, Cross Street Church, Paterson; and in 1878, Port Jervis, N. Y., where he closed his life and labors, Feb. 16, 1880. Dr. Crane was a clear, thorough, and able writer; a gentle and painstaking instructor, a powerful temperance advocate, an exemplary Christian gentleman, and a successful minister. His authorship embraces, *Essay on Dancing* (1848):—*The Right Way; or, Practical Lectures on the Decalogue* (1853):—*Popular Amusements* (1869):—*Arts of Intoxication* (1870):—*Holiness the Birthright of all God's Children* (1874):—*Methodism and its Methods* (1875); besides being a frequent contributor to the *Methodist Quarterly Review, The Christian Advocate*, and periodicals. See *Minutes of Annual Conferences*, 1880, p. 37; Simpson, *Cyclopædia of Methodism*, s. v.

Crane, Nathaniel M., a Presbyterian minister, was born at West Bloomfield, N. J., Dec. 12, 1805. He was converted when about fifteen years of age; and, after spending two years in the Bloomfield Academy, entered Williams College, Mass., and was two years in the Theological Seminary at Allegheny, Pa., and one year in that at Auburn, N. Y. In 1836 he was ordained by the Cayuga Presbytery, and sent to India as a missionary, where he remained for seven years; returning to America he preached as a supply through Western Pennsylvania until his death, Sept. 21, 1859. See Wilson, *Presb. Hist. Almanac*, 1861, p. 83.

Crane, Origen, a Baptist minister, was born at Mansfield, Conn., July 26, 1804. Without taking a collegiate course he graduated at the Newton Theological Institution in 1836; soon after was ordained at Newton Upper Falls, Mass., remaining for three years (1836–1839), and then removed to Weston, where he was pastor fourteen years. He was for some years an agent of the American and Foreign Bible Society, and for a time was a supply at New England Village, Grafton, and West Sutton. He died at New England Village, April 20, 1860. See Cathcart, *Baptist Encyclop.* s. v. (J. C. S.)

Crane, Robert E., a Wesleyan Methodist minister in Nova Scotia, was born at Grand Pré (Horton) in 1818. He entered the ministry in 1846; became a supernumerary in 1867; and died in Halifax, June 28, 1872. See *Minutes of Conference of Eastern British America*, 1872, p. 9.

Crane, Robert H., a Wesleyan Methodist missionary, was a native of Nova Scotia. He labored in his native province from 1818 until 1832, and afterwards in the West Indies, principally St. Vincent, on which he died, at Kingstown, Feb. 3, 1839. See *Minutes of the British Conference*, 1839, p. 431.

Crane, Silas Axtelle, D.D., an Episcopal minister, was born at Berkeley, Mass., Oct. 21, 1799. He graduated from Brown University in 1823, taught one year, and was then tutor of mathematics in the university (1824–1828). He studied theology under Rev. Dr.

N. B. Crocker, of Providence, R. I.; was ordained deacon in 1832; was rector of St. Stephen's Church in Middlebury, Vt. (1833–1837), and then removed to St. Louis, Mo., to take the presidency of Kemper College. After two years he became rector of St. Luke's Church, in East Greenwich, where he died, July 16, 1872. (J. C. S.)

Crane, Simeon Harrison, a Presbyterian minister, was born at Newark, N. J., March 8, 1800. He graduated (from what college is uncertain) in 1823; studied theology for two years at Princeton Theological Seminary; was ordained Aug. 11, 1827; stated supply at Bethel, Ky., from 1827 to 1831; agent for the Board of Domestic Missions in 1831; stated supply at Lebanon, O., from 1833 to 1839; agent for New Albany Seminary, Ind., in 1840; and died in Lexington, Ky., Aug. 30, 1841. See *Gen. Cat. of Princeton Theol. Sem.* 1881, p. 44.

Crane, William Croes, D.D., a Protestant Episcopal clergyman, was born at Bridgeton, N. J., in 1814. He received a military education at West Point, N. Y.; was ordained deacon in 1837; for several years, until 1856, was rector in Centreville, Md.; subsequently, for a short time, in Baltimore; and at St. Andrew's Church, Jackson, Miss., from 1858 until his death, March 21, 1877. See *Prot. Episc. Almanac*, 1878, p. 168.

Craner, François Regis, a Swiss writer of the Jesuit order, was born at Lucerne in 1728. After the suppression of his order, he taught ancient literature at the gymnasium of his native city, where he died in 1806, leaving a German translation of the *Æneid* of Virgil (1783):—and *Dramas*, gathered from Swiss history. See Hoefer, *Nouv. Biog. Générale*, s. v.

Craner, Thomas, an English Particular Baptist, was pastor in Bedfordshire till the people fell into doctrinal error; in 1756 he settled at Jewin Street, London. In 1760 the Church removed to Red Cross Street, where he preached till his death, March 18, 1773, in the fifty-seventh year of his age. He published, *A Declaration of the Faith and Practice of the Church of Christ:—A Scripture Manual*, besides four separate *Sermons*. See Wilson, *Dissenting Churches*, iii, 320.

Cranford, James, an English divine of the 17th century, was born at Coventry, Warwickshire, where his father was a divine and schoolmaster of great note. He was educated at Oxford, beneficed in Northamptonshire, and afterwards removed to St. Christopher's, London. He died in 1657, leaving *The Teares of Ireland* (Lond. 1642, 12mo):—*Sermon on Heresies* (1646). He was a laborious preacher, an exact linguist, a subtle disputant, and an orthodox but charitable theologian. See Fuller, *Worthies of England* (ed. Nuttall), iii, 288[e].

Crankshaw, John Weir, an English Wesleyan minister, was born at Adlington, near Bolton. He was converted at nine; began to preach at sixteen; spent three years at the Didsbury Institution; took his first circuit in 1847; spent fifteen years in the active work; and died at Bristol, Jan. 22, 1869, in the forty-fourth year of his age. See *Minutes of the British Conference*, 1869, p. 18.

Cranley, Thomas, D.D., an Irish prelate, although a native of England, was a fellow of Merton College, warden of New College, and for a time chancellor of the University of Oxford. He was consecrated to the archiepiscopal see of Dublin in 1397. In 1398 he had letters of protection on proceeding to foreign parts in the service of the king, and in the following year had power to treat with the Irish. He was several times appointed lord chancellor. In 1417 he went to England, and died at Farringdon May 25 of that year. See D'Alton, *Memoirs of the Archbishops of Dublin*, p. 151; Fuller, *Worthies of England* (ed. Nuttall), iii, 207.

Cranmer, E. H., a Methodist Episcopal minister, was born in 1812. He was converted in 1838, and in 1840 joined the Genesee Conference; served the Church with much success as pastor and presiding elder for many years until his health failed; and died Oct. 8, 1880. See *Minutes of Annual Conferences*, 1881, p. 327.

Cranston (Cranstoun, or **Cranstoune)** is the family name of several Scotch clergymen.

1. John (1), took his degree at the University of St. Andrews in 1611; was presented to the living at South Leith, Edinburgh, in 1620; transferred to Liberton in 1624; back to South Leith, first charge, in 1627; and died in 1629, aged about thirty-eight years. See *Fasti Eccles. Scoticanæ*, i, 99, 104, 115.

2. John (2), took his degree at Edinburgh University in 1685; was appointed to the living at Crailing in 1692, and ordained; transferred to Ancrum in 1704, and died Oct. 17, 1748, aged eighty-four years. See *Fasti Eccles. Scoticanæ*, i, 485, 493.

3. John (3), was licensed to preach in 1730; presented to the living at Ancrum as assistant and successor to his father in 1733, and ordained; and died Jan. 17, 1790, aged eighty-four years. See *Fasti Eccles. Scoticanæ*, i, 485.

4. Michael, was appointed the first Protestant minister at Selkirk in 1580; transferred to Liberton in 1585; transferred to Cramond in 1590; in 1596 was imprisoned for stirring up a tumult and uproar in Edinburgh. His opinions changed greatly as he advanced in life. He died in 1631. See *Fasti Eccles. Scoticanæ*, i, 114, 132, 539.

5. Robert, took his degree at the University of St. Andrews in 1609; was presented to the living at Kettle or Lathris in 1626, in succession to his father; transferred to Scoonie in 1630; was a member of the assembly in 1638, and died in 1643, aged about fifty-four years. See *Fasti Eccles. Scoticanæ*, ii, 495, 558.

6. Thomas, was appointed to Borthwick in 1567, as the first Protestant minister there; transferred to Liberton in 1569; to Peebles in 1571; returned to Liberton in 1574; removed to Ashkirk in 1579, and to Liberton in 1580; retransferred to Liberton in 1582, and died in Edinburgh in 1585. See *Fasti Eccles. Scoticanæ*, i, 113, 114, 235, 266, 542.

7. William, was promoted from being regent at the University of St. Andrews; appointed to the living at Kettle in 1589; was a member of the general assemblies of 1590, 1597, and 1602; subscribed the protest against introducing episcopacy in 1606; deprived in 1620; again presented to Kettle in 1623 by the king, but resigned before May, 1626, and died in January, 1633, aged seventy-seven years. See *Fasti Eccles. Scoticanæ*, ii, 495.

Cranston, Robert, an Irish Wesleyan minister, was born in the county Cavan, Aug. 1, 1785. He became a Christian in his eighteenth year, and an itinerant in 1811. After preaching for sixteen years, he retired on account of bodily affliction, and died July 12, 1836. In the Irish Conference of 1816, he, with seven other ministers, was reprehended for administering the Lord's Supper to the people of his charge. See *Minutes of the British Conference*, 1836; Smith, *Hist. of Wesl. Meth.* iii, 23–25.

Cranston, Walter, a minister of the Protestant Episcopal Church, was born at Newport, R. I., Dec. 12, 1789. Having studied under John Fraser, in Newport, and graduated at Harvard College in 1810, he took a voyage to the island of Trinidad, and, returning in 1811, went to Charleston, S. C., and afterwards to Cambridge for study. In the autumn he was appointed Greek tutor in the university, and held the position until 1815, studying theology meanwhile. Part of the time he officiated as lay-reader in the Episcopal Church at Cambridge. Jan. 20, 1815, he was ordained deacon. After resigning his tutorship he went to Savannah, Ga., and became pastor of Christ Church in the fall of 1815. The next year he was ordained presbyter, and returned to Savannah to resume his pastoral duties. On two occasions, when yellow fever invaded the city, he remained at his post. His health failing, he went to Middletown, Conn., and died there, July 25, 1822. See Sprague, *Annals of the Amer. Pulpit*, v, 580.

Cranz, Friedrich Alexander Leopold, a Protestant theologian of Germany, was born May 12, 1807, at Berlin. He studied there and in Halle, was ordained in 1833, and appointed military preacher at Torgau. In 1840 he was called as first military preacher to Posen, was in 1846 member of consistory, and in 1854 general superintendent of the province of Posen, and died Aug. 26, 1878. He was one of the most faithful leaders of the Evangelical Church in his country. (B. P.)

Crapsey, Jacob, a Free-will Baptist minister, was born in 1767. He was baptized in Ontario, N. Y., in 1822; soon after was ordained, and for ten years engaged in the work of preaching the gospel. He removed to Royalton in 1826, where he died in October, 1832. See *Free-will Baptist Register*, 1834, p. 65. (J. C. S.)

Crapster, William Thomas, a Unitarian minister, was born Feb. 29, 1824, near Lisbon, Md. In 1851 he entered Princeton Theological Seminary, but graduated from the divinity school of Harvard University in 1856. He was licensed by the Boston Association in 1854, and ordained an evangelist June 16, 1857, and preached occasionally in various places, both in the North and South. He died Feb. 5, 1879. See *Necrol. Report of Princeton Theol. Sem.* 1879, p. 55.

Crashaw, John, an English Wesleyan minister, was born at Cheetham Hill, Manchester, in 1811. He was converted at seventeen, appointed to his first circuit in 1834, to his last (Kettering) in 1869, and died suddenly, May 22, 1870. He wrote, *Important Truths in Simple Verse*:—*Lectures to Children* (Lond. 1853, 18mo):—*Conversations about Wesley*:—*Facts about Boys for Boys*. See *Minutes of the British Conference*, 1870, p. 34.

Crashaw, Richard, an English clergyman and poet, was born in London, and educated at the Charterhouse, and at Pembroke Hall, Cambridge, of which he became a fellow in 1637. He took orders and became distinguished as an eloquent preacher, but was ejected in 1644 for refusing to take the covenant. He then removed to France and embraced Romanism. Having been reduced to great pecuniary distress, he received, through the influence of Henrietta Maria, the positions of secretary to one of the cardinals and canon of the church of Loretto. He died about 1650. Among his best known pieces are, *Hymn to the Name of Jesus*:—*Music's Duel*:—*Lines on a Prayer-book*; and some of his translations. His poetry consisted principally of religious invocations and translations of rare merit from the Latin and Italian. See Chalmers, *Biog. Dict.* s. v.; Allibone, *Dict. of Brit. and Amer. Authors*, s. v.

Crashaw, William, an English clergymen, father of Richard Crashaw, was preacher at the Temple, London, at the beginning of the 17th century, and a violent opponent of Romanism. He published, *Roman Forgeries, and Falsifications of Authors* (1606):—*Newes from Italy of a Second Moses*, etc. (1608):—*Fiscus Papalis* (1617):—*The Jesuites Gospel, written by themselves, Laid Open and Reproved* (1641); and other works. See Allibone, *Dict. of Brit. and Amer. Authors*, s. v.

Crashfield, Richard, an English martyr, was burned at Norwich in 1557, because he refused the doctrines and ceremonies of the Romish Church. See Fox, *Acts and Monuments*, viii, 398.

Crasselius, Bartholomäus, a Lutheran minister of Germany, was born at Wermsdorf, near Glauchau, Feb. 21, 1677. He was a pupil of A. H. Franke, and died while pastor at Düsseldorf, Nov. 10, 1724. He composed about nine hymns, of which has been translated into English, "Heiligster Jesu, Heilgungsquelle," by Mills, in *Horæ Germanicæ*, p. 287: "Most holy Jesus! Fount Unfailing," and "Dir, dir Jehovah will ich singen," by Winkworth (*Chorale Book for England*, No. 117): "Jehovah, let me now adore Thee." See Koch, *Gesch. des deutschen Kirchenleides*, iv, 418 sq. (B. P.)

Crasset, Jean, a French ascetic theologian of the Jesuit order, was born at Dieppe, Jan. 3, 1618. He taught in the colleges of his order, distinguished himself as a preacher, and died at Paris, Jan. 4, 1692. His principal works are, *Méthode d'Oraison* (Paris, 1673):—*Méditations pour tous les Jours de l'Année* (ibid. 1678; translated into German, Dutch, Italian, Spanish, and Latin):—*Le Chrêtien en Solitude* (ibid. 1683; latest ed. 1860):—*La Douce et Sainte Mort* (ibid. 1681):—*Dissertation sur les Oracles des Sibylles* (ibid. 1678, 1684):—*Vie de Madame Hélyot* (ibid. 1683):—*Histoire de l'Église du Japon* (ibid. 1689, 1715); this work is largely gathered from that of Solier upon the same subject, published in 1627:—*La Foi Victorieuse de l'Infidélité et du Libertinage* (ibid. 1693):—*Des Congregations de Notre-Dâme Erigées dans les Maisons des Jésuites* (ibid. 1694):—*Abrégé de la Vie de Claude Hélyot*, at the beginning of the *Œuvres Spirituelles de M. Hélyot* (ibid. 1710). See Hoefer, *Nouv. Biog. Générale*, s. v.; Wetzer u. Welte, *Kirchen-Lexikon*, s. v.

Crasso, Damiano, a Dominican of Rivoli, in Piedmont, who died at Pavia in 1515, is the author of *Commentarius super Jobum*:—*De S. Joannis Affinitate et Consanguinitate cum Christo Domino*. See Niger, *De Scriptor. Flor.*; Echard, *De Scriptoribus Ordinis Dominicanorum*; Jöcher, *Allgemeines Gelehrten-Lexikon*, s. v. (B. P.)

Crasso, Francesco, an Italian prelate and jurist, was of an ancient family of Milan. He studied law, and practiced in his native city in 1528. He afterwards fulfilled various public functions. Pius IV appointed him prothonotary and governor of Bologna, and in 1565 he was made cardinal. He died at Rome, Sept. 1, 1566, leaving, *Novæ Constitutiones* (1541):—*Orationes* (1541, 1559):—*Commentaria in Jus Civile*:—*Carmina*. The poems of Crasso are found in the *Rime della Signora Tullia d'Aragona* (Venice, 1560). See Hoefer, *Nouv. Biog. Générale*, s. v.

Cratès of Thebes, a Cynic philosopher, son of Ascondus, flourished in the 4th century B.C. He went to Athens, where he became a disciple of Diogenes, and subsequently one of the most distinguished of the Cynics. He was at Thebes in 307 B.C. Crates was heir to a large fortune, which he bestowed upon his native city, or, according to one account, he placed in the hands of a banker, with instructions to give it to his sons in case they should become fools, but if they became philosophers, to bestow it upon the poor. He was in the habit of visiting every house in Athens and rebuking its inmates, from which circumstance he acquired the name of the "door-opener." In spite of the poverty to which he had reduced himself, and notwithstanding his ugly and deformed figure, he gained the affections of Hipparchia, the daughter of a family of distinction. She refused many wealthy suitors, and because of the opposition of her parents threatened to commit suicide. She finally gained the consent of her parents and was married to Crates. He wrote a book of fourteen letters on philosophical subjects, and some tragedies of an earnest and philosophical character, all of which have been lost. See Smith, *Dict. of Greek and Roman Biog. and Myth.* s. v.; *Encyclop. Brit.* (9th ed.) s. v.

Crato is a probably imaginary "bishop of the Syrians," asserted by Prædestinatus (i, 33) to have been a successful antagonist of the heresy of Theodotus.

Craton is set down in old martyrologies as a martyr at Rome, celebrated Feb. 15.

Crauford (or **Craufurde**). See Crawford.

Craven, Braxton, D.D., LL.D., a minister of the Methodist Episcopal Church South, was born in Randolph County, N. C., Aug. 26, 1822. He studied in the Quaker school at New Garden, and afterwards at Union Institute (now Trinity College), of which he became principal in 1842. He was licensed to preach in 1840, and entered the North Carolina Conference in 1857. With the exception of two years in the pastorate, all his active life was spent at the head of Trinity College. He died at his post, Dec. 7, 1882. See *Minutes of Annual Conferences of the M. E. Church South*, 1882, p. 110.

Craven, Isaac N., a minister of the Methodist Episcopal Church South, was born in North Carolina, Aug. 15, 1806. He removed to Georgia in early life, was converted, joined the Methodist Episcopal Church, and was licensed to preach in 1832. He became a member of the Florida Conference in 1847. He united with the East Texas Conference in 1867, and subsequently became a member of the North Texas Conference. He died Aug. 6, 1881. See *Minutes of Annual Conferences of the M. E. Church South*, 1881, p. 347.

Craven, Wesley R., a minister of the Methodist Episcopal Church South, was born in Randolph County, N. C., April 15, 1856. His parents removed the following year to Missouri, where he was converted at fifteen years of age. He was licensed to preach in 1877, and the same year entered the St. Louis Conference on trial. He died near Richwoods, Aug. 4, 1881. See *Minutes of Annual Conferences of the M. E. Church South*, 1881, p. 367.

Craw, Paul, a Bohemian martyr, was taken at St. Andrews by bishop Henry, and delivered over to the secular power to be burned, for holding opinions contrary to the Church of Rome. He was burned in 1431. See Fox, *Acts and Monuments*, iii, 600.

Craw, Peter, a Scotch clergyman, tutor in the family of Robert Veitch, was licensed to preach in 1802, and presented to the living at St. Boswell's (Presbytery of Selkirk) in 1810. He died March 21, 1834, aged sixty years. See *Fasti Eccles. Scoticanæ*, i, 553.

Crawford (occasionally written **Crauford**, or **Crawforde**) is the family name of a number of Scotch clergymen.

1. Alexander, took his degree at Edinburgh University in 1647; was licensed to preach in 1652; was minister at Dornock in 1662, and deprived by the privy council the same year. He was still living in June, 1689. See *Fasti Eccles. Scoticanæ*, i, 616.

2. Archibald, was the first Protestant minister at Kilmaurs, called in 1567, and transferred to Stevenston in 1569. In 1574 Dalry and Kilbirnie were under his care, where he continued in 1601, and afterwards resigned. See *Fasti Eccles. Scoticanæ*, ii, 177, 186.

3. Charles, was licensed to preach in 1659, and presented to the living at Ecclesmachan in 1661. He died in July, 1682. See *Fasti Eccles. Scoticanæ*, i, 184.

4. Dugald, was licensed to preach in 1781; ordained the same year as deputy-chaplain to a regiment in the Dutch service; became assistant at Kilmory; was presented to the living at Saddell and Skipness in 1799, and transferred to Kilmory in 1815. He was drowned, March 5, 1821, aged sixty-eight years. He published three single *Sermons*, and *Mental Tooth-pick for the Fair Sex*. See *Fasti Eccles. Scoticanæ*, iii, 48.

5. George (1), took his degree at Edinburgh University in 1618; was appointed to the living at West Kilbride in 1632, and was deposed in 1648 for conniving at slander and sin in his parishioners, and selling his horse on a Sabbath-day. See *Fasti Eccles. Scoticanæ*, ii, 190.

6. George (2), was licensed to preach in 1704; called to the living at Symington, Ayrshire, in 1708; ordained in 1709; transferred to Stonykirk in 1711; and admitted in 1712. He died in January, 1730. See *Fasti Eccles. Scoticanæ*, i, 772; ii, 145.

7. George (3), son of the professor of moral philosophy at St. Andrews, was licensed to preach in 1826; presented to the living at Cults in 1828, and ordained in 1829. He died Nov. 5, 1831, aged thirty years. A volume of his *Miscellaneous Discourses* was published in 1832. See *Fasti Eccles. Scoticanæ*, 485, 486.

8. Hugh, took his degree at Glasgow University in 1648; was deprived by the privy council in 1662; indulged by the privy council in 1672, and appointed to Riccarton; cited to appear before the privy council in 1677, and before his cautioners in 1681; afterwards had a charge in Ireland; was recalled in 1687 to New Cumnock, and admitted to the living in 1688. He died in May, 1692, aged about sixty-four years. See *Fasti Eccles. Scoticanæ*, ii, 105, 135.

9. James, was licensed to preach in 1781; elected to the living at Newark in 1784; ordained in 1785, and promoted to Lochwinnoch in 1802 on the choice of the parishioners. He died May 17, 1814, aged sixty-four years. See *Fasti Eccles. Scoticanæ*, ii, 226, 255.

10. John, took his degree at Glasgow University in 1631; was admitted to the living at Lamington in 1645; was a member of the Commission of Assembly in 1649, and continued in 1662; summoned before the synod in 1664 for not conforming, and indulged by the privy council in 1669. He died Aug. 7, 1674, aged sixty years. See *Fasti Eccles. Scoticanæ*, i, 224.

11. Matthew, took his degree at the University of Edinburgh in 1662, and studied afterwards at Utrecht; was licensed privately to preach in 1671; charged before the synod in 1674 with keeping conventicles, and for non-appearance was termed rebel, but could not be found; was called by the Presbyterians at Eastwood in 1679, and entered on the living there; was at the first meeting of synod after toleration in 1687; a member of the assembly in 1690, and is said to have had a principal part in settling the affairs of the Kirk at that period of transition. He died in December, 1700, aged about fifty-nine years. He published three works against popery, one in Latin, and left in MS. a *History of the Church of Scotland*. See *Fasti Eccles. Scoticanæ*, ii, 312.

12. Patrick, took his degree at Edinburgh University in 1681; was licensed to preach in 1689; called to the living at Dailly in 1691, and ordained. He died in June, 1710, aged about forty-nine years. See *Fasti Eccles. Scoticanæ*, ii, 107.

13. Robert, was licensed to preach in 1824; appointed to the living at Kirkpatrick-Irongray in 1832, and ordained assistant in that parish; joined the Free Secession in 1843, and was admitted minister at the Free Church, Virginhall, in 1844. He died at Penpont, Aug. 7, 1856, aged fifty-seven years. See *Fasti Eccles. Scoticanæ*, i, 594.

14. Thomas Jackson, D.D., youngest son of the professor of moral philosophy at St. Andrews, took his degree at that university in 1831; was licensed to preach in 1834; was presented to the living at Cults the same year, and ordained; transferred to Glammis in 1838; promoted to St. Andrew's Church, Edinburgh, in 1844; appointed convener of the General Assembly's committee on psalmody in 1845, and for missions in 1850, which he held until 1854; was convener of the Home Missionary Committee in 1858; admitted professor of divinity at Edinburgh University in 1859, and elected moderator of the General Assembly in 1867. He died at Genoa, Italy, in 1875. Dr. Crawford published, *Reasons for Adherence to the Church of Scotland* (1843):—*Presbyterianism Defended against Prelacy and Tractarianism* (1853):—*The Fatherhood of God Considered* (1866):—*The Doctrine of Holy Scripture respecting the Atonement* (1871):—and some single *Sermons*. See *Fasti Eccles. Scoticanæ*, ii, 486; iii, 771, 772.

15. William (1), took his degree at Edinburgh University in 1641; was presented to the manse and living at Ladykirk in 1651; conforming to episcopacy, he was collated to the living in 1662, but deposed in August, 1690, for drunkenness, he having been so charged fifteen years before. He died in 1695, aged eighty-four years. See *Fasti Eccles. Scoticanæ*, i, 442.

16. William (2), was born at Kelso in 1676; took

his degree at Edinburgh University in 1700; was licensed to preach in 1712, called to the living at Wilton, and ordained in 1713. He died May 28, 1737. He published a sermon, *Christ the Power of God*, etc. (1731): —*A Short Manual against Infidelity* (1734). His *Works* were also printed (Edinb. 1748, 2 vols.). See *Fasti Eccles. Scoticanæ*, i, 517.

17. WILLIAM (3), D.D., was licensed to preach in 1787; appointed to the living at Straiton in 1791, and ordained. Having been appointed professor of moral philosophy at the University of St. Andrews, he resigned his charge in 1816, and died Sept. 23, 1822, aged sixty years. See *Fasti Eccles. Scoticanæ*, ii, 144.

Crawford, Alexander, a Baptist minister, was a native of Argyleshire, Scotland. He united with the Independent (Congregational) Church of the Isle of Arran at nineteen, went to Edinburgh to study under Haldane and Ewing, and was immersed. In 1811 he emigrated to Yarmouth, N. S., where he remained three years. In 1814 he removed to Prince Edward's Island, and labored with success in planting Baptist churches throughout the island. He died in March, 1828, aged forty-two. He published *Believer Immersion as Opposed to Unbeliever Sprinkling* (1827). See Bill, *Hist. of the Baptists in the Maritime Provinces*, p. 662.

Crawford, Alexander William. See LINDSAY, *Lord.*

Crawford, Andrew Jackson, a minister of the Methodist Episcopal Church South, was born in Tennessee. He fought in the battle of New Orleans, in the war of 1812; embraced religion in his young manhood, and became a member of the Tennessee Conference in 1821. He was sent out by the United States government as a surveyor of lands in the Cherokee nation, and at the same time as missionary to the Indians. In 1835 he removed to Alabama, served some years as register of the land-office at Demopolis, and then united with the Alabama Conference. He spent his last years in retirement at his home in Marengo County, where he died in July, 1866. See *Minutes of Annual Conferences of the M. E. Church South*, 1866, p. 41.

Crawford, David Black, M.D., a Baptist minister, was born in South Carolina in 1794. He was licensed to preach in the Cumberland Presbyterian Church, but changed his views and united with the Baptist Church, and was inducted into the ministry in 1839. He served as pastor the Mound Bluff Church, and the Albion and Antioch churches in Mississippi, near Vicksburg, and also practiced medicine quite successfully. He died Aug. 27, 1849. See Sprague, *Annals of the Amer. Pulpit*, vi, 834.

Crawford, Edward, a Presbyterian minister, was licensed to preach by the Presbytery of Hanover in 1777; on Oct. 27 of the same year became pastor at Sinking Spring and Spreading Spring, Va., and some time after 1786 at Glade Spring and Rocky Spring, Tenn., where he remained until 1803. See Alexander, *Princeton College in the 18th Century*.

Crawford, George M., a Presbyterian minister, was born in Abingdon County, Va., June 4, 1796. He was licensed and ordained by the Abingdon Presbytery in 1822, and preached for six years in Virginia and Kentucky. In 1839 he joined the Lexington Presbytery, Mo., and labored for some time as a missionary in that state with great zeal and ability. He died June 4, 1858. See Wilson, *Presb. Hist. Almanac*, 1860, p. 120.

Crawford, George W., A.M., a Methodist Episcopal minister, was born in Orange County, Ind. He removed to Green County in 1833, was converted in his youth, graduated at Asbury University in 1851, and in 1854 entered the North-western Indiana Conference, in which he filled important charges until his death, Aug. 9, 1859. See *Minutes of Annual Conferences*, 1859, p. 297; Simpson, *Cyclop. of Methodism*, s. v.

Crawford, Gilbert, a Presbyterian minister, was born in Scotland. He studied at Princeton Theological Seminary one year (1821); was licensed by the Presbytery of New Brunswick in 1822; subsequently ordained, and served as supply at Le Roy, N. Y., and as pastor at Buffalo from 1827 to 1829; supply at Le Roy again in 1830, at Albion in 1833, and pastor soon after until 1835; supply of the First Church at Lockport for two years; went to Milwaukee, Wis., back again to New York, and preached at Albion, Boone Centre, and Le Roy up to 1846. He died in 1848. See *Gen. Cat. of Princeton Theol. Sem.* 1881, p. 35.

Crawford, Henry Ellet, a Presbyterian minister, was born in Orange County, N. C., Dec. 1, 1832. He graduated at Hanover College, Ind., in 1859, and at Princeton Theological Seminary in 1862; was ordained, in 1863, pastor of Pleasant and Jefferson churches, in the bounds of the Madison Presbytery, Ind. He died Feb. 5, 1866. See Wilson, *Presb. Hist. Almanac*, 1867, p. 128.

Crawford, James (1), a Presbyterian minister, was born in Rockbridge County, Va., Nov. 28, 1794. He graduated at New Jersey College in 1826, and Princeton Theological Seminary in 1829; was ordained missionary in 1828; was first pastor at Delphi, Ind., and then supply at Hopewell and Nayburn, also preaching at Graysville, until 1851. He subsequently became a member of the Presbytery of Vincennes, and died at Morning Sun, Ia., July 18, 1872. See *Gen. Cat. of Princeton Theol. Sem.* 1881, p. 44; *Presbyterian*, Aug. 10, 1872

Crawford, James (2), a Methodist Episcopal minister, was born at Salem, N. Y. He was converted in childhood; licensed to exhort at the age of eighteen; in 1838 to preach, while a student at the Oneida Conference Seminary, and admitted to the Indiana Conference. With the exception of a three years' rest as supernumerary, from 1866 to 1869, he labored zealously until his death in 1872. See *Minutes of Annual Conferences*, 1872, p. 90.

Crawford, James B., a Methodist Episcopal minister, was born at Durham, Me., Dec. 22, 1828. He was converted at eleven; obtained his education at Kent's Hill; began preaching in 1852, and in 1856 entered the East Maine Conference. He commenced his labors at Bucksport Seminary in 1859, and was connected with that institution until his death, March 31, 1869. See *Minutes of Annual Conferences*, 1869, p. 145.

Crawford, James Y., a minister of the Methodist Episcopal Church South, was born in South Carolina in 1802. He was converted in 1818; admitted into the Holston Conference in 1820; located from ill-health in 1836; was readmitted in 1848, and labored faithfully until his death in 1850. See *Minutes of Annual Conferences of the M. E. Church South*, 1850, p. 272.

Crawford, John (1), a Methodist Episcopal minister, was born in Fayette County, Pa., Sept. 28, 1799. He was converted when about sixteen; licensed to preach in 1820; in 1821 entered the Pittsburgh Conference, and in it continued to labor until his death, Feb. 29, 1832. See *Minutes of Annual Conferences*, 1833, p. 214.

Crawford, John (2), a Methodist Episcopal minister, was born at White Plains, N. Y. He commenced his ministry in 1835, served various important charges in New York and its vicinity, and died while on a visit to his son in London, O., Sept. 28, 1880. See *Minutes of Annual Conferences*, 1881, p. 81.

Crawford, John B., a minister of the Reformed (Dutch) Church, was born at Crawford, N. Y., in 1814. He graduated from Rutgers College in 1836, and from New Brunswick Seminary in 1839; was licensed by the Classis of Orange the same year; was pastor at Middletown Village, Monmouth Co., N. J., from November, 1839, to October, 1840, when he died. See Corwin, *Manual of the Ref. Church in America*, 3d ed. p. 224.

Crawford, John H., a minister of the German Reformed Church South, was born in Carroll County, Md., July 23, 1801. He was received into the Church under the Rev. Jacob Geiger; studied theology at Carlisle, Pa., under the Rev. Dr. Lewis Mayer; was ordained in 1828, and sent as a missionary to North Carolina, where he labored faithfully and with great success up to the time of his removal to Augusta County, Va., where he died, Oct. 9, 1864. See Harbaugh, *Fathers of the Ref. Church*, iv, 219-223. (D. Y. H.)

Crawford, Joseph, a Methodist Episcopal minister, entered the travelling connection in 1797. He occupied many of the most important appointments in the New England and New York Conferences, and had great success; but in 1820 was expelled from the New York Conference, for some cause now unknown, after which he entirely disappeared. See *Minutes of Annual Conferences*, 1797-1820; Sprague, *Annals of the Amer. Pulpit*, vii, 99; Stevens, *Hist. of the M. E. Church*, iv, 49, 63, 312.

Crawford, Nathaniel Macon, D.D., a Baptist minister, was born near Lexington, Oglethorpe Co., Ga., March 22, 1811. He graduated from the University of Georgia in 1829, was admitted to the bar of that state, but did not enter upon the practice of the law, having been chosen professor of mathematics in Oglethorpe University, which position he held until 1841. About that time he became a Baptist, received license to preach in 1843, and was ordained in 1844. For the next three years he was pastor, first in Washington, Ga., and then in Charleston, S. C. In 1847 he became professor of Biblical literature in Mercer University, Ga.; in 1854 was elected president of the university; in 1857 was called to the chair of mental and moral philosophy in the University of Mississippi, and soon after in the Western Theological Seminary at Georgetown, Ky. In the autumn of 1858 he returned as president to Mercer University, but during the civil war accepted the presidency of the Baptist Institution at Georgetown, Ky., remaining there until 1871, when he resigned on account of impaired health. He died at Atlanta, Ga., Oct. 27, 1871. Dr. Crawford took a high rank, both as a scholar and as a preacher, in the South. He published a few works, in which were exhibited the results of his scholarship and the charms of a graceful style. (J. C. S.)

Crawford, Oshea W., a Free-will Baptist minister, was born at Brunswick, Me., in November, 1809. When he was eight years of age his parents removed to Chautauqua County, N. Y. He became a Christian at fifteen, was licensed to preach in 1829, and ordained in 1834. He preached in Canada West, New York, Pennsylvania, Ohio, and Michigan, and died at Chesterfield, Lucas Co., O., March 10, 1846. See *Free-will Baptist Register*, 1850, p. 78. (J. C. S.)

Crawford, Peter, a Baptist minister, was born in Virginia in 1809. He began to preach about 1831; studied in what is now Richmond College, Va.; in 1835 established a school, which became the Judson Female Institute, at Marion, Ala.; for some time taught in Central Female College, Miss., and from 1866 to 1871 was president of a female college at Keachi, De Soto Parish, La. He died April 25, 1873. See Cathcart, *Baptist Encyclop.* p. 291. (J. C. S.)

Crawford, William, D.D., an Irish clergyman, was ordained minister of Strabane in 1766. In 1784, upon the request of the synod of Ulster, he undertook the instruction of candidates for the ministry in logic, mathematics, and philosophy, and afterwards enlarged the course of instruction to that of a college course. In 1798 he became pastor at Hollywood, where he died in 1801. Dr. Crawford was a man of considerable learning and great application, but his religious views were decidedly anti-evangelical. He was the author of *Remarks on Lord Chesterfield's Letters:—History of Ireland* (2 vols.):—and published two *Sermons*, besides translations from *Turretine's Dissertations on Natural Theology*. See Reid, *Hist. of the Presb. Church in Ireland*.

Crawford, William H. (1), a minister of the Methodist Episcopal Church South, was born in Greene County, Ga., March 31, 1825. He was converted at the age of fourteen; licensed to preach in 1844; in 1845 was admitted into the Georgia Conference, and labored diligently until his death, July 15, 1847. See *Minutes of Annual Conferences of the M. E. Church South*, 1847, p. 137.

Crawford, William H. (2), a minister of the Methodist Episcopal Church South, was born in Giles County, Va., Dec. 12, 1842. He was converted when a boy; licensed to preach in 1869; in 1873 joined the Holston Conference, and labored therein faithfully until his health failed, a year before his death, which occurred in Watauga County, N. C., March 2, 1880. See *Minutes of Annual Conferences of the M. E. Church South*, 1880, p. 144.

Crawley, Arthur R. R., a Baptist missionary, was born at Sydney, Cape Breton, in 1831. He graduated from Acadia College, N. S., in 1849, and from the Newton Theological Institution in 1852. Under the auspices of the American Baptist Missionary Union, he sailed to Henzada, Burmah, in December, 1853, and in the following October commenced his labors there, achieving great success. He made a visit to the United States in 1868, and another in 1872. He died Oct. 9, 1876. See *Amer. Baptist Magazine*, lvii, 180. (J. C. S.)

Crawley, Sarah, an English minister of the Society of Friends, was born at Hitchin, Hertfordshire, in 1717. She was converted in early life. itinerated as a preacher through different parts of Great Britain and Ireland, and died in London in February, 1799. See *Piety Promoted*, iii, 288. (J. C. S.)

Crayer (or **Cræyer**), GASPAR DE, a very eminent Flemish painter, was born at Brussels in 1582, and studied for a short time under Raphael van Coxie of that city. One of his best pictures, for the refectory of the abbey of Affleghem, represents *A Centurion Dismounting to Worship the Saviour*. His principal painting is at Brussels, in the Church of Notre Dame, *Christ Appearing to Mary Magdalene;* others in different churches are, *The Assumption*, *The Descent of the Holy Ghost*, and *The Resurrection*. He died at Ghent, Jan. 27, 1669. See Hoefer, *Nouv. Biog. Générale*, s. v.; Spooner, *Biog. Hist. of the Fine Arts*, s. v.

Creagh, Peter (1), D.D., an Irish prelate, was appointed to the see of Cork in 1676; imprisoned in 1680; about 1686 translated to the archdiocese of Tuam; and promoted to the archbishopric of Dublin, March 9, 1693. In 1695 the acts were revived, prohibiting the foreign or domestic education of Catholics, and in 1697 all the Popish prelates, vicars-general, deans, monks and others, who exercised ecclesiastical jurisdiction in Ireland, were ordered to depart before May 1, 1698. Whatever was the promise of the earlier period of Creagh's administration, it was soon overcast by the succession of Anne. He was obliged to flee to the continent, and died at Argentina (Strasburg), in 1705 or 1707. See D'Alton, *Memoirs of the Abps. of Dublin*, p. 457; Brady, *Episcopal Succession*, i, 338; ii, 91.

Creagh, Peter (2), an Irish prelate, was made titular bishop of Avaro in 1745, bishop of Waterford in 1750, and died in 1774. See Brady, *Episcopal Succession*, ii, 74.

Creaghead. See CRAIGHEAD.

Creak, Alexander, an English Congregational minister, was born in London, April 16, 1785, and was converted in 1801. He studied first in Hackney College, and then in Homerton College in 1809; entered the pastorate at Burnham Westgate, Norfolk, in August, 1810; resigned in November, 1813; was pastor at Yarmouth from April, 1814, until the failure of his health in 1842, and died Sept. 1, 1848. See (Lond.) *Cong. Year-book*, 1848, p. 220.

Creak, Henry Brown, A.M., an English Congregational minister, was born at Yarmouth, March 25, 1821. He was converted early in life; studied in a German university, and at Spring Hill College, Birmingham; was ordained at Atherstone in 1845; was professor in Airedale College from 1848 to 1863, and died Feb. 10, 1864. See (Lond.) *Cong. Year-book*, 1865, p. 230.

Cream-box is a vulgar name for a *chrismatory*.

Creamer, JOHN, a Methodist Episcopal minister, was born at Middletown, Conn., March 19, 1791. He was left an orphan at the age of ten; converted at eighteen; and in 1816 entered the Philadelphia Conference, wherein he continued with acceptance and usefulness until his death, April 25, 1827. See *Minutes of Annual Conferences*, 1827, p. 542; *Methodist Magazine*, x, 376.

Crease, WILLIAM, an English Congregational minister, was born at Stirling, and educated by the United Presbyterian Church. He became pastor at Wilmslow, Cheshire, in 1844, and labored there very successfully until December, 1849. In the spring of 1850 he removed to Hazelgrove, but died in May of the same year, in the fortieth year of his age. See (Lond.) *Cong. Year-book*, 1850, p. 93.

Creath, WILLIAM, a Baptist minister, was born in Nova Scotia, Dec. 25, 1768, of Presbyterian parents. He was converted when about seventeen years old, removed to North Carolina at twenty, joined a Baptist Church, and soon after commenced to preach, his labors being greatly blessed. For the last fifteen years of his life he gave himself very largely to itinerant work. He died suddenly at Edenton, N. C., Aug. 11, 1822. See *Latter-day Luminary*, iv, 63. (J. C. S.)

Creaticŏlæ (*creature-worshippers*) were a Christian sect which arose in the 6th century, headed by Severus of Antioch, who maintained that the body of Christ was corruptible, but in consequence of the Godhead dwelling in it was never corrupted. See APHTHARTODOCETÆ.

Creda (Credan, or **Credānus)** is the name of two early English ecclesiastics:

1. An abbot of Mercia, A.D. cir. 775.

2. Abbot of Evesham, between Almund, A.D. 783 or 787, and Tintferth, A.D. 803.—Smith, *Dict. of Christ. Biog.* s. v.

Credence. We add the following particulars from Walcott, *Sac. Archæol*, s. v.:

"It either takes the form of a little table covered with a linen cloth—at Brabourne it is on the south side, and formed of black marble, with a cross in a circle carved on it—or is made like an aumbry in the wall. In some churches a second table held the mass vestments of the bishop. The wall credence is often connected with a drain, is rare in the 12th (one occurs at Lausanne), but is usual in the following century. Sometimes it occurs on the north and south sides of an altar; often it is divided by a thin slab of stone. When the pope celebrates on Easter-day there are three credences—two on the epistle side, one containing the deacon's plate, the second supporting two candles and necessaries required by the sacristan. The third, or pope's credence, is on the gospel side, where, at the end of the Creed, the sacristan washes the sacred vessels, drinks of the wine and the water, and finally, at the offertory, tastes the particles from which the hosts are prepared, at the command of the cardinal-deacon, as a precaution against poison. The first use of credences in the Roman ritual occurs in the time of Leo X, in 1516, and apparently was introduced when the custom of personal offering fell into desuetude."

Credi, LORENZO ANDREA DI (called *Sciarpelloni*), a reputable Florentine painter, was born about 1452, and studied under Andrea Verocchio at the same time with Leonardo da Vinci. He painted many Madonnas and Holy Families. He died about 1536. See Hoefer, *Nouv. Biog. Générale*, s. v.; Spooner, *Biog. Hist. of the Fine Arts*, s. v.

Credŭla. See ARISTO.

Cree, Hamilton, a Methodist Episcopal minister, was born near Carmichael, Pa., in 1811. He was received into the Pittsburgh Conference in 1838, retired after thirteen years' labor, and died at his home in Brooke County, W. Va., Sept. 21, 1880. See *Minutes of Annual Conferences*, 1880, p. 248.

Cree, John, an Associate minister, was a native of Scotland, and came to the city of New York in 1791. He was ordained in 1792, and afterwards settled in Ligonier valley, near Pittsburgh, where he died after a few years. See Sprague, *Annals of the Amer. Pulpit*, IX, iii, 32.

Cree Version OF THE SCRIPTURES. There are two dialects of the Cree language, the difference between them consisting of the uniform substitution of certain consonants for others. One is called the Moose Fort, or East Main Cree, the other the Red River Cree. A complete Bible in the Eastern dialect for the Cree Indians in the Hudson's Bay Territories was printed in 1861, at the expense of the British and Foreign Bible Society, in syllabic characters, the translation having been made by the Rev. W. Mason of the Church Missionary Society. In the Western dialect, the gospels of Mark and John, together with other parts of the New Test. and the Psalms, were printed, in the Roman character, since 1855, the translation having been made by archdeacon Hunter, for the benefit of the Cree Indians of the Saskatchewan valley, in Rupert's Land, who had also reduced the Cree to a written system. Up to March 31, 1882, altogether 33,590 copies were distributed. See *Bible of Every Land*, p. 448. (B. P.)

Creech, Thomas, an English poet and clergyman, was born near Sherborne, Dorsetshire, in 1659, and entered at Wadham College, Oxford, in 1675. In 1683 he was elected probationer fellow of All-Souls' College. Having taken orders in 1699, he was presented to the living of Welwyn, in Hertfordshire. He put an end to his life in June, 1700. See Chalmers, *Biog. Dict.* s. v.; Allibone, *Dict. of Brit. and Amer. Authors*, s. v.

Creech, William, a Scotch clergyman, studied at Edinburgh University; became tutor to George Cranstoun; was licensed to preach in 1733; called to the living at Newbattle in 1738; ordained in 1739, and died Aug. 21, 1745, aged forty years. See *Fasti Eccles. Scoticanæ*, i, 296, 297.

Creed. The following is the Greek text of the *Apostles' Creed:*

Πιστεύω εἰς ΘΕΟΝ ΠΑΤΕΡΑ, *παντοκράτορα, ποιητὴν οὐρανοῦ καὶ γῆς.*

Καὶ (εἰς) 'ΙΗΣΟΥΝ ΧΡΙΣΤΟΝ, *υἱὸν αὐτοῦ τὸν μονογενῆ, τὸν κύριον ἡμῶν, τὸν συλληφθέντα ἐκ πνεύματος ἁγίου, γεννηθέντα ἐκ* Μαρίας *τῆς παρθένου, παθόντα ἐπὶ* Ποντίου Πιλάτου, *σταυρωθέντα, θανόντα, καὶ ταφέντα, κατελθόντα εἰς τὰ κατώτατα, τῇ τρίτῃ ἡμέρᾳ ἀναστάντα ἀπὸ τῶν νεκρῶν, ἀνελθόντα εἰς τοὺς οὐρανούς, καθεζόμενον ἐν δεξιᾷ θεοῦ πατρὸς παντοδυνάμου, ἐκεῖθεν ἐρχόμενον κρῖναι ζῶντας καὶ νεκρούς.*

Πιστεύω εἰς τὸ ΠΝΕΥΜΑ ΤΟ "ΑΓΙΟΝ, *ἁγίαν καθολικὴν ἐκκλησίαν, ἁγίων κοινωνίαν, ἄφεσιν ἁμαρτιῶν, σαρκὸς ἀνάστασιν, ζωὴν αἰώνιον.* 'Αμήν.

Dr. Schaff, in his *Creeds of Christendom* (N. Y. 1877, 3 vols.), which is the latest, and in many respects the most complete, treatise on ecclesiastical symbolics, arranges the Apostles' Creed as in pages 162, 163.

Dr. Heurtley, in his valuable collection of creeds of the Western Church, which has been supplemented by two "University Programmes" by Dr. C. J. Caspari, professor of theology at the Norwegian University, published at Christiana in 1866 and 1869, traces the growth of the creed (as far as it can be traced) through Tertullian and Cyprian; then we must take a leap from Novatian (A.D. 250) to Rufinus, bishop of Aquileia (A.D.

390), the intermediate space of one hundred and forty years affording only one stepping-stone, furnished by the notes of the belief of Marcellus of Ancyra, which he delivered on his departure from Rome. The date of this is A.D. 341. We might have expected Marcellus to exhibit his belief in the words of the creed of Nicæa; the fact that he used another symbol is interesting for more reasons than one. It comes to us in Greek, and with the assurance that he had received it from the Scriptures, and been taught it by his forefathers in the Lord; by which he must have meant that he regarded it as in entire agreement with the Scriptures. The creed of Ancyra, then, must in substance have accorded nearly with the creed of Rome as we learn it from Rufinus, differing from it only in the following points, viz.: it omits the name *Father* in the first article; it reads "born of the Holy Ghost and of the Virgin Mary;" and at the end there is added the clause "eternal life." The annexed table (taken from Smith's *Dict. of Christ. Biog.* s. v.) shows the principal forms of the Apostles' Creed in Latin, the variations being printed in italics.

AQUILEIAN CREED.	OLD ROMAN CREED.	MODERN ROMAN CREED.
Credo in *Deo Patre omnipotente, invisibili et impassibili*	Credo in Deum Patrem omnipotentem	Credo in Deum Patrem omnipotentem, *creatorem caeli et terrae*
et in Christo Jesu unico Filio ejus Domino nostro	et in Christum Jesum unicum Filium ejus Dominum nostrum	et in *Jesum Christum* Filium ejus unicum Dominum nostrum
Qui natus est de Spiritu Sancto ex Maria Virgine	Qui natus est de Spiritu Sancto ex Maria Virgine	qui *conceptus* est de Spiritu Sancto *natus* ex Maria Virgine
crucifixus sub Pontio Pilato et sepultus	crucifixus sub Pontio Pilato et sepultus	*Passus* sub Pontio Pilato crucifixus *mortuus* et sepultus
descendit in inferna		descendit ad inferna
tertia die resurrexit a mortuis	tertia die resurrexit a mortuis	tertia die resurrexit a mortuis
ascendit in caelos	ascendit in caelos	ascendit *ad* caelos
sedet ad dexteram Patris	sedet ad dexteram Patris	sedet ad dexteram *Dei* Patris *omnipotentis*
inde venturus est judicare vivos et mortuos	inde venturus est judicare vivos et mortuos	inde venturus est judicare vivos et mortuos
et in Spiritu Sancto	et in Spiritum Sanctum	*Credo* in Spiritum Sanctum
sanctam ecclesiam	sanctam ecclesiam	sanctam ecclesiam *Catholicam*
		sanctorum communionem
remissionem peccatorum	remissionem peccatorum	remissionem peccatorum
hujus carnis resurrectionem	carnis resurrectionem	carnis resurrectionem
		vitam aeternam

Creek Version. See MUSKOKEE.

Creeping to the Cross (so called). Alcuin mentions that on Good Friday a cross was prepared before the altar, and kissed in succession by the clergy and people. Sometimes it was laid on a cushion in a side-chapel. By Ælfric's Canons (957), the faithful were required to pay their adoration, and greet God's rood with a kiss. "We humble ourselves to Christ herein," Cranmer says, "offering unto him, and kissing the cross, in memory of our redemption by Christ on the cross." The practice was forbidden in 1549, but was observed at Dunbar in 1568 by the congregation, bare-legged and barefooted. During the ceremonial the hymns "Pange, lingua," and "Vexilla regis prodeunt," were sung, followed by the "Improperia," or reproaches, an expansion of Mal. iii, 3, 4.

Creichton. See CRICHTON.

Creigh, Patrick, a Scotch clergyman, was minister at Ratho in 1565; was three times complained of for neglect of his ministerial duty; suspended from his ministry in 1567, and ordered to make his repentance at Edinburgh. He was settled at North Berwick in 1568, but deposed the same year; was again admitted by the assembly in 1572 to read prayers at Haddington. See *Fasti Eccles. Scoticanæ*, i, 139, 341.

Creigh, Thomas, D.D., a Presbyterian minister, was born in Landisburg, Perry Co., Pa., Sept. 9, 1808. He graduated from Dickinson College in 1828; was soon afterwards converted, and studied theology under Rev. Geo. Duffield, D.D., and at Princeton Seminary; was licensed by the Presbytery of Carlisle; ordained pastor of the Upper West Conococheague Church at Mercersburg, Pa., in 1831, and continued there with great zeal, fidelity, and usefulness until his sudden death, April 21, 1880. See *Necrol. Report of Princeton College*, 1881, p. 37. (W. P. S.)

Creighton, James, an early Methodist preacher, was born at Moyne Hall, near Cavan, Ireland, in 1739. He studied at a grammar-school in Cavan, graduated in 1764 at Trinity College, Dublin, and, on October 28, the same year, was ordained a deacon in the cathedral church of Kilmore. Creighton confesses that at that time he had no experimental knowledge of the way of salvation, and that the bishop had warned him against preaching the doctrines of the Methodists. About 1776 he was converted through the reading of some of the writings of Wesley and Fletcher. He then commenced itinerating through Ireland, often preaching amid persecution and danger. In 1783 he was appointed by Wesley resident clergyman of the City-road Chapel, London, where he officiated until the infirmities of age compelled him to retire. In 1784 he assisted Wesley and Coke in the ordination of Whatcoat and Vasey; he also participated in the consecration of Coke as bishop for the United States of America. From 1790 to 1792 he was editor of the *Arminian Magazine*. He died at Hackney, London, Dec. 26, 1819. Creighton published, *Dictionary of Scripture Proper Names, with a Preliminary Dissertation* (commended by Dr. A. Clarke), 1807:—*Elegiac Stanzas on the Death of Charles Wesley:—Dialogue on the Death of John Wesley:—Fénelon's Dialogues:—Thuckford's History of the World.* Dr. Osborn (*Outlines of Wesleyan Bibliography*, Lond. 1869) enumerates eighteen separate publications. See Sandford, *Memoirs of Wesleyan Preachers* (N. Y. 1843), p. 51 sq.; Stevenson, *City-road Chapel* (Lond. 1872, 8vo), p. 147–149, 282; Stevens, *Hist. of Methodism*, ii, 214, 297; Smith, *Hist. of Wesl. Meth.* i, 478 sq.; ii, 276, 277.

Creighton (or **Crighton**), **Robert**, *Sen.*, D.D., an English prelate, was born in 1593, and educated at Trinity College, Cambridge. He became prebendary of Lincoln in 1631, prebendary of Wells in 1632, dean of Wells in 1660, and bishop of Bath and Wells in 1670; and died Nov. 21, 1672, leaving some *Sermons* and *Translations*. See Le Neve, *Fasti;* Allibone, *Dict. of Brit. and Amer. Authors*, s. v.

Creighton, Robert, *Jun.*, D.D., an English divine, was born in 1639. He became famous for his skill in church music, and was installed precentor of Wells in 1674. He died in 1736. The celebrated anthem, "I will arise and go to my Father," is by him, and he also published a volume of *Sermons* (1720). See Allibone, *Dict. of Brit. and Amer. Authors*, s. v.

Creizenach, MICHAEL, a Jewish rabbi of Germany, was born at Mayence, May 16, 1789. After a thorough study of the Talmud and the Jewish Scriptures, he began to read German, devoting all his leisure to the Kantian philosophy, while at the lyceum of his native place. In 1813 he opened a private seminary, which he conducted until 1825, when he was called as professor to the Philanthropinum at Frankfort-on-the-Main, where he died August 5, 1842. His main work is שֻׁלְחָן עָרוּךְ, or *Encyklopaedische Darstellung des mo-*

COMPARATIVE TABLE OF THE

AS RELATED TO THE APOSTLES'

THE APOSTLES' CREED. (Rome.) About A.D. 340. Later additions are in *italics.*	IRENÆUS. (Gaul.) A.D. 170.	TERTULLIAN. (North Africa.) A.D. 200.	ORIGEN. (Alexandria.) A.D. 230.	CYPRIAN. (Carthage.) A.D. 250.	NOVATIAN. (Rome.) A.D. 250.
I believe	We believe	We believe	[We believe in]	I believe	We believe
1. in GOD THE FATHER Almighty, *Maker of heaven and earth;*	1. . . . in ONE GOD THE FATHER Almighty, who made heaven and earth, and the sea, and all that in them is;	1. . . . in ONE GOD, the Creator of the world, who produced all out of nothing . . .	1. ONE GOD, who created and framed everything . . . Who in the last days sent	1. in GOD THE FATHER;	1. in GOD THE FATHER and Almighty Lord;
2. And in JESUS CHRIST, His only Son, our Lord;	2. And in one CHRIST JESUS, the Son of God [our Lord];	2. And in the Word, his Son, JESUS CHRIST;	2. Our Lord JESUS CHRIST . . . born of the Father before all creation . . .	2. in his Son CHRIST;	2. in the Son of God, CHRIST JESUS, our Lord God;
3. who was *conceived* by the Holy Ghost, born of the Virgin Mary;	3. Who became flesh [of the Virgin] for our salvation;	3. Who through the Spirit and power of God the Father descended into the Virgin Mary, was made flesh in her womb, and born of her;	3. born of the Virgin and the Holy Ghost . . . made incarnate while remaining God . . .		
4. *suffered* under Pontius Pilate, was crucified, *dead*, and buried;	4. and his suffering [under Pontius Pilate];	4. Was fixed on the cross [under Pontius Pilate], was dead and buried;	4. suffered in truth, died;		
5. *He descended into Hades;* the third day he rose from the dead;	5. and his rising from the dead;	5. rose again the third day;	5. rose from the dead;		
6. He ascended into heaven, and sitteth on the right hand of *God* the Father *Almighty;*	6. and his bodily assumption into heaven;	6. was taken up into heaven and sitteth at the right hand of God the Father;	6. was taken up . . .		
7. from thence he shall come to judge the quick and the dead.	7. and his coming from heaven in the glory of the Father to comprehend all things under one head, . . . and to execute righteous judgment over all.	7. He will come to judge the quick and the dead.			
8. And *I believe* in THE HOLY GHOST;	8. And in THE HOLY GHOST.	8. And in THE HOLY GHOST, the Paraclete, the Sanctifier, sent by Christ from the Father.	8. THE HOLY GHOST, united in honor and dignity with the Father and the Son.	8. in THE HOLY GHOST;	8. in THE HOLY GHOST (promised of old to the Church, and granted in the appointed and fitting time).
9. the holy *Catholic* Church; *the communion of saints;*					
10. the forgiveness of sins;				10. I believe the forgiveness of sins,	
11. the resurrection of the body;	11. And that Christ shall come from heaven to raise up all flesh, . . . and to adjudge the impious and unjust . . . to eternal fire,	11. And that Christ will, after the restoration of the flesh, receive his saints			
12. *and the life everlasting.**	12. and to give to the just and holy immortality and eternal glory.	12. into the enjoyment of eternal life and the promises of heaven, and judge the wicked with eternal fire.		12. and eternal life through the holy Church.	

* The Roman Creed, according to Rufinus (390), ends with *carnis resurrectionem;* but the Greek version of the Roman Creed by Marcellus (341), with ζωὴν αἰώνιον.

saischen Gesetzes (4 vols.); a work which called forth many criticisms from the orthodox party. See Fürst, *Bibl. Jud.* i, 190 sq.; Kayserling, *Bibliothek jüdischer Kanzelredner*, i, 384 sq.; Jost, *Michael Creiznach*, in the *Jahrbuch für Israeliten* (Vienna, 1843), ii, 79 sq.; Jost, *Gesch. d. Juden. u. s. Sekten*, iii, 361. (B. P.)

Crell, Michael, a German Protestant theologian, who lived in the early half of the 17th century, was minister at Altenburg, and wrote, *Spicilegium Poeticum* (Leipsic, 1629):—*Anagramatismorum Sylloge II* (1631):—*Breviarium Etymol. N. T.* (Altenburg, 1645):—*Syllabus Græco-Biblicus* (ibid. 1646; Rauneburg, 1663):—also some works on the Holy Scriptures.—See Hoefer, *Nouv. Biog. Générale*, s. v.

Crell, Paulus, a Lutheran theologian of Germany, was born at Eisleben, Feb. 5, 1531. He was doctor and professor of theology at Wittenberg; was called in 1568 as provost to Meissen, and died there, May 24, 1579. He prepared an *Evangelien-Harmonie*, and wrote, *Opus Concordantiarum:—Tractatus de Justificatione:—Commonefactio de Verbis Symboli:—Credo Remissionem Peccatorum et de Dicto Pauli:—Gratia Salvati Estis:—Spongia de Definitione Evangelii.* See Freheri, *Theatrum Eruditorum;* Jöcher, *Allgemeines Gelehrten-Lexikon*, s. v.; Winer, *Handbuch der theol. Lit.* i, 166. (B. P.)

Crell, Spinovius Christoph, a German Socinian theologian, son of Michael, was successively pastor of Unitarian churches in Poland, Silesia, and Prussia. He died Dec. 12, 1680, leaving, *De Virtute Christiania et Gentili*, published in the series of *Éthiques* of his father.

ANTE-NICENE RULES OF FAITH,

CREED AND THE NICENE CREED.

GREGORY. (Neo-Cæsarea.) A.D. 270.	LUCIAN. (Antioch.) A.D. 300.	EUSEBIUS. (Cæsarea, Pal.) A.D. 325.	CYRIL. (Jerusalem.) A.D. 350.	NICÆNO-CONSTANTINOPOLITAN CREED. A.D. 325 and 381.†
[We believe in] 1. ONE GOD THE FATHER;	[We believe in] 1. ONE GOD THE FATHER Almighty, Maker and Provider of all things;	We believe 1. in ONE GOD THE FATHER Almighty, Maker of all things visible and invisible;	We believe 1. in ONE GOD THE FATHER Almighty, Maker of heaven and earth, and of all things visible and invisible;	We [I] believe 1. in ONE GOD THE FATHER Almighty, Maker of *heaven and earth, and of* all things visible and invisible;
2. one LORD, . . . God of God, the image and likeness of the Godhead, . . . the Wisdom and Power which produces all creation, the true Son of the true Father . . .	2. And in one Lord JESUS CHRIST his Son, begotten of the Father before all ages, God of God, Wisdom, Life, Light . . .	2. And in one Lord JESUS CHRIST, the Word of God, God of God, Light of Light, Life of Life. the only-begotten Son, the first-born of every creature, begotten of God the Father before all ages; by whom all things were made;	2. And in ONE LORD JESUS CHRIST, the only-begotten Son of God, begotten of the Father before all ages, very God, by whom all things were made;	2. And in one Lord JESUS CHRIST, the *only-begotten* Son of God, begotten of the Father *before all worlds;* [God of God], Light of Light, very God of very God, begotten, not made, being of one substance with the Father (ὁμοούσιον τῷ Πατρί), by whom all things were made;
	3. who was born of a Virgin, according to the Scriptures, and became man . . .	3. who for our salvation was made flesh and lived among men;	3. who was made flesh, and became man;	3. who, for us men, and for our salvation, came down *from heaven,* and was incarnate *by the Holy Ghost and* [*of, ex*] *the Virgin Mary,* and was made man;
	4. who suffered for us;	4. and suffered;	4. was crucified, and was buried;	4. He *was crucified for us under Pontius Pilate, and* suffered, *and was buried;*
	5. and rose for us on the third day;	5. and rose on the third day;	5. rose on the third day;	5. and the third day he rose again, *according to the Scriptures;*
	6. and ascended into heaven, and sitteth on the right hand of God the Father;	6. and ascended to the Father;	6. and ascended into heaven, and sitteth on the right hand of the Father;	6. and ascended into heaven, *and sitteth on the right hand of the Father;*
	7. and again is coming with glory and power, to judge the quick and the dead;	7. and will come again with glory, to judge the quick and the dead.	7. and will come again in glory, to judge the quick and the dead; whose kingdom shall have no end;	7. and he shall come *again, with glory,* to judge the quick and the dead; *whose kingdom shall have no end;*
8. one HOLY GHOST, . . . the minister of sanctification, in whom is revealed God the Father, who is over all things and through all things, and God the Son, who is through all things—a perfect Trinity, not divided nor differing in glory, eternity, and sovereignty . . .	8. And in THE HOLY GHOST, given for consolation and sanctification and perfection to those who believe . . .	8. We believe also in THE HOLY GHOST.	8. And in one HOLY GHOST, the Advocate, who spake in the Prophets.	8. And [I believe] in THE HOLY GHOST, *the Lord, and Giver of life, Who proceedeth from the Father* [*and the Son, Filioque*], *who with the Father and the Son together is worshipped and glorified, who spake by the Prophets.*
			9. And in one baptism of repentance for the remission of sins;	9. *And* [I believe] *in one holy Catholic and Apostolic Church;*
			10. and in one holy Catholic Church;	10. *we* [I] *acknowledge one baptism for the remission of sins;*
			11. and in the resurrection of the flesh;	11. *and we* [I] *look for the resurrection of the dead;*
			12. and in life everlasting (ζωὴν αἰώνιον).	12. *and the life of the world to come* (ζωὴν τοῦ μέλλοντος αἰῶνος).

† The words in *italics* in the last column are additions of the Second Œcumenical Council (381); the words in brackets are Western changes.

See Hoefer, *Nouv. Biog. Générale*, s. v.; Jöcher, *Allgemeines Gelehrten-Lexikon*, s. v.

Crell, Wolfgang, a German Protestant theologian, was professor of metaphysics and theology at Frankfort-on-the-Oder. He died July 8, 1664, leaving, *De Difficultate Cognoscendæ Veritatis*. See Hoefer, *Nouv. Biog. Générale*, s. v.; Jöcher, *Allgemeines Gelehrten-Lexikon*, s. v

Crellin, HENRY, a Methodist Episcopal minister, was born in Philadelphia, Pa., March 19, 1820. He was converted in his twentieth year; removed to Iowa in 1854, and in 1856 entered the Iowa Conference, wherein he labored until his death, Jan. 1, 1867. See *Minutes of Annual Conferences*, 1867, p. 208.

Cremation, the burning of human corpses, was probably the general practice of the ancient world, with certain important exceptions. In Egypt dead bodies were embalmed; in Judæa they were buried in sepulchres; and in China they were buried in the earth. In Greece only suicides, unteethed children, and persons struck by lightning were denied the right to be burned; while at Rome, from the close of the republic to the end of the 4th century A.D., burning on the pyre or *rogus* was the general rule. Even the Jews used cremation in the vale of Tophet when a plague came; and the modern Jews of Berlin and the Spanish and Portuguese Jews at Mile-End cemetery have been among the first to welcome the lately revived process. Cremation is still practiced over a great part of Asia and America, but not always in the same form. Thus, the ashes may be stored in urns, or buried in the earth, or thrown to the wind, or smeared with gum on the heads of the mourners. In one case the three processes of embalming, burning, and burying are performed; and in another, if a member of the tribe die at a great distance from home, some of his money and clothes are nevertheless burned by the family. It is claimed by some that the practice of cremation in modern Europe was at first stopped, and has since been prevented in a great measure, by the Christian doctrine of the resurrection of the body; partly, also, by the notion that the Christian's body was redeemed and purified. The very general practice of burying bodies in the precincts of a church in order that the dead might have the benefit of the prayers of persons resorting thither, and the religious ceremony which precedes both European burials and Asiatic cremations, have given the subject a religious aspect. The question is also a sanitary one, and has attracted very considerable attention lately.

For the last ten years many distinguished physicians and chemists in Italy have warmly advocated the general adoption of cremation, and, in 1874, a congress called to consider the matter at Milan resolved to petition the Chamber of Deputies for a clause in the new sanitary code, permitting cremation under the supervision of the syndics of the commune. In Switzerland there are two associations in support of the cause. In 1797 cremation began to be discussed by the French Assembly, under the Directory, and the events of the Franco-Prussian war have again brought the subject under notice. The military experiments at Sedan, Châlons, and Metz, of burying large numbers of bodies with quicklime, or pitch and straw, were not successful, but very dangerous. The municipality of Vienna has formally made cremation permissive. There is a propagandist society, called the *Urne*, and the main difficulty for the poor seems to be the cost of carrying the bodies five miles. To overcome this a pneumatic tube has been proposed. Dresden, Leipsic, and Berlin are the centres of the German movement. In England Sir Henry Thompson first brought the question prominently before the public, and in 1874 started the cremation society of London. Its object is to introduce, through the agency of cemetery companies, and parochial and municipal authorities and burial-boards, some rapid process of disposing of the dead, "which cannot offend the living and shall render the remains absolutely innocuous." His problem was this: "Given a dead body, to resolve it into carbonic acid, water, and ammonia, rapidly, safely, and not unpleasantly." Relying on the facts connected with recent burial legislation, he pointed out that in the neighborhood of cemeteries there is a constantly increasing risk of contaminated air and water. The problem he solved by the Siemens process of cremation. The British authorities also have had to interfere in the management of the Hindû cremations, so as to reduce the cost and perfect the sanitary arrangements of the process.

Among the practical methods of cremation which have recently been attempted are those of Dr. Polli, at the Milan gas-works, and Prof. Brunetti of Padua. The former obtained complete calcination of dogs in two hours, by the use of coal-gas mixed with atmospheric air, applied to a cylindrical retort of refracting clay, so as to consume the gaseous products of combustion. The ashes remaining were five per cent. by weight of the material before cremation. The latter used an oblong furnace of refracting brick, with side doors to regulate the draught, and above a cast-iron dome, with movable shutters. The body was placed on a metallic plate suspended on iron wire. The noxious gases, which were generated in the first part of the process, passed through a flue into a second furnace, and were entirely consumed. The process required four hours. In the ordinary Siemens regenerative furnace only the hot blast is used, the body supplying hydrogen and carbon; or a stream of heated hydrocarbon mixed with heated air is sent from a gasometer supplied with coal, or other fuel, the brick or iron cased chamber being thus heated to a high degree before cremation begins (*Encycl. Brit.* 9th ed. s. v.). The subject has also been agitated in America, two societies having been organized here for cremation of corpses, and occasional instances have occurred; but the ovens and other apparatus have been as yet but moderately patronized.

The operation, as carried on at one of the best-constructed furnaces, is thus described by an eye witness:

> "Cremation is erroneously supposed to be a burning of the body. It is not. No flame whatever touches the flesh or bones from the beginning to the end of the process. It is properly and strictly *incineration*, or reduction of the human frame to ashes; an absorption of all the gaseous elements carried on inside a fire-clay retort, three feet in diameter and seven in length. As the door of the retort is opened the inrushing air cools it from white to red heat, and the whole interior is filled with a beautiful rosy light. The body, decently clad as for burial, is laid in a crib, which is covered with a clean white sheet soaked in alum. The crib is then put into the retort. The sheet retains its original position and conceals the form until nothing but the bones are left—and these gently crumble into dust. The relatives then receive a few pounds of clean, pure ashes in an urn, which can be placed in any cemetery, public or private, in a vault or church niche, or disposed of as personal choice may dictate."

This process is certainly a great improvement upon the rude and tedious operation of the ancient Romans and the modern Hindûs, consisting of a roasting of the corpse upon an immense pile of wood, filling the air with smoke and the noxious fumes of burning flesh. It is also claimed by its advocates to be much more economical than ordinary burial. Could the prejudice naturally entertained against it, especially by Christians, as a heathenish and barbaric custom, be overcome, there is no telling how popular the practice might yet become. See Eassie, *Cremation of the Dead* (Lond. 1875), a valuable work; Vegmann Ercolani, *Cremation the most Rational Method of Disposing of the Dead* (Zurich, 1874, 4th ed.); Reclam, *De le Crémation des Cadavres;* Sir Thomas Browne, *Hydriotaphia, or Urn-burial* (1658); Walker, *On Graveyards* (Lond. 1839); Pietra Santa, *La Crémation des Morts en France et a l'Étranger;* Brunetti, *La Cremazione dei Cadaveri* (Padua, 1873). See BURIAL.

Crementius (or **Clementius**) is the name of two early Christians:

1. A sub-deacon of Carthage, in connection with Cyprian (*Epist.* viii).

2. A canonized martyr at Saragossa, about A.D. 304, in the persecution of Diocletian, at the time when Dacian was governor of Spain, having fought twice in the arena, and retired without staining it by his blood (Prudentius, *Peristeph.* hymn v, in Migne's *Patrol. Lat.* lx, 982; Ruinart, *Acta Sincera Martyrum*, p. 468; Ceillier, iii, 44).—Smith, *Dict. of Christian Biography*, s. v.

Cremer, BERNHARD SEBASTIAN, a Reformed theologian of Germany, was born in 1683, taught theology and antiquities at Harderwick, and died Sept. 14, 1750. In his exposition of the Scriptures he carried out to the utmost extreme the system of Cocceius (q. v.). He wrote, *Prodromus Typicus in V. et N. T. Loca* (Amsterdam, 1720):—*Prophetico-Typicarum Exercitationum ex V. T. Tetras* (ibid. 1723):—*In Legem Naziræorum* (ibid. 1727):—*Summa Theologia Supernaturalis* (Harderwick, 1722):—*Antiquitates Mosaico-Typicæ* (ibid. 1733):—*De Arca et Shechina, Igne Sacro et Oleo Unctionis* (1737):—*Œdipus Evangelicus Sacrarum Antiquitatum* (Amsterdam, 1745). See Moser, *Jetztleb. theol. Unparth. Kirchenhistorie*, iii, 1129; Jöcher, *Allgemeines Gelehrten-Lexikon*, s. v.; Hoefer, *Nouv. Biog. Générale*, s. v. (B. P.)

Cremona, NICCOLO DA, a reputable Italian historical painter, flourished at Cremona about 1518. In Santa Maria Maddalena Monachi, at Bologna, is a picture by this artist, of *The Taking Down from the Cross*, dated 1518.

Cremonese, IL. See CALETTI.

Cremonini, GIOVANNI BATTISTA, an Italian painter, was born at Cento, and flourished about 1600. His best works are at Bologna: *The Assumption*, in Santa Maria della Vita; *The Annunciation*, and the *Death of St. Francis*, in San Francesco. He died in 1610.

Creolese Version OF THE SCRIPTURES. This language, a kind of broken Dutch, with a rather Danish orthography, is the language of the black population of the Danish West Indies. The New Test. in Creolese was printed in 1781, by order of the Danish government. Another edition was printed at Copenhagen in 1818, by the Danish Bible Society. The grammar of this language has been treated by De St. Quentin, *Introduction à l'Histoire de Cayenne Grammaire Créole* (Paris, 1872). (B. P.)

Crephagenētēs, a deity worshipped at Thebes, in Egypt, and supposed to have been the same as *Cneph* or *Kneph*.

Crépin and **Crépinien**. See CRISPIN.

Crescas (or **Kreskas**), CHASDAÏ BEN-ABRAHAM, a Spanish rabbi, was born at Barcelona about 1340, and died in 1410 at Saragossa. He was the scion of a noble family, and stood high in reputation at the royal court and among the rabbinical authorities of his time, who solicited his opinion on momentous questions. In 1391 he witnessed the fanatical persecution of the Jews in Spain, in which he lost his son. He is the author of a polemical work, entitled מַאֲמָר, "On the Dogmas of Christianity," with a refutation of the same, treating of (1) original sin; (2) redemption; (3) incarnation; (4) virginity of Mary; (5) eucharist, etc., written in Spanish, and translated into Hebrew by Joseph ibn-Shem-Tob. Another work of his is *Or Adonai*, אוֹר אֲדוֹנָי, "light of the Lord," a logical masterpiece of the dogmatics of Judaism, published at Vienna in 1860. See Fürst, *Bibl. Jud.* ii, 209; De' Rossi, *Dizionario Storico* (Germ. transl.), p. 173, and *Bibl. Judaica Antichristiana*, p. 24, 29; Grätz, *Gesch. d. Juden*, viii, 32 sq., 98 sq., 410 sq.; Jost, *Gesch. d. Juden. u. s. Sekten*, iii, 84; Finn, *Sephardim*, p. 393; Lindo, *History of the Jews in Spain*, p. 268; Frankel, *Monatsschrift*, 1867, p. 311 sq.; especially Joël, *Don Chasdai Creska's Religionsphilosophische Lehren* (Breslau, 1866). (B. P.)

Crescens is the name of several early Christians:

1. The disciple of St. Paul, afterwards bishop in Galatia, variously commemorated on June 27 or April 15.

2. One of the seven sons of St. Symphorosa, martyr at Tivoli under Hadrian, commemorated July 21 or June 27.

3. Or Crescentius, martyr at Tomi, commemorated Oct. 1.

4. Crescens, Paulus, and Dioscorides were three boy martyrs of Rome, commemorated May 28.

5. Bishop of Cirta, in Numidia, now Constantine. Crescens is a particularly common name on monuments of Cirta (8th Suffrag. in Syn. Carth. sub. Cyp. vii, A.D. 256).

Crescentia is the name of two Christian saints:

1. A martyr in Sicily under Diocletian, commemorated June 15.

2. A virgin, whose tumulus was near Paris, in a place where a stone bears the inscription: "Hic Requiescit Crescentia Sacrata Deo Puella;" but nothing more is known of her. She is commemorated Aug. 19. See Gregory of Tours, *De Gloria Confess.* cap. 105, in Migne's *Patrol. Lat.* lxxi, 904.

Crescentiānus is the name of several early saints: (1) Martyr in Sardinia, commemorated May 31; (2) martyr in Africa, commemorated June 13; (3) martyr in Campania, commemorated July 2; (4) martyr at Augustana, commemorated Aug. 12; (5) martyr at Rome, under Maximian, commemorated Nov. 24 or March 16.

Crescentio (or **Crescentius**), martyr at Rome, commemorated Sept. 17.

Crescentius was a controversialist on the subject of the Easter celebration of the 4th century (Epiph. *Hæres.* 70, 9, in the *Patrol. Græc.* xlii, 555, § 821; Ceillier, iii, 105). See also CRESCENS (3); CRESCENTIO.

Cresconius (or **Crisconius**) is the name of several early Christian ecclesiastics:

1. Bishop of Villa Regia, in Numidia, at the end of the 4th century. He deserted his see and seized on that of Tubia, or Tubuna. The third Council of Carthage, A.D. 397, passed a decree ordering his return to his own see (can. 38), which he entirely disregarded. The secular arm was called in with as little effect. At the Council of Carthage, A.D. 401, the primate of Numidia was ordered to summon Cresconius before the next general council, and to depose him if he failed to appear (*Cod. Canon. Eccl. Afric.* can. 77). But no mention is made of him at the Council of Milevum, A.D. 402; and if he is the same who appears as bishop of Tubuna at the Conference of Carthage, in 411 (*Prim. Cognit.* c. xxi), he must have carried the day (Labbe, *Concil.* ii, 1072, 1096, 1172, 1377; Tillemont, xiii, 305).

2. A monk of Adrumetum, mentioned by Augustine (*Epp.* 214, 215).

3. An African bishop, who, about 690, at the request of the "pontifex" Liberinus or Liberius, published a systematized collection of the apostolic canons and those of the early councils, and the decretals of the popes from Siricius to Gelasius, as an improvement upon an earlier work of the kind by Fulgentius Ferrandus. Both are printed by Migne, *Patrol.* lxxxviii. The author has often been confounded with the Latin poet Flavius Cresconius Corippus.

Crésol, LOUIS, a French scholar of the Jesuit order, was born in 1568, in the diocese of Tréguier. He taught classics, philosophy, and theology successively; was for fifteen years secretary of the general of his order at Rome; and died Nov. 11, 1634. His principal works are *Theatrum Veterum Rhetorum* (Paris, 1620):—*De Perfecta Oratoris Actione et Pronunciatione* (ibid. eod.):—*Mystagogus Hominum* (ibid. 1629, 1638):—*Anthologia Sacra* (ibid. 1632, 1638). See Hoefer, *Nouv. Biog. Générale*, s. v.

Crespel, EMMANUEL, O. S. F., an eminent Roman Catholic missionary, was a native of Belgium. In 1723 he left Avesnes, in Hainault, and arrived at Quebec in October, 1724. Being ordained March 17, 1726, he went as chaplain with Lignery's expedition against the Foxes. He was next stationed at Niagara, Fort Frontenac, and Crown Point, suffering greatly in his winter service at the last-named place. Being recalled to France, he sailed from Quebec, Nov. 3, 1736, but was shipwrecked on the way, and barely escaped death. He returned to Quebec, and was pastor at Soulanges till 1738, when he finally returned to Europe. His *Letters*, describing his perils in America, were published in French, at Frankfort, in 1742; soon appeared in German, and an English translation was issued in London in 1797. Dr. Shea published another version in his *Perils of the Ocean and Wilderness.* See *Cath. Almanac*, 1873, p. 50; De Courcy and Shea, *Hist. of the Cath. Church in the U. S.* p. 474.

Crespet, PIERRE, a French theologian of the order of Celestines, was born at Sens in 1543. He was elevated to the first positions of his order, and was an active partisan in Church and State; but finally withdrew from politics. He succeeded in obtaining a priory in Vivarais, where he died in 1594. His principal works are, *Discours sur la Vie et Passion de Sainte-Catherine*, in verse (Sens, 1577):—*La Pomme de Grénade Mystique* (Paris, 1586, 1595; Rouen, 1605):—*Deux Livres de la Haine de Satan*, etc. (Paris, 1590):—*Commentaires de*

Bernardin de Mendoce des Guerres de Flandre et des Pays-Bas (ibid. 1591). See Hoefer, *Nouv. Biog. Générale*, s. v.; *Biog. Universelle*, s. v.

Crespi (or **Crespy**), an Italian engraver, practiced the art about 1705. There are a few plates by him, among which is *The Descent from the Cross*, after Cignani.

Crespi, Benedetto (called *il Bustino*), a painter of Como, flourished about the middle of the 17th century. Some of his works are in the churches of Como.

Crespi, Daniele, a Milanese historical and portrait painter, was born in 1590, and studied under Gio. Battista Crespi, and afterwards under Procaccini. Among the best works of this artist are, *The Descent from the Cross*, and his celebrated set of subjects from the life of St. Bruno, at the Certosa. He died in 1630. See Hoefer, *Nouv. Biog. Générale*, s. v.; Spooner, *Biog. Hist. of the Fine Arts*, s. v.

Crespi, Giovanni Battista (called *il Cerano*), an Italian painter, was born at Cerano, near Novara, in 1557. He visited Rome and Venice, and subsequently settled at Milan, where he was patronized by the duke-cardinal Federigo. One of his best productions was *The Baptism of St. Agostino*, in San Marco, at Milan. He died in 1633. See Hoefer, *Nouv. Biog. Générale*, s. v.; Spooner, *Biog. Hist. of the Fine Arts*, s. v.

Crespi, Giovanni (or Giuseppe) Maria (called *il Spagnuolo*, from the finery of his dress), a Bolognese painter, was born in 1665, and studied under Canuti and Cignani. He executed a number of works for the churches of Bologna, among which are *The Last Supper; The Annunciation; The Temptation of St. Anthony; St. John Preaching;* and *The Crucifixion.* He died in 1747. See Hoefer, *Nouv. Biog. Générale*, s. v.; Spooner, *Biog. Hist. of the Fine Arts*, s. v.

Crespi, Giovanni Pietro (called also *de Castoldi*), a reputable Italian painter, flourished about 1535, at Milan, and left some specimens of his genius in the Church of Santa Maria de Busto.

Crespo, Francisco, a Spanish Benedictine, who died Sept. 25, 1665, in his eighty-second year, was abbot of Montferrat, general visitor of his congregation, and professor of theology at Salamanca, and wrote, *Tribunal Thomisticum de Immaculatæ Deiparæ Conceptu* (Barcelona, 1657). See Hoefer, *Nouvelle Biographie Générale*, s. v.; Jöcher, *Allgemeines Gelehrten-Lexikon*, s. v.

Cressell, Edward, an English Congregational minister, was born at Hackney, April 4, 1830. In April, 1853, he was received as an agent of the London City Mission; subsequently labored in the Leadenhall Street and Holborn Hill districts for over eleven years; was some time evangelist of Claremont Chapel, which led to his entrance into the ministry. He was pastor at Houghton, in Hants, for five years; next at Hatton, Norfolk, from 1875 until his death, Nov. 21, 1880. See (Lond.) *Cong. Year-book*, 1881, p. 366.

Cresselle (Fr. for *rattle*) is a wooden instrument used instead of bells in some places, to summon the people to service during Passion week. It is supposed to represent Christ praying upon the cross, and inviting all to embrace his doctrine. Similar instruments are in use among the Turks, in consequence of their strong prejudice against the sound of bells. See Clapper.

Cresset is an oil-lamp in which the wick floats about upon a small circle of cork. Anciently, English churches were often lighted by this sort of lamp, and the side-chapels of cathedrals were likewise so illuminated.

Cressett, Edward, an English prelate, became dean of Hereford in 1736, was consecrated bishop of Llandaff Feb. 12, 1749, and died Feb. 13, 1755. He published some single *Sermons*. See Le Neve, *Fasti*; Allibone, *Dict. of Brit. and Amer. Authors*, s. v.

Cressey, E. H., D.D., a Protestant Episcopal clergyman, was rector, for many years, in Auburn, N. Y., but removed in 1859 to Castleton. In 1860 he took charge of St. Paul's, Stapleton; in 1862 removed to Newburg, as rector of two churches in that vicinity; in 1864 was assistant minister of the Church of the Annunciation, New York city; and the following year became pastor of Trinity Church, Trenton, N. J., where he died, Sept. 20, 1866. See *Prot. Episc. Almanac*, 1867, p. 101.

Cressey, E. W., a Baptist minister, was born at Sharon, Vt., July, 1808. He was converted in his nineteenth year, and after obtaining what education he could, was ordained as an evangelist at Garland, Me., in November, 1837. He preached at Sangerville in 1838 and 1839; in 1841 became pastor in Vassalborough; in 1850 was located at Wabash, Ind.; in 1852 organized a Church at Rolling Stone, near Winona, Minn.; in 1853 at Minneapolis; in 1854 at Prescott, Wis.; and afterwards, at churches in Hastings, Pine Island, and Roscoe, in Minn. In 1865 he became pastor at Richfield. The last ten years of his life were spent in Minneapolis, where he died, Sept. 15, 1883. See Millet, *Hist. of the Baptists of Maine; Chicago Standard*, Oct. 18, 1883. (J. C. S.)

Cressey, George Washington, a Congregational minister, was born at Rowley, Mass., in December, 1813. He graduated from Bowdoin College in 1835, and from the Andover Theological Seminary in 1838; was ordained in 1840 at Kennebunk, Me., where he remained nearly twelve years; and was stated supply at Buxton Centre, until his death, Feb. 12, 1867. See *Hist. of Bowdoin College*, p. 473. (J. C. S.)

Cressey, Hugh. See Cressy.

Cressey, Isaac, a Baptist minister, was born at Fairfax, Vt., Dec. 22, 1807. He was converted early, and in 1841 engaged in preaching at Keene, N. H.; in 1845 was ordained in Berkshire, Vt.; subsequently labored at Sanbornton, N. H., Johnson and Waterbury, Vt.; and died in the last-named place, Aug. 3, 1855. See *Watchman and Reflector*, Aug. 16, 1855. (J. C. S.)

Cressey, Timothy Robinson, a Baptist minister, was born at Pomfret, Conn., Sept. 18, 1800. He graduated from Amherst College in 1828; studied theology two years (1828–30) at the Newton Theological Institution; was ordained June 5, 1830; served as pastor in Columbus, O., from 1834 to 1842; was agent of the American and Foreign Bible Society from 1843 to 1846; pastor at Indianapolis, Ind., from 1846 to 1852; at St. Paul, Minn., from 1852 to 1854; missionary of the American Baptist Home Mission Society; pastor at Hastings, Minn.; chaplain of a regiment of United States volunteers from 1861 to 1863; pastor at Kendalville, Ind., from 1864 to 1866; at Indianola, Ia., from 1868 to 1870; and died at Des Moines, Aug. 30, 1870. (J. C. S.)

Cresson, Sarah, a minister of the Society of Friends, orthodox, was born at Philadelphia, Pa., in 1771; began to preach at the age of nineteen; removed to Haddonfield, N. J., in 1807; and died at Woodbury, Sept. 23, 1829. See *Memorials, etc., for Pennsylvania*, 1879, p. 197.

Cresswell, Daniel, D.D., an English divine and mathematician, was born in 1776; became a fellow of Trinity College, Cambridge; was proctor of the university in 1813, and tutor in 1814. He died in 1844. His publications include several mathematical works, and *Sermons on Domestic Duties* (1829). See Allibone, *Dict. of Brit. and Amer. Authors*, s. v.

Cresswell, Henry, an English Congregational minister, was born at Wallingford, Berks, Dec. 18, 1804. He was educated at Hoxton Academy and at Highbury; in 1828, on leaving college, he became pastor at Ipswich, where he remained three years; then at Guildhall Street, Canterbury, for five years, as co-pastor, and afterwards in sole charge, until his death, Dec. 1, 1879. See (Lond.) *Congregational Year-book*, 1882, p. 291.

Cressy, Council of (*Concilium Christiacum*), was held in Ponthieu, A.D. 676, or at Autun, A.D. 670, the canons being headed with the name of Leodegarius, bishop of Autun: passed several canons, but, among others, one exacting, on pain of episcopal condemnation, from every priest, deacon, subdeacon, or "clericus," assent to the "Athanasian faith."

Cressy, Charles, a Methodist Episcopal minister, was born at Corinth, Me., July 7, 1841. He was educated at the East Maine Conference Seminary; spent several years in teaching; entered the Upper Iowa Conference in 1870, and continued in the active work until his death, at Hampton, Dec. 21, 1881. See *Minutes of Annual Conferences*, 1882, p. 314.

Cressy (or **Cressey**), *Sir* **Hugh Paulin**, a Roman Catholic clergyman, was born at Wakefield, Yorkshire, England, in 1605. He was educated at the free grammar-school of his native town, and at Merton College, Oxford; in 1626 was elected a fellow of his college; subsequently took holy orders and became chaplain to Thomas, lord Wentworth, and afterwards to Lucius, lord Falkland, who promoted him to the deanery of Laughlin, and a canonry of Windsor. He travelled in Italy, and in 1646, while at Rome, embraced the Roman Catholic faith. He resided for seven or more years in the college of Douay, where he changed his name to *Serenus de Cressey*. After the Restoration he came to England, and became chaplain to the queen. Shortly before his death, which took place in 1674, he retired to Grinstead, in Sussex. He published, *Narrative of the Conversion unto Catholic Unity of Hugh Paulin* (Paris, 1647, sm. 8vo; 1653, 8vo; the last ed. contains an answer to J. P., author of the preface to lord Falkland's work on infidelity):—*Sancta Sophia* (Douay, 1657, 2 vols. 8vo):—*R. C. Doctrines no Novelties* (1663, 8vo):—*Church Hist. of Brittany* (1668, fol.; completed only to about 1350). See *Church of England Magazine*, March, 1845, p. 162; Allibone, *Dict. of Brit. and Amer. Authors*, s. v.; Hoefer, *Nouv. Biog. Générale*, s. v.

Crest (Lat. *crista*), the ornamental finishing which surmounts a screen, canopy, or other similar subordinate portion of a building, whether a battlement, open carved work, or other enrichment: a row of Tudor-flowers is very often used in late Perpendicular work. The name is sometimes applied to the top stones on the parapet and other similar parts of a Gothic building, usually called the capping or coping. The finials of gables and pinnacles are also sometimes called crests. *Crest-tiles* were often made with a row of ornaments, resembling small battlements or Tudor-flowers, on the top, and glazed, and still are so occasionally, but in general they are quite plain. Frequently these ornaments were formed in lead when the ridge of the roof was covered with that material, as at Exeter Cathedral.

Crests on Exeter Cathedral.

Crestey, Pierre, a French philanthropist, was born at Trun, near Argentan, Nov. 17, 1622. He was rector of Barenton, and distinguished himself by his zeal in founding establishments of public utility, the principal of which are, a hospital at Barenton, a house of hospitable monks in the same place, a similar house at Vimoutiers, an Hôtel-Dieu at Bernay, and a seminary at Domfront. He died at Barenton, Feb. 23, 1703. See Hoefer, *Nouv. Biog. Générale*, s.v.; *Biog. Universelle*, s.v.

Cresti. See Passignano.

Creti, Donato, an Italian painter, was born at Cremona in 1671, and studied under Pasinelli at Bologna, where he resided, and painted a number of pictures for the churches there, the best of which is *The Adoration of the Magi*, in the Mendicanti. He died at Bologna in 1749. See Hoefer, *Nouv. Biog. Générale*, s.v.; Spooner, *Biog. Hist. of the Fine Arts*, s. v.

Cretin, Joseph, a Roman Catholic bishop, was born at Lyons, France, in 1800. He came with bishop Loras to America, and succeeded Petiot among the Winnebagoes, where he built a church and school, which failed in competition with the state schools in 1848. On Jan. 26, 1857, he was consecrated first bishop of St. Paul, Minn. After great exertions for the promotion of the interests of his diocese, bishop Cretin was struck down with apoplexy, Feb. 22 following. See De Courcy and Shea, *Hist. of the Cath. Church in the U. S.* p. 641.

Crétineau-Joly, Jacques, a French historian, was born Sept. 23, 1803, at Fontenay, in Vendée, and was educated at Paris, at the seminary of St. Sulpice. When nineteen years of age he was appointed professor of philosophy, but, before entering upon his duties, he travelled in Italy and Germany. He died Jan. 3, 1875. He edited several politico-religious journals, and is the author of *Histoire de la Compagnie de Jésus* (Paris, 1844-46, 6 vols.; 3d ed. 1851):—*Clement XIV et les Jésuites* (ibid. 1847):—*L'Église Romaine en Face de Révolution* (ibid. 1852, 2 vols.):—*Le Cardinal Consalvi* (ibid. 1864, 2 vols.):—*Bonaparte, le Concordat de* 1801 *et le Cardinal Consalvi* (ibid. 1869). See Hoefer, *Nouv. Biog. Générale*, s. v. (B. P.)

Creutziger (Lat. *Cruciger*), **Caspar**, a German Protestant theologian, son of another of the same name, was born at Wittenberg, March 19, 1525. Having been expelled from his professorship there because he had embraced the doctrines of Calvin, he was called as preacher to Cassel, where he died, April 16, 1597, leaving *De Justificatione et Bonis Operibus*, and some polemical works. See Hoefer, *Nouv. Biog. Générale*, s. v.; Jöcher, *Allgemeines Gelehrten-Lexikon*, s. v.

Creutziger, Felix, a Polish reformer of the middle of the 16th century, was superintendent of the evangelical congregation of Little Poland, and influential in bringing about the union of the Bohemians in that country, especially enlisting count Ostroro in that movement. See Sandomir Agreement.

Creutziger, Georg, was born at Merseburg, Sept. 24, 1575; studied at Leipsic and Wittenberg; became professor and doctor of theology at Marburg; and died July 8, 1637, leaving *Harmonia Quatuor Linguarum Cardinalium*. See Jöcher, *Allgemeines Gelehrten-Lexikon*, s. v.

Crevey, Thomas, a Scotch clergyman, was born at Old Aberdeen, Sept. 8, 1644; took his degree at King's College there in 1663; was presented to the living at Newhills in 1679; became synod-clerk; protested against the assembly's committee for the north in 1694; was deprived for adultery in 1695, and went to Ireland. See *Fasti Eccles. Scoticanæ*, iii, 507.

Crewe, Nathaniel, LL.D., an English prelate, was born at Stean, Northampton, Jan. 31, 1633, and in 1652 admitted commoner of Lincoln College, Oxford, where he was chosen fellow in 1655-56. He entered into holy orders July 2, 1664, and, April 29, 1669, was installed dean of Chichester; in 1671 was elected bishop of Oxford, and consecrated July 2; was translated to Durham, Oct. 22, 1674; in 1686 was appointed one of the commissioners in the new ecclesiastical commission erected by king James, and held several other important offices during his life. He was a very great benefactor to Lincoln College, of which he had been fellow and rector. He died Sept. 18, 1721. See Chalmers, *Biog. Dict.* s. v.; Allibone, *Dict. of Brit. and Amer. Authors*, s. v.

Crewenna, an Irish *saint*, is said to have been one of the companions of St. Breaca from Ireland to Cornwall in the 5th century, but the hagiologies of this period are very uncertain.

Crews, HOOPER, D.D., a Methodist Episcopal minister, was born near Pruetts Knob, Barren County, Ky., April 17, 1807. He was converted in 1824, licensed to preach in 1828, and joined the Kentucky Conference in 1829. After five years he was transferred to the Illinois Conference, in which he served Springfield, Danville District, and Galena. In 1840 he became a member of the Rock River Conference, in which his appointments were as follows: Chicago, Chicago District; Mount Morris District; Chicago District; agent for Rock River Seminary, Galena; Clark Street, Chicago; First Church, Rockford; Rockford District; Joliet; Chicago District; Indiana Avenue, Chicago; Embury Church, Freeport; Batavia; First Church, Rockford, and Oregon, Ill., where he died, Dec. 21, 1880. Dr. Crews was a delegate to four general conferences. During the year 1862 he was chaplain of the 100th Illinois regiment. He was sound in theology, logical in methods, and preached with power. See *Minutes of Annual Conferences*, 1881.

Creyghlon. See CREIGHLON.

Crichton (occasionally written **Creichtoun**), the family name of several Scotch clergymen and prelates:

1. DAVID, LL.D., was teacher in a school at Anstruther Easter; then English master at the Madras College, St. Andrews; licensed to preach in 1833; appointed to the chapel of ease, Inverbrothock, in 1838; joined the Free Secession in 1843; and had a son, Andrew, minister of the Free New North Church, Edinburgh. See *Fasti Eccles. Scoticanæ*, iii, 809.

2. GEORGE, was made bishop of Dunkeld in 1527, also keeper of the privy-seal, and died Jan. 24, 1543. He was not much skilled in matters of religion. See Keith, *Scottish Bishops*, p. 94.

3. JAMES (1), D.D., took his degree at Glasgow University in 1655; was admitted to the living at Kilbride in 1663; deprived at the Revolution; was dean of the faculty of Glasgow University from 1679 to 1689, and died in April, 1692, aged about fifty-seven years. See *Fasti Eccles. Scoticanæ*, ii, 290.

4. JAMES (2), D.D., studied at Edinburgh University; was licensed to preach in 1798; presented to the living at Wamphray in 1799; ordained in 1800; transferred to Holywood in 1805, and died July 26, 1820. See *Fasti Eccles. Scoticanæ*, i, 583, 666.

5. JOHN, took his degree at the University of St. Andrews in 1619; was called as colleague to the living at Abercorn in 1622; transferred to Campsie in 1623; to Paisley in 1629; was deposed in 1638 for Arminianism, etc.; petitioned the presbytery in 1649 to be restored, he being a chaplain in the army. He was afterwards stationed at Dublin. See *Fasti Eccles. Scoticanæ*, i, 164; ii, 53, 196.

6. JOSEPH, was licensed to preach in 1776; presented to the living at Carstairs in 1785, and ordained in 1786; transferred to Ceres in 1793, and died Feb. 15, 1849, aged ninety-five years. See *Fasti Eccles. Scoticanæ*, i, 164; ii, 319, 478.

7. PATRICK (1), was born at Nauchton; took his degree at Edinburgh University in 1600; was presented to the vicarage of Forgand in 1606, but changed it for that of Ruthven in 1609; and continued in 1644. See *Fasti Eccles. Scoticanæ*, iii, 759.

8. PATRICK (2), was licensed to preach in 1758; presented to the living at Glendevon in 1765, but was kept in suspense and refused admission to the charge till 1770. The presbytery denied him ordination in 1771, and he resigned in 1774. See *Fasti Eccles. Scoticanæ*, ii, 768.

9. ROBERT (1), nephew of bishop George Crichton, was promoted to the see of Dunkeld in 1550, where he continued until put out by the reformers, at least as late as Dec. 22, 1561. He is said to have been appointed a commissioner for divorcing the earl of Bothwell from lady Jane Gordon. See Keith, *Scottish Bishops*, p. 96.

10. ROBERT (2), took his degree at the University of St. Andrews in 1625; was admitted to the living at Essie-with-Nevay before 1637, and died before Aug. 1, 1665, aged about sixty years. See *Fasti Eccles. Scoticanæ*, iii, 747.

11. WILLIAM, took his degree at Edinburgh University in 1649; was called to the living at Bathgate in 1654, and ordained; his ministry was inhibited in 1655, and he was removed by the synod in 1660; was indulged by the privy council in 1672, but refused; returned in 1687, and opened a meeting-house and formed a presbytery; was a member of the assembly in 1690; elected moderator in 1692; transferred to Falkirk the same year; promoted to Tron Church, Edinburgh, in 1695; again elected moderator in 1697; resigned in 1707, and died Nov. 27, 1708, aged seventy-seven years. See *Fasti Eccles. Scoticanæ*, i, 56, 167, 186.

Crickett, James, an English Congregational minister, was born in London in 1789. He became a wealthy merchant, and on retiring was ordained at Ramsbury, Wiltshire; afterwards removed to Adderbury, Oxfordshire, where he preached many years gratuitously. He died at Portland Isle, in February, 1863. See (Lond.) *Cong. Year-book*, 1865, p. 232.

Crickett, John, an English Wesleyan minister, commenced his ministry in 1780; preached in England and Ireland for twenty-six years, became a supernumerary in 1805, and died Dec. 11, 1806. See *Minutes of the British Conference*, 1807; Smith, *Hist. of Wesl. Meth.* ii, 444, 445.

Crida, an obscure Welsh saint, was probably one of the devotees who settled in Cornwall, but others think the name merely a corruption of *Credanus* (q. v.).

Crigler, A. I., a Lutheran minister, son of Rev. John J. Crigler, was born in Ralls County, Mo., March 24, 1840. In 1871 he graduated from Wittenburg College, O., and subsequently from Wittenburg Theological Seminary; was licensed by the Miami Synod, and for two years served as a home missionary in Iowa; for several succeeding years he preached at Knoxville, Ia.; afterwards removed to Colorado, but soon returned to Knoxville; again went to Colorado, and then to Missouri, and died at Millard, Jan. 16, 1880. See *Lutheran Observer*, Feb. 13, 1880.

Crigler, John Jefferson, a Lutheran minister, was born in Madison County, Va., March 1, 1811, and spent his childhood in Boone County, Ky. At forty-five years of age he began the study of theology under Rev. D. Harbaugh and professor J. Y. Harris; was licensed to preach May 19, 1856, by the synod of Kentucky, and served as pastor in Dearborn County, Ind.; in 1858 removed to Sullivan County, Mo., and labored there ten years in missionary work; was pastor, in 1874, of Johnston's Grove Church, in Story Co., Ia., besides acting as missionary to neighboring congregations. He died at Knoxville, Marion Co., March 11, 1877. See *Lutheran Observer*, March 30, 1877.

Crinesius, CHRISTOPH, a Lutheran theologian of Germany, was born in 1584 at Schlackenwald, in Bohemia, was at first court-preacher at Gschwend and Grub, on the borders of Styria, then deacon and professor of theology and Oriental languages at Altdorf, and died Aug. 28, 1629, leaving *Lexicon Syriacum:—Exercitationes Hebraicæ Quinque:—De Fide Catholica Petri:—Gymnasium Syriacum:—Epistola ad Romanos et Titum*

Syriaca:—Analysis Nov. Testamenti:—Lingua Samaritana:—Gymnasium Chaldaicum:—Lexicon Chaldaicum:—De Confusione Linguarum, etc. See Steinschneider, *Bibliogr. Handbuch*, s. v.; Jöcher, *Allgemeines Gelehrten-Lexikon*, s. v.; Hoefer, *Nouv. Biog. Générale*, s. v. (B. P.)

Crinīti Fratres (*long-haired brethren*) was a name under which Augustine censures the Mesopotamian monks for wearing long hair, against the rule of the Roman Catholic Church.

Crinsoz (de Bionens), Theodore, a Swiss Protestant theologian, was born in 1690, at Nyon, near Geneva. He had undertaken a new translation of the Bible, but the clergy of Geneva, wishing, without doubt, to be revenged upon him because he had refused to sign the Formula of Concord, would not permit him to publish it. He died about 1750, leaving *Job, Traduit en Français* (Rotterdam, 1729):—*Les Psaumes, Traduits en Français* (Ivuerdun, eod.):—*Essai sur l'Apocalypse* (eod.), and some polemical works. See Hoefer, *Nouv. Biog. Générale*, s. v.

Cririe, James, D.D., a Scotch clergyman, born at Newabbey in 1752, was a cattle-herd, but fond of reading, and largely self-taught; became master of the grammar-school at Wigton in 1777; was promoted to the rectorship of the high-school at Leith in 1787, where he introduced the monitorial system; licensed to preach in 1791; became a master in the high-school at Edinburgh in 1795; presented to the living at Dalton in 1801, and died Jan. 5, 1835. He was master of several Continental languages, a Fellow of the Society of Scottish Antiquaries in 1795, and filled their office of Latin secretary from 1799 to 1815. He published, *Sketches in Verse Descriptive of Scenes Chiefly in the Highlands* (1803). See *Fasti Eccles. Scoticanæ*, i, 646.

Criscuolo, Giovanni Andrea (or **Angelo**), an Italian painter, the younger brother of Giovanni Filippo, was instructed in the school of Marco da Siena. He painted a number of works for the Neapolitan churches, among which are *The Stoning of Stephen*, in San Stefano; and the picture of the *Virgin and Infant, with St. Jerome*, dated 1572. He died about 1580.

Criscuolo, Giovanni Filippo, an Italian painter, was born at Gaeta about 1495, and studied under Andrea da Salerno. He painted a number of fine works for the churches of Naples, particularly an altarpiece in Santa Maria della Grazia, representing the *Virgin and Infant in the Clouds, with Saints below;* and the *Adoration of the Magi*, in Santa Maria del Rosario. He died at Naples in 1584.

Crisēnus, a Scotch saint mentioned in the legend of St. Andrews as a companion of St. Regulus (q. v.).

Crismond, John M., a minister of the Methodist Episcopal Church South, was born and reared in Baltimore, Md. He was converted in youth, and in 1836, removing to Abingdon, Va., was licensed to preach, and in 1837 entered the Holston Conference, continuing to labor with zeal and fidelity until his death, April 27, 1875. See *Minutes of Annual Conferences of the M. E. Church South*, 1875, p. 155.

Crisp, Alfred, an English Congregational minister, was born at Leeds, Oct. 2, 1809. He was converted in early manhood, ordained to the ministry in London in 1850, and continued to labor at home and in the surrounding villages until 1853, when he became pastor at Alfreton, Derbyshire. He removed, in 1857, to the Channel Islands, first to Jersey, and afterwards to Guernsey, where he remained until his death, April 24, 1867. See (Lond.) *Cong. Year-book*, 1868, p. 265.

Crisp, Edmund, an English Congregational minister, was born at Hertford, June 26, 1796, of pious Nonconformist parents. In 1816 he entered the Missionary College at Gosport; in 1821 was ordained at Hertford and set sail for Madras, India, where he labored seven years, and then, removing to Combaconum, toiled seven years longer, until his health failed and he returned to England. In 1840 he again sailed for India, and became tutor at the college for training native pastors, at Bangalore. In 1848 Mr. Crisp finally returned to England because of sickness, travelled one year in aid of the missionary cause, preached four years at Grantham, travelled six years as representative of the Religious Tract Society, and, becoming one of the Association secretaries, settled at Ealing, where he remained until his death, Nov. 6, 1877. See (Lond.) *Cong. Year-book*, 1878, p. 311.

Crisp, George Steffe, an English Congregational minister, was born at Wrentham, Suffolk, March 8, 1786. He was converted early, studied at Wymondley Academy, and settled at Lowestoft in 1808. He resigned his pastorate in 1817, removed to Aldwinckle, Northamptonshire, and in 1821 resumed the pastorate at Lowestoft, where he continued until 1832. He died May 30, 1863. See (Lond.) *Cong. Year-book*, 1864, p. 205.

Crisp, Joseph Hemus, an English Congregational minister, was born at Nottingham, June 17, 1782. He was converted at nineteen; became class-leader and local preacher in the New Connection Methodist Church; and in 1804 was called to the regular ministry, being appointed first at Hull, and afterwards at Dewsbury. In 1807 he entered the Independent College at Idle, and in 1810 became pastor of the Congregational Church at Brighouse, near Halifax. He retired to Ashby-de-la-Zouch in 1840, and there died, Jan. 12, 1869. See (Lond.) *Cong. Year-book*, 1810, p. 282.

Crisp, Samuel, an English minister of the Society of Friends, was born at Norfolk about 1667. He received a collegiate education, took orders in the Established Church, and for a time was a parish curate and chaplain in a private family. While he was residing in London, in 1700, he united with the Friends. Not long after he opened a boarding-school at Stepney, near London. He died there April 7, 1704. Mr. Crisp published, *The Present State of Quakerism in England* (1701):—*A Libeller Exposed:*—also three *Letters*, on similar subjects. See *Friends' Library*, xiii, 149-163. (J. C. S.)

Crisp, Stephen, an English minister of the Society of Friends, was born at Colchester about 1640. For thirty-five years he travelled and preached in many parts of England, Scotland, Holland, Germany, and the Low Countries. His life was one of much hardship. He died June 28, 1692. Among his writings, which are numerous, though none of them are long, may be mentioned, *A Word of Reproof to the Teachers of the World*, etc.:—*A Description of the Church of Scotland:—An Epistle to Friends, concerning the Present and Succeeding Times:—A Plain Pathway Opened to the Simple Hearted:—An Alarm in the Borders of Spiritual Egypt*. See *Friends' Library*, xiv, 275. (J. C. S.)

Crisp, Thomas, an English Dissenting minister, was born in 1738. He was educated under Dr. Conder; first settled at Colchester; thence removed to Ringwood, and afterwards to Hertford; but, though a man of excellent character and of a peaceable spirit, he met with great trouble and opposition in every place. He at last returned to the home of his nativity, and died suddenly, near Wrentham, in 1806. He published, *The Charge at the Ordination of Sir Harry Trelawney*. See (Lond.) *Theological and Biblical Magazine*, February, 1806, p. 79.

Crisp, Thomas S., D.D., an English Baptist minister, was born at Beccles, Suffolk, in 1788. He received his education in an Independent college and in one of the Scotch universities; became teacher in the Baptist College, Bristol; in 1818 was associated with Rev. Dr. Ryland as pastor there; and upon the death of the latter was elected president of the college. He died at Cotham, Bristol, June 16, 1868. His scholarship is said to have been of a superior character, although he was singularly diffident. See *Appleton's Annual Cyclopædia*, viii, 594; Cathcart, *Baptist. Encyclop.* s. v. (J. C. S.)

Crispi, Geronimo, an Italian prelate, was born at Ferrara, Sept. 30, 1667. He pursued his studies in his native city; became doctor of law in 1696; then was ordained priest, and soon after archdeacon. In 1708 he was appointed auditor of the rota, and in 1720 archbishop of Ravenna. He left this see for the patriarchate of Antioch, and in 1743 was appointed archbishop of Ferrara, where he died in 1746, leaving, *Discorsi ed Imni Sacri* (Rome, 1720):—*Discorsi ed Imni Sacri Altri* (Ravenna, 1722):—*Compendium Vitæ Clementis XI* (ibid. 1723):—*Decisiones Rotæ Romanæ* (Urbino, 1728). See Hoefer, *Nouv. Biog. Générale*, s. v.

Crispi, Scipione, a Piedmontese painter, was born at Tortona, and practiced the art from 1592 to 1599. His works are, *The Visitation of the Virgin to Elizabeth*, in San Lorenzo, at Voghera; and an altar-piece at Tortona, of *Sts. Francesco and Domenico*.

Crispīna, *Saint*, commemorated Dec. 5 (or Dec. 3), is said to have been an illustrious matron of Thagura, who was put to death A.D. 304, under Aulesius, proconsul at Thebaste, in Africa, and rejoiced in her torture as a Christian (Augustine, *in Psalm.* cxx, 13; cxxxvii, 3; *Serm.* 354, cap. 5, 44).

Crispīnus was the name of several early Christians, besides St. Crispin (q. v.):

1. A bishop, martyred at Astyagis, commemorated Nov. 19.

2. A presbyter of Lampsacus, his native city, who wrote, about A.D. 337, a life of bishop Parthenius (given in the Bollandists, s. a.; see also Cave, *Hist. Lit.* i, 204; Tillemont, vi, 288).

3. A Donatist bishop of Colama, addressed A.D. 399 and 406 by Augustine (*Epist.* 51 [172], 60 [173]).

Crispion, archdeacon to Epiphanius, mentioned as archbishop of Salamis cir. A.D. 368 to 403 (Sozom. viii, 15; Migne, *Patrol. Græc.* lxvii. 1555, § 345; Ceillier, vi, 380.

Crispŏlus (or **Crispŭlus**), a martyr in Sardinia, is commemorated May 30.

Crispus, a presbyter, martyr at Rome under Diocletian, is commemorated Aug. 18.

Crist, Jacob B., a Lutheran minister, was born in Berks County, near Reading, Pa., Nov. 11, 1798. Removing to Harrisburg, Va., he joined the Methodist Church, and in the fall of 1824 was licensed as a preacher; for one year was pastor of the Warm Springs Circuit; was selected as travelling companion to bishop McKendree three years; and for several years agent for the Sunday-school Union and the American Colonization Society. He afterwards joined the Lutheran Church; became agent for the Illinois College and for the Education Society; in 1850 pastor at Mount Joy, Lancaster Co., Pa., which he served three years; and then successively pastor at Kishacoquillas, Mifflin Co.; Sinking Valley, Blair Co.; Jenner Charge, Somerset Co.; Antis, Blair Co.; supplying, also, the Church at Freeport, Armstrong Co. For a time he was agent for Pennsylvania College. In May, 1870, he removed to Altoona for rest; and afterwards went to Antis Charge, from which he retired in 1875. He died at Altoona, April 28, 1881. See *Lutheran Observer*, xlix, No. 21.

Cristēta, martyr in Spain, is commemorated Oct. 27.

Cristiŏlus, a Welsh saint of the 6th century, is the reputed founder of Llangristiolus in Anglesey, and Eglwys Wrw, and Penrydd in Pembrokeshire (Rees, *Welsh Saints*, p. 220).—Smith, *Dict. of Christ. Biog.* s. v.

Cristobolo, a Grecian architect, flourished about the middle of the 15th century, and was employed by Mohammed II to erect a mosque at Constantinople, on the ruins of the Church of the Holy Apostles. which he did successfully.

Cristofori, Fabio, and **Pietro Paolo**, Italian artists, father and son, the former of whom flourished in 1658, and the latter died in 1740, deserve great credit for the perfection which they attained in the mosaic art. They executed in concert several admirable works in the Basilica of St. Peter's, among which are *The Communion of St. Jerome;* and *The Baptism of Christ.* See Spooner, *Biog. Hist. of the Fine Arts*, s. v.

Critan is the name of several Irish *saints:*

1. Son of Illadhon, commemorated May 11, at Achadh-finnich, on the river Dodder, County Dublin, where they are probably interred. Colgan affirms that he was the *Credan, Cridan*, or *Critan* who was one of the many pupils whom St. Petroc had during his residence in Ireland (Todd and Reeves, *Mart. Doneg.* p. 125; Colgan, *Acta Sanctorum*, p. 585, c. 4; 586 n.).

2. Bishop of Aendruim, or Nendrum (now called Mahee Island, in Strangford Lough), commemorated May 17, whose death is given at A.D. 638 by the Irish Annalists (O'Donovan, *Four Masters*, i, 256 n., 257; Reeves, *ut sup.* p. 148).

3. Of Móin-Miolan, commemorated Feb. 7 with Lonan and Miolan or Mellan, all sons of Daire; buried at Cluain-feart-Molua (now Confertmulloe or Kyle, in the barony of Upper Ossory, Queen's County) (Colgan, *ut sup.* p. 58 n.; O'Donovan, *ut sup.* i, 207 n.).

4. Certronnach, of Bennchar (Bangor), commemorated Sept. 16. In *Mart. Doneg.* (Todd and Reeves, p. 251) he is called cellarer of St. Comgall of Bangor, and is said to have got the name *Certronnach* because he used to divide fairly. His mother was Eithne, daughter of Saran, son of Colgan, and sister of Ronan. He died A.D. 669 (O'Donovan, i, 280 n., 281).

Critchlow, Benjamin C., D.D., a Presbyterian minister, was born Dec. 14, 1807. He pursued his literary studies at Western University, Pittsburgh, Pa., and graduated at Western Theological Seminary in 1836. His first pastorate was Slippery Rock and New Brighton; his next Beaver and New Brighton; but, after a few years, he left Beaver and confined his labors to Brighton. In 1876 he accepted a call to the Church of Greenville, Mercer County, but resigned in the spring of 1881. After this he occasionally preached at Stoneborough, Mercer County, and at Rochester, until his death, April 21, 1882. See *Presbyterian Banner*, April 26, 1882.

Critchton, Andrew, LL.D., a minister and author in the Established Church of Scotland, was born in December, 1790, in the parish of Kirkmahoe, Dumfriesshire. He received his education at the Dumfries Academy and the University of Edinburgh, became a licensed preacher, and was for some time engaged in teaching in Edinburgh and North Berwick. In 1823 he published his first work, the *Life of the Rev. John Blackader*, which was followed by the *Life of Colonel J. Blackader*, and *Memoirs of the Rev. Thomas Scott.* To *Constable's Miscellany* he contributed four volumes, viz., *Converts from Infidelity*, and a translation of Koch's *Revolutions in Europe.* In the *Edinburgh Cabinet Library* he wrote the *History of Arabia* and *Scandinavia, Ancient and Modern*, each in two volumes. He commenced his connection with the newspaper press in 1828 by editing the *Edinburgh Evening Post.* In 1830 he conducted the *North Briton*, and in 1832 he undertook the editorship of the *Edinburgh Advertiser*, in which employment he continued till June, 1851. He contributed extensively to periodicals; among others, to the *Westminster, Tait's Edinburgh Magazine*, the *Dublin University, Frazer's Magazine*, the *Church Review*, and the *Church of Scotland Magazine and Review.* He was a member of the Presbytery of Edinburgh, being ruling elder of the congregation of Trinity College Church, and sat in the General Assembly of the Church of Scotland as elder for the burgh of Cullen, for three years previous to his death, which occurred in Edinburgh, Jan. 9, 1856. See Hardwicke, *Annual Biography*, 1856, p. 198.

Crithomancy (Gr. κριθή, *barley*, and μαντεία, *divination*) was a species of fortune-telling by means of the dough of the barley-meal cakes used in sacrifice.

Criticism, Biblical. We add a few items to the account given in vol. ii:

The textual examination of the New Test. in particular has received a powerful stimulus by the labors of the Anglo-American Committee on Bible Revision, who had necessarily to reconsider the Greek text. Although they have not directly put forth any new edition, yet the results of their criticism have been embodied in *The Greek Testament, with the Readings adopted by the Revisers of the Authorized Version* (Oxford, 1881, 12mo), which may be regarded as the most mature and impartial fruit of the combined scholarship of the times, and probably nearer the autograph than any other text extant. Almost simultaneous with this appeared the *Greek Testament* prepared by Drs. Westcott and Hort (Oxford, 1881, 12mo), which, with its additional volume of critical remarks, has been republished (Harpers, N. Y. 1882 sq.) under the able editorship of Dr. Schaff, who has also added a *Companion*, consisting of illustrative matter, largely bearing upon the revision.

Meanwhile Tregelles and Tischendorf each lived just long enough to complete their valuable critical editions, and the *Prolegomena* to that of the latter is in process of issue at Leipsic (vol. iii, pt. 1, 1884). These nearly exhaust the elements of critical comparison.

A fierce attack has been made by some scholars, especially opposed to Bible revision, on the conclusions arrived at in the foregoing productions. It has been claimed that they unnecessarily depart from the *textus receptus*, and unduly lean upon the few great uncial MSS., to the exclusion of all other copies and to the neglect of the early versions. This objection leaves room for doubt whether the Greek text to be finally accepted has yet been constructed. But these are valuable contributions toward this final result, and we may hope that ere long another *Griesbach* will arise, capable of surveying the whole field with broad and accurate scholarship and impartial judgment. Meanwhile we may rejoice at the immense advance already made towards this desirable end.

See Reuss, *Bibliotheca Novi Testamenti Græci* (Brunswick, 1872), containing the most complete list of printed editions up to that time; Hammond, *Outlines of Textual Criticism* (Oxford, 1872, 1876); Mitchell, *Critical Hand-book* (Andover and Lond. 1880); Field, *Notes on Select Passages of the Greek Testament* (Oxford, 1881, giving gentle criticisms of the revisers); Burgon, *New Testament Revision* (in the [Lond.] *Quar. Rev.* Oct. 1881, Jan. and April, 1882; reprinted together, Lond. and N. Y. 1883), a sweeping condemnation of the Revision Committee; and the exhaustive monograph of Hall, *Critical Bibliography of the Gr. Test. published in America* (Phila. 1883).

Crittenden, Samuel Worcester, a Presbyterian minister, was born at North Adams, Mass., Feb. 22, 1824. After devoting some time to the study of law, he commenced a theological course in the Union Theological Seminary in 1852, continuing it one year at Princeton, and graduating at Union in 1855. He was ordained April 29, 1856, over the Gilead Presbyterian Church, Carmel, N. Y.; was pastor at Clifton, S. I., in 1858 and 1859, and subsequently at Darby, Pa., from 1862 to 1865, until he received the appointment of corresponding secretary of the American and Foreign Christian Union. After occupying this post five years, he was financial agent of the Presbyterian Hospital, Philadelphia, in 1871 and 1872, and died in that city March 2, 1884. See *N. Y. Observer*, March 6, 1884. (W. P. S.)

Crivelli (Crevilli, or **Crivilli), Carlo,** a Venetian painter, flourished from 1450 to 1486, and studied under Jacobello del Fiore. He has a fine altar-piece at the Osservanti, in Macerta; and in San Sebastiano, at Venice, two pictures, representing *St. Fabian* and *The Marriage of St. Catharine*. See Hoefer, *Nouv. Biog. Générale*, s. v.; Spooner, *Biog. Hist. of the Fine Arts*, s. v.

Crivelli, Vittorio, a Venetian painter, probably a brother of Carlo, painted some altar-pieces in the churches of Monte San Martino, and in San Giovanni at Venice, in 1489 and 1490.

Croatian Version. See Slavonic Versions.

Croce, Santa di Gerusalemme (Ital. *the Holy Cross of Jerusalem*), is one of the seven great basilicas of Rome. It was founded by Constantine in 331. It is particularly remarkable for the immense number of relics which it contains, all of which are exhibited on certain days, especially the fourth Sunday in Lent, for reverence and adoration of devotees. All who attend the services at that church on that day are entitled to certain indulgences; and all who share in the masses celebrated are entitled to the release of one soul from purgatory. See Seymour, *Pilgrimage to Rome*. See Basilica.

Crocefisso Santissimo (Ital. *most holy crucifix*) is a wooden cross at Naples, which is remarkable as having been said to have thanked Thomas Aquinas for his beautiful and salutary writings. It belonged to the church of St. Dominic the Great.

Crochet, James, a Free-will Baptist minister, was born at Gorham, Me., in 1817. He was converted in Lewiston, and ordained February, 1846; for three years was pastor at North Yarmouth and Pownal; preached about a year and a half at Falmouth, afterwards went to Buxton, and finally to Scarborough, where he died, Jan. 16, 1854. See *Free-will Baptist Register*, 1855, p. 88. (J. C. S.)

Crochett, John, a Baptist minister, was born at Stratham, N. H., July 15, 1766. He was converted in 1791, licensed to preach in 1792, ordained at Sanbornton, Sept. 3, 1794, and remained pastor there until his death, Feb. 11, 1833. (J. C. S.)

Crochford, W., an English Baptist minister, was born at Keysoe, Bedfordshire, in 1758. For many years he served as pastor, without charge, at Great Gidding, in Huntingdonshire, and died in August 1836. See (London) *Baptist Hand-book*, 1837, p. 16. (J. C. S.)

Crocius, Johann Georg, a Protestant theologian of Germany, was born at Cassel, Jan. 26, 1629. He pursued his studies at Groningen, became doctor at Basle in 1656, fellow professor of theology at Marburg in 1657, titular professor in 1661, and died July 13, 1674, leaving, *De Natura Objecto et Necessitate Logices* (Bremen, 1644):—*De Elementis in Genere et in Specie* (Cassel, 1647):—*De Animæ Rationalis Ortu* (ibid. 1648, 1649):—*De Judæis* (Gröningen, 1650):—*De Angelis* (Leyden, 1651):—*De Baptismo* (Marburg, 1656):—*De Sanctis* (1662):—*De Communione sub Utraque* (ibid. 1663). See Hoefer, *Nouv. Biog. Générale*, s. v.

Crocius, Ludwig, a Reformed theologian, who died at Bremen, Dec. 7, 1655, is the author of *De Perseverantio Sanctorum*:—*De Vera Religione et Catholica Ecclesia*:—*Examen Calvinistarum Descriptionis D. M. Hoei Austriaci*;—*Assertio Confessionis Augustanæ*:—*Comm. in Titum*:—*Apodeixis Parænetica ad Judæos per Orbem Dispersos de Messia*. See Jöcher, *Allgemeines Gelehrten-Lexikon*, s. v.; Fürst, *Bibl. Jud.* i, 192.

Crockat(t). See Crocket.

Crocker, Asahel B., a Reformed (Dutch) minister, was born at Cambridge, N. Y., in 1813. He graduated from Union College in 1839; spent one year in Princeton Theological Seminary; was licensed by the Presbytery of Troy; was pastor at Glenville, N. Y., from 1842 to 1848; East Congregational Church, N. Y. city, thereafter until his death in 1840. See Corwin, *Manual of the Ref. Church in America* (3d ed.), p. 224.

Crocker, Nathan Bourne, D.D., a Protestant Episcopal minister, was born at Barnstable, Mass., July 4, 1781. He graduated at Harvard College in 1802, and began the study of medicine, which, however, he soon abandoned for theology, and acted as lay reader at St. John's Church, Providence. Becoming deacon in 1803, he accepted the rectorship of that church. On account of failing health he resigned his charge in 1804, but resumed it Jan. 1, 1808, and remained in it until his death, Oct. 19, 1865. Dr. Crocker was a member of the Standing Committee of the Diocese of Rhode Island during his entire rectorship, excepting one year; deputy to the General Convention from 1808 to 1862; and a member of the Board of Fellows of Brown University for nearly fifty years. See *Amer. Quar. Church Rev.* Jan. 1866, p. 669.

Crocker, Thomas, a Baptist minister, was born in North Carolina in 1786, and for more than thirty years was a very successful preacher in Wake, Warren, Granville, and Franklin counties. He died Dec. 8, 1848. See Cathcart, *Baptist Encyclop.* p. 296. (J. C. S.)

Crocker, William Goss, a Baptist missionary, was born at Newburyport, Mass., Feb. 10, 1805. He graduated from the Newton Theological Institution in 1834, and was ordained at Newburyport, Sept. 25 of the same year, proceeding at once to Africa, where he arrived Aug. 12, 1835. He entered with great zeal into his work, and was a most devoted and laborious missionary for seven years. He succeeded in reducing the Bassa language to writing, and prepared also a *Bassa Spelling-book*, and quite a number of hymns in the same tongue. He returned to the United States in 1842, remaining a year and a half, when he re-embarked for Africa, and arrived at Monrovia, Liberia, Feb. 23, 1844, but died the next day. (J. C. S.)

Crocket (also written **Crockat** or **Crockatt**) is the family name of several Scotch clergymen:

1. James, took his degree at the University of St. Andrews in 1674; was licensed to preach in 1678; presented to the living at Caputh in 1683; continued in 1689; deprived by the privy council in 1701, and removed to Morinty. See *Fasti Eccles. Scoticanæ*, ii, 796.

2. John (1), was licensed to preach in 1703; called to the living at Dallas in 1708, and ordained; and died April 21, 1748. See *Fasti Eccles. Scoticanæ*, iii, 179.

3. John (2), was licensed to preach in 1739; called to the living at Parton in 1743; ordained in 1744; and died July 20, 1760, aged forty-five years. See *Fasti Eccles. Scoticanæ*, i, 720.

4. John (3), was licensed to preach in 1803; presented to the living at Kirkgunzeon in 1809, and ordained; and died June 20, 1867, in his ninetieth year. He had a clear and vigorous intellect, correct taste, a wonderfully retentive memory, and was a good scholar. See *Fasti Eccles. Scoticanæ*, i, 587.

Southwell Minster, A.D.1320.

Crockets (Fr. *croc*=a hook), projecting leaves, flowers, or bunches of foliage, used in Gothic architecture to decorate the angles of spires, canopies, pinnacles, etc.; they are also frequently found on gables, on the weather-mouldings of doors and windows, and

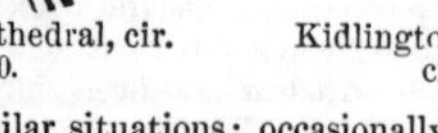
Hereford Cathedral, cir. 1250.

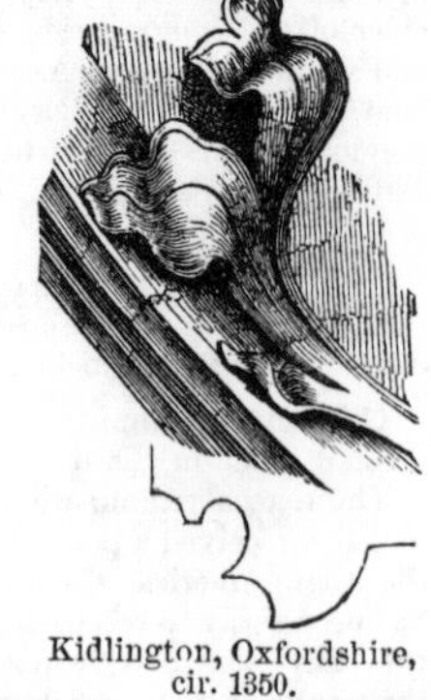
Kidlington, Oxfordshire, cir. 1350.

in other similar situations; occasionally they are used among vertical mouldings, as at Lincoln Cathedral, where they run up the mullions of the windows of the tower, and the sides of some of the arches, but they are not employed in horizontal situations. They are used in suites, and are placed at equal distances apart: the varieties are innumerable. The first instances of crockets are to be found late in the Early English style; they mostly consist either of small leaves or rather long stalks, or bunches of leaves curled back something like the head of a bishop's pastoral crook. *Decorated* crockets vary considerably; the most usual form is that of a broad leaf with the edges attached to the moulding on which it is placed, and the middle part and point raised.

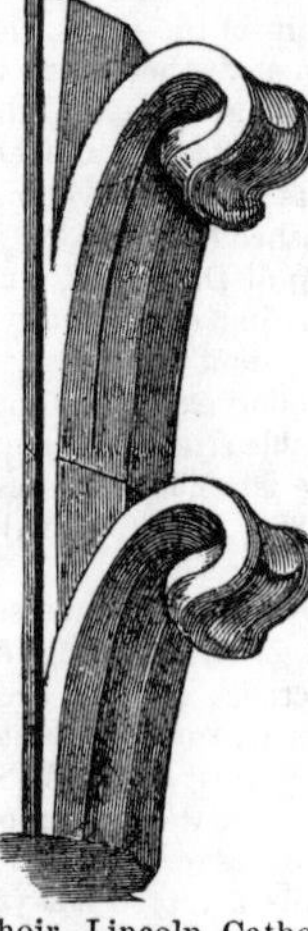
Choir, Lincoln Cathedral, cir. 1200.

In the *Perpendicular* style this is the most prevalent form, but they are not unfrequently made like flat, square leaves, which are united with the mouldings by the stalk and one edge only. In a few instances, animals and figures are used in place of crockets, as in Henry the Seventh's chapel.

Litcham, Norfolk, cir. 1450.

Crockhay, Gertrude, an English martyr, was a native of St. Catharine's, near London. She would not attend mass, and closed her doors upon the priests when they came to see her. She was taken, examined, and condemned to be burned; but died April 13, 1528, before the time fixed for her execution. See Fox, *Acts and Monuments*, viii, 726.

Crocota was a dress of women among the ancient Greeks and Romans. It was more especially worn at the festival of the *Dionysia*, and also by the priestesses of *Cybele*.

Crocquet. See Croquet.

Crocus, Cornelius, a Dutch theologian and scholar, a native of Amsterdam, was appointed rector of the Latin schools of his native city, and labored zealously to inspire his pupils with a love for the Catholic religion. At the age of fifty he went to Rome, entered the Jesuit society, and died there in 1550. His principal works are, *Farrago Sordidorum Verborum* (Cologne, 1520):—*De Fide et Operibus* (Antwerp, 1531):—*Disputatio contra Anabaptistas* (ibid. 1535):—*Josephus Castus* (ibid. 1548):—*Paraclesis ad Capescendam Sententiam Josephi Casti* (ibid.):—*De Vera Ecclesia* (Cologne, 1548). See Hoefer, *Nouv. Biog. Générale*, s. v.; Jöcher, *Allgemeines Gelehrten-Lexikon*, s. v.

Croes, John, a minister of the Protestant Episcopal Church, was born Sept. 22, 1787. Ordained deacon in 1809, and subsequently a priest, he began his labors in the ministry in St. Peter's Church, Freehold, N. J.; was thence transferred to Christ Church, Shrewsbury, and afterwards to Christ Church, Middletown. After a few months spent in New Brunswick, he became rector of St. Paul's Church, Paterson, where he remained three years. During the following two years he was in Newark, and the two years succeeding he assisted his father, the bishop of New Jersey, in Christ Church, New Brunswick. He became rector of that parish at the death of his father, and continued there for eight years. In Keyport he founded and served St. James's Church nine years, at Brown's Point, erecting the building on his own land and by his own gifts and collections. He finally made his residence at Brooklyn, N. Y., where, and in adjoining places, he was busily employed until his death, Aug. 18, 1849. See *Amer. Quar. Church Rev.* 1849, p. 446.

Croes, Robert B., D.D., a Protestant Episcopal clergyman, brother of the foregoing, was born at Sweedsborough, N. J., in 1800. He graduated from the General Theological Seminary (N. Y.), and was ordained in 1823. For a number of years he was rector of a church in New Brunswick, N. J., which he left about the year 1859, and removed to New York. He returned, however, in 1861, to New Brunswick, still retaining his connection with the diocese of New York, without regular work; in 1866 he resided at Boyd's Corners, N. Y. Subsequently he removed to Yonkers, and died there, July 22, 1878. See *Prot. Episc. Almanac*, 1879, p. 168.

Croft, Gabriel, an English Congregational minister, was born at Great Eccleston, Lancashire, Jan. 31, 1791. He entered Hackney Academy in 1811, and about three years later was ordained at Pickering, Yorkshire, where he labored until 1850; afterwards living without charge at Ripon, Eccleston, Kirkham, Garstang, and finally at Preston, until his death, Nov. 14, 1868. See (Lond.) *Cong. Year-book*, p. 241.

Croft, *Sir* **Herbert** (1), an English clergyman, was educated at Christ Church, Oxford, and became a member of Parliament in the latter end of queen Elizabeth's reign. After he had lived fifty-two years as a Protestant he became a Roman Catholic, went to Douay, and had an apartment in the monastery of the English Benedictines as a lay brother of the order. He died April 10, 1622, leaving *Arguments to Show that the Church in Communion with the See of Rome is the True Church* (1619). See Chalmers, *Biog. Dict.* s. v.; Allibone, *Dict. of Brit. and Amer. Authors*, s. v.

Croft, Herbert (2), D.D., an English prelate, son of the foregoing, was born Oct. 18, 1603, at Great Milton, near Thame, Oxfordshire. He was educated in the English college of the Jesuits at St. Omer's, and at Oxford; entered into orders, and became minister in Gloucestershire, and rector of Harding, in Oxfordshire. In August, 1639, he was made a prebendary of Salisbury Cathedral, in 1640 of Worcester, and the year after canon of Windsor. In 1644 he was nominated dean of Hereford, to which see he was promoted Dec. 2, 1661. About 1667 he became dean of the royal chapel, which position he held until 1669. In 1675, when the quarrel with the Nonconformists was at its height, he published a piece entitled *The Naked Truth, or the True State of the Primitive Church* (4to), which created some controversy and excited an uncommon degree of attention. He resigned his bishopric some years before his death, which occurred May 18, 1691. He published some single *Sermons*, and *The Theory of the Earth* (1688). See Chalmers, *Biog. Dict.* s. v.; Allibone, *Dict. of Brit. and Amer. Authors*, s. v.

Croft, *Sir* **Herbert** (3), an English clergyman, was born in London in 1751, and educated at University College, Oxford. He took orders in 1782, succeeded to a baronetcy in 1797, and died in 1816. His publications include, *A Brother's Advice to his Sisters* (1775):—*Love and Madness* (1780):—*Fanaticism and Treason* (eod.):—*The Literary Fly* (eod.):—and other works. See Allibone, *Dict. of Brit. and Amer. Authors*, s. v.

Croft, Joel, a Methodist Episcopal minister, was born at Phillipstown, Putnam Co., N. Y., Feb. 11, 1820. He was converted at the age of sixteen; soon after entered the academy at Peekskill; also began a private theological course; received license to preach in 1842, and in 1845 joined the New York Conference, of which he remained a worthy and acceptable member until his decease, March 27, 1879. See *Minutes of Annual Conferences*, 1879, p. 28.

Croft, Joseph, an English Congregational minister, was born at Great Eccleston, near Preston, Lancashire, Jan. 5, 1802. He studied at Rotherham College, became pastor at Ripon in 1827, and labored there with eminent success for more than forty years. After 1868 he lived in retirement until his death, June 20, 1879. See (Lond.) *Cong. Year-book*, 1880, p. 317.

Crofts, Edward, an English Wesleyan minister, was born near Stamford in 1817. He was educated at the Hoxton Theological Institution, appointed to his first circuit in 1839, became a supernumerary in 1870, and died at Manorbier, near Tenby, July 2, 1873. See *Minutes of the British Conference*, 1873, p. 36.

Crofts, Henry Only, D.D., an English Methodist preacher, was born in the city of Lichfield, Sept. 8, 1813. At seventeen he began to preach, at twenty-two entered the New Connection ministry, and after spending four years in England, joined the Rev. J. Addegman in the newly established mission in Canada, of which he was the general superintendent for ten years. Returning to England in 1851, he travelled in nine of the leading circuits with zeal and success. He became a supernumerary in 1879, but continued to preach as he was able, until his death at Manchester, Jan. 21, 1880. Dr. Crofts was president of the conference in 1861, and the author of a volume of *Sermons*. See *Minutes of the Conference*.

Crofts, John, an English Wesleyan minister, was born in 1798. He was converted when about seventeen, entered the ministry in 1820, labored in Jamaica, Turk's Island, West Indies, Bermuda (1830–33), and Harbor Island, returned home in 1835, travelled English circuits until his retirement in 1854, and died at Sandbach, Cheshire, Dec. 31, 1857. See *Minutes of the British Conference*, 1858.

Crofts, Matthew Henry, an English Baptist minister, was born at Upton, Northamptonshire, in 1801. He was converted at twenty-nine years of age, at once began to preach, notwithstanding his defective education, and in 1834 became pastor in Ramsey, Huntingdonshire, where he remained until 1852. He then removed to Andover, Hants Co., and was pastor there till his death, Feb. 20, 1856. See (Lond.) *Baptist Handbook*, 1856, p. 46. (J. C. S.)

Croggon, Walter Oke, an English Wesleyan minister, was born of Baptist parents, at Penryn, Cornwall. He was converted in his nineteenth year, and in 1817 entered the ministry; was stationed successively in Cornwall (1817–22), at Charenton, France (1823 sq.), Zante, Ionian Isles (1827), Kingswood, England (1834), and London, as superintendent of schools (1836–49). He died at Sittingbourne, Kent, Jan. 30, 1854, in the sixty-third year of his age. See *Minutes of the British Conference*, 1854; *Wesl. Meth. Mag.* 1833, p. 241, 1854, p. 478.

Croï, François de, a French Protestant controversialist of the beginning of the 17th century, was pastor at Uzes, and the author of several works, the best-known of which is his treatise *Les Trois Conformités* (1605). See Hoefer, *Nouv. Biog. Générale*, s. v.

Croï, Jean de, a Protestant theologian and scholar, son of François Croï, was born at Uzes. He was successively pastor at Béziers and Uzes, and for some years professor in the Protestant Academy of Nismes. He died at Uzes, Aug. 31, 1659, leaving, among other works, *Observationes in quædam Origenis, Irenæi et Tertulliani Loca* (Geneva, 1632):—*In Novum Fœdus Observationes* (ibid. 1646):—*La Vérité de la Religion Reformée* (1645, 1650):—*Augustin Supposé* (1656). See Hoefer, *Nouv. Biog. Générale*, s. v.; Jöcher, *Allgemeines Gelehrten-Lexikon*, s. v.

Croine (or **Crone**) is the name of several female Irish saints, of whom the following are the best known:

1. A virgin, commemorated Jan. 27. She was of the race of Maine, son of Niall of the Nine Hostages, and was venerated at Cill-croine (Kilcron) in Ui-Maine, County Galway; but beyond this we have no information.

There were others of the same name, and the ruins of the Church of St. Croine, virgin, of Kill-Crony or Kilcroney, in the parish of Kilmacanoge, bar. Rathdown, County Wicklow, still exist in the disused churchyard. At Jan. 27 the *Mart. Tallaght* has the feast of "Croni Innse Locha Crone" (Todd and Reeves, *Mart. Doneg.* p. 29; Colgan, *Acta Sanctorum*, p. 267 n.; O'Hanlon, *Irish Saints*, p. 455, 456; Kelly, *Cal. of Irish Saints*, p. xiii).

2. Beg (Little), of Tempull-Croine, virgin, commemorated July 7, was the daughter of Diarmaid, son of Garvan, of the race of Conall Gulban, son of Niall of the Nine Hostages. She is given as *Cronia* by Colgan, among the saints descended from Conall Gulban, the parent-stem of St. Columba, and her church was situated in Tyrconnel (Todd and Reeves, *Mart. Doneg.* p. 189; Colgan, *Tr. Thaum.* p. 480 n.).

Croiset, Jean, a French ascetic theologian of the Jesuit order, born at Marseilles, was for a long time rector of the House of the Novitiate of Avignon, and governed it with much regularity and mildness. He died at Avignon, Jan. 31, 1738. His principal works are, *Vie de Marie-Madeleine de la Trinité* (1696):—*Vie des Saints pour tous les Jours de l'Année* (Lyons, 1723, 1742):—*Parallèle des Mœurs de ce Siècle et de la Morale de Jean Croiset* (ibid. 1735):—*Exercices de Pieté pour les Dimanches et Fêtes* (ibid. 1736, 1747, 1764, 1804; also under the title, *Année Chrétienne*, Toulouse, 1812):—*Illusions du Cœur* (Lyons, 1736, 1748):—*Heures et Réglements pour les Pensionnaires Jésuites* (ibid. 1739):—*Devotion au Sacré Cœur de Jésus Christ* (Paris, 1741):—*Retraite Spirituelle pour un Jour de Chaque Mois* (Lyons, 1822):—*Réflexions Chrétiennes* (ibid. 1823):—*Méditations.* See Hoefer, *Nouv. Biog. Générale*, s. v.; Jöcher, *Allgemeines Gelehrten-Lexikon*, s. v.

Croius. See Croï.

Croix, Claude la. See Lacroix.

Croix, Jean de la Sainte. See Cruz, (*Saint*) Juan de la.

Croker, Thomas, an English martyr, was a bricklayer in Gloucester, who was burned May 12, 1556, for his faithful adherence to Christ. See Fox, *Acts and Monuments*, viii, 144.

Crole, Anthony, an English Independent minister, was born at Fettercairn, Scotland, in 1740. He studied at Trevecca College, was ordained, in 1766, pastor at Cumberland Street, London; began a new church at Pinner's Hall, but removed in 1797 to Founder's Hall, and died July 3, 1803. He published the *Sermon* at the opening of Cheshunt College, and issued two other works. See Wilson, *Dissenting Churches*, ii, 294-301.

Croll, Alfred De Long, a Lutheran minister, was born in Berks County, Pa., June 25, 1838. He studied at Kutztown, at Reading, and at Freeland seminary; graduated in 1862 from Gettysburg Theological Seminary; in 1863 was ordained by the Ministerium of Pennsylvania, and took charge of a congregation near Lykens. After several years he united with the Synod of East Pennyslvania, resigned his charge, organized new congregations at Lyons, Millerstown, Hereford, and Pleasantville, also acting as pastor at Mohrsville with extraordinary success. He died at Lyons, June 19, 1876. See *Lutheran Observer*, July 7, 1876.

Croll, Robert, a Scotch clergyman, took his degree at Marischal College, Aberdeen, in 1767; was schoolmaster of the parish of Inverbervie in 1771; licensed to preach in 1779; appointed to the living there in 1780; ordained assistant and successor, and died June 3, 1820, aged eighty years. See *Fasti Eccles. Scoticanæ*, iii, 860.

Cromacius. See Chromatius.

Croman. See Cronan.

Cromar, Andrew, a Scotch clergyman, was licensed to preach in 1820; presented to the living at Oathlaw in 1830; ordained in 1831; and died Nov. 10, 1835, aged forty years. See *Fasti Eccles. Scoticanæ*, iii, 780.

Crombach (or **Crumbach**), Hermann, a German historian and antiquarian of the Jesuit order, was born at Cologne in 1598. He taught in various colleges of his order, devoted himself to researches upon the ecclesiastical history and antiquities of his native country, and died Feb. 7, 1680, leaving *Ursula Vindicata* (Cologne, 1647; augmented ed. 1674):—*Primitiæ Gentium* (ibid. 1654):—*Vita P. D. Jacobi-Marlo Harstii* (ibid. 1655):—*Auctarium Sanctæ Ursulæ Vindicatæ* (ibid. 1669):—*Chronographica Descriptio Omnium Parochiarum ad Archi-dioceseos Coloniensis Hierarchiam Pertinentium*, in the *Bibliotheca Coloniensis* of Joseph Hartzeim (ibid. 1747). See Hoefer, *Nouv. Biog. Générale*, s. v.; Jöcher, *Allgemeines Gelehrten-Lexikon*, s. v.

Crombie, Andrew, a Scotch clergyman, was presented to the vicarage of Knockbain in 1592; transferred to Chanonry about 1594, and to Rosemarkie in 1596; back to Kilmuir Wester in 1597, and again to Rosemarkie in 1599; appointed by the assembly of 1600 to visit the bounds of Murray; and continued in February, 1630. See *Fasti Eccles. Scoticanæ*, iii, 274, 283.

Crombie, James, D.D., a Scotch clergyman, took his first degree at the University of St. Andrews in 1752; was licensed to preach in 1757; presented to the living at Lhanbryde in 1760; accepted a call to Belfast, but resigned in 1770; and died March 1, 1790, aged about fifty-eight years. He published a *Sermon* (Belfast, 1781). See *Fasti Eccles. Scoticanæ*, iii, 167, 168.

Crombie, William, a Scotch clergyman, took his degree at the University of St. Andrews in 1753; was licensed to preach in 1759; ordained in 1761 minister of a Presbyterian congregation at Wisbeach, England; presented to the living at Kirkcudbright in 1765; transferred to Spott in 1769; and died Jan. 6, 1789. He published *The Soul's Perpetual Progress towards Perfection* (1768). See *Fasti Eccles. Scoticanæ*, i, 382, 691.

Cromcruah (or **Cromernach**) was one of the first idols of the Irish, and was made of pure gold, and surrounded by twelve brazen images. Its worship still existed at the introduction of Christianity into Ireland.

Crome, a name common to several Lutheran theologians, of whom we mention the following:

1. Carl Petrus Theodor, was born in 1821, and died Aug. 15, 1874. He was a strict Lutheran, who wrote and fought for his Church. He published, *Christliches Kirchen- und Haus-Gesangbuch* (2d ed. Elberfeld, 1861):—*Gebetbuch für evangelisch-lutherische Christen* (2d ed. ibid. 1860):—*LXXV Psalmen aus dem heiligen Psalter ausgewählt und geordnet* (ibid. 1856):—*Die Wahrheit des Unions-Lutherthums* (ibid. eod.). See Zuchold, *Bibl. Theol.* i, 250 sq.

2. FRIEDRICH ADOLPH, was born Feb. 21, 1757, at Rehburg; was in 1799 superintendent at Eimbeck, in 1823 at Jeinsen, and died March 1, 1825. He published, *Versuch einer Vervollkommnung der geistl. Beredtsamkeit* (Hanover, 1825). See Winer, *Handbuch der theol. Lit.* ii, 64.

3. FRIEDRICH GOTTLIEB, was born in 1775 at Eimbeck, and died as doctor of theology and superintendent at Lüneburg in 1838. He wrote, *Probalia haud Probabilia* (Leyden, 1824):—*Beiträge zur Erklärung des Neuen Testament* (Göttingen, 1828):—*Geographisch-historische Beschreibung des Landes Syrien* (ibid. 1834). See Winer, *Handbuch der theol. Lit.* i, 87, 150; Zuchold, *Bibl. Theol.* i, 251. (B. P.)

Cromer, GIULIO (called *il Croma*), a painter of Ferrara, was born in 1572, studied under Domenico Mona, and died in 1632. He painted *The Presentation*, and *The Death of the Virgin*, in the Scala, at Ferrara.

Cromernach. See CROMCRUAH.

Cromm, ADRIAN, a Dutch Jesuit, was born in 1591 at Arschot, in the Netherlands, and died at Brussels, May 2, 1651. He wrote, *Psalmi Davidis cum Compendiosa Paraphrasi*:—*Evangelia Historico Ordine Concordiæ in Modum Digesta*. See Andreæ, *Bibliotheca Belgica*; Alegambe, *Bibliotheca Scriptorum Societatis Jesu*; Jöcher, *Allgemeines Gelehrten-Lexikon*, s.v. (B. P.)

Crompton, SAMUEL, an English Wesleyan minister, began his pastorate in 1813, became a supernumerary in 1847, and died at Unsworth, near Bury, July 6, 1866. See *Minutes of the British Conference*, 1866, p. 38.

Cromwell, James O., a Methodist Episcopal minister, began his itinerant life in 1780; served various circuits in the Middle States, namely, Sussex, 1780; East Jersey, 1781; Fluvanna, 1782; Pittsylvania, 1783; Kent, 1784; Port Roseway, 1785; was sent as missionary to Nova Scotia in 1786; and located in 1793. See *Minutes of Annual Conferences*, 1780-85; Sprague, *Annals of the Amer. Pulpit*, vii, 103; Stevens, *Hist. of the Meth. Episc. Church*, ii, 82, 88, 128, 188, 379.

Cromwell, James W. H., a Methodist Episcopal minister, was born at Majorville, N. B., Oct. 23, 1843. He removed to Frederickton in 1862, where for a few years he taught school; received license to preach in 1869; and in 1870 joined the East Maine Conference, wherein he continued laborious until his death, Aug. 23, 1874. See *Minutes of Annual Conferences*, 1875, p. 79.

Cromwell, Oliver, who deserves notice here as one of the great politico-religious characters of Great Britain, was born in the town of Huntingdon, April 25, 1599. His father was Robert Cromwell, of a family possessed of a baronetcy, and his mother being a daughter of Sir Richard Stewart, efforts have often been made to show that he was connected with the royal family. He is said, by unfriendly authorities, to have spent a dissolute and extravagant youth, interrupted by serious misgivings, which brought him at last to stern self-condemnation, and resulted in a Puritanic piety. He was educated at the Huntingdon grammar-school, and was admitted, April 22, 1616, a commoner of Sidney-Sussex College, Cambridge; but on the death of his father, in June, 1617, he left the university, and began the study of law in London. When twenty-one years old he married Elizabeth, the daughter of Sir Thomas Bourchier, and thus, both by descent and alliance, he was a member of the higher country-gentleman class, or of the nobility, as it would be termed in other European countries. In that age, however, refinement was only kept up by attendance at court, and Cromwell, who lived away from town and followed country pursuits, became a man of rustic deportment. Though he had been elected to the brief parliament of 1628, it was not till 1640 that he was known in the House of Commons, and Sir Philip Warwick, who observed his rise, has left a curious notice of his personal appearance.

Mask of Cromwell, taken after death.

"His apparel was a plain cloth suit, which seemed to have been made by an ill country tailor. His hat was without a hat-band. His stature was of good size; his sword stuck close to his side; his countenance swollen and reddish, his voice sharp and untunable, and his eloquence full of fervor." He had been for some years establishing an influence with the Puritan party, who frequented his house and bowed to his strong judgment. He showed his great business capacity in the struggle of the Long Parliament, but it was not until the parliament raised a military force, to which he brought a troop of horse, that his powers of organization and command were fully developed. He speedily rose to authority as lieutenant-general of the horse, and when he was specially exempted from the self-denying ordinance, so that he could both deliberate in parliament and hold command, he became the most powerful man in the country. He showed his eminent sagacity in reconstructing the army, and infusing into it high spirit along with stern discipline. At the battle of Naseby, in 1645, it was seen, in the signal destruction brought on the well-officered royal army, how effectively he could strike with the weapon he had constructed. His military policy throughout was to despise secondary means and ends, but to invest himself with overwhelming power and crush his enemy. He saw the large share which artillery must bear in warfare, and anticipated modern generals in fostering that destructive arm. His repeated victories over the royalists, his establishment of the predominance of the army over parliament, and of the Independents over the Presbyterians, his relentless exertions to bring Charles I to the block, and his dismissal of the parliament, are all great events in the history of the day, which cannot be narrated with sufficient distinctness without much detail. In 1649 he conducted an exterminating war in Ireland, instigated by the ferocious principle that whatever human being opposed him should be put to death. In Scotland, where he saw there were more suitable materials for the sort of government he desired, he was rather a pacificator than an oppressor. Dec. 16, 1653, he took the title of Lord Protector, and became virtually king of Britain, and one who submitted to very little constitutional restraint. Cromwell died Sept. 3, 1658, and the revolution which he had conducted speedily came to an end. He was buried in Westminster Abbey, but in 1661 his remains were dug up and treated with ignominy. How far he was sincere in the religious convictions by which he professed to be led has been matter of debate, and modern writers have by turns decried him as a usurper and lauded him as a liberator. That he was under powerful religious impulses cannot be doubted; the question arises as to the extent to which, by their power alone, and by no promptings of worldliness, he was driven on in his ambitious career. He was an enlightened internal reformer, and established many ministerial improvements, and it cannot be questioned that the line of public policy which has made England famous since, was inaugurated during his administration.

Cromwell, William, an English Baptist minister, was born about 1800, and united with the Church at Beckington; began to preach in two or three churches in Bath, and became pastor in Wood Street; soon afterwards of Providence Chapel, and finally of Ebenezer Chapel. He died April 13, 1854. See (Lond.) *Baptist Handbook*, 1855, p. 47. (J. C. S.)

Cron, Joseph Anton, a Roman Catholic theologian, was born at Podersam, in Bohemia, Sept. 29, 1751. He was for some time professor of polemics and dogmatics at Prague; and in 1822 became doctor of theology and capitulary at Ossegk, where he died, Jan. 20, 1826, leaving *Beiträge zur Methodik der Kirchengeschichte* (Prague, 1795). See Winer, *Handbuch der theol. Lit.* i, 530. (B. P.)

Cron, William, a Scotch clergyman, a native of Dumfriesshire, was tutor in the family of sir P. A. Irving; licensed to preach in 1812; presented to the living at Menmuir in 1824; ordained in 1825, and died May 4, 1859. See *Fasti Eccles. Scoticanæ*, iii, 843.

Cronan (**Croman**, or **Chronan**) is a very frequent name in Irish hagiologies, and has several synonyms, as *Cuaran*, *Mochuaroc*, and frequently *Mochua*, *Cron* and *Cua* having in Irish the same meaning.

1. Son of Cummain, of Sliabh Eibhlinne, in Munster, commemorated May 4. Ænghus associates him with Siollan the deacon. His church was among the Slieve-Phelim mountains, County Tipperary (Todd and Reeves, *Mart. Doneg.* p. 120, n., 121).

2. See CUARAN.

3. Commemorated Nov. 11, probably son of Sinell, of the race of Coindri, son of Fergus, of the clan Rudhraidhe. Colgan calls him the brother of St. Beodan, Baitan, or Mobaoi (Dec. 13), Carnan, etc., and St. Ænghus calls his mother Sina. He died of the Yellow Plague in A.D. 664 (Colgan, *Acta Sanctorum*, p. 219, n.[6]; 598, c. 3; O'Donovan, *Four Masters*, i, 277).

4. Son of Ualach, abbot of Clonmacnoise, commemorated July 18. He died in 637 or 638.

5. Abbot of Airdne (Arran Isles, in Galway Bay), commemorated March 8, the same day as a Scottish saint, "Cronan the Monk."

6. Abbot of Benuchar (Bangor), 680-691, and commemorated Nov. 6. He is called "filius cucalnæi" = "Mac Cuchuailne."

7. Abbot of Cluain-dolcain (now Clondalkin, in the county of Dublin), probably in the 8th century. His father was Lughaidh, of the royal line of Erin, and his mother was Carner of Cluain-dasaileach; his brothers were Bædan (q. v.), etc.

8. Abbot and martyr of Glais-mor (Clashmore), commemorated Feb. 10. His father is said to have been Mellan, and he lived among the Desii of Munster, about the end of the 6th century.

9. An obscure saint of Lismore, who died about 718, and is commemorated June 1.

10. Abbot of Fearrea (Ferns), and perhaps bishop of Luachair, who died in 653, and is commemorated June 22.

11. Priest of Maghbile (now Moville, near Newtownards, in County Down), commemorated Aug. 7, addressed by pope-elect John IV on the Paschal controversy (Bede, *Eccles. Hist.* ii, c. 19), in A.D. 640.

12. Of Roscrea, commemorated April 28, who flourished about A.D. 625. He was a native of Ely O'Carrol in Munster, his father being Odran, of that sept, and his mother Coemri, of the sept of Corcobaschin, a district in the west of the present County Clare. Taking with him his maternal cousin St. Mobai, he spent some years traversing Connaught, and then, returning to his native province, built a cell near Loch Crea, at a place called Seanross, now Corbally (O'Donovan, *Four Masters*, i, 412 n.). As this place was so secluded (desertus et avius) St. Cronan afterwards left it, and built his great church by the highway at Roscrea, in the county of Tipperary, where he had one of the most famous schools in Ireland. There, in piety and works that make for peace with God and man, he spent the remainder of his days, the honored friend of Fingen, king of Munster, and the willing advocate of the oppressed.

13. Of Tuaim-greine (now Tomgraney, in the barony of Upper Tulla, County Clare), commemorated Oct. 19. This saint appears twice in the *Mart. Doneg.*, first in the original hand at Oct. 19; and next in the second hand, on the authority of Mar. O'Gorman, at Nov. 1. Among the saints of the family of St. Colman of Kilmacduach (Feb. 3), or house of the Hy-Fiachrach, Colgan gives "St. Cronan, son of Ængus, son of Corbmac, etc., Feb. 20 or Oct. 19;" and *Mart. Doneg.* at Feb. 20 also mentions that there is a Cronan with this pedigree (Todd and Reeves, *Mart. Doneg.* p. 55, 279, 293; Colgan, *Acta Sanctorum*, p. 248, c. 2).

14. "Beg" of Ændruim (Nendrum), bishop, commemorated Jan. 7. His name appears third among the bishops of the Scots in the north of Ireland to whom, with priests and others, pope John IV, when yet but pope-elect, A.D. 640, addressed the famous letter on the Paschal question and the Pelagian heresy (see No. 11 above). The Irish *Annals* generally place his death in A.D. 642, and the *Ann. Tigh.*, perhaps more accurately, in A.D. 643; but Lanigan (*Eccl. History of Ireland*, ii, 412) is mistaken in calling him "bishop of Antrim" (Reeves, *Eccl. Ant.* p. 10, n., 63, n., 148-150, 187-197; O'Hanlon, *Irish Saints*, i, 95, 96).

There is another Cronan Beg, who, however, is usually known as Cronbeg (q. v.).

15. "Clairenech" (i. e. *flat-faced*), commemorated Jan. 29. Under Seighin it is stated "the three Clairenechs were Cronan, Baeithin, and Seighin."

Cronānus. See MOCHUA.

Cronbeg, an Irish *saint*, abbot of Cluain-mic-nois (Clonmacnoise), is commemorated April 6. According to Tighernach, he succeeded Forcren in 686, and died A.D. 694, but the other *Annals* place the dates rather earlier. He is also designated by the double diminutive Cron-an-beg (Cronan-beg). See Todd and Reeves, *Mart. Doneg.* p. 97; O'Conor, *Rer. Hib. Script.* ii, 214, 217; iv, 65; O'Donovan, *Four Masters*, i, 291, 297.—Smith, *Dict. of Christ. Biog.* s. v.

Crone. See CROINE.

Cronin, JOHN W., a Methodist Episcopal minister, was born in Harford County, Md., about 1813. He was converted at an early age, and in 1837 entered the Baltimore Conference, wherein he labored until his death, Oct. 3, 1845. See *Minutes of Annual Conferences*, 1846, p. 9.

Cronius is the name of two early Christians:

1. An ecclesiastic who accompanied Athanasius to Tyre, and signed his letter to the church of that place (Athan. *ad Constant.* i, 797); perhaps the same as the bishop of Metole in the list given by Meletius (ibid. 789).

2. A presbyter and solitary, visited by Palladius A.D. 394 (who was afterwards bishop of Helenopolis in Bithynia), and about the same time by Petronius (afterwards bishop of Boulogne, and canonized). He was a disciple and interpreter to St. Anthony, and lived in the deserts of Egypt. He was canonized (Pallad. *Hist. Laus.* cap. 7, § 713; *De Vitis Patrum*, vii, cap. 19, ap. Migne, *Patrol. Lat.* lxxiii, 1041, 1122, 1126; Ceillier, vii, 485; x, 161).

Crook, Enoch, an English Baptist minister, was born at Bath, Dec. 11, 1797. He was converted at eighteen years of age; studied at Bradford Academy; was ordained March 11, 1823, at Crewkerne, Somersetshire, and in 1834 went to Battersea, where he continued as pastor until his death, June 28, 1837. See *English Baptist Magazine*, 1837, p. 381-384; (Lond.) *Baptist Handbook*, 1838, p. 22. (J. C. S.)

Crook, John (1), an English minister of the Society of Friends, was born in Bedfordshire in 1617. After being a justice of the peace, he joined the Friends about 1654; preached in Bedfordshire and the neighboring counties; suffered imprisonment in London, Huntingdon, Aylesbury, and Ipswich; afterwards itinerated in Hertfordshire, and died Feb. 26, 1699. See *Friends' Library*, xiii, 202, 292; Evans, *Piety Promoted*, i, 169. (J. C. S.)

Crook, John (2), an English Wesleyan minister, was born near Leigh, Lancashire, in 1742. He entered the army and was converted while quartered at Limerick; afterwards became a class-leader in Liverpool, and the society there sent him, in 1775, as a missionary to the Isle of Man, whose inhabitants were in a heathenish state of immorality. Amid discouragement and persecution he planted Methodism in that island, and in 1782 was appointed to the Lisburn Circuit, in counties Down and Antrim, and thereafter labored in Ireland, except another term of service in the Isle of Man, from 1786 to 1788, and 1798. During the latter part of his life he preached in England. He died at Scarborough, Dec. 27, 1805. See *Wesl. Meth. Mag.* 1808, p. 3, etc.; *Minutes of the British Conference*, 1806; Stevens, *Hist. of Meth.* ii, 325; iii, 202; Smith, *Hist. of Wesl. Meth.* i, 391, 451; ii, 429; Rosser, *Hist. of Wesl. Meth. in the Isle of Man* (Lond. 1849), p. 48 sq.

Crook, John David Weaver, a minister of the Methodist Episcopal Church South, was born in Orangeburg District, S. C., Oct. 6, 1820. He joined the Church when about twenty-two, labored several years as a local preacher, and in 1851 was admitted into the South Carolina Conference. He died May 1, 1866. See *Minutes of Annual Conferences of the M. E. Church South*, 1866, p. 20.

Crook, Robert, an English Congregational minister, was born about 1770. He was converted in 1789; studied under the Rev. Mr. Reader at Taunton; settled at Kingsbridge, Devonshire; afterwards removed to Newton Abbot, where he remained pastor for nearly half a century. He resigned in 1835, and removed to Chudleigh, where he died, May 10, 1850. See (Lond.) *Cong. Year-book*, 1850, p. 94.

Crook, William (1), one of the patriarchs of Irish Methodism, was born at Cabystown, County Fermanagh, December, 1784. He was received into the ministry in 1804; became a supernumerary in 1851; resided in Dublin and Belfast, and died in the former city, May 4, 1862, being at the time senior minister in the Irish Conference. Mr. Crook published a pamphlet in 1823, entitled, *A Few Plain Proofs that the Church of England is not Calvinistic*. See *Memorials of Rev. Wm. Crook* (Lond. and Dublin, 1863), by his son, Rev. Wm. Crook; *Minutes of the British Conference*, 1862, p. 36.

Crook, William (2), a minister of the Methodist Episcopal Church South, was born in Chester District, S. C., in 1805. He was converted in 1821, licensed to preach in 1825; admitted into the South Carolina Conference; and died Nov. 25, 1867. See *Minutes of Annual Conferences of the M. E. Church South*, 1867, p. 113.

Crooke, George Alexander, D.D., D.C.L., a Protestant Episcopal clergyman, graduated from Trinity College, Dublin, Ireland, and was ordained deacon in 1854, and presbyter in 1855. About 1858 he resided in Philadelphia, Pa.; the following year was made rector of St. Peter's Church, Lewes, Del.; in 1860, of St. John's Church, Northern Liberties, Philadelphia, continuing until 1864. The following year he returned to his former parish, in Lewes, and remained until 1867, when he became assistant minister in St. James's Parish, Philadelphia. Subsequently he resided several years in that city, without charge, and died there, April 18, 1877. See *Prot. Episc. Almanac*, 1878, p. 168.

Crooker, Samuel, a minister of the Bible Christians, was born in North Devon, England, in October, 1808. He was converted in 1833; went to his first circuit, Ringsash, in 1840, but left in discouragement. Two years afterwards he was stationed at Chard, where scores of conversions cheered him. After twenty-two years of effective work he settled at Dunster, Somerset, where he died, May 1, 1881. See *Minutes of the Sixty-third Annual Conference of the Bible Christians.*

Crookes, William (1), a Scotch clergyman, took his degree at Glasgow University in 1619; was licensed to preach in 1625; became assistant minister at Leswalt in 1631; was presented to the living at Kilmaurs in 1638; continued in 1650; went to Ireland; was minister at Ballykelly, from which he was obliged to remove, and had assistance in money from the kirk session at Torphichen in 1659, and charity in 1662. He died in 1697, aged about ninety years. See *Fasti Eccles. Scoticanæ*, ii, 178.

Crookes, William (2), an English Wesleyan minister, was born at Barlborough, Derbyshire, Jan. 18, 1803. He was converted when seventeen; entered the ministry in 1825; was appointed to Jamaica, W. I., in 1827; returned home after eleven years of successful labor, and exercised his ministry in England for upwards of thirty years; became a supernumerary in 1871, first at Merthyr-Tydvil, afterwards in Chesterfield; and died at Old Whittington, Chesterfield, May 9, 1879. See *Minutes of the British Conference*, 1879, p. 38.

Crooks, David, a faithful minister of the German Reformed Church, was born March 12, 1820. He studied at Mercersburg, Pa.; was licensed by the classis of Zion in 1838; subsequently went to North Carolina, where he was ordained as pastor at Davidson; and, after some years, removed to Lincoln, where he died, Jan. 24, 1859. See Harbaugh, *Fathers of the Ref. Church*, iv, 317–320. (D. Y. H.)

Crooks, John, a Scotch clergyman, took his degree at Glasgow University in 1643; was called to the living at New Luce in 1646; admitted in 1647; transferred to Ballantrae in 1658; and died after Feb. 15, 1661. See *Fasti Eccles. Scoticanæ*, i, 753, 767.

Crooks, John Conrad, a minister of the Methodist Episcopal Church South, was born in Greenup County, Ky., about 1824. He was converted in early life; entered the local ministry in 1855; acquired a good education; devoted several years to school-teaching; and in 1866 united with the Western Virginia Conference, wherein he labored with unsurpassed acceptability and success till his death, March 2, 1875. See *Minutes of Annual Conferences of the M. E. Church South*, 1875, p. 15.

Crookshank, William, D.D., a Scotch Presbyterian minister, took his first degree in one of the Scotch universities; went to London, and was ordained pastor of the Scotch Church, Swallow Street, in January, 1734. He was a man of learning, but in 1767 fell under the censure of the Church, removed into the country, and died July 28, 1769, when more than seventy years old. In 1749 he published, in two volumes, *The History of the State and Sufferings of the Church of Scotland, from the Restoration to the Revolution.* He also published an English translation of *Witsius on the Covenants*, and five separate *Sermons*. See Wilson, *Dissenting Churches*, iv, 46; Allibone, *Dict. of Brit. and Amer. Authors*, s. v.

Crookshanke, John, a Scotch clergyman, was licensed to preach in 1624; appointed assistant to his father-in-law in 1625; called to the living at Redgorton in 1626, and ordained; joined the Protestors in 1651; continued in March, 1661; and he is said to have been "slain at Pentland." See *Fasti Eccles. Scoticanæ*, ii, 655.

Croom, M. G., a Methodist Episcopal minister, was born in 1820. He was converted when quite young, and was first a member of the African M. E. Church. In 1871 he joined the North Carolina Conference, in which he served as pastor and presiding elder until his death, at Wilmington, March 17, 1881. See *Minutes of Annual Conferences*, 1882, p. 72.

Crop is a name for the top or finial of a pyx (q. v.).

Croquet (or **Crocquet**), André, a French Dominican, was born at Douay, and was first prior of the monastery of Hasnon. He was doctor of theology, and died in 1580, leaving, *Commentarius in Epistolam Pauli ad Romanos* (Douay, 1577):—*Enarratio Epistolæ ad Hebræos* (ibid. 1578):—*Catechetes Christianus* (ibid. 1575; Lyons, 1593):—*Paraphrasis sive Conciones in Septem Psalmos Pœnitentiales* (Douay, 1579). See Hoefer, *Nouv. Biog. Générale*, s. v.: Jöcher, *Allgemeines Gelehrten-Lexikon*, s. v.

Crosbie, Alexander, a Scotch clergyman, born at Merkland, was licensed to preach in 1804; presented to the living at Buittle in 1807; ordained in 1808; and died Dec. 3, 1847, aged seventy years. See *Fasti Eccles. Scoticanæ*, i, 704.

Crosbie, John Geddes, A.M., a Scotch clergyman, was called to Birmingham in 1824; ordained by the Glasgow Presbytery in 1825; resigned his English charge in 1826; was presented to the living at Fenwick in 1828; resigned in 1836, in consequence of a change of opinion, and left the Scotch Church. He died June 16, 1838. See *Fasti Eccles. Scoticanæ*, ii, 170.

Crosbie, William Glendonwyne, a Scotch clergyman, took his degree at Edinburgh University in 1828; was licensed to preach in 1829; appointed to the living at Parton the same year; ordained in 1830; and died March 18, 1845, aged thirty-eight years. See *Fasti Eccles. Scoticanæ*, i, 720.

Crosby, Benjamin, an English Wesleyan missionary, was sent to Sierra Leone in 1834, and died April 24, 1837, aged twenty-nine years. See *Minutes of the British Conference*, 1837.

Crosby, Daniel, a Congregational minister, was born in Hampden, Me., Oct. 8, 1799. He graduated from Yale College in 1823, and completed his theological course at Andover in 1826; became pastor at Conway in 1827, and of Winthrop Church, Charlestown, in 1833; in 1842 entered upon the editorial duties at the Mission House in Boston, and died Feb. 28, 1843. He published a small work on the *Character of Christ*, and several *Sermons*. See Sprague, *Annals of the Amer. Pulpit*, iv, 822.

Crosby, Jewett Vernon, a Presbyterian minister, was born at Staunton, Va., July 8, 1816. He graduated from Hampden-Sidney College in 1837, taught for a time, spent one year in Union Theological Seminary, Virginia, then became stated supply at Manning's Neck, N. C., and Jerusalem, Va., in 1843; was ordained evangelist by the Presbytery of East Hanover, Sept. 23 of the same year; preached at Southampton and Smithfield, Va., until 1847; afterwards at Bardstown, Ky.; from 1848 to 1860 was pastor of that church, at the same time being principal of the female academy there; stated supply at Midway and Clear Creek until 1864; was also principal of Rose Hill Female Academy; thereafter stated supply and principal of the female academy at Bardstown, until his death, Nov. 14, 1877. See *Gen. Cat. of Princeton Theol. Sem.* 1881, p. 136.

Crosby, John (1), an English Wesleyan minister, was born at Whitby in 1755. He was converted in 1774, under the preaching of a Church of England minister, and in 1783 Wesley appointed him to a circuit. He labored with great success for twenty-eight years, travelling eighteen circuits, finally settled at Bolton as a supernumerary, and died there, March 29, 1816. See *Wesl. Meth. Mag.* 1819, p. 3; *Minutes of the British Conference*, 1816.

Crosby, John (2), a Congregational minister, was born at Bangor, Me., in 1803. He graduated from Bowdoin College in 1823; taught for a year in Hallowell; graduated from Andover Theological Seminary in 1827, and, June 11, 1828, was ordained pastor in Castine; resigned in 1831; labored for a year in Pennsylvania as agent of the American Colonization Society; then went to Savannah, Ga., and subsequently to Barbadoes, where he died, May 26, 1833. See *History of Bowdoin College*, p. 261, 262; *Trien. Cat. of Andover Theol. Sem.* 1870, p. 74. (J. C. S.)

Crosby, John (3), an English Wesleyan minister, was born at Powis House, near Kirbythorpe, Westmoreland, Aug. 9, 1804. He was converted in 1819; in 1829 was sent to Penrith as supply; the following year to Appleby, and in 1831 to Kendal, where he died, Jan. 3, 1832. See *Wesl. Meth. Mag.* 1834, p. 493; *Minutes of the British Conference*, 1832, p. 111.

Crosby, Joshua, A.M., a Congregational minister, was ordained pastor in Enfield, Mass., Dec. 2, 1789, and died in 1838. See Sprague, *Annals of the Amer. Pulpit*, ii, 142.

Crosby, Stephen, a Congregational minister, was born at Thompson, Conn., about 1795. He entered Brown University, but graduated from Union College, Schenectady, N. Y., in 1816 or 1817; pursued his theological studies there under president Nott; in June, 1819, was ordained pastor in Spencer, Mass., and dismissed May 31, 1825. Subsequently he was pastor in East Granby, Conn.; next in the western part of New York, and finally in or near Norwich, Conn., where he died in 1839. See *Hist. of Spencer*, p. 100. (J. C. S.)

Crosby, Thomas (1), an English Baptist historian, was born about 1700. For some time he was at the head of an institution for the education of boys. He was a deacon of the Church of which Dr. Gill was pastor. His great work was his *History of English Baptists, from the Reformation to the Beginning of the Reign of George I* (Lond. 1738–40, 4 vols. 8vo). See Haynes, *Baptist Cyclop.* p. 168. (J. C. S.)

Crosby, Thomas (2), an English Wesleyan Methodist minister, was born at Stockwith, March 25, 1816. He was converted at eighteen, received into the ministry in 1842, and died at Haslingden, June 28, 1875. See *Minutes of the British Conference*, 1875, p. 28.

Crosdale, John, D.D., a Protestant Episcopal clergyman, was rector for many years in Newtown, Md., and also of Pocomoke and Coventry parishes. He died at Newtown, March 11, 1878. See *Prot. Episc. Almanac*, 1879, p. 168.

Croser, John P., a distinguished Baptist philanthropist, was born in that part of Springfield now called West Dale, in Delaware Co., Pa., Jan. 13, 1793. At the age of fifteen he united with the First Baptist Church in Philadelphia, and at twenty-eight commenced the struggle of life, which eventuated in a career of great success in business. Mr. Croser's interest in the kingdom of Christ early developed itself, and was exhibited in labors and contributions to the Bible and tract societies, the temperance and anti-slavery causes, foreign missions, and especially in the cause of education. He subscribed liberally in aid of the Lewisburg University, gave ten thousand dollars to the American Baptist Publication Society for a Sunday-school Library Fund, and five thousand dollars to purchase books for poor ministers. As wealth increased, so did his benevolence grow more expansive, and his donations flowed in a steady stream in every direction. He died March 11, 1866. He perpetuates his memory through the fifty-thousand-dollar memorial fund for missions among the colored people of the country, and through the theological institution at Upland, Pa., which bears his name. See Dr. J. Wheaton Smith's *Life of J. P. Croser*. (J. C. S.)

Crosier, Samuel B., a Methodist Episcopal minister, was born at Halifax, Vt., in 1812. He was converted at the age of twenty; soon after received license to preach; in 1851 was admitted into the Black River

Conference; became a superannuate in 1868, and died at Clyde, N. Y., Dec. 31, 1870. See *Minutes of Annual Conferences*, 1871, p. 128.

Cross. The statement of Bede relating to the four kinds of wood of which the cross of Christ was made—the upright of cypress, the cross-piece of cedar, the head-piece of fir, and the foot-support of box—departs from the Eastern tradition, which substitutes olive and palm for the two latter varieties of wood. See CROSS, CHRIST'S.

Engraved Stone of the Earliest Period.

The private use of crosses, or representations of the cross, is highly uncertain before Constantine, though Martigny refers to Perret for certain stones, apparently belonging to rings, on which the cross is engraved, and which appear to be of date prior to Constantine. It seems probable that the use of the monogram prevailed before and during his time, with sacrificial meaning attaching more and more to the cruciform in the Christian mind. See MONOGRAM OF CHRIST.

The following engravings illustrate the various forms which this symbol of Christianity assumed in early times. See CRUCIFIX; INSCRIPTIONS.

Cross on a Single Tomb in the Callixtine Catacomb.

The term "station-cross" is derived from the Roman military term *statio*, and applied to a large cross on the chief altar, or in some principal part of a church, but occasionally removed or carried in procession to another spot, and then constituting a special place of prayer. Processional crosses may be traced to the use of the Labarum in Constantine's army, and also to his substitution of the cross for the dragon, or placing it above the dragon on standards of cohorts, etc. See STATION.

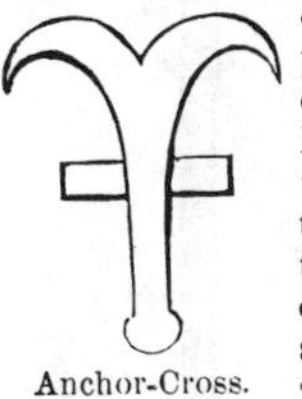
Anchor-Cross.

CROSS, as an architectural ornament in churches and religious edifices, was almost always placed upon the points of the gables, the form varying considerably, according to the style of the architecture and the character of the building; many of these crosses are extremely elegant and ornamental; it was also very frequently carved on gravestones, and was introduced in various ways among the decorations of churches.

Warmington, Northants, A.D. 1250.

A small cross (which was often a *crucifix*) was placed upon the altar, and was usually of a costly material, and sometimes of the most elaborate workmanship, enriched with jewels; crosses were also carried in religious processions upon long staves.

Merton College Chapel, A.D. 1450.

A large cross with the figure attached, called the *rood*, was placed over the main entrance of the chancel in every church.

It was formerly the custom in Great Britain, as it still is in Roman Catholic countries, to erect crosses in cemeteries, by the road-side, and in the market-places and open spaces in towns and villages, of which numerous examples remain, though, with the exception of the market crosses, most of them are greatly defaced: those in cemeteries and by the way-side were generally simple structures, raised on a few steps, consisting of a tall shaft, with sometimes a few mouldings to form a base, and a cross on the top; in some instances they had small niches or other ornaments round the top of the shaft, below the cross; the village crosses appear generally to have been of the same simple description, but sometimes they were more important erections. Market crosses were usually polygonal buildings with an open archway on each of the sides, and vaulted within, large enough to afford shelter to a considerable number of persons; of these good examples remain at Malmesbury, Salisbury, Chichester, Glastonbury, etc. Crosses were also erected in commemoration of remarkable occurrences, of which Queen Eleanor's crosses are beautiful examples; these are memorials of the places at which her corpse rested each night on its journey to Westminster for interment.

Churchyard Cross, Waterperry, cir. 1320.

The cross was a favorite form for the plan of churches, and great numbers are built in this shape, the Western churches mostly following the Latin form of cross, the Byzantine churches following the Greek form, i. e. with the chancel, nave, and two transepts all of equal length.

CROSS OF ABSOLUTION was a metal cross, inscribed with a papal absolution, buried in graves. Specimens have been found at Meaux, Mayence, Périgueux, and Bury St. Edmund's. One of a bishop, cir. 1088, is preserved at Chichester.

CROSS, ADORATION OF. See ADORATION OF THE CROSS.

CROSS, APPARITION OF THE, *at Jerusalem*, about the third hour of the day, in the time of Constantius, in the year 346, is commemorated May 7 in the Byzantine and Ethiopic calendars.

CROSS OF BOUNDARY (WAYSIDE, and SANCTUARY). Crosses engraved on boundary stones are mentioned as early as 807; and standing crosses for the same purposes are frequently alluded to in old English cartularies. Near Hereford there is a good example, of the 14th century. At Bury and Beverley, the whole precinct was distinguished at the cardinal points of the compass by tall crosses. In Cornwall and the Isle of Man crosses are very common; in the former region they sometimes have a rounded head. One at Towednack has a curious double-incised cross, like a patriarchal cross, which may mark the boundary of a religious house. St. Burian's has a church-yard cross of the 13th or 14th century; and at a little distance a sanctuary cross, with a crucifix. At Battel, as late as the 17th century, the boundaries were marked by watch crosses. There is a wayside cross, of the 14th century, in Burleigh Park.

CROSS OF CALVARY is a cross on three steps. These steps are said by some writers to signify the three theological virtues—faith, hope, and charity.

CROSS OF CONSECRATION. See CONSECRATION CROSS.

CROSS CROSSLET is a cross with equal arms, each of the ends of which is terminated by another cross.

CROSS, GREEK, a cross in which the vertical and transverse parts are of equal length.

CROSS, INCENSING THE, is a ceremony by which all crosses to be erected in Roman Catholic countries, in public places, high-roads, and cross-ways, as well as on the tops of chapels, are prepared previous to erection. Candles are first lighted at the foot of the cross, after which the celebrant sits down before it and delivers a discourse to the people on its manifold virtues. Then he sprinkles the cross with holy water, and afterwards with incense, and at the close of this ceremony candles are set upon the top of each arm of the cross.

CROSS, LATIN, is a cross the transverse beam of which is placed at one-third distance from the top of the perpendicular portion.

CROSS OF MALTA is a cross of eight points, the badge of the knights of Malta. The points are said to symbolize the eight beatitudes (Matt. vi).

CROSS, MARKET, is an erection of stone, commonly vaulted, supported on four or more pillars, and entered by arched apertures on each side, surmounted by a cross, usually built in the centre of the cross-streets, for the shelter of persons attending market. Many curious and remarkable ancient specimens exist; e. g. at Glastonbury, Chichester, Malmesbury, and Winchester. All these are of Pointed architecture.

CROSS, MEMORIAL, was a beautiful structure of stone, erected near Durham, in memory of the victory of the Red Hills, and called Neville's Cross, while an humbler crucifix of wood marks the spot on which the monks had stood, praying for the rout of the Scots.

CROSS, ORDEAL OF THE, is a mode of trial anciently practiced among the Anglo-Saxons. The accused person brought eleven compurgators to swear to his innocence. Two pieces of wood, on one of which the cross was delineated, were placed under a cover, and he was to choose one of these. If he took the one with the cross, he was regarded as innocent; if the other, guilty. This species of ordeal was abolished about A.D. 820, as exposing the sacred symbol to profanation.

CROSS, PAPAL, is a cross with three transverse beams, the upper one less wide than the second, and the second less wide than the third.

Spanish Example of a Cross Pectoral.

CROSS, PECTORAL, is a cross of precious metal worn round the necks of Roman Catholic and Greek bishops, attached to a chain, symbolizing to the faithful authority and jurisdiction. It was worn by St. Alphege in the 11th century.

CROSS FOR PREACHING. Crosses, at which sermons were delivered, existed on the north side of Norwich and Worcester cathedrals and St. Paul's, and on the south at Hereford. A beautiful example remains in the Dominican monastery at Hereford. St. Oswald used to preach at the cemetery cross of Worcester.

CROSS OF PRELATES (or CROSIER). Of this episcopal emblem we give the following additional particulars from Walcott, *Sac. Archæol.* s. v.:

"It reminded bishops of their duty, as the pastoral staff was for the direction of the laity. The archiepiscopal cross of Canterbury was distinguished from the processional cross (which had but one) by two crucifixes, behind and before. The double-crossed patriarchal cross, so called, formed by the addition of the scroll, was used in Greece, but in the West is merely a conventional and arbitrary invention of painters (it resembles, however, the cross of Lorraine); and the triple-barred cross of the pope is equally modern and unauthorized. The cross was carried by a subdeacon in front of pope Leo IV, when he rode on horseback, according to the custom of his predecessors. The archbishop of Ravenna was allowed to have his cross borne before him throughout his province, and within three miles of Rome. Augustine entered Canterbury with a cross borne before him; Thomas à Becket was preceded by his silver cross; and St. Anselm refused to allow the archbishop of Dublin such a privilege in England; while archbishop Peckham, in 1279, excommunicated all persons selling victuals to the archbishop of York, if the latter persisted in having his crosier carried in state within the province of Canterbury. After the 9th century, legates apostolic were permitted to enjoy this distinction; and in the 12th century it was extended to metropolitans who had received the pall; but in the 13th century it became common to all archbishops. Innocent III and the Council of Lateran, in 1215, granted the use of the banner of the cross to be carried before the patriarchs of Alexandria, Antioch, and Jerusalem, except in the city of Rome. The cross-bearing is a prerogative, not an act of jurisdiction, but simply a sign of honor and reverence due to a dignity. The bishop of

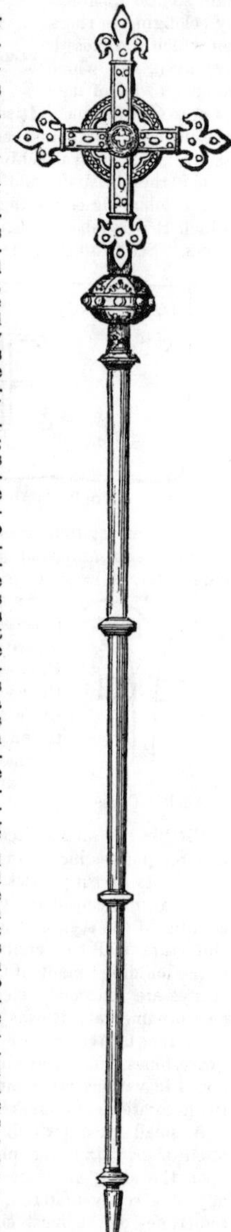

Crosier.

Lucca wears the pall, and, like the bishop of Pavia, has his cross carried before him by grant of Alexander II, 1070; his canons walk mitred in processions, like cardinals. The kings of Hungary also carry the cross, in memory of king Stephen, to whom it was granted, in 1000, by pope Sylvester II. The archbishop of Nazareth had the right of using the cross everywhere; and the archbishop of Toledo throughout Spain. In 1452 Booth, of York, by a compact made in 1353, gave an image of himself to Canterbury, having carried his cross within the province. The bishop of Funchal, on certain days, has a crosier carried before him, instead of the staff, in memory of the see having once been metropolitan. The pope never carries a crosier, unless he should be in the diocese of Treves, where St. Peter is said to have given his staff to its first bishop, Eucherius. The reason is, that the bend at the top of a crosier betokens restricted jurisdiction, while the pontiff claims unlimited sovereignty. It is certain, however, that originally he received a *ferula*, or staff, at his inauguration. The bishop of Capetown was the first colonial metropolitan who carried a crosier. There is a fine crosier of the 15th century at Toledo, which cardinal Mendoza, in 1492, planted on the Alhambra; and another, with enamel work, at Cologne. Ragenfroi's cross, of the 12th century, with Goliath in the head, is at Goodrich Court; a third, with enamel and figures, is in the British Museum."

CROSS, Red or Blue, is the mark set on houses infected, in times of plague.

CROSS, Reliquary, is a box of precious metal, in the form of a cross, so arranged as to receive particles of the relics of the saints.

CROSS of the Resurrection of Christ is a tall, slight cross, to the top of which is affixed a floating pennon of white, charged in its turn with a scarlet or crimson cross.

CROSS, Screen (or Rood). A cross on or above the altar is one of the legal *ornamenta* of the same; and the cross, with the figure of our Lord attached, can be

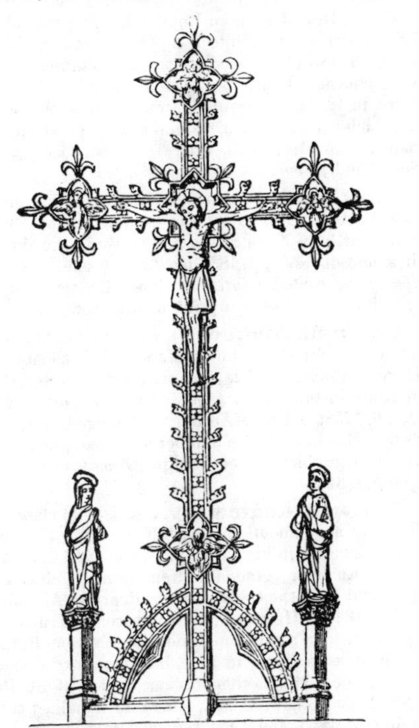

14th-century Cross, on a Chancel-screen.

erected in sculpture over the altar, or as an important part of the rood-screen. Anciently, almost every English church owned its rood-cross, with the figures of Mary and John on either side.

CROSS, Sign of the, is a signal current among Christians, made in the West by drawing the three fingers of the right hand from the forehead to the breast, and from the left to the right shoulder. The use of this sign is a very ancient Christian practice, possibly as old as Christianity itself. Minutius Felix asserts that it was a badge of faith among the primitive disciples; and Tertullian, long before material crosses were in use, tells us that "upon every motion, at their going out or coming in, at dressing, at their going to bath, or to meals, or to bed, or whatever their employment or occasion called them to, they were wont to *mark* their foreheads with the sign of the cross; adding, that this was a practice which tradition had introduced, custom had confirmed, and which the present generation received upon the credit of that which went down before them" (Tertullian. *De Coron. Mil.* c. iii). The following is the ordinary Oriental mode of making the *sign of the cross.* The tips of the thumb and the two forefingers of the right hand are brought together (the third and fourth fingers being folded in the palm of the hand). The hand is then lifted, and the three finger-tips brought into contact with the middle of the forehead; it is then brought down to the chest, and moved transversely upwards to the right shoulder; and, lastly, horizontally to the left. The meaning of the act is thus explained by certain mystical Eastern writers. The conjunction of the three finger-tips signifies in one action the equality and unity of the Three Persons of the Holy Trinity; the raising of the hand to the forehead signifies that God the Word was in heaven glorified together with the Father and the life-giving Spirit from all eternity. The descent of the hand to the waist or breast denotes that this same God came down from heaven to the earth, and was incarnate by the Holy Spirit in the womb of the ever-virgin Mary, thus becoming man for our salvation; the motion upward to the right shoulder symbolizes that he has reascended into heaven, and is sitting at the right hand of God the Father; the horizontal motion, from right to left, that our blessed Saviour's arms were stretched out on the cross to make atonement for the sins of the world; that he is gathering together into one body the faithful out of all nations, and that at the last day he will set the righteous on his right hand and the wicked on his left. After the joined fingers have touched the left shoulder some Easterns lay the open palm on the left breast over the heart and bow the head. This is reputed as a declaration of devotion to the cause, and submission to the will, of the divine Master.

CROSS, Weeping, is one at which penance was performed.

Cross, Abijah, a Congregational minister, was born in Massachusetts in 1793. He graduated from Dartmouth College in 1821; studied in Andover Theological Seminary in 1823; was ordained March 4, 1824; was pastor at Salisbury, N. H., until 1829; at West Haverhill, Mass., stated supply until 1831, and pastor until 1853; without charge at the same place thereafter until his death, July 16, 1856. See *Trien. Cat. of Andover Theol. Sem.* 1870, p. 67.

Cross, Coleman Harwell, a minister of the Methodist Episcopal Church South, was born in Giles County, Tenn., Oct. 5, 1833. He was converted in 1857, and in the same year entered the Tennessee Conference, in which he successfully labored to the close of his life, Aug. 9, 1860. See *Minutes of Annual Conferences of the M. E. Church South*, 1860, p. 212.

Cross, David, a Free-will Baptist minister, was born at Wilmot, N. H., Jan. 22, 1786. He was converted at thirty years of age, soon after began to preach, and died in Newark, Vt., June 22, 1870. See *Free-will Baptist Register*, 1871, p. 81. (J. C. S.)

Cross, John, a Presbyterian minister, styled by Dr. Brownlee "a Scottish worthy," was received as a member of the New Jersey Synod in 1732, and settled at a place called The Mountains, back of Newark. The remarkable revival in his congregation, in 1734 and 1735, is noticed in Edwards's *Thoughts on Revivals*. He was the minister of Baskingridge and Staten Island, and one of the first members of the New Brunswick Presbytery. He was wonderfully successful as a revivalist. Whitefield was refreshed by meeting with him, and they labored together at Baskingridge and the vicinity. Cross afterwards fell into sin, and it is not known where he died. (W. P. S.)

Cross, Joseph Gould, a Methodist Episcopal minister, was born in Onondaga County, N. Y., Jan. 12, 1840. He was converted at the age of nine; removed to Illinois with his father early in life; spent four years in school at Evanston; and in 1867 was admitted into the Rock River Conference, wherein he labored with marked success until his death, May 28, 1870. See *Minutes of Annual Conferences*, 1870, p. 275.

Cross, Joshua L., a Baptist minister, was born in Tennessee in 1822. He joined the Church in 1847, was ordained in October of that year, and began his work in western Tennessee in 1848, visiting the churches in Henderson County, and acting as pastor at Unity until the close of 1849; after which he labored in Fayette County, other parts of western Tennessee, and in parts of northern Mississippi for a number of years. In 1869 his labors were divided between the churches at Byhalia and Olive Branch, until his death, March 11, 1870. See Borum, *Sketches of Tenn. Ministers*, p. 113. (J. C. S.)

Cross (*née Fisher*), **Mary**, an English minister of the Society of Friends, was born in the north of England about 1623. She appeared as a minister in 1652, and was imprisoned and even whipped for addressing public assemblies during her travels in the south of England. Subsequently she visited the West India Islands and North America, in 1658. In 1662 she married William Bayley, and in 1678 John Cross, of London; but finally came to America, and resided on the banks of the Ashley River, near Charleston, S. C., where she died, about 1700. See Bowden, *Hist of the Soc. of Friends in America*, i, 38-41. (J. C. S.)

Cross, Robert, a Presbyterian minister, was born near Ballykelly, Ireland, in 1689. He was licensed by the synod in 1717; preached some time in New Castle, Pa., and became pastor there in 1718; was ordained March 17, 1719; in September, 1723, was called to Jamaica, N. Y.; in 1737 to Philadelphia; resigned June 2, 1758, and died in that city, Aug. 9, 1766. (W. P. S.)

Cross, Walter, A.M., an English Independent minister, studied in Scotland and Holland, and settled as pastor in Rope-maker's Alley, Moorfields, London, in 1675. He preached at Utrecht in 1685; returned to London, and died there in 1701. He published two *Sermons*, and in 1698 *A Treatise on the Art of Expounding Scripture by the Points called Accents*. See Wilson, *Dissenting Churches*, ii, 535.

Cross, William, an English Wesleyan missionary, was converted at the age of twenty-one; in 1827 was sent to New Zealand, in 1829 to the Friendly Islands, and in October, 1835, with Cargill, to the cannibals of Fiji. He remained at his post until his death, Oct. 15, 1842. The story of his trials and dangers and marvellous successes may be found in the *Life of Cross*, by John Hunt (Lond. 1846, 12mo). See *Minutes of the British Conference*, 1844; Moister, *Hist. of Wesleyan Missions*, 1858.

Cross, William G., a minister of the Methodist Episcopal Church South, was born in Morgan County, Va., Jan. 17, 1822. He experienced religion at the age of twenty-two; united with the Baltimore Conference in 1846; became a superannuate in 1873; and died Aug. 4 of the same year. See *Minutes of Annual Conferences of the M. E. Church South*, 1874, p. 4.

Cross-alphabets is a name applied to certain characters made by the pope at the dedication of churches. A pot of ashes is provided, which, in the course of the ceremony, is strewed in two lines, each about a span in breadth, in the form of a cross, transversely from angle to angle of the church. During the chanting of the *Benedictus* the pontiff scores with the point of his pastoral staff on one of these lines the Greek alphabet, and on the other the Latin.

Cross-week. The days of the rogation were so called in 1571; the name formerly designated the week in which the finding of the Holy Cross, May 3, was kept.

Crosse, John, A.M., an English divine, was born in 1737. For upwards of thirty years he was vicar of Bradford, Yorkshire, and died there June 17, 1816. See (Lond.) *Christian Observer*, July, 1816, p. 485.

Crossett, Cortes Z., a Methodist Episcopal minister, was born in Danbury, N. H., Sept. 17, 1853. He was converted in 1875, joined the West Wisconsin Conference in 1877, and labored at Necedah, Ellsworth, and Pepin, where he died, Sept. 17, 1881. See *Minutes of Annual Conferences*, 1881, p. 319.

Crossette, Robert, a Presbyterian minister, was born in Massachusetts. He graduated from Bangor Theological Seminary, was settled for a time at Dennysville, Me., and afterwards served churches in New Hampshire, Massachusetts, New Jersey, and Pennsylvania. In 1868 he removed to College Hill, O., where he died, June 24, 1872. See *Presbyterian*, July 6, 1872.

Crossley, David, an English Baptist minister, a co-laborer in early life of John Bunyan as a preacher, became pastor in 1705 at Curriers' Hall, Cripplegate, London, and years afterwards retired into the country, where he eventually kept a school, and died about 1743. See Wilson, *Dissenting Churches*, ii, 572. (J. C. S.)

Crossley, John, an English Congregational minister, was born at White Hall, Over Darwen, Nov. 20, 1790. He was converted when about fourteen years of age; educated himself; was ordained at Tosside, Yorkshire, in 1820; afterwards labored at Horwich, Buxton, and Lichfield; and then, resigning the regular ministry, removed to Farnworth, where he died, Oct. 23, 1864. See (Lond.) *Cong. Year-book*, 1865, p. 232.

Crosthwaite, Thomas, an English Wesleyan missionary, was accepted by the Conference in 1830; labored partly in Nova Scotia and partly in the West Indies, and died May 1, 1836, aged thirty-one. See *Minutes of the British Conference*, 1836; Cooney, *Autobiog. of a Wesleyan Missionary* (Montreal, 1856), p. 234.

Croswell, Andrew (1), a Congregational minister, was born in Charlestown, Mass. He graduated from Harvard College in 1728; was ordained in Groton, Conn., in 1736; installed over a new society in Boston, Mass., Oct. 6, 1738, and died April 12, 1785, aged seventy-six years. He published a number of *Sermons* and controversial pamphlets. See Sprague, *Annals of the Amer. Pulpit*, i, 322.

Croswell, Andrew (2), an Episcopal clergyman, was born at Falmouth, Mass., July 9, 1822. He studied at the academy in his native place and at Phillips Academy in Andover; graduated from Brown University in 1843, and from the theological seminary at Alexandria, Va., in 1846. He was ordained deacon the same year, took charge of a mission station in Johnston, R. I., was ordained a presbyter in 1848, had charge of a Church in Chicopee, Mass., then became rector of St. Paul's Church in Brunswick, Me., where he remained till the spring of 1853, and then removed to Newton Lower Falls, Mass., and was rector of St. Mary's Church in that place three years. He afterwards resided in Cambridge for a time; out of his efforts grew St. James's parish, North Cambridge, of which he was rector till the spring of 1871. He died on Cushing's Island, near Portland, June 30, 1879. See *Brown University Necrology*, 1879, 1880; *Prot. Episc. Almanac*, 1880, p. 171. (J. C. S.)

Croswell, Harry, D.D., a Protestant Episcopal

clergyman, was born at West Hartford, Conn., June 16, 1778. He was ordained deacon in 1814, and presbyter in 1815. He began his ministerial work in Christ Church, Hudson, N. Y., in May, 1814, and on Jan. 1 of the following year commenced his services in Church Street, New York city, and was instituted rector of the parish Feb. 22, 1816. For more than forty years he was rector of Trinity Church, New Haven, Conn., and died there, March 13, 1858. See *Amer. Quar. Church Rev.* 1858, p. 173.

Crouch, Benjamin T., *Sr.*, a minister of the Methodist Episcopal Church South, was born in New Castle County, Del., July 1, 1796. He joined the Church in 1816; received license to exhort in 1818; and in 1819 was licensed to preach, and admitted into the Ohio Conference. On the formation of the Kentucky Conference, in 1820, he became one of its members. He took a superannuate relation in 1827, re-entered the effective ranks in 1830, and continued faithful until 1856, when he again became a superannuate and took charge of a school at Goshen, Oldham Co., Ky., where he died, April 26, 1858. See *Minutes of Annual Conferences of the M. E. Church South*, 1858, p. 3.

Crouch, Benjamin T., *Jr.*, a minister of the Methodist Episcopal Church South, was born and reared in Kentucky. He embraced religion early in life, and in 1851 entered the Memphis Conference. After two or three years of useful service, he went as missionary to California, subsequently returned to the regular work of the Memphis Conference, wherein he was faithful until the beginning of the Rebellion, when he became chaplain in the Confederate army, and was shot in the battle of Thompson's Station, Middle Tennessee, in 1863. See *Minutes of Annual Conferences of the M. E. Church South*, 1863, p. 434.

Crouch, Christopher J., a Methodist Episcopal minister, was born in Cecil County, Md., Jan. 1, 1811. He joined the Church when about eighteen; received license to exhort in 1831, and in 1833 entered the Philadelphia Conference, wherein he served with zeal and fidelity until 1868, when he became a supernumerary. He was post-chaplain in the Union army two years, and died Feb. 4, 1874. See *Minutes of Annual Conferences*, 1874, p. 34.

Crouch, John F., a Methodist Episcopal minister, was born in Cecil County, Md., May 27, 1804. He embraced religion at fifteen; was licensed to exhort in 1826; to preach in 1831; and in 1833 entered the Philadelphia Conference; was a supernumerary seven years, and died Sept. 23, 1852. See *Minutes of Annual Conferences*, 1853, p. 173.

Crouch, William, an English minister of the Society of Friends, was born at Penton, in Hampshire, April 5, 1628. In 1656 he joined the Friends in London, and by his preaching and pecuniary help did much to sustain their then feeble cause. He died Nov. 13, 1710. See *Friends' Library*, xi, 287-331. (J. C. S.)

Crouched (or **Crutched**, i. e. *crossed*) **Friars** were a religious order, called also *Crosiers* or *Crossbearers*, which was founded in the 4th century, in honor of the discovery of the Cross by the empress Helena. They came to England in 1244, and carried in their hand a staff, on the top of which was a cross. They had monasteries at London, Ryegate, and Oxford.

Crouched-mas-day is the festival in the Greek Church in honor of the erection of the cross. From this feast, which occurred on Sept. 14, the Eastern Church commenced to calculate its ecclesiastical year.

Crouseilhes, Pierre Vincent, *baron Dombidau de*, a French prelate, born at Pau, July 19, 1751, became grand-vicar at Aix, and afterwards canon of the cathedral. He went abroad during the Revolution, and after his return to France was appointed bishop of Quimper, April 21, 1805, and distinguished himself by his zeal for the imperial government. He also employed himself actively in the promotion of missions. He died June 29, 1823, leaving several *Mandements*, addressed to refractory Britons, the object of which was the celebration of the victories of Napoleon. See Hoefer, *Nouv. Biog. Générale*, s. v.

Crowder, Thomas, a minister of the Methodist Episcopal Church South, was born in Wake County, N. C., Sept. 22, 1797. He was piously trained, and received a liberal education; was converted in 1819, and in 1821 entered the Virginia Annual Conference, in which he did good service until his death, in December, 1852. See *Minutes of Annual Conferences of the M. E. Church South*, 1853, p. 445; Sprague, *Annals of the Amer. Pulpit*, vii, 654.

Crowe, George H., a Protestant Episcopal clergyman, began his ministry in 1867, as assistant minister in St. Michael's Church, New York city, and died Sept. 28, 1868. See *Prot. Episc. Almanac*, 1869, p. 109.

Crowe, John, an English Wesleyan minister, was born at Coventry, converted young, entered the ministry in 1815, became a supernumerary in 1855, and died while on a visit to Bourton, near Shaftesbury, Oct. 13, 1857, in the sixty-fourth year of his age. See *Minutes of the British Conference*, 1858.

Crowe, John Finley, D.D., a Presbyterian minister, was born in Green County, Tenn., June 17, 1787. In 1812 he entered Transylvania College, in Kentucky; iu 1815 was licensed by the Lexington Presbytery, and soon after accepted a call to Shelbyville, where he labored until 1833. He was professor in Hanover College, Ind., until about 1855, and died Jan. 17, 1860. Dr. Crowe was a man of sound judgment and deep piety. As a teacher, he was ranked among the first. See Wilson, *Presb. Hist. Almanac*, 1861, p. 84.

Crowe, William, an English Baptist minister, was born at Braintree in December, 1796. He was converted at sixteen; studied with Dr. Bogue of Gosport, and was appointed a missionary to Quilon, in the Bombay presidency. After laboring four years, he returned to England; preached, for a time, at Lutterworth; in Kingston, Surrey, nine years; in Worcester, sixteen years; and then resided, without charge, in Hammersmith, until his death, Nov. 27, 1872. See (Lond.) *Baptist Hand-book*, 1873, 253. (J. C. S.)

Crowell, Churchwell Anderson, a minister of the Methodist Episcopal Church South, was born in Mecklenburg County, N. C., Sept. 15, 1806. He was converted in 1825; licensed to exhort in 1826; to preach in 1828; in 1829 united with the South Carolina Conference; was transferred to the Georgia Conference in 1850, and in 1867 to the South Georgia Conference, laboring faithfully until his death, Jan. 10, 1872. See *Minutes of Annual Conferences of the M. E. Church South*, 1872, p. 681.

Crowell, Jesse T., a Methodist Episcopal minister, was born at Villanova, Chautauqua Co., N. Y., April 2, 1839. He was converted in boyhood, and notwithstanding a partial loss of eyesight, acquired much knowledge; was licensed to preach, after a year's study at Wyoming Seminary; entered the Wyoming Conference in 1862, and labored with great success until 1868, when his health failed. He died Feb. 18, 1869. See *Minutes of Annual Conferences*, 1869, p. 111.

Crowell, William, D.D., a Baptist minister, was born in Middlefield, Mass., Sept. 22, 1806. He was carefully educated, and began to preach in early manhood. In 1838 he became editor of *The Christian Watchman*, and conducted that paper with distinguished ability. In 1848, the journal being united with *The Christian Reflector*, Dr. Crowell occupied a pastorate in Waterville, Me., for a year or two, and then for several years was the editor of *The Western Watchman*, at St. Louis. About 1860 he became a pastor in central Illinois, and was officially connected for a time with Shurtleff College, at Alton. He died at Flanders, N. J., Aug. 19, 1871. Dr.

Crowell was the author of several works, among the best known and most valuable of which are, *The Church Member's Manual*, and a *History of Baptist Literature*, which he prepared for the Missionary Jubilee volume. (J. C. S.)

Crowley, Ann, an English minister of the Society of Friends, was born at Shillingford, Oxfordshire, in 1765. She was converted at sixteen, and at twenty-six "first came forth as a minister." In 1796 she removed to Uxbridge, and labored in that vicinity until her death, April 10, 1826. See *Piety Promoted*, iv, 289. (J. C. S.)

Crowley, Robert, an English divine and poet, was born in Gloucestershire or Northamptonshire, and educated at Magdalen College, Oxford, where he was elected probationer fellow in 1542. In the beginning of the reign of Edward VI he settled in London, there carried on the trade of printing and bookselling, and preached often, being in orders. Eventually several benefices were bestowed upon him, among which were the archdeaconry and a prebend in Hereford, both of which he resigned in 1567, a prebend in St. Paul's, the rectory of St. Peter le Poor, and the vicarage of St. Giles's, Cripplegate. He died June 18, 1588, leaving, among other works, *The Voice of the Last Trumpet, blown by the Seventh Angel:—Pleasure and Pain, Heaven and Hell:—The Four Usual Notes of Christ's Church* (1581, 4to). See Chalmers, *Biog. Dict.* s. v.; Allibone, *Dict. of Brit. and Amer. Authors*, s. v.

Crown of Christian Princes. From the portraits on their coins, it appears that the early emperors adopted the *diadem*, or simple fillet, worn either simply or encircling the helmet with which their head was covered. The coins of Constantine the Great depict

Constantine and Heraclius. (From Ferrario, *Costumi.*)

him wearing diadems or fillets of various kinds; some ornamented with gems; some enriched with a double row of pearls, with the loose ends of the fillet hanging down over his shoulders. Sometimes he wears a helmet surrounded by a diadem, with a cross in front. This combination is also seen on the coins of Gratian, Valentinian II, Theodosius, and the emperors Leo and Basil. Heraclius, A.D. 610-641, is represented as wear-

Justinian and Theodora. (From Mosaics at San Vitale, Ravenna.)

ing a helmet encircled by a gemmed diadem with pendent ends, and a cross above the forehead. The combination of the diadem with the *tiara* was borrowed from the Orientals, among whom it had been in use from ancient times. It was worn by Zenobia, and was adopted by her conqueror, Aurelian. It is seen in medals, under the form of a peaked cap ornamented with gems, rising from a jewelled diadem or fillet, tied behind. The cap, in later times, assumed the popular name of *tuphan*, the origin of the modern *turban*. Zonaras describes the emperor Basil, in the 9th century, as wearing a "tiara," popularly known as "tuphan." Another form of the imperial head-gear was a low-crowned cap, apparently destitute of diadem or any special distinction of royalty. This was known as Camelaucium (q. v.). Constantine appears in this cap on his triumphal arch in Rome, and in an illumination from a MS. of the 9th century, representing the Council of Nicæa. Justinian, in the mosaics of the sanctuary of San Vitale, at Ravenna, has his head covered with a jewelled cap, while the empress Theodora wears a tiara surrounded with three circlets of gems. Strings of pearls and other gems hang down from each.

Tuphan. (From Ferrario.)

Constantine. (From his Arch at Rome.)

The diadem, in its original form of a linen or silken ribbon or fillet, gradually went out of use from Justinian's time, and was replaced by a flexible band of gold, sometimes adorned with a band of pearls and precious stones, representing the old "diadem." The name

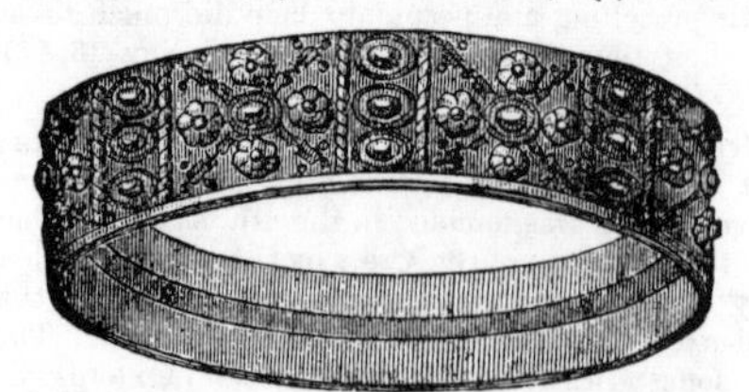

Diadem. (From Ferrario.)

"crown" was in use for the imperial symbol as early as the time of Constantine. This circlet was closed by a cap of rich stuff decorated with gems. In the time of Constantinus Porphyrogenitus the royal treasury contained circlets or *stemmata* of various colors, white, green, and blue, according to the enamel with which they were coated. These circlets decorated with gems are mentioned by Claudian in connection with the two sons of Theodosius, Arcadius and Honorius, towards the end of the 4th century.

The most ancient examples of crowns are those long preserved in the treasury of the cathedral of Monza, in Lombardy, belonging to the early part of the 7th century. These crowns were three in number: (1) the so-called *Iron Crown*, "Corona Ferrea;" (2) the crown

Iron Crown of Lombardy. (At Monza Cathedral.)

of Agilulf; and (3) that of Theodelinda. Agilulf's crown was taken to Paris as a prize of war by Napoleon I, in 1804, by mistake for the Iron Crown, and was stolen from the "Cabinet des Médailles," in which it was deposited, and melted down. See Coronation.

CROWN, *as a Christian Emblem*, being the symbol of victory and recompense (Rev. ii, 10; 2 Tim. iv, 8), became the token of martyrdom; first, the cross was

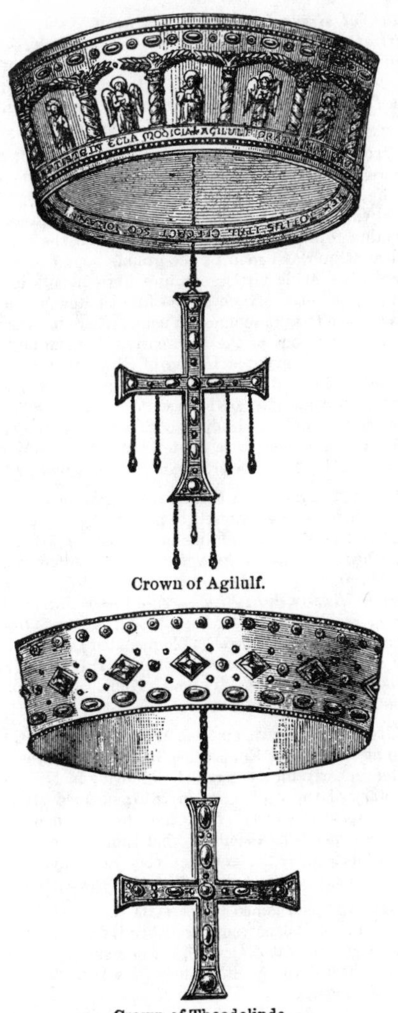

Crown of Agilulf.

Crown of Theodelinda.

crowned, and then crowns of laurel, flowers, palm, or precious metal were suspended or carved over the tombs of martyrs and confessors. Sometimes the divine hand offers the crown; sometimes two crowns are represented, for a virgin martyr; or doves carry crowns of olive, emblems of peace bought by the martyr's triumph; or the palm and cross are associated, to represent the merit, the labor, and prize. Hence came the hanging crown of light; and the "oblations," the representation of the Blessed offering their crowns to the Redeemer. The Christian emperors gave their soldiers crowns of laurel, adorned with the monogram of Christ.—Walcott, *Sac. Archæol.* s. v.

CROWN OF CHRISTIANS. See AUREOLE.

CROWN, CLERICAL. See CORONA CLERICALIS.

CROWN, DEDICATED. See CORONA VOTIVA.

CROWN, FUNERAL, was made of leaves and flowers, among the Greeks generally of parsley, which was usually wreathed around the head of a dead person before interment. Floral wreaths were often placed upon the bier, or scattered on the road along which the funeral procession was to pass, or twisted round the urn in which the ashes were contained, or the tomb in which the remains were laid.

CROWN OF LIGHT. See CORONA LUCIS.

CROWN, NATAL, was that which it was customary to suspend at the threshold of a house in which a child was born. At Athens, when the child was a boy, the natal crown was of olive; when a girl, of wool; while at Rome they were of laurel, ivy, or parsley.

CROWN, NUPTIAL, was one with which persons just entering into the bonds of matrimony were decked. Newly married persons of both sexes among the Hebrews wore crowns upon their wedding-day. Among the early Christians the act of crowning the parties was the commencement of the marriage ceremony. This was done by the priest with due solemnity. On the eighth day the married pair presented themselves again in the church, when the minister, after an appropriate prayer, took off the nuptial crown and dismissed them with his solemn benediction. The ceremonies of coronation and dissolving the crowns are still observed in the Greek Church. The crowns used in Greece are of olive branches twined with white and purple ribbon; but in Russia they are of gold and silver, or, in country places, of tin, and are preserved as the property of the Church. Among the Jews, nuptial coronation continued until the beginning of the war under Vespasian; and crowns of roses, myrtle, and ivy are still used in Jewish marriages in many places. See CORONA NUPTIALIS; MARRIAGE.

CROWN, RADIATED, is one with rays apparently emanating from it, and used by the ancient Romans to place upon the heads of the images of their gods or deified heroes.

CROWN, SACERDOTAL, was worn by the priests or *sacerdotes* of the ancient Romans when engaged in offering sacrifices. It was formed of different materials, sometimes of olive, sometimes of gold; but the most ancient sacrificial garland used by the Romans was made of ears of corn.

CROWN, SUTILE, was composed of any kind of flowers sewed together, and used by the Salii (q. v.) at their festivals.

CROWN OF TAPERS. See CORONA LUCIS.

CROWN, VOTIVE. See CORONA VOTIVA.

Crowns (Heb. תָּגִּין, *taggin*) is a name given to points or horns with which certain letters in the MSS. used in the Jewish synagogues are decorated, and which distinguish them from the MSS. in ordinary use. The rabbins affirm that God gave them to Moses on Mount Sinai, and that he taught him how to make them. See TITTLE.

Crownse, ADAM, a Lutheran minister, was born at Sharon, N. Y., in 1798. He studied the classics and theology at Hartwick Seminary, graduating in 1823; the same year was licensed by the New York Ministerium, and began to preach in Sharon and Rhinebeck (then Guilderland), where he remained over twenty years. He was thereafter pastor at Middleburg, and subsequently returned to Guilderland. He died in May, 1865. See *Lutheran Observer*, Aug. 25, 1865.

Crowson, ELIJAH L., a minister of the Methodist Episcopal Church South, was converted at twenty, labored many years as a local preacher, and in 1854 entered the Little Rock Conference. He became superannuated in 1867, and died Jan. 3, 1868. See *Minutes of Annual Conferences of the M. E. Church South*, 1868, p. 274.

Crowther, Jonathan (1), an early English Methodist minister, was converted in youth, and labored for thirty-eight years in the Wesleyan connection. In 1819 he was chosen president of the English Conference, and in 1820 of the Irish Conference. He died June 8, 1824. He is the author of *Portraiture of Methodism* (1811), and a number of minor works of the same character. See *Minutes of the British Conference*, 1824, p. 472; Osborn, *Meth. Literature*, s. v.

Crowther, Jonathan (2), an English Methodist minister, son of Timothy, and nephew of the above and of Robert, was born at St. Austell, Cornwall, July 31,

1794. He was converted in youth, and educated at Kingswood School. In 1814 he began to preach, and in 1823 was appointed head-master of that school, having already held the same office at Woodhouse Grove. He afterwards served several important circuits, until he was called in 1837 to the superintendency of the Wesleyan missions in Madras, where he labored with great efficiency. In 1843 he returned to home work in England, and in 1849 was appointed classical tutor in the Wesleyan Theological Institution at Didsbury, where he remained until his death, Jan. 11, 1856. He published several *Sermons* and other pamphlets. See *Minutes of the British Conference*, 1856, p. 202.

Crowther, Robert, an English Wesleyan minister, was born at Booth-town, near Halifax, in 1762. He was converted at about the age of fifteen, was received by the conference in 1789, and continued to travel until 1830, when he became a supernumerary at Rochdale. He died there Jan. 19, 1833. See *Minutes of the British Conference*, 1833; *Wesl. Meth. Mag.* 1834, p. 881 sq.

Crowther, Samuel, A.M., an English divine, was born in London, Jan. 9, 1769. He was educated at Croydon Free-school and Winchester College; became fellow of New College, Oxford; was ordained in 1792 to the curacy of East Bergholt, Suffolk, and removed in 1795 to Barking, Essex. In 1800 he received the united livings of Christ Church, Newgate Street, and St. Leonard's, Foster Lane; and was shortly after chosen one of the lecturers of St. Botolph, Bishopgate. March 27, 1825, he was seized with apoplexy, and he died Sept. 28, 1829. See (Lond.) *Christian Guardian*, Nov. 1829, p. 440.

Crowther, Thomas, a Presbyterian minister, was born at Bridlington Quay, England, July 7, 1840. He graduated from Columbia College, N. Y., in 1858; spent about four years in teaching; one in Princeton Seminary (1863); and graduated from Union Seminary, N. Y., in 1865. He was licensed by the Presbytery of New York, April 18, 1866, and ordained an evangelist in 1867; went to Southfield Congregational Church, New Marlborough, Mass., as a supply, and was installed Jan. 23, 1868; next at Pittsfield, in 1872; and in 1875 was called to Brooklyn, N. Y., first as pastor of the Memorial Presbyterian Church, and then as pastor of the First Presbyterian Church, where he died, Oct. 10, 1877. See *Necrol. Report of Princeton Theol. Sem.* 1878, p. 62.

Crowther, Timothy, an English Wesleyan minister, was born near Halifax in 1757. He was converted at the age of twenty-two, under the ministrations of a clergyman of the Church of England; entered the ministry in 1784, became a supernumerary in 1815, and died March 25, 1829. See *Minutes of the British Conference*, 1829.

Crowther, William, an English Baptist minister, was born at Gomersal, Yorkshire, April 2, 1816. He was baptized in 1834; spent the greater part of his ministerial career as a supply and occasional preacher, while continuing in business at his native place; but eventually accepted the pastorate of Rehoboth Chapel, Lockwood, where he died in 1882. See (Lond.) *Baptist Hand-book*, 1883, p. 257.

Croxall, Samuel, D.D., an English clergyman, was born at Walton-upon-Thames, in Surrey, and received his education at Eton School and St. John's College, Cambridge. He probably was ordained about 1713. Soon after leaving the university he was instituted to the vicarage of Hampton, in Middlesex, and afterwards, in February, 1731, to the united parishes of St. Mary Somerset and St. Mary Mounthaw, in London. He was also chancellor, prebendary, canon residentiary, and portionist of the church of Hereford. In 1732 he was made archdeacon of Salop and chaplain to the king, and in February, 1734, obtained the vicarage of Sellack, in Herefordshire. He died Feb. 13, 1752. The following are some of his works: *Two Original Cantos, in Imitation of Spenser's Fairy Queen, as a Satire on the Earl of Oxford's Administration:—The Vision:—The Fair Circassian* (1722, 4to). He was the author of *Scripture Politics* (1735, 8vo). His latest publication was *The Royal Manual.* See Chalmers, *Biog. Dict.* s. v.; Allibone, *Dict. of Brit. and Amer. Authors*, s. v.

Croy (or **Crouy**), Gustave Maximilien Juste, *prince de*, a French prelate, was born at the chateau of the Hermitage, near Vieux Condé, Sept. 12, 1773. From early youth he exhibited great piety and an inclination towards preaching. He entered the ecclesiastical calling as canon of the grand chapter of Strasburg. His noble birth gave him high honors in the Church, but at the time of the French Revolution he was obliged to take refuge at Vienna, where he was one of the four canons of the Lichtenstein foundation. In 1817 he was appointed bishop of Strasburg; in 1821 succeeded the cardinal of Perigord as grand-almoner of France; became peer of France in 1822; in 1824 was transferred from the bishopric of Strasburg to the archbishopric of Rouen; was made cardinal in 1825, and died in 1844. See Hoefer, *Nouv. Biog. Générale*, s. v.

Crozet, Thomas, a French theologian of the order of Recollets, devoted himself to preaching, resided for a long time at Madrid, and died at Avignon in 1720. He published, *Consejos de la Sabiduria Recapitulacion de las Maximas*, etc. (Marseilles, 1690):—*Maximes Morales:—Histoire de la Bienheureuse Vierge Marie* (ibid. 1695); republished under the title *La Mystique Cité de Dieu:—Censura Censuræ* (Cologne, 1697):—*Introduction aux Vertus Morales et Héroïques* (Brussels, 1722):—*Indiculus Universalis* (Lyons, 1705). See Hoefer, *Nouv. Biog. Générale*, s. v.

Crozier, Robert, an Irish Wesleyan minister, was born at Trory, near Enniskillen, in 1765. He was converted in early life; entered the ministry in 1793; was secretary of the conference in 1815; pleaded strongly for the right of societies to receive the sacraments during the famous discussions at that time; retired to his native place in 1822; and died very suddenly, Nov. 3, 1856. See *Minutes of the British Conference*, 1857.

Cruaidh, surnamed Cos-fhada (i. e. *Longlegs*), an Irish saint of Bolana (now probably Ballina, in Tipperary), commemorated Oct. 26, is represented as having been appealed to by St. Moling (q. v.) for help in a case of danger.

Crucifix. It is necessary to distinguish between the use of this figure as an object or instrument of devotion, and that of pictorial or other representations of the Crucifixion as a scene. Every variety and combination of the arts of sculpture, mosaic, painting, and engraving has been applied to this great subject from early times, and to all parts of it; and this distinction is one of principle as well as convenience.

If the end of the 5th century be considered the beginning of the Middle Ages, the public representation of the Crucifixion may be said to be a mediæval usage in point of time. Martigny claims for France the honor of having possessed the first public crucifix-painting which ever existed; for which he refers to Gregory of

Upper Half of Crucifixion MS. of Rabula.

Theodelinda's Crucifix.

Tours, and which he says must have been at least as old as the middle of the 6th century. But he says,

Antique Blasphemous *Graffito* of the Crucifixion.

probably with great correctness, that all the most eminent Crucifixions known were objects of private devotion, instancing the pectoral cross of queen Theodelinda, and the Syriac MS. of the Medicean Library at Florence. The official or public use of the cross as a symbol of redemption begins with Constantine, though, of course, it had been variously employed by all Christians at an earlier date. See CROSS.

Crucifixes, according to Guericke, did not appear in churches till after the 7th century. Such images, probably, in the early days of the Church, would produce too crude and painful an effect on the Christian imagination, and to that of the more hopeful pagan they would be intolerable; not only because his feelings would recoil from the thought of the punishment of the cross, but from superstitious terror of associating the "unhappy tree" with a Divine Being. The *Graffito Blasfemo* of the Palatine illustrates this; but Christian teachers may have refrained from any addition to the cross, as a symbol of divine humiliation and suffering, from purely charitable motives.

Perpendicular of the Vatican Cross.

The cross itself may have been felt to be temporarily unwelcome to persons in certain stages of conversion.

Cruciger. See CREUTZIGER.

Cruden, the name of several Scotch clergymen:

1. DAVID, D.D., took his first degree at Marischal College, Aberdeen, in 1764; was licensed to preach in 1768; presented to the living at Nigg in 1769; and died Nov. 18, 1826, aged eighty years. He published, in 1821, *Observations on the Conduct of a Minister;* also *An Account of the Parish.* See *Fasti Eccles. Scoticanæ*, iii, 511.

2. GEORGE, took his degree at Marischal College, Aberdeen, in 1791; became schoolmaster in that city; was licensed to preach in 1805; became a teacher of mathematics at Aberdeen; was presented to the living at Logie-Buchan in 1817; and died Sept. 11, 1850, aged seventy-six years. He published, *Historical Evidence of the Fulfilment of the Promise, "Lo, I am with you always,"* etc. (1823):—*Account of the Parishes of Old Deer and Logie-Buchan.* See *Fasti Eccles. Scoticanæ*, iii, 610.

3. WILLIAM, was born at Pitsligo in 1725; took his degree at Marischal College, Aberdeen, in 1743; became a teacher of English at Montrose; was licensed to preach in 1752; called to the living at Logie in 1753, and ordained; presented to the living in 1759; resigned, on being called to the Relief Meeting-house, Glasgow, in 1767; was elected minister of the Scots Church, Crown Court, London, in 1773, where he continued till his death, Nov. 5, 1785. His publications were, *Hymns on a Variety of Divine Subjects* (1761):—*Sermons on Evangelical and Practical Subjects* (1787). See *Fasti Eccles. Scoticanæ*, iii, 838; Wilson, *Dissenting Churches*, iv, 9.

Crudup, JONAH, a Baptist minister, was born in Wake County, N. C., June 5, 1791; ordained in August, 1813, and was pastor of several churches in North Carolina for about fifty years. Mr. Crudup was a preacher of surpassing eloquence, and was a member of Congress from 1821 to 1823. He died May 20, 1872. See Cathcart, *Baptist Encyclop.* p. 299. (J. C. S.)

Cruet (*Urceolus, amula, burette*) is a vase for holding the water and wine used at holy communion. John de Garlande, writing cir. 1080, says there should be two cruets—one for wine, the other for water. The ancient cruets were very rarely of crystal or glass, generally of enamelled copper, and, in consequence, about the 14th century, were distinguished by the letters V and A to mark their contents. Several ancient examples are preserved—one of the 13th century, at Paris; one, in the form of an angel, of the 14th century, at Aix-la-Chapelle; and another of the 14th or 15th century in the same cathedral, silver gilt. Sometimes the handle

Cruets.

was made in the form of a dragon. After the time of the Renaissance the cruets were made of transparent material; there was one at Grandmont Abbey, however, of crystal, mounted in silver, of the 13th century, with an eagle engraved upon it. A cruet for oil, in bronze, used at the coronations of the emperors, and shaped like an antique bust, is preserved in the treasury of Aix-la-Chapelle. Four of silver, of the 9th century, are preserved in the Vatican; they are of classical form. See AMA; AMPULLA.

Crüger, Johann, a German composer of Church music, was born April 9, 1598, at Gross-Breese, near Guben, in Brandenburg. He studied at Wittenberg, was in 1622 organist at St. Nikolai, in Berlin, and died there, Feb. 23, 1662. He wrote, *Præcepta Musicæ Practicæ Figuralis* (Berlin, 1625):—*Synopsis Musica* (ibid. 1630):—*Quæstiones Musicæ* (1650); and composed, besides, many chorals, which are still in use in the German Church. He also published, *Neues Gesangbuch augsburger Konfession* (ibid. 1640):—*Geistliche Kirchenmelodien* (Leips. 1649):—*Psalmodia Sacra* (1658):—*Praxis Pietatis* (eod.). See Koch, *Geschichte des deutschen Kirchenleides*, iv, 99 sq.; Grove, *Dict. of Music*, s. v. (B. P.)

Crüger, Theodor, a Lutheran theologian of Germany, was born in 1694 at Stettin, in Pomerania. He studied at Jena and Wittenberg; was in 1721 rector at Lucka, in Lower Lusatia; in 1727, pastor at Kirchhain; in 1732, superintendent at Colditz, and in 1735 at Chemnitz. He was made doctor of theology in 1737, and died June 1, 1751, leaving, *Schediasma Historicum*, etc. (Wittenberg, 1719):—*De Successione Pontificum Romanorum* (ibid. 1723):—*Heptalogos in Ara Crucis* (Frankfort, 1726):—*De Veterum Christianorum Disciplina Arcani* (Wittenberg, 1727):—*Introductio in Christologiam Moralem* (Dresden, 1732), etc. See Mosers, *Jetztlebende Theologen;* Winer, *Handbuch der theol. Lit.* i, 634; Jöcher, *Allgemeines Gelehrten-Lexikon*, s. v. (B. P.)

Crugot, MARTIN, a Protestant theologian of Germany, was born at Bremen, Jan. 5, 1725. Under Iken and Nonne he prepared himself for the ministry, without attending any university. In 1746 he accepted a call to Herford; in 1747 went to Carolath; in 1748 was called as second preacher to Blomberg, but returned again to Carolath, where he died, Sept. 5, 1790, leaving *Sermons*, besides some ascetical works, as, *Morgen- und Abendgedanken* (Züllichau, 1777):—*Das Wesentliche in der Christlichen Sittens- und Glaubenslehre* (Sajan, 1776):—*Der Christ in der Einsamkeit* (Breslau, 1761; 5th ed. 1779). See Döring, *Die gelehrten Theologen Deutschlands*, i, 288 sq. (B. P.)

Cruickshank (or **Cruikshank**) is the family name of several Scotch clergymen:

1. ALEXANDER, was licensed to preach in 1748; presented to the living at Mearns in 1752; and died Jan. 22, 1791, aged sixty-seven years. See *Fasti Eccles. Scoticanæ*, ii, 228.

2. GEORGE (1), studied at Marischal College, Aberdeen; was schoolmaster for a time; licensed to preach in 1735; called to the living at Arbroath in 1737, and ordained in 1738; transferred to Kinnell in 1748; and died Nov. 12, 1753. He published, *Answers to the Queries of Mr. Maitland*. See *Fasti Eccles. Scoticanæ*, iii, 786, 801.

3. GEORGE (2), took his degree at Marischal College, Aberdeen, in 1771; was schoolmaster at Inveravon, and assistant minister at Rothes; appointed to the living there in 1788, and ordained; and died June 15, 1838, aged eighty-five years. See *Fasti Eccles. Scoticanæ*, iii, 226.

4. JAMES (1), D.D., son of the rector of Banff Academy, took his degree at King's College, Aberdeen, in 1806; was licensed to preach in 1812; ordained in 1816 as assistant at Turreff; presented to the living in 1821; transferred to Fyvie in 1843; and died April 12, 1858, aged seventy years. See *Fasti Eccles. Scoticanæ*, iii, 648.

5. JAMES (2), was licensed to preach, and presented to the living at Manor in 1833 and ordained; transferred to Stevenston in 1843. See *Fasti Eccles. Scoticanæ*, i, 251.

6. JAMES ALEXANDER, son of the minister at Glass, became schoolmaster of that parish in 1822; took his degree at King's College, Aberdeen, in 1823; was licensed to preach in 1827, appointed assistant at Mortlach the same year, and ordained; presented to the living in 1837. He was one of the majority who joined in ordaining the presentee to Marnoch in 1841, against the wish of the assembly. He was living in 1863. See *Fasti Eccles. Scoticanæ*, iii, 211.

7. JOHN, a native of Culsalmond, took his degree at King's College, Aberdeen, in 1789; was licensed to preach in 1795; presented to the living at Glass in 1799; and died Dec. 20, 1841, aged seventy-four years. See *Fasti Eccles. Scoticanæ*, iii, 200.

8. THOMAS, was the first Protestant minister at Kinloch; called to the living in 1567, presented in 1573, and in 1574 had three other places in charge. He continued in 1590. See *Fasti Eccles. Scoticanæ*, ii, 807.

9. WILLIAM, was licensed to preach in 1740; called to the living at Ruthven in 1743; ordained in 1744; and died July 14, 1756. See *Fasti Eccles. Scoticanæ*, iii, 759.

Cruikshank, William, a Reformed (Dutch) minister, was born in 1798, at Salem, N. Y. He graduated from Union College in 1821, studied theology in New Brunswick Theological Seminary, entered the ministry in 1824, and was settled on Long Island, at Flatlands and New Lots (1825-34). In 1835 he founded the Reformed Church at Newburg, N. Y., and was its pastor until 1838. For several years thereafter he was without charge, on account of ill-health, and only served as stated supply in the retired church of Mamakating from 1849 until his death in 1854. Mr. Cruikshank was an eloquent and powerful preacher, of logical mind and impressive delivery, possessed of a voice of great power and flexibility, and graceful in appearance and manners. He was the author of a standard tract published by the American Tract Society, entitled *David Baldwin, or, the Miller's Son*, also of a printed sermon on the *Intermediate State*. While without pastoral care, he published a series of papers under the heading of *Washington's Body-Guard*. See Corwin, *Manual of the Ref. Church in America*, 3d ed. p. 225. (W. J. R. T.)

Cruimmin, an Irish *saint*, commemorated June 28, was the son of Corbmac, of the race of Tadhg, and of Darerca, the sister of St. Patrick. The latter placed him in charge of some relics at Lecain (now Leckin), and he lived as bishop there till an extreme old age. By some he is confounded with St. Cruemus, and by others with St. Cruimthor Nathi (festival on Aug. 9), who prophesied St. Fechin's greatness.

Cruimther (dimin. *cruimtheran*), an Irish word for presbyter or *priest*, often occurring in the calendars prefixed to proper names.

Cruimtheris, a daughter of king Longobardus, placed by St. Patrick in a cell on Mt. Kenngobha, to the east of Armagh (now Ballyboley Hill, in Antrim), and was there occupied in making ecclesiastical embroidery

Cruithnechan (otherwise called *Caritanus*, by way of diminutive), an Irish *saint*, commemorated March 7, flourished about the beginning of the 6th century. He was the son of Cellachan, and, after marrying and having children, renounced the world, with his three daughters. He baptized St. Columba in the Church of Tulach-Dubglaise (now Temple-Douglas, in Donegal).

Crum, George Cramer, a Methodist Episcopal minister, was born at Winchester, Va., June 29, 1809. At seventeen he removed to Hillsborough, O., where he was converted in 1827, licensed to preach in 1831, and received into the Ohio Conference the same year. During his long service in the itinerant ranks he served many of the best charges in his conference. He was a member of the Cincinnati Conference from its organization in 1852 until the close of his life. He was superannuated in 1877, and died in Xenia, March 4, 1882. See *Minutes of Annual Conferences*, 1882, p. 321.

Crum, John, a Methodist Episcopal minister, was born at Elizabeth, Allegheny Co., Pa., Dec. 25, 1809. He united with the Seceder Church in early manhood, about a year afterwards was converted, and soon joined the Methodists in Ashtabula County, O. He entered the Erie Conference in 1836, and travelled with but slight intermission until his death at Volant, Pa., Jan. 10, 1882. See *Minutes of Annual Conferences*, 1882, p. 316.

Crume, Moses, a Methodist Episcopal minister, was converted in 1785, in Shenandoah County, Va.; emigrated to Kentucky later; was licensed to preach in 1793, and labored in that capacity until 1808, when he entered the Western Conference. In 1823 he became superannuated, and thus continued until his death in 1839. See *Minutes of Annual Conferences*, 1840, p. 52.

Crump, John, an English Nonconformist divine, became minister at Maidstone about 1653, and was ejected for nonconformity in 1662. He published *The Great Supper* (1669). See Allibone, *Dict. of Brit. and Amer. Authors*, s. v.

Crump, John Henry, A.M., an English Congregational minister, was born at Coventry, March 15, 1803. In 1822 he entered the Congregational College at Hoxton; in 1826 became pastor at Weymouth; in 1838 chaplain of the Protestant Dissenters' Collegiate School at Mill Hill, Middlesex, and in 1847 removed to Lechlade, Gloucestershire, where he died Feb. 14, 1849. He wrote a beautiful memoir of his friend, Rev. Thomas C. Everett. See (Lond.) *Evang. Magazine*, 1849, p. 225.

Crump, Joseph, an English Wesleyan minister, was born at Dudley in 1800. He was converted in early life, began his ministry in 1825, retired to his native place in 1860, and died June 5, 1862. See *Minutes of the British Conference*, 1862, p. 31.

Crumpton, Thomas, an English Baptist minister, was born near Tenbury, Worcestershire, in December, 1780, or January, 1781. He was baptized about 1800, and, for many years, was officially connected with "The Baptist Itinerant and Missionary Societies," "The Sunday-school Union," and other kindred institutions. In September, 1840, he commenced a six years' pastorate at Shrewsbury. He died at Leeds, Sept. 25, 1868. See (Lond.) *Baptist Hand-book*, 1869, p. 138. (J. C. S.)

Crunnmhael is the name of several old Irish saints. See also Conamhail.

1. Also called *Cruindmael-Erbuilg*, son of Ronan, of the sept of the Hy-Cennsealch, ruled for three years as chief of the clan, and then became a monk at Clonard, in Meath. He was a special friend of St. Lasrean, bishop of Leighlinn, and died A.D. 650. He is commemorated June 22.

2. Abbot after Dubhdabbhoireann at Clonard, A.D. 787 till his death in 793, and also for some time at Druim-Ineasglainn (now Dromiskin, in Louth). He has no festal day.

Cruse, Christian, D.D., a Protestant Episcopal clergyman, was born in Philadelphia, Pa., June 27, 1794, of Danish parents. He graduated from the University of Pennsylvania in 1815; was appointed professor in that institution in 1831, but resigned in 1833; was ordained in 1842; became rector of Trinity parish, Fishkill, N. Y., in April, 1846; resigned in 1851; soon after became librarian of the General Theological Seminary, and devoted himself to the study of ancient languages. He died in New York city, Oct. 5, 1865. In Syriac, Hebrew, and Greek, Dr. Cruse was one of the most learned men in his Church. See *Amer. Quar. Church Rev.* January, 1866, p. 669.

Crusenius, Nicolaus, prior of the Augustinian monasteries at Brussels and Antwerp, and general visitor of his order in Austria and Bohemia, who died at Vienna in 1629, is the author of *Monasticon Augustinianum*, etc. (Munich, 1623). See Winer, *Handbuch der theol. Lit.* i, 705; Jöcher, *Allgemeines Gelehrten-Lexikon*, s. v. (B. P.)

Crusius, Magnus, a Lutheran theologian, was born in Schleswig, Jan. 10, 1697. He studied at Kiel, was in 1723 called to Copenhagen, and accompanied as chaplain the Danish ambassador to France. In 1731 he was appointed to the pastorate at Bramstedt, in Holstein, in 1733 first preacher and member of consistory at Flensburg, in 1735 professor of theology at Göttingen, where he also took, in 1737, the degree of doctor of divinity. In 1747 he was made general superintendent at Harburg, and died Jan. 6, 1751. He is the author of *De Senectute Heroica Veterum Christianorum* (Harburg, 1721):—*Prologi Origenis in Evangelia SS. Matt., Lucæ et Joannis* (Göttingen, 1735):—*De Resurrectione Spirituali* (ibid. 1738):—*De Mysterio Silentii et Clamoris* (ibid. eod.), etc. See Mosers u. Neubauer, *Jetztlebende Theologen;* Heinsius, *Kirchen Historie*, iv; Strodtmann, *Neues Gelehrtes Europa*, v; Jöcher, *Allgemeines Gelehrten-Lexikon*, s. v.; Winer, *Handbuch der theol. Lit.* i, 897. (B. P.)

Cruso, Timothy, A.M., an English Nonconformist minister, was born in 1655. He was educated for the ministry, first in a dissenting academy, and then at one of the universities of Scotland; and was pastor of a church which met in Crutched Friars, London, where he continued to the close of his life, Nov. 26, 1697. Mr. Cruso was chosen one of the preachers of the Merchants' Lecture at Pinner's Hall, and his sermons there verify the high eulogium given him by all for his great ability. See Bogue and Bennet, *Hist. of Dissenters* (2d ed.), i, 467; (Lond.) *Theol. and Bibl. Mag.* Oct. 1805, p. 383; Wilson, *Dissenting Churches*, i, 56.

Crux Ansata. See Cross.

Cruz (*Saint*), Juan de, a Spanish ascetic theologian, whose family name was *Yesiez*, was born in 1542 at Ontiveros, in Old Castile. At twenty-one he became a Carmelite at the monastery of Medina del Campo, and aided St. Theresa in reforming the monks, who eventually, however, through enmity, took him to Toledo, where he was imprisoned for nine months, and then was released through St. Theresa's interposition. He afterwards founded and controlled some monasteries. In 1591 he encountered new persecutions, and was banished to the convent of Pegnuela, upon the Sierra Morena, but obtained the liberty of retiring to the convent of Ubeda, where he died, Dec. 14, 1591. He was beatified in 1675, and canonized in 1726. He wrote, *Noche Obscura del Alma:—Subida del Monte Carmelo:—Cantico Espiritual entro le Alma y Chrysto, su Esposa:—Llama de Amor Viva;* and other works in Spanish. His works, collected and published for the first time at Barcelona in 1619, were translated into French by P. Cyprian (Paris, 1641); by P. Louis of St. Theresa (ibid. 1665); by P. Maillard (ibid. 1694); and in Latin by P. Andrew de Jesus (Cologne, 1639). They are written in an obscure and mysterious style. See Hoefer, *Nouv. Biog. Générale*, s. v.; *Encyclop. Brit.* (9th ed.) s. v.

Cryer, Thomas, an English Wesleyan missionary, was born at Bingley, Yorkshire, in 1800. He was converted at twenty, and in 1829 was sent as a missionary to India. He labored in Bangalore, Madras, Negapatam, and Manargoody. During an interval from missionary labor (1840–41) he was stationed at Dewsbury, England. He was appointed to Madras in 1852, arrived in that city Oct. 1, and died Oct. 5. See *Minutes of the British Conference*, 1853, p. 186.

Crypt. Of this important form of church architecture we give additional details from Walcott, *Sac. Archæol.* s. v.:

"The earliest crypts which we possess are those of Hexham and Ripon. They have several entrances; one used exclusively by the priest serving at the altar, the others for the ascent and descent of the worshippers, and opening into a chapel containing relics and a recess for an altar. In the wall are niches, with funnel-headed openings for lamps. At Winchester, a low, arched doorway, below the screen of the feretory, led down to the relic chamber, which was in consequence called the Holy Hole. In later times, aumbries and secret hiding-places for plate and treasures were generally provided. In the 11th, 12th, and 13th centuries crypts became developed into magnificent subterranean churches, like those of Canterbury, Gloucester, Rochester, Worcester, Winchester; St. Peter's, Oxford; Bayeux, Chartres, Saintes, Auxerre, Bourges, Holy Trinity, Caen; St. Denis, Ghent; Fiesole, Padua, Florence, Pavia, Palermo, and Modena. The earlier examples are of moderate dimensions, resembling cells, as in the pre-Norman examples at Lastingham, at St. Mellon, at Rouen, of the 4th century; St. Maur, and Faye la Vineuse. After the 14th century the crypt was replaced by lateral chapels built above ground. In fact, all crypts —called in some places the crowds—the shrouds, or undercroft—were built to put Christians in remembrance of the old state of the Primitive Church before Constantine. The crypts of the Duomo and San Ambrogio, Milan, Parma, and Monte Cassino, are still used as a winter choir; and the parish church of St. Faith, in the shrouds of St. Paul's, was occupied until the Great Fire. Several of the largest cathedrals, built on unfavorable sites for excavation, as Durham and Chichester, have no crypt. The crypts of Winchester, Rochester, Gloucester, Worcester, and Canterbury were all made before 1085; and after that date the construction of crypts was laid aside, except where they were a continuation of existing buildings, as at Canterbury and Rochester. There is, however, an exceptional Early English example under the Lady Chapel of Hereford, and one of Decorated date at Waltham. A curious Decorated contrivance for constructing a crypt in an earlier church, which was never designed to have one, may be seen at Wimborne Minster, where the crypt under the presbytery lies open to the aisles. At Bosham and Dorchester (Oxon) there is a small crypt in the south alley of the nave, under a raised platform, for an altar or chapel, which is only another specimen, on a much smaller scale, of the same principle which, at Lubeck, Hildesheim, Naumburg, Halberstadt, Rochester, and Canterbury, left the crypt floor on a level almost with the nave, and raised the choir-level to a great height, enclosing it with stone screens. At Christchurch and Gloucester there was a crypt under each corner of the cross, except the western one. At Auxerre and Bourges the crypt, like the subterranean church of Assisi, was useful as a constructional arrangement to maintain the level of the choir. Occasionally the crypt assumes rather the character of a lower church, as in the Sainte-Chapelle (Paris), Eton, and St. Stephen's, Westminster. There is no example of a crypt in the Peninsula or Ireland, and Scotland possesses only one, at Glasgow. At Westminster, Glasgow, and Wells there is a crypt under the chapter-house, which contained an altar. The crypt was frequently lighted brilliantly on great festivals, and its chapels were constantly thronged with pilgrims and visitors, so that at present we can hardly portray to ourselves, in their cheerless desolation, that once they were much frequented places of prayer."

Crypta seems to have been sometimes used in Christian times as synonymous with "cemetery." We may, however, mark this distinction between the two words, that "cemetery" is a word of wider signification, including open-air burial-grounds, while "crypta" is strictly limited to those excavated beneath the surface of the ground.

We sometimes meet with the expression *cryptæ arenarum*, or *cryptæ arenariæ* (i. e. "of the sand-pits"), in connection with the interment of Christian martyrs. These would seem to indicate the galleries of a deserted pozzuolana pit, as places of sepulture. But though the subterranean cemeteries very frequently had a close connection with these quarries, and were approached through their adita, the sand-pits themselves were seldom or never used for interment, for which, indeed, they were unfit, without very extensive alteration and adaptation. The passages referred to, which are chiefly found in the not very trustworthy *Acts of the Martyrs*, have probably originated in a confusion between the catacombs themselves and the quarries with which they were often so closely connected.—Smith, *Dict. of Christ. Antiq.* s. v. See CATACOMBS.

Crystallomancy (Gr. κρυστάλλος, *crystal, glass*, and μαντεία, *divination*) is a species of divination by means of a mirror or enchanted glass, in which future events were said to be represented or signified by certain marks or figures.

Cseles, MARTIN, a Hungarian theologian, was born at Rosenthal, Jan. 23, 1641. He took holy orders in 1657, and afterwards went to Rome as pontifical penitentiary. Returning to his country, he was appointed provost of Raab and Presburg. During the civil troubles which broke out in Hungary he fell into the hands of the Rakotzki party, who held him prisoner for a year. He died at Patak, Jan. 14, 1709, leaving, *Educatio Historico-Chronologica de Episcopatu Transylvaniæ:—Descriptio Amplitudinis Episcopatus Sirmiensis*. See Hoefer, *Nouv. Biog. Générale*, s. v.

Ctesiphon, a Roman (probably) to whom St. Jerome writes from Bethlehem (*Epist.* 133, ed. Vall.) on the question of Pelagianism, on which Ctesiphon had written to ask his opinion.

Ctesiphon (*on the Tigris*), COUNCIL OF (*Concilium Ctesiphonense*), was held A.D. 420, under Taballaha, archbishop of Seleucia, on the opposite bank of the river. Here the Nicene faith was received, and with it the canons to which the consent of the rest of the Church westward had been given.

Ctibor, JOHN (called *Cotwa*), a Moravian theologian, was canon of Brünn, of Olmutz, and of Prague, dean of Sinczna in 1615, and provost of Lutomierz. He died in 1637. He wrote in the Bohemian language. His principal work is directed against the Protestants, and is entitled *Larve*. His sermons were also esteemed. See Hoefer, *Nouv. Biog. Générale*, s. v.; *Biog. Universelle*, s. v.

Ctistolătræ (κτιστολάτραι, called also, from their founder, *Gajanitæ*) were a subdivision of the *Aphthartodocetæ* (q. v.), themselves a sect of the Monophysites, who, in opposition to the *Aktistetæ*, taught that the body of Christ was created. See Hagenbach, *Hist. of Doctrines*, i, 281, Clark's translation; Dorner, *Person of Christ*, div. ii, vol. i, p. 131; Herzog, *Real-Encyklop.* **ix**, 749.

Cuach. See COCCA.

Cuan (**Cuanna**, **Cuanan**, or **Cuannache**; diminutive of *Cu*, "a hound;" Lat. *Cuanus*) is a name of several Irish saints:

1. Of Airbhre in Hy-Cennsealach, Leinster, commemorated July 10, is thought to have succeeded St. Brogan (q. v.) in the abbacy of Mothel, Waterford.

2. Of Cluain-mor (now Clonmore, Carlow), commemorated Oct. 15, is thought to have accompanied St. Moliny (q. v.).

There is another Cuan, "of Ath-eascrach" (now probably Ahasragh, in Galway), who died A.D. 788 or 793, and is commemorated also on Oct. 15.

3. Son of Tigher-nach, of the race of the Nine Hostages, and brother of Sts. Begbile, Colman, and Conna, is commemorated March 2, and lived about the close of the 6th century.

There are also Cuan-Cam and Cuan the anchoret of Lilcah (not identified), who both died A.D. 743; also Cuan of Imleach-Jubhair (Emly), who died A.D. 787; and Cuan of Louth, who died in 823.

Cuanan GLINNE, an Irish *saint*, commemorated Feb. 3, was abbot of Maghbile (now Moville. County Down, and died in 747.

Cuanghas MAC DALL (i. e. *blind boy*, although he afterwards received his sight), an Irish *saint*, commemorated March 13, succeeded St. Pulcherius as abbot of Liathmore (Leamokevoge, in Tipperary), and died in 747.

Cuanna (or **Cuanda**) is the name of several early Irish saints:

1. Abbot of Killchuanna (now Kilcoona, in Galway) and Lismore, celebrated Feb. 4, is said to have been born at the close of the 6th century, his mother being Meda (Finmeda or Conmania), daughter of Fingen, and his father unknown, while his brother was St. Carthach of Rahen. Many miracles are related of him, and he died about 650. See Colgan, *Acta Sanctorum*, p. 249 sq.

2. Son of Miodhavn of Rosco, celebrated April 10, is of obscure and confused history, but seems to have died in 721. See Forbes, *Scott. Saints*, p. 10; Kelly, *Irish Saints*, xxi.

3. Surnamed "the Blind;" celebrated March 11, is thought to have been the son of Tulan, and is said to have been miraculously taught music by St. Patrick.

Cuānus. See MOCHUA.

Cuaran (**Koran, Cronan, Mochuaroc**, or **Crovinus**), an early Irish saint (surnamed *the Wise*), commemorated Feb. 9, is said to have been born in Munster, being the son of Nethservan, of a noble family, and became a bishop, but of what place is unknown. He seems to have flourished about A.D. 570, and is therefore different from Cronan of Lismore.

Cuba, in pagan mythology, was the tutelary goddess of sleepers, especially of children.

Cuba, an early Saxon presbyter, attested a charter of archbishop Ethelheard, A.D. 805.

Cubbitt, GEORGE, an English Wesleyan minister, was born at Norwich, in December, 1791. He joined the Church in 1808, at Sheffield, whither his family had removed. He commenced his ministry in 1813; labored in Carbonear and St. John's, Newfoundland, from 1816 to 1818; in Glasgow, Scotland, in 1819, and from 1820 to 1835 in Boston, Oxford, Bristol, Sheffield, Huddersfield, and London. From 1836 to the end of his life he was editor of the conference office publications. In 1839 he replied to the attacks on Methodism made by Daniel O'Connell in the Manchester newspapers. *The Times* spoke highly of Cubbitt's answers. He died after three days' illness, Oct. 13, 1850. Cubbitt wrote *Conversations on the Miracles of Christ* (18mo):—*Conversations on the Parables*, and other minor publications. He was one of the acutest and ablest of Wesleyan theologians. During the latter part of his life he lived as a recluse. See *Minutes of the British Conference*, 1851; Smith, *Hist. of Wesl. Meth.* iii, 438, 439.

Cubero, PEDRO, a Spanish missionary and traveller, was born in 1645, near Calatayud, in Aragon. He commenced his travels at the age of twenty-five, going from Saragossa to Paris, afterwards visited Rome, Venice, Vienna, Constantinople, Warsaw, Moscow, Astrakhan, Kasbin, Ispahan, Shiraz, Laar, Surat, Goa, Malacca, Manilla, and Mexico, returning to Europe after a nine years' absence, and published an account of his missions in Spanish (Madrid, 1680; Saragossa, 1688). Cubero was the first traveller who made the tour of the world from west to east, and in part by land. His work gives a detailed account of the steppes of Astrakhan, of the deserts of Persia, and of Manilla. See Hoefer, *Nouv. Biog. Génèrale*, s. v.; *Biog. Universelle*, s. v.

Cubert. See CUDBERTH.

Cubicŭlum is a term used in early Christian architecture in two senses.

1. We find it employed to denote what we should now call the side chapels of the nave of a church. The first instance of its use in this sense is in the writings of Paulinus of Nola, who describes the church erected at Nola, and particularizes these side chapels, which were evidently novel features in church arrangement. There were four on each side of the nave, beyond the side aisles, with two verses inscribed over the entrances. Their object was to furnish places of retirement for those who desired to pray or meditate on the word of God, and for the sepulchral memorials of the departed. They differed from the side chapels of later ages in containing no altars, as originally there was but one altar in a church. Paulinus also speaks of these chapels under the name of *cellæ* or *cellulæ*, e. g., when speaking of a thief who had concealed himself in one of them all night. Perhaps the earliest existing example in Rome of such a chapel attached to the body of a church is that of St. Zeno in the Church of Santa Prassede, built by pope Paschal I about A.D. 817.

2. The word *cubiculum* is likewise employed to designate the family grave chambers in the subterranean cemeteries at Rome. In addition to the ordinary places of interment in the ambulacra, the catacombs contain an immense number of sepulchral chambers or cubicula, each enshrining a larger or smaller number of dead, as well in table tombs and arcosolia, as in loculi pierced in the walls. These were originally family burial-places, excavated and embellished at the expense of the friends of the departed, and from the date of their first construction served for the celebration of the eucharistic feast and agape, on the occasion of the funeral, and its successive anniversaries. In times of persecution they may have supplied places of religious assembly where the faithful might gather in security for the celebration of the holy mysteries, at the graves of the departed martyrs and others whose fate they might be soon called to share by sealing their testimony with their blood. The name *cubiculum* is of exclusively Christian use as applied to places of interment. From inscriptions in which the term occurs, Marchi infers "that in the 4th century the persons named caused that their own cubicula should be excavated at their own expense. Each cubiculum was of sufficient dimensions to serve for several generations of the respective families. If it proved insufficient loculi were added at a greater or less distance from the cubiculum." Sometimes we find the arch of an arcosolium of the 1st century cut through and used as a door or entrance to a second cubiculum excavated in its rear, the original sarcophagus being removed and carried to the back of the chapel that other bodies might be placed near it.

Cubiculum in the Catacomb of St. Agnes. (With Seats Hewn out of the Rock.)

The number of these sepulchral chambers is almost beyond computation. Marchi reckons more than sixty in the eighth part of the catacomb of St. Agnes. In that of St. Callixtus they amount to some hundreds. They are equally frequent in the other cemeteries. Their form is very varied. In the catacomb of St. Callixtus, with very few exceptions, they are rectangular, and that appears to have been the earlier shape. But there are examples of many other forms, triangular, pentagonal, hexagonal, octagonal, circular, and semicircular. The roof is sometimes a barrel vault, sometimes a coved ceiling, nearly flat; in one instance, it expands into a lofty dome, lighted by a *luminare*. Both the roof, the vaults, and the recesses of the arcosolia are

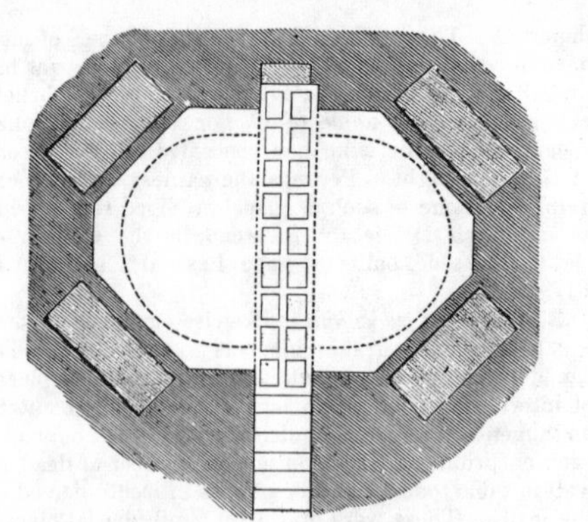

Plan of Cubiculum. (From Catacomb of St. Callixtus.)

generally coated with stucco, and richly decorated with religious paintings. In the later restorations the walls are often veneered with plates of costly marble. See PLATONIA. In a very large number of examples the *Good Shepherd* occupies the centre of the ceiling, the surrounding lunettes containing *Adam and Eve after the Fall, The History of Jonah, The Sacrifice of Abraham, Moses Striking the Rock, The Three Children in the Furnace, The Visit of the Wise Men to Christ, The Raising of Lazarus, The Healing of the Blind Man, The Paralytic Carrying his Bed, The Miracle of the Loaves,* and other scenes from the limited cycle of Scriptural subjects to which early Christian art confined itself, treated with a wearisome uniformity; embellished with palm branches, vines laden with grapes, the dove, the peacock, and other familiar Christian symbols. The

Section of Cubiculum. (From Catacomb of St. Callixtus.)

walls of the chamber were also similarly decorated. See FRESCOES. The vault is in some cases supported by columns, either cut out of the tufa, or formed of brick coated with stucco. Light and air were not unfrequently admitted by means of a shaft communicating with the surface of the ground, called *luminare.* A chamber so lighted was known as a *cubiculum clarum.* These cubicula were very frequently double, one on either side of the gallery, and, as we have just noticed, in some instances a luminare was sunk in the centre so as to give light to both. The cubicula, generally speaking, are of small dimensions, and are incapable of containing more than a very limited number of worshippers. But there are also found halls and chambers of much larger proportions, which have been considered by the chief Roman Catholic authorities on the subject to have been constructed for the purpose of religious assemblies. These are distinguished by Marchi, by an arbitrary nomenclature, into *cryptæ*, for the smaller, and *ecclesiæ*, for the larger, excavations. See CATACOMBS.

Cubitt, JAMES, an English Baptist minister, was born at Neateshead, Suffolk, in 1808. He graduated from Stepney College in 1834, and the same year became pastor of the Church at Ilford, Essex. In 1837 he removed to Stratford-on-Avon, in 1841 to Bourton-on-the-Water, remaining there seven years, and then was pastor at Thrapston, Northamptonshire, for twelve years. In 1861 he became one of the tutors in Mr. Spurgeon's Metropolitan Tabernacle, Southwark, but in 1863 was compelled to desist from all occupation, and died Aug. 5 of the same year. See (Lond.) *Baptist Hand-book*, 1865, p. 121. (J. C. S.)

Cuboirne (**Coubran**, or **Cubran**), an Irish saint, commemorated Nov. 10, is said to have died as abbot of Cillarhaidh (now Killeigh, in King's County), A.D. 762.

Cubrĭcus. See MANES.

Cucojo, the head of a heretical Syrian sect of Valentinians in the latter part of the 2d century (Ephrem. *Contra Hæreticos*, xxii, 485 b, in Assemani, vol. ii).

Cucufas, an early martyr at Barcelona, celebrated July 25.

Cuculla was a hood worn by Benedictine monks and nuns, equivalent to the later *cowl* (q. v.).

Cucŭlus, an epithet of an unknown disciple of Alcuin.

Cucumellum, a flagon or bowl belonging to the altar in early Christian churches, which was used probably for containing the communion wine. See Bingham, *Antiq.* bk. viii, chap. vi, sect. xxi. Compare AMA.

Cudaman, an early Saxon abbot, attested a charter of Ethelheard, archbishop of Canterbury, A.D. 805.

Cudbert (**Cudberct**, or **Cudbrictus**). See CUTHBERT.

Cudberth (or **Cubert**), an early English abbot of the see of Canterbury, died A.D. 777.

Cudburg (or **Cudbuch**). See CUTHBURG.

Cudda, an early English abbot of Mercia, cir. A.D. 742.

Cuddy, JAMES BILLINGSLEY, a Methodist Episcopal minister, was born in Baltimore County, Md., Aug. 16, 1836. He was converted at sixteen; studied one year at Manchester Academy, and two at Dickinson Seminary, Williamsport; received license to exhort in 1857; and in 1860 entered the East Baltimore Conference, wherein he served until his death, Aug. 2, 1874. See *Minutes of Annual Conferences*, 1875, p. 32.

Cuddy, MACGILLA. See ARCHDEKIN, RICHARD.

Cudrādus, a presbyter of the Church of Lindisfarne, A.D. 793 (Alcuin, *Epist.* 5).

Cudred (or **Cudret**). See CUTHRED.

Cudsuida. See CUTSUIDA.

Cuduald, abbot of the monastery of Oundle (Undalum), in North Hants, A.D. 709 (Bede, *Eccles. Hist.* v, 19).

Cue—. See QUE—.

Cueilly, OLIVIER DE, a French theologian, was born at Laval in 1565. He became a Dominican at the convent there, and afterwards went to Paris, where he taught several branches of theology. He died about 1620, leaving *Interprétation sur les Premiers Chapitres du Prophète Ézéchiel* (Paris, 1611):—*Les Fléaux de Dieu* (ibid. 1613). See Hoefer, *Nouv. Biog. Générale*, s. v.

Cuenburh (**Cenburg**, **Quenburga**, etc.), sister of Ina, king of Wessex, co-foundress of Wimburn Abbey with her sister, is perhaps also the same as the abbess *Caenburga*, probably of Wimburn, A.D. cir. 718.

Cuernert, DIRK (or THEODORE VAN), a Dutch engraver, was born at Amsterdam in 1522, and lived chiefly at Haarlem, where he was more noted for religious controversy than for attainments in the art

He died in 1590. The following are his chief works: *The Descent from the Cross; Joseph Explaining his Dream; Joseph Interpreting the Dreams of his Fellow-Prisoners; Job Reproached by his Wife; Balaam and his Ass.*

Cueuret (or **Curet**), PIERRE, a French theologian, who lived about the middle of the 16th century, was canon of the Church of Mans, and chaplain of the duke of Mayenne, who intrusted him with important matters. He wrote, *La Fleur de Prédication selon Saint Éphrem* (without date), from the Latin of Ambrose the Camaldule. According to La Croix du Maine, we are indebted to Cueuret for the first edition of the *Triomphant Mystère des Actes des Apôtres*, of Arnoul and Simon Criban, published in 1537. See Hoefer, *Nouv. Biog. Générale*, s. v.

Cueva, MARTIN DE LA, a Spanish grammarian of the order of Cordeliers, lived in the middle of the 16th century. He wrote *De Corrupto Docendæ Grammaticæ Latinæ Genere* (Anvers, 1550). See Hoefer, *Nouv. Biog. Générale*, s. v.

Cufa, an abbot of the diocese of Winchester, who attested an act of the Council of Clovesho, Oct. 12, 803.

Cuff, JOHN HARCOMBE, an English Congregational minister, was born near Chard, Somerset, in 1790. He was educated at the Western Academy, Axminster; in 1812 commenced his ministry at Wellington, Somerset, and continued it there until his death, November, 1846. See (Lond.) *Evang. Magazine*, August, 1847, p. 401.

Cuffee, PAUL, a native Indian preacher of the Shinnecock tribe of Indians on Long Island, was born in 1757, and was for thirteen years in the employ of the New York Missionary Society. He died March 7, 1812.

Cuganaeich. See CONGAN.

Cui—. See QUI—.

Cuichelm, an early English prelate, was consecrated seventh bishop of Rochester by archbishop Theodore, but deserted the see (Bede, *Hist. Eccles.* iv, 12).

Cuirbin. See CERBAN.

Culan (**Colan**, or **Dachualen**), a doubtful Irish *saint*, given by Colgan (*Acta Sanctorum*) under Feb. 18.

Culbertson, JAMES, a Presbyterian minister, was born in Franklin County, Pa. He was educated at Cannonsburg College, and installed at Zanesville, O., in 1812, where, after a long and useful service, he died suddenly, Feb. 23, 1847. (W. P. S.)

Culcheth, WILLIAM, an English Wesleyan minister, was born at Daventry in 1810. He was converted early in life, admitted into the ministry in 1833, and died July 26, 1852. See *Minutes of the British Conference*, 1852.

Cull, HUGH, a Methodist Episcopal minister, and an eminent local preacher for nearly sixty years, died near Richmond, Ind., Aug. 30, 1862, in his one hundred and fifth year. See *Appleton's Annual Cyclopædia*, 1863, p. 672.

Cullen, Gavin, a Scotch clergyman, born in Lanarkshire, was licensed to preach in 1821; presented to the living at Balmaclellan in 1825, and ordained; and died Jan. 18, 1844, aged fifty years. See *Fasti Eccles. Scoticanæ*, i, 697.

Cullen, John, an English Wesleyan minister, was born at Newark, Nottinghamshire, Oct. 25, 1786. He commenced his ministry in 1809, became a supernumerary in 1851, settled at Wellingborough, and died April 15, 1863. See *Minutes of the British Conference*, 1863, p. 20.

Cullen, John Edward, an English Congregational minister, first cousin of cardinal Cullen, was born at Gort, in the west of Ireland, May 10, 1794. He was early designed by his parents for the priesthood, and educated for that purpose in Dublin, but his study of the Scriptures led him to renounce the Roman Catholic faith. He resolved to commence preaching at once at Omagh, in the north of Ireland, and at the same time was engaged as private tutor in the family of James Buchanan, Esq., father of president Buchanan of the United States. Persecution from the Catholics induced him to remove to London, where he maintained himself by teaching in schools and private families. About 1820 he was ordained, and preached successively at Caistor, in Lincolnshire; Flocton, in Yorkshire; Fairford, in Gloucestershire; Lacock, in Wiltshire; Boroughbridge, in Yorkshire; Burwell, in Cambridgeshire; and, lastly, at Fordham, until 1856, where he died, Dec. 30, 1878. He published *The Voice of Truth*. See (Lond.) *Cong. Year-book*, 1880, p. 318.

Cullen, Paul, an eminent Roman Catholic prelate, was born April 27, 1803, at Prospect, in Ireland. He studied at the college in Carlow; went in 1820 to Rome, where he completed his education. In 1828 he received the degree of doctor of theology; was rector of the Irish college at Rome, and in 1849 was appointed archbishop of Armagh. In 1851 he was transferred to Dublin, where he opened, in 1854, the Catholic high-school, whose first rector was John Newman. In 1869 he was made cardinal. He died Oct. 24, 1878. His *Pastoral Letters* and other *Writings of Cardinal Cullen* (edit. Moran) were published in 1883. See Brady, *The Episcopal Succession in England, Scotland, and Ireland*, i, 345; Bellesheim, in Wetzer u. Welte's *Kirchen-Lexikon*, s. v. (B. P.)

Cullingford, JOHN, an English Wesleyan preacher, entered the ministry in 1825, and was sent as a missionary to the West Indies. Being seized with illness in 1845, he left Trinidad for Barbadoes, and died there, March 4, 1846, in the forty-sixth year of his age. See *Minutes of the British Conference*, 1846.

Cullum, *Sir* JOHN, an English clergyman and an accomplished antiquary, was born in 1733, and educated at St. Catharine Hall, Cambridge, where he became a fellow in 1758. In April, 1762, he was presented to the rectory of Hawstead, in Suffolk; and in December, 1774, instituted to the vicarage of Great Thurlow. He died Oct. 9, 1785. His *History of the Parish of Hawstead and Hardwick House* was originally published as the twenty-third number of the *Bibliotheca Topographica Britannica*. See Chalmers, *Biog. Dict.* s. v.; Allibone, *Dict. of Brit. and Amer. Authors*, s. v.

Culmer, RICHARD, an English clergyman of Kent, is represented by Wood (*Fasti Oxonienses*) as "an ignorant person, and with his ignorance one of the most daring schismatics in all that country." He published, *Cathedrall Newes from Canterbury* (1644):—*Minister's Hue and Cry* (1651):—*Lawless Tithe Robbers Discovered* (1655). See Allibone, *Dict. of Brit. and Amer. Authors*, s. v.

Culshaw, JOSEPH, an English Wesleyan minister, was born of Roman Catholic parents at Ormskirk, Sept. 25, 1856. In 1877 he entered the Richmond Theological School; early in 1879 began circuit-work at the diamond fields, South Africa; and the year following removed to Kronstadt, in Orange Free State. He was drowned Feb. 8, 1880. See *Minutes of the British Conference*, 1881, p. 60.

Culter was a knife used by the ancient pagans in slaughtering victims at the altars of the gods. It usually had one edge, a sharp point, and a curved back.

Cultrarius (Lat. *culter*, a knife) was the person who killed the victims which were sacrificed to the gods by the heathens of ancient times. The presiding priest never performed this service himself, but appointed one of his attendants to the office of *cultrarius* for each occasion.

Culver, Aaron L., a Methodist Episcopal minister, was born at Dobb's Ferry, N. Y., Feb. 19, 1841. He was converted at twelve; after studying at Claverack in 1859 or 1860, labored for four years as a local preacher, and then in the New York Conference, till his death in 1878. See *Minutes of Annual Conferences*, 1878, p. 43.

Culver, Cyrus, a Methodist Episcopal minister, was born at Chester, Mass., in 1780. He was converted in early life; labored several years as a local preacher; in 1811 entered the New York Conference; in 1827 became a supernumerary, in 1830 a superannuate, and died March 11, 1846. See *Minutes of Annual Conferences*, 1846, p. 29.

Culver, Newell, a Methodist Episcopal minister, was born at Pomfret, Vt., July 13, 1811. He joined the Church in January, 1833, and in July of the same year was received on trial into the New Hampshire Conference. He continued in the active work, except for three years (1849–52), until 1871, when his health failed. He died Sept. 22, 1882. See *Minutes of Annual Conferences*, 1883, p. 84.

Culverwell, Ezekiel, an English Puritan divine, published a *Treatise on Faith* (Lond. 1629):—*A Blessed Estate* (1633):—*Meditations* (1634). See Allibone, *Dict. of Brit. and Amer. Authors*, s. v.

Cuman was an abbot of Glastonbury, England, A.D. 800–802.

Cumanus (or **Conanus**) was second abbot of Abingdon, died A.D. 784.

Cumberland, Denison, an Irish prelate, became bishop of Clonfert in 1763, and was translated to Kilmore in 1772. He published some single *Sermons*. See Allibone, *Dict. of Brit. and Amer. Authors*, s. v.

Cumbertus (or **Tumbertus**), was abbot of Glastonbury, England, A.D. 744–753.

Cumin (**Cumian, Cumeanus, Cumeneus**, or **Cummein**), was the name of about a score of Irish saints, of whom but few are clearly identifiable.

1. Son of Dubh, and abbot of Druimdruith, commemorated Jan. 12.

2. Bishop of Bobbio, commemorated Aug. 19, died after seventeen years of piety, at the age of ninety-five, about A.D. 744.

3. A poet of Connor, about the middle of the 7th century.

4. Otherwise called *Cadhan*, commemorated June 1, seems to have been the son of Cronchu, son of Ronan, of the race of Corbmac Cas, and to have lived about A.D. 738.

5. Surnamed *Fin*, "the Fair," commemorated Feb. 24, is thought to be the same as the son of Ernan, of the district of Tyrconnell, who retired to the monastery of Hy. He probably became abbot A.D. 657, and died in 699. He is famous as the earliest biographer of St. Columba.

6. Surnamed *Foda*, "the Tall," of Cluainferta-Brenainn (now Clonfert), commemorated Nov. 12, was the son of Fiachna, of the royal line of West Munster. He was born about A.D. 590, and his original name was *Aedh*. He seems to have been a man of great learning, and wrote a hymn in praise of the apostles and evangelists (edited by Todd, *Book of Hymns*, i, 81). He died A.D. 662.

Cumin, John. See Comin.

Cumin, Robert, a Scotch clergyman, was born in 1660; called to the living at Riccarton in 1694; ordained in 1695, and died April 8, 1739. See *Fasti Eccles. Scoticanæ*, ii, 136.

Cumine, Andrew, a Scotch clergyman, was teacher at the grammar-school in Irvine in 1696; called to the living at Largs in 1701, and died July 4, 1762, aged eighty-eight years. See *Fasti Eccles. Scoticanæ*, ii, 253.

Cumine, John, a Scotch clergyman, son of the foregoing, was licensed to preach in 1739; called, in 1742, to be assistant to his father at Largs, and died Jan. 31, 1743. See *Fasti Eccles. Scoticanæ*, ii, 253.

Cumine, William, a Scotch clergyman, originally schoolmaster of Fraserburgh, was licensed to preach in 1754; presented to the living at Tyrie in 1761; ordained in 1762; transferred to Ruthen in 1772, and died Feb. 8, 1800, in his eightieth year. See *Fasti Eccles. Scoticanæ*, iii, 639, 643.

Cuming (or **Cumming**) is the family name of many Scotch clergyman. For others of later date see Cumming.

1. Alexander (1), was licensed to preach in 1672; called to the living at Dallas the same year, and died May 24, 1681. See *Fasti Eccles. Scoticanæ*, iii, 179.

2. Alexander (2), was licensed to preach, and presented to the living at Moy-and-Dalarossie in 1680, and ordained. Though a Jacobite, he continued after the Revolution in 1688, and died April 27, 1709. See *Fasti Eccles. Scoticanæ*, iii, 268.

3. Alexander (3), was bursar to the presbytery in 1684 and 1685; minister at Liberton in 1689; deprived the same year for not praying for the king and queen, and died at Edinburgh, April 26, 1713, aged sixty years. See *Fasti Eccles. Scoticanæ*, i, 115.

4. David, born at Relugas, took his degree at King's College, Aberdeen, in 1667; succeeded his brother as schoolmaster at Turrif, and then in the living at Edenkeillie in 1672, and was ordained; received into communion in 1694; was one of the ministers appointed in 1699 to visit the Highland parishes of Moray, and died at the end of the same year, aged about fifty-two years. See *Fasti Eccles. Scoticanæ*, iii, 183.

5. George (1), took his degree at King's College, Aberdeen, in 1619; was appointed to the living at Dallas in 1624, and ordained; in 1631 was charged before the presbytery with making railing verses, found among the people, which he denied on oath; was the only minister in the presbytery who refused to subscribe the Covenant in 1638; officiated as synod clerk in 1643; was a member of the Commissions of Assembly in 1644 and 1645; and subscribed the marquis of Huntly's bond in 1646. He died before May 3, 1648, aged about forty-nine years. See *Fasti Eccles. Scoticanæ*, iii, 179.

6. George (2), took his degree at King's College, Aberdeen, in 1647; became schoolmaster at Elgin, where he was obtruded on the grammar-school by the magistrates, in 1649, without the consent of the presbytery; was licensed to preach in 1655; called to the living at Urray in 1658, and died in 1705, aged about seventy-eight years. See *Fasti Eccles. Scoticanæ*, iii, 305.

7. George (3), born at Elgin, took his degree at King's College, Aberdeen, in 1667; was licensed to preach in 1674; presented to the living at Essil in 1676, and ordained. He died Sept. 20, 1723, aged about seventy-six years. His two sons, Archibald and George, both settled as clergymen in England. See *Fasti Eccles. Scoticanæ*, iii, 170.

8. John (1), born at Relugas, took his degree at King's College, Aberdeen, in 1661; became schoolmaster at Turrif; was presented to the living at Edenkeillie in 1688, and ordained; transferred to Auldearn in 1672; resigned in 1682, and settled at Cullen. He died at Edenkeillie, Feb. 9, 1689, aged forty-eight years. His son John was the first regius professor of divinity and church history in the Edinburgh University. See *Fasti Eccles. Scoticanæ*, iii, 183, 246, 673.

9. John (2), took his degree at King's College, Aberdeen, in 1663; was licensed to preach in 1668; called to the living at Birnie in 1670, and ordained; instituted in 1671; deprived in 1690 for nonconformity; went to Ireland, where he is said to have joined the Romish Church. See *Fasti Eccles. Scoticanæ*, iii, 159.

10. John (3), was called to the living at Sandsting-and-Aithsting in 1701; ordained in 1702; falling under censure, was reproved by the synod in 1704. He died May 21, 1731. See *Fasti Eccles. Scoticanæ*, iii, 428.

11. John (4), son of the minister at Edenkeillie, studied theology at Glasgow University; was called to the living at Eyemouth in 1708, and ordained; transferred to Humbie in 1715, and died Feb. 26, 1754, aged seventy-four years. See *Fasti Eccles. Scoticanæ*, i, 338, 437.

12. JOHN (5), D.D., was born in 1685, in Ireland; educated in a Scotch university; removed to England, and was chosen pastor at Cambridge. In 1714 the court designed the overthrow of dissent by act of parliament, and Mr. Cuming resisted that act by publishing *The Corruptions and Defections of the Present Times as to Matters of Religion.* In 1715 he wrote and published *Remarks on Dr. Bentley's Sermon on Popery.* In 1716 he took charge of the Scotch Church at Founder's Hall, Lothbury, London. In 1717 he preached a *Sermon to Controvert One on the Kingdom of Christ*, published by bishop Hoadley. He took an active part in the Salter's Hall Synod in 1719, in defense of the Trinity, and was one of the signers. He preached and published a sermon on the subject, which, in 1722, he defended by a bulky volume *On the Authority of Scripture Consequences in Matters of Faith.* In 1724 he published the *Funeral Sermon of Benjamin Robinson.* He died Sept. 7, 1729. See Wilson, *Dissenting Churches*, ii, 487.

13. MICHAEL, took his degree at the University of St. Andrews in 1659; became a chaplain; was licensed to preach in 1663; appointed to the living at Drainy in 1666; declined to take the test in 1681, but was returned to his ministry in 1683, and died in March, 1695. See *Fasti Eccles. Scoticanæ*, iii, 161.

14. PATRICK (1), was presented by the king to the parsonage of Dallas and vicarage of Alderne in 1576, which he resigned before February, 1586; was transferred to Urquhart in 1578, his former parishes being conjoined. See *Fasti Eccles. Scoticanæ*, iii, 173, 178.

15. PATRICK (2), born at Relugas, took his degree at Edinburgh University in 1670; became minister to a Presbyterian congregation in Dublin; was called to the living at Ormiston in 1689; ordained in 1690, reserving the liberty to return to Ireland. He was a member of the General Assembly in 1690, and was appointed with principal Dunlop, in 1694, to get the royal sanction to hold the General Assembly, which had been interrupted. He had the care of all the churches, was a constant friend to all young ministers and scholars, and a most instructive and cheerful companion. He died March 10, 1731, aged eighty-one years. See *Fasti Eccles. Scoticanæ*, i, 302.

16. PATRICK (3), D.D., son of the minister of Relugas, took his degree at Edinburgh University in 1716; became chaplain to lord justice Clerk (Grange); was licensed to preach in 1720; appointed to the living at Kirkmahoe the same year, and ordained; transferred to Lochmaben in 1725, and to the Collegiate Church, second charge, Edinburgh, in 1732; elected moderator of the General Assembly several times, and died April 1, 1756, aged eighty years. He was distinguished for erudition, liberal sentiments, and extensive benevolence. His talents as a speaker gave him great influence, and, patronized by the Argyll family, then holding in their hands the government of Scotland, he acquired the chief management of the affairs of the Church in Scotland from the year 1751. His sons, Robert and Patrick, were professors in the universities of Edinburgh and Glasgow. See *Fasti Eccles. Scoticanæ*, i, 15, 588, 642.

17. PATRICK (4), D.D., was born in 1695; in 1737 became professor of church history in the University of Edinburgh, and was also one of the ministers of the city, having been ordained when but seventeen years old. He resigned his professorship in 1762, in favor of his son. Soon after his removal to Edinburgh he became the leader of the Church party known as the *Moderates.* He was several times moderator of the assembly, and died April 1, 1776, at Rybreas, in the parish of Edenkeillie. Dr. Cuming was a man of extensive historical and critical knowledge; and as a preacher, equalled by few, having an easy, fluent, neat, and elegant style. See *Annals of the Church of Scotland* (1739-1766), i, 319.

18. ROBERT, took his degree at King's College, Aberdeen, in 1680; was licensed to preach, and admitted to the living at Urquhart-and-Glenmorriston in 1686, and ordained. He died before April 8, 1730, aged about seventy years. See *Fasti Eccles. Scoticanæ*, iii, 120.

19. WILLIAM (1), took his degree at King's College, Aberdeen, in 1622; was licensed to preach, but not settled; complained of to the synod in 1624 for marrying irregularly at Inverness, but continued in the ministry. See *Fasti Eccles. Scoticanæ*, iii, 344.

20. WILLIAM (2), took his degree at King's College, Aberdeen, in 1661; was appointed to the living at Dores in 1663, and ordained; removed in 1664; called to Halkirk in 1677, and continued in 1688. See *Fasti Eccles. Scoticanæ*, iii, 262, 362.

21. WILLIAM (3), brother of the minister at Riccarton, was licensed to preach in 1693; called to the living at Caterline in 1708, ordained in 1709, and died in 1717. See *Fasti Eccles. Scoticanæ*, iii, 877.

Cumings, ABIJAH PRESTON, a Presbyterian minister, was born at Dover, N. Y., July 4, 1803. He graduated from Union College in 1832; studied theology for two years in Princeton Theological Seminary; was licensed by the Presbytery of New Brunswick, Oct. 21, 1835; was editor of the *New York Observer* from 1836 to 1871, and died at Nice, France, May 13, 1871. See *Gen. Cat. of Princeton Theol. Sem.* 1881, p. 88.

Cumma was abbot of Abingdon, England, about A.D. 725-737.

Cumman is the name of two early Irish virgins and saints:

1. Commemorated July 6, seems to have been twin-sister of Ethne and daughter of Cormac, of the royal race of Ireland, and flourished about A.D. 560.

2. Commemorated May 29, apparently of the Ards (County Down), and of the royal race of Erin, before A.D. 800.

Cummian (often confounded with St. *Cumin* [q. v]), an early Irish ecclesiast of unknown parentage, was probably educated in St. Columba's monastery at Durrow, and had his church at Kilcomin (King's County). He is known for his zeal in the Paschal controversy, and a letter of his is extant on the subject, written A.D. 634 (given in Usher, *Works*, iv, 430). He is also thought to be the author of an abridgment of the penitential Psalms (in Fleming, *Collect. Sacra*, p. 197).

Cumming, Alexander, a Scotch clergyman, was licensed to preach in 1828; presented to the living at Dunbarnie in 1833; ordained in 1834; joined the Free Secession in 1843, and became minister at Gorbals Free East Church in 1853. His publications were, a *Lecture*, a *Sermon*, and *An Account of the Parish.* See *Fasti Eccles. Scoticanæ*, ii, 634.

Cumming, Andrew, a minister of the Methodist Episcopal Church South, was born in Hawkins County, Tenn., Nov. 18, 1817. He was converted and joined the Methodist Episcopal Church in 1833, and three years later removed with his father's family to Illinois. There he was licensed to preach in 1843, joined the Illinois Conference, and was transferred immediately to the Arkansas Conference. At the division of the Church the following year he became a member of the southern branch. He was a member successively of the Indian Mission, the East Texas, and the North Texas conferences. He became superannuated in 1864, and died at Turner's Point, Texas, Oct. 6, 1882. See *Minutes of Annual Conferences of the M. E. Church South*, 1882, p. 145.

Cumming, David B., a minister of the Methodist Episcopal Church South, was born at Mercersburg, Pa., June 3, 1796. He was converted in 1818, licensed to preach in 1819, and entered the Tennessee Conference in 1821. In 1823 he was ordained deacon, and transferred to Holston Conference in 1824. In its bounds he travelled until 1834, excepting three years that he was a supernumerary, being agent for the American Bible Society. From 1834 to 1838 he had charge of the Indian Mission work of that conference. He was transferred in 1838 to the Arkansas Conference, within the bounds of which he served during the next six years. From 1845 until his death he was a member of the Indian Mission Conference. From 1872 to 1879 he was superannuated. He was the pioneer of Methodism among the Wyandottes, the Senecas, the Delawares, the Creeks, and Cherokees. He served three terms as presiding elder, and was a delegate to the General Conference of 1854. His death occurred in McDonald County, Mo., Aug. 25, 1880. See *Minutes of Annual Conferences of the M. E. Church South*, 1880, p. 151.

Cumming, Francis H., D.D., a Protestant Episcopal minister, was born at New Haven, Conn., Oct. 28, 1799. His literary and theological studies were pursued under Rev. Dr. Rudd of Elizabeth, N. J.; and he was ordained deacon in 1819, and priest in 1820. He remained a year in his first cure in Binghamton, N. Y.; was then called to St. Luke's, Rochester, officiating there during nine years; spent one year in Reading, Pa., and one in Le Roy, N. Y.; became secretary, agent, and editor of the Protestant Episcopal Sunday-school Union, removing to New York meanwhile, and holding these offices for the space of four years. He was the first rector of Calvary Church, New York city; in 1839 entered upon the duties of rector of St. Andrew's, Ann Arbor, Mich., continuing there four years; became rector in 1843 of St. Mark's Church, Grand Rapids, which post he held until his death, Aug. 26, 1862. He was chaplain of the 3d regiment Michigan Infantry, and twenty-five years represented the diocese of Michigan in the General Convention. Possessed of great energy of character, and a mind well stored, he was by no means an ordinary man. See *Amer. Quar. Church Rev.* April, 1863, p. 150.

Cumming, Hooper, D.D., a Presbyterian minister, was born in New Jersey. He graduated from Princeton College in 1805, and from Andover Theological Seminary in 1810; was ordained in 1811; preached in the Second Presbyterian Church of Newark, N. J., from 1811 to 1814; at Schenectady, N. Y., from 1815 to 1817; in the Third Presbyterian Church, Albany, from 1817 to 1822; and in the Vandewater-street Church, New York city, in 1822 and 1823. He went to Charleston, S. C., in 1824, and died there, Dec. 18, 1825. See *Trien. Cat. of Andover Theol. Sem.* 1870, p. 17.

Cumming, James, a Methodist Episcopal minister, was a member of the Holston Conference, and died in 1868 or 1869. See *Minutes of Annual Conferences*, 1869, p. 264.

Cumming, John (1), a Scotch clergyman, a native of Kilmarnock, was licensed to preach in 1795; became assistant minister at Dundee, and afterwards librarian at Glasgow; was presented to the living at Fraserburgh in 1814, ordained in 1815, and died Jan. 25, 1857, aged eighty-four years. See *Fasti Eccles. Scoticanæ*, iii, 628.

Cumming, John (2), D.D., an eminent minister of the Scotch Church, was born in Aberdeenshire, Nov. 10, 1810. He went to London in 1833; became minister of the Church in Crown Court, and through life maintained his connection with the Established Kirk, having no sympathy with the cause which led Chalmers to forsake it. He died in London, July 6, 1881. Dr. Cumming was equally noted as an opponent of the Church of Rome and as a believer in the speedy advent of Christ. He was a clear thinker and an able preacher, possessing much learning and vivid imagination, which rendered him interesting to those even who did not accept his peculiar views. In 1872 he preached before the queen on "Communion between Heaven and Earth," and was personally thanked by her majesty for his effort, with which she professed herself greatly pleased. His church was not large enough to hold the vast crowds which attended his ministry. The writings of Dr. Cumming were very numerous, among which we notice, *The Church of Scotland:—Apocalyptic Sketches:—Lectures on the Seven Churches:—Lecture on the Miracles:—Lecture on the Parables:—Lecture on Daniel:—The Finger of God:—Christ our Passover:—The Comforter:—A Message from God:—The Great Sacrifice:—Christ Receiving Sinners:—Is Christianity from God?—Sabbath Morning Readings on Genesis:—On Exodus:—On Leviticus:—Benedictions:—Voices of the Night:—Of the Day:—Of the Dead:—God in History:—Infant Salvation:—Baptismal Font:—Lectures for the Times:—Christian Patriotism:—The Communion Table;—Almost Protestant:—The Church Before the Flood:—Liberty:—Equality:—Fraternity:—The Revolutionists:—The True Charter:—The True Succession:—Exposition of Psalm xci:—Occasional Discourses:—Thanksgiving, an Exposition of Psalm ciii:—Our Father; a Week's Family Prayers:—An Edition of the Pulpit Psalm-book, Church of Scotland:—An Edition of Fox's Book of Martyrs:—An Edition of Albert Barnes's Notes:—Translation of Bonaventura's Psalter of the Blessed Virgin:—Discussion on Protestantism with Daniel French, Esq.:—The Tent and the Altar:—Daily Family Devotion*, etc. See Allibone, *Dict. of Brit. and Amer. Authors*, s. v. (W. P. S.)

Cumming, John A., a minister in the Methodist Episcopal Church South, was born in Buncombe County, N. C., Nov. 23, 1826. He embraced religion at an early age; and in 1849 was licensed to preach, and received into the Indian Mission Conference. He began his labors among the Indians on the Shawnee and Delaware Mission under great disadvantages. On the change of boundaries he became a member of the St. Louis Conference, in which he ended his days in 1859 or 1860. See *Minutes of Annual Conferences of the M. E. Church South*, 1860, p. 205.

Cumming (or **Cuming**), **Moses**, an Irish Presbyterian minister, was ordained over the First Dromore Church in 1784, and removed to Armagh in 1796, where he died in 1816. For many years he was clerk of the synod of Ulster. See Stuart, *Armagh*, p. 498; Reid, *Hist. of the Presb. Church in Ireland.*

Cumming, Paxton, a Methodist Episcopal minister, was born in Rockingham County, Va., Feb. 12, 1808. He experienced religion at sixteen; and the same year was licensed to preach, and admitted into the Holston Conference. In 1828 he located, because of ill-health; subsequently removed to Illinois, and in 1837 entered the Illinois Conference. In 1838 he became superannuated, and died Aug. 21, 1839. See *Minutes of Annual Conferences*, 1840, p. 53.

Cummings, Archibald, a minister of the Church of England, appeared before the vestry of Christ Church, Philadelphia, Pa., Sept. 9, 1726, with an appointment to that church from the bishop of London, and was accordingly received as rector, a position which he held until his death, in April, 1741. See Sprague, *Annals of the Amer. Pulpit*, v, 88.

Cummings, Asa, D.D., a Congregational minister, was born at Andover, Mass., Sept. 29, 1790. He graduated from Harvard College in 1817, and from Andover Theological Seminary in 1820; was ordained pastor at Yarmouth, Me., in 1821, where he remained until 1829, and then removed to Portland, as proprietor and editor of the *Christian Mirror*. Here, for thirty years, he labored most faithfully, and by his pen, through the columns of his paper, he was the instrument of largely increasing the efficiency of the Congregational churches of the state. He wrote the interesting and useful *Memoirs of Edward Payson.* His death occurred suddenly, on the steamer *George Law*, on his way home from Aspinwall, June 5 or 6, 1856. See *Boston Advertiser*,

July 16, 1856; *Trien. Cat. of Andover Theol. Sem.* 1870, p. 41. (J. C. S.)

Cummings, Charles (1), a Presbyterian minister, was an Irishman by birth, and came to America in early manhood. It is believed that he obtained most of his education in this country. He was licensed by the Hanover Presbytery, April 18, 1767, as preacher at North Mountain, Va., where he remained for five years. He died March, 1812. See Sprague, *Annals of the Amer. Pulpit*, iii, 285.

Cummings, Charles (2), a Baptist minister, was born at Seabrook, N. H., Sept. 23, 1777. He removed in early life to Dublin, where he was converted, and was baptized July 16, 1797. In 1805 he was licensed, and in 1810 was ordained at Sullivan, where he remained fifteen years, during a part of the time preaching in Keene, and also laboring as a missionary throughout the state. He was next pastor in Hillsborough, afterwards in Marlborough, and finally in Swanzey. He died in Roxbury, Mass., Dec. 27, 1849. (J. C. S.)

Cummings, Cyrus, a Methodist Episcopal minister, was born at Bridgewater, N. H., April 23, 1791. He experienced religion in 1809, received license to exhort in 1810, and in 1811 entered the New England Conference. In 1816 he located at North Yarmouth, Me.; in 1818 removed to West Cumberland; in 1848, to Portland; in 1852 was admitted into the Maine Conference as a superannuate, laboring as chaplain to the poor, until his death in 1859 or 1860. See *Minutes of Annual Conferences*, 1860, p. 114.

Cummings, Henry, D.D., a Unitarian minister, was born at Tyngsborough, Mass., Sept. 25, 1737. He graduated at Harvard College in 1760, and began the study of theology; in 1762 preached as a candidate at Billerica, and in November accepted a call from the Church to become their pastor. He resigned his charge in 1814, and died Sept. 5, 1823. Dr. Cummings was appointed delegate to the convention which framed the Constitution of Massachusetts. In 1795 he preached the annual sermon before the convention of ministers in Massachusetts, and the same year delivered the Dudleian lecture in Harvard College. He published a great number of *Sermons*. See Sprague, *Annals of the Amer. Pulpit*, viii, 55.

Cummings, Jacob, a Congregational minister, was born at Warren, Mass., Dec. 5, 1792. He studied at Phillips Academy; graduated at Dartmouth College in 1815; taught at the Hampton, N. H., Academy; was ordained in 1824 at Stratham, and remained there for eleven years. His other pastorates were Sharon, Mass., in 1835; Southborough, in 1838; Hillsborough Bridge, N. H., in 1843; and Exeter, where he died, June 20, 1866. See *Cong. Quarterly*, 1867, p. 40.

Cummings, Jeremiah W., D.D., a Roman Catholic divine, was born in Washington, D. C., April 5, 1824. His father was a lieutenant in the United States navy, and died when on a cruise in the Mediterranean sea when Jeremiah was young. His mother became a Catholic, and sent her son to a seminary established at Nyack-on-the-Hudson by bishop Dubois, whence he went to the Propaganda College, Rome, where he received the highest honors. In 1847 he returned to America, and was for a time stationed at the old St. Patrick's Cathedral, Mott Street, New York city. Thence he went to a temporary church at Madison Avenue and Twentieth Street, and finally built St. Stephen's Church, Twenty-eighth Street, of which he remained pastor until his death, Jan. 4, 1866. Dr. Cummings was well known as an effective preacher, a popular lecturer, a graceful poet, and an elegant writer. He was the author of *Italian Legends:—Spiritual Progress:—Hymns and Songs for Catholic Schools:—The Silver Stole.* He wrote and corrected many articles on Catholic subjects for the first edition of *Appleton's Cyclopædia.* He was a genial gentleman, and of great popularity among all classes. See (N. Y.) *Cath. Annual*, 1881, p. 54.

Cummings, Preston, a Congregational minister, was born in Seekonk, Mass., May 1, 1800. He spent his early life in Attleborough, where he fitted for college, and graduated from Brown University in 1822. He studied theology with Dr. Calvin Park; was ordained at Lebanon, N. Y., Aug. 22, 1825; dismissed in February, 1827; was pastor in Dighton, Mass., from Dec. 26 following until Oct. 5, 1835; of the North Church, Wrentham, from July 6, 1836, to Jan. 1, 1838; and at Buckland from 1840 to 1848. He resided in Leicester from 1851 to 1871, and thereafter in Holden, where he died April 8, 1875. Mr. Cummings compiled a valuable *Dictionary of Congregational Usages and Principles.* See *Hist. of Meriden Association*, p. 183. (J. C. S.)

Cummings, Seneca, a Presbyterian minister, was born at Antrim, N. H., May 16, 1817. He graduated from Dartmouth College in 1844, began his theological studies at Lane Seminary the same year, and completed them at Union Seminary in 1847; was ordained a Congregational minister, Sept. 30, the same year; became a missionary to Foo-Chow, China, in 1848; returned to the United States in 1856, and died at New Ipswich, N. H., Aug. 12 of that year. See *Gen. Cat. of Union Theol. Sem.* 1876, p. 45.

Cummings, Stedman, a Free-will Baptist minister, was born at Washington, Vt., Nov. 10, 1806. He was converted when fourteen years of age, ordained in 1825, and labored as an evangelist in Vermont and Canada. In 1854 he went West, and about 1870 removed to Kansas, where he preached occasionally. He died at Kirwin, Kansas, Oct. 19, 1883. See *Morning Star*, May 14, 1884. (J. C. S.)

Cummins, Alexander, a Methodist Episcopal minister, was born in Albemarle County, Va., Sept. 3, 1787. He embraced religion in his twentieth year, and in 1809 entered the Western Conference. With the exception of one year's intermission as supernumerary he labored zealously until early in 1823, when he became superannuated. He died Sept. 27 of that year. See *Minutes of Annual Conferences*, 1825, p. 474; *Meth. Mag.* vii, 225.

Cummins, Asa, a Methodist Episcopal minister, was born at Thompson, Windham Co., Conn., Sept. 1, 1762. He was converted in his twenty-fifth year, licensed to preach in 1797, and in 1802 entered the itinerant ranks, and began travelling the Albany and Saratoga circuits. His latter years were in connection with the Oneida Conference, as a superannuate. He died Sept. 5, 1836. See *Minutes of Annual Conferences*, 1836, p. 411.

Cummins, Charles, D.D., a Presbyterian minister, was born at Strasburg, Pa., July 15, 1776, of Scotch-Irish Presbyterian parents. He graduated from Dickinson College in 1799, was licensed to preach by the New Castle Presbytery in 1801, and in 1804 was ordained pastor of the churches of Chestnut Level and Little Britain. In 1808 he accepted a call from a church in Florida, Orange Co., N. Y., where he remained until his death, Jan. 9, 1863. (W. P. S.)

Cummins, Charles P., M.D., a Presbyterian minister, was born in Franklin County, Pa., in 1803. He graduated from Jefferson Medical College, Philadelphia, and practiced medicine in his native county until 1836; was licensed by the Carlisle Presbytery the same year, and installed pastor of Dickinson Church, where he remained until 1843. He was pastor of the Presbyterian Church of Clarion, Clarion Co., from 1847 to 1862, and died March 22, 1865. See Wilson. *Presb. Hist. Almanac*, 1866, p. 100.

Cummins, Francis, D.D., a Presbyterian minister, was born at Shippensburg, Pa., in 1752, of parents who had been Presbyterians in Ireland. He graduated from the college called "Queen's Museum," in North

Carolina, in 1776, and engaged for several years afterwards in teaching; was licensed to preach by the Presbytery of Orange, in Mecklenburg County, Dec. 15, 1780, and in 1782 accepted a call from Bethel Church, in York District, S. C. He was never long stationary in any one field. He labored about one year in North Carolina, twenty-four years in South Carolina, and twenty-five years in Georgia. He died Feb. 22, 1832. See Sprague, *Annals of the Amer. Pulpit*, iii, 418.

Cummins, Frederick P., a Protestant Episcopal clergyman, entered the ministry in 1871, doing service as a missionary, in connection with which he was rector of St. John's Church, Crawfordsville, Ind. The following year he was rector, not only of St. John's, but also of St. Philip's Church in Covington, which two parishes he served until his death, Jan. 17, 1874. See *Prot. Episc. Almanac*, 1875, p. 144.

Cummins, George David, D.D., senior bishop of the Reformed Episcopal Church, has already been noticed under that denomination in Vol. VIII. We here add that he was born near Smyrna, Del., Dec. 11, 1822; graduated from Dickinson College in 1841 was a preacher in the Methodist Church for two years; joined the Protestant Episcopal ministry, and was ordained presbyter in 1847. For six years he was rector of Christ Church, at Norfolk, Va., and afterwards of St. James's Church, at Richmond; Trinity Church, Washington, D. C.; and St. Peter's Church, Baltimore, Md. In 1866 Mr. Cummins was elected assistant bishop of the diocese of Kentucky. Seven years thereafter bishop Cummins withdrew on acconnt of the Romanizing tendencies of the Episcopal Church, and founded the Reformed Episcopal Church, of which he was made the first bishop, in December, 1873. He died suddenly, June 26, 1876, at his residence in Lutherville, Baltimore Co., Md. Bishop Cummins was emphatically a Low-Churchman, of broad and evangelical views, of dignified and commanding presence, a ready and clear thinker, and a free pulpit orator and platform speaker. See *Memoir*, by his wife (N. Y. 1878).

Cummins, John, an English Congregational minister, was born in Manchester, April 11, 1804. He was converted in youth, and in due time, after a preparation for village preaching, being recommended to the London Missionary Society, was sent to Madagascar as an artisan missionary. Soon after his arrival Mr. Cummins was compelled to leave, in consequence of the death of king Radama, and the accession of queen Ranavalona to the throne. Returning to England, he settled at Smallbridge, and afterwards successively at Blackpool, Holbeck, Kirkheaton, and Stubbin-Elsecar, where he labored fourteen years, and then retired to Sheffield, where he died, May 29, 1872. See (Lond.) *Cong. Year-book*, 1873, p. 321.

Cummins, V. C., a minister in the Methodist Episcopal Church South, was born in Harrison County, Ky., in May, 1848. He joined the Church in 1863, was educated at the Kentucky Wesleyan University, and in 1872 connected himself with the Kentucky Conference, in which he labored until his death, July 20, 1875. See *Minutes of Annual Conferences of the M. E. Church South*, 1875, p. 223.

Cumner, JOHN, a Methodist Episcopal minister, was born in Massachusetts, about 1789. He was licensed to preach in 1826, and in 1833 entered the Maine Conference, in connection with which he labored, with the exception of a three years' location, until his death, Feb. 5, 1861. See *Minutes of Annual Conferences*, 1861, p. 109.

Cun—. See under CYN—.

Cundiff, WILLIAM, a Methodist Episcopal minister, was converted in 1824, licensed to exhort in 1825, in 1826 to preach, and was admitted into the Kentucky Conference. In 1830 he removed to Illinois, and in 1837 joined the Illinois Conference. He died in 1839 or 1840, aged about thirty-five. See *Minutes of Annual Conferences*, 1840, p. 54.

Cundinomarca was the goddess of love of the Mexicans, in whose temple religious and secular assemblies were held.

Cunego, Aloysio, an Italian engraver, the elder son and scholar of Domenico, was born at Verona in 1757, and resided principally at Leghorn, where he executed two works, *St. Margaret* and *Mary Magdalene*.

Cunego, Domenico, an Italian engraver, was born at Verona in 1727. He went to England and engraved the following plates: *Three Subjects of the Creation*, from the Sistine Chapel; *The Birth of St. John Baptist; The Prodigal Son; St. Cecilia Receiving the Palm of Martyrdom*. He died at Rome in 1794. See Hoefer, *Nouv. Biog. Générale*, s. v.; Spooner, *Biog. Hist. of the Fine Arts*, s. v.

Cunegonda (or **Kinge**), *Saint*, daughter of Bela IV, king of Hungary, and granddaughter of Theodore Lascaris I, emperor of Constantinople, married Boleslas, called *the Chaste*, king of Lesser Poland, but lived, like her husband, in a state of complete continence, devoting herself to the sick in the hospitals. After her husband's death, in 1279, she retired to a monastery at Sandecz, and died there, July 24, 1292. She was canonized by Alexander VIII in 1690. See Hoefer, *Nouv. Biog. Générale*, s. v.

Cungar, an early English anchorite, is said to have been the son of a prince at Constantinople, and went to Britain about A.D. 71, establishing a monastery in Congresbury (named from him), on the Yeo, and afterwards one in the north of Wales.

Cungi (**Congi**, or **Cugni**), three painters, brothers—GIOVANNI BATTISTA, LEONARDO, and FRANCESCO—were natives of Borgo San Sepolcro, where they flourished in the middle of the 16th century. They were chiefly employed in the churches and convents in their own country, especially in the Church of San Rocco and the convent of the Osservanti at San Sepolcro.

Cunha, *Don* **Rodrigo da**, a Portuguese prelate and writer, was born at Lisbon in 1577. He first studied with the Jesuits, then went to Coimbra; after being admitted to the Royal College of St. Paul, took orders, and familiarized himself especially with canonical jurisprudence. He was promoted in 1615 to the bishopric of Portalegre, and some years later to that of Oporto. In 1626 he occupied the archiepiscopal see of Braga. He also became primate of an important part of the peninsula, and occupied the archbishopric of Lisbon from 1635, where he gave further proof of his patriotism and love of independence when the revolution of 1640 placed the duke of Braganza upon the throne. In the absence of the new sovereign, he was chosen by the people governor of the kingdom. He died at Lisbon Jan. 3, 1643. We are indebted to this prelate for an *Ecclesiastical History of Oporto, Braga, and Lisbon*, in which he was aided by Pontaleo de Ciabra (Oporto, 1623, 1742). See Hoefer, *Nouv. Biog. Générale*, s. v.

Cunha (or **Cugna**), **Theodosius da**, an Augustinian and professor at Coimbra, who died April 26, 1742, is the author of, *Prœmialia Theologia Universæ:—Tractatus de Incarnatione, de Advocatione, de Resurrectione*. See Keller, in Wetzer u. Welte's *Kirchen-Lexikon*, s. v. (B. P.)

Cuniberct. See CYNEBERT.

Cunibert (**Hunibert**, or **Chunebert**), bishop OF COLOGNE in the 7th century, was born in the bishopric of Trier. He was made bishop in 623, and died in 663. He took an active part in the religious and political affairs of his time. Under Sigebert III and Childeric II he exercised a great influence. See *Gallia*

Christiana, iii; Gelenius, *De Adm. Magnitudine Coloniæ* (Cologne, 1645); Rettberg, *Kirchengeschichte Deutschlands*, i, 296; Hefele, in Wetzer u. Welte's *Kirchen-Lexikon;* Wagsnmann, in Herzog's *Real-Encyclop.* s. v. He is set down as a saint in Usuard's *Martyrology*, Nov. 12. (B. P.)

Cunibert of England, bishop and confessor, commemorated April 25, was educated at the monastery of Balmerino, in Fifeshire, and eventually betook himself as a recluse to the desert, where he died, about A.D. 690.

Cuniliati, Fulgente, an Italian theologian of the Dominican order, was born at Venice in 1685. He taught successively philosophy and theology, distinguished himself as a preacher, and became vicar-general of his order. He died Oct. 9, 1759, leaving several lives of saints and works of devotion, for which see Hoefer, *Nouv. Biog. Générale*, s. v.

Cunina, in Roman mythology, was a goddess who especially gave protection to new-born children; hence her name, from *Cuna*, the cradle.

Cuningham (also spelled **Cuninghame**, **Cunyngham**, etc.), the family name of many Scotch clergymen. See also Cunningham.

1. Adam, was licensed to preach in 1831; presented to the living at Eskdalemuir in 1835, and ordained in 1836; transferred to Crailing in 1843. See *Fasti Eccles. Scoticanæ*, i, 635.

2. Alexander (1), took his degree at the University of St. Andrews in 1631; was presented by the king to the living at Ettrick in 1641; refused to conform to episcopacy in 1662, and settled on his estate at Hyndhope, where his descendants resided two centuries afterwards. His son Alexander was minister to Venice, and was author of the *History of Great Britain, from* 1688 *to the Accession of George I*, translated from the Latin in 1787 by Dr. William Thompson. See *Fasti Eccles. Scoticanæ*, i, 546.

3. Alexander (2), took his degree at Glasgow University in 1646; was admitted to the living at Glasserton before 1664, and died before 1674. See *Fasti Eccles. Scoticanæ*, i, 731.

4. Alexander (3), took his degree at Edinburgh University in 1663; was appointed to the living at Colmonell in 1666; transferred to Monkton in 1676; ousted by the people at the Revolution in 1688, and died in 1692, aged about forty-nine years. See *Fasti Eccles. Scoticanæ*, i, 756; ii, 128.

5. Alexander (4), born at Glengarnock, was appointed to the living at Dreghorn in 1695, and ordained. He died in August, 1712, aged forty-seven years. See *Fasti Eccles. Scoticanæ*, ii, 164.

6. Charles (1), was licensed to preach in 1729; presented to the living at Tranent in 1739; ordained in 1740, and died April 4, 1793, aged ninety-one years. See *Fasti Eccles. Scoticanæ*, i, 360.

7. Charles (2), was licensed to preach in 1795; presented to the living at Lundie and Fowlis in 1797; ordained in 1798; transferred to Dailly in 1806, and died Aug. 10, 1815. See *Fasti Eccles. Scoticanæ*, ii, 108; iii, 718.

8. David (1), was in orders prior to the Reformation, and in 1562 was the first Protestant minister at Lanark, with a pension for life provided by the pope's bull from Rome. He was transferred to Lesmahago in 1570, thence to Cadder in 1572, and in 1574 had Monkland and Leinzie in charge; was joint visitor for Clydesdale, Renfrew, and Lennox in 1576, and was one of those who drew up the heads of policy in the second book of discipline. He was elevated to the bishopric of Aberdeen in 1577, the first of the reformed religion. He was commissioner for Aberdeen and Banff in 1578; accused of scandal in 1586; appointed visitor of King's College in 1594, and died Aug. 30, 1600. See *Fasti Eccles. Scoticanæ*, ii, 49, 306, 327; iii, 462, 466, 884, 887.

9. David (2), took his degree at Glasgow University in 1600; was presented to the living at Dunscore in 1609; was a member of the Court of High Commission in 1610, and again in 1619; transferred to Percietown in 1613, and continued there in 1631. See *Fasti Eccles. Scoticanæ*, i, 578; ii, 272, 345.

10. David (3), took his degree at Glasgow University in 1650; was admitted to the living at Cambuslang in 1663, and died about 1688. See *Fasti Eccles. Scoticanæ*, ii, 272, 273.

11. Gabriel (1), took his degree at Glasgow University in 1632; was admitted to the living at Kilsyth in 1637, and died in September, 1665, aged about fifty-four years. See *Fasti Eccles. Scoticanæ*, ii, 72.

12. Gabriel (2), took his degree at Glasgow University in 1642; was presented to the living at Dunlop in 1648; deprived in 1664 for not conforming to episcopacy, but restored in 1672. In 1674 he was charged with being a conventicle preacher; was called before the privy council in 1677 for not obeying the rules; and in 1683 was denounced, put to the horn, his movable goods seized, and his stipend given to the widow of another minister; but returned to his living in 1687, and was restored by act of parliament in 1690. He preached the opening sermon of the first General Assembly after the Revolution; was on the committee for visiting colleges, and died in May, 1691, aged about sixty-nine years. See *Fasti Eccles. Scoticanæ*, ii, 166.

13. George, was born April 24, 1766; licensed to preach in 1790; for some time taught in an academy at Westruther; presented to the living at Dunse in 1797, and ordained. He died suddenly, Jan. 9, 1847.

14. Hugh, was licensed to preach in 1781; presented to the living at Tranent as successor to his uncle Charles in 1784, and died July 20, 1801. He published *A Short Explanation of the Ten Commandments:—Sermon on the Death of his Mother:—Account of the Parish.* See *Fasti Eccles. Scoticanæ*, i, 360.

15. James (1), took his degree at Glasgow University in 1579; was reader at Dumbarton in 1585 and 1586; was appointed the first Protestant minister at Bonhill in 1588; continued in 1591; transferred to Cardross in 1596, and died before May 10, 1603, aged forty-four years. See *Fasti Eccles. Scoticanæ*, ii, 346.

16. James (2), took his degree at Glasgow University in 1602; was presented to the living at Buchanan in 1604; transferred to Dunlop in 1606, thence to Cumnock in 1608; was a commissioner to reside at Edinburgh for the ministers at the Tables in 1637; a member of the Commissions of Assemblies in 1643 and 1644, and died about the latter date, aged sixty-three years. See *Fasti Eccles. Scoticanæ*, ii, 103, 166, 348.

17. James (3), took his degree at the University of St. Andrews in 1648, residing in Edinburgh; was called to the living at Lasswade in 1659, and ordained; deprived by act of parliament in 1662, after the Restoration. See *Fasti Eccles. Scoticanæ*, i, 290.

18. James (4), took his degree at Edinburgh University in 1701; was licensed to preach in 1709; called to the living at Smailholm in 1710, and ordained. He died May 12, 1743, aged about sixty-two years. See *Fasti Eccles. Scoticanæ*, i, 532.

19. John (1), was admitted to baptize and solemnize marriages at Kirkmichael, in 1567; presented to the vicarage of Kirkcudbright-Innertig in April, 1571, where he was probably reader; promoted to the living at Dailly in 1574; admitted in 1575, having also Girvan and Kirkoswald under his care; removed to Girvan as the first Protestant minister there in 1590; continued in 1608, and died before April 6, 1612. See *Fasti Eccles. Scoticanæ*, ii, 106, 116.

20. John (2), took his degree at Glasgow University in 1595; was admitted to the living at Houston in 1599; transferred to Kilallan in 1602, thence to Dalry in 1604, and died in April, 1635, aged about sixty years. See *Fasti Eccles. Scoticanæ*, ii, 161, 214, 217.

21. John (3), took his degree at Glasgow University in 1621; was admitted to the living at Lecropt in

1627, and resigned in 1637. See *Fasti Eccles. Scoticanæ*, ii, 732.

22. JOHN (4), was presented to the living at Old Cumnock in 1647, and admitted; refusing to conform to episcopacy after the Restoration, in 1662, was confined to his parish, and died in October, 1668. See *Fasti Eccles. Scoticanæ*, ii, 103.

23. JOHN (5), was born at Enterkin; took his degree at Glasgow University in 1665; became curate to the bishop of the diocese, and was called to the living at Parton. He was accused before the privy council, in 1676, of holding conventicles at Bladenoch, Glenluce; was ousted by the people in 1689, and deprived by act of parliament, in 1690, restoring Presbyterian ministers. He died the same year, aged about forty-five years. See *Fasti Eccles. Scoticanæ*, i, 719.

24. JOHN (6), was licensed to preach in 1755; called to the living at Dalmellington in 1756, and ordained; transferred to Monkton and Prestwick in 1762, and died May 28, 1774, aged forty-four years. See *Fasti Eccles. Scoticanæ*, ii, 110, 129.

25. JOHN MACPHERSON, A.M., was licensed to preach in 1809; presented to the living at Newtyle in 1815, and ordained; transferred to Kinglassie in 1818, and died Sept. 8, 1847, aged sixty years. His son Hugh was a clergyman in the Church of England, near Durham. He published *A Short Address to the Congregation at Kirkcaldy* (1845). See *Fasti Eccles. Scoticanæ*, ii, 549; iii, 758.

26. PATRICK, took his degree at Edinburgh University in 1666, residing in Hawick; was licensed to preach in 1684; presented to the living at Lochrutton the same year, and ordained; transferred to Kirktown in 1687, and died about 1706. See *Fasti Eccles. Scoticanæ*, i, 504, 595.

27. RICHARD, son of the minister at Dreghorn, was licensed to preach in 1730; called to the living at Symington in 1733, and ordained. He died Nov. 4, 1760, aged fifty-six years. See *Fasti Eccles. Scoticanæ*, ii, 145, 146.

28. ROBERT (1), took his degree at Glasgow University in 1608; was licensed to preach in 1617; admitted to the living at Hawick in 1625; was a member of the General Assembly in 1638, of the Commission in 1647, and died after Oct. 8, 1656. See *Fasti Eccles. Scoticanæ*, i, 496.

29. ROBERT (2), took his degree at Edinburgh University in 1642; was admitted to the living at Ashkirk in 1649; deprived after the Restoration by act of parliament in 1662; indulged by the privy council in 1669; suspended again, but restored in 1689, and continued in 1690. See *Fasti Eccles. Scoticanæ*, i, 542.

30. ROBERT (3), took his degree at Edinburgh University in 1689; was licensed to preach in 1693; called to the living at Wilton in 1694, and ordained; joined with three others in 1703 in a dissent against an act of the synod on the government of the Church; was transferred to Hawick in 1712; went to Cornwall, England, for his health, in July, 1721, and died Aug. 5, 1722, aged about fifty-four years. See *Fasti Eccles. Scoticanæ*, i, 498, 517.

31. SAMUEL, secretary to his cousin, the archbishop of St. Andrews, in 1591, and afterwards schoolmaster at Forgan; was licensed to preach in 1611; presented to the living at Ferryport-on-Craig in 1615; subscribed to the covenant at Edinburgh in 1638, but was deposed for insufficiency, and died before Oct. 1, 1641. See *Fasti Eccles. Scoticanæ*, ii, 427.

32. WILLIAM (1), was appointed to the living at West Kilbride in 1658; deprived by the privy council in 1662, and died in January, 1669. See *Fasti Eccles. Scoticanæ*, ii, 190.

33. WILLIAM (2), was licensed to preach in 1681; presented to the living at Lochwinnoch in 1683, and deprived in 1689 for disloyalty to the king and queen. See *Fasti Eccles. Scoticanæ*, ii, 225.

34. WILLIAM (3), took his degree at the University of St. Andrews in 1692; was licensed to preach in 1700; called to the living at Kembach in 1702, and ordained; and died before Nov. 20, 1728, aged about fifty-seven years. See *Fasti Eccles. Scoticanæ*, ii, 433.

35. WILLIAM (4), son of the foregoing, took his degree at the University of St. Andrews in 1725; had a bursary; was licensed to preach in 1731; presented to the living at Mouswald in 1736; ordained in 1737; transferred to Durrisdeer in 1743; thence to Sanquhar in 1753; and died Aug. 25, 1758. See *Fasti Eccles. Scoticanæ*, i, 659, 674, 684.

36. WILLIAM BRUCE, was licensed to preach in 1831; presented to the living of Prestonpans in 1833, and ordained. He joined the Free Secession in 1843. He published, *Collegiate Education versus Collegiate Extension* (1850):—*Friendly Hints*, a tract:—*An Account of the Parish.* He was living in 1860. See *Fasti Eccles. Scoticanæ*, i, 353.

Cunison (or **Cunisone**), the family name of several Scotch clergymen:

1. ALEXANDER, son of John (2), was called to the living at Kilfinichen and Kilvickeon in 1706, and ordained in 1707. He was bitten by a mad dog, and caused himself to be bled to death, Nov. 15, 1717. See *Fasti Eccles. Scoticanæ*, iii, 84.

2. JOHN (1), born at Dunkeld, took his degree at the University of St. Andrews in 1615; was presented to the living at Dull in 1624; and died before Jan. 4, 1682, aged about eighty-six years. See *Fasti Eccles. Scoticanæ*, ii, 818.

3. JOHN (2), took his degree at the University of St. Andrews in 1644; was admitted to the living at Killin before 1650; transferred to Kilbride, Arran, in 1655; deprived by act of Parliament in 1662; returned to the living in 1687; was restored by act of Parliament in 1690; was a member of the General Assembly the same year; transferred to Killean and Kilchenzie in 1692; resigned on account of old age in 1697, but lived in Killean till his death. See *Fasti Eccles. Scoticanæ*, ii, 824; iii, 41, 45.

4. JOHN (3), took his degree at the University of St. Andrews in 1676; was admitted to the living at Dull in 1682; and died in August, 1693, aged about fifty-eight years. See *Fasti Eccles. Scoticanæ*, ii, 818.

Cunnera. See CAINNER.

Cunningham, Alexander, a Presbyterian minister, was born in Mercer, Pa., Jan. 21, 1815. He graduated at Washington College in 1840; studied theology at the Western Theological Seminary; was licensed by the Presbytery of Erie, Sept. 4, 1842; ordained by the same, Oct. 5, 1843, and installed pastor of the churches of Gravel Run and Washington. He was released from this charge in 1851, and dismissed to the Presbytery of Allegheny. He died at Whitestown, Sept. 5, 1874. See *Hist. of the Presbytery of Erie.*

Cunningham, Alexander Newton, D.D., a Presbyterian minister, was born near Jonesborough, Tenn., March 16, 1807. He graduated at Washington College, Tenn., in 1826, and at Princeton Theological Seminary in 1830; was licensed by New Brunswick Presbytery, April 28 of the same year; preached at Montgomery, Ala., from 1833 to 1836; at Augusta, Ga., from 1838 to 1842; was stated supply at Franklin, Tenn., from 1844 to 1858; also founded the Franklin Institute. He preached in Shelbyville from 1859 to 1862; then volunteered as chaplain in the Southern army, and labored in the hospitals at Montgomery, Ala.; from here he returned to Franklin, and was professor in the Female Institute. In 1874 he became pastor in Fayetteville, and in Aberdeen, Miss., where he continued until his death, Sept. 5, 1878. He was an excellent preacher and industrious student. See *Necrol. Report of Princeton Theol. Sem.* 1879, p. 26.

Cunningham, Amor D., a Methodist Episcopal minister, was born in Ripley County, Ind., July 12, 1833. He experienced religion and entered Brookville College in his nineteenth year, spent some years in school-teaching, and finally entered the Indiana Conference. In 1860 he assumed the editorship of the *Daily Indiana American*, and afterwards served some time as chaplain of the Fifth Indiana Cavalry. In 1862 he was transferred to the North-west Indiana Conference; subsequently was elected president of Northern Indiana College; and died Aug. 9, 1868. See *Minutes of Annual Conferences*, 1868, p. 250.

Cunningham, James, a Methodist Episcopal minister, was born in Philadelphia, Nov. 30, 1811. He was converted in 1829, licensed to exhort in 1832, joined the Philadelphia Conference in 1834, and labored therein until his death, in 1881. See *Minutes of Annual Conferences*, 1882, p. 71.

Cunningham (or **Cunnyngham**), **Jesse**, a minister in the Methodist Episcopal Church South, was born on the French Broad River, East Tenn., Oct. 25, 1789. He united with the Church at the age of nine; was converted in 1807; received license to preach in 1810; entered the Holston Conference in 1811, and continued his labors until his death, July 10, 1857. See *Minutes of Annual Conferences of the M. E. Church South*, 1857, p. 753.

Cunningham, John K., a Presbyterian minister, was born in Pennsylvania. He was a student in Jefferson College, and graduated from Princeton Theological Seminary in 1827; was licensed by the Presbytery of New Brunswick, April 23, 1828; ordained and became stated supply at Montour, Pa., in 1829, and then pastor from 1830 to 1838; pastor at Island Creek, O., from 1840 to 1852; stated supply at Wayne and Chester in 1854 and 1855; and died at Wooster in the latter year. See *Gen. Cat. of Princeton Theol. Sem.* 1881, p. 49.

Cunningham, John Whitfield, D.D., a Presbyterian minister, was born in Salem, Tenn., in 1805. He graduated from Washington College in 1823, and from Princeton Theological Seminary in 1824; was professor of Biblical literature and exegesis in Hanover Seminary, Ind.; and stated supply at Middle Fork from 1831 to 1834; was ordained by the Presbytery of Salem in the latter year; pastor at Jonesborough, Tenn., until 1845; stated supply of Second Church, Knoxville, for one year; pastor of Second Church, La Porte, Ind., from 1846 to 1849; agent of the American Home Missionary Society from 1859 to 1862; stated supply at Nora and Lena, Ill., for three years; labored for the Presbyterian missions in Illinois from 1865 to 1867; was stated supply for a Congregational Church in Naperville until 1871, and died there, Feb. 8, 1874. See *Gen. Cat. of Princeton Theol. Sem.* 1881, p. 57.

Cunningham, John William, an English clergyman, was born in London, Jan. 3, 1780. He graduated at St. John's College, Cambridge; was curate of Ripley, in Surrey; afterwards of Clapham; and in 1811 vicar of Harrow, where he remained to the close of his life, about 1861. Mr. Cunningham was editor of the *Christian Observer* eight years, beginning with 1850; and was an earnest advocate of the missionary and Bible societies. See (Lond.) *Christian Observer*, November, 1861, p. 878.

Cunningham, Joseph Parker, a Presbyterian minister, was born in Greene County, Ga., Jan. 21, 1799. He was educated in Transylvania University, Ky., and graduated from Princeton Theological Seminary in 1821; was licensed to preach by the New Brunswick Presbytery in 1822; in 1824 was ordained pastor of Concord Church by South Alabama Presbytery; in 1832 became stated supply at Mt. Pisgah, Ky., and died there in 1833. See Sprague, *Annals of the Amer. Pulpit*, iv, 60; *Gen. Cat. of Princeton Theol. Sem.* 1880, p. 26.

Cunningham, Nathaniel Pendleton, a Methodist Episcopal minister, was born in Pendleton County, Va., Aug. 1, 1807. He was converted in 1825; received license to preach in 1827; in 1829 entered the Baltimore Conference; and in 1837 was transferred to the Illinois Conference, wherein he served till his death, July 7, 1848. See *Minutes of Annual Conferences*, 1848, p. 283.

Cunningham, Oscar F., a minister in the Methodist Episcopal Church South, was born in Grayson County, Va., May 1, 1813. He embraced religion in his youth; was licensed to preach in his twenty-first year; and in 1835 united with the Holston Conference. After travelling several years he located, but subsequently was made presiding elder, in which office he continued nearly to the close of his life, June 15, 1848. See *Minutes of Annual Conferences of the M. E. Church South*, 1848, p. 169.

Cunningham, Richard, a Baptist minister, was born in Halifax, N. S., in 1812. He began to preach in 1828; was ordained pastor at Wilmot Mountain, March 25, 1829; and remained there about twenty years. He was subsequently pastor at Digby, N. S., and died Jan. 15, 1858. See Cathcart, *Bapt. Encyclop.* p. 300. (J. C. S.)

Cunningham, Robert, a Methodist Episcopal minister, was born in Butler County, Pa. He joined the Church in 1841, and in 1848 entered the Pittsburgh Conference, wherein he toiled until he became superannuated, in 1870. He died April 8, 1872. See *Minutes of Annual Conferences*, 1873, p. 41.

Cunningham, Robert M., D.D., a Presbyterian minister, was born in York County, Pa., Sept. 10, 1760. He removed with his father to North Carolina when he was in his fifteenth year; graduated at Dickinson College, Pa., in 1789; was licensed to preach by the Presbytery of South Carolina in 1792; in 1802 removed to Lexington, Ky., and became pastor of the Church at that place, where he remained until 1822. He died July 11, 1839. See Sprague, *Annals of the Amer. Pulpit*, iv, 58.

Cunningham, Timothy, a Free-will Baptist minister, was born in March, 1756. He served in the Revolutionary war; was converted in 1790, and commenced preaching soon after. He was ordained Jan. 25, 1804, by the Edgecomb Quarterly Meeting, Me., and, after a ministry of great usefulness, died, Jan. 16, 1836. See *Free-will Baptist Register*, 1837, p. 67. (J. C. S.)

Cunningham, T. M., D.D., a Presbyterian minister, was called to succeed Dr. Duncan, in the Church which bore the latter's name in Baltimore, Md., but declined, and was ordained pastor of the Presbyterian Church in St. Louis, Mo. After some years he removed as pastor to Indianapolis, and thence to the Alexander Church, Philadelphia. For the benefit of his health he went to San Francisco, Cal., and became pastor of the Central Church. He identified himself with the Presbyterian Theological Seminary there, and crossed the Continent several times in its behalf. He died at Oakland, Cal., Feb. 22, 1880. He was a preacher of distinguished ability, and his sermons were eloquent and powerful. See (San Francisco) *Occident*, March, 1880. (W. P. S.)

Cunningham, William, a Presbyterian minister, was born at Blairsville, Pa., June 14, 1827. He graduated from Jefferson College in 1852; spent three years teaching at Harrodsburg, Ky.; studied one year at the Western Theological Seminary at Allegheny, Pa., and graduated from Princeton Seminary in 1858. He was licensed by the Presbytery of Blairsville, June 17, 1857. In June, 1858, he went as supply to Blairsville; served as chaplain to a regiment of Pennsylvania Volunteers one year; after which he devoted himself to study and occasional preaching until 1863, when he went West. He served as stated supply Prospect Church, in the Presbytery of Peoria, and then the Church of Princeville, until 1865, teaching at the same time. Returning to Pennsylvania, he became pastor of Fairfield and Union churches, in the Presbytery of Blairsville. He died April 21, 1879. See *Necrol. Report of Princeton Theol. Sem.* 1880, p. 44.

Cunningham, William Madison, D.D., a Presbyterian minister, was born in Jonesborough, Tenn., June 28, 1812. He was a student of Washington College; graduated from Princeton Theological Seminary in 1833; was ordained by the Lexington Presbytery, June 26, 1835; served as pastor at Lexington, Va., until 1840; stated supply at Chattanooga, Tenn., for a short time; pastor at La Grange, Ga., from 1841 until his death, March 3, 1870. See *Gen. Cat. of Princeton Theol. Sem.* 1881, p. 75.

Cunningham, W. I. W., a Methodist Episcopal minister, was born in Indiana about 1830. He was converted in early life; educated in part in Asbury (now De Pauw) University; engaged in teaching for a time, and began preaching in 1858. After supplying a circuit in the North-west Wisconsin Conference, he was received into the travelling ranks, where he continued for six years, then took a supernumerary relation, and the next year was transferred to the Minnesota Conference, in which he labored until compelled to take a superannuated relation. He died April 3, 1882. See *Minutes of Annual Conferences*, 1882, p. 318.

Cunred, became abbot of the monastery of Sts. Peter and Paul (afterwards St. Augustine's) at Canterbury, in 803, and died in 823.

Cunuberthus. See CYNIBERCT (2).

Cunuulfus. See CYNEWULF.

Cunyngham. See CUNINGHAM, CUNNINGHAM.

Cuoenburg, an English abbess in Mercia, A.D. 811.

Cup OF BLESSING, a cup which was blessed among the Jews in ceremonial entertainments, or on solemn occasions. Paul employs the expression (1 Cor. x, 16) to describe the wine used in the Lord's supper.

CUP, EUCHARISTIC. See CHALICE.

CUP OF SALVATION, an offering, probably a libation of wine poured on the victim sacrificed on thanksgiving occasions, which the Jews of Egypt offered in their festivals for deliverance (2 Macc. vi, 27).

Cupé, PIERRE, a French theologian, who lived in the latter half of the 18th century, was rector of Bois, in the diocese of Saintes, and wrote *Le Ciel Ouvert à Tous les Hommes* (1768), a work reputed to be profane. See Hoefer, *Nouv. Biog. Générale*, s. v.

Cupella, in Christian archæology, is a small sepulchral recess for children, in the catacombs. At present we have only one instance of its use, which is given by Marchi (*Monumenti Primit.* p. 114). The inscription upon it records the burial of her two children, Secundina and Laurentius, by their mother Secunda. The solecisms in grammar and orthography of which it is full show that Secunda was a person of humble rank. The stone is preserved in the Museum Kircherianum.

Cupella is evidently the diminutive of *cupa*, explained to mean "urn," "sepulchral chest." This sense is a derivative one, from its classical meaning of a large cask, butt, or vat. It appears in pagan inscriptions but rarely. The use of the word survived until later times. The idea has been propounded that we may find in *cupella*, as a place of Christian burial, the etymology of the word *capella*, chapel, which has so long perplexed philologists, and of which no satisfactory derivation has ever yet been discovered. The architectural term *cupola* is another form of the same root.

Cupellomancy, divination by means of cups. The practice is very ancient. It was known in Egypt in the time of Joseph (Gen. xliv, 5), and is still practiced in England, among the ignorant, who profess to "read" in cups a sign of future events. See DIVINATION.

Cuper, WILLEM, a Flemish historian of the Jesuit order, was born at Antwerp in 1686, and died Feb. 2, 1741, leaving *De Patriarchis Constantinopolitanis* (Antwerp, 1733). Cuper aided in collecting the *Acta Sanctorum* of the Bollandists, July and August. See Hoefer, *Nouv. Biog. Générale*, s. v.

Cupīdo (*Cupid*), in Roman mythology, was the god of loving *desire*, a translation of the Greek πάθος. The name is more poetical than mythical, and usually he is identified with *Amor* (q. v.).

Cupola (Ital.), a concave ceiling, either hemispherical or of any other curve, covering a circular or polygonal area; also a roof, the exterior of which is of either of these forms, more usually called a dome, and in Latin *tholus*.—Parker, *Gloss. of Architect.* s. v.

Cupples is the family name of several Scotch clergymen:

1. GEORGE (1), son of the minister of Kirkoswald, was licensed to preach in 1752; appointed to the living at Swinton in 1754, and ordained. He died Sept. 14, 1798, aged seventy-one years. See *Fasti Eccles. Scoticanæ*, i, 447.

2. GEORGE (2), son of the minister of Swinton, was licensed to preach in 1807; became assistant at Dunbar; was presented to the living at Legerwood in 1811; ordained in 1812; elected presbytery clerk in 1825; transferred to the second charge, Stirling, in 1833; admitted in 1834; joined the Free Secession in 1843; and was admitted minister to the Free Church, Kilmadock, the same year. He died May 1, 1850, aged sixty-four years. See *Fasti Eccles. Scoticanæ*, i, 529; ii, 682.

3. WILLIAM, took his degree at Glasgow University; was licensed to preach in 1717; presented to the living at Kirkoswald in 1719; and was the first in Scotland who gave in a letter of acceptance with the presentation, according to the act of Assembly. He was ordained in 1720, and died March 17, 1751, aged about sixty-one years. He published *The Experiences of John Stevenson, Land-laborer of Dailly* (1729). See *Fasti Eccles. Scoticanæ*, ii, 121.

Cupra, in Roman mythology, was the name of Juno among the Etrurians. She had a temple at Firmum Picenum, in Asia.

Cura (*care*), in Roman mythology, was an allegoric deity of which a fable is told. In thought, she was sitting by the shore of the sea, and watching the waves. Unconsciously to herself, her fingers formed out of clay a form—and behold! it was man. She begged Jupiter to give him life, which he did, but required that the man should belong to him, to which Cura was opposed, as she had formed him, and, moreover, the earth, from which he had been taken, would not agree. Saturn, as judge, said: Jupiter shall receive the body after death, Cura shall have it during life, and his name shall be *homo* (man), because he was taken from *humus* (the earth).

Curaçāo is an island of the Caribbean Sea, belonging to the Dutch. A large proportion of the population consists of free negroes, and for their benefit the Netherlands Bible Society published in 1846 the Gospel of Matthew, to which, since 1865, the Gospel of Mark has been added by the American Bible Society.

Curae (*cares*), in Roman mythology, were revenging goddesses, who lived at the entrance to Tartarus.

Curate. We add an account of the *history* of this office from Walcott, *Sac. Archæol.* s. v.:

"Until the 4th and 5th centuries in the East there were country curates, and Cyprian mentions town clergy. In the large cities, from the 4th to the 5th century, in the East and at Rome, the churches had their own priests, who instructed the people, the communion being given only in the cathedral. In the beginning of the 4th century pope Marcellus established twenty-five titles for preparatory instruction before baptism and reconciliation of penitents. In the Greek Church cardinal priests discharged the same duty. In the beginning of the 5th century the bishop sent the eucharist for distribution to the parish priests: then by degrees the latter received power to reconcile penitents in case of necessity and heretics in danger of death, in the absence of the bishop; to visit the sick, to administer extreme unction, and to choose singers. In the 7th century the number of assistant clerks was augmented or diminished according to the condition of the Church revenues, as in the 6th century they had received authority to celebrate in their churches and oratories, chapels of ease required by the increase in the numbers of the faithful. The bishops gradually regarding them as fellow-workers, subordinated their assistants to them in all things touching divine worship and burial. It was not until the close of the 16th century, in England, that the word was restricted to assistant clergy, deputies, or substitutes. In France the latter are still called vicars. In England, in the Middle Ages, the distinction was drawn between temporary and perpetual curates."

Curcach (Corcair, or Quorrair) is the name of several Irish virgin saints, of whom only two are clearly traceable:

1. Commemorated March 8 or Aug. 8, is said to have been the sister of St. Finnian and daughter of Corpreus, of a princely family in Ulster, and to have lived in the middle of the 6th century.

2. Commemorated July 21 as the patron saint of Kilcorkey, in County Roscommon.

Curchus, a deity of the ancient inhabitants of Prussia, who was believed to preside over eating and drinking, on which account they offered to him their first-fruits, in his honor kept up a continual fire, and every year, breaking his old statue, erected a new one.

Curcneus. See CORCAN.

Curcodemus, an ancient deacon commemorated in Usuard's *Martyrology* as a martyr at Auxerre on May 4.

Curdie, JAMES, a Scotch clergyman, took his degree at Edinburgh University. He was licensed to preach in 1821, ordained in 1825 as missionary at Tarbert, presented to the living at Gigha and Cara in 1826, and admitted in 1827. He was there in 1860. See *Fasti Eccles. Scoticanæ*, iii, 41.

Cure BY FAITH. See FAITH-CURE.

Curētæ, in Greek mythology, were originally priests of the orgiastic Jupiter cultus on Crete. They were armed, and their worship consisted in weapon-dances. The latter was also the case with the Corybantes and with the Idæan Dactyles; therefore these three classes were eventually confused. According to Strabo, those Curetæ who were among the oldest inhabitants of Ætolia were different from the above.

Cureus, JOACHIM, a Protestant theologian and philosopher of Germany, was born at Freistadt, in Silesia, Oct. 22, 1532. He studied at Wittenberg, and in 1554 was rector in his native city. He then went to Padua and Bologna for the study of medicine, and after his return, in 1559, settled as physician at Glogau, where he took an active part in the introduction of the Reformation, but in the spirit of his friend Melanchthon. He died at Glogau, Jan. 21, 1573. One year after his death his *Exegesis Perspicua*, etc., appeared, which caused the deposition and expulsion of all Philippistic theologians by August of Saxony, because he believed them to be the authors of the same. See Grusinger, *Commentatio de Joach. Cureo* (Marburg, 1853); Heppe, *Geschichte des deutschen Protestantismus* (ibid. eod.), ii, 422 sq., 467-494; Herzog, *Real-Encyklop.* s. v. (B. P.)

Curia, FRANCESCO, a Neapolitan painter, was born in 1538, and was a pupil of Gio. Filippo Criscuolo; afterwards visited Rome, where he studied the works of Raphael. On his return to Naples he painted for the churches there. His masterpiece was a grand picture of *The Crucifixion*, in the Chiesa della Pieta. He died in 1610.

Curial (or Curiel), JUAN ALFONSO, a Spanish Benedictine, was professor of theology at Salamanca, where he died, Sept. 28, 1609. After his death were published *Lecturæ in D. Thomæ Aq.* 1, 2 (Douay, 1618; Antwerp, 1621): — *Controversiæ in Diversa Loca S. Scripturæ* (Salamanca, 1611). See Le Mire, *De Script. Sæc.* xvii; Nic. Antonio, *Biblioth. Hisp.* i, 631; Hurter, *Nomenclator*, i, 275; Langhorst, in Wetzer u. Welte's *Kirchen-Lexikon*, s. v. (B. P.)

Curig. See CYRICUS.

Curio was the president of a *curia* or ward in ancient Rome. His office was to officiate as priest. There were thirty *curiones*, and over these was a *curio maximus* or chief priest.

Curitan is the name of two early Irish saints:

1. Abbot and bishop of Rosmeinn, commemorated March 16, was one of those who assisted in releasing certain women of Erinn from bondage.

2. Of Kilmore, commemorated Aug. 9.

Curnan, an early Irish saint, commemorated Jan. 6, was bishop of Kilcoman, and was the son of Sinell, of the race of Coinan, in Ulster.

Curnock, NEHEMIAH, an English Wesleyan minister, was born at Bristol in 1810. He united with the Church at thirteen; began to preach at an early age; entered the ministry in 1834, and died July 26, 1869. He was known as "the children's preacher." He published a work entitled *The Father of Methodism* (Lond. 1847, 18mo). See *Minutes of the British Conference*, 1869, p. 27; Stevenson, *Wesleyan Hymn-book and its Associations* (Lond. 1870), p. 315.

Curradi (or Currado), FRANCESCO, a Florentine historical and portrait painter, was born in 1570, and studied under Battista Naldini. His *Magdalene*, and *The Martyrdom of St. Thecla*, in the Florentine galleries, are considered his best. He died in 1661. See Hoefer, *Nouv. Biog. Générale*, s. v.; Spooner, *Biog. Hist. of the Fine Arts*, s. v.

Curran, RICHARD AUGUSTUS, D.D., a Presbyterian minister, was born at Mifflintown, Pa., July 15, 1808. He graduated from Washington College in 1834, and from Princeton Theological Seminary in 1837; became stated supply at Millville, N. J., and Gallipolis, O., in 1838; Cassville, Ga., in 1839. He was ordained an evangelist by the Presbytery of New Jersey the same year, and became stated supply at Cedarville, N. J., and pastor in 1842; at Shavers Creek Church, Pa., in 1849; Cottage Church in 1854, and dismissed in 1859, on being appointed professor of Pottstown Cottage Seminary. He afterwards became stated supply and teacher at Huntington, Ind.; pastor at Minerva, O., in 1872; at Bethlehem, Pa., in 1874, and dismissed in 1875. He died at Bourbon, Ind., March 26, 1883. See *Necrol. Report of Princeton Alumni*, 1884. (W. P. S.)

Currelly, CHARLES, an English Wesleyan preacher, was born at Devonport, Jan. 4, 1806. He was converted at fifteen; began to preach in 1827; was received by the conference in 1830; and retired to Bristol in 1862, where he died, Sept. 29, 1868. See *Minutes of the British Conference*, 1869, p. 10.

Currie is the family name of numerous Scotch clergymen:

1. HENRY, a native of Kinross-shire, was licensed to preach in 1793; presented to the living at Carsphairn in 1802, and ordained; and died suddenly, Dec. 9, 1815, aged sixty-three years. See *Fasti Eccles. Scoticanæ*, i, 707.

2. JAMES (1), took his degree at Edinburgh University in 1645; was called to the living at Shotts in 1649, and ordained; deprived by act of Parliament in 1662; cited before the privy council in 1669 for keeping conventicles, but escaped censure by not appearing; accepted indulgence in 1672, thereby offending his parishioners, who forsook the church; was again cited in 1677 and in 1684 for keeping conventicles; refused to read the proclamation of thanksgiving for the escape of the king from the Rye-house plot, and was imprisoned in 1685; was returned to his charge at Shotts in 1687, and died before Jan. 24, 1693. See *Fasti Eccles. Scoticanæ*, ii, 297, 298.

3. James (2), took his degree at Edinburgh University in 1695; was licensed to preach in 1697; called to the living at Hoddam in 1700, and ordained; and died Feb. 25, 1726, aged fifty-two years. See *Fasti Eccles. Scoticanæ*, i, 621.

4. James (3), son of the minister at Hoddam, received a bursary in Glasgow University in 1741; was presented to the living of Kirkpatrick-Fleming in 1745; ordained in 1746; transferred to Middlebie in 1763; and died Oct. 24, 1773, aged fifty-seven years. See *Fasti Eccles. Scoticanæ*, i, 622, 624.

5. James (4), was licensed to preach in 1809; elected to the living at Catrine in 1815; ordained in 1816; and deposed in June, 1836, for intoxication. See *Fasti Eccles. Scoticanæ*, ii, 141.

6. John (1), took his degree at Edinburgh University in 1629; was called to the living at Culter in 1636; was deposed in 1653, but restored by the synod in 1661. He died in reduced circumstances. See *Fasti Eccles. Scoticanæ*, i, 218.

7. John (2), a native of Ochiltree, was called to the living at Oldhamstocks in 1694; ordained in 1695; transferred to Elgin in 1697, but not confirmed; transferred to Haddington in 1704; elected moderator of the General Assembly in 1709, and died June 18, 1720. See *Fasti Eccles. Scoticanæ*, i, 313, 377.

8. John (3), took his degree at Glasgow University in 1695; was licensed to preach in 1699; called to the living at Old Monkland in 1700, and ordained; and died in 1741, aged about sixty-six years. See *Fasti Eccles. Scoticanæ*, ii, 293.

9. John (4), took his degree at Edinburgh University in 1699; was licensed to preach in 1705; called to the living at Kinglassie the same year, and ordained. He adhered to the protest against loosing the four seceders in 1733, and died Sept. 22, 1765, aged about eighty-six years. He published *A Sermon at the Opening of the Synod* (1733); and seven separate works in vindication of the Church. See *Fasti Eccles. Scoticanæ*, ii, 548.

10. John (5), son of the minister of Old Monkland, took his degree at Glasgow University in 1725; was licensed to preach in 1730; called to the living at New Monkland in 1732; ordained in 1733, and died April 19, 1758. See *Fasti Eccles. Scoticanæ*, ii, 295.

11. John (6), a native of Dumfriesshire, was licensed to preach in 1816; presented to the living at Murroes in 1821, and ordained. He assumed the name of *Irving* in 1846, and died July 20, 1863. See *Fasti Eccles. Scoticanæ*, iii, 729.

12. William, took his degree at Edinburgh University in 1742; was licensed to preach in 1744; called to the living at Scone, but set aside in 1747; called and ordained assistant and successor to his father at Kinglassie in 1750; and died March 11, 1770, aged forty-eight years. See *Fasti Eccles. Scoticanæ*, ii, 548.

Currie, A. H., a Protestant Episcopal clergyman, entered the ministry about 1866, and throughout his life remained in the diocese of Virginia. In 1870 he was living in Warminster; in 1871 became rector of Tillotson Parish, residing at Glenmore; and continued in this rectorship until his death, Oct. 17, 1878. See *Prot. Episc. Almanac*, 1880, p. 171.

Currie, Robert O., D.D., a (Dutch) Reformed minister, was born of Scotch parentage, in 1806. He graduated from Rutgers College in 1829, and from New Brunswick Theological Seminary in 1834. His only settlement as a pastor was at New Utrecht, L. I., from 1835 to 1866, when he died. His mind was remarkable for clearness, precision, and strength; his learning was varied, accurate, and thorough. He was an excellent classical and Biblical scholar. As a preacher, he was instructive, direct, fervid, and strong. He wrote much for the religious periodical press. His only volume is a well-written memoir of his former pastor and friend, the Rev. Richard Sluyter. See Corwin, *Manual of the Ref. Church in America*, s. v. (W. J. R. T.)

Currier, John, a Free-will Baptist minister, was born at Meredith, N. H., May 13, 1809. He was converted at twenty-three; licensed to preach by the Durham Quarterly Meeting in May, 1838; and was ordained in January, 1842. Soon after he removed to Thornton, where he preached but a short time, and died Nov. 2, 1843. See *Free-will Baptist Register*, 1844, p. 75. (J. C. S.)

Curry, Hiram M., a Methodist Episcopal minister, was born in Adams County, O., April 7, 1818. He was converted in early life; in 1848 was admitted into the Ohio Conference; was transferred in 1863 to the Cincinnati Conference, and died March 3, 1874. See *Minutes of Annual Conferences*, 1874, p. 102; Simpson, *Cyclop. of Methodism*, s. v.

Curry, J. M., a Baptist minister, was born at Canning, N. B. He was appointed to a mission in Miramichi in 1860; ordained in 1864, at Norton; was pastor at Northampton, Rockland, South Richmond, Hampton, and Upham; and labored at Kars, Wickham, McDonald's Corner, Hammond Vale, Peticodiac, North River, and Shediac, all in New Brunswick. He died at Hillsborough, Feb. 8, 1880, aged forty-nine. See *Baptist Year-book for Maritime Provinces*, 1880; Bill, *Fifty Years with the Baptists*, p. 569.

Curry, Thomas M., a Methodist Episcopal minister, was born at Yorktown, Westchester County, N. Y., Feb. 13, 1831. He was converted at twenty-one; studied in the New York Conference Seminary; in 1856 entered the New York Conference, and died Sept. 17, 1868. See *Minutes of Annual Conferences*, 1869, p. 90.

Curry, William F., a Presbyterian minister, was born at Paris, Bourbon Co., Ky., July 23, 1800. He was educated at Transylvania University, Lexington; licensed by the New York Presbytery in 1822, and sent as a missionary to the northern part of Georgia, where his labors were abundantly blessed. About 1830 he was appointed general agent for the Home Missionary Society of northern Ohio. He died May 19, 1861. See Wilson, *Presb. Hist. Almanac*, 1862, p. 179.

Cursōrēs, Ecclesiæ, were messengers employed in the early Christian Church, in times of danger, to give private notice to each member of the time and place of holding meetings for worship. It was also the term used to denote messengers sent from one country to another upon the important affairs of the Church.

Cursŭālēs Equi (*post-horses*), i. e. horses belonging to the "public course;" called also for shortness *cursus*, "course." The Roman posting or postal system —the distinction between the two belongs to a late stage of civilization—was established by Augustus. According to the *Secret History* of Procopius, the day's journey consisted of eight posts, sometimes fewer, but never less than five. Each stable had forty horses, and as many stablemen. Bingham gives a quite incorrect idea of the system in describing the *cursuales equi* as being simply impressed for the army and exchequer. The early Christian emperors made minute laws regulating these messengers, and some of them evince their regard for the life and comfort of the animals. The clergy were exempt from this service, and from the tax for it. See Smith, *Dict. of Christ. Antiq.* s. v.

Cursus is the original name of the breviary (q. v.) in the Romish Church. The same term was used to denote the Gallican liturgy, which was used in the British churches for a long period, until the Roman liturgy came to be employed. See Liturgy.

Curtain (*cortina, aulæum, velum; βῆλον, παραπέρασμα, καταπέτασμα, ἀμφίθυρον*). Curtains were used in ancient churches for the following purposes: (1) to hang over the outer doorway of the church; (2) to close the doorway between the nave of the church and the sanctuary, or perhaps rather to fill the open panels or *cancelli* of the door, during the time of the consecration of the eucharist; (3) to fill the space between the pillars of the ciborium, or canopy of the altar; (4) curtains were also used in baptisteries.

Curtchew (**Cutchou**, or **Cowslan**) is apparently an early Scottish name for ST. CONSTANTINE (q. v.).

Curteis, THOMAS, D.D., an English divine, one of the prebendaries of the cathedral at Canterbury in 1755, rector of Sevenoaks, in Kent, of St. Dionis Backchurch, London, and one of the proctors in convocation for the diocese of Rochester, died April 28, 1775. See *Annual Register*, 1775, p. 209.

Curtenius, ANTONIUS, a Reformed (Dutch) minister, was born in Holland in 1698, and came to America in 1730. He was pastor at Hackensack until 1737; at Hackensack and Schraalenburgh until 1755; Brooklyn, Flatlands, Bushwick, Flatbush, New Utrecht, and Gravesend in 1756, when he died. See Corwin, *Manual of the Ref. Church in America*, 3d ed. p. 226.

Curti, Francesco, a Bolognese engraver, was born in 1603, and studied under Cherubino Alberti. The following are his principal plates: *The Virgin and St. Catherine; The Virgin Teaching the Infant Jesus to Read; The Marriage of St. Catherine; The Infant Christ Sleeping*. He died about 1670. See Hoefer, *Nouv. Biog. Générale*, s. v.; Spooner, *Biog. Hist. of the Fine Arts*, s. v.

Curti, Pietro, an Italian Hebraist of the Jesuit order, who was born in Rome in 1711, and died there April 4, 1762, was regarded as one of the best metaphysicians of his time. He taught Hebrew in the Roman College, and published several dissertations on difficult passages of Scripture, especially *Christus Sacerdos* (Rome, 1751):—*Sol Stans* (ibid. 1754):—*Sol Retrogradus* (ibid. 1756). See Hoefer, *Nouv. Biog. Générale*, s. v.

Curtice, CORBAN, a Congregational minister, was born at Windsor, N. H., Feb. 11, 1809. He studied at Hancock Academy, and graduated from Gilmanton Seminary in 1843; Oct. 5 of that year was ordained pastor of Northfield and Sanbornton Bridge (the latter now Tilton), N. H., and was dismissed May 3, 1870. The next three years he was acting pastor at Boscawen, and thereafter resided at Tilton, without charge, until his death, Feb. 19, 1881. See *Cong. Year-book*, 1882, p. 26.

Curtis, Chandler, a Baptist minister, was born at Wallingford, Conn., in 1795. In 1835 he went to the Indian country, under the direction of the American Baptist Board of Foreign Missions. The field of his labors was among various Indian tribes, from the Choctaws, on Red River, to the Omahas, far to the northwest. After five years' service he removed to Griggsville, Ill., in 1842 to Massachusetts, was pastor for two years in Westminster, and died July 27, 1881. He published, in 1866, *The Mystery of Iniquity*, and two volumes on *Christianity Delineated*. See *The Watchman*, Sept. 8, 1881. (J. C. S.)

Curtis, Daniel, an English Baptist minister, was born in London in 1799. He was converted in youth; baptized at Blandford Street Church in 1815, of which he was deacon for many years; and in 1827 assisted in forming a new Church for the Rev. J. Foreman, in Dorset Square. Being an occasional preacher for some years, Mr. Curtis was ordained pastor at Homerton Row, in August, 1837, and died July 26, 1853. See (Lond.) *Baptist Hand-book*, 1854, p. 48.

Curtis, David, a Baptist minister, was born at East Stoughton, Mass., Feb. 17, 1782. He graduated from Brown University in 1808; was pastor at two different times in Pawtuxet, R. I., and for one year postmaster of the village. For two years he preached in Harwich, Mass., and for about the same time at New Bedford; lived eight years in Abington, serving part of the time as pastor. His next pastorates, of two years each, were at Fisksville and Chepacket, both in Rhode Island. The last twenty-five years of his life were spent in his native place, and he died there, Sept. 12, 1869. See Fuller, *History of Harwich*, p. 226. (J. C. S.)

Curtis, Grandison, a minister in the Methodist Episcopal Church South, was born in Ohio, July 22, 1818. He joined the Baptists in early life; removed to the Pacific coast in 1850; in 1862 joined the Methodist Episcopal Church South; soon after was licensed to preach, and continued as a local preacher until 1871, when he entered the Columbia Conference, wherein he labored till his death, which occurred near La Grande, Union Co., Or., Jan. 21, 1873. See *Minutes of Annual Conferences of the M. E. Church South*, 1873, p. 908.

Curtis, Harvey, D.D., a Presbyterian minister, was born at Adams, N. Y., May 30, 1806. He graduated from Middlebury College, Vt., in 1831; studied the next year at Princeton Theological Seminary; was ordained pastor of the Congregational Church in Brandon, Vt., Feb. 18, 1836; in 1843 accepted a call from a Presbyterian Church in Madison, Ind., and remained there eight years. In 1852 he was called to the First Presbyterian Church in Chicago; in 1858 was elected to the presidency of Knox College, Ill., and died at Galesburg, Sept. 18, 1862. See Wilson, *Presb. Hist. Almanac*, 1863, p. 292; *Gen. Cat. of Princeton Theol. Sem.* 1881, p. 81.

Curtis, Henry, a Baptist minister, was born at Illston, Leicestershire, England, Oct. 11, 1800. He came to the United States in 1812; resided first in Otsego County, N. Y., and afterwards in the city of New York, where he joined the Baptist Church, and was licensed to preach, March 10, 1824. The same year he was ordained at Harpersville, N. Y.; in 1832 he became pastor of the Church in Bethany, where he remained fourteen years. He did much evangelical labor in Wayne County, during a period of thirty-five years, and thirteen churches were more or less under his pastoral care. He died about 1860. See Cathcart, *Baptist Encyclop.* p. 302. (J. C. S.)

Curtis, James, an English Methodist preacher, was born at Westwoodside, Lincolnshire, in 1797. Removing to Sheffield, he was converted at the age of seventeen, and devoted himself to Church work. In 1822 he entered the New Connection ministry, and for thirty-three years travelled in twenty-two circuits, most of them important ones. He became a superannuate in 1855, and died in the city of York, March 8, 1874. See *Minutes of the Conference.*

Curtis, John, a Wesleyan missionary, after spending three years in the theological institution at Richmond, England, was in 1868 appointed to Honduras, Central America, where he labored in various circuits. He returned to England in impaired health, and was ordained at the Conference of 1872. He was next appointed to Turk's Island, Bahama district, but was seized with pulmonary disease, and died at sea, on his homeward voyage, Aug. 6, 1874. See *Minutes of the British Conference*, 1875, p. 34.

Curtis, John D., a Methodist Episcopal minister, was born at Plymouth, England, Feb. 29, 1816. He came to Philadelphia, Pa., with his parents, when but three years of age; began preaching at the age of twenty; in 1837 united with the Philadelphia Conference; in 1876 became superannuated, and retired to the city of Wilmington, where he died, July 25, 1877. See *Minutes of Annual Conferences*, 1878, p. 22.

Curtis, Jonathan, a Congregational minister, was born at Randolph, Mass., Oct. 22, 1786. He graduated from Dartmouth College in 1811; was ordained at Epsom, N. H., in 1815; dismissed in 1825. His other charges were Sharon, Mass., Pittsfield, N. H., and South Woodstock, Conn. He died at Chicopee, Mass., Jan.

27, 1861. Mr. Curtis published several *Sermons* and *Addresses*. See *Cong. Quarterly*, 1861, p. 352.

Curtis, Joseph, an English Baptist minister, was born at Exeter in 1815. He labored as an evangelist while yet a layman in the Established Church; afterwards became a Baptist, gave up business entirely, and devoted himself to gratuitous labors from place to place, visiting the cottages, where he read, prayed, and conversed, announcing at each house his intention of preaching in the open air. He was some time pastor at St. Mary Ottery, and at Cranford, Middlesex. He died near Devoran, Cornwall, Dec. 18, 1878. See (Lond.) *Baptist Hand-book*, 1880, p. 294.

Curtis, Joseph E., a Presbyterian minister, was born at Wethersfield, Conn., Oct. 9, 1789. He graduated from Williams College, Mass., in 1815, and went to Virginia, where he was licensed by Hanover Presbytery in 1828, and installed pastor of Powhatan Church, remaining there until 1842. He died at Montrose, March 1, 1859. See Wilson, *Presb. Hist. Almanac*, 1860, p. 69.

Curtis, Joseph Wait, a Congregational minister, was born in Vermont. He graduated from Dartmouth College in 1811; was ordained, July 5, 1816, pastor at North Yarmouth, Me.; preached at Warren, O., from 1820 to 1832; was chaplain of Vermont penitentiary for two years; missionary in Canada in 1835; without a charge in Vermont the next year; and pastor at Hadley, Mass., from 1836 until his death, March 16, 1857. See *Trien. Cat. of Andover Theol. Sem.* 1870, p. 28.

Curtis, M. Ashley, D.D., a Protestant Episcopal clergyman, was rector for several years, until about 1856, in Society Hill, S. C. Shortly after he was rector of St. Matthew's Church, Hillsborough, N. C., and in this pastorate he remained until his death, in April, 1872. See *Prot. Episc. Almanac*, 1873, p. 133.

Curtis, Otis Freeman, a Congregational minister, was born in Hanover, N. H., July 6, 1804. He studied at Kimball Union Academy; read theology with Rev. William A. Chapin at Craftsbury, Vt.; and was ordained an evangelist Oct. 23, 1828. He was pastor at Barton and Irasburg the two following years; evangelist in Derby and other towns in northern Vermont (Barre, Peacham, Glover, Plainfield) from 1830 to 1835; preached in Canton (Ill.), Chicago, Racine, Kenosha, Waukesha, and Milwaukee; Shopiere from 1848 to 1850; installed at Emerald Grove, Wis., May 6, 1851; dismissed May 1, 1863; preached at Versailles, N. Y., among the Seneca Indians, from 1864 to 1867; was acting pastor at Dover, Ill., until 1874; without charge at Emerald Grove until 1878; and died at David City, Neb., July 1, 1879. See *Cong. Year-book*, 1880, p. 16.

Curtis, Reuben B., a Methodist Episcopal minister, was born in Lisbon, Me. He was converted in 1830, in 1845 joined the Maine Conference, in 1862 was transferred to the Wisconsin Conference, in 1868 became superannuated, and died May 21, 1872. See *Minutes of Annual Conferences*, 1872, p. 119.

Curtis, Thomas, D.D., a Baptist minister and educator, was born in England, and came to America about 1845, being then over fifty years of age. He preached for some time in Charleston, S. C., and eventually established a school for young ladies at Limestone Springs. He lost his life on a steamer that was burned on the Potomac in 1858. See Cathcart, *Baptist Encyclop.* s. v.

Curtis, Thomas F., D.D., a Baptist minister, was born in England in 1816. He was educated in the South Carolina University, and pursued his theological studies under the direction of his father, the Rev. Thomas Curtis, D.D. After several years' pastorate over a church near Boston, he was called to a professorship in Lewisburg University, Pa., where he remained until 1865. In 1867 he took up his residence in Cambridge, Mass., where he died in 1872. Dr. Curtis published a volume on *Inspiration*. He is also author of a work on *Communion*, and another entitled *Progress of Baptist Principles in the Last Hundred Years*. (J. C. S.)

Curtis, Timothy, an English Wesleyan minister, a native of Yorkshire, was sent in 1830 to Jamaica, and died at Falmouth, on that island, Dec. 24, 1854, in his forty-ninth year. See *Minutes of the British Conference*, 1855.

Curtis, William, a Congregational minister, was born in Hoxcy, Lincolnshire, England, May 15, 1798. He first united with the Primitive Methodist Church and entered its ministry; came to Illinois in 1830, and joined the Methodist Episcopal Church, but withdrew in 1832; then organized a church at Albion, and was ordained its pastor; and eventually five other churches. He died June 15, 1877.

Curtis, William A., a Protestant Episcopal clergyman, graduated from the General Theological Seminary, N. Y. He was rector of St. Peter's Church, Hobart, for many years, until his death, in Norwich, Conn., Oct. 31, 1862. See *Prot. Episc. Almanac*, 1863, p. 94.

Curtiss, Caleb, a Congregational minister, graduated from Princeton College, studied theology, and was ordained pastor at Charlton, Mass., in 1761. He was dismissed in 1776, after which he represented the town in the Provincial Congress, and served in other public capacities. He died March 21, 1802. See Alexander, *Princeton College in the 18th Century*.

Curtiss, Claudius G., a Methodist Episcopal minister, was born in Niagara County, N. Y., Jan. 16, 1823. He was converted in his twentieth year, and immediately joined the Methodist Episcopal Church. In 1854 he removed to Markham, Canada, where he was licensed to preach by the Canada Wesleyan Church. In 1860 he united with the Evangelical Association, was ordained, and appointed to Seneca charge. In 1867 he returned to the Methodist Episcopal Church, and was received as a member of the East Genesee Conference. He took a supernumerary relation in 1881, and retired to his home in Hammondsport, where he died, Aug. 18, 1882. See *Minutes of Annual Conferences*, 1882, p. 320.

Curtiss, Samuel Ives, a Congregational minister, was born at Meriden, Conn., March 5, 1803. He studied in the preparatory department of the Bangor Theological Seminary, and in 1832 graduated from Yale Divinity School. In November of that year he was ordained pastor in East Hampton, remaining there five years. From 1837 to 1839 he was acting pastor in West Woodstock, four years acting pastor at Union, and from April 12, 1843, regular pastor until his death, March 26, 1880. See *Cong. Year-book*, 1881, p. 20.

Curtiss, William M., a minister in the Methodist Episcopal Church South, was born at Norway, Herkimer Co., N. Y., Aug. 6, 1798. He received a liberal education; went to Mississippi when about twenty-two, and engaged in teaching; joined the Church in 1821; and in 1822 was licensed to preach, and admitted into the Mississippi Conference. In 1837 he located; in 1855 re-entered the effective ranks; in 1861 became superannuated, and died Feb. 9, 1863. See *Minutes of Annual Conferences of the M. E. Church South*, 1864, p. 495.

Curtius, SEBASTIAN, a Reformed theologian of Germany, doctor and professor of theology at Marburg, where he died, May 30, 1684, is the author of *Radices Ling. S. Hebr.* (Weimar, 1629, 1645, 1649; Amsterdam, 1652):—*Manuale Hebræo-Chald. Lat. Belgicum* (Frankfort, 1668):—*Kleiner Juden Katechismus* (Cassel, 1650). See Jöcher, *Allgemeines Gelehrten-Lexikon*, s. v.; Steinschneider, *Bibliogr. Handbuch*, s. v.; Wolf, *Bibl. Hebræa*, ii, 551; Fürst, *Bibl. Jud.* i, 193 (where the first two works are erroneously ascribed to *Cursius*). (B. P.)

Curvius. See CUARAN.

Curwen, Hugh, an Irish prelate, was a native of

Westmoreland, and became dean of Hereford in 1541. On Oct. 20, 1555, he became archbishop of Dublin; in 1557 was constituted one of the lords-justices of Ireland; in June, 1559, was appointed keeper of the great seal of Ireland; in 1560 was one of the spiritual lords, who sat in the Parliament; in 1563 was again constituted lord-chancellor; in 1567 procured his translation to Oxford, and spent one year there. He died at Swinbrook in November, 1568. See D'Alton, *Memoirs of the Archbishops of Dublin*, p. 235.

Curwen, John, an English Congregational minister, was born at Heckmondwike, Yorkshire, Nov. 14, 1816. He was early brought to Christ; was educated at Coward College, and at University College, London; became assistant minister in the Church at Basingstoke in 1838; in 1841 co-pastor at Stowmarket, Suffolk; in 1844 pastor at Plaistow; resigned in 1867, on account of ill-health, and devoted himself to the improvement of Church music, establishing a printing and publishing business for that purpose. He died May 26, 1880. He published, *The Little Tune-book Harmonized:—The Child's Own Hymn-book:—The Standard Course of the Tonic-sol-fa Method:—How to Observe Harmony:—The Teacher's Manual:—Musical Statics:—Constructive Exercises in Elementary Musical Composition:—Musical Theory*, and other works. See (Lond.) *Cong. Year-book*, 1881, p. 366.

Curwen, Spedding, an English Congregational minister, was born at Whitehaven, Cumberland, Jan. 19, 1790. He was brought up in the Established Church, but joined the Independents at Leeds, and was soon engaged in speaking at weekly prayer-meetings and at adjacent villages on Sunday evenings, and finally became a student in Rotherham College. He was ordained at Heckmondwike in December, 1814; was called to the Church at Cottingham, near Hull, in 1819, also preaching on Sunday evenings at Fish Street Chapel; and accepted a call from the Church at Barbican, London, in 1824. While there he, with others, founded the Christian Instruction Society. In 1828 he went to Frome, Somersetshire, where he labored for eleven years; in 1838 he settled for a few months at Newbury, whence he was called by the new society at Castle Street, Reading, and there remained until his death, Jan. 9, 1856. See (Lond.) *Cong. Yearbook*, 1857, p. 173-175; *Evangelical Mag*. March, 1856.

Curwin, George, a Congregational minister, son of Hon. Jonathan Curwin, was born at Salem, Mass., May 21, 1683. He graduated from Harvard College in 1701; was ordained in Salem, as colleague to the Rev. Mr. Noyes, May 19, 1714; and died Nov. 23, 1717. See Sprague, *Annals of the Amer. Pulpit*, i, 254.

Cusa (Cusan, or **Cusanus)**, an early English abbot of the Wicii, in the latter part of the 8th century.

Cusari, The Book of. See Jehudah (*Ha-Levi*) *ben-Samuel*.

Cushen, Samuel, a Methodist Episcopal minister, was born in Frederick County, Md., March 21, 1796. He joined the Church at the age of eighteen, and in 1818 entered the travelling ministry, wherein he labored as his health would permit until his decease, in July, 1825. See *Minutes of Annual Conferences*, 1825, p. 475; *Methodist Magazine*, vii, 366.

Cushing, Caleb, a Congregational minister, was born at Scituate, Mass. He graduated from Harvard College in 1692; was ordained pastor of the First Church in Salisbury, Mass., Nov. 9, 1698. The Rev. Edmund Noyes became his colleague, Nov. 20, 1751. Mr. Cushing died Jan. 25, 1752, aged eighty years. See Sprague, *Annals of the Amer. Pulpit*, i, 453.

Cushing, Christopher, D.D., a Congregational minister, was born at Scituate, Mass., May 3, 1820. In 1844 he graduated from Yale College; spent one year in Yale Divinity School, and in 1847 graduated from Andover Theological Seminary. In February, 1849, he was ordained pastor of the Edwards Church, Boston, and remained there until April, 1851; from September following until September, 1868, was pastor in North Brookfield; for ten years, from 1867, was secretary of the American Congregational Union; from January to July, 1879, treasurer of the Massachusetts Home Missionary Society; from 1867 to 1875 one of the editors of the *Congregational Quarterly*, and was its sole editor and proprietor during the succeeding three years. In 1855 he became one of the overseers of the Charity Fund of Amherst College; from 1852 to 1863 he prepared and published the *Annual Reports* of the Brookfield Auxiliary Foreign Missionary Society. He also published many *Sermons* and *Addresses*. He died Oct. 23, 1881. See *Cong. Year-book*, 1882, p. 26.

Cushing, Jacob, D.D., a Congregational minister, son of Rev. Job Cushing, of Shrewsbury, Mass., graduated from Harvard College in 1748; was ordained pastor in Waltham, Nov. 22, 1752; and died Jan. 18, 1809, aged seventy-nine years. See Sprague, *Annals of the Amer. Pulpit*, i, 514.

Cushing, James Royal, a Congregational minister, was born at Salisbury, N. H., Nov. 24, 1800. He studied at the Thetford (Vt.) Academy; graduated from Bangor Theological Seminary in 1828; the next year, Aug. 12, he was ordained pastor of the Church in Boxborough, Mass., where he remained until June 10, 1833; the next two years was city missionary in Boston; from June, 1835, until April, 1844, pastor in East Haverhill; from November following until May, 1854, pastor in Wells, Me. After this he was acting pastor in the following places: Taunton, Mass., until 1861; North Rochester till 1869; Cotuit Port the next year; Waquoid, 1871-74; subsequently resided without charge at East Haverhill until his death, June 11, 1881. See *Cong. Year-book*, 1882, p. 27.

Cushing, Job, a Congregational minister, was born at Hingham, Mass. He graduated from Harvard College in 1714; was ordained first pastor of the Church in Shrewsbury, Dec. 4, 1723; and died Aug. 6, 1760, aged sixty-seven years. See Sprague, *Annals of the Amer. Pulpit*, i, 514.

Cushing, Jonathan, a Unitarian minister, was born at Hingham, Mass., in 1690. He graduated from Harvard College in 1712; was ordained at Dover, N. H., Sept. 18, 1717; and died March 25, 1769. See Sprague, *Annals of the Amer. Pulpit*, viii, 74.

Cushing, Jonathan Peter, a Presbyterian minister, was born at Rochester, N. H., March 12, 1793. He studied at Phillips Academy, Exeter; graduated from Dartmouth College in 1817; went to Virginia, and became connected with Hampden-Sidney College, first as a tutor, then as a professor, and after the death of Dr. Hodge, in 1820, as president, in which office he continued until the close of his life, April 25, 1835. See Sprague, *Annals of the Amer. Pulpit*, iv, 524.

Cushing, Perez Lincoln, a Baptist minister, was born in Boston, Mass., March 6, 1822. He graduated from Brown University in 1849; spent one year at the Newton Theological Institution, and was ordained in 1852. For six years thereafter he was chaplain of the Reform School at Westborough; and subsequently, for twelve years, of the State Almshouse at Bridgewater. He was also a teacher at Middleborough for a time. He died at Santa Barbara, Cal., March, 14, 1875. See *Newton General Catalogue*, p. 39. (J. C. S.)

Cushing, Samuel A., a Methodist Episcopal minister, was born at Brattleborough, Vt., Jan. 24, 1812. In 1831 he entered the ministry, and the following year joined the Vermont and New Hampshire Conference, where he served eleven charges in New Hampshire. His health failing, he became superannuated, supplying, for a season, East Cambridge. Taking a transfer in 1844 to New England Conference, he filled four more pastorates; and from 1859 was again a superannuate.

During the Rebellion he entered the work of the Christian Commission, until himself prostrated by disease, which terminated his life at Waltham, Mass., March 10, 1881. See *Minutes of Annual Conferences*, 1881, p. 83.

Cushman, Chester Lemuel, a Congregational minister, was born at Stafford, Conn., March 29, 1831. He graduated at Amherst College in 1856; was ordained pastor at Townshend, Vt., Dec. 22, 1859; dismissed Oct. 15, 1866; became pastor at Ludlow and Phillipston, Mass., and at Ludlow Mills; and died April 21, 1880. See *Minutes of Gen. Convention of Vermont*, 1881, p. 49.

Cushman, Elisha, a Baptist minister, son of Rev. Elisha Cushman, was born at Hartford, Conn., July 4, 1813. In March, 1836, he commenced, with Mr. Isaac N. Bolles, the publication of what was subsequently known as the *Hartford Courier*, a political newspaper. In March, 1838, he began a religious paper, the *Christian Secretary*, the organ of the Baptists in Connecticut, which had been discontinued for a short time. In the autumn of 1839 he became a Christian, and united with the First Baptist Church in Hartford. Soon after this he retired from the editorship of the political paper, of which he had had charge, and confined his attention to the *Secretary*. In April, 1840, he was licensed to preach, and was ordained pastor of the Baptist Church in Willington, Sept. 30 of the same year. He now gave up his editorial work, and devoted himself to his Church, of which he remained pastor for five years, when, in consequence of ill-health, he resigned. In a year or two his health was so far restored that he was able to resume his ministerial work, and in April, 1847, he accepted a call to the pastorate of the Church at Deep River, where he continued for several years. He afterwards acted as pastor of the Church in West Hartford for some time, and returned, at length, to his former position as editor of the *Christian Secretary*, for a season, performing the duties of pastor of the Church at Bloomfield. His death occurred at Hartford, Jan. 4, 1876. See the *Cushman Genealogy*, p. 408; Turnbull, in the *Christian Secretary*, Jan. 12, 1876. (J. C. S.)

Cushman, Isaac Jackson, a Presbyterian minister, was born in Ohio. He graduated from the Miami University, Oxford, O., in 1858, and entered the Theological Seminary at Xenia; was licensed to preach by the Chillicothe Presbytery in 1859, and in 1860 was ordained by the Cincinnati Presbytery pastor at Murdock, where he remained till his death, Aug. 26, 1881, at the age of forty-nine. (W. P. S.)

Cushman, Isaac Somes, a Methodist Episcopal minister, was born at New Gloucester, Me., in 1823. He graduated from Bowdoin College in 1844; subsequently from the Medical School of the same college; and for three years practiced medicine in Saco. In 1851 he entered Concord Biblical Institute, and in 1853 joined the New England Conference. During the civil war he was chaplain of the Thirty-third Massachusetts Regiment, and afterwards surgeon of the First Massachusetts Cavalry. In 1864 he re-entered the pastorate in the Maine Conference; and in 1867 was transferred to the New England Conference, in which he continued until his sudden death, Sept. 6, 1870. See *Minutes of Annual Conferences*, 1871, p. 87.

Cushman, Job, a Congregational minister, was born at Kingston, Mass., Jan. 17, 1797. He studied at the Kingston Grammar School; graduated from Brown University in 1819; studied theology with Calvin Park, D.D., and was ordained in Springfield, N. H., July 6, 1825, where he remained pastor three years. During 1828 and 1829 he was acting pastor in Bristol; the next two years in Sullivan; 1832 in Westford, Conn.; from 1833 to 1835 in North Wrentham (now Norfolk), Mass.; until 1839 pastor in Prescott; from 1841 to 1843 acting pastor in Tolland; from 1852 to 1854, in Palmyra, Pewaukee, and Watertown, Wis.; from 1856 to 1859 in Truro and North Truro, Mass.; until 1861 in Marlborough, Vt.; 1862 in Plymouth, Mass. From 1863 to 1867 he resided in Plymouth without charge, and thereafter in Grinnell, Ia. He died Aug. 5, 1878. He published, *Address on Washington's Birthday* (1835):—*The Law of God:—The Living and the Dead:—Revivals of Religion Desirable:—The Blessedness of Living in the Present Age:—A Complaint; Appeal to Churches of the Old Colony* (1871). See *Cong. Year-book*, 1879, p. 40.

Cushman, Ralph, a Presbyterian minister, was born in Massachusetts in 1792. He graduated from Williams College in 1817, and from Andover Theological Seminary in 1820; was ordained Nov. 16, 1821; travelled as a home missionary in Kentucky from that time to 1824; and then settled at Pittsford, N. Y., until 1826, and at Manlius until 1830, when he acted for a year as an agent for the American Home Missionary Society; and removing to Ohio the same year, died at Wooster, Aug. 27, 1831. See *Presbyterianism in Central N. Y.* p. 504; *Trien. Cat. of Andover Theol. Sem.* 1870, p. 41.

Cushman, Richards, a Congregational minister, was born in Massachusetts in 1819. He graduated from Brown University in 1844, and studied one year thereafter in Andover Theological Seminary; was ordained in 1847 a missionary for the Foreign Evangelical Society to Hayti, where he remained until his death, June 7, 1849. See *Trien. Cat. of Andover Theol. Sem.* 1870, p. 175.

Cushman, Robert Woodward, D.D., a Baptist minister, son of Job Cushman, a lineal descendant of Robert Cushman, of the Pilgrim Fathers, was born at Woolwich, Me., April 10, 1800. For some time he was engaged in the watchmaking and jewelry business. Having become a Christian, and fitted for college, he entered Columbian College, Washington, D. C., and graduated in 1826. By his own efforts he paid his way while procuring an education, yet took a high rank as a scholar. He was ordained, August, 1826, pastor of the Baptist Church in Poughkeepsie, N. Y., and a little more than a year afterwards removed to Philadelphia. In 1828 he established "a young ladies' institute" of a high order, still constantly employed as a preacher, and for a time was the editor of the *Christian Gazette*. In the various organizations for religious work, established by his denomination, he took an active interest. He was one of the early and warm friends of the American Baptist Publication Society. After nearly twelve years of labor in Philadelphia, he was called to the pastorate of the Bowdoin Square Church, in Boston, and was installed July 8, 1841. In the winter of 1847–48 he went to Washington, to take charge of the E Street Baptist Church in that city during the temporary absence of its pastor, Rev. G. W. Samson. He remained in Washington, and established a ladies' school, which he conducted for five years, and then returned to Boston, to become the principal of the "Mount Vernon Ladies' School." In 1863 he retired from active life on account of impaired health, and spent his closing years in Wakefield, Mass., where he died, April 7, 1868. (J. C. S.)

Cushman, Rufus Spaulding, D.D., a Congregational minister, was born at Fairhaven, Vt., Aug. 31, 1815. He studied at Castleton Seminary; graduated from Middlebury College in 1837; was a teacher in Pickens County, Ala., in 1838 and 1839, and in Lowndes County, Miss., in 1840. He became a member of Lane Theological Seminary in 1841, and graduated from Auburn Theological Seminary in 1843; was ordained at Orwell, Vt., Dec. 21 of the same year; dismissed May 7, 1862; May 28 following was installed over the Church at Manchester, and died May 18, 1877. See *Gen. Cat. of Auburn Theol. Sem.* 1883, p. 265.

Cushny, Alexander (1), a Scotch clergyman, took his degree at King's College, Aberdeen, in 1774; became schoolmaster of Foveran; was licensed to preach in 1782; presented to the living of Oyne in 1786, and ordained; and died Feb. 1, 1839, aged eighty-five years.

Two of his sons were ministers — Dr. Alexander, at Rayne; Robert, at Bellie. See *Fasti Eccles. Scoticanæ*, iii, 597.

Cushny, Alexander (2), D.D., a Scotch clergyman, took his first degree at Marischal College, Aberdeen, in 1805; commenced teaching in his youth; was presented to the living at Strachan in 1814; ordained in 1815; transferred to Rayne in 1820; elected synod clerk in 1825; deposed in 1842 by the assembly, with others, for holding communion with the deposed ministers at Strathbogie, but the sentence was reversed in five months. His knowledge of business, intrepidity, and straightforward conduct were of great service in defeating the plans of the non-intrusion party in the synod. He had a son, John, minister of Speymouth. See *Fasti Eccles. Scoticanæ*, iii, 542, 600.

Cushny, Robert, a Scotch clergyman, took his degree at Marischal College, Aberdeen, in 1826; was licensed to preach in 1831; presented to the living at Insch in 1836, and ordained assistant and successor; transferred to Bellie in 1843, and continued in 1860. See *Fasti Eccles. Scoticanæ*, iii, 582.

Cusighe, Simone da, an old painter of the Venetian school, flourished at Cusighe, a place near the city of Belluno, from 1382 to 1409. There is a good altarpiece executed by him in his native place. See Spooner, *Biog. Hist. of the Fine Arts*, s. v.

Cusp (Lat. *a spear-point*), the projecting points forming the featherings or foliations in Gothic tracery, arches, panels, etc.; they came into use during the latter part of the Early English style, at which period they were sometimes worked with a small leaf, usually a trefoil, on the end. When first introduced, the cusps sprang from the flat under-surface or soffit of the arch, entirely independent of the mouldings, and this method was sometimes followed in Decorated work; but they very soon began to be formed from the inner moulding next the soffit (usually either a splay or a hollow), and this continued to be the general practice until the expiration of Gothic architecture. Some of the richest examples may be found in Lincoln Cathedral. See Panel.

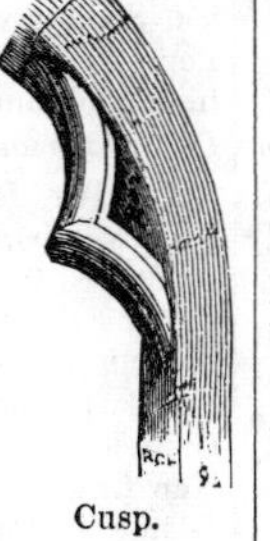
Cusp.

In the *Decorated* and *Perpendicular* styles they were frequently ornamented at the ends, either with heads,

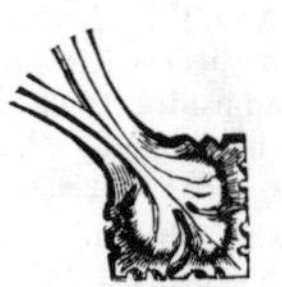
Crosby Hall.

Screen, Lincoln Cathedral.

leaves, or flowers, and occasionally with animals.—Parker, *Gloss. of Architect.* s. v. See Foils.

Custōdēs Archivōrum (*keepers of the records*) were the same as the *Ceimeliarchs* (q. v.).

Custōdēs Ecclesiæ (*keepers of the church*) were, in ancient ecclesiastical use, either those otherwise called *Ostiarii*, one of the inferior orders in the early Church, or, more probably, perhaps, the same officers who are sometimes distinguished as "elders of the Church," and whose duties corresponded in certain points with those of the modern Churchwarden (q. v.).

Custōdes Locōrum Sanctōrum (*keepers of the holy places* of Palestine), so called because of their relation to our Lord's earthly history: e. g. Bethlehem, Mount Golgotha, the Holy Sepulchre, Mount Olivet. Such an office was probably occasioned by the custom which arose among Christians in early times of visiting these places for purposes of piety and devotion; and that the function of these "keepers" was accounted a religious service appears from their having been exempted, by a statute of Theodosius, in the same manner as ecclesiastics generally, from personal tribute, out of regard to this their special employment.—Smith, *Dict. of Christ. Antiq.* s. v.

Custos (*warden*) is specially the treasurer or chief sacristan in a foreign cathedral. See Custos Arcæ.

There were anciently also various others thus designated: the *custos ordinis*, one of the great monastic officers, the third and fourth priors, who acted as the rounds; the *custos feretri*, the shrine-keeper; the *custos operis* or *fabricæ*, the canon in charge of repairs of the building, in secular cathedrals; the four *custodes* at Exeter, attendants in the sacristy, bell-ringers, and marshalmen in processions; and the *custos puerorum* at Salisbury, a canon who had the supervision of the choristers.—Walcott, *Sac. Archæol.* s. v.

Custos Arcæ (*keeper of the chest*) was a name given to the archdeacon, as having charge of the treasury of the Church, and the care of dispensing the oblations of the people. In this capacity Cæcilian was accused by the Donatists of having prohibited the deacons from carrying any provision to the martyrs in prison. The fourth Council of Carthage directs the bishop not to concern himself personally in the care and government of widows, orphans, and strangers, but to commit the duty to his archpresbyter or archdeacon.—Smith, *Dict. of Christ. Antiq.* s. v.

Cusworth, Joseph, an English Wesleyan minister, was born near Rotherham, Yorkshire. He was converted in Sheffield in 1804; in 1807 was received into the ministry; from 1843 was governor of Kingswood School, and to him is due the erection of the noble building at Lansdown, Bath; and for twenty-seven years was one of the treasurers of the Home Mission and Contingent Fund. He died March 19, 1857, in the seventy-first year of his age. See *Minutes of the British Conference*, 1857.

Cuthbald was a monk and at length abbot of Medeshamstede (afterwards Peterborough) in 680, and a man of great piety and wisdom. See also Cuduald.

Cuthberht was a presbyter of Lichfield, A.D. 803.

Cuthbert, archbishop of Canterbury, was born in Mercia, of noble parents, and was high in favor with the king. In 736 he was appointed to the see of Hereford, and in 741 was translated to the see of Canterbury, and proceeded to Rome soon after. He seems to have agreed with Boniface, that the centre of unity must be the see of Rome, and was ambitious of establishing this principle in the Church of England. He obtained the permission of the king to convene a synod, which in 747 met at Clovesho, and there he carried many of his points; but the proposal to bring the Anglican Church under subjugation to the see of Rome, although noticed, was very quietly evaded. We hear very little of the provincial labors of Cuthbert after this council. He died in 758. See Hook, *Lives of the Archbishops of Canterbury*, i, 217 sq.

Cuthbert was also the name of two early English abbots:

1. Of Malmesbury, in the latter part of the 8th century.

2. Of Jarrow and Wearmouth, in the same century. He was a disciple of Bede, and several of his *Letters* are extant. See Smith, *Dict. of Christ. Biog.* s. v.

Cuthbert, Hayhurst, an English minister of the Society of Friends, was born in Yorkshire about 1632, and was among the first in that county who embraced the principles of the Quakers. Soon after reaching his majority he became an accredited minister. More than once during the next few years he was subjected to great hardship on account of his religious opinions, being several times thrown into prison. In 1682 he accompanied William Penn to America, and is said to have been "an instrument, in the divine hand, of comfort and consolation to his brethren under their new circumstances." He died at his residence in Bucks County, Pa., in January, 1683. See Bowden, *Hist. of the Friends in America*, ii, 106. (J. C. S.)

Cuthbert, James (1), a Scotch clergyman, was licensed to preach in 1707; called to the living at Culross in 1708, and ordained. He died Oct. 1, 1715. He published, *The Counter-Querries Querried* (1712):—*A Letter on the Danger of Considering the Influence of the Spirit as a Rule of Duty.* See *Fasti Eccles. Scoticanæ*, ii, 586.

Cuthbert, James (2), a promising young missionary of the British Wesleyans, embarked for West Africa in November, 1864, and died at Lagos, on his way to Abeokuta, Feb. 22, 1865. See *Minutes of the British Conference*, 1865, p. 31.

Cuthbertson, Alexander, a Scotch clergyman, was licensed to preach in 1817; became assistant to Rev. Dr. Somerville of Jedburgh; was presented by the king to the living of Edrom in 1823, and ordained. He died June 4, 1849, aged fifty-six years. See *Fasti Eccles. Scoticanæ*, i, 436.

Cuthbertson, John, an Associate Reformed minister, was born in Scotland in 1720. He studied for the ministry under the Rev. John McMillan, the father and founder of the Reformed Presbytery of Scotland; emigrated to America in 1752, and for more than twenty years was the only Reformed Presbyterian minister in this country, having charge of the small Reformed Presbyterian societies scattered over the thirteen colonies. He entered cordially into the union in 1782, and, after this, his field of labor was restricted to his own immediate charge, Octorara, Pa., where he died, March 10, 1791. See Sprague, *Annals of the Amer. Pulpit*, IX, iv, 7.

Cuthbertson, Robert, LL.D., a Scotch Congregational minister, was born at Paisley, Nov. 15, 1805. He was educated at the University of Glasgow, and at the Divinity Hall of the United Secession Church; was licensed to preach in 1830, and ordained pastor of the Chalmers Street Church, Dunfermline, in 1833. He resigned in 1843; joined the Congregationalists in 1845, and became pastor at Cleckheaton in 1852; retired to Leeds in 1869, and continued to reside there until his death, Dec. 17, 1881. See (Lond.) *Cong. Year-book*, 1883, p. 274.

Cuthburg (Cudburg, Cudburh, Cuthbritha, or Cuthburga), sister of Ina, king of Wessex, was the foundress and first abbess of Wimburn, cir. A.D. 705. She had been the wife of Alfred, king of Northumberland, and a nun at Barking. She is commemorated Aug. 31.

Cuthbyhrt. See CUTHBERT.

Cuthfrith was the twelfth bishop of Lichfield, about A.D. 765–769.

Cuthill, ALEXANDER, a Scotch clergyman, was licensed to preach in 1809; called to the second charge at Ayr in 1814, and ordained. He died Feb. 17, 1852, leaving, *Public Sins Aggravated by the Enjoyment of Great Public Blessings* (1843):—*Discourses on Practical Religion* (Ayr, 1851, 2 vols. 8vo):—*An Account of the Parish.* See *Fasti Eccles. Scoticanæ*, ii, 95.

Cuthman (Cutmen, or Cutmanus), *Saint*, commemorated Feb. 8, was an English monk at Stenninga or Steyning, in Essex, in the 9th or 10th century. The Bollandists relate many curious legends of him.

Cuthred is the name of several early English ecclesiasts:

1. An abbot, probably of Mercia, in the middle of the 8th century.

2. An abbot of Hereford, A.D. 803.

3. A presbyter, probably of Kent, A.D. 808. See Smith, *Dict. of Christ. Biog.* s. v.

Cuthwin (Cuthuuinus) is the name (1) of the first bishop of Leicester, appointed in 679; also (2) of the eighth bishop of Dunwich, about the middle of the 8th century. See also CUTHBERT.

Cutler, Abel, a Congregational minister, was born in Massachusetts. He graduated from Williams College in 1807, and from Andover Theological Seminary in 1810; was acting as home missionary in 1815, and may have been so previously; was ordained Oct. 24, 1816, as pastor at Yarmouth, remaining until 1833; was not afterwards settled, nor in regular service, and died at Northampton, Feb. 27, 1859. See *Trien. Cat. of Andover Theol. Sem.* 1870, p. 17.

Cutler, Calvin, a Presbyterian minister, was born at Guildhall, Vt., in 1791. He graduated from Dartmouth College in 1819; became pastor of the Church in Windham, N. H., April, 1828, and died in 1844. See Sprague, *Annals of the Amer. Pulpit*, iv, 414.

Cutler, Elbridge Gerry, a Congregational minister, was born in Maine. He studied theology one year in Andover Theological Seminary as a member of the class of 1839; was a student in Harvard College; graduated from Yale Divinity School in 1839; was stated supply at Phippsburg, Me., in 1840 and 1841; was ordained Jan. 15, 1842; and was pastor at Belfast from that year until his death at Reading, Pa., April 28, 1846. See *Trien. Cat. of Andover Theol. Sem.* 1870, p. 140.

Cutler, Lyman, a Congregational minister, was born in Massachusetts in 1827. He graduated from Dartmouth College in 1847, and from Andover Theological Seminary in 1850; was installed Jan. 22, 1851, at Pepperell; and was pastor of Eliot Church, Newton, from 1854 until his death, April 28, 1855. See *Trien. Cat. of Andover Theol. Sem.* 1870, p. 183.

Cutler, Rufus Putnam, a Congregational minister, was born at Hamilton, Mass., July 11, 1815. He graduated from Yale College in 1840, and from the Divinity School of Harvard University in 1844; in 1846 became pastor of the Second Unitarian Congregational Society of Portland, Me.; in 1854, of the First Unitarian Church in San Francisco, Cal.; and in 1859 returned to New England. He preached for a few months at Staten Island; in 1869 took charge of a church in Charleston, S. C.; in October, 1872, sailed for Europe, and on his return voyage, in August, 1873, he was struck with partial paralysis. He died in Brooklyn, N. Y., Dec. 9, 1877. See *Obituary Record of Yale College*, 1878.

Cutler, Stephen H., a Methodist Episcopal minister, was born at Montpelier, Vt., Nov. 1, 1802. He was converted at eighteen; in 1827 was licensed to preach, and admitted into the New Hampshire Conference, wherein he labored to the close of his life, May 22, 1834. See *Minutes of Annual Conferences*, 1834, p. 283.

Cutsuida (or **Cudsuida**) was abbess of Worcester, probably at the end of the 7th century.

Cuttell, HENRY MARTYN, a preacher of the United Methodist Free Church, was born at Sheffield, Yorkshire, April 27, 1839, where his father was a godly local preacher. He was converted under the ministry of the Rev. James Caughey, an American evangelist; for a short time was a local preacher; in 1861 began to travel as a minister in the Free Methodist Church; and died suddenly, Sept. 4, 1868. See *Minutes of the Twelfth Annual Assembly.*

Cutter, EDWARD FRANCIS, D.D., a Congregational minister, was born at Portland, Me., Jan. 20, 1810. He graduated from Bowdoin College in 1828, and from Andover Theological Seminary in 1831; was ordained pastor of the Second Church in Warren, Me., May 8, 1833; dismissed May 8, 1846; Sept. 23 of the latter year was installed pastor at Belfast, and resigned in October, 1855, but was not regularly dismissed until a year afterwards. During 1856 and 1857 he was editor of the *Christian Era.* The next two years he was acting pastor at

Beardstown, Ill., and then, from 1859 to 1863, resided in Belfast, Me., without charge. At Rockland he was acting pastor from 1863 to 1871, and at Andover during 1873. Excepting one year in California, he resided, after this, without charge, in Belfast. At two periods he was recording secretary of the General Conference of Maine, viz. 1844-48 and 1851; from 1868 to 1880, secretary of the Maine Congregational Charitable Society; from 1842 to 1857, trustee of the Maine Missionary Society; from 1873, an overseer of Bowdoin College. His death occurred in Charleston, S. C., March 27, 1880. Mr. Cutter wrote largely for religious periodicals, and besides various sermons and essays, he published, *Pastoral Conversations* (1846):—*Day of Judgment and Day of Salvation:—Household Instruction.* See *Cong. Year-Book*, 1881, p. 20.

Cutting, Leonard, a minister of the Protestant Episcopal Church, was born at Great Yarmouth, England, in 1724. When seventeen years of age he was admitted to Pembroke College, Cambridge University, and received his degree of A.B. in 1747. He came to Virginia, and became overseer of a plantation, and subsequently of a large farm in New Jersey. He was appointed tutor in the college at New York in 1756, and professor of the Greek and Latin languages and of moral philosophy. From November, 1757, to March, 1758, during the absence of president Johnson, Mr. Cutting had charge of the institution, and again in 1759. Having prepared for the ministry in the meantime, he resigned his professorship in October, 1763, and went to England for ordination. He was appointed missionary to Piscataqua (now Stelton) and New Brunswick, N. J., by the Society for the Propagation of the Gospel in Foreign Parts. In 1766 he became rector of St. George's Church, Hempstead, L. I., conducting a classical school at the same time. His next pastorate was at Snow Hill, Md., in 1784, whence, in 1785, he removed to Christ Church, in Newbern, N. C., and thence, after eight years, to New York city. In September, 1792, he was a member of the General Convention, and was secretary of the House of Bishops. He died in New York, Jan. 25, 1794. See Sprague, *Annals of the Amer. Pulpit*, v, 223.

Cutting, Sewell Sylvester, D.D., a Baptist minister, was born at Windsor, Vt., Jan. 19, 1813. He united with the Church in 1827, and commenced the study of law at the age of sixteen, but subsequently decided to prepare for the ministry. He was fitted for college at South Reading, now Wakefield, Mass.; spent two years in Waterville College, now Colby University, and two years at the University of Vermont, where he graduated with the highest honors of his class in 1835. He was ordained March 31, 1836, as pastor of the Church in West Boylston, Mass., and not long after was called to the Church in Southbridge, where he remained from 1837 to 1845. He next took editorial charge of *The Baptist Advocate*, in New York city, afterwards called the *New York Recorder*. For a short time he was corresponding secretary of the American and Foreign Bible Society, and for a year or two was engaged in editorial work in connection with the *Watchman and Reflector* of Boston and the *Christian Review*. In 1853 he once more became editor of the *New York Recorder*, which, as consolidated with the *Baptist Register*, became subsequently *The Examiner*. In 1855 he became professor of rhetoric and of history in the University of Rochester; in 1868, secretary of the American Baptist Educational Commission; in 1879, secretary of the American Baptist Home Mission Society. After serving one year, he went abroad, and did not enter again upon any public position. His death took place Feb. 7, 1882. Among the best known of the publications of Dr. Cutting are his *Struggles and Triumphs of Religious Liberty*, and his *Historical Vindications of the Baptists* (Bost. 1858). See Cathcart, *Baptist Encyclop.* p. 305. (J. C. S.)

Cuttriss, William, an English Baptist minister, was born in 1784. He was converted at sixteen; pursued a course of theological study under Dr. Ryland, at the Bristol College, and was ordained in 1808 as pastor of the Church at Arnsby, Leicestershire. In 1818 he removed to Ridgemont, Bedfordshire, and died there, Dec. 16, 1829. See (Lond.) *Baptist Magazine*, 1830, p. 409. (J. C. S.)

Cutulf was abbot of Evesham about A.D. 780.

Cutzupītæ (August. *Ep.* 53; *De Unit. Eccl.* 6) is probably a corruption for *Cutupritæ*, i. q. *Cotopitæ* or *Gotispitæ*, a name given to the heretics called Circumcelliones (q. v.).

Cuutfert. See Cuthfrith.

Cuvier, Charles Chrétien Léopold, a French Protestant theologian, was born Oct. 24, 1798. He studied at Montbéliard and Strasburg; in 1821 was appointed professor of history at the royal college of Strasburg, in 1824 professor of history at the university there, and occupied this latter position for nearly forty years. In 1859 he was elected dean of the faculty, but in 1860 resigned his professorship on account of broken health. On his retirement he was decorated with the cross of the legion of honor, and appointed honorary dean. The remainder of his life he spent in writing and improving the religious state of the Church. He died April 17, 1881, at Montbéliard. He published, *Exposition de la Doctrine Évangélique* (Paris and Strasburg, 1834):—*Esquisse sur les Écrivains Sacrés des Hébreux* (1843):—*Le Petit Catéchisme de Luther* (1846):—*Précis de l'Histoire des Missions Chrétiennes* (eod.):—*La Venue du Sauveur* (eod.):—*Les Souffrances et le Triomphe du Sauveur* (eod.):—*Conseils et Consolations de l'Expérience; Cours d'Études Historiques* (1860-80). He also edited *Recueil de Psaumes et Cantiques*, and a new edition of *La Liturgie de la Confession d'Augsburg.* See Zuchold, *Bibl. Theol.* i, 254; Lichtenberger, *Encyclop. des Sciences Religieuses*, s. v. (B. P.)

Cuyck, Henry Van, a Dutch theologian and scholar, was born in 1546 at Kuilenburg. For fourteen years he taught philosophy at Louvain. After having been vicar-general of the archbishop of Malines, he became bishop of Ruremond in 1596, and won the reputation of being a prelate both pious and instructive. He died Oct. 7, 1609. His principal works are, *Orationes Panegyricæ* (Antwerp, 1575):—an edition of the works of Cassianus (ibid. 1578):—*Speculum Concubinariorum Sacerdotum, Monachorum, Clericorum* (Cologne, 1599; Louvain, 1601):—*Epistolæ Parœneticæ.* See Hoefer, *Nouv. Biog. Générale*, s. v.; Jöcher, *Allgemeines Gelehrten-Lexikon*, s. v.

Cuykendall, E. Nelson, a Methodist Episcopal minister, was born in 1826. He was converted in 1842; licensed to preach in 1847; in 1848 entered the Oneida Conference; in 1857 became superannuated, and died Sept. 4 the same year. See *Minutes of Annual Conferences*, 1858, p. 89; Simpson, *Cyclop. of Methodism*, s. v.

Cwenburh. See Cuenburh.

Cwiffen, a Welsh saint of the 7th century, commemorated June 3, was founder of Llangwyfen, in Denbighshire, and patron of Tudweilig, in Carnarvonshire (Rees, *Welsh Saints*, p. 304).

Cybar (or **Cibar**; Lat. *Eparchius*), a French anchorite, at first entered the monastery of Sedaciac, in Perigord, but afterwards secluded himself in a cell near Angoulême, where he was patronized by Aptonius II, the bishop of Angoulême, who ordained him priest. As he became popular, disciples flocked to him for instruction, and a monastery sprung up. He died July 1, 581, having occupied his cell for thirty-nine years. He is commemorated July 1. See Smith, *Dict. of Christ. Biog.* s. v.

Cybi [pronounced *Kubby*] (Lat. *Chebius*, or *Kebius*), a Welsh saint, was a younger cousin of St. David. He was present at the synod of Brefi, and his memory, near

Llanddewi Brefi, the place where it was held, is preserved in the name of the Church of Llangybi. The churches of Llangybi, near Caerleon, and Llangybi, in Carnarvonshire, were founded by him. He is especially distinguished as founder of a society at Caergybi or Holyhead, in Anglesey. As presiding over this he was styled, according to the practice of the time, a bishop, though he never had authority over a diocese. The day of commemoration is variously given as Nov. 6 and Nov. 8.

Cyclus Anni. See Calendar.

Cyclus Paschalis. See Easter.

Cyfeilach, bishop of Glamorgan, was killed A.D. 756.

Cyfyw (or **Cwynllyw**), a Welsh saint of the 6th century, was patron of Llangyfyw, near Caerleon (Rees, *Welsh Saints*, p. 233).

Cyhelyn was ninth metropolitan of Caerleon, according to the *Iolo MSS.* of E. Williams (Stubbs, *Register*, p. 154).

Cylinnius, a Gallic bishop, is addressed in conjunction with bishop Proculus by Augustine "and the other fathers of Africa." The letter begs them to receive back Leporius, who had been banished for Pelagian opinions, but had not changed his mind. See Smith, *Dict. of Christ. Biog.* s. v.

Cyma (Gr.), an undulated moulding, of which there are two kinds: *cyma recta*, which is hollow in the upper part, and round in the lower; and *cyma reversa*,

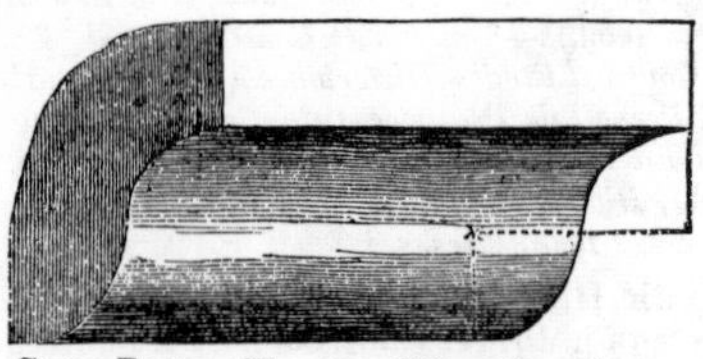

Cyma Recta. Theatre of Marcellus, Rome.

called also the ogee, which is hollow in the lower part and round in the upper. The term cyma, without an adjective, is always considered to mean a cyma recta. It is usually the upper member of Grecian and Roman entablatures, excepting in the Tuscan and Doric orders,

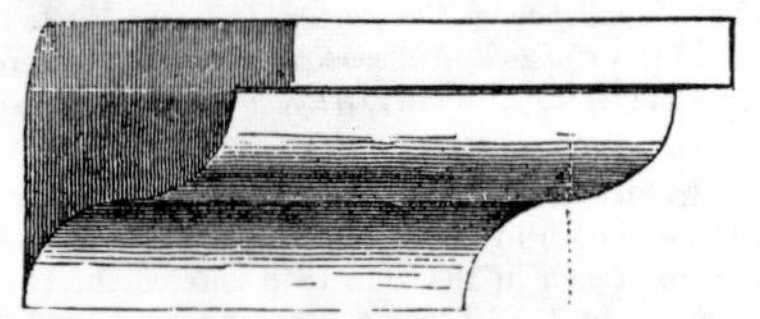

Cyma Reversa, or Ogee. Temple of Antoninus and Faustina, Rome.

and in classical architecture is very rarely used in any but a horizontal position, except over pediments. In the Norman style this moulding is not very often met with, but in Gothic architecture it is frequent, especially in doorways, windows, archways, etc., but the proportions are generally very different from those given to it by the ancients, and it is called an ogee. An example of a *quirked* cyma is given under Ogee.—Parker, *Gloss. of Architect.* s. v. See Column.

Cymatium. This is not easy to define, but it may be called a capping moulding to certain parts and subdivisions of the orders in classic architecture: the projecting mouldings on the upper part of the architrave (except in the Doric order, where it is denominated *tenia*), the corresponding moulding over the frieze, and the small moulding between the corona and cyma of the cornice, are each called by this name; the small moulding, also, which runs round the upper part of the modillons of a cornice, is their cymatium; and the upper moulding of the abacus of the Roman Doric capital is likewise so called; the upper mouldings which serve as a cornice to pedestals have occasionally the same name. —Parker, *Gloss. of Architect.* s. v.

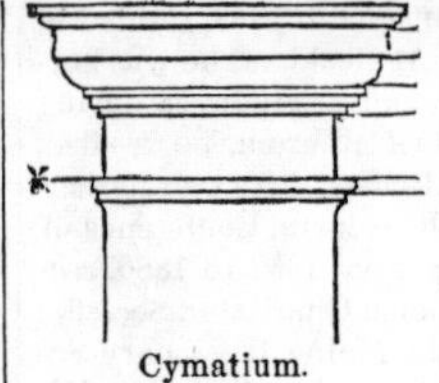

Cymatium.

Cymatius was bishop of Gabala, or perhaps Paltus, in Syria Prima, A.D. 341-362. It is supposed that he is one of the bishops who assisted Lucifer, bishop of Cagliari, in his sudden consecration of Paulinus, presbyter of Antioch, chief of the Eustathian party. See Smith, *Dict. of Christ. Biog.* s. v.

Cymbălum. This word is occasionally used for a bell, or some other sonorous instrument used instead of a bell. Thus Gregory the Great (*Dialogue*, i, 9) speaks of a cymbalum; and Durandus (*Rationale*, i, 4, § 2) of monks being called to the refectory by the sound of a cymbalum which hung in the cloister. See Smith, *Dict. of Christ. Biog.* s. v. See Cymbal.

Cyn-. See Cun-; Kin-; Kyn-.

Cynan was sixth metropolitan of Caerleon, according to *Iolo MSS.* of E. Williams (Stubbs, *Regist.* p. 154).

Cynbryd, a Welsh saint of the 5th century, founder of Llanddulas, in Denbighshire, was slain by the Saxons at Bwlch Cynbryd. He is commemorated March 19 (Rees, *Welsh Saints*, p. 144).

Cynddilig, a Welsh saint of the 6th century, is commemorated on Nov. 1 in the parish of Llanrhystud, in Cardiganshire (Rees, *Welsh Saints*, p. 281).

Cyndeyrn, son of Arthog ab Ceredig, was a Welsh saint of the 6th century, and patron of Llangyndeyrn, formerly subject to Llandyfaelog, in Carmarthenshire. He is commemorated on July 25 (Rees, *Welsh Saints*, p. 211).

Cyne-. See Cyni-.

Cyneberht (**Cyniberct**, **Cuniberct**, or **Kinbert**; Lat. *Chumbrechus*) is the name of two early British bishops:

1. The fourth bishop of the Lindisfari, in the see of Siduacester. His exact date is not known, but is between 706 and 733. It was from him that Bede received his information on the ecclesiastical history of Lindsey.

2. The twelfth bishop of Winchester, was present at the legatine synod of 787. Between 799 and 801 he went to Rome with the archbishop, and as his successor appears in 803. He probably remained or died abroad.

Cyneberthus. See Cumbertus.

Cynebryht. See Cyneberht.

Cyneburgh (or **Cyneburga**). See Cyniburga.

Cynedrid (**Cynedryd**, **Cynedrytha**, or **Cynedritha**). See Cynethrith.

Cynegius was præfect of the Prætorians at Rome, A.D. 384–390. In A.D. 384 the emperor Theodosius sent him a rescript at the request of Marcellinus and Faustinus, two presbyters of the Luciferian faction, enjoining that the Luciferians should have the same religious liberty as the Catholics, and highly praising some of their representatives. The seventh and eighth letters of Gregory of Nyssa are addressed to this Cynegius, in behalf of Synesius and Alexander, two accused persons.

Cynegyslus. See Cengille.

Cyneheard (or **Kinehard**) was the eighth bishop of Winchester, in the ancient lists. According to the *Anglo-Saxon Chronicle* he was appointed in 754, and his name is found appended to charters from 755 to 766. His death was probably prior to 788, the date given by some MSS. of Florence. Two letters of Cyneheard to

Sullus are preserved among the letters of Boniface (*Mon. Moguntina*, ed. Jaffé, Nos. 110, 121).

Cyneheardus was a presbyter who attested a donation by Dunuuald to the church of St. Peter and St. Paul (afterwards St. Augustine, at Canterbury).

Cyneswitha (**Cynesuith, Cynesuuith, Kynesuith, Kynesuuith, Kyneswith,** or **Kineswitha**), an English saint, was a daughter of Penda, king of Mercia, and his queen Cynwise or Cyneswith. Her sister Cyniburga and three of their five brothers, Ethelred, Merewald, and Mercelinus, were also reckoned saints. She had been betrothed to Offa, king of the East Angles, but gave him up to become a nun in her sister's convent, "Kineburgae Castrum" or "Castre." Both the sisters were present at the hallowing of Medeshamstede (afterwards called Peterborough), in the reign of their brother Wulfhere, and their names are attached to his charters. They were both buried in their own convent, and in the 11th century their remains were removed to Peterborough.

Cynethrith was an English abbess of some religious house belonging to bishop Wilfrid. In A.D. 709 she received the silk robe on which his dead body had been laid, and through which a miracle is said to have been wrought.

Cyneualc (or **Cynehualc**). See Coinwalch.

Cyneulfus. See Cynewulf.

Cyneuulf (**Cynewulf, Cynwulf, Cymwlf, Chenewlf,** or **Kimuulf**; Lat. *Cynewulfus. Cyneuulfus*, *Conuulfus*, *Cunuulfus*, *Conwulfus*, *Cinewlfus*, or *Kineulfus*) was consecrated bishop of Lindisfarne, A.D. 740. In 750 he fell under the displeasure of Eadberht, king of Northumbria, for giving shelter to prince Offa, who had taken sanctuary at Lindisfarne. The monastery was besieged, and Cynewulf imprisoned at Bamborough, the charge of his diocese having been delegated to Friothubert, bishop of Hexham. He was released, and in A.D. 780, worn out with years and labor, made Higbald his deputy in the bishopric, with the assent of the congregation. He spent the remainder of his days in retirement, and died 783.

Cynfab, an early Welsh saint, was patron of Capel Cynfab, formerly in the parish of Llanfair ar y Bryn, in Carmarthenshire. He is commemorated on Nov. 15 (Rees, *Welsh Saints*, p. 307).

Cynfarch Oer, a Welsh saint of the 5th century, was a chieftain in North Britain. He is the reputed founder of Llangynfarch, in Maelor, Flintshire, a church destroyed by the Saxons in the battle of Bangor, A.D. 603 (Rees, *Welsh Saints*, p. 168).

Cynfarwy, an early Welsh saint, was patron of Llechgynfarwy Church, in Anglesey. He is commemorated Nov. 7 (Rees, *Welsh Saints*, p. 307).

Cynfelyn ab Bleiddyd, a Welsh saint of Bangor Deiniol, in the 6th century, was founder of Llangynfelyn, in Cardiganshire (Rees, *Welsh Saints*, p. 260).

Cynfran, a Welsh saint of the 5th century, was founder of Llysfaen, in Rhos, Denbighshire, and patron of the well there named Ffynnon Cynfran (Rees, *Welsh Saints*, p. 144).

Cynfyw (or **Cynyw**), a Welsh saint of the 6th century, is reputed founder of the church of Llangynyw, in Montgomeryshire (Rees, *Welsh Saints*, p. 233).

Cyngar (or **Cungar**) is the name of a number of early Welsh saints, whom it is difficult to identify. An account of them is given in Rees, *Welsh Saints*, p. 183, 211, 232.

Cyngen, son of Cadell and prince of Powys, in the 6th century, was reckoned among the Welsh saints for the patronage he afforded them, and for his liberal endowments to the Church. A church at Shrewsbury was dedicated to him.

Cynhafal, a Welsh saint of the 7th century, founded Llangynhafal, in Denbighshire. He is commemorated Oct. 5 (Rees, *Welsh Saints*, p. 295).

Cynhaiarn, a Welsh saint of the 6th century, was patron of Ynys Cynhaiarn, a chapel under Cruccaith, in Carnarvonshire (Rees, *Welsh Saints*, p. 275).

Cyni-. See Cyne-.

Cynibaldus, an English abbot, attested two charters of Cuthred, king of Wessex, A.D. 749. See Smith, *Dict. of Christ. Biog.* s. v.

Cyniberct (**Cyneberht,** or **Kinbert**; Lat. *Cunnberthus*). See also Cyneberht.

1. Abbot of Hrentford or Redbridge. He baptized, A.D. 686, the two sons of Arvald, king of the Isle of Wight, before they were put to death by Caedwalla (Bede. *H. E.* iv, 16).

2. A deacon of Cuthbert. He was archbishop of Canterbury, and is mentioned in a letter from Boniface to his master (Boniface, *Epp.* ed. Giles, i 139).

Cynibill, brother of bishops Cedda and Ceadda, and of the presbyter Caelin, was a presbyter to Cedda. Bede gives his participation in the consecration of a site for the monastery of Lastingham (*H. E.* iii, 1).

Cyniburga (**Kineburga,** or **Kinneburga**), a Welsh saint, born in the latter part of the 7th century, was a daughter of Penda, the pagan king of Mercia, and sister of Cyneswitha (q. v.). She married Alfrid, king of Northumbria, but left him "pro amore Dei," and entered the monastery which her brothers Wulfhere and Ethelred, kings of Mercia, constructed, and which was called after her "Kineburgæ Castrum" or "Castre." The two sisters were both present at the consecration of Medeshamstede, in the reign of their brother Wulfhere, and signed the charter; and it is said that in the 11th century Aelfsi, abbot of this monastery (then called Peterborough), removed their bodies from Castre, where they died, to Peterborough. The account of these sisters resembles that of Cuenburga and Cuthburga, sisters of Ina, king of Wessex. See Smith, *Dict. of Christ. Biog.* s. v. See Cuenburga.

Cynidr, a Welsh saint of the 5th century, was the possible founder of Llangynidr and Aberyscir, two churches in Brecknockshire (Rees, *Welsh Saints*, p. 148, 149).

Cynifrid (or **Cynifrith**), abbot of Gilling, County of York, in Gaetlingum, was brother of Ceolfrid, abbot of Jarrow and Wearmouth. He died in the pestilence of A.D. 664.

Cynimund (or **Cynemund**) was a monk of Lindisfarne, and afterwards of Jarrow, in the time of Bede, who describes him as "fidelissimus mihi nostræ ecclesiæ presbyter."

Cynin, a Welsh saint of the 5th century, was founder of Llangynin, near St. Clears, in Carmarthenshire, and said to have been a bishop (Rees, *Welsh Saints*, p. 144, 145).

Cynllo, a Welsh saint of the 5th century, was founder or patron of three churches in north Radnorshire, Nantmel, Llangynllo, and Llanbister (Rees, *Welsh Saints*, p. 12, 133).

Cynmur, a Welsh saint of the 6th century, was one of the companions of St. Teilo after his return from Armorica (Rees, *Welsh Saints*, p. 253).

Cynog (or **Cynawg**), son of Brychan, was a Welsh saint in the 5th century, of eminent sanctity. He was patron of several churches in Brecknockshire, among which are Defynog, Merthyr Cynog, and Llangynog (Rees, *Welsh Saints*, p. 138, 139).

Cynog (**Cynoc, Cinauc, Cinnauc, Kenauc,** or **Kinochus**) was bishop of Llanbadarn, and afterwards successor of David, at St. David's. He died A.D. 606.

Cynon was a Welsh saint of the 6th century. He accompanied Cadfan to Bardsey, where he was made chancellor of the monastery. He is the reputed founder of the church of Tregynon, in Montgomeryshire, and the patron of Capel Cynon, subject to Llandyssilio Gogo, in Cardiganshire (Rees, *Welsh Saints*, p. 215).

Cynred (Lat. *Cynredus*). See COENRED.

Cynudyn, a Welsh saint of the 6th century, was dean of the college of Padarn, at Llanbadarn Fawr. It has been suggested that a stone in the church-yard of Llanwnws, in Cardiganshire, inscribed "Canotinn," may have been a monument to his memory (Rees, *Welsh Saints*, p. 261).

Cynulf was one of four presbyters from the diocese of Dunwich, attesting an act of the Council of Clovesho, Oct. 12, 803.

Cynwulf. See CYNEWULF.

Cynwyd (or **Cynwydion**), a Welsh saint of the 6th century, was a member of the congregation of Cattwg, and presumed founder of Llangynwyd Fawr, in Glamorganshire (Rees, *Welsh Saints*, p. 208, 270).

Cynwyl, a Welsh saint of the 6th century, was one of the sons of Dunod, Dinothus, or Dinott, and co-founder with him of the monastery of Bangor Iscoed. He is himself deemed the founder of Cynwyl Gaio, the church of a parish adjoining that of Llanddewi Brefi; of Cynwyl Elfed, in Carmarthenshire; and of Aberporth, in Cardiganshire. He is commemorated on April 30 (Rees, *Welsh Saints*, p. 206, 260).

Cynyw. See CYNFYW.

Cyprian is the name of several early saints and others:

1. A magician of Antioch, who is said to have been hired by one Idas to make a Christian virgin, Justina, enamoured of him, but was converted himself, and was martyred with her at Damascus, under Decius, or at Nicomedia, under Diocletian. The whole story is very probably a figment. He is the pretended author of the confession of Cyprian, found in some MSS. He has been confounded with the great Cyprian by Prudentius (*De Steph.* p. 13), and by Gregory Nazianzen (*Orat.* 18).

2. A saint of Corinth, who is commemorated March 10 among the disciples of Quadratus, and of whom a romantic story is told, which is absurd. His martyrdom, if there be any reality in it, must belong to the persecution of Diocletian.

3. A learned presbyter, to whom Jerome writes from Bethlehem (Letter 140, ed. Vall.), expounding Psa. xc.

4. A deacon, mentioned by Jerome (Letter 112, ed. Vall.) as the bearer of three letters from Augustine to him, at Bethlehem.

5. Saint, and bishop of Bordeaux. He was the sixth bishop of that diocese, and took part in the Council of Agde (506) and the synod of Orleans under Clovis I (511). He appears to have succeeded St. Gallicinus after the interregnum caused by the Arian troubles.

6. Saint, and third bishop of Toulon. He was second patron of that city, and belonged to the principal family in Montelieu, Marseilles. He flourished in the time of Anastasius, Justinus, and Justinianus, emperors, of Clovis, king of the Franks, and of Childebert, his son. He was born probably in 475 or 476, and ordained at thirty years of age by St. Cæsarius of Arles, of whom he was a disciple. Cyprian was present at the fourth Council of Arles, A.D. 524. In 527 he subscribed to the Council of Carpentras, and the synodical letter to Agrœcius, bishop of Antipolis. In A.D. 529 he came to the third synod of Vaison. In the same year he took part in the second synod of Orange, and was sent by Cæsarius to the council of the bishops beyond the Isar, at Valentia, where he outshone all in scriptural and patristic knowledge. After the conquest of the Arian Goths, Cyprian went to the fourth Council of Orleans, A.D. 541. After the death of Cæsarius, he remained in the bishopric in peace. But soon afterwards Alboin, king of the Goths, invaded Gaul with a large army, and devastated all the cities of Gallia Narbonensis with fire and sword. His soldiers butchered the people, and killed many bishops. They found Cyprian, together with his friends Mandrianus and Flavianus, in the church, cast them out, and killed them (Aug. 556). Such is the account of his death given by Guesnayus in *Annal. Massil.*, but the Bollandists say that he was not martyred, but died a happy death, A.D. 549. He is commemorated on Oct. 3. He wrote a *Life of Cæsarius of Arles*, in 530.

7. Saint, and abbot of Périgueux. He was also called *Subranus.* He took the religious habit in a monastery of which the abbot's name was Savalon, and having been a model to the whole community, retired to a solitude near the Dordogne, where he built a hermitage, which afterwards gave rise to the little town of St. Cyprien. He died towards the end of the 6th century, and Gregory of Tours recounts legends of several appropriate wonders, calling him a man of magnificent piety. He is commemorated Dec. 9.

8. A monk of Monte Cassino in the time of the emperor Constantinus VI and the empress Irene. He composed a Sapphic hymn on the miracles of St. Benedict, in twenty-four stanzas, to be sung on his festival.

9. A saint and martyr, lies buried in the Church of St. Francis, Boulogne, and is commemorated March 10.

10. A saint, and author of a poem on the resurrection, at the end of the works of Tertullian.

11. A bishop martyred with Justina. He is commemorated Sept. 26.

12. A martyr in Africa under Humeric, commemorated Oct. 12.

Cyprian, Ernst Solomon, a Lutheran theologian of Germany, was born Sept. 22, 1673, at Ostheim, in Franconia. He studied at Jena and Helmstädt, was in 1699 professor extraordinarius of philosophy, and in 1700 rector of the gymnasium academicum at Coburg. In 1713 he was called to Gotha as member of consistory, became vice-president in 1735, and died Sept. 19, 1745. He was one of the few defenders of Lutheran orthodoxy during the 18th century, and wrote, *Historie der Augsb. Confession* (Gotha, 1730; 3d ed. 1736):—*Allgemeine Anmerkungen über Arnold's Kirchen- und Ketzer Historie* (Helmstädt, 1700; 3d ed. 1701):—*Dissertatio de Omophorio Episcopor. Græcorum* (1698):—*De Propagatione Hæresium per Cantilenas* (Coburg, 1708; Jena, 1715):—*Tabularium Ecclesiæ Rom. sec. xvi*, etc. (Frankfort, 1743):—*Ueberzeugende Belehrung vom Ursprung und Wachsthum des Papstthums* (Gotha, 1719, etc.). See Fabricius, *Historia Bibliothecæ Fabricianæ*, iv, 455; Fischer, *Leben E. S. Cyprians* (Leipsic, 1749); Schulze, *Leben Herzog Friedrichs II, von Gotha* (1851); Herzog, *Real-Encyklop.* s. v.; Lichtenberger, *Encyclopédie des Sciences Religieuses*, s. v.; Döring, *Die Gelehrten Theologen Deutschlands*, i, 297 sq.; Winer, *Handbuch der theol. Lit.* i, 20, 127, 328, 381, 533, 534, 544, 614, 639, 669, 678, 737, 738, 755, 849, 860. (B. P.)

Cyprianus, JOHANNES, a Lutheran theologian, was born at Rawicz, in Poland, Oct. 24, 1642. He studied at Jena and Leipsic, was in 1678 licentiate, in 1699 doctor, and in 1710 professor of theology at Leipsic. In 1715 he was appointed canon of Zeitz and Meissen, and finally senior of the university. He died March 12, 1723, leaving, *De Voce* שאל *et* ᾅδης:—*De Fundamento Ecclesiæ Evangelicæ:—De Apostasia a Christo et Ejusdem Gratia Instituta per Opera Legatia:—De Propagando Evangelio ad Gen. iv, 26:—De Nomine Christi Ecclesiastico* ἰχθύς:—*De Baptismo Proselytarum Judaico.* See Jöcher, *Allgemeines Gelehrten-Lexikon*, s. v. (B. P.)

Cyprus, COUNCIL OF (*Concilium Cyprianum*), held A.D. 401, at the instigation of Theophilus of Alexandria, which prohibited the reading of the works of Origen. See Smith, *Dict. of Christ. Antiq.* s. v.

Cyr. See CYRICUS.

Cyra. See CIAR.

Cyriăca was a martyr, A.D. 282, and is commemorated July 7.

Cyriacus, the name of a number of saints, martyrs, and others. See also CHRYSE; CYRICUS.

1. A martyr who, with his brother Theodulus, was put to death in the time of Hadrian. They are commemorated May 2.

2. A deacon of Rome. He is said to have suffered martyrdom there early in the 4th century, under Maximin. His commemoration is given variously March 16, Aug. 8, and July 15; the first, probably, being the festival of his martyrdom, the second, of the removal of his bones by pope Marcellus, the last, of a church dedicated to his name.

3. A disciple of Marcellus of Ancyra.

4. A saint, commemorated in the menology of Basil as a man of Jerusalem, martyred with his mother by Julian the Apostate, his right hand being first cut off because his writings had made so many converts.

5. Bishop of Adana, in Cilicia. He was present at the Council of Constantinople in 381, and, by the permission of Diodorus of Tarsus, his metropolitan, remained behind on its separation to instruct Nectarius, who had been unexpectedly raised from the rank of a layman to the archiepiscopal see of Constantinople. He was one of the three bishops commissioned by the council to convey their synodal letter to Damasus and the other bishops of the West.

6. See CYRICUS 1.

7. A presbyter of Antioch, addressed along with Castus and Valerius and Diophantes by Chrysostom (*Ep.* 22, 62, 66, 107, 130, 222), and alone by his exiled fellow-presbyter Constantius in a letter wrongly ascribed to Chrysostom (*Ep.* 241).

8. A deacon who, together with Paul, accompanied the deputation of bishops who conveyed to Rome Chrysostom's letter to Innocent, in 404 (Pallad. p. 11). He was unable to join his namesake, bishop Cyriacus, and his companions, in Rome in 405, his health not permitting him to take a long voyage (*Ep.* 148).

9. A bishop, apparently resident at Constantinople. He was a friend and correspondent of Chrysostom. From a letter to Olympias (*Ep. ad Olymp.* 12) it is evident that he had sufficient influence to change the place of Chrysostom's exile. Two letters of Chrysostom to Cyriacus are extant.

10. A bishop of Synnada, in Phrygia, friend and fellow-sufferer of Chrysostom, who, together with Eulysius, bishop of Apamea, embarked with him when expelled from Constantinople, in June, 404, and accompanied him on the first stages of his journey. The whole party was arrested at Nicæa on suspicion of complicity in the conflagration at Constantinople, and thrown into chains. After a few days, Cyriacus and Eulysius were separated from Chrysostom and brought back and imprisoned at Chalcedon (Pallad. p. 38; Sozom. viii, 22). While they were in prison Chrysostom wrote them a consolatory and encouraging letter (Chrysost. *Ep.* 147). Being acquitted of the charge, Cyriacus was sent back to Constantinople, but was driven from the city by the law enforcing communion with Arsacius, Theophilus, and Porphyry. He fled to Rome, where he arrived towards the beginning of 405. He laid the statement of his own and Chrysostom's troubles before Innocent, his oral account being confirmed by the letters brought a few days afterwards by Eulysius (Pallad. p. 11). He accompanied the unfortunate western deputation to Constantinople in 406, and shared in the ill-treatment to which they were subjected (Chrysost. *Ep.* 156; Pallad. p. 13). He and his eastern colleagues were seized and put on board a vessel, and it was reported that they had been drowned. But they were purposely reserved by their enemies for insult and ill-usage. They were conveyed to places of exile in the most remote and desolate parts of the empire. Cyriacus was imprisoned in the Persian fortress of Palmyra, eighty miles beyond Emesa.

11. Bishop (*Quiragos* or *Shahag*) of Daik, in Persarmenia, about A.D. 390–411 (Faustus Byzantinus, vi, 11, in Langlois, *Coll. Hist. Arm.* i, 309).

12. A sub-deacon of the Church of Macedonia, A.D. 414.

13. A bishop in Thessaly in the time of pope Boniface I. In a letter to Rufus, bishop of Thessalonica, Boniface tells him that he has separated from his communion Cyriacus, among other bishops, unless they obtain pardon through Rufus.

14. Bishop of Lodi (A.D. 451, 452). Bearer of the synodal letter of the Council of Milan in A.D. 451 to pope Leo the Great.

15. One of the two deacons appointed to summon the bishops to the sessions of the Council of Chalcedon.

16. Bishop of Tyana. He supported the demand of Julian and Severus for the condemnation of the Council of Chalcedon, and the Tome of Leo, but in 518 turned completely round and signed the "relatio" to John, the patriarch of Constantinople, drawn up at the synod that met in that city, which asked for the restoration of the names of Leo of Rome, and Euphemius and Macedonius of Constantinople to the diptychs, and the condemnation of Severus and the other impugners of the decrees of Chalcedon. In the Latin acts he appears as "Dominicus" (Labbe, *Concil.* iv, 1586; v, 167; Le Quien, i, 400).

17. Abbot of St. Andrew's at Rome, employed by Gregory the Great about A.D. 593 in the conversion of the Barbaricini in Sardinia.

18. Martyr at Tomi, commemorated June 20.

19. The anchorite (A.D. 448–557), commemorated Sept. 29.

Cyriacus OF CARTHAGE, who lived in the 11th century, in the time of Gregory VII, was one of the last Christian bishops of North Africa. He was highly esteemed by Gregory, who also recommended to him Sevandus, archbishop of Hippo Regius. See Jaffé, *Regesta Pontif.* ad ann. 1076, June; Gregorii VII, *Registr.* iii, 19 sq.; Wagenmann, in Herzog's *Real-Encyklop.* s. v. (B. P.)

Cyricius (**Quiricus**, or **Syricus**) was bishop of Barcino (Barcelona) in Spain, about 662. He wrote two letters to Ildefonsus of Toledo, in the first of which he thanks him, in language almost blasphemous in the extravagance of its praise, for having sent him his work on the *Virginity of the Blessed Virgin Mary*. In the second, he entreats him to devote his time to the elucidation of obscure passages of Holy Scripture.

Cyricus (**Cyr**, or **Curig**; Lat. *Cericus* or *Quiricus*), is also the name of three early Christian martyrs.

1. A martyr of Tarsus, in Cilicia, about 304. There is little doubt that this is the martyr *Cyriacus*, who, with his mother Julitta, suffered in the Diocletian persecution. St. Cyricus was venerated in the east of Scotland at an early period. He is to be distinguished from the Pictish king Cyric, Grig, or Gregorius, who had his chief residence at Dunottar, in the 9th century. He is commemorated June 16.

2. A martyr who suffered by drowning in the Hellespont, commemorated Jan. 3.

3. A martyr at Antioch, commemorated June 16.

Cyril (Lat. *Cyrillus*) is the name of several persons in the early Church, besides those mentioned in vol. ii:

1. A bishop of Antioch, who succeeded Timæus A.D. 283, and held the see to A.D. 304, when he was succeeded by Tyrannus. Eusebius speaks of him as his contemporary. During his episcopate Dorotheus attained celebrity as an expounder of Scripture (Euseb. *H. E.* lib. vii, c. 32; *Chronicon* ad ann. 4 Probi). According to an obscure tradition he suffered martyrdom at the commencement of Diocletian's persecution, and is commemorated in the Roman martyrology July 22.

2. An intruding bishop of Jerusalem who, followed by Baronius and Touttée, was thrust into the see of his great namesake during his deposition, in succession to Herennius. The two Cyrils are identified by some.

3. A presbyter or bishop of Palestine, to whom Jerome had delivered a written confession of his faith. Jerome refers to this when applied to for proof of his orthodoxy.

4. A martyr of Heliopolis, in Syria, a deacon who suffered for the faith in the time of Julian, having previously displayed great zeal in the destruction of idols, in the reign of Constantine. He is commemorated March 20.

5. A bishop in Armenia, reconciled by St. Basil to the Church at Satala in 372.

6. Deacon to St. Hilary of Arles, by whom he was wonderfully cured, after having had his foot bruised by the fall of a large stone.

7. Bishop of Adana, in Cilicia Prima. He was one of the Antiochene party at the Council of Ephesus, A.D. 431. He signed the remonstrance against the opening of the council by Cyril of Alexandria, before the arrival of John of Antioch and his companions, as well as the sentence of deposition passed by them on Cyril and his adherents. He also took part in the synod of Tarsus, A.D. 434.

8. Bishop of Cœla, in Thrace, in the 5th century. In conjunction with Euprepius, bishop of Byza, he opposed at the Council of Ephesus (431) the custom of one bishop holding two or three sees, then prevalent in Europe. The council authorized the custom, but afterwards special bishops were given to several towns.

9. Fourteenth bishop of Treves. He rebuilt the cell of St. Eucherius, near Treves, which lay burned and deserted. There he placed the bodies of the first three bishops of Treves, and his own remains were deposited with them after his death, which occurred about 458. He is commemorated May 19.

10. Bishop of Gaza, one of the prelates who signed the synodal letter of John of Jerusalem to John of Constantinople, condemnatory of Severus of Antioch and his followers, A.D. 518.

11. Of Scythopolis (Bethshan), so called from his birthplace, a hagiologist, flourished cir. 555. His father, John, was famous for his religious life. Cyril commenced an ascetic career at the age of sixteen. On leaving his monastery to visit Jerusalem and the other holy places, his mother charged him to put himself under the instruction of John the Silentiary, by whom he was commended to the care of Leontius, the abbot of the monastery of St. Euthymius, who admitted him as a monk in 542. Thence Cyril passed to the Laura of St. Saba, where he commenced his sacred biographies with the lives of St. Euthymius and St. Saba, deriving his information from the elder monks who had seen and known those holy men. He also wrote the life of St. John the Silentiary, and other biographies, affording a valuable picture of the inner life of the Eastern Church in the 6th century. They have been unfortunately largely interpolated by Metaphrastes.

12. A bishop and martyr, apparently in Egypt, commemorated July 9.

13. A martyr at Philadelphia, in Asia Minor, commemorated Aug. 1.

Cyrilla was a martyr under Claudius, and daughter of Decius. She is commemorated Oct. 28.

Cyriltonas, a Syriac hymn-writer, lived about the end of the 4th century. His name, as well as his hymns, have only become known of late. A German translation of his hymns, with introduction and notes, was published by Bickell in 1872, at Kempten. See Streber, in Wetzer u. Welte's *Kirchen-Lexikon*, s. v. (B. P.)

Cyrinus (or **Quirinus**) is the name of several early ecclesiasts and martyrs. See Cyricus.

1. Bishop of Chalcedon. He was an Egyptian by birth, and a relative of Theophilus, patriarch of Alexandria. In 401 he accompanied Chrysostom as a friend in his visitation of Ephesus and the Asiatic churches; but for some unexplained reason he became from this time his most virulent enemy, accusing him of pride, tyranny, and heresy. He was prevented from taking part in the opening of the proceedings against that father, at Constantinople, in 403, by a bishop stepping upon his foot, producing a painful wound, which inflamed and gangrened, eventually producing his death. He was present, however, at the synod of the Oak, and never relaxed his persecution of Chrysostom, being one of the four bishops who, after his recall, took his condemnation on their own heads. His death, in 405, after twice resorting to amputation and enduring great suffering, was regarded by the friends of the persecuted father as a mark of the vengeance of Heaven.

2. A German Benedictine, also called *Aribo.* He became abbot of St. Dionysius, at Schlechdorf, and in 760 the fourth bishop of Freising, in Bavaria. He died in 783. Cyrinus wrote the life of St. Corbinianus, the first bishop of Freising.

3. A martyr at Rome under Claudius. He is commemorated March 25.

4. A martyr at Rome under Diocletian, commemorated April 26.

5. A martyr at Milan under Nero, commemorated June 12.

Cyrion (1), bishop of Doliche, one of the subscribers to the Semi-Arian Council of Seleucia. (2) Presbyter and martyr, commemorated Feb. 14.

Cyrus is the name of several early bishops:

1. Of Berœa, succeeded Eustathius as bishop of that city in 325. He was persecuted, on account of his orthodoxy, by the Arian party, and deposed by Constantius.

2. Bishop of Tyre, was present at the Council of Ephesus in 431. He was a leading member of the party of John of Antioch and the Oriental bishops, against Cyril of Alexandria, and was chosen as one of the deputation to wait on Theodosius II to lay a complaint of the illegality of his proceedings, but being indisposed, Macarius of Laodicea took his place. He was deposed by Cyril in the name of the council.

3. Bishop of Aphrodisias, and metropolitan of Cairo. He was born of Christian parents, and was a monk when elevated to the bishopric. He was conspicuous at the Council of Ephesus, in 431, for his vacillation, signing one day the act for the deposition of Nestorius, and on the next an appeal to the emperors against the legality of the acts of the council. Although still greater weakness of character was shown when, at the "Robber's Synod" in 449, he signed the act of condemnation of Flavian and Eusebius, yet he stood so high that in 456 he was specially exempted from the operation of a general law by the emperor, on account of his great merits.

4. Bishop of Phasis, in Colchis, and afterwards patriarch of Alexandria, 630-641. Although the plans of Heraclius for the union of the monophysite party with the Church were at first unacceptable to him, he afterwards gave them his hearty support, and was rewarded by elevation to the patriarchate of Alexandria. He now succeeded in effecting a temporary union of the Egyptian monophysites, known as Theodosians, with the Catholic body. But the agreement being such that both parties claimed a victory, it could not be lasting. Although counselled by pope Honorius I to give less attention to theological refinements, and more to true godliness, Cyrus called a council at Alexandria, which adopted the *Ekthesis* published by Heraclius in 639. This met with no better success than the former agreement, and in the midst of these distractions the Saracens invaded Egypt under Amron, in June, 638. Heraclius appointed Cyrus præfect of Egypt, and gave him the conduct of the war. Cyrus prevailed on Amron to withdraw his forces by the promise of an annual tribute, and the hand of the emperor's daughter Eudocia. Indignant at these terms, Heraclius summoned the patriarch to Constantinople. His life would not have been spared but for the siege of Alexandria by Amron. He was sent back to negotiate, but arrived too late. The city fell after fourteen months' siege, Dec. 22, 640, and Cyrus died some time in 641.

5. Forty-third patriarch of Constantinople, 705–711. He was formerly a recluse at Amastris, and had predicted to Justinian II his restoration to the imperial dignity. He was deposed by the monothelite emperor Bardanes, on his accession to the throne in 711, and confined in the monastery of Chora, which he had founded.

6. A martyr in 292. He was a wonder-worker, but not mercenary. His death is commemorated Jan. 31, and his translation June 28.

Cyrus-Florus. See PAULUS SILENTIARIUS.

Cyzicus, COUNCIL OF (*Concilium Cyzicēnum*), held A.D. 376, according to Mansi, being the meeting of Semi-Arians mentioned by Basil in his letter to Patrophilus, and spoken of as a recent occurrence. "What else they did there I know not," says he; "but thus much I hear, that having been reticent of the term *Homoousion*, they now give utterance to the term *Homoiousion*, and join Eunomius in publishing blasphemies against the Holy Ghost.

Cyzicus, THE MARTYRS OF, are commemorated April 29 (al. 28).

Czechowitzky, MARTIN, a Socinian teacher and preacher, who died at Lublin in 1608, is the author of *Synopsis Justificationis Nostræ per Christum:—De Auctoritate Sacræ Scripturæ:—De Pædobaptistarum Origine:—Dialogi xiii de Variis Religionis Articulis.* He also translated the New Test. into Polish, which he published, with notes. See Sandii *Bibl. Antitrinit.*; Witte, *Diarium Biographicum*; Jöcher, *Allgemeines Gelehrten-Lexikon*, s. v.; Winer, *Handbuch der theol. Lit.* i, 184. (B. P.)

D.

Dabaiba, an idol of the inhabitants of Panama. This goddess was of mortal extraction, and, having led a virtuous life on earth, was deified after death, and called by those idolaters *the mother of God.* They sacrificed slaves to her, and worshipped her by fasting three or four days together, and by acts of devotion, such as sighs, groans, and ecstasies.

Dabbasheth. Tristram (*Bible Places*, p. 252) thinks this is "the modern *Duweibeh*," "between Jokneam (Keimûn) and the sea, along the south boundary of Carmel," thus making the line of Zebulun include the crest of Carmel, and doubtless referring to *Khurbet ed-Duweibeh*, which the Ordnance Map lays down at one and one half miles north-west from Tell-Keimûn, and which the *Memoirs* (i, 311) describe as "heaps of stones, well cut and of good size, apparently Byzantine work;" but Trelawney Saunders (*Map of the Old Test.*) adopts the suggestion of *Jebâta*, as in vol. ii, p. 638, described in the *Memoirs* (i, 274) as "a small mud hamlet in the plain, said only to contain eighty souls."

Dabbs, RICHARD, a Baptist minister, was born in Charlotte County, Va. He was pastor first at Ash Camp, afterwards in Petersburg; in 1820, in Lynchburg; subsequently, in Nashville, Tenn. He died May 21, 1825. See Cathcart, *Baptist Encyclop.* p. 306. (J. C. S.)

Daberath. The *Memoirs* (i, 363) accompanying the Ordnance Map of Western Palestine contain the following additional notice of this place: "*Deburieh*—a small village built of stone, with inhabited caves; contains about two hundred Moslems, and is surrounded by gardens of figs and olives. It is situated on the slope of the hill. Water is obtained from cisterns in the village." "It has several Protestant families, the fruits of the English Church mission" (Tristram, *Bible Places*, p. 235).

Daberna (**Taberna**, or **Ferna**), GIUSEPPE, a Sicilian theologian, was born at Camerata in 1599. He was a Capuchin friar, and died in 1677, leaving, *Dissertazione della Scienza per Bene Finire* (Messina, 1652):—*Harmonia della Biblia* (ibid. 1656):—*Ceremonie per Celebrare la Messa* (Palermo, 1669):—*Il Vocabulario Toscano*:—also some religious works in Italian. See Hoefer, *Nouv. Biog. Générale*, s. v.

Dabheog, of Lough Derg, an Irish or Welsh saint, commemorated Jan 1.

Dabillon, ANDRÉ, a French theologian, and for a time a Jesuit, became grand-vicar of Caumartin, bishop of Amiens, then rector of Magné, Saintonge, and died there about 1664, leaving, *La Divinité Défendue*:—*Le Concile de la Grace*, etc. A collection of his works was printed at Paris, 1645. They were attributed to Barcos, nephew of John Duvergier of Hauranne, abbot of St. Cyran, in the *Histoire Ecclésiastique* of Dupin. See Hoefer, *Nouv. Biog. Générale*, s. v.

Dabis (or **Debis**), a Japanese deity, of which a large image of brass stood in the road from Osaka to Sorungo, which was consulted every year by a spotless virgin.

Dabius (**David**, otherwise called **Dobi**, **Biteus**, or **Mobiou**), an Irish priest and saint, preached with great success in his own country and in Alba, and was patron saint of Domnach Cluana, now Donachcloney, in the county of Down, and of Kippen, in Scotland, where a famous church was dedicated under his patronage, by the name of *Movean*. We still have Kippendavie besides Dunblane. To him, probably, more than to St. David or Dewi of Wales, are the Celtic dedications to St. David to be assigned. He is commemorated July 22.

Dablon, CLAUDE, a French Jesuit missionary in Canada, New York, Michigan, and Wisconsin, was born in 1618. He began a mission at Onondaga in 1655, and in 1668 established another at Sault Ste. Marie and one among the Foxes. In 1670 he became superior of the Canada missions. He died in Quebec, Sept. 20, 1697. He wrote the *Relation de la Nouvelle France*, 1671–79 (printed partly at the time and partly later; reprinted, N. Y. 1810).

Dabney, JOHN B., LL.D., a Protestant Episcopal clergyman, began his ministry in 1862 by officiating in Campbell County, Va., serving in Moore Parish, where subsequently he became rector, and remained in that position until his death, April 23, 1868. See *Prot. Episc. Almanac*, 1869, p. 109.

Daboi is one of the snakes of Africa worshipped by the Widahs; it is attended by maidens as its priestesses, who, with the snake, receive great respect.

Dabonna is often given in the lists of nephews and nieces of St. Patrick, but much doubt rests on all his kindred. See DURERCA.

Dabrecog (or **Da-Breccoc**), of Tuam-dreman, is an Irish saint, commemorated on May 9; probably the same given by some on this day as *Dubricin* or *Dabricin*.

Dabud. See DAVID, 1.

Dace, JOHN, an English Wesleyan missionary, was born at Wednesbury in 1754. He was converted young; in 1806 offered himself as a missionary to the West Indies; and died at St. Bartholomew, Sept. 3, 1821. See *Minutes of the British Conference*, 1822.

Dachiarog, "the saint of Airigul," is cited as a prophet. He may have been the Ulster saint *Ciaroc*, *Ciarog*, or *Mochuaroc*, who, with Breccan, was one of "the two heroes of purity who love Christ faithfully."

Dachonna is a very common name in the list of saints, either as *Conna* and *Connan*, or with the prefixes of veneration *Da* or *Do* and *Mo*. It was the baptismal name of St. Machar (q. v.).

The most famous saint of this name is commemorated May 15. He was bishop of Connor, and of the race of Eoghan, son of Niall. "St. Dachonna the pious, bishop of Condere," died in 726.

Dachsel, GEORG CHRISTOPH, a German Hebraist and theologian, a native of Alt-Leisnig, pursued his studies at Leipsic, took his degrees, and became minister at Lechnitz in 1712, and at Geringswalde in 1729, where his death occurred in 1742. He wrote, *De Unctione Elisæi* (Leipsic, 1708):—*Biblia Hebraica Accentuata* (ibid. 1729). See Hoefer, *Nouv. Biog. Générale*, s. v.

Daciānus (1), a persecuting officer in Spain, in 303 or 304, under Diocletian and Maximian. He was noted for his severity in carrying out their orders, especially against bishops, presbyters, and all ordained ministers. (2) One of the forty-nine martyrs of Carthage in 304, in the persecution by Diocletian under the proconsul Anulinus. (3) Metropolitan of Byzacene, in Africa, in the 6th century. A rescript was addressed to him by Justinian I in 541.

Dacius, *Saint*, bishop of Milan, was called to that see in 527. He exhorted the inhabitants of that city to defend themselves against the Goths, and on its capture took refuge at Corinth. He afterwards went to Constantinople, where the emperor, Justinian, who had published a constitution prejudicial to the clergy, wished him to sign it, but the prelate stoutly refused. He died February, 552. A MS. history, found in the library of Milan, is falsely attributed to Dacius. St. Dacius is commemorated Jan. 14. See Hoefer, *Nouv. Biog. Générale*, s. v.

Dacriānus is the name of a supposed Benedictine abbot. He is the reputed author of *Speculum Monachorum* and *Spiritualis Vitæ Documenta*, ascribed to the 8th century. The name was probably feigned by Ludovicus Blosius, an abbot of the 16th century.

Dactȳli Idaei, in Greek mythology, were dæmons, to whom was accredited, in Asia Minor, especially near the Trojan mountain Ida, the first discovery of metallurgy, and who received divine worship. Their origin and real signification were not known even in the most flourishing period of Grecian and Roman art. It is only surmised that they received their name from their dexterity of finger (δάκτυλος), and from the mountain Ida. Their number is variously reckoned at from ten to one hundred.

Dactyliomancy (Gr. δακτύλιος, *a ring*, and μαντεία, *divination*), a species of augury practiced among the ancient Greeks and Romans, performed by suspending a ring from a fine thread over a round table, on the edge of which were marked the letters of the alphabet. When the vibration of the ring had ceased, the letters over which the ring happened to hang, when joined together, gave the answer to the inquirer. See DIVINATION.

Dacūnus is the name of a saint who was one of the anchorites said to have come with St. Petrock to Bodmin, one of the most sacred sites in Cornwall, in the 6th century.

Dadas, with Quintilian, was a disciple of Maximus the reader, at Dorostolus of Macedonia. They were martyred under Maximian, and are commemorated April 28.

Daddi, Bernardo, an Italian painter, was born at Arezzo, and flourished in the middle of the 14th century. He studied under Spinello Aretino, and was elected a member of the company of painters at Florence in 1355. He was celebrated in his day, and some of his works are still preserved in the churches of that city. He died there in 1380.

Daddi, Cosimo, an Italian painter, was born at Florence, where he flourished from about 1600 to 1630. He has several pictures in the monastery of San Lino, in that city, representing scenes from the *Life of the Virgin*. In the church of San Michaele there is still an altar-piece representing the patron saint of that church defeating the apostate angels. Daddi died in 1630.

Dadès, in one of the Gnostic systems, is the archon of the fourth heaven.

Dadgah, in Persian mythology, is the place of justice, a small temple of fire of the Guebres. There is no fire-chapel in it, with a separate altar, but the fire burns on the ground, in distinction from the larger temple Derimber, which can only he built on selected sites, and must have a fire-chapel with an altar.

Dado. (1) Bishop of Amiens, is placed after Deodatus, about the end of the 7th century. (2) First abbot of Rodez. He lived in the 8th century, and built with his own hands a cell at a place called Conchæ. His first disciple was Medraldus, who succeeded him as abbot and obtained the "privilegium" from Louis' the Pious. Dado then retired to a more remote place called Grandevabrum. See AUDOENUS.

Dadswell, JAMES, an English Congregational minister, was born at Woolwich, Sept. 5, 1823. He embraced religion in his eighteenth year, and in 1856 was ordained at Caversham Hill, near Reading, where he labored until his death, July 19, 1865. See (Lond.) *Cong. Year-book*, 1866, p. 244.

Dadu Pant'his, one of the Vaishnava (q. v.) sects in Hindostan. They originated with Dadu, a cotton-cleaner by profession, who is supposed to have flourished about A.D. 1600. Having been admonished by a voice from heaven to devote himself to a religious life, he retired to Baherana mountain for that purpose, and after some time disappeared, leaving no traces of his whereabouts. His followers believed him to have been absorbed into the deity. The members of this sect are divided into three classes: 1. The *Vivaktas*, religious characters who go bareheaded, and have but one garment and one water-pot. 2. The *Nagas*, who carry arms, and are ready to use them for hire. 3. The *Bister Dhavis*, who follow the ordinary occupations of life. The sect is said to be very numerous in Marwar and Ajmere. Their chief place of worship is at Naraiva. See Gardner, *Faiths of the World*, s. v.

Dadūchi, the torch-bearers in the Eleusinian Mysteries, whose duty was to offer prayers and sing hymns to Ceres and Proserpine. They passed the lighted torch from hand to hand, in commemoration of Ceres searching for her daughter Proserpine by the light of a torch which she had kindled at the fires of Ætna.

Dædæ Tængri, in Thibetan mythology, was a famous race of spirits, existing previous to the visible world, but who became limited through the creation of the world, without their being subject to the laws of death. As there were many who had reached this limit, but still did not die, dissatisfied with their doubtful destiny, they left their thrones and flitted about in the heavens until they came to the kingdom of Assurian spirits.

The latter were continually in disunity, and the arrival of the Dædæ Tængri strengthened one party to such an extent that a war resulted which lasted many millions of years.

Daeghelm is believed to have been abbot of Bardney. He signed the act of the Council of Clovesho, Oct. 12, 803.

Daelman, KAREL GHISLAIN, a Belgian theologian, was born at Mons in 1670. He became successively doctor, doctor-regent, and professor of theology at Louvain, rector of the university, president of the college of Adrian, and canon of St. Peter, in the same city; then canon of St. Gertrude, at Nivelles. He died at Louvain, Dec. 21, 1731, leaving, *Thèses sur le Système de la Grace* (Louvain, 1706): — *De Actibus Humanis*: — *Théologie Scolastico-Morale* (1738; republished several times); also some *Oraisons Latines*. See Hoefer, *Nouv. Biog. Générale*, s. v.

Dæmonology *of the later Jews*. This subject is inextricably involved with their angelology, although, strictly speaking, *angels* are good spirits and *dæmons* bad ones. The views of the later Jews are thus summed up by a recent writer (*Supernatural Religion*, i, 128 sq.):

"In the apocryphal book of Tobit, the angel Raphael prescribes, as an infallible means of driving out the amorous dæmon Asmodeus, fumigation with the heart and liver of a fish; and the angel describes himself as one of the seven holy ones that present the prayers of saints to God. The book of Enoch relates the fall of the angels through love for the daughters of men, and gives the names of twenty-one of them and their leaders: Jequin was he who seduced the holy angels; Ashbeël gave them evil counsel and corrupted them; Gadreël seduced Eve, and also taught the children of men the manufacture and use of murderous and military weapons; Penemuë taught them many mysteries, also the art of writing; Kaodeja taught them all the wicked practices of spirits and dæmons, including magic and exorcism. The offspring of the fallen angels and the daughters of men were giants whose height was three thousand cubits, and they are the dæmons still working evil on the earth. Azazel taught men various arts, such as making bracelets and ornaments; Uriel is the angel of thunder and earthquakes; Raphael of the spirits of men; Raquel executes vengeance on the world and the stars; Michael is set over the saints; Sarathael over the misled souls of men; Gabriel over serpents, Paradise, and the cherubim. All the elements of nature are presided over by special spiritual beings. Philo Judæus and the Talmud are full of similar notions; an angel of the sun and moon is described in the *Ascensio Isaiæ*."

Daes, JAMES, a Scotch clergyman, who "came out from Linlithcowe," officiated in Anstruther in January, 1585; in June confessed he had not entered the Reformed Kirk in proper order; in August accepted a call to commence a new kirk in Ersilton in March, 1586; officiated at Anstruther in 1588; was a member of the assemblies of 1595 and 1602; presented to the living by the king in 1611; called before the Court of High Commission in 1620; resigned before Jan. 4, 1633, and died before June 20, 1643. See *Fasti Eccles. Scoticanæ*, i, 124, 523.

Dafrosa was martyred with her husband, Fabian, under Julian, at Rome. She is commemorated Jan. 4.

Dagaeus. See DAIGH.

Dagamundus (or **Dagamodus**) was ninth abbot of the monastery of St. Claudius, on Mount Jura. His rule began in the last of the 6th, and covered the first quarter of the 7th century.

Dagāmus was an Irish bishop and confessor, who flourished at the close of the 6th and the beginning of the 7th century. He was a strict maintainer of traditional rites, giving way with great difficulty to the reasoning of Augustine, and refused to eat even in the same house with the Roman bishops. His commemoration is variously given as March 22 and May 29.

Dagan, bishop of Inbher Daoile, now Ennereilly, in the barony of Arklow, County Wicklow, was the son of Colman, of the race of Labhraidh Lorc. His three brothers were saints, and he was progenitor of the men of Leinster. He was educated at Liathmore, under St. Mochoemoc or Pulcherius, and after visiting Rome became abbot of Inbher Daoile. He was a leader in the Paschal controversy, and although mentioned as intractable, is said to have been of a peculiarly mild disposition. He is perhaps the same as *Dagamus* (q. v.). He was born between 565 and 570, and died Sept. 13, 641. Both March 12 and Sept. 13 are given as his festival.

Dagg, JOHN L., D.D., a Baptist minister, was born at Middleburg, Loudon Co., Va., Feb. 13, 1794. He was converted in 1809, baptized in 1816, ordained in 1817; for several years preached to churches in his native state, and in 1825 became pastor of the Fifth Baptist Church in Philadelphia. He removed to Tuscaloosa, Ala., in 1836, and for eight years was principal of the Alabama Female Athenæum. In 1844 he was elected president of Mercer University, Ga., where he also gave instruction in theology. He resigned his office in 1856, and died June 11, 1884, at Haynesville, Ala. He published, *Manual of Theology* (1857): — *Treatise on Church Order* (1858): — *Elements of Moral Science* (1859): — *Evidences of Christianity* (1868), and several minor works, some of them of a controversial character. See Cathcart, *Baptist Encyclop.* p. 306. **(J. C. S.)**

Daggal. See DAJAL.

Daggett, Levi, *Jr.*, a Methodist Episcopal minister, was born at Troy, N. H., in 1820. He was converted in 1841, and after a few months' preaching united with the Providence Conference. He died April 18, 1857. See *Minutes of Annual Conference*, 1858, p. 39.

Daggett, Oliver Ellsworth, D.D., a Congregational minister, was born at New Haven, Conn., Jan. 14, 1810. He graduated from Yale College in 1828; and subsequently studied in the Law School and the Divinity School. He was pastor of the South Church in Hartford, from April 12, 1837, to June 23, 1843; in Canandaigua, N. Y., from January, 1845, to October, 1867; for three years of Yale College Church and Livingston professor of divinity in the college; and from February, 1871, to September, 1877, pastor of the Second Church in New London, Conn.; and subsequently resided in Hartford without charge. He died Sept. 1, 1880. See *Cong. Year-book*, 1881, p. 21.

Dagĭla was wife of a steward of Huneric, king of the Vandals. Under the persecution of Genseric, she several times confessed her faith. In A.D. 483, under Huneric, she was flogged with whips and staves till she was exhausted, and then exiled to a barren desert, whither she went with cheerfulness. They afterwards offered to send her to a less frightful place, but she preferred to remain where she was.

Dagin, FRANCESCO (called *il Capella*), an Italian painter, was born at Venice in 1714, and studied under Giovanni Battista Piazzetta. He was elected a member of the Academy at Venice. One of his best works is *St. George and the Dragon*, in the parochial church of San Bonate, in Bergamo. He died in 1784.

Dagnus. See DECIUS.

Dago, eleventh bishop of Orleans and successor of St. Flosculus, lived about the end of the 5th or beginning of the 6th century.

Dágoba (Sanscrit, *dá*, *dátu*, or *dhátu*, an osseous relic, and *geba*, or *garbha*, the womb) is a conical structure surmounting relics among the Buddhists. These buildings are sometimes of immense height, of circular form, and composed of stone or brick, faced with stone or stucco. They are built upon a platform, which again rests upon a natural or artificial elevation, and is usually reached by a flight of steps. Of the relics preserved in them, the most conspicuous objects are generally vessels of stone or metal. They commonly contain a silver box or casket, and within that, or sometimes by itself, a casket of gold. Within these vessels, or sometimes in the cell in which they are placed, are found small pearls, gold buttons, gold ornaments and rings, beads, pieces of white and colored glass and crystal, pieces of clay or stone with impressions of figures, bits of bone and teeth of animals, pieces of cloth, and bits of bark. The dagobas are held in the utmost respect by the Buddhists, on account of the relics in them. See Gardner, *Faiths of the World*, s. v.; Wilson, *Ariana Antiqua;* Hardy, *Eastern Monachism*, p. 217 sq.

Dagobertus (or **Radabertus**) was the twentieth archbishop of Tarentaise, and lived about the end of the 8th century.

Dagonel, Pierre, a French theologian, was born on the island of Lifu, in the Pacific Ocean, in 1585. He entered the Jesuit order Aug. 2, 1605, taught philosophy for four years, and became prefect of the College of Dijon. He died at Pont-à-Mousson, Dec. 7, 1650, leaving *Traité des Indulgences* (Nancy, 1626):—*Le Chemin du Ciel* (ibid. 1627):—*Les Dévotes Pensées* (Paris, 1631):—*Dosithée* (ibid. eod.):—*L'Échelle des Saints* (ibid. 1638):—*Le Miroir des Riches* (ibid. 1641):—*Les Devoirs du Chrétien* (Lyons, 1643 and 1647). See Hoefer, *Nouv. Biog. Générale*, s. v.

Daguerre, Jean, a French theologian, was born at La Ressorce, at the foot of the Pyrenees, in 1703. He established and directed, for fifty-two years, a seminary there, founded a convent of nuns at Hasparren, and died in 1788, leaving *Abrégé des Principes de Morale* (Paris, 1773, 1819, 1823). See Hoefer, *Nouv. Biog. Générale*, s. v.

Daguet, Pierre Antoine Alexandre, a French theologian, was born at Baumes-les-Dames (Franche-Comté), Dec. 1, 1707. He belonged to the Jesuit order, and when it was dissolved, withdrew to Besançon, where he died in 1775, leaving *Exercices Chrétiens des Gens de Guerre*, etc. (Lyons, 1749):—*Considérations Chrétiennes pour Chaque Jour du Mois* (ibid. 1758):—*Exercices du Chrétien* (ibid. 1759):—*La Consolation du Chrétien* (ibid.). See Hoefer, *Nouv. Biog. Générale*, s. v.

Dagum, in Lamian religion, is the official dress of the priests among the Mongolians. It is a large cloak or mantle, made of yellow silk, striped with red, and with a collar, also of red.

Dagur (or **Dag**, i. e. *day*), according to the Norse mythology, is the son of Dellingur (twilight), the third husband of Not (night), the daughter of Niörf (darkness), a giant who had his habitation in Jotunheim. Dagur and Not were adopted by Alfadur, who gave them each two stallions and two wagons, with which to journey around the earth once a day. Not rides with her steed Rhimfaxi (dark mane) in advance. The earth is wet every morning from the foam (dew) running from the steed. Dagur's steed is called Skinfaxi (bright mane); from his shining mane everything becomes light.

Dahl, Johann Christian Wilhelm, a Lutheran theologian of Germany, was born Sept. 1, 1771, at Rostock. In 1778 he began his studies at his native place, and after having completed them at Jena and Göttingen, returned as lecturer to Rostock in 1797. In 1802 he was made professor of Greek literature, and in 1804 professor of theology; in 1807 he took his degree as doctor of theology, presenting for his thesis, *De αὐθεντίᾳ Epistolarum Petrinæ Posterioris atque Judæ*. He died April 15, 1810. He published, *Amos, neu übersetzt und erläutert* (Göttingen, 1795):—*Observationes Philologicæ atque Criticæ ad quædam Prophetarum Minorum Loca* (Neu-Strelitz, 1798):—*Chrestomathia Philoniana* (Hamburg, 1800-1802, 2 vols.):—*Lehrbuch der Homiletik* (Leipsic, 1811). See Winer, *Handbuch der theol. Lit.* i, 91, 223, 226, 798; ii, 60, 97; Döring, *Die Gelehrten Theologen Deutschlands*, i, 304 sq.; Fürst, *Bibl. Jud.* i, 194. (B. P.)

Dahler, Jean George, a Franco-German Protestant theologian, was born at Strasburg, Dec. 7, 1760, and died while professor of theology and Old Testament exegesis there, June 29, 1832. He wrote, *Animadversiones in Versionem Græcam Proverbior. Salom. ex Veneta S. Marci Bibliotheca Nuper Editam* (Strasburg, 1786):—*De Librorum Paralipomenum Auctoritate atque Fide* (ibid. 1819):—*Die Denk- und Sittensprüche Salomos* (ibid. 1810):—*Jérémie Traduit sur le Texte Original, Accompagné de Notes* (ibid. 1825-1830, 2 vols.). See Winer, *Handbuch der theol. Lit.* i, 52, 79, 212, 219, 859; Fürst, *Bibl. Jud.* i, 194; Lichtenberger, *Encyclopédie des Sciences Religieuses*, s. v. (B. P.)

Dahlman, John Jacob William, a German Reformed minister, was born at Elberfeld, Rhenish Prussia, June 29, 1801. He became a member of the German Reformed Church in Elberfeld in 1845; came to New York in 1848, and in 1851 was licensed to preach. He was pastor at Lancaster, Erie Co., N. Y., in 1852, and in 1853 at Arnheim, Brown Co., O. In 1858 he removed East, and was for a time pastor of a German Presbyterian congregation at Jamaica, L. I. He served the Reformed Church at Melrose, N. Y., from 1861 to 1863, when he took charge of the congregation in Glassborough, N. J., for six years, and then removed to Bridesburg, Pa., where he labored several years. His health failing, he divided his remaining days between Collegeville, Montgomery Co., and Philadelphia, where he died, Aug. 1, 1874. See Harbaugh, *Fathers of the Germ. Ref. Church*, v, 112.

Dahman, in Persian mythology, is a pure and holy genius, whose favor cannot be secured by sacrifices, but only by prayers and good deeds. The Persians made thirty prayers to this spirit for their relations, and, in consequence, sixty sins unto death were forgiven the dead. Dahman is the most noble benefactor of the inhabitants of heaven, as also of the human souls going there. His first work is to take the soul and bring it into the presence of God, after which it is entirely safe.

Dahme, Georg Christian, a Lutheran theologian of Germany, was born Oct. 8, 1739, at Jeinsen, a village in the province of Hanover. After being for some time court chaplain at the city of Hanover, he was appointed in 1792 general superintendent at Celle, and died while member of consistory and dean of Bardowieck, June 20, 1803. He published, *Predigten* (Brunswick, 1775):—*Sieben kleine exegetische Aufsätze* (Göttingen, 1791). See Döring, *Die deutschen Kanzelredner des* 18. *und* 19. *Jahrhunderts*, p. 24 sq. (B. P.)

Dähne, August Ferdinand, a Protestant theologian of Germany, was born at Leipsic, Oct. 26, 1807. He commenced his academical lectures at Halle in 1831, was in 1835 professor extraordinarius there, and died Nov. 30, 1878, leaving, *De Præscientiæ Divinæ cum Libertate Humana Concordia* (Leipsic, 1830):—*De Γνώσει Clementis Alexandrini* (ibid. 1831):—*Geschichtliche Darstellung der jüdisch-alexandrinischen Religions-Philosophie* (Halle, 1834, 2 vols.):—*Entwickelung des Paulinischen Lehrbegriffs* (ibid. 1835):—*Die Christuspartei in der apostolischen Kirche zu Corinth* (ibid. 1841). See Zuchold, *Bibl. Theol.* i, 257; Fürst, *Bibl. Jud.* i, 194; Winer, *Handbuch der theol. Lit.* i, 295, 418, 522, 888. (B. P.)

Dahomey, Religion of. Dahomey forms a kingdom of considerable extent in the interior of Western Africa, behind the Slave Coast. The centre of its religious and political system is a superstitious veneration for the person of their monarch, whom the natives regard as almost a divinity. It is even accounted criminal to believe that the king eats, drinks, and sleeps like ordinary mortals. It is needless to say that his orders are implicitly obeyed, however unreasonable or tyrannical they may be.

Fetish (q. v.) worship prevails here, as in all other parts of Western Africa, the *leopard* being their sacred animal. The public sacrifice to this animal consists of a bullock; but private sacrifices of fowls, and even goats, are common, and are offered with great ceremony. When a man dies his principal wives and some of his favorites are offered in sacrifice on his tomb. The priesthood is taken from the higher classes, even some of the royal wives and children being found in the sacred order. To reveal the sacred mysteries and incantations, the knowledge of which is limited to the priestly office, is visited with certain death. See Forbes, *Dahomey and the Dahomans;* Wilson, *Western Africa.*

Daiboth, a Japanese idol of great popularity, is of monstrous height, sits in the middle of his pagoda on a table altar raised but a little from the ground, and with his hand, which is as long as the body of an ordinary man, touches the roof. He has the breasts and face of a woman, and black, woolly, crispy locks; and is encircled on all sides with gilded rays, on which are placed a great number of images representing the inferior idols of the Japanese.

Daiching, in Lamian mythology, is the god of war among the Mongolians, Thibetians, and Mantchoorians. He is represented in full uniform, surrounded by trophies, and his figure is used to decorate the army-banners, also carried as a badge. All success in war is ascribed to him, and it is believed that his presence is a preventive against all harm.

Daigh (or **Dega**; Lat. *Dageus*), an Irish bishop of the 6th century, was son of Cairell, of the race of Eoghan. He was a pupil of St. Finnian of Clonard, and, after he became a priest, gave the viaticum to St. Mochta of Louth. He was a skilful artificer, and was said to pass his days in reading, and carving iron and copper, and his nights in transcribing manuscripts. The construction of three hundred bells and three hundred crosiers of bishops and abbots, with the transcription of three hundred copies of the gospels, is attributed to him. He died A.D. 587. His chief festival was Aug. 18, although Feb. 19 is given as a minor festival.

Daikoku, in Japanese mythology, is one of the four deities of wealth. He is the giver of happiness and prosperity, for with the hammer which he holds he can change everything he touches, and get anything he desires. He sits on a keg of rice, and beside him is a bag in which he preserves his treasures, and out of which he dispenses to his worshippers whatever they need.

Daill, THOMAS, a Scotch clergyman, entered as exhorter in 1568; signed the articles drawn up by the synod in 1572; was reader from 1574 to 1576, and died Feb. 19, 1586. See *Fasti Eccles. Scoticanæ*, i, 382.

Daillé, PIERRE, a clergyman of the French Reformed Church, was born in 1649, and removed to America in the latter part of the 17th century. He had ministered in the early Huguenot settlements in Massachusetts for some time, when the Reformed Dutch Church in New York engaged him, in 1683, to preach to the French Reformed Church in that city, as colleague of Henricus Selyns. After 1792, he devoted himself to itinerant missionary work among the Huguenots, preaching occasionally at New Paltz, in Ulster Co., N. Y., for several years; also at New Rochelle, Westchester Co., and on Staten Island. In 1696 he became the minister of the French Reformed Church in Boston, where he died, May 20, 1715. See *Col. Hist. of N. Y.* iii, 651, and *Mass.* ii, 52; DeWitt, *Hist. Discourse*, p. 36; Corwin, *Manual of the Ref. Church in America*, p. 228. (W. J. R. T.)

Daily, WILLIAM M., D.D., LL.D., a Methodist Episcopal minister, was born at Coshocton, O., in 1812. He spent his childhood on a farm in Franklin County, Ind.; learned all he could at the accessible schools by the time he was fifteen; then began teaching; was converted; commenced preaching the next year, and in 1831 entered the Indiana Conference. In 1836 he was stationed at Bloomington, and graduated at Indiana State University. In 1838 he was transferred to the Missouri Conference, and stationed at St. Louis. Soon after he was elected a professor in St. Charles College. In 1840 he returned to Indiana, broken in health, and suffering from hemorrhage of the lungs. In 1843 he re-entered the active ranks as pastor at Madison, Ind.; in 1844 and 1845 was chaplain in the United States Congress; then again entered the regular work; was elected president of Indiana State University in 1853; and in 1862 appointed hospital chaplain at St. Louis, which position he held until 1865, when he went South as special mail-agent. In 1869 he connected himself with the Louisiana Conference, and served the Church as presiding elder till his decease, in January, 1877. See *Minutes of Annual Conference*, 1878, p. 6.

Daily Celebration *of the Holy Communion* is mentioned in Acts ii, 42–46; and by Tertullian, Cyprian, Irenæus, Ambrose, Gregory, and Stephen of Autun, and is provided for in the Church of England.

Daily Prayer. See DAILY SERVICE.

Daily Preface is the preface used on all ferial days in the Church of England, immediately before the *Sanctus*, in the service of the holy communion.

Dai-Nitz No-Rai, in Japanese mythology, is the great form of the sun, a god of the air and light, he from whom all light, even that of the sun and stars, comes. He is represented seated on a cow. See AMA-NO WATTA.

Dains-leif, in Norse mythology, is the sword of king Högni, the father of the sorceress Hildur. The sword had been made by dwarfs, and had the attribute that, once unsheathed, it must shed blood, and that the wounds made by it were incurable. The war, which originated between Högni and Hedin, from the seizure of Hildur, will continue, by the force of this sword and Hildur's strategy, to the end of the world.

Daira, in Greek mythology, "the omniscient," a divine being in the Eleusinian Mysteries, mother of Eleusis, by Mercury, is declared one sometimes with Venus, sometimes with Ceres, also with Juno and Proserpina.

Dairchell (or **Dairchella**), an Irish bishop of Glendalough, was the son of Curetai. He died in 678, and is commemorated May 3.

Daire (or **Daria**) is the name of several saints given in the Irish calendars, but sufficient cannot be found to give them a well-defined individuality or place in history.

Dairi, the spiritual head or supreme pontiff of the Shinto (q. v.) religion of Japan. At one time he combined in his own person the offices of secular and ecclesiastical ruler of the country. Towards the end of the 16th century, however, the temporal power was taken from him, leaving him only the spiritual. His position is one of great dignity, and he attempts to maintain it with suitable display. The descendants of the royal family all belong to his court, and have now become so numerous that they are obliged to labor at the most humble occupations to maintain their outward dignity. The person of the Dairi is regarded as very sacred, even as above all mortal imperfection. When he dies, the next heir (of whatever age or sex) succeeds to the office thus made vacant. At such a time he is said to renovate his soul, that is, to be renewed in the form of his successor. The Dairi confers all titles of honor, and canonizes the saints.

Dais is (1) tabernacle work, canopies; (2) the raised platform for the principal table in the hall, hence called the high table; (3) the canopy over a president's chair. The stall-like seat of the archbishop of Canterbury remains at Mayfield, and forms the centre of the table.

Dajak Version OF THE SCRIPTURES. The Dajak is spoken in Borneo. A translation of the New Test. was commenced by missionaries of the Rhenish mission in 1843, and completed in 1846. It was printed under the superintendence of Mr. A. Hardiland, at the Cape of Good Hope. This version is written in a dialect of the Dajak called Poelopetak, which prevails almost over the whole south side of Borneo. A new and revised edition was published in 1859. (B. P.)

Dajal, the name which Mohammed gave to the antichrist or false Christ, whose appearance he regarded as one of the ten signs which should precede the resurrection. The prophet thus describes him: "Verily he is of low stature, although bulky; and has splay feet, and is blind, with his flesh even on one side of his face, without the mark of an eye, and his other eye is neither full nor sunk into his head. Then, if you should have a doubt about Dajal, know that your cherisher (God) is not blind." He describes him as coming with deceptions, and displaying miraculous power. He succeeds for a certain time, until the advent of Christ shall put an end to him and his followers.

Dakhani Version OF THE SCRIPTURES. The Dakhani is a dialect of Hindostanee current in the Madras presidency, and is used by the Mohammedans. The first parts of Scripture, Genesis and the four gospels, were published about the year 1862, to which were added, in 1868, the other parts of the New Test. (B. P.)

Dakin, Ann, wife of John Dakin, was a minister of the Society of Friends, and died in Charlotte, Vt., March 28, 1861, aged fifty-nine years. She became a member when about twenty-two years of age, and for many years was an acceptable minister. In 1850, however, she withdrew from the society, but towards the close of her life reunited with the Friends. See *Amer. Annual Monitor*, 1862, p. 42.

Dakin, Joseph, an English Wesleyan minister, was born at Castleton, Derbyshire. He commenced his ministry in 1811, worked hard, and died suddenly at Thirsk, Jan. 8, 1818, aged thirty-one years.

Dakins, William (1), one of the translators of King James's Bible, was educated at Westminster School and Trinity College, where he became a junior fellow Oct. 3, 1593, and senior fellow the following March. In 1601 he was made Greek lecturer of that college, and in 1604 was chosen professor of divinity in Gresham College. He died in February, 1607. He was one of two who translated the epistles of St. Paul and the canonical epistles, but did not live to see the work completed. See Chalmers, *Biog. Dict.* s. v.; Allibone, *Dict. of Brit. and Amer. Authors*, s. v.

Dakins, William (2), D.D., an English clergyman, published a translation of the *History of Catherine, Empress of Russia* (1798, 2 vols.), and several single *Sermons.* See Allibone, *Dict. of Brit. and Amer. Authors*, s. v.

Dakota Version OF THE SCRIPTURES. Till the year 1839 no edition of any portion of the Scripture was printed for the Dakota or Sioux Indians. But in 1879 the entire Bible, the work of the Revs. Th. S. Williamson and S. R. Riggs, was given to the Dakota people. Forty years these two missionaries spent in their work, each laboring separately, but having the translation carefully read and freely criticised by the other. (B. P.)

Dakpa-zamo, in Lamian mythology, is one of the most frightful divisions of hell. It belongs to the eight regions into which hell (Gnielva) is divided; and in this place the damned are tortured by fire until the pain kills them, but immediately they awake to new life and new tortures.

Daksha, in Hindû mythology, is a powerful uncreated spirit, sprung from Brahma's thumb, and therefore one of the ten rulers of all beings. He had no son, but fifty daughters by his wife Prassudi, the daughter of Suayambhu. These daughters were given away in marriage that they might bear him sons. Twenty-seven of the same were given to Chiandra, the god of the moon; thirteen to Kasyapa, Brahma's grandson; seven to Darma, the god of justice and benevolence; of the remaining three, Akni received one, Werotren another, and the last and most beautful, Shakti, was given to Siva. The ten rulers, of whom Daksha was one, gave a great feast once, to which all the gods were invited. When Daksha entered the gods all arose out of respect to him, save Siva, who remained seated. Daksha then insulted him, without Siva saying anything. Some time thereafter Daksha invited all the gods to another festival, but overlooked Siva and his wife Shakti. Although Siva sought to persuade her not to go, Shakti went to the festival, and was treated with insult. She then said she would lay aside the body she received from Daksha, and take on another. This took place, and she was born as Parwadi; but Siva, in anger over his loss, tore a hair from his head, out of which there came a giant, who cut off Daksha's head, set his house on fire, and burned his head up with it. The gods prayed Siva's forgiveness, which was granted. But as Daksha's head did not exist, he placed a goat's head in its stead.

Dakshinas, or *right-hand form* of worship among the Hindûs, that is, when the worship of any goddess is performed in a public manner, and agreeably to the *Vedas* or *Puranas.* The only ceremony which can be supposed to form an exception to the general character of this mode is the *Bali*, an offering of blood, in which rite a number of animals, usually kids, are annually decapitated. In some cases life is offered without shedding blood, when the more barbarous practice is adopted of pummelling the poor animal to death with the fists; at other times blood only is offered, without injury to life. Such practices are not considered orthodox.

Daladá, the left canine tooth of Buddha, the most celebrated relic in the possession of his followers. To preserve this, the only portion which remains of the body of the holy sage, a temple has been erected, in which it is deposited, being placed in a small chamber, enshrined in six cases, the largest of them being upwards of five feet in height, and formed of silver, on the model of a dágoba (q. v.). The same shape is preserved in the five inner ones, two of them being inlaid with rubies and other precious stones. The relic itself "is a piece of discolored ivory or bone, slightly curved, nearly two inches in length, and one in diameter at the base; and from thence to the other extremity, which is rounded and blunt, it considerably decreases in size." The history of this venerable relic is given by Hardy, in *Eastern Monachism*, p. 224 sq.

Dalai-Lama, the great high-priest of the inhabitants of Tartary and Thibet. See LAMAISM.

Dalberg, Adolphus, prince-abbot of Fulda, founded, in 1734, in this celebrated abbey, a Catholic university. See Hoefer, *Nouv. Biog. Générale*, s. v.

Dalberg, Wolfgang de, chamberlain of Worms, was raised to the dignity of archbishop and of elector of Mentz. He died in 1601. See Hoefer, *Nouv. Biog. Générale*, s. v.

Dalbey, JOEL, a Methodist Protestant minister, was born in Ohio, June 1, 1810. He was converted in early life; in 1828 licensed to preach in the Methodist Episcopal Church; in 1859 joined the Methodist Protestant Church, and thereafter labored successively on various circuits in Ohio and Pennsylvania. In 1841 he was elected president of the Pittsburgh Conference, and in 1843 to the presidency of the Muskingum Conference; in 1846 was transferred to the Ohio Conference, but in 1851 removed to St. Charles County, Mo., and settled on a farm. He next entered the Illinois Conference, and in 1860 joined the North Iowa Conference, in which he labored until his death, Nov. 22, 1869. See Bassett, *History of the Meth. Protestant Church*, p. 379.

Dalbhach (Lat. *Dalmacius*), an Irish saint of Cuil-Collainge, lived about the first half of the 7th century. He was of the race of Oilill Flaunbeg, a disciple of St. Abban and a friend of St. Caiman. He was a strict performer of penance, and it is said that "he never touched his hand to his side as long as he lived." He is commemorated Oct. 23.

Dalbin, JEAN, a French theologian, was born at Toulouse about 1530, and was appointed archdeacon of the cathedral of that city. He wrote several religious and controversial works, the principal of which are, *Discours*, etc. (Paris, 1566; Avignon, 1567):—*Le Sacrement de l'Autel* (Paris, 1566):—*Opuscules Spirituels* (ibid. 1567):—*La Marque de l'Église* (ibid. 1568). See Hoefer, *Nouv. Biog. Générale*, s. v.

Dalby, William, an English Wesleyan minister, was born at Sutton-Bonnington, Nottinghamshire, June 10, 1783. He united with the Methodist society at the age of seventeen, entered the ministry in 1807, became a supernumerary at the end of forty-four years, took up his abode at Wisbeach, Cambridgeshire, and labored until his death, March 12, 1860. See *Minutes of the British Conference*, 1860.

Dalby, William Lee, a minister of the Methodist Episcopal Church South, was born in Northampton County, Va., July 6, 1825. He was licensed to preach in 1848; joined the Virginia Conference in 1852; and labored until his death, Feb. 7, 1866. See *Minutes of Annual Conferences of the M. E. Church South*, 1866, p. 7.

Dalcho, FREDERICK, M.D., a Protestant Episcopal minister, was born in London, England, in 1770, of Prussian parents. He received a classical and medical education in Baltimore, Md., and obtained a physician's commission in the American army. In 1799 he resigned and removed to Charleston, S. C. About 1807 he became editor of the *Charleston Courier;* but in 1811 was appointed lay-reader in St. Paul's Parish, Colleton; in 1814 was ordained deacon of the Protestant Episcopal Church, and became pastor of the same parish; June 12, 1818, he was admitted to the priesthood; and Feb. 23, 1819, elected assistant minister of St. Michael's Church in Charleston. He died there, Nov. 24, 1836. His principal publication is, *Historical Account of the P. E. Church in South Carolina*. He also wrote, *The Divinity of our Saviour:—The Evidence from Prophecy*, etc.; and was the projector, and for a long time the principal conductor, of the *Gospel Messenger*. See Sprague, *Annals of the Amer. Pulpit*, v, 560.

Dale, Abner, a German Reformed minister, was born near Boalsburg, Centre Co., Pa., Nov. 17, 1829. He graduated from Marshall College in 1852, and from the theological seminary at Mercersburg in 1856. Soon after he was ordained pastor at Fairview, Butler Co.; and from 1860 to 1866 he served successively Rimersburg and Mercer Mission. His health failing, he was without a charge for several years, but finally accepted a call again to Fairview, and labored there until his death, Jan. 16, 1875. See Harbaugh, *Fathers of the Germ. Ref. Church*, v, 189.

Dale, Hervey Smith, a Baptist minister, was born at Danvers, Mass., in 1812. He graduated from Brown University in 1834, and from Union Theological Seminary in 1841; was ordained the same year, and settled at Newport, O., until 1851; was pastor at Lebanon for several years, from 1852; in 1856 became agent for the Western Baptist Educational Society; and died in Cincinnati in 1857. See *Gen. Cat. of Union Theol. Sem.* 1876, p. 19.

Dale, I. A., a Baptist minister, was born in De Kalb County, Tenn., in 1825. He united with the Church in 1849; the same year was licensed to preach; ordained in June, 1853; labored in the southern part of Illinois; and died at Sandoval, Jan. 18, 1875. See *Minutes of Ill. Anniversaries*, 1875, p. 7. (J. C. S.)

Dale, James Wilkinson, D.D., a Presbyterian minister, was born at Odessa, Del., Oct. 16, 1812. He received his preparatory education in Philadelphia under Mr. Cleanthus Felt; graduated from the University of Pennsylvania in 1831, and began the study of law in Philadelphia. In the fall of 1832 he entered Andover Theological Seminary; joined the middle class in Princeton Theological Seminary in the fall of 1833; the next year returned to the seminary at Andover, and graduated in 1835. He was licensed by Andover Association, April 16, visited the churches of Long Island, and those of eastern Massachusetts the year following, presenting the missionary cause, and was ordained at Dracut, Aug. 29, 1837, as an appointee of the American Board of Commissioners for Foreign Missions; but the financial condition of the society preventing it from sending him abroad, he studied medicine in the University of Pennsylvania, graduating April 6, 1838, and supplying at the same time the Fifth and the Fifteenth Presbyterian churches in that city. He was an agent of the Pennsylvania Bible Society, and labored for it throughout the state for the next seven years; was pastor of Ridley and Middletown churches, Delaware County, from May 17, 1846, to April 8, 1858; at Media, in the same county, from Oct. 26, 1866, to Aug. 3, 1871; and at Wayne from Sept. 28, 1871, to Oct. 23, 1876. He died at Media, April 19, 1881. Dr. Dale published many works, the chief of which are a masterly series on *Baptism* (Phila. 1867-1874, 4 vols. 8vo), in opposition to the views of Baptists. Prof. A. C. Kendrick reviewed the volume entitled *Classic Baptism*, in the *Baptist Quarterly*, April, 1869; Prof. Broadus his *Patristic and Christic Baptism*, in the same *Review*, 1875, p. 245; and Dr. Whitsitt gave a general reply to Dr. Dale's works in the *Baptist Quarterly*, April, 1877. See also the scholarly and valuable book by David B. Ford, entitled, *Studies on the Baptismal Question, including a Review of Dr. Dale* (Bost. 1879, 8vo).

Dale, Jeremiah, a Baptist minister, was born in Danvers, Mass., in 1787. He was converted at the age of eighteen; in 1816 removed to Zanesville, O.; in 1823 was ordained, and performed much itinerant service, both in Ohio and Virginia; in the spring of 1831 returned to Danvers, where he died, Sept. 4 of that year. See *Christian Watchman*, Sept. 16, 1831. (J. C. S.)

Dale, Jonathan, an English Congregational minister, was born at Goostrey, Cheshire, Aug. 11, 1827. He joined the Wesleyans; studied at Richmond College; was preacher for nearly four years at Leicester; then united with the Independents; and in 1855 became pastor at Hallaton and Slawston, in Leicestershire. In 1859 he removed to Heanor; and in 1867 became pastor of the united churches of Repton and Barrow, where he remained until his death, May 29, 1872. See (Lond.) *Cong. Year-book*, 1873, p. 322.

Dale, Samuel, a Methodist Episcopal minister, was a member of the Delaware Conference, and after many years of active service died at Middletown, Del., Nov. 16, 1873, aged seventy-three. See *Minutes of Annual Conferences*, 1873, p. 77.

Dale, Thomas, an English divine and poet, was born in London in 1797. He was educated at Cambridge, ordained in 1823, and after several successive appointments as curate and lecturer, was professor of English literature in London University from 1828 to 1830. In 1835 he became vicar of St. Bride, Fleet Street; in 1836 professor of English literature in King's College, London; resigned in 1839; in 1843 was made canon of St. Paul's; and in 1870 dean of Rochester. He died May 14 of the same year, leaving several volumes of *Sermons* and *Poems*.

Dalen, CORNELIS VAN, a Flemish engraver, was born at Antwerp about 1640, and was called *the Younger* to distinguish him from his father. He was a pupil of Cornelis Visscher, and executed a number of pictures after his style, among which are, *The Adoration of the Shepherds; The Virgin with the Infant Jesus.* See Hoefer, *Nouv. Biog. Générale*, s. v.; Spooner, *Biog. Hist. of the Fine Arts*, s. v.

Dalfinus, bishop or archbishop of Lyons, flourished in the middle of the 7th century. It is said that when Wilfrid made his visit to Rome, he was hospitably entertained by Dalfinus, who became warmly attached to him and wished to make him his heir. On his return in 658 he tarried at Lyons three years, during which time Dalfinus, with eight other bishops, was put to death by Baldhild, widow of Clovis II, king of the Franks. She was afterwards a canonized saint, and the story is inconsistent with her character.

Dalgairns, JOHN BERNARD, an English priest of the Oratory, was born Oct. 21, 1818. He studied at Oxford, became an adherent of Dr. John Henry Newman, shared with him the monastic life in Littlemore, near Oxford, assisted him in the edition of *Lives of British Saints*, became a Roman Catholic in 1843, and received holy orders at Langres, in France. He then went to Rome, and after his return to London he became a member of the Oratory there, and died April 8, 1876. Besides contributions to the *Dublin Review* and *Contemporary Review*, he wrote *The Sacred Heart* and *Holy Communion.* See Bellesheim, in Wetzer u. Welte's *Kirchen-Lexikon*, s. v. (B. P.)

Dalgardno, WILLIAM, a Scotch clergyman, graduated at King's College, Aberdeen, in 1651; officiated at Walls and Flota for two years; was admitted to the living in 1657, and resigned on account of his age in 1699. See *Fasti Eccles. Scoticanæ*, iii, 404.

Dalgarno, Andrew, a Scotch clergyman, graduated at King's College, Aberdeen, in 1660; became helper to John Jamesone at Tyrie; and was recognised as incumbent in 1692, 1693, and 1694 by William, lord Saltoun. See *Fasti Eccles. Scoticanæ*, iii, 643.

Dalgarno, George, a Scotch clergyman, was admitted in March, 1685, to the living at Fyvie, and died in 1717. See *Fasti Eccles. Scoticanæ*, iii, 658.

Dalgarno, William, a Scotch clergyman, graduated at King's College, Aberdeen, in 1646; was ordained minister at Penicuick in November, 1656; collated in October, 1662; transferred to Kirkmahoe in 1663; continued April 27, 1664; transferred to Mauchline in 1665; presented by the king to Dunsyre in 1669; transferred to St. Fergus in 1678; admitted April 18; and died in 1696, aged about seventy years. See *Fasti Eccles. Scoticanæ*, i, 222, 305, 587; iii, 404, 639.

Dalgleish (or **Dalgleische**), the family name of numerous Scotch clergymen:

1. ALEXANDER (1), was accepted and sent to preach the gospel to the heathen, but died on the way, between Montserrat and Darien, in November, 1699. See *Fasti Eccles. Scoticanæ*, i, 400.

2. ALEXANDER (2), was licensed to preach in July, 1688; called to the living at Abercorn in June, 1689; ordained Jan. 1 following; called to Dunfermline, April 7, 1697; transferred to Linlithgow, May 3, 1699; and died May 30, 1726. See *Fasti Eccles. Scoticanæ*, i, 161, 165.

3. COLIN, graduated at Edinburgh University in 1670; was called to the living at Parton in 1675, translated to Old Luce in 1684, and became a papist about 1686. See *Fasti Eccles. Scoticanæ*, i, 719, 766.

4. DAVID, graduated at the University of St. Andrews in 1599; was an expectant there in 1608; was appointed to the living at Cupar, second charge, in 1614; ordained in 1617; presented to the living at Aberdour in 1636; transferred to the first charge at Cupar in 1642; was injured in a journey to Edinburgh, and died May 7, 1652, aged about seventy-three years. See *Fasti Eccles. Scoticanæ*, ii, 461, 464.

5. JOHN (1), graduated at the University of St. Andrews in 1662; was licensed to preach in 1667; became chaplain to William, earl of Roxburgh, who presented him, in March, 1672, to the living at Roxburgh, to which he was ordained in March, 1673; was without a cure till 1688, when he was appointed to Queensferry; transferred to Roxburgh in 1690, and to Old Machar in 1696; continued at Roxburgh through infirmity in January, 1698, but transferred to Dundee in 1700, and died after Nov. 1, 1715, aged seventy-four years. See *Fasti Eccles. Scoticanæ*, i, 198, 470, 690; iii, 692.

6. JOHN (2), graduated at Edinburgh University in 1672; was called to the living at Kirkcudbright in 1683; transferred to Strathaven after 1684, and died at Edinburgh in June, 1699, aged about forty-seven years. See *Fasti Eccles. Scoticanæ*, i, 690; ii, 262.

7. NICOL, regent in St. Leonard's College, St. Andrews; was appointed minister to the second charge at St. Cuthbert's in 1581; tried by the privy council in 1584, and convicted of concealing treasonable correspondence, and a scaffold was erected for his execution, but he was pardoned, released, and returned to his charge; transferred in September, 1588, and settled at Pittenweem in 1589; became chaplain to the countess of Forfar. He took an active share in the business of the Church; was a member of the assemblies in 1589, 1590, 1591 (when he was elected moderator), 1592, 1593, 1595, 1597, and died in 1608. See *Fasti Eccles. Scoticanæ*, i, 123; ii, 454, 469.

8. ROBERT (1), son of Alexander, minister at Linlithgow, was licensed to preach in 1719; called to the living of the second charge at Linlithgow in 1720; transferred to the first charge in 1726; presented to the living in January, 1727, and died Aug. 9, 1758, aged sixty-four years. He left two sons, Robert and William, in the ministry. See *Fasti Eccles. Scoticanæ*, i, 162, 163.

9. ROBERT (2), D.D., son of the minister at Ferryport, was born June 5, 1731; graduated at the University of St. Andrews in 1750; licensed to preach in 1756; presented by the king as successor to his father at Ferryport-on-Craig, in December, 1759; ordained in May, 1760; resigned his charge in November, 1794, and died April 19, 1803. He published *An Account of the Parish.* See *Fasti Eccles. Scoticanæ*, ii, 428.

10. WALTER, graduated at Edinburgh University in July, 1661; was licensed to preach, and admitted to the living at Girthon in October, 1665; transferred to Tongland in 1666, and to Westerkirk in 1668; deprived on account of the test in 1682, and died at Inzeholm in February, 1688, aged forty-seven years. See *Fasti Eccles. Scoticanæ*, i, 637, 713, 724.

11. WILLIAM, son of a skipper of Queensferry, graduated at Glasgow University in June, 1707; became bursar there in 1710; studied theology under Dr. Mark; at Leyden; was licensed to preach in 1717; called to the living at Carnbee the same year, and ordained in 1719; transferred to Ferryport-on-Craig in 1739; succeeded to the family estate in Scotscraig, and died there Aug. 6, 1759, aged seventy years. See *Fasti Eccles. Scoticanæ*, ii, 414, 428.

Dalham, FLORENTIUS (or FLORIAN), an Austrian geometrician, doctor of theology, and librarian at Salzburg, was born July 22, 1713, at Vienna, where he also acted for some time as professor of philosophy, and died Jan. 19, 1795. He is the author of *Concilia Salisburgensia Diocesana* (Augsburg, 1788, fol.). See Winer, *Handbuch der theol. Lit.* i, 663; Hoefer, *Nouv. Biog. Générale*, s. v.

Daliell, John, a Scotch clergyman, graduated at Edinburgh University in 1610; was licensed to preach in 1614; became a schoolmaster at Prestonpans; was presented to the living at Prestonkirk in 1619; continued July, 1669, and died before Nov. 3, 1682. See *Fasti Eccles. Scoticanæ*, i, 378.

Daliell, Mungo, a Scotch clergyman, graduated at Glasgow University in 1603; was presented to the vicarage of Coldingham by the king; transferred to the living at Cranshaws in 1615; continued, but the charge was vacant in 1652. See *Fasti Eccles. Scoticanæ*, i, 409.

Daling, Alexander, a Scotch clergyman, was licensed to preach in November, 1739; called to the living of Cleish in February, and ordained in July, 1743; was one of three suspended from sitting in synods or presbyteries or general assemblies, regarding the settlement of Inverkeithing; was released in June, 1765, and died Aug. 11, 1790, aged seventy-eight years. See *Fasti Eccles. Scoticanæ*, ii, 582.

Daling, William, a Scotch clergyman, son of the foregoing, was licensed to preach in July, 1786; ordained assistant minister to his father at Cleish, in October, 1788; succeeded in 1790, and died Nov. 18, 1835, in his eightieth year. See *Fasti Eccles. Scoticanæ*, ii, 583.

Dalkiel, in later Hebrew dæmonology, is a fallen spirit, whose office is to wield a fiery switch, with which he drives the lost to the seventh region of hell.

Dall, Henry, a Scotch clergyman, graduated at the University of St. Andrews in July, 1699; was called to the living at Kirkcaldy, second charge, in August, and ordained in November, 1704; transferred to the first charge in October, 1711, and died in February, 1724, aged about forty-five years. See *Fasti Eccles. Scoticanæ*, ii, 516, 519.

Dall, John, a Scotch clergyman, graduated at the University of St. Andrews in July, 1663; became chaplain to the laird of Duninald; was presented to the living of Kinnaird in September, 1676, and died in 1698, aged about fifty-five years. See *Fasti Eccles. Scoticanæ*, iii, 829.

Dall, Robert, an English Wesleyan minister, was converted at the age of seventeen, entered the itinerancy under Wesley in 1772, labored in Great Britain, Ireland, and the Isle of Man with great success, became a supernumerary, and died Oct. 10, 1828, aged eighty-one years. See *Minutes of the British Conference*, 1829.

Dall, William (1), a Scotch clergyman, was called to the living at Barrie in September, 1720; ordained the month following, and died Sept. 27, 1775. See *Fasti Eccles. Scoticanæ*, iii, 792.

Dall, William (2), a Scotch clergyman, was licensed to preach in 1727, called and ordained to the living at Monifieth in 1738, and died May 25, 1762. See *Fasti Eccles. Scoticanæ*, iii, 725.

Dallan Forgaill (properly **Eochard, Eigeas**, or **Righ Eigeas**), of Cluain Dallain, an Irish saint of the 6th century, was the son of Colla, of the race of Colla Nais, who was monarch of Ireland, A.D. 323–326. He was born on the borders of Connaught and Ulster, at a place called Masrige and Cathrige Sleacht, afterwards Teallach Eathach. He was early recognised as the royal poet, and the greatest scholar in Ireland. In his day the bards had become very turbulent and annoying to royalty, and because king Aedh refused their requests, they threatened to satirize him in their bardic lays. The king issued a decree of banishment. At a convention of the estates of the nation, which met at Drumceatt (now Daisy Hill, in the county of Londonderry), the question of the bards coming up, St. Columba pleaded successfully for their retention, as a useful body. In gratitude to St. Columba, Dallan composed the *Amhra Cholumcille*, or "Praises of St. Columba," which, though largely glossed, remains to this day. It

is written in very old and almost unintelligible Irish. It was long used as a charm, and the reciting of it was believed to be a safeguard in danger, and a sure remedy in blindness, Dallan himself having, it is said, received his sight on the completion of his poem at St. Columba's death. He is also said by Colgan (*Acta Sanctorum*, 204) to have composed other panegyrics in praise of St. Senan of Iniscathey and St. Conall of Iniscail, which had the same wonderful effects. He is said to have been made chief Ollamh, or special master of education and literature, at the reformation then inaugurated in Ireland. In or about the year 594 Dallan was killed by the pirates on the island of Iniscail (now Inishkeel, in Gweebara Bay, County Donegal), and was buried in the church of St. Conall of Iniscail, where his memory was long held in great veneration. He is popularly connected with several churches, as with Maighin, a church in Westmeath; Killdallain, now Killadallan or Kildallan, in the diocese of Kilmore, County Cavan; Disert-Dallain; Tullach-Dallain, in the diocese of Raphoe; and Cluain-Dallain, now Clonallan, in the diocese of Dromore, County Down. He is commemorated Jan. 29.

Dallas, Alexander, a Scotch clergyman, was licensed to preach in 1700, called and ordained to the living at Kinnell in 1703, and died Jan. 20, 1705. See *Fasti Eccles. Scoticanæ*, iii, 800.

Dallas, Alexander R. C., an English divine, was admitted as a gentleman commoner at Worcester College, Oxford, in 1820; in 1821 accepted the curacy of Radley; became bishop of Jamaica in 1824; was appointed chaplain to the Rev. Dr. Sumner in 1826; entered upon the ministry at Wonston in 1828, where he continued about forty years, and died Dec. 12, 1869. Mr. Dallas was a powerful advocate of the missionary cause, and a great champion of anti-Catholicism in Ireland. He was the author of, *A Voice from Heaven to Ireland:—Practical Sermons on the Lord's Prayer:—Pastoral Superintendence, its Motive, Detail, and Support:—Curates' Offering:—Village Sermons:—Miracles of Christ:—Parables of Christ:—Progress and Prospects of Romanism:—Scriptural View of the Position of the Jews:—Cottager's Guide to the New Testament*, and many other valuable works. See (Lond.) *Christian Observer*, February, 1872, p. 98; Allibone, *Dict. of Brit. and Amer. Authors*, s. v.

Dallas, James, a Scotch clergyman, was licensed to preach in 1786; missionary at Stornoway, and schoolmaster there in 1787; schoolmaster at Kincardine in 1791; presented to the living at Contin in 1792, but his ordination delayed for a year on false charges; ordained in August, 1793, and died Sept. 18, 1825, aged seventy-one years. See *Fasti Eccles. Scoticanæ*, iii, 294.

Dallas, John (1), a Scotch clergyman, was admitted to the living at Tain before July 4, 1649, and continued Oct. 5, 1658. See *Fasti Eccles. Scoticanæ*, iii, 309.

Dallas, John (2), a Scotch clergyman, was born at Budzet; admitted to the living of Ardersier before April, 1665; deprived by Act of Parliament in April, 1690; intruded in 1691, and died about 1693. See *Fasti Eccles. Scoticanæ*, iii, 244.

Dallaway, James, an English clergyman, was born at Bristol in 1763, and educated at Trinity College, Oxford. He became rector of South Stoke, in Sussex, in 1799, and vicar of Leatherhead, Surrey, in 1801. He was for some time chaplain and physician to the British embassy at the Porte, and gave much attention to antiquarian pursuits. He died in 1834. His publications include *Letters of Bishop Rundell to Mrs. Sandys* (1789, 2 vols.):—*Constantinople, Ancient and Modern* (1797):—*Notices of Ancient Church Architecture in the 15th Century* (1823), and other works, chiefly of antiquarian interest. See Allibone, *Dict. of Brit. and Amer. Authors*, s. v.

Dallewell, John, an English Baptist missionary, was born in Sunderland, Nov. 14, 1816. For a time he was a Methodist local preacher, but in 1836 united with the Scotch Baptist Church in his native town. In December, 1840, he was publicly set apart for evangelical work in Jamaica, and embarked for the field of his labor in January, 1841, but died there Oct. 11 following. See (Lond.) *Baptist Hand-book*, 1842, p. 35. (J. C. S.)

Dallicker (*De la Cour*), Frederick, a German Reformed minister, was born Feb. 2, 1738. He was licensed in 1757; was pastor at Amwell, N. J., until 1770; Rockaway Valley, Alexandria, and Foxenburgh, until 1782; at Goshenhoppen, Pa., until 1784, and died at Faulkner Swamp, Jan. 5, 1799. See Harbaugh, *Fathers of the Germ. Ref. Church*, ii, 382.

Dalliston, John, an English Baptist minister, was born in Bury St. Edmunds in 1815. He was early converted, and united with the Church in his native place; was ordained pastor at Sibile Hedingham, in Essex, and was drowned Aug. 30, 1843. See (Lond.) *Baptist Handbook*, 1844, p. 16. (J. C. S.)

Dalmacius. See Dalbhach.

Dalmahoy, James, a Scotch clergyman, was an exhorter at Cambuskenneth in 1567, when the Reformed faith came in; reader there in 1574, with four other places in charge in 1576, and continued in 1580. See *Fasti Eccles. Scoticanæ*, ii, 696.

Dalmàsio, Lippo Scannabecchi (called *Lippo dalle Madonne*), an Italian painter, was born in Bologna. He was a pupil of Vitale da Bologna, and as early as 1376 far surpassed all his contemporaries. There is a picture, painted by him, of *The Virgin*, in the Church of San Petronio, at Bologna. He died about 1410. See Hoefer, *Nouv. Biog. Générale*, s. v.; Spooner, *Biog. Hist. of the Fine Arts*, s. v.

Dalmata, Anton, a Croatian theologian, who lived in the latter half of the 16th century, wrote, *Bekenntniss des Glaubens die Carol V*, etc. (Tübingen, 1562; a translation made in collaboration with Primus, Truber, and Stephen Consul):—*Novum Testamentum Croatice* (Trau, 1562 or 1565). See Hoefer, *Nouv. Biog. Générale*, s. v.

Dalmatia, Council of (*Concilium Dalmaticum*). Held in 1199, by John, chaplain to pope Innocent III, and Simon, his sub-deacon, both legates of the Roman see. In this council the Church of Dalmatia submitted itself to the authority of Rome. Twelve canons were published.

1. Enjoins that a bishop convicted of taking any fee for ordination shall be deposed forever.
4. Directs that the secrecy of confession shall be kept inviolate under pain of deposition.
8. Condemns those lay persons who present to benefices, and those of the clergy who receive them at the hands of the laymen.
10. Excommunicates husbands who forsake their wives, without waiting for the judgment of the Church.
11. Forbids the ordination of bastards, and of the sons of priests.
12. Forbids the ordination of any one as priest under thirty years of age.

The acts are subscribed by seven bishops, besides the legates and the archbishop Dominicus.—Labbe, *Concil.* xi, 7; Landon, *Manual of Councils*, s. v.

Dalmatic. Although this is described as a species of long-sleeved tunic, there are fair grounds for believing that *in its original form* the dalmatic, as worn by men, was a short-sleeved or sleeveless tunic, equivalent to the colobion. This is shown by the way in which the two words are used synonymously, as in Epiphanius. Again, in the edict of Diocletian fixing the maximum price of articles throughout the Roman empire, the two words are used as equivalents. We first meet with the dalmatic as a secular dress, of a stately or luxurious character, worn by persons in high position. Thus there would necessarily be something exceptional in the use of it; and then, like other articles of Roman apparel, it became adopted by the Church as a vestment for ecclesiastics. Lampridius charges Commodus with unseemly behavior in that he appeared in the streets in a dalmatic. If at this time it had short sleeves, there would be an obvious unseemliness in a person of rank being seen abroad without an upper garment. Others, who hold that even then the dalmatic was a long-sleeved dress, refer the cause of the censure to the implied effeminacy of the wearer. The edict of Diocletian furnishes us with much interesting information as to the different varieties of this garment in use in the Roman empire at the end of the 3d century, A.D. It was made of various materials, wool, silk, linen; sometimes the ornamental stripe was present, sometimes absent. Dalmatics both for men's and women's use are mentioned. Three different qualities are given for each sex, the price varying both according to the quality and the place of manufacture. In later times the dalmatic was worn by sovereigns at their coronation and on other great occasions. See Coronation.

The ideas, then, of dignity and stateliness were associated with the dalmatic as a secular dress. The earliest notice of its ecclesiastical use is, if the document be genuine, in the *Acta Martyrii* of St. Cyprian. Here, where the vesture is evidently that *ordinarily* used by the bishop (if, indeed, a distinction between the every-day dress of the Christian ministry and that used in divine service had yet arisen), we find first the under linen garment, over this the dalmatic, and finally the birrus or cloak. Pope Sylvester I (A.D. 335) ordered that deacons should for the future wear dalmatics instead of colobia. Whether a new vestment was introduced or the existing one modified, the result was the introduction of a long-sleeved in the place of a short-sleeved tunic. Walafrid Strabo (859) says that when the priests began to use chasubles, dalmatics were permitted to the deacons, but "at that time the permission was not given to all to do what now almost all bishops and some priests think they may do; namely, wear a dalmatic under the chasuble." It is noticeable that this ordinance had special reference to deacons, and that the dalmatic was in some special way associated with the local Church of Rome. Thus, when Cæsarius, bishop of Arles, visited Rome, pope Symmachus granted him, as a special distinction, the privilege of wearing the pallium (q. v.), and to his deacons that of dalmatics, after the Roman fashion. Also Gregory the Great, in a letter to Aregius, bishop of Vapincum, accords to him and his archdeacon the sought-for privilege of wearing dalmatics. Indirect evidence pointing to the same result may be gathered from the fact of the absence of any mention of the dalmatic in the acts of the fourth Council of Toledo (A.D. 633), among the regulations as to the dress of the Christian ministry, showing that this vestment was not one then in use in Spain. The dalmatic thus being a vestment which even in the West had *primarily* only a local acceptance, we are prepared to find that

Mosaic in the Church of San Vitale at Ravenna, exhibiting Ancient Forms of the Dalmatic.

in the East there is nothing which, strictly speaking, answers to it. The "sticharion," however, is the representative of the general type of white tunic, which, under whatever name we know it, alb, dalmatic, or tunicle, is essentially the same dress.

One or two further remarks may be made in conclusion, as to the ornamental stripes [see CLAVUS] of the dalmatic. As to the color of these, it is stated by Marriott that he had met with exclusively black stripes in all ancient pictures of ecclesiastical dalmatics prior to the year 600, as in the well-known Ravenna mosaic (see above), the earliest exception being a mosaic of the date 640, in which the apostles have red stripes on their tunics. The red or purple stripes afterwards became common, and are spoken of as worn back and front; but whether this was the case with the original type of the dress may perhaps be doubted. Further, these ornamental stripes are found on the borders of the sleeves; and on the left side, in later days, was a border of

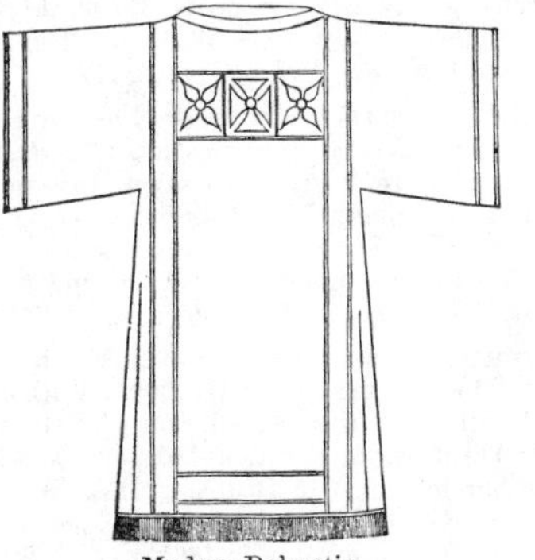

Modern Dalmatic.

fringe, for which various writers have found appropriate symbolical reasons.

Dalmatin, GEORG, a Slavonic theologian and Orientalist, lived in the latter half of the 16th century. In 1568 he translated the Bible of Luther into his native language. The printing of this translation was intrusted to John Manlius, who established the first printing-house at Laybach, and was completed at Wittenberg in 1584. After repairing to Dresden, in order to thank the elector of Saxony for having permitted the printer to take charge of this operation, Dalmatin went to perform pastoral duties at St. Khazaim, in 1585. Being exiled in 1598 by the Catholics, who called him abusively *Cavale* (Kobila, "the preacher"), he found an asylum at the house of the baron of Ansperg, who lodged him in a vault placed under the stables of the château, and afterwards called the *Trou.* See Hoefer, *Nouv. Biog. Générale*, s. v.; Chalmers, *Biog. Dict.* s. v.

Dalmatius (or **Delmatius**), the name of early ecclesiastics:

1. A martyr under Maximian, commemorated on Dec. 5.

2. Censor at Antioch, commissioned by Constantine the Great to inquire into a charge brought by the Arians against Athanasius, of having murdered Arsenius. Dalmatius wrote to the archbishop to prepare his defence.

3. Monk and abbot near Constantinople, often called *Dalmatus*, and commemorated Aug. 3. He exerted a powerful influence at the time of the Council of Ephesus (431), against Chrysoretes the chamberlain and the Nestorian party at the court of Theodosius II. His influence arose from his eminent piety, his strength of character, and his fiery zeal. Under Theodosius the Great he had served in the second company of Guards, was married, and had a family. Feeling a call to a monastic life, he left his wife and children, except a son Faustus, and went to receive instruction from the abbot Isaac, who had dwelt in the desert from his infancy. Isaac, at his death, made him Hegumenus, or superior of the monastery, under the patriarch Atticus. Consulted by councils, patriarchs, and emperors, he remained in his cell forty-eight years without quitting it. After the Nestorian party at Ephesus had deposed Cyril and Memnon, bishop of Ephesus, and imprisoned them, news of their distress reached him by secret conveyance. While he prayed he believed that he heard a great voice summoning him forth from his retreat. Accompanied by the monks of all the monasteries, with their abbots at their head, he appeared before the palace. The abbots were admitted with him to the imperial presence. The outcome was that the emperor came to a knowledge of the truth from Dalmatius, as the council acknowledged, and ordered a deputation of each party to appear before him.

4. Bishop of Cyzicum. The archbishop had nominated Proclus, but the people, according to the canons, chose the monk Dalmatius. He was present at Ephesus in 431.

5. *Saint*, third bishop of Rodez, from 524 to 580. He was present at the Council of Clermont in 525, at the first Council of Arvernum in 535, and at the Council of Orleans in 541. Dalmatius was once condemned to death for the faith, at Brives-la-Gaillarde. St. Anstites interceded for him with the tribune who had condemned him, but his intercession was of no avail, and Dalmatius was actually led out to execution. Anstites then prayed for him, the execution was hindered by some extraordinary atmospheric phenomena, and the condemned man lived to a good old age. He is commemorated Nov. 2.

6. *Saint*, a French prelate of the Benedictine order, and regular priest of Grasse or Notre Dame of Orbieu. He assisted, in 1068, at the Council of Gerona, in which four canons were passed against those who had repudiated their wives in order to espouse others, against simony, and incestuous marriages, disorders then very common. Dalmatius was elected archbishop of Narbonne in September, 1081, and presided in September, 1086, at the council held in the abbey of St. Étienne of Bagnols. He died at Rieux, Jan. 17, 1097. See Hoefer, *Nouv. Biog. Générale*, s. v.

Dalmătus. See DALMATIUS, 3.

Dalrymple (written also **Dalrumpill**, etc.), the family name of several Scotch clergymen:

1. ANDREW, graduated at Glasgow University in 1646; was called to the living of Auchinleck in 1650; deprived by the privy council in 1662; accused of preaching and baptizing irregularly in 1669; fined half his salary for not keeping the Restoration festival in 1673, and died in June, 1676, aged fifty years. See *Fasti Eccles. Scoticanæ*, ii, 96, 139.

2. DAVID, a natural son of lord Dromore, was schoolmaster of Kettle in November, 1692; licensed to preach in 1696; appointed and ordained minister at Dundurcos in May, 1698; and died Feb. 23, 1747. See *Fasti Eccles. Scoticanæ*, iii, 221.

3. JAMES, was reader at the first General Assembly, in 1560, "though qualified to preach and administer the sacraments;" entered Beltyn in 1568; the same year was presented to the living of Ayr, and died in 1580. See *Fasti Eccles. Scoticanæ*, ii, 84.

4. JOHN, graduated at Edinburgh University in June, 1697; was licensed to preach in 1702; called and ordained to the living at Morham in April, 1704; resigned in January, 1706; and died in Edinburgh, Feb. 10, 1716, aged thirty-six years. See *Fasti Eccles. Scoticanæ*, i, 340.

5. ROBERT, son of David, was licensed to preach in December, 1728; presented to the living at Dallas in June, 1748; ordained in February, 1749; deposed in April, 1763, for fornication; the sentence was revoked in 1776. He died March 20, 1778. See *Fasti Eccles. Scoticanæ*, iii, 179.

6. WILLIAM, D.D., was born at Ayr, Aug. 29, 1723; licensed to preach in 1745; called to the second charge at Ayr in August, and ordained in December, 1746; transferred to the first charge in May, 1756; was moderator of the General Assembly, May, 1781; and died Jan. 28, 1814. He was a man of meek temper, warm zeal, amiable manners, and sincere piety. He published, *Three Sermons* (Glasgow, 1776):—*Family Worship Explained* (1787):—*A History of Christ* (eod.):—*Sequel* to the same (1791):—*The Mosaic Account of the Creation* (1794):—*Meditations and Prayers* (1795):—*Legacy of Dying Thoughts* (1796):—*Solomon's Ethics; or the Book of Proverbs made Easy* (1799):—*The Scripture Jewish History* (1803):—*An Account of the Parish*. See *Fasti Eccles. Scoticanæ*, ii, 89, 92.

Dalrymple, Edwin A., D.D., a Protestant Episcopal clergyman, was born in Baltimore, Md., in 1818. He was educated at St. Mary's College, Baltimore, and then studied theology at the Alexandria Episcopal Seminary. His first charge was Old Church, Hanover County, Va., and the church at New Kent Court-house. He then became rector of the high-school near Alexandria, where he was eminently successful for several years; visited Europe, and afterwards resided in Baltimore as the president of the School of Letters of Maryland. He was for many years one of the examining chaplains of the diocese, and rector of the House of Refuge at the time of his death, Oct. 30, 1881. For many years, up to 1874, he taught school in the University Buildings on Mulberry Street, Baltimore.

Dalrymple, Samuel B., a Protestant Episcopal minister, was ordained deacon in 1856, and presbyter the following year; and was rector of Grace Church, Honesdale, Pa., at the time of his death, Oct. 27, 1863, at the age of thirty years. See *Amer. Quar. Church Rev.* Jan. 1864, p. 669.

Dalrymple, William H., a Baptist minister, was born at Watertown, Mass., Feb. 20, 1808. He studied at the South Reading Academy, and at the Newton Theological Institution two years (1833-35); was ordained at South Abington, Mass., April 29, 1835, where he remained until 1837; was pastor at Northborough from 1838 to 1840; at South Gardiner from 1840 to 1842; in Woodville from 1844 to 1846; agent of the American Peace Society from 1846 to 1848; pastor at Barnstable in 1849 and 1850; at Fitzwilliam, N. H., from 1851 to 1853; Hudson, from 1855 to 1858; Stratham, from 1860 to 1862; and thereafter at Haverhill, Mass., where he died, Sept. 10, 1879. See *Gen. Cat. of Newton Theol. Inst.* p. 16. (J. C. S.)

Dalrymple, William Miller, a Methodist Episcopal minister, was born in Philadelphia, Feb. 2, 1824. He was converted at the age of nineteen, began preaching in 1852, and in the following year entered the Philadelphia Conference, in which he labored until his death, June 27, 1875. See *Minutes of Annual Conferences*, 1876, p. 50.

Dalton, Jacob, an English Independent minister, was educated at Mile End by Dr. Conder, and was ordained in 1766. He was settled first at the Silver Street Church, London; at Christmas, 1769, he removed to Coventry as assistant to Patrick Simpson, and was chosen sole pastor in 1773. He gave way to drinking, and sank into obscurity. In 1772 he published a volume of fifteen *Sermons*. See Wilson, *Dissenting Churches*, iii, 113.

Dalton, John, D.D., an English clergyman, was born in 1709 at Dean, Cumberland, and was educated at Lowther, Westmoreland, and at Queen's College, Oxford, where he was preacher for some years. In 1750 he was presented to the rectory of St. Mary, at Hill. He died at Worcester, July 21, 1763, leaving a volume of *Sermons* (1757):—*Two Epistles* (1744, 4to, written in 1735):—and some single *Sermons*. See Chalmers, *Biog. Dict.* s. v.; Allibone, *Dict. of Brit. and Amer. Authors*, s. v.

Daly, DANIEL, an Irish Dominican, was born in County Kerry in 1595, and as a monk adopted the name of *Dominicus a Rosario*. He was educated at Tralee and in Flanders; attained considerable reputation for his great learning; was invited to Lisbon to assist in founding a monastery for the Irish Dominicans, and was elected its first superior. In 1655 he was appointed ambassador to Louis XIV of France, by the duke of Braganza, to negotiate a treaty of alliance and affinity between the two courts. He died at Lisbon, June 30, 1662. One book only of his is known, *Initium, Incrementum, et Exitus Familiæ Giraldinorum* (Lisbon, 1655, 8vo). See Chalmers, *Biog. Dict.* s. v.; Allibone, *Dict. of Brit. and Amer. Authors*, s. v.

Dalzeil, ANDREW, a Scotch clergyman, was licensed to preach in July, 1734; presented to the living of Stonykirk; ordained in September, 1739; and died Nov. 22, 1755. See *Fasti Eccles. Scoticanæ*, i, 772.

Dalzell, NINIAN, a Scotch clergyman, was the first Protestant minister at Dumfries in 1567; removed to Caerlaverock in 1574, with three other places in charge; became a schoolmaster at Dumfries; renounced the Protestant faith; corrupted the youth sent to his care; was deposed by the assembly of 1579; and died April 21, 1587. See *Fasti Eccles. Scoticanæ*, i, 567, 573.

Daman, JOSEPH BROOKS, a Baptist minister, was born at Hanover, Mass., Nov. 13, 1809. Without a college education, he took the full course of study at the Newton Theological Institution (1838-41); and was pastor of churches in West Dedham, Mass., Woonsocket, R. I., East Killingly and Lyme, Conn., and Lake Village, N. H., where he died, in 1865. (J. C. S.)

Damascène, a French preacher at the close of the 18th century, was a Minorite of the Franciscan order, and provincial of the Recollets of Paris, He wrote, *Discours sur les Évangiles* (Paris, 1698, 1699):—*Discours Ecclésiastiques et Monastiques* (ibid. 1708). See Hoefer, *Nouv. Biog. Générale*, s. v.

Damberger, JOSEPH FERDINAND, a German scholar, was born at Passau, March 1, 1795. He studied at different universities, was made a priest in 1818, and joined the Jesuit order in 1837. In 1845 he was made professor of history at Lucerne, and died May 1, 1859, leaving *Fürstentafel der Europäischen Staatengeschichte*, (Regensburg, 1830):—*Synchronistiche Geschichte der Kirche und Welt im Mittelalter* (ibid. 1850-1863, 15 vols., the concluding vols. being edited by Rattinge). See Janner, in Wetzer u. Welte's *Kirchen-Lexikon*, s. v. (B. P.)

Damchuk, in Mongolian mythology, is a green horse, the steed of the god Maidari, the last Burchan, who descended to earth in order to exalt men again to their former duration of life, their virtue, and their beauty. The green horse is a great idol (Dolon Erdeni), which, with six other idols, is placed on the altars of the Mongolian temples.

Dame, FRIEDERICH, a Lutheran theologian of Germany, was born in Holstein, July 22, 1567. He studied at Rostock and Königsberg; was in 1592 rector at Itzehoe; in 1594, deacon at Flensburg; in 1600 pastor, and in 1604 provost there. He died Dec. 18, 1635, leaving *Voluntate Dei erga Genus Humanum*:—*De Resurrectione Mortuorum*:—*Apodixis de Animæ Immortalitate*, etc. See Moller, *Cimbria Literata*; Jöcher, *Allgemeines Gelehrten-Lexikon*, s. v. (B. P.)

Damhnat was an Irish saint of Sliabh Betha, now Slieve Beagh, in Tyrone. She is commemorated June 13.

Damia, a goddess among the ancients, said to be the wife of Faunus. She was so chaste that she never saw nor heard any other man than her own husband. Her sacrifice, which was always offered in private houses, with windows and doors shut, was called Damium. No man, nor picture of a male, was suffered to be present, nor were women allowed to reveal what passed.

Damian (*Damianus*, or *Damiani*, *Petrus*), Hymns of. Of these the following have become especially known: *Gravi me terrore pulsas, vitæ dies ultima.* "This awful hymn," says Mr. Neale, "is the *dies iræ* of individual life. The realization of the hour of death is shown, not only by this hymn, but by the commendatory prayer, used from his (the author's) time in the Roman Church, which begins, 'To God I commend thee, beloved brother; and to him whose creature thou art I commit thee.'" In the translation of Mr. Neale the first stanza runs thus:

> "O what terror in thy forethought,
> Ending scene of mortal life!
> Heart is sickened, veins are loosened,
> Thrills each nerve, with terror rife,
> When the anxious heart depicteth
> All the anguish of the strife!"

Another translation, given by P. S. Worsley, in *Lyra Messianica*, runs thus:

> "Heavily with dread thou loomest, last day of my earthly life;
> Heart and melting veins within me shudder at the mortal strife,
> When I would inform my spirit with what horrors thou art rife."

Another hymn is his *Crux mundi benedictio*, which Mr. Neale rendered—

> "O Cross, whereby the earth is blest,
> Certain Redemption, Hope, and Rest,
> Once as the Tree of Torture known,
> Now the bright gate to Jesu's Throne."

Better known is his *Ad perennis vitæ fontem*, "the noblest he has left us," and which, in R. F. Littledale's translation in *Lyra Mystica*, reads thus:

> "For the fount of life eternal is my thirsting spirit fain,
> And my prisoned soul would gladly burst her fleshly bars in twain,
> While the exile strives and struggles on to win her home again."

See Trench, *Sacred Latin Poetry*, p. 277 sq., 315 sq.; Rambach, *Anthologie christlicher Gesänge*, p. 238, 241; Daniel, *Thesaurus Hymnologicus*, i, 116, 224; iv, 291; Mone, *Hymni Lat. Med. Ævi*, i, 422; Neale, *Mediæval Hymns*, p. 52 sq. (B. P.)

Damiani, Felice, an eminent Italian painter, was born at Gubbio, and flourished from 1584 till 1616. He studied under Benedetto Nucci, and painted principally for the churches in his native city. His most esteemed work is the *Baptism of St. Augustine*, in the church of that saint, at Gubbio, painted in 1594. Another is the *Decapitation of St. Paul*, in San Recavati, at Castel-Nuovo. About 1596 he decorated two chapels in the Church of the Madonna de Lumi, at San Severino, with scenes from the life of the Virgin and the infancy of Christ. See Hoefer, *Nouv. Biog. Générale*, s. v.; Spooner, *Biog. Hist. of the Fine Arts*, s. v.

Damiani, Johann, a Hungarian theologian, was born at Tuhegli, June 21, 1710. In 1726 he went to Rome, studied at Fermo under the auspices of pope Benedict XIII, and on March 5, 1735, he entered orders. Returning to Rome, he was welcomed by pope Clement XII, who proposed him for the canonship of Presburg. He occupied various other positions in the ecclesiastical hierarchy, and died about 1780. His principal works are. *Doctrina veræ Christi Ecclesiæ* (Ofen, 1762):—*Justa Religionis Coactio*, etc. (ibid. 1765). This was a treatise concerning means for bringing dissenters into the Romish Church. See Hoefer, *Nouv. Biog. Générale*, s.

Damiani, Wilhelm Friederich, a Hungarian theologian, brother of the foregoing, was born Jan. 18, 1714. After having studied at Fermo he was chosen by Clement XII for primate of the kingdom. He died at Presburg, June 17, 1760, leaving *Synopsis vitæ Missionis Miraculorum et Evangeliorum Martini Lutheri et Joannis Calvini* (Ofen, 1761);—*Synopsis Doctrinæ Martini Lutheri et Joannis Calvini* (ibid. eod.). See Hoefer, *Nouv. Biog. Générale*, s. v.

Damiānus, the name of several early Christians:

1. A missionary sent by pope Eleutherius to Britain.

2. Bishop of Sidon, was a member of the synod at Antioch in 444, and also of the Council of Chalcedon in 451, when he gave his vote for the deposition of Dioscorus.

3. A companion of St. Regulus. One of the churches of St. Andrews was dedicated to him. He is commemorated June 1.

4. Fifth bishop of Rochester, was consecrated by archbishop Deusdedit about 655.

5. *Saint*, bishop of Ticinum (now Pavia), where he was born; and, while a presbyter, attended the synod held by Mansuetus, archbishop of Milan, against the Monothelites, in 679. He was deputed by the synod to draw up an exposition of faith to be sent to the emperor, which was received by acclamation in the Council of Constantinople in 680. He succeeded Anastasius the latter year as bishop, and died in 710.

Damini, Pietro, an Italian historical painter, was born at Castel-Franco in 1592, and studied under Giovanni Battista Novelli. There are many of his works in Castel-Franco, Vicenza, Crema, and Padua. In the church of Il Santo, at Padua, is his principal work, *The Crucifixion, with the Virgin Mary and St. John.* In the monastery of the Padri Serviti, at Vicenza, are several of his works, representing scenes from the life of St. Filippo. He died at Venice in 1631. See Hoefer, *Nouv. Biog. Générale*, s. v.; Spooner, *Biog. Hist. of the Fine Arts*, s. v.

Damiron, Jean Philibert, a French philosopher, was born in 1794, at Belleville. He was professor of philosophy at Paris, and died in 1862, leaving, *Cours de Philosophie* (Paris, 1842):—*Essais sur l'Histoire de la Philosophie en France au Dix-septième Siècle* (1846, 2 vols.):—also *Au Dix-huitième Siècle* (1862, 2 vols.):—and *Au Dix-neuvième Siècle* (3d ed. 1834). See Franck, *Moralistes et Philosophes* (Paris, 1872); Lichtenberger, *Encyclop. des Sciences Religieuses.* (B. P.)

Damm, Christian Tobias, a Lutheran theologian of Germany, was born at Geithain, in Saxony, Jan. 9, 1699. He studied at Halle, where he also for some time acted as teacher at the orphanage. In 1730 he was called to Berlin as con-rector at the Kölnische gymnasium, was made in 1742 pro-rector, and finally rector. He died May 27, 1778, having published, *Brief des Apostel Jacobi, übersetzt mit Anmerkungen* (Berlin, 1747):—*Das Neue Testament von neuem übersetzt und mit Anmerkungen begleitet* (ibid. 1764, 1765, 3 vols.); a work which caused his deposition from office, because he therein advocated Socinian doctrines:—*Vom historischen Glauben* (ibid. 1772):—*Betrachtungen über die Religion* (ibid. 1773). See Meusel, *Gelehrtes Deutschland;* Jöcher, *Allgemeines Gelehrten-Lexikon*, s. v.; Winer, *Handbuch der theol. Lit.* i, 171. (B. P.)

Damm, Georg, a Lutheran theologian of Germany, was born at Rostock in 1633. In 1663 he was deacon at St. Mary's, in that city; in 1667, pastor of the Altstadt, in Königsberg, and member of consistory, the same year taking his degree as doctor of theology at Greifswalde. He died May 11, 1679. He wrote, *De die Omnium Primo:—De Ritu Baptizandi super Sepulchra:—De Officio Pastorali Elenchtico ex Joh. xvi*, 8. See Arnold, *Historie der Königsbergischen Universität;* Jöcher, *Allgemeines Gelehrten-Lexikon*, s. v. (B. P.)

Damoetas. See Riculphus.

Damon, David, D.D., a Congregational minister,

was born in 1781. He graduated from Harvard College in 1811; was settled at Lunenburg in 1815, and died in 1843. He published one or two *Sermons*, and an *Address on Temperance*, delivered at Amesbury, Mass., in 1829. (J. C. S.)

Dampierre, Antoine Esmonin de, a French ascetic writer, was born at Beaune in January, 1743. He was successively counsellor and president à mortier at the parliament of Burgundy, president of the chamber in the royal court of Dijon, 1811, and member of the general council of the Cote d'Or, 1817. He died Sept. 11, 1824, leaving, *Verités Divines pour le Cœur et l'Esprit* (Lausanne, 1823):—*Historique de la Révolution* (Dijon, 1824). See Hoefer, *Nouv. Biog. Générale*, s. v.

Da Mula. See Amulio.

Damȳsus, in Greek mythology, was the swiftest of the giants, whose body was employed by the centaur Chiron, in order to strengthen that of Achilles.

Dan, Thomas, an English minister of the Society of Friends, was born at Nutfield, Surrey, in 1704, and became a preacher in 1734. The field of his labors was chiefly in England. He died Feb. 23, 1769. See *Piety Promoted*, ii, 433. (J. C. S.)

Dana (*a gift*), the term used by Buddhists of Ceylon to denote alms. Alms given to priests are restricted to four articles only—robes, food, a pallet to lie upon, and medicine or sick diet. Almsgiving is the first of virtues among the Buddhists, and superior to the observance of all the precepts. It brings a greatly increased reward in a future birth, including, if the duty be properly discharged, both wealth and attendants.

Dana, Asa J., a Methodist Episcopal minister, was born at Pultneyville, Ontario County, N. Y., March 24, 1820. He was converted in his twelfth year; received license to exhort in 1838, to preach in 1839, and the same year united with the Oneida Conference, wherein he labored zealously till his death, Oct. 5, 1857. See *Minutes of Annual Conferences*, 1858, p. 88.

Dana, Charles B., D.D., a Protestant Episcopal clergyman, was rector, for many years, of Christ Church, Fairfax Parish, Alexandria, Va., and remained in that office until 1860, when, after residing for a short time without charge in that place, he removed to Port Gibson, Miss., as rector of St. James's Church. In 1866 he went to Natchez, as rector of Trinity Church, of which he was incumbent at the time of his death, Feb. 25, 1873, aged sixty-six years. See *Prot. Episc. Almanac*, 1874, p. 138.

Dana, Gideon, a Congregational minister, was born at Oxford, Mass., Sept. 11, 1805. In 1830 he graduated from Brown University, and in 1836 from Bangor Theological Seminary—although part of his professional studies were pursued at Princeton, N. J. For a time he preached at North Falmouth, Mass.; Jan. 3, 1838, he was ordained pastor at South Amherst, where he remained until 1840. Subsequently, for four years, he labored in Holyoke, and was one year in the service of the American Tract Society. He preached in Harmar, O., from 1845 to 1850; spent several months in the service of the Western Seamen's Friend Society, and then took charge of the Second Presbyterian Church at Delaware. He removed to Strongsville in June, 1852, and in November, 1855, to Oberlin, as agent for the American and Foreign Christian Union. From 1859 to 1861 he served the Church in Bucyrus; in June, 1863, removed to Wauseon, but in 1868 returned to Oberlin, where he died, May 9, 1872. See *Cong. Quarterly*, 1873, p. 323.

Dana, James, D.D., a Congregational minister, was born at Cambridge, Mass., in 1735. He graduated from Harvard College in 1753, and remained there as a resident-graduate several years. In 1758 he was ordained pastor at Wallingford, Conn., notwithstanding the opposition of the Consociation on doctrinal grounds, and a church quarrel ensued, which was not healed until about 1772. When the Revolutionary struggle began, Mr. Dana became very popular on account of his decided stand for American liberty. Rev. James Noyes became his colleague in May, 1785. Four years after, Dr. Dana was called to the pastoral charge of the First Church in New Haven, and retired in December, 1805. He died in New Haven, Aug. 18, 1812. See Sprague, *Annals of the Amer. Pulpit*, i, 565.

Dana, Joseph, D.D., a Congregational minister, was born at Pomfret, Conn., Nov. 2, 1742. He graduated at Yale College in 1760; was ordained over the South Church in Ipswich, Mass., in 1765, and continued pastor there until his death, Nov. 16, 1827. Dr. Dana published several *Sermons* and *Addresses*. See Sprague, *Annals of the Amer. Pulpit*, i, 597; *Cong. Quarterly*, 1859, p. 42.

Dana, Simeon, M.D., a Free-will Baptist minister, was born at Lebanon, N. H., December, 1876. After practicing medicine some years, he began preaching in New Hampshire, and divided his time between his own church, that in Holderness, and that in North Holderness. He died Sept. 28, 1853. See *Free-will Baptist Register*, 1855, p. 89. (J. C. S.)

Dana, William Coombs, D.D., a Presbyterian minister, was born at Newburyport, Mass., Feb. 13, 1810. He graduated from Dartmouth College in 1828; was then employed in teaching, became a student in Andover Theological Seminary, and also in Columbia Seminary; was licensed, and spent a part of a year in Princeton Theological Seminary. He was ordained Feb. 14, 1836, pastor of Central Church, Charleston, S. C.; and died there, Nov. 30, 1880. He published a translation of Fénelon on the *Education of Daughters* (1831):—*A Transatlantic Tour* (1845):—*The Life of the Rev. Daniel Dana*, his father (1860); and compiled a volume of *Hymns*. See *Gen. Cat. of Princeton Theol. Sem.* 1881, p. 98.

Danace, a name given to the obolus, or coin which the ancient Greeks were wont to place in the mouth of the dead, to pay Charon for carrying them in his boat across the Styx to Hades.

Danavandri, in Indian mythology, is the god of the healing art, a special incarnation of Vishnu. There are no separate temples built for him (pagodas), but his image, a statue representing an old, bearded man, reading in a book, is erected on Vishnu's altar. He was produced when the gods turned the Mandar mountain into the sea of milk, to prepare amrita. Then he came out from the sea with a vessel which contained this ambrosia.

Danavas, in Hindû mythology, a numerous train of evil spirits, who often caused destructive wars, and were in continual discord with the kingdom of Indra. Twice Vishnu delivered his sovereign from the control of the dæmons, and Ihumanta also once came to his assistance.

Danax, the reader, of Aulon in Illyria, fled with the sacred vessels from a rustic riot against the Christians to a place by the sea, five miles from the town, but his enemies pursued him, let themselves down to him by ropes, bade him sacrifice to Bacchus, and, as he would not, cut him down with their swords and cast him into the sea, Jan. 16 (year not specified).

Dance, Matthew Maze, a Methodist Episcopal minister, was born in Dinwiddie County, Va., Jan. 29, 1790. He was converted about 1807; spent the next five years in teaching and study; entered the Virginia Conference in 1812, and was appointed to the Bertie Circuit; in 1814 became private secretary to bishop Asbury; located in 1822, settled in Prince Edward County, and died there, March 8, 1873. See *Minutes of Annual Conferences of the M. E. Church South*, 1873, p. 789.

Dance of Death is a series of pictures in which Death, portrayed as a skeleton, is the principal figure, and represents all the animation of a living person, sometimes amusingly ludicrous, and at others mischievous, but always busily employed. It is interesting, as it exhibits the costumes of all ranks and conditions of life at the period. Hans Holbein painted a dance of death in the royal galleries at Whitehall. There was also a fine example in the cloisters of the chantry chapel of St. Anne, called the Pardon Church House, on the north side of St. Paul's, in London, which dated from the reign of Henry V; and others were painted in the cloisters of the Holy Innocents at Paris, at Basle and Lubeck in the 15th century, at Minden in the 14th century; and at Dresden, Leipsic, and Annaberg. In the 14th century it is alluded to in the "Vision of Piers Plowman," and has been said to have been acted as a spiritual masque by clerks. Prior speaks of "imperial death leading up Holbein's dance." Possibly it was a memorial of a fatal plague as well as a moral lesson.

It was known also under the title of the *Dance Macabre*, either from an imaginary poet of Germany called Macabar, who was said to have written the appropriate distichs placed under each set of figures, or more probably from the hermit saint of Egypt, Macarius, who is still portrayed on pictures in Greek monasteries, as he was frequently introduced. The English name was *Dance of Poulì's* (St. Paul's).

Dancel, Jean Charles Richard, a French prelate and theologian, was born in 1761 at Cherbourg. He went to Paris; entered the society called the Robertines; was admitted to the Sorbonne as *socius;* obtained a chair of philosophy; in 1792 went to England, and there taught mathematics; returned to France in 1801, after the concordat; entered the chapter of Coutances; became grand-vicar, then rector of Valognes and archdeacon in 1805. Oct. 28, 1827, he was consecrated bishop of Bayeux, and distinguished himself by his zeal for the extension of seminaries. He died April 20, 1836, leaving *Apologie du Serment Civique* (1790). See Hoefer, *Nouv. Biog. Générale*, s. v.

Danckwerts, Hermann, a Lutheran theologian of Germany, was born April 4, 1814, at Plate. He studied at Göttingen; was in 1843 pastor at Bienenbüttel; in 1855, superintendent at Börry; in 1860, pastor at Göttingen, and finally superintendent there. He died July 26, 1881. He was an excellent preacher, who led many in the way of righteousness. (B. P.)

Dandam, in Hindû mythology, is a staff with seven ash knots, which the Sanjasi, or Indian saints, carry, and whose knots they must daily moisten with water from the Ganges, whereby they are protected against all influences of evil dæmons.

Dandavatren, in Hindû mythology, is a new birth and the third incarnation of the giant-dæmon Eruniakassiaben, one of the two Daidyas. He was subdued and slain by Vishnu, according to the Avatera.

Dandesuren, in Hindû mythology, was a holy penitent and favorite of Siva, who commanded the same worship to be paid to this saint as is given to the god himself. Therefore Dandesuren's statue stands in the temple of Siva, side by side with that of the great destroyer.

Dandini, Cesare, an Italian painter, was born at Florence in 1595, and studied successively with Curradi, Passignano, and Cristofano Allori. He executed many pictures and altar-pieces for the churches and convents at Florence. He died in 1658. See Hoefer, *Nouv. Biog. Générale*, s. v.; Spooner, *Biog. Hist. of the Fine Arts*, s. v.

Dandini, Ottaviano, an Italian painter of the middle of the 18th century, was the son of Pietro, by whom he was instructed. There are several of his works in the convents and churches at Florence, highly praised. There are some paintings of sacred subjects by him, in the Church of San Lorenzo; also in the Church of Santa Maddalena, at Pescia. See Hoefer, *Nouv. Biog. Générale*, s. v.; Spooner, *Biog. Hist. of the Fine Arts*, s. v.

Dandini, Pietro, an Italian painter, was born at Florence in 1646, and received instruction in the art when but four years of age, from Valerio Spada. He afterwards travelled through Italy, studying the best masters, and at the same time executed a number of paintings for the churches and convents of Florence. One of his most important works was the cupola in the church of Santa Maria Maddalena. In the Church of Santa Maria Maggiore is his picture of *St. Francisco.* He died in 1712. See Hoefer, *Nouv. Biog. Générale*, s. v.; Spooner, *Biog. Hist. of the Fine Arts*, s. v.

Dandis, one of the Vaishnava (q. v.) sects among the Hindûs, and a legitimate representative of the fourth Asrama or mendicant life, into which the Hindû is believed to enter after passing the previous stages of student, householder, and hermit. A Brahmin, however, does not require to pass through the previous stages, but is allowed to enter at once into the fourth order. The Dandi is distinguished by carrying a small dand or wand, with several projections from it, and a piece of cloth dyed with red ochre, in which the Brahminical cord is supposed to be enshrined, attached to it; he shaves his hair and beard, wears only a loin-cloth, and subsists upon food obtained ready dressed from the houses of the Brahmins once a day only, which he deposits in the small clay pot that he always carries with him. They are generally found in cities, collected, like other mendicants, in *maths.*

Dandolo, Faustino, a Venetian theologian, was born about 1379. He was successively apostolic prothonotary, legate *a latere*, and governor of Bologna; and died in 1449, leaving *Compendium pro Catholicæ Fidei Instructione.* There has also been attributed to him *Tractatus de Beneficiis; Responsa Quædam Juridica.* See Hoefer, *Nouv. Biog. Générale*, s. v.

Dandy, James H., a Methodist Episcopal minister, was born in Ireland, Sept. 8, 1798. He entered the Philadelphia Conference in 1826, and, by subsequent changes in the conference lines, was a member, first of the New Jersey, and afterwards of the Newark Conference. From 1857 to 1873 he sustained a supernumerary relation, and in the latter year was superannuated. He died in 1882 or 1883. See *Minutes of Annual Conferences*, 1883, p. 84.

Dane, Francis (1), a Congregational minister, was partly educated in England, and completed his theological studies in America. About 1648 he became pastor in Andover, Mass. In March, 1682, the Rev. Thomas Barnard became his assistant. During the witchcraft frenzy in 1692, it is said that intimations of Mr. Dane's implication served somewhat to check the delusion, as it was not believed that so pious a man could be in league with the devil. He died Feb. 17, 1699, aged eighty-one years. See Sprague, *Annals of the Amer. Pulpit*, i, 198.

Dane, Francis (2), a Methodist Episcopal minister, was born at Andover, Mass., May 1, 1782. He was converted in early life, and in 1810 joined the New England Conference, wherein he preached until 1840, when he superannuated. He was afterwards twice honored by being elected to the Massachusetts State Legislature. He died Oct. 16, 1864. See *Minutes of Annual Conferences*, 1865, p. 42.

Dane, John, a Congregational minister, was born at Andover, Mass. He graduated from Dartmouth College in 1800; was ordained pastor of the Church in Pittston, Me., Feb. 16, 1803, and was dismissed on account of gross immoralities in 1804. See Sprague, *Annals of the Amer. Pulpit*, ii, 379.

Danedi, Giovanni Stefano (called *Montalto*), a Milanese painter, was born at Treviglio in 1608, and studied under Cavaliere Morazzone. He executed many works in the churches and convents of Milan, among them *The Martyrdom of St. Justina*, in the Church of Santa Maria Pedone. He died at Milan in 1689.

Danedi, Giuseppe, an Italian painter, brother of the foregoing, was born at Treviglio in 1618, and studied under Guido Reni, at Bologna. He went to Turin, and executed some admirable pictures for the churches of that city, among them the fine altar-piece representing *The Massacre of the Innocents.* He died in 1688.

Danès, Pierre, a French scholar and bishop, was born at Paris in 1497. When quite young, he entered the College of Navarre, where he was appointed first professor of Greek in 1530. In 1545 he was present at the Council of Trent, and his address, which he delivered there in the following year, was printed at the instance of Francis I. When Henry II ascended the throne, he appointed Danès, in 1547, as tutor to the dauphin, afterwards Francis II. In 1548 he was elected to the see of Lavaur, and died at St. Germain des Prés, April 23, 1577. He wrote a number of historical works and addresses. See *Abrégé de la Vie du Cel. Pierre Danès* (Paris, 1731); Jöcher, *Allgemeines Gelehrten-Lexikon*, s. v.; Hoefer, *Nouv. Biog. Générale*, s. v. (B. P.)

Danès, Pierre Louis, a Flemish theologian, was born at Cassel, Flanders, in 1684. He taught philosophy at Louvain, was rector of St. James's at Antwerp in 1714, graduate-canon at Ypres in 1717, then president of the episcopal seminary, and penitentiary. In 1732 he returned to Louvain, and succeeded to Daelman in the chair of philosophy. He died at Louvain, May 28, 1736, leaving *Institutiones Doctrinæ Christianæ* (Louvain, 1713 and 1768; this is an abridgment of an excellent theological work):—*Orationes et Homiliæ* (ibid. 1735):—*De Fide, Spe et Charitate* (ibid. eod.). See Hoefer, *Nouv. Biog. Générale*, s. v.

Danforth, A. H., a Baptist minister, was born in 1818. Immediately upon completing his educational course at Hamilton in 1847, he went as missionary to Assam, India, but after eleven years labor there, ill-health obliged him to return, and he settled with the Baptist Church at Milestown, Pa., where he labored as pastor three years, and where, after serving the Christian Commission some time in the Army of the Potomac, he died Feb. 13, 1864. See *Appleton's Annual Cyclopædia*, 1865, p. 633.

Danforth, Francis, a Congregational minister, was born in New Hampshire in 1794. He graduated from Dartmouth College in 1819, and from Andover Theological Seminary in 1822; was ordained June 11, 1823; pastor at Greenfield, where he remained until 1831; at Winchester until 1839; of the First Church of Hadley, Mass., until 1842; was without charge until 1844; was at Byron and Medina, N. Y., in 1845; stated supply of the Presbyterian Church at Clarence from 1846 to 1852, and thereafter without charge at the same place until his death, Jan. 29, 1854. See *Trien. Cat. of Andover Theol. Sem.* 1870, p. 50.

Danforth, John, a Congregational minister, son of Rev. Samuel Danforth, Sr., was born Nov. 5, 1660. He graduated at Harvard College in 1677; was ordained the seventh minister of the Church in Dorchester, June 28, 1682, and occupied that position until his death, May 26, 1730. He left several published discourses, among them two *Sermons on the Earthquake in* 1727. (J. C. S.)

Danforth, R. Edmund, a Methodist Episcopal minister, was born at Merrimac, N. H. He was converted in 1854; received license to exhort and to preach in 1855; and in 1856 entered the Biblical Institute at Concord, N. H., where he remained two years, meantime joining the New Hampshire Conference, in which he labored till his death, June 28, 1863. See *Minutes of Annual Conferences*, 1864, p. 75.

Danforth, William Burke, a Congregational minister, was born at Barnard, Vt., Feb. 21, 1849. He studied at Royalton Academy, graduated at Dartmouth College in 1871, and from Yale Divinity School in 1874; was ordained pastor of the Church in Gilead, Conn., July 9 of the same year, and died there July 4, 1875. See *Cong. Quarterly*, 1876, p. 423.

Dangerfield, Joan, an English martyr, was the wife of the godly William Dangerfield, and on account of her faithfulness to her religion she was taken from her home, with a child only fourteen days old, and cast into prison amid thieves and murderers. She remained there for some weeks, when she was taken to the place of execution and burned, with three other martyrs, in 1556. See Fox, *Acts and Monuments*, viii, 251.

Dangerfield, William, an English martyr, was a citizen of Wootton-under-Edge, not far from Bristol. He was suspected by some of his adversaries, and put into prison, where he remained until his legs were almost fretted off with irons. After much suffering he recanted, against the advice of his wife, who was a prisoner at the same time; he had no sooner quitted the jail, than, his conscience upbraiding him, he began to pray for forgiveness, for which he was soon put to the stake and burned, in 1556. See Fox, *Acts and Monuments*, viii, 251.

Dani, ELDAD HA-. See ELDAD HAD-DANI.

Danicie, GEORG, a famous Servian linguist, was born at Neusatz, April 4, 1825. In 1856 he was appointed librarian at Belgrade, in 1859 professor at the lyceum there, and in 1853 professor of Slavic philology at the college. In 1867 he went to Agram, where he was made secretary of the academy. In 1873 he was recalled to Belgrade, but in 1877 he went again to Agram to continue his large Serbo-Croatian dictionary, which was published by the academy. He died Nov. 17, 1882. His chief work lies in his linguistic publications concerning the Servian language, but he also holds an honorable position on account of his excellent translation of the Old Testament into the Servian language. (B. P.)

Daniel (sometimes **Danihel**) was the name of a number of early bishops and presbyters:

1. Presbyter, said to have been martyred in Persia, Feb. 21, in the thirty-fifth year of Sapor (A.D. 344), with a virgin, whose name in Chaldee meant Rose, after five days' torture and three months' interrogation, according to brief acts given from a Vatican MS. by Assemani (*Mart. Orient.* p. 103.)

2. One of the abbots of Scetè in Egypt, in the 4th or 5th century. He was a disciple of Paphnutius, and served him in the capacity of deacon at the altar. He is the speaker in the fourth of the Collationes of Johannes Cassianus, who had met him during a tour in Egypt.

3. A disciple of the solitary Arsenius, about 445, who performed for him the duties of hospitality to strangers arriving at his cell.

4. Bishop at a council assembled by Cyril at Alexandria about A.D. 430, for the condemnation of Nestorius. He was one of the four bishops selected to carry to Constantinople the letter written by Cyril in the name of this council, together with the letter of pope Celestine in the name of a Roman council on the same subject.

5. A presbyter at Alexandria, sent in A.D. 438 to Acacius, bishop of Meletina, Theodotus of Ancyra, and Firmus of Cæsarea, with a credential letter by Cyril of Alexandria, to show them the situation of affairs and the reply he proposed to send to the Oriental bishops at Antioch.

6. Bishop of Charræ (Haran) in Mesopotamia, in the middle of the 5th century. He was the nephew of the celebrated Nestorian, Ibas, bishop of Edessa, who consecrated him. He voted against Athanasius in the council held at Antioch in 444. Charges were preferred against him by a synod held at Berytus, and his disorderly and licentious life being proven, he was anathematized by Dioscorus at the Latrocinium of Ephesus.

7. See DEINOL WYN.

8. A deacon mentioned in the will of St. Perpetuus, archbishop of Tours. He lived about the end of the 5th century.

9. Bishop of Theodosiopolis (or Rhæsina) in Mesopotamia, in the middle of the 6th century. He wrote works against the errors of "the Marcionites, Manichees, Chaldæans, and astrologers."

10. Abbot of the monastery afterwards known as St. Médard's, at Soissons. The monastery was founded by Clotaire I of the Franks about 560, and at its dedication, in 562, Daniel became its first abbot. He is said to have been a disciple of St. Maurus of Glaufeuille, and to have obtained the privilege of immunity from pope John III.

11. Saint and bishop of Cenn-Garadh (now Kingarth, on the island of Bute, in the Firth of Clyde). He is commemorated Feb. 18.

12. A monk of the 7th century, who wrote at the monastery of Rhaitu the *Life of John Climacus*, abbot of Mount Sinai (605).

13. Bishop of Salach, in Mesopotamia. He lived in the 8th century, and wrote a *Commentary on the Psalms*.

14. Succeeded Aribertus as fifteenth archbishop of Narbonne. He was one of twelve Gallic bishops present at the Roman council held in the Lateran basilica under pope Stephen IV, A.D. 769, concerning the election of the pope and the cultus of sacred images. The principal event recorded of his episcopate was his holding a synod in the basilica of Sts. Justus and Pastor at Narbonne, on June 27, 788 (Baluze, Petrus de Marca), or 791 (*Gall. Christ.*), attended by the bishops of the provinces of Narbonne and Tarragona, which were then united, and by those of the neighboring provinces of Arles, Vienne, Aix, and Eause. Three subjects were discussed. (1) The heresy taught by Felix, bishop of Urgel, concerning the adoption of the Son of God, and this was in all probability condemned, though there is no distinct information on that point. (2) The state of the church of Ausona (Vich), the capital of the province of Tarragona, which had formerly lost its episcopal see through the invasion of the Moors, and been ecclesiastically annexed to Narbonne. It was decided that it should remain in this subjection until the pagans were expelled, after which it should have a bishop of its own. (3) A dispute with Winedurus, bishop of Elne, as to jurisdiction over the *Pagus Redensis*, in the Pyrenees, and this was decided in Daniel's favor. The exact date of his death is not known, although Nebridus succeeded him.

Daniel, *Saint*, OF AFRICA, was provincial of the order of Minorites of Calabria. In 1221 he embarked for Africa, at the head of a mission composed of brothers Samuel, Angelus, Donno, Ugolino, Leo, and Nicolas. for the purpose of laboring for the conversion of the Moors. They landed at Ceuta and commenced preaching. The people seized them, and led them to Mohammed the Green, king of Morocco; this prince despoiled them, scourged them, threw them into prison, and finally beheaded them, Oct. 8, 1221. They suffered martyrdom with joy and courage. Some years after, the child-prince of Portugal, son of king Alfonso the Fat, obtained their bodies of the king of Morocco, and presented them to Spain. In 1516, pope Leo X added them to the number of saints. Their festival is celebrated Oct. 13. See Hoefer, *Nouv. Biog. Générale*, s. v.

Daniel DE SAINT JOSEPH (properly *Joseph le Gouverneur*), a French theologian, was born at St. Malo

in 1601. He entered the novitiate of the Carmelites of Rennes at the age of fifteen, and nine years afterwards taught philosophy at Caen, and subsequently theology, with great repute. He became provincial of his order in the province of Toulouse, and died at Guildo, Feb. 5, 1666, leaving *Vie de Saint André Corsin* (Rennes, 1630):—*Manuel de la Confrérie de la Sainte Famille de Jésus* (Angers, 1640):—*Le Théologien Français sur le Mystère de la Sainte Trinité* (1643, 1658):—*Panégyriques* (1660). See Hoefer, *Nouv. Biog. Générale*, s. v.

Daniel DE SAINT-SEVER, a French theologian, who lived in 1625, was a Capuchin of the province of Guienne. He taught theology, was possessed of a good memory, and was versed in nearly all the languages. He wrote, *De Decensu Christi ad Inferos* (Lyons, 1618, in Latin and French):—*De Collatione et Disputatione cum Nomansensibus et Septimaniis Factionis Calvinianæ* (Avignon, 1625). See Hoefer, *Nouv. Biog. Générale*, s. v.

Daniel DE LA VIERGE (properly *Audenærde*), a Belgian theologian, was born at Hamme, near Dendermonde, Flanders, in 1615. He obtained his education at the house of the Carmelites, whom he joined in 1632. He was successively lecturer on theology, master of novices, prior of the convents of Brussels and Malines, and twice provincial. He distinguished himself by his piety and charity, and died Oct. 24, 1678, leaving a large number of works, among which we notice, *The Art of Confession* (Brussels, 1649, in Flemish):—*Demonstration of the True Church* (ibid. eod., in Flemish):—*Epitome Vitæ Sancti Petri Thomæ*, etc. (Antwerp, 1659):—*Vita Sancti Eliæ Prophitæ* (Frankfort, 1670). See Hoefer, *Nouv. Biog. Générale*, s. v.

Daniel, FESTIVAL OF, a festival celebrated by the Greek Church on Dec. 17, in memory of the prophet Daniel, and the three young Hebrews who were cast into the fiery furnace.

Daniel, Ebenezer, an English Baptist minister, was born at Burford, in Oxfordshire, Oct. 14, 1784. He was converted when a child, and baptized at the age of seventeen. He became a student in Bristol College in 1802; was ordained, in 1808, as pastor at Brixham, Devonshire; in 1812 removed to Luton, Bedfordshire; was designated as a missionary to Ceylon, Feb. 17, 1830; reached his station Aug. 14 following, and labored until his death, June 2, 1844. See (Lond.) *Baptist Magazine*, 1846, p. 137, 201. (J. C. S.)

Daniel, Elizabeth, a minister of the Society of Friends, was born at Salem, N. J., in 1709, and early in life was called into both the Church and the ministry. She sometimes travelled in sections of Pennsylvania and Maryland, and died Oct. 30, 1760. See *Piety Promoted*, iv, 416–418. (J. C. S.)

Daniel, Gabriel, a French ecclesiastical writer, was born at Rouen in 1649. When eighteen years of age he joined the Jesuits. After he had taught for some years in the college at Rouen with great success, his superiors sent him to Paris as librarian of the "domus professæ" of his society, where he died in 1728. His most important work is *L'Histoire de France* (Paris, 1713, also 1755–60, 3 vols.), against which Mezerai wrote his *Observations Critiques*:—also *Recueil de Divers Ouvrages Philosophiques, Théologiques, Apologétiques et Critiques* (ibid. 1724, 3 vols.). See Lichtenberger, *Encyclop. des Sciences Religieuses*, s. v.; Jöcher, *Allgemeines Gelehrten-Lexikon*, s. v.; *Encyclop. Brit.* (9th ed.) s. v. (B. P.)

Daniel, Herbert, an English Congregational minister, was born near Pontypool, March 30, 1801. He was converted at the age of eighteen; received his ministerial training at Pontypool and at Abergavenny; and was ordained pastor at Maesycwmwr in 1832. In 1837 he formed a church in Pontypool, and in 1841 another in Cefnycrib. He died Oct. 26, 1874. See (Lond.) *Cong. Year-book*, 1875, p. 320.

Daniel, Hermann Adalbert, a Protestant theologian of Germany, was born at Köthen, Nov. 18, 1812. He studied at Halle; was in 1843 assistant tutor at the school there; in 1844, inspector adjunctus, with the title of professor; and died at Leipsic, Sept. 13, 1871. He published, *Commentationis de Tatiano Apologeta Specimen* (Halle, 1835):—*Tatianus als Apologet* (ibid. 1837):—*Hymnologischer Blüthenstrauss* (ibid. 1840):—*Theologische Controversen* (ibid. 1843). But his main works, which have made his name known beyond the limits of his own country, are, *Codex Liturgicus Ecclesiæ Universæ* (Leipsic, 1847–55, 4 vols.; vol. i, *Codex Liturgicus Ecclesiæ Romano-Catholicæ*, 1847; vol. ii, *Cod. Lit. Ecclesiæ Lutheranæ*, 1848; vol. iii, *Cod. Lit. Ecclesiæ Reformatæ atque Anglicanæ*, 1851; vol. iv, *Cod. Lit. Ecclesiæ Orientalis*, 1855):—*Thesaurus Hymnologicus* (Halle, 1841–46, 5 vols.). See Zuchold, *Bibl. Theol.* i, 258. (B. P.)

Daniel, James Taylor, a minister of the Bible Christians, was born in Devon, England, March 5, 1838. He was converted when twenty years of age; for two years labored with great acceptability and usefulness as a local preacher on the Holsworthy Circuit, and in 1864 entered the itinerant ministry. After thirteen years of successful labor, he died suddenly, May 2, 1877. See *Minutes of the Conference*, 1877.

Daniel, John, a Methodist Episcopal minister, was born in Philadelphia, Pa., in 1807, of Quaker parents. He was converted in early youth, licensed to preach in 1828, and in 1832 joined the Indiana Conference, in which he rendered effective service until 1852, when he was transferred to the California Conference. He at length became superannuated, and died Oct. 19, 1880. See *Minutes of Annual Conferences*, 1881, p. 316.

Daniel, Mark, an English Wesleyan minister, was converted in early life, began to preach in 1794, and died Feb. 21, 1821, aged fifty-five years. See *Minutes of the British Conference*, 1821.

Daniel, Robert, a Bible Christian minister, was born in the parish of St. Austell, Cornwall, England. He was converted in 1824, and entered the ministry in 1833. His health failed in 1838, and he died Dec. 11, 1839.

Daniel, Robert T., a Baptist minister, was born in Middlesex County, Va., June 10, 1773. He removed to North Carolina; in 1802 united with the Church at Holly Springs, Wake Co., and was ordained in 1803. He labored as an itinerant evangelist in different parts of North Carolina, Virginia, Mississippi, and Tennessee; and died in Paris, Tenn., Sept. 14, 1840. See Cathcart, *Baptist Encyclop.* p. 306. (J. C. S.)

Daniel, Walter (Lat. *Gualterus*), a Cistercian of England, who died about the year 1170, is the author of, *De Conceptione B. Mariæ:—De Virginitate Ejusdem:—Expositio Super-* "*Missus est Angelus*":—*De Onere Jumentorum Austri Esa. xxx*, 6, in two books. See Pitseus, *De Scriptoribus Angliæ;* De Visch, *Bibliotheca Scriptorum Ordinis Cisterciensis;* Jöcher, *Allgemeines Gelehrten-Lexikon*, s. v. (B. P.)

Daniels, Amos, a Free-will Baptist minister, was born at Hartford, Conn., in 1787. He was converted in August, 1806, and joined the Methodists, among whom he was a preacher for about eight years; but afterwards united with a Free-will Baptist Church, and was ordained in 1822. He labored much among the feeble churches, and for twenty-five years was the pastor of the Virgil and Dryden Church, N. Y. He died at his residence in Vestal, April 29, 1873. See *Morning Star*, Dec. 24, 1873. (J. C. S.)

Daniels, Edmund, an English Congregational minister, was born at Waltham, near Canterbury, in 1837. He early united with the Wesleyan Methodists, and, before reaching his sixteenth year, was an acceptable lay preacher. After studying at Didsbury College, he was appointed to Hereford, Cornwall, and Norfolk. In 1866 he joined the Congregationalists, and labored at Tyldesley, Hollingworth, and Bolton. In 1874 he removed to Felling, near Gateshead, and finally to Byker, where he died, April 26, 1878. See (Lond.) *Cong. Year-book*, 1879, p. 308.

Daniels, Henry, an English Wesleyan minister, was born at Ecclesfield, near Sheffield, in 1802. He was converted in early life; commenced his ministry in 1828; spent thirty-seven years of toil, almost entirely in the counties of Devon and Cornwall; and died at St. Austell, Nov. 8, 1869. See *Minutes of the British Conference*, 1870, p. 21.

Daniels, John H., a Baptist minister, was born in Caroline County, Va., Jan. 15, 1811. He was converted in 1832, ordained in 1833, and preached in Kentucky about three years; in 1836 settled in Cass County, Ill., and preached for the churches of Princeton, Richland, Sangamon Bottom, and other places; thence removed to Bath, Mason Co., where he preached until his death, May 20, 1881. See *Minutes of Ill. Anniversaries*, 1881, p. 25. (J. C. S.)

Danish Version OF THE SCRIPTURES. See SCANDINAVIAN VERSIONS.

Danker, GEORGE, a Methodist Episcopal minister, was born near Bremen, Germany, in 1794. He was converted in 1824; immediately became an earnest exhorter, for which he was severely persecuted; labored some years as a city missionary with marked success; came to America in 1836, and settled in Marietta, O., where for some time he preached with large success for the Lutheran Church. About three years later he united with the Cincinnati Conference, and in it continued faithful and laborious until 1859, when he became superannuated, and retired to Marietta, where he died, March 4, 1861. See *Minutes of Annual Conferences*, 1861, p. 166.

Danley, LEROY C., a minister of the Methodist Episcopal Church South, entered the Kentucky Conference in 1840; travelled circuits until 1849, when he located; was readmitted in 1855; became supernumerary in 1859, superannuated in 1860, and died July 27, 1873. See *Minutes of Annual Conferences of the M. E. Church South*, 1873, p. 861.

Dann, CHRISTIAN ADAM, a Lutheran theologian of Germany, was born at Tübingen, Dec. 24, 1758, where he also prepared himself for the ministry. In 1793 he was appointed deacon at Göppingen; in 1794, assistant at Stuttgart; in 1819, pastor at Mössingen; and in 1824 again at Stuttgart, as archdeacon at the Stiftskirche. In 1825 he became pastor at St. Leonhard, and died March 19, 1837. His writings, mostly ascetical brochures, are enumerated in Zuchold, *Bibl. Theol.* i, 258–260. See also Winer, *Handbuch der theol. Lit.* ii, 257, 332, 367, 374; Herzog, *Real-Encyklop.* s. v.; Hofacker, *Denkmal der Liebe* (Stuttgart, 1837); Albert Knapp, in his *Christoterpe* (1847); M. A. Knapp, *Sechs Lebensbilder* (1875). (B. P.)

Dannah. For this place Lieut. Conder at first strongly advocated the modern *Domeh* [see DUMAH], two miles north of ed-Dhoheriyeh (*Quar. Statement* of the "Pal. Explor. Soc." Jan. 1875, p. 55); but he has since more plausibly suggested (*Bible Hand-book*, p. 408; *Tent-work*, ii, 336) *Idhnah*, which, however, is north-west instead of south-west from Hebron. See JEDNA.

Dannecker, ANTON VON, a Roman Catholic theologian of Germany, was born in 1816 in Rathshausen. In 1841 he was made priest, in 1845 chaplain, and in 1849 pastor at Stuttgart. In 1860 he became a member of the Rottenburg chapter, which he also represented from 1868 to 1876 in the house of representatives at Würtemberg. In 1856 and 1857 he acted as theological counsellor to the Würtemberg ambassador at Rome, and died while capitulary and papal prelate at Rottenburg, June 6, 1881. (B. P.)

Danneil, JOHANN FRIEDRICH, a Lutheran theologian of Germany, who died while member of consistory and pastor of St. Ægidius at Quedlinburg, Feb. 10, 1772, is the author of *Kräftige Trostgründe der Religion wider die Schrecken des Todes* (Helmstädt, 1749):—*Der Gottesacher, die Auferstehung, und das Gericht* (Quedlinburg, 1760). See Hamberger, *Gelehrtes Deutschland;* Jöcher, *Allgemeines Gelehrten-Lexikon*, s. v. (B. P.)

Dannelly, JAMES, a minister of the Methodist Episcopal Church South, was born in Columbia County, Ga., Feb. 4, 1786. He was converted at the age of thirty, and in 1818 received license to preach and was admitted into the South Carolina Conference, in which he labored faithfully, with but two years' intermission as superannuate, until 1838, when he again became superannuated. He died April 28, 1855. See *Minutes of Annual Conferences of the M. E. Church South*, 1855, p. 627; Simpson, *Cyclop. of Methodism*, s. v.; Sprague, *Annals of the Amer. Pulpit*, vii, 606.

Dannemayr, MATHIAS, a Roman Catholic theologian of Germany, was born Feb. 13, 1741, at Oepfingen, in Würtemburg. He studied at Freiburg, and was appointed in 1773 professor of church history there. In 1786 he was called to Vienna, but exchanged his position for that of a custos in the university library, on account of feeble health, in 1803. He died July 8, 1805, leaving *Introductio in Historiam Ecclesiæ Christianæ Universam* (Friburgi, 1778):—*Historia Succincta Controversiarum de Librorum Symbolicorum Auctoritate inter Lutheranos Agitatarum* (ibid. 1780):—*Institutiones Eccles. N. T.* (1783):—*Institutiones Ecclesiasticæ Novi Testamenti* (Viennæ, 1788; 2d ed. 1806). See Döring, *Die gelehrten Theologen Deutschlands*, i, 308 sq.; Winer, *Handbuch der theol. Lit.* i, 529, 541; Hoefer, *Nouv. Biog. Générale*, s. v. (B. P.)

Danni-Devaru (*Cold-water gods*), a title given by the Badagas of India to the Mahalinga idols, which were supposed to enable their priests to walk upon hot coals as if they were cold water.

Danov, ERNST JACOB, a Lutheran theologian of Germany, was born March 12, 1741, at Redlau, near Dantzic. He studied at Helmstädt, and was in 1766 appointed rector of the Johannes school at Dantzic. He accepted a call as professor extraordinarius of theology to Jena in 1768, and drowned himself March 18, 1782, leaving *De Vera Verborum Sermonis Hebraici Natura* (Sedan, 1740):—*De Choreis Sacris Ebræorum* (Greifsw. 1766):—*De Vera Natura et Indole Verbi* ל״א (Sedan, 1768):—*De Gloria Christi* (Jenæ, 1769):—*Institutiones Theologiæ Dogmaticæ* (ibid. 1772–76):—*De Episcopis Tempore Apostolorum* (ibid. 1770):—*Explanatio Locorum Scripturæ S. Divinitatem Jesu Christi Probantium* (ibid. 1774):—*Jesus Christus Filius Dei* (1776, 1777, 2 parts):—*Progr. Super Integritate Scripturæ* (ibid. 1777):—*De eo, quod in Religione vim Rationis Superat* (ibid. 1778–81). See Döring, *Die gelehrten Theologen Deutschlands*, i, 310 sq.; Winer, *Handbuch der theol. Lit.* i, 22, 298, 383, 447; Fürst, *Bibl. Jud.* i, 195; Steinschneider, *Bibliog. Handbuch*, s. v.; Lichtenberger, *Encyclop. des Sciences Religieuses*, s. v.; Herzog, *Real-Encyklop.* (2d ed.) s. v.; Hoefer, *Nouv. Biog. Générale*, s. v. (B. P.)

Dante, GIROLAMO, a Venetian painter, was a scholar of Titian, and painted from his own designs. There is a fine altar-piece, by him, in the Church of San Giovanni Nuovo at Venice. He flourished in the first part of the 16th century. See Spooner, *Biog. Hist. of the Fine Arts*, s. v.; Hoefer, *Nouv. Biog. Générale*, s. v.

Dantecourt, JEAN BAPTISTE, a French theologian, was born in Paris, June 24, 1643. He joined the regular canons of St. Geneviève at St. Augustin, Sept. 8, 1662; was appointed chancellor of the University of Paris in 1680; and pastor of St. Étienne-du-Mont in 1694. He retired to St. Geneviève in 1710, and died at Paris, April 5, 1718, leaving *Les Augustins et Les Bénédictins aux États de Bourgogne:*—*Défense de l'Église* (Paris, 1689). See Hoefer, *Nouv. Biog. Générale*, s. v.

Dantforth, CHARLES, a Presbyterian minister, was born at Rupert, Vt., Aug. 23, 1800. He graduated from Williams College in 1826; studied at Auburn Seminary; was licensed by the Presbytery of Cayuga in 1829, and ordained an evangelist; soon after went to Ohio and Indiana; labored several years in the bounds of the presbyteries of Miami and Chillicothe; in 1838 became a member of the Presbytery of Erie; in 1840 removed to Springfield, Pa.; afterwards resided at Oberlin, O., preaching as he was able, until his death, April 29, 1867. See *Hist. of the Presb. of Erie.*

Danti, Girolamo, an Italian painter, was born at Perugia in 1547. There are some of his works in the Church of San Pietro, in his native city. He died in 1580. See Spooner, *Biog. Hist. of the Fine Arts*, s. v.

Danti, Ignazio, a Dominican friar, was born at Perugia in 1537. He painted four subjects from the New Test. by order of pope Gregory XIII. He died at Rome in 1586. See Spooner, *Biog. Hist. of the Fine Arts*, s. v.

Dantine, FRANÇOIS, a learned Benedictine monk of the congregation of St. Maur, was born at Gourieux, in the diocese of Liege, April 1, 1688. He studied at Douay, taught in various schools of France, and died Nov. 3, 1746. He edited an improved edition of Ducange's *Glossary* in 1736; assisted Clemencet in the great work *L'Art de Vérifier les Dates*, and wrote a *Traduction des Psaumes* (Paris, 1739, 1740). See *Biog. Universelle*, s. v.

Danukobi, in Hindû mythology, is a celebrated pool, or bath, which Vishnu dug for himself and Siva. It lies near Pondicherry, on the peninsula this side of the Ganges, near a large temple of Siva. The spot is sacred for another reason. It was the place where the ape-king Hanuman met Rama, when they both undertook the journey to Ceylon. This bath is visited by innumerable parties of pilgrims; whoever bathes in it is purified from all sin, but he must bring water from the Ganges with him to wash the Lingam of the pagoda, and he is obliged to sleep on the bare earth, without covering, during the entire pilgrimage.

D'Anvers, HENRY, an English Baptist, born of respectable parents, was a colonel in the Parliamentary army in 1646, governor of Stafford, and a magistrate well-beloved of the people, as he refused bribes. He became a Baptist during the Commonwealth, and after the Restoration made over his estates to trustees to save their confiscation by his persecutors. In 1663 he was joint-pastor of a Church in Aldgate. In 1674 the government offered a reward for his apprehension, and he was sent prisoner to the Tower; but his wife procured his release in 1675. He afterwards defended the duke of Monmouth, and for safety fled to Holland, where he died in 1686. In 1674 he published a *Treatise on Baptism*, which made him many adversaries. Some of his brethren defended him against his antagonists. He also published, *A Treatise of the Laying on of Hands, with the History Thereof* (1674). In another book, called *Theopolis*, he fully considers "the Dragon, the Beast, and False Prophet." He was a worthy man, of unspotted life. See Wilson, *Dissenting Churches*, i, 393; Benedict, *Hist. of the Baptists;* Haynes, *Baptist Cyclop.* i, 13–16.

Danzer, JAKOB, a Roman Catholic theologian of Germany, was born March 4, 1743, at Lengenfeld, in Suabia. He joined the order of the Benedictines at Isny; was in 1784 professor of moral and pastoral theology at Salzburg, but had to resign his position in 1792 on account of his liberal tendencies. In 1795 he was second canon at Buchau, and died there Sept. 4, 1796. He published, *Anleitung zur christlichen Moral* (Salzburg, 1787-91, 1792, 3 vols.):—*Ueber den Geist Jesu und seine Lehre* (ibid. 1795, 1797):—*Beiträge zur Reformation der* *christlichen Theologie* (Ulm, 1793):—*Magazin zur Verbesserung des dogmatischen Lehrbegriffs der Katholiken* (1794). See Döring, *Die gelehrten Theologen Deutschlands*, i, 315 sq.; Winer, *Handbuch der theol. Lit.* i, 316, 702; Hoefer, *Nouv. Biog. Générale*, s. v. (B. P.)

Daola, a Tonquinese idol, who presides over travellers.

Daon, Roger François, a French theologian, was born at Briqueville, diocese of Bayeux, in 1679. He became a priest in 1699; taught theology at Avranches; was afterwards made governor of the smaller seminary at Rennes; and was successively superior of the seminaries of Avranches, Senlis, Caen, and Seez, where he died, Aug. 16, 1749, leaving *Le Tribunal de la Pénitence*, etc. (Paris, 1738):—*Pratique du Sacrement* (Caen, 1740):—*Méthodes des Conférences Spirituelles*, etc. (ibid. 1744):—*La Conduite des Âmes* (Paris, 1753):—*Cathéchisme pour les Ordinants*, etc.:—*Instruction à l'Amour de Dieu*:—*Réglements de Vie pour un Prêtre.* See Hoefer, *Nouv. Biog. Générale*, s. v.

Daphnomantia, in Greek paganism, was the art of prophesying from the twig of a laurel-tree. It was thrown into the fire, and its crackling and bending was carefully noticed, from which the answer was concluded as given by Apollo. See Divination.

Daphnus, second bishop of Vaison, lived in the time of Constantine the Great (cir. 314). He came to the Council of Arles with Victor, an exorcist, at the order of the emperor. See Smith, *Dict. of Christ. Biog.* s. v.

Dapp, Raymund, an evangelical minister of Germany, was born Sept. 22, 1744, at Geislingen, near Ulm, and died May 1, 1819, near Berlin. He is the author of *Gemeinnütziges Magazin für Prediger* (Berlin, 1805-1816, 7 vols.):—*Predigtbuch für christliche Landleute* (ibid. 1797):—*Kurze Predigten und Predigtentwürfe* (1793-1805, 6 vols.):—*Gebetbuch für christliche Landleute* (1786, 1799). See Zuchold, *Bibl. Theol.* i, 261; Win.., *Handbuch der theol. Lit.* ii, 39, 174, 193, 380. (B. P.)

Dara, in Lamaism, was the name of two goddesses who sprang from two tears of Jashik, which he let fall over the fearful destiny of the damned. They were personifications of love and sympathy.

Dararians, the name of a heretical Mohammedan sect, derived from their founder Darari. They flourished on the coast of Syria and in the district of Lebanon. Darari was an impostor, who came from Persia to Egypt about A.D. 1000, and endeavored to persuade the people that the caliph Hakem was God. For this blasphemy he was put to death by the indignant people.

Darbelin was an Irish saint, given as one of the four virgin daughters of Mac Iaar, living at Cill-nā-ninghen, now Killininny, County Dublin. They were Darinnill, Darbelin, Cael, and Coimgheall. She is commemorated Oct. 26.

Darbile (or **Derbhiledh**), an Irish saint, was daughter of Cormac, son of Brecchius. She was accepted as patron saint of the descendants of Amhalghaidh, son of Fiachra, in the place of St. Corbmac. She flourished about the middle of the 6th century, and is also known as Darbile and Derivla of Irras. The church in which she lived, died, and was buried is in Mullet, barony of Erris, County Mayo, She is commemorated Aug. 3 and Oct. 26.

Darboy, Georges, a French ecclesiastic, was born Jan. 16, 1813. He became teacher of philosophy and theology at the Seminary of Langres in 1839, bishop of Nancy in 1859, and archbishop of Paris in 1863. He was a firm opponent of papal infallibility in the Vatican Council, but yielded to the decision of the majority. He was arrested by the Communists April 5, 1871, and when the government troops entered the city he was shot at St. Roquette, May 24 following. Among his most important works are *Les Saintes Femmes* (1850):—*Les Femmes de la Bible* (5th ed. 1859):—*La Vie de St. Thomas à Becket* (2d ed. 1860). See Wetzer u. Welte, *Kirchen-Lexikon*, s. v. (B. P.)

Darby, Deborah, a minister of the Society of Friends, in England, travelled with her fellow-minister, Rebecca Byrd, in the principality of Wales, in 1784. Subsequently, in 1793, both embarked for America, and spent three years there preaching the Gospel. She died in 1810. See *The Friend*, viii, 357.

Darby, John Nelson, who was born in London, Nov. 18, 1800, and died at Bournemouth, April 28, 1882, is noted as the head of the Darbyites or Plymouth Brethren (q. v.). He is also known on the Continent by his writings, which have been translated into German, and for which see Zuchold, *Bibl. Theol.* i, 261 sq. (B. P.)

Darby, M. W., a Protestant Episcopal clergyman, was rector of Grace Church, Montrose, Ia.; at the time of his death, at Port Jervis, N. Y., July 20, 1878. See *Prot. Episc. Almanac*, 1879, p. 168.

Dare, James, an English minister, originally a Methodist, joined the Congregationalists about 1872, and was appointed to Rutherglen and Wahgunyah, Victoria, where he labored until his death, Jan. 13, 1876. See (Lond.) *Cong. Year-book*, 1877, p. 353.

Darerca, a reputed Irish saint, is said to have been the sister of St. Patrick. Her father was Calphurnius, a British nobleman, and her mother Conchessa, a sister or niece of St. Martin of Tours. Colgan says that she bore to two husbands, Conis and Restitutus, seventeen sons, who were bishops, and two daughters, who were virgins. In her old age she devoted herself to God, and took charge of the altar vestings, with her sisters Lupita and Tigrida. Later writers have thrown discredit upon the whole story. She is commemorated March 22.

Daret, Jean, a Benedictine monk, was born at Mantes in 1667. His opposition to the bull *Unigenitus* made him famous in his day, and he composed controversial writings which are now forgotten. He also assisted Mabillon in his great works. He died Jan. 3, 1736. See Hoefer, *Nouv. Biog. Générale*, s. v.

Daret, Pierre, a French engraver, was born in Paris in 1610. The following are some of his principal works: *St. John Sitting in the Desert; The Virgin Suckling the Infant; St. Peter Delivered from Prison; The Entombing of Christ; The Holy Family, with an Angel Presenting Fruit to the Infant Jesus; The Dead Christ, with the Marys; The Virgin and Infant.*

Darg, Patrick, a Scotch clergyman, was minister at Fordyce in 1599; had letters of "dispositure and mortification" from the advocate, Edinburgh, in September, 1629, and died about 1662. See *Fasti Eccles. Scoticanæ*, iii, 666.

Darg, Walter, a Scotch clergyman, graduated at King's College, Aberdeen, in 1623; was the first minister at Deskford after it was separated from Fordyce in 1630; was suspended in 1650, and deposed in 1651 for insufficiency; was accused of marrying persons irregularly in 1666 and 1674. See *Fasti Eccles. Scoticanæ*, iii, 674.

Dargavel, John, a Scotch clergyman, graduated at Edinburgh University in 1665; was presented to the living at Southdean in August of that year; transferred to Prestonkirk in 1670, and collated thereto in March; accused Sept. 1, 1670, of fornication. See *Fasti Eccles. Scoticanæ*, i, 378, 512.

Daria, wife of Nicander, martyr in Mœsia, under Maximus, in the persecution of Galerius, bravely encouraged her husband to martyrdom; and when the judge sneeringly said that she only wanted another husband, she offered to die first. She was sent to prison, but was released before her husband's death, and was present. See Smith, *Dict. of Christ. Biog.* s. v.

Darida, in Hindû mythology, was a powerful dæmon, who challenged Siva to battle. The latter implored Vishnu's help, who came out of Siva's eye in the form of the eight-headed giantess, Bradrakali, and slew the dæmon.

Darinnill, an Irish saint of Cill-na-ninghen, was one of the virgin daughters of Mac Iaar. She is commemorated Oct. 26. See DARBELIN.

Darius, a martyr at Nicæa, commemorated Dec. 19.

Darkin, CHARLES, an English Baptist minister, was born about 1800. He was converted at the age of seventeen; joined Dr. Cox's Church, Mare Street, Hackney; entered Stepney College; became pastor at Woodstock, Oxfordshire, in June, 1826; and in 1841 removed to Cirencester, where he died in 1853. See (Lond.) *Baptist Hand-book*, 1854, p. 49. (J. C. S.)

Darley, THOMAS, a Methodist Episcopal minister, a native of England, entered the travelling ministry in 1801; located in 1806, but continued his labors with characteristic zeal and fidelity until 1814, when he was readmitted into the Georgia Conference, and therein continued till his death, April 16, 1832. See *Minutes of Annual Conferences*, 1833, p. 215.

Darling, the family name of several Scotch clergymen:

1. ANDREW (1), graduated at Edinburgh University in 1670; was presented by the king to the living at Stitchel; ordained May 1, 1683; deprived by the privy council in 1689 for not praying for the king and queen; and deposed for drunkenness in 1692. See *Fasti Eccles. Scoticanæ*, i, 474.

2. ANDREW (2), a native of Galashiels, graduated at Edinburgh University in 1693; was ordained minister at Hoddam, Oct. 13, 1696; transferred to Kinnoul before December, 1697; admitted in January, 1698, and died Aug. 12, 1731, aged fifty-nine years. See *Fasti Eccles. Scoticanæ*, i, 620; ii, 648.

3. HUGH, graduated at Edinburgh University in July, 1696; licensed to preach in August, 1699; called to the living at Innerwick in April, and ordained in August, 1700. He died at Edinburgh, Sept. 29, 1701, aged about twenty-five years. He had two brothers in the ministry, Andrew and Robert. See *Fasti Eccles. Scoticanæ*, i, 375.

4. JAMES, son of the minister at Ewes, was called in January, and ordained, in March, 1734, minister at Kinkell; transferred to Kintore in January, 1738, and died March 29, 1742. See *Fasti Eccles. Scoticanæ*, iii, 585, 589.

5. PETER, graduated at Edinburgh University in 1695; was licensed to preach in 1697; called and ordained in June, 1698, to the living at Boyndie; and died in 1730, aged about fifty-five years. See *Fasti Eccles. Scoticanæ*, iii, 671.

6. ROBERT, graduated at Edinburgh University in July, 1685; had a unanimous call to the living at Ewes; was ordained Nov. 20, 1694; called to Gask in 1699, but declined, and died Dec. 1, 1716, aged forty-seven years. See *Fasti Eccles. Scoticanæ*, i, 636.

Darling, David, an English Congregational minister, was born in 1785. In 1816 he was sent by the London Missionary Society to Eastern Polynesia; and after laboring for sixteen years in the Society Islands, went to the Marquesas and took part in the translation of the Scriptures into the language of that group. He afterwards removed to Tahiti, where he continued to labor until 1859, when he retired, on account of age and infirmity, to Sydney, and died there, Dec. 6, 1867. See (Lond.) *Cong. Year-book*, 1869, p. 234.

Darlugdach (Dardulacha, Derlughach, or **Derlugdacha)**, abbess of Kildare, has a Scotch, Irish, and possible Continental connection. She succeeded her mistress, St. Brigida, in the abbacy of Kildare, about 523, and died a year afterwards. A romantic story is told of her early history by Baring-Gould, *Lives of the Saints*, ii, 22.

Darnalt, JEAN, a French theologian, lived about 1618. He was priest of St. Croix at Bordeaux, and wrote, *La Vie de Saint Mommolin* (Bordeaux, 1618):—*Statuta et Decreta Reformationis Congregat. Bened.* etc. (Paris, 1605). See Hoefer, *Nouv. Biog. Générale*, s. v.

Darney, WILLIAM, an English Wesleyan preacher, commenced his itinerancy (according to Hill, *Alphab. Arrangem.*) in 1742, and was instrumental in raising several societies in the North of England, which for some time were called "William Darney's Societies." For an account of his maltreatment bv mobs see *Wesl. Meth. Magazine*, 1842, p. 619 sq.; Stevens, *Hist. of Methodism*, ii, 131. He finally settled in Colne, Lancashire, but preached as he was able, until his death in 1779 or 1780. He published, *A Collection of Hymns* (Leeds, 1751, 12mo, pp. 296):—*The Fundamental Doctrines of Holy Scripture*, etc. (Glasgow, 1755, 16mo). See Atmore, *Meth. Memorial*, 1801, p. 100.

Darney was rather Calvinistic in his creed, fearless of danger, and extensively useful. His doggerel hymns greatly annoyed the good taste of Wesley. One of them was spun out to one hundred and four stanzas. "A hard Scotchman," Everett calls him. See *Wesl. Centenary Takings* (Lond. 1841, 3d ed.), i, 321; Jackson, *Life of Charles Wesley* (N. Y.), p. 451-453; Christopher, *Epworth Singers and other Poets of Methodism* (N. Y. and Lond. 1874), p. 213-215; Wesley, *Works* (Lond. 3d ed.), xii, 305; xiii, 188, 191.

Daroczi, GEORG, a Transylvanian theologian of the Jesuit order, lived in the first part of the 17th century, and wrote, *Ortus et Progressus Collegii Societatis Jesu Claudio-Politani* (Clausenburg, 1736). See Hoefer, *Nouv. Biog. Générale*, s. v.

Daronatsi, PAUL, an Armenian abbot, was born in 1043, in the province of Daron. He was noted for his profound knowledge of philosophy and theology. He died in 1123, leaving a letter, which he wrote (1101) in favor of the Monophysites against Theophistes (printed at Constantinople in 1752; Galanus has inserted from it about twenty passages in his *Conciliatio*):—also a *Treatise against the Greek Church:—A Commentary on Daniel*. See Hoefer, *Nouv. Biog. Générale*, s. v.

Darroch, the family name of several Scotch clergymen:

1. DUGALD, graduated at Glasgow University in 1638; was admitted to the living at Kilcalmonell and Kilberry in 1641; had a recommendation in 1646 to the committee of Money; was transferred to Campbelton in 1649; appointed the same year one of the translators of the Shorter Catechism into Irish; intrusted with the translation of the *Brief Sum of Christian Doctrine* in 1660, and had to translate the Second Book of Kings into Irish, as part of the whole Bible; was deprived by the privy council in 1662, and died about 1664 or 1665. See *Fasti Eccles. Scoticanæ*, iii, 35, 43.

2. JOHN (1), graduated at Glasgow University in 1625; was minister at Jura and Colonsay in 1639; deposed in September, 1646, "for preaching to and gross compliance with rebels," and died before May 9, 1649. See *Fasti Eccles. Scoticanæ*, iii, 53.

3. JOHN (2), was a student in Glasgow University in 1665; recommended for license to preach in 1669, and called that year to the living at Kilcalmonell and Kilberry; had charge of a Presbyterian congregation at Glenarm, Ireland, in 1687; was a member of the General Assembly in 1690; recalled to Kilcalmonell in 1691; transferred to Craigneish in May, 1692, and died in May, 1730. See *Fasti Eccles. Scoticanæ*, iii, 43, 44.

4. MAURICE, had charge of the parish of Kilcalmonell in 1629, and died March 10, 1638, aged sixty-three years. See *Fasti Eccles. Scoticanæ*, iii, 43.

5. ROBERT, graduated at Glasgow University in 1579; was chosen minister at Kilmarnock in 1580; was a member of the General Assembly in 1581; regent in Glasgow University in 1583; transferred to Stonehouse in 1585, and to Kilbride in 1586; had the parsonage of

Torrens presented to him by the king in 1587; was appointed in 1592 to give information against the Papists; in 1597 was a commissioner to consider grievances; in 1606 was chosen constant moderator for the presbytery, but died the same month, aged about forty-eight years. See *Fasti Eccles. Scoticanæ*, ii, 289, 302, 357.

6. WILLIAM, son of the minister of Craigneish, studied theology in Glasgow University; was licensed to preach in 1700; called to the living at Kilchrenan and Dalavich in 1701; deposed in January, 1710, for neglect of family worship, and afterwards became mentally deranged. See *Fasti Eccles. Scoticanæ*, iii, 71.

Darrow, Francis, a Baptist minister, was born at Waterford, Conn., in 1779. He was converted under the preaching of his grandfather, Zadoc Darrow; was ordained, in 1809, assistant in Waterford; in 1827 became sole pastor, and remained until his death, in November, 1850. See *Watchman and Reflector*, Nov. 21, 1850. (J. C. S.)

Darrow, Nathan, a Presbyterian minister, was ordained and settled at Homer, N. Y., Jan. 2, 1803; went to Cleveland in 1808, and afterwards to Vienna, O., where he resided till his death. See *Presbyterianism in Central N. Y.* p. 505.

Darrow, William V., a Methodist Episcopal minister, was born in Camden County, N. J., March 20, 1819. He joined the Church in 1842; received license to exhort in 1849, to preach in 1850, and in 1851 was admitted into the New Jersey Conference, wherein he labored till his death, Jan. 24, 1856. See *Minutes of Annual Conferences*, 1856, p. 28.

Darrow, Zadoc, *Sr.*, a Baptist minister, was born Dec. 25, 1728. He was ordained pastor in Waterford, Conn., in 1769, and his influence extended throughout the eastern part of the state. He died in 1827. See Cathcart, *Baptist Encyclop.* p. 308; Sprague, *Annals of the Amer. Pulpit*, vi, 109.

Darrow, Zadoc, *Jr.*, a Baptist minister, was born at New London, Conn., June 11, 1768. He was converted at the age of seventeen, baptized in March, 1788, and licensed in 1792. In 1807 he removed to Chenango County, N. Y., where he preached to three different churches; in 1819 went to Missouri, lived in St. Louis three years, and in 1823 purchased a tract of land and settled in the vicinity of Rock Spring, Ill.; was publicly ordained Aug. 22, 1824, and removed in 1849 to Collinsville, where he died July 18 of that year. See *Minutes of Ill. Anniversaries*, 1849, p. 6. (J. C. S.)

Darshan, Moses. See MOSES HA-DARSHAN.

Darshan, Simon. See CARA, SIMEON.

Darstius, G. H., a German Reformed minister, was settled pastor in Bucks County, Pa., about the year 1731, preaching in both the Dutch and German languages. In 1748 he removed to Holland. See Harbaugh, *Fathers of the Germ. Ref. Church*, ii, 375.

Darte, FREEMAN, a Free-will Baptist minister, was born at Salisbury, N. Y., Aug. 22, 1803. He was converted in 1832; joined the Church in 1834; not long after commenced to preach, and was pastor in Erie and Cattaraugus counties. He died suddenly, Jan. 22, 1883. See *Morning Star*, Feb. 14, 1883. (J. C. S.)

Daruj, in Persian mythology, was a division of the evil dæmons, brought forth by Ahriman, as opposed to the creations of light from Ormuzd.

Darvands, in Zendic mythology, are six evil spirits created by Ahriman, in opposition to the Amshaspands of Ahuramazda. Their names were Akomano, Ander, Samva, Nasatyas, Taric, and Zaric. These were mostly the same as the deities of the Vedas, only changed into dæmons by the Zends.

Darwinism. See EVOLUTION.

Dasa-bala is a term employed to denote ten *attributes* or modes of wisdom possessed by Buddha. They are as follows: "1. The wisdom that understands what knowledge is necessary for the right fulfilment of any particular duty in whatsoever situation; 2. That which knows the result or consequences of *karma*, or moral action; 3. That which knows the way to the attainment of *nirwana*, or annihilation; 4. That which sees the various *sakwalas* or systems of worlds; 5. That which knows the thoughts of other beings; 6. That which knows that the organs of sense are not the self; 7. That which knows the purity produced by the exercise of the *dhyanas*, or abstract meditation; 8. That which knows where any one was born in all his former births; 9. That which knows where any one will be born in all his future births; 10. That which knows how the results proceeding from *karma*, or moral action, may be overcome" (Hardy, *Manual of Buddhism*).

Dasa-dandu are ten *prohibitions* which are enjoined upon the Buddhist monks, to be studied during their novitiate, as follows: "1. The eating of food after mid-day; 2. The seeing of dances or the hearing of music or singing; 3. The use of ornaments or perfumes; 4. The use of a seat or couch more than a cubit high; 5. The receiving of gold, silver, or money; 6. Practicing some deception to prevent another priest from receiving that to which he is entitled; 7. Practicing some deception to injure another priest, or bring him into danger; 8. Practicing some deception in order to cause another priest to be expelled from the community; 9. Speaking evil of another priest; 10. Uttering slanders in order to excite dissension among the priests of the same community. The first five of these crimes may be forgiven, if the priest bring sand and sprinkle it in the court-yard of the *wihara;* and the second five may be forgiven after temporary expulsion" (Hardy, *Eastern Monachism*, p. 28).

Dasa-sil are ten *obligations* which must be repeated and meditated upon by the Buddhist priest three hours a day during his novitiate. They are as follows: "1. I will observe the precept, or ordinance, that forbids the taking of life; 2. I will observe the precept, or ordinance, that forbids the taking of that which has not been given; 3. I will observe the precept, or ordinance, that forbids sexual intercourse; 4. I will observe the precept, or ordinance, that forbids the saying of that which is not true; 5. I will observe the precept, or ordinance, that forbids the use of intoxicating drinks, that leads to indifference towards religion; 6. I will observe the precept, or ordinance, that forbids the eating of food after mid-day; 7. I will observe the precept, or ordinance, that forbids attendance upon dancing, singing, music, and masks; 8. I will observe the precept, or ordinance, that forbids the adorning of the body with flowers, and the use of perfumes and unguents; 9. I will observe the precept, or ordinance, that forbids the use of high or honorable seats or couches; 10. I will observe the precept, or ordinance, that forbids the receiving of gold or silver" (Hardy, *Eastern Monachism*, p. 24).

Daser, LUDWIG HERCULES, a Lutheran minister of Germany, was born at Affalterbach, April 4, 1705. He studied at Tübingen, was in 1735 pastor at Schwaickheim, and died in 1765, leaving, *De Origine et Auctorite Punctorum Hebraicorum Divina* (Tübingen, 1728):—*De Augustiniana Decalogi Divisione* (ibid. 1733):—*Vertheidigung der Integritatis Textus Hebraici Veteris Testamenti* (Heilbronn, 1764). See Fürst, *Bibl. Jud.* i, 197; Steinschneider, *Bibliogr. Handbuch*, s. v.; Jöcher, *Allgemeines Gelehrten-Lexikon*, s. v.; Hoefer, *Nouv. Biog. Générale*, s. v. (B. P.)

Dash, FREDERICK H., an English Congregational minister, was born at Gosport, Hants, Dec. 25, 1854. He entered Hackney College in 1874; in 1879 became pastor at Bungay; was ordained Jan. 27, 1880, and died Oct. 30 following. See (Lond.) *Cong. Year-book*, 1881, p. 369.

Dashiell, Alfred H., D.D., a Presbyterian minister, was born in Maryland, Aug. 2, 1793. He graduated at the University of Pennsylvania; was ordained by the Presbytery of Philadelphia; became successively pastor of the Mariners' Church, Philadelphia; of First Church, Jacksonville, Ill.; president of a female academy, Nashville, Tenn.; pastor Presbyterian Church, Franklin; for nineteen years at Shelbyville; and finally resided in Brooklyn, N. Y., until his death, March 18, 1881. See Norton, *Hist. of the Presb. Church in Ill.*

Dashiell, Benjamin D., a minister of the Methodist Episcopal Church South, was born at Vienna, Md., Sept. 21, 1831. He removed with his parents to Texas in 1837; was licensed to preach in 1852; admitted into the Texas Conference on trial the same year; located in 1867; re-entered the conference in 1869, continuing in the itinerant ranks until 1880; and died Jan. 14, 1882. See *Minutes of Annual Conferences of the M. E. Church South*, 1882, p. 120.

Dashiell, George, a Protestant Episcopal minister, was born at Stepney, Somerset Co., Md.; was admitted to orders, and preached in Delaware, in South Sassafras Parish, Kent Co., Md., in Chester, and in St. Peter's, Baltimore. In 1816 he set up an independent church, claiming and exercising the authority to ordain others. He died in New York city in April, 1852. He was distinguished for his eloquence. See Sprague, *Annals of the Amer. Pulpit*, v, 313.

Dashiell, Robert Laurenson, D.D., a Methodist Episcopal minister, was born in Salisbury, Md., June 25, 1825. He was converted at the age of fifteen; graduated from Dickinson College in 1846, and in 1848 entered the Baltimore Conference. His fields of labor were West River Circuit, Md., and Loudon, Va.; four years at Union and Wesley chapels, in Washington; 1856 and 1857, Eutaw Street, and 1858 and 1859, Charles Street, Baltimore; 1860 and 1861, Central Church, Newark, N. J.; 1862 and 1863, Trinity, Jersey City; 1864 to 1866, St. Paul's, Newark; 1867, First Church, Orange; in nearly all of which he had large and lasting revivals. In 1868 he was elected president of Dickinson College; resigned in 1872, and was made presiding elder of Jersey City district; but, in May of that year, was chosen missionary secretary, which office he continued to hold to the close of his life, March 8, 1880. Dr. Dashiell was a man of extraordinary gifts and graces, and left a rare record of success. His spirit was free and genial, his temperament poetical, his nature radical, his zeal outspoken, his friendship lavish. See *Minutes of Annual Conferences*, 1880, p. 38; Simpson, *Cyclop. of Methodism*, s. v.

Dasius. (1) A soldier, in the time of Diocletian and Maximian, at Dorostolus, where it was the custom to offer a human sacrifice to Saturn on Nov. 20. He, being selected for the purpose, preferred to die as a Christian, which meant dying by torture. (2) A martyr at Nicomedia, with Zoticus, Gaius, and twelve soldiers. He is commemorated Oct. 21.

Dasnami Dandis (*ten-named Dandis*), among the Hindûs, are the primitive members of the order of Dandis (q. v.), who refer their origin to Saukara Achárya (q. v.). There were *ten* classes of mendicants descended from this remarkable man, only three of whom have so far retained their purity as to entitle them to be called Saukara's Dandis. They are numerous, especially in and about Benares; and to these the chief Vedanti writers belong. The remaining members of the Dasnami class, who have degenerated from the original purity of practice which distinguished the primitive Dandis, are still religious characters, only they have given up the use of clothes, money, and ornaments; they prepare their own food, and admit members from any order of Hindûs, whereas the original Dandis admit only Brahmins.

Dass, Ishuree, a Presbyterian minister, was born at Futtehpoor, India, in 1826. He was educated in the mission-school there, and, on a visit to America, entered Lafayette College, Easton, Pa., but was compelled to return to his native land without graduating. He continued his studies with the English missionaries, and, in 1865, was licensed by Furruckabad Presbytery, and stationed at Futtehpoor, where he died, May 2, 1867. He wrote a prize essay on *Female Education in India.* See Wilson, *Hist. Presb. Almanac*, 1868, p. 83.

Dassel, Christian Conrad, a Lutheran theologian of Germany, was born at Harkesbüttel, March 16, 1768. In 1794 he was teacher at Hanover, in 1796 preacher at Schloss-Ricklingen, in 1800 at Hohenbostel, and in 1806 first preacher at Stadthagen, where he died, in 1826. He wrote: *Ueber den Verfall des öffentlichen Religionscultus in theologischer Hinsicht* (Neustadt, 1818):—*Der hannöverische Landeskatechismus als Lese- und Erbauungsbuch* (Hanover, 1800):—*Commentar über der hannöverischer Landeskatechismus* (Göttingen, 1811). See Winer, *Handbuch der theol. Lit.* i, 496; ii, 219; Zuchold, *Bibl. Theol.* i, 264. (B. P.)

Dassier, Lazare, a French preacher, lived about 1685. He was of the order of St. Dominic, and published a number of *Sermons*, for which see Hoefer, *Nouv. Biog. Générale*, s. v.

Dassov, Nicolaus, a Lutheran theologian of Germany, was born at Hamburg, Dec. 11, 1639. At Greifswald, where he took the degree of doctor of theology, he was also professor, senior of the theological faculty, member of consistory, and pastor of St. Mary's. He died Aug. 8, 1706, leaving: *De Prima Nicolaitarum Hæresi:*—*De Vento Pentecostali:*—*De Glorificatione Christi.* See Moller, *Cimbria Litterata;* Jöcher, *Allgemeines Gelehrten-Lexikon*, s. v. (B. P.)

Dassov, Theodor, a German theologian, brother of Nicolaus, was born at Hamburg. He studied at Giessen and Wittenberg; was in 1678 professor extraordinarius of Oriental languages, and in 1689 professor ordinarius at the latter place, where he also took his degree as doctor of theology, in 1699. He accepted a call to Kiel, and died Jan. 6, 1721, while general superintendent of Holstein and provost of Rendsburg. He wrote: *Avis Ungue Sect. Inque Sacrific. Oblat.* (Wittenberg, 1697):—*De Emphasi Sacrarum Vocum ex Vet. Hist. Hebr. Repet.* (Kiel, 1714):—*De Jure Finium ex Pandect. Talmudic.* (Wittenberg, 1735):—*De Ritibus Mesusæ* (ibid. 1714): *Dissidium Pontif. Rom. et Hebr.* (ibid. 1735)—*Imagines Hebræorum Rerum, quæ Nostra Ætate Circumferunt* (ibid. 1735):—*Rabbinismi, Philol. s. Ancillant.* (1674):—*Diatribe in Judæos de Resurrectione Mortuorum* (1675):—*Vota Monastica et Nasiræorum* (1736):—*Scholia Criticorum* (1707). See Moller, *Cimbria Litterata;* Jöcher, *Allgemeines Gelehrten-Lexikon*, s. v.; Winer, *Handbuch der theol. Lit.* i, 143, 202, 604; Fürst, *Bibl. Jud.* i, 197; Steinschneider, *Bibliogr. Handbuch*, s. v. (B. P.)

Datan, in Slavonic mythology, was a god of the Poles, who was said to dispense blessings, prosperity, and plenty, especially in fruits of the field.

Dathe, Hieronymus, a Lutheran theologian of Germany, was born at Hamburg, Feb. 4, 1667. He studied at Giessen and Wittenberg; was in 1694 provost and superintendent at Kemberg, in 1700 at Annaberg, and died, a doctor of theology, June 14, 1707, leaving, *De Sacramento Baptismi, de Peccato et Libero Arbitrio:*—*Orationes de Patientia Christi.* See Moller, *Cimbria Litterata;* Jöcher, *Allgemeines Gelehrten-Lexikon*, s. v. (B. P.)

Dathevatsi, Gregory, an Armenian theologian, who lived in the middle of the 14th century, was monk in a monastery at Dathev. After having studied under the celebrated John Orodnetsi, he taught theology and philosophy. He died in 1410, leaving about twenty works, of which the best known is a *Book of Questions*, printed at Constantinople, and held to be heretical.

There was also another Gregory Dathevatsi, who was martyred in the 17th century by the Kurds; and this one, according to the opinion of Sérpos, is commemorated in the Armenian liturgy. See Hoefer, *Nouv. Biog. Générale*, q. v.

Dati, Leonardo (1), an Italian theologian, was born at Florence about 1360. He entered the order of the Dominicans, and became celebrated for learning and piety. He was sent, in the year 1400, to the Council of Constance. After having accomplished diplomatic missions to the king of Bohemia, in 1409, and the emperor Sigismund, in 1413, he was elected general of his order in 1414; and died in April, 1425, leaving several theological works, the only ones of which that have been printed are, *Sermones de Petitionibus* (Lyons, 1518, 8vo):—*Sermones de Flagellis Peccatorum* (ibid. eod. 4to). See Hoefer, *Nouv. Biog. Générale*, s. v.

Dati, Leonardo (2), an Italian theologian, was born at Florence in 1408. He was canon at Florence, and afterwards secretary to popes Calixtus III, Pius II, Paul II, and Sixtus IV. He was appointed, in 1467, bishop of Massa, and died at Rome in 1472, leaving in MS. many works in prose and verse. Mehus published thirty-three of his *Letters* (Florence, 1742, 8vo). See Hoefer, *Nouv. Biog. Générale*, s. v.

Datius, bishop of Milan, was consecrated about 527. He brought ruin upon his countrymen by the part he took in instigating the revolt of Liguria from Vitiges, the Gothic king of Italy. When Milan was sacked by the Goths he fled to Constantinople. In 547 he united with pope Vigilius in opposing Justinian's condemnatory edict of the three articles, by refusing to sign it; and the two controversialists took refuge in the church of St. Peter, at Constantinople, in 551, from which the imperial troops vainly endeavored to drag the pope by force. A second refuge was taken in the church of St. Euphemia, at Chalcedon, where the pope, afraid to leave his asylum, appointed Datius one of his representatives in the approaching discussions. Datius died about 555. See Smith, *Dict. of Christ. Biog.* s. v.

Datīva was a female martyr in Byzacium, Africa, in 484; commemorated Dec. 6, with seven others.

Dativus is the name of several early Christians of eminence:

1. Bishop of Badæ, in Numidia, a frontier post towards the Gætuli, was the author of several epistles.

2. Seventh bishop of Limoges, succeeded Adelphius in the latter part of the 3d century. He was deposed at the end of nineteen years, during the persecution of Diocletian.

3. A celebrated senator, was martyred under Diocletian, at Carthage, in 304. He and forty-eight others were surprised while worshipping at Abitina, and, after severe torture, died—some from starvation. He is commemorated on Feb. 11. See Smith, *Dict. of Christ. Biog.* s. v.

Datta (or **Dattatreya**), an incarnation of a portion of Vishnu, and therefore venerated by the Vaishnavas (q. v.). He was also eminent for his practice of the Yoga, and hence is held in high estimation by the Yogis (q. v.).—Gardner, *Faiths of the World*, s. v.

Daubenton, Guillaume, a French Jesuit, born at Auxerre in 1648, went to Spain as confessor to Philip V; was sent back in 1706, but returned in 1716. He died in 1723, leaving *Oraisons Funèbres* and a *Vie de Saint François Régis*. See Hoefer, *Nouv. Biog. Générale*, s. v.

Daubentonne (or **Dabentonne**), Jeanne (called also *Pieroime Daubenton*), a French female fanatic, born in Paris, was burned there, July 5, 1372, for setting herself up as a prophetess at the head of the *Turlupins* or "Brothers of the Company of Poverty." See Hoefer, *Nouv. Biog. Générale*, s. v.

D'Aubigné. See Merle.

Daüble, G., a Baptist missionary, was born in Switzerland about 1820. Under the auspices of the Basle Missionary Society, he was laboring in Dacca, Bengal, when he became a Baptist, and was baptized at Tezpur, on the Brahmaputra, Assam, Feb. 4, 1850; and appointed a missionary at Nowgong, on the other side of the river. He died March 21, 1853. See *The Missionary Jubilee*, p. 245. (J. C. S.)

Daubus, Charles, a French Protestant ecclesiastic and philosopher, born at Auxerre, was for some time minister at Nérac. Among several productions, he wrote, *L'Échelle de Jacob* (St. Foy, 1626, 8vo):—*L'Ébionisme des Moines* (12mo):—*Bellarmin Réformé* (1631, 8vo). See Hoefer, *Nouv. Biog. Générale*, s. v.

Daûd, an Arabic philosopher, son of Nassir, belonged to the tribe of the Thaï, died A.D. 770. See Hoefer, *Nouv. Biog. Générale*, s. v.

Daudé, Pierre (1), a French Protestant theologian, was born at Marvejols (Lozère), Sept. 26, 1654. He studied theology at Puylaurens, and went in 1680 to England, where he completed his studies; was active for some time in the evangelical ministry, and for twenty-eight years was clerk of the exchequer. He died in London, Jan. 29, 1733, leaving several transitory pieces (Amsterdam, 1730). See Hoefer, *Nouv. Biog. Générale*, s. v.

Daudé, Pierre (2), a French Protestant divine, nephew of the foregoing, was born at Marvejols (Lozère) in 1681, and died in England, May 11, 1754, leaving the following works, which were published anonymously, *Vie de Michel de Cervantes, Trad. de L'Espagnol de Mayans y Siscar* (Amsterdam, 1740, 2 vols.):—*Traité de la Foi, Traduit du Latin de Burnet* (ibid. 1729). According to Barbier and Burnet, he co-operated in the publication of the *Bibliothèque Historique*, 1733–47. See Hoefer, *Nouv. Biog. Générale*, s. v.

Dauderstadt, Christoph, a Lutheran theologian of Germany, was born at Naumburg in 1580. He studied at Leipsic and Wittenberg, was in 1605 con-rector at Zeitz, in 1608 rector, in 1612 at Saleck, and in 1617 pastor at Skeuditz. In 1625 he went to Freiburg, and died in 1654. He wrote, *Apodixis Messiæ*:—*Passio Secundum Quattuor Evangelistas*:—*Meditat. Septem Verborum Christi in Cruce*:—*Anti-Christus Orientaliis.* See Schamelius, *Naumburgum Literatum*; Jöcher, *Allgemeines Gelehrten-Lexikon*, s. v. (B. P.)

Daughaday, Thomas, a Methodist Episcopal minister, was born in Baltimore County, Md., in 1777. He was converted young; in 1798 entered the Baltimore Conference; travelled in Maryland, Virginia, and Pennsylvania until 1802, when he located; but re-entered the effective ranks in 1805, and labored to the close of his life, Oct. 12, 1810. See *Minutes of Annual Conferences*, 1811, p. 192.

Daugherty, James, D.D., a Congregational minister, was born in Park, near Lairmount, County Londonderry, Ireland, April 9, 1796. He came to America in 1819, and went to South Hero, Vt. After preparatory studies with the Rev. Asa Lyon, and in St. Albans' Academy, he graduated from the University of Vermont in 1830, studying theology with Rev. O. S. Hoyt, of Hinesburg, and also with W. Smith, D.D., of St. Albans. He was ordained as an evangelist, Jan. 18, 1832, and for some time labored for the Colonial Missionary Society; was also a teacher at Frost Village and Shefford, Canada; was installed at Milton, Vt., Sept. 28, 1836, and dismissed July 5, 1848. He next was agent for the Foreign Evangelical Society one year; then acting pastor at Fairfax, Vt., from 1849 to 1851. Nov. 12, 1857, he was installed at Johnson; dismissed March 12, 1867, and remained there without charge until his death, June 10, 1878. (W. P. S.)

Daughtry, Josiah B., a minister of the Methodist Episcopal Church South, joined the Tennessee Conference in 1816; became superannuated in 1845; entered the Mississippi Conference in 1850; again became superannuated in 1853; and died late in that year or early in 1854. See *Minutes of Annual Conferences of the M. E. Church South*, 1854, p. 529.

Daullé, JEAN, an eminent French engraver, was born at Abbeville in 1707, and settled in Paris, where he was admitted a member of the Academy in 1742. He died there, April 23, 1763. The following are some of his principal plates: *The Magdalen; Diogenes with his Lantern*. See Hoefer, *Nouv. Biog. Générale*, s. v.; Spooner, *Biog. Hist. of the Fine Arts*, s. v.

Daumer, GEORG FRIEDRICH, a Roman Catholic convert of Germany, was born at Nüremberg, March 5, 1800. He commenced studying theology at Erlangen, where he belonged to the so-called pietists. The lectures of Schelling made him give up theology, which he exchanged at Leipsic for philology. In 1822 he was appointed teacher at the Latin school, and in 1827 at the gymnasium of his native place. In 1833 he resigned his position, joined in 1858 the Roman Catholic Church, and died Dec. 14, 1875, at Würzburg. He published, *Urgeschichte des Menschengeistes* (Nürnberg, 1827):—*Philosophie, Religion und Alterthum* (1833):—*Ueber die Entwendung ägyptischen Eigenthums heim Auszug der Israeliten aus Egypten* (ibid.):—*Polemische Blätter, betreffend Christenthum, Bibelglauben und Theologie* (ibid. 1834):—*Züge zu einer neuen Philosophie der Religion und Religionsgeschichte* (ibid. 1835):—*Anthropologismus und Kriticismus der Gegenwart* (ibid. 1844):—*Die Stimme der Wahrheit in den religiösen und confessionellen Kämpfen der Gegenwart* (ibid. 1845):—*Sabbath, Moloch und Tabu* (ibid. 1839):—*Der Feuer- und Molochdienst der alten Hebräer* (Braunschweig, 1842):—*Die Geheimnisse des christlichen Alterthums* (Hamburg, 1847, 2 vols.):—*Die Religion des neuen Weltalters* (ibid. 1850, 3 vols.):—*Meine Conversion Ein Stück Seelen- und Zeitgeschichte* (Mayence, 1859). See Zuchold, *Bibl. Theol.* i, 265; Fürst, *Bibl. Jud.* i, 197 sq.; Lichtenberger, *Encyclop. des Sciences Religieuses*, s. v.; Hoefer, *Nouv. Biog. Générale*, s. v. (B. P.)

Daun, GEORGE, a Scotch clergyman, graduated at King's College, Aberdeen, in 1772; was schoolmaster at Alves; licensed to preach in 1778; appointed to the living at Insch in 1790, and died May 21, 1821, aged seventy years. See *Fasti Eccles. Scoticanæ*, iii, 582.

Dauney, Francis (1), a Scotch clergyman, graduated at Marischal College, Aberdeen; was licensed to preach in June, 1742; called to the living at Lumphanan; ordained in June, 1743; transferred to Banchory-Ternan in June, 1758; and died April 2, 1800, aged eighty-one years. See *Fasti Eccles. Scoticanæ*, iii, 523, 536, 537.

Dauney, Francis (2), a Scotch clergyman, was licensed to preach in May, 1709; called to the living at Keithhall and Kinkell in 1710; transferred to Kemnay in 1719, and died Nov. 7, 1745. See *Fasti Eccles. Scoticanæ*, iii, 585, 588.

Daurès, LOUIS, a French theologian, was born at Milhau (Rouergue) in 1655. He became a Dominican, went to Paris, and founded there the community of penitence called St. Valère, in the suburb of St. Germain, with the object of gathering together young girls who had been led into debauchery. He died there, May 10, 1728, leaving *L'Église Protestante Détruite par Elle Même* (Paris, 1689, 12mo). See Hoefer, *Nouv. Biog. Générale*, s. v.

D'Aurolt, ANTHONY. See AVEROLT, ANTHONY.

Dausas was a martyr in Persia in 361. He was one of the captives carried away by Sapor II when he took Bezabde or Phœnicia. Heliodorus, the bishop, being taken ill, consecrated Dausas, and gave him charge over all the captives who had escaped the rack. When they assembled to worship, it was reported to the king that they met to curse him, and the Christians, to the number of three hundred, were collected, and commanded to embrace fire-worship or die. Dausas encouraged his flock, telling them that they would be delivered from bondage and restored to their country. Two hundred and sixty-five of them were slain, twenty-five apostatized, and the fate of the other ten is unknown. See Smith, *Dict. of Christ. Biog.* s. v.

Dausque (or **Dausquey**; Lat. *Dausquius*), a French scholar, was born at St. Omer, Dec. 5, 1566. He joined the Jesuits, but left them in 1610, and became canon of Tournay. He died about 1636, leaving, among other works, *Basilii, Seleuciensis Episcopi, Homiliæ* (Heidelberg, 1604; transl. from the Greek, with notes):—*Scutum Duplex*, etc. (Douay, 1610):—*Sancti Pauli Sanctitudo* (Paris, 1627):—*Sancti Josephi Sanctificatio extra Uterum* (Lyons, 1671). See Hoefer, *Nouv. Biog. Générale*, s. v.

Daut, JOHANN MAXIMILIAN, a journeyman shoemaker of Frankfort-on-the-Main, was one of those enthusiasts who appeared after the beginning of the 18th century, and proclaimed the coming judgment of God. At the divine behest, as he said, he wrote, in 1710, his *Helle Donnerposaune*, in which he cries the woe especially over Frankfort and the Roman empire. Only a small number will be saved for the marriage-feast of the Lamb, after Turks, Jews, and heathen have been converted. Against the Lutheran clergy he was especially severe. Expelled from Frankfort, he went to Leyden, where he soon had a conflict with Ueberfeldt, against whom he wrote, calling his adherents "Judas brethren." He was afterwards, however, again on good terms with Ueberfeldt. In and about Ulm he succeeded with his notions, in consequence of which the magistrate issued an edict against these meddling preachers, and prohibited the reading of Daut's writings, to which also belonged his *Geistliche Betrachtungen*, published in 1711. John Frick, a pastor and professor of theology, who was appointed to bring him back from his errors, succeeded in his mission, and again reconciled him with the Church. See Walch, *Rel. Streitigkeiten in der lutherischen Kirche*, ii, 794; v, 1051; Pfaff, *Introductio in Hist. Theol.* ii, 372; Burger, *Exercitatio de Sutoribus Fanaticis* (Leipsic, 1730); Fuhrmann, *Handbuch der Rel. und Kirchengeschichte*, s. v.; Hagenbach, in Herzog's *Real-Encyklop.* s. v.; Jöcher, *Allgemeines Gelehrten-Lexikon*, s. v. (B. P.)

Davcina, an early Chaldæan goddess, the wife of Hea, and the mother of Marduk. She has been supposed to represent the earth in a female form, as Hea was the god of the waters. Her analogue was the Phœnician goddess *Bohu*.

Davenport, Addington, a clergyman of the Church of England, graduated from Harvard College in 1719, and went to England for ordination. For a while he was pastor of the Church in Scituate, Mass.; he became assistant rector of King's Chapel, Boston, April 15, 1737; and in May, 1740, rector of Trinity Church in the same city. He died there, Sept. 8, 1746. See Sprague, *Annals of the Amer. Pulpit*, v, 122.

Davenport, Benjamin, an English Baptist minister, was born at Bourneheath, Bromsgrove, in 1826. He was converted at seventeen; joined the Baptist Church at Holy Cross, and began to preach at Catshill and Stony Stratford. He settled as pastor at Brington, Northamptonshire, in 1854, and died July 30, 1857. See (Lond.) *Baptist Hand-book*, 1858, p. 49.

Davenport, Ebenezer, a Congregational minister, graduated from Princeton College, was settled over the First Church at Greenwich, Conn., in 1767, and remained there until his death in 1773.

Davenport, James, an eccentric Presbyterian minister, was born at Stamford, Conn., in 1716. He graduated from Yale College at the age of twenty-two. In 1738 the Philadelphia Presbytery gave Maidenhead and Hopewell leave to call him, but he preferred to settle at Southold, L. I., and was ordained by a council, Oct. 26, 1738. He was not an eloquent speaker, and in preaching exhausted himself, exhibiting strange contortions of face, and a strange, singing tone, which was imitated by many Baptists of the South. Whitefield, who met him in 1740, styles him "one of the ministers whom God had sent out, a sweet, zealous soul." Davenport had considerable success in Southold, and was the means of a great revival in Baskingridge, N. J., where he preached for a season. He visited Connecticut in 1741. At Stonington, one hundred persons were converted by his first sermon. Twenty of the Niantic Indians were converted under his preaching at East Lyme, and many of the Mohegan tribe, also. At New Haven he came into conflict with the pastor. He was afterwards arrested at Ripton for disorderly proceedings and carried to Hartford, where he sang all night in prison. The grand jury presented him as a defamer of the ministry; he was treated as insane, and carried to his home. In March, 1743, he went to New London and organized a separate church, his followers making a bonfire of religious books and fine clothing. After a severe illness, his mind underwent a change; he bewailed his errors, and in July, 1744, made ample retraction. In 1746 he became a member of the New Brunswick Presbytery. Having recovered his health, he spent two months, in 1750, in Virginia, and also labored with some success at Cape May, N. J. He was called to Maidenhead and Hopewell, and was installed Oct. 27, 1754. As moderator of the synod of New York he preached the opening sermon, which was printed with the title *The Faithful Minister Encouraged.* He remained pastor for three years, but his labors were not greatly blessed. Many of the extravagances charged against him were untrue, coming from scoffers and worldly men. Davenport died in 1757, and was buried in the New-Light graveyard, near Pennington, N. J. (W. P. S.)

Davenport, John, a Presbyterian minister, was ordained by the Presbytery of Suffolk, June 4, 1775, and served the congregation in Southold, L. I., for two years. On Aug. 12, 1795, he was settled at Deerfield, N. J., but resigned in 1805. He died July 13, 1821. See Alexander, *Princeton College in the 18th Century.*

Davenport, Robert Dunlevy, a Baptist missionary, was born in Williamsburg, Va., March 25, 1809. He studied at the Virginia Baptist Seminary; was ordained at Richmond in August, 1835; received his appointment as a missionary to labor among the Siamese in September following, and arrived in Bangkok in July, 1836. Being a practical printer, he took with him a press, types in Chinese and Siamese, and a lithographic press, and was the means of doing great good, by the publication of religious literature for the people for whose spiritual welfare he was laboring. At the end of about nine years' service he returned to America on account of his health, and died at Alexandria, La., Nov. 24, 1848. (J. C. S.)

Davenport, Silas D., a Protestant Episcopal clergyman, was rector, in 1857, in Wadesborough, N. C., whence he removed to Corpus Christi, Texas, in 1861, and subsequently, in 1865, performed missionary work at Waco. In 1866 he was rector of Trinity Church, in Marshall, whence he removed to Dallas in 1868, as rector of St. Matthew's Church, and there remained until his death, Jan. 1, 1877. See *Prot. Episc. Almanac,* 1878, p. 168.

Daveyro, Pantaleon, a Portuguese monk, who lived at the end of the 16th and the beginning of the 17th century. He made a journey to Jerusalem, of which he published an account, under the title, *Itinerario de Terra Sancta* (Lisbon, 1593). Diego Tavares published of it a much more enlarged edition (ibid. 1683). See Hoefer, *Nouv. Biog. Générale,* s. v.

David. Among the Egyptians, an archimandrite, or any head of a monastery, of whatever rank, was called *David;* so that, when a monastic head gave letters of commendation to any one, he subscribed himself as "*David* illius loci" (Gratian, *De Formatis,* quoted by Ducange).

David, a frequent name in early Christian history. See also Dabius.

1. One of the four luminaries of the Barbeliot system. See Dades.

2. A bishop of the 5th century. About 440 he carried a letter from Leo the Great to the bishop of Mauritania, and is praised by the pope.

3. A deacon, and treasurer of the Church of Edessa, was one of the witnesses produced by the presbyters against Ibas before Photius of Tyre. His testimony was rejected by the judges.

4. This is a common form of the Irish Dabi, Mobi, etc. The most famous of the name was David, called sometimes "Legate of all Ireland," who succeeded St. Dubhthach as bishop of Armagh in 548. He died in 550.

5. A martyr, together with three boys, is commemorated June 25.

6. Of Thessalonica, is commemorated June 26.

7. King of Ethiopia, commemorated Sept. 7.

8. King of the Jews, commemorated variously: Sept. 30 (*Cal. Armen.*); Dec. 19 (*Cal. Ethiop.*); Dec. 29 (*Mart. Rom. Vet.*).

9. Commemorated with Constantine, Oct. 2.

David, a Scotch prelate, was chamberlain to the king, and was consecrated bishop of St. Andrews on St. Vincent's day, Jan. 22, 1233, by William, Gilbert, and Clement, bishops of Glasgow, Caithness, and Dumblane. In 1242 he held a provincial council at Perth; and in 1249 performed the ceremony of anointing king Alexander III, at Scone. He died at Northampton in 1253. See Keith, *Scottish Bishops,* p. 16.

David, another Scotch prelate, was bishop of Argyle in 1330 and 1350. See Keith, *Scottish Bishops,* p. 287.

David, a Carmelite of the 15th century, was born in Cherbury, Shropshire. Leland says he was *Theologiæ copritione clarus.* Going over to Ireland he was made bishop of Dromore (1427–29). He wrote some books, but they are not mentioned by Bale (*De Scriptoribus Brit.*) nor by sir James Ware (*De Scriptoribus Hibernicis*), so they were few or obscure. Returning to England, he died, and was buried in the Carmelite monastery at Ludlow in 1420. See Fuller, *Worthies of England* (ed. Nuttall), iii, 64.

David Almasser, a Jew of Moravia, who lived about the end of the 12th century, professed to be the Messiah. He pretended to make himself invisible at pleasure; and the ignorant Jews submitted to his call and followed him in masses. The governor (who was alarmed by the agitation) promised him pardon if he would surrender himself to his hands. David did so with confidence, and was put in prison. He escaped, however, and the Jews, being threatened with severe fines, delivered up David, who this time no more escaped either the eye or the hand of the executioner. See Hoefer, *Nouv. Biog. Générale,* s. v.

David Alrui (*Alroy* or *el-Roi,* i. e. "the seeing;" also called *Menahem ben-Solomon*) is known in Jewish history as one of the false Messiahs who arose from time to time. About the year 1160 he appeared among the Persian Jews, and proclaimed himself as sent from God to free the Jews from the Mohammedans and to bring them back to Jerusalem. David brought trouble upon his countrymen, and his timely death—his father-in-law had invited David to a supper, and while in a state of drunkenness the latter was beheaded—stopped the persecution of the sultan against the Jews. Disraeli has taken this historical event as the plot of his *Alroy.* See Lent, *De Judæorum Pseudomessiis* (2d ed. Herborn,

1697), p. 52 sq.; Grätz, *Geschichte der Juden*, vi, 291 sq.; Rohling, in Wetzer u. Welte's *Kirchen-Lexikon*, s. v.; Hoefer, *Nouv. Biog. Générale*, s. v. (B. P.)

David BEN-ARJE LÖW. See LIDA, DAVID DE.

David BEN-GEDALJA *ibn-Jachja*. See IBN-JACHJA, DAVID.

David BEN-ISAAC *de Pomis*. See POMIS, DAVID DE.

David BEN-JEHUDA (*Leon*). See MESSER, LEON.

David GANS. See GANS, DAVID.

David HA-KOHEN *de Lara*. See LARA, DAVID DE.

David OPPENHEIM. See OPPENHEIM, DAVID.

David PROVENZALE. See PROVENZALE, DAVID.

David RUBENI (also called *David Leimlein*), a fanatical Jew, lived at the end of the 15th and in the first part of the 16th century. It was said that he frequently remained without food for sixty days; professed to come from the east of Tartary; and announced the advent of the Messiah for the year 1500. Accordingly, in 1499, he pretended to have received a divine command to lead the Jews back to the land of their fathers; and when some were preparing to go to the Holy Land, David was under the necessity of declaring that God was displeased with their sins, and had therefore retarded the accomplishment of his promise. Pope Clement VII, who favored the Israelites, honored David with much distinction. David went to Lisbon, and there succeeded in bringing back to Judaism Solomon Molcho, who had become a Christian, and who occupied the position of secretary to the king of Portugal. Solomon was both an orator and a scribe, and thus afforded great help to David. The two together happened to be present at Mantua when Charles V passed through the city. Solomon was so imprudent as to ask the emperor for an audience, hoping to convert him to Judaism; but the only result was that he was compelled to mount the funeral pile. David was seized at the same time, and sent to Spain, where he died a few days afterwards. His death did not undeceive the Jews, who believed for a long time that he returned every week to visit his wife, who was in Italy. See Hoefer, *Nouv. Biog. Générale*, s. v.

David, Charles, a French engraver, was born in Paris about 1600. The following are some of his best prints: *Christ Shown to the People by Pilate; The Virgin and Infant, with Angels; The Virgin, with St. Bernard.* See *Biog. Universelle*, s. v.; Spooner, *Biog. Hist. of the Fine Arts*, s. v.

David, Claude, a French Benedictine of the society of St. Maur, was born at Dijon in 1644, and died Nov. 6, 1705. He composed several works on the subject of ecclesiastical scholarship, one only of which has been printed: *Dissertation sur Saint Denys l'Aréopagite.* See Hoefer, *Nouv. Biog. Générale*, s. v.

David, François Anne, a French engraver and editor, was born in Paris in 1741; was a pupil of Le Bas; and died in his native city, April 2, 1824. The following are some of his principal religious works: *Adam and Eve in Paradise; David with the Head of Goliath.* He also published many volumes, including an illustrated Bible. See Hoefer, *Nouv. Biog. Générale*, s. v.; Spooner, *Biog. Hist. of the Fine Arts*, s. v.

David, Jacques, a French poet and theologian, who was born at Annecy, and lived about 1536, was judge at Vélay, and left *Historia Dedicationis Ecclesiæ Podii Aniciensis in Vallavia*, etc. (Avignon, 1516); three royal songs, four ballads, and ten roundelays, in praise of the Virgin Mary, with an orison (Lyons, 1536). See Hoefer, *Nouv. Biog. Générale*, s. v.

David, Jean (1), a Belgian theologian, was born at Courtrai in 1546. He was pastor of St. Martin's, at Courtrai; joined the Jesuits in 1581; was successively rector of the colleges of Courtrai, Brussels, and Ghent, and died at Antwerp, Aug. 9, 1613. His numerous ascetic works are written in Latin and Flemish, including *Veridicus Christianus* (Antwerp, 1601):—*Extinctorium Famosæ Facis Hollandiæ* (ibid. 1602):—*Alvearium Romanæ Ecclesiæ* (ibid.):—*Arcanum Hæreticum* (ibid.):—*Labyrinthum Hæreticorum* (ibid. 1605):—*Occasionis Arreptæ ac Neglectæ Typus* (ibid. eod.):—*Paradisus Sponsiac Sponsæ* (ibid. 1607):—and many others. See Hoefer, *Nouv. Biog. Générale*, s. v.

David, Jean (2), a French canon, was born at Carcassonne, and flourished about 1672. He was commendatory of the abbey of the Bons-Hommes, near Angers, and was sent to Rome on a mission by Louis XIV, where he died. His principal works are, *Du Jugement Canonique des Évêques* (Paris, 1671):—*Réponse aux Remarques de M. de Launoy* (ibid. eod.). See Hoefer, *Nouv. Biog. Générale*, s. v.

David, Jerome, a French engraver, brother of Charles, was born at Paris in 1608. The following is a list of some of his principal works: *Adam and Eve Driven from Paradise; The Assumption of the Virgin; St. Francis of Paula.* He etched forty-two plates from the designs of Montano, of churches, tombs, and altars at Rome. See Hoefer, *Nouv. Biog. Générale*, s. v.; Spooner, *Biog. Hist. of the Fine Arts*, s. v.

David, John Baptist, a Roman Catholic bishop, was born near Nantes, France, in 1760. He was made a priest of St. Sulpice in 1784; came to America with Flaget and Badin in 1792 as missionary in Maryland; in Kentucky in 1811 sq.; was bishop of Mauricastro *in partibus* and coadjutor of Bardstown in 1819; and died June 12, 1841. See De Courcy and Shea, *Hist. of the Cath. Church in the U. S.* p. 70, 125.

David, Lodovico Antonio, an Italian painter, was born at Lugano in 1648, and studied under Cavaliere Cairo and Ercole Procaccini at Milan. He became a painter of eminence, and executed many works for the churches and convents at Milan and Venice. In the Church of San Silvestro, in Venice, is a *Nativity* by this artist, which is especially commended. He died about 1730. See Hoefer, *Nouv. Biog. Générale*, s. v.; Spooner, *Biog. Hist. of the Fine Arts*, s. v.

David, Nicolas Joseph, a French theologian, was born near Bayeux. He was professor in the college of Montaigu and canon of St. Marcel, and died at Paris, Aug. 5, 1784, leaving *Réfutation du Système d'un Philosophe Cartésien* (Paris, 1729). See Hoefer, *Nouv. Biog. Générale*, s. v.

Davidge, JAMES, an English Baptist minister, was born at Motcomb, Dorsetshire, Oct. 14, 1803, of Wesleyan parents, and was blind from his birth. At the age of fifteen he was placed in the blind asylum at Bristol to learn the trade of basket-making. Returning to his native village, he awakened much interest as "The Blind Preacher." Being also a musician and poet, he composed his own hymns and tunes, after singing which, his preaching was especially attractive to his hearers. Having become a Baptist, he was ordained at Iwerne Minster, July 25, 1833, where he continued till his death, Jan. 6, 1872. See (Lond.) *Baptist Hand-book*, 1873, p. 255. (J. C. S.)

Davidi, FRANCISCUS, a German Socinian, was born in Transylvania about 1510. At first a zealous Romanist, he became a Protestant, and defended the Lutheran doctrines against the Zwinglians. He soon joined the latter, and finally became a Socinian, through the influence of Georg Blandrata, who also succeeded in causing the removal of the Lutheran court-preacher, Dionysius Alesius, and putting Davidi in his place. Davidi's influence over prince Sigismund was so great that he was appointed superintendent of Transylvania. When the synod at Torda was held, in 1568, Davidi openly declared that Jesus Christ was nothing but a man, without any claim to adoration. Being accused of intrigues against the state, he was condemned to imprisonment in the fortress at Detva, where he died, June 6, 1579. Some of his published writings are found in the *Bibli-*

otheca Fratrum Polonorum. See Jöcher, *Allgemeines Gelehrten-Lexikon*, s. v.; Lichtenberger, *Encyclopédie des Sciences Religieuses*, s. v. (B. P.)

Davids, Arthur Lumley, a Jewish writer, was born in London in 1811, and died July 17, 1832. Before he was twenty, he delivered a lecture in the presence of the "Society for the Cultivation of Hebrew Literature," on *The Philosophy of the Jews*, replete with deep learning and profound research, and published in 1833. He also wrote a *Grammar of the Turkish Language, with a Preliminary Discourse on the Language and Literature of Eastern Nations* (London, 1832), a work which called forth the most unqualified praise from the most competent judges of the subject. See Fürst, *Bibl. Jud.* i, 202. (B. P.)

Davidson (occasionally written **Davidsone** or **Davidsoune**), the family name of a large number of Scotch clergymen:

1. Adam, graduated at Edinburgh University, June 28, 1697; was licensed to preach Dec. 7, 1698; called to the living at Essie-with-Nevay, Aug. 27, 1701; ordained Dec. 30, 1702, and died Oct. 24, 1720, aged forty-one years. See *Fasti Eccles. Scoticanæ*, iii, 747.

2. Alexander (1), was licensed to preach in 1740; called to the living at Traquair; ordained in 1744; and died July 20, 1759. See *Fasti Eccles. Scoticanæ*, i, 258.

3. Alexander (2), was licensed to preach in 1758; presented to the living at Stenton in 1766; ordained in February, 1767; and died Jan. 24, 1801, aged seventy years. See *Fasti Eccles. Scoticanæ*, i, 384.

4. Alexander (3), was licensed to preach in 1802; presented to the living of Gargunnock in 1809; ordained in 1810; transferred to Slamannan in August, 1826; and died Oct. 29, 1855, leaving a son, Thomas, in the ministry. See *Fasti Eccles. Scoticanæ*, i, 201; ii, 705.

5. Alexander (4), a native of Dyke, graduated at King's College, Aberdeen, in 1826; became teacher in the family of Irvine of Schivas; was licensed to preach in 1831; elected to the living at Northesk in 1838; ordained in 1839; resigned in 1843; and died April 5, 1858, aged fifty-three years. See *Fasti Eccles. Scoticanæ*, i, 288.

6. Alexander Dyce, D.D., was tutor in the family of James Blaikie, provost of Aberdeen; was licensed to preach March 31, 1830; presented by the town council to the living of the South Church in June, 1832, and ordained in August; transferred to the West Church, April 14, 1836, and joined the Free Secession June 15, 1843. He published four *Sermons* (Aberdeen, 1836–1848):—*The Position and Duties of Christ's Church* (ibid. 1844):—*Lectures on the Book of Esther* (Edinburgh, 1859). See *Fasti Eccles. Scoticanæ*, iii, 465, 479.

7. Archibald, D.D., son of the minister at Crawfordjohn, was presented to the living at the second charge, Paisley, and ordained Sept. 7, 1758; transferred to Inchinnan Sept. 30, 1761; was appointed principal of the University of Glasgow, but resigned in October, 1786, and died July 7, 1803. See *Fasti Eccles. Scoticanæ*, ii, 201, 221.

8. David (1), D.D., native of Fowlis-Wester, was baptized in February, 1750; licensed to preach in August, 1773; ordained Jan. 2, 1776; became assistant to Mr. Robert Walker, of Monzie; was presented to the living at Kippen in May, 1776; transferred to Dundee in July, 1782; and died Dec. 22, 1825, aged seventy-five years. See *Fasti Eccles. Scoticanæ*, ii, 731; iii, 694.

9. David (2), was licensed to preach in February, 1792; presented to the living at Cumbernauld, and ordained, Sept. 17, 1801; and died April 11, 1814, aged forty-seven years. See *Fasti Eccles. Scoticanæ*, ii, 63.

10. David (3), son of the minister at Dundee, studied theology at Edinburgh University; was licensed to preach July 31, 1822; unanimously elected the first minister of the church of Broughty Ferry, Oct. 25, and ordained Dec. 13, 1827; joined the Free Secession, Aug. 22, 1843, and died three days afterwards, aged forty-one years. He published a *Sermon* (1830). See *Fasti Eccles. Scoticanæ*, iii, 726.

11. Duncan, was promoted from being regent in Aberdeen University, and presented by the king, in February, 1574, to the living at Rathen, as the first minister; in 1593 Lonmay was under his care. He was moderator of the assembly in August, 1597, and continued in 1601. See *Fasti Eccles. Scoticanæ*, iii, 637.

12. Elliot William, was licensed to preach in 1788; appointed by the king assistant and successor to his father, Isaac, in September, 1789, and died Aug. 21, 1846, aged eighty years. See *Fasti Eccles. Scoticanæ*, i, 746.

13. George (1), graduated at Edinburgh University in June, 1658; was admitted to the living at Rerrick in 1664; transferred to Anwoth in 1666, and to Whitsome in 1668; continued in October, 1684; and died before Feb. 5, 1686. See *Fasti Eccles. Scoticanæ*, i, 450, 693, 721.

14. George (2), graduated at King's College, Aberdeen, March 31, 1809; was licensed to preach Nov. 22, 1814; ordained in March, 1819, as missionary at Berriedale; presented Feb. 22, and admitted June 15, 1820, to the living at Latheron; and joined the Free Secession, March 24, 1843. He published *An Account of the Parish.* See *Fasti Eccles. Scoticanæ*, iii, 364.

15. George Ramsay, was licensed to preach June 25, 1823; presented by the earl of Kintore, in March, 1828, to the living at Drumblade, and ordained May 8; translated to lady Glenorchy's Church, Edinburgh, July 14, 1842; joined the Free Secession, June 28, 1843. He published, *Privilege and Duty; a Pastoral Address to Lady Glenorchy's Congregation* (Edinburgh, 1845):—*Britain's Past Policy, Penitence, and Pledge*, a sermon (ibid. 1857):—*An Account of the Parish.* See *Fasti Eccles. Scoticanæ*, iii, 653.

16. Henry, was born at Eckford in 1687; graduated from Edinburgh University in 1705; was licensed to preach in March, 1712; and ordained minister at Galashiels in December, 1714. He was one of twelve ministers who petitioned the General Assembly, in 1721, against the *Marrow of Modern Divinity*, for which they were scoffingly called the Twelve Apostles. About 1735 he adopted the principles of the Independents, but retained his living till his death, Oct. 24, 1756. He published three *Sermons;* and *Letters to Christian Friends* (Edinburgh, 1811). See *Fasti Eccles. Scoticanæ*, i, 550.

17. Hugh, was licensed to preach in March, 1799; appointed schoolmaster at Maybole in 1811; presented in January, and ordained April 24, 1817, minister at Eaglesham; and died April 27, 1829, aged fifty-six years. See *Fasti Eccles. Scoticanæ*, ii, 65.

18. Isaac, D.D., minister of a Presbyterian church at Ratcliffe Highway, London, graduated from Edinburgh University in 1775; was admitted minister at Sorbie the same year; transferred to Whithorn in 1794; and died Dec. 26, 1810. See *Fasti Eccles. Scoticanæ*, i, 745, 749.

19. James, graduated at the University of St. Andrews in March, 1580; was presented to the vicarage of Wigton in 1590, and Kirkmadryne in 1596; transferred to Whithorn about 1599; continued in 1606, and adhered with forty-one others to the protestation against the introduction of episcopacy. He died before April 17, 1617. See *Fasti Eccles. Scoticanæ*, i, 729, 746.

20. John (1), was appointed the second Protestant minister at Hamilton in 1567, and had charge, also, of Dawserff, Dalyell, Cambusnethan, and Blantyre, in 1574; was a member of the assembly in 1581; appointed by the secret council, in March, 1589, one of the commissioners for the maintenance and defence of true religion, and continued in 1596. See *Fasti Eccles. Scoticanæ*, ii, 257.

21. John (2), graduated at the University of St. Andrews; was settled at Liberton in 1579, and was a commissioner of the General Assembly of 1581. He wrote a poetical tract against the regent, James, earl of Morton, in 1579, and wept when the earl forgave him; was appointed by the General Assembly of 1582 to pronounce sentence of excommunication against the archbishop of Glasgow, and was "nothing affrayed," but was threatened with a violent death, so was guarded to the kirk for ten Sundays. In 1583 he boldly admonished the king "to forbear his often swearing," and the same year had to advise him "to beware of innovations in the court." He fled to England in April, 1584, to escape the rage of his enemies. He refused in 1588 to be again settled at Liberton, but was appointed to St. Giles's parish church, Edinburgh, in 1589; was moderator of the synod and of the General Assembly that year; appointed to the second charge, Holyrood house, in 1590; was a member of the assembly, 1591; preached in the New Kirk, Edinburgh, 1592, was transferred to Prestonpans in 1595; presented to the vicarage in 1597; appointed by the assembly a visitor of five presbyteries; and died before Sept. 5, 1604, aged about fifty-six years. He built the kirk and manse at his own expense; and left all his property to support the school which he founded, "for teaching Latin, Greek, and Hebrew, and instructing the youth in virtue and learning." He published, *Dialogue Betwixt a Clerk and a Courtier* (1573):—*Ane Breif Commendation of Vprightnes* (4to, eod.):—*D. Bancroft's Rashness in Rayling against the Church* (1590):—*Memorial of the Life and Death of Robert Campbell and his Wife* (1595):—*Some Helps for Young Scholars in Christianity* (1602):—*Discovery of the Unnatural and Traitorous Conspiracy of Scottish Papists* (1593):—*Apologie*, and several *Letters*:—*Short Form of Morning and Evening Prayer*. See *Fasti Eccles. Scoticanæ*, i, 7, 87, 114, 349.

22. JOHN (3), graduated at the University of St. Andrews in 1582; was appointed the second Protestant minister at Comrie in 1588; removed to Muthill in 1589; was a member of the General Assembly, 1590, and one of forty-two ministers who signed a protest to parliament against the introduction of Episcopacy in 1606; moderator of the Presbytery in 1590; and died April 7, 1607, aged about forty-five years. See *Fasti Eccles. Scoticanæ*, ii, 752, 779.

23. JOHN (4), graduated at the University of St. Andrews in 1628; was presented to the living of Southdean in July, 1635. Refusing to conform to Episcopacy, was confined to his parish in 1662; and was deposed in July, 1666, for fornication. See *Fasti Eccles. Scoticanæ*, i, 512.

24. JOHN (5), son of the minister at Crawford-john, was licensed to preach in January, 1743; called in January, and ordained May 7, 1745, minister at Old Kilpatrick; and died May 19, 1793. He published *An Account of the Parish*. See *Fasti Eccles. Scoticanæ*, ii, 362.

25. PATRICK (1), graduated at Edinburgh University in 1587; was appointed minister at Auchterarder in 1591, having also Monyvaird in charge in 1593; presented by James VI to the living at Muckart in 1594; and continued in April, 1620. See *Fasti Eccles. Scoticanæ*, ii, 746, 776.

26. PATRICK (2), D.D., a native of Scotstown, became schoolmaster of Keith-hall; was licensed to preach in April, 1771; became assistant to Mr. Robert Farquharson, minister of Chapel Garioch; was presented to the living at Kemnay, and ordained June 19, 1776; transferred to Rayne in February, 1778, and died May 21, 1819, aged seventy-five years. He published *An Account of the Parish*. See *Fasti Eccles. Scoticanæ*, iii, 588.

27. PATRICK (3), youngest son of William, minister at Inverury, graduated at Marischal College, Aberdeen, April 1, 1806; became schoolmaster of Kintore; was licensed to preach in July, 1814; presented to the living at Insch in 1821; ordained May 8, 1822; and died Nov. 17, 1858, aged sixty-eight years. See *Fasti Eccles. Scoticanæ*, iii, 582.

28. ROBERT (1), graduated at Edinburgh University in July, 1628; was a member of the commission of assembly in 1647; and died in November, 1657, aged about fifty years. See *Fasti Eccles. Scoticanæ*, i, 383.

29. ROBERT (2), was licensed to preach in February, 1708; became chaplain to lady Blantyre; was called to the living at Crawford-john in December, 1712; ordained in November, 1713; and died Jan. 7, 1749, aged sixty-seven years. He left two sons, Archibald and John, in the ministry. See *Fasti Eccles. Scoticanæ*, ii, 322.

30. THOMAS (1), studied theology at Glasgow University; was licensed to preach by the Scotch Presbytery at London, Dec. 12, 1700; received by the Presbytery at Edinburgh, 1702, elected sole lecturer in the Tron Church, Edinburgh, Sept. 11, 1706; commissioned chaplain by queen Anne at Stirling castle, and ordained Oct. 18, 1709; promoted to Whitekirk in 1713; transferred to Dundee, Jan. 5, 1732; and died Nov. 27, 1760, aged eighty-two years. His son Hugh became rector of Kirkby, in Yorkshire; and his son Thomas Randall was minister at Inchture, then at Stirling. See *Fasti Eccles. Scoticanæ*, i, 386; ii, 685; iii, 689.

31. THOMAS (2), studied at the universities of Aberdeen and Glasgow; became schoolmaster at Dores in 1819; was licensed to preach, and ordained minister at Kilmalie, April 4, 1826; made missionary at Tarbert, April 15, 1829; presented to Salen in December, 1835; joined the Free Secession, May 24, 1843. See *Fasti Eccles. Scoticanæ*, iii, 113, 114.

32. WILLIAM (1), graduated at the University of St. Andrews in 1595; was appointed to the living at Reay in 1601; transferred to Farr before 1607; and continued in 1608. See *Fasti Eccles. Scoticanæ*, iii, 350, 366.

33. WILLIAM (2), graduated at the University of St. Andrews in 1603; was an expectant in the synod in 1611; admitted to the living of Auchindoir and Kearn before November, 1633; was a member of the General Assembly in 1639; and continued April 16, 1667. See *Fasti Eccles. Scoticanæ*, iii, 548.

34. WILLIAM (3), a native of Kintore, was minister at Rathen in 1603; present at the Aberdeen Assembly in July, 1605, contrary to the king's order; confessed his error to the privy council in October, and was admonished and returned to his charge. He was admitted a burgess and guild-brother of Aberdeen, Aug. 1, 1620; was a member of the commission of assembly, 1645; and died in 1657. See *Fasti Eccles. Scoticanæ*, iii, 638.

35. WILLIAM (4), had been a minister in Ireland who fled at the time of the insurrection in 1641. After a stay in England and the south of Scotland, he was invited to the living at Canisbay in 1652, and admitted Feb. 17, 1655; transferred to Birsay Oct. 18, 1666; lost his sight May 25, 1673, and died after Sept. 9, 1690. See *Fasti Eccles. Scoticanæ*, iii, 358, 393.

36. WILLIAM (5), graduated at King's College, Aberdeen, July 12, 1660; and was admitted to the living at Killearnan, Feb. 25, 1669. See *Fasti Eccles. Scoticanæ*, iii, 281.

37. WILLIAM (6), a native of Aberdeenshire, became schoolmaster of Navar; was licensed to preach Aug. 19, 1741; called to the living at Lethnot and Navar, and ordained Sept. 25, 1746; and died March 12, 1775, aged seventy-three years. See *Fasti Eccles. Scoticanæ*, iii, 833.

38. WILLIAM (7), graduated at King's College, Aberdeen, April 23, 1751; became schoolmaster at Inverury in June, 1751; was licensed to preach Feb. 14, 1759; ordained assistant minister, and successor at Inverury, Sept. 6, 1767; and died Jan. 19, 1799, aged sixty-eight years. He left two sons in the ministry, William and Patrick. See *Fasti Eccles. Scoticanæ*, iii, 583.

39. WILLIAM (8), was ordained in October, 1762, minister of the Presbyterian congregation, Castlegarth, Newcastle-on-Tyne; presented in January, and admitted in May, 1801, to the living at Mordington; and died June 24, 1804, aged sixty-eight years. See *Fasti Eccles. Scoticanæ*, i, 445.

Davidson, Adoniram Judson, a Baptist minister, was baptized in 1858; licensed to preach in 1873; matriculated at Acadia College in 1872; preached for a while in 1873 at Isaacs Harbor, and in 1874 undertook a mission to Eatonville, N. S., and died at his home in Portaupique, Jan. 14, 1876, aged thirty-three years. See *Baptist Year-book of N. S., N. B., and P. E. I.*, 1876, p. 36.

Davidson, Alexander, a Protestant Episcopal clergyman, entered the ministry in 1867; became assistant minister of St. George's Church, Newburgh, N. Y., but served only a short time, and died Sept. 29, 1870. See *Prot. Episc. Almanac*, 1871, p. 118.

Davidson, Asbury, a minister in the Methodist Episcopal Church South, was born in Tennessee in 1810. He was admitted into the Tennessee Conference in 1831; served as presiding elder in the Memphis Conference during 1842 and 1844; was transferred to the Mississippi Conference in 1845; located and removed to Texas in 1851; joined the Texas Conference in 1855, and died Dec. 21, 1868. See *Minutes of Annual Conferences of the M. E. Church South*, 1869, p. 385.

Davidson, Benjamin, an English Oriental scholar, was born of Jewish parentage. In 1845 he was in connection with the British Society for the Propagation of the Gospel among the Jews, and in 1847 was appointed principal of the college founded by that society for training missionaries for the Jews. He died in London in 1871. Besides assisting in the edition of the *Englishman's Hebrew and Chaldee Concordance*, he is the author of the *Analytical Hebrew and Chaldee Lexicon:—Syriac Reading Lessons, with Analysis:—Chaldee Reading Lessons:*—and joint author of *Arabic Reading Lessons.* But his *chef-d'œuvre* is his posthumous work, *A Concordance of the Hebrew and Chaldee Scriptures* (Lond. 1876), the most complete Hebrew concordance hitherto issued. The order of the books is here retained uniformly, and also that of the personal inflections of the verb. The suffixes are, moreover, expressed in detail. At the end of the volume a list of particles is given. (B. P.)

Davidson, C. B., D.D., a Protestant Episcopal clergyman, entered the ministry in 1867, becoming pastor of Grace Church, Indianapolis, Ind.; in 1870 resided in Springfield, O., where he assumed the rectorship of Christ Church; in 1873 became rector of St. John's Church, Cincinnati; and died in December, 1874, aged fifty-eight years. See *Prot. Episc. Almanac*, 1874, p. 145.

Davidson, James H., a Methodist Episcopal minister, was born in Westmoreland County, Pa., in 1836. He was converted in early life; removed to Indiana in 1856; received license to preach soon after; in 1859 entered the South-eastern Indiana Conference; in 1861 enlisted in the Seventieth Regiment Indiana Volunteers; served in the army one year; re-entered the itinerancy, and continued until his death, June 18, 1866. See *Minutes of Annual Conferences*, 1866, p. 205.

Davidson, James I., a Methodist Episcopal minister, was born near Newcastle-on-Tyne, Northumberland, England, Dec. 14, 1824. He was converted at the age of eight; conducted prayer-meetings at ten; began to exhort and preach at twelve; became a regular licensed preacher among the Wesleyans when but sixteen; in 1849 emigrated to America; in 1850 settled in Quincy, Ill.; in 1851 entered the Illinois Conference; in 1862 was appointed chaplain of the Seventy-third Regiment Illinois Volunteers, but afterwards became successively captain, major, and lieutenant-colonel; returned to the pastorate, and continued until his death, Jan. 10, 1870. See *Minutes of Annual Conferences*, 1870, p. 235.

Davidson, John Edward, a Presbyterian minister, was born in Fairfield District, S. C., June 16, 1827. He graduated from Princeton Theological Seminary in 1853; was ordained an evangelist by the Presbytery of Tombigbee, Dec. 17 of the same year; became pastor at Minden, Ala., in 1854, and died there Oct. 30 of that year. See *Gen. Cat. of Princeton Theol. Sem.* 1881, p. 178.

Davidson, Joseph T., a Presbyterian minister, was born in Fairfield District, S. C., April 11, 1818. He was licensed to preach by the Presbytery of Red River, Jan. 7, 1841; ordained, in 1854, pastor at Homer, La.; supported his family by teaching and working on the farm; organized several churches and saw many revivals; and died at Homer, Oct. 21, 1881. See *S. W. Presbyterian*, Nov. 1, 1881. (W. P. S.)

Davidson, Robert, D.D., a Presbyterian minister, only son of Rev. R. Davidson, D.D., second president of Dickinson College, was born at Carlisle, Pa., Feb. 23, 1808. He graduated from Dickinson College in 1828, and from Princeton Theological Seminary in 1831; the following year took charge of the McChord (or Second) Church of Lexington, Ky., was ordained there in March, 1832, and became distinguished for his pulpit eloquence and his earnest work as a pastor. In 1840 he became president of Transylvania University, Kentucky; in 1842 was appointed superintendent of public institutions, but after holding that office a short time and declining a professorship in Centre College and the presidency of Ohio University, he accepted the pastoral charge of the First Presbyterian Church in New Brunswick, N. J., May 4, 1843. In 1859 he became pastor of the Spring Street Church, New York city. From 1864 to 1868 his pastoral charge was the First Church of Huntington, L. I., and he afterwards resided in Philadelphia, Pa., until his death, April 6, 1876. Dr. Davidson served the General Assembly as its permanent clerk from 1845 to 1850. For a quarter of a century he was a member of the Board of Foreign Missions; for ten years a director of Princeton Seminary, and in 1869 was one of the delegates to the General Assembly of the Free Church of Scotland. He was a frequent contributor to the periodical literature of the day. He published a large number of pamphlets, sermons, etc., and wrote several able articles for the *Princeton Review.* He was also the author of a number of volumes, the largest and best known of which is his *History of the Presbyterian Church in Kentucky.* "He was a man of fine culture, a scholar, a writer of great purity and elegance. As a minister of Christ he won and maintained to the end a high position." See *Necrol. Report of Princeton Theol. Sem.* 1877, p. 26.

Davidson, Thomas Leslie, D.D., a Baptist minister, was born in Edinburgh, Scotland, Sept. 6, 1825. He went to Canada in 1833; in 1841 united with the Church; in 1843 entered the Baptist College in Montreal; in August, 1847, was ordained pastor in Pickering, Ont., continuing there till December, 1850, when he went to the city of Brantford, and remained there till April, 1860. During this pastorate he baptized three hundred and eight persons, and built two churches. He was at the same time editor of the *Canadian Messenger*, now the *Canadian Baptist*, assuming that position in 1854. In 1857 he was chosen secretary of the Baptist Missionary Convention of Ontario, and held the office for fifteen successive years. He was afterwards pastor at St. George (1860–66), Elgin (1866–73), and Guelph (1873–77). For one year after leaving the last place he was general financial and travelling secretary of the Ontario Baptist Convention. His last pastorates were in Chatham and Tiverton, Ont. In 1858 he published a work on *Baptism and Communion.* He died in October, 1883. See Cathcart, *Baptist Encyclop.* p. 308; *Chicago Standard*, Oct. 25, 1883. (J. C. S.)

Davidson, W. Fayette, a Protestant Episcopal clergyman, was a deacon for several years in the diocese of Pennsylvania; in 1858 officiated in Philadelphia for a short time, and then removed to Suffolk, Va., where he died, Dec. 24, 1859. See *Prot. Episc. Almanac*, 1861, p. 98.

Davie, Alexander, a Scotch clergyman, studied at the University of St. Andrews; was presented by the king to the living at Inchture in 1799, and ordained in August of that year; libelled by the presbytery in 1811, but the charge was withdrawn; the parishioners brought a new charge against him in 1812, which, after three years' litigation, was declared "not proven," in May, 1815. He died Sept. 3, 1840, aged seventy-seven years. See *Fasti Eccles. Scoticanæ*, iii, 700.

Davie, John, a Scotch clergyman, intruded in the living at Strickathrow in 1701, and again in November, 1715, "coming in with near eighty men under arms, with beating drums and flying colors, and preached a little." He continued till February, 1716, and was deposed in October following, at which time he was factor to James, earl of Southesk. See *Fasti Eccles. Scoticanæ*, iii, 850.

Davie, J. T. M., a Reformed (Dutch) minister, came from the Presbytery of North River in 1853; served the Church at Flatlands, L. I., from 1853 to 1861, and died in 1862. See Corwin, *Manual of the Ref. Church in America*, 3d ed., p. 230.

Davies, Benjamin (1), D.D., an English Independent minister, son of an Independent minister in Wales, was educated at Carmarthen, settled first at Abergavenny, and was tutor of an academy there. In 1783 he went to London as pastor at Fetter Lane, and tutor in the Homerton Academy. He was one of the six Merchant Lecturers from 1783. He filled his varied duties with great respectability and accceptance till his health failed, and he died after July, 1795. He published several *Sermons*. See Wilson, *Dissenting Churches*, iii, 462, 463.

Davies, Benjamin (2), a Welsh Baptist minister, was born at Llangan, Carmarthenshire, in 1777. He was baptized in 1795; had a good education; was ordained at Ffynon in 1792, and after a life of great usefulness died there, Aug. 16, 1828. See (Lond.) *Baptist Magazine*, 1829, p. 181. (J. C. S.)

Davies, Benjamin (3), an English Baptist minister, was born at Dorchester, Aug. 31, 1833. He was converted at the age of sixteen; for a few years was engaged in secular business, but in October, 1854, became pastor of the Church in South Chard, Somersetshire; in eighteen months removed to Linsdale, and preached till the close of 1858, when he went to Greenwich, where he was pastor until his sudden death, May 11, 1872. See (Lond.) *Baptist Hand-book*, 1874, p. 265. (J. C. S.)

Davies, Daniel (1), a Welsh Baptist minister, was born in Pembrokeshire in 1814. He graduated from Pontypool College in 1841; became co-pastor with Rev. Robert Williams at Ruthin, Denbighshire, for a few years; pastor at Llanelly, near Abergavenny, for twelve years, and afterwards at Cowbridge, Glamorgan, until his death, Dec. 14, 1867. See (Lond.) *Baptist Handbook*, 1869, p. 139. (J. C. S.)

Davies, Daniel (2), an English Congregational minister, was born at Maelgrove, Pembrokeshire, in 1780. He was early converted to Christ; ordained at Rhesycae, Flintshire, in 1808; five years later removed to Cardigan, and remained there until his death, Jan. 18, 1867. See (Lond.) *Cong. Year-book*, 1868, p. 266.

Davies, Daniel (3), an English Congregational minister, was born at Hawey Mill, Radnorshire, April 17, 1787. He was converted when very young; trained for the ministry at Wrexham College; was ordained at Sarnau, Montgomeryshire, where he labored ten years; thence removed to Wollerton, Salop, where he continued until his death, March 20, 1865. See (Lond.) *Cong. Year-book*, 1866, p. 245.

Davies, Daniel (4), an English Congregational minister, was born at Castle Villa, Pembrokeshire, in 1791. He joined the Church at the age of eighteen; began preaching in the following year; in 1812 entered Abergavenny Academy; in 1819 was ordained co-pastor at Trefgarn and Penybont; afterwards had oversight of the churches at Gower, Glamorganshire, at Winslow, again at Penybont, and finally at Zion's Hill, Pembrokeshire, where he died, Sept. 28, 1859. See (Lond.) *Cong. Year-book*, 1860, p. 181.

Davies, Daniel (5), D.D., a Welsh Baptist minister, was born in Carmarthenshire, Dec. 15, 1797. He became blind at the age of seven; studied for a time in the Liverpool College for the Blind, and for a short period was a preacher among the Welsh Presbyterians. At the age of twenty-three he became a Baptist, and for five years was pastor of a Welsh Church in London, when he removed to Bethesda, Swansea, and there had charge of the church for thirty years. In 1855 he removed to Cardigan, where he was pastor for several years. He died in Glamorganshire, but the exact date does not appear. See Cathcart, *Baptist Encyclop.* p. 309. (J. C. S.)

Davies, Daniel (6), a Welsh Baptist minister, was born in Carmarthenshire in 1805. He joined the Church at the age of thirteen; in 1830 became pastor at Lixworn, Flintshire, where he remained seventeen years, and at Penyfron and Halkin, until his death, May 30, 1859. See (Lond.) *Baptist Hand-book*, 1861, p. 97. (J. C. S.)

Davies, David (1), a Welsh Congregational minister, was born at Clifforch, Cardiganshire, February, 1791. He joined the Church when very young; entered the Presbyterian College at Carmarthen in his seventeenth year; was co-pastor at Carnarvon two years, and then at Pant-teg and Peniel, near Carmarthen, until his death, July 31, 1864. He was president of the college at Carmarthen twenty-one years. See (Lond.) *Cong. Year-book*, 1865, p. 233.

Davies, David (2), a Welsh Baptist minister, son of the Rev. Benjamin Davies, was born at Denant, March 2, 1794. He was brought up a carpenter, converted under the last sermon of his father in 1812, and soon began to preach. He studied under Rev. Micah Thomas, at Abergavenny, and afterwards at Stepney College, London. In 1822 he was chosen assistant minister at Evesham; subsequently was pastor at Haverfordwest; and after being for some years tutor of the college at that place, died there, March 19, 1856. See (Lond.) *Baptist Hand-book*, 1856, p. 6.

Davies, David (3), a Welsh Congregational minister, was born in Llanybydder, Carmarthenshire, in June, 1798. He joined the Church at the age of fifteen; before he was twenty, through the request of the Church, began preaching; was ordained at New Inn, near Pontypool, in 1823, where he continued to preach until his death, Dec. 12, 1875. See (Lond.) *Cong. Yearbook*, 1877, p. 353.

Davies, David (4), a Welsh Congregational minister, was born at Blaenpantyvi, in the parish of Troedyroer, in 1806. He was converted about 1822, while attending the Neuaddlwyd Academy; in 1828 began preaching, and was ordained pastor at Capel-y-reu-cellan; in 1839 removed to Lampeter, where he labored till his death, Dec. 17, 1871. See (Lond.) *Cong. Year-Book*, 1873, p. 322.

Davies, David (5), a Methodist Episcopal minister, was born at Newtown, Montgomeryshire, Wales, June 10, 1807. He embraced religion in early life; received license to preach at the age of sixteen; came to America in 1831, and in 1833 united with the Oneida Conference. He became so affected by blindness that he was obliged to retire from all active work in 1873, and died Feb. 2, 1878. See *Minutes of Annual Conferences*, 1878, p. 67.

Davies, David (6), a Welsh Congregational minister, labored eleven years, and then suffered two years of indisposition and inability to perform his pastoral duties, when he died at Glantâf, Glamorganshire, July 16, 1851, at the age of forty years. See (Lond.) *Cong. Year-book*, 1851, p. 214.

Davies, David (7), a Welsh Baptist minister, was born at Culycwm, Carmarthenshire, in 1813. He began to preach in 1836; entered Pontypool College in 1841; in 1844 was ordained pastor of the Old Church at Waintrodau, Bedwas, where he ministered with great acceptance and success for twenty years. His next pastorate was with the Charles Street Church, Newport, Monmouthshire; and his last with the Church in Bedwas, where he died, Jan. 11, 1872. See (Lond.) *Baptist Hand-book*, 1873, p. 256. (J. C. S.)

Davies, David Milton, a Welsh Congregational minister, was born near Lampeter, Cardiganshire, Nov. 23, 1827. He joined the Church in 1840; studied two years at Hanover, and four years at Brecon College; was ordained at Hay, Brecon, in 1853; about a year later became pastor at Wern and Penycae, in Cardiganshire, where he labored with great zeal and success until 1858, then removed to Llanfyllin, Montgomeryshire, and remained until his death, June 7, 1869. For some years he was one of the responsible editors of the *Dysgedydd*, a denominational monthly. See (Lond.) *Cong. Year-book*, 1870, p. 283.

Davies, David Rowland, a Congregational minister, was born in Ystradfellte, Glamorganshire, South Wales, in 1809. In 1843 he emigrated to America, and was ordained June 17 as pastor of the Church at Brady's Bend, Pa., where he died, Aug. 15, 1881. See *Cong. Year-book*, 1882, p. 28.

Davies, Ebenezer, F.G.S., an English Congregational minister, was born at Ruthin, North Wales, April 3, 1808. He was educated at Rotherham College, and settled at Tabernacle Chapel, Stockport, in 1838. After one year of unexampled success, he accepted a call of the London Missionary Society to go to New Amsterdam, in Berbice, British Guiana, where he labored faithfully until 1848. He then returned to England, and became the minister of a chapel in London, where he remained twenty-four years. His last years were spent in Southport. He died at Bryniach, Ruthin, Feb. 3, 1882. See (Lond.) *Cong. Year-book*, 1883, p. 275.

Davies, Edward (1), a Welsh Baptist minister, was born in 1769. He began to preach in 1789, and finally was pastor of the English and Welsh Church at Maesteg, Glamorganshire, where he died, Nov. 8, 1843. See (Lond.) *Baptist Hand-book*, 1844, p. 16. (J. C. S.)

Davies, Edward (2), a Welsh Congregational minister, was born at Llanrhaiadr-y-Mochnant, May, 1786. He was converted in youth; began his ministry in 1815, at Capel Helyg and Rhoslan; in 1822 became pastor of the churches at Penystryt and Maentwrog; relinquished his pastoral work in 1856, but continued to preach in different places till near his death, at Trawsfynydd, Jan. 5, 1872. See (Lond.) *Cong. Year-book*, 1873, p. 323.

Davies, Edward (3), A.M., an English Congregational minister, was born near Newport, Shropshire, March 15, 1796. He was converted at sixteen years of age; in March, 1813, joined the Church at Harwood; entered North Wales Academy, at Llanfyllin, in January, 1817; in 1820 was appointed tutor of classics, and in January was ordained as co-pastor, at Newtown, Montgomeryshire, and as pastor of the neighboring church of Bwlchyfridd. In 1839 he removed with the academy to Brecon, retaining his office as classical tutor until his death, Feb. 25, 1857. See (Lond.) *Cong. Year-book*, 1858, p. 196.

Davies, Evan (1), an English Congregational minister, was born at Hengwm, Cardiganshire, in 1805. He was carefully trained as a Calvinistic Methodist; experienced conversion in early manhood in London, whither he had gone to engage in business; joined the Congregationalists; studied at Neuaddlwyd Academy, and at the Western Academy; and settled as minister first at Great Torrington, North Devon, for a short time; was sent by the London Missionary Society, after ordination, in 1835, to Penang, China, where he devoted himself incessantly to the study of the Chinese language, established a Christian school for native children, and preached to the English soldiers stationed there. Mr. Davies returned to England in 1840, travelled as missionary agent until 1844, when he accepted the oversight of the Congregational Church in Richmond, Surrey. In 1857 he removed to Heywood, Lancashire, remained there two years, then went to Dalston, and finally to Hornsey, where he died, June 18, 1864. Mr. Davies was the author of the following works: *China and her Spiritual Claims:—Memoirs of the Rev. Samuel Dyer:—An Appeal to the Reason and Good Conscience of Catholics:—Lectures on the Sabbath;* and editor of the following works: *Letters of the late Rev. Samuel Dyer to his Children; Lectures on Christian Theology*, by the late Rev. Dr. Payne; and *The Works of the late Rev. Dr. Edward Williams of Rotherham.* His notes on *Original Sin* and *Baptism*, which appear in his edition of Dr. Williams's works, evince great power as a thinker. See (Lond.) *Cong. Year-book*, 1865, p. 234.

Davies, Evan (2), a Welsh Wesleyan minister, was born at Cellan, near Lampeter, in November, 1819. He was converted in 1839, entered the ministry in 1846, and died at Llangollen, Jan. 11, 1877. See *Minutes of the British Conference*, 1877, p. 27.

Davies, Francis Barton, a minister of the Methodist Episcopal Church South, was born in Savannah, Ga. He was converted in early life; began his ministry in the Holston Conference, but afterwards gave up preaching for a time, on account of failing health; in 1866 again entered the itinerant ranks in the North Georgia Conference, in which he labored until his death, at Decatur, April 25, 1881, in the forty-seventh year of his age. See *Minutes of Annual Conferences of the M. E. Church South*, 1881, p. 332.

Davies, George, an English Wesleyan missionary, was sent out by the British Conference in 1863 to West Africa, where, after a few months of earnest and useful labor, his health failed. Returning to his native land, he was appointed in 1865 to the South Bristol Circuit; but died at Cardiff, Aug. 3, 1866, in the twenty-fifth year of his age. See *Minutes of the British Conference*, 1866, p. 39.

Davies, George Palmer, an English Congregational minister, was born at Narberth, Pembrokeshire, April 30, 1826. He was educated at Carmarthen and Homerton colleges, and at the age of twenty-four entered upon the pastorate of the Church at Wandsworth, where he remained three years. Retiring to recuperate his failing health, he sojourned in Bonn and subsequently in Berlin, pursuing his theological studies. He refused the chair of theology at Carmarthen College, and accepted the agency of the British and Foreign Bible Society in south Germany. For several years he lived in Frankfort; but in 1869, having been called to superintend the entire work of the Bible Society in Germany and Switzerland, he removed to Berlin, where he continued to reside until his death, April 23, 1881. He wrote, *Erinnerungsblätter von Freundeshand* (Berlin, 1881). See (Lond.) *Cong. Year-book*, 1882, p. 292.

Davies, Henry (1), a Welsh Baptist minister, was born at Llanggloffan, Pembrokeshire, in 1783. He began to preach at the age of nineteen or twenty; studied two years at Abergavenny College; and in 1811 was chosen co-pastor in his native town, where he remained until his death, Aug. 23, 1862. For twenty-eight years he was secretary of the association in his shire. See (Lond.) *Baptist Hand-book*, 1863, p. 113. (J. C. S.)

Davies, Henry (2), an English Wesleyan minister, was born at Barnstable, Oct. 23, 1799. He was converted at sixteen; was appointed to the West Indies in 1821; returned to England in 1824; was henceforth engaged in the home work; became a supernumerary in 1855; re-entered the itinerancy in 1859; retired in 1865; and died in Cambridge, Jan. 19, 1870. See *Minutes of the British Conference*, 1870, p. 22.

Davies, Henry (3), an English Congregational minister, was born in London in 1817. He studied at Newport Pagnel Academy; preached successively at Godmanchester, Ryde, and Lavenham; and died March 22, 1877. See (Lond.) *Cong. Year-book*, 1878, p. 312.

Davies, Henry (4), a Welsh Congregational minister, was born at Bwlch-y-gwynt, Carmarthenshire, May 21, 1820. He joined the Church at the age of fifteen; began preaching in the following year; studied for the ministry at Frood-Vale Academy; and was ordained in 1842 at Bethania, Llanon, where he labored successfully until his death, Feb. 1, 1871. See (Lond.) *Cong. Year-book*, 1872, p. 311.

Davies, Howell, a Welsh Baptist minister, was born at Trelech in 1818, and brought up an Independent. In 1844 he was immersed and began to preach. In 1850 he removed to Maestig, Glamorganshire; and, while keeping a school, and serving as pastor over the Baptist Church there, he died, April 25, 1866. See (Lond.) *Baptist Hand-book*, 1866.

Davies, Isaac (1), a Welsh Baptist minister, was born near Corwen, Oct. 21, 1817. He studied at the college in Bradford in 1843; became pastor of the united churches of Swanwick and Riddings, in Derbyshire; in November, 1850, removed to Cupar-Fife, Scotland; and in September, 1853, to Newcastle-on-Tyne, where he remained three years, and died July 19, 1860. See (Lond.) *Baptist Hand-book*, 1862, p. 106. (J. C. S.)

Davies, Isaac (2), a Welsh Wesleyan minister, was born at Mynydd-bach, Carmarthen. He united with the Methodist society in early life; preached for some time in the Welsh language; was accepted for the ministry in 1857, and sent to Ireland, where he labored six years; was appointed to an English charge in 1863; and died suddenly at Chipping-Norton, Oxfordshire, April, 1868. See *Minutes of the British Conference*, 1868, p. 24.

Davies, Jacob, an English Baptist minister, was born at Newtown, Montgomeryshire, Wales, Feb. 22, 1816. He was converted and baptized at the age of seventeen, and soon afterwards began to preach. In 1840 he entered Bradford College; and in 1844 was sent out to Ceylon by the Baptist Missionary Society; in 1847 his health failed, but he continued to labor as he had strength till his death, at Colombo, in April, 1849. See (Lond.) *Baptist Hand-book*, 1850, p. 44.

Davies, James Adams, a Presbyterian minister, was born in York District, S. C., May 20, 1829. He was converted in early life; educated in Davidson College, N. C.; graduated from the theological seminary at Columbia, S. C., in 1855, when he was licensed by the Bethel Presbytery; was ordained, in 1857, pastor of Beersheba Church, and died at Yorkville, March 18, 1867. See Wilson, *Presb. Hist. Almanac*, 1868, p. 325.

Davies, James E., a Presbyterian minister, was born in Mecklenburg County, N. C., Oct. 20, 1787. He was converted in 1800; in 1818 removed to Illinois, and was licensed to preach by the Illinois Presbytery; became pastor at Hopedale, and died there, Oct. 22, 1862. See Wilson, *Presb. Hist. Almanac*, 1863, p. 414.

Davies, John (1), D.D., a Welsh clergyman and antiquary, was born in the latter part of the 16th century in Denbighshire, and educated by William Morgan, afterwards bishop of St. Asaph, and at Jesus College, Oxford. He was rector of Malloyd, in Merionethshire, and canon of St. Asaph. He was a fine Greek and Hebrew scholar. The time of his death is unknown. His works are, *Antiquæ Linguæ Britannicæ* (1621, 8vo):—*Dictionarium Latino-Britannicum.* He also assisted in translating the Bible into Welsh, in that correct edition which came out in 1620. See Chalmers, *Biog. Dict.* s. v.; Allibone, *Dict. of Brit. and Amer. Authors*, s. v.

Davies, John (2), D.D., an English clergyman and an eminent critic, was born in London, April 22, 1679. He was educated at the Charterhouse School and Queen's College, Cambridge, where he took the degree of A.B. in 1698; was chosen a fellow of his college in 1702, and became proctor in 1709. In 1711, having distinguished himself by several learned publications, he was collated to the rectory of Fen-Ditton, near Cambridge, and to a prebend in the Church of Ely, taking the same year the degree of LL.D. In 1716 he was chosen master of Queen's College. He died March 7, 1732. Dr. Davies was not the author of any original work, but employed himself in publishing some correct editions of Greek and Latin authors of antiquity. See Chalmers, *Biog. Dict.* s. v.; Allibone, *Dict. of Brit. and Amer. Authors*, s. v.

Davies, John (3), an English Congregational minister, was born in Piccadilly, London, March 4, 1792. He studied at Hoxton College; was first settled at Bath, but soon accepted an invitation to Rodborough, Gloucestershire, where he remained a considerable period; was for many years pastor of the Rev. George Whitefield's chapel in Bristol; resigned on account of ill-health; remained some years without a charge, and then accepted a co-pastorate at Taunton. He afterwards settled at Oswestry, where he remained six or seven years, and then became pastor of the Independent chapel at Welshpool, where he died in March, 1851. See (Lond.) *Cong. Year-book*, 1851, p. 213.

Davies, John (4), an English Congregational minister, was born at Llangyfni, Carmarthenshire, Wales, Aug. 30, 1769. He joined the Calvinistic Methodists in 1786; studied at Trevecca and Cheshunt colleges; was ordained at Spa Fields in 1796; settled first at Handsworth, and subsequently at Tetbury, Ludgershall, and Whitstable; in 1829 retired to Reading, but was soon after urged to accept the pastorate at Bracknell, Berkshire; thither he removed, and, after fourteen years of earnest labor, was disabled by paralysis, and died March 2, 1861. See (Lond.) *Cong. Year-book*, 1862, p. 227.

Davies, John (5), an English Congregational missionary, was born in 1771. He left England, May 5, 1800, and arrived at Tahiti, Polynesia, July 10, 1801, when the island was sunken in barbarism and idolatry. On account of the fierce war that broke out in Tahiti in 1808, he was obliged to retire to Huaheine; after remaining there a year, went to Port Jackson, which he reached Feb. 17, 1810; returned to Tahiti in September, 1811; but in 1818 again removed to Huaheine, and thence to Papara in 1820, where he labored till his death in 1856. See (Lond.) *Cong. Year-book*, 1857, p. 175.

Davies, John (6), a Welsh Wesleyan minister, was born in Flintshire in 1784. He joined the Methodist society at the age of sixteen; entered the ministry in 1806, and died Dec. 21, 1845. See *Minutes of the British Conference*, 1846.

Davies, John (7), a Welsh Congregational minister, was born at Esgerfynwent, Carmarthenshire, in 1799. He was converted at the age of ten; studied six years at Carmarthen College, beginning in 1819, supplying, meanwhile, several vacant churches; was ordained in 1826, at Summerfield Chapel, Neath, Glamorganshire; resigned in 1838, but continued to preach at various places to the time of his death, Aug. 3, 1862. See (Lond.) *Cong. Year-book*, 1864, p. 206.

Davies, John (8), a Methodist Episcopal minister.

was born in Liverpool, England, March 5, 1799. He was converted at the age of nine; became a local preacher nine years later; emigrated to New York city in 1827, where for years he did valiant work as a city missionary; and in 1836 entered the New York Conference, wherein he labored until his death, July 2, 1876. See *Minutes of Annual Conferences*, 1877, p. 42.

Davies, John (9), a Congregational minister, was born Sept. 9, 1800, near Aberystwith, Cardiganshire, Wales. He was converted at fourteen years of age; soon after joined the Church at Woolwich; at the age of sixteen entered the college at Llanfyllin; was pastor at New Cross, Deptford, four years; and in October, 1826, became pastor at Daventry, where he remained till his death, June 27, 1857. See (Lond.) *Cong. Year-book*, 1858, p. 197.

Davies, John (10), a Welsh Congregational minister, was born at Cilianaeron, Cardiganshire, April, 1805. He joined the Church very early in life; studied at the Presbyterian College, Carmarthen; was ordained pastor at Bwlchyffridd, Montgomeryshire; twelve years later retired to Llanwnog, and preached occasionally at various places till his death, June 24, 1872. See (Lond.) *Cong. Year-book*, 1873, p. 322.

Davies, John (11), an English Congregational minister, previously a Methodist local preacher at Ebenezer, Newport, Pembrokeshire, was ordained pastor at Gideon, April 19, 1843; resigned in 1871, but was able for some time to preach occasionally; and died Aug. 22, 1880, in the seventy-first year of his age. See (Lond.) *Cong. Year-book*, 1881, p. 369.

Davies, John (12), a Welsh Congregational minister, was born in the parish of Mothvey, Carmarthenshire, May 1, 1823. He was converted in his twelfth year; began to preach when but sixteen; completed a course at Brecon College; was ordained at Llanelly, Brecknockshire, in 1846; became pastor at Aberaman in 1854; in 1863 removed to Cardiff, and in 1868 resigned his Welsh charge, and became pastor of an English congregation which he had organized in Cardiff; in which capacity he continued till his death, May 8, 1874. He edited the *Bierniad*, a Welsh quarterly, from its commencement in 1860 until a few months of his death. See (Lond.) *Cong. Year-book*, 1875, p. 321.

Davies, John (13), a Congregational minister, was born in Wales in 1824. He was a student at Bala College, Merionethshire; was ordained pastor at Conway, Dec. 19, 1849; subsequently served at Henryd, where he remained until 1859; then was installed pastor at Amwythiz, and in 1864 at Ruthya. From 1868 to 1879 he was engaged in farming, and in the latter year arrived in America. From January, 1880, he was acting pastor in Mineral Ridge, O., until his death, Feb. 9, 1881. See *Cong. Year-book*, 1882, p. 28.

Davies, John (14), a Baptist minister, was born in Birmingham, England, April 11, 1837. He was educated at Rawden College, Yorkshire, ordained in 1862 in his native city, where he was pastor of the Bond Street Church five years; came to the United States in 1867, and for four years took charge of the Church in South Norwalk, Conn. In 1872 he became pastor of the Central Church, Norwich, where his health suddenly failed, Dec. 28, 1879. He returned to England, and died in Birmingham, April 19, 1880. See *The Christian Secretary*, April, 1880. (J. C. S.)

Davies, John (15), a Welsh Congregational minister, was born at Maesteg, Glamorganshire. He was brought up in the British school in his native town, and then became a pupil-teacher in Aberdare; afterwards entered the Normal College at Swansea as assistant master, whence he went to the Carmarthen Presbyterian College. Sept. 4, 1871, he was ordained pastor of the English Church at Maesteg and the Welsh Church at Zoar, but, owing to failing health, gave up his charge and became master of the Llangadog Grammar-school, in which position he died, May 21, 1879, at the age of thirty-five. See (Lond.) *Cong. Year-book*, 1880, p. 319.

Davies, John (16), a Welsh Baptist minister, was born at St. George's, near Cardiff, Sept. 17, 1851. He joined the Church at the age of fifteen, and early decided to enter the ministry, preaching his first sermon when about eighteen. In 1872 he entered Cardigan Grammar-school, and afterwards spent three years in Haverfordwest College. In June, 1876, he became pastor of the Baptist Church at Penycae, North Wales, where he labored diligently until 1879. He then went to Porth, Rhondda Valley, Glamorganshire; and died June 9, 1880. See (Lond.) *Baptist Hand-book*, 1882, p. 300.

Davies, John David, an English Congregational minister, was born at Braintree, Essex, Feb. 10, 1829. He was converted when about eighteen years old; studied at Hackney College; was settled at Blakeney, Gloucestershire, seven years; was sent by the Colonial Missionary Society to Melbourne in 1863, and was soon called to the pastorate at Kew, in the vicinity. After three years he returned, in ill-health, to England; and accepted the pastorate at Wareham, Dorset, where he continued until his death, March 4, 1871. See (Lond.) *Cong. Year-book*, 1872, p. 312.

Davies, John Jordan, an English Baptist minister, was born at Cardigan, Wales, and brought up in the Church of England, but changed his views, was baptized, and studied for the ministry at the Baptist College in Bristol. He was successively pastor at Bath; in 1828 at Tottenham, London; in 1849 at Luton, Bedfordshire, where he died, Oct. 4, 1858.

Davies, John Le Roy, a Presbyterian minister, son of the Rev. John B. Davies, was born in Chester District, S. C., Nov. 3, 1799. He received a thorough academic education; graduated from the University of North Carolina in 1821, and from Princeton Theological Seminary, N. J., in 1824; was licensed by the New Brunswick Presbytery, and ordained by Bethel Presbytery, then in connection with the synod of North Carolina, June 7, 1827. His first charge was Catholic Presbyterian Church, in Chester District, S. C., where he labored for eleven years; in 1839 he became pastor of Prospect and Centre churches, in Concord Presbytery, N. C.; in 1845 gave up the latter; in 1850 returned to South Carolina, and supplied several churches in his native region; in 1859 visited Arkansas, and, returning to South Carolina, died June 16, 1860. See Wilson, *Presb. Hist. Almanac*, 1861, p. 85.

Davies, John Philip, a Welsh Baptist minister, was born at Bangor, Cardiganshire, March 12, 1786, and was the son of Rev. David Davies, a clergyman of the Established Church. In his fifteenth year he began to frequent meetings of Dissenters, and at length, with his father's reluctant consent, joined the Baptists, in his eighteenth year. He became pastor at Holywell, in North Wales, and shortly afterwards of a small congregation of Welsh Baptists in Liverpool, but after a time removed to London; soon returned to Wales and became pastor at Ferryside, Carmarthenshire. After several years he took up his residence at Tredegar Iron Works, Monmouthshire, where he died, Aug. 23, 1832. See (Lond.) *Baptist Magazine*, 1836, p. 271. (J. C. S.)

Davies, Jonathan, a Welsh Congregational minister, was born near Neuaddlwyd, Cardiganshire, Oct. 26, 1802. He joined the Church in his youth; studied at Neuaddlwyd Academy; in 1828 became pastor at Harwood, Flintshire; soon afterwards he removed to Carergwil, where he labored until 1860, when he retired to Abergele, Denbighshire, and there died, May 24, 1871. See (Lond.) *Cong. Year-book*, 1872, p. 311.

Davies, Joseph, a Welsh Baptist minister, was born at Bettws, Cardiganshire, in February, 1803. He was baptized and joined the Church at ten years of age; was first pastor at Eardisland for two years, then at Whilestone, Hereford, from 1829 until his death, Aug. 12, 1850.

Davies, Joshua, a Welsh Congregational minister, was born near Newcastle Emlyn, Carmarthenshire, in 1837. He joined the Church in his youth; studied at the Congregational College at Bala; was ordained at Newmarket, Flintshire, in 1863, and labored there until his death, July 5, 1869. See (Lond.) *Cong. Year-book*, 1870, p. 284.

Davies, J. F., a Welsh Baptist minister, son of Rev. Daniel Davies (1), was born at Cwmdu, in the parish of Talley, Carmarthenshire, April 4, 1848. He was baptized by his father at the age of fifteen; studied for three years at the college of Haverfordwest; was recognised as pastor at Abernant, Aberdare, in August, 1869; and died May 26, 1872. See (Lond.) *Baptist Hand-book*, 1873, p. 256. (J. C. S.)

Davies, J. G., a Welsh Congregational minister, was born in Brecknockshire in 1832. He joined the Church in early life; studied at Brecon Independent College; and in 1867 was ordained at Penywern, Dowlais, where he labored until his death, Jan. 21, 1870. See (Lond.) *Cong. Year-book*, 1871, p. 310.

Davies, Miles, a Welsh clergyman, in the beginning of the 18th century, was born in Tre'r-Abbot, in Whiteford parish, Flintshire. He was a vehement foe to popery, Arianism, and Socinianism, and of the most fervent loyalty to George I and the Hanoverian succession. He went to London and published a few works, among which are his *Athenæ Britannicæ* (1715, 8vo):—and *A Critical History of Pamphlets* (1715). Little else is known of him. See Chalmers, *Biog. Dict.* s. v.; Allibone, *Dict. of Brit. and Amer. Authors*, s. v.

Davies, Owen, a Welsh Wesleyan minister, was born at Wrexham in 1752. He was converted through Methodist instrumentality; became a local preacher in London, and in 1789 was sent by Wesley to Manchester. He next travelled the Bedford, Lynn, Bristol, Northampton, Chester, Oxford, and Penzance circuits, until, in 1800, he was sent to North Wales. He preached there for fifteen years, and was often called "the Welsh bishop." He was superintendent of the Liverpool circuit for two years, and died Jan. 30, 1830. See *Wesl. Meth. Magazine*, 1832, p. 389, 469, 541; Smith, *Hist. of Wesl. Methodism*, ii, 359-395; *Minutes of the British Conference*, 1830.

Davies, Philip, an English Baptist minister, was born at Whitchurch, Hampshire, Oct. 21, 1773. After his conversion he joined the Independent Church at Reading, and in 1802 the Baptist Church there; soon after became pastor in Oakingham; in 1808 removed to his native town, where he labored until his death, Sept. 7, 1840. See (Lond.) *Baptist Hand-book*, 1841, p. 32. (J. C. S.)

Davies, Philip L., a Baptist minister, was born in Wales in 1831; baptized at the age of fourteen, in Blaenem, Monmouthshire; soon after came to Pottsville, Pa., and began to preach to the Welsh people. For three years he was a student in the University of Lewisburgh, and was ordained, Dec. 25, 1859, pastor at Carbondale, where he remained three years, and then took charge of the English Church at Blakeley. In 1863 he became pastor in Camden, N. J., resigning after a seven years' successful ministry, to become the successor of Rev. Dr. John Dowling, in the Berean Church, New York city, where he died, July 30, 1875. See Cathcart, *Baptist Encyclop.* p. 1305. (J. C. S.)

Davies, Rees, a Welsh Independent minister, was born at Lanwrtyd, Brecknockshire, in 1773. He was educated at the Presbyterian College, Carmarthen; in 1801 was ordained in Mill Street, Newport, where he remained till 1828; and afterwards continued to preach occasionally until his death, in February, 1839. See (Lond.) *Evangelical Magazine*, 1839, p. 598.

Davies, Richard (1), a Welsh minister of the Society of Friends, was born at Welshpool in 1635. He was educated in the Church of England; in 1667 became a Friend, and was more than once imprisoned. He frequently made missionary tours through different parts of Great Britain; in 1674 was brought into intimate relations with George Fox, and died Jan. 22, 1707. See *Friends' Library*, xiii, 1. (J. C. S.)

Davies, Richard (2), a Wesleyan Methodist missionary, was born in Pembrokeshire, South Wales, Oct. 24, 1812. He was converted under the Methodists; accepted by the conference in 1837; spent one year at the theological institution; sailed for Jamaica in October, 1838; preached at Savana La Mar, Bath, and Port Antonio, and died Nov. 1, 1844. See *Wesl. Meth. Magazine*, 1847, p. 1041; *Minutes of the British Conference*, 1845.

Davies, Richard P., a minister of the Methodist Episcopal Church South, was born in Shrewsbury, England, March 12, 1833. He emigrated to Canada with his parents when twelve years old; was converted among the Wesleyans in 1852; removed to Louisiana and joined the Church South in 1855; received license to preach in 1858; went to Lewisville, Ark., in 1860; and in 1863 entered the Little Rock Conference, in which he labored zealously until his death by assassination, Feb. 24, 1871. See *Minutes of Annual Conferences of the M. E. Church South*, 1871, p. 619.

Davies, Robert, an English Congregational minister, was born at Carnarvon, Wales, Sept. 9, 1815. He joined the Church at twelve years of age; after studying at the college at Blackburn, was ordained at Ripley, in Hampshire; three or four years later removed to Bilston, near Wolverhampton; after twelve years resigned; became pastor at Merton, in Surrey, March 3, 1861; in 1872 resigned, and removed to Bath, where he died, June 1, 1879. See (Lond.) *Cong. Year-book*, 1880, p. 320.

Davies, Samuel, a Welsh Wesleyan minister, a native of Flintshire, was converted early, called into the ministry in 1807, became a supernumerary at Holywell in 1846, and died at Denbigh, May 7, 1854. He wrote many valuable books. See *Minutes of the British Conference*, 1854.

Davies, Samuel Ambrose, an English Congregational minister, son of Rev. Edward Davies, was born at Ipswich in 1800. He entered Wymondley Academy in 1816; labored first at Lindfield, Sussex, a few years, and then was ordained at Enfield, where he ministered twenty years, and died Feb. 20, 1865. See (Lond.) *Cong. Year-book*, 1866, p. 246.

Davies, Sneyd, D.D., an English clergyman, was born at Shrewsbury, and educated at Eton and King's College, Cambridge, taking his degrees in 1737 and 1739. He was collated to the canonry of Lichfield in 1751; soon after presented to the mastership of St. John's Hospital, Lichfield; was also archdeacon of Derby, and rector of Kingsland, in Herefordshire. He died Feb. 6, 1769. He wrote several of the anonymous imitations of Horace in Duncombe's edition (1767), and at the end of volume four is given the character of the ancient Romans, from a poem by him, entitled, *The Progress of Science*. See Chalmers, *Biog. Dict.* s. v.; Allibone, *Dict. of Brit. and Amer. Authors*, s. v.

Davies, Stephen, a preacher of the United Methodist Free Church, was born at Camborne, Cornwall, Jan. 7, 1816. He was converted at nineteen, and joined the Methodists; entered the ministry of the Methodist Free Church in 1852, and died at Ripley, Derbyshire, July 18, 1874. See *Minutes of the 17th Annual Assembly*.

Davies, Theophilus, an English Congregational minister, was born at Hanover Chapel Parsonage, near Abergavenny, Oct. 19, 1798. His father, the Rev. Emmanuel Davies, being the pastor of the Church at Hanover, he was early led to Christ, and commenced preaching in his seventeenth year. He entered the Western Academy in 1816, and settled at Hazlegrove, near Stockport, in 1821; afterwards at Stourbridge, Worcestershire, where he was ordained, Sept. 5, 1826; in 1835 removed to Ludlow, in 1852 to Newton-le Willows, Lancashire, and from there to Hungerford, Berkshire, in 1857; resigned in 1865, and preached occasionally until his death at Hereford, Nov. 7, 1879. See (Lond.) *Cong. Year-book*, 1880, p. 321.

Davies, Thomas (1), a missionary of the Church of England, was born at Kington, Herefordshire, Dec. 21 (O. S.), 1736. His father settled in the town of Litchfield, Conn., and the son graduated from Yale College in 1758; and, after three years of theological study, was ordained in England in August, 1761; returned to America under the auspices of the Society for the Propagation of the Gospel in Foreign Parts, and preached at New Milford, Roxbury, Sharon, New Preston, and New Fairfield—to which Litchfield was soon added. He also held occasional services in Washington, Kent, Cornwall, Salisbury, Great Barrington, and Woodbury. He died in New Milford, Conn., May 12, 1766. See Sprague, *Annals of the Amer. Pulpit*, v, 265.

Davies, Thomas (2), an English Baptist minister, was brought up a stone-mason; delivered a lecture on Monday evenings, in Angel Alley, London; was minister at Petticoat Lane about fourteen years, and died very suddenly, June 15, 1763. See Wilson, *Dissenting Churches*, iv, 426.

Davies, Thomas (3), a Welsh Congregational minister, was born in the parish of Llangeler, Carmarthenshire. He joined the Church at the age of nineteen, and, after preaching some years in his own neighborhood, was ordained at Pentreath, Isle of Anglesey, in 1825; afterwards ministered at Festeniog, Aberdaron, and Moelfro, and retired to Bodfford, where he died, April 26, 1865. See (Lond.) *Cong. Year-book*, 1866, p. 246.

Davies, Thomas (4), a Welsh Congregational minister, was born in the parish of Trelech, Carmarthenshire, in 1820. He joined the Church at the age of sixteen; in his twenty-first year began to preach; entered Brecon College in 1843, and in 1847 was ordained at Llandilo, Carmarthenshire, where he labored until his sudden death, Oct. 28, 1873. See (Lond.) *Cong. Year-book*, 1874, p. 321.

Davies, Thomas Frederick, a Congregational minister, was born in 1793. He graduated at Yale College in 1813; spent the two following years teaching in New Haven, meantime pursuing his theological studies; was licensed to preach in 1816; in 1817 was ordained at Huntington; in 1819 removed to New Haven, became the editor of the *Christian Spectator*, and several years later was connected with the *Religious Intelligencer*. From 1829 to 1839 he was pastor of the Church at Green Farms, now Westport; the next ten years resided in New Haven, and died at Westport, Feb. 16, 1865. See *Appleton's Annual Cyclop.* 1865, p. 634.

Davies, William (1), a Welsh Congregational minister, was born at Caerlem, Devonshire, Dec. 24, 1785. He was converted in youth; began to preach at the age of seventeen; studied under a private instructor at Glandwr, and in the same way completed his theological training at Pembroke; was ordained in his twenty-first year at Fishguard, South Wales, where he labored until 1865, when he resigned the regular pastorate. He died Jan. 4, 1875. See (Lond.) *Cong. Year-book*, 1876, p. 325.

Davies, William (2), a Welsh Wesleyan minister, was born at Llanfyllin, Montgomeryshire, in 1787. He was converted at the age of eighteen; in 1809 commenced his ministry, the last fifteen years of which were spent near Brecon, where he died, Oct. 15, 1869. See *Minutes of the British Conference*, 1870, p. 19.

Davies, William (3), a Welsh Congregational minister, was born in the neighborhood of Penrhywgaled, Cardiganshire, Dec. 31, 1792. He was converted in his twentieth year; educated at Neuaddlwyd and Llanfyllin academies; ordained in 1822 at Llangollen; and in 1826 removed to Rhydyceisiaid, where he died, June 17, 1861. See (Lond.) *Cong. Year-book*, 1862, p. 227.

Davies, William (4), a Welsh Baptist minister, was born at Coedcanlass, Pembrokeshire, May 1, 1795. In March, 1816, he was converted and baptized at Haverfordwest, and soon afterwards began to preach in country places. In 1819 he entered Stepney College, and supplied the church at Hailsham during a vacation. The aged pastor resigned in his favor, and he settled there, after various trials from ill-health. In 1838 he removed to Canterbury, and there died, Jan. 25, 1851. See (Lond.) *Baptist Hand-book*, 1852; (Lond.) *Baptist Magazine*, 1851, p. 429.

Davies, W. Pollard, an English Congregational minister, was born at Coventry, July 3, 1791. He joined the Church at the age of sixteen; entered Hoxton Academy about a year later; was ordained at Wellingborough when about twenty-one years old; labored eight years at that place; removed into Devonshire, where he remained some time without a charge; served at Plymouth eight years; was pastor at Ashburton eleven years; resided some time at Petworth; preached at Putney six years, and finally retired to Leamington, where he died, March 13, 1872. See (Lond.) *Cong. Year-book*, 1873, p. 324.

Davies, W. R., an English Baptist minister, was born in 1800. He joined the Church in his youth; preached occasionally in Pembrokeshire, Wales, and in 1838 became pastor at Dowlais, Glamorganshire, where he died, Aug. 1, 1849. See (Lond.) *Baptist Hand-book*, 1850.

Davikna, the Accadian goddess of nature, spouse of Hea.

Davila, Francisco, a Spanish theologian, was born at Avila, of a noble family, and took the habit of the Dominicans. He followed, in 1596, his cousin, the cardinal Davila, to Rome, where Clément VIII appointed him to the Congregation of the Index. Davila distinguished himself in the dispute which arose at that time between the Dominicans and the Jesuits. He died in 1604, leaving, *De Gratia et Libero Arbitrio* (Rome, 1599):—*De Confessione per Litteras* (Douay, 1623). See Hoefer, *Nouv. Biog. Générale*, s. v.

Davis, Absalom, a minister in the Methodist Episcopal Church South, was born in Wayne County, Ky.; was converted in manhood; labored several years as a local preacher, and in 1852 entered the Louisville Conference, wherein he continued until his death, Sept. 30, 1858. See *Minutes of Annual Conferences of the M. E. Church South*, 1858, p. 8.

Davis, Absalom L., a minister in the Methodist Episcopal Church South, was born in Tennessee, May 10, 1812. In early life he removed to Indiana, where he was converted and united with the Methodist Episcopal Church. In 1864 he joined the Methodist Episcopal Church South, in Illinois, and in 1867 became a member of its Illinois Conference. He died at De Soto, Ill., April 20, 1882. See *Minutes of Annual Conferences of the M. E. Church South*, 1882, p. 40.

Davis, Alpheus, a Methodist Episcopal minister, was born in Paris, Oneida Co., N. Y., Dec. 11, 1793. He was converted at the age of thirteen; in 1816 admitted into the travelling ministry; in 1820 became superannuated, and died Oct. 8 the same year. See *Minutes of Annual Conferences*, 1821, p. 362.

Davis, Amos, a minister in the Methodist Episcopal Church South, was born in Bullock County, Ga., in 1829. He was converted and licensed to preach in 1854; became a member of the Florida Conference subsequently, and labored until his death, March 16, 1864.

See *Minutes of Annual Conferences of the M. E. Church South*, 1864, p. 522.

Davis, Aquilla, a Methodist minister, was born in Berks County, Pa., Oct. 20, 1834. He was converted in his twentieth year; entered the ministry of the United Brethren in 1859; in 1866 became a minister of the Evangelical Association, and died in Ogle County, Ill., April 11, 1879. See *Evangelical Messenger.*

Davis, Arthur, a minister in the Methodist Episcopal Church South, was born in Stewart County, Tenn., Feb. 17, 1811. He was reared under Baptist influence; converted in 1830, and joined the Methodists; received license to preach in 1831; in 1870 was transferred from the Memphis Conference to the White River Conference, and died in April, 1879. See *Minutes of Annual Conferences of the M. E. Church South*, 1879, p. 117.

Davis, Caleb Bailey, a Baptist minister, was born at Wrentham, Mass., July 3, 1807. Without taking a college course, he studied theology at the Newton Theological Institution from 1834 to 1837; was ordained pastor in Paris, Me., June 27, 1838, and died at Portland, Jan. 12, 1855. (J. C. S.)

Davis, Charles S., a Methodist Episcopal minister, was employed in 1835 as teacher in Hammondsport, N. Y.; in 1838 admitted into the East Genesee Conference; located and resided near Havana, N. Y., from 1850 to 1861; eventually became a superannuate, and died Nov. 5, 1870, in his sixtieth year. See *Minutes of Annual Conferences*, 1871, p. 158.

Davis, Claiborne Albert, D.D., a Cumberland Presbyterian minister, was born in Hardin County, Tenn., Nov. 8, 1825. While he was quite young his parents removed to Illinois, and subsequently the family went to St. Louis County, Mo. The Platte Presbytery received him as a candidate for the ministry in October, 1845; in April, 1846, he was licensed as a probationer; and in April, 1847, ordained. The first six months he devoted to missionary work, chiefly in the cities of St. Joseph and Platte; in 1847 he became pastor in Platte; in 1851 in Lexington; in 1859 succeeded Rev. Dr. A. M. Bryan as pastor in Memphis, Tenn., where he died, Oct. 19, 1867. Dr. Davis was recognised as one of the foremost preachers in that city. The General Assembly appointed him, in May, 1866, a delegate to the General Assembly of the Presbyterian Church South. See Baird, *Biographical Sketches*, 2d series, p. 380.

Davis, C. B., a minister of the Methodist Episcopal Church South, was born in Muhlenburg County, Ky., July 19, 1815. He embraced religion in his seventeenth year, and very early entered the ministry of the Methodist Episcopal Church. His itinerant life was all spent in the Tennessee Conference, first in the Methodist Episcopal Church, then, after 1844, in the Methodist Episcopal Church South. He died at McMinnville, Tenn., June 3, 1882. See *Minutes of Annual Conferences of the M. E. Church South*, 1882, p. 50.

Davis, C. C., a Methodist Episcopal minister, was born at New Springfield, Mahoning Co., O., in October, 1833. He was converted in his twenty-first year; received license to preach in 1856; and in 1860 entered the Pittsburgh Conference, in which he labored until within a short time of his death, Oct. 17, 1866. See *Minutes of Annual Conferences*, 1867, p. 70.

Davis, Daniel Gateward, D.D., a colonial bishop of the Church of England, was educated at Pembroke College, Oxford; graduated in 1814; after filling various offices in the Church at home, was consecrated in Westminster Abbey as bishop of Antigua, West Indies. in 1842, and died in London, Oct. 25, 1857. See *Amer. Quar. Church Rev.* 1858, p. 623.

Davis, David, a Baptist minister, born in Pembrokeshire, South Wales, in 1707, but was brought to America in 1710. He was pastor of the Welsh Tract Baptist Church at Pencader Hundred, New Castle Co., Del., from May 27, 1748, until his death, Aug. 19, 1769. See Sprague, *Annals of the Amer. Pulpit*, vi, 117.

Davis, Ebenezer, an English Baptist minister, son of the Rev. Richard Davis of Walworth, was born in 1800. He was baptized at fifteen, and for some years followed mercantile pursuits, preaching occasionally. In 1834 he was chosen pastor at Deal, Kent; afterwards had a pastoral charge at Lewes, Romford, Wycombe, and Southsea; and finally settled at Belvedere, Kent, where he had a stroke of paralysis in 1868, and died Oct. 23, 1870. See (Lond.) *Baptist Hand-book*, 1872.

Davis, Edward, D.D., a Protestant Episcopal minister, who died at South Ballston, N. Y., Nov. 19, 1863, aged fifty-nine years, was the founder and first rector of the parish of Calvary Church, Burnt Hills, N. Y. See *Amer. Quar. Church Rev.* January, 1864, p. 669.

Davis, Edward le, an English engraver, was probably born in Wales, and went to France, where he learned the art of engraving. He returned to his native country and settled in London about 1670. The following are some of his plates: *St. Cecilia, with Angels; Ecce Homo; The Holy Family.* See Spooner, *Biog. Hist. of the Fine Arts*, s. v.

Davis, Eliel, an English Baptist minister, was born at Folkestone, Kent, June 5, 1803. At nineteen years of age he went to London as a draper's assistant, and joined the Church under Joseph Toimey. He began to preach in the villages, and entered Stepney College in 1826. In 1828 he became a pastor in the Isle of Wight; in 1834 removed to Lambeth; in 1841 to Eye, in Suffolk; in 1842 to St. Ives, where he suddenly died, March 29, 1849. See (Lond.) *Baptist Hand-book*, 1850, p. 41.

Davis, Elnathan (1), a Baptist minister, was born in Maryland in 1739. In 1757 he moved to North Carolina, and was ordained in 1764; labored in that state thirty-four years, and then went to South Carolina, where he served his Master in the ministry till his death, the date of which does not appear. See Cathcart, *Baptist Encyclop.* p. 311. (J. C. S.)

Davis, Elnathan (2), a Congregational minister, was born at Holden, Mass., Aug. 19, 1807. He graduated from Williams College in 1834; studied two years at the Theological Institute of Hartford; and, having been appointed missionary to South Africa by the American Board of Commissioners for Foreign Missions, was ordained at his native place, Nov. 9, 1836. Changing his plans, he afterwards engaged in home missions in south Michigan and north Indiana. In 1845 he labored in the American Peace Society; in September, 1846, was installed pastor at Ashburnham, Mass.; in 1849 was sent as a delegate to the World's Peace Convention in Paris; in 1850 became secretary of the American Peace Society; for fourteen years was pastor in Fitchburg, Mass.; then, for a time, secretary of the American Missionary Association; and from 1869 to 1879 pastor in Auburn, Mass., where he died, April 9, 1881. See *Hist. Cat. of Theol. Inst. of Conn.* 1881, p. 15. (J. C. S.)

Davis, Emerson, D.D., a Congregational minister, was born at Ware, Mass., July 15, 1798. He graduated from Williams College in 1821; studied theology with Dr. Griffin while tutor there; was preceptor at Westfield Academy until February, 1836; ordained pastor in Westfield the same year, and remained there until his death, June 8, 1866. Dr. Davis was a member of the Massachusetts Board of Education. See *Cong. Quarterly*, 1859, p. 52; 1866, p. 315.

Davis, Francis Henry, a Baptist minister, was born at Kingsville, O., July 17, 1837. He graduated from the University of Rochester in 1860, and from the Theological Seminary there in 1865; was pastor at White Pigeon, Mich., from 1865 to 1867, and at Napoleon thereafter until his death, April 2, 1872. See *Gen. Cat. of Rochester Theol. Sem.* p. 27. (J. C. S.)

Davis, Franklin, a Congregational minister, was born at Bangor, Me., Jan. 24, 1816. He graduated from Bowdoin College in 1839, and from Bangor Theological Seminary in 1845; was ordained pastor at Warren, Me., Oct. 6, 1847; in 1849 became acting pastor at East Orrington; in 1854 at Alton, N. H.; in 1856 at North Wrentham (now Norfolk), Mass.; in 1860 at Berkley; in 1864 at Newington, N. H.; and from 1876 at Tamworth, until his death, which occurred on a railroad train at Ipswich, Mass., Oct. 26, 1882. See *Cong. Year-book*, 1883, p. 21.

Davis, Frederick Bruce, a Protestant Episcopal clergyman, entered upon his ministry in 1868 as missionary in Lancaster and Clarendon, S. C.; in 1870 was rector of St. Mark's, in Clarendon, and also in charge of the Church of the Holy Comforter in Sumter, where he remained until 1872; and then removed to Union as rector of the Church of the Nativity. He died Jan. 21, 1873. See *Prot. Episc. Almanac*, 1874, p. 138.

Davis, Garret, a minister in the Methodist Episcopal Church South, was born about 1814. He was converted about 1835 in Lexington, Ky., and in 1841 entered the Kentucky Conference, wherein he served to the close of his life, July 18, 1844. See *Minutes of Annual Conferences of the M. E. Church South*, 1846, p. 56.

Davis, George, an English Baptist minister, was born in the Forest of Dean in 1823. He was converted in early life; became a Primitive Methodist preacher for several years; in 1846 changed his views and was publicly immersed; for three years studied theology at Monmouth; settled over the Church at Tetbury; and was ordained in 1850. His health failed a year afterwards, and he died March 22, 1852. See (Lond.) *Baptist Hand-book*, 1853, p. 43.

Davis, George Atherton, a Presbyterian minister, was born at Lunenburg, Vt., Jan. 3, 1813. He graduated from Dickinson College in 1838; taught in Maryland from 1839 to 1841; graduated from Union Theological Seminary in 1844; in April, 1845, was pastor at Hanover College, Va., and died there, Oct. 9, 1846. See *Gen. Cat. of Union Theol. Sem.* 1876, p. 32.

Davis, George S., a Protestant Episcopal clergyman, was for many years rector of St. Paul's Church, Medina, O. In 1870 he became rector of Grace Church, Ravenna, to which parish was added, in 1872, Christ Church, in Kent; the next year he was missionary at Kinsman and Niles; in 1877 he removed to Cleveland, as missionary at large, an office which he continued to hold until his death, in May, 1880. See Whittaker, *Alm. and Directory*, 1881, p. 172.

Davis, George W. (1), a Methodist Episcopal minister, was born in Morgan County, Ga., in 1808. He was converted in 1824, and in 1828 entered the Georgia Conference, in which he labored to the close of his life, Nov. 27, 1832. See *Minutes of Annual Conferences*, 1833, p. 215.

Davis, George W. (2), a Free-will Baptist minister, was born in Greenbrier County, Va., Jan. 12, 1830. At the age of nineteen he removed to the state of Illinois; was converted in June, 1856; licensed in March, 1857, by the Walnut Creek Quarterly Meeting; went in October of that year to Hillsdale, Mich., to study, preaching at the same time; was ordained April 29, 1860; returned to Illinois, and died at Kewanee, May 5, 1861. See *Free-will Baptist Register*, 1862, p. 91. (J. C. S.)

Davis, Gustavus Fellowes, D.D., a Baptist minister, was born in Boston, Mass., March 17, 1797. He was converted about 1813; began at once to preach; was ordained June 13, 1816, at Preston, Conn.; in 1818 removed to South Reading (now Wakefield), Mass.; in 1829 became pastor of the First Church in Hartford, Conn., and died Sept. 17, 1836. See *Christian Secretary*, September, 1836. (J. C. S.)

Davis, G. B., a Baptist minister, was born in Delaware in 1792. He was converted in 1814; removed to Illinois in 1834 as agent for the American Bible Society; subsequently was financial agent of Shurtleff College, and pastor of the Bunker Hill Church, Ill.; afterwards labored to promote the interests of the Indian Mission Association in Tennessee and Alabama; and died near Bunker Hill, Ill., Aug. 29, 1852. See *Minutes of Ill. Anniversaries*, 1852, p. 9. (J. C. S.)

Davis, Henry (1), D.D., a Congregational educator, was born at East Hampton, N. Y., in 1771. He graduated from Yale College in 1796; for seven years was tutor in Williams and Yale colleges; professor of Greek in Union College from 1805 to 1810; president of Middlebury College, Vt., from 1810 to 1817; president of Hamilton College, Clinton, N. Y., from 1817 to 1833, and died there, March 7, 1852. His published works are his *Inaugural Address*, on assuming the presidency of Hamilton College, and a *Sermon* which he preached before the American Board of Commissioners for Foreign Missions. See Allen, *Amer. Biog.* s. v. (J. C. S.)

Davis, Henry (2), D.D., a Baptist minister, was born at Charlton, Saratoga Co., N. Y., April 23, 1800. Early in life he moved to the city of New York; subsequently was engaged in teaching at Ogden, Monroe Co., where he was converted, and joined the Baptist Church in the fall of 1818; graduated from the theological institution at Hamilton, June 7, 1827, and the next day was ordained at Bridgewater. For a time he labored as a missionary in Detroit, Mich., and planted the first church of his denomination in that city. His other pastorates were, Palmyra, N. Y., Brockport, Jordan, Cannon Street, New York city, Second Church, Rochester, Columbus, O., New Corydon and Rock Island, Ill. He died at Danville, Ill., Aug. 21, 1870. See *Minutes of Ill. Anniversaries*, 1870, p. 69. (J. C. S.)

Davis, Henry Edward, an English theologian, was born at Windsor, Middlesex, July 11, 1756, studied at Balliol College, Oxford, and died Feb. 10, 1784, leaving *Examination of Gibbon's History*. See Chalmers, *Biog. Dict.* s. v.

Davis, Henry M., a Protestant Episcopal clergyman, was employed as a missionary at Islip, N. Y., in 1853; in 1857 became rector of St. John's Church, in that place; in 1861 rector of the Church of Charity Foundation, Brooklyn; in 1864 missionary at St. Paul's Church, Salem, N. Y., of which subsequently, in 1872, he became rector, and so remained until his death, Sept. 29, 1875, at the age of sixty-six years. See *Prot. Episc. Almanac*, 1876, p. 150.

Davis, Isaac G., a Free-will Baptist minister, was born at Stanstead, Canada East, March 1, 1819. He was converted at the age of seventeen; in 1838 commenced to preach; was licensed June 22, 1839; ordained at Huntington, Vt., Sept. 26, 1840; entered the Biblical School at Lowell, Mass., laboring, meantime, at Roxbury; for a few years was at Portsmouth and Deerfield, N. H., and on a missionary tour in Nova Scotia and New Brunswick; in 1848 went to the West, and with the exception of a year or two spent in Elgin, Ill., devoted himself to missionary labors in Boone and McHenry counties, and as pastor in Fayette, Wis., where he died in December, 1862. See Barrett, *Memoirs of Eminent Preachers*, p. 249. (J. C. S.)

Davis, Jairus E., a Free-will Baptist minister, was born in New England in 1813, and was one of the early missionaries of his denomination in New York and the Western states. He died at North Reading, Mich., Dec. 3, 1870. See *Free-will Baptist Register*, 1871, p. 82. (J. C. S.)

Davis, James, a Baptist minister, was born at Hopkinton, N. H., Nov. 6, 1772. He graduated from Dartmouth College in 1798; was ordained as an evangelist in 1804; in 1816 was immersed; ordained as a Baptist evangelist Nov. 14, 1816, at Lyme, Conn.; preached in various places, but chiefly devoted himself to missionary and educational causes, and died May 28, 1821. See *Baptist Missionary Magazine*, new series, iii, p. 201, 208. (J. C. S.)

Davis, John (1), a Baptist minister, was born at Pennypack, Pa., Sept. 10, 1721. He was licensed to preach in 1756; the same year became pastor at Winter Run, Harford Co., Md., where he remained until his death in 1809. See Sprague, *Annals of the Amer. Pulpit*, vi, 69.

Davis, John (2), a Baptist minister, was born in New Castle County, Del., in 1737. He graduated at Philadelphia College in 1763; was licensed to preach in 1769; in 1770 was called to the pastorate of the Second Baptist Church of Boston, and died Dec. 13, 1772. See Sprague, *Annals of the Amer. Pulpit*, vi, 117.

Davis, John (3), an English Wesleyan minister, was born at Dursley, Gloucestershire, Oct. 27, 1780. He joined the Methodist Society at the age of seventeen, entered the ministry in 1802, became a supernumerary in 1845, and died May 16, 1852. See *Minutes of the British Conference*, 1852.

Davis, John (4), A.M., a Baptist minister, was born in Liverpool, England, Nov. 8, 1803. He studied at Horton College, Bradford; was ordained pastor at Portsea, Hampshire, Jan. 13, 1829; was minister to several churches, the last of which was Port Mahon, Sheffield. In 1845 he came to New Jersey; became pastor of a church; afterwards accepted an agency for the American and Foreign Bible Society; visited the provinces, and in 1853 succeeded Burton in the pastorate at Yarmouth, N. S. After a short period of ministry at St. George, N. B., he became pastor at Charlottetown, P. E. I., and remained there until his death, Aug. 14, 1875. See Cathcart, *Bapt. Encyclop.* p. 314.

Davis, John C. C., a minister in the Methodist Episcopal Church South, was born in Lewis County, Ky., March 2, 1832. He removed with his parents to Buchanan County, Mo., in 1837; was converted in 1850; in 1853 was admitted into the Missouri Conference; became superannuated in 1874, and died March 11, 1875. See *Minutes of Annual Conferences of the M. E. Church South*, 1875, p. 239.

Davis, John N., a Methodist Episcopal minister, was born in Mecklenburg County, N. C., Nov. 11, 1804. He was converted in 1832; received license to preach, and entered the South Carolina Conference in 1834; in 1840 became superannuated, and died in June, 1844. See *Minutes of Annual Conferences*, 1845, p. 591.

Davis, John R., a Methodist Episcopal minister, was born in Carteret County, N. C., in 1812. In 1837 he joined the Methodists; received license to exhort in 1841, to preach in 1843, and in 1845 entered the North Indiana Conference; in 1860 became superannuated, and died May 17, 1877. See *Minutes of Annual Conferences*, 1878, p. 54.

Davis, John Wheelwright, a Presbyterian minister, was born at Newburyport, Mass., June 4, 1800. He was licensed by the Philadelphia Presbytery in 1834; labored as a home missionary in various parts of the state of New York; subsequently became an agent for the American Tract Society in Philadelphia, and died there, Aug. 5, 1867. See Wilson, *Presb. Hist. Almanac*, 1868, p. 196.

Davis, Joseph (1), an English Baptist minister, was born at Chipping-Norton, Oxfordshire, in August, 1627. He was converted in early life; was baptized at Coventry, and experienced bitter persecution from the civil authorities. He died in London, Feb. 16, 1706, leaving a work entitled *My Last Legacy*, which was printed in 1720. See Crosby, *Hist. of the English Baptists*, iii, 180. (J. C. S.)

Davis, Joseph (2), a Free-will Baptist minister, was born at Madbury, N. H., in 1792. He was converted at the age of eighteen; united with the Church in 1819; was ordained July 4, 1824; and died in Effingham, Dec. 14, 1843. See *Free-will Baptist Register*, 1845, p. 75. (J. C. S.)

Davis, Joseph (3), an English Baptist minister, the son and grandson of ministers, was born in Liverpool, Oct. 7, 1807. He was baptized at the age of nineteen; entered Horton College in 1827; became pastor at Church-street, Blackfriars; resigned in 1841, and removed to Manchester, where he was pastor of York-street chapel only eighteen months; then settled at Arnesby, Leicestershire, in 1843; removed to Kent-street chapel, Portsea, in 1854; and to Romford in 1866, where he was stricken with paralysis in 1879, and died Oct. 23, 1881. See (Lond.) *Baptist Hand-book*, 1882, p. 301.

Davis, Joseph Hoomes, a minister in the Methodist Episcopal Church South, was born in Gloucester County, Va., April 13, 1809; was converted in his fourteenth year; educated in the academies of Gloucester and Northumberland, and in 1836 entered the Virginia Conference, in which he labored till his death, May 8, 1879. See *Minutes of Annual Conferences of the M. E. Church South*, 1879, p. 105.

Davis, J. W., a Methodist Episcopal minister, was born at Tyringham, Berkshire Co., Mass., April 30, 1791. He was converted in 1809; removed to Ohio in 1816, and in 1825 entered the Pittsburgh Conference; in 1828 was transferred to the Erie Conference, and, after two years, located; at the close of four years again entered the effective ranks; became superannuated in 1845, and died in January, 1854. See *Minutes of Annual Conferences*, 1854, p. 409.

Davis, Nathan, a Protestant minister and African traveller, was born in 1812. For a time he edited the *Hebrew-Christian Magazine*, and afterwards took charge of a congregation. In 1856 the earl of Clarendon, secretary of state, sent him to the East, to explore the site of ancient Carthage. He died Jan. 6, 1882. He published, *Tunis* (1841):—*A Voice from North and South Africa* (1844):—*Wanderings in Belât Ejjareed* (1854, 2 vols.):—*Arabic Reading Lessons* (1855):—*Carthage and her Remains* (1861):—*Ruined Cities within Numidian and Carthaginian Territories* (1862). (B. P.)

Davis, Nimrod R., a Methodist Episcopal minister, was born near Kingston, Roane Co., Tenn., Sept. 28, 1814. He was converted in 1834; soon after received license to exhort and to preach; removed to Kentucky in 1847, and entered the Kentucky Conference as supply, in which he labored until he became a supernumerary, and finally a superannuate. He died April 18, 1879. See *Minutes of Annual Conferences*, 1880, p. 31.

Davis, Peter, a minister of the Society of Friends, was born in England in 1680, and educated as a Presbyterian. In 1716 he united with the Friends, and was a well-known preacher in that denomination, at first in Westerly, R. I., but eventually in England and France. The proverb, "Honesty is the best policy," is said to have originated with him. He died Feb. 29, 1776.

His successor was his son PETER, "a man of deep piety and peculiar gifts, noted for his laconic and forcible addresses, who died Jan. 22, 1812, at the age of one hundred and one years and seven months." See *R. I. Biographical Cyclop.* p. 88. (J. C. S.)

Davis, Richard (1), an Irish divine, was born in 1649, and died in 1741. He published a *Letter to a Roman Catholic Friend* (Lond. 1694):—*The Truly Catholic and Old Religion* (Dublin, 1716); and other works. See Allibone, *Dict. of Brit. and Amer. Authors*, s. v.

Davis, Richard (2), an English Baptist minister, was born in 1776. For several years he was pastor of the Church at Middleton Cheney, but eventually became insane, and died in March, 1838. See (Lond.) *Baptist Hand-book*, 1838, p. 26. (J. C. S.)

Davis, Richard Montgomery, a Presbyterian

minister, was born about 1796. He served in the war of 1812; joined the Church in 1822; graduated from Union College in 1828, and from Auburn Theological Seminary in 1831; was ordained the same year; in 1835 took charge of the church in Springfield, N. Y.; afterwards preached in Bridgewater, and died June 13, 1842. See *Presbyterianism in Central N. Y.* p. 510.

Davis, Robert, an English Congregational minister, was born at Emsworth, Hampshire, April 19, 1791. He joined the Church in 1810; became a student at Gosport in 1811; was ordained at Totton in 1818; in 1821 removed to Crondall; in 1825 to Spalding, where his stay was very brief; afterwards preached successively at Tamworth, Earlshilton, in Leicestershire; Wellingborough, Turvey, Brackley, in Northamptonshire; Sawston, Cambridgeshire; and finally retired to his native town, where he died, April 16, 1871. See (Lond.) *Cong. Year-book*, 1872, p. 313.

Davis, Rowland, LL.D., an Irish divine, was born near Cork in 1649, and educated at Trinity College, Dublin. Having entered into holy orders, he was made dean of Cork, and was afterwards vicar-general of the diocese. He died in 1721, leaving two sermons, entitled *Christian Loyalty* (1716, 4to), and a *Charity Sermon* (Dublin, 1717, 8vo). See Chalmers, *Biog. Dict.* s. v.

Davis, Samuel (1), a Methodist Episcopal minister, was born at New Holland, Lancaster Co., Pa., Oct. 7, 1793. He was converted in 1812, and in 1814 entered the travelling connection of the Baltimore Conference, wherein he toiled faithfully to the close of his life, Sept. 16, 1822. See *Minutes of Annual Conferences*, 1823, p. 401; *Meth. Magazine*, v, 439.

Davis, Samuel (2), an English Congregational minister, was born at Leominster, March 17, 1803. He studied at Highbury; preached two years at Bilston, Staffordshire, then removed to Needham Market, where he was ordained as co-pastor in 1834; in 1841 removed to Bow, afterwards to Barnet, where he continued to labor until within a few months of his death, July 8, 1865. See (Lond.) *Cong. Year-book*, 1866, p. 247.

Davis, Samuel Chalmers, a Protestant Episcopal clergyman, was born in Baltimore, Md. For several years he was a Methodist preacher; was ordained in 1837; in 1839 became rector of William and Mary's parish, St. Mary's County; removed to New York in 1844, and after serving in several places went back to Maryland in 1849; officiated in Holy Trinity and Ascension parishes, Carroll County; also in Trinity parish, Charles County; in 1852 returned to New York, and died there, May 8, 1862, aged fifty-six years. See *Amer. Quar. Church Rev.*, April, 1863, p. 148.

Davis, Samuel H. (1), a Presbyterian minister, was residing in Delaware in 1692; the scene of his labors in the ministry from 1705 onwards, was the churches planted by Mr. Makemie in Maryland, and those in their immediate vicinity. He finally succeeded Mr. Hampton as minister of Snow Hill, and died in the summer of 1725. See Sprague, *Annals of the Amer. Pulpit*, iii, 3.

Davis, Samuel H. (2), a Presbyterian minister, was born in Frederick County, Md., Oct. 14, 1833. He graduated from Hampden-Sidney College, Va., in 1853; studied theology at Union Seminary; was licensed by the Presbytery of Baltimore in 1856; preached at Amelia and Namozine, Va., and died July 19, 1858. See Wilson, *Presb. Hist. Almanac*, 1860, p. 70.

Davis, Samuel S., D.D., a Presbyterian minister, was born in Ballston, N. Y., July 12, 1793. He entered Union College at Schenectady, but graduated at Middlebury College in 1812; took charge of an academy at Castleton, Vt.; in the fall of 1815 entered Princeton Seminary, but before the close of the year went to act as tutor at Union College; returned again in 1817, and graduated in 1819. He was licensed by the Presbytery of Albany, Oct. 12 of the same year; soon afterwards was commissioned to collect funds for a seminary in North Carolina, which was eventually located at Columbia, S. C. He was ordained at Albany, Aug. 12, 1821; became pastor at Darien, Ga., Dec. 16 of the same year; after two years went to Camden, S. C.; in 1833 accepted an appointment as agent of the General Assembly's Board of Education; in 1841 and 1842 was professor of Latin in Oglethorpe University, Milledgeville, Ga.; from 1845 to 1851 served at Camden, S. C., a second time, and died June 21, 1877. See *Necrolog. Report of Princeton Theol. Sem.* 1878, p. 9.

Davis, Seth, a Protestant Episcopal clergyman, was born at Providence, R. I., July 18, 1802. He graduated at Hobart College in 1827; took the course at the General Theological Seminary; was ordained deacon in 1833, officiating at Seneca Falls, N. Y.; became rector of Trinity Church, Cleveland, O., where he was ordained presbyter, and remained four years; returned to western New York, laboring in several parishes, and a part of the time engaged in teaching; in 1854 went to Connecticut, and took charge of the parishes in Woodbury, North Haven, and Northford; in 1857 was pastor at Monroe, where he died, July 6, 1862. See *Amer. Quar. Church Rev.*, April, 1863, p. 149.

Davis, Silas Newton, a Cumberland Presbyterian minister, was born in Livingston County, Ky., May 28, 1808. The Anderson Presbytery received him Nov. 14, 1827; shortly after he entered a theological school conducted by Rev. Richard Beard, D.D., at McLemorsville, Tenn.; Sept. 11, 1828, he was licensed as a probationer; the following year was appointed to what was called the Livingston district; after spending the summer in study at Cumberland College, was ordained in the fall of 1830; until 1834 his time was chiefly spent in itinerant work in Tennessee; for several years he was pastor of the Elkton Congregation; in 1850 he removed to Cumberland College, and died Sept. 26, 1854. See Beard, *Biographical Sketches*, 2d series, p. 321.

Davis, Stephen (1), an English Baptist minister, was born at Andover, Hampshire, Oct. 30, 1783. He was converted at thirteen years of age; baptized in London in 1802; began to preach at twenty, and became an evangelist in Ireland in 1816. He afterwards was the travelling agent of the Irish Baptist Society, and as such visited America in 1832 and 1833. In 1837 he located in London, and visited over England and Scotland as the advocate of the society till 1845, when gout obliged him to resign, and he continued to preach, as he had strength, till his death, Feb. 3, 1856. See (Lond.) *Baptist Hand-book*, 1856, p. 47.

Davis, Stephen (2), a Methodist Episcopal minister, was born in Gloucester County, Va., about 1765. He travelled about seven years in the itinerant connection, and died in August, 1795. See *Minutes of Annual Conferences*, 1796, p. 66.

Davis, Stephen Joshua, an English Baptist minister, was born at Woolwich, Kent, in 1805. He was converted in his youth; studied at Bristol College in 1826; attended the ministry of Rev. Robert Hall; first settled at Weymouth; was called to London in 1837; was many years secretary of the Baptist Home Missionary Society and of the Irish Missions, and in 1863 settled as pastor at Aberdeen, Scotland, where he died, May 11, 1866. See (Lond.) *Baptist Hand-book*, 1867, p. 132.

Davis, Sylvester, a Baptist minister, was born at Royalton, Mass., in 1809. He was converted in 1830; studied at Hamilton, N. Y.; was ordained at Evans Mills; subsequently settled in Cassville, and in February, 1851, went to the Sandwich Islands, where he died, Feb. 5, 1852. See *Amer. Baptist Register*, 1852, p. 416. (J. C. S.)

Davis, Thomas (1), an English Baptist minister was born at Newport, Isle of Wight, about 1730. He was converted at Woolwich, Kent, joined the Church there, was called as pastor to Reading, Berkshire, and died Dec. 27, 1796. See *Rippon's Register*, ii, 514. (J. C. S.)

Davis, Thomas (2), a Protestant Episcopal clergyman, was admitted to orders in England in September, 1773; came to America; settled in Norfolk parish, Va.; in 1792 was in St. Stephen's parish; in 1795 became rector of Christ Church, Alexandria, and died there some time before 1810. See Sprague, *Annals of the Amer. Pulpit*, v, 406.

Davis, Thomas Frederick, D.D., a Protestant Episcopal bishop, was consecrated in St. John's Chapel, New York city, as bishop of South Carolina, Oct. 17, 1853, resided at Camden, and died Dec. 2, 1871. See *Prot. Episc. Almanac*, 1872, p. 127.

Davis, Thomas F., *Jr.*, a Protestant Episcopal clergyman, was rector in 1853 at Henderson, N. C.; in the following year became assistant minister of Grace Church, Camden, S. C., in which position he remained until his death in 1866. See *Prot. Episc. Almanac*, 1867, p. 101.

Davis, William (1), a Baptist minister, was born in Orange County, Va., Jan. 7, 1765. He was immersed at a Baptist Church in Orange County, called "Blue Run," in his fifteenth year; soon after began publicly to exhort; at sixteen became a soldier in the Revolutionary army, and was wounded in the head. He was licensed to preach in 1788; ordained in Georgia in 1793; served one church in Elbert County twenty-three years; that at Beaver Dam twelve years; Clark's Station nineteen years; and died Oct. 31, 1831. See Campbell, *Georgia Baptists*. (J. C. S.)

Davis, William (2), an English Congregational minister, was born in London, June 15, 1788. He studied at Southampton; entered Hoxton Academy in 1814; in 1818 became pastor at Hastings, and died Jan. 19, 1855. He published, *The True Dignity of Human Nature:—Immortality*. See (Lond.) *Cong. Year-book*, 1856, p. 210.

Davis, William (3), a Canadian Methodist preacher, was born in Dublin, Ireland, June 5, 1851. In 1854 his parents emigrated to Toronto, Canada. He was converted in 1869, under the Primitive Methodists, and began to preach; was accepted by the Bible Christians in 1873; travelled in several circuits; and died April 19, 1880, at Palmyra, Canada.

Davis, William C., a Presbyterian minister, was born in 1760. He was received as a candidate under the South Carolina Presbytery in 1786; licensed in 1787; accepted a call from the Nazareth Church in 1788; ordained in 1789; in 1806 became pastor at Bullock Creek, S. C.; was deposed April 3, 1811, for erroneous doctrine; and died Sept. 28, 1831. See Sprague, *Annals of the Amer. Pulpit*, iv, 122.

Davis, William F. P., a German Reformed minister, was born in Paradise, York Co., Pa., Oct. 1, 1831. He completed his classical and theological studies at Lancaster in 1863; the same year was licensed and ordained; for some time was pastor at New Oxford, in Adams County; then of the Sinking Spring charge, in Berks County; and died at Reading, June 11, 1883. (D. Y. H.)

Davis, William H., a Baptist minister, was born in Jasper County, Ga., Aug. 18, 1826; graduated from Mercer University in 1853; was ordained the same year, and settled in Burke County, Ga. For seven years (1868–75), besides preaching, he was engaged in teaching in the Hepzibah High-school; and died Sept. 18, 1879. See Cathcart, *Baptist Encyclop.* p. 316. (J. C. S.)

Davison, John, a Canadian Methodist minister, was born near Newcastle-on-Tyne, England, Nov. 23, 1799. He was a member of the first Primitive Methodist Society formed in Newcastle, and at nineteen years of age made his first attempt at preaching. In March, 1823, he was appointed, with certain others, to the Shields and Sunderland missions. Afterwards he was appointed to the Hexham Station. Subsequently he travelled on seventeen stations, extending over a period of twenty-four years. In 1849 he went to Canada as superintendent of missions. He resided in Toronto three years; then, after filling four appointments, he was in 1859 appointed general missionary secretary and book-steward, which brought him to Toronto again, where he continued to reside until his death, March 1, 1884. In 1840 Mr. Davison compiled the journals of William Clowes, and in 1854 published the life of that evangelist. He commenced a monthly paper, *The Evangelist*, which in 1858 was merged into the *Christian Journal*, and had the charge of it until 1866. He also compiled the first *Book of Discipline* of the Canadian Methodists. See (Toronto) *Christian Guardian*, March 19, 1884.

Davison, John Wiles, a Methodist Episcopal minister, was born in Cambridgeshire, England, Dec. 17, 1810. He was converted at the age of thirteen; emigrated to Wilkesbarre, Pa., in 1838; in 1840 joined the Oneida Conference; about 1856 removed to Illinois, and in the following year connected himself with the Rock River Conference. He became a superannuate in 1870, and died Jan. 12, 1876. See *Minutes of Annual Conferences*, 1876, p. 151.

Davke (the female Earth), in Græco-Babylonian mythology, was the wife of Aos, and the mother of the demiurgus Bel. She was also called *Davcina*.

Davy, William, an English divine, was born about 1743. He studied at the Exeter Free Grammar-school; graduated from college, and became curate at Lustleigh; was presented to the living of Winkleigh, Devon, and died June 13, 1826. He published *System of Divinity* (Exeter, 1785, 6 vols. 12mo; 1825, 2 vols. 8vo; 1827, 3 vols. 8vo; Lustleigh, 1796–1807, 26 vols. 8vo). See (Lond.) *Annual Register*, 1826, p. 258; Allibone, *Dict. of Brit. and Amer. Authors*, s. v.

Davys, George, D.D., a bishop of the Church of England, graduated at Christ College, Cambridge, in 1803, and became a fellow; subsequently was curate of Littlebury, and in 1814 of Chesterford; afterwards of Swaffham Prior; removed to Kensington, and was appointed tutor to the princess Victoria; was advanced to the see of Peterborough in 1839, and died April 18, 1864, aged eighty-four years. In theology Dr. Davys belonged to the evangelical section of his church, although he took no part in theological controversy. See *Amer. Quar. Church Rev.* July, 1864, p. 326.

Daw, John, a Scotch clergyman, took his degree at St. Salvador's College, St. Andrews, in 1663; became chaplain to the laird of Duninald; was presented to the living at Kinnaird; admitted Sept. 28, 1676; and died in 1698, aged about fifty-five years. See *Fasti Eccles. Scoticanæ*, iii, 829.

Dawes, Mark, an English Wesleyan minister, was born at Ridgway, near Sheffield. He was converted early; entered the ministry in 1809; and died at Birstall, June 1, 1844, in the fifty-ninth year of his age. See *Minutes of the British Conference*, 1844, p. 13.

Dawkes, Clendon, an English Baptist minister, was said to be a native of Wellingborough. He settled in early life at Wapping, about 1719, but in 1726 took charge of a newly formed church in Collier's Rents, Southwark. About 1734 he was chosen afternoon preacher at Devonshire Square, but on the dissolution of that society in 1751, removed to Hemel-Hempstead, Herts, where he died, Dec. 8, 1758. See Wilson, *Dissenting Churches*, i, 531.

Daws, Josiah, a Baptist minister, was born in Callaway County, N. C., in 1826. His family moved to Tennessee in 1827. He was baptized in 1849, ordained in 1851 or 1852, and, for three years, was pastor of the Antioch Church. In 1857 he moved to Kentucky, and preached two years for the Columbus Church, and four years for the Cane Run Church. During the war he resided in Tennessee, but at its close returned to Kentucky, and died at Rutherford, Tenn., March 1, 1872. See Borum, *Sketches of Tenn. Ministers*, p. 200. (J. C. S.)

Dawson, Benjamin, LL.D., an English Presbyterian minister, grandson of a clergyman ejected in 1662, took his degree at Glasgow; settled at Congleton, Cheshire, in 1752; removed to St. Thomas's Church, Southwark, about 1754; in 1759 joined the Church of England, became rector of Burgh, Suffolk, and died in July, 1814, aged eighty-five years. He published, *Lectures in Defence of the Trinity* (1764):—*Dialogue on the Question of Liberty and Necessity* (1780):—two tracts on *The Intermediate State*:—*An English Dictionary on a New Plan*. See Wilson, *Dissenting Churches*, iv, 315-317.

Dawson, Charles Cornelius, an English Baptist minister, was born at Shenfield, Essex, Nov. 13, 1817. He was converted at twenty, and was baptized by the Rev. W. Upton; sailed for Ceylon in 1840, and for some time did the printing at the mission press there; afterwards took charge of the station at Matura, till his health failed, and sailed for England Feb. 10, 1850, but was never again heard of. See (Lond.) *Baptist Hand-book*, 1851, p. 54.

Dawson, James (1), a Scotch clergyman, son of Rev. John Dawson, took his degree at Edinburgh University, Nov. 9, 1722; studied divinity at Glasgow University in 1725; was licensed to preach the same year; presented to the living at Langton, and ordained Aug. 18, 1727; transferred to the West Kirk, St. Cuthbert's, Edinburgh, Jan. 31, 1733; and died Jan. 22, 1735, aged thirty-three years. See *Fasti Eccles. Scoticanæ*, i, 122, 419.

Dawson, James (2), a preacher of the United Methodist Free Church, was born at Lowmore, Clitheroe, Lancashire, in 1842; was sent to the Free Methodist Sunday-school, where he was converted; in 1861 became a local preacher, and in 1864 a home missionary. He travelled in three circuits, and died in the autumn of 1868. See *Minutes of the 13th Annual Assembly*.

Dawson, John (1), a Scotch clergyman, took his degree at Edinburgh University, July 9, 1694; was called in May, 1698, to Langton; ordained July 14 following; and died in November, 1726, aged about fifty-three years. See *Fasti Eccles. Scoticanæ*, i, 419.

Dawson, John (2), an English Wesleyan minister, was a native of Portsmouth. He was converted in early life; received into the ministry in 1833, and died at New Cross, Deptford, Sept. 6, 1875. See *Minutes of the British Conference*, 1876, p. 14.

Dawson, John Edmonds, D.D., a Baptist minister, was born in Washington County, Ga., March 7, 1805. He united with the Church in 1827; was ordained Jan. 14, 1835; and died Nov. 18, 1860. His ministerial life was spent chiefly in the middle and western parts of the state, and he rose to the highest rank as a preacher. See Cathcart, *Baptist Encyclop.* p. 1298. (J. C. S.)

Dawson, Joseph, an English Wesleyan minister, was born at Wimeswould, Leicestershire, Feb. 28, 1847. He was converted at twenty-one; appointed to Cardiff in 1875; and died Feb. 13, 1877. See *Minutes of the British Conference*, 1877, p. 29.

Dawson, Robert, a Scotch clergyman, had the gift of a bursary in Edinburgh University in November, 1747; was licensed to preach in November, 1752; became assistant to Mr. Archibald Lundie, minister of Salton; was presented by the king to the living at Stow; ordained Sept. 25, 1759; and died March 23, 1809, aged eighty-one years. He published *An Account of the Parish*. See *Fasti Eccles. Scoticanæ*, i, 534.

Dawson, Samuel, a minister in the Methodist Episcopal Church South, was born in Rockingham County, Va., Nov. 10, 1798. He joined the Church about 1814, and entered the Mississippi Conference in 1841, wherein he labored as health permitted until his death, in 1858. See *Minutes of Annual Conferences of the M. E. Church South*, 1858, p. 35.

Dawson, Samuel G., a Baptist minister, was born in Virginia in 1834. He was converted when young; in May, 1859, was ordained near Marietta; about four years afterwards engaged in missionary work in East Toledo; was chosen secretary of the convention in January, 1875, and died Sept. 5 following. See Cathcart, *Baptist Encyclop.* p. 317. (J. C. S.)

Dawson, Thomas, a Baptist minister, was born in England in 1790. He was, in early life, an officer in the English army; but, at the age of twenty-five, was baptized, and came to the United States in 1818. The following year he was ordained, and soon after sent as a missionary to the Cherokees in North Carolina. After their removal by the government, he went to South Carolina, and for twenty years preached among the mountains, and was a missionary among the colored people on the coast. He died June 29, 1880. See Cathcart, *Baptist Encyclop.* p. 317. (J. C. S.)

Dawson, William (1), an eminent Wesleyan lay-preacher, was born at Garforth, Yorkshire, March 30, 1773, and died suddenly at Colne, June 5, 1841. He was at first a member of the Established Church; became a local preacher in 1801; and, making his home at Barnbow, near Leeds, went up and down the kingdom, preaching, raising collections, speaking at missionary meetings, followed sometimes from town to town by colliers and yeomen; having congregations so large that he was compelled to preach in the open air. One who heard him says, "The effect of his sermons on the immense and eager audiences I never saw before nor expect to see again. Not a man, woman, nor child could resist him; and there was so much Scripture in his representations, and all said in honor of Christ, that the speaker, with the sacred, magic wand, was hid in the glory of his divine Redeemer" (Wakeley, *Heroes of Methodism*, p. 360). Dr. George Smith considers him "the most eminent lay-preacher that has ever appeared in Methodism;" and Adam Clarke exclaimed, "What an astonishing mind he has." He "possessed a strong, highly original, noble and generous mind, with an equally catholic spirit, and his whole character was as transparent as the light, and warm as the sun's own ray; and although not an educated man in the strictest sense of the term, much less refined, yet he possessed, along with earnest, manly sense, and a vigorous intellect, striking originality and a rich power of conception, which, although not free from occasional eccentricity, bespoke the man of true genius." Dawson published an address on the death of Rev. William Bramwell, short memoirs, speeches on passing events; and a volume of his private letters—tender, faithful, forcible, graceful—a "spiritual treasury," was edited by Everett, and issued in London in 1842. See Everett, *Memoirs of William Dawson* (Lond. 1842, pp. 547); West, *Sketches of Wesleyan Preachers*, p. 299 sq.; Stevens, *Hist. of Methodism*, iii, 179-184, 271, 275; Smith, *Hist. of Wesleyan Methodism*, iii, 452-454 (see Index); *Minutes of the British Conference*, 1841, p. 137.

Dawson, William (2), an English Wesleyan minister, nephew of the foregoing, was born at Ancaster, near York, Oct. 19, 1807. He was converted at the age of sixteen; entered the ministry in 1830; was appointed to his last circuit (Holmfirth) in 1858, and died Aug. 19 of the same year. See *Minutes of the British Conference*, 1859.

Dawson, William (3), an English Congregational minister, son of Rev. James Dawson, was born in Vizagapatam, a sea-port of Orissa, India, Jan. 16, 1816. He was converted early; studied at Madras, and began his ministry in 1838, as an assistant missionary, first at

Cuddapah, and afterwards at Tripassore. In 1845 he was ordained pastor at Chicacole, and in 1851 removed to Vizianagram, where he labored until ill-health caused his resignation in 1874. In 1875 he embarked, with many friends, for England; but on May 5 died and was buried at sea. Mr. Dawson compiled a Telugu *Hymn-book*, and several tracts. See (Lond.) *Cong. Year-book*, 1876, p. 327.

Dawson, William James, an English Wesleyan minister, was born at Portsea, Feb. 19, 1816. He joined the Church in 1831; was received into the ministry in 1838; became a supernumerary at Freemantle in 1872; and died April 5, 1880. See *Minutes of the British Conference*, 1880, p. 28.

Day, Andrew, a minister of the Methodist Episcopal Church South, was born in Gibson County, Ind., July 22, 1816. He was converted in 1836; joined the Mississippi Conference in 1838, in which he labored forty-two years; and died at the residence of his son, in Lexington, Miss., May 8, 1880. See *Minutes of Annual Conferences of the M. E. Church South*, 1880, p. 175.

Day, George (1), a Roman Catholic prelate of the 16th century, was born in Shropshire, and was successively scholar, fellow, and provost of King's College, Cambridge, which office he retained with the bishopric of Chichester, to which he was consecrated in 1543. He was a most pertinacious Romanist, for which he was deprived of his benefice under Edward VI, and restored by queen Mary. He died in 1556. See Fuller, *Worthies of England* (ed. Nuttall), iii, 59.

Day, George (2), an English Baptist minister, was born at Wincanton in 1788. He was pastor first of an Independent church in his native town; subsequently of a Baptist church in the same place; and died March 10, 1858. See (Lond.) *Baptist Hand-book*, 1861, p. 98. (J. C. S.)

Day, George Tiffany, D.D., a Free-will Baptist minister, was born at Concord (now Day), Saratoga Co., N. Y., Dec. 8, 1822. While a lad, he went into a cotton factory at Hebronville, Mass. At the age of twelve he lived for a time with an elder brother, and subsequently at Lonsdale, R. I. He was converted in the winter of 1839-40, and was baptized by Rev. Martin Cheney, of Olneyville, with whose church he united. Two years afterwards he became a student in the Smithville Seminary, and subsequently went to the theological school of his denomination at Whitestown, N. Y. Dec. 1, 1846, he commenced preaching in Grafton, Mass., and was ordained at Olneyville, May 20, 1847. In the spring of 1851 he became principal of Geauga Seminary, in Ohio, at the same time taking charge of the church there, until, in July, 1852, he removed as pastor to Olneyville, R. I., also serving as one of the editors of the *Free-will Baptist Quarterly*. In April, 1857, he visited Europe, and on his return was called to the Roger Williams Church, in Providence, where he remained about nine years. At once he secured a high place among the ministers of the city. In 1866 he again visited Europe, and extended his trip to the Holy Land. The remainder of his life was spent as editor of the *Morning Star*. He died in Providence, May 21, 1875. See Bowen, *Memoir*. (J. C. S.)

Day, George W., a Baptist minister, was born in Russell County, Va., Feb. 15, 1807. He joined the Methodists Feb. 24, 1838, but soon after united with the Baptists; was licensed in La Grange, Tenn., April 14, 1839, and engaged in itinerant labors in the Big Hatchie Association; was ordained Oct. 17, 1841, and for several years was pastor of the Big Black Church, near Denmark, Madison Co., Tenn., also having charge of the Bethlehem Church in Hardeman County, for ten years, as well as of several others in Tennessee; and finally of the churches at Maple Springs, Denmark, and Ararat—all in Madison Co., and Woodland, Haywood Co. He died in August, 1881. See Borum, *Sketches of Tenn. Ministers*, p. 191. (J. C. S.)

Day, Ira, a Free-will Baptist minister, was born at Burlington, Otsego Co., N. Y., Oct. 6, 1818. When about thirteen years old he joined the Congregational Church at Plainfield, N. Y.; in 1856 removed to Willet, where he joined the Free-will Baptists, and where he was subsequently licensed and ordained pastor. Finally he occupied the same relation in Fabius for three years, and died there, July 29, 1883. See *Morning Star*, Nov. 7, 1883. (J. C. S.)

Day, Isaac D., a Methodist Episcopal minister, was born at Petersburg, Pa., April 9, 1809. He was converted in his sixteenth year; in 1849 entered the Cincinnati Conference; two years later was transferred to the Ohio Conference, wherein he labored until his death, which occurred March 30, 1856. See *Minutes of Annual Conferences*, 1856, p. 113.

Day, Israel, a Congregational minister, was born at Attleborough, Mass.; ordained over the Church in Killingly, Conn., in 1785; dismissed in 1826; and died in Killingly, Dec. 10, 1831. See *Cong. Quarterly*, 1860, p. 185.

Day, Jeremiah, a Congregational minister, was born at Colchester, Conn., Jan. 25 (O. S.), 1737. He graduated from Yale College in 1756; taught a school in Sharon until Dec. 1, 1757, when he began the study of theology with the Rev. Dr. Joseph Bellamy; after a year and a half taught school again about two years in Esopus, N. Y.; settled on a farm on Sharon mountain, still continuing his studies; and in 1766 and 1767 was representative in the General Assembly. Not long after, he resumed his theological studies under the Rev. Cotton Mather Smith, and, after preaching at Danbury and other places, was ordained pastor at New Preston, Jan. 31, 1770. In the fall of 1788 he made a missionary tour through western Vermont. In 1794 he made another tour, this time to the settlements on the Delaware, in the state of New York, and on the Susquehanna, in Pennsylvania. From the establishment of the *Connecticut Evangelical Magazine*, in 1800, he was one of the editors until the close of his life, at Sharon, Sept. 12, 1806. See Sprague, *Annals of the Amer. Pulpit*, i, 688.

Day, John, an English clergyman, was born in Aldersgate Street, London, in 1566, and was educated at St. Alban's Hall, Oxford; in 1588 was elected a fellow of Oriel College; entered into holy orders, and became a favorite preacher in the university; travelled three years previous to 1608, when he obtained the vicarage of St. Mary's, in Oxford; and died at Thurlow, Suffolk, in 1627. He published some sermons, among which the best are *Conciones ad Clerum* (Oxon, 1612, 1615):—also *Commentaries on the First Eight Psalms* (ibid. 1620). See Chalmers, *Biog. Dict.* s. v.; Allibone, *Dict. of Brit. and Amer. Authors*, s. v.

Day, John Steele, a Methodist Episcopal minister, was born at Guildhall, Essex Co., Vt., June 4, 1816. He was converted at the age of fifteen, and licensed to preach in 1839; in 1843 joined the New England Conference, in which he became a superannuate in 1848; in 1851 resumed effective work; in 1878 took a supernumerary, and, in 1880, a superannuated relation; and died at Winthrop, Mass., March 1, 1882. See *Minutes of Annual Conferences*, 1882, p. 92.

Day, Joshua, a Baptist minister, was born at Reading, Berkshire, England, in 1837. He came to the United States in 1863, and took up his residence in Gloversville, N. Y.; soon after entered the ministry, settling first at Northville, and removing afterwards to Newark; he became pastor of the North Baptist Church, and subsequently of the Calvary Church, in Albany, where he died, June 20, 1877. See *Baptist Weekly*, June 28, 1877. (J. C. S.)

Day, Jotham, a Baptist minister, was born in

Maine about 1790; was ordained in Kennebunkport in 1821; in 1828 became pastor of the Second Church in Lisbon; and after 1836 preached for the Second Church in Bowdoin as a supply. See Millett, *Hist. of the Baptists of Maine*, p. 441. (J. C. S.)

Day, J. C., a Lutheran minister, was born at Germantown, Pa., Oct. 10, 1808. He was a student at Gettysburg in 1834; was licensed to preach in 1836; first labored at Friesburg, N. J.; then for ten years was pastor at Saddle River and Ramapo; six years in Churchtown, N. Y.; and for nineteen years in New Germantown, N. J.; removed, without charge, to Mount Vale, and died there, March 25, 1882. See *Lutheran Observer*, April 28, 1882.

Day, Mark, an English Wesleyan minister, was born near Dewsbury, Yorkshire. He was converted at the age of seventeen; commenced his ministry in 1808; and died at Huddersfield, June 30, 1823, aged thirty-eight years. See *Minutes of the British Conference*, 1823.

Day, Mulford, a Methodist Episcopal minister, was born at New Providence, N. J., April 8, 1801. He was converted in 1819; in 1833 entered the Philadelphia Conference; subsequently was transferred to the New Jersey Conference, and in it labored until his death, June 26, 1851. See *Minutes of Annual Conferences*, 1852, p. 28.

Day, Pliny Butts, D.D., a Congregational minister, was born at Chester Village (now Huntington), Mass., April 21, 1806. He entered the academy at Amherst in 1828; graduated from Amherst College in 1834, and from Andover Theological Seminary in 1837; during the winter months of his senior year at Andover performed missionary work among the Catholics in Canada. The First Congregational Church in Derry, N. H., installed him pastor, Oct. 4, 1837, and he continued there for more than thirteen years. During the summer of 1851 he visited Europe, and his letters of travel were published in the *Congregational Journal*. On his return he became pastor at Hollis, N. H., July 7, 1852, and remained until his death, July 6, 1869. He was remarkable for saintliness of character, superior business capacity, and thoughtful discourses. See *Cong. Quarterly*, 1871, p. 431.

Day, Reuben, a Baptist minister, was born Feb. 11, 1809, in Russell County, Va. In 1827 he removed to Tennessee; in 1841 united with the Church in Savannah, Hardin Co.; was licensed to preach in 1842; ordained in November the same year, and acted as pastor in Savannah in 1843; spent 1844 in missionary work, in West Tennessee; had a short pastorate at Cotton Grove, in Madison Co.; took charge, in 1846, of the Pleasant Plains Church, where he remained seven years; afterwards served several churches in Madison, Henderson, Gibson, and Hardeman counties, for ten or fifteen years, including Cane Creek and Liberty Grove. He died in 1880. See Borum, *Sketches of Tenn. Ministers*, p. 197. (J. C. S.)

Day, Richard (1), an English martyr, was burned at the stake for the defence of the Gospel, with three others, in June, 1558, at Islington. See Fox, *Acts and Monuments*, viii, 467.

Day, Richard (2), an English clergyman and printer, was educated at Eton School and King's College, Cambridge, where he became a fellow about 1571, and, being ordained, supplied the place of minister at Ryegate, in Surrey. He afterwards turned his attention principally to printing. He translated Fox's *De Christo Triumphante Comœdia* (1579), and wrote a preface and conclusion to the *Testaments of the Twelve Patriarchs*. See Chalmers, *Biog. Dict.* s. v.; Allibone, *Dict. of Brit. and Amer. Authors*, s. v.

Day, Robert (1), an English Baptist minister, was born at Milverton, Somersetshire, July 2, 1721. He was converted at the age of nineteen; two years later united with the Church at Row Green, Wellington; in 1743 commenced his studies at Bristol, preaching occasionally to neighboring churches; was ordained pastor in Wellington April 8, 1747, and died there, April 1, 1791. See Rippon, *Register*, 1791, p. 260. (J. C. S.)

Day, Robert (2), an English Wesleyan minister, was born at Dewsbury, Nov. 8, 1794. He was converted in 1809; called to the ministry in 1820; became a supernumerary in 1859; resided at Lowestoft, and died March 27, 1864. See *Minutes of the British Conference*, 1864, p. 20.

Day, Samuel, a Congregational minister, was born at Wrentham, Mass., April 14, 1808. He graduated from Williams College in 1833; for a time taught in Wrentham and at Troy, N. Y.; preached for two years in West Troy; Sept. 23, 1840, was ordained pastor in Wolcottville, Conn., remaining until June, 1845; eight years following was agent of the American and Foreign Christian Union; then became acting pastor at Bellows' Falls, Vt., in 1854; Princeton, Ill., in 1859; Amboy, in 1860; chaplain of the 8th Regiment Illinois Volunteers in 1862; in 1866 removed to Ann Arbor, Mich., without charge, and died in Brooklyn, N. Y., April 3, 1881. See *Cong. Year-book*, 1882, p. 28.

Day, Samuel Stearns, a Baptist minister, was born in Leeds County, Ont., in 1808. He joined the Baptists in 1825; graduated from the theological institution at Hamilton, N. Y., in 1835; was appointed by the Missionary Union to labor in the East, in August of the same year, and arrived in Calcutta the February following; in 1837 went to Madras for purposes of study, and in due time entered upon his work among the Teloogoos. In 1840 he went to Bellore, and, with the exception of a short visit to his native country in 1845, labored most faithfully for eighteen years among the native tribes, after which he once more returned in broken health to the United States, and died at Cortlandville, N. Y., in October, 1871. See *Baptist Missionary Magazine*, November, 1871. (J. C. S.)

Day, Simon, an English Wesleyan minister, was born in 1745. He was converted while at a boarding-school at Bristol; soon began to preach in the village of Somerset; in 1766 was appointed for Cornwall, but after a while retired from the ministry; in 1779 again entered the itinerant work; in 1817 became a supernumerary at Frome, and died March 17, 1832. See *Minutes of the British Conference*, 1832.

Day, Warren, a Congregational minister, was born at Sharon, Vt., Oct. 1, 1789. He graduated from Dartmouth College in 1814; preached at Richmond, N. Y., from 1816 to 1828; at Orangeville, two years; at Enfield, from 1838 to 1844; at Richmond, from 1845 to 1850; resided at Wawatosa, Wis., from 1854 to 1863, and died at Richmond, N. Y., May 19, 1864. See *Cong. Quarterly*, 1865, p. 207.

Day, William (1), an English prelate, brother of George Day, bishop of Chichester, was admitted to King's College, Cambridge, in 1545; became proctor of Cambridge in 1558; was made, by queen Elizabeth, provost of Eton and dean of Windsor; and made bishop of Winchester, which office he enjoyed scarcely a year, dying of extreme old age in 1596. Unlike his brother, he was a zealous Protestant. See Fuller, *Worthies of England* (ed. Nuttall), iii, 60.

Day, William (2), an English divine, was born about 1765. He was ordained to the curacy of Dewsbury, Yorkshire, in 1788, where he remained six years and a half; thence removed to Bengeworth, Worcestershire, in which he spent a similar period; in 1801 became assistant to the Rev. T. T. Biddulph, at St. James's, Bristol, with whom he continued till 1810, when he was preferred to the vicarage of St. Philip's by the corporation, at the same time laboring at other places in the vicinity. He died Sept. 7, 1832. See (Lond.) *Christian Guardian*, November, 1832, p. 425.

Dayken, Alexander, a German martyr, who had been the means of doing much good in other countries, went to Dornick, and for preaching there to the people was apprehended, beheaded, and burned, in 1562. See Fox, *Acts and Monuments*, iv, 394.

Dayton, A. C., a Baptist minister, was born at Plainfield, N. J., Sept. 4, 1813. He joined the Presbyterians at the age of twelve, graduated from the New York City Medical College, and, after practicing a short time, went to Florida for his health; three years afterwards removed to Vicksburg, Miss.; in 1852 united with a Baptist Church, and began at once to preach; subsequently became an agent of the Bible Board of the Southern Baptist Convention, residing in Nashville, Tenn., where he was the associate editor of the *Tennessee Baptist*, at the same time writing *Theodosia*, also *Infidel's Daughter*, and several other books for Sunday-schools. During the civil war he was engaged in teaching and in literary pursuits, until his death at Perry, Ga., June 11, 1865. See Cathcart, *Baptist Encyclop.* p. 319. (J. C. S.)

Dayton, Ezra Fairchild, a Presbyterian minister, was born at Mendham, N. J., June 6, 1808. He graduated from New Jersey College in 1826; was principal of an academy in Baskingridge, from 1826 to 1829; spent part of a year in Princeton Seminary; was ordained an evangelist by the Presbytery of Newark, Jan. 14, 1834; was stated supply at Augusta, from 1833 to 1836; at Sparta, from 1837 to 1839, and died there in October of the latter year. See *Gen. Cat. of Princeton Theol. Sem.* 1881, p. 76.

Daza, Antonio, a Spanish theologian and ecclesiastical historian, was born at Valladolid, and lived about 1625. He took the habit of the Franciscans, became overseer of the convent at Valladolid, minister of the province of Concepcion, and commissary-general of his order under Gregory XV. He wrote, *Las Chronicas de la Orden de S. Francisco* (Valladolid, 1611):—*Historia de las Llagas de S. Francisco* (Madrid, 1612):—*Vida de sor Juana de la Cruz, de la Terzera Orden de S. Francisco* (ibid. 1613):—*Exercicios Espirituales* (translated into Italian by Antiodocco, Rome, 1616):—*La Purissima Conception de Nuestra Senora* (Madrid, 1621):—*Vida de Pedro Regalado* (ibid. 1627). See Hoefer, *Nouv. Biog. Générale*, s. v.

Dead, Beating the. See Chibbut Hak-keber.

DEAD, Book of the. See Ritual of the Dead.

DEAD, Burning of the. See Cremation.

DEAD, Communion of the. The practice of placing the eucharist within the lips of the dead prevailed in all parts of the Church for some centuries. This and the baptism of the dead were forbidden by councils. Gregory Nazianzen utters a serious warning against them. Even when the better sense of the Church rejected the more revolting usage, the custom continued in a form hardly less superstitious, of placing a portion of the consecrated bread upon the breast of the corpse to be interred with it, as a charm against the attacks of malignant spirits.

DEAD, Festival of the. See All-Souls' Day.

DEAD, Prayer for the. See Mass.

DEAD, Treatment of the See Burial; Funeral.

Dealtry, Thomas, D.D., a missionary bishop of the Church of England, was born at Nottingley, near Pontefract, in 1795, and was the son of James Dealtry, descended from the ancient family of Dealtry of Lofthouse Hall, near Wakefield, Yorkshire. He was educated at St. Catharine's Hall, Cambridge, where he graduated as LL.B. in 1828; was created archdeacon at Calcutta in 1835, and held that office until consecrated bishop of Madras, in 1849. He died March 4, 1861, leaving *Sermons* on various occasions. See *Amer. Quar. Church Rev.* 1861, p. 396.

Deambulatoria (or **Deambulacra**) were covered porticoes for walking in, more particularly those surrounding a church. They were sometimes of two stories, and occasionally contained altars. The term is also used for the walks of a cloister (q. v.).

Dean, Henry, archbishop of Canterbury, was born about 1430, and was probably educated at St. Mary's College, Oxford, but also studied at Cambridge. He seems to have been one of the black canons, and was prior at Llanthony, in Monmouthshire, before 1481. On Sept. 13, 1494, he was constituted lord chancellor of Ireland; was consecrated bishop of Bangor, Oct. 6, 1496, where he accomplished wonders in the way of restoring cathedrals, and rebuilding the palace. He was translated to the see of Salisbury, Aug. 23, 1499, and was at the same time appointed registrar of the Order of the Garter. He occupied the see of Salisbury little more than a year. During this time he received the great seal, under the title of lord-keeper. He was appointed to the see of Canterbury about 1501. His health began to fail in 1502, and he died Feb. 15, 1503. See Hook, *Lives of the Abps. of Canterbury*, v, 500 sq.

Dean, Paul, a noted Universalist and Unitarian minister, was born at Barnard, Vt., in 1789. He held the doctrine of the Restorationists, and was pastor of churches in Boston and Easton, Mass. He died at Framingham, Oct. 1, 1860. He published numerous *Sermons*, etc.

Dean, William, an early Presbyterian minister, was educated at the Log College, N. J.; was taken on trial by the New Brunswick Presbytery, Aug. 3, 1741; licensed Oct. 12, 1742, and was sent to Neshaminy and the Forks of Delaware, a region inhabited by the Lenape, or Delawares, and other tribes. In 1745 he went with Byram of Mendham into Augusta County, Va., where a great awakening attended their labors, and continued until 1751. He was ordained, in 1755, pastor of the Forks of Brandywine, and received a call also from Timber Ridge and the Forks of James River, but it was not put into his hands. He died July 9, 1758. (W. P. S.)

Deane, James, a judge and missionary to the Indians of New York, was born at Groton, Conn., Aug. 20, 1748, and graduated at Dartmouth College in 1773. He having been associated in religious work among the Six Nations at the age of twelve, after leaving college was sent as a missionary to the Canadian Indians, and used his influence in the interests of peace. He served in the Revolution with the rank of major, and acted as interpreter at Fort Stanwix. After the war he was long a judge in Oneida County, N. Y., and held other important offices. He died at Westmoreland, in that county, Sept. 10, 1823.

Deane, Samuel (1), D.D., a Congregational minister, was born at Norton, Mass., July 30, 1733. He graduated from Harvard College in 1760; was settled in 1764 at Falmouth, as colleague to the Rev. Thomas Smith, and died Nov. 12, 1814. See Sprague, *Annals of the Amer. Pulpit*, ii, 327.

Deane, Samuel (2), a Congregational minister, was born March 30, 1784, at Mansfield, Mass., and graduated from Brown University in 1805. In 1810 he became pastor of the Second Congregational Church in Scituate, where he remained until his death, Aug. 9, 1834. He published a *History of Scituate* (1831), besides several poems and sermons.

Deasuil (Celt. *deas*, "the south," and *suil*, "a way"), a Druidical ceremony consisting in pacing thrice round an earthen walk, which encompassed the temple externally, and which is still visible at Stonehenge (q. v.). The route represented the course of the sun, being from the east southward to the west. This custom, as a religious rite, is of great antiquity, and very extensive. The benediction of the Deasuil was long used in Ireland, Wales, and the Scottish Highlands, and is said to be at present not entirely extinct.—Gardner, *Faiths of the World*, s. v. See DRUIDS.

Debir, in the mountains of Judah. Lieut. Conder gives an extended argument (*Quar. Statement* of the "Pal. Explor. Fund," Jan. 1875, p. 49 sq.) in favor of locating this place at the modern *ed-Dhoheriyeh* [see DANNAH, vol. ii, p. 672], which may be summed up thus: (1) Both names signify *the back*, i. e. ridge, of the mountains, on which this place is conspicuous; (2) it has ancient remains, consisting of cave dwellings, wells, and cisterns; five old roads lead from it, and large stones, at the distance of about three thousand cubits around it, seem to mark the limits of a Levitical city; (3) there are fine springs in the neighborhood, namely, those of Seil Dilbeh, six miles west of Juttah, which feed a brook that runs several miles. To this identification Tristram (*Bible Places*, p. 61) and Trelawney Saunders (*Map of the O. T.*) accede. The argument, however, is rather specious than strong: (1) The names do not agree in etymology, and the resemblance in meaning is very doubtful; (2) the ruins show, indeed, an ancient site, but not necessarily the one in question, and the Levitical bounds are particularly dubious; (3) the springs are too distant to indicate any special connection with this locality, which, moreover, is farther from Hebron than we should expect.

De Blois, François Louis. See BLOSIUS.

De Blois, Stephen W., D.D., a Baptist minister, was born in 1827 at Halifax, N. S. He graduated from Acadia College in June, 1846; studied theology at Newton; was ordained Feb. 26, 1854, in Chester; and in 1855 became pastor of the First Church in Horton, where he remained twenty-seven years. He died at Wolfville, Feb. 4, 1884. See Cathcart, *Baptist Encyclop.* p. 322. (J. C. S.)

Debo (or **Bebo**) was the twenty-second bishop of Avignon, about 429. He was previously a senator of advanced years, universally beloved for his justice, mildness, and every good work. In 433 he restored the Church of St. Paul, which had been destroyed by the Vandals, and afterwards dedicated it to Sts. Peter and Paul.

De Bollandt, SEBASTIAN. See BOLLANDUS.

Debris, NICOLAS, a French doctor of theology in the 16th century, was one of the four theologians whom Charles IX sent to the Council of Trent. He wrote, *Instruction à Supporter les Adversités du Monde* (Paris, 1542):—*Bref Aiguillon à Aimer l'État de Religion Chrétienne*, etc. (ibid. 1544). See Hoefer, *Nouv. Biog. Générale*, s. v.

Decalvatio (*making bald*). See CORPORAL INFLICTIONS; PUNISHMENTS.

Decanātus (or **Decania**), (1) the office of a dean; (2) the district of a rural dean; (3) sometimes a farm or monastic grange, in late charters.

Decăni (or **Deans**), an order of men instituted in the 9th century, to assist the bishops in the inspection of their dioceses. Seven of the most enlightened men of the congregation were appointed, under the name of *decani*, to take charge of the rest. See DEAN.

Decanicium was the pastoral staff borne before the patriarch of Constantinople on solemn occasions, delivered to him in the first instance by the emperor. Pancirolus, however, states that it was a silver mace.

Decanĭcum (**Decania**, or **Decanica**) was an ecclesiastical prison in which criminal clerks were incarcerated by their ecclesiastical superiors. The word is derived from the *decani*, who were jailers. By a false etymology it is sometimes written *dicaincum* and *diaconicum*. The clergy, instead of being beheaded or hung for misdemeanors, had suspended from their necks the gospels and the cross, and were imprisoned in one of the decanica of the church. The heretics, by a decree of Arcadius and Honorius, were deprived, with other buildings, of the decanica. See Smith, *Dict. of Christ. Antiq.* s. v.

Decănus. See DEAN.

De Capella, ANDREW. See CAPELLA.

Decentius, (1) bishop of Leone, in Spain, was present at the Council of Elvira, A.D. 300 or 301; (2) bishop of Eugubium, in Umbria, about 416. Among the epistles of Innocent I is a letter of praise addressed to him.

De Champs, VICTOR, cardinal-archbishop of Mechlin, was born Dec. 6, 1810, at Melle. He was a follower of Lamennais, and in the spirit of his teacher wrote for different political periodicals, but in 1832 betook himself to the study of theology. He joined the Redemptorists at St. Trond; soon became famous as a pulpit orator; went on a pilgrimage to Rome in 1850; in 1865 was raised to the episcopal see of Namur, and in 1867 to the archiepiscopal see of Mechlin; and in 1875 was made cardinal, probably for his advocacy of papal infallibility. Bishop De Champs was especially severe against the free-masons, and proved himself a decided Ultramontanist. He died Sept. 29, 1883. (B. P.)

De Charms, RICHARD, a minister of the New Jerusalem Church, was born in Philadelphia, Pa., in 1797. In early life he was a printer; graduated at Yale College in 1826; the year previous studied Swedenborgianism under Thomas Worcester, D.D., at the same time superintending the publication of the *New Jerusalem Magazine;* continued his theological researches in Baltimore, Md., and there began to preach in 1828, his first sermon, considered a masterpiece, being published, and afterwards reprinted in London. Its title was *The Paramount Importance of Spiritual Things.* After a year of pastoral labor in Bedford, Pa., he went to London, studied under Rev. Samuel Noble, and on returning, in 1832, became pastor of the First New Jerusalem Church in Cincinnati, O., and conducted a periodical called *The Precursor.* Subsequently he preached in Philadelphia, Baltimore, and New York. In his latter days he devoted much attention to various mechanical contrivances and inventions of his own. He died March 20, 1864. He was the author of *Sermons Illustrating the Doctrine of the Lord:—Series of Lectures Delivered at Charleston, S. C.:—The New Churchman:*—and *Freedom and Slavery in the Light of the New Jerusalem.* See *Appleton's Annual Cyclop.* 1864, p. 598.

Decius, (1) eighth bishop of Macon, is assigned by Severtius to the period from 599 to 612; (2) succeeded Deodatus as eleventh bishop of Macon, in the latter part of the 7th century and the beginning of the 8th.

Decker, Christian August Heinrich, a Lutheran minister, was born Oct. 13, 1806, at Husum, in Schleswig, and studied theology at Kiel and Berlin. In 1833 he was appointed collaborator at the Meldorf school, and ten years later, in 1843, was called to the pastorate at Klein-Wesenberg, near Lubeck. In 1863 he was called to Leezen, near Segeberg, and in 1875 to the Thumbye and Struxdorf pastorate, in Angeln. He died June 11, 1884. He was a very active man, and a stanch defender of his Church. He wrote, *Ordnung des Gottesdienstes und der Kirchlichen Handlungen*, etc. (Altona, 1845):—*Die Revolution in Schleswig-Holstein* (Hamburg, 1850):—*Ueber Gustav-Adolphs-Verein und Bekenntniss* (ibid. 1861). See Zuchold, *Bibl. Theol.* i, 266; Luthardt's *Allgemeine Evangelisch-Lutherische Kirchenzeitung*, 1884, No. 42. (B. P.)

Decker (or **Deckher**), **Conrad**, a Dutch theologian of the order of the Jesuits, taught at Heidelberg, and died in 1620, leaving, *De Papa Romano et Papissa Romana:—De Proprietatibus Jesuitarum*, etc. See Hoefer, *Nouv. Biog. Générale*, s. v.

Deckers, JAN, a Flemish theologian, was born at Hazebrouck about 1559. He studied at Douay, became a Jesuit at Naples, taught, at Douay and Louvain, philosophy and theology, and became chancellor of the university at Gratz and rector of the college at Olmütz, in Moravia. He died at Gratz in 1619. His principal works are, *Tabula Chronographica* (1605):—*Theologicæ Dissertationes*, etc. (Paris, 1699):—*Tabula Expansa Ephemeridum*. See Hoefer, *Nouv. Biog. Générale*, s. v.

Declan (or **Deglan**) (1) was an Irish saint, who wrought with St. Virgilius, St. Rupert, and others in the evangelization of Bavaria, and died at Frisengen, Dec. 1, about the middle of the 8th century; (2) bishop of Ardmor, was a son of Erc and Deitsin, or Dethidin. Through his father he could boast of royal ancestry. He was born at Decies, in the county of Waterford, and probably died about the middle of the 7th century. He is commemorated July 24.

Decorated Style. See GOTHIC ARCHITECTURE.

Decret, CLAUDE, a French theologian and moralist, was born at Tournus in 1598. He joined the Jesuits in 1614, and became professor of philosophy and of belles-lettres at Châlons, and afterwards rector of the college in the same town. He died at Paris, April 10, 1668, leaving *La Véritable Veuve* (Paris, 1654). See Hoefer, *Nouv. Biog. Générale*, s. v.

Decretists, one of the two parties into which the students of canon law in the 12th century were divided in consequence of the general recognition at that period of the supreme authority of the pope. The name is taken from the title of a work, *Decretum Gratiani*, which formed the basis of their studies in ecclesiastical law. Neander says, "The zeal with which the study of civil and ecclesiastical law was pursued had, however, this injurious effect, that the clergy were thereby drawn away from the study of the Bible, and from the higher, directly theological, interest, and their whole life devoted solely to these pursuits." The opposite party were called Legists. See Neander, *Hist. of the Church*, iv, 203 sq.

Decrētum (or **Decretālè**) is the letter of the clergy and people of a city, sent to the metropolitan and the comprovincial bishops, signifying the election of a bishop of their city, whom they required to be consecrated. Gregory of Tours says that in the choice of Mauritius the electors could not come to one *decretum*. The name is also given to a form to be read by the deacon when a bishop is "designated." The difference between this and the foregoing *decretum* appears to be that the one was sent by the hands of some official of the vacant see immediately on the election of the bishop; if, thereupon, the pope gave his assent, the bishop became technically *designate*, and the deacon of his church read the *decretale* or petition for consecration.

Decumānus (or **Degeman**) was a Welsh saint, who lived a hermit on the seashore at the place called from him St. Decuman's, near Watchet, in Somersetshire. His well was long pointed out there, and a chapel existed in the parish of Wendron, near Helstone, in Cornwall, which was dedicated to him. He is said to have died Aug. 27, 706.

Deda was a presbyter and abbot of Peartaneu (Bardney), in the province of the Lindissi. He is the authority of Bede for what he states concerning the early evangelization of Lincolnshire, and the multitude of people baptized in the Trent by bishop Paulinus in the presence of king Edwin. Beda calls him a faithful man.

Defensor, (1) the first bishop of Angers. Nothing is known of his birth or age. (2) A monk of the monastery Ligugè, which St. Martin founded on the river Calin, not far from Poitiers. He lived about the end of the 7th century or the beginning of the 8th. He was a diligent student of the fathers, and by his scholarly habits acquired the title of "Grammarian." He made extracts and compiled a book entitled *Scintillarum, seu Sententiarum Catholicorum Patrum*. The work is divided into eighty chapters, and treats of the principal Christian virtues. It has appeared, according to Possevin, in three editions: Antwerp, 1550; Venice, 1552; Cologne, 1554.

Defensor ECCLESIÆ. See ADVOCATE OF THE CHURCH.

Dega. See DAIGH.

Degenkolb, KARL FRIEDRICH, a German theologian, was born at Weissenfels, July 12, 1682. He studied at Leipsic, became deacon in 1716, archdeacon in 1723, pastor at Stolpen in 1729, and died in 1747. His principal works are *Kirch-Regierunge Gottes im Alten und Neuen Testament* (Bautzen, 1715):—*Einleitung in die politische Historie* (Pirna, 1716):—*Wider die Atheisten, Materialisten, Juden, Türken und Heiden* (1722):—*Grundriss der Theologie* (Dresden, 1731). See Hoefer, *Nouv. Biog. Générale*, s. v.

Degin, bishop of Menevia. See DAVID, ST.

Deguerry, GASPARD, a French priest, was born at Lyons in 1797. Having completed his studies in the college of Villefranche, he was in 1820 ordained priest. In 1824 he preached at Lyons, in 1825 and 1826 at Paris, and in the year following Charles X appointed him chaplain of the sixth regiment of the royal guards. After the revolution in 1830 Deguerry resumed preaching again. On his return from Rome, in 1840, he was made canon of Notre Dame, then archpriest, and finally curate of St. Eustatius in 1845 and of St. Magdalene in 1849. He refused the bishopric of Marseilles, offered to him by Napoleon III, but accepted a call as religious instructor of the prince in 1868. Being taken prisoner by the communists, March 18, 1871, he was shot at La Roquette. He wrote, *Éloges de Jeanne d'Arc* (1828, 1856):—*Histoire de l'Ancien et du Nouveau Testament* (1846):—*Vie des Saints* (1845):—and Sermons on the Lord's Prayer, preached at the Tuileries in 1866. See Lichtenberger, *Encyclop. des Sciences Religieuses*, s. v. (B. P.)

Deharbe, JOSEPH, a German Jesuit, was born in 1800 at Strasburg. In 1817 he joined his order, and was professor at the college of Brieg, in Switzerland, where he educated most of the Jesuits, who since 1848 have acted as missionaries in Germany. He died Nov. 8, 1871, at Maria-Einsiedeln, leaving, *Gründliche und leichtfassliche Erklärung des katholischen Katechismus* (1857-63, 5 vols.):—*Die vollkommene Lebe Gottes* (Ratisbon, 1856):—*Examen ad Usum Cleri* (2d ed. 1849; 3d ed. 1866). (B. P.)

Deicŏlae (*worshippers of God*) was a name sometimes applied to *monks*.

Deicŏlus (**Deel, Deicola**, or **Dichuill**) of Lure was a saint and abbot. He went with St. Columban from Britain to Burgundy, and shared his fortunes at Luxeuil. He was a uterine brother of St. Gallus. Bodily weakness hindered him from following Columban into exile, and although left to perish in the brushwood near the monastery, he found his way to the place where Lutra or Lure now stands, in Burgundy, and built his cell there, which eventually grew into a large and flourishing monastery. He is said to have been visited by the Roman pontiff. After ten years at Lure, seeing death approaching, he appointed Columbinus his successor, and, retiring to greater seclusion, died Jan. 18, 625. His chief festival has always been on that day of the year.

Deifĕrus. See DIER.

Deihl, MICHAEL, a Lutheran professor, was born near Greencastle, Franklin Co., Pa., in March, 1819. He attended a classical school, in his native town, in 1838; graduated from Pennsylvania College in 1844, and then pursued the course in the Gettysburg Theological Seminary. In 1846 he accepted an appointment to the chair of ancient languages in Wittenberg College, Springfield, O., which position he held until 1868, when impaired health compelled him to resign. In connection with his labors as professor, he took charge of churches at different times in several places near Springfield. He died there, March 29, 1869. In 1859 he published a *Biography of Dr. Ezra Keller*, first president of Wittenberg College. See *Pennsylvania College Book*, 1882, p. 220.

Deiniolen (Deiniol ab, Deiniol Ail, or **Deiniol Fab)** was a Welsh saint of the 6th century. He was a son of Deiniol, first bishop of Bangor. He succeeded his father as second abbot in the monastery at that place, and is said to have founded the church of Llandeiniolen, in Carnarvonshire, in 616. He is commemorated Nov. 23.

De Koven, James, D.D., a Protestant Episcopal clergyman, was born in Middletown, Conn., Sept. 19, 1831. He graduated from Columbia College and the General Theological Seminary; in 1857 took charge of the Church in Delafield, Wis.; and in 1859 removed to Racine, as rector and warden of the university there. In 1875 he was elected bishop of Illinois, but declined. For many years he was a delegate to the General Convention. He died at Racine, March 19, 1879. Dr. De Koven was noted for his High-Church views. A posthumous volume of his *Sermons* was published by Dr. Dix (N. Y. 1880). See *Protestant Episcopal Almanac*, 1880, p. 171.

De la Basse, Eli. See Basse, Eli.

De la Harpe, Henri, D.D., a distinguished Swiss theologian, was born at Bordeaux, France, in 1809. He pursued his studies in Edinburgh, and gained the first prize in natural philosophy in 1828. The year following he went to Geneva, and finally graduated from the theological seminary of Montauban. In 1832 and 1833 he studied in the seminary just founded by D'Aubigné and his compeers. In 1837 he was called to the chair of Old-Test. exegesis and criticism, which place he filled until the day of his death, in December, 1880, and never consented to receive any compensation for his valuable services. He succeeded D'Aubigné as president of the theological seminary. Professor La Harpe was a broad as well as a deep scholar. He was more or less master of twenty languages. A short time before his death he completed the translation of the Old Test. into French, a work on which he had been engaged twenty-five years. He was president of the Geographical Society of Geneva and the editor of its *Journal*. See *N. Y. Observer*, Jan. 6, 1881. (W. P. S.)

De Lasky, John. See Lasko.

Delatōres (*Informers*, sometimes called *Calumniatores*) were those unfaithful brethren in the early Church, who, for money or favor from the civil authorities, betrayed the Christians into the hands of their persecutors. Titus issued an edict forbidding slaves to inform against their masters, or freedmen against their patrons. It is not wonderful that during and immediately after the days of persecution the informer was regarded with horror. Thus the Council of Elvira, A.D. 305, excommunicated, even on his deathbed, any informer who had caused the proscription or death of the person informed against; for informing in less important cases, the informer might be readmitted to communion after five years; or, if a catechumen, he might be admitted to baptism after five years. The first council of Arles, A.D. 314, reckons among "traditores" not only those who gave up to the persecutors the Holy Scriptures and sacred vessels, but also those who handed in lists of the brethren; and respecting these the council decrees that whoever shall be discovered, from the public records, to have committed such offences shall be solemnly degraded from the clerical order. The capitularies of the Frank kings cite the canon of Elvira. The same capitularies enjoin bishops to excommunicate "accusers of the brethren;" and, even after amendment, not to admit them to holy orders, though they may be admitted to communion. There is attributed to pope Hadrian I a decree: "Let the tongue of an informer be cut out, or let his head be cut off." Precisely the same is found in the Frank capitularies, and nearly the same in the Theodosian code.

Delaune, Thomas, an English Baptist minister and author, was born of Roman Catholic parents in Ireland, near the commencement of the 17th century. He was educated in his native country; was converted in youth; subsequently was teacher in a grammar-school in London, and was ordained as a Baptist minister. The nonconformists of England being invited by Dr. Calamy, at the time one of the chaplains of Charles II, to make a statement of the reasons which led them to dissent from the Established Church, with the assurance that they would be candidly taken into consideration, Delaune published his famous *Plea for the Nonconformists* (1684, 4to); it passed through twenty editions. The author was severely punished by torture, mutilation, fine, and imprisonment in Newgate, where, after a time, he died. His other works are, *Truth Defended*, etc. (Lond. 1667):—*Survey of Joseph Whiston's Book on Baptism* (1676):—*The Present State of London* (1681):—*A Key to Open Scripture Metaphors* (1682, 2 vols. fol.). See Hayne, *Church Transplanted*, p. 169.

Delaune, William, D.D., an English divine, became president of St. John's College, Oxford, in 1698, prebendary of Winchester in 1702, vice-chancellor of Oxford University the same year, Margaret professor of divinity at Oxford in 1715, and died May 23, 1728. He published *A Sermon* (1702):—and *Twelve Sermons* (1728). See Allibone, *Dict. of Brit. and Amer. Authors*, s. v.; Le Neve, *Fasti*, vol. i.

Delaware Version of the Scriptures. This dialect of the Algonquin stock was spoken at the time of the discovery of America, between the Hudson and the Susquehanna rivers, by the Delaware and Minsi tribes. In 1818 the Rev. Christian Frederick Dencke, a Moravian missionary stationed at New Fairfield, in Upper Canada, forwarded a translation of the Epistles of St. John to the board of the American Bible Society, which has been published. (B. P.)

Delbrück, Johann Friedrich Theophil, *the elder*, a German theologian, was born at Magdeburg, Aug. 22, 1768. He studied theology at Halle, was made professor of the gymnasium in his native town, and became rector in 1797. From 1800 to 1809 he had charge of the education of the Prussian princes, and was then appointed member of the privy council. He filled several other offices, and lastly had the superintendence of Zeitz (archbishopric). He died July 4, 1830. See Hoefer, *Nouv. Biog. Générale*, s. v.

Delegātus. See Legate.

Delfino, Giovanni Pietro, an Italian ecclesiastic, was born at Brescia in 1709. He studied theology at Venice, was appointed archpriest of San Zenone, and died in 1770, leaving, *Il Tempio d. Dio* (Brescia, 1760):—*Ragionamento*, etc. (in the *Opuscoli Scientifici* of Calogera). See Hoefer, *Nouv. Biog. Générale*, s. v.

Delfino, Pietro, an Italian theologian, was born at Venice in 1444. He joined the Camaldules at the age of eighteen, was elected vicar-general of his order in 1479, and general in 1480, holding this position, at times with much opposition, until 1515. He died Jan. 15, 1525, leaving *Epistolæ* (Venice, 1724). See Hoefer, *Nouv. Biog. Générale*, s. v.

Delfinone, Girolamo, a very eminent artist in pictorial embroidery, flourished at Milan about 1495. He executed a number of subjects from sacred history, some of which represent the history of the Virgin. See Spooner, *Biog. Hist. of the Fine Arts*, s. v.

Delisle, Joseph, a French theologian, was born at Brainville, in Bassigny, about 1690. He served for some time in the French army, joined the Benedictines at St. Vanne in 1711, taught at the abbey of Moyenmoutier, then at St. Maurice, in Valais; was appointed abbot of St. Leopold at Nancy, and died at St. Mihiel, Jan. 24, 1766, leaving, *Vie de M. Hugy* (Nancy, 1831):—*L'Obligation de Faire l'Aumône* (Neufchâteau, 1736):—*Le Martyre de la Légion Thébaine* (Nancy, 1737):—*Histoire du Jeûne* (Paris, 1741):—*Histoire de l'Abbaye de St. Mihiel* (Nancy, 1758). See Hoefer, *Nouv. Biog. Générale*, s. v.

Delitzsch, Johann, eldest son of Dr. Franz Delitzsch, was born at Rostock, Aug. 3, 1846. He studied at Erlangen, Tübingen, and Leipsic, and published as his doctorate dissertation *Die Gotteslehre des Thomas von Aquino*, in 1870. Two years later he commenced his academical career at Leipsic by presenting his *De Inspiratione Scripturæ Sacræ*. In 1874 he published in the *Studien und Kritiken* an essay, *Zur Quellenkritik der ältesten Kirchlichen Berichte über Simon Petrus und Simon Magus*, which was followed in 1875 by his *Lehrsystem der römischen Kirche*. He was now made professor extraordinarius at the Leipsic University. In 1876 he published Oehler's *Lehrbuch der Symbolik*, but in the same year his health gave way, and he died, Feb. 3, at Rapallo, near Genoa. See Schürer, *Theologische Literatur-zeitung*, 1876, p. 141 sq. (B. P.)

Deliverers, a Christian sect mentioned by Augustine as having arisen about A.D. 260, and who derived their name from the doctrine, which they maintained, that upon Christ's descent into hell infidels believed, and all were delivered from thence.

Dell, William, M.D., an English Baptist minister, was born about 1600. Soon after graduation from the University of Cambridge, he took orders in the Established Church, and officiated in the parish of Yelden, Bedfordshire. In 1645 he became chaplain in the army, and in 1649 was appointed master of Caius College, Cambridge, but was ejected by the act of uniformity. The precise time of his death we have not been able to ascertain. Dr. Dell published several sermons and essays, the most important of which were eventually issued as his *Select Works* (London, 1773, 8vo). See Hayne, *Baptist Cyclopædia*, i, 195. (J. C. S.)

Dellingur (*twilight*), in Norse mythology, was the third husband of Norf's daughter, Not (*night*); the shining son of this couple was Dagur, or Dag (*the day*).

Dellius, Godfriedus, a minister of the Reformed Church in Holland, was sent to America in 1683 as assistant to the Rev. Gideon Schaats, in Albany. Mr. Dellius was also an active missionary among the Mohawk Indians. The last ten years of his pastorate exhibit a record of political complications, and his name appears very often in the *Documentary History of N. Y.*, the *Colonial History of N. Y.*, and other records of the time. Of his last days we have no notice. See also Corwin, *Manual Ref. Church in America;* Dr. Rogers's *Historical Discourse*, p. 17. (W. J. R. T.)

Delmare, Paulo Marcelli, an Italian theologian, was born at Geneva in 1734. He was converted from Judaism by a priest of his native city, and received baptism in 1753. He entered the clerical ranks, and, after spending several years in missionary work, was called in 1783 to teach theology at Florence; and died Feb. 17, 1821, leaving several controversial treatises, for which see Hoefer, *Nouv. Biog. Générale*, s. v.

Demarest, Cornelius T., a (Dutch) Reformed minister, graduated at Columbia College, N. Y., in 1804; studied theology with Dr. Solomon Froeligh; was pastor at White House, N. J., from 1808 to 1813, and at English Neighborhood from 1813 to 1824, when he seceded to the True Reformed Church, giving occasion to a celebrated lawsuit as to the Church property (see Taylor, *Annals of the Classis of Bergen*, p. 261–285). His ministry in the True Reformed Church continued until his decease in 1863, his last eleven years being spent as pastor of the Church in King Street, New York. He published *A Lamentation over the Rev. Solomon Froeligh*, with copious historical notes. See Corwin, *Manual of the Ref. Church in America*, p. 69. (W. J. R. T.)

Demeter. See Ceres.

Demetria, a daughter of Faustus, and martyr at Rome under Julian; commemorated June 21.

Demetrius. (1) A martyr at Thessalonica, A.D. 296; commemorated Oct. 8 or Oct. 26. (2) Bishop and martyr at Antioch with Anianus, Eutosius, and twenty others; commemorated Nov. 10. (3) *Saint;* commemorated Dec. 22, with Honoratus and Florus. (4) Patriarch of Alexandria, A.D. 231; commemorated March 8 and Oct. 9. (5) Demetrius and Basilius; commemorated Nov. 12.

Demetrius Pepanus, a Greek theologian, was born on the island of Chios about 1620. He was sent to Rome to finish his studies, and entered into orders, but was released from his vows on account of his health. He returned to his native land, but left the island of Chios with his wife and children in 1655, and it is supposed that he perished in a shipwreck. All his theological writings were intended to bring back the Greek schismatics to the Catholic Church. They were discovered at Chios by the English consul Stellio Rafaelli, and were published under the title *Demetrii Pepani Domestici Chii Opera quæ Reperiuntur* (Rome, 1781, 2 vols.). See Hoefer, *Nouv. Biog. Générale*, s. v.

Demetrius of Sunium, a Cynic philosopher, was educated in the school of the sophist Rhodius. He spent a considerable part of his life at Corinth, being an opponent of Apollonius of Tyana, and first became famous during the reign of Caligula (A.D. 37–41). The emperor, wishing to secure the philosopher to his party, sent him a large present; but Demetrius refused it with indignation, saying, "If Caligula wishes to bribe me, let him send me his crown." Vespasian banished him for his insolence, but he derided the punishment. He lived to an advanced age, and Seneca observes that nature had brought him forth to show mankind how an exalted genius may live uncorrupted by the vices of the world. See Smith, *Dict. of Greek and Rom. Biog. and Myth.* s. v.; *Encyclop. Britan.* (9th ed.) s. v.

Demme, Hermann Christoph Gottfried, a Lutheran theologian, was born Sept. 7, 1760, at Mülhausen, where, in 1796, he acted as superintendent. In 1801 he was called as general superintendent to Altenburg, and died there, Dec. 21, 1822. He wrote, *Beiträge zur reinen Gottesverehrung* (Riga, 1792):—*Predigten über die Sonn- und Festtagsevangelien* (Gotha, 1808):—*Neue Reden zur Todtenfeier in Altenburg gehalten* (ibid. 1817). He is also the author of several romances, under the pseudonym of *Karl Stelle*, besides numerous hymns. See Döring, *Die deutschen Kanzelredner der* 18. *und* 19. *Jahrhunderts*, p. 26 sq.; Winer, *Handbuch der theol. Lit.* ii, 93, 133, 160, 166, 173, 238, 294, 326, 337, 341, 398; Hoefer, *Nouv. Biog. Générale*, s. v. (B. P.)

Democrĭtus was one of the ablest and least known of the Greek philosophers, whose position lies on the border-line between the mythical sages of the elder time and the historic founders of Greek philosophy. His personal career is shadowy and uncertain; his speculations are fragmentary and dislocated; his works have been lost, or only survive in brief and disconnected fragments; his tenets are well known, but have often been exaggerated or distorted. His influence on later philosophy has not always been duly appreciated; but it has been scarcely inferior to that of Socrates and the Socratic school. His characteristic doctrines were transmitted by underground currents to widely diffused sects. They have special claims to present consideration for their marked congruity with the rationalistic and agnostic schemes now in vogue. In all ages there is an unbroken traduction of earlier opinions, and an intimate connection between the accepted theories and the contemporaneous conditions of the societies in which they prevail. In both respects, the philosophy of Democritus was notable in the æra of its manifestation, and it may be of great service for the elucidation, in both, of the philosophical distemperature of the respective periods.

I. *Life.*—The dates of the birth and death of Democritus, and his length of days, are entirely uncertain, though he may be regarded as later than Anaxagoras, and contemporaneous with Socrates. He appears to have been born at Abdera about B.C. 460, and to have died about B.C, 357. He is variously stated to have attained ninety, ninety-nine, one hundred, one hundred and four, one hundred and eight, and even one hundred and nine years. He was the son of Hegesistratus (by some named Damasippus, by others, Athenocritus), who was said to have entertained Xerxes on his flight from Salamis. Fables clustered round his name. Three autobiographical notices survive. The first states that he was forty years younger than Anaxagoras; the second, that the *Little Diacosmus* was composed "seven hundred and thirty years after the taking of Troy;" the third, "that he had traversed more countries than any of his countrymen" (Herodotus would be included); "that he had known the greatest diversities of climate and soil, and had heard many sages; that he had never been surpassed in geometrical diagrams and demonstrations, not even by the Egyptian Arpedonaptæ, with whom he had lived five years." Very little information is contained in these statements.

The death of his father left Democritus with an ample inheritance. He is reported to have taken the smallest share in the distribution of the property, as it was in ready money, immediately available for the travels which he promptly undertook. The rest of the estate he abandoned to his brothers. If this were the case, the epigrammatic observation of Horace would be deprived of its point (1 *Epist.* xii, 12).

Many legends were current in regard to the travels of Democritus among the Ethiopians, Egyptians, Chaldæans, Persians, and even Indian Gymnosophists. A very pretty story is told of an imaginary visit to the king of Persia; but the same tale is told, in slightly altered form, in many lands. Darius was inconsolable for the loss of his queen. Democritus promised to recall her from the dead, if he were supplied with all things needed for the avocation. Whatever was required was furnished in abundance; but one thing more was demanded—the names of three persons who had never felt sorrow, to be inscribed on the tomb.

Democritus visited Athens (*Fragm. Promisc.* 7). He is reported to have resided there—to have known Socrates—but to have kept himself wholly unknown; "Constantem hominem et gravem! qui glorietur, a Gloria se abfuisse" (Cicero, *Tusc. Disp.* V, xxxvi, 104). His whole career is a fabric of fables (Aul. Gell. *Noct. Att.* X, xii, 8). He is alleged to have shut himself up in tombs, that he might be free from interruption and distraction of mind. As Bayle suggests, the advantages of such a procedure are questionable. Bayle also characterizes as a "silly story" the tradition that he put out his eyes in order to promote his meditations (Cicero, *De Fin.* v, 29); Cicero prudently appends "*vero falsone*" as a restriction to his statement.

Democritus returned from his long travels enriched with great and varied knowledge, but stripped of means, which had been expended on his journeys. Thenceforth he may have been dependent upon his brother Damastes for support. The tradition represented that he was summoned before the magistrates of Abdera, for infringing the laws by living without visible means of support. In his defence, he read before them his Μέγας Διάκοσμος. They were so much charmed by it that they presented him with five hundred talents, and decreed that he should be buried at the public expense. His want of means was due to no incapacity for gaining a livelihood, but to his being engrossed in his studies. He had gained an acquaintance with the language of birds, and knew all secrets, like the wondrous women of Eastern story. He anticipated the recent wisdom of "weather forecasts" and "weather probabilities," and could tell when it would rain and when it would clear up. He might have made a brilliant speculator, for, on one occasion, foreseeing a disastrous season for olives, and that oil would bear a high price, he monopolized all the olives that could be procured (Pliny, *Hist. Nat.* xviii, 28). His only design, however, was to show that he could easily make money if he desired to do so. His poverty was deliberately accepted, and was welcome from his contempt of wealth. It was borne with joyous exhilaration; he was always seen with a smile on his face, and, hence, was designated "the laughing philosopher." Later philosophers supposed that he laughed at the vanities of life, and the weaknesses of mankind: "Adeo nihil illi serium videbatur, quæ serio gerebantur" (Seneca, *De Ira.* ii, 10; *De Tranquill. Animi*, xxii). His long life passed away in the serene and sedulous prosecution of his speculative and physical investigations. It must have been diligently employed, if he composed the multitude of works which were generally accredited to him. Death came at last at his bidding, though it spared him till life became wearisome. He was represented as having starved himself to death:

> "Sponte sua lito caput obvius obtulit ipso."
> (Lucret. iii, 1052.)

He delayed his end for three days with the smell of bread or honey, at the request of his sister, the priestess of Ceres, who was unwilling that the festival in progress should be contaminated by death in the family.

II. *Works.*—A list of sixty treatises by Democritus is given by Diogenes Laërtius, on ethical, physical, mathematical, musical, technical, and miscellaneous topics. These were arranged by Thrasyllus in Tetralogies, as was done by him, also, in regard to the works of Plato. An attempt has been made by Mullach to restore this distribution. Such a proceeding must be purely conjectural, as data are absent for even probable conclusions. Of these manifold volumes, only three hundred and twenty genuine fragments have been saved. These are, for the most part, extremely brief; the longest of them being on the subject of agriculture. They are inadequate to enable us to judge directly of either the literary or philosophical merits of the author. The testimonies of the ancients must, therefore, pass unchallenged. It is strong evidence of his high capacity that he received the designation of πένταθλος from the Greeks, and was termed *vir magnus imprimis*, by Cicero. He was equally esteemed for his style, for his learning, and for his bold speculation. Plato proposed that his books should be burned, a proposal which may have sprung from jealousy, but arose more probably from thorough antipathy to his doctrines and apprehension of their pernicious effects. Many treatises were falsely ascribed to Democritus. From these may have been derived the forty-six spurious fragments gathered by Mullach.

III. *Philosophy.*—In the time and country of Democritus, philosophy still retained much of that indistinctness of character which had appertained to it when it signified nothing more than the earnest pursuit of knowledge. It was still thoroughly unsystematic. If logical inquiries had been already inaugurated, they had not yet assumed a fixed and coherent form.

The philosophy of Democritus may be divided into ethical and physical: the former embracing acute practical observations; the latter comprehending, as was the wont of early speculation, such theology as comported with his schemes—in both respects showing some connection with Parmenides and the Eleatics, though it might be erroneous to imagine any positive affiliation. The Eleatics had rendered philosophy too ideal and too impalpable. The Ionic school, in aiming at simplicity of doctrine, had fallen into narrow and arbitrary fantasies. A more tangible speculation than the Eleatic, a more thorough and acceptable exposition than the Ionic, was in demand. This requirement Leucippus and his successor, Democritus, consciously or unconsciously, endeavored to supply. The intellectual current ran in the direction of the atomistic philosophy. As all the writings of Leucippus were early lost, and as his opinions are only known through their development by his illustrious follower, the consideration of his views will be implicated with the appreciation of the doctrines of Democritus.

The ethical philosophy of the laughing sage seems to have been of a purely practical cast, and to have been, in the main, the application of keen judgment to the ordinary conduct of life; thus approximating to the aphoristic wisdom of the early "Wise Men." Examples of such prudence are frequent, even in the scanty relics remaining, and have been compactly presented by Zeller: "Truth dwells in the bottom of a pit;" "Much learning is often mere folly" (*Fr.* 139-141); "The world is a stage, life a passage: you came, you saw, you departed;" "Fortune is an idol fashioned by the unwisdom of men" (*Fr.* 14). Here is the origin of the celebrated moral of Juvenal:

> "Nos te,
> Nos facimus, Fortuna, deam, cœloquo locamus."

"Not the act only, but the disposition, should be regarded" (*Fr.* 109); "Good and evil grow from the same root. Evil does not proceed from the gods, but from the blindness and malice of men" (*Fr.* 12, 13). The urgency of habitual self-restraint (*Fr.* 75), and of contentment (*Fr.* 24, 27, 29), are associated with the characteristic aim of the ethics of Democritus, the attainment of *εὐθυμία* (*Fr.* 20), healthy tranquillity. This serene temper may be compared with the Peripatetic *εὐδαιμονία*, or with the modern pursuit of "happiness," which is just as vague, as unsatisfactory, and as unscientific as any of its predecessors. Such tranquillity, however, explains the designation of Democritus as *rideus*, and points towards the simple virtues of daily life. The ethical tone of Democritus is as innocent and pure as was his own conduct.

The physical philosophy of Democritus is the most characteristic, and has been the most influential and enduring branch of his speculations. It provides the mould for his psychological assumptions, and for his ethical conclusions. The negation of immaterial realities, or agnosticism in regard to them, necessitates a spectral phenomenalism and a dim universe. Democritus held that there was only one principle—the *plenum* or *μεστόν*, and the *vacuum* or *κενόν*:

> "Omnis, ut est, igitur, per se Natura, duabus
> Consistet rebus; nam *Corpora* sunt et *Inane*."
> (Lucret. i, 420, 421; see Sext. Empir. *Adv. Math.* vii, 135-139.)

The assertion of a *vacuum* was inevitable, as long as the existence, elasticity, and interpenetrability of gaseous fluids were unknown. The *plenum* was composed of an infinite number of *atoms* (*indivisibilia*) moving freely in infinite space—for space, or the extension of the universe, was regarded as infinite:

> "Nam medium nihil esse potest, ubi Inane locus quo
> Infinita."
> (Lucret. i, 1069; comp. Aristot. *De Cœlo*, iii, 4.)

In this infinite space were contained an infinite number of worlds. The atoms were solid, impenetrable, homogeneous in quality, diverse in size and shape, though infinitesimal in magnitude (Aristot. *Met.* i, 4; Cicero, *De Fin.* I, vi, 17). They are eternal, immutable, and imperishable. Their origin is inscrutable, and beyond the domain of legitimate investigation (Aristot. *Phys.* vii, 1). The atoms possessed of themselves an incessant downward motion. The differences of size and shape produced contacts and combinations. The whole process of nature was a cycle of compositions, decompositions, and recompositions (Lucret. ii, 1000). Nothing was lost; nothing was gained. *Omnia mutantur, nil interit.* There are indications that Democritus attributed spontaneous motion, or a sort of rudimentary vitality, to atoms. The ceaseless and intricate movement of the atomic particles in space generated a gyrating motion of the incoherent mass—*Δίνη*—a whirl. This universal circumvolution probably suggested the vortices of Des Cartes (see DES CARTES), and furnishes a prelude to the modern nebular hypothesis. These eddies hurl the atoms with various collisions, winnow the subtile from the gross, and induce coherence in diversified conjunctions, whence arises, by further and modified concrescences, the endless multiplicity of things (Cicero, *Acad. Qu.* iv, 38). By this restless circulation all things have been produced, and all the vicissitudes of things. The rapidity of the orbicular motion kindles the stars, and lights up the heavenly bodies. Through the effects of this motion the earth is permeated by fiery action and quickening heat. The matters of which it is compounded originate from the dissimilar forms and magnitudes of the atoms, which are round in fire, and differ in size and shape in air, earth, and water.

The microcosm accords with the macrocosm. Man is of like constitution with his habitation. Of this inexplicable marvel of the universe neither definition nor determination is attempted. He, too, is a postulate. He is accepted for what he is, or is supposed to be. He is a compound of water and mud. His life, or soul, is a fine, diffused, and segregated fire; vital sparks of atomic, not of heavenly, flame. This is extinguished by death, and perishes with the body. All bodies are mortal, but all are renascent, *in formis mutatis.* This seems only a rude and tentative way of indicating the doctrine now generally received, of the permanence and transmutation of matter:

> "Semper motus connectitur omnis,
> Et vetere exoritur semper novus ordine certo."

Knowledge itself is the result of physical agitation. It is of two kinds: that derived directly from the mind, and that obtained from the senses. It is not obvious with what meaning the term "mind" is employed, whether as intuitive, or as reflective, or as reproductive. The conceptions of Democritus were by no means definite on the subject. The same vagueness and fluitancy attend all the tenets of Democritus not confined to purely physical topics. Perceptions are excited by effluxes—*ἔδωλα*—projected from the things perceived (*Fr.* 14, 40). Democritus, however, recognised sound as the vibratory motion of the air. Knowledge obtained through the senses—*sensus tenebricosi* (Cicero, *Acad.* IV, x, 31)—was deceptive, *σκοτίη κρίσις*. That from reason, *γνώμη γνησίη*, merited credence, if definite and clear. Nevertheless, there could be no true knowledge, *ἐτεῇ οὐδὲν ἴδμεν περὶ οὐδενός*. How could it be otherwise with a system which made being and non-being equally existent, *μὴ μᾶλλον τὸ δὲν ἢ τὸ μηδὲν εἶναι*.

With such principles, physical and psychological, no real theology was possible. Yet Democritus was unwilling, or unable, to sever himself entirely from the popular belief. He was thus involved in an inconsistency, perhaps inevitable, which is strangely illustrated by a corresponding incongruity in Comte's *Positivism.* He did not absolutely exclude divinity from the universe, but he reduced it to a vague and empty superstition, which was rather a vague rehabilitation of popular fantasies than a reputable development of philosophy. Cicero deemed it more accordant with the stupidity of his countrymen than with his own acumen. His gods were idols, fashioned out of the thinnest and subtilest atoms; and sometimes revealed themselves, especially in the dark. They were earthly ghosts! "The earth hath bubbles as the water hath; and these are of them." They were gigantic spectres, of human form, though far transcending human stature. Like goblins, fays, and peris, they were mortal; but their duration exceeded the span of human life. They had voices, and could utter sounds intelligible to men; and they foretold future events. Such divine personages could not be the object of any theology, and in no respect detracted from the materialism of the school. The theology was a pretence or a mockery.

IV. *His Influence.*—Democritus is entitled to be placed by the side of Aristotle and Plato, in regard to the effect produced on later ages by his speculations. This effect, if less immediate and less ennobling than the action of the Peripatetic and Academic systems, has been more lasting in its specific character. If less stimulant to the highest intellectual aspirations, it has the merit of having more effectually moulded the procedures of scientific research. The physical philosophy of Epicurus was entirely deduced from it, with such alterations as gave the pretence of originality, and not of mere revival. Still, it was fully absorbed into Epicureanism, and so obviously as to be incapable of being ignored. "What is in the physics of Epicurus which does not descend from Democritus?" asks Cicero (*De Nat. Deor.* I, xxv, 73; xliii, 120). "Democritus, formed by Leucippus, left his inheritance of folly to Epicurus;" observes Lactantius (*Div. Inst.* iii, 17; comp. *De Ira Dei*, x). Wherever Epicureanism spread, through Hellenic lands and through the empire of Rome, the doctrines of Democritus were accepted—the *sancta Democriti Sententia* (Lucret. iii, 372), though modified by the derivative school. Their influence was not limited to the ancient world. They reappeared with Gassendi in the 17th century. They were revived in partial and disguised form in the atomic theory of Dalton, and in the nebular hypothesis. They recur in more than their pristine vigor and exclusiveness in modern agnosticism, and in current physical schemes. The atomic speculations of Democritus are a rudimentary type of evolutionism, and of kindred dreams. It has already been stated that they furnished some of the notable suppositions of Des Cartes. They may be discerned in the *System of Positive Philosophy.* How thoroughly they are the progenitors, or, at least, the precursors of recent scientific devices, is manifested by the marvellous harmony of such opinions with the brilliant poem of Lucretius. This harmony is profoundly and instinctively felt. Its recognition is shown by the recent renewal of the earnest study of Lucretius; and by the numerous editions of his work, and the brilliant or recondite essays upon it, which have been welcomed in late years. For these reasons, the views of Democritus, and his place in the development of philosophy, cannot be safely disregarded in estimating either ancient or modern thought.

V. *Literature.*—Besides the historians of ancient philosophy, and especially Brücker, Ritter, and Zeller, the following special treatises may be advantageously consulted: Magnenus, *Democritus Reviviscens* (Paris, 1646); [in 1655, Peter Borel promised a treatise in 3 vols. fol., *De Vita et Philosophia Democriti*]; Bayle, *Dict. Hist. et Crit.* s. v.; Göding, *Diss. de Democrito et ejus Philosophia* (Upsala, 1703); Geffers, *Quæstiones Democriteæ* (Göttingen, 1829); Burchardt, *Democr. Phil. de Sensibus Fragm.* (Minden, 1830); *Fragm. der Moral des Abd. Democrits* (ibid. 1834); Papencordt, *De Atomorum Doctrina* (Berlin, 1832); Hemisöth, *Democriti de Anima Doctrina* (Bonn, 1835); Müllach, *Democriti Operum Fragmenta*, etc. (Berlin, 1846), which alone is sufficient for all ordinary purposes; Johnson, *Der Sensualismus des Demokrit.* (Plauen, 1868); Müllach, *Fragmenta Democriti, apud Fragmenta Philosophorum Græcorum*, tom. i (Paris, 1875). (G. F. H.)

Democritus, *Saint,* lived at Sinnada, in Africa, and is commemorated July 31, with Secundus and Dionysius.

Demōnax, the most distinguished of the later cynics, flourished in the 2d century of our æra. He probably lived in the time of Hadrian (A.D. 117-138), though the exact dates of his birth and death are unknown. Lucian, his only contemporary biographer, represents him as a wise and good man, and writes his history avowedly as an example for the imitation of the young of his own time. He was by birth a Cyprian, and removed to Athens, where he joined the cynic school, chiefly out of respect to the memory of Diogenes. He seems to have been free from the austerity and moroseness of the other members of his sect, but valued their indifference to outward circumstances. He was exceedingly popular at Athens, and was, no doubt, an amiable, good-humored man; but contributed nothing more to philosophy than his predecessors. He died when nearly a hundred years old, and was buried with great magnificence.

Dendrites, a name given to those Greek monks in the 12th century who passed their lives on high trees.

Dendrophŏri. See COLLEGIUM DENDROPHORIUM.

Denis (ST.), COUNCIL OF (*Concilium ad Sanctum Dionysium*). Held near Paris A.D. 768; a Frankish council of bishops and nobles, at which Pepin le Bref divided his kingdom between his sons Charlemagne and Carloman.

Denison, Edward, D.D., an English prelate, born in 1801, was educated at Oriel College, Oxford, and in 1826 elected to a fellowship at Merton College. He succeeded to the vicarage of St. Peter's-in-the-East, Oxford, and in March, 1837, to the see of Salisbury. He died at Portsmouth, March 6, 1854. In politics the bishop was a Whig, but he was constitutionally timid; and hence, while his administration was unexceptionable, it can hardly be characterized as energetic. See *Amer. Quar. Church Rev.* 1854, p. 464.

Denison, Samuel D., D.D., a Protestant Episcopal clergyman, born in Boston in 1810, was ordained deacon in 1845; for eight years thereafter engaged in missionary work in Texas, and at Great Barrington, Mass.; in 1853 elected secretary and general agent of the Foreign Committee, continuing in office until 1864; recalled October, 1868, to December, 1870; again, March to May, 1873; and again, December, 1875, to November, 1876; and died at White Plains, N. Y., Sept. 3, 1880. See Whittaker, *Almanac and Directory*, 1881.

Denne, Henry, an English Baptist minister, was born about 1600; educated at Cambridge University; took orders in the Church of England in 1630; and was ten years the parish minister at Pyrton, in Hertfordshire. In 1641 he preached the visitation sermon, in which he lashed some of the clergy for their vices; in 1643 he embraced Baptist views, was immersed in London, and began to preach at Bell Alley. He was imprisoned for preaching against infant baptism. Rev. Daniel Featly was in the same prison at the same time for opposing the Baptists. Being persecuted for his preaching, Denne entered the army, where he gained great reputation. In 1658 he had a two days' discussion with Dr. Gunning, on baptism, in St. Clement's Church, London. He defended himself with so much learning that one party said he was an Antinomian, the other party that he was an Arminian. He died about 1661. He published six works of a controversial character, between 1643 and 1658. See Wilson, *Dissenting Churches*, ii, 440.

Denne, John, D.D., an English divine and antiquary, was born at Littlebourne, May 25, 1693. He studied in the free schools of Sandwich and Canterbury, and at Corpus Christi College, Cambridge, where he became fellow in April, 1716; was ordained deacon the same year, and priest Sept. 21, 1718; soon after was nominated by the college to the perpetual cure of St. Benedict's Church, in Cambridge; whence he was preferred, in 1721, to the rectory of Norton-Davy, in Northamptonshire; but this he exchanged, Sept. 30, 1723, for the vicarage of St. Leonard, Shoreditch, in London; in 1725 he was appointed preacher of Mr. Boyle's lecture, and continued so for three years. He was promoted to the archdeaconry of Rochester, July 22, 1728; in July, 1729, was instituted to the vicarage of St. Margaret's, Rochester; but this he resigned to take possession of the rectory of Lambeth, Nov. 27, 1731. He died Aug. 5, 1767. The following are some of his sermons: *A Concio ad Clerum* (1745):—*Articles of Inquiry for a Parochial Visitation* (1732):—*A Register of Benefactions to the Parish of Shoreditch* (1745). See Chalmers, *Biog. Dict.* s. v.; Allibone, *Dict. of Brit. and Amer. Authors*, s. v.

Denton, Richard, a Presbyterian minister, was born in the north of England. He was among the first of the Puritans who came to America. The records show that he settled in Weathersfield, Conn., about the middle of the 17th century; thence he went to Hempstead, L. I.; and subsequently served the Church in Jamaica. He has been called the father of the Presbyterian Church in America. (W. P. S.)

Denton, Thomas, an English clergyman, was born at Seberham, Cumberland, in 1724, and was educated at Queen's College, Oxford, where he took his master's degree, June 16, 1752. Soon after leaving college he became curate to the pastor at Netherby, at Arthuret, and Kirkandrews. He died at Ashted, in Surrey, June 27, 1777. He wrote two poems, *Immortality* (1755, 4to):—*The House of Superstition* (1762). See Chalmers, *Biog. Dict.* s. v.; Allibone, *Dict. of Brit. and Amer. Authors*, s. v.

Denys, *Saint.* See DIONYSIUS.

Denzinger, HEINRICH JOSEPH DOMINICUS, a Roman Catholic theologian, was born Oct. 16, 1819, at Liege; ordained in 1844; and in 1848 appointed professor of exegesis at Würzburg. In 1854 he was called to the chair of dogmatics, and died June 19, 1883. He belonged to the ultramontanist party of the Church, and wrote, *Kritik der Vorlesungen von Thiersch über Katholicismus und Protestantismus* (Würzburg, 1847, 1848):—*Ueber die Echtheit des bisherigen Textes der ignatianischen Briefe* (1849):—*Enchiridion Symbolorum et Definitionum*, etc. (5th ed. 1874):—*Die Lehre von der unbefleckten Empfängniss der sel. Jungfrau Maria* (1854; 2d ed. 1855):—*Vier Bücher von der religiösen Erkenntniss* (1856, 2 vols.):—*Ritus Orientalium*, etc. (1863, 1864, 2 vols.). He was also consulter of the *Congregatio de Propaganda Fide pro Rebus Orientalibus.* (B. P.)

Deodand (Lat. *Deo*, "to God," *dandus*, "given"), a thing given or forfeited to God in consequence of its having caused the death of a human being. If a cart, for instance, should crush a man to death it would become a *deodand*, that is, to be distributed to the poor by the royal almoner, by way of expiation or atonement for the death which it has caused. See Exod. xxi, 28.

Deo Dicātus, a term applied to those engaged in religious service.

Deo Gratias (*Thanks be to God*), a response of the people in the liturgy, derived from the apostolic use of the phrase (1 Cor. xv, 57; 2 Cor. ii, 14). According to the Mozarabic rite the people said "Deo gratias" at the naming of the passage to be read as the "prophecy" in the liturgy. Bona speaks of it being used instead of "Amen," or "Laus tibi Christe," when the gospel was ended. Augustine notices it as a common mode of greeting among the monks, for which they were ridiculed by the Agonistici among the Donatists. It was sometimes used by way of acclamation on other occasions.

Depéry, JEAN-IRÉNÉE, a French prelate and bibliographer, was born at Chalex, near Gex, March 16, 1796. He was first professor of rhetoric at Chambéry, then vicar-general of the diocese of Belley, and afterwards bishop of Gap. He left several works on hagiology and similar subjects, for which see Hoefer, *Nouv. Biog. Générale*, s. v.

Deportatio is a term for carrying a bishop in a chair by his fellow-bishops, on his way to be enthroned. It was customary in the Gallican Church. A "chairing" of the bishop on the shoulders of certain persons of rank, the first time he entered his cathedral, was customary in several of the French churches in the middle ages.

Depositio (*in Hagiology*). In martyrologies the word is applied to the death-day of a saint. This meaning is given it by Maximus in the sermon *De Depositione S. Eusebii*, and strongly held by Papebroch in his *Conatus Chronologico-Histor. ad Calal. Pontiff. Roman.*

The word was doubtless used also to designate the day on which the relics were entombed.

Deprecatory. *Literæ Deprecatoriæ* are "letters of request" given by presbyters who were unable to grant the formal "dimissory letters" of the bishops. See DIMISSORY LETTERS.

Deputātus. In the Greek Church those not ordained, but nominated, to the minor services of the Church were called: the Theori, those in charge of the sacred vestments; the Camisati, those attending to the vessels in the altar-service; and *Deputati*, those who, carrying lighted tapers, in the processions preceded the deacon who bore the book of the gospels or the oblations. They corresponded to the "taper-bearers" of the Latin Church. See ACOLYTI. When necessary, they cleared the way for the bishop through the crowded church.

Deputies, Dissenting. See DENOMINATIONS, THE THREE; and DISSENTERS.

Derling, JOHANN THEOPHIL, a German theologian, was born at Aschersleben, Feb. 14, 1697; visited a large part of Germany; became minister and inspector of the gymnasium at Halberstadt; and died July 21, 1771. His principal works are, *De Consuetudine Preponendi Ænigmata apud Veteres* (Halle, 1720):—*De Servis Litteratis* (ibid.):—*De More Inurendi Stigmata Vetustissimo* (ibid.). See Hoefer, *Nouv. Biog. Générale*, s. v.

Derlington, JOHN DE, D.D., an Irish prelate, was born at Derlington (now Darlington), in the diocese of Durham, and was a Dominican friar. He was confessor to king Henry III; was promoted to the see of Dublin in September, 1279, and consecrated archbishop the following April. He died March 29, 1284. See D'Alton, *Memoirs of the Archbishops of Dublin*, p. 104.

De Ronde. See RONDE.

De Sanctis, LUIGI, a Protestant theologian, was born at Rome, Dec. 31, 1808, and when twenty-three years of age was ordained priest. He lived for some time at Viterbo and Genoa, where he greatly distinguished himself; and when he returned to Rome, he was appointed member *Qualificatore della Suprema S. Inquisizione*, and curate of the parish called *Maddalena alla Rotonda.* Being suspected by the inquisition of heterodoxy, an investigation was made concerning him. The reading of the Bible, however, brought about his final rupture with the Church, and, assisted by a Scotch minister, he left Rome, Sept. 10, 1847. Pope Pius IX, who was greatly attached to De Sanctis, had a letter written to him by cardinal Ferretti, inviting him to return. But it was in vain; "I swear before God, that in leaving Rome I had no other object in view than the salvation of my soul," such was his reply. At Malta he published, *Il Cristiano Cattolico*:—*La Confessione*, etc. In 1850 he went to Geneva, where he joined the Evangelical Church; and, when Italy was opened to the work of evangelization, he was appointed preacher by the Waldensian Church. A difference of opinion caused him to join the Plymouth Brethren at Turin, with whom he was connected for six years. The experience made in this connection led him back to the Church which was dear to him, and which appointed him professor of the Waldensian theological school at Florence, where he also edited *L'Eco della Verità.* He died Dec. 31, 1869. See *Biografia di Luigi de Sanctis* (Firenze, 1870); Comba, in Lichtenberger, *Encyclop. des Sciences Religieuses,* s. v. (B. P.)

Des Bois *de Rochefort,* ÉLÉONORE MARIE, a French prelate, was born at Paris in 1739; became doctor of the Sorbonne, vicar-general of La Rochelle, rector of St. André-des-Arts, at Paris, and finally constitutional bishop of Amiens. He also presided at the Assemblée Législative, and was one of the editors of the *Annales de la Religion.* He died in 1807, leaving, among other works, *Lettres Pastorales et Mandements* (Paris, 1800). See Hoefer, *Nouv. Biog. Générale,* s. v.

Descensus, a word applied to the *vault* beneath the altar, in which are placed the relics of the saints.

Desecration *of churches and altars.* This phrase denotes the pollution of a church or altar by the committing in it of homicide or other revolting crime, or by a removal of the relics deposited there at its consecration, so as to require "reconciliation" before service could be conducted there again.

Deseriz (or **Dericius**), JOSEPH INNOCENT, a Hungarian prelate, was born at Neitra in 1702. He taught belles-lettres, and afterwards theology, in the seminary of Raab; was called to Rome and made cardinal, employing his time in literary pursuits and embassies. He finally settled at Waitzen, in Hungary, where he continued his literary work until his death, in 1765, leaving several treatises on the ecclesiastical history of his native country, for which see Hoefer, *Nouv. Biog. Générale,* s. v.

Desert, CHURCH OF THE, a title sometimes applied to persecuted bodies of Christians, especially the Huguenots; in allusion to the vision in Rev. xii, 6.

Desertion OF THE CLERICAL LIFE. To abandon a religious life, after having once been initiated into the sacred duties, was considered a crime worthy of excommunication or other severe punishment. The Council of Chalcedon (A. D. 451), the Council of Angers (A.D. 453), the first Council of Tours (A.D. 461), a Breton council (date unsettled, probably about A.D. 555), the Council of Frankfort (A.D. 794), all decreed against the offence. Under Justinian's code, a cleric guilty of deserting his service was punished by being made a *curialis,* i. e. one charged with the burdens of the state—a political beast of burden. In a letter of pope Zacharias (A.D. 741-752) to king Pepin of France, he threatens any deserter with an anathema unless he repent and return.

Desgallards (Lat. *Gallasius*), NICOLAS, a Swiss Protestant theologian, was born in 1520. He became a citizen of Geneva in 1551, and pastor of a church in the neighborhood in 1553. He was sent to Paris in 1557, and founded a French church in London in 1560. He attended at the colloquy of Poissy with his friend Theodore de Beza, and presided at the synod of Paris, in 1565. In 1571 he was chosen by the queen of Navarre as her preacher. Calvin esteemed him very highly, and engaged him as secretary. Ancillon says that he worked with Beza on the history of the Reformed churches of France. Desgallards died about the year 1580, leaving, *Pro Gul. Favello et Collegiis Ejus,* etc. (Geneva, 1545):—*Traité de la Cêne* (ibid. eod.):—*Traité contre les Anabaptistes et les Libertins* (ibid. 1549):—*La Forme de Police Ecclésiastique Instituée à Londres en l'Église Française* (1561):—*De la Divine Essence de Jésus Christ, contre les Nouveaux Ariens* (Lyons, 1566). Desgallards also translated a great many of Calvin's works into French. See Hoefer, *Nouv. Biog. Générale,* s. v.

Deshays, JEAN BAPTISTE (called *Le Romain*), an eminent French painter, was born at Rouen in 1729, and studied under Colin de Vermont and Restout. In 1751 he drew the grand prize of the Academy. He went to Rome and remained three years, and on his return was admitted to the Royal Academy, in 1758. Among his chief productions are *The Martyrdom of St. Andrew,* and *The Death of St. Benedict.* He died at Paris, Feb. 10, 1765. See Hoefer, *Nouv. Biog. Générale,* s. v.; Spooner, *Biog. Hist. of the Fine Arts,* s. v.

Desiderāta, a name sometimes applied to the sacraments, as being desired by all Christians.

Desiderius. (1) Bishop of Vienne, martyr at Lyons; natal day, Feb. 11. According to Ado, he suffered martyrdom on May 23, and was translated Feb. 11. (2) Bishop of Ferrara; day of death, May 23. (3) The reader, martyr at Naples under Diocletian, with Januarius the bishop, and others; commemorated Sept. 19.

Desjardins (or **van den Bogaerten**), MARTIN, an eminent Dutch sculptor, was born at Breda, Holland, in 1640. He was received into the Academy of Paris at the age of thirty-one; and died in Paris in 1694. Among his numerous productions were six groups for the Church of the Mazarin College, representing the fathers of the Greek and Roman churches. See Spooner, *Biog. Hist. of the Fine Arts,* s. v.; Hoefer, *Nouv. Biog. Générale,* s. v.

Deslyons, JEAN, a French theologian, was born at Pontoise in 1615. He studied at Paris, entered the ministry, and was made doctor in the Sorbonne. On Sept. 11, 1638, he became dean of Senlis, and continued in office till his death, May 26, 1700. For a list of his numerous writings, see Hoefer, *Nouv. Biog. Générale,* s. v.

De Sola, Abraham, a Jewish rabbi, son of the following, was born in London, England, Sept. 18, 1825. Having completed his academical as well as theological studies, he accepted in 1847 a call from the Portuguese Hebrew Congregation of Montreal, Canada. In 1848 he was appointed professor of Hebrew and Shemitic literature in M'Gill College, which also conferred on him the degree of doctor of laws. He died at New York city, June 6, 1882. See Morais, *Eminent Israelites of the Nineteenth Century,* p. 53 sq. (B. P.)

De Sola, David Aaron. See SOLA, DAVID AARON.

Desplaces, LOUIS, an eminent French engraver, was born in Paris in 1682, and died in 1739. The following are his best prints: *The Martyrdom of St. Peter; The Purification.* See Hoefer, *Nouv. Biog. Générale,* s. v.; Spooner, *Biog. Hist. of the Fine Arts,* s. v.

Despotĭcæ is the name applied by the Greeks to the greater festivals of the Church, generally reckoned as twelve in number.

Despuig (*y Daneto*), *Don* ANTONIO, a Spanish prelate, was born at Palma, on the island of Majorca, March 31, 1745, of a family allied to the ancient kings of Aragon. At the end of his studies he was provided with a canonicate, and appointed to travel in France, Germany, Holland, and England, to acquaint himself with the different cities where the general councils of the East had been held. He remained for a time at Rome in 1778, then visited Calabria, Sicily, Malta, Venice, and came back to Rome in 1785, with the title of an auditor of the rota for the kingdom of Aragon. Having been appointed bishop of Orihuela by Charles IV in 1791, he was transferred, in 1795, to the archbishopric of Valencia, and in 1796 to Seville. He afterwards fell into political complications abroad, but, returning to Spain in 1798, was made councillor of state, resigning the archbishopric of Seville and receiving in exchange several rich benefices. He took part in the Conclave of Venice in 1800, and was made cardinal by Pius VII. He also shared the captivity of that pontiff in France from 1809 to 1812, and died at the baths of Lucca, May 30, 1813. See Hoefer, *Nouv. Biog. Générale,* s. v.

Dessler, WOLFGANG CHRISTOPH, a German hymn-writer, was born at Nuremberg, Feb. 11, 1660, and died while head-master of the grammar-school of his native place, March 11, 1722. Of his many hymns we mention those which have been translated into English, as, *Wie wohl ist mir, O Freund der Seele* ("O Friend of souls, how well with me," in *Lyra Germanica*, i, 147):—*Mein Jesu, den die Seraphinen* ("My Jesus, if the Seraphim," *ibid.* ii, 78):—*Ich lass dich nicht, Du musst mein Jesus bleiben* ("I leave thee not, thou art my Jesus ever," in *The Breaking Crucible*, by J. W. Alexander):—*Frisch, frisch hindurch mein Geist* ("Courage, my heart, press cheerly on," in *Christian Singers of Germany*, p. 277):—*Oeffne mir die Perlenpforten* ("How the pearly gates unfold," in *Lyra Germanica*, ii, 234). See Koch, *Geschichte des deutschen Kirchenliedes*, iii, 531 sq. (B. P.)

Destūr, in the old Persian religion, was the high-priest in every place inhabited by Parsees, who was lawgiver and judge throughout his whole district. He received one tenth of the income of the faithful.

Desubas. See MAJAL, MATHIEU.

Desverges, MARIE JOSEPH ADOLPHE NOËL, a French Orientalist, was born at Paris in 1805, where he also pursued his Oriental studies. He was a member of the Asiatic Society, and corresponding member of the Academy of Inscriptions. He died at Nice, Jan. 2, 1867, leaving, *Vie de Mohammed d'Aboulfeda*, in Arabic, with a French translation (1837):—*Histoire de l'Afrique sous la Domination Musulmane* (1841):—*L'Étrurie et les Étrusques* (1864, 2 vols.). For the *Univers Pittoresque* he prepared that part which treats of Abyssinia and Arabia. (B. P.)

Deti, GIOVANNI BATTISTA, an Italian ecclesiastic, was born at Florence in 1581. He was a kinsman to Clement VIII, who sent him to the gymnasium at Rome. Deti distinguished himself by his studies and learning, so that at the age of seventeen years he was made a cardinal. Some time after he was appointed dean of the sacred college. He died in 1630, leaving *Relatio Facta in Consistorio Coram Urbano VIII*, etc., which was printed in the collection of the Bollandists. See Hoefer, *Nouv. Biog. Générale*, s. v.

Deusdĕdit (originally *Frithona*), archbishop of Canterbury, was a West Saxon by birth. His education seems to have been good, but the place where he prosecuted his studies is unknown. He was consecrated March 26, 657, and gave entire satisfaction to the people of Canterbury. He died in 644. See Hook, *Lives of the Archbishops of Canterbury*, i, 130 sq.

Deutinger, MARTIN, a Roman Catholic philosopher, was born in 1815 at Langenpreising, in Upper Bavaria. In 1837 he was ordained priest, in 1844 became teacher at Freising, and in 1846 professor of philosophy at Munich. In 1847 he was exiled to Dillingen, in 1852 was placed on the list of retired teachers; and died Sept. 8, 1864. He published, *Verhältniss der Kunst zum Christenthum* (Freising, 1843):—*Grundlinien einer positiven Philosophie* (Regensburg, 1843-53, 7 vols.):—*Bilder des Geistes in Kunst und Natur* (ibid. 1849-51, 3 vols.):—*Geist der christl. Ueberlieferung* (1850, 2 vols.):—*Principien der neueren Philosophie und der christl. Wissenschaft* (1857):—*Das Reich Gottes nach des Apostels Johannes Lehre* (Freiburg, 1862, 2 vols.):—*Renan und das Wunder* (Munich, 1864). (B. P.)

Deutsch, David, a Jewish rabbi, who died at Sohrau, in Upper Silesia, July 31, 1873, is the author of, *Der Prophet Habakuk, mit hebräischem Commentar und deutscher Uebersetzung* (Breslau, 1837):—*Rücksprache mit allen Gläubigen des rabbinischen Judenthums* (ibid. 1842):—*Zur Würdigung der Braunschweiger Rabbiner Versammlung* (ibid. 1845):—*Protestation gegen die Versammlung* (ibid. 1846, in Hebrew and German). He also published a German translation of the polemical work, entitled *Chizuk Emunah*, of Abraham Troki (q. v.) (2d ed. 1875). See Fürst, *Bibl. Jud.* i, 207 sq. (B. P.)

Deutsch, Emanuel Oscar Menahem, a Jewish writer, nephew of the foregoing, was born at Neisse, in Silesia, Oct. 28, 1829. He studied at Berlin, and in 1855 was appointed assistant in the library of the British Museum, a position which he held until his death, which took place at Alexandria, in Egypt, May 12, 1873. He was a contributor to *Chambers's Encyclopædia*, Smith's *Dictionary of the Bible*, and Kitto's *Cyclopædia of Biblical Literature*. Besides, he contributed to various periodicals, especially the *Quarterly Review*, for which he wrote an article entitled, *What is the Talmud?* (Oct. 1867), which attracted great attention, and was soon translated into other languages. See the article TALMUD in this Cyclopædia (vol. x, p. 172 sq.). Nineteen of his papers were published after the author's death, under the title *Literary Remains* (Lond. 1874, reprinted in New York). See Morais, *Eminent Israelites of the Nineteenth Century*, p. 57 sq. (B. P.)

Deutsch, Siegmund Hermann, a missionary among the Jews, was born of Jewish parentage in 1791, at Peiskretscham, in Upper Silesia. Besides a Talmudical, he also received a secular education, and at the age of twenty-one was enrolled among the students of the Breslau University, where he devoted himself entirely to mathematics and astronomy. To avoid a lengthened military service, he early volunteered for the Prussian army, and in a short time was made an artillery officer. The rising in Greece enkindled his youthful energy and ardor, and, with a few like-minded companions, he left for that country. In 1824 he came back to Berlin, and attended the sermons of the famous Gossner. Having publicly professed his faith in Christianity, he attended the lectures of the distinguished Neander. In 1828 he was appointed to labor among the Jews at Warsaw, and in 1830 was stationed at Breslau, where he also attended the theological lectures of the different professors. In 1833 he again returned to Warsaw, and remained till 1853, when this field had to be given up, in consequence of an imperial ukase. From Poland, Mr. Deutsch went to Nuremberg, to labor there among the Jews. He died Oct. 1, 1864. See *The* (Lond.) *Jewish Herald*, 1864; Delitzsch, *Saat auf Hoffnung* (Erlangen, 1864), II, iii, 33 sq. (B. P.)

Deutschmann, JOHANN, a German Protestant theologian, was born at Jüterbogk, Aug. 10, 1625. He studied and received his degrees at Wittenberg. In 1652 he was appointed assistant of the faculty of philosophy; in 1665 travelled through Germany, Denmark, and the Netherlands; in 1657 was appointed privat-docent; and in 1662 professor extraordinary. This theologian loved particularly to dispute, and had, says Jöcher, his head full of odd notions, especially on the identity of the religion of Adam with that of the Lutherans. He died Aug. 12, 1706, leaving an immense number of publications, of which the principal are, *De Libris Scripturæ Apogryphis* (Wittenberg, 1682):—*De Petra ad Matt. xvi. 18*:—*Biblicum Abelis Theologiæ Compendium* (ibid. 1709):—*Panoplia Conversionis Augustanæ* (ibid. eod.):—*Analysis et Exegesis Compendii Hutteni* (ibid. eod.):—*Theologia Positiva Adami Protoplasti* (ibid. eod.). See Hoefer, *Nouv. Biog. Générale*, s. v.

Devas, the generic name for gods among the Hindûs. Throughout the Vedic period they were mere shapeless abstractions. It is true that human properties were frequently ascribed to them; it was even believed that gods are ultimately mortal, and can only purchase an exemption from the common lot by drinking of the potent *amrita*, or draught of immortality, that is, the *soma* (q. v.). But in the later period, when Brahminism had been introduced, the devas became more completely humanized, assumed a definite shape in the imagination of the worshipper, and exhibited all the ordinary signs of individuality. They were all regarded as inferior to the one Great Spirit, who is the primal source of being, and of whom the devas are no more than scintillations of majesty. They are worshipped, according to a Hindû writer, in order that men's minds may be composed, and led by degrees to the essential unity. The devas have their dwelling-place in *Meru*, the local heaven of the Hindûs. They are of different degrees of rank, some of them being superior, others inferior. *Devas* or *Dewas* are also the deities of the Buddhists, whether denoting the divine persons on the earth, or in the celestial regions above. There are numberless dwellings of the devas in the *lokas* or spheres above the earth. For an account of these see Hardy, *Manual of Buddhism*.

Devatas, gods worshipped by ordinary Hindûs, such as Rama, Krishna, Siva, Kali, and others.

De Veil, Carolus Maria, D.D., an English Baptist, was a Jew, born at Metz, Lorraine, and educated in Judaism; but, by comparing the Old with the New Test., became a Christian. His father tried to kill him with a sword, but he escaped, and became a canon-regular of the Augustines, at Melun, and professor of divinity in the University of Anjou, where he took his degree. In 1672 was published his *Commentary on St. Mark and St. Luke*, in defence of the Church of Rome. Being employed to write against the Huguenots, he was led to embrace Protestantism, fled to Holland, abjured popery in 1677, and finally went to England, where he was kindly received by several bishops, and admitted to holy orders in the English Church. He published a *Commentary on Solomon's Song, and the Minor Prophets*, which secured him high favor and patronage, and the bishop of London gave him free access to his library. There coming into contact with the leading Baptists, he joined their body, but thereby forfeited all his Church friends excepting Dr. Tillotson. He became pastor in Gracechurch Street, and brought much honor to the denomination. In 1684 was published his *Literal Explanation of the Acts of the Apostles*, in Latin, then translated it into English. De Veil afterwards practiced medicine for his maintenance; but the Baptists allowed him a yearly stipend till his death. See Wilson, *Dissenting Churches*, i, 205.

De Veil, Louis de Compeigne, an English theologian and author, of the same family as the foregoing, embraced the Romish religion in early life, but afterwards renounced it for the Protestant faith, left France, where he had been the king's interpreter of Oriental languages, and went to England in 1679, where he immediately joined the Established Church. He published several books exhibiting considerable learning, chiefly relating to Jewish literature. See Bogue and Bennett, *History of Dissenters*, 2d ed. i, 477.

Gnostic Representation of the Devil.

Devil, IN ART. Representations of the devil as the final tormentor of men belong to mediæval rather than to primitive art. Probably the earliest existing representation of hell is in the mosaics of Torcello, as that painted by Methodius, even if its story be true, has perished. In early art the devil generally appears in the form of a serpent as the tempter of man in this world. Didron, however, in the *Iconographie du Serpent*, mentions a gnostic combination of human and serpentine form, with leonine head and face, derived from the ancient Egyptian symbol of a lion-headed serpent. The human, being predominant, appears an anticipation of the personified serpent of the middle ages.

The Gothic or mediæval representations seem to begin in Italy with the fiend in the *Chase of Theodoric*, which, till lately destroyed by gradual and wanton mischief, adorned the front of San Zenone in Verona.

In the Laurentian MS. of Rabula (A.D. 587) there is an extraordinary representaion of the dæmoniacs of Gadara, just delivered from their tormenting spirits, who are fluttering away in the form of little black humanities of mischievous expression.

Antique Representation of Expelled Dæmons.

Devil Worship. The ancient Hebrews are distinctly charged with this sin in Deut. xxxii, 17, "They sacrificed unto devils, not to God." In later times they spoke of all false gods as devils, in consequence of the hatred which they bore to all kinds of idolatry, and we find them calling the chief deity of the Phœnicians *Beelzebub* (q. v.), the prince of devils.

Among the aboriginal races of India, remnants of which are still to be found in what are called the Hill tribes, inhabiting the forests and mountain fastnesses, devil-worship has always been widely prevalent. The evil spirits among these people are propitiated by means of bloody sacrifices and frantic dances. This form of worship also prevails in one form or another in Ceylon, on the coast of Malabar, among the Ugrian races of Siberia, and the Hill tribes on the south-western frontier of China. Devil-worship is also charged against the Yezidees (q. v.). See SHAMANISM.

De Vinne, DANIEL, a veteran Methodist Episcopal minister, was born of Roman Catholic parents, in Londonderry, Ireland, Feb. 1, 1793. Being led providentially into a Methodist watch-meeting, in Albany, N. Y., he was converted Jan. 2, 1810. He then began to study various branches of liberal learning, in which he soon became proficient, and engaged in teaching school in Brooklyn. In October, 1818, he went to New Orleans as a missionary, entered the Mississippi Conference in 1819, and was a member of the General Conference of 1824, at which time he was transferred to the New York Conference. Here he labored until his strength gave way, and he retired after forty years of active service. He died at Morrisania, N. Y., Feb. 10, 1883. See *Minutes of Annual Conferences*, 1883, p. 91; *Memorial* (N. Y. 1883).

Devoti, GIOVANNI, an Italian theologian, was born at Rome in July, 1744. At the age of twenty he was made professor of canon law in the college there, and published, the following year, a treatise called *De Notissimis in Jure Legibus*. He was made bishop of Anagni in 1789, and also of Carthage, *in partibus infidelium;* next secretary of briefs to the princes, and camerarius, and finally consulter to the Congregation of the Immunity. He accompanied Pius VII to France, at the consecration of the emperor Napoleon, and was subsequently connected with the prelates of the society of the Index. He died at Rome, Sept. 18, 1820. His principal work is entitled *Institutiones Canonicæ* (Rome, 1785; often reprinted). Devoti also undertook a *Jus Canonicum Universum*, of which only three volumes have been published (Rome, 1803, 1804, 1817). See Hoefer, *Nouv. Biog. Générale*, s. v.

Dewales, the name given to temples in Ceylon in which Brahminical deities are worshipped. Entrance to them is forbidden to Europeans. "In the sanctum are the armlets or foot-rings of Pattiné, or the weapons of the other deities, with a painted screen before them; but there are no images, or none that are permanently placed; in some of the ceremonies temporary images are made of rice, or of some other material equally perishable."—Hardy, *Eastern Monachism*, p. 201.

Dewa-lokas, the six celestial worlds which the Buddhists believe to be situated between the earth and the Brahma-lokas. In these worlds, where there are numberless mansions inhabited by the Devas (q. v.), perfect happiness is enjoyed. See Hardy, *Eastern Monachism.*

Dewar, Daniel, LL.D., a Scotch clergyman, a native of Glen-Dochart, was educated at an Independent college in England; licensed by the presbytery of Mull in November, 1812; ordained missionary at Strontian, Sept. 24, 1813; elected minister at Greyfriars' Church, Aberdeen, July 13, 1814; admitted to the professorship of moral philosophy in King's College, June 4, 1817, which he held in conjunction with the living of Greyfriars; promoted to Tron Church, Glasgow, in 1819; made principal of the university and Marischal College, Aberdeen, and resigned his charge in November, 1832. He died at Over-Durdie, May 28, 1867, in his eightieth year. See *Fasti Eccles. Scoticanæ*, ii, 12; iii, 476.

Dewey, Orville, D.D., a Unitarian minister, was born March 28, 1794. He graduated at Williams College in 1814; studied theology at Andover from 1816 to 1819, and soon after was Dr. Channing's assistant. In 1823 he became pastor of the Unitarian Church at New Bedford, Mass., and in 1835 came to the Second Unitarian Church at New York. Ill-health led him to resign his pastorate in 1848, and to retire to his farm in Sheffield, Mass. There he prepared two courses of lectures for the Lowell Institute in Boston. From 1858 to 1862 he was pastor of the new South Church in Boston. He died at Sheffield, March 21, 1882. Dr. Dewey published, *Letters on Revivals:—Discourses on Human Nature:—The Two Great Commandments*, in sermons (N. Y. 1876). (B. P.)

De Witt, Thomas, D.D., an eminent Reformed (Dutch) minister, was born at Kingston, N. Y., Sept. 13, 1791. He graduated from Union College in 1808; studied theology under Brodhead and Froeligh; also at New Brunswick Seminary in 1812, and was licensed by the Classis of New Brunswick in the same year; was pastor at Hopewell and New Hackensack from Nov. 24, 1812, to 1825; at Hopewell from 1825 to 1827; at New York from 1827 to 1874; was editor of the *Christian Intelligencer* from 1831 to 1843, and died May 18, 1874. Dr. De Witt took great interest in the various benevolent enterprises of his day, especially the Bible and Tract societies, and was greatly honored and revered by all classes of men and denominations of Christians. He was one of the vice-presidents of the Historical Society for thirty years, and president from 1870 to 1872. Dr. De Witt was a Christian minister of singular purity and simplicity. His numerous writings, chiefly on religious biography, history, and practice, are enumerated in Corwin's *Manual of the Ref. Church in America* (3d ed.), p. 239 sq.

De Witt, William R., D.D., a Presbyterian minister, was born at Rhinebeck, N. Y., Feb. 25, 1792. He was converted in 1810, and educated at Schenectady College and the Associate Reformed Seminary. In 1818 he accepted a call to become pastor of the Presbyterian Church in Harrisburg, Pa., where he remained till his death, Dec. 23, 1867. Dr. De Witt was eminently a Christian preacher. See Wilson, *Presb. Hist. Almanac*, 1868, p. 196.

De Wolfe, Charles, D.D., an eminent Wesleyan minister, was born at Wolfville, N. S., May 30, 1815. He secured a liberal education; commenced the study of law in Halifax; was converted under Dr. Crawley; united with the Methodists strongly against the wish of his parents, and in 1837 left Halifax for England, having been recommended by the Nova Scotia district to the British Conference. He received his theological training at Hoxton, London; was ordained in City Road Chapel, Sept. 14, 1838; sailed for his native land, and ministered in Halifax, Windsor, Charlottetown, Petite Rivière, Shelburne, and Sackville. In 1861 he was appointed the first theological professor in the institution at Sackville, N. B. In 1863 he was chosen president of the Conference of Eastern British America. He at length became a supernumerary, took up his residence in his native village, and died there, June 9, 1875. Dr. De Wolfe was a typical gentleman—cultured, refined. He was a man of great catholicity and of large-hearted sympathy for the poor and the suffering. His preaching was intellectual, yet fervent, and a rich treat to all. See *Minutes of the Nova Scotia Conference*, 1875, p. 7.

Dews, *in Persian Mythology.* The Dews of the teachings of Zoroaster are not personifications of the good, but of the physical and moral evil, formed to combat with the beings of light created by Ormuzd. Thus Ahriman set over against the seven Amshaspands of Ormuzd the seven Erzdews. From these, the highest beings of the kingdom of darkness, downward, there is just as great a number of harmful dæmons as of good, friendly genii. The supreme Dews have creative powers; their names are Ahriman, Ashmoph, Eghetash, Boshasp, Astujad, Tarik, Tosius; also the following, Ander, Savel, Tarmad, and Zarej. Many others are mentioned in the poetical and moral works of the Persians. An exceptional class are the Peris—light, airy beings of extraordinary beauty, living in the upper regions on the perfume of the flowers. They are fallen spirits, but the way to paradise is open to them, as also to Ahriman, if they reform.

Dexter, Flavius Lucius, a Spanish theologian, the son of St. Pacian, bishop of Barcelona, lived about the year 400. He was appointed, at the age of thirty, præfect of the prætorium, by the emperor Honorius, but soon resigned this dignity and retired to his native country, where he was made governor of Toledo. He wrote a *Chronicle*, of which Jerome speaks. This chronicle was for a long time supposed to be lost, when the Jesuit Jerome de Higuera announced that he had discovered a MS. in the library of Fulda. This MS. was brought by Torialba to Calderon, who published it under the title *Fragmentum Chronici F. L. Dextri, cum Chronico Marci Maximi*, etc. (Saragossa, 1619; reprinted in Seville in 1627, in Lyons the same year, and by Nicholas Antonio in his *Bibliotheca Hispana Vetus*). It is generally supposed, however, that the *Chronicle* published by Calderon was a manufacture of Higuera. See Hoefer, *Nouv. Biog. Générale*, s. v.

Dexter, Henry V., D.D., a Baptist minister, was born at Wayne, Me., April 3, 1815. He graduated from Waterville College, now Colby University, in 1842, and from the Newton Theological Institution in 1845. He was ordained in Brookline, Mass., Sept. 7, the same year, and was pastor of the Second Baptist Church in Calais, Me., until 1854. His next pastorate was in Augusta, until 1860, and a second time in Calais. For two years (1870–72) he was at Kennebunkport, and then accepted a call to Baldwinsville, Mass., where he died, July, 1884. See Cathcart, *Baptist Encyclop.* p. 332. (J. C. S.)

Deza, Diego, a Dominican and second grand-inquisitor of Spain, was born in 1444 at Toro, in Leon. In 1479 he succeeded Peter of Osma as professor of theology in the University of Salamanca; in 1494 was made bishop of Zamora; in 1496 bishop of Salamanca; in 1497 was elevated to the episcopal see of Jaen, which he occupied till 1500, when he was appointed bishop of Palencia. In 1505 he became archbishop of Seville, after having been previously appointed successor of Torquemada; and in 1523 was made archbishop of Toledo and primate of Spain. While on his way to Toledo he died, June 9, 1523, leaving *Defensorium Thomæ Aquinatis* (Seville, 1491; Paris, 1514). A complete edition of his works was published at Madrid in 1576. See Llorente, *Histoire de l'Inquisition d'Espagne* (Paris, 1818), i, 289 sq., 330 sq.; iv, 253 sq.; Prescott, *History of the Reign of Ferdinand and Isabella* (Lond. 1862), i, 359; ii, 291, 319; Hefele, *Cardinal Ximenes* (2d ed. Tübingen, 1851), 276 sq., 351 sq., 359; Rodrigo, *Hist. Verdadera de la Inquisicion* (Madrid, 1877); ii, 116 sq., 205 sq., 235 sq., 245 sq.; Gams, *Zur Geschichte der spanischen Staatsinquisition* (Regensburg, 1878), p. 56 sq.; Hundhausen, in Wetzer u. Welte's *Kirchen-Lexikon*, s. v. (B. P.)

Deza, Pedro, a Spanish prelate, was born at Seville, Feb. 24, 1520. He studied at Salamanca, where he obtained a chair as professor of law; afterwards became official of Compostella, auditor of Valladolid, archdeacon of Calatrava, member of the inquisition, and finally president of Grenada in 1569. He obtained the cardinal's hat in 1578, went to Rome two years later, and died there, Aug. 27, 1600. See Hoefer, *Nouv. Biog. Générale*, s. v.

Dharma, the teachings of Gotama Buddha, or the system of truth among the Buddhists. It is one of the three gems or great treasures which they prize above all other objects. It consists of several portions, which, when collected together, were divided into two principal classes, called *Suttani* and *Abhidhammani*. These are again divided into three collections, called, in the Singhalese, *Winaya*, or discipline; *Sutra*, or discourses; and *Abhidharma*, or pre-eminent truths. These collections are called *Pitakas*, one version of which consists of about four thousand five hundred leaves. These are bound up in various sizes to suit the convenience of those using them. The Dharma is literally worshipped, and the books are usually kept wrapped up with the utmost care in cloth. Whenever the Buddhist speaks of these sacred books he adds an epithet of honor. Sometimes they are placed upon a rude kind of altar by the road-side, that those who pass by may put money upon it in order to obtain merit. The Dharma is considered as perfect, having nothing superfluous and nothing wanting.—Hardy, *Eastern Monachism*, p. 167, 192. See BANA.

Diab, the law of retaliation among the Mohammedans, the nearest relative of a murdered person having the right to claim the price of blood from the murderer. The directions of the Koran on this subject are as follows: "Retaliation is commanded you in cases of murder—a freeman for a freeman, a slave for a slave, and a woman for a woman. But he who shall pardon a murderer shall obtain mercy from God; and when a man shall have pardoned a murderer, he shall no longer have it in his power to exact retaliation from him."

Diacænism (Gr. διά, *through*, and καινός, *new*), a name formerly given by the Greek Church to the week after Easter, as being the Renovation or first week of the festival of our Saviour's resurrection. On the fifth day of that week the patriarch of Constantinople, along with the bishops and principal clergy, were formerly accustomed to begin the day's services with a ceremony in the imperial palace in honor of the emperor.

Diaconia. (1) The name given to the places where food and alms were distributed to the poor by the deacons of the Church of Rome, consisting of a hall in which the distributing took place, and an oratory or chapel annexed. Over each *diaconia* a deacon presided, and the archdeacon superintended them all. The original diaconia has given place to another plan, where the hall is dispensed with, and the chapel has become a church; of these there are now fourteen, each assigned to a cardinal-deacon. (2) The word was also used, as by Gregory the Great (*Ep. ad Joann.* 24), for that part of the deacon's office which consisted in dispensing food and money to the poor. (3) The word was used for monastic almsgiving in the earlier days of monachism.

Diaconĭca, certain short prayers in the liturgy recited by the deacons, called also εἰρηνικά, as being prayers for *peace*.

Diaconoftchins, a sect of *Raskolniks* (q. v.), or dissenters from the Russo-Greek Church. They derived their name from the διάκονος or deacon Alexander, their founder. He belonged to the Church at Veska, but separated from it in 1706, in consequence of a dispute which had arisen relative to some ecclesiastical ceremonies.

Diadŏchus, bishop of Photia or Photice (Epirus), lived about 460. Photius says (*Cod.* 201) that he had read a book of this bishop, containing ten definitions and a hundred chapters. Although this book has not come down unto our time, yet we have a translation from the Greek into Latin, made by the Jesuit Turrien under this title, *S. Diadochi Episcopi Photices, Capita Centum de Perfectione Spirituali*, etc. (Florence, 1570; reprinted several times); but there is no evidence as to its authenticity. See Hoefer, *Nouv. Biog. Générale*, s.v.

Diagoras OF MELOS, a Greek philosopher, was surnamed the Atheist, and lived in the time of Socrates and Aristophanes. He must have removed from his native island to Athens before the performance of the *Clouds* of Aristophanes, B.C. 423, for he is alluded to in that piece as one well known to the Athenians. He attacked the Eleusinian mysteries, and ridiculed the popular religion. He was a disciple of Democritus of Abdera. In 411 he was accused of impiety, but the real trouble was his politics. He left the city, fearing the result of a trial, and was condemned to death by the court. He died at Corinth. His works are lost.

Diana, BENEDETTO, an eminent Venetian painter, flourished in the latter part of the 15th and first part of the 16th century. He excelled in architectural pieces, and found considerable employment in the churches of his native city. Some of his pictures are much admired, particularly his altar-piece of *St. Lucia*, in the Church of the Apostoli.

Dianæus (or **Dianius**), bishop of Cæsarea, in Cappadocia, B.C. cir. 340-362, a saintly man, but of weak judgment and vacillating character.

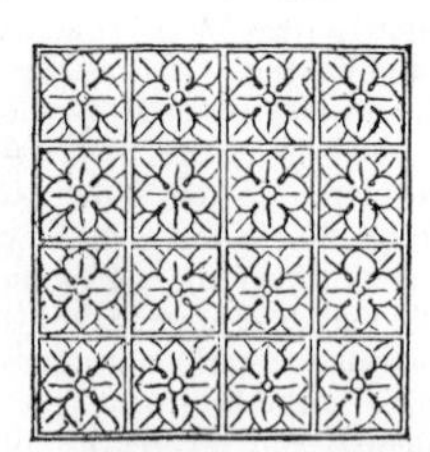

Monument of William de Valence, Westminster.

Diaper-work (or **Diapering**), *in Architecture*, an ornament of flowers applied to a plain surface, whether carved or painted; if carved, the flowers are entirely sunk into the work below the general surface; they are usually square, and placed close to each other, but occasionally other forms are used, as in the choir-screen of Canterbury; this kind of decoration was first introduced in the Early English style, when it was sometimes applied to large spaces, as in WestminsterAbbey and Chichester Cathedral; in the Decorated style it was also extensively employed. An example may be seen in the illustration of part of one of the Eleanor Crosses given under CANOPY. In the Perpendicular style diapering was used only as a painted ornament, and, as no attention has been paid to the preservation of such decorations, but few specimens remain. The origin of the name has been a source of dispute, but it is generally supposed to be taken from a kind of cloth worked in square patterns, which was then very commonly used. This cloth was called "Dyaper" i. e. D'Ypres, from the chief manufactory being at Ypres, in Belgium.

Diapsalma, a mode of singing sometimes adopted in the early Christian churches, in which the priests led the psalmody and the people sang responses.

Diarmaid (Lat. *Dermitius*), a very common name in Ireland, and borne by many of the saints: some of these are simply placed upon a day in the calendars, with or without their father's name and the place of dedication, while others have a few particulars preserved by history or tradition. Several of them are enumerated by Smith, *Dict. of Christ. Biog.* s. v.

Diatĭmus, bishop of Lymirus, in Lycia, who, with other of the Lycian prelates, wrote to Basil, (*Epist.* 403, 420) in 375, expressing their desire to separate themselves from the heterodox Asiatic bishops as well as to enter into communion with him.

Diaz, Diego Valentino, an eminent Spanish painter, lived at Valladolid, and executed many works for the churches and convents of that city. He founded the House of Mercy, or Hospital for Orphans, and died in 1660.

Diaz, Juan, a Spanish martyr, was born at Cuença, in Castile. While a student at Paris, he became a convert to Protestantism, in 1540. In 1545 he left Paris for Geneva, with a recommendation to Calvin. From Geneva he went to Strasburg, where he was held in high esteem by Martin Bucer; at the latter's request, Diaz accompanied him to the diet of Ratisbon, December, 1545. Pietro Malvenda, who was present at Ratisbon, tried everything to bring Diaz back to the Church of Rome, but in vain. At last Malvenda succeeded in influencing Diaz's brother Alfonzo to commit fratricide. Alfonzo, who was an officer at the papal court, hastened from Rome, and perpetrated the foul deed at Neuburg-on-the-Danube, March 27, 1546. In Germany this fratricide produced general horror; but the emperor Charles V and the pope approved of it, and the murderer was not punished. He however committed suicide at Trent in 1551. Diaz wrote a confession of faith, *Christianæ Religionis Summa*, which was published at Neuburg in 1546, and put into the index by Pius IV in 1564. It was reprinted at Strasburg in 1692 and 1694, and Zurich in 1763. It was translated into French by Crespin, *Confession de Foy, qui est un Sommaire de la Religion Chrétienne* (1565; a Spanish translation was published in 1865):—*Summa de la Religion Cristiana.* In the epistolary part of Calvin's works are found several letters of Diaz, addressed to Calvin in 1545 and 1546. See Beza, *Icones* (Geneva, 1580); Bayle, *Dict. Hist.* ii,312; Boehmer, *Spanish Reformers of Two Centuries, from* 1520 (Lond. 1874), p. 185-216; Picheral-Dardier, in Lichtenberger's *Encyclop. des Sciences Religieuses*, s. v. (B. P.)

Diblik, in Slavonic mythology, was a goddess of *fire.*

Dibon OF GAD. This place has lately acquired a great archæological celebrity in consequence of the discovery there of the famous Moabitic stone of king

Ruins of Dibon.

Mesha (q. v.). The following is Tristram's description of the locality (*Land of Moab*, p. 147):

"Dibon is a twin city, upon two adjacent knolls, the ruins covering not only the tops, but the sides, to their base, and surrounded by one common wall. Close under both knolls, on the west, runs a little wady, in which, after the late rains, we found a puddle of water here and there; and beyond the wady the even plain ceases, and the country becomes rocky and undulating. All the hills are limestone, and there is no trace of any basalt but what has been carried here by man. Still, there are many basaltic blocks, dressed, and often with lime on them, evidently used in masonry; and we found a few traces of carvings on other stones. The place is full of caverns, cisterns, vaulted underground storehouses, and rude semicircular arches, like the rest." (For plan of the ruins, see cut on following page.)

Dibric. See DUBRICIUS.

Dicaiophỹlax (Gr. δίκαιος, *just*, and φύλαξ, *a keeper*), an officer in the Greek Church who takes care of the Church's title and her charters.

Dicasius, bishop of Tabia, in Galatia Prima (cir. A.D. 314-325).

Dicastillo, JUAN DE, a Spanish Jesuit, was born in 1585 at Naples; joined his order in 1600; was professor of theology and philosophy at Murcia, Toledo, and Vienne, and died in 1653 at Ingolstadt. He wrote, *De Justitia et Jure*, etc. (Antwerp, 1641):—*De Incarnatione* (ibid. 1642):—*De Sacramentis* (1646-52, 3 vols.):—*De Juramento* (1662). See Langhorst, in Wetzer u. Welte's *Kirchen-Lexikon*, s. v. (B. P.)

Dice. The playing at dice or other games of chance has always been discountenanced by the Church. The *Pædagogue* of Clement forbids it. Apollonius denounces the Montanists for it, asking whether prophets play at dice. The *Apostolical Canons* forbid the practice, under pain of degradation or excommunication. The Council of Eliberis (A.D. 305) and the Trullan Council (at the close of the 7th century) both forbade it. Justinian denounced games of chance, and even the being present at them, affixing a penalty to the act by the clergy, of suspension and seclusion in a monastery for three years. The account Jerome gives of Synesius alleging his own propensity to gambling as

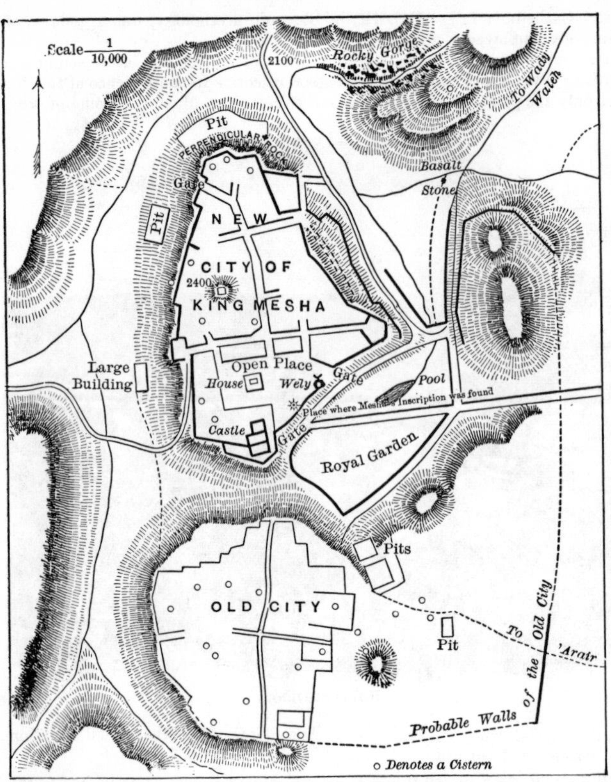

Plan of the Ruins of Dibon. (From the *Zeitschrift des Paläst. Vereins*, 1879, i.)

a reason for not being made bishop, and the account of the accusation by certain nuns of the convent of St. Radegund at Poictiers against their abbess, for dicing, and other references of like character, show that the habit was nevertheless all too frequent in the Church.

Dicerium, a double wax taper used by the bishops of the Greek Church in the benediction of the book of the gospels lying on the holy table. The *dicerium* was held to typify the two natures of Christ, while the *tricerium* symbolized the Trinity.

Dichu, an Irish saint, son of Trichem, of Sabhall, the first disciple of St. Patrick, in Ulster, A.D. cir. 432. He is commemorated April 29.

Dick, Robert, D.D., a Scotch clergyman, son of Rev. James Dick, minister in Glasgow, was proposed on trial for the ministry, July, 1746; licensed to preach Jan. 14, 1747; presented to the living at Lanark in September, 1748, and a settlement ordered by the Assembly, May 15, 1750. On presenting himself for ordination in September, he was refused admission to the Church, a mob having carried off the keys, and he was ordained in the Tron Church, Glasgow. Another mob prevented his entry into the church on Sunday, in October, and he preached at Lee, with the approval of the presbytery. In August, 1754, he was transferred to New Greyfriars' Church, Edinburgh; was translated to the Old Church, but changed to Trinity College Church, April 26, 1758; was appointed in May, 1760, a commissioner to visit the Highlands and select suitable places for missionaries under the royal bounty. He did not go, however, and died Aug. 24, 1782, aged sixty years. He was one of the most able and distinguished ministers of his day. He published two single *Sermons* (Edinb. 1758, 1762):—*The State of the Case* (ibid. 1763). See *Fasti Eccles. Scoticanæ*, i, 38, 70; ii, 308.

Dickenson, E. W., D.D., a Baptist minister, was born at Salem, N. J., Jan. 28, 1810. He graduated from the Hamilton Institution in 1835; was ordained at Poughkeepsie in 1836, and continued as pastor there for forty years. His other pastorates were at Danvers, Mass., Burlington, N. J., Elmira, N. Y., Lewisburg, and Marcus Hook, Pa., in which place he resided fourteen years. He died Dec. 8, 1875. See Cathcart, *Baptist Encyclop.* p. 382. (J. C. S.)

Dickerson, James Stokes, D.D., a Baptist minister, was born in Philadelphia, Pa., July 6, 1825. He graduated from Madison University in 1848; soon after was associated with Dr. M. B. Anderson in the management of *The New York Recorder*, and was subsequently connected with *The Chronicle*. His pastorates were at Wilmington, Del., Pittsburgh, Pa., and South Boston, Mass. He died March 21, 1876, in Chicago, where he had gone to connect himself with *The Standard*. See *Memoir* (N. Y.). (J. C. S.)

Dickey, Ebenezer, D.D., a Presbyterian minister, was born near Oxford, Chester Co., Pa., March 12, 1772. He graduated from the University of Pennsylvania in 1792, was licensed by the First Associate Reformed Presbytery of Pennsylvania in 1794; in 1796 was settled over the united congregations of Oxford and Octorora, Pa. His connection with the last charge lasted only four years, and that with Oxford until his death, May 31, 1831. See Sprague, *Annals of the Amer. Pulpit*, iv, 133.

Dickey, John Miller, D.D., a Presbyterian minister, was born at Oxford, Pa., Dec. 15, 1806. He prepared for college at Oxford and Milton; graduated from Dickinson College in 1824, and from Princeton Theological Seminary in 1827; was licensed by the New Castle Presbytery, Oct. 17, 1827, and ordained by the same, May 19, 1830. He preached the first year under a commission from the Board of Domestic Missions in the north-eastern counties of Pennsylvania, and then labored in Georgia and Florida. Having accepted a call to become pastor of the Church at New Castle, Del., he was ordained; next went to Oxford and Upper West Nottingham, Pa.; for fifteen years, while pastor, was also principal of the Oxford Female Seminary, and died March 21, 1878. Dr. Dickey was deeply interested in many philanthropic and educational institutions. See *Necrolog. Report of Princeton Theol. Sem.* 1878, p. 12.

Dickinson, Baxter, D.D., a Presbyterian minister, was born at Amherst, Mass., April 14, 1795. He united with the Congregational Church there in 1811; graduated from Yale College in 1817, and from Andover Theological Seminary in 1821; was pastor of the Congregational Church in Longmeadow, from 1823 to 1829; of the Third Presbyterian Church in Newark, N. J., from 1829 to 1835; professor in Lane Theological Seminary from 1835 to 1839; in Auburn Theological Seminary from 1839 to 1847; in Andover Theological Seminary in 1848; secretary of the American and Foreign Christian Union, Boston, Mass., from 1850 to 1859; resided at Lake Forest, Ill., from 1859 to 1868, and thereafter in Brooklyn, N. Y., until his death, Dec. 7, 1875. Dr. Dickinson was one of the acknowledged leaders in the New-school Presbyterian Church, and was moderator of the assembly of that Church in Philadelphia, in

1839. He was a man of fine scholarship, a thorough teacher, and a preacher of unusual ability. See *Presbyterian*, Dec. 18, 1875; *Gen. Cat. of Auburn Theol. Sem.* 1883, p. 257.

Dickinson, Charles, an Irish prelate, was born in August, 1792, at Cork, Ireland. He graduated, in 1815, from Trinity College, Dublin, with distinction; in 1819 was appointed assistant chaplain of the Magdalen Asylum, and three years later at the Female Orphan House, where he continued for nine years; next became one of the archbishop of Dublin's chaplains; in July, 1833, was appointed to the parish of St. Ann's, Dublin; in 1840 was made bishop of Meath, and died July 12, 1842. See *The Church of England Magazine*, Aug. 1846, p. 107.

Dickinson, Moses, a Presbyterian minister, was born at Springfield, Mass., Dec. 12, 1695. He graduated from Yale College in 1717, and his first charge was Hopewell, N. J., where his labors were attended by extraordinary revivals, and his first appearance at the synod was in 1722. In 1727 he removed, as pastor, to Norwalk, Conn. On the death of his brother Jonathan, he completed the latter's second *Vindication of the Sovereignty of Grace.* Early in 1764 he sought an assistant in William Tennent, Jr., the son of the patriarch of Freehold, N. J., but during the closing years of his life, after Tennent's removal, he pursued his work alone. He died May 1, 1778. (W. P. S.)

Dickinson, Richard William, D.D., a Presbyterian minister, was born in the city of New York, Nov. 21, 1804. He graduated from Yale College in 1823; studied two years thereafter in the theological seminary at Princeton, N. J.; was licensed to preach by the Second Presbytery of New York, March 5, 1828; ordained an evangelist Oct. 24 following; settled over the Presbyterian Church at Lancaster, Pa., Oct. 18, 1829; resigned in 1833 on account of injured voice; spent the following winter in Florida, and the next season in foreign travel, and then resumed preaching on his return to New York city, where he supplied the pulpit of the Market Street Dutch Church from 1834 to 1835. In 1836 he became pastor of the Bowery Presbyterian Church, but resigned the April following; was installed over the Canal Street Presbyterian Church, Oct. 22, 1839; resigned in 1844; in November, 1859, was invited to take charge of the Mount Washington Valley Church, and acted as its pastor for about thirteen years. He died at Fordham, Aug. 16, 1874. See *Obituary Record of Yale College*, 1875; *Gen. Cat. of Princeton Theol. Sem.* 1881, p. 44.

Dickson, Charles, a Scotch clergyman, studied at Edinburgh University; was licensed to preach Dec. 6, 1821; presented to the living at Wamphray in November, 1824; was ordained May 5, 1825, and died May 10, 1853. He published, *The Case of Blind Bartimeus Considered and Illustrated:—Baptismal Regeneration Tested by the Scriptures*, etc.:—*An Account of the Parish.* See *Fasti Eccles. Scoticanæ*, i, 666.

Dickson, Cyrus, D.D., a Presbyterian minister, was born in Erie County, Pa., Dec. 20, 1816. He graduated at Jefferson College, and was ordained, in 1839, pastor at Franklin. After remaining there several years, he received a call from Wheeling, W. Va., where he labored earnestly and successfully until he was called to Baltimore, in 1856, as pastor of Westminster Presbyterian Church, remaining there fourteen years. In 1870 he was elected secretary of the Presbyterian Board of Home Missions, in which office he performed the great work of his life. In 1870, on the reunion of the Presbyterian Church, he was appointed permanent clerk of the General Assembly, which office he held at the time of his death, Sept. 11, 1881. See *Baltimore Presbyterian*, Sept. 16, 1881. (W. P. S.)

Dickson, the family name of several Scotch clergymen:

1. David (1), A.M., was regent in Glasgow University; admitted assistant minister at Irvine, March 31, 1618; proposed for Edinburgh in October, 1620; deprived by the High Court of Commission, Jan. 10, 1622, and confined in Turriff for opposing the Articles of Perth, but permitted to return in July, 1623. In the discharge of his official duties he secured the esteem of the gentry, nobles, and parishioners. For employing two of his countrymen in 1637, who were under Irish Episcopal ban, he was again tried by the High Commission. The same year he refused to accept the service-book attempted to be obtruded. He was a member of the assembly in 1638, appointed chaplain to the Ayrshire regiment in 1639, and the same year was elected moderator of the General Assembly. He was translated to the professorship of divinity in Glasgow University, Jan. 30, 1640; admitted to the Cathedral Church, Glasgow, May 18, 1640, but attended only one meeting of session, and a commissioner was appointed, March 29, 1649, to appear against his translation to Edinburgh. He was appointed to the second charge at Edinburgh, April 12, 1650, and held the professorship of divinity in conjunction. He was elected, a second time, moderator of the General Assembly, July 21, 1652; deprived in October, and died in December, 1662, aged seventy-eight years. As a preacher, he was the most popular and powerful of his day, and his services at Irvine were crowned with wonderful success. He took a foremost part at the Glasgow Assembly in 1638, in the overthrow of episcopacy. When the Church divided into Resolutioners and Protesters, he took part with the former. He published, *A Treatise on the Promises* (Dublin, 1630):—*Explanation of the Epistle to the Hebrews* (Aberdeen, 1635):—*Expositio Analytica Omnium Apostolicarum Epistolarum* (Glasgow, 1645):—*True Christian Love*, in verse (1649):—*Exposition of the Gospel of Matthew* (Lond. 1651):—*Explanation of the Psalms* (ibid. 1653-55, 3 vols.):—*Therapeutica Sacra* (Edinb. 1656; transl. ibid. 1664):—*A Commentary on the Epistles* (Lond. 1659):—*Prælectiones in Confessionem Fidei* (fol. transl.):—*Truth's Victory over Error* (Lond. 1658):—several pamphlets in the disputes with the doctors of Aberdeen (4to), and some in defence of the public resolutions. *The Directory for Public Worship* was drawn up by him, with the assistance of Alexander Henderson and David Calderwood, and *The Sum of Saving Knowledge*, by him, in conjunction with James Durham. He also published some minor poems: *The Christian Sacrifice*, and *O Mother Dear, Jerusalem.* See *Fasti Eccles. Scoticanæ*, i, 27; ii, 8, 153.

2. David (2), D.D., a native of Kilbucho, graduated at Edinburgh University, May 22, 1734; was licensed to preach, Aug. 16, 1744; presented to the living at Newlands in June, 1755, and ordained March 31, 1756; deposed March 2, 1763, but restored in June; suspended from the ministry, and finally deposed, April 22, 1767; contested his claim for stipend, and obtained decision in his favor in February, 1768. He died April 9, 1780, aged seventy years. He published *A Letter to the Rev. Mr. Kinloch* (Edinburgh, 1750):—*A Letter to the Rev. John Adams* (ibid. eod.). See *Fasti Eccles. Scoticanæ*, i, 253.

3. David (3), third son of the preceding, was educated at the parish school of West Linton, the grammar-school at Peebles, and the universities of Glasgow and Edinburgh. He was licensed to preach in August, 1775; appointed assistant and successor at Liberton, and ordained May 1, 1777; transferred to Bothkennar, April 23, 1783; was brought forward as a candidate for St. Cuthbert's in 1785; accepted a call to Canongate Chapel of Ease, Oct. 1, 1795, as the first minister there; was transferred to Trinity College, Edinburgh, Feb. 27, 1799; promoted Nov. 30, 1801, to New North Church, and died Aug. 3, 1820, aged sixty-six years. He published four single *Sermons* (Edinburgh, 1779-1819):—*Sermons Preached on Different Occasions* (ibid. 1818):—*Gospel Tidings:—An Account of Bothkennar.* See *Fasti Eccles. Scoticanæ*, i, 33, 69, 91, 226; ii, 695.

4. David (4), D.D., eldest son of the foregoing, was educated at the parish school of Bothkennar, and at Edinburgh University; was licensed to preach in December, 1801; called in January, and ordained March 10, 1802, minister of the second charge, Kilmarnock; presented to St. Cuthbert's, Edinburgh, March 29, 1803, and died July 28, 1842, aged sixty-two years. He was indefatigable and zealous in promoting benevolent and missionary societies, and was secretary of the Scottish Missionary Society for many years. He published five single *Sermons* (Edinburgh, 1806-31):—*Discourses Doctrinal and Practical* (1837):—edited *Memoir of Miss Fanny Woodbury* (1826):—*Sermons by the Rev. W. F. Ireland, D.D.* (1829):—*Lectures and Sermons by the Rev. George B. Brand* (1841), and communicated several articles to the *Edinburgh Cyclopædia, Christian Instructor*, and other periodical works. See *Fasti Eccles. Scoticanæ*, i, 127; ii, 177.

5. Robert, D.D., was licensed to preach Dec. 4, 1782; presented by the magistrates and kirk session to the living of the second charge, South Leith, in January, and ordained July 17, 1787; translated to the first charge, Sept. 29, 1790, and died Jan. 25, 1824, aged sixty-five years. His discourses were marked by Scriptural research, a vigorous understanding, a chaste, nervous style, and an energetic expression. See *Fasti Eccles. Scoticanæ*, i, 102, 103, 108.

Dicterium. See Pulpit.

Dictinius, a Priscillianist, whose writings are condemned by Leo the Great (*Epist.* xv, 16), at length recanted, and was restored to the Church.

Dictionaries, Biblical, Theological, and Ecclesiastical. We continue here our account of the leading works of this kind which have appeared since the article in volume II was printed.

New editions of the great cyclopædias of Herzog and Wetzer u. Welte are now in course of publication, continued since the death of the principal editors, the former by Plitt and Hauch, and the latter by Hergenwöthe and Kaulen. The works have been almost entirely rewritten and greatly improved, but they still retain the excellences and defects of the former edition as to contents and manner of treatment.

Meanwhile a very extensive work of a similar character, *Encyclopédie des Sciences Religieuses*, has been edited by F. Lichtenberger (Paris, 1877-82, 13 vols.), which is Protestant, slightly rationalistic and scholarly, but rather adapted to popular use than to profound or minute research.

Dr. Philip Schaff has prepared a condensed and modified translation of Herzog's work, with many fresh articles, under the title of *Religious Encyclopædia* (New York and Edinburgh, 1881-84, 3 vols.). Except in size, it partakes of the qualities, both excellent and otherwise, that characterize its great original. Notwithstanding the American additions, it still is strongly Germanic in its range and method. The Biblical portion of the work is comparatively scant, and the biographical relatively preponderant. As a natural consequence of its origin, the chief excellence lies in the historical department, although, of course, it has room for little more than an abstract from the copious stores of Herzog. It is to be regretted that the plan of the work does not include cuts, which so often aid in the illustration, especially of archæological subjects. Nevertheless it is a valuable and convenient compendium of religious knowledge, and well adapted to the wants of such as cannot afford a more extensive work, yet desire something beyond the brief unscientific manuals heretofore current.

Dr. Joseph Schäfler, *Handlexikon der Katholischen Theologie* (Ratisbon; begun in 1880 and still in course of publication), is to be completed in four volumes. Its treatment of topics is fresh, its tone liberal, its arrangement good. It is altogether a very satisfactory work on Roman Catholic theology, for general use.

Dr. J. Hamburger, *Real-Encyklopädie für Bibel und Talmud* (Strelitz, 1866-83. Division I, treating of Biblical topics, was completed in 1867; Division II, of Talmudical subjects, in 1883. A second and improved edition of Division I is to appear in the near future). This work, prepared by a Jewish rabbi of Germany, has a conceded value in the department of Jewish, and also of general, archæology, and has no serious competitor.

Dr. Daniel Schenkel, *Bibel-Lexikon* (Leipsic, 1868-75, 5 vols. 8vo, illustrated). This work is characterized by thoroughness and independence, and is designed to meet the demand for a Biblical and Theological Dictionary of small compass, and suited to the general Church-public of Protestant Germany. It is liberal or slightly rationalistic in its treatment of subjects, as might be expected in the work of its corps of collaborators.

Dr. Eduard C. A. Riehm, *Handwörterbuch des Biblischen Altertums* (Bielefeld and Leipsic, 1875-84, 8vo, illustrated), is the work of a number of conservative German scholars, and forms an excellent manual, more like English Bible Dictionaries in its range and execution than any other.

H. Zeller, *Biblisches Wörterbuch* (2d and improved edition, Gotha, 1866). A useful manual, of limited compass.

Dr. F. X. Kraus, *Real-Encyklopädie der Christlichen Alterthümer* (Freiburg, 1880 sq., still incomplete). The scope of this work embraces the first six centuries of the Christian æra. Its articles are copiously illustrated with wood-cuts, mostly taken from Martigny's *Dictionnaire des Antiquités Chrétiennes.* The work is, upon the whole, a valuable compilation. Its authors are of the Roman Catholic faith.

Dr. William Smith's *Dictionary of Christian Antiquities* (Lond. 1875-80, 2 vols.), and his *Dictionary of Christian Biography* (ibid. 1877 sq.; to be completed in four vols., of which three have already been issued), have been prepared, with the aid, in the former work, of Prof. Cheatham, and, in the latter, of Prof. Wace, on the same comprehensive and scholarly plan as his *Dictionaries of Classical Antiquities and Biography;* but they only come down to the time of Charlemagne.

Potter's Complete Bible Encyclopædia, edited by Rev. W. Blackwood, D.D., LL.D. (Phila. 1873 sq., 3 vols. 4to), includes many theological and biographical articles; and is intended for popular use. It is superbly, but not always appropriately, illustrated.

J. H. Blunt, *Dictionary of Doctrinal and Historical Theology* (Lond. 1872, imperial 8vo), and *Dictionary of Sects, Heresies*, etc. (ibid. 1874), are useful preparations from a High-Church point of view.

M. E. C. Wolcott, *Sacred Archæology* (Lond. 1868, 8vo), contains interesting notices of ecclesiastical art and institutions, especially relating to the Anglican Church.

F. G. Lee, *Glossary of Liturgical and Ecclesiastical Terms* (Lond. 1877, 8vo, illustrated), is chiefly occupied with description of sacred vestments and appurtenances, all from a High-Church standpoint.

Parker's Glossary of Terms used in Architecture (Lond. 1845, 4th ed. 3 vols. 8vo, copiously illustrated) is a very convenient and useful summary of details relating to architectural science, including churches particularly.

Dida, seventh abbess of the Benedictine convent of St. Peter, Lyons, in the time of bishop Fucualdus.

Dido, (1) the twenty-sixth bishop of Poictiers, cir. A.D. 673; (2) the thirty-second bishop of Nogent, in the 8th century; (3) the thirty-seventh bishop of Tours, A.D. 742-744.

Didymia, fourth abbess of the convent of Sante-Croix, at Poictiers, in the 6th century.

Didy̆mus, a martyr at Alexandria, A.D. 304, and commemorated April 28, is said to have been a Christian teacher there, and to have been beheaded for aiding the escape of Theodora, a Christian girl, from a fate worse than death, on account of her faith.

Diecmann, Johann, a German philologist and theologian, was born at Stade, June 30, 1647. He studied at Giessen and Wittenberg, and was appointed president of the college in his native place, superintendent of the duchies of Bremen and Weser, and later professor of theology in the university of Kiel. He died at Kiel, July 4, 1720, leaving several dissertations, enumerated in the sixth volume of the *Historia Bibliothecæ Fabricianæ*. See Hoefer, *Nouv. Biog. Générale*, s. v.; Chalmers, *Biog. Dict.* s. v.

Diedo, Giovanni, an Italian theologian, born at Bassano in 1487, filled with distinction the highest functions in the Augustinian order, and died at Bologna in 1553, leaving, *Catechismus de Arte Neapolitana* (Rome, 1547):—*Commentarii in Pauli Epistolas ad Timotheum* (1553):—*Expositiones in Epistolas Petri, Jacobi et Judæ*, etc. See Hoefer, *Nouv. Biog. Générale*, s. v.

Diefenbach, Martin, a German theologian, born at Frankfort-on-the-Main in 1661, devoted himself to the conversion of the Jews, and published on this very subject two volumes in German, with a Latin title *Judæus Convertendus* (Frankfort, 1696):—*Judæus Conversus* (1709). He died in 1709. See Hoefer, *Nouv. Biog. Générale*, s. v.

Diego de Deza. See Deza.

Diego de Yepes, a Spanish prelate and historian, was born at Yepes, near Toledo, in 1531. He joined the order of the Hieronymites, and became successively bishop of Albarracin, confessor of the king, Philip II, and bishop of Tarragona. He died in 1614, leaving, *Historia de la Persecucion de Ingalaterra* (Madrid, 1599):—*Vida de la Madre Teresa de Jesus* (ibid. eod.; Saragossa, 1606):—*De la Muerte del Rey Felipe Segundo* (Milan, 1607). See Hoefer, *Nouv. Biog. Générale*, s. v.

Diego, Francisco Garcia, D.D., a Roman Catholic prelate, who had for some time directed the missionaries as præfect, was on April 27, 1840, appointed first bishop of California, residing at Santa Barbara, where he at once prepared to erect a Franciscan monastery and a theological seminary, as well as a cathedral and residence; but the income of the "Pious Fund" of California—created at the time of the Jesuit missions there (1642 sq.) by charitable benefactors—was withheld, as the Mexican government had appropriated the property in which it was invested. In 1844, however, he obtained a grant of thirty-five thousand acres of land, by means of which he established a college at Santa Iñez mission. Diego died at Santa Barbara, April 30, 1846. See De Courcy and Shea, *Hist. of the Cath. Church in the United States*, p. 693.

Diepenbeck, Abraham van, an eminent Flemish painter, was born at Bois-le-Duc in 1607, and died at Antwerp in 1675. He seems first to have practiced painting on glass. Some of his efforts of this kind are still admired in Amsterdam, particularly the windows in the cathedral, on which he painted the works of mercy, and those of the Church of the Dominicans, which are embellished with representations from the life of St. Paul. Several pictures by this master were brought to the United States some years ago, and sold for enormous prices. One of these, the *Mocking of Christ*, was a most admirable performance. See Spooner, *Biog. Hist. of the Fine Arts*, s. v.; Hoefer, *Nouv. Biog. Générale*, s. v.

Diepenbrock, Andreas van, a Finlandish theologian, was born at Riga, Nov. 2, 1624, studied at Marburg and Giessen, fulfilled various ecclesiastical functions, and died in his native place, April 4, 1698, leaving, *De Ente et Potentia*:—*De Judicio Contradictionis Formalis in Disciplinis Realibus Exercitæ* (1698). See Hoefer, *Nouv. Biog. Générale*, s. v.

Dier (**Dihenfyr**, or **Deiferus**), a Welsh saint, died about A.D. 664, and is commemorated Nov. 21.

Dieringer, Franz Xavier, a Roman Catholic theologian of Germany, was born at Rangendingen, in Hohenzollern, Aug. 22, 1811. In 1835 he was ordained priest, in 1840 was made professor of dogmatics at Speyer, in 1843 at Bonn, and in 1853 became a member of the chapter at Cologne. In 1856 he was spoken of as a candidate for the Paderborn bishopric, in 1864 for the Treves and in 1866 for the Cologne bishoprics; but his name was always erased from the list by the government as a "persona minus grata." When, in 1869, the perplexities of the Vatican council commenced, he belonged to those who regarded the declaration of the papal infallibility as non-opportune. When, finally, the infallibility of the pope was adopted by the council, he retired from his office, and died Sept. 8, 1876, at Veringendorf, in Hohenzollern, leaving, *System der göttlichen Thaten des Christenthums* (Mayence, 1842, 2 vols.; 2d ed. 1857):—*Kanzelvörtrage an gebildete Katholiken* (1844):—*Leben des heiligen Karl Borromäus* (Cologne, 1846):—*Lehrbuch der Katholischen Dogmatik* (Mayence, 1845; 5th ed. 1866):—*Das Epistelbuch der Katholischen Kirche, theologisch erklärt* (ibid. 1863, 3 vols.):—*Laienkatechismus über Religion, Offenbarung und Kirche* (ibid. 1855). (B. P.)

Dierkens, Petrus, a Flemish theologian, was born at Ghent; entered the Dominican order in 1620, and taught both philosophy and theology at Louvain. He was, in succession, doctor of theology, school director, and vicar provincial of Lower Germany, and died Aug. 3, 1675, leaving, *Exercitia Spiritualia* (Ghent, 1659):—*De Vita Contemplativa*, etc. (ibid. 1663):—*De Obligationibus Regulæ et Constitutionum* (ibid. 1667). See Hoefer, *Nouv. Biog. Générale*, s. v.

Dies, used, like the English "day," to designate a festival: (1) *Dies Adoratus*, Good Friday. (2) *Dies Ægyptiaci*, certain "unlucky days" supposed to have been discovered by the ancient Egyptians from astrological calculations, and marked in the calendars, but their observance was forbidden. (3) *Dies Boni*, used to designate festivals. (4) *Dies Consecrati*, the four days at Christmas observed as festival days, on which no courts were to be held. (5) *Dies Magnus Felicissimus* used for Easter-day; *Dies Magnus*, also used for the Last day. (6) *Dies Natalis*, birthday. (7) *Dies Neophytorum*, the eight days of special observance, from Easter-day to its octave, during which the newly baptized wore white garments. (8) *Dies Palmarum* (or, *In Ramis Palmarum*), Palm Sunday. (9) *Dies Sancti*, the forty days of Lent. (10) *Dies Scrutinii*, the days on which candidates for baptism were examined, especially Wednesday in the fourth week of Lent. (11) *Dies Solis, Dies Lunæ*. See Week. (12) *Dies Tinearum* or *Murium*, certain days when ceremonies were performed to avert the ravages of moths or mice. (13) *Dies Viridium*, Thursday of holy week in some ancient German calendars; "Green Thursday" in modern German ones. See Maunday Thursday. (14) *Dies Votorum*, a wedding-day among the Lombards.

Dies (or **Diaz**), Gaspar, a Portuguese painter, sometimes called "the Portuguese Raphael," flourished about 1525, and was instructed in the school of Michael Angelo at Rome. On his return to Portugal he executed, by order of the king, a number of excellent pictures for the churches. In 1534 he painted his celebrated *Descent of the Holy Spirit* for the Church of the Miseracordia. He died at Lisbon in 1571. See Hoefer, *Nouv. Biog. Générale*, s. v.; Spooner, *Biog. Hist. of the Fine Arts*, s. v.

Diesbach, Johann, a German Jesuit, was born at Prague in 1729, became successively professor at Olmütz, Brunn, Prague, and Vienna, and died in 1792, leaving a few scientific and historical works, for which see Hoefer, *Nouv. Biog. Générale*, s. v.

Diest, Heinrich, a German theologian, was born at Altena, in Westphalia, in 1595. He studied at Dortmund, Siegen, and Basle, and continued his studies at

Heidelberg; but was obliged to leave that city at the time of the religious disputes, and returned to Basle, to pass his examinations for the doctor's degree, in 1621. Until 1624 he lived at Leyden as a private teacher. He was appointed minister of the Gospel at Emmerich, and in 1629 professor of theology and Hebrew in the University of Harderwick. In 1641 he went to Deventer in the same capacity, and died there in 1673, leaving, among many other works, *De Ratione Studii Theologici* (Harderwick, 1634):—*Oratio Inauguralis* (Deventer, 1640): —*Funda Davidis* (1646):—*Pedum Davidis* (1657). See Hoefer, *Nouv. Biog. Générale*, s. v.

Diestel, LUDWIG VON, a Protestant doctor and professor of theology in Germany, was born at Königsberg, Sept. 28, 1825. He studied at Berlin, Bonn, and at his native place. In 1851 he commenced his theological lectures at Bonn, and was, in 1858, appointed university-preacher and professor of theology. In 1862 he was called to Greifswalde, in 1867 to Jena, and, after Oehler's death, in 1872, to Tübingen, where he died, May 15, 1879. A few months before his death he had been ennobled. Besides his contributions to the *Studien und Kritiken*, Herzog's *Real-Encyklopædie* (1st ed.), and Schenkel's *Bibel-Lexikon*, he published, *Der Segen Jakobs in Gen. xlix historisch erläutert* (Braunschweig, 1853):—*Geschichte des alten Testaments in der christlichen Kirche* (Jena, 1868), a "magnum opus:"—*Die Sintflut und die Flutsagen des Altertums* (1871; 2d ed. 1876). (B. P.)

Diēta, the ecclesiastical *Cursus* or daily office.

Dietelmair, JOHANN AUGUSTIN, a Lutheran theologian of Germany, was born April 2, 1717, at Nuremberg. He studied at Altdorf and Halle, was in 1741 afternoon-preacher at his native place, and in 1744 deacon there. In 1746 he was called to Altdorf as professor of theology. He opened his lectures with an address, *De eo, quod Difficile est in Munere Doctoris Academici et Præcipue Theologi.* In the same year he took the degree of doctor of theology. He died April 6, 1785. He wrote, *Antiquitas Codicis Alexandrini Vindicator* (Halle and Magdeburg, 1739):—*De Religione Christiana Philosophiæ Nomine a Veteribus Compellata* (Altdorf, 1740):—*De Descensu Christi ad Inferos Literaria* (Nuremburg, 1741, 1762):—*De Serie Veterum Doctorum in Schola Alexandrina* (Altdorf, 1746):—*De ἀποκαταστάσει πάντων Scripturaria et Fanatica* (ibid. 1746): —*De Fragmento Clementis Romani*, etc. (ibid. 1749). See Döring, *Die gelehrten Theologen Deutschlands*, i, 325 sq.; Winer, *Handbuch der theol. Lit.* i, 20, 136, 599, 605, 889; Fürst, *Bibl. Jud.* i, 208. (B. P.)

Dietenberger, JOHANN, a German Dominican and doctor of theology, who died in 1534, while canon and inquisitor-general of Mentz and Cologne, is the author of a German translation of the Bible, published at Mentz in 1534 (revised by C. Ulenberg, Cologne, 1630; and again by the theologians of Mentz, ibid. 1662). He also wrote, *De Divortio* (ibid. 1532):—*De Votis Monasticis* (1524):—*De Apostasia*:—*De Præceptorum et Consiliorum Differentia*:—*In Defensionem Sacrificii Missæ*. See Jöcher, *Allgemeines Gelehrten-Lexikon*, s. v.; Lichtenberger, *Encyclop. des Sciences Religieuses*, s. v.; Hoefer, *Nouv. Biog. Générale*, s. v. (B. P.)

Dietl, GEORG ALOYS, a Roman Catholic theologian of Germany, was born Feb. 19, 1752, at Pressath, in the Upper Palatinate. In 1784 he was appointed pastor at Berg, near Landshut; in 1801 he was called to Landshut as professor, where he died, May 27, 1809, leaving, *Predigten* (Munich, 1786, 1802):—*Homilien über die sonntäglichen Evangelien* (ibid. 1789; 4th ed. 1829). See Winer, *Handbuch der theol. Lit.* ii, 139; Döring, *Die deutschen Kanzelredner des* 18. *und* 19. *Jahrhunderts*, p. 34 sq. (B. P.)

Dietlen, JOHANNES, a Lutheran minister of Germany, was born Sept. 13, 1790, at Leipheim, in Bavaria. In 1818 he was sub-rector of the Latin school at Schwabach; in 1824, pastor of Volksratshofen, near Memmingen; in 1838, pastor primarius and dean at Wassertrüdingen; in 1842, he was called to Beiersdorf, and died Sept. 15, 1866, leaving, *Geschichtliche Darstellung der Gründung der christlichen Kirche*, etc. (Nuremberg, 1838):—*Unser Glaube ist der Sieg*, against Ronge, Ghillany, and others (Erlangen, 1849). See Zuchold, *Bibl. Theol.* i, 280; Delitzsch, *Saat auf Hoffnung* (Erlangen, 1864), ii, 140 sq. (B. P.)

Dietpold (or **Dietbold**), THEOBALD, a German prelate, born in 1189, was bishop of Passau; made with Frederic Barbarossa the journey to the Holy Land; and died on his return home, leaving *Epistola ad Taganonem*. See Hoefer, *Nouv. Biog. Générale*, s. v.

Dietrich OF APOLDA (or THURINGIA), a German Dominican, born at Apolda, near Jena, is the author of a *Life of St. Elizabeth of Thuringia* (printed in Canisius, *Antiq. Lectiones*, ed. Basnage, iv, 113; preface and supplement in Mencken, *Script. Rerum Germ. x*). He also wrote the *Life of St. Dominic*. See Hefele, in Wetzer u. Welte's *Kirchen-Lexikon*, s. v. (B. P.)

Dietrich OF MÜNSTER (or OSNABRÜCK), a famous German preacher and ascetical writer, was born about the year 1435, at Münster, in Westphalia, and died at Louvain, Dec. 11, 1515, leaving, *De Passione Domini*:—*De Exercitatione Interiore*:—*Manuale Simplicium*. But the book which is best known of his writings is his *Christenspiegel*, a catechism, containing also prayers and meditations, which was printed very often. See *Der Katholik*, 1860, i, 584 sq.; Nordhoff, *Dietrich Cölde und sein Christenspiegel*, in Pick's *Monatsschrift für rheinisch-westfälische Geschichtsforsthung*, 1875, i, 67 sq.; Evelt, in Wetzer u. Welte's *Kirchen-Lexikon*, s. v. (B. P.)

Dietrich (or **Dietricy**), **Christian Wilhelm Ernst**, a German artist, was born at Weimar, in Saxony, Oct. 30, 1712, and studied under Alex. Thiele. He was sent by the king, with a pension, to Italy. He painted scriptural and historical subjects well, his chief pictures being *Lot and his Daughters; Abraham Going to Sacrifice Isaac; The Nativity; The Adoration of the Shepherds; The Taking Down from the Cross; St. Jerome Writing; Christ Appearing to Magdalene; The Flight into Egypt; The Circumcision.* He died at Dresden, April 24, 1774. See Hoefer, *Nouv. Biog. Générale*, s. v.; Spooner, *Biog. Hist. of the Fine Arts*, s. v.

Dietrich, Franz Eduard Christoph, a Protestant theologian and Orientalist of Germany, was born July 2, 1810, at Strauch, in Saxony. In 1839 he commenced his lectures at Marburg, and died there while professor of theology, Jan. 27, 1883, leaving, *Abhandlungen für semitische Sprachforschung* (Leipsic, 1844): —*De Sermonis Chaldaici Proprietate* (Marburg, 1838): —*Codicum Syriacorum Specimina* (ibid. 1855):—*Zwei sidonische Inschriften* (ibid. eod.):—*De Psalterii usu Publico et Divisione in Ecclesia Syriaca* (ibid. 1862):—*Morgengebete der alten Syrischen Kirche* (ibid. 1864):—*De Cruce Ruthwellensi* (ibid. 1865):—*De Sanchoniathonis Nomine* (ibid. 1872). He also edited two editions of Gesenius's *Manual Lexikon* (5th and 7th eds. 1855-68). (B. P.)

Dietrichstein, FRANZ, *prince of*, a Roman Catholic prelate of Germany, was born at Madrid, Aug. 22, 1570. After studying philosophy at Prague and theology at Rome, he became successively canon of Olmütz, camerarius of pope Clement VIII, and legate *à latere* at several marriage ceremonies of royal families. While president of the imperial council of state, he opposed the enforcement of the royal letters in Moravia, which were of a tolerant character; and after he had expelled Boeskay, a Hungarian rebel, he was himself driven away by the Moravian insurgents; but after Bohemia was pacified he brought back into the bosom of the Church of Rome the Protestants of Moravia, and instituted the order of the Piarists. Ferdinand II nominated him prince, in 1631, in return for the services which he had rendered both to the State and the Church. He died at

Brünn, in Moravia, Sept. 19, 1636, leaving discourses on the saints, some statutes upon the reform of the clergy and the people, a treatise on controversy, and some poems, sacred and profane. His *Life*, written by Voigt, was published, with notes and a supplement, by Schwalbe (Leipsic, 1792). See Hoefer, *Nouv. Biog. Générale*, s. v.

Dietz, FRIEDRICH WILHELM, a Protestant theologian, was born at Dillenburg in 1817, studied at Göttingen and Herborn, was in 1842 vicar at Diez, in 1844 con-rector at the gymnasium there, in 1852 pastor at Diez, in 1856 second preacher at Wiesbaden, in 1868 first pastor and court-preacher at Biebrich-Mosbach, and died in 1880. (B. P.)

Dietzel, JOHANN JACOB, a Lutheran minister of Germany, was born Aug. 7, 1808, at Rennweg, near Nuremberg. He studied theology and philology at Erlangen, and after having taught for ten years in different colleges, was appointed in 1842 third pastor of the Church of the Holy Ghost at Nuremberg, where he labored until his death, June 20, 1876. He took a great interest in the mission among Jews and heathen, and promoted the kingdom of Christ everywhere. (B. P.)

Dietzsch, AUGUST, a Protestant theologian of Germany, who died while professor of theology at Bonn, March 4, 1872, is the author of *Adam und Christus, Rom. v*, 12-21 (Bonn, 1871). (B. P.)

Diggers, a term of reproach applied to the Waldenses (q. v.), because they were subjected to such persecution that they were compelled to dig caverns in the earth in which to hold meetings for worship.

Digna, the name of two Christian martyrs: (1) The servant of St. Afre, with whose remains she was burned at Augsburg while attempting to convey them away; commemorated Aug. 5. (2) A virgin of Tabana, executed at Cordova in 853, along with St. Felix, by the Moors; commemorated June 14.

Dignitary, a term used in England to denote one who holds cathedral or other preferments to which jurisdiction is annexed.

Dignĭtas, a classical term, gradually applied to offices, was purely secular at first. In the process of time, when ecclesiastics were appointed to secular offices, the people began to speak of "dignities" in the Church. First applied to the lower ranks, the term was finally used for all Church officials, i. e. pope, cardinal, patriarch, archbishop, metropolitan, bishop, etc. According to Ducange, in ecclesiastical parlance, "when a benefice included the administration of ecclesiastical affairs with jurisdiction, it was called a dignity."

Dike, Daniel and **Jeremiah.** See DYKE.

Dilapidations, in English law, is the name given to the waste committed by the incumbent of an ecclesiastical living. By the general law a tenant for life has no power to cut down timber, destroy buildings, etc. (voluntary waste), or to let buildings fall into disrepair (permissive waste). See *Encyclop. Brit.* (9th ed.) s. v.

Dillard, RYLAND THOMPSON, D.D., a Baptist minister, was born in Caroline County, Va., in November, 1797. He was educated at Port Royal, served in the war of 1812, removed to Kentucky, studied law, and practiced for a time in Winchester; was ordained in 1824, and for forty-seven years served as pastor of the Church at East Hickman, and for more than thirty years of this period had the pastoral charge of the Church at David's Forks. He was superintendent of public instruction for Kentucky in 1842-48. His death occurred Nov. 26, 1878. See Cathcart, *Baptist Encyclop.* p. 334. (J. C. S.)

Diller, JACOB W., D.D., a Protestant Episcopal clergyman, was born at Lancaster, Pa., in 1810. He was ordained deacon in 1834 and presbyter in 1835. With the exception of four years as rector of St. Stephen's Church in Middlebury, Vt., his entire ministry was spent in St. Luke's, Brooklyn. He was lost in the burning of the steamer *Seawanhaka*, off Randall's Island, N. Y., June 28, 1880, aged seventy years. See Whittaker, *Almanac and Directory*, 1881.

Dillingham, FRANCIS, an English divine, was born at Dean, Bedfordshire; became a fellow in Christ College, Cambridge; was an excellent linguist and subtle disputant; was chosen in 1607 one of the translators of the Bible, being on the 1 Chron.-Eccles. committee; was richly beneficed at Wilden, Bedfordshire, and died there. See Fuller, *Worthies of England* (ed. Nuttall), i, 170; Anderson, *Annals of the English Bible* (ed. Prime), p. 406.

Dima (Dimma, or **Dioma,** dimin. *Dimmog*, Lat. *Dimanus, Dimaus*, etc), the name of several Irish saints (commemorated respectively on March 9, May 12, June 27, July 19), besides the bishop of Condeire (Connor), about A.D. 640, commemorated Jan. 6.

Diman, JEREMIAH LEWIS, D.D., a Congregational minister, was born at Bristol, R. I., May 1, 1831. He studied under Rev. James N. Sikes, of Bristol; graduated from Brown University in 1851; and, after spending two years in Germany, entered Andover Theological Seminary, from which he graduated in 1856. On Dec. 9 of the latter year he was ordained over the First Church in Fall River, Mass.; in 1860 he became pastor of Harvard Church, Brookline; and from 1864 until the close of his life, Feb. 3, 1881, he was professor of history and political economy in Brown University. From 1873 he was a corresponding member of the Massachusetts Historical Society. Among his published addresses is *The Historic Basis of Belief*, one of the Boston lectures (1870):—*Historical Address at the 200th Anniversary in Bristol, R. I.* (1880):—*The Theistic Argument as Affected by Recent Theories* (1881). He edited the third and fifth volumes of the Narragansett Club publications, containing "John Cotton's answer to Roger Williams" and "John Fox digg'd out of his Burrowes." A posthumous volume, entitled *Orations and Essays, with Selected Parish Sermons*, was published in 1881. See *Cong. Year-book*, 1882, p. 28.

Dimesses, an order of nuns, consisting of young maids and widows, founded in the state of Venice in the 16th century by Dejanata Valmarana, the wife of a civilian of Verona. Rules for their observance were laid down by a Franciscan named Anthony Pagani, in 1584. Their habit was either black or brown woollen, as the wearer might choose.

Diminutos, a name used to denote those persons whose confessions before the inquisition (q. v.) were defective and imperfect. There were three kinds of *diminutos*, who were condemned to die: 1. Those who, having accused themselves after being imprisoned, or, at least, before sentence of condemnation had passed upon them, had consequently time to examine themselves and make a complete declaration. 2. Those who did not confess till after sentence of condemnation had passed upon them. 3. Those who did not confess until they were given up to the confessors. These were never afterwards put to the torture, and could only be delivered from death by naming all their accomplices without a single exception.

Dimmick, LUTHER FRASEUR, D.D., a Congregational minister, was born at Shaftesbury, Vt., Nov. 15, 1790. He graduated from Hamilton College in 1816, and from Andover Theological Seminary in 1819; was ordained pastor of the Church in Newburyport, Mass., the same year; and died suddenly, May 16, 1860. He was remarkable for his gentleness and sympathy; was a sound preacher and able scholar, and his long pastorate was very successful. He published a *Historical Discourse.* See *Cong. Quarterly*, 1860, p. 370.

Dimœrĭtæ (so called from δίς, *twice*, and μοίρα, a *part*, because they only recognised two thirds of the nature of Christ, the human soul and body, denying the divine nature), another name for the APOLLINARIANS (q. v.), who were subdivided into various sects, as Vatalians, Synusiasts, Polemians, Valentinians, etc.

Dimpna (or **Dympna**), a virgin martyr of Ireland, probably in the 7th century, commemorated May 15.

Din (Arab. *practice*) is the second of the two parts into which Islamism is divided, faith and practice. The *din*, or practice, consists of, 1, prayers and purifications; 2, alms; 3, fasting; and, 4, pilgrimage to Mecca.

Dina Chariyawa, a manual of daily observances to be attended to by Buddhist priests in Ceylon. For the contents of this manual see Hardy, *Eastern Monachism*, p. 24 sq.

Dindorf, GOTTLIEB IMMANUEL, a Lutheran theologian of Germany, was born Aug. 10, 1755, at Rotta, near Wittenberg. He studied, at Leipsic, philosophy, theology, and ancient languages; was in 1786 professor of philosophy, in 1791 professor of Hebrew and cognate languages, and died Dec. 19, 1812, leaving, *Maxima Versionum Difficultas in Linguarum Dissimilitudine Sita Est* (Leipsic, 1783):—*In Epistolam Syriacam Simeonis Beth-Arsamensis de Barsauma*, etc. (ibid. 1788):—*Quomodo Nomen* קהלת *Salomoni Tribuatur?* (ibid. 1791): *Recitationes in Evangelium Johannis* (ibid. 1796):—*Novum Lexicon Linguæ Hebraico-Chaldaicæ*, etc. (1801-4). See Döring, *Die gelehrten Theologen Deutschlands*, i, 331 sq.; Winer, *Handbuch der theol. Lit.* i, 248, 250, 267; Fürst, *Bibl. Jud.* i, 209; Steinschneider, *Bibliog. Handbuch*, s. v. (the latter two call him erroneously Theophilus Immanual). (B. P.)

Dinet, GASPARD, bishop of Mâcon, who lived about 1617, wrote *Ordonnances Synodales de Mascon* (Lyons, 1602). See Hoefer, *Nouv. Biog. Générale*, s. v.

Dingolvinga, COUNCIL OF (*Concilium Dingolvingense*), held at Dingolfing, on the river Isar, in Bavaria, A.D. 772, under Tassilo, duke of Bavaria, passed thirteen canons upon discipline and reformation of manners. —Smith, *Dict. of Christ. Antiq.* s. v.

Dini, PIETRO, an Italian prelate, was born at Florence about 1570. He studied belles-lettres, and, while young, was made member of the Academy de la Crusca. In 1621 he succeeded cardinal Bondini, his uncle, in the archiepiscopal see of Fermo, and died in 1625. His fine library, which was particularly rich in Italian MSS. of the 13th and 14th centuries, has now passed over to the Bibliotheca Magliabecchiana. See Hoefer, *Nouv. Biog. Générale*, s. v.

Dinooth (Lat. *Dinōthus*), a Welsh saint, was abbot of Bangor between A.D. 500 and 542. He was originally a North British chieftain, and founded a monastery, the remains of which still exist in Flintshire.

Dinwiddie, JAMES LEMONTE, D.D., an Associate Reformed minister, was born in Adams County, Pa., Feb. 23, 1798. He graduated from Washington College in 1816, and took a theological course in 1817 and 1818. Being a popular preacher, he received many calls from vacant congregations; but accepted one from Mercer, Pa., and labored there fourteen years. In 1834 he took charge of a Presbyterian congregation in Philadelphia. After continuing in this connection about seven years, he returned to his mother Church, and was again received as a member of the Presbytery of Monongahela in 1841. Shortly after this he was installed pastor of the Second Associate Reformed Church of Pittsburgh. In 1842 he was elected to the professorship of Biblical literature and sacred criticism in the theological seminary of the Reformed Church at Allegheny, and died in 1849. See Sprague, *Annals of the Amer. Pulpit*, IX, iv, 154.

Dio, in Slavonic mythology, were birds of misfortune, the *Harpies* of the Slavs.

Diocesan Synods were ecclesiastical conventions which the patriarchs of the ancient Christian Church had the privilege of summoning whenever occasion required. They consisted of the metropolitans and all the provincial bishops.

Diocles, a martyr at Histrias (Istria), commemorated May 24.

Diodati, ALEXANDRE AMÉDÉE EDOUARD, pastor and professor at Geneva, was born in 1789. He belonged to one of those Protestant families which settled at Geneva. In 1811 he entered upon the duties of the sacred ministry, and was actively engaged therein at several stations till the year 1839, when he was appointed professor of ethics. In the following year he was given the chair of apologetics and pastoral theology, which he retained till his death in 1860. Of his many writings we mention, his French translation of *Chalmers's Sermons* (Paris, 1825):—*De l'Enseignement Primaire: le Père Girard* (in *Bibl. Univ.* July and August, 1830):—*Essai sur le Christianisme, Envisagé dans ses Rapports avec la Perfectibilité de l'Être Moral* (Geneva and Paris, 1830):—*Discours Religieux* (ed. by M. Coulin, Paris, 1861):—*Méditations sur des Textes de l'Épître aux Ephésiens* (ibid. 1863). See Viguet, in *Le Chrétien Évangélique* (1860, p. 353); Naville, in *Bibliothèque Universelle* (Feb. 1861); Coulin, in Lichtenberger's *Encyclop. des Sciences Religieuses*, s. v. (B. P.)

Diodōrus. (1) A presbyter and martyr at Rome under Valerian (A.D. 251); commemorated Dec. 1 (or Jan. 17 or Oct. 25). (2) A martyr at Perga, in Pamphylia; commemorated April 22 (or Feb. 26). (3) Bishop of Tyre, A.D. 381, whose inquiry of Epiphanius of Salamis led the latter to compose his treatise on the gems in the high-priest's breastplate.

Diodŏtus, a saint of Africa; commemorated with Anesius, March 31.

Diogĕnēs, the most noted of the Cynics, was born about 412 B.C. He was the son of Icesias, a money-changer of Sinope, in Pontus. One account states that they were detected in adulterating coin, and that father and son were compelled to leave their native city. But according to another account, Icesias died in prison, and Diogenes fled to Athens with a single attendant, whom, upon his arrival, he dismissed with the remark, "If Manes could live without Diogenes, why not Diogenes without him?" Thereupon he discarded all superfluities of dress and utensils, retaining only a wooden bowl, his cloak, and his wallet. The first of these, however, was also relinquished, on seeing a boy drink from the hollow of his hand. He now went to Cynosarges, the seat of the famous Antisthenes, where he cheerfully endured all the abuse heaped upon him by his master and fellow-disciples. Thus introduced to the favorable consideration of the Cynics, and willing to endure any hardship for the sake of wisdom, he soon outstripped his master in learning and extravagance of life. The story that he took up his abode in a cask belonging to the temple of Cybele does not rest upon unquestioned evidence. But that he was accustomed to inure himself to the vicissitudes of the weather by rolling himself in the hot sand in summer, and embracing statues covered with snow in winter, are facts resting on the best of authority. At Athens he was held in great esteem. He ridiculed and despised all intellectual pursuits which did not directly and obviously tend to some immediate and practical good. He abused literary men for reading about the evils of Ulysses, and neglecting their own; musicians for stringing the lyre harmoniously while they left their minds discordant; men of science for troubling themselves about the moon and stars while they neglected what lay immediately before them; orators for learning to say what was right, but not to practice it. His numerous witty apothegms are handed down by Diogenes Laertius, and generally display that unwise contempt for the common opinions and pursuits of men which is so unlikely to reform them.

Diogenes was making a voyage to Ægina, when the ship was taken by pirates, and he carried to Crete and sold as a slave. When interrogated as to his trade, he answered that he understood no trade but "to govern men," and begged to be sold to a man "that wanted a master." Such a purchaser was found in the person of Xeniades of Corinth, over whom he acquired great influence, receiving from him his freedom, and being appointed to take charge of the education of his children. He remained in the house of Xeniades during the remainder of his life. He is believed to have died in 323 B.C. It was during his residence at Corinth that the celebrated meeting between him and Alexander the Great is said to have taken place. The king is reported to have begun the conversation by saying, "I am Alexander the Great;" to which the philosopher replied, "And I am Diogenes the Cynic." The king then inquired whether he could do anything to oblige him. But the only request Diogenes had to make was that Alexander should stand from between him and the sun. The king is said to have admired the Cynic so much that he said, "If I were not Alexander, I should wish to be Diogenes." He appears never to have returned to Athens. The mode of his death is unknown, although various stories have been repeated concerning it. His own desire was that his body should be thrown to the beasts of the field, but Xeniades gave him an honorable interment. At Corinth there was a pillar erected to his memory, on which rested a dog of Parian marble. He has been charged with indecencies of various kinds, which have cast a stain upon his memory; but there is no certain foundation for much that has been said, and the conduct of the later Cynics was such as to reflect discredit on the very name. The Cynics answered arguments by facts. When some one was arguing in support of the Eleatic doctrine of the impossibility of motion, Diogenes rose and walked. See Smith, *Dict. of Greek and Rom. Biog. and Myth.* s. v.; *Encyclop. Britannica*, 9th ed. s. v.; Ueberweg, *Hist. of Philos.* i, 94.

Diogenes. (1) A saint in Macedonia, commemorated April 6. (2) A presbyter of Alexandria in the 4th century, said to have been personally maltreated by Basil of Ancyra. (3) A liberal friend of Chrysostom in his exile, A.D. 404. (4) A bishop of Seleucobelus, in Syria, who attended the council at Ephesus, A.D. 431. (5) A digamist bishop ordained by Alexander of Antioch. (6) A bishop of Cyzicus (A.D. 449–451), present at the councils of Ephesus and Chalcedon.

Diogeniānus, third bishop of Alby, A.D. cir. 407; one of the most notable prelates of his age.

Diogĕnus, the name of two saints: (1) Bishop of Geneva, lived, according to some, about the end of the 3d century, while others maintain that he was present at the Council of Aquileia in 381. (2) Bishop of Grenoble, succeeded St. Domninus about the end of the 4th century.

Diomēdēs, a Christian physician of Tarsus, martyred at Nicæa, A.D. 288, and commemorated June 9 or Aug. 16.

Dionysia. (1) Virgin martyr at Lampsacus, A.D. 250, together with Peter, Andrew, and Paul; commemorated May 15. (2) Martyr in Africa in the 5th century, with seven others; commemorated Dec. 6.

Dionysius. (1) Martyr in Lower Armenia with Amelianus and Sebastian; commemorated Feb. 8. (2) Martyr; commemorated with Ammonius, Feb. 14. (3) Martyr at Aquileia, with Hilarius, Tatian, Felix, and Largus; commemorated March 16. (4) Saint, uncle of Pancratius; commemorated May 12. (5) Bishop and confessor under Constantius; deposition at Milan, May 25. (6) Martyr at Sinnada, with Democritus and Secundus; commemorated July 31. (7) Saint, of Phrygia; commemorated Sept. 20. (8) Bishop of Paris, martyr with Rusticus and Eleutherius, probably in A.D. 272; commemorated Oct. 9. (9) Pope, under Claudius II; deposition at Rome, Dec. 26 or 27. (10) Martyr, with Petrus and Lampsacensus; commemorated May 18. (11) One of the Seven Sleepers of Ephesus; commemorated Oct. 22. (12) Sixth bishop of Vienne, in France, thought to have been martyred A.D. 193; commemorated May 9. (13) Three young men of the same name, martyred at Tripoli, March 24, A.D. 304. (14) A disciple of Quadratus, and a martyr at Corinth, probably under Diocletian. (15) Two of this name martyred together at Cæsarea, under Diocletian. (16) Fifteenth bishop of Mentz for twenty-six years, in the beginning of the 4th century. (17) Saint, bishop of Milan after Protasius, A.D. 346. (18) Bishop of Lydda, present at the Council of Constantinople, A.D. 381. (19) Eleventh bishop of Tours, a native of Burgundy, seems to have died about A.D. 513. (20) Bishop of Ascalon, who attended the third synod of Jerusalem, A.D. 536. (21) Bishop of Seleucia Pieria in the middle of the 6th century.

Diopĕtus, first bishop of Orleans, about the middle of the 4th century.

Diŏra (**Diera**, or **Deora**), thirteenth bishop of Rochester, cir. A.D. 775–781.

Dios, a hermit under Theodosius the Great; commemorated July 19.

Dioscorĭdēs, one of the three boy-martyrs of Rome. See CRESCENS.

Dioscŏrus. (1) Martyr under Numerian; commemorated Feb. 25. (2) The Reader, martyr in Egypt; commemorated May 18. (3) Martyr under Decius at Alexandria, with Heron, Arsenius, and Isidorus, commemorated Dec. 14.

Diotallevi, FRANCESCO, an Italian prelate and theologian, was born at Rimini in 1579. He studied at Rome, was appointed bishop of San Angelo di Lombardi at Naples, and then sent to Poland as nuncio, where he remained seven years. He died on his journey home to Rome in 1620, leaving *De Concensu Dei ad Actus Liberos Voluntatis* (Lyons, 1611), and a treatise *De Usuria*, which is in MS. See Hoefer, *Nouv. Biog. Générale*, s. v.

Dipavali, a Hindû festival in honor of Vishnu (q. v.). It was instituted to commemorate an exploit of the god when in the form of Krishna (q. v.). A certain *Ratjasja* had taken captive sixteen thousand virgins, but Krishna slew him and set them at liberty. In this celebration the Hindû holds a festival during the day, and the houses are illuminated at night.

Dippers, a name sometimes given to the *Dunkers* (q. v.), or German Baptists, on account of their mode of baptism.

Diptych (*τὰ δίπτυχα*) contained especially the names of bishops, whether living or dead. The primary custom would seem to be, that they were read after the oblation of the bread and wine, and before the consecration. (1) Sometimes they were read by the deacon. (2) In some churches it would appear that the subdeacon recited the names on the diptychs behind the altar. (3) Frequently the priest himself repeated the names. (4) A curious plan is that mentioned by Fulcuin, where the subdeacon whispered the names to the priest. (5) We find even that in some cases the tablets were merely laid upon the altar, with the names of the offerers and benefactors, of whom the priest made general mention.

In the church of Ravenna, a chasuble was made to serve the purpose of a diptych.

The name of diptych was also given to registers in which were entered, as occasion required, the names of newly baptized persons, as then first becoming members of the Christian family.

Of all extant specimens, the one which is usually called

Ordinary Diptych.

the "Diptych of Rambona, in Picenum," is the most ancient and extraordinary. It contains a medallion of the First Person of the Trinity above, with the sun and moon below on the right and left of the cross, personified as figures bearing torches. There are two titles, EGO SUM IHS NAZARENUS, in rude Roman letters, with a smaller label, REX JUDEORUM, over the cross. The nimbus is cruciform, the waistcloth reaches almost to the knees, the navel is strangely formed into an eye. The Virgin and St. John stand under the arms of the cross. But the distinguishing detail is the addition of the Roman wolf and twins below the cross, with the words ROMULUS ET REMULUS A LUPA NUTRITI. This wonderful ivory is now in the Vatican Museum (see Murray's *Hand-book*), and is in the most ancient style of what may be called dark-age Byzantine art, when all instruction and perception of beauty are departed, but so vigorous a sense of the reality of the fact remains as to render the work highly impressive.

Diptych of Rambona.

Diraidh (or Deoraid), two Irish saints: (1) Of Eadardruim (now Drum, in Athlone, County Roscommon), commemorated Jan. 13, seems to have lived about the close of the 5th century. (2) Bishop of Ferns, succeeded Maldogar, A.D. 677, and died in 690. He is commemorated July 27.

Dirdan, a Welsh saint of the 5th century.

Directāneus, any psalm, hymn, or canticle said in the service of the Church in monotone.

Dirnberger, Franz, a Roman Catholic theologian of Germany, was born at Bamberg in 1809. From 1834 to 1845 he was professor at Regensburg; from 1845 to 1854 director of the Georgianum and professor of pastoral theology at Munich; and thereafter at Eichstädt, until his death, Feb. 25, 1875. (B. P.)

Dirûk, an Armenian theologian, was the son of Moses Koun, of the city of Zarishat, in the province of Vanant, and was born about the end of the 4th century. He was one of the eminent writers and scholars of the school founded by Mesrob. He entered into sacred orders, and gained a great reputation by his works and his zeal for patriotic religion, having deeply studied the Syriac, Greek, and Latin languages. He died about the year 460, leaving a number of works, among which may be cited a life of the patriarch Sahak, homilies, and also his works on the Holy Scriptures. See Hoefer, *Nouv. Biog. Générale*, s. v.

Dirying, a Welsh saint of the 6th century.

Disciplina Arcani, a term of post-Reformation controversy, is applied to designate a number of modes of procedure in teaching the Christian faith, akin to one another in kind, although differing considerably in character; which prevailed from about the middle of the 2d century until the natural course of circumstances rendered any system which involved secrecy or reserve impossible. So far as these were defensible, they arose out of the principles (1) of imparting knowledge of the truth by degrees, and in methods adapted to the capacity of the recipients; and (2) of cutting off occasion of profaneness or of more hardened unbelief by not proclaiming the truths and mysteries of the faith indiscriminately, or in plain words, or at once, to unbelievers. The deeper Christian doctrines were withheld from those out of the Church, and the mass of those within. The secrets of the initiations into the churchly orders were likewise diligently kept from the laity. This was the foundation of that to which the word was afterwards applied. See Arcani.

Discofĕræ, a name for the sisters who bring the dishes to the table at the convents of the nuns.

Discommunicants, those who neglect to partake of the holy communion, a habit early and constantly condemned by the Christian Church.

Disibode. See Dysibod.

Disk, Winged, with pendant crowned uræi, carrying the cross of life, was an emblem placed over the doorways to the Egyptian temples, and is supposed to represent the progress of the sun in the heavens from east to west. As a form of the solar deity it was a symbol of the god Horus likewise, and was regarded by the Egyptians as the protecting or benevolent spirit, the *Agathodæmon* of the Greeks. Its analogue was in some respects the *Ferohir* of the Assyrians, and perhaps the Spirit of the Sun of the Cabalists.

Dîs Manĭbus (*to the gods the Manes*). The letters *D. M.* are sometimes found inscribed in the catacombs. Boldetti, together with others of the earlier school of antiquaries, claimed that they stood for "Deo Maximo;" but De' Rossi has doubtless advanced the more correct theory, i. e. that they stand for "Diis Manibus" (*dedicated to the deified shades of the departed*), which was a heathen motto, but was inscribed upon the Christian tombstones, and shows how slowly people relax the customs of their ancestors.

Disney, John (1), a learned English divine, was born at Lincoln in 1677, and was educated at a grammar-school and at Middle Temple. After acting as a magistrate for twenty years, he was ordained a minister of the Established Church in 1719, and the same year was presented with the vicarage of Croft and the rectory of Kirby-super-Baine, both in his native county. In 1722 he was instituted to the vicarage of St. Mary, in Nottingham, where he remained until his death, Feb. 3, 1729-30. His principles of religion were orthodox in regard to points of doctrine and articles of faith; in respect to the principles of others, they were truly catholic. The following are a few of his numerous publications: *Primitiæ Sacræ* (Lond. 1701, 1703):—*A Sermon Preached in the Parish Church of St. Botolph's*, Aldgate, London, Nov. 22, 1719:—and six other occasional *Sermons*. See Chalmers, *Biog. Dict.* s. v.; Allibone, *Dict. of Brit. and Amer. Authors*, s. v.

Disney, John (2), D.D., an English Unitarian minister, was born in 1746, and educated at Peterhouse, Cambridge. After taking orders he was presented to the vicarage of Swinderby, Lincolnshire, and appointed chaplain to bishop Law. In 1782 he resigned his preferments in the Episcopal Church, and, removing to London, became first assistant and afterwards sole minister of the Unitarian chapel in Essex Street. He resigned in 1804, and died Dec. 26, 1816. Dr. Disney published, *Memoirs of Dr. Sykes* (1785, 8vo):—*of Dr. Jartin* (1792, 8vo):—*of T. H. Hollis* (1780, 2 vols. 4to; new ed. 1808, 4to):—*Sermons* (1793-1816, 4 vols. 8vo). See (Lond.) *Annual Register*, 1816, p. 225; Allibone, *Dict. of Brit. and Amer. Authors*, s. v.; Wilson, *Dissenting Churches*, iii, 488.

Disputatio, a discussion on Scripture, enjoined by some monastic rules.

Disputations, a name sometimes given to sermons, in the ancient Church, from the controversial character which they often necessarily assumed.

Dissen, Heinrich von, an ascetic writer, was born Oct. 18, 1413. He studied at Cologne, and received holy orders at Osnabrück. He soon joined the Carthusians of Cologne, and died there, Nov. 26, 1484, leaving, *Sermones Dominicales* (4 vols.):—*Postillæ in Evangelia* (2 vols.):—*Expositiones in Evangelia Dominicalia*:—*Psalterium de S. Trinitate*, etc.:—*De Præsentatione B. Mariæ Virg.*:—*De Laude Ordinis Carthusianorum*:—*Expositio Super Librum Apocalypsis S. Joannis*:—*Expositio in Symbolum S. Athanasii et Orationem Dominicam.* See Hartzheim, *Biblioth. Colon.* p. 116; Petreji, *Biblioth. Carthus.* (Cologne, 1609), p. 127; Kessel, in Wetzer u. Welte's *Kirchen-Lexikon*, s. v. (B. P.)

Diterich, Johann Samuel, a Lutheran theologian of Germany, was born Dec. 15, 1721, at Berlin; studied at Frankfort and Halle, and was in 1748 appointed third preacher at St. Mary's. In 1751 he became second preacher, and on the death of his father succeeded him as *primarius*. In 1770 he was appointed member of the superior consistory, and died Jan. 14, 1797, leaving, *Cogitationes Philosophicæ de Precibus Continuis* (Frankfort, 1742):—*Kurzer Entwurf der christl. Lehre* (Berlin, 1754), besides a number of sermons and ascetical discourses. See Döring, *Die gelehrten Theologen Deutschlands*, i, 334 sq.; Winer, *Handbuch der Theol. Lit.* ii, 86, 226, 289, 295, 339. (B. P.)

Dittenberger, Theophor Wilhelm, a Protestant theologian of Germany, was born April 30, 1807, at Theningen, in the Breisgau; studied at Heidelberg and Halle, and was in 1831 pastor at Baden. In 1832 he was privat-docent at Heidelberg, and in 1836 professor and university-preacher there. In 1852 he was called to Weimar, where he died, May 1, 1871. He published, *Ueber Predigerseminarien* (Heidelberg, 1835), which effected the establishment of a theological seminary at Heidelberg:—*Conspectus Introductionis in Theologiam Homileticam* (ibid. 1836). Besides a great many sermons, which he published from time to time, he edited the *Zeitschrift für deutsch-protestantische Kirchen-Verfassung.* See Zuchold, *Bibl. Theol.* i, 284 sq. (B. P.)

Dittrich, Joseph, bishop of Corycus and apostolical vicar of Saxony, was born at Marschen, in Bohemia, April 25, 1794. He received holy orders at Leitermitz in 1818; in 1824 went to Leipsic as director of the Catholic schools there; three years later took charge of the schools at Dresden; in 1831 was appointed court-preacher; in 1845 was made cathedral dean of Budissin or Bautzen, and in 1846 apostolical vicar of Saxony. The same year he was raised to the episcopal see, and died Oct. 5, 1853. See Forwerk, *Geschichte der Katholischen Hofkirche zu Dresden* (Dresden, 1851); Hefele, in Wetzer u. Welte's *Kirchen-Lexikon*, s. v. (B. P.)

Diucholl (Dicholl, Duchoil, etc.), the name of several Irish saints: (1) Son of Neman, commemorated Dec. 25. (2) Of Cluain-braein (near Louth), commemorated May 1. (3) Derg, son of Nessan, of Inisfaithlenu (now Ireland's Eye, off Howth, County Dublin), in the 6th or 7th century; commemorated March 15.

Diuma (or **Dwina**), first bishop of the Mercians, was a Scot (or Irishman), consecrated A.D. 655, and died shortly afterwards.

Dius. (1) The thirty-first bishop of Jerusalem, A.D. 190, succeeding Narcissus, and followed by Germanus. (2) A monk of Antioch, cir. A.D. 413; commemorated July 19. (3) Saint, of Cæsarea, commemorated July 12. (4) Martyr under Maximinus at Alexandria, with Peter, bishop of Alexandria, Faustus the Presbyter, and Ammonius; commemorated Nov. 26.

Dius Fidius (*Medi-fidi*), a god of the Sabines, adopted by the Romans, and regarded as the god of integrity or good faith; hence he was frequently sworn by. He was said to be the son of Jupiter, and was often confounded with Hercules.

Divitiānus, bishop of Soissons about the beginning of the 4th century, is said to have been the grandson of St. Sinicius, and is commemorated as a saint on Oct. 5.

Divolé (or **Divoley**), Pierre, a French theologian, was born at Auxerre at the beginning of the 16th century; became doctor in theology at Paris; entered the order of the preaching brothers, among whom he achieved great distinction; and died in 1568, leaving, for posthumous publication, *Instructions et Sermons pour tous les Jours de Carême*, etc. (Paris, 1576):—*Deux Sermons de la Sainte Messe et Cérémonies d'Icelle* (ibid. 1581). See Hoefer, *Nouv. Biog. Générale*, s. v.

Dixon, James, D.D., an eminent minister of the British Wesleyan Connection, was born at Donington Castle, Leicestershire, Oct. 28, 1788. He became an earnest Methodist at the age of twenty; studied theology four years; was received into the ministry in 1812; served as a missionary at Gibraltar, in 1829; and discharged with unvarying vigor a ministry of over half a century in England. He was elected president of the Conference in 1841, and representative to the General Conference of the Methodist Episcopal Church at Pittsburgh, Pa., in 1848. Being smitten with incurable blindness in 1856, he became a supernumerary in 1863, and died at Bradford, Yorkshire, Eng. (where he took up his residence), Dec. 28, 1871. Dr. Dixon had one of the most powerful and accomplished minds that ever graced the British Conference. In the meridian of his life his preaching was a fine example of the philosophical style; his sermons elaborated with care, dealing with great principles and logical sequences, expatiating upon the harmonies of the Gospel economy, and invested with an air of grandeur and an imposing mental attitude, and full of thought. Later in life there was a rich and sweet simplicity in his ministrations. With Watson and other lights of the Conference, he advocated the abolition of slavery in the West Indies, and some of his speeches on this subject were high examples of a burning logic and eloquence. He was a most bitter opponent of Romanism, and used the influence of his powerful voice and pen in opposing its advances as well as the granting of constitutional privileges to its adherents. He took deep interest in public affairs, and had strong political views (he was a Tory). He was one of the defenders of Dr. Bunting during the "Warren" discussions. His powerful and sanctified mind, noble character, frank, genial, sincere, and serene piety, shining from out of the darkness of his deep affliction, made him to be venerated and loved throughout the whole Connection. Dr. Dixon published *Methodism in its Origin, Economy, and Present Position* (Lond. 1843; N. Y. 1853), besides a large number of sermons, lectures, and biographical sketches, for which see Osborn, *Wesleyan Bibliography*, s. v. His own life has been written by his son, Rev. R. W. Dixon (Lond. 1874).

Dixon, Joseph, D.D., Roman Catholic primate of Ireland, was for some years a professor in Maynooth College, and in 1852 was appointed to the see of Armagh, where he died, April 29, 1866. He was greatly beloved by his people, and highly respected by Protestants of all denominations. See *Appleton's Annual Cyclop.* 1866, p. 592.

Dlugosz (Lat. *Longinus*), JOHN, the historian of Poland, was born at Brzesnica in 1415, studied at Nouy-Korczyn and the University of Cracow, and was designated for the archbishopric of Lemberg, but died May 29, 1840, before consecration to the high office. He wrote, *Historiæ Poloniæ Libri XIII ab Antiquissimis Temporibus Usque ad Annum* 1480:—*Episcopatus Smogorzoviensis et Pizzinensis, quae Runi Wratislaviensis, Ecclesiarum Historiæ et Acto* (ed. Lipf, Breslau, 1847):—*Vitæ Episcoporum Posnaniensium* (Brunsberg, 1604). A new edition of Dlugosz's works was published by Przezdziecki (Cracow, 1863). See Stemmer, in Wetzer u. Welte's *Kirchen-Lexikon*, s. v. (B. P.)

Doak, Archibald Alexander, D.D., a Presbyterian minister, was born in Washington County, Tenn., July 13, 1815. He graduated from Washington College, Tenn., in 1833, and from Princeton Theological Seminary in 1835; was ordained by the Holston Presbytery in 1839; in 1841 became professor in Washington College; and in 1856 professor of ancient languages in East Tennessee University. His health declined in 1861, and he retired to private life in Clarksville, where he died, May 26, 1866. See Wilson, *Presb. Hist. Almanac*, 1867, p. 429.

Doak, Samuel, D.D., a Presbyterian minister, was born in August, 1749, of Irish extraction. He graduated from the College of New Jersey in 1775; was licensed to preach by the Hanover Presbytery, Oct. 31, 1777; in 1785 established Martin Academy (which in 1795 became Washington College), and continued to act as its president until 1818. He died Dec. 12, 1830. See Sprague, *Annals of the Amer. Pulpit*, iii, 394.

Doban, a Scottish saint, commemorated April 12, seems to have been one of St. Boniface's companions in Germany, and eventually bishop of Treves, cir. A.D. 751.

Dobbins, ROBERT, a Methodist Protestant minister, was born in Pennsylvania, April 20, 1768. He was converted in youth, and early began evangelistic labors among his neighbors, especially the poor. His early ministerial service was in the Methodist Episcopal Church. In 1829 he seceded and took an active part in the organization of the Methodist Protestant Church, and in 1830 entered its itinerancy. The circuits which he served were Port William, Highland, Washington, Rehoboth (now Lynchburg), Xenia, and Springfield, all in Ohio. He died Jan. 13, 1860. Mr. Dobbins was endued with a vigorous mind and constitution. His meek, earnest spirit commanded great respect. He once represented his county (Greene) for two years in the Ohio Legislature. See Bassett, *Hist. of the M. P. Church*, p. 338; Caddy, *Life and Times of Robert Dobbins* (Cincinnati, 1868).

Dobbs, C. E. W., D.D., a Baptist minister, was born at Portsmouth, Va., Aug. 12, 1840. He learned the printer's trade, and became editorially connected with the press of Norfolk and Portsmouth. In 1859 he united with the church at Greensborough, N. C., and the year following entered the theological seminary at Greenville, S. C. (since removed to Louisville, Ky.). Having completed his studies, he preached for a few years in the Court Street and Fourth Street churches in Portsmouth. In 1866 he removed to Kentucky, and for several years preached for churches in Madison County; became pastor of the church in Bowling Green, remaining there six years, and then went to Dayton. His last settlement was in Madison, Ind. For a considerable time he was secretary of the Southern Baptist Convention, and of the General Association of Kentucky. He died July, 1884. Dr. Dobbs wrote much for the periodical press, and published one or two small books. See Cathcart, *Bapt. Encyclop.* p. 338. (J. C. S.)

Dobda (or **Dubhda**), an Irish saint, commemorated April 15, seems to have been bishop of Chiem-see, in Upper Bavaria, cir. A.D. 748, and assistant of St. Virgilius as bishop of Salzburg, cir. A.D. 756.

Dobie, JAMES, D.D., a Scotch clergyman, was licensed in Northumberland; received by the Presbytery of Kelso; presented to the living at Mid-Calder in January, and ordained July 27, 1773; transferred to Linlithgow, May 31, 1792; and died November 10, 1826, aged eighty years. He published a *Sermon Preached after the Death of Lord President Blair and Viscount Melville* (Edinburgh, 1811):—*An Account of the Parish.* See *Fasti Eccles. Scoticanæ*, i, 162, 176.

Dobrila, GEORG, a Greek prelate, was born April 16, 1812, at Antignano, in Istria. In 1837 he received holy orders; in 1842 was made doctor of theology at Vienna; shortly afterwards was called as chaplain and catechist to Trieste, where in 1849 he was appointed rector and professor at the Episcopal seminary. In 1854 he was made dean, in 1857 raised to the bishopric of Trieste and Capo d'Istria, and died Jan. 13, 1882. (B. P.)

Doc (Lat. *Docæus*), JEAN, a French prelate, was a Benedictine monk of the abbey of Saint-Denis, near Paris, also doctor of theology and canonical law, as well as an excellent preacher. He was elevated to the dignity of a grand-prior of Saint-Denis, and in 1557 was placed in the episcopal see of Laon. He died in 1560, leaving *De Æterna Filii Dei Generatione* (Paris, 1554):—*Homiliæ per Annum* (Antwerp, 1640). See Hoefer, *Nouv. Biog. Générale*, s. v.

Docampo, GONSALVO, a Spanish prelate and native of Madrid, lived for a long time in Italy and was the favorite of Clement VIII; became canon of Seville, archdeacon of Niebla, bishop of Cadiz, and finally archbishop of Lima, Peru, in 1623. He died in 1626, leaving *Del Govierno del Peru*:—*Una Carto Pastoral a Todas los Curas de Almas de su Arzobispado.* See Hoefer, *Nouv. Biog. Générale*, s. v.

Doctor. We here give an alphabetical list of such additional epithets as were given to some doctors of the middle ages, although some of them were not public teachers:

Doctor abstractionum, acutus et illuminatissimus, to Francis of Mayroni (Marojus), who died in 1323;
acutissimus, to Francis d'Albescola della Rovere (afterwards pope Sixtus IV), died in 1484;
acutus, to Gabriel Vasquez, a Jesuit, died in 1604;
admirabilis (*mirabilis*), to Roger Bacon, died in 1294;
amœnus, to Robert of Cownton, died about 1340;
angelicus, communis, also *cherubicus*, to Thomas Aquinas, died in 1274;
authenticus, to Gregorius de Rimini, died in 1358;
authoratus, copiosus, fundatissimus et solidus, to Richard of Middleton, died about 1300;

Doctor beatus et fundatissimus, to Ægidius de Colonna, died in 1316;
bonus, to Walther Brinkeli, died about 1310;
cherubicus, see *angelicus;*
christianissimus, to Johannes Gersonus, died in 1429;
christianus, to Nicolaus of Cusa, died in 1464;
clarus, to Louis de Montesinos, died in 1621;
clarus et subtilis, to Dionysius the Younger, of the 14th century;
collectivus, to Landulf Caracciole, died in 1351;
columna, to William of Champeaux, died in 1121;
communis, see *angelicus;*
contradictionum, to John Wessel, died in 1489;
conspicuus et planus, to Walther Burleigh, died after 1337;
copiosus, see *authoratus;*
divinus, ecstaticus, to John of Ruysbroeck, died in 1381;
doctorum, to Anselm of Laon, died in 1117;
dulcifluus, to Anton Andreæ, died about 1320;
ecstaticus, to Dionysius de Leewis of Rickel, died in 1471;
ecstaticus, see *divinus;*
elegans et facundus, to Peter Aureoli, died in 1322;
eminens, to St. John of Matha, died in 1213;
evangelicus, to John Wycliffe, died in 1384;
excellentissimus, to Anton Corsetti, died in 1503;
eximius, to John Tisserius, died about 1564; and Francis Suarez, died in 1617;
facundus, see *elegans;*
famosissimus, to Peter Alberti, died about 1426;
famosus, to Bertrand de la Tour, died in 1334;
fundamentalis, subtilis et perspicacissimus, to John Faber of Bordeaux, died about 1350;
fundatissimus, see *authoratus* and *beatus;*
fundatus, to William Verus (de Waria), died about 1270;
illibatus, to Alexander Alamannicus of the 15th century;
illuminatissimus, see *abstractionum;*
illuminatus, to Raymond Lullus, died in 1315;
illuminatus et sublimis, to John Tauler, died in 1361;
illustratus, to Francis Picenus (de Marchia) of the 14th century;
illustris, or *illustratus*, to Adam of Morisco, died about 1308;
inclytus, to William Mackelfield, died about 1300;
ingeniosissimus, to Andrew of Neufchâteau, died about 1300;
invincibilis, to Petrus Thomas of the 14th century;
invincibilis et singularis, to William Occam, died about 1347;
irrefragabilis, fons vitæ, monarcha theologorum, to Alexander Hales, died in 1243;
magnus, universalis, to Alanus of Ryssel, died in 1202;
marianus, to Anselm of Canterbury, died in 1109; and John Duns Scotus, died in 1308;
mellifluus, to St. Bernard, died in 1153;
mellifluus alter, to Ælred, died in 1166;
mirabilis, see *admirabilis;*
mirabilis, to Anton Perez, the Jesuit, died in 1649;
moralis, to Gerhard Eudo (Odonis), died in 1349;
notabilis, to Peter of Ryssel;
ordinatissimus, or *ornatissimus*, to John de Barsolis, died about 1347;
ornatissimus et sufficiens, to Peter de Aquila, died about 1344;
pacificus et proficuus (*profitabilis*), to Nicholas Bonetus, died in 1360;
perspicacissimus, see *fundamentalis;*
perspicuus, see *conspicuus;*
planus, see *conspicuus;*
planus et utilis, to Nicholas de Lyra, died in 1341;
præclarus, to Peter of Kaiserslautern, died about 1330;
præstantissimus, to Thomas Netter of Walden, died in 1431;
proficuus and *profitabilis*, see *pacificus;*
profundus, to Thomas of Bradwardin, died in 1349;
profundissimus, to Paul of Venice, died in 1428; Gabriel Biel, died in 1495; and John Alfons Curiel, died in 1609;
refulgidus, to Peter Philargi (afterwards pope Alexander V), died in 1410;
resolutissimus, to William Durandus de S. Pourçain, died in 1332;
resolutus, princeps Averroistarum, to John Baco, died in 1346;
scholasticus, to Peter Abelard, died in 1142; Gilbert de la Porée, died in 1154; Petrus Lombardus, died in 1164; Peter of Poictiers, died in 1205; and Hugo de Castro Novo, who died after 1322;
seraphicus, to Bonaventura, died in 1274; sometimes, also, attributed to St. Francis of Assisi, who died in 1226;
singularis, see *invincibilis;*
solemnis, to Henry Goethals of Ghent, died in 1293;
solidus, see *authoratus;*
speculativus, to Jacobus of Viterbo, died in 1308;
sublimis, see *illuminatus;*
sublimis, to Francis de Bachone, died in 1372; and John of Courte-Cuisse, who died about 1425;
subtilis, to John Duns Scotus, died in 1308;
Doctor subtilis, see *clarus* and *fundamentalis;*
subtilissimus, to Peter of Mantua of the 14th century;
succinctus, to Francis of Arcoli, who died about 1340;
sufficiens, see *ornatissimus;*
summus doctorum, to Peter of Belle-Perche, who died in 1308;
universalis, to Albertus Magnus, who died in 1280:
universalis, see *magnus;*
utilis, see *planus;*
venerandus, to Walfried de Fontibus, who died after 1240.

See Streber, in Wetzer u. Welte's *Kirchen-Lexikon*, s. v. (B. P.)

Doctor audientium (*teacher of the hearers*), the instructor of the *audientes* (q. v.), or lowest order of catechumens in the early Church. They were simply catechists.

Doctors, CHRIST *in Conference with.* The subject is represented in a fresco of the first cubiculum of the Callixtine catacomb. Our Lord is on a lofty seat in the midst, with hand upraised in the act of speaking; the doctors on his right and left, with some expression of wonder on their countenances. The only sarcophagus besides that of Junius Bassus, which *indisputably* contains this subject, is said by Martigny to be in San Ambrogio, at Milan. In this representation Christ is placed in a stall or *edicule* above the surrounding figures, which are seated, while two palms stand by him, one on either side. He holds in his hand a book or scroll, which is partly unrolled, while the doctors have closed theirs. In Allegranza, tav. i, a mosaic from San Aquilino of Milan represents the Lord's elevated seat on a rock, with the divine lamb below, referring to Rev. v, "able to open the book." On his right and left are Joseph and Mary in the attitude of adoration. Perret gives a copy of a very skilful painting from the catacombs, which places two doctors on the Lord's right hand, who are expressing attention and wonder, and Joseph and Mary on the other, with looks of patient waiting for him. The fine diptych of the 5th century at the cathedral of Milan, and that of Murano, also represent our Lord sitting, with the doctors standing before him. His appearance here is more mature than the Gospels warrant. Below his

Diptych of Murano.

feet is a figure, supposed to represent Uranus, or the firmament of the heavens (Psa. xviii, 9).

Doctrīna ADDÆI. See ADDÆI DOCTRINA.

Doctrīna DUODĔCIM APOSTOLŌRUM. See TEACHING OF THE TWELVE APOSTLES.

Doctrinaires is the common name of two religious associations which originated, independently of each other, in Italy and France. In Italy the movement began under pope Pius IV, and the association was established by Marcus de Sedis-Cusani, who associated with himself some persons for the purpose of instructing the people, more especially the children, in the catechism.

Priest of the Christian Doctrine in Italy.

Pope Gregory XIII approved of this society, called *Padri della Dottrina Christiana*. In France the association of the *Pères de la Doctrine Chrétienne* was founded by Cæsar de Bus, priest and canon of Cavaillon, in 1592, and was confirmed by pope Clement VIII. See Helyot, *Histoire des Ordres Monastiques* (Paris, 1714–19), iv, 232-252; Herzog, *Real-Encyklop.* s. v.; Lichtenberger, *Encyclop. des Sciences Religieuses*, s. v. (B. P.)

Docus. See CADOC.

Dod, Albert Baldwin, D.D., a Presbyterian minister, was born at Mendham, N. J., March 24, 1805. He graduated at Princeton College in 1822; spent about four years teaching near Fredericksburg, Va.; was licensed to preach in the spring of 1828 by the Presbytery of New York; and in 1830 appointed to the mathematical professorship in the college of Princeton, where he labored till his death, Nov. 20, 1845. Professor Dod published several articles in the *Biblical Repertory*, one of which, on "Transcendentalism," attracted great attention, and was printed in a separate pamphlet. He was a man of very great ability as a writer and debater, and was very popular as a professor among his pupils. His sermons dealt with principles and strove to convince the understanding and rule the convictions. See *Index to Princeton Rev.* 1825–1868.

Dod, John, an English divine, was born at Shotledge, Cheshire, in 1547; was bred in Jesus College, Cambridge; by nature a witty, by industry a learned, by grace a godly, divine; successively minister of Hanwell, in Oxford, Fenny Compton, in Warwick, Canons Ashby and Fawsley, in Northamptonshire, though for a time silenced in each of them, and died, after a holy life in troublesome times, in 1645. When his mouth was shut by the authorities he instructed as much as before by his holy demeanor and pious discourse. His chief production was an *Exposition of the Ten Commandments* (Lond. 1606), whence he is often styled *the Decalogist.* See Fuller, *Worthies of England* (ed. Nuttall), i, 278; Chalmers, *Biog. Dict.* s. v.

Dod, William Armstrong, D.D., a Protestant Episcopal clergyman, appears in the ministry in 1859, residing at that time in Princeton, N. J., and became rector of Trinity Church in that place. This office he held until 1866, but he continued to reside in Princeton until his death, Dec. 3, 1872, aged fifty-six years. See *Prot. Episc. Almanac*, 1874, p. 138.

Dodd, Charles (or *Richard Tootle*), a Roman Catholic clergyman, resided at Harvington, in Worcestershire, England, and died there about 1745. His most celebrated work is a *Church History of England* (Brussels, 1737–42, 3 vols. fol.), several editions of which have appeared. See Chalmers, *Biog. Dict.* s. v.; Allibone, *Dict. of Brit. and Amer. Authors*, s. v.

Dodge, Orrin, D.D., a Baptist minister, was born in Litchfield County, Conn., in 1803. He was baptized by Bishop Griswold, and received his early religious training in the Protestant Episcopal Church. In 1815 he removed to central New York, attending school and working on a farm. From the age of seventeen to twenty-six he taught school; for three years was in a public position in West Troy, and then for several years in active mercantile business. Being converted in 1831, he was licensed in 1833, and ordained at Sand Lake, in May, 1834, remaining there three years. His other pastorates were Maysville, nine years, West Troy, two years, and Ballston, two years. In 1848 he was appointed secretary for missions for the New York Baptist Convention, and, about a year after, agent for collecting funds for the American Baptist Missionary Union, in which position, through a long term, he exhibited rare executive abilities. For five years he was laid aside from his labors by paralysis, and died at the residence of his daughter, in the city of New York, May 17, 1884. See Cathcart, *Bapt. Encyclop.* p. 340. (J. C. S.)

Dodge, William Earl, an eminent philanthropic elder in the Presbyterian Church, was born at Hartford, Conn., Sept. 4, 1805. He came to New York in 1818 and entered a dry-goods store as an errand boy and clerk, and, after remaining nine years, set up business for himself in the same line; but in 1833 entered into partnership with his father-in-law, Anson G. Phelps, and continued in the same business until his death, Feb. 9, 1883. Mr. Dodge was supposed to have left a fortune of upwards of five million dollars. He was either a president or director of many companies and societies. President Lincoln appointed him on the famous Indian Commission. He was a member of the Thirty-ninth Congress, of the Peace Commission of 1861, and of the Loyal League Commission, delegate to the World's Christian Alliance, and president for three terms of the Chamber of Commerce. He resigned the presidency of the Republican Union because of its deriving part of its revenue from the sale of liquor, and of a railroad company because of its violation of the Sabbath. Few have done more for the cause of temperance than Mr. Dodge. He was actively engaged in every benevolent enterprise, and gave upwards of one hundred thousand dollars a year to benevolent objects. (W. P. S.)

Dodo. (1) Abbot of St. Genulfus in Bourges, died cir. A.D. 850. (2) Called also *Odo*, abbot of St. Martial at Limousin, about the middle of the 9th century. (3) The twenty-first bishop of Toul, at the beginning of the 8th century.

Dodolinus (called also *Dolinus*, *Laudolenus*, and even *Boholinus*), a French saint, bishop of Vienne about the middle of the 7th century, is commemorated on April 1.

Dodwell, WILLIAM, D.D., an English clergyman, born at Shottesbrook, in Berkshire, June 17, 1709, was educated at Trinity College, Oxford, where he took his master's degree in 1732. He was rector of Shottesbrook and vicar of Buckleberry and of White-Waltham; became a canon of the cathedral church at Salisbury, and was promoted to the archdeaconry of Berks by Bishop Thomas. He died Oct. 21, 1785. The following are some of his publications: *Two Sermons on the Eternity of Future Punishment*:—*Visitation Sermon on the Desirableness of the Christian Faith* (Oxford, 1744):—*Two Sermons on Rational Faith* (ibid. 1745):—*Dissertation on Jephthah's Vow* (London, 1745):—*Sermon on St. Paul's Wish* (Oxford, 1752), and many other single sermons. See Chalmers, *Biog. Dict.* s. v.; Allibone, *Dict. of Brit. and Amer. Authors*, s. v.

Dogfan, a Welsh saint, slain in the 5th century by the pagan Saxons, is commemorated July 13.

Doggett, DAVID SETH, D.D., a bishop of the Methodist Episcopal Church South, was born in Lancaster County, Va., June 26, 1810. He was educated at the University of Virginia, and intended to follow the legal profession, but after his conversion gave it up for the ministry; on leaving college taught school a year in Orange County, Va., and in 1829 entered the Virginia Conference. That year he was sent to Roanoke Circuit, N. C.; in 1830 to Mattamuskeet Circuit, in the same state; in 1831 to Petersburg, Va.; in 1832 to Lynchburg; in 1834 to Trinity Station, Richmond; in 1835 to Petersburg; in 1836 to Norfolk; in 1838 to Lynchburg; in 1839 to Charlotteville, acting meanwhile as chaplain to the University of Virginia; and in 1840 was chaplain to Randolph-Macon College, and pastor of the town in which the college was then located. From 1841 to 1846 he was professor of mental and moral philosophy in the same institution. In 1847 he was again sent to Lynchburg; in 1849 to Washington Street Station, Petersburg; in 1851 to Richmond; in 1853 to Granby Street Station, Norfolk; in 1855 edited the *Review*; in 1856 went to Washington, D. C.; in 1858 was presiding elder of the Richmond District; in 1862 served Broad Street Station, and in 1864 Centenary Church. In 1865 he was associate editor with Rev. John E. Edwards, D.D., of the *Episcopal Methodist*, in Richmond; and in April, 1867, was elected to the Episcopacy. He continued to reside in the same city, and executed the duties of his high office with great zeal, devotedness, and success until his death, Oct. 27, 1880. It is thought he hastened his decease by overtaxing himself responding to extra calls in the summer of 1880. See *The Quarterly Review of the M. E. Church South*, Jan. 1881, p. 109; Simpson, *Cyclop. of Methodism*, s. v.

Dogura (or **Jumboo**) Version *of the Scriptures*. This dialect is spoken in the mountainous or northern districts of Lahore, and east of the river Chenab and of Cashmere. A version of the New. Test. in Dogura was undertaken in Serampore in 1814, and left the press in 1826. (B. P.)

Dohrn, Johann Albert Bernhard, a distinguished Orientalist of Germany, was born in 1805 at Scheuerfeld, near Coburg. He studied theology at Halle and Leipsic, but afterwards turned his attention exclusively to the languages of the East. In 1826 he was appointed professor of Sanscrit in the University of Kharkov, in Russia. Six years later he was called to the chair of Asiatic history and geography in the Oriental Institute at St. Petersburg, which he resigned in 1843 to become senior librarian of the imperial public library. He died in 1881. He published in 1846 *Das Asiatische Museum der Kaiserlicher Akademie der Wissenschaften*, and in 1852 *Catalogue des Manuscrits et Xylographes Orientaux*. His last undertaking was an elaborate work on the migration of the ancient Huns in Taberistan. (B. P.)

Dolben, John (1), D.D., an English clergyman and archbishop of York, born at Stanwick, in Northamptonshire, March 20, 1625, was educated at Westminster school, being admitted a king's scholar in 1636, and in 1640 elected to Christ Church, Oxford. He was ordained about 1652; in 1660 presented to the rectory of Newington-cum-Britwell, in Oxfordshire, in the gift of the archbishop of Canterbury; in 1662 appointed archdeacon of London, and presented to the vicarage of St. Giles, Cripplegate, but resigned both in a short time to take the deanery of Westminster. In 1666 he was consecrated bishop of Rochester, and allowed to hold the deanery of Westminster *in commendam;* translated to the see of York in 1683, and became an ecclesiastical governor of that place. He died April 11, 1686. See Chalmers, *Biog. Dict.* s. v.; Allibone, *Dict. of Brit. and Amer. Authors*, s. v.

Dolben, *Sir* **John** (2), D.D., an English clergyman, was made prebendary of Durham, April 2, 1718. He published a sermon, *Concio ad Clerum*, on Heb. xii, 1 (1726). See Allibone, *Dict. of Brit. and Amer. Authors*, s. v.

Dolcino, leader of the Apostolici (q. v.), was born in the diocese of Novara. He was the son of a priest, joined the Apostolici in 1291, and became their leader in 1300, after the death of Segarelle. On behalf of his sect he wrote three works, of which the third is entirely lost, but of the first two there are some extracts in the *Additamentum ad Historiam Dulcini*. The first was written in 1300, at Dalmatia, and is addressed to the scattered members of the sect as well as to all Christians. He distinguishes four stages, *status*, in the development of the divine life on earth. The first begins with the patriarchs, the second with Christ and his apostles, the third with pope Silvester and the emperor Constantine the Great, and the fourth with Segarelle and himself. Each stage was good in itself, but degeneration called forth a new one, for the better. The fourth stage was to last to the end of the world. Dolcino also made some predictions, which proved a failure, yet in spite of this the people did not lose confidence in him. There are, indeed, in his works both true religious enthusiasm and a sharp sense of the corruption of the Church; but both are blurred by the whims of a sensuous and ill-regulated imagination. Dante (*Inferno*, xxviii, 55 sq.) puts him on the same level with Mohammed. See *Historia Dulcini* and *Additamentum*, in Muratori, *Script. Rerum Ital.* ix, 425 sq.; Mosheim, *Geschichte des Apostelordens*, in his *Ketzergeschichte* (Helmstädt, 1748), p. 193 sq.; Schlosser, *Abälard und Dulcin* (Gotha, 1807); Baggiolini, *Dolcino e i Patareni* (Novara, 1838); Krone, *Fra Dolcino und die Patarener* (Leipsic, 1844); Döllinger, *Der Weissagungsglaube und das Prophetenthum in der christlichen Zeit*, in Riehl's *Histor. Taschenbuch*, 1871; Schmidt, in Plitt-Herzog, *Real-Encyklop.* s. v.; Lichtenberger, *Encyclopédie des Sciences Religieuses*, s. v. (B. P.)

Dolera, Clemente, a Genoese prelate and theologian, was born at Moneglia in 1501. He was a Franciscan, and became general of his order. In 1557 Paul IV made him cardinal, with the title of *Sainte-Marie de Ara Cœli*, and bishop of Foligno. He died at Rome, Jan. 6, 1568, leaving, *Compendium Catholicarum Institutionum* (Rome, 1562):—*De Symbola Apostolorum:—De Sacramentis:—De Præceptis Divinis:—De Peccatis et Eorum Differentiis:—De Consiliis Evangelicis:—De Cœlibatu Sacerdotum:—De Œcumenico Concilio*, etc. See Hoefer, *Nouv. Biog. Générale*, s. v.

Dolichiānus (or **Dulichianus**), twenty-ninth bishop of Jerusalem, about the last quarter of the 2d century.

Dolium, a convenient generic term for the various representations of casks and large vessels which occur frequently in early Christian art, and have symbolic meaning very generally attributed to them. As they are usually found on tombs, they are taken as empty, representing the body when the soul has fled from it. The close juncture of the staves in some of the casks has been thought to indicate Christian unity.

Casks. (From the Catacombs.)

Dollendorp, Johann (or Heinrich von), a German theologian, was a professed monk of the convent of the Carmelites of Cologne and doctor of the University of Paris. He taught in that capital in 1339, became provincial of his order for Germany in 1351, and gained great reputation both as a theologian and as a preacher. He died at Cologne in 1375, leaving, *Super Sententias:—Sermones de Tempore:—Sermones de Sanctis*, etc. See Hoefer, *Nouv. Biog. Générale*, s. v.

Doller, Johann Lorenz, a Roman Catholic theologian of Germany, was born Oct. 3, 1750, at Bretten. In 1768 he joined the order of Jesuits at Mayence, and in 1772 was appointed professor at Heidelberg. In 1779 he resigned on account of feeble health, and died Jan. 30, 1820. He published, *Zeugnisse aller Jahrhunderte* (Frankfort-on-the-Main, 1816):—*Luther's Katholisches Monument* (ibid. 1817). See Döring, *Die gelehrten Theologen Deutschlands*, i, 339 sq.; Winer, *Handbuch der Theol. Lit.* i, 405, 465. (B. P.)

Dolphin, *in Christian Art.* The dolphin has been used from an early date in several senses, representing either the Lord himself, the individual Christian, or abstract qualities, such as those of swiftness, brilliancy, conjugal affection, etc.

The Dolphin as an Emblem.

Dolz (Lat. *Dolscius*), PAUL, a German theologian and Græcist, was born at Plauen, in 1526. He studied at the University of Wittenberg. Melanchthon, who was his instructor, took him into his friendship, and helped him to obtain a place at the gymnasium of Halle. Dolscius attached himself closely to the cause and the doctrines of the famous reformer. He also studied medicine, and wrote Greek with facility. The city of Halle appointed him burgomaster, and later inspector of the churches, schools, and salt-wells. He died there, March 9, 1589. His principal works are, *Confessio Fidei Exhibita Augustæ Græce Reddita* (Basle, 1559):—*Psalmi Davidis Græcis Versibus Elegiacis Redditi* (ibid. 1555). See Hoefer, *Nouv. Biog. Générale*, s. v.

Dom, a title of respect given to the Benedictines and canons, being the abbreviation of *dominus*, which was the Latin for the mediæval *ser* (sieur), and *sir* of the Reformation, and was applied to non-graduate priests. The A.B. of Cambridge is now designated "dominus," but the A.M., as at Oxford, is "dominus magister," and the D.D. "dominus doctor."

Domenec, MICHAEL, D.D., a Roman Catholic bishop, was a native of Spain. He joined the American mission of Lazarists while studying for the priesthood, was ordained at Cape Girardeau, Mo., and for many years served as pastor at Germantown, Pa. On Dec. 6, 1860, he was consecrated bishop of Pittsburgh, as successor to Dr. O'Connor, resigned. On Jan. 11, 1876, his diocese being divided, the new see of Allegheny was created, to which Domenec was translated. His health soon after failing, he went to Europe, and after visiting Rome, resigned his see, and died at Tarragona, Spain, Feb. 5, 1878, aged sixty-five years. As a bishop Domenec was esteemed for his energy, charity, self-devotion, and zeal. See De Courcy and Shea, *Hist. of the Cath. Church in the U. S.* p. 302.

Domenichi (or **de Domenico**), an Italian prelate and theologian, was born in Venice in 1416. He taught logic at Padua, theology at Bologna and Rome, and was appointed bishop of Torcello in 1448. Paul II transferred him to the see of Brescia, and Sixtus IV appointed him governor of Rome. Domenichi died at Brescia in 1478, leaving, *De Reformationibus Romanæ Curiæ* (Brescia, 1495):—*De Sanguine Christi* (Venice, 1557):—*De Dignitate Episcopali* (Rome, 1757). He also published an edition of the *Moralia* of Gregory the Great (ibid. 1475). See Hoefer, *Nouv. Biog. Générale*, s. v.

Domenichino. See ZAMPIERI, DOMENICO.

Domestic ("belonging to the house or household") has several ecclesiastical senses: (1) *Domestici* are all who belong to the "household of faith." (2) In the East, the principal dignitary in a church choir after the "chief singer." There was one on each side of the choir, to lead the singers in antiphonal chanting. (3) *Domesticus Ostiorum* ("of the doors"), the chief doorkeeper at Constantinople. See Smith, *Dict. of Christ. Antiq.* s. v.

Domingo DE JESUS MARIA, a Spanish theologian, was born at Calatayud (Old Castile), May 16, 1559. He taught first among the Carmelites of the ancient observance, and afterwards took the habit of the barefooted Carmelites. Being called to Rome about 1590, he was raised to the highest offices of his order, and was engaged by the pope in various important embassies. Besides Greek and Latin, Domingo knew nearly all living languages. He died at Vienna, Feb. 16, 1630, leaving, *Sentenze Spirituali* (Paris, 1623):—*Argumenta Psalmorum Divini* (Rome, eod.):—*Alia Argumenta Psalmorum* (ibid.):—*La Concordia Espiritual* (Bruxelles, 1626; translated into French under the title, *De la Théologie Mystique*):—*De la Protection de la Vierge* (Paris, 1645):—*Directoire pour Bien Mourir*:—*Vie du Frère Alexis de Saint-Bernard, Polonais*, etc. See Hoefer, *Nouv. Biog. Générale*, s. v.; Bonif. Müller, *Leben und Werken d. Dominicus a Jesu Maria* (Vienna, 1878).

Dominic, *Saint* (surnamed *Loricatus*, from the iron coat of mail which he constantly wore next to his skin), a famous Italian hermit, who died at Fonta Vellano (Umbria), Oct. 14, 1060, had passed through all the clerical degrees and then devoted himself to a life of soliary penance and extreme austerity, inflicting lashes upon himself daily, and hourly reciting certain Psalms.

Dominic OF FLANDERS, a theologian, went to Italy when very young; entered the order of the Dominicans, and taught theology at Bologna, where he died in 1500. He wrote several books on scholastic philosophy, for which see Hoefer, *Nouv. Biog. Générale*, s. v.

Dominic OF THE HOLY TRINITY, a French theologian, was born at Nevers, Aug. 4, 1616. He belonged to a nobleman's family, and in 1634 joined the Carmelites in Paris. He was sent to Rome to teach; then went to Malta as inquisitor, but came back to Rome again. In 1656 he was made general of his order, and pope Clement X appointed him qualifier of the holy office. He died at Rome, April 7, 1687, leaving, *De Anno Jubilæi* (Rome, 1650):—*Bibliotheca Theologica*, etc. (ibid. 1665–76, 7 vols.). See Hoefer, *Nouv. Biog. Générale*, s. v.

Dominic OF JERUSALEM, a converted rabbi, was born in 1550. He was made doctor at Safet, in Galilee, where he lectured on the Talmud, and became physician to the sultan. In 1600 he was converted to Christianity at Rome, where he taught Hebrew. He translated the New Test. into Hebrew. See Hoefer, *Nouv. Biog. Générale*, s. v.

Dominic OF ST. GEMINIAN, a famous canonist of the 15th century, was a native of San Geminiano, in Florence. After completing his studies, he became in 1407 vicar-general to the bishop of Modena, took part in 1409 in the synod of Pisa, and was for many years professor at Bologna, where he died. He wrote, *Commentaria Propria Diligentissime Castigata in Decretum* (edited by P. Albignac, Venice, 1504):—*Commentarius in Sextum* (Venice, 1558, 1579):—*Consilia et Responsa* (Leyden, 1533; Venice, 1550). Comp. Schulte, *Geschichte der Quellen und Literatur des canonischen Rechts*, ii, 295 (Stuttgart, 1877); Streber, in Wetzer u. Welte's *Kirchen-Lexikon*, s. v. (B. P.)

Dominic OF ST. THOMAS, a Portuguese theologian, was born at Lisbon, and lived about the year 1674. He belonged to the Dominican order, and became successively prior, royal preacher, doctor, and professor of theology. He wrote *Summa Theologiæ* (Lisbon, 1690), containing a long statement of the nature and origin of the inquisition. See Hoefer, *Nouv. Biog. Générale*, s. v.

Dominĭca, the *Lord's day*, not the Sabbath. See SUNDAY.

Dominĭca, a matron saint, commemorated Jan. 8.

Dominica GAUDII (*the Lord's day of joy*), a name given by some of the ancient Christian writers to *Easter Sunday*. The Roman emperors were accustomed on that day, as a token of joy, to grant a release to all prisoners except those guilty of great crimes.

Dominican. We add the following particulars from Walcott, *Sac. Archæol.* s. v.:

"The rule, a modification of that of St. Austin, was strict abstinence from flesh; fasts of seven months' duration, from Holy Cross Day to Easter, and on all Fridays; maintenance wholly by the alms of the faithful; the use of woollen clothes only; and at first a mere white tunic and scapular, without a cowl. In time this rigor was abated, and they wore a white serge tunic, a black cappa or cloak, and a hood for the head; and their simple, unadorned chapels became magnificent churches, rich in every ornament of architecture, color, and carving. From their devotion to the Blessed Virgin, they called themselves at first, until the pope forbade it, *Brothers of the Virgin Mary;* and they always had a Madonna and crucifix in their cells. There was a general chapter held annually. The superior was called master of the order, and the greater officers, priors and superiors. The order was instituted for preaching at home and for missions to the heathen; it has produced one thousand four hundred and fifty-eight cardinals. It used to take mere children and enroll them before the conventional age of probation. They held that the Virgin was conceived in original sin, consecrated Saturdays to her honor, and were, in scholastic theology, stout Thomists. Their preaching-cross remains at Hereford, their refectory at Canterbury, the nave of the church and other buildings may be seen at Norwich, and part of their convent at Lynn, Beverley, and Gloucester. There were three divisions of the order—the preaching friars, who occupied a convent; cloistered nuns; and the militia of Jesus Christ, who engaged in actual war on heretics; they afterwards admitted brethren and sisters of the Penitence of St. Dominic, who were approved in 1360 by Innocent VI. Bishop Pecock says they evaded their rule, which forbade them to touch money, by counting with a stick. The early Dominican churches were plain, without images, carvings, or pictures, and provided with only one bell. The use of the organ was not common. Women were not allowed to sit in the choir-aisles, and large high screens parted off the friars from the congregation, for whose use, at the elevation of the host, windows were opened in these partitions. The lay brothers sat apart. Occasionally their churches, as at Venice and Pistoia, were cruciform, but usually terminated in a square end; the naves of Perugia and Spoleto are aisleless, but sometimes they had narrow recesses, as at Ghent, or lateral chantries for altars; or, as at Pisa, Sligo, Brecon, Kilmallock, Gloucester, and Roscommon, a single aisle for the accommodation of the congregation at sermons; lateral chapels were added at a later date. Apsidal choirs occur at Monza, Milan, Toulouse, Antwerp, Oberwesel; and at Paris, Agen, and Toulouse the church was double, consisting simply of two aisles of equal length. At Louvain and Norwich the nave has aisles of the usual size. The choirs had no aisles. The chapter-house at Toulouse was apsidal, and had three aisles. This order prays more than any other for the dead, the friars chanting the 'De Profundis' every time they pass through the cloister."

Dominican Monk of Convers.

Dominican Nun, with Cape.

Dominici, Giovanni, an Italian prelate and theologian, was born at Florence about 1356, entered the Dominican order, and became a famous teacher of theology and canon law; also distinguished himself as a preacher; went on an embassy to Rome in 1406; was made bishop of Ragusa in 1407, and cardinal in 1408 (which preferments led to a violent controversy), and died at Buda in 1419, leaving several minor productions, for which see Hoefer, *Nouv. Biog. Générale,* s. v.

Dominĭcus (1), *Saint,* bishop of Cambray, cir. A.D. 540; (2) bishop of Carthage in the time of Gregory the Great; (3) bishop of Civita Vecchia, A.D. 601; (4) the eleventh bishop of Carpentras, A.D. 640–645; (5) the fifth bishop of Amiens, A.D. 721; (6) seventh bishop of Sion (Sedunum), A.D. 516.

Dominius, third bishop of Geneva in the first half of the 5th century.

Domĭnus (or **Domnus,** in later Gallican documents), equivalent to "saint," the same as the *mar* of the Chaldæan Christians, was at first a title of the abbot, afterwards of his sub-officials, and in the Middle Ages of monks generally. It has been applied to saints, bishops, and to the pope.

Domio, a martyr, was bishop of Salona, in Dalmatia, and is commemorated April 11.

Domitiānus, (1) abbot of Lyons; deposition July 1; (2) martyr at Philadelphia, in Arabia; commemorated Aug. 1; (3) deacon and martyr at Ancyra, in Galatia, with Eutyches; commemorated Dec. 28; (4) *saint,* abbot of Rambach-de-Joux, in the diocese of Lyons, in the 4th or 5th century; commemorated July 1; (5) seventh bishop of Geneva, about A.D. 470; (6) seventh bishop of Cologne, A.D. 535; (7) twelfth bishop of Angers, cir. A.D. 557–568; (8) *saint,* bishop of Maestricht in the middle of the 6th century, of whom some legendary miracles are told, is commemorated May 7; (9) metropolitan bishop of Ancyra, one of the Acephali, wrote to pope Vigilius *On the Origenian Controversy,* A.D. 554 (see Migne, lxvii, 532, 627); (10) bishop of Melitene and metropolitan of Armenia, cir. A.D. 564, was a well-read scholar, and an eminent saint. He was a relative of the emperor (Maurice), and one of his principal officers. After he had become a widower he consecrated himself to the service of God, and was raised to the see of Melitene, a city of Armenia. In 589 Maurice sent him to Chosroes II, king of Persia, who was dethroned by his subjects. Domitianus assisted the defeated monarch with his counsels, and did not neglect anything to convert him, but without success, so that finally he wrote about him to pope Gregory. Domitianus came back to Constantinople, where Maurice kept him near, as his adviser and minister, assigning him even the guardianship of his children, but the prelate died before the emperor, in 602. The body of Domitianus was transferred to Melitene, and as Theophylact says, "God attested his holiness by various miracles." He is commemorated Jan. 10.

Domitilla, a virgin martyr at Terracina, in Campania, under Domitian and Trajan; commemorated May 7 (or 12).

Domitius, (1) martyr in Syria, commemorated July 5; (2) martyr in Phrygia, under Julian, commemorated Aug. 7; (3) *saint,* a confessor and ecclesiastic near Amiens, before the middle of the 8th century; he resigned his office, and lived the rest of his days as a hermit. His relics were transferred in 1279 to the Cathedral of Amiens. He is commemorated Oct. 23.

Dommerich, Johann Christoph, a Lutheran theologian of Germany, was born Dec. 25, 1723, at Bückeburg. He studied at Halle; for some time acted as tutor in the orphanage there; in 1747 was appointed morning preacher at his native place, but in the following year accepted a call to Helmstädt; in 1749 became rector at Wolfenbüttel, and in 1759 professor of metaphysics at Helmstädt, where he died, May 28, 1767. He wrote, *Meditationes Philosophicæ et Theologicæ* (Lemgo, 1744):—*Commentatio Theologica* (Helmstädt, 1748):—*De Fœdere Baptismali* (ibid. 1749):—*Theologisches Compendium* (Halle, 1759):—*Gedanken über den Skepticismus* (Braunschweig, 1767). See Döring, *Die gelehrten Theologen Deutschlands*, i, 341 sq.; Jöcher, *Allgemeines Gelehrten-Lexikon*, s. v. (B. P.)

Domnina (or **Domnia**), *Saint*, was of a noble family of Antioch. Having become a widow, she professed Christianity with her two daughters, Bernice and Prosdoce, and on the outbreak of the persecution by Diocletian, the three retired to Edessa. They were seized and ordered to Antioch; but on reaching a river near Hierapolis, they took each other by the hand, precipitated themselves into the water, and were drowned. Their bodies were taken from the river and brought to Antioch, where Chrysostom testifies that they were in his time. They are commemorated April 14.

Domnīnus, (1) martyr at Thessalonica, under Galerius, commemorated March 30; (2) martyr at Cæsarea, with several others, under Maximin, Nov. 5, 307; commemorated Oct. 9; (3) *saint*, bishop of Digne, in Gaul, in the beginning of the 3d century; commemorated Feb. 13; (4) bishop of Marcionopolis, in Mœsia Inferior, cir. A.D. 360; (5) sometimes called *saint*, bishop of Grenoble at the Council of Aquileia; (6) *saint*, twenty-second bishop of Vienne, in France, about the middle of the 6th century.

Domnŏlus (or **Domus**), (1) *Saint* (otherwise called *Andelain*), a confessor of Auxerre, is commemorated Oct. 21; (2) *saint* (otherwise called *Anolet, Dampnolet, Tonnolein*, etc.), is said to have been a prince of Limosin, where his body was originally buried in the Church of St. Gregory, near the monastery of St. Andrew, but was taken outside the city in 1534; commemorated July 1; (3) *saint*, tenth bishop of Le Mans, appointed by Clothaire, A.D. 559, and died Dec. 1, 581, after a life of great virtue; (4) *saint*, twenty-ninth archbishop of Vienne, France, in the beginning of the 7th century; noted for redeeming Christian captives; commemorated June 16; (5) twelfth bishop of Macon, France, cir. A.D. 732-743.

Domnŭlus, bishop of Marseilles in the 7th century

Domnus is the name of three ancient bishops of Antioch: (1) son of Demetrianus, appointed by the Council of Antioch, A.D. 269, without the voice of the clergy or people, and was installed in office three years later by a decree of the emperor. He held the see only a few years; (2) nephew of John of Antioch, on whose death in 441 he was elected bishop, and attained great popularity. He was afterwards involved in the Athanasian controversy, and after many vicissitudes was finally expelled from the see, and retired to the laura of St. Euthymius of Palestine, A.D. 452; (3) a Thracian, appointed by Justinian in 546, and occupied the see fourteen years.

Domnus is also the name of (1) one of the forty-three solitaries who lived in the 4th century, at Raithu, in the caverns of Sinai, and were attacked about A.D. 373, by the Blemmyes; Domnus died of his wounds, and is commemorated Jan. 14; (2) bishop of Apamea, present at the Council of Chalcedon, A.D. 451; (3) bishop of Elne (Helena) before A.D. 568; a man of great sanctity; (4) bishop of Messana (also called *Donus*) in the 7th century; (5) pope. See Donus; (6) forty-first bishop of Avignon, died about A.D. 743.

Domo (or **Dromo**), twenty-ninth abbot of Chartres, in the 7th century.

Donadeus, twelfth bishop of Gap, present at the synod of Narbonne in A.D. 788.

Donald (Lat. *Donevaldus*), a Scotch *saint*, commemorated with his nine daughters, July 15.

Donātā, of Scillita, a martyr at Carthage, with eleven others, commemorated July 17.

Donatiānus, (1) *Saint*, a martyr at Nantes, with his brother Rogantius, cir. A.D. 299; commemorated May 24; (2) bishop and confessor in Africa, under Hunnericus, commemorated Sept. 6; (3) bishop of Claudii Forum at the Council of Rome, A.D. 313; (4) *saint*, a bishop and confessor of Châlons-sur-Saône, cir. A.D. 346, commemorated Aug. 7; (5) *saint*, a bishop of Rheims (commonly called St. Donas), A.D. 360-390, a Roman by birth, commemorated Oct. 14; (6) bishop of Telepte, in Africa, presided at the council there, A.D. 418.

Donatilla, a virgin martyr, in Africa, with Maxima and Secunda, under Gallienus, commemorated July 30.

Donato, Luigi, an Italian theologian, was born in Venice, became bishop of Bergamo, and died in 1484, leaving, among other works, *Commentaries on the Master of Sentences;* also *Sermons*, etc. See Hoefer, *Nouv. Biog. Générale*, s. v.

Donatus. (1) Martyr at Rome with Aquilinus and three others; commemorated Feb. 4. (2) Martyr at Concordia with Secundianus, Romulus, and eighty-six others; commemorated Feb. 17. (3) Martyr at Carthage; commemorated March 1. (4) Martyr in Africa, with Epiphanius the bishop, and others; commemorated April 7 (or 6). (5) Martyr at Cæsarea, in Cappadocia, with Polyeuctus and Victorius; commemorated May 21. (6) Bishop and martyr at Aretium, in Tuscany, under Julian; commemorated Aug. 7. (7) The presbyter and anchorite in a district on Mount Jura, in Belgic Gaul; commemorated Aug. 19. (8) Martyr at Antioch, with Restitutus, Valerianus, Fructuosa, and twelve others; commemorated Aug. 23. (9) Martyr at Capua, with Quintus and Arcontius; commemorated Sept. 5. (10) Martyr with Hermogenes and twenty-two others; commemorated Dec. 12. (11) Bishop of Eurœa, in Vetus Epirus, cir. A.D. 387. (12) Bishop of Tysedis, in Numidia, in the 4th century. (13) Donatist bishop of Bagaia, in the 4th century. (14) Bishop of Nicopolis, in Vetus Epirus, cir. A.D. 425-433. (15) Twenty-fifth bishop of Avignon, in the middle of the 5th century. (16) One of the four bishops from Africa at the Council of Rome, A.D. 487. (17) Bishop of Besançon, born in 592 or 594, and died in 651; commemorated Aug. 7. (18) The name of two Irish saints (probably Lat. for *Donagh*); one, bishop of Lupia (now Leece, near Naples), in the 7th century; the other, bishop of Fiesole, in Tuscany: both commemorated Oct. 22. (19) Patriarch of Grado, A.D. 717-730. See also Dunan; Dunchaidh.

Dondi (*Dall' Orologio*), Francesco Scipione, an Italian prelate and theologian, was born in January, 1756. He studied at the college of Modena; in 1807 was called to the bishopric of Padua; and died Oct. 6, 1829, leaving many archæological works, for which see Hoefer, *Nouv. Biog. Générale*, s. v.

Donelson, Park Shattuck, D.D., a Methodist Episcopal minister, was born at Colerain, Mass., April 17, 1825. He was converted in 1835; accepted the call to the ministry in 1842; graduated from the Michigan University in 1849, and spent the next two years in the theological school at Auburn, N. Y. He joined the Michigan Conference in 1851, and served two years as professor of ancient languages in Albion College. The next two years he was pastor at Lansing, when he was elected president of the Ohio Wesleyan Female College, at Delaware, O., and in that capacity served seventeen years. The last ten years of his life were spent in the pastorate, in the Central Ohio Conference. He was twice a delegate to the General Conference, and a delegate to the First Œcumenical Conference (London, 1881). He died in Dexter, Mich., May 6, 1882. See *Minutes of Annual Conferences*, 1882, p. 327; *Gen. Cat. of Auburn Theol. Sem.* 1883, p. 287.

Doni (*d'Attichi*), Louis, a French prelate and writer,

of Italian extraction, was born in 1596; entered the order of the Minorites in 1616, was made co-rector of their house in Paris, later provincial of Burgundy, bishop of Riez in 1628, and died at Autun, July 2, 1664, leaving a number of works, chiefly historical and biographical, for which see Hoefer, *Nouv. Biog. Générale*, s. v.

Donin, Ludwig, an ascetic writer, was born in 1810 at Tiefenbach, in Lower Austria. In 1833 he was made priest; and from 1835 to his death, Aug. 20, 1876, he discharged his pastoral duties at St. Stephen's, in Vienna. See Kaulen, in Wetzer u. Welte's *Kirchen-Lexikon*, s. v. (B. P.)

Donjon (Donjum, or **Duisson)**, Geoffroi de, a noted French crusader, was elected tenth grand-master of the order of St. John of Jerusalem in 1191, and the same year distinguished himself in the battles at Arsuf and Ramleh. See Templars.

Donnan, the name of several Scotch *saints:* (1) Abbot of Egg, massacred A.D. 627; commemorated April 17. (2) Priest of Inis-aingin, in Loch Rilh, about the middle of the 6th century; commemorated Jan. 7 (also April 29 and Aug. 10). (3) Deacon with his brother St. Ciaran, at Cluain; commemorated Aug. 11.

Donnell, Robert, a Cumberland Presbyterian minister, was born in Guilford County, N. C., in April, 1784. In 1806 he was given authority to preach, and in 1809 penetrated into northern Alabama and organized several congregations in that new country. In October, 1811, he was ordained. Previous to 1817 he labored chiefly as an itinerant minister; after that date he settled first in Madison County, Ala., where he resided about two years, and then settled ten miles from Athens, Limestone Co. Although at this time engaged in agricultural pursuits, he still was laboriously employed as a minister. The General Assembly of 1831 appointed him one of five missionaries to western Pennsylvania. About 1830 he began to labor in Nashville, and, as a result, Cumberland Presbyterianism was introduced into that city. For the purpose of organizing a congregation, he went to Memphis in 1845, and labored there several months. Shortly after, he succeeded the Rev. George Donnell as pastor of the congregation at Lebanon, Tenn., and remained until February, 1849, when he removed to Athens, Ala., where he died, May 24, 1855. Mr. Donnell published, in the latter part of his life, a small volume entitled *Thoughts.* When the first General Assembly met, in 1829, at Princeton, Ky., he preached the opening sermon; and in 1837 he was moderator of that body. For a considerable time he was regarded as the leader of the southern portion of the Church. See Beard, *Biographical Sketches* (1st ser.), p. 101.

Donnolo, Sabbathai, an Italian Hebrew writer, was born at Oria, near Otranto, in 913. At the time when Oria was plundered by the Mohammedans of the Fatimite kingdom, he was taken captive with his parents. While the latter were taken to Palermo and Africa, Donnolo was redeemed at Trani. Destitute of all means for support, he paved his own way by studying medicine and astrology, in which branches he soon became famous. Though a practitioner of medicine—for he was physician to the Byzantine viceroy Eupraxios—he owes his reputation to his erudite works on astronomy. He wrote, *Sefer Tachkemoni* (ס' תחכמוני), a commentary on the Boraita of Samuel of Nehardea, in which he embodies what he had personally learned in the East about the zodiac and the constellations, and the horoscopes of astrology, as well as what he had read in the writings of Greek, Arabian, and Indian astronomers:—*Zophnath Paaneach* (ס' צפנת פענח), an astronomical commentary on the book *Jezirah*, the introductory portion of which is printed in Geiger's *Melo Chofnayim* (Berlin, 1840):—*Sefer Hammazaloth* (ס' המזלות), an astrognosy. See Grätz, *Gesch. d. Juden*, v, 316; Etheridge, *Introduction to Hebrew Literature*, p. 281; Steinschneider, *Jewish Literature*, p. 181; Fürst, *Bibl. Jud.* i, 211; Geiger, *Sabb. Donnolo*, in *Melo Chofnayim*, p. 95-99; Fürst, in *Literatur- und Kulturgeschichte der Juden in Asien*, i, 49; Jellinek, *Der Menschals Gottes Ebenbild von R. S. Donolo* (Leipsic, 1854); De' Rossi, *Dizionario Storico*, p. 89 (Germ. transl.). (B. P.)

Donortius, a Scotch prelate, was bishop of the see of Aberdeen about 1016. He died in 1098. See Keith, *Scottish Bishops*, p. 102.

Donoso, Josef, an eminent Spanish painter, was born at Consuegra in 1628, and studied in the school of Juan Carreno for six years. He executed a large number of works for the churches and public edifices of Madrid, among which are those in the Convent de la Victoire, viz., *The Canonization of St. Peter of Alcantara;* six large pictures from the life of St. Benedict; *The Conception; The Last Supper.* He died in 1686. See Spooner, *Biog. Hist. of the Fine Arts*, s. v.

Donus (or **Domnus**) **I**, seventy-ninth pope, was born at Rome, and was made pontiff Nov. 1, 676. In 677 he obtained from Constantine Pogonatus the revocation of the edict which exempted the archbishopric of Ravenna from the jurisdiction of the holy see. Reparatus, who was then archbishop, had the prudence to submit, and thus to make an end to the schism of Ravenna. Donus restored the Basilica of St. Paul, and adorned the atrium of the Church of St. Peter, which was called the Paradise. Some Church historians give Donus I the title *saint.* He died April 11, 678. See Hoefer, *Nouv. Biog. Générale*, s. v.

Donus (or **Domnus**) **II**, according to some, the one hundred and thirty-seventh pope, was elected pontiff in 974, after the expulsion of Benedict VI, and by influence of the counts of Tusculum. His pontificate, however, is very obscure. He is set down as having died Dec. 19, 975. See Popes.

Doolittle, Justus, a Presbyterian missionary, was born in Rutland, N. Y., June 23, 1824. He graduated from Hamilton College in 1846, and from Auburn Theological Seminary in 1849; was ordained at Auburn the same year, and served as missionary in Foochow, Tientsin, and Shanghai, until 1869, and in 1872 and 1873. Thereafter he resided at Clinton, N. Y., until his death, June 15, 1880. He is the author of *Social Life of the Chinese* (1865, 2 vols.):—*Vocabulary and Hand-book of Chinese Language* (1873). See *Gen. Cat. of Auburn Theol. Sem.* 1883, p. 277. (B. P.)

Doorga. See Durga.

Doors of Churches. The principal outer doors of a church seem to have been in ancient times at the west, if the church was so built that the altar was at the east end, or, at any rate, in the end facing the altar. In a basilican church of three aisles there were for the most part three western doors. In Constantine's great "Church of the Saviour," at Jerusalem, the three doors faced the east. The great Church of St. Sophia, at Constantinople, had nine doors between the narthex and the nave. As these were covered with silver, not only were they called the "Silver Doors," but the same term came to designate the corresponding doors of other churches, although not so decorated. The great western doors of the nave were called the "Royal Gates;" and when the church had a narthex, the western doors of this were also called "Royal Gates." The "Beautiful Gates" were supposed by Goar to be the gates which separate chorus and trapeza; by Ducange, those which separate nave from narthex; and by Neale, the outer gates of the narthex. The "Angelic Gate" was one which allowed a person to enter the trapeza so as to draw near the choir.

Dora. *Sister.* See Pattison, Dorothy Wyndlow.

Dorbene (surnamed *the Tall*), an Irish *saint*, commemorated Oct. 28, was abbot of Iona, and died in 713.

Doré, PIERRE (Lat. *Petrus Auratus*), a French theologian, born at Orleans about 1500, joined the Dominicans at Blois in 1514, was admitted into the Sorbonne in 1532, became prior of his monastery in 1545, and directed for a long time the college at Châlons-sur-Marne. He was court-preacher, and acquired great celebrity by his violent denunciations of the Protestants. He died at Paris, May 19, 1559, leaving many writings with odd titles and contents. See Hoefer, *Nouv. Biog. Générale*, s. v.

Doremus, *Mrs.* SARAH PLATT (*née* **Haines**), a noted philanthropic member of the Reformed (Dutch) Church, was born in New York city, Aug. 3, 1802. She was manager and director of more benevolent and religious institutions than any other woman in the country, if not in the world. In 1828 she set on foot a mission for the suffering Greeks. She was the patron of the City Prison Association, and of many institutions for the relief of women and children, as well as of the city Bible and Tract Societies. To her Dr. Sims went with his noble idea of a hospital for women, which she took hold of and carried through. Her house was a model of a Christian home, and it was a hospitable resort for missionaries on their way to distant fields, or returning with broken health, not only of her own Church, but of every other. Early, while yet it was dark, she might have been seen on her way to market to procure food for the asylums under her motherly care. The crown of her work was the organization of the Women's Missionary Society, out of which has grown similar associations all over the land, auxiliary to the Board of Foreign Missions, and from which go contributions to China, India, Japan, and Africa. When others in the hot season sought the seaside for rest and recreation, she stood by her post and labored night and day for her widely extended charge. She died at her residence in New York, Jan. 29, 1877. (W. P. S.)

Doren, WILLIAM HOWARD VAN, a Presbyterian clergyman, was born in Orange County, N. Y., March 2, 1810. He was a graduate of Columbia College and of the Western Theological Seminary, Allegheny, Pa. In 1836 he was licensed to preach by the Louisville Presbytery, and shortly afterwards spent two years in missionary work. In 1839 he accepted a call to the Reformed Church in East Brooklyn, L. I., of which he was pastor eleven years. He also took charge of a mission church in New York city, now known as the Thirty-fourth Street Church, and afterwards of the Second Church at St. Louis. In 1865 he removed to Chicago, and in 1878 to Indianapolis, Ind., where he died, Sept. 8, 1882. He is the author of *A Suggestive Commentary on Luke, with Critical and Homiletical Notes* (N. Y. 1868, 2 vols.):—*A Suggestive Commentary on St. John* (Lond. 1879, 2 vols.):—*A Suggestive Commentary on St. Paul's Epistle to the Romans* (1870, 2 vols.). (B. P.)

Doria, a martyr, with Chrysanthus, under Numerian, commemorated March 19.

Doria, Giovanni Pamfili, an Italian prelate, was born at Rome, Nov. 11, 1751. He was made archbishop at the age of twenty, and was sent on an embassy to Madrid, and afterwards as nuncio to France. On his return to Rome he was made cardinal, with the title of *Sainte-Marie*. In April, 1798, when the French entered Rome, he was arrested, but was soon released, and retired to his family at Genoa. He was eventually appointed financial intendant to the papal court. See Hoefer, *Nouv. Biog. Générale*, s. v.

Doria, Sinibaldo, an Italian prelate, was born at Genoa, Oct. 21, 1664. After enjoying successively various offices at Rome, he was called to the archiepiscopacy of Patras, Dec. 11, 1711; to that of Benevento, May 21, 1731; was declared cardinal on Sept. 24 following, and died at Benevento, Dec. 4, 1733. See Hoefer, *Nouv. Biog. Générale*, s. v.

Dorigny, Louis, an eminent French painter and engraver, was born at Paris in 1654. He went to Rome, and after remaining there four years, executed the grand altar-piece for the Feuillants at Foligno. He afterwards visited Venice, where he remained ten years. The work which does him most honor is the cupola of the cathedral at Trent. He died at Verona in 1742. See Spooner, *Biog. Hist. of the Fine Arts*, s. v.; Hoefer, *Nouv. Biog. Générale*, s. v.

Dorigny, Nicolas, a celebrated engraver, was born at Paris in 1657, and studied in Italy twenty years. In 1711 he went to England to do some fine work. He returned to Paris in 1724, where he died in 1746. The following are some of his most capital prints: *St. Peter Walking on the Sea; The Virgin and Infant, with St. Charles Borromeo, and St. Liborius; The Adoration of the Magi; The Birth of the Virgin; The Trinity; St. Francis Kneeling before the Virgin and Infant; St. Peter and St. John Healing the Lame Man at the Gate of the Temple.* See Spooner, *Biog. Hist. of the Fine Arts*, s. v.; Hoefer, *Nouv. Biog. Générale*, s. v.

Dorland (or **Dorlant**), PIERRE, a Belgian theologian, was born at Diest (Brabant), took the habit of the Carthusian friars at the monastery of Zelhem, became prior of that house, and died Aug. 25, 1507. He wrote many works on practical piety, for the principal of which see Hoefer, *Nouv. Biog. Générale*, s. v.

D'Orléans (*de la Mothe*), LOUIS FRANÇOIS GABRIEL, a French prelate, was born at Carpentras, Jan. 15, 1683, of an ancient family of Vicenza, called *Aureliani*. He pursued his studies with the Jesuits, and became successively canon of Carpentras, grand vicar of Arles, administrator of the diocese of Senez, and finally bishop of Amiens in 1733, an office which he filled with great ability. He died there, July 10, 1774, leaving *Lettres Spirituelles* (Paris, 1777). Abbé Dargnies has published his *Mémoires* (Mechlin, 1785). See Hoefer, *Nouv. Biog. Générale*, s. v.

Dorman, THOMAS, a Roman Catholic writer of the 16th century, was born at Amersham, Buckinghamshire, England. He was educated at Berkhamstead School (Protestant, founded by Dr. Incent), Hertfordshire; afterwards became a Romanist, fled to the Continent during the Protestant ascendency, and there wrote a book *Against Alexander Nowel, the English Calvinist:—A Proof of Certain Articles in Religion Denied by M. Jewell* (Antwerp, 1564, 4to):—*Disproof of Mr. Alex. Nowell's Reproof* (ibid. 1565, 4to):—*A Request to Mr. Jewell*, etc. (Lond. 1567, 8vo). See Fuller, *Worthies of England* (ed. Nuttall), i, 211; Wood, *Athen. Oxon.*

Dormans, JEAN DE, cardinal-chancellor and guardian of the seals under the kings John II and Charles V, was born at Dormans (Champagne). He founded at Paris, May 16, 1370, the college called De Beauvais, from the name of his diocese, and died in that city, Nov. 7, 1373. See Hoefer, *Nouv. Biog. Générale*, s. v.

Dormitory. It was the primitive custom for all the monks of a monastery to sleep in one large dormitory. Not until the 14th century was the custom introduced of using separate sleeping-cells. By the rule of Benedict all were to sleep in one room, if possible, with the abbot in their midst, or in larger monasteries ten or twenty, together with a dean. Only the aged, the infirm, and the excommunicated were excepted from this arrangement. Each monk was to have a separate bed. They were to sleep clothed and girded. The room was kept under lock and key until morning. In the first fervor of monastic zeal it was a common practice to sleep on the bare ground—afterwards on mats. A fire was kept burning in the room all night. The sleeping-room for stranger monks was usually close to the great dormitory and the chapel. See Smith, *Dict. of Christ. Antiq.* s. v.

Dorner, Isaac August, one of the most prominent evangelical theologians of Germany, was born in the village of Neuhausen-ob-Eck, in Würtemberg, June 20, 1809, being the son of a Lutheran clergyman. He was educated at Tübingen, acted as pastor in his native place, and subsequently travelled in Holland and England. He became successively professor of theology in the universities of Tübingen (1838), Kiel (1839), Königsberg (1840), Bonn (1847), Göttingen (1853), and in 1857 at Berlin, where he died, July 12, 1884. He was a councillor of the upper consistory, a distinguished contributor to Herzog's *Encyklopädie*, and co-editor of the *Jahrbücher für Deutsche Theologie*. The first great work of Dr. Dorner, and that which at once gave him celebrity, was his *Entwicklungsgeschichte von der Person Christi* (Stuttgard, 1839, 1846; Berlin, 1854, 4 vols. 8vo), translated by D. W. Simon in Clark's "Foreign Theological Library," and entitled *History of the Development of the Person of Christ* (Edinburgh, 1859, 5 vols. 8vo). In its first form it was a single volume of moderate size. Subsequently he made it by far the most learned and extensive discussion of the theme which has ever been undertaken. It is critical as well as historical. A vast amount of collateral matter, of great importance to the theological student, is incidentally interwoven in its chapters. In this work, as everywhere, Dorner shows himself in cordial sympathy with evangelical truth, yet bound to no traditional formulas in which that truth has been set forth in times past. The book is a fine example of the mingling of intellectual freedom with due reverence, and of the spirit of science with genuine devoutness. The *Geschichte der Protestantischen Theologie* (Leipsic, 1867), translated as *History of Protestant Theology* (Edinburgh, 1871–72, 2 vols.), referring particularly to Germany, is a work of more popular interest than the treatise just referred to. It surveys the Reformation, in its sources and phenomena, and in its consequences, on the doctrinal side. In the earlier chapters is to be found a profound as well as discriminating exposition of the cardinal truth of justification by faith, in its relation to the authority of the Scriptures. What is meant by "Christian consciousness," and what rights pertain to it, are instructively unfolded. A volume less known than either of those noticed above is the *Collection of Essays*, which embrace some of the most valuable of the briefer contributions of Dorner to theological literature. The extended paper, in which he treats of the *Attributes of God*, is a masterly handling of this topic. But the crowning work of his life was the *System of Christian Theology*, which called forth the praise and admiration of all enlightened and unprejudiced judges. When, in 1873, the Evangelical Alliance met in New York, Dorner was one of the European delegates. He combined profound learning, critical penetration, and power of generalization with an earnest Christian spirit. He was thoroughly trained in the ancient and modern schools of philosophy, and gave evidence, on his first appearance before the public, of his ability to defeat the pantheistic Hegelians with their own weapons, and thus to do most important service to German theology. This service he faithfully rendered, and lifted up theology to the rank of a science, pointed out the path of reconciliation between knowledge and faith, and raised up a body of defenders and expounders of Christianity against the philosophical and critical infidelity on the continent of Europe. Besides the works mentioned above, Prof. Dorner published a number of treatises mentioned in Zuchold, *Bibl. Theol.* i, 289 sq. (B. P.)

Dornex, an inferior kind of damask, anciently used for church vestments, altar-hangings, etc., originally manufactured at Doornick (Tournay), in Flanders.

Dorōna. "Indus et Dorona" are commemorated as *saints* Dec. 19.

Dorothea, a virgin martyr with Theophilus at Cæsarea, in Cappadocia, under Diocletian; commemorated Feb. 6.

Dorotheanisses is the name of the members of a society formed for the care of neglected girls. In order to protect such girls against immoral influences and to get them used to work, a society of Christian young ladies and women was formed at Rome in 1830. St. Dorothea was chosen as the patroness of the society, and the rules and regulations of the same were printed at Rome in 1836. Pope Gregory XVI sanctioned, in 1841, the movement, which soon made rapid progress in Lombardy and Venice. As the sisters had not only to take care of these neglected girls, but also to educate them, pope Pius IX confirmed them in 1860 as the *Teaching-sisters of St. Dorothea*. See Kaulen, in Wetzer u. Welte's *Kirchen-Lexikon*, s. v. (B. P.)

Dorotheus. (1) Martyr with Castor at Tarsus, in Cilicia; commemorated March 28. (2) Martyr with Gorgonius at Nicomedia, under Diocletian; commemorated Sept. 9. There are two other saints of the same name commemorated on this day—one, an anchorite of Thebes, in Egypt, cir. A.D. 395; the other, a founder of a monastery at Trebizond, in the 11th century, over which he is said to have presided many years; but there appears to be some confusion in the name, perhaps by an identification with one or more of the four archimandrites of Palestine who are reported under this name. (3) First abbot of Lyons, in France, in the 3d century. (4) A deacon of Antioch, A.D. 372. (5) A presbyter sent by Basil to seek help from the Roman bishops, A.D. 373. (6) An Arian bishop (also called *Theodorus*) of Antioch during the Melitian schism, A.D. 376. (7) Abbot of a nunnery in Athribia (Egypt), cir. A.D. 431. (8) A monk of Alexandria, banished by the emperor Anastasius, cir. A.D. 502, for writing a book in favor of the decrees of the Council of Chalcedon. (9) Bishop of Thessalonica, A.D. 515–20. (10) A monk (also called *Droctovæus*) of great virtue, appointed abbot of St. Vincent (France) A.D. 559.

Dorpat Esthonian. See Esthonian.

Dorr, Benjamin, D.D., a Protestant Episcopal divine, was born at Salisbury, Mass., March 22, 1796, and graduated at Dartmouth College in 1817, after which he studied law and then theology. He was ordained deacon in 1820 and presbyter in 1823. He was rector of the united churches of Lansingburg and Waterford, N. Y., from 1820 to 1829; rector of Trinity Church, Utica, until 1835; and general agent for the domestic committee of the Board of Missions until 1837, when he became rector of Christ Church, Philadelphia. He died Sept. 18, 1869. His publications include, *History of the Pocket Prayer-book* (written by itself):—*Churchman's Manual:—Prophecies and Types:—Invitation to the Holy Communion:—Travels in the East*, and other works. See Allibone, *Dict. of Brit. and Amer. Authors*, s. v.

Dorrance, John, D.D., a Presbyterian minister, was born at Kingston, Pa., Feb. 28, 1800. He graduated from New Jersey College in 1823, and from Princeton Theological Seminary in 1826; was licensed by the Mississippi Presbytery the same year; was pastor at Baton Rouge, La., till 1830; then at Wysox, Pa.; July 8, 1833, was called to Wilkesbarre, and died there, April 18, 1861. See *Gen. Cat. of Princeton Theol. Sem.* 1881, p. 44.

Dorrellites, a religious sect, followers of one Dorrell, who disseminated his doctrines at Leyden, Mass., about the close of the last century. He pretended to be a prophet sent to supersede the Christian dispensation and to introduce a new one, of which he was to be the head. The creed of this sect, according to the statement of Dorrell, was as follows: "Jesus Christ, as to substance, is a spirit, and is God. He took a body, died, and never rose from the dead. None of the human race will ever rise from their graves. The resurrection spoken of in Scripture is only one from sin to spiritual life, which consists in perfect obedience to God. Written revelation is a type of the substance of the true revelation which God makes to those whom he raises from spiritual death. The substance is God revealed in the soul. Those who have it are perfect, are incapable of sinning, and have nothing to do with the Bible. Neither prayer nor any other worship is necessary. There is no law but that of nature. There is no future judgment. God has no forethought, no knowledge, of what passes in the dark world, which is hell, nor any knowledge of what has taken place or will take place in this world."

Dorsal (or **Dossal**) (Lat. *dorsum*, and Fr. *dos*, "the back"). (1) The hinder part of a stall. (2) The hanging behind the choir stalls, or an altar, and rendered *tapecium*. It is made of satin or damask, and should have a representation of the Crucifixion embroidered on it; or, if there be a crucifix on the altar, there should be depicted one of the joyful mysteries. At St. Alban's, at the close of the 11th century, it was wrought with the martyrdom of the saint; and two others, in the 12th century, represented the Prodigal Son and the Traveller who Fell among Thieves. Some heraldic tapestries were in use behind the stalls of Exeter. Possibly dorsals were the origin of the linen pattern on panelling.

Dorsten, Johann von, an Augustinian theologian of the 15th century, was professor of theology and philosophy at Erfurt, where he died in 1481. Of his many writings, only the *Tractatus sive Collatio Synodalis de Statutis Ecclesiarum* (Erfurt, 1489), and *Determinatio de Cruore Miraculoso Jesu Christi* (Leipsic, 1510), were published. A list of his works is given in Ossinger, *Biblioth. August.* p. 299. See also Hartzheim, *Bibl. Col.* p. 167; Fabr.-Mansi, iii, 359; Kaulen, in Wetzer u. Welte's *Kirchen-Lexikon*, s. v. (B. P.)

Dorymĕdon, a martyr with Trophimus and Sabbatius, A.D. 278; commemorated Sept. 19.

Dosi, Girolamo, a distinguished Italian architect, was born at Carpi in 1695, instructed in the school of Fontana, where he soon attained distinction, and was appointed state architect by Clement XII. Among his best works are the cathedrals of Albano and Velletri, and the basilica of Santa Maria Maggiore. He died at Carpi in 1775. See Spooner, *Biog. Hist. of the Fine Arts*, s. v.; Hoefer, *Nouv. Biog. Générale*, s. v.

Dositheus. (1) Bishop of Seleucia Pieria, transferred to Tarsus, A.D. 415. (2) An obscure hermit near Jerusalem, in the 6th century, according to some later martyrologies, and commemorated Feb. 23.

Dothan. The latest description of this interesting site is by Lieut. Conder (*Tent-work in Palestine*, i, 107):

"By noon we reached Dothan, the scene of Joseph's betrayal by his brethren, and halted under a spreading fig-tree beside a long cactus hedge. Just north of us was the well called Bîr-el-Hŭfîreh ('Well of the Pit'), and east of us a second, with a water-trough, thus accounting for the name Dothan, 'two wells.' Above the wells on the north rises the shapeless mound where the town once stood, and on the west spread the dark-brown plain of 'Arrâbeh, across which runs the main Egyptian road—the road by which the armies of Thothmes and Necho came up from the sea-coast, and by which the Midianitish merchants went down with their captive. The cattle stood by the well, huddling in the shade, waiting to be watered, and rude cowherds and goatherds gathered around us in groups, which were, no doubt, not far different in dress or language from Joseph's brethren four thousand years ago."

Tell-Dothân, from the South. (From a Photograph by the Editor.)

Dotto, abbot of the Orkneys, died A.D. 502; commemorated April 9.

Doub, Peter, D.D., a minister in the Methodist Episcopal Church South, was born in Stokes County, N. C., March 12, 1796. He received an early religious training, but a very limited education; experienced religion in 1817; in the following year united with the Virginia Conference; spent his latter years in connection with the North Carolina Conference, and died Aug. 24, 1869. See *Minutes of Annual Conferences of the M. E. Church South*, 1869, p. 310; Simpson, *Cyclop. of Methodism*, s. v.

Doubdain, Jean, a French traveller, was canon of St. Denis in France. In 1651 he sailed from Marseilles for Jaffa, and arrived at Jerusalem, March 30, 1652. He thereafter visited Bethlehem, Jericho, Mt. Carmel, Haifa or Caiphas, Galilee, Nazareth, Canaan, Mt. Tabor, Acre, and Sidon, thence home, by way of Genoa, through Italy, and back to St. Denis, Nov. 22, 1652. He wrote an account of his travels under the title, *Le Voyage de la Terre Sainte* (Paris, 1661, 1662, and 1666). Doubdain died about the year 1670. See Hoefer, *Nouv. Biog. Générale*, s. v.

Doufflest (or **Duffeit**), Gerhard, an eminent Flemish painter, was born at Liege, Aug. 16, 1594. He studied in the school of Rubens, at Antwerp, and afterwards went to Italy. There is an admirable picture by this artist, representing the *Elevation of the Cross*, at

Liege. He died in 1660. See Hoefer, *Nouv. Biog. Générale*, s. v.; Spooner, *Biog. Hist. of the Fine Arts*, s. v.

Dougal, a Scotch prelate, was bishop of the see of Dunblane about 1390. See Keith, *Scottish Bishops*, p. 176.

Dougherty, JAMES, D.D., a Congregational minister, was born at Park, near Lairmount, County Londonderry, Ireland, April 9, 1796. In 1819 he came to South Hero, Vt. After studying with Rev. Asa Lyon, and in St. Albans Academy, he entered the University of Vermont, graduating in 1830. He subsequently studied theology, and was ordained Jan. 18, 1832, as an evangelist, and for some time served in the employ of the Colonial Missionary Society, performing duty also as teacher in Frost Village and Shefford, Quebec. After preaching a year, he was installed pastor at Milton, Vt., Sept. 28, 1836, and served until July 5, 1848. About this time, for one year, he was agent for the Foreign Evangelical Society. From 1849 to 1851 he preached in Fairfax, Vt. From November, 1857, to March, 1867, he was pastor in Johnson, where he resided subsequently without charge, until his death, June 10, 1878. For some time he served as superintendent of schools in Milton and Johnson, and was also trustee of the Bakersfield and Johnson academies. See *Cong. Year-book*, 1879, p. 41.

Douglas, Alexander, a Scotch prelate, was minister at Elgin about seventeen years, and promoted to the see of Moray in 1606. He died at Elgin, in May, 1623. See Keith, *Scottish Bishops*, p. 152.

Douglas, John (1), a Scotch prelate, was a Carmelite friar, afterwards chaplain to the earl of Argyle, and finally the first Protestant bishop of the see of St. Andrews. He became rector of the University of St. Andrews, Nov. 30, 1570. See Keith, *Scottish Bishops*, p. 39.

Douglas, John (2), D.D., a Scotch clergyman, son of George Douglas of Parkhead, graduated at Edinburgh University in February, 1602; became chaplain of the North British Regiment in the Low Countries; was ordained in Stirling Kirk in February, 1606; admitted to the living of the second charge at St. Andrews in 1621; transferred to Crail in 1625; was a member of the commission for the maintenance of Church discipline, Oct. 21, 1634, and died before Oct. 22, 1635, aged about fifty-four years. See *Fasti Eccles. Scoticanæ*, ii, 394, 417.

Douglas, Robert (1), a Scotch prelate, was born in 1626, and received his education at King's College, Aberdeen. He began preaching about 1650, at Laurencekirk, in the Mearns; then ministered at Bothwell, Renfrew, and Hamilton, from which place he was made dean of Glasgow; soon after elected to the bishopric of Brechin, and consecrated to that office in 1682. In 1684 he was translated to the see of Dunblane, where he continued until deprived by the revolution. He died at Dundee, Sept. 22, 1716. See Keith, *Scottish Bishops*, p. 168, 183.

Douglas, Robert (2), D.D., a Scotch clergyman, son of John Douglas, minister of Jedburgh, was licensed to preach Sept. 5, 1769; presented to the living at Galashiels in March, and ordained in July, 1770. He died Nov. 15, 1820, aged seventy-three years. He was assiduous in promoting the manufactures and the interest of his parishioners, by his advice and pecuniary assistance. He published *Observations on the Nature of Oaths, and the Danger of Multiplying Them* (1783):—*General View of the Agriculture of Roxburgh and Selkirk* (Edinburgh, 1798):—*An Account of the Parish.* See *Fasti Eccles. Scoticanæ*, i, 551.

Douvre, THOMAS DE, an English prelate of French descent, was born at Bayeux in 1027. He was treasurer of the cathedral of that city when William the Conqueror conferred upon him, in 1070, the archbishopric of York. He reconstructed the cathedral of that city,

and composed a treatise on *Chants*, which was accepted by several churches. In order to settle the quarrel between the sees of York and Canterbury, which had arisen on the subject of the pre-eminence, he joined with his adversary, Lanfranc, in arbitration before the pope. The affair came back before William, who decided in favor of Canterbury, in 1072. Douvre died in 1100.

There was another THOMAS DOUVRE, archbishop of York from 1109 to 1114, who is said to have been a relative of the foregoing.

Dove, *in Christian Art*. As a symbol of the believer, the dove of course has chief reference to two texts of Scripture, belonging to different yet harmonious trains of thought. One is Matt. x, 16, "Be ye wise as serpents and harmless as doves;" the other, Psa. lv, 6, "O that I had wings like a dove, then would I flee away and be at rest." The passages in Cant. i, 15; ii, 14; v, 2; vi, 9, refer to the Church, and therefore may be taken as referring simply to all faithful souls.

Doves on a Tomb.

The dove with the olive evidently refers to the flood.

Noah's Dove. (From the Catacombs.)

As an emblem of the Third Person of the Trinity, the carved or painted figure of the dove appeared from a very early period in all baptisteries (see Luke, iii, 22).

Baptismal Dove. (From the Catacomb of Pontianus, 7th Century.)

For the eucharistic dove, see COLUMBA.

Dove, THOMAS, D.D., an English prelate, was born in London, and bred a "lanquam" (a fellow's fellow) in Pembroke Hall, Cambridge. He afterwards became an eminent preacher, "and his sermons," says Fuller, "substantial in themselves, were advantaged by his comely person and graceful elocution." Queen Elizabeth was much pleased with him, and in 1589 preferred him dean of Norwich, advancing him in 1600 to the bishopric of Peterborough. He died in 1630. See Fuller, *Worthies of England* (ed. Nuttall), ii, 359; *Church Hist. of England*, bk. xl, an. 1630, par. 17.

Dow, Anthony, D.D., a Scotch clergyman, eldest son of Rev. David Dow, of Dron, was born Nov. 4, 1762; licensed to preach Nov. 30, 1785; called to the living at Kilspindie in August, 1788, and ordained Feb. 12, 1789; appointed presbytery clerk Sept. 18, 1799, which he resigned in 1811; was transferred to Kirkpatrick-Irongray in 1818, and died July 17, 1834. He published *An Account of Kilspindie.* See *Fasti Eccles. Scoticanæ*, i, 594; ii, 644, 645.

Dowling, John, a Baptist minister, was born at Pevensey, England, May 12, 1807. When sixteen years of age he became a Christian, and joined the Eagle Street Church, London. For eight years (1825-32) he was engaged in teaching, and became the author of three school-books. At the end of this period he removed with his wife and children to the United States, and in 1832 was ordained in Catskill, N.Y.; but a short time afterwards was called to the pastorate of the Second Baptist Church in Newport, R. I., and subsequently to the Pine Street, now the Central Baptist Church, Providence. He next preached for a Church in New York, holding its meetings in Masonic Hall. In 1844 he became pastor of the Berean Church in the same city, where he continued for several years, and then preached to a Church meeting in Hope Chapel, on Broadway, which has since become the Calvary Baptist Church on Twenty-third Street. For about four years (1852-56) he was pastor of the Sansom Street Church in Philadelphia. In 1856 he returned to the Berean Church, New York. For a time he preached for the Second Baptist Church in Newark, N. J., and subsequently supplied the pulpit of the South Baptist Church in New York. He died July 4, 1878. Dr. Dowling's occasional published sermons and discourses were well received, and one of them, *The Value of Illustration*, had a wide circulation. His principal work was his *History of Romanism* (New York, 1845), which passed through many editions. Besides these works, Dr. Dowling wrote and compiled, *A Vindication of the Baptists* (8vo):—*An Exposition of the Prophecies Supposed by William Miller to Predict the Second Coming of Christ* (1840, 18mo):—*A Defence of the Protestant Scriptures*, etc. (1843):—*Judson's Offering* (18mo):—*Conference Hymn-book:—Baptist Noel's Work on Baptism:—Works of Lorenzo Dow:—Conyears Middleton:—Memoir of Jacob Thomas:—Translation from the French of Dr. Cotes.* See Williams, *Memorial Discourses;* Allibone, *Dict. of Brit. and Amer. Authors*, i, 516, 517. (J. C. S.)

Downes, Henry, D.D., an Irish prelate, became bishop of Killala in 1716; was translated to Elphin in 1720, to Meath in 1724, and to Derry in 1726. He published *Sermons* (1697-1725). See Allibone, *Dict. of Brit. and Amer. Authors*, s. v.

Downes, Robert, an Irish prelate, was bishop of Leighlin and Ferns. He published a *Sermon* (1750). See Allibone, *Dict. of Brit. and Amer. Authors*, s. v.

Downham, John, younger son of William Downham, bishop of Chester, was born in Chester; graduated at Cambridge; became a preacher in London in the church behind the Exchange, and died, very aged, about 1644. He wrote *The Christian Warfare*, and numerous other works, for which see Allibone, *Dict. of Brit. and Amer. Authors*, s. v.

Downham, William, an English prelate, was archdeacon of Brecknock in 1559, became bishop of Chester in 1561, and died Dec. 3, 1577. See Le Neve, *Fasti Eccles. Anglicanæ*, iii, 258.

Downing, Calybute, an English divine, was born in 1606, and in 1623 became a commoner of Oriel College, Oxford. After entering into orders he held the vicarage of Hackney, near London, with the parsonage of Hickford, in Buckinghamshire. He joined the parliamentary party, became a great promoter of their designs, and in a sermon preached before the artillery company, Sept. 1, 1640, delivered this doctrine: "That for the defence of religion and reformation of the Church, it was lawful to take up arms against the king." After this he became chaplain to lord Roberts's regiment, and in 1643 was one of the assembly of divines. He died in 1644. His writings are scarce. See Chalmers, *Biog. Dict.* s. v.; Allibone, *Dict. of Brit. and Amer. Authors*, s. v.

Downman, Hugh, an English clergyman, physician, and poet, was born at Newton House, in the village of Newton St. Cyres, Devonshire, in 1740, and educated at the grammar-school of Exeter, and Balliol College, Oxford. He was ordained in 1762, but had little attachment to the Church. He turned his attention to the study of medicine, and wrote a number of poems, which indicate some share of poetical taste. He died at Exeter, Sept. 23, 1809. See Chalmers, *Biog. Dict.* s. v.; Allibone, *Dict. of Brit. and Amer. Authors*, s. v.

Doxarians (or **Aposchists**), a sect spoken of by John of Damascus as disregarding the ecclesiastical ceremonies of the times; probably meaning the Paulicians (q. v.).

Doxology. The exact periods of the origin of the liturgical doxologies are unknown, owing to the scantiness of early Christian literature. But it may be safely conjectured that, in their earliest forms, they came into use soon after the circulation of the Gospel narratives. The "Gloria in Excelsis" is unquestionably of Eastern origin. Liturgical speculators have ingeniously discovered a reference to its existence in very early writers. It has frequently been assumed that it was, in fact, "the hymn" which Christians sang on all solemn occasions, including such as are referred to in Acts xvi, 25; 1 Cor. xiv, 26; and Col. iii, 16. The origin and history of the "Gloria Patri," or lesser doxology, is even more obscure than that of the "Gloria in Excelsis," and in its present shape it is the result of the Arian controversies concerning the nature of Christ.

Doyen, Gabriel François, an eminent French painter, was born at Paris in 1726, and at the age of twenty gained the grand prize of the Royal Academy. In 1748 he went to Rome, and there studied the works of the great masters. He afterwards visited Venice, Bologna, and Parma, and after his return to Paris, in 1753, he executed his celebrated picture, representing *A Group of Persons Attacked by the Plague*, for the Church of St. Roch, and painted the chapel of St. Gregory-aux-Invalides. He died at St. Petersburg, June 5, 1806. See Spooner, *Biog. Hist. of the Fine Arts*, s. v.; Hoefer, *Nouv. Biog. Générale*, s. v.

Doyle, Mary, a philanthropist of the Society of Friends, eldest daughter of Edward Doyle, of Ferns, Ireland, was compelled early in life to earn her own livelihood. In 1796 she and her sister Anne, with their small savings, opened a shop in Ballytore, Ireland. They prospered until the rebellion of 1798, when the military plundered them of their provisions and outlaws robbed them of their money. After the rebellion their business prospered again. Mary was skilful in medical knowledge, and devoted herself to the relief of the poor. Anne died in 1822. Her sister continued to devote herself to works of charity, and died April 6, 1834, aged seventy-one years. See *The Friend*, viii, 167.

Dozy, Reinhart, a famous Dutch Orientalist, was born at Leyden, Feb. 21, 1820. From 1850 to 1883 he was professor at the university of his native city, and was known as one of the best Arabic scholars. He died April 29, 1883. In 1845 he published *Dictionnaire Détaillé des Noms et des Vêtement chez les Arabes* (Amsterdam), for which he received a prize from the Netherlandish Institute of Sciences. Of his other works, we mention *Scriptorum Arabum Loci de Abbadidis* (Leyden, 1846-63, 3 vols.):—*Commentaire Historique sur le Poëme d'Ibn-Abdoun* (ibid. 1848):—*Histoire des Musulmans d'Espagne* (ibid. 1861, 1881, 4 vols.; Germ. transl.

in 2 vols. 1874):—*Catalogus Codicum Orientalium Bibliothecæ Lugduno-Batavæ* (ibid. 1851, 2 vols.):—*Notices sur Quelques Manuscrits Arabes* (ibid. 1847–51). His last work is his *Supplément aux Dictionnaires Arabes* (1877–81, 2 vols.), one of the most important in the department of Arabic lexicography. (B. P.)

Drach, DAVID PAUL, a Jewish convert to Christianity, was born at Strasburg in 1791. In 1808 he acted as rabbi, and was for some time member of the Jewish central consistory at Paris. In 1823 he joined the Church of Rome with his four children, and in 1827 went to Rome, where he was appointed librarian at the Propaganda, and died there in 1865. He published, *Lettres d'un Rabbin Converti aux Israëlites* (Rome, 1833; transl. into German by Z. Baumblatt, under the title *Katholicismus und der Judaismus*, Frankenthal, 1841):—*Du Divorce dans la Synagogue* (Rome, 1840):—*Harmonie Entre l'Église et la Synagogue* (Paris, 1844, 2 vols.). He also assisted in the publication of the fifth edition of the *Bible de Vence* (ibid. 1748, 14 vols.; 1827–33, 5th ed. 27 vols.):—*Le Livre Yashar, Traduit* (ibid. 1858). (B. P.)

Draconarius denotes the bearer of the military standard, on which a dragon was represented. When Constantine placed the Christian symbol on the military ensigns instead of the dragon, the name outlived the change, and the standard-bearer was still called *draconarius*. Sometimes we find the ancient symbol joined to the new, the dragon being placed beneath the cross. In the Christianized empire this name came to signify the official who carried a standard or banner in ecclesiastical processions. The name was sometimes also given to the cross-bearer.

Dracontia were dragon-temples found in Asia Minor, Epirus, North Africa, Gaul, and Britain. They were formed of immense stones, set upright in rows. They had probably a reference to the Deluge, and destructive agents under the form of monster serpents.

Drake, Benjamin M., D.D., a minister of the Methodist Episcopal Church South, was born of devout parents in Robeson County, N. C., Sept. 11, 1800. He was converted in 1818; in 1820 joined the Tennessee Conference; in 1821 was transferred to the Mississippi Conference; became president of Elizabeth Female Academy in 1828, which position he held four years, and then resumed his place in the regular Conference work. In 1854 he was elected president of Centenary College, and died in 1860. Dr. Drake's whole life was an illustration of the saving power of grace. He was meek and dignified, cheerful and firm, able, energetic. See *Minutes of Annual Conferences of the M. E. Church South*, 1860, p. 227; Simpson, *Cyclop. of Methodism*, s. v.

Drake, Cyrus Bryant, D.D., a Congregational minister, was born at Weybridge, Vt., Aug. 18, 1812. He graduated from Middlebury College in 1834, and from Andover Theological Seminary in 1837. His only pastorate was in the Church at Royalton, Vt., of which he was ordained pastor Oct. 12, 1837, and died in office. In 1846 a bronchial affection induced him to resign, but the resignation was not accepted, although he spent ten months as secretary of the Vermont Domestic Missionary Society. Twice he was unable to preach, during 1857–59 and 1862–71, but his people refused to part with him. In 1852 he was elected moderator of the General Convention, and was its corresponding secretary during 1856 and 1857. He served his native state as a member of the Constitutional Convention, and in 1870 was elected to the Legislature. His death occurred April 21, 1878. See *Cong. Year-book*, 1879, p. 42.

Drake, Samuel, D.D., an English clergyman, published *Sermons*, etc. (1670–1724), and a new edition of Parker's *De Antiquitate Britannicæ Ecclesiæ* (1729). See Allibone, *Dict. of Brit. and Amer. Authors*, s. v.

Dramas, CHRISTIAN. There is little evidence that sacred dramas were ever acted till after the time of Charlemagne. A pictorial and dramatic representation of the facts of the Nativity is implied in many of the descriptions shortly after this time. See MYSTERIES.

Drane, ROBERT BRENT, D.D., an Episcopal minister, was born in what is now the District of Columbia (then Maryland), Jan. 9, 1797. He fitted for college at Phillips Academy, Andover, Mass.; graduated at Harvard College in 1824; had charge, for a few years, of a classical school in Salem, Mass.; and was settled as a minister in Hagerstown, Md., several years. In 1836 he became rector of St. James's Church, in Wilmington, N. C., and continued in office until 1843, when he took charge of a small college near Louisville, Ky. Subsequently he returned to his old parish in Wilmington, where he continued in office till his death, Oct. 16, 1862. See *Necrology of Harvard College*, p. 472. (J. C. S.)

Drant, THOMAS, an English divine and poet of the 16th century, was educated at St. John's College, Cambridge, where he took his degree of bachelor of divinity in 1569. In the same year he was admitted to a prebend in the cathedral of Chichester, June 27; July 2, to one in St. Paul's; and, March 9 following, was installed archdeacon of Lewes. He probably died in 1578. He translated Ecclesiastes into Latin hexameters (1572, 4to), and published some Latin poetry, printed at Paris. He also published some *Sermons*. See Chalmers, *Biog. Dict.* s. v.; Allibone, *Dict. of Brit. and Amer. Authors*, s. v.

Draper, Bourne Hall, LL.D., a Baptist minister, was born at Cumnor, near Oxford, England, in 1778. He studied in the school connected with Christ Church College, Oxford; became an apprentice to the Clarendon Press; joined the Baptist Church; pursued a course of theological study at the Bristol College; in 1804 was ordained pastor of the Church at Chipping Norton, Oxfordshire, where he remained about five years; removed as pastor to Coseley, Staffordshire; accepted a call to the Church in Southampton in 1820, and died there Oct. 12, 1843. In 1816 Dr. Draper wrote the hymn

> "Ye Christian heroes, go proclaim
> Salvation in Immanuel's name."

See *National Baptist*, March 3, 1881. (J. C. S.)

Draper, Daniel James, a prominent Methodist minister of Australia, was born at Wickham, Hampshire, Aug. 28, 1810. He was converted in early life; received into the British Conference in 1834; appointed to Australia in 1835; labored in New South Wales, Adelaide, Victoria, etc.; filled important offices; was made president of the Australasian Conference in 1859; visited his native land, as representative to the British Conference, in 1864, and, upon his return voyage to Australia, perished, by the foundering of the steamship *London*, in the Bay of Biscay, January 11, 1866. See Symons, *Life of D. J. Draper* (Lond. 1870); *Minutes of the British Conference*, 1867, p. 41; Stevenson, *City Road Chapel*, p. 235, 282.

Draucius, fourth bishop of Therouanne, in France; died probably cir. A.D. 667.

Draupner, in Norse mythology, was a golden ring, sent by Baldur from the infernal regions to his father Odin. It had been made by the dwarf Sindri, and possessed the miraculous attribute that every ninth night eight equally large gold rings dropped from it.

Drausin (or **Drosin**; Lat. *Drausius* or *Drautio*), *Saint*, bishop of Soissons, was born in Soissonnais about 606. He was the son of Leudomar and of Rachilda, who placed him under the guidance of St. Ansaricus, bishop of Soissons, who admitted him among the number of clerks in 649. He became archdeacon of Soissons in 652, and replaced in the episcopal see bishop Bartholin, who was accused of simony. In 657 Dausin built the abbey of St. Pierre de Rotonde, near

Compiègne. He died in 667, and is commemorated March 5.

Dreams *in Christian History.* The attempt to foretell the future by the interpretation of ordinary dreams was not condemned by the early Church; rather it was acknowledged that dreams might be made the vehicle of divine revelation. But some of the old heathen practices by which men sought to acquire supernatural knowledge in dreams, such as sleeping in an idol's temple wrapped in the skin of a sacrifice, or under the boughs of a sacred tree, were distinctly condemned.

Drechsler, JOHANN GABRIEL, a Protestant theologian of Germany, born at Wolkenstein, in Saxony, taught philosophy at Halle, and died Oct. 20, 1677, leaving, *Manuductio ad Poesin Hebraïcam:—Compendium Chronologico-historicum:*—also *De Larvis Natalitiis Christianorum* (Leipsic, 1683), under the anagram of *Chressulder.* See Hoefer, *Nouv. Biog. Générale,* s. v.

Dreisbach, JOHN, a prominent minister of the Evangelical Association, was born in Northumberland County, Pa., June 5, 1789; received on trial by the conference in 1807; in 1814 appointed the first presiding elder of that body; located in 1821; in 1828 and 1829 was a member of the Pennsylvania House of Representatives; in 1851 removed to Ohio; in 1854 became editor of the *Evangelical Messenger* at Cleveland; resigned in 1857, and died Aug. 20, 1871. Mr. Driesbach was regularly a delegate to the General Conference, and in 1816 prepared *The Spiritual Psaltery,* for a long time the standard hymn-book of his denomination. See *Albright and his Colaborers,* p. 277.

Drelincourt, Henri, the brother of Laurent, was born at Paris about 1630. He was first advocate and afterwards minister at Gien, and then at Fontainebleau. He died in 1683, leaving a collection of *Sermons.* See Hoefer, *Nouv. Biog. Génèrale,* s. v.

Drelincourt, Laurent, son of Charles (q. v.), was born at Paris in 1625. After having completed his studies at Saumur, he was called to the Reformed Church at La Rochelle. He was ordained in 1651 by his father, and fully justified by the sanctity of his life and his Christian humility the confidence which the people of La Rochelle had placed in him. In 1660 he was obliged to leave that place in consequence of an edict which prohibited Protestant families, who had not already resided there before the year 1628, to live there. He accepted a call to Niort, where he died, June 2, 1680, leaving, *Le Saint Ministère de l'Évangile* (1651):—*Sermon sur les Noces de Cana* (1657):—*La Salutaire Lever du Soleil de Justice* (1665):—*Les Étoiles de l'Église et les Chandeliers Mystiques* (1677):—*Sonnets Chrétiens* (often reprinted). See Lichtenberger, *Encyclop. des Sciences Religieuses,* s. v.; Hoefer, *Nouv. Biog. Générale,* s. v. (B. P.)

Dresde, FRIEDRICH WILHELM, a Lutheran theologian of Germany, was born at Naumburg, March 4, 1740; studied at Leipsic; was in 1772 appointed professor of Oriental languages at Wittenberg, and in 1778 professor of theology there; and died March 10, 1805, leaving, *De Immortalitate Animæ, Patriarchis non Ignota* (Leipsic, 1764):—*De Anno Judaico* (ibid. 1766):—*Votum Jephthæ* (ibid. 1767):—*Triga Commentationum Acadd. Critic.* (ibid. 1773):—*In Diversitatem Lectionis Codicis Hebræi,* etc. (ibid. 1776):—*In Castiganda Lectione Massoretica* (ibid. 1778):—*Elementa Sermonis Ebraici* (ibid. 1779, 1790):—*De Usu Pentateuchi Samaritani* (ibid. 1783):—*Le Libro Fœderis* (1790-92, 7 parts):—*De Vera vi* עולם (ibid. 1793, 1794):—*De Notione Spiritus S. in Codice Hebraico* (ibid. 1797). See Döring, *Die gelehrten Theologen Deutschlands,* i, 345 sq.; Winer, *Handbuch der theol. Lit.* i, 129, 226, 270, 399, 436; Fürst, *Bibl. Jud.* i, 212. (B. P.)

Dress, CHRISTIAN. In the primitive days Christians probably took little thought for raiment. They generally wore the ordinary dress of their station and country. A strong feeling was prevalent against luxury, display, and immodesty in apparel. Nevertheless, even in the 1st century, "gay clothing" was found in Christian assemblies. Tertullian likens those who adorn themselves with costly articles to the woman "arrayed in purple and scarlet color" spoken of in the Apocalypse. The pope also, in several councils, declared against extravagant dressing. Pope Zacharias decreed (A.D. 743) that bishops, priests, and deacons should not use secular dress, but only the sacerdotal tunic; and that when they walked out, whether in city or country—unless on a long journey—they should wear some kind of upper garment or wrapper. The second Council of Nice, in the year 787, condemns bishops and clerics who distinguish themselves by the richness and brilliant colors of their dress. So Tarasius, patriarch of Constantinople, bade his clergy abstain from golden girdles, and from garments bright with silk and purple, prescribing girdles of goats' hair, and tunics decent but not gorgeous. The Council of Aix (A.D. 816) inveighs against personal ornament and splendor of dress in the clergy, and exhorts them to be neither splendid nor slovenly.

Dresser, CHARLES, D.D., an Episcopal clergyman, was born at Pomfret, Conn., Feb. 24, 1800. He graduated from Brown University in 1823; spent some time in Virginia, as tutor in private families; studied theology under bishop Meade, by whom he was ordained; removed to Springfield, Ill., as rector there; subsequently was employed by bishop Chase in the business department of Jubilee College, in which institution he was, for a time, a professor; and died there March 25, 1865. (J. C. S.)

Dreux, PHILIPPE DE, bishop of Beauvais, went twice to the Holy Land (1178 and 1190) to fight the infidels, and on his second visit remained a captive at Bagdad for some time. After his return he turned his arms against the English, fell into their hands in 1197, and was put by king Richard into a close prison. Pope Celestine III interposed with the king of England for his deliverance, but Richard declined, in a humorous reply. The bishop being finally set free, turned his arms, in 1210, against the Albigenses, and in 1214 he appeared on the field of Bouvines as one of the heroes of the day. He died in his diocese in 1217. See Hoefer, *Nouv. Biog. Générale,* s. v.

Drevet, Pierre, an eminent French engraver, was born at Lyons in 1663, and after having studied under Germain Audran in his native city, went to Paris to complete his preparation. The following are his best prints: *Abraham's Sacrifice; The Annunciation; The Adoration of the Shepherds; The Crucifixion.* He died at Paris in 1738. See Spooner, *Biog. Hist. of the Fine Arts,* s. v.

Drevet, Pierre Imbreh, was born at Paris in 1697. He is claimed by his countrymen to have been one of the greatest engravers of any age or country. He died at Paris in 1739. The following are some of his best works: *Adam and Eve after their Transgression; Rebekah Receiving Abraham's Presents; The Holy Family; The Entry of Christ into Jerusalem; The Resurrection; The Presentation in the Temple; Christ in the Garden of Gethsemane.* See Spooner, *Biog. Hist. of the Fine Arts,* s. v.; Hoefer, *Nouv. Biog. Générale,* s. v.

Drew, DANIEL, for many years a noted capitalist and railroad director in New York, and mentioned here for his acts of Christian munificence, was born at Carmel, Putnam Co., N. Y., July 29, 1797. When fifteen years old he enlisted as a substitute in the state militia, and with the bounty money as a capital, became a cattle-drover. In 1829 he opened a cattle yard in New York; in 1834 went into the steamboat business; became a stock-broker and banker in 1844. In middle life Mr. Drew united with the Methodist Episcopal Church, of which he ever after remained an humble and faithful member. In 1866 he founded Drew Theological Seminary at Madison, N. J., by a gift of $500,000, paying over to its trustees in all not far from $750,000. He gave $250,000 for the founding of the Drew Seminary for Young Ladies, at Carmel. He also built a fine church at his native place, and another at Brewsters; in addition, he freely gave to many other benefactions. Mr. Drew was remarkably bold and successful in his enterprises, but, to use his own words, he "got caught at last," and in 1876 was a poor man. He died Sept. 18, 1879, regretting chiefly his inability to carry out his benevolent enterprises. See Simpson, *Cyclop. of Methodism ; Christian Advocate* (N. Y.), 1879, p. 616.

Dreyer, Christian, a Lutheran theologian of Germany, was born Dec. 22, 1610, at Stettin. He studied at Jena, Wittenberg, Rostock, and Königsberg. In the latter place he was also appointed professor of theology and first court-preacher, and died there, Aug. 3, 1688. Of his many writings we name, *De Principiis Fidei Christianæ:—De Corpore et Sanguine Christi in S. Eucharistia Præsente:—De Justificatione et Certitudine Gratiæ ex Job ix*, 20, 21:—*De Primatu Romani Pontificis: —De Igne Purgatorio, quem Redit Romana Ecclesia.* See Jöcher, *Allgemeines Gelehrten-Lexikon*, s. v.; Winer, *Handbuch der theol. Lit.* ii, 496. (B. P.)

Drisius, Samuel, of Leyden, was pastor of the Holland Church in London until, in 1652, he was called and removed to the Reformed (Dutch) Church in New York city, where he ministered until his death in 1682. Once in every month he preached to the Waldenses on Staten Island. He was the colleague of the elder Megapolensis for twelve years, and is said, like him, to have been very intolerant towards those who dissented from his religious views. At their instance governor Stuyvesant issued a proclamation against conventicles, under which fines and imprisonment were inflicted upon those who disobeyed the order. The Dutch West India Company, however, soon rebuked and rectified these unwarranted proceedings. Mr. Drisius was an accomplished scholar and linguist. See Corwin, *Manual of the Ref. Church in America*, p. 74; De Witt, *Hist. Discourses*, p. 35 36, 69. (W. J. R. T.)

Droctigisilius, fifteenth bishop of Soissons, towards the end of the 6th century.

Droctoaldus, *Saint*, fourteenth bishop of Auxerre, died in November, cir. A.D. 532.

Droctoveus, the abbot, was a disciple of Germanus, the bishop; his decease at Paris is commemorated March 10.

Drogon (1), a French prelate, said to have been the natural son of Charlemagne, became in 820 abbot of Luxeuil, where, under his direction, science and art flourished. In 829 he was made bishop of Metz. He was drowned in a river while fishing, in 855 or 857. See Hoefer. *Nouv. Biog. Générale*, s. v.

Drogon (2) (or **Drocon**), a French prelate, was made bishop of Beauvais in 1030. In 1035 he founded the convent of St. Symphorien-les-Beauvais. The king of France, Henry I, in one of his diplomas qualifies him as a "vir divinæ religioni totus mancipatus." He died at Beauvais, April 21, 1047. See Hoefer, *Nouv. Biog Générale*, s. v.

Drogon (3), a French cardinal and theologian, was born in Champagne, entered the Benedictine order, became prior of St. Nicolas of Rheims, and in 1128 was elected abbot of St. Jean de Laon. Pope Innocent II called him to Rome in 1130, and made him bishop of Ostia and cardinal. He died in 1138, leaving several treatises printed in the *Bibliotheca Patrum* (Paris, 1644), i, 565. See Hoefer, *Nouv. Biog. Générale*, s. v.

Droma, in Norse mythology, was the second strong chain which the Asas had made to bind the wolf Fenris. He allowed himself to be bound with it, but when he shook himself it flew in pieces.

Dromic, a term applied to Oriental churches of the apsidal or basilican form, from their similarity to a race-course. The original St. Sophia, at Constantinople, was of this style.

Drops, Festival of the, a ceremony observed by the Copts on June 12, annually, because on that day the drops of dew fall which are believed to lead to the rise of the Nile. As soon as this dew has fallen, the water begins to be corrupt, and assumes a greenish color, which increases more and more till the river appears as a lake covered over with moss. This lasts from twenty to forty days. As soon as the green color is gone, the river becomes red and very muddy. The Copts called the drops of dew the benediction of heaven, and believed that the Almighty sent down Michael the archangel to infuse these sacred drops into the Nile that it might begin to rise, and at length irrigate and fertilize their country. See Nile; Nilus.

Drosis, a virgin, probably of Antioch, in Syria, burned for her faith (as mentioned by Chrysostom, ii, 688), and commemorated Sept. 22.

Drostan (Throstan, Drustan, or **Dunstan)**, a Scotch saint, commemorated Dec. 14, is said to have been of royal blood, and abbot of Holywood, and afterwards of Glenesk, in Forfarshire, about the end of the 6th century.

Droste-Hülshoff, Clement August, *Baron* von, a professor of canon law, was born at Colsfeld, in February, 1793. He studied theology and philosophy at Münster, where Hermes was his teacher. From 1814 to 1817 he was professor at the Münster Gymnasium. When called to Berlin by the government, he betook himself to the study of canon law, resigned his position at Münster, and commenced his lectures at Bonn in 1822. He died at Wiesbaden, Aug. 13, 1832. He published, *Lehrbuch des Naturrechts und der Philosophie* (Bonn, 1823; 2d ed. 1831):—*Ueber das Naturrecht als eine Quelle des Kirchenrechts* (ibid. 1822):—*Religionsphilosophische Abhandlungen* (ibid. 1824):—*Grundsätze des gemeinen Kirchenrechts der Katholiken und Evangelischen in Deutschland* (Münster, 1828-33, 2 vols.). (B. P.)

Drottes (or **Drotner**, also **Diar**) were the heathen Teutonic priests in ancient Germany and Britain. Their office was confined to certain families, and was hereditary in its transmission; but they appear to have been far inferior both in wealth and power to the Druids. They enjoyed peculiar privileges in virtue of their sacred calling; being exempted from war, prohibited from appearing in arms, and even from mounting a horse. The Teutonic pagans had also an order of priestesses, who served in the temples of their female deities; and Friga (q. v.) was attended by kings' daughters, and ladies of the highest rank of nobility. Some of these consecrated females were consulted as infallible oracles, and held in the greatest veneration, as if they themselves were divinities.

Drouais, Jean Germain, a distinguished French painter, was born in Paris, Nov. 25, 1763, and instructed by his father. He gained the grand prize of the Royal Academy by his admirable picture of *The Canaanitish Woman at the Feet of Christ.* He died at Rome, Feb. 13, 1788. See Spooner, *Biog. Hist. of the Fine Arts*, s. v.; Hoefer, *Nouv. Biog. Générale*, s. v.

Dructegangus. (1) Third abbot of Gorze, in the diocese of Metz, died A.D. 769. (2) Eighth abbot of Jumièges, in Normandy, A.D. 753.

Druigen, an Irish saint, commemorated March 6, was a sister of St. Brigida (q. v.).

Drum, Sacred, an instrument of magical incantation formerly in use among the native Laplanders. It was made of the body or trunk of a pine or hollow birch, which could be found only in particular spots, and every part of which, both trunk and branches, had the remarkable peculiarity of being inflected from the right to the left. The drum was constructed of one entire piece of wood, hollowed out in the middle. The upper part, which was flat, was covered with skin, and the lower part, which was convex, was so constructed that after they made two long openings in it the wood between served as a handle. The rims, which kept the skin tight in a kind of circular form, were not exactly round, but rather oval. Upon the skin thus stretched on the head of the drum, the Laplanders painted various figures in red, which seemed to be of somewhat hieroglyphical character. There were added to this copper rings of various patterns, to be used in incantations. The hammer with which the drum was beaten was made from the horn of a reindeer.

Drumm, John H., M.D., D.D., a Protestant Episcopal clergyman, was born in Dublin, Ireland, in 1827; graduated from the New York Medical College in 1852; was ordained deacon in 1857, and presbyter in 1863; in 1857 officiated in Brookville, Ind.; in 1859, was rector of St. James's Church, Dundaff, Pa.; in 1862, of St. James's Church in Bristol; in 1875, of St. Mark's Church, New Britain, Conn.; in 1877 he was in San Saba, Tex., but returned in the following year to Bristol, Pa., where he died, March 5, 1879. See *Prot. Episc. Almanac*, 1880, p. 171.

Drummond, E. A. H., D.D., an English divine, who was born in 1758 and died in 1830, published, *Sermons* (1792):—*Catechetical Questions Prior to Confirmation* (Lond. 1813). See Allibone, *Dict. of Brit. and Amer. Authors*, s. v.

Drummond, George, D.D., a Scotch clergyman, descended from the family of Hawthornden, was licensed to preach in July, 1761; presented to the living at Dunbarton in August, 1765; ordained May 1, 1766; and died Feb. 14, 1819, aged eighty-one years. He was a man of high respectability, deep erudition, and eminent worth. He published *An Account of the Parish*. See *Fasti Eccles. Scoticanæ*, ii, 370.

Drummond, James, D.D., a Scotch clergyman, third son of Rev. James Drummond of Deanstown, was probably born at Fowlis, Perthshire, in 1619; graduated at St. Andrews' University in 1645; was appointed to the living at Auchterarder about 1650; transferred to Muthill in 1656; promoted to the bishopric of Brechin in 1684, retaining the parish of Muthill in conjunction, which he resigned in 1686. He had a pension from James II of one hundred pounds sterling, in December, 1685; signed an address to the king in November, 1688, just before his majesty's abdication, and preached for the last time in the cathedral, April 14, 1689, three days after episcopacy had been abolished. When deprived, he resided for four years in Slain's Castle, with John, earl of Errol, and died in 1695. He was a good and pious man, diligent in his office, read the Scriptures daily in the original; and while his chief and patron, the earl of Perth, was zealous to promote popery, he was as strenuously and determinedly opposed to popery as any one in the kingdom. See *Fasti Eccles. Scoticanæ*, ii, 747, 780; iii, 891; Keith, *Scottish Bishops*, p. 169.

Drummond, William Hamilton, D.D., a scholar, poet, and divine, died in Dublin, Ireland, Oct. 16, 1865, aged eighty-seven years. He was the author of poems on the Battle of Trafalgar, the Giant's Causeway, etc.; and prepared also a translation of Lucretius. See *Appleton's Annual Cyclop.* 1865, p. 675.

Drunkenness. Denunciations of this vice are contained both in the Old and New Test. St. Paul expressly includes drunkards among those who shall not inherit the kingdom of heaven. This vice became peculiarly shameless at Rome about the time of the Christian æra. The surrounding nations, too, were drunkards. Drunken habits were to afford a presumption against a person accused before the Church courts. Still, the vice flourished among the Christians. Jerome warns the priests never to smell of wine. Revellings and drunkenness were deemed allowable in commemorating the martyrs. The first distinct Church enactment against drunkenness appears in the canons of the Council of Tours. The West, however, seems to have been the chief home of gluttony and drunkenness. A canon of the Council of Autun, A.D. 670, enacted that no gluttonous or drunken priest should touch the sacrament or say the mass under pain of losing his dignity. The Council of Berkhamstead enacted that if a priest be so drunk that he cannot fulfil his office he should be deposed by the bishop. In regard to drunkenness in the Church in Britain, Boniface says: "It is also said in your parishes drunkenness is a too common evil, so that not only do the bishops not forbid it, but themselves, drinking too much, become intoxicated, and compel others to do so, offering them larger beakers." In the Carlovingian period civil penalties or disabilities began to be inflicted for drunkenness. See Temperance.

Drury, Asa, D.D., a Baptist minister, was born July 26, 1802. He graduated from Yale College in 1829, and for two years following was rector of the Hopkins Grammar-school at New Haven; was ordained as an evangelist in the Baptist ministry, Sept. 14, 1834; was professor of languages in Denison University, Granville, O., and held the office one year, 1836; for three years (1836-39) was professor of Greek in Cincinnati College; the year following a professor in what is now Colby University, Waterville, Me.; then returned to Cincinnati College; after a time became principal of the classical school connected with the Baptist Theological Institute at Covington, Ky., and at the same time professor of ecclesiastical history and Greek literature; for several years was principal of the high-school, and superintendent of schools in Covington; and spent the last four years of his life in St. Anthony, Minn. where he was pastor of a Baptist Church. He died March 18, 1870. (J. C. S.)

Drusus, a martyr at Antioch with Zosimus and Theodorus; commemorated Dec. 14.

Druys (Lat. *Drusius*), John, a Belgian canon, was born at Cumptich, near Tirlemont, in 1568. He studied at St. Trond, at Namur, and at Louvain; joined the order of Premonstrants at the abbey of du Parc, near Louvain, May 29, 1588; taught theology there; in 1604 became deputy for the states of Brabant, and the following year vicar of the *circarii* of Brabant and Friesland. He was charged by archduke Albert with several missions in connection with ecclesiastical discipline; appointed *circarius* in Spain in 1630; and finally was counsellor of the state. He died at Brussels, March 25, 1634, leaving, *Visitatio Almæ Universitatis Lovaniensis* (Louvain, 1617):—*Exhortatio ad Candidi Ordinis Præmonstratensis Religiosos* (ibid. 1621):—*Statuta Candidi et Canonici Ordinis Præmonstratensis Renovata*, etc. (ibid. 1628). See Hoefer, *Nouv. Biog. Générale*, s. v.

Druzbicki, Caspar, a Jesuit, was born in 1589 at Sieradz, in Poland, and died at Posen in 1662. He wrote *De Variis Passionis Christi Meditandi Modis* (Lublin, 1652):—*Fasciculus Exercitationum*, etc. (Cracow, 1662):—*Tribunal Conscientiæ*, etc. (ibid. 1672):—*In Dominicas Totius anni Considerationes* (1679):—*Lapis Lydius*, etc. (1699; a German translation was published in 1739; a more recent one is that by Ratte, 1884). A complete edition of his works was issued at Ingolstadt in 1732, 2 vols. fol., under the title *Venerabilis P. Gasparis Druzbicki Opera Omnia*. See *Encyklop. Koscielna*, iv, 355; Lüdke, in Wetzer u. Welte's *Kirchen-Lexikon*, s. v. (B. P.)

Dryads (from *δρύς, an oak*), female deities of an inferior rank, who presided over woods. They were much more fortunate than the Hamadryads, having the liberty of walking about, and even surviving the destruction of the trees over which they presided. They also had the liberty of marrying. The poets frequently confound the Dryads, Hamadryads, and Naiads.

Dryander, HERMANN, a Lutheran theologian of Germany, was born Dec. 22, 1809, at Halle, where he also pursued his theological studies. In 1834 he was appointed deacon at the church "Unsere Lieben Frauen" there, in 1876 first preacher, and died as superintendent and member of consistory, Feb. 15, 1880. See *Zum Gedächtniss Dr. Hermann Ludwig Dryander's* (Halle, 1880). (B. P.)

Dualla Version OF THE SCRIPTURES. In this language, which is spoken in the Cameroons district, West Africa, some portions of the Old and New Test. has been translated by the Rev. A. Saker, of the Baptist Missionary Society. The grammar has been treated by Saker in *Grammatical Elements of the Dualla Language* (1855). (B. P.)

Dubbs, JOSEPH S., D.D., a German Reformed minister, was born at Upper Milford, Lehigh Co., Pa., Oct. 16, 1796. His early education was received at a Quaker school, and, after studying theology four years under Rev. F. L. Herman, D.D., he was licensed to preach in 1822. He received the charge of Windsor and Weiss churches, Berks County, in June, the same year, and was ordained in 1823. In 1824 the Eppler's Church, and in 1826 the Hains Church, were added to his charge, of which he remained pastor until 1831. From this period until 1861 he was pastor of the Allentown, Egypt, Union, and Jordan churches. That year he resigned the charge of the Allentown Church, which had increased to twelve hundred members, continuing to preach to the remaining three until 1866, when he retired from active labor, and removed to Allentown, where he died, April 14, 1877. He was conscientious in the discharge of duty, and acquired an unusual degree of popularity. Dr. Dubbs was a frequent correspondent of the German periodicals of his Church, and the author of several popular German hymns. See Harbaugh, *Fathers of the Germ. Ref. Church*, v, 239.

Du Bec, PHILIPPE, a French prelate, was born in 1524. He was appointed bishop of Vannes in 1559, and six years later passed to the diocese of Nantes. He was one of those prelates who held the place of ecclesiastical peers at the coronation of Henry IV in 1589. The same year he was called to the archbishopric of Rheims, and in the year following he received the title of commander of the order of the Holy Ghost. But the bulls were not forwarded before the end of three years, on account of the differences of Henry IV with the court of Rome. Du Bec died in 1605. He left a collection of *Sermons*, and a French translation of the *Treatise of the Widows of St. Ambrose* (Paris, 1590). See Hoefer, *Nouv. Biog. Générale*, s. v.

Dubhan is the name of two Irish saints: (1) A priest, about the middle of the 7th century, commemorated Nov. 11. (2) A pilgrim in the County Wexford, commemorated Feb. 11.

Dubhdalethe is the name of three abbots of Armagh, in Ireland, one in the 8th century, and two in the 10th and 11th; also of an abbot of Kilskeery, County Meath, who died A.D. 750.

Dubhthach (or **Duach**) is the name of three Irish saints: (1) A bishop of Armagh, A.D. 497–513; commemorated Feb. 5. (2) A companion of Moling (q. v.), commemorated Oct. 7. (3) Priest of king Leogaire, converted by St. Patrick, A.D. 433.

Dubois, Benjamin, a Reformed (Dutch) minister, descended from the French Huguenots who settled on Staten Island to escape the persecutions of Louis XIV, was born in 1739. He studied theology under Rev. J. H. Goetschius, was licensed by the American Classis in 1764, and for sixty-three years was pastor of the united Reformed Dutch churches of Freehold and Middletown, in Monmouth Co., N. J. During the Revolutionary war he was foremost among the defenders of liberty, and often preached to his people upon their duty during the struggle. He died in 1827. See Marcellus, *Hist. Discourse;* Corwin, *Manual of the Ref. Church in America*, p. 75. (W. J. R. T.)

Dubois, Gérard, a French Church historian, was born at Orleans in 1629. He became a member of the congregation of the Oratory in 1650, and taught rhetoric there several years. He wrote the concluding volume of the *Ecclesiastical History* of Le Cointe, including a life of the latter (1683). He was commissioned by Harlay, archbishop of Paris, to undertake a *History of the Church of Paris*, the first volume of which (1690) carries it down to 1108. Du Bois died at Paris, July 1, 1696, leaving the second volume unfinished. It was completed by fathers La Ripe and Desmolets (1710), and brings the history down to 1364. See Landon, *Eccles. Dict.* s. v.; Hoefer, *Nouv. Biog. Générale*, s. v.

Dubois, Gualterus, a distinguished minister of the Reformed (Dutch) Church, was born at Streefkerk, in Holland, in 1666, and graduated from the University of Leyden in 1697, when he was licensed to preach the Gospel. His father, Rev. Peter Dubois, was a very eminent minister of the Church of Holland, settled in Amsterdam, the one hundredth in succession from the Reformation. The son came to America, when twenty-eight years old, as the colleague of dominie Selyns in the Dutch Church of New York, where he ministered fifty-one years with great acceptance and ability. He was a man of noble presence, of amiable spirit, and dignified bearing; a diligent student and expounder of God's Word, whole books of the Bible being left among the subjects of his pulpit instructions, in his elaborate and beautiful manuscripts; also a strong advocate of the independence of the Reformed Church in America from foreign control, especially in the matter of ministerial education and ordination, although he died before this question reached its crisis in the disruption of the Church. His death, which followed a brief illness, in his eightieth year, called forth universal expressions of public grief and respect for his character and services. He was regarded more as "a bishop among the Dutch churches than as the pastor of a single organization." See De Witt, *Memorial;* Smith, *Hist. of New York;* Corwin, *Manual of the Ref. Church in America*, s. v.; Taylor, *Annals.* (W. J. R. T.)

Dubois, Jean (1), a reputable French sculptor, was born at Dijon in 1626. Among other excellent works, he executed the statues of St. Stephen and St. Medard, and the tomb of Pierre Odebert, in the cathedral of Dijon; the grand altar and the *Assumption of the Virgin*, in the Church of Notre Dame. The statue of the Virgin is considered his masterpiece. He died Nov. 29, 1694. See Hoefer, *Nouv. Biog. Générale*, s. v.; Spooner, *Biog. Hist. of the Fine Arts*, s. v.

Dubois, Jean (2) (*Joannes à Bosco*, otherwise *Olivarius*), a French preacher, was born about the middle of the 16th century. After living for some time as a Celestine monk, he obtained permission of the pope to become a soldier, and in that capacity acquitted himself so well as to obtain the favor of king Henry III, who styled him "the emperor of monks." When peace was restored, he quitted the profession of arms and returned to his cloister. He was a favorite preacher, and was selected by Henry IV to be one of his ordinary chaplains; and so highly esteemed by cardinal Seraphin Olivier that he adopted him, gave him his name and arms, and obtained for him the Cistercian abbey of Beaulieu, in Argonne. He was a strenuous opponent of the Jesuits, and on June 6, 1610 (Trinity Sunday), declaimed against them, and especially against the books of Mariana and Bécan, in the Church of St. Eustachius. For this, when he went to Rome, as agent extraordinary for Louis XIII, he was, Nov. 11, 1611, thrown into prison, where he died, after fifteen years' confinement, Aug. 28, 1626. He wrote, among other works, *Floriacensis Bibliotheca Benedictina*, etc. (Lyons, 1605, 8vo). See Landon, *Eccles. Dict.* s. v.; Hoefer, *Nouv. Biog. Générale*, s. v.

Dubois, Jean Antoine, a French missionary, one of the directors of the seminary of foreign missions, member of the Asiatic societies of Paris and London, and of the Literary Society of Madras, was born in 1765 at St. Remèze (Ardèche). About 1791 he went to Mysore to preach Christianity, his principal residence being at Pettah, near Seringapatam. After thirty-two years of sojourn in India, he returned to Europe with the strong conviction that in the actual state of affairs the conversion of the Hindûs was impossible. This opinion, which he advanced in his *Letters on the State of Christianity in India* (Lond. 1823), became in England the object of very lively attacks. He died at Paris, Feb. 7, 1848. For the list of Dubois' other writings, see Hoefer, *Nouv. Biog. Générale*, s. v.

Dubois, John, a Roman Catholic prelate, was born in Paris, France, Aug. 24, 1764, and ordained in 1787. He came to America in 1791; labored in Maryland and Virginia; founded Mount St. Mary's College and Seminary, Baltimore, Md., in 1807; succeeded John Connolly as bishop of New York in 1826, and died in that city, Dec. 20, 1842. He was highly revered in his own denomination. See De Courcy and Shea, *Hist. of the Cath. Church in the U. S.* p. 70, 104, 397 sq.

Dubric (or **Dyfrig**), archbishop of Caerleon, distinguished in the story of king Alfred of England as famous for sanctity, was the grandson of Brychan, king of Brecknockshire, and appears to have been the first bishop of Llandaff, about A.D. 470, and to have died in 522. His bones were transferred in 1120 to the new cathedral on the island of Enlli or Bardsey, where they had been originally interred. His death is commemorated Nov. 4, and his translation May 29.

Duchacet, Henry William, D.D., a minister of the Protestant Episcopal Church, entered upon public life as a physician in New York city; but about 1824 he was ordained, and after having filled several other important positions, in 1833 accepted the rectorship of St. Stephen's parish, Philadelphia, where he died Dec. 13, 1865, aged sixty-eight years. For many years he was a leading member of the standing committee of the diocese, and was associated with most of its religious societies. By his agency a great charity was inaugurated, the Burd Asylum for Orphans; and he had planned an asylum for disabled clergymen, having already taken the preliminary steps for its establishment, when his sudden death frustrated his design. See *Amer. Quar. Church Rev.* April, 1866, p. 126.

Ducks, *in early Christian art.* These birds occur repeatedly in the bass-reliefs of the Duomo at Ravenna, on the great piers at the east end, and at the same place in the Church of San Giovanni Evangelista. The reason for their use is unknown, but has been supposed to be either on account of the bright colors or because domesticated in the monasteries.

Ducreux, Gabriel Marie, a French historian, dean at Auxerre and afterwards at Orleans, was born at the latter place, June 27, 1743, and died there Aug. 24, 1790. He is known as the author of *Les Siècles Chrétiens* (Paris, 1775, 9 vols.; German translation by Fischer, Vienna and Landshut, 1781-90):—*Pensées et Reflexions* (Paris, 1765, 2 vols.). See Hefele, in Wetzer u. Welte's *Kirchen-Lexikon*, s. v. (B. P.)

Dudd, eleventh bishop of Winchester, between 781 and 785.

Dudley, John, an English clergyman, became a prebendary of Lincoln in 1724, was installed archdeacon of Bedford, June 11, 1731, and died about 1745. He published a few single *Sermons*. See Allibone, *Dict. of Brit. and Amer. Authors*, s. v.

Dudley, William, an English prelate of the 15th century, son of John Dudley, the eighth baron of Dudley, Staffordshire, was educated at University College, Oxford, thence preferred dean of Windsor, and afterwards for six years bishop of Durham. He died in London in 1483, and was buried in Westminster. See Fuller, *Worthies of England* (ed. Nuttall), iii, 131.

Dudüng, Claudius Antony, a Swiss prelate, was appointed to the bishopric of Lausanne in 1716, and died June 16, 1745, leaving *Status seu Epocha Ecclesiæ Aventicensis* (1724). See Hoefer, *Nouv. Biog. Générale*, s. v.

Duff, Alexander, D.D., a Scotch clergyman and missionary, was born at Pitlochrie, Perthshire, April 25, 1806. He was carefully educated in the Established Church of Scotland; graduated from the University of St. Andrews, was ordained Aug. 12, 1829, and the same year sailed for India with his wife. The vessel was wrecked on the voyage, and on arriving at Calcutta he was advised by the English residents not to begin operations until an imposing church structure should be reared. Nevertheless, he rented a small house in that city, and commenced a school for the instruction of the natives. In 1832 three Brahmins were baptized, an event which produced a profound impression upon all classes. In 1834 Dr. Duff's health gave way, and he returned home for recuperation. He attended the General Assembly of the Scottish Church, and delivered a powerful address in behalf of the great cause in which he was engaged. He returned to India in 1840, and entered a larger and much more suitable building for school purposes, which had been erected in his absence. When the disruption of the Scotch Church took place in 1843, Dr. Duff cast in his lot with the Free Church, though by this act he forfeited the use of all the mission property. He leased a building and continued his labors, the number of his pupils having increased to eight hundred. A church was erected which cost $50,000. Contemplating a visit to his native land in 1853, Dr. Duff made an extensive tour throughout India, that he might by personal observation make himself acquainted with the condition and wants of the people, and lay them before the churches at home. Before his embarkation, the people raised $25,000, and in addition to this $50,000 were subscribed in Great Britain for the erection of buildings for educational and missionary purposes. In 1854 he visited the United States and Canada. Wherever he preached, vast crowds were assembled to listen to his thrilling descriptions of the land of his work and adoption. After his return home he was elected moderator of the General Assembly. His health being feeble, he visited the Mediterranean shores, made a trip to Palestine, and returned to India considerably improved. He was appointed by a member of the British cabinet to draft a constitution for the India University, and was chosen dean of the faculty, and also elected a member of the syndicate. During all this time his own college in Calcutta progressed rapidly. In 1865 there were on the rolls more than eighteen hundred and seventy-four students. Other schools in different places under his supervision contained upwards of three thousand pupils. In consequence of failing health he was obliged to return again to Scotland, not without the same tokens of respect and esteem. He was elected professor of evangelical theology in the new college of the Free Church, Edinburgh, and here his last labors were performed. He died at Sidmouth, Devonshire, England, Feb. 12, 1878. See his *Life*, by Dr. G. Smith (Edinburgh, 1880). (W. P. S.)

Duff, David, D.D., a Scotch clergyman, graduated at the University of St. Andrews in 1802; was licensed to preach May 5, 1805; presented to the living at Moulin the same year, and ordained Feb. 21, 1806; promoted to Kenmore, March 29, 1831; and was in 1869 Father of the Church, being then about ninety years old. See *Fasti Eccles. Scoticanæ*, ii, 812, 824.

Duff, John, D.D., a Scotch clergyman, was licensed to preach in March, 1793; presented by the earl of Mansfield in February, 1796, to the living at Kinfauns; ordained Jan. 19, 1797, and died March 8, 1816, aged forty-eight years. See *Fasti Eccles. Scoticanæ*, ii, 646.

Duff, Robert, D.D., a Scotch clergyman, son of the Rev. William Duff of Kinedar, graduated at King's College, Aberdeen, March 29, 1756; was licensed to preach in October, 1762; presented to the living at Kinedar in succession to his father, and ordained Sept. 18, 1765. He died, having been more than seven years Father of the Synod, Oct. 31, 1825, aged eighty six years. See *Fasti Eccles. Scoticanæ*, iii, 663

Duffield, George, D.D., a Presbyterian divine, was born at Strasburg, Lancaster Co., Pa., July 4, 1794, and educated at the University of Pennsylvania. He was for many years pastor of Presbyterian churches in Philadelphia, New York, and Detroit, and was an active leader of the New School movement. He died at Detroit, Mich., June 26, 1868. His publications include *Spiritual Life:—Dissertation on the Prophecies:—Millenarianism Defended:—Claims of Episcopal Bishops Examined*, and other works. See Allibone, *Dict. of Brit. and Amer. Authors*, s. v.

Du Fossé, Pierre Thomas, a French writer, was born at Rouen in 1634. He was educated at Port Royal des Champs, and the impressions which he received there attached him more and more to his teachers, so that no persecution could prevail upon him to change his views. He was associated with Tillemont, Lemaistre, Arnaud, D'Andilly, and others. When imprisoned in 1666 in the Bastile, he found there De Sacy, who was a great comfort to him. He died in 1698, leaving *Vie de Barthélemy des Martyrs* (Paris, 1663):—*Vie de Thomas de Cantorbéry* (1674):—*Étude sur Tertullien et Origène* (1675):—*Vie des Saints*, comprising only the months of January and February:—also commentaries on Numbers, Deuteronomy, Joshua, Ruth, Psalms, and the Gospels. His *Mémoires* were published at Utrecht in 1739. See Lichtenberger, *Encyclop. des Sciences Religieuses*, s. v. (B. P.)

Duguesnay, Alfred, a French Roman Catholic prelate, born at Rouen in 1814, was for many years pastor of the Church of St. Laurent, in Paris, made bishop of Limoges in 1871, and died Sept. 15, 1884.

Duhlhajja, the last of the four sacred months of the Mohammedans, the month in which the pilgrimage to Mecca is performed.

Duilech (or **Doulach**), an Irish saint of Clochar, near Dublin, commemorated Nov. 17.

Duinsech, an Irish virgin of Loch-Cuan, in Ulster, commemorated Aug. 6.

Duitsch, Christian Solomon, a Protestant minister, was born of Jewish parentage at Temesvar, in Hungary, in 1734. According to the fashion of that time, his education was entirely Talmudical. In 1760 he received the degree of "morenu," or rabbinical doctor; and being the son-in-law of a wealthy Jew, he had everything that an ambitious Jew could desire. He devoted the whole of his time to the study of the Talmud and the Midrashim, but many a passage treating of the Messiah, repentance, and conversion led him to a diligent examination of Christianity. Without entering upon the history of his inner struggles, which is given in his interesting *De wonderlijke Leidinge Gods* and *Het Veroolg van de wonderlijke Leidinge Gods* (Amsterdam, 1767–69; new ed. Nijkerk, 1870), we will state that on June 25, 1767, he was openly baptized at Amsterdam. Duitsch now betook himself to the study of theology, and having been duly prepared, entered the Utrecht University, where he attended the theological lectures for six years. On April 16, 1776, he passed his examination; and a year later, April 14, 1777, was elected pastor at Mydrecht, where he died, Nov. 15, 1797. He wrote, *Israëls Verlossinge en cenwige Behoudenis* (Amsterdam, 1769–93). See Fürst, in Delitzsch's *Saat auf Hoffnung*, 1875, p. 3 sq. (B. P.)

Duke, Richard, an English divine and poet, was educated at Westminster School and Trinity College, Cambridge, where he became a fellow about 1682. Having been ordained, he was presented to the rectory of Blaby, in Leicestershire; in 1687 made a prebendary of Gloucester; and in 1688 chosen a proctor in convocation for that Church, and was chaplain to queen Anne. In 1710 he was presented to the living of Witney, in Oxfordshire. He died Feb. 10 of the same year. He published three *Sermons* in his lifetime, the first, on *The Imitation of Christ*, preached before the queen in 1703; the other two were preached in 1704. See Chalmers, *Biog. Dict.* s. v.; Allibone, *Dict. of Brit. and Amer. Authors*, s. v.

Dula, a martyr at Nicomedia, commemorated March 25.

Du Lau, Jean Marie, a French prelate and theologian, born Oct. 30, 1738, was general agent of the clergy, and became archbishop of Arles in 1775. Having opposed the French Revolution, he was arrested, after Aug. 10, and imprisoned in the convent of the Carmelites, in Rue de Vaugirard, where he was assassinated, Sept. 2, 1792. He wrote, *Adresse au Roi* (Paris, 1792):—*Recueil de Mandements et Lettres Pastorales* (Arles, 1795). His complete works were published by Jacques Constant (ibid. 1817). See Hoefer, *Nouv. Biog. Générale*, s. v.

Dulcidius (also **Dulcius**, **Doux**, or **Doucis**). (1) *Saint*, third bishop of Agen, in the province of Bordeaux, probably in the 5th century, is commemorated Oct. 17; (2) eighteenth bishop of Anicium (le Puy en Velay), A.D. 705; (3) tenth bishop of Toul, between A.D. 532 and 539; (4) a Spanish prelate of the 9th century, was a priest at Toledo, when he was sent, in 883, by Alfonso III of Castile, to Abub-Ali, the chief of the Saracens, and on his return was raised to the see of Toledo. Joseph Pellicer published, as a work of Dulcidius, an old chronicle written in Latin (Barcelona, 1663). See Hoefer, *Nouv. Biog. Générale*, s. v.

Dülcken, Anton, a Carthusian monk and ascetic writer, was born at Cologne about 1560, and died as prior of the Carthusians at Freiburg, Oct. 1, 1623. His works are mostly translations of ascetical writings, originally written in Italian, Spanish, and French. See Hartzheim, *Bibliotheca Colonnensis*, p. 20; Petreji, *Bibliotheca Carthus.* p. 10; Kessel, in Wetzer u. Welte's *Kirchen-Lexikon*, s. v. (B. P.)

Dulianists, a sect of Arians, so called from using the word δοῦλος to describe the relation of the Son to the Father.

Dulkaada, one of the four sacred months of the Mohammedans. This month is sacred as being devoted to preparation for the pilgrimage to Mecca.

Dullaphel, an Arabian legendary prophet, said to have existed before Christ, and to have restored twenty thousand persons to life at one time.

Dumbness. The *Apostolical Canons* excommunicate any cleric who mocks the deaf, dumb, or blind. These three classes are excluded from the episcopate, not as defiled, but that the proceedings of the Church should not be hindered. The capacity of the dumb to receive the sacraments or accept a penance was the subject of some controversy. A whole work of Fulgentius is devoted to the question of the validity of the baptism of an Ethiop catechumen after the loss of his voice, and he concluded that it was entitled to the same validity as that of an infant. This view prevailed in the Church. Among other canonical authorities, the first Council of Orange, A.D. 441, enacted that a person suddenly losing his voice might be baptized or accept a penance, if his previous will thereto could be proved by the witness of others, or his actual will by his nod. So the second

Council of Arles (A.D. 452) to the same effect as regards baptism. According to one of Ulpian's *Fragments*, the dumb could not be a witness nor make a testament. By a constitution of Justinian, A.D. 531, deaf mutes were declared incapable of making a will or codicil, or conferring a freedom, unless the infirmity should not be congenital, and they should have learned to write before it occurred, in which case they could exercise these rights by writing under their own hand. The dumb were in all cases allowed to do so by such writing. It was, however, held by the old law that the dumb, as well as the deaf and blind, could lawfully contract marriage, and become subject to dotal obligations. Deaf mutes were held excused from civil honors, but not from civic charges. But the dumb might lawfully decline a guardianship or curatorship.

Dumont, A. H., D.D., a Presbyterian minister, was born in New York in 1798. He was educated at Columbia College, and studied theology in the seminary at New Brunswick, N. J. His first pastorate was near Albany, N. Y.; in 1841 he became pastor of the Presbyterian Church at Morristown, N. J.; in 1845 he removed to Newport, R. I., where he devoted himself to the interests of education, and perfected the public-school system which Newport to this day enjoys. He died July 5, 1865. See Wilson, *Presb. Hist. Almanac*, 1866, p. 100.

Dun (Lat. *Dunnus*), eleventh bishop of Rochester, A.D. 741.

Dunan (Lat. *Donatus*), an Irish prelate, was bishop of Dublin, and by the aid of Sitric, the king, built the Cathedral of the Holy Trinity, afterwards called Christ Church, in that city, in 1038. He died May 6, 1074. See D'Alton, *Memoirs of the Abps. of Dublin*, p. 26.

Dunbar, Columba, a Scotch prelate, was dean of the Church of Dunbar about 1411. He was promoted to the see of Moray in 1429, and died in 1435, while on his return from the Council of Basle. See Keith, *Scottish Bishops*, p. 143.

Dunbar, Gavin (1), a Scotch prelate, was dean of Moray in 1488, and continued there till March 18, 1503, when he was made archdeacon, and lord-register of St. Andrews, which offices he filled fifteen years, and then became bishop of Aberdeen, in 1518. He died March 9, 1532. It is said that this bishop was the first to advise Hector Boece to write his history of Scotland. He built a bridge over the river Dee, consisting of seven arches, and endowed a hospital for twelve poor men, with a preceptor, in 1531. See Keith, *Scottish Bishops*, p. 119.

Dunbar, Gavin (2), a Scotch prelate, was early preferred to the priory of Whitehern, in Galloway, and at the same time became instructor to the young king James V. He was made bishop of Glasgow Dec. 22, 1524; in 1526 one of the privy council, and Aug. 21, 1528, lord chancellor, continuing in this last office until 1543. Having then some leisure time, he built the stately gate-house at his episcopal palace in Glasgow. He died April 30, 1547. See Keith, *Scottish Bishops*, p. 256.

Dunbar, William (1), a Scotch poet and monk, was born at Salton, East Lothian, about 1465, and educated at the University of St. Andrews. He afterwards became a Franciscan, and travelled in Scotland, England, and France, as a preacher. He was for some time in the diplomatic service of James IV, and resided at his court as a pensioner. He died in 1530. His poetry began to be made known to the public about the beginning of the last century. His principal allegorical poems are, *The Thistle and the Rose:—The Dance of the Seven Deadly Sins through Hell:*—and *The Golden Terge*. Critics speak in the highest praise of his poetry, some of them placing him in the very front rank of Scottish poets. See Allibone, *Dict. of Brit. and Amer. Authors*, s. v.; Chalmers, *Biog. Dict.* s. v.

Dunbar, William (2), D.D., a Scotch clergyman, was tutor in the family of M'Neill; licensed to preach in 1804; presented to the living at Applegarth, and ordained May 7, 1807; nominated moderator of the Assembly in 1839, but declined the honor, and died Jan. 6, 1861, aged eighty-one years. He published, in the *Naturalist's Library*, "The Natural History of Bees" (Edinb. 1840):—and *An Account of the Parish of Applegarth*. See *Fasti Eccles. Scoticanæ*, i, 644.

Duncan, a Scotch prelate, was bishop of Dunkeld in 1351, and also in 1354. He probably died in that see in 1363. See Keith, *Scottish Bishops*, p. 84.

Duncan, Alexander, D.D., a Scotch clergyman, brother of David, minister at Stow, was licensed to preach Jan. 7, 1735; called to the living at Traquair, and ordained assistant and successor, Sept. 12, 1738; transferred to Smailholm, Oct. 26, 1743; and died Sept. 29, 1795, aged eighty-six years. He published, *A Preservative against the Principles of Infidelity* (Edinb. 1774):—*The Devout Communicant's Assistant* (Berwick, 1792):—*The Evidence of the Resurrection of Jesus*, a sermon (Edinb. 1783):—*The History of the Revolution of* 1688 (ibid. 1790):—*Miscellaneous Essays* (1799):—*An Account of the Parish of Smailholm*. See *Fasti Eccles. Scoticanæ*, i, 257, 532.

Duncan, Andrew, D.D., a Scotch clergyman, son of Patrick, minister at Tibbermore; was licensed to preach in July, 1778; presented to the living at Auchterarder, and ordained Sept. 6, 1781; elected Presbytery clerk in November, 1784, which office he held to Jan. 3, 1792; transferred to Ratho Feb. 1, 1803; elected principal clerk to the General Assembly May 21, 1807; elected moderator to the General Assembly in May, 1824, and died July 29, 1827, aged seventy-one years. He published, *The Benefits of Christianity*, a sermon (Edinb. 1806):—*An Account of Auchterarder*. See *Fasti Eccles. Scoticanæ*, i, 141; ii, 748.

Duncan, Daniel, D.D., an English clergyman, wrote *Collects upon the Principal Articles of the Christian Faith, according to the Order of the Catechism of the Church of England* (1754):—and other religious tracts. He died in 1761. See Chalmers, *Biog. Dict.* xii, 447; Allibone, *Dict. of Brit. and Amer. Authors*, s. v.

Duncan, Henry, D.D., a Scotch clergyman, third son of Rev. George Duncan, was educated first at home, then at an academy at Dumfries, and completed his studies successively at the universities of St. Andrews, Glasgow, and Edinburgh, at the last of which he was associated with Henry Brougham, Horner, and Petty (Marquis of Lansdowne). He was licensed to preach in August, 1798; presented to the living at Ruthwell in May, and ordained Sept. 19, 1799; was elected moderator of the General Assembly in May, 1839; joined the Free Secession, and signed the deed of demission, May 24, 1843; and died Feb. 19, 1846, aged seventy-one years. He superintended the education of many young gentlemen in the manse, with that of his own family; formed an auxiliary Bible society in Dumfries in 1810; and founded a parish savings bank. Among his numerous publications are, *A Pamphlet on the Socinian Controversy* (Liverpool, 1791):—three separate *Sermons:*—six separate *Letters* on popular passing events:—*An Essay on the Nature and Advantages of Parish Banks* (1815):—*The Young South Country Weaver:—William Douglas* (Edinb. 1826, 3 vols.):—*Account of the Runic Monument at Ruthwell Manse* (1833):—*Sacred Philosophy of the Seasons* (Edinb. 1835, 4 vols.). He originated and wrote for the *Edinburgh Christian Instructor;* likewise the *Dumfries and Galloway Courier*, and edited it for seven years, being the principal proprietor thereof. He also edited, for a time, the *Dumfries Journal*. See *Fasti Eccles. Scoticanæ*, i, 626, 627.

Duncan, John (1), D.D., an English clergyman, son of Dr. Daniel Duncan, was born in 1720, and educated at St. John's College, Oxford. In 1745 and 1746 he was chaplain to the king's regiment, and was present at various battles in Scotland. In 1768 he was presented to the college living of South Warnborough, Hants, which he held forty-five years. He died at Bath, Dec. 28, 1808. His publications include an *Essay on Happiness*, a poem:—*Address to the Rational Advocates of the Church of England;* and other works. See Chalmers, *Biog. Dict.* xii, 447; Allibone, *Dict. of Brit. and Amer. Authors*, s. v.

Duncan, John (2), LL.D., a Scotch Presbyterian, preached successively at Maidstone, in Kent; at Tadley, Hampshire; and at Wimborne, in Dorset. He removed to London about 1790, and was chosen minister at the Peter Street Church, Soho, where he remained some years in the present century. See Wilson, *Dissenting Churches*, iv, 37.

Duncan, John (3), LL.D., a Scotch clergyman, was ordained, April 28, 1836, the first minister of the Church extension parish of Milton, presbytery of Glasgow; resigned his parish work in October, 1840; was set apart as missionary to the Jews, May 16, 1841; joined the Free Secession in 1843, and was appointed professor of Oriental languages in the college at Edinburgh the same year. He died Feb. 26, 1870. Dr. Duncan published a *Lecture on the Jews*, and *Letters* in the *Home and Foreign Missionary Record.* See *Fasti Eccles. Scoticanæ*, ii, 45; *Life*, by David Brown (Edinburgh, 1872).

Duncan, John (4), D.D., a Baptist minister, was born in Scotland, Oct. 14, 1812. He was converted at the age of fourteen, while attending an academy at Huntley, and became a member of an Independent Church in his native place. He came to the United States in early manhood, and joined a Baptist church in Troy, N. Y. The Church in Stillwater licensed him to preach, Sept. 29, 1838, and he was ordained in Cohoes, May 22, 1839. He had two or three pastorates in the state of New York, and then in Lowell, Mass., for several years. In 1854 he was called to the First Church in Camden, N. J., and next to South Boston, his ministry here being between five and six years. His other pastorates were in West Cambridge and Fall River, Mass.; Brooklyn, N. Y.; Essex, Conn.; and Mansfield, Mass. April 5, 1883, his health suddenly gave way, and he died July 28, 1884. See *The Watchman*, Aug. 14, 1884. (J. C. S.)

Duncan, Robert (1), a Scotch clergyman, was born at Edinburgh in February, 1699; graduated from Edinburgh University in June, 1718; after studying theology, went to the Continent as a tutor to the brother of the earl of Rothes, and pursued the study of divinity and law at the University of Groningen, where he ruptured a blood-vessel internally, but, recovering, was promised advancement to remain. He preferred to return to Scotland, and was licensed at Edinburgh, in October, 1726. During his preaching at St. Cuthbert's Church, in Edinburgh, he strained his voice, from which cause his complaint returned; after resting, he was called to the living at Tillicoultry in October, 1727, and ordained Jan. 25, 1728. He died May 18, 1729. He prepared for publication *An Exposition of the Epistle to the Hebrews* (Edinburgh, 1731). See *Fasti Eccles. Scoticanæ*, ii, 740.

Duncan, Robert (2), D.D., a Scotch clergyman, was licensed to preach March 27, 1776; presented to the living at Dundonald in April, and ordained Sept. 11, 1783; and died April 14, 1815. He published, *Infidelity the Growing Evil of the Times*, a sermon (Ayr, 1794): —*An Account of the Parish of Dundonald.* See *Fasti Eccles. Scoticanæ*, ii, 113.

Duncan, William Cecil, a Baptist minister, was born in the city of New York, Jan. 24, 1824; graduated from Columbia College in 1844, and from the theological department of Madison University in 1846; became editor of the *Southwestern Baptist Chronicle* at New Orleans, and pastor of the First Baptist Church there. In 1851 he became professor of ancient languages in the University of Louisiana, and in 1853 pastor of the Coliseum Baptist Church in the same city. He died there, May 1, 1864. Among his published writings are a work on baptism and a translation of Von Rhoden's *John the Baptist.* See *Appleton's Annual Cyclop.* iv, 366; Cathcart, *Baptist Encyclop.* p. 349. (J. C. S.)

Dunchadk (Lat. *Donatus*), an Irish saint, commemorated May 25, was the son of Cennfaedlakh, and abbot of Hy, A.D. 706.

Duncker, Hans Gottfried Ludwig, a Protestant theologian of Germany, was born at Hamburg, Aug. 17, 1810. He studied at Göttingen and Berlin. In 1836 he commenced his academical lectures at Göttingen; was, in 1843, professor extraordinarius, and in 1854, ordinarius; and died, doctor of theology and member of consistory, Nov. 7, 1875. He is the author of, *Historiæ Doctrinæ de Ratione, Quæ Inter Peccatum Originale et Actuale Intercedit* (Göttingen, 1837):—*Des heiligen Irenæus Christologie* (ibid. 1843):—*Zur Geschichte der christl. Logoslehre* (ibid. 1848). See Zuchold, *Bibl. Theol.* i, 299. (B. P.)

Duncombe, John, an English clergyman, was born in 1730, and educated at Benet College, Cambridge, where he was chosen fellow in 1750; and, in 1753, ordained at Kew chapel, and appointed to the curacy of Sundridge, in Kent, after which he became assistant preacher at St. Anne's, Soho. In 1757 he was presented to the united livings of St. Andrew and St. Mary Bredman, in Canterbury, where he settled, and in 1766 became one of the six preachers in the cathedral. He died in 1785. His publications in both prose and poetry are very numerous. See Chalmers, *Biog. Dict.* s. v.; Allibone, *Dict. of Brit. and Amer. Authors*, s. v.

Dundemore, Stephen de, a Scotch prelate, was the descendant of an ancient family in Fifeshire, and is by some called *Dundee.* He was chancellor of the see of Glasgow, and afterwards, in 1317, elected bishop; but, being an enemy to the English interest, king Edward II would not consent to his appointment. He was never consecrated, but is said to have died on his way to Rome. See Keith, *Scottish Bishops*, p. 242.

Dundumore, Thomas de, a Scotch prelate, was bishop of Ross in 1309, and, together with the other bishops, recognized the title of king Robert Bruce to the crown of Scotland in the same year. See Keith, *Scottish Bishops*, p. 187.

Dunkan, John, a Scotch prelate, was elected bishop of the Isles, May 21, and consecrated Nov. 25, 1375. He died in 1380. See Keith, *Scottish Bishops*, p. 304.

Dunkarton, Robert, a reputable English mezzotint-engraver, was born about 1744. He executed a large number of plates in London, among which are the following: *Lot and his Daughters; Christ and the Disciples at Emmaus;* and four subjects from the life of Joseph. See Spooner, *Biog. Hist. of the Fine Arts*, s. v.

Dunkel, Johann Gottlob Wilhelm, a Reformed theologian of Germany, was born at Köthen, Sept. 28, 1720. He studied at Halle, and received the degree of doctor of philosophy in 1739. In 1744 he was pastor at Diebzig, near Köthen, and in 1748 at Wulfen and Dronen, in the county of Anhalt-Köthen. He died Sept. 8, 1759, leaving, *Historisch-kritische Nachrichten von verstorbenen Gelehrten* (Köthen, 1753-60, 3 vols.):—*Theod. Dassovii de Vacca Rufa Opusculum* (Leipsic, 1758). See Döring, *Die gelehrten Theologen Deutschlands*, i, 347 sq. (B. P.)

Dunlap, James, D.D., a Presbyterian minister, was born in Chester County, Pa., in 1744; educated at New Jersey College; licensed to preach by the Donegal

Presbytery in 1776; in 1803 called to the presidency of Jefferson College, Cannonsburg, Pa.; in 1812 resigned on account of increasing infirmities, and died Nov. 12, 1818. See Sprague, *Annals of the Amer. Pulpit*, iii, 422.

Dunlap, William, an eminent American painter, was born at Perth Amboy in 1766. He commenced painting portraits in crayons at the age of sixteen. The next year he spent some time near Princeton, N. J., then the headquarters of Washington. Here he saw the general often, and painted his portrait and that of his wife. He resided three years in London, and returned to America in 1787. In 1821 he began the picture of *Christ Rejected*, at New York. He afterwards painted the *Bearing of the Cross* and the *Calvary*, which was considered his best production, and gained him considerable reputation. Mr. Dunlap wrote a *History of the Rise and Progress of the Arts in the United States* (1834, 2 vols. 8vo), and a *History of the Stage in the United States* (2 vols. 8vo). He died in 1835. See Spooner, *Biog. Hist. of the Fine Arts*, s. v.

Dunlop, William, an English clergyman, was born in Glasgow in 1692. In 1712 he went to Utrecht, where he spent two years, and in 1716 was promoted to be regius professor of divinity and church history. He often preached in the churches at Edinburgh. He died there in 1720. His works are *Sermons* (2 vols. 12mo), and an *Essay on Confession of Faith*. See Chalmers, *Biog. Dict.* s. v.; Allibone, *Dict. of Brit. and Amer. Authors*, s. v.

Dunn, Robinson Potter, D.D., a Presbyterian minister, was born at Newport, R. I., May 31, 1825. He graduated from Brown University in 1844, with the honors of his class, and from Princeton Theological Seminary in 1848. He was licensed the same year, and began preaching in the First Presbyterian Church, Camden, N. J. In 1851 he was called to the chair of rhetoric and English literature in Brown University. He died at Newport, R. I., Aug. 28, 1867. Dr. Dunn was a frequent contributor to the *Princeton Review* and *Bibliotheca Sacra*; and translated and edited one volume of Lange's *Commentary on the Old Test.* See Wilson, *Presb. Hist. Almanac*, 1868, p. 84.

Dunn, Samuel, a veteran Methodist Episcopal minister, was born at Mevagissey, Cornwall, England, Feb. 13, 1798. He was converted at fourteen years of age, licensed in 1817, and in 1819 joined the Conference at Bristol. In 1822 he went as missionary to the Shetland Isles, in response to an appeal from Adam Clarke. After an eminently successful missionary work, he returned and served the following circuits: Newcastle-on-Tyne, Rochdale, Manchester, Sheffield, Lancaster, Edinburgh, Camborne, Dudley, Halifax, Newcastle-on-Tyne, Nottingham. In 1849 he was expelled, with two others, as the result of the "Fly-sheet Controversy," which event had no bearing upon his moral character, but was the occasion of one of the largest secessions from English Wesleyanism. A fine church was built for him at Camborne, which he served from 1850 to 1861. In 1862 he became pastor of a church in Sheffield, where he remained until 1864. In 1865 he came to America and preached in pulpits that were opened to him. He joined the New York East Conference in 1867, and became superannuated the same year, in which relation he continued until his death, Jan. 24, 1882. His life was one of great usefulness. See *Minutes of Annual Conferences*, 1882, p. 76.

Dunster, Charles, an English clergyman, was rector of Petworth, Sussex. He published some works on literary criticism, and *Observations on Luke's Gospel* (1805):—*On Matthew's Gospel* (1806); and other works. See Allibone, *Dict. of Brit. and Amer. Authors*, s. v.

Dupanloup, Felix Antoine Philibert, a French prelate, was born at St. Félix (old department of Mont Blanc), Jan. 3, 1802. He studied at Paris, was ordained priest, and acquired the reputation of a good preacher and catechist. In 1841 he was appointed professor of sacred eloquence in the theological faculty of Paris, and attracted to the Sorbonne large audiences. Archbishop Affre appointed him grand vicar, and he also held several court offices. He was appointed bishop of Orleans in 1849, and died Oct. 11, 1878. Dupanloup was an earnest advocate of education, morality, and piety, occupying in these regards the high position of conservative progress. On the establishment of the Roman republic he wrote a pamphlet upon the temporal sovereignty of the pope. In 1850 he published the first volume of a work entitled *De l'Éducation*, which has been greatly admired. In 1854 he took the place of Tissot in the Académie Française. On the occasion of the re-erection of the statue of Joan of Arc at Orleans he delivered an eloquent panegyric on that heroine. His writings are enumerated in Hoefer, *Nouv. Biog. Générale*, s. v.; Vapereau, *Dict. des Contemporains*, s. v.; and were published collectively as *Œuvres Choisies* (Paris, 1873-75, 7 vols.).

Duperron, Jacques Davy, a French prelate, nephew of another of the same name, was grand chaplain to Henrietta, queen of England, and bishop of Angoulême and of Évreux. He died Feb. 9, 1649. He published the controversial works of his uncle.

Dupont, Jacques Marie Antoine Célestin, a French prelate, was born at Iglesias, Sardinia, Feb. 2, 1792, of a French family settled there. He studied first at Villa Franca, next in the seminary at Nice, and finally in that of St. Irenæus, at Lyons, where he was ordained priest in 1814; became private secretary to cardinal Colonna d'Istria, devoted himself to the study of the law, and was received as *doctor in utroque* at the University of Turin, April 10, 1815. In 1821 he was appointed canon of Sens, in 1822 one of the vicars-general of the same diocese, in 1823 bishop *in partibus* of Samosata, and bishop of St. Dié, May 9, 1830; was raised to the metropolitan see of Avignon, May 1, 1839; in 1841 he was transferred to the bishopric of Bourges, made cardinal in 1847, and died May 27, 1859. See Hoefer, *Nouv. Biog. Générale*, s. v.

Duport, James, D.D., son of the following, a learned Græcist, was born in 1606; educated at Westminster school and Trinity College; became professor of Greek at Cambridge in 1632; prebend in Lincoln Cathedral in 1641; dean of Peterborough in 1664; master of Magdalen College, Cambridge, in 1668; rector of Aston-Flamville and Burbach about 1672, and died July 17, 1679, leaving numerous classical works on ancient literature, for which see Chalmers, *Biog. Dict.* s. v.

Duport, John, D.D., an English divine, was born at Sheepshead, Leicestershire. He was fellow, then master, of Jesus College, Cambridge, once proctor (1580) and three times vice-chancellor of that university (1590 sq.), and prebendary of Ely (1609). He died in 1617. He was one of the translators of the king James version of the Bible.

Duprat, Antoine, a French prelate, was born at Issoire, Auvergne, Jan. 17, 1463; educated first in a Benedictine abbey, and finally under the direction of archbishop Boyer, who was his relative; was soon raised to civil office, including the presidency of Parliament, and eventually became chancellor under Francis I. He was ordained priest in 1516, soon after made archbishop of Sens, later cardinal, and died July 8, 1535. See Hoefer, *Nouv. Biog. Générale*, s. v.

Duprat, Guillaume, a French prelate, son of the preceding, was born in 1507; became bishop of Clermont in 1528, and distinguished himself among the French members of the Council of Trent. He died in his castle of Beauregard in 1560. See Hoefer, *Nouv. Biog. Générale*, s. v.

Dupre, John, D.D., an English divine, was born about 1753, and died in 1835. He published *Sermons*

(1782–87, 2 vols.):—*Discourses* (1815, 2 vols.). See Allibone, *Dict. of Brit. and Amer. Authors*, s. v.

Dupreau (Lat. *Prateolus*), GABRIEL, a French theologian, was born at Marcoussis in 1511. He taught theology at the College of Navarre, and distinguished himself by the zeal with which he opposed the doctrines of Luther and Calvin. He died at Péronne, April 19, 1588, leaving, *Du Devoir d'un Capitaine*, translated from the Latin of Claude Cotereau (Poitiers, 1547):—*De la Puissance et Sapience de Dieu*, etc., translated from the Greek (Paris, 1557):—*Des Faux Prophètes* (ibid. 1564):—*La Synagogue de l'Antechrist* (ibid. eod.):—and especially *De Sectis Hæreticorum* (ibid. 1569), with others, for which see Hoefer, *Nouv. Biog. Générale*, s. v.

Du Puis, MATTHIAS, a French missionary, was born in Picardy; took the habit of a Dominican at Paris, March 23, 1641, and was sent in 1644 into the mission fields of America. He remained at Guadaloupe until 1650, when he returned to France, and lived successively at Caen, Langres, and Orleans, at which last place he died, about 1655, leaving a work on his mission (Caen, 1652). See Hoefer, *Nouv. Biog. Générale*, s. v.

Du Puy, Hugues, a French crusader, went to Palestine in 1096 with his wife (the sister of Éverard de Poisieu) and three sons. He was one of the chief captains of the Christian army. See Hoefer, *Nouv. Biog. Générale*, s. v.

Du Puy, Raymond, nephew of the preceding, second grand-master of the Knights of Malta, was born in Dauphiny about 1080. He entered the Hospital of St. John at Jerusalem, and after having attended on the poor and the sick pilgrims there for more than twenty years, was elected president about 1121. Du Puy organized the Knights of Malta into a military body, designed to defend the holy places against the infidels. Then his order was divided into three classes, of which the first comprised all noblemen, the second the priests and chaplains, and the third, under the name of *serving brothers*, private persons. He gave them, at the same time, rules, which were confirmed by the pope in 1127. He contributed very strongly to the taking of Ascalon in 1154, and defeated with his chevaliers the sultan at the battle of Noureddin. He died in 1160, from the effect of the wounds which he received in this latter engagement. He has been placed among the number of the saints of the order of Malta. See Hoefer, *Nouv. Biog. Générale*, s. v.

Duquesne (*d'Icard*), ARNAUD BERNARD, a French theologian, was born at Paris in 1732; became doctor in the Sorbonne, vicar-general of Soissons, and treasurer of the Bastile, and died in his native city in 1791, leaving, *Retraite Spirituelle* (Paris, 1772):—*L'Évangile Médité* (ibid. 1773):—*L'Année Apostolique* (ibid. 1791):—*Les Grandeurs de Marie* (ibid. eod.). See Hoefer, *Nouv. Biog. Générale*, s. v.

Duquesnoy, FRANCIS (called *the Fleming*), a reputable sculptor, was born at Brussels in 1594, and went to Italy while young for instruction in the art. His statue of *St. Susanna*, for the Church of the Madonna at Loretto, has been highly extolled. For the basilica of St. Peter's he executed a colossal statue of *St. Andrew*, which is one of the finest productions of modern art. He died at Leghorn in 1646. See Hoefer, *Nouv. Biog. Générale*, s. v.; Spooner, *Biog. Hist. of the Fine Arts*, s. v.

Duran. See PROFIAT.

Durand, a French Benedictine, was born about 1012 at Neubourg, in the diocese of Évreux. He was the nephew of Gérard, abbot of St. Vandrille, and while young adopted the rule of St. Bernard at Rouen, where he studied philosophy, music, and theology, so that he became well known among the prelates of Normandy for his learning. William the Bastard sent him to take charge of the abbey of St. Martin of Troarn, in 1059, where he distinguished himself for the maintenance of ecclesiastical discipline. He had a very fine and strong voice, and composed many chants and anthems. Durand died about 1089, in his own abbey, leaving only a dogmatic treatise entitled *Du Corps et du Sang de Jésus Christ* (preceded by about nine hundred hexameter verses, and printed in the *Bibliotheca Maxima Patrum*, xviii), besides two brief epitaphs. See Hoefer, *Nouv. Biog. Générale*, s. v.

Durand (*de Maillane*), PIERRE TOUSSAINT, a famous French jurist, was born at St. Remy, in Provence, in 1729, and died at Aix in 1814. He defended the rights of the Gallican Church against the pretensions of the Roman see, and published *Dictionnaire de Droit Canonique* (Avignon, 1761, and since):—*Institutes du Droit Canonique* (translated from the Latin of Lancelot, Lyons, 1770, 3 vols.):—*Les Libertés de l'Église Gallicane* (ibid. 1771, 5 vols.). See Lichtenberger, *Encyclop. des Sciences Religieuses*, s. v. (B. P.)

Durant, Henry, LL.D., a Congregational minister and teacher, was born at Acton, Mass., June 18, 1802; studied at Phillips Academy, Andover, and graduated from Yale College in 1827; for two years thereafter was principal of the Garrison Forrest Academy, in Baltimore Co., Md.; and in 1829 became tutor in Yale College. While in this position he pursued the course of study in the theological seminary, and graduated in 1833. Dec. 25 of that year he was ordained pastor of the Byfield Church (Newbury), and was dismissed therefrom in 1849. Meanwhile, in 1847 and until 1851, he was principal of Dummer Academy, in Byfield. In April, 1853, he went to California, and in June following opened the school in Oakland, and was its principal until it became the College of California in 1854. It was merged in the University of California in 1869. Up to that date Dr. Durant had been professor of ancient languages. From 1870 to 1872 he was president of the university, but, at the latter date, illness compelled him to resign. He died in Oakland, Jan. 22, 1875. See *Cong. Quarterly*, 1876, p. 423.

Durant, John, an English nonconformist divine, was born in 1620, and ejected in 1662. He published, *Salvation of the Saints* (1653):—*Six Sermons* (1655):—*Spiritual Seamen* (eod.):—*Comfort and Counsel* (1658); and other works. See Allibone, *Dict. of Brit. and Amer. Authors*, s. v.

Durbin, JOHN PRICE, D.D., an eminent Methodist Episcopal minister, was born in Bourbon County, Ky., in 1800. He was converted in his eighteenth year; served some time as local preacher; but, because of his vehement style of delivery, his health gave out, and obliged him to resort to conversational preaching in the cabins of his neighbors. In 1820 he entered the Ohio Conference, and was appointed to Greenville Circuit; and now, on the saddle, he began his search for knowledge, struggling through various books, including the English, Latin, and Greek grammars, until 1822, when he was stationed on a circuit twelve miles from Oxford, the seat of the Miami University, which institution he immediately attended. In 1825 he entered the Cincinnati College, where he completed his course, and received the degree of A.M. After being seven years in the ministry, he was elected professor of languages in Augusta College, Ky., which position he held two years. His health then failing, he was appointed agent for the college, and in its behalf visited the Eastern cities. His eloquence made him famous, and soon his name was sufficient to call together thousands. In 1832 he was elected to the editorship of the *Christian Advocate*, in New York; in 1834 was transferred to the New York Conference, and elected president of Dickinson College, at Carlisle, Pa.; in 1836 was transferred to the Philadelphia Conference, of which he remained a member during life. In 1842 and 1843 he travelled in Europe and the East, and published, as the result, four volumes of *Observations*. In 1844 he was a delegate to the General Conference, where he took an active part, and exhibited great ability in the contest concerning slavery. Having vacated his office in Dickinson College, he, in 1850, was appointed as missionary secretary, and, under his control, Methodist Episcopal missions were extended into China, India, Germany, Switzerland, Norway, Denmark, Sweden, Bulgaria, Italy, and South America; and the Church entered upon a new æra of princely giving. He died Oct. 18, 1876. Besides the above books of travel, Dr. Durbin edited the American edition of Wood's *Mosaic History of the Creation, with Notes* (8vo); and contributed largely to various periodicals. See *Minutes of Annual Conferences*, 1877, p. 33; Simpson, *Cyclop. of Methodism*, s. v.

Düre, Georg van der (better known as *Georgius Aportanus*), the reformer of East Frisia, was born at Zwolle, and died at Emden in 1526. He was the first who openly opposed the Catholic Church at Emden in 1519, and preached against her from the same pulpit in which the doctrine of Rome was defended. Düre's influence caused all priests to be expelled from the Roman Catholic churches, and Emden became the nucleus from which Protestant missionaries were sent to the Netherlands. See Meinders, *Kerkelijke hervorming*, p. 395; Ypey en Dermont, *Geschiedenis der ned. hervormde Kerk*, i, 34; Harkenroht, *Oostfriesche oorsprongkelijkheden*, i, 135, 146 sq.; ii, 609, 697; Eggerik Beninga, *Chronyk van Oostfriesland*, p. 602; Wiarda, *Ostfriesische Geschichte*, ii, 313 sq., 324 sq.; Alberdingk Thijm, in Wetzer u. Welte's *Kirchen-Lexikon*, s. v. (B. P.)

Durel (or **Durell**), John, D.D., a learned English divine, was born at St. Helier's, in the isle of Jersey, in 1625, and educated at Merton College, Oxford, and at Saumur, France. He was minister at St. Malo, but came to England, and was very instrumental in establishing the new Episcopal French Church in London, in which he officiated for some years. In April, 1663, he was made prebendary in the cathedral of Salisbury, and, Feb. 11 following, succeeded to the canonry of Windsor. July 1, 1668, he was installed into the fourth prebend of Durham, and in 1677 was given the deanery of Windsor. He had also the living of Witney, in Oxfordshire, conferred upon him. He died June 8, 1683. His works are numerous. See Chalmers, *Biog. Dict.* s. v.; Allibone, *Dict. of Brit. and Amer. Authors*, s. v.

Düren, Councils of (*Concilium Duriense*), held at Düren, near Aix-la-Chapelle. 1. In A.D. 748, under Pepin, who called a synod, for the restoration of churches, and for the relief of the poor. 2. In A.D. 761, a national council under Pepin. 3. In A.D. 775, under Charlemagne. 4. In A.D. 779, under Charlemagne. The council, composed of bishops, nobles, and abbots, passed twenty-four capitula upon discipline, one of which enforces payment of tithes.

Durfee, Calvin, D.D., a Congregational minister, was born at Pittsfield, Mass., Oct. 6, 1797. He studied at Lenox Academy; graduated at Williams College in 1825; studied theology with Dr. Woodbridge of Hadley; was ordained in Hunter, N. Y., April 21, 1828, and served that church until August, 1835. From March 2, 1836, until July 15, 1851, he was pastor in South Dedham (now Norwood), Mass.; from 1851 to 1855, acting pastor in Brooklyn, O.; from 1855 to 1858, financial agent of Williams College; from 1854 to 1856, a trustee of Western Reserve College; from 1860 to 1865, acting pastor in South Williamstown, and continued to reside at Williamstown until his death, Nov. 20, 1879. He was also a member of the New England Historic Genealogical Society. Besides publishing various discourses and other pamphlets, he issued a *History of Williams College* (1860):—*Williams' Obituary Record*, fourteen pamphlets (1866–79):—*Biographical Annals of Williams College* (1871). See *Cong. Year-book*, 1880, p. 17.

Dûrga, one of the principal forms in which the consort of Siva (q. v.), the Hindû god, is represented. She is possessed of great power, being endowed with the distinctive attributes of all the gods. She is generally represented with *ten arms*, each of which is supplied with a warlike weapon. She obtained the name of Dûrga in the following manner: In remote ages, a giant named Durga, having performed austerities of extraordinary merit in honor of Brahma, obtained his blessing, and with it great power. He conquered the three worlds; dethroned all the gods except the Trimurti; banished them from the heavens to the forests, and compelled them to worship him. Religion was abolished, and the Brahmins forsook the reading of the Vedas. The gods, in their distress, applied to Siva for assistance, and he prevailed upon Parvâti, his wife, to attempt the destruction of the giant. She undertook

Figure of Dûrga.

the task. Durga set out to meet her with a grea. army, while she prepared to receive his attack with a thousand arms. A great conflict ensued, in which the giant and all his forces were destroyed. The gods immediately ascended their hitherto vacant thrones, and, in return for so signal a deliverance, immortalized the victory by transferring to the conquering goddess the name of *Dûrga*. She is extensively and enthusiastically worshipped throughout Eastern India. The wealthy natives have images of Dûrga in their houses, made of gold, silver, brass, copper, crystal, stone, or mixed metal, which are daily adored. Her *ten-armed* figure is approached with the utmost reverence. On either side images of her two sons are usually placed, and around her are commonly represented a multitude of demigoddesses, the companions of Dûrga in her wars. She is regarded as the patroness of thieves and robbers, who hold her in great veneration. For this reason the Dakvits or bandits of Bengal are scrupulous in their devotions to her, and before setting out on their marauding excursions dedicate to her a portion of the spoils to be taken. See Kali; Parvati.

Dûrga Pûjah, an annual festival celebrated among the natives of eastern India, in honor of the goddess Dûrga (q. v.). It lasts fifteen days, twelve of which are devoted to *preparation* and three to *worship*. For these occasions multitudes of images are prepared, of a composition of wood, hay, clay, or other light and cheap material. They vary from a few inches to fifteen or twenty feet in height, but are usually of the size of a human body. The first part of the ceremony consists in the consecration of the idols, at the completion of which the spirit of Dûrga is supposed to enter the image. Then the worship of the goddess commences with great energy and intense devotion. Every conceivable ceremony, gyration, carousal, dance, and sacrifice is performed for three days and three nights. On the morning of the fourth day the idols are unconsecrated, and the goddess dismissed from her earthly habitation. The owners now carry these images forth to the banks of the Ganges, where, after various rites and ceremonies, the carriers suddenly make an assault upon them, violently break them in pieces, and cast their broken fragments into the depths of the river. See HINDÛISM.

Durie, ANDREW, a Scotch prelate, was made abbot of Melrose about Sept. 24, 1527, and became bishop of Galloway in 1541. He probably died in September, 1558. See Keith, *Scottish Bishops*, p. 278.

Durinn, in Norse mythology, was one of the most famous and oldest dwarfs, whom Odin endowed with human form and powers of mind. He and Mödsognir were excellent workmen in metals.

Duriotōrus, sixth bishop of Rennes, about the middle of the 7th century.

Dursch, JOHANN GEORG MARTIN, a Roman Catholic theologian of Germany, was born in 1801. Having acted as professor of the gymnasium at Ehingen-on-the-Danube for fourteen years, he was in 1842 preacher at Wurmlingen, and in 1850 at Rottweil, where he died, Feb. 22, 1881. He published, *Geschichte der christl. Religion und Kirche* (Ehingen, 1834):—*Das Verhältniss der Schule zu Kirche und Staat* (Ulm, 1838):—*Aesthetik* (Stuttgard, 1839):—*Allgemeiner Commentar über die Psalmen* (Carlsruhe, 1842):—*Symbolik der christlichen Religion* (Tübingen, 1858, 2 vols.):—*Der Symbolische Charakter der christlichen Religion und Kunst* (Schaffhausen, 1860). See Winer, *Handbuch der theol. Lit.* ii, 313; Zuchold, *Bibl. Theol.* i, 300. (B. P.)

Dutch Version OF THE SCRIPTURES. Dutch (sometimes styled "Low Dutch," to distinguish it from "High Dutch," or German) is the language spoken by all classes in Holland. It is also used to a great extent in South Africa, more or less in Java, the Moluccas and the other Dutch colonies, and among the Dutch colonists in the United States. The first Dutch version was probably the one published at Delft in 1477, under the title *De Bybel dat nive Testament.* 2 *Deele . . . wol overgheset ut den Latine in Duytsche* (fol.). There is no doubt that this edition was followed by others, for in the edict published Oct. 14, 1529, at the command of Charles V, three editions of the New Test. are mentioned, which were condemned. In 1528 there was published by W. Vorstmann, at Antwerp, *De Bibel Tgeheele oude ende nieuwe Testament met grooter naersticheyt na dem Latijnschen text gecorrigeret.* This is said to have been the second of the editions of the Bible condemned by Charles V, because they were designed for Catholics. In 1535 H. Petersen published, at Antwerp, *Dey bibel Tgeheele oude ende Nieuwe Testament, met groter neersticheyt ghecorrigeert.* In 1560 N. Bieskens van Diest published *Der Bibel inhoudende dat oude ende Nieuwe Testament*, and in 1563 L. Kindern published another edition, in which 1 John v, 7, is wanting. This edition is remarkable as having been printed *op de Nordsee.* In 1565 was published at Emden, in folio, *Biblia dat is de gantsche Heylighe Schrifft grondelick ende trouwelik, verduytschet, met verklaringhe duysterer woorden, redenen en spreucken, ende verscheyden lectien.* This is a translation of Luther's version, known under the name of *Uylenspiegels-Bijbel*, or *Deux-des-Bijbel*, according to the glosses in Ecclus. xix, 5 and Neh. iii, 5. In 1571 was published *Biblia dat is de gantsche Heylighe Schrifft, grondelic ende trouwelick verduytschet. Met verklaringhe duysterer woorden, redenen en spreucken, ende verscheyden Lectien die in andere loflike ouersettinghen ghevondem, ende hier aen de Cant toe ghesettet zyn.* This edition is very rare, having been printed at Ghent under the Spanish sway. In the same year the necessity of procuring an improved version was publicly discussed, but it was not until the famous Synod of Dort, in 1618–19, that actual preparations were made for immediate commencement of the work. For the translation of the Old Test. were chosen John Bogerman (1576–1637), first professor of theology at Franeker, a very learned and able man, but odious to the Remonstrants for his translation of Beza's severe treatise, *De la Punition des Hérétiques*, his polemical work against Grotius, and his arbitrary bearing as president of the great synod; Willem Baudart, pastor at Zutphen; Gerson Bucer, author of *De Gubernatione Ecclesiæ*, which drew upon him the hatred of James I. For the translation of the New Test. and Apocrypha were chosen Jacobus Rolandus, minister at Amsterdam; Hermanus Faukelius (1569–1621), minister at Middelburg, and Petrus Cornelii, minister at Enkhuysen. As substitutes for the Old Test. company were chosen Antonius Thysius, professor at Harderwyk, afterwards at Leyden; Jacobus Rolandus and H. Faukelius, as above named. Those for the New Test. were Festius Hommius, minister at Leyden; Antonius Walæus, professor at Leyden, and Jadocus Hoingius, rector of the academy at Harderwyk. Besides the translators, there were appointed revisers on the nomination of the delegates from the different provinces. These were—

A. FOR THE OLD TESTAMENT.

Gelderland.—Antonius Thysius.
South Holland.—Johannes Polyander, professor at Leyden.
North Holland.—Petrus Plancius, eminent for his scientific attainments.
Zeeland.—Jadocus Larenus, minister at Flushing.
Friesland.—Sibrandus Lubbertus, professor at Franeker, famous for his skill in controversy against Bellarmine, Socinus, Grotius, and others.
Overyssel.—Jacobus Revius, rector of a college at Leyden.
Groningen.—Francis Gomar (1563–1641), professor of theology.

B. FOR THE NEW TESTAMENT.

Gelderland.—Sebastian Damman, minister at Zutphen.
South Holland.—Festus Hommius.
North Holland.—Gosuinus Geldorpius.
Zeeland.—Antonius Walæus.
Friesland.—Bernardus Fullenius, minister at Leeuwarden.
Overyssel.—Johannes Langius, but he removing from the province the next year, Kaspar Sibelius of Deventer was put in his place.
Groningen.—Ubbo Emmius, professor at Groningen.

A petition was presented to the states-general, requesting them to undertake the expense of the work. The translators of the Old Test. commenced their work at Leyden in 1626, and completed it in 1632; those of the New Test. commenced in 1628, and completed in 1634. Each book was printed as soon as finished, and a copy was sent to each of the revisers. The revision of the Old Test. was begun in 1633, and completed in 1634. The revisers of the New Test. commenced their undertaking in the latter year. None of the translators long survived the completion of the work. The first edition of this version was published at Leyden, by Paulus Aerthz van Ravensheyn, in 1637, under the title *Biblia dat is . . . des ouden en des nieuwen Testaments. Nu eerst door Last der Hoogh-Mog Heeren Staten General . . . en volgens het Besluyt van de Synode Nationael, gehouden tot Dordrecht, inde Jaeren* 1618 *ende* 1619. Without giving the titles, we will only mention that meanwhile at least six other editions were published. That the version published in 1637 was repeatedly issued is a matter of course. When the first edition was published the Remonstrants were opposed to the translation; but when they had carefully examined it, they were so struck with its faithfulness and accuracy that they adopted the Old Test. as their own. After the lapse of more than forty years, a version of the New Test. was executed expressly for their use by Christian Hartsoeker, an Arminian minister at Rotterdam, and was published at Amsterdam, by Hendrick en Dirk, in

1680, under the title *Het Nieuwe Testament of verbondt Uit het Grieksch op nieuws vertaelt door Christian Hartsoeker Bedinaer de H. Evang. in de remonstrantsche gemeinte tot Rotterdam. Met byvajing van eenige Korte aenteekningen.* This version, although professedly a new translation from the Greek, chiefly followed that of the synod. For a long time the Lutherans and Mennonites used the translation of Nicolaus Biestkens, first published in 1560; but in 1648 M. A. Viszcher prepared *Biblia, Dat is de gantsche H. Schrifture vervattende alle de Boecken des Ouden ende des Nieuwen Testaments. Van nieuws uyt D. M. Luthers Hoog-Duytsche Bibel in onse Nederlandsche tale getrouwelyck over-geset, tot dienst van de Christelyoke Gemeynten donveränderde Augsburgische Confessie in dese Nederlande* (Gedruct t'Amsterdam by Rieuwert Dircksz van Baardt). The title-page is followed by an engraving, representing Martin Luther holding in his hand the Augsburg Confession. Below the engraving the following lines are printed in Latin and Dutch:

> "Roma orbem domuit, Romam sibi Papa subegit,
> Viribus illa suis, fraudibus iste suis.
> Quanto iste major Lutherus, major et illa,
> Istum illamque uno qui domuit calama."

This Bible, also called Viszcher's Bible, was henceforth used by the Lutherans, and contains, besides all the prefaces, Luther's marginal readings.

In 1717 a New Test. was published at Amsterdam, the printing having been done at the expense of Peter I of Russia; in 1721 another edition was published, also at the expense of the emperor, in five volumes. The Dutch translation is printed on one column, the other having been left blank, because the emperor intended to have the Russian version printed on it.

In 1825 a new translation, in the modern style and orthography, by the learned Prof. Van der Palm, of Leyden, was published; and though not adopted in churches, it is greatly esteemed and extensively used.

A revised edition of the established version was published in 1834; the orthography introduced was that according to the system of Prof. Siegenbeek, which had received the sanction of the government. This system has, however, fallen into disrepute, and was not adopted in subsequent editions. Within a recent period the Netherlands Bible Society appointed a commission to modernize the orthography of the Bible, and the alterations which were introduced, both in spelling and in some points of grammar, were considerable. All the editions printed now by that society are with these alterations.

The British and Foreign Bible Society also issued several editions of the authorized Dutch version. The first edition, consisting of five thousand copies of the New Test., appeared in 1809, and other editions of the entire Bible followed since. The total number of copies issued by the British and Foreign Bible Society up to March 31, 1884, amounted to 1,823,338, besides five thousand copies of the New Test. with English. The Netherlands Bible Society has distributed, since its formation in 1815, altogether 1,530,844 copies. (B. P.)

Duthac, a Scotch prelate, was bishop of Ross, and was of a noble family. He probably died in 1249, and is commemorated as a saint March 8. See Keith, *Scottish Bishops*, p. 186.

Dutherius, third bishop of Nicæa, in France, is said to have been slain by the Vandals A.D. 483 or 493.

Duthracht. (1) A female Irish saint, commemorated Oct. 25, is variously called also *Durach* and *Drachna.* (2) An Irish saint, commemorated May 16, is said to have been abbot of Liathdruim.

Duttenhofer, Christian Friedrich, a Lutheran theologian of Germany, was born Feb. 3, 1742, at Nürtingen, in Würtemberg. He studied at Tübingen and Leipsic; was in 1771 deacon at Beilstein; in 1777, pastor at Grunau; and, in 1780, fourth preacher at St. Nicolaus, in Heilbronn; in 1800, was made senior of the ministry, and in 1806 the Helmstädt University honored him with the theological doctorate. He died March 17, 1814, leaving, *Untersuchungen über Pietismus* (Halle, 1787):—*Predigten* (Heilbronn, 1792):—*Geschichte der Religionsschwärmereien* (ibid. 1796-99, 3 vols.; 2d ed. 1802):—*Versuch über den letzten Grundsatz der christlichen Sittenlehre* (Tübingen, 1801):—*Betrachtungen über die Geschichte des Christenthums* (Heilbronn, 1813). See Döring, *Die gelehrten Theologen Deutschlands*, i, 349 sq.; Winer, *Handbuch der theol. Lit.* i, 335, 484, 486, 732; ii, 93, 208. (B. P.)

Duval, André, a French theologian, was born at Pontoise, Jan. 15, 1564, and died at Paris, Sept. 9, 1638. He enjoyed the favor of cardinal Du Perron, and through his influence he was called to the theological chair in Paris. For some time he was also superior-general of the Carmelites of France, and dean of the theological faculty at Paris. He wrote, *De Potestate Ecclesiæ* (Paris, 1612):—*De Romani Pontificis Potestate* (ibid. 1614):—*De Summi Pontificis Auctoritate* (1622). See Lichtenberger, *Encyclop. des Sciences Religieuses*, s. v.; Hoefer, *Nouv. Biog. Générale*, s. v. (B. P.)

Duval (*de Dampierre*), **Charles Antoine Henri**, a French prelate, was born at the castle of Hans in 1746, and became, by marriage, lord of Dampierre-le-Château. He exercised the functions successively of grand-vicar, canon, and archbishop of Paris until 1791; but, as he would not take the constitutional oath, he was incarcerated until 1794. Eight years after, he was nominated by the first consul to the bishopric of Clermont, and, in 1811, was called to the national council at Paris, in which he took part with the majority who resisted the will of the emperor. In 1814 Louis XVIII appointed him member of the commission of affairs of the Church of France; in 1828 he signed the memoir against the ordinances of June. His Christian charity had won him the affections and the respect of his flock. He died in 1833. See Hoefer, *Nouv. Biog. Générale*, s. v.

Duval, Jean, a French prelate and Orientalist, was born at Clamecy (Nivernais) in 1697. Having finished his studies, he entered, in 1615, the order of the barefooted Carmelites, adopting the name of *Bernard de Sainte-Thérèse*, afterwards went to the East as a missionary, and was appointed bishop of Bagdad in 1658. He died at Paris, April 10, 1669, leaving some very important works on the Oriental languages, which have remained in MS. See Hoefer, *Nouv. Biog. Générale*, s. v.

Duvoisin, Jean Baptiste, a French prelate, was born at Langres, Oct. 16, 1744. Being vicar-general of the bishop of Laon, he refused to take the oath of allegiance to the civil authority, and emigrated to Brunswick. In 1802 he returned to France, was made bishop of Nantes, and enjoyed the confidence of the imperial family to a high degree. Duvoisin died July 9, 1813, leaving, among other works, *Dissertation Critique sur la Vision de Constantin* (1774):—*Autorité des Livres de Moïse* (1788):—*Démonstration Évangelique*, with an *Essai sur la Tolérance.* See Lichtenberger, *Encyclop. des Sciences Religieuses*, s. v.; Hoefer, *Nouv. Biog. Générale*, s. v. (B. P.)

Duzak, a place, according to the ancient Persian system of religion, where Ahriman, the devs, and the souls of the wicked are thoroughly cleansed and purified by fire, after which they are restored to the divine favor.

Dvalin, in Norse mythology, was a dwarf who possessed a knowledge of the art of making swords for battle.

Dwight, Harrison Gray Otis, D.D., a missionary of the American Board of Commissioners of Foreign Missions, was born at Conway, Mass., Nov. 22, 1803. He graduated from Hamilton College in 1825 and from Andover Theological Seminary in 1828, and in 1830 sailed for the East. After spending two years exploring the field, he settled as missionary at Constantinople in 1832, and there remained nearly thirty years, preaching, superintending schools, and editing a religious paper. He also published a very popular book entitled *Christianity Brought Home from the East.* He was killed by a railroad accident in Vermont, Jan. 25, 1862. See *Appleton's Annual Cyclop.* 1862, p. 662.

Dwija (*twice born*), an appellation given to a Hindû Brahmin after his investiture with the sacred cord. See CORD, INVESTITURE WITH THE.

Dwynwen, a Welsh saint, patroness of lovers, appears to have lived in the 5th century, and is commemorated Jan. 25.

Dwywan is the Noah of the British islands. He and his wife Dwywach are the progenitors of the new-born human race. The sea, Llyon, broke from its bounds and flooded the world. The two, Dwywan and his wife, saved themselves in a sailless, but well-constructed, vessel, made by God himself, and took on board a male and a female of every kind of animal. The ship drifted to Britain, from which country the whole world was again peopled.

Dyava, in Hindû mythology, is the goddess of air; every Brahmin offers her daily a little butter and a few hairs from the forehead of a holy cow.

Dyce, ALEXANDER, oldest son of a general in the East India Company's service, was born in George Street, Edinburgh, June 30, 1797, and received his bachelor's degree at Oxford in 1819. Between 1822 and 1825 he served two curacies, and died May 9, 1869. His publications were chiefly in the line of literary criticism. Besides editions of Greene, Webster, Shirley, Middleton, Skelton, Beaumont and Fletcher, Marlowe, Peele, Bentley, Collins, Pope, Akenside, Beattie, and others, he published a new and complete edition of the *Works of William Shakespeare* (1853-58, 6 vols. 8vo). See Allibone, *Dict. of Brit. and Amer. Authors*, s. v.

Dyer, George, an English Baptist minister and antiquary, was born in London, March 15, 1755, and educated at Cambridge. He preached at Oxford for some years, and then removed to London in 1792. He died March 2, 1841, leaving, *An Inquiry into the Nature of Subscription to the Thirty-nine Articles* (1790):—*Poems and Critical Essays on Poetry* (1802, 2 vols.):—*History of the University and Colleges of Cambridge*, etc. (1814), and other works. See Allibone, *Dict. of Brit. and Amer. Authors*, s. v.

Dyer, Mary, one of the martyrs among New England Friends, was born in Rhode Island. During a visit to England she joined the Friends, and was recognised as a minister in that denomination. Returning to America she began to preach in Boston, from which place she was expelled in 1657, and subsequently, in 1658, from New Haven. In visiting four Friends imprisoned in Boston she was thrown into jail, in 1659, but was soon discharged, and returned to her home. Soon, however, she came again to Boston, was arrested, cast into prison, tried, and condemned to death a second time. At the gallows she was reprieved. In March, 1660, she once more visited Boston, was arrested, tried, condemned, and hanged April 1 following. See *History of Friends in America*, vol. i, chap. xi. (J. C. S.)

Dyer, William, an English Nonconformist divine, who late in life became a Quaker, was born about 1636, ejected in 1662, and died in 1696. He published *Sermons*, etc. (1663-83). See Allibone, *Dict. of Brit. and Amer. Authors*, s. v.

Dyfnan, a Welsh saint of the 5th century, was the son of Brychan, and is commemorated April 23.

Dyfnog, a Welsh saint of the 7th century, is commemorated Feb. 13.

Dyke, Daniel (1), an English Baptist, born at Epping, Essex, about 1617, took his degree at Cambridge University, and soon became known for his great learning and useful preaching, thereby securing a valuable living at Great Hadham. In 1653 he was made one of Oliver Cromwell's chaplains, but refused Church preferment at the Restoration in 1660, and preferred persecution with the Dissenters. In 1668 he was chosen joint pastor with William Kiffin, at Devonshire Square, and continued a faithful laborer there until his death, in 1688. His modesty prevented him from printing anything, but he joined others in writing three controversial tracts, and he edited a volume of *Sermons* by his father. See Wilson, *Dissenting Churches*, i, 433-435.

Dyke, Daniel (2), an English Puritan divine, was educated at Cambridge. He was minister at Coggeshall, Essex, and at one time settled at St. Albans. He was suspended in 1588, and died in 1614. His writings (some of them posthumously published) include *Self-Deceiving* (1614):—*Repentance* (1631):—*Six Evangelical Histories* (1617). See Allibone, *Dict. of Brit. and Amer. Authors*, s. v.

Dyke, Jeremiah, an English Puritan divine, father of Daniel (1), was minister at Epping, Essex, in 1609, and died in 1620. He wrote various sermons and theological treatises (1619-40), and the *Worthy Communicant* (1642). See Allibone, *Dict. of Brit. and Amer. Authors*, s. v.

Dymond, JONATHAN, a noted English moralist, was born at Exeter in 1796, and became a member of the Society of Friends. He was a linendraper. In 1823 he published *An Inquiry into the Accordancy of War with the Principles of Christianity.* He died May 6, 1828. In 1829 his *Essay on the Principles of Morality and on the Private and Political Rights and Obligations of Mankind* was published (2 vols. 8vo). See Allibone, *Dict. of Brit. and Amer. Authors*, s. v.

Dynămis (*power*), in the system of Basilides, as described by Irenæus (i, 24), is named, together with Sophia (*wisdom*), as following Nous (*mind*), Logos (*reason*), and Phronesis (*thought*) in the series of emanations from the unborn Father.

Dynamius. (1) Bishop of Angoulême, A.D. 450. (2) Third bishop of Béziers, about the middle of the 15th century. (3) Thirteenth bishop of Avignon, A.D. 605-627. (4) Thirty-fifth bishop of Avignon for twenty-three years, in the early part of the 7th century.

Dyothelites (δυοθελῆται), a name given to those orthodox Christians in the 7th century who held that there were two wills in Christ, a divine and a human, in opposition to the *Monothelites* (q. v.). The sixth œcumenical council (i. e. the third Œcumenical Council of Constantinople), called by the emperor Constantine Pogonatus in A.D. 680, asserted the doctrine of two wills in Christ in the following terms: "Two wills and two natural modes of operation united with each other, without opposition or change, so that no antagonism can be found to exist between them, but a constant subjection of the human will to the divine." The champions of monothelism were anathematized, as well as the patriarchs of Constantinople and the pontiff Honorius. The monothelite doctrine was placed in the ascendency in 711, but two years later Anastasius II ascended the throne and established dyothelism, whereupon the monothelites fled the country.

Dyscolius, sixth bishop of Rheims, about A.D. 346.

Dysen, in Norse mythology, are feminine protecting spirits in general. The name has a threefold signification: (1) it is often identical with the Walküres; (2) it is used of goddesses of destiny, good or evil; (3) it has reference specially to Freya, who was thus honored by calling her the goddess, and sacrifice was made to her in the middle of winter by the Dyssablot, so called from this service.

Dysibod (Disibod, or **Disen)**, an Irish prelate,

was born in Ireland, and was ordained a priest at the age of thirty. He was some time afterwards made bishop, some say of Dublin. When he had governed his see ten years he was compelled to resign it, in 675. He then left Ireland, and travelled into Germany, going from place to place preaching the Gospel, for ten years. At last he arrived at a high, woody mountain, where he settled. He drew many of the order of St. Benedict to him, and founded a monastery on this mountain, which was called Mount Disibod, since changed into Dissenberg. He died there, July 8, in the eighty-first year of his age. His life was written by the abbess Hildegardis. See D'Alton, *Memoirs of the Abps. of Dublin*, p. 20.

Dyzĕmas. (1) *Dismes*, *decimæ*, tithe-day. (2) The name of the penitent thief in the apocryphal gospel. His fellow is called Gesmas or Gestas, and the soldier Longinus, from his spear (*lonche*).

E.

Eaba, abbot of Malmesbury, in the 8th century.

Eadbald (Lat. *Ædboldus*), 12th bishop of London, A.D. 796.

Eadbert (i. e. *Albert* or *Adalbert*). (1) Bishop of Lindisfarne, A.D. 688; died May 6 (his day of commemoration), A.D. 698. (2) Ninth bishop of London (sometimes called *Filbrith*), cir. A.D. 772–788. (3) Abbot of Reculver (called also *Heahbert*), A.D. 747. (4) Abbot of Mercia, A.D. 747. (5) Abbot of Sherborn, A.D. 803. (6) First bishop of the South Saxons, A.D. 711. (7) Fifth bishop of the Middle Angles at Leicester, A.D. 764–787.

Eadburga (i. e. *Ethelburga*). (1) Daughter of Aldwulf, king of the East Angles, was abbess of Repton, in the 7th century. (2) Widow of Wulfhere, king of Mercia, was second abbess of St. Peter's, Gloucester, A.D. 710–735.

Eadfrid (i. e. *Alfred*). See EADFRITH.

Eadgar (i. e. *Edgar*). (1) Third bishop of Lindisfarne, cir. A.D. 706–731. (2) Tenth bishop of London, A.D. 787–796.

Eadhed, a priest of Oswy, king of Northumbria; ordained by Deusdedit in 664, consecrated bishop of Lindsey in 678, and transferred to Ripon soon afterwards.

Eadie, JOHN, D.D., LL.D., a distinguished divine of the Presbyterian Church in Scotland, was born at Alva, Stirlingshire, May 9, 1810. He graduated from the University of Glasgow, studied at the Divinity Hall of the Secession Church (United Presbyterian), and in 1835 was ordained pastor of the Cambridge Street Church, Glasgow, in which he speedily attained great eminence and usefulness. He was regarded as the leading representative of the denomination to which he belonged and of the city which has always been its stronghold. As a preacher he was distinguished for his hard common-sense and occasional flashes of happy illustration, for his masculine piety, deep earnestness, and breadth of sympathy, both intellectual and emotional. He was frequently called to other important charges, but was too strongly attached to Glasgow to leave. In 1836 he removed with his congregation to a new and beautiful church at Lansdowne Crescent, where his influence continued unabated until his death, June 3, 1876. Dr. Eadie bore the reputation of extensive and profound scholarship, and in 1843 was appointed by the Church to the chair of hermeneutics and the evidences of natural and revealed religion in Divinity Hall. As a critic he was acute and painstaking, as an interpreter eminently fair-minded. In the pulpit, as in the professor's chair, his strength lay in the tact with which he selected the soundest results of Biblical criticism, whether his own or that of others, and presented them in a clear and connected form with a constant view of their practical bearing. If this last fact gave a non-academic aspect to some of his lectures, it rendered them not less interesting and probably not less useful to his auditors. Being engaged in two distinct offices, either of which were sufficient to claim all his energies, he nevertheless found time for an amount of work in a third sphere, of which the same thing may be said. Most of his works were connected with Biblical criticism and interpretation, some of them being designed for popular use and others being more strictly scientific. To the former class belong his contributions to the *Biblical Cyclopædias* of Kitto and Fairbairn, his edition of Cruden's *Concordance*, *Oriental History*, and his discourses. The *Life of Dr. Kitto* obtained a deserved popularity, also his *Dictionary of the Bible for the Young*, *Lectures on the Bible to the Young*, etc. His last work, the *History of the English Bible* (1876, 2 vols.), will probably be the most enduring memorial of his ability as an author. He is the author of valuable expositions on the Greek text of Galatians, Ephesians, Philippians, Colossians, and Thessalonians. See his *Life*, by Brown (Lond. 1878). (W. P. S.)

Eadred (or **Heardred**), bishop of Hexham, consecrated Oct. 29, 797, died in 800.

Eadric, second abbot of St. Albans, A.D. 796.

Eadsige, archbishop of Canterbury, of whose parentage and birthplace nothing seems to be known. The earliest mention of him presents him as one of the chaplains of Canute; he was then a secular, and, of course, in priest's orders. He was consecrated bishop of St. Martin's in 1035; was translated to the see of Canterbury in 1038, and repaired to Rome for the pallium. On his return home, in 1043, he was called upon to officiate at the coronation of Edward the Confessor—the memorable event of his life. He died in 1050. See Hook, *Lives of the Abps. of Canterbury*, i, 489 sq.

Eadulf (or **Aldwulf**, Lat. *Adulphus*). (1) Eighth bishop of Lindsey, A.D. 796–836. (2) Fifteenth bishop of Lichfield, cir. A.D. 803–816.

Eagle, IN CHRISTIAN SYMBOLISM. St. Gregory considered this bird to typify the contemplative life; other fathers regarded it as an emblem of resurrection (Psa. ciii, 5). It is the symbol of St. John the Evangelist, as it soars up to heaven and the sun; and he dwells in his Gospel and the Revelations specially on the divine discourses and the celestial glory of the Sun of Righteousness. It also represented the regeneration of the neophyte; the resurrection of the Saviour (says St. Ambrose); and renewing of the soul on earth, as glory hereafter will renew body and soul; the power of grace when it is portrayed drinking at a chalice. or in combat with a serpent, the type of evil.

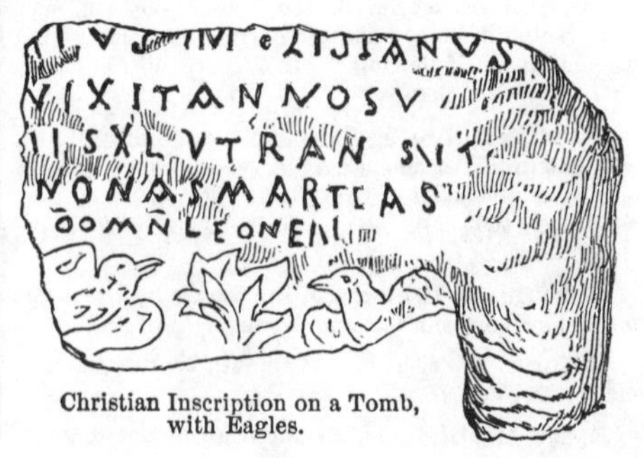

Christian Inscription on a Tomb, with Eagles.

EAGLE, AS AN ARCHITECTURAL TERM, is used to designate a brazen or wooden lectern, the upper portion of which represents an eagle with outstretched wings, on the back of which is a book-rest. Many ancient examples of such lecterns remain in collegiate and cathedral churches, and a great number of new specimens have been made for use after the old models. See LECTERN.

Eagleton, WILLIAM, D.D., a Presbyterian minister, was born in Maryville, Tenn., March 25, 1796. He was educated in Maryville College, and studied theology in the South-western Theological Seminary, at the same place. In 1827 he was licensed by the Union Presbytery, and soon after was elected professor in Maryville College. In 1829 he accepted a call to the Church in Murfreesborough, where he remained till his death, March 28, 1866. See Wilson, *Presb. Hist. Almanac*, 1867, p. 431.

Eames, JAMES HENRY, D.D., a Protestant Episcopal minister, was born at Dedham, Mass., Nov. 29, 1814. The first two years of his college course were spent at King College, Bristol, Tenn., and the last two at Brown University, where he graduated in 1839. He pursued his theological studies with Rev. John Bristed, of Bristol, R. I., was ordained deacon in December, 1841, and presbyter in 1842; was rector of Ascension Church, in Wakefield, for about four years, when he took charge of St. Stephen's Church in Providence, remaining there until 1850, and then engaged in missionary labor in Rhode Island; became rector of St. Paul's Church, Concord, N. H., in 1858, and held that position until his death, which occurred in the harbor of Hamilton, Bermuda, Dec. 10, 1877. For many years Dr. Eames was chaplain to the asylum for the insane, and performed a large amount of missionary work in New Hampshire. Three times he travelled in Europe, and spent part of several winters in Bermuda. (J. C. S.)

Eanbald (or **Enbald**). (1) The pupil and successor of Albert in the archiepiscopal see of York, A.D. 782. He was very vigorous in the administration of his diocese, and died at a monastery called Etlete (or Edete), Aug. 10, 796. (2) Called also *Heantbald*, succeeded the foregoing as archbishop of York, and his history is given with considerable detail by Alcuin. He appears to have died A.D. 812.

Eanbert, bishop of Hexham, cir. A.D. 800–806.

Eanfrith, fifth bishop of Elmham, A.D. 736.

Eanswitha (or **Enswida**), a British saint, commemorated Aug. 31, was the daughter of Eadba, king of Kent, and lived a virgin, in a nunnery founded by her, at Folkestone, where she died, some say in 640, others in 673.

Eardulf (Lat. *Ardulphus*). (1) Bishop of East Anglia (Dunwich) in 747. (2) Twelfth bishop of Rochester, cir. A.D. 762.

Earle, Jabez, D.D., an English Independent minister, was born about 1676, and educated among the Dissenters. He was assistant to the Rev. Thomas Reynolds, at the Weigh-House, London, in 1699; and in 1707 removed to Hanover Street, where he ministered more than sixty years, and died in 1768, leaving a number of *Sermons* and theological treatises, etc. (1706–35; new ed. 1816, 8vo). See Chalmers, *Biog. Dict.* s. v.; Allibone, *Dict. of Brit. and Amer. Authors*, s. v.; Wilson, *Dissenting Churches*, i, 169; ii, 6, 492, 508, 530.

Earle (or **Earles**), **John**, an English prelate, was born at York in 1601, and entered Merton College, Oxford, in 1620. He became chaplain and tutor to prince Charles, and chancellor of the cathedral of Salisbury. On the Restoration he was made dean of Westminster, and consecrated bishop of Worcester in 1662. In September, 1664, he was transferred to the see of Salisbury. He died Nov. 17, 1665, leaving *Microcosmography* (Lond. 1628, 8vo; 6th ed. 1630, 12mo). See Chalmers, *Biog. Dict.* s. v.; Allibone, *Dict. of Brit. and Amer. Authors*, s. v.

Earlom, RICHARD, a pre-eminent English engraver, was born in London in 1742, and was the pupil of Cipriani. He died in 1822. The following are some of his principal plates: *The Holy Family; Mary Magdalene Washing the Feet of Christ; David and Bathsheba; The Repose; The Virgin and Infant; The Infant Jesus Sleeping; The Presentation in the Temple; The Virgin and Infant with St. John.* See Spooner, *Biog. Hist. of the Fine Arts*, s. v.

Early, JOHN, D.D., a bishop of the Methodist Episcopal Church South, was born in Bedford County, Va., Jan. 1, 1786, of Baptist parents. He was converted in 1804; licensed to preach in 1806; and in 1807 entered the Virginia Conference, wherein he continued laboriously and faithfully till 1815, when the growing necessities of his family obliged him to locate and engage in secular business. In 1821 he re-entered the effective ranks, and labored with marvellous success until 1846, when he connected himself with the Church South, and devoted his energies to establishing and operating the Southern Book Concern. In 1854 he was elected to the episcopacy; in 1866 was granted a superannuated relation, and died in Lynchburg, Nov. 5, 1873. Bishop Early was full of the missionary spirit, and everywhere awakened missionary zeal; was one of the chief founders of Randolph-Macon College; was a man of great energy and devotedness, and held a high position in the esteem of the Church. See *Minutes of Annual Conferences of the M. E. Church South*, 1873, p. 914; Simpson, *Cyclop. of Methodism*, s. v.

Earnulph. See ARNULPH.

Ears, TOUCHING OF. In holy communion it seems to have been the custom to touch the organs of sense with the moisture left on the lips after receiving the cup.

Earulfus, abbot and confessor, commemorated Dec. 29.

East, PRAYER TOWARDS THE. See BOWING; ORIENTATION.

Eastburn, MANTON, D.D., LL.D., a bishop of the Protestant Episcopal Church, was born in England, Feb. 9, 1801, being brother of James W., the poet. His parents came to America when he was a boy. He graduated from Columbia College, New York, in 1817, and in due time thereafter from the General Theological Seminary in the same city. He was ordained assistant minister of Christ Church in 1822; became rector of the Church of the Ascension in 1827; was consecrated bishop of Massachusetts Dec. 29, 1842; and died in Boston, Sept. 12, 1872. Bishop Eastburn published several addresses and essays, and edited Thornton's *Family Prayers*. See Drake, *Dict. of Amer. Biog.* s. v.; *Prot. Episc. Almanac*, 1873, p. 133.

Easter-candle. See PASCHAL TAPER.

Easter-eggs. The egg was the symbol of creation in Egypt, and of hope and the resurrection among early Christians; and the custom of giving colored pasch eggs on Easter morning is found in the East, in the Tyrol, in Russia, in Greece, in many parts of England, where it may be traced back to the time of Edward I, and was observed at Gray's Inn in the reign of Elizabeth. In France the pasch egg is eaten before any other nourishment is taken on Easter day. Tansy pudding, according to Selden, is a memorial of the bitter herbs eaten by the Jews; and peculiar cakes in some places formed the staple fare on this day. Paul II issued a form of benediction of eggs for England, Scotland, and Ireland. Henry VIII received a paschal egg in a case of silver filigree from the pope. The Jews regarded the egg as a symbol of death.—Walcott, *Sac. Archæol.* s. v. See EGG.

Easterwine (or **Eosterwini**), coadjutor-abbot of Wearmouth, was the nephew of Benedict, the founder of that monastery, and was born in 650. At the age of twenty-four he renounced his secular prospects, was ordained in 679, and devoted himself with singular humility and affection to the duties of his recluse life. He died March 7, 686.

Eastlake, *Sir* CHARLES LOCK, an English painter, was born at Plymouth in 1793. He studied under Fuseli at the Royal Academy, and at the Louvre, in Paris. He went to Rome in 1817, and remained there many years. In 1841 he was appointed secretary to the royal commission on fine arts; from 1843 to 1847 was keeper of the National Gallery; and in 1850 was knighted, made president of the Royal Academy, and director of the National Gallery. He died in Pisa, Dec. 23, 1865. Among his most noted works are, *Christ Weeping over Jerusalem; Pilgrims Arriving in Sight of Rome; Christ Blessing Little Children; Hagar and Ishmael*, and the *Raising of Jairus's Daughter.* He wrote *Materials for a History of Oil Painting*, and *Contributions to the Literature of the Fine Arts* (posthumous; edited by lady Eastlake). A *History* of his life was published by lady Eastlake in London in 1870.

Easton, THOMAS, D.D., a Scotch clergyman, graduated from Glasgow University; was licensed to preach in June, 1807; presented by lord Douglas to the living of Kirriemuir in 1809, and ordained March 22, 1810. He died April 5, 1856, aged seventy-nine years. In him learning, knowledge, modesty, and moral worth were combined with meekness and piety. He published six different works, chiefly of a local theological character. See *Fasti Eccles. Scoticanæ*, iii, 777.

Eata (or **Ecka**). (1) First bishop of Hexham, A.D. 678, and the fifth of Lindisfarne, 681-685, was originally from Northumbria, and abbot of Old Melrose; he died Oct. 26, 686. (2) An anchorite of Crayke, in Yorkshire, who died in 767.

Eaton, Asa, D.D., a Protestant Episcopal minister, was born at Plaistow, N. H., July 25, 1778. His preparatory studies were begun at the age of twenty-one, and he graduated from Harvard University in 1803. On Oct. 23 of the same year Christ Church invited him to act as lay-reader, and he continued in this position until 1805, when he was ordained, and remained rector until 1829. In that year he became city missionary, laboring among the destitute until 1837. From 1837 to 1841 he was connected with St. Mary's Hall, a young ladies' school at Burlington, N. J. Then he returned to Boston, but without a regular charge, and died there, March 24, 1858. See *Amer. Quar. Church Rev.* 1858, p. 341; *Necrol. of Harvard College*, p. 178.

Eaton, George W., D.D., LL.D., a distinguished Baptist scholar, was born near Huntingdon, Pa., July 3, 1804, and graduated from Union College, Schenectady, N. Y., in 1829. Upon his graduation he was appointed tutor, which position he held a year or two. In 1831 he became professor of languages in Georgetown College, Ky., and in 1833 professor of mathematics and natural philosophy at Hamilton College. He subsequently filled the professorships of ecclesiastical and civil history, and of systematic theology, and was appointed president of Madison University and of the Hamilton Theological Seminary, holding the latter position until his death, Aug. 3, 1872. Dr. Eaton was a man of the widest and warmest sympathies, earnest in his convictions, and able to maintain them with fervid eloquence. (J. C. S.)

Eaton, Horace, D.D., a Presbyterian minister, was born in Sutton, N. H., Oct. 7, 1810. He studied at Phillips Academy, Andover, Mass., and graduated from Dartmouth College in 1839 and from the Union Theological Seminary in 1842. For six years he was pastor of the Sixth Presbyterian Church in New York city, and thereafter of the First Presbyterian Church in Palmyra, N. Y., until his death, Oct. 21, 1883. See *Providence Journal*, Oct. 23, 1883. (J. C. S.)

Eaton, Joseph, a veteran Baptist minister, was born at Wells, Me., June 22, 1743. He was converted at the age of twenty-two, licensed to preach in 1793, and in 1798 was ordained pastor of the Church in Wells, the service being performed in Berwick. After his resignation, in 1820, Mr. Eaton was engaged for several years in evangelistic labors in the section of the country in which he lived. His death took place in December, 1831. See Millett, *History of the Baptists in Maine*, p. 442. (J. C. S.)

Eaton, Joseph H., LL.D., a Baptist minister, brother of Rev. G. W. Eaton, D.D., was born in Berlin, Delaware Co., O., Sept. 10, 1812. He graduated from the Hamilton Literary and Theological Institution (now Madison University) in 1837, and for three years thereafter was engaged in teaching. He was elected professor in 1841, and in 1847 president of what is now Union University, Murfreesborough, Tenn. His ordination took place in 1843, and he was pastor of the Church in the same place, having also the oversight of several county churches. His health broke down under these excessive labors, and he died, Jan. 12, 1859. See Cathcart, *Baptist Cyclop.* p. 358. (J. C. S.)

Eaton, Peter, D.D., a Unitarian minister, was born at Haverhill, Mass., March 25, 1765. He studied under the Rev. Phineas Adams, graduated from Harvard College in 1787, taught a school for one year at Woburn, and then passed some time in the study of theology. Having received license, he preached his first sermon in Boxford, Jan. 10, 1789, and in October following was installed as pastor there. In 1819 he preached the annual sermon before the Legislature of Massachusetts, and in 1820 resigned his charge at Boxford. In 1845 he removed to Andover, where he remained until his death, in April, 1848. Dr. Eaton published many valuable *Sermons.* See Sprague, *Annals of the Amer. Pulpit*, viii, 222.

Ebal, MOUNT. We extract some additional particulars from Lieut. Conder's *Tent Work in Palestine*, i, 88:

"There are three curious places on Ebal: one of which is a rude stone building, enclosing a space of fifty feet square, with walls twenty feet thick, in which are chambers. The Samaritans call it part of a ruined village, but its use and origin are a mystery. It resembles most the curious monuments near Hizmeh, called the 'Tombs of the Sons of Israel.' The second place is the little cave and ruined chapel of Sitt Eslamîyeh, 'The Lady of Islam,' who has given her name to the mountain. It is perched on the side of a precipice, and is held sacred by the Moslems, who have a tradition that the bones of the saint were carried hither through the air from Damascus. The third place is a site the importance of which has not been previously recognised. It is a little Moslem Mukâm, said once to have been a church, called 'Amâd ed-Dîn, the 'Monument of the Faith.' The name thus preserved has no connection with Samaritan tradition, but it is undisputed that the sacred places of the peasantry often represent spots famous in Bible history. It is therefore perhaps possible that the site thus reverenced is none other than that of the monumental altar of twelve stones from Jordan, which Joshua erected, according to the Biblical account, on Ebal, and not on Gerizim, as the Samaritans believe, charging the Jews with having altered the names (Deut. xxvii, 4). The hill-top on which this monument stands is called Râs el-Kâdy, 'Hill of the Judge.' It was here that the Crusaders placed Dan, the site of Jeroboam's Calf Temple, and the present name may perhaps be connected with this theory, Dan ('the Judge') being translated into the Arabic Kâdy ('Judge'), just as it has been at the true Dan, now Tell el-Kâdy, at the source of the Jordan." (See illustration on opposite page.)

Ebarcius. (1) Sixteenth bishop of Nevers, cir. A.D. 696. (2) Thirty-third bishop of Tours, cir. A.D. 696.

Ebasius, bishop of Vicus Aterii, in Byzacia, Africa, cir. A.D. 641-649.

Mount Ebal.

Ebba (**Æbha**, or **Ebbe**), abbess of Coddingham, in Berwickshire, was daughter of Ethelfrid, king of Northumbria, and sister of St. Oswald. In A.D. 679 her convent was burned, and she died Aug. 25 (her festal day), 683.

Ebbo, *Saint*, twenty-ninth bishop of Sens, was born at Tonnerre (Burgundy). He was of a noble family, but entered the monastery of Saint-Pierre-le-Vif; was elected abbot of it, and soon succeeded his uncle, St. Gericus, bishop of Sens. He spent the latter part of his life in a hermitage at the village of Arce, where he died in 750. He is commemorated Aug. 27. See Hoefer, *Nouv. Biog. Générale*, s. v.

Ebbo (Lat. *Ebulus*), twenty-ninth bishop of Limoges, cir. A.D. 752.

Ebeling, Christian, a Lutheran theologian of Germany, was born at Bückeburg, Nov. 3, 1668. He studied at Jena; was in 1697 professor of philosophy at Rinteln; in 1708 professor of ethics, and in 1714 doctor and professor of theology. He died Sept. 3, 1716, leaving *De Mysterio Trinitatis* (Lemgo, 1714):—*Ethicæ Christianæ Compendium* (ibid. 1715):—*Examen Concilii Tridentini* (ibid. 1716):—*Theologia Homiletica* (ibid. eod.). See Strieder, *Hessische Gelehrten Geschichte;* Jöcher, *Allgemeines Gelehrten-Lexikon*, s. v. (B. P.)

Ebeling, Johann Justus, a German theologian, was born at Elze, Aug. 27, 1715. He studied at Helmstädt; was appointed in 1740 pastor at Garmessen, and became in 1753 superintendent at Luneburg, where he died, March 2, 1783. His principal works are, *Andächtige Betrachtungen*, etc. (Hildesheim, 1747):—*Sünden der Menschen* (Lemgo, 1748): *Heilige Wahrheiten des Glaubens*, etc. (Luneburg, eod.):—*Erbauliche Betrachtungen*. See Hoefer, *Nouv. Biog. Générale*, s. v.

Ebendorffer (*de Haselbach*), THOMAS, a Roman Catholic theologian, who died in 1464, is the author of *Commentarius in Evangelium Johannis:*—*Expositio Symboli Apostolorum:*—*De Casibus Excommunicationis:*—*De Novem Alienis Peccatis:*—*Commentarius in Esaiam*. See Jöcher, *Allgemeines Gelehrten-Lexikon*, s. v.; Hoefer, *Nouv. Biog. Générale*, s. v. (B. P.)

Ebenezer. On the strength of Jerome's location of this spot, near Bethshemesh, Lieut. Conder proposes (*Tent Work in Palest.* ii, 336) to identify it with the present *Deir Arbân*, two miles east of Ain-Shems, "a large village on the lower slope of a high ridge, with a well to the north, and olives on the east, west, and north" (*Memoirs* of Ordnance Survey, iii, 24).

Eberhard, MATTHIAS, a Roman Catholic prelate, was born at Treves, Nov. 1, 1815. He studied at the clerical seminary of his native place, and received holy orders in 1839; in 1840 became chaplain of St. Castor's, at Coblentz; was called in 1843 as episcopal secretary to Treves, and appointed the same year professor of dogmatics at the clerical seminary there. In 1850 he became member of the chapter, and was consecrated in 1862 bishop of Treves. After Arnold's death, in 1864, his name was stricken from the list of candidates as *persona regi minus grata*, but he was elected in 1867 by the chapter. In 1869 and 1870 he was at Rome as member of the Vatican Council. The Prussian "Folk-Laws" brought him in 1873 in conflict with the government, and as he could not pay the fines, he was imprisoned in 1874. He died May 5, 1876, leaving *De Tituli Sedis Apostolicæ*, etc. (Treves, 1846). (B. P.)

Eberle, CHRISTIAN GUSTAV, a Lutheran minister of Germany, was born in 1813, and died Dec. 9, 1879, at Ochsenbach, in Würtemberg. He published, *Luthers Glaubensrichtung* (Stuttgard, 1858):—*Luther ein Zeichen dem widersprochen wird* (ibid. 1860):—*Luthers Evangelien-Auslegung aus seinen homiletischen und exegetischen Werken* (ibid. 1857). See Zuchold, *Bibl. Theol.* i, 302. (B. P.)

Ebermann, VITUS, a German Jesuit, was born in 1597. In 1620 he joined his order, was professor of philosophy and theology at Mayence and Würzburg, and died April 8, 1675, leaving *Bellarmini Controversiæ Vindicatæ:*—*Parallela Ecclesiæ Veræ et Falsæ:*—*Anatomia Calixtina:*—*Irenicum anti-Calixtinum:*—*Irenicon Catholicon Helmstadiensi Oppositum:*—*Bellarminus Vindicatus* (4 vols.):—*Justa Expositio cum Lutheranorum Doctoribus*. See Jöcher, *Allgemeines Gelehrten-Lexikon*, s. v.; Alegambe, *Bibliotheca Scriptorum Societatis Jesu*. (B. P.)

Ebert, SAMUEL, a Lutheran minister of Germany, was born at Leipsic, Oct. 17, 1747; studied theology there; was appointed deacon at Taucha, near Leipsic; and in 1791 preacher of St. George's, at his native place. He died Aug. 8, 1807, leaving *Homiletisches Magazin über die evangelischen Texte* (Leipsic, 1780):—*Homiletisches Magazin über die epistolischen Texte* (ibid. 1782; 2d ed. 1792):—*Homiletisches Magazin für die Passionszeit* (ibid. 1783):—*Homiletisches Magazin über den Katechismus Lutheri* (ibid. 1791). See Döring, *Die gelehrten Theologen Deutschlands*, s. v. (B. P.)

Eberus, PAUL, D.D., a German clergyman, was born at Kitzingen, in Franconia, Nov. 8, 1511, and was educated at Anspach. He was appointed to the professorship of philosophy in 1544, and in 1556 to that of Hebrew; in 1558 he gathered a Church in Wittenberg. He died Dec. 20, 1589. Some of his works are, *Expositio Evangelion:* — *Dominicalium Calendarium Historicum* (Wittenb. 1550, 8vo, reprinted at Basle the same year).

Eblis, the name given to the *devil* by the Mohammedans.

Ebon Version OF THE SCRIPTURES. Ebon is the most southerly of the Marshall Islands. These islands are the second group of Micronesia, beginning from the east with the Gilbert Island. The first Scripture in this language was from the gospel of Matthew, chaps. v to xi. This translation was printed at Ebon, between 1858 and 1860. The work was done by the pioneer missionaries, Revs. E. T. Doane and G. Pierson. A version of Mark, prepared by Mr. Doane, was printed at Honolulu in 1863. The Rev. B. G. Snow prepared for the press the gospels of Matthew and John, and the Acts, and revised Mark for a reprint. In 1871 he prepared the gospel of Luke and a revision of Matthew for the press. In 1877 Genesis was issued from the mission press at Ebon, translated by J. F. Whitney, who also resumed the work on Romans, left unfinished by Mr. Snow, and translated the epistles from 1 Corinthians through Philippians. These were printed at the New York Bible House in 1882, together with the book of Genesis and the three epistles of John. The Rev. E. M. Pease, who joined the mission in 1877, has resumed the work of translation of the rest of the New Test. (B. P.)

Eboras, a Persian presbyter, martyred with Miles, a bishop, and Seboa, a deacon, during the reign of Sapor II (A.D. 346); and commemorated Nov. 13.

Eborīnus, sixteenth bishop of Toul, cir. A.D. 664.

Ebrbuharites, an order of monks among the Mohammedans, who derived their name from their founder, Ebrbuhar, the scholar of Nacshbendi, who came from Persia to Europe in the 14th century to propagate their faith. They professed to surrender all care about worldly concerns, and to give themselves wholly up to the contemplation of eternal objects. They were esteemed heretics by the Mohammedans generally, because they refused to go on pilgrimage to Mecca, alleging that the journey was unnecessary, as they were permitted in secret vision, while sitting in their cells, to behold the holy city.

Ebregesĭlus, ninth bishop of Cologne, A.D. 590.

Ebregesius, *Saint*, twenty-fourth or twenty-fifth bishop of Liege, A.D. 618-623; commemorated March 28.

Ebremundus. See EVREMOND.

Ebrigisĭlus, twenty-third bishop of Meaux, about the end of the 7th century.

Ebroinus, forty-second bishop of Bourges, A.D. 810.

Ebrulfus. See EVROUL.

Ebulus (**Evolius**, **Eubrelus**, or even **Ermilius**). (1) Third bishop of Limoges, A.D. 89. (2) Sixth bishop of Avignon, A.D. 202.

Eccard, JOHANNES, a celebrated composer of Church music, was born at Mühlhausen, on the Unstrut, Prussia, in 1553. Having received some instruction in music at home, he became, at the age of eighteen, the pupil of Orlando di Lasso at Munich. In 1574 he was again at Mühlhausen, where he resided four years, and edited, together with Johann von Burgk, his first master, a collection of sacred songs called *Crepundia Sacra Helmboldi* (1577). He was for some time engaged in a private family, and in 1583 became assistant conductor, and twelve years later first chapel-master, at Königsberg. In 1608 he became chief conductor of the elector's chapel in Berlin, and died in 1611. Eccard's works consist exclusively of vocal compositions, such as songs, sacred cantatas, and chorales for four or five, and sometimes for seven, eight, or even nine voices. They are instinct with a spirit of true religious feeling, and possess an interest above their artistic value. Eccard's setting of "*Ein feste Burg ist unser Gott*" is still regarded by the Germans as their representative national hymn. Eccard and his school are in the same way inseparably connected with the history of the Reformation. Of his songs a great many collections are extant. See *Encyclop. Brit.* (9th ed.) s. v.; Grove, *Dict. of Music*, s. v.

Ecclesiā (*the Church*), one of the eight primary æons in the system of Valentinus (q. v.), and held to be the archetype of the lower one on earth. The Gnostics likewise had a heavenly Church, but not a distinct being. This notion is evidently a corruption of the Scriptural idea of the heavenly Jerusalem, and tendencies to a fanciful separation of the Church triumphant and the Church militant are noticeable in the *Shepherd* of Hermas (Vis. ii, 4) and in Clement's *Second Epistle to the Corinthians* (chap. xiv).

ECCLESIA APOSTOLĬCA, a name applied by some of the early fathers to the Church of Rome, on account of the prevalent belief that the apostles Peter and Paul both taught at Rome, and honored the Church by their martyrdom.

ECCLESIA MATRIX (*Mother Church*), a name given in ancient times to the cathedral church, to which all the clergy of a city or diocese belonged.

Ecclesiæ Causidĭci (*Church lawyers*), the name formerly applied to ecclesiastical chancellors. See CHANCELLOR.

Ecclesiarch, in the East, was the sacrist, who had general charge of the church and its contents, and summoned the people by bells or other means. The minor ecclesiastical officials were under his authority.

Ecclesiasterion, a term sometimes used in early times to denote the church building as distinguished from the *ecclesia*, or members of the Christian Church.

Ecclesiastes, BOOK OF. A somewhat fuller discussion of the points relating to the *authorship* of this composition is appropriate, in view of the confident assertion of many critics, especially in Germany, that the contents forbid its ascription to Solomon. We might fairly offset these opinions of modern scholars by that of the ancient Hebraists, certainly in nowise their inferiors, who seem to have found no such difficulty even in the linguistic peculiarities of the book as to require a later than the Solomonic age for its production. The direct evidence of the writer himself, in the opening verse, has not been fairly treated by these rationalizing critics, for while most of them are compelled to admit that "the Preacher, the son of David, king in Jerusalem," can only point to Solomon, they yet evade the argument as if this were merely a *nom de plume;* and Plumptre (*Cambridge Bible*, introd. ad loc.) does not hesitate to compare this with the pious fraud in the apocryphal book of "The Wisdom of Solomon." The attempt to justify this pseudonym by the modern practice of fictitious authorship will apply very well so far as the assumption of the fancy title *Koheleth* is concerned, but is a total failure as to the more definite addition "son of David, king in Jerusalem;" for such a precise and misleading designation is unprecedented in the history of trustworthy literature. The book is either Solomon's or a forgery.

The anonymous author of *The Authorship of Ecclesiastes* (Lond. 1880, 8vo) has nearly exhausted the arguments in favor of the Solomonic date, as derived from a comparison of Solomon's other writings, and he extends the inquiry into the minutiæ of style and phraseology with a thoroughness that ought to shake the confidence of the holders of the opposite view. As to alleged Aramaisms in Ecclesiastes, there are certainly none more decided than appear in Deborah's ode (Judg. v; pure Chaldaism יְרַד, ver. 13; so בַּר, Psa. ii, 12).

Delitzsch, in his *Commentary* on this book (Clark's translation, Edinb. 1877, p. 190 sq.) has collected a formidable "list of the Hapaxlegomena, and of the Words and Forms in the Book of Koheleth belonging to a more recent Period of the Language" than Solomon; and this has been pointed to by later critics generally as conclusive against the Solomonic authorship. The writer of the above monograph justly remarks (p. 32), "A cursory glance at the list, however, seems sufficient to shake one's confidence in it; and if it be faithfully scrutinized, it shrinks down to almost nothing." Accordingly he examines several of these words, as specimens, and shows conclusively that they do not sustain the position. It is worth our while to analyze this "list," and we shall see what a slender basis it affords for the conclusion based upon it. There are ninety-five of these words enumerated by Delitzsch, of which, by his own showing, fifteen (besides one which he has overlooked) are found, in the same form and sense, more or less frequently, in writings of the early or middle Hebrew (Moses to Isaiah), and may therefore be set aside as wholly irrelevant. Of the rest, twenty-six words occur elsewhere only in the Talmudic writers or the Targums, in the same form and sense, and therefore, if they prove anything, prove entirely too much, for they would argue a rabbinical date, which we know is impossible, since the Sept. translation of Ecclesiastes, now extant, carries the original up to the time of the Ptolemies at least. Still further we may reduce the list by excluding nineteen words which appear in substantially the same or some closely cognate form in confessedly earlier writers, and thirteen others which are used by them in a slightly different sense. Deducting all these immaterial peculiarities, there remain only twenty-one words, or less than one fourth in the list, that are really pertinent to the question. Of these, again, eleven are found in this book only (strictly *hapaxlegomena*), and therefore determine nothing as to its age, being such forms as, for aught we know, might have been employed by any writer. Once more, we ought in fairness to exclude certain particles and dubious forms (רְאוּת, רְעוּת, אִלּוּ, בְּכֵן), which are vague and inconclusive. The actual residuum available thus dwindles down to six words only, namely, בָּטֵל (xii, 3), זְמָן (iii, 1), כָּשֵׁר (x, 10; xi, 6), פֵּשֶׁר (viii, 1), פִּתְגָּם (ibid.), and רַעְיוֹן (i, 17; ii, 22; iv, 16), which is no greater number than can be pointed out in Job and some other pre-exilian books. None of these half-dozen words is sufficiently distinctive in known origin and history to determine the date of the writing. The evidence is too negative. They are not like some modern terms, which we can trace to a specific source and occasion when they were first coined or introduced. The cognate dialects exhibit all of them in the same or similar signification, and of most of them (perhaps even the last two are no exceptions) the Hebrew itself has the root in no very remote sense. They are neither foreign nor technical terms.

The same line of argument is applicable to the peculiar inflections and constructions adduced by Delitzsch in the same connection. They have been greatly exaggerated in relative number and importance. That the book of Ecclesiastes is singular in many of its forms and phrases no one can doubt, but that these peculiarities are such as specially belong to the *later* Hebrew has not been made out. We have several books written in the post-exilian period, but *Koheleth* does not wear their impress, either in general or in particular. The only other book in the canonical Hebrew Scriptures analogous to it in teaching is Proverbs, and we have nothing in apocryphal Jewish literature that compares with it, except perhaps "The Wisdom of Solomon," which is only extant in Greek (being apparently the original), and was evidently modelled after *Koheleth*. That Solomon was a perfectly classical writer is not to be assumed, either from his æra or what else we know of him. The effort to express philosophical ideas in the inadequate Shemitic tongue may well explain many of the harsh terms and strange constructions of Ecclesiastes. Certainly we gain nothing by attributing the book to some unknown writer of some indefinite age, concerning whom nothing can be proved or disproved. Subjective arguments on a question of authorship are of the most deceptive character, as the well-known attempt to determine who wrote *The Letters of Junius* has proved. One good historical statement, whether made in the writing itself or by traditionary testimony, outweighs all such speculative and conjectural dicta. Until some candidate better accredited than Solomon shall be brought forward, in deserting him we shall be forsaking the substance for a shadow.

Ecclesiastĭcæ Res. (1) The term is used, in a wide sense, to denote all matters belonging to the Church, as opposed to things secular or worldly. It also indicates the priestly office and duties. It is likewise used in reference to "spiritual" things, immaterial or material. To the former class belong the invisible gifts and graces bestowed by God upon the soul; to the latter, the outward acts or objects connected with such gifts, as the sacraments and other religious rites. From this it is sometimes applied to the vestments of ministers, as well as to the beneficent institutions over which the Church has jurisdiction. (2) The narrower sense of the term designates the property of the Church.

Ecclesiastical Commission, in English law, is a standing body invested with very important powers, under the operations of which extensive changes have been made in the distribution of the revenues of the Church of England. In 1835 two committees were appointed "to consider the state of the several dioceses of England and Wales, with reference to the amount of their revenues and the more equal distribution of episcopal duties, and the prevention of the necessity of attaching by commendam to bishoprics certain benefices with cure of souls; and to consider also the state of the several cathedral and collegiate churches in England and Wales, with a view to the suggestion of such measures as might render them conducive to the efficiency of the Established Church, and to ascertain the best mode of providing for the cure of souls, with special reference to the residence of the clergy on their respective benefices." Upon the recommendation of these committees a permanent commission was appointed by 6 and 7 Will. IV, c. 77, for the purpose of preparing and laying before the king in council such schemes as should appear to them to be best adapted for carrying into effect the alterations suggested in the report of the original commission and recited in the act. The first members of this commission were the two archbishops and three bishops, the lord-chancellor and the principal officers of state, and three laymen named in the act. By a later act (3 and 4 Vict. c. 113), all the bishops, the chiefs of the three courts at Westminster, the master of the rolls, the judges of the Prerogative Court and Court of Admiralty, and the deans of Canterbury, St. Paul's, and Westminster, were added to the commission; and power was given to the crown to appoint four and the archbishop of Canterbury to appoint two additional lay commissioners, who are required to be "members of the United Church of England and Ireland, and to subscribe a declaration to that effect." Five are a quorum; but two bishops at least must be present at any proceeding under the common seal of the commission, and if only two are present they can demand its postponement to a subsequent meeting. Paid commissioners, under the title of Church estates' commissioners, are also appointed—two by the crown and one by the archbishop of Canterbury. These three are the joint treasurers of the commission, and constitute, along with two members appointed by the commission, the Church estates' committee, charged with all business relating to the sale, purchase, exchange, letting, or management of any lands, tithes, or hereditaments. The schemes of the commission having, after due notice to persons affected thereby, been laid before the queen in council, may be ratified by orders, specifying the times when they shall take effect; and such orders, when published in the *London Gazette*, have the same force as acts of Parliament. See *Encyclop. Brit.* (9th ed.) s. v.

Ecclesiastical Law. See Canon Law.

Ecclesiastĭcus. (1) Any person in orders, whether major or minor. (2) Isidore of Seville speaks of a clerk occupying his due position in the hierarchy as an "ecclesiastical clerk," in distinction from an irregular clerk. (3) Those who were so connected with a Church as to be unable to leave its service were called in a special sense "ecclesiastical men." They were not slaves.

Ecclesiecdĭci (*Church lawyers*), the chancellors (q. v.) of bishops.

Ecclesius. (1) Bishop of Ravenna, A.D. 522-533. (2) Bishop of Chiusi (Clusium), A.D. 600-602.

Ecdĭci (ἔκδικοι), certain officers appointed in consequence of the legal disability of clergy and monks to represent the Church in civil affairs. See Advocate of the Church.

Ecdicius. (1) An intruding bishop of Parnasus (Cappadocia Tertia), A.D. 375. (2) Bishop of the island of Tenos, in the Ægean, A.D. 553.

Ecfrith, fifth abbot of Glastonbury, A.D. 719–729.

Echi (Lat. *Echea* or *Achea*), an Irish saint, sister of St. Patrick, is commemorated Aug. 5.

Echlech, an Irish saint, son of Daighre and brother of Caemhan, is commemorated Aug. 14.

Echtach (Lat. *Ectacia*), an Irish virgin saint, is commemorated Feb. 5.

Echtbrann, abbot of Glendalough, County Wicklow, died A.D. 795.

Eckard, Heinrich, a Lutheran theologian of Germany, was born at Wetter, in Hesse, Oct. 19, 1582. He studied at Marburg; was in 1601 pastor at Wildungen, in Waldeck, and in 1608 professor at Giessen; in 1610 he was superintendent at Frankenhausen, and in 1616 general superintendent at Altenburg, where he died, Feb. 22, 1624, leaving, *Quæstiones de Quibus inter Augustanæ Confessionis Theologos et Calvinianos Disceptatur*:—*Theologia Calvinianorum*:—*Compendium Theologiæ Patrum*:—*Isagoge in Catechismum Lutheri*:—*Analysis Epistolæ Johannis*:—*De Causa Meritoria Justificationis contra Piscatorem*:—*De Ordine Ecclesiastico et Politico.* See Jöcher, *Allgemeines Gelehrten-Lexikon*, s. v.; Winer, *Handbuch der theol. Lit.* i, 436. (B. P.)

Eckard, Heinrich Martin, a Lutheran theologian of Germany, was born at Gossleben, in Thuringia, in 1615, and died April 14, 1669, pastor primarius and general superintendent at Alefeld, in Hildesheim, leaving, *Disputatio de Trinitate* (Rinteln, 1654):—*De Prædestinatione* (ibid. 1655):—*De Natura et Principio Theologiæ* (ibid. 1657):—*De Sacramentis in Genere, et in Specie de Baptismo et Eucharistia* (ibid. 1660):—*De Peccati Origine* (ibid. 1661):—*De Spiritu* (ibid. 1662):—*De Divinitate Christi contra Photinianos* (ibid. 1664):—*De Vera et Reali Corporis et Sanguinis Christi in Eucharistia Præsentia* (ibid. 1669). See Dollen, *Lebenbeschreibung der Rintelschen Prof. Theol.*; Strieders, *Hessische Gelehrten Geschichte*; Jöcher, *Allgemeines Gelehrten-Lexikon*, s. v. (B. P.)

Eckhard, Albert, a Lutheran theologian of Germany, was born at Wetter, in Hesse, in 1577. He studied at Marburg, was in 1607 superintendent at Hildesheim, and died there, Aug. 6, 1609, leaving, *Disput. de Conciliis contra Rob. Bellarminum* (Marburg, 1597):—*De Descensu Christi ad Inferos* (ibid. 1599):—*De Spiritu Sancto* (ibid. eod.):—*De Sanctæ Trinitatis Mysterio* (ibid. 1605):—*An Semel Justificati Spiritum Sanctum Amittere Possint* (Giessen, 1607):—*An Christo θεανθρώπῳ Secundum Humanam Naturam dona Vere Divina et Infinita sint Collata?* (Hildesheim, 1608). See Strieders, *Hessische Gelehrten Geschichte*; Jöcher, *Allgemeines Gelehrten-Lexikon*, s. v. (B. P.)

Eckhard, Paul Jacob, a Lutheran theologian of Germany, was born at Jüterbogk, Dec. 6, 1693. He studied at Zerbst, Quedlinburg, and Wittenberg; was appointed in 1728 deacon at St. Nicolai, in his native city, and died there, March 6, 1753, leaving, among other works, *Werdische Kirchen-Historie* (Wittenberg, 1739). See Jöcher, *Allgemeines Gelehrten-Lexikon*, s. v. (B. P.)

Eckhard, Tobias, *the elder*, was born at Delitzsch in 1558. In 1614 he was con-rector at Naumburg; in 1624 rector, and in 1634 pastor, at Gross-Jena, where he died, May 9, 1652. See Jöcher, *Allgemeines Gelehrten-Lexikon*, s. v. (B. P.)

Eckhard, Tobias, *the younger*, was born at Jüterbogk, Nov. 1, 1662. He studied at Wittenberg, where he also lectured after completing his studies. In 1691 he was called as con-rector to Stade, in 1704 to Quedlinburg, and died there, Dec. 13, 1737, leaving, *De Immutabilitate Dei* (Wittenberg, 1683):—*De Signo S. Pauli Epistolarum ad 2 Thess. iii*, 17 (ibid. 1687):—*De Paulo Athleta ad 1 Cor. ix*, 26 (ibid. 1688):—*De Athenis Superstitiosis ad Actor. xvii*, 22, 23 (ibid. eod.):—*De Spiritu, Principe Æris ad Ephes. ii*, 2 (ibid. eod.):—*De Christi Servatoris Resurrectione Rom. i*, 4, *Alterius Nomine Scripta* (ibid. eod.):—*De Funesto Judæ Exitu* (ibid. 1689):—*De Facto Hielis cum Dispendio Duorum Filiorum Hierichuntem Ædificantis ad 1 Reg. xvi*, 34 (ibid. eod.):—*De Fonte Hæresium ad Col. ii*, 8 (ibid. 1691):—*De Justificationis in V. ac N. Test. Ratione Una et Eadem* (ibid. eod.), etc. See Jöcher, *Allgemeines Gelehrten-Lexikon*, s. v.; Winer, *Handbuch der theol. Lit.* i, 132, 394. (B. P.)

Eckley, Joseph, D.D., a Congregational minister, was born in London, England, Oct. 11 (O. S.), 1750. When about seventeen years of age his father moved with his family to America, and settled in Morristown, N. J. Soon after his arrival Joseph was sent to the College of New Jersey, from which he graduated in 1772; and, in order to prosecute his theological studies, he remained at Princeton. May 7, 1776, he was licensed to preach by the Presbytery of New York. The Old South Church, Boston, having been reorganized, after the dispersion occasioned by the Revolution, chose him for their pastor in 1778; and he was ordained Oct. 27, 1779. In 1808 he was provided with a colleague, Rev. Joshua Huntington. He died in Boston, April 30, 1811. In temperament Dr. Eckley was ardent. Although frequently called upon to preach on important occasions, he was not remarkable as a speaker, being inclined to abstraction and possessed of an unmusical voice. See Sprague, *Annals of the Amer. Pulpit*, ii, 137.

Ecleston, Thomas, a Franciscan of the 14th century, was born at Eclestone, Cheshire; was bred a Franciscan in Oxford, and died in 1340. He wrote a book on the succession of the Franciscans in England, with their works and wonders, from their first coming in to his own time, dedicating the same modestly to a fellow-friar. Another work of his is, *De Impugnatione Ordinis sui per Dominicanos.* See Fuller, *Worthies of England*, i, 276.

Economist (a *steward*), called by Possidius provost of the church-house, was a priest, as stated by Isidore Pelusiotes, appointed by the Council of Chalcedon in 451, and elected by the clergy in the East, to discharge the same duties as devolved on a mediæval treasurer, provost of canons, and almoners in an English cathedral. In the Western Church he is mentioned in the 4th century, and was a deacon at Milan in the time of Ambrose. His office was contemporaneous with the restriction of an archdeacon to spiritual duties. In the vacancy of the see, by the councils of Chalcedon and Trent, he acted as receiver-general and administrator of the episcopal revenues. At Kilkenny, St. David's, and Exeter, as now at Windsor, he received the capitular rents, and at Westminster provided the common table and paid the servants' wages. At Hereford two economists, or bailiffs, rendered half-yearly accounts of the great commons.

Econŏmus. See Œconomus.

Ecphonēsis (ἐκφώνησις), that portion of an office which is said audibly in contrast with that which is said silently; especially the doxology, with which the secret prayers generally conclude.

Ecrar (*confession of sins*). The duty of confession of sins is reckoned by Mohammedans to be the fifth capital and fundamental article of their religion. It is the doctrine of the Koran that God will pardon those who confess their sins.

Ecstatĭci, a kind of diviners among the ancient Greeks, who were wont to fall into a trance in which they continued a considerable time, deprived of all sense and motion, and on their recovery they gave marvellous accounts of what they had seen and heard. In Roman Catholic countries, also, many stories have been told of individuals who have been in a state of *ecstasis*, or trance, during which they are said to have seen and conversed with the Virgin Mary and other saints.

Ectenia (*ἐκτενία*). The liturgies of Basil and Chrysostom begin with a litany, sometimes known by this name. It may also refer to the length or the earnestness of the supplication. Litanies of a similar form are also found in the hour-offices. See LITANY.

Ectypomata (*ἐκτυπώματα*) were gifts of a peculiar kind, which began to be made to churches probably about the middle of the 5th century. They are first mentioned by Theodoret, who tells us that when any one obtained the benefit of a signal cure from God in any member of his body, such as his eyes, hands, or feet, he then brought his *ectypoma*, the image or figure of the part cured, in silver or gold, to be hung up in the church as a memorial of divine favor. Such a practice prevailed among the ancient Greeks and Romans, and also among the Egyptians. The same custom was known among the Philistines, as we may infer from the case of the "golden emerods" and mice (1 Sam. vi, 4). In Roman Catholic countries representations of parts of the body healed are often seen suspended upon the walls of churches.

Ed. See SARTABA.

Edburg. See EADBURGA.

Edda. See NORSE MYTHOLOGY.

Eddius (i. e. *Æddi*, surnamed *Stephen*), a noted singer in Kent, a friend of Wilfrid, archbishop of York, A.D. 720.

Eddo, sixth bishop of Curia Rhætorum (now Chur, of Grisons), cir. A.D. 500-530.

Eddy, THOMAS MEARS, D.D., a distinguished Methodist Episcopal minister, son of Rev. Augustus Eddy, was born in Newtown, Hamilton Co., O., Sept. 7, 1823. He received a careful religious training; consecrated himself to the Saviour very early in life; and in 1842 entered the Indiana Conference, filling its most important appointments. In 1856 he was elected editor of *The Northwestern Christian Advocate.* During his editorial career of fourteen years, this periodical increased from a weekly issue of fourteen thousand to about thirty thousand copies. At its close he re-entered the pastorate, in connection with the Baltimore Conference. In 1872 he was elected missionary secretary, and as such was very laborious and successful to the close of his life, Oct. 7, 1874. Dr. Eddy was a clear, logical, pathetic preacher; a forcible, sprightly writer; a genial companion, and a devout man. See *Minutes of Annual Conferences*, 1875, p. 17; Simpson, *Cyclop. of Methodism*, s. v.

Edel, J. Löw, a famous Talmudist, who died at Slonim in 1827, is the author of עיר הים, or *Disquisitions on the Haggadas in the Talmud and Explanations of the Haggadic Interpretation of the Scripture* (Ostrok, 1835):—שפה לנאמנים, a Hebrew grammar (Lemberg, 1793):—also *Philosophical Derashas*, or homilies (1802):—*Commentaries* on Maimonides' introduction to the Talmudic tract Tohoroth, etc. See Fürst, *Bibl. Jud.* i, 220 sq.

Edelburg. See ETHELBURGA.

Edeles, SAMUEL ELIESER, a Talmudist of the 16th century, rabbi at Ostrok, Lublin, etc., is the author of glosses and novellas on Talmudic treatises, for which see Fürst, *Bibl. Jud.* i, 221; De' Rossi, *Dizionario Storico*, p. 95 (Germ. transl.), s. v. Eideles. (B. P.)

Edelinck, GERARD, a celebrated Flemish engraver, was born at Antwerp in 1627, studied under Cornelis Galle, and was subsequently elected a royal academician. He died at Paris in 1707. The following are some of his principal works: *The Holy Family, with St. John, St. Elizabeth, and Two Angels; The Holy Family, where St. John is Presenting Flowers to the Infant Jesus; The Virgin Mary at the Foot of the Cross; Mary Magdalene, penitent, Trampling on the Vanities of the World; St. Louis Prostrating himself before a Crucifix.* See Spooner, *Biog. Hist. of the Fine Arts*, s. v.

Edeling, CHRISTIAN LUDWIG, a Lutheran theologian of Germany, was born in 1678 at Löbejün, near Halle. He studied at Halle, and was the tutor of the famous count Zinzendorf. In 1706 he was appointed rector at Gröningen, and in 1710 was made assistant of the pastor primarius Müller at Schwanebeck, near Halberstadt, whom he succeeded in 1723. He died Sept. 18, 1742, leaving some fine hymns still used in the German Church: "Auf, auf, mein Geist, betrachte," "Christen erwarten in allerlei Fällen." See Koch, *Geschichte des deutschen Kirchenliedes*, v, 219 sq. (B. P.)

Edelmann, Gottfried, a Lutheran minister of Germany, was born Dec. 20, 1660, at Marolissa, in Upper Lusatia. He studied at Leipsic; was first pastor at Holzkirch, in his native province; in 1693 accepted a call to Lauban, and died there in 1724, leaving a number of hymns. See Hoffmann, *Laubanische Prediger-Historie*, p. 287; Koch, *Geschichte des deutschen Kirchenliedes*, v, 448 sq. (B. P.)

Edelmann, Hirsh, a Jewish scholar of Germany, who died at Berlin, Nov. 21, 1858, is the author of סדר ההגדה, or the *Narrative for the Jewish Passover*, with critical notes and scholia (Königsberg, 1845). He also published the *Jewish Prayer-book*, with glosses and scholia (ibid.); and edited *The Song of Solomon*, with Obadja Seforno's commentary (Dantzic, 1845). See Fürst, *Bibl. Jud.* i, 222. (B. P.)

Eden. The locality of Paradise has recently been investigated afresh by Friedrich Delitzsch (*Wo lag das Paradisus*, Leipsic, 1881), who places the garden of Eden in that part of Northern or Upper Babylonia which immediately surrounds the site of Babylon itself. He associates the name *Eden* with the non-Shemitic *edin* ("plain"), instead of the well-received Hebraic derivation, and compares the Accadian name *Kardunias* ("garden of the God Dunias"), of the district around Babylon. He regards "the river going forth from Eden to water the garden" as that system of watercourses, with one general current, which irrigated the isthmus between the Tigris and the Euphrates at its narrowest point, just above Babylon. The other two of the four principal "heads" of the stream he thinks were perhaps half-natural, half-artificial, *canals* flowing out of the Euphrates—the Pallokopas on the west, and the Shat-en-Nil on the east. He has not actually found in the Chaldæan records the names Pishon or Gichon, but he believes the former to be the Accadian *pisan* ("water-vessel"), and the latter is supposed to be the Babylonian *Gughan dê*, possibly pointing to one of these canals. The precariousness of this identification is evident at a glance, and well comports with the fanciful character of many of that learned Orientalist's interpretations. See PARADISE, in this volume.

Edēnus, sixteenth bishop of Meaux, cir. A.D. 552.

Eder. Lieut. Conder proposes (*Tent Work in Palest.* ii, 336) to identify this with the present *Khurbet el-Adar*, three miles south of Gaza, consisting only of "ruined rubble cisterns and traces of a town, with immense masses of broken pottery forming mounds at the site" (*Memoirs* of the Ordnance Survey, iii, 251); but the location seems out of place if the list in Joshua begins at the east.

Eder, GEORG, a Roman Catholic writer, was born at Freysingen in 1524, and studied at Cologne. He was the spiritual adviser of the emperor Ferdinand I, and died May 19, 1586, leaving, *Œconomia Bibliorum seu Partitionum Theologicarum*, etc. (Cologne, 1568; Venice, 1572):—*Compendium Catechismi Catholici* (Cologne, 1570):—*De Fide Catholica* (1571):—*Malleus Hæreticorum* (Ingolstadt, 1580):—*Matæologia Hæreticorum* (ibid. 1581). See Jöcher, *Allgemeines Gelehrten-Lexikon*, s. v. (B. P.)

Edes, Henry, D.D., a Unitarian minister, was a native of Boston, and graduated from Harvard College in 1799. He was ordained and installed pastor of the First Church in Providence, R. I., July 17, 1806; dismissed in June, 1832, and died in 1851. See Sprague, *Annals of the Amer. Pulpit*, viii, 95.

Edesius, a martyr, commemorated April 5. See Ædesius.

Edessa, Martyrs of, under Trajan (A.D. 114), especially the bishop, Barsimæus (according to some), and Sabellius, together with Barbea, the sister of the latter; commemorated together on Jan. 30.

Edeyrn, a Welsh saint, commemorated Jan. 6, was a bard of royal descent, who embraced a monastic life in the early days of British Christianity.

Edgeworth, Roger, a Roman Catholic divine, was born at Holt Castle, on the borders of Wales. He was educated at Oxford, elected fellow of Oriel College in 1507, and soon after ordained. About 1519 he was appointed canon successively at Salisbury, Wells, and Bristol; in 1554 chancellor of Wells, and also vicar of St. Cuthbert's Church, to which he was admitted Oct. 3, 1543. He died in 1560, leaving a volume of *Sermons* (Lond. 1557, 4to). See Chalmers, *Biog. Dict.* s. v.; Allibone, *Dict. of Brit. and Amer. Authors*, s. v.

Edhameis (also *Ædhamais, Eadhamais*, etc.), an Irish saint, daughter of Ædh, is commemorated Jan. 18.

Edhemi, a monastic order among the Mohammedans, founded by Ibrahim ibn-Edhem, who died at Damascus, A.D. 777. His disciples say that he was a slave, a native of Abyssinia, that he always desired to please God, regularly read the Koran in the mosques, and prayed day and night with his face to the ground. Edhem established a strictly ascetic order, who gave themselves much to prayer and fasting, and professed to discourse with Enoch in the wilderness.

Edhniuch (Lat. *Egnacius*), an Irish priest, son of Ere, and abbot of Liath, died A.D. 767.

Edibius. (1) Saint, bishop of Soissons, A.D. 451, is commemorated Dec. 10. (2) Sixth bishop of Amiens, in 511.

Edictius (**Edicius**, or **Hecdicus**), said to have been thirty-fourth bishop of Vienne (France), A.D. 678; commemorated Oct. 23.

Edilfym, eleventh bishop of Llandaff, died in the latter part of the 7th century.

Edmondson, Jonathan, A.M., an English Wesleyan minister (nephew of Jonathan Catlow, an early Methodist preacher, who withdrew a short time before his death on account of a disagreement with Wesley on the doctrine of sin in believers; cousin of James Catlow, who died when about taking orders in the Church of England, and of Samuel Catlow, a Socinian minister, and father of Jonathan Edmondson, of the Wesleyan Conference), was born at Keighley, Yorkshire, March 24, 1767. He was converted in 1784, was sent by Wesley to the Epworth Circuit in 1786, and retired a supernumerary at Portsmouth in 1836. He died July 7, 1842. Dr. Edmondson was eminently a holy and laborious minister, and was highly esteemed by his brethren. In 1814 he was made one of the general secretaries of the Missionary Society, in which office he labored beyond his strength. In 1818 he was elected president of the conference sitting in Leeds. He was a voluminous reader, a diligent student, a lucid expositor, an evangelical preacher, and a faithful pastor. During his busy ministry he wrote some valuable books: *Short Sermons on Important Subjects* (Lond. 1807, 1829, 2 vols. 8vo):—*A Concise System of Self-government* (ibid. 1815; 3d ed. 1834, 12mo):—*Sermons on the Nature and Offices of the Holy Ghost* (ibid. 1823; 2d ed. 1837):—*Essay on the Christian Ministry* (ibid. 1828, 12mo):—*Scripture Views of the Heavenly World* (ibid. 1835, 12mo; 3d ed. 1850, 18mo):—*Elements of Revealed Religion* (1839, 12mo). See *Wesl. Meth. Mag.* 1850, p. 1, 113; *Minutes of the British Conference*, 1842.

Edmundson, William, a noted minister of the English Society of Friends, was born in Westmoreland in 1627. He was apprenticed in York as a carpenter, served in the army under Cromwell, but resigned in 1652, and in 1653 became an earnest Quaker. Subsequently he resided at Antrim, Ireland, and in the spring of 1654 removed to County Armagh, devoting himself to secular pursuits. He established meetings at his own house, and soon after, in company with John Tiffin, from England, went through Ireland preaching. Subsequently he visited England and urged George Fox to send preachers into Ireland, and when some of these arrived he accompanied them through the country. Having been made a minister himself, he preached in public places with great effect. At Armagh he was thrown into prison, and subsequently was brought before the justices at the Sessions Court, who ordered his release. In 1655 he travelled into Leinster, holding meetings in most of the towns. At Finagh the innkeepers refused to lodge him because he was a Quaker. At Belturbet his meeting was broken up, many of his followers were arrested, and he was put in the stocks in the market-place, but eventually was triumphantly acquitted. For several months he suffered confinement in a dungeon at Cavan, where he nearly lost his life from suffocation. Being set at liberty, he visited the North of Ireland. While preaching at Londonderry, on a market-day, he was arrested and imprisoned. In 1661 the persecution of the Quakers was renewed with increased violence, and he was incarcerated at Maryborough. He made three voyages to North America and the West Indies between 1670 and 1684, and died June 30, 1712. See *The Friend*, vi, 167; Reid, *Hist. of the Presb. Church in Ireland.*

Edoldus (or **Heldoaldus**), twenty-fourth bishop of Meaux, about the close of the 7th century.

Edrei *of Naphtali.* Lieut. Conder suggests (*Tent Work in Palest.* ii, 366) for this site that of the present *Yâter*, situated a mile and a half north of Beit-lîf (Heleph), and described as "a small stone village, containing about three hundred Metawêleh, situated on a hill-top, with olive-trees and arable land adjacent, having a pool and many cisterns and a spring near it;" also as containing rock-cut tombs, two ruined watch-towers, and other signs of antiquity (*Memoirs* to the Ordnance Survey, i, 203, 260). The place is not far from Hazor (if at Hazzûr), and on the extreme western confines of the tribe.

Edris (*the student*), one of the appellations of the prophet Enoch among the Mohammedans. He was the third of the prophets, and, according to the Arabians, the greatest that flourished in the antediluvian world. They represent him as having been commissioned to preach to the Cainites, but they rejected his teaching; and in consequence he waged war upon them and made them slaves to the true believers. He is also said to have ordered the faithful to treat all future infidels in the same way, being thus the originator of religious wars and of the persecution of infidels. To Edris the Arabians attribute the invention of the pen, the needle, the sciences of astronomy and arithmetic, and the arts of magic and divination. He is alleged to have written thirty treatises, only one of which survives to the present time—*The Book of Enoch*, an apocryphal work, held in great esteem by the Arabians. See Gardner, *Faiths of the World*, s. v.

Edson, THEODORE, D.D., LL.D., an Episcopal clergyman, was born at Bridgewater, Mass., Aug. 24, 1793, being descended fifth in the line from Samuel Edson, who came to Salem soon after the landing of the Pilgrims at Plymouth, and was one of the original fifteen proprietors of the town of Bridgewater. Theodore received his academic education at the Andover Phillips Academy; graduated at Harvard College in 1822; studied theology with the Rev. Dr. Jarvis of Boston; and in March, 1824, conducted the first religious service in East Chelmsford, now Lowell, after John Eliot, the apostle to the Indians. In April of the same year ground was broken for St. Anne's Church, which was consecrated in March, 1825, at which time Dr. Edson was admitted to full orders. From that time until within a few days of his last illness he conducted the services of that Church "with dignity, solemnity, and impressiveness." He died in Lowell, after a long, useful, and singularly devoted life, June 25, 1883.—*Boston Advertiser*, June 26, 1883. (J. C. S.)

Edward, *Saint*, was the son of Edgar, king of the Saxons, and the beautiful Ethelfleda, who died shortly after his birth, in 961. In 975, when Edgar died, Edward, a pious youth, was elected to the crown, much to the discontent of Elfrida, his step-mother, who wished her own son, Ethelred, on the throne. In 979 (or 978), Edward was poisoned at Corfe Castle, by his own people, according to Henry of Huntingdon, or, as was probable, by order of Elfrida, as Florence of Worcester and William of Malmesbury record. Malmesbury says that a light from heaven shone over his grave at Wareham, and wonders were wrought there and miracles of healing; and that Elfrida, at length terrified and conscience-stricken, retired to the convent of Wherwell to repent of her wickedness. The young Edward was not a martyr for the Christian faith; but being a good youth, and unjustly and cruelly slain, the people looked upon him as a saint and called him Edward the martyr; and so he has a place in the Anglican and Roman martyrologies. He is commemorated on March 18. His body was afterwards translated to the minster at Shaftesbury (June 20), and his translation is set down on Feb. 18. See Baring-Gould, *Lives of the Saints*, iii, 324 (March 18); Butler, *Lives of the Saints* (March 18); Fuller, *Worthies of England*, i, 453; Green, *Hist. of English People*, i, 96; Knight, *Pop. Hist. of England*, i, 147, 148.

Edward, a Scotch prelate, was formerly a monk of Coupar in Forfarshire, and was promoted to the see of Brechin about 1260. It is said that he walked through the whole kingdom, with Eustathius, abbot of Aberbrothock, preaching the gospel wherever he came. See Keith, *Scottish Bishops*, p. 160.

Edwards, Jonathan, D.D., an English divine and able writer against Socinianism, was born at Wrexham, Denbighshire, in 1629, and in 1655 became a servitor of Christ Church, Oxford, where he was admitted A.B., October, 1659. He was rector of Kiddington, Oxfordshire, which he exchanged, in 1681, for Hinton, Hampshire; was elected principal of Jesus College in 1686, and treasurer of Llandaff in 1687. He held other important offices, and died July 20, 1712. His publications are, *Remarks upon Dr. Sherlock's Examination of the Oxford Decree*, etc. (Oxford, 1695, 4to):—*A Preservative against Socinianism* (in 4 parts):—*A Vindication of the Doctrine of Original Sin* (Oxford, 1711, 8vo). See Chalmers, *Biog. Dict.* s. v.; Allibone, *Dict. of Brit. and Amer. Authors*, s. v.

Edwards, Peter Cuthbert, a Baptist minister and educator, was born near Society Hill, S. C., Feb. 8, 1819. He was converted in early life, studied in South Carolina College, and graduated from the theological institution at Newton, Mass., in 1844. After studying for a time in the Union Theological Seminary, New York city, he became, in 1845, professor of Biblical literature and exegesis in Furman Theological Institution; and on the removal of the seminary from Fairfield District, S. C., to Greenville, he was appointed professor of ancient languages, which office he filled with rare ability until his sudden death, May 15, 1867. See *Gen. Cat. of Newton Theol. Institution.* (J. C. S.)

Edwardston, THOMAS, an English divine of the 14th century, was so named from his birthplace in Suffolk; was educated at Oxford; became an Augustinian in Clare; was a great scholar; and acted as confessor to Lionel, duke of Clarence, whom he attended to Italy; returned to his native country, and died at Clare in 1396. Pits thinks he had an archbishopric in Ireland; but this is disowned by the judicious sir James Ware (*De Scriptoribus Hiberniæ*, ii, 126). Perhaps Edwardston was temporarily intrusted with an archbishopric in Italy. See Fuller, *Worthies of England* (ed. Nuttall), iii, 167.

Edwen, a female saint of Saxon descent, is commemorated in Wales on Nov. 6.

Eed el-korban (*festival of the sacrifice*), a festival celebrated among the Persian Mohammedans in honor of the patriarch Abraham. The day before the feast about four hundred camels are collected from the neighboring country, and the first that rises, after resting, is chosen for the sacrifice, shot, and speared. See Gardner, *Faiths of the World*, s. v.

Egan, MICHAEL, a Roman Catholic prelate, was recommended to the pope, by archbishop Carroll, for the see of Philadelphia, June 17, 1807, as "a man about fifty, endowed with all the qualities to discharge with perfection the function of the episcopacy, except that he lacks robust health, large experience, and eminent firmness in his disposition. He is a learned, modest, humble priest, who maintains the spirit of his order in his whole conduct." He was accordingly appointed October 28, 1810. During his short episcopacy the Sisters of Charity were (in 1814) established in his city. Egan died July 22, 1814, and was succeeded by Maréchal. See De Courcy and Shea, *History of the Catholic Church in the United States*, p. 214–217.

Egara, COUNCIL OF (*Concilium Egarense*), was held A.D. 615 at Egara (now Terassa), in Catalonia, to confirm the enactments of Osca and Huesca seventeen years before. Twelve bishops, a presbyter, and a deacon subscribed to it.

Egbald. (1) Abbot, probably of Peterborough, A.D. 671. (2) Abbot of Waltham (probably Hampshire), early in the 8th century. (3) Tenth bishop of Winchester, A.D. cir. 778.

Egbert, bishop of Lindisfarne, A.D. 803–821.

Egbo, an idol worshipped by the natives of Old Calabar, in Western Africa. It is a human skull stuck upon the top of a stick, with a few feathers tied to it. One of these idols is yet found in almost every house where the inmates adhere to their former idolatry.

Egdūnus, a presbyter, martyr at Nicomedia with seven others, A.D. 303; commemorated March 12.

Egemonius (**Ægemonius**, or **Ignomus**), bishop of Autun, died A.D. 374.

Eger, AKIBA MOSES, a famous rabbi and Talmudist, who died at Posen, Oct. 12, 1839, is the author of various disquisitions and novellas on Talmudic treatises. See Fürst, *Bibl. Jud.* i, 224; Kämpf, *Biographie des hochberühmten, hochseligen Herrn Akiba Eger* (Lissa, 1838). (B. P.)

Egerēdus, bishop of Salamanca, A.D. 646.

Egeria (or **Ægeria**), in Roman mythology, was an Italian spring-nymph, protecting deity of the city of Rome, who lived in the sacred woods of the Camenæ, and blessed the peaceful, wise ruler Numa by her useful advice. She is said by some to have been the wife of Numa. When the king died she retreated from

Rome, and was so overcome with sorrow that Diana, out of sympathy, changed her into a spring, which has her name.

Egers, Samuel Levi, a rabbi at Brunswick, where he died, Dec. 3, 1842, is the author of several novellas on Talmudic treatises and homilies upon Sabbatical sections of the Pentateuch. See Fürst, *Bibl. Jud.* i, 224. (B. P.)

Egerton, John, an English prelate, was born Nov. 30, 1721; educated at Eton school; admitted a gentleman commoner in Oriel College, Oxford, May 20, 1740; ordained deacon in Grosvenor Chapel, Westminster, Dec. 21, 1745, and the following day priest. He became pastor of the Church at Ross, in Herefordshire, and Jan. 3, 1746, was collated to the canonry of Cublington, in the Church of Hereford, where he was promoted to the deanery on July 24, 1750. July 4, 1756, he was consecrated bishop of Bangor, at Lambeth; Nov. 12, 1768, translated to the see of Lichfield and Coventry, with which he held a prebend and residentiaryship in St. Paul's, and also the two preferments before mentioned, Ross and Cublington. He was elected to the see of Durham on July 8, 1771, and after enjoying several important positions, died in London, Jan. 18, 1787. See Chalmers, *Biog. Dict.* s. v.; Allibone, *Dict. of Brit. and Amer. Authors*, s. v.

Egg, *as a Christian symbol.* Marble eggs have been found in the tombs of some of the saints, and egg-shells occasionally in the loculi of the martyrs, a relic of the celebration of the Agapæ. As a Christian symbol it signified the immature hope of the resurrection; the use of it on Easter doubtless has reference to this idea.

EGG, Mundane. In the cosmogonies of many heathen nations, both ancient and modern, the *egg* occupies a very prominent place, representing the world in its transition from the chaotic to the fully organized and orderly condition. In the Rig-Veda of ancient Hindûism the supreme spirit is represented as producing an egg, and from the egg is evolved a world. At a later period Brahma is said to have deposited in the primordial waters an egg shining like gold. In ancient Egypt we find Cneph, the creator, producing an egg, the symbol of the world. In the Sandwich Islands an eagle is represented as depositing an egg in the primordial waters, and among the Finns an aquatic bird. In the ancient Celtic legends the mundane egg was produced by a serpent, which had no sooner brought it forth than it hastened to devour it. But while the mundane egg represents the world in its first creation, it is often found also as emblematic of its renovation, after having been purified by fire. So Herodotus relates that the phœnix buried the body of its father in a mass of myrrh of the form of an egg. Similar fables are related as to the origin of man.

Eghlionna, an Irish virgin saint of Cashel, commemorated Jan. 21.

Egica, bishop of Segontia (Siguenza), A.D. 655.

Egidio (or **Egiel**), an early missionary, lived in A.D. 964. He was bishop of Tusculum (Frascati), and was sent to Poland about 972 by pope John XIII to propagate the Catholic religion and to regulate its exercises. Egidio sent for prelates from Germany, France, and Italy, and divided them among the new churches. He erected the first archbishoprics and seven bishoprics. See Hoefer, *Nouv. Biog. Générale*, s. v.

Egidius (or **Ægidius**), nineteenth bishop of Rheims, A.D. 565, not to be confounded with the popular St. Giles (q. v.), was a liberal benefactor of his Church, but one of the most ambitious and intriguing prelates of his time, and was finally deposed for treason.

Egila. (1) Bishop of Osma, cir. A.D. 633-656. (2) Bishop of Eliberi, about the end of the 8th century; supposed to be the same mentioned by Adrian I in the Adoptionist controversy.

Egilward (or **Egilbert**), fifth bishop of Würzburg, A.D. 803.

Egino. (1) Twenty-first bishop of Constance, A.D. 781-813. (2) Bishop of Verona in 796; retired in 799 to the monastery of Reichenau, and died there in 802.

Eglof, sixth bishop of Dunwich, in the latter part of the 8th century.

Egoaldus, twenty-fifth bishop of Geneva, in the 7th century.

Egremont, William (otherwise called *Egumonde, Egmund*, or *William of Stamford*), an English prelate, was born at Egremont, Cumberland, in the 14th century. He journeyed towards the south, fixed himself at Stamford, became an Augustinian monk and doctor of divinity, went beyond the seas, was made by the pope *episcopus Pissinensis*, and held the suffraganship under Henry Beaufort, bishop of London. He flourished under Richard II, A.D. 1390, and left many learned works. See Fuller, *Worthies of England* (ed. Nuttall), i, 345.

Egrilius, a martyr at Cæsarea, in Cappadocia, commemorated Nov. 2.

Egwald, abbot of Tisbury, in Wiltshire, A.D. 759.

Egwin, said to belong to the royal family of Mercia, was made bishop of Worcester in 692, and died Dec. 30, 717. The following three works are attributed to him: a *History of the Foundation of Evesham:*—a *Book of Visions:*—and a *Life of Aldhelm.* See Smith, *Dict. of Christ. Biog.* s. v.; Allibone, *Dict. of Brit. and Amer. Authors*, s. v.

Egwulf, seventh bishop of London, A.D. 745.

Egyptians, Gospel of. See Gospels, Spurious.

Ehinger, Elias, a Lutheran theologian of Germany, was born Sept. 7, 1573. He studied at Wittenberg and Tübingen, and was in 1597 court-preacher at Albertsberg, in Lower Austria. Being obliged to leave the country on account of intolerance, he went in 1605 to Rothenburg, on the Tauber, was made rector there, and accepted a call in 1607 to Augsburg. In 1629 he had to leave that place also, and went to Schul-Pforta, in Saxony. Being recalled to Augsburg, he stayed there only a short time, and went in 1635 to Regensburg, where he died, Nov. 28, 1653. He is the author of a large number of writings, of little value for our time. See Jöcher, *Allgemeines Gelehrten-Lexikon*, s. v.; Brucker, *Commentarius de Vita et Scriptis Ehingeri* (1724). (B. P.)

Ehinger, Johann, grandfather of Elias, was born at Lauingen in 1488. For some time he was a monk, but professed the Evangelical religion, and in 1537 became preacher at St. Stephen's, in Augsburg. Being obliged, on account of his religion, to leave the place in 1551, he became general superintendent of Pfalz-Neuburg, assisted in introducing the evangelical doctrine into the Palatinate, and died at Augsburg in 1572, having been recalled there in 1555, after the treaty of Passau had been signed. See Brucker, *Vita Eliæ Ehingeri;* Jöcher, *Allgemeines Gelehrten-Lexikon*, s.v. (B. P.)

Ehoarn, a hermit-martyr in Brittany, cir. A.D. 520, slain in his cell in the diocese of Vannes by robbers, and commemorated Feb. 11.

Ehrenfeuchter, Friedrich August Eduard, an Evangelical theologian of Germany, was born at Leopoldshafen, near Carlsruhe, Dec. 15, 1814. He studied at Heidelberg, and in 1845 was appointed professor and university-preacher at Göttingen, where he died, March 20, 1878. He is the author of *Theorie des christlichen Cultus* (Hamburg and Gotha, 1840):—*Entwickelungsgeschichte der Menschheit* (Heidelberg, 1845):—*Zeugnisse aus dem akademischen Gottesdienste zu Göttingen* (Göttingen, 1849):—*Zur Geschichte des Katechismus* (ibid. 1857):—*Praktische Theologie* (ibid. 1859):—*Christenthum und die moderne Weltanschauung* (ibid. 1876). He also contributed to different reviews and periodicals. See Wagenmann, in Herzog-Plitt, *Real-Encyklop.;* Lichtenberger, *Encyclop. des Sciences Religieuses*, s. v.; Zuchold, *Bibl. Theol.* i, 309. (B. P.)

Ehrhardt, Sigismund Justus, a Lutheran theologian, was born at Gemünd, Sept. 21, 1733. He studied at Erlangen, Jena, and Halle. In 1754 he was preacher at Markt Burg-Pressach, in Franconia, but the intolerance of the Roman Catholics obliged him to leave the place, and he went to Halle and Berlin, where he gave private lessons. In 1768 he was appointed deacon at Steinau, and died June 6, 1793, pastor at Besching, in the Silesian principality of Wohlau. He wrote, *Commentatio de Claudii Tiberii Neronis* (Coburg, 1752): *Commentationes II de Latinitate S. Pauli* (Schleusingen, 1755). See Döring, *Die gelehrten Theologen Deutschlands*, s. v. (B. P.)

Ehrlich, Johann Gottlieb, a Lutheran minister of Germany, was born at Rabenau, in Saxony, in 1719. He studied at Leipsic, where he also lectured for some time; in 1753 was appointed pastor at Poppendorf, and in 1760 preacher at Wezdorf, in Thuringia. He died March 4, 1779, leaving, *De Quadragesimæ Jejunio* (Leipsic, 1744):—*De Erroribus Pauli Samosateni* (ibid. 1745): —*De Genuina Voce* אבוס *Significatione* (ibid. eod.):—*De Opprobrio Ægypti Ablato* (ibid. eod.). See Jöcher, *Allgemeines Gelehrten-Lexikon*, s. v. (B. P.)

Ehrlich, Johann Nepomuk, a Roman Catholic theologian, was born at Vienna in 1810. In 1827 he joined the Piarists, received holy orders in 1834, and was in 1836 professor of philosophy, history, and literature at the gymnasium in Krems. In 1850 he was called to Gratzen as professor of ethics, and in 1856 to the chair of fundamental theology at Prague, where he died, Oct. 23, 1864. He wrote, *Ueber das christliche Princip der Gesellschaft* (Prague, 1856):—*Fundamental-Theologie* (ibid. 1859). (B. P.)

Ehrmann, Daniel, a Jewish rabbi, was born at Muttersdorf, in Bohemia, in 1818, and studied at Prague. In 1843 he was rabbi at Kuttenplan, in 1844 at Hohenems, and in 1852 he accepted a call to Böhmisch-Leipa. In 1860 he resigned his position and retired to Prague, where he died, Dec. 12, 1882. He published, *Betrachtungen über jüdische Verhältnisse* (Buda, 1841): —*Gebete für jüdische Frauenzimmer* (Prague, 1842):—*Geschichte der Cultur und der Schulen unter den Juden* (ibid. 1846):—*Die Bibel nach ihrem ganzen Inhalte dargestellt* (Feldkirch, 1852; Prague, 1854):—*Das Buch Esther übersetzt* (Prague, 1861):—*Geschichte der Israeliten* (Brünn, 1869; 2d ed. 1873):—*Aus Palästina und Babylon* (Vienna, 1880). See Fürst, *Bibl. Jud.* i, 225; Kayserling, *Bibliothek jüd. Kanzelredner*, ii, 320; Lippe, *Bibliographisches Lexikon*, p. 90 sq., 590 sq. (B. P.)

Eibeschütz. See Eybenschütz.

Eicetæ, an order of Syrian monks in the 9th century, who held dancing to be an essential part of divine worship, and engaged in this exercise in their public services. They defended their practice by the example of Miriam at the Red Sea and of David at the removal of the ark. They met with few imitators, but John of Damascus thought it best to expose their error.

Eichelberger, Lewis, D.D., a Lutheran minister, was born in Frederick County, Md., Aug. 25, 1803. At an early age he attended the school in Frederick under the care of David F. Schaeffer, D.D. Subsequently he was taken to Georgetown, D. C., and entered Rev. Dr. Carnahan's classical school. He graduated from Dickinson College, Carlisle, Pa., in 1826, and with the first class at the Gettysburg Theological Seminary. On Oct. 21, 1828, he was licensed to preach. His first charge was the Lutheran Church in Winchester, Va., in connection with which he also served three other congregations. In the spring of 1833 he resigned the pastorate in Winchester, but still preached to the three neighboring churches. At this period he opened a female seminary in Winchester, which he successfully conducted for several years. He temporarily edited a political weekly journal, and for a time the *Evangelical Lutheran Preacher*, afterwards merged in the *Lutheran Observer*. In 1849 he was elected professor of theology in the Lexington (S. C.) Lutheran Seminary, where he labored for nine years. In 1858 he returned to Winchester, devoting himself to literature. At this time he began his *History of the Lutheran Church*. Among other offices of trust to which he was elected by the synod he was a trustee of Pennsylvania College and a director of the Gettysburg Theological Seminary. He died Sept. 16, 1859. See *Evangelical Review*, xiv, 293.

Eichhorn, Anton, a Roman Catholic theologian of Germany, was born in 1809. He received holy orders in 1832, was in 1836 professor of the gymnasium at Braunsberg, and in 1838 professor of theology at the Lyceum there. In 1851 he became a member of the chapter at Frauenburg, in 1855 vicar-general, and in 1866 was appointed dean. He died Feb. 27, 1869, leaving *Der ermländische Bischof und Cardinal Stanislaus Hosius* (Mayence, 1854–55, 2 vols.). (B. P.)

Eichhorn, Paul, a Lutheran theologian, was born at Eckau, in Courland, in 1599. He studied theology in Germany, was in 1621 preacher at Grenzhof for the Lettish population, in 1634 German preacher at Mittau, and in 1636 superintendent of Courland. He died at Mittau, Aug. 8, 1655, leaving, *Widerlegung der Abgötterei und nichtigen Aberglaubens* (Riga, 1627):—*Reformatio Gentis Letticæ in Ducatu Curlandiæ* (ibid. 1636):—*Historia Lettica* (Dorpat, 1649). The duke Jacob of Courland sent him to the conference held at Thorn, where he also signed the *Positiones Theologorum Augustanæ Confessionis*, Oct. 25, 1645. See Kallmeyer, in *Ueber die religiösen Vorstellungen der alten Völker in Lett- und Estland* (Riga, 1857); Brockhaus, *Conversationslexikon*, s. v. (B. P.)

Eichler, Christian Gottlob, a Lutheran theologian, who died at Leipsic, March 10, 1785, is the author of *Disp. de Mose, Candidato regni Ægyptii* (Leipsic, 1733):—*De Patientia Jobi* (ibid. 1744):—*Visio Eliphazi* (ibid. 1751). See Jöcher, *Allgemeines Gelehrten-Lexikon*, s. v. (B. P.)

Eichstädt, Heinrich Carl Abraham, a Lutheran theologian, was born at Oschatz, Aug. 7, 1771. He was for some time professor of philosophy at Leipsic, but accepted a call to Jena, where he died in 1849. He is the author of *Super Flaviano de Jesu Christo Testimonio* (Jena, 1841–45):—*Flaviani de Jesu Christo Testimonii Αὐθεντία* (ibid. 1840–41):—*De Dictione Scriptorum Novi Testamenti* (ibid. 1843):—*Parabola Jesu Christi de Œconomo Improbo* (ibid. 1847). See Zuchold, *Bibl. Theol.* i, 312; Winer, *Handbuch der theol. Lit.* i, 3, 107, 254, 562, 573, 575, 804, 861, 894. (B. P.)

Eigen, the first female saint of Wales, was the daughter of Caractacus, and taken to Rome by Claudius to grace his triumph over Britain.

Eikin, in Norse mythology, is one of the rivers flowing around the land of the gods. It is supplied from the dewdrops which fall from the horns of the reindeer Aeykthyrner.

Eilĕtum (εἰλετόν). According to Germanus of Constantinople it represents the linen cloth in which the body of Christ was wrapped when laid in the tomb. The chalice and paten are placed on it when the priest has unfolded it, immediately before the deacon warns the catechumens to depart.

Eilmar, Georg Christian, a Lutheran theologian of Germany, was born at Mühlhausen, Jan. 6, 1665, and studied at Wittenberg. In 1689 he was called to the pastorate at Graba, near Salfeld; was in 1691 deacon at Langensalza, in 1696 superintendent at Heldrungen, and in 1698 was made doctor of divinity and pastor primarius at his native place, where he died, Oct. 20, 1715. He wrote, *De Valore Interpretationis Vulgatæ* (Wittenberg, 1687):—*De Consensu Orthodoxo de Christo* (ibid. 1698), etc. See Jöcher, *Allgemeines Gelehrten-Lexikon*, s. v. (B. P.)

Eilunny, a Welsh saint in the first half of the 7th century.

Eimbetha (or **Einbetta**), *Saint*, a virgin, commemorated Sept. 16, is said to have been one of the companions of St. Ursula.

Eimhin (**Emir**, or **Evin**), an Irish *saint*, son of Eoghan, and bishop of Ros-glas and Ros-mic-Triuin, A.D. 580, is commemorated Dec. 22.

Einari (or **Einarsen**), GISSUR, an Icelandish theologian, lived about the middle of the 16th century. He studied at Hamburg and Wittenberg, where he heard Luther and Melanchthon, and in 1540 was elected bishop in place of Paulson. In 1541 the government granted the ministers the privilege of marriage, of which they had been deprived since 1272, and this innovation occasioned many disputes. During these troubles Einari died. Such was the animosity against him that by order of the bishop, Jon Areson, his body was disinterred and his ashes scattered to the winds. He left a translation of the Proverbs of Solomon in Norwegian (Holar, 1580). See Hoefer, *Nouv. Biog. Générale*, s. v.

Einem, Johann August Christoph von, a Lutheran theologian of Germany, was born at Osterweddingen, near Magdeburg, Nov. 25, 1730. He studied at Halle, and in 1754 was appointed teacher at a high-school in Berlin. In 1759 he was also appointed preacher at Trinity Church there, and in 1768 accepted a call to the pastorate at Genthin. He died Oct. 24, 1810, leaving, *De Pelagianismo æque ac Fanaticismo ab Ecclesia Jesu Christi Arcendo* (Halle, 1762):—*Praktische Lebensbeschreibungen verstorbener und nachlebender Geistlichen* (Stendal, 1787). His best work, however, is his continuation of Mosheim's Church history. See Döring, *Die gelehrten Theologen Deutschlands*, s. v.; Winer, *Handbuch der theol. Lit.* i, 535; ii, 52. (B. P.)

Einem, Johann Just von, a Lutheran theologian of Germany, was born at Göttingen, Aug. 11, 1685. In 1712 he was rector at Bergen, in 1728 pastor at Osterweddingen, near Magdeburg, and died in 1744. He wrote, *Anweisung zum Studiren aus Lutheri Schriften gezeigt* (Magdeburg, 1727):—*Anweisung zur Hermeneutik aus Lutheri Schriften* (ibid. eod.):—*Melanchthoniana* (Helmstädt, 1730):—*Introductio in Bibliothecam Græcam J. A. Fabricii* (Magdeburg, 1733):—*Introductio in ejusdem Bibliothecam Latinam* (ibid. 1734). See Mosers, *Jetztlebende Theologen;* Jöcher, *Allgemeines Gelehrten-Lexikon*, s. v. (B. P.)

Einhard (or **Eynardus**), *Saint*, a solitary of Altona, in Westphalia, is commemorated March 25.

Einhorn, DAVID, a Jewish rabbi, was born at Dispeck, in Bavaria, Nov. 10, 1809. He attended the rabbinical school at Fürth, and the universities of Erlangen, Würzburg, and Munich. At the latter place he took his degree as doctor of philosophy in 1834. His first charge was at Hopstadten, and while officiating there he attended the second conference of Reform Jews at Frankfort-on-the-Main, in 1845. A little later he succeeded Holdheim (q. v.) as chief rabbi of Mecklenburg-Schwerin. In 1851 he was called to Pesth by the Reformed congregation, where he advocated extreme measures for those days; his liberalism aroused the dissatisfaction of the government, and his temple was closed. In 1855 he landed at Baltimore, and was appointed rabbi of the *Har Sinai* congregation there. His known opposition to slavery aroused the ire of the Baltimoreans, in the days of '61, and he was called to Philadelphia by the Reform congregation. In 1866 he went to New York to take charge of the temple "Adas Jeshurun," which in 1873 was consolidated with the "Anshe Chesed," under the name of "Beth El." On July 12, 1879, he retired from his office, and died Nov. 2 of that year. He published, *Das Prinzip des Mosaismus*, etc. (Leipsic, 1854):—*Olath Tamid* (Baltimore, 1856). After his death two volumes of *Sermons* were published. See Morais, *Eminent Israelites of the 19th Century* (Philadelphia, 1880). (B. P.)

Einsiedel, GEORG HANBOLD, a German divine and statesman, was born in 1521. He studied theology, and was one of the zealous hearers of Luther, Melanchthon, and Scharf, defending the Reformation with his word and with the sword in the war of Schmalkalden. He was counsellor of the princes Moritz and August der Starke, of Saxony, from 1576 to 1586. Einsiedel died in 1592. See Hoefer, *Nouv. Biog. Générale*, s. v.

Eirenica (εἰρηνικά). (1) The name given to the earlier clauses of the great litany in the Greek liturgies, as being prayers for peace. (2) See PACIFICÆ.

Eisenlohr, JOHANN JACOB, a Lutheran theologian of Germany, was born Nov. 3, 1656, at Reutlingen. He studied at Tübingen and Wittenberg, and was pastor and superintendent at his native city from 1680 to 1702. In the latter year he was called to Durlach, where he died, June 14, 1736. He wrote, *De Scientia Dei Media:—De Gratia Dei Præveniente:—Philologemata Sacra in Varia Sacræ Scripturæ Loca:—De Theologia in Genere:—De Principio Theologiæ Cognoscendi:—De Theologiæ Objecto, seu de Christiana Religione.* See Jöcher, *Allgemeines Gelehrten-Lexikon*, s. v. (B. P.)

Eisenschmid, LEONHARD MARTIN, a Protestant theologian of Germany, was born at Ingolstadt, Nov. 5, 1797, of Roman Catholic parentage. In 1818 he was professor at Neuburg, in 1822 at Munich, and in 1824 at the Aschaffenburg gymnasium. In 1828 he joined the Evangelical Church, was made rector of the gymnasium at Schweinfurt, and died May 27, 1836. He wrote, *Unterschied der römisch-katholischen und der evangelisch-protestantischen Kirche* (Leipsic, 1828):—*Das römisch-katholische Messbuch* (Neustadt, 1829):—*Ueber die Versuche neuerer Zeit*, etc. (ibid. eod.):—*Die Gebräuche und Segnungen der römisch-katholischen Kirche* (ibid. 1830):—*Ueber die Unfehlbarkeit des ersten allgemeinen Concils zu Nicäa* (ibid. eod.):—*Ueber die Unfehlbarkeit der allgemeinen Concilien der Katholischen Kirche* (ibid. 1831). See Zuchold, *Bibl. Theol.* i, 315; Winer, *Handbuch der theol. Lit.* i, 346, 626, 664, 695. (B. P.)

Eisenstadt, MEÏ BEN-ISAAC, a famous Talmudist, was born in Lithuania in 1670. He was rabbi at Eisenstadt, Hungary, and died there in 1744, leaving novellas on some Talmudic treatises, and homilies on the Pentateuch and the five Megilloth (i. e. Esther, Song of Songs, Lamentations, Ruth, and Ecclesiastes). See Fürst, *Bibl. Jud.* i, 227; Zipser, in *Literatur Blatt des Orient*, 1847, xii, 24. (B. P.)

Eisiteria, sacrifices which the senate at Athens were accustomed to offer to Zeus and Athena before they commenced the public deliberations of each session. Libations were offered, and a festival was held.

Eisler, TOBIAS, a German theologian, was born at Nuremberg, April 2, 1683. He received a careful education; studied law at Altorf and at Halle, was appointed secretary to the duchess of Saxe-Eisenach, afterwards returned to Nuremberg, and abandoned the law to devote himself to the education of the poor. At Helmstädt he founded a school for poor boys, and another for girls. Eisler was strongly pietistic. He died at Helmstädt, Oct. 8, 1753. For the chief among his numerous works see Hoefer, *Nouv. Biog. Générale*, s. v.

Eithne (or **Ethnea**), the name of several Irish saints. (1) Daughter of Bait, of the barony of Nethercross, County Dublin, in the 7th century, is commemorated March 29. (2) Daughter of king Laeghaire, A.D. 432, commemorated Jan. 11 and Feb. 26. (3) Virgin, daughter of Cormac or of Marcius, in the 6th century, commemorated July 6.

Eitzen, Paul de, a Lutheran theologian of Germany, was born at Hamburg, Jan. 25, 1522. He studied at Wittenberg, under Luther and Melanchthon, in 1544 became rector at Cöln, in Brandenburg, in 1555 superintendent at his native place, in 1562 first court-preacher at Schleswig, and in 1576 professor at the gymnasium there. He refused to sign the *Formula Concordiæ*, which caused him much trouble. In 1593 he resigned his offices, and died Feb. 25, 1598. His writings are mentioned in Jöcher, *Allgemeines Gelehrten-Lexikon*, s. v.; see also Greve, *Memoria Pauli ab Eitzen Instaurata* (Hamburg, 1744). (B. P.)

Ekron. The latest description of this important place is by Lieut. Conder (*Tent Work in Palestine*, ii, 174):

"North-east of Makkedah, Ekron still stands, on low rising ground—a mud hamlet, with gardens fenced with prickly pears. There is nothing ancient here, any more than at Ashdod or Jamnia; but one point may be mentioned which is of some interest. Ekron means 'barren,' yet the town stood in the rich Philistine plain. The reason is, that north of the Sorek valley there is a long, sandy swell reaching to the sea-coast—an uncultivated district, now called Deirân, the Arabic name being equivalent to its old title, *Daroma;* Ekron stands close to this dry, barren spur, and above the fertile corn-lands in the valley."

Elah. We extract some interesting details concerning this noted valley from the latest description, that of Lieut. Conder (*Tent Work in Palestine*, ii, 187, 190):

"The Great Valley of Elah (Wâdy es-Sunt) is the highway from Philistia to Hebron; it has its head not far from Terkûmieh, and runs down northwards, past Keilah and Hareth, dividing the low hills of the Shephelah from the rocky mountains of Judah; eight miles from the valley-head stands Shochoh, and Wâdy es-Sunt is here a quarter of a mile across; just north of this ruin it turns round westward, and so runs, growing deeper and deeper, between the rocky hills covered with brushwood, becoming an open vale of rich corn-land, flanked by ancient fortresses, and finally debouching at the cliff of Tell es-Sâfieh. About two and a half miles south of the great angle near Shochoh there is a very large and ancient terebinth, one of the few old trees of the species along the course of the valley, which took its Hebrew name of Elah from them. This terebinth is towards the west side of the vale, just where a small tributary ravine joins Wâdy es-Sunt; and near it are two ancient wells, not unlike those at Beersheba, with stone water-troughs round them; south of the ravine is a high, rounded hill, almost isolated by valleys, and covered with ruins, a natural fortress, not unlike the well-known Tells which occur lower down the Valley of Elah."

"Two points require to be made clear as to the episode of David's battle with Goliath; one is the meaning of the expression Gai or 'ravine;' the other is the source whence David took the 'smooth stones.' A visit to the spot explains both. In the middle of the broad, open valley we found a deep trench with vertical sides, impassable except at certain places—a valley in a valley, and a natural barrier between the two hosts; the sides and bed of this trench are strewn with rounded and water-worn pebbles, which would have been well fitted for David's sling. Here, then, we may picture to ourselves the two hosts, covering the low, rocky hills opposite to each other, and half hidden among the lentisk bushes; between them was the rich expanse of ripening barley and the red banks of the torrent, with its white, shingly bed; behind all were the distant blue hill-walls of Judah, whence Saul had just come down. The mail-clad champion advanced from the west, through the low corn, with his mighty lance perhaps tufted with feathers, his brazen helmet shining in the sun; from the east, a ruddy boy, in his white shirt and sandals, armed with a goat's-hair sling, came down to the brook, and, according to the poetic fancy of the rabbis, the pebbles were given voices, and cried: 'By us shalt thou overcome the giant.' The champion fell from an unseen cause, and the wild Philistines fled to the mouth of the valley, where Gath stood towering on its white chalk-cliff, a frontier fortress, the key to the high-road leading to the corn-lands of Judah, and to the vineyards of Hebron." (See cut on next page.)

Ekron. (From Thomson's *Southern Palestine and Jerusalem.*)

Eladius (or **Heladius**), *Saint*, fourth bishop of Auxerre, cir. A.D. 387, is commemorated May 8.

Elaeth (surnamed "the king"), a Welsh bard and saint of the 6th or 7th century, is commemorated Nov. 10.

Valley of Elah. (From Thomson's *Southern Palestine and Jerusalem.*)

Elair (Lat. *Helarius*), an Irish saint, anchorite, and scribe of Loch-Crea, died A.D. 807, and is commemorated Sept. 7.

Elapius, fifteenth bishop of Poictiers, cir. A.D. 535–540.

Elasippus, a Cappadocian martyr in the reign of Aurelian, with his triplet brothers, Melassippus and Speusippus, is said to have been a horse-breaker by profession, to have been converted at twenty-five years of age, and to have been burned in a furnace. They are commemorated Jan. 17.

Elasius (or **Elaphius**), *Saint*, seventeenth bishop of Châlons-sur-Marne, died cir. A.D. 580, and is commemorated Aug. 19.

Elbodus, *Saint*, bishop of Bangor, A.D. 755–809, induced the people of North Wales to use the Roman cycle of Easter.

Elchanan BEN-MENACHEM. See PAULUS OF PRAGUE.

Eldad, the name of two Welsh saints. (1) Son of Arth, of the 7th century. (2) Son of Geraint, afterwards bishop of Gloucester, A.D. 600–634, slain by the pagan Saxons.

Eldad HAD-DANI, a famous Jewish traveller, flourished about 880–890. In his interesting but fabulous narrative, *Sefer Eldad had-Dani*, he pretends to tell of the remnants of the ten tribes, their laws, customs, and their condition. His narrative has been translated into Latin by Genebrard, into French by Carmoly, and into Judæo-German by Men. ben-Salomo. Extracts are given by Bartolocci in *Biblioth. Magna Rabbinica*, i, 101, and Eisenmenger, *Neuentdeckses Judenthum*, ii, 527–539. See Fürst, *Bibl. Jud.* i, 230 sq.; Zunz, *Gottesd. Vorträge der Juden*, p. 139; Landauer, in *Literaturblatt des Orients*, 1846, p. 121 sq.; Rapaport, *Bikkure ha-ittim*, 1824, p. 63, 68. (B. P.)

Eldhrimner, in Norse mythology, is the iron pot in which the boar Sährimner, in Walhalla, is cooked, which after every meal revives, in order, on the following day, to be slaughtered and served up again by the cook Andhrimner.

Eldridge, JOSEPH, D.D., a Congregational minister, was born at Yarmouth, Mass., July 18, 1804. After a preliminary course at Phillips Academy, he graduated from Yale College in 1829, and in 1832 from Yale Divinity School. He was ordained pastor of the Church at Norfolk, Conn., April 25, 1832, and continued to serve in that parish until Nov. 2, 1874. He died there, March 31, 1875. From 1847 he was a member of the corporation of Yale College; from 1867 of the American Board for Foreign Missions. See *Cong. Quarterly*, 1876, p. 424.

Eldunen (or **Elduuen**), fifteenth bishop of St. Davids.

Eleazar, a teacher of the Maccabees, is commemorated as a saint, Aug. 1 (July 29).

Eleazar BEN-ARAK, a famous Jewish teacher of the 1st century of our æra, was one of the most celebrated disciples of Jochanan ben-Zachai (q. v.). One of his recorded maxims is found in *Aboth*, ii, 19: "Be quick to study the law, and know what thou shouldst return in answer to the Epicurean, and remember before whom thou laborest; for the master who employed thee is faithful, and will recompense thee the reward of thy toil." As a teacher, he was so highly esteemed that to attend his lectures was regarded like fulfilling a commandment (*Cholin*, fol. 106). See Hamburger, *Real-Encyclop.* ii, 155 sq.; Bacher, in Frankel-Grätz's *Monatsschrift*, 1882, p. 241. (B. P.)

Eleazar BEN-AZARIA, a Talmudic teacher of the 1st century of our æra, belonged to a noble priestly family. When Gamaliel the younger was deposed at Jabneh, Eleazar was elected president of the college, although only seventeen years of age. One of his first measures was to remove the doorkeeper and give free admission to the college to all, whereas Gamaliel had excluded every disciple who was not "the same inwardly as outwardly." It is added that when anything is recorded as having happened בו ביום "on that day," the occasion of Azaria's accession is referred to; and the day is described as one in which all the pending controversies were decided. When Gamaliel was reinstated, Ben-Azaria acted as vice-president, and, according to the Talmud, matters were so arranged that on three Sabbaths in the month Gamaliel acted as president, whereas the fourth was given to Eleazar. Hence the saying: "Whose Sabbath is it? The Sabbath of rabbi Eleazar ben-Azaria." A saying of his is recorded in *Aboth*, iii, 26: "No Torah, no culture; no culture, no Torah; no wisdom, no fear of God; no fear of God, no wisdom; no knowledge, no discernment; no discernment, no knowledge; no meal, no Torah; no Torah, no meal." See Hamburger, *Real-Encyclop.* ii, 156 sq.; Bacher, in Frankel-Grätz's *Monatsschrift*, 1883, p. 6 sq. (B. P.)

Eleazar BEN-AZKARI (or ASKARI), a rabbi of the 16th century, is the author of an exposition of the six hundred and thirteen precepts, ספר חרדים (Venice, 1601; Zolkiew, 1778; Brünn, 1795). See Fürst, *Bibl. Jud.* i, 65. (B. P.)

Eleazar BEN-CHISMA, a disciple of the famous rabbi Akiba (q. v.), was noted alike as a Talmudist and an astronomer. His recorded maxim (*Aboth*, iii, 28), "Qinnim and Pitche Nidda are essentials of the Torah; canons of astronomy and geometry are after-courses of wisdom," shows his delight in astronomical and mathematical problems. See Bacher, in Frankel-Grätz's *Monatsschrift*, 1883, p. 538. (B. P.)

Eleazar BEN-JEHUDA. See ELIEZER BEN-JUDAH.

Eleazar BEN-SHAMNA, a Jewish teacher of the 2d century, was a pupil of the famous rabbi Akiba. During the persecution by Hadrian he went to Nisibis, in Babylonia. His recorded maxim was: "Let the honor of thy disciple be dear unto thee as the honor of thine associate; and the honor of thine associate as the fear of thy master; and the fear of thy master as the fear of heaven" (*Aboth*, iv, 17). See Hamburger, *Real-Encyclop.* ii, 159. (B. P.)

Eleazar BEN-YISHAI, a converted Jew of the 17th century, is the author of a *Brief Compendium of the Vain Hopes of the Jews' Messias* (Lond. 1652). See Wolf, *Bibl. Hebræa*, iv, 786; Jöcher, *Allgemeines Gelehrten-Lexikon*, s. v. (B. P.)

Eleazar HAK-KALIR. See KALIR, ELEASAR HA-.

Eleazar OF MODIN, a Jewish teacher of the 2d century. He was a relative of Bar Cochab, and not only upheld his messianic pretensions, but also stimulated the religious energy and encouraged the hopes of the defenders of Bethar. Weighed down by years and emaciated by fasts, the aged ascetic was daily to be seen on the ramparts, where, clad in sackcloth and covered with ashes, he would, in the sight of all, implore heavenly aid with tears and by continual fastings. As long as the defenders of Bethar saw Eleazar at his post they felt secure under the canopy of his piety, and in the assurance of divine aid. Even the treacherous Samaritans felt the awe of his presence, and were wont to say that Bethar could not be taken "so long as this cock remained to crow in ashes." At last one of them succeeded in rendering Eleazar an object of suspicion to Bar Cochab, who rudely pushed the old man aside with his foot. Eleazar fell to the ground a corpse. His recorded maxim is: "He that profanes things sacred, and contemns the festivals, and annuls the covenant of Abraham our Father, and acts barefacedly against the Torah, even though he be a doer of good works, has no portion in the world to come" (*Aboth*, iii, 17). See Hamburger, *Real-Encyclop.* ii, p. 161 sq.; Bacher, *Die Agada der Tanaiten*, in Frankel-Grätz's *Monatsschrift*, 1882, p. 529 sq. (B. P.)

Eleazarus, a martyr at Lyons, with his eight children and Minervius; commemorated Aug. 23.

Electi, a name sometimes applied to Christians in the early ages of the Christian Church.

Among the Manichæans, the term denoted the higher or more holy of the two classes into which believers were divided, the lower being styled simply "auditores."

Electoral College is a committee of clergy and notables convened to elect bishops and other clergy, as a means of avoiding the tumult of a popular election, following the advice of Clement of Rome and the Council of Laodicea.

Eledanus, legendary bishop of Dumbarton, said to have been appointed by king Arthur, A.D. 519.

Eleemosynarius. (1) See ALMS. (2) The word also designates the "executor" of a will, when distributed for pious purposes.

Eleëson. See KYRIE.

Elements, EUCHARISTIC. The Latin word *elementa* does not appear to have been used in this technical sense in the early ages of the Church, though it is a very natural word to express the component parts of anything. The unconsecrated elements on the altar are called, in Eastern liturgies, "the Mysteries;" the bread alone, "the Seal," from its being divided by lines in the form of a cross. When the elements have been placed on the altar they acquire other names, having more distinct reference to sacrifice, as "the Lamb," or "the First-born." The elements are also called "symbols," "types," "visible forms," as outward representations of inward and spiritual grace.

Throughout the Church, bread and wine have always been recognised as the elements in the eucharist, with but few exceptions. An obscure sect, called the Artotyritæ, added cheese to the bread. Some sects used no wine, but water alone; while others used wine in the evening service, but not in the morning.

I. *Composition of the Bread.*—The Church has been unanimous in using wheat as the material for the bread, it being regarded as the superior grain. The great controversy has been, Shall the bread be leavened or unleavened? The principal arguments bearing on this question are the following: It has generally been assumed in the West that the Last Supper was eaten at the feast of the Passover, and that therefore the bread used was unleavened, which was the only kind the Jews were allowed to eat at that time. But it is contended by some writers of the Greek Church that the Last Supper was held on the 13th Nisan, when leavened bread was still used; and there is no direct statement, either in the New Test. or in the writings of the early fathers, to indicate that unleavened bread was used; on the contrary, the fact that only "bread" was mentioned would lead to the inference that only common bread was meant. Justin Martyr simply speaks of bread, and as he is giving a particular description of the Christian rites, it seems most probable that he would have mentioned the fact had any particular kind of bread been used. Epiphanius says that the Ebionites, in imitation of the saints in the Church, celebrate mysteries yearly in the Church with unleavened cakes. Innocent I sent to the bishops leavened bread, said to have been called by him "fermentum," in distinction from the unleavened. Cyprian, and still later, Isidore of Seville, in their discussions, leave out all mention of leaven as an ingredient in the eucharistic bread, which they would hardly have done had it been in use. But Alcuin (A.D. 790) says that the bread should be perfectly free from leaven of any kind. Rabanus Maurus (A.D. 819) likewise directs that the bread should be unleavened according to the Hebrew custom. It has been inferred by some that the eucharistic bread was introduced between the latter part of the 9th and the 11th centuries, for the reason that Photius of Constantinople (A.D. 867) never mentioned the use of unleavened bread; while Michael Cærularius, also patriarch of Constantinople (A.D. 1054), frequently does. The silence of Photius would only show that either the use of it was unknown to him, or that he regarded it as a thing of no consequence. But John Maro, writing, at any rate, before the Trullan Council, says that those who made the eucharistic offering in leavened bread reproached the Western churches, the Armenians, and the Maronites, with offering "unleavened cakes," which were not bread at all; a clear proof that the Western churches generally, in the 7th century, were thought to agree with the Maronites and the Armenians in this respect.

On the whole, then, there is distinct evidence that

unleavened bread was used in the eucharist by the Latins, and by some eastern sects, in the 7th and 8th centuries; and there is strong evidence that it was used in the 3d. In the orthodox Eastern Church, there can be no doubt that leavened bread has been used from a very early period indeed; if not from the very first, at any rate from the time when Judaizing sects insisted on using unleavened cakes, like those of the Passover, in the Lord's Supper.

The Syrian Christians, besides the leaven which is common to almost all Oriental communions, mix with the bread a little oil and salt, a practice which they defend by many mystical reasons. The modern Greeks eagerly advocate the mixture of salt, which (they say) represents the life; so that a sacrifice without salt is a dead sacrifice.

In regard to the character of the bread, the sixth canon of the Council of Toledo (A.D. 693) enacts that no other bread than such as is whole and clean and especially prepared shall be placed on the altar of the Lord.

The form of the loaf used by the Jews was round, and somewhat less than an inch thick, and six or eight inches in diameter. Oblates were frequently used, and impressed with a cross.

II. *Composition of the Cup.*—With regard to the element of wine there has been less controversy, though it is an interesting and unsettled question whether the cup was mixed at the institution of the sacrament by our blessed Lord himself. Lightfoot (*Temple Service*, i, 691) says that he that drank pure wine performed his duty; so that, although it seems probable that our Lord used the mixed cup, yet it is not certain that he did so. The Babylonian Talmud calls water mixed with wine "the fruit of the vine;" but it would appear that the same term is used for pure wine in Isa. xxxii, 12; Hab. iii, 17; so that nothing positive can be ascertained from the use of that term. On the whole, it seems probable that our Lord used a mixed cup, and it is acknowledged on all hands that, with the exception of a few heretics, the Church used wine mixed with water. Justin Martyr and Cyprian both justify the mixing of the two. The third Council of Carthage orders "that in the sacrament of the body and blood of the Lord, nothing else be offered but what the Lord himself commanded, that is, bread, and wine mixed with water." The African code, both Greek and Latin, has this same canon. The liturgies of James and Mark contain like words, while the liturgies of Basil and Chyrsostom order the deacon to put wine and water into the cup before the priest places it on the altar. In like manner, in some form or another, the mixing is mentioned in the liturgies of Ethiopia, Nestorius, Severus, of the Roman and the Gallican churches. A peculiar rite of the Byzantine Church is the mixing of hot water with the wine. In the liturgy of Chrysostom, after the fraction of the oblate, the deacon, taking up the vessel of boiling water, says to the priest, "Sir, bless the boiling water;" the priest then says, "Blessed be the fervency of thy saints forever, now and always, and for ages of ages;" then the deacon pours a small quantity of the boiling water into the chalice, saying, "The fervency of faith, full of the Holy Spirit. Amen." The principal deviations from the received practice of the Church in this matter have been the opposite usages of the Aquarians and Ebionites, who used no wine at all in the eucharist, and of the Armenians, who mixed no water with the wine.

Some in the 7th century offered milk for wine in the eucharist; others communicated the people not with wine pressed from grapes, but with the grapes themselves.

A peculiar instance of an addition to the cup is the dropping of milk and honey into it, according to the Roman rite, on Easter eve, the great day for the baptism of catechumens.

The wine in use in the Church has in general been red, apparently from a desire to symbolize as much as possible the blood of our Lord. Various mystical reasons have been given for the mixture of the water with the wine. Besides the presumption that our Lord used the mixed cup at the first institution, the liturgies generally allege as a further reason that blood and water flowed from his pierced side. In the comment on Mark, ascribed to Jerome, another is given: that by one we might be purged from sin, by the other redeemed from punishment. Alcuin (*Epist.* 90) finds in the three things, water, flour, and wine, which may be placed on the altar, a mystical resemblance to the three heavenly witnesses of 1 John v, 7.

Elenara (or **Elevara**), a virgin martyr with Sponsaria, in Gaul, in the reign of Diocletian, is commemorated May 2.

Elenog, a Welsh saint of the 7th century.

Eleph. Lieut. Conder identifies this place with the present village of *Lifta*, west of Jerusalem (*Quar. Report* of the "Palest. Explor. Fund," Jan. 1881, p. 51), a site which he elsewhere (*Tent Work in Palest.* ii, 339) assigns to Nephtoah (q. v.).

Elephantus, eleventh bishop of Uzes, A.D. 810.

Elephas, said to have been seventh bishop of Valence, at the close of the 6th century.

Eleri (or **Melcri**), the name of two Welsh saints. (1) Daughter of Brychan, in the middle of the 5th century. (2) Daughter of Dingad, at Pennach (Denbighshire), at the end of the 6th century.

Elerius, a Cambrian monk (different from the martyr in Jersey), died cir. A.D. 660, and is commemorated June 13.

Eleshaan, an Ethiopian king, hermit, and saint (commemorated in Rome, Oct. 22; in Ethiopia, May 15), concerning whom the early hagiographers tell discordant stories, seems to have lived in the 6th century.

Eleuchadius, bishop of Ravenna, A.D. 100-112, commemorated Feb. 14, is said to have been originally an eminent Platonic philosopher, converted by Apollinaris on a visit to Rome.

Eleusius, bishop of Cyzicus, one of the most influential members of the Semi-Arian party in the second half of the 4th century, was a man of high personal character. At the instance of Acacius he was deposed, A.D. 360, but returned the next year, and finally seems to have fallen under the general condemnation of the Macedonian heretics, A.D. 383.

Eleutherius. (1) Bishop of Illyricum, martyred together with his mother, Anthia, in the reign of Hadrian; commemorated April 13 or 18. (2) One of the fourteen bishops (sees not named) who composed the synod of Diospolis (Lydda), A.D. 415. (3) Bishop of Geneva in the 5th century. (4) *Saint*, eighth in the list of bishops of Terracina, cir. A.D. 443; commemorated Sept. 6. (5) Bishop of Chalcedon at the time of the council, A.D. 451. (6) Said to have been elected patriarch of Alexandria by the orthodox party, A.D. 484. (7) *Saint*, commemorated Feb. 20, was third bishop of Tournay in the 8th or 9th century. (8) *Saint*, fifteenth bishop of Auxerre, A.D. 532-561, commemorated Aug. 16. (9) Bishop of Cordova, A.D. 589. (10) The first known bishop of Salamanca, A.D. 589. (11) Bishop of Lucca, A.D. 680. (12) Martyr in Persia under Sapor II, commemorated April 13. (13) Soldier and martyr at Nicomedia, under Diocletian, commemorated Oct. 2. (14) Martyr at Paris, A.D. 272; commemorated Oct. 9. (15) Martyr at Tarsus, in Bithynia, commemorated Aug. 4. (16) A martyr at Byzantium, A.D. 311. (17) Abbot of St. Mark's, Spoleto, in the 6th century. (18) Exarch of Ravenna, cir. A.D. 616-620.

Eleutheropolis. For a copious exhibit of the antiquities of *Beit-Jibrin*, see the *Memoirs* accompanying the Ordnance Survey (iii, 266 sq.).

Eleuthĕrus, martyr at Cæsarea, in Cappadocia, perhaps under Hadrian, commemorated Sept. 27.

Elevation of the Host. The lifting up of the paten and consecrated element of bread was instituted by pope Honorius III (cir. 1210), and he directed that it should be adored when elevated, or carried to the sick, the people reverently bowing. Casalius quotes as his authority for this custom Psa. lxxii, 16. Anastasius Sinaita alludes to this ceremony; and it appears as early as, perhaps, the fourth century in the Greek Church; it has been traced in England in the 11th, in France in the 12th, and in Germany and Italy before the 13th century. Thomas Aquinas and Bonaventura mention the elevation of the paten only; the elevation of the chalice was of later date. The ringing of little bells at this time was introduced by William of Paris, and generally enjoined by Gregory XI.

Elevation of the Host. (From an Old Illumination.)

Elf (old Scandinavian, *Alfar;* Anglo-Saxon, *Ælf;* Danish, *Elv;* German, *Alp;* apparently meaning *white*), in Norse, British, and German popular superstitious belief, is a being between deity and man. The Edda names three classes of elves: *Light, Dark*, and *Black;* the first of whom inhabit the pure regions of light, the second mountain-grottoes and caves, the third the infernal regions. But this threefold division seems to have been soon abandoned for a dualism. Snorre Sturleson (died 1241) says: "In Alfheim there live the people of Light-Alfs, and under the earth are the Dark-Alfs, both entirely different from each other in appearance and powers; the former shining with a brightness that eclipses the sun, the latter darker than pitch." The light elves are cheerful, pleasant beings, sometimes visible, sometimes invisible; they enjoy the company of men and gods. On the contrary, the dark elves shun the light, and only leave their gloomy habitations at night; and in case the sun finds them still on earth, they become petrified by his rays. The dark elves are greatly misformed. They have monstrous noses and bellies, bones thin as a spindle, bald or horned heads. However, they are quite skilful, and not only expert in all powers of magic, but possess a rare knowledge in all metallic works; but with all their labors there is always an accompanying curse. The dwelling of these is ever in the thickest darkness; but they light up their dismal habitations by means of brilliant precious stones and shining metals. Some dwell in stones, others in the earth, still others in the sea. They eagerly steal unbaptized children of Christians, rear them in their earthen or rocky dwellings, and bring some of their own hateful, malformed children as substitutes, which can only be got rid of by rubbing their feet with fat and roasting them over the fire. The child cries unmercifully, whereupon the elves return and bring back the stolen child, in order to save their own from the tortures. The light elves are entirely different in every respect; justice and fairness are sacred to them. They never harm any one; even when they have been wronged they only revenge themselves by teasing. They find great pleasure in associating with Christians. As they have human forms and are extraordinarily beautiful, it is not seldom that they form intimate relations with men. If children follow from such intimacy, these must be bathed entirely in the sacred water for baptism, as otherwise they will not be endowed with immortal souls. The time of the elves' appearance is after sundown, in cheerful, summer moonlight nights; then they often appear in swarms, to enjoy themselves and follow every imaginable sport. Their favorite pastime is the dance; they pass whole nights occupied with this amusement, and wherever in the field or pasture a company of elves have danced, there the grass grows greener and fresher. We are accustomed to suppose the elves to be very small, but they can take on any form or size they choose. Sometimes they are hateful, sometimes beautiful; sometimes large, at other times small; just as suits their purpose. The Scots and Irish still hold to the belief that their respective countries are pre-eminently loved and visited by the elves. The most pleasant and animating stories may be found there relating to these beings; and whenever a cloud of dust is seen to rise from the road, the people, believing that the elves are changing their dwelling-places, bow in reverence before them. They often teach men their arts of magic; and, although the information they impart is very meagre, still the persons so instructed become powerful, and are feared and dreaded. Music is loved by the elves above everything else, and although their music is simple, still it exerts upon man a most wonderful influence. The piece of music entitled "Elf-king" forces every listener, and even the table and chairs, to dance as long as the music lasts; but the player cannot stop playing, for the arm and hand using the instrument is likewise charmed and bewitched: either he must play the piece backward exactly, or somebody must come from behind and cut the strings of the violin. Some have said that the elves are angels banished from heaven, who have not sunk into hell, and in this respect there is great similarity between them and the peris of the Persians. The latter are also pleasant, supernatural beings, but deprived of heaven, still not banished to hell. The elves often, in their songs, express a hope of a coming deliverance; this song immediately becomes a weeping and wailing if any one is so cruel as to disturb them in their hopes. The belief in elves has given German poets of modern days material for the loveliest and most animating representations. Compare the fable "The Elves," in Ludwig Tieck's book *Phantasus;* also the novel of the same, entitled *Die Vogelscheuche;* and especially a passage in the story of "Cordelia," by A. Treuburg (Friedrich Vischer), in the *Jahrbuch schwäbischer Dichter*, by Mörike and Zimmermann. Some myths of dwarfs, witches, sprites,

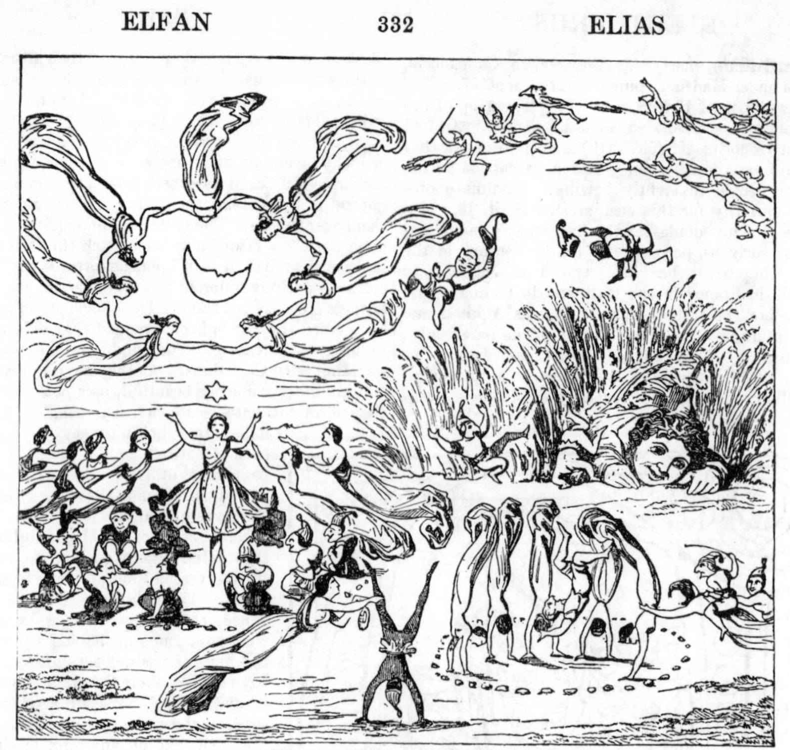

Elves in their Moonlight Antics.

etc., make all these appear as the nearest relatives of elves.

Elfan (Lat. *Alvanius*) appears in the legend of king Lucius, in his application to pope Eleutherus for Christian instruction, and is said in Welsh writers to have been abbot of Glastonbury; by others, of London, in the 2d century.

Elfeio (or **Ailvym**), a Welsh saint of the 9th century.

Elffin (*Elphinus*), a Welsh saint of the college of St. Illtyd in the beginning of the 6th century.

Elfleda (or **Ælbfled**), abbess of Whitby (born A.D. 655, died at the age of fifty-nine), commemorated Feb. 8, was daughter of Oswy, king of Northumbria, and a friend of St. Cuthbert.

Elga, *Saint*, a Welsh hermit, said to have been born in Devonshire and taken by pirates to Ireland, but to have escaped to Bardsey, off Carnarvonshire. His remains were removed to Llandaff in 1120.

Elgu, a Welsh saint of the 6th century.

Elhæarn (or **Ælhaiarn**), a Welsh saint of Carnarvonshire, is commemorated Nov. 1.

Eliab, deacon and martyr of Ethiopia, A.D. 375, is commemorated Dec. 2.

Elian, a Welsh saint, confused with St. Hilary, is celebrated in August.

Elias (or **Helias**). (1) Bishop of Lyons, second after Irenæus. (2) Bishop of Sedunum (Setten), in the Valais, about the beginning of the 5th century. (3) A Syrian bishop who endeavored to dissuade Nestorius from his heresy. (4) Bishop of Bolandus, in Lydia, A.D. 451. (5) Bishop of Seleuco-belus, on the Orontes, A.D. 458. (6) Bishop of Majorca, A.D. 484. (7) Bishop of Cæsarea, in Cappadocia, deposed by Anastasius I before A.D. 512. (8) A martyr of the 5th century, commemorated Jan. 14. (9) Prior of a nunnery in Athribis, in the Delta, said to have been remarkably sanctified from carnal passion by a dream. (10) A solitary near Antinoüs, in the Thebaïd, in the 4th century. (11) A hermit near the Dead Sea, noted for hospitality. (12) Abbot of a monastery in Syria, celebrated for his holiness and wisdom. (13) Abbot of Isania, near Antioch, near the close of the 6th century.

Elias (Armen. *Eghia*). (1) Patriarch OF ARMENIA, was born at Arjich. He was bishop of the Peznounians, and was raised to the dignity of a patriarch in 703, after the death of Sahag or Isaac III. He showed himself as one of the most violent adversaries of the Council of Chalcedon. At this time, the princess who governed the Aghovans (Albanians) took pains to make her subjects adopt the doctrine of the Council of Chalcedon, and to unite them with the Romish Church; but this displeased the nobility, at whose suggestion Elias wrote three letters to the bishop and to the princess, in order to induce them to renounce the enterprise. But as these remonstrances remained without effect, he resorted to violence and persecution. The Arabians were then masters of Armenia, and the patriarch addressed himself to the emir, or kaliph, accusing his adversaries of forming a conspiracy with the emperor of the Greeks, in order to escape from the authority of the Moslems. In consequence Nerses and the princess were laid in chains, by the order of Omar II, and a new bishop was given to the Albanians. Elias died A.D. 718. (2) Occupied the patriarchate from A.D. 760 to 797, with the exception of an interval, during which he was expelled by the patriarch Theodoret. See Hoefer, *Nouv. Biog. Générale*, s. v.

Elias HAL-LEVI *ben-Benjamin* OF CONSTANTINOPLE, who flourished in the 16th century, is the author of a ritual for the Jewish congregations in Greece, printed at Constantinople in 1602. He also wrote various Talmudic decisions. See Fürst, *Bibl. Jud.* i, 236 sq.; Jöcher, *Allgemeines Gelehrten-Lexikon*, s. v. (B. P.)

Elias, bishop OF JERUSALEM. (1) A.D. 494-513. He was an Arab by birth, and received his education in one of the Nitrian monasteries; but being expelled by Timothy Ælurus in A.D. 457, he took refuge with St. Euthymius. He afterwards resided in a cell at Jericho. He was a strict ascetic, and took an active part in the

Athanasian controversy, in consequence of which he was finally banished to Ǽla, on the Red Sea. (2) Cir. A.D. 760–797. He was for a time deposed on the charge of image-worship, brought by Theodorus, an ambitious monk, in 763. He was represented at the second General Council at Nice, in 787, by John, a priest, and Thomas, a prior of the convent of St. Arsena, near Babylon, in Egypt, who also represented the patriarchs of Alexandria and Antioch. (3) Died about 907. In 881 he sent a letter to Charlemagne; likewise, also, to the prelates, princes, and nobles of Gaul. A Latin translation of the letter (it is not probable that the original was in this language) may be found in the *Spicilegium* of D'Achery (Paris, 1723, vol. iii).

Elias MISRACHI. See MISRACHI.

Elias MONTALTO. See MONTALTO.

Elias BEN-MOSES *Ashkenasi*. See LOANZ.

Elias BEN-MOSES *Baal-Shem*. See LOANZ.

Elias BEN-MOSES *Beshitzi*. See BESHITZI, ELIAS.

Elias BEN-MOSES *de Vidas*. See VIDAS, ELIAS.

Elias OF RADNOR. See WILLIAM OF RADNOR.

Elias BEN-SALORNO *Abraham hak-Kohen*, who died in 1729, is the author of שבט מוסר, or *Ethics*, in fifty-two chapters (Constantinople, 1692):—מדרש אליהו, a *Commentary on Midrash Rabba* (ibid. 1693):—מדרש אליהו על אסתר, a *Commentary and Homilies on Esther* (Smyrna, 1759). He also wrote cabalistic treatises, comments upon the hagadoth of the Palestinian Talmud, etc. See Fürst, *Bibl. Jud.* i, 238; Jöcher, *Allgemeines Gelehrten-Lexikon*, s. v. (B. P.)

Elias OF TREKINGHAM, a monk of the 13th century, was born at Trekingham, Lincolnshire—a village since depopulated—was a monk of Peterborough, doctor of divinity in Oxford, a learned man, and a great lover of history, writing a chronicle from A.D. 625 to 1270, when he probably died. See Fuller, *Worthies of England* (ed. Nuttall), ii, 287.

Elias WILNA. See WILNA.

Elias, Apocalypse of. Under this title an apocryphal work was current in the 2d century, from which, according to Origen (*Homily* 35 on Matt. xxvii, vol. iii, 916), the Pauline quotation "Eye hath not seen," etc. (1 Cor. ii, 9), is said to have been taken. The same was repeated by Zacharias Chrysopolitanus (*Harmoniæ Evangelicæ*, ch. 166); and by Georgius Syncellus, who writes that it was taken ἐκ τῶν ᾽Ηλία ἀποκρύφων. This view was, however, early controverted by Jerome, who, referring to 1 Cor. ii, 9, says: "Solent hoc loco Apocryphorum quidam deliramenta sectari, et dicere quod de Apocalypsi Eliæ testimonium sumtum sit, cum in Esaia juxta Hebraicum ita legatur: A sæculo non audierunt neque auribus perceperunt" (*Epistola* 101 *ad Pammachium;* comp. also, on Isa. lxiv, 4 *in lib. xvii in Isaiam*, iv, 761, ed. Vallars.). It is probably the same work which is rejected in the *Apostolic Constitutions*, vi, 16, and in the *Synopsis Sac. Script.* ascribed to Athanasius, ii, 154. See Fabricius, *Codex Pseudepigraphus*, i, 1072; Smith, *Dict. of Christ. Biog.* s. v. (B. P.)

Elidius. (1) *Saint*, from whom one of the Scilly Isles was named, now corrupted into St. Helen's Isle. He is also called *St. Lyde*, and is sometimes confounded with Eligius, bishop of Noyon. (2) Martyr in Auvergne, under Childeric II (A.D. 674); commemorated Jan. 25.

Eliezer BEN-ISAAC of Worms, who flourished in the 11th century, is the author of an ascetic work entitled, ארחות חיים, also called צואת ר' אליעזר הגדול, *The Testament of Rabbi Eliezer the Great*. It was edited by Chajim Cesarini, Constantinople, 1519, and often since. In a Judæo-German translation it was published at Amsterdam in 1649. See Fürst, *Bibl. Jud.* i. 233. (B. P.)

Elifantus (or **Alephantus**), thirty-third archbishop of Arles, near the close of the 8th century.

Elijah, the prophet, is commemorated as a saint July 4 (July 20, Nov. 27).

Elijah HAB-BABLI (i. e. *the Babylonian*), a Jewish rabbi, who flourished in Babylonia in the 10th century, is the author of an haggadic work, entitled תנא דבי אליהו. It was first published at Venice in 1550; latest edition at Warsaw in 1883. Comp. Zunz, *Gottesdienstliche Vorträge* (Berlin, 1832), p. 112–117; Fürst, *Bibl. Jud.* i, 235. (B. P.)

Elijah BACHUR. See ELIAS LEVITA.

Elijah BEN-CHAYIM of Constantinople, who flourished in the beginning of the 17th century, is the author of אמרי שפר, or *Homilies on the Pentateuch* (Venice, 1630):—מים חיים, or *Decisions* (ibid. 1647). See Fürst, *Bibl. Jud.* i, 236; Jöcher, *Allgemeines Gelehrten-Lexikon*, s. v.; De' Rossi, *Dizionario Storico* (Germ. transl.) p. 95. (B. P.)

Elined (**Ǽlivedha, Luned**, or **Enid**), a Welsh virgin *saint*, commemorated Aug. 1, was daughter of earl Ynywl and granddaughter of Brychan, in Brecknockshire, and is said to have been slain for refusing marriage with a prince.

Elinga, FRANCIS JANSSENS, a Dominican, who died at Bruges, Nov. 22, 1715, is the author of *Auctoritas Thomæ Aquinatis:—Suprema Romani Pontificis Auctoritas:—Doctrina de Romani Pontificis Auctoritate et Infallibilitate:—Dissertationes Theol. Selectæ:—Summa Conciliorum Barth. Carranzæ Aucta et Additionibus Illustrata.* See Jöcher, *Allgemeines Gelehrten-Lexikon*, s. v. (B. P.)

Eliot, Jared, M.D., a Congregational minister, son of Rev. Joseph Eliot, was born at Guilford, Conn., Nov. 7, 1685. While Yale College was yet located at Killingworth, he graduated from it in 1706. In October, 1709, he was ordained pastor of the Killingworth Church, as successor to the Rev. Mr. Pierson, and retained this position until his death, April 22, 1763. From 1730 to 1762 he was a fellow of Yale College. In 1722, the day after commencement at Yale, a number of prominent men assembled in the college library to consider a paper signed by some of the leading clergymen of Connecticut, among whom was Dr. Eliot, in which doubts regarding the validity of Presbyterian ordination were expressed. In October following, according to arrangement, the divine right of Episcopacy was discussed before a large number of clergy and laity. As the result, some avowed themselves Episcopalians, while Dr. Eliot and others were convinced of the truth of Presbyterianism. It is said of him that he was the chief physician of his time in the colony, being eminent also as a botanist and as a scientific agriculturist. Through him the white mulberry was introduced into Connecticut, and with it the silkworm, concerning which he published a treatise. In 1761 he received a gold medal from a society in London for his process of extracting iron from black sand, for he was likewise a mineralogist. His linguistic acquirements were also of a superior order. His agricultural tastes led him to devise various ways for draining swamps and reclaiming marshes, and he published several essays on agriculture. A large number of farms in the colony belonged to him. So conscientious, however, was he as a clergyman that he never omitted preaching on the Sabbath during forty successive years. Benjamin Franklin frequently visited him, and the two maintained a correspondence. Socially he was very agreeable, and among his people he was regarded as a great preacher. A few of his sermons were published. See Sprague, *Annals of the Amer. Pulpit*, i, 270.

Eliot, John, D.D., a Unitarian minister, was born in Boston, May 31, 1754. He prepared for college in the North Grammar-school in Boston, and in 1772 graduated from Harvard College. Soon after his graduation he took charge of a school in Roxbury, where he remained one year. He studied theology at Cambridge. In 1775 he commenced his labors as a preacher at Dover. In 1776 he received an earnest request from several leading members of the Episcopal Church at Halifax, N. S., to become an assistant to their aged pastor, but declined. He officiated for a short time as chaplain to the recruits of colonel Marshall's regiment, then raised in Boston for the expedition to Canada. After this he passed several months at Littleton as the assistant of Rev. Daniel Rogers, and during the winter of 1778-79 supplied the First Church in Salem. In 1779 he was ordained and installed pastor of the New North Church in the same town. In 1804 he was chosen a member of the corporation of Harvard College. He was also a member of most of the literary and charitable societies in Boston and vicinity, and in some of them he held important offices. Dr. Eliot died Feb. 14, 1813. He published several single *Sermons*. See Sprague, *Annals of the Amer. Pulpit*, viii, 92.

Elisæus. (1) Bishop of Arezzo, A.D. 713. (2) Bishop of Bologna, cir. A.D. 716. (3) Thirtieth bishop of Noyon, A.D. 747. (4) Forty-third bishop of Auch, about the close of the 8th century. (5) A Scotch prelate, promoted to the see of Galloway about 1405, and still holding that office in 1412.

Elisha, the prophet, is commemorated as a saint in various Christian calendars on June 14 (Oct. 12, Oct. 16).

Elisha OF ARMENIA. (1) Elected patriarch A.D. 936, after the death of Theodorus (Asdouadzadour) I, and established the seat of his administration at Agathomar, on lake Van. His enemies deposed him by means of intrigues and betrayals in 941, and he died A.D. 943. (2) Born A.D. 1451. Being first bishop of Erivan and then vicar-general of the patriarch of Armenia, he became patriarch in 1503, after the death of Thaddæus I, and ruled with wisdom. He was well versed in theology, rhetoric, and sacred history. He died in 1575, leaving in MS. a *Commentary on Genesis:—Life of St. Gregory*, in verse:—and forty-five *Sermons*. See Hoefer, *Nouv. Biog. Générale*, s. v.

Elisha BEN-ABUJA (surnamed *Acher*, i. e. "the other one," after his apostasy) was a pupil of the famous rabbi Akiba (q. v.). He was the son of a wealthy citizen of Jerusalem, and was early initiated in the study of the law, but afterwards apostatized from Judaism. It is related of him that while attending the Jewish college he had often been noticed to carry with him writings of the "Minim" (probably of Gnostics), and that he had even been in the habit of quoting Greek poetry. One of the most intimate friends and pupils of Elisha was the famous rabbi, Meïr (q. v.), who seized every opportunity to invite his friend to return into the bosom of the synagogue—a proposition to which Elisha refused to accede, as forgiveness could not be granted to one who had so wantonly abused the gifts bestowed upon him. When Acher lay on his deathbed, Meïr hastened to his side, and renewed, this time effectually, his solicitations on this subject. Legend has it that Meïr spread his cloak over the grave of Acher; a cloud of smoke rose from it, and Meïr turned away with the somewhat blasphemous application of Ruth iii, 13, "Tarry this night (of time), and it shall be in the morning (of immortality) that he the All-merciful will deliver and ransom thee; but if he be unwilling, then I will redeem thee." See Hamburger, *Real-Encyklop.* ii, 168 sq.; Bacher, in Frankel-Grätz's *Monatsschrift*, 1884, p. 234 sq.; Jellinek, *Elischa ben-Abujja, genannt Acher* (Leipsic, 1847). (B. P.)

Elisha GALICHO. See GALICHO.

Elissæus. (1) Bishop of Diocletianopolis, in Palestine, A.D. 359. (2) A priest condemned to slavery by the Council of Seville (A.D. 619), for ingratitude to his bishop.

Elithur, the name of three saints in the Irish calendar, at April 25, May 12, and Dec. 23.

Elivager, celebrated rivers which occupy a conspicuous place in the cosmogony of the ancient Scandinavians. They are the source whence came the original cosmical matter or substance from which the worlds were formed, as well as the giants and men. See NORSE MYTHOLOGY.

Elizabeth. (1) Mother of John the Baptist, commemorated Feb. 10. (2) A wonder-worker of Constantinople, commemorated April 24.

Elkanah BEN-JEROCHAN BEN-ABIGDOR, a Jewish writer of the 15th century, is the author of a cabalistic work entitled, קנה חכמה וקנה בינה, which was first published at Prague in 1610:—ס׳ הפליאה, also called ס׳ סתרי תורה, a cabalistic Midrash on Gen. v, 29, published first in 1784. See Fürst, *Bibl. Jud.* i, 239 sq.; Jöcher, *Allgemeines Gelehrten-Lexikon*, s. v. (B. P.)

Ella, bishop of Siguenza (Segontia), cir. A.D. 680-685.

Ellbrigh, abbess of Cluain-Bronaigh (Clonbroney, County Longford), died A.D. 785.

Ellendorf, JOHANN OTTO, a Roman Catholic writer, was born at Wiedenbrück, in Westphalia, in 1805. In 1826 he was rector at the gymnasium of his native place, and in 1841 was called to Berlin as professor of jurisprudence. He wrote, *Der heilige Bernhard von Clairvaux* (Essen, 1837):—*Die Katholische Kirche Preussens* (Rudolstadt, 1837):—*Thomas Becket* (Essen, 1838):—*Die Karolinger* (ibid. 1838, 1839, 2 vols.):—*Die Moral und Politik der Jesuiten* (Darmstadt, 1840):—*Das Primat der römischen Päpste* (ibid. 1841, 1846, 2 vols.):—*Ist Petrus in Rom gewesen?* (ibid. 1841):—*Die Stellung der spanischen Kirche*, etc. (ibid. 1843). See Zuchold, *Bibl. Theol.* i, 316 sq. (B. P.)

Ellenius, abbot of Llancarvan, A.D. 570-577

Eller, MORITZ M., a Jewish preacher, was born at Mannheim in 1801. He studied at Bonn and Heidelberg. From 1834 to 1844 he was teacher at the Maier-Michel-David Free School in Hanover, accepted in the latter year a call as rabbi to Celle, and died Jan. 4, 1848. See Heimbürger, *M. M. Eller nach seinem Leben und Wirken, nebst einigen Vorträgen des Verewigten* (Celle, 1848); Kayserling, *Bibliothekjüdischer Kanzelredner*, ii, 248. (B. P.)

Elli, abbot of Whitton, in the 6th century.

Ellingwood, JOHN WALLACE, D.D., a Congregational minister, was born at Beverly, Mass., May 2, 1782. For several years he pursued the business of a silversmith, relinquishing that occupation in 1810 to enter the Andover Theological Seminary. In 1812 he was ordained over the Church in Bath, Me., where he labored with great fidelity and success until 1843, when ill-health compelled him to resign his charge. He died at Bath, Aug. 19, 1860. Dr. Ellingwood was a man of great wisdom and prudence, firmness and independence of opinion, benevolence and self-control; he took a deep interest in the great religious and moral enterprises of his day, and held responsible positions on the Boards of his Church. Eight revivals of religion resulted from his labors. Three of his sermons were published in 1851. See *Cong. Quarterly*, 1860, p. 420.

Elliott, Charles, D.D. See vol. iii, p. 1042.

Elliott, David, DD., LL.D., a Presbyterian minister, was born in Sherman's Valley, Perry Co., Pa., Feb. 6, 1787. To the age of sixteen he had only the educational advantages of the rural district in which he lived; but in 1802 he entered the classical school in Tuscarora Valley, and in the spring of 1804 went to another in the town of Mifflin, where he spent one year. In 1805 he became an assistant of Rev. Matthew Brown, in the academy of Washington, at the same time making preparation to enter the junior class of Dickinson College, where he graduated Sept. 28, 1808. He studied theology with Rev. John Linn, Rev. Dr. Culbertson, of Zanesville, O., and Rev. Joshua Williams, D.D., of Newville, Pa. He was licensed to preach as a probationer by the Presbytery of Carlisle, Sept. 26, 1811; and Feb. 19, 1812, received a call to settle as pastor of the Church of Mercersburg, where he served until Oct. 29, 1829. His second pastorate was at Washington, lasting until 1836. For a time he was acting president of Washington College and professor of moral philosophy. In 1836 the Assembly called him to take a professorship in the Western Theological Seminary of Pennsylvania. In 1849 he was again solicited to become president of Washington College, but declined. He was often sent as a member to the General Assembly, and was moderator of the synod in 1831, 1834, and 1838. He died March 18, 1874. Dr. Elliott was successful as a preacher and pastor, a thorough student, successful educator, wise in the management of all affairs in the assembly, equal to the most trying crisis, a man greatly loved and honored by all. See Brownson, *Memorial*.

Elliott, James H., D.D., a Protestant Episcopal clergyman, brother of bishop Elliott of Georgia, was born in Charleston, S. C., in 1819; ordained deacon in 1849; ministered successively at Beaufort, Grahamville, St. Michael's, Charleston, Madison, Ga., and St. Paul's, Charleston; was editor of the *Christian Witness*, Boston, from 1868 to 1870; and died at Charleston, June 11, 1877. See *Prot. Episc. Almanac*, 1878, p. 168.

Elliott, Jared Leigh, D.D., a Presbyterian minister, was born in Washington, D. C., June 24, 1807. Most of his boyhood was spent as a sailor. He afterwards studied in the academy at Princeton, N. J.; graduated from the College of New Jersey in 1831; spent two years at Auburn Theological Seminary, N. Y.; then one year in Princeton Theological Seminary; was licensed by the Presbytery of New York, April 13, 1834; and was ordained an evangelist by the Presbytery of Philadelphia, Oct. 26, 1835. His successive fields of labor were, as stated supply at Poughkeepsie, N. Y., 1834; of the Mariners' Church, Philadelphia, Pa., 1835; of the first and second churches of Washington, and of the Church at Frederick, Md., 1836–39; chaplain in the U. S. Navy, 1849; army, 1861–81. He made many long sea-voyages, and was attached to the South Arctic Exploring Expedition in 1840. Dr. Elliott died at Washington, D. C., April 16, 1881. See *Necrol. Report of Princeton Theol. Sem.* 1882.

Ellis, Clement, an English divine, was born in 1630, near Penrith, in Cumberland, and was educated at Oxford. In 1693 he was appointed a prebendary of Southwell. He died in 1700. He published a number of sermons and theological treatises (1661–1700), and some were issued after his death: *Discourse on the Parable, with an Account of his Life and Writings* (1704, 8vo):—*The Scripture Catechist*. See Chalmers, *Biog. Dict.* s. v.; Allibone, *Dict. of Brit. and Amer. Authors*, s. v.

Ellis, William, an English Congregationalist minister, was born at Wisbeach, Aug. 29, 1794. Being converted when quite young, he offered his services to the London Missionary Society; was educated for mission work at Gosport, and, in January, 1816, was sent to Tahiti, the largest of the Society Islands. In 1822 he went to the Sandwich Islands, and greatly assisted in establishing Christianity there, preaching frequently in Hawaiian; he assisted in the arrangement of the alphabet; wrote the first hymns; baptized the first convert, the queen-mother, Keo-puo-lani; and shortly afterwards preached her funeral sermon. In 1824 his wife's health gave way and compelled their return to England. He went by way of Boston, and spent three months in the northern states, rendering great service to the American Foreign Mission Board by telling the story of the Hawaii mission. For six years after his arrival in England Mr. Ellis was agent of the London Missionary Society among the county auxiliaries. In 1841 broken health compelled him to resign official life, and he settled at Hoddesdon to the quiet duties of a country pastor. In 1862 he went to Madagascar, reorganized the mission which had been nearly ruined by the persecutions of the late queen, saw the native church and its agencies resettled on a healthy system, the schools reopened and the press at work, and in 1865 returned to Hoddesdon, where he died, July 9, 1872. Mr. Ellis published, *Missionary Narrative of a Tour through Hawaii, or Owhyhee* (Lond. 1826, 8vo; 4th ed. 1827, 8vo):—*Polynesian Researches* (1829, 2 vols. 8vo; last ed. 1853, 4 vols. 12mo):—*Vindication of the South Sea Missions* (1831, 8vo):—*History of Madagascar* (1832, 2 vols. 8vo):—*History of the London Missionary Society* (1844, 8vo), and other valuable works. See (Lond.) *Cong. Year-book*, 1873, p. 325; Allibone, *Dict. of Brit. and Amer. Authors*, s. v.; *Life*, by his son (Lond. 1873).

Elloc, an Irish saint of Killmalloch, is commemorated July 13 (or 24).

Elltin. (1) An Irish saint of Shancoe, County Sligo, commemorated Jan. 11. (2) A confessor of Kinsale, commemorated Dec. 11.

Ellwood, Thomas, a Quaker writer of some reputation, was born at Crowell, near Thame, in Oxfordshire, in August, 1639, where he was educated. He united with the Friends in 1658; became a preacher, and died March 1, 1713. The following are some of his publications: *Forgery no Christianity* (1674, 12mo):—*The Foundation of Tithes Shaken* (1682, 1720, 8vo; Wickham, 1690, 4to):—*Sacred History* (1705–09). He was an intimate friend of Milton. After perusing the MS. of *Paradise Lost*, he returned it to the author with the remark, "Thou hast said much here of Paradise lost, but what hast thou to say of Paradise found." To this timely hint the world is indebted for *Paradise Regained*. See Chalmers, *Biog. Dict.* s. v.; Allibone, *Dict. of Brit. and Amer. Authors*, s. v.

Elmacin (or **Elmakyn**), George, an Egyptian historian, known in the East by the name of *Ibn-Amid*, was born in 1223. He was a Christian, and occupied the place of *ketib*, or secretary, at the court of the sultans of Egypt, an office usually filled by Christians. In 1238 he succeeded his father, Yaser el-Amid, who had held the office of secretary to the council of war under the sultans of Egypt for forty-five years. Elmacin died at Damascus in 1273. He wrote a *History of the Saracens*, consisting of annals which extend from the time of Mohammed to the year 1117. It is principally occupied with the affairs of the Saracen empire, but contains some passages relating to the eastern Christians. It was published, in Arabic and Latin, at Leyden, in 1625. Other editions have also appeared. See *Encyclop. Brit.* 9th ed. s. v.

Elmendorf, Anthony, D.D., a (Dutch) Reformed minister, was born in Ulster County, N. Y., in 1813; graduated from Rutgers College in 1836, and from the New Brunswick Theological Seminary in 1839. The first eight years of his ministry were passed in quiet country churches (Hurley, N. Y., 1840, Hyde Park, 1843). He then removed to Brooklyn, and after three years of earnest work in the new Church on Bedford Avenue (1848–51), started in his own house the Sunday-school and congregation of the North Reformed Church, Brooklyn, which is the monument of his courageous, indefatigable, and successful labors. Worn out with toil and feeble health, he resigned his charge but a few months before his death, which occurred in 1866. He was a careful sermonizer, a diligent student, and an eloquent preacher. His pastoral efficiency was wonderful. (W. J. R. T.)

Elmenhorst, Heinrich, a Lutheran theologian, was born Oct. 19, 1632, at Parchim, in Mecklenburg, studied at Leipsic and Wittenberg, and accepted a call in 1660 to Hamburg, where he died May 21, 1704. He is the author of *Geistliche Lieder* (Hamburg, 1681):—*Geistreiche Lieder* (ibid. 1700). See Molleri, *Cimbria Literata* (Copenh., 1744), ii, 183 sq.; Schröder, *Lexikon der Hamburgischen Schriftsteller*, vol. ii; Wezel, *Hymnopoetica*, iv, 103 sq.; Koch, *Geschichte des deutschen Kirchenliedes*, v, 365 sq.; Jöcher, *Allgemeines Gelehrten-Lexikon*, s. v. (B. P.)

Elmerus (or **Ermelius**), patron saint of a church at Molhanium, diocese of Liege, is assigned to the 7th or 8th century, and commemorated Aug. 28.

Elmo, *Saint.* See ERASMUS.

Elmsley, PETER, D.D., an English scholar and divine, was born in 1773, and educated at Westminster School and at Merton College, Oxford. In 1798 he was presented to Little Horkesley, a small chapelry in Essex, but becoming master of a fortune by the death of an uncle, he devoted himself to literary studies, and particularly to Greek literature. He lived for a while in Edinburgh, where he was intimately associated with the founders of the *Edinburgh Review*, and contributed to that periodical several articles. He also edited with consummate ability several classical works. In 1816 he made a voyage to Italy in search of manuscripts, and passed the winter of 1818 in researches in the Laurentian library at Florence. The next year he was appointed to assist sir Humphry Davy in the unavailing task of trying to decipher some of the papyri found at Herculaneum. He died March 8, 1825. Dr. Emsley was one of the most accomplished Greek scholars of his day. See *The New Amer. Cyclop.* vii, 111; (Lond.) *Annual Register*, 1825, p. 232; Hart, *English Literature*, p. 439.

Eloæus (or **Æloæus**), one of the seven ruling spirits in the Ophite (q. v.) system.

Elodia, a virgin martyr with Nunilo at Osca (Huesca); commemorated Oct. 22.

Eloi, *Saint.* See ELIGIUS.

Elon. Lieut. Conder (*Tent Work in Palest.* ii, 336) proposes to identify this site with that of *Beit Ello*, a village marked on the *Ordnance Map* (sheet xiv) at eleven miles northeast of Jimzu (Gimzo), in a plain, without any traces of antiquity; and Tristram (*Bible Places*, p. 51) concurs in this location, which, however, is without the boundaries of Dan. But *Elon-beth-hanan*, which is probably the same place, the former identifies much more plausibly with *Beit Anân*, which is laid down at two and a quarter miles south of *Beit-ur el-Foka* (Upper Bethhoron), and described (*Memoirs* to the Survey, iii, 16) as "a small village on the top of a flat ridge; near the main road to the west are the remains of a khan, with water, and about a mile to the east is a spring. It was a fief of the Holy Sepulchre in the 12th century."

Eloquius, abbot of Lagny, commemorated as a saint Dec. 3, was a Hibernian or Scot who accompanied St. Fursey to Belgium as a missionary about the middle of the 7th century.

Elotherius (or **Eleutherius**), twenty-seventh bishop of Avignon, A.D. 475.

Elpedephŏrus, bishop of Cuiculis or Cuizis in Numidia, A.D. 349.

Elpenipsa, one of the forty-eight martyrs of Lyons (q. v.).

Elpidiphŏrus and companions, martys in Persia, A.D. 320; commemorated Nov. 2.

Elpidius. (1) Bishop and martyr in Cherson under Diocletian, commemorated March 8. (2) Bishop of Comana in Cappadocia, A.D. 325. (3) Bishop of Palestine, A.D. 347. (4) Bishop of Satala in Armenia, deposed A.D. 360. (5) Bishop of a maritime town in the East, A.D. 375, excommunicated by Eustathius. (6) Bishop of Dionysia in Bostra, A.D. 381. (7) Bishop of Laodicea in Syria, deposed A.D. 404 for attachment to the cause of Chrysostom, but restored in 414. (8) Bishop of Lyons, cir. A.D. 424. (9) Two bishops of Thermæ in Galatia, one A.D. 451, the other A.D. 692. (10) Saint, first of the four recorded bishops of Atella in Campania, cir. A.D. 400. (11) A bishop who, with eleven companions, is commemorated Sept. 1. (12) Bishop of Damietta, who fled to Constantinople, A.D. 487, to escape the Eutychians. (13) Bishop of Volterra, A.D. 501. (14) Bishop of Ancyra in the early part of the 6th century. (15) One of four brothers, all Spanish bishops in the first half of the 6th century. (16) Bishop of Thebæ in Thessaly, A.D. 531. (17) Bishop of Catania, cir. A.D. 580. (18) A bishop, probably of some eastern see, censured by Gregory the Great, A.D. 597. (19) Bishop of Tarazona (Turiasso), A.D. 633–638. (20) Bishop of Astorga, A.D. 654. (21) Patron saint of the town of St. Elpidia in Pisenum, said by some to have been a Cappadocian by birth, and to have died A.D. 393. (22) Abbot of the monastery founded by Timotheus in Cappadocia, where he died before A.D. 420. (23) Archimandrite of Constantinople, A.D. 448. (24) Surnamed *Rusticus*, a deacon of Lyons, a skilful physician, and a friend of Ennodius, in the time of Theodoric, king of the Ostrogoths; the author of some poems still extant (see Migne, *Patr. Lat.* lxii, 545). (25) Martyr under Julian with several others, commemorated Nov. 16.

Elpidophorus. (1) An apostate during the persecution by the Vandal king Hunneric, A.D. 484. (2) Bishop of Anastasiopolis in Caria, A.D. 553.

Elpis (*hope*), one of the æons in the system of Valentinus (q. v.).

Elpis, a (mythical) martyr, daughter of Sophia; commemorated with her sisters, Pistis and Agape, Sept. 17.

Elstob, WILLIAM, an English clergyman and antiquary, was born at Newcastle-upon-Tyne, Jan. 1, 1673, and was educated at Eton and Catharine Hall, Cambridge. In 1696 he became a fellow of University College. In 1792 he was appointed rector of the united parishes of St. Swithin and St. Mary Bothan, London. In 1703 he published an edition of Ascham's Latin letters. He died in 1714. The following are some of his publications: *An Essay on the Great Affinity and Mutual Agreement between the Two Professions of Law and Divinity* (Lond. 8vo):—*Sermons* (1704, 4to):—*A Translation into Latin of the Saxon Homily of Lupus, with Notes by Dr. Hickes* (1701).

Elswich, JOHANN HERMANN, a Lutheran divine, was born at Rendsburg, in Holstein, June 19, 1684, and was educated at Lubeck, Rostock, Leipsic, Jena, and Würtemberg, at which last university he took his master's degree. In 1717 he was invited to become pastor of the Church of Sts. Cosmo and Damian, at Stade. He died there, June 10, 1721. For a list of some of his works, see Chalmers, *Biog. Dict.* s. v.; Jöcher, *Allgemeines Gelehrten-Lexikon*, s. v.

Eltekeh. Lieut. Conder suggests (*Tent Work in Palest.* ii, 336; see *Quar. Statement* of "Palest. Explor. Fund," January, 1881, p. 51) that this is the present *Beit Likia*, which is laid down on the Ordnance Map one and three quarter miles south-west of *Beit-ur el-Tahta* (Lower Bethhoron), and described in the *Memoirs* to the Survey (iii, 16) as "a small village on a main road at the foot of the hills, supplied by cisterns; with ancient foundations among the houses;" and in this identification Tristram concurs (*Bible Places*, p. 51).

Eltinge, WILHELMUS, D.D., a Reformed (Dutch) minister, was born near Kingston, N. Y., in 1778, graduated at Princeton College in 1796, and pursued theological studies with Dr. Theodorick Romeyn at Schenectady, N. Y. He was licensed in 1798, and passed his long ministry at Paramus, N. J. From 1799 to 1811 he likewise served the adjoining church of Saddle River, and from 1816 to 1833 the First Church of Totown, now Paterson. He resigned the latter in 1850, and died in 1851. Dr. Eltinge was a man of respectable attainments, and of great firmness and decision. He was a very prominent actor in the ecclesiastical troubles in Bergen County which led to the secession in 1822, and the organization of the "True Reformed Dutch Church," of which he was a strong and life-long opponent. See Corwin, *Manual of the Ref. Church in America*, p. 255. (W. J. R. T.)

Elton, Romeo, D.D., a Baptist minister and scholar, was born at Burlington, Conn., in 1790. He graduated from Brown University in 1813, engaged in teaching for two or three years; was ordained at Newport, R. I., June 11, 1817; became pastor of the Second Baptist Church there, but resigned in 1822 on account of his health, and two years after was settled in Windsor, Vt. Being professor of Greek and Latin in Brown University, he spent about two years abroad, chiefly in Germany, in study, and assumed his chair in 1827. He retired from his office in 1843, and in 1845 took up his residence in Exeter, in the south of England, where he remained twenty-two years; then removed to Bath, where he lived two years, during all which period he preached almost constantly in the vacant pulpits of Baptist and Independent churches, and wrote for the press. For several years he was one of the editors of the *Eclectic Review*. He returned to America in 1869, and died in Boston, Mass., Feb. 5, 1870. He left by his will, among other bequests, one of $20,000 to Brown University to establish a professorship of natural theology, and nearly as much to Columbian University to establish a professorship of intellectual and moral philosophy. Among his published writings may be found an edition of Callender's *Century Sermon*:—a volume of *President Maxcy's Remains* (1844):—and a *Life of Roger Williams* (1853). (J. C. S.)

Elurion, an Egyptian bishop, A.D. 347.

Elvetus, bishop of Arezzo, A.D. 775.

Elwandus, bishop of Treviso, in 452.

Elwert, Eduard, an evangelical theologian of Germany, was born at Cannstadt, Feb. 22, 1805. In 1830 he commenced his academical career at Tübingen, was in 1836 appointed professor at Zurich, and from 1839 to 1841 acted as professor at Tübingen. Bodily infirmities obliged him to retire from his academic activity, and he accepted the pastorate at Mötzingen. In 1850 he was placed at the head of the Schönthal Seminary, where he labored until 1864, when he was obliged to retire entirely from active work. He died June 9, 1865, at his native place, having published, *De Antinomia Joh. Agricolæ* (Zurich, 1836):—*Annotationes in Gal. ii*, 1-10, etc. (Tübingen, 1852):—*Quæstiones et Observationes ad Philologiam Sacram N. Test. Pertinentes* (ibid. 1860). He also contributed to several theological reviews. See Kübel, in Herzog-Plitt, *Real-Encyklop.* s. v.; Zuchold, *Bibl. Theol.* i, 318. (B. P.)

Elwin (or **Alunus**), *Saint*, one of Breaca's companions in her voyage from Ireland to Cornwall; commemorated Feb. 22.

Elwoed, abbot of St. Illtyd's (now Lantwit Major), in the 6th century.

Elwog (Lat. *Eluogus*), bishop of Llandaff, in the second half of the 8th century.

Elwystyl (or **Elgistil**), suffragan bishop of Llandaff, in the first half of the 6th century.

Ely, Alfred, D.D., a Congregational minister, was born at West Springfield, Mass., Nov. 8, 1778. Leaving a clerkship at the age of twenty-one, he prepared for college at the Hartford (Conn.) grammar-school, and graduated from the College of New Jersey in 1804. After a tutorship at the college for one year, he was ordained over the Church in Monson, Mass., in 1806, where he was an active minister for thirty-six years, and died July 6, 1866. Dr. Ely was an able preacher and theologian, and his ministry was greatly blessed to the spiritual and moral elevation of his people. Twenty-one of his sermons and addresses were published. See *Cong. Quarterly*, 1867, p. 137.

Ely, David, D.D., a Congregational minister, was born at Lyme, Conn., July 7 (O. S.), 1749. In 1769 he graduated from Yale College; in October, 1771, was licensed to preach; and Oct. 27, 1773, was ordained colleague with Rev. Jedediah Mills in Huntington, Conn. He died there, Feb. 16, 1816. During the Revolution he was a zealous patriot. Though he made no pretensions to style, he had a talent for communicating the truth, which strongly impressed it upon the memory. His facility and felicity in quoting Scripture were excelled by few. About a hundred pupils were prepared by him for Yale College. From 1778 he was a member of the corporation of Yale; was, for a long time, secretary of the same, and one of the prudential committee. See Sprague, *Annals of the Amer. Pulpit*, ii, 4.

Ely, Samuel Rose, D.D., a Presbyterian minister, was born at West Springfield, Mass., Dec. 29, 1803. He graduated from Williams College in 1830, studied theology for two years in Princeton Theological Seminary, and was ordained by the Presbytery of Westchester, N. Y., Dec. 4, 1834. He served as pastor at Carmel, from 1834 to 1836; at Easthampton, from 1836 to 1846; at Brooklyn, in 1850; and as stated supply at Roslyn, from 1853 until his death, May 11, 1873. See *Gen. Cat. of Princeton Theol. Sem.* 1881, p. 82.

Elymas, a presbyter, martyred in Persia under Decius; commemorated April 22.

Elysium, in Greek and Roman mythology, is the abode of the blessed. According to Homer, it lies in the mild sunlight, this side of Oceanus; whether it is an island or not is not mentioned. Hesiod speaks of islands of the blessed, where on the Oceanus river the heroes live in peace, and where the earth yearly brings forth three harvests of fruits. According to Pindar, the citadel, Kronos (Saturn), is on the islands of the blessed. Here cool, refreshing sea-breezes blow, gold-glittering flowers bloom on the trees, and along the springs. The heroes decorate their persons with them. They only reach this blessed abode who pass a threefold test in Hades and on earth by keeping themselves unstained by crimes. Besides Rhadamanthus, whom Kronos selected as his successor, Pindar mentions Peleus, Cadmus, and Achilles as being here. Virgil gives another description of the Elysium: "Laughing æther fills the fields with a purple light; a distinct sun and distinct stars shed their light upon them." Æneas there finds those who received wounds in battling for their country, priests who led a spotless life, sacred poets who sung the worth of Phœbus, discoverers who benefited mankind by their arts, etc.

Elzevir is the name of a family, the members of which are known by their publications of theological works, more especially of the New Test. Louis Elzevir, who had embraced Calvinism in France, had to leave his country in 1580, and went to Leyden, where he established a book-store, which soon became known by the publication of Drusii *Ebraicarum Quæstionum libri duo* (1583). The descendants of Louis established themselves at Utrecht, Amsterdam, and at other places. His grandson, Isaac, was appointed in 1620 university printer at Leyden, and this privilege remained with the family until 1712. The Elzevirs published such works as La Pegrère's *Præadamitæ*, in 1655, and Richard Simon's *Histoire Crit. du Vieux Testament*, in 1680, which the Church of Rome tried to suppress. What assures the Elzevirs an honorable place in the history of theology is the fact that they issued several editions of the Greek New Test., which became popular and authoritative for a long period. The preface to the second edition, published in 1633, boldly proclaims, "Textum ergo habes, nunc ab omnibus receptum; in quo nihil immutatum aut corruptum damus;" hence the name *textus receptus*, or commonly received standard text. All the Holland editions were scrupulously copied from the Elzevir text, and Wetstein could not get authority to print his famous Greek Test. (1751-52) except on condition of following it. See Bernus, in Lichtenberger's *Encyclop. des Sciences Religieuses*, s. v.; but more especially Alphons Willems's *Histoire et Annales Typographiques* (Brussels and Paris, 1880, 2 vols.), where a history of the Elzevir family and a list of their publications is given. (B. P.)

Ema (or **Ama**), a martyr, with six other nuns, captives with Eliabus (q. v.), commemorated May 22.

Emant, of Cluain, an Irish saint, said by some to have been a bishop; commemorated July 1.

Emanuel BEN-SALOMO. See IMMANUEL.

Emanus, slain by thieves at Chartres in the 6th century, is said to have been a Cappadocian pilgrim to Rome and other cities of Italy; commemorated May 16.

Ember Days. These are days of fasting occurring quarterly, in commemoration of the seasons (Lat. *quatuor temporum*, whence by contraction the German *Quatember*, and the English *Ember*). We find them at an early period associated with the invoking of God's blessing on each of the four seasons in turn, and the special striving by prayers and fasting to merit such blessings. They were celebrated at Nativity, Easter, Epiphany, and Pentecost. About the time of Gelasius they were selected as the most fitting for the ordination of the clergy. In the Eastern Church there is no trace whatever of an observance of the Ember seasons. The passage of Athanasius, which some have quoted in support of a different conclusion, merely proves the existence of a fast at Pentecost. As regards the Gallican Church, the Ember seasons do not seem to have been established much before the time of Charlemagne. The second Council of Tours (A.D. 567), in prescribing the fasts to be observed by monks, makes no mention whatever of the fasts of the four seasons. The observance of the Ember days is purely a Western institution. It was, doubtless, at first a rite merely of the local Roman Church, whence it gradually spread throughout the West. The history of the development of the custom is probably thus: Fasts were celebrated at the times of Lent, Pentecost, and the Nativity; these periods would roughly correspond with three of the four seasons, and thus some bishop of Rome, Leo or one of his predecessors, may have conceived the idea of making them symbolize the return of the seasons, and so added the one necessary to complete the four. It would soon come to pass, then, that they would be spoken of as originally ordained with that view; the length of celebration settled, the fasts then became associated with the seasons, and were regarded as independent of Lent, etc. Thus they might occasionally fall outside of these seasons, and finally such irregularity may have caused the settlement of the matter as at present.

Embla, in Norse mythology, was the first woman created by the Asas, from a tree-trunk (*Embla*, "the pine," while *Ask*, "the ash," was the name of the first man). She was endowed with feeling, motion, spirit, life, the senses of hearing and seeing, and was gifted with the power of speech. By Ask, her husband, she became mother of the human race.

Embolism (also *Embolis* and *Embolum*). (1) An inserted prayer; the name given to the prayer which in almost all ancient liturgies follows the Lord's prayer, founded on one or both of the two last petitions. It is so called because it is interposed there, and what had been already asked in the Lord's prayer is expanded, and it is more clearly expressed what evils we seek to be delivered from, viz. past, present, and future. There are also added the names of the saints by whose intercession we strengthen our prayers, viz. the Virgin Mary, Peter, Paul, and Andrew. The embolism was usually repeated by the priest in a low voice, symbolizing the silence during the period that our Lord lay in the grave; but in the Ambrosian rite it was always pronounced aloud. This practice, which has left very faint traces in the Western Church, holds a more important place in Oriental liturgies. The embolism is not, however, found in the liturgies of Chrysostom and Basil, but appears in those of James, Mark, and Theodore the Interpreter, as well as in the Armenian, Mozarabic, and Coptic Basil. As examples of the shorter embolism we give that of the Church of Jerusalem:

> "And lead us not into temptation, O Lord, the Lord of Hosts, who knowest our infirmity; but deliver us from the Evil One, and his works, and every assault and will of his, for the sake of Thy Holy name which is called upon our lowliness;"

and the Syriac Liturgy of St. James:

> "O Lord our God, lead us not into temptation, which we devoid of strength are not able to bear, but also with the temptation make a way of escape, that we may be able to bear it, and deliver us from evil, through Jesus Christ," etc.

(2) Embolism also designates the excess of the solar year over twelve lunar months, commonly called the *Epact*.

Embŏlus, a covered portico or cloister; in ecclesiastical language a cloister surrounding the external walls of a church, serving as an ambulatory in hot, rainy, and dirty weather, and also affording a convenient passage for the priests and ministers of the church from the *bema* and *diaconicum* to the *narthex*. These porticos were generally vaulted, and highly ornamented with mosaic pictures. Such porticos were found at St. Sophia, Constantinople; St. Michael, at Anaplus; and the Deipara, at Jerusalem.

Emden, JACOB ISRAEL, a Jewish writer of Germany, was born in 1696, and died at Altona in 1776. He is the author of numerous treatises, among which are, בית אל, a ritual for the whole year (Altona, 1745, 4 parts, and often; latest ed. Lemberg, 1860):—*A Life of Jon. Eybenschütz*, entitled, בית יהונתן (Altona, 1752):—מטפחת ספרים, *The Wrapper of Books* (ibid. 1763); a critique on the Sohar:—צצים ופרחים *On the Fundamental Doctrines of the Cabala* (ibid. 1756):—תורת הקנאות, *A Collection of Accounts Referring to Sabbathai Zewi, his Pupils and Adherents* (ibid. 1752; Lemberg, 1870). See Fürst, *Bibl. Jud.* i, 240 sq.; Grätz, *Geschichte der Juden*, x, 396 sq.; Ginsburg, *The Kabbalah*, p. 141 sq.; Jost, *Geschichte des Judenthums u. s. Sekten*, iii, 194, 252, 308; Fürst, *Jacob Emden*, in *Literaturbl. des Orients*, 1846, c. 442; also the art. EYBENSCHÜTZ. (B. P.)

Emeran, *Saint*. See EMMERAN.

Emerentiāna, a virgin martyr at Rome, A.D. 304, foster-sister of St. Agnes; commemorated Jan. 23.

Emeria, daughter of St. Patrick, and abbess of Clonbroney, commemorated July 11.

Emeric. See EYMERIC.

Emerīnus (or **Eamenus**), bishop of Limoges in the 3d century.

Emerĭta. (1) Supposed sister of the British king Lucius, whom she followed in his missionary journeys; she was martyred at Coir of the Grisons in Switzerland, and is commemorated Dec. 4. (2) Virgin martyr at Rome, cir. A.D. 257, commemorated Sept. 22.

Emeritense, CONCILIUM. See MERIDA, COUNCIL OF.

Emerĭtus. (1) Donatist bishop of Julia Cæsarea (now Shershell) in Morocco, largely concerned in the Council at Carthage, in June, A.D. 411. (2) Bishop of Macri, in Mauritania, banished by the Council of Carthage, A.D. 484. (3) Eleventh archbishop of Embrun, A.D. 585-610. (4) A reader and martyr at Abitina, in Africa, A.D. 303, commemorated Feb. 11 or 12.

Emerius. (1) Eighth bishop of Saintes, A.D. 562 or 563, and seated by order of king Charibert, although irregularly elected. (2) *Saint*, son of St. Candia, and first abbot of Banyoles, in Catalonia, A.D. 739, commemorated Jan. 27.

Emery, SAMUEL MOODY, D.D., an Episcopal minister, was born in West Newbury, Mass., in 1803, and graduated from Harvard College in 1830. He was ordained by the bishop of Connecticut in 1836, and was called to be rector of the Church in Portland, where he remained in the discharge of his ministerial and parochial duties for the long period of thirty-seven years. Having resigned in 1873, he did not accept another pastorate, but after a time removed to his native place, where he resided about ten years, and died Aug. 16, 1883. See *Boston Advertiser*, Aug. 18, 1883. (J. C. S.)

Emeterius AGRICOLA (*St. Madir* or *Matinus*), is said to have suffered martyrdom near Barcelona, cir. A.D. 680; commemorated March 3.

Emetherius (or **Hæmaterius**), martyr at Calahorro, on the Ebro, commemorated March 3.

Emigdius, first bishop and tutelary saint of Ascolin, in Picenum, suffered martyrdom A.D. 303 or 304, and is commemorated Aug. 5.

Emĭla. (1) Bishop of Barcelona, cir. A.D. 600-615. (2) Bishop of Mentesa, consecrated before A.D. 589. (3) Bishop of Ilici (Elche), A.D. 688. (4) Last bishop of Coimbra under the Goths, A.D. 693. (5) Deacon and martyr at Cordova, under the Saracens, commemorated Sept. 5.

Emiliānus (or **Æmilianus**). (1) First bishop of Valence, in Gaul, A.D. 374. (2) Eleventh bishop of Vercelli, cir. A.D. 500, commemorated Sept. 11. (3) Twenty-second bishop of Vercelli, A.D. 653. (4) Patriarch of Grado, A.D. 749. (5) An Irish bishop, patron of Faenza, in the north of Italy. (6) A hermit in the forest of Ponticiacum, in Auvergne, who died at the age of ninety, in A.D. 538. (7) Called *San Millan*, one of the most famous of Spanish saints, is said to have been born about 473 in Old Castile, and to have been converted by a dream while a shepherd; instructed by St. Felix; fixed his hermitage first at Verdeyo, afterwards in the remotest parts of Burgos, where he passed forty years of ascetic life; was drawn into public life by Didymus, bishop of Tarrazona, and ordained a presbyter; but his utter unworldliness drew upon him the odium of his colleagues, and he finally withdrew to a monastery near Vergegium, where he died, after the most rigorous asceticism, cir. A.D. 572. He is commemorated Nov. 12. His *Life* was written by St. Braulio (who died in A.D. 657), and first published by Sandoval in 1601. There is much legend connected with him. (8) Abbot of Lagny, cir. A.D. 648, commemorated March 10. (9) Martyr in Numidia, A.D. 259, commemorated April 29. (10) Martyr at Dorostorum, in Mœsia, under Julian, commemorated July 18. (11) Deacon, martyred at Cordova, is commemorated Sept. 17. (12) Presbyter and confessor in Tarragona, commemorated Nov. 12.

Emilius (or **Æmilius**). (1) Martyr at Capua under Diocletian, commemorated Oct. 6. (2) A bishop, father of Ia, who was married to Julian of Elana. (3) *Saint*, bishop of Beneventum, A.D. 405; perhaps the same with No. 2.

Eminentius, a Donatist bishop in A.D. 411.

Emitericus (or **Emiterius**), twelfth bishop of Tarentaise, in the middle of the 7th century.

Emmaus, of Luke xxiv, 13. The Sinaitic MS. here reads, one hundred and sixty furlongs, which has been eagerly seized upon as confirming the identification with Nicopolis; but Tischendorf in his last edition of the MS. does not adopt the reading, and the distance as stated by Josephus (*War*, vii, 6, 6) confirms the number sixty. Lieut. Conder is inclined to fix the site of this Emmaus at *Khurbet el-Khamasa*, eight miles from Jerusalem towards Beit-Jibrin, containing ruins of an ancient church (*Memoirs* to the Ordnance Survey, iii, 36).

A full description of the interesting remains at Amwâs (the Emmaus of 1 Macc. iii, 40) is given in the *Memoirs* accompanying the Ordnance Survey (iii, 63 sq.).

Emmaus, now Amwâs. (From Thomson's *Southern Palestine and Jerusalem.*)

Emmerich, Anna Katharina, a German visionary, was born at Flansk (duchy of Münster), Sept. 8, 1774. In 1802 she joined the Augustinians of Dulmen. She had visions when quite young, and in 1798 declared that she had seen Jesus Christ placing on her forehead a crown of thorns. On the suppression of her convent she retired to a private house, where she became subject to new visions, during which she claimed to have received the *stigmata* of the crucifixion, and a cross-mark on her chest. The facts were investigated in 1813 by a physician and an ecclesiastical commission, who seem to have been convinced of their reality, and recorded them, in 1814, in a journal of Salzburg. She died Feb. 9, 1824. See Hoefer, *Nouv. Biog. Générale*, s. v.

Emmerich, Frédéric Charles Timothée, a French theologian, was born at Strasburg, Feb. 25, 1786. After a journey through Germany he went to Paris, and on his return to Strasburg in 1809 was appointed superior of the College of St. Thomas, and professor of ancient languages in the gymnasium, whence he was transferred in 1812 to the Protestant school, and to the theological faculty in 1819. He died June 1, 1820, leaving, *De Evangeliis secundum Hebræos, Ægypteos atque Justinum Martyrem*:—*Choix de Sermons* (1824). See Hoefer, *Nouv. Biog. Générale*, s. v.

Emmerling, Christian August Gottfried, a Lutheran theologian of Germany, was born June 6, 1781. He studied at Leipsic, was in 1805 catechist, and in 1810 preacher there; in 1811 became assistant to the pastor of Probstheyda, near Leipsic, and in 1814 was appointed to the pastorate of that place. He died Jan. 22, 1827, leaving, *De Paulo Felicem Institutionis suæ Successum Prædicante*, 2 *Cor*. 2, 14–17 (Leipsic, 1809):—*C. A. Th. Keilii Elementa Hermeneutices Novi Testamenti* (ibid. 1811):—*Pauli Epistola ad Corinthios posterior* (ibid. 1823). See Döring, *Die gelehrten Theologen Deutschlands*, s. v.; Winer, *Handbuch der theol. Lit*. i, 107, 260. (B. P.)

Empereur, Constantine Le. See L'Empereur.

Emphotium (ἐμφώτιον) is one of the names for the white robe with which persons were invested at baptism. The name is no doubt derived from the "enlightening" attributed to the baptismal ceremony. See Baptism.

Emphytensis (ἐμφύτενσις) is a contract by which the beneficial ownership of real property is transferred by the proprietor to another, either for a term of not less than ten years, or for a life or lives, or in perpetuity, in consideration of an annual payment. It differs from letting in that it applies only to real property, and must last for at least ten years; while in letting only the use and enjoyment of produce is transferred. It is unlike feudal tenure in that it requires periodical payment, not personal service.

Ecclesiastical emphytensis is a contract by which property belonging to a church, monastery, or other religious foundation, is granted. It requires the assent of the bishop, and must be for the benefit of the body granting it. This precaution is taken to check the alienation of church property. See Alienation.

Empie, Adam, D.D., a Protestant Episcopal minisister, was born at Schenectady, N. Y. He graduated from Union College; studied medicine at Columbia College; then studied theology; was ordained deacon in 1809, and his first charge was in Hempstead, L. I., where he also taught the classics; became pastor of St. James's, Wilmington, Del., in 1811; in 1814 received an appointment as chaplain and professor of rhetoric in the United States Military Academy, West Point, N. Y.; became rector again at St. James's parish, Wilmington, in 1815; president of the College of William and Mary, Virginia, in 1827; resigned the presidency in 1836; was temporarily principal of the diocesan school at Raleigh, N. C.; removed in 1837 to Richmond, Va., becoming rector of St. James's, where he remained until declining health compelled his retirement. He returned to Wilmington in 1859, and died there Nov. 6, 1860, aged seventy-five years. Dr. Empie led a laborious life. He represented his church in Virginia on several occasions in the General Convention. Among his literary remains is a volume of *Sermons*, published in 1856. See *Amer. Quar. Church Rev*. 1861, p. 698.

Empire, Roman. See Roman Empire.

Emporagius, Eric Gabriel, a Swedish theologian, studied at Upsal, and taught physics there in 1637, and theology in 1641; was received as doctor by that faculty in 1647, and in 1654, after having filled other ecclesiastical positions, was appointed bishop of Strengnäs. He died March 14, 1674, leaving, among other writings, *Admonitio Consolatoria*, etc. (Upsal, 1629):—*De Rerum Duratione* (ibid. 1631):—*Hexialogicæ* (ibid. 1636):—*De Disciplina Ecclesiastica* (Stockholm, 1661). See Hoefer, *Nouv. Biog. Générale*, s. v.

Empyrean (Gr. ἐν, *in*, and πῦρ, *fire*), a name sometimes given to heaven, the special residence of deity, from the burning splendor with which it is supposed to be invested.

Enam. Lieut. Conder suggests (*Tent Work in Palest*. ii, 336; comp. *Quar. Statement* of the "Pal. Explor. Fund," Jan. 1881, p. 51) for this place "the ruin *Allin*, in the low hills south-west of Jerusalem," meaning apparently the insignificant *Khurbet 'Alia* marked on the ordnance map at three and one quarter miles south-west of Bethlehem, but there is nothing striking in the identification.

Enander, Samuel, a Swedish prelate, was born at Eneby in 1607. After fulfilling several ecclesiastical function, she was appointed bishop of Linköping. He died in 1670. His principal works are, *De Intellectu et Voluntate Hominis* (Upsal, 1629):—*De Sensibus Interioribus* (ibid. 1632):—*De Mundo* (ibid. 1634). See Hoefer, *Nouv. Biog. Générale*, s. v.

Encheirium (ἐγχείριον) is the napkin with which the priest wipes his hands, and which he wears at the girdle. Germanus of Constantinople describes it as above, and says that "to have a napkin at the girdle is typical of him who washed his hands and said, 'I am innocent' (Matt. xxvii, 24)."

Encolpium (ἐγκόλπιον) is a portable reliquary, worn around the neck. Such ornaments are of the highest antiquity. Chrysostom speaks of particles of the true cross, encased in gold, being suspended from the neck. The pectoral cross (q. v.), worn by the bishops, was also called *Encolpium*. Such are first mentioned by Gregory the Great. He sent one to Theodelinda containing a fragment of the cross; it still exists at Monza, and is used by the provost of that ancient church when he officiates pontifically. Two amulets, given to this princess by the same pontiff for the use of her children, are preserved in the treasures of Monza. From Gregory we also learn that filings from St. Peter's chains were sometimes enclosed in golden keys. Gregory himself had sent one of these consecrated keys to Childebert, king of the Franks, to protect him from all evils. See Reliquary.

Pectoral Cross.

Encratis, *Saint*. See Engratia.

Endemann, Samuel, a Reformed theologian of Germany, was born March 18, 1727, at Carlsdorf. He studied at Marburg and Rinteln, was in 1750 preacher at Jesberg, in Hesse, and in 1753 at Hanau. In 1766 he was appointed member of consistory, and in 1767 became professor of theology and Hebrew at the gymnasium in the latter place. In 1782 he accepted a call as professor of theology to Marburg, and died there May 31, 1789, leaving, *Institutiones Theologiæ Dogmaticæ* (Hanover, 1777, 2 vols.):—*Institutiones Theologiæ Mo-*

ralis (Frankfort, 1780, 2 vols.):—*Compendium Theologiæ* (ibid. 1782):—*Sciagraphia* (Marburg, 1783):—*Compendium Theologiæ Moralis* (Frankfort, 1784). His *Compendium Theologiæ Dogmaticæ* was edited and published by A. J. Arnoldi (Hanover, 1790). See Döring, *Die gelehrten Theologen Deutschlands*, s. v.; Winer, *Handbuch der theol. Lit.* i, 305, 313. (B. P.)

Endowment, in ecclesiastical phrase, is the property given by the founder of a church for its maintenance, including the pay of the clerks. Justinian compelled those who built churches to endow them; without competent provision for support no clerk was ordained to any church; whoever desired a parish church on his estate was to set apart a landed endowment for its clerks (A.D. 541); a bishop was not to consecrate a church until the endowment of it had been regularly secured by a deed or charter (A.D. 572); founders of churches were to understand that they had no further authority over property which they had given to the Church, but that both the Church and its endowment were at the disposition of the bishop, to be employed according to the canons (A.D. 633). According to the ninth Council of Toledo, A.D. 655, a bishop was not to confer on any monastic church in his diocese more than a fiftieth part of the Church funds; and on a non-monastic church, or church designed for his own burial-place, not more than a one-hundredth part. The royal confirmation was required if one who held a fief from the king endowed a church.

Endress, CHRISTIAN, D.D., a Lutheran minister, was born in Philadelphia, Pa., March 12, 1775. He graduated from the University of Pennsylvania in 1790; in 1792 was appointed tutor in the same university; preached his first sermon at Zion's Church, Philadelphia, in 1793; in 1795 was elected principal of the Congregational school of Zion and St. Michael; in 1801 resigned and removed to Easton, having accepted a call to the Lutheran Church in that place, and while there preached frequently to neighboring congregations. Until 1799 he was subject to the superintendence of the minister or ministers of the Church in Philadelphia, but at the last-mentioned date he received a license from the ministerium of Pennsylvania, and was ordained at Reading in 1802. In 1815 he was chosen pastor of the Lutheran congregation at Lancaster, and died there in September, 1827. See Sprague, *Annals of the Amer. Pulpit*, IX, i, 107; *Evangelical Review*, vi, 22.

Énée, a French prelate and theologian, was notary or secretary to Charles the Bald, and was famed for his honesty and merit. In A.D. 853 he was elected bishop of Paris. On June 14, 859, he assisted at the Council of Savonnières, near Toul; in 861 at that of Pitres-sur-Seine, near Rouen; in 862 at that of Soissons; in 864 at the second at Pitres-sur-Seine; in August, 866, at that of Soissons, and October, 867, that of Troyes. He was also at the Council of Verberie on April 24, 869; in August, the same year, at that of Pitres-sur-Seine; and finally, in May, 870, at that of Attigny. After various other services to the Church and State, Énée was made abbot of St. Denis and grand chancellor of the palace. He died Dec. 27, 870, leaving a book against Photius and the errors of the Greeks (printed in vol. vii of the *Spicilegium* of D'Achery and in vol. viii of Labbe and Cossart's *Concilia*). See Hoefer, *Nouv. Biog. Générale*, s. v.

Engadine, UPPER AND LOWER VERSION. See ROMANESE VERSION.

En-gannim *of Judah*. For this site Lieut. Conder suggests (*Tent Work in Palest.* ii, 336; comp. *Quar. Statement* of the "Pal. Explor. Soc." Jan. 1881, p. 51) the small ruin called *Khurbet Um-Jina*, laid down on the Ordnance Map on the south edge of Wady Surar, about three fourths of a mile south-west of Ain-Shems (Beth-shemesh), and in this identification Tristram concurs (*Bible Places*, p. 48).

Engastrimythi (Gr. ἐν, *in*, γαστήρ, *the belly*, and μῦθος, *an utterance*), a name given to the priestesses of Apollo, from a species of ventriloquism which they practiced, speaking from within, while not the slightest motion of the lips could be observed. The voice was supposed to proceed from a spirit within the body of the Pythoness (q. v.).

En-gedi. See ZIZ.

Engel, Arnold, a Dutch poet and theologian, was born at Maestricht in 1620. He belonged to the Jesuits, taught theology, and died at Prague in 1676, leaving several works in Latin verse, for which see Hoefer, *Nouv. Biog. Générale*, s. v.

Engel, Moritz Erdmann, a Lutheran theologian of Germany, was born at Plauen, July 29, 1767, where he also died, Feb. 10, 1836. He wrote, *Geist der Bibel für Schule und Haus* (13th ed. Leipsic, 1846):—*Die Religion nach Vernunft und Schrift* (8th ed. Plauen, 1848):—*Die Augsburgische Confession als des Evangeliums Kern und Zeugniss* (Leipsic, 1830). See Zuchold, *Bibl. Theol.* i, 320; Winer, *Handbuch der theol. Lit.* ii, 232, 248, 261, 266, 316, 368. (B. P.)

Engelbert *the Frank*. See ANGILBERT.

Engelbrechtsen (or **Engelberts**), CORNELIS, an old Dutch painter, was born at Leyden in 1468, and studied the works of Hans van Eyck. The following are some of his noted pieces: *The Taking down from the Cross; Abraham about to Sacrifice Isaac; Scenes from the Life of the Virgin*. His best work, however, was an altar-piece in the Church of St. Peter, at Leyden, representing the *Adoration of the Lamb*, as described in the Apocalypse. He died at Leyden in 1533. See Spooner, *Biog. Hist. of the Fine Arts*, s. v.; Hoefer, *Nouv. Biog. Générale*, s. v.

Engelcken, Heinrich Ascanius, a Lutheran theologian of Germany, was born at Rostock, Aug. 15, 1675. He studied at the universities of his native place and Leipsic, was in 1704 professor at Rostock, in 1713 superintendent and pastor of St. George's at Parchim, and died Jan. 13, 1734. He published a number of theological dissertations. See Jöcher, *Allgemeines Gelehrten-Lexikon*, s. v. (B. P.)

Engelcken, Hermann Christoph, a Lutheran theologian of Germany, was born at Jennervitz, in Mecklenburg, June 9, 1679. He studied at different universities, was in 1709 pastor of St. John's at Rostock, in 1710 doctor of divinity, and in 1716 professor of theology there. He died Jan. 2, 1742, leaving, *Miraculum Dilacerati a Simsone Inermi Leonis*:—*De Deo Israelis Perditore ad Hos. xiii*, 9:—*Vindicatio Psalm. ciii, cxlv, et cxlix*:—*De Dogmate Transubstantiationis*:—*De Resurrectione Mystica*:—*De Gentilium Salute non Speranda*:—*De Expulsione Principis Mundi Joh. xii*, 31:—*De die Christi Viso ab Abrahamo, Joh. viii*, 56:—*De Paulo Christi Cognitionem Omnibus aliis Rebus Anteponente*:—*De Jesaia de Vita Christi Resuscitati Vaticinante cap. liii*, 8. See Jöcher, *Allgemeines Gelehrten-Lexikon*, s. v.; Neubauer, *Nachricht von jetztlebenden Gottesgelehrten*, s. v.; Steinschneider, *Bibl. Handbuch*, s. v. (B. P.)

Engelen (Lat. *Angelis*), WILLEM VAN, a Dutch theologian, was born at Bois-le-Duc, Sept. 1, 1583. He commenced his studies in his native town, and finished them at Louvain, under the direction of Rausin, Follega, and Malderus. In 1606 he taught both Greek and philosophy at the College of Porc; was received into orders in 1607; in 1614 appointed canon of St. Pierre and professor of morals; in 1616 elected president of the College of Viglius, and was made doctor of theology on Oct. 11 of the same year; in 1646 became president of the College of Pope Adrian VI; in 1648 was appointed to the bishopric of Ruremond, but died at Louvain, Feb. 3, 1649, without having received his bulla from Rome. He was celebrated in dogmatical theology and scholastics, and vigorously opposed the doctrines of Jansenius.

He left, *Den Deckmantel des Catholyckenaems*, etc. (Louvain, 1630), which specially attacked Vaët, Udemans, van Swalmen, and Everwyn:—*Relation des Troubles à Louvain*, etc. (1641):—*Protestatio Theologarum Lovani* (1642). See Hoefer, *Nouv. Biog. Générale*, s. v.

Engelgrave, Assuerus, a Belgian monk, brother of the following, was born at Antwerp. He took the habit of a Dominican there, and gained great reputation as a preacher in Brabant and Flanders. He died in the prime of life, July 21, 1640, leaving *Conciones Variæ*. See Hoefer, *Nouv. Biog. Générale*, s. v.

Engelgrave, Hans Baptist, a Belgian theologian, was born at Antwerp in 1601. He joined the Jesuits in 1619, assisted at the ninth general assembly of the society at Rome, became rector of the College of Bruges, was twice provincial of Flanders, and finally superior of the house at Antwerp, where he died, May 3, 1658, leaving, *Meditationes in Omnes Dominicas* (Antwerp, 1658):—*Dominicales et Festivales* (Cologne, 1659). See Hoefer, *Nouv. Biog. Générale*, s. v.

Engelgrave, Hendrik, a Belgian theologian, brother of the preceding, was born at Antwerp in 1610. He joined the society of Jesus in 1628; became successively director and then præfect of the lower classes; directed for fifteen years several convents; became rector of the colleges of Oudenarde, Cassel, and Bruges, being surnamed the *Magazine of Sciences*, on account of his extended knowledge; and died at Antwerp, March 8, 1670, leaving, *Cœleste Pantheon* (Cologne, 1647):—*Lux Evangelica*, etc. (Antwerp, 1648; inserted in the Index at Rome on July 27, 1686, but reprinted several times):—*Cœleste Empyreum* (Cologne, 1668):—*Meditatien ofte Saete Bemerkingen* (Antwerp, 1670):—*Divum Domus Facta*, etc. (Cologne, 1688):—*Commentaria in Evangelia Quadragesimæ* (ibid. 1725):—and several pieces of poetry in Latin, 4to. See Hoefer, *Nouv. Biog. Générale*, s. v.

Engelhardt, Daniel. See ANGELOCRATOR.

Engelhardt, Moritz von, a Lutheran theologian of Germany, was born July 8, 1828, at Dorpat, where he also completed his theological studies. Being advised by his teachers, Philippi, Th. Harnack, and K. F. Keil, to pursue an academical career, he went to Erlangen, where he attended the lectures of Hofmann, Thomasius, and Delitzsch; then to Bonn, where Rothe and Dorner were his teachers, and finally to Berlin, where Hengstenberg lectured. Thus prepared, he returned to his native city, taking the magister-degree by presenting his monograph on *Valentin Ernst Löscher nach seinem Leben und Wirken* (Dorpat, 1853; 2d ed. 1856), and commenced his lectures as a privat-docent. In 1855 he was appointed professor of Church history, and in the following year was made doctor of theology on presenting his *De Tentatione Christi*. In 1864 he published his *Schenkel und Strauss, Zwei Zeugen der Wahrheit*, and in 1878 *Das Christenthum Justins des Märtyrers* (Erlangen; reviewed in Schürer's *Theol. Literaturzeitung*, 1878, 632 sq.). In 1880 his *Sermons*, delivered at the university church, were published, and in 1881 *Die ersten Versuche zur Aufrichtung des wahren Christenthums in einer Gemeinde der Heiligen* (Riga). He died Dec. 5, 1881. See Lichtenberger, *Encyclop. des Sciences Religieuses*, s. v. (B. P.)

Engelschall, CARL GOTTFRIED, a Lutheran theologian of Germany, was born May 5, 1675. He studied at Leipsic and Wittenberg, was in 1698 pastor at Embskirchen, in Bavaria, in 1701 archdeacon at Reichenbach, and in 1707 court-preacher at Dresden. He died March 23, 1738, leaving many ascetical writings. See Jöcher, *Allgemeines Gelehrten-Lexikon*, s. v. (B. P.)

Engenhagen, HEINRICH, a Lutheran theologian of Germany, was born at Lübeck, April 26, 1615. In 1643 he was appointed deacon at St. James's, in his native place, became its pastor in 1662, and died Sept. 1, 1685. See Jöcher, *Allgemeines Gelehrten-Lexikon*, s. v. (B. P.)

Engeström, JOHANN, a Lutheran doctor of theology, of Sweden, and bishop of Lund, who was born in 1699, and died May 16, 1777, is the author of *Grammatica Hebræa Biblica* (Lund, 1734). See Jöcher, *Allgemeines Gelehrten-Lexikon*, s. v.; Steinschneider, *Bibliographisches Handbuch*, s. v. (B. P.)

Enghein, FRANÇOIS D', a Belgian theologian, was born at Brussels in 1648. He took the habit of a Dominican at Ghent, and finished his studies at Louvain, where he was made doctor of theology, Jan. 21, 1685, and taught successively philosophy and theology. Having become director of the studies of his order, he assisted at the chapter-general which assembled at Rome in 1694, and after a very long sojourn with pope Clement XI, came back in 1703 to take up again his functions at Louvain. In 1706 he refused the bishopric of Antwerp, and retired to Ghent, where he spent the rest of his days in study, and died Nov. 9, 1722, leaving, *De Potestate Ecclesiastica* (Cologne, 1685):—*Auctoritas Sedis Apostolicæ* (ibid. 1689):—*Vindiciæ Adversus Avitum Academicum*:—*De Doctrina S. Thomæ ad Gratiam Efficacem* (Louvain, 1703):—*Contra Constitutionem Sedis Apostolicæ Unigenitus* (Ghent, 1715). See Hoefer, *Nouv. Biog. Générale*, s. v.

Engil, a word which very frequently occurs in the Koran, and denotes the Gospel or New Test. as distinguished from the *Taourat*, the Law or Old Test. Mohammedans generally understand by *Engil*, as used in the Koran, an imaginary gospel, which they say was sent by God from heaven to Jesus Christ, and of which nothing remains but what is cited in the Koran; while the gospel which is in the hands of Christians they regard as corrupted.

Engilbert. See ANGILBERT.

England, JOHN, a Roman Catholic prelate, was born in Cork, Ireland, Sept. 23, 1786, and was educated at Carlow. He was ordained priest Oct. 9, 1808, and appointed lecturer at the North Chapel in Cork, and chaplain of the prisons. In May, 1808, he began the publication of a monthly magazine called *The Religious Repertory*. He was made president of the theological college of St. Mary in 1812, and in 1817 parish priest at Brandon; 1820, was appointed bishop of the new diocese of Charleston, S. C., where he established an academy and theological seminary, and taught in both of them. He went to Rome in 1832, and was appointed by the pope apostolic legate to Hayti. He died at Charleston, April 11, 1842. Bp. England founded several religious and charitable institutions at Cork, and left a number of writings, most of which appeared in the periodical press. A complete edition of his works was prepared by bishop Reynolds (Baltimore, 1849, 5 vols. 8vo).

Englert, Johann, a Lutheran theologian of Germany, was born at Schweinfurt, Dec. 29, 1688. He studied at Leipsic, was in 1713 preacher at Oberdorf, and in 1715 sub-deacon at his native place. In 1725 he was appointed professor of theology and of Hebrew at the gymnasium there, and in 1732 he succeeded his father, Johann Matthäus (q. v.), as pastor primarius and inspector of the gymnasium, and died Feb. 25, 1751. He published, *Disp. de Paschate Jesu Christu Ultimo* (Schweinfurt, 1725; Jena, 1726):—*Disp. de Singulari Dei Providentia Circa Scholas* (Schweinfurt, 1734):—*Quæstiones in Tria Prima Capita Geneseos* (ibid. 1744). See Jöcher, *Allgemeines Gelehrten-Lexikon*, s. v.; Neubauer, *Jetztlebende Theologen*, s. v. (B. P.)

Englert, Johann Matthäus, a Lutheran minister of Germany, was born Jan. 14, 1661, at Schweinfurt; studied at Giessen, Leipsic, and Wittenberg; was in 1687 called to his native place as teacher of the high-school; in 1709, accepted the appointment as deacon, and died in 1732, pastor primarius and inspector of the gymnasium. He is the author of several hymns. See Wezel, *Anal. Hymn.* i, 53 sq.; Koch, *Geschichte des deutschen Kirchen-*

liedes, v, 410 sq.; Jöcher, *Allgemeines Gelehrten-Lexikon*, s. v. (B. P.)

Englert, Johann Wilhelm, was born at Schweinfurt, Dec. 10, 1706, where he was also appointed pastor of St. Saviour in 1732. In 1737 he was made subdeacon of St. John's, in 1751 deacon and professor of theology, in 1754 archdeacon, and in 1764 pastor primarius and inspector of the gymnasium. He died in 1768, leaving, among other treatises, *Disp. de Indulgentiæ Judæorum Paschalis Tempore Modoque* (Giessen, 1731). See Jöcher, *Allgemeines Gelehrten-Lexikon*, s. v. (B. P.)

English Nuns, a society founded in the 17th century, by Maria Ward, and originally intended for the education of youth. The first convent was established at St. Omer; there were soon others opened at Rome, in other parts of Italy, and in Munich. Doubts concerning the orthodoxy of the opinions held by the founder led to their suppression by Urban VIII in 1630. Yet they were not destroyed, and were formally re-established by Clement XI in 1703. Aside from education, they also devoted themselves to the care of the sick. The congregation recognises three degrees: noble ladies, civilian maidens, and serving sisters; yet they make no difference in their dress or mode of life. The superiors are always chosen from the first degree. See Herzog, *Real-Encyklop.* s. v.

Engratia (Encratis, or **Eugracia)**, a Spanish saint, lived at Saragossa in 304. She was persecuted as a Christian under the emperors Diocletian and Maximin Hercules, and suffered, as reported by Prudentius, most fearful tortures. Nevertheless Engratia "recovered with the time," and in spite of her wounds died at an advanced age. Her relics are preserved at Saragossa, and she is commemorated April 16. See Hoefer, *Nouv. Biog. Générale*, s. v.

Engstfeld, Peter Friedrich, a German hymn writer, was born June 6, 1793, at Heiligenhaus, near Elberfeld, and died Oct. 4, 1848. His hymns are published in *Zeugnisse aus dem verborgenen Leben* (Essen, 1840; 2d ed. 1846). See Koch, *Geschichte des deutschen Kirchenliedes*, vii, 296 sq. (B. P.)

En-haddah. As the modern representative of this site Lieut. Conder suggests (*Tent Work in Palest.* ii, 336; comp. *Quar. Statement* of the "Pal. Explor. Fund," Jan. 1881, p. 51) *Kefr Adân*, on the south edge of the plain of Esdraelon, three miles north-west of Jenin (Engannim), which the *Memoirs* to the Ordnance Survey (ii, 45) describe as "a village of moderate size on the slope of the hills, built of stone, with olives below and a well on the west. This appears to be the *Kefr Outheni* of the Talmud, a village on the border between Samaria and Galilee (Mishna, *Gittin*, vii, 7)."

En-hakkore. Lieut. Conder is inclined to find this spot in a series of springs to which he gives the name of *'Ayûn Kâra* (*Tent Work in Palest.* ii, 336), and which are laid down on the Ordnance Map three and one half miles north-west of Ain-Shemis (Beth-shemesh). But the identification is precarious. See Lehi.

Enimia (or **Emmia**), *Saint*, a Frankish princess, lived in 631. She was, according to some hagiographers, the sister or daughter of king Dagobert I. She retired about 631 into the mountains of Gévaudan, near the source of the Tarn, and constructed there a double monastery for both sexes. After having been consecrated by St. Llare, bishop of Javoux (now Mende), Enimia took the title of an abbess, and died in the government of her communities. She is commemorated Oct. 6. See Hoefer, *Nouv. Biog. Générale*, s. v.

Enjedin, Georg, a Transylvanian Socinian, who was born about 1550, and died Nov. 28, 1597, superintendent of the Socinian congregations in Transylvania, is the author of, *Explicatio Locorum Scripturæ Vet. et Novi Test. ex quibus Trinitatis Dogma Stabiliri Solet:—Explicatio Locorum Catechesis Raccoviensis.* See Jöcher, *Allgemeines Gelehrten-Lexikon*, s. v. (B. P.)

Enna (Lat. *Endeus*) is the name of several Irish saints, the most noted of whom was the son of Conall Derg, chief of the Oriels, whom he succeeded on the throne, and became a famous warrior. Being suddenly converted to Christianity, he renounced the throne, and after studying in the monastery of Mansenus, in Britain, thence went to Rome, and, returning to his native land, became abbot of Aran, in Killeany bay, where he probably died, cir. A.D. 542. He is commemorated March 21.

Ennathas, *Saint*, a virgin, martyred in Palestine under Diocletian, by being scourged through the streets of Cæsarea, and then burned. She is commemorated Nov. 13.

Ennemond, *Saint.* See Annemondus.

Enoch, the translated patriarch, is commemorated in some calendars of saints on Jan. 22 or July 19.

Ens (or **Enzo**), **Giuseppe**, called *the Younger*, was a court painter to Ridolfo II, and flourished about 1660. In his celebrated *Tomb of Christ*, at Ognissanti, he styled himself *Jos. Heinsius.* He gained such an immense reputation in his time for his pictures, that pope Urban VIII made him a chevalier of the Order of the Holy Cross. He painted several altar-pieces for the churches of Venice. See Spooner, *Biog. Hist. of the Fine Arts*, s. v.

Ens, Jan, a Protestant theologian of Holland, was born at Quadyck in West Frisia, May 9, 1682. He studied at Leyden, was in 1720 professor of theology at Utrecht, where he died, Jan. 6, 1723, leaving, *Bibliotheca Sacra:—Aanmerkinger over Iesaias xi en xii:—Oratio Inauguralis de Persecutione Juliani.* See Jöcher, *Allgemeines Gelehrten-Lexikon*, s. v.; Winer, *Handbuch der theol. Lit.* i, 332. (B. P.)

Entalma (ἔνταλμα) is the Greek name of the document by which a bishop confers on a monk the privilege of hearing confessions.

Enthronistic Letters were letters anciently addressed by newly installed bishops to foreign bishops, announcing their promotion to the episcopal office, and giving an account of their faith and orthodoxy. They received in return letters of peace and Christian fellowship. A failure to send such messages was regarded as an indication of a withdrawal from communion with the rest of the Christian world.

ENTHRONISTIC Sermon is the sermon preached by a bishop on the occasion of his enthronization (q. v.).

Enthronization. (1) The solemn placing of a bishop on his throne. See Bishop.

(2) The word is also used to designate the placing or "enthroning" of relics of the saints in the altar of a church, on consecration. See Consecration of Churches.

(3) The installation of a presbyter is sometimes designated by the same word.

Enthusiastæ. Those who pretended to prophesy by the motion of an indwelling dæmon, which they thought to be the Holy Spirit. See Euchites.

Entrance. Two of the most remarkable ceremonies of the Eastern Liturgies are the Lesser and the Greater Entrance—that of the word and that of the sacrament.

I. *The Lesser Entrance* is the bearing in of the book of the gospels in solemn procession.

> "Then the priest and the deacon, standing before the holy table, make three genuflections. Then the priest, taking the holy book out of the Gospels, gives it to the deacon; and so, going out by the north side, with lights going before them, they make the lesser entrance."

That is, the deacon and priest pass from the sanctuary into the chapel of the prothesis, which is to the north of it, and so out into the body of the church, where, by a devious path, they return to the holy doors, which are open; the volume, often decorated with great magnificence, is laid on the holy table, whence it is again taken to the ambo, when the gospel is to be read.

This "Entrance" corresponds to the carrying of the gospel by the deacon to the ambo or rood-loft in the Western Church, once a rite of great importance; for the book was preceded not only by tapers, but by a crucifix.

II. *The Greater Entrance.* This ceremony has, like others, been developed from very small beginnings into great prominence and magnificence.

The liturgy of St. James simply alludes, in passing, to the bringing in of the elements. St. Mark's liturgy is even more vague.

In the Armenian rite the celebrant lies prostrate before the altar while the Great Entrance is made; in this rite (anomalously) the elements are spoken of as the body and blood of Christ *before* consecration.

In the much more developed rite of Constantinople, after the chanting of the Cherubic hymn, the ceremony proceeds as follows:

During the previous part of the eucharistic office, the elements have remained on the table in the chapel of the prothesis. At the proper point, the deacon censes the altar and the sanctuary, and then goes before the priest into the prothesis. The priest then lifts the "aer," or covering, from the chalice and paten, and lays it on the deacon's shoulder, and then places upon it the paten, covered with the asterisk and veil. The deacon takes hold of these with his left hand, bearing the censer in his right; the priest takes the chalice and follows the deacon, and so, preceded by tapers, they move round to the holy doors, as in the lesser entrance. In great churches, where there are dignified clergy and many attendants, this procession is one of great magnificence. Where there is but a single priest and no deacon, he bears the paten on his shoulder, supporting it by his left hand, and the chalice in his right hand before his breast.

In the Coptic St. Basil, the Great Entrance is made at the very beginning of the liturgy; the directions for it are very curious and minute.

"The priest goes to the Takaddemet (Prothesis) from which he shall take the lamb (i. e. loaf), looking attentively that there be no flaw in it.... When he hath all that he needs, the lamb, the wine, and the incense,... he takes the lamb in his hand and wipes it lightly, as Christ the Lord was first washed with water before he was presented to Simeon the priest; then he shall bear it round to the altar in his hands, as Simeon bare him round the temple. At last the priest shall lay it down on the altar and shall place it on the paten, which signifies the cradle; and shall cover it with a linen cloth, as the Virgin did at his Nativity."

A deacon seems to have borne the cruet. See INTROIT.

Entry INTO JERUSALEM. This event in our Lord's life is very frequently represented in the earlier art of the Christian Church, occurring on some of the first sarcophagi, though not, it seems, in fresco or mosaic in the catacombs or elsewhere, except in an ancient mosaic of the Vatican, and one from the basilica at Bethlehem. The earliest MS. representation of it is probably that in the Rabula or Laurentian Evangeliary. The treatment is almost always the same; the Lord is mounted on the ass, sometimes accompanied by her foal, and the multitude with their palm-branches follow, or lay their garments before him. His right hand is generally raised in the act of blessing. The multitude frequently raise their hands in thanksgiving. In one of the oldest MSS. of the New Test. in existence, the Gregorian Evangeliary of St. Cuthbert, the Lord is represented mounted on an ass, and bearing a large whip—evidently with reference to the scourge of small cords used in the expulsion of buyers and sellers from the temple. There is a certain variety in the examples taken from the different carvings. Sometimes Zacchæus is represented in the "fig or sycamore tree" behind the Lord, as if to call attention to the beginning of his last journey at Jericho.

Christ's Entry into Jerusalem. (From the Sarcophagus of Junius Bassus.)

Entychites, a sect of the followers of Simon, who, according to Clemens Alex. (*Stromata*, vii, 17; p. 900), derived this name from their promiscuous (ἐντυγχάνω) sexual intercourse at the night meetings. Others write the name *Eutychites* or *Euchites*.

Envy was always reckoned an odious sin, and one of the first magnitude; but there are no distinct penalties attached to it, inasmuch as, before it could bring a man under public discipline, it required to be displayed in some outward and vicious action, which received its appropriate punishment.

Eonus (or **Æonius**), a French saint, was of noble birth, and became bishop of Arles, A.D. 492. He assisted, Sept. 2, 499, at the conference between the Catholic bishops of Burgundy and the Arian prelates at Lyons, in the presence of Gondeband, king of Burgundy, who favored Arianism. About the same time Eonus was involved in the dispute with Avitus of Vienne, concerning the primatial right of their respective churches, which was brought before pope Symmachus, and finally decided in favor of the see of Arles. Eonus was allied with Ruricius of Limoges, and with Pomerus, abbot of Arles, and has left us his correspondence with those saints. He died Aug. 16, 502, and is commemorated on Aug. 30. See Hoefer, *Nouv. Biog. Générale*, s. v.; Smith, *Dict. of Christ. Biog.* s. v.

Epact. In determining the epact we either find the number of days required to make up the lunar to the solar year, and so the numeral of the moon's age on Jan. 1, or, with Scaliger, we may use March 1, which comes to the same thing, and has the advantage of avoiding the ambiguity of leap-year. The old Latin cycles of eighty-four years indicated Easter by means of the epacts of Jan. 1, and the day of the week on which Jan. 1 fell.

The method of determining the months (lunar) was as follows: For the first month of the year, that month was taken whose age was expressed by the epact. The day of December on which it commenced is found by subtracting the epact (when more than one) from thirty-three. The first month was always counted full, then hollow and full succeeded by turns, so that the last month in the year, in a common lunar year, was hollow, in an intercalary year full. From the last begins the new moon of the following year.

The Easter new moon being found, Easter-day was, according to the Latin rules, that Sunday which fell on or next after the 16th of the moon, not therefore later than the 22d of the moon. The choice of the month was determined thus: New moon must not be earlier than March 5, and full moon not later than March 21; the first of these rules sometimes having to give way to save the violation of the latter.

The following rule is given for the epact of Jan. 1, viz., multiply the golden number by eleven, and divide the product by thirty, the remainder is the epact. But this rule will not give the epacts mentioned above, which were constructed as we have just described—with a saltus lunæ, or addition of twelve after the 19th year of the cycle, etc.

Ephes-damnum. The ruined site, *Damûn*, proposed by Van de Velde for this place does not appear on the *Ordnance Map;* and Lieutenant Conder suggests as an identification (*Tent Work in Palestine*, ii, 336), a place in the same general vicinity called *Beit-Fased*, lying one and three quarter miles south of Beit-Nettîf.

Ephesus, SEVEN SLEEPERS OF. See SEVEN SLEEPERS.

Ephŏri (Gr. *ἔφοροι, inspectors*), a name sometimes applied by ancient Christian writers to bishops.

Ephraim BEN-SIMSON, a Jewish rabbi, who flourished at the beginning of the 13th century in France, is the author of a commentary on the Pentateuch. Excerpts are made from it by Azulai in his נחל קדומים, and in תורה אור. See Fürst, *Bibl. Jud.* i, 223; De' Rossi, *Dizionario Storico*, p. 94 (Germ. transl.). (B. P.)

Ephrem (or **Ephraim**), patriarch OF ANTIOCH, a Greek theologian, was born in the second part of the 5th century. If the epithet of *Amidian* (ὁ 'Αμίδιος), which Theophanes gives him, indicates the place of his birth, he was born at Amida, in Armenia, near the source of the Tigris. He first had civil employments, and under the reign of Justin I obtained the high dignity of a count of the Orient. In the years 525 and 526 Antioch was almost wholly destroyed by earthquakes, and by fires, which were the consequences of them. The inhabitants, who were touched by the compassion which Ephrem showed for their disasters, and by the help which he extended to them, appointed him successor to the patriarch Euphrasius, who was buried under the ruins of the city. All the writers on Church history praise his conduct as a patriarch, his charity towards the poor, the zeal and vigor with which he opposed heretics. Not satisfied with condemning, in a synod at Antioch, those who tried to revive the errors of Origen, he also wrote divers treatises against the Nestorians, the Eutychians, the Severians, the Acephali, and in favor of the Council of Chalcedon. Towards the end of his life he was forced by the emperor Justinian to subscribe to the condemnation of three of the decrees of the Council of Chalcedon, which he had there so warmly defended. Ephrem died A.D. 545. His works are known to us only by their analysis, which Photius has given in his *Bibliotheca;* they made together three volumes, which were consecrated to the defense of the dogmas of the Church, and particularly of the decrees of the Council of Chalcedon. The first volume contained a letter to Zenobius, advocate of Emessa, and member of the sect of the Acephali; letters to the emperor Justinian; to Anthimus, bishop of Trapezus; to Dometianus Syncleticus, metropolitan of Tarsus; to Brazes the Persian, and to others. The acts of a synod (*συνοδιχὴ πρᾶξις*) were kept by Ephrem, on the subject of certain heterodox books, panegyrics, and other discourses. The second volume contained a treatise in four books, in defense of Cyril of Alexandria, and of the Synod of Chalcedon, against the Nestorians, the Eutychians, and responses on the theological subjects to the advocate Anatolius. See Hoefer, *Nouv. Biog. Générale*, s. v.; Smith, *Dict. of Christ. Biog.* s. v.

Ephrem, patriarch OF ARMENIA, was born at Sis in 1734. The objects of his study were poetry, eloquence, theology, history, and chronology. The pope appointed him bishop *in partibus*, on account of his talent and of the influence which he possessed with the united Armenians. After the death of his brother, Gabriel, in 1771, he was raised to the patriarchal see of Sis, and died in 1784, leaving, *Explanation of the Psalms of David: — Collection of Sacred and Profane Poetry: — A Poem on Genesis: — Rules of Armenian Versification: — Collection of Letters*, both in prose and in verse: — *Chronological History of the Armenian Patriarchs of Cilicia.* See Hoefer, *Nouv. Biog. Générale*, s. v.

Ephrem, *Saint*, bishop OF MYLASA, in Caria, lived anterior to the 5th century, and is commemorated Jan. 24 at Leuca, near Mylasa, where he had been interred. See Hoefer, *Nouv. Biog. Générale*, s. v.

Epictētus, a Roman Stoic philosopher, was born at Hierapolis, Phrygia, in the 1st century, and while young was a slave of Epaphroditus. When he became a freedman is not known. He was involved in the proscription by which Domitian banished all philosophers from Rome, and retired to Nicopolis, in Epirus, where he opened a school of Stoic philosophy, and held those conversations which have been preserved in the *Manual* and philosophical lectures, compiled from his discourses by his pupil Arrian. His teachings are summed up in the formula, "Bear and forbear." Recognizing only will and reason, his highest conception of life was to be passionless under whatever circumstances. "Man," he said, "is but a pilot; observe the star, hold the rudder, and be not distracted on thy way." He is supposed to have committed nothing to writing.

Epigonatium (*ἐπιγονάτιον*), a portion of the sacerdotal habit, used in both the Greek and Roman churches, consisting of an appendage somewhat resembling a small maniple, on the right side hanging from the girdle. In the Roman Church it is worn only by the pope. In the Greek Church it is borne by all bishops, and consists of brocade, velvet, or some stiff material, a foot in dimensions, with a cross wrought upon it, and tassels hanging from the three lower corners. It is not used in the English Church. See VESTMENTS.

Epigŏnus, a heresiarch, was a disciple of Noëtus, and came to Rome about A.D. 200, and there propagated his master's opinions. See NOËTIANS.

Epilenæa, sacred games celebrated among the ancient Greeks in the time of vintage, before the invention of the wine-press. They contended with one another in treading the grapes, who should soonest press out the *must*, in the meantime singing the praises of Dionysus, and begging that the *must* might be sweet and good.

Epimanicia, the maniples or hand-pieces of the priests of the Greek Church. They are provided with *epimanicia* for both arms, while the *maniple* (q. v.) of the Romish priesthood is worn on the left hand alone.

Epinicion, a triumphal hymn used in the communion service of the early Church. It consisted of the words, "Holy, holy, holy, Lord God of Hosts!" It has sometimes been confounded with the *Trisagion* (q. v.).

Epiphanians, a branch of the CARPOCRATIANS (q. v.).

Epiphanias, bishop OF ARMENIA, lived in the latter part of the 7th century. After having been one of the most distinguished scholars of the patriarchal school, he retired into a desert near Tevin, whence he was taken to discharge the functions of abbot of the monastery of Sourp Garabed (St. John the Baptist), in the province of Daron, to which dignity was joined the title of bishop of the Mamigonians, borne by Epiphanias for twenty years. In A.D. 629 he assisted at the Council of Garin (Erzerûm), and wrote, *The History of the Monastery of Sourp Garabed: — The History of the Council at Ephesus: — Commentary on the Psalms of David and on the Book of Proverbs: — Sermons.* See Hoefer, *Nouv. Biog. Générale*, s. v.

Epiphanius, fourteenth bishop and fifth patriarch OF CONSTANTINOPLE, A.D. 520–535, seems to have been a quiet and prudent person, well fitted for that violent age, when the great popular sedition occurred in that city (A.D. 531), and when the emperors prescribed the policy of the Church. His letters to pope Hormisdas are extant, also the sentence of the court which he held against Severus and Peter (Migne, *Patrol. Græc.* lxxxvi, 783 sq.).

Epiphanius OF JERUSALEM, a Greek hagiographer, lived probably in the 12th century. Allatius (*De Symeonum Scriptis*, p. 106) and Fabricius (*Codex Apogryph.* n. 2) have given an extract from the *Life of the Virgin* by this author; the entire work has been published since in the *Anecdota Literaria* of Amodutius. Epiphanius is also the author of a *History of St. Andrew*, the apostle (Allatius, *De Symeonum Scriptis*, p. 90), and of a *Description of Jerusalem* (published by Ferdinand Morelli in his *Expositio Thematum*, Paris, 1620, and by Allatius, *Σύμμιχτα*). A MS. in the Bodleian Library contains a treatise entitled *Epiphanii Monachi et Presbyteri, Character B. Virginis et Domini Nostri*, which differs from the *Life of the Virgin* cited above, but seems to be by the same author. The same is also true of the MS. entitled *De Dissidio quatuor Evangelistarum Circa Resurrectionem Christi*, which is found in the same library. See Hoefer, *Nouv. Biog. Générale*, s. v.

Epiphanius THE YOUNGER, bishop of Constantia, lived about the end of the 7th century. He was represented at the third General Council of Constantinople, in A.D. 680, by the bishop of Trimithus. Several of his discourses attributed to St. Epiphanius belong probably to this Epiphanius or to a bishop of Constantia, also called Epiphanius. This latter is the author of a letter of congratulation, which was addressed to the patriarch John, who was restored to the see of Constantinople in 867. See Hoefer, *Nouv. Biog. Générale*, s. v.

Episcŏpa, a name sometimes given in the early Church to the wife of a bishop. The word is used in this sense in the second Council of Tours, where it is said that if a bishop have not a wife there shall no train of women follow him.

Episcŏpæ, a name given to the deaconesses (q. v.) of the ancient Christian Church.

Episcopate, the office of a bishop (q. v.).

Episcŏpi Senātus (*bishops of the senate*), a name given in the canon law to the chapter of a cathedral (q. v.).

Episcopissæ, a name sometimes given to the deaconesses of the early Church.

Episcŏpus Judæorum (*bishop of the Jews*). The Jews of England, under the first Norman kings, had over them an officer under this title, licensed by the crown, who judged and ruled them according to their own law.

Episcopus Regionarius, a bishop in the early Church, whose labors were confined to no particular place, but who wandered about from one district to another.

Episēmon (*ἐπίσημον*, i. e. *distinguished*), a cabalistic word much used in the Gnostic system of Marcus, and hinted at by several of the early Church fathers.

Episozomĕne (*ἐπισωζομένη*), a name given by the Cappadocian Christians to Ascension day (q. v.), probably because on that day our salvation was perfected.

Epistemonarch (Gr. *ἐπίσταμαι*, *to know*, *ἄρχων*, *a ruler*), an officer in the Greek Church, whose duty it is to guard the doctrines of the Church, and to examine all matters relating to faith.

Epistle, the first lesson in the communion service of the Church of England, deriving its name from the circumstance that it is generally taken from the apostolic epistles; though sometimes from the Acts, and occasionally from the Old-Test. writings. The form was derived from that of the Greek and Latin churches, where it was usually denominated the "Apostle." It has been in use in the English Church since the time of Augustine of Canterbury, a period of twelve hundred years. See Hook, *Church Dict.* s. v.; Staunton, *Eccles. Dict.* s. v.

Epistler, an ecclesiastical officer mentioned in the canons of the Church of England, and in the injunctions of queen Elizabeth, whose duty it was to read the Epistle in collegiate churches. He was required to be dressed in a cope. The office is now obsolete.

Epistŏlæ Synodĭcæ, a name sometimes given to *enthronistic letters* (q. v.), but more generally used to indicate the circular letters by which a primate summoned a council of the Church in ancient times.

Epitrachelion (Gr. *ἐπί*, *upon*, and *τράχηλος*, *the neck*), a vestment of the Greek ecclesiastics, which, instead of being put round the neck like a scarf, is joined at the centre, and has an orifice left at its upper end that it may be passed over the head. See STOLE.

Eponamon, a name given by the natives of Chili, in South America, to the *devil*, as being strong and powerful.

Epulōnēs, a special order of priests among the ancient Romans. They were first appointed B.C. 198, to preside at the *Epulum Jovis* (q. v.) and similar feasts, and were usually three in number, although they were at one time seven and at another ten.

Epŭlum Jovis (*the feast of Jupiter*), a festival of the ancient Romans, held in honor of the father of the gods. At these the gods themselves were supposed to be present; for their statues were brought on rich beds, with their *pulvinaria* or pillows, and placed at the most honorable part of the table as the principal guests. The care of this apparatus belonged to the *epulones* (q. v.).

Equiria (Lat. *equus*, "a horse"), two festivals celebrated by the ancient Romans, the one in February, the other in March, in honor of Mars, the god of war, at which horse-racing was the principal amusement.

Equitius, bishop of Hippo Diarrhytus, notoriou for his turbulence, against whom the Council of Carthage, A.D. 401, took steps towards a deposition.

Eraclius. See HERACLIUS.

Erard (*Eberhard*), a Bavarian bishop, lived about 679. He was the brother of St. Hidulphus, archbishop of Treves, and assisted him in the administration of his see. He was consecrated originally bishop of Ardagh, in Ireland, but finally of Ratisbon, yet without a stationary location. He is often given the title of *the Blessed*, and is commemorated Jan. 8 (also Jan. 6, Feb. 9, April 14, and Oct. 8). See Hoefer, *Nouv. Biog. Générale*, s. v.; Smith, *Dict. of Christ. Biog.* s. v.

Erasmus, *Saint* (commonly called *Elmo*, also *Ermo*), was bishop of some see near Antioch, and is said to have returned to Firmiæ, in Campania, and then to have suffered martyrdom under Diocletian. The acts of this saint, given by the Bollandists, are entirely apocryphal. It is pretended that the body of Erasmus was preserved at Gaeta, with the exception of some parts which were given to the monastery of Mt. Cœlius at Rome, and some to those of St. Orestes. St. Erasmus is invoked by the sailors on the Mediterranean against tempest and other danger, and for this reason they have given his name to an electric phenomenon which often appears on top of the masts of vessels during a storm. He is also the patron saint against the stomach-ache, on the tradition that he suffered martyrdom by evisceration. He is commemorated June 2 (or 3). See Jameson, *Sacred and Legendary Art*, p. 699.

Erasmus, JOHANNES, a Dutch theologian, lived in 1593. He was very learned, even according to the testimony of his adversaries. He knew Hebrew well, and had corrected Tremellius and Junius's version of the prophets. Having been appointed rector at Antwerp, he confessed the doctrine of the Unitarians, but William, prince of Orange, prevented his making proselytes, aud obliged him to leave Holland. Erasmus first retired to Poland, and then into Transylvania, where the Unitarians made him minister at Claudiopolis, on the condition, however, that he would not teach that the Son of God was created before all other things. Erasmus had a great conference on this subject with Faustus Socinus. He went from Claudiopolis to Cracow, and asked permission of the Unitarians to explain his reasons for not believing "that Jesus Christ was not at all the Son of God before his birth by his mother." Socinus was appointed to answer him. The disputation lasted two days, but ended in the satisfaction of neither party. See Hoefer, *Nouv. Biog. Générale*, s. v.

Erath, Augustin, a Roman Catholic theologian of Germany, was born Jan. 28, 1648, near Augsburg. In 1679 he was appointed professor of theology at Dillingen, and died Sept. 5, 1719. He is the author of many writings, enumerated in Jöcher, *Allgemeines Gelehrten-Lexikon*, s. v. (B. P.)

Erăto, in Greek mythology, was one of the nine muses; her songs were so touching and charming that they moved even the most callous hearts to love; hence also her name (from ἔρος, *love*). She is said to have been the first to compose *elegies* or plaintive verse. She is generally represented with the lyre on her arm and a plectrum in her hand.

Figure of Erato.

Erbkram, Heinrich Wilhelm, a Protestant theologian of Germany, was born July 8, 1810, at Glogau. For his academical career he prepared himself at the Wittenberg Seminary, and commenced his theological lectures at Berlin in 1838. In 1855 he accepted a call to Königsberg, and died there, Jan. 9, 1884. He is best known as the author of *Geschichte der protestantischen Sekten im Zeitalter der Reformation* (Hamburg and Gotha, 1848). (B. P.)

Erc (Lat. *Hercus*) is the name of several Irish saints, the chief of whom was bishop of Slane, of royal descent, who died A.D. 512, aged about ninety years, and is commemorated on Nov. 2.

Erchembert (or **Erchempert**), an Italian historian, was descended from the dukes of Benevento. The castle of Pilau, where he resided with his father, Adelgair, was taken in August, 881, by Pandonulf, count of Capua, and Erchembert was carried away a prisoner, but escaped and took the habit of a monk at the convent of the Benedictines of Monte Cassino. At the age of twenty-five he was elected abbot of a convent near by; but was driven from it by Arnulf, and returned for the rest of his days to his cell. He wrote a *Chronicle*, or an extended history of the Lombards, which is believed to be lost, although an abridged edition, from 774 to 888, as a continuation of the work of Paul Diacre, was published by Antonio Caracioli (Naples, 1626); by Camillo Peregrini, in his *Historia Principum Longobardorum*, etc. (ibid. 1643). There is also attributed to Erchembert, *De Destructione et Renovatione Cassiensis Cœnobii:—De Ismaelitarum Incursione:—Vida Landulfi I, Episcopi Capuæ*, extending from 851 to 879, in verse:—*Acta Translationis Corporis St. Matthæi, Apost.* See Hoefer, *Nouv. Biog. Générale*, s. v.

Ercnat (or **Herenat**), an Irish saint, commemorated Jan. 8 and Oct. 30, was a virgin of Duneane, A.D. 460, who died, it is said, of love for St. Benigius, but revived, and spent her days in preparing and embroidering sacred vestments.

Erdaviraph, an impostor who flourished in Persia in the 3d century, and was considered the real restorer of the doctrines of the Magi. He professed to have fallen into a deep sleep, during which his soul made the journey to paradise, being seven days on the way.

Erĕbus (ἔρεβος, *darkness*), in Greek mythology, is the infernal region, the subterranean, chaotic night; being represented as son of Chaos and Caligo. Erebus does not seem to be identical with Tartarus. His descendants are the following, by Night: Age, Death, Fate, Abstinence, Dreams, Epiphron, Clotho, Lachesis, Atropos, the three Parcæ, Dispute, Evil, Malice, Nemesis, Euphrosyne, Friendship, Sympathy, Styx, and Sleep.

Erembert, *Saint*, eleventh bishop of Toulouse, was born at Villiolicorte, near Poissy. He became a monk in 648 at the abbey of Fontenelle, which then was directed by Wandregisilus. Being appointed by Clothaire III to the see of Toulouse, about 656, he governed it twelve years with prudence, and then resigned, and dwelt for some time at his native home, but finally retired to the monastery of Fontenelle, where he died in 671 or 678. He is commemorated May 14. See Hoefer, *Nouv. Biog. Générale*, s. v.; Smith, *Dict. of Christ. Biog.* s. v.

Erendiganus, Rufi, a Swiss theologian, lived in the second part of the 17th century. He was a Capuchin, and definitor and provincial of his order. He wrote, *Manuductio Sacerdotis* (Lucerne, 1674):—*Calendarium Spirituale* (ibid. 1698):—*Revelationes S. Brigittæ* (ibid. 1699):—*Speculum Animarum Thomæ de Kempis* (ibid. eod.). See Hoefer, *Nouv. Biog. Générale*, s. v.

Erevantsi, Melkhiseth (i. e. *Melchisedech of Erivan*), an Armenian doctor, was born in 1559 at Vejan. He early devoted himself to monastical life, and after studying under the famous doctor Nersês Peghlow about fifteen years, left his monastery, which was situated in the isle of Lim, in the centre of the lake of Van, in order to visit Armenia. He planted a great number of institutions of education, and returned to his monastery. The patriarch, Moses III, sent him out again as director of the patriarchal school of Echmiadzin. He died at Erivan in 1631, leaving several MSS. on grammatical, rhetorical, and philosophical subjects. See Hoefer, *Nouv. Biog. Générale*, s. v.

Ergas, Joseph *ben-Immanuel*, a Jewish rabbi, who flourished at Leghorn in the 18th century, is the author of ס׳ שומר אמונים, a *Philosophy of Religion and Cabala*, written in the form of a dialogue (Amsterdam, 1736):—ס׳ מבוא פתחים, *Introduction to the Science of the True Cabala* (ibid.):—a collection of decisions, שו״ת דברי יוסף (Leghorn, 1742). See Fürst, *Bibl. Jud.* i, 247; Jöcher, *Allgemeines Gelehrten-Lexikon*, s. v. (B. P.)

Erhard, Thomas Aquinas, a German theologian of the order of the Benedictines, who lived in the first part of the 18th century, wrote, *Gloria S. Benedicti* (Augsburg, 1720):—*Opus Rhetoricum:—Die Bibel Lateinisch und Deutsch* (ibid. 1726):—*Manuale Biblicum* (1724):—*Polycrates Gersensis*, etc. (1729):—*Commentarius in Universa Biblia* (Augsburg, 1735):—*De Imitatione Christi* (about 1739):—*Concordantiæ Bibliorum Wessofontanæ* (Augsburg, 1751). See Hoefer, *Nouv. Biog. Générale*, s. v.

Eribert, archbishop of Milan, A.D. 1015, took a prominent part in the intrigues that then divided Italy. He was a noted warrior, and established a military order of the *Humiliati*, which subsisted till 1570. See Hoefer, *Nouv. Biog. Générale*, s. v.

Eric of Brandenburg, twenty-sixth archbishop of Magdeburg, was son of John I, elector of Brandenburg, and was elected in 1278. He had a stormy administration, and died in 1295. See Hoefer, *Nouv. Biog. Générale*, s. v.

Eris (ἔρις, *strife*), in Greek mythology, was the personification of *Discord*, the daughter of Night. When the deities were merrily assembled at the wedding of Peleus and Thetis, Eris threw an apple among them, bearing the inscription "To the most beautiful." Juno, Venus, and Minerva claimed it. Had Jupiter decided in favor of one he would have incurred the bitter enmity of the others, and hence he refused to announce his opinion; therefore Paris was authorized to decide. Power and greatness, wisdom and fame, offered by the earnest goddesses, had no influence with him; for Venus promised him the most beautiful woman of Greece as a possession. That goddess therefore received the prize of beauty; Paris carried off Helena, the Trojan war was the result, and all the deities took a part in it: Juno and Minerva as enemies of the Trojans; Venus, Apollo, and Mars on the side of those against whom war was made.

Erkenwald, the fourth bishop of the East Saxons, whose episcopal see was London, was brother of St. Ethelburga, and is said to have been born at Stallington, in Lindsey, of a noble family. From Bede we learn that he was already noted for sanctity when raised to the episcopate in 676. He died in 690, and is commemorated April 30 as the founder of St. Paul's (where his remains were interred), and also of one or two monasteries.

Erkiglit, in Greenland mythology, are the spirits of war, living on the east side of the country, cruel, and enemies of man. They are represented as large men with animal heads. Probably this superstition came from an ancient tradition, which gives to the northern coast of Greenland very warlike inhabitants, who sometimes pressed to all parts of the island in plundering and devastating expeditions, and destroyed all living beings.

Erlkönig, in Norse mythology, is probably akin to *Elfkönig*, the ruler of the ethereal beings which are called elves (q. v.). He is not dangerous to grown persons, but often abducts children of Christians before they are baptized, not from any evil motive, but because he takes a great joy in them, and because the elves generally glory in coming into contact with human beings. He is represented as an unusually large, bearded man, with a shining crown and a wide, trailing mantle.

Erloersortok, in Greenland mythology, is the ruler of the air, the evil principle. He is cruel and cunning; waylaying those who are on the way to heaven, and lives on their vitals, which he tears from them.

Ermelendis (or **Hermelinda**), *Saint*, was born at Odenca, near Louvain, about 550. She was of a rich family of Brabant, and was but twelve years old when she resolved to consecrate herself to God. Some time later her parents tried to induce her to marry, but she cut off her own hair in their presence and hid herself in the solitudes of the vicinity. She only left her cell, with bare feet, when she assisted at the divine services. Two young men, brothers, and lords of the place, having designs upon her chastity, Ermelinde retired to a more secluded place called Meldric (now Meldaert), near Hugard (Brabant), and subsisted there on fruits and herbs till her death, about A.D. 595. Forty-eight years afterwards her obscure tomb was discovered, and a chapel was erected over it, which has since perished. She is commemorated on Oct. 29. See Hoefer, *Nouv. Biog. Générale*, s. v.; Smith, *Dict. of Christ. Biog.* s. v.

Ermenaire (*Hermenarius*), twenty-sixth bishop of Autun, A.D. 678, piously buried the mutilated remains of his predecessor, St. Léger.

Ermenfrid, abbot of Cuisance, in Franche-Comté, entered monastic life, about 627, at Luxeuil; and coming into possession, by inheritance, of the monastery at Cuisance, restored it, and died there in old age. He is commemorated on Sept. 25. See Smith, *Dict. of Christ. Biog.* s. v.

Ernan (also *Mernoc*), the name of several Irish saints, one of whom was uncle, and two others nephews, of St. Columba.

Ernest OF SAXONY, forty-first archbishop of Magdeburg, was elected to that see Jan. 19, 1476; but the pope declined at first to consecrate him, and he had a long contest with Adolphus of Anhalt and the citizens of Magdeburg before he secured quiet possession of the see. He died Aug. 3, 1513. See Hoefer, *Nouv. Biog. Générale*, s. v.

Ernesti, Günther Gottlieb, an Evangelical preacher of Germany, was born June 25, 1759, at Coburg. He studied at Jena, was for some time employed by the minister for ecclesiastical affairs at Hildburghausen, and died there, June 28, 1797, being court-preacher at the time. Most of his publications were sermons. See Döring, *Die Gelehrten Theologen Deutschlands*, s. v. (B. P.)

Ernesti, Heinrich Friedrich Theodor Ludwig, a Lutheran theologian of Germany, was born May 27, 1814, at Brunswick. He studied at Göttingen; was in 1838 deacon at his native place, in 1842 pastor at Wolfenbüttel, in 1843 superintendent, in 1850 member of consistory, and in 1858 general superintendent, and died at Wolfenbüttel, Aug. 17, 1880. He published *Expositions on Luther's Smaller Catechism* (1861), which is used in many places as the official manual for religious instruction. He also wrote, *Ursprung der Sünde nach Paulinischen Lehrbegriff* (Göttingen, 1862, 2 vols.):—*Die Ethik des Apostels Paulus* (3d ed. ibid. 1880). His earliest work was *De Præclara Christi in Apostolis Instituendis Sapientia atque Prudentia* (ibid. 1834). See Zuchold, *Bibl. Theol.* i, 332 sq. (B. P.)

Ernesti, Jakob Daniel, a German Protestant theologian, was born at Rochlitz, Dec. 3, 1640. He studied till the age of fifteen under his father, Daniel, and then at Leipsic and Altenburg, and became, in 1663, minister of the gospel at Eybitsch, rector at the gymnasium of Altenburg in 1678, deacon in 1683, archdeacon in 1685, and finally consistorial assessor in 1705. He died Dec. 15, 1707. His principal works are, *Prodromus Apanthismatum* (Altenburg, 1672):—*Selecta Historica Rariorum Casuum* (ibid. 1680). See Hoefer, *Nouv. Biog. Générale*, s. v.

Ernesti, Johann Christian, a Lutheran theologian of Germany, was born Feb. 13, 1695. He studied at Wittenberg and Leipsic, and died superintendent in Langensalza, in 1770. A list of his writings is given in Jöcher, *Allgemeines Gelehrten-Lexikon*, s. v. (B. P.)

Ernesti, Johann Christoph, a Lutheran theologian of Germany, was born Jan. 11, 1662. He studied at Wittenberg, and died there doctor of theology, Aug. 11, 1722, leaving *Disputationes de Bibliis Polyglottis*:—*De Antiquo Excommunicandi Ritu*:—*De Dialogis Doctorum Veteris Ecclesiæ*:—*De Absoluto Reprobationis Decreto*. See Jöcher, *Allgemeines Gelehrten-Lexikon*, s. v.; Fürst, *Bibl. Jud.* i, 247. (B. P.)

Ernesti, Johann Heinrich Martin, a Lutheran theologian of Germany, was born Nov. 26, 1755, at Mittwitz, near Cronach, and died at Coburg, May 10, 1836. He wrote, *Irene*. (Sulzbach, 1828):—*Ueber Censur- und Bücherverbote*, etc. (Leipsic, 1829):—*Der Kirchen-Staat* (Nuremberg, 1830). See Zuchold, *Bibl. Theol.* i, 333; Winer, *Handbuch der theol. Lit.* i, 610; ii, 321, 322. (B. P.)

Eromangan Version OF THE SCRIPTURES. This language is spoken in the island of Eromanga, one of the New Hebrides group. The version of Luke's gospel, which was published in 1864, was begun by the Rev. G. N. Gordon, who was cruelly massacred by the natives in 1860. The work was completed by his brother, the Rev. James I. The latter has since translated the book of Genesis, which was printed at Sydney in 1868, and was followed by Matthew's gospel in 1869, at London. In 1878 the Acts of the Apostles, which were translated by the Rev. H. A. Robertson, were published at the request of the New Hebrides mission at Sydney. These are at present the only parts of the Scripture translated into this language. (B. P.)

Erovaz, grand priest to the gods of Armenia. He was the brother of Erovant II, who intrusted him with the direction of the supreme national cultus, and also placed in his care the fortress of Pacaran, the ecclesiastical capital of Armenia. Sempad the Pacratide, who had taken possession of that place after the death of Erovant, drowned Erovaz in the river Akhourian, A.D. 88, and took away his treasures and his five hundred slaves. See Hoefer, *Nouv. Biog. Générale*, s. v.

Erskine, Charles, a cardinal of Scotch descent, was born at Rome, Feb. 13, 1753. After entering the profession of a lawyer when still quite young, he attained a rare knowledge of Latin and philosophy, and was honored by Pius VI, who himself had been a lawyer. During the French revolution, Erskine was sent on an embassy to London by that pontiff, remained there for eight years, and when he came back to Italy under Pius VII received the cardinal's hat. When afterwards he went to Paris he was welcomed by the consular government. Erskine died March 19, 1811. See Hoefer, *Nouv. Biog. Générale*, s. v.

Erskine (or **Areskine**), **Henry**, a Scotch divine, one of the youngest of the *thirty-three* children of Ralph Erskine of Shielfield, was born at Dryburgh in 1624, where he received his early education. He took his master's degree at the University of Edinburgh in 1645, was ordained to the ministry by the Presbyterians in England, to the living at Cornhill, in Durham, but was soon ejected by the act of uniformity, in 1662, and returned to his own country. But the persecutions carried on then in Scotland required him to take refuge in Holland. In 1687, when king James's toleration was proclaimed, Mr. Erskine embraced it; and on the re-establishment of the presbytery in 1690, he was appointed minister of Chirnside, in Berwickshire. He died Aug. 10, 1696. He never published any of his works. See Chalmers, *Biog. Dict.* s. v.; *Fasti Eccles. Scoticanæ*, i, 427, 451.

Erskine (or **Erskyn**), **John**, a Scotch clergyman, of Dun, knight, son of John Erskyne, of Dun, was born about 1508; studied first at the University of Aberdeen, then on the Continent. Having imbibed the doctrines of the Reformation, he taught them to the son of Alexander Straton, a neighbor who paid the forfeit of his life for his opinions, at Edinburgh, in August, 1534. He led many other persons to embrace the new principles, and secured for them safety and protection. When the English invaded Montrose, in 1548, Erskine, supported by his townsmen, repulsed them with a loss of eight hundred of the invaders. He lived a retired life till John Knox appeared, in 1555, when he joined him at Edinburgh, took part with his followers in their public services, and was coadjutor with Knox till a secession took place. He was one of the eight appointed by parliament, in 1557, to witness the marriage of the queen with the dauphin of France. On his return, in 1558, he assisted in forming a Church of the Reformation, became an exhorter, drew up an address to the queen-dowager against the Romanists, with whose dissimulations, in 1559, the people at Perth became so enraged that they attacked the monasteries, and cast down the images, sparing only the places of worship through the influence of Erskine and Knox. He was nominated by the lords and barons, in July, 1560, the first minister at Montrose under the Reformation, sat in the first General Assembly, 1560, and was appointed superintendent of Angus and Mearns, in 1561. Of the first fifty-six General Assemblies, he attended forty-four, and was the moderator over five of them, three times in succession. He was a member of the convention at Leith in 1571; had to summon principals, and three regents of the university, and try them for teaching popery, in 1567 and 1569, and on their refusal to accept the new faith they were deprived by the privy council. He several times offered his resignation, which was always declined, and he died March 12, 1589, having been second only to Knox in accomplishing and securing the work of the Reformation. He governed his portion of the Church with singular wisdom and authority, disallowing all innovations. He was a man of courage, zeal, learning, prudence, generosity, and liberality. He compiled and published part of the *Second Book of Discipline*. See *Fasti Eccles. Scoticanæ*, iii, 887.

Erskine, Thomas, of Linlathen, Scotland, a writer on theology and religion, was born Oct. 13, 1788. After being educated at the high-school of Edinburgh and at Durham, he attended the literary and law classes of the University of Edinburgh, and in 1810 became a member of the Edinburgh faculty of advocates. On the death of his elder brother, in 1816, he succeeded to the family estate of Linlathen, near Dundee, and retired from the bar, spending the remainder of his life in the discussion—either by conversation, by letters, or by literary publications—of the most important religious questions. He died at Edinburgh, March 20, 1870. His principal works are, *Remarks on the Internal Evidence for the Truth of Revealed Religion* (1820):—an *Essay on Faith* (1822):—and the *Unconditional Freeness of the Gospel* (1828). These have all passed through several editions, and have also been translated into French. He also wrote, *The Brazen Serpent* (1831):—*The Doctrine of Election* (1839):—a posthumous work entitled *Spiritual Order and Other Papers* (1871), and various essays. Two volumes of his *Letters*, edited by William Hanna, D.D., with reminiscences by dean Stanley and principal Shairp, appeared in 1877. See *Encyclop. Brit.* 9th ed. s. v.

Erskine, William, a Scotch nominal prelate, was minister of Campsey and commendator of Paisley. He was a titular bishop of Glasgow in 1585, but was never consecrated. He held the office but two years. See Keith, *Scottish Bishops*, p. 262.

Erthal, Franz Ludwig von, a German prelate, was born at Lohr-on-the-Main, Sept. 16, 1730. He studied law at Würzburg, and when thirty-three years of age became a member of the chapter there. The emperor Joseph II appointed him to several high positions, and in 1779 he was made prince-bishop of Bamberg and Würzburg. His government was in every respect an excellent one. He died Feb. 16, 1795, leaving, *Zeit und Pflicht der Christen* (Würzburg, 1793):—*Reden an das Landvolk* (Bamberg, 1797). See Schmid, in Herzog-Plitt's *Real-Encyclop.* s. v.; *Geschichte der Katholikirche Deutschlands* (Munich, 1872); Bernhard, *Franz Ludwig von Erthal* (Tübingen, 1852). (B. P.)

Erwin, Alexander R., D.D., a minister of the Methodist Episcopal Church South, was born in Louisiana, Jan. 12, 1820, of pious Baptist parents. He joined the Methodist Episcopal Church in 1839; was licensed to preach in 1840, and in 1842 entered the Tennessee Conference. In 1848 he was appointed president of Clarksville Female Academy; in 1854 re-entered the regular work; in 1859 was appointed president of Huntsville Female College, and died Jan. 10, 1860. Dr. Erwin was manly and dignified in appearance, humble and cheerful in spirit, extensive in knowledge, and energetic in labor. See *Minutes of Annual Conferences of the M. E. Church South*, 1860, p. 212.

Erythraeus, Joachim (1), a Lutheran theologian, was born Dec. 13, 1637, at Bela, in Upper Hungary. He studied at Wittenberg, and was for some time archdeacon in his native country. When the evangelical preachers had to leave Hungary, he went to Pomerania, and was appointed pastor at Stettin, where he died, March 21, 1699. He wrote, *Dissert. de Attributis Dei*:—*Synopsis Biblica Stilo Ligato Scripta*:—*Breviarium Biblicum*:—*Apodemica Sacra*:—*Expositio Con-*

fessionis Augustanæ. See Jöcher, *Allgemeines Gelehrten-Lexikon,* s. v. (B. P.)

Erythraeus, Joachim (2), son of the foregoing, was born Jan. 28, 1663. With his father he went to Pomerania, was in 1688 deacon, and in 1700 succeeded his father. He died April 28, 1703. See Jöcher, *Allgemeines Gelehrten-Lexikon,* s. v. (B. P.)

Erythropel, a name common to several Lutheran ministers of Germany:

1. DAVID RUPERT, was born March 30, 1653, at Hanover, and studied at Jena. In 1679 he was court-preacher at his native place, in 1685 member of consistory, in 1698 superintendent, in 1706 first court-preacher, and died Dec. 22, 1732. He wrote, *De Montibus Pietatis:—De Ministris Ecclesiarum Augustanæ Confessionis.* See Jöcher, *Allgemeines Gelehrten-Lexikon,* s. v.

2. DAVID WILHELM, son of the above, was born at Hanover, June 20, 1687. He studied at different universities, and after his return commenced his ministry in his native city in 1710. He was intrusted with the highest ecclesiastical positions, and died in February, 1758. He wrote, *De Fatis Calicis Eucharistici* (Helmstädt, 1708).

3. GEORGE, was born at Hanover in 1607, studied at Rinteln and Jena, and died in his native city in 1669.

4. MARTIN, was born at Hanover in 1610. He studied at Helmstädt and Marburg, was in 1634 pastor at Darmstädt, in 1648 court-preacher and general superintendent, and died June 1, 1655. He wrote, *Pathologica Christi Prophetica* (Marburg, 1640):—*Thesaurus Connubialis,* or *Geistlicher Eheschatz in Predigten* (ibid. 1641).

5. RUPERT, father of Martin, was born in 1556, studied at Leipsic and Wittenberg, and was in 1584 conrector at Hanover. In 1585 he was made pastor of the Church of the Holy Cross, in 1596 of St. George's, and died Oct. 7, 1626. He wrote, *Analysis Logica in Epistol. et Evangel. Dominic. Pericopas:—Postilla Methodica in Epistol. et Evangelia:—Theologia Apostolica et Methodica,* or exposition on the epistles of Paul, Peter, James, Jude, John, and the epistle to the Hebrews:—*Harmonia Historica IV Evangelistarum:—Catena Aurea in Harmon. Evangel.* See Jöcher, *Allgemeines Gelehrten-Lexikon,* s. v. (B. P.)

Esaias OF EGYPT, who lived about the end of the 4th century, was abbot of some monastery in that country, and left a large number of MSS., nearly all in Greek. Assemani cites some in Arabic and Syriac, but these are probably translations from the Greek. Several have been published, viz., *Chapters on the Ascetic and Quiet Life* (Κεφάλαια περὶ ἀσκήσεως καὶ ἡσυχίας), in Greek and Latin, in the *Thesaurus Asceticus* of Peter Possin (Paris, 1684):—*Præcepta seu Concilia Posita Tironibus* (Augsburg, 1759):—*Orationes,* a Latin translation of twenty-nine discourses, or rather apothegms, published by Franc. Zini, with other ascetical writings by St. Nilus and other theologians (Venice, 1574):—*Dubitationes in Visionem Ezechielis,* in MS. in the royal library of the Escurial in Spain, has been described by Montfaucon, but it has not been printed. It is doubtful if all these works are by the same author, as there may have been several writers of this name in Egypt. See Hoefer, *Nouv. Biog. Générale,* s. v.; Smith, *Dict. of Christ. Biog.* s. v.

Escalante, JUAN ANTONIO, a reputable Spanish historical painter, was born at Cordova in 1630, and studied under Francisco Rizi. There are a number of his works in the churches of Madrid, which are highly praised, among which is a fine picture of *St. Catharine,* in San Miguel; and an altar-piece representing *The Dead Christ,* with other figures, in the Church of Espiritu Santo. He died at Madrid in 1670. See Hoefer, *Nouv. Biog. Générale,* s. v.; Spooner, *Biog. Hist. of the Fine Arts,* s. v.

Eschenbach, ANDREAS CHRISTIAN, a German divine and philologist, was born at Nuremberg, March 24, 1663, and was educated at Altdorf, where, in 1684, he received the poetic crown. He went to Jena and taught the classics with considerable reputation. He travelled through Germany and Holland, and on his return assisted his father in the Church of Wehrd, in Nuremberg. In 1691 he was appointed inspector of the schools of Altdorf, and in 1695 was recalled to Nuremberg as deacon of the Church of St. Mary, and professor of eloquence, poetry, history, and the Greek language in St. Giles's College, to which office, in 1705, was added that of pastor of St. Clare. He died Sept. 24, 1722. Some of his philological dissertations were printed in 1700, in the *Syntagma Secundum Dissertationum Philologicarum* (Rotterdam, 8vo). His *Epigenes sive Commentarius in Fragmenta Orphica,* was published at Nuremberg (1702, 4to). He translated into German, Allix on *The Truth of the Christian Religion,* and on *The Coming of the Messiah.* See Chalmers, *Biog. Dict.* s. v.; Jöcher, *Allgemeines Gelehrten-Lexikon,* s. v.

Eschenburg, Bernhard, a Lutheran theologian of Germany, who died at Lübeck, Sept. 30, 1832, is the author of, *Versuch einer Geschichte der öffentlichen Religionsvorträge* (Jena, 1785). See Winer, *Handbuch der theol. Lit.* i, 628; ii, 57. (B. P.)

Eschenburg, Johann Joachim, a Lutheran hymn-writer of Germany, was born Dec. 7, 1743, at Hamburg, and died at Brunswick, Feb. 29, 1820. He is the author of twelve hymns. See Jördens, *Lexicon deutscher Dichter und Prosaisten,* vi, 768–798; Schröder, *Lexicon der Hamburgischen Schriftsteller,* vol. ii; Koch, *Geschichte des deutschen Kirchenliedes,* vi, 237 sq.; Winer, *Handbuch der theol. Lit.* ii, 290. (B. P.)

Eschenmayer, ADAM CARL AUGUST, a German philosophical writer, was born July 4, 1768, at Neuenburg. In 1811 he was made professor of philosophy at Tübingen, but retired in 1836 from his academical position to Kirchheim, and died there, Nov. 17, 1852. He wrote, *Die Philosophie in ihrem Uebergange zur Nichtphilosophie* (Erlangen, 1803):—*System der Moralphilosophie* (Stuttgart, 1818):—*Religionsphilosophie* (Tübingen, 1818–24, 3 vols.):—*Die Hegelsche Religionsphilosophie verglichen mit dem christlichen Prinzip* (ibid. 1834), written against Hegel:—*Der Ischariotismus unserer Tage* (ibid. 1835), written against the *Life of Jesus,* by Strauss:—*Charakteristik des Unglaubens, Halbglaubens und Vollglaubens* (ibid. 1838):—*Grundriss der Naturphilosophie* (ibid. 1832):—*Grundzüge der christlichen Philosophie* (Basle, 1840):—*Organon des Christenthums* (Stuttgart, 1843):—*Sechs Perioden der christlichen Kirche* (Heilbronn, 1851). See Lichtenberger, *Encyclop. des Sciences Religieuses,* s. v.; Winer, *Handbuch der theol. Lit.* i, 286, 288, 429, 551, 594; ii, 10; Zuchold, *Bibl. Theol.* i, 336. (B. P.)

Eschius. See VAN ESCHE.

Eschrakites (*enlightened*), a Mohammedan sect who give themselves to contemplation. Their meditations pertain chiefly to God, whom they, unlike the other Mohammedans, believe to be a trinity of persons. Wherever the Koran conflicts with their doctrines they consider it abrogated. They hold in utter contempt the gross notions of Mohammed concerning the sensual pleasures of paradise, and consider man's supreme happiness to consist in the contemplation of divinity. This is one of the most respectable of the Mohammedan sects, resembling more nearly than any other, both in faith and practice, ordinary Christians.

Escobar, Bartolomeo de, a Spanish missionary, who spent his life and fortune in pious labors, was born at Seville in 1562. He became a Jesuit in the West Indies, where he lived seventeen years, and afterwards spent three years at Lima, dying there in 1624, and leaving, *Conciones in Quinquagesima* (Lyons, 1617):—*Conciones de Festis Domini* (Paris, 1624):—*Conciones super Omnes Beatæ Virginis Festivitates* (ibid. eod.):—*Ser-*

mones de la Concepcion (Oviedo, 1622). See Hoefer, *Nouv. Biog. Générale*, s. v.

Escobar (*del Carro*), **Juan**, a Spanish theologian, was born at Puente de Cantos (Andalusia); taught law with success at the College of Santa Maria and at the University of Seville; became afterwards inquisitor at Murcia and at Cordova, and died at Madrid after 1642, leaving, *De Puritate Sancti Officii Inquisitionis*, etc. (Lyons, 1637):—*De Utroque Foro* (Cordova, 1642):—*De Confessariis*, etc. (ibid. eod.):—*De Horis Canonicis* (ibid. eod.):—*Antilogia*, etc. (ibid. eod.). See Hoefer, *Nouv. Biog. Générale*, s. v.

Escobar, Marina de, a Spanish foundress of religious orders, was born at Valladolid, Feb. 8, 1554. Although the daughter of rich parents, she refused marriage. She had visions very frequently, in which Sts. Gertrude, Brigitta, and Mathilda appeared to her. In 1582 a number of women desired to share her mode of living, and retired under her guidance to a monastery, to which she gave the name of *Recollection of St. Bridget*. She died June 9, 1633. Her *Life*, begun by P. Del Puente, was finished by P. Cachupin, the provincial of the Jesuits of Castile (Madrid, 1665). See Hoefer, *Nouv. Biog. Générale*, s. v.

Escobar, Pedro Suarez de, a Spanish theologian, was born at Medina; belonged to the order of the Hermits of St. Augustine, and went into Spanish America, preaching the Catholic faith in Mexico. He became successively first theologian of the cathedral of that city, præfect of the province, and bishop of Guadalaxara. He died at Tlaicapan in 1591, leaving, *Escata del Paraiso Celestial:—Silva de la Perfeccion Evangelica:—Relox de Principes:—Sermones de los Evangelios de Todo et Año* (Madrid, 1601). See Hoefer, *Nouv. Biog. Générale*, s. v.

Escuara. See BASQUE SPANISH.

Esdaile, JAMES, D.D., a Scotch clergyman, became a tutor in the family of Mr. Christie, of Durie; was licensed to preach in June, 1803; presented by the town council to the second charge at Montrose in June, and ordained Aug. 14, 1805; promoted to the East Church, Perth, Oct. 18, 1810; resigned his charge, which was accepted June 15, 1844, after securing a bond from the magistrates for an annuity of £200, having discharged the duties of his office with great ability and a high degree of acceptance and usefulness. He died Jan. 8, 1854, aged eighty years. He published, *Christian Theology* (Edinb. 1823):—*Apocraphy*, for the Perthshire Bible Society (1826):—*A Letter to the Rev. W. A. Thomson* (Perth, eod.):—*Lectures on the Shorter Catechism* (ibid. 1829):—*Civil and Religious Institutions Necessarily and Inseparably Connected* (ibid. 1833):—*The Voluntary Church Scheme without Foundation in Scripture, Reason, or Common-sense* (ibid. 1834):—*The Spirit, Principles, and Reasoning of the Voluntaries Exposed* (ibid. eod.), with various articles in the *Edinburgh Encyclopædia*. See *Fasti Eccles. Scoticanæ*, ii, 619; iii, 848.

Esdras (Armen. *Ezr* or *Ezras*), catholicos or universal patriarch of Armenia, was born at Parhajnaguerd (in the province of Ararat). He was educated from his childhood in the patriarchal palace, and after having filled the office of doorkeeper to St. Gregory the Illuminator, was elected to succeed the patriarch Christopher III, who died A.D. 628. A short time after that the emperor Heraclius, on his return from his expedition against Chosroes II, king of Persia, stopped at Garin, formerly called Theodosiopolis and now Erzerûm, and undertook to unite the Armenian Church with the Greek. To this end he tried to conciliate the affections of the Armenians who had submitted to his rule. He gave them as governor-general a very popular man, the prince Mjej Cnouni; he treated the patriarch with distinction, and gave him a part of the city of Goghp. At the order of the emperor, Esdras called together a council (A.D. 629) in the city of Garin, where a great number of bishops, doctors (vertabeds), and Armenian princes, likewise several Greek doctors, came together. During the conference of one month, the reunion of the two churches was decreed. The Council of Chalcedon was recognised as the fourth General Council, and it was concluded that the feast of the nativity of Jesus Christ is to be celebrated separately from that of his baptism. Most of the Perso-Armenian bishops adhered to the decisions of the council. Many of the theologians who had attached themselves to the anathematized doctrines received Esdras very coldly when he came back to Tevin, the seat of his administration, and loudly disapproved his last acts. The chief of this party, John Maïragometsi, was ill-treated by order of the patriarch and sent into exile as a heretic. Esdras died in 689, of sorrow, it is said. He has been differently judged by his compatriots; the historians John VI Catholicos and Michael Asori (or the Syrian) call him ignorant, while the Armenians unitedly reverence him as a saint. During his time Armenia was ravaged by the Arabs, who massacred thirty thousand people in the city of Tevin. Nerses III, bishop of Daïk, succeeded Esdras. See Hoefer, *Nouv. Biog. Générale*, s. v.

Esger, HANS, a Dutch theologian and hebraist, was born at Amsterdam, Jan. 2, 1696. He was preacher at Ost- and Wester-Blocker, at Naarden, Middelburg, and finally at Amsterdam. In 1755 he was called as professor of Hebrew antiquities at Leyden, where he had been teaching theology before, and died there, May 28 of same year, leaving, *Mosis Maimonidis Constitutio de Siglis* (Leyden, 1727):—*Oratio de Supremo Ecclesiæ Doctore* (ibid. 1740):—*De Regimine Ecclesiæ* (ibid. 1741):—*De Fontibus Theologiæ* (ibid. 1751). See Hoefer, *Nouv. Biog. Générale*, s. v.

Eshbili, YOM-TOB *ben-Abraham*, a famous Talmudist of the 13th century, is known for his novellas on almost all the treatises of the Talmud. These novellas, or חדושים, are highly appreciated by Talmudic scholars, and are therefore often reprinted. A complete list of them is given by Fürst, *Bibl. Jud.* i, 248–250. (B. P.)

Eshean. For this Biblical site Lieut. Conder suggests (*Memoirs* to the Ordnance Survey, iii, 313) the present ruined village *es-Simia*, lying three and a half miles southwest of Juttah.

Eskild, a Swedish prelate, succeeded to the see of Lund, although his election was forbidden by king Eric Ermund, against whom he took arms while only bishop of Röskilde. He finally retired to the monastery of Clairvaux, in France, where he died, Sept. 6, 1181. See Hoefer, *Nouv. Biog. Générale*, s. v.

Eskilli, NICOLAUS, a Swedish theologian, was born July 4, 1588. He studied at different universities of Germany, and was in 1611 rector at Calmar. The war between Sweden and Denmark put a sudden stop to his activity, but he resumed it in 1623. He died Feb. 17, 1650, leaving, *Disp. Synodalis de Scriptura Sacra* (Colmar, 1629):—*De Jehovah Elohim* (ibid. 1632):—*De Persona et Officio Christi* (ibid. 1633):—*De Creatione et Providentia* (ibid. 1635):—*Disputationes Octo Synodales* (ibid.). See Jöcher, *Allgemeines Gelehrten-Lexikon*, s. v. (B. P.)

Eskuche, BALTHASAR LUDWIG, a Reformed theologian of Germany, was born at Cassel, March 12, 1710; studied at Marburg; was in 1734 preacher and professor at Rinteln, and died March 16, 1755, leaving, *De Naufragio Paulino* (Bremen, 1730):—*De Requie Pauli in Melita* (Magdeburg, 1731):—*De Festo Judæorum Purim* (Marburg and Rinteln, 1734):—*In Orationem Paulinam in Areopago* (Rinteln, 1735–40):—*De Festo ξυλοφορίων* (ibid. 1738):—*Disp. ad Oraculum Jerem. xxxi*, 22 (ibid. 1739):—*De Muliere Bethaniensi* (ibid.):—*Erläuterung der heiligen Schrift aus morgenländischen Reisebeschreibungen* (ibid. 1745, 2 vols.):—*Observationes Philolog. Crit. in Nov. Test.* (ibid. 1748–54). See Jöcher, *Allgemeines Gelehrten-Lexikon*, s. v.; Winer, *Handbuch der theol. Lit.* i, 134; Fürst, *Bibl. Jud.* i, 250. (B. P.)

Esora (Judith iv, 4) is thought by Lieut. Conder (*Tent Work in Palest.* ii, 336; comp. *Quar. Statement* of the "Pal. Explor. Fund," January, 1881, p. 52) to be the present "village *Asîreh*, north of Shechem," meaning, doubtless, what is laid down on the *Ordnance Map* as *Asîret el-Hatob*, three miles north of Nablûs, but not noticed in the *Memoirs* accompanying the Survey.

Espagne, JEAN D', a French Protestant theologian, was born in Dauphiny in 1591; became pastor at Orange in 1620, but soon left France, and was successively minister in Holland and at London, where he died, April 25, 1659, leaving English translations of some small treatises, especially *Les Erreurs Populaires en Points de la Religion*, etc. (La Haye, 1639):—*La Manducation du Corps de Christ* (ibid. 1640):—*L'Usage de l'Oraison Dominicale* (Lond. 1646). See Hoefer, *Nouv. Biog. Générale*, s. v.

Espence (Lat. *Espencœus*), CHARLES D', a French theologian, was born of noble parents at Châlons-sur-Marne, in 1511, and became a doctor of the Sorbonne and rector of the University of Paris. Cardinal de Lorraine employed him in various important cases. He distinguished himself in the assembly of Orleans in 1560, and at the Conference of Poissy in 1561. He died Oct. 5, 1571, leaving, *Institution d'un Prince Chrétien* (Lyons, 1548):—*Traité des Ouvrages Clandestins*:—*Des Commentaires sur les Épitres de Saint-Paul à Timothée et à Tite*, full of long discussions on hierarchy and ecclesiastical discipline; also several controversial treatises, some in French and others in Latin. All these were collected at Paris in 1619. See Hoefer, *Nouv. Biog. Générale*, s. v.

Espinac, PIERRE D', a French prelate, born early in the 16th century, was the son of Pierre d'Espinac, lieutenant of the king in Burgundy. He became canon-count, then dean of the Church of Lyons, and finally archbishop there, after the death of his uncle, Antoine d'Albon, in 1574. The clergy chose him as their orator in the assembly of Blois, and he became chief of the deputation of the Catholics at the celebrated deputation of Suresne. He died Jan. 9, 1599, leaving, besides addresses on the above occasions, *Exhortation au Peuple de Lyon* (1583):—*Un Bréviaire*:—*Des Poesies Françaises* (not printed). See Hoefer, *Nouv. Biog. Générale*, s. v.

Espinay, André d', a French prelate, was successively archbishop of Arles and of Bordeaux, cardinal-archbishop and count of Lyons, and aided Charles VIII in his war in Brittany. He died at Paris, Nov. 10, 1500. See Hoefer, *Nouv. Biog. Générale*, s. v.

Espinay, Charles d', a French bishop, born of an ancient family of Brittany about 1530, became commendatory abbot of Tronchet, of St. Gildas du Bois, and prior of Gahard and of Bécherel, was appointed in 1558 bishop of Dol, but before being consecrated assisted at the Council of Trent. He was active in the ecclesiastical troubles of his time, and died in September, 1591. See Hoefer, *Nouv. Biog. Générale*, s. v.

Espinay, Jacques d', a French prelate, was apostolical prothonotary of the holy see, and succeeded by his intrigues in being appointed bishop of St. Malo, Jan. 9, 1450. Nicholas V transferred him, March 18 following, to the see of Rennes, but the duc of Brittany, Pierre II, violently opposed these changes. In the end, Espinay was deprived even of his patrimony, and although suffering from the gout was confined in a prison, where he died, Jan. 9, 1482. See Hoefer, *Nouv. Biog. Générale*, s. v.

Espinel, VICENTE, a Spanish writer and ecclesiastic, was born at Ronda, in the province of Granada, about 1551. He was educated at Salamanca, and served as a soldier in Flanders. His ecclesiastical position seems to have been that of chaplain at Ronda, but he resided chiefly at Madrid. He died about 1634. He is now chiefly noted for his romance of *Marcos de Olregon*, a work delineating Spanish manners. He was also a poet of some reputation. There is a good English translation of his *Marcos de Olregon*, by Algernon Langton (Lond. 1816, 2 vols.). See *Encyclop. Brit.* 9th ed. s. v.

Espinosa, DIEGO DE, a Spanish prelate and statesman, was born at Martininos de las Posadas (old Castile), in 1502. He studied civil and canonical law, which he taught when very young at Cuença; then became auditor at Seville, and director of the royal council of Navarre. Philip II appointed him some time afterwards grand inquisitor of Spain, superintendent of the negotiations and affairs of Italy, and finally bishop of Siguenza. In 1568 Espinosa received the cardinal's hat. In the exercise of his high functions he was remarkable for his equal severity against iniquitous judges and heretics. He died Sept. 5, 1572. See Hoefer, *Nouv. Biog. Générale*, s. v.

Esquimaux Version OF THE SCRIPTURES. The Esquimaux are a people dispersed over the northern coast of North America, inhabiting the shores of all the seas, bays, gulfs, and islands of the Arctic Ocean, from the Atlantic to the Pacific. They are also found on the Atlantic side of the continent, along the coast of Labrador, as far south as the fiftieth degree of latitude; and are likewise to be met with on the opposite coast of America, along the shores of the Pacific, from Behring Strait to Mount St. Elias, in the sixtieth degree of latitude. Moravian missionaries were the first who proclaimed the glad tidings of the Gospel in these inclement regions. The first part of the New Test. which was published in that language was the gospel of John, and three years later, in 1813, the British and Foreign Bible Society published the other three gospels. Other parts soon followed, till in 1826 the entire New Test. was given to that benighted people. Of the Old Test. different parts were published from time to time, till in 1871 the entire Bible was printed for the Esquimaux. The language has been treated in modern times by Kleinschmidt, in *Grammatik der grönlandischen Sprache* (Berlin, 1871). See GREENLANDISH VERSION. (B. P.)

Estaing, François, a learned and charitable French prelate, was born Jan. 6, 1462. He was bishop of Rhodez, and constructed the tower of the cathedral at his own expense. He died Nov. 1, 1529. See Hoefer, *Nouv. Biog. Générale*, s. v.

Estaing, Joachim, bishop of Clermont, died in 1650, and had as his successor in his diocese his brother Louis, who was almoner to Anne of Austria. See Hoefer, *Nouv. Biog. Générale*, s. v.

Estampes. See ÉTAMPES.

Este, Ippolito d', an Italian prelate, son of duke Ercole I, was born in 1479. He was appointed cardinal at the age of fifteen years by pope Alexander VI. He is accused of having given orders for putting out the eyes of his natural brother, Giulio d'Este, through jealousy. He was the political counsellor and lieutenant of his brother Alfonso, who had become duke of Ferrara in 1505. He contributed to the destruction of the Venetian fleet, Dec. 22, 1509. Cardinal d'Este had received a very careful education, and possessed extensive knowledge, particularly of mathematics. He died in 1520. See Hoefer, *Nouv. Biog. Générale*, s. v.

Este, Juan Baptista d', a convert from Judaism, who flourished in the beginning of the 17th century in Portugal, is the author of *Consolaçon Christiana* (Lisbon, 1616):—*Dialogo entre Discipulo e Mestre Catechizante*, in one hundred chapters (ibid. 1621). See Fürst, *Bibl. Jud.* i, 258; Wolf, *Bibl. Hebr.* i and iii, 810; Jöcher, *Allgemeines Gelehrten-Lexikon*, s. v. (B. P.)

Estella, DIEGO D', a Spanish ascetic writer, was born at Estella in 1524. After studying at the universities of Toulouse and Salamanca, he entered the monastic life, and gained the confidence of Philip II, who called him his consulting theologian. He died Aug. 1, 1578, leaving *De la Vida del Evangelista San Juan*

(Lisbon, 1554):—*De la Vanidad del Mundo* (Salamanca, 1574):—*In Evangelium Lucæ* (Alcala de Henares, 1578). See Hoefer, *Nouv. Biog. Générale*, s. v.

Estes, DANIEL GORDON, D.D., a Protestant Episcopal clergyman, graduated from the General Theological Seminary; officiated in St. Louis, Mo., in 1853, and in the following year became rector. In 1857 he resided in Amesbury, Mass.; subsequently became rector of St. James's Church in that place, and continued to serve that parish until 1872. He died Aug. 9, 1873, aged fifty-three years. See *Prot. Episc. Almanac*, 1874, p. 138.

Esthonian Version. See REVAL ESTHONIAN VERSION; RUSSIA (VERSIONS OF).

Estori HAP-PARCHI *ben-Moses*. See PARCHI ESTORI.

Estouteville, GUILLAUME, a French prelate, was born before 1403. He studied at the University of Paris, entered early the Benedictine order, and was raised to the highest dignity, being successively bishop of Maurienne, Digne, Beziers, Ostia, Velletri, and Port-Sainte-Rufin, and also archbishop of Rouen. He had, among other abbeys, those of St. Ouen de Rouen, of Jumiéges, of Montebourg, and of Mont St. Michel, together with the priories of St. Martin-des-Champs, at Paris, Grand Pré, and Beaumont en Auge (Normandy). In 1437 he was made cardinal-priest by Eugenius IV, with the title of *Silvestre et Martin des Monts*. He was legate in France under Nicholas V, and took part in the election of four pontiffs. In 1477 Sixtus IV appointed him chamberlain of the Church of Rome. D'Estouteville died dean of the sacred college, Dec. 22, 1483. He bestowed his immense wealth on several ecclesiastical and literary institutions. See Hoefer, *Nouv. Biog. Générale*, s. v.

Estrées, César d', a French prelate, was born at Paris, Feb. 5, 1628. When quite young he was appointed bishop of Laon. Louis XIV charged him several times with negotiations, in which he showed a profound knowledge of the affairs of the Church and of those of the State. D'Estrées obtained the cardinal's hat in 1674. In 1680 he resigned the bishopric of Laon in favor of his nephew, and went to Rome on public affairs. He was eventually made abbot of St. Germain-des-Prés, and died dean of the French Academy, Dec. 18, 1714. See Hoefer, *Nouv. Biog. Générale*, s. v.

Estrées, Jean d', a French prelate, was born in 1666, and became abbot of St. Claude. Louis XIV sent him on an embassy to Portugal in 1692, and finally to Spain in 1703. In January, 1716, he was appointed archbishop of Cambray, and died March 3, 1718, without being consecrated. See Hoefer, *Nouv. Biog. Générale*, s. v.

Etam. The rock thus designated in the account of Samson's exploits (Judg. xv) is regarded by Lieut. Conder (*Quar. Statement* of the "Pal. Explor. Fund," Jan. 1875, p. 12) as the remarkable chasm or cave near the present *Beit-Atâb*, eight miles west by north from Bethlehem, and described in the *Memoirs* accompanying the Ordnance Survey (iii, 23) as a cavern some two hundred and fifty feet long, with an average height of five to eight feet and a width of about eighteen feet; entered at the east end by a vertical shaft called "the well," six by five feet wide and twenty feet deep. The village is a small one, standing on a bare knoll of rock some sixty to one hundred feet above the surrounding ridge, with cisterns to the houses, and a few traces of antiquity. The place is in the vicinity of Samson's adventures, and the identification is accepted by Tristram (*Bible Places*, p. 48).

Etam of Simeon (1 Chron. iv, 32) will in that case be a different place, for which Lieut. Conder suggests (*Tent Work in Palest.* ii, 336) the present ruin *Aitûn*, laid down on the *Ordnance Map* at eight miles south by east from Beit-Jibim, and described in the accompanying *Memoirs* (iii, 278) as "a mound with foundations; a square cell is cut in the rock opposite the ruin on the south."

Etam of Judah (2 Chron. xi, 6), as still different, has been confirmed at Wady Urtas by the recovery of the name in *Ain-Atân*, a spring on the hillside, south-east of the pools of Solomon (el-Burak), one of the four that feed the reservoirs (*Memoirs* to the Ordnance Survey, iii, 90).

Étampes-Valençay, Achille d', a French prelate and general, was born at Tours in 1589. He was for a long time a valiant captain of the Knights of Malta. At the siege of Montauban he attracted the attention of Louis XIII, who assigned him a company of cavalry in his regiment. After the capture of La Rochelle, where he commanded as vice-admiral, he became major-general. Immediately after the restoration of peace he returned to Malta. Pope Urban VIII charged him with the command of the pontifical troops against the duke of Parma, and as a reward gave him the cardinal's hat. The new prelate showed as much vigor in the council as he had at the head of the army. He was involved in a contest between Mazarin and the court of Rome. He died in that city in 1646. See Hoefer, *Nouv. Biog. Générale*, s. v.

Étampes-Valençay, Léonor d', a French prelate and theologian, brother of the preceding, was born about 1585. He entered the ministry, and obtained, while quite young, the abbey of Bourgueil-en-Vallée, which he represented as deputy to the Estates-general of 1614. In 1620 he succeeded his cousin Philippe Hurault in the see of Chartres, and in 1647 was transferred to the archbishopric of Rheims. He signalized himself in the assembly of the clergy of 1636 by maintaining the royal authority. He died at Paris in 1651, leaving a poem in Latin, in honor of the Virgin (Paris, 1605):—a *Ritual*, for the diocese of Chartres (ibid. 1627). See Hoefer, *Nouv. Biog. Générale*, s. v.

Etchen (**Echeus**, or **Etlan**), commemorated Feb. 11 in the Irish and Scotch calendars, was bishop of Cluain-foda, in Meath, of royal descent, originally a physician. He seems to have been born cir. A.D. 490, to have lived on the borders of Ossory, and died A.D. 578.

Eternālès, a Christian sect, supposed to have arisen about A.D. 260, deriving their name from their belief in the eternity of the world. They maintained that the earth will continue in its present state, even after the resurrection of the dead.

Eternity of the World. See COSMOGONY.

Ethelbert. (1) *Saint*, king of the East-Angles, beheaded in 792 (rather 794) by order of Offa, king of Mercia, and venerated May 20 as the patron of Hereford. (2) *Saint*, martyred with his brother, St. Ethelred, at the court of their cousin Egbert, king of Kent, in the 7th century, and commemorated on Oct. 17. (3) Archbishop of York (called also *Adalbert*, and usually *Albert*), a kinsman and pupil of archbishop Egbert, and the teacher of Alcuin, was consecrated to the see April 24, 767, and in 773 pope Adrian sent him the pallium. He made an excellent archbishop, continuing his frugal habits, and devoting himself to the interests of the Church. In 780 he appointed Eanbald his coadjutor, and died at York, Nov. 8, 781 or 782. (4) Bishop of Withem, in Galloway, consecrated June 10, 777; died Oct. 16, 797.

Ethelburga is the name of several early English abbesses, one of whom is especially entitled *saint*. She was sister to Erkenwald, bishop of London; was by him appointed first abbess of the nunnery at Barking, Essex, which he built and endowed. Here she led a very austere life, and died in 676. She is commemorated on Oct. 11.

Ethelgar, archbishop of Canterbury, was educated at Glastonbury, where he was a favorite pupil. In 964 he was appointed abbot of Newminster at Winchester, and on May 2, 980, he was consecrated to the see of Selsey.

For more than eight years Ethelgar was bishop of Selsey. In 988 he was translated to the see of Canterbury. All hopes and expectations seem to have been disappointed by his death, Dec. 3, 989. See Hook, *Lives of the Abps. of Canterbury*, i, 428 sq.

Ethelhard, archbishop of Canterbury, does not seem to have figured in history until his consecration to that see, July 21, 793. His first public act was to assist in nominating representatives to attend the council which the emperor Charlemagne had called to assemble at Frankfort, one of the most important councils ever held in the West. His administration was one of success and satisfaction to his people. He was especially instrumental in securing, in 802, the pope's recognition of the sovereign rights of the see. He died May 12, 805. See Hook, *Lives of the Abps. of Canterbury*, i, 255 sq.; Smith, *Dict. of Christ. Biog.* s. v.

Ethelnoth, archbishop of Canterbury, was the son of Egelmaer, the earl, and was a Glastonbury man. He obtained the grant of additional privileges for the monastery from Canute, and is reported to have written its history. He was first a monk of Glastonbury, then dean of Canterbury, and chaplain to Canute, the king. Other preferment he declined until a vacancy occurred in the see of Canterbury. In 1020 the see was vacant, and Ethelnoth was nominated by the king as primate of England. Having settled his affairs in Canterbury, he made provision for a temporary absence, and proceeded to Rome in 1022, where he was received with distinction by Benedict VIII. From Rome he went to Pavia to visit the tomb of St. Augustine of Hippo. Ethelnoth seems to have been a church restorer. He repaired substantially the cathedral, which his predecessors had only patched over. He displayed both firmness and discretion during his administration. He died in October, 1038. See Hook, *Lives of the Abps. of Canterbury*, i, 478 sq.

Ethelred, archbishop of Canterbury, is said to have been bishop in Wiltshire before his appointment to Canterbury in 870. He was educated at the monastery of St. Augustine. After his appointment to the see, he went immediately to Rome for the pallium, as was required in those days. During Ethelred's administration it is said that Cameliac came to Canterbury to be consecrated by him to the see of Llandaff. This plainly shows that the spiritual supremacy of the English Church already extended, at least, over the south-eastern part of Wales. In the episcopate of Ethelred, the same Church gave proof of its revived energy, by opening a communication with the Christians of the far East, especially with those then existing in India. These things occurred towards the close of Ethelred's life. He was cordial in his co-operation with the king, and took many steps towards the reformation of the Church. To him also is due, at least, the merit of carrying into effect the will of the sovereign. He died in 889. See Hook, *Lives of the Abps. of Canterbury*, i, 298 sq.

Ethelred. See AILRED.

Ethelreda, *Saint*. See AUDRY, ST.

Ethelwold (Lat. *Ædilualdus*), bishop of Lindisfarne, cir. 724–740, was originally a servant under St. Cuthbert, and afterwards abbot of Melrose, and lived through many vicissitudes in those days of peril. He is commemorated on Feb. 12.

Ether is identified by lieutenant Conder (*Tent Work in Palestine*, ii, 336) with a ruined site, *el-Atr*, one mile north-west of Beit-Jibrin; but it is doubtful if the territory of Simeon extended so far north. Van de Velde's *Tell Athan*, "a little to the north-east of Beersheba," which is adopted by Tristram (*Bible Places*, p. 42), does not appear on the *Ordnance Map*.

Ethiopian Church. See ABYSSINIAN CHURCH.

Ethiopian Monks. Monasticism spread rapidly up the Nile into Ethiopia, and gained as strong a hold there as in Egypt or Syria, if not a stronger. All the monasteries in Ethiopia professed to obey the so-called "Rule of Antony," but with different observances. An attempt at reformation, such as invariably recurs in the life of a monastic order, was made in the 7th century; Tecla-Haimanot being the second founder or Benedict of Ethiopian monasticism. He endeavored to consolidate the system under a superior-general, second in ecclesiastical rank only to the patriarch of Ethiopia, who was to visit and inspect the monasteries personally or by proxy. Several of them, however, preferred to retain their independence, like Congregationalists. Monks swarmed in Ethiopia long after the first fervor of asceticism; and the constitution of the Ethiopian Church was monastic. The story of a military order of monks, like the knights-templar, originating in the 4th century, is purely fabulous. See Helyot, *Dict. des Ordres Religieux*, ii, 222 sq.

Ethiopian Monk.

Ethnophrŏnēs (from ἔθνος, *a nation*, and φρονέω, *to think*), a name sometimes applied to the heretics of the 7th century, who sought to combine pagan customs and ceremonies with Christianity.

Etsbega, a dignitary of the Abyssinian Church, next in authority to the Abuna (q. v.).

Etu, an object of worship in the islands of the Pacific, consisting of some bird, fish, or reptile, in which the natives believed a spirit resided. For an account of this worship see Williams, *Missionary Researches*.

Eucadires, priests of the ancient Carthaginian deities, also called *Abadires* (q. v.).

Eucherius, the thirty-second bishop of Orleans, was born there, of noble parents, towards the close of the 7th century; devoted himself early to a monastic life at Jumiéges; was elected to the see on the death of his uncle, in 717; administered it with remarkable success, but was banished to Cologne, in 732, by Charles Martel, apparently for resisting a confiscation of the Church revenues; and died at a place near Liege in 738 (or 742). He is commemorated Feb. 20.

Euchomĕni (from εὔχομαι, *to pray*), a name sometimes applied to those of the catechumens (q. v.) who remained to receive the minister's prayers and benedictions. See GENUFLECTENTES.

Eudes DE ROUGEMONT, sixty-eighth bishop of Besançon, belonged to one of the oldest families of Burgundy, and succeeded, Feb. 9, 1269, Guillaume de La Tour. He fell into a quarrel with his people, in 1279, concerning the expenses of the see, which resulted in his discomfiture. He died June 23, 1301. See Hoefer, *Nouv. Biog. Générale*, s. v.

Eufronius. See EUPHRONIUS.

Eugenius, a Catholic bishop OF CARTHAGE, was elected to that see in 480 or 481. In 483 he was banished by the Arian party to Tripoli, where he remained until 484, when he returned to his diocese. But the next king banished him to Gaul, where he remained the rest of his life. He died at Vienne, Sept. 6, 505. He left *Expositio Fidei Catholici* (printed in Migne, *Patrol. Lat.* lviii). See Chalmers, *Biog. Dict.* s. v.; Smith, *Dict. of Christ. Biog.* s. v.

Eugenius, bishop OF TOLEDO, the second of that name, was first a clerk of the Church there, and on being chosen bishop, retired to Saragossa in a monastery; but being discovered, was brought back to Toledo, and ordained in 646. He presided at the councils held at Toledo in the years 653, 655, and 656, and died in 657. He was the author of several works, particularly a treatise on the Trinity, two books of miscellanies, and one in prose and verse, which were published by father Sirmond at Paris (1619, 8vo; also in 1696; Venice, 1728, in the *Bibliotheca Max. Patrum;* Lyons, 1677, xii, 345). See Chalmers, *Biog. Dict.* s. v.; Smith, *Dict. of Christ. Biog.* s. v.

Eukteroi Oikoi (*εὐκτήριον, an oratory,* and *οἶκος, a house*), a name sometimes applied to ancient Christian churches.

Eulogium, the consecrated bread of the Greek Church.

Eulysius, bishop of Apamea, in Bithynia, one of Chrysostom's most loyal adherents, banished to Mizpah, beyond Bosrah, in Syria, A.D. 406.

Eumenides. See FURIES.

Euphemia, *Saint*, of Chalcedon, suffered martyrdom in the time of Galerius, cir. A.D. 307. Her anniversary is Sept. 16.

Euphemius (by some *Euthymius*), third patriarch of Constantinople, A.D. 489–496, was a learned historian and orthodox presbyter of that city, but became involved in the jealousies between the Greek and Roman ecclesiastics, and was finally deposed by the emperor Anastasius. He died in 515.

Euphrasia (or **Euphrosyna**), daughter of Paphnutius of Alexandria, early in the 5th century, fled from home to avoid marriage, and was received into a neighboring monastery, where, under the assumed name of *Smaragdius*, she concealed her sex for thirty-eight years. Her father meanwhile visited her, without recognising her, and was converted to Christianity. On her death-bed she discovered herself to him, and he became a monk. She is commemorated by the Latins, Feb. 11; by the Greeks, Sept. 25.

Euphrates, a heretic of the 2d century, was the founder of the sect of Ophites or Serpentarians, one of whose dogmas was, that the serpent by which our first parents were deceived was either Christ himself or Sophia (*wisdom*) concealed under that form, for which reason they paid a kind of divine honor to certain serpents kept for that purpose. In most points he adhered to the Oriental or Gnostic philosophy, of two opposite principles, with the æons and other dreams of those sects. Origen did not consider the disciples of Euphrates as Christians, but as calumniators of Jesus Christ.

Euphronius (or **Eufronius**). (1) Bishop of Antioch, intruded by the Arian party, A.D. 332–334. (2) Bishop of Colonia, in Armenia; afterwards metropolitan of Nicopolis, A.D. 375. (3) Ninth bishop of Autun, not long before A.D. 452; commemorated Aug. 3. (4) The eighteenth bishop of Tours, A.D. 555–572, who resisted the violent encroachments of the civil power, died in his seventieth year, and is commemorated Aug. 4.

Eurōpa, in Greek mythology, was the famous beloved of Jupiter, for whose sake he transformed himself into a bull, and took her on his back to Crete, where she gave birth by him to Minos, Rhadamanthus, and Sarpedon. According to Homer, she was a daughter of Phœnix and Perimede; but later writers make her the daughter of the Phœnician king Agenor and Telephassa. Agenor, on learning of her abduction, sent out all his sons in search of her, with the command not to return without her. As they did not discover her, the sons settled in strange countries, and thus the father lost all his children. Europa married Asterion, the

Antique Stone Figure of Europa.

king of Crete, who brought up her children as wise, just men, so that they became the judges of the infernal regions. She was worshipped on Crete. The myth doubtless represents the passage of colonists across the Hellespont from Asia to Europe.

Eurus, in Greek mythology, is the east, or, rather, south-east, wind, bringing to the Greeks close, damp

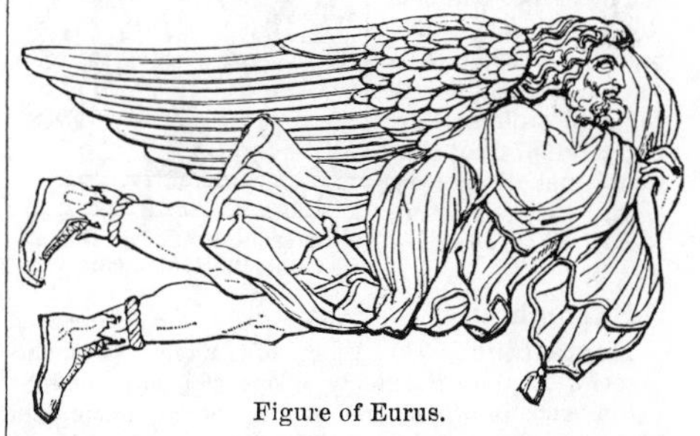

Figure of Eurus.

weather, and heavy storms. Therefore he is represented on the tower of the winds with flowing hair, tangled beard, and of surly aspect. See EAST WIND.

Eusebia, *Saint*, abbess of Hamay or Hamaige, daughter of Adalbrand, a Frankish lord, and of St. Rictrude, was born in 637. She was educated by her grandmother, St. Gertrude, abbess of Hamay (Hamaticum), and was elected to succeed her in 649; but as she was only twelve years old, Rictrude, who at that time was abbess of Marchiennes, let her come into her convent with her whole community, by order of the king, Clovis II. Eusebia, who could not forget her monastery of Hamaige, therefore rose secretly in the night with one of her friends, and went there to chant the service, and came back the following morning to Marchiennes. Her mother found this out, however, gave her a severe chastisement, and engaged many bishops and abbots to remonstrate with her, but they found her inflexible, and advised Rictrude to leave her at liberty. When only thirteen years old, Eusebia returned to Hamaige as abbess, and governed her community with humility, mildness, and prudence. She died in 660, and is commemorated March 16. See Hoefer, *Nouv. Biog. Générale*, s. v.; Smith, *Dict. of Christ. Biog.* s. v.

Eusebius, the name of a very great number of early Christian ecclesiastics, of whom we mention a few of the most noted. (1) Fifth bishop of Antibes, cir. A.D. 549–554. (2) Bishop of Cæsarea, in Cappadocia, A.D. 362–370, a friend of Gregory Nazianzen. (3) The twenty-second bishop of Milan, A.D. 449–465. (4) Bishop of Pelusium, cir. A.D. 431–457. (5) Bishop of Tarragona, cir. A.D. 610–632. (6) Bishop of Valentinianopolis, in proconsular Asia, deposed for scandalous acts, A.D. 400. (7) Presbyter of Rome, A.D. 538, commemorated as a confessor Aug. 14. (8) Presbyter of Cremona, a friend of St. Jerome.

Representation of St. Eustachius, by Domenichino.

Eustachius (or **Eustathius**, said to have been named *Placidius* before his conversion), a noted saint, is commemorated by the Latins Nov. 2, and by the Greeks Sept. 20, as a military martyr, along with his wife Theopista, and his two sons, Agapius and Theopistus, at Rome, under Hadrian, A.D. 118. His *Acts* are evidently spurious, but his martyrdom is undoubted. Many churches are dedicated to him, especially one in Rome, and one in Paris. Baronius thinks he may have been the Placidus who was a general under Titus (Josephus, *War*, iii, 4; iv, 187), but that would make him very aged. See Jameson, *Sacred and Legendary Art*, p. 792.

Eustachius, GIOV. PAUL. See NOLA PAUL.

Eustathius. (1) Abbot of Luxeuil (Franche-Comté), born in Burgundy about 560, succeeded St. Columbanus in 610, labored as a missionary among the Varasci in 616, and died in 625; commemorated March 29 (by others Oct. 11). (2) Bishop of Attalia, resigned in 431. (3) Bishop of Berytus, in Syria, ejected for time-serving heresy, in 457. (4) Patriarch of Alexandria, 801–805.

Eustochius. (1) Fifth archbishop of Tours, 443–460, is commemorated as a saint, Sept. 19. (2) Patriarch of Jerusalem, 544–556.

Eustorgius, bishop of Milan, 512–518.

Antique Figure of Euterpe.

Eustrates, one of a class of martyrs to whom a festival is dedicated in the Greek Church on Dec. 13.

Eustratius, a Greek theologian, who lived in the 6th century, wrote a treatise on *The Condition of the Soul of Man after Death*, printed for the first time by Leo Allatius, in the *De Occidentalium atque Orientalium*. The author has been identified with Eustathius, the biographer of Eutychius, of the 6th century.

Eustratius, bishop of Nice, flourished in the beginning of the 12th century, and was noted for his polemic writings in divinity, and his philosophical works. His Greek commentaries on Aristotle's *Analytica*, and on his *Ethica*, are still extant; the former published at Venice in 1534, the latter at the same place in 1536, and at Paris in 1543.

Euterpe, in Greek mythology, one of the muses, who presided over lyric poetry. See cut below.

Eutherius, bishop of Tyana, an earnest Nestorian, was an acknowledged leader of that party in the Council of Ephesus (A.D. 431), and for some time afterwards. He was ultimately banished to Scythopolis, and thence to Tyre, where he died. He wrote a treatise, usually published with the works of Athanasius.

Euthymius, abbot of Pharan, in Judæa, was born in Melitene (Armenia) in 377. He was educated under bishop Otreius, who ordained him priest, and intrusted him with the direction of the monasteries of Melitene. In 406 he went to Palestine, and retired into a cell near Jerusalem. Soon after he was joined by a great number of recluses, who chose him as their superior. His authority extended over several monasteries. Euthymius converted to Christianity a large number of Arabians, and brought back to the orthodox Church several Nestorians and Manichæans. Through his entreaty also the empress Eudoxia, the wife of Theodosius the younger, entered into the bosom of the Catholic Church. There was also attributed to Euthymius the power of performing miracles. He died in 473. After his death he was revered as a saint, first in the East, and then in the West. See Hoefer, *Nouvelle Biographie Générale*, s. v.; Smith, *Dictionary of Christian Biography*, s. v.

Eutropius, bishop of Valencia, in Spain, towards the end of the 6th century, originally abbot of the monastery of Servitanum, was associated with the most influential Spanish ecclesiastics of his time.

Eutuchites (from εὐ, *good*, and τίχη, *fortune*), a heretical sect mentioned by Theodoret as belonging to the 3d century. They held that our souls were placed in our bodies only to honor the angels who created them, that we ought to be afflicted at nothing, and to be equally pleased with vice and virtue. They also taught that Christ was the son of an unknown god.

Eutychianus, a celebrated monk in the mountains separating Phrygia and Bithynia, in the time of Constantine the Great.

Eutychius. (1) Bishop of Eleutheropolis (Hebron), in Palestine, in the middle of the 4th century, was deposed for semi-Arianism. (2) Sub-deacon of Alexandria, martyred by the Arians, A.D. 356. (3) The last-known exarch of Ravenna, A.D. 727–751.

Evagrius. (1) Orthodox bishop of Constantinople for two months in 370. (2) Bishop of Antioch, cir. A.D. 388–392.

Evaldus, a Scotch prelate, was appointed the first bishop of the see of Argyle in 1200, by bishop John. See Keith, *Scottish Bishops*, p. 284.

Evangel (Gr. εὐαγγέλιον, *good tidings*), a name often applied to the gospel. Hence the term *evangelical* (q. v.).

Evangelical Adventists. See ADVENTISTS, EVANGELICAL.

Evangelista, the name given in the Greek Church to the deacon who reads the gospels in the course of divine service.

Evangelists, THE FOUR, *Representations of, in Christian Art.* The adoption of the four creatures of the apocalypse (iv, 6) as images of the evangelists does not seem to have taken place generally, or is not recorded on Christian monuments, before the 5th century. It involves, of course, a peculiarly impressive connection between the beginning of the visions of Ezekiel and the unveiling of heaven to the eyes of John. The application of each symbol to each writer may be referred

St. Matthew.

to Jerome on Ezekiel i. Matthew has the man, as beginning his gospel with the Lord's human genealogy;

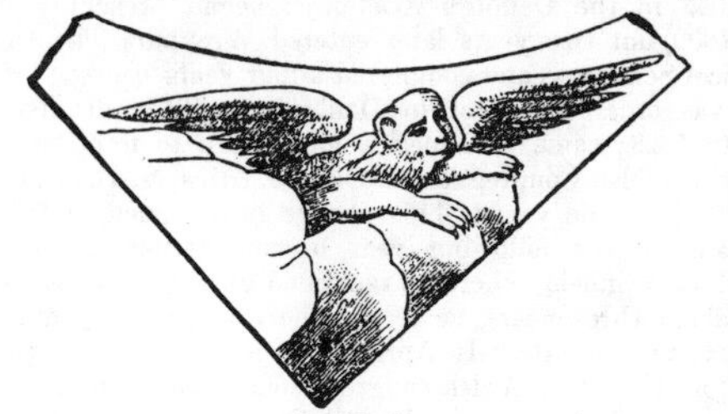
St. Mark.

Mark the lion, as testifying the Lord's royal dignity, or as containing the terrible condemnation of unbelievers

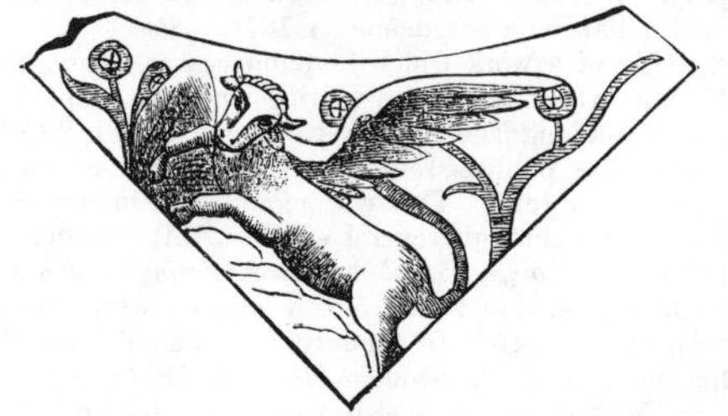
St. Luke.

at the end of his gospel; Luke the ox, as he dwells on the priesthood and sacrifice of Christ; John the eagle,

St. John.

as contemplating the Lord's divine nature. Ingenuity and devotion have done their utmost on this subject for centuries, with little result. The accompanying emblematical figures are found in the chapel of San Satiro, in Milan. See Martigny, *Dict. des Arch. Chrétienne*, s. v.; Jameson, *Sacred and Legendary Art*, p. 132 sq.

Evangelists. In the British census of 1851 four congregations returned themselves as worshipping under this name, probably to avoid being identified with any sect.

Evans, Benjamin, D.D., an English Baptist minister, was born at Bilston, Staffordshire, May 13, 1803. As a boy his thirst for knowledge was intense, and he excelled in drawings on Staffordshire pottery-ware. He was converted in his youth, joined the Baptists, and at twenty entered Horton College, Bradford, Yorkshire. In 1825 he accepted an invitation as pastor over a very small Church at the seaport of Scarborough, where, for forty years, he preached four sermons, held five prayer-meetings, and conducted three Bible-classes weekly. He formed a new Baptist Ministerial Association, which sent out a young man from Horton College to represent the Baptist cause in Germany. He also founded the first Baptist church in Brussels. He effectually resisted the levying of Church rates in Scarborough on Independents; took a leading part in the anti-Corn-Law League, and in the anti-State-Church Associations, and was the founder and first secretary of the Mechanics' Institute in the town; the Archæological Society and Museum owes much of its success to his efforts. He was the founder of the Society for the Education of Ministers' Sons, and its president; the founder of the Theological College at Bury, and professor of ecclesiastical history in it; and he also established and edited *The Baptist Record*, a quarterly journal. Among his published works are, *The Enlarged History of Scarborough:—The History of Horton and Rawdon Colleges:—The History of the Early English Baptists* (2 vols.):—*Modern Popery:—Hints to Young Christians:—Life of Wickliffe:—History of the German Reformation:—Lectures on Ecclesiastical History:—The Religious State of Belgium*, and about a score of pamphlets on popular topics. He was the father of the *Freeman* newspaper, and a contributor to half a dozen Baptist magazines. He died suddenly, April 6, 1871. See (Lond.) *Baptist Hand-book*, 1872.

Evans, C., D.D., a Welsh Baptist minister, was born at Llannwchllyn, Merionethshire, June 22, 1781. He was baptized in early life, began to preach in 1809, was two years in the Abergavenny Academy, and then for seven years pastor of the small Church of Llannefyd and Llansannan. In 1823 he removed to Cefnmawr, which was his residence for thirty-five years, during twenty-nine of which he was pastor of the Church in that place. Considering the imperfection of his early education, he became a more than ordinarily cultured scholar, and wrote, *The Peculiar Tenets of the Baptists*, and *A History of the Baptists, Based on the Fundamental Principles of their System.* He died March 28, 1864. See (Lond.) *Baptist Hand-book*, 1865, p. 121. (J. C. S.)

Evans, Evan (1), D.D., a minister of the Church of England, is supposed to have been a native of Wales. He was sent to Philadelphia, Pa., by the bishop of London, in 1700. Five years before, a church had been built there, and of this he took charge. Through his instrumentality churches were formed at Chichester, Chester, Maidenhead, Concord, Evesham, Montgomery, Radnor, and Oxford, places all within a radius of forty miles. After four years of service at Philadelphia, he asked for and received an assistant. In 1707 he visited England, and urged that a bishop should be sent over to the colonies. In 1709 he returned to his charge in Philadelphia, and in 1711 it was found necessary to enlarge the church edifice. Resigning, he again visited England in 1716, and on his return to America accepted an appointment to Oxford and Radnor, a part of his former field, and remained there until 1718, when he resigned his mission, removed to Maryland, to St. George's parish, then in Baltimore, now Harford, County, and on every alternate Sabbath officiated in the adjoining parish, over twenty miles distant. He died in October, 1721. See Sprague, *Annals of the Amer. Pulpit*, v, 22.

Evans, Evan (2), a Welsh divine and poet, was born at Cynhawdren, in Cardiganshire, about 1730, and was educated at Jesus College, Oxford. After taking orders in college, he officiated as curate in several places, particularly Newick, in Kent, Llanvair Talhaiarn, in Denbighshire, and Towyn, in Merionethshire. He died at his birthplace in 1790. He published *Dissertatio de Bardis* (1764, 4to), and translated into Welsh two volumes of *Tillotson's Sermons.* See Chalmers, *Biog. Dict.* s. v.; Allibone, *Dict. of Brit. and Amer. Authors*, s. v.

Evans, James, the celebrated Canadian missionary among the Indians, brother of Rev. Ephraim Evans, D.D., entered upon the missionary work at St. Clair, Ont., in 1834. He labored at Rice Lake, Credit, Ancaster, and other places. To his mental vigor and indomitable perseverance the Indians are indebted for many advantages. Not the least of these is a written and printed character of their language, invented by Evans. He left behind him many papers, both in print and manuscript—a private journal, translations, Indian vocabularies, letters, etc. He died suddenly, while on a visit to England, at Keelby, Lincolnshire, Nov. 23, 1846. Evans was a warm friend, a man of gênius, an enterprising explorer, a devoted missionary, and an humble Christian. See *Minutes of the British Conference*, 1847, p. 462; Carroll, *Case and his Contemporaries* (see index, vol. v).

Evans, James Harrington, a Baptist minister of John Street Chapel, London, was born about 1785. He died about 1849. His works are, *Dialogues on the Trinity* (Lond. 1819, 8vo):—*Sermons on the Spirit of Holiness* (1839, 4th ed. 12mo). See Allibone, *Dict. of Brit. and Amer. Authors*, s. v.

Evans, John, LL.D., a Baptist minister, was born about 1767, at Usk, Monmouthshire. He was pastor of a congregation of General Baptists, Worship Street, London, from 1792 to 1827, and died in the latter year, leaving a number of theological sermons and other works, for a list of which see Watt, *Bibl. Brit.*, and the *Gentleman's Magazine*, XCVII, i, 369. He published, in 1797, *An Attempt to Account for the Infidelity of the Late Mr. Gibbon.* His best-known work is a *Brief Sketch of the Different Denominations into which the Christian World is Divided* (1794). See Allibone, *Dict. of Brit. and Amer. Authors*, s. v.

Evans, Jonathan, an English Congregational minister, was born at Coventry about 1748. He was converted in 1778 or 1779, and shortly after began to work with much earnestness for the salvation of his irreligious neighbors. In 1782 he turned his attention more particularly to the parish of Foleshill, near Coventry, and was so successful as to purchase, in 1784, a building for a place of worship, and eventually a chapel was built. In 1796 a church was formed, chiefly of those who were the fruits of his ministry, of which he was ordained pastor, April 4, 1797. He died Aug. 31, 1809. Mr. Evans was a plain, earnest preacher, and very successful in winning souls. He was the author of three fine hymns, commencing, "Come, thou soul-transforming spirit," "Hark! the voice of love and mercy," "Let saints on earth their anthems raise." See (Lond.) *Evangelical Magazine*, 1847, p. 128.

Eveillon, Jacques, a French theologian, and grand-vicar of Angers under Messrs. Fouquet, Miron, De Reuil, and Arnaud, was born at Angers in 1572, and obtained his preferments in consequence of his superior knowledge of ecclesiastical laws and customs. He died at Angers in 1651. He was the author of an excellent treatise, *Des Excommunications et des Monitoires* (1672). See Chalmers, *Biog. Dict.* s. v.; Hoefer, *Nouv. Biog. Générale*, s. v.

Eveleigh, John, D.D., provost of Oriel College, Oxford, and prebendary of Rochester (1781), was born in 1747. He died Dec. 10, 1814, leaving *The Trinity* (1791):—*Sermons Preached before the University of Oxford* (1792):—*Plurality of Persons in the Godhead Proved* (1797). See Allibone, *Dict. of Brit. and Amer. Authors*, s. v.

Everett, James, a noted English Methodist preacher, was born at Alnwick, Northumberland, May 16, 1784. He was converted when about nineteen years of age, joined the Wesleyans, soon began to preach, in 1806 was called into the regular work at Sunderland, and afterwards occupied important appointments in the Conference until 1821, when he became a supernumerary; but in 1828 resumed an efficient relation for a few years, and then retired as a superannuate to the city of York. In 1847 the celebrated "Fly Sheets" appeared in the Wesleyan connection, strongly inveighing against its administration; and their authorship being charged upon Mr. Everett, and he not denying it, he was expelled in 1848 from the ministry, together with Revs. James Dunn and Walter Griffith, who united in forming what has since been known as the Methodist Free Church (q. v.). Mr. Everett died in Sunderland, May 10, 1872. He is the author of several publications, chiefly biographical.

Everett, Robert, D.D., a Congregational minister, was born in Gronant, North Wales, Jan. 2, 1791. He studied under Rev. Thomas Jones, of Newmarket, also in the Denbigh Academy; began preaching in 1809, but two years later entered Wrexham Theological Seminary, and completed a four years' course. He was ordained pastor in Denbigh in 1815; dismissed in 1823; came to America and began to minister to the Welsh Congregational Church, Utica, N. Y., in July of the same year. This charge he resigned in 1832, and in the following year became acting pastor at East Winfield, where he remained until 1835, when, for about three years, he served the Presbyterian Church at Westernville. In April, 1838, he was installed pastor of the two Welsh congregations of Steuben, a position which he retained until the close of his life, although, during the last few years, he preached only occasionally. He died there, Feb. 25, 1875. The Welsh people in the United States gave him eleven hundred dollars as a testimonial in 1871. *Stenographia* is the title of a work which he published at Denbigh in 1816, in which shorthand writing was first adapted to the Welsh language. Sixty editions of his *First Catechism* were published in Wales, being first issued at Denbigh in 1822. This was republished in America, and passed through several editions. At Steuben he published a *Larger Catechism;* also *Arveinydd*, an aid to reading Welsh, of which fifteen editions were printed prior to his death. In January, 1840, he published the first number of *Y Cenhadwr Americanaidd* (The American Missionary), a Welsh Congregational monthly, which was edited, after his death, by his son. In 1843 he published *Y Dyngarwr* (The Philanthropist), devoted to emancipation and temperance; and from 1850 to 1852 he edited *Y Detholydd* (Eclectic). Two Welsh hymn-books, published in 1839 and 1846, were in large part prepared by Dr. Everett. See *Cong. Quarterly*, 1876, p. 425; 1877, p. 314.

Everton, Silvester de, an English prelate of the 13th century, took his name from Everton, a village in Bedfordshire. He received the lord chancellorship of England in 1246, and was very skilful in customs of chancery. The next year he was consecrated bishop of Carlisle. With the rest of the English bishops he boldly requested of Henry III that all foreigners and insufficient persons might be put out of their bishoprics. The king retorted on the bishops, singling out Silvester as to the point of insufficiency. Everton lost his life by a fall from a horse, in 1254. See Fuller, *Worthies of England* (ed. Nuttall), i, 168.

Evigilātor, an officer in Greek monasteries, whose duty it was to waken the monks for nocturnal and matutinal services. Another officer of the kind was the *excitator*, who had to waken a monk asleep in church.

Evocatio, a religious ceremony observed by the ancient Romans when besieging a town, in which they solemnly called upon the deities of the place to forsake it and come over to their assistance. They usually attempted to bribe the gods by promising them temples and festivals.

Evodius, according to tradition, the first bishop of Antioch, after A.D. 42.

Evolution. The important relations which the scientific subject has assumed to religious literature justifies us in a more copious and particular treatment than was appropriate under the general head of DEVELOPMENT (q. v.).*

I. *Definition.*—Evolution in its widest sense, and viewed from the scientific standpoint, is the continuous transformation and differentiation of an identical substance. More specifically, it is the continuous unfolding of a material existence according to such method that constituent parts which were germinal or potential become actual and functional, and according to such an order that the primitive existence is successively more differentiated, with parts progressively more and more specialized in structure and function. It is the passage from the homogeneous to the heterogeneous. It implies continuity and unity of existence. It also implies persistence of the fundamental conception embodied in the primitive substance, so that, however diversified, all its parts still conform to a changeless type. It is a mode which reveals itself transcendentally as the necessary product of mind; it reveals thought as all-pervading and all-enduring throughout the material realm in which the law of evolution finds its exemplification.

Whether the phenomena of the natural world come into existence under a method conformable to the above definition of evolution is a question of fact, to be decided by investigation of the phenomena.† This question of fact falls, therefore, strictly within the domain of natural science. Whatever verdict may be pronounced at this tribunal can never be invalidated by any *à priori* considerations, nor by any delineation of supposed consequences or implications of the verdict. Nor can it be set aside as proceeding from incompetent authority, since no authority in a question of fact can be conceived more competent than that of a body of witnesses who have surpassed all others in the study of that about which they testify. For our present purpose we must ascertain, therefore, what are the determinations of natural science in reference to the nature of the successions of phenomena in the natural world. Does science find a material continuity running through these successions; or does it find them marked by interruptions, discontinuity, and new beginnings?

II. *History of Opinion.*—In searching for the best judgment of mankind in reference to the question of material continuity in the natural world we ought to cite first the opinions of thinkers antedating the epoch when scientific research had supplied material for a proper demonstration of the doctrine. As all philosophizing on the laws of nature must, of necessity, be grounded on an observation of nature more or less extensive and more or less exact, so the opinions of the ancient philosophers, however slender the basis of their inductions, must be regarded as essentially scientific. Science had not yet been distinguished from philosophy. Theories as to the origin of the world and of organic existence were in vogue some centuries before the Christian æra. The hylozoism of the Ionian physicists conceived a primordial matter endowed with generative or transmutative powers through which cosmic forms, successively differentiated, came into being. The speculation presents analogies with the modern one of Buffon. Heraclitus, about 500 B.C., taught the doctrine of a perpetual flux of things, involving ceaseless conflicts between opposites, in the midst of which individual things survive, by superior fitness, the processes of destruction and renovation. A developmental mode of cosmic origins was taught by Anaxagoras of Clazomenæ (Aristotle, *Physica*, viii, 1) about 500 B.C. He supposed the primitive condition of things to be a heterogeneous commixture of substances without order or motion. This continued an indefinite period, when the mind began to act upon it by instituting a revolving motion at a single point. This propagated itself into the surrounding realm, and led to the separation of the elementary contraries, fire and air, water and earth. The process was repeated in the resulting masses, and thus, by continuous differentiation of likes and unlikes, the actual constitution of the world resulted (Ueberweg, *Hist of Philos.* i, 66). The views of Leucippus and Democritus, about 430 B.C., contemplated a gradual evolution of things. They held that immensity was eternally filled with atoms actuated by an eternal motion. These, in disposing themselves according to size, produced collisions which originated vortical motions. These, extending farther and farther, led to the formation of worlds. Such views were extended by Epicurus and the Roman Lucretius; and long afterwards, similar theories, but with more theistic leanings, were entertained by Torricelli, Galileo, and Gassendi. The Greek atomists attributed the lateral motions of the atoms to choice—a conception of the animated nature of atoms which was revived in the monads of Gassendi, Leibnitz, Rosmini, Campanella, Bruno, and Maupertuis; and reproduced in the conscious atoms and molecules of Häckel, Elsberg, and other moderns. The evolution of the cosmic system through the intervention of vortices was undertaken in the well-known theory of Descartes (*Principia Philosophiæ*, 1644); and Kepler made use, also, of a vortical movement in the matter of a primitive chaos, but invoked the Empedoclean conception of attractions and repulsions for the initiation of the primitive motions. The speculations of Swedenborg (*Principia Rerum Naturalium*, 1733-34) also posited vortical atomic motions, which expanded to cosmical movements and led to the differentiation of worlds. These various speculations (more fully set forth in Winchell's *World Life, or Comparative Geology*, pt. iv), opened the way for the better-defined and better-defended nebular cosmogonies of Kant and his successors. The evolution of the earth's physical features by means of fire and water was first undertaken by Leibnitz (*Protogæa*, etc., 1749, first, in abstract, in *Acta Eruditorum*, Leipzig, 1683). These eminent thinkers, whom, in this connection, we can only mention, all conceive the earth and the solar system to have originated through the progressive differentiations of a primitive chaotic matter. This is the conception of modern evolution.

Meantime the notion of a material continuity in the successions of the organic world was repeatedly shadowed forth. Empedocles taught the progressive origination of organic forms. Aristotle maintained that immanent divine mind determines in nature a tendency towards improvement and perfection. Lucretius held that the races of men, however diverse, are derived from a common origin, and this through the continual survival of those best fitted for the environment. In later times, Sir Mathew Hale (*Primitive Origination of Mankind*, 1677, p. 211), enumerates distinctly the results of the struggle for existence in the animal. De Maillet (*Telliamed*, Amsterdam, 1748), attempted to explain how animal forms undergo transmutation through the influence of changed environment; and Lamarck (*Philosophie Zoölogique*, new ed. 1873) to this influence added the principle of use and disuse, and admitted also an underlying inherent conatus towards beneficial change. These very concise references to the history of opinion may be supplemented by a perusal of the article on "Evolution" in the *Encyclopædia Britannica*, and by a study of the later works to be mentioned in the progress of this article. Within our restricted limits it will be more profitable to proceed to an outline of the evidences of evolution as at present understood.

III. *The Scientific Evidences.*—1. *Inorganic Evolution.* The processes of change in the topographical and hydrographical features of the earth's surface are so familiar that we almost fail to note the fact that these re-

* We present, unmodified, the facts and positions of our esteemed correspondent on this subject, who views it in a scientific aspect, although we dissent from some of his conclusions.—ED. See SCEPTICISM, in this volume.

† Not speculatively viewed, however, but in the light of all the evidence, both natural and revealed.—ED.

cent transformations are but the last terms of a series of changes which have moulded the globe and imparted to it the features that complete its fitness for the reception of organic populations. But, in fact, the filling and drainage of a pond or lakelet in a human lifetime is the same kind of work as that which spread the deposits of the prairies of the Mississippi, the *tchornosjom* of southern Russia, the pampas of Buenos Ayres, and the steppes of southern Siberia. The alluvial sediment left by a Mississippi overflow of this year is only one of the succession of contributions which, in ages past, have formed the entire delta of the great river. The delta grows; ocean sediments accumulate; the hillsides waste; the mountains wear out; whole shore-lines rise or sink; and the integration of these minute annual changes between vast limits of time shows that all the grander features of our planet have grown into existence by progressive transformations of the original matter. All this is obvious.

So it is obvious that the observed and admitted tenor of events implies an ancient course of change, in times so remote that the conditions had not yet approximated to those revealed in the human period. The pages of geological science enumerate those changes. It is not necessary to assume that all or any of the conclusions of science are exact in reference to the particular events of the geological past; it cannot be doubted, however, that research has successfully shown that the present is the outcome of the past, and that the rocks and waters and gases which we observe are only a transformed portion of the material of the primeval world. The actual earth has passed, by material continuity, from a primitive state, in which all its physical conditions were extremely different from the present. Its mountains, rivers, islands, and seas have progressively come into existence. Its different portions have become more and more differentiated. It was once more homogeneous. It has undergone a real evolution.

But the geognostic data which pass before our observation disclose the primitive world in a process of emergence from a molten state. The world's history has been a history of cooling; and there are numerous indications that the actual records of geology note only the last stages of the world's cooling history. We have not the space at command, nor is it necessary, to enter into an enumeration of the grounds on which science has traced terrestrial evolution backward to a nebular state, and even to a remoter one, in which the matter of the whole solar system is disclosed in a process of common evolution, under the action of the same forces as enter into the transformations of the earth's surface in these times, before human eyes. That our planetary system has had a nebular history is almost unanimously admitted by the science of the present. The chief divergences of opinion concern only some details of that history. This conclusion implies a material continuity through the totality of the changes. Rocks and ocean and atmosphere have *grown* out of fire-mist and nebula. World-life is a grand spectacle of evolution, and it illustrates continuity and unity of method on a scale of vastness which is deeply impressive. The details of the evolution must be sought in special works (see Winchell, *World Life*, 1883). The conception of modern nebular theory is itself an evolution. It was first shadowed forth by the Greek and mediæval thinkers already quoted. It began to assume a consistent and modern aspect at the hands of Immanuel Kant (*Allgemeine Naturgeschichte und Theorie des Himmels*, 1755, and a prize essay, read in 1754 before the Berlin Academy of Science). Sir William Herschel's nebular researches disclosed the apparent existence of enormous patches of chaotic world-stuff, which seemed to undergo a process of differentiation into stars and planets (see sundry memoirs, read before the Royal Society of London between 1783 and 1818, but especially in 1784, 1785, 1791, 1795, 1811, and 1814; also Sir John Herschel, *Observations of Nebulæ and Clusters of Stars at Slough*, 1825–33; *Phil. Trans.* Nov. 21, 1833). Laplace, in apparent ignorance of Kant's remarkable speculation, brought the conception of nebular cosmogony to a rigorously scientific statement (*Exposition du Système du Monde*, 1796); and the general form of his theory enters into the most recent cosmological speculations, though the progress of discovery and of thought has necessitated slight modifications, and has greatly extended the scope of the grand generalization. That which for years was known as "the nebular hypothesis"* has strengthened into a nebular theory, accepted now with almost the same confidence as the Newtonian theory of universal gravitation. This is the verdict of science on a question in its own appropriate field. No dissent from the outside is deserving of consideration; though, of course, exceptions taken by a scientific minority must be honestly examined. For a discussion of alleged difficulties of nebular cosmogony, see Winchell's *World Life*, p. 153–198.

According to this conclusion, the cosmic realm is the grandest conceivable exemplification of the method of evolution pursued in nature. This evolution guides and determines all the ulterior details of inorganic history. The total inorganic universe, as we know it, is the final outcome of the method of efficient activity revealed in nature, and it has been exerted upon identical portions of matter from the dawn of cosmical history to the present. The question of fact, so far as concerns inorganic nature, can no longer be agitated.

2. *Organic Evolution.*—This is a greater and more serious question. Does a material continuity run through the succession of organic types which have appeared and disappeared in the history of the world? Are the higher species of the modern world descended from the lower species of the ancient world? Are the diversified types derived from a common ancestry? Is man's bodily organism the outcome of genealogical descent? That these queries must be answered affirmatively seems to be the inevitable conclusion from an enormous amount of modern research. The proofs are numerous and diverse; but we may range them along five lines of argumentation, converging towards the conclusion.

(1.) *Ontogeny.*—By this we mean the history of the individual. This, beyond all controversy, is an evolution. The succession of changes from the beginning of conscious life to maturity is great, but they are wrought in the same identical being. Still greater ontogenetic transformations may be traced back through

* The "nebular theory" here referred to is based upon the supposition that the universe originally existed in the form of gaseous vapor diffused by intense heat throughout space, and that all the heavenly bodies have resulted from this by rotation and gradual condensation through cooling off. Most or all the phenomena which they exhibit, such as sphericity, orbital and axial revolution, together with earthquakes and volcanoes (as showing the still liquid central mass), are thought to be best explained on this hypothesis, and the fact that nebulæ are yet discovered in the starry spaces is held as confirmatory of it. On the other hand, some of these nebulæ have already been resolved by powerful telescopes into a mass of separate stars, and the presumption is therefore strong that such is the composition of all of them. Comets are too little known to be of much weight in the argument. Many astronomical facts, however, are decidedly antagonistic to the "nebular" view, such as the want of ascertainable ratio between the magnitudes, distances from the sun and periods of revolution of our own planets and the obliquity of their orbits, some celestial bodies actually moving in the opposite direction. Experiments with the spectrum show that they are not all composed of the same elements. Moreover it is impossible to see, if space were at first filled with incandescent gas, where the excessive heat could have radiated to. For these and other reasons some of the ablest astronomers, Proctor for example, wholly discard the theory as insufficient and disproved. The question is a purely scientific one, of no especial interest to the theologian, so long as the origination of matter, motion, and life, with their laws and properties, be attributed to the divine fiat. But the attempt to identify the processes of the nebular theory of cosmogony with any part of the narrative in the first chapter of Genesis is exegetically preposterous. Whatever therefore may become of that theory, Moses is not responsible for it, and revelation has nothing to do with it.—Ed.

embryonic life to the earliest changes wrought in the fertilized ovum. The unfertilized ovum is itself only a transformed epithelial cell, and consists of yolk, germinative vesicle, and germinative dot. The successive transformations of these elements bring into view, first, the faint outlines of the most fundamental structures, as vertebræ, spinal marrow and brain, heart and digestive structures, then the complete details, and finally the accessory structures belonging to the perfected form. The particulars of the history are too technical to be enumerated in this place. This succession of embryonic transformations in a higher vertebrate reveals a wonderful case of characteristic evolution, beginning in a cell and ending in a complicated animal structure. But the most impressive significance of the history will be mentioned in another connection. For details, see Balfour, *A Treatise on Comparative Embryology* (1880, vol. i); Kölliker, *Entwickelungsgeschichte des Menschen und der höheren Thiere* (1876); Foster and Balfour, *Elements of Embryology* (1874, vol. i, on the chick); Häckel, *Anthropogenie* (1874); Packard, *Life Histories* (1876); and, further, the important works of Häckel, Owen, Bischoff, Parker, Remak, Agassiz, Clark, Reichert, von Baer, etc.

(2.) *Morphology.*—The forms of animals and plants are said to be similar in proportion to their affinities; but the implications of the statement are seldom appreciated. Among men, family resemblances are understood to signify blood relationship more or less remote. All men of the same race possess so many points of resemblance that every one admits their common descent from the same original parent. All mankind, according to the doctrine of evolution, however diverse in feature or endowment, must have descended from a common primitive human ancestry. But when we speak of two so-called species of the cat family, say the leopard of Africa and the panther of Asia, the popular opinion is that they are primordially distinct; though their resemblances are vastly closer than those of the Bushman and his neighbor, the Cape Englishman, the denial of whose kinship we resent. In fact, these two cats are so closely similar that some zoologists unite them in one species. If pronounced one species, popular opinion would assign them a common descent; if two species, it would hold them primordially distinct. Yet the animals, with all their characteristics, remain the same, whatever view may be taken of the systematic value of their slight distinctions. Now the question of consanguinity is one of fact, not depending on the opinion which may be entertained respecting differences.* Whatever that opinion may be, it continues manifest that we have a better reason for ascribing these cats to a common ancestry than for doing this with a Congo African and a blonde Scandinavian. But suppose we compare the leopard and the tiger—two distinct species by all admissions. The nature of their resemblances is precisely the same as in the other case, and only a little less in degree. To admit the common descent of the leopard and panther is to compel, at the risk of inconsistency, the admission of the common descent of the leopard and the tiger. When we assent to the consanguineous relation of two recognised species the whole proposition, in all its breadth, is conceded, that not only all cats, but all mammals, are derived from some primitive stock; and the divergences existing have been acquired during the progress of the generations. But since mammals present so many graduations towards birds, in egg-laying ornithorhynchus and echidna, towards reptiles in the chelonians, and fishes in the cetaceans, we cannot refuse a common descent to mammals and all other vertebrates. This admission brings the whole animal kingdom with it, for some tunicates and cephalopods would be admitted close kin to some of the lowest vertebrates. Indeed, if we compare any two representatives of the animal kingdom, however divergent, we shall find that they resemble each other in more points than the number of their differences; and the argument for their common descent is of the same nature as in the case of the negro and Scandinavian. This, then, is an indication of the nature of the argument from morphology—and we can only present the indication (for further details, see works on zoology and botany). Some striking animal portraits may be found in Johnson, *Natural History* (2 vols. 8vo); Cassell, *Natural History* (1883, 6 vols. 8vo); Knight, *Animated Nature* (2 vols. 4to); Brehm, *Thierleben* (9 vols. 8vo). Details of structure in Owen, *Comparative Anatomy* (3 vols. 8vo); Häckel, *Generelle Morphologie der Organismen* (vol. i); Gegenbaur, *Grundriss der vergleichenden Anatomie* (8vo); Huxley, *Manual of the Anatomy of Vertebrated Animals* (8vo), etc.

(3.) *Palæontology.*—The doctrine of the descent of all living species from a common remote ancestry implies that in former times the divergences of organic types were less than at present. Such a retral convergence of genealogical lines is precisely what palæontology shows. Within historic times this convergence is almost imperceptible; but as soon as we enter the æons of geology no fact is more conspicuous. To take an example which has been much bruited, the domestic horse, now so widely differentiated from five-toed quadrupeds, we find that in the age immediately preceding the present true horses lived, in which the rudimentary second and fourth digits, or splint bones, of the modern horse were more developed. Further back were horses with the same bones terminated by dangling hooflets. Still further back were horses having these hooflets more developed, and reaching the ground. But these horses had other splint bones, the rudimentary condition of a first digit, and in remoter times these rudiments are found terminated by dangling hooflets, and in still remoter, by functional hoofs. So we trace the succession of equine types back to a four-toed quadruped which, when we consider the corresponding divergences in the teeth, tibiæ, and other structures, we should hesitate to group with modern horses, if they were not connected by a gradation so gentle that we find no place to draw the dividing line.* The ancient four-toed horses are connected with a type of five-toed predecessors by a similar kind of relationship. The equine succession leads back, therefore, to a five-toed quadruped. If we take the modern ox or sheep or pig or camel or rhinoceros, we shall be able to trace back similarly a succession which leads towards a primitive five-toed quadruped; and in every case such quadruped approximates the form which stands at the beginning of the equine succession. The details of facts establishing such a generalization are accessible to all readers in the writings of Leidy, Cope, Marsh, Gaudry, Owen, Huxley, and other palæontologists. See Cope's memoirs in reports of surveys under Hayden and Wheeler, and briefer papers in *American Naturalist;* Marsh, in *American Journal of Science* (ser. iii); Leidy, *U. S. Geol. Survey of the Territories* (vol. i); *Ancient Fauna of Nebraska* (1853); "Extinct Mammalia of Dakota and Nebraska," in the *Jour. Acad. Nat. Science* (Phila. 1869, vol. vii). In a manner precisely similar the two types of modern birds—"flying" and "running"—may be traced back along two successional lines, to Mesozoic Saurian reptiles. So, progress has been made in tracing lines of succession among invertebrate animals and plants. The facts show what the doctrine of descent requires, a gradual convergence backward of all the lines of organic succession.

But, if these successions are genealogical,† there must have been uninterrupted continuity along each line. The chain connecting the past and the present exhib-

* But on this question we have, in the book of Genesis, *historical* proof which cannot safely be neglected; and it is more definite than the scientific.—Ed.

* But there does not seem to be a particle of proof that these latter races were *genetically* or actually derived from the former ones. On the contrary, these very differences—all the evidence we possess on the subject—go to show that they are not their offspring.—Ed.

† This *genealogy* is, in our view, a pure assumption.—Ed.

ited no missing links. It is the attempt of palæontology to discover traces of all the links; but obviously the attempt is more difficult than to find all the fragments of a meteorite which exploded in the sky before the Christian æra. The work of palæontology is necessarily incomplete; the relics of many types which once contributed to the continuity of the successions worked out remain undiscovered. There are, indeed, many missing links in our knowledge; but the tenor of discovery is such as to imply that no missing links interrupted the continuity of the actual successions. Every year's acquisition of new facts narrows the great gaps, and closes up some of the smaller ones. Some successions are already reconstructed with marvellous completeness; beyond question much more is destined to be accomplished; and we may logically forecast the future state of the evidence and anticipate the conclusion. So we reason from palæontology, and it seems entirely logical to conclude that in the actual life-history of our planet the successions of specific forms were nicely graduated from the rude and generalized types of the remote past to the large-brained and highly specialized types of the present. But this admission does not establish any genetic connections running through the several series. Each species may still have resulted from a special origination. Only the presumptions to be drawn from embryology and morphology suggest genetic descent in palæontology. The facts of palæontology might be as they are, with every species a primordial and persistent form; but the establishment of these graduated successions establishes what must have been the fact on the theory of common descent, and constitutes a link in the chain of argument.

(4.) *Variability.*—Is it within the economy of nature that organic types shall undergo indefinite secular variation, or maintain essential permanence? Within the historic period few undomesticated species are known to have varied to any marked extent; but all those domesticated have become differentiated, and sometimes to a striking extent. The different breeds of horses, cattle, dogs, fowls, and pigeons differ to such an extent that many of them, but for our knowledge of their common origin, would be set down by any naturalist as distinct species. They are distinct species in the same sense as the jaguar and the ounce and the panther are distinct. The elder Agassiz, though no evolutionist, used to proclaim the different races of men as widely distinct as the different families of monkeys. The suggestion that these divergences have not arisen in a state of nature seems to possess no relevancy, for it is still shown that the aptitude to vary is possessed by nature's organisms. Moreover, the influences brought to bear on these animals through man's treatment are the same in kind as those which sometimes arise from natural operations; they only differ in intensity, and thus accelerate changes for which nature fitted, and perhaps destined, the being. Finally, the changed forms result from the same kind of action of the same physiological forces as are in play in animals uninfluenced by domestication. Only powers like those of digestion, respiration, growth, and adaptation have been employed in the development of these varieties, and these are the functional activities of all animals. It would seem, therefore, that the results of domestication may be fairly appealed to as tests of the permanence of species. (See Darwin, *Animals and Plants under Domestication.*)

But it appears that great variations sometimes occur among animals and plants in a state of nature. Conflicts between individuals and conflicts with physical conditions are influences continually making their impressions on the organism. These are not causes, but only conditions, of organic change. By the law of adaptation the forces of the organism effect such changes as changed environment demands. The same species of birds, mammals, and molluscs, in their wide range across a continent from east to west, and from north to south, are found to vary according to the latitude, longitude, altitude, and other circumstances. A thorough knowledge of such variations in North America has led to the merging of large numbers of once accepted species (Allen, *Proc. Bos. Soc. Nat. Hist.* xv, 156; xvi, 276; *Bull. Mus. Comp. Zoöl.* ii, No 4, p. 345, Aug. 1876; *Amer. Naturalist,* Oct. 1876, p. 625; Baird, *Mem. National Acad.* Jan. 1863; *Amer. Jour. Sci.* II, xli, Jan., March, and May, 1863; Ridgeway, *Amer. Jour. Sci.* III, iv, 454, v, 415). Similar extreme variability is observed in many invertebrate species, both recent and extinct. Häckel, in a remarkable work on calcareous sponges, has reached the conclusion that all the forms belong to one species, so gradual are the transitions between the several nominal species (*Die Kalkschwämme,* 1872, 2 vols. 8vo). Many forms of fossil shells formerly regarded as distinct species have more recently been united, simply because series of intermediate forms became known. Hilgendorf has traced minutely the secular variations of a species of *Planorbis* (*Ueber Planorbis multiformis in Steinheimer Süsswasserkalk*), and Hyatt has extended these studies (*Proc. Amer. Assoc.* 1880, and "Anniversary Mem." in *Bost. Soc. Nat. Hist.* 1880). Similar work has been done among Palæozoic brachiopods.

The influence of changed environment is sometimes accelerated by human intervention. The axolotl, permanently gill-bearing in its native elevated home, loses its gills when kept near the sea-level, and becomes a land salamander. In Japan certain leeches and planarians have become adapted to land life, and a fish, even (*Periophthalmus*), frequents the land and seems in a transition state. Certain brine shrimps are reported by Schmaukevitch as undergoing important structural changes in the course of a few generations, when the brine is gradually freshened; and return to the original state as the salinity is again restored (*Zeitsch. wiss. Zoölogie,* xxv, Suppl. i, 1875, p. 103, pl. 6; *Annals and Mag. Nat. Hist.* March, 1876; ib. xxix, 429–494, 1877. See, also, *Contributions to a Knowledge of the Influence of External Conditions of Life upon the Organization of Animals,* transl. in Hayden's twelfth *Ann. Rep.* pt. i, 473–514. But compare Verrill, *Proc. Amer. Assoc.* 1869, 230; *Amer. Jour. Sci.* II, xlviii, 244, 430; Packard, *Amer. Jour. Sci.* III, ii, 108). The domestic cat on the Pribilov Islands becomes thickened, short, losing the tail, and undergoing great change of voice. Certain domestic pigs in Texas are well known to have become solid-hoofed.

Through hybridity, also, probably, result forms divergent from recognised species. Among cultivated plants hybrids are not uncommon. In the wild state the number of reputed hybrid forms may be judged from a glance through any manual of botany. (See also, Hooker, *Flora of New Zealand;* Candolle, "Étude sur l'Espèce," in the *Bibliothèque Univ. de Genève,* Nov. 1862; Hooker and Thomson, *Flora Indica,* vol. i, "Introductory Essay," London, 1855; Gray, *Amer. Jour. Sci.* II, xxi, 134; Naudin: *Hybridity in the Vegetable Kingdom*). Among animals, fertile hybridity, as well as infertile, is pretty well established.* From the hare and the rabbit has arisen a self-sustaining hybrid now extensively employed in Europe for food. Fertile hybrids of the common and Chinese geese are extensively reared in India, as also in England; while several generations of the hybrid from the mallard and muscovy ducks are reported living in Mt. Auburn cemetery (Brewer, *Proc. Bos. Soc. Nat. Hist.* 21 Jan. 1874). Carl Vogt reports fertile hybrids of the wolf and dog, as also of the goat and sheep, and the latter is confirmed by Häckel; Von Tschudi and Vogt both report the same of the goat and steinbock, and of the fox and dog. The same is alleged of the buffalo and bison. Without relying on the intervention of hybridity, enough has been observed of the power of organic forms to adapt themselves permanently to the perma-

* But we believe this is true only to a very limited extent, and the fertility very rarely extends to successive generations.—Ed.

nent changes of the environment to fully establish the conclusion that it is the economy of nature to permit structural variations without limits.* If a full survey of the facts to which we have too briefly alluded justifies the conclusion, as we think it does, then no bar exists to the conclusion that the successions of Palæontological types have arisen through the continued variation of primitive forms; and that the latter, also, may have arisen through variation and descent from one primordial, life-endowed being. This extreme conclusion, however, is not at all necessary to the proof of a method of evolution in the world, since the genealogical lines may have proceeded from any such number of beginnings as the state of the observed relationships may allow.

(5.) *Comparative Embryology.*—A careful study of the aspects of the developing embryo of a higher vertebrate, as indicated above, under "Ontogeny," shows that it reaches, in ascending order, a succession of stages which may be enumerated and defined. Now the facts to which we wish to direct attention particularly, constitute a series of significant parallelisms. (a) *Ontogenetic parallelism.* Research shows that every higher vertebrate passes through the same embryonic stages, and no divergences revealing the characteristics of class, genus, and species make their appearance until the development is well advanced. To a certain stage the human embryo cannot be distinguished from that of a fish; at later stages, it diverges successively from the embryo of reptiles, birds, quadrupeds, and quadrumana. The embryo chick is absolutely undistinguishable from the embryo of man until about the sixth day of incubation. Even invertebrates pursue a course of development closely parallel with that of the earlier stages of the mammalian embryo. (Häckel, *Natürliche Schöpfungsgeschichte*, xi Vortrag; *Anthropogenie*, xiii-xix Vorträge; Balfour, *British Assoc.* Address, 1880, *Nature*, xxii, 418). (b) *Taxonomic parallelism.* The succession of aspects presented by the mammalian embryo is identical with that shown in the gradations of living animals. The disappearance of the nucleus of the egg results in a simple cytode, which is paralleled in the living world by *Protamœba*, the lowest known animal. The new-formed nucleus gives the ovum the character of *Amœba*. The "morula" mass resulting from the divisions of the yolk is paralleled by *Labyrinthula.* The spheroid formed of a single layer of cells corresponds to the larves of *Planula.* The invagination of this, forming a two-walled spheroid or urn ("gastrula") is paralleled by the larves of *Protascus.* The four-layered, elongated form answers to the worm *Turbellaria.* The fibrous, semi-tubular cranium and gelatinous spine are found adult in the lancelet. The gill-arches of the embryo are permanent in the dog-fish and other sharks. The tailed condition represents the maturity of the reptile. So, without further particulars, it may be broadly asserted that the gradations of living animals are pictured in the successive stages of the mammalian embryo. (See especially Häckel and Balfour, as cited; Baer, *Nachrichten über Leben und Schriften*, 1865.) The principle has, indeed, found useful application in some cases, in determining the relative rank of animals. (c) *Palæontological parallelism.* It was amply shown by the elder Agassiz that the geological succession of organic types presents an order identical with that of the classificatory arrangement of animals. (See especially, *Essay on Classification.*) This has been more fully illustrated by Häckel (see citations above). Owing, however to the recognised imperfection of our knowledge of extinct life, this parallelism is less detailed than the others. We know specifically, however, that the primitive form, *Eozoön*, must have been akin to *Amœba* and *Labyrinthula;* that the turbellarian grade was reached in *Scolithus*, of the Potsdam sandstone; that the shark type was attained in the Upper Silurian and Devonian; the transition from aquatic to terrestrial creatures, in the Amphibia of the Coal Measures, with some advance in the Trias; that reptiles succeeded in the Mesozoic, and birds appeared on their decline; that the lowest mammalian types existed in the Jurassic, and higher types followed through the Tertiary; that the lowest four-handed animals were of Lower Eocene age, and that tailed monkeys, anthropoid apes, and men followed in due order.

The established facts of comparative embryology show a prolonged and detailed succession of organic conceptions literally three times repeated. The doctrine of chances demonstrates that this must result from some mutual dependence and connection among them. The palæontological succession must result from the order of succession under a law of development as primitively exemplified in the evolution of the individual. In the latter, each successive stage arises demonstrably by continuity with the preceding. The palæontological series consists of the final terms of many genetically related embryonic series successive in the extinct world. The taxonomic series consists of the final terms of many genetically related embryonic series simultaneous in the actual world. All the terms in each series are therefore materially connected through the embryonic series of which they are several parts.*

IV. *Evolution Theories.*—While most evolutionists believe that the intellectual and moral elements of man are, equally with the material organism, the outcome of a long process of improvement, Mr. A. R. Wallace holds that both body and mind of man may have arisen in a different manner. (Wallace, *Contributions to the Theory of Natural Selection*, Am. ed. 1871; Address at Glasgow *Meeting Brit. Assoc.* 1871, *Amer. Jour. Sci.* III, xiii, 377), while St. George Mivart limits the exception to man's psychic nature (*Genesis of Species*, 1871; *Lessons from Nature*, 1876). The majority of evolutionists maintain that man's body is so intimately identified in structure with that of lower animals that it is incredible that it has not participated in the common history. As to his psychic nature, it is held to be identical in many of its manifestations with the natures of brutes, and a strong presumption hence arises that even man's highest powers exist germinally in the lower animals.

The speculations of theorists concern chiefly the causes, conditions, and instrumentalities on which organic evolution depends. De Maillet, in a work whose title (*Telliamed*, 1748) was an anagram of the author's name, represents that organic beings possess an aptitude for structural changes, and that changes arise when, under changed conditions, the animal puts forth efforts to exercise changed functions. Lamarck (*Philosophie Zoölogique*, 1809; new ed. by Martins, Paris, 1873) maintained that primitive rudiments of the great divisions of the organic kingdoms arose by *spontaneous generation;* that these were endowed with an *inherent tendency* to improvement, which becomes effective especially through *use and disuse* of organs, while the influence of *external conditions* determines use and disuse. The author of the *Vestiges of Creation*, 1844, suggested that life first appeared on our planet "in simple germinal vesicles," "produced by some chemico-electrical operation," and that successive steps of advance were effected "through the agency of the ordinary process of generation." The conditions under which this process resulted in an improved being were presented, he thought, in abnormally *prolonged gestation.* Next, the principle of *natural selection* was suggested simultaneously by Charles R. Darwin and A. R. Wallace (*Jour. Linnæan Soc.* London, August, 1858; preceded by Wallace's paper in *Ann.* and *Mag. Nat. Hist.* September, 1855), and this

* We submit that these very limited variations do not prove a capacity for unlimited variation.—Ed.

* The force of this argument, however, seems to us to be wholly invalidated by two facts: 1. No instance of the propagation of one species of animal by parents of another, has been historically found; 2. The embryo in every instance stops at the precise point prescribed by its specific character; and becomes either an abortion or a monster if it fails to reach it.—Ed.

was most industriously and ably elaborated and illustrated by Darwin in a subsequent series of publications which have constituted an epoch in the history of scientific thought (*Origin of Species*, 1859; *Variations of Animals and Plants*, 1868; *The Descent of Man*, 1871; *Expression of the Emotions*, 1872; *Insectivorous Plants*, 1875; *Effects of Cross- and Self-Fertilization*, 1876, and numerous other works and memoirs bearing more or less directly on the question of natural selection). This theory is not to be identified with the broad doctrine of evolution, as is commonly done. It assumes that a method of evolution exists in nature, and undertakes to explain by what means and agencies it is carried on. Recognising the fact that a perpetual struggle exists among individuals for existence, and for most favorable conditions of existence, and that the strongest always succeed the best, while the feeblest tend to perish, the obvious and necessary inference is drawn that the species is perpetuated by its best representatives, and thus undergoes continual improvement, precisely as when man intervenes to improve the breeds of domestic animals. Darwin inclined at first to consider this tendency a full explanation of organic progress, but later he admitted other influences, including, like Lamarck, an inherent nisus towards improvement, and the effects of use and disuse of organs. For an ampler exposition of the doctrine, see the article "Darwinism" in the *Encyclopædia Americana*. That a process of natural selection goes on, and that its tendency is what Darwin claims, all must admit. But there is a growing belief that organic advances and relapses require an appeal also, to other conditions, instrumentalities, and causes. For instance, professor Parsons, of Harvard, inclined to regard specific variation as the result of *extraordinary births* (*Amer. Jour. Science*, July, 1860, II, xxx, 1), and soon afterwards Richard Owen advanced an almost identical idea (*Anat. of Vertebrates*, chap. xl; *Amer. Jour. Science*, II, xlvii, 33). Galton's theory seems to be the same (*Hereditary Genius*, 1869, p. 363–383). Kölliker varied this conception by suggesting *heterogeneous generation* through agamic and parthenogenic reproduction—a profound misapprehension of proper generation (*Ueber die Darwin'sche Schöpfungsgeschichte*, 1864). Huxley, while accepting Darwinism for what it is worth, has indicated some qualifications and additions (*Lay Sermons, Addresses, and Reviews*, 1862; *On the Origin of Species*, 1863; *Critiques and Addresses*, 1869, etc.). He holds particularly that nature sometimes makes *considerable jumps;* that the process of natural selection *goes on among the molecules* of the organism, and that there exists an *inherent tendency of organization to vary*. The latter point he emphasizes. Alpheus Hyatt, in 1868, pointed out that degradational metamorphoses in the old age of the individual, or the type, could not rationally be referred to natural selection, which acts in the contrary direction. An *internal law* fixes the duration of the species as of the individual. Specific advance he attributes to habitual *acceleration of embryonic development*. In the advanced age of species the reverse takes place, and thus the decline of a species reproduces, in inverted order, the succession of types which appeared during the rise of the species (*Mem. Boston Soc. Nat. Hist.* 1867, i, pt. 2; *Amer. Naturalist*, June, 1870, iv, 230; *Fossil Cephalopods, Museum Comparatur Zoöl.* Cambridge, 1872). Professor E. D. Cope varied this conception by attributing the recession of organic types to the influence of retarded development (*Synopsis of Cyprinidæ of Penn.* 1866; "Origin of Genera," in the *Proc. Acad. Nat. Science*, Phila. October, 1868; "The Hypothesis of Evolution," in *Lipp. Mag.* 1870, and *University Series*, New Haven, 1873; "The Method of Creation of Organic Types," in the *Proc. Acad. Nat. Science*, Phila. 1871, and other papers). Probably the suggestions based on rate and duration of embryonic changes are all available. At the same time it is quite conceivable that the principle of natural selection obtains in embryonic life, both in conditions immediately present with the embryo and those external conditions which produce them—the circumstances surrounding the female parent, or even the male. This becomes intelligible on the basis of some such theory as Spencer's "Physiological Units," Darwin's "Pangenesis," Elsberg's "Plastidule Hypothesis" (*Proc. Amer. Assoc.* 1874, 1876), Häckel's "Perigenesis" (*Die Perigenesis*, 1876; *Die heutige Entwickelungslehre*, etc., 1879; *Nature*, Oct. 4, 1877, and *Pop. Scien. Monthly Suppl.*), or Brooks' "Law of Heredity" (New York, 1883). Still, it must be admitted that in some cases widely variant forms, as in the Ancon breed of sheep, arise suddenly where, to all appearance, some other condition not yet known determines the divergence. We think also it must be finally admitted that the organism is affected by an implanted destination or law, which bends it constantly towards conformity to the environment, and employs the several agencies mentioned for the accomplishment of this result. In the history of the world the environment has undergone a progressive differentiation and improvement. Organization has advanced correspondingly. When the environment remains persistent, or deteriorates, organic forms persist or even deteriorate to a corresponding extent. If, however, no existing theory of organic evolution proves final, the fact of organic evolution remains highly probable.

V. *Limitations of the Doctrine.*—We have stated, preliminarily, that the question of evolution is simply one of fact. In ascertaining whether a method of evolution is a fact in the natural world, we are not concerned in anything outside of this simple inquiry. It is of no import whether the result is effectuated by necessity or free-will, by inherent forces, by implanted forces or external forces, by material forces or spiritual forces, by mediate action or immediate action. We are not even concerned in determining what conditions are favorable, what instrumentalities are employed, whether the action is prenatal or postnatal, whether through embryonic development, prolonged, accelerated, or retarded. All these questions are interesting—some of them may be important. The human mind cannot be restrained from investigating them. But it is important to understand clearly that a verdict on any one of these questions does not bear on the antecedent question of fact. If the fact exists, different persons may explain and interpret it differently. The explanation falls within the domain of science; the interpretation touches philosophy and theism. Scientific explanations are already various—each probably partial. Interpretations may be materialistic or spiritualistic—that will depend on the antecedent philosophy of the thinker. They may be theistic or atheistic—that depends on the predisposition of the interpreter. Philosophic and theological opinions must rest on other grounds. The fact of a method of evolution in the world is not responsible for them.

More categorically, we may state: (1) The fact of evolution implies nothing in respect to causation. It throws no light on secondary cause or first cause. It does not imply the evolution of life from inorganic matter. It knows nothing of beginnings; it discovers only a method of continuance; the beginning may have been a creation by fiat. It knows nothing of the cause or causes of continuance; it may be by immanent divine agency. (2) There is no assumption of inherent forces or necessary activities, or eternal matter. It is allowable to deny inherent forces and necessary actions, and hold to the creation of matter and force, and even to the identification of natural force with the divine volition. (3) There is no implication concerning the nature or origin of mind. It may arise with each distinct organism; it may arise only in the human organism. (4) Nothing is implied concerning the interpretation of the activities going forward in the organism. We are at liberty to affirm that they imply choice, selection, intelligence. We are at full liberty to trace intelligence in the methods of the inorganic world, or to affirm that the all-embracing method of evolution is itself the highest possible manifestation of intelligence and unity. (5) We may also, if we please, maintain that the method of the world and the collocations of the world imply determination and motive. Thus, in brief, the limitations of the essential doctrine of evolution are such that, in spite of the speculative views of some evolutionists, the full acceptance of the doctrine does not conflict with any fundamental conception of Christian theology.

VI. *Literature.*—Many of the most important original works have been cited in the progress of this article. Some other titles may be added: Spencer, *First Principles of Philosophy; Principles of Biology;* Gray, *Darwiniana* (1878); Romanes, *The Scientific Evidences of Organic Evolution* (1882), Chapman, *The Evolution of Life* (1873); Semper, *Animal Life as Affected by the Natural Conditions of Existence; Die Verwandtschaftsbeziehungen der gegliederten Thiere* (1875); Lankester, *Degeneration, a Chapter in Darwinism* (1880); Lindsay, *Mind in the Lower Animals* (1879); Seidlitz, *Beiträge zur Descendenz-Theorie* (1876); Fritz Müller, *Für Darwin* (eod.); Zacharias, *Zur Entwickelungstheorie* (eod.); Jacoby, *Études sur la Sélection dans ses Rapports avec l'Hérédité chez l'Homme;* Canestrini, *Teoria di Darwin Criticamente Exposta* (Milan, 1880); Du Prel, *Der Kampf ums Dasein am Himmel;* Faivre, *La Variabilité des Espèces* (1868); Weismann, *Studien zur Descendenz-Theorie* (1876); Ribot, *Heredity;* O. Schmidt, *Descent and Darwinism* (1875); H. Müller, *Die Befruchtung der Blumen durch Insecten* (1873; an Engl. translation, 1883); *Alpenblumen und ihre Befruchtung durch Insecten* (1881); Fechner, *Einige Ideen zur Schöpfungs- und Entwickelungsgeschichte der Organismen;* Mivart, *Man and Apes* (1874); Bastian, *Evolution and the Origin of Life;* Roux, *Der Kampf der Theile im Organismus* (1881); Cazelles, *Outline of the Evolution Philosophy* (1875). On the interpretation of evolution: Dreher, *Der Darwinismus und seine Stellung in der Philosophie* (1877); von Giżycki, *Philosophische Consequenzen der Lamarck-Darwin'schen Entwickelungstheorie* (1876); R. Schmidt, *Die Darwin'schen Theorien und ihre Stellung zur Philosophie, Religion, und Moral* (eod.; id. Engl. translation); Henslow, *The Theory of the Evolution of Living Things, and the Application of the Principles of Evolution to Religion* (1873); Leconte, *Religion and Science;* Simcox, *Natural Law* (1877); Wright, *Philosophical Discussions*, especially p. 97-266; Weismann, *Ueber die letzten Ursachen der Transmutationen* (1876); Spiller, *Die Urkraft des Weltalls nach ihrem Wesen und Wirken* (eod.); Schneider, *Der thierische Wille* (1880); Romanes, *Animal Intelligence* (1883); *Mental Evolution in Animals* (eod.); Savage, *The Religion of Evolution* (1877); Beale, *Life Theories, their Influence upon Religious Thought* (1871); Winchell, *The Speculative Consequences of Evolution* (1881); *Sparks from a Geologist's Hammer*, p. 301-385 (eod.), p. 301-385; Beckett, *On the Origin of the Laws of Nature.* Critical and adverse writings: von Hartmann, *Wahrheit und Irrthum im Darwinismus* (1875); Wigand, *Der Darwinismus u. die Naturforschung Newtons u. Cuviers* (1874-77, 3 vols.); Virchow, *Die Freiheit der Wissenschaft im modernen Staat* (1877; Engl. translation); Semper, *Häckelismus in der Zoölogie* (1876); Michaelis, *Anti-Darwinistische Beobachtungen* (1877); Mivart, *Lessons from Nature, as Manifested in Mind and Matter* (1876); *Contemporary Evolution* (eod.); Agassiz, *Contributions to the Natural History of the U. S.* vol. i, Introduction; *Amer. Jour. Science*, July, 1860; Dawson, *The Story of the Earth and Man* (1873); Hodge, *What is Darwinism?*; Barrande, *Trilobites* (1871); *Cephalopodes* (1877); *Brachiopodes* (1879). A monthly journal of highest ability, devoted to evolution, is *Kosmos*, Stuttgart. (A. W.)

Evovæ is an artificial word made out of the vowels in the words "sæculorum Amen," which occur at the end of the Gloria Patri. Its object was to serve as a kind of *memoria technica* to enable singers to render the several Gregorian chants properly; each letter in evovæ standing for the syllable from which it is extracted. It must be borne in mind that psalms, etc., were sung under antiphons, and that the music of the antiphon, being constructed in a particular "mode" or "scale," such as Dorian, Phrygian, and the like, the chant or "tone" ("tune") to the psalm, being not intended to represent a full stop or close, might (and usually did) not end on the final belonging to the mode, leaving that for the concluding antiphon: thus different forms of the same mode or tone would arise, and these were called evovæ, and sometimes by other names. This only applies to the latter half (cadence) of the chant, as in the "mediation" (at the middle of the verse of a psalm) scarcely any variety was admitted, except such as arose from local use. Thus, in the various works on the subject, and in service books, varieties of endings are to be found of greater or less antiquity. See Smith, *Dict. of Christ. Antiq.* s. v.

Evremond (Lat. *Ebremundus*), *Saint*, was born at Bayeux of a noble family; married a high-born lady, but suddenly devoted himself to a monastic life in Fontenay; afterwards became abbot of Mont Maire, in the diocese of Seez, and died about A.D. 720 (others say before 584). He is commemorated June 10. See Smith, *Dict. of Christ. Antiq.* s. v.; Guérin, *Les Petits Bollandistes*, vi, 553.

Evroul (Lat. *Ebrulfus*). (1) Saint, was brought up at the court of Childebert I and his successor, was noted for his learning and wealth, but renounced all for a monk's life, and founded the monastery of St. Evroul d'Ouche (Uticus), in the diocese of Lisieux (Neustria), where he died in 596. He is commemorated Dec. 29. (2) The eighteenth bishop of Noyon and Tournay, died A.D. 621 (according to others, before 575). (3) Saint, is said to have been abbot of the monastery of St. Fuscien-aux-Bois, near Amiens, probably near the close of the 6th century. He is commemorated July 26.

Ewald, Christian Ferdinand, an Episcopal minister and famous missionary among the Jews, was born of Jewish parentage, Sept. 14, 1802, at Maroldsweisach, near Bamberg. At the age of twenty he joined the Christian Church, studied at Basle, and was in 1826 licensed to preach the gospel. In 1829 he was called to London, and having duly prepared for missionary work, he connected himself in 1832 with the London Society for Propagating the Gospel among the Jews. In 1836 he was ordained by the bishop of London, having been previously in Lutheran orders. There are but few of the society's missionaries whose sphere of labor has been so lengthened in duration or so wide in extent. For nearly ten years he labored with great devotedness in one of the most trying portions of the Jewish mission field—the north coast of Africa—at Algiers, Tunis, Tripoli, and other large towns. In 1839 he left Tunis for a time and proceeded to Leghorn, and in 1841 finally left Tunis to accompany the first Anglican bishop, Dr. Alexander, to Jerusalem as his chaplain, and for some ten years was earnestly engaged in the Holy City. An account of the work is given in his *Missionary Labors in the City of Jerusalem.* In 1851 ill-health compelled him to leave the East, and, being appointed principal of the home mission, he took up his abode in London. In 1872 a general debility of constitution rendered it necessary for him to resign his position. He died August 9, 1874. The University of Erlangen, of which Ewald was a graduate, on the publication of his German translation of the Talmudic treatise *Aboda Sarah*, in 1856, conferred upon him *de religione Christiana inter barbaras gentes propaganda optime merito, linguarum orientalium gnarrissimo*, the diploma of a doctor in philosophy, and the archbishop of Canterbury conferred upon him, in 1872, the degree of bachelor of divinity, as stated in the diploma, in consideration "of his uprightness of life, sound doctrine, and purity of morals; of his proficiency in the study of divinity, of Hebrew and Oriental languages and literature; and also of his missionary labors and eminent services in the promotion of Christianity among the Jews." (B. P.)

Ewald, Georg Heinrich August, one of the most learned Orientalists of our century, was born at Göttingen, Nov. 16, 1803. In 1820 he entered the university of his native city, and three years later received the degree of doctor of philosophy. After teaching for some time at the Wolfenbüttel gymnasium, he returned in 1824 to Göttingen, became *repetent* at the university, and in 1827 was made professor. In 1837 he was expelled from his position for having signed, with six other professors, a protest against the revocation of the liberal constitution of 1833, which Ernest Augustus, king of Hanover, effected. In 1829 and 1836 he had visited France and Italy, and now (in 1838) he visited England. In the same year he was appointed professor at Tübingen, where he remained for ten years. The bitter feuds with his colleagues made his stay there very unpleasant, and it was a relief when, in 1848, he was recalled to Göttingen. In 1867 he refused to take the oath of allegiance to the king of Prussia, and this refusal was punished by his exclusion from the faculty of philosophy, although he was still allowed his salary and the privilege of lecturing. This latter privilege was withdrawn in 1868, on account of utterances against the king. He died of heart disease, May 4, 1875. Ewald's writings have found about as many admirers abroad as at home. The value of much of his learning is seriously impaired by his dogmatic spirit. His independence often degenerates into self-conceit. His violent rationalism is conspicuous. His literary activity began in 1823, with the *Composition der Genesis Kritisch untersucht*, and only closed with an autobiography written during the last months of his life, which has not been published. Of his many writings we mention, *De Metris Carminum Arabicorum* (Brunswick, 1825):—*Das Hohelied Salomo's übersetzt und erklärt* (1826; 3d ed. 1866):—*Libri Wakedii de Mesopotamiæ Expugnatæ Historia pars* (1827):—*Kritische Grammatik der Hebr. Sprache* (eod.), subsequently enlarged, and *Ausführliches Lehrbuch der Hebr. Sprache des Alten Testaments* (1844; 8th ed. 1870; Engl. transl. by Nicholson, Lond. 1836; of the syntax alone, from 8th ed. by Kennedy, Edinb. 1879):—*Hebräische Sprachlehre für Anfänger* (1842; Engl. transl. from 3d ed. by Smith, Lond. 1870):—*Abhandlungen zur orientalischen und biblischen Literatur* (1832):—*Grammatica Critica Ling. Arab.* (1831-33, 2 vols.):—*Die poetischen Bücher des Alten Bundes* (1835-39; 3d ed. 1868; Engl. transl. Lond. 1880 sq.):—*Propheten des Alten Bundes* (1840, 1841; 2d ed. 1867, 1867, 3 vols.; Engl. transl. Lond. 1876-81, 5 vols.):—*Geschichte des Volkes Israel* (1843-59, 7 vols.; 3d ed. 1868; Engl. transl. corresponding to vol. i-iv):—*History of Israel* (Lond. 1867-74, 5 vols.):—*Die Alterthümer des Volkes Israel* (1848; Engl. transl. *Antiquities of Israel*, Lond. 1876):—*Die drei ersten Evangelien übersetzt und erklärt* (1850):—*Das äthiopische Buch Henokh* (1854):—*Das vierte Buch Ezra* (1860):—*Die Sendschreiben des Apostels Paulus übersetzt und erklärt* (1857):—*Die Johanneischen Schriften* (1861, 1862):—*Die Bücher des Neuen Testaments* (1870, 1871):—*Die Theologie des Alten und Neuen Bundes* (1870-75, 4 vols.):—*Jahrbücher der biblischen Wissenschaft*, i-xi, 1848-61, containing a number of essays which are still very valuable. In connection with L. Dukes he published, *Beiträge zur Geschichte der ältesten Auslegung des Spracherklärung des Alten Test.* (1844, 3 vols.). See Herzog-Plitt, *Real-Encyklop.* s. v.; Lichtenberger, *Encyclopédie des Sciences Religieuses*, s. v.; Zuchold, *Bibl. Theol.* i, 341-344; Fürst, *Bibl. Jud.* i, 261; Steinschneider, *Bibl. Handbuch*, s. v. (B. P.)

Ewe Version OF THE SCRIPTURES. The Ewe or Ewegbe (also called *Eipe, Aijigbe, Krepe, Dahomey*) language is spoken on the west coast of Africa, at and beyond the river Volta. The Rev. B. Schlegel, of the Bremen Missionary Society, began to translate the Holy Scriptures into this language in the year 1858, and the Bremen Bible Society undertook the printing of the same. In 1861 the four gospels were published. In 1874 the British and Foreign Bible Society published, at the request of the Bremen mission, St. Paul's epistles, which were translated by the Rev. Mr. Ulerz, and in 1878 the entire New Test. was issued from the press. Several books of the Old Test. have also been published, as Exodus, Joshua to Ruth, and Samuel. Up to March 31, 1884, there were distributed 4500 portions of the Old Test. and 3000 portions of the New Test. For the study of the language, see Schlegel, *Schlüssel zur Ewe Sprache* (Stuttgart, 1857). (B. P.)

Ewh, GEORG, a Lutheran minister, was born in 1828, at Kirchberg, in Rhenish Prussia. He studied theology at Bonn and Berlin, came to America in 1866, and was appointed pastor of the Lutheran Church (St. Matthew's) at Jersey City, N. J., where he died, April 7, 1881. (B. P.)

Ewing, Alexander, D.C.L., a Scotch bishop, was born in Aberdeen, March 25, 1814. He was educated at a private school in Chelsea and at the University of Edinburgh, but, owing to his delicate health and ample inheritance, he did not adopt a profession on leaving school. He began preparation for the ministry in 1836, and entered into priest's orders in 1841, when he took charge of the Episcopal congregation at Forres. He remained in this position until 1846, when he was elected first bishop of the newly restored diocese of Argyll and the Isles, the duties of which office he discharged till his death, May 22, 1873. His theological views were communicated to the world in the form of letters to the newspapers, pamphlets, special sermons, essays contributed to the series of *Present Day Papers*, of which he was the editor, and a volume of sermons entitled *Revelation considered as Light*. He also published the *Cathedral or Abbey Church of Iona* (1865). See *Memoir*, by Ross (1877); *Encyclop. Brit.* (9th ed.), s. v.

Ewing, Greville, D.D., a Scotch clergyman, was born in Edinburgh in 1767; educated at the high-school; apprenticed to an engraver, but when of age studied theology at Edinburgh University; became tutor to the family of Mr. Lockhart, of Castle Hill; was licensed to preach Sept. 5, 1792, and his talents made him popular from the first. He was nominated by the trustees as minister of lady Glenorchy's chapel, Edinburgh, in June, 1792, and ordained colleague in October, 1793. Aided by Robert Haldane, Esq., he proposed to organize a select company for propagating the gospel in Bengal, but the East India Company was hostile to the movement. He established the *Missionary Magazine* for Scotland, the first religious periodical in that country. He resigned his charge, Dec. 26, 1798; became minister to a large congregation at the Tabernacle, Glasgow, in May, 1799, under the auspices of Mr. Haldane, and presided over a seminary for training pious young men for the ministry for two and a half years with considerable success. Differences having arisen with Mr. Haldane, he resigned, and in 1811 became senior tutor to a new theological seminary belonging to the Congregational Union, and continued to discharge the duties with praiseworthy fidelity till obliged by debility to resign. He died Aug. 2, 1841. He published five single *Sermons;* several controversial works; *A Greek Grammar, and Greek and English Scripture Lexicon* (Edinb. 1802, 1812):—*Facts and Documents respecting the Connections between Robert Haldane and Greville Ewing* (1809):—*An Essay on Baptism* (1823):—*Memoir of Barbara Ewing* (1829), with many smaller works. See *Fasti Eccles. Scoticanæ*, i, 80, 81.

Excellents. See GAONS.

Excision, an ecclesiastical sentence among the Jews, whereby a person was separated or cut off from his people. See BAN; EXCOMMUNICATION.

Exclusiva, in ecclesiastical law, means the right,

claimed by Austria, France, and Spain, to exclude each one candidate at a papal election. This right has never been formally acknowledged by the curia, but the claim has always, since the 15th century, been complied with by the conclave, although the Jesuits, shortly before the death of Pius IX, asserted that this right should no more be granted, since these states were no longer Catholic, in the old sense of the word, but tolerant rather. See Häberlin, *Römisches Conclave* (Halle, 1769), p. 152 sq.; *Ueber die Rechte der Regierungen beim Conclave* (Munich, 1872); Bonghi, *Pio IX e il Papa Futuro* (Milan, 1877), p. 47-58; Mejer, in Herzog-Plitt, *Real-Encyklop.* s. v.; Smith, *Dict. of Christ. Antiq.* s. v. (B. P.)

Exedra, a name sometimes given by St. Augustine to the *ambo* (q. v.). It is often used in ancient writers as synonymous with the *apsis* (q. v.).

Exiteria, sacrifices offered by the ancient Greek generals before setting out on any warlike expedition. They were of the nature of divination, to ascertain whether the enterprise was to be successful or disastrous.

Exocatacœli, a name given to several officers of the Church at Constantinople, high in authority, and in public assemblies taking precedence of the bishops. Originally they were priests, but afterwards only deacons. The college of the *exocatacœli* corresponded to the college of cardinals (q. v.) at Rome.

Exocionites (Ἐξωκιονῖται), a name applied to the Arians (q. v.) of the 4th century, who, when expelled from Constantinople by Theodosius the Great, retired to a place outside the city. The name occurs in the records of Justinian, and frequently in the chronicle of Alexandria.

Exoteric. See ESOTERIC.

Exothouměni (ἐξωθούμενοι), the first of the four classes of *catechumens* (q. v.) in the early Church. They were instructed privately outside the Church, and prevented from entering into the Church until they were more fully enlightened.

Expectatives, a term employed in the 14th century, when the French pontiffs residing at Avignon assumed to themselves the power of conferring all sacred offices, by which means they raised immense sums of money, calling forth the bitterest complaints from all the nations of Europe. Expectatives were abolished by the Council of Constance, March 25, 1436. See EXPECTANCY.

Expilly, LOUIS ALEXANDRE, a French prelate, was born Feb. 24, 1742, at Brest. He studied at Paris, and was made bachelor of divinity there; was nominated pastor of St. Martin of Morlaix; in 1789 became deputy of the states-general; was consecrated bishop of the department of Finistère, Feb. 24, 1791, and shared the fate of twenty-five of his colleagues, who were beheaded, May 22, 1794, for having taken an appeal to the department of the West against the national convention. See Hoefer, *Nouv. Biog. Générale*, s. v.

Exsufflation, a part of the ceremony of baptism in the ancient Christian Church, in which the candidate stood with his hands stretched out towards the West, and struck them together; then he proceeded thrice to exsufflate or spit, in defiance of Satan. See BAPTISM.

Extispĭces (Lat. *exta*, entrails, and *specio*, to look), a name sometimes given to the ancient *haruspices* (q. v.), because it was their duty carefully to examine the entrails of the victims offered in sacrifice.

Exucontians (Ἐξουκόντιοι), a name given to the class of Arians called Aëtians (q. v.), because they affirmed that the Son of God might be called God and the Word of God, but only in a sense consistent with his having been brought forth from non-existence. See ARIANS; SEMI-ARIANS.

Eybenschütz, JONATHAN, a Jewish rabbi, was born at Cracow in 1690. He was not only a very learned Talmudist, but especially a follower of the cabalistic system of the pseudo-Messiah Chayon, whom he had met at Prague in 1726. At the age of twenty-one Eybenschütz was president of a rabbinical college at Cracow, which soon became very famous. From year to year the number of his pupils increased, and he was soon recognised as a great authority. His position shielded him from the ban which was to be pronounced upon the followers of Sabbathai Zewi (q. v.) and Chayon. To avoid all suspicion, Eybenschütz himself pronounced the ban upon all the followers of the pseudo-Messiah, and in 1728 the congregation of Prague appointed him preacher. In 1740 he accepted a call to Metz, and in 1750 he went to Altona. It seemed as if with him an evil spirit had entered that place, which divided the German and the Polish Jews. When Eybenschütz came there, the famous Jacob Emden (q. v.) lived there, and, like his father, who had proscribed Chayon and his followers, regarded himself as the keeper of orthodoxy. An opportunity was soon offered to Emden whereby his vanity and his desire for heresy-hunting should be satisfied. At the time when Eybenschütz came to Altona there was an epidemic in that city. Since every rabbi was regarded as a sort of magician, the new-comer was expected to put a stop to the disease. Eybenschütz prepared amulets, which he distributed among the people. For curiosity's sake one was opened, and lo! in it was written: "O thou God of Israel, who dwellest in the beauty of thy power, send down salvation to this person through the merit of thy servant Sabbathai Zewi, in order that thy name, and the name of the Messiah Sabbathai Zewi, may be hallowed in the world." This amulet came into the hands of Emden. Eybenschütz denied all connection with the adherents of Sabbathai, and as he had already gained a great influence, it was believed; at least, everybody kept quiet. But Emden was not quiet, and finally the ban was pronounced against Eybenschütz. The matter was brought before the king, Frederic V of Denmark, who decided in favor of Emden. Eybenschütz lost his position as rabbi of the congregation. As his best friends left him, in his perplexity he finally went to a former pupil of his, Moses Gerson Kohen, who after his baptism had taken the name of Karl Anton (q. v.). Anton wrote an apology in behalf of his teacher, which he dedicated to the king of Denmark. This, and other influences, had at last such effect that the whole affair was dropped, and Eybenschütz was elected anew as rabbi of the congregation. The Jewish community, however, became divided, and this division lasted as long as both Eybenschütz and Emden were alive. Eybenschütz died in 1764, and was followed twelve years later by his opponent Emden. Both are buried in the Jewish cemetery of Altona. Eybenschütz wrote, ס׳ אהבת יהונתן, sermons and comments (Hamburg, 1766):—אלון בכות, homiletical comments upon the Lamentations (ibid. 1765), etc. See Fürst, *Bibl. Jud.* i, 261 sq.; De' Rossi, *Dizionario Storico*, p. 96 (Germ. transl.); Grätz, *Gesch. d. Juden*, x, 385 sq., note 7, p. liv; Jost, *Gesch. d. Juden. u. s. Sekten*, iii, 250 sq., 309 sq.; Jöcher, *Allgemeines Gelehrten-Lexikon*, s. v. (B. P.)

Eyck, HUBERT and JOHN VAN, two brothers, were Flemish painters, and natives of the small town of Maeseyck, on the river Maes. Hubert was probably born in 1366, and John in 1370. They established themselves at Bruges. They are said by some writers to have been the discoverers of oil painting. They generally painted in concert until the death of Hubert. Their most important work was an altar-piece with folding-doors, painted for Jodocus Vyts, who placed it in the Church of St. Bavon, at Ghent. The principal picture in this curious production represents the *Adoration of the Lamb*, as described by St. John in the Revelation. On one of the folding-doors is represented *Adam and Eve*, and on the other *St. Cœcilia*. In the sacristy of the cathedral at Bruges is preserved a picture painted by John in 1436, representing the *Virgin and Infant*, with St. George, St. Donatius, and other saints. Hubert died Sept. 18, 1429, and John in July, 1440. See Hoefer, *Nouv. Biog. Générale*, s. v.; Spooner, *Biog. Hist. of the Fine Arts*, s. v.

Eyckens, PETER, an eminent Flemish historical painter, was born at Antwerp in 1599, and was chosen director of the academy at Antwerp. His principal works in that city are, *The Last Supper*, in the Church of St. Andrew; *St. Catherine Disputing with the Pagans*, in the cathedral; and *St. John Preaching in the Wilderness*, in the Church of the Convent called Bogaerde. At Mechlin, in the Church of the Jesuits, were two of his most admired works. He died in 1649. See Hoefer, *Nouv. Biog. Générale*, s. v.; Spooner, *Biog. Hist. of the Fine Arts*, s. v.

Eyre, WILLIAM, an English Calvinistic divine, was born in Wiltshire about 1613, and entered the University of Oxford in 1629. In 1654 he was minister of St. Edmund's Church, Salisbury, and was ejected for nonconformity in 1662. He died in 1670. He published, *Epistola ad Vaserium de Textus Hebraici Variantibus Lectionibus* (1652):—*The True Justification of a Sinner Explained* (1654); in Latin, under the title of *Vindiciæ Justificationis Gratuitæ* (eod.). See Allibone, *Dict. of Brit. and Amer. Authors*, s. v.

Eytel, FRIEDRICH HERMANN, a Lutheran minister of Germany, was born Feb. 11, 1819, at Esslingen. He studied at Tübingen, was in 1856 pastor at Höfingen, in 1861 at Maichingen, where he died, April 21, 1869. He published *Psalter in Modernem Gewande* (Stuttgard, 1862; 2d ed. 1866). See Koch, *Geschichte des deutschen Kirchenliedes*, vii, 306. (B. P.)

Ezan, a hymn used in Mohammedan countries by the *Muezzin* (q. v.), or public crier, who chants it from the minarets of the mosques in a loud, deep-toned voice, summoning the people to their devotions. The proclamation is as follows: *God is great*, four times repeated; *I bear witness that there is no god but God*, twice repeated; *I bear witness that Mohammed is the prophet of God*, twice repeated; *Come to the temple of salvation*, twice repeated; *God is great, God is most great; there is no God but God, and Mohammed is his prophet.* At the morning prayer the muezzin must add, *Prayer is better than sleep*, twice repeated.

Ezekiel, a Jewish Greek writer, who lived a century before Christ, is the author of a dramatic poem after the manner of Euripides, on the *Deliverance of Israel from Egypt*, entitled ἐξαγωγή. Fragments of this poem are preserved in the *Præparatio Evangelica* of Eusebius (ix, 28, 29), and in the *Stromata* of Clement of Alexandria (i, 23, p. 414). They are given by Delitzsch in his *Zur Geschichte der jüdischen Poësie* (Leipsic, 1836), p. 211-219. The best edition of them, with translation and notes, is by Philippson (Berlin, 1830), entitled Ἐζεκιήλου τοῦ τῶν Ἰουδαϊκῶν τραγῳδιῶν ποιήτου ἐξαγωγή, etc. See Etheridge, *Introduction to Hebrew Literature*, p. 114; Edersheim, *History of the Jewish Nation*, p. 563 sq.; Herzfeld, *Gesch. des Volkes Israel*, ii, 491, 517-519, 579 (Leipsic, 1863); Fürst, *Bibl. Jud.* i, 264; Smith, *Dict. of Christ. Biog.* s. v.; Jöcher, *Allgemeines Gelehrten-Lexikon*, s. v. (B. P.)

Ezengatsi, George (Armen. *Keore*), an Armenian doctor, was born about 1338. He was a disciple of the celebrated John Orodnetsi, and a friend of Gregory Dathevatsi. He was one of the greatest theologians of his century, and professor in a monastery near Ezenga. He wrote, *Instructions how to Administer the Sacraments of Marriage and Baptism*:—*Explications of the Homilies of St. Gregory Nazianzen*:—*A Commentary on the Apocalypse*:—fourteen *Sermons*. There is also attributed to him a *Commentary on Isaiah*. All these works remain in MS. See Hoefer, *Nouv. Biog. Générale*, s. v.

Ezengatsi, John (Armen. *Hovan*), surnamed *Blûz* and *Torzoretsi*, the last of the classical writers and fathers of the Armenian Church, studied under Parzerpetsi, became *vastabed* (priest and doctor), and retired to the monastery of Torzor. In 1281 he travelled through Armenia, and went on a pilgrimage to Jerusalem. On his return he was made patriarch and head of the school of Hromgla. Soon after he retired to a monastery on Mt. Sebouh, and wrote his *Treatise on Grammar*. In 1284 he went to Tiflis, and gained great celebrity as a preacher. He died in 1326, leaving numerous other works, for which see Hoefer, *Nouv. Biog. Générale*, s. v.

Eznik (or **Eznag**), GOGHPATSI (i. e. native of Kolp), a theologian, and one of the best writers of Armenia, was born in 397. He was well versed in the Syriac and Greek languages, so that his masters, the patriarchs Isaac and Mesrob, gave him a mission to Edessa in 425, then to Constantinople, to collect and translate into Armenian the works of the Church fathers. Eznik became still later bishop of the province of Parcrevant and of the country of the Arsharounikhi. In 449 he attended the national council of Ardachad, which refused to embrace the religion of Zoroaster. Eznik died about 478, leaving, besides some homilies and short treatises, a work entitled *The Destruction of False Doctrines* (first published in the original Armenian at Smyrna, in 1762; and in a better form in the *Collection of Armenian Classics*, Venice, 1826; translated into French by Vaillant de Percival, Paris, 1833). See Hoefer, *Nouv. Biog. Générale*, s. v.; Smith, *Dict. of Christ. Biog.* s. v.

Ezra, Abraham ibn-. See ABEN-EZRA.

Ezra, Moses ibn-, *ben Jacob*, a Jewish writer, was born about 1070, and died about 1139. He is considered one of the most finished of Hebrew poets, but is equally celebrated as a Talmudist and professor of Greek philosophy. Although, like his brother poets, he excelled in sacred song, he also tuned his lyre as an inhabitant of the West, and sang at times of love, but more often in praise of the beauties of nature, which in later times was even acknowledged by Alexander von Humboldt (*Cosmos*, iii, p. 119), who praised his sublime description of natural scenery. His works are remarkable not only for the intrinsic excellence of the matter, but also for the purity, sweetness, and æsthetic grace of their style. His *selichoth*, or penitential hymns, are greatly esteemed by the Jews, who give to Ibn-Ezra the epithet of *has-salach*, or the "selichoth poet," par excellence. He wrote hymns for festival and other occasions, entitled זמירות ותחנונים, in the Sephardim ritual:—*Diwan R. M. ben-Ezra*, a collection of poems, lyrical, occasional, and devotional:—*Sefer ha-tarshish*, or *Sefer Anak*, ס׳ התרשיש or ס׳ ענק; this poem is called *Tarshish*, from the number of its stanzas—1210:—*Sefer Arugath Hab-bosem*, ס׳ ערגת הבשם, the "Garden of Spices," on the philosophy of religion, after the manner of Saadiah's *Emunoth*, in seven chapters, fragments of which have been published by Dukes, after a Hamburg MS. in Zion ii, p. 117 (Frankfort-on-the-Main, 1842, 1843):—*Tokacha*, תוכחה, a penitential hymn, reprinted by Asker, in his *Book of Life*, with an English translation (Lond. 1849). See Fürst, *Bibl. Jud.* i, 257 sq.; De' Rossi, *Dizionario Storico* (Germ. transl.), p. 11; Grätz, *Geschichte der Juden*, vi, 123 sq.; Delitzsch, *Zur Geschichte der jüd. Poësie*, p. 45, 168; Jost, *Gesch. d. Juden. u. s. Sekten*, ii, 414; Sachs, *Religiöse Poësie der Juden*, p. 69 sq., 276 sq.; Zunz, *Literaturgeschichte der synag. Poësie*, p. 202, 412, 585, 614; *Synagogale Poësie*, p. 21, 133, 228 sq.; Kimchi, *Liber Radicum* (ed. Biesenthal and Lebrecht), p. xxxvi sq.; Kämpf, *Nichtandalusische Poësie andalusischer Dichter*, p. 192-216; Dukes, *Moses ben-Ezra* (Altona, 1839); *Rabbinische Blumenlese*, p. 58. (B. P.)

F.

Faber, Ægidius, a Carmelite monk, who died at Brussels in 1506, is the author of, *De Origine Religionum:—De Testamento Christi in Cruce:—Commentarii in Evangelia, Epistolas Pauli, Librum Ruth et Job.* See Jöcher, *Allgemeines Gelehrten-Lexikon*, s. v. (B. P.)

Faber, Frederick William, D.D., an English clergyman and hymn-writer, was born at Calverley, Yorkshire, June 28, 1814. He was educated at Harrow and the University of Oxford, where he became a fellow of University College in 1837. About this time he gave up his Calvinistic views and became an enthusiastic admirer and follower of John H. Newman. In 1841 he travelled on the Continent, and on his return published *Sights and Thoughts in Foreign Churches and among Foreign Peoples*, a work of great merit. He now became rector of Elton, in Huntingdonshire, but soon proceeded again to the Continent to study the methods followed by the Roman Catholic Church. Returning to Elton he devoted himself earnestly to his parish, but was constrained to adopt the Romish faith in 1845. On leaving Elton his parishioners sobbed out, "God bless you, Mr. Faber, wherever you go." He founded a religious community at Birmingham, called Wilfridians, after the name Wilfrid, which Faber assumed. The community was ultimately merged in the oratory of St. Philip Neri, of which father Newman was the head; and in 1849 a branch of the oratory was established in London, over which Faber presided until his death, Sept. 26, 1863. He was a voluminous writer, although it is mainly as a hymn-writer that he will be known in the future. Among his finest compositions of this class are, *The Greatness of God; The Will of God; The Eternal Father; The God of my Childhood; The Pilgrims of the Night; The Shadow of the Rock.* Besides the work above mentioned, he published, previous to his conversion to Romanism, *Tracts on the Church and the Prayer-Book* (1839):—*A Sermon on Education* (1840):—*The Cherwell Water-Lily and other Poems* (1840):—*The Styrian Lake*, etc. (1842):—*Sir Lancelot*, a poem (1844):—*The Rosary*, etc. (1845), and several other papers. After his conversion he published, *Catholic Hymns:—Essay on Beatification and Canonization* (1848):—*The Spirit and Genius of St. Philip Neri* (1850):—*Catholic Home Missions* (1851):—*All for Jesus* (1854):—*Growth in Holiness* (1855):—*The Blessed Sacrament* (1856):—*The Creator and the Creature* (1857):—*The Foot of the Cross, or Sorrows of Mary* (1858):—*Spiritual Conferences* (1859), and other works. The only complete edition of his *Hymns* is the one published by Richardson & Son in 1861 (2d ed. 1871). His *Notes on Doctrinal and Spiritual Subjects* were edited by father Bowden, and issued after Faber's death. See his *Life and Letters*, by father Bowden; *Early Life*, by his brother; *Encyclop. Brit.* 9th ed. s. v.

Faber, Georg, a Lutheran theologian, was born at Uffenheim, in Franconia, in 1579, and studied at Wittenberg. In 1606 he was preacher at Lichtenau, in 1616 at Nüremberg, where he died, July 16, 1634. He is the author of, *Institutiones Grammaticæ Hebraice* (Nüremberg, 1626):—*Lectionis Hebr. Institutio* (Anspach, 1608). See Jöcher, *Allgemeines Gelehrten-Lexikon*, s. v.; Fürst, *Bibl. Jud.* i, 265; Steinschneider, *Bibliogr. Handbuch*, s. v. (B. P.)

Faber, Johann Gottlieb, a Lutheran theologian of Germany, was born at Stuttgart, March 8, 1717. He studied at Tübingen, and was appointed professor there in 1748. In 1767 he was made member of consistory and abbot of Alpirsbach. He died at Stuttgart, March 18, 1779, leaving, *De Naturalismo Morali* (Tübingen, 1752):—*De Anima Legum* (ibid.):—*De Principe Christiano* (ibid. 1753):—*De Miraculis Christi* (ibid. 1764):—*Meletema Philosophicum* (ibid. 1765):—*De Diversis Fontibus Tolerantiæ* (ibid. 1769):—*Theologia Dogmatica* (Stuttgart, 1780). See Döring, *Die gelehrten Theologen Deutschlands*, i, 392 sq.; Winer, *Handbuch der theol. Lit.* i, 685; Jöcher, *Allgemeines Gelehrten-Lexikon*, s. v. (B. P.)

Faber, Matthias, a Jesuit, was born Feb. 24, 1587, at Altomünster, in Bavaria. In 1607 he entered the German College at Rome, received holy orders there, and returned to Germany in 1611. In 1637 he went to Vienna and joined the Jesuits, and died at Tyrnau, in Hungary, in 1653. He is the author of a homiletical work entitled, *Concionum Opus Tripartitum*, which has often been published (latest ed. Ratisbon, 1879). Besides he wrote, *Rerum Naturæ Descriptio* (Dillingen, 1607). See Jöcher, *Allgemeines Gelehrten-Lexikon*, s. v.; *Literarischer Handweiser für das Katholische Deutschland*, 1880, No. 266. (B. P.)

Faber, Philip, a Franciscan, and professor of theology at Padua, where he died, Aug. 28, 1630, is the author of, *De Primatu Petri et Pontificis Romani:—De Censuris Ecclesiasticis:—De Prædestinatione.* See Jöcher, *Allgemeines Gelehrten-Lexikon*, s. v.; Winer, *Handbuch der theol. Lit.* i, 460. (B. P.)

Fabiola, a Roman lady of an illustrious family. Being married first to a man who became lost in debauchery, she divorced herself from him, and being then but little acquainted with the commands of the gospel, she married a second husband of the same sort as the first. For this act she was excluded from the communion of the Church, to which she eventually returned, after public penitence, with extreme humility. She spent all her fortune for the relief of the poor, and for the establishment of a large hospital at Rome. In A.D. 395 she went to Palestine, and visited Jerome at Bethlehem. The invasion of the Huns into Palestine forced her to leave that country, and she returned to Italy, where she continued to consecrate her life to continual exercises of piety and charity. Fabiola died Dec. 29, 399. See Hoefer, *Nouv. Biog. Générale*, s. v.; Smith, *Dict. of Christ. Biog.* s. v.

Fabre, Jean, a French preacher, was born at Tarascon, in Provence, about 1370. He entered the order of the Carmelite friars in 1390, and preached with success in divers churches in Provence. Pope Martin V appointed him archbishop of Cagliari in 1423. Fabre governed his diocese for seventeen years. Having been made patriarch of Cæsarea, he resigned his archiepiscopacy, and ended his days in retirement about the year 1442. His sermons have been collected under the title of *Homiliæ Sacræ*. See Hoefer, *Nouv. Biog. Générale*, s. v.

Fabricius, Johannes (1), a German theologian, was born at Nüremberg in 1560, and was successively instructor and pastor there for forty-eight years, being enthusiastically attached to the doctrines of Melanchthon. He died in 1636, leaving *De Dignitate Conjugii* (1592). See Hoefer, *Nouv. Biog. Générale*, s. v.

Fabricius, Johannes (2), son of the preceding, a German theologian, was born at Nüremberg, March 31, 1616. He studied at Jena, Leipsic, Wittenberg, and finally at Altorf, where he became professor of theology. In 1649 he was appointed preacher in his native city, and died there about 1690. For his works, which are not now of much interest, see Hoefer, *Nouv. Biog. Générale*, s. v.

Fabricius, Theodosius, a Lutheran theologian of Germany, was born at Nordhausen, Aug. 11, 1560. He studied at Wittenberg, was in 1584 deacon there, and in 1586 superintendent at Herzberg. He died at Göttingen, Aug. 7, 1597, leaving *Compendium Doctrinæ*

Christianæ:—Harmonia Passionis et Resurrectionis Christi:—Loci Communes ex Scriptis Lutheri. See Jöcher, *Allgemeines Gelehrten-Lexikon*, s. v.; Fürst, *Bibl. Jud.* i, 265. (B. P.)

Fabronius, HERMANN, a Reformed theologian of the 17th century, is the author of a didactic poem entitled, *Christiades*, i. e. *Israelis in Terram Sanctam Introductio per Mosen, et in Cœlum per Jesum Christum:—Concordia Lutherano-Calvinistica:—Weissagung Daniels von Verwüstung der Stadt Jerusalem.* See Jöcher, *Allgemeines Gelehrten-Lexikon*, s. v.; Fürst, *Bibl. Jud.* i, 265. (B. P.)

Facilides, VICTORIN GOTTFRIED, a Lutheran theologian, was born in 1777 at Mittweida, in Saxony. He was for some time pastor at Rochlitz, in Bohemia, and from 1835 superintendent at Oschatz, where he died, Dec. 31, 1841. He wrote, *De εὐκαιρίας Homileticæ Observatione* (Leipsic, 1830), and also published a number of sermons. See Zuchold, *Bibl. Theol.* i, 348; Winer, *Handbuch der theol. Lit.* ii, 65, 173, 174, 176, 177. (B. P.)

Faculty Court, a court of the archbishop of Canterbury, which grants dispensations to marry, to eat flesh on days prohibited, to hold two or more benefices, etc. The officer of this court is called the master of faculties. See FACULTY.

Faes, JOHANN, a Lutheran theologian of Germany, was born at Lüneburg, Feb. 11, 1646. In 1675 he was pastor at Steigerberg, in the county of Hoya, in 1682 at Minden, in 1687 at Stade, and died there in 1712. He wrote, *De Jubilæis Pontificum Romanorum:—Exercitatio in Cartesii Meditationes:—Anatome Bullæ Jubilææ Universalis Anni* 1700:—*Expositio in Epistolam ad Philemonem.* See Jöcher, *Allgemeines Gelehrten-Lexikon*, s. v.; Winer, *Handbuch der theol. Lit.* i, 631. (B. P.)

Fagan, LUKE, D.D., an Irish prelate, was translated from the diocese of Meath to the see of Dublin in 1729. In 1733, probably the last of Dr. Fagan's life, the act was passed (7 Geo. II, c. 6) whereby converts from the Roman Catholic faith, whose wives were of that persuasion, or whose children were educated in it, were prohibited, under severe penalties, from exercising the office of justices of the peace. This prelate did not in any way distinguish himself. See D'Alton, *Memoirs of the Abps. of Dublin*, p. 466.

Fage, DURAND, one of the French *Illuminati* (q. v.), was born at Aubais, in Languedoc, in 1681. After the suppression of the Camisards in 1705, he submitted to the Church authorities, and was taken across the frontier to Germany, whence he passed to Holland, and in 1706 went to London. He died, probably, in England about the middle of the 18th century, leaving a work entitled *Théâtre Sacré des Cévennes* (Lond. 1707, 12mo); reprinted under the title *Les Prophètes Protestants* (Paris, 1847, 8vo).

Fahlcrantz, CHRISTIAN ERIK, a Lutheran theologian of Sweden, was born Aug. 30, 1790. In 1829 he was professor of theology at Upsala; in 1849 was elevated to the episcopal see at Westeräs, and died Aug. 6, 1866. He was one of the editors of the *Ecklesiastik-Tidskrift*, and published a collection of his writings (Orebro, 1863–66, 7 vols.). (B. P.)

Faigaux, FRANÇOIS LOUIS, a French Protestant theologian, was born at Yverdun, in Berne, in 1707. He studied at Basle, where he was also preacher for some time. In 1751 he was called as French preacher to Cassel, where he died, Oct. 20 the same year, leaving, *Religion du Cœur* (Rotterdam, 1736):—*Sermons Diverses* (Hague, 1740):—*Adversus Dilationem Conversionis* (Marburg, 1743):—*Les Paroles de la Vie Éternelle* (Schwabach, 1743; Cassel, 1752):—*Sur la Folie de l'Athéisme* (Schwabach, 1749):—*Le Petit Catéchisme de Heidelberg* (ibid. 1752). See Jöcher, *Allgemeines Gelehrten-Lexikon*, s. v. (B. P.)

Faillon, MICHEL ÉTIENNE, a French theological and historical writer, was born at Tarascon in 1799. He became a Sulpician of Paris, and was sent to Montreal in 1854 as visitor of the houses of that congregation in America. He died in Paris, Oct. 25, 1870. His literary work was confined chiefly to subjects connected with the history of Canada. His publications include a *Life of Margaret Bourgeoys*, foundress of the Congregation Sisters (1852):—*Life of Madame d'Youville*, foundress of the Gray Sisters (eod.):—*Life of the Venerable Mr. Olier* (1853):—*Life of Mlle. Maure*, foundress of the Hôtel Dieu (1854):—*Life of Mlle. le Ber*, the recluse (1860):—and a very extended *History of the French Colony in Canada* (1865–66, 3 vols. 4to), only a small part of his plan.

Fainche, an Irish virgin saint, commemorated Jan. 1, was sister of St. Ennea, of noble lineage, and greatly aided him in his religious labors. See Smith, *Dict. of Christ. Biog.* s. v.

Fairbairn, PATRICK, D.D., a Scotch Presbyterian minister, was born at Halyburton, Berwickshire, Scotland, Jan. 28, 1805. He was educated in the school at Greenlaw, and sent to College at Edinburgh; licensed to preach in 1826; in 1830 went to the Orkney Islands with a family who had large possessions there, and was shortly after ordained pastor of the island parish of North Ronaldshay, where he labored six years. While there he translated Steiger on 1 Peter, for Clark's *Theological Library*, and began the study of typology. In 1837 he removed to Glasgow, where for three years he was pastor of one of the churches erected in connection with the church-building scheme of Dr. Chalmers; in 1840 he was installed pastor of the parish of Salton, East Lothian, where he was when the disruption of the Scottish Church occurred, and he continued in the Free Church there until 1852, when he was appointed first assistant professor, and shortly after professor of divinity in the Free Church College at Aberdeen. In 1856 he was transferred to Glasgow, being the first professor appointed to the Free Church Theological College, and the next year was elected principal of the same. In 1867 he was appointed a delegate from the Free Church of Scotland to visit the churches in America. He died suddenly at Glasgow, Aug. 6, 1874. Dr. Fairbairn's literary productions were numerous. Besides editing the *Imperial Bible Dictionary* (2 vols. 8vo), the following may be noted: *An Exposition of the First Epistle of St. Peter* (1836, 2 vols. 12mo):—*Typology of Scripture* (Edinb. 1845–47, 2 vols. 8vo; Phila. 1853, 8vo):—*Commentary on the Psalms*, translated from Hengstenberg (1845–48, 3 vols. 8vo):—*Jonah; His Life, Character, and Mission* (1849, 12mo):—*Ezekiel and the Book of his Prophecy* (1851, 8vo):—*The Revelation of St. John*, translated from Hengstenberg (Edinb. 1851, 3 vols. 8vo):—*Prophecy*, etc. (1856, 8vo):—*Hermeneutical Manual* (1858, 8vo):—*Pastoral Epistles* (1874):—*Pastoral Theology* (posthumous, 1875):—*Law in Scripture* (1868). See *Fasti Eccles. Scoticanæ*, i, 366; ii, 44; iii, 411. (W. P. S.)

Fairchild, ASHBEL GREEN, D.D., an eminent Presbyterian minister, was born at Hanover, N. J., May 1, 1795, and was piously trained by a widowed mother. At the age of thirteen he commenced his classical studies at Morristown; in November, 1812, entered the senior class in Princeton College, and graduated in September, 1813. In January, 1814, he made a public profession of religion, and united with the Presbyterian Church of Hanover; and in June of the same year entered the Theological Seminary at Princeton. He was licensed to preach by the Presbytery of New Jersey in April, 1816, and in September following he left the seminary and entered upon a missionary tour of six months in North Carolina, as assistant to Rev. Dr. Hall. Returning home in April, 1817, he spent two months in a missionary field in the north-western part of his native state. In September of the same year he entered upon another missionary tour, under the direction of the Western Missionary Society, spending three months on the waters of the Monongahela, and then three months on the upper branches of the Allegheny. He was taken under the care of the Presbytery of Redstone, April 21, 1818, and was appointed stated supply to the congregation of George's Creek for half his time; on July 1 following was ordained as an evangelist in Pittsburgh; July 2, 1822, installed pastor of the churches of George's Creek, Morgantown, and Greensborough, Va., and for the first three years was obliged to make up the deficiency in his salary by teaching; in April, 1827, he was installed pastor of the Tent Church, Pa., where he served for thirty-six years. He died there, June 30, 1864. In Dr. Fairchild the dignity and the simplicity of the Gospel ministry were most beautifully combined and exemplified. Besides frequent contributions to the weekly religious press, he published *The Great Supper:—Scripture Baptism:—Unpopular Doctrines:*—and *What Presbyterians Believe*, all issued by the Presbyterian Board of Publication. See *Gen. Cat. of Princeton Theol. Sem.* 1881, p. 16; Nevin, *Presb. Encyclop.* s. v. (H. O. R.)

Fairfowl (or **Fairfull**), Andrew, a Scotch prelate, was born at Dunfermline, Dec. 14, 1606; graduated from the University of St. Andrews in 1623; early became chaplain to the earl of Rothes; minister at Leslie in 1632; afterwards at North Leith, and at Dunse in 1636. He was preferred to the see of Glasgow, Nov. 14, 1661, by king Charles II, and was consecrated in June, 1662. He died at Edinburgh, Nov. 2, 1663. See Keith, *Scottish Bishops*, p. 265; *Fasti Eccles. Scoticanæ*, ii, 378, 549.

Fairlie (or **Fairly**), James, A.M., a Scotch clergyman, was promoted from regent in the Edinburgh University; admitted to the living at South Leith in 1625; transferred to the professorship of divinity in Edinburgh University in 1629; presented to the collegiate or second charge, Greyfriars Church, Edinburgh, in 1630; resigned July 28, 1637, having been elected bishop of Argyll, but was deposed by the assembly in 1638. He failed in his suit to obtain the living of Largo and other parishes, was recommended by the Commission of Assembly, and accepted in March, 1644, as minister at Lasswade, and was presented to that living by the king in 1645. He died in February, 1658, aged about seventy years. He published *The Muses' Welcome*, two poems. See *Fasti Eccles. Scoticanæ*, i, 45, 105, 289.

Fairy (variously derived from the Celtic, *faer*, "to charm;" Old English, *fere*, "a companion;" from *faran*, "to go;" Persian, *peri;* Arab. *feri;* but probably rather from the Lat. *fatum*, through the mediæval *fatare*, "to enchant;" the French *faer*, thence *faerie*, "illusion"), an illusory or imaginary being, properly female, of supernatural but limited power, common to the popular belief of most European countries. The *fay* of romance resembles the Greek *nymph*, generally represented as a damsel of almost angelic loveliness, who seduced knights into enchanted isles and palaces. Fairy-land was supposed to be sometimes underground, at others amid wildernesses, or even in the ocean. The English sprite, or male fairy, Shakespeare's *Puck*, called "Robin Goodfellow," corresponds to the German "Knecht Ruprecht," the Scotch "brownie," and the French "esprit folet," or "gobelin" (goblin), and the Cornish "pixy." See Elf.

Everything known of fairies in the way of sayings and fables came from the Romance people. There were at first only three of these beings, but soon their number swelled to seven, and later to thirteen. Since their number was seven, these are six good and one evil, likewise later twelve good, the thirteenth evil. This, probably, is a result of the influence of Christianity, which sought to bring the fairies, as heathen deities, therefore spirits of darkness, into disrepute, which, however, could not be accomplished at once. They are spoken of as superhuman, long-lived female beings, sometimes good, sometimes bad; the former adorned with all the charms of body and spirit, exceedingly beautiful and young, perfect mistresses of all female arts, and ever ready to help the down-trodden, to lead the lost in the right path, by their gift of sorcery to make the impossible possible, and to use this power as becomes the perfect will of a divine being. The evil fairies are the opposite, but have no power to undo the work of other similar beings. In the French Pyrenees it is believed that if flax be laid on the threshold of a fairy grotto, they immediately change it into the finest thread. On New Year's day the fairies visit the houses whose inmates believe in them, and bring fortune in their right hand and misfortune in their left. In a room a table is spread for them, a white cloth on it, a loaf of bread, with a knife, a white shell full of water or wine, and a candle. The windows and doors are then thrown open, and he who shows the greatest hospitality may hope for a rich harvest, but he who neglects this duty may fear the greatest disasters. On New Year's morning the family surround the table, the father breaks the bread and distributes it, whereupon it is eaten as breakfast; then all wish each other a happy New Year. In the Highlands of Scotland it is thought dangerous to speak out the name of a fairy on the mountains which they inhabit. The fairies are able assistants at births; therefore they are often taken as god-parents, and a place is reserved for them at the table. In Franche-Comté there is known a *Fée Arie*, who appears at country festivals during the harvesting season, and rewards the diligent reapers; she drops fruit from the trees for good children, and during the Christmas season she distributes nuts and cake, similar to the German *Frau Holda*. Again, the fairies appear as giant-maidens, carrying huge rocks on their heads and in their aprons, while with the other hand they turn the spindle. On Saturdays the power of the fairies leaves them; they therefore take all kinds of forms on this day, and try to elude the gaze of all eyes. They can hide in a tree, in a horse, in a sword, in a mantle, and this is the origin of the belief that such things are "gefeyt," that is, possessed of a fairy.

For the literature of the subject see Shakespeare, *Midsummer-Night's Dream;* Perrault, *Contes de ma Mère l'Oye* (1697); Keightly, *Fairy Mythology* (Lond. 1860); and Scott's writings.

Faith-cure, a popular name for certain sudden and remarkable cases of recovery in recent times, claimed to have been effected by the power of faith in God alone, without the use of any medicine or physical remedy. We cite a few notable cases from the public prints:

"New Haven, Conn., *March* 27.—A remarkable faith-cure is reported from the village of Noank. Mrs. Fannie S. Spencer, the wife of ex-Representative John R. Spencer, has for many years been a victim of the opium habit and asthma. Her family is one of the wealthiest and most reputable in eastern Connecticut. She is now sixty-five years old. Over forty years ago she suffered from an attack of ill-health, and her physician prescribed opium. She is of a nervous temperament. The use of the drug as a medicine developed an appetite for it, to which she gave way. She was also a great snuff-taker, and in addition there was the asthmatic trouble which the drug was used to relieve. All the local doctors agreed that an opium habit of forty years' standing was an in-incurable disease. One day about a week ago two or three of Mrs. Spencer's friends met at her residence, and a season of prayer was determined upon. Prayers were offered and continued with earnestness by those present for some time. It was during this period that Mrs. Spencer says she experienced a peculiar sensation of mind and body unlike anything she had ever felt before. She calls it the 'Blessings of the Holy Spirit.' From that moment she dates her complete cure, and she and her friends declare she has not since touched opium nor snuff, nor has she felt any desire for them, and she has been entirely free from the asthmatical trouble."—*N. Y. Times*, March 28, 1884.

"Cleveland, *June* 29.—A strange case of faith-cure came to light here to-day. It is that of Miss Rebecca Kerby, who has been on an invalid's bed forty years, in a farm-house just out of Chardon, a small town near here. During that time she has been on her feet but twice, and then only at the expense of great suffering. For twenty-eight years she has not sat up, and yet it is told of her that on Monday, after prayer and an exercise of faith, she arose from her bed, sat in a chair for an hour, and was able to walk once across the room."—*The Tribune* (N. Y.), July 1, 1884.

"Mrs. Emily J. Wimpy, wife of John A. Wimpy, a resident of the village of Norcross, twenty miles from the city of Atlanta, Ga., who had not been able to walk upon the ground for twenty-two years in consequence of extreme physical weakness and suffering, was enabled to rise and walk and go about and do as others do without any assistance, being restored to her former state of good health. This was done through the faith that God was able and would heal her by divine power. The fact is attested and reported through the press by Rev. W. A. Parks, a presiding elder of the North Georgia Conference of the M. E. Church South, who was present and witnessed it."—*The Way of Holiness*, quoted in *The Law and Gospel*, Paris, Ill., December, 1884.

Many similar instances might easily be collected. In fact, there is a regular hospital, conducted by Dr. Cullis, of Boston, where patients of nearly all sorts repair for healing by means of simple prayer and faith, with no other outward sign than mere touch.* Professions of a like ability are put forth by several religious bodies, especially what is known as the "Irvingite," or Catholic Apostolic Church (q. v.).

With regard to all these statements we have to remark:

1. It is not impossible nor incredible that miracles should take place in modern times, provided that suitable occasions of necessity should arise. God is undoubtedly as able to effect them now as anciently. The only question is one of fact; and that is further limited to this inquiry: Do these phenomena take place through natural law—whether bodily or mental, or both combined—or are they the supernatural results of direct divine power in answer to believing prayer?

2. The evidence in most of the cases certainly, and probably in all, if the circumstances were detailed, is decidedly in favor of the former, or natural solution. It will be observed that they are chiefly if not wholly of such a chronic character that the mind of the patient has largely to do with their existence and continuance. *They are nervous diseases*, functional and not organic derangements. We have yet to hear of an acute malady, a well-defined fever, a settled consumption, a broken limb, or a positive lesion of any kind being cured in this manner. With the older prophets, with Christ and his apostles, all these and much more marked disabilities were just as readily healed as any. There was nothing done in a corner, nor was there the least opportunity to doubt the absolute divine power. There is generally—we might say invariably—an air of mystery and collusion about these cases, which justly lays them open to suspicion. Until, therefore, more palpable and *bona fide* examples shall be adduced, we hold ourselves justified in doubting that these cures are anything more than the effect of the imagination upon highly susceptible systems.

3. At the same time we fully and gladly admit that earnest faith and prayer have an influence upon divine providence, which may lead to a cure that would not take place without them. This is through a special blessing upon the means used, or upon the person, without any particular medical means. But this is a very different thing from the peculiar claim set up in the cases adduced. See MIRACLE; PRAYER.

4. The prerequisite of "faith" on the part of the subjects applying for these cures is a suspicious circumstance; for they are required not only to believe that the Lord is able to perform the cure (which no Christian doubts), but that he is also willing to do it, and even that he actually *will* do it, which they have no right to assume. This is more than Jesus demanded, for the leper only said, "Lord, *if* thou wilt thou canst," and the question asked on another occasion was, "Believe ye that I am able?" Confidence enough to induce the patient to come to our Lord, or in friends to bring him, of course was necessary; but a fixed conviction that the cure was positively about to be wrought was not demanded. When it is said that "He could not do many mighty works because of their unbelief," in a certain place, it merely denotes this indisposition to apply to him. There never was a failure, however desperate the case, when this simple condition of asking was complied with. A larger measure of belief than this in such matters we judge to be *presumption* rather than wholesome faith.

5. The champions of "faith-cure" generally appeal to James v, 14, 15, as a standing proof-text for the correctness of their position; but most of them pay little or no attention to the precise and express stipulations there made about "calling for the *elders of the church*," and "anointing with oil;" and they lay the whole stress

---

* The institution referred to is "The Faith-Cure House," which is part of a system of *Faith-Work*, established by Charles Cullis, M.D., at Grove Hall, Boston Highlands, in 1864, and now including in addition (according to the 19th *Annual Report*, 1883), "The Consumptives' Home, with its accommodation for eighty patients; the Spinal Cottage, with its four incurable cases of spinal disease; two Orphans' Homes, with their twenty-nine children; the Deaconesses' Home, for workers; Grove-Hall Church and the Little Chapel for the Dead;" besides the "Willard Tract Repository and Faith-Training College," in the city of Boston, branches in New York, Philadelphia, California, a Cancer Home at Walpole, Mass., a college at Boydton, Va., for colored people, and a mission in India. The whole involved an expenditure for that year of $37,353.91, and for the nineteen years, $589,770.86; entirely raised by voluntary contributions, without personal solicitation. The Faith-Cure House was dedicated in 1882, after an expenditure of $4,303.77, raised in a similar manner. None of these institutions have any permanent fund or resources except the free-will offerings of friends from time to time. Many remarkable cures, it is claimed, have been effected through these instrumentalities—"cancers, tumors, paralysis, spinal diseases, consumption, chronic rheumatism" (see the cases in Dr. Cullis's two little volumes, entitled *Faith-Cures*, published in 1879 and 1881 at his Repository); but they require careful sifting in the light of medical science before they can properly be adduced to show any direct or preternatural divine interference. It is but just to say that this last assertion is scarcely made in its bold or full form by the advocates of the system; although their language, at least in the popular impression, seems to imply such a view. Of the numerous cases recited in these small volumes no scientific or exact statement is made, and in most instances the real nature of the disease is not disclosed at all, or very vaguely. A few are apparently examples of incipient consumption, cancer, or other dangerous and violent maladies. There are some of affections of the eyes, ears, and other special organs; but the symptoms are equally indefinite. Most are nervous disorders. Failures are not reported. The whole narrative, except in its pious sentiment, reads very much like the popular advertisements of cures by patent medicines. In nearly every example it is easy to trace the beneficial influence of hope upon the nervous system of the patient, as the probable mainspring of the recovery. That devout gratitude to God should be experienced by the subjects of these changes was certainly proper and natural; but it does not follow that they were correct in their opinion as to the particular channel or medium of the cure. There is nothing decidedly preternatural or supernatural about one of them. Nearly every physician of extensive practice has witnessed equally remarkable restorations in which no distinctively divine claim was set up. Nevertheless the facts are doubtless stated by Dr. Cullis with substantial truth, and if invalids may be cured in that way, it is certainly a very convenient and economical method of practice. There have been some other institutions in this country, however, that have attempted to imitate his plan, so far at least as to discard medical treatment; but they have been such woful failures that the civil law has been invoked in order to save their victims from death by criminal neglect. Providence commonly blesses only judicious physical means to beneficial physical results.

There are several similar establishments in Europe, the most noted of which are one at Männedorf, near Zurich, in Switzerland, established by Dorothea Trudel, and since her death, in 1862, carried on by Samuel Teller, and one at Bad Boll, in Würtemberg, Germany, established by a Lutheran clergyman, and since his death carried on by his sons. These are Christian retreats for a temporary sojourn of patients laboring under various diseases of body or mind, at a nominal charge for board, or, in the case of the poor, entirely free, where many remarkable cures are said to have been effected by prayer alone without medicine. As statistical reports are seldom or never issued by these institutions, which are all conducted on the voluntary plan, it is impossible to exhibit or analyze their results accurately.

upon "the prayer of faith." This, however, as the whole passage shows, is not the petition of the patient merely, nor of a self-constituted committee or a few volunteers, but of the regular ecclesiastical authorities, duly and formally convoked for that purpose. Most judicious expositors hold that this refers to the exercise of the miraculous "gift of healing" enjoyed by some early believers as a special endowment of the apostles, and that the direction has therefore ceased to be pertinent in later times. Such has been the practical comment of the Evangelical Church, departed from only by a few ecclesiastical bodies (with whom the experiment has been a signal failure), and by the Roman Catholics (who pervert it to teach "extreme unction"). See ANOINTING.

Fakone, a district in Japan in which there is situated a lake, at the bottom of which the Japanese believe is found a purgatory for children. On the shore of this lake are built five small wooden chapels, in each of which sits a priest beating a gong, and howling a *nimanda*. *Fakone* is also the name of a temple in Japan, famous for its relics. It contains the sabres of the heroic Camis (q. v.), still stained with the blood of those slain in battle; the vestments which were said to have been worn by an angel, and which supplied the place of wings; and the tomb of Joritomo, the first secular emperor of the Japanese.

Falck, NATHANIEL, a Lutheran theologian of Germany, was born at Dantzic, Oct. 11, 1663. He studied at Rostock and Wittenberg, and died at Stettin, Aug. 18, 1693, leaving, *De Dæmonologia Recentiorum Autorum Falsa:—Septinarium Sacrum Concionum Sacrarum*, etc. See Jöcher, *Allgemeines Gelehrten-Lexikon*, s. v. (B. P.)

Falco, JUAN CONCHILLAS, a reputable Spanish painter, was born at Valencia in 1651, and studied in the school of Mario. He was much employed for the churches and private collections, and died in 1711. See Spooner, *Biog. Hist. of the Fine Arts*, s. v.

Falconer, Colin, a Scotch prelate, was born in 1623, studied the liberal arts at St. Leonard's College, and graduated from the University of St. Andrews in 1645. He became a clergyman in 1651, and ministered to the parish of Essil, in the diocese of Moray, and a few years afterwards at Forres, where he continued until promoted to the bishopric of Argyle, Sept. 5, 1679, whence he was translated to the see of Moray, Feb. 7, 1680. He died at Spynie, Nov. 11, 1686. See Keith, *Scottish Bishops*, p. 154, 292; *Fasti Eccles. Scoticanæ*, iii, 152, 169, 177, 446, 452.

Falconer, John, D.D., a Scotch clergyman, son of Dr. David Falconer, graduated at Edinburgh University in 1679; became chaplain to the family of Wemyss; was admitted to the living at Carnbee, May 23, 1683, but deprived by the privy council in 1689 for not praying for the king and queen. He was consecrated a bishop of the Non-Jurant Church at Dundee, April 28, 1709, having the district of Brechin assigned to him in 1720. He died at Inglismadie, July 6, 1723, aged about sixty-four years. He wrote a tract describing the various covenants of God. See *Fasti Eccles. Scoticanæ*, ii, 413.

Falconer, Thomas, a learned layman, was born at Chester, England, in 1736, and died Sept. 4, 1792. He published, *Devotions for the Sacrament of the Lord's Supper* (1786):—*Chronological Tables from Solomon to the Death of Alexander the Great* (1796). See Chalmers, *Biog. Dict.* s. v.; Allibone, *Dict. of Brit. and Amer. Authors*, s. v.

Falconet, ÉTIENNE MAURICE, an eminent French sculptor, was born at Paris in 1716, and studied in the school of Lemoine. In 1754 he was admitted to the Royal Academy, and was afterwards appointed professor and rector. Among his most important works in sculpture are *Christ's Agony*, *The Annunciation*, and *Moses* and *David*, in the Church of St. Roch, at Paris, also *St. Ambrose*, in the Church of the Invalides. He died in 1791. See Hoefer, *Nouv. Biog. Générale*, s. v.; Spooner, *Biog. Hist. of the Fine Arts*, s. v.

Falk is a name common to many Jewish rabbis:

1. JACOB JOSHUA, who died at Frankfort-on-the-Main in 1756, is the author of novellas on different treatises of the Talmud, for which see Fürst, *Bibl. Jud.* i, 271 sq.

2. JOSHUA BEN-ALEXANDER *hak-Kohen*, who died about 1620, was rabbi at Lemberg, and wrote commentaries on the Jewish ritual, entitled דרישה ופרישה; he also wrote *derashas* on the Pentateuch. See Fürst, *loc. cit.* p. 272; De' Rossi, *Dizionario Storico* (Germ. transl.), p. 103.

3. JOSHUA BEN-JOSEPH, who died in 1648, was rabbi at Cracow, and wrote discussions on some Talmudic treatises. See Fürst, *loc. cit.* p. 273 sq.

4. JOSHUA of Lissa, was rabbi at Hamburg, and wrote under the title עמק יהושע, i. e., *The Valley of Joshua*, expositions on sections of the Pentateuch. See Fürst, *loc. cit.* p. 273; De' Rossi, *loc. cit.* p. 103; Jöcher, *Allgemeines Gelehrten-Lexikon*, s. v. (B. P.)

Falk, LUDWIG, a Reformed theologian of Germany, was born in 1801. He was first pastor at Landshut, afterwards first preacher at the Reformed Cathedral Church in Breslau, and member of the Silesian consistory. He died at Waldau, near Liegnitz, Aug. 20, 1872, leaving a volume of sermons, entitled *Alles in allen Christus* (Breslau, 1843). See Zuchold, *Bibl. Theol.* i, 349. (B. P.)

Falling away OR FROM GRACE. See APOSTASY; BACKSLIDE; PERSEVERANCE.

Fan, ECCLESIASTICAL. See FLABELLUM.

Fancourt, SAMUEL, a dissenting minister, and the originator of circulating libraries in London, was born in 1678, and died in 1768. He published several *Sermons* and theological treatises in 1720. See Chalmers, *Biog. Dict.* s. v.; Allibone, *Dict. of Brit. and Amer. Authors*, s. v.

Fano, Fidelis a, an Italian writer, was born Dec. 24, 1838, at Fano, Italy. In 1855 he entered the order of the Franciscans, and was ordained priest in 1862. Having been called to Rome in 1870, he published there *Bonaventuræ Doctrina de Pontificis Primatu et Infallibilitate:—Ratio Novæ Collectionis Operum S. Bonaventuræ* (1874). After having ransacked almost all the European libraries with a view to editing a new and critical edition of Bonaventura's works, for which he seemed to have been specially adapted, he died Aug. 12, 1881, at the College of St. Bonaventura in Quaracchi, near Florence. His notes, comprising several folio volumes, are in the hands of P. Ignatius, one of the first assistants of Fidelis, who will probably bring about the publication of the works of the *doctor Seraphicus*. (B. P.)

Fano, Menachem Asaria di, a Jewish rabbi, who died at Mantua in 1620, is famous alike for his Talmudic and Cabalistic lore. Most of his writings are on the Cabala, for which see Fürst, *Bibl. Jud.* i, 274 sq.; De' Rossi, *Dizionario Storico* (Germ. transl.), p. 103 sq.; Wolf, *Bibl. Hebræa*, i, No. 772; iii, No. 1447. (B. P.)

Fanon. (1) A head-dress worn by the pope when he celebrates mass pontifically. It is described as a veil variegated, like the Mosaic ephod, with four colors, symbolizing the four elements, put over the head after the pope was vested with the alb, and tied round the neck, forming a kind of hood, the tiara or other head-dress being put on above

Fanon.

it. The lower part was concealed by the *planeta.* The annexed figure is from a small brass statue on the doors of the oratory of St. John Baptist at the Lateran. At the "Foot-washing" the "Roman Ceremonial" directs that the pope should wear the *fanon* alone without the mitre. (2) The napkin or handkerchief, used by the priest during the celebration of the mass to wipe away perspiration from the face, etc., properly called *facitergium.* (3) In later times the white linen cloth in which the laity made their oblations at the altar. The word is sometimes erroneously spelled "favones." (4) A still later use of the word is for the church banners employed in processions. This is perhaps not earlier than the French and German writers of the 11th century. (5) The strings or lappets of the mitre.

Fansaga, COSIMO, an eminent Italian sculptor and architect, was born at Clusone, near Bergamo, in 1591, and visited Rome and studied sculpture and architecture under Pietro Bernini. The façade of the Church of Santo Spirito de' Neopolitani is the only work by him in that city. He, however, built and adorned a number of altars in Naples. Among his principal works are the façades of the churches of San Francesco Saverio, Santa Teresa degli Scalzi, and San Domenico Maggiore. He died in 1678. See Hoefer, *Nouv. Biog. Générale*, s.v.; Spooner, *Biog. Hist. of the Fine Arts*, s.v.

Fanti Version OF THE SCRIPTURES. Fanti is a language spoken in the neighborhood of Cape Coast Castle, in West Africa. The Fanti people are supposed to number about two millions, of whom about five thousand are able to read. At present the four gospels only are circulated, the translation having been made but recently (it is first mentioned in the annual report of the British and Foreign Bible Society for 1884), by a Mr. Parker, a very able native minister of the Wesleyan Church, whose father was a fetish worshipper. The version, chiefly made from the Authorized English Version, compared with the Otji translation, was submitted to a number of ministers for revision, and finally passed at the annual district meeting by a vote of the whole of the ministers. (B. P.)

Fara (or **Burgundofara**), *Saint*, daughter of Chagneric, a high official of the court of Theodebert, king of Austrasia, early became a nun at Meaux in 614, and afterwards abbess of a convent near that place. She died in 655, and is celebrated Dec. 7.

Fardh, a term by which the Mohammedans describe what is clearly declared in the Koran; and they consider any one an infidel who rejects it.

Farinato, PAOLO, *degli Uberti*, an eminent Italian painter, was born at Verona in 1522, and studied some time under Nicolo Golfino. Among his principal works which are at Verona are three pictures in Santa Maria in Organo, representing *St. Michael Discomfiting Lucifer*, the *Mothers Presenting their Children to Constantine*, and the *Murder of the Innocents.* In San Tommaso is a picture of *St. Onuphrius.* One of Farinato's finest paintings is the *Descent from the Cross*, in the Church of the Cappucini. He painted a number of other pictures for different churches. He died in 1606. See Spooner, *Biog. Hist. of the Fine Arts*, s.v.; Hoefer, *Nouv. Biog. Générale*, s.v.

Farlatti, DANIELE, an Italian Jesuit, was born at San Daniele in Friuli in 1690. He studied at Bologna, was for some time at Rome, and in 1722 was called to Padua to assist Riceputi in preparing his history of the Illyrian Church. For twenty years he arranged the material, and after Riceputi's death, in 1742, he commenced the publication of the work, of which he edited four volumes, while four more volumes were published after his death, April 23, 1773, by Coleti. The title of the work is *Illyricum Sacrum* (Venice, 1751–1819, 8 vols.). The fifth volume contains a biography of Farlatti. See Jöcher, *Allgemeines Gelehrten-Lexikon*, s.v. (B. P.)

Farmer, RICHARD, D.D., a learned English divine, was born at Leicester in 1735, and educated at Emmanuel College, Cambridge, of which he became master in 1775. He subsequently became vice-chancellor and principal librarian of the university, and obtained prebends at Lichfield and Canterbury. He exchanged the latter for a canonry at St. Paul's. Both an English and Irish bishopric were offered him and declined. He died in 1797. In 1766 he issued proposals for publishing a history of the town of Leicester, from the MSS. of Thomas Staveley. He found the work too laborious, and gave his materials to John Nichols, who published it under the title, *History and Antiquities of Leicester* (1795–1811). See Chalmers, *Biog. Dict.* s.v.; Allibone, *Dict. of Brit. and Amer. Authors*, s.v.

Farnham, NICHOLAS OF. See FERNHAM.

Farnsworth, BENJAMIN F., D.D., a Baptist minister and distinguished educator, was born about 1790. He graduated from Dartmouth College in 1813; for a short time was editor of the *Christian Watchman;* and in 1826 was chosen first principal and professor of theology in the New Hampton Literary and Theological Institution. In 1836 he was called to the presidency of Georgetown College, Ky., but shortly after went to Louisville, where he established the Prather Grove Seminary. Subsequently he was elected president of Union University, Murfreesborough, Tenn., and then of the Memphis University. He died near Lexington, Ky., May 4, 1851. See *Amer. Baptist Register*, 1852, p. 416. (J. C. S.)

Faro (or **Burgundofaro**), *Saint*, was born in Burgundy about 592, being the son of Agneric, one of the principal officers of Theodebert, king of Austrasia, and was educated at the court of that prince. In 613 he went over to Clotaire II, by whom he was highly esteemed. He then renounced the world, with the consent of his wife Blidechilde, received the clerical tonsure in Meaux, and was elected bishop of that city in 627. He administered his diocese with great zeal, died in 672, and was buried in the abbey of Sainte-Croix, near Meaux. He is commemorated Oct. 28. See Hoefer, *Nouv. Biog. Générale*, s.v.; Smith, *Dict. of Christ. Biog.* s.v.

Faroese Version OF THE SCRIPTURES. See SCANDINAVIAN VERSIONS.

Farolfus, MICHAEL ANGELO, a native of Crete, who died March 6, 1715, joined the Minorites and studied at Padua. He was chaplain to pope Alexander VIII, and was elevated to the episcopal see at Trau, in Dalmatia, by Clement XI. He wrote, *Conciones in Sacellis Pontificis Habitæ:—Synopsis Controversiarum Græcorum cum Latinis:—Pro Canonisatione B. Jacobi de Marchia* (3 vols.). The latter work made him lose the favor of the Roman see and the cardinalate, which was designed for him. See Jöcher, *Allgemeines Gelehrten-Lexikon*, s.v. (B. P.)

Farquharson, JAMES, F.R.S., LL.D., a Scotch clergyman, son of the excise officer at Coull, was born in 1781; graduated at the University and King's College, Aberdeen, in 1798; was appointed schoolmaster of the parish the same year; presented by the prince regent to the living at Alford in August, and ordained Sept. 17, 1813. He died Dec. 3, 1843. His attainments in meteorological science were of a very high order, and he was a frequent contributor to various learned periodicals, and corresponded with most of the learned men in Europe. He published, *A New Illustration of the Latter Part of Daniel's Last Vision and Prophecy* (Lond. 1838):—*The Native Forests of Aberdeenshire:—Noah's Ark:—The Aurora Borealis:—The Currency:—An Essay on Cutting Grain with the Scythe*, in the *Transactions of the Highland Society:*—besides many papers in the *Philosophical Transactions:*—also *An Account of the Parish.* See *Fasti Eccles. Scoticanæ*, iii, 547.

Farr, ALFRED A., a Methodist Episcopal minister, was born in Middlebury, Vt., Aug. 29, 1810. He joined the Church in 1826, and in 1839 entered the Troy Conference, wherein he labored earnestly and faithfully as a pastor, chaplain, and missionary until 1869, when he became superannuated. He died Nov. 4, 1874, honored as a sort of "veteran reserve" in all useful labor. See *Minutes of the Annual Conferences*, 1875, p. 65.

Farrar, ABRAHAM ECCLES, an English Wesleyan minister, was of a family somewhat distinguished in clerical lists. His father (John) was a Methodist minister, who died in 1837; his younger brother was president of the British Conference in 1870, and is the author of *Dictionary of the Bible* and other valuable works; his elder son, Wesley, entered the Wesleyan ministry in 1846, and his youngest son is canon of Durham and author of the *Critical History of Free Thought*. Abraham E. was born at Sowerby, a village overhanging the vale of Todmorden, April 20, 1788. From 1797 to 1801 he was at the Kingswood School. Soon after his return home he gave his heart to God. He was articled to an attorney at Sunderland, but in 1807 was received into the ministry. His first field was Holderness, where this talented and refined young man was subjected to all the humiliating trials that mobs and persecuting rectors made the order of the day with the early Methodist preachers (Stevens, *Hist. of Methodism*, iii, 211 sq.; Smith, *Hist. of Wesl. Meth.* ii, 451 sq.). He served the Church faithfully, and was intrusted by it with important offices. While the fire of youth was still burning upon the altar, and the gravity of age and the maturity of intellect gave evidence of long years of usefulness, he was suddenly called away. On April 1, 1849, in great pain, he preached an anniversary sermon in the East London Circuit, and died one week thereafter. Farrar was amiable, courteous, diligent, and sympathetic. He had a mind of critical, reflective, and analytical power. He wrote, *The Condemner of Methodism Condemned* (1814):—*Religious Instruction of Children Enforced* (1820):—*The Juvenile Bible-class Book* (1825):—*The Benefits of Messiah's Advent*, a sermon (1842):—*Sketches of Popular Antiquities for the Young* (1850). See *Minutes of the British Conference*, 1849; Stevenson, *City Road Chapel*, p. 322; *Wesl. Meth. Mag.* 1849, p. 543, 986; 1853, p. 305; *Wesleyan Takings*, i, 346.

Faselt, CHRISTIAN, a Lutheran theologian of Germany, who died April 26, 1694, while pastor and superintendent at Liebenwerda, in Saxony, is the author of *Diss. de Imperio Hominis in Hominem:—De Origine Falsi:—De Unctura Christi Sepulcrali:—De Vita Solitaria:—De Primo Avium in Gen. i*, 20. See Jöcher, *Allgemeines Gelehrten-Lexikon*, s. v. (B. P.)

Fassel, HIRSCH B., a Jewish rabbi, was born at Boskowitz, in Moravia, in 1801. He was for some time preacher at Prossnitz, in Moravia; and from 1851 until his death, in December, 1883, at Gross-Kaniza, in Hungary. He wrote, *Das mosaisch-rabbinische Civilrecht* (Gross-Kaniza, 1852-54, 2 vols.):—*Das mosaisch-rabbinische Gerichtsverfahren* (ibid. 1858):—*Die mosaisch-rabbinische Tugend- und Rechtslehre* (ibid. eod.):—*Das mosaisch-rabbinische Strafrecht und strafrechtliche Gerichtsverfahren* (ibid. 1870). He also published a *Catechism of Judaism*, *Sermons*, and some minor treatises. See Fürst, *Bibl. Jud.* i, 277; Lippe, *Bibliographisches Lexikon* (Vienna, 1881), p. 98 sq. (B. P.)

Fassi, Guido. See CONTE.

Fast OF THE HOLY APOSTLES, a fast observed by the Greek Church in imitation of the apostles, who, they suppose, prepared themselves by fasting and prayer for going forth to proclaim the gospel message. This fast commences the week after Whitsuntide, and continues till the festival of St. Peter and St. Paul.

Fast Synods, a name given to Christian synods in ancient times, which met on fast weeks.

Fasti, the sacred books of the ancient Romans, in which were recorded the *fasti dies*, or lawful days—days on which legal business might be transacted before the prætor without impiety. These *fasti* contained a full enumeration of the months and days of the year, the various dates belonging to a calendar, and the several festivals arranged under their appropriate dates. Before the adoption of the practice of preparing such tables, it was customary for the priests to proclaim the different festivals, for the information of the people.

Faté (or **Efatese**) **Version** OF THE SCRIPTURES. This language is spoken on the island of Faté, or Sandwich island, the centre of the New Hebrides. In 1865 the gospel of Mark was translated by the Rev. D. Morrison of Errakor, and printed at Sydney in 1866. From the annual report of the British and Foreign Bible Society for 1866 we subjoin the following:

"The history of the gospel in Faté has been peculiar and interesting. For about a quarter of a century our brethren of the London Missionary Society have had native teachers from Samoa and Raratonga laboring on this island. Several of those devoted men were barbarously murdered by the natives; several more of them fell victims to the sickly climate, and some of them left the island to recruit their enfeebled health elsewhere. At times as many as six or eight stations were occupied by teachers, but, owing to the above causes, for the last ten or twelve years only one, or, at times, two stations could be kept open; the others relapsed to heathenism. But in one of these stations, *Errakor*, the chief and the whole people embraced Christianity; and although at one time for two years they had no teacher living among them, they held fast to their profession, while the rest of the island was heathen. Errakor was like an oasis in the desert. Six years ago we settled two Aneityum teachers on Faté. One of them died about three years ago; the other died in August last. This year we reopened one of the old stations, and settled three teachers from Mare. Eighteen months ago, when we settled Mr. Morrison at Errakor, he found a population of one hundred and sixty, all Christian. Of these sixty were Church members. There is another station at Pango, about three miles distant, occupied by teachers, where the chief and a part of the people are Christians. Mr. Morrison has had no accessions as yet from the heathen; but there is evidently a softening process going on around, and from the growing intelligence and increased vigor of Christian character observable at Errakor, there can be little doubt that from this centre the Word of God will soon sound forth to the regions beyond, till all Faté shall receive the gospel of salvation."

In 1870 the gospel of John was printed at Auckland, New Zealand, the translation having been made by the Rev. James Cosh. This gospel was followed by the translation of that of Luke and the book of Genesis. In 1880 the Acts of the Apostles were also printed, the translation having been made by the Rev. J. W. Mackenzie. (B. P.)

Fates. See PARCÆ.

Fathers OF THE CHRISTIAN DOCTRINE, an order of monks collected in France by Cæsar de Bus in the 16th century, who employed themselves in instructing the ignorant, and especially the young. It was approved by Clement VIII in 1597. Another order, bearing a similar name and having a like object, was formed in Italy about the same time by Marcus Cusanus, a knight of Milan, and was approved by Pius V and Gregory XIII. See DOCTRINAIRES.

FATHERS OF THE ORATORY. See ORATORY, PRIESTS OF THE.

FATHERS OF SOMASCHO, a name given to the clerks (regular) of St. Majuli, from the town Somascho, where their first general resided. See SOMASCHIANS.

Fatihat (*preface* or *introduction*) is the title of the first chapter of the Koran, which consists only of the following short prayer: "Praise be to God, the Lord of all creatures, the most merciful, the king of the day of judgment. Thee do we worship, and of thee do we beg assistance. Direct us in the right way, in the way of those to whom thou hast been gracious; not of those against whom thou art incensed, nor of those who go astray."

Fatima, the daughter of Mohammed, was born at Mecca in 606, five years before her father assumed the office of a religious reformer. At the age of fifteen she was married to Ali, the cousin of Mohammed, of whom she was the only wife. She died in 632. The Arabian dynasty of the Fatimites, which from 909 to 1171 ruled over Egypt and the northern part of Africa, and latterly over Syria and Palestine, claimed to be descended from Fatima. The religious tenets of their adherents differed considerably from those of the orthodox Mohammedans, and in time they sought to give to the Koran an allegorical interpretation, so as to avoid obedience to its literal precepts. The Shiites, including the Mohammedans of Persia, hold both Ali and Fatima, as well as the twelve Imams, in the utmost veneration, while they regard Abubeker, Omar, and Othman as usurpers of the caliphate. They venerate Fatima as a saint, and the Shiites afford us the only instance which occurs in Islamism of giving religious honor to a woman. She was one of the four women whom the prophet regarded as perfect.

Faudoas, PIERRE PAUL, *Baron de*, a French prelate, was born at Lalanne, April 1, 1750, of a noble family in reduced circumstances. Having entered into orders, he became titulary of the abbey of Gaillac in 1788. During the revolution he was obliged to emigrate, and, returning to France, found himself compromised in some conspiracies of the royalists, but was advanced to the bishopric of Meaux in January, 1805. Thereafter he attached himself strongly to the emperor. Louis XVIII, on his restoration, left him in a sort of disgrace until his death in 1819. See Hoefer, *Nouv. Biog. Générale*, s. v.

Fauns, a species of demi-gods, inhabiting the forests, called also *Sylvani, satyrs.* They were sons of Faunus and Fauna, or Fatua, king and queen of the Latins, and, though accounted semi-divine, were supposed to die after a long life. They were Roman deities, unknown to the Greeks, and were represented with

Faun.

horns on their heads, pointed ears, and crowned with branches of the pine, while their lower extremities resembled those of the goat. Later, when Greek mythology was introduced, they were often confounded with Pan. They were of a musical and voluptuous character. Female fauns are also spoken of.

Faust, Isaac, a Lutheran theologian of Germany, was born at Strasburg, June 10, 1631, and died there, a doctor and professor of theology, Nov. 20, 1702. He wrote dissertations in Latin on various passages of Scripture. See Jöcher, *Allgemeines Gelehrten-Lexikon*, s. v. (B. P.)

Faust, Johann, brother of Isaac, was born at Strasburg, Sept. 22, 1632, and died there July 1, 1695, a doctor and professor of theology. He wrote monographs in Latin on several Scriptural subjects. See Jöcher, *Allgemeines Gelehrten-Lexikon*, s. v. (B. P.)

Fausta, a virgin martyr under Galerius, A.D. 305, was the daughter of rich parents, and noted for her Christian activity. She is commemorated Sept. 20 or Jan. 2.

Faustiānus. See FAUSTINUS.

Faustīnus, the name of numerous early bishops and several martyrs, of the latter of whom we here notice: (1) A soldier under Commodus, put to death cir. A.D. 182, for refusing to offer sacrifice; commemorated Aug. 7. (2) Put to death under Diocletian, at the seventh milestone from Rome; commemorated July 29. The catacomb of Generosa, where he was buried, has lately been discovered. (3) A presbyter, put to death with his brother Jovita, at Brixia, in Italy, under Hadrian, commemorated Feb. 15.

Fausto, BARTOLOMEO A SANTO, a Cistercian of Sicily, who died at Naples in 1636, is the author of, *De Pœnitentia:—De Horis Canonicis:—De Sacris Indulgentiis:—Speculum Confessariorum:—Thesaurus Confessariorum*, which were republished in three volumes, under the title of *Theologia Moralis.* See Jöcher, *Allgemeines Gelehrten-Lexikon*, s. v. (B. P.)

Faustus, the name of numerous early bishops and martyrs, among whom we notice here: (1) A presbyter and archimandrite of Constantinople, active in the Eutychian controversy, A.D. 448–451. (2) An Italian, confided in childhood by his parents to St. Benedict of Monte Casino, sent A.D. 543 to assist in founding the monastery of Glanfeuil, in Anjou, where he remained forty-six years. He is commemorated Feb. 15.

Favaronibus, AUGUSTIN DE (also called *Augustinus Romanus*), archbishop of Nazareth and Barletta, who died in 1443, was a native of Rome. He wrote annotations on the Revelation and St. Paul's epistles, also some treatises, as *De Peccato Originali:—De Potestate Papæ:—De Perfecta Justitia Militantis Ecclesiæ:—De Potestate Principum in Collatione Bonorum Suorum Ecclesiis Facta.* His *De Sacramento Unitatis Jesu Christi et Ecclesiæ, De Christo Capite et Ejus Inclyto Principatu*, and *De Charitate Christi Circa Electos et Ejus Infinito Amore*, were rejected by the Council at Basle in 1435. See Jöcher, *Allgemeines Gelehrten-Lexikon*, s. v. (B. P.)

Faye, Antoine de la. See LAFAYE.

Faye, Jean de, a French prelate, was born in the second part of the 12th century, of a noble family of Touraine. He was dean at the cathedral church of Tours, when, in 1208, he was called to the metropolitan see of that city by the majority of the suffragan bishops, but with much opposition. He introduced the Minims into the city of Tours. He had great disputes with Maurice, bishop of Mans, whom he suspended from his pastoral functions; and excommunicated Pierre Mauclerc for persecuting Étienne, bishop of Nantes. De Faye died April 23 or 26, 1228. See Hoefer, *Nouv. Biog. Générale*, s. v.

Fayet, JEAN JACQUES, a French prelate, was born at Mende, July 26, 1787; studied law at Paris; entered the Minorite order at St. Sulpice, and there directed the catechismal exercises. In 1811 he was ordained; became principal of the college of Mende in 1814; was made chevalier of the Legion of Honor; went on a mission through the country; joined the editorial staff of *Le Conservateur;* went to Rouen as grand-vicar; in 1832 became assistant to the archbishop there; bishop of Orleans in 1842; and died April 4, 1849. See Hoefer, *Nouv. Biog. Générale*, s. v.

Fayumi Saadiah. See SAADIAH.

Febronia, a virgin martyr at Nisibus, in Mesopotamia, under Diocletian, A.D. 304; commemorated June 25.

Fébure (or **Fèvre**), **Michel** (also called *Justinien de Tours*), a French Capuchin missionary and Orientalist, was born about 1640. For eighteen years he travelled in Syria, Mesopotamia, Chaldæa, Assyria, Kurdistan, Arabia, Palestine, etc. There are no details of his life, but he left some very curious and valued works, especially *Overo Descrittione della Turchia* (Rome, 1674); translated later into French, German, and Spanish):—*Objectiones Muhameticæ adversus Catholicos* (ibid. 1679):—*Christian Doctrine*, in Arabic:—*Théâtre de la Turquie* (Paris, 1682). See Hoefer, *Nouv. Biog. Générale*, s. v.

Fébure, Nicolas le, a French Dominican, was born in 1588. He studied at Paris, was in 1631 prior of his convent at Chartres, and died at Rochelle in 1653, leaving *Expositio Doctrinæ Orthodoxæ*:—*Manuale Ecclesiasticum Historicum*. See Echard, *De Scriptoribus Ordinis Dominicanorum*; Jöcher, *Allgemeines Gelehrten-Lexikon*, s. v. (B. P.)

Fébure, Turriane le, a Jesuit, was born at Douay, France, in 1608, and died there, June 28, 1672. He published, *Opuscula Varia*:—*Elogia Sanctorum*. See Jöcher, *Allgemeines Gelehrten-Lexikon*, s. v. (B. P.)

Fécamp (Lat. *Fiscanus* or *Fiscanum*), a place in Normandy, known for its famous abbey, which was dedicated to the Holy Trinity. It was founded in 658 by the count of Caux, but was destroyed in 841 by the Normans. Duke Richard I of Normandy had it rebuilt, and it was dedicated in 1006 as a Benedictine abbey to the Holy Trinity. The abbey lasted till the 18th century. See Busserolle, *Recherches-historiques sur Fécamp* (Paris, 1859); Fallue, *Histoire de la Ville et de l'Abbaye de Fécamp* (Rouen, 1841); Berger, in Lichtenberger's *Encyclop. des Sciences Religieuses*, s. v. (B. P.)

Feckenham, JOHN DE, was the last abbot of Westminster, and at the age of eighteen went to Gloucester Hall, Oxford, where he was educated. His right name was *Howman*. He was the last mitred abbot who sat in the House of Peers. He published a few controversial pieces. See *Biog. Brit.*; Dodd, *Christ. Hist.*; Strype, *Cranmer*; *Athen. Oxon.* He was continually employed in doing good to the persecuted Protestants of his day, but was afterwards, to the disgrace of the crown, imprisoned himself, and died a captive in Wisbeach Castle, in the Isle of Ely, in 1585. See Chalmers, *Biog. Dict.* s. v.; Allibone, *Dict. of Brit. and Amer. Authors*, s. v.

Feddersen, JAKOB FRIEDRICH, a Lutheran theologian of Germany, was born July 31, 1736, at Schleswig. He studied at Jena; was in 1760 preacher to the duke of Holstein-Augustenburg; and in 1769 third preacher of St. John's, at Magdeburg. In 1777 he was called to Brunswick, and in 1788 accepted a call to Altona, where he died at the end of the same year. He published a number of sermons, which are enumerated in Döring, *Deutsche Kanzelredner*, p. 55 sq. See also Koch, *Geschichte des deutschen Kirchenliedes*, vi, 296 sq.; Winer, *Handbuch der theol. Lit.* ii, 252, 257, 321, 325, 328, 364, 383, 385. (B. P.)

Fehmel, AMANDUS GOTTHOLD, a Lutheran theologian of Germany, was born July 30, 1688. He studied at Leipsic, and died, July 22, 1721, doctor and professor of theology at Hildburghausen, leaving *De Catacumbis Romanis*:—*De Errorum Criteriis circa Religionem Communibus*:—*De Criteriis veræ Religioni Communibus*:—*De Consiliis Irenicis, Unionem Ecclesiæ, Evangelicæ cum Romana Concernentibus*:—*De Constitutione Unigenitus*. See Jöcher, *Allgemeines Gelehrten-Lexikon*, s. v. (B. P.)

Fehre, SAMUEL BENJAMIN, a Lutheran theologian of Germany, who died Oct. 28, 1772, is the author of *Die zwei Thiere in der Offenbarung Johannis* (Chemnitz, 1754):—*Der Weissagung in der Offenbarung Johannis* (Frankfort, 1757):—*Ueber Hane's Kirchengeschichte des neuen Testaments* (Leipsic, 1768):—*Ueber Hane's Entwurf*, etc. (ibid. 1770). See Meusel, *Gelehrtes Deutschland*; Jöcher, *Allgemeines Gelehrten-Lexikon*, s. v.; Zuchold, *Bibl. Theol.* i, 350. (B. P.)

Fehse, JOHANN HEINRICH, a Lutheran theologian of Germany, who was born at Hamburg, June 10, 1725, and died in 1777, is the author of *Explicatio Dicti Paulini ad Gal. i*, 8 (Rostock, 1744):—*Die Lehre von der Salbung Christi* (ibid. 1755). See Meusel, *Gelehrtes Deutschland*, s. v.; Jöcher, *Allgemeines Gelehrten-Lexikon*, s. v. (B. P.)

Fei, ALESSANDRO (called *del Barbiere*), a reputable Florentine historical painter, was born in 1538 (or 1543), and studied successively under Ridolfo Ghirlandajo, Pietro Francia, and Tommaso Manzuoli. His works may be seen in the churches of Florence, Pistoja, and Messina. One of his most esteemed pictures is in the Church of Santa Croce at Florence, representing the *Scourging of Christ*. See Hoefer, *Nouv. Biog. Générale*, s. v.; Spooner, *Biog. Hist. of the Fine Arts*, s. v.

Feigerle, IGNATIUS, a Roman Catholic theologian and prelate of Germany, was a Moravian by birth. In 1818 he received holy orders; was in 1823 professor of theology at the lyceum in Olmütz; in 1827 first rector of the newly founded university there; in 1830 professor at the Vienna University; in 1831 court chaplain; and in 1840 court preacher there. In 1852 he was consecrated as bishop of St. Pölten, and died Sept. 27, 1863. He wrote, *Historia Vitæ SS. Thomæ a Villanova, Thomæ Aquinatis et Laur. Justiniani* (Vienna, 1839):—*Predigt-Entwürfe* (ibid. 1835, 3 vols.; 3d ed. 1844):—*Predigten über die heilige Messe* (ibid. 1844).—*Der geistige Kampf in Predigten* (ibid. 1861, translated also into Italian). (B. P.)

Feilire OF ÆNGUS THE CULDEE. The word *feilire*, derived from "feil," the Irish equivalent of "vigils," is applied to the metrical festology composed by Ængus the Culdee about the year 780. It is the most ancient of five martyrologies belonging to Ireland. It consists of three parts: (1) Five quatrains invoking a blessing on the poet and his work; (2) a preface of two hundred and twenty quatrains; and (3) the festology itself, in three hundred and sixty-five quatrains, for every day in the year.

Feilmoser, ANDREAS BENEDICT, a Roman Catholic theologian of Germany, was born at Hopfgarten, in the Tyrol, in 1777. He took holy orders in 1800, and was for some time professor of theology at Innspruck. In 1821 he was called to Tübingen, where he died, July 20, 1831. Besides contributing to the *Tübingen Theologische Quartalschrift*, he wrote *Einleitung in die Bücher des Neuen Bundes* (Innspruck, 1810; Tübingen, 1830). See Winer, *Handbuch der theol. Lit.* i, 13, 75; Lichtenberger, *Encyclop. des Sciences Religieuses*, s. v. (B. P.)

Feki, THE BLIND MEN OF, an order of blind devotees in Japan, instituted in A.D. 1150. There is a legend that their founder, Feki, was captured by Joritomo. The captive, though kindly treated, not being able to look upon his captor without an irresistible desire to kill him, plucked out his eyes and presented them to Joritomo. There is another more ancient but less numerous order of the blind, claiming as its founder a son of one of the emperors of Japan, who cried himself blind at the death of his beautiful princess. This last society is composed of none but ecclesiastics; the other consists of secular persons of all ranks. They are not supported by alms, like many other devotees, but most of them are mechanics, who earn their own living.

Felbinger, JEREMIAS, a Socinian, who was born at Brieg, in Silesia, April 27, 1616, was for some time rector at Cöslin, in Pomerania, and afterwards chorister at the princely school in Stettin. On account of his Socinian tendencies he had to give up his position, and went to Holland, where he died in 1687. He wrote, *Demonstrationes Christianæ* (1653):—*Die Lehre von Gott*, etc. (1654):—*Epistola ad Christianos unum Altissimum Deum, Patrem*, etc. (1672). He also translated into German the *Confessio Fidei Christ. edita Nomine Ecclesiar. quæ in Polonia unum Deum Profitentur* (1653):

—and made a translation of the New Test. from the Greek into German (Amsterdam, 1660). See Winer, *Handbuch der theol. Lit.* i, 169, 333, 419; Jöcher, *Allgemeines Gelehrten-Lexikon*, s. v. (B. P.)

Felde, Albert zum, a Lutheran theologian of Germany, was born Sept. 9, 1675, at Hamburg. In 1704 he was pastor at Tönningen; in 1709 pastor, and doctor and professor of theology at Kiel, where he died, Dec. 27, 1720, leaving *Institutiones Theologiæ Moralis:—Analecta Disquisitionum Sacrarum:—Politica Sacra:—De Enallage Scripturæ Sacræ:—Dialogus cum Tryphone verum esse Justini Martyris Fœtum:—De Cultu imaginum Anti-Christiano:—Decas Observationum Sacrarum ex Patribus Apostolicis.* See Winer, *Handbuch der theol. Lit.* i, 127; Jöcher, *Allgemeines Gelehrten-Lexikon*, s. v.; Moller, *Cimbria Litterata.* (B. P.)

Felder, Franz Carl, a Roman Catholic theologian of Germany, was born Oct. 6, 1766. He studied at Dillingen, where Sailer was among his teachers. In 1789 he took holy orders, and in 1794 became pastor at Waltershofen, where he died, June 1, 1818. He published, *Festpredigten* (Ulm, 1804–5, 2 vols.):—*Kleines Magazin fur Katholische Religionslehrer* (Constance, 1806–8, 3 vols.):—*Neues Magazin für Katholische Religionslehrer* (1809–16, 8 vols.):—*Literaturzeitung für Katholische Religionslehrer* (Landshut, 1810–16, 7 vols.):—*Gelehrten-Lexikon der Katholischen Geistlichkeit Deutschland und der Schweiz* (ibid. 1817; the second and third vols. were edited by Waitzenegger, 1820–22). See Döring, *Die gelehrten Theologen Deutschlands*, i, 397 sq.; Winer, *Handbuch der theol. Lit.* i, 12, 856; ii, 42, 112, 151. (B. P.)

Feldhoff, Friedrich August, a Lutheran theologian of Germany, was born at Elberfeld, Nov. 19, 1800. He studied at Heidelberg and Berlin; was for some time assistant to the Lutheran pastor of his native place, and accepted a call to Nymwegen, in Holland, in 1823. In 1828 he was called to Wupperfeld, and died Jan. 8, 1844. He wrote, *Die Zeitenlinie der heiligen Schrift* (Frankfort, 1831):—*Ueber die Jahre der Geburt und Auferstehung unseres Herrn* (ibid. 1832):—*Die Völkertafel der Genesis* (Elberfeld, 1837):—*Gnomen zur Geschichte des vier Weltalter* (Barmen, 1840):—*Christliche Gedichte* (ibid. eod.):—*Feierklänge* (ibid.). See Koch, *Geschichte des deutschen Kirchenliedes*, vii, 197 sq.; Zuchold, *Bibl. Theol.* i, 352. (B. P.)

Félice, Guillaume Adam de, professor and dean of the Protestant faculty of Montauban, was born at Otterberg in 1803. He studied at Strasburg; was in 1836 pastor at Bolbec; in 1838 was called to the chair of ethics and homiletics at Montauban, and in 1865 was made dean of the faculty. In 1870 he retired from public activity, and died at Lausanne, Oct. 23, 1871. Félice was a very excellent preacher. Besides his contributions to *Les Archives du Christianisme, L'Espérance, New York Observer*, and the *Evangelical Christendom*, he published, *Essai sur l'Esprit et le But de l'Institution Biblique*, a prize essay (Paris, 1823):—*Appel d'un Chrétien aux gens de Lettres* (ibid. 1841; Germ. transl. by Dielitz, Berlin, 1843):—*Histoire des Protestants de France* (4th ed. Toulouse, 1861; translated into four different languages). See Pédezert, *G. de Félice, Professeur et Prédicateur;* Recolin, in Lichtenberger's *Encyclop. des Sciences Religieuses*, s. v.; Zuchold, *Bibl. Theol.* i, 352 sq. (B. P.)

Felician, *Saint*, was arrested at Rome for being a Christian, in company with his brother Primus. The two were brought before the emperor Maximian Hercules, who, on their refusing to sacrifice to idols, condemned them to be publicly scourged. He then sent them to Promotus, the judge of Normentum, a city four or five leagues distant from Rome. Promotus not being able to shake their resolution, beheaded them both, in the year 286 or 287. Moréri says that "the acts of these martyrs do not seem authentical;" however it be, the Church honors their anniversary on June 9. See Hoefer, *Nouv. Biog. Générale*, s. v.

Felician, a noted Donatist bishop of Musti, somewhere in Africa, deeply implicated in the controversy concerning Prætextatus, at the close of the 4th century, and finally deposed. See Smith, *Dict. of Christ. Biog.* s. v.

Feliciano, Porfirio, an Italian prelate and poet, was born in the canton of Vaud in 1562. He was educated in philosophy, mathematics, jurisprudence, belles-lettres, and wrote very fine Latin. Being at first attached to cardinal Salviati, he became secretary to pope Paul V, who appointed him bishop of Foligno, where he died, Oct. 2, 1632. He left *Rime Diverse, Morali, Espirituali* (Foligno, 1630), and several volumes of letters in Latin and Italian. See Hoefer, *Nouv. Biog. Générale*, s. v.

Felicianus, Hispalensis, a Spanish Capuchin, who died between 1730 and 1740, is the author of *Instructio vitæ Spiritualis Brevis et Clara* (Seville, 1696; Madrid, 1700):—*Cantiones Spirituales* (Seville, 1698):—*Officium Parvum SS. Trinitatis* (1700):—*De Fontibus Salvatoris* (1708):—*Lux Apostolica* (1716). See Bern a Bononia, *Bibl. Capucc.;* Jöcher, *Allgemeines Gelehrten-Lexikon*, s. v. (B. P.)

Félicien de Sainte-Magdeleine, a French Carmelite monk, was born in the beginning of the 17th century, at Nantes. He taught theology in his native town and at Bordeaux; afterwards became prior of Agen; and at last definitor of the province of Touraine. He distinguished himself by his great knowledge and regular habits. Being suspected as a Jansenist, he returned to Nantes, where he died in 1685, leaving *Defensio Providentiæ Divinæ* (Bordeaux, 1657, 3 vols.):—*Nova Eloquentiæ Methodus* (Paris, 1666). See Hoefer, *Nouv. Biog. Générale*, s. v.

Felix is the name of a very large number of early Christians, among whom we notice the following: (1) Bishop of Aptunga, apparently in proconsular Africa; prominent in the controversy concerning the ordination of Cæcilianus (q. v.) to the see of Carthage, early in the 4th century. (2) The apostle of the East Angles and first bishop of Dunwich; died cir. A.D. 647, and commemorated as a saint March 8. (3) Donatist bishop of Idisia, in Numidia, in 361; guilty of great excesses. (4) *Saint*, bishop of Nantes, in Brittany, in 550; died Jan. 6, 582; commemorated July 7. (5) First bishop of Nuceria (or Nocera), in Umbria, in 402. (6) Archbishop of Ravenna in 708; carried to Constantinople and blinded, but afterwards restored, and died Nov. 25, 724. (7) Metropolitan bishop of Seville; confirmed by the Council of Toledo near the close of the 7th century. (8) Bishop of Siponto; addressed by Gregory the Great in 591 and 593. (9) Bishop of Treves in 386; resigned about 398. (10) Bishop of Tubzoca, martyred under Diocletian in 303, and commemorated as a saint Oct. 24. (11) Abbot of a little monastery in Byzacena, to which Fulgentius (q. v.) retired early in the 6th century. (12) Surnamed *Octavius*, a reader, of Abutina, in Africa, martyred at Carthage under Anulinus, the proconsul, with Dativus (q. v.), and commemorated as a saint Feb. 12. (13) A native of Scilita, martyred at Carthage under Severus (A.D. 200 or 202), along with Perpetua (q. v.) and others; commemorated July 17.

Felix of Cantalicio, *Saint*, an Italian monk, was born at Cantalicio, Umbria, in 1513. He took the habit of a Capuchin, in 1543, at Ascoli. In 1546 he was sent to Rome as a mendicant friar. During a plague which desolated Rome in 1580, Felix made himself remarkable by his truly Christian zeal; as also during a famine in 1585. In spite of his privations and penances he lived to the age of seventy-four. Urban VIII beatified him Oct. 1, 1625; Innocent X commenced his canonization Feb. 6, 1652, and Clement XI finished it, May 8, 1709. See Hoefer, *Nouv. Biog. Générale*, s. v

Felix OF VALOIS. See VALOIS, FELIX OF.

Fell, SAMUEL, D.D., a learned English divine, was born in the parish of St. Clement Danes, London, in 1594, and was educated at Christ Church, Oxford. In 1626 he was made Margaret professor of divinity, and had a prebend at Worcester. He was then a Calvinist, but, renouncing that system, he was made dean of Lichfield in 1637, and in 1638 dean of Christ Church. He was appointed vice-chancellor in 1645, which office he retained until 1647. He died Feb. 1, 1648-49. He published *Primitiæ; sive Oratio Habita Oxoniæ in Scholia Theologiæ*, Nov. 9, 1626. See Chalmers, *Biog. Dict.* s. v.; Allibone, *Dict. of Brit. and Amer. Authors*, s. v.

Fellon, THOMAS BERNARD, a French Jesuit, was born at Avignon, July 12, 1672, and died March 25, 1759. He published, *Paraphrase des Psaumes:—Traité de l'Amour de Dieu Selon François de Sales* (Nancy, 1754, 3 vols.). See Lichtenberger, *Encyclop. des Sciences Religieuses*, s. v.; Jöcher, *Allgemeines Gelehrten-Lexikon*, s. v. (B. P.)

Fels, a name common to several Protestant theologians:

1. JOHANN HEINRICH, who was born at Lindau in 1733, and died in 1790, is the author of *Diss. de Varia Confessionis Tetrapolitanæ Fortuna* (Göttingen, 1775). See Winer, *Handbuch der theol. Lit.* i, 332.

2. JOHANN MICHAEL, professor of theology and preacher at St. Gall, was born there in 1761, and died Sept. 21, 1833. He is the author of, *Die Kirchliche Trennung der Confessionen* (St. Gall, 1829):—*Denkmal schweizerischer Reformatoren in Vorlesungen* (ibid. 1819). See Winer, *Handbuch der theol. Lit.* i, 359, 748.

3. SEBASTIAN, was born Sept. 20, 1697, at Kempten, in Suabia. He studied at Halle and Jena, and died at Lindau, May 18, 1749, leaving *De Protestantium Justificatione* (1718). See Jöcher, *Allgemeines Gelehrten-Lexikon*, s. v. (B. P.)

Fels, Christian Lebrecht, a Jewish convert of Prague, was born in 1640, and died at Hamburg in 1719. He was professor of Hebrew at various universities and gymnasia, and wrote, מראה דרך היהודים, i. e. *Hodegus Judæorum* (Leipsic, 1703):—*Brevis et Perspicua via ad Linguam Sanctam* (Sondershausen, 1697):—*Brevis et Perspicua via ad Accentuationem* (Wittenberg, 1700). See Fürst, *Bibl. Jud.* i, 278 sq.; Steinschneider, *Bibliographisches Handbuch*, s. v.; Wolf, *Bibl. Hebr.* i, 1009; Jöcher, *Allgemeines Gelehrten-Lexikon*, s. v.; Roi, *Die Evangelische Christenheit und die Juden* (Carlsruhe, 1884), i, 116 sq. (B. P.)

Felton, NICHOLAS, D.D., an English prelate, was born at Yarmouth, in Norfolk, in 1563, and educated at Pembroke Hall, where he became fellow Nov. 27, 1583. He was rector of St. Mary-le-Bow, Jan. 17, 1595, and some time of St. Antholin's, London. He was elected master of Pembroke Hall, June 29, 1616, and admitted rector of Great Easton, in Essex, Oct. 23 following; in the same year collated to a prebend in St. Paul's, and in 1617 promoted to the see of Bristol, to which he was consecrated Dec. 14. In 1618 he was nominated to the bishopric of Coventry and Lichfield, but translated to Ely March 11 of that year. He died Oct. 5, 1626. See Chalmers, *Biog. Dict.* s. v.

Feltus, HENRY J., D.D., a Protestant Episcopal clergyman, was born in 1775. He was a native of Ireland, and came to America when quite a young man. Having been for some time a preacher in another communion, he was admitted into the ministry of the Protestant Episcopal Church about 1798. He officiated for a period at Easton, Pa., when he became rector of Trinity Church, Sweedsborough, N. J., whence he was called, in 1808, to the rectorate of St. Ann's Church, Brooklyn, L. I., and thence, in 1824, to that of St. Stephen's Church, New York city. He died Aug. 24, 1828. Dr. Feltus was distinguished for piety, and fidelity in the discharge of all his ministerial duties. He was humble and affectionate, and much beloved and respected by his congregation. See *The Christian Journal* (N. Y.), 1828, p. 287.

Felwinger, JOHANN PAUL, a German theologian, was born at Nüremberg in 1616. Having been professor at Altdorf, he took part in the religious controversies of the time, and distinguished himself by his zeal against the writings of the Socinians, in opposition to whom he put forth, *Anti-Ostorodus:—Defensio pro A. Grawero contra Smalzium*. He died in 1681. See Hoefer, *Nouv. Biog. Générale*, s. v.

Fen, JOHN, a Roman Catholic divine of the 16th century, was born at Montacute, Somersetshire. He was educated at New College, Oxford, where he continued till ejected by the queen's commissioners for his zeal for Romanism. He was then schoolmaster at Bury St. Edmund's, till removed on the same account. He fled to Flanders, thence to Italy, and at last fixed his residence at Louvain, where he died in 1613. He wrote and translated many books, living to celebrate his fiftieth year of exile beyond the seas. See Fuller, *Worthies of England* (ed. Nuttall), iii, 106; Allibone, *Dict. of Brit. and Amer. Authors*, s. v.

Feneberg, JOHANN MICHAEL, a German Jesuit, was born Feb. 9, 1751, at Oberndorf, in Switzerland. In 1773 he was professor at the gymnasium in Ingolstadt, in 1795 preacher at Seeg, in 1805 at Vöhringen, near Ulm, where he died, Oct. 12, 1812. Feneberg is the author of several hymns, which breathe an evangelical spirit, and are found in Fuchs, *Sammlung Erbaulicher Lieder* (Kempten, 1812). See Sailer, *Aus Fenebergs Leben* (Munich, 1814); Koch, *Geschichte des deutschen Kirchenliedes*, vi, 553 sq. (B. P.)

Fenner, WILLIAM, a minister of the Church of England, was born Jan. 31, 1831, at Southwark. In 1854 he entered the college of the London Jews' Society, and in 1857 was appointed lay missionary among the Jews of the duchy of Posen. In 1860 Mr. Fenner was to reopen the mission in Tunis, and was ordained by bishop Tomlinson of Gibraltar. He died at Tunis, July 22, 1874. (B. P.)

Fenouillet (or **Fenoillet**), PIERRE DE, a French prelate, was born at Annecy (Savoy), studied there, entered into orders, became theological tutor at Gap, and then went to Paris, where he became preacher to Henry IV. In 1607 he was nominated bishop of Montpellier, and in 1609 assisted at the Council of Narbonne; but he became so zealous for Romanism that the Protestants complained of his rigor, and he abandoned his diocese and joined the royal army, July 2, 1621. He was afterwards busy in commissions until his return to his diocese, Sept. 20, 1636. In 1652, being sent to Paris on some religious matters, he died there, Nov. 23, leaving a number of addresses, for which see Hoefer, *Nouv. Biog. Générale*, s. v.

Fenris (or **Fenrir**), in Scandinavian mythology, was a wolf, the frightful son of the evil Loke and the giantess Angerbode. The Asas knew the danger that threatened them from the children of this pair, therefore they brought Fenris up, in order to moderate his wildness, which was so great that only one Asa, the strong and wise Tyr, could bring food to him. The gods attempted to bind him, and laid two huge chains on him, Leding and Droma, but when he stretched himself they flew apart. Then the Asas ordered a band to be made, which appeared to be of silk, but was composed of the beard of a woman, the root of a mountain, the breath of a fish, the saliva of a bird, and the muscles of a bear; this was called Gleipner. It was light, but the wolf did not allow it to be laid on him, and he had become much stronger since tearing the two chains. The Asas began to persuade him, telling him that if he did not expose himself to some danger he would never become renowned; the band was certainly stronger than it appeared to be, but they would loose him in case he were too weak. "If I do not free myself," Fenris answered, "I know what awaits me; therefore let it not touch my feet. There must be some magic in play; but if you are honest, let one of you lay his hand into my throat as an assurance of your sincerity." After much persuasion, Tyr assented to lay his hand into the wolf's throat; the band was adjusted, but when Fenris wanted to stretch himself, he found that the band gradually contracted. Then the Asas laughed, except Tyr, for his hand had been bitten off. Since that time Tyr is one-handed. They might have killed the monster, but the sanctity of the place forbade it. They therefore took one end of the band, called Gelgia, drew it through a rock, Gjol, and with the aid of another rock, Twite, they hammered the first still deeper into the earth, and as Fenris wanted to devour all who came near him, they put a sword into his throat, so that the handle lay in the upper, the blade in the lower jaw, and Fenris was made harmless. His body has grown so that by opening his mouth he touches heaven and earth. Eventually he will free himself, unite with his sister, the Midgardsnake, and with the sons of Surtur, in war against the Asas, devour the sun, and even the god Odin; but finally the god Allvadur will tear his throat so far apart that he will die. Odin will come from his grave, and the world will be renewed. Fenris had two sons, Skoll and Hate, by the giantess Grige. Skoll persecutes the sun, Hate devours the moon. See NORSE MYTHOLOGY.

Fenton, ROGER, D.D., an Anglican clergyman of the 16th century, was born in Lancashire, became fellow of Pembroke Hall, Cambridge, and was the laborious, pious, beloved, and learned minister of St. Stephen's, Walbrook, London. He was a friend of Dr. Nicholas Felton, collegiates and city ministers together. Fenton died in London in 1615, in his fiftieth year, leaving a treatise against usury. See Fuller, *Worthies of England* (ed. Nuttall).

Fenwick, Benedict Joseph, a Roman Catholic bishop, was born at Leonardstown, Md., Sept. 3, 1782. He was made bishop of Boston, Mass., Nov. 1, 1825, a diocese which then had only three priests. He enlarged his cathedral, established schools, started a theological seminary, introduced the Sisters of Charity through Ann Alexis in 1832, saw the first synod of Boston assembled in 1842, the erection of a new see of Hartford in 1844, founded the College of the Holy Cross at Worcester, through the Jesuits, the great Catholic university of New England, and died in Boston after an energetic episcopate, Aug. 11, 1846, prudent, learned, and charitable. See De Courcey and Shea, *Hist. of the Cath. Church in the U. S.* p. 509.

Fenwick, Edward, a Roman Catholic bishop, was a native of Maryland, long a Dominican missionary in Kentucky, and was consecrated the first bishop of Cincinnati, Jan. 13, 1822, a see which then included Ohio, Michigan, and Wisconsin. He built churches throughout his vast diocese, dedicated the Cathedral of Cincinnati in 1826, called in the aid of the Sisters of St. Dominic, Sisters of Charity, and the Poor Clares, founded in his city the Athenæum, now St. Xavier's College, and in 1831 established the *Catholic Telegraph*, the oldest of American Catholic papers. Edward Fenwick died of cholera at Wooster, O., Sept. 26, 1832. See De Courcey and Shea, *Hist. of the Cath. Church in the U. S.* p. 547.

Fenwick, Michael, an eccentric preacher, connected with the early Methodist movement in England, commenced to preach in 1750, and travelled some time with Wesley, until the latter, on account of Fenwick's peculiarities, dismissed him. He almost idolized Wesley, and imitated him so accurately in speaking, praying, preaching, and writing, that it was difficult to discriminate between them. Though imprudent, his courage and zeal for Methodism never changed. He was not given a circuit, nor was he acknowledged as a preacher for several years before his death. Yet he always attended the place of the annual conference, and continued there during its session, though he was not permitted to be present in conference after 1784. The conference allowed him a pittance annually, and he had many generous friends in different parts of the kingdom, in the house of one of whom he lived (in Bridlington) for some years before his death, in 1797. See Atmore, *Meth. Memorial*, s. v.

Feologild, archbishop of Canterbury, was consecrated June 9, 832, to that see, but died Aug. 29 following. He had formerly been abbot of one of the Kentish monasteries. See Hook, *Lives of Abps. of Canterbury*, i, 283 sq.; Smith, *Dict. of Christ. Biog.* s. v.

Feralia, a festival of the ancient Romans, observed annually in honor of the manes of deceased friends and relations. It was instituted by Numa, and lasted eleven days. The family and acquaintances of the deceased went to the graves and walked round them, offering up prayers to the gods of the infernal regions in behalf of their dead friends. An entertainment was then prepared and placed on a great stone, and of this the dead were supposed to partake. During the entire days of the feast no marriages were allowed to be celebrated, and the worship of the other deities was suspended, all their temples being shut.

Ferat, in Mohammedanism, is separation from God, the greatest and severest punishment for the damned.

Ferber, JOHANN JACOB, a Protestant theologian of Germany, was born at Strasburg in 1673. He studied at different universities, and died at his native place, Feb. 12, 1717, shortly after he was called there as professor of theology. He wrote, *De Certitudine Theologiæ Naturalis* (Wittenberg, 1708):—*De iis quæ in Philosophia Morali Eximia Sunt* (ibid. 1709):—*De Theologia Experimentali* (ibid. 1711):—*De Principio Cartesii de Omnibus est Dubitandum* (ibid. 1716). See Jöcher, *Allgemeines Gelehrten-Lexikon*, s. v. (B. P.)

Ferdinand. See FERNANDO.

Ferdinand, PHILIP, a Jewish convert, was a native of Poland. He was professor of Hebrew at Oxford and Cambridge, instructed the famous Scaliger in the Talmud, and died in 1598. He wrote, קול יי״, *Haec sunt Verba Dei*, in which he treats of the Jewish precepts, laws, feasts, etc. (Canterbury, 1587). See Fürst, *Bibl. Theol.* i, 279; Wolf, *Bibl. Hebr.* i, No. 1832; iii, No. 1832; Jöcher, *Allgemeines Gelehrten-Lexikon*, s. v.; Roi, *Die Evangelische Christenheit und die Juden* (Karlsruhe, 1884), p. 186 sq. (B. P.)

Fergus, *Saint*, a primitive Scotch bishop and confessor, commemorated Nov. 15 to 18, was probably of Irish birth, and passed through Scotland from the west southward, planting churches and converting the natives to Christianity. See Smith, *Dict. of Christ. Biog.* s. v.

Ferguson, Colin, D.D., a Protestant Episcopal minister, was born in Kent County, Md., Dec. 8, 1751. A Scotch schoolmaster became interested in him as a pupil and took him to Edinburgh, paying the expenses of his education at the university. In 1782 he was an instructor in the Kent County School at Chestertown, Md. When Washington College, the oldest in the state, was organized in 1783, he was chosen professor of languages, mathematics, and natural philosophy, and held the position till 1793, when he was appointed president. After studying theology, he was admitted to deacon's orders, Aug. 3, 1785, to priest's, Aug. 7 of the same year, and became rector in St. Paul's Parish, Kent County, Md., where he served until 1799. In 1804 he retired to his farm, near Georgetown Cross Roads, where he spent the rest of his life. He died March 10, 1806. Of the General Convention of 1789, which framed the constitution of the Church, he was an active member. He was more distinguished as a scholar than as a preacher. See Sprague, *Annals of the Amer. Pulpit*, v, 342.

Ferguson, James, LL.D., a Scotch clergyman.

born in Dolphinton, studied at the United College, and graduated at the University of St. Andrews in 1763; was licensed to preach in October, 1768; presented to the living at Dolphinton in September, 1772, and ordained April 7, 1773; transferred to Pettinain, Feb. 22, 1780, and died May 18, 1803, aged fifty-six years, much esteemed for his literary abilities. He published *An Account of the Parish of Pettinain.* See *Fasti Eccles. Scoticanæ*, i, 221; ii, 332.

Ferguson, Robert, D.D., LL.D., an English Congregational minister, was born in Glasgow, May 12, 1806; educated at Hoxton College, and entered upon his ministry at Haddington about 1830. He afterwards preached at Leicester, Finchingfield, Stepney, Stratford, ten years at Ryde, beginning with 1849, and then, returning to London, undertook the charge of Portland Chapel, St. John's Wood, but resigned six years later in order to devote his energies more directly to the establishment of the Pastors' Retiring Fund, of which he was one of the original founders. He died March 27, 1875. As a preacher Mr. Ferguson was in a marked degree argumentative and rhetorical, though not to the exclusion of the practical. As a writer he was elegant, persuasive, and forcible. Among other interesting productions of his pen are, *Sacred Studies:—Consecrated Heights:—The Penalties of Greatness:—Sacrifice:—Family Prayers.* He was for some time editor of the *Eclectic Review*, and the *Free Church of England Magazine.* He was elected a fellow of the Antiquarian Society in 1854, and in the same year became a member of the Royal Irish Academy. He took great interest in the advancement of workingmen, and wrote for their benefit popular histories of England and Scotland. See (Lond.) *Cong. Year-book*, 1876, p. 331.

Fergusson, James, D.D., a Scotch clergyman, born in Blair-Athol, was licensed to preach March 29, 1809; ordained by the Presbytery of Dalkeith, Dec. 7, 1813, as assistant at Inveresk; presented to the living at Beath by the earl of Moray in March, 1815, admitted May 4 of the same year, and died March 19, 1866, aged eighty-four years. He published *An Account of the Parish.* See *Fasti Eccles. Scoticanæ*, ii, 578.

Fergussone, David, a Scotch clergyman, born in Dundee, was nominated by the lords of the privy council to be the first Protestant minister at Dunfermline, in 1560. He was a member of thirty-nine assemblies, from June, 1563, to May, 1597, and moderator in those of 1572 and 1578. In 1567 Rossyth was under his care, and in 1574 Carnock and Baith were added. In 1576 he was appointed visitor of the churches in the diocese from Forth to Tay and from the Ochils to Dunkeld. He died Aug. 23, 1598, at an advanced age. Though not educated at a university, yet from his good taste, lively fancy, piety, and integrity, he was highly useful in improving and enriching the Scottish language, and he was a favorite with all classes. He took a lively share in ecclesiastical affairs, wrote a diary of historical notes, and had a valuable library of books of theology and natural history. He wrote, *An Answer to the Epistle written by Renat Benedict* (Edinb. 1563); a *Sermon* preached at Leith in 1572, and *Scottish Proverbs Gathered Together* (ibid. 1641). Some of his tracts were printed by the Bannatyne Club in 1860. See *Fasti Eccles. Scoticanæ*, ii, 565.

Feriæ (*holidays*), a name given by the ancient Romans to all peculiar seasons of rejoicing, including sacred festivals or days consecrated to any particular god. The *feriæ* were of several classes. Some of the public festivals were regularly observed, and the date of their occurrence was marked in the *Fasti* (q. v.). Such were termed *Feriæ Stativæ* or stated holidays. Other public festivals were held annually, but not on any fixed day, and received the name of *Feriæ Conceptivæ.* The most solemn class of holidays were those appointed by the public authorities to be observed in consequence of some great national emergency or impending public calamity, and received the name of *Feriæ Imperativæ.* No lawsuits were allowed to be conducted during the public *feriæ*, and the people were strictly enjoined to abstain from work under penalty of a fine. The introduction of Christianity into Rome, and especially its adoption as the religion of the state, led to the abolition of the *feriæ* and the substitution of Christian festivals.

FERIÆ Latīnæ, a festival instituted by Tarquinius Superbus, or perhaps at an earlier period, in honor of the alliance between the Romans and the Latins. It was held on Mt. Alba, and was originally dedicated to the worship of *Jupiter Latiaris.* The festival continued for several days, usually five or six. An ox was generally offered in sacrifice by the consul then in office, amid the assembled multitudes, who engaged in rejoicings of all kinds. The two days immediately following the festival were considered sacred, and on them no marriages were celebrated. This festival was observed until the 4th century.

FERIÆ Sementīvæ, a festival of the ancient Romans, observed during a single day in seed-time, for the purpose of praying for the blessing of the gods upon the seed sown.

Ferings, Richard de, an Irish prelate, was promoted and consecrated to the see of Dublin in 1299. Immediately after his consecration he made that conveyance of Church lands alluded to by Carte in the introduction to his *Life of Ormond.* This caused some disturbance, but archbishop Ferings finally succeeded in bringing about an agreement in 1300. In 1303 he constituted the churches of Stagonil and Tipperkevin prebends of St. Patrick's Cathedral. In 1304 he renewed the privileges granted by his predecessors to the dean and chapter of St. Patrick's, and particularly the exemption of their prebendal churches from visitations by the archdeacon or dean. He did not succeed in his administration, and died Oct. 18, 1306, while on his way from Rome. See D'Alton, *Memoirs of the Abps. of Dublin*, p. 114.

Fernald, Mark, a veteran minister of the Christian denomination, was born March 9, 1784, in Kittery, Me. He learned the trade of a carpenter, and at different times in his youth went to sea; but was converted in 1807, and united with a Free-will Baptist Church. The following year he began to preach, at once engaged in itinerant labor, and was ordained Sept. 20, 1809. For several years he was a travelling preacher, chiefly in New England. He became regular pastor at York in April, 1818, but gradually became identified with the body called "Christians." He died at Kittery, Dec. 29, 1851, where he had been pastor for thirty-six years. See his *Life*, written by himself. (J. C. S.)

Fernald, Woodbury Melcher, a Universalist minister, was born at Portsmouth, N. H., March 21, 1813. He began his ministry in Nashua in 1835, received ordination the following year, and in 1838 moved to Cabotville (now Chicopee), Mass. In 1840 and 1841 he was located in Newburyport; then three years in Stoneham; in 1845 removed to Boston; embraced Swedenborgianism, and was ordained a preacher of that faith. He published, the same year, a work entitled *The Eternity of Heaven and Hell Confirmed by Scripture, and Grounded in the Realities of the Human Soul:—Compendium of the Theological and Spiritual Writings of Swedenborg* (1854):—*God in His Providence* (1859):—*Memoirs and Reminiscences of the late Professor Bush* (1860):—*First Causes of Character* (1865):—a posthumous volume of *Sermons*, found marked for publication at his decease, was issued under the title, *The True Christian Life, and How to Attain It* (1874). He died in Boston, Dec. 10, 1873. Mr. Fernald was a voluminous and vigorous writer; a sincere, pure, and spiritually-minded man; and possessed of a metaphysical turn of mind. See *Universalist Register*, 1875, p. 124.

Fernandez, Alfonso, a Spanish Dominican, was born in 1573 at Placentia, and died after 1627. He is the author of *Historia Ecclesiastica de Nuestros Tiempos:—Concertatio Prædicatoria pro Ecclesia Catholica contra Hæreticos, Gentiles, Judæos et Agarenos.* See Echard, *De Scriptoribus Ordinis Dominicanorum;* Antonii *Bibliotheca Hispanica;* Jocher, *Allgemeines Gelehrten-Lexikon*, s. v. (B. P.)

Fernandez, Antonio, a Spanish Jesuit, was born at Coimbra, where he also died, May 14, 1628. He was for some time missionary in the East Indies, and after his return was preacher at Lisbon. He wrote, *Commentar. in Visiônes Veteris Testamenti cum Paraphrasibus Capitum.* See Antonii *Bibliotheca Hispanica;* Jöcher, *Allgemeines Gelehrten-Lexikon*, s. v. (B. P.)

Fernando DE TALAVERA, a Spanish prelate and theologian, was born at Talavera-la-Reyna (Old Castile) in 1445. He was a Hieronymite monk, became bishop of Avila, confessor and counsellor of Ferdinand V, the Catholic, and of his wife Isabella. He encouraged them particularly in their enterprise against the Moors, which finally led to the surrender of Grenada. He obtained the archiepiscopacy of that city, and labored very zealously in the propagation of the Catholic religion. The biographers pretend that he died in sanctity, May 14, 1507, and that several miracles took place at his tomb. He wrote, *Provechosa Doctrina de lo que Debe Saber Todo Fiel Christiano:—Avisacion de las Maneras de Pecados:—El Restituir y Satisfacer:—De Como Demos de Comulgar:—Ceremonial Detodos los Oficios Divinos*, in Latin and Spanish:—and divers other works. See Hoefer, *Nouv. Biog. Générale*, s. v.

Fernham, NICHOLAS OF (or *Nicolas de Ferneham*), was born at Farnham, Surrey, and was educated as a physician at Oxford. He became a student in Paris, and there gained great esteem, being accounted *famosus Anglicanus* (Matthew Paris, 1229). Here he continued until the university was in effect dissolved through the discords between the clergy and people. He lived for some years in Bologna, and on his return home became physician to Henry III, who at last made him bishop of Chester. Fernham became bishop of Durham in 1241, which see he also resigned in 1249. He wrote many books "of the practice in physic and use of herbs," and died at Stockton in private life in February, 1258. See Fuller, *Worthies of England* (ed. Nuttall), iii, 206.

Ferquhard, a Scotch prelate, was made bishop of the Isles, and presented to the temporality of this see, and to the commendamry of Icolumkill, May 24, 1530. He resigned the bishopric into the hands of the pope, in favor of Roderic Maclean, in 1544. See Keith, *Scottish Bishops*, p. 306.

Ferranti, Decio and **Agostino**, two miniature painters, very celebrated in their day, flourished at Milan in 1500. In the cathedral at Vigevano are three of their works, consisting of a *Missal*, a *Book of the Four Evangelists*, and a *Book of the Epistles*, illuminated with miniature pictures and ornaments in the most exquisite taste. See Spooner, *Biog. Hist. of the Fine Arts*, s. v.; Hoefer, *Nouv. Biog. Générale*, s. v.

Ferrara (*d'Este*), IPPOLITO. See ESTE.

Ferrari, Bartolommeo (by some erroneously called *Ferrera*), a noted Italian monk, was born at Milan in 1497, of one of the first families there. He was left an orphan in youth, but distinguished himself by his piety and charity. In connection with Antonio-Maria Zaccario de Cremona and Giacomo-Antonio Morigia, a nobleman of Milan, he instituted the congregation of the Regular Clerks of St. Paul, sanctioned in 1530 under Clement VII, and confirmed three years afterwards by Paul III. Ferrari was elected superior in 1542, but governed his order two years only. The Barnabites (by which name his order was commonly known) spread over Germany, Bohemia, Savoy, France, etc., teaching in the principal universities. Soon afterwards women likewise united themselves into communities, and were called *Angelice*, observing the rules of the Barnabites, under the direction of the same fathers; but the discipline of this religious order did not keep its original purity very long. Ferrari died in November, 1544. See Hoefer, *Nouv. Biog. Générale*, s. v.

Ferrari, Gaudenzio (also called *Gaudenzio Milanese*), an eminent Italian painter, was born at Valdugia, in the territory of Novara, in 1484, and was probably a scholar of Pietro Perugino. Among his principal works was the cupola of Santa Maria, in Saronno. His picture of *St. Christopher*, in the church of that saint, at Vercelli, is greatly admired. In the same church are several other pictures of his, representing scenes in the life of Christ, including *Mary Magdalene* and the *Passion.* There are many other paintings of his elsewhere. He died in 1550. See Hoefer, *Nouv. Biog. Générale*, s. v.; Spooner, *Biog. Hist. of the Fine Arts*, s. v.

Ferréol is the name of several French saints. (1) A presbyter and martyr of Besançon, suffered with Ferrutio in the time of Irenæus; commemorated June 16. (2) Martyr at Vienne, under Maximian, cir. A.D. 304, and commemorated Sept. 18, was a military tribune who befriended the Christians. (3) Fifth bishop of Uzes, said to have been born of a noble family in Narbonne, was educated by Roricus, bishop of Uzes, whom he succeeded in 553. He labored for the conversion of the Jews, and was once temporarily banished by king Childebert under false suspicion. He died in 581, and is commemorated Jan. 4. (4) Fourteenth bishop of Limoges, is said to have died in 595, and is commemorated Sept. 18. (5) Thirteenth bishop of Grenoble, is said to have been martyred A.D. 683, and is commemorated Jan. 12 (or 16).

Ferrie, WILLIAM, D.D., a Scotch clergyman, was promoted from the professorship of civil history, St. Andrews; presented by the earl of Balcarras to the living at Kilconquhar in April, 1813, which he held in conjunction, as agreed to by the assembly, and was ordained Feb. 3, 1814. He died June 7, 1850, aged sixty-seven years. He was an energetic and laborious minister, whom Dr. Chalmers characterized as "the best minister in Fife, and the worst professor." He published, *A Catechism on the Evidences of Revealed Religion, with Questions on Natural Religion* (Edinburgh), a *Sermon* preached at Kilconquhar in 1842, and *An Account of the Parish.* See *Fasti Eccles. Scoticanæ*, ii, 438.

Ferrin, CLARK ELAM, D.D., a Congregational minister, was born at Holland, Vt., July 20, 1818. In 1845 he graduated from the University of Vermont, and, after teaching two years in Georgia, graduated in 1850 from Andover Theological Seminary. He was ordained Dec. 9 following, at Barton, Vt., and remained with that Church until Dec. 13, 1854. From Feb. 9, 1856, until Sept. 7, 1877, he was pastor in Hinesburg, and in Plainfield from February, 1878, till his death, June 27, 1881. During twenty-four years he was a member of the corporation of the Vermont University. In 1858 and 1859 he represented Hinesburg in the State Legislature. He was the author of several pamphlets. See *Cong. Yearbook*, 1882, p. 30.

Ferris, ISAAC, D.D., LL.D., an eminent Reformed (Dutch) minister, was born in New York city, Oct. 3, 1799. He graduated from Columbia College in 1816, and from the New Brunswick Theological Seminary in 1820; was licensed by the Classis of New Brunswick in the same year, and became pastor there in 1821; at Albany in 1824; Market Street, New York city, in 1836; and was then chosen chancellor of New York University, and professor of moral philosophy and evidences of revealed religion in 1852. After laboring seventeen and a half years, he was made emeritus, with the college debt paid and four professorships endowed. In 1870 he retired from active labors, and remained thus till his death, June 16, 1873. As a preacher, Dr. Ferris was clear, discriminating earnest, and practical; and as an administrator he has seldom been equalled. He was very successful as a pastor, possessing personal magnetism which gained for him friends, and made him a centre of influence. He had a noble, well-balanced, fully-disciplined, and broad mind. His nature was kind, and his benevolence large, yet he could be stern and positive when necessary. He was deeply pious, and this trait shone forth on all occasions. Many of his sermons and addresses have been published, and some of them delivered before various religious societies are of permanent historical interest. See Corwin, *Manual of the Ref. Church in America*, 3d ed. p. 258.

Ferus, GEORG, a Bohemian Jesuit, was born in 1585, and died Jan. 21, 1655. He translated from the Latin into the Bohemian language the *Lives of Ignatius Loyola and Francis Xavier:—The Glory of Ignatius*, by Nicol. Lancitius:—*The Spiritual Praxis*, by Nicol. Spondratus, etc. See Alegambe, *Bibliotheca Scriptorum Societatis Jesu;* Jöcher, *Allgemeines Gelehrten-Lexikon*, s. v. (B. P.)

Fervers, in Zendic mythology, constitute the third rank of celestial deities, being the souls of every object that had life, to which, therefore, prayers were offered; a species of celestial *manes*.

Fesole, CONGREGATION OF, an order of monks, founded about 1386 by Charles of Montegranelli, who lived among the mountains of Fesole. They were also called Mendicant Friars of St. Jerome. The order was approved by Innocent VII, and confirmed by Gregory XII and Eugenius IV. See Gardner, *Faiths of the World*, s. v.

Fessel, DANIEL, a Lutheran theologian of Germany, was born in Saxony in 1599; studied at Wittenberg, was in 1625 court preacher to the widow of the elector of Brandenburg, in 1630 superintendent and member of consistory at Cüstrin, and died Oct. 17, 1676, leaving, *Adversaria Sacra:—Theatrum Theologico-Politico Historicum:—Promptuarium Biblicum:—Theosophiæ Mysticæ Nucleus:—Regnum Christi et Diaboli Mysticum:—Christus Mysticus*. See Winer, *Handbuch der theol. Lit.* i, 189; Jöcher, *Allgemeines Gelehrten-Lexikon*, s. v. (B. P.)

Fessler, JOSEPH, a Roman Catholic theologian and bishop, was born Dec. 2, 1813, at Lochau, in Vorarlberg, Austria, and studied at Brixen and Innspruck. In 1837 he received holy orders, and was promoted in 1839 as doctor of theology at Vienna. In 1841 he was made professor of Church history and of canon law at Brixen, and in 1852 was called to Vienna. In 1862 he was appointed bishop of Nyssa *in partibus*, and in 1865 succeeded Feigerle as bishop of St. Pölten. At the Vatican council he was first secretary. He died April 25, 1872, leaving, *Ueber die Provincial-Synoden und Diöcesan-Synoden* (Innspruck, 1849):—*Institutiones Patrologiæ* (1850–52, 2 vols.):—*Das Kirchliche Bücherverbot* (Vienna, 1858):—*Die Protestantenfrage in Oesterreich* (ibid. 1861):—*Vermischte Schriften* (Freiburg, 1869):—*Die wahre und falsche Unfehlbarkeit der Päpste* (Vienna, 1871). See Erdinger, *Joseph Fessler* (Brixen, 1874); Zuchold, *Bibl. Theol.* i, 354; *Literarischer Handweiser für das Kathol. Deutschland*, 1872, p. 212. (B. P.)

Fest, JOHANN SAMUEL, a Lutheran theologian of Germany, was born in Thuringia, Feb. 28, 1754. He studied at Leipsic, was in 1784 preacher at Trachenau, near that city, and died there, Nov. 16, 1796, leaving, *Ueber die Vortheile der Leiden und Widerwärtigkeiten des Lebens* (Leipsic, 1784; 2d ed. 1787; translated also into Dutch). His other publications are of no importance. See Döring, *Die gelehrten Theologen Deutschlands*, i, 399 sq.; Winer, *Handbuch der theol. Lit.* i, 426, 861; ii, 160, 196, 383, 385, 386. (B. P.)

Fête Dieu (*Feast of God*, the French name for *Corpus Christi*), a solemn festival observed in the Romish Church on the Thursday after the octave of Whitsuntide, for the performing of a peculiar kind of worship to our Saviour in the eucharist. The festival is said to have originated with pope Urban IV in 1264; but in consequence of the political commotions of the time, the bull appointing it was not universally obeyed. It was confirmed, however, by the Council of Vienne, in 1311, and further solemnized by pope John XXII, in 1316.

Feti, DOMENICO, an able Italian painter, was born at Rome in 1589; was a scholar of Lodovico Cardi, and afterwards studied the works of Giulio Romano at Mantua. There is a picture by him, representing the *Miraculous Feeding of the Multitude*, which is highly commended. Some of his other principal works are: *Christ Praying in the Garden; Christ Presented to the People by Pilate; Christ Crowned with Thorns;* and *The Entombment*. Feti died at Venice in 1624. See Hoefer, *Nouv. Biog. Générale*, s. v.; Spooner, *Biog. Hist. of the Fine Arts*, s. v.

Fetiāles, a college of ancient Roman priests, supposed to have been instituted by Numa, whose duty it was to see that, in all transactions with other nations, the public faith should be maintained inviolate. In case of any injury from a neighboring nation, four *fetiales* were despatched to claim redress. One of these was chosen to represent the four. This deputy then proceeded to the court of the injuring tribe or nation, delivered his message, and waited thirty days for an answer. On his return the government would proceed in accordance with the message he brought, and in case of a declaration of war it became the duty of the *fetial* deputy to return at once to the border of the offending country, and, throwing a spear pointed with iron or smeared with blood, to make a solemn declaration of war in the name of the Roman people upon the inhabitants of that land.

Fetish (from the Portuguese *fetisso*, "magician," and *fetisseira*, "witch"), is a general name for the deities of the negroes of Guinea; each differing, according to the direction of his masoucki or priest. The natives of Africa ascribe all their good-fortune to these gods, and make libations of palm wine in their honor. Some birds, the sword-fish, and certain stones are considered fetishes. These deities are worshipped at the foot of certain trees, are adored as household gods, and carried about by the devotees.

Fetva, in Mohammedanism, is a declaration that a public act is in conformity with the Koran. The right of granting this sanction belongs to the Sheik ul-Islâm, who usually consults the college of Ulemas before making a decision. No act of the Turkish government will be readily obeyed without the fetva, because not necessarily binding on the faithful. It has sometimes been used to dethrone sultans, and deliver them over to the fury of the Janizaries. The privilege was resisted by Mourad IV, who boldly beheaded the Sheik ul-Islâm for opposing his will.

Feuardent, FRANÇOIS, a French controversialist, a member of the order of the Discalceati (q. v.), and doctor of the Paris University, was born at Coutances, Dec. 1, 1539. In 1576 he was made doctor of theology, and died, guardian of the monastery at Bayeux, Jan. 1, 1610. He was a severe opponent of the Protestants, and a sort of Ishmael against his own co-religionists, when they differed from him. He wrote, *Theomachia Calvinistica:—Divins Opuscules et Exercices Spirituels de S. Ephrem, mis en Français:—Censura Ecclesiæ Orientalis de Præcipuis Nostri Sæculi Hæreticorum Dogmatibus Hieremiæ Constantinop. Patriarchæ:—De Sacrorum Bibliorum Autoritate, Veritate, Utilitate, Obscuritate et Interpretandi Ratione:—Biblia Sacra cum Glossa Ordinaria:—Reponses aux Doutes d'un Hérétique Converti:—Antidota Adversus Impias Criminationes, quibus Antiquissimos et Sapientissimos Ecclesiæ Africanæ Doctores Tertullianum et Cyprianum Vexant Lacerantque Lutherani et Calvini:—Homiliæ 25 in Librum Jobum*. See Bayle, *Dictionnaire Historique Critique;* Winer, *Handbuch der theol. Lit.* i, 341; Jöcher, *Allgemeines Gelehrten-Lexikon*, s. v.; Hoefer, *Nouv. Biog. Générale*, s. v. (B. P.)

Feuerbach, LUDWIG ANDREAS, a German philosopher, was born at Landshut, Bavaria, July 28, 1804. He studied theology and philosophy at Heidelberg and Berlin. In 1828 he began to lecture on philosophy at Erlangen, and opened his lectures with a dissertation, *De Ratione una, Universali, Infinita*. In 1830 he published, anonymously, *Gedanken über Tod und Unsterblichkeit*, in which he denied the belief in immortality. As this book closed to him all and every academic advancement, he retired to Bruckberg, where he spent most of his life. In 1833 he published *Geschichte der neueren Philosophie von Bacon von Verulam bis Spinoza;* in 1837, *Darstellung, Entwickelung und Kritik der Leibnitzschen Philosophie;* in 1838, *Pierre Bayle nach seinen für die Geschichte der Philosophie und Menschheit interessantesten Momenten*. In 1839 he joined the so-called left wing of the Hegelian school, became a very bitter opponent of his former master, and published *Kritik der hegelschen Philosophie*, in the *Berliner Jahrbücher*. Feuerbach now attempted an independent development in the direction of naturalism, or, rather, materialism. In his principal work, *Das Wesen des Christenthums* (Leipsic, 1841; Eng. transl. by George Eliot, Lond. 1853; new ed. 1881; Russian transl. by Philadelph Theomachoff, Lond. 1861), he defines God as a mere projection into empty space of the human *ego*, as an image of man, and religion as a simple psychological process, as an illusion. In 1848 he once more lectured publicly at Heidelberg; but, when the revolutionary movement completely failed, he again retired to private life. Feuerbach died Sept. 13, 1872. His writings comprise ten volumes (Leipsic, 1845-66; 3d ed. 1876). See Grün, *Ludwig Feuerbach in seinem Briefwechsel und Nachlasse* (Leipsic, 1874, 2 vols.); Beyer, *Leben und Geist Ludwig Feuerbachs* (ibid. 1873); Schaller, *Darstellung und Kritik der Philosophie L. Feuerbachs* (1847); Schaden, *Ueber den Gegensatz des theistischen und pantheistischen Handpunkts* (1848); Frantz, *Ueber den Atheismus* (1844); Haym, *Feuerbach und die Philosophie* (1847); Bartholmay, *Histoire Critique des Doctrines Religieuses de la Philosophie Moderne* (1855), ii, 377; Matter, in Lichtenberger's *Encyklop. des Sciences Religieuses*, s. v.; Zuchold, *Bibl. Theol.* i, 355. (B. P.)

Feuerborn, JUSTUS, a Lutheran theologian of Germany, born in Westphalia, Nov. 13, 1587, was for some time court preacher at Darmstadt, afterwards professor at Marburg, and died at Giessen, doctor and professor of theology, Feb. 6, 1656. He wrote, *Kenosigraphia Christologica:—Succincta Epitome Errorum Calvinianorum:—Expositio Epistolæ Pauli ad Galatas:—Theologia Jobœa:—Syntagma Disquisitionum Sacrarum*. See Winer, *Handbuch der theol. Lit.* i, 353; Freher, *Theatrum Eruditorum;* Jöcher, *Allgemeines Gelehrten-Lexikon*, s. v. (B. P.)

Feuerlein, a name common to several Lutheran theologians, viz.:

1. CONRAD, was born Nov. 29, 1629, in Franconia, studied at different universities, and died at Nuremberg, May 29, 1704. His publications are mostly sermons.

2. CONRAD FRIEDRICH, son of Friedrich, was born at Nuremberg, July 15, 1694, and died there Aug. 22, 1742.

3. FRIEDRICH, brother of Johann Conrad, was born at Nuremberg, Jan. 10, 1664, and died there Dec. 14, 1716.

4. JACOB WILHELM, son of Johann Conrad, was born at Nuremberg, March 23, 1689. He studied at various universities; was in 1715 professor at Altdorf, in 1736 at Göttingen, and died there May 10, 1776. He wrote, *De Dubitatione Cartesiana Perniciosa* (Jena, 1711):—*An Existentia Dei sit Veritas Indemonstrabilis* (Altdorf, 1717):—*Philosophemata Potiora Recognitionum Clementi Romano Falso Attributarum* (ibid. 1728):—*De Scriba Evangelico, ad Math.* xiii, 52 (ibid. 1730):—*De Libero Arbitrio* (ibid. eod.):—*De Historia August. Confessionis* (ibid. 1731):—*De Axiomate, ex Nihilo Nihil Fit* (ibid. 1732):—*De Voce* ברא (ibid. 1733):—*De Christo, Novo Legislatore* (ibid. 1739):—*De Jejunio Antepaschali* (ibid. 1741):—*Bibliotheca Symbolica Evangelica Lutherana* (Göttingen, 1752). This is only a partial list of his many writings, the titles of which occupy five and a half columns in Jöcher. See Göttens, *Gelehrtes Europa*, 2, 3; *Beiträge zur Historie der Gelahrtheit unserer Zeiten*, v; Moser and Neubauer, *Jetztlebende Theologen;* Wills, *Nürnberger Gelehrten-Lexikon;* Pütter, *Gel. Geschichte von Göttingen*, p. 115; Winer, *Handbuch der theol. Lit.* i, 317, 339, 456, 598, 602, 842, 861, 889.

5. JOHANN CONRAD, son of Conrad, was born Jan. 5, 1650, and died superintendent at Nördlingen, March 3, 1718. His publications are mostly sermons.

6. JOHANN JACOB, son of Conrad, was born at Nuremberg, May 9, 1670, and died there May 30, 1716. See Jöcher, *Allgemeines Gelehrten-Lexikon*, s. v.; and *Supplement* to Jöcher, s. v. (B. P.)

Feustking, JOHANN HEINRICH, a Lutheran theologian of Germany, was born at Stella, in Holstein, March 7, 1672. He studied at Rostock and Wittenberg; was in 1697 superintendent at Jessen; in 1703 provost at Kemberg; in 1706 court preacher at Zerbst; in 1709 professor of theology at Wittenberg; in 1712 first court preacher and member of consistory at Gotha, where he died, March 23, 1713. He wrote, *Pastorale Evangelicum:—Historia Colloquii Jeurensis* (Zerbst, 1707). See Moller, *Cimbria Litterata;* Winer, *Handbuch der theol. Lit.* i, 763; Jöcher, *Allgemeines Gelehrten-Lexikon*, s. v. (B. P.)

Feutrier, JEAN FRANÇOIS HYACINTHE, *count*, a French prelate, was born at Paris, April 2, 1785. After studying at St. Sulpice, he entered into orders, and was soon appointed, by cardinal Fesch, general secretary of the great almonry of France. He was active in politico-religious affairs under Napoleon. On the restoration of royalty he was appointed rector of La Madeleine, where he did many good works. In 1826 he was made bishop of Beauvais, and in 1829 a count and peer of France. He died at Paris, June 27, 1830. See Hoefer, *Nouv. Biog. Générale*, s. v.; Lichtenberger, *Encyclop. des Sciences Religieuses*, s. v.

Feyerabend, MAURUS, a Roman Catholic theologian of Germany, was born Oct. 7, 1754. In 1777 he took holy orders; was for some time teacher in the monastery at Ottobeueren, in Suabia; when it was closed in 1802, lived in literary retirement, and died March 8, 1818. He translated into German the *Epistles of Gregory the Great* (Kempten, 1807):—his *Homilies* (ibid. 1810):—and the *Writings of Cyprian* (Munich, 1817). See Döring, *Die gelehrten Theologen Deutschland*, i, 404 sq.; Winer, *Handbuch der theol. Lit.* i, 906, 907. (B. P.)

Fiac, an Irish saint, commemorated Oct. 12, was bishop of Sleibhte (now Sletty), and is said to have been consecrated by St. Patrick. There are two hymns attributed to him; one (probably genuine) entitled *The Praise of St. Patrick:*—another (probably spurious), *The Hymn on St. Brigida*. See Smith, *Dict. of Christ. Biog.* s. v.

Fiancels, a ceremony of betrothal as practiced in the Romish Church, after which an oath was administered to the man, by which he bound himself "to take the woman to wife within forty days, if holy Church will permit."

Fibus, BARTHOLOMÄUS, a Roman Catholic theologian, was born at Aix-la-Chapelle, Aug. 24, 1643. In 1662 he joined the Jesuits; was for some time professor of theology at Cologne, and died there, Feb. 13, 1706. He wrote, *Apologia pro Conscientiis Infirmis* (Cologne, 1682):—*De Radice Damnatorum Propositionum ab Alexandro VII et Innocentio II* (ibid. 1682):—*Via Veritatis et Vitæ contra Atheos, Paganos, Judæos*, etc. (ibid.

1696):—*Demonstratio Tripartita Dei adversus Atheos, Gentiles*, etc. (ibid. 1702). See Harzheim, *Bibl. Colon.;* Jöcher, *Allgemeines Gelehrten-Lexikon*, s. v. (B. P.)

Fichte, Immanuel Hermann von, a German philosopher, the son of Johann Gottlieb Fichte, was born at Jena, July 18, 1797. Although he had given himself to the study of philosophy, he was at first teacher in the gymnasium at Saarbrück, afterwards at Düsseldorf, and in 1835 at Bonn as professor of philosophy. In 1842 he was called to Tübingen, and died there, Aug. 9, 1879, having been ennobled by the king of Würtemberg in consideration of his great merits. His career as teacher and writer may be divided into two epochs. The first begins with his *Beiträgen zur Characteristik der neueren Philosophie* (1829), and especially with his *Ueber Gegensatz, Wendspunkt und Ziel heutiger Philosophie* (1832). During this period we find him in close connection with the Leipsic professor Weisse, with whom he labored for the destruction of the Hegelian system, out of which he tried to bring forth a speculative theism free from all rationalism. With his *Speculative Theologie* (1846), and *System der Ethik* (1850–53, 2 vols.), he closes this phase of development to give himself entirely to psychological speculation. To this second period belong his *Anthropologie* (1856; 3d ed. 1876), *Psychologie* (1864–73, 2 parts), and a number of monographs. His *Vermischte Schriften zur Philosophie, Theologie und Ethik* (1869) contain a part of his essays contributed to the *Zeitschrift für Philosophie und philosophische Kritik*, which he edited alone from 1837 to 1847. The ground character of his philosophy was a positive religious one, directed against all and every kind of materialism. See *Neue Evangelische Kirchenzeitung*, 1879, p. 585 sq.; Matter, in Lichtenberger's *Encyclop. des Sciences Religieuses*, s. v.; Zuchold, *Bibl. Theol.* i, 356. (B. P.)

Ficoroni, Francesco di, a famous Italian antiquary, who was born at Lugano in 1664, and died at Rome, Jan. 25, 1747, is the author of, *Osservazioni Sopra l'Antichita di Roma Descritte nel Diario Italico di Montfaucon* (Rome, 1709);—*Memorie piu Singolari di Roma e sue Vicinanze* (ibid. 1730):—*Le Vestigie e Rarita di Roma Antica, e le Singolarita di Roma Moderna* (ibid. 1744, 2 vols.). See Jöcher, *Allgemeines Gelehrten-Lexikon*, s. v.; Hoefer, *Nouv. Biog. Générale*, s. v. (B. P.)

Fidanque, Jacob *ben-Abraham*, a Portuguese rabbi of Hamburg, who died at London, Aug. 4, 1709, is the editor of Solomon ben-Melech's מכלל יופי (Amsterdam, 1685), and of Abarbanel's commentary on the former prophets (Hamburg, 1687). See Fürst, *Bibl. Jud.* i, 280; Jöcher, *Allgemeines Gelehrten-Lexikon*, s. v. (B. P.)

Fide, Jerome a Sancta. See Jerome a Sancta Fide.

Fiedler, Caspar, a Lutheran theologian, was born at Rochlitz, in Bohemia, Oct. 20, 1649, and died there, May 15, 1719. He was an ascetic writer. See Heynen, *Beschreibung von Rochlitz;* Jöcher, *Allgemeines Gelehrten-Lexikon*, s. v. (B. P.)

Fiedler, Constantin, a Lutheran theologian, was born at Dantzic, March 6, 1579, and died at Rostock, Oct. 21, 1644. See Jöcher, *Allgemeines Gelehrten-Lexikon*, s. v. (B. P.)

Fiedler, Ferdinand Ambrosius, a Lutheran theologian of Germany, was born Oct. 18, 1737, at Vienna. He joined the Augustinians, and after having received holy orders, was for some time professor of apologetics and canon law. In 1767 he left the monastery, went to Leipsic and Hamburg, and in the latter place joined the Evangelical Church. In 1772 he was appointed court-preacher at Ludwigslust, and in 1773 received the degree of doctor of divinity. In 1774 he was made superintendent at Doberan, and died at Altona, June 26, 1780. He wrote, *Der Proselyt* (Leipsic, 1768–71, 3 vols.):—*De Ecclesia Repræsentante* (Bützow, 1773):—*Geschichte aller Ceremonien der römisch-Katholischen Kirche* (Leipsic, 1777–85, 2 vols.). See Döring, *Die gelehrten Theologen Deutschlands*, i, 406 sq.; Winer, *Handbuch der theol. Lit.* i, 626; Jöcher, *Allgemeines Gelehrten-Lexikon*, s. v. (B. P.)

Field, Benjamin, an English Wesleyan minister of marked ability, was born at Sevenoaks, Kent, in 1823. He was converted when twelve years of age, under the ministry of Thomas Collins, became a local preacher at the age of sixteen, was accepted as a candidate for the ministry in 1843, spent three years at the Richmond Theological Institution, and July 2, 1846, was ordained; a few days after, with Glanville and Morris, sailed as a missionary to India. For this work he had every qualification except that of physical adaptability to the climate, and he was soon stricken with fever. Returning to England, he travelled the Chatteris (1850), Luton, Bradford, Hackney, City Road, London, and Penzance (1864) circuits until he was compelled to desist through disease. In December, 1865, he embarked for Melbourne, Australia, where he spent the rest of his brief life. He edited the *Wesleyan Chronicle* for a year (1868). Mr. Field died in the city of Melbourne, Sept. 1, 1869. His piety and earnestness were successful in winning souls, and his love for God, superior abilities, and accumulated sorrows, won for him the love of all. Field wrote, *Life of Mrs. C. E. Martin* [his sister] (1862, 24mo):—*The Penitent's Inquiry*, an admirable tractate, which has had a large circulation in England and Australia:—*The Student's Hand-book of Christian Theology*, an excellent treatise (Melbourne, 1868; enlarged ed., with a biographical sketch by Rev. John C. Symons, Lond. 1870, 12mo). Among the shorter presentations of a systematic Wesleyan theology this latter work is probably unsurpassed. See Symons, *Memoir*, s. v.; *Minutes of the British Conference*, 1870, p. 12; *Wesl. Meth. Magazine*, 1870, p. 1026.

Field, Edward, an English prelate, was born in 1801. He studied at Rugby and Queen's College, Oxford, where he gained a Michel fellowship, was appointed public examiner in 1827, and was consecrated bishop of Newfoundland in 1844. He died June 8, 1876. See *Appleton's Annual Cyclop.* 1876, p. 633.

Fierte, a privilege enjoyed formerly by the archbishops of Rouen, in Normandy, in consequence of the miraculous deliverance which St. Romanus is said to have had from a dragon which infested the neighborhood. The saint took with him a condemned malefactor, and repaired to the haunts of the monster. He then stripped off his stole, bound it around the neck of the dragon, and ordered the criminal to lead it into the town, where it was burned in the presence of the assembled inhabitants. In reward for his bold feat the malefactor obtained his pardon; and in order to keep up the remembrance of this wonderful deliverance, a custom was long preserved in the district of bestowing pardon on Ascension day upon a criminal, if he would only assist to carry in procession the shrine called the *fierte* of St. Romanus.

Fiesco, Cattarina. See Catharine of Genoa.

Fiesco, Giorgio, an Italian prelate, was archbishop of Genoa when pope Eugenius IV appointed him cardinal-priest, with the title of St. Anastasia, and bishop of Ostia. Nicholas V gave him the legation of Liguria. Giorgio Fiesco enjoyed the favor of Calixtus III and of Pius II. He died at Rome, Oct. 11, 1461, but his body was transferred to Genoa. See Hoefer, *Nouv. Biog. Générale*, s. v.

Fiesco, Giovanni, an Italian prelate, was bishop of Vercelli, and was appointed cardinal-priest, with the title of St. Mark, in 1378, by pope Urban VI, who was very fond of him, and charged him with several important missions. Fiesco died in 1384. See Hoefer, *Nouv. Biog. Générale*, s. v.

Fiesco, Guglielmo, an Italian prelate, was born in Genoa, and was the nephew of pope Innocent IV, who made him, in December, 1244, cardinal-deacon, with the title of St. Eustachius. The same pontiff gave him the protectorate of the Augustinians, and placed him at the head of some troops in 1254, to operate against France. Guglielmo came back to Rome after the death of his uncle, and took part at the election of pope Alexander IV, on Dec. 12 of that year. He died in 1256, and was buried in the Church of San Lorenzo. See Hoefer, *Nouv. Biog. Générale*, s. v.

Fiesco, Luca, an Italian prelate, was appointed in 1298 cardinal-deacon, with the title of St. Mary in Via Lata, by pope Boniface VIII. Luca proved his gratitude Sept. 9, 1303, by delivering Anagni from an insurrection. On Jan. 6, 1309, he was at Aix-la-Chapelle, and assisted as legate-extraordinary of pope Clement V, in the coronation of the emperor Henry VII of Luxemburg. John XXII sent him as legate to England. Fiesco died in 1336, and was buried in the metropolitan church of Genoa. See Hoefer, *Nouv. Biog. Générale*, s. v.

Fiesco, Luigi, an Italian prelate, succeeded his uncle Giovanni through the favor of pope Urban VI, and was appointed, in 1385, cardinal-deacon, with the title of St. Adrian. Boniface IX nominated Luigi legate of the holy see in Romagna, and obtained by his instrumentality the submission of several cities, among them Anagni. In 1404 Luigi refused to recognise Cosmo de Migliorati (Innocent VII), who had been chosen by seven cardinals in place of Boniface IX. He put himself under the jurisdiction of the pope at Avignon, Pedro de Luna (Benedict XIII), whom he abandoned in 1409 or 1410, to join Pietro Philargi (Alexander V). The successor of this latter pontiff, Baldassare Cossa (John XXIII), appointed Luigi governor of Bologna. In 1414 he attended at the Council of Constance, and in 1417 at the election of Ottone Colonna (Martin V). He was sent by this pontiff as a legate into Sicily, and returned to Rome, where he died, April 3, 1423. See Hoefer, *Nouv. Biog. Générale*, s. v.

Fiesco, Niccolo, an Italian prelate, was bishop of Fréjus and of Toulon. On the recommendation of Louis XII, pope Alexander VI appointed him, in May, 1503, cardinal-priest of St. Nicolas *inter imagines*, afterwards with the title of the Twelve Apostles. Some time later Niccolo obtained the archbishopric of Embrun, and also that of Ravenna. According to the account of his contemporaries, he was a just and liberal counsellor of popes Alexander VI, Julius II, and Adrian VI. It is said that he refused to be a candidate for the papacy in competition with Giulio de' Medici (Clement VII), the successor of Adrian VI. Fiesco died June 14, 1524. See Hoefer, *Nouv. Biog. Générale*, s. v.

Fiesole, Giovanni da. See Angelico.

Fifyne, Thomas de, a Scotch prelate, was probably a dignitary in the Church of Ross before his promotion to the bishopric of that see in 1274. See Keith, *Scottish Bishops*, p. 187.

Fijian Version of the Scriptures. This language is spoken in the Fiji islands (q. v.). The principal dialect is that of Bau, and a translation of the New Test. was made into this idiom by the late Rev. J. Hunt, in concert with other Wesleyan missionaries. The work was completed in 1849. In 1854 the British and Foreign Bible Society printed an edition of five thousand Fijian New Tests., and in 1858 the same society issued an edition of five thousand gospels. In the meantime the missionaries employed in the Fiji Islands were diligently engaged in the translation of the Old Test., which they completed in 1854. The printing of the work was commenced in England under the joint supervision of the Rev. Mr. Calvert, a long resident in the islands, and the editorial superintendent of the British and Foreign Bible Society, in the year 1857. As Mr. Calvert, however, was compelled to return to his missionary station, the work was left in an unfinished state. The printing was consequently suspended, and a new editor was appointed by the Wesleyan Missionary Society, to whom the examination of the unfinished part of the text was confided, in order that such revision might be introduced as was necessary to secure harmony in grammatical construction and orthography. The Rev. H. B. Lyth having been selected for this important duty, finished the work in 1864, and the committee of the British and Foreign Bible Society announced to its supporters in the report for 1865 the completion of the entire Bible in the language of Fiji, a work upon the preparation of which a vast amount of care and anxious study had been expended. The following account of the reception of the Scriptures in Fiji, soon after their arrival, will be read with interest:

"How the natives rejoiced at the sight of the complete Bible! When I told them that the vessel was in with the Bibles on board, they wanted me to start off at once to fetch them. On receiving them, being greatly excited myself, I walked through Bau with a copy. I took it to the school, and to the king's house, followed by a troop of youngsters, who shouted as we went along, 'Here is the Bible complete—look at it, look at it!' On showing the copy to the king, he asked if we had plenty. I told him we had sufficient for all the preachers in Fiji. 'But,' said he, 'what about us chiefs who can read, and wish to have the whole book; can we not get a copy?' He was satisfied when I told him he should have one." (Report for 1866.)

The extensive circulation of the Fijian Scriptures made it necessary to print, in 1866, two editions of the New Test., consisting together of six thousand five hundred copies, and in 1870 another supply of three thousand copies. A revised edition of the Fijian Bible was published by the British and Foreign Bible Society in 1883. According to the annual report of this society, there were circulated up to March 31, 1884, fifty-five thousand and eight parts of the Bible. For linguistic helps, see Hazlewood, *A Compendious Grammar of the Feejeean Language*, and his *Feejeean and English and English and Feejeean Dictionary*. (B. P.)

Fikenscher, Georg Wolfgang August, a Lutheran theologian of Germany, was born Aug. 28, 1773, at Bayreuth, and died there Sept. 4, 1813. He wrote, *De Pontificum Eccles. Christ. Maximor. Potestate* (Nuremberg, 1813). See Winer, *Handbuch der theol. Lit.* i, 679. (B. P.)

Fikenscher, Karl Christoph Christian, a Lutheran theologian of Germany, born at Culmbach, Nov. 30, 1798, became pastor of St. Sebaldus at Nuremberg, and died in 1858. Besides a number of sermons, he published, *Geschichte des Reichstags zu Augsburg im Jahre* 1530 (Nuremberg, 1830):—*Biblisch-Praktische Auslegung des Evangelium Johannis* (ibid. 1831-34, 3 vols.):—*Die Protestantische Kirche gegen Herrn Weihbischof Wittmann in Regensburg vertheidigt* (ibid. 1832). See Zuchold, *Bibl. Theol.* i, 357 sq.; Winer, *Handbuch der theol. Lit.* i, 752; ii, 23, No. 135, 155, 307. (B. P.)

Fikoosan, a mountain in Japan, to which an order of Jammabos or monks go in pilgrimage once a year; an extremely difficult task, on account of the precipices with which it abounds. This mountain is believed to be a test of the character of a man, for if a wicked person should undertake the pilgrimage, the devil would enter into him on his first attempt to ascend the hill. See Jammabos.

Filastre (or **Fillastre**), Guillaume, the name of two French prelates, uncle and nephew.

1. Born in 1347 or 1348 at La Suze (Maine), studied at the University of Angers, became dean of Rheims, where he also taught theology and mathematics, and founded a library; took an active part in the politico-religious movements of his day; was made prior of St. Ayoub, archbishop of Aix (in Provence), and in 1411 cardinal. He died at Rome, Nov. 6, 1428. See Hoefer, *Nouv. Biog. Générale*, s. v.

2. Born probably in Maine, early entered the Benedictine order, became prior of Sermaise, abbot of St. Thierry in Champagne; was received as doctor at Louvain in January, 1436; made bishop of Verdun, Sept. 30,

1437, but after many turmoils exchanged his see for that of Tournay in 1452, and died at Ghent, Aug. 22, 1473, leaving *La Toison d'Or*, a treatise on that order, of which he had been chancellor (published at Paris, 1517; Troyes, 1530). See Hoefer, *Nouv. Biog. Générale*, s. v.

Filipowski, HERSCHELL, a Hebrew scholar, was born in Poland in 1817. In 1840 he went to England, and received an appointment as teacher of Hebrew and Oriental languages in the Jews' College, Finsbury Square, London. Subsequently he became connected with the Colonial and Standard Life offices of Edinburgh, remaining in that city a number of years, and died July 12, 1872. Filipowski is especially known as the editor of older Jewish works, such as of Abraham bar-Chiyah's *Sepher Haïbur*, which treats of the mathematical and technical chronology of the Hebrews, Nazarites, Mohammedans, etc. (Lond. 1851): — Menahem ben-Saruk's *Machbereth*, מחברת, or first Hebrew lexicon (1854):—Azarja de' Rossi's *Sepher Mazreph Lakesseph* or *Dissertatio Critica de Aetate Mundi* (Edinb. eod.):—Abraham Saccuto's *Liber Juchassin*, ס' יוחסין (Lond. 1857). He also published *Sepher Ha-asiph*, or treatises pertaining to the exegesis of the Old Test. (Leipsic, 1849), and *Sepher Moëd Moädim*, or a Hebrew and Roman almanac (Lond. 1846). See Fürst, *Bibl. Jud.* iii, 84 sq.; Morais, *Eminent Israelites of the* 19*th Century* (Phila. 1880), p. 71 sq. (B. P.)

Filippi, SEBASTIANO (called *Bastianino*), an eminent Italian painter, was born at Ferrara in 1532, and was instructed by his father, Camillo. When eighteen years of age he went to Rome and entered the school of Buonarotti. His great work in the Cathedral of Ferrara, representing the *Last Judgment*, established his fame. Among his best works are the *Martyrdom of St. Catherine*, in the church dedicated to that saint; and the *Adoration of the Magi*, in Santa Maria de Servi. He painted also the *Virgin and Infant; St. John*, and the *Dead Christ supported by Angels*. Filippi died in 1602. See Spooner, *Biog. Hist. of the Fine Arts*, s. v.

Filles de Dieu (*Daughters of God*), an order of nuns in France who devote themselves to visiting the sick. They repeat the Penitential Psalms once a week. Another religious order bearing the same name was formed in the 13th century, which afterwards became merged in the order of *Fontevrault* (q. v.).

Filliuccius (or **Figliucci**), VINCENTE, a Jesuit of Sienna, was born in 1566, and died professor of theology at Rome, April 5, 1622, leaving *De Christianis Officiis et Casibus Conscientiæ* (Lyons, 1626, 2 vols.):—*Synopsis Universæ Theologiæ* (ibid. 1628):—*De Statu Clericorum, de Beneficiis, de Pensionibus, de Spoliis, de Clericorum Vita et Simonia, de Alienatione Rerum Spiritualium*. See Moréri, *Dictionnaire;* Alegambe, *Bibliotheca Scriptorum Societatis Jesu;* Le Mir, *De Scriptoribus Societatis Jesu;* Jöcher, *Allgemeines Gelehrten-Lexikon*, s. v.; Lichtenberger, *Encyclop. des Sciences Religieuses*, s. v. (B. P.)

Fillmore, Glezen, D.D., a Methodist Episcopal minister, was born in Bennington, Vt., Dec. 22, 1789. He received license to preach in 1809, spent the following years as a local preacher, and in 1818 entered the Genesee Conference and was appointed to Buffalo and Black Rock. There were then about fifteen hundred inhabitants in Buffalo, and no church edifice. He leased a lot on what is now Franklin Street, forty-eight days later had on it a house of worship, and two years later reported eighty-two members. His next appointment was to the presiding eldership of Erie District, which stretched from Lake Ontario to Meadville, Pa., and on which his labors were extremely severe and his support exceedingly meagre. In 1830 and 1831 he was pastor of the first and only Methodist Episcopal Church in Rochester. A camp-meeting held in Henrietta had such an effect upon Rochester that nine hundred people professed conversion. The last four years of his active ministry were spent as presiding elder of Buffalo District. In that city, as pastor and presiding elder, he labored twenty-one years. He belonged to the Genesee Conference fifty-four years, and to the Western New York two years, during the last fifteen holding a superannuated relation. He took an active part in the establishment of the Genesee Wesleyan Seminary, Lima, N. Y., and was chosen four times as a delegate to the General Conference. He died in Clarence, Jan. 26, 1875. See *Minutes of Annual Conferences*, 1875, p. 158; Simpson, *Cyclop. of Methodism;* Stevens, *Hist. of the M. E. Church*, iv, 268.

Fillmore, Isaac Otis, D.D., a Presbyterian minister, was born July 15, 1816, at Sennett, N. Y. He graduated with honor at Union College in 1840, and soon after entered Princeton Seminary, where he spent nearly two years in study. He was licensed to preach by the Presbytery of Troy, Feb. 18, 1842; ordained and installed at Cambridge, Washington Co., by the same presbytery, Sept. 15, 1843; labored there twelve years, and was next at Batavia two and a half years; then became pastor of the Park Central Church, Syracuse, for seven years; in 1866 took charge of the Church at Knowlesville, where he labored four years, and then went to California, and for two years preached at San Francisco, Marysville, and other important places. After this he returned to the East, preached (1873–74) at Jordan, N. Y., and then at Green Island, Albany Co., where he died, Oct. 22, 1875. See *Necrol. Report of Princeton Theol. Sem.* 1876, p. 24.

Finan, *Saint*. See FINNAN.

Finbar. See BARRFINN.

Finckel, SAMUEL, D.D., a Lutheran minister, was born at Jonestown, Lebanon Co., Pa., Feb. 22, 1811. In 1825 he began preparations for the ministry under the direction of Rev. John Stein, of Jonestown; in 1827 continued his studies at Gettysburg; in July, 1831, was employed as tutor in the Dauphin Academy, Harrisburg; in 1832 was licensed to preach, and in the following year was ordained pastor of the churches in Middletown and Greensburg. For more than three years he resided in Taneytown, Md.; about three years in Middletown, Pa.; four years in Germantown, and nearly three years in Cumberland, Md. Then for twenty-three years he was pastor of the German Evangelical Church in Washington, D. C. Resigning this charge on account of advancing age, he subsequently gathered an English congregation in Memorial Hall, in the same city, to whom he ministered about two years. In 1848, in addition to his pastoral labors in Washington, he was employed as a clerk in the quartermaster-general's office. He died in Washington, Feb. 13, 1873. See *Fifty Years in the Lutheran Ministry*, 1878, p. 235.

Findlay, John (1), D.D., a Scotch clergyman, was born in Glasgow, Sept. 26, 1751; graduated at Glasgow University; was licensed to preach Aug. 2, 1780; presented to the living at the High Church, Paisley, ordained March 14, 1781, and died March 25, 1821. He was a warm friend of the Bible, missionary, and school societies, and aided by his advice the formation of auxiliary societies at Paisley and Renfrew. He was grave and cheerful in conversation, uniformly correct in language and matter, yet lively, entertaining, and instructive. He published *Sermons*, preached before the London Missionary Society (Lond. 1799). See *Fasti Eccles. Scoticanæ*, ii, 207.

Findlay, John (2), D.D., a Scotch clergyman, was licensed to preach May 7, 1800; called to the living at Norriestown in March, and ordained June 16, 1803; promoted to St. Paul's Church, Perth, in August, 1807, and died April 4, 1846, aged sixty-six years. He published an address, annexed to a sermon (Glasgow, 1803). See *Fasti Eccles. Scoticanæ*, ii, 619, 728.

Findlay, Robert (1), D.D., a Scotch clergyman,

son of Rev. Thomas Findlay, minister at Prestonkirk, graduated at Edinburgh University, Dec. 10, 1734; was licensed to preach July 5, 1738; called to the living at Inch, April 3, and ordained July 26, 1739; engaged in business at London, Nov. 18, 1761, and died March 30, 1782. See *Fasti Eccles. Scoticanæ*, i, 758.

Findlay, Robert (2), D.D., a Scotch clergyman, was licensed to preach Oct. 5, 1743; called to the living at Stevenston in March, and ordained Aug. 23, 1744; transferred to Galston April 29, 1745; promoted to the Town Church, Paisley, Feb. 20, 1754; transferred to the north-west quarter, Glasgow, Jan. 29, 1756; being admitted professor of divinity in the Glasgow University, he resigned his parish duties and charge, Jan. 1, 1783. He died June 15, 1814, aged ninety-three years. Dr. Findlay published, *Vindication of the Sacred Books* (1770):—*Psalmody* (1763). See *Fasti Eccles. Scoticanæ*, ii, 26, 116, 187, 203; Allibone, *Dict. of Brit. and Amer. Authors*, s. v.

Fingask, THOMAS DE, a Scotch prelate, was employed in divers embassies to England during the captivity of king David II, and was bishop of Caithness in 1348 and 1357. He died in 1360. See Keith, *Scottish Bishops*, p. 213.

Finlay (1), a Scotch prelate, was bishop of Dunblane in 1406 and 1408. He died in 1419. See Keith, *Scottish Bishops*, p. 176.

Finlay (2), a Scotch prelate, was a Dominican friar, and chaplain to Murdoch, duke of Albany, in 1425. Upon the fall of the duke this prelate went to Ireland, and there died. He was probably for a time bishop of Argyle. See Keith, *Scottish Bishops*, p. 287.

Finlay, John, D.D., a Baptist minister, was born in the parish of Loudoun, Ayrshire, Scotland, March 10, 1794. He was educated in the Scottish Kirk; graduated from the University of Glasgow in 1810; was converted under the ministry of Dr. Chalmers; came to America in 1817, and, soon after landing at Savannah, went to Augusta, Ga., where he was elected rector of Richmond Academy. He was licensed by the Harmony Presbytery, and, for a time, preached in the "Brick Church" in Augusta; subsequently went to New York, where, uniting with Dr. Arch. McClay's Church, he was licensed as a Baptist preacher; soon after was ordained in Albany, N. Y., where he was pastor until called to the First Church in Baltimore, in 1821. In 1835 he removed to Jackson, Tenn., preaching and teaching for a time until a church was formed. Subsequently he went to Louisville, Ky., where he was pastor a year and a half; then returned to Jackson; next went to Middleton, O., then to Lebanon, and in the fall of 1849 to Memphis, Tenn., where he remained till the spring of 1852. He died at Greenville, on the Mississippi, about 1860. See Borum, *Sketches of Tenn. Ministers*, p. 254, 263. (J. C. S.)

Finlayson, JAMES, D.D., a Scotch clergyman, professor of logic in the Edinburgh University, which office he held in conjunction with his benefice, was formerly tutor in the family of Sir William Murray; presented to the living at Borthwick, Aug. 30, 1786, and ordained April 6, 1787; transferred to Lady Yester's Chapel of Ease, Edinburgh, June 8, 1790; promoted to Old Greyfriars Church in that city, Dec. 25, 1793; transferred to the High Church, Feb. 27, 1799; unanimously elected moderator of the General Assembly, May 20, 1802; appointed almoner to the king the same year, but resigned the office soon afterwards, and died Jan. 28, 1808, in his fiftieth year. His life exhibited an example of self-prompted merit, unblemished purity, and elevated virtue; while to his generous aid not a few were indebted for their promotion in life. He was deeply interested in the welfare of the Church, and skilled in the management of her affairs. He published, *Argument in Support of Chapels of Ease* (fol. 1798):—*Preaching, a Means of Promoting the General Progress of Human Improvement* (Edinburgh, 1801):—*Sermons* (ibid. 1809, 8vo):—*Life of Dr. Blair*, with Blair's *Sermons*, vol. v. See *Fasti Eccles. Scoticanæ*, i, 24, 44, 63, 64, 268.

Finney, CHARLES G., an eminent Congregational minister, was born at Warren, Conn., Aug. 29, 1792. In early manhood he left his father's farm in western New York, and began the study of law in Adams, Jefferson Co., but shortly abandoned it for the ministry, to which he was ordained in 1824, with comparatively little previous theological training. He soon became noted as an evangelist, and great revivals attended his preaching everywhere. In 1835 he became a professor in Oberlin College, O., where he continued as teacher, pastor, and president (1852–66), with brief tours as a revivalist in England (1848, 1851), until his death, Aug. 16, 1875. He was eminently successful in religious labors for the conversion of sinners, which were conducted with great fervor and earnestness, very much after the manner of Methodists. Mr. Finney wrote, *Lectures on Revivals* (Boston, 1835, and many editions since):—*Lectures to Professing Christians* (Oberlin, 1836):—*Sermons on Important Subjects* (N. Y. 1839):—*Lectures on Systematic Theology* (Oberlin, 1846, and later). See *Autobiography* (N. Y. 1876); OBERLIN THEOLOGY.

Finnish Version. See RUSSIA, VERSIONS OF.

Finotti, JOSEPH M., a Roman Catholic divine, was born in Ferrara, Italy, in 1817, and educated at the Jesuit College, Rome. Being induced, in 1845, by professor Ryder, of Georgetown College, to come to America, Finotti was ordained at Georgetown; in 1850 was pastor of St. Mary's Church, Alexandria, Va.; in 1852 left the Society of Jesus, and went to Boston, Mass., where he was for three years editor of the Boston *Pilot*, was also pastor of Brookline, Brighton, and other missions, and afterwards at Arlington, near Boston. He resided for a time at St. Mary's Seminary, near Cincinnati, O., from there he went to Omaha, Neb., and finally to Central City, Col., in 1877, of which parish he had charge until his death, Jan. 10, 1879. Finotti was a lover of books, most of his time being spent in his library, and he was constantly writing. He published, *A French Grammar* (in Italian):—*A Month of Mary* (1853):—*Life of Blessed Paul of the Cross* (1860):—*Italy in the Fifteenth Century*:—*Diary of a Soldier* (1861):—*The French Zouave* (1863):—*Herman, the Pianist* (ibid.):—*The Spirit of St. Francis of Sales* (1866):—*Works of Rev. Arthur O'Leary*:—*Life of Blessed Peter Cleaver*, etc. Most of these works are translations, or were edited by him. His greatest work, never completed, was his *Bibliographia Catholica Americana*, being a list of all the Roman Catholic books published in the United States, with notices of their authors and epitome of their contents. The first part, bringing the list down to 1825, was published in 1872. One of the projects of Finotti was the introduction into schools of a well-arranged series of Christian classics. See (N. Y.) *Catholic Annual*, 1880, p. 44.

Fire, HOLY, *of the Greek Church*, a fire kindled by the Greek and Armenian monks in the Church of the Holy Sepulchre at Jerusalem, under pretense of a miracle, on Saturday of the Greek Easter week, amid the wildest enthusiasm of the multitude, and the utmost confusion and uproar; so much so that many are trampled to death in the crowd. Dr. Wolff, in his *Missionary Journal*, relates that the Greek metropolitan declared in reference to this pretended miracle, "The holy fire was known in the time of the Greek emperors; it was then seen in the Holy Sepulchre, and also in the time that the Crusaders were in possession of the place. Many of the Latin historians mention it. From the time of the invasion of the Turks till now, the holy fire has been seen both by believers and unbelievers." See Herschell, *Visit to my Fatherland in* 1843.

FIRE ORDEAL. See ORDEALS.

FIRE, PILLAR OF. See PILLAR OF CLOUD.

Firkowitsch, ABRAHAM, a Karaite scholar, was born Sept. 27, 1786, at Lootsk, in Volhynia, and died June 7, 1874, at Shufut-Kale, in the Crimea. He is known for his zeal in collecting old manuscripts concerning the history of the Karaite Jews. The collected material he published in *Massa u-Meriba* (Eupatoria, 1838), and *Abne Sikkaron* (Wilna, 1872). Many of his manuscripts and epigraphs he sold to the Imperial Library at St. Petersburg. Although Firkowitsch was highly esteemed among his co-religionists, yet some doubts were raised as to the genuineness of some of his pretended dates, said to be found on tombstones and in manuscripts. What was a mere supposition while he was alive became a certainty after his death. Scholars like Strack and Harkavy examined his investigations, and proved that Firkowitsch was guilty of wilful forgeries, by which he deceived the literary world. See Jellinek, *Abraham Firkowitsch* (Vienna, 1875); Harkavy, *Abr. Firkowitsch's Altjüdische Denkmäler in der Krim* (St. Petersburg, 1876); Deinard, *Biography of Firkowitsch* [in Hebrew] (Warsaw, 1875); but especially Strack, *A. Firkowitsch und Seine Entdeckungen* (Leipsic, 1876). (B. P.)

Firmament, *in Christian Art.* This seems to be represented usually by a male figure supporting an arch (see cut under DOCTORS), but occasionally likewise by a female figure in a similar position (Martigny, *Dict. des Antiq. Chrétiennes*, s. v.).

Probable Antique Christian Representation of the Firmament.

Firmin, the name of several early saints and ecclesiastics, of whom we particularize: (1) Bishop of Amiens, a native of Pampeluna, ordained as a missionary bishop of Gaul, died probably A.D. 303, and commemorated Sept. 25. (2) *Saint*, fourth bishop of Uzes, born in Narbonne of noble parentage, cir. A.D. 516; trained by his uncle, Poricus, early ordained, and consecrated bishop A.D. 538; died in 553, and commemorated Oct. 11.

Firmin, GILES, an English Nonconformist divine, was born in Suffolk in 1617, and educated at Cambridge. He was ordained, and became minister at Shalford, in Essex, where he continued until he was ejected, in 1662, by the act of uniformity. He died in 1697, leaving several sermons and theological treatises (1652 sq.), the best of which is *The Real Christian.* See Chalmers, *Biog. Dict.* s. v.; Allibone, *Dict. of Brit. and Amer. Authors*, s. v.

Firmus is the name of several early Christians, of whom we particularize: (1) A martyr with Rusticus at Verona, A.D. 304; commemorated Aug. 9. (2) Bishop of the Cappadocian Cæsarea, deposed by the Oriental party, and died A.D. 439. He left a number of letters, first published by Muratori, *Anecdot. Græc.* (Patav. 1707), also by Migne, *Patrol.* lxxvii, 1477. See Smith, *Dict. of Christ. Biog.* s. v.

Fisch, GEORGE, D.D., a French theologian, commonly known as "Pastor Fisch," was born at Nyon, canton of Vaud, Switzerland, July 6, 1814. He studied at Lausanne, was for some time preacher of a small German congregation at Vevay, till in 1846 called to Lyons, France, to become an assistant preacher to Adolphe Monod, whom he subsequently succeeded. In 1855 he went to Paris as successor of Louis Bridel, and died July 3, 1881, at Vallorbe, Switzerland. Fisch took an active part in the Constitutional Synod of 1849, which formed the union of the Evangelical churches of France. From 1863 till his death he was president of the Synodal Commission, and thus directed the work of the Free churches. When, in 1856, the Evangelical Alliance was founded, he became the very soul of the branch of this society in France, and attended the meetings at London, Paris, Berlin, Geneva, Amsterdam, and New York. He was particularly interested in the South-Africa mission among the Bassutos, in Mr. McAll's mission in Paris, and in every way he advanced the cause of the Gospel. See Lichtenberger, *Encyclop. des Sciences Religieuses*, s. v. (B. P.)

Fischart, JOHANN (called also *Mentzer*, from his native place, Mayence), a Lutheran hymn-writer, was born about 1547. He studied law, and for some time practiced it at Frankfort-on-the-Main. From there he went to Strasburg, and died in 1589. Many of his hymns are found in the hymn-books of the 16th and 17th centuries. A copy of his *Gesangbüchlein*, published in 1576, has been found in the British Museum at London, by professor Max Müller, and from a copy made by him, with the assistance of Herr von Bunsen, an edition was published at Berlin in 1849. See Gödecke, *Grundriss der deutschen Dichtung* (Hanover, 1849), i, 386-398; Vilmar, *Zur Literatur Fischarts* (Marburg, 1846); Weller, *Neue Originalpoesien Joh. Fischarts* (Halle, 1859); Gervinus, *Geschichte der poetischen Nationalliteratur der Deutschen*, 3d ed. iii, p. 131; Kurz, *Geschichte der deutschen Literatur*, 4th ed. iv, p. 26; Koch, *Geschichte des deutschen Kirchenliedes*, ii, 279 sq., 487 sq. (B. P.)

Fischer, Augustin, a Roman Catholic theologian of Germany, was born April 12, 1766. He was for some time teacher at the Augustinian monastery in Erfurt, accepted a call in 1813 as court-preacher and sub-regent of the seminary at Aschaffenburg, and died in 1816, leaving *Lehrbuch der christlichen Religion*, etc. (Erfurt, 1802; 6th ed. 1826). See Winer, *Handbuch der theol. Lit.* ii, 242. (B. P.)

Fischer, Carl Gottlieb, a Lutheran theologian of Germany, was born Oct. 9, 1745. He studied at Königsberg, where Kant's lectures greatly influenced him. In 1778 he was appointed pastor of the royal hospital at Königsberg, and died there, Sept. 19, 1801, leaving *Homilien über merkwürdige Erzählungen aus der Geschichte Jesu* (Königsberg, 1799, 3 vols.). See Döring, *Deutsche Kanzelredner*, p. 58 sq.; Winer, *Handbuch der theol. Lit.* i, 118, 232, 293. (B. P.)

Fischer, Christoph (1), a Lutheran theologian of Germany, who died as court-preacher and general superintendent at Zell, in 1597, wrote *Erklärungen* on the passion, resurrection, and ascension of Christ, on the Psalms, on Luther's catechism, etc. See Jöcher, *Allgemeines Gelehrten-Lexikon*, s. v. (B. P.)

Fischer, Christoph (2), a Roman Catholic theologian, teacher of the Greek language and of hermeneutics of the New Test. at Prague, where he died, Jan. 13, 1791, is the author of, *Die heiligen Schriften des Neuen Testaments übersetzt mit Erklärungen* (Prague, 1784; Treves, 1794):—*Institutiones hermen. Novi Testamenti* (Prague, 1788). See Winer, *Handbuch der theol. Lit.* i, 107, 174. (B. P.)

Fischer, Erdmann Rudolph, a Lutheran theologian of Germany, was born Nov. 28, 1687, was in 1721 preacher at Coburg, in 1758 general superintendent there, and died June 1, 1776. He wrote, *Comm. de θεοδρόμοις Veteris Ecclesiæ Legatis* (Coburg, 1717):—*Vita Jo. Gerhardi* (Leipsic, 1723):—*Die unveränderte Augsburgische Confession* (Coburg, 1730, 1755):—*De Eligenda inter Christianos Religione Dissidentes* (ibid. 1734):—*Cypriani Dissertationes Varii Argumenti* (ibid. 1755):—*Hieronymi Epist. ad Nepotianum* (ibid. 1758). See Moser and Neubauer, *Jetztlebende Theologen;* Meusel, *Gelehrtes Deutschland;* Jöcher, *Allgemeines Gelehrten-Lexikon*, s. v.; Winer, *Handbuch der theol. Lit.* i, 20, 30, 613, 860. (B. P.)

Fischer, Friedrich, a Lutheran theologian of Germany, was born in 1558. In 1586 he was rector at Grimma, and accepted a call in 1594 to Bautzen, where he died, in 1623, leaving, *Decalogus*, or thirty-eight sermons on the decalogue (Bautzen, 1608):—*Oratio Dominica*, or fifteen sermons on the Lord's Prayer (ibid. 1611):—*Misteriodidascalia*, or twenty-two sermons on baptism and the Lord's supper (Wittenberg, eod.):—*Pædagogia Christiana*, or twenty sermons on the catechism (ibid. 1613). See Ober-Lausitzer, *Merkwürdigkeiten;* Jöcher, *Allgemeines Gelehrten-Lexikon*, s. v. (B. P.)

Fischer, Gottfried Angelus, a Roman Catholic theologian of Germany, was born at Munich, Nov. 5, 1768. He was for some time professor of philosophy and history at the gymnasium of his native place, received in 1817 a call as pastor to Niedervichbach, in Bavaria, and died in 1836. He wrote, *Lehre der Katholischen Kirche* (Munich, 1819):—*Predigten über die acht Selig preisungen* (ibid. 1834):—*Vollständiges Katholisches Religionslehrbuch* (ibid. 1822, 1829):—*Lese- und Gebetbuch für junge Katholische Christen* (Augsburg, 1827). See Winer, *Handbuch der theol. Lit.* i, 465; ii, 120, 243, 373. (B. P.)

Fischer, Gottlob Eusebius, a Lutheran theologian of Germany, was born May 23, 1769, at Golssen, in Lower Lusatia. In 1797 he was deacon, in 1801 archdeacon, in 1810 pastor at Ranis, in 1819 superintendent at Sangerhausen, and died in 1849, leaving, *Predigtentwürfe über freie Texte* (Eisleben, 1835, 1836, 2 vols.):—*Christliches Predigtbuch* (Sangerhausen, 1836):—*Christliche Betstunden* (Neustadt, 1834–36, 4 parts):—*Jesus Christus, eine Erzählung für verständige Kinder* (Leipsic, 1794):—*Kirchliche Catechisationen* (Neustadt, 1828–31, 4 vols.):—he also worked up the New Test. part to Dinter's *Die Bibel, als Erbauungsbuch für Gebildete* (ibid. 1832). See Winer, *Handbuch der theol. Lit.* ii, 56, 74, 84, 144, 189, 257, 271, 354; Zuchold, *Bibl. Theol.* i, 360 sq. (B. P.)

Fischer, Jacob Benjamin, a Lutheran theologian of Germany, general superintendent of Livonia, who died Nov. 3, 1744, deserves to be mentioned for the great interest he took in having the Bible given to his people in their vernacular. The first Livonian or Lettish Bible was edited by his father, John, who died in 1705. The care of the second edition devolved on Jacob Benjamin, and it was printed at Königsberg in 1739. (B. P.)

Fischer, Johann Friedrich, a Lutheran theologian of Germany, was born at Coburg, Oct. 10, 1724, became rector of the Thomas school at Leipsic, and died there, Oct. 17, 1799. He published, *Commentatio de Statu et Jurisdictione Judæorum Secundum Leges Rom. Germ.* (Strasburg, 1763):—*Prolusiones de Verss. Græc. Vet. Test.* (Leipsic, 1772):—*Prolusiones de Vitiis Lexicorum Novi Test.* (ibid. 1772–90):—*De Chaldaicis Onkelosi Jonathanæque Versionibus Vet. Test.*, etc. (ibid. 1775):—*De Versione Librorum Divinorum Novi Test. Vulgata* (ibid. 1776):—*Clavis Reliquiarum Vers. Græcar. V. Test. Aquilæ, Symmachi*, etc. (ibid. 1758). See Fürst, *Bibl. Jud.* i, 282; Winer, *Handbuch der theol. Lit.* i, 48, 125, 127, 128, 129, 130, 192. (B. P.)

Fischer, Johann Michael, a Lutheran theologian of Germany, was born at Coburg, March 21, 1682. He studied at Leipsic, was in 1709 rector at his native place, in 1714 preacher at the Holy Cross Church, and died March 1, 1724, leaving *De Solemnis Veteris Ecclesiæ Antepaschalibus* (Leipsic, 1704). See *Unschuldige Nachrichten*, 1725, p. 1041; Winer, *Handbuch der theol. Lit.* i, 617; Jöcher, *Allgemeines Gelehrten-Lexikon*, s. v. (B. P.)

Fischer, Ludwig Eberhard, a Lutheran theologian of Germany, was born Aug. 6, 1695. He studied at Tübingen, was in 1727 preacher at Zavelstein, in 1732 at Stuttgart, and took a prominent part in the religious as well as political welfare of his country. He died in 1773, leaving several hymns, which are found in the Würtemberg hymn-book. See Moser, *Schwäbische Merkwürdigkeiten*, p. 372; Koch, *Geschichte des Deutschen Kirchenliedes*, v, 85 sq. (B. P.)

Fischer, Samuel, a Reformed theologian, who died at Aarberg, in Switzerland, in 1831, is the author of, *Geschichte der Reformation in Bern* (Berne, 1827):—*Geschichte der Disputation und Reformation in Bern* (ibid. 1828). See Winer, *Handbuch der theol. Lit.* i, 811. (B. P.)

Fischlin, Ludwig Melchior, a Lutheran theologian of Germany, was born in 1672 at Hausen, near Brackenheim, in Würtemberg, studied at Tübingen, and died Aug. 11, 1729. He wrote, *Theatrum Mysterii ἀποκαταστάσεως πάντων* (Ulm, 1710, 2 vols.). See Jöcher, *Allgemeines Gelehrten-Lexikon*, s. v.; Winer, *Handbuch der theol. Lit.* i, 856. (B. P.)

Fisen, Bartholomew, a Jesuit, was born at Liege in 1591, and died at Lisle, June 26, 1649. He is the author of, *Origo Prima Festi Corporis Christi* (Liege, 1628):—*Historia Ecclesiæ Leodiensis* (ibid. 1642, 1696, 2 vols. fol.). See Winer, *Handbuch der theol. Lit.* i, 619, 825; Jöcher, *Allgemeines Gelehrten-Lexikon*, s. v. (B. P.)

Fish, *in Christian Art.* The fish is a symbol of almost universal occurrence in the painting and sculpture of the primitive Church. Like the dove or the lamb, it is used in more than one sense; but its nonscriptural or anagrammatic meaning was perhaps the most popular. See Ichthys. At so early a period as the middle of the 2d century, and under the continual dangers of persecution, the use of such a symbol for the person of the Lord was perfectly natural, as it would attract no notice from the outer world; and in the same manner, with even more obvious reasons, the form of the cross was frequently disguised up to the time of

Antique Lamp with Christian Symbol and Monogram.

Constantine. But the mystic senses assigned to the emblem by various fathers often seem to the modern mind somewhat gratuitous and ill-founded. See FISHERMAN.

Bronze Tessera given to the newly baptized.

Fish, Henry, A.M., an English Wesleyan minister, was born at Hooton-Pagnell, near Doncaster, Aug. 5, 1802. He joined a class in his eighteenth year, was accepted by the conference as a candidate for the ministry in 1823, became a supernumerary at Kettering in 1847, was a happy and useful servant of the Church during his long retirement, and died Jan. 16, 1879. He was a powerful preacher. "He had a quick discernment of the meaning of the text, and a faculty of clear, logical arrangement; and the Gospel which he proclaimed with noble eloquence and intense earnestness wrought deep conviction in the hearts of his hearers and turned many to righteousness, some of whom have ranked among the most gifted and devoted sons of Methodism." Mr. Fish published, *Truth of the Christian Religion* (Bristol, 1839):—*Natural Theology* (ibid. 1840):—*The Workings of Popery* (Lond. 1845):—*Methodism the Work of God* (Bristol, 1839):—*Death of Rev. Maximilian Wilson* (Lond. 1857):—*Purchase of the Truth* (Hull, eod.):—*Memorials of Mrs. Parson Cooper, of Dunstable* (Lond. 1845, 8vo):—*Joseph Pearson* (Bath, 1849, 12mo):—*John Wild, of Armley* (Lond. 1863, 18mo):—*Romanism* (Hull, 1836, 8vo):—*Movements of the Oxford Tractarians* (Lond. 1842, 8vo):—*Doctrines of the Oxford Tractarians* (ibid. 1841, 8vo):—*Chapters on the Teaching of the Roman Catholic Church* (ibid. 1853, 12mo):—*The Class-leaders' Manual* (ibid. 1849, 18mo):—*The Present Agitation in the Wesleyan Methodist Connection* (3d ed. ibid. 1851, 12mo):—*Rev. Evan Lewis, B.A.* (Cong.), *and the Wesleyan Methodists* (ibid. 1863, 2 vols. 12mo). He also edited, with an introduction, *A Poetical Version of the Psalms of David*, by Charles Wesley (ibid. 1854, 8vo). He was for many years a contributor to Methodist periodical literature. See *Minutes of the British Conference*, 1879, p. 24; *Wesl. Centenary Takings*, i, 307; Osborne, *Methodist Bibliography*, p. 102.

Fish, Henry Clay, D.D., a Baptist minister, was born at Halifax, Vt., Jan. 27, 1820; graduated from Union Theological Seminary, N. Y., in 1845; was ordained, June 26 of that year, over the Church in Somerville, N. J., and in January, 1851, became pastor of the First Church in Newark, which office he held till his death, Oct. 2, 1877. Dr. Fish was the author of several works, among them, *Primitive Piety Revived* (Boston, 1855):—*Pulpit Eloquence of the Nineteenth Century* (N. Y. 1856, 1877):—*The Hand-book of Revivals* (Boston, 1874). His *Bible Lands Illustrated* (Hartford, 1876), was the outcome of a tour in the Holy Land. See *Gen. Cat. of Union Theol. Sem.* 1876, p. 36; (N. Y.) *Examiner*, Oct. 1877; Cathcart, *Baptist Encyclop.* s. v. (J. C. S.)

Fish, John H., D.D., a Protestant Episcopal clergyman, graduated from the General Theological Seminary, N. Y.; in 1853 was employed as chaplain in the United States army, at San Saba; in 1854 served in the same capacity at Jefferson Barracks, Mo.; in 1868 was removed to Fort Rice; in 1871 to Fort Randall, Dak., and there remained until within a short time of his death, which occurred at Montclair, N. J., Oct. 21, 1878, at the age of sixty-six years. See *Prot. Episc. Almanac*, 1879, p. 168.

Fish, Simon, a zealous promoter of the English reformation, was born in Kent, educated at Oxford, and died about 1531. He published, *The Supplicacyon for the Beggars*, a satire upon bishops, abbots, priors, monks, friars, and the popish clergy in general (1526):—*The Sum of the Scriptures*, from the Dutch (1530). See Chalmers, *Biog. Dict.* s. v.; Allibone, *Dict. of Brit. and Amer. Authors*, s. v.

Fisher, Abiel, D.D., a Baptist minister, was born at Putney, Vt., June 19, 1787. He graduated from the University of Vermont in 1811; studied theology with Rev. Nathaniel Kendrick; was ordained an evangelist in Brandon, June 15, 1815; was pastor in Bellingham, Mass., twelve years; in West Boylston, three years; and subsequently in Sturbridge, Mass., Pawtuxet, R. I., and Swansea and Sutton, Mass. He died at West Boylston, in the summer of 1862. He was one of the "fathers" of the Baptist denomination in Massachusetts, and held in high esteem. See Cathcart, *Baptist Encyclop.* p. 295. (J. C. S.)

Fisher, George H., D.D., a Reformed (Dutch) minister, graduated from Columbia College in 1821, and from the New Brunswick Theological Seminary in 1825; was licensed by the Classis of New Brunswick in the same year; was pastor at North Branch until 1830; at Fishkill until 1835; at Hudson until 1841; at Broome Street, New York city, until 1855; at Utica until 1859; at Hackensack, Second Church, from 1864 to 1870, and was then made pastor emeritus. He died at the last-named place, Nov. 23, 1874. As a preacher, Dr. Fisher stood for years in the foremost rank in his denomination, being fluent in speech, clear in statement, and tender in manner. He was for six years secretary of the Board of Domestic Missions for the eastern department, and published, *Divine Providence Proved and Illustrated*, in the *National Preacher* (1848). See Corwin, *Manual of the Ref. Church in America*, 3d ed. p. 260.

Fisher, James, one of the four leaders of the secession from the Established Church of Scotland, and professor of divinity to the Associate (Burgher) Synod, was born at Bar, Scotland, Jan. 23, 1697. He commenced his curriculum in Glasgow in 1712, and closed it in St. Andrews in 1716; and then entered the Divinity Hall in the University of Edinburgh, where he continued six sessions. He was licensed to preach in 1722, and for some time supplied pulpits within the bounds of the presbytery. His first parish was at Glenisla, Forfarshire, and in 1725 he removed to Kinclaven. In 1732 he took an active part in denouncing the encroachments of the British legislature on the ecclesiastical liberties of Scotland, before the General Assembly, which soon resulted in his being suspended from the ministry. Mr. Fisher, with his other dissenting brethren, shortly afterwards constituted themselves into a presbytery, and with their respective congregations thus formed *The Associate Presbytery.* After various fruitless endeavors on the part of the General Assembly to induce Mr. Fisher to return to the Established Church, he, in 1741, was ejected from the church and manse of Kinclaven, whence he removed to Glasgow in response to a unanimous call from a newly organized Church holding his views, which he served continuously for over thirty years. He died Sept. 28, 1775. Mr. Fisher was somewhat under the middle size, well proportioned, had a lively, affectionate, cheerful countenance, easy and alert in all his movements, was neat in dress, and orderly and punctual in all his affairs, an habitual early riser, and a conscientious, diligent student. His published works are, *The Inestimable Value of Divine Truth*, (Edinb. 1739):—*Christ Jesus the Lord, Considered as the Inexhaustible Matter of Gospel Preaching* (ibid. 1741):—*The Character of a Faithful Minister of Christ* (ibid. 1752):—*The Assembly's Shorter Catechism Explained by Way of Question and Answer* (Glasgow, 1753, pt. i, 8vo; pt. ii, 1760):—*Christ the Sole and Wonderful Doer in the Work of Man's Redemption* (ibid. 1755), and a few reviews. See *Memorials of Alexander Moncrieff* and *James Fisher*, in the *United Presbyterian Fathers*, 1849, p. 9; *Fasti Eccles. Scoticanæ*, ii, 802.

Fisher, John, D.D., an English prelate, was born in 1748. He received his early education at Peterborough and at St. Paul's School, London; in 1766 was admitted at Peterhouse, Cambridge, where he took the degree of A.B. in 1770; in 1773 was elected a fellow of St. John's College, and in the same year proceeded A.M., in 1780 B.D., and in that year was appointed tutor to his royal highness prince Edward, afterwards duke of Kent. In 1781 he was nominated chaplain to the king, and appointed one of the deputy clerks of the closet; and in 1783 elected a fellow of the Society of Antiquaries. In 1785, his attendance upon prince Edward ceasing upon his royal highness going to Germany to finish his education there, he went to Italy for his health; but was recalled from Naples in 1786, and appointed by the king a canon of Windsor; he resigned his canonry in 1803, on being promoted to the see of Exeter; at the end of the same year was appointed preceptor to the princess Charlotte of Wales; in 1807 translated to the see of Salisbury, which position he held until his death, May 8, 1825. Bishop Fisher was an accomplished scholar and a sound divine; but owing to the numerous duties which devolved upon him he had but little leisure to devote to literary pursuits. He published a number of sermons delivered by him on special occasions, which possess superior merit. See *The* (Lond.) *Annual Register*, 1825, p. 247.

Fisher, Jonathan Parker, D.D., an English divine, was born about 1757. He was matriculated May 7, 1774; proceeded A.M. Oct. 10, 1780; B.D. May 22, 1802; and grand compounder May 14, 1807. He died in 1838, being at the time sub-dean and canon-residentiary of Exeter Cathedral, and rector of Farringdon, Devonshire. See *The* (Lond.) *Christian Remembrancer*, September, 1838, p. 568.

Fisher, Nathaniel, a Protestant Episcopal clergyman, was born at Dedham, Mass., July 8, 1742. He graduated from Harvard College in 1763, and soon after the beginning of the revolution was in the service of the Society for the Propagation of the Gospel in Foreign Parts, as a schoolmaster at Granville, Nova Scotia. Having crossed the Atlantic for ordination in 1777, he was admitted to orders by the bishop of London, Sept. 25; not long after arrived at Nova Scotia as a missionary to the churches at Annapolis and Granville, and remained there till 1781. In the following year he was invited to the rectorship of St. Peter's Church, Salem, Mass.; but on arriving in that commonwealth he was arrested as a subject of Great Britain, and imprisoned. On taking the oath of fidelity to the new government he was released. His ministry in Salem covered a period of thirty years, until his death, Dec. 20, 1812. Mr. Fisher actively promoted the organization of the Protestant Episcopal Church in Massachusetts, and was secretary of the first convention of the churches of Massachusetts and Rhode Island in 1784. In 1790 he was one of those chosen to frame the constitution for the government of the Protestant Episcopal churches in Massachusetts; elected a member of the first standing committee of the diocese, and was one of the persons appointed to publish the revised Book of Common Prayer. A volume of Mr. Fisher's *Sermons*, edited by judge Joseph Story, was published after his death. His style of preaching was compact, dignified, and vigorous. See Sprague, *Annals of the Amer. Pulpit*, v, 328.

Fisher, Peter S., a pious and successful German Reformed minister, was born in Berks County, Pa., Oct. 11, 1804; studied theology under the Rev. Dr. F. L. Herman; was licensed and ordained in 1826, and placed over some congregations in the vicinity of Harrisburg. After laboring there with great acceptance for seven years, he removed to Centre County, where he proved himself a faithful servant of Christ, and enjoyed the undiminished confidence of the people up to the time of his removal to Bucks County in 1857. Here he labored with his usual zeal, prudence, and success. Mr. Fisher always manifested a deep interest in the various benevolent operations of the Church, especially in the cause of orphans. He died very suddenly, May 22, 1873, universally esteemed. He is thought to have preached about ten thousand sermons, added to the Church some fifteen hundred members, and solemnized two thousand marriages. See *Ref. Church Mess.*, June 4, 1873. (D. Y. H.)

Fisher, Samuel R., D.D., a prominent minister of the (German) Reformed Church, was born at Norristown, Pa., June 2, 1810. From his earliest childhood he evinced a spirit of piety, and became a full member of the Church when only fourteen years of age. About this time he entered the family of his pastor, the Rev. George Wack, in part as servant-boy and partly as student. Here he remained five years. In 1829 he matriculated at Jefferson College, Cannonsburg, and graduated in 1834. Soon afterwards he began the study of theology in the Seminary of the Reformed Church, then located at Carlisle. He was licensed to preach in 1836, and became pastor of the Reformed Church in Emmittsburg, Md. He remained here only about three years, when, in 1840, he became identified with the Publication Society of the Reformed Church, located at Chambersburg, Pa. In 1864 the establishment was removed to Philadelphia, where Dr. Fisher continued his labors, with slight changes, as editor-in-chief of the *Reformed Church Messenger* and superintendent of the publication interests of the Church. He died at Tiffin, O., whither he had gone to attend the General Synod, June 5, 1881. During a period of forty years or more, Dr. Fisher acted as stated clerk of the Synod of the Reformed Church in the United States. The duties of this office he performed with scrupulous exactitude and fidelity. In the meantime, also, he filled other stations of honor and responsibility, serving for many years as a member of the board of visitors of the theological seminary and as treasurer of the board of education. In every position which he occupied he rendered full and complete satisfaction. He was a man of good natural endowments, fine culture, and great skill in the practical application and use of his acquirements. He was also noted for his extraordinary energy of character, perseverance, sterling integrity, and wonderful endurance. The amount of work which he accomplished was enormous. Besides the large amount of writing done as editor of the *Messenger* and stated clerk of the Synod, he published, *Exercises on the Heidelberg Catechism:—Heidelberg Catechism Simplified:—Family Assistant*, a book of devotions:—*The Rum Plague*, translated from the German. He was also a frequent contributor to the *Guardian* and the *Mercersburg Review*. See *Ref. Church Mess.*, June 15, 1881. (D. Y. H.)

Fisher, Samuel Ware, D.D., LL.D., a Presbyterian minister, was born at Morristown, N. J., April 5, 1814. His father was an eminent Presbyterian minister in that town, his church being one of the largest in the state. Samuel graduated at Yale College in 1835; studied theology two years at Princeton, N. J., and one year at Union Seminary, New York. Shortly afterwards he was ordained pastor in West Bloomfield, N. J. Here he remained a little more than four years, and then was installed, Oct. 13, 1843, over the Fourth Presbyterian Church of Albany, N. Y. From Albany he removed to Cincinnati, O., and became pastor of the Second Presbyterian Church and successor of Dr. Lyman Beecher, entering upon the duties of his office in April, 1847. Here he had a brilliant and eminently successful ministry. A series of sermons preached by him to young men, *Three Great Temptations*, published in 1852, went through six editions. In the fall of 1858 he was inaugurated president of Hamilton College, N. Y., and remained in office eight years. He was installed pastor of the Westminster Church of Utica, Nov. 15, 1867, and remained four years in that position. His death took place at College Hill, near Cincinnati, O., Jan. 18, 1874. See *Biog. Encyclop. of Ohio*, p. 55; *Gen. Cat. of Union Theol. Sem.* 1876, p. 13. (J. C. S.)

Fisherman, *in Christian Art.* By this emblem our Lord and his disciples are frequently depicted on ancient monuments. The net is more rarely represented than the hook and line; but the net of St. Peter, with the Lord fishing with the line, is a device of the papal signets. At San Zenone, in Verona, the patron saint is thus represented, and this subject, with those of Abraham's sacrifice, Noah's ark, and others, on the bronze doors and marble front of that most important church, are specially valuable as connecting the earlier Lombard carvings with the most ancient and scriptural subjects of primitive church-work. This symbol, like the vine, is adopted from pagan decorations, which, of course, proves its antiquity.

Symbolical figure of the Divine or Apostolic fisher. (From an early representation.)

Delineation of a fisherman drawing forth a huge fish from the waters at Horeb. (From the Callixtine Catacomb.)

Fiske, Nathan, D.D., a Congregational minister, was born at Weston, Mass., Sept. 9, 1733. He graduated from Harvard College in 1754; became pastor May 28, 1758, in the Third Precinct, Brookfield, and died there, Nov. 25, 1799. He had a genius for progressive improvement. His preaching was practical, and yet abounded in the beauties of literary composition. Besides several sermons, two volumes of his essays, entitled *The Moral Monitor*, are among his published works. See Sprague, *Annals of the Amer. Pulpit*, i, 571.

Figure of the Lord holding in his hand a large fish, as if just drawn from the sea. (From an antique glass cup.)

Fitch, Chauncey W., D.D., a Protestant Episcopal clergyman, was for a number of years rector of the church in Piqua, O.; in 1861, of St. Stephen's Church, Terre Haute, Ind.; in 1864, of St. Paul's Church, Jeffersonville, and chaplain of the military hospital at that place; in 1866 was appointed post-chaplain at Fort Wayne, Detroit, Mich., a position which he continued to hold until 1875, when he removed to Jeffersonville, Ind., and died there, July 13, 1878, aged seventy-seven years. See *Prot. Episc. Almanac*, 1879, p. 168.

Fitch, Elijah, a Congregational minister, was born at Windham, Conn., in 1746, and graduated from Yale College in 1765. After preaching for a time in Franklin, Mass., he was ordained, Jan. 15, 1772, at Hopkinton, as colleague with Rev. Samuel Barrett, who died the December following, when Mr. Fitch became sole pastor of the church. He remained in office until his death, Dec. 16, 1788. He was a fine scholar and poet, as well as an excellent minister. See *Hist. of Mendon Association*, p. 117. (J. C. S.)

Fitton, James, one of the founders of the Roman Catholic Church in New England, was born in Boston, Mass., in 1803, and was confirmed by the first bishop of Boston, Dr. Cheverus. He attended the first Catholic school in New England, under Rev. Dr. Matignon, and was for a while teacher in the seminary attached to the old church in Franklin, where he had for one of his pupils, Dr. Williams, archbishop of Boston. He was ordained to the priesthood by Bishop Fenwick, Dec. 23, 1827. In 1829 he was sent on a mission to the Passamaquoddy Indians, in Maine, the same year to New Hampshire and Vermont, and soon established his headquarters at Hartford, Conn., where he purchased the first Catholic church, established the *Catholic Press*, and extended his labors to every county in Connecticut. He established what is now the College of the Holy Cross, at Worcester, Mass., and helped build the Catholic cause at Northampton, Providence, R. I., Newport, and other places in those two states. In August, 1855, he was transferred to East Boston, Mass., where he founded four parishes. He also established several schools. He died in Boston, Sept. 15, 1881. Mr. Fitton compiled *The Triumph of Religion*, edited the *Manual of St. Joseph*, a prayer-book, and was the author of a *History of the Catholic Church in New England* (1872). "His work is seen in the whole history of Catholicity in New England. No page can be written without his impress upon it. Wisdom filled his works; wisdom completed them. In life he seemed to us what he really was, a model priest" (Bishop Healy). See (N. Y.) *Catholic Annual*, 1883, p. 74.

Fitz, Daniel, D.D., a Congregational minister, was born in New Hampshire in 1795; graduated from Dartmouth College in 1818, and from Andover Theological Seminary in 1825; was ordained June 28, 1826, pastor of South Church, Ipswich, Mass., and died there, Sept. 2, 1869. See *Trien. Cat. of Andover Theol. Sem.* 1880, p. 64.

Fitz-Geffrey (or **Fitz-Geoffroi**), Charles, an English clergyman, was born in Cornwall about 1575; educated at Broadgate-hall, Oxford; became rector of St. Dominic's, in his own county, and died in 1636. He was an excellent Latin poet. His publications are, *Affaniæ sive Epigrammata*, lib. iii, and *Cenotaphia*, lib. i (1601):—a religious poem called the *Blessed Birthday* (1634, 1636). He also published some *Sermons*. See Chalmers, *Biog. Dict.* s. v.; Allibone, *Dict. of Brit. and Amer. Authors*, s. v.

Fitzgerald, Gerald, D.D., Hebrew professor in Dublin University; published *Originality and Permanence of the Biblical Hebrew* (1796):—*A Hebrew Grammar*, for the use of the students of the University of Dublin (1799). See Allibone, *Dict. of Brit. and Amer. Authors*, s. v.

Fitzherbert, Thomas, a zealous Roman Catholic, was born in Staffordshire in 1552; educated at Oxford; in 1614 became a Jesuit at Rome, and was rector of the English college in that city for twenty-three years. He died in 1640, leaving a treatise concerning *Policy and Religion* (1606–10), and several *Tracts in Defence of the Church.* See Allibone, *Dict. of Brit. and Amer. Authors*, s. v.

Fitz-James, François, *Duc de*, a French prelate and theologian, was born at Saint-Germain-en-Laye, June 9, 1709. He renounced his family dignities to enter the clerical life at the age of eighteen, and was appointed abbot of Saint Victor in 1727. He became bishop of Soissons in 1739, and afterwards succeeded cardinal of Auvergne, as first almoner of Louis XV. This prelate taught the rigid doctrines of Jansenism. He died at Soissons, July 19, 1764, and after his death his works were published under the title, *Œuvres Posthumes* (1769–70, 3 vols.). See Hoefer, *Nouv. Biog. Générale*, s. v.

Fitz-James, Richard, an English prelate, and a distinguished benefactor of Merton College, Oxford, was a native of Somersetshire. He went to Oxford about 1459, and in 1465 was elected probationer fellow of Merton College; in 1473 was proctor; in March, 1484, vicar of Minehead, and about the same time rector of Aller, in Somersetshire. In May, 1496, he was consecrated bishop of Rochester, from which, January, 1503, he was translated to Chichester, and in March, 1505, to the see of London. He died Jan. 15, 1522.

Fitz-Jocelin, REGINALD, an English prelate, was the son of Jocelin, bishop of Salisbury, and was born in 1141. Early in life he was appointed archdeacon of Salisbury; when thirty-three he was elected to the important see of Bath and Wells, in 1174. He accompanied the archbishop-elect of Canterbury to Rome soon after, and was consecrated at the Church of St. John de Maurienne, in Savoy, by Richard, archbishop of Canterbury. On his return to England he was enthroned in great state. There was some opposition to this appointment. Reginald appears to have been a weak, well-meaning man, probably under the influence of his associates. In 1191 he was very unexpectedly elected to the see of Canterbury. Reginald sent to Rome for the pallium, and would have gone himself had he not been detained by illness. Meantime his illness increased, and he said "It is God's will that I should not be an archbishop, and my will submits to his." He died Dec. 26, 1191. See Hook, *Lives of the Abps. of Canterbury*, ii, 574 sq.

Fitzpatrick, JOHN BERNARD, D.D., a Roman Catholic bishop, was born of Irish parents, in Boston, Mass., Nov. 1, 1812. He received his education at Boston, the College of Montreal, and the Sulpitian Seminary, Paris. He was ordained priest in 1840, in 1844 was consecrated coadjutor-bishop of Boston, and in 1846 succeeded bishop Fenwick in the episcopacy. He died Feb. 13, 1866.

Fitz-Ralph, RICHARD, an Irish prelate, is supposed to have been born in Devonshire. He was educated at Oxford, and in 1347 was created archbishop of Armagh. He was a strenuous opponent of the mendicant orders; and being in London at a time when a warm contest was carried on between the friars and secular clergy, about preaching, hearing confessions, etc., he delivered several sermons, in which he laid down nine conclusions against the mendicants. Upon complaint made by the latter to the pope, Richard was ordered to appear at Avignon, which he did, and well defended his views. Miracles were attributed to him after his decease, in 1360, and a fruitless application for his canonization was made to Boniface IX. He wrote, *Sermones ad Crucem Londinensem* (1356):—*Adversus Errores Armenorum* (Paris, 1612):—*Defensio Curatorum adversus Fratres Mendicantes*, etc. (Paris, 1496):—*De Laudibus S. Deiparæ*. Bayle says that he translated the New Test. into Irish.

Fitzsimon, Henry, a zealous Jesuit, was born at Dublin in 1569, educated at Oxford, and died in 1644. He published a *Justification of the Mass* (1611):—a *Catalogue of the Irish Saints* (1621), and some other theological treatises in defence of his faith. See Chalmers, *Biog. Dict.* s. v.; Allibone, *Dict. of Brit. and Amer. Authors*, s. v.

Fitzsimon, Patrick, D.D., an Irish prelate, was dean of Dublin, and was appointed to the see of Dublin in 1763, having previously been parish priest of St. Audeon's. He filled this see six years, and died in Francis Street, Dublin, in 1769. His life seems to have been so unobtrusive and purely ecclesiastical as to leave no materials of interest for a memoir. See D'Alton, *Memoirs of the Abps. of Dublin*, p. 471.

Fitzsimon, Walter, an Irish prelate, was a bachelor of civil and canon law, a learned divine and philosopher, precentor of St. Patrick's Church, whose chapter he represented as proxy in a parliament of 1478. On June 14, 1484, he was appointed to the see of Dublin, and consecrated in St. Patrick's Cathedral, Sept. 26 following. In 1487 this prelate was one of those who espoused the cause of Lambert Simnel, and were accessory to his coronation in Christ Church. In 1488 Fitzsimon was permitted to renew his allegiance, and receive pardon through Sir Richard Edgecombe. In 1492 this prelate was made deputy to Jasper, duke of Bedford. While in this situation he endeavored to promote industrious habits among the more indolent of the people. In 1496 he held a provincial synod in the Church of the Holy Trinity, on which occasion an annual contribution for seven years was settled by the clergy of the province, to provide salaries for the lecturers of the university in St. Patrick's Cathedral. In May of the same year he granted to John Alleyne, dean of St. Patrick's, license to build a hospital for the relief of poor Catholics. In 1508 he was deputy to Gerald, earl of Kildare, and in 1509 lord-chancellor. He died May 14, 1511, at Finglass. See D'Alton, *Memoirs of the Abps. of Dublin*, p. 171.

Fix, CHRISTIAN GOTTHELF, a Lutheran theologian, was born at Chemnitz, June 5, 1761, and died there, Jan. 6, 1809. He published, *Der Kursächsische Kirchenstaat vor der Reformation* (Freiburg, 1806, 1807, 3 vols.):—*Abriss der Kursächsischen Kirchen- und Consistorialverfassung* (Leipsic, 1795, 2 vols.):—*Geistliche Statistik vom Königreich Sachsen* (Giessen, 1800). See Winer, *Handbuch der theol. Lit.* i, 800. (B. P.)

Flabellum (*fan;* Gr. ῥιπίδιον). Among the evidences of the Eastern origin of the Christian religion is the use of this implement during the celebration of the eucharist. Having its birthplace and earliest home in a climate teeming with insect life, where food exposed uncovered is instantly blackened and polluted by swarms of flies, it was natural that the bread and wine of its sacramental feast should be guarded from defilement by the customary precautions. The *flabellum* having been

Greek Flabellum. Armenian Flabellum.

once introduced among the furniture of the altar for necessary uses, in process of time became one of its regular ornaments, and was thus transferred to the more temperate climates of the West, where its original purpose was almost forgotten.

The earliest notice of it as a liturgical ornament is in the *Apostolical Constitutions*, which direct that after the oblation, before and during the prayer of consecration, two deacons are to stand, one on either side of the altar, holding a *flabellum* made of thin membrane (parchment), or of peacock feathers, or of fine linen, and quietly drive away the flies and other small insects, that they strike not against the vessels. In the liturgies also of Chrysostom and Basil, the deacons are directed to fan the holy oblations during the prayer of consecration. This fanning ceased with the Lord's Prayer, and was not resumed. Early writers furnish many notices of the use of the *flabellum* as an essential part of the liturgical ceremonial. Moschus (*Prat. Spirit.* 196), when narrating how some shepherd boys near Apamea were imitating the celebration of the eucharist in childish sport, is careful to mention that two of the children stood on either side of the celebrant, vibrating their handkerchiefs like fans.

As the deacons were the officers appointed to wave the fan over the sacred oblations, its delivery constitutes a part of many of the Oriental forms for the ordination to the diaconate. After the stole has been given

Deacon fanning the Infant Saviour Seated on the Knees of his Mother. (From a gilded glass found in the Catacombs.)

and placed on the left shoulder, the holy fan is put into the deacon's hands, and he is placed "at the side of the holy table to fan;" and again, the deacon is directed to take the fan and stand at the right side of the table, and wave it over the holy things. See cut under ELEVATION OF THE HOST.

Although there is no mention of the *flabellum* in the

Liturgical Flabellum of the Abbey of Tournus.

Latin ritual books, there is no doubt that it was used by the Western Church at an early time. The fan appears to have gradually fallen into disuse there, and to have almost entirely ceased by the 14th century. At the present day, the only relic of the usage is in the magnificent fans of peacocks' feathers carried by the attendants of the pope in solemn processions on certain great festivals.

Though the original intention of the fan was one of simple utility, various mystical meanings collected round it. Reference has been already made to the idea that these feather fans typified the cherubim and seraphim surrounding the holy throne. Germanus also holds (*Contemp. Rev. Eccles.* p. 157) that the vibration of the fans typifies the tremor and astonishment of the angels at our Lord's Passion. We find the same idea in a passage from the monk Job, given by Photius, who also states (*Cod.* v, 25) that another purpose of the vibration of the fans was the raising of the mind from the material elements of the eucharist, and fixing them on the spiritual realities.

See Martigny, *De l'Usage du Flabellum;* Bingham, *Christ. Antiq.* viii, 6, § 21; xv, 3, § 6; Bona, *Rer. Liturg.* i, 25, § 6; Augusti, *Christl. Archäol.* iii, 536 sq.; *Archæol. Jour.* v, 200; xiv, 17; Smith, *Dict. of Christ. Antiq.* s. v.

Flaccilla (sometimes written *Placilla or Placidia*), an early Christian empress, was a Spaniard by birth, or rather, perhaps, daughter of Antonius (præfect of Gaul); was married to Theodosius I, in 376, by whom she had several children. She was a woman of great virtue and charity; died apparently in 385, and is commemorated as a saint in the Greek Church on Sept. 14.

Flaccillus (written also *Flacillus, Placillus, Flacitus, Placetus,* and *Placentius*), Arian bishop of Antioch, A.D. 333–342.

Flachs, SIGISMUND ANDREAS, a Lutheran theologian of Germany, was born Nov. 21, 1692, studied at Leipsic, where he was also adjunctus of the philosophical faculty, and died at Leisnig, in Saxony, in 1745, leaving, *De Restitutendis Duobus Versibus Jos.* 21 (Leipsic, 1714):—*De Casu Stellarum in Fine Mundi* (ibid. 1718):—*De Vocibus ἅπαξ λεγομένοις in Epistola Jacobi* (ibid. 1727):—*Einleitung zur Augsburgischen Confession* (ibid. 1730). See Winer, *Handbuch der theol. Lit.* i, 272; Fürst, *Bibl. Jud.* i, 282; Jöcher, *Allgemeines Gelehrten-Lexikon*, s. v. (B. P.)

Flacksenius, Jacobus, a Finnish theologian and physician, a native of Mackyla, was provost of the cathedral of Abo. In 1665 he taught logic and metaphysics in that same city; in 1679 he lectured on theology, and died in 1696, leaving, *Institutiones Pneumaticæ* (Abo, 1664):—*Collegium Logicum* (ibid. 1678). See Hoefer, *Nouv. Biog. Générale*, s. v.

Flacksenius, Johann, a Lutheran theologian and prelate of Finland, was born at Mackyla in 1636. He studied at the University of Abo, of which he became secretary in 1665. Still later he was successively connected with the faculty of philosophy, professor of mathematics in 1669, and pastor in 1682. Finally he became bishop of Wiborg, and died July 11, 1708, leaving, among other works, *Oratio Funebris in Abitum M. Andreæ Thuronis*, etc. (Abo, 1665):—*De Ecclesia Ejusque Subjecto*, etc. (1689):—*Sylloge Systematum Theologiæ*, etc. (ibid. 1690):—*Chronologia Sacra* (ibid. 1692):—*Harmoniæ Evangelicæ* (ibid. 1701). See Hoefer, *Nouv. Biog. Générale*, s. v.

Flaget, BENEDICT JOSEPH, a Roman Catholic prelate, was born at Courtenay, Auvergne, Nov. 7, 1763. He entered the Sulpitian seminary at Clermont, and after his ordination was received into the society of St. Sulpice. As the troubles of the French revolution came on he offered himself to bishop Carroll for service in America, and arrived in Philadelphia, Nov. 7, 1793. His first mission was at Vincennes, Ind., one of the oldest French settlements in the West, whence he was recalled in 1795 to assume a professorship in Georgetown College. On Nov. 4, 1810, he was consecrated bishop of the new diocese of Bardstown. His zealous labors extended to St. Louis and New Orleans. He established a seminary in his new diocese, and by the aid of priests like David, Elder, Byrne, and the Dominican and Jesuit fathers, institutions arose to meet the needs of his flock. In 1832 his resignation of his see was accepted, but, with Dr. Chalrat as coadjutor, he was reinstated. Bishop Flaget then visited Rome, when the pope urged him to travel through France and Northern Italy, to commend the Association for the Propagation of the Faith. Cures said to have been effected by his prayers added to the force of his reputation. Returning to Kentucky, he resumed his toilsome labors. After his see was removed to Louisville, Dr. Chalrat resigned, and M. J. Spalding, afterwards the learned archbishop of Baltimore, succeeded him. Bishop Flaget closed his long and laborious life, Feb. 11, 1850. See *Cath. Almanac*, 1872, p. 57; De Courcy and Shea, *Hist. of the Cath. Church in the United States*, p. 70, 538.

Flambard (or **Passeflabere**), RANULPH (or RALPH), an English prelate, and justiciar under William Rufus, was a Norman of low birth, who came to England in the train of William the Conqueror, in 1066. He took holy orders, obtained several Church preferments, was appointed chaplain to the bishop of London, and made prebendary of St. Paul's. He afterwards entered the service of William II, who made him his chaplain. By his unscrupulous artifices with the king he raised himself to the highest places in Church and State. He seems to have been the first man to apply feudalism to the estates of the Church. He suggested that they should be considered as fiefs or benefices held of the king, which at every vacancy should devolve to the crown till the vacancy was supplied. After the death of Lanfranc the king gave himself up unreservedly to Flambard. The justiciar obtained for himself the custody of the vacant abbeys of Winchester and Chertsey, the bishopric of Lincoln, and the archbishopric of Canterbury. His oppressive measures brought him into such odium that an attempt was made in 1099 to murder him at sea, which, however, proved unsuccessful. He was then rewarded with the see of Durham, for which he was obliged to pay the king £1000. On the death of William II, in 1100, he was imprisoned in the Tower, "the first man," says Freeman, "recorded to have dwelled as a prisoner in the Conqueror's fortress." In February of the following year he managed to escape from his prison, and fled to Normandy. There he joined duke Robert, instigated him to invade England, whither he returned with him. He was afterwards restored to his see, and appears to have attended to his duties faithfully the rest of his life. He completed his cathedral, built Norham castle, and fortified Durham. He endowed the college of Christchurch, and founded the priory of Motitsford. He died Sept. 5, 1128. See *Encyclop. Brit.* 9th ed. s. v.

Flaminia, the name of a young priestess, who assisted the *Flaminica* in her sacred duties. This was also the name given to the house of the *Flamen Dialis*, from which no one could carry out fire except for sacred purposes.

Flaminĭca, the wife of the *Flamen Dialis* (see FLAMEN), or priest of Jupiter, among the ancient Romans. She was put under the same restrictions as her husband, and if she died he was compelled to resign his office. She sacrificed a ram to Jupiter on each of the *Nundinæ* (q. v.).

Flaminio (originally *Tarrabini*), MARCO ANTONIO, an eminent Italian poet, was born at Seravalle, in 1498, studied philosophy at Bologna, attached himself to various ecclesiastics, and died at Rome, Feb. 18, 1550, judge of St. Peter. He was appointed secretary for the Council of Trent, but, being of a friendly disposition towards Luther and his work, he refused to accept the appointment. He wrote several poetical works, especially, *In Librum Psalmorum Brevis Explanatio* (Venice, 1545). See Winer, *Handbuch der Theol. Lit.* i, 207; Fürst, *Bibl. Jud.* i, 282; Jöcher, *Allgemeines Gelehrten-Lexikon*, s. v.; Chalmers, *Biog. Dict.* s. v.; Hoefer, *Nouv. Biog. Générale*, s. v. (B. P.)

Flanders, CHARLES WORTHEN, D.D., a Baptist minister, was born at Salisbury, Mass., in February, 1807. He graduated at Brown University in 1839; pursued his theological studies with Rev. John Wayland, D.D. (a brother of Dr. F. Wayland), then pastor of the First Baptist Church in Salem; was ordained over the First Baptist Church in Danvers, Nov. 11, 1840, remaining there for nearly ten years, when he took charge of the First Baptist Church at Concord, N. H.; and subsequently was pastor of Baptist churches in Kennebunkport, Me., and Westboro and Beverly Farms, Mass. He died at Beverly, Aug. 2, 1875. (J. C. S.)

Flaviānus, the second of that name, bishop of Antioch, A.D. 498–512, was weak and vacillating in moral character, originally a monk at Tilmognon, in Cœle-Syria, later nuncio of the Church of Antioch at the imperial court in Constantinople, and was deposed in consequence of the Monophysite troubles at Alexandria, ending his life in banishment, A.D. 518. See Smith, *Dict. of Christ. Biog.* s. v.

Fleck, FERDINAND FLORENS, a Lutheran theologian of Germany, was born at Dresden, April 5, 1800, and died, doctor and professor of theology, at Leipsic, in 1849, leaving, *De Regno Christi* (Leipsic, 1826):—*De Regno Divino* (ibid. 1829):—*Otium Theologicum* (ibid. 1831):—*Wissenschaftliche Reise*, etc. (ibid. 1835–38, 2 vols.):—*Die Vertheidigung des Christenthums* (ibid. 1842):—*System der christlichen Dogmatik* (ibid. 1847):—*Der Fortschritt des Menschengeschlechts* (Giessen, 1848). He also edited *Testamentum Novum, Vulgatæ Editionis*, etc. (Leipsic, 1840). See Winer, *Handbuch der Theol. Lit.* i, 440; Zuchold, *Bibl. Theol.* i, 363. (B. P.)

Fleetwood, JOHN, D.D., probably an assumed name for the author of the *Christian Prayer-book* (Lond. 1772):—*Christian Dictionary* (1773):—*Life of Christ* (often printed, and formerly very popular):—and *Lives of the Apostles, John the Baptist, and the Virgin Mary* (Glasgow, 1813). See Allibone, *Dict. of Brit. and Amer. Authors*, s. v.

Flekeles, ELEAZAR *ben-David*, a Jewish rabbi, was born at Prague in 1754, and died there in 1826, leaving אַהֲבַת דָּוִד, a disquisition and criticism of the sect of the Sabbathæans in Prague, (1800):—עוֹלַת צִבּוּר, a collection of derashas, in which he vents his ire against the translators of the Bible, especially against the school of Moses Mendelssohn (1787):—מְלֶאכֶת הַקֹּדֶשׁ, on the holy names of God in the Scripture (1812). See Fürst, *Bibl. Jud.* i, 283 sq.; Spitz, זִכָּרוֹן אֱלְעָזָר, or *Biography of Flekeles* (Prague, 1827). (B. P.)

Flemael (Fr. *Flémalle*), BERTHOLET, an eminent Flemish painter, was born at Liege in 1614, and was a pupil of Gerard Doufflest, at Liege, whence he went to Italy, and studied the works of the great masters. He soon gained distinction, and was invited to Florence by the grand duke of Tuscany, to do some work. He went to Paris, and painted for the cupola of the Carmelites, *Elijah taken up into Heaven*, and *Elisha Receiving the Mantle of the Prophet*. He also painted the *Adoration of the Magi*, for the sacristy of the Augustines. He returned to his native city in 1647, and was employed in many important works for the churches, the first of which was *The Crucifixion*, for one of the collegiate chapels, which gained him great reputation. Some of his other principal works are, *The Elevation of the Cross; The Assumption of the Virgin; The Conversion of St. Paul; The Raising of Lazarus*, and *The Crucifixion*. He was elected a member, and subsequently a professor, of the Royal Academy at Paris. He died at Liege in

1675. See Spooner, *Biog. Hist. of the Fine Arts*, s. v.; Hoefer, *Nouv. Biog. Générale*, s. v.

Fleming, Alexander (1), D.D., a Scotch clergyman, son of a farmer in Hawkwood, was born July 30, 1747; licensed to preach March 28, 1780; presented by the duke of Hamilton to the living at Hamilton, second charge, and ordained Nov. 17, 1785; appointed one of the king's chaplains in ordinary in Scotland, Sept. 7, 1799, and died May 28, 1830. See *Fasti Eccles. Scoticanæ*, ii, 261.

Fleming, Alexander (2), D.D., a Scotch clergyman, graduated at Glasgow University; was licensed to preach Jan. 20, 1801; elected by the parishioners to the living at Neilston, Paisley, in June, and ordained Sept. 27, 1804. The parishioners, in 1826, refused to take the sittings by auction, which led to protracted litigation, ending in an appeal to the House of Lords in April, 1834. The assembly publicly thanked Mr. Fleming, in 1833, for his zeal, labors, and great exertions in the cause. The want of increased accommodation being felt in many other places gave rise to the appointment of a committee of the assembly in May, 1828, for Church accommodation, which merged in May, 1835, into that of the committee for Church extension, and has led to the erection of more than one hundred and fifty additional churches and parishes. Dr. Fleming died June 10, 1845, aged seventy-four years. His publications were numerous, and treated chiefly of Church matters in controversy at the time, one of which related to the building and endowing of churches. He printed *An Historical Lecture on Teinds* (1835):—a *Sermon* preached at the admission of Rev. R. Stevenson (1836):—*A Letter to Sir Robert Peel* (1842):—*An Account of the Parish of Neilston.* See *Fasti Eccles. Scoticanæ*, ii, 231, 232.

Fleming, Caleb, D.D., a distinguished English Independent minister, was born at Nottingham in 1698, and studied classical and scientific subjects and mathematics under able teachers in Nottingham and London. The bishops of Winchester and Carlisle made him handsome and liberal offers to enter the Church, but his preference was for nonconformity, and he accepted a pastorate in Bartholomew Close in 1738, with a small salary. He objected to a confession of faith and to the imposition of hands. In 1753 he was appointed to succeed Dr. Foster as minister at Pinner's Hall. Here he labored till his death, July 21, 1779. His published works are mostly of a controversial character, the first issued in 1729, the last in 1775, and they are fifty in number. They show much learning and research, but his doctrines were Socinian in character, and they imbittered his temper and kept him in a continual atmosphere of contention and disputation. See Wilson, *Dissenting Churches*, ii, 283.

Fleming, John (1), D.D., a Scotch clergyman, son of William F., minister of Houston, was licensed to preach April 24, 1734; called in January to the living at Kilmalcolm, ordained June 23, 1737, and died June 30, 1787, aged seventy-five years. He was distinguished for his talents, knowledge, conduct, and piety, which commanded the highest esteem and respect. See *Fasti Eccles. Scoticanæ*, ii, 251.

Fleming, John (2), D.D., a Scotch clergyman, son of Alexander, of Bathgate, was born Jan. 10, 1785; licensed to preach April 22, 1806; called to the living at Bressay in August, and ordained Sept. 22, 1808; transferred to Flisk, Cupar, in 1810, and admitted April 18, 1811; promoted to Clackmannan, Sept. 4, 1832; admitted professor of natural philosophy in the university and King's College, Aberdeen; but in 1843, having become identified with the Free Church, he resigned his position, and two years later became professor of natural science in the Free Church College of Edinburgh. He died Nov. 18, 1857. His writings were chiefly scientific. See *Fasti Eccles. Scoticanæ*, ii, 251, 494, 697; iii, 424, 697.

Fleming, Patrick, an Irish Roman Catholic ecclesiastic and writer, was born at Louth, April 17, 1599. He was appointed lecturer of divinity at Prague, where he remained until the city was besieged by the elector of Saxony in 1631, when he was murdered. He published *Collectanea Sacra*, or *Lives of Irish and Scotch Saints* (1667). See Chalmers, *Biog. Dict.* s. v.; Allibone, *Dict. of Brit. and Amer. Authors*, s. v.

Fleming (or **Flemmynge**), **Richard**, an English prelate, and the founder of Lincoln College, Oxford, was born at Crofton, in Yorkshire, about 1360, and educated at University College, Oxford. In 1406 he was presented to the prebend of South Newbold, in the Church of York, and in 1407 was proctor of the university. In 1415, being rector of Boston, in Lincolnshire, he exchanged his prebend of South Newbold for that of Langford, in the Cathedral Church of York, and in April, 1420, was promoted to the see of Lincoln. In 1428 he executed that decree of the Council of Constance which ordered that the bones of Wycklif should be taken up and burned. He died at Sleford, Jan. 25, 1431.

Fleming, Thomas (1), D.D., an Irish prelate, of the family of the barons of Slane, was a Franciscan friar, and for some time a professor of theology in Louvain. He was made archbishop of Dublin, Oct. 23, 1623. In conformity with a proclamation issued by lord Falkland, in April, 1629, the archbishop and mayor of Dublin seized upon several priests in that city in the act of saying mass, their ornaments were taken from them, the images battered and destroyed, and the priests and friars were delivered up to the soldiers. Between the years 1633 and 1640, Dr. Fleming's life appears to have been passed in the unobtrusive exercise of his ecclesiastical duties. In 1640 he presided at a provincial council, which was held at Tycrogher, in the county of Kildare. In 1642 archbishop Fleming, being much annoyed with the affairs of the country, sent the Rev. Joseph Everard to appear as his proxy at the synod of the Roman Catholic clergy, which met at Kilkenny in May of that year. On June 20, 1643, archbishop Fleming and the archbishop of Tuam were the only prelates who signed the commission authorizing Nicholas, viscount Gormanston, Lucas Dillon, Sir Robert Talbot, and others, to treat with the marquis of Ormond for the cessation of arms. In July, 1644, he was present at the general assembly, when the oath of association was agreed upon, whereby every confederate swore to bear true faith and allegiance to the king and his heirs, to maintain the fundamental laws of Ireland, the free exercise of the Roman Catholic faith, and to obey the orders and decrees of the supreme council. In 1649 he was one of those who signed the declaration, at Clonmacnoise, reconciling all former differences. In October, 1650, this prelate, in person, at Galway, signed the document authorizing Dr. Nicholas French, bishop of Ferns, and Hugh Rochfort, to treat and agree with any Catholic prince, state, republic, or person as they might deem expedient for the preservation of the Catholic religion. He died about 1666. See D'Alton, *Memoirs of the Abps. of Dublin*, p. 390.

Fleming, Thomas (2), D.D., a Scotch clergyman, a native of Kirkmichael, was educated at the parish-school of Blairgowrie, at the grammar-school, Perth, and at the universities of St. Andrews and Edinburgh. He became tutor to Robert Haldane, of Airthrey, and his brother, who were the founders of the Tabernacle Church; was licensed to preach Nov. 5, 1777; called March 4 to the living at Kirkmichael, and ordained April 29, 1779; transferred to Kenmore July 4, 1780, and presented to the living by the earl of Breadalbane; promoted to Kirkcaldy by George III, in July, 1788; transferred to Lady Yester's Chapel of Ease in Edinburgh, April 17, 1806, and died July 19, 1824, aged seventy years. He was characterized by enlightened piety, holy deportment, the diligent discharge of public and private duty, and the strenuous opposition he gave to infidelity and vice. The benevolent institutions of Edinburgh reaped much advantage from his friendly counsels and aid; he gave particular attention to the affairs of George Heriot's Hospital, the Orphan Hospital, the Edinburgh Education Society, and the Christian Knowledge Society. He published three single *Sermons* (1790-1809):—*Sermons* (Edinburgh, 1826):—*A Remarkable Agitation of the Waters of Loch Tay* (Trans. Royal Soc. Edinb.):—*An Account of the Parish of Kirkcaldy*:—*Memoir of Robert Cathcart, Esq., of Drum.* He translated the Shorter Catechism into Gaelic, and assisted in revising the translation of the Scriptures into Gaelic. See *Fasti Eccles. Scoticanæ*, i, 64; ii, 516, 804, 824.

Fleming, William, D.D., a Scotch clergyman, a native of Strathaven, studied at Glasgow University; was licensed to preach April 28, 1818; became assistant in succession to the Rev. Dr. Pollock, of Govan, and Dr. Taylor, of St. Enoch's, Glasgow; was presented by George IV, in February, 1826, to the living at Westruther, and ordained May 11; transferred to Old Kilpatrick in August of the same year. Having been elected professor of Oriental languages in Glasgow University, he resigned his benefice Oct. 23, 1832, and died March 3, 1866, aged seventy-four years. See *Fasti Eccles. Scoticanæ*, i, 537; ii, 362.

Flemish Version OF THE SCRIPTURES. This is merely a dialectic variety of the Dutch. It is spoken in East and West Flanders, in Antwerp, and in part of Limburg. It is also spoken in the arrondissements of Brussels and Louvain, in Brabant, and even in parts of the neighboring departments of France. The first printed edition of the Belgic or Flemish Bible appears to have been that published at Delft in 1477, and again at Gouda in 1479. Other editions were printed at Antwerp in 1518 and 1525. In 1526 another translation of the Scriptures into Belgic was made by several learned men, and published at Antwerp. The next edition was that of the Old Test. by William Vosterman, published at Antwerp in 1528; the New Test. was published in 1531, and again in 1533. This edition was followed by others, almost too numerous to be here specified. Many of these editions were afterwards prohibited by the Inquisition, and their continued publication was suspended by the edict of Charles V, in 1546. In spite of this edict, certain divines of the University of Louvain, among others Nicholas von Wingh, a regular canon of Louvain, undertook the revision and correction of the Belgic version according to the last revision of the Vulgate, and this revised edition was published under the sanction of the emperor, at Louvain and Cologne, in 1548. After numerous editions of this version had been issued at Antwerp, it was revised and corrected by the doctors of Louvain, according to the text of the Vulgate, as revised by order of pope Clement VIII. This revised translation was printed by Plantin, at Antwerp, in 1599; again at Cologne in 1604, and at Antwerp in 1626; and it may, perhaps, be regarded as the standard Flemish version. Several other revised editions of this version followed. In 1717, Algidius Wit, a Ghent divine, published another version of the Belgic Scriptures, and about the same time another translation was commenced by Andrew Scurrius, at Gorcum. Two volumes were printed at Utrecht in 1715-17, but the death of the translator, in 1719, put an end to the work, when he had carried it only as far as the Second Book of Kings. It is said to be in the purest dialect of the Flemish. Another Flemish translation, according to the Vulgate, was printed at Antwerp in 1717, and again at Utrecht in 1718. In 1820, in accordance with the wishes of the people, permission was given by the archbishop of Malines to print an edition of the Flemish New Test., translated by Maurenhof. This appeared at Brussels about 1821; an edition of the whole Bible was printed at the same time from the Louvain edition of 1599. In 1837 the British and Foreign Bible Society published an edition of the Flemish Testament under the superintendence of her agent, Mr. W. P. Tiddy, then residing at Brussels. Soon other editions of the Test., and an edition of the entire Bible followed. Of late the British and Foreign Bible Society has undertaken a revision of the Flemish New Test., and in the report for 1877 we read that pastor De Jonghe has, "at the request of the committee, undertaken a new translation of St. Matthew's gospel from the Greek into Flemish, with the assistance of M. Matthyssen, of Antwerp. This new version has been ordered, not so much in deference to the wishes of the Belgian Protestant clergy, who make use of the Dutch states-general version, but from a desire not to be restricted in the Flemish to the Louvain translation, which was made from the Vulgate at the end of the 16th century, but to have a version made directly from the original. M. Matthyssen is also superintending a new edition of the Louvain Test., in which the orthography will be conformed to that now in general use, and adopted by the Belgian government." Of the revised edition the four gospels and Acts are now circulated. Up to March 31, 1884, the British and Foreign Bible Society had disposed of 248,075 parts of the Flemish Bible version. (B. P.)

Flessa, JOHANN ADAM, a Lutheran theologian of Germany, was born Dec. 24, 1694. He studied at Altdorf, was in 1723 professor at the gymnasium in Bayreuth, and in 1727 court-deacon to the margrave George Friedrich Carl. In 1741 he was called as professor of theology and director of the gymnasium at Altona, and died at Oldenburg, Oct. 11, 1775. He wrote, *De Beneficiorum Fundamento in Futurum, ex* 1 *Tim.* 6, 19 (Altdorf, 1716):—*Diss. Theses Theologico-Ecclesiasticæ* (Bayreuth, 1731):—*De Illo Paulino* ὀρθοτομεῖν *ad* 2 *Tim.* 2, 15 (ibid. 1733):—*De Fatis Babylonis* θεοπνευστίας *Prophetarum Testibus* (Altona, 1748). See Döring, *Die gelehrten Theologen Deutschlands*, 1, 412 sq. (B. P.)

Fletcher, Charles, a Methodist Episcopal minister, was born near Leeds, Yorkshire, England, Jan. 10, 1811. He was converted in 1827, licensed in 1829, and was for several years a local preacher in England and America. He joined the New York East Conference in 1852, filling the stations of Summerfield Church, Brooklyn; Birmingham and Bridgeport, Conn.; Seventh Street and Twenty-seventh Street, New York city; Mamaroneck, New York; Meriden, Conn.; Sands Street, Brooklyn; First Church, New Haven; Pacific Street, Brooklyn. He served full terms as presiding elder of Long Island South and New York East Districts. Death closed his successful ministry, April 20, 1880. He was an excellent preacher, and people of mature judgment and scholarship and of cultivated taste, sat under his ministry with delight. See *Minutes of Annual Conferences*, 1881, p. 79.

Fletcher, David, A.M., a Scotch prelate, second son of Andrew, of Dundee, graduated at the University of St. Andrews in 1625; was elected by the town council to the second charge, or collegiate church, at Edinburgh, and admitted May 22, 1635; in 1638 was assaulted and maltreated by several women for refusing to obey some unruly people in the city; was deposed by the commission of assembly, Jan. 1, 1639, for disobeying the General Assembly at Glasgow, and reading and defending the service-book; but restored by the General Assembly in August following; was admitted to the living at Melrose, Feb. 4, 1641; was a member of the commission of assembly in 1645 and 1647; and promoted to the bishopric of Argyll in 1662, yet retaining his benefice in conjunction till his death in March, 1665, aged about sixty years. See *Fasti Eccles. Scoticanæ*, i, 14, 560.

Fletcher, Giles, an English theologian and poet, nephew of bishop Richard Fletcher, was born about 1588; educated at Cambridge; entered into orders, and became in 1617 rector of Alderton, Suffolk, which position he retained till his death in 1623. Besides some minor effusions, he is thought to have been the author of *Christ's Victory and Triumph over Death*, a poem of considerable celebrity (Cambridge, 1610, 4to; 1632, 1640, 1783; improved ed. by Grosart, Lond. 1869).

Fletcher, Horace, D.D., a Baptist minister, was born at Cavendish, Vt., Oct. 28, 1796; graduated from Dartmouth College; studied law, and practiced it in his native village; became a teacher in the academy at North Bennington; was licensed, and in 1843 called to a pastoral charge in the latter place, and so continued until his death at Townshend, Nov. 26, 1871. (J.C.S.)

Fletcher, Joshua, D.D., a Baptist minister, was born at Kingsbury, Washington Co., N. Y., April 27, 1804; graduated from what is now Madison University in 1829; shortly after was ordained pastor of a Church in Saratoga, where he remained until 1848. His other pastorates were in Amenia and Cambridge, in Southington, Conn., and Wallingford, Vt. He died at Wallingford, May 8, 1882. See Cathcart, *Baptist Encyclop.* p. 400. (J. C. S.)

Fletcher, Richard, D.D., an English prelate, was probably a native of Kent; graduated from Trinity College in 1563; in September, 1572, was instituted to the prebend of Islington; in 1585 received that of Sutton-Longa, in the Church of Lincoln; in 1589 was promoted by Queen Elizabeth to the bishopric of Bristol; in 1592 was translated to Worcester, and about two years after to the see of London. He died in London, June 15, 1596.

Fleuriau, Louis Gaston, a French prelate, was born in Paris in 1662. After he had been canonist successively of Chartres, abbot of Moreilles, and treasurer of St. Chapelle, he was appointed, in 1698, bishop of Aire, and transferred in 1706 to the episcopal see of Orleans. On his entry into the city he delivered eight hundred and fifty-four debtors from the prison. He died Jan. 11, 1733, leaving, *Ordonnances Règlements et Avis Synodaux* (Orleans, 1736):—*Histoire de l'Entrée de Louis Gaston Fleuriau d'Annenonville* (Paris, 1707):—*Discours Académique* (Orleans, eod.). See Hoefer, *Nouv. Biog. Générale*, s. v.

Fleury (Lat. *Floriacum*), a French town, famous for its Benedictine abbey, was situated in the department of Loiret-on-the-Loire, not far from Sully. The abbey was founded about the year 640, and, after the bones of St. Benedict were transported there in 653, it became very famous. The school founded there by St. Odo was soon known as a seat of learning. The monastery, with its library, was destroyed in 1652 by the Calvinists. See Rocher, *L'Histoire de l'Abbaye Royale de St.-Benoît-sur-Loire* (Orleans, 1865); Berger, in Lichtenberger's *Encyclop. des Sciences Religieuses*, s. v. (B. P.)

Fleury, André Hercule de, a French statesman and prelate, was born at Lodève, June 22, 1653; studied early at the College of Clermont, in Paris, and afterwards at that of Harcourt; entered into political life, was made bishop of Fréjus about 1707, but left that position in 1715 for the abbey of Tournus, and afterwards for that of St. Stephen, in Caen; in 1726 was made cardinal, and died at Paris, Jan. 29, 1743. See Hoefer, *Nouv. Biog. Générale*, s. v.

Flexman, Robert, D.D., an English Presbyterian minister, was born at Great Torrington, Devonshire, Feb. 22, 1707-8. He studied for the ministry at Tiverton Academy; in 1730 was ordained at Modbury; next spent five years at Crediton, and four years at Chard, and settled at Bradford, Wilts, in 1739. In 1747 he removed to Rotherhithe, London. In 1783 his health failing, he resigned, and the Church was dissolved, but he continued the morning lecture at St. Helen's. He afterwards preached occasionally as health permitted. His published works were varied. He was a man of prodigious memory, which secured him the task of compiling the general index to the journals of the House of Commons from 1660 to 1697. He published sermons, tracts, and several important biographical sketches of distinguished ministers. He died June 14, 1795. See Wilson, *Dissenting Churches*, iv, 361-366.

Flimmer, Johannes, a Lutheran theologian and hymn-writer, was born in 1512. In 1537 he was preacher at Augsburg, in 1553 at Strasburg, and died there in 1578. See Rittelmeyer, *Die evang. Kirchenliederdichter des Elsasses* (1855); Koch, *Geschichte des deutschen Kirchenliedes*, ii, 278 sq. (B. P.)

Flins (or **Flinz**), in Slavonic mythology, was a manly, bearded figure on a large flint stone (whence the name). The figure is very thin, so that it was held as a skeleton in some places, and thus made this the god of death among the Slavs. From several attributes of the accompanying figure it has been concluded that

Figure of Flins.

the black, burned staff indicates a torch, significant of the resurrection. The animal standing by was said to be a lion, because by his loud roaring he would raise the dead.

Flint, Ephraim, D.D., a Congregational minister, was born at Lincoln, Mass., Nov. 29, 1828. He attended Lawrence Academy at Groton; graduated from Williams College in 1851; the next year was principal of the academy in Westfield, and held the same position in 1855. Meantime (1853-54) he was in charge of Orleans Academy. From 1856 to 1862 he was principal of the high-school in Lee; and thereafter until 1865 occupied the same position in Lynn. Subsequently he was a resident student at Andover, was ordained pastor of the church in Hinsdale, Sept. 19, 1867, and died Nov. 28, 1882. See *Cong. Year-book*, 1883, p. 22.

Flint, James, D.D., a Unitarian minister, was born at Reading, Mass., Dec. 10, 1779. He studied under the Rev. Eliab Stone, and graduated from Harvard College in 1802; was engaged for a year or two as principal of an academy at Andover; then became a student of theology under the Rev. Joshua Bates, of Dedham. In due time he was licensed to preach; was ordained pastor of the Congregational society in East Bridgewater, Oct. 29, 1806; resigned in 1821; was installed Sept. 19 of that year over the East Society in Salem, and died there, March 4, 1855. His publications consisted chiefly of single sermons. See Sprague, *Annals of the Amer. Pulpit*, viii, 407.

Flipart, Jean Jacques, a reputable French engraver, was born at Paris in 1723, instructed by his father, Jean Charles, became a member of the Royal Academy, and died in 1789. The following plates, among others, are by him: *The Holy Family; Adam and Eve after their Fall; Christ Curing the Paralytic.* See Spooner, *Biog. Hist. of the Fine Arts*, s. v.; Hoefer, *Nouv. Biog. Générale*, s. v.

Flittner, Johann, a Lutheran theologian and hymn-writer of Germany, was born Nov. 1, 1618. He studied at different universities, was in 1646 deacon at Grimmen, near Greifswalde, and died at Stralsund, Jan. 7, 1678. His hymns are published in *Himmlisches Lust-*

Gärtlein (Greifswalde, 1661). See Mohnike, *Hymnologische Forschungen* (Stralsund, 1830), ii, 1 sq.; Jöcher, *Allgemeines Gelehrten-Lexikon*, s. v.; Koch, *Gesch. des deutschen Kirchenliedes*, iii, 442 sq.; iv, 128; viii, 232. (B. P.)

Flora, in Roman mythology, was the goddess of flowers, whose lively festivals were celebrated on April 27. Her first temple was dedicated to her in Rome by the Sabine king Titus Tatius. Her festival, called Floralia, was instituted in the year of the city 516. It was celebrated by plays, dancing, and midnight debauches. The accompanying figure, after an antique statue, may be found in the museum at Naples.

Figure of Flora.

Florence of Worcester, an English monk and chronicler, lived during the end of the 11th and beginning of the 12th century. He acquired a great reputation for learning, and died June 5, 1118. He wrote a *Chronicle*, which begins with the creation of the world and ends with the year of his death. That part of the work which relates to contemporary events is one of the most valuable of existing authorities. The chronicle was continued from 1118 to 1141 by an anonymous writer. The most accessible edition is a translation, with notes, by Thomas Forester, in Bohn's Antiquarian Library. See *Encyclop. Brit.* 9th ed. s. v.

Florentina, a Spanish saint, commemorated June 20, was sister of Leander, Isidore, and Fulgentius, and became a nun and superior of the convent near Astigis (Ecija) about the close of the 6th century.

Florentius, a Scotch prelate, was elected to the see of Glasgow in 1202, but was never consecrated. He died at Rome. See Keith, *Scottish Bishops*, p. 236.

Florez, Alphonso de, a Spanish Jesuit, who died Dec. 11, 1660, is the author of, *De Inclyto Agone Martyrii*, etc.:—*In Cap. xxiv Ecclesiastici*. See Alegambe, *Bibliotheca Scriptorum Societatis Jesu;* Jöcher, *Allgemeines Gelehrten-Lexikon*, s. v. (B. P.)

Florez, Enrique, a Spanish historical scholar, was born at Valladolid, Feb. 14, 1701. He entered the order of St. Augustine, taught theology at the University of Alcala, and published a *Cursus Theologiæ* (1732–38, 5 vols. 4to). He afterwards devoted himself exclusively to historical studies, and died at Madrid in May or August, 1773. He wrote, *Clave Historial* (1743): —*La España Sagrada* (1747–49), a vast compilation of local ecclesiastical history, which obtained a European reputation, and of which twenty-nine volumes appeared in the author's lifetime, and others by later hands at subsequent dates:—and other works of less importance. See Hoefer, *Nouv. Biog. Générale*, s. v.

Florinus, a presbyter of the Church of Rome, degraded for heresy in the latter part of the 2d century (Euseb. *Hist. Eccl.* v, 15, 20).

Floriot, Pierre, a French theologian, was born in the diocese of Langres in 1604. He became curate of Lais, a parish near Paris, and finally confessor of the nuns of Port-Royal-des-Champs. He died Dec. 1, 1691, leaving, *La Morale du Pater* (Rouen, 1672):—*Homélies sur les Évangiles* (Paris, 1677):—*Traité de la Messe* (ibid. 1679):—*Recueil de Pièces Concernant la Morale Chrétienne* (Rouen, 1745). See Hoefer, *Nouv. Biog. Générale*, s. v.

Floris, Frans, an eminent Flemish painter, was born at Antwerp in 1520, and studied sculpture under his uncle, Claude de Vriendt, until he was twenty, when he turned his attention to painting, and entered the school of Lambert Lombard. He afterwards went to Rome and studied there several years. He was favored with the especial patronage of the counts of Hoorn and Egmont, and was received into the academy at Antwerp in 1559. His most esteemed work is, *The Last Judgment*, painted for the Church of Notre Dame, at Brussels, and now in the Museum there; in the Museum at Antioch is his next best work, *The Fall of Lucifer*. He died in 1570. See Spooner, *Biog. Hist. of the Fine Arts*, s. v.; Chalmers, *Biog. Dict.* s. v.

Flörke, Wilhelm, a Lutheran theologian of Germany, who died Aug. 6, 1874, pastor at Toitenwinkel, near Rostock, is the author of, *Die Lehre vom tausendjährigen Reiche* (Marburg, 1860):—*Vom hochwürdigen Sakramente* (Breslau, 1869):—*Die letzten Dinge in Vorträgen* (Rostock, 1866):—*Das Summ-episcopat, seine Bedeutung und sein Fall* (Hanover, 1872). (B. P.)

Floss, Heinrich Joseph, a Roman Catholic theologian of Germany, was born July 29, 1819, at Wormersdorf, near Rheinbach; received holy orders in 1842; commenced his academical career at Bonn in 1854, and died a professor of theology there, May 4, 1881, leaving, *Geschichtliche Nachrichten über die Aachener Heiligthümer* (Bonn, 1855):—*Die Papstwahlen unter den Ottonen* (Freiburg, 1858):—*Die Uebertragung der heiligen Dreikönige von Mailand nach Köln* (Cologne, 1864): —*Das kloster Rolandswerth bei Bonn* (ibid. 1868). (B. P.)

Flowers, Festival of, a classical festival of the Hindûs, celebrated by the Rajpoots during nine days, in honor of Gauri, the wife of *Mahadeva* or *Iswara*. It takes place at the vernal equinox, the ceremonies commencing on the entrance of the sun into Aries, which is the opening of the Hindû year. Clay images are formed of Gauri and Siva, which are immediately placed together. A small trench is then opened in the earth, in which barley is sown. The ground is irrigated, and artificial heat supplied until the grain begins to germinate, when the women with joined hands dance round the trench, invoking the blessing of Gauri upon their husbands. After this the young barley is taken up and presented by the women to their husbands, who wear it in their turbans. Various ceremonies are then performed during several days within the houses, at the close of which the images are richly adorned and carried in a grand procession.

Flügel, Gustav Lebrecht, a German Orientalist, was born Feb. 18, 1802, at Bautzen, in Saxony, and studied theology and philology at Leipsic. He continued his Oriental studies at Vienna under Hammer-Purgstall, and at Paris under De Sacy. In 1851 Flügel was called to Vienna to prepare a catalogue of the Oriental manuscripts of the imperial library. His main work is the *Lexicon Bibliographicum et Encyclopædicum a Haji Khalfa Compositum*, which he published with a Latin translation and commentary, at the expense of the Oriental Translation Fund of London (Lond. and Leipsic, 1835–58, 7 vols.). He also edited an elegant edition of the Koran (Leipsic, 1834, 1841, 1858), and published *Concordantiæ Corani Arabicæ* (ibid. 1842). Of his other writings we mention, *Geschichte der Araber* (1832–40, 3 vols.; 2d ed. 1864):—*Al-Kindi, genannt der Philosoph der Araber* (ibid. 1857):—*Mani, seine Lehren und seine Schriften* (ibid. 1862):—*Die grammatischen Schulen der Araber* (ibid. eod.):—*Geschichte der Araber bis auf den Sturz des Chalifats von Bagdad* (2d ed. 1864), besides contributions to German reviews and cyclopædias. Flügel died at Dresden, July 5, 1870. After his death, Rödiger and Müller published his edition of *Kitâb al-Fihrist*, of Ibn-al-nadin (1871–72, vols. i and ii). See Dugat, *Histoire des Orientalistes* (Paris, 1870), ii, 91, 291; Lichtenberger, *Encyclop. des Sciences Religieuses*,

s. v.; Brockhaus, *Conversations-Lexikon* (13th ed.), vi, 927 sq. (B. P.)

Flügge, Christian Wilhelm, a Lutheran theologian of Germany, was born Dec. 7, 1773, at Winsen, in Lüneburg; studied at Göttingen, where he also lectured after completing his studies; in 1801 took charge of the pastorate of Scharnebeck, in Lüneburg, and died June 21, 1828, leaving, *Geschichte des Glaubens* (Leipsic, 1794–1800, 3 vols.):—*Versuch einer Geschichte der theolog. Wissenschaften* (Halle, 1796–98, 3 vols.):—*Darstellung des bisherigen Einflusses der Kantischen Philosophie* (Hanover, 1796):—*Einleitung in die Geschichte der theologischen Wissenschaften* (Halle, 1799):—*Einleitung in das Studium und in die Literatur der Religions- und Kirchengeschichte* (Göttingen, 1801):—*Die Himmelfahrt Jesu* (Hanover, 1808). See Döring, *Die gelehrten Theologen Deutschlands*, i, 416 sq.; Winer, *Handbuch der theol. Lit.* i, 5, 509, 529, 562, 604, 634, 779. (B. P.)

Fobes, Perez, LL.D., a Congregational minister, was born at Bridgewater, Mass., Sept. 21, 1742. He graduated from Harvard College in 1762, then taught school, studied theology, and, Nov. 19, 1766, was ordained pastor at Raynham. During the Revolution he was the outspoken friend of liberty, and, notwithstanding his feeble health, volunteered as chaplain in the army in 1777. The president of Brown University, Dr. Manning, having been elected to Congress in 1786, Mr. Fobes was chosen vice-president, and soon after became professor of natural philosophy. These positions, however, did not affect his pastoral charge, and he still resided at Raynham. From 1795 until his death, Feb. 23, 1812, he was a fellow of the university. In 1796 he was called to the supervision of Bristol Academy, to which institution he rendered important aid. The American Academy of Arts and Sciences numbered him among its members. As a preacher, he had more than a common reputation; his sermons were carefully prepared, and were marked by their perspicuous style. In the pulpit his manner was earnest and accompanied by considerable action. His success as a teacher grew out of his rare talent in communicating knowledge. See Sprague, *Annals of the Amer. Pulpit*, i, 645.

Fobian, Moses, a Jewish writer, who flourished in Greece in the 16th century, published the book of Job with a Neo-Greek translation in Hebrew letters, אִיּוֹב עִם תַּרְגּוּם רוֹמָאנִי (Constantinople, 1576):—the Proverbs of Solomon in the same manner (ibid. 1548):—the Pentateuch, with a Neo-Greek and Spanish translation (ibid. 1547; Ferrara, 1583). See Fürst, *Bibl. Jud.* i, 285 sq. (B. P.)

Fock, Johann Georg, a Lutheran theologian of Germany, was born Nov. 16, 1757, at Neuenmünster, in Holstein. For some time superintendent of the evangelical congregations in Austria and pastor at Vienna, he was called in 1796 to Kiel, where he died, Aug. 23, 1835. He published, *Sammlung einiger Kanzelvorträge* (Vienna, 1791):—*Oeffentliche Religiöse Vorträge* (ibid. 1793):—*Anleitung zur gründlichen Erkenntniss der christlichen Religion* (ibid. 1794; 6th ed. 1834). See Winer, *Handbuch der theol. Lit.* ii, 93, 178, 205, 208, 221, 273; Zuchold, *Bibl. Theol.* i, 366. (B. P.)

Focus, the ancient Roman *hearth*, which was dedicated to the Lares (q. v.) of each family. The domestic hearth was looked upon with such veneration that to swear by the royal hearth was accounted the most sacred oath among the Scythians. On the occasion of religious festivals the hearth was adorned with garlands.

Fodhail, Ben-Aiadh, Abou Ali, a Mohammedan saint and ascetic, was born at Abiwerd (Khorassan) or at Samarcand. He commenced by being a thief on the highway, then he studied the works of Coufa, and settled at Mecca, where he died in the year 187 of the hegira (A.D. 803). He is the reputed author of a large number of sentences and replies, some of which may be mentioned here: "God," said he, "multiplies the afflictions of those whom he loves, and the worldly prosperity of those whom he hates;" "Actions of piety which are performed through ostentation are the actions of pagans;" "It is better to be affectionate to one's equals and to try to be agreeable to them, than to spend the night in prayer and the day in abstinences." Fodhail had one day refused the presents of the caliph, Haroun al-Raschid; his companions remarked to him that he ought to have accepted these gifts in order to distribute them among the poor; but he answered, "If this money had been legally acquired, it would have been legal to accept it." Fodhail laughed but once after his conversion, and that was when he heard of the death of his son, "for," said he, "what pleases God, pleases me also." See Hoefer, *Nouv. Biog. Générale*, s. v.

Foering, Christian Frederick, an early Reformed (Dutch) minister, was born in Hanover, Germany, in 1736, and studied theology under professor Weyberg. His father died in the military service of his country, and his mother brought him, when he was but seven years old, to New York. Afterwards they settled in Philadelphia. He became a school-teacher, then a surveyor, and at last a minister, being licensed in 1770 by the Classis of New York, in the Reformed Dutch Church. He was settled in Germantown, Pa., in 1771; in the German Reformed Church, New York, from 1772 to 1774; and in the Dutch Reformed Church, Hillsborough, or Millstone, N. J., from 1774 to 1779, where he died, March 29 of the latter year. Mr. Foering was of a devout and fervid spirit, and preached in German, Dutch, or English. He was one of the original trustees of Rutgers College. During the American Revolution he espoused the cause of his adopted country with patriotic zeal. See the Millstone *Centennial Hist. Discourse*, by Rev. E. F. Corwin, one of his successors, p. 47–55; Corwin, *Manual of the Ref. Church in America*, p. 83. (W. J. R. T.)

Foinard, Frédéric Maurice, a French theologian, who died at Paris in 1743, is the author of, *Explications du Sens Littéral et Spirituel de la Genèse* (2 vols.):—*Projet pour un nouveau Bréviaire Ecclésiastique* (1720):—*Breviarium Ecclesiasticum* (2 vols.):—*Les Psaumes traduits*, etc. (1742). See Moréri, *Grand Dict. Historique*, iv, 110, 230; Jöcher, *Allgemeines Gelehrten-Lexikon*, s. v.; Lichtenberger, *Encyclop. des Sciences Religieuses*, s. v. (B. P.)

Foix, Paul de, a French prelate, was born in 1528; became first a magistrate, and was engaged in royal commissions; but in 1576 was made archbishop of Toulouse, and in 1579 went as ambassador to Rome, where he died about the end of May, 1584. See Hoefer, *Nouv. Biog. Générale*, s. v.

Foix, Pierre de, cardinal and archbishop of Arles, was born in 1386. Pope Benedict XIII sent him as a legate to the Council at Constance, and he greatly promoted the cause of Martin V, who, after his election, sent him as his legate to the king of Aragon. In 1429 he convened a council at Tortosa, and the then pending differences were harmonized by him. In 1457 he attended the provincial council at Avignon. He died in 1464. See Lichtenberger, *Encyclop. des Sciences Religieuses*, s. v.; Jöcher, *Allgemeines Gelehrten-Lexikon*, s. v. (B. P.)

Folcher, John, a Swedish theologian, was a native of Calmar. He studied at Upsal and at Giessen, became master of arts in 1693, licentiate in theology in 1696, professor of philosophy at Calmar in 1698, and of theology at Pernau in 1701. His sympathies with the doctrines of the Pietists involved him in violent controversies, so that he had to flee to Stockholm at the time of the taking of Livonia by the Russians. He then retired to an estate which he possessed in Scania. In 1723 he came back to Stockholm, where he found again the same opposition. He died in 1729, leaving, *De Spiritu Animali* (Upsal, 1689):—*De G. Fabio Cunc-*

tatore (Giessen, 1693):—*Δοχιμασία Veri Hominis Christiani*, etc. (ibid. 1696):—*Streitschriften mit Broems, Gezelius und Humble.* See Hoefer, *Nouv. Biog. Générale*, s. v.

Foley, THOMAS, D.D., a Roman Catholic bishop, was born in Baltimore, Md., March 6, 1822. He graduated from Mount St. Mary's College in 1840, studied theology for six years, was ordained priest, Aug. 16, 1846, served missions in Montgomery County, in a few months was called to St. Patrick's Church, Washington, D. C., in 1848 was appointed secretary to archbishop Eccleston, and in 1851 was made chancellor. In 1864 bishop Spalding of Baltimore selected him as chancellor, and in 1867 as vicar-general. He was appointed to the see of Chicago, Nov. 19, 1869, was consecrated March 27, 1870, and died there Feb. 19, 1879. "In point of person and dignified bearing, Foley was one of the best specimens of a thoroughbred Churchman on this continent. He was a fine pulpit orator, possessed great executive ability, and was beloved by all for his piety and charity." See (N. Y.) *Catholic Annual*, 1880, p. 41.

Foligno, AGNOLA DE, an Italian nun, was born at Foligno (duchy of Spoleto). She made herself famous by an exalted piety from her early life, but married a nobleman of her native town, yet did not discontinue her religious practices. Being left a widow in the prime of life, she entered a convent of the third order of St. Francis, and connected herself closely with Ubertino de Casal, a monk of the same order, who was famous for his mysticism. According to Ubertino's report, it was Agnola who guided him into the way of salvation, sustaining him by her example and advice. She assisted him also in writing the *Arbor Vitæ Crucificæ Jesu* (Venice, 1485), a rare and singular book, in which the authors pretend that Jesus himself was the founder of their order. Agnola submitted cheerfully to flagellations and macerations the most painful, saying, "that the surest mark of love is to suffer freely for the one who is loved." She composed a book, giving an account of her various temptations by the evil spirit, published at Paris in 1538, under the title, *Theologia Crucis.* She died Jan. 4, 1309. See Hoefer, *Nouv. Biog. Générale*, s. v.

Foliot, Gilbert, a monk of Cluny, was abbot of Gloucester in 1139, and bishop of Hereford in 1148. He was also bishop of London in 1163. He died in 1188, leaving *Expositio in Cant. Canticorum* (ed. Junius, 1638). See Allibone, *Dict. of Brit. and Amer. Authors*, s. v.

Foliot, Robert, cousin of bishop Gilbert Foliot, was a native of Devonshire. According to Bale (*De Scriptoribus Brit.* cent. iii, No. 8), he lived for a long time in France, where he got the surname of Robertus Melodunensis (Robert of Melun). He was first tutor to Becket, by whose favor he succeeded his kinsman in the see of Hereford. He wrote several books, of which that on *The Sacrament of the Old Law* is the most remarkable. According to bishop Godwin (*Lives of the Bishops*) Robert de Melun (also bishop of Hereford) was a distinct person from Robert Foliot, and the latter was advanced bishop after the death of Becket. He is also called the archdeacon of Oxford. He died in 1186. See Fuller, *Worthies of England* (ed. Nuttall), i, 404.

Fonda, JESSE, an early Reformed (Dutch) minister, was born at Watervliet, N. Y., in 1786. He was converted in youth, and graduated from Union College with honor, in 1806. The Classis of Albany licensed him to preach in 1809, his theological course having been pursued with some neighboring ministers. He then began a course of systematic and thorough study, which gave high tone to his future ministry. His first settlement was at Nassau, from 1808 to 1813, in connection with the adjacent church of Schodack. His reputation grew so rapidly as a preacher that he was called in the latter year to the First Church of New Brunswick, N.J. Here he sustained himself with marked ability in the presence of the professors and students of the college and theological seminary. In 1817 he removed to the large and flourishing church at Montgomery, N. Y., where he labored until his decease in 1827. Mr. Fonda published several pamphlets upon subjects of current interest, and was the author of a valuable practical volume upon *The Sacraments*, which elicited considerable discussion as to his views of the nature of the baptism of John the Baptist; viz. that it was not Christian baptism. See *Magazine of Ref. Dutch Church*, November and December, 1827, ii, 228, 263, 340; Steele, *Centennial Discourse*; Corwin, *Manual of the Ref. Church in America*, s. v. (W. J. R. T.)

Fonseca, Aaron and **Isaac Diaz**, two brothers of Portuguese descent, were both strict adherents of orthodox Judaism. When they found that the teachings of the Bible were not in harmony with those of the rabbins, they questioned them with regard to their doubts, which finally had the result that on Feb. 28, 1712, they were both excommunicated from the Jewish community. In the eyes of the Christians they were suspected of being Atheists, and to counteract this suspicion the two brothers appealed to the pastor of the Reformed Church, Hero Sibersma, requesting him to examine them. He did so, and openly declared them to be true believers in the Old Test. A more diligent study of the Old Test. in the light of the New brought them to the knowledge of the Messiah, and six months after their excommunication from the synagogue they were received into the Church. The two brothers published, in the Dutch language, in 1714, the reasons for their apostasy from Judaism. See Fürst, *Bibl. Jud.* i, 286; Kalkar, *Israel u. die Kirche*, p. 64; Jöcher, *Allgemeines Gelehrten-Lexikon*, s. v.; Le Roi, *Die Evangelische Christenheit und die Juden* (Carlsruhe, 1884), p. 415 sq. (B. P.)

Fonseca (*Soares*), **Antonio da** (better known by the name of *Antonio das Chagas*), a celebrated Portuguese theologian, was born at Vidigueira, June 25, 1631. He studied at the University of Evora, and after the death of his father engaged as a simple soldier, but having killed a man in a duel, fled to Brazil. At Bahia he was reformed from a life of licentiousness by reading a treatise of F. Luiz da Granada, and from that time resolved to become a Franciscan. He returned to Europe, and, after some relapses of faith, joined the order of St. Francis of Evora, May 18, 1662. Afterwards he studied theology at Coimbra, established a seminary at Torres-Vedras in 1678, and there died, with the reputation of sanctity, Oct. 20, 1682, leaving the following works, posthumously published: *Faiscas de Amor Divino* (Lisbon, 1683):—*Obras Espirituaes* (ibid. 1684, 1687, in 2 parts):—*O Padre nosso Commentado* (1688):—*Espelho do Espirito em que deve verse e Comporse a Alma* (1683):—*Escola da Penitencia* (1687):—*Sermoes Genuinos* (1690), besides a number of ascetical writings still in MS. See Hoefer, *Nouv. Biog. Générale*, s. v.

Fonseca, Juan Rodriguez de, a Spanish prelate, was born at Toro in 1451. He became successively dean of Seville, bishop of Badajoz, of Cordova, of Valencia and Burgos, and archbishop of Rosana. He accomplished several diplomatic missions. While dean of Seville he was charged with the ordering of the armament destined for the discovery of the New World. Being consulted before on the project of Christopher Columbus, he treated the great navigator as a visionary. He never forgave him for having succeeded, and let pass no occasion for doing him harm, especially after the death of Isabella, when Fonseca, being charged with the management of affairs regarding the New World, pursued with all his hatred the family of Columbus. He was less hostile to Fernando Cortez and to La Casas, who challenged and obtained, in 1520, the dissolution of the council of which this prelate was president. Being a hard man, fanatic and passionate, Fonseca became a great friend of the inquisitor Torquemada. He died at Burgos, March 4, 1524. See Hoefer, *Nouv. Biog. Générale*, s. v.

Font, Baptismal. The material in the Western Church was, as a rule, stone; frequently porphyry, or other rich marbles. In the Eastern Church the font was usually of metal or wood, and seldom or never possessed any beauty (Neale, *Eastern Church*, i, 214).

The usual form of the font was octagonal, with a mystical reference to the eighth day, as the day of our Lord's resurrection, and of regeneration by the Spirit (comp. Ambros. *Epist.* 20, 44). The piscina is sometimes found of a circular form, and is occasionally, though very rarely (as at Aquileia) hexagonal. Gregory of

Font in the Baptistery at Aquileia.

Tours (*De Glor. Martyr.* lib. i, c. 23) speaks of a font in the shape of a cross, in Spain. The form of a sepulchre is stated to have been sometimes adopted, in allusion to the Christian's burial with Christ in baptism (Rom. iv, 4).

The piscina usually formed a basin in the centre of the baptistery, rather beneath the level of the pavement, surrounded with a low wall. It was entered by an ascent and descent of steps. According to Isidore Hispal. (*Orig.* xv, 4; *De Div. Off.* ii, 24) the normal number was seven; three in descent, to symbolize the triple renunciation of the world, the flesh, and the devil; three in ascent, to symbolize the confession of the Trinity, and a seventh, "septimus . . . qui et quartus," at the summit of the enclosing wall, for the officiating minister to stand on. But the rule concerning the number was not invariable. At Nocera, the number of steps is five, two in ascent, and three in descent. The descent into the piscina of St. John Lateran is by four steps.

FONT, Consecration of. In the 4th century, the ceremony of blessing the water to be used in baptism was already regarded as of high antiquity (see Basil the Great, *De Spiritu Sancta*, 27; Ignatius, *Ad Ephes.* 18; Irenæus, *Hæres.* i, 21, § 4; Tertullian, *De Baptismo*, 4; Cyprian, *Epist.* 70, 71; Sedatus of Thuburbum, *Sententiæ Episc.* 18, in Cyprian's *Works;* Cyril of Jerusalem, *Catech.* iii, 3; Ambrose, *De iis qui Initiantur*, 5). Probably the earliest form extant, which cannot be assumed with certainty to be older than the beginning of the 4th century, is that of the *Apostolical Constitutions* (vii, 43), in which the priest, after a recitation of the mercies of God, analogous to the preface of the eucharistic office, proceeds, "Look down from heaven, and sanctify this water, and grant grace and power that he who is baptized according to the command of thy Christ may with him be crucified and die, and be buried and rise again to the adoption which is in him, by dying unto sin, but living unto righteousness." Compare Dionysius Areop. *Hierarch Eccles.* c. 2.

Another ceremony, the pouring in of chrism, generally so as to form a cross on the surface of the water, was probably of later introduction, though it is found at least as early as the 6th century.

Amalarius (*De Eccl. Off.* i, 25) expressly mentions insufflation as one of the rites in exorcism (q. v.). After the expulsion of the evil spirit by exorcism, he simply says, "munitur aqua crucis signaculo," not distinctly mentioning the pouring in of chrism in the form of a cross.

In the Gregorian *Sacramentary* (p. 71-73) is mentioned another rite, that of plunging tapers into the water to be consecrated. Two lighted tapers are carried before the bishop to the font; after the benediction, the aforesaid two tapers are plunged into the font, and the bishop "insufflates" on the water three times. After this the chrism is poured into the font, and the children are baptized. The ceremony mentioned by

Consecration of the Baptismal Water by a Taper. (From a Pontifical of the 9th Century.)

Amalarius (*De Eccl. Off.* i, 25), of plunging the tapers of the *neophytes* into the font, seems to be distinct from this.

See Martene, *De Rit. Ant.*; Binterim, *Denkwürdigkeiten;* Probst, *Sakramente u. Sakramentalien;* Smith, *Dict. of Christ. Antiq.* s. v.

Fontaine, Nicolas, a French theologian, was born at Paris in 1625. At the age of twenty he joined the Port-Royalists, and soon became intimately acquainted with Nicole, Arnauld, De Sacy, and others. In 1666 he was imprisoned with De Sacy. After his release he lived at different places, and finally died at Melun, Jan. 28, 1709. He wrote, *Histoire de l'Ancien et du Nouveau Testament* (Paris, 1670):—*Psaumes de David* (1674):—*Explication du Nouveau Testament* (1675, 4 vols.; 1685, 2 vols.):—*Vies des Patriarches* (1683):—*Vies des Prophètes* (1693):—*Dictionnaire Chrétien* (1691, 1712):—*Sermons de St. Grégoire de Nazianze* (1693, 2 vols.):—*Homélies de St. Chrysostôme, sur les Epîtres de St. Paul* (7 vols.), besides other works. He is best known by his posthumous work, *Mémoires pour Servir à l'Histoire de Port-Royal* (Cologne, 1736). See Lichtenberger, *Encyclop. des Sciences Religieuses*, s. v.; Jöcher, *Allgemeines Gelehrten-Lexikon*, s. v.; Hoefer, *Nouv. Biog. Générale; Biog. Universelle*, s. v. (B. P.)

Fontana, Carlo, a famous Italian architect, was born in 1638, and died at Rome in 1714. He wrote, *Il Tempio Vaticano*, etc. (Rome, 1694, fol.):—*Descrizione della Capella del Fonte Baptismale nella Basilica Vaticana* (ibid. 1697). See Winer, *Handbuch der theol. Lit.* i, 814; Jöcher, *Allgemeines Gelehrten-Lexikon*, s. v.; Hoefer, *Nouv. Biog. Générale*, s. v. (B. P.)

Fontana, Domenico, an eminent Italian architect, was born near lake Como in 1543; studied architecture at Rome, and while there was employed to erect the chapel of the Persepio in Santa Maria Maggiore. The pope, being desirous of raising an obelisk in the square of St. Peter's, collected about five hundred mathematicians, engineers, and learned men, among whom Fontana's plan was approved, and with the assistance of one hundred and forty horses and eight hundred men, he removed this immense mass, weighing about 750,000 pounds. For this undertaking he was created a knight of the Golden Spur, and a Roman nobleman. He afterwards erected other obelisks in Santa Maria Maggiore. He died at Naples in 1607. See Spooner, *Biog. Hist. of the Fine Arts*, s. v.; Hoefer, *Nouv. Biog. Générale*, s. v.

Fontana, Francesco Ludovico, an Italian prelate, was born Aug. 28, 1750, at Casala Maggiore (duchy of Milan); entered the Barnabite order in 1767; eventually became professor of eloquence in the College of Milan, where he acquired great fluency in the Greek language; in 1804 he accompanied Pius VII to France, and on the return of the pope to Rome was made cardinal, March 8, 1816, placed at the head of the congregation of the Index, still retaining his title as superior-general of the Barnabites. He died at Rome, March 19, 1822. See Hoefer, *Nouv. Biog. Générale*, s. v.

Fontana, Lavinia, an eminent Italian painter, daughter of Prospero Fontana, was born at Bologna in 1552, and studied under her father. She painted a number of works for the Bolognese churches, of which the best are, *The Miracle of the Loaves; The Annunciation;* and *The Crucifixion.* She subsequently went to Rome, where she practiced portrait-painting with great success. She died at Rome in 1614. See Hoefer, *Nouv. Biog. Générale*, s. v.; Spooner, *Biog. Hist. of the Fine Arts*, s. v.

Fontana, Prospero, an eminent historical and portrait painter, was born at Bologna in 1512, and studied under Francucci. His masterpiece is at Bologna, in Santa Maria della Grazie. In the same church is an admirable picture of *The Annunciation*, by him. He also executed the *Descent from the Cross*, in the Bolognese Academy. He died in 1597. See Hoefer, *Nouv. Biog. Générale*, s. v.; Spooner, *Biog. Hist. of the Fine Arts*, s. v.

Fontanés, FERDINAND, a French Protestant theologian, was born at Nîmes, May 15, 1797. He studied at Geneva, and entered the ministry in 1821. While discharging his ministerial duties at his native place, there occurred, in 1824, a vacancy in the theological faculty at Montauban. Fontanés made an application, and passed such an excellent examination that his appointment became a matter of course. Rumors from Nîmes having reached the faculty as to some liberal opinions of the candidate, it was thought best to prepare a theological formula which Fontanés was to sign. But he refused to do this on conscientious grounds. In 1826 he succeeded M. Olivier Desmont at Nîmes, and died there, Jan. 9, 1862. Of his writings we mention, besides his many articles in the *Évangéliste: Catéchisme Évangélique* (8th ed. 1867):—*Histoire Sainte*, in questions and answers (4th ed. 1866):—*De l'Unité Religieuse dans l'Église Réformée de France* (1844):—*De la Lutte Engagée dans les Églises Protestantes* (1842). See Lichtenberger, *Encyclop. des Sciences Religieuses*, s. v. (B. P.)

Fontinalia, a festival celebrated annually among the ancient Romans on Oct. 13, when the wells were adorned with garlands, and flowers thrown into them.

Foote, Charles Henry, D.D., a Presbyterian minister, was born at Lenox, Mass., June 17, 1825. He prepared for college at Rochester, N. Y.; graduated from Williams College in 1849; taught one year at the academy at Mendon; studied law one year; graduated from Princeton Theological Seminary in 1854; was licensed by the New Brunswick Presbytery, and afterwards ordained pastor of the Second Presbyterian Church of that city. After an earnest and successful pastorate of three and a half years, he removed to the West; in 1866 was installed pastor at Jerseyville, Ill.; next at Cairo, in 1868; over the North Church of St. Louis, Mo., in 1871; over the Walnut Street Church, Evansville, Ind., in 1876, and at Ionia, Mich., in 1879, where he died, June 28, 1880. See *Necrol. Report of Princeton Theol. Sem.* 1881, p. 72. (W. P. S.)

Foote, James, D.D., a Scotch clergyman, son of the Rev. James Foote, minister of Fettercairn, graduated from Marischal College and the University, Aberdeen, March 31, 1798; was licensed to preach July 25, 1804; presented by king George III to the living at Logie, and ordained Dec. 21, 1809; promoted to the third charge at Aberdeen in November, 1824, and admitted June 23, 1825; joined the Free Secession May 24, 1843, and died June 25, 1856, aged seventy-four years. He published four single *Sermons* (Dundee, 1813; Lond. 1819):—*Lectures on the Gospel by Luke* (Glasgow, 1838, 6 vols.):—*Pastoral Letter to the Congregation of the Free East Church* (Aberdeen, 1844):—*A Treatise on Effectual Calling* (Edinb. 1846):—*A Sermon in the Free Church Pulpit* (vol. i). See *Fasti Eccles. Scoticanæ*, iii, 473, 838.

Foote, William Henry, D.D., a Presbyterian minister, was born at Colchester, Conn., Dec. 20, 1794. He entered Yale College in the junior year; spent some time teaching, and then entered and studied for one year in Princeton Theological Seminary. Having been licensed by the Presbytery of Winchester in October, 1819, he preached at various missionary stations in Virginia until June, 1822, when he organized and afterwards became pastor of a church in Woodstock. In November, 1824, he became pastor of the congregations of Mount Bethel, Springfield, and Romney; about 1838 agent of the Central Board of Foreign Missions, laboring within the bounds of the synods of Virginia and North Carolina. While thus engaged, he gathered the materials for his volumes, afterwards published, of *Sketches, Historical and Biographical, of the Presbyterian Church in Virginia and North Carolina.* In 1845 he returned to his old charge in Romney, and continued till 1861. During the war he was occupied in lower Virginia as agent for Hampden-Sidney College, also in supplying vacant pulpits, and in Petersburg, during Grant's siege, as chaplain to the hospital. He returned to Romney and Springfield (now in West Virginia), and labored till his death, Nov. 22, 1869. See *Obituary Record of Yale College*, 1870; *Gen. Cat. of Princeton Theol. Sem.* 1881, p. 27.

Footprints, MONUMENTAL. Sepulchral slabs have been found in the catacombs and elsewhere incised with footprints. The two feet as a rule point the same way, though sometimes, but rarely, they are turned in opposite directions. A slab in the Kircherian Museum bears two pairs of footprints pointed contrary ways, as of a person going and returning (fig. 1). Some of these slabs

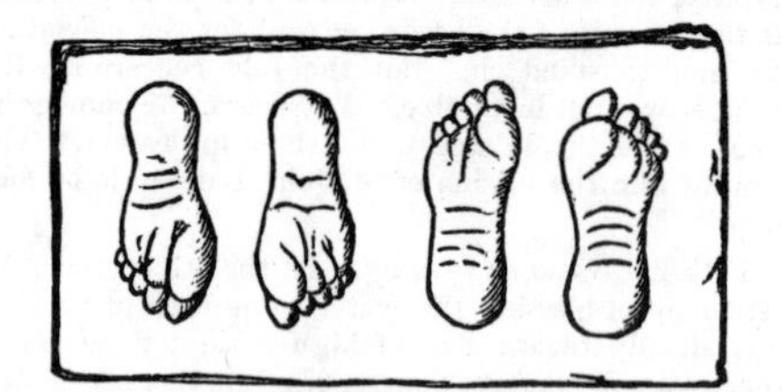

Fig. 1.—Monumental Slab with Footprints. (In the Kircherian Museum.)

are certainly Christian, though the fact in other cases is uncertain. A slab given by Boldetti, inscribed with JANUARIA IN DEO at one end, bears the sole of a foot, with IN DEO incised upon it, at the other. Perret gives a slab erected by a Christian husband to his wife, with a pair of footprints incised on it, not bare, as is customary, but shod in shoes or sandals. Sometimes, but more rarely, we find a single foot seen in profile.

The signification of this mark is much controverted. Some regard the footprint as the symbol of possession, denoting that the burial-place had been purchased by the individual as his own. This view is based on a false etymology. The idea that a sense of their loss and a deep regret and affection for the departed was thus indicated is a mere romantic fancy. More may be said for the view, that as such emblems were sometimes dedicated as votive offerings by travellers on their return from a journey, they were intended on a Christian slab to indicate a holy thankfulness for the safe completion of the earthly pilgrimage of the departed. Another, more prosaic, but by no means improbable, interpretation, especially of a single foot, is that it was a thank-offering for recovery from gout or other disease affecting the foot.

The same emblem is frequently found on seal rings. The sole of the foot bears sometimes the name of the owner, e. g. FORTVNIVS (Boldetti, p. 506; Perret, vol. iv, pl. xi, No. 4); JVSTVS (Aringhi, ii, 698; Agincourt, *Sculpt.* pl. viii, No. 23), from the catacomb of St. Agnes; sometimes a Christian motto or device, e. g. SPES IN DEO (fig. 2) (Perret, u. s. No. 5), and the monogram of

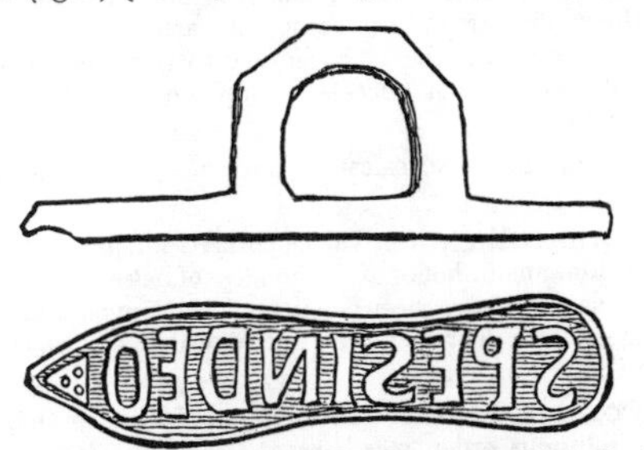

Fig. 2.—Seal-ring in the Form of a Footprint. (In the Kircherian Museum.)

Christ (ib. No. 6). In an example given by Perret (vol. iv, pl. xxiii, No. 21), we see the stamp of such a seal bearing the sole of a foot, with PAVLI incised on it, five times repeated on the mortar in which a gilt glass had been imbedded, in the catacomb of St. Sixtus.

Forbes, Alexander, a Scotch prelate, was rector of Fettercairn, in Mearns, and was promoted to the see of Caithness, Nov. 12, 1606, where he sat until he was translated to Aberdeen in 1615. See Keith, *Scottish Bishops*, p. 217.

Forbes, Alexander Penrose, D.C.L., a Scotch bishop, was born in Edinburgh, June 6, 1817. He was educated at the Edinburgh Academy, the University of Glasgow, and Haileybury College. In 1836 he went to Madras, India, but finding the climate unfavorable to his health, was obliged after two or three years to return to England. He then entered Brasenose College, Oxford, graduated in 1844, was ordained in the English Church, and held an English curacy. In 1846 he became vicar of St. Saviour's, Leeds, and in the following year was appointed bishop of Brechin. Being prosecuted for heresy, on account of some opinions set forth in his primary charge, delivered and published in 1857, he was acquitted with "a censure and an admonition." He died at Dundee, Oct. 8, 1875, leaving treatises on the Nicene Creed, the Thirty-nine Articles, various commentaries and devotional works, discourses, and reviews. See *Encyclop. Brit.* 9th ed. s. v.

Forbes, George, D.D., a Scotch clergyman, second son of the minister at Leochel, graduated from Marischal College and the university, Aberdeen, March 31, 1797; was licensed to preach July 12, 1803; presented in November following to the living at Strathdon, and ordained March 1, 1804; resigned his cure in November, 1829, and retired from the ministry Jan. 27, 1830. He died suddenly, Feb. 16, 1834, aged fifty-five years. He discharged the duties of his ministry with zeal, and his labors were crowned with eminent success. See *Fasti Eccles. Scoticanæ*, iii, 565.

Forbes, John, a Scotch clergyman, third son of William Forbes of Corse, was born about 1566; studied at San Salvator's College, and took his degree from the University of St. Andrews in 1583; was admitted to the living at Alford in 1593. He was commissioned in 1605 to wait upon the king to inform his majesty what the assembly of Aberdeen had done in opposition to the royal pleasure, he having been the moderator. The privy council condemned him to be imprisoned, first in Edinburgh castle, then in the castle at Blackness. In 1606, he, with five others, was tried at Linlithgow on the charge of treason, declining to acknowledge the authority of the privy council, and banished, Oct. 23, 1606, for life. He went to Sedan in 1607, became the minister to the British merchants at Middleburgh, laid the foundation of a Scottish church there in 1611, removed to the church at Delft in 1621, was displaced by order of the British government, and died about 1634. He published, *The Saint's Hope, and its Infallibleness* (1608):—*Two Sermons* (eod.):—*A Treatise Tending to the Clearing of Justification* (1616, 4to):—*A Treatise how God's Spirit may be Discerned from Man's Spirit* (Lond. 1617):—*Four Sermons on 1 Tim. vi* (1635, 4to):—*Certain Records Touching the Estate of the Kirk in* 1605, 1606:—*Three Letters to James VI* (1851). See *Fasti Eccles. Scoticanæ*, iii, 545.

Forbes, Lewis William, D.D., a Scotch clergyman, graduated at the university and King's College, Aberdeen, March 29, 1811; was licensed to preach July 4, 1815; presented to the living at Boharm in June, and ordained Aug. 20, 1816; elected moderator of the General Assembly in May, 1852, and died Jan. 8, 1854, aged sixty years. He occupied a prominent position in the Church in the North, was most exemplary in the discharge of his duties, and much esteemed. He published the sermon he preached at the opening of the General Assembly in 1853, and also *An Account of the Parish of Boharm.* See *Fasti Eccles. Scoticanæ*, iii, 228, 898.

Forbes, Patrick, a Scotch clergyman, son of the Rev. Francis Forbes of Grange, graduated from Marischal College and the university, Aberdeen, in 1793; was appointed schoolmaster of the parish of Boharm, May 1 following; licensed to preach by the Presbytery of Strathbogie, May 3, 1797; presented to the living at Boharm in May, and ordained Aug. 14, 1800; promoted to Old Machar, second charge, April 25, 1816; was elected moderator of the General Assembly in May, 1829, and died Oct. 13, 1847, aged seventy-two years. He published *Considerations on the Constitution of the Church of Scotland* (Edinb. 1841), and translated *Principles of Interpretation of the Old Testament*, by J. H. Pareau, in the *Biblical Cabinet*, vol. viii. See *Fasti Eccles. Scoticanæ*, iii, 220, 488, 898.

Forbin-Janson, CHARLES AUGUSTE MARIE JOSEPH, *Comte de*, a French prelate, was born in Paris, Nov. 3, 1785; early became a politician, but shortly after entered the seminary of St. Sulpice; was ordained in 1811; immediately became grand-vicar of the diocese of Chambéry; was consecrated bishop of Nancy and Toul in 1824; during the political dangers following he took refuge in Canada, but returned to France, and died near Marseilles, July 12, 1844. See Hoefer, *Nouv. Biog. Générale*, s. v.

Ford, James, D.D., a Scotch clergyman, graduated from Edinburgh University, April 14, 1743; was licensed to preach Nov. 26, 1746; ordained July 31, 1751, as minister to the congregation at Warnford; presented by the earl of Lauderdale to the living at Lauder; admitted Sept. 27, 1753, and died Sept. 24, 1810, aged eighty-six years. He published two single *Sermons* (1777–78), and *An Account of the Parish of Lauder.* See *Fasti Eccles. Scoticanæ*, i, 521.

Ford, Simon, a divine and Latin poet of some notoriety, was born in East Ogwell, Devonshire, in 1619, and educated at Magdalen Hall, Oxford. In 1651 he was vicar of St. Laurence, Reading, of Northampton in

1659, and in 1685 of Old Swinford, Worcestershire. He died in 1699. He was one of the translators of *Plutarch's Morals*, printed in 1684, and published a number of sermons, Latin poems, etc., from 1646 to 1696, a list of which will be found in *Athen. Oxon.* See Chalmers, *Biog. Dict.* s. v.; Allibone, *Dict. of Brit. and Amer. Authors*, s. v.

Fordicidia, a festival celebrated annually in the month of March among the ancient Romans. It was instituted by Numa, in consequence of a general barrenness which happened to prevail among the cattle. The name was derived from the sacrifice of a *Forda*, that is, a cow with a calf.

Fore-jotre, in Norse mythology, was the principal Jote, i. e. the oldest giant, the forefather of the ancient Forjontnian deities, who ruled over Scandinavia prior to the Asas, and were driven out by Odin. Their history lies so far in the past that little is known of them save their name; but from this we deduce a mythology personifying nature. Fore-jotre had three sons: Æger, the sea; Kare, the air; Loge, the fire; and one daughter: Ran, theft. This last was the wife of Æger, and by him she had nine daughters: Himingläfa, the heaven-threatening; Dufa, the deep; Blodugadda, the bloodthirsty; Heffring, the rising; Udur, the falling; Raun, the rustling; Bylgia, the storm; Dröbna, the threatening; Kolga, the flood. Kare, the air, produced Frosta, the frost; the latter produced Snio-hingamble, the icy snow. Loge, the third son of Fore-jotre, married Glod, the flame; and by him she had Einmiria, the coal, and Eisa, the ashes. See NORSE MYTHOLOGY.

Foreman, ANDREW, was prothonotary apostolic in Scotland in 1499, in 1501 was promoted to the see of Moray, and together with it held in commendam the priories of Pittenweem in Scotland, and of Cottingham in England. About 1506 he was appointed by king James IV as his ambassador, to procure a personal conference between him and Henry, king of England. In 1514 he was translated to the see of St. Andrews, and in 1517 was also perpetual commendator of the monastery of Dunfermline. He died in 1522. See Keith, *Scottish Bishops*, p. 35, 146.

Formalists, a sect of thinkers which arose in the 12th century, as a compromise between the doctrines of the *Nominalists* and *Realists.* They professed to hold an intermediate place between the two parties, abstracting the forms of things, and assigning to them the place of universals. Duns Scotus is said to have originated *formalism*, although the elements of the doctrine were to be found in the writings of mediæval philosophers anterior to his time.

Forman, AARON PARKER, D.D., a Presbyterian minister, was born Nov. 12, 1827, in Ralls County, Mo. He was converted at the age of eleven; graduated from Centre College, Ky., in 1849, with the highest honors of his class, and from Princeton Theological Seminary in 1853; preached that year in Hannibal, Mo., and in March, 1854, was ordained pastor there. In 1864 he was called to St. Joseph, where he acted with great prudence, fidelity, and zeal. In 1870 broken health compelled him to resign, and travel in Minnesota and Colorado; and after serving in the Price Street Church, St. Louis, Mo., in March, 1872, he became pastor of the Church in Canton, Miss. He died at Courtland, Ala., Oct. 14, 1875. Dr. Forman was a man of great gentleness and amiability of character, combined with unusual firmness and sound judgment; an excellent scholar, a popular preacher, and a beloved pastor. See *Gen. Cat. of Princeton Theol. Sem.* 1881, p. 178. (W. P. S.)

Formosans, RELIGION OF THE. Formosa is a large island in the China Sea, called in Chinese *Tai-Wan*, 245 miles in length from north to south, and about 100 miles in breadth at the broadest part, containing an area of 14,982 square miles. The religion of the islanders is polytheistic in its character, there being recognised among them a plurality of deities, two of whom are regarded as supreme, one of them residing in the north, and the other in the east. The one is a guardian of men, the other, who is a goddess, the guardian of women. They acknowledge also another deity who resides in the north, and is an evil spirit. There are two gods of war, a god of health, a god of forests, and a god of cornfields. They have also household gods, who preside over the several departments of nature. The worship of the gods, which consists of invocations, sacrifices, and libations, is conducted by priestesses called *Juibas*, who work themselves up to a frenzy, or fall into a trance, during which they pretend to hold familiar intercourse with the gods. The Formosans acknowledge the immortality of the soul, and always erect a bamboo hut for the dwelling of the spirit of a departed relative or friend. They also hold to future rewards and punishments, but have no idea of the resurrection of the body. An attempt was made by the Dutch in the 17th century to Christianize the island, but without success. They are now in gross heathenism.

Formula, in ecclesiastical phrase, is a profession of faith.

Fornacalia, a festival celebrated among the ancient Romans in honor of the goddess of baking, *Fornax.* It is said to have been instituted by Numa, and the time of its celebration was announced every year by the Curio Maximus.

Fornari, Maria Victoria, an Italian foundress of a religious order, was born at Genoa in 1562. She was married to Angelo Strate, by whom she had five children, who all devoted themselves to the Church. After the death of her husband, she instituted the order of the *Celestial Annonciades*, which had over a hundred houses in Italy, Germany, and France. The nuns were dressed in white robes, with a light blue shawl. She died Dec. 15, 1617. See Hoefer, *Nouv. Biog. Générale*, s. v.

Fornari, Niccolo, an Italian prelate, was born at Rome, Jan. 23, 1788. He studied with ardor, was received into orders, and devoted himself to instruction in theology. Pope Gregory XVI made him nuncio to Brussels. He was afterwards appointed a chief commissioner of the congregation of studies. Fornari was made cardinal *in petto*, Dec. 21, 1846, and proclaimed as such Sept. 30, 1850. He was for some time papal nuncio at Paris, where he died, June 15, 1856. See Hoefer, *Nouv. Biog. Générale*, s. v.

Forrest, JOHN, D.D., a Presbyterian minister, was born at Edinburgh, Scotland, Sept. 19, 1799. He graduated from Edinburgh University, studied theology, received a call from the Scotch Presbyterian Church of Charleston, S. C., in June, 1832, and being ordained by the Edinburgh Presbytery, was in due time installed pastor. He continued there until his death, which occurred in July, 1879. (W. P. S.)

Forrester, WALTER, a Scotch prelate, was first a canon of the Church of Aberdeen, next was made secretary of state, and then promoted to the bishopric of Brechin in 1401, where he was still ruling in 1415. See Keith, *Scottish Bishops*, p. 163.

Forsete, in Norse mythology, was a son of Baldur, and Nanna, the lovely daughter of Nef. He was the god of peace, union, and friendship; pacifying every quarrel. A beautiful palace called Glitner, resting upon golden pillars, and covered with silver shingles, was his throne, which constituted the most righteous judgment-seat of the world.

Förstemann, CARL EDUARD, a Lutheran theologian of Germany, secretary at the university library in Halle, who died in 1847, published, *Brück's Geschichte der Religionshandlung* (in the *Archiv für die Geschichte der Kirchl. Reformation*, Halle, 1831):—*Urkundenbuch* *zu der Geschichte des Reichstages zu Augsburg im Jahre* 1530 (1833, 2 vols.):—*Zehn Briefe Dr. Johann Forster's an Johann Schradi* (Nordhausen, 1835):—*Luther's Testamente aus den Jahren* 1537 *und* 1542 (ibid. 1846):—*Denkmale dem Dr. M. Luther von der Hochachtung und Liebe seiner Zeitgenossen errichtet* (ibid. eod.):—*Luther's Tod und Begräbniss im Jahre* 1546 (ibid. eod.). See Winer, *Handbuch der theol. Lit.* i, 741, 752; Zuchold, *Bibl. Theol.* i, 367. (B. P.)

Forster, Froben, a German philosopher and ecclesiastic, was born Aug. 30, 1709, at Königsberg. He studied at Regensburg, where he also joined the Benedictines, and took holy orders in 1733. In 1744 he was called to Salzburg, but in 1747 was recalled to his monastery, and became its prior in 1750. In 1762 he was made abbot, and died Oct. 11, 1791. He wrote, besides philosophical treatises, *De Scripturæ Sacræ Vulgata Editione* (Salzburg, 1748), and edited *Alcuini Opera* (ibid. 1777, 4 vols. fol.). (B. P.)

Förster, Heinrich, D.D., an eminent Roman Catholic prelate of Germany, was born Nov. 24, 1800, at Gross-Glogau. He studied at Breslau, and received holy orders in 1825. While chaplain and pastor at Landshut, his pulpit abilities became known, and he was called, in 1837, as cathedral-dean to Breslau. When bishop Diepenbrock died in 1853, Förster was appointed as "persona gratissima" his successor. At the Vatican council he belonged to the opposition party, but finally yielded, and accepted the dogma of infallibility. Not obeying the so-called May-laws of the Prussian government, he was deposed, in 1875, from his office, and fled to the castle in Johannisberg, in Austro-Silesia, where he died, Oct. 20, 1881. He is the author of, *Lebensbild Diepenbrocks* (Breslau, 1869):—*Predigten* (ibid. 1851, 7 vols.; 5th ed. Ratisbon, 1878):—*Pastoral Letters* (Breslau, 1880, 2 vols.). See Franz, *Heinrich Förster, Fürstbischof von Breslau, ein Lebensbild* (Breslau, 1875). (B. P.)

Forster, Johann, a Lutheran theologian of Germany, was born Dec. 25, 1576. He studied at Leipsic, was in 1599 preacher there, in 1601 rector at Schneeberg, in 1609 professor of theology at Wittenberg, and in 1613 general superintendent and president of the consistory at Mansfeld. He died Nov. 17, 1613, leaving, *Systema Problematum Theologicorum*:—*Vindiciæ Lutheri*:—*Comment. in Jesaiam*:—*Thesaurus Catecheticus*:—*Comment. in Jeremiam Ejusque Threnos*:—*Medulla Capitis* 53 *Jesaiæ Disputationibus* 5 *Expressa*:—*Passio Christi Typica ex Psalmis et Prophetis*, etc. See Jöcher, *Allgemeines Gelehrten-Lexikon*, s. v. (B. P.)

Förster, Johann Christian, a Lutheran theologian of Germany, was born at Auerstädt, in Thuringia, Oct. 6, 1754. He studied at Leipsic, was in 1782 afternoon-preacher at Naumburg, and in 1794 cathedral-preacher there; in 1800 accepted a call as superintendent to Weissenfels, and died there at the end of that same year. He published a number of ascetical books. See Döring, *Die gelehrten Theologen Deutschlands*, i, 418 sq.; Winer, *Handbuch der theol. Lit.* ii, 132, 207, 213, 224, 252, 331, 366, 394. (B. P.)

Forsyth, John Alexander, LL.D., a Scotch clergyman, son of John Forsyth, graduated from the university and King's College, Aberdeen, in 1786; was licensed to preach Oct. 13, 1790; presented by the king to the living at Belhelvie, in succession to his father, in January, 1791, and ordained Aug. 24 following. He died June 11, 1843, aged seventy-four years. To his knowledge of theology and the pastoral office he added a profound knowledge of chemistry, and was of great service to the British government in the manufacture of gunpowder. He was the discoverer, in 1805, of the percussion-lock, which was afterwards universally adopted, both in the army and by sportsmen; but he never received any public reward. See *Fasti Eccles. Scoticanæ*, iii, 495.

Fortiguerra, Niccolo (1), a Dominican of Sienna, was born in 1180, made bishop of Aleria in 1264, and died in 1270, leaving *Postillæ in IV Prophetas Majores, in IV Evangelia, in Epistolas Pauli et in Apocalypsin*:—*Comment. in Dionysium de Divinis Nominibus*:—*De Duabus in Christo Naturis*:—*De Cœlibatu*. See Jöcher, *Allgemeines Gelehrten-Lexikon*, s. v. (B. P.)

Fortiguerra (or **Forteguerri**), **Niccolo** (2), an Italian cardinal of the 15th century, who rendered important military and diplomatic service to popes Eugenius IV, Nicholas V, Pius II, and Paul II, and was a liberal patron of learning, died at Viterbo in 1473, aged fifty-five years.

Fortiguerra, Niccolo (3), an Italian prelate and poet, surnamed *the Younger*, to distinguish him from an ancient member of his family, the cardinal of the same name, was born at Pistoja, Nov. 25, 1674. While still young, he showed quite a disposition for poetry; but after he had been made doctor, in 1695, he went to Rome, and distinguished himself there by his knowledge. He accompanied into Spain the papal legate, Zondadari, and on his return to Rome became honorary chamberlain to Clement XI, canon of Santa Maria Maggiore, and referendary of two chancelleries. About the same time he was admitted into the academy of the Arcades, under the name of *Nidalmo Tiseo*. In 1715 he improvised a poem in the manner of Berni, Du Pulci, and Ariosto. He died Feb. 17, 1735, leaving several orations, addresses, and other minor pieces, for which see Hoefer, *Nouv. Biog. Générale*, s. v.

Fortius, Johannes, a convert from Judaism, who lived in the 16th century, is the author of a Hebrew grammar, entitled ס' דקדוק (Prague, 1570):—*De Mystica Litterarum Significatione* (part of it reprinted in Kircher's *Œdipus Ægyptiacus*, Rome, 1652–54). See Fürst, *Bibl. Jud.* i, 287; Steinschneider, *Biblogr. Handbuch*, s. v.; Jöcher, *Allgemeines Gelehrten-Lexikon*, s. v. (B. P.)

Fortlage, Arnold Rudolph Karl, a German philosopher, was born June 12, 1806, at Osnabrück. He first studied theology at Göttingen and Berlin, but, attracted by Hegel's lectures, betook himself entirely to the study of philosophy, which he continued in 1829 at Munich, under Schelling. In the same year he commenced his philosophical lectures at Heidelberg; in 1845 he was at Berlin, and in the following year accepted a call to Jena, where he died, Nov. 8, 1881. Of his works we mention, *Die Lücken des Hegel'schen Systems der Philosophie*, etc. (Heidelberg and Leipsic, 1832):—*Philosophische Meditationen über Plato's Symposion* (Heidelberg, 1835):—*Aurelii Augustini Doctrina de Tempora* (ibid. 1836):—*Genetische Geschichte der Philosophie seit Kant* (Leipsic, 1852):—*Das System der Psychologie als empirischer Wissenschaft aus der Beobachtung des innern Sinnes* (ibid. 1855, 2 vols.):—*Acht Psychologische Vorträge* (Jena, 1869):—*Sechs Psychologische Vorträge* (1870):—*Vier Psychologische Vorträge* (1874):—*Beiträge zur Psychologie als Wissenschaft aus Spekulation und Erfahrung* (Leipsic, 1875), as a supplement to his *System*. His position concerning the philosophy of religion Fortlage had already defined in the *Darstellung und Kritik der Beweise für das Dasein Gottes* (Heidelberg, 1840). The belief in God is not a matter of rational persuasion, but rests entirely on moral motives. Religion is essentially a moral state, and only the translation of this state into the idea is the dogma of God's existence. Philosophic speculation had the peculiar fate that it commenced with the secondary factor of the religious consciousness, and found itself, and this against its own will, only towards the end driven back to the other. This turn, so rich in consequences, commenced with Kant—after him the philosophy of religion, instead of advancing, has only been protracted. But Kant, too, needs to be supplemented: the purely transcendental belief, emanating from a moral and religious need, asks for precise points from which it connects with the material world; it necessarily wishes to know the places, where upon entering into the world, it can suppose the efficiency of the character of its moral persuasion, in accordance with reason and experience. This is the gap which Fortlage endeavored to fill out in his lectures on the philosophy of religion. Besides these works he wrote, *Das musikalische System der Griechen*, etc. (Leipsic, 1847):—the article "Griechische Musik," in Ersch and Gruber's *Allg. Encyklopädie*, lxxxi, 175-245 (ibid. 1863):—*Die Gesänge Christlicher Vorzeit* (Berlin, 1844, containing translations of Greek and Latin hymns):—*Vorlesungen über die Geschichte der Poësie* (Stuttgart, 1839). (B. P.)

Förtsch, MICHAEL, a Lutheran theologian of Germany, was born July 24, 1654, at Wertheim, in Franconia, studied at different universities, was in 1695 professor at Tübingen, in 1705 professor at Jena, and died April 24, 1724. He published, *Commentarius ad Ambrosii Libros de Officiis:—Institutio Isagogica de Justitia et Jure:—De Origine, Veritate, et Immutabili Rectitudine Juris Naturalis*, etc.:—*Vindiciæ Doctrinæ de Divina Scripturæ Sacræ Inspiratione:—Dissertationes ad Ezech. iii*, 17-19; *Hos. v.* 6; *Matt. xix*, 28; *x*, 22; *Rom. i*, 4; *i*, 17; *i*, 19, 20; *viii*, 14; *viii*, 21; *Tit. i*, 1, 2; *Hebr. ii*, 10, 11, etc. See Köcher, *Schediasma de Vita, Scriptis, ac Meritis Fœrtschii in Ecclesiam* (1725); Jöcher, *Allgemeines Gelehrten-Lexikon*, s. v. (B. P.)

Fortunātus, an Italian hagiographer, was born at Vercellæ in the beginning of the 6th century. He has been confounded sometimes with Fortunatus Venantius. He merited by his knowledge the surname of the *Philosopher of the Lombards*, and was elevated to the episcopate; it is not known, however, in what diocese. He was obliged to leave his church, but for what reason is unknown; retired to France, where he bound himself in friendship with St. Germanus, bishop of Paris; and died at Chelles, near Paris, about 569. He wrote the *Life of St. Marcellus*. The *Life of St. Hilary* has also been attributed to him. See Hoefer, *Nouv. Biog. Générale*, s. v.; Smith, *Dict. of Christ. Antiq.* s. v.

Fortunatus's (VENANTIUS) **Hymns**. Fortunatus is the author of the following hymns: *Vexilla Regis Prodeunt* (q. v.), translated into English ("The royal banners forward go") by Neale, in *Mediæval Hymns and Sequences* (Lond. 1867), p. 6:—*Quem Terra, Pontus, Æthera* (English translation, "The God whom earth and sea and sky," in *Hymns Ancient and Modern*):—*Pange Lingua, Gloriosi* (q. v.):—*Crux Benedicta Nitet* (the original is found in Trench, *Sacred Latin Poetry*, p. 130 sq., and an English translation, "The blessed cross shines now to us," in *Lyra Messianica*, p. 220 sq.):—*Salve, Festa Dies, toto Venerabilis Ævo* (q. v.):—*Agnoscet Omne Sæculum*, on the nativity of Christ:—*Tibi Laus Perennis Author*, on baptism. "The poetry of Venantius Prudentius," says Mr. Yule (*Dict. of Christ. Biog.* s. v.), "represents the expiring effort of the Latin muse in Gaul. Even the poet himself felt the decadence not merely of language, but of thought, which characterizes his verse,

> 'Ast ego sensus inops...
> Fæce gravis, sermone levis, ratione pigrescens,
> Mente hebes, arte carens, usu rudis, ore nec expers'
> (*Vit. St. Martin*, v. 26-28),

and it is difficult to dissent from the severe judgment he has passed upon himself. His style is pedantic, his taste bad, his grammar and prosody seldom correct for many lines together. Two of his longer poems, however, display a simplicity and pathos which are foreign to his usual style. One of these treats of the marriage of Galesuintha, sister of Brunehart, with Chilperic; the other is the elegy upon the fall of Thuringia. For what is of real merit in these two pieces we are in all probability indebted to the genius of Rhadegund rather than to any sudden access of inspiration in the poet himself." See Trench, *Sacred Latin Poetry;* Daniel, *Thesaurus Hymnologicus*, i, 168 sq.; Bormann, *Ueber das Leben des Lateinischen Dichters Fortunatus* (Fulda, 1848). (B. P.)

Fortune, in Roman and Greek mythology, "chance." This goddess, called *Tyche* by the Greeks, was represented at Ægira, in Achaia, in a small temple, by the horn of Amalthæa, and a small winged Cupid, which signified that the love-affairs of men were furthered more by fortune than by beauty. Pindar, therefore, called her one of the Parcæ, or goddesses of destiny. The Fortuna of the Romans had temples in various parts of the city, and in several cities of the empire, those at Antium (Horace, *Od.* i, 35) and Præneste being the most celebrated.

Antique Statue of Fortune.

Fortunio, AGOSTINO, an Italian member of the order of the Camaldules, who lived in the 16th century, is the author of, *Historiarum Camaldulensiam Libri* 3 (Florence, 1575):—*Historiar. Camald. pars Posterior* (Venice, 1579):—*De Origine Ordinis Camaldulensis* (Florence, 1592). See Winer, *Handbuch der theol. Lit.* i, 714; Jöcher, *Allgemeines Gelehrten-Lexikon*, s. v. (B. P.)

Forty Martyrs. (1) This number of soldiers is commemorated on March 9, as having suffered under Licinius in 320, at Sebaste, in Armenia. (2) Another set of forty martyrs is commemorated on May 20, as having suffered in Persia, A.D. 375. (3) Forty virgins are said to have suffered on Dec. 24, under Decius, at Antioch, in Syria.

Foscarari (Lat. *Forsherarius*), EGIDIO, an Italian Roman Catholic prelate, was born at Bologna, Jan. 27, 1512. He entered the Dominican order, and in 1544 became prior and inquisitor at his native place, and afterwards bishop of Modena. He was imprisoned for heresy by Paul V, but vindicated by Pius IV. He entered the Council of Trent in 1561, in which he assisted Forerius and Leonardo Marini in preparing the catechism, and correcting the missal and breviary. He died at Rome, Dec. 23, 1564. He was frugal, modest, and austere, and devoted much time and money to the poor and to the reclamation of the vicious classes.

Foss, ARCHIBALD CAMPBELL, a Methodist Episcopal minister, son of Rev. Cyrus Foss, was born at Phillipstown, N. Y., March 6, 1830. He spent two years of his youth as clerk in a dry-goods store in New York city; entered Amenia Seminary at the age of seventeen; became highly honored for his scholarly and Christian character; received license to preach; entered the Sophomore class of Wesleyan University at the age of nineteen; supported himself by teaching during vacations; graduated in 1852, and immediately joined the New York Conference. His appointments were: Lenox, 1852 and 1853; Morrisania, 1854 and 1855; Thirtieth Street, New York city, 1856 and 1857; St. Paul's, 1858 and 1859; the next year with Dr. McClintock, Tarrytown, but labored there only a few weeks, when, being appointed to the professorship of Latin and Hebrew in Wesleyan University, he repaired thither, and there continued two years; Poughkeepsie District, 1862 to June, 1865; Thirtieth Street, New York city, July, 1865, to 1867, and finally to Sing Sing, in 1868, where he labored one year, and then retired from the effective ranks and sailed to Europe. In 1869 he preached one month in Florence, Italy, and another in Lausanne, Switzerland. Early in 1870 he left his pleasant Swiss home for a tour through the principal cities of Italy. He returned to Clarens,

Switzerland, March 3, thoroughly worn out with fatigue, and prostrated with gastric fever, and after a few days of suffering died. Mr. Foss was pre-eminently independent and original. He was brave and self-reliant, a wise and safe counsellor, generous, yet cautious, patient, painstaking, able, and eminently successful. See *Minutes of Annual Conferences*, 1870, p. 97.

Fossarii (or **Fossōres**), the term by which the *grave-diggers* or sextons of the early Church were designated. The term *fossor* is of frequent occurrence in the inscriptions of the catacombs. The most common appearance of the term is in the later epitaphs, which testify to the purchase of graves from individuals of this class. The burial of the departed was probably at first a work of Christian charity, performed without fee or reward by their surviving brethren. Afterwards, when the Church had become more numerous, it was

Fresco of Fossor in the Cemetery of Callistus.

He wears a tunic marked with *gammadia* on its hem, carries a pick over his right shoulder, and a lamp in his left hand, and is surrounded by a heap of levers, picks, and other tools employed in his work. Above is the inscription: "Diogenes Fossor in pace depositus Octabu Kalendas Octobris."

carried out at the public expense under the special care of the presbyters of the "titles" of Rome. When Christianity became the established religion, the *fossores* evidently established a kind of property in the catacombs, which authorized them to sell graves either to living persons for their own burial, or to the friends of the deceased. This state of things seems to have had a widespread but transient existence. A fossor's pick has been discovered by De' Rossi in the cemetery of Callistus, much oxidized, but still recognizable. See Martigny, *Dict. des Antiq. Chrétiennes*, s. v.

Fosse, Charles de la, an eminent French painter, was born at Paris in 1640, studied under Charles le Brun, and having gained the prize of the academy, was sent to Italy with the royal pension. On his return to Paris he was immediately taken into the service of Louis XIV, and painted four fine pictures for the apartments of the Tuileries. His next work was a fresco painting in the chapel of St. Eustache, representing *Adam and Eve*, and the *Marriage of the Virgin*. In 1693 he was elected a royal academician. The following are some of his best paintings at Versailles: *The Sacrifice of Iphigenia; The Infant Moses Saved from the Nile; The Resurrection; The Nativity; The Adoration of the Magi.* He died at Paris in 1716. See Spooner, *Biog. Hist. of the Fine Arts*, s. v.

Fosta, in North German mythology, was a goddess worshipped by the Frisians. She stands in close union with Hertha, the goddess of the earth. Both are goddesses of peace, and it is singular that they appear armed. In the temple of Fosta, on Helgoland, she was represented with bow and arrow at her back, a helmet on her head, five arrows in her left hand, and four ears of corn in her right. She was worshipped in Holstein and Denmark.

Foster, Eden Burroughs, D.D., a Congregational minister, grandson of Rev. Eden Burroughs, D.D., of Hanover, N. H., was born at Hanover, May 26, 1813. He studied at Kimball Union Academy; graduated from Dartmouth College in 1837, and spent one year at Andover Theological Seminary. From Aug. 18, 1841, to Jan. 7, 1847, he was pastor in Henniker. After supplying the church in Pelham for several months, he was installed pastor of it, June 21, 1848, and remained until January, 1853; thereafter was pastor of the John Street Church, Lowell, Mass.; in 1861 at West Springfield; and in May, 1866, was reinstalled at Lowell, where he died, April 11, 1882. After 1875 he was assisted by a colleague. Among his publications are the following: *Sermons on Baptism* (1843):—*Duty of Young Men* (1850). See *Cong. Year-book*, 1883, p. 22.

Fothad, a Scotch prelate, was deprived in the first year of his administration of the see of St. Andrews (952), by king Indulfus. He died in 961 or 962. See Keith, *Scottish Bishops*, p. 6.

Fotherby, Martin, D.D., dean of Canterbury, was born at Great Grimsby in 1559, educated at and became a fellow of Trinity College, Cambridge. In 1596 was prebendary of Canterbury, and in 1618 bishop of Salisbury. He died March 12, 1619, leaving *Four Sermons* (1608):—*The Clearing of Four Truths against Atheists* (1622). See Chalmers, *Biog. Dict.* s. v.; Allibone, *Dict. of Brit. and Amer. Authors*, s. v.

Fothergill, George, D.D., an English divine, was born at Lockholme, in Ravenstonedale, in 1705, and educated at Oxford, where he became fellow. He was elected principal of Edmund Hall, Oct. 17, 1751, vicar of Bramley soon after, and died Oct. 5, 1760. His works were published in 1756, 1757, 1758, and some *Sermons* in 1761 and 1762. See Chalmers, *Biog. Dict.* s. v.; Allibone, *Dict. of Brit. and Amer. Authors*, s. v.

Foullon, Jean Erard, a French Jesuit, and rector of the college at Huy, who was born at Liege in 1608, and died Oct. 25, 1668, is the author of, *Jonas Typus Hominis a Deo Fugientis:—Compendium Historiæ Leodicensis:—Comment. Historici et Morales ad Duos Libros Maccabæorum.* See Winer, *Handbuch der theol. Lit.* i, 825; Jöcher, *Allgemeines Gelehrten-Lexikon*, s. v.; *Biog. Universelle*, s. v. (B. P.)

Foulques (Lat. *Fulco*), a French prelate, was born about 850, and educated in the church at Rheims, where he was eventually a canon. He afterwards became abbot of St. Beitun, and in March, 883, archbishop of Rheims. He greatly improved the diocese, but at length became so deeply involved in the political convulsions of the times that he was assassinated in 900. See Hoefer, *Nouv. Biog. Générale*, s. v.

Foulques (surnamed *the Great*), a French writer of sacred history, was born in the first part of the 11th century. He was the thirty-first abbot of Corbie; assisted as such at the Council of Rheims in 1049, and at the Council of the General States in 1065, at Corbie. He is noted for his long contest for the privileges of his Church against two bishops of Amiens. He died in 1095. See Hoefer, *Nouv. Biog. Générale*, s. v.

Fountayne, John, D.D., an English clergyman, was born at Merton, near Doncaster, about 1714. He was educated at Catherine Hall, Cambridge, of which he became fellow; and was successively prebendary of Salisbury, canon of Windsor, and dean of York. Twice in his life, if not oftener, he might have been advanced to the episcopal bench, but declined it. He died Feb. 14, 1802. He was exemplary in the discharge of every relative and social duty; hospitable, benevolent, and a lover of good men. See *The* (Lond.) *Christian Observer*, February, 1802, p. 144.

Fouquet (or **Foucquet**), Louis, a French prelate, who died in 1703, bishop and count of Agde, and master of the royal oratory, became involved in trouble, and finally retired from his diocese. See Hoefer, *Nouv Biog. Générale*, s. v.

Four Crowned Martyrs. See CORONATI QUATUOR.

Four Rivers. See RIVERS, THE FOUR.

Fourmont, MICHEL, a famous French Orientalist, was born at Herblay, Sept. 28, 1690, and died at Paris, Feb. 5, 1746. He was professor of Syriac at the royal college in Paris, and member of the Academy of Inscriptions. Many of his dissertations are found in the *Mémoires* of the academy. See Lichtenberger, *Encyclop. des Sciences Religieuses,* s. v.; Freret, *Éloge de l'Abbé Fourmont,* in *Hist. de l'Académie des Inscriptions,* xviii, 432; Jöcher, *Allgemeines Gelehrten-Lexikon,* s. v.; Hoefer, *Nouv. Biog. Générale,* s. v.

Fournier (*baron de la Contamine*), MARIE NICOLAS, a French prelate, was born at Gex (Ain), Dec. 27, 1760; educated in Paris; became professor of theology at Orleans; after the Revolution went to Paris as a preacher; was appointed (1805) chaplain, afterwards almoner to the emperor, and bishop of Montpellier, July 15, 1806; was nominated, in 1817, for the archbishopric of Navarre, but was not confirmed, and died at Montpellier, Dec. 29, 1834. See Hoefer, *Nouv. Biog. Générale,* s. v.

Fowler, Charles James, LL.D., a Scotch clergyman, was licensed to preach by the Aberdeen Presbytery in 1828; elected minister of the church at Roxburgh Place, Morningside, Edinburgh, and ordained Aug. 7, 1834; transferred to St. Luke's, Glasgow, Feb. 22, 1837; promoted to Ratho, Dec. 22, 1842, and died at Torquay, England, March 16, 1866. He published *The Right Improvement of Divine Judgments* (a sermon, 1851):—lectures on *The Evidences of Revealed Religion,* on *Infidelity,* and on *Sabbath-Schools:—A Preface to Watson's Apology for the Bible.* See *Fasti Eccles. Scoticanæ,* i, 131; ii, 45.

Fowler, Joseph, an eminent English Wesleyan minister, was born at Little Horton, near Bradford, Yorkshire, May 18, 1791. He was educated at the Bradford Grammar-school, converted under the preaching of John Crosse, vicar of Bradford, and in 1811 admitted into the ministry. In 1848 he was elected secretary of the conference, and it was owing to failure of health that he was not elected president in 1849 or 1850. He died, after acute suffering, in the Chapel-house, City Road, London, March 17, 1851, being the only preacher who has died there since Wesley. Joseph Fowler was an able preacher, a judicious superintendent, an unwearied pastor, and a large-hearted friend. He was the leader of the liberal section of the conference. See Stevenson, *City Road Chapel,* p. 324 sq.; *Wesl. Meth. Magazine,* 1851, p. 400, 918; 1852, p. 242; *Minutes of the British Conference,* 1851; *Wesl. Takings* (Lond. 1841), i, 351.

Fowler, Philemon Halsted, D.D., a Presbyterian minister, was born at Albany, N. Y., Feb. 9, 1814. He received his preparatory education at the academy in his native place; graduated from Hobart College, Geneva, in 1832, and for one year was tutor in that institution; was licensed by the Albany Presbytery, Oct. 15, 1835; graduated from Princeton Theological Seminary in 1836; served as pastor elect the Second Presbyterian Church of Washington, D. C.; and in 1839 was installed in Elmira, N. Y., where he remained until 1850. In 1851 he became pastor of the First Presbyterian Church of Utica, where he labored till 1874. In 1866 he was made a member of the Joint Committee on Reunion, on the part of the New School General Assembly; in 1869 was elected moderator of the General Assembly. He died Dec. 19, 1879. Dr. Fowler was the author of a number of published sermons and small volumes, his largest work being his *History of Presbyterianism in Central New York* (1877). He was a member of the American Board of Commissioners for Foreign Missions, a trustee of Hamilton College, and a director of Auburn Theological Seminary. He was widely known and honored for his personal qualities. He preached Christ with great directness and fidelity. See *Necrol. Report of Princeton Theol. Sem.* 1880, p. 23.

Fowler, Robert, D.D., an Irish prelate, was prebendary of Westminster, and received his education at Trinity College, Cambridge, where he took the degree of bachelor of arts in 1747, master of arts in 1751, and in 1771 was promoted to the see of Killaloe and Kilfenora. In 1773 he was ordered by the House of Lords to preach before them at Christ Church on Oct. 2; translated to the see of Dublin, Dec. 22, 1778; in 1782 was one of twelve spiritual peers who protested against the bill for the relief of the Dissenters; in 1789 concurred with fourteen others in protesting against the memorable address of the Irish House of Lords to the prince of Wales. He died at Bassingbourne Hall, near Dunmow, in Essex, Oct. 10, 1801. See D'Alton, *Memoirs of the Abps. of Dublin,* p. 347.

Fowler, William Chauncey, LL.D., a Congregational minister, was born at Killingworth (now Clinton), Conn., Sept. 1, 1793. He graduated from Yale College in 1816, and then spent a year as private tutor in a family in Fauquier County, Va.; resumed his position as rector of the grammar-school in New Haven, beginning also the study of theology under Professor Fitch. In 1819 he was appointed tutor in the college, and Aug. 31, 1825, was ordained pastor of the Congregational Church in Greenfield, Mass. In 1827 he was dismissed, to accept the professorship of chemistry and natural history in Middlebury College, Vt., where he remained until 1838, and then went to Amherst College, Mass., as professor of rhetoric. He resigned this position in 1843, but continued to reside in Amherst till 1858, when he removed to Durham, Conn., and died there, Jan. 15, 1881. From the time of his resignation as professor, he was engaged in preparing various works for the press. In 1845 he edited the university edition of Webster's *Dictionary.* He next prepared three volumes, composing a series of English grammars, entitled *The English Language in its Elements and Forms.* In 1858 he published *Memorials of the Chaunceys;* in 1863 *The Sectional Controversy;* in 1866 a *History of Durham;* in 1872 a *Treatise on Local Law in Massachusetts and Connecticut;* and later several collections of essays. In 1850 he was elected to the Massachusetts legislature from the town of Amherst. He represented the 18th district of Connecticut in the state senate in 1864. See *Obituary Record of Yale College,* 1881.

Fox, CHARLES M., LL.D., a Protestant Episcopal clergyman, of the diocese of Illinois, was rector of St. Paul's Church, Brooklyn, N. Y., in 1870. He died Sept. 4, 1871. See *Prot. Episc. Almanac,* 1872, p. 127.

Fox-worship, a species of idolatry practiced only among the Japanese, who seem to be in doubt as to whether the fox is a god or a devil. If a Japanese feels himself in need of supernatural aid, he sets out a platter of rice and beans as an offering to his fox, and if on the following day some of it has disappeared, this is looked upon as a favorable omen. There are in Japan two species of foxes, very much like the ordinary foxes of Europe and America, and, from the immunity they enjoy, they are great nuisances. See Gardner, *Faiths of the World,* s. v.

Fraction, a technical name for the act of breaking the bread in the celebration of the holy eucharist. There are three kinds of fraction in use at present; though only the first of them is essential to the sacrament, and can be traced with certainty to the infancy of the Church: (1) a fraction illustrative of the words of institution, and therefore a direct imitation of our Lord's action; (2) purely symbolical fractions after the consecration has been completed; (3) the necessary fraction for the distribution of the bread among the communicants. For the illustration of each of these in the various rituals, see Smith, *Dict. of Christ. Antiq.* s. v.

Frähn, Christian Martin, a famous German Orientalist, numismatician, and historian, was born at Rostock, June 4, 1782, where he also pursued his Oriental studies. In 1807 he was appointed professor of Oriental languages at Kasan, and in 1815 chief librarian and director of the Asiatic Museum at St. Petersburg, where he died, Aug. 16, 1851. He published, among other works, *Recensio Numorum Muhamedanorum* (St. Petersburg, 1826), to which must be added his *Opuscula Posthuma* (ed. by Dorn, ibid. 1855-77, 2 vols.):—*Ibn Fosslans und anderer Araber Berichte über die Russen älterer Zeit* (ibid. 1823):—*Topographische Uebersicht der Ausgrabungen von altem arabischen Gelde in Russland* (ibid. 1841):—*Curarum Exeget. et Crit. in Nahumum prophet. Specimen* (Rostock, 1806):—*De Chasaris* (St. Petersburg, 1822). See Hoefer, *Nouv. Biog. Générale*, s. v. (B. P.)

Franceschini, Baldassare (called *il Volterrano*), an eminent Italian painter, was born at Volterra in 1611, and studied under Matteo Roselli and Gio. de San Giovanni. Among his great frescos is the cupola of the Cappella Niccolini, in the church of Santa Croce at Florence; and in the vault of a chapel of Santa Maria Maggiore is a picture of *Elias*, which is considered a grand production. He died in 1689. See Hoefer, *Nouv. Biog. Générale*, s. v.; Spooner, *Biog. Hist. of the Fine Arts*, s. v.

Franceschini, *Cav.* **Marc' Antonio**, an eminent Italian painter, was born at Bologna, April 5, 1648, and was instructed in the school of Gio. Battista Galli. The principal works of this master at Bologna are a ceiling in the Palazzo Ranuzzi; *The Death of St. Joseph*, in Corpus Domini; *St. Francis of Sales Kneeling before the Virgin and Infant*, in La Madonna di Galeria; a fine picture of *The Annunciation*, at the Institute. At Rimini, in the Church of the Augustines, is a fine picture of *St. Tommaso Giving Alms to the Poor*. Franceschini died Dec. 24, 1728. See Hoefer, *Nouv. Biog. Générale*, s. v.; Spooner, *Biog. Hist. of the Fine Arts*, s. v.

Francesco, Medico, an Italian convert from Judaism, who lived at Mantua in the 17th century, is the author of, אִגֶּרֶת, or *Epistola in Lingua Hebr., Chald., Syriaca*, etc. (Mantua, 1630; transl. into Germ. by Chrys. Dudulæus, Nuremberg, s. a.). See Fürst, *Bibl. Jud.* i, 287; Wolf, *Bibl. Hebr.* iii, 951. (B. P.)

Franchi, Antonio, a reputable Italian painter, was born at Lucca, July 14, 1634, studied under Baldassare Franceschini, and settled at Florence. He painted a number of works for the churches, among which his picture of *Christ Giving the Keys to St. Peter*, in the parochial church of Caporgnano, at Lucca, is considered his masterpiece. He died July 8, 1709. See Hoefer, *Nouv. Biog. Générale*, s. v.; Spooner, *Biog. Hist. of the Fine Arts*, s. v.

Franchi, Guglielmo, an Italian convert from Judaism, of the 16th century, is the author of שמש לשון הקדש, or a Hebrew grammar in the Italian language (Bergamo, 1591, and often):—*Alphabetum Hebraicum*, or a Hebrew reader (Rome, 1596). See Fürst, *Bibl. Jud.* i, 287; Jöcher, *Allgemeines Gelehrten-Lexikon*, s. v.; Steinschneider, *Bibliogr. Handbuch*, s. v.; Wolf, *Bibl. Hebr.* iii, 237. (B. P.)

Franchini, Giovanni, an eminent Italian ecclesiastical historian, was born at Modena, Dec. 28, 1633. Having entered the order of the Minorites, he became theologian to Francis II, duke of Modena. He died in his native city, April 4, 1695, leaving several works on the history of his order, for which see Hoefer, *Nouv. Biog. Générale*, s. v.

Francis. See Francesco; François.

Francisci, Erasmus, a Lutheran hymn-writer, was born Nov. 19, 1627, at Lübeck, and died at Nuremberg, Dec. 20, 1694. Some of his hymns are still to be found in German hymn-books. See Molleri, *Cimbria Litterata*, i, 178-184; Wezel, *Hymnopœographia*, i, 227-233; Jöcher, *Allgemeines Gelehrten-Lexikon*, s. v.; Koch, *Geschichte des deutschen Kirchenliedes*, iii, 526 sq. (B. P.)

Franciscis, Alessandro di, an Italian Dominican of the 16th century. Being of Jewish origin, he was also called *Hebræus* or *Hebræinus*. He was vicar-general and procurator of his order, in 1594 received the episcopal see at Forli, but resigned his office in 1597, and retired to Rome, where he died about 1600. He wrote a commentary on Genesis and on Exodus, 1-20, which is still in manuscript in the Vatican library. See Jöcher, *Allgemeines Gelehrten-Lexikon*, s. v.; Ughelli, *Italia Sacra*, ii, 629; Delitzsch, *Wissenschaft, Kunst, Judenthum*, p. 292. (B. P.)

Franck, Johann, a Lutheran hymn-writer of Germany, was born June 1, 1618, at Guben, in Lower Lusatia, and died June 18, 1677. His hymns belong to the gems of German hymnology. Some of his spiritual songs have also been translated into English. See Wezel, *Hymnop.* i, 164 sq.; Pasig's introduction to his edition of Franck's *Hymns* (Grimma, 1846); Jentsch, *Johann Franck von Guben* (Guben, 1877); Koch, *Gesch. des deutschen Kirchenliedes*, iii, 278 sq. (B. P.)

Franck, Sebastian. See Francus.

Franck, Solomon, a Lutheran hymn-writer of Germany, was born March 6, 1659, at Weimar, and died July 11, 1725. Some of his hymns are still in use in the German Church. They were edited by Schauer, *Sol. Franck's Geistliche Lieder* (Halle, 1855). See Wezel, *Hymnop.* i, 217 sq.; Koch, *Geschichte des deutschen Kirchenliedes*, v, 420 sq. (B. P.)

Francke, August, a Lutheran theologian of Germany, was born in 1792. He commenced his ministerial work in 1816, was in 1821 preacher at Dresden, in 1828 court-preacher there, and died in 1859. He published, *De Fide Christo Habenda* (Dresden, 1830):—*Das Altarfest des evangelischen Christen* (ibid. 1834):—*Geschichte des biblischen Offenbarungs Glaubens* (ibid. 1830):—*Das Leben Jesu* (Leipsic, 1839; 3d ed. 1842):—*Die Grundlehren der Religion Jesu* (ibid. 1848). He also published a number of sermons. See Winer, *Handbuch der theol. Lit.* i, 445; Zuchold, *Bibl. Theol.* i, 371 sq. (B. P.)

Francke, Christoph, a Lutheran theologian of Germany, was born at Nuremberg, Oct. 26, 1642. He studied at different universities, commenced his academical career at Kiel in 1665, and died professor and librarian, Feb. 11, 1704, leaving, *Specimen Controversiarum Ecclesiæ Lutheranæ cum Remonstrantibus*:—*Exercitationes anti-Wendelianæ et anti-Limborchianæ*:—*Brevis et Liquida Demonstratio Deitatis Christi, Jonæ Slichtingio Opposita*. See Jöcher, *Allgemeines Gelehrten-Lexikon*, s. v.; Winer, *Handbuch der theol. Lit.* i, 353. (B. P.)

Francke, Georg Samuel, a Lutheran theologian of Germany, born Sept. 7, 1763, was in 1806 preacher at Sonderburg, in 1810 doctor and professor of theology at Kiel, and died March 28, 1840. He published, *Entwurf einer Apologetik der Christl. Religion* (Altona, 1817):—*De Historia Dogmatum Arminiorum* (Kiel, 1814):—*Commentat. Quædam Theologicæ de Librorum Vet. Test.* (1788):—*Ueber die neuren Schicksale des Spinozismus* (1808):—*Theologische Encyklopädie* (Altona, 1819). See Winer, *Handbuch der theol. Lit.* i, 3, 386, 765; Fürst, *Bibl. Jud.* i, 290. (B. P.)

Francke, Johann, a Lutheran theologian of Germany, was born in 1650. He studied at Leipsic, had several pastorates in Pomerania, and died April 17, 1723. He published, *Lux Tenebrosa*, etc.:—*Tenebræ Lucidæ*, etc.:—*Commentarius in Psalmos*:—*Prophetia Amosi, Nahumi, Habacuci, Sophoniæ, Obadiæ, Haggai, Malachiæ*:—*Ministerium Accentuum Ebræorum*. See Jöcher, *Allgemeines Gelehrten-Lexikon*, s. v.; Fürst, *Bibl. Jud.* i, 288. (B. P.)

Francklin, Thomas, D.D., an English clergyman,

was born in 1721, and in June, 1750, was chosen Greek professor of Cambridge. He was preferred to the livings of Ware and Thundrich in 1757, and to that of Brasted in 1776. He died in 1784. He published, separately, translations from Phalaris, Cicero, Sophocles, and Lucian (1749–81). See Chalmers, *Biographical Dictionary*, s. v.; Allibone, *Dict. of Brit. and Amer. Authors*, s. v.

Franco, Alfonso, an eminent painter of Messina, was born in 1466. His best pictures were in Messina, a *Taking Down from the Cross*, in the Church of San Francesco di Paolo, and the *Dispute of Christ with the Doctors*, in San Agostino. He died in 1524.

Franco, Battista (called *il Semelei*), an eminent painter and engraver, was born at Venice in 1498. He went to Rome and studied the works of Michael Angelo. He painted in fresco the choir of the Metropolitan Church at Urbino; and a picture in oil representing the *Virgin and Infant, between St. Peter and St. Paul.* There are several easel pictures from the life of Christ in the cathedral at Osimo. The following are some of his works; *Moses Striking the Rock; Abraham Meeting Melchisedec; Abraham about to Sacrifice Isaac; The Israelites Gathering Manna in the Desert; St. Jerome Holding a Skull; The Virgin and Infant with St. John; St. John the Baptist; The Adoration of the Shepherds, with Angels in the Clouds.* He died in 1561. See Hoefer, *Nouv. Biog. Générale*, s. v.; Spooner, *Biog. Hist. of the Fine Arts*, s. v.

François, Claude, a French ecclesiastic, was born at Paris in 1559, and made his profession at the abbey of the Benedictines of St. Vannes, March 21, 1589. In 1606 he aided in effecting a radical reformation within his congregation, revised the principal articles, and became a deputy to Monte-Cassino to consult the constitutions of that monastery. In 1610 he was sent to Paris to secure the approval of the new regulations by the ecclesiastical superiors and Louis XIII, and frequently served as president of his congregation. He died at St. Mihiel, Aug. 10, 1632, leaving several works relating particularly to the affairs of his order, for which see Hoefer, *Nouv. Biog. Générale*, s. v.

Frank, a name common to several Lutheran hymnwriters, of whom we mention the following:

1. Michael, was born March 16, 1609, and died Sept. 24, 1667. His hymns are collected in *Geistliches Harpffenspiel* (Coburg, 1657), and *Geistlicher Lieder erstes Zwölf* (ibid. 1662). See Koch, *Geschichte des deutschen Kirchenliedes*, iii, 435 sq.

2. Peter, a brother of Michael, was born Sept. 27, 1616, studied at Jena, was preacher in 1645, and died July 22, 1675. See Koch, *ut sup.*, p. 441 sq.; Ludovici, *De Hymnis et Hymnopolis Hennebergicis*, p. 21; Wezel, *Hymnopœographia*, i.

3. Sebastian, oldest brother of the three, was born Jan. 18, 1606, and died April 12, 1668. He suffered very much from the miseries of the Thirty Years' War. See Ludovici, *De Hymnis*, etc.; Winterfeld, *Der evang. Kirchengesang*, ii, 468–472 (Berlin, 1845); Koch, *ut sup.*, p. 431 sq. (B. P.)

Franke, Karl Christian Lebrecht, a Protestant theologian of Germany, was born Nov. 24, 1796, and died May 1, 1879, at Halle, doctor and professor of theology. He wrote, *De Diei Dominici Apud Veteres Christianos Celebratione* (Halle, 1826):—*Geschichte der Hallischen Reformation* (ibid. 1841). Besides, he published sermons, for which see Winer, *Handbuch der theol. Lit.* i, 617; ii, 36, 174; Zuchold, *Bibl. Theol.* i, 373 sq. (B. P.)

Fränkel, David (1), a Jewish author of Germany, born at Berlin in 1779, was director of the Jewish schools at Dessau, and died in 1865. He published, *Zeitschrift zur Beförderung der Kultur und Humanität unter der jüd. Nation* (1806–1840):—*Gemeinnützige Blätter für Wissenschaft, Schule und Leben* (Dessau, 1835):—*Die Lage der Juden in der ältern und neueren Zeit* (ibid. 1808). With M. H. Bock he translated the Pentateuch and Joshua into German (ibid. 1815). See Fürst, *Bibl. Jud.* i, 291. (B. P.)

Fränkel, David (2) *ben-Naftali Hirsch*, a Jewish rabbi, who was born at Dessau in 1707, and died at Berlin in 1767, is the author of a commentary on several treatises of the Jerusalem-Talmud. See Fürst, *Bibl. Jud.* i. 290 sq. (B. P.)

Frankel, Zacharias, a Jewish theologian, was born at Prague, Oct. 18, 1801. He studied in the University of Pesth, and received the degree of doctor of philosophy in 1831. In the spring of 1832 he was intrusted with the district-rabbinate of Leitmeritz, in Bohemia, and in the temple at Teplitz, his seat of office, the service received a new cast, owing to the German sermon which he was the first to introduce in the Bohemian synagogue. In 1836 he was called to Dresden as chief rabbi for Dresden and Leipsic. At Dresden, Frankel battled for justice at the bar of public opinion, and secured for the Jews the right of citizenship by his *Die Eidesleistung der Juden in theologischer und historischer Bedeutung* (Dresden, 1840; 2d ed. 1847), followed by *Der gerichtliche Beweis nach mosaisch-talmudischen Rechte* (Berlin, 1841), which promoted the cause of his Prussian co-religionists. In 1854 Frankel was called to Breslau to organize the Jewish theological seminary, whose director he became. He died at Breslau, Feb. 13, 1875. In the Christian world he is known as the author of, *Vorstudien zur Septuaginta* (Leipsic, 1841):—*Ueber den Einfluss der Palästinischen Exegese auf die Alexandrinische Hermeneutik* (ibid. 1851):—*Ueber Palästinische und Alexandrinische Schriftforschung* (Breslau, 1854). Of other works we mention, *Hodegetica in Mischnam Librosque cum ea Conjunctos* (in Hebrew, Leipsic, 1859):—*Additamenta* to the preceding work (also in Hebrew, ibid. 1865):—*Grundlinien des mosaisch-talmudischen Eherechtes* (Breslau, 1859):—*Entwurf einer Geschichte der Literatur der nachtalmudischen Responsen* (ibid. 1865):—*Introductio in Talmud Hierosolymitanum* (Hebrew, ibid. 1870):—*Targum der Propheten* (ibid. 1872). He also intended to publish a new edition of the Jerusalem-Talmud, with notes; of this, however, only two treatises, Berachoth and Peah, were printed (Vienna, 1874). In connection with other learned Jews, he published *Zeitschrift für die Religiösen Interessen des Judenthums* (Berlin, 1844–46, 3 vols.); and in 1851 he commenced his *Monatschrift für Geschichte und Wissenschaft des Judenthums*, which is still continued by Grätz and Frankel. See Fürst, *Bibl. Jud.* i, 294; Zuchold, *Bibl. Theol.* i, 374; Morais, *Eminent Israelites of the 19th Century* (Philadelphia, 1880), p. 81 sq. (B. P.)

Frankenberg, Abraham *von*, a German nobleman, an adherent of Jacob Böhme, was born June 24, 1593. He studied at Breslau, where he became acquainted with Böhme's writings. The latter's philosophy influenced him so much that he now betook himself entirely to mystic contemplations, and in order to do this with greater effect, he retired to his country-seat. He died June 25, 1652. For his writings and hymns see Arnold, *Ungarteiische Kirchen- und Ketzer-Historie*, ii, 410 sq.; Wezel, *Hymnopœographia*, iv; *Weimarisches Jahrbuch*, 1854, p. 157–160; Jöcher, *Allgemeines Gelehrten-Lexikon*, s. v.; Koch, *Geschichte des deutschen Kirchenliedes*, iii, 287 sq. (B. P.)

Frankfurter, Naftali, a Jewish rabbi of Germany, was born Feb. 13, 1810, at Oberndorf, in Würtemberg; studied at Heidelberg and Tübingen, was rabbi at Braunsbach, accepted in 1840 a call to Hamburg, and died there, April 13, 1866, leaving, besides *Sermons*, *Stillstand und Fortschritt* (Hamburg, 1841):—*Die Verantwortlichkeit des Volkslehrers im jetzigen Israel* (ibid. 1844). In connection with Berthold Auerbach he published *Gallerie der ausgezeichneten Israeliten* (Stuttgart, 1838). See Kayserling, *Bibliothek jüdischer Kanzelredner*, i, 278 sq.; *Allgemeine Zeitung des Judenthums*, 1866, col. 266; Fürst, *Bibl. Jud.* i, 296. (B. P.)

Frankland, Benjamin, A.B., one of the men representing the scholarship of the English Wesleyan Connection, was born at St. Ives, Cornwall, in May, 1819. He was a descendant of Dr. Benjamin Frankland, eminent as the great Puritan schoolmaster of his time (see Dr. Halley's *Puritanism in Lancashire*, etc.), the son of Rev. Benjamin Frankland, and brother of Rev. W. Joseph Frankland. He was educated at the Woodhouse Grove School (1829-33), and the University of Dublin (1837 sq.); and was for ten years tutor at Woodhouse Grove, and six months master at Wesley College, Sheffield. He was converted when eighteen years of age, entered the ministry in 1845, and throughout his various circuits, from Diss, in 1845, to Islington, London, in 1863, his ministry was greatly prized, especially by the thoughtful and cultivated, and his personal character won profound and affectionate esteem. In 1864 he succeeded J. Gilchrist Wilson as assistant editor of the *Wesleyan Methodist Magazine* and other connectional publications, and on the death of the lamented Thornton, in 1865, the entire duties of editorship devolved on him, shared however, in 1868, by the appointment of a colleague, Benjamin Gregory. This position he held until his unexpected death after a short illness, Jan. 17, 1876. Besides his scholarly contributions to the *Magazine*, Frankland wrote, *Outlines of Literary Culture* (Lond. 1853, 12mo):—*Intuitionalism* (ibid. 1861, crown 8vo):—*Of Israel, but not Israel* (Exeter, 1859, 12mo):—*The Wesleyan Conference* (Lond. 1852, 8vo). See *Wesl. Meth. Magazine*, 1876, p. 192, 742, 844; *Minutes of the British Conference*, 1876, p. 19.

Frankland, Thomas, an English divine, was born in Lancashire in 1633, and was educated at and became a fellow of Brazenose College, Oxford. He became a preacher, afterwards a physician, and died in 1690. His published works are, *The Honors of the Lords Spiritual Asserted* (1681):—*The Annals of King James I and King Charles I* (eod.). See Chalmers, *Biog. Dict.* s. v.; Allibone, *Dict. of Brit. and Amer. Authors*, s. v.

Franzoni, Luigi, an Italian prelate, was born at Genoa, March 29, 1789; studied under the direction of Zanobi Benucci; was ordained priest in 1814; became first an urban missionary, bishop of Turin in 1831, and died March 26, 1862. He was an avowed champion of Ultramontanism, for which he was imprisoned in 1850, and took refuge in Lyons. See Hoefer, *Nouv. Biog. Générale*, s. v.

Fraser, Edward, a talented colored Wesleyan preacher, was born a slave in the island of Barbadoes. He was in youth so appreciated by his master that he was given a good education and made his confidential clerk. Converted in Bermuda, becoming a local preacher and called into the ministry in 1827, he was given his liberty at the request of the British Wesleyan Conference, and labored in several of the West Indian islands. As a preacher, he was thoughtful, calm, dignified, clear in exposition and powerful in application. He moved with dignity and grace among the people of his charge, training the young, comforting the sick, and relieving the poor. On perplexing questions his well-balanced mind and clear, logical views made him powerful among his brethren. He was for eighteen years district secretary. For the cause of missions and education he twice visited England, where the memory of his noble pulpit and platform deliverances are still remembered. At the annual missionary meeting in Exeter Hall, London, in his visit of 1837-38, he delivered a powerful address. He died at Grateful Hill, Jamaica, in 1872, aged seventy-four years. See *Minutes of the British Conference*, 1872, p. 41; Smith, *Hist. of Wesl. Methodism*, iii, 366, 367; Everett, *Wesleyan Centenary Takings*, ii, 14.

Fraser, James, D.D., a Scotch clergyman, graduated from the university and Marischal College, Aberdeen, in 1771; was licensed to preach Feb. 3, 1779; presented to the living at Drumoak in November, 1785, ordained June 15, 1786, and died Jan. 31, 1828, aged seventy-two years. He published *An Account of the Parish of Drumoak*, and edited *Lectures on the Pastoral Character of Principal George Campbell* (1811). See *Fasti Eccles. Scoticanæ*, iii, 498.

Fraser, Paul, D.D., a Scotch clergyman, a native of Inverness, graduated from the university and King's College, Aberdeen, April 30, 1755; was ordained by the Presbytery of Lorn, Sept. 2, 1761, as missionary at Glencoe, from which he was removed to that of Fort William; was admitted minister of the parish of Craignish in 1765; transferred to the second charge, Inverary, May 28, 1789, admitted June 17, and died "Father of the Church," Oct. 2, 1827, aged ninety-five years. For a time he held the chaplaincy of the 98th Foot regiment, and the 5th regiment of Fencibles. He published *An Account of the Parish of Inverary*. See *Fasti Eccles. Scoticanæ*, iii, 4, 6.

Fraterculi. See Fratricelli.

Fratzscher, Heinrich Wolfgang, a Lutheran theologian of Germany, born at Erfurt, Nov. 12, 1694, studied at Halle, was in 1720 magister at Erfurt, in 1738 professor, accepted in 1744 a call as general-superintendent of the duchy of Coburg, and died July 14, 1757. He wrote, *De Jeremia et Vaticinio Ejus* (Halle, 1712):—*De Necessitate et Utilitate Lectionis Script. Sacræ in Fontibus* (Erfurt, 1738). See Jöcher, *Allgemeines Gelehrten-Lexikon*, s. v. (B. P.)

Frauenstädt, Christian Martin Julius, a German philosopher, was born April 17, 1813, at Bojanowo, in the duchy of Posen. He studied theology and philosophy at Berlin and published, in 1838, *Die Freiheit des Menschen und die Persönlichkeit Gottes*, which was followed in 1839 by *Die Menschwerdung Gottes nach ihrer Möglichkeit, Wirklichkeit und Notwendigkeit.* In his *Studien und Kritiken zur Theologie und Philosophie* (Berlin, 1840), he examined the philosophy of religion of Steffen, and with his *Schelling's Vorlesungen in Berlin* (ibid. 1842), he placed himself in opposition to the *Philosophie der Offenbarung.* In 1846 he made the acquaintance of Schopenhauer, and became his most ardent admirer. In 1848 he published his *Ueber das wahre Verhältniss der Vernunft zur Offenbarung* (dedicated to Schopenhauer), followed by other works in which he advocated more or less the system of his friend, whose works he also edited (Leipsic, 1873-74, 6 vols.; 2d ed. 1877). Frauenstädt died at Berlin, Jan. 13, 1879. See Brockhaus, *Conversations-Lexikon* (13th ed.), s. v.; Zuchold, *Bibl. Theol.* i, 377. (B. P.)

Fravashis, certain fetichistic spirits worshipped by the early inhabitants of Media.

Fravitta (Phravittas, Flavita, or **Flavianus)**, twenty-third bishop of Constantinople, A.D. 489, is said to have acquired his position by a remarkable fraud, having been originally a presbyter of the Church of St. Thecla, in the suburbs of that city. He died within four months, and the trick was exposed.

Frazer, John (1), a Scotch prelate, was abbot of Melrose, and promoted to the see of Ross in 1485. He was witness to an agreement between the community of Linlithgow and the priory of St. Andrews in 1497, and was one of the king's privy council in 1506. He died Feb. 5, 1507. See Keith, *Scottish Bishops*, p. 189.

Frazer, John (2), D.D., a Methodist Episcopal minister, was born in Ireland in 1803. He was a descendant of the celebrated Scotch Frazer family, which gave so many distinguished officers to the British army. At the age of seventeen he sailed to the United States and entered the woods of Maine as a lumberman. In 1831 he joined the New York Conference, and began his itinerant career on the shores of lake Champlain. For twenty-five years he continued to preach in that region, then embraced in the Troy Conference. His appointments were Middlebury, Poultney, and Grand Isle in Vermont; Albany, Troy, Schenectady, Lansingburg, and two terms as presiding elder in New York. In 1856 failing health induced him to remove to Ohio, where he joined the Ohio Conference, and was stationed as presiding elder three years each in Columbus and Zanesville. In 1866 he was transferred to the Southern Illinois Conference, and stationed first at Alton, then at Brighton, and last at Lebanon, where he died, Feb. 17, 1871. Dr. Frazer was a man of the purest character, a scorner of all hypocrisy and double-dealing; thoroughly read in theology, was powerfully fluent, and an eminently successful revivalist. See *Minutes of Annual Conferences*, 1871, p. 231.

Frazer, William, a Scotch prelate, was promoted to the see of St. Andrews in 1279, and was consecrated at Rome by pope Nicholas III, June 14, 1280. About the same time he was lord chancellor and witness to king Alexander III. In 1288 he was chosen to be one of the regents of the kingdom, and after the death of queen Margaret he yielded a forced submission to Edward I of England. He died at Arteville, Sept. 13, 1297. See Keith, *Scottish Bishops*, p. 20.

Freda was a god of war among the Frisians, who was worshipped with another similar figure, Weda, which caused the Romans to make a comparison with Castor and Pollux. They appear armed, with wings projecting from their shoulders.

Frédégaire (Lat. *Fredegarius*), a French ecclesiastical historian of the middle of the 7th century, has left a chronicle of France, and of Burgundy in particular, from Gregory of Tours to his own time (published as a sequel to the works of the former, Basle, 1568, 8vo, and later).

Freder, Johannes (1), a Lutheran theologian and hymn-writer of Germany, was born Aug. 29, 1510, at Cöslin, in Pomerania. He studied at Wittenberg, was in 1537 called to Hamburg, in 1547 to Stralsund, in 1549 to Greifswalde, and in 1556 to Wismar, where he died, Jan. 25, 1562. See Jöcher, *Allgemeines Gelehrten-Lexikon*, s. v.; Koch, *Geschichte des deutschen Kirchenliedes*, i, 421 sq.; Mohnicke, *Johannes Frederus Leben und geistliche Gesänge* (Stralsund, 1840); Zuchold, *Bibl. Theol.* i, 377. (B. P.)

Freder, Johannes (2), son of the preceding, was born at Hamburg, Jan. 6, 1544. He studied at Wittenberg and Rostock, was professor of theology at the latter place, and died in 1604. He edited Dav. Chytræi *Summa Doctrinæ de Vera Dei Agnitione:—Explicatio Articulorum Symboli Apostolici de Filio Dei:—Liber de Spir. Sanct. Divinitate*. He wrote, *Theses de Prædestinatione Hominum in Christo ad Vitam et Salutem Æternam*. See Jöcher, *Allgemeines Gelehrten-Lexikon*, s. v.; Molleri, *Cimbria Litterata*. (B. P.)

Frederick III OF SAXONY (usually styled *the Wise*), was born at Torgau, Jan. 17, 1463, and succeeded his father Ernest as elector, in 1486. He is chiefly known as the founder of the University of Wittenberg, and the friend of Luther, whom he carried off for safety to the Warburg; but he had not the courage to establish the reformed faith in his dominions. He became administrator of the empire in 1519, and declined the imperial crown. He died May 5, 1525. See the literature by Klüppel, in Plitt-Herzog's *Real-Encyklop.* s. v. See LUTHER.

Frederick III OF THE PALATINATE (called *the Pious*), was born Feb. 14, 1525, succeeded his father, John II, in 1556, as palatine of Simmern, and Otto Henry as elector-palatine in 1559. In 1537 he married a Lutheran princess, and adopted the Reformed faith, which in 1560 he introduced into his dominions, despite an effort in 1566 to secure an imperial edict against him. He died Oct. 26, 1576. See the literature in Plitt-Herzog's *Real-Encyklop.* s. v. See REFORMATION.

Fredet, PIERRE, D.D., a Roman Catholic priest, was born at Sehasat, France, about 1801; educated at Clermont; became a member of the Society of St. Sulpice, and came to Baltimore in 1831, where, till his death, Jan. 1, 1856, he was attached to St. Mary's Seminary. He is said to have been a diligent and thorough student, and a voluminous writer. See Hough, *Amer. Biog. Notes*, p. 149. (J. C. S.)

Frédol, BÉRENGER DE (called *the Elder*), a French prelate, was born at the château de la Vérune about 1250; became successively canon at Béziers, Narbonne, and Aix, bishop of Béziers, Oct. 28, 1294, and cardinal in 1305. He was employed by the pope in several literary and diplomatic functions, and died at Avignon, June 13, 1323, leaving a few works on canon law, for which see Hoefer, *Nouv. Biog. Générale*, s. v.

Free Christian Brethren, the name under which one congregation in Scotland is returned in the British census of 1851.

Free Methodist Church. See METHODISTS, FREE.

Freeman, Bernardus, a Reformed (Dutch) minister, was born in Westphalia, and licensed there; came to America in 1700; was refused by the Church at Albany for want of education; became a missionary to the Mohawks (1700-5); preached at various places on the western end of Long Island, and died in 1743. He was a man of great natural ability, and the author of several works in the Mohawk language, for which see Corwin, *Manual of the Ref. Church in America*, 3d ed. p. 265.

Freeman, George W., D.D., missionary bishop of the Protestant Episcopal Church in the south-west, was born at Sandwich, Mass.; taught a large boarding-school in Warrenton, N. C.; was ordained rector of Christ Church, Raleigh, where he remained for many years; then of Emmanuel Church, New Castle, Del.; consecrated bishop Oct. 26, 1844, in Philadelphia, Pa., and died at Little Rock, Ark., April 29, 1858, aged sixty-nine years. See *Amer. Quar. Church Rev.* 1858, p. 340.

Free-thinking Christians, a sect which arose in London in 1796, professing to be a Christian Church founded on the principles of free inquiry. They were originally a body of Universalists, who separated from their congregation by rejecting the doctrine of the trinity, the atonement, and many other doctrines held by orthodox Christians generally. Their next step was to dispense with the sacraments, and deny the immateriality of the soul. Finally, they rejected the Scriptures, and abolished all forms of worship, though still holding their meetings on the Sabbath as a matter of convenience. They assembled for purposes of discussion and debate on religious and social questions.

Fregoso, FEDERIGO, an Italian prelate, was born at Genoa about 1480; early took religious orders; became bishop of Gubbio in 1507; fled on account of political troubles to Rome, but returned to Genoa in 1513; was of great service in the civil war ensuing; made cardinal in 1539, and died at Gubbio, July 13, 1541.

Freia, in Norse mythology, was the most excellent among the Asas next to Frigga, the wife of Odin, being daughter of the dark Niord and the shady Skade. Freia was the goddess of the moon, in the ancient Scandinavian religion of nature. Later she was the goddess of love. She favors suitors, and finds great pleasure in songs, which she teaches to the scalds. She loves spring and flowers, and is gracious to the elves. In order to secure greater swiftness she makes use of a pair of falcon wings, which she allows other deities to use. The glittering necklace which the dwarfs presented to her is called *Brising*. Freia was married to Odur, and had two daughters by him: Hnos (beautiful) and Gersemi (attractive). Some time after, Odur made a journey, and as he did not return, Freia sought him, travelling through many countries, and assuming different names: Mardöl, Horn, Gefion, Syr, Vanadys; but it was all useless. She therefore shed bitter tears, which were changed into gold. Her journey made her known in all lands, and she was worshipped under various names. In North Germany, Denmark, Friesland, and Saxony, she retained the name Freia. She was represented with helmet, armor, bow, and sword, above in male, below in female dress. Odin receives valiant warriors into Valhalla; Freia receives all virtuous and lovely women into her heavenly dwelling, Folkvangur. She herself loves mostly to stay in her hall, Sesrumner, and has melancholy thoughts about her departed husband, Odur. The Swedes dedicated a number of temples to her, among which that at Upsala was the most celebrated. Her name is connected with the German verb "freien," *to woo*, and the sixth day of the week, Friday, is named after her.

Freind, Robert, D.D., an English clergyman, was born in 1667; educated principally at Westminster; elected to Christ Church, Oxford, in 1686; engaged in the famous controversy about the epistles of Phalaris, and died in 1751, leaving some Latin and English poetry, for which see Bentley, *Nichols's Collection*. He also published a *Sermon*, preached before the House of Commons (1711), and *Cicero's Orations* (1724). See Chalmers, *Biog. Dict.* s. v.; Allibone, *Dict. of Brit. and Amer. Authors*, s. v.

Freir (or **Frey**), in Norse mythology, was the son of Niord; the latter became one of the Asas, after showing his power to perform wonders. Freir's mother was Skade. His sister Freia represents the moon, and correspondingly he represents the sun. Freir is called the most excellent of the Asas. He rules over the rain and sunshine, and must be invoked for fruitful years and for peace. He presides over wealthy people, gives to maidens their lovers, and restores to women their husbands, when taken in battle. Freir once seated himself on the throne Hlidskialf, from which he could look over the whole world. This throne was designed only for Odin, and Freir was immediately punished for the liberty he took by becoming enamoured of a Jote maiden, namely, the beautiful Gerdur, daughter of the mountain-giant, Gymer, and of Aurboda. When he came home, he neither ate nor drank, nor said anything. A consuming melancholy fell upon him, and no one dared to talk with him. Even his father Niord asked his servant, Skirner, to find out what was the trouble. Freir said he loved the beautiful Jote maiden, and could not live without her any longer. Skirner then went out to woo Gerdur for him, after he had asked Freir for his trusty sword, which had been made by dwarfs, and possessed the singular faculty of killing of itself after it had once been drawn. Freir gave it to him, and thus, when he was attacked by the powerful Beli, he was forced to slay him with the horns of a reindeer. Skirner brought back the favorable answer that after nine nights Gerdur would appear to him. Then Freir said, "I cannot wait so long, for a single night is longer than a whole month." Gerdur is the northern light personified. Freir lives with her in Alfheim. As god of the sun, he also possesses the gold-colored boar, Gullinbursti. Besides this he owns the horse Blodughofi. He also has a skilful air-vessel, called Skidbladnir, made by dwarfs, the sons of Yvold. Oaths are given in Freir's name, in which case usually a boar is sacrificed to him, and a ring dipped in its blood, which is held by the swearer, who says: "So help me, Freir, Niord, and the mighty Asas!"

Freitag, Augustine M., a Redemptorist preacher, was born in Hanover, of Lutheran parentage, in 1836. At the age of sixteen he joined the Roman Catholic Church, and commenced his preparatory studies for the priestly office at Göttingen. After coming to America, he completed his studies at Cumberland, Md., and joined the Redemptorists. He was ordained priest in 1863, and assigned to duty in New York city. After serving there for some years he was transferred to Boston, Mass. In 1882 he returned to New York city, became assistant-rector of St. Alphonso's, and died there July 26 of the same year. (B. P.)

Fréminet, Martin, an eminent French painter, was born at Paris in 1567. He produced a fine picture of *St. Sebastian*, at Paris, when very young; afterwards visited Rome and studied the works of Michael Angelo; spent fifteen years in Italy, then returned to Paris in the reign of Henry IV, who appointed him his painter, and employed him in the chapel at Fontainebleau, the ceiling of which represents subjects from the Old and New Testaments, among them *Noah and his Family Entering the Ark*, and *The Annunciation*. He died at Paris, June 16, 1619. See Hoefer, *Nouv. Biog. Générale*, s. v.; Spooner, *Biog. Hist. of the Fine Arts*, s. v.

Frémont, Charles, a French monk, was born at Tours in 1610; entered the order of Grammont at the age of eighteen, and conceived the idea of bringing back the monks to the rigor of their primitive rule. Despite his superiors, through the protection of cardinal Richelieu, he succeeded in establishing the ancient discipline, not only in the house of Thiers, in Auvergne, which citizens had founded for him in 1650, but also in six or seven other houses, which had become nearly ruined. He died in 1689, leaving *La Vie, la Mort et les Miracles de Saint-Étienne, Confesseur, Fondateur de l'Ordre de Grammont* (Dijon, 1647). See Hoefer, *Nouv. Biog. Générale*, s. v.

French-Basque Version. See Basque French.

French Version of the Scriptures. The British and Foreign Bible Society, since its inception of Bible-work in France and the French-speaking countries, circulated the translations of Martin, Osterwald, and De Sacy; the latter for the use of Roman Catholics. In 1869 the same society published a revised edition of Osterwald's New Test. The object of this edition was to bring it as far as possible into conformity with the original editions, and to do away with the needless alterations which have been introduced by various printers or editors. On the same basis the Old Test. was published in 1871. In 1875 the Rev. Arnold Bovet addressed a communication to the agent of the British and Foreign Bible Society in Germany, the subject of which was the present condition and character of the French Protestant versions. In how far Mr. Bovet's suggestions were carried out we do not know, but in the report for the year 1877 we read: "The committee have been busy throughout the year in remedying certain minor defects in several of the French editions, in order to make them more perfect and more uniform. Several new versions of the Scriptures in French have been urged on the committee, but they did not see their way to the adoption of any of them; they hope, however, that the present activity in Bible translating and revision may lead to the production of a version more accurate and more acceptable to the French people than any which they now possess." From the annual report published in 1884 it appears that the *Societé Biblique de France* had undertaken a revision of Osterwald, and that this revised recension has also been adopted by the British and Foreign Bible Society. The report reads thus: "The committee have resolved to adopt the recently revised version of Osterwald. The revision of the New Test. was completed by Mons. Frossard in 1869. A conference of pastors at Paris appointed a commission to examine the version, and they expressed the wish in the following year that the *Societé Biblique de France* should publish it. In 1868 a committee, consisting of MM. Bruston, H. Kruger, W. Monod, and M. Byse began the revision of the Old Test. In 1877 the number of revisers was raised from four to thirteen, namely, professors Bois, Bruston, Chapuis, and Coussivat, and pastors Le Savoureux, Kruger, Monod, Laufer, Bornand, Byse, Favez, Frossard, and Monnier. All the books of the Old Test. were revised at least twice, the greater part three times, and some (Psalms, Daniel, Hosea, Joel, Amos, etc.) four times. The direction of the work was intrusted to pastor Frank Vermeil, with whom were associated MM. Matter and Frossard. In 1879 the publication commenced. Since then 17,000 of the 8vo and 16mo Bibles have been sold, and 150,000 copies of the revised New Test. since its publication. The basis of the revision of the New Test. was the *Textus Receptus*. The committee of the British and Foreign Bible Society, in taking up this latest revision of Osterwald's version, have the hearty approval of the *Societé Biblique de France*."

The British and Foreign Bible Society has also undertaken since 1879 the printing of De Sacy's Bible, collated with the folio of 1759, and with alternative readings from the originals for all passages liable to misconstruction.

Outside of the Bible societies, there were published *La Sainte Bible, Texte de la Vulgate, Traduction Française en Regard, avec Commentaires Théol., Moraux, Philol., Histor., etc., Rédigés d'Apres les Meilleurs Travaux Anciens et Contemp.* (Paris, 1869–82, 16 vols.). In this Bible work, the commentaries of German, French, English, and American scholars have been made use of. Thus, Alexander's *Commentary on Isaiah*, Lyman Abbott's *New Test., The Speaker's Commentary*, the works of Alford, Wordsworth, Ellicott, and even Smith's *Dict. of the Bible* have been perused. Besides this work of Roman Catholics, we must mention the Protestant Bible work by Reuss, *La Bible. Traduction Nouvelle avec Introductions et Commentaires* (Paris, 1874–81, 16 parts). The different parts have the following titles, besides the *Préface et Introduction Générale* and *Table Générale des Matières:* I. *Histoire des Israélites Depuis la Conquête de la Palestine jusqu'à l'Exil* (*Livres des Juges, de Samuel et des Rois*); II. *Les Prophètes*, 2 vols.; III. *L'Histoire Sainte et la Loi* (*Pentateuque et Josué*), 2 vols.; IV. *Chronique Ecclésiastique de Jérusalem* (Chron., Ezra, Neh.); V. *Poésie Lyrique* (*Le Psautier, les Lamentations, le Cantique des Cantiques*); VI. *Philosophie Religieuse et Morale des Hébreux* (*Job, les Proverbes, l'Ecclésiaste, l'Ecclésiastique, la Sapience, Contes Moraux* [*Jonas, Tobit, Susanne, Pages du Roi Darius*], *Baruch, Manassé*); VII. *Littérature, Politique, et Polémique* (*Ruth, Maccabées, Daniel, Esther, Judith, le 3me Livre des Maccabées, l'Histoire du Bel et du Serpent, l'Épitre de Jéremie*); VIII. *Histoire Évangélique* (*Synopse des Trois Premiers Évangiles*); IX. *La Théologie Johannique* (*Évangile et Épitres*); X. *L'Histoire Apostolique* (*Actes des Apôtres*); XI. *Les Épitres Pauliniennes*, 2 vols.; XII. *Les Épitres Catholiques;* XIII. *L'Apocalypse*.

Last, but not least, we mention the new translation of the Old Test. from the Hebrew text by the Rev. Dr. Louis Segond, published at Geneva in 1874 (2d ed. Nancy, 1877; 3d ed. Geneva, 1879), and the new translation of the New Test. from the Greek, published in 1879. His work has been accepted by the University Press, Oxford, England. This version is regarded as a decided improvement upon all others, and as worthy of national official use. In 1878 appeared *La Bible Annotée par une Société de Théologiens et de Pasteurs*, fasc. i (*Ancien Testament, les Prophètes I*), Neufchâtel. (For a review of this part comp. Diestel, in Schürer's *Theol. Literaturzeitung*, 1879, col. 217). (B. P.)

French, John W., D.D., a Protestant Episcopal clergyman of the diocese of Maryland, graduated from the General Theological Seminary of New York, was for some years rector in Washington, D. C.; in 1857 was chaplain at the Military Academy, West Point, N. Y.; in 1866 was appointed professor of moral philosophy in the same institution, and continued there until his death, July 7, 1871. See *Prot. Episc. Almanac*, 1872, p. 127.

French, William, D.D., an English clergyman, was born in 1786, and educated at Caius College, Cambridge. In 1820 he was master at Jesus College, and canon of Ely in 1832. He died in 1849, leaving *New Translations of the Proverbs of Solomon* (1831):—*New Translations of the Book of Psalms* (1842). See Allibone, *Dict. of Brit. and Amer. Authors*, s. v.

Frensdorff, Solomon, a Jewish writer, and professor at the Israelitish teachers' seminary in Hanover, who died in 1880, is the author of, *Fragmente aus der Punctations- und Accentlehre der hebräischen Sprache* (Hanover, 1847):—*Die Massora Magna nach den ältesten Drucken* (ibid. 1875, of which only the first part, *Die Massora in alphabetischer Ordnung*, was published). He also edited the masoretic work, אכלה ואכלה (ibid. 1864), a description of which is given under *Oclah ve-Oclah* in this *Cyclopædia*. (B. P.)

Frenzel, a name common to several German authors, of whom we mention:

1. Abraham, was born in November, 1656, at Kosel, studied at Wittenberg, and died April 15, 1740, at Schönau, near Bernstadt. He wrote, *De Originibus Linguæ Sorobicæ, libri iv* (Bautzen, 1693–96):—*De Diis Slavorum et Soroborum in Specie* (published in Hoffmann's *Scriptores Rerum Lusaticorum*, 2 vols.):—*De Vocabulis Propriis Sorobicis Pagorum* (published also in Hoffmann's work). Besides, he left in manuscript a *Dictionary of the Wendish Language*, works on the manners of the people of Upper Lusatia (extracts from which were published by Muka under the title *Frenceliana*, in *Casopis Mácisy Serbskeje*, Bautzen, 1880–82). See Jöcher, *Allgemeines Gelehrten-Lexikon*, s. v.

2. Michael, born Feb. 2, 1628, studied at Leipsic, was pastor at Kosel, and died June 29, 1706. He translated the New Test. into the Wendish language, also the Psalms, and Luther's catechism. See Jöcher, *Allgemeines Gelehrten-Lexikon*, s. v.

3. Michael, *Jr.*, brother of Abraham, was born Feb. 14, 1667, studied at Wittenberg, and died as deacon at Hoyerswerda, Feb. 11, 1752. He wrote *Dissertatio de Idolis Slavorum* (Wittenberg, 1691).

4. Solomon Gotthold, son of Michael, *Jr.*, who was born in 1701, and died deacon at Hoyerswerda, March 22, 1768, is the author of a *Wendish Catechism* (Löbau, 1738). See Jöcher, *Allgemeines Gelehrten-Lexikon*, s. v. For the family Frenzel see Schubert, *Chronik der Geschlechter Frenzel und Schletter* (Dresden, 1843). (B. P.)

Fresco, or wall-painting in water-colors, was very common in the early ages of the Christian æra, and was gradually introduced into sacred places, especially churches and the catacombs, portions of it still remaining. The subjects are usually Scriptural, though sometimes purely ideal. (See illustration on p. 417.) For the details see Smith, *Dict. of Christ. Antiq.* s. v. See Painting.

Fresnoy, Charles Alphonse du, a very eminent French painter, was born in Paris in 1611, and studied in the school of François Perrier, after which he visited Italy. In 1656 he returned to his native city, where he painted, among other works, a fine picture of *St. Margaret*, for the church of that name. He died in Paris in 1665. He was occupied during a long period of his life in preparing for publication his admirable poem on art, *De Arte Graphica*, which was issued after his death. See Spooner, *Biog. Hist. of the Fine Arts*, s. v.; Hoefer, *Nouv. Biog. Générale*, s. v.

Freudentheil, Wilhelm Nicholas, a Lutheran theologian of Germany, was born at Stade, in Hanover, June 5, 1771. He studied at Göttingen; was in 1792 professor of literature and history at Zelle; in 1796 subrector; in 1805 con-rector; in 1809 rector at Stade; in 1816 was called as deacon to Hamburg; in 1828 was pastor at the Church of the Holy Ghost, and was honored in 1841 by his *alma mater* with the theological doctorate. He died March 7, 1853. Besides his *Commentatio de Codice sacro more*, etc. (Göttingen, 1791), he contributed some fine specimens to German hymnology. See Winer, *Handbuch der theol. Lit.* i, 108; Schröder, *Lexicon der Hamburger Schriftsteller*; Geffcken,

Cubiculum in the Cemetery of St. Callistus.

Biographical Introduction to Freudentheil's Poems (Hamburg, 1854); Koch, *Geschichte der deutschen Kirchenliedes*, vii, 71 sq. (B. P.)

Frey, Franz Andreas, a Roman Catholic theologian of Germany, was born July 20, 1763, at Bamberg, where he also studied, and took holy orders in 1787. In 1795 he commenced his lectures on canon law at the university of his native place, and died there, June 24, 1820. He published, *Disp. Theses theol. de Religione, nec non de Principiis Theologicis* (Bamberg, 1787):—*Kritischer Commentar über das Kirchenrecht für Katholiken und Protestanten* (ibid. 1812–20, 3 vols.). See Döring, *Die Gelehrten Theologen Deutschlands*, i, 435 sq.; Winer, *Handbuch der theol. Lit.* ii, 9; Zuchold, *Bibl. Theol.* i, 380. (B. P.)

Frey, Jean Jacques, an eminent Swiss engraver, was born at Lucerne in 1681, and after acquiring the elements of his art in his own country, went to Rome, where he studied for some time under Arnold van Westerhout. The following are some of his many plates: *The Holy Family; St. Jerome; St. Joseph Presenting Cherries to the Infant Christ; St. Andrew Kneeling before the Cross; St. Bernard; The Adoration of the Shepherds; The Archangel Michael.* He died at Rome in 1752. See Hoefer, *Nouv. Biog. Générale*, s. v.; Spooner, *Biog. Hist. of the Fine Arts.* s. v.

Freyenmoet (or **Frymuth**), John Caspar, a Reformed (Dutch) minister, was born in Switzerland in 1720, came to America in his youth, and lived at what is now Port Jervis, N. Y., then the centre of the Dutch churches situated on the Delaware river—Minisink, Walpeck, Smithfield, and Mahackemack—which sent him to Holland to be educated for the ministry and ordained as their pastor. He returned in 1741, and ministered to them until 1756. His great popularity as a preacher, and his deep piety and zeal, created an active strife for his services between the churches referred to and those in Ulster County. He removed to Columbia County in 1756, and continued until his death, in 1778, the acceptable and useful minister of the churches of Kinderhook, Claverack, Livingston Manor, Red Hook, and Schodack. He favored the ordination of ministers in this country, and was a conservative in the early Coetus party, but indignantly withdrew when they proposed to organize a classis. His social qualities were of a high order, and his prudence and skill in settling delicate ecclesiastical cases brought him into frequent request upon official commissions. See Slauson, *Hist. Discourse at Port Jervis;* Zabriskie, *Centennial Discourse at Claverack;* Corwin, *Manual of the Reformed Church in America*, s. v. (W. J. R. T.)

Freytag, Georg Wilhelm Friedrich, a German theologian and scholar, was born at Lüneburg, Sept. 19, 1788, and educated in philology and theology at the University of Göttingen. From 1811 to 1813 he acted as theological tutor there, then went to Königsberg as sub-librarian; in 1815 became a chaplain in the Prussian army, in which capacity he visited Paris; afterwards resigned his chaplaincy, and remained in Paris to prosecute his Oriental studies under De Sacy. In 1819 he was appointed professor of Oriental languages at Bonn, and continued in that position until his death, Nov. 16, 1861. Besides publishing a compendium of Hebrew grammar (*Kurzgefasste Grammatik der hebräischen Sprache*, 1835), and a treatise on Arabic versification (*Darstellung der Arabischen Verskunst*, 1838), Freytag edited two volumes of Arabic songs (*Hamasæ Carmina*, 1828–52), and three of Arabic proverbs (*Arabum Proverbia*, 1838–43). His principal work, however, was his *Lexicon Arabico-Latinum* (1830–37), which rapidly superseded the earlier lexicons. See *Encyclop. Brit.* 9th ed. s. v.

Fricco, in Norse mythology, was the third god with Odin and Thor, who were worshipped in the great temple at Upsala (then the capital of Sweden). According to the latest researches he is one with *Freir*.

Friday, the Mohammedan weekly Sabbath, commencing at the preceding sunset. The Mohammedans regard it as the chief of all days. The public services, which occupy only a portion of the day, the rest being devoted to business and recreation, commence at noon, and besides the usual prayers there are additional ceremonies performed, including the reading and reciting of parts of the Koran from the reading-desk, and the delivery of sermons from the pulpit by the Imams.

Friderici, Jeremias, a Lutheran theologian of Germany, was born at Leipsic in 1696, studied in the same city and became master of arts, catechist, and preacher, and died there, Sept. 6, 1766. He wrote, *De Hosea Propheta* (Leipsic, 1715):—*De Daniele* (ibid. 1716):—*De Zacharia* (ibid. 1718):—*De Ezechiele* (ibid. 1719):—*De Deo, Patriarchæ Jacobi* (ibid. 1729):—*Sixtini Amamæ Parænesis* (ibid. 1730). See Jöcher, *Allgemeines Gelehrten-Lexikon*, s. v. (B. P.)

Friderici, Johann Christoph, a Lutheran theologian of Germany, was born June 25, 1730, at Tempelburg, in Pomerania, studied at Halle, and was for some time military chaplain. In 1760 he was called to the pastorate at Neustadt-Magdeburg, and in 1768 to Göttingen. In 1770 he was appointed general superintendent and first pastor at Clausthal, but five years later he accepted a call to Hamburg, where he died, Aug. 12, 1777. Besides a number of sermons, he published *Specimen Inaugurale Theologicum de Virtute vere Christiana* (Kiel, 1776; Germ. transl. by Thiess, Hamburg, 1779). See Döring, *Die gelehrten Theologen Deutschlands*, i, 448 sq.; Jöcher, *Allgemeines Gelehrten-Lexikon*, s. v. (B. P.)

Frideswida (Fredeswithe, Frithswith, etc.), an early English saint, is said to have been a king's daughter, who fled to Oxford to escape marriage, and founded a convent there about the time of Bede. She died about 735, and is commemorated on Oct. 19.

Fried-Ailek, in the mythology of the Laplanders, is that one of the three supreme gods who superintended Friday. He was the companion of the sun, and allowed no works on that day; sacrifices, however, could reconcile him.

Friedemann, Friedrich Traugott, a Lutheran theologian of Germany, born March 30, 1793, was in 1820 rector at Wittenberg, in 1823 rector at Brunswick, in 1828 director at Weilburg, and died in 1839. He wrote, *De Summa Christianæ Doctrinæ* (Wittenberg, 1821; transl. by Fried. Beck, Leipsic, 1823):—*Christlich-religiöse Anregungen* (Weilburg, 1837). See Winer, *Handbuch der theol. Lit.* i, 369; ii, 378; Zuchold, *Bibl. Theol.* i, 383. (B. P.)

Friedenthal, Marcus Beer, a Jewish writer of Germany, was born at Gross-Glogau in 1779, and died at Breslau, Dec. 5, 1859. He wrote, עקרי אמונה, *Ueber die Dogmen des Jüdischen Glaubens* (Breslau, 1816–18, 3 vols.):—יסוד הדת (1821–23, 7 vols.), a kind of apology of Judaism, which was followed by a supplement, entitled החכמה התבונה והדת (ibid. 1843–46). See Fürst, *Bibl. Jud.* i, 299 sq. (B. P.)

Friederich, Gerhard, a Protestant theologian of Germany, born Jan. 2, 1779, was in 1812 preacher at Bornheim, in 1816 at Frankfort-on-the-Main, and died there in 1860. He published, *Reden der Religion und dem Vaterlande geweiht* (Frankfort, 1817–19, 2 vols.):—*Christliche Vorträge* (3d ed. Hanau, 1833, 2 vols.):—*Christus an die Herrscher und das Volk* (Frankfort, 1831):—*Das Christenleben* (Stuttgart, 1836):—*Religion und Kirchenthum* (Giessen, 1842), etc. See Winer, *Handbuch der theol. Lit.* i, 408; ii, 99, 159, 172, 315, 321, 336, 364, 366, 374, 379, 403; Zuchold, *Bibl. Theol.* i, 383–385. (B. P.)

Friedlieb, Philipp Heinrich, a Lutheran theologian of Germany, who died at Stralsund, Sept. 10, 1663, wrote, *Theologia:—Angelologia:—Anthropologia:—Christologia:—Ecclesiologia:—Medulla Theologiæ Theticæ, Polemicæ et Moralis:—Theologia Biblica seu Exegetica:—Phosphorus Biblicus*, etc. See Jöcher, *Allgemeines Gelehrten-Lexikon*, s. v.; Witte, *Diarium Biographicum*. (B. P.)

Frimel, Johannes (1), a Lutheran theologian of Germany, was born at Breslau, in Silesia, Nov. 2, 1606. He studied at different universities, was deacon at Wittenberg in 1631, preacher in his native city in 1647, and died Feb. 5, 1660. He wrote, *Proba Fidei Evangelica:—De Cœlo Beatorum:—De Legitima Vocatione Lutheri:—De Verbo Dei Scripto*. See Jöcher, *Allgemeines Gelehrten-Lexikon*, s. v.; Winer, *Handbuch der theol. Lit.* i, 759. (B. P.)

Frimel, Johannes (2), son of the foregoing, born at Wittenberg, Nov. 20, 1632, studied at different universities, was deacon at Breslau in 1660, archdeacon in 1676, and died Nov. 13, 1688. He wrote *De Bona Conscientia*. See Jöcher, *Allgemeines Gelehrten-Lexikon*, s. v. (B. P.)

Frind, Anton Ludwig, a Roman Catholic historian, was born Oct. 9, 1823, at Hainspach, in Bohemia. In 1847 he received holy orders, was in 1851 catechist, in 1852 professor at the gymnasium in Leitmeritz; in 1859 was made director of the gymnasium at Eger, and in 1869 canon of the chapter at Prague. In 1879 he was transferred to the episcopal see of Leitmeritz, and died Oct. 28, 1881. His main work is *Kirchengeschichte Böhmens* (Prague, 1864–78, 4 vols., the last volume coming down to the year 1561). Besides, he published, *Katholische Apologetik für gebildete Christen* (3d ed. ibid. 1877):—*Geschichte der Bischöfe und Erzbischöfe von Prag* (ibid. 1873):—*Der heilige Johannes von Nepomuk* (ibid. 1879). (B. P.)

Frisch, Johann, a Lutheran theologian, who died while preacher at Altona in 1692, wrote, *Disp. Historico-Theologica de Waldensibus* (Wittenberg, 1659):—*Historischer Tagweiser, oder Anweisung dessen, wassich in der Christenheit zugetragen* (ibid. 1675). See Thiessens, *Hamb. Gelehrten Geschichte*; Jöcher, *Allgemeines Gelehrten-Lexikon*, s. v. (B. P.)

Frisch, Johann David, a Lutheran theologian of Germany, born Aug. 21, 1676, was in 1701 deacon at St. Leonhard, in Stuttgart, in 1714 preacher, in 1720 general-superintendent, in 1726 member of consistory, and died Jan. 8, 1742. He wrote, *Neuklingende Harfe Davids*, or a commentary on the Psalms:—*De Origine, Diis et Terra Palæstinorum*. See Jöcher, *Allgemeines Gelehrten-Lexikon*, s. v.; Fürst, *Bibl. Theol.* i, 304. (B. P.)

Frisch, Johann Friedrich, a Lutheran theologian of Germany, was born Dec. 26, 1715. He studied at Leipsic, and died there as pastor of St. George's, Nov. 4, 1778. He wrote, *Commentatio Philologica de ἀντιφάσει Nulla*, etc. (Freiberg, 1740):—*De Vero Sensu et Genuina Ratione Legis Divinæ, Deut. xxii*, 10 (Leipsic, 1744):—*De Muliere Peregrina apud Hebræos* (ibid. eod.):—*De Levi cum Matthæo non Confundendo* (ibid. 1746):—*Apocalyptischer Catechismus* (1773). See Jöcher, *Allgemeines Gelehrten-Lexikon*, s. v.; Fürst, *Bibl. Jud.* i, 304; Winer, *Handbuch der theol. Lit.* i, 566. (B. P.)

Frisch, Samuel Gottlob, a Lutheran theologian of Germany, was born March 22, 1765, at Freiberg. He studied at Leipsic, was for some time deacon at Mutshen, in Saxony, morning preacher at Freiberg, and after 1822 court preacher at Dresden, where he died, April 21, 1829. Of his publications we mention, *Lucæ Commentarium de Vita, Dictis Factisque Jesu et Apostolorum* (Freiberg, 1817; reprinted in Rosenmüller's *Commentationes Theologicæ*, i, 272 sq.). See Döring, *Die gelehrten Theologen Deutschlands*, i, 450 sq.; Winer, *Handbuch der theol. Lit.* i, 87; ii, 94, 163, 204. (B. P.)

Frisius, Simon, an eminent Dutch engraver, was born at Leeuwarden, in Friesland, about 1580. He is regarded as the first who brought etching to perfection. The following are some of his principal works: *The Descent of the Holy Ghost; The Assumption of the Virgin; The Virgin Suckling the Infant.* See *Biog. Universelle*, s. v.; Spooner, *Biog. Hist. of the Fine Arts*, s. v.

Fritsch, Johann Heinrich, a Lutheran theologian of Germany, was born at Quedlinburg, Feb. 3, 1772. He studied at Halle, and was in 1795 preacher at his native place. In 1804 he was appointed first preacher of St. Benedict's; in 1817 he received the degree of doctor of theology from the Königsberg University; in 1821 was made superintendent, and died Jan. 1, 1829. He published some homiletical works, for which see Döring, *Die gelehrten Theologen Deutschlands*, i, 456 sq.; Winer, *Handbuch der theol. Lit.* i, 496, 863; ii, 36, 46, 56, 67, 123, 153, 296; Zuchold, *Bibl. Theol.* i, 386. (B. P.)

Frizon, Pierre, a French historian and theologian, was born in the diocese of Rheims, in the latter part of the 15th century. He was a Jesuit for some time, and taught in the colleges of that society; but left it to enter the University of Paris, where he was made doctor in 1623. He was admitted to the College of Navarre in 1624, and became in 1635 grand-master of it. He died in July, 1650 or 1651, leaving, *La Moyens pour Discerner les Bibles Françaises Catholiques* (Paris, 1621):—*Gallia Purpurata* (ibid. 1638), against which Baluze wrote his *Anti-Frizonius* (Toulouse, 1652). See Jöcher, *Allgemeines Gelehrten-Lexikon*, s. v.; Hoefer, *Nouv. Biog. Générale*, s. v. (B. P.)

Friuli, Council of (*Concilium Forojuliense*), was held A.D. 796 (*not* 791), as Pagi shows, under Paulinus, patriarch of Aquileia, whose letter to Charlemagne, formerly misconnected with the synod of Altino, A.D. 802, assigns three causes for its meeting: (1) the orthodox faith; (2) ecclesiastical discipline; and (3) recent outrages, probably by the Huns. The first of these is explained in his speech, which is an elaborate apology for the reception into the Western creed of the clause "and the Son," which Charlemagne had attacked, and the pope vindicated, the second Nicene Council two years before for not having in theirs; Paulinus himself endeavoring to prove both right. The resemblance between parts of this speech and the Athanasian creed has been remarked, and is very close. Besides it is observable that all priests are required to commit to memory the entire exposition of "the Catholic faith," with which he concludes: while, for everybody else, the learning by heart of the Creed and the Lord's Prayer is prescribed. Of the canons, the 1st threatens simony; the 2d drunkenness; the 4th and 5th deprecate secular employments and amusements for the clergy. By the 10th, a divorced person is forbidden to marry again till the former partner dies; and by the 13th all are inhibited from working on Sundays and holidays. See Smith, *Dict. of Christ. Antiq.* s. v.; Landon, *Manual of Councils*, s. v.

Fro, in Norse mythology, is a deity of the second grade, worshipped by the Goths and Danes as the ruler of the winds. He received bloody, often human, sacrifices, which he himself instituted. According to other accounts, black animals were sacrificed to him by the Danish king, Hadding, which later were replaced by human sacrifices; they are called *Froablot*. Others make Fro the same with *Freir* (q. v.).

Froeligh, Solomon, D.D., a Reformed (Dutch) minister, was born at Red Hook, N. Y., in 1750. He studied theology with Dr. Theodorick Romeyn and Rev. J. H. Goetschius, and was licensed to preach in 1774. His first pastoral charge was on Long Island, in the churches of Jamaica, Newtown, Oyster Bay, and Success (1775-76). He was an ardent patriot during the Revolutionary War, and was compelled to flee from his congregations when the British occupied Long Island. From 1776 to 1780 he supplied the churches of Fishkill and Poughkeepsie, and at the end of the war was pastor at Hillsborough and Neshanic, N. J. In 1786 he removed to the united churches of Hackensack and Schraalenbergh; was appointed by the General Synod lector in theology in 1792, and in 1797 professor of theology, an office which he held until 1822. The churches over which he was last settled had long been in difficulties, which were not quieted by his coming among them; and, in 1822, he seceded, with four other ministers in the North, Messrs. Brokaw, Palmer, Toll, and Wyckoff, who had previously been suspended for contumacy, and they organized what was called "The True Reformed Dutch Church." A small number of disaffected congregations and ministers afterwards joined them. In 1823 Dr. Froeligh was suspended by the General Synod from his professorship and from the ministry, for schism and contempt of ecclesiastical authority, and for promoting divisions in the Church. His own letters proved that he had for many years contemplated this secession. After this he continued to minister to the two churches which had seceded with him, as their pastor, until his decease, Oct. 8, 1827. For a full history of these events, see *Annals of the Classis of Bergen*, by Benjamin C. Taylor, D.D., p. 188-233; also autobiographical notes incorporated in Rev. C. T. Demarest's *Lamentation over Rev. Solomon Froeligh, D.D.* Dr. Froeligh was neither very learned nor gifted with genius, but was a man of unquestioned ability and respectable attainments in the old theology. In his early ministry he was useful and blessed with considerable success. See also Corwin, *Manual of the Ref. Church in America*, s. v.; *Minutes of General Synod*, 1823; *Memoir*, by Peter Labagh, D.D., p. 129-135. (W. J. R. T.)

Frohberger, Christian Gottlieb, a Lutheran theologian of Germany, was born July 27, 1742, at Wehlen, near Pirna, in Saxony. He studied at Halle and Leipsic, and was in 1774 preacher at Rennersdorf, near Herrnhut. In 1820 he retired from the ministry, and died Jan. 29, 1827. He published some ascetical works, for which see Döring, *Die gelehrten Theologen Deutschlands*, i, 461 sq.; Winer, *Handbuch der theol. Lit.* i, 774; ii, 130; Zuchold, *Bibl. Theol.* i, 389; Koch, *Gesch. des deutschen Kirchenliedes*, vi, 289 sq. (B. P.)

Frohne, Johann Adolph, a Lutheran theologian of Germany, was born Jan. 11, 1652. He studied at Jena, where he also lectured for some time. In 1678 he accepted a call as rector to Lemgo, was in 1680 preacher there, and succeeded his father in 1691 as preacher at Mühlhausen. In 1692 he went to Giessen, and presented for the degree of theologiæ licentiatus, *De Fide ut Dispositione Meritoria ad Justificationem contra Pontificios.* In 1693 he received the theological doctorate, and died Nov. 12, 1713. He published, *Gründlicher Beweis des geistlichen Priesterthums* (Mühlhausen, 1703, against which Eilmar wrote his *Gründliche Erörterung der Lehre von dem geistlichen Priesterthum*, 1704):—*Recht des geistlichen Priesters* (written against Eilmar, 1705):—*Theologia Definitiva* (Frankfort-on-the-Main, 1707). See Walch, *Bibl. Theol.* ii, 765 sq.; Jöcher, *Allgemeines Gelehrten-Lexikon*, s. v. (B. P.)

Fromman, Andreas, a German philosopher, was born at Coburg, Aug. 11, 1591, and died March 26, 1666. He wrote, *Dissertationes 6 de Stultitia Atheismi, ad Psa. xiv*:—*De Metu Pauli ad 2 Cor. xi*, 3:—*De Fide Pontificiorum Explicata et Implicata, Formata et Informi.* See Jöcher, *Allgemeines Gelehrten-Lexikon*, s. v. (B. P.)

Frommann, Erhard Andreas, a Lutheran theologian of Germany, was born Nov. 8, 1722. He studied at Coburg and Altdorf, was in 1756 professor of Greek and Oriental languages at Coburg, and died Oct. 1, 1774. He wrote, *De Cultu Deorum ex ὀνοματοθεσίᾳ Illustri* (Altdorf, 1745):—*De Hermeneuta Veteris Ecclesiæ* (ibid. 1747):—*De Syntaxi Linguæ et Præcipue Ebraicæ* (ibid.

eod.):—*De Lingua Profunda ad Esa. xxxiii*, 19; *Ezech. iii*, 5, 6 (ibid. 1748):—*De Opinata Sanctitate Linguæ Ebraicæ* (Coburg, 1756):—*De Sacris Judæorum* (ibid. 1759):—*An Variæ Lectiones ad Codicem V. Test. ex Mischna Collogi Possint* (ibid. 1760):—*De Ecclesiæ Christianæ Reformatione Judæis Utili* (ibid. 1761):—*Disp. Spec. Topices Pauli in Fide Salvifica ex Vet. Test. Probanda* (ibid. 1762):—*De Feminis Quibusdam quæ Evangelii Veritatem Tempore Reformationis Sacrorum Scriptis Defenderunt* (ibid. 1764):—*De Canone Hermeneutico* (ibid. 1767). See Jöcher, *Allgemeines Gelehrten-Lexikon*, s. v.; Winer, *Handbuch der theol. Lit.* i, 21, 132. (B. P.)

Frommann, Georg Carl, a Lutheran theologian of Germany, was born April 9, 1809, at Lauten, near Coburg. He studied theology at Jena, Bonn, and Berlin, with Bleek, Nitzsch, Schleiermacher, and Neander for his teachers. He commenced his theological lectures at Jena, and his *Darlegung des johanneischen Lehrbegriffs*, published in 1833 in the *Studien und Kritiken*, proved him to be a worthy pupil of his teachers. In 1837 he was appointed professor of theology, and in 1839 published his *Darlegung* in an extended form, in consideration of which the Rostock University honored him with the doctorate of theology. In the same year he was called as pastor to St. Peter's, in St. Petersburg, where he labored for twenty-five years, accompanied with great blessing. In 1865 he resigned his position, and made Berlin his residence, where he lectured as honorary professor. In 1868 he was recalled to St. Petersburg as general superintendent, but in 1876 was paralyzed, and returned as an invalid to Jena, never to resume again his work. He died Dec. 5, 1879. He also wrote, *De Disciplina Arcani, quæ in Vetere Ecclesia Christiana Obtinuisse Fertur* (Jena, 1833). See Zuchold, *Bibl. Theol.* i, 390. (B. P.)

Fronteau, Jean, a French archæologist and controversialist, was born at Angers in 1614. After completing his studies in his native city, he took the habit of a regular canon in the abbey of Toussaint, at Angers. He was called to Paris in 1634, and engaged to teach philosophy, and then theology, at the abbey of St. Genevieve, and was made chancellor of the University of Paris. Being suspected, however, of Jansenism, he was exiled to the diocese of Angers in 1661, but soon called back to Paris, where he remained until his death, April 17, 1662. He wrote, *Summa Totius Philosophiæ* (Paris, 1640):—*Thomas à Kempis Vindicatus* (ibid. 1641):—*De Jure Episcoporum* (1659):—*Φιλοτησία Veterum* (1640). See Hoefer, *Nouv. Biog. Générale*, s. v.

Fröreisen, Isaac, a Lutheran theologian and professor of theology at Strasburg, who died June 5, 1632, is the author of, *De Aug. Confess. Materia, Fundamento et Forma*, etc.:—*Scutum Catholicæ Veritatis pro Invenienda Vera in his Terris Militante Ecclesia*:—*Dissertationes contra Weigelianos*:—*Apologeticus contra Carolum Sachsium Calvinistam*:—*Vindiciæ Synopticæ pro Sacro Geneseos Codice contra Bellarminum*:—*De Angelis Bonis, ad Matth. iv.* 11:—*De Ædificio Spirituali ad* 1 *Cor. iii*, 11-13. See Witte, *Diarium Biographicum*; Jöcher, *Allgemeines Gelehrten-Lexikon*, s. v. (B. P.)

Fröreisen, Johann Leonhard, a Lutheran theologian, was born May 9, 1694. He studied at Giessen and Jena, was in 1724 professor of theology at Strasburg, and died Jan. 13, 1761, leaving, *Disp. de Ostracismo* (Strasburg, 1711):—*De Pœnitentia Dei* (ibid. 1714):—*De Infelici Divitis Felicitate ad Luc. xvi*, 19:—*De Characteribus Veræ Reformationis* (Jena, 1717):—*De Charlataneria Theologorum* (Strasburg, 1735):—*De Domesticis Pastorum Visitationibus* (ibid. eod.). See Moser, *Jetztlebende Theologen*; Strodtmann, *Jetztlebende Gelehrte*; Jöcher, *Allgemeines Gelehrten-Lexikon*, s. v. (B. P.)

Frosch, Johann, the reformer of Augsburg, originally belonged to the Carmelites. In 1516 he was made licentiate of theology at Wittenberg, under the presidency of Luther, and in 1517 prior of the Carmelite monastery at Augsburg. When Luther openly broke with the Church of Rome, Frosch, too, began to preach the pure gospel at Augsburg, and in 1522 he was appointed by the city council as evangelical preacher. In 1527 he held a disputation with the Anabaptists at Augsburg, and in 1531 was dismissed by the council because it leaned towards Zwinglianism. Frosch went to Nüremberg, and died there in 1533. See Jöcher, *Allgemeines Gelehrten-Lexikon*, s. v.; Koch, *Gesch. des deutschen Kirchenliedes*, i, 405; ii, 475. (B. P.)

Frossard, Benoît Daniel Emilien, a French theologian, youngest son of Benjamin Sigismond (q. v.), was born June 26, 1802, at Paris. At the age of fifteen he was sent to England, where he came into direct relationship with some distinguished members of the Friends, who made a lasting impression upon him. Having returned to France, he studied theology at Montauban, and presented as his thesis for the degree of bachelor of divinity, *Accord entre le Récit de Moëse sur l'Âge du Genre Humain et les Phénomènes Géologiques*. In 1825 he was called to Nîmes, and in 1847 was appointed director of the seminary which was to be established beside the theological university at Montauban. In 1848 he resigned his position, and made his home at Bagnères-de-Bigorre, at the foot of the Pyrenees, where he died, Jan. 25, 1881. His great zeal for the Protestants scattered about the Pyrenees was so effective and so laborious that he was styled "the apostle of the Pyrenees." He wrote, *L'Ami de la Famille*:—*Les Archives Évangéliques*:—*La Vie Réelle*:—*Le Livre des Faibles*:—*Le Catéchisme Biblique*. See Lichtenberger, *Encyclop. des Sciences Religieuses*, s. v.; Zuchold, *Bibl. Theol.* i, 391. (B. P.)

Frothaire, a French prelate, was born in the second part of the 8th century. He was educated at the monastery of Garze, became abbot of St. Evre, at Toul, and bishop of that city in 813. During the revolt of Bernard, he proved himself faithful to the cause of Louis le Débonnaire, and took an important part in several councils which judged the rebel bishops. He left twenty-one letters, which were published by André Duchesne, in his *Historiæ Francorum Scriptores*, ii. See Hoefer, *Nouv. Biog. Générale*, s. v.

Fructuosus, an early martyr, commemorated Jan. 21, was bishop of Tarragona in the 3d century, and burned alive during the Diocletian persecution. See Smith, *Dict. of Christ. Biog.* s. v.

Frymuth. See Freyenmoet.

Fryxell, Andres, a Swedish historian, was born Feb. 7, 1795, at Hasselskoj, in Dalsland. In 1822 he was teacher, in 1828 rector of the Marien school at Stockholm, in 1833 professor, and in 1836 pastor at Sunne, one of the largest parishes of Sweden. In 1840 he was received into the Stockholm Academy, and in 1845 made doctor of theology. He died March 21, 1881. He is known as the author of *Berichte aus der Schwedischen Geschichte*, of which more than forty volumes have been published since 1823. (B. P.)

Fuchs, Adolph Friedrich, a Lutheran theologian of Germany, was born Dec. 27, 1758, at Neuenkirchen, in Mecklenburg-Strelitz. He studied at Göttingen, was in 1778 con-rector at the gymnasium in Prentzlau, in 1781 rector of the cathedral-school at Ratzeburg, and in 1810 superintendent of the Güstrov diocese. He died April 13, 1828, leaving *Der Brief Pauli an die Römer* (Stendal, 1789):—*Progr. in qua Ratione ad Reliquos de Libri Hagiographorum* (Rostock, 1797). See Döring, *Die gelehrten Theologen Deutschlands*, i, 466 sq. (B. P.)

Fuchs, Gottlieb Daniel, a Lutheran theologian of Germany, who died at Stuttgart in 1783, is the author of *Bibliothek der Kirchenversammlungen des* 4 *und* 5 *Jahrhunderts* (Leipsic, 1780-1784, 4 vols.). See Winer, *Handbuch der theol. Lit.* i, 659. (B. P.)

Fuchs, Karl Heinrich, a Lutheran theologian of Germany, who was born in 1762 at Heidelberg, and died at Munich in 1842, is the author of, *Annalen der Protest. Kirche im Königreich Bayern* (Nüremberg, 1819-23):—*Allgemeine Uebersicht des Zustandes der Protest. Kirche in Bayern*, etc. (Anspach, 1830);—*Die Einführung der Kirchenvorstande* (Nüremberg, 1822):—*Die Evangelische Kirche, ihre Bekenntnisse und Gottesdienstlichen Handlungen* (ibid. 1829):—*Annalen der Protest. Kirche im Königreich Bayern* (Munich, 1839-43). See Winer, *Handbuch der theol. Lit.* i, 785; ii, 20, 72, 77, 79, 100, 195; Zuchold, *Bibl. Theol.* i, 392 sq. (B. P.)

Fuchten, JOHANN, a Protestant theologian, was born at Antwerp, Nov. 26, 1568, became pastor at Hildesheim in 1602, and died at Helmstädt, Nov. 26, 1622, professor and doctor of theology. He edited, *Paschasii Ratberti Testimonia SS. Patrum de Genuino Eucharistiæ Intellectu Usuque*:—*Ejusdem Libri II de Spiritu S.*:—*Sancti Augustini Sententias ex Omnibus ejus Operibus a S. Prospero Excerptas*, etc. See Witte, *Diarium Biographicum*; Jöcher, *Allgemeines Gelehrten-Lexikon*, s. v.; Winer, *Handbuch der theol. Lit.* i, 911. (B. P.)

Fuga, FERDINANDO, an eminent Italian architect, was born at Florence in 1699, and studied under Gio. Battista Fugini. In 1725 he was sent to Naples by cardinal Giudire, to erect a chapel in his palace. He also erected the Church della Morte, in the Strada Giulia. He died at Florence, Feb. 7, 1782. See *Biog. Universelle*, s. v.; Spooner, *Biog. Hist. of the Fine Arts*, s. v.

Führich, JOSEPH VON, a Bohemian painter, was born at Kratzau in 1800. His admiration for the pictures in the wayside chapels of his native country led him to attempt a sketch of *The Nativity* for the Christmas festival in his father's house. He became the pupil of Bengler in the Academy of Prague in 1816, and in 1826 went to Rome, where he added three frescos to those executed by Cornelius and Overbeck in the Palazzo Massimi. In 1831 he finished the *Triumph of Christ*, now in the Raczynski Palace at Berlin. In 1834 he became custos, and in 1841 professor of composition in the Academy of Vienna. After this he completed the monumental pictures of the Church of St. Nepomuk, and (1854-61) the vast series of wall-paintings which cover the inside of the Lerchenfeld Church at Vienna. In 1872 he was pensioned, and made a knight of the order of Francis Joseph. He died March 13, 1876. "Führich has been fairly described as a 'Nazarene,' a romantic religious artist, whose pencil did more than any other to restore the old spirit of Dürer and give new shape to countless incidents of the gospel and scriptural legends." His principal works are his illustrations of Tieck's *Genofeva*, *The Lord's Prayer*, *The Triumph of Christ*, *The Road to Bethlehem*, *The Succession of Christ*, according to Thomas à Kempis, *The Prodigal Son*, and the verses of the Psalter. See *Encyclop. Brit.* 9th ed., s. v.

Fuhrmann, WILHELM DAVID, a Protestant theologian of Germany, was born at Soest, May 15, 1764, was in 1806 preacher at Hamm, and died Jan. 20, 1838. He is the author of, *Handbuch der theol. Literatur* (Leipsic, 1818-21, 2 vols.):—*Handbuch der neuesten theol. Literatur* (Barmen, 1835):—*Handwörterbuch der christl. Religions- und Kirchengeschichte* (Halle, 1826-29, 3 vols.):—*Christliche Glaubenslehre in alphabetischer Ordnung* (Leipsic, 1802):—*Christliche Morallehre für den Kanzelgebrauch in alphabetischer Ordnung* (ibid. 1797-1803, 5 vols.). See Winer, *Handbuch der theol. Lit.* i, 6, 295, 538; ii, 56; Zuchold, *Bibl. Theol.* i, 395. (B. P.)

Fulborn, STEPHEN DE, an English prelate of the 13th century, was born at Fulborn, Cambridgeshire. In 1274 he became bishop of Waterford and lord treasurer of Ireland; hence he was preferred archbishop of Tuam, and was also chief-justice of Ireland. He is reported to have given to the Church of Glastonbury, England, "indulgences of an hundred days," probably, as Fuller suggests, so many days to all in his province who went on a pilgrimage to that place—"an over-papal act for a plain archbishop." He died in 1288, and was buried in Trinity Church, Dublin. See Fuller, *Worthies of England* (ed. Nuttall), i, 228.

Fulcran, saint and bishop, was a native of Lodeve, archdiocese of Narbonne, France, in the 10th century, and from his childhood exhibited marked piety. He was educated by Theodoric, bishop of Lodeve, who ordained him. On the death of Theodoric, the city elected Fulcran to be his successor, and he was consecrated at Narbonne by archbishop Imerick, Feb. 4, 949. His zeal and humility endeared him to his flock, as did also his abundant charity in time of famine. For a harsh word ("The man deserves to be burnt") spoken of a bishop who had fallen into heresy, and whom he heard was actually burned by the people, he was filled with remorse, twice went to Rome to do penance, tore the clothes from his back, bade his companions beat him through the streets with thorn branches, and made his confessions in the Church of St. Peter. When near his death, multitudes poured to Lodeve to receive his blessing. Fulcran died in 1006. He is celebrated in the Gallican martyrology (Feb. 13), and his life has been written by bishop Bernard Guido, compiled from ancient notices and lives of this saint, published by Bollandus. See Baring-Gould, *Lives of the Saints*, ii, 294.

Fulford, FRANCIS, D.D., a Canadian prelate, was born at Sidmouth, England, in 1803, and educated at Exeter College, Oxford, of which he became a fellow in 1825. He held prominent positions in the Church of England, and in 1850 became lord-bishop of Montreal and metropolitan of Canada. He died in Montreal, Sept. 9, 1868. His writings include *Sermons*:—*Progress of the Reformation*:—and other works.

Fulke OF STAMFORD, was born in Somersetshire, made treasurer of St. Paul's, London, and then by papal bull declared archbishop of Dublin in 1256. He died in his manor of Finglas in 1271, and was buried in St. Mary's chapel, of the Church of St. Patrick. See Fuller, *Worthies of England* (ed. Nuttall), iii, 94.

Fulla (or **Volla**), in Scandinavian mythology, was a goddess, the sister and companion of the goddess Freia.

Fuller, Nicholas, a learned English divine, was born at Southampton in 1557, and educated at a free school in the same place, and at Hart Hall, Oxford. He became rector of Allington, Wiltshire, prebend of Salisbury, and rector of Bishop Waltham, Hampshire. He died in 1622. His works are *Miscellanea Theologica, lib. iii* (Heidelberg, 1612):—*Miscellanea Sacra* (1622). See Chalmers, *Biog. Dict.* s. v.; Allibone, *Dict. of Brit. and Amer. Authors*, s. v.

Fuller, Richard, D.D., an eminent Baptist minister, was born at Beaufort, S. C., April 22, 1804. He studied under Rev. Dr. Brantly, entered Harvard University in 1820, but on account of ill-health left it during his junior year, and became a lawyer in his native state. In 1832 he was converted, under the preaching of Rev. Daniel Barker, joined the Baptist Church, was ordained the next year pastor at Beaufort, and in 1847 removed to Baltimore to take charge of the Seventh Baptist Church. In 1836 he visited Europe, and during his pastorate at Beaufort was engaged in a controversy with bishop England on the Roman Catholic claims, as well as with Dr. Wayland on the slavery question. He died in Baltimore, Oct. 20, 1876. Dr. Fuller was an eloquent preacher, an admirable pastor, and a noble specimen of Christian manliness and power. Besides *Letters* on the above controversies and several *Sermons*, he published an *Argument on Close Communion* (1849), and was one of the editors of the *Baptist Hymn-book*. See Cathcart, *Baptist Encyclop.* s. v.; Drake, *Dict. of Amer. Biog.* s. v.; *Life*, by Cuthbert (N. Y. 1879).

Fulrad (Lat. *Folredus*), an early French prelate, the son of wealthy parents in Alsace, became fourteenth abbot of St. Denis, in Paris, about 750, and was for many years ambassador of kings and popes, who conferred upon him the most special privileges. He died in 784. See Smith, *Dict. of Christ. Biog.* s. v.; Hoefer, *Nouv. Biog. Générale*, s. v.

Fulton, WILLIAM, D.D., a Protestant Episcopal clergyman, officiated, after his ordination, in Fremont, O.; about 1859 removed to Chicago, Ill.; and in 1860 to Cedar Rapids, Ia., where he became rector of Grace Church; in 1864 of All-Hallow's parish, Snow Hill, Md.; in 1870 of Spring Hill parish, Salisbury, where he died, Dec. 6, 1877, aged forty-nine years. See *Prot. Episc. Almanac*, 1879, p. 168.

Fumel, JEAN FELIX HENRI DE, a French prelate, was born at Toulouse in 1717; studied at St. Sulpice; was consecrated bishop of Lodeve in 1750; distinguished himself by his episcopal ability, his ardent charity, and his attachment to the authority of the Church, and died Jan. 2, 1790. He wrote several funeral orations. See Hoefer, *Nouv. Biog. Générale*, s. v.

Funeral Service, that part of the liturgy which the Church of England appoints to be read at the burial of the dead. It is said to have been of very great antiquity, and was used both in the Eastern and Western churches. This service is read over all the dead indiscriminately, with the exception of those who die unbaptized, of self-murderers, and those who die under the sentence of the greater excommunication.

Furies (Eumenides or **Diræ)**, mythical personages, either daughters of Nox and Acheron, of Terra and the blood of Saturn, of the Earth and Darkness, of Eris, that is, Contention, or of Jupiter. Their names were Alecto, Megæra, and Tisiphone. Some add a fourth, called Lyssa; though others recognise but one Fury, called Adrastia, daughter of Jupiter and Necessity, and the avenger of all vice. Their office was to force persons guilty of crimes committed in secret to confess their guilt. They punished their incorrigible subjects with insanity. They were represented as of vast size, old, squalid, and terrible to behold. They wore a dark robe with a serpent as a girdle. The uncultured age took pains to connect everything horrible with these frightful forms: eyes emitting flame, snake-hairs, claw-hands, with viper scourges. Their dwelling-place is an iron palace in the infernal region, where they torture those who arrive in Tartarus without being reconciled to the gods. With the progress of civilization the myths of these deities had many changes; the bloody pictures disappeared, and in their place were substituted the Eumenides (q. v.)

Furinalia, an annual festival celebrated by the ancient Romans in honor of the obscure goddess Furina. It was observed towards the end of July, and the services were conducted by a flamen.

Furini, FRANCESCO, an eminent Italian painter, was born at Florence in 1604, and studied in the schools of Passignano and Roseli, and then went to Rome. Among his finest works was a picture of *The Three Graces*, in the Palazzo Strozzi. He painted a number of large works for the churches, the best of which are at Borgo San Lorenzo, near Florence, representing *St. Francis Receiving the Stigmata*, and the *Conception of the Virgin*. He died in 1649. See Spooner, *Biog. Hist. of the Fine Arts*, s. v.

Fürst, JULIUS, an eminent Hebrew scholar of Germany, was born May 12, 1805, at Zerkowo, in the duchy of Posen. He studied at different universities, and after having taken his degree as doctor of philosophy, took up his abode at Leipsic, where he commenced his lectures at the university in 1839. In 1864 he was made professor, and died Feb. 9, 1873. He published, *Lehrgebäude der aramäischen Idiome* (Leipsic, 1835):—*Perlenschnüre aramäischer Gnomen und Lieder* (1836):—*Concordantiæ Librorum Sacrorum Veteris Testamenti* (1837-40):—*Hebräisches und Chaldäisches Handwörterbuch* (1857-61, and often; English translation by S. Davidson, Lond. 1864; 3d ed. 1867):—*Geschichte der bibl. Literatur* (1867-70, 2 vols.):—*Der Kanon des Alten Testaments* (1868, 2 vols.):—*Kultur- und Litteraturgeschichte der Juden in Asien* (vol. i, 1849):—*Geschichte des Karäerthums* (1862-65, 3 vols.):—*Bibliotheca Judaica* (1848-63, 3 vols.). See Kayserling, *Bibliothek jüdischer Kanzelredner*, ii, 285; Zuchold, *Bibl. Theol.* i, 396 sq.; Etheridge, *Introduction to Hebrew Literature*, p. 483; Morais, *Eminent Israelites of the 19th Century*, p. 89 sq. (B. P.)

Fürstenthal, JACOB RAFAEL, a Hebrew scholar, was born in 1781, and died at Breslau, Dec. 16, 1855. He published, *Selichoth*, or the penitential prayers, with a German translation and Hebrew commentary (Breslau, 1823-24, 2 vols.):—he also translated into German Pakuda's (q. v.) חובת הלבבות, or, *Duties of the Heart* (ibid. 1835):—Maimonides' *More Nebuchim* (only the first part, Krotoschin, 1839):—Aboab's *Menorath ha-maor* (ibid. 1843). A very valuable work of his is *Rabbinische Anthologie* (Breslau, 1834). See Fürst, *Bibl. Jud.* i, 307 sq., where a complete list of his works is given. (B. P.)

Fürstenberg, Ferdinand von, a German prelate, was born at Bilstein, in Westphalia, Oct. 21, 1626. Dedicated to the Church from infancy, he became canon of Hildesheim, and finally *camererie segreto* of pope Alexander VII. He was chosen bishop of Paderborn, April 20, 1661, and took possession the following October. He administered his diocese with a remarkable spirit of equity, encouraged public instruction, caused new school buildings to be erected, attended to a careful distribution of instruction, preached successfully in behalf of various missions, and raised for this object 101,740 thalers. In 1678 he became bishop of Munster, after having been the coadjutor of his predecessor, also vicar-general of the pope for the countries of the North. He died June 26, 1683, leaving some poems and other works. See Hoefer, *Nouv. Biog. Générale*, s. v.

Fürstenberg, Franz Egon von, a German prelate, was born at Strasburg, May 27, 1662. He was minister to the elector of Cologne, Maximilian Henry. His attachment to Louis XIV led him to contribute to the formation of the Ligue de Rhin, contracted in view of the peace between the king and several electors of Germany. In 1661 he induced the elector of Cologne to leave to the disposal of the king of France the places of Nuiz and of Kaiserwerth. He was appointed bishop of Metz in 1658, but in 1663 resigned this position for that of Strasburg. He devoted himself to recovering from the hands of the Lutherans certain domains which formerly belonged to the Church of Strasburg. This prelate died April 1, 1682, a little after the re-establishment of the Catholic faith in the Cathedral of Strasburg, and after the recall of the canons in accordance with the submission of Strasburg to the king of France. See Hoefer, *Nouv. Biog. Générale*, s. v.

Fürstenberg, Wilhelm Egon von, surnamed *Prince William*, brother of Franz, was born in 1629. Like his elder brother, he was counsellor to the elector of Cologne, Maximilian Henry, and declared himself a partisan of France. Incensed at this, the emperor removed him, Feb. 13, 1674, then imprisoned him successively at Vienna and at Neustadt. Fürstenberg did not regain his liberty until after the peace of Nimeguen. Called to the bishopric of Metz in 1663, he resigned the following year. He was appointed bishop of Strasburg on the death of his brother in 1682. He then committed to the Jesuits the direction of a seminary and college founded by him. In 1686, through the representation of the French government, he received from pope Innocent XI the hat of a cardinal. He was elected coadjutor of Maximilian

Henry, elector of Cologne, Jan. 7, 1688; but the court of Rome, then at variance with the court of France, did not ratify this election, and another candidate, prince Clement of Bavaria, bishop of Ratisbon, superseded him. In compensation for this he received of Louis XIV the abbey of St. Germain-des-Près, where he went to dwell. He died at Paris, April 10, 1704. See Hoefer, *Nouv. Biog. Générale*, s. v.

Fuss (Lat. *Fusius*), ADAM, a Lutheran theologian of Germany, was born July 28, 1580, studied at Jena and Leipsic, and died in 1648. He published, *Compendium Dictionarium Hebr. Germanicum* (Leipsic, 1632):—*Horologium Schickardi Germ.* (ibid. eod.). See Fürst, *Bibl. Jud.* i, 310; Jöcher, *Allgemeines Gelehrten-Lexikon*, s. v. (B. P.)

Füssli, JOHANN CONRAD, a Reformed theologian of Germany, who was born at Zurich in 1707, and died in 1775, is the author of, *Thesaurus Historiæ Helveticæ* (Zurich, 1735):—*Nachricht von der Zürchischen Uebersetzung des Josephus* (ibid. 1736):—*Comment. ad Rom. v*, 13 (ibid. 1738):—*Diss. Apologetica pro Davide Rege Adv. Obtrectationes P. Baelii* (ibid. 1741):—*Beiträge zur Erläuterung der Reformations-Geschichte des Schweitzerlandes* (ibid. 1741–53):—*Epistolæ ab Ecclesiæ Helveticæ Reformatoribus vel ad eos Scriptæ* (ibid. 1742):—*Dissertatio de Fanaticis Sec. xi in Italia* (Berne, 1761):—*Neue und unpartheiische Kirchen- und Ketzer-Historie der mittlern Zeit* (Frankfort, 1770):—*De Genuina Albigensium et Waldensium Distinctione* (in the *Misc. Lips.* part 10). See Jöcher, *Allgemeines Gelehrten-Lexikon*, s. v.; Winer, *Handbuch der theol. Lit.* i, 576, 747, 810. (B. P.)

Futtafahi, in the mythology of the South Sea islands, is the mightiest among the gods of the sea, whom the inhabitants of the Friendly Islands worship. Many sacrifices of fruits and flowers are given to him and his wife Faikuwa.

Fyfe, ROBERT A., D.D., a Baptist minister, was born of Scotch parents, Oct. 20, 1816, at Saint-Philippe, near Montreal. He studied at Madison University, N. Y., and graduated at the Newton Theological Institution in 1842; was ordained at Brookline, Mass., and was pastor in Perth, Can., the same year. In 1843 he removed to Montreal to take a position as professor in the college there; next year became pastor of a Church in Toronto; in 1848 was again pastor in Perth; about 1850 removed to Warren, R. I.; in 1853 to Milwaukee, Wis.; in 1855 to Toronto again, over the Bond Street Church; in 1860 was elected president of the Canadian Literary Institute at Woodstock, and died there, Sept. 4, 1878. Few Baptist ministers in Canada have accomplished more for the denomination which he so ably represented than Dr. Fyfe. See Cathcart, *Baptist Encyclop.* s. v. (J. C. S.)

Fylfot (or **Fytfot**), i. e. *fourfooted*, a term used to describe a mystical cross, made from the combination, in a cruciform arrangement, of four Greek gammas, thus (fig. 1), or thus (fig. 2); occasionally the small γ was

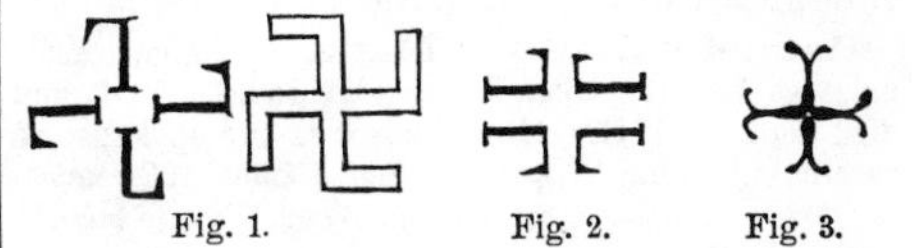

Fig. 1. Fig. 2. Fig. 3.

employed, thus (fig. 3). It was also called *Gammatium* (*Γαμμάτιον*), the Greek term for this mystical device. Its use formed a part of the ancient Secret Discipline in the primitive Church. See GAMMADIA.

Funeral Pall, a covering for the coffin during the procession to church, during the service in church, and until the coffin is afterwards placed in the grave. Anciently palls were either of violet or black, adorned with a cross, and sometimes richly embroidered with flowers, heraldic devices, or figures of saints.

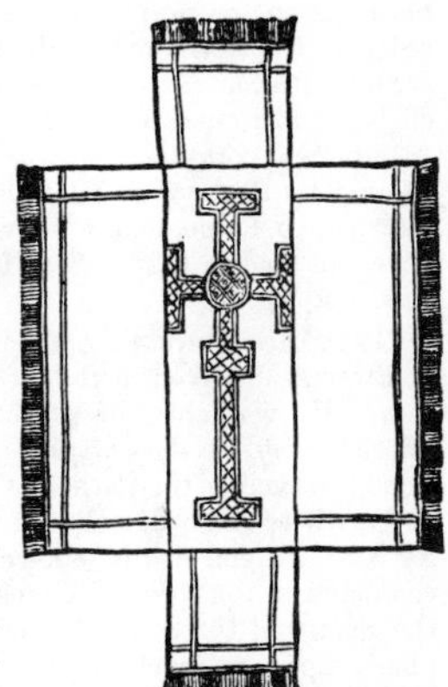

Funeral Pall of the 16th Century.

Fylla, in Norse mythology, was one of the Asas who live with Frigga, in Wingolf, in the palace Fensaler. She is very beautiful, has long, flowing hair, and delicate color of skin. A golden band on her forehead characterizes her as a goddess, and she is the confidential adviser of the wife of Odin, as well as her private maid.

G.

Gabăta (or **Gabbatha**), properly a *bowl;* hence a pensile lamp of similar form, for a church, made of different metals—gold, silver, brass, and electrum. These lamps were frequently embossed, or decorated in bass-relief, and ornamented with lilies, heads of gryphons or lions, or even fashioned in the form of these animals. Like the *coronæ* used for lighting, they very often had crosses attached to them.

An Ancient Gabata.

Gabbai, Isaac ibn-, a Jewish writer, who flourished at Leghorn at the beginning of the 17th century, is the author of כף נחת, or, a commentary on the Mishna (Venice, 1614, and often). See Fürst, *Bibl. Jud.* i, 311; Jöcher, *Allgemeines Gelehrten-Lexikon*, s. v. (B. P.)

Gabbai, Meïr ibn-, a Jewish writer of Italy, in the 16th century, is the author of, דרך אמונה, a cabalistic work, which treats of the ten sephiroth (Padua, 1563; latest edition, by Goldberg, Berlin, 1850):—עבדת הקדש, also מראות אלהים, a cabalistico-philosophical work (Mantua, 1545):—תולעת יעקב, cabalistic explanations of the Jewish prayers (Constantinople, 1560). See De' Rossi, *Dizionario Storico* (Germ. transl.), p. 107 sq.; Fürst, *Bibl. Jud.* i, 311 sq. (B. P.)

Gabriel, FESTIVAL OF, is celebrated by the Greek Church on March 26, in honor of the archangel Gabriel.

Another holy day, called the *Festival of Sts. Gabriel and Michael*, is held in honor of the two archangels, on Nov. 1, by the Greek Church.

Gabriel (surnamed *Severus*), a Greek prelate, born in Monembasia in 1577, was ordained bishop of Philadelphia, at Constantinople, by the patriarch Jeremiah. Seeing that his church contained few Greeks, he withdrew to Venice, where he was bishop of the Greeks living there. His writings were published by Simon, under the title, *Fides Ecclesiæ Orientalis* (in Greek and Latin, 1671). They comprise two treatises, one relating to the sacraments, the other entitled *Apologia*, published for the first time at Venice in 1600. See Hoefer, *Nouv. Biog. Générale*, s. v.

Gabrielli, a heretical prelate, lived in the latter half of the 17th century. He belonged to the Roman branch of the Gabrielli family. Actions both foul and strange have been imputed to him, such as making sacrifices of human blood at the reunions of his friends. Francis Picchitelli, called also Cecco Foligname, had been sent to assassinate the marquis of Buffalo, but the emissary being seized, exposed his accomplices, among them Gabrielli, who was confined in a convent of Monte Cassino, and deprived of his income. Afterwards he was conducted to the château of Perugia by the order of Innocent XI. See Hoefer, *Nouv. Biog. Générale*, s. v.

Gabrielli, Giovanni Maria, an Italian cardinal, was born at Citta-da-Castello, Jan. 10, 1654, and died Sept. 17, 1711. He is known as the apologist of cardinal Sfondrati's works. See Jöcher, *Allgemeines Gelehrten-Lexikon*, s. v.; Hoefer, *Nouv. Biog. Générale*, s. v. (B. P.)

Gabrielli, Giulio, an Italian prelate, was born at Rome, Aug. 20, 1748; became bishop of Sinigaglia, and cardinal-priest, Feb. 23, 1801, and on March 27, 1808, pro-secretary of state under Pius VII. On account of his incessant recriminations, Gabrielli was arrested by order of Napoleon, and on June 17 was superseded by cardinal Pecca. After the removal of the pope, Gabrielli went to France, and was banished to Saumur. In 1813 he was permitted, with several other cardinals, to accompany the pope to Fontainebleau. He afterwards returned to Rome, where he was likely to be elected pope, but died in 1822. See Hoefer, *Nouv. Biog. Générale*, s. v.

Gabrino, Augustino, an Italian fanatic, was born at Brescia, and lived in the latter half of the 17th century. He was chief of a sect of fanatics called the *Chevaliers of the Apocalypse*. He declared his intention of defending the Catholic Church against the antichrist whose reign he believed to be approaching. He gave as ensigns to his followers a sabre and staff of command in the form of a cross, a sparkling star, and the names of three angels, Gabriel, Michael, and Raphael, upon their clothing. They numbered about twenty-four, mostly artisans. On Palm Sunday of 1694, Gabrino rushed, sword in hand, upon the ecclesiastics, claiming their homage. He was accordingly imprisoned as a madman. A number of his proselytes were arrested upon the confessions of one of them, and the rest dispersed. See Hoefer, *Nouv. Biog. Générale*, s. v.

Gack, Georg Christoph, a Lutheran theologian, was born at Hof, in Bavaria, in 1793, and died at Sulzbach in 1851. He wrote, *De Presbyteriorum Constitutione*, etc. (Sulzbach, 1823):—*Geschichte des Herzogthums Sulzbach* (Leipsic, 1847). See Winer, *Handbuch der theol. Lit.* ii, 19, 215; Zuchold, *Bibl. Theol.* i, 399. (B. P.)

Gadara (now *Um-Keis*). For a recent and full account of the present condition of this interesting site, see Merrill, *East of the Jordan* (N. Y. 1881), p. 145 sq.

Gadara (Um-Keis). (From Thomson's *Central Palestine and Phœnicia.*)

Gadsden, Christopher P., D.D., a Protestant Episcopal clergyman, was assistant minister in Charleston, S. C., for many years, until 1859, when he became rector of St. Luke's Church in that city. He was a member of the standing committee of his diocese, a member of the board of missions to the colored men and freedmen of South Carolina, and a deputy to the General Convention. He died July 24, 1871, aged forty-five years. See *Prot. Episc. Almanac*, 1872, p. 127.

Gaelic Version of the Scriptures. This language is spoken in the Highlands and Western Isles of Scotland. It was not till the year 1767 that a New Test. in the Gaelic tongue was provided for the Scotch Highlanders in the translation of the Rev. James Stuart of Killin. The work was published at the expense of the Society in Scotland for Promoting Christian Knowledge. The first edition consisted of 10,000 copies, and a larger edition of 21,500 copies was issued by the same society in 1796. The next step of the society was to obtain a Gaelic version of the Old Test. To facilitate the work, the Old Test. was divided into four parts, two of which were allotted to the Rev. Dr. John Stuart, of Luss, the son of the translator of the New Test.; a third part, also, afterwards fell to his share, although it had in the first instance been executed by another hand. The remaining fourth part, consisting of the prophetical books, was translated by the Rev. Dr. Smith, of Campbelltown, and, on its completion, was found to differ altogether in style and execution from the other portion of the Bible translated by Dr. Stuart. The whole version was completed for the press in 1801. In consequence of many complaints concerning the discrepancy in style between the prophetical and the other books, the society resolved in their next edition to subject the prophetical books to a thorough revision, that they might be rendered conformable to the other parts of the version. This plan was effected in 1807, and 20,000 copies of the Old together with the New Test. were printed at Glasgow, under the care of the Rev. Alexander Stewart, of Dingwall. In the same year the British and Foreign Bible Society published, in London, an edition, consisting of 20,000 Bibles and 10,000 Testaments, but not being sufficient to satisfy the urgent demands for more copies, from time to time other editions followed. The total number of Gaelic Bibles and Testaments printed by the British and Foreign Bible Society up to March 31, 1884, was 160,126. This number, however, does not include a supply of 50,500 Bibles and Testaments furnished to the Highlanders by other societies between 1810 and 1829. See *Bible of Every Land*, p. 158. (B. P.)

Gaetano, Antonio, an Italian prelate, was born in 1566. He was archbishop of Capua, for several years nuncio at Vienna and Madrid, and died in 1624. He was learned, and handled satire with much ability. See Hoefer, *Nouv. Biog. Générale*, s. v.

Gaetano, Bonifacio, an Italian prelate, was bishop of Cassano in 1599, vice-legate of Urban, cardinal in 1606, archbishop of Tarentum in 1613, and finally legate of Romagna. He died June 29, 1617, leaving some sermons. See Hoefer, *Nouv. Biog. Générale*, s. v.

Gagarin, Ivan S., a Jesuit, was born in Russia in 1814. For some time he held an appointment in the Russian diplomatic service, and joined his order in 1843. Afterwards he devoted a good deal of attention to the differences between the Eastern and Western churches, and published as the result of his studies a considerable number of books and *brochures* in the French language, the best known of these being, *Le Clergé Russe:—Les Églises d'Orient:—Le Pape:—L'Église Russe et les Rascolniks:—Les Jésuites en Russie.* He co-operated with some of his countrymen in founding the excellent Slavonic library in Paris, known as the *Musée Slave*, which, since the expulsion of the Jesuits from France, in 1880, has been located in the Rue de Sèvres. Gagarin died at Paris, July 20, 1882. (B. P.)

Gagliardi, Achille, an Italian Jesuit, who died at Modena, July 6, 1607, is the author of *Breve Compendio Intorno alla Professione Christiana:—De Disciplina Hominis:—Explicatio Instituti Societatis Jesu:—Meditationes pro Omnibus Hominum Statibus.* See Alegambe, *Bibliotheca Scriptorum Societatis Jesu;* Jöcher, *Allgemeines Gelehrten-Lexikon*, s. v. (B. P.)

Gagliardi, Paolo, a canon at Brescia, where he died, Aug. 16, 1742, is known as the editor of *Veterum Brixiæ Episcoporum Philasterii et Gaudentii Opera* (Brixen, 1738):—*Gaudentii Sermones* (Padua, 1720; Augsburg, 1757). See Jöcher, *Allgemeines Gelehrten-Lexikon*, s. v.; Winer, *Handbuch der theol. Lit.* i, 875, 906. (B. P.)

Gagnatius. See CAGNAZZO.

Gagnée (Gagni or **Gaigny)**, JEAN DE (Lat. *Gagnæus*), a French theologian, was born in Paris. Having been made treasurer at the College of Navarre, he commenced, about 1524, the study of theology, which he was called to teach in 1529. He then translated the *Livre des Sentences.* In 1531 he became rector of the university, and was made doctor of theology. Being called to the court of Francis I, he copied rare manuscripts in the royal library. Having become almoner and preacher of the king, Gagnée made use of his influence for the maintenance of the privileges of the university. He died in 1549, leaving, *Commentarius Primasii Uticensis in Epistolas S. Pauli* (Latin and French; Paris and Lyons, 1537):—a translation from Latin to French of the *Sermons of Guerrie*, abbot of Igny:—*Davidici Psalmi* (Paris, 1547):—*Paraphrasis in Epistolam ad Romanos* (ibid. 1533, 1633):—*Scholia in Evangelia quatuor et in Actus Apostolorum* (ibid. 1552, 1631, and in the *Biblia Maxima* of John de la Haye, ibid. 1643):—*Hendeca Syllabus de Sanctissimo Christi Corpore in Eucharistia.* See Hoefer, *Nouv. Biog. Générale*, s. v.

Gahan, WILLIAM, D.D., an eminent Roman Catholic divine, was born in Dublin, Ireland, June 5, 1732. On Sept. 18, 1749, he joined the hermits of St. Augustine in Dublin, and the year after was sent to the convent of the order at Louvain, to complete his ecclesiastical studies at the university. Here he was promoted to the priesthood, May 25, 1755. He returned to Ireland and was made curate of the Church of St. Paul, Dublin, where he was in labors abundant. He died there, Dec. 6, 1804. His best known writings are, *Sermons:—History of the Church:—The Christian Guide to Heaven:—Catholic Devotions.* See *Cath. Almanac*, 1875, p. 50.

Gaillard DE LONJUMEAU, a French prelate, was the person who conceived the idea of a grand dictionary of universal history, the execution of which he confided to Moréri, his almoner. For the compilation of this work he made numerous researches in various countries, and especially in Rome, in the library of the Vatican. It was to Gaillard de Lonjumeau that Moreri dedicated the first edition of this work, undertaken in the province, and published at Lyons in 1674. Gaillard was bishop of Apt from 1673 to 1693. He died in 1695. See Hoefer, *Nouv. Biog. Générale*, s. v.

Gaillard, Georg, a Carmelite of Cologne, who died in 1687, is the author of *Sacrificium Vespertinum Tripartitum*, etc. (Cologne, 1682):—*Trifœdus Marianum*, etc. (ibid. 1683, 1687). See Harzheim, *Bibl. Colonensis;* Jöcher, *Allgemeines Gelehrten-Lexikon*, s. v. (B. P.)

Gain (*de Montaignac*), FRANÇOIS DE, a French prelate, was born Jan. 6, 1744, at the chateau of Montaignac. He was at first almoner of the king and grand vicar of Rheims, and in 1782 became bishop of Tarbes. He was strongly opposed to the innovations of the assembly, and retired to Spain in 1790. Nevertheless, in 1791 he came to Tarbes to protest in a public sermon against the new order of things, and to explain his refusal of the oath. The French conquests obliged him to flee to Portugal, and at the time of the concordat he resigned, Nov. 6, 1801. He died near Lisbon in 1806, leaving fifty-seven writings upon ecclesiastical matters. See Hoefer, *Nouv. Biog. Générale*, s. v.

Galatino, PIETRO DI, a Franciscan of the 16th century, professor of theology and philosophy at Rome, is the author of *De Arcanis Catholicæ Veritatis*, etc. (Ortona di Mare, 1518, and often):—*Opus de Theologia:—Commentaria in Apocalypsin:—De Ecclesiæ Catholicæ Institutione, Deformatione et Reformatione:—Ostium Apertum seu de recta Sacræ Scripturæ Interpretatione*, etc. See Fürst, *Bibl. Jud.* i, 314; Wolf, *Bibl. Hebr.* i, 971; Jöcher, *Allgemeines Gelehrten-Lexikon*, s. v. (B. P.)

Galberry, THOMAS, a Roman Catholic bishop, of the order of St. Augustine, was placed in the see of Hartford, Conn., March 19, 1876. He zealously continued the work of his predecessors till the summer of 1878, when, his health failing, he set out for a convent of his order near Philadelphia. He became so ill in the cars that he was removed to a hotel in New York, where he died, Oct. 17 of the same year. See De Courcey and Shea, *Hist. of the Cath. Church in the U. S.* p. 5, 7.

Gale, George Washington, D.D., a Presbyterian minister, was born in North East, N. Y., Dec. 3, 1789. He graduated from Union College in 1814, studied theology one year thereafter at Princeton Seminary, was licensed by Hudson Presbytery in September, 1816, and ordained pastor at Adams, Jefferson Co., N. Y., in 1819, where he remained till 1823. In 1827 he founded the Oneida Manual Labor Institute at Whitesborough, and in 1832 Knox College, at Galesburg, Ill. He died there, Sept. 13, 1862. See Wilson, *Presb. Hist. Almanac*, 1863, p. 296; *Gen. Cat. of Princeton Theol. Sem.* 1881, p. 18; Nevin, *Presb. Encyclop.* s. v.

Gale, Nahum, D.D., a Congregational minister, was born at Auburn, Mass., March 6, 1812. He studied at Phillips Academy, Andover, graduated from Amherst College in 1837, and four years after from the East Windsor Theological Seminary. He was ordained at Ware, June 22, 1842, of which church he was pastor until 1851, when he became professor of ecclesiastical history and the pastoral charge in the East Windsor Seminary, retaining that position until 1853. On Sept. 1 of that year he was installed pastor of the Church at Lee, and died in Newburyport, Sept. 18, 1876. Among his published works are, *Pilgrims' First Year in New England* (1857):—*Memoir of Rev. Bennett Tyler, D.D.* (1859):—*Conversion Through Personal Effort* (1866):—*Prophet of the Highest* (1873). See *Cong. Quarterly* 1877, p. 416.

Galen, CHRISTOPH BERNHARD MATTHÆUS VAN, a German prelate and general, was born in Westphalia in 1604. Having completed his studies, he travelled in various parts of Europe, entered as colonel the service of the elector of Cologne, and made, from 1637 to 1647, several campaigns against the French and Swedes. At the treaty of peace at Münster, he accepted a canonship in that city, afterwards obtained the provostship, and in 1650 was elected bishop-prince. The inhabitants objected to some of his regulations, and he was obliged to adopt special measures to compel their obedience. In 1664 he was chosen one of the general directors of the army of the empire against the Turks. Returning to his bishopric, he allied himself in 1665 with Charles II, king of England, against the people of Holland, but Louis XIV interposed between the belligerent parties.

In 1672 Galen took arms against the states-general, but Leopold I of Germany obliged him to make a treaty with them in 1674. This bishop, fierce and war-loving, died at Huy, Sept. 19, 1678. See Hoefer, *Nouv. Biog. Générale*, s. v.

Galesi, Dominico, an Italian prelate, lived in the latter half of the 17th century. He was bishop of Kuvo, and wrote *Ecclesiastica in Matrimonium Potestas, adversus Jo. Launoi Doctrinam*, etc. (Paris, 1677), which was followed by a reply from Launoy. See Hoefer, *Nouv. Biog. Générale*, s. v.

Galesni (Lat. **Galesinius**), Pietro, a learned Italian ecclesiastical antiquary and apostolical notary, who died about 1590, devoted most of his time to researches in ecclesiastical history. He endeavored to correct and illustrate the *Roman Martyrology*, by remodelling it and adding a number of new facts concerning the saints. He wrote the *Lives of the Saints of Milan* (1582), and a *Commentary on the Pentateuch* (1587). See Chalmers, *Biog. Dict.* s. v.

Galiczon, Gatien de, a French theologian, was born at Angers, Oct. 27, 1658. Having received the degree of doctor of civil and canon law at the age of twenty, he entered into orders; in 1688 was made canon and chorister at St. Martin of Tours; shortly after official and grand vicar; but his close attention to his duties threw him into a dangerous illness. He returned to Angers and there recovered his health. Persuaded that the sparing of his life was a miracle, he consecrated himself more wholly to the service of God. In 1707 he was appointed bishop of Agathocles and coadjutor of the bishop of Babylon. He started for Persia, and died there soon after his arrival at Ispahan, Sept. 27, 1712. He wrote some works, for which see Hoefer, *Nouv. Biog. Générale*, s. v.

Galilæum is the name given to the catechumenal oil in the Greek Church. It is considered as sanctified by drops of *Meirun* or holy *chrism* (q. v.) which are mixed with it.

Galilei, Alessandro, an eminent Florentine architect, was born in 1691. He resided seven years in England, and on his return to Tuscany was appointed state architect by Cosmo III. He was invited by Clement XII to Rome, where he erected three superb monuments of art, the façades of S. Giovanni de' Fiorentini and S. Giovanni Laterano, and the Corsini chapel in the latter edifice. He died in 1737. See Hoefer, *Nouv. Biog. Générale*, s. v.; Spooner, *Biog. Hist. of the Fine Arts*, s. v.

Galla, *Saint*, was a daughter of Symmachus, a Roman noble, who died in the former part of the 6th century; she became a widow while very young, and took the veil at St. Peter's monastery. She is commemorated Oct. 5.

Galla Version of the Scriptures. The Galla language is spoken by the Gallas (q. v.). While Dr. Krapf resided in Shoa, between the years 1839 and 1842, he translated the gospels of Matthew, Luke, and John, the epistle to the Romans, and the book of Genesis. The gospel of Matthew and five chapters of the gospel of John were printed in Roman letters, the copies being designed for distribution among the Galla tribes around Shoa, where the Church Missionary Society contemplated the establishment of a mission. The opposition of the Abyssinian priesthood led, however, to the abandonment, in 1844, of the Shoa mission, and the station was accordingly transferred to the Wanika country, whence it was hoped that opportunities for a wider dissemination of the Bible than that originally contemplated by the society might accrue. But these hopes have been doomed to be disappointed. Of late the translation of the Bible into the Galla language has again been taken up by the Rev. Dr. Krapf, and among the translations published, the British and Foreign Bible Society announced, for the year 1876, the New Test. in Galla, printed in Amharic characters. Besides the New Test. there are also printed the books of Genesis and Exodus, the latter having left the press in 1877. For the study of the language, see Tutschek, *Dictionary and Grammar of the Galla Language* (Munich, 1844–45). (B. P.)

Gallæus, Servatius, a Reformed preacher of Holland, who died near the end of the 17th century, is known as the editor of Lactantius's works, published at Leyden in 1660; he also edited the *Sibylline Oracles* (Amsterdam, 1687–88), and wrote *Dissertationes de Sibyllis Earumque Oraculis* (ibid. 1688). See Jöcher, *Allgemeines Gelehrten-Lexikon*, s. v.; Winer, *Handbuch der theol. Lit.* i, 908. (B. P.)

Galland, Thomas, an English Wesleyan minister, was born at Hull. He was converted at the age of fifteen, under the ministry of W. E. Miller, and being designed for the ministry of the Church of England, was sent to Cambridge, where he graduated as master of arts. He entered the Methodist ministry, but still prosecuted his studies. He was one of the advanced liberal members of the Conference, but, with independence of thought, he deferred to the peace and unity of the Church. With unbending principles, he was tender and charitable towards others; with great vigor of intellect, he was simple, frank, and ingenuous; with an anxious desire for the freedom of the Church, he had a fixed concern for Christian order. He was a leader in the institution of that body and of its spiritual government, and ably advocated all its great interests. His ministry, which began in 1816, was evangelical, ardent, and powerful; and he was withal a diligent and faithful pastor. He died suddenly at Hull, May 12, 1843, aged forty-nine years. Galland was wealthy and liberal. As a pulpit expositor of Scripture, he was, perhaps, without an equal in his day. See *Minutes of the British Conference*, 1843; Stevenson, *City-Road Chapel*, p. 266; Smith, *Hist. of Wesl. Meth.* iii, 35, 229, 244, 350, 355, 412, 419, 478, 479; Everett, *Wesl. Centenary Takings*, vol. ii, sketch 9.

Gallardo, Matteo, a reputable Spanish painter, resided at Madrid in 1657. There is a picture of Christ, and several of the Virgin, by him, which are highly commended. See Spooner, *Biog. Hist. of the Fine Arts*, s. v.

Galle, Philip, an eminent Dutch engraver, was born at Haarlem in 1537, and early established himself at Antwerp. The following are some of his prints: *Solomon Directing the Building of the Temple*; a set of prints of subjects from the Old and New Test.; *Abraham Sacrificing Isaac; Christ with the Two Disciples at Emmaus*. He died in 1612. See Hoefer, *Nouv. Biog. Générale*, s. v.; Spooner, *Biog. Hist. of the Fine Arts*, s. v.

Gallemart, Joannes de, a Roman Catholic theologian, who died at Douay in 1625, doctor and professor of theology, is known as the editor of *Canones et Decreta Concil. Trid.* (Cologne, 1620). See Jöcher, *Allgemeines Gelehrten-Lexikon*, s. v.; Winer, *Handbuch der theol. Lit.* i, 319. (B. P.)

Galli, priests of Cybele (q. v.) among the ancient Romans, who received the worship of this goddess from the Phrygians. They were selected from the lowest class of society, and were allowed at certain times to ask alms from the people. The chief priest among them was called *Archigallus*.

Gallican Councils: councils held in France, but at some place unknown.

I. A.D. 355, at Poitiers or Toulouse, possibly. St. Hilary, writing to the Easterns, A.D. 360, says he, five years before, with the bishops of France, withdrew from the communion of the Arian bishops Ursacius and Valens, and of Saturninus of Arles, who had espoused their cause. The opening chapters of his work addressed to Constantius are thought to have emanated from this council.

II. A.D. 376. There seems a reference to one such in a law of that year, dated Treves, of the Theodosian code; but it is not known where or for what object.

III. A.D. 444, in which Hilary of Arles presided, and Chelidonius of Besançon, where this council may have met, therefore, was accused of being husband of a widow, and deposed. On appealing, however, to St. Leo he was restored, as having been condemned on a false charge. Both their letter to him and his answer are preserved among his epistles.

IV. A.D. 678, at some place unknown; when St. Leodegar or Leger, bishop of Autun, was degraded as having been accessory to the death of king Childeric II five years before.

V. A.D. 678 or 679, against the Monothelites; as appears from the reference made to it by the Gallican bishops subscribing to the Roman synod under pope Agatho, preserved in the 4th act of the 6th council, but they do not say where.

VI. A.D. 796, at Tours possibly, where Joseph, bishop of Mans and a suffragan of Tours, was deposed for cruelty.

VII. Three more councils may be grouped under this head, usually called Councils of Auvergne, but this name is misleading, as it means the town formerly so called, not the province. When the town changed its name to Clermont, councils held there subsequently were styled by its new name, while the earlier retained its old. We save confusion, therefore, by classing them under Gallican. Of these the first met Nov. 8, A.D. 535, in the second year of king Theodebert, and passed sixteen canons, to which fifteen bishops, headed by Honoratus, metropolitan of Bourges, subscribed; his suffragan of Auvergne subscribing second. Their canons deprecate lay influences in the appointment of bishops, and lay interference between bishops and clergy. No furniture belonging to the Church may be used for private funerals or marriages. The appointment of Jews as judges, and marriages between Jews and Christians, are denounced. Presbyters and deacons marrying are to be deposed. In a collective note to king Theodebert, the bishops entreat that neither the clergy, nor others, living in his dominions may be robbed of their rightful possessions, and in their fifth canon they declare all spoliations of Church property null and void, and the spoilers excommunicated wherever it occurs. Several other canons are given to this council by Burchard. The second, A.D. 549, was attended by ten bishops, but only to receive the canons passed at the 5th Council of Orleans. The third, A.D. 588, was occupied solely with a dispute between the bishops of Rhodes and Cahors.

Gallifiet, Joseph, a French theologian, was born in 1663, near Aix (Provence). He entered the Jesuit order, became rector, then provincial, of the College of the Trinity, at Lyons, where he had completed his studies, and was regarded as the principal promoter of the devotion to the Sacred Heart of Jesus. In 1723 he became assistant to the general of the Jesuits at Rome. He died about 1740, leaving several works on devotion, for which see Hoefer, *Nouv. Biog. Générale*, s. v.

Gallim. Lieut. Conder suggests (*Tent-Work in Palest.* ii, 336) as a representative of this site the present *Beit-Jâla*, doubtless meaning the place of that name a few miles south of Jerusalem (see Zelah); but the passage in Isaiah (x, 30) requires a position north of that city.

Galloche, Louis, a reputable French historical painter, was born at Paris in 1670, and studied under Louis Boullonge. He was a member of the Royal Academy. Among his works are the *Departure of St. Paul from Miletus*, in the Church of Notre Dame; *The Good Samaritan*, and *The Resurrection.* He died in 1761. See Hoefer, *Nouv. Biog. Générale*, s. v.; Spooner, *Biog. Hist. of the Fine Arts*, s. v.

Gallonius, Antonius, a priest of the congregation of the oratory, was a native of Rome, and died there in 1605. His works were numerous, but he is chiefly known by his *Trattato degli Instrumenti di Martirio*, etc. In 1591 he published his *History of the Virgins: — The Lives of Certain Martyrs* (1597).

Gallucci, Angelo, an Italian Jesuit, was born at Macerata in 1593, became a famous preacher, professor of eloquence in the College of Rome, and died Feb. 28, 1674, leaving some *Sermons* and other works, for which see *Biog. Universelle*, s. v.

Gallucci, Tarquinio, an Italian Jesuit, was born at Sabina in 1574, became professor of rhetoric, and finally rector of the Greek College in Rome, and died there July 28, 1649, leaving some commentaries on classical works.

Gallus, *Saint* (1), sixteenth bishop of Clermont-Ferrand, was born in that city (Auvergne) about 489, of patrician parents. In order to escape marriage, he took refuge at the monastery of Cornon (Cronom or Cournom), and there embraced the monastic life. St. Quintianus, then bishop of Auvergne, ordained him deacon, kept him near himself, and drew him into literary pursuits. Later, Thierry, king of Austrasia, attracted Gallus to his court. Here he remained until 527, when St. Quintianus died, and Gallus was elected to succeed him. He distinguished himself by his gentleness and charity. Being uncle of St. Gregory of Tours, he took charge of the education of his nephew. St. Gallus assisted at the first two councils of Clermont-Ferrand, Nov. 8, 535 and 549, as well as at the second, third, fourth, and fifth of Orleans—June 23, 533; May 7, 538; Aug. 31, 541; and Oct. 28, 549. The hagiographers affirm that he possessed the gift of miracles. By his prayers he arrested the flames which threatened the destruction of the city, and at another time delivered the citizens from the fearful ravages of disease. He died about 553, and his body is preserved in the Church of Notre Dame du Port, at Clermont-Ferrand. He is honored by the Church July 1. See Hoefer, *Nouv. Biog. Générale*, s. v.; Smith, *Dict. of Christ. Biog.* s. v.

Gallus, *Saint* (2), twenty-third bishop of Clermont-Ferrand, lived in the 7th century. He was elected in 650, and is honored as a saint in his diocese on Nov. 1. He wrote a *Lettre Adressée à Saint Didier, évêque de Cahors*, which Ussher falsely attributes to St. Gall of Hibernia. See Hoefer, *Nouv. Biog. Générale*, s. v.; Smith, *Dict. of Christ. Biog.* s. v.

Gallus, Nicolas (properly *Hahn*), a Lutheran theologian of Germany, was born at Köthen, June 21, 1516. He studied at Wittenberg, was in 1542 deacon at Ratisbon, which place, however, he had to leave on account of the Interim (q. v.). He went to Wittenberg to occupy the pulpit of Cruciger, who was prevented from discharging his ministerial functions by sickness. From Wittenberg Gallus went to Magdeburg, but returned again to Ratisbon in 1553, and died there in 1570. In connection with Flacius (q. v.), Gallus opposed the Interim and Osiander, and defended his Church against the intrusion of all and every error. See Salig, *Vollständige Historie der Augsburgscher Confession*, ii, 1008 sq.; Jöcher, *Allgemeines Gelehrten-Lexikon*, s. v.; Lichtenberger, *Encyclop. des Sciences Religieuses*, s. v.; Herzog-Plitt, *Real-Encyklop.* s. v. (B. P.)

Gallus, Robertus, a French mystic, lived at Orange in 1291. He derived his name from his French origin, and was provincial of a monastic order. According to Ouden, he was very pious, but of little note. He believed himself endowed with the gift of revelation, and wrote several works in this line. The only one which has come down to us was published at Paris in 1513, at the house of Henry Stephens, under the editorship of Le Fevre of Étaples, and is entitled *Liber Trium Virorum* (namely, Hermas, Uguelin, and Robert Gallus himself), *et Trium Spiritualium Virginum* (the princesses Hildegarde, Élisabeth, and Mechtilde). See Hoefer, *Nouv. Biog. Générale*, s. v.

Gally, HENRY, D.D., an English divine, was born at Beckenham, Kent, in August, 1696, and was educated at Benet College, Cambridge. In 1724 he was chosen lecturer of St. Paul's Covent-garden, and in the same year was instituted to the rectory of Wavendon or Wanden, in Buckinghamshire. The king preferred him to a prebend in the Cathedral of Gloucester in 1728, and three years later to one in Norwich. He died Aug. 7, 1769. He was the author of two sermons on the *Misery of Man*, preached in 1723:—*The Moral Character of Theophrastus*, translated from the Greek, with notes:—*A Critical Essay on Characteristic Writing:*—*Sermon* before the House of Commons. See Chalmers, *Biog. Dict.* s. v.; Allibone, *Dict. of Brit. and Amer. Authors*, s. v.

Galon (also called *Guallo*, *Gualla*, or *Gualo*), GIACOMO, an Italian prelate, was born at Vercelli prior to 1150. He was canon-regular at Paris, and occupied from 1173 to 1185 the episcopal see of his native city. He distinguished himself by his zeal and virtue, and pope Innocent III accorded to him, in recognition of this, the cardinalate. Galon had charge of a mission in Languedoc, where he displayed great intolerance towards the Albigenses. He afterwards went to England on a diplomatic mission. Later, pope Honorius III sent him to the emperor Frederick II, to secure aid for the Christians in Palestine against the Mussulmans. Galon died at Vercelli in 1227. See Hoefer, *Nouv. Biog. Générale*, s. v.

Galura, BERNHARD, prince-bishop of Brixen, was born Aug. 21, 1764. He was for some time preacher at Freiburg, made suffragan bishop and vicar-general at Feldkirch in 1820, in 1829 consecrated prince-bishop of Brixen, and died in 1856. He wrote, *Diss. de Traditione altero Revelationis fonte* (Freiburg, 1790):—*Die Ehre der heiligen Messe* (4th ed. Augsburg, 1827):—*Biblische Geschichte der Welterlösung durch Jesum den Sohn Gottes* (ibid. 1806):—*Die ganze Katholische Religion* (ibid. 1796–99, 5 vols.):—*Gebet- und Betrachtungsbuch für Christen* (6th ed. 1836, etc.). See Winer, *Handbuch der theol. Lit.* i, 61, 403, 456, 673; ii, 241, 259, 267, 272, 346, 352, 368, 386. (B. P.)

Galvam (or **Galvao**), **Francisco Fernando**, a Portuguese orator, was born at Lisbon in 1554. He entered the ecclesiastical ranks, and acquired great renown as a preacher. He was regarded as a classical writer in Portugal. To the vigorous study which gained for him the title of doctor of theology, he added the gift of a powerful memory. He died in 1610. His works have appeared under the following titles: *Sermoes do Doutor Francisco-Fernando Galvão Arcediago de Cerveira* (Lisbon, 1611):—*Sermoes dos Festas dos Santos* (ibid. 1613):—*Sermoes dos Festas do Christo* (ibid. 1616). He had as editor a writer of merit, Amados Vieira. See Hoefer, *Nouv. Biog. Générale*, s. v.

Galvam (or **Galvao**), **João**, *count of Arganil*, was a warlike Portuguese prelate, born at Evora in the 15th century. He was the son of Ruy Galvao, secretary of Alfonso V, and succeeded his father. He became prior of the convent of the Augustines, and in 1451 accompanied princess Leonora, as she went to be married to the emperor Frederick III. On his return, in 1461, he became bishop of Coimbra. Alfonso V sent him ten years later to Africa. At Arzilla and Tangier he fought so valiantly that the king conferred upon him the title of count of Arganil, which title ever afterwards belonged to the bishop of Coimbra. The archbishopric of Braga being vacant, Galvao was called to it by Sixtus IV in 1480. He died Aug. 5, 1485, at a very advanced age. He left in manuscript, *Jornada da Emperatriz Dona Leonor*. See Hoefer, *Nouv. Biog. Générale*, s. v.

Gamaches, PHILIPPE DE, a French theologian, was born in 1568. The faculty of theology made him doctor in 1598, and the same year he became professor of positive theology in the Sorbonne. He acquired a high reputation for profound learning and incorruptible independence of judgment. He died at Paris, July 21, 1625. His commentaries upon Thomas Aquinas, published under the title, *Theologia Scolastica, Speculativa, Practica* (Paris, 1627), were highly esteemed. See Hoefer, *Nouv. Biog. Générale*, s. v.

Gamaliel BEN-JEHUDAH (surnamed *Bathraah*, i. e. the Last) terminated the long dynasty of the house of Hillel. Though styled patriarch, yet his power was hardly more than nominal. The Jewish population of Palestine had lost their preponderant influence by dispersion; and the stronger the foreign synagogues became, the less were they disposed to appeal to the patriarchal see, though its existence was still regarded with a certain complacency. But the thing itself was now to end. The emperor Honorius had inhibited the transfer of contributions from the West to the patriarchal coffers at Tiberias; and Gamaliel himself, under the charge of contumacy, in the erection of synagogues contrary to the imperial law, by an edict of Theodosius was stripped of his secular title of "præfect" in the year 415 (*Cod. Theod.* vi, 22). It may be that this is the same Gamaliel whom Jerome mentions (*Epist.* 57, § 3) as an enemy of Hesychius. Gamaliel died without an heir, and thus, with his death, this shadow of dignity, which he retained in Jewish circles, entirely passed away. See Etheridge, *Introduction to Jewish Literature*, p. 139 sq.; Smith, *Dict. of Christ. Biog.* s. v. (B. P.)

Gamaliel, a Scotch prelate, was an Englishman by birth, consecrated by Roger, archbishop of York, and promoted to the see of the Isles in 1181. See Keith, *Scottish Bishops*, p. 298.

Gambara, Giovanni Francesco, an Italian prelate, nephew of Uberto, was born at Brescia, Jan. 17, 1533. He was son of Giovanni Brunero II, count of Prato Albuino, who rendered great service to the house of Austria, and distinguished himself among the Latin poets of his time. Giovanni, after having been educated at Perugia and Padua, was sent to the court of Charles V. He afterwards returned to Rome, performed various offices under Julius III and Pius IV, and was made cardinal in 1561. Pius V appointed him bishop of Viterbo. He died at Rome, May 5, 1587. See Hoefer, *Nouv. Biog. Générale*, s. v.

Gambara, Lattanzio, an eminent Italian painter, was born at Brescia in 1541, and was instructed in the school of Girolamo Romanino. His greatest and most studied production is his fresco in the dome of the cathedral at Parma, representing subjects from the life of Christ. Some of his other admired works are, *Cain Slaying Abel; Moses and the Brazen Serpent; Samson and Delilah; Judith with the Head of Holofernes; Jael and Sisera; The Taking Down from the Cross.* He died in 1574.

Gambara, Uberto, an Italian prelate, was born at Brescia, near the close of the 15th century. He was the son of Gian. Francesco, count of Prato Albuino, who abandoned the side of the Venetians after the battle of Chiara in 1509, and joined the French in order to save the city of Brescia, his native place. This desertion irritated the Venetians against him, but they were appeased through the intervention of pope Leo X, a particular friend of the count. This pontiff called the young Uberto to himself, and sent him as nuncio to Portugal. Clement VII sent him to solicit, in 1527, the aid of the king of England against Charles V. Gambara acquitted himself with success in this mission, and on his return was appointed bishop of Tortona. Paul III made him cardinal in 1539, and confided to him the legations of Parma and Placentia. In this position Gambara adroitly favored the designs of the Farnese, and afforded them much aid, by placing them in possession of these principalities. He died at Rome, Feb. 14, 1549. See Hoefer, *Nouv. Biog. Générale*, s. v.

Gamelia, the name applied to a sacrifice among the ancient Greeks, which the parents of a girl about to be married were accustomed to offer to Athena (q. v.), on the day before the marriage. In time the word came to be applied to marriage solemnities in general.

Gameline, a Scotch prelate, was archdeacon and lord-chancellor of St. Andrews in 1250. He was made bishop of St. Andrews in 1255, on St. Thomas's day, and consecrated on St. Stephen's day of the same year. Here he continued until his death in 1271. See Keith, *Scottish Bishops*, p. 18.

Gammadia (γαμμάδια, for γαμμάτια), a cruciform ornament, embroidered on the borders or woven into the texture of ecclesiastical vestments, both in the West and East. It takes its name from being composed of four capital *gammas* (Γ) placed back to back, thus ⅃ L forming a voided Greek cross. The *gammas* ㄱ Γ were also sometimes placed face to face, so as to constitute a hollow square, in the centre of which a cross was inscribed. Vestments so decorated were known by the name of *polystauria* (πολυσταύρια). See FYLFOT.

Ganach. See IBN-GANACH.

Ganapatyas, the worshippers of *Ganesa* (q. v.). They can scarcely be considered as a distinct sect, Ganesa being worshipped by all the Hindûs as having power to remove all difficulties and impediments. Hence, they never commence a journey or engage in any important work without invoking his protection. Some, however, pay this god more particular devotion, and therefore may be considered as specially entitled to be called *Ganapatyas*.

Ganesa, a Hindû deity, was the son of Siva and Parvati. He is considered the god of prudence, who removes all hinderances, and corresponds to the Greek *Hermes*, or the Roman *Mercury*, the great teacher and presiding deity of authors. Ganesa is always addressed as "that god upon whose glorious forehead the new moon is painted with the froth of Ganga." He is generally represented sitting cross-legged, with four arms and hands, and having the head and proboscis of an elephant. Ganesa had formerly six classes of worshippers; in the present day he cannot boast of any exclusive adoration, although he shares a kind of homage along with all the other gods. See PULEAR.

Ganga Sagor, a sacred island among the Hindûs, situated at the union of the great western or holiest branch of the Ganges with the Indian ocean. It is low, flat, and swampy, yet it is one of the most celebrated places of pilgrimage in India, on account of the peculiar sacredness of the waters at this point. On the island stands a ruinous temple dedicated to Kapila, the founder of the Sankhya system. This temple is usually occupied by a few disciples of Kapila, and crowds repair thither twice every year, at the full moon in November and in January, to perform obsequies for the benefit of their deceased ancestors, and to practice various ablutions in the sacred waters. As many as 300,000 pilgrims have resorted to this sacred spot from all parts of India in a single year.

Gangas, the idolatrous priests of the inhabitants of Congo, in western Africa. They acknowledge one Supreme Being, but worship also a number of subordinate deities who preside over the different departments of nature. These priests teach the people to worship their deities by various rites and ceremonies, but chiefly by donations of food and clothing, which they appropriate to their own use. They make the people believe that they can bring down blessings upon them, avert judgments, cure diseases, and dispel witchcraft.

Gangauf, THEODOR, a Roman Catholic theologian of Germany, was born Nov. 1, 1809, at Bergen. In 1833 he received holy orders, in 1836 joined the Benedictines at Augsburg, was in 1842 professor of philosophy and philology at the Augsburg Lyceum, in 1848 rector of the same, and died Sept. 15, 1875. He was a follower of Günther's philosophical system, and wrote, *Die Metaphysische Psychologie des heil. Augustin* (1844-47):—*Augustin's Principien über das Verhältniss von Glauben und Wissen* (1851):—*Augustin's Lehre von Gott dem Dreieinigen* (1865). (B. P.)

Gang-days. See ROGATION.

Ganinnanses (from Singhalese *gana*, an assembly), a name applied in Ceylon to the novices as well as the priests among the Buddhists.

Ganj Bakshis, a division of the Sikhs (q. v.) in Hindustan, who are said to have derived their name from their founder. They are few in number and of little importance.

Gannett, EZRA STILES, D.D., a Unitarian minister, was born at Cambridge, Mass., May 4, 1801. He was educated at Phillips Academy, Andover, and Harvard College, where he graduated in 1820. He then spent three years in the Cambridge Divinity School, and was ordained colleague-pastor with Dr. William E. Channing, June 24, 1824. He remained in that charge until his death, Aug. 28, 1871. He founded *The Scripture Interpreter*, edited for some years *The Monthly Miscellany*, and was joint editor with Dr. Alvan Lamson (1844-49) of *The Christian Examiner*. He also published numerous discourses.

Gänsbacher, JOHANN BAPTIST, a German composer of church music, was born at Sterzing, in Tyrol, in 1778. He was educated under various masters until 1802, when he became the pupil of the celebrated Abbate Vogler. Through this connection he became acquainted with Weber and Meyerbeer, and a friendship sprung up among the three young musicians which was dissolved only by death. Gänsbacher was director of the music of St. Stephen's Cathedral, Vienna, from 1823 until his death, July 13, 1844. His compositions consist chiefly of church music, including not less than seventeen masses, besides litanies, motets, offertories, etc. He also wrote several sonatas, a symphony, and one or two minor dramatic compositions. See *Encyclop. Brit.* 9th ed. s. v.

Gansbert, a French monk, and celebrated reformer of various monasteries, was born in the early half of the 10th century, of a noble family. The record of the foundation of the abbey of Bourgueil, in 991, mentions him as the abbot of St. Julien of Tours at that period. He was also simultaneously abbot of Bourgueil-en-Vallée, of St. Pierre de la Couture, at Mons, of Maillegais, and of Marmoutiers. The *Histoire Littéraire de la France* states that he reformed these monasteries, and that he established a great number of charters, which we are unable to mention. About 1000 he went to Rome, and obtained of pope Sylvester the confirmation of the privileges of St. Julien. In 1001 he engaged in important discussions with a certain knight named Gautier, upon the subject of the immunities of Bourgueil. The same year he received of queen Bertha various manors. He died at Bourgueil, Sept. 27, but there is much uncertainty about the year, some making it 1006, others 1007. See Hoefer, *Nouv. Biog. Générale*, s. v.

Gantesviler, JOHANN JACOB, a Lutheran theologian, born at Basle in 1631, was professor at Herborn in 1650, in 1665 at Hanau, in 1678 at Duisburg, and died March 25, 1691. He wrote, *Mysterii Urim et Thummim Delineatio* (Hanau, 1674):—*Scrutinium Theologicum de Loquela Angelorum* (Duisburg, 1682). See Strieder, *Hessische Gelehrten Geschichte; Miscell. Duisburg*, i, 550; Jöcher, *Allgemeines Gelehrten-Lexikon*, s. v. (B. P.)

Gaon (גָּאוֹן, *excellence*) is the academic title of the Jewish presidents of the colleges of Sora (q. v.) and Pumbaditha (q. v.). The title originated, according to the Jewish historian Grätz, cir. A.D. 658. When Ali, the son-in-law and vizier of Mohammed, was elected caliph (A.D. 655), and the Islamites were divided into two parties, one for and the other against him, both the Babylonian Jews and the Nestorian Christians decided in his favor, and rendered him great assistance. Ali rewarded rabbi Isaac, then president of the college of Sora, with the title "Gaon." Accordingly, the word is either of Arabic or Persian origin, and properly belonged to the presidents of the Sora college, who alone bore the appellation at the beginning. The president of the subordinate sister college at Pumbaditha was called the *head of the college*, ריש מתיבתא, by the Babylonians, and the appellation *Gaon*, whereby the presidents were sometimes styled, obtained at first among the non-Babylonian Jews, who were not thoroughly acquainted with the dignities of the respective colleges in Babylon. It was only after the year 917, when Pumbaditha became of equal importance with Sora, and especially when, after the death of Saadia (q. v.), the college at Sora began to decay altogether, and Pumbaditha continued alone to be the college of the doctors of the law, that the presidents of its college, like those of Sora, were described by the title of Gaon. The period of the Gaonim comprises the time from A.D. 658 to 1040, and is divided into that of the *First Gaonim*, from A.D. 658 to 760, and that of the *Later Gaonim*, from A.D. 760 to 1040. The only literary productions of the First Gaonastic Period are the *Sheëltoth* of rabbi Acha of Shabcha, which combine all the different characteristics of the study of the rabbis, viz., Halacha, Midrash, Talmud, and Responsa, arranged according to the sections of the Pentateuch, explaining their respective laws and observations by means of extracts from the Babylonian Talmud, and original compositions in the favorite form of questions and answers (שאלתות). To this period also belongs the beginning of the Neo-Hebrew poetry, or the so-called *Piut* (פיוט), a term obviously taken from the Greek, and the poet was, in like manner, called *peïtan* (פיטן, ποιητής). Now these *piutim* (פיוטים), written either in the form of the *acrostic* or arrangement of words, strophes, and lines, or *rhyme* (חרוז) or *metre* (מקצב), are to be found in the *Machsorim* or synagogue rituals of the different countries, and consist of *Keroboth* (קרובות, i. e. that part of the morning service which comprehends the first three benedictions) for the morning prayer; *Penitential Prayers* (סליחות); *Elegies* (קינות); *Hosannas* (הושענות); *Petitions* (בקשות), etc.

Of the literati among the later Gaonim, we notice Mar Zemach I, ben-Paltoj, of Pumbaditha (872–890), the author of a Talmudic lexicon called "Aruch," which however, is not the same as the Aruch of Nathan ben-Jechiel (q. v.). Zemach's lexicon has not yet come to light. Excerpts were published by Rappaport, from the collection made by Saccuto in the Hebrew essays and reviews, called *Bikkure ha-ittim* (Vienna, 1830), xi, 81 sq. Other excerpts were published by Geiger in *Zeitschrift d. D. M. G.* (Leipsic, 1858), xi, 144. Zemach is also supposed to be the author of the chronological account of the Tanaïm and Amoraïm (סדר תנאים ואמוראים), which was edited by Luzzatto in the Hebrew *Essays* (Prague, 1839), iv, 184. Contemporary with Paltoj was Nachshon ben-Zadok (q. v.) of Sura, A.D. 881–889. Another writer of this period was *Simeon of Kahira or Misr*, in Egypt, who composed a compendium of the most important halachoth from both Talmuds, with the title *Great Halachoth* (הלכות גדולות), about the year 900. To this period also belongs Ibn Koreish (q. v.) and Saadia (q. v.). With the latter's death the last sunset light of the Soranic academy had passed away, and about the year 948 the school had to be closed. In order to secure its further existence, four young men were sent out, never to return again, to interest their rich co-religionists in this old school of learning. The young men fell into the hands of a Spanish corsair. Among these captives was Moses ben-Chanoch (q. v.). While the Soranic school was closed, that of Pumbaditha was presided over before its final close by two men, Sherira Gaon (q. v.) and Hai ben-Shirira (q. v.).

With the exception of the authors we have named already, the great mass of the Gaonastic literature is anonymous. We mention the *Midrash Espa* (מדרש אספה), on part of the book of Numbers; the *Midrash Haskem* (מדרש השכם); the chronicle, entitled *History of the Maccabees of Joseph ben-Gorion*, which is a translation of an Arabic book of the Maccabees, the *Tarich al-Makkabaïn, Jussuf ibn-Gorgon.* This book, says Dr. Grätz, was afterwards translated by an Italian Jew, who, by his additions to it, displayed great skill in his Hebrew style, and which translation is generally known under the title, *Josippon* (q. v.). Besides the *Josippon* or *Pseudo-Josephus*, we must mention an ethical midrash, entitled *Tana debê Eliahu, or Seder Eliahu* (סדר אליהו תנא דבי אליהו), the *Midrash Tanchuma* or *Tanchuma Jelamdenu.* (B. P.)

Garafolus, Gabriel, an Augustinian monk of Italy, who died at Spoleto in 1433, wrote *Adversus Hæreses:—Adversus Fratricellos:—Sermones in Evangelia.* See Ughelli, *Italia Sacra*; Jöcher, *Allgemeines Gelehrten-Lexikon*, s. v. (B. P.)

Garcaeus, Johannes, a Lutheran theologian of Germany, was born Dec. 13, 1530, at Hamburg. He studied at Wittenberg, was in 1557 professor of theology and pastor at Greifswalde, in 1562 superintendent and first preacher at Brandenburg, and died Jan. 22, 1575. He wrote, *De Erigendis Figuris Cœli* (Wittenberg, 1556):—*De S. Laurentio Martyre* (ibid. 1562):—*De S. Joanne Baptista* (ibid. eod.):—*De Magis ex Oriente* (ibid. eod.):—*De S. Martino Episcopo Turonensi* (ibid. 1563):—*Confessio Orthodoxa de Spiritu Sancto* (1565):—*De Infanticidio Herodis* (ibid. eod.):—*Collatio summi Pontificis V. et N. T.* (Leipsic, 1574). See Thiess, *Hamburg Gelehrten-Lexikon;* Jöcher, *Allgemeines Gelehrten-Lexikon*, s. v. (B. P.)

Garcin (*de Tassy*), Joseph Héliodore Sagesse Vertu, a famous French Orientalist, was born Jan. 20, 1794, at Marseilles. In 1817 he went to Paris, where he studied under Sylvestre de Sacy. The latter especially interested him in the vulgar Arabic spoken by the Mussulmans of India, and to this he devoted himself entirely. A chair for Hindustani was especially created for him at the college in Paris; he succeeded Talleyrand as member of the Academy of Inscriptions, in 1838, and after Mohl's death, in 1876, he was made president of the Asiatic Society. Garcin de Tassy died Sept. 2, 1878. He published, *Rudiments de la Langue Hindoustani* (Paris, 1829; with appendices, 1843):—*Rudiments de la Langue Hindouï* (ibid. 1847):—*Les Ouvres de Wali, Célèbre Poète du Dekkan* (with a translation, 1834):—*Les Aventures de Kamrup* (ibid. eod.):—an edition of the *Pend-Nameh* of Saadi, "Mantik ul-Ataïr" (*Le Language des Oiseaux*):—*Doctrines et Devoirs des Musulmans* (from the Arabic, 1827–40):—*Poésie Philosophique et Religieuse des Persans* (1857):—*Rhétorique et Prosodie de l'Orient Musulman* (1873). (B. P.)

Gardiner, John, D.D., an English divine, was born about 1756. He was educated at Tiverton, whence he went to the University of Glasgow, where he studied civil law. He then entered himself in the Middle Temple, with a view to qualify for the bar. An irresistible impulse induced him to exchange the law for the Church, and in consequence he repaired to Wadham College, Oxford. In 1781 he took possession of the vicarage of Shirley and rectory of Brailsford, in the county of Derby, the presentation to which had been purchased by his father, with whom he afterwards resided for some years at Wellington, performing gratuitously the duty of curate in that parish. In 1789 he undertook the same office at Taunton, and there continued till his father, in 1796, purchased for him the Octagon Chapel at Bath, where he officiated till his death in 1838. He also served as a magistrate for the county of Somerset. Dr. Gardiner published a number of occasional *Discourses* (1793-1811), and a volume of *Sermons* (Bath, 1802, 8vo). See *The Christian Remembrancer* (Lond.), Sept. 1838, p. 568; Allibone, *Dict. of Brit. and Amer. Authors*, s. v.

Gardiner, John Sylvester, D.D., a Protestant Episcopal minister, was born at Haverford-West, South Wales, in June, 1765. At the age of five years he was sent to America to the care of his grandfather, then a resident of Boston, where he attended school, and after three or four years returned to his father, who was attorney-general on the island of St. Christopher, W. I. Shortly after, John was sent to England, where, from 1776 to 1782, he was a pupil of the famous Dr. Parr. After this he visited his father in the West Indies, and in 1783 went to Boston, which became his permanent home. Partly under the tutorship of his father and partly under that of judge Tudor, he studied law, but abandoned it to enter the ministry, officiating as lay-reader at Pownalboro', Me., and studying theology. He was ordained deacon in New York city, Oct. 18, 1787, and presbyter, Dec. 4, 1791. For a while he preached at St. Helena, Beaufort, S. C., and then was elected, in 1792, assistant to Dr. Parker, rector of Trinity Church, Boston. A meagre support compelled him to teach school. He was chosen rector of the church, April 15, 1805, vice Dr. Parker, made a bishop. After many years of service his health became impaired, and he made a voyage to Europe to recuperate, but died at Harrowgate, England, July 29, 1830. He was a member of the Anthology Club, which published the *Monthly Anthology and Boston Review*. Among his literary remains are a large number of published *Sermons*, *Addresses*, etc. See Sprague, *Annals of the Amer. Pulpit*, v, 363.

Gardiner, Richard, an English divine, was born at Hereford in 1591, educated at the school there, and at Christ Church, where he was canon in 1629. In 1630 he was chaplain to Charles I. He died in 1670. He published several *Sermons* (1659). See Chalmers, *Biog. Dict.* s. v.; Allibone, *Dict. of Brit. and Amer. Authors*, s. v.

Garibald (Lat. *Gariobaldus, Gaiavaldus, Goibaldus, Herbaldus*, etc.), appointed bishop of Ratisbon by St. Boniface, A.D. 739, is commemorated Jan. 8. See Smith, *Dict. of Christ. Biog.* s. v.

Garlande, Étienne, a French prelate, was priest, archdeacon of Paris, chancellor of the kingdom, and at length seneschal. Forced, at the end of seven years, to resign these functions, as they were incompatible with the ecclesiastical calling, he transferred them to Amaury of Montfort, count of Evreux, without the consent of the king, who seized his chateau at Livry as a punishment, but afterwards consented, about 1129, to receive Garlande and Amaury into his favor, on condition that they should resign their claims to the office of seneschal. Garlande died in 1150, at Orleans, where he had consecrated his nephew, Manasses, bishop. See Hoefer, *Nouv. Biog. Générale*, s. v.

Garnet, Henry Highland, D.D., a colored Presbyterian minister, was born in New Market, Kent Co., Md., April 15, 1815, of parents who escaped from slavery, in 1824, to New Hope, Pa., and the next year came to New York city, where the lad went to school, and at the same time served as a cook. In 1831 he entered a high-school; in 1835 went to Canaan Academy, N. H.; next year to Oneida Institute, N. Y.; in 1840 settled as a teacher in Troy; studied theology under Dr. Beman; was licensed to preach in 1842, and the next year installed pastor of the Liberty Street Presbyterian Church in that city. The same year he delivered an eloquent speech in Buffalo, before the Liberty Party convention. He addressed the state legislature in January, 1844, and in 1846 he presided at the Delevan Temperance Union, at Poughkeepsie. About this time the late Gerrit Smith appointed him an agent for the purpose of distributing a large gift of lands in this state among colored men. In 1850 Dr. Garnet was invited to lecture in England, made an address in Exeter Hall, and was elected a delegate to the Peace Congress held at Frankfort-on-the-Main. At its conclusion he travelled through Bavaria, Prussia, and France. In 1852 he was sent by the United Presbyterian Church of Scotland as a missionary to Jamaica, West Indies. While there he received a unanimous call to the pulpit of the Shiloh Presbyterian Church, then at Prince and Marion Streets, New York, and soon became the leader of the colored population in that city. In 1861 he revisited England, as the president of the African Colonization Society, but soon returned, and volunteered as chaplain to the colored troops at Riker's Island. He early took an active interest in the poorer people of his race, and organized several charitable societies which care for all the colored people who try to support themselves. Dr. Garnet was the first colored man who, on any occasion, spoke in the national capitol, where he preached on Sunday, Feb. 12, 1865, in the hall of the House of Representatives. In April of that year he was called by the Fifteenth Street Presbyterian Church of Washington, D. C., and accepted the call, staying there several years. Again he returned to his former church, the Shiloh, and was its pastor until the autumn of 1881, when he accepted the appointment of United States minister and consul to Liberia. He died at Monrovia, Africa, Feb. 13, 1882. See *The* (N. Y.) *Tribune*, March 11, 1882.

Garnham, Robert Edward, an English divine, was born at Bury St. Edmunds, May 1, 1753, and educated at Trinity College, Cambridge. He was ordained deacon March 3, 1776, and soon after entered into the curacies of Nowton and Great Welnatham. He was ordained priest, June 15, 1777; in 1793 became college preacher at Cambridge, and in November, 1797, was advanced into the seniority, but resigned in 1789. He died June 24, 1802. His writings were numerous, but all anonymous.

Garnier, Jean, a French Reformed theologian, was born at Avignon in the beginning of the 16th century, and died at Cassel, in January, 1574. He succeeded Pierre Bruly, or Brulius (q. v.), as pastor of the French Church in Strasburg, which was founded by Calvin in 1538. He rejected with disdain the Interim (q. v.), which Charles V was about to introduce in Strasburg in 1549. He left the city, but returned in 1552, to leave it again in 1555. In 1559 he was appointed professor of theology at Marburg, and three years later court-preacher at Cassel. He published *Confession de la Foy Chréstienne de Strasbourg* (Strasburg, 1549, 1552; transl. into English, Lond. 1562):—*De Epistola Pauli ad Hebræos Declamatio* (Marburg, 1559). See Strieder, *Hist. Litt. de la Hesse;* Haag, *La France Protestante*, vol. v; Jöcher, *Allgemeines Gelehrten-Lexikon*, s. v.; Dardier, in Lichtenberger's *Encyclop. des Sciences Religieuses*, s. v. (B. P.)

Garretson, John, D.D., a minister of the Reformed (Dutch) Church, was born at Six-Mile Run, N. J., Nov. 9, 1801. He graduated from Union College in 1823, and from the New Brunswick Theological Seminary in 1826; was licensed by the Classis of New Brunswick, and became missionary to Kinderhook Landing (Stuyvesant) and Columbiaville, N. Y., the same year; at Middleburg in 1827; at Schraalenburg, N. J., in 1833; at Brooklyn, N. Y., organizing the Central Church there, in 1836; at Belleville, N. J., in 1837; corresponding secretary of the Board of Domestic Missions in 1849; pastor at Canastota, N. Y., in 1859; at Owasco Outlet in 1861; at Esopus in 1865; also stated supply at St. Remy; at Lawrenceville, Pa (Presbyterian), in 1866; at Cortlandtown, N. Y., in 1869; then two years without a charge, until he became rector of Hertzog Hall in 1874, where he died in 1875. He was clear and discriminating as a preacher, wise in counsel, and of broad and well-wrought plans for the advancement of the Church. See Corwin, *Manual of the Ref. Church in America*, 3d ed. p. 280.

Garrison, William Lloyd, a leading abolitionist, was born at Newburyport, Mass., Dec. 12, 1804. His mother was early left a widow, and poor, so that the son, after various attempts at learning a trade, was at length apprenticed to a printer in his native town, where he soon began to write for the journals, and in 1826 became proprietor of the *Free Press*. This not succeeding financially, he started in 1827 the *National Philanthropist*, in the advocacy of moral reforms, and in 1831 the *Liberator*, a fierce opponent of slavery, which was continued till the act of emancipation during the civil war. He was often in personal peril by the violence of the friends of slavery. He visited England several times in furtherance of his principles, and was received there with great enthusiasm. He died May 24, 1879. He published *Sonnets and Other Poems* (1848), and a selection from his *Speeches and Writings* (1852).

Garth, the greensward or grass area between, or within, the cloisters of a religious house.

Garth, Helvicus, a Lutheran theologian of Germany, was born Dec. 18, 1579. He studied at Marburg and Strasburg, and died at Prague, Dec. 5, 1619. He wrote, *De Invocatione Sanctorum:—De Judice Controversiarum:—Comment. in Nahum et Habakuk:—Theologiæ Jesuitarum Præcipua Capita:—De Articulis Controversis Inter Lutheranos et Calvinianos:—Acta et Post-Acta Colloquii Pragensis:—De Providentia Dei in Vocatione Doctorum et Ministrorum Ecclesiæ.* See Jöcher, *Allgemeines Gelehrten-Lexikon*, s. v.; Witte, *Memoriæ Theologorum.* (B. P.)

Gartland, Francis Xavier, a Roman Catholic bishop, was born in Dublin in 1805; ordained in Philadelphia in 1832; consecrated bishop of Savannah, Ga., Nov. 10, 1850, and died of yellow fever in that city, Sept. 20, 1853. See De Courcy and Shea, *Hist. of the Cath. Church in the U. S.* p. 167.

Gärtner, *Herr* von, an eminent German architect, was born at Coblentz in 1792, and while young visited Italy, France, and Spain. He afterwards settled at Munich, and was appointed by Louis I professor of architecture in the Royal Academy of Fine Arts in that city. In 1822 he was appointed director of the state manufactory of porcelain and glass paintings. He erected a number of edifices at Munich, among which were the university, the triumphal gate, the clerical seminary, and the Church of St. Louis. After the departure of Von Cornelius to Berlin, Von Gärtner became director of the Academy of Fine Arts, having formerly been nominated chief architect and inspector-general of the plastic monuments. He died in 1847.

Garuda, the sacred bird of Vishnû (q. v.), as the eagle was the bird of Jupiter. Garuda was worshipped by the Vaishnavas (q. v.) in the golden age of Hindû idolatry.

Gaspari, Johann Baptist von, a German historian, was born in 1702, and died at Vienna in 1768. He wrote, *De Tridentinis Antiquitatibus:—De Protestantium Germanorum in Catholicos Gestis:—Breviarium Vitæ S. Theodori Episc. Salisburgensium* (published by his brother Lazaro, Venice, 1780). See L. Gaspari, *Della Vita, Degli Studii e Degli Scritti di Gio. Batt. de Gaspari* (Venice, 1770); Jöcher, *Allgemeines Gelehrten-Lexikon*, s. v. (B. P.)

Gasparin, Agénor, *Comte de*, an eminent layman of the French Protestant Church, was born at Orange (France), July 12, 1810. He studied law at Paris and took an active part in French politics, and in 1842 he represented Bastia in the House of Deputies. Religious subjects, however, engrossed a large share of his attention. In 1843 he published *Intérêts Généraux du Protestantisme Français*, and in 1846 *Christianisme et Paganisme* (2 vols.). In 1848 he attended the general synod of the Reformed churches of France, and maintained with Frederick Monod the necessity of a well-defined creed for that Church. The last twenty-three years of his life he spent in Switzerland, and there he wrote his *Les Écoles du Doute et l'École de la Foi:—Un Grand Peuple qui se Rèleve* (1861):—*L'Amérique devant l'Europe* (1862), directed against slavery. He also delivered lectures on religious topics, and in every way promoted the cause of religion. He died May 8, 1871. Some of his works were also translated into German, and of his *L'Amérique devant l'Europe* an English translation was published in New York (3d ed. 1863). See Maville, *Le Comte Ag. de Gasparin* (Geneva, 1871); Borel, *Le Comte Ag. de Gasparin* (Paris, 1879; Engl. transl. N. Y. 1880); Lichtenberger, *Encyclop. des Sciences Religieuses*, s. v.; Zuchold, *Bibl. Theol.* i, 400. (B. P.)

Gass, Joachim Christian, a Protestant theologian of Germany, was born May 26, 1766. He studied at Halle, was in 1795 military chaplain, in 1807 preacher at Berlin, in 1810 professor of theology at Breslau, and died there, Feb. 19, 1831. A friend and pupil of Schleiermacher, Gass also represented the theology of his master. As a member of consistory, he took an active part in the ecclesiastical affairs of his province. He wrote, *Erinnerung an den Reichstag zu Speier in Jahre* 1529 (Breslau, 1829):—*Jahrbücher des Protestantischen Kirchen- und Schulwesens von und für Schlesien* (1817–20, 4 vols.):—*Ueber das Wesen der Kirchenzucht* (1819):—*Ueber den Religionsunterricht in den obern Classen der Gymnasien* (1828):—*Ueber den christl. Cultus* (1815). See Schleiermacher, *Briefwechsel mit Gass* (Berlin, 1852); Lichtenberger, *Encyclop. des Sciences Religieuses*, s. v.; Plitt-Herzog, *Real-Encyclop.* s. v.; Winer, *Handbuch der theol. Lit.* i, 751, 808; ii, 21, 38, 74, 75, 157, 167, 169, 179. (B. P.)

Gasser, Vincent, a Roman Catholic prelate, was born in the Tyrol in 1809. In 1836 he was professor of theology at Brixen, member of parliament in 1848, bishop of Brixen in 1856, and prince-bishop in 1859. He died in 1879. He was the head of the Tyrolese Ultramontanists, and allowed the Jesuits to use their influence in the universities and schools. (B. P.)

Gastaldi, Geronimo, an Italian prelate, was born at Genoa in the early part of the 17th century, of an ancient Genoese family. He embraced the ecclesiastical calling, and went to Rome. In 1656, Gastaldi, already a prelate, was designated for the perilous position of general commissary of the hospitals, and was afterwards appointed general commissioner of public health, and so faithfully did he perform his duties that he secured the archbishopric of Benevento, the cardinalate, and the legation to Bologna. Several monuments erected at his expense at Rome and Benevento attest his charity and munificence. He gave his observations concerning contagious diseases in a work which was published at Bologna in 1684, the year previous to his death, suggesting certain precautions and remedies. See Hoefer, *Nouv. Biog. Générale*, s. v.

Gastaud, François, a French theologian, was born at Aix about 1660. He entered the congregation of the Oratorio at the age of fourteen, but after five years withdrew, having studied philosophy at Marseilles and theology at Arles. He was ordained priest, and for several years preached at Paris with great success. His brother, a distinguished advocate, having died about 1700, abbé Gastaud, after two years of study, was appointed counsellor to the parliament of Aix, and obtained a license to practice from the court of Rome. He also succeeded well in this, and in 1717 gained an important suit against the Jesuits. This affair, together with his predilection for the Jansenists, made enemies who attacked him, and whom he repulsed with great violence. Being banished to Viviers in 1727, and recalled in about eight months, he was again banished in 1731 to the same place, where he died in 1732. Some of his principal works are, *Homélies sur l'Épître aux Romains* (Paris, 1699):—*Le Politique des Jésuites Démasquée* (without date). See Hoefer, *Nouv. Biog. Générale*, s. v.

Gastromancy (from γαστήρ, *the belly*, and μαντεία, *divination*), a mode of divination practiced among the ancient Greeks, by filling certain round glasses with pure water, placing lighted torches round them, then praying to the deity in a low, muttering voice, and proposing the question which they wished answered. Certain images were now observed in the glass, representing what was to happen.

Gataker, Thomas, a divine of the 16th century, son of William Gataker, was born at Gatacre Hall, Shropshire. He studied law at the Temple, London, during the reign of Mary, and was often present at the examination of persecuted people. Their hard usage and patience influenced him in their favor, which his parents perceived, and immediately sent him to Louvain to reinstate him in the Catholic faith. This did not seem to have the desired effect, although afterwards he appears to have become reconciled to his father. He studied theology, was educated at Oxford, became pastor at St. Edmund's, Lombard Street, London, and died in 1593, leaving a learned son of the same name. See Fuller, *Worthies of England* (ed. Nuttall), iii, 56.

Gates, Holy, the name given to the folding gates in the centre of the *iconostasis*, or screen, which, in the modern Greek churches, separates the body of the church from the holy of holies. The *holy gates* are opened and shut frequently during the service, part of the prayers and lessons being recited in front of them and part within the adytum.

Gath. In the *Quarterly Statement* of the "Palest. Explor. Fund," Oct. 1880, p. 211 sq., there is an extended paper on the site of this important city, which Mr. Trelawney Saunders strongly argues was located at *Khurbah Abu-Gheith*, at the head of Wady el-Hesy (here called el-Muleihah), which falls into the Mediterranean between Gaza and Hebron; whereas Lieut. Conder gives substantial reasons for rejecting this location, and in favor of *Tell es-Safieh*, the *Blanche-Garde* of the Crusaders. This place is described in the *Memoirs* accompanying the Ordnance Survey (ii, 440).

Gath (Tell es-Safieh). (From Thomson's *Southern Palestine and Jerusalem.*)

Gatian, *Saint*, apostle of Touraine, was born at Rome, according to the ancient annalists. His arrival among the Gauls took place, according to Gregory of Tours, under the consulate of Decius and Grotus, i. e., in 250 or 251. When he presented himself at the metropolis of Lyons he did not find the pagans, for the most part, very docile. He preached during the day in the city or in the country round about, choosing to address the lower class, and at night concealed himself from the violence of enemies. The city of Tours reverenced him as the chief of its bishops. He labored for fifty years to diffuse the Christian faith, and at the time of his death, which occurred Dec. 20, 301, the Church of Tours was founded. See Hoefer, *Nouv. Biog. Générale*, s. v.; Smith, *Dict. of Christ. Biog.* s. v.

Gatti, Bernardo (called *Soiaro*), an eminent Italian painter, was born at Cremona, and was a scholar of Correggio. Some of his best works are his *Repose in Egypt*, in St. Sigismund's, at Cremona; *Christ in the Manger*, at St. Peter's, in the same city; and the *Dead Christ*, in the Magdalene, at Parma. A great number of his works have been taken to other countries, particularly to Spain. He died in 1575. See Hoefer, *Nouv. Biog. Générale*, s. v.; Spooner, *Biog. Hist. of the Fine Arts*, s. v.

Gatti, Giovanni Andrea, a Sicilian prelate, was born at Messina in 1420. He entered the Dominican order, and, while young, taught in their convent at Messina, excelling all his contemporaries in philosophy and theology, civil and canonical law, belles-lettres and eloquence, Greek, and especially familiar with Latin and Hebrew. To his extensive knowledge was added a very remarkable memory. From Messina he went to Rome as professor. Florence, Bologna, and Ferrara enjoyed successively his lectures, which had become celebrated throughout all the scholastic world. He was among the most familiar friends of Bessarion, who caused him to be appointed, in 1468, commendatory abbot of two Benedictine convents in Sicily. According to Fontana, he had already performed the functions of inquisitor in the diocese of Messina. Ferdinand I conferred upon him the bishopric of Cefalu, and employed him in various missions to the holy see. The sovereign pontiff promised him the bishopric of Catania by apostolic letters of Dec. 18, 1477; but king Ferdinand objected, and Gatti resigned it. He returned to Cefalu and devoted himself to the administration of his diocese. Feeling that death was near, he resigned his functions in 1483, and went to end his days at the convent of Messina, where he commenced his religious life. He died in 1484, and was interred in the Cathedral of Messina. Mongitore attributes to him some works, which are preserved in MS. at the monastery of St. Dominic, Palermo. See Hoefer, *Nouv. Biog. Générale*, s. v.

Gattola, Erasmus, an abbot of Monte Cassino, was born at Gaeta in 1662, and died May 1, 1734. He wrote *Historia Abbatiæ Casinensis*, etc. (Venice, 1734, 2 vols.). See Winer, *Handbuch der theol. Lit.* i, 712; Jöcher, *Allgemeines Gelehrten-Lexikon*, s. v. (B. P.)

Gaucher, *Saint*, was born at Meulan, Normandy, in 1060. At the age of eighteen, under the direction of Raigner, he resolved to devote himself to prayer and to the austerities of penitence in solitude. Upon the invitation of Humbert, canon of Limoges, he went to Limousin, and there dwelt in a hermitage in the forest of Chavaignac. At the end of three years he obtained from the canons of St. Étienne of Limoges authority to build a monastery in a place known as Salvatius, later as Aureil, which was conducted according to the regulation of St. Augustine. Shortly after Gaucher established a monastery for women, near this. Aureil, becoming celebrated for its sanctity and for the miracles of St. Gaucher, became the retreat of St. Stephen of Muret, St. Lambert (founder of the Abbey de la Couronne, afterwards bishop of Angoulême), and St. Faucher. Gaucher, at that time an octogenarian, returning from Limoges, where he had held an assembly concerning the affairs of his convent, a false step caused him to strike his head violently against a stone, which place is still called *Le Pas de St. Gaucher*, and where a chapel was erected. This accident caused his death three days later at Aureil (1140), whither he had been carried. He was canonized by pope Celestin III, and his remains placed in a shrine by Sebrand, bishop of Limoges, Sept. 18, 1194. In Limousin and Normandy his festival is celebrated April 9. See Hoefer, *Nouv. Biog. Générale*, s. v.

Gaudenzio, Paganini, a Roman Catholic theologian of Italy, was born at Poschiavo, in the canton of Grisons, about 1595. In 1627 he was professor at Pisa, and died Jan. 3, 1649. He wrote, *De Dogmatibus et Ritibus Veteris Ecclesiæ Hæreticorum*:—*De Dogmatum Origenis cum Philosophia Platonis Comparatione*:—*Della Morte di S. Giovanni Evangelista Discorsidue*, and other works. See Winer, *Handbuch der theol. Lit.* i, 899; Jöcher, *Allgemeines Gelehrten-Lexikon*, s. v.; Hoefer, *Nouv. Biog. Générale*, s. v. (B. P.)

Gaudied, with large beads. Every decade or tenth large bead in the rosaries representing a Paternoster is a gaud; each smaller bead stands for an Ave Maria.

Gaudiōsus, *Saint*, bishop of Tarazona, in Arragon, under king Gundemar, was noted for his bold profession of the orthodox faith. He died in 530, and is commemorated on Nov. 3.

Gaudlitz, Gottlieb, a Lutheran theologian, was born in Saxony, Nov. 17, 1694. He studied at Leipsic, was magister in 1717, catechist in 1721, pastor of St. Thomas in 1741, doctor of divinity the same year, and died Feb. 20, 1745, leaving, *Disputationes de Epistolis Christi ἐμψύχοις*:—*De Justificatione Dei coram Hominibus*:—*De Christo Exegeta*:—*Das Leben Ahabs, Königs in Israel*, etc. See Jöcher, *Allgemeines Gelehrten-Lexikon*, s. v. (B. P.)

Gauffier, Louis, an eminent French painter, was born at Rochelle in 1761, and studied under Taraval. In 1784 he carried off the grand prize of the Academy for his picture of the *Syrophenician Woman.* He went to Rome with the royal pension, and produced several pictures which greatly increased his reputation. Among his other works are *The Roman Matrons Sending their Jewels to the Senate, The Angels Appearing to Abraham*, and *Jacob and Rachel.* He died at Florence, Oct. 20, 1801. See Hoefer, *Nouv. Biog. Générale*, s. v.; Spooner, *Biog. Hist. of the Fine Arts*, s. v.

Gaulli, Giovanni Battista (called *Baciccio*), an eminent Italian painter, was born in 1639, and was instructed in the art in Genoa, after which he went to Rome, where he studied the works of the best masters. The ceiling of the Church del Gesu, at Rome, is his most celebrated performance, representing St. Francis Xavier taken up to heaven. The following are some of his principal pictures: *The Madonna and Infant; The Death of St. Saverio.* He also gained reputation by painting the angels in the dome of St. Agnes. He died in 1709.

Gault, Jean Baptiste, a French prelate, was born at Tours, Dec. 29, 1595. He and his elder brother, Eustache, having in view the ecclesiastical calling, pursued their studies at Le Flèche, then at Paris, and finally at Rome. After a sojourn of eighteen months in the latter city they returned to France, and entered the congregation of the Oratorio. Jean received the order of priesthood at Troyes, and directed successively the houses of his order at Langres, Dijon, and Le Mans. He was also charged with various apostolic missions to Spain and Flanders. His brother, who had shared all his religious labors, was appointed bishop of Marseilles, but died, March 13, 1639, before receiving his bulla from Rome, and Jean was appointed to succeed him. The latter showed remarkable zeal for the reform of his diocese, for the relief of the poor, for the restoration of captives, and for the conversion of galley-slaves. A premature death removed him from his diocese, May 25, 1643. The clergy of France demanded his beatification at Rome in 1645. Eustache Gault was the author of a book entitled *Discours de l'État et Couronne de Suède* (Le Mans, 1633). See Hoefer, *Nouv. Biog. Générale*, s. v.

Gaulter, John, an eminent English Wesleyan minister, was born at Chester, March 21, 1764. He was converted by remarkable providences, and called to the ministry by Wesley in 1785. He was president of the conference in 1817. In 1835 he was laid aside by a stroke of paralysis, and died at Chelsea, London, June 19, 1839. He had a vigorous understanding, a remarkably retentive memory, and a vivid imagination. In 1812 Gaulter revised and republished Rev. David Simpson's *Plea for Religion and the Sacred Writings.* See *Minutes of the British Conference*, 1839; Stevenson, *Hist. of City Road Chapel*, p. 560 sq.

Gaultier, Jacques, a French Jesuit, was born in 1562, and died at Grenoble, Oct. 14, 1636, professor of theology and Hebrew. He wrote, *Tabula Chronographica Status Ecclesiæ Catholicæ*:—*Anatomia Calvinismi*:—*Index Controversiarum ad Evangelia Accommodata.* See Alegambe, *Bibliotheca Scriptorum Societatis Jesu;* Jöcher, *Allgemeines Gelehrten-Lexikon*, s. v. (B. P.)

Gaupp, Carl Friedrich, a Protestant theologian of Germany, and professor of theology, who died at Berlin in 1863, is the author of *Die Römische Kirche* (Dresden, 1840):—*Die Union der Deutschen Kirchen* (Breslau, 1843):—*Die Union in der Kirche* (ibid. 1847):—*Praktische Theologie* (Berlin, 1848, 2 vols.). See Zuchold, *Bibl. Theol.* i, 401. (B. P.)

Gaupp, Jacob, a Protestant theologian of Germany, was born Feb. 13, 1767, at Hirschberg, and died at Liegnitz, in Silesia, Aug. 19, 1823. He wrote, *Beiträge zur Befestigung des Reiches der Wahrheit in Predigten* (Breslau, 1798):—*Predigten* (Glogau, 1801):—*Briefe eines Menschenfreundes an bekümmerte und leidende Mitmenschen* (ibid. 1800–9, 3 vols.):—*Religiöses Erbauungsbuch einer christlichen Familie* (Leipsic, 1812). See Winer, *Handbuch der theol. Lit.* ii, 94, 163, 384, 391. (B. P.)

Gauri, Festival of. See Flowers, Festival of.

Gauthier, François Louis, a French theologian, was born at Paris, March 29, 1696. He was rector of Savigny-sur-Orge, and performed for fifty-two years the pastoral functions with great zeal and charity. He died at Paris, Oct. 9, 1780, leaving, *Reflexions Chrétiennes sur les huit Béatitudes* (Paris, 1783). See Hoefer, *Nouv. Biog. Générale*, s. v.

Gauthier, Jean Baptiste, a French theologian, was born at Louviers in 1685. He was for a long time connected with Colbert, bishop of Montpelier, whose instructions and mandates he published. After the death of that prelate he settled at Paris. He died Oct. 30, 1755, near Gaillon, leaving a large number of works, directed especially against the Jesuits and infidels. See Hoefer, *Nouv. Biog. Générale*, s. v.

Gauthier, Nicolas, a French controversalist, was born at Rheims in the last quarter of the 16th century. Having renounced the Church of Rome, he went to Sedan for the study of theology; but suddenly left that place and the Protestant Church, and wrote, *Descouverte des Fraudes Sedanoises* (Paris, 1618):—*Réponse* *à l'Avertissement de J. Cappel* (Rheims, 1618):—*Les Livres de Babel Huguenote* (ibid. 1619). See Lichtenberger, *Encyclop. des Sciences Religieuses*, s. v.; Hoefer, *Nouv. Biog. Générale*, s. v. (B. P.)

Gautier de Coutances (Lat. *de Coustantiis* or *de Coustantia*), a prelate of Normandy, was born about 1140. Little is known of his life prior to 1173, when he was vice-chancellor of England and canon of Rouen. He was regarded with favor by the king of England, who, in 1177, confided to him a mission to the count of Flanders, and in 1180 sent him with an embassy to the court of the young king, Philip Augustus. Gautier, who added to his other ecclesiastical honors the canonship of Lincoln and the archdeaconship of Oxford, greatly desired the bishopric of Lisieux, but did not obtain it. A vacancy, however, occurring, he was made bishop of Lincoln, and soon after passed to the metropolitan see of Rouen. From this time the name of the archbishop of Rouen is continually mingled with the politics of the day. In 1188 he agreed to accompany king Henry II on the crusade. In return for services rendered to prince Richard, Gautier was invested with the regency of the kingdom, Oct. 8, 1191. After an absence from his diocese of four years, in which time he had obtained the liberty of the king, who had been a prisoner in Germany, he had to appease some difficulties between the canons and citizens of Rouen. In 1194 the churches of Normandy suffered greatly from the war between the kings of France and England. Gautier defended vigorously the ecclesiastical rights, and sent an interdict to Normandy, which, however, he was unable to sustain. In 1200 he had charge of promulgating, conjointly with the bishop of Poitiers, the interdict sent by Peter of Capua against the king of France. In 1204, Philip Augustus becoming master of Normandy, Gautier solemnly delivered to him the attributes of the ducal crown. He died Nov. 6, 1207. There remain to us only a few letters of Gautier, scattered among the cotemporary annalists. It was said that he also wrote a history of the crusade of Richard, but nothing remains of it. See Hoefer, *Nouv. Biog. Générale*, s. v.

Gautier de Mortagne (Lat. *Walterus de Mauritania*), a French theologian, was born at Mortagne, in Flanders, in the early part of the 12th century. He taught rhetoric at Paris, in one of the schools established upon the St. Genevieve mountain. But he soon gave up belles-lettres for theology and philosophy, and taught these two sciences at Rheims, Lyons, and other places. From 1136 to 1148 he had as disciple Jean de Salisbury. In 1150 he was canon of Laon, and became successively dean, and bishop of that church. He died at Laon in 1173. He wrote five short theological treatises in the form of letters, which occupy twenty pages in the *Spicilegium* of D'Achery. The more interesting of these letters is addressed to Abelard, who claimed to explain philosophically the mysteries of Christianity. See Hoefer, *Nouv. Biog. Générale*, s. v.

Gauzlin, a French prelate, natural son of Hugh Capet, became abbot of Fleury after the death of Abbon in 1005. He sent to Brittany the monk Felix to reform the monasteries. At the death of Dagbert, bishop of Bourges, in 1020, he was raised to the dignity of prelate in this vacancy; but the opposition of the inhabitants hindered him for a long time from taking possession of his see, and only through the intervention of the pope, Benedict VIII, he entered upon these duties in 1014. In 1022 he was at the Council of Orleans, which condemned the heresiarch Stephen, and in 1024 at the Council of Paris, where he debated the question of the apostleship of St. Martial. He died in 1030. See Hoefer, *Nouv. Biog. Générale*, s. v.

Gavardo, Niccolo, a Roman Catholic theologian, who died at Rome, June 12, 1715, is the author of, *Theologia Exantiquata juxta Doctrinam S. Augustini* (Naples, 1683-96, 6 vols.):—*Quæstiones de Hierarchia Ecclesiæ Militantis* (ibid. 1690):—*Philosophia Vindicata ab Erroribus Philosophorum Gentilium* (Rome, 1701, 4 vols.). See Argelati, *Bibl. Mediol.*; Jöcher, *Allgemeines Gelehrten-Lexikon*, s. v. (B. P.)

Gavaston, Juan, a Spanish Dominican, who died at Alicante in 1625, is the author of, *Vida de S. Vinc. Ferrer*:—*La Regla de la Tercera Orden de Predicadores*:—*De la Frequencia de la Communion*:—*Flor de los Santos de la Orden de Predicadores*:—*De los Privilegios Dados para la Fiede Apostolica a la Orden de los Predicadores.* See Antonii *Bibliotheca Hispanica*; Echard, *De Scriptoribus Ordinis Dominicanorum*; Jöcher, *Allgemeines Gelehrten-Lexikon*, s. v. (B. P.)

Gavio, Giacomo Raimondo, an Italian Carmelite, who died in 1618, is the author of, *Commentaria in Psalmum*:—*Expositiones in Genesin*:—*Expositiones in epist. ad Ephesios*:—*Sermones per Adventum, de Sanctis, Dominicales*:—*De Arte Prædicatoria.* See Oldoin, *Athenæum Romanum*; Jöcher, *Allgemeines Gelehrten-Lexikon*, s. v. (B. P.)

Gay, Ebenezer (1), D.D., a Congregational minister, was born at Dedham, Mass., May 4, 1718; graduated from Harvard College in 1737; was ordained pastor of the First Church in Suffield, Conn., Jan. 13, 1742; and died in March, 1796. See Sprague, *Annals of the Amer. Pulpit*, i, 537.

Gay, Ebenezer (2), a Congregational minister, was born in Suffield, Conn.; entered Harvard College, but transferred his membership to Yale, from which he graduated in 1787, and of which he was tutor from 1790 to 1792; was installed as colleague pastor with his father over the First Church in Suffield; and retired from the active ministry several years before his death, which occurred in February, 1837, aged seventy-one years. See Sprague, *Annals of the Amer. Pulpit*, i, 1, 537.

Gayatri, the holiest verse of the Vedas (q. v.). It is addressed to the sun, to which it was daily offered up as a prayer, in these words: "Let us meditate on the adorable light of the divine sun; may it guide our intellects. Desirous of food, we solicit the gift of the splendid sun, who should be studiously worshipped. Venerable men, guided by the understanding, salute the divine sun with oblations and praise" (Colebrooke, *Translation*). The substance of this prayer is thus given by professor Horace Wilson: "Let us meditate on the sacred light of that divine sun, that it may illuminate our minds."

Gaza. Full descriptions of this ancient and still important city may be found in Porter's *Handbook for Syria*, p. 271 sq.; and Bädeker's *Palestine*, p. 312 sq. The latest is that of Conder (*Tent-Work*, ii, 169 sq.):

> "This ancient city, the capital of Philistia, is very picturesquely situated, having a fine approach down the broad avenue from the north, and rising on an isolated hill a hundred feet above the plain. On the higher part of the hill are the governor's house, the principal mosque (an early Crusading church), and the bazaars. The green mounds traceable round this hillock are probably remains of the ancient walls of the city. Gaza bristles with minarets, and has not less than twenty wells. The population is now eighteen thousand, including sixty or seventy houses of Greek Christians. The Samaritans in the 7th century seem to have been numerous in Philistia, near Jaffa, Ascalon, and Gaza. Even as late as the commencement of the present century, they had a synagogue in this latter city, but are now no longer found there. There are two large suburbs of mud cabins on lower ground, to the east and northeast, making four quarters to the town in all. East of the Serai is the reputed tomb of Samson, whom the Moslems call 'Aly Merwân or "Aly the enslaved." On the northwest is the mosque of Hâshem, father of the prophet. The new mosque, built some forty years since, is full of marble fragments from ancient buildings, which were principally found near the sea-shore. The town is not walled, and presents the appearance of a village grown to unusual size; the brown cabins rise on the hillside row above row, and the white domes and minarets, with numerous palms, give the place a truly Oriental appearance. The bazaars are large and are considered good." (See illustration on following page.)

Gazel, love songs with which the Mohammedan

Gaza. (From Thomson's *Southern Palestine and Jerusalem.*)

dervishes called Bactashites (q. v.) salute every one they meet. They are applied allegorically to the divine love. See CANTICLES.

Gazith (גָּזִית, *hewn*, i. e. of squared stones), a place in which the Jewish Sanhedrim sat. It was a building erected of hewn stone after the second temple was finished, half of it being within the court and half within the *chêl*, and, therefore, half of it was holy and half common. See SANHEDRIM; TEMPLE.

Gazophylacium (γαζωφυλάκιον), the treasury outside the Church, among the early Christians, in which the oblations or offerings of the people were kept. The word also denotes the chest in the temple at Jerusalem in which the valuable presents consecrated to God were kept; and it was sometimes applied to the apartments of the temple used for storing the provisions for sacrifice and the priests' portion. See CHURCH; TEMPLE.

Gazzaniga, FRANZ PETER MARTIN, a Roman Catholic theologian, who lived in the second half of the 18th century at Vienna, is the author of, *Prælectiones Theologicæ* (Vienna, 1775–79, 5 vols.):—*Theol. Dogmatica in Syst. Redacta* (Ingolstadt, 1786):—*Theol. Polemica* (Vienna, 1778–79, 2 vols., Mayence, 1783). See Winer, *Handbuch der theol. Lit.* i, 306, 342. (B. P.)

Gebauer, CHRISTIAN AUGUST, a German hymnist, was born Aug. 28, 1792, at Knolelsdorf, in Saxony. He was professor at Bonn in 1828, and died at Tübingen, Nov. 18, 1852. He published, *Blüthen religiösen Sinnes* (Heidelberg, 1821; 3d. ed. 1843):—*Luther und seine Zeitgenossen* (Leipsic, 1827):—*Simon Dach und seine Freunde* (Tübingen, 1828):—*Erbauliches und Beschauliches aus Gern. Tersteegen ausgewählt* (Stuttgart, 1845):—*Heilige Seelenlust Geistliche Lieder und Sprüche von Spee, angelus Silesius und Novalis* (ibid. 1845). See Koch, *Geschichte des deutschen Kirchenliedes*, vii, 290 sq. (B. P.)

Gebhard, Brandanus, a Lutheran theologian of Germany, was born in 1704 at Greifswalde, studied there, and died at Stralsund, June 18, 1784. He wrote, *Disp. de Acquirenda Vitæ Sanctitate* (Greifswalde, 1738):—*Gedanken von der Versöhnung* (1745):—*De Gustu Morali in Psa. cxix, 66* (Stralsund, 1751). See Meusel, *Gelehrtes Deutschland;* Jöcher, *Allgemeines Gelehrten-Lexikon*, s. v. (B. P.)

Gebhard, Brandanus Heinrich, a Lutheran theologian of Germany, was born at Brunswick, Nov. 16, 1657. He studied at Jena, was in 1686 professor of Oriental languages at Greifswalde, professor of theology in 1702, and died Dec. 1, 1729. He wrote a commentary on the minor prophets:—*Vindiciæ Novi Testamenti contra R. Isaac ben Abraham:—Comment. in Zephaniam contra Abarbanelem ·—Comment. in Epistolas Judæ:—Usus Cabalæ in 3 Priora Capita Geneseos:—Vindiciæ Nominis* τετραγραμμάτου יהוה *ab Abusu:—Diss. de Consensu Judæorum cum Christo in Doctrina de Lege:—De Gog et Magog:—Enarratio Cantici Deboræ et Baruch:—De Messiæ Spiritualitate ex Voce Schiloh*, etc. See Jöcher, *Allgemeines Gelehrten-Lexikon*, s. v.; Fürst, *Bibl. Jud.* i, 319; Winer, *Handbuch der theol. Lit.* i, 272. (B. P.)

Gebhard, John G., an eminent German and Dutch Reformed minister, was born at Waldorf, Germany, Feb. 2, 1750. He received his classical education at the University of Heidelberg, and completed his theological studies at Utrecht, in Holland, where he was licensed in 1771. The same year he emigrated to America, and officiated in the German churches of Whitpain and Worcester, Pa., for three years. In 1774 he removed to New York city, as pastor of the German Church, and in 1776 accepted the call of the Dutch Reformed Church of Claverack, Columbia Co., where he continued until his death, Aug. 16, 1826. Mr. Gebhard mastered the Low Dutch tongue in three months so as to be able to preach in it. He founded the Washingtonian Institute of Claverack in 1777, and was its principal for many years. He was a spirited, earnest, and pathetic preacher, a good theologian, a leader in educational movements, a great lover of peace, a sagacious, prudent adviser, having full control of himself, and large influence over a wide region of country. He threw the whole weight of his character and office into the cause of his adopted country during the Revolutionary war. See Harbaugh, *Fathers of the Germ. Ref. Church*, ii, 293; Zabriskie, *Claverack Centennial;* Corwin, *Manual of the Ref. Church in America*, s. v.; *Magazine of the Ref. Dutch Church*, Oct. 1826, p. 232. (W. J. R. T.)

Gebser, AUGUST RUDOLPH, a Lutheran theologian of Germany, was born Jan. 19, 1801, in Thuringia. In 1823 he commenced his academical career at Jena, was in 1828 professor of theology, in 1829 professor, superintendent, and first cathedral preacher at Königsberg, and died at Halle, June 22, 1874. He wrote, *De Explicatione Sacræ Scripturæ, Præsertim Novi Testamenti e Libro Zendavesta* (Jena, 1824):—*De Oratione Dominica* (Königsberg, 1830):—*Der Brief des Jacobus übersetzt und ausführlich erklärt* (Berlin, 1828):—*Commentatio de Primordiis Studiorum Fanaticorum Anabaptistarum* (Königsberg, 1830):—*Bibliotheca Latina Vet. Poetarum Christianorum* (Jena, 1827):—*Vollständige Geschichte des Thomas Münzer und der Bauernkriege in Thüringen* (1831):—*Geschichte der Domkirche zu Königsberg und des Bisthums Samland* (1835). See Zuchold, *Bibl. Theol.* i, 405 sq.; Winer, *Handbuch der theol. Lit.* i, 110, 247, 272, 767, 809, 880. (B. P.)

Gedaliah, FAST OF, a Jewish fast observed on the third day of the month *Tisri*, in memory of the murder of Gedaliah (q. v.), son of Ahikam.

Gedalja IBN-JACHJA. See IBN-JACHJA, GEDALJA.

Geddes, ANDREW, a reputable Scotch portrait-painter, was born at Edinburgh about 1789, and was early instructed in the art in the academy there. In 1814 he visited London. About 1825 he was elected an associate of the Royal Academy, and in 1828 visited Italy, Germany, and France. On his return he painted an altar-piece for the Church of St. James at Garlic Hill; also a picture of *Christ and the Samaritan Woman.* He died in 1844. See Spooner, *Biog. Hist. of the Fine Arts,* s. v.

Gederah (or **Gederothaim**) of Joshua xv, 36. Lieut. Conder regards this as agreeing with the position of the ruin *Jedireh*, nine miles south of Ludd (*Memoirs* to the Ordnance Survey, iii, 43). But this is perhaps better suited to the requirements of Gederoth (Josh. xv, 41), which Conder (*Tent-Work*, ii, 336), locates at *Katrah*, in Wady Surar.

Gedicke, LAMPERTUS, a Lutheran theologian of Germany, was born at Gardelegen, in Saxony, Jan. 6, 1683. He studied at Halle, was military chaplain in 1709, and died at Berlin, Feb. 21, 1735. He wrote, *Primæ Veritates Oder Grundsätze der christl. Religion* (Berlin, 1717):—*Historischer Unterricht von dem Reformationswerke Lutheri* (ibid. 1718):—*Erklärung der Lehre von der wahren Gegenwart des Leibes und Blutes Christi* (ibid. 1722):—*Christliche und bescheidene Vertheidigung der Lutherischen Lehre* (1724):—*Amica Collatio de Æstimatione Rationis Theologica cum Henr. van Bashuysen* (1726). See Dunkel, *Nachrichten*, iii, 312; Jöcher, *Allgemeines Gelehrten-Lexikon*, s. v.; Koch, *Geschichte des deutschen Kirchenliedes* iv, 414 sq. (B. P.)

Gedik, SIMON, a Lutheran theologian of Germany, was born Oct. 31, 1551. He studied at Leipsic, was in 1573 pastor of St. John's there, in 1574 professor of Hebrew, and died at Meissen, Oct. 5, 1631. He is the author of many ascetical works. See Witte, *Diarium Biographicum;* Bayle, *Dictionnaire Historique Critique;* Jöcher, *Allgemeines Gelehrten-Lexikon*, s. v. (B. P.)

Geer, EZEKIEL G., D.D., a Protestant Episcopal clergyman, was chaplain at Fort Snelling, Minn., for many years, until 1860, when he was transferred to Fort Ripley; in this position he remained until 1867. Shortly after, he removed to Minneapolis, where he resided without official duty until his death, Oct. 13, 1873, aged eighty years. See *Prot. Episc. Almanac*, 1874, p. 139.

Gegoberga (or **Segoberga**) (Lat. *Cæcilia*, or *Clara*), *Saint*, said to have been a daughter of St. Romaric, whose convent she built; succeeded (cir. A.D. 626) St. Macteflede as second abbess of the double monastery of Habend (afterwards Remiremont or Romberg), on the top of a hill in the Vosges, near the Moselle. She is commemorated Aug. 12. See Smith, *Dict. of Christ. Biog.* s. v.

Gehe, CHRISTIAN HEINRICH, a Lutheran theologian of Germany, was born at Dresden in 1752, and died Sept. 4, 1807. He wrote, *De Providentia Dei in Errorum Hæresiumque Notis* (Leipsic, 1776):—*De Utilitate et Necessitate Conjungendæ Historiæ Religiosæ cum Ipsa Institutione Religionis Christianæ* (Dresden, 1783):—*Sylloge Commentationum Philologici et Theologici Argumenti* (Leipsic, 1792):—*Imago Boni Doctoris Evangelici* (1792):—*De Argumento quod pro Divinitate Religionis Christianæ ab Experientia Ducitur* (1796). See Döring, *Die gelehrten Theologen Deutschlands*, s.v. (B.P.)

Gehrig, JOHANN MARTIN, a Roman Catholic theologian, was born May 29, 1768, at Baden. In 1798 he received holy orders, in 1809 he was pastor at Ingolstädt, in 1818 at Aub, in Franconia, and died Jan. 14, 1825. He published, *Neue Sonn- und Festtagspredigten* (Bamberg, 1805–1807, 4 vols.):—*Neue Festpredigten* (ibid. 1809):—*Materialien zu Katechesen über die christliche Glaubenslehre* (ibid. 1813):—*Allerneueste Predigten für das ganze katholische Kirchenjahr* (ibid. 1814–16, 4 vols.):—*Predigten auf alle Sonntage im Jahre* (ibid. 1820, 2 vols.):—*Die zehn Gebote Gottes im Geiste und Sinne Jesu aufgefaset* (ibid. 1820; 2d ed. 1824):—*Betrachtungen über die Liedensgeschichte Jesu* (ibid. 1821):—*Die sieben Sacramente der katholischen Kirche* (ibid. eod.; 2d ed. 1825):—*Katechesen über die christlich katholische Glaubenslehre* (ibid. 1823), etc. See Winer, *Handbuch der theol. Lit.* ii, 145, 346, 347, 360, 373, 402; Döring, *Die gelehrten Theologen Deutschlands*, s. v. (B. P.)

Geiger, ABRAHAM, a Jewish rabbi of Germany, was born at Frankfort-on-the-Main, May 24, 1810. He studied at Heidelberg and Bonn, and won the prize for an essay on a question proposed by the Bonn philosophical faculty, *On the Sources of the Koran*, which was printed in 1833 with the title, *Was hat Mohamed aus dem Judenthum aufgenommen?* In November, 1832, he was invited to fill the rabbinical chair at Wiesbaden, which he quitted in 1838 for Breslau. In 1863 he was elected chief rabbi in his native town, which appointment he held until 1869, when he was called to Berlin, where he died, Oct. 23, 1874. As early as 1835, Geiger published his *Wissenschaftliche Zeitschrift für jüdische Theologie*, which was discontinued in 1847. In 1862 he began the *Jüdische Zeitschrift*, a periodical devoted to Jewish literature, but important also for the Christian student. In addition to this he published monographs on Maimonides, on the exegetical school of the rabbis in the north of France, on Elijah del Medigo, and on many other learned Jews of the Middle Ages. He contributed also to Hebrew periodicals numerous articles on Rabbinical literature, as well as to the *Journal of the German Oriental Society*, chiefly on Syrian and Samaritan literature. His *Reading-book on the Mishnah* is full of grammatical and lexicographical notes of the highest importance for the appreciation of the particular dialects of the Mishnah and the Talmud. His main work, however, *Urschrift und Uebersetzungen der Bibel* (1857), which advocates the theory that the Sadducees derived their name from the high-priest Zadoc, contains the results of twenty years' study, and is still very important for Biblical criticisms, especially in reference to the Samaritan text of the Pentateuch, and to that of the Septuagint. Geiger, from the very outset of his career, belonged to the party who were anxious to reform the Jewish synagogue in accordance with the necessities of the age, without, however, entirely breaking with the traditions of the past; and though a reformer of the Reformers, yet in his *Das Judenthum und seine Geschichte* (1865–71, 3 vols.), Geiger shows himself a narrow-minded and bigoted Jew, by making Jesus a follower of rabbi Hillel, and by asserting that "Jesus never uttered a new thought." After his death, Ludwig Geiger, a son of Abraham, published *Nachgelassene Schriften* (Berlin, 1875–77, 5 vols.), containing some older essays, formerly published, and other material from Geiger's manuscripts. See Fürst, *Bibl. Jud.* i, 324 sq.; Steinschneider, in *Magazin für die Literatur des Auslandes* (Berlin, 1874); Berthold Auerbach, in *Die Gegenwart* (1874, No. 45); Morais, *Eminent Israelites of the Nineteenth Century* (Philadelphia, 1880), p. 92 sq.;

Lichtenberger, *Encyclop. des Sciences Religieuses*, s. v. (B. P.)

Geishüttner, JOSEPH, a Roman Catholic theologian of Germany, was born in Austria in 1764, and died Jan. 5, 1805, professor of ethics and pastoral theology at Linz. He wrote, *Theologische Moral in einer wissenschaftlichen Darstellung* (Augsburg, 1804, 3 vols.):—*Versuch einer wissenschaftlichen und populären Dogmatik* (edited by F. X. Geher, Vienna, 1819). See Winer, *Handbuch der theol. Lit.* i, 316; Döring, *Die gelehrten Theologen Deutschlands*, s. v. (B. P.)

Geissel, JOHANNES VON, a Roman Catholic prelate of Germany, was born Feb. 15, 1796. In 1818 he received holy orders, was in 1819 professor and religious instructor at the gymnasium in Speier, in 1822 member of the chapter, in 1836 dean, and in 1837 bishop of Speier. In 1842 he became the coadjutor of the archbishop of Cologne, in 1846 his successor, and died Sept. 8, 1864. Geissel was one of the main promoters of Ultramontanistic ideas in Germany, especially in Prussia, and the pope acknowledged his endeavors by making him cardinal in 1850. Geissel's writings and addresses were published by Dumont (Cologne, 1869-76, 4 vols.). See Remling, *Kardinal von Geissel, Bischof von Speier und Erzbishof von Köln* (Speier, 1873); Baudri, *Der Erzbishof von Köln, Johannes Kardinal von Geissel und seine Zeit* (Cologne, 1882). (B. P.)

Geissenhainer, FREDERICK W., D.D., a Lutheran minister, son of Rev. Frederick W. Geissenhainer, a distinguished Lutheran preacher, was born at New Hanover, Montgomery Co., Pa., June 28, 1797. He came to New York city with his father, at an early age, and was licensed as a minister in 1818. His first pastorate was at Vincent, Chester Co., Pa., where he remained ten years. Fourteen years following he was pastor of St. Matthew's Church (English), in Walker Street, New York city. The congregation of Christ Church at length became the possessor of the property of St. Matthew's, and took that name. Dr. Geissenhainer then founded a new organization, and established the Church known as St. Paul's. The preaching was in a hall on Eighth Avenue; but the church was erected in 1842, on the corner of Sixth Avenue and Fifteenth Street, mainly through the liberality of Dr. Geissenhainer himself. It was a large and handsome stone structure. The organization began with eleven poor families, but speedily increased to 1500 communicants. During the last three years of his life he was aided by an assistant minister. As a preacher, he was terse, vigorous, and powerful, having complete control of the English and German languages. He died in New York city, June 2, 1879. See *Lutheran Observer*, July 4, 1879.

Gejrroed, in Norse mythology, was a mighty giant who once outwitted the cunning Loke, but at last fell by the power of Thor.

Gelbke, JOHANN HEINRICH, a Protestant theologian, and vice-president of the superior consistory at Gotha, where he died, Aug. 26, 1822, is the author of, *Der Naumburger Fürstentag* (Leipsic, 1793):—*Kirchen- und Schulverfassung des Herzogthum Gotha* (Gotha, 1790-99, 3 vols.):—*Nachricht von der deutschen Kirche in Genf* (ibid. 1799). See Winer, *Handbuch der theol. Lit.* i, 762, 804, 813. (B. P.)

Gelder, ARNAULD VAN, an eminent Dutch painter, was born at Dort in 1645, and acquired the elements of design under Samuel van Hoogstraeten, but afterwards went to Amsterdam and entered the school of Rembrandt. Among his principal historical works are a picture at Dort, representing *Solomon on his Throne, Surrounded by his Soldiers*; at the Hague, *A Jewish Synagogue*. His master-piece was a picture at Dort, representing *Bathsheba Entreating David to Leave his Kingdom to Solomon*. His last work was the *Sufferings of Christ*. He died at Dort in 1727. See Hoefer, *Nouv. Biog. Générale*, s. v.; Spooner, *Biog. Hist. of the Fine Arts*, s. v.

Geldersman, VINCENT, a reputable Flemish painter, was born at Mechlin in 1539. Among his best works is a picture of *Susanna and the Elders*, and a *Descent from the Cross*, in the cathedral at Mechlin.

Gelent, NICOLAS, bishop of Angers, was born about 1220. In 1260 he succeeded Michael de Villoyreau, and during each of the thirty years of his episcopacy he held synods, whence emanated the statutes which D'Achery has collected in his *Spicilegium*, and which are of interest as giving a knowledge of the customs of that period, and of the abuses of all kinds which the episcopal authority strove in vain to repress. Gelent died Feb. 1, 1290. See Hoefer, *Nouv. Biog. Générale*, s. v.

Gelhouen (or **Gheylouen**), ARNAULD, a Dutch theologian, was born at Rotterdam, and lived at the close of the 15th century. He was canon of the Augustinian order, at the monastery of Volnert, where he died in 1442. He wrote a moral treatise, entitled Γνῶθι σεαυτόν, *Sive Speculum Conscientiæ* (Brussels, 1476), which was the first book issued from the press of the Frères de la Vie, who introduced the art of typography at Brussels. See Hoefer, *Nouv. Biog. Générale*, s. v.

Gelpke, Christian Friedrich, a Protestant theologian of Germany, who died in 1845, is the author of, *Vindiciæ Originis Paulinæ ad Hebræos Epistolæ* (Leyden, 1832):—*Parabola Jesu de Œconomo Injusto Luc. 16 Interpretata* (Leipsic, 1829):—*Symbola ad Interpretat. Loci Act. xiv*, 3-13 (ibid. 1812):—*Jesus von Sich* (ibid. 1829):—*De Familiaritate, quæ Paulo Apostolo cum Seneca Philosopho Intercessisse Traditur* (ibid. 1813):—*Sammlung einiger Fest- und Casual-Predigten* (ibid. 1830). See Zuchold, *Bibl. Theol.* i, 413 sq.; Winer, *Handbuch der theol. Lit.* i, 90, 248, 251, 434, 551, 570; iii, 149. (B. P.)

Gelpke, Ernst Friedrich, a Protestant theologian of Germany, born in 1807, was professor of theology at Berne, and died Sept. 2, 1871. He published, *Evangelische Dogmatik* (Bonn, 1834):—*Ueber die Anordnung des Erzählungen in den synoptischen Evangelien* (Berne, 1839):—*Die Jugendgeschichte des Hernn* (ibid. 1841):—*Kirchengeschichte der Schweiz* (1856-61, 2 vols.). See Zuchold, *Bibl. Theol.* i, 413; Winer, *Handbuch der theol. Lit.* i, 302. (B. P.)

Gélu, JACQUES, a French prelate, was born in the diocese of Treves about 1370. He studied at Paris, where his talents attracted the attention of the duke of Orleans, the brother of Charles VI, who took him into his service. After the assassination of his master by the duke of Bourgogne, Gélu entered the service of the king, was in 1407 president of the parliament of the Dauphiné, and in 1414 archbishop of Tours. He attended the council at Constance, and was also present at the conclave held in 1417. In 1420 he went to Spain, being intrusted by the dauphin with a mission. In 1421 he left Naples, retired to his episcopal seat, and died Sept. 17, 1432. When, in 1429, he was asked by the court of France concerning the validity of the revelations of Jeanne d'Arc, he spoke very favorably of her divine mission, and remarked that God has revealed himself more than once to virgins, as, for example, to the sibyls. See Martène, *Thesaurus III*; Boulliot, *Biogr. Arden.* (1830), i, 430; Paumier, in Lichtenberger's *Encyclop. des Sciences Religieuses*, s. v.; Hoefer, *Nouv. Biog. Générale*, s. v. (B. P.)

Gematria, a word borrowed from the Greek, either corresponding to γεωμετρία or γραμματεία, denotes, among the Cabalists, a rule according to which the Scripture was explained. The idea of this rule was, since every letter is a numeral, to reduce the word to the number it contains, and to explain the word by another of the same quantity. Thus, from the words,

"Lo! three men stood by him" (Gen. xviii, 2), it is deduced that these three angels were *Michael, Gabriel,* and *Raphael,* because והנה שלשה, *and lo! three men,* and אלו מיכאל גבריאל ורפאל, *these are Michael, Gabriel, and Raphael,* are of the same numerical value, as will be seen from the following reduction to their numerical value of both these phrases:

ו ה נ ה ש ל ש ה
5+300+30+300+5+50+5+6=701

ל ו מ י כ א ל ג ב ר י א ל
30+1+10+200+2+3+30+1+20+10+40+6+30

ו ר פ א ל א
+1+30+1+80+200+6=701.

From the passage, "And all the inhabitants of the earth were of one language" (Gen. xi, 1), is deduced that all spoke *Hebrew;* שפה being changed for its synonym לשון, and הקדש=5+100+4+300=409, is substituted for its equivalent אחת=1+8+400=409. Or the word צמח in the passage, "For behold, I will bring forth my servant, the *Branch*" (Zech. iii, 8), must mean the Messiah; for it amounts numerically to the same as מנחם "Comforter" (Lam. i, 16)=138. So יבא שילה in the passage, "The sceptre shall not depart from Judah, nor a lawgiver from between his feet, until *Shiloh come,*" amounts numerically to the same as משיח=358; hence *Shiloh* must be the Messiah. See CABALA. (B. P.)

Gembicki, LAURENCE, archbishop and grand-chancellor of Poland, was born about 1550. He commenced his studies at Posen, and completed them at Ingolstadt. He was sent as ambassador to Rome to pope Clement VIII. Returning to Poland, he was made bishop of Kulm or Chelmno, and in 1609 became grand-chancellor of the crown. In 1613 he obtained the bishopric of Kuïavia, and in 1616 was made archbishop of Gnesen, and primate of the kingdom, the highest ecclesiastical dignity in Poland. He died in 1624, leaving *Exhortatio ad Principem Wladislaum, cum a S. R. M. Omnium Inclyte Regni Poloniæ Ordinum Consensu,* etc. See Hoefer, *Nouvelle Biographie Générale,* s. v.

Gems, *in Ecclesiastical Art.* Precious stones were employed in very early times for a great variety of ecclesiastical purposes, some articles, such as chalices, etc., being made wholly of stones more or less precious, and others, such as altars, etc., being decorated therewith. The most artistic purpose, however, was their use for seals, especially by engraving emblems of a religious character, chiefly taken from Scripture, particularly the fish, the dove, the lamb, a ship, or some other emblematic device. Occasionally a historical subject is attempted. The monogram of Christ almost always appears on them.

Gem of Red Jasper, representing the Good Shepherd, with two Dogs, and the inscription IAHN (perhaps for *Jah* is his *name*).

Gem of Red Jasper, representing a saint (perhaps Agnes) kneeling before an executioner.

Gnostic Gem of White Chalcedony, representing portrait of Christ.

Dove, with olive-twig in beak, perched upon a wheat-sheaf (an emblem of the Church), having for supporters a lion and a serpent.

GEMS, THE THREE SACRED, among the Buddhists, are Buddha, the sacred books, and the priesthood. Their worship is universal among the Buddhists, and they constitute the sacred triad in which these people place all their trust. The assistance they derive from the triad is called *sarana* (protection), which "is said to destroy the fear of reproduction, or successive existence, and to take away the fear of the mind, the pain to which the body is subject, and the misery of the four hells." "By reflecting on the three gems, scepticism, doubt, and reasoning will be driven away, and the mind become clear and calm. See Hardy, *Eastern Monachism,* p. 166, 209.

Gence, JEAN BAPTISTE MODESTE, a French ascetic writer, was born June 14, 1755, at Amiens, and died at Paris, April 17, 1840. He was keeper of the archives, and inspector of the national printing department. He published, *Dieu l'Être Infini* (Paris, 1801):—*Editions ou Traductions Françaises de l'Imitation de Jésus-Christ* (published in the *Journal des Curés,* Sept. 14, 20, 28, 1810):—*Considération sur la Question Relative à l'Imitation de Jésus-Christ* (1812):—also *Notice Biographique des Pères et Auteurs Cités par Bourdaloue* (Versailles, 1812), contributed to the fifth edition of the *Dictionnaire de l'Académie Française,* and edited with Mons. Mounard *Méditations Religieuses* (Paris, 1830 sq., 16 vols.). See Le Bas, *Dict. Encyclop. de la France;* Rabbe, *Vieilh de Boisjolin et Sainte-Preuve; Biogr. des Contempor.*; Michaud, *Biog. Universelle;* Maulvault, in Lichtenberger's *Encyclop. des Sciences Religieuses,* s. v. (B. P.)

General Baptists. See BAPTISTS.

Generation, ETERNAL, is a term used as descriptive of the Father's communicating the divine nature to the Son. On this subject we excerpt the following remarks from Buck's *Dict. of the Bible,* ed. Henderson:

"The Father is said by some divines to have produced the Word, or Son, from all eternity, by way of generation; on which occasion the word *generation* raises a peculiar idea: that procession which is really effected in the way of understanding is called generation, because, in virtue thereof, the Word becomes like him from whom he takes the original; or, as St. Paul expresses it, the figure or image of his substance; i. e. of his being and nature. Hence it is, they say, that the second person is called the Son; and that in such a way and manner as never any other was, is, or can be, because of his own divine nature, he being the true, proper, and natural Son of God, begotten by him before all worlds. Thus, he is called his *own Son* (Rom. viii, 3), his *only begotten Son* (John iii, 16). Many have attempted to explain the manner of this generation by different similitudes; but as they throw little or no light upon the subject, we shall not trouble the reader with them. Most modern divines believe that the term *Son of God* refers to Christ as mediator; and that his sonship does not lie in his divine or human nature separately considered, but in the union of both in one person (see Luke i, 35; Matt. iv, 3; John i, 49; Matt. xvi, 16; Acts ix, 20, 22; Rom. i, 4). It is observed that it is impossible that a nature properly divine should be *begotten,* since begetting, whatever idea is annexed to it, must signify some kind of production, derivation, and inferiority; consequently, that whatever is produced must have a beginning, and whatever had a beginning was not from eternity, as Christ is said to be (Col. i, 16, 17). That the sonship of Christ respects him as mediator, will be evident, if we compare John x, 30, with John xiv, 28. In the former it is said, 'I and my Father are one;' in the latter, 'My Father is greater than I.' These declarations, however opposite they seem, equally respect him as he is the Son; but if his sonship primarily and properly signify the generation of his divine nature, it will be difficult, if not impossible, according to that scheme, to make them harmonize. Considered as a distinct person in the Godhead, without respect to his office as mediator, it is impossible that, in the same view, he should be both *equal* and *inferior* to his Father. Again, he expressly tells us himself that 'the Son can do nothing of himself; that the Father showeth him all things that he doth; and that he giveth him to have life in himself' (John v, 19, 20, 26). These expressions, if applied to him as God, not as mediator, will reduce us to the disagreeable necessity of subscribing either to the creed of Arius, and maintain him to be God of an inferior nature, and thus a plurality of Gods, or of embracing the doctrine of Socinus, who allows him only to be a God by office. But if this title belong to him as mediator, every difficulty is removed. Lastly, it is observed, that though Jesus be God, and the attributes of eternal existence ascribed to him, yet the two attributes, *eternal* and *son*, are not once expressed in the same text as referring to eternal generation. This dogma, held by systematic divines, according to which our Lord was the Son of God, with respect to his divine nature, by communication from the Father, who on this account is called πηγὴ θεότητος, *the Fountain of Deity*, is of considerable antiquity. It was customary for the fathers, after the Council of Nice, to speak of the Father as ἀγέννητος, and to ascribe to him what they termed *generatio activa;* and of the Son as γεννητός, to whom they attributed *generatio passiva*. According to them it was the essential property of the Father eternally to have the divine nature of or from himself, so that, with respect to him, it was underived; whereas it was the property of the Son to be eternally begotten of the Father, and thus to derive his essence from him. To this mode of representing the relations of these two persons of the Trinity, as it respects their essence, it has justly been objected, that it necessarily goes to subvert the supreme and eternal Deity of the Son, and to represent him as essentially derived and inferior; a doctrine nowhere taught in the Scriptures. Some prefer saying that it was not the divine nature that was communicated to the Son, but only distinct personality; but this can scarcely be said to relieve the difficulty. In regard to this and all similar subjects, the safest way is to abstain from all metaphysical subtleties, and rest satisfied with the Biblical mode of representation. That Christ is the Son of God in a sense perfectly unique, and that he was from eternity God, are *truths* which the Scriptures clearly teach, but *wherein*, in that sense, his filiation consisted, is a subject on which they are entirely silent. Every attempt to explain it has only furnished a fresh instance of darkening counsel by words without knowledge."

See Owen, *Person of Christ;* Pearson, *Creed;* Ridgley, *Body of Divinity*, 3d ed. p. 73, 76; Gill, *Body of Divinity*, i, 205, 8vo ed.; Lambert, *Sermons*, ser. 13, text John xi, 35; Hodson, *Eternal Filiation of the Son of God;* Watts, *Works*, v, 77; also Dr. A. Clarke, Watson, Kidd, Stuart, Drew, and Treffry on the subject. Compare SON OF GOD.

Genesia (γενέσια, *birthday-gifts*), were offerings mentioned by Herodotus, and probably consisting of garlands, which the ancient Greeks were accustomed to present at the tombs of their deceased relatives on each annual return of their birthdays.

Genesius, *Saint*, twenty-fifth bishop of Clermont, in Auvergne (A.D. 656-662), belonged to a family of distinguished rank among the nobles of Auvergne. He renounced the advantages of his birth in order to enter upon the ecclesiastical calling. His learning and his piety caused his elevation to the episcopal see of his province, left vacant by the death of the bishop Proculus. After five years he resolved to embrace the monastic life, and accordingly set out for Rome in the disguise of a simple pilgrim. His miracles betrayed his retreat. He returned to his church, and performed his duties with extraordinary wisdom and devotion. He applied all his power against the heresies of Novatian and Jovinian, founded the abbey of Moulieu, as well as the hospital of St. Esprit, at Clermont, and the Church of St. Symphorien, where he was interred, and which from that time bore his name. He is honored June 3. The Bollandists have published his deeds, and combated the authenticity of other acts collected by various authors. See Hoefer, *Nouv. Biog. Générale*, s. v.; Smith, *Dict. of Christ. Biog.* s. v.

Genesius, *Saint*, thirty-eighth bishop of Lyons, was prior of the celebrated abbey of Fontenelle, founded in the 7th century. He employed himself in repairing several monasteries, among which were those of Corbie and Fontenelle. On being made archbishop of Lyons, he showed great ability in that office, but finally retired to the abbey of Chelles, where he died in 679. He is honored Nov. 3. See Hoefer, *Nouv. Biog. Générale*, s. v.; Smith, *Dict. of Christ. Biog.* s. v.

Genethlia (γενέθλια, *birthday-feasts*), the festivals among the early Christians held on the anniversary of the death of any martyr, terming it his *birthday* (q. v.), as being the day on which he was born to a new and higher state of being.

Genga, Bartolomeo, an eminent Italian architect, son of Girolamo Genga, was born at Urbino in 1518, and was instructed by Vasari and Ammanati, after which he visited Rome. He erected the church of San Pietro, at Mondovi, which surpasses, says one master, any other edifice of its size in Italy. He died at Malta in 1558. See Hoefer, *Nouv. Biog. Générale*, s. v.; Spooner, *Biog. Hist. of the Fine Arts*, s. v.

Genga, Girolamo, an Italian painter and eminent architect, was born at Urbino in 1476, and studied successively under Luca Signorelli and Pietro Perugino. Most of his works have perished, but mention is made of some historical subjects in the Petrucci palace at Siena: *The Resurrection* and *The Assumption.* As an architect he gained considerable eminence, and was more employed in this capacity than as a painter. At Pesaro he restored the court of the palace, built the Church of San Gio. Battista, and erected the façade of the cathedral. He died in 1551. See Hoefer, *Nouv. Biog. Générale*, s. v.; Spooner, *Biog. Hist. of the Fine Arts*, s. v.

Genius, in Roman mythology. The belief in invisible protecting spirits, or beings who care for the welfare of single persons, is found among many people and nations, but nowhere was the doctrine of genii so perfect as in Rome; there there was a distinct belief in deities, who were given to every man from the time of birth. These deities were worshipped partly on general festive days, partly each for himself. Thus a genius was especially a protecting spirit of man. This belief extended still further; every important work and object had its genius or genii.

GENIUS OF THE EMPEROR. In the early centuries of the Church, one of the tests by which Christians were detected was, to require them to make oath "by the genius or the fortune of the emperor;" an oath

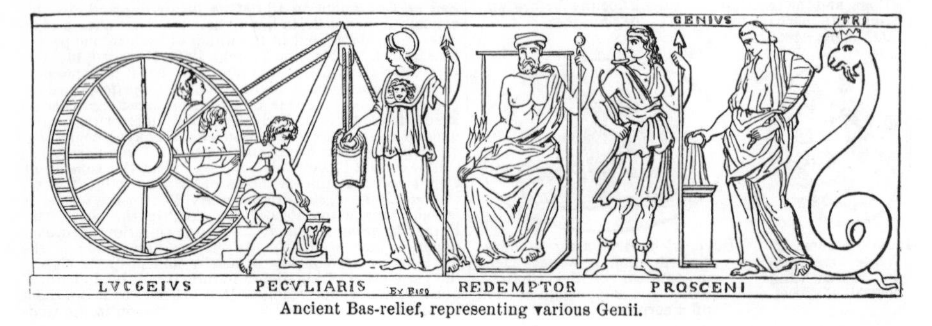

Ancient Bas-relief, representing various Genii.

which the Christians, however willing to pray for kings, constantly refused, as savoring of idolatry. Thus Polycarp was required to swear by the fortune of Cæsar; and Saturninus adjured Speratus, one of the martyrs of Scillita, "at least swear by the genius of our king;" to which he replied, "I do not know the genius of the emperor of the world."

The Genius of Eternity carrying to Heaven the Deified Figures of Antoninus Pius and his Wife Faustina. (From a Monument at Rome.)

Minucius Felix reprobates the deification of the emperor, and the heathen practice of swearing by his "genius" or "dæmon;" and Tertullian says that, although Christians did not swear by the genius of the Cæsars, they swore by a more august oath, "by their salvation." We do not, says Origen, swear by the emperor's fortune, any more than by other reputed deities; for (as some at least think) they who swear by his fortune swear by his dæmon, and Christians would die rather than take such an oath.

Gen-Ko, a Buddhist monk, was born at Sak-Syou about A.D. 1132. He introduced a new Buddhist doctrine into Japan, which soon attracted a great number of disciples. A woman of the court of the mikado was converted to this religion, which circumstance provoked great excitement, and a sentiment of hatred, mingled with an impetuous desire for vengeance in the heart of the mikado. Gen-Ko was banished, one of his most ardent disciples put to death, and others persecuted. He died A.D. 1212. See Hoefer, *Nouv. Biog. Générale*, s. v.

Gensel, JOHANN CHRISTIAN, a Lutheran theologian of Germany, was born at Annaberg, Dec. 2, 1702. He studied at Wittenberg, Leipsic, and Jena, was preacher in his native place in 1727, superintendent in 1748, and died Sept. 6, 1762. He published, *Observationes Sacræ* (Leipsic, 1733; 2d ed. 1750):—*Diss. ad Locum Pauli* 2 *Cor. xii*, 4 (1749):—*De Revelationibus et Revelationum Modis* (eod.). See Dietmann, *Chursächsische Priester;* Jöcher, *Allgemeines Gelehrten-Lexikon*, s. v. (B. P.)

Genssler, WILHELM AUGUST FRIEDRICH, a Protestant theologian of Germany, was born March 7, 1793. In 1814 he was con-rector at the lyceum in Saalfeld, in 1817 second court-preacher and professor at the gymnasium there, in 1821 first court-preacher at Coburg, in 1826 general superintendent there, and died in 1847. He wrote, *Vita Joannis Aquilæ* (Jena, 1816):—*Christliche Amtsreden an festlichen Tagen gehalten* (Coburg, 1820):—*Die Säcularfeier der augsburgschen Confession* (ibid. 1830):—*Geistliche Reden bei verschiedenen Amtsverrichtungen* (Leipsic, 1836):—*Die Herzogliche Hofkirche zu Ehrenburg in Coburg* (Coburg, 1838). See Zuchold, *Bibl. Theol.* i, 416; Winer, *Handbuch der theol. Lit.* i, 803; ii, 149, 167. (B. P.)

Gentile, LUIGI PRIMO, a reputable Italian painter, was born at Brussels in 1606; acquired the elements of design and then visited Italy, where he gained a high reputation. He resided at Rome for thirty years, and was admitted to the Academy of St. Luke in 1650. Among his works are the picture of *St. Antonio*, in San Marco, at Rome; also *The Nativity* and *St. Stefano*, in the Cappuccini at Pesaro. One of his best productions is a picture of *The Crucifixion*, in the chapel of the Trinity, in the Church of St. Michael at Ghent. He died at Brussels in 1657.

Genual. See EPIGONATION.

Genuflection (*bending of the knee*) indicates a temporary rather than a permanent act of adoration; even as it describes a bending of one knee and not of both.

Genzken, KARL ERNST BERNHARD, a Lutheran theologian of Germany, was born Dec. 5, 1811, at Rostock. From 1836 to 1846 he was pastor at Molin, and afterwards at Schwarzenbach, where he died, Nov. 9, 1882. He wrote, *Ueber die vornehmsten Einwürfe wider das Werk der Bibelverbreitung* (Schönberg, 1839):—*Festpredigten* (Lüneburg, 1841):—*Das gute Recht unserer kirchlichen Symbole* (Leipsic, 1851):—*Erklärung des kleinen Katechismus Martin Luthers* (4th ed. Lüneburg, 1860):—*Entwürfe zu Beichtreden* (Leipsic, eod.). See Zuchold, *Bibl. Theol.* i, 417. (B. P.)

Geoffrey OF COLDINGHAM, an ecclesiastical Anglo-Norman historian, lived at the commencement of the 13th century. A monk at Durham, he obtained the position of sacristan in the priory of Coldingham, in Scotland. He wrote *A Short History of the Church of Durham, from* 1152 *to* 1214, which work was first published by Wharton. Raine has given a more complete edition in his *Historiæ Dunelmensis Scriptores Tres* (1839). See Hoefer, *Nouv. Biog. Générale*, s. v.

Geoffrey (or **Stephen**) OF LLANDAFF, was brother of Urban, and was consecrated bishop of that see in 1107. He wrote a *Life* of the Welsh saint Telivous, or Teilo, and is said to have composed the register of the Church of Llandaff, published by Rev. W. J. Rees, for the Welsh Manuscript Society, in 1840. See Hoefer, *Nouv. Biog. Générale*, s. v.; Allibone, *Dict. of Brit. and Amer. Authors*, s. v.

Geoffroi BABION, a French ecclesiastical writer, lived at the commencement of the 12th century. He was one of the most celebrated scholastics, or master professors, of the school of Angers. He succeeded in this office Marbode, who was ordained bishop of Rennes in 1096. Little is known of his life, excepting that under his direction the school of Angers flourished, and that he still lived in 1110. There is no foundation for the belief of Pits, that Geoffroi was English. There is a commentary preserved in the abbey of Citeaux with this inscription, *Gaufridi Babuini super Matthæum.* See Hoefer, *Nouv. Biog. Générale*, s. v.

Geoffroi DE BAR (Lat. *Gaufridus de Barro*), a French prelate, was born in the early part of the 13th century. Doctor of theology, canon, archdeacon, and, after 1273, dean of the Church of Paris, he was appointed cardinal by pope Martin IV, March 23, 1281. He died at Rome, Aug. 21, 1283. For mention of his writings, see Hoefer, *Nouv. Biog. Générale*, s. v.

Geoffroi DE BEAULIEU, a French hagiographer, was born near the commencement of the 13th century. He entered the Dominican order, and more than twenty years performed the functions of almoner, confessor, and intimate counsellor to Louis IX, whom he accompanied in the crusade of 1248, sharing his captivity, and with whom he returned to France in 1254. He also took part in the crusade of 1270, and assisted at the last moments of Louis IX. Returning to France, he wrote, by order of pope Gregory X, the life of the saintly king. He died about 1274. Geoffroi was not a polished historian; he was a religious hagiographer, who kept within the bounds of collecting the religious customs, the prayers, the confessions, the austerities of the monarch, and all the acts of piety and charity which gained for him the title of saint. See Hoefer, *Nouv. Biog. Générale*, s. v.

Geoffroi COU DE CERF (*Collum Cervi*), a French

prelate, was born in the latter half of the 11th century. He embraced the religious life, and was successively prior of St. Nicaise of Rheims, and abbot of St. Medard of Soissons. When Abelard was confined in this abbey, Geoffroi loaded him with kindness, and the illustrious philosopher caused the remembrance to be handed down to posterity. Geoffroi revived the love and culture of letters in the convents of the order of St. Benedict, preaching in all the re-establishment of monastic discipline. In 1131 he was elected bishop of Chalons, at the wish of St. Bernard, his friend. Nine years later he assisted at the Council of Sens, and, in spite of his affection for Abelard, he could not but adhere to the judgment passed against him by this assembly. He died May 27, 1143. Of three letters written by him, the first is found in the *Bibliotheca Cluniacensis* of Duchesne, the second in the *Spicilegium* of D'Achery, and the third in the *Miscellanea* of Baluze. For other works see Hoefer, *Nouv. Biog. Générale*, s. v.

Geoffroi D'EU, a French prelate, was born at Eu near the close of the 12th century. He pursued his studies at the University of Paris, where he first took the degree of doctor of theology, then that of doctor of medicine. He was appointed canon of the Church of Amiens, and in 1222 was raised to the episcopal see of that city. He patronized the celebrated architect, Robert de Luzarches, and caused the work on the cathedral of Amiens to be completed in 1288. Geoffroi died at Amiens, Nov. 25, 1236. See Hoefer, *Nouv. Biog. Générale*, s. v.

Geoffroi DE LÈVES, a French prelate, was born in the latter half of the 11th century. After the death of Yves, bishop of Chartres, the chapter of this Church elected Geoffroi to succeed him. Count Thibault, indignant at this election, concerning which he had not been consulted, drove the new bishop from the city, and pillaged the houses of the canons who had given him their votes. Robert of Arbrisselles appeased the count, and Geoffroi, a peaceable possessor of his bishopric, was consecrated at Rome by Pascal II, in 1116. He assisted at several councils, and distinguished himself by his eloquence. He had a contest with Geoffroi of Vendôme, relative to the privileges of this abbey. If we may credit Abelard, the bishop of Chartres was the only one, at the Council of Soissons, in 1121, who did not approve the rigor of which he was the object. Nevertheless, twenty years later, he signed the condemnation of this philosopher. In 1127 he accompanied Étienne de Senlis, bishop of Paris, to Rome, and in 1132 he received the authority of legate, in which position he was obliged to combat the partisans, in Aquitania, of the antipope Anacletus, and, with the aid of St. Bernard, succeeded in restoring to the subjection of pope Innocent, duke William, whom the bishop of Angoulême had involved in the schism. He received from the holy see various missions for the extirpation of schism and heresy, and always conducted himself in an irreproachable manner in the exercise of these functions. He died Jan. 24, 1149. Some of his letters and charters have been collected in the *Gallia Christiana*. See Hoefer, *Nouv. Biog. Générale*, s. v.

Geoffroi DU LOROUX, a French prelate, was born at Le Loroux (Loratorium), a town of Touraine, near the close of the 11th century. He distinguished himself by his knowledge of theology, and it is believed that he publicly taught this science at Poitiers. In 1131 St. Bernard wrote to engage him to publicly take the part of Innocent II against Anacletus. In 1136 he was elected bishop of Bordeaux. Allied in friendship with Gilbert de La Porree, bishop of Poitiers, he attempted to preserve him at the Council of Rheims, in 1148, from ecclesiastical censure. Two years before he had presided, as legate of the holy see, at the Council of Beaugency, where the divorce of Louis the Younger and Eleonore was published. He died at Bordeaux, July 18, 1158. Five letters of his remain, addressed to Suger, and collections by Duchesne, *Scriptores*, iv, 500–506, etc. Some manuscript sermons are attributed to him, and a commentary on the first fifty Psalms of David, which appears to belong to Geoffroi de Vendôme. See Hoefer, *Nouv. Biog. Générale*, s. v.

Geoffroi DE PÉRONNE, a French theologian of the 12th century, was one of the twenty-nine persons commendable for their birth and knowledge, whom Bernard, on his voyage to Flanders about 1146, decided to embrace the religious life at Clairvaux. Geoffroi became, later, prior of this abbey, and refused the bishopric of Tournay. He still lived in 1171. For mention of his works, see Hoefer, *Nouv. Biog. Générale*, s. v.

Geoffroi DE VENDÔME (Lat. *Gaufridus Vindocinensis*), a French cardinal, was born at Angers in the latter half of the 11th century, probably of one of the important families of Anjou. Being placed while very young in the monastery of La Trinité de Vendôme, he there distinguished himself by his firmness of character and the extent of his knowledge, so that he was promoted from the rank of novitiate to the dignity of abbot, Aug. 21, 1093. The year following he went to Rome, where Urban II made him a cardinal, with the title of *St. Prisque*. In 1094 he was at Saumur among the prelates charged by the pope with acquitting Foulques of Anjou. In 1095 he assisted at the Council of Clermont, and in 1097 was found at the Council of Saintes. In 1115 Geoffroi engaged in a quarrel with the abbot of St. Aubin of Angers. The legate Umbald called him, in 1126, to the Council of Orleans, but he responded to him that an abbot of Vendôme, vassal of the holy see, obeyed the orders of the pope, and not those of a bishop or any other apostolic mandatory. He was endowed with brilliant qualities, and would have occupied the highest positions in the Church had he been less imperious and sullen. He died at Angers, March 26, 1132. His writings were collected and published, in 1610, by P. Sirmond. This collection offers five books of letters, six treatises upon various dogmatic subjects, hymns, and sermons. The matter which he most often treated of was that of investitures. A *Commentaire sur les Psaumes* is unpublished. See Hoefer, *Nouv. Biog. Générale*, s. v.

Geoffroi (or **Godefroi**) DE ST. VICTOR, a French ecclesiastical writer of the 12th century, was canon of the abbey of St. Victor, at Paris, but information concerning his life is wanting, except that he taught literature and philosophy for a long time before retiring to the cloister. Some regard him as the same person as a sub-prior of St. Barbe, bearing the same name, and of whom several letters were published by D. Martene. Various works of the canon of St. Victor exist in manuscript at the Imperial Library; for further mention see Hoefer, *Nouv. Biog. Générale*, s. v.

Geoffroi DU VIGEOIS, a French chronicler of the 12th century, was born at Clermont d'Excideuil (Périgord) about 1140. He was educated at Limoges, and there received the monkish consecration in 1159, was ordained priest at Benevent, abbey of Marche du Limousin, in 1167, by Gerand, bishop of Cahors, and appointed prior of Vigeois, in Lower Limousin, June 14, 1178. The details of his life are found only in his history, and in a most important one upon the history of Perigord and Limousin. See Hoefer, *Nouv. Biog. Générale*, s. v.

Geomancy (from γῆ, *the earth*, and μαντεία, *divination*), one of the four kinds of *divination* (q. v.) mentioned by Varro.

George is the name of numerous early ecclesiastics, among whom we specify: (1) The second patriarch of Alexandria by that name, A.D. cir. 611; (2) first patriarch of Antioch by that name, A.D. cir. 645; (3) patriarch of the Nestorians, A.D. 660; (4) second patriarch of Antioch by that name, A.D. cir. 680; (5) the forty-fourth bishop of Constantinople, and first patriarch of that name, A.D. 678–683.

George AMYRUZA, an ecclesiastical writer, was born

at Trebizond near the commencement of the 15th century. He was esteemed by John Palæologus II, emperor of Constantinople, whom he accompanied to the Council of Florence in 1439. On his return to Trebizond, he performed historical duties for David, the emperor. After the taking of Trebizond by the Turks, in 1461, he was in favor with the sultan, Mahomet II, and obtained an important place in the seraglio. He died about 1465, having embraced Mohammedanism. He wrote a work entitled, *Ad Demetrium Nauplis Ducem*, etc., directed against the union of the two churches, from which Allatius has given extracts in his *De Consensu Utriusque Ecclesiæ*. See Hoefer, *Nouv. Biog. Générale*, s. v.

George of Cyprus (afterwards called *Gregory*), patriarch of Constantinople, was born in the early part of the 13th century. He occupied an important position at Constantinople at the time of the accession of Andronicus Palæologus the elder, in 1282. He was a man of learning and eloquence, and revived the Attic dialect, which had for a long time fallen into disuse. Under the reign of Michael Palæologus, father of Andronicus, he was in favor of the union of the Greek and Latin churches, which Michael greatly desired. But the accession of Andronicus, who was opposed to this union, modified his sentiments. At the death of Joseph, Andronicus was called to the vacant see. The emperor, desiring to put an end to the existing troubles concerning the *procession* of the Holy Ghost, and a schism caused by the deposition of Arsenius, patriarch of Constantinople in 1266, wished to place a layman in the position; therefore George was rapidly advanced through the various degrees of monk, deacon, priest, and consecrated patriarch in April, 1283, under the name of Gregory. The Armenians at first refused to recognise him, and at length were excommunicated by him. He severely prosecuted the adherents of John Beccus, or Veccus, ex-patriarch, and zealous advocate of the union of the Greek and Latin churches, which sentiment appeared particularly dangerous to Gregory. He expressed his opinions upon this subject in a book, entitled, Ἔχθεσις τοῦ τόμου τῆς πίστεως, which excited so much opposition that he was obliged to abandon his see in 1289, and accordingly retired to a monastery. He died the following year, and his death is believed to have been caused by chagrin. For mention of numerous other works, see Hoefer, *Nouv. Biog. Générale*, s. v.

George (*Saint*), surnamed Mthatsmidel, abbot of Mtha-Tsminda, was born in Thrialet about 1014. He was at the age of seven years consecrated to the monastic life. Carried to Constantinople by the Greeks, who took him prisoner in 1021, he remained there twelve years, and obtained a thorough knowledge of the sciences and the Greek language. Returning to Georgia, he entered a monastery, from which he went forth privately to make a pilgrimage to Jerusalem, and afterwards to Mt. Athos, where in seven years he translated a large part of the Bible into the Georgian language. The remainder of his life was spent in analogous occupation. He composed a life of St. Euthymius, some theological treatises, and translated a large number of works of the Greek fathers. About 1051 he became abbot of the Georgian convent of Mt. Athos, called Mtha-Tsminda, which he repaired with the funds furnished by the emperor Constantine Monomachus. King Bagrad IV offered him the bishopric of Mingrelia, but he declined, and even abandoned the office of abbot, retiring to a monastery in Taurus. In 1059, king Bagrad put him in charge of the education of his son, George II. St. George died about 1072. His festival is celebrated June 28 or 29. See Hoefer, *Nouv. Biog. Générale*, s. v.

George of Nicomedia, a Byzantine theologian, who lived in the latter half of the 9th century, was keeper of the archives of the great church of Constantinople. He was the friend and correspondent of Photius, and became archbishop of Nicomedia. Several of his homilies and three of his hymns are found in the *Novum Auctarium* of Combefis, vol. i. Combefis confounded the author with George the Pisidian. Among the unpublished works of George we mention a chronicle, but it is difficult to distinguish between this and the chronicles of the other Georges. See Hoefer, *Nouv. Biog. Générale*, s. v.

George the Sinner (Ἁμαρτωλός), a Byzantine chronicler, lived near the middle of the 9th century. He wrote a chronicle which extended from the creation down to the reign of Michael III, son of Theophilus and Theodora. This man must not be confounded with other Georges who also wrote chronicles, as George Cedrenus, George Syncellus, George of Nicomedia, and George the Monk. The chronicle of George was copied by Cedrenus, Theophanus, and Michael Glycas. See Hoefer, *Nouv. Biog. Générale*, s. v.

George (*Keorkh*) **I**, patriarch of Armenia, succeeded Soghomon A.D. 792. He died in 795, and was succeeded by Joseph II. See Hoefer, *Nouv. Biog. Générale*, s. v.

George II, patriarch of Armenia, was born at Karnhi. Educated in the patriarchal palace, he was raised to the patriarchate in 876, after the death of Zachary III. He was a prudent man, who governed well his Church. He was one of the principal signers of the petition addressed to the caliph, requesting the title of king for the prince Achod, governor of Armenia. Being sent as ambassador by Sempad, successor of Achod, to Afshin, the Arab general who came to invade Armenia, he was retained as a captive, and did not regain his liberty until near the conclusion of the treaty, and by means of a ransom. He died in 897. He is the author of a letter addressed to John, a Syrian patriarch, in which he exposes the rites of the Armenian Church. His successor was Machdots II (*Elivardzetsi*). See Hoefer, *Nouv. Biog. Générale*, s. v.

George III was born at Lorhi, and occupied the patriarchal see of Armenia from 1071 to 1073. When Gregory II had abdicated, in order to retire to the Black Mountain, in the Taurus, George, who had been his secretary, was elected patriarch. Irritated because a great number of priests still addressed Gregory II as the true patriarch, he treated with great severity those who denied the regularity of his election. Being deposed in 1073, he retired to Tarsus, where he soon after ended his days. Gregory II took the place which George III had occupied for two years. See Hoefer, *Nouv. Biog. Générale*, s. v.

Georgel, Jean François, a French ecclesiastic and diplomatist, was born at Bruyères, Lorraine, Jan. 19, 1731. He entered the Jesuit order, taught, with some success, rhetoric and mathematics, in the colleges of Pont-à-Mousson, Dijon, and Strasburg, and later became secretary to Rohan, ambassador to Vienna. In 1774 he became vicar-general, and administered the diocese of Strasburg. He afterwards retired to Freiburg, and occupied himself in editing his *Mémoires*, until the grand-prior of Malta called him to his aid. He refused a bishopric, preferring the office of vicar-general of Vosges, and a quiet dwelling in the little village of Bruyères, where he died, Nov. 14, 1813, leaving six volumes of memoirs in MS., published by his nephew (Paris, 1817 or 1820). See Hoefer, *Nouv. Biog. Générale*, s. v.

Georges (or **Georgen**), an ecclesiastic of the diocese of Metz, was vicar of the parish of St. Eucaire of that city, in 1788. He died about 1848, while holding the position of grand chorister of the cathedral of Nancy. See Hoefer, *Nouv. Biog. Générale*, s. v.

Georges, Dominique, a French theologian, was born at Cutri, near Longwy, Lorraine, in 1613. He completed his course of philosophy at the College of the Jesuits at Pont-à-Mousson, entered orders, and was appointed, in 1637, curate of Circourt. Some time after he returned to Paris, went into the community of St. Nicolas-du-Chardonnet, and later into the abbey of the reformed Cistercians. At the age of forty years he was placed in charge of the abbey of Val Richer. In 1664 he was sent with the abbot of La Trappe to Rome, to solicit a general reform of the order of Citeaux. On his return he established this reform in his abbey at Val Richer, which was a course of such extreme austerity that many were unable to follow it, and he was obliged to modify it. He died Nov. 8, 1693. See Hoefer, *Nouv. Biog. Générale*, s. v.

Georgi, Christian Sigmund, a Lutheran theologian, was born at Luckau, July 20, 1701. He studied at Wittenberg, and commenced his academical career in 1723, was professor of philosophy in 1736, professor of theology in 1743, and was honored with the doctorate of divinity in 1748. He died Sept. 6, 1771, leaving *De Chaldæosyrismis, Rabbinismis et Persismis* (Wittenberg, 1726):—*De Ebraismis, Novi Test.* (ibid. 1726–27):—*De Dialecto Novi Testamenti* (ibid. 1730):—*De Idioticismis Novi Test.* (ibid. eod.):—*De Puritate Novi Test.* (ibid. 1731):—*De Latinismis Græcæ Novi Fœderis* (ibid. 1732):—*Vindiciæ Novi Testamenti ab Ebraismis* (eod.):—*Hierocriticus Novi Testamenti* (1733):—*De* סופרים *ad Varios Vet. et Novi Test. Locos Illustrandos* (1734), etc. For a full list of his writings, amounting to seventy-two, see Döring, *Die gelehrten Theologen Deutschlands*, s. v.; Jöcher, *Allgemeines Gelehrten-Lexikon*, s. v. (B. P.)

Georgian Version. See Russia, Versions of.

Georgio, Adolph a S., a Piarist, was born in 1681, in Moravia. In 1695 he joined his order, was its general in 1724, and died as bishop of Raab, Nov. 24, 1743. He wrote, עד אלוף, i. e. teacher and witness (Frankfort, 1711; a work written in Hebrew for the conversion of the Jews, which he had formerly published in Latin at Vienna, 1709):—*Die Psalmen Davids mit einer Erklärung und Phraseologie des Hebräischen Textes* (Vienna, 1737). See Jöcher, *Allgemeines Gelehrten-Lexikon*, s. v. (B. P.)

Georgius, Ambinias, a Capuchin preacher, who died at Paris in 1657, is the author of *Tertullianus Redivivus* (Paris, 1646–50, 3 vols.):—*Theologia Pauli Trina* (ibid. 1649–50, 3 vols.). See Bernard à Bononia, *Bibl. Capuccinorum;* Jöcher, *Allgemeines Gelehrten-Lexikon*, s. v. (B. P.)

Georgius, Dominicus, the younger, librarian to cardinal Imperialis, and chaplain to pope Benedict XIV, died at Rome, Aug. 20, 1747. He wrote, *De Antiquis Italiæ Metropolibus* (Rome, 1722):—*De Liturgia Romani Pontificis* (1731, 2 vols.):—*De Monogrammate Christi* (1738):—*Annalium Ecclesiasticorum Cæs. Ba onii* (Lucca, 1740):—*Vita Nicolai V Pont. Maximi ad Fidem Veterum Monumentorum*, etc. (1742):—*Martyrologium Adonis Archiepiscopi Viennensis* (1745). See Baumgarten, *Hallische Bibliothek*, vi, 436; Jöcher, *Allgemeines Gelehrten-Lexikon*, s. v.; Winer, *Handbuch der theol. Lit.* i, 539, 675, 813, 914. (B. P.)

Georgius, Ignatius, a Benedictine, who flourished in the first half of the 18th century, is the author of *Paulus Apostolus in Mari* (Venice, 1730). See Baumgarten, *Merkwürdige Bücher*, viii, 157; Walch, *Bibl. Theol.* iii, 454; Jöcher, *Allgemeines Gelehrten-Lexikon*, s. v.; Winer, *Handbuch der theol. Lit.* i, 569. (B. P.)

Gerald, abbot and bishop of Mayo, is believed to have been of Saxon lineage, and to have accompanied Colman from Lindisfarne in 664. He is commemorated on March 13.

Geraldini, Alessandro, a Neapolitan prelate, first bishop of Hispaniola, afterwards San Domingo, then Hayti, was born in 1455 at Amelia (Umbria). He belonged to a noble family, and devoted himself to the service of Spain. His brother having been sent on a mission to Francis II, duke of Brittany, Alessandro accompanied him, and remained in France until September, 1488. On his return to Spain he was appointed tutor of the princesses, and obtained aid for Christopher Columbus for his voyage of discovery. He was afterwards charged with several diplomatic missions. He first obtained the bishopric of Volterra, then of Monte Cervino (1494). In 1520 he was appointed to the bishopric of Hispaniola. He immediately repaired to his new diocese, where he employed himself with true evangelical zeal until his death, which occurred in 1525. For mention of his works, see Hoefer, *Nouv. Biog. Générale*, s. v.

Gerard of Douay, third son of Wantur III, lord of Douay, lived in the 13th century. He was priest and canon of the Church of Senlis, and bishop of Chalons-sur-Marne. He met at Douay, Oct. 17, 1206, with the bishops of Arras and Tournay, in order to remove the body of St. Amé, which the three bishops bore upon their shoulders from the Church of St. Amé of Douay to a small hill situated on the outskirts of a city upon the road to Arras. He was one of the benefactors of the abbey of Cheminon, to which he left a goodly number of manuscripts. He resigned his bishopric in 1215, and retired to the abbey of Toussaint, near Chalons, where he died some years later. See Hoefer, *Nouv. Biog. Générale*, s. v.

Gerard (*Saint*) of Hungary, was born in the Venetian States, and while very young entered a monastery. By the permission of his superiors he set out for Jerusalem to visit the Holy Sepulchre, and passing through Hungary, the king, St. Stephen, touched by his piety, gave to him the bishopric of Chonad. He distinguished himself by his apostolic zeal and his great strictness. After the death of St. Stephen he suffered great persecution, and was at last assassinated by order of a nobleman of the country. In Roman martyrology he is styled the apostle of Hungary. His death occurred Sept. 24, 1047. See Hoefer, *Nouv. Biog. Générale*, s. v.

Gerard of Liege, a Dominican, was born about 1220. He aided in the establishment of the Fête-Dieu, and died about 1270. He wrote several religious works. *De Doctrina Cordis* gained great popularity, as attested by the large number of manuscripts. It was published several times, and translated into French by W. Caoult (Douay, 1601; Lyons, 1608). His *Sermons* and *De Testamento Christi*, with others of his writings, are forgotten. See Hoefer, *Nouv. Biog. Générale*, s. v.

Gerard (*Saint*) of Toul, was born in 935, of a patrician family. While very young he entered the chapter of St. Peter of Cologne, his native city, in order to pursue his studies, and at the age of twenty-eight was promoted to the episcopal see of Toul. Consecrated at Treves in 968, and enthroned the same year, he led an upright, charitable, and studious life, and devoted himself very closely to the instruction of the numerous pupils under his care. He labored throughout his diocese, scattering the word of God, and aiding those of his subjects who were impoverished by war or pestilence. He spent as little time as possible at the imperial court, notwithstanding the wish of Otho II to the contrary. He visited Rome, and in company with twelve persons who travelled on foot in procession, went from Toul to the tomb of the apostles Peter and Paul, the principal object of their devotion. On his return to Rome he found the nobility had risen up against the episcopal power, which he had committed to the hands of his brother. Gerard died April 22, 994, was canonized fifty-seven years afterwards, and pope Leo IX, Oct. 22, 1051, removed his remains. See Hoefer, *Nouv. Biog. Générale*, s. v.

Gerard of Zutphen (or de Zerbolt), a Dutch ascetic writer, a disciple of Gerard Groot, was born in 1367, and reared in the society of the Brothers of Common Life. He died in 1398, leaving two treatises: *De Reformatione Virium Animæ*, and *De Spiritualibus Ascensionibus* (Paris, 1492; Cologne, 1579; and in the *Bibliothèque des Pères*, Cologne, 1618). See Hoefer, *Nouv. Biog. Générale*, s. v.

Gerard, John. See Gerhard, Johann.

Gerards, Mark, a reputable Flemish painter, engraver, and architect, also an illuminator and a designer, flourished about 1560. He went to England about 1580, and was appointed painter to queen Elizabeth. As a designer, he executed a set of fourteen plates on the *Passion of Christ*. He died in 1598. He is said to have been an able architect, but none of his works are mentioned.

Gerasĭmus, a celebrated anchorite of Palestine towards the middle of the 5th century, was a native of Lydia, who embraced the views of Theodosius of Jerusalem, but was restored to the true faith by Euthymius. He founded a large laura near the Jordan, characterized by extreme austerity, and died there, March 5, A.D. 475.

Geraud, *Saint*, born at Aurillac about 855, of one of the most powerful families of Auvergne, was lord of the southern part of Upper Auvergne, and his domains extended nearly to Perigord and Aquitania. He devoted himself to the study of sacred books, and finally desired to withdraw to a cloister and devote all his wealth to the Church of Rome, but was deterred from this by Gansbertus, bishop of Cahors. In 894 he founded, at Aurillac, a convent, under the control of the Benedictines, and attempted in vain the building of a cathedral. His piety led him to undertake numerous pilgrimages to the tombs of St. Peter and St. Paul. He is said to have made seven voyages to Rome, and to have traversed Upper Italy. Returning from one of these journeys, he died at St. Cirgues, near Figeac, Oct. 3, 909, having freed all his slaves. His kindness and benevolence gained for him a great reputation, and legends attribute to him a great number of miracles, performed both during his life and after his death. See Hoefer, *Nouv. Biog. Générale*, s. v.

Gerber, Christian, a German theologian, was born at Görnitz, March 27, 1660. He studied at Zeitz and Leipsic, and having completed his education at Dresden, became pastor of Roth-Schönberg in 1685, and at Lockwitz in 1690. He continued his studies, at the same time practicing medicine. His last years were full of religious controversies. He died March 24, 1731. His principal works are, *Historie der Kirchen-Ceremonien in Sachsen* (Dresden, 1723):—*Historie der Wiedergebornen in Sachsen* (ibid. 1725, 1726, 4 parts):—*Geheimnisse des Reiches Gottes* (2 parts). See Winer, *Handbuch der theol. Lit.* i, 627; ii, 364; Jöcher, *Allgemeines Gelehrten-Lexikon*, s. v.; Koch, *Geschichte des deutschen Kirchenliedes*, iv, 275 sq. (B. P.)

Gerberoy, Richard de, a French prelate, was in 1192 dean of the church at Amiens, and in 1204 became bishop of that see. It was during his episcopacy, in 1206, that the head of John the Baptist is reputed to have been conveyed from Constantinople to Amiens by a crusader named Wallon de Sarton. He died in 1210. One of his contemporaries, Richard de Fournival, attributes to him various works, among others, a book entitled *De Quatuor Virtutibus et de Ave Maria*, which appear to be lost. See Hoefer, *Nouv. Biog. Générale*, s. v.

Gerbet, Olympe Philippe, a French prelate, was born in 1798. He lent his aid to the journal *L'Avenir* until it was censured by Gregory XVI, and wrote for *L'Université Catholique*, a monthly review, founded by M. Bonnetty, a series of articles on the philosophy of religion which were quite noteworthy. He was for a long time vicar-general of M. de Salinis (bishop of Amiens), was appointed bishop of Perpignan, Dec. 19, 1853, consecrated June 29 of the following year, and died in 1864. He become known to the public as one of Lamennais' assistants in editing the journal *L'Avenir* in 1830; but before that time he had already published *Des Doctrines Philosophiques sur la Certitude dans ses Reports avec les Fondements de la Théologie* (Paris, 1826). In 1831 he published, *Coup d'Œil sur la Controverse Chrétienne*, and *Considérations sur le Dogme Général de la Piété Catholique*. More important is his *L'Esquisse de Rome Chrétienne* (1844–50, 3 vols.). See *L'Université Catholique* (1833–34); Lamennais, *Affaires de Rome* (Paris, 1835); Arboux, in Lichtenberger, *Encyclop. des Sciences Religieuses*, s. v. (B. P.)

Gerbi, Evangelista, a Franciscan of Pistoja, who died at Rome, Feb. 3, 1593, is the author of, *Della Conversione del Peccatore* (Florence, 1578):—*Il Cinque Giorni della Creazione* (1579):—*Breve Esposizione del Salmo lxvii* (1579):—*Sermoni xv sopra il Salmo cix* (Rome, 1583):—*Lezioni xii sopra Abacuc Profeta* (1585):—*Lezioni sopra la Cantica* (1589). See Zaccaria, *Bibl. Pistoj.*; Jöcher, *Allgemeines Gelehrten-Lexikon*, s. v. (B. P.)

Gere, John Avery, D.D., a Methodist Episcopal minister, was born at Chester, Mass., April 8, 1799. He was converted in 1820; joined the Baltimore Conference in 1823; and in it, as well as in the East Baltimore and Central Pennsylvania Conferences, served the most responsible appointments. He was a delegate four times to the General Conference, viz., 1840, 1844, 1852, 1872. He died at Shickshinny, Pa., June 3, 1874. Mr. Gere was fearless, yet humble, a man of prayer and power, strong in intellect, and energetic. See *Minutes of Annual Conferences*, 1875, p. 31; Simpson, *Cyclop. of Methodism*, s. v.

Geree, John, a Puritan divine, born in 1600, was minister of St. Alban's in 1645, in 1649 of St. Faith's, London, and died in Ivy Lane, Paternoster Row, in February of same year. He published, *Vindiciæ Ecclesiæ Anglicanæ* (1644), some *Sermons*, etc. See Chalmers, *Biog. Dict.* s. v.; Allibone, *Dict. of Brit. and Amer. Authors*, s. v.

Gerhard, Karl Theodor, a Lutheran theologian of Germany, was born at Breslau, Sept. 17, 1773. In 1800 he was pastor at his native place, and remained there until his death, Nov. 25, 1841. He published, *Predigten* (Breslau, 1835, 2 vols.):—*Gebete am Morgen und Abend* (1839). See Winer, *Handbuch der theol. Lit.* ii, 136, 257, 373; Zuchold, *Bibl. Theol.* i, 419. (B. P.)

Gerhardt, David Gottfried, a Lutheran theologian of Germany, was born May 9, 1734. He studied at Halle, was preacher at Breslau in 1759, pastor primarius and professor in 1778, member of consistory in 1780, and died Aug. 30, 1808. He wrote, *De Auctoritate Archæologiæ* (Halle, 1757):—*Dictum Johanneum* 1 *Epist.* 5, 7 (Breslau, 1764), besides a number of *Sermons*. See Döring, *Die deutschen Kanzelredner*, p. 62 sq.; Winer, *Handbuch der theol. Lit.* i, 271; ii, 290. (B. P.)

Gerhauser, Johann Balthasar, a Roman Catholic theologian of Germany, was born Sept. 24, 1766, and died at Dillingen in 1823, a professor of theology and director of the clerical seminary there. He wrote, *Ueber die Psalmen* (Munich, 1817):—*Charakter und Theologie des Apostels Pauli* (Landshut, 1816). See Winer, *Handbuch der theol. Lit.* i, 81, 294. (B. P.)

Gerizim, Mount. We extract some further particulars from Bädeker's *Syria and Palest.* p. 334.

"Mt. Gerizim rises to a height a little less above the sea-level than Mt. Ebal (which is 2986 feet high). It is composed almost entirely of nummulitic limestone (tertiary formation). The summit consists of a large plateau, extending from north to south, at the north end of which are the ruins of a castle. The building, as a castle, was probably erected in Justinian's time, although the walls, five to ten feet thick, consisting of drafted blocks, may possibly belong to a still older structure. The castle forms a large square, and is flanked with towers. On the east side are remains of several chambers, one of which has a Greek cross over the door. Near the burial-

Mt. Gerizim, from the North-east.

ground to the north-east rises the Moslem wely of *Skeik Ghânim*, and on the north side of the castle there is a large reservoir. Of the church which once stood here, the lowest foundations only are extant. It was an octagonal building with an apse towards the east, having its main entrance on the north, and chapels on five sides. To the south of the castle are walls and cisterns, and there is a paved way running from north to south. Some massive substructions a little below the castle, to the south, are shown as the stones of the altar which Joshua is said to have erected here (viii, 30–32). In the centre of the plateau the Samaritans point out a projecting rock as having once been the site of the altar of their temple. Over the whole mountain-top are scattered numerous cisterns and smaller paved platforms, resembling the places of prayer on the area of the Haram at Jerusalem. The whole surface bears traces of having once been covered with houses. Towards the east there are several paved terraces. At the south-east corner, the spot where Abraham was about to slay Isaac is pointed out. Near it, to the north-west, there are some curious round steps. The summit commands a noble prospect: to the east lies the plain of El-Mukhna, bounded by gentle hills, with the village of Askar lying on the north side, and that of Kefr Kullin on the south; farther to the east is Rûjib. The valley to the south is Wady Awarteh, to the east, in the distance, rise the mountains of Gilead, among which Neby Osha towers conspicuously. Towards the north the Great Hermon is visible, but the greater part of the view in this direction is shut out by Mt. Ebal. Towards the west the valleys and hills slope away to the blue band of the distant Mediterranean."

The following description of this memorable site is from the most recent and trustworthy account (Conder, *Tent Work in Palest.* i, 62 sq.):

"South of Nâblus rises the rocky and steep shoulder of Gerizim. The mountain is L-shaped; the highest ridge (2848.8 feet above the sea) runs north and south, and a lower ridge projects westwards from it. The top is about 1000 feet above the bottom of the valley east of Shechem. As compared with other Judæan mountains, the outline of Gerizim is very fine; the lower part consists of white chalk, which has been quarried, leaving

Ruins on Mt. Gerizim. (From Thomson's *Central Palestine and Phœnicia.*)

huge caverns visible above the groves which clothe the foot of the hill. Above this formation comes the dark-blue nummulitic limestone, barren and covered with shingle, rising in ledges and long slopes to the summit. The whole of the northern face of the mountain abounds with springs, the largest of which, with ruins of a little Roman shrine to its genius, was close to our camp.

"In ascending to the summit of the western spur of Gerizim, by the path up the gully behind our camp, the contrast was striking between the bright green of the gardens, dotted with red pomegranate blossoms, and the steel-gray of the barren slope. Riding eastwards and gradually ascending, we first reached the little dry stone enclosures and the oven used during the Passover. There are scattered stones round, but no distinct ruins of any buildings; the place is called Lôzeh or Luz, but the reason of this appears to have escaped notice. The title is of Samaritan origin, and is due to their view that Gerizim is the real site of Bethel or Luz, the scene of Jacob's vision.

"The highest part of the mountain is covered by the ruins of Justinian's fortress, built A.D. 533, in the midst of which stands Zeno's church, constructed in A.D. 474. The foundations alone are visible, showing an octagon with its entrance on the north, and remains of six side chapels; the fortress is a rectangle, 180 feet east and west, 230 north and south, with towers at the corners; that on the south-west being now a little mosque dedicated to Sheik Ghanim, who is, according to the Samaritans, Shechem the son of Hamor. The fortress walls are built of those constantly recurring drafted stones which are often loosely described as Jewish or Phœnician masonry, though the practiced eye soon discriminates between the original style of the temple at Jerusalem, and the rude rustic bosses of the Byzantines and Crusaders.

"A large reservoir exists, north of the castle which is called El Kŭl'ah in Arabic, and below this a spur of the hill projects, artificially severed by a ditch and covered with the traces of a former fortress. This is perhaps the station of the Roman guards, who thus prevented the Samaritans from approaching Gerizim, for it commands the north-eastern ascent to the mountain.

"Of the ancient Samaritan temple, probably the only relics are the remains of massive masonry known as the 'Ten Stones' ('Asherah Balatât), near the west wall of Justinian's fortress. They are huge blocks rudely squared, forming one course of a foundation, the north-west corner of which was laid bare by captain Anderson's excavation in 1866. There are two courses, and the lower one contains thirteen stones; this course, however, was not formerly visible, and the Samaritans considered ten stones alone to lie buried, and to be those brought from Jordan at the time of Joshua—thus supposing some supernatural agency sufficient to carry such huge blocks up a steep slope 1000 feet high, to say nothing of the journey from the Jordan. Under these stones, as before noticed, the treasures of the old temple are supposed to lie hidden.

"South of the fortress is one of those flat slabs of rock which occur all over the summit. It shelves slightly down westward, and at this end is a rock-cut cistern. The whole is surrounded by a low, drystone wall. This is the Sacred Rock of the Samaritans, and the cave is traditionally that in which the tabernacle was made. At the time of my second visit some peasants were using the Sacred Rock as a threshing-floor. Rude stone walls extend on every side, and farther south there is a curious flight of steps leading down east. They are called the 'seven steps of Abraham's altar,' and just beneath them, on the edge of the eastern precipice at the southern extremity of the plateau, there is a little trough cut in the rock resembling the Passover oven. This the Samaritans suppose to be the site of Abraham's sacrifice of Isaac, for their version of the story reads 'Moreh' instead of Moriah, and makes Gerizim the scene of the patriarch's trial."

Full archæological details may be found in the *Memoirs* accompanying the Ordnance Survey (ii, 187 sq.). See SAMARITANS, MODERN.

Gerkrath, LUDWIG, a Roman Catholic theologian and philosopher, who died at Braunsberg, Jan. 1, 1864, is the author of a monograph on *Francis Sanchez* (Vienna, 1860), and *De Connexione quæ Intercedit Inter Cartesium et Paschalium* (Braunsberg, 1862). (B. P.)

Gerlac, PETERSSEN (Lat. *Gerlacus Petri*), a Dutch ascetic writer, was born at Deventer, in Overyssel, in 1377. While very young he entered the house of the regular canons of Windesheim, near Deventer, where he took his vows, and although offered higher positions, he refused all except that of sacristan. He died in 1411. He distinguished himself by his piety, his life being one of prayer and meditation. A work was published some time after his death, entitled, *Alter Thomas de Kempis* (Cologne, 1616), and under the title of *Gerlaci Soliloquia Divina*, in a collection entitled, *Sacra Orationis Theologia*, of Pierre Poiret. John de Gorcum translated it into Flemish, and published it at Bois-le-Duc in 1613 and 1621. See Hoefer, *Nouv. Biog. Générale*, s. v.

Gerlach, Gottlob Wilhelm, a German professor of philosophy, was born Nov. 4, 1786, at Osterfeld, near Zeitz. For some time private lecturer at Wittenberg, he was called, in 1818, as professor of philosophy to Halle, and died Oct. 5, 1864. He wrote, *Grundriss der Religionsphilosophie* (Halle, 1818):—*Grundriss der philosophischen Tugendlehre* (ibid. 1820). See Winer, *Handbuch der theol. Lit.* i, 286, 288. (B. P.)

Gerlach, Stephan, a Lutheran theologian of Germany, was born at Knittlingen, Dec. 26, 1546, studied at Tübingen, was in 1578 professor of theology there, and died Jan. 30, 1612. He wrote, *Comment. in Epistolas Paulinas*:—*Disp. contra Jesuitas et Calvinianos*:—*De Contemplatione Cœnæ Domini*, etc. See Jöcher, *Allgemeines Gelehrten-Lexikon*, s. v.; Adam, *Vitæ Eruditorum.* (B. P.)

Gerland (or **Garland**), a French theologian, was born in Lorraine about 1100. He was invested with a canonship about 1130, and employed as schoolman in the collegiate church of St. Paul at Besançon. He was a very superior scholar for his time, and especially won admiration in discussions. He fell into the heresy of Berenger. From 1148 he disappears from history, and it is supposed that he died about 1150. Dom Rivet (*Hist. Lit.* vii, 156) has confounded this Gerland with another Gerland, bishop of Girgenti. His most important work is, *Candela Studii Salutaris*, or according to other manuscripts, *Candela Evangelica*, which under this last title was published at Cologne in 1527. See Hoefer, *Nouv. Biog. Générale*, s. v.

Gerling, CHRISTIAN LUDWIG, a Lutheran theologian of Germany, was born Nov. 11, 1745, at Rostock In 1769 he was university preacher in his native place, in 1771 professor of theology, in 1777 pastor primarius at Hamburg, and died Jan. 13, 1801. He wrote, *De Cognitione Dei Rerumque Divinarum Analogica* (Göttingen, 1769):—*De Concordia Rationis et Fidei* (ibid. 1770):—*Abriss der Vorlesungen über die Dogmatik* (ibid. 1771):—*Diss. Inaug. Selecta* (ibid. 1776). See Döring. *Die gelehrten Theologen Deutschlands*, s. v. (B. P.)

Germain, MICHEL, a French Benedictine of the congregation of St. Maur, who died Jan. 29, 1694, is the author of, *Tradition de l'Église Romaine sur la Prédestination* (Cologne, 1687, 2 vols.), and in connection with Mabillon he published *Musæum Italicum* (Paris, 1687). See Winer, *Handbuch der theol. Lit.* i, 600, 872; Jöcher, *Allgemeines Gelehrten-Lexikon*, s. v. (B. P.)

German Councils (*Concilium Germanicum*), i. e. councils celebrated in Germany, but at places unknown.

I. A.D. 743, probably, being the first of five said to have met under St. Boniface, by his biographer, but great obscurity hangs over their date, number, and canons, to say the least. In the preface to this council it is Carloman, mayor of the palace, who speaks, and its seven canons, besides running in his name, form the first of his capitularies. Certainly, the first of them, constituting Boniface archbishop over the bishops of his dominions, cannot have been decreed but by him. True, there is a letter from Boniface to pope Zachary, requesting leave for holding a synod of this kind, which was at once given; and in another, purporting to be from Boniface to archbishop Cuthbert, three sets of canons are quoted as having been decreed by the writer, of which these form the second. Still, even so, when and where were the other two sets passed?

II. A.D. 745, at Mayence possibly, where Aldebert and Clement were pronounced heretics, and Gervilion of Mayence deposed, to be succeeded by Boniface.

III. A.D. 747, at which the first four general councils were ordered to be received. Possibly the tenth of the letters of pope Zachary may relate to this.

IV. A.D. 759, at which Othmar, abbot of St. Gall, was unjustly condemned.

German Ebenezer Society, a body of Lutheran dissenters, who emigrated from Prussia to America some years ago, and settled near Buffalo, N. Y. They number somewhat more than one thousand souls, and hold their property in common. They are exceedingly careful as to religious observances, and very strict in keeping the Sabbath.

German Evangelical Association OF THE WEST, a sect of German Protestants in America corresponding to the United Evangelical Church of Germany. It was instituted at St. Louis, Mo., May 4, 1841, by seven ministers of the United Church of Germany. The object in view in forming this body is stated in the first paragraph of the revised statutes as follows: "The object of the association is, to work for the establishment and spread of the Evangelical Church in particular, as well as for the furtherance of all institutions for the extension of the kingdom of God. By the Evangelical Church we understand that communion which takes the Holy Scriptures of the Old and New Tests. as the Word of God, and our only infallible rule of faith and practice, and commits itself to that exposition of the Scriptures laid down in the symbolical books of the Lutheran and Reformed churches, chiefly the Augsburg Confession, Luther's Catechism, and the Heidelberg Catechism, so far as these agree; and where they differ, we hold alone to the relevant passages of Scripture, and avail ourselves of that freedom of conscience which prevails on such points in the Evangelical Church." It will thus be seen that the main purpose is to unite in one body the Lutheran and the German Reformed churches.

German Theology. See THEOLOGY, GERMAN.

German Version OF THE SCRIPTURES. By way of supplement we add the following. It is a well-known fact that, during his life, Luther made changes and corrections in each new edition of the Bible translation he published. His last edition, that of 1545, was by everybody acknowledged to contain some errors, and among these was the omission of twelve whole verses. The issue in 1546, one year after his death, contained a number of changes from that of a year earlier. For nearly two centuries Luther's translation was published only by private individuals, who could and did introduce a number of changes and deviations from the last edition of the translation. The result was that, gradually, the Christians of Germany became convinced that a return to the authentic shape of Luther's own translation should be made. The first movement in this direction was made by the Canstein Bible Institute, founded in 1712 at Halle. This institute in many, but not in all, places restored the original text of Luther, and was followed by the various Bible societies. Finally, in the year 1857, the German Bible societies decided to go to work in a systematic manner towards the attainment of this object. The Canstein Institute took the lead, and the German ecclesiastical authorities co-operated and aided in the work. A twofold object was proposed; first, to put the orthographical and grammatical features of the translation into modern shape; and secondly, which was the main thing, to restore a harmonious text. The first of these tasks was intrusted to the hands of Dr. Frommann, of Nüremberg, the greatest authority on the language of Luther's day. For the second object, two committees of theologians were appointed, one for the New Test., which did its work in 1865 and 1866, and published it in 1867, and one for the Old Test., which worked from 1871 to 1882. The leading scholars of Germany, as Nitzsch, Twesten, Riehm, Beyschlag, Köstlin, Meyer, Brückner, Schlottmann, Tholuck, Kamphausen, Kleinert, Bertheau, Delitzsch, Thenius, Diestel, Grimm, and others, constituted these committees. The result of years of scholarly toil was published at Halle, under the title, *Die Bibel, oder die ganze Heilige Schrift des Alten und Neuen Testaments nach der deutschen Uebersetzung Dr. Martin Luthers. Erster Abdruck der im Auftrage der deutschen evangelischen Kirchenkonferenz Revidirte Bibel* (*Sogenannte Probebibel*), in 1883. This book is now in the hands of the churches for criticisms, which were to be sent in by the fall of 1885; but the time has been lengthened by the Prussian authorities one year. Then the revision will receive its final shape, and will eventually be published by all the Bible societies of the German empire. In order to facilitate the examination of the work, the revisers have printed in "fat" or spaced letters, i. e. German italics, all those passages where Luther's original version differs from the modern editions, and also where the committees have made an entirely new rendering. The former class of passages are distinguished from the latter by having small hyphens before and after them. Like the revised English Test., this *Probe-Bibel* is criticised by the wise and unwise, and has already created not a small library of essays on the subject of revision. Some are dissatisfied on dogmatical grounds, others because the revisers did not act more radically. The last word has not yet been spoken.

Various other German translations have been given in commentaries and separately, but they are all of private authority. (B. P.)

Germanus, a Scotch prelate, was probably the first bishop of the Isles, and was appointed by St. Patrick, the apostle of Ireland, in 447. To him the cathedral church of the Isle of Man, within the precincts of Peel Castle, is dedicated. See Keith, *Scottish Bishops*, p. 295.

Germanus, archbishop of Patras, one of the promoters of the Greek insurrection, was born about 1771 at Dimizana, in Arcadia, and died in 1827. He was secretary and deacon to the metropolitan of Argolis, then to Gregory V, patriarch of Constantinople, and finally to the archbishop of Cyzicus. In 1806 he became archbishop of Patras. When Ali Pasha provoked the insurrection of the Greeks, Germanus put himself at the head of the insurgent party, and ever since his name has been connected with the history of that period. In the interest of Greece he went in 1822 to Italy. He sought the protection of the great powers then assembled at the Verona Congress. When the provisional government was created, Germanus was appointed minister of religious affairs, and held this office till his death. See Pouqueville, *Histoire de la Régénération de la Grèce*; Philimon, *History of the Greek Insurrection;* Goudas, *Contemporary Biographies* (Athens, 1872, the last two works written in Greek); Moshakis, in Lichtenberger, *Encyclop. des Sciences Religieuses*, s. v. (B. P.)

Germar, FRIEDRICH HEINRICH, a Protestant theologian of Germany, was born at Holstein, Sept. 29, 1776. He was rector at Glückstadt in 1802, court preacher at Augustenborg in 1809, and died in 1859. He published, *Beitrag zur allgemeinen Hermeneutik* (Altona, 1828):—*Die pan-harmonische Interpretation der heiligen Schrift* (Leipsic, 1821):—*Die hermeneutischen Mängel der sogenannten grammatisch-historischen Interpretationen* (Halle, 1834):—*Ueber die Vernachlässigung der Hermeneutik in der Protestantischen Kirche* (ibid. 1837):—*Kritik der modernen Exegese* (ibid. 1839):—*Die alte Streitfrage: Glauben oder Wissen?* (Zurich, 1856). See Zuchold, *Bibl. Theol.* i, 422; Winer, *Handbuch der theol. Lit.* i, 109, 110. (B. P.)

Germer (*St.*) DE FLAY (*Germarus of Flaviacum*), in the district of Beauvais, is said to have been born of a noble Frankish family at Giviarandra or Warandra, on the Itta, about A.D. 610. He married a noble lady, and founded a monastery near Flaviacum; but retired, cir. A.D. 648, to the monastery of Pentallum, near Rouen, of which he became abbot. Later he withdrew to a cave near the Seine, where he was ordained presbyter, but finally returned to Flaviacum, over which he presided till his death, Sept. 24, 658. See Smith, *Dict. of Christ. Biog.* s. v.

Germon, Bartholomæus, a Jesuit of Orleans, was born June 17, 1663, and died there, Oct. 2, 1718. Besides his *De Veteribus Hæreticis, Ecclesiastic. Codicum Corruptoribus* (Paris, 1713), he made himself known by his controversy with Mabillon, against whose work, *De Arte Diplomatica*, he wrote. See Le Long, *Bibl. de la France;* Winer, *Handbuch der theol. Lit.* i, 92; Jöcher, *Allgemeines Gelehrten-Lexikon*, s. v. (B. P.)

Germonio, Anastasio, an Italian canonist and jurist, was born in Piedmont in March, 1551. He belonged to the ancient and noble family of Cena. For some reason unknown he ceased his studies at the age of thirteen, and did not resume them until he was twenty-two. He studied civil and ecclesiastical law at the University of Padua, under John Manuce and Pancirole. He then went to Turin, where he received the doctorate at the hand of Pancirole himself. He was soon after called to the chair of canonical law. Germonio accompanied Jerome, archbishop of Turin, to Rome, and enjoyed great consideration at the pontifical court under popes Sixtus V, Urban VII, Gregory XIV, Innocent IX, and Clement VIII. He was charged with compiling and annotating the Decretals. Duke Charles Emmanuel recalled him to Piedmont, and appointed him, in 1608, archbishop of Taranto, and some years later sent him as ambassador to Philip III, king of Spain. Germonio died while on this mission, at Madrid, Aug. 4, 1627. He wrote a number of works, and published one edition at Rome in 1623. See Hoefer, *Nouv. Biog. Générale*, s. v.

Gerner, Herric, a Danish prelate, was born at Copenhagen, Dec. 9, 1629. He studied in Holland and England, and became, at first, pastor at Berkerod. When this city fell into the hands of the Swedes, Gerner took to flight, then entered into an arrangement with Stenwinkel for retaking the fortress of Cronenberg. He was captured by the Swedes, and finally condemned to death, but escaped by the payment of a large ransom. At the establishment of peace in 1660, Gerner resumed his pastoral duties. In 1693 he was appointed bishop of Viborg in Jutland. He died in 1700. Among his works we notice *Hesiod*, translated into Danish (Copenhagen, 1670). See Hoefer, *Nouv. Biog. Générale*, s. v.

Gernler, Lucas, a Protestant theologian, was born at Basle, Aug. 19, 1625. He was professor of theology at his native place, and died Feb. 9, 1675. He wrote, *Diss. in Confessionem Helveticam:—Syllabus Controversiarum Theologiæ:—Prælectiones in Prophetiam Danielis:—De Sacra Cœna ad* 1 *Cor. x*, 15–17:—*De Justificatione:—De Adoptione Fidelium Divina:—De Glorificatione.* See Hoffmann, *Lexikon Universale;* König, *Bibliotheca Vetus et Nova;* Freher, *Theatrum Eruditorum;* Jöcher, *Allgemeines Gelehrten-Lexikon*, s. v. (B. P.)

Gerondi, Jonah *ben-Abraham* (surnamed *ha-Chasid*, i. e. "the Pious"), a Jewish rabbi of the 13th century, who died at Toledo in 1263, is the author of אגרת התשובה, or, a treatise on repentance and asceticism (Cracow, 1586, and often):—שערי תשובה, on repentance (Constantinople, 1511):—ס׳ היראה, on the fear of God (ibid. eod.; Judeo-German translation, Freiburg, 1583):—דת הנשים, on the precepts to be observed by women (Cracow, 1609):—ס׳ אסור והתר, on things allowed and prohibited (Ferrara, 1555):—פרוש על פרקי אבות, a commentary on the *Pirke Aboth* (edited after a MS. by Dolizki, Berlin, 1848). See Fürst, *Bibl. Jud.* i, 327 sq.; De' Rossi, *Dizionario Storico* (Germ. transl.), p. 113. (B. P.)

Gerondi (or *Gerundensis*), Moses. See Nachmanides.

Gerontius, a Latin prelate, lived in the 4th century of the Christian æra. He was deacon of Milan under St. Ambrose. One day he related that he had seen in a dream the female dæmon, Onoscelis (ὀνοσκελίς, a spectre with ass's legs). Ambrose heard of this and condemned him to do penance. Instead of obeying, Gerontius went to Constantinople, made friends at court, and obtained the bishopric of Nicomedia. Ambrose protested against this ordination, and urged Nectarius, patriarch of Constantinople, to depose the new bishop. Although Nectarius did not do this, two years later it was accomplished by Chrysostom, who visited Asia in 399. The inhabitants of Nicomedia, whose love he had gained by his pleasing manners and his charity, complained bitterly at this, and the result was that the number of enemies of the patriarch was augmented, and Gerontius figured at the synod of 403 as one of the accusers of Chrysostom. See Hoefer, *Nouv. Biog. Générale*, s. v.; Smith, *Dict. of Christ. Biog.* s. v

Gerontius, a heretical archimandrite of Palestine, about the middle of the 5th century, was finally expelled from his monastery, and spent the rest of his days in homeless misery. See Smith, *Dict. of Christ. Biog.* s. v.

Gerrard (called *Gerard of St. John*), an old Dutch painter, was born at Haarlem about 1460, and entered the school of Albert van Ouwater. In the Church of St. John, at Haarlem, he executed pictures of the *Crucifixion*, the *Descent from the Cross*, and the *Resurrection*, which were esteemed superior to any productions of the time. He died in 1488. See Spooner, *Biog. Hist. of the Fine Arts*, s. v.

Gersdorf, Christoph Gotthelf, a Lutheran theologian of Germany, who died Dec. 12, 1834, is the author of *Beiträge zur Sprach-Charakteristik der Schriftsteller des Neuen Testaments* (Leipsic, 1816). See Winer, *Handbuch der theol. Lit.* i, 132. (B. P.).

Gershom ben-Jehuda (commonly called *Rabbenu Gershom*, or *the Ancient*, also *Maor hag-Golah*, i. e. "the light of the Exile") was born in France about the year 960, and died in 1028. He is the reputed founder of the Franco-German rabbinical school, in which the studies of the Babylonian college were earnestly revived. He is the founder of monogamy among the Jews, and wrote a commentary on the Talmud, and some hymns and a penitential prayer, which are extant in the *Machsor*, or Festival Ritual of the Jews. See Fürst, *Bibl. Jud.* i, 328; De' Rossi, *Dizionario Storico* (Germ. transl.), p. 114; Grätz, *Gesch. der Juden*, v, 364 sq.; Braunschweiger, *Geschichte der Juden in den Romanischen Staaten*, p. 32 sq.; Jost, *Gesch. d. Juden. u. s. Sekten*, ii, 388; Etheridge, *Introduction to Hebrew Literature*, p. 283 sq.; Steinschneider, *Jewish Literature*, p. 69; Zunz, *Literatur gesch. d. synagogalen Poësie*, p. 238; *Synagogale Poësie*, p. 171–174; Delitzsch, *Zur Gesch. der jüd. Poësie*, p. 51, 156; Frankel, *Monatsschrift* (1854), p. 230 sq. (B. P.)

Gershon, *Chaphet* ben-Moses, a Venetian rabbi, who lived in the latter half of the 17th century, was endowed with precocious erudition, and died at about the age of seventeen. He wrote *Jad Charosim* (Venice, 1700). See Hoefer, *Nouv. Biog. Générale*, s. v.

Gershon ben-Salomon, a Spanish rabbi, native of Catalonia, who lived in the latter half of the 13th century, was the father of rabbi Leon da Bañolas (Ralbag), and wrote *Shaar Hash-Shamayim* (first printed at Venice, 1547; in four parts). The first treated of the four elements; the second, of astronomy; the third, the heavens and earth, according to the principles of Averroes; the fourth, of theological matters. See Hoefer, *Nouv. Biog. Générale*, s. v.; Fürst, *Bibl. Jud.* i, 329.

Gerson, Christianus, a Lutheran minister of Germany, was born of Jewish parentage, Aug. 1, 1569, at Recklinghausen, in the then electorate of Cologne. He received his rabbinical education at the seats of learning in Fulda and Frankfort-on-the-Main. For a long time he supported himself and his family by instructing in Hebrew. While at Essen, a poor Christian woman brought her New Test. to him, which she pawned. Out of curiosity he commenced reading that book, which finally resulted in his conversion. He left his family and went to Brunswick, where he applied to the duke Heinrich Julius, begging that through his influence he might be instructed in the full truth of the Christian religion, and be baptized. He was received into the Church of St. Martin, at Halberstadt in 1600, and took the name of *Christianus.* He remained a considerable time at Halberstadt, and then went to the University at Helmstadt, aided by a munificent stipend from the duke. At the university he instructed the students in Hebrew and rabbinical literature, corresponded with Buxtorf and Wagenseil, and even received a call from the king of Denmark to Copenhagen, as teacher of Hebrew and rabbinical literature at the university. In 1612 he was ordained, was appointed deacon, and afterwards pastor at Berg, in the principality of Anhalt, and died Sept. 25, 1627. Gerson's son, whom the Jews had concealed for five years, also became a Christian, while his wife, who resisted the truth, was divorced from him in 1605 through the consistory of Wolfenbüttel. Gerson is the author of *Jüdischer Talmud. Der fürnehmste Inhalt des Talmuds und dessen Widerlegung* (Goslar, 1607; 6th ed. 1698, transl. into Danish and French):—חלק *der talmudische Jüdenschatz* (Helmstadt, 1610). See Fürst, *Bibl. Jud.* i, 329 sq.; Wolf, *Bibl. Hebræa,* i, 1008; iii, 976 sq.; Kalkar, *Israel und die Kirche,* p. 94; Le Roi, *Die evangelische Christenheit und die Juden* (Leipsic, 1884), i, 117 sq.; Jöcher, *Allgemeines Gelehrten-Lexikon,* s. v. (B. P.)

Gerson, Jean, a French theologian, brother of Jean Charlier, was born at Gerson about 1384. He went, as did his brother, to pursue his studies at Paris, at the College of Navarre, where he was admitted to the number of students of theology in 1404. His love of solitude led him to enter the order of Celestins. He took the vows in 1409, at the monastery of the Holy Trinity, at Limay, near Mantes. After having performed the duties of sub-prior in various communities of his order, he was found at a convent in Lyons, where he gave a refuge to his older brother. This token of attachment was due to the chancellor, who sincerely loved him. Jean Gerson was at the time of his death prior of the house of Lyons, and carried with him to the tomb the reputation of a saint. He died in 1434, leaving, *Epistola ad R. P. Anselmum, Cœlestinum, de Operibus Joannis, Cancellarii, Fratris sui,* in vol. i of the works of chancellor Gerson. The homonymy of these two brothers caused *Tractatus de Elevatione Mentis in Deum,* etc., to be attributed to one of them, but it belonged to Jean Nyder, a German Dominican, who died in 1440. See Hoefer, *Nouv. Biog. Générale,* s. v.

Gersonides, Magister Leo. See Ralbag.

Gervais, prior of St. Generic, in the diocese of Mans, and a French historian, lived in the 13th century. All that is known of him is that, at the request of Robert of Thorigny, who became abbot of Mont St. Michel, he wrote a *History of the Counts of Anjou and of Maine.* After remaining for a long time unpublished, it was inserted in the *Recueil des Historiens de la France,* xii, 532, from a manuscript in the Imperial Library, belonging to the monastery of St. Victor. Gervais de St. Generic is often confounded with Gervaise of Canterbury. See Hoefer, *Nouv. Biog. Générale,* s. v.

Gervaise, Nicolas, a French missionary and prelate, brother of François Armand, was born at Paris about 1662. He chose the ecclesiastical calling, and before the age of twenty had attached himself to the mission at Siam. Here he remained four years, and became acquainted with the language, religion, customs, literature, legislation, and history of that people. On his return he published the result of his observations. He brought to France two sons of the king of Macassar, and after presenting them at court, gave them as far as possible a French education. He was afterwards rector of Vannes. The provost of Suèvre-pres-Mer yielded to him his charge, which position Gervaise held for a long time, and during this time he published a great part of his works. Annoyed with the idea of proselytism, in 1724 he went to Rome, and obtained the title of bishop of Horren. Soon after his consecration he gathered together a number of clergymen, embarked with them for Central America, and commenced his labors upon the shores of the Aquira, one of the tributaries of the Orinoco. But they were assailed and massacred by the Caribs, Nov. 20, 1729. He left several works. See Hoefer, *Nouv. Biog. Générale,* s. v.

Gerwyn, *Saint.* See Berwyn, St.

Géry, André Guillaume, a French monk and orator, was born at Rheims, Feb. 17, 1727. He entered the congregation of St. Genevieve in 1742, taught philosophy and theology in the colleges of his order, preached with success at Paris, and became successively rector of St. Leger at Soissons, and of St. Irenæus at Lyons. He was elected general superior of his order in 1778. His long intimacy with two prelates not in subjection to Rome, MM. De Fitz-James and Montazet, led to his being suspected of Jansenism. He died in October, 1786. His sermons were collected and published at Paris in 1788. He also wrote *Dissertation sur le Véritable Auteur de l'Imitation de Jésus-Christ* (Paris, 1758). See Hoefer, *Nouv. Biog. Générale,* s. v.

Gesenius, August, a Lutheran theologian of Germany, born in 1718, was in 1744 professor of Greek at Helmstädt, in 1748 general superintendent and first preacher, and died Jan. 6, 1773. He wrote, *Prunis in Capite Inimici* (Göttingen, 1740):—*Christum Decoro Gentis suæ Accommodasse* (Helmstädt, 1744):—*Historia Passionis Jesu Christi Harmonica* (Wolfenbüttel, 1745):—*Opiniuncula de* חבלי שאול *ad* 2 *Sam. xxii,* 5 (1746):—*In Verba Christi Marc. iv,* 12, *et Luc. viii,* 10 (eod.). See Meusel, *Gelehrtes Deutschland;* Jöcher, *Allgemeines Gelehrten-Lexikon,* s. v. (B. P.)

Gesenius, Friedrich, a Lutheran theologian of Germany, who died in 1687, is the author of, *Lapis Lydius Sacrarum Scripturarum:—Irenæus Philalethes Explicatio Verborum Sacræ Cœnæ:—Quod Verba S. Cœnæ κατὰ τὸ ῥητόν sint Intelligenda:—Examen Religionum:—Ungleichheit der Päbstichen Traditionen mit der Bibel.* See Witte, *Diarium;* Jöcher, *Allgemeines Gelehrten-Lexikon,* s. v. (B. P.)

Gess, Wolfgang Friedrich, a Protestant theologian of Germany, born at Stuttgart, Jan. 24, 1751, was in 1787 deacon, in 1799 superintendent at Neustadt, in 1814 general superintendent at Heilbronn, and died Oct. 3 of that year. He published, *Briefe über einige theologische Zeitmaterien* (Stuttgart, 1797):—*Merkwürdigkeiten aus dem Leben und Schriften Hincmars,* etc. (Göttingen, 1806):—*Worte des Trostes und der Erbauung bei Begräbnissen* (Stuttgart, 1799). See Winer, *Handbuch der theol. Lit.* i, 397, 578, 917; ii, 388. (B. P.)

Gessel, Bernhard Friedrich, a Protestant theologian of Germany, was born April 6, 1811, at Dantzic, studied at Königsberg, where Herbart especially attracted him. In 1838 he was called as military preacher to Thorn, in West Prussia, and died there, March 14, 1881. Gessel belonged to the Liberals of the Protestant Church. He wrote very little. See Zuchold, *Bibl. Theol.* i, 435. (B. P.)

Gessner, Georg, a Swiss theologian, was born in 1764 at Diebendorf, near Zurich. He was for some time professor at his native place, in 1828 superintendent, in 1837 resigned his position, and died in 1839. He published, *Nikodemus oder die Lehre Jesu vom geistigen Gottesreiche* (Zurich, 1814):—*Der sichere Gang durchs Leben* (Stuttgart, 1826):—*Schicksale der Wahrheit unter den Menschen* (1818–20):—*Christliches Handbuch* (Zurich, 1817):—*Der Christen-Glaube in seiner Fruchtbarkeit* (Stuttgart, 1835). See Zuchold, *Bibl. Theol.* i, 435; Winer, *Handbuch der theol. Lit.* i, 863, 864; ii, 198, 200. 208, 228, 327, 332, 357, 359, 384, 392. (B. P.)

Gessner, Solomon, a distinguished Swiss poet and engraver, was born at Zurich, April 1, 1730, and is principally known by his poem on the *Death of Abel.* Among his works are several vignettes and other ornaments for his *Death of Abel* and his *Pastorals.* They are dated 1769, 1771. He died March 2, 1788. See Hoefer, *Nouv. Biog. Générale,* s. v.; Spooner, *Biog. Hist. of the Fine Arts,* s. v.

Gesta Pilati. See NICODEMUS, GOSPEL OF.

Geyser, SAMUEL GOTTFRIED, a Lutheran theologian of Germany, was born Jan. 12, 1740, at Görlitz. He studied at Wittenberg, was in 1771 professor of theology and Oriental languages at Revel, in 1777 at Kiel, and died June 15, 1808. He wrote, *Dissertationes Tres de usu Patrum* (Wittenberg, 1765):—*Poetæ Græci Antiquiores, Interpretis Sacrarum Litterarum Magistri* (ibid. 1768):—*De Dubitationibus contra Historiam Reditus Jesu Christi* (Kiel, 1778):—*Aphorismi Ethici in usum Scholarum* (ibid. 1789). See Döring, *Die gelehrten Theologen Deutschlands,* s. v. (B. P.)

Gezelius, Georgius, a Swedish biographer, was born in 1736. Like others of his name, he devoted himself to the ecclesiastical calling, became archdeacon of Lillkyrka in Norway, and later almoner to the king of Sweden, Gustavus III. He died May 24, 1789. With several learned men of his country, he wrote, *Fårsök tit et Biographisk Lexikon* (Stockholm and Upsal, 1776). In 1780 he added a supplementary volume. This work was revised and published without the name of the author, under the title, *Biografisk Lexicon* (Upsala, 1838). See Hoefer, *Nouv. Biog. Générale,* s. v.

Gezelius, Joannes (1), a Swedish prelate, was born Feb. 3, 1615, in the parish of Gezala, from which he derived his name. He was professor of theology at Dorpat, Livonia, which at that time belonged to Sweden. Promoted successively to various dignities in the Church, he was appointed in 1664 bishop of Abo, in Finland, where he died, Jan. 20, 1690. He commenced a Swedish commentary upon the Bible, which he left incomplete. See Hoefer, *Nouv. Biog. Générale,* s. v.

Gezelius, Joannes (2), a Lutheran bishop of Sweden, son of the foregoing, was born in 1647 at Dorpat. In 1674 he was professor of theology at Abo, in 1684 superintendent at Narva, in Esthonia, succeeded his father in 1690 as bishop of Abo, which position he resigned in 1713, and died April 10, 1718. He wrote, *Nomenclator Adami ad Genes. ii,* 19, 20 (Abo, 1667):—*De Instinctu Sacrificandi in Gentilibus* (1670):—*De Defensione Jehosuæ contra Satanam, ex Zachar. iii,* 1, 2 (1676):—*Fasciculus Homileticarum Dispositionum* (1693):—*Decisiones Casuum Conscientiæ* (1689). He also completed a commentary upon the Bible, which was commenced by his father. See Hoefer, *Nouv. Biog. Générale,* s. v.; Jöcher, *Allgemeines Gelehrten-Lexikon,* s. v.; Winer, *Handbuch der theol. Lit.* i, 185. (B. P.)

Gezer. This locality has recently been discovered in *Tell Jezer* (*Mound of Jezer*), lying near the village of Abû Ghôsh. The following account of it is from Conder (*Tent Work in Palest.* i, 11 sq.):

"The origin of the title [Gezer, i. e. *cut off,* or *isolated*] is at once clear, for the site is an outlier—to use a geological term—of the main line of hills, and the position commands one of the important passes to Jerusalem. As is the case with many equally important places, there is not much to be seen at Gezer. The hillside is terraced, and the eastern end occupied by a raised foundation, probably the ancient citadel. Tombs and wine-presses, cut in rock, abound, and there are traces of Christian buildings in a small chapel, and a tomb, apparently of Christian origin.

"Beneath the hill on the east there is a fine spring, which wells up in a circular ring of masonry; it is called 'Ain Yerdeh, or the 'Spring of the Gatherings,' and its existence is a strong argument in favor of the antiquity of the neighboring site. . . .

"A most interesting and curious discovery was made in 1874 at Gezer. M. Ganneau was shown by the peasantry a rude inscription deeply cut in the flat surface of the natural rock. It appears to be in Hebrew, and to read 'Boundary of Gezer' [supposed by him to mark the limits of this as a Levitical city], with other letters, which are supposed to form the Greek word Alkiou. M. Ganneau has brought forward an ingenious theory that Alkios was governor of Gezer at the time this boundary was set, and he supports it by another inscription from a tomb on which the same name occurs. This theory might seem very risky, were it not strengthened by the discovery of a second identical inscription close to the last, containing the same letters, except that the name Alkiou is written upside down. In both, it is true, the letters are hard to read, being rudely formed, but they are deeply cut, and of evident antiquity, while it can scarcely be doubted that the inscription is the same in both cases. M. Ganneau attributes them to Maccabæan times; it is curious that they should thus occur in the open country, at no definite distance from the town, and unmarked by any column or monument. Altogether they are among the many archæological puzzles of Palestine, and their origin and meaning will probably always remain questionable."

A full description of the locality and ancient remains, with a topographical map, may be found in the *Memoirs* to the Ordnance Survey, ii, 417 sq.

Ghajat, ISAAC IBN-. See IBN-GIATH, ISAAC.

Ghase, one of the three kinds of Mohammedan ablutions. Three rules are observed in its performance: 1. Those who do it must resolve to please God. 2. The body must be thoroughly cleansed. 3. The water must touch the whole skin, and all the hair of the body. The *sonna* (q. v.) requires five additional circumstances: 1. That the Bismillah (q. v.) be recited. 2. That the palms of the hands be washed before the vessels are emptied in the washing-place. 3. That before the prayers some lustration should be made with peculiar ceremonies. 4. That to cleanse the surface of the body the skin should be rubbed with the hand. 5. That all this be continued to the end of the ablution.

Ghat, a flight of steps leading down from a Hindû temple to the waters of the Ganges or other sacred stream. It is often constructed at great expense, and highly ornamented, being regarded as the most sacred part of the building.

Ghazi Khan, a holy Mussulman, who first subdued the country of Dinagepore, India, to the Moslem power. His integrity and humanity gained him the worship, not only of the Moslems, but even of the Hindûs themselves, who often perform long pilgrimages to his tomb at Sheraghat.

Ghazipore was the favorite residence of Ghazi Khan (q. v.). The place is remarkable for a sect of Brahmins who reside in it, practicing religious ceremonies in great secrecy. They resemble in their faith and practice the ancient Pythagoreans. They hold to the doctrine of the emanation of the soul, and many others different from the ordinary Hindûs, but keep the knowledge of their religious forms a profound secret.

Gheëz. See ETHIOPIC.

Gheg ALBANIAN VERSION. See ALBANIAN VERSION.

Gheyn (or **Ghein**), JAMES, *the elder,* an eminent Flemish designer and engraver, was born at Antwerp in 1565, and was instructed by his father. The following are some of his prints: *The Life and Passion of Christ; The Four Evangelists; The Adoration of the Trinity; Christ Preaching to the Jews; The Annunciation; A Repose in Egypt.* He died in 1615. See Hoefer, *Nouv. Biog. Générale,* s. v.; Spooner, *Biog. Hist. of the Fine Arts,* s. v.

Ghiberti, LORENZO, a Florentine painter, and very eminent statuary, was born in 1378, and instructed by Starnina. About 1398 he went to Rimini, and was much engaged in painting on one of the doors of the baptistery of San Giovanni. His masterpiece was the *Offering up of Isaac.* He completed three statues of *St. John the Baptist, St. Matthew,* and *St. Stephen,* for the Church of San Michele; two bas-reliefs for the baptistery of the cathedral of Siena. All these works are still preserved. The reliquary of St. Zenobius and the two doors are, to this day, among the finest specimens of the art in Italy. He died in 1455. See Hoefer, *Nouv. Biog. Générale*, s. v.; Spooner, *Biog. Hist. of the Fine Arts*, s. v.

Ghongor, in Lamaism, is one of the supreme gods of Thibet. He is a mighty protector of the earth, the sacred doctrines and morals, but because of his cruelty he is counted among the eight frightful Burchanes. He has a horrible head with open mouth, three large flaming eyes, and coral-strings made of skulls hanging about his neck. He carries in his six arms all kinds of murderous instruments, and rides an elephant.

Giabarians, a Mohammedan sect who denied the free agency of man, and taught that God is the author of all the actions of man, whether good or bad.

Giacobazio, Clemente, an Italian prelate, nephew of Domenico, was born in the latter half of the 15th century. He became canon of St. Peter of the Vatican, bishop of Massano, secretary of Paul III, and auditor of the sacred palace. In 1536 he was made cardinal, with the title of St. Anastasius, and soon after sent on a mission to Charles V. Called in 1539 to the legateship of Perugia and Ombria, he, in the performance of these duties, died at Perugia, Oct. 7, 1540. See Hoefer, *Nouv. Biog. Générale*, s. v.

Giacobazio (Lat. *Jacobatius*), **Domenico**, an Italian prelate, was born at Rome in 1443. Destined to a religious calling, he studied particularly canonical law and ecclesiastical history. He became auditor of the rota, and was successively bishop of Lucera, of Massano, and of Grossetto. After having served the Church under Sixtus IV, Innocent VIII, Alexander VI, Pius III, Julius II, and Leo X, he was appointed by the last-named pope, cardinal, with the title of St. Bartholemy de Insula, in 1517. At the death of Adrian VI, he would have been elected pope but for the French party. He died at Rome, July 2, 1527. He wrote, *A Treatise on Councils*, in Latin, which is not highly esteemed on account of its inexactness. This treatise forms the last volume of the collection of Labbe. The first edition appeared at Rome in 1538. See Hoefer, *Nouv. Biog. Générale*, s. v.

Giacomelli, MICHEL ANGELO, titulary archbishop of Chalcedon, was born in 1695, at Pistoja. He was for some time librarian to cardinal Fabroni, and then to cardinal Colligola. He died in 1774. He wrote, *Tract. Benedicti XIV de Festis Jesu Christi* (Padua, 1745):—*S. Giov. Grisostomo del Sacerdozio Libri VI Volgarizzati* (Rome, 1757):—*Omilia di S. Crisostomo* (ibid. 1758):—*Philonis Episcopi Enarratio in Canticum Canticorum* (ibid. 1772). See Jöcher, *Allgemeines Gelehrten-Lexikon*, s. v.; Winer, *Handbuch der theol. Lit.* i, 617. (B. P.)

Giattino, GIOVANNI BATTISTA, a Jesuit and professor at Rome, was born at Palermo in 1601, and died Nov. 19, 1682. He translated into Latin Pallavicini's *Istoria del Concilio de Trento* (Antwerp, 1670, 3 vols. fol.), and published *Orationes Sacræ XXIV*. See Winer, *Handbuch der theol. Lit.* i, 667; Jöcher, *Allgemeines Gelehrten-Lexikon*, s. v. (B. P.)

Gibbethon is identified by lieut. Conder (*Tent Work*, ii, 337) with *Kibbieh*, the position of which he does not indicate, and by Tristram (*Bible Places*, p. 51) with "the ruin *Geibuta*, north of Jaffa."

Gibbon, JOHANN, a Jesuit, and rector of the Jesuit college at Treves, was born in 1544, at Whinton, England, and died Dec. 3, 1589. He wrote, *Disputatio de Sanctis et de Communione Eucharistiæ sub una Specie:—Confutatio Virulentiæ Disputationis Georgii Schon:—Concertatio Ecclesiæ Catholicæ in Anglia*. See Jöcher, *Allgemeines Gelehrten-Lexikon*, s. v. (B. P.)

Gibbons, Orlando, an eminent English composer of church music, was born at Cambridge in 1583, and at the age of twenty-three was appointed organist of the Chapel Royal. He died in 1625. He composed the tunes for George Wither's translation of *Hymns and Songs of the Church*, and many other pieces of church music. See Chalmers, *Biog. Dict.* s. v.; Allibone, *Dict. of Brit. and Amer. Authors*, s. v.; *Encyclop. Brit.* 9th ed. s. v.

Gibbons, Richard, a learned English Jesuit, who was born at Winchester in 1549, and died in 1632, published *F. Riberæ Com. in Duodecim Prophetas Minores* (1612), and several other works. See Chalmers, *Biog. Dict.* s. v.; Allibone, *Dict. of Brit. and Amer. Authors*, s. v.

Gibeah OF BENJAMIN. Lieut. Conder strongly impugns (*Quar. Statement* of the "Palest. Explor. Fund," April, 1874, p. 61) the identification of this place with *Tuleil el-Fûl*, but this view is retained by Tristram (*Bible Places*, p. 118).

Gibel, ABRAHAM, a Lutheran theologian, who died in 1629 at Burg, pastor primarius, is the author of, *De Genuina Lexicographiæ Chaldaicæ Constitutione* (Wittenberg, 1606):—*Grammatica Linguæ Hebr.* (1603):—*Artificium Accentuum* (eod.):—*Strigilis* 120 *Errorum Bellarmini* (1605):—*Explicatio Loci Jerem. xxxiii*, 16. See Jöcher, *Allgemeines Gelehrten-Lexikon*, s. v.; Fürst, *Bibl. Jud.* i, 334; Steinschneider, *Bibliog. Handbuch*, s. v. (B. P.)

Gibeon. A full description of this place, especially of the numerous rock-hewn tombs in its vicinity, is given in the *Memoirs* accompanying the Ordnance Survey, iii, 94 sq.

GIBEON, POOL OF (2 Sam. ii, 13). The following interesting account of the waters in the vicinity of Gibeon is given by lieut. Conder (*Quar. Statement* of the "Palest. Explor. Fund," October, 1881, p. 255 sq.):

"El-Jîb, the modern village, occupies the north end of a detached hill some 200 feet high, surrounded by broad, flat corn valleys on every side. The inhabitants state that the old city stood on the south part of the hill; and here, in the sides of the natural scarps which fortify the site, we visited and explored some twenty rock-cut tombs. There are eight springs on the hill, the largest, or the last, being one of the finest supplies of water in this part of Palestine. One of the springs is called el-*Birkeh* (corresponding to the בְּרֵכָה or 'pool' of the above passage), and flows into a rock-cut tank measuring eleven feet by seven, the water issuing from a small cave. This place is south-west of the village, and close to the main road east and west through Gibeon. The pool is cut in the face of a cliff, and has a wall of rock about three and a half feet high on the west. Above it grows a pomegranate tree, and near it are tombs in the cliff.

The Pool in Gibeon.

Gibeon. (From Thomson's *Central Palestine and Phœnicia.*)

"It is possible, however, that the great spring ('Ain el-Belled) is the place intended in the episode of Joab's encounter, as it wells up in a chamber some thirty feet long and seven feet wide, reached by a descent of several steps, and there is said to be a passage with steps leading up from the back of the cave to the surface above. As the water is some five feet deep, and the passage is now stopped up, we did not attempt to enter it. It is clear, however, that a door of some kind once existed at the present entrance to the cave, and it would appear that the inhabitants of Gibeon were thus able to close their spring below, and to obtain access to it from above within the city. The spring in question, like many of the famous fountains in Palestine, is held sacred by the Fellahin. An earthenware lamp is occasionally lighted in the chamber. Close by is a little rock chamber with a rude masonry wall."

Giberti, GIOVANNI MATTEO, bishop of Verona, was born at Palermo in 1495, and died in 1543. He was one of those prelates who, before the Council of Trent, showed a serious interest in the reform of the Church, drawing his inspiration from Pietro Caraffa, with whom he was intimately acquainted. Thus Giberti insisted upon a better preparation and stricter examination of the clergy, and though his efforts were of no avail on account of the opposition from the clergy, yet he exercised considerable influence on Carlo Borromeo (q. v.). Giberti wrote, *Constitutiones Gibertinæ:* — *Costituzioni per le Monache:—Capitoli di Regolazione Fatta sopra le Stepe:—Monitiones Generales:—Capitoli Della Società di Carita:—Edicta Selecta:—Lettere Scielte.* See Ballerini's biography of Giberti, in the introduction to the latter's works, which were published under the title, *J. M. Giberti Opera* (Verona, 1733, 1740); Kerker, in the *Tübinger Quartalschrift*, 1859, fasc. 1; Reumont, *Geschichte der Stadt Rom.* vol. iii[6]; Benrath, in Plitt-Herzog, *Real-Encyclop.* s. v.; Jöcher, *Allgemeines Gelehrten-Lexikon*, s. v. (B. P.)

Gibieuf, a French theologian, was born at Bourges in the latter half of the 16th century. He was educated by the cardinal de Berulle, studied theology, and received the degree of doctor at the Sorbonne in 1612. The previous year he had, with four other priests, under the direction of Peter de Berulle, then also a simple priest, formed the nucleus of the congregation of the Oratorio. His general, who had introduced into France the order of Carmelites, made Gibieuf his vicar-general. He was at the same time commendatory of Juilly, a house then occupied by the canons regular. The laxity which characterized these monks led him to seek their reform from the cardinal De la Rochefoucauld. The house of Juilly was united with that of St. Genevieve, and later to the congregation of the Oratorio. It is claimed that, owing to modesty, he refused the bishopric of Nantes. He died at the seminary of St. Magloire, of which he was first superior, June 6, 1650. He wrote, *De Libertate Dei et Creaturæ* (Paris, 1630):—*La Vie et les Grandeurs de la Très-Sainte Vierge* (ibid. 1637):—*Catéchèses de la Manière de Vie Parfaite* (posthumous, ibid. 1653). He was allied with the most learned and distinguished men of his time. See Hoefer, *Nouv. Biog. Générale*, s. v.

Gibon is the name of a remarkable idol-temple in Japan. It is a large but narrow building, in the middle room of which stands a huge idol surrounded by many others of smaller dimensions. Around this temple are thirty or forty smaller temples, all arranged in regular order.

Gibson, EDWARD THOMAS, M.R.A.S., M.S.B.A., an English Baptist minister, was born at Falmouth, Nov. 11, 1818. He was educated at the naval school at Greenwich, and when about fourteen years of age entered the navy, which, however, he speedily relinquished. He was converted at the age of seventeen, and some years afterwards began study for the ministry at Bradford Baptist College. In 1854 he became pastor of the church at Guilsborough, Northamptonshire. In 1859 he accepted an invitation to the pastorate of the Baptist Church at Crayford, Kent, which he served for eighteen years. Failing health forced him to resign his charge, Oct. 7, 1877. He died at Brockley, Jan. 21, 1880. He was a diligent student, especially of the Oriental languages, of several of which he possessed a surprising knowledge. He contributed some translations to Spurgeon's *Treasury of David.* See (Lond.) *Baptist Hand-book*, 1882, p. 303.

Gickniahores, hermits of the Armenian Church (q. v.), who pass their lives in meditation on the tops of the rocks.

Giddinge, GEORGE P., D.D., a Protestant Episcopal clergyman, was rector in Quincy, Ill., for a number of years previous to 1857. In that year he became rector in Booneville, Mo., remaining there until 1859, when he removed to Palmyra as principal of a female school. He died May 1, 1861. See *Prot. Episc. Almanac*, 1862, p. 92.

Giese, GOTTLIEB CHRISTIAN, a Lutheran theologian of Germany, born Nov. 21, 1721, at Crossen, in

Brandenburg, was preacher in 1745 at Kesselsdorf, in Silesia, in 1755 deacon at Görlitz, in 1774 archdeacon there, and died Dec. 28, 1788. He wrote, *Historische Nachricht von der Bibelübersetzung Martin Luthers* (Altdorf, 1771):—*Von Luther's Verdiensten und seiner Gehülfen um die Katechismen* (Görlitz, 1782). See Winer, *Handbuch der theol. Lit.* i, 167; ii, 213. (B. P.)

Gieseler, Georg Christoph Friedrich, a Lutheran theologian of Germany, was born at Lahde, May 1, 1760. In 1791 he was pastor at Petershagen, near Minden, where the famous church-historian, Johann Karl Ludwig Gieseler (q. v.), was born. In 1803 he was first preacher at Warther, near Bielefeld, and died March 14, 1839, a doctor of theology. He wrote, *Das Abendmahl des Herrn. Ein liturgischer Versuch* (Bielefeld, 1835). See Winer, *Handbuch der theol. Lit.* ii, 9; Zuchold, *Bibl. Theol.* i, 438; Hoefer, *Nouv. Biog. Générale*, s. v. (B. P.)

Gifford, Andrew, D.D., an eminent English Baptist minister, was born at Bristol, Aug. 17, 1700, being the son of Rev. Emanuel Gifford, Baptist pastor there. He was converted in early life; studied at an academy in Tewkesbury, and under the direction of Rev. Dr. Ward of Gresham College; he was settled at Nottingham about two years, and then removed to his native place as assistant to Rev. Bernard Firkett. In December, 1729, he removed to London as pastor of the Little Wild Street Church. For many years Mr. Gifford acted as chaplain in the family of Sir Richard Ellys. In 1734 he visited Edinburgh, where he was honored with the freedom of the city. In 1757 he was appointed assistant librarian of the British Museum, which position he held until his death, June 19, 1784. His private collection of coins was one of the most curious in Great Britain. His attendance at the museum did not render him inattentive to his pastoral duties. For a period of twenty-four years he preached, in connection with several ministers of the Independent denomination, once a month, the Sabbath evening lecture at St. Helen's Church. As a preacher, he was full of animation. See Rippon, *Memoir; Amer. Bapt. Magazine*, new series, v, 353. (J. C. S.)

Gifford, Richard, an English clergyman, was born in 1725, and was rector of North Okendon, Essex, in 1772. He died in 1807. He wrote remarks on Kennicott's *Dissertation on the Tree of Life in Paradise:—Outlines of an Answer to Dr. Priestly's Disquisitions on Matter and Spirit.* See Allibone, *Dict. of Brit. and Amer. Authors*, s. v.

Giftschütz, Friedrich, a Roman Catholic professor of theology, who was born in 1748, and died at Vienna, June 5, 1788, is the author of, *Vorlesungen über die Pastoraltheologie* (Vienna, 1785; 5th ed. 1811). See Winer, *Handbuch der theol. Lit.* ii, 34. (B. P.)

Giggäus, Anton, of Milan, who died in 1632, is the author of, *R. Salom. Aben Esræ et R. Levi Ben-Gerson Commentaria in Proverbia Salomonis Latine Conversa* (Milan, 1620):—*Thesaurus Linguæ Arabicæ* (ibid. 1632, 4 vols.):—*Institutiones Linguæ Chaldaicæ et Thargumicæ.* See Argelati, *Bibl. Mediolanensis;* Jöcher, *Allgemeines Gelehrten-Lexikon*, s. v. (B. P.)

Gil of Santo Ireno (Lat. *Ægidius Lusitanus*), one of the propagators of the Dominican order, was born in the diocese of Visco in 1184. He was the son of don Rodrigo Pelago, governor of Coimbra, and one of the grand officials of the crown. He completed his studies at Coimbra, and while still young possessed two priories and three canonships in the chapters of Braga, of Coimbra, and of Ydanha. He neglected theology, and devoted himself to physics and medicine; went to Paris to perfect himself in these sciences, and there received the degree of doctor. In 1224 or 1225 he resigned all, entered the Dominican order, became a model of Christian virtue, and rapidly reached the highest honors of his order. In 1249, at a convocation of his order at Treves, he resigned his provincialship of Spain. He used his influence in re-establishing harmony between the king, don Sancho II, and his brother, the young Alfonso. He died at Santarem, May 14, 1265. Some churches of Portugal honor him as a saint, and the bishops of Visen have fixed his festival on the Sabbath after the Ascension. See Hoefer, *Nouv. Biog. Générale*, s. v.

Gilbee, Earle, D.D., an English divine, was descended from a highly respectable family in Kent. He was educated at the Charter-House, where for a considerable time he was a head scholar. From thence he entered University College, Oxford, where he graduated in due course. His first exercise of the ministry was in London, where he served a Church for some years. In the year 1795 he was instituted to the living of Barby, in Northamptonshire, which he held till his death, Oct. 2, 1813. He distinguished himself as a diligent, faithful, and successful minister of Christ. He was a firm friend of the British and Foreign Bible Society, and much rejoiced in witnessing the establishment of an auxiliary institution in the county of Northampton in 1812. Dr. Gilbee was a man whose piety was deep, and whose benevolence endeared him to all who needed his help. It was his meat and drink, whether in the pulpit or out of it, to lessen human misery and produce happiness. See *The* (Lond.) *Christian Observer*, February, 1814, p. 65.

Gilbert, *Saint*, a member of the noble family of Auvergne, was first abbot of a monastery which bore his name in the diocese of Clermont. He passed his youth at the courts of Louis the Gross and Louis the Younger, and was reckoned among the bravest and most pious knights of his time. After preaching in behalf of the second crusade, he accompanied the king to the Holy Land. The unfortunate results of the expedition threw a profound sadness into the heart of Gilbert, who attributed it to the sins of the crusaders. He resolved to consecrate himself entirely to a monastic life, with the approval of his wife and daughter. Having consulted the bishop of Clermont and the abbot of Dilo, he gave half of his goods to the poor, and reserved the remainder for building two monasteries, one for men and the other for women. The latter was established at Aubeterre, under the invocation of St. Gervais and St. Protais. His wife, Petronille, assumed the management, and at her death his daughter, Ponce, succeeded her. Gilbert retired to a place named Neuf Fontaines. He there constructed a monastery, was elected abbot, and ruled with great wisdom. On one side of the monastery was a large hospital for the sick and infirm. He died June 1, 1152, and at his request was interred in the hospital cemetery. The third abbot caused his remains to be transferred to the church. Robert of Auxerre published the life of St. Gilbert in his *Chronique.* See Hoefer, *Nouv. Biog. Générale*, s. v.

Gilbert (1), a Scotch prelate, was bishop of Dunkeld for about twenty years, but when he took his seat is unknown. He was bishop there in 1220, and also in the twenty-eighth year of the reign of king Alexander II. He died in 1236. See Keith, *Scottish Bishops*, p. 79.

Gilbert (2), a Scotch prelate, was elected to the see of Galloway in 1235, and was probably consecrated with the High Church of York the same year. He died in 1253. See Keith, *Scottish Bishops*, p. 272.

Gilbert (3), a Scotch prelate, was a native of Galloway, and was promoted to the see of the Isles in 1321. He probably died in 1326. See Keith, *Scottish Bishops*, p. 301.

Gilbert, surnamed Crispinus, a Benedictine of Normandy, who died in 1114, is the author of, *Altercatio Synagogæ et Ecclesiæ:—Comment. in Esaiam et Jeremiam:—Homiliæ in Canticum Canticorum:—De Casu Diaboli.* See Balæus *De Scriptoribus Britanniæ;* Pitsius, *De Scriptoribus Angliæ;* Oudin, *De Scriptoribus Ecclesiasticis;* Jöcher, *Allgemeines Gelehrten-Lexikon,* s. v. (B. P.)

Gilbert OF HOLLAND, flourished A.D. 1200, a scholar and divine, took his name from a district in Lincolnshire. He was invited by St. Bernard to live with him at Clairvaux, became his scholar, continued Bernard's sermons, writing forty-six in a style scarcely discernible from Bernard's. Abbot Trithemius, the German, speaks of Gilbert as a learned and eloquent author. See Fuller, *Worthies of England* (ed. Nuttall), ii, 286.

Gilbert, bishop OF LONDON, who died in 1134, is the author of, *Glossæ in Vetus et Novum Testamentum:—Comment. in Jobum, Threnos Jeremiæ et Aliquot Psalmos:—Homiliæ in Cantica Salomonis:—Comment. in Prologos S. Hieronymi super Biblia,* which works are still in MS. On account of his great learning, Gilbert was styled *Universalis.* See Oudin, *De Scriptoribus Ecclesiasticis;* Jöcher, *Allgemeines Gelehrten-Lexikon,* s. v. (B. P.)

Gilbert OF WESTMINSTER, a scholar of the first part of the 12th century, was first a monk, then abbot of Westminster. He gave himself up to the study of divinity under the guidance of Anselm, archbishop of Canterbury, attained to great knowledge of the Scriptures, studied in France, visited Rome, and on his return is reported to have had a disputation with a learned Jew, which afterwards he reduced to the form of a dialogue, and, publishing it, dedicated it to St. Anselm. He died in 1117, and was buried in Westminster. See Fuller, *Worthies of England* (ed. Nuttall), ii, 424.

Gilbert Island Version OF THE SCRIPTURES. This version is designed for the people of Gilbert islands, Micronesia. In 1869 the first parts of this version, which was prepared by the Rev. Hiram Bingham, of Honolulu, were published by the American Bible Society. The version of the entire New Test. was published in 1872, which proved to be a great boon to that benighted people, for soon a new edition was needed, which was published after a careful revision by the original translator in 1878. (B. P.)

Gildersleeve, BENJAMIN, D.D., a Presbyterian minister, was born near Norwalk, Conn., Jan. 5, 1791. He graduated from Middlebury College, Vt., in 1814; the same year removed to Georgia, and began to teach in Mount Zion Academy; in 1817 he entered Princeton Seminary, and remained there a little over one year; in 1819 commenced editing a paper called *The Missionary;* in 1820 was ordained by Hopewell Presbytery, at Athens, Ga.; in 1826 removed to Charleston, S. C., and became editor of *The Christian Observer,* which post he held until 1845; then he removed to Richmond, Va., where he was sole editor of *The Watchman and Observer,* and then co-editor of *The Central Presbyterian.* During his residence in Richmond he preached wherever he found an open door, especially in the Virginia penitentiary. He died June 20, 1875. At seventy-five blindness began to come upon him, and he then applied himself to the memorizing of large portions of Scripture and the best hymns, that he might be able to continue his ministry long after his eyesight was gone. In all places where he could find hearers he was abundant in labors. See *Necrol. Report of Princeton Theol. Sem.* 1876, p. 8.

Gile, SAMUEL, D.D., a Congregational minister, son of major Ezekiel Gile, was born at Plaistow, N. H., July 23, 1780. He graduated from Dartmouth College in 1804; studied theology under Rev. Jonathan French; was ordained pastor of the Church in Milton, Mass., Feb. 18, 1807; and died in October, 1826. See Sprague, *Annals of the Amer. Pulpit,* i, 580.

Gilfillan, GEORGE, a minister of the Scotch Presbyterian Church, was born in Scotland, Jan. 30, 1813. He was educated at the Glasgow College and at the United Secession Hall. His first call was to a congregation at Schoolwynd, Dundee, where he continued his pastoral labors until his death, Aug. 13, 1878. In 1842 he began to write sketches of the principal characters of the day, for newspapers, and they were afterwards printed in book form under the title of *The Gallery of Literary Portraits.* This was followed by two other series of the same character. In 1850 he published *The Bards of the Bible,* which has been severely criticised for its grandiloquent style. He edited an edition of *Bryant's Poems,* and among his other works are, *The Book of British Poets, Ancient and Modern,* and *The Martyrs, Heroes, and Bards of the Scotch Covenant.* He also published, *The Grand Discovery:—History of a Man:—Christianity and our Era:—A Discourse on Hades:—*and *Five Discourses on the Abuse of Talent.* He finally edited a splendid library edition of the *Popular Poets of Britain,* with notes. (W. P. S.)

Gill, Alexander, D.D., an English clergyman, was born in London in 1597, and was educated at Trinity College, Oxford. In 1635 he became head master of St. Paul's school. While usher of St. Paul's he had charge of the education of John Milton. He died in 1642. See Chalmers, *Biog. Dict.* s. v.; Allibone, *Dict. of Brit. and Amer. Authors,* s. v.

Gill, Henry, D.D., an English Congregational minister, was born at Tiverton, Devonshire, in 1823. He was led to an early decision for Christ; entered Hackney College in 1844, and at the close of his curriculum, in 1848, became pastor at Haverhill, Suffolk. In 1864 he accepted an invitation from the committee of the Bible Society to visit its auxiliaries in North America. This mission occupied him more than eighteen months, in which he proved himself admirably adapted for the work. On his return to England, he was appointed one of the London district secretaries, his chief duties being connected with the Sunday-schools of all denominations in and around the metropolis. He died at Lewisham, Nov. 4, 1870. Dr. Gill was industrious, affectionate, acceptable, and successful in all his labors. In addition to a few tracts and pamphlets, he published, *Early at the Temple,* and *The True and Beautiful.* See (Lond.) *Cong. Year-book,* 1871, p. 311.

Gillane, JOHN, was consecrated a bishop in the Episcopal Church of Scotland in 1727, and bishop of Dunblane in 1731. See Allibone, *Dict. of Brit. and Amer. Authors,* s. v.

Gilles DE ROYE (Lat. *Ægidius de Roya* or *Roia*), a French chronicler and theologian, was born at Roye, Picardy. While very young he entered the ranks of the Cistercians, and was sent to Paris to complete his studies. He received the degree of doctor of theology, and taught for nineteen years in various colleges of the order of St. Bernard. He was then appointed abbot of Royanmont, Picardy. At the age of sixty he resigned these functions, and retired to the convent of the Dunes, Belgium, where he remained eighteen years, devoting his time to meditation and study. He died at the abbey of Sparmaille, near Bruges, in 1478. He wrote, *Opus Vastum Chronodromi seu Chronici,* an abridgment of the history of John Brandon, a monk of Dunes, remaining in manuscript. Gilles de Roye carried it down to 1463, and it was continued by Adrian of Budt, of the same convent, down to 1479. Andrew Schot discovered it about twenty years later, and it was published by Sweert (Frankfort, 1620). He also left some commentaries upon the *Master of Sentences.* See Hoefer, *Nouv. Biog. Générale,* s. v.

Gilles, JEAN, a French prelate, was born in Normandy. He studied theology and law at Paris, and became chanter of the metropolitan church there. Almost alone among the high clergy of France, Gilles refused to acknowledge Clement VII (Robert of Geneva). He abandoned his benefice, and retired to Italy to Urban VI, who made him provost of Liege and auditor of the Rota. He was afterwards sent by the sacred college as nuncio to Rheims, to Treves, and to Cologne. In 1405 Innocent VII made him cardinal, with the title of St. Cosmo and St. Damian. He assisted at the conclave, Nov. 30, 1406, which elected Gregory XII, but abandoned that pontiff when he discovered that the latter held his own interests as paramount to those of the Church, and that he rejected the means proposed for the termination of the schism (1408, 1409). Gilles returned to France, where he died about 1418. He left some fragmentary writings. See Hoefer, *Nouv. Biog. Générale*, s. v.

Gillespie, Thomas, father of the Relief Church in Scotland, was born at Clearburn, near Edinburgh, in 1708. He received a careful religious training, was educated at Edinburgh, Perth, and Northampton, licensed to preach in 1740, and ordained in England in January, 1741. In August following he settled as pastor of Carnock, where he continued with unwearied diligence and much success till 1752, when he was deposed from the Church of Scotland. He, however, continued actively engaged in preaching, first, in the churchyard of Carnock, beside the church which had so often echoed to his voice; but he was soon obliged to leave this spot and betake himself to another, from which he was speedily driven, and at last was compelled to take his position on the public highway, where, during the whole summer and autumn, he proclaimed the Gospel to immense multitudes of people. In the following September he removed to Dunfermline, where, in 1753, the Relief Church was founded. He continued with unabated zeal till his last sickness, which soon closed his life, Jan. 19, 1774. Mr. Gillespie was a man of truly apostolic excellence. Conscience was the power that bore sway in his soul. His intellectual abilities were excellent, but his goodness was his greatness. See *United Presbyterian Fathers*, p. 217; *Fasti Eccles. Scoticanæ*, ii, 580.

Gillet, Eliphalet, D.D., a Congregational minister, was born at Colchester, Conn., Nov. 19, 1768. After graduating from Dartmouth College in 1791, he taught school in Wethersfield. Under the direction of Rev. Dr. Spring, he studied theology at Newburyport. In August, 1795, he was ordained pastor of the Church in Hallowell, Me. At his own request he was dismissed from this charge in May, 1827. He died there, Oct. 19, 1848. Dr. Gillet was the pioneer of Congregationalism in that section of the state. When the Maine Missionary Society was organized in 1807, he was chosen its secretary, which office he filled until the close of his life. The cause of home missions had in him an earnest friend. His mind was of a superior order, and was highly cultivated. Addicted to metaphysical discussions, he was a ready, logical, and keen debater. See Sprague, *Annals of the Amer. Pulpit*, ii, 377.

Gillet, Louis Joachim, canon and librarian at the abbey of St. Genevieve, in Paris, was born July 28, 1680. In 1717 he was pastor at Mahon, in the Malo bishopric, but resigned his position in 1740. He died Aug. 28, 1753, leaving *Nouvelle Traduction de l'Historien Joséphe* (published after his death, 4 vols., 1756). See Jöcher, *Allgemeines Gelehrten-Lexikon*, s. v.; Winer, *Handbuch der theol. Lit.* i, 157. (B. P.)

Gillett, Ezra Hall, D.D., a Presbyterian minister, was born at Colchester, Conn., July 5, 1823. He graduated from Yale College in 1841, and from Union Theological Seminary, N. Y., in 1844. He remained a resident licentiate until 1845, when he was ordained pastor of the Presbyterian Church at Harlem. He continued in this charge, an efficient and successful pastor, until 1870, when he accepted the appointment of professor in the New York University, and occupied that position until his death, Sept. 2, 1875. Dr. Gillett wrote, besides frequent articles for the periodical press, a *Life of Huss* (1861):—*History of the Presbyterian Church* (1864):—*Moral System* (1875). (W. P. S.)

Gillette, Abram Dunn, D.D., a Baptist minister, was born at Cambridge, Washington Co., N. Y., Sept. 8, 1807. He studied in the preparatory department of Hamilton Institution, graduated from Union College, was ordained in Schenectady, and in May, 1831, became pastor of the Baptist Church in that place, where he remained four years, then removed to Philadelphia, and became pastor of the Sansom Street Church. In 1839, the Eleventh Street Church (Philadelphia) having been formed under his leadership, he became its pastor, holding that office until 1852, when he accepted a call to Calvary Church, as it is now called, in New York city. In 1864 he removed to Washington, D. C., and was pastor of the First Church in that city five years. He then went to England, where he delivered a series of lectures to the students of Mr. Spurgeon's college, and, for a time, was the stated supply of a Church near London. For two years after his return (1872–74), he was corresponding secretary of the American and Foreign Bible Society. From 1874 to 1879 he was pastor at Sing Sing, N. Y., which was his last regular pastorate. He died at his summer home, Bluff Head, on the shore of lake George, Aug. 24, 1882. Dr. Gillette was the author of several memorial volumes, and frequently contributed to various journals. See *The Watchman*, Aug. 31, 1882. (J. C. S.)

Gillette, Charles, D.D., a Protestant Episcopal clergyman, was born at Granby, Conn., in 1813. He graduated from Trinity College, Hartford, in 1838; soon after became one of the professors in the Virginia High School, near Alexandria; and afterwards a student in the theological seminary in that city. He was ordained in 1842, and in October of that year was sent out as a missionary to Texas; established himself at Houston, and successfully labored there and in the regions adjacent until the close of 1851. During the next five years he had charge of the diocesan school and of St. Paul's College. In 1856 he accepted the rectorship of St. David's Church, Austin, from which he removed to St. Paul's Church, Steubenville, O. He died in 1869. See *Amer. Quar. Church Rev.* Jan. 1870, p. 634.

Gillot, Jacques, canon of St. Chapelle, at Paris, who died in January, 1619, originally dean of the Church at Langres, is the author of *Instructions et Missives des Rois tres Chrétiens de France* (Paris, 1607; new and enlarged edition by P. Dupuy, 1654). See Jöcher, *Allgemeines Gelehrten-Lexikon*, s. v.; Winer, *Handbuch der theol. Lit.* ii, 668; Hoefer, *Nouv. Biog. Générale*, s. v. (B. P.)

Giloh. Lieut. Conder thinks (*Memoirs* to the Ordnance Survey, iii, 313) that this may be represented by the ruined site *Jâla*, which the Map lays down at three and a quarter miles north-west of Hebron; but he admits that we should not expect a location so far north.

Gimle, in Norse mythology, is *heaven*, or the most charming of all regions of the spirit world. As the ancient Scandinavians considered warlike plays and drinking the greatest of all joys, so also this imperishable heaven is furnished with weapons and golden drinking-horns. It is the eternal dwelling-place of Allfadur, the seat of all the good and pious, who there partake of undisturbed blessedness. At the destruction of the world, Walhalla, the ordinary seat of the deities, Asgard, and all that belongs to it, will be destroyed; even the still higher heaven, Aundlang, and the next highest seat of the light-spirits, Vidblain, will perish; but Gimle, extending high above all these, will not even be touched by the frightful Ragnarokr (destroyer), but will stand with the eternal god, to receive the valiant warriors and the slain asas.

Ginnunga-gap, the gulf of delusion, a vast, void abyss, which the ancient Scandinavians believed to be the primeval state of the material creation. Into this capacious gulf, light as imponderable ether, flowed from the south the envenomed streams of Elivagar (q. v.), and the farther they retired from their source the more the temperature became reduced, and at last the fluid mass congealed in Ginnunga-gap.

Ginzel, JOSEPH AUGUSTIN, a Roman Catholic theologian of Austria, was born in 1804 at Reichenberg, studied at Vienna, was in 1834 professor of ethics, in 1843 professor of Church history and canon law at the clerical seminary in Leitmeritz, Bohemia, and died June 1, 1876. He wrote, *Legatio Apostolica Petri Aloysii* (Würzburg, 1840):—*Geschichte der Kirche* (Vienna, 1846-47, 2 vols.):—*Die canonische Lehrweise der Geistlichen* (Ratisbon, 1852):—*Handbuch des neuesten in Oesterreich geltenden Kirchenrechtes* (Vienna, 1857, 2 vols.):—*Geschichte der Slawenapostel Cyrill* (Leitmeritz, eod.):—*Bischof Hurdalek* (Prague, 1873):—*Kirchen-historische Schriften* (Vienna, 1872, 2 vols.). See Zuchold, *Bibl. Theol.* i, 440 sq.; *Literarischer Handweiser für das Katholische Deutschland*, 1876, col. 288. (B. P.)

Giocondo, GIOVANNI, an eminent Italian architect and engineer, was born at Verona in 1435, went to Rome when quite young, and studied with great attention the models of antiquity. After the death of Bramante, at Rome, he was declared architect of St. Peter's. By this work, and many others, he gained great fame. He died at a very advanced age. See Hoefer, *Nouv. Biog. Générale*, s. v.; Spooner, *Biog. Hist. of the Fine Arts*, s. v.

Giöll, in Scandinavian mythology, was a river which separated the land of shades from earth. It was crossed by a bridge of gold.

Giona, GIOVANNI BATTISTA. See BATTISTA.

Giordano, LUCA (called *Fa Presto*), an eminent Italian painter, was born at Naples in 1632, and was instructed in the school of Giuseppe Ribera. He spent some time at Rome, where he improved rapidly. There is a picture by him in the palace at Madrid, representing *The Nativity*, which, from its excellence, is often taken for a production of Raphael. In 1692 he was appointed painter to the king of Spain. He executed the sacristy of the cathedral at Toledo; the vault of the royal chapel at Madrid. In 1702 he went to Naples, where he had so many commissions that he could scarcely fulfill them. He painted an altar-piece in the Church of the Ascension, at Naples, which is considered one of his best works. Probably no artist ever produced as many pictures as he did. He died at Naples, Jan. 12, 1705. The following are some of his excellent productions: *Elijah calling Fire from Heaven; The Virgin and Infant Jesus; St. Joseph and St. John; Magdalene Penitent; The Adulteress before Christ; Christ Disputing with the Doctors; St. Anne Received into Heaven by the Virgin.* See Hoefer, *Nouv. Biog. Générale*, s. v; Spooner, *Biog. Hist. of the Fine Arts*, s. v.

Giorgi, ANTONIO AUGUSTINO, an Italian philologist, was born in 1711 at Santo Mauro, near Rimini. He entered the order of St. Augustine in 1727, and became procurator-general of his order, which position he occupied for eighteen years. He destroyed the old scholastic routines which controlled the schools directed by the Augustinians. His zeal for the maintenance of a pure faith led him to take part in various theological discussions, and near the close of his life he sustained a lively controversy against P. Paulin, of St. Bartholomew, concerning the religion of the Brahmins. He taught theology in various places, especially at the grand college of Rome, whither he was called by pope Benedict XIV. This pontiff charged him with making the apology for the *History of Pelagianism* of cardinal Noris. Being satisfied with the manner in which this was executed, he confided to the author the direction of the Angelican library, and admitted him to the number of learned men whom he consulted upon ecclesiastical affairs. Giorgi had studied eleven languages, among which we may mention Greek, Hebrew, Chaldee, Samaritan, and Syriac. But his erudition was more varied than profound. He died at Rome, May 4, 1797. He wrote a number of works, for which see Hoefer, *Nouv. Biog. Générale*, s. v.

Giorgione. See BARBARELLI.

Giotto, ANGIOLOTTO (called *Ambrogiotto* and *Giotto di Bondone*), a famous ancient Italian painter and architect, was born at Vespignano, near Florence, in 1276. One of his earliest works is a picture of *The Annunciation*, which is considered very beautiful. He was highly honored, and his works were in great demand. The noble families of Verona, Milan, Ravenna, Urbino, and Bologna were eager to possess his works. In 1316 he was employed at Padua to paint the chapel of the Nunziata all' Arena. In 1325 he was invited to Naples by king Robert, to paint the Church of Santa Chiara, which he decorated with subjects from the New Test. and the *Mysteries of the Apocalypse*. He was also distinguished in the art of mosaic, and executed the famous *Death of the Virgin*, at Florence. As an architect he erected the bell-tower of Santa Maria del Fiore. He died at Florence, Jan. 8, 1336. See Hoefer, *Nouv. Biog. Générale*, s. v.; Spooner, *Biog. Hist. of the Fine Arts*, s. v.

Giovanni (BATTISTA) DI TOLEDO, an eminent Spanish sculptor and architect, flourished about 1550. He visited Rome for improvement, and acquired great reputation. He was invited to Naples by the viceroy, don Pietro di Toledo, who appointed him state architect. He erected the Church of San Giacomo degli Spagnuoli. This work gained for him such a reputation that Philip II appointed him architect of all the royal works of Spain. He removed to Spain in 1559, and began the erection of the Escurial three years later. He continued to superintend this work until his death in 1567.

Giovanni DI MATTEO (or *Matteo di Giovanni*), an eminent Sienese painter, flourished from 1450 to 1491. He painted first in his native city in fresco. His masterpiece was the *Murder of the Innocents*, a subject which he repeated both at Siena and at Naples. Some of his paintings are still to be found in the collections of noble houses at Siena.

Giovanni DI PAOLO, a reputable painter of Siena, flourished about 1457. There are some of his works in the churches at Siena. His *Descent from the Cross*, in the Osservanza, painted in 1461, is considered good.

Giovanni DA PISA, an eminent Italian sculptor and architect, the son of Niccolo da Pisa, flourished during the early part of the 14th century. He erected the public cemetery at Pisa, at Naples the façade of the cathedral, and at Siena the tribune of the cathedral. He executed many works at Arezzo, Orvieto, Perugia, Pistoja, and elsewhere.

Girac, FRANÇOIS (*Bareau de*), a French prelate, was born at Angouleme in 1732. Destined from his infancy for the ecclesiastical calling, he was appointed successively vicar-general of the diocese of Angouleme, dean of the cathedral, and sent by the ecclesiastical province of Tours to the assembly of the clergy in 1765. His uprightness and conciliatory spirit led to his being called soon after, in 1766, to the bishopric of St. Brieuc, and three years later to that of Rennes, where he remained until the Revolution. Being then forced to go into exile, he attached himself successively to prince de Metternich, and Stanislas Poniatowski, last king of Poland. Returning to France, Girac, who counted thirty-five years in the episcopacy, sent in his resignation, in view of his long labors and feeble health, and accepted a canonship in the chapter of St. Denis. He died Nov. 29, 1820. See Hoefer, *Nouv. Biog. Générale*, s. v.

Girard la Pucelle (Lat. *Giraldus Puella*), professor of ecclesiastical law at Paris in the 12th century, and bishop of Coventry. He took a lively part in the contests which St. Thomas of Canterbury sustained against the king of England, and after a life full of agitation, having for a long time resided at Cologne, he went to England, was appointed bishop, and died soon after, in 1184. Many of his contemporaries bestow great praise upon his knowledge of theology, philosophy, and jurisprudence; but none of his works remain. See Hoefer, *Nouv. Biog. Générale*, s. v.

Girard, François, a French ecclesiastic, was born about 1735 at La Guillotiere (at that time dependent upon Dauphiny, and still one of the suburbs of Lyons). He established himself in Paris, where he was appointed, in 1781, rector of the parish of St. Landry. At the commencement of the revolution he showed great enthusiasm for the new ideas, and was one of the first rectors of Paris to submit to the civil constitution of the clergy. These patriotic sentiments gave him a kind of popularity, which, after the suppression of his church, in 1791, caused his election to one of the episcopal vicarages of bishop Gobel. Two years later the convention appointed him to assist Marie Antoinette in her last moments, and to conduct her to the scaffold. Appointed canon of the Church of Notre Dame, at Paris, after the restoration of Catholic worship, at his own expense he repaired the chapel and gave an annuity for its preservation. He died at Paris, Nov. 7, 1811. An anonymous treatise, entitled *Instruction sur la Constitution Civile du Clergè*, etc., published at Paris in 1791, is cited by Barbier in his *Dict. des Anonymes*, No. 8721, and given to an author named Gérard. See Hoefer, *Nouv. Biog. Générale*, s. v.

Girard (*de Ville-Thierry*), **Jean**, an ascetical writer of Paris, where he died in 1709, is the author of, *Le Véritable Pénitent:—Le Chemin du Ciel:—La Vie des Vierges:—Des Gens Mariés:—Des Veuves:—Des Religieux:—Des Religieuses:—Des Riches:—Des Pauvres:—Des Saints:—Des Clercs:—Le Chrétien Étranger sur la Terre:—Traité de la Flatterie:—Traité de la Médisance:—Vie de Jésus-Christ dans l'Eucharistie:—Le Chrétien dans la Tribulation:—La Vie de S. Jean de Dieu*. See Jöcher, *Allgemeines Gelehrten-Lexikon*, s. v.; Hoefer, *Nouv. Biog. Générale*, s. v. (B. P.)

Girard, Stephen, an American philanthropist, was born at Bordeaux, France, May 21, 1750. He began life as a sailor at the age of thirteen, and ten years later became a master and captain. He settled in Philadelphia, Pa., in May, 1777, and began his eminently successful mercantile career. During the prevalence of the yellow fever in Philadelphia in 1793, 1797–98, raging with unwonted violence, Mr. Girard devoted himself personally, fearless of all risks, to the care of the sick and the burial of the dead, not only in the hospital, of which he became manager, but throughout the city, supplying the sufferers with money and provisions. Two hundred children, whose parents died of the fever, were in a great measure intrusted to his care. In 1812 he purchased the building and a large part of the stock of the old United States bank, and commenced business as a private banker, with a capital of $1,200,000, which was afterwards increased to $4,000,000. During the war of 1812 he rendered valuable services to the government by placing at its disposal the resources of his bank, and subscribing with unexampled liberality to its loans. He died Dec. 26, 1831. He contributed liberally to all public improvements, and erected many handsome buildings in the city of Philadelphia. He was profuse in his public charities, but exacting to the last fraction due him. Notwithstanding his extraordinary attentions to the sick, he never had a friend. He was a freethinker in religion, and an ardent admirer of Voltaire and Rousseau. Although he was uneducated, his success in business had been such that his property at the time of his death amounted to about $9,000,000. Of this vast estate he bequeathed only $140,000 to his relatives. The remainder was devoted to various public charities, including hospitals, asylums, schools, etc.; $500,000 to the city of Philadelphia; $300,000 to the state of Pennsylvania; and his principal bequest, which was $2,000,000, besides certain other property, together with a plot of ground in Philadelphia, for the erection and support of a college for orphans. The most minute directions were given in regard to the buildings to be erected, and the admission and management of the inmates. He required that the pupils be instructed in the purest principles of morality, but they must be left free to adopt such religious tenets as their matured reason may lead them to prefer. No ecclesiastic, minister, or missionary of any sect whatever is allowed to hold any connection with the college, or even be admitted to the premises as a visitor. The officers and instructors of the institution are eighteen in number, and the inmates about five hundred.

Girardet, Jean, a reputable French painter, was born at Luneville, Dec. 13, 1709, instructed in the school of Claude Charles, and after spending some time there went to Italy, where he remained eight years studying the works of the great masters. There are many of his works at Metz, Verdun, and other cities of Lorraine. His *Descent from the Cross*, in one of the churches at Nancy, is considered his best production. He died at Nancy, Sept. 2, 1778. See Hoefer, *Nouv. Biog. Générale*, s. v.; Spooner, *Biog. Hist. of the Fine Arts*, s. v.

Girardon, François, an eminent French sculptor, was born at Troyes (Champagne), March 16, 1628, studied with care the statues in the churches of Troyes, and produced a picture of *The Virgin*, which was much admired. In 1657 he was admitted to the Academy at Paris; in 1659 was appointed professor; became director in 1674, and chancellor in 1695. There are many of his productions in France. The mausoleum of cardinal Richelieu, in the Church of the Sorbonne, was considered his masterpiece. He died in 1715. See Hoefer, *Nouv. Biog. Générale*, s. v.; Spooner, *Biog. Hist. of the Fine Arts*, s. v.

Giraud, Pierre, a French cardinal, was born at Montferrand, Aug. 11, 1791. Belonging to an ancient family, he was designed for the magistracy, but at the age of fifteen went to the seminary of Clermont to study philosophy, and while there developed a taste for belles-lettres and ancient classics. In October, 1812, he entered the seminary of St. Sulpice, where he studied theology and the sacred Scriptures. Three years later he was ordained priest. In 1818 he was sent as a missionary to Auvergne. He was rector of the cathedral of Clermont in 1825, when he was invited to preach during Lent at the Tuileries. A royal ordinance appointed him to the see of Rodez, Jan. 9, 1830. He was one of the signers of a criticism concerning certain propositions taken from the *Avenir*, and sent to the court of Rome by the archbishop of Toulouse. He was appointed archbishop of Cambray, Dec. 4, 1841. He was made cardinal, June 11, 1847, and Jan. 4, 1849, went to Gaeta, where Pius IX was a refugee. It was supposed with some reason that he was commissioned by MM. de Falloux and Drouyn de Lhuys to induce the pope to accept the hospitality of France. He died at Cambray, April 17, 1850. The works of Giraud have been collected and published several times. The third edition appeared in 1852. See Hoefer, *Nouv. Biog. Générale*, s. v.

Girdle, Ecclesiastical (*ζώνη*, *balteus*, or *cingulum*), a cord of linen, silk, worsted, or other material, with tassels at the extremities, by which the alb is bound round the waist of him who assumes it. It is fastened on the left side. When putting it on, the cleric says the following prayer, or one equivalent to it in terms: "Præcinge me, Domine, zona justitiæ, et constringe in me dilectionem Dei et proximi." This cincture is as old as the days of St. Gregory the Great; formerly ample in size, and broad, and often adorned with gold and gems. In the 6th century it was first reduced to its present narrow dimensions. It represented the cord with which our Lord was bound; and alludes to Luke xii, 35; Eph. vi, 4; 1 Pet. i, 13.

Girdle of St. Austin, FRATERNITY OF THE, a devotional society of the Roman Church. The girdle which they wear is made of leather, and they allege that it was worn by the Virgin Mary, John the Baptist, and many patriarchs and prophets.

Girdle of St. Francis. See FRANCIS, ST., FRATERNITY OF THE GIRDLE OF.

Girdlestone, CHARLES, a minister of the Church of England, was born March 6, 1797, and graduated at Oxford in 1818. He became successively fellow of Balliol College, university examiner, vicar of Sedgeley (Staffordshire) in 1826, rector of Alderley (Cheshire) in 1837, of Kingswinford (Staffordshire) in 1847, and died April 28, 1881, at Weston-super-Mare. He was a voluminous writer on theological subjects, from the Low-Church point of view, and published, among other religious works, *A Family Commentary on the Bible* (1832-42):—*The Book of Psalms*, according to the two authorized translations, in parallel columns, with marginal notes (1836):—*Christendom Sketched from History in the Light of Holy Scriptures* (1870). (B. P.)

Girodet-Trioson, ANNE LOUIS, an eminent French painter, was born at Montargis, Feb. 5, 1767, studied under David, and at the age of twenty gained the prize of the Academy for his picture of *Joseph's Meeting with his Brethren.* He gained great eminence in France by his picture of *The Deluge.* Many of his works are in the private collections of France. He died at Paris, Dec. 9, 1824. See Hoefer, *Nouv. Biog. Générale*, s. v.; Spooner, *Biog. Hist. of the Fine Arts*, s. v.

Giron (*Garcias de Loyasa*), *Don* PEDRO, a Spanish prelate and scholar, was born at Talavera in 1542. He was the son of Pedro Giron, member of the Council of Castile. He pursued his philosophical and theological studies at Alcala. Being appointed canon of Toledo, he became archdeacon of Guadalaxara on the withdrawal of his uncle, Lopez de Carnajel. In 1585 Philip II called him to his court as almoner and master of the chapel, and a little later intrusted to him the teaching of his little son, don Philip. In 1596 cardinal Albert of Austria appointed him grand-vicar of the archbishopric of Toledo. In 1598 he obtained the title of archbishop of the diocese which he governed. He died Feb. 22, 1599, leaving some works, for which see Hoefer, *Nouv. Biog. Générale*, s. v.

Gisbert, Blaise, a French Jesuit, born at Cahors, Feb. 21, 1657, and died Feb. 28, 1731, is the author of, *Le bon Gout de l'Éloquence Chrétienne* (Lyons, 1702):—*Éloquence Chrétienne dans l'Idée et dans la Pratique* (1714; with Zenfant's notes, Amsterdam, 1728; Germ. transl. by J. Val. Kornrumpf, Leipsic, 1740). See Winer, *Handbuch der theol. Lit.* ii, 61; Jöcher, *Allgemeines Gelehrten-Lexikon*, s. v. (B. P.)

Gisbert, Jean, a French canonist, was born at Cahors, Jan. 2, 1639. He entered the Jesuit order Oct. 2, 1654; for fifteen years taught rhetoric and philosophy at Tours; then theology for eighteen years at Toulouse, and afterwards became provincial of Languedoc. He died Aug. 5, 1711, leaving, among other works, *In Summam Sancti Thomæ Quæstiones* (1670):—*Vera Idea Theologiæ* (Toulouse, 1676; revised and enlarged, 1689):—*Scientia Religionis Universa* (vol. i, Paris, 1689). See Hoefer, *Nouv. Biog. Générale*, s. v.

Gitano (or Spanish Gypsy) Version OF THE SCRIPTURES. This version is intended for the gypsies (Gypsy being in Spanish *Gitano*). For the history of these people, and the translation of the gospel of St. Luke for them, compare the article *Gypsies.* In consequence of a fresh demand for the book, the translator has re-translated his former work, which was printed in 1873. Some copies have been sent out to Spain, and satisfactory tidings have been received concerning their acceptance among the gypsies.

Giustiniani, Agostino, an Italian Orientalist of the preaching order, was born at Genoa in 1470. At the age of fourteen years he entered the convent of the Dominicans of Santa Marie del Castello, at Genoa. By the authority of the doge and the archbishop of Genoa, his parents sent him to Valencia, in Aragon, where he contracted a serious disease. This caused him to again adopt his former project, and he returned to Pavia, took the Dominican habit in 1488, and changed his Christian name from *Pantaleon* to *Agostino.* The study of Greek, Arabic, Hebrew, and Chaldee so absorbed his attention that he neglected theology and philosophy, and indifferently performed his duties as preacher and confessor. He taught in several schools of his order, but in 1514 resigned his duties as professor in order to devote himself exclusively to the editing of a polyglot Bible. Being appointed bishop of Nebbio, in Corsica, he assisted in 1516-17 at the Lateran council, and contested some articles of the concordat with Francis I and Leo X. The cardinal having fallen into disgrace, the bishop of Nebbio withdrew to Boniface Ferrier, bishop of Ivrea. Francis I, then ruler of the country of Giustiniani, invited him to remain in his kingdom. The king increased his pension, and appointed him professor of Hebrew in the University of Paris. Giustiniani was the first who taught this language there. He remained five years in France, during which time he made a voyage to the Netherlands and England, where he met with Erasmus and Thomas Morus. Recalled to his diocese by certain affairs, he remained there most of the time until his death, which occurred while returning from Genoa to Corsica, in 1586. He wrote a number of works, for mention of which see Hoefer, *Nouv. Biog. Générale*, s. v.

Giustiniani, Angelo, an Italian prelate, was born on Scio in 1520. He joined the Franciscan order, went to Italy provided with valuable manuscripts, taught theology at Padua and Genoa, and accompanied cardinal Ferrara to France. Giustiniani took part in the discussion of Poissy, then was appointed grand almoner of the duke of Savoy, and bishop of Geneva. He assisted at the Council of Trent. Pope Pius IV confided to him an important negotiation with the king of France, in which he acquitted himself well. In 1578 he was obliged to resign his bishopric on account of a violent attack of gout. He died Feb. 22, 1596, leaving *Commentarii in Quædam Capita Sancti Johannis*:—*Sermones.* See Hoefer, *Nouv. Biog. Générale*, s. v.

Giustiniani, Fabiano, an Italian prelate and theologian, was born at Lerma, a diocese of Genoa, in 1578. His father changed his original name of *Taranchetti* for that of *Giustiniani*, having been adopted by a family of that name, not wishing to take part in the conspiracy of Luigi Fieschi. In 1597 he entered the congregation of St. Philip of Neri, and was placed in charge of the library of Santa Maria de Vallicelli, and he there formed a taste for study. In 1616 he was appointed bishop of Ajaccio, at which place he died, Jan. 3, 1627. He wrote *Index Universalis Materiarum Biblicarum* (Rome, 1612). This work contains many bibliographical errors. He also wrote other works. See Hoefer, *Nouv. Biog. Générale*, s. v.

Giustiniani (*of Chios*), **Leonardo,** an Italian prelate of Genoese origin, lived in 1453. He was archbishop of Mitylene when that island was taken by the Turks. He left a letter upon the subject of the taking of Constantinople, addressed to pope Nicholas V, and some other works, for which see Hoefer, *Nouv. Biog. Générale*, s. v.

Giustiniani, Orazio, an Italian cardinal and theologian, was born at Genoa near the close of the 16th century. He was of that branch of the Giustiniani family to which the isle of Chios belonged. Having studied theology at Rome, he entered, at the age of twenty-five years, the congregation of priests of St. Philip of Neri, and advanced rapidly to the higher positions of his order. Urban VIII appointed him first librarian of the library of the Vatican. He was charged with an important negotiation with the patriarch of Constantinople, and acquitted himself so much to the satisfaction of the pope that he bestowed upon him as a reward the bishopric of Montalto, in 1640. He restored harmony between the bishops of Montalto and the inhabitants of that place. In 1645 Innocent X appointed him bishop of Nocera, and the year following he was made cardinal, with the title of St. Onuphrius. Soon after the pope chose him as his grand penitentiary. He became again first librarian of the Vatican library, and died at Rome in 1649. See Hoefer, *Nouv. Biog. Générale*, s. v.

Giustiniani (*Di Moniglia*), **Paolo**, an Italian prelate and commentator, was born at Genoa in 1444. He was the son of Pietro Pellegro Giustiniani, ambassador to the duke of Milan. At the age of nineteen years Paolo entered the order of Minorite preachers. Some years later he was made doctor of theology, and elected prior of the convent of St. Dominic, at Genoa. In 1484 he was regent of the studies of his order at Perugia. When, at the death of Sixtus IV, the Genoese were expelled from the States of the Church, Giustiniani returned to his native country and devoted himself to preaching. In 1486 he was elected provincial of Lombardy, and in 1489 Innocent VIII chose him as master of the sacred palace. This pontiff confided to him several important missions, and in 1494 appointed him inquisitor-general of all the Genoese possessions. In 1498 Alexander VI made him apostolic commissary, and authorized him, with the governor of Rome, to examine a large number of Christians accused of heresy. In this he distinguished himself by the severity of his judgments. He was one of the judges who, in September, 1498, condemned Pietro d' Aranda, bishop of Calaharra, and steward of the pope, to perpetual imprisonment as guilty of Judaism and other errors. He was recompensed for his zeal by the gift of the bishopric of Scio, and being sent as legate to Hungary. He died at Buda in 1502, leaving commentaries upon some of the books of the Bible. See Hoefer, *Nouv. Biog. Générale*, s. v.

Gladiators, *Christian Views Concerning.*—Some pagan moralists expressed more or less strongly their disapprobation of the gladiatorial shows, as being inhuman and demoralizing; but they were too popular to be checked by such remonstrances; and nothing effectual was done to stop them until they were opposed and finally suppressed by the intervention of Christian principles and Christian heroism.

The Church expressed its abhorrence of these barbarous games as soon as it came in contact with them, not only by discountenancing attendance at them, but by refusing to admit gladiators to Christian baptism. Charioteers, racers, and many others are included in the same condemnation; probably because the public exhibitions in which they took a part were more or less connected with idolatry. For the same reason such persons, if they had already been received into the Church, were to be punished by excommunication.

The first imperial edict prohibiting the exhibition of gladiators was issued by Constantine in A.D. 325, just after the Council of Nice had been convened. Forty years later, Valentinian forbade that any Christian criminals should be condemned to fight as gladiators; and in A.D. 367 he included in a similar exemption those who had been in the imperial service about the court.

In the year 404, while a show of gladiators were exhibiting at Rome in honor of the victories of Stilicho, an Asiatic monk named Telemachus, who had come to Rome for the purpose of endeavoring to stop this barbarous practice, rushed into the amphitheatre, and strove to separate the combatants. The spectators—enraged at his attempt to deprive them of their favorite amusement—stoned him to death. But a deep impression was produced. Telemachus was justly honored as a martyr, and the emperor Honorius, taking advantage of the feeling which had been evoked, effectually put a stop to gladiatorial combats, which were never exhibited again.

Gladstanes, George, a Scotch prelate, was a native of Dundee, and minister at St. Andrews; was preferred by the king to the see of Caithness in 1600; and thence was translated to the see of St. Andrews in 1606, but was not consecrated until 1610. He was called commissioner for uniting the two kingdoms in 1604. He died May 2, 1615. See Keith, *Scottish Bishops*, p. 41-217.

Glaire, Jean Baptiste, a French Orientalist, was born at Bordeaux, April 1, 1798, and died in 1879. He published, *Lexicon Manuale Hebraïcum et Chaldaïcum* (1830; new ed. 1843):—*Principes de Grammaire Hébraïque et Chaldaïque* (1832; 3d ed. 1843):—*Chrestomathie Hébraïque et Chaldaïque* (1834, 3 vols.):—*Torath Mosché, le Pentateuque* (1836-37, 2 vols.):—*Introduction Historique et Critique aux Livres Saints* (1836, 6 vols.; 2d ed. 1843):—*Les Livres Saints Vengés* (1845, 2 vols.; 2d ed. 1874, 3 vols.):—*La Bible selon la Vulgate* (1863):—*Dictionnaire Universel des Sciences Ecclésiastiques* (1868, 2 vols.), besides contributing to the *Encyclopédie du XIX Siècle*, *Encyclopédie Catholique*, and *Biographie Catholique*. See Lichtenberger, *Encyclop. des Sciences Religieuses*, s. v. (B. P.)

Gläsener, Justus Martin, a Lutheran theologian of Germany, was born Oct. 8, 1696, at Hildesheim. He studied at Helmstädt and Halle, was in 1727 preacher at his native place, and took the degree of doctor of theology in 1733. On account of controversies with his superiors and colleagues, he was deposed from his office, and died at Vienna, Jan. 22, 1750. He wrote, *De Intercessione Beatorum Particulari*:—*De Dracone Insigni Regum Ægyptiorum ad Ezech. xxix–xxxii*:—*Specimen anti-Judaicum de Genuino Judæorum Messia*:—*De Demonstratione Spiritus S. Jesum esse Verum Messiam*:—*Diatribe Philologica de R. Simeone Filio Jochai, Auctore Libri Sohar*:—*Diss. de Trinitate Rabbinorum et Cabbalistarum non Christiana sed Mere Platonica.* See Neubauer, *Nachricht von jetztlebenden Gottesgelehrten*; Jöcher, *Allgemeines Gelehrten-Lexikon*, s. v.; Winer, *Handbuch der theol. Lit.* i, 422. (B. P.)

Glauch, Andreas, a Lutheran theologian of Germany, was born at Leipsic, April 17, 1637. In 1666 he was superintendent at Bitterfeld, in 1668 pastor in Merseburg, in 1679 archdeacon at Leipsic, and died July 11, 1681. He published, *Schediasma de usu Concordantiarum Biblicarum* (Leipsic, 1668):—*De Adventu Messiæ*:—*De Corona Christi Spinea*:—*De Victu Jo. Baptistæ*:—*De Rege Agrippa*. See Winer, *Handbuch der theol. Lit.* i, 109; Fürst, *Bibl. Jud.* i, 335; Jöcher, *Allgemeines Gelehrten-Lexikon*, s. v. (B. P.)

Gleich, Johann Andreas, a Lutheran theologian of Germany, was born at Gera, Sept. 30, 1666. He studied at Wittenberg, was in 1690 deacon at Torgau, in 1696 court-preacher at Dresden, in 1722 member of consistory, and took the degree as doctor of theology in 1724. He died Aug. 1, 1734, leaving, *Diss. de Liturgiis Orientalibus* (Wittenberg, 1724):—*De S. Eucharistia Moribundis et Mortuis Olim Data* (1690):—*Annales Ecclesiasticæ* (Dresden, 1730, 3 parts), etc. See Winer, *Handbuch der theol. Lit.* i, 602, 632, 800; Fürst, *Bibl. Jud.* i, 336; Jöcher, *Allgemeines Gelehrten-Lexikon*, s. v. (B. P.)

Gleig, George, LL.D., a Scotch prelate, was born at Boghall, Kincardineshire, May 12, 1753, and educated at King's College, Aberdeen. He took orders in his twenty-first year, and was ordained to the pastoral charge of a congregation at Pittenweem, Fifeshire, whence he removed in 1790 to Stirling. He was twice chosen bishop of Dunkeld, but the opposition of the primate rendered the election null. In 1808 he was consecrated assistant and successor to the bishop of Brechin, in 1810 was preferred to the sole charge, and in 1816 was elected primate of the Episcopal Church of Scotland. He died at Stirling, in February, 1839. He was a frequent contributor to the *Monthly Review*, the *Gentleman's Magazine*, the *Anti-Jacobin Review*, and the *British Critic*. He also wrote several articles for the third edition of the *Encyclopædia Britannica*, and on the death of the editor, Colin Macfarquhar, in 1793, was engaged to edit the remaining volumes. He also published, *Directions for the Study of Theology* (1827):—various *Sermons*, and other works. See Walker, *Life of Bishop Gleig* (1879); *Encyclop. Brit.* 9th ed. s. v.

Glendoning, Matthew, a Scotch prelate, was a canon of Glasgow, and was afterwards made bishop of that see in 1389. He appears to have sat there until his death in 1408. See Keith, *Scottish Bishops*, p. 246.

Glöckner, Hieronymus Georg, a German philosopher, was born at Freiberg in 1715. He studied at Leipsic, was in 1741 bachelor, in 1742 magister, and in 1754 professor of philosophy. He died Feb. 5, 1757. Besides his contributions to Teller's *Bible-Work*, and translation of Calmet's *Biblical Dictionary* into German, he wrote, *De Libertate Dei Adversus Recentiores Quosdam Philosophos:—De Wetstenianæ ἑρμηνείας in N. Test. Vitiis* (Leipsic, 1754). See Jöcher, *Allgemeines Gelehrten-Lexikon*, s. v.; Winer, *Handbuch der theol. Lit.* i, 133. (B. P.)

Glöckner, Johann, a Reformed minister of Germany, was born Aug. 21, 1667. He studied at Marburg, and died at Rinteln, Dec. 29, 1716, professor of Greek and preacher there. He wrote, *Disp. in Genes.* i, 24, 25:—*De Gemina Accentuatione Decalogi:—De Cognitione Dei Naturali*. See Strieder, *Hessische Gelehrten Geschichte*; Jöcher, *Allgemeines Gelehrten-Lexikon*, s. v. (B. P.)

Glörfeld, Christian Benedict, a Protestant theologian, was born in 1747 at Bernau, in Brandenburg, and died there, June 24, 1809, provost and first preacher. He published, *Der Katechismus Luthers Erklärt* (Berlin, 1791):—*Predigten über freie Texte* (ibid. 1793):—*Gespräche über biblische Erzählungen und Gleichnisse* (ibid. 1795, 1798). See Döring, *Die gelehrten Theologen Deutschlands*, s. v.; Winer, *Handbuch der theol. Lit.* ii, 163, 213, 271. (B. P.)

Glossa Ordinaria, the common exegetical manual of the Middle Ages. It consisted of short explanatory remarks, compiled by Walafrid Strabo, following for the most Rabanus Maurus.

Glover, Livingston M., D.D., a Presbyterian minister, was born at Phelps, Ontario Co., N. Y., in 1820, and, after having received the necessary training, entered the Western Reserve College, graduating in 1840. He afterwards graduated at Lane Theological Seminary, and was ordained pastor of the Presbyterian Church at Jacksonville, Ill., where he labored with great success for upwards of thirty years. He was a delegate of the General Assembly to the Free Church of Scotland. He died at Jacksonville, July 15, 1880. See (N. Y.) *Observer*, July 20, 1880. (W. P. S.)

Gloves (*χειροθήκη, gantus*). It would seem that gloves, in the strict sense of the word, were unknown to the early Greeks and Romans (Casaubon, *Animadv. in Athen.* xii, 2). That they were in use, however, among the ancient Persians appears from Xenophon (*Cyropæd.* viii, 8, 17). The European custom of wearing them seems to have originated with the German nations, as the Teutonic origin of the common Latin word for them clearly shows: and although, as an ecclesiastical vestment, properly so called, gloves do not appear till the 12th century (the first extant mention of them in that character being as late as A.D. 1152), they had been used for centuries as articles of practical convenience. Thus we find them mentioned in the life of St. Columbanus, by Jonas Bobbiensis (formerly included among the works of Bede, c. 25). In this instance, the gloves are spoken of as used "for purposes of labor," but sometimes they were obviously of a costly natures, for in the will of Riculfus, bishop of Helena (ob. A.D. 915), in a long list of valuable articles, he mentions "one pair of gloves" (Migne, *Patrol.* cxxxii, 468).

Gloves symbolized the hiding of iniquity by the merits of our Saviour, and recalled the blessing upon Jacob when he wore gloves of skins. William of Wykeham's gloves are preserved at New College, Oxford. Candidates for degrees in medicine formerly gave gloves to the graduates of the faculty in that university, in return for their escort to the doors of the convocation house. Bishop Ken contributed to the rebuilding of St. Paul's the cost of his consecration dinner and a hundred pairs of gloves. At St. Andrew's, Holborn, the clergy were given gloves at Easter, and some noblemen used to send a pair to any bishop or dean whom they heard preach. In 1636 the University of Oxford presented gloves to the members of the royal family and king Charles I.

Glück, Ernest, a Lutheran theologian, was born in Saxony, Nov. 10, 1652. He studied at Wittenberg and Leipsic, and accepted a call extended to him by the general superintendent, John Fischer, in 1673, to Livonia. On his settlement in Livonia he was grieved to find that the people were still destitute of the Scriptures in their vernacular tongue. He therefore applied himself assiduously to the task of producing a translation of the entire Scriptures from the sacred originals; and with this object in view he repaired to Hamburg, there to qualify himself for the undertaking, by studying Hebrew under Edzardi, the celebrated Hebraist. After his return from Hamburg, in 1680, he was appointed military-preacher at Dünamünde, where he also adopted Catharine Badendiek, afterwards empress of Russia, as his daughter. In 1683, Glück was appointed pastor at Marienburg, in Livonia, and translated the Bible into the Lettish, which was published at Riga in 1689, the New Test. having been published in 1685. When Marienburg was taken by Peter the Great (Aug. 6, 1702), Glück was transported with other citizens as prisoners to Moscow. Owing, however, to the fact that he had been the foster-father of Catharine, he was soon released, and was appointed inspector of all the high-schools of Moscow. Here he studied the Russian language, and commenced a translation of the New Test. into the Russian tongue. He died, however, May 5, 1705, before finishing his task. (B. P.)

Glückselig, August Legis, an archæologist, who died at Prague, Jan. 28, 1867, is the author of *Christus-Archäologie* (Prague, 1862). See Zuchold, *Bibl. Theol.* i, 447. (B. P.)

Glycas, Michael (Μιχαήλ ὁ Γλυκᾶς), a Byzantine historian, probably of the 12th century, was a native either of Constantinople or Sicily (hence called *Siculus*). He wrote some letters to the last Constantine, and a *History* (Βίβλος χρονική), in four parts, from the Creation to the death of Alexis I Comnenus (1118), first published in a Latin translation by Leunslavius (Basle, 1572, 8vo; best ed. by Bekker, in the Bonn collection of the Byzantines, 1836, 8vo).

Glycis, John (Ἰωάννης ὁ Γλύκις), or perhaps *Glycas* (Γλυκᾶς), was patriarch of Constantinople from 1316 to 1320. He was regarded as a man of great wisdom and oratorical skill. Nicephorus, who was his pupil, praised him greatly. At length, enfeebled by age and disease, Glycis resigned the dignity of patriarch, and retired to the monastery of Cynotissa. Being an elegant and correct writer, he attempted to purify the Greek language from the barbarisms with which it was surcharged. For mention of his works see Hoefer, *Nouv. Biog. Générale*, s. v.

Gobat, Samuel, D.D., missionary bishop of Jerusalem, was born Jan. 26, 1799, at Cremine, a village near

Munster, in the canton of Berne. In 1821 he entered the missionary seminary at Basle, and in 1824 went to Paris for the purpose of continuing his Oriental studies, particularly Arabic, under the celebrated Sylvester de Sacy. In 1825 he entered into the service of the Church Missionary Society at London, and in the year following embarked upon his mission to Abyssinia. But owing to the unsettled state of that country, he could not begin operations until 1830, and left in 1832. He returned in 1834, but sickness prevented his working, and so, in September, 1836, he returned to Europe. From 1839 to 1842 he was at Malta, assiduously engaged in revising the Arabic Bible, and other learned labors. In 1842 he went to Basle, afterwards to Berne, and returned again in 1845 to Malta, to inaugurate and take charge of the Malta Protestant College. Soon after he had opened the college, Mr. Gobat received an intimation that the king of Prussia had expressed an anxious desire to nominate him to the Anglican episcopate in Jerusalem. He was much surprised at the intelligence, but felt bound in conscience not to refuse the call, without violating his principles of being "obedient to the Lord in all things." "Wherefore," were his words, "I felt persuaded that the call was from God; and herein I ground my hope, that God will bless me, and make me a blessing." On Sunday, July 5, 1846, Mr. Gobat was consecrated at Lambeth as bishop of the United Church of England and Ireland in Jerusalem. His work in the Holy City, during the thirty-three years which he spent there, was very successful and vigorous. His annual letters from the Holy City were always looked for with interest, and read with the deepest attention. In the last letter, published in 1877, he stated that there were thirty-three Protestant schools in Judea, Samaria, Galilee, and beyond Jordan, containing between 1200 and 1500 children of both sexes. He died at Jerusalem, May 5, 1879. He wrote *A Journey of Three Years in Abyssinia* (Lond. 1847). See Lichtenberger, *Encyclop. des Sciences Religieuses*, s. v.; *S. Gobat, his Life and Work*, by the earl of Shaftesbury (Lond. 1884). (B. P.)

Göbel, Karl, a Protestant theologian of Germany, was born Feb. 18, 1808, at Solingen. He studied at Erlangen and Berlin, and was in 1837 appointed pastor at Altwied, near Neuwied-on-the-Rhine. In 1845 he was appointed successor to professor Krafft, at Erlangen, and in 1857 he was called to Posen as pastor of St. Peter's, and member of consistory. He died there April 24, 1881, a doctor of theology and member of the upper consistory. He published, *Der heilige Rock, ein evangelisches Zeugniss* (Neuwied, 1845):—*Evangelisches Zeugniss gegen die Irrlehren des Ghillany und Johannes Ronge* (Erlangen, 1849):—*Osterbeute Heilsgütern Christlicher Hoffnung* (2d ed. 1860):—*Stephanus, der Prediger des Gottes der Herrlichkeit* (1853):—*Das alte Testament gegen Vorurtheile und Missverständnisse der Gebildeten unserer Zeit vertheidigt* (1865). See Zuchold, *Bibl. Theol.* i, 447. (B. P.)

Göbel, Sebastian, a German theologian, was born at Dresden in 1628. He was at first pastor of the Church of Nicolaï, at Leipsic, then abbot of the convent of Bergen, near Magdeburg, in 1669. He died in 1685, leaving *Methodologia Homiletica*:—*De Pactis et Fœderibus Dei cum Hominibus*:—*Christianæ Vitæ Regulæ*:—*Thesaurus Evangelicus*:—*Cibus Fœminarum Cœlistis, seu Sacrum Orandi et Cantandi Libellus*. See Hoefer, *Nouv. Biog. Générale*, s. v.

Godard (or **Gildard**), bishop of Rouen, was born at Salency, near Noyon, about 460. According to some hagiographers, he was son of Nectar, a Roman lord, and twin brother of St. Medard, but the earliest records contain no such information. As successor to Radbod, he received the priesthood at the hands of the bishop of Vermand, then the capital of the Vermandois. He was elected bishop of Rouen near the close of the 5th century, and brought many idolaters to the Christian faith. He aided in the conversion of Clovis I, together with his co-laborers St. Remy, St. Woast, and St. Medard. In 511 he assisted at the first Council of Orleans. He discovered in St. Laudus an especial talent, although but twelve years of age, and consecrated him bishop of Coutances. The theologians attributed this to divine revelation. He died at Rouen, June 8, about 530, and was interred in the Church of the Virgin, but his remains were afterwards reinterred in the abbey of St. Medard, at Soissons, under the reign of Charles the Bald, which probably led to the conclusion that Godard was brother of Medard. These two saints are honored on June 8. According to Mabillon, Fortunatus wrote the life of these two saints, but it is uncertain. See Hoefer, *Nouv. Biog. Générale*, s. v.

Goddard, Kingston, D.D., a Protestant Episcopal clergyman, a graduate of the General Theological Seminary, was rector for several years in Philadelphia, until 1859, when he became rector of Christ Church in Cincinnati, O. In 1862 he returned to Philadelphia as rector of St. Paul's Church. In 1866 he removed to Port Richmond, N. Y., as rector of St. Andrew's Church, where he remained until the close of his life, Oct. 24, 1875, at the age of sixty-three years. See *Prot. Episc. Almanac*, 1876, p. 150.

Goddard, William Stanley, D.D., an English clergyman, was born in 1757. He was rector of Repton, Derby, and died in 1845. He published a *Sermon* on the visit of the bishop of Winchester (1811):—*Sermon* at the consecration of bishop Howley (Lond. 1814). See Allibone, *Dict. of Brit. and Amer. Authors*, s. v.

Godeberta, *Saint*, was born at Boves, near Amiens, about 640. She was consecrated by St. Elogius, bishop of Noyon, in the presence of Clotaire III (from 655 to 659). The hagiographers say that she established a society of twelve women, whom, with untiring devotion, she instructed according to the strict rules of the gospel, and by her own virtuous example. By her faith she is said to have arrested the flames, and when a violent pestilence attacked Noyon, she caused its cessation by assembling the citizens together in penitence. She died about 700. Her remains were for a long time in the cathedral of Noyon. She was canonized, and her memory is honored April 11. See Hoefer, *Nouv. Biog. Générale*, s. v.; Smith, *Dict. of Christ. Biog.* s. v.

Godehard, *Saint*, bishop of Hildesheim, was born at Ritenbach, in Bavaria, in 961. He was educated at the court of the archbishop Frederic of Salzburg. and when thirty-one years of age entered the monastery of Nieder-Altaich, and became its abbot in 997. His excellent administration of the monastery attracted the attention of the emperor Henry II, who charged him with reforming the monasteries of Hersfeld, Tegernsee, etc., and having succeeded in this task, he returned to his own monastery in 1012. When Bernward, the bishop of Hildesheim, died, he was made his successor, in 1022, and died May 5, 1038. He was canonized by Innocent III in 1131. His festival is on May 4. See Blum, *Geschichte des Fürstenthums Hildesheim*, ii, 108 sq.; Lüntzel, *Geschichte der Stadt und Diöcese Hildesheim*, p. 195 sq.; Pertz, *Monumenta Germ. Hist.* xi, 165 sq.; Wattenbach, *Deutsche Geschichts-Quellen im Mittelalter*, ii, 16-23; Uhlhorn, in Plitt-Herzog's *Real-Encyclop.* s. v.; Paumier, in Lichtenberger's *Encyclop. des Sciences Religieuses*, s. v. (B. P.)

Godelive DE GHISTELLES, *Saint*, a martyr of the 11th century, was born at Ghistelles, in Flanders. She was religiously trained from her youth at the château of Long Fort, in Boulonnais. She was married to Bertolf, who at last caused her to be put to death. Her festival is on July 6. Legend attributes to her many miracles, and her life was written by Dragon, priest of Ghistelles, one of her contemporaries. Another, published in German, was entitled *Godelive Boeck*, in Gothic characters, ornamented with coarse wood engravings. This book was translated and published by Louis de

Baecker (Bruges, 1849). See Hoefer, *Nouv. Biog. Générale*, s. v.

Godescard, Jean François, a French ecclesiastical writer, was born at Rocquemont, near Rouen, March 30, 1728. He was successively secretary of the archbishop of Paris, prior of Notre Dame de Bon Repos, near Versailles, canon of St. Louis du Louvre, and prior of St. Honorius, at Paris, where he died, Aug. 21, 1800. He wrote, *Vies des Pères, des Martyrs, et des Autres Principaux Saints* (from the English of Alban Butler, Villefranche and Paris, 1763, 1783, 1784), containing a large number of anecdotes which, true or doubtful, afford philosophers, historians, and hagiographers interesting information:—*De la Mort des Persecuteurs* (with historical notes translated from the Latin of Lectance, Paris, 1797):—*Fondements de la Religion Chrétienne* (translated from the English of Challonner):—*Table Alphabétique* (of the *Mémoires de Trévoux* down to 1740), and several theological works. See Hoefer, *Nouv. Biog. Générale*, s. v.

Godet *des Marais*, Paul de, a French prelate, was born at Talcy, near Blois, in June, 1649. He completed his studies at the Seminary of St. Sulpice, Paris, and became bishop of Chartres, confessor of madame Maintenon, and superior of the royal house of St. Cyr. On his promotion to the episcopacy he gave all his revenue to the poor. Nov. 21, 1695, he condemned several propositions taken from the works of madame Guyon and P. Lacombe. He claimed also to bring Fénélon to a recantation. In 1697 he signed, with the cardinal of Noailles and Bossuet, a declaration which was sent to Rome, by which he condemned the *Maximes des Saints*. He founded four seminaries and schools for the instruction of the young. He died Sept. 25, 1709. See Hoefer, *Nouv. Biog. Générale*, s. v.

Godwin, Thomas, D.D., an English prelate, was born at Oakingham, in Berkshire, in 1517, and was educated at Magdalen College, Oxford. In 1565 he was made dean of Christ Church, Oxford, and had also a prebend in the Cathedral of Lincoln. In 1566 he was promoted to the deanery of Canterbury. In 1576 he was one of the ecclesiastical commissioners. He was consecrated bishop of Bath and Wells in September, 1584. He died Nov. 19, 1590. Among the Parker MSS. in Benedict Church, Cambridge, is a sermon which he preached before the queen at Greenwich, in 1566, concerning the authority of the councils and fathers.

Goerce, Hugh William, was a Dutch theologian and physician. After receiving the degree of doctor of medicine, he practiced at Middelburg, where he acquired a great reputation. He understood very well the dialects of north Europe, and the classical languages, and occupied his leisure with archæology and translating several ancient authors. He died at Middelburg about 1643. For further mention of his works, see Hoefer, *Nouv. Biog. Générale*, s. v.

Goetschius, John Henry, a Reformed (Dutch) minister (son of a German minister who was sent over, probably in 1728, from the fatherland, to labor among the Germans in and around Philadelphia), was born in 1718, in Switzerland, studied in the University of Zurich, and under Rev. G. H. Dorstius, in Pennsylvania, who, with Rev. J. T. Frelinghuysen, licensed and ordained him in 1738. He was settled successively in North and South Hampton, Pa. (1738), in Jamaica, Newtown, and vicinity, on Long Island (1740), and at Hackensack and Schraalenburgh, N. J. (1748), where he died, Nov. 14, 1774. The validity of his ordination having been questioned, he was newly examined and reordained in 1748, under the authority of the Classis of Amsterdam, by the Cœtus. But while men disputed, God honored his faithful services, both before and after his second ordination, with frequent and great revivals. His whole ministry was contemporaneous with the agitation of the vexed question of education and ordination in this country, and especially in his last and longest pastorate in New Jersey, were the churches divided and troubled by its unfortunate developments. When the church was locked against him on Long Island, he preached on the steps, or under the trees, or in barns, or in private dwellings. It is related that on one Sabbath the chorister, who in those days announced the Psalms and hymns, gave out the entire 119th Psalm to be sung, to prevent his preaching. Once, when in danger of forcible resistance to his entering the church at Hackensack, he girded on his sword, and with it entered the pulpit, for in those days it was not unusual for clergymen to wear a sword, and carry it into the pulpit and place it behind them during the service. Yet Mr. Goetschius was a man of peace, a learned, pious, godly, faithful, and eminently successful preacher of the gospel in troublous times. He was also the theological instructor of a number of young men who rose to eminence and power in the Church, and who were the apostles of a liberal and independent ecclesiastical polity. Among these were professor Romeyn, the younger Frelinghuysens, Leeydt, and others. He was one of the original trustees of Rutgers College, and a leader in the forward movements of his denomination. "He was below the middle size, of a vigorous constitution, abrupt in speech, but his language was clear and expressive." One of his pupils, Dr. Solomon Froeligh, describes him as "a gentleman of profound erudition, a thoroughbred Calvinist, and an accomplished theologian." See Corwin, *Manual of the Ref. Church in America*, s. v.; Taylor, *Annals of Classis of Bergen*, p. 180; *Autobiography of Dr. S. Froeligh*. (W. J. R. T.)

Gohren, Adolph Wilhelm *von*, a Lutheran theologian, was born May 13, 1685, at Copenhagen. He studied at Kiel and Jena, was preacher at the latter place in 1722, member of consistory in 1725, and rector at Hamburg in 1731. He died July 24, 1734. Besides translating into German Buddeus's work, *De Atheismo et Superstitione* (Jena, 1723), he wrote *Disp. Inaug. Theologica de Fermento Pharisæorum* (1728). See Thiess, *Hamburger Gelehrten-Geschichte;* Jöcher, *Allgemeines Gelehrten-Lexikon*, s. v. (B. P.)

Gokei, long strips of white paper, emblems of the divine presence of the Camis (q. v.) among the Japanese. They are kept in little portable *mias* in all Japanese houses.

Goldberg, Beer, a Jewish writer, was born in 1801 in Poland. In 1840 he went to Berlin, in 1847 to London, in 1852 to Paris, and died there, May 4, 1884. He published, *Chofes Matmonim sive Anecdota Rabbinica* (Berlin, 1845):—*Jesod Olam*, edited for the first time after an old MS. (1848):—*Sefer ha-Rikmah*, of Ibn-Gemach (Frankfort, 1856):—*Sefer Taggin*, a masoretic work, edited in connection with Barges:—*Risalat*, or Ibn-Koreish's treatise on the use of the study of the Targums (Paris, 1867):—*Sefer ha-Sichronoth*, or a Hebrew concordance, by Elias Levita, edited after a Paris manuscript (Frankfort, 1874). See Fürst, *Bibl. Jud.* i, 337. (B. P.)

Golden, T. C., M.D., D.D., a Methodist Episcopal minister, was born in England, April 16, 1818. He emigrated to America in 1849, settled near Kingston, Wis., and the year following entered the Wisconsin Conference, wherein he successively served Cascade, Sheboygan Falls, Omro, and Fond du Lac, two years each. He was then transferred to the West Wisconsin Conference, and stationed at La Crosse. When the North-west Wisconsin Conference was formed he became a member of it, and was appointed presiding elder of La Crosse district from 1859 to 1862; elected a delegate to General Conference in 1860; Eau Clair district from 1863 to 1866; delegate to General Conference in 1864; located from 1865 to 1869; readmitted to the Upper Iowa Conference in 1870, and for three years was stationed at Mount Vernon, and then was appointed presiding elder of Vinton district. He died May 29, 1879. See *Minutes of Annual Conferences*, 1879, p. 50.

Golden Age is a term used in the Greek and Roman mythology to denote the reign of Saturn (q. v.), when justice and innocence were supposed to have prevailed throughout the earth, and the soil to have produced all that was necessary for the subsistence and enjoyment of mankind.

Goldhorn, David Johann Heinrich, a Lutheran theologian of Germany, was born at Leipsic, July 31, 1810, and died there, professor of theology, Dec. 21, 1874. In connection with Gersdorf, he published, *Bibliotheca Patrum Ecclesiasticorum Latinorum Selecta* (Leipsic, 1838):—wrote besides, *Commentatio Historico-Theologica de Summis Principiis Theologiæ Abælardæ* (eod.):—*Die theologische Literatur des Jahres* 1840 *und* 1841 (1842–44). See Winer, *Handbuch der theol. Lit.* i, 862, 874, 914; Zuchold, *Bibl. Theol.* i, 448. (B. P.)

Goldhorn, Johann David, a Lutheran theologian of Germany, was born Sept. 12, 1774. After having served at different places as preacher, he was called to Leipsic in 1835 as professor of theology, and died Oct. 23, 1836. He published, *Exkurse zum Buche Jonas* (Leipsic, 1803):—*De Puerorum Innocentia in Sermonibus Sacris*, etc. (1828):—*Predigten und Kasualreden* (3 vols.). See Winer, *Handbuch der theol. Lit.* i, 23, 83, 869; ii, 36, 66, 98, 172; Zuchold, *Bibl. Theol.* i, 448 sq. (B. P.)

Goldsborough, Godfrey, D.D., an Anglican bishop of the 16th century, was born in Cambridge, bred in Trinity College (pupil of archbishop Whitgift), became afterwards fellow thereof, prebend of Hereford in 1585, archdeacon of Salop in 1589, was consecrated bishop of Gloucester in 1598, and died March 26, 1604. See Fuller, *Worthies of England* (ed. Nuttall), i, 231.

Goldschad, Gotthelf Conrad, a Lutheran minister of Germany, was born May 18, 1719. He studied at Wittenberg, was in 1744 regent of the Kreutzschule at Dresden, in 1750 rector of St. Anne, and died in 1767. He wrote, *De Mandato Christi Jo. xxi*, 15–17 (1750):—*Chorus Musicus Gloriam Christi Celebrans ex Ps. lxviii*, 26 (1751):—*Septem Spiritus ante Dei Thronum ex Apoc. i*, 4 (1752):—*De Præfectis Pacificis et Exactoribus Justis Ecclesiæ a Deo Promissis ex Esaiæ lx*, 17 (1755):—*Salomonis de Juventutis Institutione Consilium ac Pretium ex Prov. xxii*, 6 (1760):—*Historische Nachricht von der Annen Kirche vor Dresden* (1763). See Jöcher, *Allgemeines Gelehrten-Lexikon*, s. v. (B. P.)

Goldsmith, John, D.D., a Presbyterian minister, was born at Riverhead, N. Y., April 10, 1794. He graduated from the College of New Jersey in 1815, and from Princeton Theological Seminary in 1819; was ordained a minister by the Presbytery of New York, Nov. 17, the same year; preached at Newtown, L. I., thereafter until his death, April 6, 1854. See *Gen. Cat. of Princeton Theol. Sem.* 1881, p. 22.

Goldwell, James, LL.D., an English prelate of the 15th century, was born at Great Chart, Kent, educated in All-Souls' College, Oxford, promoted prebend of Hereford in 1461, dean of Salisbury in 1463, secretary to king Edward IV, and at last made bishop of Norwich in 1472. He repaired the church at Great Chart, and founded a chapel on its south side. He died Feb. 15, 1498. See Fuller, *Worthies of England* (ed. Nuttall), ii, 137.

Goldwell, Thomas, an English prelate, was born at Goldwell, parish of Great Chart, Kent. Being a Benedictine, he was by queen Mary preferred bishop of St. Asaph's in 1558, but quitted the land in the first year of queen Elizabeth's reign, and, going to Rome, induced the pope to grant indulgences to those who made a pilgrimage to the well of St. Winifred, in his diocese. He died in Rome about 1581. See Fuller, *Worthies of England* (ed. Nuttall), ii, 137.

Golod, John, an Armenian patriarch of Constantinople, was born at Bales, and educated in the monastery of Amerdolu. During his patriarchate three churches belonging to the Armenians of Constantinople, which had been burned down, were rebuilt with taste and elegance. He also built several schools. The only writing of which he is the author is a profession of faith which he addressed to the papal court at Rome. He sought to re-establish the harmony between the national Armenians and the united Armenians or Roman Catholics. He was accused of softness by his people, and seeing that the preaching of the missionaries gave occasion to troubles, he closed their churches. Golod died in 1741. See Hoefer, *Nouv. Biog. Générale*, s. v.

Goltz (Lat. *Goltzius*), Hendrik, a pre-eminent Dutch engraver and painter, was born at Mülbrecht, in the duchy of Juliers, in 1558, and studied engraving under Theodore Cuernhert. He afterwards visited Italy, and studied the works of Raphael, Michael Angelo, and P. da Caravaggio. He began painting at the age of forty-two, and executed a number of fine pictures, the first of which was the *Crucifixion, with the Virgin Mary and St. John*. As an engraver, he was far more distinguished: his prints number over five hundred. The following are some of the principal: *The Life and Passion of Our Saviour; Christ and the Apostles; The Circumcision; The Adoration of the Magi; The Wise Men's Offering; The Temptation of St. Anthony; The Holy Family; The Nativity; The Murder of the Innocents; The Annunciation; The Last Supper; The Fall of Adam and Eve; The Dead Christ Supported by an Angel.* Goltz died at Haerlem in 1617. See Hoefer, *Nouv. Biog. Générale*, s. v.; Spooner, *Biog. Hist. of the Fine Arts*, s. v.

Gomarists, a name sometimes applied to the Calvinists in Holland in the 17th century, after Francis Gomar (q. v.), an eminent opponent of the Arminians in the synod of Dort.

Gomez, Juan, a reputable historical painter of Madrid, was born about 1550. He painted several subjects from the life of St. Jerome; also the large picture of the *Martyrdom of St. Ursula*. He restored the *Annunciation* and the *St. Jerome Penitent*, by F. Zucchero, which Philip II had rejected and ordered to be retouched. He died in 1597. See Hoefer, *Nouv. Biog. Générale*, s. v.; Spooner, *Biog. Hist. of the Fine Arts*, s. v.

Gomidas, an Armenian patriarch, was born at Aghtsits, in the canton of Arakadzodn. He was bishop of the Mamigonians, when he was elected patriarch in 617. After the death of John III, Gomidas erected a magnificent church, dedicated to St. Hripsimia. He died in 625, leaving *Nerpogh Hripsimia* ("Hymn in honor of St. Rhipsime"), which is still contained in the Armenian liturgy. See Hoefer, *Nouv. Biog. Générale*, s. v.; Smith, *Dict. of Christ. Biog.* s. v.

Gondi Version of the Scriptures. This dialect is spoken by the Gonds, one of the most remarkable of the hill-tribes in North-west India. In 1872 the Gospel according to Matthew, as translated by the Rev. Mr. Dawson, was printed at Allahabad, to which the gospel of Mark was added in 1874. See Driberg and Harrison, *Narrative of a Second Visit to the Gonds of the Nerbudda Territory, with a Grammar and Vocabulary of their Language* (1849).

Gondi, Pierre de, a cardinal-bishop of Paris, was born in 1533. He studied jurisprudence at Toulouse, and theology at Paris. Before 1569 he was bishop of Langres and grand-almoner of Catherine de Medici. In the following year he became bishop of Paris. A short time after the death of his brother, Henry III sent him to Rome to ask of the pope permission to alienate from the revenues of the clergy 50,000 gold florins. During the league, the Spaniards sought in vain to draw him into their party. He refused the cardinal's hat which Sixtus V offered to him in 1588, except on consent of the king. He died Feb. 17, 1616. See Hoefer, *Nouv. Biog. Générale*, s. v.

Gondrin, Louis Henry *de Pardaillan de*, a French prelate, was born at the castle of Gondrin, in the diocese of Auch, in 1620. He studied at the College of La Flèche, at the University of Paris, and in the Sorbonne. Being a relative of the bishop of Sens, Octavius of Bellegarde, he was appointed his coadjutor in 1645, and succeeded him the following year. He was one of the first who censured the *Apology of the Casuists*. In 1653 he signed the letter of the assembly of the clergy to pope Innocent X, in which the prelates recognised only the five famous propositions of Jansenius. He disapproved of the conduct of his niece, Mme. de Montespan, at the court. He died at the abbey of Chaulnes, Sept. 20, 1674, leaving letters and pastoral ordinances. See Hoefer, *Nouv. Biog. Générale*, s. v.

Gonnelieu, Jérôme de, a French Jesuit, was born at Soissons, Sept. 8, 1640. At the age of sixteen he joined his order, and died at Paris in 1717. He wrote, *De l'Essence de la Vie Spirituelle* (Paris, 1701):—*De la Presence de Dieu qui Renferme tous les Principes de la Vie Intérieure* (ibid. 1703):—*Méthode pour Bien Prier* (1710):—*Pratique de la Vie Intérieure* (eod.):—*Le Sermon de Notre-Seigneur à ses Apôtres Après la Cène* (1712). For a long time there was attributed to him a translation of the *Imitation of Christ*, which was published at Nancy in 1712, for which edition he only wrote the prayers and the application at the end of each chapter. The work of translation was, in fact, made by a printer and member of the Paris parliament, Jean Cursor, who published it for the first time in 1673 under his own name. But the ambiguous title of the edition published in 1712, *Imitation de Jésus-Christ, avec des Pratiques et des Prières, par le P. de Gonnelieu* (Nancy), led to the error of palming the authorship of the translation upon Gonnelieu; and in spite of the testimony of Calmet, Barbier, and Brunet against this authorship, the error has been perpetuated, and Gonnelieu's name continued to figure in the new editions published in 1818, 1822, and 1856. See Jöcher, *Allgemeines Gelehrten-Lexikon*, s. v.; Lichtenberger, *Encyclop. des Sciences Religieuses*, s. v. (B. P.)

Göntgen, Jonathan Gottlieb, a Protestant theologian of Germany, was born Jan. 13, 1752, at Frankfort-on-the-Main, and died there, May 7, 1807. He published, *Der Schriftforscher* (Leipsic, 1787–89, 3 vols.):—*Luther's Kleiner Katechismus* (ibid. 1791):—*Reden bei der Vorbereitung zur christlichen Feier des heiligen Abendmahls* (ibid. 1800). See Winer, *Handbuch der theol. Lit.* ii, 183, 213; Döring, *Die gelehrten Theologen Deutschlands*, s. v. (B. P.)

Gonthier, François Auguste Alphonse, a Protestant theologian, was born at Yverdon, Dec. 21, 1773. He studied at Lausanne, was in 1805 pastor at Nîmes, and died at Nyons in 1834. He published, *Lectures Chrétiennes* (1824):—*Mélanges Évangéliques:*—*Lettres Chrétiennes:*—*Petite Bibliothèque des Pères de l'Église*. See Montet, *Dict. des Génevois et des Vaudois*, etc. (Lausanne, 1877); *Archives du Christianisme* (1834); *Bibliothèque Universelle* (1861); Lichtenberger, *Encyclop. des Sciences Religieuses*, s. v.; Winer, *Handbuch der theol. Lit.* ii. 335. (B. P.)

Gonthier, Jean Baptiste Bernard, a French theologian, was born at Dijon, and died there, June 1, 1678. He wrote, *Reglement du Séminaire de Langres* (Langres, 1663):—*Le Grand Catéchisme du Diocèse de Langres* (Dijon, 1664):—*Exercice du Chrétien pour le Matin et le Soir* (ibid. eod.):—*Le Directeur Portatif* (ibid. 1662, 1674). See Papillon, *Bibl. des Auteurs de Bourgogne;* Jöcher, *Allgemeines Gelehrten-Lexikon*, s. v. (B. P.)

Gonzaga, Ercole de, an Italian cardinal, born in 1505, was the son of John Francis II, duke of Mantua. After he had studied at Bologna under the direction of Pomponacius, he was appointed bishop of Mantua in 1520, six years afterwards was made cardinal, and called to the archbishopric of Tarragona. In 1540 he took in his hands the direction of the government of the duchy of Mantua. In 1562 he was appointed by pope Pius IV to preside at the Council of Trent as first legate of the holy see, but he died March 2, 1563, leaving a catechism in Latin, published for the pastors of Mantua. He composed also a treatise on *De Institutione Vitæ Christianæ*, in MS. In the library of Este there are two volumes of letters written by him during 1559. See Hoefer, *Nouv. Biog. Générale*, s. v.

Gonzaga, Pirro de, an Italian cardinal, was born in the second part of the 15th century. He contributed to the deliverance of pope Clement VII, who had been kept in prison by Charles V. The pope rewarded him by appointing him a cardinal, and archbishop of Modena in 1527. He died in 1529. See Hoefer, *Nouv. Biog. Générale*, s. v.

Gonzaga, Scipione de, an Italian cardinal, was born Nov. 21, 1542. Cardinal Ercole de Gonzaga educated him with much care, and at the age of sixteen Scipione had perfectly acquired the ancient languages. He then studied philosophy at the University of Padua. In 1563 he founded in that city the Academy of the Eterei, of which he remained the protector during the remainder of his life. Finally he entered into the ministry, and was appointed patriarch of Jerusalem. In 1587 he received the cardinalate from pope Sixtus V. He was the intimate friend of Tasso. He died Jan. 11, 1593, leaving several pieces in verse, which were published among others, in 1567, of the Academy of the Eterei. In 1597 the abbot Marotti published *Commentarii de Vita sua*, memoirs written in Latin by Gonzaga. See Hoefer, *Nouv. Biog. Générale*, s. v.

Gonzaga, Sigismondo de, an Italian captain and cardinal, was born in the second part of the 15th century. In his military career he distinguished himself as a clever general. In 1505 he was made cardinal by Julius II, whom he defended with considerable energy against his numerous enemies. In 1511 he was appointed bishop of Mantua, and died there in 1525. See Hoefer, *Nouv. Biog. Générale*, s. v.

Gonzalvo, Martin, a Spanish religious impostor of the 14th century, was born at Cuença, and called himself the archangel Michael, to whom God had reserved the place of Lucifer, and who would some day fight against antichrist. The Inquisition burned him, but his disciple, Nicolas de Calabrois, sought to represent him after his death as the Son of God, and preached that the Holy Spirit would become incarnate, and that at the day of judgment Gonzalvo would deliver by his prayers all the condemned. De Calabrois also perished in the flames. See Hoefer, *Nouv. Biog. Générale*, s. v.

Gon-Zoar, Kin-Zo, a Japanese Buddhist monk, was born in 758, in the district of Taka-Tki, a province of Yamato. One day his mother saw in a vision an august being embracing her in his arms, and shortly afterwards she bore this son. In his twelfth year he entered a hermitage. About the year 796 he commenced the publication of a commentary in eight parts, of Fats-Ke-gyô (in Chinese Fa-Hoa-King), or sacred book of the Japanese. After his death in 827, he received the name of *So-dzyo*. He is famous in Japan for having possessed such a high degree of knowledge on the Buddhistic dogmas, and among others for having fixed the actual order of the Japanese alphabet. See Hoefer, *Nouv. Biog. Générale*, s. v.

Good Sons, Order of, a religious congregation of the third order of St. Francis, was founded in 1615, at Armantieres, a small town in Flanders, by five pious artisans. In 1626 they adopted the third rule of St. Francis. The order progressed gradually, and in 1670 consisted of two congregations, that of Lisle being added to the first one formed. Shortly after a third was formed at St. Omer, and Louis XIV gave them the direction of various public hospitals. They practiced great austerity, and used the discipline of the scourge three times a week.

Goode, WILLIAM H., D.D., a Methodist Episcopal minister, was born in Warren County, O., June 19, 1807. He began school-teaching at the age of seventeen, in Green County; afterwards removed to Madison, Ind., where he continued teaching, and studied law; was admitted to the bar before he was twenty-one; experienced religion about this time; at the age of twenty was elected president of Gallatin County Seminary, Port William, Ky., which position he held for two years; then returned to Indiana and followed farming seven or eight years; was licensed to preach in 1835; in 1836 entered the Indiana Conference, and was appointed to Lexington Circuit. A few months later he was elected principal of the New Albany Seminary. Subsequently he was sent to Jeffersonville and Indianapolis stations; in 1842 was appointed presiding elder of South Bend District, but in the middle of the year was transferred to the Arkansas Conference, and appointed to Fort Coffee Academy and mission, Choctaw nation, where he remained till 1845. In 1844 he formed the Indian Mission Conference, and became a member of it. In 1845 he was transferred to the North Indiana Conference. He afterwards labored on Peru District, four years on Greencastle District, and four years on Indianapolis District; was appointed to Richmond Station in 1853; then had charge of the entire territory between Texas and Nebraska, and the Mississippi and the Rocky Mountains. His subsequent appointments were in the same region until 1860, when he was transferred to the Western Iowa Conference, and appointed to Lowden District; Council Bluffs District in 1861; in 1862 was retransferred to the North Indiana Conference, and appointed to Union Chapel (now Grace Church), Richmond. Thereafter he served on various districts, and finally (1877-79) became superannuated. He died in Richmond, Ind., Dec. 16, 1879. Dr. Goode possessed a very high order of intellect, a deep religious character, great pulpit power, was a born leader of men, eminent for uncompromising integrity, and entirely free from inordinate ambition. See *Minutes of Annual Conferences*, 1880, p. 71.

Goodell, WILLIAM, a Congregational minister, was born at Windsor, N. Y., Oct. 25, 1792. For some years he was a merchant, first in Providence, R. I., then in Wilmington, N. C., and afterwards in Alexandria, Va. In 1827 he became editor of the *Weekly Investigator*, at Providence, R. I. Two years after he went to Boston, his paper having been consolidated with the *National Philanthropist*, published there. In 1830 he began editing the *Genius of Temperance*, in New York city, and later he was editor of the *Emancipator*. From 1836 to 1842 he edited the *Friend of Man*, at Utica, N. Y.; in 1843 was at the head of a paper in Whitesboro', called the *Christian Investigator*, and it was in that year that he organized a Congregational church in Honeoye, on anti-slavery and temperance principles, to which congregation he ministered for eight years, although he declined ordination. When he returned to New York, in 1853, he became editor of the *Radical Abolitionist*, afterwards called the *Principia*. In 1865 he removed to Bozraville, Conn., and supplied the Church in that place. From 1870 he resided in Janesville, Wis. He died Feb. 14, 1878. Besides a large number of pamphlets, principally on the subject of slavery, he published three larger works, viz.: *The Democracy of Christianity* (1850, 2 vols.):—*History of Slavery and Anti-slavery* (1852):—*American Slave Code* (1853). See *Cong. Yearbook*, 1879, p. 42.

Goodenough, JOHN JOSEPH, D.D., a Church of England divine, was born in 1780. He graduated at New College, Oxford, in 1801; in 1812 was appointed head master of the Bristol Free Grammar-school, which failed under his administration. He held one or two small pieces of preferment, together with his mastership, before taking the family living of Broughton Pogis, Oxfordshire, in 1845, at which place he died, April 22, 1856. See Hardwicke, *Annual Biography*, 1856, p. 214.

Goodford, CHARLES OLD, D.D., a Church of England divine, was born in Somerset in 1812, and educated at Eton and Cambridge (A.B. 1836). He was for many years assistant master at Eton; became head master in 1853, and succeeded Dr. Hawtry as provost in 1862. He held the rectory of Chilton Canteloo from 1856, and died May 9, 1884.

Goodrich, WILLIAM HENRY, D.D., a Presbyterian minister, was born in New Haven, Jan. 19, 1823, being the son of Rev. C. A. Goodrich, D.D., grandson of Noah Webster, LL.D., and great-grandson of Rev. Elizur Goodrich, D.D. He graduated at Yale College in 1843, and Yale Divinity School in 1847, and was tutor in Yale College two years. After making the tour of Europe, he accepted, in 1850, a call to the pastoral charge of the Congregational Church of Bristol, Conn., where he remained four years. He was then called to the pastorate of the Presbyterian Church of Binghamton, N. Y., where he remained till 1858, and then removed to Cleveland, O., as pastor of the First Presbyterian Church, where his work was marked by very great success. In 1872, after securing the settlement of the Rev. H. C. Haydn as associate pastor, he left for a visit to foreign lands, that thus his health might be restored; but he died at Lausanne, Switzerland, July 11, 1874. As a preacher, Dr. Goodrich was seldom speculative and theoretical, never dogmatic nor sectarian, but eminently spiritual and practical. A very strong point in his character was his downright, never-failing commonsense. He was remarkable for insight into the character of all with whom he had to do.

Goodsell, Buel, a veteran Methodist Episcopal minister, was born at Dover, N. Y., July 25, 1793. He was converted at the age of sixteen; in 1814 was received into the New York Conference, and served Granville Circuit, Mass. and Conn.; in 1815, Stowe Circuit, Vt.; in 1816, Chazy Circuit, N. Y.; in 1817, Middleburgh, Vt.; in 1818-19, St. Alban's Circuit; in 1820-21, Chazy Circuit, N. Y.; in 1822, Charlotte Circuit, Vt.; in 1823-26, Champlain District; in 1827, Fitchtown, N. Y.; in 1828-29, Schenectady; in 1830-31, New York city; in 1832-33, Troy; in 1834-37, Troy District; in 1838-39, John Street, New York city; in 1840-41, North Newburgh; in 1842-43, White Plains; in 1844-45, York Street, Brooklyn; in 1846-47, Willett Street, New York city; in 1848-49, Norwalk, Conn.; in 1850-51, Hempstead, L. I.; in 1852-53, New Rochelle, N. Y.; in 1854, East Brooklyn, L. I.; in 1855-58, Long Island District; in 1859-60, Greenpoint, Brooklyn; in 1861-62, Rockaway, L. I.; and thereafter East Chester and City Island, N. Y., until his death, May 4, 1863. Mr. Goodsell was a laborious, faithful, and successful minister. See *Minutes of Annual Conferences*, 1864, p. 88.

Goodsell, Dana, a veteran Presbyterian minister, was born at Bradford, Conn., Aug. 28, 1803. He entered Princeton Seminary in 1827, and remained there over two years; began a year's service in Mississippi as agent of the American Sunday-school Union, Oct. 8, 1830; and in the autumn of 1836 was laboring at Lowell, Mass. He was ordained and installed as pastor at Plainfield, Sept. 27, 1837, and dismissed Sept. 25, 1839; was next installed pastor at South Amherst, Mass., April 21, 1841, and after laboring there with much acceptance, was dismissed Nov. 12, 1846. Subsequently to 1847 he travelled in the West and South, in the service of the American Tract Society, preaching to destitute churches, and distributing religious books. In failing health he next went to North Carolina, where he accumulated much property, which was lost on the opening of the civil war in 1861. He then returned to the North, and henceforth spent most of his time in Philadelphia, where he preached as opportunity offered, and engaged in other Christian labor. In his old age he lost the remainder of his property and was cast upon the charity of the world. Becoming very feeble, he was taken, June 17, 1874, to "The Old Man's Home" in West Philadelphia, where he died, Feb. 19, 1876. Mr. Goodsell was a man of strong intellect and firm convictions, wonderfully gifted in prayer, quiet and devoted. See *Necrol. Report of Princeton Theol. Sem.* 1877, p. 24.

Goodspeed, EDGAR JOHNSON, D.D., a Baptist minister, was born in Johnsburgh, Warren Co., N. Y., May 31, 1833. He studied in the academy at Glenn's Falls, spent part of one year at Union College, Schenectady, and graduated from the University of Rochester in 1853, and from the Rochester Theological Seminary in 1856. Immediately he was ordained pastor of the Central Baptist Church in Poughkeepsie, and in the fall of 1858 removed to Janesville, Wis., in the same capacity, where he had eminent success. On the formation of the Second Baptist Church of Chicago, in 1864, he was called to be its pastor, and for several years labored with great constancy and success. In the winter of 1870 and 1871 he was suddenly prostrated by asthma, and spent several months in Europe. On his return he received for his colleague his brother, Rev. T. W. Goodspeed; and in 1876 was forced to resign. He next spent a year and a half at New Market, N. J., in entire rest and freedom from care, and then accepted a call to the Central Church of Syracuse, N. Y. In 1879 he took charge of the Benedict Institute, Columbia, S. C., with the hope that a milder climate would benefit his health. The school largely increased under his administration; but in the midst of his usefulness he died, June 12, 1881. He was a member of the board of trustees of the Chicago University and of the Theological Seminary. He was editor of *Cobbin's Commentary on the Bible*, and wrote *The Wonderful Career of Moody and Sankey in Great Britain and America:—The Life of Jesus, for Young People:—The Lives of the Apostles, for the Young:—The Great Fires in Chicago and the West:—A History of the Centennial.* See *Chicago Standard*, June 23, 1881. (J. C. S.)

Goodwillie, THOMAS, D.D., a Presbyterian minister, was born in Barnet, Caledonia Co., Vt., Sept. 27, 1800. His parents were natives of Scotland, and emigrated to the United States in 1788. He graduated fromDartmouth College, N. H., in 1820. In 1823 was licensed by Cambridge Presbytery, and in 1826 installed pastor of the Presbyterian Church of Barnet. He was a man of large experience, and an accomplished scholar. He travelled extensively through Europe in order to recuperate his health, as well as to study the workings of Catholicism. He was a life member of the American Bible Society. Dr. Goodwillie died Feb. 11, 1867. He possessed good natural ability, carefully cultivated and improved by study and intercourse with men. See Wilson, *Presb. Hist. Almanac*, 1868, p. 265.

Goodwin, Benjamin, D.D., an English Baptist minister, was born at Bath, Oct. 10, 1785, educated at the Blue School, began to learn Latin, Greek, and Hebrew while an apprentice, but went to sea, and was pressed into the navy. In 1802 he returned to Bath, was converted, and joined the Church in 1803. In 1805 he became an itinerant evangelist, and in 1808 settled as pastor at Chipping-Sodbury. In 1811 he removed to Dartmouth, and in 1815 to Great Missenden, Bucks. In 1822 he was appointed classical professor at Horton, where he continued to labor with untiring vigor during many years. In 1828 he entered heartily into the controversy on popery, in 1830 delivered lectures against "colonial slavery," and in 1834 lectured on the atheistic controversy. In 1838 he became pastor of the Baptist Church at Oxford, and took a leading part in reconciling the differences which had arisen in the Serampore mission. In 1842 he took part in the jubilee at Kettering of the founding of the Baptist missions. In 1843 he exposed the evil tendency of Dr. Pusey's teaching on the eucharist. In 1846 he returned to Bradford; in 1850 was chairman of the London meeting of the Baptist Union; in 1853 enlarged and redelivered his lectures on atheism; in 1855 he removed to Rawdon; at the age of eighty joined in the Baptist Union meeting; in 1868 he wrote two elaborate essays on the *Future State*, and died Feb. 20, 1871. See (Lond.) *Baptist Hand-book*, 1872.

Goodwin, William H., D.D., LL.D., a Methodist Episcopal minister, was born at Goodwin's Point, Tompkins Co., N. Y., June 12, 1812. He was converted at nineteen years of age, and the next year entered the Genesee Conference. His appointments were: first in his native place, then Ovid, Catharine, Brockport, East Rochester, Lyons, Canandaigua, Vienna, and Penn Yan. In 1848, on the division of the conference, he became a member of the East Genesee Conference, wherein he served Lyons, East Rochester, Elmira, Geneva, Hornellsville District, Elmira District, Rochester District, Geneva, Clifton Springs, Rushville, Ovid, and in 1874 Dryden, where his health failed, and where he died, Feb. 17, 1876. Mr. Goodwin was chosen state senator from Ontario and Livingston counties in 1854; and in 1865 was appointed regent of the University of New York. He was, in personal appearance, very prepossessing, tall, well developed, noble; in character, frank, generous to a fault; had a voice rarely equalled in depth, fulness, and sweetness; imagination fertile and chaste; a mind of great natural strength, finely cultured in logic and rhetoric; and a sincere enthusiasm that overcame all obstacles. See *Minutes of Annual Conferences*, 1876, p. 138; Simpson, *Cyclop. of Methodism*, s. v.

Gopis, in Hindû mythology, are the nine beautiful maidens who accompanied the youthful Krishna, and with him danced at night on the plains of Agra. Krishna is the Apollo, and these Gopis are the muses of the Hindûs. The number nine might be doubtful, were not Krishna represented riding on an elephant, which is artistically composed of the forms of these Gopis.

Görcke, HERMANN MORITZ, a Lutheran theologian of Germany, was born Sept. 26, 1803, and died March 6, 1883, at Zarben, in Pomerania. He is the author of *Bibel-Jahr* (Berlin, 1857-60, 4 vols.). See Zuchold, *Bibl. Theol.* i, 451. (B. P.)

Gordon, Adam, a Scotch prelate, was dean of Caithness and minister at Pettie, and was bishop of the see of Caithness. When he was made bishop is not known. He died at Elgin, June 4, 1528. See Keith, *Scottish Bishops*, p. 214.

Gordon, Alexander (1), a Scotch bishop, was first rector of Fetteresso, in the shire of Mearns, next chanter or precentor of the see of Moray, and was consecrated bishop of Aberdeen about 1517. He died June 29, 1518. See Keith, *Scottish Bishops*, p. 119.

Gordon, Alexander (2), a Scotch prelate, was made bishop of the Isles Nov. 21, 1553; from this see he was translated to that of Galloway in 1558. In 1570 he preached in John Knox's pulpit, at Edinburgh. In 1576 he was a judge in the Court of Session. He died in the same year. See Keith, *Scottish Bishops*, p. 279, 307.

Gordon, John (1), a Scotch prelate, was made bishop of Galloway Feb. 4, 1688, and consecrated at Glasgow. After the revolution he followed king James to Ireland, and then to France, and while at St. Germain's read the liturgy of the Church of England to all Protestants who came to hear. See Keith, *Scottish Bishops*, p. 283.

Gordon, John (2), D.D., F.S.A., a Church of England divine, was born at Whitworth, Durham, in 1725. He was a graduate of Emanuel College, Cambridge,

Ancient Representation of the two Gorgons, Stheno and Euryale, complaining to Neptune of the Fate of their Sister Medusa.

where he took the degrees of A.B. in 1748, A.M. in 1752, and D.D. in 1765, at Peterhouse; and was elected a fellow of Emanuel College in 1751. At his decease, which occurred Jan. 19, 1793, he was precentor and archdeacon of Lincoln, and rector of Henstead, Suffolk. He was the author of a *New Estimate of the Manners and Principles of the Times*, 3 parts:—*Occasional Thoughts on the Study of Classical Authors* (1762):—and two *Sermons* preached at Cambridge. See (Lond.) *Annual Register*, 1793, p. 69.

Gordon, Thomas, a noted religious writer, was born in Kirkcudbright, Galloway, Scotland, about 1684, and had a university education. While young he went to London, at first as a teacher, and afterwards as a writer, becoming widely known for his political and religious articles and pamphlets. He died July 28, 1750. He published, *Tacitus Translated into English* (1728-31):—*The Independent Whig, or a Defence of Primitive Christianity* (1732):—*Sallust Translated into English* (1744):—two collections of tracts: I. *A Cordial for Low Spirits* (1750); II. *The Pillars of Priestcraft and Orthodoxy Shaken* (eod.). See Chalmers, *Biog. Dict.* s. v.; Allibone, *Dict. of Brit. and Amer. Authors*, s. v.

Gordon, Thomas Patterson, D.D., a Presbyterian minister, was born in Monongahela City, Washington Co., Pa., July 23, 1813. He graduated from Jefferson College, Canonsburg, in 1834, and from the Theological Seminary at Allegheny in 1837; was licensed by Ohio Presbytery, and ordained pastor of the Buffalo Church in Cumberland, where he labored till 1842 with great acceptance. In 1846 he was appointed an agent for the Board of Domestic Missions, but the same year became pastor at Allegheny, Pa.; in 1850 he removed to Wellsville, O.; in 1856 became pastor of the Sixth Church, Pittsburgh, Pa.; in 1857 removed to Terre Haute, Ind., and died there, Aug. 15, 1865. See Wilson, *Presb. Hist. Almanac*, 1867, p. 150.

Gordon, William (1), a Scotch prelate, was bishop of Aberdeen about 1556, and died there in 1557. See Keith, *Scottish Bishops*, p. 122.

Gordon, William (2), D.D., an English clergyman and historian, was born at Hitchin, Hertfordshire, in 1729, and educated at a Dissenting academy near London. He was pastor of an Independent Church at Ipswich, and was subsequently successor to Dr. David Jennings, in the church at Old Gravel Lane, Wapping. He removed to America in 1770, and became minister of the Third Church, Roxbury, Mass. In 1781 he returned to England, and preached both at St. Neots, Huntingdonshire, and at Ipswich. He died at the latter place, Oct. 19, 1807. He published sermons, etc., 1772, 1775, 1777, 1783:—*An Abridgment of Jonathan Edwards' Treatise on the Religious Affections*:—*A History of the Rise, Progress, and Establishment of the Independency of the United States of America* (1788). See Chalmers, *Biog. Dict.* s. v.; Allibone, *Dict. of Brit. and Amer. Authors*, s. v.

Gorgons, in Greek mythology, were daughters of Phorcys and Ceto, of extraordinary beauty, but because of their pride were changed by the gods into snake-haired monsters. Their heads were covered with dragon-scales, they had teeth like hyenas, brazen hands, and wings. Their appearance was so horrible that all who saw them were transformed into stone. Their names were: Stheno, Euryale, and Medusa; the latter is usually called Gorgo. The first two were immortal, Medusa was not. When Perseus was ordered to get the head of the Gorgon, only Medusa could have been meant. See MEDUSA.

Gorham, NICHOLAS, an eminent Dominican of the 14th century, was born at Gorham, near St. Alban's, Hertfordshire, educated at Merton College, Oxford, went to France when a young man, spent the rest of his life there, and died in Paris about 1400. "Many and learned are his books," says Thomas Fuller, "having commented on almost all the Scriptures, and no hands have fewer spots of pitch upon them who touched the superstition of that age" (*Worthies of England*, ed Nuttall, ii, 51).

Göring, CHRISTIAN CARL ERNST, a Lutheran theologian, who died June 18, 1866, at Windsheim, in Bavaria, is the author of, *Mitgabe für's Leben* (4th ed. Nüremberg, 1848, 2 parts):—*Täglicher Wandel des Christen*, etc. (4th ed. Nördlingen, 1854):—*Morgen- und Abendsegen des Christen* (4th ed. 1858):—*Passions-Buch* (1856):—*Kern des teutschen Liederschatzes* (1828), etc. See Zuchold, *Bibl. Theol.* i, 451 sq.; Koch, *Geschichte des deutschen Kirchenliedes*, vii, 51 sq. (B. P.)

Gorionides. See JOSEPH BEN-GORION.

Gorlov, STEPHEN, a philologist, was born in Prussia, Dec. 27, 1619. He studied at Königsberg, was in 1647 professor of Hebrew there, and died Aug. 19, 1678. He wrote, *Disp. de Christo Filio Æterni Patris*:—*De Detorsionibus et Exceptionibus Nonnullis Judæorum in Lippmanni Nizzachon*:—*De Confusionis Linguarum Origine et Modo*:—*De Initio Decalogi Exod. xx*, 1:—*De Protevangelio Gen. iii*, 15:—*De Sono Tubarum Sanctuarii*. See Jöcher, *Allgemeines Gelehrten-Lexikon*, s. v.; Fürst, *Bibl. Jud.* i, 339. (B. P.)

Gorran, NICOLAS DE, a French theologian, was born probably in 1230. After having begun his studies with the preaching friars of Le Mans, he went to the college of Saint Jacob, at Paris; became immediately afterwards one of the lecturers of the college, and, having gained some reputation in the pulpit, was appointed confessor to the king of Navarre, son of Phillippe the Bold. Gorran died in 1295. He wrote some commentaries or postils on the Holy Scriptures, and sermons, a few only of which were published. See Hoefer, *Nouv. Biog. Générale*, s. v.

Görres. See GOERRES.

Gorsius, PETRUS, a French Jesuit, was born in 1590, and died at Beziers, April 27, 1661. He is the author of, *Meditationes in Omnes Dominicas et Festa Totius Anni:—Explicatio in Proverbia Solomonis:—Explicatio in Ecclesiastem:—Explicatio in Ecclesiasticum:—Explicatio in Librum Sapientiæ.* See Alegambe, *Bibliotheca Scriptorum Societatis Jesu;* Jöcher, *Allgemeines Gelehrten-Lexikon,* s. v. (B. P.)

Gorskius, Jacobus, a Polish Roman Catholic theologian, and archdeacon at Gnesen, who died June 17, 1585, is the author of, *De Usu Legitimo Eucharistiæ:—De Baptismo Prædestinatorum:—Animadversiones in Theologos Würtemberg:—Adversus Apostatam Christ. Francken.* See Staravolscius, *Scriptorum Poloniæ Centuria;* Ghilini, *Teatro d' Uomini Letterati;* Jöcher, *Allgemeines Gelehrten-Lexikon,* s. v. (B. P.)

Gosains (or **Goswami**) are the Hindû priests of Ekliñga, in Rajasthan. They all wear a crescent in the forehead—the distinguishing mark of the faith of Siva. It is not uncommon to find Gosains, who have made a vow of celibacy, following secular pursuits, such as the mercantile and military professions. Some of these are among the richest merchants of India, while the soldiers possess lands, and beg or serve for pay when called upon.

Goscelin, a Benedictine of St. Bertin, in Artois, who went to England in 1049, and died at the monastery of St. Augustin, in Canterbury, is the author of, *Historia Minor de Vita S. Augustini, Cantuar. Archiepiscopi:—Historia Major de Vita S. Augustini,* etc. See Foppens, *Bibl. Belgica,* i, 379 (1739); *Histoire Littéraire de France,* viii; Wright, *Biogr. Brit.* i, 518, 521 (1842); Jöcher, *Allgemeines Gelehrten-Lexikon,* s. v.; Lichtenberger, *Encyclop. des Sciences Religieuses,* s. v. (B. P.)

Goslawski (Lat. *Goslavius*), Adam, *of Bebelno,* an adherent of Socinus, lived in Poland in the first part of the 17th century, and wrote works in Latin (Rakow, 1607, 1620). Their object is to refute the system of Keckerman and of Martin on the divinity of Jesus Christ. See Hoefer, *Nouv. Biog. Générale,* s. v.

Goslicki, Wawrzyniec (Lat. *Goslicius, Laurentius Grimalius*), a learned Polish ecclesiastic, was born about 1533, and educated at Cracow and Padua. He took orders in the Roman Catholic Church, and was successively appointed bishop of Kaminietz and Posen. He was active in public affairs, and was frequently engaged in political matters. Through his influence the Jesuits were prevented from establishing their schools at Cracow. He was also a strenuous advocate of religious toleration in Poland. He died Oct. 31, 1607. His principal work is *De Optimo Senatore,* etc. (Venice, 1568), of which there are two English translations, *A Commonwealth of Good Counsaile,* etc. (1607), and *The Accomplished Senator, done into English by Mr. Oldisworth* (1733). See *Encyclop. Brit.* 9th ed. s. v.

Gosman, John, D.D., a Reformed (Dutch) minister, was born in New York city in 1784. He graduated from Columbia College in 1801, and studied theology with Drs. Alexander Proudfit and John M. Mason; was licensed by the Presbytery of Washington in 1804, and supplied the Presbyterian churches of Lansingburg, etc., until 1808, when he became pastor at Kingston, to which, for three years, Hurley was attached. In 1835 he removed to the Second Reformed Church, Philadelphia, Pa., but remained only one year. After this he officiated as a stated supply in Port Byron Presbyterian Church (1838–41), and Coeymans and New Baltimore. In 1842 he became pastor of the Reformed Church, in Hudson, and remained eleven years, resigning on account of years and health. But he could not be idle even in his retirement, and so again resumed pastoral work in the little country charge of Flatbush, Ulster Co., in 1854. He resigned in 1859, and died in 1865. Dr. Gosman was a man of commanding presence and genial manners, gifted with brilliant genius, artless as a child, generous and disinterested, full of vivacity and cheerfulness, humorous and witty, transparent, sincere, and attractive. His mind was quick, active, philosophical, and powerful, and his reading covered a wide range in literature and theology. In the pulpit he often exhibited a rare and wonderful eloquence. His sermons were filled with apt illustrations, governed by almost faultless taste, and enriched by his knowledge of the best authors and of our English tongue. His memory was uncommonly retentive. His style was rich, terse, accurate, nervous, strong, and beautiful. In every good work he was a leader. See *Memorial Addresses and Tributes;* Corwin, *Manual of the Ref. Church in America,* s. v. (W. J. R. T.)

Gospel, Book of the, the name of the volume from which the lessons were read. We extract an account of it from Walcott, *Sac. Archæol.* s. v. See Evangelistarium.

"This volume, usually splendidly illuminated and bound in jewelled covers, always stood on the altar upon a stand, and the latter is called in 1640, in England, a desk: with degrees of advancement, in 1558 it stood in the midst of the altar. Two tapers, according to Amalarius, were carried before the gospeller to represent the light of the gospel in the world, and other candles, signifying the law and the prophets, were extinguished, to show their accomplishment in the gospel. In St. Augustine's time the gospel was read on the north side, in allusion to the prophetical verse, Jer. iii, 12; and the old sacramentaries added, because it is preached to those cold in faith; but at Rome, because the men sat on the south side, and the women on the north, the deacon turned to the former, as mentioned by Amalarius, probably in allusion to 1 Cor. xiv, 35. The Gemma Animæ speaks of reading from the north side as a new custom, but it is prescribed by the use of Hereford and Seville. In some parts of England, however, the south side was still observed as late as the 15th century. When the epistle was read on the lowest, the gospel was read on the upper choir steps from a lectern; on principal festivals, Palm Sunday, and the eves of Easter and Pentecost, they were read in the rood-loft. As at St. Paul's, in cathedrals of the new foundation, also, and in all cathedrals, by the canons of 1603, a gospeller and epistolar, or deacon and subdeacon, who are either minor canons or priest-vicars, are appointed; they are to be vested 'agreeably' to the celebrant or principal minister, that is, in copes. In 1159 all these were to be canons at York, by pope Alexander III's order. Anastasius I, c. 405, ordered all priests to stand and bow reverently at the reading of the gospel. In the 6th century the people stood at the reading of both these lections, but standing was retained at the gospel only, in deference to Him that speaketh therein. At the end of the epistle the words are said, 'Here endeth the epistle," but no such form follows the gospel, because it is continued in the creed. The custom of saying 'Glory be to thee, O Lord,' prescribed before the gospel in Edward VI's First Book, and saying after it 'Thanks be to God for his holy gospel,' is as old as the time of St. Chrysostom. In Poland, during a time of idolatry, prince Mieczlaus ordered in 968 that at mass, as a sign of Christian faith, while the gospel was reading every man should draw his sword

Ancient Book of the Gospels.

half out of his scabbard, to show that all were ready to fight to death for the gospel. There was a curious English mediæval superstition of crossing the legs when the gospel from the first chapter of St. John was read. The Gospel oak was the tree at which the gospel was read in the Rogation processions."

Gospels, APOCRYPHAL (or SPURIOUS). By way of supplement we add the following. At an early period two classes of these works were noted: first, such as have reference to the infancy of Christ, or *Evangelia Infantiæ;* and, secondly, such as speak of his passion, or *Evangelia Passionis Jesu Christi.* The following are now extant:

1. *Protevangelium Jacobi*, or, according to its title in the manuscripts, *The History of James concerning the Birth of Mary* (Ἡ ἱστορία Ἰακώβου περὶ τῆς γεννήσειος Μαρίας). See Tischendorf, *Evangelia Apocrypha* (Leipsic, 1853), p. 1-49; Wright, *Contributions to the Apocryphal Literature of the New Testament, Collected and Edited from Syriac MSS. in the British Museum* (Lond. 1865).

2. *Evangelium Pseudo-Matthæi sive Liber de Ortu Beatæ Mariæ et Infantia Salvatoris.* See Thilo, *Codex Apocryphus New Test.* p. 337-400; Schade, *Liber de Infantia Mariæ et Christi Salvatoris* (Halle, 1869); Tischendorf, *l. c.* p. 50-105.

3. *Evangelium de Nativitate Mariæ*, which seems to be but another form of 2. See Tischendorf, *l. c.* p. 106-114.

4. *Historia Josephi Fabri Lignarii.* See Tischendorf, p. 115-133.

5. *Evangelium Thomæ.* Tischendorf, who discovered different recensions, gives a threefold text, two in Greek, and one in Latin. The Greek titles are (1), Θωμᾶ ἰσραηλίτου φιλοσόφου ῥητὰ εἰς τὰ παιδικὰ τοῦ Κυρίου: (2) Σύγγραμμα τοῦ ἁγίου: (3) Ἀποστόλου Θωμᾶ περὶ τῆς παιδικῆς ἀναστροφῆς τοῦ Κυρίου. The Latin title is, *Tractatus de Pueritia Jesu Secundum Thomam.* A Syriac text with an English translation was published by Wright (Lond. 1875).

6. *Evangelium Infantiæ Arabicum.* See Tischendorf, p. 171-202.

7. *Evangelium Nicodemi*, consisting of two separate works, (a) *Gesta Pilati* and (b) *Descensus Christi ad Infernos.* Both these works were joined together at an early date, though the combination did not receive the name it now bears until after the time of Charlemagne. The original title of the first work was Ὑπομνήματα τοῦ Κυρίου ἡμῶν Ἰησοῦ Χριστοῦ πραχθέντα ἐπὶ Ποντίου Πιλάτου, hence the Latin title, *Gesta Pilati* (in Gregor. Turon. *Hist. Franc.* i, 21, 24) or *Acta Pilati* (Justin Mart. *Apolog.* i, 35). The author of the *Acta Pilati* was probably a Jewish Christian, and the work is of some importance for the explanation and further elucidation of the canonical gospels. See Hofmann, *Leben Jesu*, p. 264, 379, 386, 396; Tischendorf, *Pilati circa Christum Judicio quid Lucis Offeratur Exactis Pilati* (Leipsic, 1855); Lipsius, *Die Pilatus-Akten* (Kiel, 1871).

The second part of the *Evangelium Nicodemi*, the *Descensus Christi ad Infernos*, or Διήγησις περὶ τοῦ πάθους τοῦ Κυρίου ἡμῶν Ἰησοῦ Χριστοῦ καὶ τῆς ἁγίας αὐτοῦ ἀναστάσεως, is of very little importance. In connection with these two works, Tischendorf gives some other apocryphal fabrications, which together form a group by themselves: namely, *Epistola Pilati*, incorporated in the apocryphal *Acts of St. Peter and St. Paul* (Greek text in Tischendorf, *Acta Apost. Apocryph.* p. 16); which is a letter, addressed to the emperor Claudius Tiberius, containing a report of the resurrection of Christ; *Epistola Pontii Pilati*, another letter by him, in which he excuses the unjustness of his verdict by the impossibility of resisting the prevailing excitement; *Anaphora Pilati*, a report on the trial, execution, death, and resurrection of Jesus; *Paradosis Pilati*, a report of the examination of Pilate before the emperor, his condemnation and execution. A forgery of later origin is the Latin *Epistola Pilati ad Tiberium* (Tischendorf, p. 411 sq.). To these *Evangelia Apocrypha*, which only constitute the smallest part of apocryphal gospels, the following must be added:

8. *Evangelium Secundum Ægyptios*, i. e. "the Gospel of the Egyptians," in use among the Encratites (Clem. Alex. *Strom.* iii, 9, p. 540 sq.; Potter, xiii, 553) and the Sabellians (Epiphan. *Hær.* lxii, 2).

9. *Evangelium Æternum*, the work of a Minorite of the 13th century, and condemned by pope Alexander IV.

10. *Evangelium Andræ*, mentioned by pope Innocent I (*Epist.* 6, *ad Exuper.*) and St. Augustine (*Contra Advers. Leg. et Prophet.* 20).

11. *Evangelium Apellis*, probably a mutilation of one of the canonical gospels.

12. *Evangelium Duodecim Apostolorum*, mentioned by Origen (*Hom.* 1 *in Luc.*); Ambros. (*Prooem. in Lucam*); Jerome (*Prooem. in Matt.*)

13. *Evangelium Barnabæ*, mentioned in the *Decretum Gelasii*, vi, 10, and in the catalogue of Anastasius Sinaita (by Credner, *Gesch. des Kanons*, p. 241).

14. *Evangelium Bartholomæi*, mentioned by Jerome, *Præf. in Matt.;* Gelasii, *Decretum*, vi, 12.

15. *Evangelium Basilidis*, mentioned by Origen, *Tract.* 26 *in Matt. xxxiii*, 34; Euseb. *Hist. Eccl.* 4, 7.

16. *Evangelium Cerinthi*, seems to have been the Gospel according to Matthew, arbitrarily remodelled, and in this mutilated shape accepted by the Carpocratians.

17. *Evangelium Ebionitarum*, of which fragments are found in Epiphan. *Hæres. xxx*, 13, 16, 21.

18. *Evangelium Evæ*, in use by some gnostics (Epiphan. *Hæres. xxvi*, 2, 3, 5).

19. *Evangelium Secundum Hebræos*, one of the oldest apocryphal productions, written in Chaldee with Hebrew letters, used by the Nazarenes, and translated into Greek and Latin by Jerome. See Nicholson, *The Gospel according to the Hebrews* (Lond. 1879).

20. *Evangelium Jacobi Majoris*, found in Spain in 1595, and condemned by Innocent XI in 1682.

21. *Joannis de Transitu Mariæ*, not published by Tischendorf.

22. *Evangelium Judæ Ischariotæ*, used by the Cainites.

23. *Evangelium Leucii.*

24. *Evangelia, quæ Falsavit Lucianus, Apocrypha* and *Evangelia, quæ Falsavit Hesychius, Apocrypha.* See Griesbach, *Prolog. in ed. Nov. Test. iii;* Hug, *Einleitung in das Neue Test.* 37, 38.

25. *Evangelia Manichæorum*, comprising

(a.) *Evangelium Thomæ*, different from the one given under 5.

(b.) *Evangelium Vivum.*

(c.) *Evangelium Philippi.*

(d.) *Evangelium Abdæ*, also called Μόδιος, i. e. *The Bushel.*

26. *Evangelium Marcionis*, a mutilation of the Gospel according to Luke, by the founder of the famous anti-Jewish sect.

27. *Mariæ Interrogationes Majores et Minores*, two works of obscene contents, used by some Gnostics.

28. *Evangelium Matthiæ*, mentioned by Origen, Jerome, Eusebius, Gelasius, and Beda.

29. *Narratio de Legali Christi Sacerdotio*, comp. Suidas, s. v. Ἰησοῦς.

30. *Evangelium Perfectionis*, used by the Basilidians and other Gnostics.

31. *Evangelium Petri* was in use in the congregation of Rhossus, in Cilicia, towards the close of the 2d century.

32. *Evangelium Philippi*, used by the Gnostics.

33. *Evangelium Simonitarum*, or as it was called by themselves, *Liber Quatuor Angulorum et Cardinum Mundi*, i. e. *Book of the Four Corners and Hinges of the World*, divided into four parts.

34. *Evangelium Secundum Syros*, probably identical with the *Evangelium Secundum Hebræos.*

35. *Evangelium Tatiani*, a compilation from the four gospels, hence also called *Diatessaron* (τὸ διὰ τεσσάρων). See Zahn, *Tatian's Diatesseron* (Erlangen, 1881).

36. *Evangelium Thaddæi*, mentioned in some MSS. of the *Decretum Gelasianum.* See Credner, *Zur Gesch. des Kanons* (Halle, 1847), p. 21.

37. *Evangelium Valentini*, which is perhaps the same as the *Evangelium Veritatis* used by the Valentinians, and differing widely from the canonical gospels.

See Hofmann, in Herzog-Plitt, s. v., *Apokryphen des Neuen Testaments;* Smith, *Dict. of Christ. Biog.* s. v. (B. P.)

Gospeller is a name applied to the priest in the English Church who reads the gospel in the communion service, standing at the north side of the altar. In some cathedrals one of the clergy is appointed specially to perform this duty; hence the name.

Göss, Karl Ernst Friedrich, a Lutheran theologian of Germany, was born June 18, 1757. In 1787 he was deacon, in 1814 pastor at Baiersdorf, near Erlangen, and died June 28, 1836. He wrote, *Der Verfall des öffentlichen Cultus im Mittelalter* (Sulzbach, 1820):—*Die Seelen-Feste* (Erlangen, 1825). See Winer, *Handbuch der theol. Lit.* i, 576, 619. (B. P.)

Gossel, Andreas Arnold, a Lutheran theologian of Germany, was born Dec. 20, 1700, in East Frisia. He studied at Halle, was preacher in 1723, in 1741 court-preacher at Aurich, in Prussia, and died Dec. 9, 1770. He published, *Das Evangelium von Christo, in dem liii Kapitel Iesaiä* (Bremen, 1733):—*Das Evangelium in dem liv Kapitel Iesaiä* (1736):—*Das Evangelisch-lutherische Kirchen Glaubensbekenntniss* (1739):—*Richtige Mittelstrasse in der Gnadenlehre der Evangelisch-lutherischen Kirche* (1747). See Neubauer, *Jetztlebende Theologen;* Jöcher, *Allgemeines Gelehrten-Lexikon*, s. v. (B. P.)

Gosset, Isaac, D.D., F.R.S., a Church of England divine, well known in London as a most intelligent purchaser and collector of books, and conspicuous at all public sales by his diminutive person, was born in 1744. He was of a refugee French family, and was the son of a modeller in wax, settled in London. He displayed from his childhood an extraordinary passion for rare books, and was educated at Exeter College, Oxford. He became eminent as a preacher, notwithstanding his personal disadvantages, but never sought or obtained a preferment. He was a good scriptural critic, and excelled as a bibliographer. He died Dec. 16, 1812. See (Lond.) *Annual Register*, 1812, p. 182.

Gosson, Stephen, an English divine and poet, was born at Kent in 1554, and was educated at Christchurch, Oxford. He became rector of St. Botolph, Bishopsgate Street, London, which post he retained until his death. He was distinguished for his opposition to the dramatic entertainments of the day. His death occurred in 1623. His publications are, *The School of Abuse* (1587):—*Plays Confuted in Five Actions:—The Trumpet of Weale.* See Chalmers, *Biog. Dict.* s. v.; Allibone, *Dict. of Brit. and Amer. Authors*, s. v.

Gossuin, an abbot of Anchin, theologian and scholastic philosopher, was born at Douai in 1086. He was one of the most distinguished students of the University of Paris, where he soon gained the reputation of an excellent grammarian and dialectician. Being admitted to the school of Joslain de Vierzy, who later became bishop of Soissons and also minister of Louis VII, king of France, he was selected by his fellow-students to bring to Abelard, the rival of his teacher, a challenge on science. On his return to his native city, Gossuin entered into orders, and became successively minister of several monasteries. He was at the abbey of Anchin when pope Innocent II charged him with the conversion of Abelard, who had been condemned to confinement and silence. Afterwards he was appointed abbot of Saint-Pierre-de-Châlons, and of Lobbes, in Hainaut, but he refused to accept. Gossuin finally accepted the abbey of Anchin, and governed wisely this opulent monastery. He assisted at the Council of Rheims in 1147, where he gained the friendship of St. Bernard. Gossuin died in 1166. See Hoefer, *Nouv. Biog. Générale*, s. v.

Goswami. See Gosains.

Goth, Bérand de, a French prelate, brother of pope Clement V, and son of Bérand I, lord of Villandrault (diocese of Bordeaux), was appointed to the archiepiscopate of Lyons in 1288. Bérand made his brother Bertrand de Goth his vicar-general. This appointment led to a long controversy. Bérand was made cardinal-bishop of Albano in 1294, by Celestine V. Boniface VIII appointed him his legate in France, to restore peace between the kings of France and England. Bérand died on his return from England, without having seen the end of the dissension, July 12, 1297. See Hoefer, *Nouv. Biog. Générale*, s. v.

Goths (*Gothones, Gotones, Guttones*, in Tacitus and Pliny), a German people, originally dwelling along the Baltic sea between the Vistula and the Oder. Their native name, *Gutthinda*, is preserved in the *Fragments* of bishop Ulphilas. The later form, *Gothi*, does not occur until the time of Caracalla. At the beginning of the 3d century they are spoken of as a powerful nation in the regions of the lower Danube, where the *Getæ* and Scythians of former times had lived, and the name of *Getæ* or Scythian is sometimes applied to them. The different tribes composing this people were: 1. The *Gothi Minores* or *Mœsogoths*, who became permanently established in Mœsia, and devoted themselves to agricultural pursuits (Jornandes, 51, 52); 2. *Gothi Tetraxitæ*, Ostrogoths of the Palus Mæotis (Procop. *Bell. Goth.* iv); 3. *Taifalæ*, in Dacia, a branch of the Visigoths (Ammian. Marcell. xvii, 13; xxxi, 3; *Eutrop.* viii, 2); 4. *Gepidæ;* 5. *Rugii;* 6. *Sciri* and *Turcilingi;* 7. *Heruli;* 8. *Juthungi;* some writers include also the Alans and Vandals among the Goths. The nation of the Goths was divided into two principal groups; the *Ostrogoths*, who occupied the sandy steppes of the East, and the *Visigoths*, who inhabited the more fertile and wooded countries of the West. Zosimus and Ammianus Marcellinus frequently mention the *Greutingi* or *Grutingi* and the *Thervingi* or *Tervingi*, concerning whom different opinions are entertained by modern writers. They were, perhaps, the leading tribes among the Ostrogoths and Visigoths respectively. The language of the Goths resembled the ancient dialect of the Franks very closely. They wore beards, and suffered their yellow hair to grow long. The royal dignity among them was hereditary.

The occupation of Dacia by this people took place during the reign of the emperor Philip (A.D. 244–249), and was immediately followed by aggressive wars against the Romans, in which Mœsia, Macedonia, and Greece suffered from their incursions, and the armies of the emperor Decius were twice defeated and destroyed. Between 253 and 269 they ravaged the coasts of Europe and Asia Minor with a fleet of which they had become possessed. Pityus, Trapezus, Chalcedon, Nicomedia, Nicæa, Prusa, Apamea, and Cius fell before their assaults: Cyzicus was destroyed; and the coast of Greece, from the south of Peloponnesus to Epirus and Thessaly was ravaged, Illyricum in particular being literally ransacked. In 269 Crete and Cyprus were swept by their destructive power, and Cassandrea and Thessalonica were besieged; but in that year the emperor Claudius defeated them in three great battles, which earned for him the name of *Gothicus*, and broke the barbarian power. A period of comparative quiet, interrupted by few and unimportant expeditions, now ensued in the history of the Goths. In 272 the emperor Aurelian ceded to them the province of Dacia. In 332 they followed their king, Araric, across the Danube, but were defeated, and concluded a peace which lasted until the family of Constantine vacated the imperial throne. In 375 vast swarms of Huns and Alans poured out of Asia and drove back the Ostrogoths upon the Visigoths, which latter people thereupon obtained permission to settle in Thrace, at that time lying desolate, the condition being imposed by the emperor Valens that they should embrace Christianity. Insolent usage, which they were called upon to endure at the hands of Roman officers, soon drove them into rebellion, however, and in the war which ensued they completely defeated the army of Valens in 378, and killed the emperor himself by burning a cottage which he had entered in his flight. From that time they exercised an important influence over the affairs of Constantinople, and were for a time regularly engaged in the service of the Roman empire. The application of the Ostrogoths for admission into the territories of the empire, when threatened by the Huns, was denied, and they were compelled to seek refuge in the mountains until after the defeat of the Huns in 453, when they obtained a settlement in Pannonia and Slavonia.

In 396 the Visigoths, led by Alaric, invaded and devastated Greece, till the arrival of the Roman general Stilicho, in the following year, compelled their retreat. In 400 they invaded Italy, but were defeated. A treaty was thereupon made between Alaric and Stilicho, which transferred the services of the former to the Western emperor, Honorius. A second invasion, occasioned by the delay of the Romans to meet the demands of Alaric for pay, and a western province as a home for his nation, took place 408-410. In 408 Rome was subjected to a severe blockade, from which it relieved itself by the payment of a heavy ransom. Refusal to comply with Alaric's demands led to a second siege, in which Ostia was occupied, Rome unconditionally surrendered, and the empire transferred to Attalus, but soon restored to Honorius. In 410 an assault upon the Visigoths, made with imperial sanction, provoked the storming and sack of the city, Aug. 24-30. After the death of Alaric the Visigoths established a new kingdom in Southern Gaul and Spain, which reached its highest prosperity during the latter half of the 5th century, but was soon afterwards harassed by the Franks, in Gaul, and wholly overthrown about two centuries later by the Saracens.

After the overthrow of the Huns the Ostrogoths in Pannonia became so powerful that the Eastern empire was obliged to purchase peace with them by large sums of money. Their king, Widemir, led his hosts into Italy, but they eventually joined the Visigoths in the West. Other bands, under various leaders, traversed the Eastern empire, and were finally settled between the Lower Danube and Mount Hæmus, in the very heart of the empire. In 487 king Theodoric, after protracted disputes with the emperor Zeno, marched upon Constantinople, whereupon that monarch, to save his capital, authorized the Goths to invade Italy and expel the usurper Odoacer. The enterprise was undertaken in 488, and completed in 493, at which time Odoacer was assassinated, and all his strongholds were in the possession of his adversary. Theodoric remained undisputed master of Italy during a prosperous reign of thirty-three years; but on his death his kingdom was attacked by foreign enemies, and became the prey of the Eastern empire, and the Ostrogoths ceased to be an independent people.

Christianity was introduced among the Goths about the middle of the 3d century, by prisoners taken in their wars, and there is evidence that a continuous tradition of orthodox Christianity existed from that time among the tribes who bordered on the Euxine. A Gothic bishop, Theophilus, was present in 325 at the Council of Nice, and even earlier Athanasius (*De Incarne. Verb.* § 51 sq.; Migne, xxv, 187 sq.; Neander, *Church History*, Engl. transl. iii, 179) alludes to the influence of Christianity over Gothic (?) barbarians; while Chrysostom (Ep. xiv; Migne, lii, 618) and Procopius (*Bell. Goth.* iv, 4; ed. Bonn. ii, 475) both speak of applications made to the emperor for a successor to recent Gothic bishops. The propagation of Christianity among the Visigoths was carried forward principally by bishop Ulphilas (q. v.), whose work, beginning in 348, was successful enough from the very first to excite the hostility of the heathen and call forth persecution. Ulphilas and many of his converts fled across the Danube and settled in the neighborhood of Nicopolis. The particular form of teaching adhered to by Ulphilas was that of Arianism, which had already taken deep root, and was yet more firmly established when Fridigern, who had rebelled against the king, Athanaric, consented to become a Christian and an Arian in order that he might secure the support of the Roman emperor, and when, as already related, the Visigoths were obliged to take refuge against the Huns in the territories of the empire ruled over by the Arian, Valens. Subsequently efforts were put forth to win them to Catholicism, especially by Chrysostom, who became patriarch of Constantinople in 398, but with little result. The Goths continued to be fanatical Arians, and became even violent persecutors after their settlement in Gaul and Spain, until the stubborn resistance of the Catholic party was strengthened by the accession of the Franks, and the Gothic king, Recared, solemnly passed over to the Catholic faith at the third Synod of Toledo in 589.

The Ostrogoths, though Arians, were not fanatical adherents of that creed, and Theodoric especially manifested a tolerant spirit towards the Catholics. Chrysostom's missionaries were zealously employed among these tribes, and achieved noteworthy successes. In the Crimea the Catholic Unilas was bishop of the Tetraxite Goths, and established a connection with Constantinople which remained unbroken until the 6th century. The district of Gotia, on the Cimmerian Bosphorus, was a diocese connected with the Byzantine Church in the Middle Ages, and the surname of Gotia was borne by the bishop of Capha as late as the 18th century.

In closing this article a few words respecting the culture of the Goths are required. The introduction of Christianity, and contact with the civilized subjects of Rome, did much to raise them above other German tribes in point of civilization. Ulphilas, in the 4th century, formed a new alphabet out of those of the Greeks and Romans, which was generally adopted by the German peoples, and is essentially the same as that still in use in Germany and known among us as the "black-letter" alphabet. His translation of the Scriptures into the Gothic language is, in the fragments which still survive, the most ancient document of the German language now extant. No other monuments of the Gothic language of considerable importance have been preserved. The Visigoths had a code of written laws, which was probably the first existing among German tribes, and the authorship of which is usually ascribed to their king, Euric, of the 5th century.

Ancient Sources.— Tacitus, *Germania;* Procopius, *Bell. Goth.;* Jornandes, *De Rebus Geticis;* Idacius of Lamego, *Chronicon;* Isidor. Hispal. *Hist. Goth.;* Cassiodorus, *Varia et Chron.*

Modern Literature.—Eisenschmidt, *De Origine Ostrogoth. et Visigothorum* (Jena, 1835); Zahn, *Ulfila's Gothische Bibelübersetze* (Weissenfels, 1805); Aschbach, *Gesch. d. Westgothen* (Frankfort-on-the-Main, 1827); Manso, *Gesch. d. Ostgothen in Italien* (Breslau, 1824); Wilhelm, *Germanien u. seine Bewohner* (Naumburg, 1823); Von Werbse, *Völker u. Volkerbündnisse d. Alten Deutschl.* (Hanover, 1825); Zeuss, *D. Deutschen u. Nachbarstämme;* Forbiger, *Handb. d. Alten Geographie* (Leipsic, 1848, vol. iii); Duncker, *Origg. Germaniæ;* Köpke, *Anfänge d. Königthums bei d. Gothen* (Berlin, 1859); Richter, *D. Weströmische Reich*, A.D. 375-388 (ibid. 1865); Bernhardt, *Gesch. Roms*, A.D. 253-313 (ibid. 1867); Krafft, *Gesch. d. Germ. Völker*, i, 1 (ibid. 1854); Waitz, *Leben u. Lehre d. Ulfila* (Hanover, 1840, 4to); Lembke, *Gesch. v. Spanien* (Hamburg, 1831, vol. i); Gibbon, *Decline and Fall of the Roman Empire;* Pallmann, *Gesch. d. Völker-*

wanderung, i, p. 62–85; Bessell, in Ersch and Gruber's *Encyklop.* s. v. *Gothen* and *Leben d. Ulfilas u. Bekehrung d. Gothen*, etc. (Göttingen, 1860); comp. J. Grimm, *Gesch. d. Deutschen Sprache.*

See also Smith, *Dict. of Greek and Roman Geography*, s. v.; *Gothi*, in Herzog *Real-Encyklop.* s. v.; Kurtz, *Manual of Christ. Hist.* Engl. transl. i, § 76.

Gothus, ANDRÆUS THOMAS, a Swedish ecclesiastic, was born at Wadstena in 1582. Having finished his studies at Upsal, he became rector at Wadstena in 1613, pastor at Aby in 1625, and soon afterwards was elevated to the rank of a provost. He died at Aby in 1657, leaving *Een Kort och waelgrund ad Rachnekonst* ("Short and Good Treatise on the Art of Counting," Stockholm, 1621):—*Thesaurus Epistolicus* (ibid. 1619, 1631):—*Theoria Vitæ Æternæ* (ibid. 1647). See Hoefer, *Nouv. Biog. Générale*, s. v.

Götschel, JOHANN CHRISTOPH FRIEDRICH, a Lutheran theologian of Germany, was born Dec. 8, 1768, at Bayreuth. He studied at Erlangen, was in 1790 pastor at Prague, in 1798 superintendent, accepted a call in 1799 to Eutin, and died Feb. 8, 1812. He wrote, *De Moralitate Ejusque Gradus Imputatione* (Erlangen, 1788):—*De Interpretatione Loci* 1 *Cor. xi*, 10 (ibid. eod.):—and *Sermons.* See Döring, *Die gelehrten Theologen Deutschlands*, s. v. (B. P.)

Götten, Gabriel Wilhelm, a Lutheran theologian of Germany, was born Dec. 4, 1708, at Magdeburg. He studied at Halle, was in 1736 pastor at Celle, in 1741 superintendent at Luneburg, in 1746 at Hanover, and died in 1781. He published sermons and other ascetical writings. See Winer, *Handbuch der theol. Lit.* i, 391; Döring, *Die gelehrten Theologen Deutschlands*, s. v.; Jöcher, *Allgemeines Gelehrten-Lexikon*, s. v. (B. P.)

Götten, Heinrich Ludwig, a Lutheran theologian of Germany, was born in Brunswick in 1677. He studied at Helmstädt, Halle, and Leipsic, was in 1706 preacher at Magdeburg, and died Aug. 5, 1737. He wrote *Anleitung, das Leiden und Sterben Christi*, and a number of *Sermons.* See Strodtmann, *Neues gelehrtes Europa*, vii, 620; Jöcher, *Allgemeines Gelehrten-Lexikon*, s. v. (B. P.)

Götten, Jacob, a Lutheran theologian of Germany, was born at Lubeck, July 26, 1629. He studied at Rostock, Leipsic, and Strasburg, and afterwards went into the Netherlands. While there he had frequent relations with the Jesuits, who, in expectation of converting him, had shut him up. But he escaped, and returned in 1653 to his native place, to preach the reformed religion. He became pastor of the church of St. John in 1658, and died Feb. 1, 1671. He wrote *Observationes Historico-theologicæ*:—*Spar-Stunden kurtzer Betrachtungen*, etc. See Hoefer, *Nouv. Biog. Générale*, s. v.

Gotter, Friedrich Gotthelf, a Lutheran theologian of Germany, was born Jan. 17, 1682, at Altenburg. He studied at Wittenberg and Jena, was in 1711 rector at Eisenberg, in 1737 pastor primarius and superintendent, and died May 21, 1746. He wrote, *De Conjugis Pilati Somnio* (Jena, 1704):—*De Græca Voce οὐρανοῦ Sive Cœli* (ibid. 1705):—*Diss. Historica de Henochia Urbe Prima* (1705):—*De Obscuritate Epistolis Pauli Falso Tributa* (1732):—*Miracula Christi ab Objectionibus Woolstonii Vindicata* (1733). See Neubauer, *Jetztlebende Theologen;* Jöcher, *Allgemeines Gelehrten-Lexikon*, s. v. (B. P.)

Gotter, Ludwig Andreas, a Lutheran hymnwriter of Germany, was born at Gotha, May 26, 1661, and died there, Sept. 19, 1735. Some of his hymns are still in use in the German Evangelical Church. See Koch, *Gesch. des deutschen Kirchenliedes*, iv, 400 sq.; Rudolph, *Gothaische Chronik*, iii, 272; Wezel, *Anal. Hymn.* ii, 22–30. (B. P.)

Gottfried (*abbot*) OF VENDÔME (hence *Vindocinensis*), who flourished about the year 1110, wrote *De Corpore et Sanguine Christi*:—*De Ordinatione Episcoporum*:—*De Simonia et Investitura Laicorum*:—*De Effectibus Baptismi, Confirmationis, Unctionis Infirmorum et S. Cœnæ*:—*De Iteratione Sacramenti*:—*De Tribus, quæ Pastori, in esse Debent, Justitia in Judico, Discretione in Præcepto, et Providentia in Consilio.* Gottfried's works were published by Sirmond, Paris, 1610. See Auber, *Historie des Cardinaux;* Cave, *Historia Literaria Scriptorum Ecclesiasticorum;* Jöcher, *Allgemeines Gelehrten-Lexikon*, s. v. (B. P.)

Gottfried, Christian Georg, a German convert from Judaism, who lived in the 17th century, is the author of *Einfältige doch gründliche Erläuterung der jüdischen Irrthümer* (Hamburg, 1693). See Wolf, *Bibl. Hebr.* iii, 976; Jöcher, *Allgemeines Gelehrten-Lexikon*, s. v.; Fürst, *Bibl. Jud.* i, 340. (B. P.)

Gottfried, Jacob, a famous German jurist, born at Geneva, Sept. 13, 1587, was professor of law in 1619, and died June 24, 1652. He wrote a commentary on the *Codex Theodosianus*, edited and published by Morillius in 1665, and by Daniel Ritter in 1736:—*Notæ in Tertulliani ad Nationes, Lib. ii*:—*De Interdicta Christianorum cum Gentilibus Communione*:—*De Statu Paganorum sub Imperatoribus Christianis*:—*Philostorgii Historiam Ecclesiasticam cum Versione et Notis*:—*Exercitationes II de Ecclesia et Incarnatione Christi.* See Niceron, *Mémoires;* Jöcher, *Allgemeines Gelehrten-Lexikon*, s. v. (B. P.)

Gottfried, Johann Christian, a German convert from Judaism (whose former name was *Benjamin Wolf*), who lived in the 18th century, is the author of מעשה ר״י, or a *Narrative of Simon the son of Yochaï*:—*Der ursprüngliche Glaube an die Göttlichkeit des Messias aus dem Sohar nachgewiesen* (translated also into Dutch, Amsterdam, 1724). See Fürst, *Bibl. Jud.* i, 340; Wolf, *Bibl. Hebr.* iii, 362; iv, 844 sq.; Jöcher, *Allgemeines Gelehrten-Lexikon*, s. v. (B. P.)

Gotthold, ISAAC, D.D., a Jewish rabbi, was born in Bamberg, Bavaria, and was in charge of a synagogue there for many years. In 1858 he came to America, and was at different times in charge of congregations in Brooklyn, Albany, and New York. For many years he taught private classes in ancient and modern languages. He died April 11, 1882, while rabbi of the Jewish synagogue in Fifty-seventh Street, New York city, aged seventy-four years.

Gotti, VINCENZIO LUIGI, an Italian cardinal, was born Sept. 5, 1665, at Bologna, where his father was a professor of law, and in 1680 his son took the habit in the convent of the Dominicans of that city. In 1684 he went to the University of Salamanca, and studied theology. In 1688, after his return to Italy, he was appointed to teach successively at Mantua, Rome, and Bologna, becoming, in 1695, professor of theology in the latter place. In 1708 he was made provincial of the Dominicans for Bologna. Pope Clement XI appointed him inquisitor of Milan; three years afterwards, however, Gotti resigned, and returned to Bologna as professor of polemics. In 1728 Benedict XIII conferred upon him the dignity of a cardinal. Benedict XIV made him his theologian, and later protector of the province of Bologna. Gotti died Sept. 18, 1742, leaving *Vera Chiesa di Jesu Christo* (Bologna, 1719):—*Colognia Theologico-Polemica* (ibid. 1727):—*Theologia Scholastico-Dogmatica* (1727):—*De Eligenda Inter Dissidentes Christianos Sententia* (Rome, 1734). See Hoefer, *Nouv. Biog. Générale*, s. v.

Göttingen. See GOETTINGEN.

Gottschalk, ruler of the Wends, and martyr, was educated in the monastery of St. Michael at Lüneburg, but left the monastery, and abandoned Christianity altogether, as soon as he heard that his father Uto, ruler of the Wends, was killed by a Saxon, about the year 1029. To revenge the death of his father, Gottschalk stirred up his countrymen to a frightfnl war against the Saxons. Gottschalk was defeated by Bernhard, duke of Saxony, and taken prisoner. He returned to Christianity, and after his release from prison went to the court of Canute the Great, spent ten years in Denmark and England, and after his return to Wendland in 1043 he united Holstein, Mecklenburg, Pomerania, and the Brandenburg marches into one powerful Wendish empire. He now became one of the most zealous missionaries in his country, translated the liturgical formulas and sermons of German missionaries into the vernacular; he built schools, churches, monasteries, and preached to his people. In spite of all his efforts, there lingered yet among his countrymen a heathenish fanaticism which found vent in an insurrection, that broke out in 1066, and in which Gottschalk was murdered on June 7. See Adam of Bremen, *Gesta Pontif. Hammab.* iii; Helmold, *Chron. Slav.* i, 20; Giesebrecht, *Geschichte der deutschen Kaiserzeit*, ii, 460 sq.; iii, 130 sq.; Hirsch, in *Piper's Kalender*, 1856; Dehio, *Geschichte des Erzbisthums Hamburg-Bremen* (1877), i, 183 sq.; Wagenmann, in Plitt-Herzog *Real-Encyclop.* s. v. (B. P.)

Gottskalcksson, ODDUR, the translator of the New Testament into Icelandic, son of the second bishop of Holum, in Iceland, was educated in Norway, and visited Denmark and Germany. The doctrines of the Reformation began to excite a general sensation throughout the north of Europe, and his own attention was forcibly arrested by the truths which were then unfolded. We are told that, for three successive nights, he prostrated himself half-naked before the Father of lights, beseeching him to open the eyes of his understanding, and to show him whether the principles of Rome or those of Luther were from heaven. The result of his prayers and meditations was a deep-rooted conviction that the cause of the reformer was the cause of God; and with the view of obtaining further information he repaired to Germany, and attended the lectures of Luther and Melanchthon. On his return to Iceland he entered the service of bishop Ogemund. The latter wished Gottskalcksson to become a priest, but he declined the offer, because, as he said, he had no voice for singing. As the servant of bishop Ogemund, he commenced the translation of the New Testament into Icelandic; and, to avoid persecution, he selected a small cell in a cow-house for his study. He completed a version in 1539; but finding it impossible, from the state of public opinion, to print it in Iceland, he sailed for Denmark, and published it at Copenhagen under the patronage of Christian III, in 1540. Besides this translation he published Bugenhagen's history of the sufferings and resurrection of Jesus Christ, and Jonä's sermons on the Catechism in Icelandic. He died in 1557. See Jöcher, *Allgemeines Gelehrten-Lexikon*, s. v. (B. P.)

Götz, George Friedrich, a Protestant theologian of Germany, was born at Hanau, April 9, 1750. He studied at Halle, became doctor of divinity and pastor primarius in his native place, and died there, Feb. 3, 1813. He published *Sermons* and some ascetical writings. See Döring, *Die gelehrten Theologen Deutschlands*, s. v.; Winer, *Handbuch der theol. Lit.* ii, 153, 157, 160, 163, 175, 179, 181, 184, 204, 206, 280. (B. P.)

Götz, Raphael, a Swiss theologian, poet, and teacher, was born at Götz of Münchhoff (Thurgovia), in 1559. He studied at Chur and Zurich, and went to Geneva in 1580, where he held a disputation on predestination, under the auspices of Theodore Beza. Two years afterwards he went to Basle, where he again showed his controversial power. In 1588 he received in Zurich the title *pædagogus alumnorum*, and in 1592 became, in the same city, professor of the New Test., and deacon at the cathedral. Four years afterwards he was made archdeacon, and thereupon introduced new religious songs into his parish. Unfortunately he gave himself up to alchemy, which brought him into debt, to escape which he fled in 1601. After wandering about for six months, he went to Marburg, where the landgrave Maurice appointed him professor of theology. He died there, Aug. 20, 1622, leaving *Tractatus Adversus Albericum Triumcuriani, de Prædestinatione:—De Peccato in Spiritum S.:—De Gratuita Electorum Salute*, etc.:—*Historia Captivitatis Babylonicæ.* See Hoefer, *Nouv. Biog. Générale*, s. v.

Götze. See GOETZE.

Gouda, JAN VAN, a Dutch Jesuit, who died Dec. 28, 1630, at Brussels, was for some time professor at Antwerp and preacher at Brussels. In his sermons he was especially severe against the Protestants, and his co-religionists styled him therefore *malleus hæreticorum* and *murus Catholicorum.* His writings are mostly directed against ministers of the Reformed Church. See Alegambe, *Bibliotheca Scriptorum Societatis Jesu;* Burmann, *Trajectum Eruditum;* Jöcher, *Allgemeines Gelehrten-Lexikon*, s. v. (B. P.)

Goudimel, CLAUDE, a French musical composer, was born about 1510 in Franche-Comté. He lived at Rome in 1540 when Palestrina studied there. In 1556 he was at Paris, and kept a note-printing establishment there. In 1562 he joined the Reformed Church, and was killed in the Huguenot massacre at Lyons, Aug. 24, 1572. He prepared the music for Clement Marot's and Theodore Beza's translation of the Psalms (1565). Some writers assert that he also composed Huguenot hymns, such as are still sung; but this is a mistake. See Fétis, *Biograph. des Musiciens;* Haag, *La France Protestante;* Douen, *Clément Marot et le Psautier Huguenot*, and the same in Lichtenberger's *Encyklop. des Sciences Religieuses*, s. v.; Grüneisen in Plitt-Herzog, *Real-Encyklop.* s. v.; Grove, *Dict. of Music*, s. v. (B. P.)

Gouffier, ADRIEN, cardinal of Boisy, had at first the title of prothonotary of Boisy, then he became bishop of Coutances in 1509. Francis I asked for the cardinal's hat for him of pope Leo X, in the conference of Boulogne, which this pontiff granted in 1515. In 1519 Gouffier obtained a charge as a legate in France. He was already grand almoner, and held the bishopric of Alby and other considerable benefices. He died in the castle of Villendren-sur-Indre, July 24, 1523. See Hoefer, *Nouv. Biog. Générale*, s. v.

Gouge *de Charpaignes*, MARTIN, a French prelate, was born about 1360, in Bourges. After the death of his brother John, who was treasurer of the duke of Berry, Martin was appointed to fill his place. He became bishop of Chartres in 1406, and was transferred to the see of Clermont-Ferrand in 1415. In 1409 he was arrested for being connected with the revolution of the palace, but on account of his great talents he soon returned to his former honors. Under the reign of Charles VII, Gouge became royal councillor. In 1425 he resigned his civil functions, but resumed them until Nov. 8, 1428. He died Nov. 25 or 26, 1444. See Hoefer, *Nouv. Biog. Générale*, s. v.

Goujet, CLAUDE PIERRE, a French theologian, was born at Paris, Oct. 19, 1697. In 1720 he was canon of St. James's in his native place, and died Feb. 1, 1767. He translated Grotius's work on the truth of Christianity into French (Paris, 1724) and other Latin works, and published *Maximes sur la Pénitence et sur la Communion* (1728):—*Bibliothèque des Auteurs Ecclésiastiques du XVIII Siècle, pour Servir de Continuation à celle de Mr. Dupin* (1736, 3 vols.):—*Histoire du Pontificat de Paul V* (1766, 2 vols.). See *Nouvelle Diction. Histor.;* Formey, *France Littéraire;* Jöcher, *Allgemeines Gelehrten-Lexikon*, s. v.; Lichtenberger, *Encyklop. des Sciences Religieuses*, s. v. (B. P.)

Goulet, ROBERT, a Roman Catholic theologian of the 16th century, is the author of *Tetramonos Evangeliorum, quorum integri Textus sub una Narrationis Serie Historico Ordine Continentur.* He also edited *Pauli Burgensis Scrutinium Scripturarum.* See Possevinus,

Apparatus Sacer; Jöcher, *Allgemeines Gelehrten-Lexikon,* s. v. (B. P.)

Goumilevski, Moses, a Russian prelate and writer, was bishop of Theodosia, and took an active part in the scholastic movement which Catherine II promoted in her empire. He died in 1792 by assassination in the Crimea, leaving several linguistic works, two funeral speeches of the prince Potemkin, several translations from the fathers of the Greek Church, and some fugitive pieces of poetry in Latin and Russian. See Hoefer, *Nouv. Biog. Générale,* s. v.

Gounja Ticquoa (*the God of Gods*), the title of the Supreme Being among the Hottentots. They say he is a good being, who does no one any hurt, and dwells far above the moon. They pay no act of devotion immediately to this god, and when asked why not, they answer that their first parents so grievously sinned against the Supreme God that he cursed them and all their posterity with hardness of heart, so they know little of him and have no inclination to serve him.

Gourlin, Pierre Sébastien, a French Jansenist writer, who died in 1775, made himself conspicuous by his opposition to the bull *Unigenitus.* He is the author of *Institution et Instruction Chrétiennes* (Naples, 1776, 3 vols.), which has often been reprinted, and which contains an exact exposition of the Jansenistic doctrine. To him is also attributed *Tractatus de Gratia Christi Salvatoris ac de Prædestinatione Sanctorum, in sex libros distributus* (1781, 3 vols.). See Lichtenberger, *Encyclop. des Sciences Religieuses,* s. v.; Hoefer, *Nouv. Biog. Générale,* s. v. (B. P.)

Gousset, Thomas Marie Joseph, a French prelate, was born at Montigny-lès-Cherlieux, May 1, 1792. He began in 1809 a course of study, and obtained in 1812 the diploma of a bachelor of letters; entered the great seminary of Besançon the same year, and became one of its most distinguished scholars and teachers of theology. Cardinal Rohan made him, in 1832, grand-vicar, and he was consecrated bishop of Perigueux Oct. 6, 1835. He was elevated to the archiepiscopacy of Rheims, May 25, 1840, and in 1851 obtained the cardinal's hat. He died at Rheims, Dec. 24, 1866, leaving *Exposition de la Doctrine de l'Église* (Besançon, 1823):—*Code Civil Commenté dans ses Rapports avec la Théologie Morale:*—*L'Immaculée Conception de la Bienheureuse Vierge* (Paris, 1855), etc. See Hoefer, *Nouv. Biog. Générale,* s. v.

Govona, Rosa, an Italian philanthropist, was born at Mondovi in 1716. Her parents were poor, and Rosa became an orphan while very young, but she supported herself by labor. One day, finding a little girl in a still worse condition than herself, she aided her and taught her to work, and the two soon formed the plan of gathering other poor little girls for a similar purpose. Rosa at length received a house from the community in the plain of the Brao, where she settled down with her company. Charles Emanuel III gave her several large buildings which had belonged to the friars, and she organized the establishment of *The Rosines.* She also established houses in other places, and in the centre of the cities of Novara, Fossano, Savigliano, Saluzzo, Chieri, and Saint Damian of Ostia. The establishment at Turin became the centre of all these houses, which still flourish. In this latter city she died, Feb. 28, 1776. See Hoefer, *Nouv. Biog. Générale,* s. v.

Gown. The ancient academical gown, always wide-sleeved, was an adoption of the monastic habit from the robe of the preaching-friars, who wore it instead of an alb. From itinerant lay preachers of the time of Elizabeth, the custom of the universities, the vanity of the richer clergy in the last century, wearing silk robes out-of-doors and then in the pulpit, and the introduction of lectures, not provided for by the rubric, the use of the gown in English pulpits took its origin. The narrow-sleeved gown, with a cross-slit for the arms, was an importation from Geneva, and called the lawyer's gown, in distinction from the wide velvet-sleeved gown still worn by other graduates, posers at Winchester, and often with an ermine hood by proctors at Oxford. Russet white and black gowns were worn by mourners at funerals.

Göz, Christian Gottlieb, a Lutheran theologian of Germany, was born Aug. 29, 1746. He studied at Tübingen, was in 1769 vicar, in 1777 preacher, at Stuttgart, and died Dec. 10, 1803. He published, *Uebung der Gottseligkeit in heiligen Betrachtungen und Liedern* (Stuttgart, 1776):—*Beitrag zur Geschichte der Kirchenlieder* (1784), and composed some hymns, which are still in use. See Koch, *Geschichte des deutschen Kirchenliedes,* vi, 309 sq. (B. P.)

Gozlin (Lat. *Gauzlenus*), a French prelate and statesman, was born about the beginning of the ninth century. According to some he was the son of Boricon, count of Anjou, and to others the natural son of Louis the Gentle. He became a monk at Rheims about 848, and soon after abbot of St. Germain-des-Près. Gozlin, like most of the abbots of that time, was also a warrior. In 858 he was made prisoner by the Normans, and had to purchase his liberty by a heavy ransom. After 855 he held the office of chancellor to Charles the Bald, and about 883 he was appointed bishop of Paris. He died April 16, 886. See Hoefer, *Nouv. Biog. Générale,* s. v.

Graal, The Holy, a name in mediæval tradition for the precious dish (*paropsis*) or cup used at the Last Supper, said also to be the vessel in which our Lord turned water into wine, and in which Nicodemus or Joseph of Arimathæa received the Saviour's blood at the crucifixion. Other legends describe it as a cup originally given to Solomon by the queen of Sheba. It often appears in the Arthurian laws, and probably arose from a Druidic origin. The Genoese claim to have it in the cathedral treasury, where it is known as Sacro Catino. It is of glass, of hexagonal form, with two handles, and is three feet nine inches in circumference. It was cracked in its removal from Paris, whither it had been taken under Napoleon. Sometimes the graal supports a bleeding spear, as on a crucifix at Sancreed Church, Cornwall. The Church is often represented holding a pennon and a graal opposite the synagogue with drooping head, and a banner of three points, the staff broken.

Grabau, Johann Andreas August, a Lutheran minister of Germany, was born March 18, 1804, at Olvenstädt, near Magdeburg. He studied at Halle, was in 1834 pastor at Erfurt, but was suspended in 1836 because he refused to accept the Prussian Agenda (q. v.). In 1839 he came, with a number of his adherents, to America, and settled at Buffalo, N. Y., where he founded a Lutheran congregation, to whom he preached till his death, June 2, 1879. Grabau was president of the Lutheran Buffalo Synod, founded the Martin Luther College, and was for some time editor of the *Kirchliches Informatorium* and of the *Wachende Kirche.* (B. P.)

Grabe, Martin Sylvester, a Lutheran theologian of Germany, was born at Weissensee (Thuringia), April 21, 1627. He studied at Königsberg, was professor there in 1660, in 1662 at Jena, in 1677 general-superintendent of Pomerania, and died at Colberg, Nov. 23, 1686. He published, among other writings, *Disp. in Gal. iv,* 4:—*in Joh. xvii,* 3:—*Contra Socinianos:*—*De Unione Duarum in Christo Naturarum:*—*De Perspicuitate Scripturæ Sacræ Ejusdemque Lectione Laicis Concedenda.* See Jöcher, *Allgemeines Gelehrten-Lexikon,* s. v. (B. P.)

Grabener, Christian Gottfried, a Lutheran theologian of Germany, was born April 15, 1714, at Freiberg. He studied at Leipsic, was in 1738 con-rector at Meissen, in 1742 rector at Dresden, and died Nov. 30, 1778, leaving *Disp. ad Genes. xii,* 6, 7 (Leipsic, 1737):

—*De Carminibus Apostolicis:*—*De Formula κύριε ἐλέεισον:*—*De Portis Cœli.* See Jöcher, *Allgemeines Gelehrten-Lexikon*, s. v.; Winer, *Handbuch der theol. Lit.* i, 612. (B. P.)

Grabener, Theophilus, father of the foregoing, was born Nov. 3, 1685. He studied at Wittenberg, was in 1711 professor at the gymnasium in Freiburg, in 1735 rector at Meissen, and died April 15, 1750, leaving *De Planctu Hadadrimmon ad Zach. xii*, 11 (Wittenberg, 1709):—*De Sacris Judæorum Peregrino in Hortis Ritu Factis* (1710):—*De Excommunicatione per Insomnia* (eod.):—*De Symbolo Israelitarum trans Jordanem Incolentium ad Jos. xxii*, 22-29 (Meissen, 1737):—*De Theophilo Episcopo Antiocheno* (1744). See Jöcher, *Allgemeines Gelehrten-Lexikon*, s. v. (B. P.)

Gräber, Franz Friedrich, a Protestant theologian, was born in 1784 in Prussia. He studied at Halle, and entered upon his ministerial duties in 1808. After he had occupied different pastorates, the king of Prussia appointed him, in 1846, a member of the general synod, and made him general-superintendent of Westphalia. In 1856 he retired from his office, and died in 1857. He published *Das Verlorene Paradies, Predigten* (Elberfeld, 1830). See Winer, *Handbuch der theol. Lit.* ii, 116; Zuchold, *Bibl. Theol.* i, 460. (B. P.)

Grace, Actual. See Actual Grace.

Grace at Meals was customary among the Jews (Lightfoot, *Horæ Hebr.* on Matt. xx, 36), and forms are contained in the Talmud (*Berachoth*, vii). Numerous examples occur in the New Test., and early Christian writers abundantly confirm the practice (Chrysostom, *Homil.* xlix; Clemens Alex. *Pædag.* ii, 4, § 44, 77; so also Tertullian, Cyprian, and others). Examples of forms occur both in the early Eastern and Western churches, and the Gelasian Sacramentary sets forth quite a number. See Smith, *Dict. of Christ. Antiq.* s. v.

Gradenigo, Giovanni Agostino, an Italian prelate, was born at Venice, July 10, 1725. He studied under the direction of Domenico dall' Onazio; entered the Benedictine order in 1744; in 1749 was called to teach philosophy at Mantua, and later canon law; in 1756 returned to Venice, where, in 1762, he founded an academy of ecclesiastical history; refused the bishopric of Corfu in 1765, but in 1770 became bishop of Ceneda, and died March 16, 1774, leaving a large number of short publications, for which see Hoefer, *Nouv. Biog. Générale*, s. v.

Gradenigo, Giovanni Gieronimo, an Italian prelate, was born at Venice, Feb. 19, 1708. While young he entered the order of the Theatines, and occupied several important chairs at the Seminary of Brescia. On Jan. 27, 1766, he was appointed archbishop of Udine. He died June 30, 1786, leaving *Lettera al Card. Quirini*, etc. (Venice, 1744):—*Lettera Istorica Critica Sopra Probabilismo* (Brescia, 1750):—*Le Cure Pastorali* (Udine, 1756):—*De Siclo Argenteo Hebræorum* (Rome, 1766), and other pieces, for which see Hoefer, *Nouv. Biog. Générale*, s. v.

Gradin, a French term for a step behind and above the level of the altar-slab, for placing the cross and candlesticks upon, so as not to interfere with the altar itself.

Gradual (*Graduālē*, *Grayl*). Strictly only the first verse of the anthem sung was thus called. The rest was technically styled the "verse." The mode of singing it was not everywhere the same, but that in which one sang alone for a while and many responded was probably in use from the very infancy of the Church. From Easter eve to the Saturday in Whitsun week inclusively the Gradual was followed, and at last supplanted, by the Alleluia. This had been long known in the West, and used, though not prescribed, on public occasions of religious joy. At Rome it was only sung on Easter day.

The *Tract* was another anthem sometimes sung after the epistle. Originally it was always from the Book of Psalms. The Tract in all probability was nothing more than the Gradual as it was chanted in seasons of humiliation. Very soon, however, a Tract was often sung after the Gradual; that is, a third verse was added to the anthem, which was sung continuously by the cantor without any assistance from the choir. The Gradual and Tract were sung from the same step of the ambo from which the epistle was read. The fact that the Gradual and Tract were both sung from the lesson-desk, and that by a single cantor detached thither, like the readers, from the choir, seems to indicate their common origin in that extended use of the Book of Psalms with the rest of Holy Scripture which we know to have prevailed during the first ages.

Graf, Anton, a Roman Catholic theologian, for some time professor of exegesis and pastoral theology in Tübingen, who died May 24, 1867, is the author of *Kritische Darstellung des gegenwärtigen Zustandes der praktischen Theologie* (Tübingen, 1840). (B. P.)

Graf, Carl Heinrich, a Protestant theologian of Germany, was born at Mühlhausen in 1815. He studied at Strasburg. In 1838 he was a teacher at Paris, was made a licentiate of theology at Strasburg in 1842, took the degree of doctor of philosophy at Leipsic in 1846, and was professor at the royal school at Meissen, in Saxony, and died July 16, 1869. He wrote, *De Librorum Samuelis et Regum Compositione Scriptoribus et Fide Historica* (Strasburg, 1842):—*Essai sur la Vie et les Écrits de J. Lefèvre d'Étaples* (ibid. eod.):—*Moslicheddin Sadi's Rosengarten* (translated from the Persian, Leipsic, 1846):—*Moslicheddin Sadi's Lustgarten* (Jena, 1850, 2 vols.):—*La Morale du Poète Persan Sadi* (1851):—*De Templo Silonensi* (Meissen, 1855):—*Der Prophet Jeremia erklärt* (Leipsic, 1863):—*Die sogenannte Grundschrift des Pentateuchs* (1869), besides a large number of essays contributed to the *Zeitschrift der Deutschen Morgenländischen Gesellschaft.* See Lichtenberger, *Encyclop. des Sciences Religieuses*, s. v.; Zuchold, *Bibl. Theol.* i, 460. (B. P.)

Graf, Johann Heinrich, a Lutheran minister, was born Nov. 19, 1797, at Lindow, in Brandenburg, Prussia. In 1823 he entered the missionary seminary at Berlin, and in 1825 the Hebrew College at London, to prepare himself as a missionary to promote the gospel among the Jews. He remained in England till 1827, when he was sent to the Rhenish provinces on a missionary journey. In the same year he was appointed to the mission-station at Posen, was ordained there in 1846, and died Dec. 5, 1867. (B. P.)

Gräfe, Heinrich, a German ecclesiastic and educator, was born at Buttstädt, in Weimar, May 3, 1802, and educated at Jena. In 1823 he obtained a curacy in the State Church at Weimar, and in 1825 was made rector of the town school at Jena. In 1840 he was also appointed extraordinary professor of the science of education in the University of Jena, and in 1842 he became head of the bürgerschule in Cassel. He afterwards occupied various positions in the educational field, and in 1849 entered the house of representatives of Hesse, and became noted as an agitator. He was imprisoned in 1852 for having been implicated in certain revolutionary movements. On his release he withdrew to Geneva, where he engaged in educational work till 1855, when he was appointed director of the school of industry at Bremen. He died in that city, July 21, 1868. His works were chiefly on educational subjects. See *Encyclop. Brit.* 9th ed. s. v.

Gräfenhain, Ferdinand Friedrich, a Lutheran theologian, was born Feb. 14, 1740. For some time deacon at Taucha, in Saxony, he was called in 1780 to Leipsic, and died March 18, 1823. He wrote *Animadversiones in loc. Epist. Pauli ad Philipp. ii*, 5-12 (Leipsic, 1802). See Winer, *Handbuch der theol. Lit.* i, 263. (B. P.)

Grafunder, David, a Lutheran theologian, who died Dec. 24, 1680, at Merseburg, is the author of, *Calligraphia Hebræa:—Grammatica Syriaca cum Syntaxi et Lexico:—Grammatica Chaldaica.* See Jöcher, *Allgemeines Gelehrten-Lexikon,* s. v.; Steinschneider, *Bibliogr. Handbuch,* s. v.; Fürst, *Bibl. Jud.* i, 342. (B. P.)

Graham, Andrew, a Scotch prelate, was elected and consecrated to the see of Dunblane, July 28, 1575. He was also pastor of the Church of Dunblane until his death. See Keith, *Scottish Bishops,* p. 180.

Graham, Archibald, a Scotch prelate, was first pastor at Rothsay, in the Isle of Bute, and from there promoted to the see of the Isles in 1680, where he continued until the revolution in 1688. See Keith, *Scottish Bishops,* p. 310.

Graham, Charles, an Irish Wesleyan missionary, was born at Tullinnagrackin, near Sligo, Aug. 20, 1750. After laboring for twenty-one years as a local preacher, he was, in 1790, appointed by Wesley as a missionary in Ireland. Few of the Irish preachers had severer trials from mobs than Graham, but he courageously met them. For six years he and Ouseley traversed Ireland together, bringing the light into its darkest quarters. Graham afterwards labored in Ulster, Armagh, Kilkenny, Wicklow, Wexford, and other places. He died suddenly near Athlone, April 23, 1824. His powerful appeals to his street congregations were pathetic, and sometimes overwhelming; the multitudes heard, trembled, and fell before him. See Stevens, *Hist. of Methodism,* iii, 131, 409 sq., 416 sq., 435; George Smith, *Hist. of Wesleyan Methodism,* vol. ii (see Index, vol. iii); William Smith, *Hist. of Wesleyan Methodism in Ireland,* p. 286; *Minutes of the British Conference,* 1824; Reilly, *Ouseley* (N. Y. 1848); Arthur, *Life of Ouseley* (Lond. and N. Y. 1876); Campbell, *Life of Charles Graham* (Dublin, 1868, 12mo; Toronto, 1869).

Graham, George, a Scotch prelate, was bishop of Dunblane in 1606, from which see he was translated to that of Orkney in 1615, where he continued until 1638. See Keith, *Scottish Bishops,* p. 181, 227.

Graham, John, D.D., an English prelate, was born in Durham in 1794. In 1834 he was appointed prebendary of Lincoln, having formerly been rector of Willingham, Cambridgeshire. At one time he was one of the chaplains of prince Albert, consort of queen Victoria. He was consecrated to the bishopric of Chester in 1848, which see he held until the close of his life, June 15, 1865. During his administration seventy-eight new churches were consecrated by him in his diocese. See *Amer. Quar. Church Rev.* April, 1866, p. 141.

Graham, Patrick, a Scotch prelate, was bishop of Brechin in 1463, and was translated to the see of St. Andrews in 1466. He undertook a journey to Rome in 1467, and while there the controversy concerning the superiority of the see of York over the Church of Scotland was renewed. He obtained sentence against that see, and that his own see should be erected into an archbishopric, and the pope also made him his legate within Scotland for three years. On his return he found the king's clergy and courtiers all opposed to his transactions. He was put in prison, where he died in 1478. See Keith, *Scottish Bishops,* p. 30–164.

Graham, Samuel Lyle, D.D., a Presbyterian minister, was born at Liberty, Va., Feb. 9, 1794. He studied under Rev. J. Mitchell, and subsequently at the New London Academy, and graduated at Washington College, Lexington, in 1814. After this he became tutor in the family of judge Nash of North Carolina. In 1818 he graduated from Princeton Theological Seminary, and was licensed to preach by the Presbytery of New Brunswick. He acted for a while as missionary in Indiana, and subsequently in Greenbrier and Monroe counties, Va. In 1821 he removed to North Carolina, and became pastor of Oxford and Grassy Creek churches. After remaining here seven years he took charge of the Oxford Church, where a gracious revival followed his labors, in 1830. In 1834 he became pastor at Clarksville and Shiloh, and in 1838 professor of ecclesiastical history in Union Theological Seminary, Va., which position he retained until his death at Prince Edward, Oct. 29, 1851. He contributed several papers to the *Princeton Review.* See *Gen. Cat. of Princeton Theol. Sem.* 1881, p. 20; Nevin, *Presb. Encyclop.* s. v. (W. P. S.)

Graham, Sylvester, a Presbyterian minister and reformer, was born in Sheffield, Conn., in 1794. From childhood he was troubled with weak digestion and rheumatism, and was compelled to abandon one employment after another on account of poor health. He finally studied at Amherst College, and became a Presbyterian preacher about 1826. In 1830 the Pennsylvania Temperance Society employed him as a lecturer. This led him to the study of human physiology, by which he became convinced that the only cure for intemperance was to be found in correct habits of living and judicious diet. This idea was set before the world in permanent form in his *Essay on Cholera* (1832), and *Graham Lectures on the Science of Human Life* (Boston, 1839, 2 vols.). He died at Northampton, Mass., Sept. 11, 1851. His other publications were a *Lecture to Young Men on Chastity:*—a *Treatise on Bread-Making,* from which we have the name "Graham bread":—and the *Philosophy of Sacred History,* of which only one volume was finished by him, and published after his death. In this work he attempted to show the harmony between the teachings of the Bible and his views on dietetics. See *Appleton's Amer. Cyclop.* viii, 142.

Grail. (1) *Gradale,* gradual, that which follows in degree, or the next step (*gradus*) after the epistle, a book containing the Order of Benediction of Holy Water, the Offices, Introit, or beginning of the Mass, the Kyrie, Gloria, Alleluia, Prose, Tract, Sequence, Creed, Offertory, Sanctus, Agnus Dei, and Communion and Post-Communion, which pertain to the choir in singing solemn mass. In France it denotes the Antiphonar, which was set on the gradus or analogium. (2) A verse or response, varying with the day; a portion of a psalm sung between the Epistle and Gospel while the deacon was on his way to the rood-loft. Their introduction into the Church is attributed variously to Celestine, 430, St. Ambrose, Gelasius, 490, or Gregory the Great, *c.* 600, who arranged the responses in order in his "Antiphonar." Rabanus says the name is derived from the custom of singing the grail on the steps of the ambon or pulpit; but others consider it to be taken from the responsory, gradation, or succession, or the altar-step. These verses were formerly chanted, either by a single voice or in chorus. When the chanter sang to the end tractim, they were called the Tract; but when he was interrupted by the choir, then the name was a Verse, Responsory, or Anthem.

Gramberg, Carl Peter Wilhelm, a Lutheran theologian of Germany, was born Sept. 24, 1797, at Seefeld, in Oldenburg, and died at Züllichau, in Prussia, March 29, 1830. He is the author of, *Die Chronik nach ihrem geschichtlichen Charakter* (Halle, 1823):—*Libri Geneseos Secundum Fontes* (Leipsic, eod.):—*Kritische Geschichte der Religionsideen des Alten Testaments* (Berlin, 1823, 1830, 2 vols.):—*Salomo's Buch der Sprüche übersetzt u. erklärt* (Leipsic, 1828). See Winer, *Handbuch der theol. Lit.* i, 79, 138, 212; Fürst, *Bibl. Jud.* i, 342; Zuchold, *Bibl. Theol.* i, 461. (B. P.)

Grammer, John, D.D., a Protestant Episcopal minister, was born at Petersburg, Va. He began the practice of law in that place some two years after graduating at Yale College. In January, 1824, he entered the Episcopal Theological Seminary at Alexandria, and on July 15, 1826, received deacon's orders. For the next ten years his life was that of a missionary. He lived upon his estate in Dinwiddie County, and preached in eight or ten of the neighboring counties. In October, 1835, his dwelling was burned down, and he removed to Lawrenceville. In 1838 he accepted a call to the parish of Halifax Court-house, and removed there, where he continued to reside till his death, March 5, 1871, aged seventy-five years. See *Obituary Record of Yale College*, 1871; *Prot. Episc. Almanac*, 1872, p. 127.

Grammlich, JOHANN ANDREAS, a Lutheran theologian of Germany, was born July 1, 1689, at Stuttgart. He studied at Tübingen and Halle, was in 1716 court-chaplain at Stuttgart, and died April 7, 1728. He wrote, *Erbauliche Betrachtungen auf alle Tage* (Stuttgart, 1724; new ed. by Böck, Breslau, 1853):—*Vierzig Betrachtungen von Christi Leiden und Tod* (Tübingen, 1722; new ed. by Koppen, 1865): also *Annotations* on the Acts of the Apostles, on the epistles of Peter, John, and James. See Jöcher, *Allgemeines Gelehrten-Lexikon*, s. v.; Zuchold, *Bibl. Theol.* i, 461 sq.; Winer, *Handbuch der theol. Lit.* i, 182; Koch, *Geschichte des deutschen Kirchenliedes*, v, 66 sq. (B. P.)

Grammont, Antoine Pierre de (1), a French prelate, was born in 1615. He entered the ministry when quite young. Alexander VII offered him the deanery of the chapter of Besançon, but he declined. Some time later he was consecrated archbishop of that see. When Louis XIV invaded Franche-Comté in 1668, Grammont made every exertion for defence. On the second invasion, six years later, he resigned at the door of his cathedral, and thereafter occupied himself by raising various schools in his diocese. He died May 1, 1698, leaving editions of the missal, of the breviary, of the ritual, and a catechism of his diocese. See Hoefer, *Nouv. Biog. Générale*, s. v.

Grammont, Antoine Pierre de (2), a French prelate, nephew of François Joseph, was born in 1685. After finishing his studies at the College of Louis-le-Grand, in Paris, he became a soldier at eighteen years of age; was wounded before Spire, and taken prisoner. Being exchanged, he received command of a regiment of dragoons, which bore his name. When peace was restored, Grammont returned to his province, where his uncle supplied him with a canonicate of the chapter of Besançon. He was nominated archbishop of that city by Louis XV, in 1735, and died Sept. 7, 1754. See Hoefer, *Nouv. Biog. Générale*, s. v.

Grammont, François Joseph de, a French prelate, nephew of Antoine (1), was coadjutor of his uncle under the title of bishop of Philadelphia, and succeeded him in the see of Besançon. He reconstructed the archiepiscopacy, and gave new editions to the breviary and the ritual, also published a collection of synodal statutes, and left his fortune to the seminary. He died Aug. 20, 1715. See Hoefer, *Nouv. Biog. Générale*, s. v.

Gramont, GABRIEL DE, a French prelate, succeeded his brother in the bishopric of Couserans, and also of Tarbes in 1522. He was sent on various diplomatic missions. In 1532 he was made bishop of Poitiers, and finally archbishop of Toulouse. He died March 26, 1534, leaving in MS. a collection of letters relating to his various embassies. See Hoefer, *Nouv. Biog. Générale*, s. v.

Gramur, in Norse mythology, was the famous sword of the hero Sigurd. It was the most excellent that had ever been made by dwarfs. Sigurd proved it in two ways: he cut in two a large piece of steel, and, behold, the sword had not even the slightest scratch; then he laid it in the river, which carried a light woolflake against it, and the latter was cut in two.

Granacci, FRANCESCO, a reputable Florentine painter, was born in 1477, and studied under Ghirlandajo at the same time with Buonarotti. Among his principal pictures are those of *St. Zanobi and St. Francis*, near the Virgin, under a lofty canopy, and *The Assumption*, in San Pietro Maggiore. He died in 1544. See Hoefer, *Nouv. Biog. Générale*, s. v.; Spooner, *Biog. Hist. of the Fine Arts*, s. v.

Granada, LUIS DE. See LOUIS OF GRANADA.

Grancolas, JEAN, a French theologian and member of the Sorbonne, was born at Paris in 1660. In 1685 he took his degree as doctor of divinity, was chaplain to the duke of Orleans, and died in 1732. He wrote, *Traité de l'Antiquité des Cérémonies des Sacréments* (Paris, 1692):—*Instructions sur la Religion, Tirées de l'Écriture Sainte* (1693):—*La Science des Confesseurs* (1696):—*L'Ancienne Discipline de l'Église* (1697):—*Heures Sacrées* (eod.):—*Traité des Liturgies* (1698): *Histoire Abrégée de l'Église de la Ville et de l'Université de Paris* (1728, 2 vols.). See Jöcher, *Allgemeines Gelehrten-Lexikon*, s. v.; Winer, *Handbuch der theol. Lit.* i, 603, 890; Lichtenberger, *Encyclop. des Sciences Religieuses*, s. v.; Hoefer, *Nouv. Biog. Générale*, s. v. (B. P.)

Grandi, GUIDO DE, an Italian member of the Camaldule order, was born in 1671 at Cremona. He studied at Rome, was professor at Florence and Pisa, and died at the latter place, July 21, 1742, leaving *Martyrologium Camaldulense*:—*Dissertationes Camaldulenses*, etc. See *Vita del Padre D. Guido Grandi, Scritta da Uno suo Discepolo*; Jöcher, *Allgemeines Gelehrten-Lexikon*, s. v.; Winer, *Handbuch der theol. Lit.* i, 714. (B. P.)

Grandidier, PHILLIPPE ANDRÉ, a French theologian, born at Strasburg, Nov. 9, 1752, entered into holy orders, was canon and keeper of the archives of the bishopric there, and died Oct. 11, 1787. He wrote, *Histoire de l'Église et des Princes-Évêques de Strasbourg* (1776, 1778, 2 vols.):—*Histoire Ecclésiastiques, de la Province d'Alsace* (1781):—*Essai Historique sur la Cathédrale de Strasbourg* (1782). Besides, he left in MS. a great deal of matter pertaining to the Church history of Strasburg, which was published in six volumes, by Liblin, under the title, *Œuvres Historiques Inédites de Grandidier* (Colmar, 1865). See Winer, *Handbuch der theol. Lit.* i, 823; Lichtenberger, *Encyclop. des Sciences Religieuses*, s. v.; Hoefer, *Nouv. Biog. Générale*, s. v. (B. P.)

Grandin, MARTIN, a French theologian, was born at St. Quentin in 1604. He commenced his studies at Noyon, continued them at Amiens, and finished them at Paris, in the college of the cardinal Le Moine, where he afterwards taught philosophy. He was doctor of the Sorbonne, and taught theology there more than fifty years. He died at Paris in 1691, leaving a work of value entitled, *Institutiones Theologicæ* (Paris, 1710). See Hoefer, *Nouv. Biog. Générale*, s. v.

Grandison, JOHN, an English prelate of the 14th century, was born at Asperton, Herefordshire. He was prebendary of Exeter and York in 1309, archdeacon of Nottingham, Oct. 12, 1310, and dean of Wells. While holding these preferments, he became chaplain to pope Clement V, who employed him as his nuncio in France, Spain, Germany, and England, where he attracted the notice of Edward III. He was consecrated to the see of Exeter, Oct. 18, 1327. He was enormously rich, founded Ottery St. Mary, built Bishop's Teignton, vaulted the nave, built the west front of Exeter Cathedral, annexed Radway to his see, and compelled all ecclesiastics in his diocese to bequeath their goods to him to complete his buildings. He died July 16, 1369. Bishop Grandison had great trouble with the archbishop of Canterbury. See Hook, *Lives of the Archbishops of Canterbury*, iii, 507; Fuller, *Worthies of England* (ed. Nuttall), ii, 74.

Grandpierre, HENRI, a Reformed theologian of France, who died at Paris while director of the missionary institute, in 1875, is the author of some ascetical works, as *Tristesse et Consolation*:—*Le Guide du Fidèle à la Table Sacrée*:—*Les Aspirations Chrétiennes*. Some of these, besides a number of his sermons, were translated into German. For a long time he edited a religious journal entitled, *L'Esperance*. See Zuchold, *Bibl. Theol.* i, 462; Lichtenberger, *Encyclop. des Sciences Religieuses*, s. v. (B. P.)

Grant (or **Graunt**), **Edward**, D.D., an eminent English scholar of the 16th century, was educated at Westminster School and Christchurch, or at Broadgates Hall, Oxford. In 1572 he was made master of Westminster School, where he continued until 1591. He was prebend of Westminster in 1577, of Ely in 1589, and died in Sept. or Oct. 1601. He published, *Institutio Græca Grammatices Compendiara* (1597):—*Græcæ Linguæ Spicilegium* (1575). See Chalmers, *Biog. Dict.* s. v.; Allibone, *Dict. of Brit. and Amer. Authors*, s. v.

Grant, Richard, an English prelate, is usually stated to have been dean of London, but this is very improbable. In 1221 he was chancellor of Lincoln, and in 1229 he was consecrated to the see of Canterbury. His episcopate was short, and it seems that he was not as discreet as he should have been, which was so needful for the time. He died Aug. 3, 1231. According to Tanner, the following works were written by Richard Grant: *De Fide et Legibus, lib. i:—De Sacramentis, lib. i:—De Universo Corporali et Spirituali, lib. i.* See Hook, *Lives of the Archbishops of Canterbury*, iii, 103 sq.

Grape, ZACHARIAS, a Lutheran theologian of Germany, was born at Rostock, Oct. 6, 1671. He studied at his native place and at Greifswalde, commenced his academical career in 1696 at Rostock, was in 1701 doctor, in 1704 professor of theology, and died Feb. 11, 1713, leaving, *Systema Novissimarum Controversiarum* (Rostock, 1705):—*Historia Literaria Talmudis Babylonici* (ibid. 1696):—*De Carthesii Methodo Convincendi Atheos:—De Quibusdam Locutionibus in Critica Edu. Leighi:—De Victore ab Edom ad Es. lxiii, 1-6:—An Talmud sit Cremendum?—An Circumcisio ab Ægyptiis ad Abrahamum Fuerit Derivata?* See Jöcher, *Allgemeines Gelehrten-Lexikon*, s. v.; Winer, *Handbuch der theol. Lit.* i, 343; Fürst, *Bibl. Theol.* i, 342; Steinschneider, *Bibl. Handbuch*, s. v. (B. P.)

Graptus. See THEODORE; THEOPHANES.

Graser, Conrad, a Lutheran theologian of Germany, was born at Königsberg, May 6, 1557. He was professor of Hebrew at the gymnasium in Thorn, West Prussia, and died Dec. 30, 1613, leaving, *Historia Anti-Christi Magni:—Apocalypseos Explicatio:—Tractatus de Principiis Veritatis Judaicæ:—Explicatio in Caput 9 Danielis.* See Adam, *Vitæ Eruditorum;* Jöcher, *Allgemeines Gelehrten-Lexikon*, s. v. (B. P.)

Graser, Giovanni Battista, an Italian theologian, was born April 2, 1718, at Roveredo (Tyrol). He taught, from 1761 to 1779, philosophy, history, patristic and theological literature in the College of Innsprück, exercised at the same time the functions of a conservator of the imperial library, and obtained in 1777 the title of a doctor of theology. In 1779 he retired to his native city, where he died in 1786. Among his writings are, *In Sermonem de Maria-Renata Saga*, etc. (Venice, 1752):—*Orazione in Morte di Gir. Tantarotti* (Roveredo, 1761):—*De Philosophiæ Moralis ad Jurisprudentiam Necessitate* (Vienna, 1767):—*De Historici Studii Amœnitate Atque Utilitate*, etc. (1775), also several poems, chants, and sonnets. See Hoefer, *Nouv. Biog. Générale*, s. v.

Grashof, JULIUS WERNER, D.D., a Protestant theologian of Germany, was born Oct. 4, 1802, at Prenzlaw, in Brandenburg, studied at Bonn theology and philology, was in 1826 preacher at Treves, in 1830 at Cologne, and in 1836 was appointed by the government as counsellor in the affairs pertaining to the Church and School of the Rhenish provinces. Grashof died June 25, 1873. He published, *Die Briefe der heiligen Apostel Jacobus, Petrus, Johannes und Judas* (Essen, 1830):—*Die Evangelien des Matthäus, Marcus und Lucas* (ibid. 1834):—*Luther's Bibel-Uebersetzung* (Crefeld, 1835). See Zuchold, *Bibl. Theol.* i, 463 sq. (B. P.)

Grasser, JOHANN JACOB, a Swiss historian and theologian, was born Feb. 21, 1579, at Basle. He studied a long time in France, and became three years later professor at Nîmes. In 1607 he received at Padua the title of a count-palatine, of a knight and Roman citizen. He then went to England, and on his return accepted, in his own country, the functions of a pastor in the village of Bernwyl, and afterwards at Basle, where he was connected with the Church of St. Theodor. He died at the latter place, March 21, 1627. Some of his principal works are, Εἰδύλλιον, *Helvetiæ Laudem Complectens*, etc. (Basle, 1598):—*De Antiquitatibus Nemansensibus* (Cologne, 1572):—*Ecclesia Orientalis et Meridionalis* (Strasburg, 1613):—*Itinerarium Historico-Politicum per Celebres Helvetiæ*, etc. (Basle, 1614):—*Chronicon der Waldenser* (1623), and other works on the history of Italy, France, England, and Switzerland. See Hoefer, *Nouv. Biog. Générale*, s. v.

Grassi, Giovanni, an eminent Italian ecclesiastic, was born at Verona, Oct. 12, 1778, and entered the Jesuit order, Nov. 16, 1799. In 1810 he was sent to Maryland to be superior of the Jesuit missions. He was recalled to Italy in 1817, and appointed to some important places of the order. He was also rector of the College of the Propaganda. He died Dec. 12, 1849. Grassi published *Various Notices on the State of the Republic of the United States*, 1818, which passed through three editions in Rome, Milan, and Turin. See *Cath. Almanac*, 1872, p. 102.

Grassi, Pietro Maria, an Augustinian monk of Vicenza, who flourished in the beginning of the 18th century, is the author of, *Narratio Historica de Ortu ac Progressu Hæresium Joh. Wiclefi* (Vicenza, 1707). See Winer, *Handbuch der theol. Lit.* i, 734. (B. P.)

Gratianus, PHILIP CHRISTOPH, a German theologian, was born July 2, 1742, at Oberroth (in Limburg). He studied at the convents of Blaubeuren and Bebenhausen, in Würtemberg, served afterwards in various ecclesiastical relations at Heilbronn (1767), at Neustadt (1773), at Offterdingen, and became in 1795 ecclesiastical superintendent and first pastor of the city of Weinsberg, where he died, Jan. 7, 1799, leaving, *De Harmonia Repræsentationum Dei Realium* (Tübingen, 1763):—*De Memoralibus Justini Martyris*, etc. (ibid. 1766):—*Ursprung und Fortpflanzung des Christenthums in Europa* (ibid. 1766):—*Pflanzung des Christenthums in den aus den Trümmern des römischen Kaiserthums*, etc. (Stuttgart, 1778):—*Grundlehren der Religion* (Lemgo, 1787). See Hoefer, *Nouv. Biog. Générale*, s. v.

Gratius, ORTWIN, a Roman Catholic theologian of Germany, was born in the 15th century, at Moltwick, in the diocese of Münster. In 1509 he became professor at the College of Kuick, at Cologne, and afterwards took holy orders. He undertook the defense of Hogstraten against Reuchlin, but was overthrown by Hutten. He died at Cologne, May 18, 1541, leaving, *Orationes Quodlibeticæ* (Cologne, 1508):—*Criticomastix Peregrinatio*, etc. (Lyons, 1511):—*Lamentationes Obscurorum Vivorum* (Cologne, 1518):—*Fasciculus Rerum Expectendarum et Fugiendiarum*, etc. (ibid. 1535; new and enlarged edition, by Brown, Lond. 1690):—*Apologia Adversus Joh. Reuchlinum:—Triumphus Jobi.* See Winer, *Handbuch der theol. Lit.* i, 666; Jöcher, *Allgemeines Gelehrten-Lexikon*, s. v.; Hoefer, *Nouv. Biog. Générale*, s. v. (B. P.)

Gratry, AUGUSTE JOSEPH ALPHONSE, *abbé*, a French theologian, was born at Lille, March 30, 1805. He studied at Paris, became director of the College of Sainte-Barbe, in that city, in 1841, and chaplain of the superior normal school in 1846. He resigned this position in 1851, and, in conjunction with the abbé Petetot, founded the Oratory of the Immaculate Conception, and gave special attention to the conversion and instruction of the Parisian youth. In 1861 he was appointed vicar-general of Orleans, and in 1863 he became professor of moral theology in the Sorbonne. He attacked Renan and the Rationalists with great vigor in 1864; and in

1867 he was elected a member of the French Academy. He withdrew from the Oratory in 1869 on account of the unfriendly attitude assumed towards him by that institution, because of his connection with father Hyacinthe and the International League of Peace. He set forth his views of the position of the two parties in the Vatican Council in two letters, in 1870, but was constrained to retract in 1872. He died at Montreux, Switzerland, Feb. 6 of the same year. His principal works are, *Étude sur la Sophistique Contemporaine* (Paris, 1851; 4th ed. 1863):—*De la Connaissance de Dieu* (1853, 2 vols.; 7th ed. 1864), which received the prize from the French Academy:—*Logique* (1853, 2 vols; 2d ed. 1858):—*De la Connaissance de l'Âme* (1858, 2 vols.):—*La Philosophie du Credo* (1861):—*Commentaire sur l'Évangile Selon Saint-Matthieu* (1863–65, 2 vols):—*La Morale et la Loi de l'Histoire* (1868, 2 vols.; 2d ed. 1871), in which he declares the French revolution to be the true regeneration of human society:—*Lettres sur la Religion* (1869):—*Les Sources de la Régénération Sociale* (1871). See Perraud, *Les Derniers Jours du Père Gratry; L'Oratoire de France au dix-septième et au dix-neuvième Siècle;* Bastide, in Lichtenberger's *Encyclop. des Sciences Religieuses*, s. v.; *Literarischer Handweiser für das Katholische Deutschland*, 1872, No. 210. (B. P.)

Gratton, John, an eminent minister of the English Society of Friends, was born near Monyash, England, about 1641. He was converted at the age of ten, and first joined the Presbyterians; afterwards attended successively the service of the Church of England, then the meetings of the Independents, and later of the Anabaptists; about 1671 united with the Friends, and began to preach, travelling extensively throughout England, often persecuted by mobs, and from 1680 to 1686 imprisoned at Derby. While there he sometimes preached from the window to the people, wrote letters of encouragement to his brethren, and prepared a small volume, entitled *The Prisoner's Vindication.* In 1707 he disposed of his estate at Monyash, and, his health failing, travelled thereafter but little. He died Jan. 9, 1711 or 1712. Among other things published by him was a *Journal of his Life.* See *The Friend*, vii, 61.

Graumann, Johann. See Poliander.

Graun, Caspar Heinrich, a Lutheran theologian, was born Feb. 2, 1659. He studied at Wittenberg, was in 1693 superintendent at Rochlitz, and died May 19, 1710, leaving, *Definitiones, Hypotheses et Propositiones Theologiæ Dogmatum:—Apodixis Aliquot Quæstionum Theologicarum:—De Gamaliele Cognomine Sene.* See Ranft, *Leben der chursächsischen Gottesgelehrten;* Jöcher, *Allgemeines Gelehrten-Lexikon*, s. v. (B. P.)

Graun, Karl Heinrich, an eminent German composer, was born at Wahrenbrück, Saxony, May 7, 1701. He sang in the choir at Dresden, and received instruction from various masters. Here he began the composition of cantatas and other sacred pieces at an early age. He was afterwards employed as tenor singer and composer at the opera-house of Brunswick, and became celebrated for his talents throughout Germany. In 1740 he became chapel-master to Frederick the Great, a position which he retained during the remainder of his life. He died at Berlin, Aug. 8, 1759. Among his sacred pieces are two settings of *The Passion*, and his oratorio *The Death of Jesus.* See *Encyclop. Brit.* 9th ed. s. v.

Gräve, Arnold, a Lutheran theologian of Germany, was born at Hamburg, June 8, 1700. He studied at Wittenberg, was preacher in 1727 in the neighborhood of his native city, accepted a call in 1737 to Hamburg, and died Nov. 18, 1754, leaving, *De eo Quantum Reformatio Lutheri Profuerit Logicæ* (Hamburg, 1717):—*De Tertulliani Testimonio de Apotheosi Christi* (1722):—*Athanasius de Morte Christi Referens* (eod.):—*De Moderatione Theologica* (1723). See Schmersahl, *Neue Nachrichten von verstorbenen Gelehrten*, ii, 473 sq.; Jöcher, *Allgemeines Gelehrten-Lexikon*, s. v. (B. P.)

Grave, Gerhard, a Lutheran theologian of Germany, was born in 1598. He studied at Rostock, Strasburg, and Jena, was in 1627 pastor at Hamburg, and died March 9, 1675, leaving, *Tabulæ Apocalypticæ:—Theologia Methodica:—Pent. Quæstionum Theologico-Historicarum:—Explicatio Ps. lxviii:—Disput. ad Joh. i*, 14:—*Disput. ad Rom. iii*, 23. See Moller, *Cimbria Litterata;* Jöcher, *Allgemeines Gelehrten-Lexikon*, s. v. (B. P.)

Grave (also **Gravius** and **Greaves**), **Thomas**, an English theologian, who died May 22, 1676, is the author of, *De Linguæ Arabicæ Utilitate et Præstantia:—Observationes in Persicam Pentateuchi Versionem:—Annotationes in Persicam Interpretationem Evangeliorum*, the last two are found in vol. vi of Walton's *Polyglot.* See Wood, *Athenæ Oxonienses;* Jöcher, *Allgemeines Gelehrten-Lexikon*, s. v. (B. P.)

Graver, Albert, a Lutheran theologian of Germany, was born April 3, 1575. He studied at different universities, was professor of theology at Jena, general superintendent at Weimar, and died Nov. 30, 1617, leaving, *Prælectiones in August. Confessionem:—Harmonia Præcipuorum Calvinianorum et Photinianorum:—Expositio Prophetæ Michæ:—Bellum Jesu Christi et Joannis Calvini:—De Deo in Carne Manifestato:—De Errore circa Doctrinam de Satisfactione Christi pro Peccatis:—De Creatione et Angelis:—De Anti-Christo Romano.* On account of his controversies with the Calvinists, Graver was styled *clypeus* and *gladius Lutheranismi.* See Winer, *Handbuch der theol. Lit.* i, 352; Jöcher, *Allgemeines Gelehrten-Lexikon*, s. v. (B. P.)

Graves, Richard, an English divine, was born in Gloucestershire in 1715, and educated at Abingdon, in Berkshire, and at Pembroke College, Oxford. He was rector of Cleverton, near Bath, and of Kilmersdon. He died in 1804. Among his best-known works are the *Festoon, or Collection of Epigrams:—Lucubrations in Prose and Verse*, published under the name of Peter Pomfret:—*The Spiritual Quixote:—Sermons on Various Subjects.* His last work was *The Invalid, with the Obvious Means of Enjoying Life.* See Chalmers, *Biog. Dict.* s. v.; Allibone, *Dict. of Brit. and Amer. Authors*, s. v.

Graveson, Ignace Hyacinthe Amat de, a French theologian, was born at Graveson, near Avignon, July 13, 1670. He joined the order of the Dominicans at the Convent of Arles at the age of sixteen, and studied theology at the College of St. Jacques, at Paris. He was made doctor in the Sorbonne, taught in the convent at Arles, went to Rome, refused the first chair in theology in the University of Turin, and returned to Arles, where he died, July 26, 1733. His works have been collected under the title of *Opera Omnia* (Venice, 1740). See Hoefer, *Nouv. Biog. Générale*, s. v.

Gravier, Jacques, a French missionary to America, arrived in Canada in 1684. He was sent at once to the Illinois region, to follow up the labors of Marquette and others. He made a canoe voyage from Kaskaskia down the Mississippi to confer with Iberville; went down a second time in 1706, and from thence to Europe. He returned in February, 1708, re-embarked, and died at sea in April of the same year. He wrote a grammar of the Illinois language, a journal of his voyage down the Mississippi in 1700, and other works, a part of which have been published. See *Appleton's Amer. Cyclop.* s. v.

Gravina, Dominico, an Italian theologian, was born at Naples in 1580. He entered the order of St. Dominic, and studied theology; taught in several convents of his order the interpretation of the Scriptures; in 1608 was advanced to the grade of a licensed theologian at Rome, where he was professor several years in the College of La Minerva, and was selected occasionally to address the pope. He died at Rome in 1643. Some of his principal works are, *Catholicæ Præscriptiones, Adversus omnes Veteres et Nostri Temporis Hæreticos* (Naples, 1619):—*Pro Sacro Fidei Catholicæ et Apostolicæ Deposito*, etc. (ibid. 1629):—*Ad Discernendas Veras a Falsis Visionibus et Revelationibus Lapis Lydius* (1638). See Hoefer, *Nouv. Biog. Générale*, s. v.

Gray, John, a Reformed (Dutch) minister, descended from the Scotch Covenanters, was born in Aberdeen, Scotland, in 1792, and educated and ordained in that country in 1815. He led in prayer at the family altar, and bought a Bible, then a costly book, with his own earnings, of which he afterwards wrote the history, called *Little Johnny and his Bible.* In 1818 he went with his wife to Russian Tartary as a Presbyterian missionary. After seven years of labor there, he returned on the death of his wife, and engaged in home mission work in England until 1833, when he removed to America, and spent the rest of his busy life chiefly as a missionary (Fallsburgh, N. Y. 1833-35; Schodack, 1835-46; Cohoes, 1847-48; Ghent, 1848-55; Cicero, 1856-57). He died in 1865. He was an almost constant contributor to the religious press, and was the author of several of the most striking tracts of the American Tract Society. He was a close observer of men and things, an acute thinker and vigorous writer, full of strong points and memorable forms of expression. His spirit, work, and life were full of Christ, and his earnestness was unwearied. See Corwin, *Manual of the Reformed Church in America*, s. v. (W. J. R. T.)

Gray, Joshua Taylor, Ph.D., an English Baptist, born at Davenport, Feb. 9, 1809, was the son of the Rev. W. Gray. He was early converted, baptized by his father at Northampton, and began to preach in his youth. He entered the Baptist College in 1827, and in 1830 was ordained pastor of the St. Andrew's Baptist Church, Cambridge. His mind not being suited to preaching, he opened a school at Brixton, but afterwards succeeded Mr. Bligh in his school near Bedford Square, London. In 1849 he became pastor of the Baptist Church at Hastings, but in 1850 was chosen classical tutor at the Baptist College, Stepney. In 1852 consumption set in; he visited New York, Boston, and Philadelphia, but was able to address only one American audience. He returned to his mother's house in Bristol, and died there, July 13, 1854. See (Lond.) *Baptist Handbook*, 1855, p. 49.

Gray, Thomas, D.D., a Congregational minister, was born in Boston, Mass., March 16, 1772. He graduated at Harvard University in 1790, and studied theology for a year there and under Dr. Stillman. After preaching at several places, he was called to Jamaica Plain, where he was ordained, March 27, 1793. In 1843 he resigned in favor of his colleague, Joseph H. Allen. He died at Jamaica Plain, June 1, 1847. Gray was an agreeable, practical preacher, although it was as a pastor he was most conspicuous. See *Christ. Examiner*, September, 1847, art. vii; Frothingham, *Funeral Sermon* (Boston, 1847).

Gray, William, an English prelate of the 15th century, was son of lord Gray of Codnor, Derbyshire. He studied at Balliol College, Oxford, then at Ferrara, Italy, where for a long time he heard the lectures of Guarinus of Verona, an accomplished scholar. The English king appointed him his procurator at the court of Rome, and he afterwards was preferred to the see of Ely, in which he sat twenty four years. In 1469 he served as lord-treasurer of England, being the last clergyman who discharged that office until the appointment of bishop Juxton (or Juxon) in 1635. He died Aug. 4, 1478, and was buried in the Cathedral of Ely. He wrote many books, which have not survived, however. See Fuller, *Worthies of England* (ed. Nuttall), i, 370.

Graziani, Ercole, *the Younger*, an eminent Bolognese painter, was born in 1688, and studied under Donato Creti. He painted an immense number of works for the Bolognese churches, among which is the celebrated picture of *St. Peter Consecrating St. Apollinare.* There are other works by him at Rome, *The Ascension* and *The Annunciation* in La Purita. He died in 1765. See Hoefer, *Nouv. Biog. Générale*, s. v.; Spooner, *Biog. Hist. of the Fine Arts*, s. v.

Greaton, Josiah, a Roman Catholic priest, was born about 1680; entered the Society of Jesus, July 5, 1708, became a professed father, Aug. 4, 1719, resided at St. Inigo's, Md., from 1721 to 1724; exercised his ministry in Philadelphia for nearly twenty years (1730-50); returned to Maryland; and died at Bohemia, Sept. 19, 1752. Greaton's name is a prominent one in the early annals of Catholicism in Philadelphia. See De Courcy and Shea, *Hist. of the Cath. Church in the U. S.* p. 200.

Greatrakes, Valentine, a famous English thaumaturgist, was born at Affane, County Waterford, Ireland, Feb. 14, 1628. At the age of thirteen he was obliged, on account of the civil troubles, to leave the College of Dublin, and take refuge with his mother in England. Some time later he fought in Ireland against the royalists, and after the disbanding of his regiment, in 1656, retired to a quiet life. He now imagined that he had received from above the power of curing the sick, which he actually proved in several cases by simply laying on his hands. This, however, drew upon him the attention of the local authorities, and being summoned before the bishop of Lismore, he was condemned, and had to abstain from his pretensions. He was afterwards called to England, where the countess Conway was afflicted by a disease which he cured. He was then called to London, where he went about daily professing to cure invalids. He excited the jealousy of the physicians, who began to write pamphlets against him, but Greatrakes did not hesitate to refer even to members of the court. He died in Ireland about 1700. See Chalmers, *Biog. Dict.* s. v.; Hoefer, *Nouv. Biog. Générale*, s. v.

Grebenitz, Elias, a Lutheran theologian of Germany, who died Dec. 31, 1689, professor of theology at Frankfort-on-the-Oder, is the author of, *De Christo ἀναμαρτήτῳ:—Theologiæ Systematicæ Propædia:—De Scriptura Probanda:—De Regeneratione:—De Scripturæ Sacræ Vero Usu:—De Auctoritate Conciliorum.* See Witte, *Diarium Biographicum;* Jöcher, *Allgemeines Gelehrten-Lexikon*, s. v. (B. P.)

Grebo Version of the Scriptures. The Grebo language is predominant in the immediate vicinity of cape Palmas, and is supposed to extend considerably into the interior. At present the Grebos enjoy the benefit of having in their own vernacular the gospels of Matthew and Luke, the Acts of the Apostles, Paul's epistle to the Romans, his first epistle to the Corinthians, and the book of Genesis. The publication of these parts of the Scriptures is due to the American Bible Society. (B. P.)

Greek Versions (*Modern*) of the Scriptures. See Romaic Version.

Greek-Turkish Version of the Scriptures. See Turkey, Versions of.

Green, Alexander L. P., D.D., a minister in the Methodist Episcopal Church South, was born in Sevier County, Tenn., June 24, 1807, and reared in Jackson County, Ala. He joined the Church in his ninth year; in 1824 was admitted into the Tennessee Conference; at the age of twenty-five was chosen a delegate to the General Conference, and was thus elected each session except one until his decease. He was one of the chief actors in securing a separation, in 1844, between the Methodist Episcopal Church North and South. For sixty years he gave his entire energies to the Church, dying in the midst of his labors, in Nashville, Tenn., July 15, 1874. Probably no man of his time made a more lasting impression upon his chosen denomination than Dr. Green. In winning souls he had but few equals. He was self-taught and self-cultured, strictly original, full of pathos, and unrivalled in descriptive ability. See *Minutes of Annual Conferences of the M. E. Church South*, 1874, p. 70; Simpson, *Cyclop. of Methodism*, s. v.

Green, Anson, D.D., a Canadian Methodist minister, was born at Middlebury, N. Y., Sept. 27, 1801. He went to Upper Canada in 1822, taught school in Prince Edward County, was called into the ministry in 1824, received on trial in 1825, ordained as elder in 1830, was presiding elder from 1832 to 1845, was book steward from 1845, superannuated from 1854 to 1859, was again book steward from 1859 to 1865, and retired finally from active service in the latter year. He was elected president of the conference in 1842 and 1863, and representative to the British Conference in 1846 and 1854. He died at his home in Toronto, Feb. 19, 1879. Dr. Green was a faithful laborer, a successful and popular preacher, and discharged with efficiency the duties of all the offices with which he was intrusted. He wrote his own *Life and Times*, a valuable book, which was published at the request of the conference. See *Minutes of the Toronto Conference*, 1879, p. 13.

Green, Georg, a Lutheran theologian of Germany, was born July 8, 1636. He studied at Wittenberg, Leipsic, and Strasburg, was for some time professor at Wittenberg, in 1678 court-preacher at Dresden, and died Aug. 22, 1691. He wrote, *Tres Disputationes de Sibyllis*:—*Duæ Disputationes de Rebus Herodis Magni*:—*De Ecclesia Bohemica*:—*De Hæresi Veterum Prædestinatianorum*:—*De Concilio Nicæano*. See Moller, *Cimbria Litterata*; Jöcher, *Allgemeines Gelehrten-Lexikon*, s. v. (B. P.)

Green, Georg Sigismund, *the Younger*, a Lutheran theologian of Germany, was born April 8, 1712, at Chemnitz. He studied at Wittenberg and Leipsic, in which latter place he also lectured in 1732. In 1736 he was rector at Meissen, in 1746 archdeacon, and died Jan. 12, 1754. He wrote, *De Luco Religioni ab Abrahamo Consecrato, ad Genes. xxxi*, 33 (Leipsic, 1735):—*De Vite in Templo Hierosolymitano a Romanis Reperta* (1737):—*De Clypeis in Loco Sacro Suspensis* (eod.):—*De Regibus Sacerdotibus* (1739; contained in *Exercitationes Philol. Antiquæ et Criticæ*, Meissen, 1744):—*De Plantatis in Domo Jehovah*:—*De Anno Quinquagesimo Dei Sacris Ministrorum*:—*De Choreis a Paulo Interdictis*:—*De Summa Decalogi*:—*De Deo Fulminatore*:—*De Vento Nuntio et Symboli Dei*, contained in *Exercitationum Sacrarum Decas Prima*. See Dietmann, *Chursächsische Priester*, vol. i; Jöcher, *Allgemeines Gelehrten-Lexikon*, s. v. (B. P.)

Green, John, an English prelate, was born about 1706 at Beverly, in Yorkshire, and became, in 1730, a fellow of St. John's College, Cambridge. In 1748 he was regius professor of divinity, and in 1750 was master of Benedict College. In 1756 he was dean of Lincoln, and bishop of Lincoln in 1761. In 1771 he was canon-residentiary of St. Paul's. He died April 25, 1779. He published ten occasional *Sermons* (1749–73):—*The Academic* (1750). See Chalmers, *Biog. Dict.* s. v.; Allibone, *Dict. of Brit. and Amer. Authors*, s. v.

Green, Lewis Warner, a Presbyterian minister, was born in Boyle County, Ky., Jan. 28, 1806, and educated at Centre College, Danville; studied one year (1831) at the Princeton Theological Seminary, was licensed by the Transylvania Presbytery, and appointed professor in Centre College. Subsequently he was elected professor of Hebrew and Oriental literature in the Western Theological Seminary, at Allegheny City, Pa., which position he occupied for many years. In 1848 he was elected president of Hampden Sidney College, Va. He died May 26, 1863. He was an eminent scholar and a lowly Christian. See Wilson, *Presb. Hist. Almanac*, 1868, p. 93; Nevin, *Presb. Encyclop.* s. v.; *Gen. Cat. of Princeton Theol. Sem.* 1881, p. 76.

Green, Thomas Hill, an English philosopher, was born in 1836. He was educated at Rugby and at Balliol College. In 1859 he took his bachelor's degree, began to study Hegel, and gave a good deal of attention to the Tübingen school, especially Baur. Among the fruits of these studies were two essays on the *Development of Dogma*. In 1866 he commenced lecturing at Balliol, and in 1878 was elected to the office of Whyte's professor of moral philosophy, and shortly after resigned his tutorship. He died March 26, 1882. For the *North British Review* he contributed, in 1866, on the *Philosophy of Aristotle*, and on *Popular Philosophy in its Relation to Life*. His main work followed in 1874, as part of a new edition of Hume's works by Green and Grose, in four volumes. The first two volumes, including the *Treatise on Human Nature*, were prefaced by lengthy introductory dissertations; one dealing with the theoretical philosophy of Locke, Berkeley, and Hume; the other with the ethical views of these writers and their contemporaries. "The former," says a writer in the *Academy*, "is a probably unequalled piece of minute and at the same time comprehensive criticism of the origins of current English philosophy." In December, 1877, professor Green began, in the *Contemporary Review*, a series of papers on "Mr. Herbert Spencer and Mr. G. H. Lewes: their Application of the Doctrine of Evolution to Thought." Besides, in several short reviews published in the *Academy*, he has made contributions of permanent value to the literature of philosophical criticism. See *Contemporary Review*, May, 1882. (B. P.)

Green, Valentine, an eminent English mezzotinto engraver, was born in Warwickshire in 1739. In 1765 he went to London and devoted himself to mezzotinto engraving, which, without the aid of an instructor, he elevated to a high degree of perfection. In 1789 he obtained the exclusive privilege from the king of Bavaria of engraving and publishing prints after the pictures in the Düsseldorf gallery, and in 1795 he published twenty-two prints from that collection. In 1767 he was elected a member of the Incorporated Society of Artists in Great Britain, and in 1774 an associate engraver of the Royal Academy. He died July 6, 1813. The following are some of his important works: *The Stoning of Stephen; The Raising of Lazarus; Christ Calling to him the Little Children; Jacob Blessing the Sons of Joseph; Daniel Interpreting Belshazzar's Dream; The Annunciation; The Nativity; The Virgin and Infant; St. John with his Lamb; The Entombing of Christ*. See Hoefer, *Nouv. Biog. Générale*, s. v.; Spooner, *Biog. Hist. of the Fine Arts*, s. v.

Greene, Abijah Emmons, D.D., a Presbyterian minister, was born at Greenfield, Saratoga Co., N. Y. Dec. 11, 1809. He was prepared for college at the academies at Johnstown and Amsterdam, N. Y.; graduated from Union College in 1834; went immediately to Princeton Seminary, and remained nearly three years; was licensed by the Presbytery of Albany, Oct. 15, 1835, and, after supplying Glenham Church, was ordained by the Presbytery of North River pastor at Cold Spring, May 16, 1838, from which charge he was released June 9, 1841. After this time he labored as stated supply successively at Highland Falls, Haverstraw, Rockland Lake, Highland Falls again, Southampton, Rensselaerville, Bleecker, and Hampstead churches, all in the state of New York, for various periods of time. After 1866 he resided, in poor health, at Highland Falls. He died in New York city, Oct. 20, 1881. See *Necrol. Report of Princeton Theol. Sem.* 1882, p. 33.

Greene, Maurice, an eminent English musician, was born in London in 1696. He composed cathedral music, and made collections with a view to its publication. Before he was twenty years old he was organist of St. Dunstan's, in 1717 of St. Andrew's, Holborn, in 1726 of the chapel royal, and of St. Paul's in 1727. He died in London, Sept. 1, 1755. See Chalmers, *Biog.*

Dict. s. v.; Allibone, *Dict. of Brit. and Amer. Authors*, s. v.

Greenlanders, Religion of the. These people, like the other Esquimaux, spiritualize all objects that surround them. The spirits are called *Innuet*, i. e. rulers. Malina and Aniunga are the rulers of the sun and moon. They were formerly men, but have been placed in the heavens. Their food changes their color, for they are sometimes red, sometimes yellow. The planets are women, who visit each other, therefore oftentimes a number are seen together. The rulers of the atmosphere are Innerterirsok and Erloersortok; the spirits of the sea Konguesetokit, and the ice-ruler, Sillagigsartok. The spirits of fire are called Ingersoit. The mountains are inhabited by great spirits and small gnomes, Tannersoit and Innuarolit. The gods of war Erkiglit, the spirits of food Nerrim Innuet, etc., are distributed everywhere, and they can be persuaded by mysterious means, only known to magicians, to become the protecting spirits of men. Such a guardian is called Torngak, but the great spirit, the ruler of all Innuets and Torngaks, is called Torngaseak. The wife or mother of this great spirit is a dreaded being; she is the daughter of the sorcerer who tore Disko (Greenland) from the mainland, and thrust it towards the north. She lives under the sea, and injures the fish-traffic. The invisible ruler of the universe, Scylla or Pirksoma, is the unimaginable, omniscient god. The Greenlanders have no divine worship with ceremonies. When a young man captures his first sea-lion, he lays a piece of fat or meat under a stone as a sacrifice, in order to insure good success in hunting. Sun and moon are sister and brother. The latter loved his sister, who was very beautiful, and he conceived the idea of putting out the lamps in winter, in order that he might caress and embrace her. She wanted to know who her lover was, and therefore covered her hands with rust, and thus blackened his face and clothes. Then she brought in the light, and, recognising her brother, she fled. The brother lighted a bundle of moss in order to find his way and follow her; the moss would not ignite, the sister escaped, and was placed in the heavens. The sun still follows her, and the dark spots which he has are the stripes made by his sister's blackened hands. Heaven, according to the Greenlanders, rests on the top of a mountain on the North Pole, about which it revolves daily. They have no knowledge of astronomy whatever, which is quite singular, as the stars and planets are the only means of reckoning time during the long half-year night. They have, however, the following theory as to the origin of thunder and lightning: Two old women, inhabiting a log cabin in heaven, are angry with each other over a dry, stretched seal-skin; as often as they strike the skin with their fists, a peal of thunder is heard. When, then, the house tumbles, and the burning rafters fall, the lightning is produced. The rain also has its explanation: The souls live in heaven on the brink of a dammed-up sea. When this sea swells, the overflowing waters form the rain. Their traditions also tell of Adam, Noah, and a flood. Kollak was the first man, from whose thumb there sprang the first woman, and from her came all human beings. When, after many years, the earth sank into the sea, only one man was left, who began a new generation. The Greenlanders have a twofold conception of souls: these are a shadow, or a breath. A dangerous journey must be made by all souls to heaven; for five days they must slide down a steep rock, which is therefore covered with blood.

Greenlandish Version of the Scriptures. As early as 1721, Hans Egede (q. v.), a Norwegian clergyman, settled at Sodthaas (latitude 64° north), and his attention was soon arrested by the abject and deplorable condition of the natives. He applied himself to the study of their language, reduced it to writing, and translated the Psalms and the Epistles of St. Paul. His son Paul completed the version of the New Test., portions of which were published at Copenhagen in 1744, followed in 1758 by an edition of the Gospels and Acts, and in 1766 by the entire New Test. This first attempt being very deficient, Fabricius, after the death of Egede (1789), undertook a new translation, which was printed in 1799. As this second attempt did not prove to be in any respect superior to Egede's version, Moravian missionaries undertook a third translation from Luther's German version, which was published in 1822 by the British and Foreign Bible Society, and in subsequent editions by the Danish Bible Society. A new and revised edition was published at Herrnhut, under the personal superintendence of several retired missionaries from Greenland, in 1851; while of the Old Test. only some portions are published. It is said that while John Beck, one of the missionaries, was engaged in transcribing the version of the four Gospels, the curiosity of the savages being excited to know what he was writing, he read to them the history of the Saviour's agony on the Mount of Olives. Some of them laid their hands upon their mouths, as is customary among them when they are struck with wonder; but one of them, named Kajarnak, exclaimed in a loud and serious tone, "How was that? Tell us that once more; for I, too, would fain be saved," and finally became converted to God. Up to March 31, 1884, the British and Foreign Bible Society had distributed 2000 New Tests., and 1200 portions of the Old Test. See Esquimaux Version. (B. P.)

Greenlaw, Gilbert, a Scotch prelate, was promoted to the see of Aberdeen in 1390, and was made chancellor of the kingdom in 1396. In 1423 this bishop was sent on an embassy to Charles VII, king of France, by Robert, duke of Albany. He died in 1424. See Keith, *Scottish Bishops*, p. 28-112.

Greenleaf, Jonathan, D.D., a Presbyterian minister, was born in Newburyport, Mass., Sept. 4, 1785. He was deprived of the privileges of an academic education, and when he felt that he was called to preach the gospel, he began the study of theology under Dr. Bruer, president of Dartmouth College, at Hanover, N. H. He was licensed to preach by the Cumberland Association at Saco, Me., in September, 1814. After having filled several important charges, he was elected corresponding secretary of the American Seaman's Friend Society in 1833, in which capacity he labored with untiring diligence until 1841. He died at Brooklyn, N. Y., April 24, 1865. Dr. Greenleaf was the author of, *Ecclesiastical Sketches of Maine:—History of the Churches of New York: —Thoughts on Paper: —The Genealogy of the Greenleaf Family:—A Doctrinal Catechism:*—and five tracts entitled, *The Missing Disciple; Experimental Religion; Sudden Death; Misery of Dying in Sin;* and *Shall I Come to the Lord's Supper?* During his connection with the Seaman's Friend Society, he also edited the *Sailor's Magazine.* He contributed many valuable articles to the religious papers. See Wilson, *Presb. Hist. Almanac*, 1866, p. 111.

Greenleaf, Patrick Henry, D.D., a minister of the Protestant Episcopal Church, was a native of Maine, and a son of the Hon. Simon Greenleaf. After graduating at Bowdoin College, he practiced law for several years; but turning his attention to the ministry, pursued his theological studies under bishop Doane, and was duly ordained. He was connected successively with the dioceses of Massachusetts, Pennsylvania, Ohio, and Indiana. For several years he was rector of St. John's, Charlestown, Mass.; also of St. Paul's, Cincinnati, O.; and in 1862 of Emanuel Church, Brooklyn, in which city he died, June 21, 1869, at the age of sixty-two years. See *Amer. Quar. Church Rev.*, Jan. 1870, p. 635.

Greenville (Granville or Grenville), Denis, D.D., an English clergyman, was born in Cornwall, and admitted commoner of Exeter College, Sept. 22, 1657.

The rectories of Easington and Elwick, in the palatine of Durham, were conferred upon him. He was installed dean of Durham in 1684, and deprived of his preferments in 1690, on account of his refusal to acknowledge William and Mary. He died at Paris in 1703, leaving several theological works, sermons, etc. (1684–89). See Chalmers, *Biog. Dict.* s. v.; Allibone, *Dict. of Brit. and Amer. Authors*, s. v.

Grees, a mediæval term, which some assert to be derived from *Gradus*, signifying "a step." It is frequently employed by old English writers to designate the altar-steps, which anciently were two only; but others were added later, until, in more recent times, high altars have been elevated on at least seven steps. There are some examples of this both in old and modern churches.

Greeting-house, a term sometimes applied in mediæval times to the chapter-house of a cathedral, where a newly-appointed bishop or dean received the greetings respectively of his flock, or the members of his cathedral. Such greetings, however, were as frequently given at the entrance of the choir, or in the sacristy. To an abbot they were sometimes tendered in the refectory, or even in the choir after the rites of installation.

Gregentius, *Saint*, bishop of Tephæ, in Arabia, was born at Soplian, "on the frontier of Asia," but other authorities say, at Milan, on Dec. 19 (his festal day). He went to Alexandria, where he embraced the life of an anchorite, and was sent to take charge of the Homerites. He propagated Christianity among the idolaters of Yemen, and is said to have died in 552. There is a book extant, giving some details of part of his life, entitled: *Τοῦ ἐν ἁγίοις Πατρὸς ἡμῶν Γρηγηντίου ἀρχιεπισχόπου γενομένον Τεφρῶν*, etc. (Migne, *Patrol. Græc.* lxxxvi, 5). See Hoefer, *Nouv. Biog. Générale*, s. v.; Smith, *Dict. of Christ. Biog.* s. v.

Gregorius, BAR-AHRUN (or BAR-HEBRÆUS). See ABUL-FARAJ.

Gregory (1), an Irish prelate, was elected to the see of Dublin, and went immediately to England, where he received his first orders as bishop, from Roger, bishop of Salisbury, Sept. 24, 1121, and was consecrated in the following October. After he had presided thirty-one years over his see, the archiepiscopal dignity was conferred upon him, at the Council of Kells. He died Oct. 8, 1161. See D'Alton, *Memoirs of the Abps. of Dublin*, p. 41.

Gregory (2), a Scotch prelate, was made bishop of Dunkeld in 1169. How long he sat is unknown. See Keith, *Scottish Bishops*, p. 73.

Gregory (3), a Scotch prelate, was bishop of Ross in 1161. He died in 1195. See Keith, *Scottish Bishops*, p. 184.

Gregory (4), a Scotch prelate, was bishop of Brechin in 1242. See Keith, *Scottish Bishops*, p. 158.

Gregory I,* OF ARMENIA (surnamed *the Mamigonian*), brother and successor of Hamazasb, having been given as a hostage to the Arabians from the time of the conquest of Armenia, was sent back into his own country in 659, to govern it, with the title of a patriarch. He relieved Bagdad from its caliphs until the year 679, when he made himself independent. But four years later he perished, in 683, in an encounter with the Khazars, who had crossed the Caucasus and invaded Armenia. He erected several buildings, among which the monastery of Arûj, near Erivan, and the monastery of Elivard are particularly distinguishable. See Hoefer, *Nouv. Biog. Générale*, s. v.

Gregory II, OF ARMENIA (surnamed *Vgaiaser* or *Martyrophilus*), a patriarch of Armenia, the son of Gregory Magisdros, died in 1105, at Garmir-Vankh, near Khesûn. He was educated under the direction of his father, and made great progress both in science and languages. He inherited, in 1058, the government of the duchy of Mesopotamia. But neither that dignity, nor the favor which he enjoyed at the court of Constantinople could make him attached to a secular life. He separated himself from his wife, sold all his goods, distributing the money among the unfortunate, and consecrated himself to the monastic life. Gregory is less remarkable as an administrator than as a protector of letters. He gathered about him Greek and Syrian scholars, whom he charged with translating a large number of works, written in their own languages. These versions were revised by Armenian scholars, who improved their style. The patriarch himself put his hand upon a translation of a martyrology. See Hoefer, *Nouv. Biog. Générale*, s. v.

Gregory III, OF ARMENIA (named BAHLAVUNI, and surnamed *the small Vgaiaser* or *Martyrophilus*), was born in 1092. After the death of his uncle Basil, he was consecrated patriarch in 1113, in conformity with the dispositions which were made by Gregory II. But several bishops found fault with the new patriarch as too young, and refused to recognise him. One among them, David of Aghthamar, was consecrated patriarch at the Council of Droroi-Vankh. But this usurpation was condemned in a council convocated in 1114 by Gregory III, and composed of two thousand five hundred bishops and doctors, who established the principle that for the election of a patriarch in the future it should be necessary to have the unanimous consent of the four archbishops. Gregory lived in good understanding with the Romish Church, and died in 1166, having arranged that his brother, Nurses IV, should become his successor. He left hymns, which are very well written, and which are still sung in the solemnities of the Armenian Church. See Hoefer, *Nouv. Biog. Générale*, s. v.

Gregory IV, OF ARMENIA (surnamed *Dgha*, i. e. "the child"), succeeded to his uncle Nurses IV in 1173. He gained the admiration of his people by his imposing manners. Being charged by the emperor Manuel Comnenus to renew the offer of uniting the churches of Armenia and Greece, he convoked a council at Tarsus in 1178, but, on account of disputes between the parties, the projected union failed of consummation. Gregory IV died in 1193, leaving, *Odanaver Oghg* (poetical lamentation), on the capture of Jerusalem by Saladin in 1187:—six *Letters*, which were addressed by him to the emperor Manuel, and the letter of convocation for the Council of Hrhomgla. See Hoefer, *Nouv. Biog. Générale*, s. v.

Gregory V, OF ARMENIA (surnamed *Mansug*, i. e. "the young," and *Kahavej*, "he who falls from on high"), succeeded his uncle, Gregory IV, in July, 1193, although yet quite young. After having administered his office about one year, he conducted himself in such a manner as to make himself odious to the nobility as well as to the clergy. He was accused before Leo II, and was put in the fortress of Gobidarh. He died in 1195. See Hoefer, *Nouv. Biog. Générale*, s. v.

Gregory VI, OF ARMENIA (surnamed *Abirad*), nephew of Gregory III, was elected after the deposition of Gregory V. The inhabitants of Great Armenia, and particularly the monks, refused to recognise him, because the place of his residence, the strong castle of Hrhomgla in Cilicia, or Little Armenia, was too far away from them. They chose as their patriarch Basil of Ani. When the persecution of the Armenians by the Greeks had broken out, Gregory VI vainly tried to bring back the emperor Alexis to principles of tolerance. Under his patriarchate the Armenian Church had a good understanding with that of Rome. He died in 1202. See Hoefer, *Nouv. Biog. Générale*, s. v.

Gregory VII, OF ARMENIA (surnamed *Anavarzetsi*), was proposed as successor to Jacob I in 1287,

* Strictly, Gregory II. See GREGORY *the Illuminator*.

but his attachment to the doctrines of the Roman Church was so great that in his stead were elected Constantine II, and afterwards Stephen IV. On the death of the latter, who was a captive in Egypt, Gregory was appointed to fill his place in 1294. The residence of his predecessors at Hrhomgla had been destroyed by the Mamelukes, and so Gregory VII selected his seat in Cilicia. His tendencies to substitute the Roman liturgy for the rites of the Armenian Church were regarded with disfavor by the monks of Great Armenia, who begged him to abstain from such unpopular innovations. Having taken the part of the prince Sempad against king Thoros, Sempad's brother, he crowned him in 1297, and placed him in subjection to the pope. Towards the end of his life, Gregory occupied himself mostly with the reunion of the Armenian and Roman churches. He died in 1306. See Hoefer, *Nouv. Biog. Générale*, s. v.

Gregory VIII, OF ARMENIA (surnamed *Khandsoghad*), succeeded Jacob III in 1411. He was a monk before his election. The inhabitants of Sis, who had poisoned his predecessor, made a conspiracy against their new chief, and were punished by the chief of the Mamelukes in Cilicia, but roused themselves again in 1418, deposing the patriarch, and putting him in a fortress, where he died shortly afterwards. See Hoefer, *Nouv. Biog. Générale*, s. v.

Gregory IX, OF ARMENIA (surnamed *Mousapegiants*), succeeded Joseph III in 1440 as patriarch. Cilicia had been continually invaded at that time by different enemies, on which account some of the bishops wished to establish the patriarchal seat in a different part of the empire, less exposed to danger, and proposed to transfer the see of Sis to the monastery of Echmiadzin. But as Gregory would not consent, they began to attack him on account of his election, which, in fact, had taken place in a small assembly. Accordingly seven hundred bishops and doctors united, in 1441, at Echmiadzin, under the presidency of Zacharias, bishop of Havuts-Tharha, and elected Gurragas, a monk of Kharabasd, in the province of Khadchperuni. The latter established himself at Echmiadzin, while Gregory continued in the city of Sis, being recognised only by the inhabitants of Cilicia. He died in 1447. See Hoefer, *Nouv. Biog. Générale*, s. v.

Gregory X, OF ARMENIA (surnamed *Magovetsi*), was elected patriarch, in 1443, to succeed Gurragas, whom Zacharias, bishop of Havuts-Tharha, had deposed. Yacoub Bey, of Erivan, governor of Armenia, imposed on him a heavy tribute, which, however, did not prevent Gregory from finding the means to repair the patriarchal church. He died in 1462. See Hoefer, *Nouv. Biog. Générale*, s. v.

Gregory XI, OF ARMENIA, was elected patriarch in 1536, after the death of Sarkis III. He died in 1541, and was succeeded by Stephen V. See Hoefer, *Nouv. Biog. Générale*, s. v.

Gregory XII, OF ARMENIA, succeeded Michael of Sebastopol as patriarch in 1562. He died in 1573, and was succeeded by Stephen VI. See Hoefer, *Nouv. Biog. Générale*, s. v.

Gregory XIII, OF ARMENIA, was born at Edessa. As he was in possession of a large fortune, the patriarch Melchisedech and his coadjutor, David, offered to transfer to him their dignity, if he would consent to pay their debts. Serapion (the former name of Gregory XIII) went to Joulfa (near Ispahan) in 1602, to negotiate with the patriarch the conditions of the arrangement, but could not settle anything. Some inhabitants of that city took him to Echmiadzin, and elected him patriarch, Aug. 14, 1603. That dignity caused Gregory the loss of his fortune. The Turks, who were on the point of being driven out of Armenia by the troops of Shah Abbas, requested the payment of all debts. Melchisedech being insolvent, they seized his successor, and forced from him all that they could get. Shah Abbas required of him an enormous sum, and delivered him to his ministers, who put him to torture, in order to force him to disclose his treasures. Under protest the patriarch retired to Van, and then to Amid, where he died of grief in 1606. The patriarchal seat, having remained vacant, was taken again by Melchisedech. See Hoefer, *Nouv. Biog. Générale*, s. v.

Gregory VII, OF ROME (Antipope). See BOURDIN, MAURICE.

Gregory OF HUNTINGDON, a monk of the 13th century, so called from the place of his nativity in Huntingdonshire, was bred a Benedictine monk at Ramsey, where he became prior or vice-abbot, a place he deserved, being one of the most learned men of his time in the languages. He wrote many comments on the Latin and Greek classics, and was proficient in Hebrew by constant conversing with the Jews. When the latter were driven from the kingdom, he purchased many of their literary treasures for his monastery at Ramsay, an institution which exceeded any other of the kind in England for its fine library, rich now especially in Hebrew books. Two hundred years after, a monk of the same monastery, John Yong, added yet more to the library of his school. Gregory was prior of Ramsey for thirty-eight years, flourishing under Henry III, and died in the reign of Edward I, about 1280. See Fuller, *Worthies of England* (ed. Nuttall), ii, 101.

Gregory, Caspar Robue, D.D., a Presbyterian minister, was born in Philadelphia, Sept. 17, 1824. He was prepared for college by his brother, Henry D.; graduated from the University of Pennsylvania in 1843; taught nearly two years in private families; graduated from Princeton Theological Seminary in 1847; was licensed by the Presbytery of Philadelphia, April 5, 1848; then taught a year, and was ordained an evangelist by the same presbytery, May 20, 1849. His first field of labor was as a missionary to the Choctaw Indians at Spencer Academy, in the Indian Territory. In 1850 he left the mission on account of ill-health. He next supplied the church at Oneida, Madison Co., N. Y., from April 20, 1851, until installed as its pastor, Feb. 9, 1852, continuing his labors until 1862; was installed pastor of the First Church of Bridgeton, N. J., May 12, 1864, and was released Oct. 7, 1873, immediately becoming professor of sacred rhetoric in Lincoln University, Pa. He died there, Feb. 26, 1882. Dr. Gregory was an earnest man, his preaching of a high quality, and as a professor was devoted and faithful. See *Necrol. Report of Princeton Theol. Sem.* 1882, p. 46.

Gregory, Henry, D.D., a minister of the Protestant Episcopal Church, was born Sept. 22, 1803, at Wilton, Fairfield Co., Conn. He graduated at Hobart College in 1826; was ordained deacon in 1829, and presbyter in 1831; officiated first in Moravia, N. Y.; was called to Calvary Church, Homer, in 1833; went as missionary to the Menomonee Indians, near Green Bay, Wis., in 1836; returned to Homer in 1838, and two years after was elected rector of St. Paul's Church, Syracuse, N. Y.; became the first rector of St. James's Free Church, in the same city, in 1848, but resigned in 1857 on account of impaired health; subsequently accepted the presidency of De Veaux College at Suspension Bridge, remaining in that position two years, when he established the Church Book Depository at Syracuse. He died there, April 5, 1866. In connection with the free church system, Dr. Gregory published, in 1850, a tract on the *Christian Tenth*. See *Amer. Quar. Church Rev.* July, 1866, p. 311.

Gregory, John, an English churchman of the 17th century, was born of humble parents at Amersham, Buckinghamshire, Nov. 10, 1607. He was educated at Christ Church College, Oxford, where for many years he studied sixteen hours a day. He became an exquisite linguist and general scholar, his modesty setting the greater lustre to his learning. He wrote notes on Dr. Ridley's book of *Civil and Ecclesiastical Law*. He was chaplain of Christ Church, and was thence preferred prebendary of Chichester and Sarum. He died at Kidlington, Oxfordshire, in 1646. His *Opera Posthuma* are faithfully set forth by John Gurgain. See Fuller, *Worthies of England* (ed. Nuttall), i, 208; Allibone, *Dict. of Brit. and Amer. Authors*, s. v.

Gregory, Samblak, a Russian prelate, was a native of Bulgaria, and became metropolitan of Kiev in 1414. He went to the Council of Constance in 1418, and died the year following. It is certain that this prelate was a Catholic, for his name is found in one of the ancient liturgies. The library of the synod of Moscow is in possession of twenty-seven *Discourses* of this metropolitan. See Hoefer, *Nouv. Biog. Générale*, s. v.

Greiling, Johann Christoph, a Lutheran theologian of Germany, was born Dec. 23, 1765. He was preacher in 1797 in Saxony, in 1805 superintendent at Aschersleben, and died April 3, 1840. He wrote, *Die Biblischen Frauen* (Leipsic, 1814, 2 vols.):—*Das Leben Jesu von Nazareth* (Halle, 1813):—*Ueber die Urverfassung der apostolischen Christengemeine* (1819):—*Versuch über das wechselseitige Verhältniss des Staats und der Kirche* (1802):—*Neue praktische Materialien zum Kanzelvortrag* (1798-1804, 6 vols.):—*Neueste Materialien* (1821-27, 6 vols.):—*Amtsvorträge* (1805). See Winer, *Handbuch der theol. Lit.* i, 162, 550; ii, 18, 20, 25, 66, 125, 164; Zuchold, *Bibl. Theol.* i, 465. (B. P.)

Greith, Karl Johann, a Roman Catholic doctor of theology and prelate, was born in 1807 at Rapperswyl. In 1863 he was made bishop of St. Gall, the second after the foundation of that diocese. He died May 17, 1882. He wrote, *Die deutsche Mystik im Prediger-Orden von 1250-1350* (Freiburg, 1860):—*Geschichte der altirischen Kirche* (ibid. 1867):—*Der heilige Gallus, der Apostel Alemanniens* (St. Gall, 1865):—*Licht und Recht zur Vertheidigung seiner bischöflichen Pflichtstellung* (Einsiedeln, 1874). (B. P.)

Gremiālè, an episcopal ornament for the breast, lap, and shoulders; originally a plain towel of fine linen, used in ordination to protect the sacred vestments from

French *Gremiale* of Purple Silk (of the 16th century).

any drops of unction that might fall in the act of anointing candidates for the priesthood. In later times it was made of silk or damask, to match the episcopal vestments, and was used in certain French dioceses both at solemn and high mass.

Grenvil, William de, an early English prelate, was born of a noble family in Cornwall; became canon of York, dean of Chichester, chancellor of England under king Edward I, and finally archbishop of York. His confirmation to this last preferment was delayed until he had paid the pope nine thousand five hundred marks, which reduced him to such poverty that he had to be relieved by the clergy of his province. He had this compensation—he was consecrated by the very hands of pope Clement V. He highly favored the Templars, but persons so greatly opposed as they were by the pope and Philip of France had more fear of losing than hope of gaining by his friendship. He was present at the Council of Vienna (1311), where he had a high place assigned him. He died at Cawood in 1315, and was buried in the Chapel of St. Nicholas, leaving the reputation of an able statesman and a good scholar. See Fuller, *Worthies of England* (ed. Nuttall), i, 309.

Grenz, Adam, a Lutheran theologian of Germany, was born at Rochlitz in 1700. He studied at Leipsic, was preacher in 1728, and died at Dresden, April 22, 1773, leaving, *Lucubratio Theologica in Joh. vii*, 48, 49 (Leipsic, 1739):—*De Apocrisiariis* (1748):—*De eo qui Major est Templo ad Matth. xii*, 6 (1752), etc. See Dietmann, *Chursächsische Priester;* Jöcher, *Allgemeines Gelehrten-Lexikon*, s. v.; Winer, *Handbuch der theol. Lit.* i, 613. (B. P.)

Greswell, Edward, an English ecclesiastical writer, was born at Manchester in 1797. He was educated at Oxford, where he became a fellow, and vice-president of Corpus Christi College. He devoted his life chiefly to theological literature. He died at Oxford, June 29, 1869. Among his more important publications are, *Expositions of the Parables and other Parts of the Gospels* (1834, 1835, 5 vols.):—*Prolegomena ad Harmoniam Evangelicam:* — *Dissertations upon the Principles and Arrangement of a Harmony of Gospels* (2d ed. 1837, 5 vols.):—*Fasti Temporis Catholici* (1852, 5 vols.). See *Appleton's Amer. Cyclop.* s. v.

Gretsch, Adrian, a Roman Catholic theologian, was born at Vienna, Oct. 11, 1752. He joined the Benedictines in 1770, was in 1784 professor of theology at Vienna, in 1796 dean of the theological faculty, and died Oct. 28, 1826, leaving eight volumes of *Sermons*. See Döring, *Die gelehrten Theologen Deutschlands*, s. v.; Winer, *Handbuch der theol. Lit.* ii, 113. (B. P.)

Greuter, Matthieu, a reputable French engraver, was born at Strasburg in 1566, and acquired the principles of the art in his native city. He went to Rome, where he settled permanently, and executed a number of plates, among which are the following: *The Virgin Seated, with the Infant Jesus and St. John; Mary Magdalene Sitting*. He died at Rome in 1638. See Hoefer, *Nouv. Biog. Générale*, s. v.; Spooner, *Biog. Hist. of the Fine Arts*, s. v.

Greuze, Jean Baptiste, an eminent French painter, was born at Tournus (Burgundy) in 1726, and studied under Grandon. He went to Paris, and produced his celebrated picture of *The Father Explaining the Scriptures to his Children*, which at once established his reputation. Many of his works have been engraved by eminent French artists. He died at Paris, March 21, 1805. See Hoefer, *Nouv. Biog. Générale*, s. v.; Spooner, *Biog. Hist. of the Fine Arts*, s. v.

Grew, Obadiah, D.D., an English clergyman, was born at Atherston, November, 1607, in the parish of Manceter, Warwickshire, and educated at Balliol College, Oxford. He was ordained in 1635; became minister of the great parish of St. Michael's, Coventry; was ejected at the Restoration for nonconformity; and died in 1698. He published some *Sermons* (1663):—and *Meditations upon the Parable of the Prodigal Son* (1678). See Chalmers, *Biog. Dict.* s. v.; Allibone, *Dict. of Brit. and Amer. Authors*, s. v.

Grial, Juan, a Spanish canonist, who flourished in the second part of the 16th century, is known as the editor of *Isidori Hispalensis Opera* (Madrid, 1599). See Winer, *Handbuch der theol. Lit.* i, 917; Antonii *Bibliotheca Hispanica;* Jöcher, *Allgemeines Gelehrten-Lexikon*, s. v. (B. P.)

Grier, John Ferguson, D.D., a Presbyterian minister, was born at Deep Run, Pa., in 1784. He graduated from Dickinson College in 1803 with the first honors of his class; studied theology privately; was licensed by the New Castle Presbytery in 1810; ordained pastor of the Church at Reading in 1814, and died June 26, 1829. See Sprague, *Annals of the Amer. Pulpit*, iii, 467.

Grier, John Nathan Coldwell, D.D., a Presbyterian minister, was born June 8, 1792, at the Forks of the Brandywine, Pa. In 1809 he graduated from Dickinson College; subsequently studied theology with his father, Rev. Nathan Grier; was licensed by the New Castle Presbytery, April 7, 1812, and engaged in preaching to vacant churches in Delaware. In 1814 he succeeded his father as pastor at the Forks of Brandywine, and after a long and fruitful ministry there, he resigned in 1873, and retired to his farm. He died at New Castle, Sept. 12, 1880. See *New York Observer*, Sept. 23, 1880. (W. P. S.)

Griesinger, Georg Friedrich *von*, a Protestant theologian of Germany, was born March 16, 1734. He studied at Tübingen, was in 1766 deacon at Stuttgart, in 1786 member of consistory, in 1799 doctor of theology, and died April 27, 1828, leaving, *De Decentia Restabilitionis Generis Humani* (Tübingen, 1758):—*De Commodis Angelorum Bonorum ex Opere Redemptionis* (1766):—*Theologia Dogmatica* (1825):—*Initia Theologiæ Moralis* (1826):—*Einleitung in die Schriften des neuen Bundes* (1799):—*Ueber die Authentie der alttestamentlichen Schriften* (1804): — *Ueber den Pentateuch* (1806):—*Die sämmtlichen Schriften des alten und neuen Testaments* (1824). See Döring, *Die gelehrten Theologen Deutschlands*, s. v.; Winer, *Handbuch der Theol. Lit.* i, 77, 78, 82, 389; ii, 297. (B. P.)

Griesinger, Johann Burchard, a Lutheran preacher of Germany, was born Dec. 17, 1638, at Worms. Being blind from his third year, he did not begin his studies until the age of nineteen. He went to the universities of Strasburg and Jena, and settled in 1686 at Königsberg, where he became famous as a preacher. He died July 15, 1701, leaving, *De Conceptu Quiditativo Immutabilitatis Dei:—De Genuina Nominis Tetragrammati.* See Hoefer, *Nouv. Biog. Générale*, s. v.

Griffet, Henri, a French Jesuit and court-preacher, was born at Moulins, Oct. 9, 1698, and died at Brussels, Feb. 22, 1771, leaving, among other works, *L'Année du Chrétien* (Paris, 1747, 18 vols.):—*Exercise de Piété pour la Communion* (ibid. 1748):—*Sermons* (Liege, 1767, 4 vols.). See *Nouv. Dict. Hist.*; Jöcher, *Allgemeines Gelehrten-Lexikon*, s. v.; Quérard, *France Littéraire;* Lichtenberger, *Encyclop. des Sciences Religieuses*, s. v.; Hoefer, *Nouv. Biog. Générale*, s. v. (B. P.)

Griffi (Lat. *Gryphius*), Leonardo, an Italian prelate, was born at Milan in 1437. In 1478 he was made bishop of Gubbio, and five years afterwards was transferred to the archbishopric of Benevento. He died at Rome in 1485, leaving (in the collection of Muratori, *Scriptores Rerum Italicarum*, xxv, 465) a small piece of poetry in hexameter, which narrates the exploits of Braccio de Perouse with Aquila. See Hoefer, *Nouv. Biog. Générale*, s. v.

Griffin, in Greek mythology, was a fabulous animal, in size like a lion, with four clawy feet, two wings, and the hooked bill of an eagle. It seems to have been an Oriental conception. This fantastic creature is the centre of a rare circle of myths, and it is mentioned by Hesiod and Herodotus as the guard of the gold in the innermost of northern Europe, which the one-eyed Arimaspes stole.

A Team of Griffins Attached to a Car of Apollo.

Griffin, Henry, D.D., an Irish prelate, was born July 10, 1786. He was originally a Roman Catholic, but entered Trinity College, Dublin, as a member of the Established Church; finished his under-graduate career, and gained a fellowship in 1811, which he held until 1829, when he became rector of Clonfeacle, in the diocese of Armagh. On Jan. 1, 1854, he was consecrated Lord Bishop of Limerick, Ardfert, and Aghadoe. He died at the University Club, Dublin, April 5, 1866. See *Amer. Quar. Church Rev.* July, 1866, p. 324.

Griffin, Nathaniel Herrick, D.D., a Presbyterian minister, was born at Southampton, L. I., Dec. 28, 1814. He graduated from Williams College, Mass., in 1834; spent two years in Princeton Theological Seminary; was a tutor in his alma mater in 1836–37; became thereafter stated supply successively at Westhampton, N. Y., and at Franklin; was ordained by the Presbytery June 27, 1839; was pastor at Delhi; acted as assistant professor in Williams College (1841–42), and as a teacher in Brooklyn (1843–46), professor of Latin and Greek in Williams College (1846–53), of Greek (1853–57), a teacher in Williamstown, Mass. (1857–68), librarian there (1868–76), and died in that place, Oct. 16, 1876. See *Gen. Cat. of Princeton Theol. Sem.* 1881, p. 99.

Griffith, David, D.D., a Protestant Episcopal clergyman, was born in New York city in 1742. His father was a native of Wales, who came to America in early life, settling on a farm on the East River. After preliminary study in his native city, David went to England and graduated in London as a student of medicine. About 1763 he returned to America, and began practice in the interior of the province of New York. A few years after he studied theology, went to England, was admitted to orders in August, 1770; soon after was sent to Gloucester County, N. J., as a missionary of the Society for the Propagation of the Gospel in Foreign Parts. From the close of 1771 until May, 1776, he was rector of Shelburne Parish, Loudon Co., Va.; when he entered the American army as chaplain of the 3d Virginia Regiment, remaining until the close of 1779. In 1780 he became rector of Christ Church, Alexandria, Va. Throughout the latter part of his life he is said to have enjoyed the confidence of General Washington, who was his parishioner for a number of years. It is reported that he was the first clergyman to propose a convention for the independent organization of the Church after the Revolution. In May, 1785, he was a member of the first convention that met in Richmond, Va., under the act of incorporation; and he was appointed a delegate to the ensuing General Convention. In May of that year he was chosen bishop, but was unable to meet the expenses of a voyage to England for consecration. Accordingly, in May, 1789, he resigned his claim to the office. He died in Philadelphia, Pa., Aug. 3, 1789. Dr. Griffith was regarded as a sound and able divine, and was universally esteemed. See Sprague, *Annals of the Amer. Pulpit*, v, 270.

Griffiths, David, a Welsh Congregational minister, was born at Glanmeilwch, Carnarganshire, Dec. 20, 1792. He was converted when about eighteen years of age, studied two years at Neuaddlwyd Academy, three at Wrexham College, and three at the Missionary College, Gosport; was ordained as missionary to Madagascar, reaching his destination in 1821. He formed the first native Christian church in that island, but after nearly fifteen years of labor, when the missionaries were compelled to leave the country, he returned to England. Two years later he received a letter from the Queen of Madagascar, permitting him to return for five years, at his own expense, in the capacity of a trader, but in reality a missionary. He was again expelled from the island, and after travelling on sea and land about the coast of Africa, and the Comoro Isles, he returned to his native country in 1842, and published a history of Madagascar, in Welsh. In 1852 he established a church in Kington, Radnorshire. About this time, learning that Madagascar was free for mission work, he, in company with Messrs. Joseph Freeman and T. W. Meller, commenced a new and improved translation of the Bible into the Malagasy language and finished it shortly before his death, which occurred at Machynlleth, March 21, 1863. Mr. Griffiths was emphatically practical. He could preach in three languages, and had a good knowledge of Greek, Latin, Hebrew, French, Chaldee, and Arabic. Besides his work on the Malagasy Bible, he translated into the language of Madagascar, *The Anxious Inquirer*, *Friend of Sinners*, *Come to Jesus*, *It is I*, and *Treatise on the Resurrection;* corrected former translations of *Pilgrim's Progress*, and several tracts; corrected and enlarged former works, *English and Malagasy Dictionary; Malagasy and English Dictionary; Vocabulary of Malagasy and English.* Besides his *History of Madagascar*, he published, *A History of Madagascar Martyrs*, in English: — *Malagasy Grammar:* — *Catechisms:* — *Hymn Book:* — *Essay on Destiny:* — *The Poor Rich Man, and the Rich Poor Man*, and several *Tracts.* Also left ready for the press, *Peep of Day*, and *Line upon Line.* See (Lond.) *Cong. Year-Book*, 1864, p. 216.

Grigg, Joseph, an English Presbyterian, was assistant minister at the Silver Street Church, London, from 1743 to 1747, at which last date he married the widow of Colonel Drew, a lady of much property, and retired to St. Albans, where he preached for his dissenting brethren occasionally. He contributed poetical pieces to several works between 1756 and 1765, when he issued a small tract of *Hymns on Divine Subjects.* These were collected in a small volume by Daniel Sedgwick, and published in 1861. Mr. Grigg died at Walthamstow, Oct. 29, 1768. One of his hymns, written when he was only ten years old, "Jesus! and shall it ever be," is still a favorite. See Gadsby, *Hymn Writers*, p. 63.

Griggs, Leverett, D.D., a Congregational minister, was born at Tolland, Conn., Nov. 17, 1808. He graduated at Yale College in 1829, was engaged for a year and a half in teaching at Mount Hope Institute, near Baltimore, Md., studied at the Andover Theological Seminary two years, and acted as tutor in Yale College for the same length of time, while pursuing his theological studies in the Yale Divinity School. He was ordained at North Haven, Oct. 30, 1833, and remained as pastor till July 30, 1845, when he accepted a call to the Chapel Street Church (now Church of the Redeemer), New Haven. After supplying the pulpit of the Second Church in Millbury, Mass., for a time, he became, in 1856, pastor of the Church, where he continued fourteen years. For a time he acted as an agent of the Western College Society. His home, during the last years of his life, was in Bristol, Conn., and he died there Jan. 28, 1883. The high esteem in which he was held in this town is indicated by the circumstance that, as a token of respect, a vote was passed exempting his property from taxation. See *The Congregationalist*, Feb. 8, 1883. (J. C. S.)

Grille (1), a metal screen, to enclose or protect any particular spot, locality, shrine, tomb, or sacred ornament; (2) a gate of metal enclosing or protecting the entrance of a religious house or sacred building; (3) the wicket of a monastery; (4) a small screen of iron bars inserted in the door of a monastic or conventual building, in order to allow the inmates to converse with visitors, or to answer inquiries without opening the door.

Grillet, Jean, a French missionary, one of the first explorers of Guiana, was born about 1630. He joined the Jesuits, and was sent out to Guiana, where he became superior of the establishment of his order until the English squadron destroyed the colony, Oct. 22, 1667. In 1674 he made an exploring tour through a part of that country, of which on his return to France he published an account. Grillet died about 1676. See Hoefer, *Nouv. Biog. Générale*, s. v.

Grimaldi, Agostino, a Genoese prelate, third son of Lambert, prince of Monaco, studied belles-lettres and theology, and became a particular friend of cardinals Bembo and Sadolet. In 1505 he was elected abbot of Lerins, and assisted in 1512 at the Council of Lateran. On account of some political offence, Francis I deprived him of all his revenues in France. Charles V indemnified him by giving him the bishopric of Majorca and the archbishopric of Oristano; he had even designated him to pope Clement VII as cardinal, but Agostino died before his promotion, probably of poison, April 12, 1532. There are extant of this prelate several letters to illustrious men of his time. See Hoefer, *Nouv. Biog. Générale*, s. v.

Grimaldi, Domenico, a Genoese prelate, was born in 1592, being the son of Giambattista Grimaldi, lord of Montaldeo. He had distinguished himself in the army when pope Pius V appointed him commissary-general of the galleys of the Church, in which capacity he took an active part in the battle of Lepanto. He afterwards entered into orders, and obtained the abbey of Mont Majour-les-Arles. In 1581 Gregory XIII gave him the bishopric of Savona, from which he was transferred, in 1584, to the see of Cavaillo, as archbishop and vice-legate. He persecuted Protestants with rigor and cruelty. He died in 1592. See Hoefer, *Nouv. Biog. Générale*, s. v.

Grimaldi, Geronimo, a Genoese statesman and prelate, occupied the principal offices of the republic, and accomplished several diplomatic missions with success. After the death of his wife, he entered into the ministry, and easily attained the first dignities of the Church. He was made cardinal, with the title of St. Georges-in-Velatro. He obtained afterwards the archbishopric of Bari, and then that of Genoa, where he died in 1543. See Hoefer, *Nouv. Biog. Générale*, s. v.

Grimaldi, Giovanni Francesco (called *Il Bolognese*), an eminent Italian landscape painter, was born at Bologna in 1606, and studied under the Caracci. He went to Rome for improvement, and soon rose to eminence. He was employed by Innocent X in the Vatican and at Monte Cavallo. He was invited to Paris by cardinal Mazarin, and was employed in the Louvre by Louis XIV. On returning to Rome he received numerous commissions, was patronized by Alexander VII and Clement IX, was twice appointed president of the Academy of St. Luke, and attained both fame and fortune. One of his best works was the *Baptism of Christ.* He died in 1680. See Hoefer, *Nouv. Biog. Générale*, s. v.; Spooner, *Biog. Hist. of the Fine Arts*, s. v.

Grimaldi, Giuseppe Maria, an Italian prelate, was born at Moncalieri (Piedmont), Jan. 3, 1754. He studied at Turin, entered the ministry, and was received as doctor of theology in the university at Turin, afterwards went to Verceil, in 1779, and was appointed canon of the cathedral there in 1782. In 1811 he assisted at the Council at Paris, and took part in the commission appointed to revise the response to the emperor. He died Jan. 1, 1830. See Hoefer, *Nouv. Biog. Générale*, s. v.

Grimaldi, Nicolo, a Genoese prelate, was born Dec. 6, 1645. He was at first clerk of the apostolic chamber, and superintendent of the streets and roads of Rome. In 1696 he became prefect of the pontifical almonry. After having made good use of these different employments, he left them to become secretary of the congregation of the bishops and regulars, in 1701. Clement XI made him cardinal, May 17, 1706, and on Sept. 14 following he was made legate of Bologna. After being prefect of the Consultus for several years, he passed over, June 8, 1716, to the order of the cardinal priests. He died Oct. 25, 1717, leaving an immense fortune. See Hoefer, *Nouv. Biog. Générale*, s. v.

Grimes, L. A., a distinguished colored Baptist minister, was born a slave at the South in 1808. While acting as a coachman in Washington, D. C., he attracted the attention and secured the friendship of the late Rev. Dr. Rollin H. Neale, then a student in that city. He soon became a good scholar and a most acceptable preacher, holding for twenty-five years the pastorate of a colored Baptist Church in Boston. He died there, March 14, 1873. Mr. Grimes took a special interest in the education of colored men as ministers of the gospel, and for several years was one of the most useful trustees of the Wayland Seminary, Washington, D. C. See *The Watchman*, March, 1873. (J. C. S.)

Grimm, Heinrich Adolph, a Protestant theologian of Germany, was born Sept. 1, 1747, at Siegen, in Prussia, and died at Duisburg, Aug. 29, 1813, doctor and professor of theology. He published, *Jonæ et Obadiæ Oracula Syriace* (Duisburg, 1805) : — *Chald. Chrestomathie mit einem vollständigen Glossarium* (1801) : — *Exegetische Aufsätze zur Aufklärung schwieriger Stellen der Schrift* (1793) : — *Der Prophet Jonas erklärt* (1789) : — *Nahum erklärt, mit Anmerkungen* (1790). See Winer, *Handbuch der theol. Lit.* i, 9, 54, 125, 192, 227, 228; ii, 267; Fürst, *Bibl. Jud.* i, 343. (B. P.)

Grindrod, Edmund, an English Wesleyan minister, was born in Clay Lane, near Rochdale, Feb. 28, 1786. The family removed to Liverpool when Edmund was young. At about the age of twenty, when assisting his father and brothers in the erection of the new exchange buildings in that city, he had a narrow escape from instant death. In 1806 he was received into the ministry, and henceforward labored on some of the most important charges. In 1826 a great revival blessed his labors in Edinburgh; in 1827, with Christian gentleness and firmness, he withstood the torrent of opposition at Leeds on the organ question; in 1832 and 1833 he was secretary of the conference; in 1834 was president of the Canadian Conference at Kingston; in 1834 and 1835, while stationed at Manchester, he again passed through a bitter conflict. In 1837 Grindrod was elected president of the British Conference at Leeds; in 1840 he went to his last appointment, fifth London or Lambeth circuit; in April, 1841, he underwent a severe surgical operation, and died May 1, 1842. He wrote, besides essays in periodicals, and several sermons, published collectively, *The Duties, Qualifications, and Encouragements of Class-Leaders* (Lond. 1831, 12mo) : — *Compendium of the Laws and Regulations of Wesleyan Methodism* (ibid. 1842, 8vo). See *Wesl. Meth. Magazine*, July, August, September, 1846; Stevenson, *City Road Chapel*, p. 318, 347; *Minutes of the British Conference*, 1842; Smith, *Hist. of Wesl. Methodism*, iii, 462 sq.

Grinfield, Edward William, an English clergyman and scholar, was born in 1784. He commenced his career as a writer in 1818. From 1827 to 1843 he published little, being employed during that time on his *Novum Testamentum Hellenisticum* (2 vols. 8vo), the design of which was to show the close connection between the Septuagint and the Greek Testament. The next five years were spent in preparing the *Scholia Hellenistica* (2 vols. 8vo). For fifty years he labored to elevate the Septuagint to its proper place as an interpreter of the Hebrew text. To this end he collected all the various editions of the book, and all the literature relating to them. In addition to the above, his publications are, *An Apology for the Septuagint*, in which its claims to Biblical and canonical authority are stated and defended (1850, 8vo), a number of sermons, and theological and other treatises. He died July 9, 1864. See Allibone, *Dict. of Brit. and Amer. Authors*, s. v.

Grinnell, Daniel T., D.D., a Protestant Episcopal clergyman, was rector of St. Paul's Church, Jackson, Mich., the most of his ministry being spent in this pastorate. For a long time he was a member of the missionary committee of his diocese. He died June 2, 1868, aged fifty-five years. See *Prot. Episc. Almanac*, 1869, p. 109.

Grischow, Johann Heinrich, inspector of the Halle Bible Society, was born in 1685. After completing his studies, he devoted his talents entirely to the work of the Bible Society, founded by the marquis of Canstein (q. v.), and died at Halle, Nov. 6, 1754. He translated into Latin Bingham's *Christian Antiquities* (1724, 10 vols.); he also translated from the German into Latin the works of Spener, Francke, Freylinghausen, etc. See Jöcher, *Allgemeines Gelehrten-Lexikon*, s. v.; Winer, *Handbuch der theol. Lit.* i, 606. (B. P.)

Griswold, Rufus Wilmot, D.D., a Baptist minister and writer, who was born Feb. 15, 1815, at Benson, Rutland Co., Vt., and died in New York, Aug. 27, 1857, was literary manager of a number of journals in several of the principal cities of the Union, such as, *The New-Yorker*, *The Brother Jonathan*, and *The New World*; in 1842 and 1843 editor of *Graham's Magazine*; and from August, 1850, to April, 1852, conducted the *International Magazine*. Besides these, he prepared numerous works, especially *The Poets of America* (1842), etc. See Allibone, *Dict. of Brit. and Amer. Authors*, s. v.; Duyckinck, *Cyclop. of Amer. Lit.* ii, 532.

Grithe-stool. See Frithstool.

Grobe, Johann Samuel, a Lutheran theologian of Bavaria, who died Dec. 23, 1837, is the author of, *Christliche Hauspostille* (Hildburghausen, 1824-34, 3 vols.) :—*Evangelischer Morgen- und Abendsegen auf alle Tage des Jahres* (1829; 2d enlarged ed. by Teuscher, 1857) : — *Gebetbuch für fromme und christliche Bürger* (1832, 2 vols.) :—*Denkwürdigkeiten aus dem Leben frommer Personen* (1822). See Winer, *Handbuch der theol. Lit.* ii, 138, 144, 363, 384, 396; Zuchold, *Bibl. Theol.* i, 468. (B. P.)

Groddeck, Benjamin, professor of Oriental languages at Dantzic, was born there in 1728, and died June 8, 1776. He wrote, *De Necessaria Linguarum Arabicæ et Hebraeæ Connexione* (Wittenberg, 1746) : —*De Natura Dialectorum ad Linguam Hebraicam et Arabicam Applicata* (1747) :—*De Vero Originum Hebræarum fonte et Utilitate* (eod.) :—*De Linguæ Hebrææ Antiquitate* (Dantzic, 1750) : — *De Litteris Hebraicis* (1751) :—*De Sensu Scripturæ Sacræ* (eod.) :—*De Punctis Hebræorum* (1753) :—*De Via ad Notitiam Interiorem Linguarum Orientalium Præsertim Hebrææ* (1757) : — *De Vera Verborum ל"ה Natura et Indole* (1760) :—*De Usu Versionum Græcarum Vet. Test. Hermeneutico et Critico* (1763). See Meusel, *Gelehrtes Deutschland*; Jöcher, *Allgemeines Gelehrten-Lexikon*, s. v.; Steinschneider, *Bibl. Handbuch*, s. v.; Fürst, *Bibl. Jud.* i, 344. (B. P.)

Groddeck, Gabriel, professor of Oriental languages at Dantzic, was born Jan. 7, 1672, and died Sept. 12, 1709. He wrote, *De Judæis Præputium Attrahentibus ad* 1 *Cor. vii*, 18 :—*Spicilegium Aliquot Librorum*

Anonymorum et Pseudonymorum qui Lingua Rabbinica Partim Impressi, Partim MS. Reperiuntur (reprinted in David Millius's *Catalecta Rabbinica*, Utrecht, 1728): *De Cæremonia Palmarum apud Judæos in Festo Tabernaculo* (Leipsic, 1694):—*Lingua Græca Matrum Linguarum Orientalium non esse* (1698):—*De Anno et Die Passionis S. Polycarpi* (1704). See Winer, *Handbuch der theol. Lit.* i, 900; Fürst, *Bibl. Jud.* i, 344; Jöcher, *Allgemeines Gelehrten-Lexikon*, s. v. (B. P.)

Groen (*van Prinsterer*), WILLEM, a Dutch statesman and historian, was born at the Hague, Aug. 21, 1801. He studied at Leyden, was appointed secretary to the king in 1827, and soon afterwards director of the royal archives; was, in the Dutch Parliament, the leader of the anti-revolutionary party, and opposed with great zeal the separation of State and Church, and emancipation of the school from the Church. He was a Christian statesman, and his idea was that Christianity should be the basis of all instruction, since the school has for its object not only the information, but also the education, of the individual. He has often been called the "Dutch Stahl," but Groen was more conspicuous in his position towards Rome than Julius Stahl (q. v.). Groen died May 19, 1876. He published, *Archives ou Correspondance Inédite de la Maison d'Orange-Nassau* (1840-55, 13 vols.):—*Handboek der Geschiedenis van het Vaderland* (Amsterdam, 1852):—*Maurice et Barnevelt, Étude Historique* (Utrecht, 1875). See Cohen-Stuart, *In Memoriam Groen van Prinsterer* (Utrecht, 1876); Saint-Hilaire in the *Revue Chrétienne Necrol.* p. 594 sq.; Lichtenberger, *Encyclop. des Sciences Religieuses*, s. v.; Plitt-Herzog, *Real-Encyklop.* s. v. (B. P.)

Groesbeck, GERARD DE, a French prelate, was born in 1508. He was first dean of the Cathedral of Liege, when Robert of Berg, prince-bishop, resigned his authority in his favor, July 22, 1563. He successfully resisted the encroachments of William of Orange into the territory. The Jesuits, whom the bishop had called for, assisted Groesbeck largely in his persecutions of the Calvinists, and made, in 1569, their first establishment at Liege. The prelate died Dec. 28, 1580. See Hoefer, *Nouv. Biog. Générale*, s. v.

Gröne, VALENTIN, a Roman Catholic theologian of Germany, who died March 18, 1882, dean and doctor of theology, is the author of *Tetzel und Luther* (2d ed. Soest, 1860):—*Begriff und Bedeutung vom Sacrament* (1823):—*Glaube und Wissenschaft* (1860):—*Abriss der Kirchengeschichte* (Ratisbon, 1869):—*Compendium der Kirchengeschichte* (eod.):—*Die Papst-Geschichte* (2 vols. 1864-66; 2d ed. 1875). See Zuchold, *Bibl. Theol.* i, 468. (B. P.)

Gros, NICOLAS LE. See NICOLAS.

Gros, PIERRE LE. See PIERRE.

Gross, Christian, a Lutheran theologian of Germany, was born at Wittenberg, Sept. 30, 1602. He studied at different universities, was preacher and professor at Stettin, general superintendent of Pomerania, and died at Stargard, July 17, 1673. He wrote, *Compendium Gramm. Hebrææ*:—*Sylloge Distinctionum Theol.*:—*De Auctoritate Pontificis Romani*:—*De Dissensu Calvinianorum et Lutheranorum*:—*De Magnitudine Adami*. See Witte, *Memoriæ Theologorum*; Jöcher, *Allgemeines Gelehrten-Lexikon*, s. v.; Fürst, *Bibl. Jud.* i, 344. (B. P.)

Gross, Johann Georg, a Swiss theologian, was born at Basle, March 28, 1581. He studied at his native place, was preacher there in 1598, professor of theology in 1612, and died Feb. 8, 1630. He wrote, *Disp. in Locum Hab. ii*, 4 (1611):—*Elenchus Controversiarum de Justificatione* (eod.):—*Libri III de Christiana Republica* (1612):—*Elenchus Controv. de Paschate Christi* (1613):—*Refutatio Descensus Localis Christi ad Inferos* (1614):—*De Bellis Christianorum et de Circumcisione Christi* (eod.):—*Thesaurus Concionum Sacrorum* (1616). See Jöcher, *Allgemeines Gelehrten-Lexikon*, s. v. (B. P.)

Gross, Johann Mathias, a Lutheran theologian of Germany, was born Sept. 8, 1676. He studied at Jena, was preacher in 1698, and died Dec. 11, 1748. His writings, numbering twenty-eight, are given by Döring, *Die gelehrten Theologen Deutschlands*, s. v. See also Jöcher, *Allgemeines Gelehrten-Lexikon*, s. v. (B. P.)

Grosse, Johann August Ludwig, a Protestant theologian of Germany, was born March 15, 1747, at Barleben, near Magdeburg. He studied at Halle, was in 1774 teacher at Klosterbergen, in 1779 preacher, and died Jan. 21, 1830. He published sermons and some ascetical writings. See Döring, *Die gelehrten Theologen Deutschlands*, s. v.; Winer, *Handbuch der theol. Lit.* ii, 83, 193, 202. (B. P.)

Grosse, Johann Friedrich August, a Lutheran theologian of Germany, was born at Zerbst, April 13, 1778. He studied at Wittenberg and Halle, was pastor in 1813, and died July 27, 1828. He published some sermons. See Döring, *Die gelehrten Theologen Deutschlands*, s. v. (B. P.)

Grosshain, GEORG, a Lutheran theologian of Germany, was born in 1601. He studied at Jena and Wittenberg, was professor at Erfurt in 1633, court-preacher at Weimar in 1637, and died Sept. 5, 1638, leaving, *De Catholica Judæorum Conversione*:—*Epitome Hermeneutices ad S. Script. Interpretationem*:—*De Consilio Pacis ad Dan. iv*, 24:—*De Conversione Judæorum ad Rom. xi*, 25, 26. See Binder, *De Vita et Meritis G. Grosshainii*; Jöcher, *Allgemeines Gelehrten-Lexikon*, s. v. (B. P.)

Grossmann, CHRISTIAN GOTTLOB LEBRECHT, a Lutheran theologian of Germany, was born Nov. 9, 1783. He studied at Jena, was in 1808 preacher at Priessnitz, near Naumburg, in Saxony, in 1823 general superintendent at Altenburg, in 1829 professor of theology and preacher at Leipsic, and died June 29, 1857. He wrote, *De Ascetis Judæorum Veterum* (Altenburg, 1833):—*De Procuratore Parabola J. Christi ex re Provinciali Illustrata* (Leipsic, 1824):—*Quæstiones Philoneæ* (1829):—*De Judæorum Disciplina Arcani* (1833-34, 2 parts):—*De Philosophia Sadducæorum* (1836-38, 3 parts):—*Philonis Judæi Anecdoton Græcum* (1856). He also published a number of sermons. See Winer, *Bibl. Theol.* i, 140, 248, 522; ii, 19, 171, 172, 174, 176, 177; Fürst, *Bibl. Jud.* i, 344; Zuchold, *Bibl. Theol.* i, 470 sq. (B. P.)

Grosvenor, CYRUS PITT, LL.D., a distinguished Baptist minister, was born at Grafton, Mass., Oct. 18, 1793. He studied first at New Salem Academy, afterwards Leorrette, graduated from Dartmouth College in 1818, and then taught three years as principal in an academy at Haverhill, and as preceptor in Amherst Academy, partly in studies preparatory to his ministry. In 1820 he entered Princeton Theological Seminary, and left in March, 1822. He was called to the Baptist Church of Charleston, May 19, 1823, was pastor of the Baptist Church, Georgetown; of Hartford, Conn.; of First Baptist Church, Boston, Mass.; of Second Baptist Church, Salem; of Sterling; of Baptist Church, Southbridge; and of Ganges, Allegan Co., Mich. Dr. Grosvenor died Feb. 11, 1879. He was editor of *The Christian Reflector*, and also of *The Christian Contributor*, published at Worcester, Mass., and at Utica, N. Y., respectively. For fifteen years he was connected as president and professor with New York Central College. In March, 1860, he went to Great Britain, and travelled extensively in England, Scotland, Wales, and Ireland, lecturing on American affairs, and preaching frequently. See *Necrol. Report of Princeton Theol. Sem.* 1879, p. 43.

Grotta, in Norse mythology, was a miraculous mill of king Frothi; it had two stones, so large that no one could turn them, but everything could be ground on it. In order to set it in motion the king had two maids, Menja and Fenja, who had come from Sweden. They were only allowed to rest so long as the cuckoo did not cry. When the sea-king, Mysingr, came, they ground out an army for Frothi; but the army was conquered, and became a prey of the strange king, who took the treasures and the mill on his ship, and ordered the maids to grind salt. This they did until midnight, and then asked the king whether he had enough, but Mysingr told them to keep on. They did this so long that the ship sank, and the sea was made salt.

Grulich, Friedrich Joseph, a Lutheran theologian of Germany, was born Dec. 15, 1766. He entered the ministry in 1795, was archdeacon at Torgau, and died Nov. 19, 1839, leaving, *Betrachtung über den neuesten Versuch, das Leben Jesu* (Leipsic, 1836):—*Ueber die körperliche Beredtsamkeit Jesu* (1827):—*Leidenserfahrung und Leidensgewinn* (1826):—*Ueber die Ironien in den Reden Jesu* (1838). See Winer, *Handbuch der theol. Lit.* i, 551, 557; ii, 388; Zuchold, *Bibl. Theol.* i, 472. (B. P.)

Grulich, Martin, a Lutheran theologian of Germany, was born in 1695. He studied at Wittenberg and Leipsic, was preacher in 1728, and died at Torgau, Nov. 30, 1772, a superintendent. He is the author of a great many ascetical works, of no importance for the present times. The titles are given in full in Jöcher, *Allgemeines Gelehrten-Lexikon*, s. v. (B. P.)

Grundig, Christoph Gottlob, a Lutheran theologian of Germany, was born Sept. 5, 1707. He entered upon his ministerial duties in 1737 as pastor at Hermannsdorf, near Annaberg, in Saxony, and died at Freiberg, Aug. 9, 1780. He is the author of a number of ascetical works mentioned by Jöcher in *Allgemeines Gelehrten-Lexikon*, s. v. (B. P.)

Grundtvig, Nicolai Frederik Severin, "the prophet of the North," was born Sept. 8, 1783, at Udby, a village in the island of Zealand. He studied theology at Copenhagen, was tutor in a private family in the island of Langeland from 1805 to 1808, teacher of history in a school at Copenhagen from 1808 to 1810, vicar to his father at Udby from 1810 to 1813, and again teacher at Copenhagen from 1813 to 1821. During those years of his youth and early manhood he lived like a monk, without being monkish. He only slept two hours, and for twenty years never in a bed. Before he was appointed to his pastorate, Grundtvig had already become known in the literary circles of his country. His earliest literary efforts were the *Teaching of Asa*, the *Songs of the Edda*, and *Religion and Liturgy*. From 1809 to 1822 he published a series of poetical and historical works—*Nordens Mythologie* (1808); *Optrin af Kämpelivets Undergang i Nord* (i. e. Fall of Heathenism in the North, a grand drama, 1809), and the translations of Saxo Grammaticus (1818–22, 6 vols.), Snorre Sturleson, and Beowulf's *Drapa*—most of them referring to the heroic age of Scandinavian history, and all of them pregnant with a peculiarly stirring life. But his theological productions, also his sermons, more especially his *Kort Begreb af Verdens Krönike i Sammenhäng*, i. e. View of the World's Chronicle (1812), attracted equal attention, as they ran out in a vehement denunciation of the frivolity with which the age had eliminated Christianity from its life. Attracted by the genius of Grundtvig, king Frederick VI, without consulting either the bishop or the consistory, appointed him pastor in Praestoe (a small town in Zealand), and in the next year he was called to the chaplaincy at the Church of our Saviour in Copenhagen. There he soon gathered a circle of friends and pupils around his pulpit, and day by day his position in the Danish Church became more and more strongly marked. In 1825 professor H. N. Clausen (q. v.), a rationalist, published his *Katholicismens og Protestantismens Kirkeforfatning, Läre og Ritus* (i. e. Church Government, Teaching, and Rites of Catholicism and Protestantism), and Grundtvig answered with his *Kirkens Gjenmäle* (i. e. Protest of the Church), in which he requested Clausen either to renounce his heresy or to give up his professorship. Within eight days, Grundtvig's Protest was three times reprinted. Clausen instituted a civil suit; Grundtvig was sentenced to pay a fine, and to publish nothing without permission of the royal censor. In 1826 he resigned his office, because he did not wish to serve a Church which seemed to give up the faith and the confession of the fathers. To this period belongs his interesting work, *My Literary Testament*. From 1826 to 1839 Grundtvig lived in literary retirement at Copenhagen. From 1829 to 1831 he visited England, edited a theological monthly, *Theologisk Maanedsskrift;* published the *Sang-Värk til den dansko Kirke* (1837; new editions, 1870–75), a collection of hymns, partly original, partly translated. Meanwhile his influence spread far beyond the capital, and the "Grundtvigians" and "Grundtvigianism" increased from day to day. He was allowed to preach in the afternoon in the German Frederiks-Church, and the number of his adherents grew more and more. In 1839 he was pastor of the Varton-hospital-Church, and there he remained till his death, which took place Sept. 2, 1872. His party made itself especially felt in 1848, and brought about those liberties in church and school which in some cases were detrimental to religion. See Hansen, *Wesen und Bedeutung des Grundtvigianismus* (Kiel, 1863); Lütke, *Kirchliche Zustände in den Skandinavischen Ländern* (Elberfeld, 1864); Pry, *N. F. S. Grundtvig, Biographisk Skizze* (Copenhagen, 1871); Kaftan, *Grundtvig, der Prophet des Nordens* (Basle, 1876); Lichtenberger, *Encyclop. des Sciences Religieuses*, s. v.; Plitt-Herzog, *Real-Encyklop.* s. v. (B. P.)

Grundy, Robert Caldwell, D.D., a Presbyterian minister, was born in Washington County, Ky., in 1809. He graduated at St. Joseph's College, Bardstown, in 1829, and at Princeton Theological Seminary in 1835. In 1836 he was licensed by the Transylvania Presbytery, and installed over the Presbyterian Church of Maysville, where he remained until 1858, when he removed to Memphis, Tenn., as pastor of the Second Presbyterian Church in that city. In 1863 he took charge of the Central Presbyterian Church in Cincinnati. He died at Dayton, O., June 27, 1865. See Wilson, *Presb. Hist. Almanac*, 1867, p. 153; *Gen. Cat. of Princeton Theol. Sem.* 1881, p. 88.

Grüneisen, Carl von, a Lutheran theologian of Germany, was born at Stuttgart, Jan. 17, 1802. He studied at Tübingen and Halle, was in 1825 military preacher and court-chaplain, in 1835 court-preacher and member of consistory, and died at his native place Feb. 28, 1878. Grüneisen took an active part in the development of the church of Würtemberg, and for sixteen years presided at the annual meetings of the Eisenach Church conferences. He wrote *Ueber bildliche Darstellung der Gottheit* (Stuttgart, 1828):—*Ueber das Sittliche der bildenden Kunst bei den Griechen* (Leipsic, 1833):—*Nicolaus Manuel, Leben und Werke* (Stuttgart, 1837):—*Ulms Kunstleben im Mittelalter* (Ulm, 1840):—*Predigten für die Gebildeten in der Gemeinde* (Stuttgart, 1835):—*Christliches Handbuch in Gebeten und Liedern* (5th ed. 1859):—*Ueber Gesangbuchsreform* (1839). In connection with Schnaase and Schnorr von Carolsfeld, he founded in 1858 the *Christliches Kunstblatt.* See Zuchold, *Bibl. Theol.* i, 474; Lichtenberger, *Encyclop. des Sciences Religieuses*, s. v. (B. P.)

Grünenberg, Johann Peter, a Lutheran theologian of Germany, was born Jan. 27, 1668. He studied at different universities, was in 1698 professor of theology at Rostock, and died Jan. 5, 1712, leaving *Doctrina Symbolica de S. Theologiæ Testibus Symbolicis:—Disputationes de Scientia Dei:—De Sabbatho Hebdomadali ad Gen. ii, 2:—De Samgare Victore ad Judic. iii, 31:—De Semine Davidis Christo ad 2 Sam. vii, 11–16:—De Timore Domini ad Prov. ix, 10:—De βιβλῳ γενέσεως ad Matt. i, 1:—De Fide Matt. Genealogica ad Matt. i, 6–11:—De Filio Dei ex Egypto Vocato ad Matt. ii, 15:—De Jesu Nazareno ad Matt. ii, 22, 23,* etc. See Jöcher, *Allgemeines Gelehrten-Lexikon*, s. v. (B. P.)

Gruppe, Otto Friedrich, a German philosopher and antiquarian, was born at Dantzic, April 15, 1804. He studied at Berlin, but as he opposed the Hegelian system of philosophy, the academical career was closed up to him, till at last, in 1844, he was made professor of philosophy. Gruppe died Jan. 7, 1876, at Berlin. He wrote *Antäus* (Berlin, 1831):—*Wendepunkt der Philosophie im* 19. *Jahrhundert* (1834):—*Gegenwart und Zukunft der Philosophie in Deutschland* (1855). These works were all directed against Hegel. Of his poetical productions we only mention, *Ruth, Tobias, Sulamith* (1857). (B. P.)

Guadagni, Bernardo Gaetano (or *John Anthony of St. Bernard*), an Italian prelate, was born at Florence, Sept. 14, 1674, being the son of Maria Magdalena Corsini, sister of pope Clement XII. He joined the barefooted Carmelites, at the convent of Arezzo, Nov. 11, 1700. He had been successively teacher of the novices, and several times prior and provincial of Florence, and was, on Dec. 20, 1724, appointed by pope Benedict XIII to the bishopric of Arezzo, and received from the hands of Clement XII the pallium on Nov. 26, 1730. In 1731 he was made cardinal, with the title of *St. Martin del Monte.* In 1732 he became vicar-general of Rome, which office he maintained until his death, after 1733. See Hoefer, *Nouv. Biog. Générale,* s. v.

Guadagnolo, Filippo, a Minorite and professor of Arabic in the college of the Sapienza at Rome, was born in 1596, and died March 27, 1656. In behalf of the Congregation de Propaganda Fidei, he translated the Bible from the Vulgate into Arabic, which was published in three volumes (Rome, 1671)—a work on which he spent twenty-seven years. See Winer, *Handbuch der theol. Lit.* i, 58; Jöcher, *Allgemeines Gelehrten-Lexikon,* s. v.; Toppi, *Bibliotheca Neapolitana.* (B. P.)

Guala (*Bichieri*), Giacomo, an Italian prelate, was born at Vercelli in the second part of the 12th century. At the age of twenty-one, after having studied canon law, he was made canon of the Eusebian Cathedral, and cardinal in the same year, by Innocent VII. In 1208 Innocent sent him to France as a legate to reform the habits of the clergy. For this purpose Guala wrote constitutions of ecclesiastical discipline. After having been commissioned also to reform the clergy of Lombardy, he was sent to Sicily to the emperor Frederic II, to persuade him to undertake a new crusade, but did not succeed. On his return to Italy he contributed to the foundation of the University of Vercelli, but died before the finishing of his establishment, May, 1227. See Hoefer, *Nouv. Biog. Générale,* s. v.

Gualdim (*-Paes*), a celebrated grand-master of the order of the Templars in Portugal, was born at Braga in the 12th century. He frequently fought against the Moors of the Peninsula. At the time of the second crusade he was provincial of the order of the Templars. During his five years' stay in the East, he distinguished himself at the siege of Ascalon in 1155; and in the following year came back to Europe, when he was made grand-master. In March, 1160, he laid the foundations of the magnificent castle of Thomar, which was henceforth to serve as the capitulary chapter of the Portuguese Templars. In 1190 a vast troop of Moorish soldiers advanced under the leadership of Yakub, son of Abu-Yussuf, against the doors of Thomar, determined to revenge upon the Templars that loss which they had suffered at Sandarem in 1147, to which the knights under Gualdim had largely contributed. But the Moors were repulsed. The Templars of Portugal were indeed a rampart to the Christian populations, and their order was respected, even though the pontiff was hostile to their convents. Gualdim-Paes died peacefully, in 1195, in his monastery. See Hoefer, *Nouv. Biog. Générale,* s. v.

Gualterio, Filippo Antonio, an Italian prelate and scholar, was born at San Quirico de Fermo, March 24, 1660. He belonged to one of the first families of Ancona. His grand-uncle sent him, in 1672, to Rome, to study at the college of Clement. Antonio studied philosophy at Rome, and law and theology at Fermo, where his grand-uncle was the archbishop. At the age of nineteen he received the degree of doctor, and about 1684 was admitted to the number of the candidates for prelates. On Feb. 17, 1700, Innocent XII intrusted him with the nonciature to France, and Clement XI conferred on him the abbey of the Trinity, the bishopric of Tmola and Todi, and in 1799 made him cardinal with the title of *Saint Chrysogonus.* In France Gualterio had connected himself with the principal scholars, had examined all the monastical and other libraries, and made a fine collection of MSS. of great value, medals, both antique and modern, and instruments of rare precision; but all these literary or scientific treasures, being embarked at Marseilles, were lost on the passage. He began new researches, and succeeded in collecting a number of elements, useful for a universal history, which he proposed to write. But when he was settled down as a legate at Ravenna, the imperial troops invaded that city and pillaged his house, by which his documents were either burned or dispersed. Later, Louis XV appointed him commander of the Order of the Holy Ghost. Cardinal Gualterio, with all his literary tastes, left no writings. He died at Rome, April 21, 1728. See Hoefer, *Nouv. Biog. Générale,* s. v.

Gualtperius, Otto, a Lutheran theologian of Germany, was born Jan. 1, 1546, at Rotenburg. He studied at Marburg, and was there professor of Hebrew and Greek in 1582. In 1593 he went to Lübeck as director of the schools, and died Dec. 24, 1624. He wrote, *Grammatica Linguæ Sanctæ:—Sylloge Vocum Exoticarum Novi Testamenti:—Collatio Præcipuarum Sacræ Geneseos Translationum,* etc. See Moller, *Cimbria Litterata;* Fürst, *Bibl. Jud.* i, 346; Jöcher, *Allgemeines Gelehrten-Lexikon,* s. v.; Seelen, *Athenæ Lubecenses.* (B. P.)

Guanzellis, Gianmaria de', an Italian prelate, was born in 1557 at Brazighella, near Faenza. He became a Dominican while still young, and taught school in various establishments of his order. Paul V chose him as a master of the sacred palace, and in 1607 he appointed him bishop of Polignano. Guanzellis died in 1619, leaving, *Index Librorum Expurgandorum in Studiosorum Gratiam Confectus* (Rome, 1607):—*Synodus Diœcesana Polymnianensis* (Bari). See Hoefer, *Nouv. Biog. Générale,* s. v.

Guard, Thomas, D.D., an eloquent Methodist Episcopal minister, was born in County Galway, Ireland, June 3, 1831. He was accepted by the Irish Conference of 1851 as a candidate for the ministry, and called to labor the same year. He was received into full connection in 1855. In 1862 he went to South Africa under the direction of the London Missionary Society, and spent nine years, chiefly at Grahamstown and Port Elizabeth. In 1871 he came to America on a visit, and at once became popular as a preacher and lecturer. On receiving an invitation to become the pastor of Mount Vernon Place Church, Baltimore, Md., he decided to make this country his home. He entered upon his pastorate in Baltimore in 1872. At the end of his term (in 1875) he became pastor of the Howard Street Church, San Francisco, Cal. In 1878 and 1879 he was pastor of First Church, Oakland, and in 1880 resumed his former relationship with the Mount Vernon Place Church, Baltimore. It was there that he closed his earthly career, Oct. 15, 1882. He was thoroughly acquainted with standard English divinity, and particularly with Methodist theology. As a lecturer and platform speaker he was almost without an equal. As a pulpit orator he was unsurpassed in his own or any age, and he could attract and hold the largest audiences of the most cultivated people. As a pastor he was not successful, and was incapable of managing business of any kind. See *Minutes of Annual Conferences,* 1883, p. 83.

Guarnacci, MARIO, an Italian prelate, was born at Volterre in 1701. He received the doctor's degree at Florence, where he pursued the course of Salvini. He was honored with the favor of Benedict XIV, who charged him to continue Chazon's *Lives of the Popes*, but he retired in 1757 to his own country. He discovered there the remains of Roman baths. He also made a collection of Etruscan antiquities, which he bequeathed to his native city. He died Aug. 21, 1785, leaving, *Dissertazione sopra le XII Tavole* (Florence, 1747):—*Vitæ et Res Gestæ Pontificum Romanorum*, etc. (Rome, 1751):—*Origini Italiche* (Volterre, 1768):—*Poesie di Zelalgo Arrasiona* (Lucca, 1769). See Hoefer, *Nouv. Biog. Générale*, s. v.

Guden, HEINRICH PHILIPP, a Lutheran theologian of Germany, was born Oct. 4, 1676. He studied at Helmstädt and Jena, was in 1700 pastor at Osterroda, took the degree as doctor of theology in 1720, was in 1722 pastor, general-superintendent, and professor at Göttingen, and died April 27, 1742. He wrote, *Manipulus Problematum ad Theologiam Naturalem Pertinentium:—De Bonifacio Germanorum Apostolo* (Helmstädt, 1720). See Winer, *Handbuch der theol. Lit.* i, 780; Jöcher, *Allgemeines Gelehrten-Lexikon*, s. v. (B. P.)

Gudenus, ANSELM FRIEDRICH VON, a Roman Catholic theologian of Germany, was born at Erfurt in 1731, and died May 16, 1789, leaving *Geschichte des ersten christlichen Jahrhunderts* (Würzburg, 1783, 2 vols.):—*Geschichte des zweiten christlichen Jahrhunderts* (ibid. 1787, 2 vols.). See Winer, *Handbuch der theol. Lit.* i, 548. (B. P.)

Güder, EDUARD, a Swiss theologian, was born June 1, 1817. He studied at Berne University, was pastor at Biel from 1842 to 1855, and thereafter pastor of the Rydeck Church, at Berne, until his death, July 14, 1882. In connection with his pastorate, he also held a professorship in his alma mater. He published, *Die Lehre von der Erscheinung Jesu Christi unter den Todten* (Berne, 1853):—*Alles und in Allen Christus* (sermons, ibid. 1857):—*Die Thatsächlichkeit der Auferstehung Christi und deren Bestreitung* (ibid. 1862). In 1855 he published the work of his teacher, Schneckenburger, *Vergleichende Darstellung des lutherischen u. reformirten Lehrbegriffes*, on account of which he was made doctor of theology by the Königsberg University. See Zuchold, *Bibl. Theol.* i, 475. (B. P.)

Guérard, ROBERT, a learned French Benedictine, was born at Rouen in 1641. He assisted Delfau in the revisal of St. Augustine's works; while thus employed, was accused of being concerned in a satirical book entitled, *L'Abbé Commendataire*, and confined in the abbey of Aimbournay, in Bugey. He took advantage of this exile to make a diligent search for ancient MSS., and discovered a great number; among others, St. Augustine's book against Julian, entitled, *Opus Imperfectum*. He was afterwards sent to Fécamp, then to Rouen, where he died, Jan. 2, 1715. He left *Abrégé de la Bible* (first published in 1707). See Hoefer, *Nouv. Biog. Générale*, s. v.

Guérech (1) (Lat. *Guerckus*, *Erechus*, or *Warochus*) was a bishop and count of Nantes. His father sent him for his education to a monastery, and he was appointed to the episcopal see at Nantes, or the first vacancy. However, a few days after having received the news of his election, Guérech learned of the death of his brother. The people had made him bishop, but by law of relationship he was made count. He pretended, nevertheless, to occupy the two positions simultaneously. He became famous by his war engagements with Conan le Tors (the crooked), count of Rennes. The death of Guérech, in 988, was thought to have been caused by poison. See Hoefer, *Nouv. Biog. Générale*, s. v.

Guérech (2), a French prelate, was born in the first part of the 11th century, being the son of Alain, count of Carnonailles. Airard, bishop of Nantes, having been expelled from his episcopal see in 1052, by the people of Nantes, was immediately replaced by Guérech, who, without attending to his consecration, occupied the episcopal palace, and took the administration of the Church. He had not even obtained canonical ordination when he went to the Council of Rheims in 1059. He also attended the disputation of Angers in 1062, and presided at the Council of Tours in 1068. He was a friend of the monks of Marmontiers, and sustained their pretensions in all the ecclesiastical assemblies. Guérech died July 31, 1079. See Hoefer, *Nouv. Biog. Générale*, s. v.

Guéranger, PROSPER LOUIS PASCAL, a French ecclesiastic, was born April 4, 1805, at Sablé-sur-Sarthe, in Le Mans. He studied at Angers and Le Mans, and received holy orders in 1827. For some time he was professor at Le Mans, and at the same time secretary to the bishop of De la Myre. With a view to restoring the order of the Benedictines in France, he retired in 1833 to the Benedictine abbey at Solesmes, where, with a number of friends, he commenced a monastic life according to the rules of St. Benedict. In 1836 he went to Rome, made his profession in 1837, and was appointed by Gregory XVI, abbot of Solesmes and president of the Benedictine congregation of France. He was opposed to the Gallican Church and her liturgies. In the spirit of his motto he published, *Institutions Liturgiques* (1840–52, 3 vols.):—*L'Année Liturgique* (1844–66, 9 vols.; translated also into German at Mayence, 1875):—*Essais sur le Naturalisme Contemporain* (1856, written against prince Albert de Broglie). When the Vatican council was opened, and the adherents of the Gallican Church insisted upon their privileges, Guéranger published *De la Monarchie Pontificale*, which was highly praised by pope Pius IX. At the time of his death, Jan. 30, 1875, Guéranger was dean of Le Mans, Nantes, and St. Denis. Besides the works already mentioned, he wrote, *Origines de l'Église Romaine* (1836):—*Histoire de Sainte Cécile* (1848; 2d ed. 1853; translated also into German, Ratisbon, 1851):—*Mémoire sur la Question de l'Immaculée Conception* (1850):—*Enchiridion Benedictinum, Complectens Regulam Vitam et Laudes*, etc. (1862):—*Les Exercises de Sainte Gertrude* (2d ed. eod.):—*Essai sur la Médaille de St. Benoît* (4th ed. 1865; Germ. transl. Einsiedeln, 1863):—*La Règle de Sainte Benoît* (1868):—*Sainte Cécile et la Societé Romaine aux deux Premiers Siècles* (1873). See *Literarischer Handweiser für das Katholische Deutschland*, 1875, col. 355 sq.; 1882, col. 323; Lichtenberger, *Encyclop. des Sciences Religieuses*, s. v. (B. P.)

Guericke, HEINRICH ERNST FERDINAND, a Lutheran theologian of Germany, was born Feb. 25, 1803. He studied at Halle, was made a doctor of philosophy in 1824, licentiate of theology in 1825, on presenting *De Schola, quæ Alexandriæ Floruit, Catechetica*, and professor of theology at Halle in 1829, in acknowledgment of his biography of *August Hermann Francke*, and his *Beiträge zur historisch-kritischen Einleitung ins Neue Testament*. In 1833 the Tübingen faculty conferred on him the degree of a doctor of theology. He was a very strict Lutheran, opposed the exertions of the Prussian government to effect a union between the Lutheran and Reformed churches, and founded, together with Rudelbach, the *Zeitschrift für die gesammte lutherische Theologie und Kirche*, in 1840, which was continued till 1878, in connection with professor Delitzsch. Guericke died Feb. 4, 1878. Besides the works already mentioned, he wrote, *Handbuch der Kirchengeschichte* (9th ed. 1867–69, 3 vols.; translated into English by W. G. T. Shedd, N. Y. 1857–63, 2 vols.):—*Allgemeine christliche Symbolik* (Leipsic, 1861):—*Historisch-kritische Einleitung in das Neue Testament* (ibid. 1843; 2d ed. 1854):—*Lehrbuch der christlich kirchlichen Archäologie* (2d ed. Berlin, 1859). See Zuchold, *Bibl. Theol.*

i, 475 sq.; Plitt-Herzog, *Real-Encyklop.* s. v.; Lichtenberger, *Encyclop. des Sciences Religieuses*, s. v. (B. P.)

Guérin (Lat. *Gairinus*), abbot of Flavigny, in Burgundy, and thirty-first bishop of Autun, was born about 626. He took part in the disputation in which his brother St. Léger, bishop of Autun, had engaged against Ebroïn, a burgomaster of Neustria, and shared with him his alternatives of triumph and of persecution. Ebroïn, having overcome his rivals, brought them before the tribunal, after having cut out their eyes. Guérin, being charged with complicity in the murder of Childeric II, was tied to a stake and stoned to death in 678. He is commemorated as a martyr on Aug. 25 and Oct. 2. See Hoefer, *Nouv. Biog. Générale*, s. v.

Guérin (or *Garin*), a French prelate, was born in 1160. He was first a friar of the order of the Hospitallers at Jerusalem, and succeeded, in 1213, to Geoffroi, bishop of Senlis. He was one of the principal counsellors of Philip Augustus. Guérin recovered Tournay from Renaud, count of Boulogne. In 1214 he assisted in the celebrated battle of Bouvines, in memory of which an abbey was founded in the diocese of Senlis, with the name of Notre-Dame de la Victoire. Louis VIII ascended to the throne in 1223, when Guérin continued his services to him as to his father, and received the title of chancellor. In 1228, two years after the death of Louis VIII, Guérin retired from the world, and entered the monastery of Châlis, where he died, April 19, 1230. See Hoefer, *Nouv. Biog. Générale*, s. v.

Guérin (*Gérin* or *Guarin*), whose surname and country are unknown, a grand master of the order of the Hospitallers of St. John of Jerusalem, succeeded Bertrand of Taxis in 1240. At this time the Templars and Hospitallers were divided; Thibaud VI, of Champagne, went to Palestine at the head of a crusade, and concluded a truce with the infidels after the loss of the battle of Gaza. The Templars subscribed to that truce. Richard of England followed next and sailed against Jaffa; he concluded a truce by which Jerusalem was to be surrendered. In that truce the Templars were entirely excluded. The grand master of the Hospitallers brought the treasure of the order to the patriarch of Jerusalem, to assist him in fortifying the walls of that city. But hardly had they made a few trenches, when all Palestine was invaded by the Koreishites. The grand masters of the Hospital and the Temple at Jerusalem, being almost without troops, resolved to conduct the inhabitants to Jaffa, while others refused to go, and tried to defend themselves, but were all cut down without mercy, or fell in open battle. Only twenty-six Hospitallers, thirty-three Templars, and three Teutonic knights escaped with their lives. The two grand masters of the two orders and a commander of the Teutonic knights lost their lives at the head of the army in 1243. Other historians say that they had only been made prisoners, and that Guérin died in 1244, in slavery. See Hoefer, *Nouv. Biog. Générale*, s. v.

Guérin, Anne Thérèse, foundress of a religious community, was born at Etables, St. Brieuc, Brittany, Oct. 2, 1798. In 1822 she joined the Sisters of Providence, an order founded at Ruillé-sur-Loire in 1806, assuming the name of Sister St. Theodore. Immediately after her profession she was appointed superior of an extensive establishment at Rennes, the object of which was to give poor children an education. Astonishing success attended her exertions among the ignorant and degraded. She was afterwards removed to Soulaines, where her educational and charitable duties were combined. Here she studied medicine. On Oct. 22, 1840, Sister St. Theodore, at the request of bishop Bruté, founded, at St. Mary's of the Woods, Vigo Co., Ind.—a very wilderness at the time—the Sisters of Providence in America. In November, 1841, she was joined by Sister St. Francis, a saintly woman, whose *Life and Letters*—the latter called "a string of exquisite pearls"—has been published. The two sisters died in 1856, within three months of each other. Mother Theodore united those rare virtues which form the perfect religious with extraordinary governing and financial abilities. The fruit of her charity and zeal is witnessed in extensive and numerous establishments, educational and charitable, spread over the Western States. See (N. Y.) *Cath. Annual*, 1881, p. 75.

Guérin, Eugénie de, a French lady eminent for her piety and devotion, was born at the ancient chateau of Le Cayla, Languedoc, Jan. 25, 1805. She lived in stirring times; even into the solitude of her country home came the agitation of political changes and religious disturbance, distressing to her as a legitimist and Catholic. Her life was an uneventful one, passed in the home of her father, busy in unselfish home ministrations. She died May 1, 1848. Her famous *Journal* is the record of her brother Maurice's life. She felt no call to write her own personal thoughts and feelings. It follows him through every mental and spiritual change, his griefs and joys, his relapse from the Roman faith and reconversion, his marriage and death, and then it closes. It tells of him at the seminary, then at La Chinaie, under the eminent Lamennais, who had left the Catholic Church, and was then in Paris. After her death, the French Academy caused the publication of this simple record, written in the quiet chamber for Maurice's eyes alone. Her *Journal and Letters* make two volumes of 400 pages each, and have gone through twenty editions in France. They have been translated into English, and republished in London and New York, edited by G. S. Trébutien, and have had an extensive sale among both Protestants and Romanists. See (N. Y.) *Cath. Almanac*, 1872, p. 42.

Guérin, Jean Baptiste Paulin, a distinguished French painter of history and portraits, was born at Toulon, March 25, 1783. There are a number of fine historical pieces, by him, mostly of Scriptural subjects, in the churches of Paris. He was professor of painting to the Maison Royale de St. Denis. He died at Paris, Jan. 16, 1855. See Hoefer, *Nouv. Biog. Générale*, s. v.; Spooner, *Biog. Hist. of the Fine Arts*, s. v.

Guerra, Giovanni (called *da Modena*), an Italian painter, designer, and architect, was born at Modena in 1544, and visited Rome at the age of eighteen, where he rose to considerable eminence. He executed a number of works for the chapels and churches during the pontificate of Sixtus V, and also made a great number of designs of subjects from the Old and New Test. As an architect, he designed the Scala Santa at Rome, and the Church of Santa Maria di Paradiso, and La Madonna delle Asse, at Modena. He died at Rome in 1618. See Hoefer, *Nouv. Biog. Générale*, s. v.; Spooner, *Biog. Hist. of the Fine Arts*, s. v.

Guevara, Juan Beltran, a Spanish prelate, was born at Medina-de-las-Torres in 1541. He was sent on a mission to Naples, and wrote for pope Paul V against the Venetians; for which that pontiff rewarded him with the bishopric of Salerno. Guevara was afterwards bishop of Badajoz, and died archbishop of Compostella, in May, 1622. His contemporaries designate him as governed by passion and given up to imagination. He wrote *Propugnaculum Ecclesiasticæ Libertatis Adversus Leges Venetiis Latas*, etc. See Hoefer, *Nouv. Biog. Générale*, s. v.

Guevara, *Don* **Juan Nino de**, an eminent Spanish painter, was born at Madrid in 1632, and was instructed in the school of Miguel Manrique. There are many of his works at Malaga, Cordova, and Granada. In the Church de la Charidad, at Malaga, is a fine picture of *The Triumph of the Cross;* and in the cathedral, *The Ascension of Christ*, and *The Assumption of the Virgin*. He died at Malaga in 1698. See Spooner, *Biog. Hist. of the Fine Arts*, s. v.; Rose, *Gen. Biog. Dict.* s. v.

Gui, the institutor of the order of the Hospitallers of the Saint-Esprit de Montpellier, seems, in 1197, to have united several religious persons, and to have written down the rules of that new institution, which was recognised and confirmed by a bull of pope Innocent III, April 23, 1198. This pontiff called Gui, with several of his co-workers, to Rome, where he charged them with the administration of the hospital of St. Mary in Saxony. The order founded by Gui had for its special object to offer hospitality to the sick, and was regarded as a military order. Gui died in 1208. See Hoefer, *Nouv. Biog. Générale*, s. v.

Gui D'AMIENS (thirty-fourth bishop) was born about the beginning of the 11th century, being the son of Ingelramne I, count of Ponthieu. He studied at the abbey of St. Riquier, and was appointed archdeacon of Amiens in 1049. The bishop of that city sent him some time afterwards to Rome, to obtain a sanction from the pope for the pretensions of the bishop. Gui returned to France without success, and was appointed bishop of Amiens in 1058. Ten years afterwards he accompanied, as almoner, Mathilde, the wife of William the Conqueror, into England. He died in 1076, leaving in Latin a piece of poetry on the battle of Hastings. See Hoefer, *Nouv. Biog. Générale*, s. v.

Gui D'AUXERRE, a French prelate, was born about the end of the 9th century, in the diocese of Sens. He was educated at the Cathedral of Auxerre, under the care of the bishop Herifrid, and became archdeacon there. He also went to the court of king Raoul and queen Emma, by whose influence he was appointed bishop of Auxerre, and was consecrated May 19, 933. He died Jan. 6, 961, leaving *Responsoria* and *Antiphonæ*, in honor of St. Julian. See Hoefer, *Nouv. Biog. Générale*, s. v.

Gui DE BOULOGNE (or D'AUVERGNE), a French prelate, was born in 1320, being the son of Robert, count of Auvergne. After having entered holy orders, he became canon and afterwards chancellor of the Church of Amiens. In 1340 he was elected archbishop of Lyons, and two years afterwards was appointed cardinal by Clement VI. That pope, having reduced the jubilee from one hundred to fifty years, sent, in 1350, Gui, with cardinal Ceccan, to Rome to reopen there the holy year. A short time afterwards Gui was sent as legate to Hungary to settle a difference which had arisen between Louis, king of Hungary, and the queen Jeannette of Naples. Some time after his return to France Gregory XI sent him to Spain, to effect a reconciliation of the kings of Castile and Portugal. He died at Lerida, Nov. 25, 1373, and was buried at the abbey of Bouchet, in the diocese of Clermont. See Hoefer, *Nouv. Biog. Générale*, s. v.

Gui DE BOURGOGNE (surnamed *Gallus*), a French prelate, was born in Burgundy about 1210. He was elected abbot of Citeaux in 1260. Two years afterwards he undertook a journey to Rome on business for his order. While there he received the promise of a cardinalate by pope Urban IV, with the title of St. Laurent *in Lucina*. Clement IV charged him with divers missions in France, Denmark, Sweden, and Germany. In 1267 he presided at the Council of Vienna. To him may be attributed the compilation of the acts of that assembly, found in Mansi, *Concilia*, xxiii, 1167–1178. Gui died at the Council of Lyons, May 20, 1274. See Hoefer, *Nouv. Biog. Générale*, s. v.

Gui DE SAINT-DENIS, abbot there, and counsellor of kings Charles V and Charles VI, was a doctor of canon and civil law, and well versed in sacred and profane letters. He assisted, in 1380, at the coronation of Charles VI, and in 1389 at the crowning of Isabella of Bavaria. He died April 28, 1398. See Hoefer, *Nouv. Biog. Générale*, s. v.

Gui (or *Guimar*) D'ÉTAMPES, a French prelate, was born about the middle of the 11th century. He studied in the famous school of Le Mans, and became the disciple of Hildebert of Lavardin. He visited afterwards several other schools, and also went to England, where he studied under the direction of St. Anselm, archbishop of Canterbury. After his return he assumed the functions of a professor under Hildebert, and succeeded him in 1097 as director at the school of Le Mans. According to the *Histoire Littéraire*, "Hildebert had more talent for composition and declamation; but Gui surpassed him in the liberal arts, which attracted to him a great concourse of students." Gui succeeded Hildebert as bishop of Le Mans in 1126, and did not cease even then to occupy himself with the instruction of the schools. He died in 1135, and left no writings. See Hoefer, *Nouv. Biog. Générale*, s. v.

Gui DE LUSIGNAN, king of Jerusalem, and first king of Cyprus, was born about 1140. He belonged to an ancient family of Limousin, which had distinguished itself in the first crusades. In 1180 he married Sibylla, the sister of Baldwin IV, king of Jerusalem, the widow of William of Montferrat. That princess brought him in dowry Ascalon and Joppa, and Baldwin, who had been attacked with an incurable disease, conferred upon Gui the government of the kingdom of Jerusalem. But his incapacity and pride made him unbearable to the lords, who disputed over the feeble remains of the Frankish power in the East. Baldwin soon began to regret his choice, and in 1183 took back the power from Gui de Lusignan to give it to the count of Tripolis. This gave occasion for a new civil war within the kingdom, which lasted till the death of Baldwin IV, in 1185. He had for his successor Baldwin V, a child of six years, the son of Sibylla and of William of Montferrat; but the youth died in 1186, shortly after his uncle, probably of poison administered to him by Gui. Having become heiress to the throne of Jerusalem, the sister of Baldwin IV announced her intention of separating from her husband, and of giving the crown to the most worthy of the French lords. She published the divorce in the Church of the Holy Sepulchre; Heraclius, patriarch of Jerusalem, pronouncing the separation. Sibylla, after having taken back the crown, gave it to Gui de Lusignan, and thus disgusted most of the French lords. Soon afterwards again Gui showed incapacity. Saladin, with his troops, continually invaded the country, and on the morning of July 4, 1187, threw himself with his Mohammedans upon a small body of Christian soldiers, who were encamped about the hill Hattin, near Lake Tiberias. Gui, with Reynold of Châtillon and other commanders were taken prisoners. Gui bought his liberty by restoring Ascalon to Saladin, and Jerusalem capitulated Oct. 2, 1187. Thus ended the Latin kingdom founded by Godfrey de Bouillon, after a duration of eighty-nine years. The only use that Gui made of his title of King of Jerusalem was in ceding it to Richard, in 1192, as a price of sovereignty over the island of Cyprus, which that prince had taken from the small Greek tyrant Isaac Comnenus; he also bound himself to pay back the twenty-five thousand marks which the Templars had given to Richard. Cyprus was devastated and nearly deserted; Gui peopled it again by drawing colonists from Armenia and Antioch. He also offered an asylum to a great number who fled from the domination of the Mohammedans in Palestine. After a peaceful reign of two years he died, in 1194, and transmitted his crown to his brother Amaury. See Hoefer, *Nouv. Biog. Générale*, s. v.

Gui DE PUY (thirty-first bishop), a French prelate, was born in the first part of the 10th century, being the son of Poulques the Kind, count of Anjou. He took holy orders, and was supplied with various abbeys and benefices. But, the Church having interdicted the holding of several offices, Gui surrendered all the other abbeys and gave back again all that he had taken away from the monasteries, holding only the abbey of Carmeri, which he administered with great regularity and order. He succeeded his brother Drogon in the episcopal see of Puy in 985, and died in 996. Gui left no works, but two pieces, which are of some interest in ecclesiastical history. The first is the manifestation by which he resigned his benefices (in Mabillon, *Annales Ord. Bened.* i, 47); the second is a diploma, relating to the foundation of the monastery of St. Peter (in the *Gallia Christiana*, iii). See Hoefer, *Nouv. Biog. Générale*, s. v.

Guibé, ROBERT, a French cardinal, was born at Vitré, being of high parentage, which contributed to his early fortune. His ambition as well as his aptitude to conduct the most difficult affairs, rendered him one of the most remarkable men of his time. Being appointed bishop of Tréguier in 1483, he obtained his bulla on May 20, but not yet having attained the age requisite to a canon, the pope intrusted the government of the diocese to a provisional administrator. In February, 1485, Guibé went to Rome on a message from duke Francis. In 1499 he returned to Brittany, to be transferred from the see of Tréguier to that of Rennes. He went to Rome a second time in 1502, and was appointed cardinal by Julius II, with the title of *St. Anastasia*, Jan. 1, 1506. On Jan. 24, 1507, he was called to the episcopal see of Nantes, but, preferring his position at Rome, he did not remain long at his new church. He was legate of Avignon in 1511. The king afterwards took away the revenues of the benefices from the cardinal, and Guibé resigned the bishopric of Nantes in favor of François Hamon, his nephew. Finally, in 1512, he assisted at the Lateran Council, and died Sept. 9, 1513. See Hoefer, *Nouv. Biog. Générale*, s. v.

Guibert, abbot OF GEMBLOUX and OF FLORENNES, was born about the year 1120, in Brabant. He lived for some time in the abbey of St. Martin, was elected abbot of Florennes in 1188, and five years later was placed at the head of the monastery of Gembloux; which communities he administered in wisdom, but resigned shortly before his death, which occurred Feb. 22, 1208. He wrote numerous works, e. g., *A Poem on St. Martin*, a *Life of St. Hildegard*, and several *Letters*, of which the majority have been published by Dom Martene, *Amplissima Collectio*, i, 916. A fire which broke out in the monastery of Gembloux at the end of the 17th century destroyed nearly all the works of Guibert. See Hoefer, *Nouv. Biog. Générale*, s. v.

Guichard, a French prelate, entered the order of the Cistercians and became abbot of Potigny, and in 1165 archbishop of Lyons, replacing thus another prelate, who had been deposed on account of his relations with the emperor of Germany. Guichard rendered important service to his Church, and died about 1180. Several of his letters have been preserved. Dom Martene has published, in *De Antiq. de Eccles. Ritibus*, iii, certain statutes which were promulgated by that archbishop, relating mostly to the divine service. See Hoefer, *Nouv. Biog. Générale*, s. v.

Guidacerio, AGATHO, an Italian Hebraist, born at Rocca-Coragio (Calabria), was still living in 1539. After having taken holy orders, he studied Hebrew at Rome under a Portuguese rabbi, and was appointed afterwards to teach that language. His life was much in danger during the year 1527, and having retired to Avignon, he found a protector in the bishop of Apt, Jean Nicolai, who took him to Paris. Guidacerio was appointed royal professor by Francis I, in 1530. He interpreted at the College of France both the Hebrew and Greek texts of the Scriptures, and wrote, *Grammatica Ebraicæ Linguæ* (Rome, 1514; Paris, 1529; under the title of *Peculium*, Paris, 1537); a dozen treatises, or commentaries on the Psalms; a commentary on the Song of Songs, with the Hebrew and Latin texts (Rome, 1524), and a commentary on Ecclesiastes (1531). See Hoefer, *Nouv. Biog. Générale*, s. v.

Guidiccioni, Giovanni, an Italian prelate and author, was born at Lucca, Feb. 25, 1500. He received a careful education, and was quite successful in his studies at the universities of Pisa, Bologna, and Ferrara, where he obtained the degree of a doctor of law, and then went to Rome, where he connected himself with the principal literary men. By recommendation of his uncle, Bartolommeo, he entered the service of cardinal Farnese, who, on becoming pope under the name of Paul III, in 1534, appointed Guidiccioni governor of Rome, and called him in the same year to the bishopric of Fossombrone. Guidiccioni was afterwards sent on various more or less important commissions. He was made governor of the marches of Ancona in 1541, and died at Macerata, in August of the same year. For his letters and other writings, see Hoefer, *Nouv. Biog. Générale*, s. v.

Guidiccioni, Christoforo, an Italian prelate and writer, was born at Lucca in 1536. After being rector of the Church of St. Synesius in that city, he was appointed, in 1578, bishop of Ajaccio, in Corsica, and died in 1582, leaving *Tragedie Trasportate Dalla Greca nell' Italiana Favella* (Lucca, 1547). See Hoefer, *Nouv. Biog. Générale*, s. v.

Guido, Fassi. See CONTE.

Guido, Reni. See RENI.

Guidonis, BERNARD, a celebrated French prelate, was born in the vicinity of Limoges, near La Roche l'Abeille, in 1260. He entered the convent of the Dominicans at Limoges, Sept. 16, 1279. In 1293 he taught theology in the convent of Alby, in 1301 was appointed prior of Castres, and in 1305 of Limoges. Guidonis went to Toulouse, in 1307, to enforce the inquisition against the Albigenses. In 1317 he was appointed procurator-general of his order at the court of Rome, and was charged by the pope, John XXII, with several negotiations, and on the conclusion of peace between France and Flanders, he was rewarded by being made bishop of Lodève (Lower Languedoc). He died Dec. 30, 1331. Some of his principal writings are, *Traités Théologiques Touchant les Articles de Foi:—Traité de la Pauvreté de Jésus-Christ:—Pratique de l'Office d'Inquisiteur:—Le Miroir des Saints:—Une Chronique des Souverains Pontifes*, etc. See Hoefer, *Nouv. Biog. Générale*, s. v.

Guignes, JOSEPH DE, a French Orientalist, father of Chrétien Louis Joseph (q. v.), was born at Pontoise, Oct. 19, 1721. He studied the Oriental languages under Fourmont, whom he succeeded in 1745. When the French Revolution broke out, Guignes was deprived of his position, and lived in great poverty. He died at Paris, March 3, 1800. Guignes, who had made the Chinese language a specialty, believed it to be related to the Egyptian. See his *Mémoire, dans Lequel on Prouve que les Chinois Sont une Colonie Égyptienne* (Paris, 1759). His main work is *Histoire Générale des Huns, des Turcs, des Mogols et des Autres Tatores Occidentaux* (Paris, 1756-58, 4 vols.). (B. P.)

Guijon, André, a French prelate and orator, was born at Autun, in November, 1548. He became grand-vicar to cardinal de Joyeuse, and afterwards bishop of Autun. He made a voyage to Rome to receive his new dignity, and returned to France in 1586. He died in September, 1631, leaving *Remontrance à la Cour de Parlement de Normandie*, etc. See Hoefer, *Nouv. Biog. Générale*, s. v.

Guijon, Jacques, a French prelate, a relative of the preceding, was born at Noyers in 1663. He entered the ministry, and, after success in teaching, died in 1739, leaving, *Apophthegmes des Saints* (Paris, 1709):—*Éloge de Rassicod* (1718):—*Longueruana* (1754):—and a very important MS. work entitled, *Réflexions sur les Mœurs des Français*. See Hoefer, *Nouv. Biog. Générale*, s. v.

Guldin, JOHN C., D.D., a prominent minister of the German Reformed Church, was born in Berks County, Pa., in August, 1799. He was ordained in 1820, and settled as pastor over some congregations in Montgomery County, where he labored successfully until 1841, when he removed to Chambersburg, taking charge of several congregations in the vicinity. After laboring here about one year, he was called to take charge of the German Evangelical Mission Church, in the city of New York. In this field he labored with great acceptance and success up to the time of his death, Feb. 18, 1863. Dr. Guldin was a man of fine talents, ardent feelings, and great energy of character. Besides his pastoral duties, he also labored in connection with the American Tract Society. He published a volume of *Sermons*, and aided in getting up a German hymn-book for the use of the Reformed Dutch Church. "He had a fellow-feeling for all in sorrow, and could speak from a sweet experience for the comfort of such." See Harbaugh, *Fathers of the Germ. Ref. Church*, iv, 158. (D. Y. H.)

Guillaume. See WILLIAM.

Guillaume, *frère*, an eminent French painter on glass, was born at Marseilles in 1475. He was a member of the order of Dominicans, and executed many excellent works in the south of France. In the cathedral at Arezzo he painted several admirable works, among which were *The Baptism of Christ*, *The Resurrection of Lazarus*, and *Christ Driving the Money-changers from the Temple.* He established a school for teaching the art of painting on glass. He died in 1537.

Guillaume, *Saint* (1), a French regular canon, was born at St. Germain, near Crépy, about 1105. After having been educated under the care of his uncle, the abbot Hugues of St. Germain-des-Prés, he became canon of the collegiate church of St. Geneviève, but, on account of the laxity in discipline among the monks, accepted the provostship of Espinac. In the interval, reform and regularity were established in the Church of St. Geneviève by the monks of St. Victor. Guillaume then returned there, and was elected sub-prior of the house in 1148. About the same time Absalon, bishop of Roeskild, in Denmark, wished to reform a monastery of regular canons on the isle of Eskild. Guillaume was sent there with three other canons, who abandoned him. After his arrival in Denmark, in 1171, he was made abbot of St. Thomas of the Paraclete. He re-established the discipline of that house, and lived under the greatest austerities until 1203. There are known of St. William more than a hundred letters, which were published in 1786, in the *Rerum Danicarum Scriptores.* See Hoefer, *Nouv. Biog. Générale*, s. v.

Guillaume, *Saint* (2), a French prelate, was born in the borough of Arthel (Nivernais). He was descended from a noble family, educated by William the Hermit, archdeacon of Soissons, who was his uncle, and became first canon of the Church of Paris and of Soissons. He entered the order of Grammont, in the diocese of Limoges, and later went over to that of the Cistercians at the abbey of Pontigny. In 1181 he was made abbot of Fontaine, dean in the diocese of Sens, and afterwards of Charlieu. There he was selected by Eudes of Sully, bishop of Paris in 1199, to occupy the episcopal see of Bourges. The epoch of his episcopate was marked particularly by the discussions with Philip Augustus, on the subject of the repudiation of queen Ingelburga. The bishop, who took the part of the queen, was threatened with exile and confiscation, but withstood the royal indignation, and Philip, having decided to take back Ingelburga, was reconciled with the prelate. Guillaume died in 1209, as he was about to march out against the Albigenses, who had propagated their doctrine as far as Berry. His body was deposited in the crypt of the basilica of St. Étienne of Bourges, and remained in that church until 1562, when the Huguenots, on their taking possession of the city, burned his remains. See Hoefer, *Nouv. Biog. Générale*, s. v.

Guillaume D'AUBERIVE, a French abbot and theologian, lived in the 12th century. In 1165 and 1180 he was at the head of the abbey of Auberive, which was of the order of Cistercians, in the diocese of Langres. He composed various books, which have remained unedited, however; there are cited among them four letters on the last judgment, and a treatise upon numbers, which reveals a profound knowledge of arithmetic. See Hoefer, *Nouv. Biog. Générale*, s. v.

Guillaume DE BEAUMONT, a French prelate, was born in 1177, being a member of the illustrious family of Beaumont. After the decease of Guillaume de Chemillé, which took place in May, 1202, Guillaume de Beaumont united the suffrages of the people and of the clergy, and was consecrated Sept. 23, 1203. In 1209 he put an end to disagreements between the monks of Ronceray and the friars of the Hospital of St. John. In 1223 he took an oath of allegiance to king Louis VIII. Finally, in 1236, he admitted the preaching friars into the city of Angers. He died in 1240. His literary works are very few, and of no importance; they are statutes which were published in 1680 by one of his successors, Henry Arnauld. See Hoefer, *Nouv. Biog. Générale*, s. v.

Guillaume DE BLOIS (surnamed *the cardinal of Champagne*) was born in 1135. In his early childhood he was recommended by his father to St. Bernard, who inspired him with the love of study and virtue. In 1164 Guillaume was elected bishop of Chartres, and in 1168 consecrated archbishop of Sens by the venerable Maurice, bishop of Paris. In the same year pope Alexander III, who was at that time in France, selected him as his legate, on the occasion of a quarrel which had broken out between Thomas, archbishop of Canterbury, primate of England, and king Henry II. Owing to the prudence and zeal with which he transacted his mission, he obtained the archiepiscopal see of Rheims. Guillaume had the honor of crowning, at Rheims, his nephew, Philip Augustus, as associate with his father, Louis the Younger. He took advantage of the credit which he enjoyed with Louis the Younger to obtain from him the regulation which granted to the archbishops the perpetual privilege of having the sole power of consecrating the kings of France, a regulation afterwards confirmed by the bull of the pope. At the beginning of the reign of Philip Augustus, Guillaume fell into disgrace, and so turned his further attention towards the court of Rome, which shortly afterwards conferred upon him the cardinal's hat, and restored him to his dignity at the French court, and his call to the ministry of the state. Guillaume died at Laon about 1202. See Hoefer, *Nouv. Biog. Générale*, s. v.

Guillaume (*Abbot*) DE ST. DENIS, was born at Gap, and lived in the 12th century. It seems that he had studied medicine before entering the monastic life. In 1178 he was placed at the head of the celebrated abbey from which he derives his name, and governed it with zeal and wisdom. But he displeased king Philip Augustus, and resigned in 1186. He was a man well instructed for his time, translating from the Latin the *Eulogy of St. Denis the Areopagite*, composed by Michael Syncellus, patriarch of Jerusalem, and a *Life of the Philosopher Secundus.* His writings remain in MS. See Hoefer, *Nouv. Biog. Générale*, s. v.

Guillaume DU DESERT (Lat. *Guilelmus* or *Willelmus*). See WILLIAM OF AQUITAINE.

Guillaume (*Saint*) DE MALAVAL, founder of the Guillemites, is supposed to have been a French nobleman who had chosen a soldier's life, and lived in dissipation. Being anxious to do penance, he went to Rome, where pope Eugenius III, in 1145, ordered him to make a pilgrimage to Jerusalem. After his return to Tuscany, in 1153, he settled in a lonely valley of the Sienna territory, in the diocese of Grosseto, where he spent his life in work and prayer. He died Feb. 10, 1157. Some time later some of his followers erected a hermitage with a chapel on the tomb of Guillaume, and from that time it became the shrine of the order of the Guillemites, who multiplied in Germany, Flanders, and France. See Hoefer, *Nouv. Biog. Générale*, s. v.

Guillaume DE MANDAGOT, a French prelate and canon, was born of an illustrious family of Lodève. He was successively archdeacon of Nîmes, provost of the Church of Toulouse, archbishop of Embrun about 1295, and was made cardinal and bishop of Palestine in 1312 by Clement V. In 1296 he was charged by Boniface VIII with composing the sixth book of the Decretals, together with Bérenger de Frédol and Richard of Sienna, to whom was added, some time later, Dinus, a professor of the Roman law at Bologna. Guillaume composed, about 1300, the *Summa Libelli Electionum*, a very peculiar work, which contains some interesting details on the Church of Toulouse. Some time afterwards it was revised by John Andreæ, and dedicated to Bérenger (Cologne, 1573). Guillame died at Avignon in November, 1321. See Hoefer, *Nouv. Biog. Générale*, s. v.

Guillaume (*Abbot*) DE MARMOUTIERS was born in the latter part of the 11th century, and was a native of Brittany. Before he had taken the cowl he was an archdeacon of Nantes. After the death of Hilgode, the monks of Marmoutiers selected him as their abbot, in 1104. Between these monks and the archbishop of Tours there existed at that time a grave dispute. Raoul, who occupied the metropolitan see, required that newly-elected abbots should, in the ceremony of consecration, offer to him the oath of fidelity. The monks refused to render that homage, declaring it to be humiliating. Guillaume having accordingly refused, Raoul brought a complaint before the pope. During the debate, which agitated the whole province of Tours, Guillaume himself went to Rome, and there was consecrated. In 1105 he returned to his abbey. In 1106 he sat at the Council of Poitiers, and vigorously attacked a certain lord Manceau, who had taken possession of the Church of Chahaignes. In 1108 he obtained of Benedict, bishop of Aleth, the Church of St. Malo of Dinan. In 1109 he pleaded before the Council of Laon against the monks of Chemillé. He was one of the most famous of the abbots of Marmoutiers, and increased its wealth considerably. He died May 23, 1124. See Hoefer, *Nouv. Biog. Générale*, s. v.

Guillaume DE PASSAVANT, a French prelate, was born in Saintonge, in the beginning of the 12th century. When Rainaud of Martigné, his cousin, was nominated archbishop of Rheims, Guillaume succeeded him in that church, and executed there the functions of an archdeacon until January, 1144. After that he was called to the episcopal see of Mans, where his name is found among the documents of the year 1145. He was proud and able to defend the privileges of the Church. Being asked by the monks of Marmoutiers to intervene in their favor against Guy de Laval, who had taken possession of one of their priories, he immediately excommunicated that powerful leader. In 1151 a vassal church (of Brûlan) had refused to give homage to its superior, the Church of La Coûture, and Guillaume ordered the rebel church to be demolished, for which he was obliged to go to Rome in order to justify his conduct. St. Bernard wrote in his favor to Hugues, bishop of Ostia, and to pope Eugenius III. Guillaume died at Yvré, in the province of Maine, Jan. 26, 1187. See Hoefer, *Nouv. Biog. Générale*, s. v.

Guillaume (*Saint*) PINCHON, a French prelate, was born in 1184, in the parish of St. Alban, of poor agriculturist parents. Being admitted in early youth as a clerk of the Church of St. Brieuc, he soon distinguished himself among his colleagues, early obtained a canonicate, and in 1220 was appointed bishop of St. Brieuc. The bishops of Brittany at that time were engaged in serious disputes with Peter Mauclerc. Guillaume being summoned to obey this formidable leader, responded by a sentence of excommunication. The reply of Peter Mauclerc was the exile of the prelate, and the imprisonment of the priests who were known as his most devoted partisans. But the court of Rome took up the defence of Guillaume, and made his exile of short duration. He had left his diocese in 1228, and returned to it again in 1231. He died in 1234. See Hoefer, *Nouv. Biog. Générale*, s. v.

Guillaume LE WALLON, an abbot of St. Arnoul of Metz. It is believed that he received instruction at the school of Liege. On the conclusion of his studies he retired to a cloister. His teacher wrote him a letter, engaging him to leave his retreat and to enter the ranks of the secular clergy, but Guillaume continued in his chosen vocation. In 1050 he succeeded Warin at St. Arnoul as abbot. In 1073 he was elected abbot of St. Remi at Rheims. Since the year 1071 that monastery had remained without a chief, and stood exposed to the ravages of archbishop Manassé. Guillaume had some warm disputes with the latter, and wished to resign. He wrote to the pope, and, not receiving any answer, set out for Rome. The pope received him kindly, and on his return archbishop Manassé relieved him. Guillaume retired to Metz, and although devoted to bishop Herman, he was so weak as to allow himself to be consecrated in his place, when the emperor Henry IV had expelled the latter from his see in 1085. The following year Guillaume went to meet the bishop, and in the presence of the chief members of the Church renounced the episcopate, and retired to the abbey of Gorze. He was intrusted with the care of the children educated there, and after some time bishop Herman gave him the abbey of St. Arnoul. He died about 1089. There are extant of Guillaume le Wallon a collection of seven letters to divers persons, one to Gregory VII, and two to archbishop Manassé, in which he reproaches him severely on account of his many vices. To him also is ascribed a fine prayer in honor of St. Augustine. See Hoefer, *Nouv. Biog. Générale*, s. v.

Guillebert, NICOLAS, a French prelate, who lived in the first half of the 17th century, is the author of, *Les Proverbes de Salomon Paraphrases* (Paris, 1626, 1637):—*Paraphrase sur l'Ecclésiaste de Salomon* (1627, 1635, 1642):—*La Sagesse de Salomon Paraphrasée* (1631):—*Paraphrases sur les Épitres de S. Paul aux Colosses, Thessaloniens, Timothée et Tite* (1635):—*Paraphrase de l'Épître aux Hébreux et des Épîtres Canoniques* (ibid. 1638). See Jöcher, *Allgemeines Gelehrten-Lexikon*, s. v. (B. P.)

Guillemin, PIERRE, a French Benedictine, who died Sept. 9, 1747, at Neuf-Chateau, in Lotharingia, is the author of *Commentaire Littéral Abrégé sur Tous les Livres de l'Ancien et du Nouveau Testament* (Paris, 1721). See Winer, *Handbuch der theol. Lit.* i, 188; Jöcher, *Allgemeines Gelehrten-Lexikon*, s. v. (B. P.)

Guilleminot, JEAN, a French Jesuit, born in 1614, joined his order in 1631, was professor of theology at Pont-à-Mousson, and died at Nancy, Nov. 24, 1680. He left, *Selectæ ex Philosophia Quæstiones* (Paris, 1671, 2 vols.):—*La Sagesse Chrétienne* (ibid. 1674):—*Selectæ Quæstiones Theologicæ* (1682, 2 vols.). See Papillon, *Bibl. des Auteurs de Bourgogne;* Jöcher, *Allgemeines Gelehrten-Lexikon*, s. v. (B. P.)

Guion, Elijah, D.D., a Protestant Episcopal clergyman, was first employed as a teacher in Carrolton, La., about the year 1853. The next year he was rector of St. James's Church, Baton Rouge; in 1860 he removed to New Orleans, where, during the war, he served as chaplain in the United States army; in 1867 was chosen rector of the Church of the Advent in Brownsville, Texas, where he also served as chaplain in the army; in 1871 was at Fort Sill, in the Indian Territory, as United States chaplain; in 1874 was appointed to the same position at Fort Gibson; in 1877 removed to Texas, and, still chaplain, went in the following year to Almaden Mines, Cal. He died in New Almaden, Jan. 17, 1879. See *Prot. Episc. Almanac*, 1880, p. 171.

Guion, John M., D.D., a Protestant Episcopal clergyman, a graduate of the General Theological Seminary, was employed as rector of the Church in Bethany, Conn., in 1853; the following year became assistant minister of a church in Baltimore, Md.; and shortly after was chosen rector of Trinity Church, Seneca Falls, N. Y., where he remained until his death, July 20, 1878, at the age of seventy-seven years. See *Prot. Episc. Almanac,* 1879, p. 168.

Guion, Thomas T., D.D., a Protestant Episcopal clergyman, was born at Bedford, N. Y., Aug. 31, 1817. He graduated at Trinity College, Hartford, Conn., in 1840. His first cure was the missionary station at Zoar. He then took charge of the parishes of St. Thomas, in Bethel, and St. James, in Danbury, which, at the end of three years, had become self-supporting, and he assumed the rectorship of them both. In 1848 he had charge of St. Mary's parish, Brooklyn, N. Y.; afterwards was rector of St. James's, Birmingham, Conn., for more than four years. In 1853 he accepted the pastorate of St. John's parish, Brooklyn, N. Y., where he was very successful, but his health failed. He died at Milford, Conn., Oct. 21, 1862. Dr. Guion was clear in his conceptions, honest in his convictions, and fearless in their avowal. See *Amer. Quar. Church Rev.* April, 1863, p. 150.

Guiragos (or **Cyriacus**) OF ARMENIA, was born at Kharabasd, in the province of Khajperuni. He resided thirty-two years in the convent of Khor-Virab, whence he received the surname *Virabetsi.* He was an humble and pious man, and well versed in the Scriptures. He was elected patriarch in 1141, when Gregory IX, patriarch of Armenia, residing at Sis (Cilicia), objected to the transportation of his seat to Echmiadzin (Greater Armenia). Guiragos was the first patriarch who resided at the latter place; he erected convents and churches there, repaired the cathedral, and broke up the schism which separated the patriarch Aghthamar from the rest of the Church. A certain Marcus, bishop of Georgia, who was dissatisfied with that reconciliation, pretended that the election of Guiragos was invalid, because he had not previously been consecrated bishop, and it was even said that he had never been baptized. Zacharias, bishop of Havuts-Tharhah, joined the enemies of the patriarch, and went to Echmiadzin to depose him in 1143, at the head of thirty bishops. Yakub-Khan of Erivan at first opposed the change, but, being bribed by Zacharias, gave him authority to renew the election. The suffrages were in favor of Gregory X, and Guiragos, who had been hiding during the excitement, retired into a convent, where he died the same year. See Hoefer, *Nouv. Biog. Générale,* s. v.

Guise, John, OF LORRAINE, cardinal, was born in 1498. He went to France, and contributed a great deal to the elevation of his brother, Claude of Lorraine, the first duke of Guise, and of his family. In April, 1536, Francis I sent him to Charles V to negotiate an agreement. About 1542 the cardinal was removed from the court, and he died May 18, 1550. He is known for his excessive liberality, by means of which he became so influential among the people. He was in possession of a number of archbishoprics in France. See Hoefer, *Nouv. Biog. Générale,* s. v.

Guise, Louis (1), OF LORRAINE, a French prelate, brother of Charles, also archbishop of Sens, and bishop of Troyes, of Metz, and of Alby, was born Oct. 21, 1527. He was made cardinal Dec. 22, 1553, and attended the election of pope Paul IV. He was so fond of conviviality that the people used to call him "the cardinal of the bottles." He died at Paris, March 24, 1578. See Hoefer, *Nouv. Biog. Générale,* s. v.

Guise, Louis (2), OF LORRAINE, a French prelate and peer, was born at Dampierre, July 6, 1555. The cardinal of Lorraine, his uncle, appointed him, in 1572, his coadjutor at the abbey of St. Denis, and made over to him at his death the archbishopric of Rheims, the abbeys of Fécamp and Montier-en-Der (1574). In 1578 he was made cardinal, and in the following year Henry III appointed him commander of the order of the Holy Spirit. A few days after he had been consecrated archbishop of St. Denis, Feb. 17, 1583, he went to Rheims to hold a provincial council, and then came back to Paris to mingle in the intrigues of the League. In 1585 he assisted at the ecclesiastical reunion of St. Germain-en-Laye. The Germans and Swiss had burned down (1587) his abbey of St. Urbin, in Champagne, in revenge for which the cardinal burned the castle of Brème, near château Thierry, belonging to the duke of Bouillon. Cardinal Guise was assassinated, Dec. 24, 1588. See Hoefer, *Nouv. Biog. Générale,* s. v.

Guise, Louis (3), cardinal of Lorraine, archbishop of Rheims, and peer of France, was born, according to some, Jan. 22, 1575, according to others in May, 1585. He obtained the abbeys of St. Denis and of Montier-en-Der, and also that of Châlis. He was never ordained, preferring brigandage, and exhibited that tendency in his later years, when he proposed to settle theological disputes by arms. In 1621 he followed the king on his expedition to Poitou, but fell sick at the siege of St. Jean d'Angely, and died shortly after (June 21, 1621). Charlotte des Essarts, countess of Romorantin, and one of the mistresses of Henry IV, is said to have been secretly married to the cardinal (Feb. 4, 1611), bearing to him three sons and two daughters. See Hoefer, *Nouv. Biog. Générale,* s. v.

Guise, William, a learned English divine, was born at Abload's or Abbey-load's Court, near Gloucester, in 1653, and was educated at Oriel College, where he was made fellow in 1674. He was ordained about 1677, and died Sept. 3, 1684. He translated into English, and illustrated with a commentary, Dr. Bernard's *Misnæ Pars Ordinis Primi Teraim Tituli Septem* (1690), and a tract, *De Victimis Humanis.* See Chalmers, *Biog. Dict.* s. v.; Allibone, *Dict. of Brit. and Amer. Authors,* s. v.

Guizot, FRANÇOIS PIERRE GUILLAUME, a noted French religious author, was born at Nîmes, Oct. 4, 1787, being the descendant of a family of Huguenot pastors. He was educated at Geneva, and studied law at Paris. During the literary period of his life (1812–30), he was successively professor of history at the Sorbonne, secretary-general of the interior, journalist, etc. To this period belong his *Du Gouvernement Représentatif et de l'État Actuel de la France* (1816):—*Des Conspirations et de la Justice Politique* (1821):—*Des Moyens de Gouvernement et d'Opposition* (eod.):—*De la Peine de Mort en Matière Politique* (1822):—*Essais sur l'Histoire de France* (1823):—*L'Histoire de la Révolution d'Angleterre* (1827, 1828, 2 vols.):—*L'Histoire de la Civilisation Depuis l'Établissement du Christianisme* (1829). With the year 1830 Guizot's political career commenced, and it was mainly due to his efforts as minister of public instruction that a reform of the educational system of France took place. In the year 1816 Guizot published his *Essai sur l'Histoire et sur l'État Actuel de l'Instruction Publique,* in which he insisted that the state had the right of managing and controlling the public instruction. This idea he now developed, and introduced many improvements, especially in the primary and higher schools. In ecclesiastical respects, Guizot was the main support of orthodoxy in the Reformed Church of France. In 1852 he was chosen president of the consistory. He was opposed to liberalism of any kind in religious matters. He was orthodox, and clung to the *Credo* of his Church. In 1872 he was obliged, on account of feeble health, to retire from the presidency of the synod. He died at Val de Bêcher, Sept. 12, 1874. Of his religious works, we mention, *L'Église et la Société Chrétienne* (1861):—*Méditations sur l'Essence de la Religion Chrétienne* (1864; Engl. translation, N. Y. 1865):—*Méditations sur la Religion Chrétienne dans ses Rapports avec l'État Actuel des Sociétés* (1865–68, 3 vols.):—*Les Vies de Quatre Grands*

Chrétiens Français (1868; Engl. translation, Lond. 1868):—*Mémoires pour Servir à l'Histoire de mon Temps* (1858-68, 9 vols.). He was one of the founders of the *Société Biblique* in 1826, of the *Société pour l'Encouragement de l'Instruction Primaire* in 1833, and of the *Société l'Histoire du Protestantisme Français* in 1857. When, in 1861, Guizot had to make a reply to the address of the new academician, Père Lacordaire, he defended and justified the papacy and the worldly power of the pope, whereas the Dominican praised Protestant America. This address of Guizot made a great stir. The Catholic papers, especially the *Univers*, rejoiced, and hoped soon to see Guizot return to the Church of Rome. But in spite of this Guizot remained in his Church, and from his words in his testament, "I die in the bosom of the Reformed Christian Church of France, in which I was born, and to have been born in which I rejoice," which have been quoted in full, we see that Guizot made all allowance to the Church of Rome, without becoming one of her members. See Mazade, *Portrait d'Histoire Morale et Politique du Temps Jacquemont, Guizot*, etc. (Paris, 1875); Madame de Witt, née Guizot, *Monsieur Guizot dans sa Famille et avec ses Amis* (ibid. 1880; English transl. Lond. and Boston); Lichtenberger, *Encyclop. des Sciences Religieuses*, s. v.; Plitt-Herzog, *Real-Encyklop.* s. v. (B. P.)

Gujerati Version OF THE SCRIPTURES. The Gujerati takes its name from Gujerat, a district of the Punjab in India, and the principal province in which it is spoken, and is said by the Serampore missionaries to be the vernacular of a territory equal in point of extent to England. On account of its wide diffusion it has been appropriately designated "the grand mercantile language of foreign Indian marts." The Serampore missionaries were the first to undertake a Gujerati version of the Scriptures. In 1807 they commenced printing the gospel of Matthew, but the work was given up. In 1813 it was resumed, and in 1820 the New Test., in Gujerati characters instead of the Sanscrit, was completed. The prosecution of this version was, however, resigned about this period by the Serampore missionaries to the agents of the London Missionary Society stationed at Surat. The Rev. Messrs. Skinner and Fyvie, of the London Missionary Society, published their version of the New Test. in 1821, at Surat. Shortly after the publication of the New Test. Mr. Skinner died, and the translation of the Old Test. was now carried on by Mr. Fyvie, and in 1823 it was completed at press. Other editions, in a revised state, rapidly followed as the demand increased. Another version of the New Test. was made by the Rev. Messrs. Clarkson and Flower, and an edition of two thousand copies was issued from the press. But it was subsequently resolved to publish an edition of the New Test. according to the old translation of the Surat edition, subject to such slight changes as might be deemed necessary. This edition was completed at the Bombay press in 1853. Meanwhile, preparations for a revised edition of the entire Gujerati Scriptures were in active progress under the care of the Bombay Auxiliary Society, and an edition of the New Test., according to this improved version, was completed at the mission-press in Surat in 1856. The Old Test. was completed in 1861. Besides these two editions, the Serampore New Test. and the Surat version, in 1860 a new edition of the Gujerati New Test., for the special use of the Parsees, was announced. It was carried through the press in Bombay, in Parsee characters, by the Rev. Dunjeebhoy Nowrojee, and published in 1862. In this edition the religious terms are those technically used in religious Parsee literature. Of the latter edition up to March 31, 1884, two thousand two hundred and forty-nine portions of Scripture were disposed of. See *Bible of Every Land*, p. 123. There exist several grammars for the study of this language: Munshi, *The Student's Companion in the Acquisition of a Practical Knowledge of English and Gujerati Grammar and Idioms* (Ahmedabad, 1869); Shapurji Edalji, *A Grammar of the Gujerati Language* (Bombay, 1867); Taylor, *A Grammar of the Gujerati Language* (ibid. 1868). (B. P.)

Guldberg, OVE HOEGH, a Danish statesman, historian, and theologian, was born Sept. 1, 1731, and died Feb. 8, 1808. He is known as the author of a *Chronology for the Books of the New Testament* (Copenhagen, 1785), and of *A Translation of the New Testament, with Annotations* (1794, 2 vols.), both published in the Danish language. (B. P.)

Gumpel, MORDECAI. See LEVISOHN.

Gunn, ALEXANDER, D.D., a distinguished minister of the Reformed (Dutch) Church, was born Aug. 13, 1785. He graduated from Columbia College in 1805, and prepared for the ministry under Dr. Henry Kollock of Princeton, and Dr. John Rodgers of New York. In 1809 he was licensed by the Presbytery of New York, and the same year took charge of the Church at Bloomingdale. He died Oct. 1, 1829. An accomplished gentleman, amiable, prudent, and a peace-maker, he was also noted for his conscientious piety and entire devotion to his work. His talents as a writer and preacher were of a very high order. Imaginative and cultivated, with good taste, ample learning, and fine abilities, he was among the most popular pulpit orators of New York. He wielded a powerful pen as a theological writer, and took a conspicuous part in some of the exciting controversies of his time. The General Synod, in 1825, appointed him to write the biography of the late Rev. John H. Livingston, D.D. See *Magazine of the Ref. Dutch Church*, December, 1829, p. 257; Corwin, *Manual of the Ref. Church in America*, s. v. (W. J. R. T.)

Gunner, JOHANN ERNEST, a Norwegian prelate and naturalist, was born in Christiana, Feb. 26, 1718. He began his studies under the direction of his father, who was a physician in that city, and went to Copenhagen to continue them. In 1742 the king gave him means to go to Halle, and afterwards to Jena, where he studied philosophy, and became a member of the faculty. On his return to Copenhagen in 1755 he was made extraordinary professor of theology in the university. In 1758 the bishopric of Drontheim was conferred upon him. He died at Christiansand, Sept. 23, 1773, leaving, *Hyrdebrev* (Drontheim, 1758):—*Klagtale over Kong Frederic V* (ibid. 1766):—also *Memoirs* in the *Norsk Videnskabernsselskabs Skrifter* (writings of the Academy of Science of Norway), etc. See Hoefer, *Nouv. Biog. Générale*, s. v.

Günther, Johann, a Lutheran theologian of Germany, was born April 17, 1660. He studied at Breslau and Leipsic, was preacher and licentiate of theology at the latter place, and died Jan. 20, 1714. His writings are for the most part directed against the Roman Catholic Church. See Ranft, *Leben der chursächsischen Gottesgelehrten*; Jöcher, *Allgemeines Gelehrten-Lexikon*, s. v. (B. P.)

Günther, Wolfgang, a Lutheran theologian, was born in Saxony in 1586. He studied at Wittenberg, was preacher in 1611 in the vicinity of Annaberg, in 1615 pastor and superintendent at Friedland, in 1626 at Spardan, and died Jan. 16, 1636. He wrote, *Analysis Trium Librorum Ecclesiæ Nostræ Symbolicorum* (Wittenberg, 1614):—*Aphorismi Theologici super Aug. Confessionem* (1615):—*Dispositio Epistolæ S. Pauli ad Romanos* (1625). See Jöcher, *Allgemeines Gelehrten-Lexikon*, s. v. (B. P.)

Güntherode, CARL VON, a Roman Catholic theologian of Milan, was born in 1740. In 1779 he was professor of Church history at Innsbrück, but soon exchanged the academical chair for the monastery, a step which he regretted, because both the monastic life and the religious views of the monks were not in harmony with his intellectual powers. More pleasant was his position as librarian to prince Esterhazy, at Vienna.

He died in 1795, leaving, *Institutio Theologiæ Naturalis* (1774):—*Diss. de Criteriis Veri et Falsi* (eod.):—*De Supremata Concilii Generalis supra Romanorum Pontificum* (1777). See Döring, *Die gelehrten Theologen Deutschlands*, s. v. (B. P.)

Güntner, Gabriel Johann Bernhard, a Premonstratensian, was born in 1804 in Bohemia, received holy orders in 1830, was in 1838 professor of exegesis at Prague, and died March 17, 1867. He wrote, *Hermeneutica Biblica Generalis Juxta Principia Catholica* (Prague, 1848; 2d ed. 1851; 3d ed. 1863):—*Introductio in Sacros Novi Testamenti Libros Histor.-Critica et Apologetica* (ibid. 1863, 2 vols.). (B. P.)

Günzburg, Aaron, a Jewish rabbi, was born at Prague in 1812. He received his rabbinical as well as classical education at his native place, and was appointed rabbi of the congregation of Libachowitz, in Bohemia. In 1846 he published, *Dogmatisch-historische Beleuchtung des alten Judenthums* (Prague), in which he boldly demanded the emancipation of the Jews, and grounded his demand on the words and promises of former Austrian emperors. In consequence of this publication he was obliged to leave his country, and came to America. He was elected rabbi at Baltimore, then at Rochester, N. Y., and last in Boston, where he died, July 19, 1873. See Fürst, *Bibl. Jud.* i, 348. (B. P.)

Gurley, Leonard B., D.D., a Methodist Episcopal minister, was born at Norwich, Conn., March 10, 1804. He moved to Ohio in youth, was converted, received into the Ohio Conference in 1828, was three years on circuits, thirteen on districts, two in agency of Ohio Wesleyan University, twenty-eight in stations, and six in retirement. He was elected to the general conferences of 1848, 1856, and 1864, and died at Delaware, O., March 26, 1880. Dr. Gurley was genial, generous, and sympathetic. He was a strong advocate of temperance, wrote and spoke for the abolition of slavery, and gave $3000 to Ohio Wesleyan University and $10,000 to the Board of Church Extension. His published poems exhibit high talent. See *Minutes of Annual Conferences*, 1880, p. 314.

Gurlitt, Johann Gottfried, a Lutheran theologian and philologist, was born at Leipsic, March 13, 1754. In 1802 he accepted a call to Hamburg as director of the Johanneum, and professor of Oriental languages at the academical gymnasium, and died June 14, 1827. Gurlitt was the teacher of the famous Church historian Neander. He wrote, *Explanatio Brevis Hymni 43 Davidis* (Hamburg, 1773):—*Kurze Geschichte des Tempelherrenordens* (1824). See Winer, *Handbuch der theol. Lit.* i, 228, 365, 375, 589, 679, 702, 722, 730; Fürst, *Bibl. Jud.* i, 348 sq. (B. P.)

Gurney, John Hampden, an English divine, son of Sir John Gurney, a baron of the exchequer, was born Aug. 15, 1802. He graduated at Trinity College, Cambridge, in 1824, was for some time curate of Lutterworth, Leicestershire, and in 1848 was presented by the crown with the rectory of St. Mary's, in Marylebone. He died March 3, 1862. Mr. Gurney was a most earnest and popular preacher, and among his published discourses are, *A Pastor's Warning*, suggested by the death of Sir Robert Peel (1850):—*The Lost Chief and a Mourning People*, on the death of the duke of Wellington (1852):—*The Grand Romish Fallacy, and Dangers and Duties of Protestants* (1854):—*Better Times and Worse* (1856), and several series of sermons. His lectures were published under the titles of, *Historical Sketches, Illustrating some Important Epochs from A.D.* 1400 *to A.D.* 1546:—*St. Louis and Henri IV*:—and *God's Heroes and the World's Heroes* (1858). Mr. Gurney was also the author of several psalm and hymn books, and of *Four Letters to the Bishop of Exeter on Scripture Readers*. See *Appleton's Annual Cyclopædia*, 1862, p. 685.

Gurney, Samuel, a distinguished member of the Society of Friends, and brother of Joseph John Gurney, was born at Eastham Hall, near Norwich, England, Oct. 18, 1786. His education closed when he was fourteen years of age, and he was apprenticed to a London banker and tea-merchant. He eventually became a partner in one of the most celebrated business firms of Lombard Street. Early in his active life he was associated with other distinguished philanthropists in efforts to improve the condition of English missions He was also the warm friend of the Bible Society and of the republic of Liberia. He was one of a deputation, representing four thousand merchants and tradesmen of London, sent to France, in 1853, in the interests of peace. He died in Paris, June 5, 1856. See *Memorials of Samuel Gurney*, by Mrs. Thomas Geldart (Philadelphia, 1859). (J. C. S.)

Güruth, Georg Samuel, a Lutheran theologian of Germany, was born Feb. 3, 1745, at Brieg, in Silesia. He studied at Königsberg, was in 1768 rector at Neustadt, in 1778 preacher at his native city, in 1792 pastor primarius at Krenzburg, and died Feb. 3, 1803. He published some ascetical writings. See Döring, *Die gelehrten Theologen Deutschlands*, s. v. (B. P.)

Gûrû, a teacher among the Hindûs, occupying in some degree the place of the *confessor* of the Middle Ages. He is looked upon as a representative and vehicle of divine power, and therefore entitled to the most implicit submission on the part of the man whose *gûrû* he is.

Gurwhal (or **Shreenagur**) is a dialect spoken in the province of Gurwhal, west of Kumaon. A translation of the New Test. was undertaken at Serampore in 1816, and was completed at press some time prior to 1832. (B. P.)

Gutbier, Ægidius, a German Orientalist, was born at Weissensee, in Thuringia, Sept. 1, 1617. He studied at different universities, was in 1652 professor of Oriental languages at Hamburg, took in 1660 his degree as doctor of theology at Giessen, and died Sept. 27, 1667. He published, *Novum Testamentum Syriacum*:—*Lexicon Syriacum*:—*Notæ Criticæ in Novum Testamentum Syriacum*:—*De Sibyllis et Earum Oraculis*. See Moller, *Cimbria Litterata*; Jöcher, *Allgemeines Gelehrten-Lexikon*, s. v. (B. P.)

Gutbier, Friedrich August Philip, a Lutheran theologian of Germany, was born in Thuringia, March 2, 1765, and died Feb. 5, 1838, superintendent and member of consistory. He published, *Summarien über das Neue Testament* (Leipsic, 1831-38, 4 vols.):—*Lehrbuch der christlichen Glaubens- und Sittenlehre* (Gotha, 1825):—*Liturgisches Handbuch zum Gebrauch für Prediger* (Leipsic, 1805). See Winer, *Handbuch der theol. Lit.* ii, 189, 215, 280; Zuchold, *Bibl. Theol.* i, 480 sq. (B. P.)

Güte, Heinrich Ernest, a Lutheran theologian of Germany, was born Sept. 13, 1754, at Bielefeld. He studied at Halle, was preacher there in 1779, magister in 1780, professor of theology in 1791, and died Dec. 6, 1805. He wrote, *De Factis Ejus Diei, quo Christus e Mortuis Resurrexit* (Halle, 1780):—*Anfangsgründe der hebräischen Sprache* (ibid. 1782; 2d ed. 1791):—*Entwurf zur Einleitung in's Alte Testament* (ibid. 1787):—*Kurze Uebersicht der vorzüglichsten Materien*, etc. (ibid. 1804). See Döring, *Die gelehrten Theologen Deutschlands*, s. v.; Winer, *Handbuch der theol. Lit.* i, 81; Fürst, *Bibl. Jud.* i, 349. (B. P.)

Gutelius, Samuel, a most estimable minister of the German Reformed Church, was born in Lancaster County, Pa. He studied under the Rev. Yost Henry Fries, was licensed and ordained in 1822, and immediately took charge of some congregations in Northumberland County. After laboring successfully in different charges, he died, July 17, 1866. "Strict honesty and integrity were leading and marked features in his life and character." Father Gutelius was a great sufferer, but his sufferings never interfered with his duties.

"He was an indefatigable worker, and a solid preacher. His sermons were always well prepared. He pleaded with his hearers like a man who expected to meet them at the bar of God. Indeed, he often reminded them of that meeting. He took a deep interest in all the benevolent operations of the Church, and was for a time connected with the publication of its periodicals. His ministry was characterized by great earnestness and success." See Harbaugh, *Fathers of the Ref. Church*, iv, 190. (D. Y. H.)

Guthrie (or **Guthry**), **Henry**, bishop of Dunkeld about 1664, died in 1676. He published *Memoirs, temp. Charles I* (Lond. 1702). See Allibone, *Dict. of Brit. and Amer. Authors*, s. v.

Guthrie, John (1), a Scotch prelate, was promoted to the see of Moray from Edinburgh, in 1623, where he continued until he was deprived with the other prelates by the Glasgow Assembly in 1638. He then lived at Spynie castle till 1640, when he was forced to surrender it to colonel Monroe, after which he retired to his own private castle of Guthrie, in the county of Angus. He died not long afterwards. See Keith, *Scottish Bishops*, p. 152.

Guthrie, John (2), D.D., an English Congregational minister, was born at Milnathort, Kinrossshire, Jan. 30, 1814. He was kept in the Church from infancy through the care of pious parents; entered Edinburgh University at the age of seventeen, where he took the degree of M.A., distinguishing himself in classics and philosophy; and in 1839 was ordained pastor of the Secession Church at Kendal. Shortly afterwards he was excommunicated from that Church for maintaining the universality of Christ's atonement. He then, with others, formed the Evangelical Union, became the professor in the Theological Hall of the new body, and held the office from 1846 to 1861. From 1848 to 1851 he held the pastorate in Glasgow, whence he removed to Greenock, where he labored successfully for eleven years. Thence he went to Tolmers Square, London, but returned to Glasgow, where he assumed the pastorate of a new church, and filled the chair of apologetics in the Theological Hall of the Evangelical Union. He died in London, Sept. 8, 1878. See (Lond.) *Cong. Year-book*, 1879, p. 316.

Guthrie, Thomas, D.D., an eminent Scottish pulpit orator, philanthropist, and social reformer, was born July 12, 1803, at Brechin, Forfarshire, where his father was a merchant and banker. He went through the curriculum of study prescribed by the Church of Scotland to candidates for the ministry, at the University of Edinburgh, and devoted two additional winters to the study of chemistry, natural history, and anatomy. Meanwhile he was licensed to preach by the Presbytery of Brechin in 1825; subsequently spent six months in Paris, studying the physical sciences. In 1830 he became pastor of the Church at Arbirlot, in his native county, and in 1837 was appointed one of the ministers of Old Greyfriars parish, in Edinburgh. Here his eloquence, combined with devoted labors to reclaim the degraded population of one of the worst districts of the city, soon won for him a high place in public estimation. In 1843 he joined the Free Church, and for a long series of years continued to minister to a large and influential congregation in Edinburgh. In 1845 and 1846 he performed a great service for the Free Church by his advocacy throughout the country of its scheme for providing manses or residences for its ministers. His zeal was not diverted in mere denominational or sectarian channels. He came forward in 1847 as the advocate of ragged schools, and to him the rapid extension of the system over the kingdom is very much to be ascribed. He also earnestly exerted himself in many ways in opposition to intemperance and other vices. He possessed great rhetorical talent, and his style was remarkable for the abundance and variety of the illustrations he used. Few public speakers have ever blended solemnity and deep pathos so intimately with the humorous, his tendency to which has more frequently than anything else been pointed out as his fault. Dr. Guthrie always displayed a generous sympathy with all that tended to progress or improvement of any kind. He was moderator of the General Assembly of the Free Church of Scotland in May, 1862, and died near Edinburgh, Feb. 23, 1873. His most important published works are, *The Gospel in Ezekiel*, a series of discourses:—*The Way of Life*, a volume of sermons:—*A Plea for Drunkards and against Drunkenness*:—*A Plea for Ragged Schools*, followed by a second and a third plea, the latter under the title, *Seed-time and Harvest of Ragged Schools*:—*The City, its Sins and Sorrows*:—*A Sufficient Maintenance and an Efficient Ministry* (Edinburgh, 1852, 8vo). He edited a new edition of Berridge's *Christian World Unmasked* (ibid. 1856, 8vo). For some years before his death he acted as editor of *The Sunday Magazine*, founded in 1864, in which year he retired from his regular ministrations. His *Autobiography and Memoir* was published by his sons (1873), and his *Works* (1873-76, 11 vols.). See also *Popular Preachers*, p. 33; Smith, *Our Scottish Clergy* (Edinb. 1848), p. 342; (Lond.) *Evangelical Magazine*, February, 1874; Allibone, *Dict. of Brit. and Amer. Authors*, s. v. (W. P. S.)

Guy. See Gui.

Guy, Thomas, an English philanthropist, founder of Guy's Hospital, was born at Southwark in 1644. After serving an apprenticeship of eight years, he began business as a bookseller in 1668. He dealt largely in Bibles, which he at first imported from Holland, but afterwards printed for himself. He became master of an immense fortune, and died unmarried, Dec. 17, 1724. In 1707 he built three wards of St. Thomas's Hospital, and aided it in other ways. He built Guy's Hospital at a cost of over £18,000, and left an endowment of £219,499. He also made other gifts and bequests for hospitals and almshouses. See *A True Copy of the Last Will and Testament of Thomas Guy, Esq.* (Lond. 1725); Knight, *Shadows of the Old Booksellers* (1865), p. 323; *Encyclop. Brit.* 9th ed. s. v.

Guyard, Bernard, a French Dominican, was born in 1601, and died at Paris, July 30, 1674, a doctor of theology and provincial of his order. He wrote, *La Vie de S. Vinc. Ferrier*:—*Discrimina inter Doctrinam Thomisticam et Jansenianam*:—*La Nouvelle Apparition de Luther et de Calvin*. See Échard, *De Scriptoribus Ordinis Dominicanorum*; Jöcher, *Allgemeines Gelehrten-Lexikon*, s. v.; Hoefer, *Nouv. Biog. Générale*, s. v. (B. P.)

Guyet, Charles, a French Jesuit, was born at Tours in 1601, taught theology fifteen years, afterwards became a preacher, and died in the same city, March 30, 1664. He is the author of *De Festis Propriis Locorum et Ecclesiarum*, etc. (Paris, 1657 fol.). See Winer, *Handbuch der theol. Lit.* i, 616 sq.; Jöcher, *Allgemeines Gelehrten-Lexikon*, s. v.; Alegambe, *Bibliotheca Scriptorum Societatis Jesu*; Bayle, *Dictionnaire Historique Critique*; Hoefer, *Nouv. Biog. Générale*, s. v. (B. P.)

Guyon, Claude Marie, a French abbot, who was born in 1701, and died at Paris in 1771, is the author of, *Histoire des Empires et des Républiques* (Paris, 1733, 12 vols.):—*Oracle de Nouveaux Philosophes* (2 vols.; against Voltaire):—*Apologie des Jésuites* (1762):—*Bibliothèque Ecclésiastique en Forme d'Instructions sur Toute la Religion* (1772, 8 vols.). See *Nouv. Dict. Hist.*; Jöcher, *Allgemeines Gelehrten-Lexikon*, s. v. (B. P.)

Guyon, Symphorien, a priest at St. Victor, in Orleans, who flourished in the 17th century, is the author of, *Notitia Sanctorum Ecclesiæ Aurelianensis* (1637), which was again published in French in 1647 under the title, *Histoire de l'Église et Diocèse, Ville et Université d'Orleans*. See Winer, *Handbuch der theol. Lit.* i, 822; Le Long, *Bibliothèque Historique de France*; Jöcher, *Allgemeines Gelehrten-Lexikon*, s. v. (B. P.)

Guzman, Ludovico, provincial of the Jesuits in Seville and Toledo, was born at Osorno, in Castile, in 1554, and died at Madrid, Jan. 10, 1605. He published *Hist. de las Missiones en la India Oriental* (Alcala, 1601 fol.). See Alegambe, *Bibliotheca Scriptorum Societatis Jesu;* Antonii *Bibliotheca Hispanica;* Jöcher, *Allgemeines Gelehrten-Lexikon*, s. v.; Winer, *Handbuch der theol. Lit.* i, 841. (B. P.)

Gyöngyösi (*di Peteny*), Paulus, a Hungarian Reformed theologian, was born in 1668. He studied in England and at Franeker, and took the degree of doctor of theology at the latter place in 1700. Having returned to his country, he was pastor of the Reformed congregation at Kaschau, but he had to leave that place in 1724, and went to Frankfort-on-the-Oder, where he was appointed professor of theology. He died there in 1743, leaving, *De Fatis Sexta Novi Testamenti Ætate* (Franeker, 1700):—*Disp. Duæ in μνημονευτικόν Amoris Christi et Christianorum* (ibid. 1700):—*Altare Pacis, pro Votis Vienicis Erectum; Aræ Pilati Galilæorum Substituendem* (Basle, 1722), written against the bishop of Agran and the Jesuit Timon, who wrote against the Protestants; the publication of this work was the cause of his leaving the country:—*De Reverentia Templorum Novi Test.* (Frankfort, 1731):—*De Mora Dei* (1733):—*Speculum* Ἐλευθερίας (1734):—*De Lapidibus Samariæ* (1736):—*De Glorificatione Christi* (1738), etc. See Moser, *Jetztlebende Theologen;* Dunkel, *Nachrichten*, iii, 725; Horanyi, *Mem. Hung.;* Jöcher, *Allgemeines Gelehrten-Lexikon*, s. v. (B. P.)

Gypcer (or **Gypsyre**, Fr. *gibecière*), (1) the mediæval term for a hanging bag; (2) a pouch or flat burse or purse, with a mouth or opening of metal, strung to the girdle, often represented in English monumental brasses.

H.

Haab, Philip Heinrich, a Lutheran theologian of Germany, was born at Stuttgart, Oct. 9, 1758, and died pastor at Schweigern, Würtemberg, in 1833. He is the author of, *Hebräische Griechische Grammatik zum Gebrauch für das Neue Testament* (Tübingen, 1815):—*Religionsunterricht durch Bibelgeschichte* (1818, 2 parts):—*Betrachtungen über die Leidensgeschichte Jesu Christi nach dem Bericht der 4 Evangelien* (Heilbronn, 1830). See Winer, *Handbuch der theol. Lit.* i, 126; ii, 254, 403; Zuchold, *Bibl. Theol.* i, 482. (B. P.)

Haag, Georg Friedrich, a Lutheran minister of Germany, who died March 19, 1875, is the author of, *Christliches Lehrbüchlein oder evangel. Katechumenen Unterricht* (Heidelberg, 1842):—*Christliches Hausbüchlein* (3d ed. 1861):—*Biblische Geschichten* (1855):—*Evangelisches Hausbuch* (eod.):—*Zeugnisse aus der lutherischen Kirche* (1861). See Zuchold, *Bibl. Theol.* i, 482. (B. P.)

Haak, Theodore, an English divine and natural philosopher, was born in 1605 at Neuhausen, near Worms, in Germany, and was educated partly in his native country, and finally at Oxford and Cambridge. He then visited some of the Continental universities, and returned to Oxford in 1629, but without taking a degree was ordained, in 1632, deacon to bishop Hall of Exeter. He gave himself up to literary pursuits, and was devoted to the interests of parliament during the rebellion. He died in London, May 9, 1690. He published the *Dutch Annotations on the Bible* (1657, 2 vols. fol.); was employed by the Westminster Assembly, and translated into Dutch several theological works. He seems to have been the first to propose the Royal Society. Some of his letters appeared in the *Philosophical Collections* (May, 1682).

Haar, in Norse mythology, was a dwarf, made of and living in stones.

Haas, Carl, a German convert to the Church of Rome, was born Oct. 18, 1804. He studied theology at Tübingen, and became a Protestant minister. In 1843 he was dismissed from the ministry, having the year before published *Die Glaubensgegensätze des Protestantismus und Katholicismus.* He joined the Church of Rome at Augsburg, in 1844, and published on that occasion *Offenes Sendschreiben an seine liebe Gemeinde*, etc., and *Protestantismus und Katholicismus.* He now set himself to write in the interest of the Church of Rome, and published *Josephs und Konrads Feierstunden* (Augsburg, 1845):—*Populäre Kirchengeschichte, mit besonderer Berücksichtigung der Reformationsgeschichte* (2d ed. 1846):—*Beleuchtung grosser Vorurtheile gegen die Katholische Kirche* (1857):—*Geschichte der Päpste* (1860):—*Die zwei Hauptfeinde des Christenthums* (1866):—*Natur und Gnade* (1867). After the Vatican council, Haas renounced again the Church of Rome, without returning to the Evangelical Church, and to justify himself, he published *Nach Rom und von Rom zurück nach Wittenberg* (Barmen, 1882). In 1881 he published *Der ungefälschte Luther nach den Urdrucken der königl. öffentl. Bibliothek in Stuttgart hergestellt.* Haas died Dec. 21, 1883. See Zuchold, *Bibl. Theol.* i, 484. (B. P.)

Haas, Carl Franz Lubert, a Reformed theologian of Germany, was born Aug. 12, 1722, at Cassel. He studied at Marburg, commenced his academical career there in 1748, was professor in 1754, and died Oct. 29, 1789. He wrote, *Diss. Historica de Meritis Philippi Magnanimi in Reformationem* (Marburg, 1742):—*De Eutichianismo et Variis Ejus Sectis* (ibid. 1746):—*Versuch einer Hessischen Kirchengeschichte* (ibid. 1782). See Döring, *Die gelehrten Theologen Deutschlands*, s. v.; Winer, *Handbuch der theol. Lit.* i, 793. (B. P.)

Haas, Nikolaus, a Lutheran theologian of Germany, was born Nov. 25, 1665. He studied at Altdorf and Leipsic, was pastor in 1686, and died July 26, 1715, leaving, *De Principiorum Moralium Existentia, Definitione et Divisione* (1683):—*De Astrologia Judiciaria* (1685):—*Heilige Unterredungen mit Gott* (1689):—*Enchiridion Catechismi Lutheri contra Papistas* (1703), besides a number of ascetical works. See Döring, *Die gelehrten Theologen Deutschlands*, s. v.; Winer, *Handbuch der theol. Lit.* i, 166; Jöcher, *Allgemeines Gelehrten-Lexikon*, s. v. (B. P.)

Habadim (or rather *Chabadim*), a subdivision of the Jewish sect of Chasidim, founded by rabbi Solomon, in the government of Mohilef, in the 18th century. The name is composed of the initial letters of the three Hebrew words, חכמה, בינה, דעת, "wisdom, intelligence, and knowledge." They may not improperly be termed the "Jewish Quietists," as their peculiarity consists in the rejection of external forms and the complete abandonment of the mind to abstraction and contemplation. Instead of the baptisms customary among the Jews, they go through the signs without the use of the element, and consider it their duty to disengage themselves as much as possible from matter, because of its tendency to clog the mind in its ascent to the supreme source of intelligence. In prayer they make no use of words, but simply place themselves in the attitude of supplication, and exercise themselves in mental ejaculations.

Habakkuk, the Hebrew prophet, is commemorated in the old Roman martyrologies on Jan. 15.

Habdalâh (הַבְדָּלָה, *distinction*), a ceremony by which the Jewish Sabbath is divided or separated from the other days of the week. It is performed after the concluding service in the synagogue, by reciting passages of Scripture and prayers, and the use of wine and spices. On Sabbath evening four benedictions are said, one over the wine, a second over the spice, the third over the light, "Blessed art thou Lord our God, king of the world, who hast created a shining light," and the last is, "Blessed art thou, Lord our God, king of the universe, who hast made a distinction (הַמַּבְדִּיל) between the holy and the common, between light and darkness, between Israel and the other nations, between the seventh day and the other six days of work; blessed be thou, O God, who hast made a distinction between the holy and the common." If for any reason a Jew is prevented from performing this ceremony, either at home or abroad, he is at liberty to substitute the following short benediction: "Blessed is he who has made a distinction between things sacred and profane." See Buxtorf, *Lex. Chald. Tal.* s. v. (B. P.)

Häberlin, GEORG HEINRICH, a Lutheran theologian of Germany, was born at Stuttgart, Sept. 30, 1644. He studied at Tübingen, became deacon in 1668, doctor and professor of theology in 1681, member of consistory and preacher in 1692, and died Aug. 20, 1699, leaving, *Specimen Theologiæ Practicæ:—Conspectus Locorum Theologicorum:—Theologia Corinthiaca in Forma Systematis Proposita:—De Principio Fidei:—De Unione Fidelium cum Christo:—De Justificatione Hominis Coram Deo:—De Satisfactione Christi:—De Chiliasmo Hodierno, Fidei Christianæ Ruina et Infidelitatis Judaicæ Firmamento*, etc. See Fischlin, *Memoria Theologorum Würtembergensium;* Jöcher, *Allgemeines Gelehrten-Lexikon*, s. v. (B. P.)

Habert, LOUIS, a French theologian and doctor of the Sorbonne, was born at Blois in 1638, and died at Paris, April 17, 1718. He is the author of, *Pratique du Sacrement de Pénitence* (Paris, 1714, 1729), better known as the *Pratique de Verdun.* He also wrote *Theologia Dogmatica et Moralis ad Usum Seminarii Catalaunensis* (Lyons, 1709-12, 7 vols.), which was attacked and condemned by Fénélon. Being opposed to the bull *Unigenitus*, Habert was exiled in 1714, and only returned to Paris after the death of Louis XIV. See Lichtenberger, *Encyclop. des Sciences Religieuses*, s. v.; Agricola, *Bibl. Eccles.* iii, 212; Jöcher, *Allgemeines Gelehrten-Lexikon*, s. v.; Hoefer, *Nouv. Biog. Générale*, s. v. (B. P.)

Habibus. See ABIBAS.

Habichhorst, ANDREAS DANIEL, a Lutheran theologian of Germany, who died at Greifswalde, Aug. 30, 1704, professor of theology, is the author of, *Tractatus de Melchisedeci Historia et Figura:—Dissertationes Exegeticæ in Illustriora Iesaiæ Loca:—Breviarium Formulæ Concordiæ et Controversiarum Syncretistico-Pietisticarum:—Dissertationes de Altari Gideonis:—De Ephod Gideonis:—De Magistratus et Suppliciorum Capitalium Constitutione Divina:—De Sanctorum cum Christo Redivivorum Resurrectione:—De Abrahamo Sola Fide Justificato:—De Iesaia Trinitatis Præcone.* See Pipping, *Memoriæ Theologorum;* Jöcher, *Allgemeines Gelehrten-Lexikon*, s. v. (B. P.)

Habitacle (Lat. *habitaculum*) (1) a residence; (2) a niche.

Hachilah, HILL OF. Lieut. Conder suggests for this spot (*Quar. Statement* of the "Palest. Explor. Fund," January, 1875, p. 47) "the high hill bounded by deep valleys north and south on which the ruin of *Yekin* now stands," and Tristram (*Bible Lands*, p. 63) coincides in this identification; but if this be the site of the ancient city *Cain* (q. v.), it can hardly be also that of Hachilah; and, in fact, the latter is not a proper name at all, as it invariably has the article (הַחֲכִילָה, as being a mere appendage of Ziph). Later, Lieut. Conder proposes another site (*Tent Work*, ii, 91): "This [hill] I would propose to recognise in the long ridge called *El-Kôlah*, running out of the Ziph plateau towards the Dead Sea desert or Jeshimon, a district which, properly speaking, terminates about this line, melting into the Beersheba plains. On the north side of the hill are the 'Caves of the Dreamers,' perhaps the actual scene of David's descent on Saul's sleeping guards." As to the "wood (*choresh*) of Ziph," he remarks (p. 89): "A moment's reflection will convince any traveller that as the dry, porous formation of the plateau must be unchanged since David's time, no wood of trees could then have flourished over this unwatered and sun-scorched region. The true explanation seems to be that the word choresh is a proper name with a different signification, and such is the view of the Greek version and of Josephus. We were able considerably to strengthen this theory by the discovery of the ruin of Khoreisa and the valley of Hiresh (the same word under another form), close to Ziph, the first of which may well be thought to represent the Hebrew Choresh-Ziph." But the latter term likewise is a mere denominative, for it takes the article (הַחֹרְשָׁה, 1 Sam. xxiii, 15, 18), and is elsewhere used plainly with reference to trees (Isa. xvii, 9; Ezek. xxxi, 3).

Hacke, NICHOLAS P., D.D., a German Reformed minister, was born in Baltimore, Md., Sept. 20, 1800. At the age of six years he was sent to a relative in Bremen, Germany, to acquire a thorough knowledge of the German language. He returned to America in 1816, and studied theology privately until 1819, when he accepted an invitation to preach to some congregations in Westmoreland County, Pa., returning to his studies the same year. He was licensed and ordained in 1819, and became pastor of the Greensburg charge, which he served fifty-eight years, and died there, Aug. 25, 1878. During the greater part of his ministry he preached exclusively in the German language. He was a student all his life, and used the English language with ease and grace. He was fully consecrated to his work, remarkable for his social powers, caring not for worldly honors, a model Christian gentleman, and faithful minister of the gospel. See Harbaugh, *Fathers of the Germ. Ref. Church*, v, 300.

Hacker, Joachim Bernhard Nikolaus, a Protestant theologian of Germany, was born Nov. 11, 1760, at Dresden. He studied at Wittenberg, and died at Zscheyla, in Saxony, Oct. 4, 1817, leaving some ascetical works, for which see Döring, *Deutsche Kanzelredner;* Winer, *Handbuch der theol. Lit.* ii, 356, 386. (B. P.)

Hacker, Johann Georg August, a Protestant theologian of Germany, was born at Dresden, Jan. 24, 1762. He studied at Wittenberg, was in 1784 preacher at Torgau, in 1790 garrison-preacher at Dresden, in 1796 court-preacher there, and died Feb. 21, 1823, leaving *Diss. Inauguralis de Descensu Christi ad Inferos* (Wittenberg, 1802), and several volumes of sermons. See Döring, *Deutsche Kanzelredner;* Winer, *Handbuch der theol. Lit.* i, 436; ii, 82, 91, 127, 161, 172, 173, 183, 366, 389. (B. P.)

Hackett, Horatio Balch, D.D., LL.D., an eminent Baptist scholar, was born at Salisbury, Mass., Dec. 27, 1808. In 1823 he entered Phillips Academy, Andover, and in 1827 Amherst College; became a hopeful Christian in 1828, and was valedictorian in 1830. He graduated from the theological seminary at Andover in 1834, spending one year meanwhile as tutor in Amherst College. The next year he occupied a position as teacher of classics in Mount Hope College, Baltimore, and became a member of the First Baptist Church in that city. He was adjunct professor of Latin and Greek in Brown University for four years (1835-39). In 1839 he was elected professor of Biblical Literature and Interpretation in Newton Theological Institution, and the same year was ordained to the Christian ministry. Two years of earnest devotion to the cultivation of the classes which came under his instruction were followed by a year spent abroad, six months of the time in earnest study in Halle, Germany, attending the lectures of Tholuck, Gesenius, Rödiger, and other eminent scholars, and four months in Berlin, enjoying the instructions, especially, of Neander and Hengstenberg. After his return to America, in 1842, he prepared an annotated edition of Plutarch's treatise on the *Delay of the Deity in the Punishment of the Wicked*, devoting also much time to the study of French, Chaldee, and Syriac, modern Greek, and Sanscrit. Two years afterwards he published a translation of *Winer's Grammar of the Chaldee Language.* The first number of the second volume of the *Bibliotheca Sacra*, January, 1845, contains his critique on the *Life of Jesus*, by Strauss. In the number of the same quarterly for January, 1846, is an able article on the *Synoptical Study of the Gospels, and Recent Literature Pertaining to it.* The next year (1847) appeared his *Exercises in Hebrew Grammar, and Selections from the Greek Scriptures to be Translated into Hebrew*, etc. The result of some of his studies in connection with the preparation of this volume may be found in the January (1847) number of the *Bibliotheca Sacra*, in the form of two articles from his pen, *The Structure of the Hebrew Sentence*, and *The Greek Version of the Pentateuch*, by Thiersch. Then came his great work, the *Commentary on Acts*, the first edition of which appeared in 1852. He then made a second visit to Europe, his journey being extended to Palestine, and on his return spending several weeks in Germany. In 1855 he published his *Illustrations of Scripture; Suggested by a Tour through the Holy Land.* Soon after, he set out upon his third foreign tour, spending six months in Athens, for the purpose of devoting himself to the study of modern Greek, and thence making excursions in different directions in Greece. In 1860 the Bible Union published his *Notes on the Greek Text of the Epistle of Paul to Philemon*, as the basis of a revision of the common English version; and a *Revised Version, with Notes.* In 1864 appeared his *Christian Memorials of the War.* During the same period he wrote thirty articles for the original edition of Dr. William Smith's *Dictionary.* In 1861 he wrote an introduction to the American edition of Westcott's *Study of the Gospels*; in the winter of 1865 he began to edit an American edition of Smith's *Dictionary of the Bible*, aided by Dr. Ezra Abbot. He was also engaged by Dr. Schaff to translate Van Oosterzee's *Commentary on Philemon*, for his edition of Lange's *Commentaries*, and Brauné's *Commentary on Philippians*, for the same series. He published in 1867 a second revised edition of *Plutarchus de Sera Numinis Veri Dicta*, with notes prepared by himself and professor W. S. Tyler, of Amherst College. Professor Hackett's connection with the Newton Theological Institution closed with its anniversary, June 24, 1868. Two years were next spent in laborious study in his favorite department, translating and revising the books of Ruth and of Judges for the Bible Union, upon the American edition of Smith's *Dictionary of the Bible*, and upon translations which he engaged to make for Dr. Schaff; also, in 1870, spending several months, once more, in the Old World. Having been appointed to the chair of Biblical Literature and New Testament Exegesis, in the Rochester Theological Seminary, he entered upon the duties of his office in the fall of 1870. The same zeal and enthusiasm which characterized his instructions at Newton marked his teachings at Rochester. Five years of work were followed by another of those vacations in which he took so much delight, a vacation passed amid the scenes of the Old World. He returned, apparently greatly refreshed and strengthened, to enter anew upon his work, when the summons suddenly came, telling him that his work was done. He died almost instantly, Nov. 2, 1875, at his own home in Rochester, N. Y. See *Memorials of H. B. Hackett*, edited by G. H. Whittemore (Rochester, 1876). (J. C. S.)

Hackett, Thomas, D.D., an Irish prelate, was bishop of Down and Connor in 1672. He was deprived for simony in 1694. He published some *Sermons* (1672). See Allibone, *Dict. of Brit. and Amer. Authors*, s. v.

Hackluit. See HAKLUYT.

Hadarniel, in the Talmud, is an angel of the heaven of fixed stars, and commander of fire; therefore more than twelve thousand flashes of lightning come from his mouth at every word he utters. He would not allow Moses to wander through the air, when the latter came, at the command of God, to receive the law. God chided him, therefore he offered his services, to go before Moses, and announce his words.

Hadassi, JEHUDA, a learned Karaite Jew, was born towards the end of the 11th century, at Jerusalem, and died between 1150 and 1160. He is the author of a great work, bearing upon the literature of the Karaite Jews, entitled, אֶשְׁכֹּל הַכֹּפֶר, also סֵפֶר הַפְּלַס, first published at Koslov, 1836. See Fürst, *Bibl. Jud.* i, 353; *Geschichte der Karäer*, ii, 211 sq.; De' Rossi, *Dizionario Storico* (Germ. transl.), p. 120. (B. P.)

Hadelin (Lat. *Hadalinus*), *Saint*, priest and confessor, who died about 690, was one of the disciples of St. Remacle, and when that saint resigned his bishopric of Fougères, that he might retire into the peaceful monastery of Stanislawow, lately founded by St. Sigebert, king of Austrasia, he took with him the pious Hadelin. Remacle sent Hadelin into Dinant, on the Meuse, in 669, and finding a quiet retreat at Celles, on the Lesse, he dwelt there in a cave, and built a little chapel, on the site of which afterwards rose a collegiate church. St. Hadelin is the patron of five churches in the diocese of Liege and Namur. His hermitage still exists, and has never been without a pious successor. The body of this saint was buried there, but was translated to Vise, in the diocese of Liege, in 1338. He is mentioned in the martyrologies of Ado, Wyon, Menardus, those of Liege, Cologne, etc. There are two ancient lives, one by Notker, bishop of Liege (971–1007). See Baring-Gould, *Lives of the Saints* (sub. Feb. 3, his day), ii, 49.

Hadeloga (or **Adaloga**), *Saint*, commemorated Feb. 2, is said to have been the first abbess of the nunnery of Kissingen, and a daughter of Charles Martel, in the 8th century.

Hadid. The modern site, *Hadithek*, is laid down on the *Ordnance Map* as three miles east of Ludd, and is described in the accompanying *Memoirs* (ii, 297; comp. p. 322) as "a moderate-sized village on a terraced tell at the mouth of a valley at the foot of the hills, with a well to the east. There are remains of a considerable town round it; tombs and quarries exist; and the mound on which the village stands is covered with pottery."

Hadith, a name given by Mohammedans to the sayings of Mohammed, which were handed down by oral tradition from one generation to another. There are said to be six authors of these traditions, among whom are Ayesha, the wife of the prophet; Abu-Horeira, his intimate friend; and Ibn-Abbas, his cousin-german. The collection of these traditions made by Khuarezmi numbers 5266 sayings, all of which the devout Mohammedan ought to commit to memory, or, where that cannot be done, to transcribe them.

Hadria. See ADRIA.

Hadrian. See ADRIAN.

Hâdshi-Khalfa (originally MUSTAFA *ben-Abdallah*, also known by the name of *Katib-Tshelebi*), a most celebrated Turkish historian, geographer, and biographer, was born at Constantinople about 1605. He was for some time secretary to the sultan, Murad IV, and died in 1658. His main production is a great biographical lexicon, *Keshful-funûn*, written in Arabic, in which he gives the titles of more than 18,000 Arabic, Persian, and Turkish works, with short biographies of the authors. It is of the greatest value, since it enumerates a great many others which seem to have been lost. Hammer-Purgstall largely used this work for his *Encyklopädische Uebersicht der Wissenschaften des Orients* (Leipsic, 1806). A complete edition of Hâdshi's text, with a Latin translation, was published by Flügel, *Lexicon Bibliographicum et Encyclopædicum* (Lond. 1835–58, 7 vols.). Hâdshi also published chronological tables, *Takwim-al-tawarikh* (translated into

Latin by Reiske, Leipsic, 1766), and a geography, *Dschihân-numâ* (Latin transl. by Norberg, Lund, 1818, 2 vols.). (B. P.)

Hadwinus, *Saint.* See CHADORNUS.

Hæmaterius. See CHELIDONIUS.

Hænir, in Norse mythology. When the Wanes and Asas, after a long war, agreed on an armistice, they exchanged hostages. The Asas got the Wane Niord, the Wanes the Asa Hænir, who was very beautiful, but had no mental gifts, and soon the Wanes ceased to respect him. Both hostages remain in the power of their enemies until the destruction of the world, when they will return to their kindred.

Haer, FRANCISCUS VAN DER, a theologian and historian of Utrecht, who died at Louvain, Jan. 12, 1632, is the author of, *Catena Aurea in IV Evangelia:—Concordia Historiæ Sacræ et Profanæ* (1614):—*Jesus Nazarenus Messias Danielis:—Biblia Sacra Vulgata:—Expositio in Epistolas Pauli:—De Sacramentis.* See Burmann, *Trajectum Eruditum;* Jöcher, *Allgemeines Gelehrten-Lexikon,* s. v. (B. P.)

Hafedah, an idol of the Adites, a tribe of Arabians who inhabited the country of Hadhramaut, in Yemen, or Arabia Felix. It was principally invoked for prosperity in travelling.

Häfeli, JOHANN CASPAR, a Protestant theologian, was born May 1, 1754, in Switzerland. He studied at Zurich, was vicar in 1773, in 1784 chaplain to the prince of Dessau, in 1793 preacher at Bremen, in 1802 professor at the gymnasium there, in 1805 superintendent at Bernburg, and died April 4, 1811. He is the author of some ascetical works. See Döring, *Deutsche Kanzelredner;* Winer, *Handbuch der theol. Lit.* ii, 47, 157, 168, 201, 204, 312. (B. P.)

Hafen, JOHANN BAPTIST, a Roman Catholic theologian, who died June 27, 1870, is the author of, *Strengkirchlichkeit und Liberalismus in der Kathol. Kirche* (Ulm, 1842):—*Behandlung der Ehesachen im Bisthum Rottenburg* (1867):—*Predigten* (1865, 3 vols.). (B. P.)

Haferung, JOHANN CASPAR, a Lutheran theologian of Germany, was born Feb. 14, 1669. He studied at Wittenberg, and died there May 17, 1744, doctor and professor of theology. He wrote, *De Defectibus Afflictionum Christi a Paulo Supplendis:—De Bileamo Incantatore et Propheta Periodica:—De Causis cur Christus Morte Crucis Voluerit Mori:—De Sanguine Jesu Christi:—De Mysterio Trinitatis, in Libris Apocryphis Obvio,* etc. See Moser, *Lexicon jetztlebender Theologen;* Freher, *Theatrum Eruditorum;* Neubauer, *Nachricht von den jetztlebenden Gottesgelehrten;* Jöcher, *Allgemeines Gelehrten-Lexikon,* s. v. (B. P.)

Hafizi (*keepers*), a name given to Mohammedans who commit the entire Koran to memory, and are on that account regarded as holy men, intrusted with God's law.

Haftorang, in Persian mythology, is the god and ruler of the planet Mars, the light-giver and health-restorer. As he is the protector of the northern region and its stars, he may be the seventh constellation, because Hafti denotes *seven.*

Hagemann, Lorenz, a Lutheran theologian of Germany, was born at Wolfenbüttel, Aug. 10, 1692. He studied at Jena, was preacher in 1719 at Bodenburg, in 1722 at Nordhausen, in 1728 at Hanover, in 1748 general superintendent, and died in 1752. He wrote *An Homerus Fuerit Philosophus Moralis?* (Jena, 1712), besides a number of ascetical works. See Döring, *Die gelehrten Theologen Deutschlands,* s. v.; Jöcher, *Allgemeines Gelehrten-Lexikon,* s. v. (B. P.)

Hagemann, Johann Georg, a Lutheran theologian of Germany, who died at Blankenburg in 1765, a superintendent, wrote *Betrachtungen über die fünf Bücher Moses* (Brunswick, 1732-44):—*Von den vornehmsten Uebersetzungen der heiligen Schrift* (Quedlinburg, 1747). See Jöcher, *Allgemeines Gelehrten-Lexikon,* s. v. (B. P.)

Hagen, FRIEDRICH CASPAR, a Lutheran theologian of Germany, who died April 13, 1741, member of consistory, court-preacher, and superintendent at Bayreuth, is the author of, *De Conventu Snobacence* (Bayreuth, 1717):—*De Θηριομαχίᾳ Pauli* (Wittenberg, 1703; also found in *Thesaurus Novus Theol. Philol.* ii, 875 sq.):—*Memoriæ Philosophorum, Oratorum, Poetarum, Historicorum,* etc. (Bayreuth, 1710):—*Die Ausgabe einer deutschen Bibel Lutheri.* See Baumgarten, *Merkwürdige Bücher,* ix, 107; Winer, *Handbuch der theol. Lit.* i, 751; Jöcher, *Allgemeines Gelehrten-Lexikon,* s. v. (B. P.)

Hagenbach, KARL RUDOLF, a Swiss theologian, was born at Basle, March 4, 1801. Besides the university of his native place, he studied at Bonn and Berlin, and in these places received the instruction of Lücke, Schliermacher, and Neander. Having returned to Basle, he commenced his academical career by presenting *Observationes Historico-Hermeneuticæ circa Origenis Methodum Interpretandæ Scripturæ Sacræ* (1823), and six years later he was made professor ordinarius in the theological faculty. For fifty years he belonged to the Basle University, and exerted a wide influence, not only as a teacher, but also as a preacher. He died June 7, 1874. Hagenbach's first important work was *Encyklopädie und Methodologie der theol. Wissenschaften* (Leipsic, 1833; 11th ed. by Kautzsch, 1884; Engl. transl. by Crooks and Hurst, as vol. iii of *Library of Biblical and Theological Literature,* N. Y. 1884):—*Lehrbuch der Dogmengeschichte* (1840; 4th ed. 1867; Engl. transl. by Beech, Edinburgh, revised and enlarged by Dr. H. B. Smith, N. Y. 1861, 2 vols.; new ed. with preface by Plumptre, Edinburgh, 1880, 3 vols.):—*Grundzüge der Homiletik und Liturgik* (1863). His largest work is the *Kirchengeschichte von der ältesten Zeit bis zum 19. Jahrhundert* (Leipsic, 1869-72, 7 vols.; that part which treats of the 18th and 19th centuries has been translated into English by Dr. Hurst, N. Y. 1869, 2 vols.):—*Œcolampad und Myconius* (Elberfeld, 1859):—*Predigten* (9 vols.). Besides, he contributed to Herzog's *Encyklopædia* and other theological reviews. See Eppler, *Karl Rudolf Hagenbach* (Güterslohe, 1875); Plitt-Herzog, *Real-Encyklop.* s. v.; Lichtenberger, *Encyclop. des Sciences Religieuses,* s. v.; Zuchold, *Bibl. Theol.* i, 487 sq. (B. P.)

Hager, E. W., D.D., a Protestant Episcopal clergyman of the diocese of central New York, was a chaplain of the U. S. Navy. At one time he was rector of All-Saints' Church, Worcester, Mass., and subsequently of St. George's Church, Utica, N. Y. He died in Chicago, Ill., July 7, 1880. See Whittaker, *Almanac and Directory,* 1881.

Hagioscope, a word used by English ecclesiastical writers to describe openings made through different parts of the interior walls of the church, generally on either side of the chancel arch, so as to afford a view of the altar to those worshipping in the aisles.

Hagiosidēron (*ἁγιοσίδηρον, holy iron*), one of the substitutes for bells still used in the East (also called *τὸ σιδηροῦν, κροῦσμα*). See SEMANTRON. It usually consists of an iron plate, curved like the tire of a wheel,

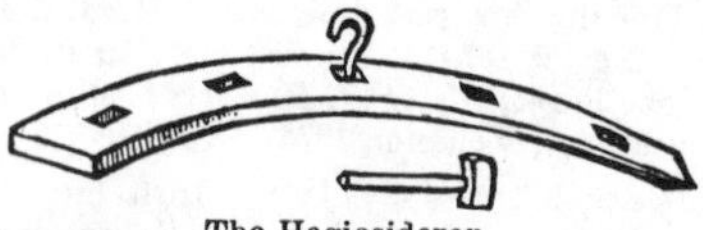

The Hagiosideron.

which is struck with a hammer, and produces a sound not unlike that of a gong. They are occasionally made of brass. See Neale, *Eastern Church,* Int. p. 217, 225; Daniel, *Codex Lit.* iv. 199.

Hagnoaldus, *Saint.* See CAGNOALDUS.

Hahn, Christoph Ulrich, a Protestant theologian of Germany, was born in 1805 at Würtemberg.

In 1833 he was deacon, in 1859 pastor at Haslach, and died Jan. 5, 1881, at Stuttgart, doctor of theology and philosophy. He organized the Evangelical Society at Stuttgart, and took a great interest in the work of missions. He published, *Der symbolischen Bücher der evangelisch-protestantischen Kirche Bedeutung und Schicksale* (Stuttgart, 1833):—*Geschichte der mittelalterlichen Ketzer, besonders im* 11., 12. *u.* 13. *Jahrhundert* (1846-50, 3 vols.):—*Handbüchlein für Kirchenälteste* (1851). See Zuchold, *Bibl. Theol.* i, 490; Winer, *Handbuch der theol. Lit.* i, 335. (B. P.)

Hahn, Hermann Joachim, a Lutheran theologian of Germany, was born in 1679 at Grabow, in Mecklenburg. He studied at Leipsic, was in 1706 deacon at Dresden, and finally preacher there. He was stabbed by a fanatical Roman Catholic, May 21, 1726. He wrote *De iis, quæ circa Receptam de Sabbatho Doctrinam, a non Nemine Nuper in Dubium Vocata sunt* (Leipsic, 1703), besides a number of ascetical works. See Jöcher, *Allgemeines Gelehrten-Lexikon*, s. v. (B. P.)

Hahn, Johann Bernhard, a Lutheran theologian of Germany, was born at Königsberg in 1685, and died there, July 8, 1755, doctor and professor of theology. He wrote, *De Appellatione Linguæ Hebrææ quæ dicitur Sancta* (Königsberg, 1715):—*De Cornubus Altaris Extremi:*—*De Festo Ebræorum Purim:*—*Introductio ad Jesaiam* (1735):—*Introductio ad Jeremiam* (1736):—*De Anno Ebræorum Jubileo* (1746):—*De* שלוים *ad Num. xi*, 31. See Jöcher, *Allgemeines Gelehrten-Lexikon*, s. v. (B. P.)

Hähn, Johann Friedrich, a Lutheran theologian of Germany, was born Aug. 15, 1710, at Bayreuth. He studied at Jena and Halle, was preacher at Klosterbergen in 1743, and military chaplain at Berlin in 1746. In 1749 he was general superintendent, in 1762 member of consistory, and died at Aurich, in East Frisia, June 4, 1789. He published sermons and other ascetical writings. See Döring, *Die gelehrten Theologen Deutschlands*, s. v. (B. P.)

Hahn, Johann Zacharias Herman, a Lutheran theologian of Germany, was born Aug. 12, 1768, at Schneeberg, in Saxony. In 1800 he was deacon at his native place, in 1804 general superintendent and member of consistory at Gera. He died Nov. 22, 1826, doctor of theology, leaving, *Politik, Moral, und Religion in Verbindung* (Leipsic, 1797-1800, 2 vols.):—*Geraisches Gesangbuch nebst Gebeten* (Gera, 1822). See Winer, *Handbuch der theol. Lit.* ii, 168, 172, 177, 291, 296. (B. P.)

Hahn, Philipp Matthäus, a Lutheran theologian of Germany, was born Nov. 25, 1739, at Scharuhausen, in Würtemberg. He studied at Tubingen, and died at Echterdingen, near Stuttgart, May 2, 1790. He was famous alike as a mechanic and theologian. A pupil of Oetinger and Bengel, he developed their theosophic system in his commentaries on different parts of the New Test., and his other writings. He published, *Betrachtungen und Predigten über die Evangelien* (Stuttgart, 1774; 5th ed. revised according to his manuscripts, 1847):—*Erbauungsstunden über den Brief an die Epheser* (published by his grandson, 1845):—*Erbauungsstunden über den Brief an die Kolosser* (1845):—*Die Lehre Jesu und seiner Gesandten* (1856):—*Die Erklärung der Bergpredigt Jesu Christi* (eod.):—*Auslegung des Briefes an die Hebräer* (ed. by Flattiol, 1859). See Plitt-Herzog, *Real-Encyklop.* s. v.; Lichtenberger, *Encyclop. des Sciences Religieuses*, s. v.; Paulus, *Philipp Matthäus Hahn* (Stuttgart, 1858); Zuchold, *Bibl. Theol.* i, 492. (B. P.)

Haï (or **Haja**) *bar-Sherira*, a Jewish rabbi, was born in 969 and died in 1035. He was the last gaon of Pumbaditha (q. v.), and was distinguished both for his personal virtues, and for an erudition which rendered him the most accomplished Jewish scholar of his time. He was a voluminous writer, and his works may be classified under the following heads: *a.* Talmudical; *b.* Exegetical; *c.* Poetical; *d.* Cabalistic; and *e.* Miscellaneous. Passing over his Talmudical works, we mention his פֵּרוּשׁ עַל תנ״ך, or commentary on the Scriptures, not extant, but cited by some of the later commentators, as Ibn-Ezra, David Kimchi, and others. *Sefer ham-measeph*, ס׳ המאסף, originally called *el-Châvi*, i. e. "the gathering," arranged alphabetically after the manner of many Arabic dictionaries, where the order is regulated by the last radical letter (e. g. רעד under *daleth*). In this dictionary, written in Arabic, which extended to the Biblical Chaldee also, the language of the Mishna, as well as a comparison of the Arabic, and sometimes even of the old Persian, was applied to the explanation of Hebrew words, as may be seen from the quotations of Ibn-Balaam (in his commentary on Numbers and Deuteronomy, preserved in Oxford, and where the dictionary of Haja is expressly called *el-Châvi*, as in Tanchûm on Judges viii, 16), Ibn-Ezra (Deut. xxxii, 39; Isa. xlvi, 8; Amos i, 27; Ps. lviii, 10; Job iv, 15; vi, 10; xiii, 27; xxi, 32), David Kimchi (in his *Book of Roots*, also in his commentary on Isa. v, 5; xxxv, 14; Jer. xii, 6; Ezek. xix, 10), Rashi (on Judg. iv, 19; Hos. iii, 4), and others. This dictionary, as well as several other treatises, is not extant. Of his poetical works, we mention *Musar haskel*, מוסר השכל, also שערי מוסר, an exposition of the Pentateuch in Arabic verse (Constantinople, 1511; Latin transl. by Mercier, Paris, 1561; and Seidel, Leipsic, 1638); *Shema Koli* (שמע קולי), i. e. "Hear my voice," in the Spanish Ritual. See Rapaport, *Biography of Hai*, in *Bikkura ha-Ittim*, x, 79-95; xi, 90-92; Steinschneider, *Jewish Literature*, p. 78, 125; and *Catalogus Libr. Hebr. in Biblioth. Bodl.* (1026-30); Fürst, *Bibl. Jud.* i, 355-358; De' Rossi, *Dizionario Storico* (Germ. transl.), p. 120 sq.; Grätz, *Gesch. d. Juden*, vi, 6-13; Geiger, *Jüd. Zeitschrift* (1862), p. 206-217, 312-314; Nascher, *Hai Gaon* (Breslau, 1867). (B. P.).

Haictites, a Mohammedan sect, who profess to believe in Christ as well as in Mohammed. They hold many of the doctrines pertaining to Christ in common with orthodox Christians. They also believe that he will come again to judge the world in the same body which he had on earth; that he will destroy Antichrist, and reign forty years, at the close of which the world will be destroyed.

Haifa, a town in Palestine, just under the northern brow of Carmel, on the shore near the mouth of the Kishon, seems to be alluded to as (near) the western terminus of Zebulon (Gen. xlix, 13, חוֹף, *chôph*, "haven;" see Deut. i, 7, "side;" Josh. ix, 1, "coasts;" in both which passages the associated geographical terms are likewise technically used as proper names). In fact the present Arabic name (properly *Chaypha*) is but the Aramaean form (חֵיפָא, *the cove*) of the Heb. word (used in the above passages only). In the Talmud the old name reappears (חיפה, *Cheyphah*, the modern form; Græcized Ἡφά: see Reland, *Palæst.* p. 718). By the Greek and Roman writers, a place called *Sycaminum* (Συκαμίνον, Hebraized שקמונה, *Sekamunah*, doubtless as a mart for *figs*) is mentioned as situated in Phœnicia, near the foot of Carmel (see Reland, p. 1024). In the Middle Ages the place was called *Porphyreon* by a strange mistake, the real town of that name being north of Sidon. It was also known as *Cayphas*, and the derivations given are very curious, either from Cephas or Caiaphas. Haifa is now a small but growing town of about two thousand inhabitants, built close upon the sandy beach, and surrounded by a shattered wall. The interior has a dreary look, which is not improved by the broken wall, and two or three rusty cannon lying about, half covered by rubbish. The only tolerable houses appear to be those of the consular agents, who abound here, as it is a frequent stopping-place, especially in foul weather, for the Levant steamers. There is a flourishing German colony in the neighborhood. The bay spreads out in front, its sandy beach sweeping gracefully along the plain to the low point on which the battlements of Acre are seen in the distance. In Haifa the Christians outnumber the Mohammedans; and there is a small community of Jews. Few remains of antiquity are visible except some tombs in the rocks; but the magnificence of former buildings is attested by the fragments of marble, granite, porphyry, and greenstone lying in the shingle on the beach. Two miles farther south-west are the remains of another large town, at the place called *Tell es-Semak*. There can scarcely be a doubt that this is the ancient Sycaminon, often confused with Haifa, but a place distinct and named from its sycamine fig-trees—a stunted specimen of which still stands near, with its little figs growing out of the stem. See Murray, *Handbook for Syria*, p. 362; Bädeker, *Palestine*, p. 348; Conder, *Tent Work*, i, 180; ii, 306. See CARMEL; KISHON.

Haight, BENJAMIN I., S.T.D., LL.D., a Protestant Episcopal clergyman, was born in the city of New York, Oct. 16, 1809. He graduated at Columbia College in 1828, and at the General Theological Seminary in the same city in 1831; was ordained that year, and became rector of St. Peter's Church in his native city; in 1834 of St. Paul's, Cincinnati; in 1837 of All-Saints', New York, and the same year likewise professor of pastoral theology in the General Theological Seminary, retaining the latter position until 1855, when he was associated with Trinity parish in the same city. He died there Feb. 21, 1879.

Hail, Mary! See AVE MARIA.

Haimo. See HAYMO.

Hair, CHRISTIAN MODES OF WEARING. In the early Church the clergy sometimes wore long hair, but the custom of cutting it short, in distinction from pagans, soon became general, and at length shaving it altogether, even to a bare spot upon the crown, was introduced as a monkish habit. See TONSURE. Penitents cut their hair short as a sign of humiliation. Laymen usually wore long hair, but ringlets were regarded as a mark of effeminacy. Women were enjoined to wear long hair, but modestly arrayed. False hair was strongly denounced.

Hair-cloth has often been worn by ascetics as a means of mortifying the flesh, especially hair-shirts. In the early church penitents were sometimes clothed with it, and candidates for baptism were often examined standing upon a piece of hair-cloth. The dying and the dead were also covered with it.

Hairetites, a skeptical Mohammedan sect, who profess to doubt everything, and to hold their minds in constant equipoise, maintaining that it is impossible to distinguish truth from falsehood. Their usual reply in discussion is, "God knows, we do not." They are, however, scrupulous in their observance of Mohammedan laws and ceremonies, both civil and religious.

Haitz, FIDELIS, a Roman Catholic theologian, was born in 1801 at Waldshut, Baden. In 1826 he was made a priest, in 1845 canon at Freiburg, and died June 9, 1873. He wrote *Die Katholische Abendmahlslehre* (Mayence, 1872). (B. P.)

Hajar EL-ASWAD, the name of the sacred black stone in the great temple of Mecca. It is supposed to have been originally an aerolite or Bætylia. See KAABA.

Haji. See HADJ.

Hakemites. See DRUSES; HAKIM.

Hakka Version. See CHINESE VERSIONS.

Hakluyt, RICHARD, an eminent English clergyman and historian, was born in London in 1553, and educated at Christ Church, Oxford. He died in 1616. He published *Divers Voyages touching the Discoverie of America, and the Islands Adjacent unto the Same* (1582). He was prebendary of Westminster in 1605, and rector of Witheringset, in Suffolk. See Chalmers, *Biog. Dict.* s. v.; Allibone, *Dict. of Brit. and Amer. Authors*, s. v.

Halak, MOUNT. Jebel *Maderah*, with which we may probably identify this mountain, lies on the south side of a wady of the same name, five miles south-west of the pass of Sufah, and is a round, isolated hill, with numerous blocks of stone on the base and summit, which Arab tradition ascribes to a destructive shower, as a punishment for inhospitality on the part of the ancient inhabitants (Palmer, *Desert of the Exodus*, p. 351).

Halal, what is permitted and sanctioned by the Mohammedan law.

Halcyon, a mythological term equivalent to *rest* or quiet, especially applied to any season of repose; a figure drawn from the so-called "halcyon days," which are a fortnight, one half before and the other after the winter solstice, during which the bird *halcyon*, or kingfisher, was fabled by the Greeks to brood, the sea remaining calm during the time of incubation. The myth originated in the classical story of Halcyone or Alcyone (Ἀλκυόνη), a daughter of Æolus and Enarete, or Ægiale, who married Ceÿx, and lived so happily with him that the two compared themselves to Jupiter and Juno, and were punished for their presumption by being changed into birds. A more literal version of the story is that Ceÿx having perished by shipwreck, Alcyone threw herself into the sea, and was metamorphosed into a kingfisher.

Halcyon Church, a denomination of Christians which is said to have arisen in the interior of the United States in 1802, who reject all creeds and confessions. They hold that there is but one person in the Godhead, and that the Father reveals himself in the personality of the Anointed. They deny eternal punishment, and believe in the annihilation of the wicked. They baptize only adults, and that in a peculiar manner. The persons to be baptized walk down into the water in procession, attended by the congregation, and accompanied with vocal and instrumental music. The ordinance is then administered in the name of the Lord Jesus Christ. They devote their children to God, not by baptism, but by dedicating them in prayer, and placing them under the guardianship of the church members.

Hale, Benjamin, D.D., a Protestant Episcopal clergyman, was born at Old Newbury, Mass., in 1797. He graduated with honor from Bowdoin College in 1818, and immediately became principal of the Saco Academy. In 1819 he entered the Andover Theological Seminary, and became a minister of the Congregational Church in 1822. The four years thereafter he spent as a tutor in Bowdoin. In 1827 he was called to Dartmouth College, N. H., as a professor, and held the office until 1835, when his professorship was abolished by the trustees of the college. He was ordained deacon in the Protestant Episcopal Church in 1828, and presbyter in 1831. After his return from a visit to the West Indies, whither he went for recuperation in the summer of 1836, he was elected to the presidency of Hobart College, in Geneva, N. Y. In 1852 he made a brief visit to Europe, and in 1856 resigned the presidency of the college, which he had held for twenty years, and afterwards lived in retirement in his native place. He died at Newburyport, Mass., July 15, 1863. Dr. Hale was the author of several scientific and professional works; but his reputation rests largely upon his work as an instructor. See *Amer. Quar. Church Rev.* Oct. 1863, p. 507.

Hale, Bernard, D.D., master of Peterhouse, in Cambridge University, was born of religious parents, and received his early education in the public school of Hartford. Afterwards he removed to Westminster, thence to Peterhouse, of which he became a fellow.

After three or four years spent in his fellowship, his father's death transmitted to him a fair estate, and he resigned his office, and thereafter lived in retirement, chiefly in Norfolk, occupied with acts of devotion and beneficence. At the Restoration he was moved by a father of the Church to enter the priesthood. Immediately several preferments were offered him, some of which he accepted, but with the understanding that whatever emoluments he reaped therefrom should be dedicated to the service of God. He largely endowed the College of St. Peter. He died about 1663. See *The* (Lond.) *Christian Remembrancer*, April, 1822, p. 208.

Hale, Enoch, a Congregational minister, brother of Nathan Hale, the Revolutionary martyr, and father of Hon. Nathan Hale, of the Boston *Daily Advertiser*, was born at Coventry, Conn., in 1754; graduated from Yale College in 1773; was ordained pastor of the Church in Westhampton, Mass., in 1779, and died Jan. 14, 1837. He was secretary of the Massachusetts General (Congregational) Association from 1804 to 1824. See *Cong. Quarterly*, 1859, p. 39; Sprague, *Annals of the Amer. Pulpit*, ii, 572.

Halenius, ENGELBERTUS, a Swedish prelate, son of Lars, was born Oct. 8, 1700, became bishop of Skara in 1753, held lively discussions with Swedenborg, and died Feb. 14, 1767, leaving some sermons, and a translation of Maimonides. See Hoefer, *Nouv. Biog. Générale*, s. v.

Hales, Alexander. See ALEXANDER ALESIUS.

Hales, Stephen, D.D., F.R.S., a Church of England divine, was born Sept. 7, 1677. He entered Corpus Christi College in 1696, graduated A.B. in 1701, A.M. in 1703, and B.D. in 1711, greatly distinguishing himself meanwhile as a botanist, anatomist, and astronomer. In 1710 he was presented to the perpetual curacy of Teddington, Middlesex, and afterwards accepted the living of Porlock, Somersetshire, which he exchanged for the living of Farringdon, Hampshire. On March 13, 1717, or 1718, he was elected a member of the Royal Society. In 1725 he published a valuable work on *Vegetable Statistics*, and in 1733 a sequel to it, entitled *Statistical Essays.* He published a very popular work on *Temperance;* and in 1739 an 8vo volume entitled, *Philosophical Experiments on Sea-water, Corn, Flesh, and other Substances.* Dr. Hales also published several sermons and many papers in the *Phil. Trans.*, etc. He died at Teddington, Jan. 4, 1761. See Masters, *Hist. of E. C. C. C.; Annual Register*, 1764, p. 42; *Gentleman's Magazine*, vol. lxix; Butler, *Life of Hildesley*, p. 362; Lysons, *Environs;* Allibone, *Dict. of Brit. and Amer. Authors*, s. v.

Hales, William, D.D., an Irish divine, was born at Cork, April 8, 1747, and educated at Trinity College, Dublin, of which he became a fellow in 1769. Afterwards he served as a college tutor, and was very popular. In due time he was ordained deacon and priest; and in 1788 was appointed to the rectory of Killesandra, in Cavan, which he held till his death, Jan. 30, 1831. Dr. Hales was eminently faithful in all the duties pertaining to the ministerial office. He was amiable and unselfish, catholic in spirit, and blameless in life. His works are, *Sonorum Doctrina* (1778):—*De Motibus Planetarum* (1782):—*Analysis Equationum* (1784):—*Observations on the Political Influence of the Doctrine of the Pope's Supremacy* (1787–88):—*The Rights of Citizens* (1793):—*The Scripture Doctrine of Political Government and Liberty* (1794):—*Methodism Inspected* (1803–5):—*Dissertations on the Prophecies Expressing the Divine and Human Character of our Lord* (1808):—*Analysis of Chronology* (1809–14; his most important publication):—*Origin and Purity of the Primitive Church in the British Isles* (1818). See *The Church of England Magazine*, March, 1842, p. 147, 164; *Memoir of Dr. Hales* in the early numbers of the *British Magazine;* Allibone, *Dict. of Brit. and Amer. Authors*, s. v.

Halhul. The modern representative of this place, *Halhûl*, is described in the *Memoirs* accompanying the Ordnance Survey (iii, 305) as "a large stone village on a hill-top, with two springs and a well; also a fine spring below ('Hin ed-Dhirweh). On the west is the mosque of Neby Yûnis, now in a partly ruinous condition, with a minaret. There are rock-cut tombs south of the village. The hills on the north have vineyards on them, and there are other tombs here also." These last are elsewhere more fully detailed (iii, 329).

Hali. For this locality Lieut. Conder accepts (*Tent Work*, ii, 377) the suggestion of the modern *'Alia*, which is laid down on the *Ordnance Map* at nine and three quarter miles south-east of Es-Zib (Ecdippa on the coast), and described in the accompanying *Memoirs* (i, 170) as "a small square building of well-dressed stone, without draft, probably of the crusades; a large number of cisterns and traces of ruins." Among the latter are added, from Guérin, a description of several sepulchral chambers containing sarcophagi. The village of Malia, which lies half a mile north-west, is thought to represent the Meltoth of Josephus (*Wars*, iii, 3, 7), and the Mahalia or Chateau du Roi of the Teutonic knights (ibid. p. 149, 155).

Haliburton, George (1), a Scotch prelate, minister of Perth, was made bishop of Dunkeld by letters royal, Jan. 18, 1602, and died in 1664. See Keith, *Scottish Bishops*, p. 98.

Haliburton, George (2), a Scotch prelate, was born in 1628, consecrated bishop of Brechin in 1678, and was translated to the see of Aberdeen in 1682, where he sat until the Revolution, in 1688. He died at his house of Denhead, in the parish of Coupar, in Angus, Sept. 29, 1715 See Keith, *Scottish Bishops*, p. 134, 168.

Halidome (or **Hallydome**), an old term for the Last Day—the general judgment.

Hall, Baynard Rush, D.D., a Reformed (Dutch) minister, was born in Philadelphia in 1798. At the age of four he was left an orphan, and heir to a large estate, which through mismanagement never came into his possession. In Union College, where he graduated in 1820, his reputation for ability and scholarship was of the first rank. He was educated with a view to the law, but Providence turned his steps to the ministry. He graduated from Princeton Theological Seminary in 1823, with bright promise of success, yet most of his life was spent in teaching. He was professor in Indiana University the same year, and taught in after-years in Trenton, Poughkeepsie, Newburgh, and Brooklyn. In 1846 he left the Presbyterian Church and joined the Reformed Church in America, but remained without charge. He died in Brooklyn, L. I., Jan. 23, 1863. Dr. Hall published in early life a valuable *Latin Grammar.* His volume entitled *The New Purchase, or Seven Years' in the West*, enjoyed great popularity. Later in life he published a work of acknowledged merit, entitled, *Teaching, a Science.* He contributed freely to the religious periodicals. See Corwin, *Manual of the Ref. Church in America*, s. v.; *Christian Intelligencer*, 1863. (W. J. R. T.)

Hall, Charles, D.D., a Presbyterian divine, was born at Williamsport, Pa., June 23, 1799. He graduated from Hamilton College in 1824; studied two years in Princeton Theological Seminary; was ordained evangelist, March 25, 1832; became secretary of the American Home Missionary Society in 1827; and so continued until his death at Newark, N. J., Oct. 31, 1853. See *Gen. Cat. of Princeton Theol. Sem.* 1881, p. 49; Nevin, *Presb. Cyclop.* s. v.

Hall, David, D.D., a Congregational minister, was born at Yarmouth, Mass., Aug. 5, 1704. He graduated from Harvard College in 1724; in November, 1728, supplied the pulpit in Sutton, and was ordained pastor Oct. 15, 1729. His church shared in the great revival of 1740. He died at Sutton, May 8, 1789. Dr. Hall was an able and faithful minister. See Sprague, *Annals of the Amer. Pulpit*, i, 357.

Hall, Edwin, D.D., a Presbyterian divine, was born at Granville, N. Y., Jan. 11, 1802. He graduated from Middlebury College in 1826; studied theology privately; taught in Middlebury for some two years; was ordained at Hebron, Aug. 27, 1830; was successively pastor at Glenn's Falls and Sandy Hill for one year thereafter; at Bloomfield, N. J., the next year; over the First Congregational Church at Norwalk, Conn., for twenty-two years, and in 1854 became professor of Christian theology in Auburn Theological Seminary, a position which he retained until his death, Sept. 8, 1877. He published several works on baptism, and other ecclesiastical subjects. See *Gen. Cat. of Auburn Theol. Sem.* 1883, p. 266.

Hall, George, an English prelate, was born in 1612, and educated at Exeter College, Oxford. He was the son of the bishop of Norwich, became prebendary of Exeter in 1639, archdeacon of Cornwall in 1641, bishop of Chester in 1662, and died Aug. 23, 1668. He published *Sermons* (1655-66). See Allibone, *Dict. of Brit. and Amer. Authors*, s. v.

Hall, Gordon, *Jr.*, D.D., a Congregational minister, was born in Bombay, India, Nov. 4, 1823. After preparatory study at Ellington, Conn., he graduated from Yale College in 1843, and from Yale Divinity School in 1847. After a term of service as tutor in the college, he was ordained pastor of the Church in Wilton, Oct. 25, 1848, and June 2, 1852, became pastor of Edwards Church, Northampton, Mass., and so continued until his death at Binghamton, N.Y., Nov. 5, 1879. From 1870 he was a corporate member of the American Commissioners for Foreign Missions; was a trustee of Williston Seminary; and from 1878 was visitor of Andover Theological Seminary. See *Cong. Year-book*, 1880, p. 20; *Obituary Record of Yale College*, 1880.

Hall, Henry, a learned English divine, was born in London in 1716, and was educated at King's College, Cambridge, where he became a fellow in 1738. In 1750 he was collated to the rectory of Harbledown, and soon after to the vicarage of Herne. He was presented to the vicarage of East Peckham in 1756, and was at the same time librarian of Lambeth. He died at Harbledown, Nov. 2, 1763. See Chalmers, *Biog. Dict.* s. v.

Hall, James, D.D., a Presbyterian minister, was born at Carlisle, Pa., Aug. 22, 1744. When he was eight years old the family moved to North Carolina, and settled in Rowan County. He was blessed with pious parents, who taught him the truths of the gospel, and thus early he was brought into the Church. He graduated at Princeton in 1774; was licensed by the Presbytery of Orange in 1775; in 1778 became pastor at Bethany, and there labored faithfully and successfully until his death, July 25, 1826. Dr. Hall was active in the scenes of the Revolutionary war. He published a few *Sermons* which he preached on national occasions. See Sprague, *Annals of the Amer. Pulpit*, iii, 381.

Hall, Jeremiah, D.D., a Baptist minister, was born at Swansey, N. H., May 21, 1805. He pursued his classical studies in the Brattleborough Academy, Vt., and his theological studies at the Newton Seminary, where he graduated in 1830. He was ordained Feb. 3, 1831, and had charge, successively, of churches in Fairfax, Westford, and Bennington; afterwards became one of the pioneer laborers of his denomination in what was then the territory of Michigan, and assisted in the organization of the Church at Kalamazoo, of which he was the pastor eight years (1835-43), and subsequently at Akron, O. (1843-45). For some time he was principal of the Norwalk Institute; then pastor in Granville (1851-53); president of Denison University (1853-63); and being a pastor for a time at Shell Rock, Ia., returned to Michigan, where he labored as occasion offered until his death, May 30, 1881. See *Gen. Cat. of Newton Sem.* p. 9. (J. C. S.)

Hall, Samuel Read, LL.D., a Congregational minister, was born at Conydon, N. H., Oct. 27, 1795. He was educated at Kimball Union Academy, and was for some years a teacher; studied theology with Rev. Walter Chapin of Woodstock, Vt.; was ordained at Concord, March 5, 1823, and remained pastor there until 1830. During this time he established and taught the first normal school in the country; afterwards became principal of the Teacher's Seminary at Andover, Mass., for six years; then took charge of Plymouth Academy, N. H. (1836-39); was pastor at Craftsbury, Vt., fourteen years; at Browington twelve years, and thereafter, with the exception of two years, when he was acting pastor in Granby, remained without charge until his death, June 24, 1877. He was moderator of the General Convention of Vermont in 1859. He published, *The Child's Assistant to a Knowledge of the Geography and History of Vermont* (1827; revised ed. 1868):—*Lectures on School Keeping* (1829):—*Lectures to Female School Teachers* (1832):—*The Child's Instructor* (eod.):—*The Arithmetical Manual* (eod.):—*Practical Lectures on Parental Responsibility, and the Religious Education of Children* (1833):—*A School History of the United States* (eod.):—*The Alphabet of Geology* (1868). He assisted president Hitchcock in the geological survey of Vermont, and a part of section vii in the published Report on Northern Vermont was prepared by him. (W. P. S.)

Hall, Thomas, a learned English Nonconformist divine, was born at Worcester, July 22, 1610, and educated at Balliol College; was master of the free school at King's-Norton, and curate of the place; and died April 13, 1665. Among his works are many controversial tracts, and commentaries on some parts of the Scriptures. See Chalmers, *Biog. Dict.* s. v.

Hall, Timothy, an English prelate, who was consecrated bishop of Oxford in 1688, and died April 10, 1690, published some *Sermons* (1684, 1689). See Allibone, *Dict. of Brit. and Amer. Authors*, s. v.

Hall, Westley, a minister of the Church of England, was one of the Oxford Methodists. Of his origin and early life nothing is known. He became one of Wesley's pupils at Lincoln College, Oxford, and joined the Methodists some time prior to Oct. 25, 1732. The date of his ordination must have been as early as 1734, as he then refused a living. He was at that time deemed a young man of "extraordinary piety, and love to souls." He married Wesley's sister, Martha, whom he afterwards abandoned, but after a very irregular and dissolute life, partly in the ministry, but chiefly as an open Deist, he became penitent, and died at Bristol, Jan. 3, 1776. See Tyerman, *The Oxford Methodists*, p. 386.

Hallahan, Margaret Mary, foundress of the congregation of St. Catherine of Sienna, was born in London, Jan. 23, 1803. From her ninth to her thirtieth year she lived at service, part of the time in Belgium. In 1834 she received her habit as a member of the Dominican order. In April, 1842, she returned to England, and began teaching at Coventry. On Dec. 8, 1845, she laid the foundation at Coventry of the first English convent of Dominican nuns, which had a hard struggle there; although at Langton (1851), Stone (1853), Stoke-upon-Trent (1857), Rhyl (1864-66), and Torquay (1864) the establishments were successful. In October, 1858, mother Margaret, accompanied by Rev. Dr. Northcote, went to Rome, in order to obtain a definite settlement as to the future government of the increasing communities. It was deemed best that they should be united in a congregation under one superioress, with one novitiate, the whole to be under the government of the order of St. Dominic. She was appointed prioress-provincial of the newly formed congregation, which afterwards received the name of St. Catherine of Sienna. Her last work was the establishment of a house at Bow, London. She died at Stone, May 11, 1868. See *Cath. Almanac* (N. Y.), 1880, p. 85.

Hallam, Robert Alexander, D.D., a Protestant Episcopal minister, was born at New London, Conn., Sept. 30, 1807. After some time spent in teaching, he graduated from the General Theological Seminary of New York city in 1832; in August of the same year was ordained deacon in Hartford, Conn., and went to Meriden as rector of St. Andrew's Church, where he was ordained presbyter, Aug. 2, 1833. He returned to New London in January, 1835, as rector of St. James's Church, a position which he held until his death, Jan. 4, 1877. In 1836 he published a volume of *Lectures on the Morning Prayer*, and a volume of *Sermons;* also, in 1871, a course of *Lectures on Moses*, and in 1873 a *History of his Parish Church.* See *Obituary Record of Yale College*, 1877.

Hallbauer, Friedrich Andreas, a Protestant theologian of Germany, was born in Thuringia, Sept. 13, 1692. He studied at Halle and Jena, was adjunctus of the philosophical faculty at Jena in 1721, professor of elocution in 1731, professor of theology in 1738, and died March 1, 1750. He wrote, *De Luthero* (Jena, 1717):—*De Ecclesia Lutherana* (ibid. 1717):—*Commentationes Philologicæ in Quædam Loca Vet. Test.* (ibid. 1721):—*Disp. in Quædam Loca Novi Test.* (ibid. eod.):—*Vindiciæ Trium Dictorum N. Test. Luc. xxiii*, 34, *Apoc. xiv*, 13, *Rom. ix*, 5 (ibid. 1736):—*Messias ex Virgine Exoriturus* (ibid. 1740):—*Comment. Theol. in Apoc. ii*, 2 (ibid. 1741):—*Filius Dei Mundi Creator et Pater Hominum* (ibid. 1746):—*De Jesu sine Patre et Matre* (ibid. 1748):—*Christus Pulcherrimus Hominum Psa. xlv*, 2 (ibid. 1749). See Döring, *Die gelehrten Theologen Deutschlands;* Winer, *Handbuch der theol. Lit.* i, 4, 736; ii, 58; Jöcher, *Allgemeines Gelehrten-Lexikon*, s. v. (B. P.)

Halley, Ebenezer, D.D., a Presbyterian minister, was born in Scotland, Aug. 1, 1801. He graduated from Edinburgh University, pursued his studies in theology under Dick and Chalmers; was ordained pastor at Leith, where he labored for ten years, and then removed to America. His first settlement was in Salem, Washington County, N. Y., as pastor of the United Presbyterian Church. After serving this Church ten years, he was called to the pastorate of the Second Street Presbyterian Church, Troy, where he remained seven years, and then became pastor of the Third Presbyterian Church, Albany. After two years he retired, in 1875, as its pastor emeritus. From 1878 he was chaplain of the State Senate. He died Oct. 31, 1881. Dr. Halley was unusually well read in classical and English literature, but his leading trait was his passion for preaching. For a great part of his ministry he followed the Scottish method of writing and memorizing; he was at the same time ready, as few are, to respond to a sudden demand for a speech or a sermon. See *New York Observer*, Nov. 10, 1881. (W. P. S.)

Halley, Robert, D.D., an English Congregational minister, was born at Blackheath, near London, Aug. 13, 1796. He joined the Church at an early age, entered Homerton College in 1816, and five years later began his ministry at St. Neot's, Huntingdonshire. On the opening of Highbury College, in 1826, Mr. Halley was chosen resident and classical tutor, which post he occupied for thirteen years. In 1834 he published a reply to Rev. James Yates's letter, which letter defended Mr. Wellbeloved's *Improved Version of the Scriptures*, entitling his reply, *The Improved Version truly Designated a Creed.* This pamphlet soon attracted special attention by its vigor, keenness of criticism, depth of scholarship, and its able handling of the Greek text. It soon found its way across the Atlantic. In 1839 he accepted a call to the pastorate of Mozley Street Chapel, Manchester, and in 1857 received an appointment to the principalship of New College, from which he retired in 1872. He spent some months at Spring Hill College, supplying a vacant chair. He was an indefatigable preacher, travelling over the whole country. He died at Betworth Park, near Arundel, Aug. 18, 1876. Dr. Halley wrote a *History of Puritanism and Nonconformity in Lancashire:*—*Lectures on the Sacraments:*—*The Lord's Supper.* See (Lond.) *Cong. Year-book*, 1877, p. 367; Allibone, *Dict. of Brit. and Amer. Authors*, s. v.

Hallier, François, a French prelate, was born at Chartres in 1595. He was doctor and professor of the Sorbonne, and syndic of the theological faculty at Paris. While at Rome in 1652 he was the main instrument of having the five propositions of Jansenius condemned. In 1656 he was made bishop of Cavaillon, and died in 1659. He wrote, *Defensio Ecclesiasticæ Hierarchiæ* (Paris, 1632):—*Monita ad Ordinandos et Ordinatos* (1634):—*De Sacris Electionibus et Ordinationibus ex Antiquo et Novo Ecclesiæ Usu* (1636, 3 vols. fol.). See Winer, *Handbuch der theol. Lit.* i, 461; Jöcher, *Allgemeines Gelehrten-Lexikon*, s. v.; Hoefer, *Nouv. Biog. Générale*, s. v. (B. P.)

Hallock, William Allen, D.D., a Congregational minister, son of Rev. Moses Hallock, was born at Plainfield, Mass., June 2, 1794. He graduated in 1819 from Williams College, and in 1822 from Andover Theological Seminary; the next three years was agent for the New England Tract Society, and in 1825 was corresponding secretary of the American Tract Society, which he was largely instrumental in founding. He was ordained in Middlefield, Mass., Oct. 5, 1836, and became honorary secretary of the Tract Society in 1870, and so continued until the close of his life in New York city, Oct. 2, 1880. He was for several years editor of the *American Messenger*, and besides several tracts, wrote and published the following:—*The Life of Harlan Page:*—*The Venerable Mayhews:*—*Life of Rev. Moses Hallock:*—*Life of Rev. Dr. Justin Edwards.* See *Cong. Year-book*, 1881, p. 24.

Halloix, Pierre, a Jesuit of Liege, was born there in 1572, and died July 30, 1856. He is the author of *Illustrium Eccl. Orient. Scriptorum Vitæ et Documenta* (Douay, 1633, 2 vols. fol.):—*Vita et Documenta S. Justini* (1622):—*Origenes Defensus, S. Origenis Vita, Virtutes et Documenta Libris IV* (Liege, 1648). See Winer, *Handbuch der theol. Lit.* i, 854, 897, 899; Jöcher, *Allgemeines Gelehrten-Lexikon*, s. v. (B. P.)

Hallowe'en, the Scotch term for the eve of the feast of All-Saints (q. v.).

Hallowmas. See All-Saints' Day.

Hallum (or **Halom**), Robert de, an English prelate of the first part of the 15th century, was of the blood royal of England, says Pits (*De Scriptoribus Britannicis*, an. 1410), but in what way is not said. He was educated in Oxford, became chancellor of that university in 1403, afterwards archdeacon of Canterbury, bishop of Salisbury, and June 6, 1411, was made cardinal. He was one of the three prelates sent to represent the English clergy in the Councils of Pisa and Constance, in which last service he died at Gotleby Castle, in 1417. See Fuller, *Worthies of England* (ed. Nuttall), iii, 323.

Hallymote (1) a sacred or holy court, presided over by an ecclesiastic; (2) a visitation by a bishop of some particular parish or church.

Halsey, Abram Oothout, D.D., a Reformed (Dutch) minister, was born in New York, Nov. 3, 1798. He graduated from Union College in 1822, and from Princeton Theological Seminary in 1827; became pastor at North and South Hampton in 1829, a position which he retained until a few months before his death at Sweedsborough, N. J., Aug. 23, 1867. He was a man of childlike, catholic spirit, and possessed a peculiar unction in prayer. He was eminent as a preacher. His theology was that of moderate Calvinism, and he held it with genuine charity towards all who differed from him. He was also a decided premillenarian, and was thoroughly versed in the literature of that question.

See Corwin, *Manual of the Ref. Church in America*, s. v. (W. J. R. T.)

Halsey, Job Foster, D.D., a Presbyterian minister, was born at Schenectady, N. Y., July 12, 1800. He received his preparatory education at Newburgh Academy; graduated from Union College in 1819; taught with his father at Newburgh; studied theology with his brother, and was licensed by the Presbytery of North River, May 1, 1823; spent from 1823 to 1826 at Princeton Seminary; was ordained by the Presbytery of New Brunswick at Freehold, N. J., June 14, 1826, and on the same day installed pastor of the Old Tennant Church in that place, where he labored until May 5, 1828; was agent in New Jersey for the American Bible Society in 1828 and 1829; in Albany, N. Y., in 1829 and 1830, for the American Tract Society, and in Pittsburgh, Pa., in 1830 and 1831, in the Sunday-school cause. He went to Allegheny City, and was installed pastor of the First Church of that city, July 1, 1831, and labored there until released, April 23, 1836. He was a professor in the Marion Manual Labor College in Missouri, in 1835 and 1836; principal of Raritan Seminary for Young Ladies, at Perth Amboy, N. J., from 1836 to 1848; was installed pastor at West Bloomfield, now Montclair, Jan. 8, 1852, where he remained until 1856; was installed pastor of the First Church of Norristown, Pa., May 11, 1856, where he labored twenty-four years. Here he died, March 24, 1882. See *Necrol. Report of Princeton Theol. Sem.* 1882, p. 12.

Halsey, Luther, D.D., LL.D., a Presbyterian minister, was born at Schenectady, N. Y., Jan. 1, 1794. After receiving a preparatory education, he graduated from Union College in 1812; then entered upon the study of medicine, but soon relinquished it for theology, and in 1816 was ordained pastor of the Presbyterian Church at Blooming Grove, Orange Co., N. Y., where his labors were blessed in the ingathering of many souls. In 1829 he was appointed professor of theology in the Allegheny Theological Seminary, and in 1837 professor of ecclesiastical history and Church polity in the Auburn Theological Seminary. In 1844 he again took charge of the Blooming Grove Church, and in 1847 accepted the chair of Church history in the Union Theological Seminary. For several of the last years of his life he occupied a retired relation. He died in New York, Oct. 29, 1880. See *New York Observer*, Nov. 11, 1880; *Gen. Cat. of Auburn Theol. Sem.* 1883, p. 279. (W. P. S.)

Hamadryads were certain rural deities in the pagan theogony, or nymphs of the woods, whose fate depended on particular trees with which they were associated.

Hambraeus, Jonas, preacher to the Swedish ambassador at Paris, and professor of Oriental languages there, was born in 1588. He studied at Upsala, Greifswald, and Rostock, was professor of Hebrew at Upsala, accompanied some noblemen on their travels in 1626, and settled at Paris as professor of Oriental languages. In 1635 he became preacher to Hugo Grotius, and died in 1665. He wrote, *Disp. de Accentibus Hebræis* (Greifswald, 1616):—*Institutio Hebraica Compendiosa* (Rostock, 1618):—*Loci Theologici Latino-Suedici* (Stockholm, 1622). He translated into Swedish the *Ethica Christiana* of Dareus (Rostock, 1618); also Erasmus's *Παράκληθις ad Christianos Omnes, ut Libenter Audiant et Legant Verbum Dei* (1620). See Hambräus, *Disp. I. et II. de Meritis ac Fatis Jonæ Hambræi* (Upsala, 1743, 1749); Moller, *Cimbria Litterata;* Stiernmann, *Bibl. Suiogothica*, p. 313; Jöcher, *Allgemeines Gelehrten-Lexikon*, s. v. (B. P.)

Hamburg, a noted city of Germany. When the reformation was introduced there in 1529, the city adopted the Church constitution prepared by Bugenhagen. This *Kirchenordnung* provided that all non-Lutherans should be excluded from the city and its territory. In 1567 members of the Anglican Church, in 1605 members of the Dutch Reformed Church, and in 1648, by the peace of Westphalia, Roman Catholics, were allowed to live in the city, but they could not become citizens, nor could they celebrate worship in public. These latter restrictions were removed by the new civil constitution of Sept. 28, 1860. The Lutheran Church is governed by a synod consisting of fifty-three members, of whom sixteen are clergymen, thirty-five laymen, and two senators, and by an ecclesiastical council consisting of nine members, viz. four laymen, three ecclesiastics, and two senators. The ecclesiastical council has the executive power, and carries out the resolutions of the synod, which meets every five years. In the year 1877, Hamburg, with a territory comprising an area of about eight square miles, had a population of 406,014, of which about eighty-nine per cent. were Lutherans, 13,796 were Jews, 7771 were Roman Catholics, and 5585 belonged to other evangelical denominations. See Plitt-Herzog, *Real-Encyclop.* s. v.; *Statistik des hamburgischen Staates* (Hamburg, 1878, part vi). (B. P.)

Hamel, Jean Baptiste du, a French philosopher and theologian, was born in 1624 at Vire, in Normandy. In 1663 he was chancellor at Bayeux, in 1666 secretary of the Academy of Sciences at Paris, and died Aug. 6, 1706. He published, *Biblia Latina Vulg.* etc. (Paris, 1706 fol.):—*Theologia Speculativa et Practica* (1691):—*Theologiæ Clericorum Seminariis Accommodatæ Summarium* (1694, 5 vols.). See Winer, *Handbuch der theol. Lit.* i, 60, 291; Jöcher, *Allgemeines Gelehrten-Lexikon*, s. v. (B. P.)

Hamelin, a French prelate of the 12th century, was the nephew of Odon, dean of St. Martin of Tours, and a scholastic of that church from the year 1186. He was elected bishop of Le Mans in December, 1190, and consecrated by pope Celestine III at Rome in the beginning of the following year. He established in all the parishes of his diocese the capitulary jurisdiction, and being devoted to the interests of the king of England, refused to render it to the French king. Upon this the revenues of the bishop were confiscated by the latter, who ordered also the suspension of the divine service in the Church of Le Mans. These troubles were settled in 1804. Hamelin abdicated about the middle of Lent, 1214, and died probably Nov. 1, 1218. See Hoefer, *Nouv. Biog. Générale*, s. v.

Hamelsveld, Ysbrand van, a former professor of theology at Utrecht, who died May 9, 1812, at Amsterdam, is the author of *Aardrijkunde des Bijbels, mit Karten* (Amsterdam, 1790, 6 vols.; Germ. transl. *Biblische Geographie, übersetzt mit Anmerkungen*, von Rudolf Jänisch, Hamburg, 1793–96):—*Allgemeene Kerkelyke Geschiedenis der Christenen* (Harlem, 1799 sq., 23 vols.). See Winer, *Handbuch der theol. Lit.* i, 149, 537; Fürst, *Bibl. Jud.* i, 360. (B. P.)

Hamet, a Mohammedan prophet, who began to teach on the western coast of Africa in 1792. He rejected the ancient doctrine of the Caliphs, introduced certain modifications into the Moslem faith, and thus gathered a number of followers. Hamet was finally killed, and his followers soon dispersed.

Hamill, Hugh, D.D., a Presbyterian minister, was born at Norristown, Pa., Feb. 28, 1810. He received his preparatory education at Norristown Academy; graduated from Rutgers College, N. J., in 1827; entered Princeton Theological Seminary in November of the same year, and left in April, 1830; then spent the winter of 1831–32 at Yale Divinity School; was licensed by the Presbytery of Philadelphia, April 30, 1830; ordained an evangelist at Buffalo, N. Y., Oct. 31, 1832; became stated supply at Black Rock (now the Breckenridge Street Church, Buffalo), from Nov. 1, 1830, until Nov. 1, 1833; began to preach at Elkton, Md., and Pencader Church, Del., where he was installed pastor by New Castle Presbytery, Jan. 21, 1834; in 1837 became connected with the High School at Lawrenceville, N. J., where he remained thirty-three

years; but about 1870 was obliged to withdraw from the work of teaching on account of impaired hearing, and in 1873 took up his residence at Newark, Del., where he spent his remaining years in study, and died Aug. 1, 1881. He was a man of fine scholarship, and his life was pure, noble, and useful. See *Necrol. Report of Princeton Theol. Sem.* 1882, p. 20.

Hamilton, Alfred, D.D., a Presbyterian minister, was born at Culpepper Court-House, Va., May 1, 1805. He was educated at Jefferson College, Pa., graduated from the Western Theological Seminary, Allegheny, in 1830; was licensed by the Ohio Presbytery, and commissioned by the Board of Domestic Missions to make a tour through Ohio, Kentucky, and Tennessee. In 1835 he accepted a call to the old church of Fagg's Manor, Chester Co., Pa., in New Castle Presbytery, where he remained for twenty-three years as pastor. He died in Chicago, Ill., Sept. 13, 1867. He was for some years associate editor of the *Northwestern Presbyterian.* See Wilson, *Presb. Hist. Almanac*, 1868, p. 103.

Hamilton, David, a Scotch prelate, was bishop of Argyle in 1506. He was witness to the grant which James, earl of Arran, made to James Hamilton, his son, of the lands of Finnart, in 1507. He also held in commendam the two abbeys of Dryburgh and Glenluce, and obtained the abbey of Sandal, in Kintyre, to be annexed to his episcopal see. He was still bishop in 1520. See Keith, *Scottish Bishops*, p. 289.

Hamilton, David Henry, D.D., a Presbyterian minister, was born at Canajoharie, N. Y., Oct. 29, 1813. He graduated from Union College in 1839; studied and practiced law in Amsterdam; graduated from the Auburn Theological Seminary in 1841; entered upon his ministry in 1843 in Trumansburg; subsequently was pastor of three other churches, in New Haven, Conn., Jacksonville, Ill., and Ripley, O. There was an interval of two years between his labors in New Haven and Jacksonville, which was spent in study at the University of Berlin, Germany. He died at Kingsborough, N. Y., July 4, 1879. As a preacher and pastor he was highly prized. He toiled incessantly, and seemed to rest in labors that would utterly break other men down. In these efforts hundreds and thousands were converted, and the churches quickened and strengthened. His *Autology*, an inductive system of mental science, a large octavo of seven hundred pages, published in 1873, is a monument not less to his industry than his mastery of philosophy, and his remarkable powers of independent, bold, sharp thinking. He had spent years in the preparation of a second volume, which he left unfinished, in which the system of theology was to be elaborated in accordance with his mental science. See *Gen. Cat. of Auburn Theol. Sem.* 1883, p. 273. (W. P. S.)

Hamilton, Gavin, a Scotch prelate, was first a minister at Hamilton, and afterwards promoted to the see of Galloway in 1606, and because the revenue was small, king James gave him the abbey of Dundrennan. He was consecrated bishop of Brechin, Oct. 20, 1610, according to the form of the Church of England. He had also a grant from the priory of Whitern annexed to the see of Galloway. Here he sat until his death, in 1614. See Keith, *Scottish Bishops*, p. 280.

Hamilton, Henry Parr, an English divine, son of Dr. Alexander Hamilton of Edinburgh, was born there in 1794, and educated at Trinity College, Cambridge, where he graduated with high honors in 1816. He held a living for several years in Yorkshire, and in 1850 was made dean of Salisbury. He died Feb. 9, 1880. Dean Hamilton published, *The Principles of Analytical Geometry:—Analytical System of Conic Sections:—Remarks on Popular Education:—The Education of the Lower Classes*, and several sermons.

Hamilton, James (1), a Scotch prelate, was reader at Petyn, in the diocese of Moray, and afterwards rector of Spot, in East Lothian. He was elected to the see of Glasgow in 1547. In 1558 he was put into the see of Argyle, and about the same time got the subdeanery of Glasgow in commendam. It is not certain whether he was ever consecrated a bishop. He became a Protestant at the Reformation. In 1565 he granted a charter to Alexander Stewart. He was still in the see in 1575. See Keith, *Scottish Bishops*, p. 289.

Hamilton, James (2), a Scotch bishop, was born in August, 1610, and ordained minister at Cambusnethan in 1634. He was then called to London by the king, and consecrated bishop of the see of Galloway in 1661. He died in 1674. See Keith, *Scottish Bishops*, p. 281.

Hamilton, James (3), M.D., an intimate friend and helper of John Wesley, was born at Dunbar, Scotland, in November or December, 1740. When about the age of eighteen he was appointed surgeon to the *Isis* man-of-war, and it was while that ship was off Malta that Dr. Hamilton became religious. His health declining after four years' service, he settled down in his native town as surgeon and apothecary, where his eminent success soon admitted him as a fellow of the Royal College of Physicians, Edinburgh. After a number of years he removed to Leeds, and subsequently, on invitation of his friends, to London, where he became physician to the London Dispensary. He followed his profession until his death, April 21, 1827. Dr. Hamilton joined the Methodist society on his return to Dunbar, and ever after continued an earnest and devoted member of the community he loved. His Christian character was peculiarly excellent. He co-operated with his friend Wesley, and his advice was sought for by the Methodist preachers, by whom he was much beloved. See *Wesl. Meth. Mag.* July and August, 1829; Stevenson, *City Road Chapel*, p. 503.

Hamilton, John (1), a Scotch prelate, was made abbot of Paisley in 1525, and went to France to pursue his studies. In 1543 he was made keeper of the privy seal, and soon after lord treasurer. He became bishop of St. Andrews the same year, and in 1545 was translated to the see of Dunkeld. Under the regency of the earl of Moray, he was accused of treason, and hanged publicly, April 1, 1570. See Keith, *Scottish Bishops*, p. 38, 95.

Hamilton, John (2), a Scotch prelate, was made bishop of Dunkeld, Oct. 19, 1686. He survived the Revolution, and died one of the ministers of Edinburgh, and sub-dean of his majesty's chapel-royal. See Keith, *Scottish Bishops*, p. 100.

Hamilton, Robert, D.D., a minister of the Church of Scotland, was a son of Dr. William Hamilton, for many years a professor in Edinburgh University, and was born and educated within its walls. He was licensed to preach by the Presbytery of Edinburgh, and served the Church of Cramond, near by, and Lady Yestor's Old Greyfriars' Church in the same city. In 1754 he was elected to the chair of divinity in the university, where he labored until failing health caused the election of Dr. Andrew Hunter as his assistant, and afterwards as his successor. Dr. Hamilton retired soon after this election, in 1779, from active work, and died April 3, 1787. He was moderator of the assembly in 1754 and 1760. See *Annals of the Church of Scotland*, 1739-66, ii, 386.

Hamilton, William, a veteran Irish Wesleyan minister, was born near Newry in 1761. He became a member of a Methodist society at the age of fourteen, in 1788 received an appointment to the Brookboro' Circuit, and for twenty-nine years labored for the evangelism of Ireland. He was the first preacher who encouraged Ouseley's extraordinary plan of labor, inducing the conference to sanction it, and to enroll the missionary on their minutes. Hamilton had superior talents; he was an effective preacher, singularly calm himself, but as singularly powerful over the passions of his hearers. His thoughts were original and often humorous; his arguments ingenious and irresistible; his style simple; the effect of his discourses sometimes magical. He worked with his might. Ouseley declared that he never saw a more indefatigable laborer. Broken down in the labors of the ministry, he was compelled to retire from the active service in 1816. He was one of the eight preachers who received a rebuke of the Irish Conference for the administration of the Lord's Supper. He died Oct. 8, 1843. See Stevens, *Hist. of Methodism*, iii, 420, 435; *Minutes of the British Conference*, 1844; Smith, *Hist. of Wesleyan Methodism*, iii, 24, 25.

Hammer, CHRISTOPH, professor of Oriental languages at Jena, who died March 19, 1597, is the author of *Pædagogus Linguarum Quinque Orientalium* (Jena, 1595). See Jöcher, *Allgemeines Gelehrten-Lexikon*, s. v.; Fürst, *Bibl. Jud.* i, 360; Steinschneider, *Bibl. Handbuch*, s. v. (B. P.)

Hammerschmid, JOHANN FLORIAN, a Roman Catholic theologian, was born May 4, 1652, in Bohemia. He was chaplain at Budweis, rector of the archiepiscopal seminary at Prague, and died there in 1737, dean and apostolical prothonotary. He wrote, *Magnalia S. Andrœ* (Prague, 1685):—*Magnalia S. Joannis Baptistœ* (ibid. 1690):—*Magnalia S. Joannis Evangelistœ* (ibid. eod.):—*Magnalia S. Matthiœ* (ibid. 1700). See Jöcher, *Allgemeines Gelehrten-Lexikon*, s. v.; Winer, *Handbuch der theol. Lit.* i, 566, 567. (B. P.)

Hammon (Josh. xix, 28). Tristram thinks (*Bible Places*, p. 293) that this is one of the mounds "just north of Alma [see UMMAH], bearing the name of *Hamûn;*" but no such name appears on the *Ordnance Map*, nor in the accompanying *Memoirs*. The *Hamûl* which has been thought to be the best modern representative of Hammon is laid down on the *Map* at one and a half miles north-east of Nakmah, as *Ain-Hamul;* which is described in the *Memoirs* (i, 157) as "a large perennial spring of good water, irrigating gardens and turning a mill near its source; a plentiful supply." No ancient ruins are noted in the immediate vicinity. Trelawney Saunders locates it (*Map of the O. T.*) at *Khurbet el-Hima*, ten miles south-east of Tyre, which consists simply of "large heaps of stones" (*Memoirs*, i, 176) without any special marks of antiquity.

Hammond, Charles, LL.D., a Congregational minister, son of Dr. Shubael Hammond, was born at Union, Conn., June 15, 1813. He studied at Monson Academy, and graduated from Yale College in 1839; entered Andover Theological Seminary, and from 1842 to 1844 attended Yale Divinity School. In the meanwhile (1839-41), he was principal of the Monson Academy, and afterwards again occupied that position (1844-1859). From this time till 1863 he was connected with the Lawrence Academy, at Groton, and then was a third time chosen principal of the Monson Academy, a position which he retained until his death, Nov. 7, 1878. He was ordained an evangelist, Oct. 5, 1855, at Tolland, Conn. He was the author of many educational articles, and published several pamphlets. See *Cong. Year-book*, 1879, p. 43.

Hammond, William, an English Calvinistic Methodist minister, was born at Battle, Sussex, Jan. 6, 1719. In 1745 he published a volume of original *Psalms, Hymns, and Spiritual Songs*. Among these were several which are found in many of our modern collections: *Lord, we come before thee now; Would you win a soul to God?* and *Awake and sing the song*. Mr. Hammond was an educated man, having been connected with St. John's College, Cambridge. Later in life he joined the Moravian Brethren, and, upon his decease, Aug. 19, 1783, was interred in their burying-ground in London. He was the author of a volume entitled *The Marrow of the Gospel*. See Belcher, *Historical Sketches of Hymns*, p. 163. (J. C. S.)

Hampulling-cloth. See AMPULLING-CLOTH.

Hamul, the angel who was regarded by the ancient Persians as the inspector of the heavens.

Hamza, in the mythology of the Druses, was a prophet of the Egyptian god Hakem, whom the Druses call their supreme deity. Hamza is an honored hero. Seven times he has come from heaven to the earth. The sacred books of the Druses call Hamza the guide of the compass, the straight road to the only salvation, the establisher of truth, the Imam of all times, the holy spirit, the final cause of all causes. He was the highest Nezir of the god Hakem. He was so highly esteemed by the latter that he ordered all angels to worship him, which they all did except Sheitun (Satan), and for this reason the latter was damned. The four other prophets, Ismael, Mahommed, Selami, and Ali, are called Hamza's wives.

Hanap, a mediæval term for a drinking-cup.

Hanau (or **Hena**), SOLOMON, a Jewish writer of the 18th century, is the author of, ס'בנין שלמה, a large Hebrew grammar (Frankfort, 1708):—ס' יסוד הנקוד, another grammatical work (Amsterdam, 1730):—צהר התבה, also a Hebrew grammar (Berlin, 1733, and often):—ס' שערי תורה, a compendium of Hebrew grammar (Hamburg, 1718):—שערי זמרה, a treatise on the Hebrew accents (1718, 1762):—מחברת שערי תפלה, a grammatical commentary on the daily prayers (1725). His works were opposed by different Jewish writers, against whom he wrote קורי עכביש and קורות ארזים (Fürth, 1744). He left a number of philological works in MS. See Fürst, *Bibl. Jud.* i, 379 sq.; Steinschneider, *Bibl. Handbuch*, s. v.; De' Rossi, *Dizionario Storico* (Germ. transl.), p. 122. (B. P.)

Hanbalites, one of the four orthodox sects of the Mohammedans, which derived its name from Ahmed Ibn-Hanbal, a devout follower of the prophet. He maintained the eternity of the Koran, and thus brought upon himself the vengeance of the caliph al-Motasem, who held that the Koran was created. Hanbal was imprisoned and scourged; but he continued to propagate his opinions until his death, which occurred about the middle of the 8th century. The Hanbalites prevail principally in the wilder districts of Arabia, their austere habits being well suited to the simple manners of the Bedouin.

Hanckel, CHRISTIAN, D.D., a Protestant Episcopal clergyman, was rector, for several years, in Charleston, S. C., and in 1858 in Radcliffborough. At this time he was president of the standing committee of his diocese, a position to which he was re-elected several successive years. In 1866 he retired from the active duties of the ministry, and in 1867 was elected honorary rector of the same church. He died in 1870. See *Prot. Episc. Almanac*, 1871, p. 118.

Hand, AARON HICKS, D.D., a Presbyterian minister, was born at Albany, N. Y., Dec. 3, 1811. He graduated from Williams College in 1831, and from Princeton Theological Seminary in 1837; was licensed by the Presbytery of New Brunswick the same year, and ordained by the Presbytery of Flint River, Ga., in 1841. He became stated supply of the churches of Roswell and Marietta in 1838, and remained until 1841. He then became pastor of the Church in Berwick, Pa., and accepted a call to the Church of Greenwich, N. J. His last charge was the Palisades Presbyterian Church, N. Y., where he remained eight years, and was in consequence of infirmity compelled to resign. His labors in all the churches of which he was pastor were attended with revivals. He died at Easton, Pa., March 3, 1880. See *New York Observer*, March 18, 1880. (W. P. S.)

Handcock, WILLIAM JOHN, noted for his labors in

connection with the French Wesleyan work under the British Conference, was born in the island of Jersey in 1813. He was converted in his nineteenth year, entered the ministry in 1838, and for five years labored in the south of France. His first circuit extended from the Alps to the Mediterranean. In 1841 he was made superintendent of the work in the Upper Alps, and his labors in those dreary regions were the most fatiguing and self-denying, and contributed to the shortening of his days. The eighteen years following 1849 were spent in the French circuits in the Channel Islands. Besides pastoral work he did much in the educational and literary line. The Wesleyan day-schools were established through his efforts, and for several years he edited the *French Methodist Magazine*, a periodical of large circulation and influence. In conjunction with one of his brethren, he prepared the new *French Hymn-Book*, completed in 1867. Failing health compelled him to seek a change of climate, and the same year he went to Birmingham. In 1868 he was appointed to the Uxbridge and Rickmansworth circuits, and died at the latter place, March 25, 1870. Handcock was studious, pious, and of unassuming manners, evangelical as a preacher, and conscientious in the discharge of his duties. He wrote, *Sommaire des Lois Organiques et Règles de Discipline des Églises Méthodistes d'Angleterre* (Guernsey, 1858, 18mo), and an *Exposition of the First Epistle of St. John* (Lond. 1861, 8vo). His biographer, in the *Wesleyan Methodist Magazine* (May, 1876, art. i) (T. J. McCartney), characterized the latter work as learned and original. See also *Minutes of the British Conference*, 1870, p. 29.

Handel, Christian Friedrich, a Lutheran theologian, who died at Neisse, Silesia, Sept. 6, 1841, a superintendent, is the author of, *Evangelische Christenlehre* (11th ed. Breslau, 1852):—*Materialien zu einem vollständigen Unterricht im Christenthum* (3d ed. Halle, 1840):—*Kurzer Inbegriff der christlichen Religionslehre* (Neisse, 1841):—*Alethosebia oder Liturgien für gebildete Gemeinden* (1824). See Winer, *Handbuch der theol. Lit.* ii, 216, 230, 281; Zuchold, *Bibl. Theol.* i, 497. (B. P.)

Handkerchief, Holy. See Veronica, St.

Handy, Isaac William Ker, D.D., a Presbyterian minister, was born in Washington, D. C., Dec. 14, 1815. A part of his early education was received from Salmon P. Chase, afterwards chief-justice of the United States. He graduated from Jefferson College, Pa., in 1834; entered Princeton Theological Seminary in November, 1835, and studied there between one and two years. He was licensed by the Presbytery of the District of Columbia, April 3, 1838; ordained by Lewes Presbytery, Nov. 22, 1838; and installed as pastor of the churches of Buckingham, Blackwater, and Laurel. He next went to Missouri to labor as a missionary, and met with much success at Warsaw and vicinity. He afterwards served the churches at Odessa, Port Penn, and Middletown, Del., where he labored two years. From 1853 for two years he was missionary on the eastern peninsula of Maryland. His next pastorate was at Portsmouth, Va. He was installed pastor of Augusta Church, in Virginia, May 13, 1870. From the division of the Church in 1861, Dr. Handy adhered throughout the rest of his life to the Southern General Assembly. During the civil war he was a prisoner for fifteen months at Fort Delaware in 1863-64. He died June 14, 1878. Dr. Handy was many years a trustee of Delaware College at Newark, Del., a member of the Presbyterian Historical Society, of the American Scientific Association, and of the Maryland Historical Society. He had a wide reputation for accurate research. See *Necrol. Report of Princeton Theol. Sem.* 1879, p. 37.

Hane, Philipp Friedrich, a Lutheran theologian of Germany, was born Feb. 2, 1696, at Belitz, in Mecklenburg. He studied at Rostock and Jena, was in 1724 librarian at Kiel, in 1730 doctor and professor of theology, and in 1733 member of consistory. He died Sept. 27, 1774, leaving, *Leben und Thaten Ignatii Loyolä* (Rostock, 1721, 1725):—*De Conciliis Lateranensibus* (Kiel, 1726):—*De Sacrorum Christianorum in Cimbria Primordiis* (1728):—*De Melanchthonis Moderatione in August. Confess. Negotio Conspicua* (1730):—*Historia Critica August. Confessionis* (1732):—*Sermones de Tempore* (1766). See Moser, *Jetztlebende Theologen;* Jöcher, *Allgemeines Gelehrten-Lexikon*, s. v.; Winer, *Handbuch der theol. Lit.* i, 328, 329, 723, 827. (B. P.)

Haneberg, Daniel Bonifacius, bishop of Spires, was born June 16, 1816, at Tanne, Bavaria. He studied at Munich, was priest in 1839, and commenced his academical career in 1840. In 1850 he entered the newly founded Benedictine monastery of St. Bonifacius, at Munich, and was made abbot in 1854. In 1861 he went to Algiers and Tunis, and in 1864 to Jerusalem. In 1868 he was called to Rome as consulter of the Romish congregation for Oriental rites, and at the same time to take part in the preparations for the Vatican Council. Like many others, he was at first opposed to the dogma of papal infallibility, but finally yielded to it. In 1872 Haneberg was appointed bishop of Spires, and died May 31, 1876. He published, *Ueber die in einer münchener Handschrift aufbehaltene arabische Psalmenübersetzung des Rabbi Saadia Gaon* (Ratisbon, 1841):—*Religiöse Alterthümer der Hebräer* (1844; 2d ed. 1869):—*Einleitung in das Alte Testament* (1845):—*Geschichte der biblischen Offenbarung* (1850; 3d ed. 1863):—*Renan's Leben Jesu beleuchtet* (1864):—*Zur Erkenntnisslehre von Ibn Sina und Albertus Magnus* (Munich, 1866):—*Canones S. Hippolyti Arabice e Codicibus Romanis* (1870). From his manuscript Schegg published *Evangelium nach Johannes übersetzt und erklärt* (1878-80, 2 vols.). See Schegg, *Erinnerungen an Haneberg* (Munich, 1877). (B. P.)

Haner, Georg, a Lutheran theologian of Germany, was born April 8, 1672. He studied at Wittenberg, was in 1736 superintendent in Transylvania, and died July 10, 1759, leaving, *De Subjecto Philosophiæ Moralis* (Wittenberg, 1691):—*De Lustratione Hebræorum* (1692):—*De Litterarum Hebraicarum Origine* (eod.):—*De Punctorum Hebræorum cum Litteris Coævitate* (1693):—*Historia Ecclesiarum Transylvanicarum a Primis Populorum Originibus ad Hæcusque Tempora* (Frankfort, 1694). See Benko, *Transylvania*, ii, 205, 429; Winer, *Handbuch der theol. Lit.* i, 839; Fürst, *Bibl. Jud.* i, 360; Jöcher, *Allgemeines Gelehrten-Lexikon*, s. v. (B. P.)

Hanifees, an orthodox Mohammedan sect, who derived their name from their founder, Abn-Hanifa, the first Moslem casuist, who flourished in the 8th century. He learned the principles and traditions of Mohammedanism from those who had lived in the time of the prophet, and was a lifelong partisan of Ali (q. v.), although now he is regarded as the chief authority of the Sonnites (q. v.). He was imprisoned for refusing to accept the office of judge, and is said to have been poisoned for resisting the execution of a severe edict against the citizens of Mosul in 767. The Hanifees are usually called the followers of reason, because they are guided chiefly by their own judgment in giving decisions, while the other Mohammedan sects adhere more closely to the letter of tradition. This is now the established faith of the Turks and Tartars, but it has branched into numerous subdivisions.

Hänlein, Heinrich Carl Alexander von, a Lutheran theologian of Germany, was born at Anspach, July 11, 1762. He studied at Erlangen and Göttingen, was in 1788 professor of theology at Erlangen, in 1808 member of consistory at Munich, in 1818 director of the Protestant superior consistory, and died at Esslingen, May 15, 1829. He wrote, *Observationes ad loca Quædam Vet. Test.* (Göttingen, 1788):—*Einleitung in die Schriften des Neuen Testaments* (Erlangen, 1794, 2 vols.; 2d ed. 1801-1803):—*Symbolæ Criticæ ad Interpretationem Vaticiniorum Habacuci* (ibid. 1795):—*Commentarius in Epistolam Judæ* (ibid. 1795-96):—*De Lectoribus*

Epistolæ Pauli ad Ephesios (ibid. 1797):—*Curæ in Libros Novi Fœderis* (1798-1804, 7 parts):—*Lehrbuch der Einleitung in die Schriften des Neuen Testaments* (1802):—*Epistola Judæ, Græce* (1804). See Döring, *Die gelehrten Theologen Deutschlands*, s. v.; Winer, *Handbuch der theol. Lit.* i, 9, 75, 103, 210, 229, 273, 556; ii, 173. (B. P.)

Hanna, Thomas, D.D., a Presbyterian minister, was born Oct. 4, 1799. He graduated at Jefferson College, Pa., in 1818; was licensed by the Chartiers Presbytery in 1820; in 1821 became pastor at Cadiz, O.; in 1850 at Washington, Pa.; and died Feb. 9, 1864. As a preacher he was clear and methodical, though his doctrines and mode of treating them was not according to the modern school. See Wilson, *Presb. Hist. Almanac*, 1865, p. 205.

Hanna, William, D.D., LL.D., a Presbyterian minister, son of Rev. Dr. Samuel Hanna, was born at Belfast, Ireland, in 1808. He received his literary and theological education at the University of Glasgow, Scotland, and entered the ministry in 1835, in which he spent a laborious and useful life, and died May 24, 1882. He wrote the biography of Dr. Chalmers, and also of Wycliffe, and an interesting history of the Huguenots, besides several other valuable works.

Hannapes, Nicolas de, a French prelate, the last of the Latin patriarchs of Jerusalem, was born at Hannapes, in the Ardennes mountains, about 1525. At the age of twelve he joined the Dominicans at Rheims, afterwards studied at the convent of St. Jacques, Paris, was ordained priest, and taught theology. He was called to Rome by pope Innocent V, where he exercised the functions of grand-penitentiary, later was selected by Nicolas IV as patriarch of Jerusalem, and in 1289 apostolic legate in Syria, Cyprus, and Armenia. Jean d'Acre was taken by the Turks, and the mission was broken up. Hannapes died in 1291, leaving, *Virtutum Vitiorumque Exempla, ex Sacris Litteris Excerpta* (Tübingen, 1533):—*Dicta Salutis Nicolai de Hannapis, ord. Prædicat.* (Mayence, 1609):—*Nicolai Patriarchæ Hyerosoly. Typicon de Jejuniis Græcorum*, etc. See Hoefer, *Nouv. Biog. Générale*, s. v.

Hannathon. For this site Tristram suggests (*Bible Places*, p. 253) *Deir Hannan*, meaning doubtless what is laid down on the *Ordnance Map* as *Deir Hanna*, three miles south-west of Mughar (the locality which we had conjectured), and thus described in the *Memoirs* (i, 364): "High walls all round the village, which is built of stone. The walls have round towers, and were built by Dhaker el-'Amr's son, S'ad el-'Amr. It is situated on the top of a high ridge, and contains about four hundred Christians. It is surrounded by olive groves and arable land. Water is obtained from cisterns and an old paved *birkeh* [pool] to the north of the village." No ancient remains are noted in the immediate vicinity. Mr. Trelawney Saunders coincides with this location (*Map of the O. T.*). Lieut. Conder, however, prefers (*Tent Work*, ii, 337) *Kefr 'Anân*, which is too far north, being five miles south-west of Sofed, and equally destitute of any traces of antiquity (*Memoirs*, i, 203).

Hannauer, Georg, a Roman Catholic theologian of Germany, was born in 1817. In 1843 he was made priest, in 1851 professor of philosophy at the Lyceum in Ratisbon, and died Jan. 11, 1868. He wrote *Ueber den Ursprung der Ideen nach Thomas von Aquin* (Ratisbon, 1855). (B. P.)

Hanneken, Menno, a Lutheran theologian of Germany, was born March 1, 1595, at Blaxen, in Oldenburg. He studied at Giessen, was in 1619 conrector at Oldenburg, in 1626 professor at Marburg, in 1646 superintendent at Lübeck, and died Feb. 17, 1671. He wrote, *Scutum Veritatis Catholicæ contra Thomam Henrici:—Synopsis Theologiæ:—Expositio Epistolæ Pauli ad Ephesios:—Doctrina de Justificatione Hominis coram Deo:—Grammatica Hebraica:—Quattuor Disput. de Augustana Confessione Invariata; Tres Disp. Hebræo-Theologicæ.* See Moller, *Cimbria Litterata*; Fürst, *Bibl. Jud.* i, 361; Steinschneider, *Bibl. Handbuch*, s. v.; Jöcher, *Allgemeines Gelehrten-Lexikon*, s. v. (B. P.)

Hanneken, Philip Ludwig, a Lutheran theologian of Germany, son of Menno, was born at Marburg, June 5, 1637. He studied at different universities, was in 1663 professor of elocution at Giessen, in 1668 doctor and professor of theology there, in 1693 professor at Wittenberg, and died Jan. 16, 1706, leaving, *Annotata Philologica in Josuam:—Declaratio Augustanæ Confessionis:—Mysterium Antichristi Ostensum:—Disputationes de Providentia, de Sessione Christi ad Dexteram Dei, de Baptismo Primarum Chiliadum ad Christum Conversarum, de Amore Dei Salutari in Judam Proditorem, de Moribus Regni Christi Illisque Oppositis Pietismo et Chiliasmo*, etc. See Moller, *Cimbria Litterata*; Fürst, *Bibl. Jud.* i, 361; Steinschneider, *Bibl. Handbuch*, s. v.; Jöcher, *Allgemeines Gelehrten-Lexikon*, s. v. (B. P.)

Hannover, Nathan, *ben-Moses*, a Jewish writer of the 17th century, is the author of יון מצולה, or a history of the persecution of the Jews in Poland, Lithuania, etc. (Venice, 1653; transl. also into Judæo-German):—שפה ברורה, a dictionary of the Hebrew language, with the corresponding German, Italian, and Latin words (Prague, 1660; an edition containing also the French was edited by Koppel ben-Wolf, Amsterdam, 1701). See Fürst, *Bibl. Jud.* i, 361 sq.; De' Rossi, *Dizionario Storico* (Germ. transl.), p. 122. (B. P.)

Hansch, Michael Gottlieb, a Lutheran theologian of Germany, was born Sept. 22, 1683. He studied at Leipsic, where he also lectured from 1709 to 1711. It was his intention to publish Kepler's manuscripts, which he had bought at Dantzic, but he only succeeded in publishing the first volume, as he could not get the support necessary for such an undertaking. Hansch died in 1752, leaving, *De Justificatione Fidelium sub Veteri Testamento, contra Paresin Coccejanam* (1702):—*De Mediis Cognoscendi Existentiam et Divinitatem Scripturæ Sacræ* (1709):—*De Fundamentali in Fide Dissensu* (eod.). See Döring, *Die gelehrten Theologen Deutschlands*, s. v.; Jöcher, *Allgemeines Gelehrten-Lexikon*, s. v. (B. P.)

Hansell, William Forde, D.D., a Baptist minister, was born in Philadelphia, Dec. 5, 1815. He graduated from Brown University in 1845, and from Princeton Theological Seminary in 1848; was ordained in 1849 in the First Baptist Church in Philadelphia, and became pastor of the Central Baptist Church in Poughkeepsie, N. Y., April 1, 1849. In April, 1853, he was released from that Church, and installed pastor of the Ninth Street Baptist Church in Cincinnati, O., Feb. 5, 1854. His services ended here July 18, 1858. For several years he resided in Philadelphia without pastoral charge. Removing to Hartford, Conn., in 1872, he preached frequently for various churches in and near that city. On going to Rainbow, a town between Hartford and Springfield, April 12, 1874, he became deeply interested in that field, remaining there and organizing a Church, which was constituted May 18, 1875. The last time he appeared in public was before the annual meeting of the Hartford Baptist Association, as the representative of that new Church. He died Nov. 26, 1875. Dr. Hansell's sermons were admirably clear; sound in doctrine, graceful in construction and expression. He dwelt specially on the person and work of the Lord Jesus Christ. See *Necrol. Report of Princeton Theol. Sem.* 1877, p. 39.

Hansen, Franz Volkmar Reinhard, a Lutheran theologian, was born in 1815. In 1843 he was pastor at Keitum, in the island of Sylt, Schleswig, but was deposed by the Danish government in 1850. From 1852 to 1862 he was court-preacher to queen Amalie, at Athens, in 1864 provost and first pastor in Schleswig, and died June 28, 1879. He is the author of, *Die Auf-*

gabe Deutschlands und die Union im Zusammenhange der Zeitgeschichte (1873). (B. P.)

Hansen, Ludwig, a Lutheran minister, was born at Hildesheim, Feb. 1, 1664. He studied at Jena, was in 1689 pastor at his native place, and died Feb. 28, 1694, leaving, *Disp. de Dæmonibus* (Jena, 1684):—*De Simplicitate Dei* (eod.):—*De Salute Majorum in Papatu* (1688). See Lauenstein, *Hildesh. Kirchenhistorie*, vii, 38; Jöcher, *Allgemeines Gelehrten-Lexikon*, s. v. (B. P.)

Hansen, Petrus, a Lutheran theologian, was born July 6, 1686, in Schleswig. He studied at Kiel, was deacon in 1714, in 1720 first pastor at Plön, Holstein, in 1729 member of consistory and superintendent, and died in 1760, leaving, *De Astuto Juliani Apostati Studio in Abolenda cum Scholis Religione Christiana* (Plön, 1733):—*Diss. Synod. de Differentia inter Religionem Naturalem et Revelatam contra Tindalium* (1733). Besides, he published a number of ascetical works. See Moser and Neubauer, *Jetztlebende Theologen;* Jöcher, *Allgemeines Gelehrten-Lexikon*, s. v. (B. P.)

Hansiz, Markus, a Jesuit and Church historian of Austria, was born April 23, 1683, at Völkermarkt, in Carinthia. He was educated in the Jesuit college at Eberndorf, studied at Vienna, and, after receiving holy orders, was for many years professor of philosophy at Gratz. His ecclesiastical researches made him conceive the idea of producing a *Germania Sacra*, after the pattern of the *Gallia Christiana* (Paris, 1656 sq.), Ughelli's *Italia Sacra* (Venice, 1717 sq.), and Wharton's *Anglia Sacra* (Lond. 1691), and he undertook a journey to Rome with a view of examining the libraries there. In 1727 he published the first volume of his *Germania Sacra: Metropolis Laureacensis cum Episcopatu Pataviensi,Chronologice Proposita* (fol.); the second volume, published in 1729, is entitled, *Archiepiscopatus Salisburgensis Chronol. Prop.;* the third volume, published in 1754, is styled, *De Episcopatu Ratisbonensi Prodromus, sive Informatio Summaria de Sede Antiqua Ratisbonensi.* The freedom with which he treated local legends roused such an opposition to him that he felt compelled to renounce literary labor in 1756, but he encouraged others to continue his work. Hansiz died Sept. 5, 1766, at Vienna, and his book was continued by Ussermann and others. See Backer, *Écrivains de la Compagnie de Jésus*, ii, 285; Werner, *Gesch. der kathol. Theologie*, p. 132; Rettberg, *Kirchen-Geschichte Deutschlands*, i, 2 sq.; Lichtenberger, *Encyclop. des Sciences Religieuses*, s. v.; Plitt-Herzog, *Real-Encyklop.* s. v. (B. P.)

Hanstein, Gottfried August Ludwig, a Lutheran theologian of Germany, was born at Magdeburg, Sept. 7, 1761. He studied at Halle, was in 1782 teacher at the cathedral-school of his native place, in 1787 preacher at Tangermünde, in 1804 member of consistory and preacher at Berlin, and died Feb. 25, 1821, doctor of theology. He published homiletical and ascetical works, for which see Döring, *Deutsche Kanzelredner;* Winer, *Handbuch der theol. Lit.* ii, 62, 94, 97, 118, 130, 148, 156, 158, 164, 168, 170, 172, 173, 175, 177, 197, 199, 203, 205, 206, 227, 233, 357; Zuchold, *Bibl. Theol.* i, 501. (B. P.)

Hanuman, the *ape-god* of the Hindûs, son of Pavan, lord of the winds. There is a reference to Hanuman in the Ramayana (q. v.), in which the monkey-chief is introduced as heading the natives of India, who had come to the assistance of Rama. In memory of this service a small pagoda is erected to his honor in the temples of Vishnu.

Haphraim. This place, according to Tristram (*Bible Places*, p. 237), "is probably represented by the little village of *el-Afuleh*, two miles west of Shunem, in the plain;" the position which we had assigned it [see Issachar], and which is adopted by Mr. Grove in Dr. Smith's *Atlas.* It is laid down on the *Ordnance Map* at two and a half miles due west of Solam, and is described in the *Memoirs* (ii, 40) as "a small village of mud in the plain, supplied by two wells. This is possibly the *Ophlah* of the lists of Thothmes III (on the temple at Karnak). Compare el-Fueh (one mile to the east). It is also mentioned by Maria Sanuto (A.D. 1321) under the name of *Afel.*" There are no other indications of antiquity. Lieut. Conder suggests (*Tent Work*, ii, 337) the identity of Haphraim with Khurbet el-Farrîyeh, which is laid down on the *Ordnance Map* far away from Shunem, at two and a half miles south of Ain-Keimûn (Jokneam), on the north edge of Mount Carmel; and is described as "a steep hillock with traces of ruins, and on the north a good spring in the valley" (*Memoir*, ii, 58, where a description and plan of the ancient tombs are given). In this latter location Mr. Trelawney Saunders coincides (*Map of the O. T.*).

Hapi. See Apis.

Happach, Johann Casimir, a Lutheran theologian of Germany, was born in 1726. He was director and professor of theology at the Coburg gymnasium in 1772, and died Aug. 11, 1783, member of consistory. He wrote, *Comm. de Calumnia Religiosa et Theologia Civili Veterum Præsertim Romanorum* (Coburg, 1749):—*De Conatibus Quibusdam Translationes Bibliorum Emendandi* (1772):—*De Papyro ad Hiob viii*, 11 (eod.):—*Explicatio Nova Cladis Bethsemiticæ*, 1 *Sam. vi*, 19 (3 parts, 1774):—*Progr. III ad Gen. xlvii*, 24 (1775):—*Progr. VI Super Quibusdam Locis Prophetæ Hoseæ* (1776, 1777). See Meusel, *Gelehrtes Deutschland;* Fürst, *Bibl. Jud.* i, 362; Jöcher, *Allgemeines Gelehrten-Lexikon*, s. v. (B. P.)

Happach, Lorenz Philipp Gottfried, a Protestant theologian of Germany, was born Jan. 6, 1742, at Hoyersdorf, near Dessau, studied at Halle, was rector and chaplain in 1764, preacher at Alten in 1772, and in 1780 at Mehringen. He died July 20, 1814, leaving *Naëmann Syrus, Illustrandum* (Bremen, 1774):—*Theologische Nebenstunden* (Dessau, 1798-1805):—*Ueber die Beschaffenheit des künftigen Lebens nach dem Tode, aus Ansichten der Bibel* (ibid. 1809-11, 2 vols.). See Döring, *Die gelehrten Theologen Deutschlands;* Winer, *Handbuch der theol. Lit.* i, 475; ii, 51. (B. P.)

Happersett, Reese, D.D., a Presbyterian minister, was born at Brandywine, Pa., July 31, 1810. He graduated from Washington College, Pa., in 1836, and from Princeton Theological Seminary in 1839; was licensed by the New Castle Presbytery the same year, and ordained in 1841. In 1844 he was appointed agent for the Board of Domestic Missions, and in this position was eminently active and useful. In 1850 he became assistant secretary of the board, and in 1859 was elected corresponding secretary. He died Oct. 2, 1866. See Wilson, *Presb. Hist. Almanac*, 1867, p. 154.

Happiness, absolutely **taken**, denotes the durable possession of perfect good, without any mixture of evil; or the enjoyment of pure pleasure unalloyed with pain; or a state in which all our wishes are satisfied; in which senses, happiness is only known by name on this earth. The word happy, when applied to any state or condition of human life, will admit of no positive definition, but is merely a relative term; that is, when we call a man happy, we mean that he is happier than some others with whom we compare him; or than the generality of others; or than he himself was in some other situation. Moralists justly observe that happiness does not consist in the pleasures of sense; as eating, drinking, music, painting, theatrical exhibitions, etc., for these pleasures continue but a little while, by repetition lose their relish, and by high expectation often bring disappointment. Nor does happiness consist in an exemption from labor, care, business, etc.; such a state being usually attended with depression of spirits, imaginary anxieties, and the whole train of hypochondriacal affections. Nor is it to be found in greatness, rank, or elevated stations, as matter of fact abundantly testifies; but happiness consists in the enjoyment of the Divine favor, a good conscience, and uniform conduct. In subordination to these, human happiness may be greatly promoted by the exercise of the social affections, the pursuit of some engaging end, the prudent constitution of the habits, and the enjoyment of our health.

Hara, one of the names of *Siva* (q. v.).

Haræus, FRANZ, a learned Dutch Catholic divine, was born at Utrecht in 1550, and educated in the academy there, after which he travelled through Germany, Italy, and Russia. He was made canon of Bois-le-Duc, then of Namur and Louvain. He died at the latter place, Jan. 12, 1632. His principal works are, *Biblia Sacra Expositionibus Priscorum Patrum Litteralibus et Mysticis Illustrata* (1630):—*Catena Aurea in IV Evangelia* (1625):—*Vitæ Sanctorum.*

Harald, a Scotch prelate, was bishop of the see of Argyle in 1228. See Keith, *Scottish Bishops*, p. 285.

Haram, a term used by Mohammedans to denote what deserves reprimand or punishment, because expressly forbidden by the law. It is the opposite of Halal (q. v.). The word *Haram* also signifies a sacred thing from which infidels are to abstain, as the temple of Mecca, or Mohammed's tomb at Medina.

Harbads, a name substituted by Zoroaster for the magi (q. v.) of the ancient Persians, and designed to denote the priests of the Guebres. See PARSEES.

Harbart, BURCHARD, doctor and professor of theology at Leipsic, was born in 1546, and died Feb. 18, 1614. He is the author of, *Theses de Smalcaldicæ Confessionis Articulis:*—*Doctrina de Conjugio:*—*Capita Doctrinam de Confessione Veræ Fidei Complectentia:*—*Capita de Lege Divina:*—*De Spiritu Sancto:*—*De Libero Hominis Arbitrio:*—*De Sacramentis in Genere:*—*De Ministerio Ecclesiastico.* See Vogel, *Leipziger Annalen;* Freher, *Theatrum Eruditorum;* Jöcher, *Allgemeines Gelehrten-Lexikon*, s. v. (B. P.)

Harcourt, Agnès d', a French nun, sister of Robert, became abbess of Longchamps, and died in 1291.

Harcourt, Guy d', a French prelate, brother of Robert, became bishop of Lisieux in 1303.

Harcourt, Louis d', a French prelate, became archbishop of Narbonne in 1452, and died Dec. 14, 1479. See Hoefer, *Nouv. Biog. Générale*, s. v.

Harcourt, Philippe d', a French prelate and statesman, was originally archdeacon of Bayeux, became bishop of that see in 1142, and died in the abbey of Le Bec about 1160. See Hoefer, *Nouv. Biog. Générale*, s. v.

Harcourt, Robert d', a French prelate and diplomat, became bishop of Coutances in 1291.

Hardenbergh, JAMES B., D.D., an eminent Reformed (Dutch) minister, was born at Rochester, N. Y., June 28, 1800. Early converted and consecrated to the ministry, he graduated from Union College in 1821, and from the Theological Seminary at New Brunswick in 1824. His first settlement was at Helderberg and Princeton, N. Y. (1824-25). He was then called to succeed Dr. Isaac Ferris, in the First Church, New Brunswick, N. J., where he remained four years (1825-29). From thence he went to Orchard Street, New York city, for a single year, when he succeeded Dr. Bethune at Rhinebeck (1830-36), and followed him again in the First Church of Philadelphia (Crown Street), where he labored successfully until 1840, and then accepted the charge of the Franklin Street, or North-west Reformed Dutch Church, in New York. Here he remained sixteen years, a healer of old dissensions, and a leader of the people to new and long prosperity. Meantime by his exertions the church edifice in Franklin Street was sold, and a new one erected in Twenty-third Street. In 1856 he resigned his pastorate to seek rest and recuperation for wasted health and strength. After a year in Europe, and two winters in the South, he preached in Savannah and Macon, Ga. Upon his return from a second visit abroad, he devoted his ample means and willing services to the founding of a city mission on the corner of Madison and Gouverneur streets, New York city. He died Jan. 24, 1870. Dr. Hardenbergh was a man of majestic frame, countenance, and bearing, handsome beyond most men, dignified, graceful, and cultivated. His preaching was earnest, evangelical, simple, direct, scriptural, and practical. "His fervor was intense. At communion seasons his face was radiant with emotion, and his tones thrilling with tenderness. He was loyal to the Church of his fathers, active in her benevolent boards, and held high rank among the first men of his period." He was a trustee of Rutgers College from 1825 till his death, and was president of the General Synod in 1842. See *Memorial Sermon*, by A. R. Thompson, D.D. (W. J. R. T.)

Hardin, ROBERT, D.D., a Presbyterian minister, was born in Greene County, Tenn., Jan. 3, 1789. He was educated in Greenville College, and studied theology privately; was licensed by Union Presbytery, ordained by French Broad Presbytery in 1814, and became pastor of the Westminster and St. Paul churches. He died in Lewisburg, Sept. 4, 1867. Dr. Hardin was considered by his brethren as a man of great moral worth and deep piety, and theological attainments far above the average. See Wilson, *Presb. Hist. Almanac*, 1868, p. 333.

Harding, NEHEMIAH HENRY, D.D., a Presbyterian minister, was born at Brunswick, Me., in October, 1794. He graduated from the University of North Carolina in 1825; spent two years in Princeton Theological Seminary; was ordained by the Presbytery of Orange, April 18, 1829; became stated supply for Milton, N. C., Bethany and Red House, and died at the former place, Feb. 17, 1849. See *Gen. Cat. of Princeton Theol. Sem.* 1881, p. 58.

Hardouim, *Saint.* See CHADŒNUS.

Hardt, ANTON JULIUS VON DER, a German theologian and Orientalist, was born at Brunswick, Nov. 13, 1707. He was professor of theology and Oriental languages at Helmstädt, and died June 27, 1785, leaving, *Epistola Rabbinica de Quibusdam Priscorum Ebræorum Rectoribus Magnificis* (Helmstädt, 1727):—*Diss. de Zereda, Gemino in Palestina et Peræa Appido* (ibid. 1728):—*De Sarepta* (eod.):—*De Judæorum Statuto Scripturæ Sensum Inflectendi* (eod.):—*Commentatio in Frontem Libri Moralis Mischnici Pirke Aboth* (eod.):—*De Jubilæo Mosis Levit. xv* (eod.):—*De Sophismatibus Judæorum in Probandis suis Constitutionibus* (1729):—*Rabbi Isaaci Aramæ Diss. Rabbinica de Usu Linguæ, cum Versione Latina* (eod.):—*Commentatio de Medrasch Symbolica Veterum Judæorum Interpretandi Ratione* (eod.):—*De Proverbio Judæorum de Camelis* (eod.):—*De Diversa Nominum Dei Jehovah et Elohim Lectione ac Scriptione* (1748):—*Grammatica Hebraica* (1775):—*De Christo Rege, ex Stirpe Davidis Oriundo* (1766):—*Pentecoste Judæorum* (1785). See Döring, *Die gelehrten Theologen Deutschlands;* Fürst, *Bibl. Jud.* i, 362; Jöcher, *Allgemeines Gelehrten-Lexikon*, s. v. (B. P.)

Hardtschmidt, JOHANN NICOLAUS, a Lutheran theologian of Strasburg, where he died in 1706, doctor and professor, is the author of, *De αὐτοχειρίᾳ Simsonis Licita ad Judic. xvi*, 30:—*De Jure Dei in Homines:*—*De Hæmorrhoidibus ad* 1 *Sam. vi*, 5:—*De Justificatione ex Fide non ex Lege, ad Galat. iii*, 11, 12:—*De Perfectione Fidelium ad Phil. iv*, 13:—*De Religione Ecclesiastica ad* 1 *Thess. v*, 21:—*De Seculo Aureo ad Apocalypsis, xx*, 5, 6:—*De Duratione Angelorum:*—*De Peccatis Electorum in Judicio Extremo non Publicandis:*—*De Mundi Æternitate:*—*Theses Theologicæ Adversus Errores Quosdam Pietisticos.* See Jöcher, *Allgemeines Gelehrten-Lexikon*, s. v. (B. P.)

Harenberg, Johann Christoph, a Lutheran theologian of Germany, was born April 24, 1696, studied at Helmstädt, and was rector at Gandersheim in 1720. In 1735 he was pastor, and accepted a call in 1745 as professor of history and antiquities to Brunswick, where he died, Nov. 12, 1774. He wrote, *Kurze Einleitung in die Æthiopische, sonderlich Habessinische alte und neue Theologie* (Helmstädt, 1719):—*De Specularibus Veterum, ad Locum* 1 *Cor. xiii*, 12 (ibid. eod.):—*Veri Divinique Natales Circumcisionis Judaicæ, Templi Salomonei, Musices Davidicæ in Sacris, et Baptismi Christianorum* (1720):—*Jura Israëlitarum in Palæstinam* (Hildesheim, 1724):—*De Articulis Suobacensibus, Fundamento Augustanæ Confessionis* (Brunswick, 1730):—*Historia Ecclesiæ Gundersheimensis Cathedralis et Collegiatæ Diplomatica* (Hanover, 1734):—*Otia Gundersheimensis, Exponendis Sacris Litteris et Historia Ecclesiasticæ Dicata, Complexa XIII Observationes* (Utrecht, 1740):—*Zwei Religionsspötter, Celsus und Edelmann* (Leipsic, 1748):—*Amos Propheta, Expositus Interpretatione Nova Latina* (Leyden, 1763):—*Aufklärung des Buches Daniel* (1773, 2 vols.). See Döring, *Die gelehrten Theologen Deutschlands;* Winer, *Handbuch der theol. Lit.* i, 21, 221, 226, 594, 722, 798; Jöcher, *Allgemeines Gelehrten-Lexikon*, s. v. (B. P.)

Hareth. Lieut. Conder argues at length (*Quar. Statement* of the "Pal. Explor. Fund," January, 1875, p. 42 sq.) against the existence of any forest in this vicinity, and therefore prefers the reading עִיר (*city*) to יַעַר (*wood*); but his reasoning is based upon a misconception (corrected in his *Tent Work*, ii, 88) of the latter word, which usually does not imply *timber*, but simply a *copse* or low brushwood. He finds the locality in question in the "small modern village of *Kharâs*, in the hills on the north side of Wady Arneba, one of the heads of the valley of Elah (Wady es-Sunt); an ancient site, with the usual indications—wells, cisterns, and rough caves in the hill-sides." It is laid down on the *Ordnance Map* seven and a half miles east of Beit-Jibrin, and two miles east of Khurbet Kila (Keilah). This identification is concurred in by Tristram (*Bible Places*, p. 43) and Trelawney Saunders (*Map of the O. T.*).

Harigara, a word which, when pronounced along with Siva and Rama, is believed by the Hindûs to bring down numberless blessings upon him who utters it. The moment these three sacred words escape from the lips, all sins are cancelled; but if they are thrice repeated, the gods are so honored that they are at a loss to find a recompense equal to the merit. Such privileged persons are no longer obliged to pass into other bodies, but are straightway absorbed in Brahm.

Harington, Edward Charles, an Anglican clergyman, was born about 1807; graduated from Worcester College, Oxford, in 1827; was appointed chancellor in 1847, in 1857 resident canon of Exeter Cathedral, and died July 18, 1881. He wrote numerous works on Church history and polity, for which see Allibone, *Dict. of Brit. and Amer. Authors*, s. v.

Hariŏli were magicians who are mentioned by ancient writers as waiting on the altars of the heathen to receive their inspiration from the fumes of the sacrifices.

Harishandis, a sect composed of *doms* or sweepers in the western province of Hindustan, the members of which are very scarce, or, perhaps, entirely extinct.

Harless, Gottlieb Christoph Adolph, a Lutheran theologian of Germany, was born at Nüremberg, Nov. 21, 1806. He studied philosophy and theology at Erlangen and Halle, and commenced his academical career at the former place in 1828. In 1836 he was appointed professor and university preacher, in 1838 he took part in starting the *Zeitschrift für Protestantismus und Kirche*, and in 1842 he published his *Christliche Ethik*, of which eight editions were printed, and which was also translated into English (Edinburgh, 1868). To this period belongs his activity as member of parliament in the Bavarian diet, where he so energetically fought for the cause of Protestantism that the ultramontane minister, Abel, deposed him from his professorship, and in 1845 sent him as member of consistory to Bayreuth. In the same year, however, he was called to Leipsic, where he labored as professor and preacher at St. Nicholai till 1847, when the king of Saxony appointed him court-preacher and vice-president of the consistory. In 1852 Harless was called to Munich as president of the Protestant superior consistory, and directed the affairs of the Protestant Church in Bavaria for twenty-five years. He died Sept. 5, 1879. Besides his *Ethik*, he published, *De Revelatione et Fide* (Erlangen, 1830):—*Commentar über den Brief Pauli an die Epheser* (1834; 2d ed. 1858):—*Die kritische Bearbeitung des Lebens Jesu von David Fr. Strauss beleuchtet* (1836):—*Theologische Encyklopädie und Methodologie* (1837):—*De Supernaturalismo Gentilium seu de via et Ratione Superstitionem a Religione Recte Distinguendi* (1838):—*Lucubrationum Evangelia Canonica Spectantium Pars I et II* (1841, 1842):—*Die Sonntagsweihe*, sermons (2d ed. 1860, 4 vols.):—*Kirche und Amt nach lutherischer Lehre* (1853):—*Die Ehescheidungsfrage* (1861):—*Das Verhältniss des Christenthums zu Kultur- und Lebensfragen der Gegenwart* (1863; 2d ed. 1866):—*Jakob Böhme und die Alchimisten* (1870; 2d ed. 1882):—*Geschichtsbilder aus der luther. Kirche Livlands* (1869):—*Staat und Kirche* (1870). See Zuchold, *Bibl. Theol.* i, 501-503; Lichtenberger, *Encyclop. des Sciences Religieuses*, s. v.; Stählin, *G. Chr. A. Harless*, in *Zeitschrift für kirchliche Wissenschaft*, 1880, ii and iii; but especially Harless's own work, *Bruchstücke aus dem Leben eines süddeutschen Theologen* (Bielefeld, 1872-75, 2 vols.). (B. P.)

Harmar, John, an English clergyman and scholar, was born about 1594, at Churchdowne, near Gloucester, and educated at Winchester School. He was appointed Greek professor in that school in 1650, and in 1659 was presented to the rectory of Enhurst, in Hampshire. He died Nov. 1, 1670. His principal works are, *Eclogæ Sententiarum et Similitudinum, e Chrysostomo Decerptæ* (Greek and Latin, with notes, 1622):—*Epistola ad Lambertum Osbaldestonum* (1649):—*A Short Catechism.* See Chalmers, *Biog. Dict.* s. v.; Allibone, *Dict. of Brit. and Amer. Authors*, s. v.

Harmon (Heb. *Harmon'*, הַרְמוֹן, probably from הָרַם, *to be high;* Sept. τὸ ὄρος τὸ Ῥομμάν; Vulg. *excelsus mons;* A. V. "the palace"), a place only mentioned in Amos iii, 4, as that to which the inhabitants of Samaria would be led forth by their Assyrian conquerors, evidently, therefore, some unknown locality of the captivity. The ancient interpretations are obviously mere etymological conjectures, chiefly by a resolution of the first part of the name into הַר, *a mountain;* and the latter into a form of מִנִּי, *Armenia*, or רִמּוֹן, *Rimmon;* which are unsuitable. Kimchi makes it equivalent to אַרְמוֹן, *a town.*

Harms, Theodor, brother of Louis (q. v.), was born in 1819. When thirty years of age he was called as missionary inspector to Hermannsburg, and succeeded his brother in 1865. In 1878 Harms put himself at the head of those ministers who left the State Church and formed separate congregations. This separation was neither in the interest of the Church nor in the interest of the great missionary work with which Harms was intrusted, and the more so as he had not those talents which would qualify him to become a party leader. Friends of Harms had, therefore, often tried to heal the breach between the State Church and the Hermannsburg Mission, but all efforts were in vain, on account of Harms being too headstrong a person. He died Feb. 16, 1885. Besides a biographical sketch of his brother Louis (5th ed. 1877), he published, *Das Hohelied kurz* *erklärt* (Leipsic, 1870):—*Der zweite Brief Petri* (1873):—*Der Psalter erklärt* (2d ed. 1870):—*Das dritte Buch Mose kurz ausgelegt* (1871):—*Der Heilsweg in 22 Predigten* (1871; 3d ed. 1877):—*Die letzten Dinge* (1872; 3d ed. 1875):—*Der Prophet Maleachi erklärt* (1878):—*Zu Jesu Füssen, Predigten* (1877). (B. P.)

Harney, Martin, a Dominican of Amsterdam, was born May 6, 1634, and died at Louvain, April 22, 1704, professor of theology. He was an opponent of the Jansenists, and wrote *L'Obéissance Raisonnable des Catholiques des Pays-Bas* (Antwerp, 1636; transl. also into Latin). See Lichtenberger, *Encyclop. des Sciences Religieuses*, s. v.; Jöcher, *Allgemeines Gelehrten-Lexikon*, s. v. (B. P.)

Harnisch, Wilhelm, a Lutheran theologian of Germany, was born at Wilsnack, Brandenburg, Aug. 28, 1786. For some time first teacher at Teachers' Seminary, in Breslau, he was called in 1822 as director to Weissenfels, and died Aug. 15, 1864, leaving, *Luther's kleiner Katechismus für die Schuljugend* (18th ed. Eisleben, 1862):—*Vollständiger Unterricht im evangelischen Christenthum* (Halle, 1831, 2 vols.):—*Entwürfe und Stoffe zu Unterredungen über Luther's kleinen Katechismus* (1841-45, 3 vols.):—*Erbauliche Betrachtungen über Luther's Katechismus* (1836):—*Die Geschichte des Reiches Gottes auf Erden* (2d ed. 1844):—*Die künftige Stellung der Schule zu Kirche, Staat und Haus* (Erfurt, 1858). See Winer, *Handbuch der theol. Lit.* ii, 70, 217, 233, 380; Zuchold, *Bibl. Theol.* i, 507. (B. P.)

Harod, Spring of. Lieut. Conder suggests for this (*Tent Work*, ii, 69) the modern *Ain el-Jema'm* ("fountain of the two troops"), described (*Memoirs* to *Ordnance Map*, ii, 81) as "a small spring of fresh water, with a considerable stream, between two larger ones,"

Ain Jalûd or Harod's Spring. (From a Photograph by the Editor.)

and laid down three miles west of Beisân. But this is to accommodate his theory of the location of Megiddo as near the Jordan. There is no good reason to desert the traditionary site of *Ain Jalûd*, which is briefly described in the same *Memoirs* (ii, 79).

Harosheth. The modern *el-Harithiyeh*, which is thought to represent the ancient site, is placed on the *Ordnance Map* nine miles south-east of Haifa, and is described in the accompanying *Memoirs* (i, 270) as "a miserable hamlet of mud; on high ground, with an open plateau to the east, and a spring below on the west ('Ain el-Ghafr). The population in 1859 is stated by consul Rogers at one hundred and twenty souls, and the tillage at twelve feddans." According to the same authority, however (i, 96), "Guérin suggests that we have the ancient name of Harosheth or *Haris*," three and a half miles south-west of Jibrin, in the north of Palestine, where "there appear to be no vestiges of ancient constructions, except a circular cistern cut in the rock. This identification is strengthened by the fact that the same word which occurs in the name Kir Haroseth, the modern Kerak, exists in the present local dialect of Moab under the same form, Harith or Haris" (*ibid.* p. 116).

Harpies (Ἅρπυιαι), in Greek mythology, were daughters of Thaumas and Electra (an Oceanid). Sometimes two, sometimes three, are mentioned, under the different names, Aëllo, Podarge, Ocypete, Celano, Thyella, Acholoë, Aëllopos, Nicothoë, and the like. In the descriptions of them there is also a great difference.

Antique Figures of the Harpies.

With Homer they are storm goddesses, fleet, but beautiful; Hesiod also calls them swift goddesses, but in Æschylus they appear as hateful, winged monsters. They were usually represented as eagles with maiden faces. At times they had human arms and legs, which ended in claws and hens' feet. They were generally sent out by the gods to punish criminals.

Harpocrătes, in Graeco-Egyptian mythology, was the name of an Egyptian deity, which originated from the words, *Har-pa-chrut*, i. e. "Har the child." This Har the Greeks usually called *Horus*, and distinguished him as Horus Harpocrates from another Horus. Both were sons of Osiris and Isis. What the ancients say about Harpocrates is quite incomplete, and therefore dark as to its significance. That he was not the god of silence, as once believed, is now fully accepted. In Rome he was worshipped as such, but probably only because he had his finger in his mouth, which is but the figurative representation of sucking, and designates him as an infant. Beans and cherries were offered to him, and on special festive days he was fed, by men, with milk, his image being carried around in procession. Among animals, scorpions, snakes, crocodiles, lions, and reindeer were sacred to him. See Horus.

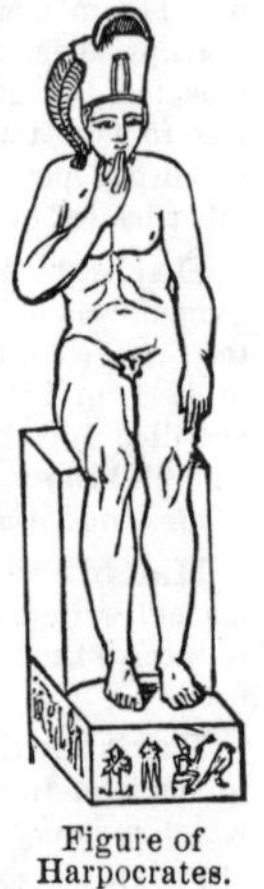

Figure of Harpocrates.

Harrison, Elias, D.D., a Presbyterian minister, was born in New York city, Jan. 22, 1790. He graduated from Princeton College in 1814, spent one year thereafter in the theological seminary there, was licensed by the New Brunswick Presbytery, ordained by the Baltimore Presbytery in 1817, and installed pastor of the First Presbyterian Church in Alexandria, Va., where he labored faithfully for forty-six years. He died Feb. 13, 1863. See *Gen. Cat. of Princeton Theol. Sem.* 1881, p. 20; Wilson, *Presb. Hist. Almanac*, 1867, p. 154.

Harrison, Jeptha, D.D., a Presbyterian minister, was born at Orange, N. J., in December, 1795. He graduated from Princeton College in 1820, and studied two years in the theological seminary there; was ordained in 1831; became stated supply at Fair Forest, S. C., in 1832, at Salem, Va., in 1835, and in 1838 became pastor of the First Presbyterian Church in Memphis, Tenn., where he labored for six years with great acceptability. He afterwards preached in Newcastle, Ky. (1844-47); Florence, Ala. (1848-50); Aberdeen, Miss. (1851-54); Burlington, Ia. (1855-58), and Fulton, Mo., where he died, Oct. 30, 1863. See *Gen. Cat. of Princeton Theol. Sem.* 1881, p. 35; Wilson, *Presb. Hist. Almanac*, 1864, p. 159; Nevin, *Presb. Encyclop.* s. v.

Harrison, John Christian, D.D., a Methodist Episcopal minister, son of Rev. Samuel Harrison of the South Carolina Conference, was born in Mecklenburg Co., N. C., Oct. 1, 1809. In 1819, with his parents, he removed to Kentucky, in 1827 was converted, became a class-leader in 1828, an exhorter in 1829, a local preacher in 1830, and later in the same year united with the Kentucky Conference. His first field of labor was Rock Castle Circuit, where he remained two years. He afterwards filled the best appointments in the conference, was presiding elder twenty-one years, occupied a seat in seven general conferences, and finally died, March 11, 1878. Mr. Harrison was a wise counsellor; had a clear, logical mind; was always affable, kind, reliable, and pure-minded, and full of faith and good works. See *Minutes of Annual Conferences*, 1878, i, 24.

Harrison, Thomas (1), an eminent English Baptist preacher, and general in the time of Cromwell, was born near Nantwich, Cheshire, England. As one of the judges selected to try king Charles, he did not shrink from what he conceived to be his duty, and gave his vote for the execution. He was the warm friend of Cromwell until the latter declared himself protector. He and his wife were baptized by immersion in 1657. At the Restoration he was arrested, tried as a regicide, and executed at Charing Cross, London, Nov. 13, 1660, his body being subjected to the most revolting treatment. See Cathcart, *Bapt. Encyclop.* s. v. (J. C. S.)

Harrison, Thomas (2), D.D., an English Independent minister, was born at Kingston-upon-Hull, Yorkshire. In his youth he removed with his parents to New England, who gave him the best education that country then afforded. He began to preach, and became chaplain to the governor of Virginia, a great enemy of Puritans. Two missionaries from England settled in Virginia, but the governor sent them out of the country. After this the Indians rose in rebellion, and murdered five hundred English persons. Those who escaped the massacre Mr. Harrison gathered into a church, but the governor became more hardened, and dismissed his chaplain, who had become too serious for him. He returned to London, where he became a popular preacher, and in 1650 succeeded Dr. Goodwin at St. Dunstan's in the East. He then removed to Broombrough Hall, where he preached continually. In 1657 he went to Ireland with Henry Cromwell, son of the protector, and preached for some years at Christ Church, Dublin. When the government changed he returned to England, resided at Chester, and preached in the cathedral till silenced in 1662. He returned to Dublin in 1663, where he had a large, respectable, and flourishing congregation. He was an agreeable and instructive preacher, and when he died, in Dublin, there was a general mourning for him in the city. He left a valuable library, including a large folio *System of Divinity* in manuscript, and published *Topica Sacra*, or Spiritual Pleadings, and a *Funeral Sermon for Lady Susanna Reynolds* (1654). See Wilson, *Dissenting Churches*, i, 221.

Harrotee Version. See HINDUWEE, DIALECTS OF.

Harsa (**Hercia**, or **Hersa**), a mediæval term, sometimes employed to describe any triangular candlestick for tapers, but more especially used to designate that which is employed in the offices of Tenebræ, in Holy Week. In it, at this service, are placed fourteen unbleached wax candles to represent the apostles and the three Marys, with one bleached wax candle to represent our Saviour. They are all extinguished in the course of the service, save the last named.

Hart, John Seely, LL.D., a Presbyterian minister, was born at Old Stockbridge, Mass., Jan. 28, 1810. He studied at Wilkesbarre Academy; graduated from Princeton College in 1830, with the highest honors of the class; the following year taught as principal of an academy at Natchez, Miss., and three years afterwards graduated from Princeton Theological Seminary. During the last two years of his course he also filled the position of tutor in the college. In 1834 he was elected adjunct professor of ancient languages in Princeton College, and filled that chair two years. He was licensed by the Presbytery of New Brunswick, Aug. 4, 1835. In 1836 he resigned his professorship in the college, purchased Edgehill School, in Princeton, and in 1842 was elected principal of the Philadelphia High School, continuing there until 1859, when he became editor of the periodicals published by the American Sunday-school Union, and in this connection began the *Sunday-school Times.* In 1862 he was elected principal of the New Jersey State Normal School, at Trenton, and held that position with distinguished usefulness and success until February, 1871. From 1864 to 1870 he also gave courses of lectures on English literature in Princeton College, where, in 1872, he was elected professor of belles-lettres and English literature, which chair he filled two years, returning in 1874 to Philadelphia, where he was engaged in literary pursuits until his death, March 26, 1877. Dr. Hart was the author of many volumes, an enthusiast in the cause of education, a devoted Sabbath-school worker, of elegant culture, accurate scholarship. During the months preceding his last illness, he had been delivering a course of popular lectures on the works of Shakespeare. He was an humble, consistent, and devout Christian. See *Necrol. Report of Princeton Theol. Sem.* 1877, p. 29.

Hart, Joseph, an English Independent minister, was born about the year 1712, of godly parents. He had a classical education, and was for many years a teacher of languages. He was long in bondage on account of his sins, but found deliverance under a sermon preached in the Moravian Chapel, Fetter-lane, London. He began to preach at the Old Meeting, St. John's Court, Bermondsey, in 1760, and afterwards settled at the Independent Chapel, Jewin Street, where his ministry was abundantly crowned, and he gathered there a prosperous Church. He would not allow either Arian or Arminian preacher in his pulpit. He died May 24, 1768, and was interred in Bunhill Fields, where twenty thousand persons are said to have been present. His hymns will live in the Church to the end of time, especially the one beginning "Come, ye sinners, poor and needy." See Wilson, *Dissenting Churches*, iii, 343; Gadsby, *Hymn Writers.*

Harte, WALTER, an English poet and divine, was born about 1700, and educated at Marlborough School and at St. Mary's Hall, Oxford, of which he became vice-principal. He was canon of Windsor in 1751, and subsequently vicar of St. Austel and of St. Blazy, Cornwall. He died in March, 1774, leaving *Poems on Several Occasions* (1727):—*Essay on Satire* (1730):—*Essay on Reason* (1735):—*A Fast Sermon* (1740). See Chalmers, *Biog. Dict.* s. v.; Allibone, *Dict. of Brit. and Amer. Authors*, s. v.

Härter, FRIEDRICH HEINRICH, a Lutheran theologian, was born Aug. 1, 1797, at Strasburg. He studied at his native place and at different German universities, was in 1823 pastor at Ittenheim, and in 1829 at Strasburg. He exercised a considerable influence in the Church and in the school, and took a great interest in the work of foreign and home missions. He died in August, 1874, leaving, besides a number of sermons, *Die Augsburgische Confession* (Strasburg, 1834). See Lichtenberger, *Encyclop. des Sciences Religieuses*, s. v.; Zuchold, *Bibl. Theol.* i, 508 sq. (B. P.)

Hartgrep, in Norse mythology, was the wife of the Danish king, Hadding, a favorite of the gods and a mighty giant. She was a powerful sorceress, feared on account of her art, and worshipped with superstitious reverence. By her assistance her husband descended alive into the infernal regions, to combat with Hela.

Hartley, Robert, a practical philanthropist, was born in England in 1795, and removed with his father to New York in 1798. He grew up with the expectation of entering the ministry, but was prevented by feeble health, and engaged in mercantile pursuits. He devoted his life to works of charity and mercy. He was the first to expose the iniquity of the "swill milk" traffic. He visited Europe and learned the various systems there in use, and on his return formed a society for the amelioration of the condition of the poor, which commanded the admiration and support of the wisest and best men in the city. He was secretary of the Hospital for the Ruptured and Crippled, and manager of the Presbyterian Hospital, Juvenile Asylum, and various other charities. He was an elder in the Madison Square Presbyterian Church, and abounded in works of piety and usefulness. He died in New York city, March 3, 1881. (W. P. S.)

Hartman, Johann Adolph, a learned German divine, was born at Münster in 1680. After being several years a Jesuit, he became a Protestant at Cassel in 1715, and was soon after made professor of philosophy and poetry. In 1722 he was appointed professor of history and rhetoric at Marpurg, and died there in 1744. His most esteemed works are, *Hist. Hassaica:—Vitæ Pontificum Romanorum Victoris III, Urbani II, Pascalis II, Gelasii II, Callisti II, Honorii II.* See Chalmers, *Biog. Dict.* s. v.

Hartmann, Christian Friedrich, a Lutheran theologian of Germany, was born at Köthen, Oct. 12, 1767. He studied at Halle, was in 1792 con-rector, and in 1796 rector, in his native place. In 1810 he was deacon of St. Agnes, in 1815 director of all the schools, and in 1822 member of consistory. He died Feb. 5, 1827, leaving, *Uebersetzung der Propheten Nahum, Habakuk, Zephania und Obadja* (Leipsic, 1791):—*Commentatio in Epistolam Judæ* (Köthen, 1793):—*De Studio Religionis Christianæ in Scholis Rite Instituendo* (ibid. 1797-98):—*Geschichte der evangelisch-lutherischen St. Agneskirche in Cöthen* (1799):—*Die biblische Geschichte mit praktischen Anmerkungen* (1802, 2 parts). See Döring, *Die gelehrten Theologen Deutschlands*, s. v.; Winer, *Handbuch der theol. Lit.* i, 273; ii, 135. (B. P.)

Hartmann, Heinrich Ludwig, a Lutheran theologian of Germany, was born Jan. 6, 1770, was in 1810 professor at the Grimma gymnasium, and died Feb. 13, 1831, leaving *Commentatio de Œconomo Improbo apud Lucam xvi,* 1-13 (Leipsic, 1830). See Winer, *Handbuch der theol. Lit.* i, 243; Zuchold, *Bibl. Theol.* i, 509. (B. P.)

Hartmann, Joachim, a Lutheran theologian of Germany, was born Jan. 1, 1715. He studied at Rostock, where he also commenced his academical career in 1739. In 1748 he took the degree of doctor of divinity, by presenting *De Actu Reprobis, Vero Redemptionis Christi Objecto*, and died Nov. 6, 1795. He published also, *De Vaticinio Simeonis Luc. xii,* 34, 35 (Rostock, 1744):—*Vindiciæ Exegeseos Dicti 2 Petri, ii,* 1 (ibid. 1754):—*Progr. Argumentorum ad Probandum pro Impœnitentia Finali Præstitam Satisfactionem ab Universalitate Gratiæ et Meriti Christi Desumtorum* (ibid. eod.):—*Jesus Nazarenus, Verus Messias* (ibid. 1757):—*Specimen Chronologiæ Biblicæ* (ibid. 1771):—*Progr. quo ad Institutum Greisbachii Textum N. T. Græcum Mutandi Quædam Exponit* (ibid. 1775). See Döring, *Die gelehrten Theologen Deutschlands*, s. v.; Winer, *Handbuch der theol. Lit.* i, 440. (B. P.)

Hartmann, Johann Melchior, a Lutheran theologian of Germany, was born Feb. 20, 1764, at Nördlingen. He studied at Jena and Göttingen, was called in 1793 to Marburg as professor of philosophy and Oriental languages, and died Feb. 16, 1827, leaving, *Commentatio de Geographia Africæ Edrisiana* (Göttingen, 1792; 2d ed. 1796):—*Anfangsgründe der hebräischen Sprache* (Marburg, 1797; 2d ed. 1819):—*Hebräische Chrestomathie* (ibid. 1797):—*Museum für biblische und orientalische Literatur* (ibid. 1807). See Döring, *Die gelehrten Theologen Deutschlands*, s. v.; Winer, *Handbuch der theol. Lit.* i, 116, 166, 277. (B. P.)

Hartmann, Julius, a Lutheran theologian of Germany, was born June 1, 1806. He served as deacon at different places in Würtemberg, and was called in 1851 to Tuttlingen. In 1877 he was made doctor of theology, and died Dec. 9, 1879, leaving, *Geschichte der Reformation in Würtemberg* (1835):—*Das Leben Jesu nach den Evangelien* (1837-39, 2 vols.):—*Johann Brenz* (1840, 2 vols.):—*Aelteste Katechetische der evangelischen Kirche* (1841):—*Erhard Schnepff der Reformator* (1870). He was also one of the editors of *Leben und ausgewählte Schriften der Väter und Begründer der luth. Kirche*, for which he wrote the life of Brenz (vol. vi of the collection, Elberfeld, 1862), and contributed to Piper's *Evangelische Kalender* and Herzog's *Real-Encyklop.* (B. P.)

Hartwell, Jesse (1), a Baptist minister, was born at Charlemont, Mass., in March, 1781. He was converted at the age of sixteen, and ordained at Sandisfield, Jan. 9, 1800. A large part of his life was spent in missionary work, under appointment from the Massachusetts Missionary Society. His tours extended beyond New England to the Black River country, N. Y., and into different sections of Pennsylvania, Ohio, and Canada. He first went to Ohio in 1815, and is believed to have baptized by immersion the first convert in the Western Reserve. He died at Perry, O., Nov. 21, 1860. See *Watchman and Reflector*, Dec. 20, 1860. (J. C. S.)

Hartwell, Jesse (2), D.D., an eminent Baptist minister, was born at New Marlborough, Mass., in 1794. He graduated with high rank from Brown University in 1819; for two years thereafter was principal of the University Grammar-school in Providence, pursuing at the same time his theological studies. He was ordained at Providence in 1821, and in 1823 went to South Carolina, and became an instructor in the Furman Theological Seminary, supplying vacant pulpits as opportunity presented. Subsequently he was settled as a clergyman in Alabama, and was an instructor in theology in what is known as Howard College, in that state. For several years he resided in Arkansas, where, as a preacher and teacher, he did good service. He became, in 1855, president of what was known as the Mt. Lebanon University, in Louisiana, and died there, Sept. 16, 1865. (J. C. S.)

Hartzheim, Caspar, a German theologian, was born at Cologne in 1678. He belonged to a distinguished family, entered the Jesuit order at Treves in 1698, and taught rhetoric, philosophy, and theology successively at Treves, Paderborn, Cologne, and other places. He died about 1750, leaving, *Custum Novæ Legis Presbyterium*, etc. (Cologne, 1717):—*Pietas in Salvatorem Mundi*, etc. (Mayence, 1728):—*Explicatio Fabularum et Superstitionum*, etc. (Cologne, 1734):—*Vita Nicolai de Cusa* (Treves, 1730):—*Solilegium Solandis Animabus Defunctorum* (Cologne, 1735; in German, 1743). See Hoefer, *Nouv. Biog. Générale*, s. v.

Hartzheim, Joseph, a German historian, was born at Cologne in 1694. At the age of seventeen he joined the Jesuits, was for some time professor of Oriental languages at Milan, afterwards professor of philosophy and theology at Cologne, and died May 17, 1763, leaving, *De Initio Metropoleos Ecclesiasticæ Coloniæ* (Cologne, 1731, 1732):—*Bibliotheca Coloniensis*, etc. (ibid. 1747):—*Catalogus Coloniensis* (ibid. 1752):—*De Edenda Collectione Conciliorum Germaniæ* (ibid. 1758): —*Concilia Germaniæ* (1759-63, 5 vols.). See Döring, *Die gelehrten Theologen Deutschlands*, s. v.; Winer, *Handbuch der theol. Lit.* i, 662; Jöcher, *Allgemeines Gelehrten-Lexikon*, s. v. (B. P.)

Haruspex, a name for Etruscan soothsayers, who divined future events from the inspection of the entrails of victims; an art afterwards introduced into Rome. See AUGUR; DIVINATION.

Harvey, *Sir* **George**, a Scottish painter, was born at St. Ninians, near Stirling, in February, 1806. He was educated in art in the Trustees' Academy at Edinburgh, and in 1826 became an associate of the Scottish Academy; in 1829 was elected a fellow, and in 1864 became its president. He received the honor of knighthood in 1867, and died at Edinburgh, Jan. 22, 1876. His best pictures are those depicting historical episodes in religious history from a puritan or evangelical standpoint, such as *Covenanters Preaching; Covenanters' Communion, John Bunyan and his Blind Daughter; Sabbath Evening; The Quitting of the Manse.* He was also equally successful in subjects not directly religious. See *Encyclop. Brit.* 9th ed. s. v.

Harvey, Joseph, D.D., a Presbyterian minister, was a native of Connecticut. While pastor of the Church at Goshen, in that state, he became deeply interested in the conversion of the Sandwich Islanders, and through his influence the first two missionaries to those islands, Messrs. Bingham and Thurston, were selected and ordained at Goshen, Sept. 28, 1819. Dr. Harvey died at Harvey, Mich., Feb. 4, 1873. See *Presbyterian*, March 1, 1873. (W. P. S.)

Hase, Christian Gottfried, a Lutheran theologian of Germany, who died at Brandenburg in 1766, is the author of, *De Messia in Jobo* (Halle, 1759):—*De Stylo Amosi Propheta et Ejus Vita* (1751):—*Versuch eines Lehrgebäudes der hebr. Sprache* (1750):—*Versuch einer Auslegung des hohen Liedes Salomonis* (1765). See Jöcher, *Allgemeines Gelehrten-Lexikon*, s. v.; Fürst, *Bibl. Jud.* i, 365; Steinschneider, *Bibl. Handbuch*, s. v. (B. P.)

Hase, Theodor, a Reformed theologian, was born at Bremen, Nov. 30, 1682. He studied at Marburg, was in 1707 professor of sacred philology at Hanau, in 1708 preacher at Bremen, in 1723 professor of theology there, and died Feb. 25, 1731. He wrote, *De Leviathan Jobi et Ceto Jonæ:—De ὀνολατρείᾳ Christianis et Judæis olim Objecta:—De Decreto Imperatoris Tiberii quo Christum Referre Voluit in Numerum Deorum:—Diss. v, de Baptismo Super Mortuis, de Aquis Hieruchintinis per Elisam Conditis, de Templo Oniæ Heliopolitano, de Jeschurune ad Deut.* xxxii, 15, and contributed largely to the *Bibliotheca Theolog. Bremensis* and *Museum Philologico-Theologicum.* His dissertations were published at Bremen in 1731, under the title, *Dissertationum et Observationum Sacrarum Sylloge.* See Winer, *Handbuch der theol. Lit.* i, 275, 279, 543; Jöcher, *Allgemeines Gelehrten-Lexikon*, s. v.; Fürst, *Bibl. Jud.* i, 365. (B. P.)

Hasenmüller, Daniel, a German philologist, was born at Eutin, July 3, 1651. He studied at Kiel and Leipsic, was in 1682 professor of Greek at the former place, in 1688 professor of homiletics, and in 1689 of Oriental languages. He died May 29, 1691, leaving, *Diss. de Linguis Orientalibus:—De Operibus Sabbathum Depellentibus:—Biblia Parva Græca:—Janua Hebraismi Aperta:*—פרקי אבות, *cum Versione Latina.* See Moller, *Cimbria Litterata;* Fürst, *Bibl. Jud.* i, 365; Jöcher, *Allgemeines Gelehrten-Lexikon*, s. v.; Steinschneider, *Bibl. Handbuch*, s. v. (B. P.)

Hasenmüller, Elias, a German Jesuit, who joined the Lutheran Church in 1587, is the author of *Historia Jesuitici Ordinis* (Frankfort, 1588, and later, Germ. transl. by Melchior Leporinus, ibid. 1594). See Winer, *Handbuch der theol. Lit.* i, 721; Jöcher, *Allgemeines Gelehrten-Lexikon*, s. v. (B. P.)

Hasert, CHRISTIAN ADOLF, a Lutheran theologian of Germany, who died Dec. 23, 1864, at Greifswalde, pastor, doctor, and professor of philosophy, published, *Predigten über die Episteln und freie Texte* (Greifswalde, 1836-37, 2 vols.):—*Ueber die Vorhersagungen Jesu von seinem Tode und seiner Auferstehung* (Berlin, 1839):—*Ueber den Religionsunterricht in Volksschullehrer-Seminarien* (Greifswalde, 1832). See Winer, *Handbuch der theol. Lit.* ii, 138, 174, 177, Zuchold, *Bibl. Theol.* i, 512. (B. P.)

Hassan, a Mohammedan teacher, was the eldest son of Ali, and the second of the twelve imâms of that line. On the death of his father, in 661, he was immediately proclaimed caliph and imâm in Irak; the former title he was forced to resign to Moawiyah, the latter or spiritual dignity he retained in reference to his followers. He was poisoned in 678 by a son of Moawiyah, as is supposed.

Hasse, Johann, a Roman Catholic theologian of Germany, was born in 1822. He studied at Breslau, and was professor of exegesis at the Pelplin seminary. In 1859 he was appointed vicar-general of the Culm diocese, in 1865 became a member of the chapter, in 1867 cathedral provost, and died Sept. 8, 1869, at Hanau, on his return from the episcopal convention which had met at Fulda. (B. P.)

Hasse, Johann Gottfried, a Protestant theologian of Germany, was born at Weimar in 1759. He studied at Jena, was in 1786 professor of Oriental languages at Königsberg, in 1788 professor of theology, and died April 12, 1806. He published, *Libri Quarti Regum Syroheptaplaris Specimen* (Jena, 1782):—*Salomo's Weisheit übersetzt mit Anmerkungen* (ibid. 1784):—*Idiognomik Davids*, etc. (ibid. eod):—*Aussichten zu küntigen Aufklärungen über das Alte Testament* (1785): —*Das andere Buch der Maccabäer neu übersetzt* (1786): —*Hebr. Sprachlehre* (1786-87):—*De Dialectis Linguæ Syriacæ* (1787):—*Lectiones Syro-Arabico-Samaritano-Æthiopicæ* (1788):—*Magazin für die biblisch-orientalische Literatur* (1788-89):—*Christus ὁ πρῶτος καὶ ὁ ἔσχατος* (ibid. 1790):—*Praktisches Handbuch der aramäischen oder syrisch-samaritanischen Sprache* (1791): —*Augustus Christi Nascituri Forsan non Ignarus* (ibid. 1805). See Döring, *Die gelehrten Theologen Deutschlands*, s. v.; Winer, *Handbuch der theol. Lit.* i, 74, 115, 200, 232, 273, 277, 280, 423, 554, 555, 617; Fürst, *Bibl. Jud.* i, 365 sq. (B. P.)

Hassel, JOHANN BERNHARD, a Lutheran theologian of Germany, was born Feb. 22, 1690, at Wolfenbüttel. He studied at Helmstadt, was preacher in his native city in 1721, general superintendent there in 1726, and died Feb. 23, 1755. His publications are but few, and without any special value for our time. See Döring, *Die gelehrten Theologen Deutschlands*, s. v.; Jöcher, *Allgemeines Gelehrten-Lexikon*, s. v. (B. P.)

Hassencamp, JOHANN MATHÄUS, a Protestant theologian of Germany, was born at Marburg, July 28, 1743. He studied at his native place and at Göttingen, was in 1769 professor of mathematics and Oriental languages at Rinteln, and died Oct. 6, 1797, leaving, *Commentatio de Pentateucho lxx Interpretum* (Marburg, 1765):—*Versuch einer neuen Erklärung der 70 Wochen Daniels* (1772):—*Der entdeckte wahre Ursprung der alten Bibelübersetzungen* (Minden, 1775):—*Annalen der neuesten theologischen Literatur und Kirchengeschichte* (1789-96, 8 vols.). See Döring, *Die gelehrten Theologen Deutschlands*, s. v.; Winer, *Handbuch der theol. Lit.* i, 9, 865. (B. P.)

Hassidæans. See ASSIDEAN.

Haswell, JAMES M., D.D., a Baptist missionary, was born at Bennington, Vt., Feb. 4, 1810. He graduated from the Hamilton Theological Seminary in 1835, and soon after was appointed missionary to Burmah, where he arrived in February, 1836. He was in the employ of the American Baptist Missionary Union for more than forty years, during which time he visited the United States, first in 1849, remaining a little more than three years, and again in 1867, making a stay of about nine months. His first work was among the Peguans, or, as they are now called, the Talaings, into whose language he translated the New Test., and issued from the press quite a number of tracts. He afterwards learned the Burmese language, and was for a long time recognised as a missionary among that people. He died Sept. 13, 1876. See *Amer. Bapt. Magazine*, lvii, 180. (J. C. S.)

Hatch, FREDERICK W., D.D., a Protestant Episcopal minister, was ordained deacon in 1810, and presbyter in 1813, and had charge, successively, of the parishes in Edenton, N. C., and Frederick, Md., after which he removed to Virginia as rector of Fredericksville parish from 1820 to 1830. While there, Thomas Jefferson was his friend and parishioner. In 1832–1836 he officiated in Christ Church, Washington, D. C., and was chaplain to the United States Senate. In the latter year he removed to Poughkeepsie, N. Y.; in 1843 to Wisconsin, taking charge of the parishes in Southport and Racine. In 1850 he went to St. Louis, Mo., in temporary charge of Christ and St. George's churches; thence travelled to California in June, 1856, laboring as a missionary in Marysville and other places. He died in Sacramento, Cal., Jan. 14, 1860, aged seventy-one years. Dr. Hatch was a fine linguist, and an indefatigable worker. See *Amer. Quar. Church Rev.* 1860, p. 180.

Hatè, in Norse mythology, was the son of the giant Gyge and the brother of Skoll; both are frightful wolves, and persecute the moon and the sun. At Ragnarokr these monsters will succeed in devouring the heavenly lights. He probably emblematizes the eclipse.

Hatfield, Edwin Francis, D.D., an eminent Presbyterian minister, was born at Elizabethtown, N. J., Jan. 9, 1807. He graduated from Middlebury College in 1829, spent two years at Andover Theological Seminary, was ordained pastor of the Second Presbyterian Church at St. Louis in 1832, in 1835 accepted a call from the Seventh Presbyterian Church, New York city, and remained its pastor for twenty-one years, enjoying a continuous season of revival, and receiving to its membership one thousand five hundred and fifty-six persons. A colony from this church, in 1856, organized a new church in the upper part of the city, and Dr. Hatfield became its pastor. He remained at this post until his health failed, and resigned in 1863. When he recovered his health he was appointed financial agent of the Union Theological Seminary, and afterwards acted as secretary of the Home Missionary Society. He died at Summit, N. J., Sept. 22, 1883. From 1846 he was stated clerk of the General Assembly, an office for which he was peculiarly fitted by his methodical habits and extensive acquaintance with the history of the Church. He was elected in 1883 moderator of the General Assembly, and performed the duties of that office with great ability. He prepared the year-book of the *New York Observer* during the time of its publication. Among his published works are, *Universalism as it Is* (1841):—*Memoir of Elihu W. Baldwin* (1843):—*St. Helena and the Cape of Good Hope* (1852):—*The History of Elizabeth, N. J.* (1868):—*The Church Hymn-book, with Tunes* (1872):—*The Chapel Hymn-book* (1873). He spent much time and labor in preparing for publication the *Minutes of the General Assembly*. See *N. Y. Observer*, Sept. 27, 1883. (W. P. S.)

Hatfield, Thomas, an English prelate, was prebendary of Lincoln (1342) and York (1343), and was promoted to the see of Durham in 1345. He died near London, May 8, 1381. He was the principal benefactor, if not the founder, of the friary at Northallerton, in Yorkshire, for Carmelites, or White Friars. See Chalmers, *Biog. Dict.* s. v.

Hatto OF VERCELLI. See ATTO.

Hauber, Eberhard David, a Protestant theologian of Germany, was born May 27, 1695. He studied at Tübingen and Altdorf, was in 1725 superintendent, member of consistory, and first preacher at Stadthagen, accepted a call in 1746 to Copenhagen as pastor of the German St. Peter's Church, and died Feb. 15, 1765, leaving, *Exegitische und moralische Gedanken über die Sünde Lot's* (Lemgo, 1732):—*Harmonie der Evangelisten* (Ulm, 1737):—*Untersuchung der Summen Geldes* 1 *Chron. xxii*, 14 (Stadthagen, 1765). See Döring, *Die gelehrten Theologen Deutschlands*, s. v.; Winer, *Handbuch der theol. Lit.* i, 429; Jöcher, *Allgemeines Gelehrten-Lexikon*, s. v. (B. P.)

Hauber, Friedrich Albert von, a Lutheran theologian of Germany, who was born Dec. 14, 1806, at Stuttgart, and died Sept. 14, 1883, at Ludwigsburg, in Würtemberg, is the author of, *Die Diener der evangelischen Kirche und die Zeit* (Stuttgart, 1849):—*Recht und Brauch der evang.-lutherischen Kirche Würtemberg's* (1854–56, 2 vols.):—*Evangelisches Hauspredigtbuch* (Ulm, 1862). See Zuchold, *Bibl. Theol.* i, 514. (B. P.)

Hauber, Johannes, a Lutheran theologian of Germany, was born Nov. 9, 1572, and died at Stuttgart, Oct. 1, 1620, doctor of theology and court-preacher. He wrote, *De Remissione Peccatorum:—De Problemate Theologico:—Utrum Philosophandi Ratio ad Materias Theologicas Adhibenda.* See Jöcher, *Allgemeines Gelehrten-Lexikon*, s. v. (B. P.)

Haudriettes, an order of Roman Catholic nuns hospitallers at Paris, founded in the reign of St. Louis, by Stephen Haudry, a secretary of that sovereign. At first it was limited to twelve poor females, but the number gradually increased, and the order was confirmed by several popes. They afterwards received the name of Nuns of the Assumption.

Hauff, the name common to several Protestant theologians:

1. CARL VICTOR, was born Sept. 2, 1752, in Würtemberg. In 1791 he was professor and preacher, in 1814 dean at Ulm, in 1816 dean and pastor at Cannstadt, and died Aug. 18, 1832, doctor of philosophy. He published, *Ueber den Gebrauch der griechischen Profanscribenten zur Erläuterung des Neuen Testaments* (Leipsic, 1796):—*Bemerkungen über die Lehrart Jesu mit Rücksicht auf jüdische Sprach- und Denkart* (Offenbach, 1798):—*Briefe den Werth der christlichen Religionsurkunde als solche betreffend* (Stuttgart, 1809–14, 3 parts):—*Die Authentie und der hohe Werth des Evangelium Johannis* (Nüremberg, 1831). See Winer, *Handbuch der theol. Lit.* i, 130, 397, 401; ii, 206; Zuchold, *Bibl. Theol.* i, 514.

2. DANIEL FRIEDRICH, was born May 30, 1749. In 1780 he was deacon at Ludwigslust, in 1801 special superintendent at Schorndorf, Würtemberg, and died April 17, 1817. He wrote, *Beweis für die Unsterblichkeit der Seele aus dem Begriff der Pflicht* (Züllichau, 1794). See Winer, *Handbuch der theol. Lit.* i, 473.

3. GOTTFRIED AUGUST, pastor at Waldenbuch, Würtemberg, who died in 1862, wrote, *Offenbarungsglaube und Kritik der biblischen Geschichtsbücher* (Stuttgart, 1843):—*Behandlung der biblischen Geschichte des alten Testaments in Volksschulen* (1850). See Zuchold, *Bibl. Theol.* i, 514. (B. P.)

Haug, Balthasar, a Protestant theologian of Germany, was born at Stammford, near Calw, July 4, 1731. He studied at Tübingen, entered upon his ministerial duties in 1757, and died at Stuttgart, Jan. 3, 1792. He published, *Diss. XII Postrema Commata Marci XVI Esse Genuina* (Tübingen, 1753):—*Der Christ am Sabbath* (1763–64, 3 vols.; 2d ed. 1778):—*De Poësi Sacra Ebræorum* (1768):—*De Motibus Terræ in Sacra Scriptura Allegatis* (1783):—*De Re Educatoria Primorum Christianorum* (1784):—*Die Alterthümer der Christen* (1785). See Döring, *Die gelehrten Theologen Deutschlands*, s. v. (B. P.)

Haug, Martin, a German Orientalist, was born Jan. 30, 1827, in Würtemberg. He studied at Tübingen and Göttingen, and commenced his academical career at Bonn in 1854. In 1856 he went to Heidelberg, to assist Bunsen in his *Bibelwerk*. In 1859 he went to India as professor of Sanscrit, returned to Germany in 1866, and accepted in 1868 a call to Munich as professor of Sanscrit. He died June 3, 1876, leaving, *Die fünf Gâthâs* (Leipsic, 1858-60, 2 vols.):—*Essays on the Sacred Language, Writings, and Religion of the Parsees* (Bombay, 1862):—*Ueber die Schrift und Sprache der zweiten Keilschriftgattung* (Göttingen, 1855):—*Ueber die Pehlewisprache und den Bundehesch* (1854):—*Essay on the Pahlavi Language* (Stuttgart, 1870):—*The Book of Arda Viraf* (Bombay and London, 1872-74). He edited and translated the *Aitareya Brahmana of the Rigveda*, his main work (Bombay, 1863, 2 vols.). Besides, he published *Ueber die ursprüngliche Bedeutung des Wortes Brahma* (Munich, 1868):—*Brahma und die Brahmanen* (1871). (B. P.)

Haul, in Norse mythology, is one of the rivers of hell, which spring from the antlers of the reindeer Æjkthyrners. Its dew flows into the spring Hwergelmer, and from this all the rivers flow.

Haulik de Váralja, GEORG, cardinal and archbishop of Agram, was born April 28, 1787, at Tyrnau, in Hungary. He studied at his native place and at Grau, was in 1812 keeper of the archiepiscopal archives at Buda, in 1814 notary of the consistory, in 1825 dean, in 1832 great provost of Agram, and in 1837 bishop there. In 1843 he was ennobled and appointed first archbishop. In 1856 he was made cardinal, and died May 11, 1869. His pastoral letters are published under the title, *Selectiones Encyclicæ Literæ et Dictiones Sacræ* (Vienna, 1850-53, 3 vols.); besides he wrote *Die Autorität, als Princip der Ordnung und des Wohlergehens in Kirche, Staat und Familie* (1865). (B. P.)

Haunold, CHRISTOPH, a German Jesuit and "præfectus studiorum" at Ingolstadt, was born at Altenthan, in Bavaria, in 1610, and died in 1689. He wrote, *Definitio pro Infallibilitate Ecclesiæ Romanæ*:—*Institutiones Theologiæ*:—*Cursus Theologicus S. Theologiæ Speculativæ Libris IV*:—*Controversiæ de Justitia et Jure Privatorum*, etc. See Alegambe, *Bibliotheca Scriptorum Societatis Jesu*; Winer, *Handbuch der theol. Lit.* i, 404; Jöcher, *Allgemeines Gelehrten-Lexikon*, s. v. (B. P.)

Haupt, CARL GERHARD, a Lutheran theologian of Germany, was born in 1778. For some time professor at the gymnasium at Quedlinburg, and also deacon, he was appointed in 1825 pastor primarius at St. Nicholai, and died Aug. 22, 1833, leaving, *Tabellarischer Abriss der vorzüglichsten Religionen und Religionsparteien der jetzigen Erdbewohner*, etc. (Quedlinburg, 1821):—*Die Religionen der Welt* (Augsburg, 1836-37):—*Handbuch über die Religions-, Kirchen-, Geistliche- und Unterrichtsangelegenheiten in Preussen* (Quedlinburg, 1822-23, 3 vols.):—*Reportorium der Predigtentwürfe der vorzüglichsten Kanzelredner* (1836):—*Biblisches Casualtext-Lexikon* (1826; new ed. by Wohlfarth, 1852):—*Casualpredigten* (1828):—*Christlicher Betaltar* (1823):—*Die Lehren der Religion, erläutert durch Beispiele aus der Bibel, aus der Weltgeschichte und dem praktischen Leben* (1829, 3 vols.):—*Biblische Real- und Verbal-Encyklopädie* (1823-28, 3 vols.). See Winer, *Handbuch der theol. Lit.* i, 512; ii, 14, 84, 123, 162, 166, 337, 363; Zuchold, *Bibl. Theol.* i, 515 sq. (B. P.)

Hauptmann, JOHANN GOTTFRIED, a Lutheran theologian of Germany, was born Oct. 19, 1712, in Saxony. He studied at Leipsic, was in 1737 con-rector at Gera, in 1742 rector and professor, and died Oct. 21, 1782, doctor of theology. He wrote, *Historia Linguæ Hebrææ* (Leipsic, 1752):—*Progr. VII ad Zach. ix*, 17 (Gera, 1756):—*Hebraici Sermonis Elementa cum Illius Historia* (Jena, 1760):—*Programm über das Alter der Vocale* (1777). See Fürst, *Bibl. Jud.* i, 367; Steinschneider, *Bibl. Handbuch*, s. v.; Meusel, *Gelehrtes Deutschland*; Jöcher, *Allgemeines Gelehrten-Lexikon*, s. v. (B. P.)

Haur, in Norse mythology, was one of the dwarfs created out of earth.

Hausen, CHRISTIAN AUGUST, a Lutheran theologian of Germany, was born at Sangerhausen, in Thuringia, Aug. 6, 1663. He studied at Wittenberg, was in 1690 deacon, in 1692 preacher at Dresden, and died Sept. 20, 1733. He is best known by his continuation of Bebel's *Memorabilia Historiæ Ecclesiast. Recentioris*, etc. (Dresden, 1731). See Winer, *Handbuch der theol. Lit.* i, 379; Jöcher, *Allgemeines Gelehrten-Lexikon*, s. v. (B. P.)

Häusle, JOHANN MICHAEL, a Roman Catholic theologian of Germany, who died at Vienna, Jan. 16, 1867, court-chaplain and professor emeritus, is known as one of the editors of *Wiener Zeitschrift für die gesammte katholische Theologie*. The history of the Vienna University he wrote for the *Freiburger Kirchen-Lexikon*. Besides, he published, *Der katholische Charakter der wiener Universität* (1864):—*Darf die wiener Hochschule paritätisch werden?* (1865). (B. P.)

Hausmeister, JACOB AUGUST, a Protestant minister of Germany, was born of Jewish parentage, at Stuttgart, Oct. 6, 1806. At the age of nineteen he joined the Christian Church at Esslingen. Shortly afterwards he entered the Basle Missionary Institute, where he remained for about six years. In 1831 the London Society for Promoting Christianity among the Jews called him as one of its missionaries. Before he left for London, he was ordained by dean Herwig, who had also received him into the Church. In 1832 he went to Strasburg as missionary, and died April 17, 1860. He published, *Merkwürdige Lebens- und Bekehrungsgeschichten* (Basle, 1835):—*Leben und Wirken des Pastors Börling* (1852):—*Der Unterricht und die Pflege jüdischer Proselyten* (Heidelberg, 1852):—*Die Judenmission*, an essay read before the Evangelical Alliance held at Paris (Basle, 1856):—*Die evangelische Mission unter Israel* (1861). See Zuchold, *Bibl. Theol.* i, 520 sq. (B. P.)

Haussa Version OF THE SCRIPTURES. Haussa is one of the most widely-extended languages of western Africa, and forms very much the medium of communication over extensive districts on both sides the rivers Niger and Chadda. The gospel according to Matthew was translated into this language prior to the year 1841, by the Rev. C. F. Schön, of the Church Missionary Society. This translation was carefully revised by the help of two natives of the Haussa country, and was printed by the British and Foreign Bible Society in 1856. Since then the following parts were put into circulation by the same society: Genesis, Exodus, gospel of John, and the Acts. See *The Bible of Every Land*, p. 412. For the study of the language, see Baikie, *Observations on the Haussa and Fulfulda Languages* (Lond. 1861); J. F. Schön, *Grammar of the Haussa Language* (ibid. 1862). (B. P.)

Hautecourt, JEAN PHILIPON DE, a Reformed theologian of Douai, was born Sept. 5, 1646. He studied at Saumur, was preacher there in 1671, professor of theology in 1677, but left France in 1685 on account of religious persecutions and went to Holland. He settled at Amsterdam in 1686, was professor of theology there, and died Oct. 30, 1715. He wrote, *De Mysterio Pietatis*:—*De Symbolo Apostolico*:—*De Peccato in Spiritum Sanctum*:—*De Primo Oraculo, Gen. iii*, 15:—*De Lege et Evangelio ad Joh. i*, 27:—*Ad Historiam Dœmoniaci a Christo Sanati, Marc. i*, 20. See Vriemot, *Series Professorum Franequeranorum*; Jöcher, *Allgemeines Gelehrten-Lexikon*, s. v. (B. P.)

Hautpoul, PAUL LOUIS JOSEPH, a French prelate, was born at the castle of Salette (Languedoc), Aug. 2, 1764. He entered into holy orders while quite young, became a priest before the time of the Revolution, and was forced to seek shelter in foreign countries. He at first emigrated to Switzerland, and afterwards to Coblentz in 1792. The family Kosen Kaski engaged him for the education of their heir, upon which abbé Hautpoul directed all his attention. He returned to France in 1818, and became almoner to the duchess of Angoulême, and after that bishop of Cahors in 1828. Being weakened by age and infirmities, he had to resign in 1842, and retired to his family at Toulouse. He died in December, 1849. See Hoefer, *Nouv. Biog. Générale*, s. v.

Hävecker, Johann Heinrich, a Lutheran theologian of Germany, was born in 1640. He studied at Helmstadt and Wittenberg, was in 1665 rector, in 1681 deacon, in 1693 pastor, and died in 1722, leaving, *De Victu et Amictu Johannis Baptistæ* (Wittenberg, 1663):—*De Mundi Ortu et Interitu* (1664):—*Morgen- und Abend-Seufzer* (1669). He also continued and edited some works of his father-in-law, Scriver (q. v.). See Jöcher, *Allgemeines Gelehrten-Lexikon*, s. v. (B. P.)

Havemann, Michael, a Protestant theologian of Germany, was born Nov. 29, 1597. He was preacher and professor at Stade, and died Jan. 12, 1672, leaving, *Hodosophia Evangelica contra Papalium Ignem Fatuum*:—*Christianismi Luminaria Magna*:—*Gamologia sive Tractatus de Jure Connubiorum*:—*Theognosia sive Theologia Antiquissima Mosaica, Prophetica, Apostolica et Rabbinica*:—*De Christianorum in Christo Perfectione et cum Christo Unione* (transl. into German by Spener). See Witte, *Diarium Biographicum*; Jöcher, *Allgemeines Gelehrten-Lexikon*, s. v. (B. P.)

Haven, Erastus Otis, D.D., LL.D., a bishop of the Methodist Episcopal Church, was born in Boston, Mass., Nov. 1, 1820, being a descendant of Richard Haven, of Puritan stock, who emigrated from the west of England, and settled in the town of Lynn, Massachusetts Bay Colony, about the year 1640. He graduated from the Wesleyan University in 1842, immediately took charge of a private academy in Sudbury, and thence went to Amenia Seminary, filling first the position of teacher of natural science, and afterwards becoming principal of the institution. In 1848 he entered upon the work of the ministry in the New York Conference, and occupied the following positions: Twenty-fourth Street (now Thirtieth Street) Church, New York city, 1848 and 1849; Red Hook Mission, N. Y., 1850 and 1851; Mulberry Street (now St. Paul's) Church, New York city, 1852. In 1853 he was elected professor of Latin in the University of Michigan, and the next year was made professor of English language, literature, and history. In 1856 he was elected editor of *Zion's Herald*, Boston, and filled the position with eminent acceptability for seven years. In 1862 and the year following he was a member of the Senate of the State of Massachusetts; from 1858 to 1863 of the state board of education, and of the board of overseers of Harvard University. In the latter year he was elected president of the University of Michigan, filling that position till 1869, when he accepted the office of president of the North-western University. Here he remained till the General Conference of 1872 elected him corresponding secretary of the Education Society. In 1874 he was called to the chancellorship of the new university at Syracuse. In 1880 he was made a bishop, and was engaged in the duties of that office at the time of his death, which occurred at Salem, Oregon, Aug. 2, 1881. Although a fine preacher and a graceful speaker, he attained chief prominence among the Methodists of America for his sound scholarship and his steadfast interest in the cause of education. His principal published works are, *The Young Man Advised* (1855):—*The Pillars of Truth* (1866):—and a *Rhetoric* (1869). He contributed largely to the periodicals of the Church, and, as editor of one of the Church papers, took no small part in the discussion of many important denominational questions.

Haven, Gilbert, a bishop of the Methodist Episcopal Church, cousin of the foregoing, was born at Malden, Mass., Sept. 19, 1821. His father, Gilbert Haven, Esq., was one of the pioneer Methodists of that place. After receiving a good common-school education he engaged in business, and early manifested such capacity as to have the most flattering offers of business connections; but feeling an ardent desire for a higher education, refused them all, prepared for college at Wesleyan University, Wilbraham, where he was converted in 1839, and in 1846 graduated at Wesleyan University, Middletown, Conn. He was immediately employed as teacher of ancient languages at Amenia Seminary, Dutchess County, N. Y., and in 1848 was elected principal of the institution. In 1851 he joined the New England Conference, wherein he served two years each at Northampton, Wilbraham, Westfield, Roxbury, and Cambridge. At the opening of the rebellion Mr. Haven was commissioned as chaplain of the Eighth Regiment of Massachusetts volunteers, served his time out (three months), then spent a year in extensive travel in Europe and Palestine, and as a result wrote and published his book on Great Britain and Western Europe, entitled *The Pilgrim's Wallet*. On his return he resumed the active ministry, and was stationed at North Russell Street, Boston, where, through his advice and influence, Grace Church was purchased. From 1867 to 1871 he was editor of *Zion's Herald*, in 1868 and 1872 was a delegate to the General Conference, and by the latter was elected to the bishopric, May 24, 1872. In this office he devoted himself earnestly to its arduous labors, and was ever conspicuous in the benevolent enterprises of the Church. He visited Mexico in 1873, and Africa in 1876 and 1877. His death at the home of his nativity, Jan. 3, 1880, was remarkably triumphant. Bishop Haven had a very extensive knowledge of books and men, a retentive and ready memory, a wonderful conversational ability, and great popularity among his personal acquaintances. He was noted for his ardent interest in reformatory enterprises, his radical opposition to slavery, and his advocacy of political and social equality. His boldly enunciated views on these subjects gave him great reputation almost wherever the English language is spoken. He was equally conspicuous for his faithful advocacy of the central doctrines of evangelical religion. He was a careful, successful pastor; a preacher of great simplicity, fluency, and power; and a vigorous and facile writer. His other publications are, *Occasional Sermons*:—*Life of Father Taylor, the Sailors' Preacher*:—*Our Next-door Neighbor; or, A Winter in Mexico*. See *Minutes of Annual Conferences*, 1880, i, 92; Simpson, *Cyclop. of Methodism*, s. v.; Daniels, *Memorials* (Boston, 1880).

Haven, Joseph, D.D., LL.D., a Congregational minister, was born at North Dennis, Mass., Jan. 4, 1816. He graduated from Amherst College in 1833, spent one year in the Union Theological Seminary, and graduated from Andover Theological Seminary in 1839. He was ordained Nov. 6 of the same year pastor of the Ashland Congregational Church, Unionville, where he remained seven years, next was pastor of the Brookline Church four years, and was then appointed professor of moral and intellectual philosophy in Amherst College. After occupying this post for eight years he was called to a professorship in the Chicago Theological Seminary, which post he occupied until his death, May 23, 1874. He is the author of a work entitled *Mental Philosophy, including the Intellect, Sensibilities, and the Will* (Boston, 1858, 12mo). (W. P. S.)

Haven, Samuel, D.D., a Congregational minister, was born in Framingham, Mass., Aug. 4, 1727 (O. S.). After graduating in 1749 from Harvard College, he was instructed in theology by Rev. Ebenezer Parkman. He was ordained, May 6, 1752, pastor of the First Church in Portsmouth, where he ministered until his death, March 3, 1806. Possessing unusual powers of oratory, he attained an extensive popularity. Although poor himself, he ministered to the destitute with a profuse liberality, especially during the Revolutionary struggle. As a means of usefulness he studied medicine, and practised gratuitously among the poor. After 1799 he only preached occasionally, and the last year and a half he was incapable of performing the duties of his office. On account of his unusual pulpit talents, his friends likened him to Whitefield. His printed sermons are numerous. See Sprague, *Annals of the Amer. Pulpit*, i, 495.

Haven, Thomas, D.D., a Unitarian minister, was born at Wrentham, Mass., in 1748. He graduated at Harvard College in 1765, was ordained pastor of the Congregational Church in Reading, Nov. 7, 1770, and died May 7, 1782. See Sprague, *Annals of the Amer. Pulpit*, viii, 133.

Haverkamp, Sigbert, a Dutch scholar, was born in 1683. He was first preacher in a small village, but was called to Leyden as professor of history and Greek, and died April 25, 1742. He published, *S. Fl. Tertulliani Apologeticus*, etc. (Leyden, 1718):—*Josephi Opera Omnia*, etc. (Amsterdam, 1726, 2 vols. fol.):—*Abudacni Historia Jacobitarum c. Annotatt. Jo. Nicolai* (Leyden, 1740). See Winer, *Handbuch der theol. Lit.* i, 102, 131, 156, 634, 912, 913; Fürst, *Bibl. Jud.* i, 366; Jöcher, *Allgemeines Gelehrten-Lexikon*, s. v. (B. P.)

Havestadt, Bernhard, a German missionary, was born at Cologne in 1715. He entered the society of the Jesuits, and devoted himself to preaching. In 1746 he was attached to the missions of Chili. He started from Hortsmar, in Westphalia, sailed from Antwerp to Lisbon, and arrived two months afterwards at Rio Janeiro, thence crossed the pampas and Andes to Chili, and reached Santiago, the capital of Chili, after a wearisome and dangerous journey of fifty-five days. He spent five years at Concepcion, thoroughly exploring the country. Having a very good knowledge of the Chilidugu dialect, he was enabled to make some few converts among the Indians. On the abolition of the Jesuit order in the Spanish states, Havestadt was arrested, June 29, 1768, and conducted to Lima, whence, by way of Panama, he returned to Europe. He died at Münster after 1778, where his *Observations* appeared (1751–77). See Hoefer, *Nouv. Biog. Générale*, s. v.

Hawaiian Version of the Scriptures. The Hawaiian is a dialect of the Polynesian language, spoken in the Sandwich Islands. When missionaries landed on the island of Hawaii, in 1820, they found a rude, illiterate people, whose language had never been reduced to writing. It was theirs to catch the fleeting sounds and give them permanent form on the printed page, and so energetically did they pursue their work, that before two years had elapsed they had begun printing in Hawaiian. To express the proper sounds of the language five vowels and seven consonants sufficed, but nine additional consonants were employed to give expression to the foreign and Bible names with which the Hawaiians would need to become acquainted. In 1826 the gospel of Matthew was prepared for press, and in 1828 a small edition of the four gospels was printed at Rochester, N. Y., at the expense of the American Board and the American Bible Society. The entire New Test. was published at Honolulu in 1832, and a second revised edition of ten thousand copies appeared in 1837. Portions of the Old Test. were also put to press from time to time, and the complete Hawaiian Bible appeared in 1839, only nineteen years after the arrival of the pioneer missionaries. Six years later it was estimated by Rev. Hiram Bingham, one of the translators, that twenty thousand Bibles and thirty thousand New Tests. had been issued, besides many thousand detached portions, and that the American Bible Society had contributed $42,420 towards this result. A bilingual Hawaiian and English New Test. was also prepared in 1857 by the American Bible Society, and of this more than ten thousand copies have been issued. See *Bible of Every Land*, p. 375. For linguistic helps, comp. Andrews, *A Dictionary of the Hawaiian Language* (Honolulu, 1865); Alexander, *A Short Synopsis of the Most Essential Points in Hawaiian Grammar* (ibid. 1864); Chamisso, *Ueber die hawaiische Sprache* (Leipsic, 1837); Bishop, *Manual of Conversation in Hawaiian and English* (Honolulu, 1854); Remy, *Ka Moslelo Hawaii. Histoire de l'Archipel Hawaiien (iles Sandwich). Texte et Traduction* (Paris, 1862). (B. P.)

Hawkins, Edward, D.D., an Anglican divine, was born in Somersetshire, England, in 1789. He was educated at Merchant Taylors' School, London, and graduated with high honors from St. John's College, Oxford, in 1811. He became a fellow of Oriel, took orders in the Church, and filled several posts in the University of Oxford with distinguished ability. In 1828 he was appointed provost of Oriel College, to which office a canonry in Rochester Cathedral and the rectory of Purleigh are annexed. He came in contact with that Catholic movement of which Oriel College is the recognised centre, and its fellows, John Henry Newman and Edward Bouvine Pusey, the leaders. He was opposed to the tractarian or "Puseyite" propaganda. His own position on theological questions was in the ranks of the liberal or "Broad" Church. Dr. Hawkins was Bampton lecturer in 1840. He edited *Milton's Poetical Works, with Notes*, published a volume of *Discourses on the Historical Scriptures of the Old Testament*, and was from 1847 to 1861 Ireland professor of exegesis in the university. He died at Oxford, Nov. 20, 1882. (W. P. S.)

Hawthorne, James, D.D., a Presbyterian minister, was born at Slabtown, Burlington Co., N. J., April 1, 1803, and in early life removed to Kentucky. He studied with Rev. A. A. Shannon, of Shelbyville; graduated from Princeton Theological Seminary in 1828; was licensed by the Presbytery of New Brunswick, Feb. 6 of that year; and Nov. 21, 1829, was ordained over the churches of Lawrenceburg and Upper Benson, in Franklin County, Ky., where he remained till April 4, 1833, after which he preached for various churches as a supply for three years. He was installed pastor of Plum Creek and Cane Run churches in Shelby County, Dec. 29, 1836; dismissed April 23, 1841, after which he supplied the Lawrenceburg Church about five years; next served the Church at Princeton for one year as a stated supply, and April 9, 1848, was installed as pastor there. For nearly thirty years he performed the duties of this pastorate with great earnestness and faithfulness. He was a man of spotless integrity, of a lovable disposition, cultivated in mind, Christlike in spirit. His long rides over rough roads in inclement seasons, while supplying weak congregations, had injured his health and laid the foundation for weakness in his later years. He died June 28, 1877. See *Necrol. Report of Princeton Theol. Sem.* 1878, p. 15. (W. P. S.)

Hawtrey, Edward Craven, D.D., an English divine, was born at Burnham, Bucks, May 7, 1789. He was educated at Eton, admitted as a scholar of King's College, Cambridge, in 1807, and three years later became a fellow of that college. In 1814 he was made assistant master of Eton College, in 1834 was appointed head master, and in 1853 was elected provost, which office he filled till his death, Jan. 27, 1862. Dr. Hawtrey, as a member of the Roxburgh Club, was well known in literary circles, and his intimate acquaintance with books enabled him to collect a library of great value. He was an accomplished scholar in the French, German, and Italian languages. His *Il Trifoglio* contains translations of poems, with a few original pieces in Greek, Italian, and German; the versions are from French and English into Greek—from Latin, English, and German into Italian—and from English into German, all executed with surprising accuracy. His administration at Eton gave evidence of superior wisdom and judgment, vastly advancing the college in classical pre-eminence. See *Appleton's Annual Cyclopædia*, 1862, p. 683.

Hay, George, D.D., a Scotch Roman Catholic prelate, was born of Episcopal parents, in Edinburgh, Aug. 24, 1729. He was destined for the medical profession, but in the midst of his studies he was summoned to join the Highland army as surgeon, in 1745. After prince Charles's defeat, he was kept three months in Edinburgh Castle, and then detained prisoner a year in London. By the act of indemnity he was set free. He was received into the Roman Catholic Church, Dec. 21, 1745, by father John Seton, S. J., of Garleton, who was on a mission to Edinburgh. On Sept. 10, 1754, he entered the Scotch College at Rome, where he completed his ecclesiastical studies and was ordained a priest. He returned to Scotland in 1759, and was sent into Banffshire, where he labored for eight years. In 1769 he was made coadjutor to bishop Grant, vicar-apostolic of Scotland. In 1771 he appeared as an author, and began that series of doctrinal, moral, and devotional works which is still popular. In 1798 he received a second coadjutor in bishop Cameron, to replace bishop Geddes, deceased. A few years afterwards, feeling his end approach, he retired to the Seminary of Aquhorties, and devoted his remaining days to devotion. He died Oct. 15, 1811. See (N. Y.) *Cath. Annual*, 1880, p. 75.

Hay, Philip Courtlandt, D.D., a Presbyterian minister, was born at Newark, N. J., July 25, 1793. He was educated at Princeton and Nassau colleges; was licensed by the New Jersey Presbytery, at Paterson, in 1820, and became pastor of the Presbyterian Church at Mendham. Subsequently he was called to the Second Presbyterian Church of Newark, where he labored faithfully for twelve years. He died Dec. 27, 1860. See Wilson, *Presb. Hist. Almanac*, 1862, p. 185.

Hay, William, D.D., a Scotch prelate, was born Feb. 17, 1647, and was educated at Aberdeen. He received holy orders from bishop Scongal, and was first settled as minister at Kilconquhar, in Fife; from here he was removed to Perth, and afterwards consecrated bishop of Moray in 1688. He died at Castlehill, near Inverness, March 17, 1707. See Keith, *Scottish Bishops*, p. 155.

Haycroft, Nathaniel, D.D., a distinguished English Baptist minister, was born near Exeter, Feb. 14, 1821. He pursued his studies at Stepney College, at Edinburgh, and Glasgow; was settled first at Saffron, then at Broadmead Chapel, Bristol, where he remained eighteen years, during which time he attained to eminent distinction among the ministers of his denomination in England. Resigning his pastorate in Bristol, he accepted a call to Leicester, and died Feb. 16, 1873. See (Lond.) *Baptist Hand-book*, 1874, p. 274.

Haye, Jean de la, a French Franciscan, was born at Paris, March 20, 1593. He was professor of philosophy and theology, court-preacher to queen Anne of Austria, and died Oct. 15, 1661. He edited the *Biblia Magna* (Paris, 1643, 5 vols.):—*Biblia Maxima* (1660, 19 vols.):—wrote *Comment. in Genesin* (3 vols. fol.):—*Apparatus Evangelicus:—Comment. in Apocalypsin*. See Witte, *Diarium Biographicum;* Winer, *Handbuch der theol. Lit.* i, 186; Jöcher, *Allgemeines Gelehrten-Lexikon*, s. v. (B. P.)

Hayer, Jean Nicolas Hubert, a French theologian, was born at Sarrelonis, June 15, 1708. He taught theology and philosophy among the Recollets, and showed himself one of the strongest defenders of the Church in his time. He died at Paris, July 16, 1780, leaving, *La Spiritualité et l'Immortalité de l'Âme* (Paris, 1758):—*Le Règle de la Foi Vengée* (ibid. 1761):—*L'Apostolicité du Ministère de l'Église Romaine* (ibid. 1765):—*Traité de l'Éxistence de Dieu* (ibid. 1774):—*La Charlatanerie des Incrédules* (1780). See Hoefer, *Nouv. Biog. Générale*, s. v.

Haymann, Christoph (1), a Lutheran theologian of Germany, was born Oct. 15, 1677, at Reichenbach, Saxony. He studied at Leipsic, and died in 1731. His ascetical writings are enumerated in Jöcher, *Allgemeines Gelehrten Lexikon*, s. v. (B. P.)

Hayman, Christoph (2), a son of the above, was born Aug. 15, 1709. He died at Meissen in 1783, doctor and professor of theology, and superintendent, leaving, *Comm. de κλήρῳ* (1746):—*Versuch einer biblischen Theologie in Tabellen* (eod.):—*Litteræ Encyclicæ in 1 Epist. ad Timoth.* (1753). See Meusel, *Gelehrtes Deutschland;* Jöcher, *Allgemeines Gelehrten-Lexikon*, s. v. (B. P.)

Haymo of Feversham, an ecclesiastic of the 13th century, was born at Feversham, Kent, studied at the University of Paris, where Leland says he was "inter Aristotelicos Aristotelissimus;" became a Franciscan, served at the Church of St. Denis, and on his return to England was made provincial of his order. His eminence in counsel led to his call to Rome, where he was chosen general of the Franciscans. Pits entitles him "speculum honestatis," yet Bale makes him an inquisitor and persecutor in Greece. At the command of pope Alexander IV he corrected and emended the Roman breviary. He died at Anagni, Italy, where the pope in person came to visit him, in 1260. See Fuller, *Worthies of England* (ed. Nuttall), ii, 150.

Haymo of Hythe, an English prelate, was born at Hythe, Kent, and made bishop of Rochester in the twelfth year of Edward II's reign, to whom he was confessor. In his native town he founded a hospital, and enlarged the episcopal palace. In his old age he resigned his bishopric, lived on his own estate, and died about 1355. See Fuller, *Worthies of England* (ed. Nuttall), ii, 135.

Haynes, J. A., D.D., a Baptist minister, was born in King and Queen County, Va., Dec. 13, 1822. He graduated from Columbian University, Washington, D.C., in 1843, was principal of Bruington Academy for a year, and then entered upon a course of medical study, receiving his degree from the Jefferson Medical College, Philadelphia, in 1846. Relinquishing his practice, he entered the Christian ministry, being licensed in 1853, and ordained in 1857. For a time he labored under the auspices of the State Mission Board, and then accepted an appointment as principal of the Clarke Female Seminary, at Berryville, Va. Subsequently he was pastor of two or three churches in Virginia, a part of the time being engaged in teaching. He died in January, 1880. See Cathcart, *Baptist Encyclop.* s. v. (J. C. S.)

Haynes, Samuel, D.D., an English clergyman, was educated at King's College, Cambridge, and was tutor to the earl of Salisbury, with whom he travelled, and who in 1737 presented him to the rectory of Hatfield, in Hertfordshire. In May, 1747, he was presented to the rectory of Clothal. He died June 9, 1752. See Chalmers, *Biog. Dict.* p. 270; Allibone, *Dict. of Brit. and Amer. Authors*, s. v.

Hayter, Thomas, an English prelate, became bishop of Norwich in 1749, bishop of London in 1761, and died Jan. 9, 1762. He published *Occasional Sermons* (1732–59). See Allibone, *Dict. of Brit. and Amer. Authors*, s. v.

Hazar-gaddah. Tristram (*Bible Places*, p. 20) coincides in the location "at *Jurrah* or *el-Ghurra*, a group of ruins on a high marl peak with steep sides, very near el-Milh, on the road to Beersheba," and so Lieut. Conder (*Quar. Statement* of the "Pal. Explor. Fund," Jan. 1875, p. 25). But more recently the latter suggests (*Tent Work*, ii, 337) *Judeideh*, the position of which he does not indicate.

Hazar-shual. The location of this place at *Saweh* is acquiesced in by Tristram (*Bible Places*, p. 20), Lieut. Conder (*Quar. Statement* of the "Pal. Explor. Fund," Jan. 1875, p. 21), but not by the latter finally

(*Tent Work*, ii, 337), nor by Trelawney Saunders (*Map of the O. T.*), who with less probability locates Jeshua (Neh. xi, 26) there. It is laid down on the *Ordnance Map* as *Khurbet Saweh*, four and a half miles north-west of Tell-Milh, and described in the accompanying *Memoirs* (iii, 409) as "a prominent hill-top, crowned with ruins, consisting of foundations and heaps of stones. The hill is surrounded by a wall built of large blocks of flint conglomerate. Other ruins of a similar kind exist in the valley beneath."

Hazelius, Ernest L., D.D., a Lutheran professor, was born at Neusalz, province of Silesia, Prussia, Sept. 6, 1777. He was educated at his native place, Klein-welke, and Barby, studying theology at Neisky in a Moravian institution, and was licensed to preach by the authorities of that Church. In 1800 he was appointed teacher of the classics in the Moravian Seminary at Nazareth, Pa., where he remained eight years, having during that period been appointed head teacher and professor of theology in the theological department. Joining the Lutheran Church, he taught, in 1809, a private classical school, and then became pastor of the united congregations of New Germantown, German Valley, and Spruce Run; also conducting a classical school at New Germantown. In 1815 the Hartwick Seminary went into operation, and he was appointed professor of Christian theology and principal of the classical department. For fifteen years he served this institution, acting also as pastor of the village church. In 1830 he became professor of Oriental and Biblical literature and German language in the Theological Seminary at Gettysburg, but resigned in 1833 to take charge of the Theological Seminary of the synod of South Carolina, holding that position from Jan. 1, 1834, until his death, Feb. 20, 1853. Among his published writings are, *Life of Luther:—Life of Stilling:—Augsburg Confession, with Annotations:—Materials for Catechization on Passages of Scripture:—History of the Lutheran Church in America.* For some time he was editor of the *Evangelical Magazine*, published at Gettysburg. He was a most accurate classical scholar, and a very successful teacher. See *Pennsylvania College Book*, 1882, p. 157.

Hazor. Of the places thus simply designated, the latest authorities make the following identifications:

1. Hazor of Naphtali (Josh. xi, 1, 10, 11, 13; xii, 19; xix, 36; Judg. iv, 2, 17; 1 Sam. xii, 9; 1 Kings ix, 15; 2 Kings xv, 29) is identified by Grove (in Smith's *Atlas*) with *Tell Huraweh*, south-east of Kedesh, and by Trelawney Saunders (*Map of the O. T.*) with *Khurbet Harrah* (evidently the same locality), which is set down on the *Ordnance Map* one and three quarter miles north-west of Lake Huleh, and described in the accompanying *Memoirs* (i, 237) as "an important ruin on a hill-top. There are considerable remains of walls of good-sized masonry and foundations, with caves, and two rock-cut tombs, with loculi. A few stones are moulded, probably door-posts or architraves. There are a number of cisterns. The principal remains are on the top and the eastern slope of the hill. A zigzag pathway formerly led down to the great spring of 'Ain el-Mellâheh." This is the location proposed by Wilson and advocated by Guérin. Lieut. Conder, on the other hand, suggests (*Tent Work*, ii, 337) *Hadîreh*, which occurs in a Jebel and Merj of that name, one and a half miles west of el-Khureibeh (Robinson's site for Hazor), lying two and a half miles south of Kedesh, and three and a half west of Lake Huleh.

Grove and Conder, however, both seem to distinguish two Hazors in the above passages, and they locate the second at *Hazzur*, a rock-cut tomb in *Khurbet Hazîreh* (ten miles west of Kedesh), where are "foundations of walls, built with large, well-dressed stones, a few small columns and broken pieces mixed up with the ruins; eight rock-cut cisterns, one rock-cut birkeh [pool], and two rock-cut tombs" (*Memoirs*, i, 239; comp. p. 223). They seem, moreover, to identify this with En-hazor (q. v.), although there is no spring there now, as there is at 'Ain el-Khurbeh, where Saunders locates the latter. This last geographer places Edrei at Hazîreh, but it should rather be identified with Khureibeh, and Hazzûr and Hazîreh will thus be left to represent a single Hazor, as the names respectively indicate. En-Hazor may then be appropriately assigned separately to *Khurbet Hazûr*, half a mile north-west of a hill of the same name, and consisting of "heaps of stones and cisterns" (*Memoirs*, i, 396), laid down five miles north-west of Yakûk, with several springs in the vicinity ('Ain el-Tahît, one and a half miles west, sufficiently copious to supply three mills; and 'Ain el-Mansûrah and 'Ain el-Diâh, one mile south). But the specific name, *'Ain Hazûr*, does not occur on the *Ordnance Map*, although several travellers speak of it here, and Tristram even says (*Bible Places*, p. 273) "This is the only Ain-Hazur."

2. Hazor of Benjamin after the Captivity (Neh. xi, 33) is identified by Grove with *Yasûr*, near Ashdod, which is out of the region indicated. It has usually been made the same with Baal-hazor (q. v.), which Conder and Saunders reasonably locate at *Tell Asûr*, four and a half miles north-east of Beitin (Bethel), "a sacred place among the peasantry, though no Mukâm exists. There is a group of fine oaks on the hill-top, sacred, apparently, to a certain Sheik Hadherah (the proper Arabic form of Hazor). The Rijâl el-Asâwir, or 'Men of 'Asur,' said to be companions of the Prophet, are also invoked by the Moslems. This appears to be a probable survival of the ancient *cultus* of Baal on this lofty summit. Here Guérin found ancient cisterns cut in the rock, and vaulted houses still standing. In the middle of the plateau was a wely, dedicated to sheik Hassan, on the site of an old church, now destroyed, of which some ruins remain, especially four fragments of columns lying on great slabs which were once the pavement of the church; besides these a capital, on which was formerly sculptured a cross of square form" (*Memoirs*, ii, 371).

Lieut. Conder, however, suggests a separate location from this for the Hazor of the post-exilian history at *Hazzûr* (*Tent Work*, ii, 119), one mile east of Neby Samwîl; a ruined site (*Memoirs*, iii, 43), four miles north-west of Jerusalem, with tombs, cisterns, and spring ('Ain Malahah) adjoining.

3. Hazor of Judah (Josh. xv, 23) is combined by Saunders with the name following (contrary to the Heb. text, which has ְו disconnective between) into the compound Hazor-Ithnan, and located at *en-Hora*, which he lays down a short distance south-east of Beersheba.

Hazor-Hadattah (Josh. xv, 25) is identified by Tristram (*Bible Places*, p. 18) with "the ruins called *Hadadah*, a watch-tower on the edge of a bluff on the high ground at the head of the Zuweirah valley, south-west of the Dead Sea." This point is beyond the bounds of the *Ordnance Map*, but is situated in the same direction as the *el-Hudeirah*, with which we have identified the place, and where Saunders locates an imaginary Hazor-Kinah (adopting the suggestion of Tristram, *Bible Places*, p. 16) and also Jagur (q. v.). See Judah.

Hea. One of the most important of all the Assyrian gods, as he combines in his numerous titles the attributes of several classic deities. His Accadian name was En-ki, or the "Lord of the World" (earth), and his Assyrian name read phonetically Ea or Hea. He unites in his offices the attributes of Pluto (Hades), of Poseidon (Neptune), and of Hermes (Wisdom). Hea, as the representative of the Greek Poseidon, was "Lord of the Abyss," *sar abzu*, and was spoken of as Hea "who dwells in the great deep." In a list of his titles he is called "Lord of the Madudu or Sailors," and it was Hea who taught Hasis Arda how to build the ark or ship (*elapu*) in which he sailed over the flood. In this character of the god of water and ocean he was associated with a female deity, Bahu, the "Void," who may be identified with the *bohu* of Genesis i, 2. Hea held dominion over a large number of spirits who dwelt in the *abzu*, or the deep. In the character of the Greek Pluto, or lord of Hades, Hea himself seldom figured, but his consort, Nin-ki-gal, the "Lady of the Great Land," appears very frequently. Hea, as lord of Hades, had the name of Nin-a-zu, and his wife was called Nin-ki-gal. But it was in the character of the god of wisdom, the "god who knows all things," that Hea figured most prominently, Nin-ni-mi-ki, "Lord of Wisdom," or, as the Accadian expressed it, the "Lord of the Bright Eye." It was Hea alone who could deliver man from the various spells and curses with which the complicated system of Chaldæan magic beset him. He also delivered Ishtar from the power of Nin-ki-gal, in the legend of her descent into Hades. Hea had for his female consort, in his character of "Lord of Wisdom," the goddess Dav-kina, the female deification of the earth, who was probably only another form of Nin-ki-gal, and resembles the classic Persephone or Proserpine; though perhaps Nin-ki-gal and Dav-kina may be better identified with Persephone and Ceres (Demeter), the "Mother and Daughter" of the Greeks.

Heacock, Grosvenor Williams, D.D., a Presbyterian minister, was born at Buffalo, N. Y., Aug. 3, 1822. He graduated from Western Reserve College in 1840, and from the Auburn Theological Seminary in 1843; was ordained pastor of the Lafayette Street Presbyterian Church in his native city, Oct. 20, 1845, and retained that position until his death, May 6, 1877. He was greatly esteemed and beloved. See *Gen. Cat. of Auburn Theol. Sem.* 1883, p. 264.

Headstone, a monument placed at the head of a grave, as a memorial of the departed. Anciently, the cross in some form or other was invariably used,

Headstone in the Churchyard at Tetsworth, Oxfordshire. Headstone in the Churchyard at Folkestone, Kent.

either simply, with floriated ends, within a circle, or in some other obvious form. During the 15th century the cruciform shape was displaced by other forms less Christian, neither artistic nor ornamental.

Healing. Touching, i. e. stroking the patient's face with both hands, to remove the scrofula, significantly called the king's evil, was practiced by the kings of France as early as Clovis or Philip I, kings of Hungary, and English sovereigns, from Edward the Confessor to queen Anne, who touched Dr. Johnson. Bradwardine says that crowds resorted to the kings of England, France, and Germany. Solemn prayer and the sign of the cross, first laid aside by James I, were used. Henry II and Edward I practiced the touch. The ceremonial took place on a progress, on Good Friday, monthly, quarterly, or at Michaelmas, Easter, and Whitsuntide, and in 1683 from All-Saints' till a week before Christmas, and from Christmas till March 1. The first form of service was drawn up in the reign of Henry VII. The gospel (Mark xvi, 14) was read while the king laid on his hands, and during another (John i, 1), at the words "the light," an angel, noble, or medal with St. Michael stamped on it was attached by a white ribbon round the neck of the patient, who had to produce a certificate of his malady, signed by the parish priest and churchwardens, and was examined by the king's surgeon-in-waiting. The faculty of healing was popularly attributed also to the ninth son of a ninth son, or the seventh son of the seventh son.

Healing-box, used for holding the chrism in extreme unction.

Healing-coin, a piece of money anciently given by kings to those persons who were "touched" for the cure of the king's evil. The coin was pierced and worn round the neck with a string or ribbon.

Healing-oil, the sacred unction, made of oil of olives and balm, for use in the sacrament of extreme unction.

Healing-pyx, the box containing the sacred oil for anointing the sick. See Pyx.

Hearing the Word of God is an ordinance of divine appointment (Rom. x, 17; Prov. viii, 4, 5; Mark iv, 24). Public reading of the Scriptures was a part of synagogue worship (Acts xiii, 15; xv, 21), and was the practice of the Christians in primitive times. Under the former dispensation there was a public hearing of the law at stated seasons (Deut. xxxi, 10, 13; Neh. viii, 2, 3). It seems, therefore, that it is a duty incumbent on us to hear, and, if sensible of our ignorance, we shall also consider it our privilege. (1) As to the manner of hearing, it should be *constantly* (Prov. viii, 34; James i, 24, 25); *attentively* (Luke xxi, 48; Acts x, 33; Luke iv, 20, 22); with *reverence* (Psa. lxxxix, 7); with *faith* (Heb. iv, 2); with an endeavor to *retain* what we hear (Heb. ii, 1; Psa. cxix, 11); with an *humble, docile disposition* (Luke x, 42); with *prayer* (Luke xviii). (2) *The advantages of hearing* are *information* (2 Tim. iii, 16); *conviction* (1 Cor. xiv, 24, 25; Acts ii); *conversion* (Psa. xi, 7; Acts iv, 4); *confirmation* (Acts xiv, 22; xvi, 5); *consolation* (Phil. i, 25; Isa. xl, 1, 2; xxxv, 3, 4). See Preaching.

Heart-burial. The heart was often buried apart from the body in the place it loved well in life, as Devorgilla founded Sweet Heart Abbey in memory of the heart-burial of her husband. Richard I's heart was buried at Rouen. Robert Bruce desired his heart to be taken to the Holy Land in lieu of his pilgrimage, and lord James Douglas carried it round his neck in a silver case, hung by a silken cord. He threw it forward in advance of his men at the great battle of Salano, and covered it with his body.

Heath, Nicholas, an English prelate, was born in London, and educated at Christ College, Cambridge. He became successively archdeacon of Stafford, bishop of Rochester (1540), of Worcester (1554), archbishop of York (1555), and chancellor of England under the reign of Mary. He was deprived of his offices because he refused to take the oath of supremacy under Elizabeth, and died at Cobham in 1560. See Hoefer, *Nouv. Biog. Générale*, s. v.

Hebdomadarii, a name anciently applied to monks from their weekly service.

Hebdŏmas Magna (*the great week*), an appellation given anciently to the week before Easter, which was observed with great solemnity. The use of this term is thus accounted for by Chrysostom: "It was called the great week, not because it consisted of longer days or more in number than other weeks, but because at this time great things were wrought for us by our Lord. For in this week the ancient tyranny of the devil was dissolved, death was extinct, the strong man was bound, his goods were spoiled, sin was abolished, the curse was destroyed, paradise was opened, heaven became accessible, men and angels were joined together, the middle wall of partition was broken down, the barriers were taken out of the way, the God of peace made peace between things in heaven and things on earth." See Chrysostom, *Hom. in Psal. cxlv. sive de Hebdomade Magna;* Bingham, *Antiq.* bk. xxi, chap. i, sec. 24.

Hebdŏmè (ἑβδόμη, *the seventh* day of the month), a festival observed by the ancient Greeks in honor of Apollo, on the seventh day of every month, because one of them was the birthday of that god. The chief place of these observances was Athens. Hymns were sung to Apollo, and the people walked in procession, carrying sprigs of laurel in their hands.

Hebè, in Greek mythology, was the daughter of Jupiter and Juno, the goddess of youth and loveliness. She is often confounded with Hygea or the goddess of health, but the latter may be recognised by her long, modest dress; Hebe, on the contrary, appears with a light apron, and half naked. Not seldom the eagle of Jupiter is found at her side. She was married to Hercules, and bore him two sons, Alexiares and Anicetus. Although she was a daughter of the supreme deities, she appears in a subordinate relation, for she not only serves all gods at the table, but harnessed the horses of Juno, when the latter advanced with Minerva against the Trojans.

Figure of Hebe. (From an ancient gem.)

Hebenstreit, Johann Christian, a Lutheran theologian of Germany, was born April 27, 1686. He studied at Leipsic, and commenced his academical career there in 1715. In 1731 he was professor of Hebrew, in 1732 doctor of divinity, in 1740 professor of theology, and died Dec. 6, 1756, leaving, *De βάκχοις ad Illustr. Ezech. viii,* 17 (Leipsic, 1713):—*De Judæo Roma Exule, ex Actor. xiv,* 1 *sq.* (ibid. 1714):—*De Sertis Convivalibus ad Ezech. viii,* 6 (ibid. eod.):—*De Pentecoste Veterum* (ibid. 1715):—*Diss. i–ix in Prophetam Malachiam* (ibid. 1731-46):—*De Maacha, a Regia Remota, ad* 1 *Reg. xv,* 13 (ibid. 1734):—*De Discrepantia et Consensu Psalmi xviii et* 2 *Sam. xxii,* 38 (ibid. 1736):—*De Ossibus Regis Edom Combustis, Amos xi,* 8 (ibid. eod.):—*De Pane Super Aquam Mittendo, Coheleth xi,* 1 (ibid. 1737):—*De Es. lxiii,* 19 *non Divellendo a Sequente Capite* (ibid. eod.):—*De Erigendis Capitibus in Adventu Messiæ, ad Ps. xxiv,* 9 *sq.* (ibid. 1741):—*De Sabbatho ante Mosaicam Legem Existente* (ibid. 1748):—*De Eliakimo, Christi Typo, Ps. xxii,* 15; *Apoc. iii,* 6 (ibid. eod.):—*Problema Exegetica ad Apoc. ii,* 4:—*Quid sit ἡ ἀγαπὴ ἡ πρώτη ab Angelo Ephesino Omissa?* (ibid. 1750):—*De Nomine Christi ἀμήν, Apoc. iii,* 14 (ibid. 1751):—*De Salomonis Idololatria ad* 1 *Reg. x,* 4–8 (ibid. 1755). See Döring, *Die gelehrten Theologen Deutschlands,* s. v.; Winer, *Handbuch der theol. Lit.* i, 231, 618; Jöcher, *Allgemeines Gelehrten-Lexikon,* s. v. (B. P.)

Hebenstreit, Johann Friedrich, a German theologian, son of Johann Paul, was doctor of theology at Leipsic in 1726, and died superintendent at Buttstadt, Thuringia, between 1760 and 1770. He wrote, *De Magorum Messiam Exosculantium Nomine, Patria et Statu* (Jena, 1709):—*De Juda Ischarioth* (Wittenberg, 1712):—*Schediasma Historico-Philologicum de Variis Christianorum Nominibus* (1713):—*De καλῷ στρατιωτῷ seu Episcopo Milite* (Leipsic, 1726):—*De Hostibus καλοῦ στρατιωτοῦ* (eod.):—*De Hæresi Carpocratianorum* (1712). See Jöcher, *Allgemeines Gelehrten-Lexikon,* s. v.; Winer, *Handbuch der theol. Lit.* i, 567, 640. (B. P.)

Hebenstreit, Johann Paul, a Lutheran theologian of Germany, was born June 25, 1664, at Neustadt-on-the-Orla. He studied at Jena, where he also commenced his academical career. In 1697 the university at Altdorf honored him with the doctorate of divinity, and in 1710 he was professor of theology at Jena. He died May 6, 1718, leaving, *Theologia Naturalis* (Jena, 1693):—*De Theologis Multiplici Calumnia Appetitis* (eod.):—*De Prædestinatione:*—*De Epiphania et Epiphaniis:*—*De Sponso in Nuptiis Canæ Galilææ:*—*De Eremitis seu Anachoretis:*—*De Johanne Eremita:*—*De Augustanæ Confessionis Nomine et Causis:*—*De Canonibus, ut Vulgo Dicuntur, Apostolicis* (1695):—*De Theologiæ Exegeticæ Natura et Constitutione:*—*De Theologiæ Exegeticæ Fine:*—*De Scripturæ S. Sensu* (1697):—*De Summa Scripturæ Sacræ Auctoritate:*—*De Peccato Originali* (1698):—*Systema Theologicum* (1707):—*De Duarum Christi Naturarum Communicatione* (1710). See Döring, *Die gelehrten Theologen Deutschlands,* s. v.; Jöcher, *Allgemeines Gelehrten-Lexikon,* s. v. (B. P.)

Hebrew Language. The central position which this "sacred tongue" occupies in Biblical literature justifies us in supplementing the article in vol. iv by a somewhat detailed exposition of some of its leading lexical and grammatical peculiarities, and in doing so we take the occasion to call attention to some features and linguistic principles not usually apprehended. These illustrate the natural simplicity no less than the profound philosophy of the language.

I. *Root Meanings.*—1. It has generally been assumed that verbs are the only primitives in Hebrew, and hence the lexicons have constantly referred all words to some verbal root. But it seems more reasonable to analogy and more consonant with fact to admit a few primitive nouns, such as אָב, *father;* אָח, *brother;* מַיִם, *water*, etc. Accordingly we find יָדָה scarcely used, except in Hiph. as a denominative from יָד, *hand,* in the sense of *stretching out the hand*, e. g. in prayer or praise.

2. A more important fact, admitted by most lexicographers, and denied of late by only a few scholars,* is that all the roots primarily seem to designate some physical act or condition, appreciable by the senses. This may be true of other languages, in the primitive forms, but it is eminently characteristic of the Hebrew. Not only were the people who used it a constitutionally poetic race, affected by and reflecting every shadow of the imagination, but their originally nomadic habits made them keenly sensitive to every accident and influence of Bedawin life. They had specific terms for pitching and striking their tents (חָנָה and נָסַע, respectively), for turning out of the road to stop at a house (גּוּר), and lodging over night (לִין), etc. They were on the constant lookout for an enemy (צָפָה), and they had a term for one of a hostile tribe (אֹיֵב as opposed to שֹׁלֵם), in distinction from personal enmity (שָׂנֵא) or individual opposition (צָרַר) The nice shades of climactic signification, which are very imperfectly developed even in the best Hebrew lexicons, are shown with graphic clearness in terms for anger: אָנַף, *to breathe hard* with the first excitement; חָרָה, *to glow* with the rising passion; חֵמָה, the *flush* of the hot blood; זָעַם, *to froth* with intense fury, etc. Attention to the ostensible sign of a root will enable us to note the steps of transition from a primitive to a derivative signification: e. g. הָגָה, *to mutter* to one's self in a brown

* We look with some distrust upon the fashion, prevalent in certain quarters, of seeking Hebrew etymons in the radicals found among the cuneiform disclosures. The dialects of the Assyrian, "Accadian," and early Babylonian are yet in too crude a state of classification and investigation to bear out much reliance upon them for such purposes, and it is doubtful if they ever will be largely available for trustworthy comparison, except in a very general manner, and for obscure roots.

study; hence *to murmur* in grudge, or *meditate* with pleasure. The constant usage of terms in a figurative sense, with an eye to their literal import, makes every word and phrase a picture, and renders even the prosiest utterances highly poetical.

3. Hebrew *synonyms*, as thus appears, have received less attention than they deserve. The lexicographers, especially Gesenius, have occasionally traced distinctions in the use of words, and have freely compared many cognate roots, resolving most of them to certain supposed essential ideas, but this last has helped very little towards a practical discrimination of their real meaning and prevalent application, and no general system of comparing verbs closely resembling each other has been instituted. Yet it is certain that in Hebrew, as in all other primitive languages, real synonyms are very rare, and in no other tongue, perhaps, are terms more distinctively employed, especially in the physical relations of life, however vaguely they may often have to be construed in their figurative and metaphysical applications. For example, the words relating to the senses are nicely correlated to each other, and finely shaded off in comparative strength. Thus שָׁמַע is *to hear* simply, the sound entering one's ears whether he will or not. But עָנָה is *to pay attention to* what is heard, as by look or gesture; hence *to answer*, as expected of one giving heed to another; and finally *to speak*, i. e. in reply to words or thoughts merely implied. Still advancing, הֶאֱזִין, a denominative from אֹזֶן, *the ear* (probably a primitive, for the root אָזַן does not occur), is *to give ear*, i. e. turn the ear in the direction of the sound, or listen, but not very intently. Finally, הִקְשִׁיב is *to prick up* the ears, i. e. use the hand for increasing the volume of sound, or hearken earnestly. So likewise רָאָה is *to see* simply, without any special effort, ἰδεῖν; but חָזָה is *to behold*, or gaze intently at some striking object, as in a vision, ὁράω or θεωρέω; and הִבִּיט is *to look at* closely, for the purpose of scrutiny or discovery, σκοπέω; while other terms are of special and narrow import, as הִשְׁקִיף, *to view*, i. e. bring into the field of vision; שׁוּר, to *peep*, as from a lurking-place; צָפָה, to *watch*, as an enemy. In addressing, קָרָא is simply to *call* out the name of a person spoken to or of; while אָמַר is to *say* something, the words being added; and דִּבֶּר is to *speak*, the language not being given; but שִׁוַּע is to *halloo*, or cry out for help; צָעַק (less strongly, זָעַק) to *shriek* from distress or danger; אָנַק to *groan* in pain or sorrow; and הָלַל merely to *talk* loud, out of folly or (Piel) in praise. Among pleasant emotions שָׂמַח is *to be glad* simply, as evinced by a quiet and satisfied demeanor; but עָלַז or עָלַץ is *to exult* with demonstrative expressions; and רָנַן *to triumph* with shouts of joy. Among unpleasant emotions יָרֵא is *to fear*, simply in a general sense; but בָּהַל is *to palpitate* with sudden alarm (Niph. *to be panic*-stricken); פָּחַד is *to be frightened* by some object of terror; עָרַץ is *to dread* an impending cause of anxiety; חָרַד *to shudder* on the surface; רָעַד *to quake* in the interior; while גִּיל and חִיל are merely to *spin round* under the influence of any violent feeling, whether *cringing* through fear, *writhing* in pain, or *jumping* for joy (especially the former word). כָּשַׁל is *to be weak in the ankles*, hence, to totter, stumble, etc.; but כָּרַע is *to bend the knees*, hence, to bow or fall; while רָבַץ is *to crouch* on the haunches, like an animal in repose. For terms denoting *forever*, there is עוֹלָם, the *vanishing point*, whether forward or backward; hence time out of mind, everlastingly; עַד, the *terminus*, a fixed point beyond which one cannot pass; and נֶצַח, the *goal* or shining mark set up as far ahead as one can well see; while תָּמִיד simply denotes *continuity*. Of negatives there is לֹא, *not*, the direct denial, οὐκ; אַל, *far from it*, the softer or deprecative disclaimer, μή; אַיִן, *by no means*, the peremptory exclusive; and בַּל, *not at all*, the absolute contradiction, οὐ μή, *omnino*. So in meteorology, עָב is a misty *scud-cloud*, so called from *obscuring* the landscape; עָנָן is a black *thunder-cloud*, so called from *veiling* the heavens; and שַׁחַק is a light *fleece-cloud*, so called from its resemblance to *dust* diffused in the sky. In brigandage מַאֲרָב is an *ambush* for a surprise; while סֵתֶר is a *covert* for security; מַחֲבֵא a *hiding-place* for secrecy; and סֹךְ or סֻכָּה merely a *lair* of wild beast, as screened by interlaced twigs. In orography and geography generally, Hebrew words are used with great precision. See TOPOGRAPHICAL TERMS.

II. *Vocalization.*—Syllabification is very simple in Hebrew, as the letters (all regarded as consonants) are the basis of articulation, and each (with the frequent exception of the quiescents) has its own vowel (expressed or implied) following. The pronunciation, indeed, is not certain, as Hebrew ceased to be a living tongue after the Babylonian exile; but the sounds of the letters probably survive in the cognate Oriental languages, especially the Arabic, and the vowels supplied by the Masoretes doubtless represent those traditionally handed down to their own times. The latter form an ingenious and apparently complicated but really simple and natural series, of which the written signs are sufficiently distinct and philosophical.

The intricate chain of vowel-changes arising in declension is remarkable for its strict conformity to the laws of the vocal organs, and euphony is its fundamental principle. The tone usually rests on the final syllable, as being in general the most significant of grammatical relations, and hence an increment, as carrying the accent, has a constant tendency to shorten the preceding part of the word. The oblique forms of nouns and verbs, including the suffixed pronouns, are thus literally *constructed*, and the balance is preserved by abbreviating the beginning. In this system two features are of prime and universal influence, namely, the semi-vocal character of the gutturals (inducing a series of peculiarities in their pointing), and the necessity of the tone for either a long closed or a short open syllable. By observing the effect of these principles and a few conventional form-signs, the grammar is wonderfully simplified and clarified.

III. *Doctrine of the so-called "Tenses."*—1. The "Præter" and the "Future." These are now well understood not to denote primarily *time*, but some other less palpable relation. The absence of a present tense is, we may remark in passing, really logical, for the present moment is but the dividing line between the past and the future, and shifts its position every instant. Ewald suggested the names "Perfect" and "Imperfect" in lieu of Præter and Future, maintaining that the former denotes a *completed* act, and the latter an *inchoate;* and some later grammarians, including Driver, in his ingenious monograph on the subject, have hastily adopted this nomenclature. But besides the inexactness of these terms in themselves, and the liability of confounding such a use with that of the corresponding tenses in English, and still more in Greek and Latin, they will be found to be essentially erroneous. As a matter of fact, in most cases, these two verb-forms indisputably designate the two relations of time, anterior and posterior; and the consummation or incipiency of the act or state is comparatively rare as an important shade of the thought. In very many, indeed, a majority of cases, such a rendering would be absurd. For example, that remarkable and pregnant announcement by Jehovah of his divine self-existence, אֶהְיֶה אֲשֶׁר

אֶהְיֶה, *I will be what I will be* (A. V. "I am that I am," Exod. iii, 14), becomes the flattest nonsense if translated "I begin to be what I begin to be." Surely this cannot be the essential conception of the tense-form in question. The true distinction is rather that the Præter marks an act or state as a matter of *fact*, or something intended to be stated as such, while the Future denotes a *conception*, or something meant to be so stated. They are respectively the objective and the subjective points of view, the actual and the imaginary, the absolute and the conditional, the indicative and the subjunctive, the independent and the relative. Out of this fundamental distinction grow all the subordinate ones, especially the *past*, as representing the only real facts, and the *future*, as being yet but a fancy. A completed act or state, as *un fait accompli*, of course thus comes in naturally under the Præter, and an inchoate one, as yet conceptual in part, falls appropriately under the Future. The use of either as "a customary Present" is but a device of grammarians in order to bring them into accord with the vague signification of that tense in other languages, especially the English. Continued or permanent action or condition is expressed in Hebrew by the participle, which is in itself always timeless. When a prophet expresses his vaticinations in the Præter (as notably in Isa. liii), his conceptions become to him realities, and he states the future as if it were already a fact. When, on the other hand, a historian uses the Future for his narrations (which less frequently occurs), he means thereby to mark the events as viewed in a subordinate relation either to his own mind (optative) or to some other events (subjunctive). The term אֶהְיֶה, therefore, in the above passage, indicates God's *revealed* attributes and character as a theme of human apprehension, while יְהוָֹה signifies his simple *self-existence*. The repetition "I conceive myself to be what I conceive myself to be," or "I am conceived to be what I am conceived to be," would then, like Pilate's phrase, "What I have written I have written," express the permanence and truthfulness of that conception. God's absolute essence is objectively incommunicable.

It would be easy to exemplify the distinction of the *independent* and the *qualified*, as represented by the two so-called "tenses" respectively. Thus, to take the first instances in Genesis: הָיְתָה (i, 2) is not the mere copula, but emphasizes the *fact* of a change having taken place in the earth; whereas יִהְיֶה and יִצְמָח (ii, 5), express the *idea* that no growth had yet been visible or observed; and יַעֲלֶה and וְהִשְׁקָה (ii, 6) denote the *appearance* of a mist, which answered these purposes. So we may render יִפָּרֵד וְהָיָה (ii, 10), "was divided *as it were*, so as to form;" יִתְבֹּשָׁשׁוּ (ii, 25), "*felt* no shame of themselves mutually." Very often in poetry the same thought is expressed in the successive hemistichs in these two forms successively, for the sake of variety; first objectively or absolutely, and then subjectively or relatively; or vice versa. The convenient subterfuge of employing the present tense in English to render these obliterates the nice shade of meaning conveyed by the original, and largely destroys its beauty and effect. A slight paraphrase is needed to bring out the delicate turn of thought. Generally some form of the Subjunctive or Potential will suffice to reproduce the graphic power of the Future. But in many (if not most) cases a real difference is intended. Thus יֶהְגֶּה (Psa. i, 2) denotes an *interior* characteristic of the saint, whereas the preceding Præters refer to his outward deportment. So even in Psa. ii, 1, 2, רָגְשׁוּ and נוֹסְדוּ state the violence of the wicked as an *act*, and the parallel Futures as of *purpose*.

2. "*Paragogic*" and "*Apocopate*" *Forms.* — The most important of the additions included under the former of these terms is the הָ appended to verbs (sometimes likewise to nouns) for the purpose of prolonging their sound, and thus naturally increasing their emphasis. With the Præter this is chiefly limited to the third person, as this alone is truly objective. With the Future, on the contrary, it is more appropriate in the first and second persons, giving the former an earnest or thorough significance, and softening the latter into a beseeching tone, an effect likewise produced when used with the Imperative.

Apocopation consists in throwing off in the Future and Imperative the loosely cemented ה final of verbs, and in dropping out the י characteristic of Hiphil. It imparts a curt or peremptory stress to the shortened form, and thus serves to distinguish the jussive from the predictive use of the third person Future. The tendency to apocopation with "vav conversive" in the Future arises from its bringing the tone forward, in consequence of the close connection with the preceding context, and especially, it would seem, on account of the particle, which (as we shall see presently) that form appears to have originally included.

3. "*Vav Conversive.*" — This peculiarity, which the Hebrew alone of all the Shemitic tongues exhibits, has been a sore puzzle to linguists, and only in recent times has received an intelligible explanation. It will serve as a crucial test of the foregoing theory of the tense-meanings. Its most usual and decided form, namely, with the Future, demands our first attention. The fact that in this case the *vav* is pointed with Pattach and the Dagesh shows the assimilation of some older consonant; in fact, there seems to have been originally some particle like an adverb more closely pointing the sequence than the simple "vav conjunctive" would have done, very much like the puerile phrase of simple story-tellers, who string each incident to the preceding by "and then." The Hebrew historian sets out with a genuine Præter (either expressed or implied), to indicate that he is stating matters of fact, but he continues his narrative with "vav conversive" and a Future to denote a consecutive series, the latter members of which he conceives and represents as depending upon the others. It is this dependent and conceptual relation that requires a Future. The incidents are all facts (as the particle implied in the pointing intimates), but not isolated or independent facts. They may or they may not be logically or causally connected, but they are viewed by the writer as historically following each other, and he designedly overlooks anything between them. After completing such a series, more or less extended, the writer begins a fresh series with another Præter, and continues it for awhile with "vav conversive" again. The whole history is thus divided off in a kind of paragraph style, and the close continuity of the subordinate statements is maintained in each paragraph. If he had used Præters with or without "vav connective" throughout, the incidents would have been merely the *disjecta membra* of history, without any positive bond of unity. The style would have been, as we say, comparatively incoherent.

The explanation of "vav conversive" with the Præter is more difficult. From the absence of any special pointing, and the less frequency of its use, we are entitled to infer its comparative unimportance. In fact, it seems to be a kind of *imitation*, by way of converse, of the "vav conversive" of the Future. A writer sets out with a Future (in form or effect), and continues the conceptual series by the Præter to indicate that he has now mentally transported himself into the region of fancy, and is describing things from that vivid impression. It thus resembles the "historic present" of many languages, in which a narrator views the scenes recounted as if actually taking place under his eye.

It can now be readily seen, in the light of the above explanation of these two "tenses," how in poetical passages (and all Hebrew is more or less poetical), the Præter and the Future (either simple or transformed by *vav*) may often be beautifully interchanged, according as the writer, for variety's sake, wishes to represent the same scene in adjoining hemistichs as either actual or conceptual; and this closer or more loose method of consecution, by means of simple *vav* or *vav conversive*, gives him a wider and nicer play of conception and expression. These are among the delicate shades of meaning which it is almost impossible to transfer to a version. For example, David says (Psa. iii, 6), "To Jehovah should I call (אֶקְרָא) [as I often have done], then he has heard me (וַיַּעֲנֵנִי);" i. e. in plain prose, Whenever I call he hears me, but in poetic fervor, When I think of myself as calling, I immediately know myself as heard.

IV. *Agglutinative Modes of Declension and Construction.*—1. *By Prefixes.*—Of these ב, ה, ו, כ, and ל are strictly inseparable, but like מ and שׁ, they probably represent original particles, as the Arabic article *el-* (which assimilates, as by a Dagesh, with the "solar letters") indicates. Whether the characteristic נ of Niphal, and the ה of its infinitive as weli as of Hiphil, Hophal, etc., had a similar origin is difficult to decide. The preformatives of the Future may be more readily traced to the full forms of the personal pronouns.

2. *By Sufformatives and Affixes.*—The personal endings of the tenses, as well as the suffixes, are clearly fragments, somewhat modified, of the pronouns which they represent. The ה directive is probably an enclitic fragment of the article as a demonstrative. The feminine ending ה was a softened form, like ה paragogic. The old constructive termination of masculine nouns was for both numbers, and the dual and plural absolute were intensive additions, like the decimal increase of the cardinal numbers. The frequent interchange of gender in the plural (notably in אָבוֹת, נָשִׁים, etc.) proves that this was a later or comparatively unimportant variation. The feminine, as the weaker, takes the place of the neuter in Greek and Latin to express the abstract.

3. *By Juxtaposition.*—Here we may enumerate three classes of amalgamation: (*a*) *compounds*, which are rare in Hebrew, except in proper names, and in cases of union by Makkeph (corresponding to our *hyphen* only in removing the principal tone); (*b*) *ellipsis*, by which connecting particles are dropped as unnecessary, especially in the terse style of poetry; and (*c*) *interchange* of the various parts of speech, which, as in English, allows nouns, particles, etc., to be freely used as adjectives, adverbs, etc., and conversely.

V. *Emphatic Position of Words.*—Here the natural order, in contradistinction from the artificial arrangement of the Latin, and the purely grammatical of the English, prevails. As with foreigners and children speaking a new language, the most important words come first (of course, after connectives, negatives, interrogatives, etc., which qualify the whole clause). Hence the predicate, as being of greater extension, precedes, and the subject or the adjective, which are but an accident of the verb or the noun, follows; except when special emphasis requires a different position, or when poetry in the parallel hemistichs calls for a pleasing variety. In this respect the Hebrew more closely resembles the Greek, which often resorts to the same expedient of emphasizing by a position near the head of the clause, like our "nominative independent." These nice shades of emphasis are difficult to render smoothly and adequately, but it might be done far more accurately than in our Authorized Version, which is habitually negligent in this respect. For the prosodiac arrangement, see POETRY, HEBREW.

Hebrew Version OF THE NEW TESTAMENT. If we may believe tradition, translations of parts of the New Test. already existed at a very early period. But as there is no certain information concerning such a version into the language of the Old-Test. Scriptures, the history of this work can only be traced back to the year 1537, when the gospel of Matthew was published in Hebrew by Sebastian Münster (q. v.). Great attention was excited by this book at the time of its appearance, on account of an ancient tradition which prevailed in the Church, that Matthew originally wrote his gospel in Hebrew. It was very evident, however, that Münster's publication, תורת המשיח, had no pretension to be regarded as the text of the sacred original, nor even as an ancient version, for the language in which it was written was not the Syro-Chaldaic, current in Palestine at the time of our Lord, but the rabbinical Hebrew in use among the Jews of the 12th century. It was, moreover, full of solecisms and barbarisms, and bore indubitable marks of having been translated either directly from the Vulgate, or from an Italian version thereof. In an apology for this work, dedicated to Henry VIII of England, Münster states that the MS. from which he printed was defective in several passages, and that he was compelled to supply the omissions as best he could from his own resources. It passed through several editions, and a Hebrew version of the epistle to the Hebrews was appended to it. Another edition of the same translation of Matthew, but printed from a more complete and correct MS. (*Recens Judœorum Penetralibus Erutum*), brought for the purpose from Italy, was published by Tillet, bishop of St. Brieux, at Paris, in 1555, with a Latin version by Mercer (*Ad Vulgatam quoad Fieri Potuit Accomodata*). The latter was published again by Dr. Herbst, under the title, *Des Schemtob ben-Schaphrut hebr. Uebersetzung des Evang. Matthaei nach den Drucken des S. Münster und J. du Tillet-Mercier* (Göttingen, 1879). In this edition the editor proves that the author of this version was none else than Shem-Tob Isaac ben-Schaphrut (q. v.), who translated this gospel for polemical purposes. Passing over the other translations of parts of the gospels, we mention the version of the four gospels into Biblical Hebrew, made by Giovanni Batista Giona (q. v.), a converted Jew, and professor of Hebrew at Rome. He dedicated it to pope Clement IX, and it was published at Rome in 1668, at the expense of the Congregation de Propaganda Fide. But this translation, as professor Delitzsch remarks, fulfilled less than might be expected from a man born at Safet, in Upper Galilee, who, besides, was a Jewish scholar. The first translation of the entire New Test. into Hebrew was made by Elias Hutter (q. v.), and published at Nüremberg in 1600 in his Polyglot Test. According to the judgment of professor Delitzsch, it is of great value, and is still worth consulting, because in many places it is very correct. A revised edition was published in London in 1661, under the superintendence of W. Robertson; but the greater part of this edition was consumed in the fire of London in 1666. A *Corrected New Testament in Hebrew* was published at London in 1798 by the Rev. R. Caddock, but it proved not to be acceptable to the Jews, for whose benefit it was published, and a new translation became a desideratum. In the meantime Dr. Buchanan brought from India a translation of the New Test., executed in Travancore, among the Jews of that country, the translator being a learned Jew. The MS. was written in the small rabbinical or Jerusalem character; the style was elegant and flowing, and tolerably faithful to the text. Dr. Buchanan deposited the MS. in the university library at Cambridge, after it had been transcribed by Mr. Yeates, of Cambridge, into the square Hebrew character. A copy was presented to the London Society for the Conversion of the Jews, and it was at one time thought that it would greatly promote the object of the society to print and circulate the production of a Jew, evidently master of his own ancient language. After much deliberation, however, a more strictly literal translation was still deemed desirable, and accordingly, in 1816, Mr. Frey and other learned Hebraists executed, under the patronage of the Jews' Society, a new edition of the New Test. In 1818 this new edition left the society's press, and was speedily followed by another issue. The British and Foreign Bible Society assisted materially in this work by purchasing at various times to a large amount. After this version had been in circulation for some time, complaints from Hebrew readers in various parts of the world were laid before the Jews' Society Committee, concerning the rendering of certain passages. To insure minute accuracy, the committee determined on a thorough revision. They consulted some of the most eminent men in Europe, and professor Gesenius was recommended to them as the first Hebrew scholar of the age. To him, therefore, the version was confided, with a request of a critique upon it, and suggestions as to alterations. Gesenius went carefully through the work as far as the Acts, and likewise through the book of Revelation. Numerous other engagements, however, compelled him to resign the task. The work, together with Gesenius's notes, was then transferred by the Jews' Committee to Dr. Joachim Neumann (q. v.), a converted Hebrew, lecturer on Hebrew at the University of Breslau. Dr. Neumann commenced the work anew, and his revision, when completed, was acknowledged to bear the stamp of diligence, accuracy, zeal, and profound scholarship. The limited funds of the society, however, prevented the publication of this valuable revision, and thus it remained for some time in MS. At this very period, the publisher of the Polyglot Bible (Mr. Bagster), requiring a Hebrew version of the New Test. for the Polyglot, applied to the Jews' Society for the critical emendations they had been amassing: the important notes of Gesenius and Neumann were in consequence handed to Mr. Bagster, and were incorporated in the new version executed for the Polyglot by Mr. Greenfield, and published in 1831. In comparing this edition of Greenfield with the second of the Jews' Society, published in 1821, the student will easily perceive that there has not been made a very great progress in the work of translation, and that neither could stand the test of criticism. The Jews' Society resolved, therefore, on a revision of the edition of 1821. A committee, consisting of Dr. M'Caul, the Rev. M. S. Alexander (afterwards bishop of Jerusalem), the Rev. J. C. Reichardt, and Mr. S. Hoga (the well-known translator of *Bunyan's Pilgrim's Progress* into Hebrew), was intrusted with the revision, which was commenced Nov. 14, 1836, and finished Feb. 8, 1838. The printing was commenced in December, 1837, and was finished in September, 1838. Duly considering and appreciating the labors of their predecessors, they endeavored to conform the Hebrew text as closely as possible to the Greek, following in most dubious cases the reading of the authorized English version; and were much pleased to find that, in very many cases, even the collocation of the Greek words furnished the best and most elegant collocation of the Hebrew. They diligently consulted the Syriac, Vulgate, German, Dutch, and French versions, but in difficulties were generally guided by the Syriac. Their desire was, as far as possible, to furnish a literal translation, remembering that it was the word of the living God which they wished to communicate. They arrived at purity of style, but always preferred perspicuity to elegance. When the revision was finished, the MS. was read through by each person privately, and then by all together, confronting it again with the Greek text. Some alterations were then suggested, and even in the reading of the proof-sheets various little amendments were made. This new edition of 1838, although a great improvement upon the former, proved by no means to be the *ultimatum*. In the year 1856 a new revision of the work was decided upon, and to the Rev. C. Reichardt (q. v.), together with Dr. R. Biesenthal, the task of revision was given. The edition of 1838 was carefully examined, and April 12, 1865, the work was completed. In 1866 the new edition, with vowels and accents, was published, which redounds to the honor of both revisers and the society. But this edition, in spite of the great amount of labor bestowed and the money spent upon it, proved itself not to be the complete *desideratum*, especially in view of the criticism concerning the text as well as the accents, which professor Delitzsch published in his Hebrew edition of St. Paul's epistle to the Romans. Considerations like these, especially the desire of realizing a hope cherished for about forty years, induced professor Delitzsch to undertake a new version of the New Test., on the basis of the *Codex*

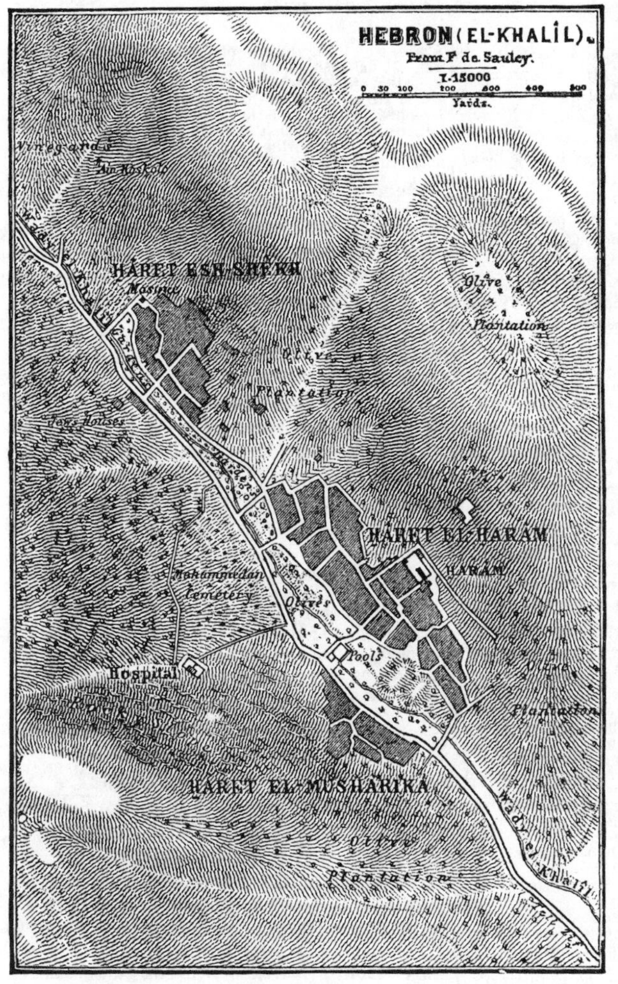

Plan of Hebron.

Hebron, as seen from the South. (From Thomson's *Southern Palestine and Jerusalem.*)

Sinaiticus. This edition was published by the British and Foreign Bible Society in 1877. In 1878 professor Delitzsch published a second edition of his translation, taking for his basis the *Textus Receptus* of the Elzevir edition of 1624, respecting the exigencies of textual criticism in all the more important cases by bracketed readings. Thus a single parenthesis, ( ), indicated a passage with weak support, although from an early date; the same with a star, (*), indicated an important varying reading; a double parenthesis, (( )), indicated a late addition to the text; and brackets, [ ], indicated words well supported by ancient testimony, but lacking in the received text. This edition also sold rapidly, and the third edition, again revised, appeared in 1880, with a slightly larger page and type. A fourth edition was published in 1881, and so also a fifth in 1883. It should be observed that during all this time the translator had the constant help of many learned friends, especially of Dr. J. H. R. Biesenthal, who had traversed the same ground himself, and of the author of the work on Hebrew tenses, Rev. S. R. Driver of Oxford. See Delitzsch, *The Hebrew New Testament of the British and Foreign Bible Society* (Leipsic, 1883). (B. P.)

Hebron. A brief but excellent description of this venerable place is given in the *Memoirs* accompanying the Ordnance Survey (iii, 305 sq.), and the latest and most complete account of the Haram enclosure there may be found in the same work (p. 333 sq.). We give some interesting particulars from Lieut. Conder's *Tent Work in Palestine*, ii, 79:

"Hebron is a long stone town on the western slope of a bare, terraced hill; it extends along the valley, and the main part reaches about seven hundred yards north and south, including the Mosque Quarter, and the Quarter of the Gate of the Corner. On the north is a separate suburb, named from the mosque of 'Aly Bukka, who died in 670 A.H.; on the south also, and west of the road, is another small suburb. The Haram stands above the middle of the main quarter. The Sultan's Pool, a large, well-built reservoir, occupies part of the valley. West of the city is an open green below the Quarantine, surrounded by hills which are covered with olives.

"The contrast between Hebron and Bethlehem is readily noticed; the town has a dead-alive appearance, and the sullen looks of the Moslem fanatics contrast with the officious eagerness of the Bethlehem Christians. There are some seventeen thousand Moslems in Hebron, according to the governor's account; and about six hundred Jews are tolerated in the Quarter of the Corner Gate. The town is the centre of commerce for the southern Arabs, who bring their wool and camel's-hair to its market. It has also a sort of trade in glass ornaments and in leather water-buckets, but the bustle and stir of Bethlehem are not found in its streets; the inhabitants seem wrapped in contemplation of the tombs of their forefathers, and boast that no pagan Frank has yet desecrated the holy shrines with his presence, or built his house in the town." (See Plan on p. 535.)

Hecatæa, apparitions which appeared during the performance of certain ceremonies in honor of the goddess Hecate (q. v.). An image of the goddess was formed of incense of Arabia, myrrh, styrax, and certain animals called ascalabotæ. These were all ground to powder, made into a paste, and moulded into an image of Hecate. Then, in the presence of this image, at midnight, under a lotus-tree, the ceremonies are duly performed, when the Hecatæa appear and assume various shapes.

Hecătè, in Greek mythology, is a mystical figure, wrapped in deep darkness, as described by Hesiod. She is called the daughter of the Titan Perses by Asteria, but the accounts vary, sometimes Jupiter, at others Tartarus, being mentioned as her father, and Juno, Ceres, Pheræa, etc., as her mother. She was the only one among the Titans who assisted Jupiter in the war with the giants; therefore she was not hurled into Tartarus, as were the others, but was endowed with great power in heaven, on earth, as well as in the infernal regions. She is usually represented triformate, from which circumstance she has the surname Tricephalus or Triceps, the three-headed. She possessed the keys to three roads, leading respectively to Hades, to heaven, and to a happy life on earth. Her work was usually at night, and therefore she has been confounded with the goddess of the moon, Selene.

Figure of Hecătè.

Hecatomb (ἑκατόμβη, from ἑκατόν, *one hundred*, and βοῦς, *an ox*), a sacrifice offered by the ancient

Greeks only on extraordinary occasions, consisting of one hundred oxen. The word is sometimes applied to an offering of other animals than oxen; and it is used occasionally to denote any large sacrifice, a definite number being used for an indefinite.

Hecht, Christian, a Lutheran theologian of Germany, was born Aug. 31, 1696, at Halle. He studied in his native place and at Leipsic; was in 1728 pro-rector of the gymnasium at Idstein, Nassau; in 1744 first pastor at Esens, in East-Frisia; and died Jan. 18, 1747, leaving, *Diss. de Sadducæismo Anna et Caiphæ:—Antiquitates Karæorum:—Varia Variorum Judicia de Synesii, Cyrenensis in Ægypto Episcopi, Fuga Istius Episcopatus:—Commentatio de Secta Scribarum sive γραμματέων.* See Winer, *Handbuch der theol. Lit.* i, 1, 451; Jöcher, *Allgemeines Gelehrten-Lexikon,* s. v. (B. P.)

Hecke, Joseph van, a Roman Catholic theologian, was born in 1795 at Bruges. In 1814 he joined the Jesuits, was for some time professor of canon law at Freiburg, Switzerland, and in Belgium, and went in 1837 to Brussels to take part in the continuation of the *Acta Sanctorum.* He wrote on Johannes Capistranus (q. v.) and Ignatius, patriarch of Constantinople (q. v.). Hecke died July 27, 1874. (B. P.)

Heckel, Johann Christian, a Protestant theologian of Germany, born at Augsburg in 1747, was deacon in his native city in 1780, and died Dec. 7, 1798, leaving, *Neues Beicht- und Communionbuch* (Augsburg, 1778, 2 vols.):—*Versuch einer theologischen Encyclopädie und Methodologie* (Leipsic, 1778), and some ascetical works. See Döring, *Die gelehrten Theologen Deutschlands,* s. v.; Winer, *Handbuch der theol. Lit.* ii, 289. (B. P.)

Heckel, Johann Friedrich, a German philologist and theologian, was born at Gera about 1640. After finishing his studies he travelled in Germany and Italy, where he connected himself with Magliabecchi and Cinelli. On his return he became successively rector of the College of Reichenbach and sub-director of the College of Rudolstadt. He spent the last days of his life at Plauen and at Oelsnitz, where he died, in 1715, leaving, *Memoria Freislebiana* (Gera, 1664):—*Dissertatio Historico-Philologico-Theologica,* etc. (Chemnitz, 1675):—*Sciagraphia Theologorum Evangelicorum* (Dresden, 1678):—*Theophili Pistorii Ornithogamelion,* etc. (ibid. eod.):—*De Constini Duobus Numis* (Frankfort, 1693):—*Manipulum Primum Epistolarum Singularium,* etc. (Plauen, 1695). See Hoefer, *Nouv. Biog. Générale,* s. v.

Hecker, Jacob Christian, a Lutheran theologian of Germany, was born in 1727. He studied at Leipsic and Göttingen, was in 1751 deacon at Meuselwitz, in Altenburg, pastor at Eisleben in 1764, and died April 14, 1779. He published, *De Oratore Sacro* (Göttingen, 1748):—*De Erroribus Vulgi in Libris Sacris* (eod.):—*De Usu Religionis Christianæ Œconomico et Civili* (Kiel, 1770). See Döring, *Die gelehrten Theologen Deutschlands,* s. v.; Jöcher, *Allgemeines Gelehrten-Lexikon,* s. v. (B. P.)

Hecker, Johann Julius, a Lutheran theologian of Germany, was born Nov. 2, 1707. He studied at Halle, was in 1735 preacher at Potsdam, in 1738 at Berlin, in 1750 member of consistory, and died June 24, 1768, leaving a few ascetical works. See Döring, *Die gelehrten Theologen Deutschlands,* s. v.; Jöcher, *Allgemeines Gelehrten-Lexikon,* s. v. (B. P.)

Hedinger, Johann Reinhard, a Lutheran theologian of Germany, was born at Stuttgart, Sept. 7, 1664. He accompanied the duke Johann Friedrich of Würtemberg as chaplain to France, was in 1692 military-preacher, in 1698 court-preacher and member of consistory, and died Dec. 28, 1704. He wrote, *De Fœdere Gratiæ:—Quæstiones Vexatæ de Testamenti Veteris Natura a Novo Discrepantia,* and some ascetical works. See Jöcher, *Allgemeines Gelehrten-Lexikon,* s. v. (B. P.)

Hedstrom, Olif G., a noted Methodist Episcopal minister, was born in Sweden in 1803, of humble parents, who gave him a fair education. When twenty-two years old he joined a band of adventurous youths, who volunteered to take two frigates from Sweden to their purchasers in one of the South American republics. After a tempestuous voyage, instead of reaching South America they landed in New York. Mr. Hedstrom soon made arrangements to return to Sweden, but on the eve of his departure was robbed of his money. He was shortly afterward led to Willett Street Methodist Episcopal Church, N. Y., experienced religion, and on reaching his Swedish home began holding Methodist class-meetings and prayer-meetings, the first ever held in that land. In 1835 he returned to New York, joined the New York Conference, and in it travelled the following circuits: Charlotte, Jefferson, Coeymans, Windham, Catskill, and Prattsville. In 1845 he was appointed to the Swedish mission, with his headquarters in the famous Bethel ship for Scandinavian seamen, foot of Carlisle Street, N. Y. He began by boarding, when possible, every incoming ship from Scandinavia or Denmark before it touched the shore, and distributing among the emigrants Bibles and tracts, telling them where they could find good temporary homes, and inviting them to the Bethel ship. In a single day he might be found in the counting-room of the rich gathering funds for the mission, far out on the deep seeking the lost sheep, at his desk answering letters from all parts of the world, at the bedside of the sick and dying, and pleading from his pulpit with the waiting throng to accept Christ. Thus he continued till his death, May 6, 1877. Mr. Hedstrom was thoroughly devoted to his work, had a simplicity of manner and fund of experimental Christianity that won the hearts of all. His religion was full of joy, and his life of success. See *Minutes of Annual Conferences,* 1878, i, 42; Simpson, *Cyclop. of Methodism,* s. v.

Heeser, Johann, a Reformed theologian, who died in 1716, is the author of *Prodomus Criticus seu Observationes Philologicæ in Omnes Voces Chaldaicas et Multas Hebraicas Veteris Testamenti* (Amsterdam, 1696, 1714):—אבן העזר *sive Lexici Philologici, Hebræo-Chaldæo Sacri, Pars I* (1714). See Fürst, *Bibl. Jud.* i, 367; Steinschneider, *Bibl. Handbuch,* s. v.; Jöcher, *Allgemeines Gelehrten-Lexikon,* s. v. (B. P.)

Hegelmayer, Thomas Gottfried, a Lutheran theologian of Germany, was born July 30, 1730. He studied at Tübingen, was in 1761 preacher, in 1777 professor of theology, and died April 13, 1786. He published, *De Sanctis Mundum et Angelos Judicaturis in* 1 *Cor. vi,* 3 (Tübingen, 1755):—*Chaldaismi Biblici Fundamenta* (1770):—*Commentatio pro loco Eusebii in Hist. Eccles. iv,* 13 (1777):—*De Peccato Originali atque Speciatim* (1778):—*Oratio in Verba Ps. cx,* 1 (1780):—*An et quo Sensu Patres Antenicæni Christum Dicerint Creaturam* (1781):—*De θεοπνευστίᾳ* (1784). See Döring, *Die gelehrten Theologen Deutschlands,* s. v.; Winer, *Handbuch der theol. Lit.* i, 110, 239, 402, 410, 422, 433, 446, 447, 596, 597. (B. P.)

Hegumĕnos (from ἡγέομαι, *to rule*), in the Greek church, the superior of a convent, the abbot or *archimandrite* of a monastery.

Heidelberg Confession. See Heidelberg Catechism.

Heidenreich, Esaias, a Lutheran theologian of Germany, was born at Lemberg, April 10, 1532. He studied at Frankfort, was preacher at Lemberg, Schweidnitz, and at Breslau. In the latter place, where he died in 1589, he was also professor of theology at the gymnasium. He published sermons on Ruth, Joshua, Joel, Amos, Obadiah, and Micah. See Jöcher, *Allgemeines Gelehrten-Lexikon,* s. v. (B. P.)

Heidenreich, Johannes, a German theologian, brother of Esaias, was born April 21, 1542, at Lemberg. He studied at Frankfort, was in 1573 doctor of theology and professor of philosophy, and finally professor of theology. He died March 31, 1617. He wrote, *Examinatio Capitum Doctrinæ Fratrum, ut Haberi Volunt, in Bohemia et Moravia:—De Patefactione Trium Personarum in Baptismo Christi Facta.* See Jöcher, *Allgemeines Gelehrten-Lexikon*, s. v. (B. P.)

Heidrun, in Scandinavian mythology, was a she-goat, said to stand above Walhalla, or the heaven of heroes, and feed on the leaves of a tree called Lærath. From her teats flows mead enough every day to supply all the heroes.

Heil, an idol of the ancient Saxons in England. This image was dashed to pieces by Austin, the English apostle, who thereupon built Cerne Abbey, on the banks of the Frome, in Dorsetshire.

Heilbronner, Jacob, a Lutheran theologian of Germany, was born Aug. 15, 1548, at Eberlingen, in Würtemberg. He studied at different universities, was in 1575 court-preacher at Zweibrücken, in 1577 doctor of theology, in 1581 general superintendent at Amberg, in 1588 court-preacher at Neuburg, Bavaria, in 1615 general superintendent at Bebenhausen, Würtemberg, and died Nov. 6, 1619, leaving, *Schwenckfeldio-Calvinismus:—Synopsis Doctrinæ Calvinianæ Refutata:—Flagellatio Jesuitica oder Jesuitische Lehre vom freiwilligen Creutz der Geisfelung.* See Winer, *Handbuch der theol. Lit.* i, 497; Jöcher, *Allgemeines Gelehrten-Lexikon*, s. v. (B. P.)

Heilbronner, Johann Christlieb, a German convert from Judaism (originally *Moses Praeger*), who lived in the 18th century, and instructed in Hebrew at different universities, is the author of *Traktat über Iesaias liii* (Tübingen, 1710):—*Klare Beweisthümer dass Jesus der wahre Messias und Gottes Sohn sei* (Dresden, 1715):—*Confutatio Exceptionum Jud. contra Genealogiam Christi, Speciatim Illarum in Chissuk Emuna* (1718; also in German). See Wolf, *Bibl. Hebr.* iii, 363; Kalkar, *Israel und die Kirche*, p. 104; Fürst, *Bibl. Jud.* i, 374; Jöcher, *Allgemeines Gelehrten-Lexikon*, s. v. (B. P.)

Heilbronner, Philip, a German divine, brother of Jacob, was born June 30, 1546. For some time a preacher, he was called in 1574 as professor of theology at the gymnasium in Lauingen, took the degree as doctor of theology in 1577, attended the colloquy at Ratisbon in 1601, and died April 17, 1616. He wrote, *Loci Communes in Epistolas ad Galatas, Timotheum et Titum:—Vaticinia Prophetarum in Locos Communes Digesta:—Postcolloquium Ratisbonense:—Antithesis Doctrinæ Petri Apostoli et Pontificis Romani:—Synopsis Variorum Hujus Temporis Errorum:—Liber de Innocentia Lutheri*, etc. See Jöcher, *Allgemeines Gelehrten-Lexikon*, s. v. (B. P.)

Heim, François Joseph, a French painter, was born at Belfort, Dec. 16, 1787. He studied in the École Centrale of Strasburg, and in 1803 entered the studio of Vincent, at Paris. In 1827 he was commissioned to decorate the Gallery Charles X in the Louvre, and completed his decorations of the conference-room of the Chamber of Deputies in 1844. He was made member of the legion of honor in 1855, and died Sept. 29, 1865. Among his paintings of religious subjects are, *Return of Jacob*, in the Musée de Bordeaux; *St. John; Resurrection of Lazarus*, in the Cathédral Autun; *Martyrdom of St. Cyr*, in St. Gervais; *Martyrdom of St. Laurence*, in Notre Dame; and his great picture of the *Massacre of the Jews*, in the Louvre. See *Encyclop. Brit.* 9th ed. s. v.

Heimdal, in Norse mythology, is the son of Odin, born of nine Jote-maidens, so that all were mothers of this god. From them he inherited beauty and greatness, from his father wisdom and power, and Odin placed him as guard of the Bifröst bridge, where he lives in a beautiful palace, Himminbiörg (heavenly castle), and gazes about to see whether mountain giants or other enemies come near the bridge. When he is awake the gods can safely slumber, for no one can approach without his knowledge. At night he can see a distance of one hundred miles, he hears the grass and hairs grow, and sleeps as little as an eagle. When enemies approach he takes his horn and makes a great noise, and the Asas and the Einheriar, and the heroes in Walhalla assemble for combat. This takes place especially at the destruction of the world. He has a surname, Gullintani (gold-tooth), from the fact that his teeth are made of gold.

Heinemann, Jeremiah, a Jewish writer of Germany, was born July 20, 1788, and died at Berlin, Oct. 16, 1855. He published, *Jedidja*, a Jewish review (Berlin, 1817–43):—*Gebete an den hohen Festen* (Leipsic, 1841):—*Katechismus der jüd. Religion* (1812):—*Sammlung der die religiöse und bürgerliche Verfassung der Juden in den Preuss. Staaten betreffender Gesetze*, etc. (1821–28):—*Allgemeines Gebetbuch der Israeliten* (1838):—*Religions- und Schulreden für Israeliten* (eod.):—*Der Prophet Iesaia*, the Hebrew text with Rashi, Chaldee, and commentary (1842):—*Der Pentateuch*, with Targum, Rashi, German translation, and Hebrew commentary (1831–33). See Fürst, *Bibl. Jud.* i, 373 sq.; Kayserling, *Bibliothek jüd. Kanzelredner*, i, 411; Winer, *Handbuch der theol. Lit.* i, 198, 523. (B. P.)

Heiner, Elias, D.D., an esteemed German Reformed minister, was born at Taneytown, Md., Sept. 16, 1810. He early connected with the Church; studied theology in the seminary of the Reformed Church at York, Pa., under the Rev. Lewis Mayer, D.D.; was licensed and ordained in 1833, and installed as pastor of the Reformed Church in Emmittsburg, Md. He was called to Baltimore in 1835, where he remained, faithfully preaching the gospel of the grace of God, to the close of his life, Oct. 20, 1863. Dr. Heiner was a man of respectable talents, good culture, deep piety, and great zeal, combined with a vast amount of practical tact. He was an acceptable preacher, and a most excellent pastor, enjoying to the last the full and unabated confidence of his people. He took a deep interest in the cause of missions, as well as in all the other benevolent operations of the Church, and did much to extend the Reformed Church in the city of Baltimore by his earnest and disinterested labors. He published the first volume of Dr. Mayer's *History of the German Reformed Church*, to which he prefixed a sketch of the author's life and labors. See Harbaugh, *Fathers of the Reformed Church*, iv, 271.

Heinrichs, Carl Friedrich Ernst, a Lutheran theologian of Germany, was born in 1798. He was ordained for the ministry in 1823, and was from 1827 pastor at Detmold. He died Dec. 30, 1882, doctor of theology and member of consistory, leaving *De iis, quæ Potissimum Contulerint ad Lutherum Sacrorum Reformatorem Sensim Effingendum* (Göttingen, 1819). See Winer, *Handbuch der theol. Lit.* i, 742. (B. P.)

Heinroth, Johann Christian Friedrich August, a German psychologist, was born at Leipsic, Jan. 17, 1773, and died there in 1843, a doctor and professor of medicine. He wrote, *Pistodice oder Resultate freier Forschung über Geschichte, Philosophie und Glauben* (Leipsic, 1829):—*Der Schlüssel zu Himmel und Hölle im Menschen* (1829):—*Die Lüge* (1834):—*Geschichte und Kritik des Mysticismus* (1830). See Winer, *Handbuch der theol. Lit.* i, 363, 483, 493, 595; Zuchold, *Bibl. Theol.* i, 531. (B. P.)

Heinsberg, Jean de, a Belgian prelate of the 15th century, was at first canon of Liege and archdeacon of Hesbaye, and became bishop of Liege at the age of twenty-three. In 1444 he resolved to go to Palestine, in pursuance of a vow, but on arriving at Venice, wrote to the bey of Tunis, and was refused permission. He died in 1459. See Hoefer, *Nouv. Biog. Générale*, s. v.

Heinsius, Johann Georg, a Lutheran theologian of Germany, who died at Reval in 1733, published *De*

Batteo Sacerdotis Magni (Wittenberg, 1719):—*Kurze Fragen aus der Kirchenhistorie des Neuen Testaments* (Jena, 1724, 6 parts; 3d ed. 1731 sq., 12 parts):—*Fragen aus der Kirchenhistorie des Alten Testaments* (ibid. eod. 3 parts). See Döring, *Die gelehrten Theologen Deutschlands*, s. v.; Jöcher, *Allgemeines Gelehrten-Lexikon*, s. v. (B. P.)

Heinson, Johann Theodor, a Lutheran theologian of Germany, was born at Hanover, July 5, 1665. He studied at Helmstädt, and continued his Oriental studies in England. In 1695 he was first preacher at Melle, in the duchy of Osnabrück, in 1698 general superintendent and court-preacher of East Frisia, accepted in 1711 a call to Hamburg, and died Sept. 21, 1726, leaving, *De Nominibus et Essentia Dei* (Helmstädt, 1690):—*De Paradiso ejusque Amissione et Custodia* (ibid. 1698). See Döring, *Die gelehrten Theologen Deutschlands*, s. v.; Fürst, *Bibl. Jud.* i, 375; Jöcher, *Allgemeines Gelehrten-Lexikon*, s. v. (B. P.)

Heiric, *Saint*, a French monk, was born about 834, at Hery, near Auxerre. It is supposed that his surname has been given to him more on account of his knowledge than for his actions. At the age of seven he was intrusted by his parents to the care of the Benedictine monks of St. Germain d'Auxerre, from whom he received his first instruction. He afterwards went to the abbey of Fulda, where he was instructed by Haimon, a disciple of Alcuin. Some time later he left Fulda to go to Ferrière, to put himself under the discipline of the abbot Lupus. He died about 881. For his numerous writings we refer to Hoefer, *Nouv. Biog. Générale*, s. v.

Hel (*cover*), in Norse mythology, was the daughter of Loke and the giantess Angerbode, sister of the wolf Fenris and the snake Jormungand. The three sisters were the most frightful creations of the infernal regions, and as the Asas knew what dangers awaited them from these monsters, they threw the snake into the sea, where she grew until she encircled the whole earth as the Midgard snake. They also chained the wolf Fenris, and placed the third child in the infernal region. There she rules over all who do not die as warriors on the battle-field. She devours men, and lives on their marrow and brain.

Figure of Hel.

Hela, in Slavonic mythology, was originally a Scandinavian deity, but worshipped also by the Wends, although in another sense, and with the attributes of an evil and angry deity. She was represented as a large woman, with a lion's open mouth. She was implored to protect from evil advice.

Held, August H. M., a Lutheran minister, was born Feb. 22, 1806, at Knoop, near Kiel, Germany. After preparatory study at Kiel he entered the College of Renzburg, and at the close of his theological course was ordained as a Lutheran minister. Instead of entering the pastoral work, he established the Held Institute at Kiel, which he conducted with signal ability for many years. In 1847 he arrived in America. For a time he was assistant pastor of St. Matthew's Church, New York city. Subsequently he founded St. Mark's Church, in Sixth Street. A division occurring in the congregation, a large portion followed him and formed the nucleus of St. John's Church, which at first held its meetings in the old Hope Chapel, and afterwards in the New York University building on Washington Square. In 1858 St. John's purchased the present church edifice in Christopher Street. For twenty-two years he was pastor of this church, and gathered about him one of the largest Lutheran congregations in New York. Two years before his death he was obliged to relinquish the pastorate on account of declining health. He died in New York city, March 31, 1881. See *Lutheran Observer*, April 8, 1881.

Held, Carl Friedrich Wilhelm, a Protestant theologian, was born in 1830 at Treptow, Pomerania. In 1852 he was repetent at Göttingen, in 1860 professor at Zurich, in 1866 at Breslau, and accepted a call to Bonn in 1867. He died May 30, 1870, leaving *De Opere Jesu Christi Salutari*, etc. (Göttingen, 1860):—*Jesus der Christ. 16 Apologetische Vorträge über die Grundlehren des Christenthums* (Zurich, 1865):—*Moderne Weltanschauung und Christenthum* (Breslau, 1866):—*Selbstzeugnisse Jesu in 15 Betrachtungen für die Suchenden unserer Zeit.* (B. P.)

Held, Christian, a German convert from Judaism, in the 17th century, was the author of, *Beweis aus der Schrift von dem dreieinigen Gott* (Kiel, 1681):—*Victoria Christiana contra Judæos* (Giessen, 1684). See Wolf, *Bibl. Hebr.* iii, 977; Fürst, *Bibl. Jud.* i, 376; Jöcher, *Allgemeines Gelehrten-Lexikon*, s. v. (B. P.)

Helding, Michael. See Sidonius, Michael.

Heleph. Of *Beit-Lîf*, which is now generally accepted as the modern representative of this place, the following is the description in the *Memoirs* (i, 201) accompanying the Ordnance Survey: "A village built of stone, containing about one hundred and fifty Moslems (Guérin says eighty Metawileh), situated on a hill-top, with a few olives and arable land. Two cisterns and a birket (pool) near by supply the water."

Helffenstein, Samuel, D.D., a prominent German Reformed minister, son of Rev. John C. Albert Helffenstein, was born at Germantown, Pa., April 17, 1775. He studied privately, partly under Rev. Mr. Stöck, and partly under Rev. Dr. Melsheimer. His theological studies he prosecuted under Rev. Dr. William Hendel, the elder, pastor of the Reformed Church on Race Street, Philadelphia. He entered the ministry in 1796 or 1797. After preaching for a short time in Montgomery County, he received a call to the Race Street Church, as successor to his theological preceptor, who died about this time. Here he labored for a period of thirty two or three years, when he retired from the active duties of the ministry, and spent the remainder of his days at his private residence in North Wales, Montgomery Co., where he died, Oct. 17, 1866. Dr. Helffenstein was a man of fine talents, thorough education, and superior pulpit abilities. He prepared a large number of young men for the ministry, and also took a deep interest in the establishment of the literary and theological institutions of the Reformed Church. In 1846 he published a work on didactic theology, which probably embodied the substance of his lectures to the students whom in earlier life he had under tuition. See Harbaugh, *Fathers of the Germ. Ref. Church*, iv, 31. (D. Y. H.)

Helgoland, in Norse mythology, was an island of the North Sea, also called *Fosetesland*, from the god Fosete. It contained only herds, sacred to the god, an altar, and a spring, to drink from which was very beneficial.

Helheim, in Norse mythology, is the kingdom of the cruel Hel (q. v.), large and extended, intersected by thirty-two rivers, which spring from the spring Hwergelmer, and one of which encircles the entire country. The gold-covered bridge, Gjalar, spans this valley. A maiden giantess, Modgudur, who keeps guard here, inquires of every one his name and family, and shows them the way to the palace of Hel. A high iron lattice surrounds the kingdom, and after having passed this, the visitor finds himself in one of the nine worlds. There are two maidens keeping guard also in Hel's palace; they have iron blood, which, when it falls to the ground, causes quarrel and war. Hel's palace contains a hall, Eliud, her table is called Hungur (hunger), Ganglate and Ganglöt are her servant and maid, Kor her bed, Blick and Böl her covering. In Helheim or Niflheim lives the evil snake, Nidhögr, which gnaws at one of the three roots of the ash-tree, Ygdrasil. There, in a cave, the dog Garmr lives, who is to bring about the death of an Asa at the destruction of the world. Helheim is not a place of punishment, but simply the dwelling-place of those who do not die of wounds on the battle-field. After the end of the world, the good are separated from the bad, the former go to eternal joy in Gimle (heaven), the latter to Nastrond.

Heling, MAURICE, a Lutheran theologian, was born in 1523 at Friedland, Prussia. He studied at different universities, was in 1550 rector at Eisleben, in 1556 superintendent at Nüremberg, and died Oct. 2, 1595, leaving, *Colloquium Evæ et Mariæ Virginis:—De Perpetua Ecclesiæ Conservatione Ministrorum:—De Argumenta Librorum Josuæ, Judicum, Ruth et 2 Librorum Samuelis et Locorum Communium Consignationes Breves.* See Zeltner, *Leben und Schriften Helings* (Altdorf, 1715); Jöcher, *Allgemeines Gelehrten-Lexikon*, s. v. (B. P.)

Helios, in Greek mythology (among the Romans *Sol*), the god of the sun, was one of the Titanides, brother of Selene and Aurora, all three children of the Titan Hyperion and the Titanid Thia. Helios rides in the wagon of the sun, drawn by four flashing steeds, borne from sea to sea, and gives the world the day. Aurora precedes, opens the sun's portals, strews roses on his path, glowing rays and golden locks undulate about his head, a light dress, woven from the breath of Zephyrus,

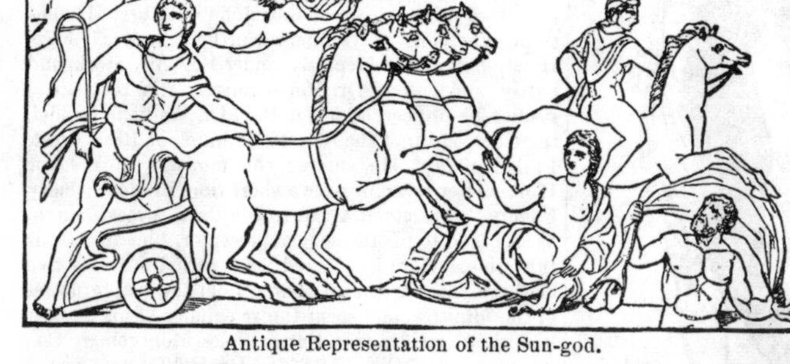

Antique Representation of the Sun-god.

flies about his hips, when he comes forth out of his palace. The latter lies in the west of the known world, where the sun sets. In order to come from here to the east, he sails back during the night in a golden canoe until he arrives again at the east. Near his palace were his herds and his gardens. As every god had a seat of worship, so Rhodes was especially sacred to Helios. Besides this the castle of Corinth belonged to him. According to Diodorus, Helios was a son of king Hyperion and his sister Basilea. The brothers of the king, fearing the latter would excel them in power, murdered him and drowned Helios.

Helkath-haz-zurim. Tristram thinks (*Bible Places*, p. 115) that a reminiscence of the battle here "seems to be preserved in a broad, smooth valley close to Gibeon [el-Jib], called *Wady el-'Aksar*, 'the vale of the soldiery.'" It runs north-west from the village.

Helladius, bishop OF CÆSAREA, in Cappadocia, succeeded his teacher, Basil the Great, in that see in 378. He attended two councils of Constantinople in 381 and 394. His life of St. Basil is cited by Damascenus, but the authenticity of that work is doubtful. See Hoefer, *Nouv. Biog. Générale*, s. v.

Helladius, bishop OF TARSUS, lived about A.D. 430. He made himself remarkable by his affection for Nestorius, and was deprived of his bishopric on that account. But it was restored to him again on the condition that he would join himself with those who pronounced the anathema against Nestorius. There are extant of him six letters. See Hoefer, *Nouv. Biog. Générale*, s. v.

Helm, JAMES ISBELL, D.D., a Presbyterian minister, and afterwards an Episcopal, was born in Washington County, Tenn., April 25, 1811. He graduated from Georgetown College, Ky., in 1833, and from Princeton Theological Seminary in 1836. He was ordained an evangelist by the Presbytery of West Tennessee, June 23, 1838; labored as a missionary in Giles County in 1837 and 1838; was pastor at Salem, N. J., in 1840; teacher at Newton in 1852; at Philadelphia, Pa., in 1853, and at Princeton, N. J., in 1855. He was reordained in the Protestant Episcopal Church in 1860; was an assistant rector in St. Mark's Church, Philadelphia, Pa., from 1860 to 1862; rector at St. Paul's Church, Sing Sing, N. Y., in 1863, and died there Oct. 15, 1880. See *Gen. Cat. of Princeton Theol. Sem.* 1881, p. 94.

Helmbreker, THEODORE, an eminent Dutch painter, was born at Haarlem in 1624, and was instructed in the school of Peter Grebber. On the death of that master he visited Rome, and spent some time in Florence and Naples. He finally settled at Rome, where he executed for the church of the Jesuits a noble landscape, in which is introduced *The Temptation of Christ in the Desert*. At Naples, in the refectory of the Jesuits' College, are three sacred subjects, most admirably executed: *Christ in the Garden; Christ Carrying his Cross;* and *The Crucifixion*. Helmbreker died at Rome in 1694. See Hoefer, *Nouv. Biog. Générale*, s.v.; Spooner, *Biog. Hist. of the Fine Arts*, s.v.

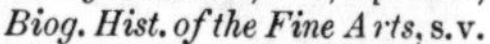

Helmer, CHARLES DOWNS, a Congregational minister, was born at Canajoharie, N. Y., Nov. 18, 1827. After spending two years in Hamilton College, he entered Yale, from which he graduated in 1852. The two years following he was a teacher in the Deaf-and-Dumb Institution in New York city. In 1857 he graduated from Union Theological Seminary. The next two years he spent in Europe. He was ordained pastor of Plymouth Church, Milwaukee, Wis., Sept. 11, 1859, from which he was dismissed, May 31, 1865; from December, 1866, to December, 1875, he was pastor of Union Park Church, Chicago, Ill.; from March, 1877, until his death, he was pastor of Tompkins Avenue Church, Brooklyn, N. Y. The degree of D.D. which was offered to him in 1875 by Beloit College, was declined. He died April 28, 1879. See *Cong. Year-book*, 1880, p. 21.

Helmich, WERNER, a Dutch Protestant divine, and one of the early promoters of the reformed religion in that country, was born at Utrecht in 1551. In 1579 he was chosen pastor of his fellow-citizens. In 1582 he was the first to preach the Protestant religion openly in the cathedral of Utrecht. He was pastor at Amsterdam in 1602, and died Aug. 29, 1608, leaving *Analysis of the Psalms* (1644).

Helmont, SEGRES JAMES VAN, a Flemish painter, the son of Matthew, was born at Antwerp, April 17, 1683, and studied under his father, also the fine works of great masters at Brussels. His principal works are in the churches at Brussels. In the Church of Mary

Magdalene is a fine picture of the *Martyrdom of St. Barbara;* in St. Michael's is the *Triumph of David;* and at the Carmelites one of his most capital works, representing *Elisha Sacrificing the Priests of Baal.* He died at Brussels, Aug. 21, 1726. See Hoefer, *Nouv. Biog. Générale,* s. v.; Spooner, *Biog. Hist. of the Fine Arts,* s. v.

Helmstadian Controversy, a name given to the controversy raised by Calixtus in the 17th century, from Helmstadt, the place where it originated. See CALIXTINES.

Helwig, Johann Andreas, a Lutheran theologian of Germany, was born Jan. 26, 1668, at Berlin. He studied at different universities, was in 1693 adjunct of the philosophical faculty at Wittenberg, in 1695 adjunct of the cathedral church at Reval, and in 1696 pastor at Narva. In 1713 he was again at Reval, and died Feb. 7, 1720, leaving, *De Nomine Missæ in Sanctorum Honorem Celebratæ* (Rostock, 1691):—*De Scepticismo Cartesii* (Wittenberg, 1692):—*De Panibus Facierum contra Witsium* (eod.):—*De Nomine Jehovah Patribus Ignoto* (eod.):—*De Simone Mago* (1693). See Gadebusch, *Liefländische Bibliothek;* Jöcher, *Allgemeines Gelehrten-Lexikon,* s. v. (B. P.)

Helwig, Jacob, a Lutheran theologian and bishop of Esthonia, who died Jan. 19, 1684, is the author of, *Disp. de Emanuele:—De Passione Christi ϑεανϑρώπου:—De Statu Exinanitonis ϑεανϑρώπου.* See Witte, *Diarium;* Jöcher, *Allgemeines Gelehrten-Lexikon,* s. v.; Fürst, *Bibl. Jud.* i, 378. (B. P.)

Hemenway, FRANCIS DANA, D.D., a Methodist Episcopal minister, was born at Chelsea, Vt., Nov. 10, 1830. He was converted in early life, graduated from the Concord Biblical Institute in 1853, taught in Newbury Seminary, where he had formerly been a pupil, joined the Vermont Conference, and in 1855 was stationed at Montpelier, where he remained two years, and then located on account of ill-health. In 1857 he removed to Evanston, Ill., as principal of a preparatory school there, and soon after was elected adjunct professor of Biblical literature in the Garrett Biblical Institute of that place. He was afterwards promoted to the chair of Biblical exegesis, and finally made professor of exegetical theology, having meanwhile become a member of the Michigan Conference, and in 1861 he was temporarily a pastor in Kalamazoo, and the following year was transferred to the Rock River Conference, and stationed in Chicago. He was a delegate to the General Conference in 1876. He died April 19, 1884. See *Minutes of Annual Conference,* 1884, p. 342.

Hemiphorium (ἡμιφόριον), a priestly upper garment, probably a short pallium (q. v.).

Hemmenway, MOSES, D.D., a Congregational minister, was born in Framingham, Mass., in 1735. He graduated from Harvard College in 1755, and after preaching at Lancaster, Boston, Townsend, and Wrentham, Mass., and at New Ipswich, N. H., for short periods, ministered a year in Wells, where he was ordained regular pastor, Aug. 8, 1759. Near the close of 1810 he was compelled to cease preaching on account of a cancer in the face, and he died in Wells, April 5, 1811. Many of his published writings are of a controversial character. See Sprague, *Annals of the Amer. Pulpit,* i, 541.

Hempel, Albert Ephraim, a Lutheran theologian of Germany, was born April 24, 1670. He studied at Leipsic and Wittenberg, was pastor at Nordhausen in 1692, licentiate of theology at Wittenberg in 1697, doctor of theology in 1711, and died March 25, 1722, leaving, *De Spinis Coronæ Christi* (Leipsic, 1686):—*De Theologiæ Onomatologia:—De τεκνοφιλίᾳ Divina ex Jer. xxxi,* 10 (Wittenberg, 1691):—*De Chiliasmo Descripto et Rejecto* (1692):—*Consilium Dei circa Hominis Creationem ex Gen. i,* 26 (1697):—*De Resurrectione Spirituali.* See Jöcher, *Allgemeines Gelehrten-Lexikon,* s. v. (B. P.)

Hempel, Christian Gottlob, a Lutheran theologian of Germany, was born in 1748, at Horburg, near Merseburg. He studied at Leipsic, and died Feb. 11, 1824. He published, *Beitrag zur richtigen Erklärung des Kryptopelagianismus* (Leipsic, 1783):—*Irrlichter und Irrgänge* (Köthen, 1790), and other ascetical works. See Döring, *Die gelehrten Theologen Deutschlands,* s. v. (B. P.)

Hempel, Ernst Wilhelm, a Lutheran theologian of Germany, was born in 1745. He studied at Leipsic. In 1769 he was university preacher at Leipsic, professor of philosophy in 1776, in 1787 professor of theology, and died April 12, 1799, leaving, *Cuinam S.S. Trinitatis Personæ, Promulgatio Legis Præcipue Tribuenda sit* (Leipsic, 1771):—*De Sapientia Dei* (1773):—*Prima Linguæ Ebrææ Elementa* (1776, 1789):—*Kurze und treue Beschreibung der Kennicotschen Bibelausgabe* (1777):—*De vera Significatione Vocabuli Semen* (1787):—*De Deo Invisibili* (1790-91, 4 parts):—*De loco Galat. iii,* 20 (1792):—*Fidem Litteris Sacris Habendam Rationi Convenienter Postulari* (1794, 4 parts). See Döring, *Die gelehrten Theologen Deutschlands,* s. v. (B. P.)

Hemphill, JOHN, D.D., an Associate Reformed minister, was born in County Derry, Ireland, in 1761. He arrived at Philadelphia shortly after the close of the American Revolution. He was a tailor by trade. He graduated at Dickinson College in 1792, was ordained at Greencastle in 1794-95, went south on a missionary tour, and returned to Greencastle in May, 1795. In 1796 he was installed pastor of Hopewell, Union, and Ebenezer, remaining in this connection until a short time previous to his death, which occurred May 30, 1832. See Sprague, *Annals of the Amer. Pulpit,* IX, iv. 62.

Hen, a name for spirits among the *Lao-Tseu,* in China. They are the souls of those who are neither good nor evil. They are generally friendly to man, and though invisible, they perform many good offices for him. The emperor puts his country under their protection, and he deposes or degrades them if they neglect their duty.

Henchman, HUMPHREY, an English prelate, was made bishop of Salisbury in 1660, bishop of London in 1663, and died Oct. 7, 1675. He published, *Diatriba Præliminaris H. Hammondi Tract. de Confirmatione Præfixa* (1661). See Allibone, *Dict. of Brit. and Amer. Authors,* s. v.

Hencke, GEORG JOHANN, a Lutheran theologian of Germany, was born in 1681. He studied at Halle, and died as preacher at Glauchau, April 12, 1720, leaving, *De Usu LXX Interpretum in Novo Testamento* (Halle, 1709):—*Introductio ad Libros Apocryphos* (1710):—*Prolegomena ad Libros Apocryphos Veteris Testamenti* (1711):—*De Textu Novi Test. Græco:—De Usu Librorum Apocryphorum Vet. Test. in Novo Testam.* (eod.). He also published a number of sermons. See Jöcher, *Allgemeines Gelehrten-Lexikon,* s. v. (B. P.)

Henckel, JOHANN OTTO, a Lutheran theologian of Germany, was born at Marburg, Nov. 22, 1636. He studied at different universities, was doctor and professor of theology at Rinteln, and died Dec. 22, 1682, leaving, *Disputationes de Peccatis:—De Ministerio Ecclesiastico:—De Latrone Converso:—De Peccato Originis:—De Omniscientia Carnis Christi:—De Schismate.* See Götz, *Elogia Theologorum;* Jöcher, *Allgemeines Gelehrten-Lexikon,* s. v. (B. P.)

Hendel, WILLIAM, D.D., an eminent German Reformed minister, son of the Rev. Dr. William Hendel, was born in Lancaster, Pa., Oct. 14, 1768. After completing his preparatory studies he entered Columbia College in New York, where he passed through a regular collegiate course. His theological studies he pursued in the seminary at New Brunswick, N. J., under the Rev. Drs. Gross and Livingston. In 1792 he was licensed to preach the gospel, and the following year ordained, and installed as pastor of the Tulpehocken charge, in Berks County, Pa. He resigned this charge in 1823, and removed to Womelsdorf, in the same county, where he died, July 11, 1846. Dr. Hendel manifested a deep interest in the cause of education, and in consequence had to suffer some persecution. See Harbaugh, *Fathers of the Ref. Church*, iii, 58. (D. Y. H.)

Henderson, Isaac J., D.D., a Presbyterian minister, was born at Natchez, Miss., Jan. 6, 1812. He graduated at Jefferson College in 1831, and from Princeton Theological Seminary in 1835. Soon after his license he spent two years as an evangelist in Mississippi, Arkansas, and Louisiana; then came to Galveston, Texas; accepted a call, and in a short time secured funds for the erection of the first Presbyterian church there. About 1850 he accepted a call to Jackson, Miss. In 1852 he went to Prytania Street Church in New Orleans, and labored over eleven years. In 1866 he began to preach at Annapolis, Md. He died Dec. 8, 1875. Dr. Henderson was faithful, practical, and interesting to all classes. See *Necrol. Report of Princeton Theol. Sem.* 1876, p. 21.

Henderson, James, M.D., a Scotch Congregational medical missionary, was born in 1830, and received a careful religious training by a pious widowed mother. He began life as a shepherd-boy, but spent several sessions at the Edinburgh University. He offered his services to the London Missionary Society, and after six months of private theological instruction, during which time he received his degree of M. D. from the University of St. Andrews, he set sail for Shanghai, China. On his arrival, in 1860, he immediately applied himself with his characteristic zeal to medical work, and his thorough devotion, united with his remarkable surgical skill, soon raised the reputation of the Chinese hospital to the highest point. In June, 1865, he was seized with fever, and died July 31 following. See (Lond.) *Cong. Year-book*, 1866, p. 258.

Henderson, Matthew H., D.D., a Protestant Episcopal clergyman, was rector for several years in Newark, N. J., until about 1856; subsequently he removed to Athens, Ga., where he became rector of Emmanuel Church, and there remained until his death, Dec. 2, 1872. See *Prot. Episc. Almanac*, 1874, p. 138.

Henderson, Robert, D.D., a Presbyterian minister, was born in Washington County, Va., May 31, 1764. Being left an orphan at an early age, he struggled hard in obtaining an education. He was licensed and ordained by the Abingdon Presbytery in 1788, and was pastor at Danbridge, Tenn., where he remained more than twenty years. He afterwards preached at Pisgah, Murfrees Spring, Nashville, and Franklin. He died in July, 1834. Dr. Henderson was a most earnest and vigorous supporter of gospel orders, especially as connected with the worship of God. See Sprague, *Annals of the Amer. Pulpit*, iii, 528.

Hengel, Wessel Albert van, a Dutch theologian, was born at Leyden, Nov. 12, 1779, where he also received his theological education. In 1803 he was pastor at Kalslagen, in 1805 at Driehuizen, in 1810 at Grootrebroek, in 1815 professor of theology at Franeker, and in 1818 professor at Amsterdam. In 1827 he was called to Leyden, and died Feb. 6, 1871. He wrote, *Annotationes in Loca Nonnulla Novi Testamenti* (Amsterdam, 1824):—*Institutio Oratoris Sacri* (Leyden, 1829):—*Commentarius Perpetuus in Epistolam Pauli ad Philippenses* (1838):—*Commentarius Perpetuus in Prioris Pauli ad Corinthios Epistolæ Caput Quintum Decimum* (1851):—*Interpretatio Pauli Epistolæ ad Romanos* (1854-59, 2 vols.):—*Five Epistles to Strauss, on his Life of Jesus* (2d ed. 1824):—*Meritorum Joannis Henrici van der Palm Commemoratio Brevis* (1840). See Winer, *Handbuch der theol. Lit.* i, 241; ii, 61, 111; Zuchold, *Bibl. Theol.* i, 535; Lichtenberger, *Encyclop. des Sciences Religieuses*, s. v. (B. P.)

Hengstenberg, Wilhelm von, a Protestant theologian of Germany, and cousin of the famous theologian, was born Feb. 9, 1804, at Elberfeld. He studied at Erlangen and Berlin, and for a number of years acted as tutor to prince William. In 1838 he entered upon his ministerial functions at Radensleben, and about the same time was ennobled. From 1841 to 1854 he was pastor at Teltow, and when the court-preacher, von Gerlach, died, Hengstenberg was appointed as his successor, in 1854, at the recommendation of the general superintendent, Dr. Hoffmann. After the latter's death he was made first court-preacher, and died Sept. 25, 1880. Hengstenberg was no writer, but he left lasting memorials in such institutions as Bethanien and Bethesda, in the capital of the German empire. He was a warm friend of the home mission, and a preacher in the true sense of the word. (B. P.)

Henich, Johann, a Lutheran divine of Germany, was born Jan. 1, 1616. He studied at different universities, was in 1643 professor of Hebrew at Rinteln, in 1651 professor of theology, and died June 27, 1671. He wrote, *Compendium Theologiæ*:—*De Veritate Religionis Christianæ*:—*Historiæ Ecclesiasticæ Partes Tres*:—*Institutiones Theologicæ*:—*De Gratia et Prædestinatione*:—*De Sanctissimo S. Trinitatis Mysterio*:—*De Veneratione Nominis Divini Jehovah*:—*De Auctoritate Antiquitatis Ecclesiasticæ et Conciliorum*:—*De Bonis Fidelium Operibus*. See Sagittarius, *Introductio ad Historiam Ecclesiasticam*; Jöcher, *Allgemeines Gelehrten-Lexikon*, s. v. (B. P.)

Henil, in the mythology of the Vandals, was a protecting god, who was worshipped under the symbol of a staff, with a hand wearing an iron ring.

Henke, Ernst Ludwig Theodor, a Protestant theologian of Germany, was born Feb. 22, 1804, at Helmstädt. He studied at Göttingen and Jena, took his degree as doctor of philosophy in 1826, and commenced the academical career at Jena in 1827 by presenting his *De Epistolæ, quæ Barnabæ Tribuitur, Authentia*. In 1828 he was appointed theological professor at the "Collegium Carolinum" in Brunswick, in 1833 was called to Jena, in 1839 to Marburg, and died there, Dec. 1, 1872. He published, *Georg Calixtus und seine Zeit* (Halle, 1853-60, 2 vols.):—*Theologorum Saxonicorum Consensus Repetitus Fidei Vere Lutheranæ* (Marburg, 1846):—*Consensus Repetitus Fidei Vere Lutheranæ* (ibid. 1847). He also contributed to the first edition of Herzog's *Real-Encyclop.*, to the *Hallische Encyclop.*, and other similar works. His lectures on the *Church History since the Reformation* were published by Gass (Halle, 1874-78, 2 vols.); those on homiletics and liturgics by Zschimmer (ibid. 1876). See Mangold, *E. L. Th. Henke, Ein Gedenkblatt* (Marburg, 1879); Plitt-Herzog, *Real-Encyclop.* s. v.; Zuchold, *Bibl. Theol.* i, 536 sq. (B. P.)

Henley, Samuel, D.D., an English clergyman, was professor of moral philosophy in the college of Williamsburg, Virginia. He was rector of Rendlesham, Suffolk, and in 1805 principal of the East India College at Hertford. He died in 1816. He published several *Sermons* (1771-1803). See Allibone, *Dict. of Brit. and Amer. Authors*, s. v.

Henneberg, Johann Valentin, a Protestant theologian of Germany, was born at Gotha, Feb. 4, 1782, and died March 18, 1831. He published, *Vorlesungen über die Leidensgeschichte Jesu* (Gotha, 1820):—*Commentar über die Geschichte Jesu Christi* (Leipsic, 1822):—*Commentar über die Geschichte des Begräbnisses Jesu* (1826):—*Homilien über die Leidensgeschichte Jesu* (Gotha, 1809):—*Die Schrift des Neuen Testaments* (1819). See Winer, *Handbuch der theol. Lit.* i, 559; ii, 61, 153, 285, 306. (B. P.)

Hennequier, Jerome, a French Dominican, was born in 1633. He studied at Douay, was professor of theology and philosophy at Cambray in 1675, and died March 13, 1712, leaving, *Cultus Mariæ Virginis Vindicatus:* — *De Absolutione Sacramentali Percipienda et Impertienda.* See Échard, *De Scriptoribus Ordinis Dominicanorum*; Jöcher, *Allgemeines Gelehrten-Lexikon*, s. v. (B. P.)

Hennequin, Aimar, a French prelate, became abbot of Épernay, and afterwards bishop of Rennes. He took an active part in the insurrection of the Parisians, May 16, 1588. In February following the duke of Mayence appointed him general counsellor of the union. On the recognition of Henry IV (March 22, 1594) the bishop of Rennes retired to his diocese, where he died in 1596, leaving, *Les Confessions de Saint Augustin* (Paris, 1577): — *Brevis Descriptio Sacrificii Missæ* (1579):—*Imitation de Jésus-Christ* (Paris, 1582). See Hoefer, *Nouv. Biog. Générale*, s. v.

Henni, John Martin, D.D., an eminent Roman Catholic prelate, was born at Obersanzen, canton Graubünden, Switzerland, June 13, 1805. He studied at the gymnasia of St. Gall and Zurich, went to Rome in 1824, and was there educated for the priesthood. In 1827 he came to America with bishop Fenwick of Cincinnati, and went to the seminary at Bardstown, Ky., where he was ordained priest, Feb. 2, 1829. He was assigned to the spiritual charge of the German-speaking Catholics of Cincinnati, and was also made professor in the Athenæum in that city, which has since developed into St. Xavier's College. He was afterwards sent as a missionary to the north-western part of Ohio. In 1834 he was brought back to Cincinnati and made pastor of the Holy Trinity Church, and vicar-general to bishop Purcell. He was a leader in everything pertaining to the welfare of the German immigrants, and in 1836 he founded and became the first editor of the *Wahrheitsfreund.* At the Fifth Provincial Council at Baltimore, in 1843, Milwaukee was made a see, and Henni was appointed its first bishop, being ordained in the Cathedral of Cincinnati, March 19, 1844. In 1847 St. Mary's Church was opened, a cathedral begun, and a hospital founded and put in charge of the Sisters of Charity. Archbishop Henni established an orphan asylum, introduced the School Sisters of Notre Dame, and built two churches. In 1855 he opened the seminary of St. Francis de Sales. Henni died Sept. 7, 1881. He left a powerful establishment, with three dioceses, 185 priests, 258 churches, 125 schools, 25 religious and charitable institutions, and 200,000 Catholics. See (N. Y.) *Catholic Annual*, 1883, p. 51; De Courcy and Shea, *Hist. of the Cath. Church in the U. S.* p. 594.

Hennig, Balthasar Gottlob, a Lutheran theologian of Germany, was born Oct. 5, 1742, not far from Leipsic. Having completed his studies, he was called as professor of Greek and Hebrew to Thorn, and died May 31, 1808, superintendent and member of consistory. He published, *De ὀρθοτομίᾳ τοῦ λόγου τῆς ἀληθέιας ad Locum 2 Tim. ii*, 15 (Leipsic, 1767):—*De Collectione Canonum et Decretorum Dionysiana* (1769):—*De Præstantia Allegoriarum Novi Testamenti* (Thorn, 1773):—*De Regno Messiæ ad Loca Psa. lxii et lxxxix* (1774):—*De Notitiis Vet. et Novi Testamenti in Doctrina Christiana* (1781): — *De Religione Christiana* (1790). See Döring, *Die gelehrten Theologen Deutschlands*, s. v. (B. P.)

Hennig, Georg Ernst Sigismund, a Lutheran theologian of Germany, was born Jan. 1, 1746, at Jauer, in Silesia. In 1776 he accepted a call to Königsberg, was professor of theology in 1802, and died Sept. 23, 1809, leaving *Glaubens- und Sittenlehre* (Königsberg, 1793), and a number of *Sermons.* See Döring, *Die gelehrten Theologen Deutschlands*, s. v. (B. P.)

Henning, Jacob, a Lutheran theologian of Germany, was born at Greifswalde, May 26, 1633. He studied at different universities, was pastor and professor of theology at his native place, and died Sept. 28, 1704, leaving, *De Sabbathi Christianorum Moralitate.* —*De Justitia Divina Essentiali:*—*De Natura Hominis ante Peccatum Integra:* — *De Omnipræsentia Humanæ Christi Naturæ:*—*De Pœnitentia, Confessione et Absolutione:*—*De Sensu Scripturæ S. Literali:*—*De Securitate Humana, ad Genes. ix*, 6:—*De Messia a Deo Percusso, ad Esaiæ liii*, 4, 5: — *De Joanne Baptista, ad Matth. iii*, 1-4:—*De Reconciliatione Nostra cum Deo per Mortem Christi ad Rom. v*, 10:—*De Pignore Hæreditatis Nostræ Sanctissimo, ad Ephes. iv*, 30:—*De Intercessione Christi Gloriosa, ad* 1 *Joan. ii*, 1:—*De Christiani Hominis Nativitate et Vita, ad* 1 *Jo. iii*, 9. See Pipping, *Memoriæ Theologorum;* Jöcher, *Allgemeines Gelehrten-Lexikon*, s. v. (B. P.)

Henrici, Daniel, a Lutheran theologian of Germany, was born at Chemnitz, April 5, 1615. He studied at different universities, was professor at Leipsic, and died March 15, 1666. He wrote, *Tractatus de Inspiratione Verborum S. Scripturæ:*—*Delineatio Christianismi:* — *Disputationes de Immanuelis Conceptione et Nativitate:*—*De Evangelio Prophetico:*—*De Baptismo ad Matth. xxvii*, 18-20:—*De Primogenitura Christi:*—*De Christo Dei et Mariæ Filio:*—*De Messiæ Officio Regio:* — *De Judiciis Ebræorum:* — *De Incarnatione Filii Dei:*—*De Religione Zwinglio-Calviniana in Articulo de S. Cœna.* See Freher, *Theatrum Eruditorum;* Jöcher, *Allgemeines Gelehrten-Lexikon*, s. v. (B. P.)

Henriques, Frey (1), a Portuguese Jesuit and missionary, who died in 1556, on the Malabar coast, left *Carta a S. Ignacio Escrita de Tanâ* (published in Italian, Venice, 1559). See Hoefer, *Nouv. Biog. Générale*, s. v.

Henriques, Frey (2), a Portuguese ecclesiastical writer, was born at Lisbon. He entered the order of the Jesuits while young, and taught theology in several colleges of his order. He died in 1590, leaving *Constituiçoes das Religiozas de Santa Martha de Lisboa.* See Hoefer, *Nouv. Biog. Générale*, s. v.

Henriques, Henrique (1), a Portuguese missionary, was born at Villa Vicoza about 1520. He was one of the first associates of the society founded by Ignatius, and was sent to the Portuguese establishments in Asia. He was well versed in different Shemitic languages. He died Feb. 6, 1600, on the coast of Malabar, leaving, *Vocabulario e Arte de Grammat. da Ling. Malabar:*—*Metho do de Confessar:*—*Doutrina Christaâ:* —*Vida de Christo, N. Senhora, e Santos:*—*Contra as Fabulas dos Gentios:*—24 *Cartas Sobre a Missão.* See Hoefer, *Nouv. Biog. Générale*, s. v.

Henriques, Henrique (2), a Portuguese theologian, was born at Oporto in 1536. He joined the Jesuits, and taught philosophy and theology in the colleges of his order at Cordova and at Salamanca; but afterwards went to the Dominicans, and became famous by his writings against the Molinists. He finally returned to the Jesuits, and died at Tivoli, Feb. 28, 1608, leaving, *Summa Theologiæ Moralis* (Salamanca, 1591; Venice, 1596):—*De Claribus Ecclesiæ*, condemned by the court of Rome:—*De Justitia Censurarum in Causa Reipublicæ Venetæ* (MSS. preserved in the Vatican, No. 5547): —also a large number of small treatises. See Hoefer, *Nouv. Biog. Générale*, s. v.

Henriquez, Crisostomo, a Spanish historian, was born at Madrid in 1594. At the age of thirteen he entered the order of the Cistercians, and afterwards he taught philosophy, theology, and history in various colleges of his community. In 1622 he was sent into the Netherlands, where the archduke Albert received him very kindly. He died at Louvain, Dec. 23, 1632, leaving more than forty works, for which see Hoefer, *Nouv. Biog. Générale*, s. v.

Henriquez, Enrico, an Italian cardinal, was born in the district of Otranto in 1701. He became successively legate to the republic of San Marino, ambassador to Philip V, king of Spain, and cardinal under Benedict XIV, and was charged with the government of Romagna. He died April 25, 1756, leaving several orations, for which see Hoefer, *Nouv. Biog. Générale*, s. v.

Henry (1), a Scotch prelate, was bishop of the see of Galloway in 1226, '27, '28, '31, '37, '40. See Keith, *Scottish Bishops*, p. 278.

Henry (2), a Scotch prelate, was abbot of Holyroodhouse, and was made bishop of Galloway in 1255. He ratified to the convent of Dryburgh all the churches granted to it within his diocese. He was bishop of Galloway in 1290. See Keith, *Scottish Bishops*, p. 273.

Henry (3), a Scotch prelate, was bishop of Galloway in 1334. See Keith, *Scottish Bishops*, p. 273.

Henry (4), a Scotch prelate, was elected and confirmed bishop of Ross, Oct. 19, 1463, and was still bishop in 1476. See Keith, *Scottish Bishops*, p. 189.

Henry OF LANGENSTEIN (also *Henricus de Hassia*), was born in Hesse about 1325. He studied at Paris, where he afterwards taught philosophy, theology, astronomy, and mathematics, and finally became vice-chancellor of the university. He was one of the leaders of the opposition to the prevailing materialism and superstition. In 1390 he accepted a call as professor in the newly founded university at Vienna, was its rector in 1393, and died in 1397. He wrote, *Consilium Pacis de Unione ac Reformatione Ecclesiæ* (in Hermann von der Hardt's *Magnum Œcum. Const. Consil.* vol. ii):—*Secreta Sacerdotum, quæ in Missa Teneri Debent.* Henry of Langenstein is now counted among the reformers before the Reformation. See Fabricius, *Bibliotheca Mediæ et Infimæ Latinitatis;* Hartwig, *Leben und Schriften Heinrichs von Langenstein* (Marburg, 1858); Plitt-Herzog, *Real-Encyclop.* s. v.; Jöcher, *Allgemeines Gelehrten-Lexikon*, s. v. (B. P.)

Henry OF SANDWICH, archdeacon of Oxford in 1259, was consecrated bishop of London in 1263. He took part with the seditious barons against king Henry III, for which he was excommunicated by Othobon, the pope's legate. He went to Rome, but did not receive absolution for seven years. He returned home, and died Sept. 16, 1273, and was buried in his own church of St. Paul's, London. See Fuller, *Worthies of England* (ed. Nuttall), ii, 135.

Henry, Caleb Sprague, D.D., a Protestant Episcopal minister and writer, was born at Rutland, Mass., Aug. 20, 1804. He graduated from Dartmouth College in 1825; studied theology at Andover in 1828, and for several years was settled as a Congregational minister at Greenfield, Mass., and Hartford, Conn. In 1835 he entered the Episcopal Church, and was appointed professor of mental and moral philosophy in Bristol College, Pa. With Dr. Hawks he established, in 1837, *The New York Review*, and from 1839 to 1852 he was professor of philosophy and history in the University of New York, a part of the time acting as chancellor. From 1847 to 1850 he was rector of St. Clement's Church in that city. He afterwards held rectorships in Poughkeepsie and Newburgh and in Litchfield, Conn., and died at Newburgh, N. Y., March 9, 1884. Professor Henry was the author of many volumes of essays, etc., the last of which, entitled *Dr. Oldham at Graystones, and His Talk There*, was published anonymously in 1860.

Henry, Robert (1), D.D., a Scotch Presbyterian divine, was born at Muirtown, St. Ninian's, Stirlingshire, Feb. 18, 1718. He was educated at the University of Edinburgh; licensed to preach in 1746, and officiated at Carlisle from 1748 to 1760, and at Berwick-upon-Tweed from 1760 to 1763. He was minister of the church of the New Greyfriars from 1763 to 1776. In 1774 he was moderator of the General Assembly of the Church of Scotland. He died Nov. 24, 1790. As an author he is best known by a *History of Great Britain* (1771, 1774, 1777, 1781, 1785, 6 vols.). See Chalmers, *Biog. Dict.* s. v.; Allibone, *Dict. of Brit. and Amer. Authors*, s. v.; *Fasti Eccles. Scoticanæ*, i, 16, 71.

Henry, Robert (2), D.D., LL.D., an Episcopal clergyman, was born at Charleston, S. C., Dec. 6, 1792. He graduated from the University of Edinburgh in 1814, was president of the College of South Carolina in 1834 and 1835, and filled in succession in that institution the chairs of logic and moral philosophy, of metaphysics and belles-lettres, and of the Greek language and literature. He died Feb. 6, 1856, leaving several *Sermons*. See Allibone, *Dict. of Brit. and Amer. Authors*, s. v.; Drake, *Dict. of Amer. Biog.* s. v.

Henry, Robert W., D.D., a Presbyterian minister, was a native of Scotland. He came to America, and became pastor in Chicago, Ill., after which he removed to New York, and was installed co-pastor with Rev. Dr. McElroy of the Scotch Presbyterian Church. He remained in this charge until called by the North Presbyterian Church, Philadelphia, Pa. He went to Europe in May, 1869, and having visited the East he was on his return home, but was smitten down by Syrian fever, and died at Alexandria, Egypt, Oct. 18, 1869. See *Presbyterian*, Nov. 13, 1869. (W. P. S.)

Henry, Symmes Cleves, D.D., a Presbyterian minister, was born at Lamington, N. J., June 7, 1797. He graduated from the College of New Jersey in 1815; studied theology for two years at Princeton Theological Seminary; was ordained evangelist by the Presbytery of Newton, May 3, 1818; became stated supply at Salem, Mass., immediately after his ordination; served as stated supply at Rochester, N.Y., in 1819; the next year of the Third Church of Philadelphia, Pa.; preached at Cranberry, N. J., from 1820 until his death, March 22, 1857. See *Gen. Cat. of Princeton Theol. Sem.* 1881, p. 20.

Hensel, JOHANN ADAM, a Lutheran minister, who died in Silesia, Feb. 2, 1778, is the author of *Geschichte der protestantischen Gemeinen in Schlesien* (Liegnitz, 1768). See Winer, *Handbuch der theol. Lit.* i, 808; Jöcher, *Allgemeines Gelehrten-Lexikon*, s. v. (B. P.)

Henshaw, JOSEPH, D.D., an English clergyman, was made prebendary of Peterborough, dean of Chichester in 1660, and bishop of Peterborough in 1663. He died March 9, 1678, leaving, *Horæ Successivæ* (1631):—*Dayly Thoughts* (1651). See Allibone, *Dict. of Brit. and Amer. Authors*, s. v.

Hensler, CHRISTIAN GOTTFRIED, a Lutheran theologian of Germany, was born March 9, 1760, in Holstein. In 1786 he was professor of theology at Kiel, resigned his office in 1809, and thereafter resided in Halle until his death, April 24, 1812. He is the author of *Bemerkungen über Stellen in der Psalmen und in der Genesis* (Hamburg, 1791):—*Erläuterung des ersten Buches Samuelis und der Salomonischen Denksprüche* (1796):—*Iesaias neu übersetzt und mit Anmerkungen* (1788):—*Bemerkungen über Stellen in Jeremias Weissagungen* (1805):—*Animadversiones in Quædam 12 Prophetarum Minorum Loca* (1786):—*Der Brief des Apostels Jakobus übersetzt und erläutert* (1801):—*Die Wahrheit und Göttlichkeit der christlichen Religion dargestellt* (1803). See Winer, *Handbuch der theol. Lit.* i, 105, 195, 217, 220, 223, 269, 272, 386; Fürst, *Bibl. Jud.* i, 384. (B. P.)

Hentenius, JOHANNES, a Dominican and professor at Louvain, where he died Oct. 2, 1566, published, *Biblia ad Vetustissima Exemplaria Recens Castigata Jussu Collegarum* (Louvain, 1547):—*Euthymii Zigabeni Commentaria in iv Evangelia* (1544):—*Œcumenii Commentarii* (1545):—*De Vera Deo Apte Inserviendi Methodo* (translated from the Spanish, 1560). See Winer, *Handbuch der theol. Lit.* i, 60, 893, 898; Jöcher, *Allgemeines Gelehrten-Lexikon*, s. v. (B. P.)

Henzi, RUDOLPH, professor of Oriental languages and of Old-Testament exegesis, who died at Dorpat in 1829, is the author of *Libri Ecclesiastæ Argumenti Brevis Adumbratio* (Dorpat, 1827). See Winer, *Handbuch der theol. Lit.* i, 82; Zuchold, *Bibl. Theol.* i, 539; Fürst (who spells the name *Henze*), *Bibl. Jud.* i, 385. (B. P.)

Heothĭna (*τὰ ἑωθινά*), in the Greek Church, designates (1) an antiphonal anthem of lauds; (2) gospels relating to the resurrection.

Hepburn, a Scotch prelate, was rector of Partoun and abbot of Dunfermline in 1515. In June of the same year he was constituted lord treasurer. In 1516 he became bishop of Moray. He died in 1524. See Keith, *Scottish Bishops*, p. 148.

Hepburn, George, a Scotch prelate, was early preferred to the provostry of Lincluden, and Feb. 9, 1503, was elected abbot of the monastery of Aberbrothock. In 1509 he was made lord treasurer, and in 1510 he was elected bishop of the see of the Isles. In 1512 he was commentator both of Arbroath and Icolumkill. This prelate was slain with the king on the unfortunate field of Flodden, Sept. 9, 1513. See Keith, *Scottish Bishops*, p. 305.

Hepburn, John (1), a Scotch prelate, was bishop of the see of Brechin in 1517, and was still there in 1532. He died in August, 1543. See Keith, *Scottish Bishops*, p. 165.

Hepburn, John (2), a Scotch prelate, was bishop of Dunblane, and one of the lords of council of session in 1467. In 1476 he assisted at the consecration of dean Livingstone to the see of Dunkeld. He was bishop of this see in 1479. He died in 1508. See Keith, *Scottish Bishops*, p. 178.

Hepburn, Patrick, a Scotch prelate, was prior of St. Andrews in 1522, and in 1524 was made secretary, in which office he continued until 1527. He was advanced to the see of Moray in 1535, and at the same time held the abbey of Scone in perpetual commendam. He was bishop of Moray still in 1561, and probably in 1568. He died at Spynie Castle, June 20, 1573. See Keith, *Scottish Bishops*, p. 150.

Hepher. This place Trelawney Saunders (*Map of the O. T.*) identifies with *Khurbet Kafir*, which the *Ordnance Map* lays down eight miles northwest of Hebron (and three miles east of Um-Burj, the neighborhood which we had conjecturally assigned), and the *Memoirs* describe (iii, 355) as "foundations and heaps of stones. It has the appearance of an old site, and an ancient road passes it."

Heppe, Heinrich Ludwig Julius, a Protestant theologian of Germany, was born at Cassel in 1820. He studied at Marburg, was in 1844 doctor of philosophy and licentiate of theology, and commenced his academical career at Marburg. In 1850 he was professor of theology, in 1864 he was honored with the doctorate of theology, and died July 25, 1879. He wrote, *Diss. de Loco Evang. Lucæ xvi*, 1-9 (Marburg, 1844):—*Thatsachen aus der Kurhessischen Kirchengeschichte* (Cassel, eod.):—*Geschichte der hessischen Generalsynoden von* 1568-1582 (1847, 2 vols.):—*Historische Untersuchungen über den Kasseler Catechismus* (ibid. eod.):—*Einführung der Verbesserungspunkte in Hessen*, etc. (1849):—*Gesch. des deutschen Protestantismus* (1852-57, 3 vols.):—*Die confessionelle Entwicklung der hessischen Kirche* (1853):—*Die confessionelle Entwicklung der altprotestantischen Kirche Deutschlands* (1854):—*Dogmatik des deutschen Protestantismus im* 16 *Jahrhundert* (Gotha, 1857, 3 vols.):—*Geschichte des deutschen Volksschulwesens* (1858-60, 5 vols.):—*Dogmatik der evang.-reform. Kirche* (1860):—*Die Bekenntnisschriften der reform. Kirchen Deutschlands* (eod.):—*Theodor Beza. Leben und ausgewählte Schriften* (1861):—*Entstehung und Fortbildung des Lutherthums* (1863):—*Philipp Melanchthon, der Lehrer Deutschlands* (1867):—*Zur Geschichte der evang. Kirche Rheinlands und Westfalens* (1867-70, 2 vols.):—*Geschichte der quietistischen Mystik in der Kathol. Kirche* (Berlin, 1875):—*Kirchengeschichte beider Hessen* (Marburg, 1876, 2 vols.):—*Geschichte des Pietismus in der Reformirten Kirche* (Leyden, 1879). See Zuchold, *Bibl. Theol.* i, 539 sq.; Lichtenberger, *Encyclop. des Sciences Religieuses*, s. v.; *Zur Erinnerung an H. Heppe* (Marburg, 1879). (B. P.)

Heracleia, a festival anciently celebrated at Athens every five years in honor of the Grecian god Heracles (q. v.).

Heraclīdēs, surnamed *Cyprus*, from his place of birth, was liberally educated, became a monk under Evagrius, and deacon at Constantinople. He was an ardent friend of Chrysostom, who caused his election as bishop of Ephesus in 401; but he was afterwards persecuted along with that eminent ecclesiastic, and finally shared his exile.

Heracliteans, the followers of the philosopher *Heraclitus* (q. v.).

Heraclius (Eraclius or **Eradius)**, bishop elect of Hippo, was designed by Augustine, Sept. 26, 426, to become his successor, but owing to some irregularity he was never inaugurated into that office, and the fall of Hippo into the hands of the Vandals abolished the see. There are attributed to Heraclius two sermons found among those of St. Augustine. See Hoefer, *Nouv. Biog. Générale*, s. v.; Smith, *Dict. of Christ. Biog.* s. v.

Heraclius (Eracle or **Everard)**, sixteenth bishop of Liege, was of a distinguished Saxon family, and was educated at Cologne under the care of Rathier, bishop of Liege. He became provost at the Collegiate Church of Bonn, and entered upon the episcopal see of Liege in 959. He devoted his attention entirely to the cause of education, establishing new schools, and placing at their head wise men, whom he called from Germany and from France. In 960 he became involved in political troubles, during which he died, in 971. There is extant of him a letter, written about 943, to Rathier, bishop of Verona, on the miraculous healing of a cancer. See Hoefer, *Nouv. Biog. Générale*, s. v.

Heranasikha (from the Singhalese, *herana*, a novice, and *sikha*, a rule or precept), a formulary required to be committed to memory by the Buddhist priest during his novitiate. It contains a number of obligations which the young priest takes upon himself.

Herberger, Valerius, a Lutheran theologian, was born at Fraustadt, Prussian Poland, April 21, 1562, and died there, May 18, 1627. He was a teacher in his native place in 1584, deacon in 1590, and pastor in 1598. His publications are still highly prized in the German Evangelical Church. He wrote, *Evangelische Herzpostille* (new ed. Berlin, 1853):—*Epistolische Herzpostille* (ibid):—*Geistreiche Stoppelpostille*:—*Magnalia Dei. De Jesu Scripturæ Nucleo et Medulla* (Halle, 1854):—*Passionszeiger* (ibid. 1858):—*Geistliche Trauerbinden*:—*Psalterparadies*:—*Erklärung des Jesus Sirach*. See Lauterbach, *Vita, Fama et Fata Valerii Herbergeri* (1708); Ledderhose, *Leben Valerius Herbergers*, in the *Sonntagsbibliothek*, vol. iv, parts 5 and 6 (Bielefeld, 1851); Specht, *Geschichte der evangelisch lutherischen Gemeinde zu Fraustadt* (1855); Plitt-Herzog, *Real-Encyklop.* s. v.; Lichtenberger, *Encyclop. des Sciences Religieuses*, s. v.; Zuchold, *Bibl. Theol.* i, 540; Jöcher, *Allgemeines Gelehrten-Lexikon*, s. v. (B. P.)

Herberne, bishop of Tours, lived about the 9th century. He had been at first custodian of the Oratory of the Seven Sleepers, a dependency of Marmoutier, afterwards abbot of that monastery, which, however, is said to have been invested by the Normans in 853. He then travelled through Gaul, but finding no safe asylum, finally reappeared in the city of Tours, where he was received as a saint. Adalard, archbishop of Tours, died in 890, and Herberne was designated to succeed him. After the desolation of Marmoutier, the Regular Canons established themselves in the deserted cloister there, and Herberne failed to drive them away. He died in 916. Some critics attributed to him the *Tractatus de Reversione S. Martini*, which was published in the *Bibliothèque de Cluny*. See Hoefer, *Nouv. Biog. Générale*, s. v.

Herberstein, Johann Carl Graf von, a German count and prelate, was born in 1722. He became bishop of Laybach in 1772, and was one of the most ardent promoters of the ecclesiastical innovations of his day. Pending negotiations with the pope for his promotion to the archbishopric, he died, Oct. 7, 1787, leaving his goods to the poor and to the normal school of his episcopal city. See Hoefer, *Nouv. Biog. Générale*, s. v.

Herbert, a Scotch prelate, was abbot of Kelso, and chancellor of the kingdom. He was consecrated bishop of Glasgow in 1147, by pope Eugenius III. He died bishop of this see, in 1164. See Keith, *Scottish Bishops*, p. 232.

Herbert, a French prelate, was born at Vouvnay, in Maine. He was at first prior of Clermont, in Maine, and then abbot of Fontaines-les-Blanches, in the diocese of Tours. Having got into a quarrel with Thibauld, count of Blois, he returned to Maine, where he became abbot of Clermont in 1179. Finally, in 1184, he was made bishop of Rennes; in 1190 he accompanied Richard, king of England, to Domfront. While at Rennes he had a difference with Andrew, lord of Vitré, whom he excommunicated until he obtained his entire submission. In 1198 the pope sent him to Bourgueil, on the frontier of Tours, to restore the good order of that monastery. He died at Rennes, Dec. 11, 1198. See Hoefer, *Nouv. Biog. Générale*, s. v.

Herbert OF BOSHAM was born at Bosham, Sussex, and being a good scholar, was a *manubus* to Thomas à Becket, archbishop of Canterbury. He was present at the murder of that prelate, and wrote an account of it. Going over to Italy, he was by pope Alexander III made archbishop of Beneventum, and in December, 1178, created cardinal. The date of his death is unknown. See Fuller, *Worthies of England* (ed. Nuttall), iii, 244.

Herbert DE LOSING, a Norman prelate, was born at Hiesmes (pagus Oximiensis), in Normandy, about the middle of the 11th century. He was a monk, and afterwards prior of the abbey of Fécamp. William Rufus called him to England in 1087, and made him abbot of Ramsey. By the royal favor, or some other means, Herbert became so rich that, in 1091, he bought from the king, for the price of 1000 livres, the bishopric of Thetford for himself, and the abbey of Winchester for his brother Robert. This most scandalous transaction was generally censured, and Herbert went to Rome to seek absolution from his simony. On his return to England he transferred the episcopal seat of Thetford to Norwich. At Thetford he founded a convent of monks of Cluny, and built a cathedral; also a monastery and two churches at Norwich, three churches at Elmham, at Lynn, and at Yarmouth. The last years of his life Herbert consecrated to the establishment of ecclesiastical discipline, thus effacing the spot upon his entry into the episcopacy. William of Malmesbury speaks of Herbert as a man of great knowledge, and Henry of Huntingdon makes mention of his writings. He died July 22, 1119. According to Bayle, he composed a book of *Sermons*, eighteen in number, two treatises, *De Prolixitate Temporum et De Fine Mundi*, monastic rules, a collection of letters, and a treatise, *Ad Anselmum*, etc., for which see Hoefer, *Nouv. Biog. Générale*, s. v.

Herbert, WILLIAM, D.C.L., an English clergyman, was born at Highclere Castle, Bucks, in 1778, and educated at Eton, and at Christ Church and Merton Colleges, Oxford. He took holy orders in 1814, was presented to the rectory of Spofforth, appointed dean of Manchester in 1840, and died in 1847. He published, *The Triumphs of Christianity:—Sermons* (1820):—*The Spectre of the Tomb*, etc. See Allibone, *Dict. of Brit. and Amer. Authors*, s. v.

Herbinius, JOHN, was born at Bitschen, in Silesia, in 1632, and was deputed by the Polish Protestant churches to those of Germany, Holland, etc., in 1664. He died in 1676. Among his works is *De Statu Ecclesiarum Augustanæ Confessionis in Polonia* (1670). See Chalmers, *Biog. Dict.* s. v.

Herbst, Ferdinand Ignatius, a Roman Catholic theologian of Germany, was born of Protestant parentage at Leipsic in 1798. He studied at Jena and Erlangen, joined the church of Rome in 1832, and was preacher at Munich, where he died, May 11, 1865. He published, *Bibliothek Christlicher Denker* (Leipsic, 1830-32, 2 vols.):—*Die Kirche und ihre Gegner* (Ratisbon, 1833):—*Antwort auf das Sendschreiben eines Gliedes der evangelischen Kirche*, etc. (Landshut, eod.). See Winer, *Handbuch der theol. Lit.* i, 351; Zuchold, *Bibl. Theol.* i, 541. (B. P.)

Herbst, Johann George, a German Benedictine, was born at Rottweil, Würtemberg, Jan. 13, 1787. In 1812 he received holy orders, was professor of theology at Ellwangen in 1814, in 1817 at Tübingen, and died July 31, 1836. He published, *Observationes Quædam de Pentateucho:—De Lingua Hebr.* הב *et* בה:—*Einleitung in die heil. Schriften des Alten Testaments* (Freiburg, 1840-42, 2 vols.). See Fürst, *Bibl. Jud.* i, 385; Lichtenberger, *Encyclop. des Sciences Religieuses*, s. v. (B. P.)

Herder, FELIX, a Swiss Reformed theologian, was born Jan. 31, 1741, at Zurich, where he studied, and finally died, Jan. 22, 1810. He published, *Predigten über die Geschichte Josephs* (Zurich, 1784):—*Versuch eines christlichen Religionsunterrichts* (edited by J. J. Hess, 1811). See Döring, *Die gelehrten Theologen Deutschlands*, s. v.; Winer, *Handbuch der theol. Lit.* ii, 229, 339. (B. P.)

Heredia, PAULUS DE. See PAULUS DE HEREDIA.

Hereford (or **Herford**), NICHOLAS, an English confessor of the 14th century, was educated doctor of divinity at Oxford, became a secular priest, declared against some practices and principles of the reigning religion, maintaining (1) that in the eucharist, after the consecration of the elements, bread and wine still remained; (2) that bishops and all clergymen ought to be subject to their respective princes; (3) that monks and friars ought to maintain themselves by their own labor; (4) that priests ought to rule their lives, not by the pope's decrees, but by the word of God. From these positions many heretical opinions were drawn by his enemies. From Oxford he was brought to London, and there, with Philip Repington, was made to recant his opinions publicly at St. Paul's Cross in 1382. Repington became a violent renegade, persecuted his party, for which he was rewarded first with the bishopric of Lincoln, then with a cardinal's cap. Hereford's recantation did not much avail him, as archbishop Arundel's jealousy kept him a prisoner all his life. We know not the date of his death. Hereford by his protest anticipated the Reformation, but he probably had not the stuff to make a Wycliffe or Tyndal. See Fuller, *Worthies of England* (ed. Nuttall), iii, 491; Fox, *Acts and Monuments*, iii, 26.

Hereford Use, a term employed to designate that rite which, taking its name from the cathedral of Hereford, was commonly used in some of the north-west counties of England, and in parts of Wales, prior to the Reformation. It differs only slightly from the use of Salisbury in the prayer of oblation and in the communion of the priest. The service-books of these rites are extremely rare. MSS., no doubt, were everywhere destroyed. Only one printed edition is known—that of Rouen, dated 1502.

Heres, MT. For this Lieut. Conder suggests (*Tent Work*, iii, 337) *Kefr Hâris*, but he gives no clew to the locality.

Herft, JOHANN BERNHARD, a Roman Catholic theologian of Germany, was born April 27, 1745. He studied at Münster, took holy orders in 1769, was in 1774 cathedral preacher at Osnabrück, canon in 1778, and dean in 1790. He died March 31, 1812. His writings are sermons. See Döring, *Die gelehrten Theologen Deutschlands*, s. v. (B. P.)

Hering, Daniel Heinrich, a Reformed theologian of Germany, was born at Stolpe, in Pomerania, Dec. 1, 1722. He studied at Halle, was in 1757 preacher at Neustadt-Eberswalde, and accepted in 1759 a call to Halle. In 1765 he went to Breslau, and died Aug. 21, 1807. He published, *De voce πορνείᾳ in Decreto Apostolico* (Halle, 1742):—*De Doctrina Bileami, Nicolaitarum et Jezabelis* (eod.):—*Von der Schule des Apostels Johannes zu Ephesus* (Breslau, 1774):—*Abhandlungen von der Schulen der Propheten* (ibid. 1777):—*Historische Nachricht von dem ersten Anfang der evangelisch-reformirten Kirche in Brandenburg und Preussen* (Halle, 1778), besides sermons. See Döring, *Die gelehrten Theologen Deutschlands*, s. v.: Winer, *Handbuch der theol. Lit.* i, 805; ii, 222; Fürst, *Bibl. Jud.* i, 385. (B. P.)

Heringa, Jodocus, a Dutch divine, who died at Utrecht in 1840, doctor and professor of theology, is the author of, *Beoordeling van de nieuwe uitgave der Prolegomena in N. Test. van J. Jac. Wetstein* (Amsterdam, 1832):—*Ueber den Begriff, die Unentbehrlichkeit und den rechten Gebrauch der bibl. kritik. aus dem Holländischen übersetzt von Beckhaus* (Offenbach, 1804):—*Ueber die Lehrart Jesu und seiner Apostel.* (from the Dutch, 1792):—*Tiental Seerredenen ter aanprijzing van christel. deugden* (Amsterdam, 1825):—*Opera Exegetica et Hermeneutica* (edited by H. E. Vinke, Utrecht, 1845). See Winer, *Handbuch der theol. Lit.* i, 43, 86, 92, 105, 130, 132, 250, 397, 399; ii, 111; Zuchold, *Bibl. Theol.* i, 543. (B. P.)

Herli-Kan, in Kalmuck mythology, is the prince of hell; a frightful and evil-minded god, the judge of men, the other gods being too merciful to judge the

Figure of Herli-Kan.

guilty. To implore his favor large sacrifices are made to him. Sixteen judges assist him, one half being males, the other half females.

Herman of Cappenberg, a Jewish convert of the 12th century, was a native of Cologne. His Jewish name was *Judah Levi.* After his conversion he entered the order of the Premonstratensians, and became abbot of Cappenberg, in Westphalia. He wrote *Opusculum de Conversione Sua*, preserved in the university library at Leipsic, and printed with Raymund Martin's *Pugio Fidei.* Herman also wrote *Vita S. Godefridi Cappenbergensis*, found in the *Acta Sanctorum* under Jan. 13. See Bartolocci, *Bibl. Rabb.* iii, 59; Kalkar, *Israel und die Kirche*, p. 85; Jöcher, *Allgemeines Gelehrten-Lexikon*, s. v.; Neander, *Kirchengeschichte*, v, 101 sq.; Wolf, *Bibl. Hebr.* i, 352; Basnage, *Histoire des Juifs* (Taylor's transl.), p. 633; Fürst, *Bibl. Jud.* i, 387. (B. P.)

Herman, Lebrecht Frederick, D.D., one of the earlier ministers of the German Reformed Church, was born in the principality of Anhalt-Köthen, Germany, Oct. 9, 1761. He prosecuted his literary and theological studies in Europe, and for a while served as assistant pastor in Bremen. In 1786 he emigrated to America, under the auspices of the synods of Holland, to aid in supplying the German churches in Pennsylvania with the means of grace. He labored for a short time in and around Easton, Pa., afterwards in Germantown and Frankford, near Philadelphia, and finally in Montgomery County. He died Jan. 30, 1848. Dr. Herman paid much attention to the training of young men for the ministry. He was in his day a prominent minister, and a learned and able theologian. See Harbaugh, *Fathers of the Germ. Ref. Church*, ii, 360. (D. Y. H.)

Hermandad, societies in Spain which were accustomed to supply victims to the Inquisition (q. v.).

Hermann, Emil, a German Protestant professor of canon law, was born at Dresden, April 9, 1812. He studied at Leipsic, where he also commenced his academical career in 1834. He was professor at Kiel in 1842, in 1847 at Göttingen, and in 1868 at Heidelberg. In 1872 he was called to Berlin as president of the Evangelical Superior Church Council (*Oberkirchenraths*), and occupied this position till 1877. He died at Gotha, April 16, 1885. Hermann published, *Johann Freiherr zu Schwarzenberg* (Leipsic, 1841):—*Autorität des kirchlichen Symbols* (Kiel, 1846):—*Ueber die Stellung der Religionsgemeinschaften im Staate* (Göttingen, 1849):—*Ueber den Entwurf einer Kirchenordnung für die Sächsische Landeskirche* (Berlin, 1861):—*Die nothwendigen Grundlagen einer die consistoriale und synodale Ordnung vereinigenden Kirchenverfassung* (ibid. 1862):—*Das staatliche Veto bei Bischofswahlen nach dem Rechte der oberrheinischen Kirchenprovinz* (Heidelberg, 1869). See Zuchold, *Bibl. Theol.* i, 545 sq. (B. P.)

Hermann, Gottlob, a Lutheran theologian of Germany, was born at Löbau, in Upper Lusatia, May 27, 1721. He studied at Leipsic, was in 1758 archdeacon at Bischofswerda, in 1759 pastor primarius at his native place, and died Jan. 2, 1789. His publications are sermons and ascetical works. See Döring, *Die gelehrten Theologen Deutschlands*, s. v. (B. P.)

Hermann, Johann Gottfried, a Lutheran theologian of Germany, was born in Saxony, Oct. 12, 1707. He studied at Leipsic, was in 1733 deacon, received a call in 1738 to Amsterdam as pastor of the German congregation, but accepted the appointment as superintendent at Plauen. In 1746 he was called to Dresden as court-preacher and member of consistory, and died July 30, 1791. He published, *De Pane Azymo et Fermentato in Cœna Domini* (Leipsic, 1739), besides a number of sermons. See Döring, *Die gelehrten Theologen Deutschlands*, s. v.; Winer, *Handbuch der theol. Lit.* i, 603. (B. P.)

Hermansen, Christen, a Lutheran theologian, was born in 1806 in Denmark, and died at Copenhagen, Oct. 19, 1882, doctor and professor of theology. For more than forty years he belonged to the university at Copenhagen, in which he lectured on the Old Test. He was one of the revisers of the Danish Bible translation. (B. P.)

Hermant, Godefroy, a French theologian, was born at Beauvais, Feb. 6, 1617. Having completed his studies, he was appointed in 1642 canon at his native place, in 1644 prior, and in 1650 doctor of the Sorbonne. In 1651 he took holy orders, and returned to Beauvais to officiate there as priest. In 1690 Hermant went to Paris to see his old friends, and on July 11 died suddenly in the street. Of his many writings we mention, *Apologie pour M. Arnauld* (1644–48):—*La Vie de Saint Jean Chrysostôme* (1664 and often):—*Vie de Saint Athanase* (1671, 2 vols.):—*Les Ascétiques de Saint Basile avec Remarques* (1671–1727):—*Vie de Saint Basile et de Saint Grégoire de Nazianze* (1674, 2 vols.):—*Vie de Saint Ambroise* (1678):—*Entretiens Spirituels sur Saint Matthieu* (1690, 3 vols.):—*Clavis Disciplinæ Ecclesiasticæ, seu Index Totius Juris Ecclesiastici* (1693). See Baillet, *La Vie de Godefroy Hermant;*

Nécrologe des plus Célèbres Défenseurs et Confesseurs de la Verité, I, iv; *Abrégé de l'Hist. Ecclés.* xii; Bayle, *Dict. Historique et Critique; Hist. Génerale de Port-Royal*, iv, viii; *Biblioth. Jansén.*; Jöcher, *Allgemeines Gelehrten-Lexikon*, s. v.; Winer, *Handbuch der theol. Lit.* i, 655, 659, 702, 728, 884, 885, 887, 902; Lichtenberger, *Encyclop. des Sciences Religieuses*, s. v.; Hoefer, *Nouv. Biog. Génerale*, s. v. (B. P.)

Hermanŭbis. Romans and Greeks sought to make their cultus accord with that of the Egyptians. Thus, Anubis of the Egyptians was confounded with Mercury of the Romans or Hermes of the Greeks, and thus there originated the compound word Hermanubis — Mercury being represented with the snake-staff, in human form, but with a dog's head, and to designate still closer the country of his worship, with a crocodile at his feet. See ANUBIS.

Figure of Hermanŭbis.

Hermengild (*Erminigildus*), Visigoth prince of Spain, was the elder of the two sons of the Arian king, Leovigeld, by his first wife, and was made governor of Baetica on his marriage. He rebelled against his father, who finally captured him about A.D. 572, and put him to death. He is commemorated as a saint by the Roman Church on April 13, as he had embraced the Catholic faith.

Hermes, Hermann Daniel, a Lutheran theologian of Germany, was born Jan. 2, 1734, in Pomerania. He studied at Halle, was teacher at Berlin in 1752, in 1766 professor at the Magdalene gymnasium in Breslau, in 1771 preacher there. In 1791 he was called to Berlin as member of the examination commission of candidates for the ministry, accepted a call as professor of theology to Kiel in 1805, and died Nov. 12, 1807. Besides several volumes of sermons, he published, *Der Christ auf dem Krankenbette* (Breslau, 1774):—*Die Lehre der heiligen Schrift* (1775-79, 3 parts):—*Schema Examinis Candidatorum S.S. Ministerii Rite Instituendi* (Berlin, 1790):—*Briefe über die Lehrbegriffe des protestantischen Kirche* (Leipsic, 1800):—*Versuch zweckmässiger Betrachtungen über die biblischen Weissagungen* (1801). See Döring, *Deutsche Kanzelredner;* Winer, *Handbuch der theol. Lit.* i, 483. (B. P.)

Hermes, Johann August, a Lutheran theologian of Germany, was born at Magdeburg, Aug. 24, 1736. He studied at Halle, was in 1757 preacher at Rettendorf, in Mecklenburg, and in 1765 at Wahren. He resigned the pastorate at the latter place on account of his liberal views, which he expressed both in the pulpit and in writing, and accepted a call in 1774 to Jericho, in the duchy of Magdeburg. In 1780 he was appointed first pastor at St. Nicholas, in Quedlinburg, and in 1799 first court-preacher. He died Jan. 6, 1822. He published, *Handbuch der Religion* (Berlin, 1779; 4th ed. 1791):—*Communionbuch* (1783, 5th ed. 1798):—*Lehrbuch der Religion Jesu* (Quedlinburg, 1798; 3d ed. 1822):—*Hat Christus auch für die zeitlichen Strafen der Sünde genug gethan?* (1792). See Döring, *Deutsche Kanzelredner;* Winer, *Handbuch der theol. Lit.* i, 9; ii, 131, 213, 282, 296, 317, 365. (B. P.)

Hermes, Johann Timotheus, a German theologian, brother of Hermann Daniel, was born in 1738. He studied at Königsberg, was for some time preacher in Silesia, accepted a call in 1772 to Breslau, and died July 24, 1821, superintendent and pastor primarius at St. Elizabeth. His publications are mostly sermons. See Döring, *Deutsche Kanzelredner;* Winer, *Handbuch der theol. Lit.* ii, 97, 141, 163, 172, 178, 341, 401. (B. P.)

Hermod, in Norse mythology, was the son of Odin, who corresponds to Mercury in the Greek system. He is a herald of the gods, distinguished by his quickness and versatility.

Figure of Hermod.

Hermogenians. See HERMOGENUS (*the heretic*).

Hermon. We give the latest account of an ascent of this remarkable mountain (Conder, *Tent Work in Palestine*, i, 261 sq.):

"We commenced the ascent of some 5000 feet about 10.30 A.M. (from Rasheyah, which is three hours distant), passing first through the fine vineyards, into which the bears often come down, from the summit, to eat grapes; thence along lanes with stone walls, passing clumps of wild rose, of oak, and of hawthorn, and honeysuckle in flower. We thus reached the bottom of the main peak, consisting entirely of gray rocks, worn by snow and rain into jagged teeth and ridges, covered with a loose shingle or gravel. It seemed impossible for horses, and still more for laden mules, to toil up; but the breeze grew fresher, and the bracing mountain air seemed to give vigor to man and beast. Resting at intervals, we gradually clambered up, passing by the little cave where the initiated Druses retire, for three or four months, and perform unknown rites. Ridge above ridge, of rock and gray gravel, appeared, each seemingly the last, each only hiding one

Mt. Hermon from Rasheyah. (From a Photograph by the Editor.)

above. Not a creature was to be seen, except an occasional vulture, and not a tree or shrub, for the snow covers all this part of the mountain till late in summer. By two o'clock we reached the summit.

"A glorious panorama repaid us for our labor. South of us lay Palestine, visible as far as Carmel and Tabor, some eighty miles away; eastward a broad plain, with detached hills on the dim horizon beyond; westward the Lebanon and the golden sea; northward, mountains as high as Hermon, Lebanon, and Anti-Lebanon. As the sun sank lower, Palestine became more distinct, and appeared wonderfully narrow. The calm, green Sea of Galilee lay, dreamlike, in its circle of dark-gray hills. Tabor was just visible to the south, and from it the plateau ran out east to the Horns of Hattin. The broken chain of the Upper Galilæan Hills, 4000 feet high, lay beneath the eye, and terminated in the Ladder of Tyre. The mole of Tyre stood out black against the gleaming water; and the deep gorge of the Litâny could be seen winding past the beautiful fortress of Belfort. Dim and misty beyond, lay the ridge of Carmel, from the promontory to the peak of Sacrifice. The white domes in Tiberias were shining in the sun, and many of the Galilæan towns, including Safed, could be distinguished. The scene presented a great contrast on the east and west. In the brown, desolate, and boundless plain to the east stood the distant green oasis of Damascus, and the white city, with its tall minarets. The flat horizon was broken only by the peaks of Jebel Kuleib, the 'Hill of Bashan,' some seventy miles away. South-east of Damascus was the terrible Lejja district, a basin of basalt seamed with deep gorges, like rough furrows, and with isolated cones, into which one appeared to look down, so distinctly were the shadows marked inside the hollow, broken craters. No trees or water relieved the dusky color; but the great dust whirlwinds were swirling slowly along over the plains, the bodies, as the Arabs tell us, of huge malignant spirits, carrying destruction in their path. At the foot of the mountain little villages were perched on the rocks, and a stream glittered in a green valley. In most of these hamlets there is a temple facing the rising sun, which appears first from behind the great plain on the east. On the west, high mountain walls, ridge behind ridge, reached out towards Beyrût, and, on the north, cedar clumps and ragged peaks, gray and dark, with long, sweeping shadows, were thrown in strong contrast against the shining sea. The sun began to set, a deep ruby flush came over all the scene, and warm purple shadows crept slowly on. The Sea of Galilee was lit up with a delicate greenish-yellow hue, between its dim walls of hill. The flush died out in a few minutes, and a pale, steel-colored shade succeeded, although to us, at a height of 9150 feet, the sun was still visible, and the rocks around us still ruddy. A long pyramidal shadow slid down to the eastern foot of Hermon, and crept across the great plain; Damascus was swallowed up by it, and finally the pointed end of the shadow stood out distinctly against the sky—a dusky cone of dull color against the flush of the afterglow. It was the shadow of the mountain itself, stretching away for seventy miles across the plain—the most marvellous shadow perhaps to be seen anywhere. The sun underwent strange changes of shape in the thick vapors—now almost square, now like a domed temple—until at length it slid into the sea, and went out like a blue spark.

"Our tent was pitched in the hollow, and six beds crowded into it. Until one in the morning we continued to observe the stars, but the cold was very considerable, though no snow was left, and the only water we had was fetched from a spring about a third of the way down, and tasted horribly of the goat-skin. In the morning I ran to the peak, and saw the sun emerge behind the distant plain, and the great conical shadow, stretching over the sea and against the western sky, becoming gradually more blunt, until it shrivelled up and was lost upon the hills beneath.

"The top of Hermon consists of three rocky peaks; two, north and south, of equal height—the third, to the west, considerably lower. On the southern peak are the ruins called Kŭsr esh-Shabîb—a rock-hewn hollow or trench, and a circular dwarf-wall, with a temple just below the peak on the south. On the plateau is a rudely-excavated cave, with a rock-cut pillar supporting the roof, and a flat space levelled above, probably once the floor of a building over the cave. Of all these objects of interest we made careful plans, as well of the shape of the summit.

"There is one remarkable natural peculiarity of Hermon still to be noticed—namely, the extreme rapidity of the formation of cloud on the summit. In a few minutes a thick cap forms over the top of the mountain, and as quickly disperses and entirely disappears."

Hernhutters. See MORAVIANS.

Herold, ADAM, a Lutheran theologian of Germany, was born May 31, 1659, at Dresden. He studied at Wittenberg, Giessen, and Kiel, was in 1683 rector at Reval, in 1692 superintendent in Saxony, and doctor of theology, and died March 2, 1711. He wrote, *Palladium Reformatorum a sua Sede cap. ix ad Rom. Destructum:—Tabula Synoptica Totius Theologiæ:—Disp. utrum Christus Ultimum Pascha Eodem an Diverso a Judæis Die Comederit:—De Judæorum Excommunicatione:—De Magis Bethlehemum Profectis.* See Ranft, *Leben der chursächsischen Gelehrten;* Jöcher, *Allgemeines Gelehrten-Lexikon*, s. v. (B. P.)

Heros (*Eros*), metropolitan bishop of Arles in the early part of the 5th century, was originally bishop of Tortosa, in Spain, but was expelled by the people from Arles in 412, and fled to Palestine, where he took part in the opposition to Pelagius. After A.D. 417 he is not heard of.

Hero-worship. See IDOLATRY.

Herrad OF LANDSPERG, an abbess of Hohenburg, or Odilienberg, an old, celebrated monastery, said to have been founded by duke Ethicot, whose daughter Odilia was the first abbess. Herrad succeeded the abbess Relindis in 1167, and died July 25, 1195. She is said to have composed the *Hortus Deliciarum*, a work containing contributions to Biblical history and to the entire field of theology. A copy of the *Hortus*, preserved at the Strasburg library, was destroyed, with other precious documents, at the bombardment of that city, Aug. 24, 1870. See Engelhart, *Herrad von Landsperg und ihr Werk Hortus Deliciarum* (Stuttgart, 1818); Le Noble, *Notice sur le Hortus Deliciarum de Herrade de Landsperg* (Paris, 1839); Piper, *Die Kalendarien der Angelsachsen und das Martyrologium der Herrad von Landsperg* (Berlin, 1862); Lichtenberger, *Encyclop. des Sciences Religieuses*, s. v.; Hoefer, *Nouv. Biog. Générale*, s. v. (B. P.)

Herregouts, HENRI, a distinguished Flemish painter of historical subjects, was born at Mechlin about 1666. There are several of his pictures in the churches of Antwerp, Louvain, and Bruges. In the cathedral at Antwerp is *The Martyrdom of St. Matthew;* and at Bruges, in the Church of St. Anne, is his masterpiece, representing *The Last Judgment.* He died at Antwerp in 1724. See Hoefer, *Nouv. Biog. Générale*, s. v.; Spooner, *Biog. Hist. of the Fine Arts*, s. v.

Herrera, Abraham de, a famous Cabalist, who died in 1639, is the author of, בית אלהים, or *Casa de Dios*, the system of the cabala in seven divisions (transl. into Hebrew by Aboab, Amsterdam, 1655; and into Latin by Rosenroth, in his *Cabbala Denudata*, vol. ii, Sulzbach, 1678):—שער השמים, or *Porta del Cielo*, also on the Cabala (Hebrew transl. by Aboab, 1655; Latin, in *Cabbala Denudata*, vol. i). See Fürst, *Bibl. Jud.* i, 386. (B. P.)

Herrera, Augustin de, a Spanish Jesuit, who died in 1649 at Seville, is the author of, *De Origine et Progressu in Ecclesia Catholica Rituum et Ceremoniarum in SS. Missæ Sacrificio:—Comment. in Syntaxi Antonii Nebrissensis.* See Alegambe, *Bibliotheca Scriptorum Societatis Jesu;* Jöcher, *Allgemeines Gelehrten-Lexikon*, s. v. (B. P.)

Herrgott, MARQUARD, a Benedictine, who died at Vienna in 1762, is the author of *Vetus Disciplina Monastica* (Paris, 1726). See Winer, *Handbuch der theol. Lit.* i, 711; Jöcher, *Allgemeines Gelehrten-Lexikon*, s. v. (B. P.)

Herrick, Marcus A, D.D., a Protestant Episcopal clergyman, was rector of the Church in Woodstock, Vt., in 1853, and so remained until 1861, when he became rector of Trinity Church, Sanbornton Bridge, N. H. In 1870 he was rector of Trinity Church, in Tilton, and continued to hold this pastorate until his death, Oct. 31, 1875, at the age of fifty-five years. See *Prot. Episc. Almanac*, 1876, p. 150.

Herrick, Robert, an English divine and eminent poet, was born in London, Aug. 20, 1591, graduated at Cambridge in 1617, and was presented to the living of Dean Prior, Devonshire, in 1629. In 1648 he was deprived by Cromwell, but was reinstated in his living by

Charles II, in 1660. He died in October, 1674. His works are, *Hesperides; or, The Works, both Humane and Divine, of Robert Herrick* (1648). To this volume was appended his *Noble Numbers* (1647). See Chalmers, *Biog. Dict.* s. v.; Allibone, *Dict. of Brit. and Amer. Authors*, s. v.

Herrmann, Christian Gotthilf Martin, a Lutheran theologian of Germany, was born at Erfurt, Feb. 8, 1765. He studied at his native city and Göttingen, was in 1789 catechist, in 1790 professor, and accepted a call in 1803 as general superintendent and member of consistory to Heiligenstadt, in Prussia. In 1816 he went back to Erfurt, was in 1817 senior of the ministry and superintendent of the Erfurt diocese, and died Aug. 26, 1823. His publications are few and of little value. See Döring, *Die gelehrten Theologen Deutschlands;* Winer, *Handbuch der theol. Lit.* ii, 236. (B. P.)

Hertenstein, Johann Friedrich, a Lutheran theologian of Germany, was born at Ulm, Aug. 11, 1676. He studied at different universities, was in 1705 teacher at his native place, in 1728 preacher at Münster, and died May 25, 1748. He is the author of, *Disp. de Juramentis:—De Cultu Divino Naturali:—De Magno Pisce, qui Jonam Vatem Deglutivit:—De Natura Theologiæ Naturalis: — De Studio Sapientiæ Veterum*, etc. See Neubauer, *Jetztlebende Theologen;* Fürst, *Bibl. Jud.* i, 387; Jöcher, *Allgemeines Gelehrten-Lexikon*, s. v. (B. P.)

Hertfelder (*von Hettingen*), Bernhard, abbot at Augsburg, was born in 1587. He studied at Rome, was prior at Salzburg, and in 1635 abbot at Augsburg. He died in 1664, leaving, *Basilica SS. Udalrici et Afræ* (Augsburg, 1653 fol.):—*Chronicon Templi et SS. Udalrici et Afræ* (eod.):—*Historia Sacrarum Reliquiarum in Basilica Udalricana* (eod., Germ. transl. by Kistler, 1712 fol.):—*Scala Cœli Meditationibus Piis et Utilibus Instructa* (1655). See *Historia Universalis Salisburgensis*, p. 255; Ziegelbauer, *Hist. Litter. Ordinis Benedictini;* Winer, *Handbuch der theol. Lit.* i, 786; Jöcher, *Allgemeines Gelehrten-Lexikon*, s. v. (B. P.)

Hertford, Council of (*Concilium Hertfordiense*, or *Herutfordiæ*), was held at Hertford, the principal borough of Herts, England, Sept. 24, 673, by Theodore, archbishop of Canterbury; the bishops of East Anglia (Bise), Rochester (Putta), Wessex (Lutherius), Mercia (Winfred), together with the deputies of Wilfred of Northumbria, and several canonists, being present. Ten canons were drawn up.

1. Commands the observance of Easter day on the Sunday after the fourteenth day of the moon in the first Jewish month.
2. Commands that no bishop shall intrude upon the parish (parochiam) of another bishop, but shall rest contented with the government of the people intrusted to him.
3. Enacts that it shall not be lawful for any bishop in any way to disturb or plunder any monastery.
4. Forbids monks to emigrate from one monastery to another without the permission of the abbot.
5. Forbids clerks to leave their own bishop and to wander about; forbids to receive them anywhere except they shall bring letters commendatory from their bishop.
6. Bishops and other clergy coming from another church to be contented with the hospitality shown to them, and not presume to perform any office in the church without the permission of the bishop of that church.
7. Orders the holding of synods twice in every year; and adds, that since many things may operate to hinder this, one shall at any rate be called every year, on the kalends of August, in the place called Cloveshooh (or Cliffshoe).
8. Orders that bishops shall take precedence according to the date and order of their consecration.
9. Declares that the question was raised, whether the number of bishops ought to be increased in proportion to the increase of the faithful, but that nothing was determined.
10. Relates to marriages: forbids all unlawful marriages; forbids incest, and to divorce a wife except for fornication; forbids a man divorced from his wife to marry another woman.

See Johnson, *Eccles. Canons*, A. D. 673; *Baronius*, A. D. 672; Labbe, *Concil.* vi, 535; Wilkins, *Concil.* i, 43.

Hertz, Jens-Michael, a Danish poet and preacher, was born July 26, 1766, at Oersloev, near Vordingborg. He was appointed bishop of Ribe in 1819, after having passed through all the decrees of the Church hierarchy. He died June 2, 1825, leaving, *Det Befriede Jerach* (in 18 cantos, Copenhagen, 1804):—*De Julio Firmico Materno* (ibid. 1817):—*Prædikener* (ibid. 1830):—*Sind in den Büchern der Könige Spuren des Pentateuch und der Mosaischen Gesetze zu finden?* (Altona, 1822):—also *Memoirs* in the *Videnskabelige Parhandlinger ved Sjællands Stifts Landemode*, I, i-iii. See Hoefer, *Nouv. Biog. Générale*, s. v.

Hervæus (or *Huvarnus*) of Brittany, an abbot of the 6th century, was the son of Huvarnion, a pious and accomplished Gallic noble, was born blind, and educated by his widowed mother for the monastic life. He built a monastery upon some land given him by Clovigonus, in the town of Laungredec, where he presided till extreme old age. He is commemorated as a saint on June 17.

Hervæus of Maine entered, about the year 1100, the Benedictine monastery at Bourg-Dieu, in Berry, and spent there about fifty years. He devoted himself entirely to the study of the Bible and fathers of the Church, and wrote commentaries, of which those on Isaiah and the Epistles of Paul have been printed (the former in 1721 and the latter in 1544, among the works of Anselm). Both are found in Migne, *Patr. Lat.* vol. 181. Hervæus belongs to those pious theologians of the early period of the Middle Ages, in whom Christianity had become a living reality, but who, fettered by the traditions of the Church, could not rid himself of the latter. See Chemnitz, *Examen Conc. Trid., de Justificatione*, art. 7, § 2; *Loci Theologici, de Justificatione*, cap. I, § 4; Frank, *Die Theologie der Konkordienformel*, ii, 54 sq.; Plitt-Herzog, *Real-Encyklop.* s. v. (B. P.)

Hervæus of Rheims was raised to that archbishopric in the year 900, and showed great energy and fidelity in its administration. He became chancellor of France in 910, and died July 2, 922. See Hoefer, *Nouv. Biog. Générale*, s. v.

Hervetus, Gentianus, a French theologian, was born in 1499 at Olivet, near Orleans. In word and writing he combated Calvinism; was present at the colloquy of Poissy and at the council of Trent. In 1562 he was made canon of Rheims, and died in 1584. Besides a great many translations, he published of his own, *Oratio ad Concilium Tridentinum* (Paris, 1556, 1563):—*Catéchisme ou Sommaire de la Foi* (1561):—*Traité du Purgatoire* (1562):—*Les Ruses et Finesses du Diable pour Tâcher à Abolir le Saint Sacrifice de Jésus-Christ* (1562). See Winer, *Handbuch der theol. Lit.* i, 888; Jöcher, *Allgemeines Gelehrten-Lexikon*, s. v.; Lichtenberger, *Encyclop. des Sciences Religieuses*, s. v. (B. P.)

Hervey, Frederick, D.D., an English prelate, fourth earl of Bristol, was born in 1730, and educated at Westminster School and Corpus Christi College, Cambridge. He was originally designed for the bar, but entered into holy orders, was promoted to the see of Cloyne in February, 1767, and translated to that of Derry in 1768. He expended most of his patrimony in liberality, and travelled extensively over Europe. He died July 8, 1803.

Herxheimer, Salomon, a Jewish rabbi, was born in 1801. He studied at Marburg, and was in 1831 elected land-rabbi of Bernburg, and died Dec. 25, 1884. He published, יסודי התורה, *Israelitische Glaubens- und Pflichtenlehre* (Minden, 1831; 27th ed. 1877):—*Praktische Anleitung zum schnellen Erlernen des Hebräischen* (Berlin, 1834; 6th ed. 1873):—תורת משה, *Der Pentateuch*, etc. (1841; 3d ed. 1865):—נביאים וכתובים, *Die Propheten und Hagiographen*, besides a number of *Sermons*. See Fürst, *Bibl. Jud.* i, 387; Kayserling, *Bibliothek Jüdischer Kanzelredner*, ii, 1 sq. (B. P.)

Herzfeld, LEVI, a Jewish writer of Germany, was born in 1810 at Ellrich, Saxony. He studied at Berlin, took the degree as doctor of philosophy in 1836, was appointed land-rabbi of Brunswick in 1842, and died in 1884. He published, *Chronologia Judicum et Primorum Regum Hebræorum* (Berlin, 1836):—קהלת, *Das Buch Koheleth* (Brunswick, 1838):—*Geschichte des Volkes Israel* (1847; 2d ed. 1863):—*Meteorologische Untersuchungen*, etc. (1863-65):—*Handelsgeschichte der Juden des Alterthums* (1879):—*Predigten* (1858; 2d ed. 1863), etc. See Fürst, *Bibl. Jud.* i, 388; Zuchold, *Bibl. Theol.* i, 547; Kayserling, *Bibl. Jüdischer Kanzelredner*, ii, 206 sq.; Morais, *Eminent Israelites of the XIXth Century*, p. 133 sq. (B. P.)

Herzlieb, CHRISTIAN FRIEDRICH CARL, a Lutheran theologian of Germany, was born Dec. 4, 1760. He studied at Halle, was in 1780 professor at the gymnasium there, in 1786 preacher at Brandenburg, and died March 19, 1794. He left several volumes of *Sermons*. See Döring, *Die gelehrten Theologen Deutschlands;* Winer, *Handbuch der theol. Lit.* ii, 137, 141, 168, 192. (B. P.)

Herzog, Eduard, a Roman Catholic theologian of Germany, was born in 1801 at Frankenstein, Silesia. In 1826 he took holy orders, and died April 17, 1867. He published, *Kanzelvorträge* (Glogau, 1855, 2 vols.):—*Der katholische Seelsorger nach seinen Amtsverpflichtungen und Amtsverrichtungen* (Breslau, 1839, 3 vols.):—*Die Verwaltung des heiligen Busssakraments* (Paderborn, 1859). (B. P.)

Herzog, Johann Jacob, D.D., a Protestant theologian of Germany, was born at Basle, Sept. 12, 1805. He entered the university of his native town in 1822, and afterwards studied at Berlin. From 1835 till 1846 he held a professorship of historical theology in the Academy of Lausanne, and was involved with his colleagues, the distinguished Vinet and Chappuis, in the struggles which resulted in the formation of the Free Church of the Canton de Vaud. Here, at Basle, he published his *Life of the Basle Reformer, Œkolampadius* (1843, 2 vols.). In 1847 Herzog was invited to fill a chair at the University of Halle, where, in 1848, he published in the university programme, *De Origine et Pristino Statu Waldensium.* In 1851 he received a commission from the Prussian government to visit Geneva, Paris, London, and Dublin, in order to investigate the sources for the history of the Waldenses. The result of this mission was his work, *Die romanischen Waldenser*, etc. (1853). At this time, also, he conceived the plan of his *Real-Encyklopædie für protestantische Theologie und Kirche*, which was published in 22 vols. from 1854 to 1868. After beginning this work he had left Halle for Erlangen, to succeed Dr. Ebrard as professor of reformed theology. In 1877 he retired from active academical duties. The last years of his life were occupied with his *Abriss der gesammten Kirchengeschichte* (1876-82, 3 vols.), and with the preparation of a second edition of his *Real-Encyklopædie*, which at the time of his death had reached the tenth volume, or the second third of the entire work. He died at Erlangen, Sept. 30, 1882. Besides the works already mentioned, he also published, *Les Frères de Plymouth et John Darby* (Lausanne, 1845):—*Bemerkungen über Zwingli's Lehre von der Vorsehung und Gnadenwahl* (in the *Studien und Kritiken*, 1839):—and a biographical sketch, *Johann Calvin* (Basle, 1843). (B. P.)

Heshbon. The following is the latest description of this once famous place (Tristram, *Land of Moab*, p. 351):

"A large piece of walling at the west end of the bold, isolated hill on which the old fortress stood, with a square block-house, and a pointed archway adjoining—a temple on the crest of the hill, with the pavement and the bases of four columns *in situ*—on the east, in the plain, just at the base of the hill, a great cistern, called by some the 'fish-pools of Heshbon,' but more probably only the reservoir for the supply of the city—these are all that remain."

General View of the Ruins of Heshbon from the North-west, with Jebel Neba in the Distance. (From a Photograph by the Editor.)

Heshmon is thought by Lieut. Conder (*Quar. Statement* of the "Pal. Explor. Fund." Jan. 1875, p. 25 sq.) to be *el-Meshash*, at the foot of the white chalk peaks of el-Ghur, three miles west of Tell-Milh, in the vicinity of Beersheba; and Tristram (*Bible Places*, p. 20) accepts the identification; but it rests merely upon a presumed order of the names.

Hesperĭdes, in Greek mythology, were daughters of Atlas and Hesperis, and are mentioned as being from three to seven in number. When Juno married Jupiter, all the gods brought presents. Earth brought forth a tree, on which grew golden apples. Juno commanded the sisters, Hesperides, to guard them. But the latter helped themselves to the apples. She therefore sent a son of Typhon and Echidna, the frightful, never-sleeping, hundred-headed dragon Ladon, to the tree, who scared everything away that approached. Hercules was sent there to get three apples out of the garden for Eurystheus. According to Diodorus, the Hesperides were daughters of Atlas, seized by Busiris, and liberated by Hercules, wherefore the latter received the desired Mela (apples) from their father voluntarily.

Hess, Carl Ernest Christoph, an eminent German engraver, was born at Darmstädt in 1755. In 1776 he settled at Augsburg, and executed several fine plates, which gained him admission to the Academy in 1780. In 1782 the elector palatine appointed him engraver to the court, and in 1787 he visited Italy for improvement. On his return to Germany he remained some time at Munich, and afterwards practiced the art with great success at Düsseldorf until 1794, when he returned to Munich. Among his esteemed productions are *The Ascension; The Holy Family; St. Jerome.* He died in 1828.

Hess, Isaac, a Jewish rabbi of Germany, father of

Mendel and Michael, was born Feb. 12, 1762, and died Aug. 9, 1827. He edited the work of his father Joseph, rabbi at Cassel, entitled בן פורת יוסף, a commentary on the Haphtaroth, homiletically arranged (Fürth, 1796), and wrote *Ueber den Eid der Juden*, etc. (Eisenach, 1824). See Fürst, *Bibl. Jud.* i, 390. (B. P.)

Hess, Mendel, a Jewish rabbi of Germany, was born March 17, 1807. He studied at Würzburg, and succeeded his father in 1827 in the rabbinate. In 1842 he settled at Eisenach, as land rabbi, but retired from his office on account of bodily infirmities, and died Sept. 21, 1872. From 1839 to 1848 he edited *Der Israelit des* 19. *Jahrhunderts*, in which he advocated reform among the Jews. He also published, *Predigten* (Eisenach, 1839-48, 3 vols.):—*Ausgewählte Predigten* (1871). See Fürst, *Bibl. Jud.* i, 390; Kayserling, *Bibliothek jüd. Kanzelredner*, ii, 153 sq. (B. P.)

Hess, Michael, a Jewish rabbi, brother of Mendel, was born April 9, 1782. He studied at Fürth and Frankfort, and was professor of the Jewish high-school at the latter place from 1806 to 1855. Hess died Feb. 26, 1860. Like his brother, he belonged to the reform party among the Jews. He published, *Freimüthige Prüfung der Schrift des Herrn Rühs über die Ansprüche der Juden an das deutsche Bürgerrecht* (Frankfort, 1816):—*Programm über den Religionsunterricht in der Schule der israelit. Gemeinde* (1821). See Fürst, *Bibl. Jud.* i, 390; Kayserling, *Bibliothek jüd. Kanzelredner*, i, 383 sq.; Stern, *Michael Hess, ein Lebensbild*, in Diesterweg's *Pädagog. Jahrbuch*, 1862, p. 1-38. (B. P.)

Hess, Salomon, a Reformed minister of Switzerland, was born at Zurich in 1763. In 1801 he was first preacher at St. Peter's, in his native place, but resigned his office in 1830, and died in 1837. He published, *Erasmus von Rotterdam nach seinem Leben und Schriften* (Zurich, 1790-92):—*Ursprung, Gang und Folgen der durch Zwingli in Zürich bewirkten Reformation* (1819):—*Anna Reinhard, Gattin und Wittwe von Ulrich Zwingli* (1819):—*Biographien berühmter Schweizer Reformatoren;* vol. i, *Lebensgeschichte des Œcolampadius* (1793); vols. ii, iii, *Lebensgeschichte des H. Bullinger* (1828-29):—*Andachten und Gebetsübung für die christliche Jugend* (1820). See Winer, *Handbuch der theol. Lit.* i, 579, 740, 748, 749; ii, 372. (B. P.)

Hesse, Johann Heinrich Gottlieb, a Lutheran theologian of Germany, was born Nov. 21, 1779. He studied at Leipsic, was preacher there in 1803, and died June 29, 1823. His best work is *Katechisationen über sittlich-religiöse Wahrheiten* (Leipsic, 1820). See Döring, *Die gelehrten Theologen Deutschlands*, s. v.; Winer, *Handbuch der theol. Lit.* ii, 269. (B. P.)

Hesse, Karl Friedrich, a Lutheran theologian of Germany, was born Nov. 5, 1706. He studied at Wittenberg, was in 1735 preacher at Dresden, in 1747 at Stolpen, in 1760 at Meissen, and died March 22, 1775. He published *Theologische Annalen für* 1731-1750 (Leipsic, 1754). See Döring, *Die gelehrten Theologen Deutschlands*, s. v.; Jöcher, *Allgemeines Gelehrten-Lexikon*, s. v. (B. P.)

Hesse, Nicolas August, a French painter, was born in Paris, Aug. 28, 1795. He studied under baron Gros at Paris, and then went to Rome, where he gained the grand prize in 1868. He acquired celebrity by his religious paintings, which may be found in various churches. He succeeded Delacroix in the Academy of Fine Arts in 1863, and died June 14, 1869.

Hessels, Jean, a Belgian controversialist, was born at Mechlin in 1522. In 1556 he was made doctor of theology at Louvain, in 1560 professor of theology, and died Nov. 7, 1566. He is the author of, *Comment. in Matthæum:*—*Comm. in Epistolas Canonicas Johannis:*—*Comm. in Priorem ad Timotheum et in Priorem Petri:*—*Explicatio in Symbolum Apostolorum:*—*Explicatio Decalogi.* See Andreas, *Bibliotheca Belgica;* Miræus, *Elogia Illustrium Belgii Scriptorum;* Jöcher, *Allgemeines Gelehrten-Lexikon*, s. v.; Hoefer, *Nouv. Biog. Générale*, s. v. (B. P.)

Hessus, Helius Eobanus, one of the most excellent Latin poets of Germany during the 16th century, was born Jan. 6, 1488, at Halgehausen, Hesse. He studied at Erfurt, was rector there in 1509, but left that place on account of the then existing troubles. In 1514 he was again at Erfurt, and in 1516 he was professor at the university. In 1526 he was called to Nuremberg, but returned to Erfurt in 1533, and accepted a call to Marburg in 1536. Hessus died Oct. 4, 1540. He deserves a place here on account of his zeal for the Reformation. He made a metrical version of the Psalms, whence Luther called him the *rex poetarum.* See Schwertzell, *Helius Eobanus Hessus, ein Lebensbild aus der Reformationszeit* (Halle, 1874); Krause, *Helius Eobanus Hessus, sein Leben und seine Werke* (Gotha, 1879). (B. P.)

Hesus, in Gallic and German mythology, was the god of war. His image had the form of a dog. The first prisoner of war was sacrificed to him. If a forest was to be dedicated, the sturdiest oak-tree was selected, and the name Hesus was cut into it.

Hesychius. (1) Bishop of Spolato, in Dalmatia, A.D. 405-429, wrote a letter of thanks to Chrysostom for his sympathy with the Eastern Church (in the works of the latter, *Ep.* 183). (2) Bishop of Castabala, in Cilicia Secunda, censured by the Council of Ephesus, A.D. 431, for opposition to Cyril. (3) Patriarch of Jerusalem, A.D. 600. (4) A noted disciple of Hilarion, and a monk of Cyprus in the middle of the 4th century, commemorated Oct. 3.

Heunisch, Caspar, a Lutheran theologian of Germany, was born at Schweinfurt. He studied at Jena, and died Oct. 18, 1690, a superintendent. He wrote, *Clavis Apocalyptica et Ezechielica* (Rothenburg, 1684):—*In Canticum Canticorum Commentarius Apocalypticus* (Leipsic, 1688). See Fürst, *Bibl. Jud.* i, 391; Jöcher, *Allgemeines Gelehrten-Lexikon*, s. v. (B. P.)

Heusde, Philip Wilhelm van, a Dutch historian and philosopher, was born June 17, 1778, at Rotterdam. He studied at Amsterdam and Leyden, was in 1804 professor at Utrecht, and died at Berne, July 28, 1839. He wrote, *Initia Philosophiæ Platonicæ* (Utrecht, 1827-36, 3 vols.; 2d ed. Leyden, 1842):—*Brieven over den Aard en de Strekking van Hooger Onderwijs* (ibid. 1829; 3d ed. 1835; Germ. transl. by Weydmann, Krefeld, 1830):—*De Socratische School* (ibid. 1834-39, 4 vols.; 2d ed. 1840-41):—*Brieven over het Beæfenen der Wijsgeerte* (1837):—*Characterismi Principum Philosophorum Veterum* (1839). After his death was published *De School van Polybius* (Amsterdam, 1841). See Rovers, *Memoria P. Heusdii Commendata* (Utrecht, 1841). (B. P.)

Heusden, Hugo Franciscus van, a Roman Catholic theologian, and vicar to the archbishop of Utrecht, died Feb. 13, 1719, leaving, *Batavia Sacra* (Brussels, 1724):—*Historia Episcopatuum Fœderati Belgii* (Lyons, 1719). See Winer, *Handbuch der theol. Lit.* i, 823 sq.; Jöcher, *Allgemeines Gelehrten-Lexikon*, s. v. (B. P.)

Heusinger, Jacob Friedrich, a Lutheran theologian of Germany, was born in 1719. He studied at Jena, was in 1750 con-rector, in 1759 rector at Wolfenbüttel, and died Sept. 27, 1778. He wrote, *Disp. de Locis Matth. xvi*, 13, 20; *Luc. vii*, 14; *Jac. ii*, 18 (Jena, 1746):—*De iv Evangeliorum Codice Græco in Biblioth. Guelferbyt.* (Wolfenbüttel, 1752). See Winer, *Handbuch der theol. Lit.* i, 101; Meusel, *Gelehrtes Deutschland;* Jöcher, *Allgemeines Gelehrten-Lexikon*, s. v. (B. P.)

Heusinger, Johann Michael, a celebrated German divine, was born in September, 1690, at Sunderhausen, in Thuringia, and was educated at Gotha, at Halle, and at Jena. He was appointed a professor at Gotha in 1730, and remained there until 1738. He died in March, 1751, leaving many historical works. See Chalmers, *Biog. Dict.* s. v.

Heusser, Meta, the best female song-writer and hymnist in the German language, was born April 6, 1797, at Hirzel, canton Zurich, where her father, Diethelm Schweizer, was pastor. In 1821 she married Dr. Heusser, an eminent physician, who died in 1859, and she herself died Jan. 2, 1876. Some of her poems appeared for the first time under the name of *Einer Verborgenen* (a hidden one). In 1857 the first volume of her poems was published, and in 1867 a second followed. In the English some of her songs are found in a little volume entitled *Hymns from the Land of Luther*, and also in Schaff's *Christ in Song*. A selection of her poems was published at London in 1875, under the title, *Alpine Lyrics*. See Koch, *Geschichte des deutschen Kirchenliedes*, vii, 377 sq. (B. P.)

Hewytt, John, D.D., an English clergyman, was minister of St. Gregory's, near St. Paul's, London. He was beheaded on Tower Hill in 1658, for a political conspiracy. He published nine select *Sermons* (1658): *Repentance and Conversion the Fabrick of Salvation*, etc., being several sermons (eod.). See Allibone, *Dict. of Brit. and Amer. Authors*, s. v.

Hexapla, an edition of the Bible prepared by Origen (q. v.).

Hey, Wilhelm, a Protestant theologian of Germany, was born March 26, 1790. He studied at Jena, was court-preacher at Gotha, and died May 19, 1854. He published, *Predigten* (Hamburg, 1830, 1832):—*Erzählungen aus dem Leben Jesu für die Jugend dichterisch bearbeitet* (1838). See Zuchold, *Bibl. Theol.* i, 552; Winer, *Handbuch der theol. Lit.* ii, 103. (B. P.)

Heyd, Ludwig Ferdinand, a Protestant theologian of Germany, who died March 6, 1842, is the author of, *Melanchthon und Tübingen* 1512–1518 (Tübingen, 1839): —*Ulrich, Herzog zu Würtemberg* (1841–44, 3 vols.). See Zuchold, *Bibl. Theol.* i, 552. (B. P.)

Heyde, Johann Daniel, a Lutheran theologian of Germany, was born April 27, 1714. He studied at Leipsic, was teacher at Gera in 1737, and died Aug. 12, 1785. His publications are sermons, partly his own, partly translations from the French of Massillon and Bourdaloue. See Döring, *Die gelehrten Theologen Deutschlands*, s. v.; Winer, *Handbuch der theol. Lit.* i, 383; Jöcher, *Allgemeines Gelehrten-Lexikon*, s. v. (B. P.)

Heym, Albert, a Protestant theologian of Germany, was born in 1801. He studied at Leipsic and Berlin, was tutor of prince Frederick Carl from 1830 to 1844, and preacher at Sakrow from 1844 to 1848. In the latter year he was appointed court-preacher at Potsdam, and he died Dec. 9, 1878. (B. P.)

Heym, Johann Gottlob, a Lutheran theologian of Germany, was born Feb. 25, 1738. He studied at Wittenberg, and died at Dolzig, in Lower Lusatia, Jan. 24, 1788. His publications are several volumes of sermons. See Döring, *Die gelehrten Theologen Deutschlands;* Winer, *Handbuch der theol. Lit.* ii, 192, 381; Zuchold, *Bibl. Theol.* i, 553. (B. P.)

Heyne, Johann, a Roman Catholic theologian of Germany, was born in 1804 at Leobschutz, Silesia. He took holy orders in 1827, acted as priest at different places till 1857, when at his own request he was made custos of the cathedral-library at Breslau, with a view of perusing the archives there. He died Oct. 28, 1871. Heyne is the author of *Dokumentirte Geschichte des Bisthums und Hochstiftes Breslau* (Breslau, 1860–68, 3 vols.). (B. P.)

Heynlin de Lapide, Johannes, one of the last eminent representatives of scholasticism, was a native of Germany. He studied at Leipsic, Basle, and Paris, and in the latter place became a doctor of the Sorbonne. In 1473 he settled at Basle, and, as a decided realist, caused, first at Basle, afterwards at Tübingen, whither he moved in 1477, so violent a contest between realism and nominalism that he finally determined to retire altogether from public life, in 1487. He spent the remainder of his life in a Carthusian monastery in Basle, and died in 1496. Heynlin wrote a commentary on Aristotle while at Paris, but it was not published until many years later, by his pupil Amerbach. He also directed the editing of the works of St. Ambrose, which were published by Amerbach in 1492. See Trithemius, *Liber de Scriptoribus Ecclesiasticis* (1494); Fischer, *Johannes Heynlin, genannt a Lapide* (Basle, 1851); Vischer, *Gesch. der Universität Basel*, p. 158 sq.; Plitt-Herzog, *Real-Encyklop.* s. v. (B. P.)

Hi, the second member of a mystic triad composed by Lao-Tseu, the celebrated Chinese philosopher. It is described as follows: "That which you look at and do not see is called *I;* that which you hearken after and do not hear is called *Hi;* that which your hand reaches after and cannot grasp is called *Wei.* These are three beings which cannot be comprehended, and which together make but one."

Hiadi, in Hindû mythology, is the collective name of the three highest castes of the Hindûs—the Brahmins, Kshetrias, and Banians—priests, warriors, and business men.

Hiadninger, in Norse mythology, are the warriors who fall in a battle, incited by the beautiful shield-maiden, Hildur. They fight until the destruction of the world.

Hicĕtæ (Ἱκέται), a sect of orthodox ascetics about the time of the emperor Marcian, who lived in monasteries, and spent their time in singing hymns, accompanied with religious dances.

Hickman, Charles, D.D., an English clergyman, was a native of Northamptonshire, and was a student of Christchurch College, Oxford, in 1667. He was minister of St. Ebbe's Church, Oxford, and lecturer of St. James's, Westminster, in 1692; subsequently rector of Hogsnorton, Leicestershire, and finally bishop of Derry in 1702. He died in 1713, leaving some *Sermons* (1680–1713). See Allibone, *Dict. of Brit. and Amer. Authors*, s. v.

Hickman, Henry, an English Nonconformist divine, was a native of Worcestershire, and educated at Cambridge. He was a fellow of Magdalen College, Oxford, was deprived at the Restoration, and became preacher to the English congregation at Leyden, where he died in 1692. He published several controversial theological treatises (1659–74), the best of which appeared without his name—*Apologia pro Ministris in Anglia (vulgo) Non-conformistis*, etc. (1664). See Chalmers, *Biog. Dict.* s. v.; Allibone, *Dict. of Brit. and Amer. Authors*, s. v.

Hickok, Milo Judson, D.D., a Presbyterian minister, was born at New Haven, Vt., Aug. 22, 1809. He graduated from Middlebury College in 1835; was professor in Delaware College three years; graduated from Union Theological Seminary, N. Y., in 1841; became a tutor in Middlebury College; and was ordained a Congregational minister, May 4, 1842. He became professor in Marietta College, O., and pastor of the Church in Harmar; two years thereafter he accepted a call as stated supply to the Presbyterian Church of Utica, N. Y., and in 1845 was installed pastor of a Church in Rochester. In 1854 he was stated supply of a Presbyterian Church in Montreal, Canada; the next year he was installed pastor of the Church in Scranton, Pa., where he remained until 1868. His health failing, he removed to Marietta, O., where he died, July 19, 1873. See *Gen. Cat. of Union Theol. Sem.* 1876, p. 19. (W. P. S.)

Hidalgo, Michael y Costillas, called the "Washington of the Mexican Revolution," was parish priest at Dolores, department of Guanajuato, Mexico. He appealed to his parishioners, raised the standard of Mexican freedom, headed the dissentients, and was proclaimed generalissimo, Sept. 17, 1810. He was joined by adherents from every side, and in six weeks was marching on Mexico city at the head of eighty thousand men. Five provinces recognised his authority.

Hidalgo, however, unfortunately halted in his advance on the capital, the royalists had time to rally, and he was utterly defeated at Puente de Calderon, Jan. 17, 1811, and after in vain endeavoring to rally the national army, was captured by treachery while endeavoring to escape to the United States. He was executed ten days afterwards. On his death, Morelos, another priest, assumed the command; a congress of forty members was called, but after the defeat and execution of Morelos, it was dissolved by general Teran, who succeeded him. The revolt was entirely quelled in 1819. Mexico gained its independence in 1822, which, amid anarchy and continual turmoil, it has retained until the present, barring the French occupation of 1862 to 1867. To-day the grateful republic of Mexico repeats in her decorations and uses on her postage-stamp the mild features of her illustrious son, the priest-patriot, Michael Hidalgo y Costillas. See (N. Y.) *Cath. Almanac*, 1876, p. 105.

Hieracites, a heretical sect which sprang up at the end of the 3d or beginning of the 4th century, founded by Hieracas or Hierax (q. v.).

Hieratic Writing, a species of sacred writing used by the ancient Egyptian priests, especially the Hierogrammatists (q. v.). It is found chiefly on the *papyri*, and is an abbreviated form of the hieroglyphic (q. v.). The matter of these manuscripts consists almost entirely of texts in reference to purely religious or scientific description, and of religious inscriptions.

Hierodiacŏni (from ἱερός, *sacred*, and διάκονος, *a deacon*), monks of the Russo-Greek Church (q. v.), who are also deacons.

Hierodūli, in Greek cultus, were persons employed in the service of a temple, especially in Syria, Phœnicia, and Asia Minor. They were females, living near temples, who hired themselves out to strangers. They were obliged to care for the decorations of the temple, knitting and cleansing the veils, wreathing the altars, etc. The priests had no other income than the presents which pilgrims to the sanctuary brought, and in order to draw as many of them as possible, the surroundings of the temple were occupied by numbers of priestesses, who gave the presents they received to the temple, as is still the case in India with the Dewadashies (Bajaderes). In Cappadocia, in the temple-woods of the Comanian goddess, Strabo met over six thousand. This custom came to Greece and Sicily, especially in connection with the worship of Venus, and many a beautiful temple was built with the money thus obtained. See DIANA; VENUS.

Hierogrammatists (from ἱερός, *sacred*, and γραμματεύς, *a scribe*), the sacred scribes among the ancient Egyptians. They employed the *hieratic writing* (q. v.), in transcribing religious writings on *papyri*, and in giving an account of religious rites and ceremonies. It was their duty also to expound the sacred mysteries as far as they were allowed to be made known to the people. They carried a wand, and were dressed in linen garments. See SCRIBE.

Hieromancy (from ἱερός, *sacred*, and μαντεία, *divination*), a species of divination among the ancient Greeks and Romans, which consisted in predicting future events by observing the various appearances which presented themselves in the act of offering sacrifices. See DIVINATION.

Hieromonăchi (from ἱερός, *sacred*, and μοναχός, *a monk*), monks of the Russo-Greek Church (q. v.), who are priests. They are considered sacred monks, and never officiate except on solemn festival occasions.

Hieronymi, WILHELM, a preacher of the German Catholics, was originally a Protestant, but joined the movement of the German Catholics in 1845, and died at Mayence, Sept. 14, 1884. He published, *Kein Papstthum! Kein Symbolzwang* (Magdeburg, 1845):—*Die Hegelianer als Lichtfreunde* (Darmstadt, 1846):—*Zeugnisse deutsch-katholischen Geistes* (1847):—*Freiheit oder Autorität*, written against bishop Ketteler (1862). See Zuchold, *Bibl. Theol.* i, 554 sq. (B. P.)

Hieronymus A SANCTA FIDE (originally *Joshua Lorki*) was a famous Talmudist and physician. When rabbi Salomon, afterwards bishop Paulus Burgensis (q. v.), had embraced and was preaching the Christian faith in Spain, Joshua Lorki wrote against him. But soon this zealous enemy of the gospel became himself an ardent confessor of the truth, and failed not to declare openly the reason which had given rise to this change in his religious opinions, by publishing two tracts against the Jews, *Probationes Novi Test. ex Vetere Testamento* (reprinted in the *Bibl. Mag. Vet. Patrum*, xxix). At the instigation of Hieronymus, who, after his baptism, entered the service of pope Benedict XIII, being appointed his physician, the famous conference was held at Tortosa (Feb. 7, 1413, to Nov. 12, 1414), under the presidency of the pope. The assembly was convened to discuss sixteen points, which were proposed by Hieronymus. Prominent among the Jewish disputants was Joseph Albo (q. v.). The result of this conference is passed over by Jewish historians with remarkable silence. According to the Christians, all the rabbis present declared themselves vanquished, and signed an act to that effect, with the exception of Albo and rabbi Ferrer. See Fürst, *Bibl. Jud.* i, 392; Kalkar, *Israel und die Kirche*, p. 28 sq.; Da Costa, *Israel and the Gentiles*, p. 328 sq. (B. P.)

Hieropoioi (from ἱερός, *sacred*, and ποιέω, *to make*), persons anciently employed at Athens to superintend the oblations and sacrifices. Ten of these officers were appointed annually, and they wore at their girdles a consecrated axe as an emblem of their office.

Higbert (*Hygbehrt*), 14th bishop of Lichfield, A.D. 779, and the only one entitled archbishop of that see. See Smith, *Dict. of Christ. Biog.* s. v.

Higgins, WILLIAM, D.D., a bishop of the Church of Ireland, was born at Greenfield, Lancaster, England, in 1793, and was educated at the Lancaster and Manchester grammar schools, and at Trinity College, Cambridge, from which he graduated in 1817. His first clerical duty in Ireland was as chaplain to the Richmond Penitentiary, in 1820, subsequently he was chaplain to the Magdalen Asylum, rector of Roscrea in 1828, vicar-general of Killaloe in 1834, dean of Limerick in 1844, bishop of Limerick in 1849, and bishop of Derry in 1853. The same year he was appointed commissioner of national education, and he succeeded bishop Plunket as an ecclesiastical commissioner. He died at Derry, July 12, 1867. See *Amer. Quar. Rev.* Oct. 1867, p. 505.

Higgs, GRIFFIN (or GRIFFITH), D.D., an English clergyman, was born at Stoke Abbot, or South Stoke, near Henley, Oxfordshire, in 1589, and was educated at Reading School and St. John's College, Oxford. In 1627 he was sent to the Hague as chaplain to the queen of Bohemia. On his return he was presented to the living of Cliffe, near Dover, and was also made chanter of St. David's. In 1638 he was made dean of Lichfield. He lost all his preferments when the Church establishment was overthrown. He died Dec. 16, 1659. His published works are, *Problemata Theologica* (1630):—*Miscellaneœ Theses Theologicœ* (eod.).

High Altar is the chief, central, or principal altar of a church. Other altars, in old documents, are often called "low altars," to distinguish them from that which is the chief altar. When there are many chapels in a church, clustering on either side of the chief chapel or chancel, the principal chancel, containing the high altar, is sometimes called the "high chancel." See ALTAR.

Highmore, JOSEPH, an English painter, was born at London in 1692, and was articled to an attorney in 1707, against his inclination. He employed his leisure hours in painting, finally commenced it as a profession, and soon met with employment. Shortly after he was commissioned by the duke of Richmond to do some work. In 1732 he visited the continent for the purpose of seeing the Düsseldorf Gallery, and two years after he went to France in order to examine the galleries there. He executed a series of pictures, which were engraved and published in 1745. Among his sacred subjects were, *The Good Samaritan; The Finding of Moses; Hagar and Ishmael.* He died in 1780. See Spooner, *Biog. Hist. of the Fine Arts*, s. v.; Rose, *Biog. Dict.* s. v.

Hiisi is the name given to the devil among the Finns. He is described as having only three fingers on each hand, but these are armed with large nails, with which he tears in pieces all who fall into his power. He is supposed to reside in the forest, whence he sends out all manner of diseases and calamities, with which he afflicts mankind.

Hildebrand, JOACHIM, a Lutheran theologian of Germany, was born Nov. 10, 1623. He studied at different universities, was in 1652 professor of theology at Helmstadt, in 1662 doctor of theology and general superintendent at Celle, and died Oct. 18, 1691. He wrote, *Diss. de Donatione Constantini Magni* (Helmstadt, 1661):—*Sacra Publica Veteris Ecclesiæ in Compendium Redacta* (1699):—*Exercit. de Veterum Concionibus* (1661):—*Rituale Baptismi Veteris, Publicis Lectionibus Olim Dicatum* (ed. Schmid, 1699):—*Rituale Eucharistiæ Veteris Ecclesiæ* (ed. Schmid, 1712):—*De Nuptiis Veterum Christianorum Libellus* (ed. Schmid, 1714), etc. See Winer, *Handbuch der theol. Lit.* i, 574, 627, 628, 630, 631, 634, 635, 638, 699; Jöcher, *Allgemeines Gelehrten-Lexikon*, s. v.; Just von Einem, *Commentarius de Vita et Scriptis Joach. Hildebrandi* (1743); Fürst, *Bibl. Jud.* i, 393. (B. P.)

Hildrop, JOHN, D.D., an English clergyman, was rector of Wath, near Rippon, Yorkshire. He died in 1756, leaving a number of sermons, theological treatises, etc. (1711-52). His miscellaneous works appeared in 1754. See Allibone, *Dict. of Brit. and Amer. Authors*, s. v.

Hile, (1) an old English word, signifying to put on a roof or cover. In old documents it is sometimes spelled "helye," "hylle," and "hyle;" (2) the covering of a church roof.

Hilgers, BERNHARD JOSEPH, a Roman Catholic divine of Germany, was born in 1803. In 1827 he took holy orders, was pastor at Siegburg in 1828, took the degree as doctor of theology at Münster in 1834, commenced his academical career at Bonn in 1835, and died Feb. 7, 1874. He published, *Ueber das Verhältniss zwischen Leib und Seele im Menschen* (Bonn, 1834):—*Symbolische Theologie* (1841):—*Kritische Darstellung der Häresien*, etc. (1837):—*Homilien* (published after his death, 1874). (B. P.)

Hilgod (or **Hilgot**), a French prelate, was at first canon of St. Genevieve, and afterwards bishop of Soissons in 1085. But grave difficulties arose against his appointment, in consequence of which he resigned about the year 1087, and retired to the monastery of Marmoutier. He died Aug. 4, 1104. See Hoefer, *Nouv. Biog. Générale*, s. v.

Hill, Benjamin M., D.D., a Baptist minister, was born at Newport, R. I., April 5, 1793. He entered the preparatory department of Pennsylvania University, but was soon called to New Orleans as a clerk; and subsequently studied medicine for a time in Philadelphia. He was converted in 1812; licensed in February, 1815; for two years preached in Leicester and Spencer, Mass.; in 1818 was ordained in Stafford, Conn., where he remained three years, and was then called to the pastorate of the First Church in New Haven, where he continued from 1821 to 1829. The next ten years of his ministry were with the First Church in Troy, N. Y. In 1840 he became corresponding secretary of the American Baptist Home Mission Society, which position he held for twenty-two years. He died in New Haven, Jan. 15, 1881. See *Christian Secretary*, Jan. 19, 1881. (J. C. S.)

Hill, Charles, D.D., a Baptist minister, was born in Kings County, Ireland, Jan. 6, 1800. In 1822 he became a student in Horton College, completing the course in two years, and then became pastor of the Church at Middleton. In 1834 he was appointed secretary of the Home Mission Society; in 1842 he became pastor of the Heneage Street Church, Birmingham, where he remained until 1851, when he removed to the United States; was pastor in Belvidere, Ill.; chaplain, for a time, in the Federal army; connected for a short period with the University of Chicago, and finally took up his residence in Belvidere, where he died in 1872. See (Lond.) *Baptist Hand-book*, 1873, p. 273. (J. C. S.)

Hill, William, D.D., an English divine, was born at Cudworth, in Warwickshire, in 1619, and educated at Merton College, Oxford. He died in 1677. He published, *Dionysii Orbis Descriptio* (1658, 1659, 1663, 1678, 1688):—*Woman's Looking-glass* (1660). See Chalmers, *Biog. Dict.* s. v.; Allibone, *Dict. of Brit. and Amer. Authors*, s. v.

Hill, William Wallace, D.D., a Presbyterian minister, was born in Bath County, Ky, Jan. 26, 1815. He prepared for college at Mt. Sterling and Paris; graduated from Centre College in 1835; entered Princeton Theological Seminary the same year, and remained two years. He was licensed by the Presbytery of New Brunswick, April 24, 1838, ordained by the Presbytery of Louisville, Oct. 3 following, and installed pastor at Shelbyville, where he served four years. He then took charge of *The Protestant Herald*, published at Bardstown, but removed it to Frankfort, as a more central place of publication. In November, 1844, he again removed with his paper to Louisville, and its name was changed to *The Presbyterian Herald*. As a religious newspaper it had few equals in the land. Its publication ceased in 1862, on account of the war. From 1845 to 1860 he was also corresponding secretary of the Western Executive Committee of the Board of Domestic Missions. He then founded Bellewood Female Seminary, near Louisville, and was its principal from 1862 to 1874. During these years he also preached more or less regularly at Plumb Creek, Middletown, and Anchorage. In 1874 he accepted the charge of the Synodical Female College at Fulton, Mo., and supplied the Presbyterian Church of that place. He left Fulton in 1877, and went to Sherman, Texas, where he commenced teaching in Austin College, preaching for the Church there at the same time. He died May 1, 1878. See *Necrol. Report of Princeton Theol. Sem.* 1879, p. 39.

Hille, WILHELM, a Lutheran theologian of Germany, was born Feb. 16, 1803. He studied at Göttingen, was from 1824 to 1833 teacher at the gymnasia in Wolfenbüttel and Helmstädt, in 1833 pastor at Marienthal, in 1834 superintendent, in 1840 general superintendent and pastor primarius at Helmstädt, and in 1845 member of consistory. In 1875 he retired from his many positions, and died Oct. 2, 1880. As Christianity had become a reality in Hille, who had freed himself from the fetters of rationalism, he became to many a leader to Christ. He published, *Oratiunculæ Synodales* (Helmstädt, 1844):—*Das Kirchenjahr* (Berlin, 1858):—*Zeugnisse von Christo* (1859). See Zuchold, *Bibl. Theol.* i, 557. (B. P.)

Hillel Manuscript. Of the ancient Hebrew MSS., now no more extant, the most famous is the codex Hillel. As to this name there is a difference of opinion. From Jewish history we know that there were two rabbis by the name of Hillel, one who lived in the first century before Christ, called Hillel I, the Great, the other who lived in the fourth century after

Christ, called Hillel II. Some, as Schickhard (*Jus Regium Hebræorum*, ed. Carpzov, Leipsic, 1674, p. 39) and Cuneus (*De Republ. Hebr.* p. 159), attributed this codex to the older Hillel; others, as David Gans, in his *Tzemach David*, Buxtorf, in *Tractatus de Punctorum Vocalium*, etc. (Basle, 1648), p. 353, attributed it to the younger Hillel. A third opinion is that this codex derives its name from the fact that it was written at Hilla, a town built near the ruins of ancient Babylon, so Fürst (*Gesch. des Karäerthums*, p. 22 sq., 138, note 14), and Ginsburg (*Levita's Massoreth ha-Massoreth*, p. 260, note 40). But none of these opinions seems to be correct. Against the first two we have the express testimony of *Abraham ben-Samuel Sakkuto* (q. v.), who, in his *Book of Genealogies*, entitled *Sepher Yuchasin*, says that when he saw the remainder of the codex (circa A.D. 1500) it was 900 years old. His words are these: "In the year 4956, on the 28th day of Ab (i. e. in 1196, better 1197), there was a great persecution of the Jews in the kingdom of Leon from the two kingdoms which came to besiege it. It was then that the twenty-four sacred books, which were written long ago, about the year 600, by rabbi Moses ben-Hillel, in an exceedingly correct manner, and after which all copies were corrected, were taken away. I saw the remaining two portions of the same, viz. the earlier prophets (i. e. Joshua, Judges, Samuel, and Kings), and the later prophets (i. e. Isaiah, Jeremiah, Ezekiel, and the twelve minor prophets), written in large and beautiful characters, which were brought to Portugal and sold in Africa, where they still are, having been written 900 years ago." Kimchi, in his grammar on Numb. xv, 4, says that the Pentateuch of this codex was extant in Toletola (בטוליטולה, *Yuchasin*, ed. Filipowski, Lond. 1857, p. 220, col. 2). From this statement it may be deduced that this codex was written about the 7th century. As to the third opinion, deriving the name from Hilla, a town near Babel, we may dismiss it as merely ingenious. A better opinion seems to be that of Strack (*Prolegomena*, p. 16), who says, "Fortasse tamen recte cogitabis eum e numero τῶν סופרים in Hispania fuisse." This is also the opinion of the famous critic Jedidja Norzi (q. v.), who remarks, on Gen. i, 5: "He was a very good Masoretic scholar, and a scribe in the city of Toletola." Whatever uncertainty may be about the derivation of its name, certain it is that this codex is very important for the criticism of the Old Test. Hebrew text, as the many quotations which we find in Norzi's critical commentary, entitled מנחת שי, published at Mantua, 1742–44, Vienna, 1813, Warsaw, 1860–66, and in Lonzano's critical work, entitled אור תורה, indicate. In the 12th century this codex was perused by the Jewish grammarian, Jaçob ben-Eleazar, as David Kimchi testifies in his grammatical work, *Michlul* (ed. Fürth, 1793, fol. 78, col. 2), and rabbi Jacob ben-Eleazar writes that in the codex Hillel, which is at Toletola, he found that the *daleth* in תִּדְרוּ was *raphe* (Deut. xii, 1); and fol. 127, col. 2, in fine, he writes: "In the codex Hillel, which is at Toletola, the word תאפה (Lev. vi, 10) is written with a *tsere*, תֵּאָפֶה, and not תֵּאָפֶה, as our present text has." We subjoin some readings of the codex Hillel:

Gen. iv, 8: In some editions of the Old Test. there is a space left between אחיו and ויהי, and is marked in the margin by פסקא, i. e. *space*. The LXX., Sam., Syr., Vul., and Jerus. Targum add, "let us go into the field." The space we have referred to is found in the editions of Buxtorf, Menasseh ben-Israel, Walton, Nissel, Hutter, Clodius, Van der Hooght. But, says Lonzano, the *piska* is a mistake of the printer, for in the MSS. which he consulted, and in codex Hillel, there is no space. The addition "let us go into the field," is not found by Symmachus, Theodotion, and Onkelos. Even Origen remarks διέλθωμεν εἰς τὸ πέδιον ἐν τῷ Ἑβραϊκῷ οὐ γέγραπται (tom. ii, 30).

Gen. ix, 29: A great many codd. and edd. read ויהיו but codex Hillel ויהי.

Gen. xix, 16: וַיִּתְמַהְמָהּ, here Lonzano remarks that the second *mem* is written with *kamets* in codd. and in cod. Hillel. In the edition of Bär and Delitzsch the word is thus written, וַיִּתְמַהְמָהּ.

Gen. xix, 20: אִמָּלְטָה נָּא. Lonzano says that נא is *raphe*, but in cod. Hillel it is written with a *dagesh*. In Bär and Delitzsch's Genesis it is written *raphe*.

Gen. xxvii, 25: וַיָּבֵא לוֹ. In cod. Hillel, says Lonzano, the accent *darga* is in the *yod*. In our editions it is in, or rather under, the *beth;* Bär and Delitzsch follow the cod. Hillel, and write וַיָּבֵא.

Gen. xxxix, 6: מַרְאֶה. Norzi remarks that the codex Hillel writes with *tsere* מַרְאֵה.

Gen. xlii, 16: הֵאָסְרוּ. In the margin of an old codex, belonging now to Dr. S. Bär, the editor of the new edition of the Old Test., in connection with professor Delitzsch, it is written בהלל האסרו, i. e. in the codex Hillel, the reading is with *segol*, הֶאסרו.

Gen. xlvi, 13: וּפֻוָּה. On this word Lonzano remarks that in Hillel and other codd. the *vav* is *raphe*, i. e. וּפֻוָה.

Exod. x, 9: וּבִזְקֵנֵנוּ. In Hillel, remarks Lonzano, it is written מלא יוד, i. e. *plene* ובזקינינו.

Exod. xxxvii, 8: כְּרוּב. In Hillel and in some other codd., remarks Lonzano, it is written with a *makkeph*.

Josh. xxi, 35, 36: Cod. Kennic. No. 357, reads in the margin לא מצינו אלו השני פסוקים בהללי, i. e. these two verses are not found in the codex Hillel. Similar is the remark in a MS. formerly belonging to H. Lotze, of Leipsic.

Prov. viii, 16: A great many codd., editions, and ancient versions, as Syriac, Vulgate, Targum, and even the Græcus Venetus, read here שפטי צדק, while the Complutensian text and other codd. read שפטי ארץ, which is also supported by codex Hillel, and is adopted in Bär's ed. of Proverbs.

These few examples will show the importance of the codex Hillel for the text of the Old Test. (B. P.)

Hilliger, Johann Zacharias, a Lutheran theologian of Germany, was born Jan. 1, 1693, at Chemnitz. He studied at Leipsic and Wittenberg, was in 1717 adjunct to the philosophical faculty at the latter place, in 1724 professor of philosophy, in 1725 superintendent at Sayda, in Saxony, and died Jan. 16, 1770. He wrote, *De Libro Recti ad Jos. x*, 15 (Leipsic, 1714):—*De ἀυλήταις ad Matth. ix*, 23 (1717):—*De Vita, Fama, et Scriptis Val. Weigelii* (1721):—*De Plagis Magnis Pharaonis ad Gen. xii*, 17 (1724):—*De Canonica Libri Esther Auctoritate* (Wittenberg, 1729):—*De Augustana Confessione Nonna Concionum Sacrarum Secundaria* (1733). See Dietmann, *Chursächsische Priester;* Jöcher, *Allgemeines Gelehrten-Lexikon*, s. v.; Winer, *Handbuch der theol. Lit.* i, 775; Fürst, *Bibl. Jud.* i, 394. (B. P.)

Hillyer, Asa, D.D., a Presbyterian minister, was born in Massachusetts, April 6, 1763. He graduated at Yale College in 1786; was ordained by the Presbytery of Suffolk, L. I., in 1788; called to Bottle Hill (now Madison), N. J., in 1789; to the First Presbyterian Church of Orange in 1801; resigned his charge when he was seventy years of age, and died at Orange, Aug. 28, 1840. During his pastorate at Orange he made a missionary tour through northern Pennsylvania and western New York, and preached the first sermon ever heard in what is now the city of Auburn. See Tuttle, *Hist. of the Presb. Church in Madison, N. J.* (New York, 1855), p. 39; Aikman, *Historical Discourse Concerning the Presbyterian Church, Madison, N. J.* (1876), p. 8.

Hilpert, Johann, a Lutheran theologian, superintendent at Hildesheim, who died May 10, 1680, is the author of, *Disquisitio de Præadamitis:*—*De Judæorum Flagellationibus:*—*De Gloria Templi Posterioris:*—*Hebræorum Philosophia Adversus Judæos:*—*De Agapis:*—*De Perseverantia Sanctorum.* See Witte, *Diarium Biographicum;* Fürst, *Bibl. Jud.* i, 394; Jöcher, *Allgemeines Gelehrten-Lexikon*, s. v. (B. P.)

Hilscher, Balthasar, a Lutheran theologian, was born April 1, 1595, at Hirschberg, Silesia. He was bachelor of theology and deacon at Leipsic, and died Sept. 13, 1630, leaving, *De Integritate Codicis Hebræi:—De Evangelio:—De Justificatione:—Disputationes de Invocatione Sanctorum, de Sanctis Angelis, de Imagine Dei:—De Hominibus in Diluvio ad* 1 *Petr. iii*, 19:—*Lutherischer Buss- und Betwecker wider den Pabst und seine Jesuiter*. See Götze, *Elogia Theologorum;* Jöcher, *Allgemeines Gelehrten-Lexikon*, s. v. (B. P.)

Hilscher, Paul Christian, a Lutheran theologian, was born March 15, 1666, at Waldheim, in Saxony. He studied at Leipsic, was in 1695 deacon at Dresden (Neustadt), in 1704 pastor there, and died Aug. 3, 1730, leaving a number of ascetical works, for which see Jöcher, *Allgemeines Gelehrten-Lexikon*, s. v.; Fürst, *Bibl. Jud.* i, 394. (B. P.)

Hilsey (or **Hildesley**), JOHN, bishop of Rochester in 1535, died in 1538, leaving, *The Manuall of Prayers; or, The Prymer in Englyshe* (1539):—*De Veri Corporis Jesu in Sacramento:—Resolutions Concerning the Sacraments*. See Allibone, *Dict. of Brit. and Amer. Authors*, s. v.

Hilten, JOHANNES, a Franciscan of Thuringia, who died in 1502, is the author of *Comment. in Apocalypsin et Danielem*. Hilton made himself famous by his so-called prophecies. See Angelus, *Bericht von Joh. Hilten und seinen Weissagungen*. (B. P.)

Hilton, WILLIAM, an English painter, was born at Lincoln, June 3, 1786. He studied in the Royal Academy School, and afterwards made a tour in Italy. In 1825 he succeeded Fuseli as keeper of the academy, and died in London, Dec. 30, 1839. Of his religious pieces the following are the principal: *Christ Crowned with Thorns*, painted in 1823, lately purchased by the academy, and regarded as his masterpiece; *The Angel Releasing Peter from Prison*, painted in 1831; *The Murder of the Innocents*, his exhibited work (1838); and *Rebekah and Abraham's Servant* (1829), now in the National Gallery. See *Encyclop. Brit.* 9th ed. s. v.

Himmel, JOHANNES, a Lutheran theologian, was born Dec. 27, 1581, at Stolpe, Pomerania. He studied at different universities, and died at Jena, March 31, 1643, doctor and professor of theology. He is the author of, *Analytica Dispositio Librorum Biblicorum:—Memoriale Biblicum Generale et Speciale cum Chronologia Biblica:—Compendium Historiæ Ecclesiasticæ a Nato Christo Usque ad Lutherum:—De Scriptura Sacra:—Commentar. in Prophetas Minores, Epistolam ad Galatas et Philemonem:—Postilla Academica in Epistolas et Evangelia Dominicalia et Festivalia:—De Canonicatu, Jure Canonico et Theologia Scholastica:—Syntagma Disputationum Theologicarum*. See Fürst, *Bibl. Jud.* i, 394; Jöcher, *Allgemeines Gelehrten-Lexikon*, s. v. (B. P.)

Hindustani Version OF THE SCRIPTURES. Hindustani (or *Urdu*), the language of "Hindu-stan," or "country of Hind," is a mixed language, and owes its formation to the intercourse of the Mohammedan invaders with the conquered natives of India. At the time of the first Mohammedan invasions, which date from the 10th century, Hinduwi, or Hindi, was the prevailing dialect in Northern India. On their permanent settlement in India the Mohammedans adopted this dialect as the medium of communication with the natives, but they greatly altered it by the introduction of words and idioms from the Persian and Arabic, their own vernacular and liturgic languages. The new dialect thence arising was called *Urdu* (camp), or *Urdu Zaban* (camp language), because the language of the Mohammedan camp and court; it was also called "Hindustani," from the geographical region through which it ultimately became diffused.

The first translation of any portion of Scripture into Hindustani seems to have been made by B. Schulze, a Danish missionary. His version of the Psalms was published by Callenberg at Halle in 1746, and the New Test. in 1758. But the most important translation that has been made into this language is that of the New Test. by the Rev. Henry Martyn, which appeared, after much delay, at Serampore in 1814. This version soon obtained such a high reputation that it led to a demand for an edition in the Devanagari (or regular Sanscrit) character, for the benefit of the Hindûs in the upper provinces. An edition in this character was published in 1817 by the Calcutta Bible Society. No subsequent editions of the Hindustani Scriptures were, however, issued in this dress, for it was found by experience that the Scriptures in the Hinduwi dialect (q. v.) were far more acceptable than in the Hindustani to the numerous class of natives who employ the Devanagari characters. For their use, as we shall have occasion to mention (see HINDUWI VERSION), Martyn's New Test. was eventually divested of its Persian and Arabic terms, and transferred into the Hinduwi idiom by Mr. Bowley.

While these editions were issued by the Calcutta Auxiliary, the publication of an edition in London had been contemplated by the British and Foreign Bible Society since the year 1815, and was published in 1819, under the superintendence of professor Lee. Four thousand copies of this edition were sent to Calcutta. The committee at the latter place now turned their attention to the publication of a Hindustani version of the Old Test. The first portion of the work published was the Pentateuch, which appeared in 1823, and in 1844 the Old Test. was completed, and editions, both in Arabic and Roman characters, were distributed. The Hindustani version of the Scriptures has undergone subsequent revision at the hands of a committee appointed for the purpose, and later editions, both of the Old and New Tests., have appeared. Some of these have been printed in the Arabic, and others in the Roman character. At present there exist four different versions in Hindustani, one by Martyn, the second by Thomasen and others, the third Yates's version, and the fourth the Benares' version, so called from the place where it was made. See *Bible of Every Land*, p. 94.

Linguistic Helps.—Garcin de Tassy, *Rudiments de la Langue Hindoustanie, avec Appendice* (Paris, 1829-33; 12th ed. 1863); Vinson, *Éléments de la Grammaire Générale Hindoustanie* (ibid. 1884); Craven, *The Popular Dictionary in English and Hindustani and Hindustani and English* (London, 1882); Dowson, *A Grammar of the Urdu or Hindustani Language; A Hindustani Exercise Book;* Fallon, *A New Hindustani-English Dictionary* (Benares, 1879); *English-Hindustani Dictionary* (1880). (B. P.)

Hinduwi Version OF THE SCRIPTURES. Hinduwi (called *Hindi* by the Serampore translators), with its various dialects, is spoken in all the upper provinces of India. Its affinity to the Sanscrit is very remarkable, and about nine tenths of its words may be traced to that language. In idiom and construction Hinduwi resembles Hindustani; the chief difference between the two dialects consists in this, that while Persian and Arabic words and phrases predominate in Hindustani, the Hinduwi is entirely free from foreign admixture, and the proper mode of writing it is in the Devanagari or regular Sanscrit characters. Beside these, the Kythi, or Kaithi, or writer's character, an imperfect imitation, and in some respects an alteration, of the Devanagari, is also used in writing and printing Hinduwi, particularly by the trading community, and it is said that of the lower class of natives there are ten who read and write in the Kythi for one who transacts business in the Devanagari.

A version into the Hinduwi language was commenced in 1802, and in 1807 the whole of the New and parts of the Old Test. were completed and ready for revision. It is one of the versions made by the late Dr. Carey. In 1811 the New Test. was published at Serampore, followed in 1813 by a second edition. A third was soon needed, and the Serampore missionaries determined to publish the version executed by the Rev. John Chamberlain. In 1819 the gospels in the Devanagari character were published, and in the following year another edition appeared in the Kaithi character. The further publication of this version was interrupted by the death of Mr. Chamberlain, and the Rev. J. T. Thompson, a Baptist missionary, long resident at Delhi, then undertook the revision of the New Test. and of the Psalms, and under his superintendence the gospels were printed in 1824. The Old Test., in Dr. Carey's translation, appeared in 1818. From time to time new editions were published in both characters by the Serampore missionary societies, each edition having been subjected to a careful revision.

There also exists another Hinduwi version of the entire Bible, known as the Bowley translation, so called from its author, the Rev. William Bowley, for many years missionary at Benares. His New Test. was completed in 1826, but the version is not a new or independent translation, but is throughout substantially the same as Martyn's Hindustani version, from which it differs chiefly in the substitution of Sanscrit for Persian and Arabic terms. Martyn's Testament was thus adapted to the use of persons speaking the Hinduwi dialect, by Mr. Bowley, agent of the Church Missionary Society at Chunar. Being unacquainted with the original languages of Scripture, he consulted the English A. V. in all passages where the Hinduwi idiom required him to alter Martyn's renderings, referring at the same time to the best commentators on Scripture. In the same manner he undertook the transference of the Hindustani version of the Old Test. into the Hinduwi dialect, following in his translation of Isaiah the one made by bishop Lowth. The idiom of the version was excellent. After all, it was felt that a revision for the purpose of conforming his version to the originals, and correcting the misapprehension of Old English idiom, was exceedingly desirable. After the formation of the North India Bible Society in 1845, this matter was taken in hand, and a revision of the New Test. undertaken. The committee consisted of Messrs. Leupoldt, Kennedy, and Schneider, and the work was carried through the press at Secundra, under the superintendence of Mr. Schneider, in 1850 and 1851. These copies of the New Test. were destroyed during the mutiny in 1857. The Rev. J. Ullmann was then sent to England to bring out a new edition, which included a revision, and the whole was completed in 1860. Soon after the revision of the New Test. a committee, consisting of Messrs. Schneider, Leupoldt, Kennedy, and Owen, was appointed to revise the Old Test. This was brought out in two volumes at the Allahabad Mission Press in 1852 and 1855. These copies, too, were destroyed in the mutiny, and another revised edition was completed under the superintendence of the former editor; of this the first volume was issued in 1866, and the second in the beginning of 1869. At present the Hinduwi version is undergoing a thorough revision. See *Bible of Every Land*, p. 100.

Linguistic Helps.—For the study of the language, see Garcin de Tassy, *Rudiments de la Langue Hindoui* (Paris, 1847); Bate, *A Dictionary of the Hindee Language;* Browne, *A Hindi Primer* (London, 1822); Etherington, *The Student's Grammar of the Hindi Language* (Benares, 1873); Kellog, *A Grammar of the Hindi Language, in which are treated the standard Hindi, Braj, and the Eastern Hindi of the Ramayan of Tulsi Das; also the Colloquial Dialects of Marwar, Kumaon, Avadh, Baghelkhand, Bhojpur, etc., with Copious Philological Notes;* Mathuráprasóda Misra, *A Trilingual Dictionary, being a Comprehensive Lexicon in English, Urdu, and Hindi, exhibiting the Syllabication, Pronunciation, and Etymology of English Words, with their Explanation in English and in Urdu and Hindi, in the Roman Character* (Benares, 1865). (B. P.)

HINDUWI, DIALECTS OF THE, AND OF CENTRAL INDIA, VERSIONS IN. The Hinduwi comprehends many dialects, strictly local and provincial, which differ from each other chiefly in the different proportions of Sanscrit, Arabic, or Persian terms entering into their composition. At a very early period translations into these different dialects were executed by the Serampore missionaries, but these translations were not afterwards reprinted; some have been practically discontinued. See *Bible of Every Land*, p. 103.

1. *Braj*, or *Brij-bhasa.* This dialect is spoken throughout the province of Agra. In 1811 the Rev. John Chamberlain, then stationed at Agra, commenced a translation of the New Test. in this dialect, and in 1813 he had finished the translation of the gospels. After much delay the New Test. was completed at press in the year 1832.

2. *Bughelcundi.* This dialect is spoken in a district between the province of Bundelcund and the sources of the Nerbudda River. A translation of the New Test. was commenced in 1814, and was published at Serampore in 1821.

3. *Canaj*, or *Canyacubja.* This dialect is spoken in the Doab of the Ganges and Jumna. A version of the New Test. was commenced in 1815 at Serampore, and completed at press in 1822.

4. *Kousulu*, or *Koshala.* This dialect is spoken in the western part of Oude. In 1820 the gospel of Matthew was printed, and nothing more since.

In addition to the Hinduwi dialects, strictly so called, there are several other *Indian dialects*, supposed to be corruptions of the general Hinduwi stock:

1. *Bikaneera.* This dialect is spoken in the province of Bikaneer, north of Marwar. The New Test. was printed at Serampore in 1823.

2. *Buttaneer*, or *Virat.* This is spoken in the province of Buttaneer, west of Delhi, and a New Test. printed in 1824 at Serampore is extant in that dialect.

3. *Harroti.* This dialect is spoken in Harroti, a province west of Bundelcund. A version of the New Test. was printed at Serampore in 1822.

4. *Juyapoora.* This is spoken in the province of Joipoor, east of Marwar and west of Agra. Only the gospel of Matthew was published at Serampore in 1815.

5. *Marwari.* This dialect is spoken in the province of Joipoor, or Marwar, north of Mewar. In this dialect the New Test. is extant since 1821.

6. *Oodeypoora.* This dialect is vernacular in the province of Mewar, or Oodeypoor. Only the gospel of Matthew has been published at Serampore in 1815.

7. *Oojein*, or *Oujjuyuni.* This dialect is vernacular in the province of Malwah of Central India. A version of the New Test. was published at Serampore in 1824. (B. P.)

Hingnoh, in the mythology of the Hottentots, is the name of the first woman, not born, but created. She is worshipped as their chief protecting goddess.

Hinton, JOHN HOWARD, an eminent English Baptist minister, was born at Oxford, March 24, 1791. He received his collegiate education at the University of Edinburgh, and having decided to enter the ministry in the Baptist denomination, began his labors at Haverford-West, where he remained for some time, and then removed to Reading. Subsequently he accepted a call to become the pastor of a large congregation worshipping in Devonshire Square, Bishopsgate, London. In 1831 he visited America. Returning to England, he once more took up his residence in Reading, where he became again a pastor, though not of the same church with which he had before been connected. Here for several years he continued to reside, until he retired from the pastorate and removed to Bristol. He died there, Dec. 17, 1873. Mr. Hinton was a somewhat voluminous writer. Among the works which he published were his *Memoirs of William Kniff*, a distinguished Baptist missionary to the West Indies:—*A History of the United States* (2 vols. 4to), of which several editions have been published:—*Theology:—Elements* *of Natural History*, besides many smaller productions on the voluntary principle in education and religion. His works have been collected in seven volumes. (J. C. S.)

Hipparchus, a martyr at Samosata, with several others, A.D. 297, under Galerius, variously commemorated March 15 and Dec. 9.

Hippocratia, a festival held by the Arcadians in honor of Poseidon (q. v.), in course of which it was customary to lead horses and mules in procession gayly caparisoned.

Hippogriff, in the mythology of the Middle Ages, was a fabulous animal, half horse, half griffin, which cleaves the air with preternatural swiftness. The Italian poet, Bojardo, seems to have invented it. Modern German poets use the name frequently for the muses' steed, *Pegasus* (q. v.).

Hirmologium (εἱρμολόγιον), an office-book in the Greek Church, consisting mainly of a collection of the Hirmoi, but containing also a few other forms.

Hirmus (εἱρμός). The Canons, which form so important a part of the Greek offices, are divided into nine odes, or practically into eight, as the second is always omitted. Each ode consists of a varying number (three, four, or five are the numbers most frequently found) of *troparia*, or short rhythmical strophes, each formed on the model of one which precedes the ode, and which is called the Hirmus. The Hirmus is usually independent of the ode, though containing a reference to the subject-matter of it; sometimes, however, the first *troparion* of an ode is called the Hirmus. It is distinguished by inverted commas (" ") in the office-books. Sometimes the first words alone of a Hirmus are given, and it is not unfrequently placed at the end of the ode to which it belongs.

Hirsch (or **Hirz**), a name common to many Jewish writers, of whom we mention the following:

1. BEN-JONATHAN *ha-Levi*, who flourished in the 18th century, is the author of נתיב הישר, a commentary on the Pentateuch, allegorical and homiletical (Dyhernfurt, 1712):—שביל הישר, glosses on Talmudic treatises (1718).

2. BEN-NISSAN, who flourished in the 18th century, wrote תפארת צבי, novellas on the Pentateuch (Amsterdam, 1755).

3. SAMUEL *ben-Samuel*, wrote a cabalistical commentary on the Pentateuch, entitled, מרגליות התורה (1788). See Fürst, *Bibl. Jud.* i, 395 sq. (B. P.)

Hirsch, Paul Wilhelm, a Jewish convert of Germany in the 18th century, who joined the Church in 1717, is the author of, מגלת תקופות, or *Entdeckung der Tekufot oder das schädliche Blut* (Berlin, 1717):—מתנת יובל, or, *Das von Gott den Christen aufs neue gewordene Jubel-Geschenk* (1718):—*Beschreibung des jüdischen Weihnachts-Festes* (1725):—*Der Juden lächerliche Zurüstung zum Sabbat* (1722):—*Beschreibung des betrübten Endes Rabban Jochanan's* (1728):—*Nachricht von der Bedeutung der beiden Redensarten: Kapore werden und Krie reissen* (1730). See Fürst, *Bibl. Jud.* i, 398; Wolf, *Bibl. Hebr.* iii, 907 sq.; Jöcher, *Allgemeines Gelehrten-Lexikon*, s. v. (B. P.)

Hirsch, Theodor, a Protestant theologian and historian of Germany, was born Dec. 17, 1806, at Dantzic. He studied at Berlin, was for some time professor at the Friedrich-Wilhelms gymnasium there, and in 1833 at Dantzic. In 1865 he was called as professor of history and librarian to Greifswalde, and died Feb. 17, 1881. He published, *Beitrag zur Reformationsgeschichte Danzigs* (Dantzic, 1842):—*Die Ober-Pfarrkirche von St. Marien in Danzig* (1843):—*Danzigs Handels- und Gewerbegeschichte unter der Herrschaft des Deutschen Ordens* (Leipsic, 1858). He also edited, with Strehlke and Töppen, *Scriptores Rerum Prussicarum* (1868 sq.). (B. P.)

Hirschel, SOLOMON, a Jewish rabbi, was born in England in 1762. He was educated in Germany and Poland, and was for some time preacher at Prenzlau, in Prussia. In 1802 he was called to London as rabbi of the synagogue in Duke's Place, but gradually his jurisdiction was extended over all the Jews of the Ashkenazi Minhag (i. e. German rite) in London, and indeed in England. It was during his time that the scattered elements formed by the English Jews were gathered into one compact mass, and the Spanish and Portuguese Jews, and the German Jews, who were formerly spoken of as two distinct "nations," became closely connected together as members of the same creed. He died Oct. 31, 1842. (B. P.)

Hirschfeld, HERMANN T., a Jewish rabbi and writer, who died at Charlottenburg, Prussia, June 10, 1884, at the age of seventy, is the author of, *De Literatura Deperdita Hebræorum; Molochsglaube und Religionsschändung* (1842):—*Tractatus Maccoth cum Scholiis Hermeneuticis et Glossario nec non Indicibus* (Berlin, 1842):—*Wünsche eines Juden* (Posen, 1846):—*Der Geist der talmudischen Auslegung der Bibel* (Berlin, 1847):—*Untersuchungen über die Religion* (Breslau, 1856):—*Ueber die Lehre von der Unsterblichkeit der Seele bei den verschiedenen Völkern* (1868). See Fürst, *Bibl. Jud.* i, 400; Zuchold, *Bibl. Theol.* i, 561. (B. P.)

Hirt, ALOYSIUS LUDWIG, a Roman Catholic divine, professor of archæology at Berlin, was born June 27, 1759, at Donaueschingen, Baden, and died June 29, 1836. He is the author of *Der Tempel Salomonis* (Berlin, 1809). See Winer, *Handbuch der theol. Lit.* i, 139; Fürst, *Bibl. Jud.* i, 400. (B. P.)

Hirzel, Heinrich, a Swiss theologian, was born at Zurich, April 17, 1818. He studied at his native place and at Tübingen, and died at Zurich, April 17, 1871, where he had been laboring since 1857. Hirzel belonged to the so-called *Protestanten-Verein*. See Lang, *Protestantische Kirchenzeitung* (May 20 and 27, 1871); Lichtenberger, *Encyclop. des Sciences Religieuses*, s. v. (B. P.)

Hirzel, Ludwig, son of Bernhard (q. v.), was born at Zurich, Aug. 27, 1801, and died April 13, 1841, professor of theology. He is the author of, *De Pentateuchi Versionis Syriacæ quam Peschito Vocant Indole* (Leipsic, 1825):—*De Chaldaismi Biblici Origine et Auctoritate Critica* (1830):—*Das Buch Hiob erklärt* (1839; 3d. ed. by Dillmann, 1869). See Winer, *Handbuch der theol. Lit.* i, 56, 124; Fürst, *Bibl. Jud.* i, 402; Zuchold, *Bibl. Theol.* i, 562. (B. P.)

Hita, RUIZ. See RUIZ.

Hitchcock, Calvin, D.D., a Congregational minister, was born at Westminster, Vt., Oct. 25, 1787, graduated from Middlebury College in 1811, and from Andover Theological Seminary in 1814. His first settlement was at Newport, R. I., where he was ordained Aug. 15, 1815. This pastorate was finished Oct. 1, 1820, and he was installed at Randolph, Mass., Feb. 28 following, and remained there for more than thirty years, the date of his dismissal being June, 1851. His residence thereafter was at Wrentham, where he died, Dec. 3, 1867. He made frequent contributions to the *Boston Recorder*, and published some *Sermons*. See *Cong. Quarterly*, 1868, p. 286.

Hitchcock, Henry L., D.D., a Presbyterian minister, was born at Benton, O., Oct. 31, 1813. He studied at the Benton Academy, graduated from Yale College in 1832, and spent some time as a student in the Lane Theological Seminary. He was licensed to preach in 1837, and installed at Morgan, O., the same year. In 1840 he began to preach at Columbus, and the next year was installed pastor there. In 1855 he was elected president of Western Reserve College, after leaving which position he lived in retirement until his death at Hudson, O., July 6, 1873. See Nevin, *Presb. Encyclop.* s. v.

Hitchcock, Samuel Austin, a philanthropic layman of the Congregational Church, was born at Brimfield, Mass., Jan. 9, 1794. On March 23, 1812, he left home in search of employment, which he found with a merchant of Dudley. In 1820 he went to Boston and entered a dry-goods firm, established for the sale of goods manufactured by the different cotton-mills—the first in New England. In 1831 he went to Southbridge as agent of the Hamilton Woollen Company. He united with the Old South Church, in Boston, June 23, 1827, and was afterwards connected with the Church in Brimfield. In 1840 he gave $10,000 to Amherst College, and this was followed by other amounts until the aggregate reached $175,000. To Andover Theological Seminary his donations amounted to $120,000. To the town of Brimfield he gave $10,000, in 1855, to establish a free school, and subsequent donations increased this to $80,000, and it was called the Hitchcock Free High-School. In 1871 he gave $50,000 to Illinois College. These are only samples of his munificence. His donations aggregated about $650,000. Mr. Hitchcock was withal a humble Christian, seeking no notoriety in the bestowal of his wealth. He died in Boston, Nov. 23, 1873. See *Cong. Quarterly*, 1874, p. 517.

Hitopadesa (*good advice*), in Hindû literature, is a famous collection of ethical tales and fables, compiled from the larger and older work called *Pancha-tantra*. It has often been printed in the original, and translated into various languages.

Hittites. All that is known concerning this important Canaanitish people, whose history is often referred to on the Egyptian and Assyrian monuments under the name *Kheta*, has been collected by Wright, *Empire of the Hittites* (Lond. 1884, 8vo).

Hittorff, JACQUES INACE, a French architect, was born at Cologne, Aug. 20, 1793. He entered the School of Fine Arts in Paris in 1810, and became architect to the government in 1818. He made a study of the remains of Greek architecture in Sicily, and followed the Greek artists in applying colors to most of his architectural designs. From 1824 he was engaged in the construction of important public buildings, of which the Church of St. Vincent de Paul is regarded as his masterpiece. He was elected to the Academy of Fine Arts in 1853, and died in Paris, March 25, 1867. His principal productions are, *Architecture Antique de la Sicile* (Paris, 1826–30, 3 vols.):—*Architecture Polychrome chez les Grecs* (1831):—*Mémoire sur Pompéi et Petra* (1866).

Hitzig, FERDINAND, a German exegetical scholar, was born at Hauingen, in Baden, June 23, 1807. He studied at Heidelberg and Halle, commenced his academical career at the former place in 1830, accepted a call to Zurich in 1832, went again in 1861 to Heidelberg as Umbreit's successor, and died Jan. 22, 1875. At Zurich Hitzig publicly announced himself in favor of calling Strauss. Though on the one hand a man without fear or hypocrisy, and on the other of a polemic temperament and caustic wit, which seemed to exclude personal piety and gentleness, yet Hitzig was of a pious nature, and not only loved the Old Test., but sought to serve the kingdom of God by his investigations. He enjoyed the esteem of his colleagues and friends, and even of his opponents. We can adopt the words of Keim, in the dedication of his *History of Jesus* (2d ed. Jan. 1875): "To the memory of F. Hitzig, the honest man without fear, the faithful friend without deceit, the pride of Zurich and Heidelberg, the bold, restless architect of Biblical science." Hitzig's earliest and by far the best work is his *Uebersetzung und Auslegung des Propheten Jesaia* (Heidelberg, 1833); his other works are, *Die Psalmen, historischer und kritischer Commentar* (1835–36, 2 vols.; new ed. 1863–65):—*Ueber Johannes Markus und seine Schriften* (Zurich, 1843):—*Urgeschichte und Mythologie der Philistäer* (Leipsic, 1845):—*Die Sprüche Salomo's* (Zurich, 1858):—*Die zwölf kleinen Propheten* (3d ed. 1863):—*Jeremiah* (1841; 2d ed. 1866):—*Ezechiel* (1847):—*Ecclesiastes* (eod.):—*Daniel* (1850):—*Das Hohelied* (1855):—*Hiob* (1874):—*Geschichte des Volkes Israel* (Leipsic, 1869). As to the value of Hitzig's commentaries and history, says Kamphausen, "If I am not mistaken, it was a want of *common-sense* which prevented this gifted and truth-loving investigator to such a remarkable degree from becoming an exemplary exegete and a trustworthy historian. Ewald was fully justified when he complained that Hitzig made that which was beautiful and tender in Solomon's song disagreeable and repulsive; that he, in an almost incredible manner, declared the first nine chapters of the Proverbs to have been the last composed, etc. But, in spite of this, Hitzig will always have a place of prominence among his contemporaries, and his works will for a long time remain a fountain of instruction and quickening to many." Hitzig also contributed to Schenkel's *Bibel-Lexikon*, to the *Zeitschrift der deutschen morgenländischen Gesellschaft*, and other periodicals. See Kneuker, in *Protestantische Kirchenzeitung* (1875, col. 181–188); Weech, in *Badische Biographien*, i, 377–380 (Heidelberg, 1875); Diestel, *Geschichte des Alten Testaments in der christl. Kirche* (Jena, 1869); Kamphausen, in Plitt-Herzog's *Real-Encyklop.* s. v.; Lichtenberger, *Encyclop. des Sciences Religieuses*, s. v. (B. P.)

Hoadly (or **Hoadley**), JOHN, D.D., an Irish prelate, was born at Tottenham, Sept. 27, 1678, and was brother to the celebrated Benjamin Hoadly, bishop of Winchester. John Hoadly was chaplain to bishop Burnet, and by him installed chancellor and canon residentiary of the Church of Salisbury, archdeacon of Sarum, and rector of St. Edmund's, and was afterwards made canon of Hereford by his brother, when bishop of that see. He was advanced, June 3, 1727, to the sees of Leighlin and Ferns. He was translated to the see of Dublin, Jan. 13, 1729. In November, 1739, Dr. Hoadly was of the privy council, when the proclamation was issued requiring all justices, magistrates, etc., to search and seize arms in possession of any papist, and to prosecute any papist who should presume to carry arms contrary to the intent of the proclamation. Dr. Hoadly adopted the system of his predecessor, and what was then styled the English interest in the country. He died at Rathfarnham, July 19, 1746. See D'Alton, *Memoirs of the Archbishops of Dublin*, p. 330.

Hobal, an idol of the ancient Arabians, was demolished by Mohammed after he had taken possession of Mecca. It was surrounded by three hundred and sixty smaller idols, each of which presided over one day of the lunar year.

Hoby, JAMES, D.D., an English Baptist minister, was born in 1788. In his youth he enjoyed the friendship and counsel of the Rev. Joseph Iviney, and in 1813 became co-pastor at Maze Pond, Southwark. In 1824 he resigned his pastoral work, and devoted his long life to the advocacy of the several Baptist funds which go to the support of the aged ministers and poorly paid pastors. He paid special attention to the claims of churches in debt, and resided successively in Birmingham, Weymouth, and Twickenham, in order to assist poor churches around each of those places. He took great interest in young ministers, and in the Foreign Missionary Society, and visited America in its behalf. He was widely esteemed and greatly beloved. He died at Caterham, Surrey, Nov. 20, 1871. See (Lond.) *Baptist Hand-book*, 1872.

Hoc agè (*do this*), a form of words solemnly pronounced by a herald when the ancient Romans were about to engage in a public sacrifice. It implied that the whole attention of the people was to be fixed on the service in hand.

Ho-Chang, a name given in China to the priests of Fo or Buddha. They strongly inculcated on their followers the worship of the *three gems*. See GEMS, THE THREE SACRED.

Höck, Heinrich, a Lutheran theologian of Germany, was born at Hamburg, Oct. 18, 1700. He studied at Giessen and Wittenberg, and died at his native place, April 26, 1779, pastor of Trinity Church. He wrote, *Das Evangelium aus den Evangeliis* (Hamburg, 1734-40, 4 parts):—*Das Siegel der Propheten in den Leiden Jesu* (1739, 1743, 2 parts):—*Beiträge zum richtigen und erbaulichen Verstande einiger Schriftstellen* (1749-52, 3 parts). See Neubauer, *Jetztlebende Theologen;* Thiess, *Hamburg. Gelehrten-Geschichte;* Jöcher, *Allgemeines Gelehrten-Lexikon*, s. v. (B. P.)

Höcker, Jonas, a Lutheran theologian of Germany, was born in 1581. He studied at different universities, was in 1609 deacon at Tübingen, in 1614 superintendent, and died June 7, 1617. He wrote, *Sylloge Utilissimorum Articulorum inter Augustanæ Confessionis Theologos et Pontificios ut et Calvinianos Controversorum:*—*Clavis Theologico-Philosophica:*—*Quæstiones Aliquot de Dignitate S. Scripturæ, de Transsubstantiatione.* See Fischlin, *Memoria Theologorum Würtembergensium;* Jöcher, *Allgemeines Gelehrten-Lexikon*, s. v. (B. P.)

Hodamo, the priest of the inhabitants of the island of Socotra, in the Indian Ocean, off the eastern coast of Africa, who worshipped the moon, for which purpose they had temples called *Moquamos.* The hodamo was chosen annually, and presented with a staff and a cross as the emblems of his office.

Hodge, Charles, D.D., LL.D., an eminent Presbyterian divine, was born in Philadelphia, Pa., Dec. 27, 1797, his father, Dr. Hugh Hodge, being an eminent physician of that city. Charles was fitted for college first at Somerville Academy, N. J., and at the age of fourteen entered Princeton, one year in advance, graduating with the highest honors in 1815. After another year of classical study, he entered the Theological Seminary at Princeton, and graduated in 1819. He was licensed by the Presbytery of Philadelphia, Oct. 21, 1819, and during the following winter preached at the Falls of Schuylkill, the Philadelphia Arsenal, and Woodbury, N. J. Being received as a licentiate from the Presbytery of Philadelphia by that of New Brunswick, July 5, 1820, he was appointed the same year to supply the churches of Georgetown and Lambertville for a number of Sabbaths during the following winter, and the next year "for Georgetown, as stated supply for one half his time during the ensuing six months;" also to supply Lambertville and Trenton First Church during parts of the years from 1820 to 1823. In May, 1820, he became assistant instructor in the original languages of Scripture in the seminary, which position he held until 1822, and was then elected by the General Assembly to the professorship of Oriental and Biblical literature. At this time he founded the *Biblical Repertory*, to which was added the title of *Princeton Review*, in 1829. In 1825 he went to Europe, and spent three years in the universities of Paris, Halle, and Berlin, returning in 1829. Dr. Hodge, after this, devoted all his hours not required in seminary duties to the conduct of his magazine, which was already beginning to take rank among American periodicals, and also to studies and researches for *A Commentary on the Epistle to the Romans*, which was published in 1835. This work was abridged in 1836, and then rewritten and enlarged in 1866. In 1840 he published *A Constitutional History of the Presbyterian Church in the United States*, in two volumes. In the same year he was transferred from the chair which he had filled for eighteen years, to that of exegetic and didactic theology, to which was united that of polemic theology, in 1851, when the incumbent, Dr. Alexander, died. In April, 1872, his friends and pupils commemorated his semi-centennial as professor in Princeton Seminary. Dr. Hodge was chosen moderator of the General Assembly—Old School—in 1846. He died in Princeton, N. J., June 19, 1878. His works, published in addition to the above, were, *Questions to the Epistle to the Romans* (1842, 18mo):—*The Way of Life* (18mo, published by the American Sunday-school Union; republished by the London Religious Tract Society, 1842):—*What is Presbyterianism?* (1856):—*Commentary on Ephesians* (N.Y. 1856, 8vo):—*Commentary on First Corinthians* (1857):—*Commentary on Second Corinthians* (1859):—*Reviews and Essays Selected from the Princeton Review* (ibid. 1857, 8vo):—*Selections from the Biblical Repertory and Princeton Review* (ibid. 8vo):—*What is Darwinism?* (1874). During this time he was busily engaged in collecting materials for his *Systematic Theology*, and also in conducting the *Review.* It is said he contributed one fifth of all the articles published in that periodical. In 1872 the *Review* was united with the *Presbyterian Quarterly* and *American Theological Review.* The *Systematic Theology*, in three volumes, large octavo, is the work of his life, and by this his power is best demonstrated, and will be transmitted to posterity. It is published in Scotland and Germany, and in all the world where Christian theology is a subject of study this work is held in the highest esteem, as the best exhibition of that system of Calvinistic doctrine known as Princeton theology. As a writer on theological, ethical, and ecclesiastical subjects, Dr. Hodge was easily at the head of all his contemporaries, and the distinguishing grace of his writings was their exquisite clearness. No one was at a loss to know what he believed and what he intended to teach, and the authority on which he relied. His theology was Biblical. In the profoundest discussions, a text of Holy Scripture is a rock on which his structure of argument rests. Therefore the rationalism of modern schools, infusing itself into his own Church and the literature of the day, was to him a shame as well as a sin, and he resented and resisted it with tremendous energy and effect; his blows were those of a giant. No man has been more persistently abused than Dr. Hodge. He has been represented as the incarnation of bigotry. Those who could not answer his arguments or detect a flaw in his logic had to fall back on the only weapon left in their artillery. No man was farther removed from intolerance, bigotry, and persecution, as all who knew him while living, and now revere and venerate him dead, know. See *Necrol. Report of Princeton Theol. Sem.* 1879, p. 9; *Memorial Discourses*, by Drs. Paxton and Boardman; *Life*, by Dr. A. A. Hodge (1880).

Hodge, John, D.D., a learned and respected English Presbyterian clergyman, was educated at Taunton for the ministry, and had his first pastoral charge at Deal, Kent. He removed to Gloucester, where he preached for some years. In 1749 he accepted a call to the church at Crosby Square, London. His energies became enfeebled with age, church members died, and he resigned in 1762 and lived in retirement, preaching occasionally till he died, Aug. 18, 1767. He bequeathed his valuable library to the Taunton Academy, where he was educated. He published a volume on *The Evidences of Christianity*, and several single *Sermons.* See Wilson, *Dissenting Churches*, i, 354.

Hodges, Richmond E., a minister of the Church of England, was born in 1836. When an apprentice in London, Mr. Hodges found an old Hebrew grammar, which fascinated his mind, and made him determine to become a Shemitic scholar. The result was that, after acting as scripture-reader for a short time, he was sent, by the Society for Promoting Christianity among the Jews, first to Palestine, then to Algeria, where he stayed until 1865. A few years afterwards he resigned his connection with the society, in order to devote himself more fully to linguistic studies. For some time he was a minister of the Reformed Episcopal Church, but a few years before his death he was ordained a clergyman of the Established Church of England. He died May 9, 1881. Mr. Hodges published *Ancient Egypt* (1861); in 1863 he brought out a new and revised edition of Craik's *Principia Hebraica;* in 1876 he published a new edition of Cory's *Ancient Fragments*, and at the time of his death he was engaged upon *An English Version of the Armenian History of Moses of Khorene.* He also assisted in the Old-Test. portion of the work known as *The Holy Bible in Paragraphs and Sections, with Emendations of the Text*, and contributed largely to the *Encyclopædia Britannica*, and to the supplement to the *English Encyclopædia.* (B. P.)

Hodgson, Francis, D.D., a Methodist Episcopal minister, was born of Wesleyan parents, in Driffield, England, Feb. 13, 1805. He sailed to the United States in his youth, and with his parents settled in West Chester, Pa., where he developed a noble manhood. He entered the Philadelphia Conference in 1828, and served consecutively, Dauphin Circuit; Elkton, Md.; St. George's, Philadelphia; Harrisburg Circuit; and Columbia. In 1836 he was transferred to the New York Conference, and stationed at Vestry Street charge; afterwards at Mulberry Street, Middletown; Hartford; and New Haven. In 1845 he received a retransfer to the Philadelphia Conference, and was sent to Trinity charge, Philadelphia; afterwards at Salem, Pa.; Harrisburg; St. Paul's, Wilmington, Del.; St. George's, Philadelphia; Union; Lancaster, Pa.; South Philadelphia District; Fifth Street, Philadelphia; and Salem, Pa. He was transferred to the Central Pennsylvania Conference in 1868, and stationed successively at Danville, Lewisburg, and Chambersburg. A superannuated relation was granted him in 1876 with the Philadelphia Conference, and he retired to that city, where he died, April 16, 1877. Dr. Hodgson was a persuasive orator, a successful preacher, a profound theologian, and a skilful polemic, as well as a man of deep piety and unwavering devotedness to the Church. See *Minutes of Annual Conferences*, 1878, p. 75; Simpson, *Cyclop. of Methodism*, s. v.

Hodur (or **Hoeder**), in Norse mythology, was a very powerful god of the Asas, but blind; the son of Odin and Frigga, therefore Baldur's brother. The latter having been made invulnerable by his mother, Loke showed the blind Hodur the small plant mistletoe, which the latter threw at Baldur, who died and was taken to Hel in the infernal regions. A third son of Odin avenged Baldur's death, by slaying Hodur and sending him to Hel. Hodur and Baldur remain good friends, because the former committed the injury involuntarily.

Hoek, Jan van, an eminent Flemish painter, born at Antwerp in 1597, was instructed in the school of Rubens, and became one of his most distinguished scholars. On returning to Flanders he was invited to Vienna by Ferdinand II, and painted the portraits of the imperial family, and some historical works for the churches and public edifices. Among his historical works is a picture of the *Deposition from the Cross*, in the Church of Our Lady, at Mechlin, highly commended. He died at Antwerp in 1650. See Hoefer, *Nouv. Biog. Générale*, s. v.; Spooner, *Biog. Hist. of the Fine Arts*, s. v.

Hoeke, Peter van, a Protestant preacher at Leyden, who lived at the beginning of the 18th century, is the author of, *Uytlegging van het Breef an de Hebreyen* (Leyden, 1693):—*Uytlegging van het Boeck Jobs* (1697):—*Uytlegging over de Propheten Nahum, Habakuk, Zephania, Haggai, Zacharia en Malachia* (1709):—*Lucubrationes in Catechismum Palatinum* (1711):—*Straets der goddelike Waerheden* (1718). See Winer, *Handbuch der theol. Lit.* i, 266; Jöcher, *Allgemeines Gelehrten-Lexikon*, s. v. (B. P.)

Hoff, Ludwig Johannes, a Lutheran minister, was born Dec. 29, 1795, at Laage, Mecklenburg-Schwerin. In 1819 he entered the missionary college of Rev. J. Jänicke, at Berlin, and in 1821 connected himself with the London Society for Propagating the Gospel among the Jews. In 1822 he was sent as missionary to Poland, and was ordained in 1824. In 1841 Hoff was stationed at Cracow, and died April 28, 1851, a faithful servant, who for nearly thirty-two years had been an active and most laborious missionary among the Jews. (B. P.)

Hoffmanists. See Hoffmann, Daniel.

Hoffmann, August Heinrich (better known as *Hoffmann von Fallersleben*), a German theologian, was born at Fallersleben, Lüneburg, April 2, 1798. After studying at Göttingen and Bonn, he devoted himself at first to theology, but afterwards betook himself entirely to the history of literature. He died Jan. 20, 1874. Hoffmann edited, in connection with Endlicher, *Fragmenta Theotisca Versionis Antiquissimæ Ev. S. Matthæi et Aliquot Homiliarum* (Vienna, 1834):—Williram's *Uebersetzung und Auslegung des Hohenliedes* (Breslau, 1827):—*Geschichte des deutschen Kirchenliedes bis auf Luther's Zeit* (1832; 3d ed. 1861):—*Ringwaldt und Benj. Schmolcke* (1833). See Winer, *Handbuch der deutschen Lit.* i, 67; ii, 287, 288; Zuchold, *Bibl. Theol.* i, 569. (B. P.)

Hoffmann, Franz, a Roman Catholic philosopher of Germany, was born at Aschaffenburg, Jan. 19, 1804. He studied at Munich, was in 1834 professor of philosophy at Amberg, in 1835 at Würzburg, and died Oct. 22, 1881. He published, *Vorhalle zur spekulativen Lehre Baader's* (Aschaffenburg, 1836):—*Spekulative Entwickelung der ewigen Selbsterzeugung Gottes, aus Franz von Baader's sämmtlichen Schriften zusammengestellt* (Amberg, 1835):—*Baader's sämmtliche Werke* (Leipsic, 1851-60, 16 vols.):—*Grundriss der allgemeinen reinen Logik* (2d ed. Würzburg, 1855):—*Baader's Blitzstrahl wider Rom* (2d ed. 1871):—*Kirche und Staat* (1872):—*Philosophische Schriften* (Erlangen, 1867-81, 8 vols.). Hoffmann, as a former pupil of Baader, contributed greatly towards propagating his master's philosophy. (B. P.)

Hoffmann, Ludwig Friedrich Wilhelm, general superintendent of Brandenburg, was born Oct. 30, 1806, in Leonberg, Würtemberg. His father was the founder of the religious colony at Kornthal (1819), and his brother, Christoph, was the originator of a movement for the colonization of Palestine. Hoffmann studied at Tübingen, where David Strauss was his fellow-student; was in 1829 vicar at Heumaden, near Stuttgart, in 1834 at Stuttgart, and accepted, in 1839, a call to Basle as inspector of the Mission Institute. He remained there for twelve years, giving himself up with great enthusiasm to his duties and to the study of the history of missions. During this period he published, *Missionsstunden und Vorträge* (Stuttgart, 1847, 1851, 1853):—*Missionsfragen* (Heidelberg, 1847):—*Die Epochen der Kirchengeschichte Indien's* (1853):—*Die christl. Literatur als Werkzeug der Mission* (eod.). From Basle he passed to Tübingen as professor; and, in 1852, he accepted the call of Frederick William IV as court-preacher to Berlin. He exerted a greater influence over the king of Prussia than any other man, in favor of ecclesiastical union. Hoffmann was an indefatigable worker, and was very influential as an evangelical preacher, sympathizing with the theology of Bengel. He died Aug. 28, 1873. He published a number of volumes of sermons under the title, *Ruf zum Herrn* (Berlin, 1854-58, 8 vols.), and *Ein Jahr der Gnade in Christo* (1864):—*Die Posaune Deutschlands* (1861-63):—*Die göttliche Stufenordnung im Alten Testament* (1854). He also contributed largely to the first edition of Herzog, etc. See Plitt-Herzog, *Real-Encyklop.* s. v.; Lichtenberger, *Encyclop. des Sciences Religieuses*, s. v.; Zuchold, *Bibl. Theol.* i, 572 sq.; *Leben und Wirken des Dr. L. Fr. W. Hoffmann* Berlin, 1878, written by his son Karl). (B. P.)

Hofmann, Johann Christian Konrad (afterwards honored by Bavaria with the title *von Hofmann*), a German theologian, was born Dec. 21, 1810, at Nuremberg. He studied at Erlangen, where the Reformed theologian, Krafft, exercised a lasting influence on Hofmann. From Erlangen he went to Berlin in 1829, at a time when Hegel, Schleiermacher, Neander, and Hengstenberg were lecturing. After teaching several years at the gymnasium in Erlangen, he became *repetent* at the university, and now devoted himself exclusively to theology. Thus he writes in 1835, "The more I occupy myself with Scripture exegesis, the more powerfully am I convinced of the certainty that the divine Word is one single work, and the more am I stimulated with the glad hope that our generation will witness the victory of the truth of inspiration. It is especially the wonderful unity of history and doctrine, which becomes clearer and clearer to me. The whole Old-Test. prophecy is but a seeing of the deepest signification of historical events and conditions. . . . It is a sheer impossibility that the prophecies of the prophets and apostles are false, while their doctrines are true; for here form and contents, fact and doctrine, are one, which is the distinguishing characteristic of revealed truth. . . . I pray God to permit me to see the Christ, now crucified by his enemies, lifted up by himself, that I may place my hands in the print of the nails, and may know him in the glory of his victory, whom I have heretofore loved in the humility of his conflict and suffering." In 1838 he commenced his academical career, and presented as his dissertation, *De Argumento Psalmi Centesimi Decimi*, in which he makes David the author of that psalm, but denies the common Messianic interpretation, by referring the psalm to the angel of Jehovah. In the year 1841 he was made professor, and published the first part of his famous work, *Weissagung und Erfüllung*. In 1842 he accepted a call to Rostock, but returned to Erlangen in 1845. His return to the latter place marked a new period of prosperity for the university, to which he devoted all his energies. He died Dec. 20, 1877. Hofmann took not only a deep interest in ecclesiastical matters, but also in political affairs, and was for several sessions a member of the Bavarian Parliament. Among Hofmann's first publications were some historical works, *Geschichte des Aufruhrs in den Sevennen unter Ludwig XIV* (1837):—*Lehrbuch der Weltgeschichte für Gymnasien* (1839; 2d ed. 1843):—*De Bellis ab Antiocho Epiphane Adversus Ptolemæos Gestis* (1835). His first effort in theology was *Die siebenzig Jahre des Jeremias und die siebenzig Jahrwochen des Daniel* (Nuremberg, 1836). Concerning this latter work he wrote to a friend: "If I am correct, I cause a great revolution in the Assyrian, Chaldæan, Egyptian, and Israelitish chronology. Jerusalem was destroyed in 605 B.C.; the seventy years of the Captivity go from 605 to 535, the sixty-two weeks of Daniel ($7 \times 62 = 434$) from 605 to 171, the sixty-third from 171 to 164. Thus the results of both investigations which I made independently from each other, agree most harmoniously with each other." *Weissagung und Erfüllung im alten und neuen Testament* (1841–44) appeared at a time when two views of prophecy prevailed; criticism explained it away as presentiment, Hengstenberg petrified it into simple prediction. Hofmann brought prophecy into closest connection with history, and treated it as an organic whole. History itself is prophecy; each period contains the germ of the future, and prefigures it. Thus the entire sacred history, in all its essential developments, is a prophecy of the final and eternal relation between God and man. The incarnation of Christ marks the beginning of the *essential* fulfilment; for the head is only the realization of the intended perfect communion with God, when it is joined with the body of believers. The word of prophecy connects itself with prophetical history, both corresponding with each other. Each event in the course of history is followed by a progress of prophecy. When God gives divers forms to the history of the Old Test., he thus exhibits the different sides which are comprehended and united in the person of Christ. Prophecy in the course of history becomes ever richer and richer in its forms, but points only to one goal—the God-man. He is then again the starting-point for new prophecy and new hope, for his appearance is the prefigurement of the final glorification of the congregation of believers. The permanent value of this work consists in the proof that the Old and New Tests. are parts of a single history of salvation; displaying the gradual realization, by divine interpositions, of redemption for the race. Between 1852 and 1856 Hofmann published his second great work, *Schriftbeweis* (2 vols.; 2d ed. 1857–60). In this work he attempted to prove the authenticity and divine origin of Christianity from its records. He lamented the usual method of doing this from single passages of Scripture, and himself sought to use the Biblical record in its entirety as one organic whole. He started from the idea that, to understand Christianity, it was not necessary to describe religious experiences, nor rehearse the doctrines of the Scriptures and the Church, but to develop the simple fact that makes us Christians, or the communion of God with man, mediated by Christ. Herein he differs fundamentally from Schleiermacher, who starts out from the sense of absolute dependence in the Christian's experience. Hofmann starts with the new birth. The results at which they arrive in their systems are therefore so entirely different. With Hofmann all is historical, with Schleiermacher, nothing. This work aroused opposition. The author had combated the doctrine of vicarious atonement, and the charge was made against him of denying the atonement altogether. Hofmann had expected opposition. For a time he kept quiet, but finally he replied in *Schutzschriften für eine neue Weise, alle Wahrheit zu lehren* (1856–59). Without continuing the controversy, Hofmann wrote his last great work, *Die heilige Schrift des neuen Testaments zusammenhängend untersucht* (1862 sq.), in which he endeavored to prove scientifically the inspiration of the Scripture and the integrity of the canon. After Hofmann's death there were published, *Theologische Ethik* (1878):—*Encyclopädie der Theologie* (edited by Bestmann, 1879):—*Biblische Hermeneutik* (edited by Volck, 1880). See Stählin, *J. Chr. K. v. Hofmann*, in Luthardt's *Allgemeine Lutherische Kirchenzeitung* (1878); Grau, *Erinnerungen an J. Chr. K. v. Hofmann* (Gütersloh, 1879); Plitt-Herzog, *Real-Encyklop.* s. v.; Lichtenberger, *Encyclop. des Sciences Religieuses*, s. v. (B. P.)

Hofmann, Leonhard, professor of Oriental languages at Jena, who died Dec. 14, 1737, is the author of, *De Ancilla Ebræa ad Ezek. xxi*, 7 (Jena, 1712):—*Disp. ad Psal. ii*, 7 (1726):—*De Singulari Hebræorum cura Sepeliendi Mortuos, ad Matt. viii*, 22 (eod.):—*De Summo Hebræorum Sacerdote ante diem Expiationis Adjurato* (1730). See Götte, *Gelehrtes Europa*, ii, 484; Jöcher, *Allgemeines Gelehrten-Lexikon*, s. v.; Fürst, *Bibl. Jud.* i, 404. (B. P.)

Hofstätter, Heinrich von, a German prelate, was born in 1805 at Aindling, in Upper Bavaria. He studied at first jurisprudence, and was already promoted in 1829 as "doctor utriusque juris," when he betook himself to the study of theology, received holy orders in 1833, and was in 1836 appointed cathedral-dean at Munich. In 1839 he was made bishop of Passau, and died May 12, 1875. (B. P.)

Hofstede de Groot, Peter, a distinguished Dutch theologian, was born Oct. 8, 1802, at Leer, in East Frisia. In 1826 he was preacher in the Reformed Church, in 1829 professor at the university in Groningen, but resigned his professorship in 1872. He died Aug. 27, 1884. Hofstede was the head of the so-called "Groningen school," the adherents of which called themselves the "Evangelicals." They represent the theologico-ecclesiastical middle-party, between the "Liberals" and the "Orthodox," and their organ, *Waarheid in Liefde*, edited by Hofstede de Groot, Pareau, and Van Oordt (1837–72), is the best exponent of this school. With Pareau, de Groot published, *Encyclopædia Theologi Christiani* (1840; 3d ed. 1851), and *Dogmatica et Apologetica Christiana* (1845). His own works are, *Theologia Naturalis* (1834; 4th ed. 1861):—*Institutiones Historiæ Ecclesiæ Christi* (1835):—*Opvoe-*

ding der Menschheid (1847):—*Kort Overzigt van de Leer der Zonde* (1856):—*Over de evangelisch-catholicke Godgeleerdheid as de Godgeleerdheid der Toekomst* (eod.):—*Het Evangelie der Apostelen tegenover de Twijfelingen en de Wijsheid der Wereld* (1861):—*Basilides, als erster Zeuge für alter und Autorität neutestamentlicher Schriften* (1868):—*Oud-catholicke Bewejung in het Licht der Kerkgeschiedenis* (1877). See Zuchold, *Bibl. Theol.* i, 577; Brockhaus, *Conversations-Lexikon*, 13th ed. s. v. (B. P.)

Hogan, WILLIAM, of some notoriety in Catholic controversies, a young priest of inferior education but good natural parts, who had been dismissed from Maynooth for a breach of discipline, left the diocese of Limerick in 1818 or 1819 for New York. He was first employed in the ministry in Albany, but left that city, against the wish of Dr. Connolly, then bishop of New York, and was temporarily installed by Rev. Dr. De Barth, administrator of the see of Philadelphia, Pa., as pastor of St. Mary's Church in that city. In December, 1820, bishop Conwell took possession of the see, and having reason to suspect Hogan's conduct in Ireland and elsewhere, withdrew his faculties. Hogan continued to officiate at St. Mary's in spite of the censure of his bishop and the refusal of the archbishop of Baltimore to entertain his appeal, the trustees of the church supporting Hogan. On Feb. 11, 1821, Conwell excommunicated Hogan, appointed other pastors, occupied the church for some months, but in the summer of that year Hogan and his party took possession of the church. Bishop England of Charleston, visiting Philadelphia, and having promised Hogan a mission in his diocese, induced Conwell to grant him power to absolve the troublesome ecclesiastic on proper submission. On Oct. 18, 1821, England absolved him; but the next day Hogan, hearkening to the advice of his trustees, retracted, said mass at St. Mary's, and resumed his functions as pastor. England then re-excommunicated him. Many of the members now deserted the interdicted church and went to St. Joseph's, where the bishop had installed William V. Harold, former pastor at St. Mary's. The two parties became more and more exasperated; the orthodox (as De Courcy and Shea term the party who went with the bishop) hoped to defeat the schismatics by electing a new board of trustees. Every male occupant of a seat was an elector. The election took place in the church on Easter Tuesday, 1822, and led to sad results. The disorder was frightful; blood was shed; and the schismatics triumphed, preserving Hogan as pastor. At the close of the year the archbishop of Baltimore (Maréchal) returned from Rome, bringing a papal brief (Aug. 2, 1822), which solemnly condemned the schismatics of St. Mary's. On Dec. 10, 1822, Hogan submitted, and received from Conwell his exeat and removal of censures. On the 14th of the same month the unhappy priest, circumvented by the trustees (it is said), objected that the authenticity of the brief had not been shown, and continued to officiate and preach at St. Mary's. He published violent pamphlets against his diocesan and bishop England, whom he sought to compromise. Hogan at length grew tired of his rebellion, left Philadelphia for the South, married, became a custom-house officer in Boston, went into the pay of the enemies of Romanism, published some books to stimulate the Know-Nothing movement (*Popery as it Was and Is*, Boston and New York, 1845:—*Nunneries and Auricular Confession*, recently reprinted at Hartford), and died in 1851 or 1852. The above account is from the standpoint of the opponents of Hogan. The historians of the Roman Catholic Church think the troubles of which Hogan was the victim were due largely to the trustee system, whose influence in the Catholic Church they deem pernicious, and it has caused many local schisms, of which this of St. Mary's was the most celebrated and scandalous, and was not healed for many years. For an account of this schism, and voluminous documents, see bishop England's *Works*, v, 109–232; De Courcy and Shea, *Hist. of Cath. Church in U. S.* p. 217.

Hogarth, WILLIAM, a celebrated painter, was born at London in 1697 or 1698, apprenticed to an engraver at an early age, and at the expiration of his apprenticeship entered the Academy of St. Martin's Lane. His first painting was a representation of Wanstead Assembly. In 1725 he engraved some prints for Beaver's *Military Punishments of the Ancients.* As a painter, he had a great facility in catching a likeness, and adopted a novel method of grouping families. He therefore devoted himself to the delineation of the calamities and crimes of private life, and the vices and follies of the age. His series of, *The Harlot's Progress; The Rake's Progress*, gained him great reputation. He was an eccentric genius, and his talents were eminently in burlesque and satire. He did not excel in historical painting, but among his principal plates there are some good works by him, representing *The Good Samaritan; The Pool of Bethesda; Paul Before Felix; Moses Brought to Pharaoh's Daughter.* He died Oct. 26, 1764.

Hoheisel, CARL LUDWIG, a German professor of Greek and Oriental languages, was born at Dantzic, Sept. 18, 1692. He studied at different universities, and died at his native place, April 7, 1732. He wrote, *Observationes Philolog.-Exegeticæ, Quibus Nonnulla δυσνόητα Esaiæ Loca Illustrantur* (Dantzic, 1729):—*Diss. I, II de Vasculo Mannæ* (Jena, 1715). See Winer, *Handbuch der theol. Lit.* i, 217; Fürst, *Bibl. Jud.* i, 404; Jöcher, *Allgemeines Gelehrten-Lexikon*, s. v. (B. P.)

Holbein, HANS, an eminent Swiss painter, designer, and wood-engraver, was born at Basle in 1498, although some think he was a native of Augsburg. He was the son and scholar of John Holbein, who settled at Basle, and resided there during the rest of his life. At the age of fifteen Hans manifested great abilities, and painted portraits of himself and his father, which were engraved in 1512. He was invited by an English nobleman to visit England, but declined the invitation. Several years afterwards he formed an intimacy with Erasmus, and painted his portrait. The latter persuaded him to go to England, and gave him a letter to Sir Thomas More. On arriving in London he sought out that nobleman, who received him with kindness, giving him apartments in his house. One day Holbein, happening to mention the nobleman who some years before had invited him to England, Sir Thomas was desirous of knowing who it was. Holbein replied that he had forgotten the title, but thought he could draw his likeness from memory; and this he did so strongly that it was immediately recognised. This peer was either the earl of Arundel or the earl of Surrey. Holbein was introduced by Sir Thomas to Henry VIII, who immediately took him into his service, assigning him apartments in the palace, with a liberal pension. On the death of Jane Seymour, Holbein was sent to Flanders to draw the portrait of Christiana, duchess dowager of Milan. He painted in oil, distemper, and water-colors. He had never practiced the last until he went to England, where he acquired the art from Lucas Corneli. There are but a few historical works by Holbein in England. The most important is that in the Surgeons' Hall, of *Henry VIII Granting the Charter to the Company of Surgeons.* At Basle are eight pictures of the *Passion of Christ;* and in the library of the University a *Dead Christ*, painted on a panel, in 1521. "It has been doubted whether the celebrated *Dance of Death* was originally designed by Holbein; but this has been occasioned by confounding the sets of prints of the *Dance of Death* engraved by Matthew Merian with the wooden cuts by Holbein, after his own designs, the originals of which are preserved in the public library at Basle." As a wood-engraver, Holbein is said to have executed some works as early as 1511, and he engraved a great many wood-cuts for the publishers of Basle, Zurich,

Lyons, and Leyden. The most important of these are a set of wood-cuts, entitled, *The Dance of Death*, which, complete, consists of fifty-three small upright plates, but is seldom found above forty-six. There are also, by Holbein, a set of ninety small cuts of subjects from the Old Test., which were published at Lyons in 1539. He made a number of designs from the Bible, which were engraved and published at Leyden in 1547. Holbein died at London in 1554. For a list of his works, see Spooner, *Biog. Hist. of the Fine Arts*, s. v.

Holcomb, Frederick, D.D., a Protestant Episcopal clergyman, officiated for many years in Trinity Church, Northfield, Conn., until 1861, when he became the minister of Christ Church, Bethlem. In 1865 he was residing in Watertown without regular pastoral work. In 1868 he officiated in Christ Church, Harwinton, in the neighborhood of Watertown, and continued in this work until his death, May 26, 1872, at the age of eighty-five years. See *Prot. Episc. Almanac*, 1873, p. 133.

Holda (or **Holla**), in German mythology, was originally a friendly goddess of the ancient heathen Germans, probably the one mentioned by Tacitus, and compared with Isis. The name is derived from the German *hold*, or *huld*, "mild." After the introduction of Christianity the goddess became a spectre, but still with friendly rather than threatening attributes. The myths about her are nowhere so spread as in Hesse and Thuringia. The popular belief in Holda (*Frau Holle*) is spread over the Rhone into Northern France and Lower Saxony. She is represented as a heavenly being, encircling the earth; when it snows she makes her bed so that the feathers fly. She enjoys seas and wells; at noon she is seen bathing and disappearing in the stream. Mortals reach her dwelling through a well. Her yearly procession on Christmas is supposed to bring fruitfulness to the country, but she also rides with the furious army, or leads it. She loves music, but her song has a sorrowful tone.

Holder, William, D.D., a learned English divine, was born in Nottinghamshire, and educated in Pembroke Hall, Cambridge. In 1642 he became rector of Blechingdon, Oxfordshire. He was canon of Ely, and of St. Paul's. He died at Amen Corner, London, Jan. 24, 1696, leaving, *Elements of Speech* (1669):—*Discourse on Time* (1691):—*Principles of Harmony* (1694). See Chalmers, *Biog. Dict.* s. v.; Allibone, *Dict. of Brit. and Amer. Authors*, s. v.

Holebeck, Laurence, an English scholar, probably a native of Lincolnshire, was bred a monk in the abbey of Ramsey, and was one of the first Hebrew scholars of his age, a language then so unknown, even to the priests, that in the reign of Henry VIII, Erasmus, with his keen wit, says, "they counted all things Hebrew which they did not understand" (*Dial. per Relig. Er.*). Holebeck made a Hebrew dictionary, counted exact in those days. Pits complains that Robert Wakefield, the first Hebrew professor at Cambridge, purloined this dictionary to his private use. Holebeck died in 1410. See Fuller, *Worthies of England* (ed. Nuttall), ii, 290.

Holiness, Beauty of, is a phrase occurring several times in the English Bible (always as a translation of the Heb. *hadrath' ko'desh*, הַדְרַת קֹדֶשׁ, *ornament of sanctity*, 1 Chron. xv, 29; 2 Chron. xx, 21; Psa. xxix, 2; cxvi, 9; in the plur. of the cognate term הָדָר, *hadár*, Psa. cx, 3), which simply denotes *splendid garments*, such as are worn on festive occasions, i. q. "holiday suit," not necessarily the sacred priestly vestments, since it is usually, if not exclusively, applied to nonsacerdotal persons.

Holl, Francis Xaver, a German Jesuit, was born at Schwandorf, Nov. 22, 1720, and died March 6, 1784, professor at Heidelberg. He published, *Statistica Ecclesiæ Germanicæ* (Heidelberg, 1779):—*Diss. Harmonia Juris Naturæ, Canonici, Civilis et Publici Germaniæ* (1782). See Weidlich, *Biographische Notizen*, iii; Jöcher, *Allgemeines Gelehrten-Lexikon*, s. v.; Winer, *Handbuch der theol. Lit.* i, 779. (B. P.)

Hollar, Wentzel, an eminent Bohemian engraver, was born at Prague in 1607, studied at Frankfort under Matthew Merian, and at the age of eighteen published his first plates, an *Ecce Homo*, and the *Virgin and Infant*. He made the tour of Germany. At Cologne he formed an acquaintance with the earl of Arundel, who took him into his employment. About this time the civil war broke out, in which Hollar became involved on the side of the royalists, and was made a prisoner by the opposite party in 1645. On obtaining his liberty he went to Flanders, and settled at Antwerp. In 1652 he returned to England, but gained little encouragement. He died March 28, 1677. There are about two thousand four hundred prints by this artist, and some of them possess considerable merit. The following are only a few of his sacred subjects: *The Virgin Suckling the Infant Jesus and Caressing St. John; The Holy Family; The Ecce Homo*, with many figures; *The Queen of Sheba Visiting Solomon; The Magdalen in the Desert Kneeling before a Crucifix*. See Spooner, *Biog. Hist. of the Fine Arts*, s. v.

Representation of Holda.

Holley, Horace, LL.D., a Unitarian minister, was born at Salisbury, Conn., Feb. 12, 1781. He was fitted for college at Williamstown, Mass.; graduated from Yale in 1803; studied law for a few months; and then commenced the study of divinity under president Dwight. He was licensed to preach in December, 1804, and was ordained and installed minister of the congregation in Greenfield, Sept. 13, 1805. He resigned this charge Sept. 13, 1808, and was installed as pastor of the Hollis Street Church, Boston, March 8, 1809. He accepted an invitation to the presidency of Transylvania University in 1818, and held that office till 1827, when he resigned it, with a view to taking charge of a seminary in Louisiana, but was attacked with yellow fever in New Orleans, and died July 31, 1827. See Sprague, *Annals of the Amer. Pulpit*, viii, 265.

Holliday, William Harrison, D.D., a Methodist Episcopal minister, was born in Berkeley County, W. Va., Aug. 31, 1835. He was converted at the age of eleven, preached his first sermon at sixteen, entered Dickinson College, Carlisle, Pa.. in 1853, and in 1855 was admitted to the Baltimore Conference. He served as junior preacher successively on Winchester, Hillsborough, and Warrenton circuits. In 1858 he was sent to Summerfield Circuit, late in that year was transferred to the Iowa Conference, and appointed to Cascade; returned a year later to the Baltimore Conference, and successively served Baltimore, South River, and Montgomery circuits, South Baltimore Station, East Washington, Winchester District, Eutaw Street, and Harford Avenue. He died March 23, 1879. Dr. Holliday was a self-sacrificing, warm-hearted, heroic, successful preacher. See *Minutes of Annual Conferences*, 1879, p. 15.

Hollingworth, Richard, D.D., an English clergyman, was vicar of Westham, and rector of St. Botolph's, Aldgate. He published six *Sermons* (1673-93), and several treatises upon the famous *Eikon-Basilikè* controversy. See Allibone, *Dict. of Brit. and Amer. Authors*, s. v.

Holmboe, Kristoffer Andreas, a Norwegian Orientalist, was born March 19, 1796. In 1825 he was professor at Christiania, resigned his office in 1876, and died April 2, 1882. He is the author of, *Traces du Budhisme en Norvége Avant l'Introduction de Christianisme* (1857):—*Bibelsk Real-Ordbog* (1868). (B. P.)

Holme, John Stanford, D.D., a Baptist minister, was born in Philadelphia, March 4, 1822, and was a descendant of John Holme, one of the first Baptists of Pennsylvania. John S. prepared for college at New Hampton, N. H.; first studied law in Philadelphia; but afterwards graduated at Madison University in 1850, and became pastor of a church in Watertown, N. Y. Four years later he was called to the pastorate of the Pierrepont Street Baptist Church, now the First, of Brooklyn, where he remained for some years, and then organized Trinity Baptist Church of New York, and was its pastor for fourteen years. He resigned that pastorate to accept that of the Riverside Baptist Church, at Eighty-sixth Street and the Boulevard, but, his health failing, he passed much of his time resting in Europe. He died at Clifton Springs, N. Y., Aug. 26, 1884. Dr. Holme was known for his literary attainments, having prepared the *Plymouth Collection of Hymns* for the Baptist churches, and compiled a popular work, entitled *Light at Evening Time*. For some time he had been a member of the staff of *The Homiletic Monthly*. See Cathcart, *Bapt. Encyclop.* s. v.

Holmes, David, D.D., a Methodist Episcopal minister, was born at Newburgh, N. Y., March 16, 1810. He was converted in his youth, and in 1834 entered the Oneida Conference, filling many of its best stations till 1855, when he was transferred to the Southern Illinois Conference. After effective labors in it of five years he was transferred to the North-west Indiana Conference, wherein he served La Porte, Delphi, and Pittsburgh. From 1861 to 1866 he was principal of Battle Ground Collegiate Institute, and in 1867 principal of North-western Indiana College. In 1868 he re-entered the regular work, and served successively Simpson Chapel, Greencastle; Brookstown; Monticello, and Battle Ground, Mich. He died Nov. 14, 1873. Dr. Holmes was a ripe scholar, an excellent logician, a thorough educator, an able preacher, and an author of merited repute. See *Minutes of Annual Conferences*, 1874, p. 93; Simpson, *Cyclop. of Methodism*, s. v.

Holmes, Obadiah, a Baptist minister, was born at Preston, Lancashire, England, in 1606, and was educated at Oxford. He arrived in America in 1639, and continued a communicant with the Congregationalists, first at Salem, and then at Rehoboth eleven years, when he became a Baptist, and joined the Baptist Church in Newport, R. I. In 1652, when the minister, Mr. Clark, sailed for England, Mr. Holmes took charge of the church in Newport, and this relation he held till his death, Oct. 15, 1682. Mr. Holmes underwent great persecution for his religious principles, being imprisoned for several months, and publicly whipped by the Puritan authorities in 1661. See Sprague, *Annals of the Amer. Pulpit*, vi, 23.

Holobolus, Manuel (Μανουὴλ Ὁλόβωλος), a Byzantine prelate and philologist, who lived in the latter part of the 13th century. From his infancy he was attached to John Lascaris, who was placed upon the throne at nine years of age, and shared with Michael Palæologus the title of emperor. When Michael ordered the young prince to be blinded and sent into exile, Holobolus, who then was still a student, could not conceal his indignation, and for this imprudence the emperor ordered that his nose and lips should be cut off. He was then imprisoned in a monastery, where he pursued his studies with so much success that he was put in charge of the younger monks in 1267. Shortly afterwards the emperor was reconciled to Holobolus, and conferred upon him the dignity of a rhetor, or lecturer on the Holy Scriptures. During the discussions which were taking place between the Greek and Latin churches, on the subject of a reunion, he opposed energetically the proposition of Michael Palæologus. He was consigned to a monastery at Nicæa in 1273. The emperor soon after brought him back to Constantinople with a cord around his neck. A long captivity did not change at all the sentiments of Holobolus, for he took part, in 1283, in the deposition of the patriarch John Veccus, a partisan of the Latin union. Holobolus left *Political Verses on Michael Palæologus*, which are cited in the *Glossarium* of Du Cange, under Ῥήτωρ and Ἑρμηνεῖαι. See Hoefer, *Nouv. Biog. Générale*, s. v.

Holocaust (ὁλόκαυστος, *wholly burned*), a kind of sacrifice wherein the whole offering was burned or consumed by fire, nothing being left for the feast. Among the heathen it was analogous to the Scripture *burnt-offering*.

Holon of Judah. For this place Lieut. Conder conjecturally proposes (*Tent Work*, ii, 337) *Beit 'Alâm*, a large ruin nine and a half miles west of Halhul, containing "foundations, caves, cistern, with heaps of stones and remains of an ancient road" (*Memoirs* of Ordnance Survey, iii, 321); and Trelawney Saunders (*O. T. Map*) locates it at *Khurbet Hanân*, two miles south-west of Hebron. The latter position is possible, but the former is not within the required group of towns.

Holtzfus, Barthold, a Reformed theologian of Germany, was born at Rügenwalde, Pomerania, Dec. 11, 1659. In 1685 he was professor of philosophy at Frankfort, in 1686 court-preacher at Stolpe, in 1696 professor, and in 1698 doctor of theology at Frankfort, and died in 1717. He wrote *De Prædestinatione, Electione et Reprobatione*, and a great many theological treatises, which were published in one volume in 1714. See Jöcher, *Allgemeines Gelehrten-Lexikon*, s. v. (B. P.)

Holtzhalb, DAVID, a Swiss theologian, was born at Zurich, April 25, 1677. He studied at his native place and at Leyden, was in 1702 professor of biblical literature at Zurich, and died Aug. 4, 1731. He wrote, *Exegesis Philologico-Theologica Psalmi xvi*:—*De Dependentia Creaturæa Deo in Esse, Fieri et Operari*:—*Exercitat Bibl. ad Jac. iv*, 5:—*De Sacra Pauli Mathematica ad Eph. iii*, 18:—*De Statutis non Bonis ad Ezek. xx*, 25:—*Typus Theologiæ Naturalis*. See Jöcher, *Allgemeines Gelehrten-Lexikon*, s. v. (B. P.)

Holtzmann, CARL JULIUS, a Protestant theologian of Germany, was born at Carlsruhe, May 6, 1804. He studied at Tübingen, was professor at the lyceum in his native place, from 1841 to 1861 preacher, and at the same time teacher in the theological seminary at Heidelberg. In 1861 he was made a prelate and a member of the higher ecclesiastical court. He was a member of the general synods held in 1861, 1867, 1871, and 1876. He died doctor of theology, Feb. 23, 1877, at Carlsruhe. (B. P.)

Holwell, WILLIAM, an English clergyman, was prebendary of Exeter in 1776, and died Feb. 13, 1798. Some of his publications are, *Beauties of Homer* (1775):—*Extracts from Pope's Translation of the Iliad* (1776):—*A Mythological, Etymological, and Historical Dictionary* (1793). See Allibone, *Dict. of Brit. and Amer. Authors*, s. v.

Holyday, BARTEN, D.D., a learned English divine, was born in the parish of All-Saints about 1593, and educated at Christchurch College, Oxford. He was chaplain to Charles I, and archdeacon of Oxford. He died in 1661. His best known works are a *Translation of Juvenal and Persius* (1673):—*Survey of the World* (1661):—*Twenty Sermons*. See Chalmers, *Biog. Dict.* s. v.; Allibone, *Dict. of Brit. and Amer. Authors*, s. v.

Holyman, JOHN, an English prelate of the 16th century, was born at Codington, Buckinghamshire, educated at New College, Oxford, became a Benedictine at Reading until that monastery was dissolved, and was preferred by queen Mary bishop of Bristol in 1554. Holyman lived peaceably, not imbruing his hands in the blood of Protestants. He died Dec. 20, 1558. See Fuller, *Worthies of England* (ed. Nuttall), i, 197.

Holzapfel, JOHANN TOBIAS GOTTLIEB, a Lutheran theologian of Germany, was born Feb. 24, 1773, at Marburg. In 1798 he was pastor and professor of Oriental languages at Rinteln, and died May 9, 1812. He wrote, *Disquis. Quisnam Ies. xi Intelligendus sit Rex Ætatem Auream Restiturus* (Rinteln, 1808):—*Obadiah neu übersetzt und erläutert* (1798):—*S. F. N. Morus: Prælect. in Epist. Pauli ad Romanos* (ed. 1794). See Fürst, *Bibl. Jud.* i, 406; Winer, *Handbuch der theol. Lit.* i, 218, 226, 256. (B. P.)

Figure of the Holzy.

Holzy, in Slavonic mythology (changed by the ancient chroniclers into *Alcis*, *Alces*, and *Altschis*), were idols of the Wends and Slavs, represented as two brothers. The giant-range of mountains seems to have been the seat of their worship. The priest who served them lived in a sacred wood, which at the same time was the dwelling-place of the gods. The Romans affirmed that the Holzy were Castor and Pollux, and that the priests wore women's dresses.

Homberg, HERZ, a Jewish writer and teacher, who died at Prague, Aug. 24, 1841, is the author of, באור לס' דברים, a commentary on Deuteronomy, prepared for and printed in Mendelssohn's *Pentateuch* (Berlin, 1783, and often):—הכורם, glosses on the Pentateuch, also printed in Mendelssohn's work:—*Ueber die moralische und politische Verbesserung der Israeliten in Böhmen* (1796):—בן־ציון, catechism for Israelites (Augsburg, 1812):—אמרי שפר, or ethics according to the Mosaic law and the Talmud (Vienna, 1802, 2 parts):—בן יקיר, or *Ueber Glaubenswahrheiten und Sittenlehren für die israelitische Jugend* (1814, and often). See Fürst, *Bibl. Jud.* i, 406. (B. P.)

Home, HENRY, *lord Kames*, a Scotch lawyer and philosopher, was born in 1696 at Kames, Berwickshire. He studied law at the University of Edinburgh, and became advocate in 1724. By a large number of publications on the subject of jurisprudence, he obtained from the beginning a large clientship; then, in 1752, he secured the post of judge at the court of sessions, and finally, in 1763, the dignity of a justice of the high court of Scotland. His taste for agriculture and metaphysics gave rise to some of his finest works. There are, among others, *Essays on the Principles of Morality and Natural Religion* (1751), in which he attempts to prove that the laws which prevail in the conduct of man have their foundation in the constitution of the human being, and are as certain and immutable as the physical laws which govern the whole system of the world:—*Elements of Criticism* (1762), in which the author tries to connect literary criticism with the principles of philosophy, very much admired, and still read:—*Sketches of the History of Man* (1773):—*The Gentleman Farmer* (1777), being an attempt to improve agriculture by subjecting it to the test of rational principles:—*Loose Hints upon Education* (1781), chiefly concerning the culture of the heart. Home died Dec. 27, 1782.

Hominicŏlæ (from *homo*, "man," and *colo*, "to worship"), a term of reproach, applied by the Apollinarians (q. v.) and others, to those who worshipped Jesus Christ.

Hommel, JOHANN CHRISTOPH, a Lutheran theologian of Germany, was born Sept. 13, 1685, at Weissenfels. He studied at Leipsic, was in 1712 bachelor of theology, in 1729 superintendent at Neustadt, and died Oct. 17, 1746, member of consistory, first court-preacher, and general superintendent of the duchy of Hildburghausen. He wrote, *Disp. in Matth. xxiv*, 29 (Leipsic, 1712):—*De Fidelibus Veteris Testamenti Extra Ecclesiam Judaicam Visibilem Dispersis*:—*De Consequentiis Evangelico-Lutheranæ Ecclesiæ ab Adversariis Falso Imputatis*:—*De Prærogativis Judæorum Vet. Test.* See Krauss, *Memorabilia von Hildburghausen*, p. 254; Jöcher, *Allgemeines Gelehrten-Lexikon*, s. v. (B. P.)

Hommius, FESTUS, a Reformed theologian, was born in 1576 at Hulst, Holland, and died July 5, 1642, a doctor of theology, preacher and præfect of the theological college at Leyden. Hommius was one of the translators of the Dutch Bible, published by the States-general, and wrote, *Collegium Anti-Bellarminianum, sive Disputationes Theologicæ pro Evangelicis contra Pontificios*:—*Harmonia Synodorum Belgicarum*. See Winer, *Handbuch der theol. Lit.* i, 182, 331; Jöcher, *Allgemeines Gelehrten-Lexikon*, s. v. (B. P.)

Honert (*Tako Hajo*), VAN DEN, a distinguished Dutch divine, was born March 6, 1666, at Norden, East Frisia. He studied at Marburg, Leyden, and Dort, was preacher in 1689, and succeeded in 1714 his former teacher, Solomon van Til, as professor of theology at Leyden. He died Feb. 23, 1740, leaving, *Voorlooper over den Brief an de Romeinen* (1698):—*Verklaaring van den Brief Pauli an de Romeinen* (Leyden, eod.):—*Beknoopte Scheets der Goddelyke Waarheeden* (1703):—*Verklaarung over Luc. vii*, 35 (1706):—*Thoge Priesterschap van Christus naar de Ordening van Melchizedek* (1712):—*Verklaaring van den cx Psalm.* (1714):—*Theologia Naturalis et Revelata* (1715):—*Diss. de Theologiæ*

Propheticæ Necessitate (1721):—*Dissertationes Historicæ:* 1. *De Creatione Mundi;* 2. *De Situ Edenis;* 3. *De Lingua Primæva* (1738). See Moser, *Lexikon der Theologen;* Winer, *Handbuch der theol. Lit.* i, 125, 199; Jöcher, *Allgemeines Gelehrten-Lexikon*, s. v. (B. P.)

Honor Cathĕdræ, an expression used in Spain in the 6th century, to denote the honorary acknowledgment which the bishops received in their parochial visitations.

Honorius, archbishop of Canterbury, was a Roman by birth, and was distinguished among his contemporaries for having been a pupil of Gregory the Great. He was chosen as the successor of Justus, to occupy the see of Canterbury. His consecration probably occurred in 627. His reign was one of long duration. He did much for England in the way of prospering her Church. The music of Canterbury, introduced by Honorius, was imitated even in the Celtic churches, and the tendency it had to promote civilization in England cannot be denied. He died at a good old age, greatly lamented by his people, and was buried at St. Augustine, Sept. 30, 653. See Hook, *Lives of the Archbishops of Canterbury*, i, 111 sq.

Honthorst, Gerard (called *Gherardo dalle Notti*), an eminent Dutch painter, was born at Utrecht in 1592. After studying under Abraham Bloemaert he visited Rome, and applied himself to the study of the works of Michael Angelo Caravaggio. He was patronized by prince Giustiniani, for whom he painted some of his best works, among which are two fine pictures of *St. Peter Delivered from Prison*, and *Christ before Pilate.* There is a torch-light scene by Honthorst, in the Church of the Madonna della Scala, at Rome, representing the *Beheading of St. John.* He died in 1660. See Hoefer, *Nouv. Biog. Générale*, s. v.; Spooner, *Biog. Hist. of the Fine Arts*, s. v.

Honyman, Andrew, a Scotch prelate, was archdeacon of St. Andrews, author of the *Seasonable Case*, and *Survey of Naphtali.* He was made bishop of Orkney in 1664, and died in February, 1676. See Keith, *Scottish Bishops*, p. 228.

Hook, Walter Farquhar, D.D., an eminent Anglican divine, son of Dr. James Hook (1771–1828), dean of Worcester, grandson of James Hook (1746–1827), organist at St. George's Chapel, Windsor, and nephew of Theodore Edward Hook (1788–1841), an eminent English author, was born in London, March 13, 1798. He graduated at Christchurch College, Oxford, in 1821, and was successively curate at Wappingham, Isle of Wight, and in Birmingham, and vicar of Trinity Church, Coventry, till 1837, when he was made vicar of Leeds. Here, during his incumbency of twenty-two years, 21 new churches, 32 parsonages, and more than 60 schools were erected in his parish, chiefly through his instrumentality. He was especially popular among the working classes. In 1859 he became dean of Chichester, and in 1862 a Fellow of the Royal Society. He was appointed chaplain in ordinary to George IV, in 1827, and retained the office under William IV and Victoria, preaching on the accession of the latter his celebrated sermon on *Hear the Church*, of which more than 100,000 copies were sold. He died Oct. 20, 1875. Dean Hook was eminently conservative in theology, and a High-Churchman. His publications are, *Church Dictionary* (7th ed. 1854, 8vo):—*Eccles. Biography* (1845–52, vols. i–viii, 12mo):—*Sermons on the Miracles* (1847–48, 2 vols. 8vo):—*Sermons on Various Subjects* (2d ed. 1844, 8vo):—*Sermons before the University of Oxford* (1847, 12mo):—*The Rights of Presbyters Asserted* (anonymous):—*Lives of the Archbishops of Canterbury*, from the Anglo-Saxon period to Juxon (Lond. 1860–77, 12 vols. 8vo):—*Disestablished Church in the United States* (Lond. 1869, 8vo). Dr. Hook's wife, a model of a saintly and beautiful character, was the author (anon.) of *Meditations for Every Day of the Year*, and *The Cross of Christ.* She died in 1871. See *Church of England Quar. Rev.* April, 1881, art. x; *Men of the Time* (Lond. 1856); *Ecl. Rev.* 4th series, xii, 502; *Fraser's Magazine*, xix, 1; *Life and Letters of W. F. Hook, D.D., F.R.S.*, by his son-in-law, W. R. W. Stephens, prebendary of Chichester (Lond. 1880).

Hooker, Edward William, D.D., a Congregational minister, son of Rev. Asahel Hooker, was born at Goshen, Conn., Nov. 24, 1794. He graduated from Middlebury College in 1814, and from Andover Theological Seminary in 1817; was ordained at Green Farms, Aug. 15, 1821, over which church he remained pastor until 1829, when he became associate general agent of the American Temperance Society, and was also editor of the *Journal of Humanity.* He was installed pastor of the Church at Bennington, Vt., Feb. 22, 1832, and was dismissed in the spring of 1844. From Aug. 25 of the latter year, for four years, he was professor of sacred rhetoric and ecclesiastical history in the Theological Institute of Connecticut, at East Windsor Hill. From 1849 to 1856 he was the regular pastor of the church at South Windsor; after which, until 1862, he served in the same relation at Fair Haven, Vt. He died at Fort Atkinson, Wis., March 31, 1875. Dr. Hooker was a trustee of Middlebury College from 1834 to 1844, and was a corporate member of the American Board of Commissioners for Foreign Missions from 1840. Among his published works are, *Life of Thomas Hooker:—Early Conversions:—Elihu Lewis*, etc.; also several pamphlets, among them, *Marks of Spiritual Declension:—Plea for Sacred Music:—Believing the Truth:—Character and Office of the Holy Spirit*, etc., with various addresses and sermons. He was also a writer for various magazines and other periodicals. See *Cong. Quarterly*, 1876, p. 427.

Hooker, Henry Brown, D.D., a Congregational minister, son of Dr. Thomas Hooker, was born at Rutland, Vt., Aug. 31, 1802. After attending the Castleton Academy, he entered Middlebury College, from which he graduated in 1821. Four years afterwards he graduated from Andover Theological Seminary. He was ordained an evangelist, Oct. 10, 1825, and for one year was a home missionary in South Carolina. From May 2, 1827, to May 17, 1836, he was pastor in Lanesboro', Mass.; from February, 1837, to June, 1858, was pastor in Falmouth; from 1857 to 1873 was secretary of the Massachusetts Home Missionary Society, and continued to assist in the office of that society until his death, July 4, 1881. From 1844 to 1851 he was a member of the Massachusetts Board of Education; from 1845 he was a corporate member of the American Board of Commissioners for Foreign Missions. The American Tract Society published eight tracts from his pen; and he also wrote three tracts for the Tract Society of Boston. He was also the author of two Sunday-school books: *Plea for the Heathen*, and *Put Off and Put On.* See *Cong. Yearbook*, 1882, p. 33.

Hooker, Herman, D.D., an Episcopal clergyman, was born at Poultney, Vt., about 1806. He graduated from Middlebury College in 1825, studied two years in Princeton Theological Seminary, and subsequently took orders in the Protestant Episcopal Church; but on losing his health became a bookseller in Philadelphia, Pa., where he died, July 25, 1865. He is the author of, *The Portion of the Soul* (1835):—*Popular Infidelity:—Uses of Adversity:—Maxims:—The Christian Life.*

Hooker, Horace, D.D., a Congregational minister and author, was born in 1793. He was a graduate of Yale College, and was remarkable for the elegance and purity of his style as a writer. He early, in connection with Rev. Thomas H. Gallaudet, LL.D., undertook the preparation of religious books for the young. Among them are, *The Youth's Book of Natural Theology*, in two parts, and a series of twelve volumes of *Bible History*; also a popular spelling-book and definer. For a period of more than twenty years he was secretary of the Connecticut Missionary Society; also for several years chaplain of the insane retreat at Hartford, where he died, Dec. 17, 1864. See *Appleton's Annual Cyclop.* 1864, p. 623.

Hoole, Elijah, D.D., an eminent Wesleyan missionary, was appointed in 1819 to Bangalore, in the Mysore country, to which, in 1823, Seringapatam was added. "He rapidly acquired an accurate knowledge of the Tamil, one of the first-fruits of which was a translation of the *Methodist Hymns.* It was thus that he laid the foundation of that proficiency as an Oriental scholar which was afterwards duly acknowledged by the Royal Asiatic Society and other learned bodies; at the same time travelling widely and laboring with unwearied diligence in his evangelical efforts, and enduring hardship as a good soldier of Christ." After nine years he returned to England sick, and was never afterwards free from pain. From 1830 to 1835 he was superintendent of schools in Ireland. Removing to London, he was, in 1834, appointed assistant secretary, and in 1836 one of the general secretaries of the Missionary Society, a position he held to the end of his life. In the administration of missionary affairs his punctuality, suavity, and diligence rendered him singularly efficient, and his unobtrusive services became more and more valuable every year. He was also honorary secretary of the British Society for the Propagation of the Gospel among the Jews, and also for the Home of the Asiatics, in London. Gentle, uniformly cheerful, Dr. Hoole was to the end of life a diligent student. He died in London, June 17, 1872, in the seventy-fifth year of his age. Dr. Hoole wrote, *Madras, Mysore, and the South of India: A Narrative of a Mission to those Countries, from* 1820 *to* 1828 (2d ed. Lond. 1844, 12mo):—*The Year-Book of Missions* (Lond. 1847, 8vo):—*The Missionary*, a poem from the Swedish, edited by Dr. Hoole (1851, 24mo):—*Byrom and the Wesleys* (1864):—*Ladies' Tamil Book* (1860). See *Minutes of the British Conference*, 1872, p. 32; Stevens, *Hist. of Methodism*, iii, 346; Osborn, *Meth. Bibliography*, p. 117.

Hooper, WILLIAM, D.D., LL.D., a distinguished Baptist minister, was born near Wilmington, N. C., Aug. 31, 1792, being a grandson of William Hooper, one of the signers of the Declaration of Independence. He graduated from the University of North Carolina, at Chapel Hill, in 1808; studied theology one year at Princeton; was appointed professor of ancient languages in his alma mater in 1817; took orders in the Episcopal Church in 1818; was rector of a church in Fayetteville from 1822 to 1824; changed his sentiments on baptism, and joined a Baptist Church; returned to the University of North Carolina, first as professor of rhetoric, and then resumed his former chair as professor of ancient languages. In 1838 he was called to South Carolina, where, for eight years, he was in the department of instruction in the Furman Institute. He was then chosen president of Wake Forest College, N. C., and held this office for six years. He was pastor in Newbern, then president of the Chowan Female Institute, and for the last years of his life was engaged in teaching at Fayetteville and Wilson. He died at Chapel Hill, Aug. 19, 1876. See *Gen. Cat. of Princeton Theol. Sem.* 1881, p. 15. (J. C. S.)

Höpfner, JOHANN GEORG CHRISTIAN, a Lutheran theologian of Germany, was born March 4, 1765, at Leipsic, and died there, Dec. 20, 1827, doctor of theology and professor of philosophy. He wrote, *In LXX Versionem Jonæ Spec.* 1-3 (Leipsic, 1787, 1788):—*De Origine Dogmatis Rom.-Pontif. de Purgatorio Nonnulla* (Halle, 1792):—*Historia Tobiæ* (1802):—*Ueber das Leben und die Verdienste des verewigten Morus* (1793). See Fürst, *Bibl. Jud.* i, 407; Winer, *Handbuch der theol. Lit.* i, 51, 194, 300, 469, 865. (B. P.)

Hopkins, Henry Harvey, D.D., a Presbyterian minister, was born in Chester County, Pa., Nov. 12, 1804. He graduated from Princeton Theological Seminary in 1832; was licensed by the Presbytery of New Castle the same year; obtained permission to labor without the bounds of the presbytery, and at once proceeded to Clinton, La. After this he went to Big Spring and Taylorsville, Ky., and served as pastor. This relation continued about nine years, and was dissolved April 2, 1844. Dr. Hopkins next took charge of two churches at Cane Run and Plum Creek, in Shelby County, and subsequently of a church at Owensboro. He died April 19, 1877. He was a devoted pastor, a wise counsellor, practical, judicious, and of large Christian experience. See *Necrol. Report of Princeton Theol. Sem.* 1878, p. 28.

Hopkins, Johns, an American philanthropist, a member of the Society of Friends, was born in Anne Arundel County, Md., May 19, 1795. He received a liberal education, and engaged in the wholesale grocery business, from which he retired in 1847 with an ample fortune. He then became president of the Merchants' Bank, and a director of the Baltimore and Ohio Railroad. He died in Baltimore, Dec. 24, 1873. Mr. Hopkins' benefactions amount in the aggregate to over $8,000,000. In 1873 he founded the Hopkins Free Hospital of Baltimore, at a cost of about $4,000,000. He also founded an orphanage for colored youth, a convalescent hospital, and the Johns Hopkins University. This institution is located at Clifton, near Baltimore, and has four hundred acres of land and an endowment of $3,000,000. Poor and deserving youth of Maryland and Virginia receive free scholarships.

Hopkins, Josiah, D.D., a Presbyterian minister, was born at Pittsford, Vt., April 26, 1785. He never attended college, though he had a good academical education. He was licensed by the Paulet Congregational Association in 1809, and was ordained pastor of the Congregational Church in New Haven, Vt., in 1811. He subsequently became pastor of the First Presbyterian Church in Auburn, N. Y. He died at Geneva, June 27, 1862. See Wilson, *Presb. Hist. Almanac*, 1863, p. 298.

Hopkins, Samuel, *Sen.*, a Congregational minister, son of John Hopkins, of Waterbury, Conn., graduated from Yale College in 1718; was ordained pastor in West Springfield, Mass., June 1, 1720, and died suddenly in October, 1755, in the sixty-second year of his age. He published *Historical Memoirs Relating to the Housatonic Indians* (1753). See Sprague, *Annals of the Amer. Pulpit*, i, 519.

Hopkins, Samuel, *Jun.*, D.D., a Congregational minister, son of the foregoing, was born in West Springfield, Mass., Oct. 31, 1729. He graduated from Yale College in 1749, and was a tutor there from 1751 to 1754; was ordained pastor at Hadley, in February, 1755, and died there, March 8, 1811. A volume of sermons was published by him in 1799. In many respects he was a remarkable man, distinguished for his good-humor, and his Calvinism was of a type opposed to Hopkinsianism. See Sprague, *Annals of the Amer. Pulpit*, i, 520.

Hopkins, Theodore Asa, D.D., a Presbyterian minister, was born at Hartford, Conn., July 25, 1805. He graduated from Yale College in 1824; studied theology privately, and was licensed by the Cayuga Presbytery, June 19, 1828. In 1829 he accepted a call from the Congregational Church at Pawtucket, Mass. His ministry there was successful and very acceptable. In 1836 he accepted a call from the First Presbyterian Church in Brooklyn, where he remained until his death, Nov. 18, 1847. See Sprague, *Annals of the Amer. Pulpit*, iv, 741.

Hoppenstedt, AUGUST FRIEDRICH LUDWIG, a Lutheran theologian of Germany, was born March 22, 1763. In 1789 he was inspector of the Teachers' Seminary at Hanover, in 1792 court-chaplain, in 1796 superintendent, in 1805 general superintendent at Harburg, in 1815 at Celle, and died April 24, 1830, doctor of theology, abbot of Loccum, and director of consistory at Hanover. He published, *Predigten* (Hanover, 1818-19,

3 vols.):—*Lieder für Volksschulen* (1793; 4th ed. 1814). See Winer, *Handbuch der theol. Lit.* i, 864; ii, 99, 171, 265, 385; Zuchold, *Bibl. Theol.* i, 585. (B. P.)

Hopper, Christopher, one of the most efficient early Methodist preachers, was born at Low-Coalburne, Ryton Parish, Durham County, England, Dec. 25, 1722. In his *Autobiography* (in Jackson's *Lives*) he gives an interesting account of his conversion under Methodist preaching, about 1743, and of his subsequent labors after 1749. For fifty years he preached throughout the land, in churches, ale-houses, cock-pits, now before a conference, then before a mob, now amid the prayers and tears of the people, then amid rotten eggs, the sound of horns and bells, brickbats, blows, and bludgeons. Four times he visited Ireland (1750, 1752, 1756, 1776, the first time with Wesley). In 1751 he and Wesley visited Scotland, the latter returning in a few days, but Hopper pressing on, and in 1759 introducing Methodism as far as Old Aberdeen and Peterhead, thus planting Methodism in North Britain. Wesley being absent from the conference at Bristol in 1780, Hopper was elected president. After 1790 he resided chiefly at Bolton, preaching till January, 1802. He died March 5 following. Hopper played an important part in British Methodism, and not merely in extending its borders. He was one of the men who gave to it Bramwell and Benson, and his melting prayers contributed to its peace and union during the critical conferences of the last decade of the 18th century (see Entwistle's *Memoirs*). He was of an original turn of mind, had fine natural abilities, was a diligent student, a pioneer preacher, and a soul-saver. See Jackson, *Early Methodist Preachers*, i, 179; Crowther, *Portraiture of Methodism*, p. 350; Stevens, *Hist. of Methodism*, i, iii (see index); Smith, *Hist. of Wesl. Methodism*, i, iii (see index); *Wesl. Meth. Magazine*, Sept. 1803; Everett, *Keen and Able Little Sketch; Wesleyan Centenary Takings* (3d ed. Lond. 1841), i, 332.

Hoppus, John, LL.D., an English Congregational minister, was born in London in 1789. He studied theology at Rotherham and Dunbar, then proceeded to the University of Glasgow, where he took his degree of M.A., and was the most distinguished pupil of his year. Thence he returned to London and took the ministerial charge of the Carter Lane Chapel, where he labored two years. He next became professor of mental and moral philosophy and logic in University College, London, which chair he occupied for thirty-six years, preaching frequently and writing extensively. He died in London, Jan. 29, 1875. The life of Dr. Hoppus was an exemplification of his oft-repeated assertion that "No service a man can render his generation is greater than this, to try to 'justify the ways of God to men.'" He wrote a masterly exposition of Bacon's *Novum Organon*, and many other treatises for the Society for the Diffusion of Useful Knowledge:—a prize essay on *Schism as Opposed to the Unity of the Church*:—a valuable pamphlet on *The Crisis of Popular Education*, as well as contributing largely to the *Psychological Journal* and *Eclectic*. See (Lond.) *Cong. Year-book*, 1876, p. 341; (Lond.) *Evangelical Magazine*, 1875, p. 281.

Hordicalia (or **Hordicidia**), an ancient Roman festival, celebrated April 15, in honor of the goddess Tellus. On these occasions thirty pregnant cows were sacrificed.

Horem. The *Hurah*, which is accepted by Conder (*Tent Work*, ii, 337) and Tristram (*Bible Places*, p. 274), but not by Saunders (*O. T. Map*), as the representative of this ancient site, is written *Khurbet el-Kûrah* on the Ordnance Map, three and a half miles north-west from Yarûn (Iron), and so in the accompanying *Memoirs* (i, 242), "heaps of stones and cisterns, on a small tell [mound]; a birkeh [pool] in the valley." This last authority suggests (i, 205) "the present ruin *Hârah*," which is laid down at two miles south-east of Tibnîn, and described (ibid. 118) as "heaps of small unhewn stones, with two olive-presses and a spring at the ruin;" an identification not adopted by Saunders.

Horey, in the mythology of the negroes in East Africa, was a dæmon, having a resemblance to the devil, whose image probably reached Abyssinia through the Christians. Those people practise circumcision in the thirteenth or fourteenth year. Before the youths are thus dedicated they are exposed to the persecution of this evil spirit, who manifests his presence by a dull, deep howl or cry. As soon as this cry is heard, victuals are prepared and placed under a tree. They are always found to have been eaten. If the food does not suffice, Horey steals a boy and devours him, keeping him in his stomach until more food is brought, whereupon he gives him up again. Many negroes affirm that they have been ten or twelve days in the stomach of this monster.

Horman (or **Horeman**), William, an English author, was born at Salisbury, Wiltshire, about 1470. He was educated at Eton and at King's College, Cambridge, was made vice-provost of Eton, where he spent the remainder of his days, and died April 12, 1535. He was one of the most general scholars of his age. He wrote on *Orthography*:—*On the Quantities of Penultimate Syllables*:—*A Chronicle, Commentaries, and Indexes to the Chronicles of Others*:—*Commentaries on Gabriel Biel's Divinity*:—*On the Divorce of Henry VIII*:—*On Cato, Varro, Columella, Palladius, De Re Rustica*. Other books he left unfinished. See Fuller, *Worthies of England* (ed. Nuttall), iii, 335; Lowndes, *Bibl. Manual*, p. 1119.

Hornblower, William Henry, D.D., a Presbyterian minister, was born at Newark, N. J., March 21, 1820. He graduated from Princeton College in 1838; studied law one year; graduated from Princeton Theological Seminary in 1842; became a missionary to "the Pines" in 1843; was ordained pastor at Paterson in 1844, and labored there with great success and usefulness until 1877, when he was elected by the General Assembly professor of homiletics, pastoral theology, sacred rhetoric, and Church government in the Western Theological Seminary, Allegheny City, Pa. He died there, July 16, 1883. See *N. Y. Observer*, July 19, 1883; Nevin, *Presb. Encyclop.* s. v.; *Necrol. Report of Princeton Theol. Sem.* 1884, p. 28. (W. P. S.)

Hornby, John, D.D., a native of Lincolnshire, bred a Carmelite, received his degree at Cambridge, flourished in 1374, and was buried at his convent in Boston. He participated in a great controversy over the priority of the Dominican and Carmelite orders, John Stock pleading for the precedency of the former, and Hornby preaching and writing for that of the latter. The judges were John Donwick, the chancellor, and the doctors of the university, and they confirmed the opinion of Hornby, under the seal of the university. Henry VIII made them friends by thrusting both out of the land. See Fuller, *Worthies of England* (ed. Nuttall), ii, 288.

Horne, Robert, an English prelate of the 16th century, was born in Durham, educated at St. John's College, Cambridge, advanced dean of Durham in 1551, and prebend of York in 1552, but in the persecution under Mary he fled to Germany, and, fixing his residence at Frankfort, became the head of the episcopal party. On returning to England he was made bishop of Winchester, Feb. 16, 1560. He was a worthy man, but ground between the papists and sectaries, who sported with his name, and twitted his person as dwarfish and deformed, apparently having no worthy cause for their opposition. He died in Southwark, June 1, 1580. He published an answer to Fuckenham's *Declaration of Scruples of Conscience* (1566), touching the oaths of supremacy. See Fuller, *Worthies of England* (ed. Nuttall), i, 482.

Horne, Thomas Hartwell, D.D., a minister of the Church of England, was born in London, Oct. 20, 1780. He was a scholar at Christ's Hospital, but did not attend the university. He was a barrister's clerk for many years; was ordained in 1819, and did parochial duty in London, chiefly at St. James's Church, Westmoreland Street, Marylebone; held an important literary appointment in the British Museum for a long time; and in 1833 the archbishop of Canterbury appointed him to his city rectory, a position which he held at the time of his death, Jan. 27, 1862. Dr. Horne was an author and editor of considerable celebrity. Among his works may be mentioned, *An Introduction to the Critical Study of the Holy Scriptures*, by which he is chiefly known (see INTRODUCTIONS):—*A Compendium of the Admiralty Laws and Regulations of the Court of Admiralty*:—*An Illustrated Record of Important Events* (in conjunction with Dr. Gillies and professor Shakespeare):—*Deism Refuted*:—*Willis's Itinerary*:—*Jewish and Christian Privileges Compared*:—*Potts's Law Dictionary*:—*Murphy's Arabian Antiquities of Spain*:—*Crosby's Gazetteer*:—*Van Leenween's Commentaries on the Dutch Law*. For other ecclesiastical and Scriptural works see Allibone, *Dict. of Brit. and Amer. Authors*, s.v. See *Amer. Quar. Church Rev.* 1862, p. 741.

Hornemann, CLAUDIUS FREES *von*, a Danish theologian, born in 1751, was in 1801 professor of theology at Copenhagen, and died in 1830. He wrote, *Specimen Exercitationum Crit. in Version. LXX Interpr. ex Philone* (i–iii, Göttingen, 1773–78):—*Observationes ad Illustrationem Doctrinæ de Canone Vet. Test. ex Philone* (Copenhagen, 1775):—*Sylloge Lectionum Variorum LXX* (1773):—*Observationes de Harmonia Linguarum Orientalium, Ebraicæ, Chaldaicæ, Syriacæ et Arabicæ* (1826–29):—*Scripta Genuina Græc. Patrum Apostolicor., Græce et Latine, Edidit* (1828, 2 vols.). See Winer, *Handbuch der theol. Lit.* i, 51, 77, 882; Fürst, *Bibl. Jud.* i, 407 sq. (B. P.)

Horner, JAMES, D.D., a minister of the Presbyterian Church in Ireland. He was Dr. McDowel's colleague in Mary's Abbey, Dublin, ordained co-pastor in 1791, and died in January, 1843. He was intrusted by the synod of Ulster with the management of much of its public business, "and was remarkable for his tact and shrewdness." He was one of the first missionary agents of the synod, and was also appointed by it on the committee for the preparation of a code of discipline. See Reid, *Hist. of the Presb. Church in Ireland*.

Horning, FRIEDRICH THEODOR, a Lutheran theologian of Germany, was born in 1809 in Alsace. In 1835 he was pastor at Grafenstaden, in 1845 at Strasburg, and died there in 1882, president of the consistory. Horning was a strict Lutheran, and founded, in 1849, the Lutheran Missionary Society. He wrote, *Evangelisch-lutherische Kirche*:—and with Rittelmeyer he published, in 1863, *Gesangbuch für Christen Augsburger Confession*. He also edited *Kirchenblatt für die Kirche Augsburger Confession*. See Lichtenberger, *Encyclop. des Sciences Religieuses*, s. v. (B. P.)

Horror, a passion excited by an object which causes a high degree of fear and detestation. It is a compound of wonder and fear. Sometimes it has a mixture of pleasure, from which, if predominant, it is denominated a pleasing horror. Such a horror seizes us at the view of vast and hanging precipices, a tempestuous ocean, or wild and solitary places. This passion is the original of superstition, as a wise and well-tempered awe is of religion. Horror and terror seem almost to be synonymous; but the former refers more to what disgusts, the latter to that which alarms us.

Horse-sacrifice, a ceremony celebrated by various ancient nations, in which a horse was offered in sacrifice to a deity, usually the sun. The Massagetæ, a great and powerful nation, whose territories extended beyond the Araxes to the extreme parts of the East, sacrificed horses to the sun. The practice prevailed in Persia in the time of Cyrus, and may have been anterior to that sovereign. Horses were sacrificed to Neptune and the deities of the rivers, being precipitated into the sea or into the rivers. The Lacedæmonians sacrificed a horse to the winds, which, by their force, carried the ashes of the victim to a distance. Among the ancient Romans a horse was sacrificed annually to Mars in the Campus Martius, in the month of October. The blood that dropped from the tail of the October horse, as it was called, was carefully preserved by the vestal virgins in the temple of Vesta, for the purpose of being used at the *Palilia* or shepherd festival. In the *Rig Veda* are two hymns in honor of the horse-sacrifice, called *Aswamedha*, which describe the horse as "bathed, and decorated with rich trappings, the variously-colored goat going before him." The horse is led three times round the sacrificial fire; he is then bound to a post and slaughtered with an ax; and the flesh is roasted on a spit, boiled, made into balls, and eaten; and finally "The horse proceeds to that assembly which is most excellent; to the presence of his father and his mother (heaven and earth). Go, horse, to-day, rejoicing to the gods, that (the sacrifice) may yield blessings to the donor." The horse-sacrifice at this day is one of the great annual ceremonies of the Hindûs.

Horsley, JOHN, an eminent English clergyman and antiquary, was born in 1685, at Mid-Lothian, and was pastor of a dissenting congregation at Morpeth. He died in December, 1731. He wrote *Roman Antiquities of Britain* (published posthumously, 1732). See Chalmers, *Biog. Dict.* s. v.; Allibone, *Dict. of Brit. and Amer. Authors*, s. v.

Horst, GEORG CONRAD, a Protestant theologian of Germany, was born June 26, 1767, and died Jan. 26, 1832, doctor of theology. He wrote, *Die Visionen Habakuks* (Gotha, 1798):—*Theurgie* (Mayence, 1820):—*Das heilige Abendmahl* (1815):—*Dämonomagie* (1818, 2 vols.):—*Mysteriosophie* (1816, 2 vols.):—*Siona* (4th ed. 1833, 2 vols.):—*Eusebia* (2d ed. 1822). See Winer, *Handbuch der theol. Lit.* i, 229, 428, 453, 599; ii, 76, 229, 332, 359, 377; Zuchold, *Bibl. Theol.* i, 588; Fürst, *Bibl. Jud.* i, 408. (B. P.)

Horton, WILLIAM, D.D., a Protestant Episcopal minister, was born at Newburyport, Mass., March 14, 1804. He graduated from Harvard College in 1824; from Andover Theological Seminary in 1827; was ordained deacon in November of that year, and presbyter Oct. 15, 1830. He was pastor at St. Paul's Church, Windsor, Vt.; in 1835 of Trinity Church, Saco, Me.; at St. Thomas's Church, Dover, N. H. (1839–47); at St. Paul's Church, Brookline, Mass. (1849); at St. Paul's Church, Newburyport (1853). He died there, Oct. 29, 1863. See *Trien. Cat. of Andover Theol. Sem.* 1870, p. 75; *Amer. Quar. Church Rev.* 1864, p. 669.

Hosah. For this place Lieut. Conder suggests (*Tent Work*, ii, 337) the present *'Ozziyeh*, meaning apparently (see *Memoirs* to Ordnance Survey, i, 51) *el-Ezziyah*, laid down at six and three quarter miles south-east of Tyre, and described (ibid. p. 48) as "a village built of stone, containing seventy Druses; situated on a ridge, with two cisterns. There are two caves to the north of it." The identification is not noted by Saunders.

Höschke, REUBEN *hak-Kohen*, a Jewish rabbi of Prague, who died in 1673, is the author of, ילקוט ראובני, a kind of midrashic collectaneum (Prague, 1660):—ילקוט ראובני הגדול, a cabalistic midrash on the Pentateuch, with extracts from Mechilta, Pesikta, Zohar, etc. (Wilmersdorf, 1681). This latter work, without any value, must be distinguished from the famous midrashic work entitled *Yalkut Shimeoni*. See Fürst, *Bibl. Jud.* i, 412 sq. (B. P.)

Hosmann, GUSTAV CHRISTOPH, a Lutheran theologian of Germany, was born May 16, 1695. He studied at Leipsic and Kiel, was deacon in 1721, and professor of theology at Kiel in 1730. In 1734 he was appointed first court-preacher, in 1749 general superintendent, and died July 10, 1766. He wrote, *Disp. Exeget. ad Gal. iii*, 19 (Kiel, 1720):—*Hypotyposis Chro-*

nologiæ Sacræ (Hamburg, 1727):—*Annotationes ad Hypotyposin Chronologiæ Sacræ* (1729):—*De Resurrectione Mortuorum a Christo Demonstrata Luc. ii*, 37, 38:—*De Baptismo Apostolorum hoc de Mysterio Sententiam Evolvens* (1732):—*Principia Theologiæ Comparativæ* (eod.):—*Chronologia Sacra Librorum V. Test. Observationibus Exegeticis Illustrata* (1734):—*Exercitationum Exegeticarum ad SS. Evangelia Fasciculi III* (1746-50):—*Chronologia Jeremiæ, Ezechielis, Haggæ, Zachariæ, Esræ et Nehemiæ* (1751):—*Historia Samuelis, Sauli et Davidis* (1752):—*Disquisitio de Æra Seleucidarum et Regum Syriæ Successione* (eod.):—*Semicenturia Observationum Sacrarum* (1753). See Moser, *Jetztlebende Theologen;* Winer, *Handbuch der theol. Lit.* i, 901; Jöcher, *Allgemeines Gelehrten-Lexikon*, s.v. (B. P.)

Hospitium, a place sometimes attached to monasteries in former times, with the view of affording temporary relief to travellers, and in which a certain number of the poor were relieved by a daily alms. It was also called a *Xenodochium*.

Hossein, the second son of Ali and Fatima, and the third of the twelve Imâms, was born A.D. 625. He endeavored to dissuade his brother Hassan (q. v.) from resigning the caliphate in favor of Moawiyah, but on finding his remonstrances unavailing, he entered heartily into the support of the new caliph, and even served in his army when the Saracens first attacked Constantinople. On the death of Moawiyah, in 679, his son Yezid succeeded, but Hossein contested the caliphate with him, having been deceived by the promise of powerful support from the professed adherents of the house of Ali. Overpowered by numbers, and deserted by many of his followers, he fell by the hand of one of Yezid's soldiers, on the 10th of the Mohammedan month Mohanem, A.D. 680. A splendid mosque was erected over the place of his burial. The place, which was named *Meshed Hossein* (the place of Hossein's martyrdom), is a favorite resort of pilgrims to this day.

Hossein's Martyrdom, Anniversary of, a religious solemnity observed both in Persia and India with extraordinary splendor. It lasts for ten days, during which the Shiites keep up continual mourning for the martyr's fate, giving themselves up to sighs and groans, fastings and tears. They abstain from shaving their heads, from bathing, and even from changing their clothes. The observances consist of a series of representations of the successive scenes in the life of Hossein, from the date of his flight from Medina to his martyrdom on the plains of Kerbela; and the exhibition of each day is preceded by the reading in a plaintive tone a portion of the history of Hossein.

Hostia, an animal among the ancient Romans which was destined for sacrifice. Sometimes the whole victim was consumed upon the altar, and at other times only the legs and intestines were burned. It was the smoke ascending from the sacrifice that was considered pleasing to the gods, hence the more numerous the animals the more pleasing the sacrifice. This was, no doubt, the reason for offering a *hecatomb*. The animal selected for sacrifice must be free from all blemishes and diseases. If it was of the larger sort of beasts the horns were marked with gold; if of the smaller sort it was crowned with the leaves of that tree which the deity for whom the sacrifice was designed was thought most to delight in.

Hotchkiss, Velona R., D.D., a Baptist minister, was born in Spafford, Onondaga Co., N.Y., June 5, 1815, and graduated from Madison University in 1838. His pastorates were in Poultney, Vt. (1839); Rochester, N.Y.; Buffalo (1849-54), also, subsequently, from 1865 until his death, and in Fall River, Mass. From 1854 to 1865 he was a professor in Rochester Theological Seminary. Dr. Hotchkiss ranked very high as a scholar and an able preacher, and was regarded as one of the strongest men in his denomination. He died in Buffalo, Jan. 4, 1882. (J. C. S.)

Hothum, William de, D.D., an Irish prelate, was born in England, but educated at Paris. In 1280 he became a Dominican friar, and was twice provincial of that order in England. He was appointed to the see of Dublin, Dec. 8, 1297; consecrated at Rome in 1298 by the pope, and died on his return, at Dijon, Aug. 27 of the same year. See D'Alton, *Memoirs of the Archbishops of Dublin*, p. 110.

Houghton, Daniel Clay, D.D., a Presbyterian minister (N. S.), was born at Lynton, Vt., in 1814. He graduated at the University of Vermont in 1840, subsequently taught a few years in Western New York, and then entered the ministry in the Methodist Episcopal Church. He was one of the founders of Genesee College, in Lima, N. Y.; was for some years professor of moral and intellectual philosophy in the college, and at the same time acted as financial agent. In 1853 he joined the Presbyterian Church, and in 1854 was appointed editor of the *Genesee Evangelist*. He died July 8, 1860. See Wilson, *Presb. Hist. Almanac*, 1861, p. 160.

House of Exposition. See Beth-Hammidrash.

House of Judgment. See Beth-Din.

House of Reading. See Beth-Hammikra.

House of the Living. See Beth-Haim.

House, Erwin, a Methodist Episcopal minister, was born at Worthington, O., Feb. 17, 1824. He was converted at the age of thirteen; graduated at Woodward College, Cincinnati, in 1846; received license to preach in 1849, and in 1865 entered the Cincinnati Conference, of which he continued a member till his death, May 20, 1875. Mr. House commenced contributing to the press as early as 1837; in 1847 was employed as assistant editor of the *Ladies' Repository*, and from March, 1851, to December, 1852, had sole editorial charge of the magazine. He published, *Sketches for the Young* (1847):—*The Missionary in Many Lands:—The Homilist:—Scripture Cabinet:—The Sunday-school Handbook*. He was a hearty advocate of temperance. As a speaker to children he had very few equals. See *Minutes of Annual Conferences*, 1875, p. 115; Simpson, *Cyclop. of Methodism*, s. v.

Hoven, Jan Daniel van, a Dutch theologian, was born Aug. 20, 1705, at Hanau. He studied at Marburg and Utrecht, was in 1728 professor at Lingen, in Westphalia, in 1739 member of consistory, in 1758 professor at Campen, and died in 1793. He wrote, *Specimen Historiæ Analyticæ* (Lingen, 1732; Amsterdam, 1734):—*Historiæ Ecclesiasticæ Pragmaticæ Specimen i-iii* (1747-52):—*Disp. de Vera Ætate Legationis Athenagoræ pro Christianis* (1752):—*Antiquitates Evangelicæ* (1758):—*Antiquitates Romanæ* (1759):—*De Vera Ætate, Dignitate et Patria Minucii Felicis* (1762), etc. See Meusel, *Gelehrtes Deutschland;* Winer, *Handbuch der theol. Lit.* i, 609, 884, 910; Jöcher, *Allgemeines Gelehrten-Lexikon*, s. v. (B. P.)

Hovey, Edmund Otis, D.D., a Presbyterian minister, was born in East Hanover, N. H., July 15, 1801. At twenty-one years of age he began his preparation for preaching the gospel, at Thetford Academy; in 1828 graduated from Dartmouth College, and in 1831 from Andover Theological Seminary. He was ordained by the Presbytery of Newburyport the same year, and sent as a missionary to Wabash, Ia. His great work was in founding and building up Wabash College, Crawfordsville, Ind., of which, in 1834, he was appointed financial agent and professor of rhetoric. Subsequently he was made professor of chemistry, mineralogy, and geology. He was also treasurer and librarian. He died there, March 10, 1877. See (N. Y.) *Evangelist*, March 29, 1877. (W. P. S.)

Howard, Bezaleel, D.D., a Unitarian minister, was born at Bridgewater, Mass., Nov. 22, 1753. He graduated from Harvard College in 1781; immediately engaged in teaching at Hingham, and at the same time pursued a course of theology under the direction of Dr. Gay. He preached his first sermon in 1783; was appointed to a tutorship at Cambridge, and during this time filled vacant pulpits in the neighborhood on the Sabbath. He accepted a call to the First Church in Springfield in November, 1784, and was ordained April 27, 1785. He resigned this charge on account of ill-health, Jan. 25, 1809. In 1819 he became pastor of a new Unitarian Church in the first parish of Springfield. He remained there until his death, Jan. 23, 1837. See Sprague, *Annals of the Amer. Pulpit*, viii, 181.

Howard, Leland, A.M., a leading Baptist minister, was born at Jamaica, Windham Co., Vt., Oct. 13, 1793. He was converted about 1810, and commenced to preach in 1812. He was a "born preacher," but placed himself under the tuition of Rev. Joshua Bradley, of the Baptist Church in Windsor, for one year, and then pursued his studies under the direction of Rev. James M. Winchell, of the First Baptist Church in Boston, Mass. He was ordained pastor in Windsor, Vt., Nov. 16, 1817, where he remained seven years, and then of the First Baptist Church in Troy, N. Y., five years, when he returned to his former pastorate in Windsor, Vt., and had charge five years. His other pastorates were Brooklyn, N. Y., Newport, R. I., Norwich, N. Y., Fifth Street Church, Troy, N. Y., Hartford, Conn., and, in 1852, he went to Rutland, Vt., and was pastor ten years. He died there, May 5, 1870. He was chaplain of the House, in the legislature of Vermont, in 1831, and of the Senate in 1861. (J. C. S.)

Howard, Leonard, D.D., an English clergyman, was rector of St. George's, Southwark, London. He died in 1767, leaving a number of *Sermons* (1736-61), and a collection of *Letters and State Papers* (1753-56). See Allibone, *Dict. of Brit. and Amer. Authors*, s. v.

Howard, Robert, an Irish Catholic prelate, was born in 1661, became bishop of Killala in 1726, of Elphin in 1729, and died about 1740. He published some *Sermons* (1738). See Allibone, *Dict. of Brit. and Amer. Authors*, s. v.

Howard, Roger S., D.D., a Protestant Episcopal clergyman, was employed, in 1857, as a teacher in Bangor, Me., and remained there until 1859, when he became rector of St. Stephen's Church, Portland. In 1861 he removed to Vermont; in 1862 became rector of Trinity Church, Rutland; in 1867 of St. James's Church, Woodstock; in 1870 president of Norwich University, and rector of St. Mary's Church, Northfield; in 1872 was called to the rectorship of the Church of the Reconciliation, Webster, Mass.; in 1879 he removed to Greenfield, where he died, April 16, 1880, aged seventy-two years. See Whittaker, *Almanac and Directory*, 1881, p. 173.

Howard, Solomon, D.D., LL.D., a Methodist Episcopal minister, was born Nov. 14, 1811. He joined the Church in 1828, graduated from Augusta College, Ky., in 1833, and entered the Ohio Conference in 1835. After eight years of successful work in the pastorate, he was for two years principal of the Ohio Wesleyan University. From 1845 to 1852 he was in educational work in Springfield, O. In 1852 he was elected president of the Ohio University, at Athens, where he remained for twenty years. He died Aug. 11, 1873, at San José, Cal. He was a delegate to the General Conference of 1856. He was emphatically an educator, and many a poor young man will remember his sympathy for him in his struggles for an education. See *Minutes of Annual Conferences*, 1873.

Howard, William D., D.D., a Presbyterian minister, was born in Philadelphia, Pa., July 28, 1814. He was among the early graduates of Lafayette College, and in 1833 became a student of theology with Dr. William Neill. He was licensed to preach in 1837, and the next year ordained pastor of the Frankford Church, now in the bounds of Philadelphia. In 1849 he removed to Pittsburgh, to take charge of the Second Presbyterian Church, where he continued to labor faithfully until his death, Sept. 22, 1876. He published occasional *Sermons*. See *Presbyterian*, Sept. 30, 1876. (W. P. S.)

Howe, George, D.D., a distinguished minister of the Southern Presbyterian Church, was born in 1802. In 1833 he was elected by the General Assembly a professor in the theological seminary at Charleston, S. C., and subsequently became president of that institution, which position he retained until his sudden death, April 15, 1883. For half a century his life had been devoted to the great work of training young men for the ministry, and though dead he yet speaks through the living lips of hundreds who went out from this school of the prophets. See (N. Y.) *Observer*, April 19, 1883. (W. P. S.)

Howe, Obadiah, D.D., an English clergyman, was vicar of Boston, Lincolnshire. He died in 1682, leaving *The Universalist Examined and Criticised* (1648):—*Sermons* (1664). See Allibone, *Dict. of Brit. and Amer. Authors*, s. v.

Howell, Thomas, an English prelate, was born at Naugamarch, Brecknockshire, educated a fellow of Jesus College, Oxford, was made canon of Windsor in 1636, bishop of Bristol in 1644, and died in 1646. He was a meek man and a most excellent preacher. See Fuller, *Worthies of England* (ed. Nuttall), iii, 515.

Howley, William, D.D., an English prelate, son of William Howley, D.D., was born Feb. 12, 1765. In his youth he attended the Winchester School, from which he went to the University of Oxford, obtaining a fellowship at New College. In 1794 he was elected fellow of Winchester College; in 1809 was appointed regius professor of divinity; and in September, 1813, succeeded Dr. Randolph as bishop of London. On the decease of Dr. Manners Sutton, in 1828, he became archbishop of Canterbury. He died Feb. 11, 1848. Besides being president of many charitable institutions, he was a fellow of the Society of Antiquaries, and a member of the Royal Society of Literature. See *Amer. Quar. Church Rev.* 1848, p. 149.

Howman, John, an English Catholic divine, was born at Feckenham, Worcestershire, about 1516, of poor parentage. He was educated by the Benedictines of Evesham, and afterwards at Gloucester College, Oxford; became chaplain to the bishop of Worcester, afterwards to Bonner, and vigorously opposed the Reformation in England. In 1549 he was imprisoned in the Tower, but was released on the accession of Mary, who made him dean of Westminster. Elizabeth offered him the archbishopric of Canterbury on condition of becoming a Protestant, but he refused, and was again imprisoned in 1560. Being released in 1563, he finally retired to the isle of Ely, and died at Wisbeach in 1585, leaving an account of his *Conference with Jane Grey* (Lond. 1554, 1626), besides some *Sermons* and a few controversial pieces.

Hoyer, Franz Heinrich, a Lutheran theologian of Germany, was born in Holstein, July 20, 1639. He studied at Helmstädt and Giessen, was in 1665 third preacher at Norden, East Frisia, in 1683 pastor primarius, and died May 20, 1699, leaving *De Usu Logices in Theologia* (Giessen, 1660):—*De Usu Metaphysicæ in Theologia* (eod.):—*De Principio Theologiæ* (eod.):—*De Deo* (eod.):—*De Quæstione Ubinam Ecclesia Lutheri Fuerit ante Lutherum* (1664), besides writing numerous ascetical works. See Jöcher, *Allgemeines Gelehrten-Lexikon*, s. v. (B. P.)

Hoyt, Nathan, D.D., a Presbyterian minister, was born at Gilmanton, Belknap Co., N. H., Feb. 27, 1793. He was educated at Cambridge, Mass., but did not enter college on account of ill-health. He was licensed by Albany Presbytery in 1823, and ordained by the same presbytery in 1826. He first labored in Troy, N. Y., as a city missionary, and on his removal to South

Carolina became pastor of the Beech Island Church. His next pastorate was in Washington, Ga., and his third and last was in Athens, where he labored with much zeal and efficiency for nearly thirty-six years. He died July 12, 1866. See Wilson, *Presb. Hist. Almanac*, 1867, p. 437.

Hoyt, Ova Phelps, D.D., a Presbyterian minister, was born at New Haven, Vt., May 26, 1800. He graduated from Middlebury College in 1821, and from Andover Theological Seminary in 1824. Soon after he was ordained pastor of the Presbyterian Church at Potsdam, N. Y., where he remained until 1830, then took the agency of the American Home Missionary Society, and resided in Utica. While there he was editor of the *Western Recorder* for a year and a half. He was stated supply at Cambridge in 1835; at Detroit, Mich., in 1839; at Kalamazoo, in 1840; district secretary of the American Board of Commissioners for Foreign Missions, in 1852; supply at Elkhart, Ia., in 1860; and from 1863 resided in Kalamazoo, Mich., until his death, Feb. 11, 1866. See Wilson, *Presb. Hist. Almanac*, 1867, p. 299.

Hreidmar, in Norse mythology. When the Asas journeyed through the world, Odin, Häner, and Loke came to a river with a waterfall. There they found a viper, devouring a salmon. Loke killed the viper, and it was brought to the village, where they sought a night's lodging of the rustic Hreidmar, who was a powerful sorcerer. Hardly had he seen the viper, when he called his two sons, Tofner and Reigen, and told them that the strangers had killed Otter (viper), their brother. Hreidmar immediately went to the Asas, who promised to pay him as much money in reparation as he desired. The sorcerer tore off the skin from the killed viper, and ordered it to be filled with red gold. Odin sent Loke into the land of the black elves to seek gold. There he found the dwarf Andwari, who gave him all the money he had in his possession. But the elf still had a small ring on his hand, which Loke ordered him to deliver with the gold. Andwari obeyed, saying, "The ring will be the death of its possessor." The hide was filled, and the ring laid on top, and thus the Asas were free from all debt. Hreidmar's sons wanted a share of the gold, but he refused them. They consulted with each other and slew their father. Now Reigen thought he might take one half, but Tofnir forbid him, ordering him to go off, or the same fate should befall him which came upon his father. Reigen fled to king Hialfrek, and became his smith. Tofnir changed himself into a snake, and guarded the gold. The smith found an avenger in Sigurd. He told the latter where Tofnir was. Sigurd dug a ditch near by where Tofnir was accustomed to get water, and waited there for him, and finally slew him. Sigurd then went to Reigen and killed him. Next he rode to Tofnir's dwelling, and took all the gold along with him. Sigurd then came to the Hinderalps; there he found a beautiful woman, who called herself Hildur, but whose real name was Brynhildur. He married her and rode to king Giuki, who had two sons, Gunnar and Högni, and one daughter, Gudrun; the latter he married, and entirely forgot Hildur. She incited Gunnar and Högni to murder Sigurd; but they, being bound together by an oath, could not become traitors to him; so the third brother, Guttorm, killed him while asleep, with a sword. King Atli, the brother of Brynhildur, married Gudrun, the widow of Sigurd. He invited Gunnar and Högni, but was anxious for their money. They hid it, whereupon he made war upon them, caught them, and killed both. Shortly after, Gudrun, to avenge the murder of her brothers, killed two of Atli's children, and gave the king some nectar to drink from the skulls of his own children. Thus eventually the whole generation of Niflungar was annihilated.

Hrugner, in Norse mythology. Thor, the mightiest of the Asas, had gone on a journey to kill magicians and giants. Odin rode on his wonderful horse Sleipner to Jotunheim, and thus came to the mightiest and most frightful of giants, Hrugner. Odin began to boast of his horse, and Hrugner, to punish him, pursued him on his own horse, Guldfaxi. Odin, however, had such a start of Hrugner that the latter could not overtake him, although he followed him to the walls of Asgard. Here the gods invited him to their drinking-bout, which invitation he accepted. He became drunk, and began to tell what wondrous things he intended to do. The Asas, tired of his boasting, mentioned Thor's name, and suddenly the mighty hero appeared, raised his frightful miölner, and inquired who had invited the boasting giant. Hrugner argued with Thor that it would be small honor to him to kill him unarmed, and challenged Thor to a duel on the boundary of Griotunagarder. This Thor accepted. The giants in Jotunheim now made a monstrous man of clay, and not finding a heart strong enough, they took out that of a horse, and called him Mokkurkalfi. Hrugner also armed himself. His head, heart, and club were all of stone. Thus armed he waited for Thor. Thor came with thunder and lightning, and threw his hammer at the giant. The latter threw his club at Thor. The two frightful weapons struck each other in the air. The stone club burst, a part falling on the earth, the other striking Thor on his head and stunning him. The hammer of Thor shattered the head of Hrugner so that he fell, his monstrous foot resting on Thor's neck. The huge man of clay fell at Thialfi's hand. None of the Asas could remove Hrugner's foot from Thor's neck until Magni, a son of Thor, came and lifted off the foot without any exertion. Thor presented him with the giant's horse, Guldfaxi.

Hu, in the mythology of the Celts, was the supreme god in Britain. He seems to have been thought very noble, for the attributes given him point to a being such as can be represented only by a pure religion. The Celts have a myth that, at the flood, he pulled the monster who caused the flood out of the water, and thus dried the earth.

Hubbard, Bela, D.D., a Protestant Episcopal minister, was born in Guilford, Conn., Aug. 27, 1739. In 1758 he graduated from Yale College, and afterwards studied theology at King's College, New York city. On Feb. 5, 1764, he was ordained deacon in the King's Chapel, London, and presbyter in St. James's Church on the 19th of the same month. Returning to America, he officiated at Guilford and Killingworth until 1767, when the Society for Propagating the Gospel in Foreign Parts appointed him missionary to New Haven and West Haven, Conn. Between these places he divided his labors equally until the Revolution; after that, until 1791, he gave only one fourth of his time to West Haven, and from that time onward his services were confined almost entirely to New Haven. Although a royalist during the Revolution, he exercised so much discretion that he was not seriously embarrassed in performing his duties. Until peace was declared, in 1783, he continued to receive a salary of £60 yearly from the society which employed him, but after that time he became entirely dependent upon his parishes. Rev. Henry Whitlock became his assistant minister in 1811—Trinity Church being the name of his parish. Dr. Hubbard died in New Haven, Dec. 6, 1812. He was not considered a brilliant man, but was distinguished for sound judgment. His style of preaching, though not animated, was earnest. See Sprague, *Annals of the Amer. Pulpit*, v, 234.

Hubbard, Benjamin H., D.D., a minister in the Methodist Episcopal Church South, was born in 1811. He was converted in early youth, licensed to preach in 1835, and shortly afterwards entered the Memphis Conference. His appointments were, Hatchie Circuit, Gallatin and Cairo, Huntsville, Ala.; Columbia, Tenn.; Trenton, Jackson, Somerville, and Athens, Ala. At the last-mentioned place he was connected with the Tennessee Conference Female Institute as president till 1852, when he was transferred to Jackson, Tenn., in connection with the Jackson Female Institute, where he died, May 2, 1853. He was a fine scholar and excellent preacher. See *Minutes of Annual Conferences of the M. E. Church South*, 1853, p. 462.

Hubbard, Isaac G., D.D., a Protestant Episcopal clergyman, for many years was rector of the church in Manchester (St. Michael's), Conn., until 1866, when he removed to Claremont, N. H., and subsequently became rector of Trinity Church in that town. At the time of his death, March 30, 1879, he had in charge Union Church, West Claremont. See *Prot. Episc. Almanac*, 1880, p. 171.

Hüber, Fortunatus, general definitor of the order of the Franciscans and provincial in Bavaria, who died at Munich, Feb. 12, 1706, is the author of, *Menologium Franciscanum* (Munich, 1698, 2 vols. fol.):—*Chronicon Triplex Trium Ordinum S. Francisci per Germaniam.* See Winer, *Handbuch der theol. Lit.* i, 718; Jöcher, *Allgemeines Gelehrten-Lexikon*, s. v. (B. P.)

Huber, Johann Nepomuk, a Roman Catholic theologian and philosopher of Germany, was born Aug. 18, 1830, at Munich, where he also studied theology and philosophy. In 1859 he was appointed professor in extraordinary and in 1864 ordinary professor of philosophy and pædagogics. His first important theological work, *Philosophie der Kirchenväter* (Munich, 1859), was placed on the *Index*, and as he did not recant, and occasionally spoke for the right of free investigation, the ultramontane party prevented his influence among the students of theology. He now betook himself to speak and to write against ultramontanism. The famous work against infallibility, *Janus, der Papst und der Concil* (Leipsic, 1869), Engl. transl. *Janus, the Pope and the Council* (Boston, 1869), is as much his work as that of Döllinger. Under the name of *Quirinus*, he published, from 1869, in the *Augsburger Allgemeine Zeitung*, his *Römische Briefe vom Concil.* Against Hergenröther's *Antijanus*, he wrote *Das Papstthum und der Staat.* The most important work of this period is his *Darstellung des Jesuitenordens nach seiner Verfassung und Doctrin, Wirksamkeit u. Geschichte* (Berlin, 1873). He also defended the principles of Christianity against materialism and the destructive tendencies related to it. Thus he wrote in 1870 a criticism on Darwin's theory, and in 1875 against Häckel, in his *Zur Kritik moderner Schöpfungslehren.* The *Alte und Neue Glaube* of Strauss found in him a severe philosophical critic in 1873, as did Hartmann the philosopher, *Des Unbewussten*, against whom he wrote *Die religiöse Frage* (1875), and *Der Pessimismus* (1876). Huber died March 19, 1879, at Munich, to the great sorrow of the Old Catholics, whose most gifted leader he was. Besides the writings already mentioned, he published, *Die cartesischen Beweise vom Dasein Gottes* (Augsburg, 1854):—*Johannes Scotus Erigena* (Munich, 1861). See Zuchold, *Bibl. Theol.* i, 590; Lichtenberger, *Encyclop. des Sciences Religieuses*, s. v.; Zierngiebl, *Johannes Huber* (Gotha, 1881). (B. P.)

Hübner, Johannes, a Lutheran theologian of Germany, was born March 17, 1668, at Tyrgau, Upper Lusatia. He studied at Leipsic, was in 1694 rector at Merseburg, in 1711 at Hamburg, and died May 21, 1731. He is best known as the author of *Zweimal* 52 *auserlesene biblische Historien*, which were published in more than one hundred editions, and were translated into other languages. This biblical history is also largely used in German parochial and Sabbath schools. (B. P.)

Hübsch, Abraham, a Jewish rabbi, was born in Hungary in 1831. He studied at Prague, where he also acted for some time as rabbi-preacher of the Meisel synagogue. In 1866 he was called to New York by the congregation Ahavath-Chesed, and died in October, 1884. Hübsch is known as the author of חמש מגלות עם תרגום סורי, i. e. *Die fünf Megiloth*, etc. (Prague, 1866). (B. P.)

Huddesford, William, D.D., an English divine, who died in 1772, was principal of Trinity College, Oxford. He published *Catalogus Liborum Manuscriptorum Viri Clarissimi Antonio a Wood* (1761). See Allibone, *Dict. of Brit. and Amer. Authors*, s. v.

Hueiteoquixqui, in Mexican mythology, was the high-priest. His word was not only advisory, but decisive. He also crowned the king. He opened the breast of the sacrifice, and tore out its heart.

Hueitequilhuitl, in Mexican religion, was one of the three great festivals, celebrated by human sacrifices, in honor of the great mother of the earth, Centeotl. It took place on the last day of the eighth month.

Huematsin, a Mexican sage, lived at Tezcuco in the 7th century, and was considered a doctor by excellence of that Athens of the New World. To him has been attributed the composition of *Teomaxtli* (the divine book), a sort of encyclopædia, which gave information, it is said, of the emigrations of the race of the Aztecs after their departure from the borders of Asia until their arrival upon the plateau of Anahuac, specifying the various halts which the invading nation was obliged to make on the borders of the Rio Giba. It has been affirmed that the *Teomaxtli* was among the Aztec books that were condemned to the fire, without being examined, by the bishop of Mexico, Zumarraga. It is possible that, in point of mythology and history, the importance of these hieroglyphic collections has been exaggerated, and so it is hardly possible now to estimate the extent of the literary losses which Mexico suffered. If the work of Huematsin had been preserved to our time, we might have some information to establish the real signification of the Mexican hieroglyphics. When we remember that the palace of Tezcuco embraced certain departments intended only for the doctors who occupied themselves with special studies, and recall what has been told of the great treasures which were stored up both at Mexico and at Tezcuco, and consecrated exclusively to the study of the kingdom of nature, it is difficult to limit the office of Huematsin to that of a simple theorist, who developed barbarian traditions and fantastic ideas. This learned Aztec seems to have derived his learning from close observation. See *Nouv. Biog. Générale*, s. v.

Hughes, John, a Wesleyan Methodist minister, nephew of John Thomas, vicar of Caerleon, Monmouthshire, was born at Brecon, County Brecon, May 18, 1776. He was educated at the grammar-school at Brecon, under the care of Rev. David Griffiths. Dr. Coke and other distinguished persons received their education at the same place and under the same master. In 1790 Hughes was converted under a sermon by John M'Kersey, and joined the Methodist Society. His parents designed him for the Established Church, but young Hughes could not conscientiously enter its ministry. In 1793 he became a resident with his uncle at Caerleon. In 1796 he was appointed by the Conference to the Cardiff Circuit. In 1800 he and Owen Davies were appointed the first missionaries in North Wales. In 1805 he was superintendent of the Welsh Mission in Liverpool. His remaining circuits were, Swansea, Bristol, Glasgow, Northwich and Warrington, Macclesfield, Newcastle-under-Lyne, etc. In 1832 he became a supernumerary at Knutsford, Cheshire. He died May 15, 1843. Hughes deliberately declined a life of ease and honor, and, contrary to the wishes of his friends, chose the toils and privations of the Methodist ministry. From this course he never swerved. He was a most diligent worker, producing, amid the pressing duties of his itinerancy, works of great and lasting value. In 1803 he published a new edition of the *Welsh Hymn-Book;* he translated part of Dr. Coke's *Commentary on the New Testament* (1809); while at Macclesfield, 1813, he wrote *A Plea for Religious Liberty*, a reply to Joseph Cook's ("Civis") *The Danger of Schism*, pamphlets which were the result of a controversy respecting the

Sunday-schools originated by David Simpson, and which were now carried on by the Methodists; *Horæ Britannicæ*, or *Studies in Early British History* (Lond. 1818, 2 vols. 8vo), a work which received the encomiums of Dr. Thomas Burgess, bishop of Salisbury, then bishop of St. Davids, of Sharon Turner, in a letter to the author, of Price, of David M'Nicoll, and of the *Eclectic Review*. It embodied the results of many years' antiquarian research, and is a work of great value. Hughes also wrote, but did not publish, a work entitled *Historical Triads; Consisting of Memorials of Remarkable Persons and Occurrences among the Cymry*, translated from the Welsh, with notes and illustrations. The manuscript has been deposited in the British Museum. He received several prizes, premiums, and medals from the Cambrian Society for his literary productions. His last work was the *Memoir and Remains of Fussell*, which he finished in 1839. See Robert Jackson, *Memoir* in *Wesleyan Methodist Magazine*, March, 1847, p. 209 sq.; *Minutes of the British Conference*, 1843; *Wesl. Meth. Magazine*, Sept. 1834, p. 669; Smith, *Hist. of Wesl. Methodism*, ii, 359, 361, 393 sq.

Hughes, Obadiah, D.D., an English Presbyterian clergyman, descended from a distinguished Puritan family, was born at Canterbury in 1695. He completed a liberal education in Scotland. He was first assistant minister, then co-pastor at Maid Lane, Southwark, and lecturer at Old Jewry. In 1721 he married the sister of the lord mayor of London, and used the riches she brought him in doing good. He was one of the preachers at Salters' Hall in 1734 against popery. He preached the funeral sermon on the death of Rev. Samuel Say, in 1743, at Westminster, and the church there called him to succeed Mr. Say in the pastorate. He suffered much from the death of friends, and himself died Dec. 10, 1751. See Wilson, *Dissenting Churches*, iv, 96.

Hugo (or **Hew**), a Scotch prelate, was a monk of Arbroath, and bishop of Dunkeld in the tenth year of king Alexander II. He was witness to a charter by king William, dated at Forfar. He died in January, 1214. See Keith, *Scottish Bishops*, p. 78.

Hugo, a cardinal, bishop OF OSTIA, was born in France, and probably, as the authors of the *Histoire Littéraire* assert, in the diocese of Beauvais. He became at first a Cistercian monk, then abbot of Trois Fontaines, in the diocese of Châlons. Pope Eugenius made him cardinal about 1151, in spite of the opposition of St. Bernard, who was sorry to lose such a man. Hugo died in 1158. To him are attributed some commentaries on the Old and New Tests., also a book on the miracles of pope Eugenius. But these indications seem to be conjectural, and it may even be supposed that they are erroneous. However, there is one of his letters which has been written on occasion of the death of Eugenius. See Hoefer, *Nouv. Biog. Générale*, s. v.

Hugues, THEODOR, a Protestant theologian of Germany, who died at Celle, July 22, 1878, doctor of theology, is the author of, *Erbauliche und belehrende Betrachtungen über das Gebet des Herrn* (Celle, 1832):—*Das Verfahren der reformirten Synode Niedersachsens*, etc. (Hamburg, eod.):—*Unionsgedanken* (1843):—*Entwurf einer vollständigen gottesdienstlichen Ordnung zum Gebrauch für evangelisch-reformirte Gemeinden* (1846): —*Die Confederation der reformirten Kirchen in Niedersachsen, Geschichte und Urkunden* (1873). See Zuchold, *Bibl. Theol.* i, 593. (B. P.)

Huitzilopochtli (also **Mexitli**), in Mexican mythology, is the supreme deity of the nation, the bloodthirsty god of war. The two sons of a widow, Coatlicue, observing that their mother was pregnant, and being afraid of the disgrace of an illegitimate birth, resolved to murder her. Just as they were in the act of doing so, Huitzilopochtli sprang out of her body, a god of war, carrying in his left hand a shield, and in his right a spear. He soon conquered his mother's murderers, and pillaged their houses. When the Aztecs left their dwelling-places, travelling for one hundred and sixty-five days, to find a more southern country, they were directed by this god, whose idol they carried before them, to the valley of Mexico. Here they built a wooden temple, which later became the site of one of stone. In this temple his image stood, frightful and terrible. The most horrible sacrifices were made in honor of this god. Hundreds of slaves and prisoners were offered to him. At the dedication of his temple, seventy thousand human beings were sacrificed, by opening the breast when yet alive, tearing out the heart, and offering it to the idol on a golden spoon. See MEXICAN RELIGION.

Hujukhu, in the mythology of the Caribbeans, is the heaven which lies above the visible heaven. There are all earthly joys in tenfold greater measure. The trees bear better fruit, the fields flowers more beautiful. Fishing is easier and less dangerous. Every man has many wives who care for him. Sickness and death are not known there.

Hukkok. *Yakûk*, the modern representation of this site, is laid down on the *Ordnance Map* three and three quarter miles north-west of the shore of the Sea of Galilee (from Khan Minyeh), and is described in the accompanying *Memoirs* (i, 364, 420) as a "stone-built village, containing about two hundred Moslems; surrounded by arable land, and situated at the foot of a hill. There is a good spring, and many cisterns are found in the village. Guérin says that, in 1875, the village was reduced to about twenty houses. There are traces of ancient remains at this village, and a rock-cut birkeh [pool] with steps leading down to it, also cut out of the rock."

Huldrer, in Norse mythology, are the mild, womanly elves, or women of the woods, who are supposed to be seen in the mountains of snow in Norway. See HOLDA.

Huller, GEORG, a Roman Catholic theologian of Germany, was born in 1812. He took holy orders in 1836, was sub-regent at Aschaffenburg in 1839, in 1865 cathedral-dean at Würzburg, and died June 22, 1870. He published *Die Idee des Göttlichen in der Wissenschaft und die sogenannte freie Wissenschaft* (Würzburg, 1867). After his death were published three volumes of his *Volkspredigten*, edited by Joseph Huller (Augsburg, 1871–73). (B. P.)

Hülsemann, WILHELM, a Protestant theologian of Germany, was born March 7, 1781, in Westphalia, and died at Iserlohn, Feb. 1, 1865, superintendent and doctor of philosophy. He published, *Die preussische Kirchenagende in Hinsicht auf die evangelische Kirche überhaupt* (Essen, 1825):—*Evangelische Hauspostille* (Düsseldorf, 1827, 2 vols.; 2d ed. 1844):—*Die Geschichte der Auferweckung des Lazarus* (Leipsic, 1835):—*Christus und die Sünderin am Jacobsbrunnen* (1837):—*Predigten und Gesänge über die Episteln der Sonn- und Festtage des Kirchenjahres* (1838, 2 vols.). See Winer, *Handbuch der theol. Lit.* ii, 275, 333, 358; Zuchold, *Bibl. Theol.* i, 594; Koch, *Geschichte des deutschen Kirchenliedes*, vii, 66 sq. (B. P.)

Hulsius, Anton, a Dutch divine, was born in 1615, at Kilda, in the duchy of Bergen. In 1644 he was preacher and professor of Hebrew at Breda, afterwards professor of theology and of Hebrew at Leyden, and died Feb. 27, 1685. He wrote, *Disputatio Epistolica cum Jacobo Abendana super Haggæi ii*, 9 (Leyden, 1666):—*Abrabanelis Comm. in LXX Hebdomadibus Danielis cum Confutatione* (1653):—*Authentia Codicis Ebræi Sacri Contra Criminationes Is. Voss Vindicata* (1662):—*Theologia Judaica* (1653):—*Nomenclator Biblicus Hebræo-Latinus* (1659):—*Compendium Lexici Hebraici* (1674):—*Liber Psalmorum Hebr. cum Annotationibus* (1650):—*Oratio de Linguæ Hebraicæ Origine et Propagatione* (1641). See Fürst, *Bibl. Jud.* i, 416 sq.; Jöcher, *Allgemeines Gelehrten-Lexikon*, s. v.; Steinschneider, *Bibl. Handbuch*, s. v. (B. P.)

Hulsius, Heinrich, a Reformed theologian of Holland, was born Oct. 10, 1654. He studied at different universities, was in 1670 doctor of theology, in 1681 professor at Duisburg, and died March 29, 1723. He wrote, *Summa Theologiæ, seu Liber de Molitione et Opere et Sabbatho Dei* (Leyden, 1683):—*Vita Ithiel, Uchal et Samuel sive in Ultima Parsemiastæ Salomonis Capita Commentarius Propheticus* (1693):—*De Vallibus Prophetarum Sacris* (Amsterdam, 1701):—*Comment. in Isrælis Prisci Prærogativas ac bona sub V. T. Dissert.* 15 *Inclusus*, etc. (1713). See Dunkel, *Nachrichten*, ii, 325; Jöcher, *Allgemeines Gelehrten-Lexikon*, s. v.; Fürst, *Bibl. Jud.* i, 417. (B. P.)

Humphrey, Heman, D.D., a Congregational minister, was born at Simsbury, Conn., March 26, 1779. He graduated from Yale College in 1805; was pastor of the Congregational Church in Fairfield from 1807 to 1817; in Pittsfield, Mass., from 1817 to 1823; president of Amherst College from 1823 to 1845; and then retired to Pittsfield, where he died, April 13, 1861. Dr. Humphrey was the author of, *Tour in France*, etc. (2 vols.):—*Domestic Education:—Letters of a Son in the Ministry:—Life and Writings of Professor W. Fiske:—Life of T. H. Gallaudet:—Sketches of the History of Revivals.* See *Appleton's Annual Cyclop.* 1861, p. 542.

Humphrey, Zephaniah Moore, D.D., a Presbyterian minister, son of Rev. Heman Humphrey, D.D., was born at Amherst, Mass., Aug. 30, 1824. He graduated from Amherst College in 1843; studied at Union Theological Seminary in 1846 and 1847; graduated from Andover Theological Seminary in 1849; preached in Milwaukee, Wis., one year thereafter; was ordained in October, 1850, pastor at Racine; became pastor of the Congregational Church in Milwaukee in 1856; of a Presbyterian Church in Chicago, Ill., in 1859; of Calvary Church, Philadelphia, Pa., in 1868; professor in Lane Theological Seminary, Cincinnati, O., in 1875; and died there, Nov. 13, 1881. He was moderator of the General Assembly of the Presbyterian Church in 1871. See *Gen. Cat. of Union Theol. Sem.* 1876, p. 55; *Trien. Cat. of Andover Theol. Sem.* 1870, p. 180.

Humphreys, Hector, D.D., a Protestant Episcopal clergyman, was born at Canton, Conn., June 8, 1797. He pursued his studies at the academy in Westfield, and graduated in 1818 from Yale College. His purpose was to enter the ministry of the Congregational Church; but, having abandoned this project, he joined the Protestant Episcopal communion, and was admitted, after due preparation, to the bar. When Washington College was established, he was elected its first professor of ancient languages. His predilection for the ministry led him to ordination, but he continued to discharge the duties of his professorship until 1831, when he was appointed president of St. John's College, Annapolis, Md. He died there, Jan. 25, 1857. Although familiar with all branches of literature, he devoted himself particularly to natural science, and he published many articles urging the application of chemistry to agriculture. See *Amer. Quar. Church Rev.* 1857, p. 146.

Hundeiker, Johann Peter, a Protestant theologian of Germany, was born in 1751, and died Jan. 26, 1836. He published, *Häusliche Gottesverehrung für christliche Familien* (Hildesheim, 1784, and later):—*Strahlen des Lichts aus den heiligen Hallen des Tempels der Wahrheit und Erkenntniss* (Leipsic, 1824):—*Häusliches Festbuch für gebildete Genossen des heiligen Abendmahls* (1821, 2 vols.):—*Weihgeschenk. Erweckungen zur Andacht in den heiligen Tagen der Einsegnung und der ersten Abendmahlsfeier* (1823; 2d ed. 1844). See Winer, *Handbuch der theol. Lit.* ii, 330, 332, 335, 367, 375; Zuchold, *Bibl. Theol.* i, 596. (B. P.)

Hundeshagen, Karl Bernhard, a Reformed theologian of Germany, was born Jan. 10, 1810, at Friedewald, Hesse. He studied at Giessen and Halle, commenced his academical career at the former place in 1830, and accepted a call in 1834 as professor in the newly founded university of Berne. In 1846 his anonymous work, *Der deutsche Protestantismus, seine Vergangenheit und seine heutigen Lebensfragen*, appeared, and fell like a flash of lightning in that troubled period. "This remarkable work," says Schaff (in his *Germany, its Universities, Theology, and Religion*, Philadelphia, 1857, p. 401), "is a manly and bold, yet well-meant and patriotic exposure of the religious, political, and social diseases of modern Germany, and represents, almost prophetically, the peculiar crisis which preceded the outbreak of the political earthquake of 1848. The author develops, first, the nature and object of Protestantism in its original form, then he traces the rise and power of recent anti-Christianity in Germany, its causes and effects, following it out even to the moral destitution of German emigrants in foreign countries; and finally he discusses the movements and questions which agitated the country in the last ten years before the revolution. He accounts for the development of modern infidelity in the bosom of German Protestantism, to a considerable extent, by the political reaction since the Congress of Vienna, which crippled the free motion of national life, violently suppressed all political discontent, and indirectly forced the bitter hostility to the existing order of things to vent itself intellectually upon the Church and Christianity. He thinks that a healthy religious life of a nation can only unfold itself on the soil of rational political freedom, as the example of England and the United States prove better than all arguments." This work made Hundeshagen's reputation, and he was at once called to Heidelberg as professor of New Testament exegesis and Church history, where he continued to labor for twenty years (1847-67). In 1867 he accepted a call to Bonn, where he spent his last years in peaceful and friendly relations with his colleagues, although a great sufferer in body. He rejoiced in the restoration of the German empire in 1870, and greeted the hour of his departure with Christian fortitude and joyfulness. He died June 2, 1873. Hundeshagen was one of the most prominent and original theologians which the Reformed Church of Germany has given in this century to the service of the Evangelical Church. His peculiar importance consisted in this, that in his own way he showed how certain features of the Reformed Church might be advantageously applied to the living Christianity of the day. He emphasized the ethical principle in Protestantism over against a mere dogmatic or critical intellectualism, and laid stress upon the social element in the Church, which was languishing by reason of its amalgamation with the State. Besides the work mentioned above, Hundeshagen published, *De Agobardi Archiepiscopi Lugdunensis Vita et Scriptis* (Giessen, 1831):—*Epistolas Aliquot Ineditas Martini Buceri, Joannis Calvini, Theodori Bezæ Aliorumque ad Historiam Ecclesiasticam Magnæ Britanniæ, Edidit* (Berne, 1840):—*Ueber den Einfluss des Calvinismus auf die Ideen von Staat und staatsbürgerlicher Freiheit* (1842):—*Die Conflikte des Zwinglianismus, Lutherthums und Calvinismus in der bernischen Landeskirche von 1522–1558* (1843):—*Die Bekenntniss-Grundlage der vereinigten evangelischen Kirche in Baden* (1851):—*Ueber die Natur und die geschichtliche Entwicklung der Humanitätsidee in ihrem Verhältniss zu Staat und Kirche* (1853):—*Der Weg zu Christo* (eod.). A collection of his essays and shorter writings was published by professor Christlieb (Gotha, 1874, 2 vols.). See Christlieb, *K. B. Hundeshagen, eine Lebensskizze* (Gotha, 1873); Riehm, in *Theolog. Studien und Kritiken*, 1874, part i; Plitt-Herzog, *Real-Encyklop.* s. v.; Lichtenberger, *Encyclop. des Sciences Religieuses*, s. v.; Zuchold, *Bibl. Theol.* i, 569 sq. (B. P.)

Hundt-Radowsky, Johann Hartwig von, a Protestant writer, was born in 1759, and died at Burgdorf, Switzerland, Aug. 15, 1835. He wrote, *Judenspiegel* (Würzburg, 1819):—*Neuer Judenspiegel* (1828):—*Die Judenschule* (1822):—*Der Christenspiegel* (Stuttgart, 1830, 3 vols.). See Winer, *Handbuch der theol.*

Lit. i, 379; Fürst, *Bibl. Jud.* i, 417; Zuchold, *Bibl. Theol.* i, 597. (B. P.)

Hungari, ANTON, a Roman Catholic priest and writer of Germany, was born at Mayence in 1809, and died Dec. 17, 1881, at Rödelheim, near Frankfort-on-the-[illegible] He published, *Christliche Reden an Sonn- und Fes[illegible]* (Mayence, 1838):—*Festtagspredigten* (Frankfort, 1841):—*Christodora* (1840):—*Gute Aussaat, Erzählungen für katholische Christen* (1867):—*Marien-Preis, erbauliche Unterhaltungen* (1866):—*Tempel der Heiligen zur Ehre Gottes* (7th ed. 1867):—*Muster-Predigten der katholischen Kanzel-Beredsamkeit* (1873–79, 12 parts). (B. P.)

Hungarian Version OF THE SCRIPTURES. The Benedictine missionaries, who, at the beginning of the 11th century, brought Christianity to the Magyars, transmitted to them also a translation of the Psalms, the gospels and epistles, as essential parts for the divine service. In the life of Margareth, daughter of king Bela IV, who died in 1271, we are told that she read the Psalms and the history of the passion of the Saviour in the Hungarian dialect—*Hungarico idiomate* (see Pray, *Vita S. Elisabethæ et B. Margar.* 1770). In consequence of the many invasions made into Hungary, only fragments of a later time have been preserved. Thus we find parts of the Old Test., translated by the Franciscans Thomas and Valentinus, in a Vienna codex, written between 1336 and 1444 (according to Révany, *Antiq. Lit. Hung.* Pesth, 1803, in the year 1450). The translation is made from the Vulgate. The four gospels are preserved in a Munich codex. Both were edited by Döbrentei, *Régi magyar nyelvemlékek* (1838), i, 3 sq.; (1842), iii, 17 sq. Psalms, Song of Solomon, and the gospels are found in a codex of the episcopal library at Stuhlweissenburg (specimens in Toldy, *Magyar N. Irodalom Törtėnete*, Pesth, 1862, i, 247). A second complete translation of the Bible was made by L. Báthory (died 1456); it is supposed that this translation is preserved in the codex Jordánszky at Grau. This codex was written in 1519, and contains Exodus vi–Judges, and all of the New Test. with the exception of the Pauline epistles. The first printed edition of the Pauline epistles, by B. Kornjáthy, was published at Cracow in 1533; the gospels, by Gabriel Pannonius Pesthinus, at Vienna in 1536; the complete New Test., by John Sylvester, was published in 1541; another in 1574. A translation of the entire Bible, from the original, which the Jesuit Stephen Szántó (Latin *Arator*) prepared towards the end of the 16th century, was never printed, whereas the translation from the Vulgate, made by the Jesuit George Káldi (*Szent Biblia, az egész Keresz-tyénségben bevött régi deák betüböl*, Vienna, 1626), is still in use among the Roman Catholics, and was often reprinted (Tyrnau, 1732; Buda, 1783; Erlau, 1862–65; the latter edition revised in accordance with modern orthography; see Dankó, *De S. Scriptura, Ejusq. Interpret. Comm.* Vienna, 1867, p. 243 sq.). A revision of Kaldi's New Test. was undertaken by a Reformed pastor in Hungary, in 1869, in behalf of the British and Foreign Bible Society. The first Protestant edition of the whole Bible appeared at Visoly, near Güns, in 1589. This is the present authorized version of Hungary. The translation was made from the originals, compared with the Vulgate and several other Latin versions, by Gaspard Caroli, or Karoli, a Magyar by birth, pastor of the Church at Güns, and dean of the Brethren of the Valley of Kaschau. He had studied at Wittenberg, where he had imbibed the principles of the Reformation. The printing was done at Visoly, where a printing-office was established for that purpose by count Stephen Bathory. The sheets, as they passed through the press, were corrected by Albert Molnar, subsequently regent of the college at Oppenheim. He afterwards subjected the whole to a careful revision, and published an improved edition at Hanau in 1608, under the title, *Biblia, az-az: Istennek O ės Ujj Testamentomában foglaltatott egész Szent irás, Magyar nyelore fordittatott Károly Gáspár által.* Molnar subsequently published other editions of the Bible, and separate editions of the New Test. The edition of 1608 is the more interesting, since it is accompanied with a Magyar translation of the Heidelberg catechism, the liturgy of the Hungarian churches, and a metrical version of the Psalms.

When the different editions were exhausted, another revision of the Hungarian Bible was undertaken by count Stephen Bethlen D'Iktar, brother to prince Gabriel Bethlen. He assembled a number of learned men to prepare the work, and established a printing-press at Warasdin. In 1657 the revision was completed, and printing was commenced; but in 1660, when the city of Warasdin was taken by the Turks, almost half of the copies were lost or destroyed. The remaining copies were saved, and taken to Claudiopolis, or Koloswar, in Transylvania, where the edition was completed in 1661. Another edition (the sixth) of the Bible was published at Amsterdam in 1684–85, by N. K. M. Totfalusi, by whom a separate edition of the New Test. and Psalms was printed during the same year. The seventh edition of the Bible was published at Cassel in 1704, edited by John Ingebrand. In 1730 an edition was published at Utrecht, *Szent Biblia, az-az: Istennek O ės Ujj Testamentomában foglaltatott egész Szent irás, Magyar nyelore fordittatott Károli Gáspár*, which was followed by others in 1737 and 1794. In Basle also an edition was published in 1751, and at Leipsic in 1776.

Another revision of the Hungarian Bible, which, perhaps, ought rather to be regarded as a new translation, was executed by Dr. Comarin, pastor of Debreczin, but he died before it could be committed to press, and the MS. was sent for publication to the celebrated Vitringa. Perhaps the edition published in Holland in 1716–17 was from this MS. The Jesuits prevented its circulation, and seized and destroyed 3000 copies.

In 1812 a Bible society was formed in Presburg, but with the exception of an edition of the Bible in 1823, no editions of the Hungarian Scriptures appear to have been published by that society. In 1814 Dr. Pinkerton found at Utrecht upwards of 2000 copies of the authorized Hungarian Bible, belonging to the above-mentioned edition of 1794. These copies were purchased by the British and Foreign Bible Society, and transmitted to Presburg for circulation.

When, in 1837, Hungary became accessible to the operations of the Bible Society, the publication of the Scriptures was commenced in Hungary itself, and the total number of Hungarian Bibles and Testaments printed by the British and Foreign Bible Society up to March 31, 1884, was 561,310.

As Caroly's Bible abounds in archaic expressions, some of which sound rude and coarse to modern ears, the British and Foreign Bible Society has of late made arrangements to secure a faithful revision. A small number of a revised New Test. was published in 1876 with the intention of eliciting the criticisms of Hungarian scholars, with a view to the settlement of the text. As the text has been fixed, the British and Foreign Bible Society published, in 1883, an edition of 10,000 New Tests. as revised by bishop Filo. See *Bible of Every Land*, p. 325. (B. P.)

Hungarian-Wendish Version. See WENDISH-HUNGARIAN VERSION, s. v.; SLAVONIC VERSIONS. By way of supplement we add that an edition of the New Test. and Psalms has been published in 1882, with a slight revision, limited to orthographical and syntactical errors, made by pastor Berke. (B. P.)

Huns. For a general description of this people and their history see vol. iv. It is the design in this place to pay some attention to particulars which are merely alluded to in the former article, and especially to examine the question of Attila's influence upon Christendom.

The name *Huns* (*Hunni*, Οὖννοι, Χοῦνοι) is a comparatively recent one in history, and its derivation is altogether uncertain. The usual theory, that it is only the Chinese *Hun-jo* transferred into the dialects of the West, is not so well established as to make it impossible, or even unlikely, that Chinese writers may have first found the name used by Byzantine historians, and appropriated it from them. It is evidently a collective name, and designates a people composed of many distinct tribes, which are mentioned in some detail by early writers.

This people belonged to the Turkish family, and can best be accounted for, so far as that portion which enters into European history is concerned, by regarding it as included among the Scythian tribes of which the later classics make mention. An Asiatic branch, whose western limits did not reach beyond the modern Turkestan, is wholly outside the scope of our inquiry. The Huns of history are first discovered as occupants of the district about the Caspian Sea, lying to the north and north-east of the Alans, who occupied the Caucasus and adjoining regions. Emerging thence, they engaged in a bloody struggle with the Alans, whom they defeated and afterward incorporated with their armies; and the allied nations then precipitated themselves on the Goths, whose territories lay beyond and contiguous to those of the Alans, and, by forcing them from their homes, produced the general irruption of barbarians into the Roman empire. In the revolt of the Goths against the empire the Huns crossed the Danube as allies of their recent enemies, and though they were for a time less conspicuous than the Goths, they were yet able to impose a tribute, under their king Rouas, upon the Romans. Bleda and Attila, the sons of Mundzuk and nephews of Rouas, succeeded the latter in 433; and after the death of Bleda, said by some authorities to have been caused by his brother, while others deny the charge, Attila became the acknowledged head of the vast hordes collected under or affiliated with the Hunnish name, and entered on a career of conquest and diplomacy which made him the most noted personage of his age, and under the embellishing hand of legend and myth has secured to him and his followers a notable place in the recollections of the world for all time. Seven hundred thousand warriors, Huns, Alans, Avars, Bulgarians, Acatzirs, and many other tribes are said to have followed him into battle. An expedition into Persia for plunder is assumed by some writers as his first distinct enterprise; but history gives clear evidence of but three campaigns conducted by Attila, all of them European wars.

1. An invasion of the Eastern or Byzantine empire in 441, in which he defeated the emperor Theodosius II in successive battles, ravaged Illyricum, Thrace, and Greece, and after several years of desultory warfare conquered a peace in 447, which gave him possession of a territory in Thrace. Having devastated the country south of the Danube, he accepted an indemnity from the emperor, and renounced all claim to its control. In addition, he exacted, however, an annual tribute and the return of deserters from his army.

2. An incursion into Gaul in 450, during which he took the towns of Treves, Metz, Rheims, Tongres, Arras, Laon, St. Quentin, Strasburg, etc. Orleans, which was the objective point of the campaign, was relieved by the Roman general Ætius when the gates had already been opened to the Huns, and pillage was beginning. Attila thereupon retreated precipitately to Châlons on the Marne, and was there attacked by the united armies of Ætius and Theodoric, the Visigoth king, and defeated in a terrible battle in which historians report a slaughter of from 252,000 to 300,000 men—the last great battle ever fought by the Romans. Returning to his possessions on the Danube, he prepared for a new campaign, which he undertook

3. In 452. The ostensible reason alleged for his incursion of that year into Italy was the refusal of the emperor Valentinian III to confer upon him the hand of his sister Honoria, accompanied by a dowry of half the empire. He crossed the Julian Alps and laid siege to Aquileia, then the second city in Italy, and at the end of three months overcame its obstinate resistance. A century later the historian Jornandes could scarcely trace the ruins of the place. Other towns were sacked, e. g. Milan, Pavia, Parma, and quite certainly also Verona, Mantua, Brescia, Bergamo, and Cremona. The whole of Lombardy was ravaged, and Attila was preparing to march on Rome when an embassy from that city, headed by Pope Leo the Great, succeeded in persuading him to a peaceful evacuation of Italy. Retiring into Pannonia by way of Augsburg, which he pillaged, he consoled himself by adding a new wife, Ildico, Hilda, or Mycolth, to the large number which he already possessed; but on the morning after this marriage he was found dead, having ruptured a blood-vessel or been foully dealt with, A.D. 453. His kingdom fell to pieces almost as soon as the great king was dead; the different nations which had followed his banner became alienated from each other, and separated, some to serve in the armies of the empire, others to seek alliance with tribes in the north and east, which were of similar race and character with themselves.

The effect of the Hunnish incursions was indirectly beneficial to Christianity. The Burgundians, for example, when threatened by Attila's uncle, Oktar or Ouptar, submitted to be baptized, in the hope that they might thus acquire power to resist the foe. The deliverance of Troyes in the Châlons campaign by the supplications of bishop Lupus, and of Rome in the following year by those of Leo the Great, convinced the mind of that and succeeding ages that piety could accomplish what armies might fail to achieve. The profound impressions wrought upon the mind of Christendom appear most clearly, however, in the legendary histories of Attila, which are preserved in three distinct currents of tradition—the Latin, Germanic, and Hungarian.

The Latin legends originated in the reaction from the panic into which Attila's conquests had thrown the whole of Europe, and sprang from ecclesiastical sources. They seek to explain his successes by exaggerating his power, and both chronology and geography are violated in the attempt to magnify his career. They describe sieges and captures which never took place, make the Hunnish army to sweep over the whole of France, derive the name of the city of Strasburg from the fancy that Attila made four roads through the city walls, and despatch the broken remnants of his army after the battle of Châlons into Spain to fight the Moors. In the title "The Scourge of God," applied to Attila, these Latin legends reach their culmination. A hermit of Champagne says to Attila before Châlons—misplaced in that province by the legend—"*Tu es flagellum Dei*—but God breaks, when he pleases, the instruments of his vengeance. God will take this sword from thee and give it to another." At Troyes Attila announces himself to St. Lupus as "the king of the Huns, the Scourge of God;" whereupon the bishop responds, "Welcome, then, scourge of the God whom I serve. Enter, and go where thou wilt." The Huns are, however, smitten with supernatural blindness, and see nothing until they have passed through the city and out at the opposite gate. Some of these legends endow Attila with diabolical attributes, sarcasm, pride, and hideous ugliness, joined with a sardonic humor, while others go to the opposite extreme, and describe him as a champion of the pope and extirpator of heresies. Some of the latter sort even represent him as preaching morality, encouraging good marriages, and portioning virtuous maidens. One reports that a great battle was fought by Attila under the walls of Rome, on the conclusion of which the dead rose again and continued the fight with great fury for three days and nights; and the location, with all its details, was afterwards pointed out.

The Germanic legends differ widely from the Latin. In them Attila is a hero, the type of royal majesty, furnished with almost superhuman bravery and strength. He is as wise as Solomon, and richer and more generous than was he. The great Theodoric and Hermanaric are always associated with him, as his inferiors. The oldest of these legends is a fragment of the 8th century at Fulda, which proves that they were circulated in the Frank dialect in Gaul during the Merovingian period. The Germanic form of Attila legend was current in England also at an early period, and receives its fullest development in the Icelandic and Scandinavian handling. The episode of Walter of Aquitaine and the *Nibelungenlied* are offshots from the primitive stock of this tradition.

The Hungarian legends associate Attila with all the phases of their early national life. Deriving the Magyar stock from Magog, the son of Japhet and king of Scythia, they trace it down to Attila and his son Arpad, the common patrons of the Magyars and Huns. When the Magyars become Christians, it is because Attila, by his docility under the hand of God, whose scourge he was, has prepared the way for their conversion through his merits. He is the inseparable patron of that people, changing when they change, and living through all the stages of their national existence.

Attila was not only a barbarian, but also a heathen, and while he fought Rome rather than the Church, and even showed regard for the sanctity of its eminent representatives, the success of his arms was universally felt to be destructive to Christianity. In the course of time, accordingly, the minds of writers, saturated with ideas derived from the churchly legends, discovered that so mighty an impersonation of the principle of evil as was Attila could be no other than Antichrist himself; and artists, under the same influence, represented him as having almost diabolical features and goat's horns. See frontispiece to Italian legend of Attila, frequently printed at Venice in the later years of the 15th century.

For the later history of the Huns, down to the time when the name and people became extinct, see the article HUNS in vol. iv.

Literature.—For the early history Ammianus Marcellinus and Priscus, especially the latter, are the principal sources. Sidonius Apollinaris notices the invasion of Gaul. Later authorities are Jornandes, Procopius, Agathius, Gregory of Tours, and Cassiodorus. Jornandes was a Goth, bitterly hostile to the Huns, and open to the charge of excessive credulity; but he is the only authority for certain portions of Attila's history.

Among modern works De Guignes's *Histoire des Huns* must be assigned the first place, as it furnishes all the speculations upon which the earliest accepted history of the Huns is based. Gibbon's account in the *Decline and Fall* (Milman's ed. vol. vi) is scarcely more than an abridgment of De Guignes's. See also Creasy, *Decisive Battles of the World* (Châlons); Neumann, *Völker des Südlichen Russlands;* Klemm, *Attila* (1827); J. v. Müller, *Attila, der Held des 5. Jahrhunderts* (1806); Herbert, *Attila, or the Triumph of Christianity* (1838); Grimm, *Deutsche Heldensagen* (Göttingen, 1829); Zeuss, *Deutsche u. Nachbarstämme* and *Ostfinnen.* Also, Bertazzolo, *Vita San Leone Primo et di Attila Flagello di Dio* (Mantua, 1614, 4to). Gibbon gives leading authorities on Attila. See the Church Histories and leading Dictionaries, etc., and the articles HUNS, LEO I, POPE, etc., in this *Cyclopædia.*

Huntingtonians, a class of Antinomians (q. v.) in England, followers of William Huntington (q. v.), a Calvinistic Methodist preacher of London. Huntington maintained that the elect are justified from all eternity, an act of which their justification in this world by faith is only a manifestation; that God sees no sin in believers, and is never angry with them; that the imputation of our sins to Christ, and of his righteousness to us, was *actual*, not *judicial;* that faith, repentance, and holy obedience are covenant conditions on the part of Christ, not on our part; and, finally, that sanctification is no evidence of justification, but rather renders it more obscure. These doctrines still continue to be taught in a number of chapels, especially in Sussex.

Hurd, Carlton, D.D., a Congregational minister, was born in New Hampshire in 1795. He graduated from Dartmouth College in 1818, and from Andover Theological Seminary in 1822; was ordained, Sept. 17, 1823, pastor at Fryeburg, Me., and died there, Dec. 6, 1855. See *Trien. Cat. of Andover Theol. Sem.* 1870, p. 51.

Hurd, Isaac, D.D., a Unitarian and subsequently a Trinitarian minister, was born at Charlestown, Mass., Dec. 7, 1785. He graduated at Harvard College in 1806; completed his theological studies at Divinity Hall, Edinburgh, Scotland; and preached his first sermon in London. He was ordained pastor of the Unitarian Society in Lynn, Mass., Sept. 15, 1813, and was dismissed May 22, 1816. Although he had so far changed his sentiments as to become an avowed Trinitarian, he was called to be the pastor of the Second (Unitarian) Society in Exeter, N. H., and was installed, Sept. 11, 1817. "Notwithstanding a conscientious difference of opinion on certain important points, he continued to enjoy the cordial respect and affection of his people." In his advanced years his society secured for him the services of colleague pastors. He died at South Reading (now Wakefield), at the residence of his son, Oct. 4, 1856. See Sprague, *Annals of the Amer. Pulpit*, viii, 446; *Necrology of Harvard College*, p. 116. (J. C. S.)

Huret, GRÉGOIRE, a reputable French engraver, was born at Lyons in 1610. The following are some of his principal plates: *Life and Passion of Our Saviour*, a set of thirty-two; *The Stoning of Stephen; St. Peter Preaching; Christ Crowned with Thorns; The Holy Family with St. Catharine.* He died at Paris in 1670. See Hoefer, *Nouv. Biog. Générale*, s. v.; Spooner, *Biog. Hist. of the Fine Arts*, s. v.

Huscanawer, a ceremony formerly practiced by the North American Indians of Virginia when they wished to prepare a candidate for the priesthood, or for enrolment among their great men. The principal men of the place where the ceremony was to be performed selected the handsomest and most vigorous youths for the purpose. They shut them up for several months, giving them no other sustenance than the infusion of certain roots, which strongly affected the nervous system. The result was that they quite lost their memory; they forgot their possessions, parents, friends, and even their language, becoming at length deaf and dumb. The purpose of this strange treatment was alleged to be to free the novices from the dangerous impressions of infancy, and to relieve the mind of all prejudice.

Husseyites, the followers of Joseph Hussey, a learned but eccentric divine, formerly of Cambridge, who held the Antinomian views of Tobias Crisp (q. v.). He maintained also the pre-existence of Christ's human soul, or, rather, of a spiritual or glorious body, in which he appeared to Adam, Abraham, and others; this body being the image of God in which man was created.

Hutangi, an apartment which is generally found in the houses of the wealthy Chinese, and devoted to ancestor-worship (q. v.). The room contains the image of the most illustrious ancestor of the family, and a record of the names of all the members of the family. Twice a year, generally in spring and autumn, the relations hold a meeting in this room, when rich presents of various kinds of meats, wines, and perfumes, with wax tapers, are laid on the table with great ceremony as gifts to their deceased ancestors.

Hutch. (1) A mediæval term for a chest, box, or hoarding-cupboard, found in use in the *Vision of Piers Plowman.* (2) This word was sometimes applied to an aumbry for the sacred vessels of the altar, as in the *Accounts of Louth Spire;* or (3) to one for the sacramental oil, baptismal shell, stoles, and towel used in baptism. (4) Any locker for books, church music, sconces, etc.

Hutchins, RICHARD, D.D., a minister of the Church of England, was Hervey's tutor, and a very faithful member of the Oxford Methodist Society. He became a fellow of Lincoln College, Dec. 8, 1720; subrector, Nov. 6, 1739; bursar and librarian, Nov. 6, 1742; rector, July 9, 1755; and died Aug. 10, 1781. His only publication is a Latin sermon, *Elucidatio Sexti Capitis Evangelii Secundum Johannem* (1847, 8vo, p. 51). "In more respects than one Dr. Hutchins continued an Oxford Methodist long after all his old friends had been dispersed." See Tyerman, *The Oxford Methodists*, p. 370.

Hutchinson, JOHN RUSSELL, D.D., a Presbyterian minister, was born in Columbia County, Pa., Feb. 12, 1807. He graduated from Jefferson College in 1826, and studied two years in Princeton Seminary. He was licensed to preach by the Presbytery of Philadelphia, April 22, 1829, and went to Mississippi the following October. He preached at Rodney, Miss.; Baton Rouge, La.; Vicksburg, Miss.; Bethel Church, Prytanea Street, and Carrolton, New Orleans, La. Jan. 1, 1834, he became connected with the College of Louisiana. In 1842 he was called to occupy the chair of ancient languages in Oakland College, Miss., which he held twelve years, and for a time, in 1851, he was acting president. In 1854 he removed to New Orleans, purchased property, and established a classical school of a high order. In 1860 he took charge of the public academy in Houston, Texas. He died Feb. 24, 1878. He was a preacher for nearly half a century, and in his prime a man of mark. See *Necrol. Report of Princeton Theol. Sem.* 1878, p. 17.

Huth, Caspar Jacob, a Lutheran theologian of Germany, was born at Frankfort-on-the-Main, Dec. 25, 1711. He studied at Jena, commenced his academical career in 1735, was professor of theology at Erlangen in 1743, and died Sept. 14, 1760, leaving, *Pauperes Spiritu* (Erlangen, 1745):—*De Schiloh Vaticinium* (eod.):—*Spes Regenitorum Viva per Resurrectionem Christi* (1746):—*Fides Matris Viventium* (1748):—*Schilo Bethlehemitanus* (eod.):—*Petrus non Petra* (1757):—*Quæstiones Theologicæ* (1758), etc. See Döring, *Die gelehrten Theologen Deutschlands*, s. v.; Jöcher, *Allgemeines Gelehrten-Lexikon*, s. v.; Fürst, *Bibl. Jud.* i, 418 sq. (B. P.)

Huth, Johann Ernest, a Lutheran theologian of Germany, who died at Altenburg, Jan. 4, 1873, superintendent, is the author of *De Loco Epistolæ Pauli ad Galatas iii*, 19, 20 (Altenburg, 1854). See Zuchold, *Bibl. Theol.* i, 600. (B. P.)

Huther, JOHANN EDUARD, a Lutheran theologian of Germany, was born Sept. 10, 1807, at Hamburg. He studied at Bonn, Göttingen, and Berlin; was in 1842 religious instructor in the gymnasium at Schwerin; in 1855 pastor at Wittenförden, near Schwerin; and died March 17, 1880, leaving, *Cyprians Lehre von der Kirche* (Gotha, 1839):—*Commentar über den Brief Pauli an die Colosser* (Hamburg, 1841):—*Der Religions-Unterricht in den Gymnasien* (Rostock, 1848). For Meyer's *Commentary* he prepared the epistles to Timothy and Titus and the Catholic epistles. See Zuchold, *Bibl. Theol.* i, 600. (B. P.)

Hutter, EDWIN W., D.D., a Lutheran minister, was born at Allentown, Pa., Sept. 12, 1813. After attending the village school he entered a printing-office. When seventeen years of age his father died, and he succeeded him as editor and proprietor of two weekly newspapers, one German, the other English. For several years he resided at Washington, D. C., as private secretary to James Buchanan, then secretary of state. Removing to Baltimore, Md., he studied theology under Dr. B. Kurtz, at the same time discharging the duties as office editor of the *Observer*. Subsequently he took charge of St. Matthew's Church, Philadelphia, the only pastorate upon which he ever entered, and which he served with great success for twenty-three years. The Northern Home for Friendless Children was founded largely through his influence. He died in September, 1873. See *Fifty Years in the Lutheran Ministry*, 1878, p. 194.

Hutterians, the followers of Hutter, an Anabaptist leader in Moravia in the 16th century. See ANABAPTISTS.

Hutton, Mancius Smedes, a Reformed (Dutch) minister, was born in Troy, N. Y., June 9, 1803. He attended the school of the famous blind teacher, Joseph Nelson, in New York city; graduated from Columbia College in 1823, and from the theological seminary at Princeton in 1826. He was licensed to preach the same year by what was then known as the Second Presbytery of New York, and acted as missionary of the Reformed (Dutch) Church in Ulster County, N. Y., in 1827 and 1828. In the latter year he was called to the Presbyterian Church in German Valley, and remained there until 1834, when he was called to the city of New York to become the colleague of the late Rev. Dr. James M. Matthews, then pastor of the South Reformed Church in Exchange Place, the church which he had attended when a boy and up to the time of leaving the city. After the great fire of Dec. 16, 1835, which destroyed most of the lower part of the city, including the Exchange Place Church, the Church divided, and the pastor went with that portion which built the edifice on the east side of Washington Square. The new church was dedicated in 1841. For many years this was one of the best-known churches in the city. The neighborhood was one of the most fashionable in the metropolis, and the congregation, a very large one, numbered among its members many of the most intelligent and wealthy of the residents of the west side. After the resignation of his colleague Dr. Hutton remained sole pastor until 1876, when the Church disbanded, caused by the removal from time to time of so many of its members to the upper part of the city. Thereafter Dr. Hutton continued without a charge until his death, April 11, 1880. Dr. Hutton was a trustee of Columbia College, a member of the Council of the New York University, president of the Board of Education of the Reformed Church for the education of young men destined for the ministry, and a director in the Bible and tract societies. By virtue of his descent from revolutionary stock, he was a member of the Society of the Cincinnati for the state of New York, and general chaplain of the society in the United States. He published a number of *Sermons* and *Addresses*, for which see Corwin, *Manual of the Ref. Church in America*, s. v.; also *Necrol. Report of Princeton Theol. Sem.* 1882, p. 15.

Hutton, Matthew (1), D.D., an English prelate, was prebend of Ely in 1560, Margaret professor of divinity in Cambridge in 1561, regius professor in 1562, master of Pembroke Hall and prebend of London the same year, dean of York in 1567, bishop of Durham in 1589, archbishop of York in 1595, and died Jan. 15 or 16, 1606.

Hutton, Matthew (2), D.D., an English prelate, was prebend of York in 1734, canon of Windsor in 1736, prebend of Westminster in 1739, bishop of Bangor in 1743, and archbishop of York in 1747. He was translated to Canterbury in 1757. He died March 19, 1758, leaving occasional *Sermons* (1741, 1744, 1745, 1747). See Allibone, *Dict. of Brit. and Amer. Authors*, s. v.

Hwergelmer, in Norse mythology, is the spring in the centre of Helheim and Niflheim, in which the drops collect that fall from the antlers of the reindeer Aeikthyrner. There are so many of them that the spring supplies thirty-seven rivers of hell. The spring is inhabited by many snakes, who gnaw at the root of the world ash-tree, Ygdrasil.

Hyacinthia, an ancient festival, celebrated annually at Amyclæ, in Greece. It lasted three days, on the first and last of which sacrifices were offered to the dead, and lamentations were held for the death of Hyacinthus, all the people laying aside their garlands and partaking only of simple cakes, with every sign of grief and mourning. The intermediate day, however, was spent in mirth and rejoicings, pæans being sung in honor of Apollo, while the youth spent the day in games of various kinds.

Hyads, a common appellation given to the seven daughters of Atlas by his wife Aethra, viz. Ambrosia, Eudora, Pasithoe, Coronis, Plexaris, Pytho, and Tyche. These virgins bewailed so immoderately the death of their brother Hyas, who was devoured by a lion, that Jupiter, out of compassion, changed them into stars and placed them in the head of Taurus, where they still retain their grief, their rising and setting being attended with extraordinary rains (ὕω, *to rain*).

Some make them the daughters of Lycurgus, born in the isle of Naxos, and translated to the skies for their care in the education of Bacchus; probably because their rains were of great benefit in forwarding the vintage.

Hyænæ, a name applied by Porphyry to the priestesses of Mithras, or the sun.

Hydriaphoria (from ὕδωρ, *water*, and φέρω, *to bear*), a ceremony in which the married alien women carried a vessel with water for the married women of Athens as they walked to the temple of Athena in the great procession of the Panathenaia.

Hydromancy (from ὕδωρ, *water*, and μαντεία, *divination*), a species of divination, in which, by the aid of certain incantations, the images of the gods were seen in the water. The practice was brought from Persia, and employed by Numa and Pythagoras.

Hydroparastătæ (Ὑδροπαραστάται), a Greek term for those who anciently pretended to celebrate the holy communion with water.

Hygden, Ranulph. See Ranulph of Chester.

Hygēa, in Greek mythology, was the goddess of health, the daughter and constant companion of Æsculapius. See Hebe.

Hyneck, Ludwig, a Lutheran theologian of Germany, was born July 4, 1795. He studied theology and philology at Leipsic, and received the degree of doctor of philosophy in 1817, on presenting his *Adnotationes in Recentioris Ævi Liberos Educandi Rationem*. In 1827 he was made licentiate of theology by the Marburg University, for writing *Quid sit quod Debeat Religioni Christianæ Sexus Muliebris Imprimis Honestior Feminarum Pars*. In 1856 he published *Geschichte des freien adelichen Jungfrauenstiftes Fischbeck und seiner Aebtissinnen*, and in 1870 he celebrated his fiftieth anniversary in the ministry, and the Marburg University honored him on that occasion with the diploma of doctor of theology. He died May 10, 1883, at Fischbeck, in the county of Schaumburg. (B. P.)

Hyperborēans, in Greek mythology, were a fabulous people, living north of the Riphaean mountain-chain, and were said to be very wise and happy, living many hundreds and even thousands of years, and at last dying by leaping into the sea. But Herodotus, Strabo, and Pliny affirm that there is nothing else meant than northern nations, and that these are extravagant accounts of ordinary human beings.

Hyporchēma, the sacred dance around the altar, which, especially among the Dorians, was wont to accompany the songs used in the worship of Apollo. It was practiced by both men and women.

Hyrokian (or **Hirrokin**), in Norse mythology, was a Jote-woman, a mighty, giant-like sorceress. She was called by the Asas to set the ship afloat upon which Baldur was to be burned. Thor was so angry that this woman excelled him in strength that he would have demolished her with his miölner had not the Asas interceded for her.

Coin of Nicæa, of the time of the emperor Lucius Verus, representing Hygea and Æsculapius, with Telesphorus.

I.

Iacchagŏgi, those who were appointed to carry the statue of Iacchus (the mystic Bacchus) in solemn procession at the celebration of the Eleusinian Mysteries (q. v.). Their heads were crowned with myrtle, and they beat drums and brazen instruments, dancing and singing as they marched along.

Iaian Version of the Scriptures. The Iaian is a dialect spoken in Uvea, one of the Loyalty islands. A translation of Luke for the twelve hundred Protestants of Uvea, and two tribes in New Caledonia, was prepared by Rev. S. Ella, and printed in 1868. Mr. Ella has continued since, assisted by a native pundit, in the preparation of the New Test., which was printed at Sydney in 1878, and to which were added the Psalms in 1879. (B. P.)

Ialdabaoth (prob. for יַלְדָּא בָּהוּת), the name given by the Ophites, in the 2d century, to the Demiurge or world-former. See Ophites.

Ibhar (or **Ebur**; Lat. *Iberius*), bishop of the island of Bergery, in Wexford Harbor, Ireland, where he died in 503, is commemorated April 23, and famous for having driven away the rats from Leinster.

Ibleam. The modern site, *Jelameh* (or *Belameh*, as Tristram, *Bible Places*, p. 221, and Conder, *Tent Work*, ii, 337, incorrectly write), is thus described in the *Memoirs* accompanying the Ordnance Survey (ii, 84): "It stands in the plain, surrounded with arable land, and is supplied by cisterns. It has a kubbeh (domed place of prayer) on the north side. This place seems not improbably the *Kaliisuna* of the lists of Thothmes, mentioned in the same group with Saanach, Anohareth, and other places on the plain (*Quar. Statement* of the 'Pal. Explor. Fund,' July, 1876, p. 147)."

Ibn-Al-Athir, an Arabian historian, was born in 1160 at Jazîrat Ibn-Omar, in Mesopotamia, and died at Mosul in 1231. He is the author of a large historical work, giving the history of the world to the year 1230, which was edited by Tornberg, under the title, *Ibn-el-Athiri Chronicon quod Perfectissimum Inscribitur* (Leyden, 1858–71, 12 vols.). (B. P.)

Ibn-Amid. See Elmacin.

Ibn-Sabba. See Sabba Ibn.

Ibn-Shem-Tob. See Shem-Tob.

Ibn-Wakkar. See Wakkar.

Ibo Version of the Scriptures. This dialect is spoken by the Ibos on the banks of the Niger, in West Africa. The first part of the New Test., the gospel of Matthew, was published in this dialect in 1859, and since that time other parts were added. Up to date there are published only eight books of the New

Test. In linguistic respects the language has been treated by J. F. Schön, in *Oku Ibo, Grammatical Elements of the Ibo Language* (1861). (B. P.)

Icelandic Version OF THE SCRIPTURES. See SCANDINAVIAN VERSIONS.

Icheri, in the mythology of the Caribbeans, are the good protecting spirits accompanying fishermen and hunters.

Icoxûs, a sect of religionists in Japan, who celebrate the festival of their founder annually in a peculiar manner. Under the impression that he who first sets foot in the temple is entitled to peculiar blessings, they all rush towards the same spot, and persons are often killed in the press.

Idalah. For this site Tristram (*Bible Places*, p. 242) and Conder (*Tent Work*, ii, 337) propose *ed-Dalieh*, on Carmel, eight and a half miles south-east of Haifa, and thus described in the *Memoirs* accompanying the Ordnance Survey (ii, 281): "A stone village of moderate size, on a knoll of one of the spurs running out of the main water-shed (or ridge) of Carmel. On the south there is a well, and a few springs on the west. On the north is a little plain, or open valley, cultivated with corn. The inhabitants are all Druses, numbered by consul Rogers in 1859 at 300 souls." But this position is entirely beyond the bounds of Zebulon, and the modern name *Dalieh* is too indefinite for identification, being likewise applied to another village on the ridge of Carmel, six and a half miles farther south-east. The site *Kefr Kireh* (proposed by Schwarz) lying one and a quarter miles south by west from Tell Keimûn (Joknean), is described in the *Memoirs* (ii, 60) as "evidently an ancient site," with traces of ruins and broken pottery on the hill and tombs in the vicinity; a good supply of water, and a small mill. The village of *Jeida* is an entirely different locality, two and a half miles west of Semunieh, and destitute of antiquities (*Memoirs*, i, 270).

Idaplan (or **Idafeld**), in Norse mythology, is the dwelling-place of the twelve great judges in Asgard, whom Odin had appointed to judge all things.

Iddera Rabba (אִדְּרָא רַבָּא), i. e. *the Great Assembly*, is the title of one of the many parts which compose the Sohar, the famous thesaurus of Jewish mysticism. It is called "Great Assembly," because it purports to give the discourses which rabbi Simon ben-Jochaï (q. v.) delivered to his disciples, who congregated around him in large numbers. Upon the summons of the Sacred Light, his disciples assembled to listen to the secrets and enigmas contained in the Book of Mysteries. Hence it is chiefly occupied with a description of the form and various members of the Deity; a disquisition on the relation of the Deity, in his two aspects of the aged and the young, to the creation and the universe, as well as on the diverse gigantic members of the Deity, such as the head, the beard, the eyes, the nose, etc.; a dissertation on pneumatology, dæmonology, etc. It concludes with telling us that three of the disciples died during these discussions. This part of the Sohar is translated in the second volume of Rosenroth's *Kabbala Denudata*. (B. P.)

Iddera Zutta (אִדְּרָא זוּטָא), i. e. *the Small Assembly*, is, like the *Iddera Rabba* (q. v.), also one of the component parts of the Sohar. It derives its name from the fact that many of the disciples of rabbi Simon ben-Jochaï had died during the course of the cabalistic revelations, and that this portion of the Sohar contains the discourses which the Sacred Light delivered before his death to a small assembly of six pupils, who still survived, and congregated to listen to the profound mysteries. It is to a great extent a recapitulation of the *Iddera Rabba*, occupying itself with speculations about the Sephiroth, the Deity, etc., and concludes with recording the death of Simon ben-Jochaï, the Sacred Light, and the medium through whom God revealed the contents of the Sohar. The *Iddera Zutta*, too, is translated into Latin by Rosenroth, in the second volume of his *Kabbala Denudata*. (B. P.)

Ide, George Barton, D.D., a Baptist minister, was born at Coventry, Vt., in 1806, his father being a well-known Baptist clergyman, Rev. John Ide, who, in 1800, had removed from New York to northern Vermont. His father gave him the best education he could secure for him, and he decided to enter the profession of law, the study of which he commenced, without having taken a collegiate course, at the age of eighteen, in the village of Brandon. He graduated from Middlebury College with the highest honors in 1830; soon after was ordained at Derby, Conn.; was invited, in 1834, to a church in Albany, N. Y.; in 1835 to the Federal Street Baptist Church in Boston, Mass.; in 1838 to the First Baptist Church in Philadelphia, Pa., and in 1852 to Springfield, Mass., where he died, April 16, 1872. Dr. Ide was one of the most distinguished ministers of his denomination. He published several works, among which were *Life Sketches of Life Truths*, and *Bible Pictures*. He also wrote several Sunday-school books. See *The Watchman*, April, 1872. (J. C. S.)

Ide, Jacob, D.D., a Congregational minister, was born at Attleborough, Mass., March 29, 1785. His pastor, Rev. Nathaniel Holman, assisted him in his preparatory studies, and he graduated from Brown University in 1809, and from Andover Theological Seminary in 1812. He was ordained Nov. 2, 1814, over the Church in West Medway, Mass., and died in office, Jan. 5, 1880, although relieved from active service in 1865. Besides numerous sermons and other literary work, he edited the works of Dr. Nathaniel Emmons, in seven volumes. See *Cong. Year-book*, 1881, p. 26.

Identism (or **Identity**), the doctrine, advocated by Fichte and Schelling, of the entire identity of God and the universe, or of Creator and creation. This ultimately coincides with Pantheism (q. v.). See Krauth-Fleming, *Vocab. of Phil. Sciences*.

Idini, the term used by the Kaffirs to denote sacrifice. Sacrifices are offered to their ancestors, and not to God; and these only in cases where they wish to avert some apprehended evil.

Idiomĕla (fully στιχηρὰ ἰδιόμελα, i. e. *peculiar strophes*) are stichera that have no periods the rhythm of which they regularly follow. They are usually said at lauds and vespers on special occasions, sometimes at the burial of a priest. See Smith, *Dict. of Christ. Antiq.* s. v.

Iduna, in Norse mythology, is the loveliest of the Asas, the goddess of eternal youth and immortality; not created or born, but existing from the beginning. She is the wife of the wise Braga, the god of the poetic art. In her keeping are the apples of rejuvenation, without which even the gods would become aged, therefore they daily eat the same.

Ifays, the wooden tablets employed by the Japanese, containing inscriptions commemorative of the dead, mentioning the date of his decease, and the name given to him since that event. The ifays are carried in the funeral procession, along with the body, to the grave, and one of them is placed over it, remaining there seven weeks, when it is removed to make way for the gravestone. Another is set up in the best apartment of the house during the period of mourning. Sweetmeats, fruits, and tea are placed before it; and morning, noon, and night food is prepared for it as for a living person. The whole household pray before it morning and evening during seven weeks, and other religious ceremonies are observed.

Iglau, TREATY OF, a celebrated compact, ratified at Iglau, in Bohemia, which closed the long-protracted war between the Hussites and the Roman Catholics. It was dated Nov. 30, 1433. See HUSSITES.

Ignispicium, a species of divination practiced by the ancient Romans, consisting of observations made on the flames ascending from the sacrificial altar.

Ijon. As a representative of this Conder suggests (*Tent Work*, ii, 337) *El-Khiam*, four and a half miles north-east from Mimas (at the great angle of the Litany); but this is an entirely modern village of about three hundred Christians and two hundred Druses (*Memoirs* accompanying the Ordnance Survey, i, 88), and the name has little resemblance. *Tell Diblin*, the more probable representative, is beyond the limits of the Ordnance Survey.

Iko-siu, the sect of the worshippers of Amidas (q. v.), the most numerous and powerful ecclesiastical body in Japan.

Ilahi (*the divine*) of Akbar was a system of philosophic deism introduced by Akbar, the emperor of Delhi, in the latter half of the 16th century. He proposed to found a new creed on the basis of universal toleration, combining in one religious body the Hindûs, Mohammedans, and Christians, along with the followers of Zoroaster. His object in establishing a new creed was both political and religious; he was the only one of the Delhi emperors who regarded India as his country, and who sought to efface from the memory of the Hindûs the fact that they were a conquered people. *Ilahi*, or the divine system, was essentially eclectic in character. The fundamental point on which Akbar insisted was the great doctrine of the Divine Unity, which he declared was but obscurely revealed in the prophets. But while he thus adopted a Mohammedan basis for his creed, he took care at the same time to declare his entire disbelief of the divinity of the Koran. From the time of his rejection of the Koran, the emperor professed himself to be an impartial inquirer after truth, and accordingly he conversed openly with the teachers of every religion. He finally decided upon a system, which was the revival of Zoroastrianism in a modified form. Having acquired sufficient influence over the theologians, doctors of the law, and learned men, to secure their public recognition of him as the sole protector of the faith, Akbar propounded his creed, which was accepted by several Hindûs and Mohammedans. Encouraged by his success, he now ordered the abolition of the old confession of Islam, "There is no God but God, and Mohammed is his prophet," and the substitution of another, "There is no God but God, and Akbar is the vicar of God." He next abrogated the five daily prayers, the ablutions, fasts, alms, and pilgrimages enjoined upon the faithful. He abolished the religious services observed on Fridays, and dismissed the muezzins. He ordered that that should be considered as clean which was declared by the Koran to be unclean. He permitted the sale of wine, and the practice of games of chance. He forbade the marriage of more than one wife, and enjoined the postponement of the circumcision of boys until twelve years of age, and even then the ceremony was to be entirely optional. He finally ordered the æra of his own accession to the throne to be used instead of the Hegira. At first he received considerable support from various sections, but his system became more and more unpopular, and, on the accession of his son Jehanghir, the empire returned to Islamism.

Ilĭcet (for *ire licet*, "you may go"), a solemn word pronounced at the conclusion of the funeral rites among the ancient Romans. It was uttered by the *præfica* or some other person at the close of the ceremony, after the bones and ashes of the deceased had been committed to the urn, and the persons present had been thrice sprinkled with pure water from a branch of olive or laurel for the purpose of purification. From the occasion on which the word *ilicet* was employed, it is sometimes used proverbially among Roman authors to signify *all is over*.

Ilithyia, in Greek and Roman mythology, is the goddess of birth, the daughter of Jupiter and Juno, born on Crete, in the Amnisian cave, and sister of Hebe, Mars, and Vulcan. Homer speaks of a number of Ilithyiæ, daughters of Juno, who send the arrow of pain, but help those in childbed. Often Ilithyia is identified with Juno, which is not strange, since Juno is the goddess of marriage. The Greek Ilithyia was also identified with Diana, probably because the latter, being the goddess of the moon, a certain influence over birth might be credited her. She is also called Lucina, or *genitalis*. Pindar and Ovid make her the daughter of Juno. In a Grecian temple erected to her she was represented as wearing a loose robe, and holding in one hand a flambeau.

Illescas, Gundisalv de, abbot of St. Frontes, Spain, who died in 1580, is the author of *Historia Pontifical y Catolica* (Salamanca, 1574; continued by L. de Bavia, M. de Guadalaxara, and J. Banos de Velasco, Madrid, 1678, 6 vols. fol.). See Winer, *Handbuch der theol. Lit.* i, 682; Jöcher, *Allgemeines Gelehrten-Lexikon*, s. v. (B. P.)

Illinos, in Chaldaic mysticism, was the second of the three primary principles of the Chaldæans, created with Anos and Aos by the uncreated from the two natural forces, the creating and conceiving principles, Asoron and Kisara.

Ilmarinen, the third of the great deities of the Finns, and the god of earth and of metals.

Imâm, a name applied by way of excellence to each of the chiefs or founders of the four principal sects of the Mohammedans.

Imâmate, the office of an Imâm, or Mohammedan priest. See Imaum, vol. iv, p. 506.

Imâms, The Twelve, the twelve Islam chiefs, according to the Persian Mohammedans, who belong to the Shiites. Ali (q. v.) is reckoned the first Imam, and immediate spiritual successor of the Prophet. Hassan (q. v.) was the second Imam, being the eldest son of Ali. He was a feeble-minded prince, and surrendered his caliphate to Moawiyah, retaining only the spiritual office. Hossein (q. v.) was the third of the line. He was succeeded by his son Ali, the fourth Imam, who, from his constancy in prayer, received the names of "the Imam of the Carpet," and "the glory of pious men." He died in 712, and was succeeded by his son Mohammed, the fifth Imam, who was a diligent student of magic, and received the name of "the possessor of the secret." The sixth Imam was Jaafar, the son of Mohammed, who was thought to be equal in wisdom to Solomon. Jaafar nominated his son Ismail his successor, but the heir-apparent having died prematurely, he named his second son Mûsa his heir. Ismail, however, had left children; hence parties arose, some holding to one as the lawful Imam, others to the other. The two sects were called *Ismailiyah* (q. v.) and *Assassins* (q. v.). The claim of Mûsa to be the seventh Imam has been generally admitted. Ali, the son of Mûsa, was the eighth Imam. He is called by the Shiites "the beloved," and his tomb, termed Meshed Ali, is a favorite object of pilgrimage. The ninth Imam was Mohammed, the son of Ali, who lived in retirement at Bagdad, where he died at an early age, leaving behind him so great a reputation for benevolence that he received the name of "the generous." His son Ali, the tenth Imam, was but a child when his father died, and having been seized by the caliph Motawakkel, who was a determined enemy of the Shiites, he was confined for life in the city of Asker, from which circumstance he is called "the Askerite." He was poisoned by order of the caliph in 868. His son and successor, Hassan, also perished by poisoning, leaving the sacred office to his son Mohammed, the twelfth and last Imam, who, at his father's death, was a child only six months old. He was kept in close confinement by the caliph, but at about the age of twelve years he suddenly disappeared; the Sonnites allege that he was drowned in the Tigris, but the Shiites deny the fact of his death, and assert that he is wandering over the earth, and will continue so to wander until the appointed period shall arrive when he shall claim and receive universal empire.

Immer, Albert, a Protestant theologian, was born Aug. 10, 1804, at Unterseen, Switzerland. He studied at Berne, was in 1838 vicar at Burgdorf, in 1840 pastor at Büren, and in 1850 professor of theology at Berne. In 1881 he retired from his professorship, and died March 23, 1884. Besides some theological essays and lectures, he published *Hermeneutik des Neuen Testaments* (Wittenberg, 1873; Engl. translation by A. H. Newman, Andover, 1877):—*Neutestamentliche Theologie* (Bonn, 1877). (B. P.)

Impanation (from *in pane*, "in the bread"), the doctrine that Christ's presence is in the bread in the Lord's supper. It is synonymous with *consubstantiation* (q. v.).

Inauguratio, the ceremony by which the ancient Romans consecrated a person or thing to the gods. It was performed by the *augurs* (q. v.), who offered prayer to the gods, asking them to show by signs whether they accepted the consecrated object. If the signs appeared favorable, the consecration was regarded as complete. The kings of Rome were inducted by the augurs as the high priests of the people; but the inauguration of the *flamens* devolved upon the college of pontiffs.

Incense-boat, a vessel for containing incense, often formed like a boat: hence its name. Examples of these are numerous in old inventories of church furniture. See Navicula.

Brazen Incense-boat, probably of the 16th century, said to have belonged to the prebendal church at Thame, Oxford.

Indagine, Johann de, a Carthusian monk of Germany, who died at Eisenach in 1475, is the author of *Commentarius in Quattuor Libros Regum*:—*De Visione Danielis cap. vii*:—*De Quattuor Sensibus Scripturæ*:—*De Potestate Ecclesiastica et de Auctoritate Papæ in Conciliis*:—*Contra Flagellatores*:—*Contra Errores Bohemorum*:—*De Cognitione Futurorum*. See Hoffmann, *Lexicon Universale*; Trithemius, *De Scriptoribus Ecclesiasticis*; Jöcher, *Allgemeines Gelehrten-Lexicon*, s. v. (B. P.)

India, Mythology of. See Hindûism.

Indix Raymi, in Peruvian mythology, is the principal one of the four known festivals of the sun, celebrated yearly in honor of the supreme deity in the Andes. It began when the sun was at its height, and moved towards the equatorial region. At the first ray of the sun all fell on their knees and worshipped the benevolent god. After this festival eight days were spent in unbroken pleasure.

Indo-Portuguese Version of the Scriptures. Indo-Portuguese is a dialect spoken by the Portuguese settlers and their descendants in Ceylon and various parts of the Indian seas. A translation of a part of the Scripture into this dialect dates back to the year 1817, when the Wesleyan missionary, Newstead, stationed at Negombo, in Ceylon, commenced a translation of the New Test. for the benefit of this people, which was printed at London in 1826. A second edition appeared at Colombo in 1831, and the Pentateuch and Psalms were printed in 1833. A revised edition of the New Test. was published in 1853. (B. P.)

Indra, in Hindû mythology, is the god of the sun, one of the twelve Adityas, the son of the god Kasyapa and Aditi, a deity of the second class, but very much worshipped. He rules over space, and is king of all genii who live in space, or in the superterrestrial paradise. Daily he rides around the earth. He sees and knows everything, for he has a thousand eyes. His wife is called Sachi, by whom he had a son, Jayanta. The mountain Meru, towards the north pole, is his dwelling-place. Amarawati is the name of his celestial city, Wardayanta is his palace, Nandana his garden. Airawat is his first elephant, and Mattala charioteer. He rules over wind and rain.

Figure of Indra.

Induction (Lat. *inductio*, from *inducere*, "to infer") is the philosophical name for the process of real inference—in other words, the act or process of reasoning from the known to the unknown, or from the limited to the unlimited. "All things that we do not know by actual trial or ocular demonstration, we know by an inductive operation. Deduction is not real inference in this sense, since the general proposition covers the case that we apply it to; in a proper deduction, the conclusion is more limited than the premises. By the inductive method we obtain a conclusion much larger than the premises; we adventure into the sphere of the unknown, and pronounce upon what we have not yet seen. . . . Accordingly, it is now considered a part of logic to lay down the rules for the right performance of this great operation." One of the greatest problems of inductive inquiry is that peculiar succession denominated cause and effect. Mill, in his *Logic*, has consequently illustrated in detail the methods to be adopted to ascertain definitely the true causative circumstance that may precede a given effect. They resolve themselves mainly into two. "One is, by comparing together different instances in which the phenomenon occurs. The other is, by comparing instances in which the phenomenon does occur, with instances, *in other respects similar*, in which it does not. These two methods may be respectively denominated the method of agreement, and the method of difference."

There are many problems growing out of the application of induction to the great variety of natural phenomena. "Thus, the great induction of universal gravity was applied *deductively* to explain a great many facts besides those that enabled the induction to be made. Not merely the motions of the planets about the sun, and the satellites about the planets, but the remote and previously unexplained phenomena of the tides, the precession of the equinoxes, etc., were found to be inferences from the general principle. This mode of determining causes is called the deductive method. When several agents unite in a compound effect, there is required a process of calculation to find from the effects of the causes acting separately the combined effect due to their concurrent action, as when the path of a projectile is deduced from the laws of gravity and of force. It is the deductive stage of science that enables mathematical calculation to be brought into play with such remarkable success as is seen in astronomy, mechanics, etc.

"The circumstance that phenomena may result from a concurrence of causes, leads to the distinction between ultimate laws and derivative or subordinate laws. Thus, gravity is an ultimate law; the movement of the planets in ellipses is but a subordinate law. These inferior laws may be perfectly true within their own limits, but not necessarily so beyond certain limits, of time, place, and circumstance. A different adjustment of the two forces that determine a planet's motion would cause a circular or a parabolic orbit; and therefore when phenomena result from a combination of ultimate laws acting under a certain arrangement, they are not to be generalized beyond the sphere where that arrangement holds. These inferior laws are sometimes mere inductions that have not been resolved into their constituent laws, and then they go under the name of 'Empirical Laws.' Thus, in the hands of Kepler, the elliptic orbit of the planets was only an empirical generalization, ascertained by the method of agreement; Newton converted it into a derivative law, when he showed that it resulted from the more general laws of gravity, etc. The earlier stages of induction present us with many of those empirical laws; in some subjects, as physiology, medicine, etc., the greater number of inductions are of this character. The cure of disease is especially an example of this: hardly any medicine can have its efficacy traced to ultimate laws of the human system. Hence the uncertainty attending the application of remedies to new cases, and also the want of success that often attends them in circumstances where we think they ought to succeed." Induction applies also to the laws of causation, to the laws of uniformities, and to those of coexistence. See Mill, *Logic*, especially book iv.

Indulgence. The use of this word by ecclesiastical writers is derived from that of the jurisconsults, who employ it to designate a remission of punishment or of taxes, especially such a general amnesty as was sometimes proclaimed by an emperor on an extraordinary occasion of rejoicing. Hence the word passed into ecclesiastical usage in the sense of a remission of penalties for offences against church discipline and order.

Usually there were four stages or degrees through which offenders had to pass before regaining communion: (1) weepers, (2) hearers, (3) kneelers, (4) bystanders; and usually several years had to be spent in each. Now the bishop, according to St. Gregory, might, in proportion to their conversion, "rescind the period of their penance; making it eight, seven, or even five years instead of nine, in each stage, should their repentance exceed in depth what it had to fulfil in length, and compensate, by its increased zeal, for the much longer time required in others to effect their cure." Eventually this system was greatly extended, until it reached the abuses that provoked the Reformation.

Indulgentia (*indulgence*), a name sometimes applied to *baptism* in the early Christian Church, as being attended, when blessed by the Holy Spirit, with absolution or the remission of sins. It was esteemed the most universal absolution and the greatest indulgence in the ministry of the Church.

Inferiæ were sacrifices which the ancient Romans offered at the tombs of their deceased relatives at certain periods, consisting of victims, wine, milk, garlands of flowers, etc.

Infirmary, MONASTIC. In his enumeration of Christian duties Benedict (*Regula*, c. 4) specifies that of visiting the sick; and elsewhere he speaks of it as a duty of primary and paramount obligation for monks, quoting the words of Christ, "I was sick, and ye ministered unto me." Beyond, however, saying that the sick are to have a separate part of the monastery assigned to them, and a separate officer in charge of them, that they are to be allowed meat and the luxury of baths, if necessary, that they are not to be exacting, and that the brethren who wait on them are not to be impatient, he gives no precise directions. Subsequently it was the special duty of the "infirmarius," the "cellerarius" (house-steward), and of the abbot himself, to look after the sick; no other monk might visit them without leave from the abbot or prior. Everything was to be done for their comfort, both in body and soul, that they should not miss the kindly offices of kinsfolk and friends; and, while the rigor of the monastic discipline was to be relaxed, whenever necessary, in their favor, due supervision was to be exercised, lest there should be any abuse of the privileges of the sick-room. The "infirmarius" was to enforce silence at meals, to check conversation in the sick-room at other times, and to discriminate carefully between real and fictitious ailments. The sick were, if possible, to recite the hours daily, and to attend mass at stated times, and if unable to walk to the chapel, they were to be carried thither in the arms of their brethren. The meal in the sick-room was to be three hours earlier than in the common refectory. The abbot might allow a separate kitchen and "buttery" for the use of the sick monks. The rule of Cæsarius of Arles ordered that the abbot was to provide good wine for the sick, the ordinary wine of the monastery being often of inferior quality. See HOSPITAL.

Informers. This class of men originated before the Christian æra, and, indeed, before the establishment of the Roman empire. When persecution arose against the Church, the informers naturally sought gain, and probably some credit with the civil authorities, by giving information against those who practiced Christian rites, since the secret assemblies of Christians for worship came under the prohibition of the Lex Julia. Tertullian states (*Apol.* c. 5) that Tiberius threatened the accusers of the Christians, but the story rests only upon his statement. He also claims M. Aurelius as a protector of Christians. Titus issued an edict, forbidding slaves to inform against their masters or freedmen against their patrons. Nerva, on his accession, republished this edict. "Jewish manners," i. e. probably Christianity, is especially mentioned as one of the subjects on which informations were forbidden. In Pliny's well-known letter to Trajan we find the informers in full work. The Christians who were brought before him were delated, and an anonymous paper was sent in, containing a list of many Christians or supposed Christians. Trajan, in his answer, though he forbade Christians to be sought out (i. e. by government officials), did not attempt to put a stop to the practice of delation; those who were informed against, if they continued in their infatuation, must be punished. In the subsequent persecutions a large part of the suffering arose from unfaithful brethren who betrayed their friends. See DELATORES.

Inge, HUGH, D.D., an Irish prelate, was born at Shepton Mallet, in Somersetshire; educated in William of Wickham's school at Winchester, and made perpetual fellow of New College, Oxford, in 1484. In 1496 he travelled in foreign countries. On his return he was successively prebendary of East Harptree, sub-chanter of the Church of Wells, warden of Wapulham, in the diocese of Lincoln, of Duttying, in Somersetshire, by the presentation of Richard the Abbot and the convent of Glastonbury, and of Weston. In 1504 he was in Rome, at which time he was one of king Henry's orators, selected to take the renunciation of all prejudicial clauses in the apostolic bulls for the translation of cardinal Hadrian to the see of Bath and Wells, and his oaths of fealty and allegiance to that monarch. In 1512 he was appointed bishop of Meath, where he remained ten years. In 1521 he was promoted to the see of Dublin. In 1527 he was made chancellor of Ireland. He repaired the palace of St. Sepulchre. He died in Dublin, Aug. 3, 1528. See D'Alton, *Memoirs of the Archbishops of Dublin*, p. 182.

Ingelram (called also by some **Newbigging**), a Scotch prelate, was rector of Peebles and archdeacon of the Church of Glasgow, and when in this office he was made chancellor by king David. He was elected and consecrated bishop of the see of Glasgow in 1164. He died Feb. 2, 1174, leaving, *Epistolæ ad Diversos:—In Evangelia Dominicalia:—Rationes Regni Administrandi*. See Keith, *Scottish Bishops*, p. 233.

Ingelramne, a German prelate, brought up in the schools of Goze and St. Anold, was made bishop of Metz in 768, being at the same time abbot of Senones. He died in 791. See Hoefer, *Nouv. Biog. Générale*, s. v.

Ingen, a hero-god of Japan, was a native of China, who lived about 1650. He was a zealous Buddhist, and was looked upon as an illustrious saint. But he was more especially venerated because, in answer to a *kito*, or special prayer which he offered, a plentiful rain had fallen in a time of drought.

Ingham, RICHARD, D.D., an English Baptist minister, was born at Stansfield, Yorkshire, in 1810. For some years he was a student at Oxford University, and afterwards in the academy of the celebrated Rev. Daniel Taylor, in London. He was baptized Nov. 20, 1829; ordained deacon of a Baptist Church, Dec. 26, 1832; licensed to preach, April 5, 1833; gave up his secular business in 1835, and pursued a course of theological study at Wisbeach; was ordained April 2, 1839, in Bradford, and remained pastor of the Tetley Street Church till November, 1847, when he removed to Louth. His next pastorate was in Halifax, from 1854 to 1862. After two or three brief pastorates in other places, he returned to Bradford and became pastor of the Infirmary Street Church. His death took place June 1, 1873. He published, in 1865, his *Hand-book on Christian Baptism*, and in 1871 his *Christian Baptism, its Subjects and Modes*. He also published his *Appeal to Friends*, on the subject of baptism. At the time of his death he had completed an extended work on the Church Establishment. Dr. Ingham filled a high place among the scholars and preachers of that branch of English Baptists with which he was identified, the "General Baptists," corresponding in most respects with the Freewill Baptists of the United States. See (Lond.) *Baptist Hand-book*, 1874, p. 277. (J. C. S.)

Inglis, Alexander, a Scotch prelate, dean of Dunkeld, archdeacon of St. Andrews, and keeper of the rolls, was chosen bishop of Dunkeld in 1483. But the pope, being displeased because he had not been consulted first, annulled the election. See Keith, *Scottish Bishops*, p. 91.

Inglis, David, D.D., LL.D., a Reformed (Dutch), and afterwards a Presbyterian minister, son of Rev. David Inglis, was born June 8, 1824. He graduated from the University of Edinburgh in 1841; studied divinity under Drs. Chalmers and John Brown; was licensed by the Presbytery of Carlisle in 1845, and came to America in 1846. He served the Presbyterian Church in the following places: Scotch Church, Detroit, Mich. (1846); stated supply at Washington Heights, New York city; Bedford, N. Y. (1847); St. Gabriel Street, Montreal, Canada, in July, 1852; Hamilton, Ontario (1855); professor of systematic theology in Knox College, Toronto (1871); pastor of Reformed Church, Brooklyn Heights (1872), where he died, Dec. 15, 1877. Dr. Inglis was a powerful and eloquent preacher of the great truths of the gospel. He was prominent in the deliberations to further the union of the different branches of the Presbyterian Church of Canada, in the success and consummation of which he greatly rejoiced. His publications are, *Exposition of International Sunday-school Lessons in Sower and Gospel Field* (1874-77):—*Historical Sermon in Commemoration of the Twenty-fifth Anniversary of the Church on Brooklyn Heights* (1875):—many contributions to the press:—*Vedder Lectures*, in course of preparation at his death. See Corwin, *Manual of the Ref. Church in America*, 3d ed. p. 317.

Inglis, James, D.D., a Presbyterian minister, was born at Philadelphia, Pa., in 1777. He graduated from Columbia College in 1795; studied theology privately, and was licensed to preach by the New York Presbytery in 1801. In 1802 he accepted a call to the First Presbyterian Church of Baltimore. He died Aug. 15, 1820. He published, *A Sermon on Fasting, Humiliation, and Prayer* (1808):—*A Missionary Sermon*, preached in Philadelphia in 1812:—and a *Discourse*, delivered in the First Presbyterian Church of Baltimore in 1814. See Sprague, *Annals of the Amer. Pulpit*, iv, 278.

Inglis, John, a bishop of the Church of England, was born in New York city, Dec. 9, 1777, where his father, Charles Inglis, D.D., was rector of Trinity Church. He received his education at King's College, Windsor. In 1800 he went to England to advance the interests of his alma mater; in 1801 he took orders, and was appointed to the mission of Aylesford. In 1816, Rev. Dr. Stanser, rector of St. Paul's, became bishop of Nova Scotia, and Dr. Inglis succeeded him as rector, and, in 1825, to the bishopric of Nova Scotia, which at that time included New Brunswick, Newfoundland, and Bermuda. He died in London, Oct. 27, 1850. See *Amer. Quar. Church. Rev.* 1851, p. 154.

Ingnersoit are the spirits of fire among the Greenlanders, and live along the strand. They were formerly human beings, but when the flood came they were changed into spirits of fire.

Ingraham, JOSEPH H., D.D., a Protestant Episcopal clergyman, was born at Portland, Me., in 1809. He entered Yale College, but did not graduate; went to Buenos Ayres, South America, as a commercial clerk; was for several years after his return a teacher; and about 1830 became professor in Jefferson College, near Natchez. While here he was widely known as a writer of novels, etc., as *The South-west, by a Yankee:—Lafitte:—Burton:—The Quadroon*, etc. About 1847 he was confirmed as a member of the Protestant Episcopal Church, at Nashville, Tenn., where he established a flourishing seminary for young ladies. He was ordained deacon in 1851, and presbyter in 1852; became missionary at Aberdeen, Miss.; afterwards was rector of St. John's Church, Mobile, Ala.; then at Riverside, Tenn.; removed to Holly Springs, in 1858, where he revived St. Thomas's Hall. He died there, Dec. 18, 1860. Besides various religious pamphlets, Dr. Ingraham was the author of, *The Prince of the House of David:—The Pillar of Fire:*—and *The Throne of David*, which were very popular. See *Amer. Quar. Church Rev.* 1861, p. 186.

Initial Hymn. See INTROIT.

Initiāti, a name applied to the faithful in the early Christian Church, as being initiated, that is, admitted to the use of sacred offices, and to the knowledge of the sacred mysteries of the Christian religion. Hence the fathers, in speaking of any doctrines which were not explained to the catechumens, were accustomed to say, "The initiated know what is said." St. Ambrose addressed a work especially to the Initiati.

Inlaga are a class of spirits whose worship forms the most prominent feature in the superstitious practices of Southern Guinea. They are the spirits of dead men; but whether good or evil, even the natives themselves do not know. The spirits of their ancestors the natives call *Abambo;* but the Inlaga are the spirits of strangers, and have come from a distance. Sick, and especially nervous, persons are supposed to be possessed with one or the other of these classes of spirits, and various ceremonies are performed to deliver them from their power. The patient is first tested by the priest, to ascertain which class of spirits has possession of him; he is then exorcised, and when sufficiently recovered, sent about his affairs, but under certain restrictions, lest his disease return.

Innes, John (1), a Scotch prelate, was consecrated bishop of the see of Moray, Jan. 23, 1407. He died April 25, 1414. See Keith, *Scottish Bishops*, p. 142.

Innes, John (2), a Scotch prelate, was dean of Ross, and bishop of the see of Caithness about 1447. He died in 1448. See Keith, *Scottish Bishops*, p. 214.

Innuarolit are mountain spirits of the Greenlanders, extraordinarily small, but quite expert.

Institor, Heinrich, a Dominican of the 16th century, is the author of *Malleus Maleficarum:—Clypeus T. R. Ecclesiæ Defensionis contra Pickardos et Waldenses:—De Plenaria Potestate Pontificis et Monarchiæ:—Replica Adversus Sententiam Christum Nonnisi sub Conditione in Eucharistia Adorandum:—Sermones XXX de Eucharistia.* See Echard, *De Scriptoribus Ordinis Dominicanorum;* Jöcher, *Allgemeines Gelehrten-Lexikon*, s. v. (B. P.)

Intercīsi dies were days, among the ancient Romans, which were devoted partly to the worship of the gods, and partly to ordinary business.

Invisibility, an attribute ascribed to God in the Scriptures. For example, Paul (1 Tim. i, 17) calls him "the king eternal, immortal, invisible." Jesus says (John i, 18) "No man hath seen God at any time." He is therefore the *invisible* God.

Ipabog, in Slavonic mythology, was an idol of the Wends, brought to light by recent antiquaries, probably worshipped on Rügen as a god of hunting.

Iperius, Joannes (surnamed "*the Long*"), a Benedictine abbot of St. Bertin, was a native of Ypres, Belgium, and died in 1383. He is the author of a *History* or *Chronicon* of his monastery, from the year 590 to 1294. It has been inserted, under the title of *Chronica, sive Historia Monasterii S. Bertini*, in the *Thesaurus Novus Anecdotorum*, etc., iii, 446 sq. (1717). He also wrote a life of Erkembod, published in the *Acta Sanctorum*, under April 12. See André, *Bibl. Belg.* ii, 669 (1739); Lichtenberger, *Encyclop. des Sciences Religieuses*, s. v. (B. P.)

Irhov, Wilhelm, a Dutch theologian, who died Nov. 18, 1760, at Utrecht, doctor and professor of theology, is the author of *Conjectanea Philol.-Crit.-Theologica in Psalmorum Titulos* (Leyden, 1728). See Winer, *Handbuch der theol. Lit.* i, 82; Fürst, *Bibl. Jud.* ii, 137. (B. P.)

Irish Presbyterian Church. See *Presbyterian Church in Ireland*, s. v. Presbyterian Churches.

Irish Version of the Scriptures. The Irish or Erse language is now little known except as the vernacular of an illiterate population, but it was once the language of literature and science. The Roman letters are often used in Erse compositions, but the Irish have an ancient alphabet of their own, for which they feel a truly national predilection. The origin of this alphabet is very uncertain; it bears some resemblance to the Anglo-Saxon, and it has been questioned whether the Saxons derived their alphabetical system from the Irish, or vice versa. In the dedication of the Irish Prayer-Book of 1608, it is confidently asserted that the Saxons borrowed their letters from Ireland.

The first printed New Test., in the Irish characters, was published in 1602. When bishop Bedell was appointed to the see of Kilmore and Ardagh, in 1629, he undertook the translation of the Old Test. Not being acquainted with the language, he commenced to study the same at the age of fifty-seven. His next measure was to secure the services of native Irish scholars, and with their help the version of the Old Test. was completed in 1640, to remain in MS. till 1681. After due examination and revision it was published in London in 1686, together with the New Test.

More than a century was suffered to roll away before any efficient measures were taken to reprint the Scriptures in Irish, until, in 1809, an edition of 2000 New Tests., conformable to the accredited version of bishop Bedell, was published in Roman characters by the British and Foreign Bible Society. Other editions followed in 1813, 1816, and 1817. In the latter year also a complete Irish Bible was issued, the version of Bedell being employed as the text of the Old Test. In the course of the following year 3000 copies of the New Test., in the Irish character, were published, and in 1828 the entire Irish Bible appeared in the vernacular. From the report of the British and Foreign Bible Society for the year 1881 we learn that a revised edition of the New Test. is to be published. In order to bring about such a revision, twenty-five interleaved New Tests. are to be placed in the hands of competent Irish scholars, and their corrections of archaisms, obsolete words, and orthographical errors will be examined by the chief reviser and editor, the Rev. James Goodman, Canon of Ross, and professor of Irish in the University of Dublin. As the first instalment of this revision the Gospel of Luke was published in 1884. See *Bible of Every Land*, p. 160. (B. P.)

Irmin (*Irmensäule, Irminsul*, etc.), in German mythology, seems to have been a principal god of the ancient Saxons. At Eresburg, now Stadtbergen, on the Dimel, the famous pillar Irmin is said to have stood, that was destroyed by Charlemagne in 772, during the Saxon wars. Might, courage, war, were all-important to the Germanic nations; therefore it is quite possible that Irmin was a god of war.

Ir-Nahash. *Deir Nakhkhâs*, the probable representative of this site, lying one and a half miles northeast from Beit-Jibrîn, is merely described in the *Memoirs* accompanying the Ordnance Survey (iii, 275), as "a ruined birkeh [pool], and a cave with two hundred and fifty niches [for burial]."

Iron. The modern representative of this site, *Yarûn*, located four miles north-west from El-Jish (Ahlab or Gischala), is described in the *Memoirs* accompanying the Ordnance Survey (i, 203), as "a stone village, containing about 200 Metawileh and 200 Christians. It is situated on the edge of a plain, with vineyards and arable lands; to the west rises a basalt top, called el-Burj [the castle], full of cisterns, and supposed to be the site of an ancient castle; there are large stones strewn about; three large birkehs [pools] and many cisterns to supply water; one of the birkehs is ruined." The remains of a large church in the village are described in detail (p. 258).

Iroquois Version of the Scriptures. This version is of very recent date. There are also Iroquois Indians in the provinces of Quebec and Ontario who do not understand the Scriptures in Mohawk published by the British and Foreign Bible Society. For the benefit of these Indians, the Four Gospels were published in 1880 at Montreal. The translation was made by chief Joseph Oncsakeural, revised by Jean Dion and the Rev. T. Laforte. Chief Joseph had all qualifications for the translation, since, in 1865, under the direction of the Roman Catholic missionaries at Oka, and with the approval of the Roman Catholic bishop of Montreal, he prepared a translation into Iroquois of the Gospels and Epistles used in the Missal. (B. P.)

Irpeel is conjectured by Conder (*Tent Work*, ii, 337), to be represented by the modern *Rafat*, as two of the radical letters are the same. This place lies one and a half miles north of el-Jib (Gibeon), and is thus described in the *Memoirs* accompanying the Ordnance Survey (iii, 13, also 155): "A small hamlet on a ridge, with a spring to the west, and many rock-cut tombs.... Traces of ruins: cisterns cut in rocks, and rough pillar-shafts, with ruins of a modern village and a Mukân.

Irvingites. See Irving, Edward; Catholic Apostolic Church.

Irwing, Karl Friedrich von, a Protestant theologian of Germany, who was born at Berlin, Nov. 21, 1728, and died there, Dec. 17, 1801, member of consistory, is the author of *Versuch über den Ursprung der Erkenntniss der Wahrheit und der Wissenschaft* (Berlin, 1781). See Winer, *Handbuch der theol. Lit.* i, 430. (B. P.)

Isaac ABRABANEL. See ABRABANEL, ISAAC.

Isaac DE ACOSTA. See ACOSTA, ISAAC DE.

Isaac ALFEZ (or ALFASS). See ALFEZ, ISAAC.

Isaac ALISSANI. See IBN-GIATH, ISAAC.

Isaac OF ANTIOCH. See ISAAC THE SYRIAN (*a*).

Isaac ARAMA. See ARAMA, ISAAC.

Isaac ATHIAS. See ATHIAS, ISAAC.

Isaac CAMPANTON. See CAMPANTON, ISAAC.

Isaac CANTARINI. See CANTARINI, ISAAC.

Isaac CARDOSO. See CARDOSO, ISAAC.

Isaac BEN-JEHUDA *ha-Levi*, a Jewish writer of the 17th century, is the author of ס' פענח רזא, a commentary on the Pentateuch, compiled from different authors (Prague, 1607). See Fürst, *Bibl. Jud.* ii, 142. (B. P.)

Isaac LAMPRONTI. See LAMPRONTI, ISAAC.

Isaac LORIA. See LORIA, ISAAC.

Isaac BEN-MOSES. See PROFIAT DURAN.

Isaac NASIR. See NASIR, ISAAC.

Isaac ONQUENIRA. See ONQUENIRA, ISAAC.

Isaac OROBIO. See OROBIO, ISAAC.

Isaac BEN-SIMEON of Prague, who lived in the 17th century, is the author of מדרש שוחר עם פרוש, i. e. the Midrash Shocher Tob (a midrash on Psalms, Proverbs, and Samuel), with short glosses (Prague, 1613):—חומש עם פרוש, i. e. the Pentateuch in Hebrew, with a Judæo-German commentary (ibid. 1608). See Fürst, *Bibl. Jud.* i, 145; De' Rossi, *Dizionario Storico* (Germ. transl.), p. 125. (B. P.)

Isaac, USIËL, a Jewish rabbi of Amsterdam, who flourished in the 17th century, is the author of מענה לשון, i. e. a Hebrew grammar (Amsterdam, 1657). See Fürst, *Bibl. Jud.* i, 145; De Barrios, *Casa de Jacob* (Amsterdam, 1683, giving a biography of Isaac Usiel). (B. P.)

Isaac Viva. See CANTARINI, ISAAC.

Isaacs, SAMUEL M., a Jewish rabbi, was born at Leeuwarden, Holland, Jan. 4, 1804. His father having emigrated to England, young Isaacs received his education there. In 1839 he came to New York to take charge of the congregation Benai Jeshurun, then worshipping in Elm Street. In 1857 he commenced the publishing of the *Jewish Messenger*, which was intended to uphold conservative Judaism against the so-called reformed party. In 1877 Isaacs retired from his ministry of the Shaare Tefila congregation, with which he had been connected since 1845, and died May 19, 1878. He was highly respected, not only by his own coreligionists, but also by Christians. (B. P.)

Isbraniki, a sect of Russian dissenters, which arose about the middle of the 16th century. The name which they assumed means the *company of the elect*, but they were reckoned by the adherents of the established religion among the *Raskolniks* (q. v.) or Schismatics. The cause of their separation was a difficulty concerning the revision of the church books. These books were printed in 1562, under the czar, John Basilides, from manuscript copies, which, being considered incorrect, were somewhat altered in their printed form. The changes introduced were regarded by some as teaching unsound doctrine, and a sect arose who adhered to the former books, and called themselves *Starovertsi*, or believers in the old faith. These dissenters, however, were comparatively few in number till about the middle of the following century, when, in consequence of a revision of the church books by the patriarch Nikon, the cry of unsound doctrine was again raised, and the number of dissenters increased. This sect was tolerated by the state under Alexander I.

Ise (or **Isje**), the name of a central province of Japan, to which the religious sect of the Shiutrists requires each of its adherents to make a pilgrimage once a year, or at least once in their life. In Isje is the grand *Mia* or temple of *Teusio-Dai-Jin*, which is the model after which all the other temples are built. Isje is a place of no natural attractions. It is rather regarded as a monument of antique poverty and simplicity. The *Mia* where the pilgrims pay their devotions is a low wooden edifice with a flat thatched roof, and on entering nothing is to be seen but a metallic mirror, which is regarded as a symbol of the deity, and some white paper, which is considered the emblem of purity of heart. The worshippers do not presume to enter this temple, but look through a lattice window from without while they say their prayers.

Ishtar, one of the chief deities of the Assyrians and Babylonians alike, although she was generically one of the deities of the second rank. She was the daughter of the moon-god Sin, and was identified by the Chaldæans with the planet Venus. She was essentially a warlike goddess, and was called the "Goddess of Battles and of Victories," in which attribute she was often represented as giving a bow to the Assyrian king in token of his victories over his foes. She was also, as the goddess of productive nature, the keeper of all the treasures of the earth, and hence was figured as Allat, the "Queen of the Spear or Divining-rod." In another form of the same principle she was the goddess of sensual indulgence. She was the special protectress of Erech, and in her character of Anna, or Nana, of Nineveh, while she was distinguished also at Arbela, another great seat of her worship, as Ishtar of Arbela. Her offices, names, and attributes were very various, and there appears to have been two Ishtars, mother and daughter, one the great nature goddess, the other the heroine of one of the mythical legends, called the "Descent of Ishtar into Hades." There is a considerable amount of confusion yet remaining to be cleared away with regard to the relations of Ishtar to Davcina, Bilit, Ashtaroth, and Izdubar; but generally the mythologies agree in making her the goddess most brought into contact with men and the under world.

Ising, JOHANN CHRISTIAN, a Lutheran theologian of Germany, was born Oct. 24, 1617, in Austria. He studied at Königsberg, and died there, July 4, 1684, cathedral deacon. He wrote *Exercitationes Histor. Chronol. Geograph. et Philol. in Pentateuchum et Josuam.* See Arnold, *Historie der königsbergischen Universität;* Jöcher, *Allgemeines Gelehrten-Lexikon*, s. v. (B. P.)

Ismailiyah, the followers of Ismail or Ismaël (q. v.).

Isoard, JOACHIM JEAN XAVIER D', a French prelate, was born at Aix, in Provence, Oct. 23, 1766. His family originated in Dauphiné, and was a very ancient one. He lost his father when he was a child, and was placed into the seminary of Aix by his mother When the Bonapartes took refuge upon the continent, they found some support in the family of Isoard. About that time he departed for Italy, and connected himself, in 1794, with the count of Provence, at Verona. On his return to his native city in the same year he associated himself with a royalist band, and, it is said, was instrumental in saving the life of Lucien Bonaparte. When Pius VII was brought as a captive to France, Isoard followed him. Napoleon proposed to him some high employments, and even a place in the senate, but he refused. After the death of cardinal Fesch, in May, 1839, Isoard was designated to replace him, June 14. He died at Paris, Oct. 8 of the same year. See Hoefer, *Nouv. Biog. Generale*, s. v.

Isochristæ (from ἴσος, *equal*, and Χριστός, *Christ*),

some followers of Origen, who were charged with maintaining that the apostles were raised to equal glory with their master. They were condemned by a council at Constantinople in 553.

Isolani, GIACOMO, an Italian legislator and cardinal, was born at Bologna. He had obtained a great reputation as a scholar, being well versed both in civil and canonical law, when, after the loss of his wife, he decided to enter the ministry. He soon became distinguished in his new position, and after he had filled several important functions, pope John XIII made him cardinal, in 1414, and left him his vicar at Rome, where he was made prisoner by the troops of Ladislas, king of Naples. Finally he was set at liberty by the efforts of Giacomo Sforça Attendole, and Felippe Maria Visconti made him governor of Genoa. He died at Milan, Feb. 19, 1431, leaving several *Consilias* and other works on law. See Hoefer, *Nouv. Biog. Générale*, s. v.

Isparetta was the supreme god of the inhabitants of the coast of Malabar. When the earth was to be created he changed himself into an egg, from which heaven and earth, and all that it contains, sprang.

Israel BEN-MOSES, a Jewish writer of the 16th century, is the author of תמים יחדיו על תהלים, a cabalistic exposition of the Psalms (Lublin, 1592, preceded by an essay on the soul):—תמים יחדיו על משלי, a cabalistic exposition of Proverbs (ibid. eod.). The essay on the soul was published separately, with a Latin translation by Voisin (Paris, 1635). See Fürst, *Bibl. Jud.* i, 149. (B. P.)

Israeli, Paul. See RICCIUS, PAUL.

Israeli, Samuel. See MOROCCO, SAMUEL ISRAELI.

Israfil, the angel who, according to the Mohammedans, will sound the trumpet which is to summon the world to judgment on the last day.

Isselburg, HEINRICH, a Protestant theologian of Germany, who died at Bremen in 1629, is the author of, *Medulla Papismi de Arce ac Judice Controversiarum Theologicarum:—Digeries Præcipuarum Controvers. inter Romanos Pontifices et Protestantes Orthodoxos:—Manuale Pauperum Spiritu:—De Jure Protestantium contra Pontif. Rom. Ejusque Concilia, Imperium atque Anathema:—Catechesis Religionis Christianæ Anatomen:—De Charitate Christiana.* See Witte, *Diarium Biographicum;* Jöcher, *Allgemeines Gelehrten-Lexikon,* s. v. (B. P.)

Isthmian GAMES, one of the great national festivals among the ancient Greeks, which derived its name from the isthmus of Corinth, where they were celebrated. They were held every third year, in honor of Poseidon, or, as some allege, every fifth year. See GAMES.

Istio, in Teutonic mythology, was one of the three sons of Mannus, and the father of one of the three races of the Germans.

Ithun, in Norse mythology, is held imprisoned under the ash-tree Ygdrasil. Probably this Ithun is identical with *Iduna,* who guards the rejuvenating apples of the gods.

Itogay, a household god among the Mongol Tartars. He is the guardian of their families, and presides over all the products of the earth. The Tartar does not presume to dine until this god and his family have been first served, by covering the mouths of the idols with grease. When the people have dined they throw out the fragments, expecting them to be devoured by some unknown spirits.

Ittur Sopherim (עִטּוּר סוֹפְרִים, *ablatio scribarum*) denotes the removal of a superfluous ו which had crept into the text. The Masorites have noticed five instances of such a superfluous ו, which has erroneously been prefixed to אחר in Gen. xviii, 5; xxiv, 55; Numb. xxxi, 2; Psa. lxviii, 26, and to the word משפטיך in Psa. xxxvi, 7. See *Nedarim,* fol. 37, col. 2; *Ochlah ve Ochlah,* sect. 217, p. 128; Lenz, *Dissertatio de Notis Masorethicis, Piska, Tikkun Sopherim et Ittur Sopherim* (Wittenberg, 1702); Werchau, *De Ablatione Scribarum* (Leipsic, 1715; reprinted in Hasæus and Ikenius's *Thesaurus,* i, 19–26); Trägard, *De Ablationibus et Ordinationibus Scribarum in Masora Notatio* (Greifswalde, 1763); Geiger, *Urschrift und Uebersetzungen der Bibel* (Breslau, 1857), p. 251–254; Strack, *Prolegomena Critica* (Leipsic, 1873), p. 86. (B. P.)

Ives, DWIGHT, D.D., a Baptist minister, was born in West Springfield, Mass., Sept. 20, 1805. He graduated at Brown University in 1835, and was ordained pastor of the First Baptist Church in Springfield, Mass., soon after. He removed to Alton, Ill., in 1836, to take charge of the Baptist church in that place, where he had a very successful ministry. The climate proving unfavorable to his health, he returned to New England, and became pastor of the Second Baptist Church in Suffield, Conn., in 1839, and continued in office until 1874. His pastorate here was one of great ability, and singularly blessed. He took a deep interest in the establishment of the Connecticut Literary Institution, a seminary of a high order, under the patronage of the Baptists of Connecticut. He resigned his pastorate in April, 1874, and removed to Conway, Mass., where he performed ministerial duties as his health would permit, until his death, Dec. 22, 1875. (J. C. S.)

Ixcuina was the goddess of love and all joys, the *Venus* of the Mexicans.

Ixīon, in Greek mythology, was the son of Antion and Perimela, king in Thessaly. He married Dia, the daughter of Deïoneus, but refused to pay the promised wedding presents to her father, wherefore the latter took possession of a number of horses of Ixion as a substitute. Ixion promised to give Deïoneus what he wanted, and caused him to fall into a cave of red-hot coals, under the pretence it was a cave of gold. It was so great a crime that no man would purify him. Jupiter did this himself, and was so pleased with Ixion that he fed him at the table of the gods. A new crime sprang up in the heart of the murderer. He longed for the love of Juno. Juno forgave him, and formed Nephele (a cloud), by whom Ixion became father of the Centaurs. Finally, Jupiter's patience becoming exhausted, he threw him into Tartarus, where he remains, tortured by the Furies, along with Sisyphus and Tantalus. His penalty is to turn a wheel which perpetually recoils.

Ixion and his Wheel.

Ixtitlon is the Æsculapius of the Mexicans, the protecting god of the medical art.

Izdubar (or **Gizdubar,** *Mass of Fire*) is, according to the newly discovered Izdubar Tablets, an early mythical Assyrian hero, who was probably a form of the solar deity. He was a great chieftain, and delivered the city of Erech when it was assailed by the giants. He had for his wife the goddess Ishtar, who proved unfaithful to him, and sent some monstrous bulls to destroy him. These animals he was enabled to slay by the assistance of his faithful friend and adviser, the deified sage Heabani, who was ultimately killed by an unknown insect or reptile, called a Tambukki. Izdubar afterwards, becoming afflicted with a cutaneous disorder, went by the advice of his boatman, Urhamsi, to seek the sage Adrahasis, who, having survived the Deluge, was supposed to be able to cure him of his malady. Adrahasis complied with his request, and related to him in considerable detail the legend of the flood. Upon returning to Erech, Izdubar set up a monument in memory alike of his cure and of the story related by his benefactor, and then, by the aid of enchantment, had the soul of Heabani raised up to commune with him. Izdubar seems after these events to have become a king, but his history is so mixed up with a mythological series of legends that his real character is uncertain, as also are, of course, his parentage and birth.

Ized, in Persian mythology, is a name of the twenty-eight good genii of the second rank, who recognize Ormuzd and his seven assistants, the Amshaspands, as their ruler. The Izeds are male and female beings of greatest purity and mildness, created by Ormuzd, the representative of the highest, invisible god, and superintend the year, the month, the day, the hour, guide men on life's journey, command the animal and vegetable world, and rule the natural laws and elements, and are in continuous combat with Ahriman and his evil spirits.

Izquierdo, Sebastiano, a Jesuit, was born at Alcaraz, Spain, in 1601. He was rector of the colleges at Murcia and Alcala, and died about 1680. He wrote, *Opus Theologicum et Philosophicum:—Praxis Exercitionum Spiritualium.* See Alegambe, *Bibliotheca Scriptorum Societatis Jesu;* Jöcher, *Allgemeines Gelehrten-Lexicon*, s. v.; Antonii *Bibliotheca Hispanica.* (B. P.)

J.

Jaabez, Isaac, a Jewish rabbi of Constantinople, who died at the beginning of the 17th century, is the author of תורת חסד, a commentary on the Hagiographa, consisting of ten different parts: 1, קדש הלולים, on the Song of Songs; 2, צמח קדש, on Ruth; 3, צדקת המים, on Lamentations; 4, שערי מדע, on Coheleth; 5, עטרת שלום, on Esther; 6, תהלות י״י, on the Psalms; 7, למודי י״י, on Proverbs; 8, יראת שדי, on Job; 9, ברכת ישרים, on Daniel; 10, חוסים מושיע, on Ezra and Nehemiah, reprinted in Moses Frankfurter's *Rabbinic Bible* (Amsterdam, 1724–27). See De' Rossi, *Dizionario Storico* (Germ. transl.), p. 133; Fürst, *Bibl. Jud.* ii, 2.

Jaabez, Joseph *ben-Abraham*, a Jewish rabbi of the 16th century, belonged to those exiles who left Spain in 1492. Jaabez settled at Adrianople, where he became rabbi preacher. He wrote מאמר האחדות, or system of Jewish dogmatics (Ferrara, 1554):—יסוד האמונה, or Dogmatics of Judaism, printed with the "system:"—אור החיים, or faith triumphant over philosophy (ibid. eod.; Amsterdam, 1781; Przemysl, 1873):—פרוש על תהלים, a commentary on the Psalms (Salonika, 1571). See De' Rossi, *Dizionario Storico* (Germ. transl.), 132 sq.; Fürst, *Bibl. Jud.* ii, 1; Jellinek, *Joseph Jaabez, eine kurze Biographie* in *Literatur-Blatt des Orients*, 1846, col. 261 sq. (B. P.)

Jaafarites, a Mohammedan sect who held in highest reverence the memory of Jaafar, the sixth of the twelve Imams. An unsuccessful attempt was made by Nadir Shah to assimilate the Persian Mohammedanism to that of the Turks, acknowledging Jaafar as the head of the new national faith. See Imams, the Twelve.

Jaazer. *Khurbet Sâr*, the probable representative of this locality, is laid down at seven miles west of Ammân, with notes of a pool, tower, and sarcophagi adjoining, on the reduced *Map* of the Ordnance Survey in the fragment published east of the Jordan; but the *Memoirs* containing details have not appeared. It is situated on the road running along the south side of Wady Sîr. Tristram says (*Bible Places*, p. 337): "It consists only of grass-grown mounds and rows of foundations at the very head of the valley, above a marshy spring, the highest source of the Seir." Merrill says (*East of the Jordan*, p. 405), "Sar we made to be 3400 feet above the sea-level;" the *Map* indicates 1390 feet.

Jabbok. *Wady Zerka*, the modern name of this stream (which must be carefully distinguished from the Zerka Maïn, farther south, near Callirrhoë), has been explored by Dr. Merrill, whose account closes thus (*East of the Jordan*, p. 381):

"Its winding course is remarkable, making it in this regard unlike any other river of Syria. The Jordan is more crooked, having almost innumerable short bends; but the Jabbok sweeps far out into the desert, then doubles back upon itself, and forces its way through a mountain. The valley is seventy or more miles in length, and is exceedingly fertile. Along its head-waters lived a great and powerful race, which existed from the earliest advent of the Hebrews in this region clear down to a period subsequent to the time of Christ. . . . Its capacities are great, because every acre can be reached by irrigating canals. Even at present it is very extensively cultivated, and contains many fine farms. On the hill-sides there are, at certain points, some unused canals, of which a few can be traced to a distance of five or eight miles."

Jabme Acco was a goddess worshipped by the Laplanders, the mother of death. Her dwelling was deep in the bed of the earth, and the departed remained with her, until their destiny was decided by the judges of the infernal regions.

Jabneel of Naphtali is identified by Conder (*Tent Work*, ii, 337), with *Yemma*, a modern village with a spring of the same name, four miles south-west of the Sea of Tiberias, but with no special signs of antiquity (*Memoirs* accompanying the Ordnance Map, i, 365).

Jabneh. The modern site *Yebnah* is located midway (four and a quarter miles) between Akir (Ekron) and the shore, and is thus spoken of in the *Memoirs* accompanying the Ordnance Survey (ii, 441): "The modern village occupies a strong position on a rounded hill, the houses being mostly of mud. The only remains of interest noted were the church in the village and the mosque west of it," which are described in detail.

Jachja, David. See Ibn-Jachja, David.

Jachja, Gedalja. See Ibn-Jachja, Gedalja.

Jachja, Joseph. See Ibn-Jachja, Joseph.

Jachmann, Johann Gottlieb, a Lutheran theologian of Germany, was born at Breslau, Jan. 8, 1727. He studied at Leipsic, was in 1752 conrector of the Magdalene Gymnasium at Breslau, in 1767 provost of St. Mary's and St. George's churches, at Oels, Silesia, and died Feb. 15, 1776. He wrote, *De Sabbatho ante Legem Mosaicam Existente* (Leipsic, 1748):—*Spicilegium Observationum in Matthæi Caput xxiv* (1749):—*Observatio Exegetica in Ies. xxvi*, 19 (1749):—*De Beringeri Editione N. Test. Germanica* (Breslau, 1757):—*De Josepho, pro-rege Ægyptiorum* (1764):—*De Justino, Martyro et Philosopho* (1765). See Jöcher, *Allgemeines Gelehrten-Lexikon*, s. v.; Fürst, *Bibl. Jud.* ii, 5. (B. P.)

Jackson, Abner, D.D., LL.D., a Protestant Episcopal clergyman, graduated from Trinity College, Hartford, Conn., in 1837, and taught there for several years.

In 1858 he was made president of Hobart College, Geneva, N. Y., and also held the Startin professorship of the evidences of Christianity. In 1867 he removed to Hartford, Conn., becoming president of Trinity College, where he was also Hobart professor of ethics and metaphysics, and continued in that position until his death, April 19, 1874, aged sixty-three years. In 1873 he was deputy from his diocese to the General Convention, and was one of the standing committee in 1871. See *Prot. Episc. Almanac*, 1875, p. 144.

Jackson, Charles Davis, D.D., a Protestant Episcopal clergyman, was born at Salem, Mass., Dec. 15, 1811. He graduated from Dartmouth College in 1833; studied theology two years in Andover Theological Seminary; was engaged in teaching several years; ordained deacon in 1841, and presbyter in 1842; served as rector of St. Stephen's Church one or two years; of St. Luke's, Staten Island, from 1843 to 1847, and thereafter of St. Peter's, Westchester County, N. Y., for more than twenty years. He died June 28, 1871. He was the author of a work on *Popular Education*, and another on *The Relation of Education to Crime*, besides *Sermons*.

Jackson, Henry, D.D., a Baptist minister, was born at Providence, R. I., June 16, 1798. He graduated from Brown University in 1817, and studied theology at Andover Theological Seminary for over a year (1821); was ordained in 1822; then took charge of a Baptist Church in Charlestown, Mass.; next of the First Baptist Church of Hartford, Conn. (1836); of New Bedford, Mass. (1839); of the Central Church, Newport, R. I. (1847), and continued there till his sudden death, March 2, 1863. See *Trien. Cat. of Andover Theol. Sem.* 1870, p. 48.

Jackson, John, D.D., an English prelate, was born in London, Feb. 22, 1811. After studying at the Reading School, under Dr. Richard Valpy, he entered Pembroke College, Oxford, where he graduated in 1833, in the first class in classics. He was appointed to the head-mastership of Islington Grammar-school in 1836. In 1846 he was made rector of St. James's Church, Piccadilly, an appointment which soon made widely known his qualities as a preacher of singularly impressive earnestness and his powers as the administrator of a large and populous district. In 1847 Dr. Jackson was appointed chaplain to the queen, and in 1845, 1850, 1862, and 1866 he was a select preacher at Oxford. In 1852 he was made canon of Bristol. In 1853 he delivered the Boyle lectures in London, and in the same year was made bishop of Lincoln. He was transferred to the see of London, Jan. 4, 1869, and died Jan. 6, 1884. Dr. Jackson published many sermons and charges, and a popular pamphlet on *The Sinfulness of Little Sins*.

Jackson, Samuel Cram, D.D., a Congregational minister, son of Rev. Dr. William Jackson, was born at Dorset, Vt., March 13, 1802. He graduated from Middlebury College in 1821, and studied for some time in the law school at New Haven, Conn.; graduated from Andover Theological Seminary in 1826; was ordained June 6 of the following year as pastor of West Church, in Andover, from which he was dismissed in September, 1850, and became assistant secretary of the State Board of Education, also acting librarian of the State Library, which office he held until 1877. He died July 26, 1878. Dr. Jackson published, *Blessings of the Year*, a sermon at West Andover, Dec. 30, 1827:—*Funeral Discourse of Rev. S. G. Pierce*, Methuen, May 10, 1839:—*Thanksgiving Sermon*, Nov. 28, 1839:—*The License Law Vindicated:—Religious Principle a Source of Public Prosperity:—The Massachusetts Election Sermon* (1843). See *Cong. Year-book*, 1879, p. 45.

Jackson, Thomas, an eminent Wesleyan Methodist minister and writer, was born at Sancton, Yorkshire, Dec. 10, 1783. He had no educational advantages in youth, but by extraordinary diligence in reading and study, continued with unabated vigor through a long life, he attained to a good degree of learning, though he was never a first-class scholar. He was converted in youth, entered the ministry in 1804, and was soon brought into notice by the wise, spirited, and faithful manner in which he discharged the various duties of a young Wesleyan minister. While at Wakefield he had a sharp contest with a Dissenting minister of Holmfirth, Rev. J. Cockin, about the "Five Points," and his *Four Letters* to that gentleman were the beginning of his long career as an author (Leeds, 1814–15, 8vo). *The Calvinistic Controversy, The Times of Charles the First, The Commonwealth and the Restoration*, the writings of Wesley, Fletcher, etc., and *The Early History of Methodism* were thoroughly studied, so that in these fields Jackson became *facile princeps*, and his works in these lines have great and enduring value. During his first year at Wakefield (1814), he read through with care nearly sixty volumes, and he never subsequently diminished the amount of his reading. From 1824 to 1843 he was editor of the *Magazine* and Book-room publications, and during these eighteen years he did an amount of ministerial and literary work that is marvellous. During the centenary year of Methodism (1838) he was made president of the conference, was requested to prepare a volume on the subject of the centenary, describing the rise, progress, and benefits of Wesleyan Methodism, and was appointed to preach the centenary sermon before the conference; yet Jackson went through all this extra work, and the great success of the movement was largely due to his pen, preaching and pleading, his godliness making itself felt through all Methodism. In 1849 he was for the second time elevated to the presidency. For nineteen years (1843–62) he was theological tutor at Richmond, being painstaking, perspicuous, comprehensive, and copious in his lectures, and "unutterably anxious to perpetuate sound doctrine." He became a supernumerary in 1861, taking up his residence in the suburbs of London, and preached and wrote as long as he was able. "His old age was beautiful. Always calm, cheerful, benign, often overflowing with kindness and love, he carried a happy influence wherever he went, and excited universal love and admiration." He died at Shepherd's Bush, near London, March 10, 1873. A list of Mr. Jackson's numerous works, which are largely contributions to Methodist biography and literature, may be found in Osborn, *Methodist Bibliography*, p. 122. See *Recollections of my Own Life and Times*, by Thomas Jackson (Lond. 1873); *Minutes of the British Conference*, 1873, p. 25; Smith, *Hist. of Wesl. Methodism* (index, vol. iii); Stevenson, *City-Road Chapel*, p. 284; *Sunday at Home* (Lond. March 28, 1874); Everett, *Wesleyan Takings*, i, 341.

Jacob, *Rabbi*, is the name of a Jewish teacher who lived in the latter part of the 2d century of our æra. We have a recorded maxim of his in the treatise *Pirke Aboth*: "This world is like a vestibule before the world to come; prepare thyself at the vestibule, that thou mayest be admitted into the hall. Better is one hour of repentance and good works in this world than all the life of the world to come; better is one hour of refreshment of spirit in the world to come than all the life of this world" (ch. iv, 23, 24). (B. P.)

Jacob Erlandsen, a Danish prelate, was originally dean of the chapter of Lund, in which capacity he attended the Council of Lyons in 1245. He afterwards became bishop of Roeskilde, and archbishop of Lund in 1253. He died May 10, 1274. See Hoefer, *Nouv. Biog. Générale*, s. v.

Jacob ben-Isaac of Prague, who died about 1628, is the author of צאינה וראינה, or a Judæo-German midrash on the Pentateuch, the five Megilloth and Haftaras (Amsterdam, 1648, and often; partly translated into Latin by Saubert, Helmstädt, 1660; Engl. transl. by Hershon, Lond. 1865); a modern imitation is the *La Semaine Israélite*, by B. Crehange (Paris, 1847). See Fürst, *Bibl. Jud.* ii, 19 sq. (B. P.)

Jacob Natta. See Natta.

Jacob SASPORTAS. See SASPORTAS.

Jacob OF VITERBO, archbishop of Naples, who died in 1308, was at first an Augustinian monk, and had the reputation of great learning. Gandolfo, in his dissertation, *De Ducentis Augustinianis*, attributes to him a large number of works, which are still unpublished. See Hoefer, *Nouv. Biog. Générale*, s. v.

Jacob, Carl, a Benedictine, who died at Salzburg in 1661, is the author of, *De Gratia Divina* (1630):—*Theoremata ex Universa Doctoris Angelici Summa* (1642):—*Verbum Dei Incarnatum* (eod.):—*De Deo Uno et Trino* (1644):—*Convivium Eucharisticum* (eod.). See *Hist. Univers. Salisburg.* p. 314; Jöcher, *Allgemeines Gelehrten-Lexikon*, s. v. (B. P.)

Jacob, Louis, a French Carmelite, was born at Chalons-sur-Saône in 1608, and died in 1670. Upon joining his order, he took the name of Louis de St. Charles. He wrote, *Bibliotheca Pontificia* (Lyons, 1643):—*Elogium Venerabilis Sororis Isaunæ de Cambri, Tornacensis Monialis S. Augustini* (Paris, 1644):—*Bibliotheca Parisina* (1645):—*Bibliographia Gallica Universalis* (1646):—*De Claris Scriptoribus Cabilonensibus Libri Tres* (1652):—*Catalogus Abbatum et Abbatissarum Benedictionis Dei, Ordinis Cisterciensis*, etc. See Cosme de St. Étienne, *Mémoire sur le P. Louis de St. Charles;* Nicéron, *Mémoires*, xl, p. 87 sq.; Lichtenberger, *Encyclop. des Sciences Religieuses*, s. v. (B. P.)

Jacobazzi (Lat. *Jacobatius*), DOMINICO, bishop of Lucera, was employed in various important affairs by Sixtus IV, and was created cardinal in 1517 by Leo X. He died July 2, 1527. He left a *Treatise on the Councils*. See Chalmers, *Biog. Dict.* s. v.

Jacobi, Adam Friedrich Ernst, a German divine, who died April 3, 1807, superintendent and member of consistory at Cranichfeld, in the duchy of Gotha, is the author of, *Neuester Religionszustand in Holland* (Gotha, 1777):—*Katechisationen über 12 auserlesene Stücke der heiligen Schrift* (Weimar, 1773):—*Religion aus der Bibel in Unterredungen aus den Hauptstellen derselben* (ibid. 1794). See Winer, *Handbuch der theol. Lit.* i, 824; ii, 270, 354. (B. P.)

Jacobi, Johann Friedrich, a Lutheran theologian of Germany, was born Jan. 16, 1712. For some time preacher at Osterode and Brunswick, he was called in 1758 as general superintendent of Lüneburg to Celle, and died March 21, 1791. He wrote a number of ascetical works. See Winer, *Handbuch der theol. Lit.* i, 23, 385, 418, 438, 488; ii, 40. (B. P.)

Jacobins, a name applied in France to the Dominicans (q. v.), because their principal convent was situated near the gate of St. James (*Jacobus*), in Paris. At the commencement of the first French revolution the meetings of its most zealous promoters were held in the hall of this convent, and from this circumstance Jacobin came to be another name for revolutionist.

Jacobites, the adherents of James II of England, particularly the non-jurors, who separated from the high Episcopal Church simply because they would not take the oath of allegiance to the new king, and who in the public services prayed for the Stuart family. They were most numerous in Scotland, but were much lessened by the defeat of the Pretender in 1745, and still more so by his death in 1788. See NON-JURORS.

Jacobites, ORDER OF, a Romish order of mendicant monks, established by Innocent III in the 13th century, but which soon ceased to exist.

Jacobs, MICHAEL, D.D., a Lutheran minister, was born in Franklin County, Pa., Jan. 18, 1808. In 1823 he entered the preparatory department of Jefferson College, Cannonsburg, from which he eventually graduated. While there he joined the Presbyterian Church. After teaching in a boarding-school several months at Belair, Md., he moved in April, 1829, to Gettysburg, where he taught mathematics in the Gettysburg Gymnasium, afterwards Pennsylvania College, in which he was elected professor of mathematics and natural science. Having studied theology privately, he was licensed to preach in the fall of 1832. He was repeatedly president and treasurer of his synod, and for a time was secretary of the General Synod. For several years he was editor of the *Linnean Record and Journal*. In 1865 his department was restricted to mathematics. The following year he withdrew from college instruction. He died July 22, 1871. Although a voluminous writer, very little of his work was published beyond a number of review articles and a small volume entitled *Notes on the Battle of Gettysburg*. See *Fifty Years in the Lutheran Ministry*, 1878, p. 228.

Jacob's Well. The following is the latest description of this spot (*Bîr Yakûb*), taken from Lieut. Conder's *Tent Work in Palestine*, i, 71. A full account is given in the *Memoirs* accompanying the Ordnance Survey, ii, 172 sq.

"The tradition of Jacob's Well is one in which Jews, Samaritans, Moslems, and Christians alike agree. There are also other reasons which lead to the belief that the tradition is trustworthy; the proximity of Joseph's Tomb and of Sychar, and finally the fact of a well existing at all in a place abounding with streams, one of which is within one hundred yards' distance. No other important well is found near, and the utility of such a work can only be explained on the assumption that it was necessary for the patriarch to have water within his own land, surrounded as he was by strangers, who may naturally be supposed to have guarded jealously their rights to the springs. By digging the well Jacob avoided those quarrels from which his father had suffered in the Philistine country, pursuing a policy of peace which appears generally to have distinguished his actions.

"The well then, as being one of the few undoubted sites made sacred by the feet of Christ, is a spot of greater interest that any near Shechem. Its neighborhood is not marked by any very prominent monument, and, indeed, it would be quite possible to pass by it without knowing of its existence. Just east of the gardens of Balâta, a dusty mound by the road half covers the stumps of three granite columns. After a few moments' search a hole is found south-west of them, and by this the visitor descends through the roof of a little vault, apparently modern. The vault stretches twenty feet east and west, and is ten feet broad, the hole in the pointed arch of the roof being in the north-east corner. The floor is covered with fallen stones, which block the mouth of the well; through these we let down the tape and found the depth to be seventy-five feet. The diameter is seven feet six

Interior of Jacob's Well.

inches, the whole depth cut through alluvial soil and soft rock, receiving water by infiltration through the sides. There appears to be occasionally as much as two fathoms of water, but in summer the well is dry. The little vault is built on to a second, running at right angles northwards from the west end, but the communication is now walled up. In this second vault there are said to be remains of a tessellated pavement, and the bases of the three columns above mentioned rest on this floor, the shafts sticking out through the roof—a sufficient proof that the vault is modern."

Jacobson, Heinrich Friedrich, a German professor of canon law, was born June 8, 1804, at Marienwerder. He studied at Königsberg, Berlin, and Göttingen, commenced his academical career at Königsberg in 1826, was professor there in 1831, and died March 19, 1868. He published, *De Codicibus Gregoriano et Hermogeniano* (Königsberg, 1826):—*Kirchenrechtliche Versuche zur Begründung eines Systems des Kirchenrechts* (1831):—*De Fontibus Juris Ecclesiastici Borussici* (1838):—*Geschichte der Quellen des Kirchenrechts des Preussischen Staats* (1837-44, 3 vols.):—*Das evangelische Kirchenrecht des Preussischen Staates und seiner Provinzen* (Halle, 1864-66, 2 vols.). See Zuchold, *Bibl. Theol.* i, 603 sq. (B. P.)

Jacobson, Israel, a Jewish rabbi of Germany, was born at Halberstadt, Oct. 17, 1768. He was one of the earliest promoters of reform among his coreligionists. In 1801 he founded an educational establishment at Seesen, in Westphalia, in which Jewish and Christian boys were taught side by side. When the kingdom of Westphalia was erected, Jacobson had the ear of the government; a consistory was established, and he was made its president. In 1805 Jacobson introduced into his synagogue an organ, German hymns, confirmation, and the German sermon. The example set by him was followed by others. When, in 1815, the kingdom of Westphalia was buried under the ruins of Napoleon's empire, Jacobson settled at Berlin, where he established again a private temple of the modern style, in which he officiated as high-priest. He died Sept. 13, 1828. See Jost, *Jacobson und die neuern Richtungen* in the *Israelitische Annalen*, i, 29 sq.; Kayserling, *Bibliothek jüdischer Kanzelredner*, i, 13 sq.; M'Caul, *Sketches of Judaism and the Jews*, p. 61 sq. (B. P.)

Jacobson, Jacob Hirsch, a Jewish ascetical writer of Germany, who died at Dresden, Jan. 10, 1885, is the author of, *Pirke Aboth oder Rabbinische Gnomologie* (Hebrew text with German translation and commentary, Breslau, 1840):—*Israelitisches Gebetbuch* (Hebrew and German, 1843):—דבר אמת ליעקב, *eine Auswahl Israelitischer Kanzelvorträge zu religiöser Belehrung und Erbauung:—Katechetischer Leitfaden beim Unterricht in der israelitischen Religion* (7th ed. 1876): —*Die Geschichten der heiligen Schriften* (3d ed. 1875). See Fürst, *Bibl. Jud.* ii, 5 sq. (B. P.)

Jacobson, William, D.D., an English prelate, was born at Great Yarmouth, Norfolk, in 1803. He matriculated at St. Edmund's Hall in 1823, migrated shortly afterwards to Lincoln College, on obtaining a scholarship there, and, in 1829, having taken his degree, became a fellow of Exeter. He was made bishop of Chester in 1865, and died at Oxford, July 12, 1884. The chief works of bishop Jacobson were his new edition of Nowell's *Catechisms*, his reprint in six volumes of the *Works of Bishop Sanderson*, and his edition of the *Remains of Clement, Ignatius, and Polycarp* (1838; 4th ed. 1866, 2 vols.). (B. P.)

Jacobus. See JAMES.

Jacobus BARADÆUS, a Monophysite bishop of Edessa, is said to have been born at Tela or Constantia, fifty-five miles east of Edessa, towards the close of the 5th century. He was early trained in the ministry, became a noted ascetic, was called to the Byzantine court, but lived there a complete recluse, and was made bishop nominally of Edessa, but virtually metropolitan, A.D. 541. Amid the disastrous and troublesome period in which he lived, his courage and energy prolonged the cause of the party to which he belonged, especially in the famous quarrel with Paul of Antioch. He died suddenly, July 30, 578. A *Liturgy* is incorrectly ascribed to him (Renaudot, *Lit. Or.* i, 332), also a *Catechesis*, largely used by the Jacobites (Cave, *Hist. Lit.* i, 524). See Smith, *Dict. of Christ. Biog.* s. v.

Jacobus SARUGENSIS, made bishop of Botnæ, a little town in the district of Sarug, in Osstroënæ, at the age of sixty-seven, A.D. 519, and who died two years afterwards, is the author of very many ecclesiastical works, both in prose and poetry, chiefly of a ritualistic or epistolary character, for which see Smith, *Dict. of Christ. Biog.* s. v.

Jacobus, MELANCHTHON WILLIAMS, D.D., LL.D., a Presbyterian minister, was born at Newark, N. J., Sept. 19, 1816. He entered the sophomore class at Princeton College in his fifteenth year, and graduated in 1834 with the highest honors. In 1835 he entered Princeton Theological Seminary, where he not only regularly graduated, but spent a fourth year in study, at the same time assisting professor J. Addison Alexander in the department of Hebrew. In 1839 he was received by the Presbytery of New York, and in September was ordained pastor of the First Presbyterian Church of Brooklyn, N. Y. At the close of his twelve years pastorate here the Church was one of the most flourishing in the city. In the fall of 1850 he made a tour through Europe, Egypt, and Palestine, and returned with greatly improved health. During his absence the General Assembly, in May, 1851, had elected him professor of Oriental and Biblical literature in the theological seminary at Allegheny, which position he accepted on his return, and was released from his pastoral charge, Oct. 21, 1851. In January, 1858, in addition to his work in the seminary, he accepted a call to the Central Church of Pittsburgh, which he served for twelve years with marked success. In 1866 he made a second tour of Europe. He was moderator of the last General Assembly of the Old School Church in 1869, and conjointly with Rev. P. H. Fowler, D.D., presided at the opening of the first reunited assembly in 1870. He presented the able report on sustentation, which was adopted by the General Assembly of 1871, and was secretary of that scheme for three years, until it was merged into the Board of Home Missions in 1874. In 1876 he was elected secretary of the Board of Education, but declined the position that he might continue in the ministry. He died Oct. 28, 1876. He had just attended a meeting of the Synod of Pittsburgh, and taken an active part in its proceedings. On the day preceding he had taught his seminary classes as usual. In 1848 Dr. Jacobus, while in Brooklyn, published the first volume of his *Notes on the New Testament*. Other volumes followed at intervals, the two volumes on Genesis appearing in 1864. These commentaries have had an immense sale, and are found among all denominations of Christians. Besides these he was the author of many other and smaller works. Dr. Jacobus stood in the front rank of the Biblical scholars of his age. As a preacher he maintained all through his ministry a high position, while on the platform his addresses were always happy and effective. He was a most energetic and persistent worker, and his industry was untiring. See *Necrol. Report of Princeton Theol. Sem.* 1877, p. 36.

Jacoby, LUDWIG S., D.D., a Methodist Episcopal minister, was born in Old Strelitz, Mecklenburg, Germany, Oct. 21, 1813. His parents being pious Jews, he was devoutly trained, and liberally educated, especially in the ancient languages. In 1835 he was baptized by a Lutheran minister. In 1838 he emigrated to the United States, and settled in Cincinnati, O., as a physician. He also devoted himself to teaching. About that time he was spiritually converted, under the preaching of Dr. Nast. In 1841 he was sent to St. Louis, Mo., to start the first German mission in that city. Desiring to labor more immediately for his countrymen, he was sent, in 1849, to Bremen, Germany, where he formed a Methodist Episcopal Society. There he continued, faithful in the various offices of presiding elder, pastor, editor, book agent, and superintendent for twenty years. He then returned to the United States, and was transferred to the South-western German Conference, and stationed at Eighth Street charge, St. Louis. In 1873 he was made presiding elder of St. Louis district, whereon he labored faithfully until near his death, which occurred in St. Louis, Mo., June 21, 1874. Dr. Jacoby's life was full of devotedness and energy, and his death full of peace and blessings. See *Minutes of Annual Conferences*, 1874, p. 88; Simpson, *Cyclop. of Methodism*, s. v.

Jacopone DE TODI. See STABAT MATER.

Jacquemont, FRANÇOIS, a French Jansenist, was born in 1757 at Boën, in the diocese of Lyons, and died at St. Étienne in 1835. He published, *Instruction sur les Avantages et les Vérités de la Religion Chrétienne* (1795):—*Avis aux Fidèles*, etc. (1796):—*Maximes de l'Église Gallicane* (Lyons, 1818). See Lichtenberger, *Encyclop. des Sciences Religieuses*, s. v. (B. P.)

Jad Hachezaka. See MAIMONIDES.

Jaenbert, archbishop of Canterbury, received his education at St. Augustine's, and was consecrated at Canterbury, Feb. 2, 766, by Egbert, archbishop of York. The great event of this episcopate is the conversion of the bishopric of Lichfield into a metropolitan see by Offa, king of Mercia, and the consequent spoliation, with the loss of dominion, authority, and dignity, of the archbishop of Canterbury. There was much to render the last years of Jaenbert's life melancholy, for the prospects of his country were gloomy in the extreme. Thwarted and discomfited to the last, Jaenbert perceived that his orders to be buried at St. Augustine's would not be obeyed by his chapter if he died without the walls of the monastery, and he therefore sought an asylum in the place endeared to him by the recollection of younger and happier days. He commanded his stone coffin to be prepared; his episcopal robes were arranged by his bedside; his soul was comforted by the psalms sung and the Scriptures read to him by brethren who could sympathize with him in his fallen fortunes. He died Aug. 11, 790. See Hook, *Lives of the Archbishops of Canterbury*, i, 242 sq.

Jaeshik, in Lamaism, was a Buddha, who brought Buddhism to Thibet, A.D. 407. Jakshiamuni, the fifth divine Burchan, and the supreme god of the Lamaites, caused him to spring forth out of the beautiful Padma-flower, knowing what sanctity he would thereby receive, and authorized him to bring about the salvation of men. Jaeshik undertook, however, only to save the men living in the snowy countries of the north; and he promised to carry out this plan with all perseverance, though his head should split into ten and his body into a thousand parts. He first descended into the kingdoms of hell, and visited the kingdom of monsters (Birid), then that of animals, of men, of evil genii, Assuri and Tägri, and there destroyed all pains and torture; for as soon as his holy mouth spoke the saving words, "Om-ma-ni-pad-mä-hum," hell no longer existed. After having accomplished so much, he began his journey on earth, and travelled through the countries beyond the mountains of snow. There also he spoke his magic words, destroyed evil, brought good from heaven, and led men to the true religion. Next he ascended into the country of the deities on the Red Mountain. There, to his consternation, he again saw many millions of beings unmercifully tortured by being bathed in the Otang Sea, or sea of fire. The tortures of these unfortunates brought forth a tear from each one of his eyes, out of which there sprang two goddesses, who promised to assist him, and, placing themselves in his eyes, their power was manifested by the glances of Jaeshik. He spoke the above-mentioned six words also here, saved the doomed, and converted them to faith in the supreme god Jakshiamuni, so that his work was almost finished. But all the saved were not yet strong in the faith, and this troubled him. He longed for the blessed land of eternal happiness, his home; and suddenly his head split into ten parts and his body into a thousand. Burchan joined the latter together again, and consoled him by saying that his body would become the holiest sanctuary of the world. The thousand parts were to become so many hands, each with one eye, and were to represent so many monarchs.

Figure of Jaeshik.

Jafè, Mardechai *ben-Abraham*, a famous Jewish author, resided in 1561 at Venice, whence, during a persecution of the Jews, he retreated to Bohemia, and became rabbi in the synagogues of Grodno, Lublin, Kremnitz, and Prague. He is the author of the *Lebushim*, a series of ten works, which hold a high place in the classics of modern Judaism. The general title of the series is לבוש מלכות, *Royal Apparel*, from Est. viii, 15; and the collection itself is sometimes called לבוש or ספר הלבושים. It consists of (1) *Lebush tekeleth*, or "the Purple Robe;" (2) *Lebush ha-chor*, or "the White Vestment;" (3) *Lebush atereth zahab*, or "the Crown of God;" (4) *Lebush butz veargaman*, or "the Vestment of fine linen and purple;" (5) *Lebush ir Shushan*, or "the Vestment of the City of Shushan." These five treatises turn upon the objects of the ritual codices of the Arba Turim of Jacob ben-Asher (q. v.), and the Shulchan Aruch of Joseph Karo (q. v.). The remaining five *lebushim* are exegetical, cabalistic, and philosophical. See Fürst, *Bibl. Jud.* ii, 7 sq.; Etheridge, *Introduction to Hebrew Literature*, p. 457; De' Rossi, *Dizionario Storico* (Germ. transl.), p. 136. (B. P.)

Jafè, Samuel, a rabbi at Constantinople in the latter part of the 16th century, is the author of homilies on the Midrashim, on the Pentateuch, and on Esther, Lamentations, and Ruth. He afterwards published them under the title of יפה תואר. He also published homilies on the haggadoth of the Palestinian Talmud. See Fürst, *Bibl. Jud.* ii, 9 sq.; De' Rossi, *Dizionario Storico* (Germ. transl.), p. 136. (B. P.)

Jaga, in Hindûism, is one of the costliest and most

honored sacrifices, which the Brahmins offer to the sun and the planets, and at which strictly no one from any other caste is allowed to be present. In the spring of the year a certain spot is selected and cleansed. A hut is built, in which several hundred Brahmins can be accommodated with seats; in the centre of this the holy pillar is erected, Mahadewa's symbol. Around this a fire is kindled by rubbing together two pieces of wood; and now all that can find room crowd into the hut. The remaining Brahmins surround the holy place, so that no profane eye desecrate the sanctuary. Then a widow is strangled (blood is not allowed to be shed); the liver is roasted with butter, divided in as many parts as there are Brahmins, and given to them on a slice of bread, which they are obliged to eat. Whoever does this is said to be specially purified and made sinless; and the Brahmin who kindled the fire and performed the sacrificial ceremony may take a part of the fire to his home, where he is to keep it constantly burning, and at his death he is permitted to have his funeral pile kindled with it, by virtue of which he enters paradise immediately, without any transmigration of his soul. Of course, under the English rule these barbarities are no longer permitted.

Jäger, JOHANN WOLFGANG, a Lutheran theologian of Germany, was born at Stuttgart, March 17, 1647, and died at Tübingen, April 2, 1720, doctor and professor of theology, chancellor, and provost. He is the author of, *Historia Ecclesiastica*, etc. (1710, 2 vols. fol.; Hamburg, 1709, 1717):—*Examen Quietismi:—Separatismus Hodiernus sub Examen Vocatus:—De Doctrina Communicationis Idiomatum:—Compendium Theologiæ Positivæ*. See Jöcher, *Allgemeines Gelehrten-Lexikon*, s. v.; Winer, *Handbuch der theol. Lit.* i, 285, 481, 579, 887. (B. P.)

Jaghatai-Turki [*Tartar*] (or **Tekke Turcoman**) **Version** OF THE SCRIPTURES. This dialect is vernacular to the Uzbek and Turkish tribes of Turkestan and Central Asia, and a version of any part of the Scriptures into it is of a very recent date. In 1879 the Rev. James Bassett had completed a translation of the gospel of Matthew, with the assistance of a mirza from Meshed. After a careful revision made at Teheran, the translator carried his version through the press in London. A new and revised edition of this gospel was again printed at Tiflis, and most of the vowel points, which were so numerous in the first edition, were omitted. (B. P.)

Jagnepawadam, in Hindûism, is the cord of the Brahmins, a sacred mark or sign of the highest caste, which no one else is allowed to carry under severe penalties. It is made of nine threads of wool, which are long enough to be wound one hundred and eight times around the hand (because of the one hundred and eight legends of Brahma). These nine threads are divided into three parts, corresponding to the three Vedas, or holy books, and they are then suspended over the right shoulder, so as to touch the hip under the left arm. This Brahmin-cord places him who carries it above the reach of the civil law.

Jagouth (or **Yaghûth**), one of the five principal gods of the ancient Arabians. He was usually represented in the form of a lion, and is mentioned by name in the Koran.

Jahed, ABÛ-OSMAN-AMRÛ, a Mohammedan doctor of the sect of the Motazelites. The name of Jahed, by which he is generally designated, is only a surname given to him on account of his brilliant eyes. He was thoroughly acquainted with Greek literature. He gained a great many adherents by his writings and eloquence. Among his theological books one is cited as being composed in favor of Ali, and containing more than a thousand traditions respecting him. The best of his works, according to Ibn-Khallican, who cites but two, is a treatise on animals, probably borrowed largely from Greek writers. Jahed died at Bussora, A.D. 869. See Hoefer, *Nouv. Biog. Générale*, s. v.

Jais, ÆGIDIUS, a Benedictine, was born at Mittenwald, Bavaria, March 17, 1750. In 1770 he joined his order, was in 1778 professor at the Salzburg Gymnasium, and in 1803 professor of theology there. In 1814 he retired from public duties, and died Dec. 4, 1822. He published, *Predigten* (Munich, 1803, 2 vols.):—*Katechismus* (Würzburg, 1811):—*Handbuch zum Unterrichte in der christ kathol. Glaubens- und Sittenlehre* (1821), and other ascetical works. See Winer, *Handbuch der theol. Lit.* ii, 112, 241, 267, 346, 378. (B. P.)

Jaish, BARUCH IBN. See IBN-JAISH.

Jakobi, ADAM FRIEDRICH ERNST, a Lutheran theologian of Germany, was born Oct. 27, 1733. He studied at Jena, acted for some time as private tutor, went in 1763 as military chaplain to Holland, and was in 1775 appointed superintendent by duke Ernest of Gotha, Jakobi died April 3, 1807. He wrote, *Diss. Theologica de Peccatis Apostolorum Actualibus* (Jena, 1754):—*Exercitatio Exegetico-Theologica de Monogamia* (Gotha. 1776), besides a number of historical and pedagogical works. See Döring, *Die gelehrten Theologen Deutschlands*, s. v. (B. P.)

Jakshiamuni, in Lamaism, is the supreme god of the Thibetians, identical with *Buddha* of India, an incarnation of Vishnu, who appears for the fourth time to save men. He is the present sovereign of the universe. After him there will yet come nine hundred and ninety-six Buddhas, before the salvation of men shall be finished. The inhabitants of Thibet, Mongolia, Tartary, China, and Japan hold him to be the only god, creator and giver of their religion.

Jalaguier, PROSPER FRÉDÉRIC, a French Protestant theologian, was born Aug. 21, 1795. Having acted as pastor at several places, Jalaguier was called in 1833 to Montauban, to fill temporarily the chair of Christian ethics. Two years later he was appointed professor of dogmatics, and occupied this office till his death at Montauban, March 22, 1864. He published, *Le Temoignage de Dieu* (1851):—*Authenticité du Nouveau Testament* (eod.):—*Inspiration du Nouveau Testament* (eod.):—*Simple Exposé de la Question Chrétienne* (1852):—*Du Principe Chrétien et du Catholicisme, du Rationalisme et du Protestantisme* (1855):—*Une Vue de la Question Scripturaire* (1863). In these works he defended with great firmness the reality of a supernatural revelation and the religious authority of the Scripture, against the writers of the *Revue de Strasbourg*. See Lichtenberger, *Encyclop. des Sciences Religieuses*, s. v. (B. P.)

Jaldabaoth. See IALDABAOTH.

Jalinder, in Hindû mythology, was one of the mighty dæmons which, sprung from Danu, are classed and recognised under the name of Danuwas. He was dreaded by all the gods, because he was unconquerable; but this was only by the marvellous virtue and purity of his wife, who favored no one in heaven or on earth. The dæmon challenged Shiva, and fought with him in Mahadewa's form, and would have come off victorious had not Vishnu come to the assistance of the god. This he did by taking on the form of a dæmon just like Jalinder, and, coming to the wife of the latter, overcame her virtue, and immediately the dæmon's strength left him, so that he was conquered and killed.

Jalkut (יַלְקוּט), i. e. collection, is the title of a Midrashic catena of traditional expositions from upwards of fifty different works of all ages, many of which are of great value. This Midrash extends over the whole Bible. The latest edition is the one published at Warsaw (1876–77). The author of the Jalkut is Simeon Cara (q. v.). (B. P.)

Jalloof Version OF THE SCRIPTURES. This dialect (also called *Jolof*, *Woloff*, *Guiluf*, etc.), is spoken by a large tribe near Bathurst, Gambia, West Africa, numbering about 50,000 souls. In 1881, the British and Foreign Bible Society, at the request of the Wesleyan Missionary Society, resolved to print a tentative edition of 500 copies of the gospel of Matthew. The translation was made by Rev. R. Dixon, of Bathurst, Gambia, who had used his version in the services, and found it was understood and liked by the people. See *Bible of Every Land*, p. 407. (B. P.)

Jam mœsta QUIESCE QUERELA is the beginning of the grand burial-hymn of Prudentius (q. v.). This hymn, which, as Trench says, is "the crowning glory of the poetry of Prudentius," brings before us the ancient worship in deserts and in catacombs, and of which Herder says that no one can read it without feeling his heart moved by its touching tones. The first stanza runs thus in the original:

"Jam mœsta quiesce querela,
Lacrimas suspendite, matres,
Nullus sua pignora plangat,
Mors haec reparatio vitæ est."

And in Caswall's translation:

"Cease, ye tearful mourners,
Thus your hearts to rend,
Death is life's beginning,
Rather than its end."

A German translation is also found in Schaff's *Deutsches Gesangbuch*, No. 468. (B. P.)

Jama, in Hindû mythology, is the ruler of a division of the infernal region (Nark), and the highest judge there, who decides whether the departed souls are to be admitted to heaven or go to hell, in which latter case they begin their wanderings through life anew. A mirror, made of pure fire, portrays to him the deeds of all men. On a golden scale, held by his assistants, he weighs human deeds, and leads those found wanting to Nark, the others to Suerga (heaven). He is a protecting spirit of virtue and justice, and the most honored companion of Shiva. Nevertheless, he is represented in a frightful appearance, with hideous features, a number of arms, heavy weapons, and riding on a black buffalo with four horns. He lives in Jamapur (city of Jama).

Jamandaga (or **Macha Alla**) was one of the supreme deities of the Kalmucks. He is represented somewhat like Herli-Kan, but differs from that deity in possessing six arms. His color is blue, and the palms of the hands and the soles of his feet are red. Flowers and skulls are his crown, and snakes his armlets and anklets, while a snake hangs over both shoulders. His girdle is a string of human heads. In one hand he holds a sceptre, in another two cords. In two he holds drinking-vessels, and in the fifth and sixth the hide of an animal. This frightful god crushes with his feet a form which has human arms and feet, but a head resembling an elephant's. This idol is also surrounded by good and evil dæmons.

Figure of Jamandaga.

Jamanduga, in Thibetanian mythology, is one of the eight fearful gods (Nadman-Dobshot), who by their might destroy evil, protect the world, and are zealously worshipped by the followers of Lamaism. Jamanduga is an emanation of the god Monsushari. Jakshiamuni, the supreme god, gave him the most hateful appearance that he could devise, in order that he might conquer the frightful Tshotshitshalba, the most dreaded of all evil dæmons, who continually seeks to destroy the world. In this form Jamanduga is of a bluish color, surrounded by flames of fire, and has ten heads, in three rows, one of which is that of a bull, another that of a goat, and the rest distorted human faces; but the last and topmost one is that of a beautiful maiden, to denote his divine nature. Twenty arms carry the deadliest weapons and instruments of torture, and with twenty feet he walks on a heap of crushed men. See JAMANDAGA.

Jamas, in the mythology of the Antilles, was the mother of the great spirit Jokahuna, whom Tonatiks sent to the earth in his stead. This goddess was worshipped on the island Quisqueja (Hayti). She had an idol there, at whose side two servants stood, one to call the gods together, when the goddess wanted to send them out to fulfil her wishes, the other to punish the disobedient.

Jambawat, in Hindû mythology, was an Avatar, an incarnation of the supreme god, in the form of a giant bear. Rama (an incarnation of Vishnu) appeared for the purpose of conquering Ravana, the giant king of Ceylon. The gods all supported the latter, with armies of apes, of bears, and other animals. Brahma gave the bears a king, Jambawat, who came out of the mouth of the god, and who possessed the spirit of Brahma. He now wished to make the expedition to Ceylon alone, but Krishna fought three days with him, until he recognised the supremacy of Vishnu (whose incarnation Krishna was). Then he followed Rama, with his entire army of bears, and assisted him in conquering Ceylon and its ruler.

James, John Thomas, D.D., an Anglican colonial bishop, was born in England in 1786. He was educated at the Charter House and at Christ Church, Oxford, became vicar of Flitton, Bedfordshire, and was elevated to the see of Calcutta. He arrived in that city, Jan. 15, 1828; on June 23 he set out on a visitation to the Upper Provinces of Bengal, and died while on his way to the island of Penang, Aug. 22 of the same year. Bishop James had acquired some celebrity as an author and traveller. He wrote *Journal of Travels in Germany, Sweden, Russia, Poland*, etc. (Lond. 1816, 4to): — *Views in Russia, Poland*, etc., prepared in colors:—*The Flemish, Dutch, and German Schools of Painting* (Lond. 1822, 8vo). See (N. Y.) *Christ. Journal*, 1829, p. 191; *Asiatic Journal*, April, 1829; *Penang Register*, Sept. 10, 1828; Lowndes, *Bibl. Manual*, s. v.; *Brief Memoirs of Bp. J. T. James* (Lond. 1830, 8vo); Darling, *Cyclop. Bib.* s. v.

James, William, D.D., a Presbyterian minister, was born in Albany, N. Y., in June, 1797. He received an academic and collegiate education, and was ordained about the 25th year of his age. He was pastor of the Second Presbyterian Church in Rochester, N. Y., from 1825 until 1830 or 1831, and then for a time of the Third Presbyterian Church in Montgomery Street, Albany. He died in 1868. See Munsell, *History of Albany*, iv, 10. (J. C. S.)

Jameson, GEORGE, an eminent Scotch portrait painter, was born at Aberdeen in 1586, and studied under Rubens and Vandyck. He died at Edinburgh, in 1644. The largest collection of his works are at Taymouth.

Jammabos, a Shinto order of mountain priests of Japan, are a kind of wandering monks, dependent on the benevolence of the people for subsistence; and from the circumstance that they go armed with swords or scimitars, they are sometimes called mountain soldiers. Their founder lived about the 6th century. He wandered about in deserts, and climbed the steepest mountains, subjecting himself to the severest privations. His followers, on entering the order, made a solemn vow to renounce all temporal advantages for the prospect of eternal happiness. In course of time they became divided into two orders, called *Tojunfa* and *Fonsaufa*. The former are obliged to go on a pilgrimage once a year to the mountain of Fikoosan (q. v.). The other order of Jammabos are obliged annually to pay a visit to the sepulchre of their founder, which is also situated on the top of a high and almost inaccessible mountain. In preparation for this hazardous undertaking, they practice frequent ablutions and severe mortifications. During their pilgrimage they eat only herbs and roots. On their return they go to Miaco, and present a gift to the general of the religious order to which they belong, who, in turn, bestows some honorable title on the pilgrim. At their original institution the Jammabos were *Shintoists*, but they have blended that form of religion with the worship of strange gods. See SHINTO.

Jammy, PIERRE, a Dominican of Languedoc, who died in 1665 at Grenoble, doctor of divinity, is best known as the editor of the works of Albertus Magnus (21 vols. fol. Lyons, 1651). See Winer, *Handbuch der theol. Lit.* i, 914; Jöcher, *Allgemeines Gelehrten-Lexikon*, s. v. (B. P.)

Jan, JOHANN WILHELM, a Lutheran theologian, was born Nov. 9, 1681. He studied at Wittenberg, was in 1713 professor of elocution, in 1714 of history, in 1719 doctor and professor of theology, and died Aug. 27, 1725. He wrote, *Judicia Eruditorum de Origine Electorum:—Historia Æræ Christianæ:—De Censu Romanorum Primo:—De Articulis Suobacensibus Augustanæ Confessionis Fundamento:—De Liturgiis Orientalibus in Doctrina de S. Eucharistia*, etc. See Jöcher, *Allgemeines Gelehrten-Lexikon*, s. v.; Winer, *Handbuch der theol. Lit.* i, 611. (B. P.)

Janes, Edwin L., a Methodist Episcopal minister, twin brother of bishop E. S. Janes, was born at Sheffield, Mass., April (his biographers say May) 27, 1807. He spent his boyhood near Salisbury, Conn., receiving the rudiments of an English education; was converted while teaching school in Columbia, N. Y.; and in 1832 entered the Philadelphia Conference. His appointments were, Asbury Church, West Philadelphia; Elizabeth, Plainfield, and Irvington, N. J.; Asbury Church, West Philadelphia; then to Haddington, Middletown, and Odessa Circuits, Del.; then Elkton and St. George's Church, Philadelphia; then was transferred to the New York Conference, and sent in turn to Mulberry Street Church; South Second Street, Williamsburgh; South Fifth Street (which was organized by him); Bridgeport and Middletown, Conn., in 1854 and 1855, presiding elder of New Haven District; South Fifth Street, Williamsburgh, three years; John Street and Forsyth Street, New York city; Flushing and Whitestone, L. I.; Summerfield Church, Brooklyn, in 1866; Central Church in 1867, and John Street, New York city, in 1868 and 1869, where he closed his pastoral life. In 1870 he was appointed district secretary or agent of the National Temperance Society and Publishing House, which office he held until his death, Jan. 10, 1875. Mr. Janes was among the foremost of saintly men; an unrivalled pastor; a man of extraordinary power in prayer; of rare eloquence in exhortation; an ingenious, instructive, effectual preacher; a sound theologian, and a devoted temperance worker. See *Minutes of Annual Conferences*, 1875, p. 51; Simpson, *Cyclop. of Methodism*, s. v.

Janes, Edmund Storer, D.D., LL.D., a bishop of the Methodist Episcopal Church, was born of highly respectable but not wealthy parents, at Sheffield, Mass., April 27, 1807. He was converted in 1820, and united with the Methodist Episcopal Church. From 1824 to 1830 he was engaged in teaching, during which time he studied law with the intention of making it the profession of his life; but in 1830 joined the Philadelphia Conference, and during the first few years of his ministry, in addition to his work as a minister and his theological studies, which were thorough if not broad, studied medicine. He was ordained deacon in 1832, and elder in 1834, and after filling various important charges was, in 1838, appointed agent for Dickinson College. In 1840 he was elected financial secretary of the American Bible Society; and in 1844 was elected to the bishopric in conjunction with bishop Hamline, they being the last of the bishops who received the vote of the undivided Church. For more than thirty-one years he discharged his duties in the episcopal office, travelling in all the states except Florida, and in most of the territories, besides being president of the Missionary Society, of the Board of Church Extension, and of the Sunday-school Union and Tract Society of the Methodist Episcopal Church, as well as being one of the managers of the American Bible Society, of the directors of the American Colonization Society, of the trustees of the Wesleyan University at Middletown, Conn., of the Drew Theological Seminary, and president of the Minard Home, Morristown, N. J. Bishop Janes was in many respects one of the most remarkable men in the history of American Methodism. He inherited the sterling mental and moral qualities of his Puritan ancestors; possessed a mind of a high order, enriched by generous culture, and disciplined by the severest training. He was a model platform speaker, ready, earnest, and impressive; a preacher of rare power, grasp, and eloquence; and an administrator of peerless activity, clearness, decision, patience, and comprehensiveness. He was a man of inflexible principle, thorough, conscientious, and untiring in labor and devotion; and a Christian of the purest humility. He died Sept. 18, 1876. See *Minutes of Annual Conferences*, 1876, p. 365; Simpson, *Cyclop. of Methodism*, s. v.; *Life*, by Dr. Ridgaway (N. Y. 1882).

Jangamas, a Hindû sect, the essential characteristic of which is wearing the Lingam (q. v.), or symbol of creative production, on some part of the dress or person. The type is of small size, made of copper or silver, and is commonly worn suspended in a case round the neck, or sometimes tied in the turban. In common with the worshippers of Siva generally, the Jangamas smear their foreheads with ashes, wear necklaces, and carry rosaries made of the *Rudráksha* seed. The clerical members of the sect usually stain their garments with red ochre. They are not numerous in Upper India; but in the south of India the Jangamas, or *Lingayets*, as they are often called, are very numerous, and the officiating priests of Siva are commonly of this sect. They are also represented as being very numerous in the Deccan. Besides the Jangama priests of Kedarnath, a wealthy establishment of them exists at Benares.

Jänisch, RUDOLPH, a Lutheran theologian of Germany, was born at Hamburg, May 22, 1750. He studied at Göttingen, was catechist in his native city, and in 1789 pastor of the Lutheran Church at Amsterdam. In 1796 he was recalled to Hamburg, and died April 7, 1826, pastor primarius of St. Catharine's. He wrote, *Cogitationes de Animi Humani Libertate* (Hamburg, 1770):—*Predigtentwürfe über die sonn- und festtäglichen Evangelien* (1797-1804, 8 parts). See Döring, *Die gelehrten Theologen Deutschlands*, s. v.; Winer, *Handbuch der theol. Lit.* i, 149. (B. P.)

Janoah, (1) OF EPHRAIM. Of *Khurbet Yanûn*, the modern representative of this place, the *Memoirs* accompanying the Ordnance Survey (ii, 395) give only this notice: "Traces of ruins above a spring." (2) OF NAPHTALI. The *Yanûh*, thought by some to represent this place, is a double village, nine and three quarter miles south-east from es-Zib (Ecdippa, or Achzib), which would fall on the border between Asher and Naphtali, and is thus described (from Guérin) in the *Memoirs* accompanying the Ordnance Survey (i, 193): "Cisterns cut in the rock, and many cut stones scattered over the soil, surrounding platforms or employed as building material, show that we are here on the site of a small ancient city, the name of which is faithfully preserved in its modern name." Lieut. Conder, however, distinguishes this locality from the Janoah of 2 Kings xv, 29 (see the *Memoirs* as above, i, 96; but no description of the place is given), which he regards as the *Janûh* lying four miles south of the Leontes (Nahr Kasimîyeh), and six and a quarter miles east of Tyre; but this would fall within the tribe of Asher.

Jansen (Lat. *Jansenius*), JACQUES, a Belgian theologian, was born at Amsterdam in 1547. He studied at Louvain, was in 1575 first president of the newly-founded Augustinian college, in 1580 professor of theology, in 1614 dean, and died July 30, 1625. He wrote, *Instructio Catholici Ecclesiastæ:—Enarratio in Exodi xv et Deuteron. xxxii:—Commentar. in Jobum:—In Nahum et Habacuc Prophetas:—In Cantica Canticorum:—In Psalmos Davidis:—In Evangelium Johannis.* See Andrea, *Bibliotheca Belgica;* Miræus, *Elogia Illustrium Belgii Scriptorum;* Jöcher, *Allgemeines Gelehrten-Lexikon*, s. v.; Lichtenberger, *Encyclop. des Sciences Religieuses*, s. v. (B. P.)

Jansens, ELINGA FRANCISCUS, a Dutch Dominican, who died in 1715, was one of the most famous canonists of his time. He wrote, *Autoritas D. Thomæ Aquinatis* (1604):—*Certissimum quid Certissimæ Veritatis pro Doctrina Doctoris Angelici:—Controversiæ in Hæreticos Opusculum* (Antwerp, 1673):—*Suprema Romani Pontificis Autoritas* (1689):—*De Romani Pontificis Autoritate et Infallibilitate* (1690):—*Forma et Esse Ecclesiæ Christi* (1702):—*Dissertationes de Principalioribus Quæstionibus hoc Tempore in Scolis Disputatis* (1707). See Lichtenberger, *Encyclop. des Sciences Religieuses*, s. v. (B. P.)

Janssens, Abraham, an eminent Flemish painter, was born at Antwerp in 1569, and at an early age executed a number of works for the churches of Flanders, which rank him among the ablest artists of the Flemish school. His paintings in the Church of the Carmelites at Antwerp, representing *The Virgin and the Infant*, and *The Entombment*, are highly commended. In the cathedral at Ghent is an *Ecce Homo*, and a *Descent from the Cross* worthy of Rubens himself. His masterpiece is the *Resurrection of Lazarus*, in the collection of the elector-palatine. He probably died in 1631. See Hoefer, *Nouv. Biog. Générale*, s. v.; Spooner, *Biog. Hist. of the Fine Arts*, s. v.

Janssens, Hans Herman, a Dutch theologian, was born in 1783, and died at Leyden in 1855, professor of exegesis and dogmatics. He published *Hermeneutica Sacra* (Liege, 1818, 2 vols.; Paris, 1851; Turin, 1858), a work which is held in high repute among Catholics, and has also been translated into French (Paris, 1827, 1833). See Lichtenberger, *Encyclop. des Sciences Religieuses*, s. v. (B. P.)

Janum. For this locality Conder suggests (*Tent Work*, ii, 337) the present *Beni Naîm*, which lies three miles east of Hebron (a position possible, perhaps, for the group of towns with which it is associated in the sacred text), with cisterns in the vicinity, and thus described (from Guérin) in the *Memoirs* accompanying the Ordnance Survey (iii, 325):

"Here I saw in many places ancient materials employed in Arab buildings. Several fragments of wall still upright in good cut stones attracted my attention. I visited a mosque which covers, according to the tradition of the people, the tomb of Lot. The coffin shown to me consists of a great wooden coffer, covered with a carpet, and probably contains the body of some modern santon revered under the name of Abraham's nephew. Around this sanctuary extends a court surrounded by a square gallery, which is itself enclosed by a wall built of stones belonging to different periods. On one of them I distinguished the trace of a mutilated cross, and one of the people told me that the mosque is supposed to have succeeded a Christian Church. It is at once a sacred edifice and a fortress, for the terraces which cover the gallery are provided with a parapet pierced with loopholes. . . . I was told by the sheik that the place used to be called *Kefr Bereik*, which confirms Robinson's identification of the place with Jerome's *Caphar Barnebo.*"

Janus, in Roman mythology, was a god, concerning whose original signification the most contrary views were held. The most commonly accepted view is that he was a deified king of ancient Italy. About his worship in Rome the following is related: Numa dedicated a sanctuary to his honor, which was opened in time of war and closed in time of peace. This goes to show that he was a god of war, as also his by-name "Quirinus." He is represented with a double face, sometimes with four heads. In his right hand he carried a staff (the symbol of augury), in his left a key (god of doors, for Janua signifies door). On his fingers the number three hundred was written on one hand, the number sixty-five on the other, designating him the god of the year.

Figure of Janus on an ancient coin.

Janvier, GEORGE WASHINGTON, D.D., a Presbyterian minister, was born of Huguenot descent at Cantwell's Bridge (now Odessa), Del., Jan. 22, 1784. In his twentieth year he joined the Presbyterian Church, and began his preparatory studies with his pastor, Rev. Dr. Read, and continued them at Princeton, but did not graduate. He was licensed by the Presbytery of New Castle, Sept. 26, 1810; spent one year in itinerant preaching; became pastor at Pittsgrove, N. J., May 13, 1812; and died there June 9, 1865. He was moderator of the Synod of New Jersey, and was a member of the Board of Foreign Missions. See Wilson, *Presb. Hist. Almanac*, 1866, p. 115.

Japan. This archipelago in eastern Asia consists of one large island, Hondo (*mainland* or *continent*), not called Nippon by the natives, but formerly so named by foreigners, three other large islands, Shikoku (*four provinces*), Kiushiu (*nine provinces*), and Yézo (*unexplored land*), a number of outlying islands, Sado, Oki, Iki, Tsushima, Awaji, Goto, etc., and the more distant groups, the Kuriles (*smokers*), Bonin (*no man's*), and Riu Kiu (*hanging fringe-tassels* or *sleeping dragon*), with nearly four thousand islets. The area of this empire, called by the natives Nihon or Nippon (*sunrise*), or Dai Nihon Koku (*great land of the sun's root*, or *origin*), is, by survey of 1874, 146,571$\frac{77}{100}$ square miles, and the population, by census of 1874, 33,623,373 souls. Hondo contains nearly 15,000,000 people, and, with the islands immediately south and next to it, may be called Old Japan (native Oyashima, *eight great islands*), because historically conquered and colonized in early times. New Japan comprises later acquisitions and colonies, such as Yézo and Riu Kiu.

The origin of the dominant race in Japan is not yet entirely clear to scholars, but traditions all point to Corea and northern Asia as the ancestral seats of that conquering race which, near the Christian æra, descended upon the land over which they saw the sun rise. They found other races on the soil whom they subdued. Many of the subjugated were doubtless of near Asian origin, like their conquerors, but there were also the straight-eyed, black-haired Ainos, who now occupy only Yézo and the Kuriles, whither they were in early times (from the 4th to the 13th century of our æra) driven. The conquerors, by the superior force both of their fetiches and dogmas, as well as of their valor, arms, and agriculture, made conquest only after long struggles. The farmers and warriors finally pacified the fishers and hunters, and established both their political rule and imported religion, Shintō, over "all within the four seas." The first mikado or emperor, deified as Jimmu Tennō (*heavenly king*), is said to have begun to reign B.C. 667, in his miya or palace-temple, near the miyako (*city*) of Kiōto—but of Japanese dates, until the introduction of almanacs and writing, with methods for keeping record of time, from China, in the 3d century and later, no one can speak with certainty, and Japanese traditions that antedate the Christian æra are chronologically worthless.

The first form of government was a rude species of feudalism, in which the mikado was suzerain, and his relatives or captains were rulers of the conquered land, which had been duly parcelled out into districts. This order of things continued until the 7th century, when the centralized system of pure monarchy, introduced from China, was carried out, and the mikado, as sole ruler, was assisted by six boards or ministries of government, and all provincial officers were appointed in and sent out from Kiōto. Several centuries were necessary to bring this method to perfection, and in the distant provinces military families who had kept the peace and put down insurrections at first made themselves necessary to the central government, and later, at the capital, transferred their energies to ambitious schemes in the palace itself. The introduction of Buddhism led the mikados to neglect the sceptre, and to become Buddhist monks, or live in gross licentiousness under cover of a professedly holy life. This paved the way for the rise of the shōguns (known later as kubo sama, "Tycoon," etc.), who gradually concentrated the powers of the executive in their own hands, while nominally the mikado was the fountain of honors. Exaggerating the mikado's "spiritual" importance for his own ends, the shōgun usurped the functions of military and civil administration, and held the army, the treasury, and the appointing power. Yoritomo, at Kamakura, in 1192, began the dual system of government, which, with slight intermissions, lasted until 1868, though Iyéyasu, at Yedo, in 1604, established the order of things in Japan with which, until 1868, foreigners have been most familiar. Side by side with this spectacle of two rulers and two capitals grew up the elaborate feudalism of Japan, which has so attracted the attention of students, and which in its perfected development was unique in Asia.

The story of the introduction of Portuguese Christianity into Dai Nippon, as given by professor Schem in volume iv, is in the main an admirable one. We note only the following needed corrections: Tanéga (*seed island*) for Yanega, Hidéyoshi for Fide Yose, Iyéyasu for Yie Yazoo, Hirado for Firando, Yedo for Yeddo, Bakafu for Rankfu, Isé for Isyay, Riobu for Ryoby, etc. We may add that, in 1877, most interesting relics—documents, books, tapestry—of the Japanese embassy to the pope were discovered, and that while in Japan, in 1873, the writer identified the place of imprisonment and burial of "Sedotti" (Jean Baptiste Sidotti), "the last Catholic priest" who, in 1709, landed in Japan, and "was never again heard of" until the Rev. S. R. Brown, D.D., unearthed the account of his inquisition and trial, written by a Japanese scholar. Further, the recently found correspondence of the Dutch superintendents of Déshima requires us to relieve the Hollanders of much of the odium resting on their names for assisting with cannon to crush the "Christian" insurrection at Shimabara, in 1627 (not "at the close of the 16th century"), in which very much fewer than seventy thousand "Christians" were either concerned or injured.

For two centuries and a half after the expulsion of the Romish priests, the supposed extirpation of Christianity, and sealing of all the doors of the empire against foreign influences, Japan rested in peace in the calm of despotism. But while the successors of Iyéyasu, in Yedo, supposed that the duarchy feudalism and national isolation were permanently established, great currents of thought began to move under the surface. These were finally to break out in floods that should sweep away the old and bring in a new æra never dreamed of by ancient or modern man in Japan. These movements were intended to effect the overthrow of the shōgun and his abasement as the emperor's vassal, the replacement of the mikado on his throne as sole ruler, the abolition of the feudal system, the disestablishment of Buddhism, and the restoration of Shintō as the state cultus. All was ready, or nearly so, for upheaval, when the squadron of American steamers, under commodore Matthew Calbraith Perry, swept into the bay of Yedo, July 8, 1853. After his treaty, and those made later by Townsend Harris, our consul-general, and European envoys, and the opening of the ports to foreign residence and commerce, the men who had wrought to undermine the shōgunate bent their energies to the expulsion of the foreigners and the dictatorial isolation of "the holy country" from the rest of the world. The advent of foreigners precipitated a crisis long preparing, and in the chaos of conflicting elements that kept the country in commotion from 1859 to 1870 foreigners resident on the soil could see little but the occasional outbursts of incendiarism, assassination, riots, and bloodshed, culminating in the civil war of 1868–70. In this the progressive party was successful. The mikado was reinstated to supreme power in the capital, which had been removed from Kiōto to Yedo (*bay-door*)—which received the new and more appropriate name, Tōkiō (*eastern capital*)—the office of shōgun was abolished, and its last incumbent retired to Shidzuoka (where he died in 1884), feudalism was abolished, and the three hundred or less petty territorial rulers or daimios were retired to private life in Tōkiō, the hereditary pensions of the military-literati, or idle privileged classes, were capitalized and extinguished, society was reconstructed on the simplified basis of "the three classes," nobles, gentry, and common people. From the centralized government in Tōkiō now proceeded the most radical measures of reform, political, social, and moral, which, in their rapidity and frequency, served to show that the mikado's advisers were making all haste to be "civilized." The goal of their agonizing race was the equality of Japan among the nations of Christendom, and the abolition of the odious extra-territoriality clause from the treaties. Dependence was not placed alone upon development of industrial and military resources, although these were carefully attended to, and wisely, for new Japan was not yet purged of the old spirit of feudalism. Several insurrections had to be quelled, one of them, the Satsuma rebellion in 1877, being on a scale which threatened for a time the very existence of the government, and cost the country twenty thousand lives and a hundred million dollars. By means of telegraphs, steamers, improved rifles, ships, and cannon, backed by the valor of peasant conscripts, led by officers of modern education, peace was won after seven months' war. Political education by means of newspapers (now two thousand in number in Japan, or more than in both Spain and Russia) and debating-clubs proceeded apace, resulting finally in the establishment of local assemblies, a franchise based on property qualification, and the solemn oath-bound promise of the mikado that, in 1890, a national parliament should be formed, and the government (changed from absolute despotism) become a limited monarchy. And this in Asia! Such is the political outlook in Japan. Let us now glance at her religious condition.

When the treaties lifted the seals from the closed doors of the empire, and missionaries from the three great divisions of the Christian Church entered Japan, the Roman Catholics searched at once for, and soon found, remnants of the 17th century converts, numbering in all probably five thousand. Preserving a few Latin words of sacred import, and some of the characteristic forms of the Roman ritual, with here and there an image or picture of the Virgin or of Jesus, these descendants of the martyrs were, despite their debased and half heathenish condition, *Kiristans.* With this advantage of historic continuity the Roman Catholics began their work simultaneously with the Russo-Greeks and American Protestants. Persecutions soon broke out, and were carried on both by the old shōgun's and the new mikado's government. The writer has a vivid recollection of seeing, on a bitter cold winter's day, in the mountains of Echizen, a gang of these wretched prisoners roped together and led by jailers while tramping in the snow to their place of duress in the volcano craters of Kaga. The intercession of diplomatists, and especially of the Rev. G. F. Verbeck, then the trusted servant of the government, and president of the Imperial University of Tōkiō, finally stopped these inhuman proceedings. Fear of the censure of Christian nations, and their threatened final refusal to expunge the extra-territoriality clause from the treaties, have compelled the Japanese to cease from persecution in every form. In 1872 the anti-Christian edicts, which, since 1600, had denounced "the corrupt sect," and promised rewards to informers, were removed. Later, both Buddhism and Shintō were disestablished, the department of religion was abolished, and the vexatious burial laws repealed, "and thus it has been brought to pass that Christianity has been, by the action of the Japanese government itself, placed upon a footing of perfect equality with the old-established and recognized religions of Japan. In other words, within twenty-five years from the first Protestant mission in the empire, Christianity secures a position before the law which it gained in ancient Rome only after the delays and persecutions of over three centuries."

About thirty Protestant missionary societies now have representatives in Japan, most of them from America. In addition to the usual methods of missionary work by the foreign teachers, the Japanese themselves carry on matters pretty much in their own way. Almost every form of Christian effort in vogue among us is quickly adopted by the Japanese brethren. Preaching services held in public halls and theatres by a number of speakers during several days in succession are very popular and effective. Social meetings for the promotion of harmony and Christian fellowship are frequently held in individual churches or unitedly by different churches or denominations. The Japanese are good public speakers, enjoying the privilege of a participation in social worship, and being emotional and sympathetic. There are few of those pauses of dead silence which so afflict our own meetings for prayer. The telegraph, now ramifying throughout Japan, often bears such messages as these, "Konnichi Mitami Kudari, Kitokwai furuu" (today the Holy Spirit has come down, and the meetings are full of fervor). Prayer-meetings held exclusively for and by women, scripture-reading leagues, young men's Christian associations, popular lecture courses, and religious periodicals, edited by native Christians, supplement the foreign missionary's work, and that of the American, Scotch, and Bible societies, and thus fill the whole land with light and truth. Old missionaries declare that the native Church members, who are very apt at first to join the Church from intellectual conviction, show a most cheering growth in spiritual knowledge. The preaching of the young licentiates or pastors, at first dealing almost exclusively with morality, becomes more spiritual, Christ and his cross being the prominent theme. The complete New Test. has now been in the hands of the Japanese for five years, and the year 1886 will, D. V., see the completed Bible in their homes. The Scriptures are published in three styles of print and diction, so that all classes may read them. Ninety thousand copies and portions of the Scriptures, and one hundred and sixty thousand tracts were distributed by the tract societies last year. Turning away from China as the mother country of knowledge and inspiration, the Japanese now look to Europe and America. A company of literary men and scholars are endeavoring to do away with the use of Chinese ideographs, and to print books and newspapers in the Roman character. Familiarity with their own phonetics, or syllabary of forty-eight letters, makes the final adoption of the Roman alphabet easy. The *Romaji-kai* is the newspaper in which they are showing how a native boy may now learn to read better in ten months than he could of old in ten years.

Much of the literary, social, political, as well as moral progress made by the Japanese, results either directly or indirectly from missionary labor, suggestion, or stimulus. In addition to their preaching, teaching, translation, and healing, they have conferred upon natives and foreigners alike a lasting benefit of incalculable importance by their aids to the mastery of the language, and their other publications. The following statistics of Christianity in Japan are from the paper read before the Osaka Conference in April, 1883:

	Protestant.	Roman Catholic.	Greek.
Bishops	—	3	—
Missionaries	145	43	5
Priests (Japanese)	—	—	11
Ordained Ministers	49	—	—
Unordained Evangelists, Catechists, etc.	100	202	106
Bible women	37	—	—
Converts	4987	26,180	8863
Contributions	$12,064	—	$4373
Schools:		3	—
Theological	7	71	—
Students	71	74	—
Mixed	39	2920	—
Scholars	1520	—	—
Boys'	9	—	—
Scholars	454	—	—
Girls'	15	—	—
Scholars	556	—	—
Sunday	109	—	—
Scholars	4132	—	—
Organized churches	93	—	148
Churches or chapels	—	80	—
Preaching places	?	—	281
Hospitals	5	—	—
In-patients	795	—	—
Dispensaries	8	—	—
Patients	24,898	—	—

Of the dangers that beset the churches of Christ in Japan we do not here speak, but refer the reader to the following recent works for a more thorough study of the country and people, and the work for Christ in the sunrise kingdom.

Literature.—Transactions of the Asiatic Society of Japan (1874–85), vol. i–xiv; Léon Pagés, *Histoire de la Religion Chrétienne au Japon;* Griffis, *The Mikado's Empire* (New York, 1876; 4th ed. 1884); *Corea, the Hermit Nation* (ibid. 1882); Bird, *Unbeaten Tracks in Japan* (ibid. 1881); Rein, *Japan* (ibid. 1884), and the works of baron De Hubner, E. Warren Clark, E. J. Reed, Isabella Carruthers, W. Gray Dixon, Henry Faulds, and others. (W. E. G.)

Japanese Version OF THE SCRIPTURES. The honor of translating the first portion of Scripture into the language of the extensive empire of Japan belongs to the late Dr. Gützlaff (q. v.). About the year 1835 three shipwrecked Japanese mariners arrived at Macao on their voyage homewards, and during the few months that they remained in that city Dr. Gützlaff availed himself of their aid in translating the gospel of John into their language. This translation was printed at Singapore about 1838. In this version the word used for God was *Gokuraku*, the term the Buddhists use for paradise or the state of supreme bliss. For *Logos* or the Word he used *Kashikoi mono*, the wise or clever person; for Holy Spirit, *Kami*. While in England Dr. Gützlaff proposed, in 1849, to the British and Foreign Bible Society, to have the Scriptures printed in the Japanese tongue. The Acts of the Apostles and the epistles of John were consequently printed according to Gützlaff's translation.

As the style of his version was found inferior, and little likely to prove acceptable to the better educated in Japan, a new translation was undertaken by Dr. Bettelheim, a medical missionary and convert from Judaism. He was sent to the Loochoo islands in 1846, and while there made a translation of the New Test. While in Hong Kong he published the gospel of Luke, under the care of the bishop of Victoria, and at the expense of the Society for Promoting Christian Knowledge. It was printed on blocks, in royal octavo size, with Gützlaff's Chinese translation at the top of the page, and Bettelheim's, in the Loochoo dialect, at the bottom, in Katakana, or the character used for scientific works. When Bettelheim left Japan in 1854 he took up his residence in Chicago, and from this place he offered, in 1860, to sell his translation to the United States government. The government, wishing to know its merits, sent a copy of one of the gospels and a grammar he had compiled to its minister resident in Japan, Mr. Harris, to be examined by scholars there and reported on. Mr. Harris not knowing what better to do, sent it to Drs. Brown and Hepburn, two missionaries, but whether from the peculiarities of the dialect, or out of very imperfect knowledge of the Japanese language at that early day of their residence there, they could not make anything out of it. So it was returned to Mr. Harris with an unfavorable report. Dr. Bettelheim, however, revised his work in Chicago, with the assistance of a Japanese, bringing it more into conformity with the pure Japanese. This revision, consisting of the four gospels and Acts, was offered to the British and Foreign Bible Society, and purchased by them. It was printed at Vienna in 1872 for that society, in the Hiragama character, which is more generally understood in Japan than the Kantakana, in which it was written.

This publication was the only direct effort made by that society as a temporary measure until something better could be prepared. The committee appointed by the missionary convention commenced its sittings in June, 1874. There were invited to meet and participate in the work of translation the Rev. R. S. Maclay, of the American Episcopal Mission; Rev. N. Brown, D.D., of the American Baptist Mission; the Rev. John Piper, of the Church Missionary Society; and the Rev. W. B. Wright, of the Society for the Propagation of the Gospel. Mr. Piper and Mr. Wright, owing to their residing at such an inconvenient distance, could not meet the committee. Dr. Nathan Brown sat with the committee about eighteen months, until January, 1876, when he resigned, and continued to prosecute the work of translation alone. The other members of the committee continued at the work of translation and revision with but slight interruption, Dr. Maclay being absent about eighteen months, owing to other duties, and Dr. Brown being compelled through ill-health to cease work in July, 1879. The committee finished their work of translation and revision of the New Test. Nov. 3, 1879, about five years and six months after they had commenced. The work was cut on blocks and published in the following order: Luke, August, 1875; Romans, March, 1876; Hebrews and Matthew (revised), January, 1877; Mark (revised), April, 1877; epistles of John, June, 1877; Acts, September, 1877; Galatians, January, 1878; John, gospel (revised), May, 1878; 1 Corinthians, August, 1878; 2 Corinthians, September, 1878; Ephesians, Philippians, 1st and 2d Thessalonians, June, 1879; Philemon, James, 1st and 2d Peter, Jude, Colossians, Revelation, April, 1880. As to the literary style of the translation—a matter of no small importance—the following statement, made by the Rev. Dr. J. C. Hepburn on the occasion of celebrating the completion of the Japanese version of the New Test., April 19, 1880, at Tokio, will be of interest:

"In this country, where, from the earliest times, the Chinese language and literature has had such a powerful influence upon the cultivation and language of the people, it was, at the very first, a matter of considerable anxiety in what literary style our work should be brought out to make it most acceptable and useful. The conclusion was not difficult to arrive at: that—avoiding on the one hand the *quasi*-Chinese style, only intelligible to the highly educated, scholarly, and comparatively very small portion of the people; and on the other hand, a vulgar colloquial, which, though easily understood, might make the Scriptures contemptible—we should choose that style which, while respected even by the so-called *literati*, was easy and intelligible to all classes. We thus adhered to the vernacular, or pure Japanese, and to a style which may be called classical, in which many of their best books intended for the common reader are written. And our more enlarged experience has given us no reason to regret our first determination, but rather to be more and more satisfied with it, and to believe that in this, as well as in many other matters, we have been under the guidance of a kind and all-ruling Providence."

The committee had assistance from several Japanese scholars, among whom Mr. Okuno and Mr. Matsuyama are mentioned. Of the latter it is said, "He has been with the committee from the first and throughout its whole work. He has been our chief dependence, assistant, and arbiter in all cases of difficulty. Whatever virtue there is in our Japanese text, it is mainly, if not altogether, owing to his scholarly ability, the perfect knowledge he has of his own language, his conscientious care, and identifying himself with the work." At present the New Test. is circulated in Japan in the following editions:

1. *The Standard, or Kanamejiri, New Testament.*—This is a republication of the New Test. completed in 1880, with such changes as the translation committee finally decided upon.

2. *The Romanized New Testament;* or, *Warera no shu Iyesu Kirisuto no Shin Yaku zen sho.*—This is the Japanese of the Standard New Test., in Roman letter. The transliteration was done by Dr. Hepburn. The *Daily Gazette* of Yokohama, Oct. 16, 1880, has the following notice concerning the editor: "The labors of this modest but excellent philanthropist and Japanese scholar in the causes of learning and Christianity in Japan are well known. His dictionary, Japanese-English and English-Japanese, was the first work of its kind published in this country, and notwithstanding the more elaborate and copious contribution of Mr. Satow, it still retains its high rank for accuracy and general usefulness. In the midst of other occupations, Dr. Hepburn has found time to add to his literary reputation a complete Romanized version of the New Test., a piece of work which can be but imperfectly estimated by its extent, which embraces six hundred and fifty-three closely printed royal octavo pages.

"Of the quality of the translation we do not feel competent to form an opinion. Dr. Hepburn's close association with the gentlemen who undertook the work is itself a guarantee of excellence; but we may, at a later time, have occasion to notice it critically.

"The American Bible Society is to be congratulated on this valuable addition to its library, and the thanks of all who desire the promotion of good works are due to those whose labor has yielded this good fruit."

3. *The Common Reader's, or Sohirakana, New Testament.*—In this the common cursive Japanese character is used, almost alone, with but very few Chinese characters. It is intended to meet the wants of the most illiterate. The first volume will appear in a few days, and the entire work will be finished, we hope, before the close of the year. It will be a volume slightly thinner than the Standard New Test. The Rev. Mr. Knox, of the Presbyterian Mission, has kindly superintended the proof-reading.

4. *The Shinkatakana New Testament.*—In this style the angular Japanese *kana* are used, with many Chinese characters. It is thought that this will be the favorite edition with the scholarly classes. It is of just about the same size as the Standard, and its cost and selling price will be the same. The proof-reading of this work has been under the supervision of Dr. Hepburn.

5. *The Chino-Japanese, or Kunten, New Testament and Psalms.*—The New Test. was prepared by the Rev. D. C. Greene, D.D., and the Psalms by the Rt. Rev. W. C. Williams, D.D. This is an adaptation of the Bridgman and Culbertson Chinese translation for the use of Japanese readers. In the words of Dr. Greene, "The word *kunten* is the name given to the diminutive characters written on the right side of the Chinese ideographs. These, which consist for the most part of the Japanese phonetic characters, serve to supply the terminations of the Japanese verbs and such particles as are not found in the Chinese construction. Besides the *kunten*, there are certain numerals and arbitrary signs placed on the left of each column, which indicate the Japanese order of thought. By the insertion of these marks, this book becomes substantially a translation into Japanese of the Chinese version above mentioned."

A commencement with the translation of the Old Test. into Japanese has also been made. Delegates of the Protestant missions in Japan met in Tokio, May 10, 1878, to consider principally plans for translating the Old Test. A permanent translation committee was arranged for, to consist of one member from each mission, to be elected by the mission itself, who are to assign the work of translating the different portions of the Old Test. to various sub-committees; and the results of their labors are to be submitted to a general revising committee, to be appointed by the permanent committee. The revision committee is made up of Drs. Hepburn,

Brown, Maclay, and the Rev. Messrs. Green and Piper. As to the progress made in the Old Test. translation, we learn from the different reports of the British and Foreign Bible Society that most of the books have been translated, and that some have already been printed. Besides the reports of the British and Foreign Bible Society, compare also the *Bible Society Record* of the American Bible Society. (B. P.)

Japhia. Its modern representative, *Yâfa*, lies one and a half miles south-west of Nazareth. It contains no ancient remains, except a few broken columns, and about thirty cisterns. For a description of the numerous grain-pits cut in the rocks see the *Memoirs* accompanying the Ordnance Survey, i, 353 sq.

Jarmuth OF JUDAH. The modern representative of this place, *Khurbet el-Yarmûk*, lies one and a half miles north-west of Beit-Nettîf, of which the *Memoirs* to the Ordnance Survey give only this meagre description (iii, 128): "Heaps of stones, foundations, and cisterns," with a reference to "section A, Jarmuth," which contains no allusion to it.

Jarrom, WILLIAM, an English Baptist minister, was born at Ely Place, Wisbeach, Cambridgeshire, July 29, 1814. After leaving school he spent some time in study at home, and in teaching the classics. He was for some time pastor of a church at Northampton, where he also conducted a school. He resigned his pastorate in 1841, but continued his school until he went as a missionary to China in 1845. While there, he labored at Ningpo with much success. He returned to England in 1851, and settled at Isleham in 1852. He removed to Kegworth in 1856, where he opened a boarding-school, and preached frequently. In 1868 he went to Barton as co-pastor, and in 1874 to West Vale, near Halifax, as pastor. He finally removed to Coningsby, near Boston, Lincolnshire, where he taught and preached until a few days before his death, Feb. 28, 1882. See *Baptist Hand-book* for 1883, p. 266.

Jattir. The modern representative of this, *Khurbet Attir*, lies four and a quarter miles south-east of ed-Dhoheriyeh, and nine and three quarter miles north of Tell Milh (Moladah), and is thus described in the *Memoirs* accompanying the Ordnance Survey (iii, 408): "Foundations, and heaps of stones; a great many caves; a ruined masonry tomb; several fallen pillar-shafts and cisterns. There is a kubbeh [dome] at the ruin, which stands on a knoll. Many of the caves have masonry arches to the doors. A large building remains, four courses of the wall being left. Below the ruins on the hill-side is a large oil-press."

Jaubert (*De Barrault*), JEAN, a French prelate and theologian, was the son of Emeri, count of Barrault, and studied at La Flèche, both philosophy and theology, as an abbot of St. Pierre de Solognac, in the diocese of Limoges. He was consecrated bishop of Bazas at Rome, in August, 1612. Two years afterwards he was at the assembly of the clergy at Paris. He had been designated as grand-almoner to Henrietta Maria of France, queen of England, but the Protestants succeeded in preventing him from getting that position. In 1630 he was appointed archbishop of Arles. He presided over the assembly of the clergy, in 1635, at Paris, where he died, July 30, 1643, leaving *Erreurs et Faussetés Remarquables* (Bordeaux, 1622-31). See Hoefer, *Nouv. Biog. Générale*, s. v.

Jauk (or **Yauk**), one of the five deified men mentioned in the Koran as having been worshipped by the ancient Arabians. They are supposed to have been antediluvians who had been distinguished for their virtues. The Arabians represent Jauk under the figure of a horse.

Javanese Version OF THE SCRIPTURES. The language spoken on the island of Java is, next to Malayan, which is distinct from it, the most polished and most cultivated of Polynesian dialects. Since A.D. 1400, when the Javanese embraced Mohammedanism, many Arabic words have been adopted, by which the native deficiency of the dialect in abstract terms has been in some measure supplied. There are two principal styles of language, called *boso kromo* and *boso ngoko*. The *boso kromo* is the higher style, used in addressing persons of superior rank, etc.; and the *boso ngoko* is the lower style, used in addressing persons of lower rank; it is also found sometimes in older writings, and in narratives, etc.

The preparation of a Javanese version was first suggested by Dr. Wm. Hunter, of Calcutta, in 1812. When the Java Bible Society was formed, in 1814, the translation was one of the first things considered, but the language was found very difficult of acquirement to Europeans. At length the Rev. Gottlob Brückner, a native of Germany, stationed as minister of the Dutch Church at Samarang, undertook the difficult task. In 1820 he commenced the translation of the New Test., which was printed in 1831 at Serampore. The translation of the Old Test. was undertaken by the Rev. Mr. Gerické, a missionary of the Netherlands Society. In 1831 he completed a version of the Psalms, which he sent to Holland, to the Netherlands Society, for publication.

Mr. Gerické also made a fresh translation of the New Test., on the basis of the preceding. The printing was conducted at the Hague, under the eyes of the translator, Professor Roorda assisting him in the correction of the proof-sheets. The revised New Test. was issued in 1848, and in 1857 the Old Test. was also published, under the auspices of the Netherlands Society. Of late, however, the British and Foreign Bible Society has undertaken to publish a revised edition, at the request of the Rev. P. Jansz of Djapara, supported by Mr. Haffenden, the society's agent in Singapore. "The people of Java," the report of the British and Foreign Bible Society for 1883 states, "are said to number 19,000,000. Of these 8,000,000 are Javanese, 8,000,000 Sundanese, and 3,000,000 Malays. From many sources the committee learn that the existing version of the Bible is full of errors, some of which give a false meaning to the passages in which they occur, and that for practical purposes it is almost worthless. Mr. Haffenden has returned from a journey in Java, where he found the want of an intelligible version of the Scriptures." This induced the British and Foreign Bible Society to authorize the Rev. Jansz, who for over thirty years has been a missionary in Java of the Baptist Society for the Propagation of the Gospel in the Netherland Colonies, and who, besides, is the author of a Javanese Grammar and Dictionary which have reached a third edition, and of several religious books in the Javanese tongue, to prepare a new version. In this work of retranslation Mr. Jansz has the aid of two educated native Christians. In its revised form the gospel of Luke was printed at Singapore in 1884. See *Bible of Every Land*, p. 369. (B. P.)

Jawas were the physicians, priests, and advisers of the small kings among the nations inhabiting Florida. They claimed to have converse with the spirits.

Jawinna, in Lettian mythology, was a friendly goddess of the ancient heathen Prussians, who blessed the sown fields with fruitfulness.

Jay, GUIDO MICHAEL LE. See LEJAY.

Jean. See JOHN.

Jeaurat, EDME, an eminent French engraver, was born in Paris about 1680, and studied under Bernard Picart. The following are some of his best works: *The Meeting of David and Abigail; John the Baptist Baptizing the Jews; The Interview between Jacob and Rachel; The Finding of Moses.*

Jebis (or **Jebisu**), in Japanese mythology, was the younger brother of the sun deity, but because he was ill-formed he was cast off by his parents. He lived by fishing, and amassed great wealth. After his death he was worshipped as god of the sea, and as one of the seven gods of wealth. He is represented as the god of waters, the protector of sailors and fishermen, sitting on a lotus-flower, or on a rock, with a line and a fish in his hands.

Figure of Jebis.

Jechiel, in the Talmud, is the supreme genius of the good genii ruling the animal kingdom. Subordinate to him are Pasiel, Gaviel, and Chamiel.

Jechiel DE PESARO. See PESARO, JECHIEL.

Jechiel NATHAN. See NATHAN BEN-JECHIEL.

Jedaja PENINI. See PENINI, JEDAJA.

Jehud. The probable representative of this place *el-Yehudiyeh*, eight and a quarter miles south by east from Yafa, is described in the *Memoirs* accompanying the Ordnance Survey (ii, 258) as "a large mud village, supplied by a pond, and surrounded by palm-trees. Mr. Drake states the population at 800 to 1000 souls. According to the Samaritans, Judah (Neby Hûdah) was buried here."

Jehuda BEN-ELIEZER, a Jewish writer of the 14th century, is the author of מִנְחַת יְהוּדָה, or a commentary on the Pentateuch, in which he especially explains difficult passages of Rashi. This commentary, in which more than one hundred Jewish authorities are quoted, was published at Leghorn in 1783. See Fürst, *Bibl. Jud.* ii, 34; De' Rossi, *Dizionario Storico* (Germ. transl.), p. 141. (B. P.)

Jehuda BEN-ILAÏ, a Tanaite of the 2d century, and teacher of the famous Judah hak-Kodesh (q. v.), was a cooper by trade. While he spent his days in manual labor, he spent his nights in persevering study. After attaining the degree of rabbi, he still labored at his trade. So far from being ashamed of this, he gloried in it, and used sometimes to have a tub or hogshead of his own workmanship brought into the lecture-room, which he used as a pulpit. His honest integrity procured him the title of *ha-chasid*, or "the Just." In the department of Scripture exposition he paid particular attention to the third book of Moses, or Leviticus, and it is considered that the book "Sifra" was first composed by him, though more fully elaborated afterwards. See Hamburger, *Real-Encyklop.* ii, 452 sq.; Bacher, *Die Agada der Tanaïten* (Strasburg, 1884), p. 101, 128, 199, 235, 246, 267, 291, 441. (B. P.)

Jehul, according to the Talmud, is the supreme genius of the genii ruling the fire. Subordinate to him are Seraphiel, Gabriel, Nuriel, Tamaël, Shimshiel, Hadarniel, and Sarniel.

Jeitteles, JUDA LÖW, a Jewish author, born in 1773, and died at Vienna, June 6, 1838, is the author of מְבוֹא לְשׁוֹן אֲרָמִית, or a grammar of the Aramæan language (Prague, 1813); besides, he translated into German, Job (Vienna, 1834), the Twelve Minor Prophets (1835), Chronicles (eod.), Samuel (1833), Ezekiel (1835), Daniel, Ezra, Nehemiah (eod.), which he published with his own comments. See Fürst, *Bibl. Jud.* i, 52. (B. P.)

Jejeebhoy, *Sir* JAMSETJEE, a Parsee philanthropist, was born in Bombay, July 15, 1783. He made voyages between India and China, and amassed a large fortune, possessing at his death about $4,000,000. As early as 1822 he released the debtors confined in the jail by paying their debts; and his donations to public objects were estimated at about $1,500,000. He received the honor of knighthood from Queen Victoria in 1842, and a gold medal in 1843. He endowed hospitals, schools, medical institutions, and other benevolent establishments. A school at Bombay for the education and support of poor Parsee children he endowed at an expense of $250,000. He built comfortable places of refuge for the convenience of travellers in various parts of the country, the causeway which unites the islands of Bombay and Salsette, the water-works at Poonah, the bridges at Earla, Parta, and Bartba, and many other public works. In 1857 he was advanced to the dignity of a baronet. He died at Bombay, April 14, 1859. A statue was erected to his memory in the town-hall of Bombay, and exposed to view Aug. 1, 1859. See Appleton's *Amer. Cyclop.* s. v.

Jejumi (*figure-treading*) is a ceremony observed annually among the Japanese, of trampling upon the crucifix, and images of the Virgin Mary and other saints. It was designed to express the abhorrence of the Japanese for the religion which the Jesuits had tried to introduce into their empire. The images were about a foot long, cast in brass, and kept in a particular box for the purpose. The ceremony took place in presence of the street officers. Each house was entered by turns, two messengers carrying the box. The images were laid upon the bare floor, and the list of the household being called, they were required in turn to tread upon them. Young children, not yet able to walk, were held in their mothers' arms, so as to touch the images with their feet.

Jekire, an evil spirit among the Japanese, which they expel by exorcism.

Jelf, RICHARD WILLIAM, an English clergyman, was born in London in 1798, and educated at Oxford, where he graduated in 1820, and became a fellow of Oriel College and a tutor. In 1826 he became preceptor in the royal family. He was made canon of Christ Church in 1831, Bampton lecturer and principal of King's College, London, in 1844. He died in Oxford, Sept. 19, 1871. Among his published works are, *Sermons, Doctrinal and Practical* (1835):—*The Means of Grace* (Bampton Lectures, 1844):—and a new edition of the *Works of Bishop Jewel* (1847-48, 8 vols.).

Jemma, the judge of the wicked after death, among the Japanese, who beholds in a large mirror all the most secret transactions of mankind. Intercession by the priests with Amidas in behalf of the sinner, and liberal presents on the part of his relatives, are sure to release him before the expiration of the allotted time for punishment. The figure of Jemma, the king of the devils, is monstrous; and on each side of him are two large devils, one acting as his secretary, and registering in a book all the sins of mankind, while the other dictates what the secretary is to record. This idol is situated in a temple of Jemma, a short distance from Miaco, in a delightful grotto. The walls are covered with frightful pictures of tortures which the wicked are supposed to undergo. This temple is resorted to by crowds of people from all parts of the country, with oblations and money in their hands, to redeem the souls from dreaded punishments. See JAMA.

Jemshid, in Iranian history, the mythical hero who led the Aryan tribes in their first emigration to Asia, and who taught them the arts of civilization. He is said, however, to have taught them idolatry also. His real name was *Yima-Khacta*.

Jenichen, GOTTLOB FRIEDRICH, a Lutheran theologian of Germany, was born March 26, 1680, and died at Leipsic, Sept. 17, 1735, professor of ethics. He is the author of *Historia et Examen Bullæ Clementis XI contra Quesnelium Emissæ* (Leipsic, 1714). See Winer, *Handbuch der theol. Lit.* i, 652. (B. P.)

Jenings, SAMUEL, a distinguished minister of the Society of Friends, was born at Coleshill, Buckinghamshire, England, about 1650, and emigrated to New Jersey in 1680, having for some time been an approved minister in his denomination. Soon after his arrival he was appointed by governor Byllinge, of New Jersey, as his deputy. This position he occupied until 1683, when the Provincial Assembly chose him governor of the colony for one year. Up to the time of his removal to Philadelphia, in 1692, he occupied the highest offices in the province. In Pennsylvania his abilities were highly appreciated, and he was nominated to the commission of the peace. When the controversy arose with George Keith (q. v.) he became one of his most zealous and active opponents, and in the early part of 1694 sailed for London as respondent in the appeal of Keith to the London Yearly Meeting, where he ably vindicated the cause of his American brethren from the aspersions of their detractor. On returning from England he removed from Philadelphia to Burlington, his former home in New Jersey. In 1702 he was appointed a member of the Provincial Council, and in 1707 was elected speaker of the assembly, "in which station he distinguished himself by a bold and fearless opposition to the arbitrary misrule of the bigoted lord Cornbury." In his spiritual vocation we are told that he was "an able minister of the gospel, and labored much therein, to the comfort and edification of many people, both in the province of New Jersey and other places. He was one of those rare individuals in whom was concentrated a variety of qualifications and mental endowments, by which, under the sanctifying power of truth, he was made eminently useful to his fellow-men, both in his ministerial and civil capacity." He died at Burlington in 1708. See Bowden, *Hist. of Friends in America*, ii, 254. (J. C. S.)

Jenkyn, T. W., D.D., a Welsh Congregational minister, was born in South Wales in 1796. He gave early evidence of earnest piety; began to preach while in his youth, studied at Homerton College, and settled first at Oswestry in 1823. While in that border-town of his native country he published *The Extent of the Atonement*, by which he acquired both literary and theological celebrity, and which led to his being appointed to the theological chair, eventually to the presidency, of Coward College. Meanwhile he removed to Stafford, and there wrote and published *On the Union of the Holy Spirit and the Church in the Conversion of the World.* In 1837 he relinquished his charge in Stafford, and, proceeding to Germany, formed friendships with the distinguished theologians of that country. When Coward College was amalgamated with Highbury and Homerton colleges, in 1850, Dr. Jenkyn's services were no longer required. Being anxious to do good, he went to Rochester, to establish a new interest in that town, and after a short visit to America returned and labored there to his dying day, May 26, 1858. Dr. Jenkyn was social in his habits, an impassioned lover of music, and no less enthusiastic in his devotion to theological science. See (Lond.) *Cong. Year-book*, 1859, p. 203.

Jennings, OBADIAH, D.D., a Presbyterian minister, was born near Baskengridge, N. J., Dec. 13, 1778. He was educated at Jefferson College, Cannonsburg. Pa. He studied law for some years, and was admitted to the bar in 1800. He joined the Presbyterian Church in 1811, was licensed to preach in 1816, by the Presbytery of Ohio, and soon afterwards accepted a call to the Presbyterian Church in Steubenville, O., where he labored with great fidelity and success for six years, and then accepted a call to Washington, Pa. In 1828 he removed to Nashville, Tenn., where he remained till the close of his life, Jan. 12, 1832. See Sprague, *Annals of the Amer. Pulpit*, iv, 549.

Jenny, ROBERT, LL.D., a Protestant Episcopal clergyman, son of archdeacon Jenny of Waneytown, in the north of Ireland, arrived in America in 1715, as a missionary of the Society for Propagating the Gospel, having been appointed assistant to the Rev. William Vesey, rector of Trinity Church, New York city. In 1722 he was transferred to Rye, and remained there until 1728, when he assumed charge of the church in Hempstead, L. I. In November, 1742, by license of the bishop of London, he became rector of Christ Church, Philadelphia, which post he held until the close of his life. His ministry covered fifty-two years. He died in January, 1762, aged seventy-five years. See Sprague, *Annals of the Amer. Pulpit*, v, 16.

Jericho. For a description of *Tell es-Sultan*, supposed to be the site of the ancient city, see the *Memoirs* accompanying the Ordnance Survey (iii, 222). The following account of the locality in general is from Conder, *Tent Work*, ii, 2 sq.:

"Reaching Jericho we were again disappointed. The long groves, which appear so charming at a distance, are entirely composed of thorny shrubs. The *dôm* or *zizyphus* grows into a tree, with small green leaves and formidable prickles; the *nebk*, another species, forms long hedges of brier, of which it is said the cruel 'crown of thorns' was woven, for which reason it is called *spina Christi.* The

Jericho, now Er-Riha. (From Thomson's *Southern Palestine and Jerusalem*).

zakkûn, or balsam-tree (*balanites*), is equally thorny, and beneath these grow poisonous nightshade and other noxious plants. The distant beauty of the groves is only a mockery, and the environs of Jericho, when reached, are as stony and unlovely as any other part of the country.

"Yet, in some respects, the place is still charming. Here, late in autumn, the sound of running water and the song of birds greeted our ears. Among the high mounds, or *tellûl*, bare and dusty, a fresh, beautiful stream was flowing from 'Ain es-Sultân, the site of the first Jericho. The great spring wells up in a stony pool, under a high hillock, and opposite to this tell is a jungle crowned by a very large castor-oil tree and other thick foliage. In this grateful shade the birds have found a retreat. The great gray shrikes (*Abu Zereik*) sit on the top branches, and the queer 'hopping thrushes,' with their tails stuck up like rapiers, bound about beneath. The bulbul also sings in the groves—a gray bird with a black head and a curious yellow patch at the root of the tail. Still more beautiful are the great Smyrna kingfishers (*Abu Nukr*), in their blue coats and chocolate-colored waistcoats, white-throated, with bills like red sealing-wax; and the gray African species (*Abu Kubeia*), which also flutters above the stream. Last, but not least, come the lovely sun-birds (*Suweid*), peculiar to the Jordan valley, darting about like little black wrens, but resplendent, when seen close, with all the colors of the prism. . . .

"There is only one natural position for a large town in the plains of Jericho, namely, the neighborhood of the beautiful fountain called 'the Sultan's Spring,' near the foot of the Quarantania precipice. Nothing can well explain the choice of a new position, but the fact that Jericho was cursed by Joshua, and that the curse was fulfilled. Thus it is by the spring that we naturally place the Jericho of Joshua's time, and this view receives confirmation from the account of the flight of the spies 'to the mountain;' for if situated in the immediate vicinity of the great crag of Kŭrŭntŭl, the city was so near that the fugitives might easily have crept through the cane jungle and thorn-groves to the shelter of one of the innumerable caverns in the face of its precipices.

"Of ancient Jericho nothing now remains but the bright spring, and the shapeless mound above it. We can hardly wonder at this when we find that even the Jericho of Herod has disappeared, and that only a vague conjecture can be made as to the position of Thrax and Taurus, the great towers which once defended it. It seems probable that this second town stood south of ancient Jericho, and even closer to the hills, for the great aqueduct which brought water, a distance of four miles, from the fine spring at the head of the wild Kelt chasm, leads just to the opening of the plain, and seems to be the only one of the numerous aqueducts which dates back to Roman times. At the mouth of the pass, also, is the rock fort called Jubr or Chubr, in which title we may recognise, as my companion, Mr. Drake, pointed out, a relic of the name Cupros, which was given to a tower above Herod's Jericho.

"Jerome tells us that there were in his day two Jerichos, and in A.D. 333, the anonymous pilgrim of Bordeaux found a town at the foot of the pass. Here also we have remains of a bridge which has the *opus reticulatum* of Roman masonry, and this, with a few strewn fragments and with two great mounds of sun-dried brick, seems all that is left of the second Jericho. The Byzantine, or 4th-century town, mentioned by Jerome as the second Jericho, is no doubt represented by the foundations and fragments of cornice and capital, over which the rider stumbles among the thorn groves east of the 'Ain es-Sultân.

"By A.D. 700 Jericho had again disappeared, and thus, in the 12th century, we find the site once more moved. The modern Erîha then springs into existence near a square tower, such as the Crusaders erected along their pilgrim roads, and a tradition of the 'Garden of Abraham' comes into existence as early as the time of Sæwulf (A.D. 1102). In the 14th century sir John Maundeville finds Jericho a little village, and Abraham's garden is then stated to be at the foot of the Quarantania. Fetellus makes the distance between Jericho and the latter mountain two miles, and thus it is pretty clear that the modern Erîha represents the site which was created in the Crusading period."

Jerusalem, Synod of, 1672. Of all synods which were held at Jerusalem since the apostles' time, this is the most important. The doctrines of Cyril Lucar (q. v.) were condemned by his successor, Cyril of Berrhoë, at the Council of Constantinople in 1638, and again by the next patriarch, Parthenius, at the Synod of Jassy in 1642. The metropolitan of Kiew, Petrus Mogilas, also found it necessary to protest against these doctrines; and his confession, *ὀρθόδοξος ὁμολογία τῆς πίστεως τῆς καθολικῆς καὶ ἀποστολικῆς ἐκκλεσίας τῆς ἀνατολικῆς*, was sanctioned, in 1643, by the patriarchs of Constantinople, Alexandria, Antioch, Jerusalem, and Moscow. Thus an effective barrier was erected against the Calvinistic invasions of the orthodoxy of the Eastern Church. Nevertheless, both the Reformed and the Roman Catholic theologians continued to hint that the Greek Church was leaning respectively either this or that way. In the controversy between the Reformed minister, Jean Claude, and the Jansenists, Nicole and Arnauld, concerning the eucharist and transubstantiation, the former alleged, in support of his views, the dogma of the Eastern Church, such as it appeared in its oldest form, and such as it had been revived by Cyril Lucar; while the latter appealed to the dogma of the Eastern Church in its œcumenical form. In 1660 the patriarch of Jerusalem, Nectarius, published a book against Claude, and in 1672 his successor, Dositheus, convened a synod at Jerusalem for the purpose of still further defending the orthodoxy of the Eastern Church. The synod was attended by sixty-eight representatives, and resulted in the so-called *Shield of Orthodoxy*, March 20, 1672, one of the most important confessional works of the Eastern Church, the full title of which is, *Ἀσπὶς ὀρθοδοξίας, ἢ ἀπολογία καὶ ἔλεγχος πρὸς τοὺς διασύροντας τὴν ἀνατολικὴν ἐκκλησίαν αἱρετικῶς φρονεῖν ἐν τοῖς περὶ θεοῦ καὶ τῶν θείων, ὡς κακοφρονοῦσιν οὗτοι αὐτοὶ οἱ Καλουῖνοι δηλονότι.* The first part is directed against the Calvinists, and contains a strong condemnation of the views ascribed to Cyril Lucar, and at the same time an adroit vindication of him personally, flatly denying that he ever held such opinions, ever wrote the books containing them, etc. The second part is critico-dogmatical, and presents a full confession of the Orthodox Greek faith in the form of a refutation of the theses of Cyril. This second part, or *σύντομος ὁμολογία*, treats in eighteen *decreta* and four *quæstiones* the following subjects: 1. Trinity; 2. The holy Scriptures and their interpretation by the Church; 3. Predestination; 4. Origin of the evil; 5. Relation of divine Providence to the evil; 6. Original sin; 7. Incarnation of the Son of God; 8. The mediatorship of Christ and the saints; 9. Faith acting in charity; 10. Church and episcopacy; 11. Church membership; 12. Infallibility of the Church; 13. Justification by faith and works; 14. Ability of the natural and of the regenerated man; 15. Seven sacraments; 16. Infant baptism; 17. Eucharist; 18. State after death. The four *quæstiones* are: 1. Can all Christians read the Bible? 2. Is the Bible conspicuous for all? 3. What constitutes the holy Scriptures? (acceptance of the apocryphal books); 4. What is to be believed concerning images and veneration of the saints? The synodical acts were first published in Greek and Latin, Paris, 1676, and again in 1678. The best editions are found in Harduin, *Acta Concil.* xi, 179 sq., and in Kimmel, *Monumenta Fidei Eccl. Orientalis* (Jena, 1850). See also Gass, *Symbolik der griechischen Kirche* (Berlin, 1872), p. 79 sq.; Schaff, *Creeds of Christendom*, i, 61-67; Plitt-Herzog, *Real-Encyklop.* s. v. (B. P.)

Jerushalmi Tanchum. See Tanchum of Jerusalem.

Jervis, William Henley, a minister of the Church of England, was born in 1813, and educated at Harrow, where he won some of the first prizes in the school at the unusually early age of fifteen, and at Christ Church, Oxford, where he took a second class in 1835. He was for some years rector of St. Nicholas, Guildford, and held, up to his death, a prebendal stall at Heytesbury—abolished by recent legislation, so that the dignity died with him, Jan. 27, 1882. Mr. Jervis, who took his wife's name some years ago, was a son of the late dean Pearson of Salisbury, and elder brother of canon Pearson of Windsor. To the general public he is best known as the author of a learned and interesting work on the *History of the Church of France, from the Concordat of Boulogne to the Close of the First Empire* (London, 1872-82, 3 vols.). (B. P.)

Jeshua. For this Biblical site Lieut. Conder proposes (*Tent Work*, ii, 338) the ruin and tell *es-Saweh*, four and a quarter miles north-west of Tell-Milh (Moladah), which is thus described in the *Memoirs* accompanying the Ordnance Survey (iii, 409): "A prominent hill-top, crowned with ruins, consisting of foundations and heaps of stones. The hill is surrounded by a wall built of large blocks of flint conglomerate. Other rocks of a similar kind exist in the valley beneath." The place proposed by Schwarz is probably *Eshua*, one and a half miles north-east of Surah (Zorah), and two and a quarter south-west of Kesla (Chesalon), "a small village near the foot of the hill, with a well to the west, and olive-trees beneath" (*Memoirs* to Ordnance Survey, iii, 25); but this is probably Eshtaol (q. v.).

Jeshua (*ha-Lewi*) BEN-JOSEF, a Jewish writer of the 15th century, is the author of הֲלִיכוֹת עוֹלָם, or a methodology of the Talmud (Constantinople, 1510, and often since). It was translated into Latin by L'Empereur, under the title, *Clavis Talmudica* (Leyden, 1635); also by Bashuysen, *Clavis Talmudica Maxima* (Hanau, 1714); and by Struve, *Logicæ Hebraicæ Rudimenta* (Jena, 1697). See Fürst, *Bibl. Jud.* ii, 64 sq. (B. P.)

Jesseans, according to Epiphanius, a name given to the early Christians, either from Jesse, the father of David, or, more probably, from the name of the Lord Jesus.

Jesse's Tomb is traditionally shown in a corner of a ruined monastery on the hillside between Hebron and Abraham's Oak (Conder, *Tent Work*, ii, 84).

Jesu dulcis memoria. See BERNARD OF CLAIRVAUX'S HYMNS.

Jeter, JEREMIAH BELL, D.D., a Baptist minister, was born in Bedford County, Va., July 18, 1802. His early education was limited. He was converted in 1821; began to preach in 1822; was ordained May 4, 1824, at High Hills Church, Sussex County, where he remained about two years; then removed to Campbell County, and became pastor of the Hill's Creek and Union Hill churches. In the autumn of 1827 he was installed pastor of Morattico Church, in Lancaster County, and subsequently of the Wicomico Church, in Northumberland County. In the latter part of 1835 he was called to the pastorate of the First Baptist Church in Richmond, where for thirteen years and a half he was eminently successful. In the fall of 1849 he was called to the Second Baptist Church in St. Louis, where he remained three years, and then returned to Richmond to become pastor of the Grace Street Church. He resigned in 1870. He became the senior editor of the *Religious Herald*, the leading organ of the Baptist denomination in the south, in 1866, and occupied that position till the close of his life, Feb. 18, 1880. Among the books of which he was the author were, *Memoirs of Rev. A. W. Clopton:—Memoirs of J. L. Shuch, Missionary to China:—Memoirs of Rev. Andrew Broaddus:—Memoirs of Rev. Daniel Witt:—Campbellism Examined:—Campbellism Re-examined*, both of these works placing Dr. Jeter among the first polemic writers of his times. The *Christian Mirror* and the *Seal of Heaven* were published by the American Tract Society. See the *Religious Herald*, Feb. 26, 1880. (J. C. S.)

Jethlah. For this place Lieut. Conder suggests (*Tent Work*, ii, 338) *Beit Tûl*, a ruined site four and a quarter miles south-east of Yalo (Ajalon), containing "foundations and a Mukam" (*Memoirs* to Ordnance Survey, iii, 86).

Jezreel. *Zer'in*, the modern representative of this noted place, is briefly described in the *Memoirs* accompanying the Ordnance Survey (ii, 88), but more graphically by Conder (*Tent Work*, i, 124):

"Crossing the valley, we see before us the site of Jezreel, on a knoll five hundred feet high. The position is very peculiar, for while on the north and north-east the slopes are steep and rugged, on the south the ascent is very gradual, and the traveller coming northwards is astonished to look down suddenly on the valley, with its two springs, one ('Ain Jâlûd) welling out from a conglomerate cliff, and forming a pool about one hundred yards long, with muddy borders; the other ('Ain Tub'aûn), the Crusaders' Fountain of Tubania, where the Christian armies were fed 'miraculously' for three days on the fish which still swarm in most of the great springs near.

"The main road ascends from near these springs and passes by the 'Dead Spring,' which was reopened by the governor of Jenîn, and now forms a shallow pool between rocks of black basalt, covered with red and orange-colored lichen, and also full of little fish; thence it passes on the east side beneath the knoll of Zer'în (Jezreel) to the plain on the south. Climbing up to the village, we are again struck by the absence of any traces of antiquity; the buildings, including the central tower, are all modern, and only the great mound beneath, and perhaps some of the innumerable cisterns, seem ancient; yet the site is

Jezreel. (From Thomson's *Central Palestine and Phœnicia.*)

undoubted, and has never been really lost. Here, from a tower, perhaps standing where the modern one is erected, the watchman could see down the broad valley of Jezreel as far as Bethshan, and watch the dust and the gleam of the armor advancing. The course of the two horsemen and of Jehu's chariot was distinctly seen beneath the hill, and the distances are sufficiently extensive to give time for the succession of events.

"On the east and south-east there are rock-cut winepresses on the rugged hills, where no doubt the 'portion of the field of Naboth' and his vineyard are to be placed —a good instance of the decay of vine cultivation in Palestine."

Jidsin-Jombaja, in Lamaism, was a young, beautiful god, a Burchan, assistant or friend of Jakshiamuni, when the latter founded his religion. He usually is placed beside the statue of the supreme god in the Lama temple, and is represented as a very soft, feminine personage, with four arms, the body light-yellow color, the dress blue. Jidsin-Jombaja was instructor of astrological and other secret sciences, and taught the wise men in these branches.

Jijelia (or **Jiemona**), in Slavonic mythology, was a youthful goddess of hunting, comparable in many things to Diana of the Romans, but wanting the hostile attributes of the latter. She was regarded as a friendly companion, and as giving success in hunting. She subdues the wild animals, drives the reindeer within range of the hunter, and favors the most courageous and most worthy; hence many young people, whose family relations were not positively known, were called her sons and daughters, in case they were beautiful and daring. She is also said to have been the goddess of love, at least, she was implored by the Slavs for children, unless she is mistaken for the similarly named Jijindla, who was worshipped as the goddess of marriage.

Jilsbog was a Wendian and Slavic deity, representing the moon, with a half-moon on the breast, and the arms raised in the form of a half-moon. He was also a god of time (his name is from *Jas*, "time"), because the Wends measured their time according to the moons.

Jinas, saints among the Jainas (q. v.) in India. A saint is called a *Jina*, as being the victor over all human passions and propensities. He is supposed to possess thirty-six superhuman attributes, four of which regard his person; eleven refer to his supernatural powers; while the remaining nineteen are of celestial origin, as the raining of flowers and perfumes, the sound of heavenly drums, and the menial offices rendered by *Indra* and the gods. The Jinas are twenty-four in number, and, although similar in their general character and attributes, are distinguished from each other in color, stature, and longevity. Two of them are red, two white, two blue, two black, the rest are of a golden hue, or a yellowish brown. In regard to stature and length of life, they undergo a gradual decrease from Rishabha, the first Jina, who was five hundred poles in stature, and lived 8,400,000 great years, to Mahavira, the twenty-fourth Jina, who had degenerated to the size of a man, and was not more than forty years on the earth.

Jins (i. e. *genii*), according to the Mohammedans, an intermediate race between angels and men. They are said to be made of fire, but with grosser bodies than the angels, to propagate their species, and, though long-lived, not to be immortal; also to have inhabited the earth previous to Adam, under a succession of sovereigns. Mohammed professed to be sent as a preacher to them as well as to men. In the Koran there is a chapter bearing their name, in which they are introduced as saying: "There are some among us who are upright, and there are some among us who are otherwise: we are of different ways, and we verily thought that we could by no means frustrate God in the earth, neither could we escape him by flight; therefore, when we heard the direction, we believed therein. There are Moslems among us, and others who swerve from righteousness."

Jirsik, Johann Valentin, a Roman Catholic prelate of Bohemia, was born June 19, 1798. In 1881 he was made bishop of Budweis, in Bohemia, and died Feb. 23, 1883. He is the author of *Populäre Dogmatik oder Glaubenslehre der katholischen Kirche*, edited by B. Schön (4th ed. Vienna, 1865):—in the Bohemian language Jirsik published *Twenty Friendly Letters Addressed to the Protestants in Bohemia* (1842). See Zuchold, *Bibl. Theol.* i, 679 sq. (B. P.)

Jisu, a god among the Japanese, whose office it is to convey souls to the infernal regions.

Joachim of Korsun, the first bishop of Novgorod. He was commissioned, in 992, by the metropolitan of Kiew, Leonce, with evangelizing the northern part of Russia, and has the honor of having planted Christianity there, and having founded the Church of St. Sophia, at Novgorod, where he died in 1030, after a useful episcopate. See Hoefer, *Nouv. Biog. Générale*, s. v.

Joan of Valois, *Saint* and *queen*, was the daughter of Louis XI of France and Charlotte of Savoy, and was born in 1456. She was plain in face and somewhat deformed, and her father, who wished a son, treated her with contempt. This dislike increased, until on one occasion the king rushed into the room to kill her, and her life was only saved by the countess of Linierès. In her twelfth year Joan was married against her will to duke Louis of Orleans, who also treated her with coldness and contempt. Louis XI died in August, 1483, and his son succeeded him as Charles VIII, under the regency of his elder sister Anne. The husband of Joan, thinking the regency ought to have been intrusted to him, endeavored to stir up an insurrection, was unsuccessful, and fled to Francis II of Brittany the bitter foe of France. War broke out, and Joan stood as an angel of peace and reconciliation between the contending parties. Twice she obtained pardon for her captured husband, and he as often returned to his perfidy. After the death of Charles VIII, April 7, 1498, the duke of Orleans ascended the throne as Louis XII. He at once obtained a divorce from pope Alexander VI, by taking an oath that his marriage with Joan was not complete. He gave her the duchy of Berry and Pontoise. She resided at Bourges, where she spent time and revenues in the exercise of charity. In 1500 she founded the order of the Annunciation for women. Joan took the habit herself in 1504, but died Feb. 4, 1505, and was buried at Bourges. Her body was torn from its resting-place in 1562, and burned by Calvinists. She is commemorated in the French martyrology on Feb. 4. Her canonization began under Clement XII, and was completed by Pius VI, in 1775, but she was venerated at Bourges from the time of her death. See Baring-Gould, *Lives of the Saints*, ii, 109.

Joasaf I, the fourth Russian patriarch, was elected Feb. 6, 1634, and died Nov. 28, 1642. He left a ritual, containing the synodal statutes of his predecessor Philaret. See Hoefer, *Nouv. Biog. Générale*, s. v.

Joasaf II, the sixth patriarch of Russia, was raised to that dignity Dec. 29, 1667. He assembled, in the first year of his patriarchate, a council to anathematize the sectaries; at this council were present Païsi, the patriarch of Alexandria and Macarius of Antioch; its principal motions are inscribed in the Slongebuik, or missal of 1668. There are extant of his works, a pastoral letter (1668):—another directed to the sectaries, entitled *Gezl Pravlenia* (reprinted in 1753):—an *Instruction on the Manner of Painting the Images* (1668):—and another on *The Manner of Behaving One's Self at the Church* (reprinted at Moscow in 1786). He died Feb. 17, 1672. See Hoefer, *Nouv. Biog. Générale*, s. v.

Jobson, Frederick James, D.D., a minister of the Wesleyan Methodist Connection, was born July 6, 1812, at Lincoln, England. He was converted in his eighteenth year, received on trial by the conference, and appointed to the Patrington Circuit in 1834. He soon became known and highly esteemed as a man of superior gifts and excellent spirit. He was a representative of the Wesleyan Church to American Methodism in 1855, and to Australia in 1860. He filled the appointment of book steward fifteen years, and was elected president of the conference in 1869. In 1880 he became a supernumerary, and died at Hull, Jan. 4, 1881. Dr. Jobson published *Chapel and School Architecture* (1850):—*America and American Methodism* (1857):—*Australia, with Notes by the Way of Egypt* (1862). As a preacher, his fine natural temper, his sound judgment, combined with a most vivid imagination, his cultivated taste, and intense earnestness fitted him for that extensive usefulness which, by the grace of God, he achieved. His talents were much in request for funeral sermons and memorial tributes for his brethren in the Methodist body. Three of such productions, to the memory of the Rev. J. Bunting, D. J. Draper, and Dr. Hannah, were published separately. See *Minutes of the British Conference*, 1881, p. 27.

Joceline, a Scotch prelate, was elected bishop of the see of Glasgow in 1174, and consecrated by Eskilus, archbishop of Lunden, in Denmark, June 1, 1175, in Charavalle. He died at Melrose in 1199. He enlarged the cathedral of Glasgow, and is said to have rebuilt it in the same state it continues, and dedicated it in 1197. See Keith, *Scottish Bishops*, p. 235.

Jocelyn (or **Joceline**) OF WELLS, an early English prelate, was born and educated at Wells, Somersetshire, of which he became the bishop in 1206, and was the first to fix the title of Bath and Wells to the old see of Glaston. The monks of Glastonbury purchased their exemption from the territory of the see by parting with four manors to the new diocese of Wells. Jocelyn, with archbishop Langton, was banished on account of obstinacy against king John. After five years exile in France he returned to his see, and devoted himself to the beautifying and enriching of his cathedral. He erected some new prebends, and to the use of the chapter appropriated many churches, increasing the revenues of the offices, and he gave three manors to the episcopal see. He, with Hugo, bishop of Lincoln, was the first founder of St. John's, in Wells, and at his own cost built a chapel at Wokey, and another at Wells. The cathedral of Wells was his masterpiece, however. He died Nov. 19, 1242. See Fuller, *Worthies of England* (ed. Nuttall), iii, 93.

Jocelyn, GEORGE BEMIS, D.D., a Methodist Episcopal minister, was born at New Haven, Conn., Jan. 3, 1824. Shortly afterwards, with his parents, he removed to Cincinnati, and from thence, in 1830, to New Albany, Ind., where he was converted at the age of fourteen. In 1842 he graduated at Indiana Asbury University. He was licensed to preach in 1843, and in the same year was admitted to Indiana Conference, and appointed to Paoli Circuit. In 1844 he was sent to Rockport, where his health soon failed; at his own request he was discontinued, and, removing to Vincennes, Ind., opened a select school. A few months later in the same year he was placed in charge of the preparatory department of Vincennes University, which position he held till September, 1849, when he returned to New Albany and opened the De Pauw Female College. In 1853 he was elected professor of mathematics and natural science in Whitewater College, and in 1855 to the presidency of the same institution. Failure of health led him to spend 1856 as agent for a western railway company, and for the Northwestern University. In 1857 he was transferred to Iowa, and appointed to Fifth Street Church, Des Moines; in 1859 to Zion Church, Burlington; and in 1861 was elected president of Iowa Wesleyan University at Mount Pleasant, serving meantime as pastor of University and Asbury Chapel. In 1864 he was elected president of Albion College, Mich., and transferred from the Iowa to the Detroit Conference. Resigning his presidency in 1869, he was transferred to the Michigan Conference, and stationed at Division Street, Grand Rapids. In 1871 he was re-elected president of Albion College, which office he sustained till his death, Jan. 27, 1877. Dr. Jocelyn possessed large natural endowments, intellectual and spiritual, which he patiently and thoroughly cultured, placing him in the foremost rank of instructors of his age. As a preacher he had few superiors in power of thought, perspicuity of style, and impressiveness of manner. See *Minutes of Annual Conferences*, 1877, p. 105; Simpson, *Cyclop. of Methodism*, s. v.

Jochanan, Isaac *ha-Lewi*. See ISAAC LEVITA.

Jochanan, Salomo, a convert from Judaism, was a native of Posen. In 1657 he was baptized at Dantzic, was in 1659 professor of Hebrew there, and died July 1, 1683. He published, *Programma de Jubilæis Hebræorum* (Dantzic, 1658):—*Demonstrationes* 38, *Jesum Christum Verum et Æternum Messiam Esse* (Frankfort, 1660):—*Der verheissene Messias* (Dantzic, 1683):—*Zertheilte Finsterniss, oder Widerlegung des Buches Fajjumi's von Israels Erlösung* (1681). See Fürst, *Bibl. Jud.* ii, 97. (B. P.)

Joel, David, a Jewish writer, was born at Schwerin, in the duchy of Posen, in 1813. After having completed his studies he was rabbi at Schwersentz and then at Krotoschin. In 1879 he was called to the Talmudic chair of the Rabbinical Seminary at Breslau, where he died, Sept. 8, 1882. He is the author of מדרש הזהר, or *Die Religionsphilosophie des Sohar* (Leipsic, 1849). (B. P.)

Joel, Heymann, a Jewish rabbi, who died at Hirschberg, in Silesia, Dec. 20, 1884, published, *Das Prinzip der Patriarchen* (Düsseldorf, 1857):—*Festpredigten für die hohen Festtage des Jahres* (2d ed. Hirschberg, 1872). (B. P.)

Joga, in Hindûism, is the world's age, according to which the whole Indian chronology is regulated. The earth, according to this system, stands 12,000 divine years, of which each contains 360 common years, together, 4,320,000 of our years. These 4,000,000 years are divided into four Jogas, which have their particular names. The first is called Krita-Joga, and lasts 4000 divine years; the second, Treta-Joga, lasting 3000 divine years; the third, Dwapar-Joga, lasting 2000 divine years; and the last is called Kali-Joga. In this we live, and it lasts 1000 divine years. Between each of these Jogas there is a twilight period, after the first, of 800 divine years, after the second, of 600 divine years, after the third, of 400 divine years, after the fourth, of 200 divine years. This entire period is called Maha-Joga, or Sadir-Joga. 1000 Maha-Jogas are 4,320,000,000 of our years, and this makes one day of Brahma. The night is equally long, together, 8,640,000,000. In this night all things are dissolved until Brahma wakes up and re-enlivens them. Such a Sadir-Joga, taken 360 times, forms a year of Brahma, namely, 3,110,400,000,000 of our years. Brahma lives 100 such years, namely, 311,040,000,000,000. After Brahma's death an equally long period of destruction follows. After 622,080,000,000,000 years Brahma comes to life again, and the circle of days and nights begin anew. The last-mentioned figure forms a day of Vishnu; 360 of these days form one of his years. His life lasts 100 such years, making a round sum of 22,394,880,000,000,000,000. Probably Shiva would have a still longer life had the Shivaites not made their god immortal.

Figure of Joguegeir.

Jogi, in Hindûism, are penitents who torture themselves, either for money or as an act of piety, in the most severe manner.

Joguegeir, in Hindû mythology, is the principal enemy of the eastern Buddha, and seems to be identical with *Dewadet*. He is represented as a child, wound about by an angry snake; although it seems not to be the child, but the snake, that is the evil dæmon, for Krishna killed the monstrous snake Kalinak, as a child, by treading on its head.

Jogues, Isaac, a French Jesuit missionary, was born in Orleans, Jan. 10, 1607. He entered the Jesuit school at Rouen in 1624, studied theology in Paris, and took orders in 1636. He was sent as a missionary to Canada the same year, and reached Quebec July 2. He labored earnestly among the Hurons and Dinoudadies for several years. In 1642, in company with father Raymbault, he went to Sault Ste. Marie to establish a mission among the Algonquins. He returned to Quebec with a party of Hurons for supplies for the mission, and on his way back fell into an ambuscade of Iroquois, when almost the whole party was killed and Jogues taken prisoner. He was now subjected to the most cruel treatment, and afterwards condemned to death. He became aware of his impending fate through the Dutch citizens of Albany, and effected his escape. He made his way to New Amsterdam (New York), and from there sailed to Europe. He returned to Canada in 1644, and in 1646 went with M. Bourdon to confirm the peace in the Mohawk castles. Peace being established, he set out, Sept. 27 of the same year, to found a Mohawk mission, but was put to death by the Mohawks at Caughnawaga (now Fonda), N. Y., Oct. 18, 1646. A *Life of Jogues*, by the Rev. Félix Martin, appeared at Paris in 1873.

Johannsen, Johann Christian Gottberg, a Lutheran theologian, was born June 20, 1793, at Nortorf, Holstein. In 1818 he was preacher at Glückstadt, was called in 1825 as pastor primarius of St. Peter's at Copenhagen, and died in 1858, doctor of theology. He published, *Aufschwung zu dem Ewigen* (Altona, 1820, 2 parts):—*Ueber die Grundsätze eines Lehrbuches der christl. Religion* (ibid. 1823):—*Religionsvorträge für denkende Verehrer Jesu* (ibid. 1828, 2 parts):—*Untersuchung der Rechtmässigkeit der Verpflichtung*, etc. (ibid. 1833):—*Die Anfänge des Symbolzwanges*, etc. (Leipsic, 1847):—*Die augsburgische Confession* (ibid. eod.). See Zuchold, *Bibl. Theol.* i, 624 sq.; Winer, *Handbuch der theol. Lit.* i, 337, 473, 751; ii, 16, 74, 100, 180, 234; Fürst, *Bibl. Jud.* ii, 99. (B. P.)

John is the name of several early Scotch prelates:

1. Consecrated bishop of the see of Glasgow in 1115. Some time after he made a visit to the Holy Land. He rebuilt and adorned the cathedral church, and consecrated it in July, 1136; divided the diocese into two archdeaconries of Glasgow and Teviotdale, set up the offices of dean, subdean, chancellor, treasurer, sacrist, chantor, and succentor, and settled a prebend upon each of them out of the donations he had received from the king. He was witness to a charter of St. David's to the monastery of Newbottle in 1140. He died May 28, 1147. See Keith, *Scottish Bishops*, p. 232.

2. A monk of Sais, in Normandy, and bishop of the see of the Isles about 1151. See Keith, *Scottish Bishops*, p. 297.

3. Consecrated (with Hugh) bishop of St. Andrews in 1178. See Keith, *Scottish Bishops*, p. 12.

4. Bishop of Caithness in 1185, and witness to king William in a donation to the abbey of Kinloss, at the time when Hugo was chancellor of the kingdom. See Keith, *Scottish Bishops*, p. 206.

5. Bishop of Galloway in 1189. He became a monk of Holyrood House in 1206, and died in 1209. See Keith, *Scottish Bishops*, p. 272.

6. Bishop of Aberdeen about 1200, and such in 1201. He died in 1207. See Keith, *Scottish Bishops*, p. 105.

7. Probably bishop of the Isles in 1226. See Keith, *Scottish Bishops*, p. 299.

8. Bishop of Dunkeld in 1356, and was still such in 1365. See Keith, *Scottish Bishops*, p. 84.

9. Probably bishop of the Isles about 1388. See Keith, *Scottish Bishops*, p. 304.

10. Bishop of Ross in 1420, and witness in the same year to a resignation made by William Graham of his barony of Kerdale into the hands of Thomas, earl of Moray. See Keith, *Scottish Bishops*, p. 189.

11. Bishop of the Isles about 1490, and privy-councillor to king James IV, from whom he received the abbacy of Icolumkill in 1507. See Keith, *Scottish Bishops*, p. 305.

12. Bishop of Argyle in 1499. See Keith, *Scottish Bishops*, p. 288.

13. *Joannes Electus Sodoren*, sat in the Parliament in 1524. See Keith, *Scottish Bishops*, p. 306.

John of Chur (surnamed *Rütberg*). From the beginning of the 14th century we often meet in the mystic writings of South Germany with the name of *Friends of God* (q. v.). One of them was John of Chur, the son of a rich merchant. Suddenly arrested in a wild career, he gave himself up entirely to mystical contemplations. He renounced all his fortune, to which he had fallen heir by the death of his father, and distributed it for benevolent purposes. He regarded suffering as a special gift of divine grace, and even evil thoughts, doubts, and impure desires he believed were to be patiently endured rather than striven against, for they were dispensed by God. He taught that the perfect man "has become one with God, when he wants nothing else except what God wills." About the year 1357 he sought to unite his friends who were of the same spirit into a society. From indications in his writings we conclude that Chur, or Coire, in the canton of the Grisons, Switzerland, was his native city. In 1365 he determined to separate himself from the bustle of the town, and in company with two friends, led by a little black dog, they went into a mountain, where they built a chapel. By and by they were joined by two others, and of these "five men," John of Chur speaks in a separate treatise. He probably died in 1382. His writings consist of letters and tracts. See Acquoy, *Het Klooster te Windesheim en Zijn Inoloed* (Utrecht, 1875); Preger, in the *Zeitschrift für die historische Theologie* (1869), i, 109 sq., 137 sq.; *Der Gottesfreund im Oberland und Nikolaus von Basel*, in the *Historisch-politische Blätter* (Munich, 1875), lxxv; *Der Gottesfreund im Oberland*, in the *Jahrbuch für schweizerische Geschichte* (Zurich, 1877); *Besuch eines Cardinals beim Gottesfreund im Oberland*, in the *Theolog. Quartalschrift* (Tübingen, 1876), iv; Jundt, *Les Amis de Dieu au Quatorzième Siècle* (Paris, 1879); Plitt-Herzog, *Real-Encyklop.* s. v. (B. P.)

John "the Constant," elector of Saxony (1525–32), one of the most zealous of the princely supporters of the Reformation, was born at Meissen, June 30, 1468. He early imbibed a love for a military life, and in several campaigns under Maximilian I, against the Hungarians and Venetians, displayed great decision and courage. When the Reformation struggle began he was already fifty years of age, but followed it up from the very beginning, and with his son, John Frederick, soon became a follower of Luther, of whose sermons he often took notes. He bade the priests of his realm preach the gospel and administer the sacraments according to the institution of Christ. At the diet of Spires, in 1526, he openly espoused the cause of Luther, in connection with the other evangelical princes. He was threatened by a league of Catholic princes, formed at Breslau in 1528, with exile from his land and people unless he delivered up Luther and restored the old order of things. He expressed his refusal to comply by marshalling his troops, which, however, it did not become necessary to use. At the second diet of Spires, in 1529, he signed a protest against the action of the majority, which forbade all religious innovations or discussions on the mass until the convention of an œcumenical council. He acknowledged obedience to the emperor, except where it conflicted with the honor of God and the salvation of souls. At the diet of Augsburg, in 1530, his conduct was heroic. In spite of all personal annoyances he stood firmly by the side of the evangelicals. In 1531 he entered into a league of defence with the evangelical princes and cities for six years, which forced upon the emperor the religious peace of Nuremberg, July 23, 1532. He died Aug. 16 of the same year. Luther preached his funeral sermon from 1 Thess. iv, 13–18, and Melanchthon pronounced a memorial address soon after in Latin. Luther honored him as a pious, sincere prince. John was a man of peace, and yet a good soldier of Christ. See Spalatin's *Biography*, in Mencke, *Script. rerum Germ.* iii, 1003 sq.; Ranke, *Deutsche Geschichte im Zeitalter der Reformation*, i–iii; Gretschel-Bülau, *Geschichte des sächsischen Volkes und Staates*, i, 419 sq.; Plitt, *Einleitung in die Augustana;* Plitt-Herzog, *Real-Encyklop.* s. v.; Lichtenberger, *Encyclop. des Sciences Religieuses*, s. v. (B. P.)

John, patriarch OF CONSTANTINOPLE, known for his connection with the measures of the emperor Michael Palæologus, looking to the union of Christendom. He at first refused his aid, and declared the Latins heretics, for which he was imprisoned. While in prison he found leisure to examine the older Greek literature concerning the dissensions of the Eastern and Western churches, and these investigations changed his mind. He was released and made patriarch, but after the death of the emperor retired to a monastery, in 1283. He was again restored, and again exiled, dying in 1298 in Bithynia. The Greek Church excludes his name from the number of the orthodox, but not the Latin Church; hence his writings are found in Leo Allatius's *Græcia Orthodoxa*, tom. i, ii. See Gass, in Plitt-Herzog, *Real-Encyklop.* s. v. (B. P.)

John OF DARLINGTON, an Irish prelate, was a native of Darlington, Durham, trained a Dominican, and a great clerk, "qui literatura pollebat excellenter et cursilio" (Mat. Paris). Henry III made him his confessor, "which argueth his piety, that so devout a prince used him in so conscientious an office." He afterwards became archbishop of Dublin, being the choice of pope John XXI, in order to settle impartially the rival claims of William de la Corner, king's chaplain, the choice of the prior and convent of Trinity Church, and of Fromund le Brun, the pope's chaplain, the elect of the dean and chapter of St. Patrick's. The pope set both aside. John was also collector of Peter's Pence in Ireland to popes John XXI, Nicholas III, and Martin IV. He wrote many books. Returning to England, he died in 1284, and was buried at Preaching Friars. See Fuller, *Worthies of England*, i, 486.

John OF FLANDERS, a Flemish prelate, was the son of Guy, count of Flanders. He became at first provost of St. Peter of Lille, and of St. Donatian of Bruges. Nicholas III provided him with the bishopric of Metz, Jan. 2, 1280, but he neglected the duties of that charge, and only took its revenues to acquire grounds at Flanders. After a short time he was appointed bishop of Liege, and took possession of his new Church, Oct. 31, 1282. In 1285 he got into difficulties with the sheriffs of Liege, and left the city, taking with him his clergy, and retiring into the borough of Huy. His exile lasted twenty-two months. After his return to Liege he made a league with his brother-in-law, the duke of Brabant, against Renaud, count of Guelders. In 1288, while hunting, according to the custom of those times, he was seized and imprisoned for five months, until he paid a ransom. He died Oct. 14, 1292. He published, in 1287, *Synodal Statutes*, collected by D. Martène, *Thes. Anecd.* iv, 829. See Hoefer, *Nouv. Biog. Générale*, s. v.

John OF THE GRATE (so-called from an iron grating which surrounded his sepulchre), *Saint*, bishop and confessor, was a Breton, born in 1098. He made rapid progress in his studies, and was made bishop of Aleth. As a bishop his life was embittered by a series of lawsuits with the monks of Marmoutiers. He wished to remove his episcopal see to the island of St. Malo, Aleth being exposed to pirates. But the monks claimed the Church of St. Malo, the pope decided in their favor, and Lucius II at length condemned John to lose his see. He then retired under the protection of St. Bernard to Clairvaux, until, on the death of Lucius, a monk of Clairvaux (Eugenius III) was elevated to the papal throne. John appealed again and was heard. His rights were restored, and the monks of Marmoutiers were obliged to cede the Church of St. Malo to the bishop. It was during his bishopric that the strange heresy of the fanatical Eon de l'Étoile (q. v.) broke out, and John tried by persuasion and instruction to disabuse of their heresy such of the enthusiasts as overran his diocese, and succeeded in converting many. John of the Grate died Feb. 1, 1163. He immediately received popular reverence as a saint, and numerous miracles are said to have augmented the reverence of the people. In 1517 Denis Brigonnet, ambassador of the king to Rome, obtained from Leo X permission for him to be commemorated in a solemn office as a confessor bishop. Monsignor Antoine Joseph des Laurents, last bishop of St. Malo but one, examined John's relics, Oct. 15, 1784. During the revolution they were ordered to be cast into the sea, but the order was countermanded, and the sexton was required to bury them in the common fosse in the cemetery. In November, 1799, M. Manet, a priest who had remained through the Reign of Terror in St. Malo, verified the relics. In a sealed box, March 7, 1823, they were deposited in their ancient shrine, and Nov. 16, 1839, by the sanction of the pope, they were finally installed with great ceremony, and are now in the Church of St. Malo. The authorities for the life of John of the Grate are Albertus Magnus of Morlaix, and the letters of Bernard and Nicholas of Clairvaux. His festival is observed as a double by the Church of St. Malo, in Brittany, and his name appears in Saussaye's supplement to the Gallican martyrology. See Baring-Gould, *Lives of the Saints*, ii, 26 (sub Feb. 1, his day).

John, a metropolitan OF KIEW, was raised to that dignity in 1164 by the patriarch of Constantinople, Lucas Chrysoberges. He is famous for his letter to pope Alexander III, of which a rare book entitled *Kirilovoi* (Moscow, 1644) gives some extracts. John died May 12, 1166. See Hoefer, *Nouv. Biog. Générale*, s. v.

John OF MONMOUTH (so called from the place of his nativity), a doctor of divinity and canon of Lincoln, was chosen bishop of Llandaff in 1296, after a vacancy in that see of seven years, the pope remitting the election to archbishop Kilwarby, who called John of Monmouth. He became a great benefactor to the bishopric, procuring for it, among other revenues, the rectory of Newland. He was a learned and pious theologian. He died April 8, 1323. See Fuller, *Worthies of England* (ed. Nuttall), ii, 434.

John Baptist OF SALERNO, a Jesuit, and friend of pope Clement XI, was born in 1670. He accompanied the nephew of the pope, Albani, to Germany and Poland as theological adviser, and succeeded in converting Frederick Augustus of Saxony to the Church of Rome. In acknowledgment of this deed John Baptist was made cardinal, and died in 1729. He is the author of *Specimen Orientalis Ecclesiæ* (Rome, 1706). See Lichtenberger, *Encyclop. des Sciences Religieuses*, s. v. (B. P.)

John, Frederick (surnamed *the Magnanimous*), elector of Saxony, son of John the Constant (q. v.), was born at Torgau, June 30, 1503. Brought up in the Church of the Reformation, he became its unwavering advocate, and, like his father, he was on terms of most intimate friendship with Luther, with whom he carried on an uninterrupted correspondence. He increased the endowment of Wittenberg University from the sequestrated revenues of convents, and in 1548 founded the University of Jena. His relations to the emperor were unpleasant. In 1536 he entered into a reaffirmation of the Smalcald league, by which the Protestant princes bound themselves to mutual protection for ten years. In 1544 the emperor Charles V was left free to give his whole attention to the affairs in Germany. A war broke out. Frederick was finally defeated, and taken prisoner at Mühlberg, April 24, 1547. He remained in prison till 1552, and died at Weimar, March 3, 1554. John Frederick remained true to the cause of the Evangelical Church in spite of his many misfortunes. See Müller, *Geschichte Johann Friedrich des Grossmüthigen* (Jena, 1765); Ranke, *Deutsche Geschichte im Zeitalter der Reformation*, iv, 190 sq.; Burkhardt, *Die Gefangenschaft Joh. Fr. d. Grossmüthigen* (1863); Plitt-Herzog, *Real-Encyklop.* s. v.; Lichtenberger, *Encyclop. des Sciences Religieuses*, s. v. (B. P.)

Johnes, TIMOTHY, D.D., a Presbyterian minister of Welsh extraction, was born at Southampton, L. I., May 24, 1717. He graduated from Yale College in 1737, was ordained by the New York Presbytery, Feb. 9, 1743, pastor at Morristown, N. J., and had great success in his ministry there, which closed with his death, Sept. 17, 1794. In 1777 general Washington, on one occasion, communed with his congregation while in the vicinity. See Sprague, *Annals of the Amer. Pulpit*, iii, 16. (W. P. S.)

Johns, Henry Van Dyke, D.D., a Protestant Episcopal clergyman, was born at New Castle, Del., in 1803, being the youngest son of the Hon. Kensey Johns, chief-justice of Delaware and United States senator. He graduated from Princeton College, afterwards studied at the General Theological Seminary, N. Y., and continued his theological studies under the direction of his brother, bishop Johns of Virginia. His ministry began at Wilmington, Del.; he was for some time rector of the Church at Frederick, Md.; thence he was called to Trinity Church, Washington, D. C.; subsequently to Cincinnati, O.; then to the rectorship of Christ Church, Baltimore, Md., where he continued until 1853, when Emanuel Church was built by a portion of his congregation, and he became its rector, a position which he occupied until his death, April 22, 1859. See *Amer. Quar. Church Rev.* 1859, p. 352.

Johns, John, D.D., LL.D., a Protestant Episcopal clergyman, was born at New Castle, Del., July 10, 1796. He graduated from the College of New Jersey in 1815; studied two years at Princeton Theological Seminary; in his eighteenth year joined the Protestant Episcopal Church, and, June 10, 1819, was ordained deacon, and in 1820 presbyter. His first parish was All-Saints' Church, Frederick, Md., and in 1829 he became rector of old Christ's Church, in Baltimore. In 1837 a new church was erected, called the Church of the Messiah, of which he was rector until he became assistant bishop of the diocese of Virginia, May 21, 1842. In 1849 he was elected president of William and Mary College, where he remained until 1854. He died at Alexandria, Va., April 5, 1876. He was a leader of the Evangelical side of his Church, and commanded admiration from men of all shades of opinion by the purity of his life and the sincerity of his convictions. See *Necrol. Report of Princeton Theol. Sem.* 1877, p. 12.

Johnson, George Henry Sacheverell, an eminent Anglican clergyman and mathematician, was born at Keswick, Northumberland, about 1808. He graduated from Queen's College, Oxford, in 1828, obtained several scholarships and a tutorship therein, became professor of astronomy in 1839, of moral philosophy from 1842 to 1845, preacher at Whitehall in 1852, dean of Wells in 1854, and died Nov. 6, 1881. He published a *Treatise on Optics* (1836):—*Sermons* (1857):—and wrote the annotations on the Psalms in the *Speaker's Commentary.*

Johnson, Samuel, a Unitarian writer, was born at Salem, Mass., Oct. 10, 1822. He graduated from Harvard College in 1843, and from Harvard Divinity School in 1846; became pastor of a "Free Church" at Lynn in 1853; in 1870 removed to Salem, and in 1876 to North Andover, where he died, Feb. 19, 1882. Although not an ordained minister, he was intimately associated with the humanitarian tendencies of modern Unitarianism, and an ardent opponent of slavery, speaking and writing eloquently on kindred subjects of reform. He published *A Book of Hymns* (1846):—*The Worship of Jesus* (1868):—and *Oriental Religions* (his principal work, vol. i, Boston, 1872).

Johnson, Samuel R., D.D., a Protestant Episcopal clergyman, graduated from the General Theological Seminary, was for many years a professor of systematic divinity there, and a prominent member and secretary of the standing committee of his diocese. In 1872 he became rector of St. Thomas's Church, Amenia Union, N. Y., and died Aug. 13, 1873. See *Prot. Episc. Almanac*, 1874, p. 138.

Johnson, William L., D.D., a Protestant Episcopal clergyman, was a graduate of the General Theological Seminary, rector in Jamaica, L. I., for at least eighteen years, and died there, Aug. 4, 1870, aged eighty years. See *Prot. Episc. Almanac*, 1871, p. 118.

Johnston, JOHN, D.D., a Presbyterian minister, was born at Crawford, Orange Co., N. Y., Jan. 28, 1778. He graduated from the College of New Jersey in 1801; studied theology privately in Princeton; was licensed by the New Brunswick Presbytery in October, 1806. In 1807 he accepted a call to the united congregations of Newburgh and New Windsor, N. Y. In 1810 he was released from the congregation of New Windsor, but remained as pastor at Newburgh until his death, Aug. 26, 1855. See Sprague, *Annals of the Amer. Pulpit*, iv, 394.

Johnstone, WILLIAM O., D.D., a Presbyterian minister, was born in Ireland, April 17, 1822, but received his education in this country. He was pastor of the Kensington Presbyterian Church, Philadelphia, Pa., for more than thirty years, and his services in every department of Church work were constant and untiring. He died suddenly, Jan. 16, 1883. See (Phila.) *Presbyterian*, Jan. 20, 1883. (W. P. S.)

Jokneam. Of *Tell Keimûn*, the modern representative of this place, a brief account may be found in the *Memoirs* accompanying the Ordnance Survey (ii, 48), and of the few remaining antiquities (p. 69). A freer description is given by Lieut. Conder (*Tent Work*, i, 131):

"North of Lejjûn the great Wâdy el-Milh runs down from the white plateau of the 'Breezy Land,' which it separates from the southern end of Carmel. Here at the mouth stands a huge tell or mound called Keimûn, on which are remains of a little Byzantine chapel, and of a small fort erected by the famous native chief Dhahr el-'Amr. The Samaritans have a curious legend connected with this site. According to them Joshua was challenged by the giants, and enclosed here with his army in seven walls of iron. A dove carried his message thence to Nabih, king of the tribes east of Jordan, who came to his assistance. The magic walls fell down, and the king of Persia, Shobek, was transfixed by an arrow which nailed him on his horse to the ground.

"The present name is a slight modification of the ancient Jokneam of Carmel, but the Crusaders seem to have been puzzled by it, and transformed Keimûn into Cain Mons, or Mount Cain, whence arose the curious legend that Cain was here slain with an arrow by Lamech, which they supposed to be the murder referred to in the Song of Lamech (Gen. iv, 23). The chapel no doubt shows the spot once held to be the site of the death of Cain, but the derivation of the name was as fanciful as that of Haifa from Cephas or from Caiaphas the high-priest."

Joktheel OF JUDAH. For this town Tristram proposes (*Bible Places*, p. 40) *Khurbet Mesheifrefeh*, near Gaza, on the ground that "the word is the Arabic equivalent of the Hebrew;" and a writer in the *Quar. Statement* of the "Pal. Explor. Fund" (January, 1881, p. 53) proposes "the large ruin *Kutlâneh*, south of Gezer, as the words are from similar roots." But both these identifications are very precarious.

Jol. See YULE.

Jolof Version. See JALLOOF VERSION.

Jolowicz, HEYMANN, a Jewish scholar, who died at Königsberg, Prussia, in 1875, is the author of, *Die fortschreitende Entwickelung der Cultur der Juden in Deutschland* (Berlin, 1841):—*Harfenklänge der heiligen Vorzeit* (Leipsic, 1846):—*Blüthen rabbinischer Weisheit* (Thorn, 1845):—*Die Himmelfahrt und Vision des Propheten Jesaia* (Leipsic, 1854):—*Die germanische Welt in ihrer Berührung mit dem Christenthume* (ibid. 1854):—*Blüthenkranz morgenländischer Dichtungen* (1860):—*Geschichte der Juden in Königsberg* (1867). See Fürst, *Bibl. Jud.* ii, 100 sq.; Zuchold, *Bibl. Theol.* i, 626. (B. P.)

Jona BEN-GANACH. See IBN-GANACH.

Jonä, SUENO, a professor of Oriental languages at Upsala, was born in 1590, and died in 1641. He published, *Elementale Theologicum*, etc. (Upsala, 1625):—*Catechesis Minor* (ibid. 1627):—*Institutionum Hebraicarum pars Elementaria*, etc. (1637):—*Institutionum Hebraicarum pars Secunda* (1638). See Stiernmann, *Bibl. Suio-Gothica*, p. 347; Jöcher, *Allgemeines Gelehrten-Lexikon*, s. v. (B. P.)

Jones, Alexander, D.D., a Protestant Episcopal clergyman, was born at Charleston, S. C., Nov. 8, 1796. He graduated from Brown University in 1814; pursued his theological studies under the direction of bishop Griswold, at Bristol, R. I.; took charge of a school for some years in Bardstown, Ky.; was ordained deacon in 1822; in 1824 became rector of Zion Church, in Charlestown, Va.; in 1851 of St. Paul's Church, in Richmond, and afterwards was settled as rector of St. Peter's Church, in Perth Amboy, N. J., where he remained seventeen years (1857–74), and then having had a stroke of paralysis, he was obliged to abandon all ministerial labor. He died at Perth Amboy, Feb. 15, 1874. "He had a high rank among the clergy of the Episcopal Church for scholarship and useful service, and was a gentleman of genial manners and refined taste." (J. C. S.)

Jones, Arthur, D.D., a Welsh Congregational minister, was born at Llanrwst, Denbighshire, Feb. 12, 1776. He was converted when about eighteen years of age, joined the Calvinistic Methodists, and soon became an exhorter and preacher. He was ordained at Bangor in 1810, where he labored earnestly as pastor; in 1815 he removed to the Welsh churches at Deptford and Woolwich, Kent; in 1823 he returned to his former charge at Bangor; in 1854 he retired to Chester, where he died, Feb. 29, 1860. He published several tracts and sermons, besides his work entitled, *Pyngeian Athrawiaethol* (doctrinal points). See (Lond.) *Cong. Year-book*, 1861, p. 215.

Jones, Inigo, an eminent English architect, was born in London in 1572. He went to Venice and studied the works of Palladio, and his reputation procured him the appointment of chief architect to Christian IV, king of Denmark, who, in 1606, brought Jones with him to England. He was induced to remain, and was appointed architect to the queen, and subsequently to Henry, prince of Wales. He invented many ingenious decorations and wonderful machines. Among his works are the palace of lord Pembroke, at Wilton, in the county of Wilts; the queen's chapel, St. James; the façades of Holyrood House; and Heriot's Hospital, Edinburgh. He died in London, July 21, 1652. A collection of Inigo Jones's architectural designs was published by Kent in 1712 and 1724. See Spooner, *Biog. Hist. of the Fine Arts*, s. v.; Hoefer, *Nouv. Biog. Générale*, s. v.

Jones, John Collier, D.D., an English divine, was born at Plympton, Devonshire, Oct. 7, 1770. He graduated from Exeter College, Oxford, June 6, 1792, and shortly after was elected to a Petrean fellowship. Entering holy orders, he became curate of Mortlake, in Surrey, but afterwards accepted a chaplainship on board the *Namur*, and was present in the action off cape St. Vincent, in 1797. In 1808 he became one of the tutors of his college; in 1812 a public examiner; select preacher in 1819; and on the death of Dr. Cole was elected to the rectorship of Exeter. Dr. Jones's other official appointments were, delegate of accounts in 1824; vice-chancellor from October, 1828, to 1832; and joint curator of the Sheldonian Theatre in 1829. He was also vicar of Kidlington, and an acting magistrate for the county of Oxford. He died in 1838. His inflexible integrity, gracefulness of manner, and kindness of disposition won for him the esteem and love of all with whom he came in contact. See (Lond.) *Christian Remembrancer*, Sept. 1838, p. 568.

Jones, John Emlyn, LL.D., a Welsh Baptist minister, was born at Newcastle Emlyn, Carmarthenshire, Jan. 8, 1820. He was baptized at the age of thirteen; received a good education; was ordained in 1852 co-pastor at Pontypridd; was then pastor in Ebbw Vale; then in Cardiff; in 1865 removed to Merthyr; in 1869 to Llandudno, North Wales, and finally returned to Ebbw Vale, where he died, Jan. 18, 1873. He was ever busy with his pen, as with his tongue, contributing largely to both the Welsh and the English newspaper press. He published Welsh translations of *Gill's Commentary* and *Hamilton's Grammar*. He wrote *Hanes Prydain Fawr am yr Haner Canrif Diweddaf* ("The History of Great Britain for the Past Half Century"). For several years he was busily engaged in writing his *Y Parthsyllydd, Sef, Haner yr Holl Fyd* ("The History of the Whole World"), one volume of which was published. See (Lond.) *Baptist Hand-book*, 1874, p. 282. (J. C. S.)

Jones, Samuel Beach, D.D., a Presbyterian minister, was born at Charleston, S. C., Nov. 23, 1811. He studied at Yale College; spent four years in Princeton Theological Seminary (1832–36); acted one year as assistant secretary of the Board of Missions; was ordained in 1837; became professor of Hebrew in the Oakland Seminary, Miss., in 1838; was pastor of the First Presbyterian Church at Bridgeton, N. J., from 1839 to 1863; preached in Fairfield from 1870 to 1875, and died at Bridgeton, March 19, 1883. See (*N. Y.*) *Observer*, March 22, 1883. (W. P. S.)

Jones, Thomas (1), D.D., an Irish prelate, was born in Lancashire, and educated at Christ College, Cambridge. His first promotion was to the chancellorship of St. Patrick's Cathedral; in 1581 he was elected its dean; in May, 1584, dean Jones was promoted to the see of Meath, and on May 12 was consecrated in St. Patrick's Church. Having presided over that see twenty-one years, he was translated to that of Dublin in 1605, and was consecrated Nov. 9 of the same year. In 1611, he, and the other archbishops of the Established Church, held a council in Dublin, wherein it was decreed that the suffragans should reside in their respective dioceses, visit all the churches, and institute such regulations as would be best calculated to prevent sectarianism and extirpate popery. In 1613 he was one of the justices in commission with sir Richard Wingfield. In 1614 he had a grant of the temporalities of the bishoprics of Kilmore and Ardagh during vacancy. During the episcopacy of archbishop Jones he repaired a great part of Christ Church. He died at his palace of St. Sepulchre's in April, 1619. See D'Alton, *Memoirs of the Archbishops of Dublin*, p. 250.

Jones, Thomas (2), an English divine, was born near Havod, Cardiganshire, Wales, April 2, 1752. He was educated at the grammar-school of Ystradmeirig, and ordained in 1774. Having labored in the curacy of Llangevelin and Eglwysvach from 1774 to 1778, he removed to Leintwardine, Herefordshire, England, thence to Longnor, Shropshire, and from this place to Oswestry. His next curacy was Loppington; and in 1785 he was appointed to the living of Creation, Northamptonshire, where he remained till the increasing infirmities of age obliged him to reign his office in 1833. He died Jan. 7, 1845. His works are, *Jonah's Portrait* (1818, 12mo; 9th ed. 1845, 8vo):—*Scripture Directory*

Joppa, from the South-west. (From Thomson's *Southern Palestine and Jerusalem.*)

(Lond. 1811, 8vo; 8th ed. 1839, 12mo):—*The True Christian* (5th ed. 1844, sq.):—*The Prodigal's Pilgrimage* (1831, 12mo; new ed. 1847, 16mo):—*Sober Views of the Millennium* (1835, 12mo):—*Fountain of Life* (3d ed. 1848, 16mo):—*Notes of Fifty-five Sermons*, edited by Rev. John Owen (1851, 12mo). See *The* (Lond.) *Christian Guardian*, July, 1845, p. 281, 329; Allibone, *Dict. of Brit. and Amer. Authors*, s. v.

Joppa. Of the modern *Yafa* (called *Jaffa* by the Europeans) a tolerably full account is given in the *Memoirs* accompanying the Ordnance Survey (ii, 275 sq.); and the description by Lieut. Conder (*Tent Work*, i, 1 sq.) contains some interesting particulars:

"The town rose from the shore on a brown hillock; the dark, flat-roofed houses climbing the hill one above another, but no prominent building breaking the sky outline. The yellow, gleaming beach, with its low cliffs and sand-dunes, stretched away north and south, and in the distance the dim blue Judæan hills were visible in shadow.

"Jaffa is called the port of Jerusalem, but has no proper harbor at present. In ancient times the 'Moon Pool,' south of the town, now silted up, was perhaps the landing-place for Hiram's rafts of cedar-wood; but the traveller passes through a narrow opening in a dangerous reef running parallel with the shore, or, if the weather is bad, he is obliged to make a long detour round the northern end of the same reef. By ten in the morning the land breeze rises, and a considerable swell is therefore always to be expected. The entrance through the reef is only sufficient for one boat, and thus every year boats are wrecked on the rocks and lives lost. It is said also that each year at least one person is killed by the sharks close to land. The little Russian steamer was anchored about two miles from shore, and rolled considerably. The decks were crowded with a motley assemblage, specimens of every Levantine nationality. Each deck passenger had his bedding with him, and the general effect was that of a great rag-heap, with human faces—black, brown, and white—legs, arms, and umbrellas sticking out of the rags in unexpected places. Apart from the rest sat a group of swarthy Bedouin, with their huge headshawls, not unlike a coal-scuttle in effect, bound with a white cord round the brow. They wore their best dresses, the black hair cloak, with red slippers. The rugged dark faces with white beards and sunscorched eyes wore a curious mixed expression of assumed dignity and badly concealed curiosity concerning the wonders of civilization surrounding them. The coloring of these various groups would have been a treat to an artist. The dull rich tints were lit up here and there by patches of red leather and yellow silk. Like all Oriental color, it was saved from any gaudiness of effect by the large masses of dull brown or indigo which predominated. The steamer was soon besieged by a fleet of

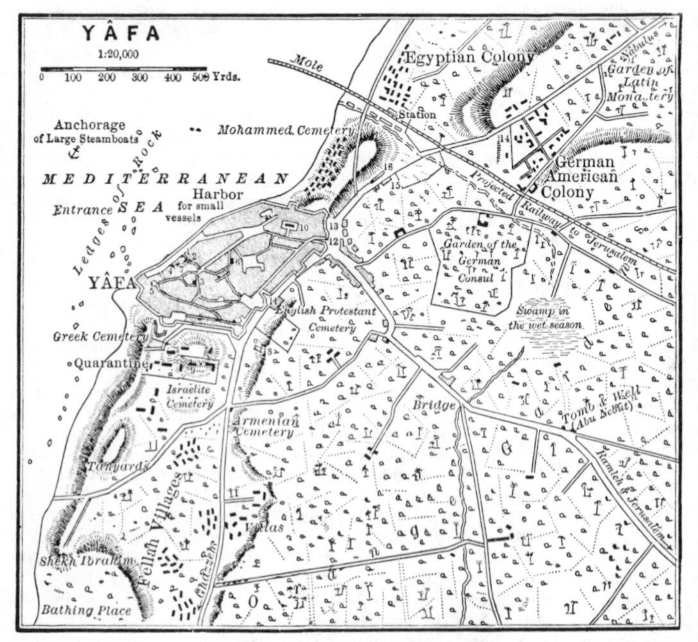

Plan of Joppa and its Environs.

long, flat boats with sturdy rowers, and into these the passengers were precipitated, and their luggage dropped in after them. The swell was so great that we were in constant danger of being capsized under the accommodation-ladder. As we rowed off, and sank in the trough of the waves, the shore and town disappeared, and only the nearest boats were visible high up on the crest of the rollers. The exciting moment of reaching the reef came next; the women closed their eyes, the rowers got into a regular swing, chanting a rude rhyme, and, waiting for the wave, we were suddenly carried past the ugly black rocks into smooth water close to the wharf. The landing at Jaffa has been from time immemorial an exciting scene. We have the terrible and graphic account of the old pilgrim (Sæwulf) who, 'from his sins or from the badness of the ship,' was almost wrecked, and who witnessed from the shore the death of his companions, helpless in a great storm in the offing. We have the account of Richard Lion-Heart springing, fully-armed, into the surf and fighting his way on shore. The little port made by the reef has been long the only place south of Acre where landing was possible; but the storms which have covered the beach with modern wrecks were equally fatal to the Genoese galleys and crusading war-ships.

"The town of Jaffa contains little of interest, though it is sufficiently striking to a new-comer. The broad effects of light and shadow are perhaps enhanced here by the numerous arched streets and the flights of steps which climb from the sea-level to the higher part of the town. The glory of Jaffa consists in its beautiful gardens, which stretch inland about a mile and a half, and extend north and south over a length of two miles. Oranges, lemons, palms, bananas, pomegranates, and other fruits grow in thick groves surrounded by old cactus hedges, having narrow lanes between them deep in sand. Sweet water is found in abundance at a moderate depth. The scent of the oranges is said to be at times perceptible some miles from land, to approaching ships. Still more curious is the fact that the beautiful little sunbird, peculiar to the Jordan valley, is also to be found in these gardens. How this African wanderer can have made its way across districts entirely unfitted for its abode, to spots separated by the great mountain chain, it is not easy to explain.

"Outside the town on the north-east is the little German colony, the neat white houses of which were built originally by an American society which was almost exterminated by fever, and finally broken up by internal differences, caused, I understand, by some resemblance in the views of the chief to those of Brigham Young. The land and buildings were bought by the thrifty German settlers, members of the Temple Society, with the views and history of which sect I became further acquainted during the following winter. See PALESTINE, COLONISTS IN.

"The soil of the Jaffa plain is naturally of great fertility. Even the negligent tillage of the peasantry produces fine harvests. The Germans ploughed deeper, and were rewarded by a crop of thistles, which to a good farmer would have been a subject of satisfaction as proving the existence of virgin soil, only requiring to be scoured by other crops for a year or two in order to yield fine harvests of corn. At this time of year, the barley had been gathered in, and only the dry stubble was left."

Jordaens, JAKOB, an eminent Flemish painter, was born at Antwerp, May 19, 1594, studied under Adam van Oort, and copied the pictures of Titian and Paul Veronese. He was employed by the king of Spain to do some important work. His paintings are very numerous, and abound in the churches and public edifices of the Netherlands. Some of the most celebrated are *St. Apollonia*, in the church of the Augustines at Antwerp; *Christ Disputing with the Doctors*, in that of St. Walburg at Furnes; *The Triumphal Entry*. He died at Antwerp, Oct. 18, 1678. There are a few other etchings by him, among which are the following: *The Flight into Egypt; Christ Driving the Traders from the Temple; The Descent from the Cross*. See Hoefer, *Nouv. Biog. Générale*, s. v.; Spooner, *Biog. Hist. of the Fine Arts*, s. v.

Jordan VALLEY. We extract some interesting particulars on this, the one great river of the Holy Land, from Lieut. Conder's *Tent Work in Palestine* (ii, 35 sq.), which summarizes the whole information in a clear and compact form. (See map on following page.)

"The Jordan Valley is not only the most remarkable feature of Palestine, but one of the most curious places in the world. It has no exact counterpart elsewhere, and the extraordinary phenomenon of clouds sweeping as a thick mist 500 feet below the level of the sea, is one which few European eyes have seen, but which we witnessed in the early storms of the spring of 1874.

"The Jordan rises as a full-grown river, issuing from the cave at Baniâs, about 1000 feet above the level of the Mediterranean. In the short distance of twelve miles it falls not less than 1000 feet, passing through the papyrus-marshes, and reaching the Huleh Lake. This lake is four miles long, and from its southern extremity to the north end of the Sea of Galilee is ten and a half miles. The second lake has been determined, by our line of levels, as 682 feet below the Mediterranean; thus in twenty-six and a half miles there is a fall of 1682 feet, or more than sixty feet to the mile.

"The Sea of Galilee is twelve and a half miles long, and thence the Jordan flows sixty-five miles, measuring in a straight line (the bends make it a good deal more) to the Dead Sea, 1292 feet below the Mediterranean. The fall in this distance is, however, not regular. Above the Jisr Mujâmi'a it is over forty feet to the mile. From the south end of the Sea of Galilee to the Dâmieh ford is a distance of forty-two miles, and a fall of only 460 feet. From the Dâmieh to the mouth of Wâdy el 'Aujeh is thirteen miles, with sixty feet fall, and thence to the Dead Sea is ten miles, with ninety feet of fall.

"It will be seen from the above that the total direct length of Jordan is about 104 miles, or only half the length of the Thames; that the fall to the Sea of Galilee is over sixty feet to the mile; thence to the Dâmieh, at first forty feet, afterwards not quite eleven feet per mile; from the Dâmieh to the 'Aujeh not much over four and a half feet to the mile; and for the last ten miles, about nine feet per mile. The break down of the immense chasm may thus be said to commence immediately north of the Sea of Galilee.

"The valley may be divided into eight sections. First, the portion between Banîas and the Huleh, where it is some five miles broad, with steep cliffs some 2000 feet high on either side and a broad marsh between. Secondly, from the Huleh to the Sea of Galilee, where the stream runs close to the eastern hills, and about four miles from the base of those on the west, which rise towards the high Safed mountains, more than 3500 feet above the lake. Thirdly, for thirteen miles from the south end of the Sea of Galilee to the neighborhood of Beisân, the valley is only one and a half miles broad west of the river, and about three on the east, the steep cliffs of the plateau of Kaukab el-Hawa on the west reaching an altitude of 1800 feet above the stream.

"South of Beisân is the fourth district, with a plain west of Jordan, twelve miles long and six miles broad, the line of hills on the east being straight, and the foot of the mountain on this side about two miles from the river. In the neighborhood of Beisân the cross section of the plain shows three levels: that of the shelf on which Beisân stands, about 300 feet below sea-level; that of the Ghôr itself, some 400 feet lower, reached by an almost precipitous descent; and that of the Zor, or narrow trench, from half to a quarter of a mile wide, and about 150 feet lower still. The higher shelf extends westward to the foot of Gilboa; it dies away on the south, but on the north it gradually rises into the plateau of Kaukab and to the western table-land above the Sea of Galilee, 1800 feet above Jordan.

"After leaving the Beisân plain the river passes through a narrow valley twelve miles long and two to three miles wide, with a raised table-land to the west, having a level averaging about 500 feet above the sea. The Beisân plain is full of springs of fresh water, some of which are thermal, but a large current of salt warm water flows down Wâdy Mâleh, at the north extremity of this fifth district.

"In the sixth district, the Dâmieh region, the valley again opens to a width of about three miles on the west, and five on the east of Jordan. The great block of the Kurn Sŭrtŭbeh here stands out like a bastion, on the west, 2400 feet above the river. Passing this mountain the seventh district is entered—a broad valley extending from near Fusâil to 'Osh el-Ghŭrâb, north of Jericho. In this region the Ghôr itself is five miles broad west of the river, and rather more on the east; the lower trench, or Zor, is also wider here, and more distinctly separated from the Ghôr. A curious geographical feature of this region was also discovered by the survey party. The great affluents of the Fâr'ah and 'Aujeh do not flow straight to Jordan, but turn south about a mile west of it, and each runs, for about six miles, nearly parallel with the river; thus the mouth of the Fâr'ah is actually to be found just where that of the next valley is shown on most maps. This curious feature was not discovered even by Captain Warren, and nothing more surprised me, in surveying the district, than the unsuspected parallel course of the streams. The whole of the valley in the seventh region is full of salt springs and salt marshes, but the Fâr'ah, flowing from the Ænon springs, is a perennial stream of fresh water.

"The eighth and last district is that of the plain of Jericho, which, with the corresponding basin (Ghôr-es-Seisebân) east of Jordan, measures over eight miles north and south, and more than fourteen across, with Jordan about in the middle. The Zor is here about a mile wide, and some 200 feet below the broad plain of the Ghôr."

Jormungand, in Norse mythology, was the Midgard-snake, the daughter of Loke and the giantess

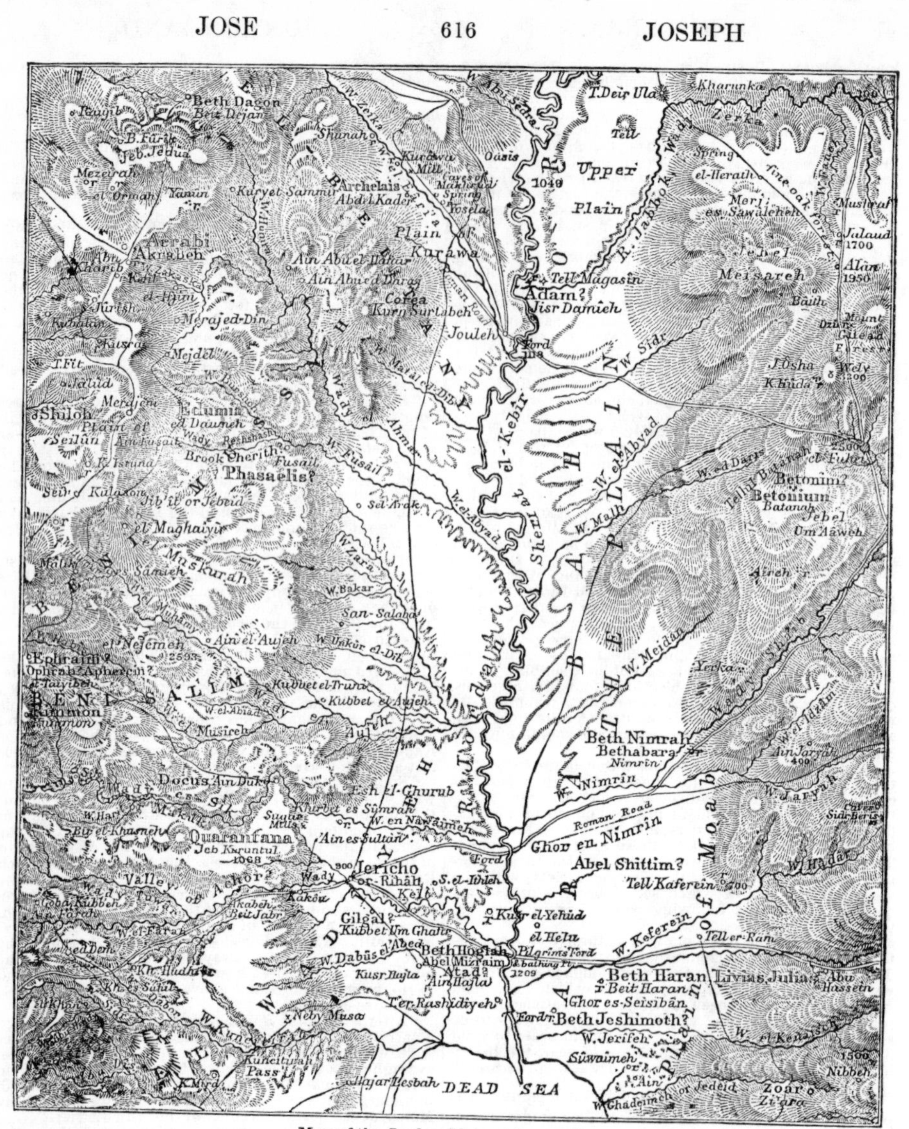

Map of the Jordan Plain at its mouth.

Angerbode, also the sister of the wolf Fenris and the blue Hela. The gods threw Jormungand into the ocean, where she grew so as to encircle the earth. When she drinks, there is low tide; when she gives back the water again, it is high tide. Thus she will live until Ragnarokr (world's end) comes. Thor will then slay her with his miölner, or hammer, but will himself be drowned in the poisonous streams issuing from her mouth.

Jose BEN-CHALEFTA (surnamed *the thinker*), a Jewish rabbi, was born at Sepphoris, in Palestine, about the year 80 A.D. Involved in the political schemes of rabbi Akiba (q. v.), he was obliged, in the year 124, to save himself from the Roman sword by fleeing to Asia Minor, from whence, on the death of the emperor Hadrian, in 136, he returned to Sepphoris, and died as the head of a school in that place, in 150. Jose's life is said to have been an edifying example of moral conduct, diligence in acquiring and communicating knowledge, and an amiable modesty and humility. "I would rather," said he, "be a learner in a school than be founder of the school. I would rather, in the fulfilment of my duty, die a bitter death, than be infamous in the too well beaten way. I would rather overdo my duty than fail in it. I would rather collect for the poor than, by distributing among them, gain consideration for myself. I would rather be unjustly blamed, than really do what is wrong." Jose is the author of a historical work, which has been preserved, and is possessed of lasting interest, the *Seder Olam* (q. v.). See Hamburger, *Real-Encyklop.* ii, 493 sq.; Bacher, *Die Agada der Tanaïten* (Strasburg, 1884), pp. 20, 87, 99, 110, 139, 207, 223, 242, 246, 247, 284, 305, 337, 381, 422, 438; Fürst, *Bibl. Jud.* ii, 107 sq. (B. P.)

Josenhaus, JOHANNES, a Protestant theologian, for some time inspector of the Basle Missionary Institute, who died Dec. 25, 1884, is the author of, *Die Herrlichkeit Jesu Christi des Sohnes Gottes* (Stuttgart, 1846):—*Bilder aus der Missionswelt* (Basle, 1858):—*Atlas der evangelischen Missionsgesellschaft zu Basel* (2d ed. ibid. 1859). See Zuchold, *Bibl. Theol.* i, 628. (B. P.)

Joseph BEN-JOSHUA *ben-Meir* (surnamed *Ha-Sefardi*, i. e. "the Spaniard"), was born in 1496 at Avignon, whither his father had retired on leaving Spain. He is the author of a historical work, entitled דִּבְרֵי הַיָּמִים, *Chronicles of the Kings of France and the Ottoman Sovereigns*, in two parts, the first from the creation till 1520, and the second of transactions from that time till 1553 (Venice, 1554; Amsterdam, 1733). Disinterested, and contemporary with those events, he must be regarded as an impartial historian. This work has been translated in part into Latin by Louis Ferrand, *Synopsis sive Conspectus Libri Hebraici*, etc. (Paris, 1670). An English translation of the whole, by C. H. Bialloblotzky, has made this interesting work accessible to English readers, *The Chronicles of R. Joseph ben-Joshua Meir, the Sephardi* (Lond. 1836, 2 vols.). See Fürst, *Bibl. Jud.* ii, 115; Etheridge, *Introd. to Hebr. Lit.* p.453; Lindo, *History of the Jews of Spain and Portugal*, p.451; Jost, *Geschichte des Judenthums*, iii, 124. (B. P.)

Josephinism. Under this term we generally understand those ecclesiastical reforms which were introduced by Joseph II, German emperor from 1780 to 1790. It was Joseph's object to form a *national Austrian Church*, congruent with the territory of the state, closely connected with the strongly centralized secular government, and as far as possible independent of Rome. As, on many points along the boundaries, Austrian dominions ranged under the authority of foreign bishops, a new circumscription of the dioceses was necessary, and it was carried out with little ceremony. A new oath of subjection to the temporal ruler was demanded of the bishops. All imperial decrees were sent to the bishops, and again by them to the pastors, who had to make them known to their flocks from the pulpit. On the other hand, no papal bulls or briefs could be published in the country without an imperial "placet." Connected with this movement was *the education of the clergy*. The theological students were forbidden to visit the "Collegium Germanico-Hungaricum" in Rome, which institute was replaced by the "Collegium Germanicum et Hungaricum" at Pavia. The philological and theological schools in the monasteries were closed, and diocesan seminaries were opened under the superintendence of an imperial committee. For the *divine services* the use of the German language was prescribed, and the Latin was abolished. Pilgrimages outside of the country were forbidden. Rules were given in respect to the luxurious ornamentation of the churches, the magnificent processions, the brilliant illuminations. *All religious orders* not engaged in preaching, teaching, or nursing the sick, were dissolved. Between 1770 and 1786 the number of monasteries sank from 2136 to 1425, and that of monks and nuns from 64,890 to 44,280. On Oct. 13, 1781, an *edict of religious toleration* was promulgated, according to which the Evangelicals of the Augsburg and Helvetic confessions obtained a limited freedom of worship. Civil disqualifications arising from denominational differences were abolished. Even the position of the Jews was improved. Previous to that edict of toleration, on May 4, an imperial decree had enacted that the oath of obedience to the pope, and the "Professio fidei Tridentinæ," usual at the distribution of degrees, were abrogated, and that the bulls "In cœna Domini" and "Unigenitus" were to be torn out of the books of the liturgy. The Roman curia became, of course, greatly alarmed at these proceedings, and in January, 1782, pope Pius VI went in person to Vienna. He was politely received without effecting any change, and the more so since the emperor had the support of the most influential prelates of Austro-Hungaria. Joseph, however, died Feb. 20, 1790, and his early death prevented his reforms from taking root. During his immediate successors the old order was again revived. See his biographies by Geissler (Halle, 1783, 15 vols.); Meusel (Leipsic, 1790); Perzl (Vienna, eod.); Huber (ibid. 1792); Heyne (Leipsic, 1848, 3 vols.); Ramshorn (ibid. 1861); Meynert (Vienna, 1862); Riehl und Reinöhl, *Kaiser Josef II als Reform. auf kirchlich. Gebiete* (ibid. 1881); Frank, *Das Toleranz-Patent Kaiser Josef's II* (ibid. 1882); Schmidt, *Kaiser Josef II* (Berlin, 1875); Leistner, *Kaiser Josef's II unvergessliche Gedanken, Aussprüche und Bestrebungen* (Vienna, 1878); Beer, *Joseph II* (in the *Neuen Plutarch*, Leipsic, 1842, vol. ix); also Ranke, *Die deutschen Mächte und der Fürstenbund* (Leipsic, 1871, vol. i); Plitt-Herzog, *Real-Encyklop*, s. v.; Lichtenberger, *Encyclop. des Sciences Religieuses*, s. v. *Joseph II*. (B. P.)

Josephites is the name of a congregation of missionary priests of St. Joseph, organized at Lyons in 1656, by a certain Cretenet, a native of Champlitte, in Burgundy, and a surgeon by profession, who consecrated himself to the service at the hospital in Lyons. The first object of these priests was to act as missionaries in the country, and then to engage in charitable works in the different colleges.

There exists also an organization of females, known as "Sisters of St. Joseph," which was instituted by the bishop of Puy in 1650. These sisters, besides doing charitable works, have to care for the hospitals, govern the houses of refuge, and are charged with the instruction of orphans and little children in the schools, and with visiting the sick. Their vows are very simple, and they can always be relieved from them by the bishop in whose diocese they live. See Hélyot, *Hist. des Ordres Monast.* viii, 186 sq.; Lichtenberger, *Encyclop. des Sciences Religieuses*, s. v. (B. P.)

Sister of St. Joseph.

Joseph's Tomb (*Kabr Yûsef*) is briefly described in the *Memoirs* accompanying the Ordnance Survey (ii, 194), and more popularly in Lieut. Conder's *Tent Work* (ii, 74) as follows:

"About six hundred yards north of the well [of Jacob] is the traditional tomb of Joseph, venerated by the members of every religious community in Palestine. The building stands east of the road from Balâta to 'Askar, at the end of a row of fine fig-trees. The enclosure is square and roofless, the walls whitewashed and in good repair, for, as an inscription on the south wall, in English, informs the visitor, it was rebuilt by consul Rogers, the friend of the Samaritans, in 1868; it is about twenty-five feet square, and on the north is another building of equal size, but older and partly ruinous, surmounted by a little dome. The tomb itself resembles most of the Moslem cenotaphs—a long block, with an arched or vaulted roof having a pointed cross section. It is rudely plastered, and some seven feet long and three feet high. It is placed askew, and nearest to the west wall of the court. A stone bench is built into the east wall, on which three Jews were seated at the time of our second visit, book in hand, swinging backwards and forwards as they crooned out a nasal chant—a prayer, no doubt, appropriate to the place.

"The most curious point to notice is, however, the existence of two short pillars, one at the head, and the other at the foot of the tomb, having shallow cup-shaped hollows at their tops. These hollows are blackened by fire, for the Jews have the custom of burning sacrifices on them, small articles, such as handkerchiefs, gold lace, or shawls, being consumed. Whether this practice is also observed by the Samaritans is doubtful.

"The tomb points approximately north and south, thus being at right angles to the direction of Moslem tombs north of Mecca. How the Mohammedans explain this disregard of orientation in so respected a prophet as 'our Lord Joseph,' I have never heard; perhaps the rule is held to be only established since the time of Mohammed. The veneration in which the shrine is held by the Moslem peasantry is, at all events, not diminished by this fact."

Joshua's Tomb. Lieut. Conder gives the local traditions on the subject as follows (*Tent Work*, i, 78):

"The 'Holy King Joshua' is said by the Samaritans to have been buried at Kefr Hâris, which they identify with Timnath Heres. This village is nine miles south of Nablûs.

"The Jewish pilgrim, rabbi Jacob of Paris, visited Caphar Cheres—presumably Kefr Hâris—in A.D. 1258, and mentions the tombs of Joshua, Nûn, and Caleb. The Samaritans also hold that Caleb was buried with Joshua, and thus we have the curious result that Jews and Samaritans agree as to the site of these tombs, both placing them within the bounds of Samaria. The crusading writers point to the same site for Joshua's tomb, and the place is marked on the map of Marino Sanuto (A.D. 1322) in the relative position of Kefr Hâris.

"The modern village has three sacred places: one of Neby Nûn, the second Neby Lush'a, the third Neby Kifl. In the first two we recognise Nun and Joshua; Neby Kifl was a historic character, but his shrine possibly occupies the place of the mediæval tomb of Caleb.

"The site of Joshua's tomb seems therefore to be preserved by an indigenous tradition at least as authentic as that of Joseph's tomb. It has been supposed that Jerome indicates a different site, but a careful reading of his account of St. Paula's journey seems to show that he also refers to the tombs at Kefr Hâris."

For another traditional site of Joshua's tomb see TIMNATH-HERES.

Jotes, in Norse mythology. These forms of Scandinavian deities seem to have a historic background. They were probably the aborigines of the north of Europe, who were driven from their possessions by the companions of Odin; hence the undying enmity between the Jotes and the Asas. Fable makes the Jotes to be monstrous giants and magicians, living in dark caves and grottos. They and the Thusses seem to have been derived from one family.

Jouffroi (Lat. *Joffredus*), JEAN DE, a French prelate, was born at Luxueil (Franche-Comté) about 1412. He studied at Dôl, Cologne, and Pavia, and taught three years in the last-named place. He assisted at the Council of Ferrara in 1438, and was engaged in several important religious and diplomatic missions. In 1430 he became bishop of Arras, and in 1461 cardinal. He died Nov. 24, 1473. See Hoefer, *Nouv. Biog. Générale*, s. v.

Jouffroy, FRANÇOIS GASPARD DE, a French prelate, was born in 1723 at the castle of Gonsans, near Besançon. He became canon of St. Claude, then bishop of Gap in 1774, and of Mans in 1778. Being elected a deputy of the states-general in 1789, he protested against the decrees of the assembly, and went into exile in 1792. He was received by the chapter of Paderborn (Westphalia), and given a revenue of six thousand two hundred florins. He died there in 1797. See Hoefer, *Nouv. Biog. Générale*, s. v.

Joulouka, in the mythology of the Antilles nations, is the monstrous spirit whose feathered head may be seen in the rainbow. See JULUKA.

Jouvenet, JEAN, an eminent French painter, was born at Rouen, Aug. 21, 1647. At the age of seventeen he went to Paris and studied with Nicholas Poussin, and at twenty-seven produced his celebrated picture of *Christ Curing the Paralytic*, in the Church of Notre Dame. Soon after he painted, in the Hospital of the Invalides, between the windows of the dome, *The Twelve Apostles, with Angels*. In 1665 he was admitted a member of the Academy, and painted for his reception the picture of *Queen Esther before Ahasuerus*—one of the finest works in the halls of the Academy. About this time he executed four pictures for the Church of St. Martin aux Champs, representing *Mary Magdalene at the Feet of our Saviour, in the House of Simon the Pharisee; Christ Driving the Money-changers from the Temple; The Miraculous Draught of Fishes; The Raising of Lazarus*. His most famous work is the *Deposition from the Cross*, painted for the Church of the Capuchins, at Paris, where he died, April 5, 1717. See Hoefer, *Nouv. Biog. Générale*, s. v.; Spooner, *Biog. Hist. of the Fine Arts*, s. v.

Jowett, Joseph, LL.D., a learned English clergyman, was born about 1750; admitted in 1769 to Trinity College; in 1773 removed to Trinity Hall, where he became assistant tutor, then fellow and principal tutor, and afterwards regius professor of the civil law, which office he retained till his death, Nov. 13, 1813. In addition to his professorship he held the living of Wethersfield, in Essex. Dr. Jowett was a scholarly man, a humble Christian, and a devoted friend of the Bible Society and kindred associations. See (Lond.) *Christian Observer*, Dec. 1813, p. 820.

Jowett, William, a Church of England divine, was born in 1789. He graduated at St. John's College, Cambridge, in 1810, and was the first clergyman of the Church of England who volunteered, in 1813, for the foreign service of the Church Missionary Society. His field of labor was in the countries in the Mediterranean, and the fruits of his observations were, *Christian Researches in the Mediterranean from* 1815 *to* 1820, and *Christian Researches in Syria and the Holy Land in* 1823 *and* 1824. He was also the author of, *Time and Temper: a Manual of Selections from Holy Scripture, with Thoughts on Education* (4th ed. 1852):—*Helps to Pastoral Visitations* (2d ed. 1848, 3 parts). From 1832 to 1840 he acted as clerical secretary to the Church Missionary Society; for many years held the Sunday evening lectureship of St. Mary's, Aldermanbury; and in 1851 succeeded the Rev. R. Bickersteth as St. John's chaplain. He died at Clapham, Surrey, Feb. 20, 1855. See Hardwicke, *Annual Biography*, 1856, p. 208.

Joy of the Law, FESTIVAL OF THE, is a name given to the ninth day of the Feast of Tabernacles among the modern Jews. On that day three MSS. of the Pentateuch are laid upon the desk, and three portions are read by three different persons, one portion from each MS., the first closing with the end of Deuteronomy. Another immediately begins with the first of Genesis, to indicate that man should be continually employed in reading and studying the word of God.

Joyce, THOMAS, a Dominican, proceeded D.D. in Oxford, and, living there, became provincial of his order both in England and Wales. From this place, without ever having any other preferment, pope Clement V created him cardinal of St. Sabine—a contradiction, as some call attention, between the friar's profession and practice. He had six brethren, all Dominicans, and Fuller, refusing to liken them to the seven sons of Sceva (Acts xix, 14), all exorcists, terms them "a week of brethren, whereof this rubricated cardinal was the dominical letter." Thomas flourished in 1310, and was buried in his convent at Oxford. See Fuller, *Worthies of England* (ed. Nuttall), iii, 12.

Juanes, JUAN BAPTISTA, an eminent Spanish painter, was born at Valencia in 1523, and studied at Rome, but afterwards settled at Valencia. He is ranked by the Spanish writers as one of the greatest artists of the glorious age of pope Leo X. Pacheco bestows upon him the highest encomiums, and Palomino Velasco does not hesitate to prefer him to Morales, or even to Raphael himself. Juanes limited himself to subjects of sacred history, and his works are entirely confined to the churches and convents of his native city. There is a fine picture by him, representing *The Baptism of Christ*, in the Cathedral of Valencia. There are three others, representing *The Nativity; The Martyrdom of St. Inez; The Burial of a Monk*. Another fine picture is a *Dead Christ*, in the Church of San Pedro. He died in 1579.

Jubilation, GIFT OF, a privilege alleged by theurgic mysticism to be granted to eminent Romish saints, by which they are enabled in their last moments to sing a triumphant death-song.

Jubin (or **Gebuin**), *Saint*, a French prelate, was the son of Hugues III, count of Dijon. Having entered the ministry, he was appointed archdeacon of the Church of Langres. In 1077 he attended the provincial Council of Lyons at Autun, became archbishop of Lyons, and died there, April 18, 1082. He is invoked in cases of gout and the stone, with which he had himself been afflicted during his life. There are extant of Jubin six letters treating of the primacy to his see, printed by Descordes, Dom Liran, Baluze, etc. See Hoefer, *Nouv. Biog. Générale*, s. v.

Judæo-Arabic Version OF THE SCRIPTURES. This is not properly a version, but Arabic in Hebrew characters. As early as 1820 the printing of an edition of the Arabic New Test. in Hebrew characters was suggested to the British and Foreign Bible Society. Nothing, however, was done for the many thousand Jews in Egypt, Tunis, and the whole north of Africa, Yemen, Syria, and Mesopotamia (to whom the Arabic is vernacular, but who seldom read or write except in Hebrew characters), until 1846, when the Bombay Auxiliary Bible Society commenced for their use an edition of the gospels of Matthew and John, with the Acts of the Apostles, and the epistle to the Hebrews, under the superintendence of the Rev. Dr. Wilson of Bombay. The work was published in 1847, and has ever since been circulated. (B. P.)

Judæo-German Version OF THE SCRIPTURES. Like the above, this is the German New Test. in rabbinical characters. The first edition of this testament was printed at Cracow in 1540; the work was executed by John Herzuge, a converted Jew, on the basis of Luther's version; but the book of Revelation is omitted. In 1820 the London Society for Promoting Christianity among the Jews undertook to furnish the German Jews with copies of the German Scriptures in rabbinical characters. The society's first edition appeared in 1820: the German text was from Luther's version, published by Meyer at Frankfort in 1819, and the transcription into rabbinical characters was made by Mr. Judah D'Allemand of London. In 1859 the British and Foreign Bible Society published the Judæo-German Old Test., under the care of Rev. R. König, and in 1869 the book of Psalms, carefully revised by Rev. W. Edwards of Breslau, was printed at Vienna. (B. P.)

Judæo-Persian Version OF THE SCRIPTURES. This is the Persian New Test. in Hebrew characters, and designed for the Jews in Persia. When, in 1841, Dr. Häberlin applied to some Christian friends for aid in imparting the Scriptures to the Persian Jews, he received in reply from Herat a copy of Martyn's Persian New Test., written in Hebrew characters, under the care of Dr. Login. Dr. Häberlin laid the version before the Calcutta committee, and they agreed to refer the matter to the British and Foreign Bible Society. The latter requested the Calcutta Society to print an edition of two thousand New Tests. in this form, and arrangements were made to have the edition printed at Calcutta, under the eye of the Rev. Dr. Yates. The death of the latter rendered this plan abortive, and after the Bombay Society had transmitted to London manuscript copies of the Judæo-Persian gospels, an edition of one thousand copies was completed at London in 1849, under the superintendence of the Rev. Dr. Wilson of Bombay. These are all the printed parts extant. (B. P.)

Judæo-Polish Version OF THE SCRIPTURES. See RUSSIA, VERSIONS OF (20).

Judæo-Spanish Version OF THE SCRIPTURES. The Judæo-Spanish is spoken by the Jews of Turkey, who are descendants of the Jews formerly settled in the Spanish Peninsula, but forcibly ejected from Spain in 1492, and from Portugal in 1497, by the merciless mandate of Ferdinand and Isabella. As to the versions of the Old Test., compare the art. ROMANIC VERSIONS. A translation of the New Test. into Judæo-Spanish was undertaken by the British and Foreign Bible Society at the suggestion of Dr. Pinkerton, and, in 1823, the Rev. Mr. Leeves, their agent in Turkey, undertook the translation which was printed in 1829 at Corfu. It was afterwards revised, and reprinted at Athens in 1844. In 1874 the British and Foreign Bible Society undertook a careful revision of the New Test., with the assistance of the Rev. J. Christie of the Scottish Missionary Society. This new edition was printed at Constantinople in 1877, and is now in circulation. The Old Test. in Judæo-Spanish, with Hebrew in parallel columns, has also been published by the American Bible Society. (B. P.)

Judd, BETHEL, D.D., a Protestant Episcopal minister, was born at Watertown, Conn., in the spring of 1776. He graduated from Yale College in 1797, and immediately entered upon his preparation for the ministry; was ordained deacon in 1798, and his ministerial life covered sixty years of activity. At different periods he was engaged in the dioceses of Connecticut, New York, Western New York, Maryland, North Carolina, and Florida, and was one of the early presidents of St. John's College, Annapolis, as well as rector of the Church in that city. Among the missionary stations was that of St. Augustine, Fla. During fifteen years he was rector of St. James's Church, New London, Conn., a charge which he resigned on being appointed president of the Episcopal Academy, Cheshire. He died at Wilmington, Del., April 8, 1858. He was a ripe scholar, and an earnest and effective preacher. See *Amer. Quar. Church Rev.* 1858, p. 342.

Judea. See JUDÆA.

Juel was the most noted festival of the Scandinavian worship, which was celebrated in the longest night as a new year's celebration. Sacrifices and vows were made to the gods for fruitfulness for the coming year. In honor of the god Freir a huge boar was butchered, and the sacrifice, called the Jula-pig or Julablot, was made in the presence of the king. A golden boar was brought into the hall, all laid their hands on it and made the most binding vows. Then four weeks of eating, drinking, dancing, and playing followed. The name *Yule* for Christmas is thought to have thus originated.

Jug. See JOGA.

Juhles, a name given to aerial spirits or dæmons among the Laplanders, from whom they receive a sort of adoration, though no statues or images of them exist. Their worship is conducted under particular trees. On Christmas-eve, and the day following, they celebrate the festival of the Juhles. On this occasion they rigidly abstain from animal food; and they carefully reserve some fragments of the food employed, which they suspend in a box behind the house, for the refreshment of the spirits.

Juigné, ANTOINE ÉLÉONORE LÉON, *Leclerc de*, a French prelate of high family, was born at Paris in 1728. He studied in his native city, became bishop of Chalons in 1764, and during the French revolution took refuge at Chambery, afterwards at Constance, and finally at Augsburg. In 1802 he returned to France, but lived privately in Paris till his death, March 19, 1811. He left some ecclesiastical works, for which see Hoefer, *Nouv. Biog. Générale*, s. v.

Julien, SIMON (called *Julian of Parma*), an eminent French painter, was born at Toulon in 1736, studied under Bardou at Marseilles, and afterwards visited Paris, where he became a pupil of Carlo Vanloo, and gained the grand prize of the Royal Academy. He then visited Rome with the royal pension, and remained in that city ten years. On returning to Paris he soon gained a reputation, and was elected an academician. Among his best performances is an altar-piece for the chapel of the archbishop of Paris, at Conflans, representing *St. Anthony in a Trance.* He died at Paris, Feb. 23, 1800. See Spooner, *Biog. Hist. of the Fine Arts*, s. v.; Hoefer, *Nouv. Biog. Générale*, s. v.

Juluka, in the mythology of the Caribbeans, is a mighty spirit, living on fish, doves, and other animals. He is of gigantic size, walks over land and sea, and his head projects far above the clouds. His forehead is decorated by a beautiful bandage, made of the feathers of the colibri, splendidly colored; this he shows morning and evening. It is the rainbow. The remainder of the body remains hid in the clouds. If this spirit does not find enough to eat he causes sickness among the inhabitants. See JOULOUKA.

Jumala, the supreme deity of the Laplanders. He was represented by a wooden idol in human form, seated on a sort of altar, with a crown on his head and a bowl in his lap, into which the devotees throw their voluntary offerings.

Jumnoutri, a village on the banks of the river Jumna, which is considered by the Hindûs as a spot of remarkable sanctity. Pilgrimage to this place from the low countries was thought to impart to the adventurer virtues almost equal to deification.

Jung, ANDREAS, a Protestant professor of Strasburg, who was born in 1793, and died in 1863, is the author of, *Geschichte des Reichstags zu Speyer in dem Jahre* 1529 (Strasburg, 1830):—*Geschichte der Reformation der Kirche in Strassburg* (ibid. eod.):—*Die öffentlichen Bibliotheken Strassburg's* (1836, 1844). See Zuchold, *Bibl. Theol.* i, 634; Schmidt, *Discours Académique Prononcé à la Mémoire de M. A. Jung* (1864); Lichtenberger, *Encyclop. des Sciences Religieuses*, s. v. (B. P.)

Junge, CHRISTIAN GOTTFRIED, a Lutheran theologian of Germany, was born at Nuremberg, Oct. 20, 1748. He studied at Altdorf, commenced his ministerial career in 1769, was in 1783 professor of theology at Jena, in 1793 pastor at his native city, and died March 27, 1814. He wrote, *De Duratione Pœnarum Infernalium*, etc. (Altdorf, 1783):—*De Pœnarum Divinarum vi Emendatrice* (eod.). Besides a number of ascetical works and sermons, he also published the third edition of Döderlein's *Summa Institutionis Theologi Christiani* (1793). See Döring, *Die gelehrten Theologen Deutschlands*, s. v.; Zuchold, *Bibl. Theol.* i, 634; Winer, *Handbuch der theol. Lit.* i, 23, 298; ii, 280. (B. P.)

Junkheim, JOHANN ZACHARIAS LEONHARD, a Lutheran theologian of Germany, was born at Anspach, Sept. 8, 1729. He studied at Göttingen, was in 1754 vicar at his native place, and two years later pastor there. In 1757 he was rector of the gymnasium in Anspach, in 1764 court-preacher, and died Aug. 17, 1790. He wrote, *De Argumento pro Religione a Constantia Martyrum* (Göttingen, 1751):—*Progr. ad* 1 *Petr. iv*, 1, 2 (1762):—*De Providentia Divina* (eod.):—*Decas Quæstionum Synodalium* (1783-90). He also published *Sermons*. See Döring, *Die gelehrten Theologen Deutschlands*, s. v.; Fürst, *Bibl. Jud.* ii, 157; Winer, *Handbuch der theol. Lit.* i, 394, 444; ii, 288. (B. P.)

Junkin, DAVID X., D.D., a Presbyterian minister, was born near Mercer, Pa., Jan. 8, 1808. He graduated from Jefferson College in 1831, and studied two years at Princeton Theological Seminary. In 1835 he was ordained pastor at Greenwich, N. J.; in 1841 became professor of belles-lettres in Lafayette College; in 1848 pastor of the F Street Church, Washington, D. C.; in 1853 at Hollidaysburg, Pa.; in 1860 chaplain at Annapolis, Md.; in 1866 pastor of the North Church, Chicago, Ill., and in the same year at Newcastle, Pa. He died at Martinsburg, W. Va., April 22, 1880. Dr. Junkin was an eloquent and successful preacher, and a ready writer, being the author of several valuable books, among which was one entitled *The Oath a Divine Ordinance, and an Element of the Social Constitution* (N. Y. 1845, 12mo). See *New York Observer*, May 6, 1880; *Gen. Cat. of Princeton Theol. Sem.* 1881, p. 83. (W. P. S.)

Justi, LEONHARD JOHANN KARL, a Lutheran theologian of Germany, was born at Münchhausen, Hesse, Dec. 5, 1753. He studied at Marburg and Göttingen, was in 1774 deacon at Marburg, and commenced his academical career in 1775. In 1779 he was professor, and succeeded his brother as first pastor of St. Elizabeth. He died May 12, 1800, leaving, *Weissagungsgesang Mosis an die Israeliten, Deut. xxxii* (Göttingen, 1774):—*De Bileami Asina Loquente ad Numb. xxii* (Marburg, eod.):—*Ueber die den Ægyptern von den Israeliten bei ihrer Abreise abgeforderten Geräthe, Exod. v*, 11, 12 (1777):—*Ueber den Genius des Sokrates* (1779). See Döring, *Die gelehrten Theologen Deutschlands*, s. v.; Fürst, *Bibl. Jud.* ii, 157; Winer, *Handbuch der theol. Lit.* i, 23. (B. P.)

Justicers, ITINERANT, officers appointed by Richard I of England to watch over the interests of the Jews residents within the kingdom. They were instructed to protect the Hebrews against all oppression, to secure them in their interests and property, to decide all controversies between them and the Christians, to keep the seal of their corporation, and the keys of their public treasury.

Justiniani, Agostino, a Dominican and bishop of Nebbio, in the isle of Corsica, was born at Genoa in 1470, and died in 1536, on the way from Genoa to Corsica. He edited, *Philonis Judæi Quæstiones et Responsiones super Genesin*:—*R. Mosis Ægyptii Ductor Dubitantium*:—*Porcheti de Sylvaticis Victoria contra Impios Hebræos*:—*Liber Jobi Veritati Hebraicæ Restitutus*, and published *Psalterium Hebr., Græc., Arab. et Chald. cum Tribus Lat. Interpretationibus et Glossis* (Genoa, 1516). See Jöcher, *Allgemeines Gelehrten-Lexikon*, s. v.; Winer, *Handbuch der theol. Lit.* i, 36; Lichtenberger, *Encyclop. des Sciences Religieuses*, s. v. (B. P.)

Justiniani, Benedetto, a Jesuit papal preacher at Rome, who died Dec. 19, 1622, at Toulouse, professor of theology, wrote *Explanationes in Omnes Epistolas Pauli* (Lyons, 1612, 2 vols.):—*Explanationes in Omnes Epistolas Catholicas* (ibid. 1621):—*Apologia pro Libertate Ecclesiastica ad Gallo-Francos*. See Jöcher, *Allgemeines Gelehrten-Lexikon*, s. v.; Winer, *Handbuch der theol. Lit.* i, 253, 268. (B. P.)

Justus, archbishop of Canterbury, accompanied Laurentius and Mellitus when they departed from Rome, in 601, to join the mission at Canterbury. He was a Roman by birth; was also first bishop of the see of Rochester. He was translated to Canterbury in 624. The great event of his short occupancy of the latter see was the extension of the Kentish mission to Northumbria. This was effected by the marriage of Edwin, the king of Northumbria, with Ethelburga, the sister of Eadbald, king of Kent. Justus consecrated Paulinus, July 21, 625, to be archbishop of York. He died Nov. 10, 627. See Hook, *Lives of the Archbishops of Canterbury*, i, 100 sq.

Juttah. Its modern representative *Yutta* is thus described in the *Memoirs* accompanying the Ordnance Survey (iii, 310):

> "A large village standing on a ridge. It is built of stone, but some of the inhabitants live in tents. The water supply is from cisterns. On the south there are rock-cut tombs, and rock wine-presses are found all around the village. The neighborhood is extremely stony. South of the village are scattered olives, which are conspicuous objects; on the west, a little lower, under a cliff, is a small olive-yard; to the south-west a few figs. The inhabitants are very rich in flocks; the village owns, it is said, 17,000 sheep, besides goats, cows, camels, horses, and donkeys. The sheik alone has 250 sheep."

K.

Kabasilas. See CABASILAS.

Kabir Panthis, among the Hindûs, are the followers of Kabir, whom they allege to have been the incarnate deity. They believe that he lived in the world three hundred years, from 1149 to 1449 A.D., and that as a child he was found floating on a lotus in a lake or pond near Benares. He is also claimed by the Moslems as a professor of their faith. The Kabir Panthis being in the main *favorers* of Vishnu, they are included among the Vaishuara sects, although they worship no Hindû deity, nor do they practice any of the Hindû ceremonies. Those, however, who have retired from the world, and given themselves to a life of seclusion, abstain from all the ordinary practices of the Hindûs, and employ themselves chiefly in chanting hymns to the invisible Kabir. They believe in one God, the creator of the world, who has a body formed of the five elements of matter, and a mind endowed with the three Gunas or qualities of being. He is free from the defects of human nature, and can assume what particular shape he will; in all other respects he does not differ from man, and the pure man, the Sádh of the Kabir sect, is his living resemblance, and after death is his associate and equal. Their moral code is brief, but judicious in the main. Humanity is the first virtue, and the shedding of blood, whether of man or animal, is regarded as a heinous crime; because life is the gift of God, and must not be violated by his creatures. Truth is another great principle of morality, and ignorance of God is attributed to falsehood. Retirement from the world is desirable, as a check upon the passions and desires. The last point in the code is implicit devotion, in word, act, and thought, to the Guru or spiritual guide. This sect is very widely diffused throughout India. It is further divided into various branches, twelve of these being traced up to the founder, among whom a difference of opinion as well as descent prevails. Of the establishments of this sect, the Kabir Chaura, at Benares, is pre-eminent in dignity, and is a constant resort for pilgrims. Their doctrines are taught in a great variety of works in different dialects of India; but the great authority to which they are wont to refer is the Vijek, which, however, gives more attention to the defects of other systems than to the explanation of its own.

Kabyle Version OF THE SCRIPTURES. The Kabyle is spoken in Algeria and Tunis, and it is only of late that a gospel in the Kabyle vernacular has been published. From the report of the British and Foreign Bible Society for 1884 we learn that, in order to secure as accurate a version as possible, Dr. G. Sauerwein was sent out to Algiers. He returned with a version of the gospel of St. John, made from the French, by an Arab who assisted Père Olivier with his Kabyle-French dictionary. Dr. Sauerwein has revised that gospel from the Greek, and, according to the report for 1885, it was passing through the press. (B. P.)

Kaddish (קָדִּישׁ), in Jewish usage, means a prayer said by a son for his deceased father or mother during the first eleven months after their death. This prayer has to be repeated morning and evening at the close of the synagogue service, and runs thus, "May his great name be exalted and sanctified throughout the world, which he has created according to his will. May he establish his kingdom in our lifetime, and in the lifetime of the whole house of Israel, soon, and in a short time, and say ye Amen, Amen. May his great name be blessed and glorified for ever and ever. May his hallowed name be praised, glorified, exalted, magnified, honored, and most excellently adored; blessed is he, far exceeding all blessings, hymns, praises, and beatitudes that are repeated throughout the world, and say ye Amen. May our prayer be accepted with mercy and kindness. May the prayers and supplications of the whole house of Israel be accepted in the presence of their Father, who is in heaven, and say ye Amen. Blessed be the name of the Lord, from henceforth and forevermore. May the fulness of peace from heaven, with life, be granted unto us, and all Israel, and say ye Amen. My help is from the Lord, who made heaven and earth. May he who maketh peace in his high heavens bestow peace upon us, and on all Israel, and say ye Amen."

Besides this Kaddish, there is also one used by the rabbins after having delivered a lecture or completed their study. This is called the "Kaddish of the Rabbins," and runs thus, "Unto Israel, their rabbins, their disciples, and all their successors, who diligently study the law, who are in this and every other place; may there be unto them, and to you, abundant peace, grace, favor, mercy, long life, enlarged maintenance, and redemption, from the presence of the Lord of heaven and earth, and say ye Amen. May the fulness of peace," etc. See Hamburger, *Real-Encyklop.* s. v. (B. P.)

Kadesh-barnea. The search for this interesting locality, and the controversy concerning its site, still continue. The most recent and enterprising explorer is H. Clay Trumbull, D.D., editor of the *Sunday-School Times*, who has written an elaborate and magnificent work on the subject (*Kadesh-Barnea, its Importance and Probable Site*, etc., New York, 1884, 8vo). After great pains, while on a trip through the Sinaitic desert, he succeeded in reaching *'Ain Kadeis*, which, in his map of the region, accompanying his volume, he locates fifty-five miles west by north of Petra, and seventy-five north-east of the castle of Nukl. His description of the spot is as follows (p. 272):

"It was a marvellous sight! Out from the barren and desolate stretch of the burning desert-waste, we had come with magical suddenness into an oasis of verdure and beauty, unlooked for and hardly conceivable in such a region. A carpet of grass covered the ground. Fig-trees, laden with fruit nearly ripe enough for eating, were along the shelter of the southern hillside. Shrubs and flowers showed themselves in variety and profusion. Running water gurgled under the waving grass. We had seen nothing like it since leaving Wady Feirân; nor was it equalled in loveliness of scene by any single bit of landscape, of like extent, even there.

"Standing out from the earth-covered limestone hills at the north-eastern sweep of this picturesque recess was to be seen the 'large single mass, or a small hill, of solid rock,' which Rowlands looked at as the cliff (*sela*) smitten by Moses, to cause it to 'give forth his water,' when its flowing stream had been exhausted. From underneath this ragged spur of the north-easterly mountain range issued the now abundant stream.

"A circular wall, stoned up from the bottom with time-worn limestone blocks, was the first receptacle of the water. A marble watering-trough was near this well—better finished than the troughs at Beersheba, but of like primitive workmanship. The mouth of this well was only about three feet across it, and the water came to within three or four feet of the top. A little distance westerly from this well, and down the slope, was a second well, stoned up much like the first, but of greater diameter; and here again was a marble watering-trough. A basin or pool of water, larger than either of the wells, but not stoned up like them, was seemingly the principal watering-place. It was a short distance south-westerly from the second well, and it looked as if it and the two wells might be supplied from the same subterranean source—the springs under the rock. Around the margin of the pool, as also around the stoned walls, camel and goat dung—as if of flocks and herds for centuries—was trodden down and commingled with the limestone dust so as to form a solid plaster-bed. Another and yet larger pool, lower down the slope, was supplied with water by a stream which rippled and cascaded along its narrow bed from the upper pool; and yet beyond this, westward, the water gurgled away under the grass as we had met it when coming in, and finally lost itself in the parching wady, from which this oasis opened. The water itself was remarkably pure and sweet; unequalled by any we had found after leaving the Nile."

Meanwhile the late indefatigable Rev. F. W. Holland, after several ineffectual attempts, had at length successfully achieved a visit to the same spot, and an account of it from his field-book is given in the *Quarterly Statement* of the "Pal. Explor. Fund" for Jan. 1884. The accompanying sketch map of his route places 'Ain Kadeis at about the same distance as above from Petra and Nukl respectively, and gives it an elevation of one thousand four hundred and eighty-five feet above the sea. The place is thus described (p. 9)

"There are three springs, two on the hill-side, and one in the bed of the wady; from the lower spring on the hill-side a good stream of water flows for about one hundred yards down the wady, forming pools at which the goats are watered; the camels go to the spring. The upper spring on the hillside is a poor one now; it is built round with large rough stones to a depth of five feet, and there is a rude stone trough here and at the lowest spring. The three springs are not more than forty yards apart. The wady, which is stony throughout, has a bed, below the springs, nearly fifteen feet deep, between stony *jorfs*. As one ascends, the mountains become lower and less steep; there is much pasturage on them; the lower strata are chalk with flints; the upper, hard limestone (nummulitic?); large masses have fallen down and lie in the valley. There are a few fig-trees and a bed of coarse grass. About fifty yards higher up the wady than 'Ain Kadeis

Vicinity of 'Ain Kadeis.

there is a deeper well with four old watering-places; there are also traces of others near."

Both these explorers strongly identify the site with Kadesh-barnea, and the conclusion has been adopted by a large number of Biblical scholars. The name and character of the place have certainly been established as coincident, but still the position is unsatisfactory. 'Ain Kadeis is nearly midway between the Arabah and the Mediterranean, and after all the arguments of Dr. Trumbull and others, this seems too far west to suit the requirements of the Scriptural account, particularly the journeys of the Israelites. Especially is the attempt to remove the well-established position of Mount Hor to some locality west of the Arabah, for the purpose of accommodating this identification (as Dr. Trumbull does not hesitate to do) too herculean an undertaking. That the comparatively late name, "Idumæa," may have been extended so as to include the region immediately south of Palestine, we may very well concede, without admitting that the older designation of "Edom" ever passed the Arabah, which is the natural and still-existing boundary. The reasoning of Dr. Trumbull to the contrary, however ingenious and learned, seems too much like a piece of special pleading for a foregone and favorite theory, and parts of it are clearly defective, especially as to the conquering march of Joshua (Josh. xv, 19, where "from Kadesh-barnea even unto Gaza," evidently marks the eastern and the western limits respectively), the alleged contradiction between the refusal of a passage by Edom to the Israelites, and their burial of Aaron on the traditional Mount Hor (for they did not thereby acquire any title or cross the territory), and the imaginary "Wall Road." See SHUR. We cannot help thinking that more thorough exploration of the north-eastern part of the Sinaitic desert will yet bring to light other oases of a similar character, and among them one still bearing the not uncommon name of Kadesh, or perhaps some trace of the distinctive term *Barnea*. Lieut. Conder expresses a similar conviction (*Quar. Statement* of the "Pal. Explor. Fund," Jan. 1885, p. 21 sq.).

Kadr, AL, the title of the ninety-seventh chapter of the Koran, which contains an account of God's sending down the Koran from heaven to Mohammed. It represents God as saying, "The night Al Kadr is better than a thousand months." Which night this is has not been definitely ascertained.

Kadroma, in Thibetanian mythology, was a goddess who, changed into an ape, married the god Cenresi, likewise an ape, and by him became the mother of the entire population of Thibet.

Kaffir Version OF THE SCRIPTURES. The Kaffir is spoken by the Kaffres (q. v.), and was reduced to writing by the Rev. W. B. Boyce, a Wesleyan missionary, who, in connection with the Revs. Wm. Shaw and W. J. Shrewsbury, commenced in 1830 a translation of the Scriptures, which was completed in the course of four years. This translation, however, formed but the basis of that eventually published, and it was not till 1841 that, after a very careful revision, the New Test. was published. A vigorous revision was again undertaken, and in 1845 the revised New Test. was published, which was used by all the missionaries laboring among the Kaffre tribes. A new and again carefully revised edition of the New Test. was completed in 1854 at the Mount Coke Wesleyan mission press, and in 1859 the entire Old Test., after a careful revision, was completed at press. In 1865 the committee of the British and Foreign Bible Society announced that the revised Kaffir Bible, which had been slowly progressing for some time under the editorial supervision of the Rev. J. W. Appleyard, was completed and ready for circulation. The features of this revised edition were, that "very laborious efforts have been made to render the work an accurate and faithful translation of the Hebrew and Greek texts; and the proficiency of Mr. Appleyard in the knowledge of the Kaffir language, combined with great critical care, afford every reasonable guarantee that this version of the Holy Scriptures will prove correct, intelligible, and idiomatic, and in all respects admirably adapted to the people among whom it will now circulate. Its appearance, after long and earnest expectation, will be hailed with peculiar satisfaction by all missionaries laboring where the Kaffir language is spoken." In 1869 the report of the British and Foreign Bible Society again announced that the translation of this Bible was about to undergo revision: "A board of revisers, which consists of representatives of the various churches in South Africa, has been formed, and its labors already commenced. The difficulty here, as in so many other cases, is to make the translation idiomatic without sacrificing the exact sense of the sacred original." In 1871 the four gospels were announced as completed, and one of them was printed as a specimen, in order to elicit further criticisms, if needful, before the text is finally settled. In 1874 the board of revisers lost one of its most valuable helpers, the Rev. J. W. Appleyard, shortly after the revision of the New Test. was completed, which was issued together with the unrevised Old Test. in 1878. The revision of the Old Test. is still in progress; from July 8, 1874, to Jan. 22, 1882, the Old Test. was revised up to Jeremiah xxvi. See *Bible of Every Land*, p. 426 sq. (B. P.)

Kager, JOHANN MATTHIAS, an eminent German painter, was born at Munich in 1566, and went to Italy while young, where he spent several years studying the best works of the great masters. He died at Augsburg in 1634. His works are chiefly in the churches and public edifices of Munich. He etched a few plates from his own designs, among which are the following: *The Adoration of the Shepherds; The Baptism of Christ by St. John; The Holy Family; St. Francis Surrounded by the Monks of his Order; The Virgin and Child in the Clouds.* See Hoefer, *Nouv. Biog. Générale*, s. v.; Spooner, *Biog. Hist. of the Fine Arts*, s. v.

Kaguru Version OF THE SCRIPTURES. The

Kaguru is a dialect spoken by a tribe of East Equatorial Africa, and in this vernacular the gospels of Matthew and Luke, together with the books of Ruth and Jonah, were published by the British and Foreign Bible Society in 1884, the translation having been made by missionary Last. (B. P.)

Kahana BAR-TACHLIFA, a Jewish writer, was born at Pum-Nahara about 330, was in 397 rector at the college of Pumbaditha, in Babylon, and died in 413. Kahana is the author of an hagadic work, entitled *Pesikta de Rab Kahana* (פסיקתא דרב כהנא), comprising a cycle of lessons both from the Pentateuch and the Prophets, for all the festivals and principal Sabbaths of the year, and embodying the traditional explanation of these portions of Scripture. This midrash was for a long time only known from citations found in the Jalkut and Aruch. In the year 1868, however, S. Bubér published, at Lyck, an edition of the *Pesikta* according to a MS. which had been found at Zefath, and copied in Egypt, with critical annotations, emendations, etc., and an elaborate introduction. See Zunz, *Gottesdienstliche Vorträge der Juden*, p. 185-226, 239-251; Fürst, *Bibl. Jud.* ii, 159 sq.; Geiger, *Jüdische Zeitschrift*, 1869, p. 187-195; Theodor, *Zur Composition der agadischen Homilien*, in Frankel-Grätz's *Monatsschrift*, 1879, p. 97-113, 164-175, 271-278, 337-339, 455-457, Grätz, *Gesch. d. Juden*, iv, 495 sq. (B. P.)

Kähler, Ludwig August, a Protestant theologian of Germany, was born March 6, 1775, at Sommerfeld, Prussia. Having completed his studies, he was appointed in 1798 preacher at Canig, near Guben, in 1809 deacon and in 1812 archdeacon at Cotbus, in 1819 member of consistory, preacher, and professor of theology at Königsberg, where he died in 1856, a doctor of theology. He published, *Christliche Sittenlehre* (Königsberg, 1833): — *Beiträge zu den Versuchen neuerer Zeit, den Katholicismus zu idealisiren* (ibid. 1828):—*Supernaturalismus und Rationalismus in ihrem gemeinschaftlichen Ursprunge*, etc. (Leipsic, 1818):—*Ueber Schwärmerei, Begeisterung, scheinbare und wahre Grösse* (Königsberg, 1820):—*Predigten über den alleinseligmachenden Glauben an den Sohn Gottes* (ibid. 1826):—*Die christliche Lehre nach der heiligen Schrift* (2d ed. 1836):—*Wissenschaftlicher Abriss der christlichen Sittenlehre* (ibid. 1835, 1836). See Zuchold, *Bibl. Theol.* i, 638; Winer, *Handbuch der theol. Lit.* i, 302, 315, 346, 368, 371, 385; ii, 22, 26, 48, 76, 157, 177, 197, 200, 234, 361; *Dr. Ludwig A. Kähler, Mittheilungen über sein Leben und seine Schriften, von S. A. Kähler* (Königsberg, 1856). (B. P.)

Kahler, Wigand, a Lutheran theologian of Germany, nephew of Johannes Kahler (q. v.), was born at Wolmar, Hesse-Cassel, March 27, 1699. He studied at Rinteln, where he also commenced his academical career, and where he died, Nov. 14, 1747, professor of theology, having taken two years previous the degree of doctor of theology at Göttingen. He wrote, *De Veris et Fictis Textus Sacri Trajectionibus*: — *De Methodo Studii Theologici*:—*De ἀποκαραδοκίᾳ τῆς κτίσεως ad Rom. viii*, 19:—*De Innocentia Dei circa Lapsum Primorum Parentum*. See Moser, *Lexikon jetztlebender Gottesgelehrten*; Neubauer, *Nachricht von jetztlebenden Gottesgelehrten*; Jöcher, *Allgemeines Gelehrten-Lexikon*, s. v. (B. P.)

Kaiomorts, in Persian mythology, as represented in the Zend-Avesta, is the first man, who proceeded out of the right hip of the bull Abudad after Ahriman had the same killed. He was both a man and a woman, the object of worship by the angels. Thus Ahriman's plan to destroy the generation which was to populate the earth did not succeed. He therefore sent a Dew, Astujad, besides a thousand other genii of the infernal region, to battle against him. Kaiomorts withstood thirty years before he succumbed. The liquids flowing from his body fructified the earth. The seed grew into an immense tree, which, instead of fruit, bore ten human pairs, one of which, Meshia and Meshiane, were the progenitors of the human race. They, too, were seduced by Ahriman, and live sinful and condemned, suffering the punishment of their sin unto the resurrection.

Kaiser, Gottlieb Philipp Christian, a Lutheran theologian of Germany, was born at Hof, May 7, 1781. In 1801 he was teacher at the gymnasium of his native place, in 1809 deacon at Münchberg, in 1814 at Erlangen, in 1816 professor of theology there, and died in 1843, member of consistory and doctor of theology. He wrote, *De Apologeticis Evang. Joannis Consiliis* (Erlangen, 1821-25):—*Grundriss eines Systems der neutest. Hermeneutik* (ibid. 1817):—*De Mosaicis Symbolis et Geniis* (ibid. 1827):—*Commentarius in Priora Geneseos Capita* (1830):—*Literärgeschichte der melanchthonischen Original-Ausgabe der augsburgischen Confession* (Nüremberg, eod.):—*Linguæ Aramaicæ Usus in Nov. Testam.* etc. (1831):—*Die biblische Theologie oder Judaismus und Christianismus* (Erlangen, 1814, 1821, 2 vols.): —*Collectivum der davidischen Könige in Jerusalem* (1823):—*Das Hohelied ein Collectivgesang auf Serubabel* (1825):—*Erläuterung der fünf Psalmbücher* (1827): —*Ueber die Ursprache*, etc. (1840). See Winer, *Handbuch der theol. Lit.* i, 87, 107, 139, 200, 213, 215, 245, 293, 301, 329, 340; ii, 20, 31, 60, 99, 172; Fürst, *Bibl. Jud.* ii, 162; Zuchold, *Bibl. Theol.* i, 640; Diestel, *Gesch. des Alten Testaments*, p. 668 sq., 697, 713 sq., 747, 755. (B. P.)

Kaiser, Nikolaus, a Lutheran theologian of Germany, was born Nov. 8, 1734. He studied at Wittenberg and Erlangen, was in 1763 rector at Redwitz, and died March 14, 1800. He published, *De Luthero Interprete* (Hof, 1768): — *De Joannis Hussii Martyrio* (ibid. 1769): — *De Infausta Muhammedis Secta*, etc. (1771):—*De Meritis Lutheri in Hymnodiam* (1772):— *De Voto Paulino 2 Cor. xiii*, 13 (1774): — *Inhalt der augsburgischen Confession* (1783). See Döring, *Die gelehrten Theologen Deutschlands*, s. v. (B. P.)

Kala Maha, the male form of the Hindû god *Siva*, in his character of Time, the great destroyer of all things.

Kalands-Brothers. See CALENDARUM FRATRES.

Kalastri Linga, in Hindû mythology, is one of the commonest representations of Siva. A pious Indian had noticed that the right eye of the god wept. Immediately he took out his right eye and put it into

Representation of Kalastri Linga.

the idol. Soon after the left eye began to run, and the friend of the god sacrificed his left eye, and, as he was blind, he made use of his foot to find the spot where this eye was to be put in.

Kalendar. See ABDAL.

Kalewa, in Norse mythology, was one of the first gods of the far north, reigning long before the Asas, a mighty giant, and father of the hunter Hiisi, an evil god, whose frightful habitation is a place of damnation.

Kali-age. See KALIYUGA.

Kalika Purana, one of the sacred writings of the Hindûs, which is chiefly devoted to a recital of the different modes of worshipping and appeasing the goddess Kali (q. v.). See PURANAS.

Kalinak, in Hindû mythology, is a monstrous thousand-headed snake. Vishnu sought to capture it, riding on his giant bird, Garndha. When the serpent saw him coming it hid in the river Jumna, whose water it poisoned. When Vishnu, in his ninth Avatar, was still a boy, he decided to deliver the world from this reptile and its offspring. The reptile encircled him with a thousand fangs, but the god walked on its heads and crushed them all but one. He then sent it to the infernal regions, where its poison is used to torture the damned.

Kalisch, MARCUS M., a Jewish writer and commentator, was born at Treptow, Prussia, May 16, 1828. He studied at Halle and Berlin, and took the degree of doctor of philosophy in 1848. In the same year he left his native country on account of political disturbances, and went to England, where he took up a permanent residence. He became secretary to chief rabbi Adler, at London. Here he published his *Historical and Critical Commentaries on Genesis, Exodus, and Leviticus* (1855-72, 4 vols.):—*Hebrew Grammar* (1863, 1865, 2 parts):—*Bible Studies: I. The Prophecies of Balaam;* or, *The Hebrew and the Heathen* (1877); II. *The Book of Jonah* (1878). Kalisch died Aug. 23, 1885. (B. P.)

Kalki (or **Kalkin**, also called **Kalighi**), the *tenth Avatar*, or incarnation of Vishnu, which is yet future, and in which he will appear at the close of the Kaliyuga (q. v.), "when the practices taught by the Vedas and the institutes of the law shall have ceased." According to the Vishnu-Purana, he will then be born "in the family of *Vishnuyasas* (i. e. possessing the glory of Vishnu), an eminent Brahmin of Sambhala village, endowed with the eight superhuman faculties. He will then destroy all the barbarians and thieves, and all whose minds are devoted to iniquity." The expectation of the Hindû, in reference to the deliverance from present evils by Vishnu, is remarkably similar to the Hebrew expectation of the coming Messiah.

Kalmuck Mythology is nearly related to that of Thibet, the latter extending through India, China, Cashmere, Tartary, and far north. But this mythology has been greatly altered and modified by climatic, social, and other circumstances. According to the fables of the Zongarian Kalmucks and Tartars, the earth was originally covered with water. A great wind-storm arose, causing such a commotion of the waters that from the ensuing chaos eighty mountains sprung up, half of which formed a great range. Seven gods descended from heaven to visit the earth, and several of them satisfied their hunger. The earth then contained honey, and not knowing its origin, two of the deities ate of the honey, and so lost the privilege of returning with the other five. They then populated the earth. There are a thousand deities, who reign alternately. Six have finished their reign; the seventh, Shak Jumeni, rules at present. Maidiri (the prophet), will follow. But before he begins, the world will come to an end, the destroyer will come, surrounded by seven suns, which will set fire to the world. A rain-storm, following, will put out the fire, and Maidiri will go to heaven to take possession of his throne. Then the earth will be entirely depopulated, all men having gone to paradise, and the inhabitants of hell will come up to inhabit it. Their spirits take possession of other animals, from the lowest insect upwards, and thus the transmigration will continue, until the worst spirit of hell shall have become human, and worthy of paradise. To reach that happy place is usually only possible at the end of each world period, but those men who have led a holy life reach the gates of paradise at death.

Kalmuckian Version. By way of supplement to the article RUSSIA, VERSIONS OF, 21, we will add that the British and Foreign Bible Society has published, in 1884, the four gospels, in the translation of professor Pozdnejeff, who is also preparing the remainder of the New Test. (B. P.)

Kalthoff, JOHANN PAUL, a Roman Catholic theologian, who died at Münster in 1839, is the author of, *Jus Matrimonii Veterum Indorum* (Bonn, 1829):—*Grammatik der Hebr. Sprache* (Ratisbon, 1837):—*Handbuch der Hebr. Alterthümer* (Münster, 1839). See Zuchold, *Bibl. Theol.* i, 643; Fürst, *Bibl. Jud.* ii, 167 sq.; Winer, *Handbuch der theol. Lit.* i, 143. (B. P.)

Kalybe. See CHAPEL.

Kama, in Hindû mythology, is the Indian god of love; verbally the word means "desire." He is the son of heaven and disappointment, and is also called the heart-entering, bodiless, restless god, surnames which are all very significant. Tenderness (Retti) is his wife, and Vassant (blooming-time) his companion, who continually fills his quiver with buds as arrow-points. His favorite residence is at Agra, for there the women are the most beautiful of all portions of India. Kama

Figure of Kama.

has a visible form, but because he disturbed Hara, the ruler of creation, in his practices, the latter burned him to ashes by one look, and since then he is called bodiless. He is represented riding on a parrot. His bow is made of sugar-cane. His arrow-points are the rosy-red blooming buds of the amra-tree. The gods sought to induce Siva to a new marriage, and therefore turned to the god of love, under whose influence Siva soon married.

Kamdeva, in Hindû mythology, is the divine cow that can fulfil all desires, produced while the Amrita was in process of preparation, by turning the mountain Mandar into the sea of milk. She was presented by Indra to the Brahmin Jamadagai, who was therefore supernatural, wealthy, and honored everywhere. An evil-minded king, Shawkawser, ruler of Ayadhya, came to him with his whole train of followers, and entertainment was given with the aid of the cow. Then he demanded the cow, which was refused, whereupon the evil king made war on the Brahmin; but the cow slew all his army, and ascended again to heaven. The king sought revenge by killing the wise Brahmin; thereupon the cow hurried to the son of the murdered Brahmin, Parasu Rama, and called him to avenge the death of his father; the cow so assisted him that the evil king was slain.

Kamisimo, a garment of ceremony among the Japanese, worn on festival and other solemn occasions. It consists of two parts, a short cloak without sleeves, called *katageno*, and a short petticoat, called *rakama*, fastened about the waist by a band.

Kämpfer, Peter Christian, a Protestant theologian of Germany, was born Nov. 13, 1702. He studied at Rostock, was in 1736 professor of metaphysics there, in 1739 deacon, and took his degree as doctor of divinity in 1749. He died May 13, 1755. His writings are, *De Usu Terminorum Ecclesiasticorum* (Rostock, 1730):—*De Litteris Atque Punctis in Scriptura Veteris Testamenti Hebraicis* (ibid. 1734):—*De Origine Atque Indole τοῦ Keri et Chetibh* (ibid. 1739):—*De Litteris, Vocalibus et Accentibus in Scriptura V. T. Hebraicis* (ibid. 1742):—*Modus Prædicationis Paulinæ per Exegesin Dicti* 1 *Cor.* ii, 4 *Sistens* (ibid. 1749). See Döring, *Die gelehrten Theologen Deutschlands*, s. v. (B. P.)

Kampfschulte, Franz Wilhelm, a Roman Catholic theologian of Germany, was born Nov. 12, 1831, at Wickede, in Westphalia. He studied at Paderborn, Münster, and Berlin, took the degree of doctor of philosophy in 1859, and commenced his academical career in Bonn, where he was also made professor in 1861. He died Dec. 3, 1872, a member of the Old Catholic Church. He published, *De Georgio Wicelio* (Paderborn, 1856):—*Die Universität Erfurt in ihrem Verhältniss zur Reformation* (Treves, 1858-60, 2 vols.):—*De Joanne Croto Rubiano* (Bonn, 1862):—*Zur Geschichte des Mittelalters* (ibid. 1864):—*Johann Calvin, seine Kirche und sein Staat in Genf* (Leipsic, 1869, vol. i). See Zuchold, *Bibl. Theol.* i, 644; *Literarischer Handweiser für das katholische Deutschland*, 1871, col. 111 sq.; 1873, col. 171 sq. (B. P.)

Kamyu-Murunu (*desire for death*), modes of suicide formerly prescribed in the Hindû Shastras (q. v.). The commonest mode is drowning in the Ganges, but sometimes the suicide submits to being buried alive. There was formerly an instrument kept by which a person could decapitate himself. It consisted of a sharp, crescent-shaped knife, with a chain and stirrup to each horn. The devotee placed the sharp edge on the back of his neck, and his feet in the stirrups, then gave a violent jerk with his legs, and his head was instantly severed from his body.

Kanah of Asher. The modern village *Kana*, which has usually been identified with this site, lies seven and a quarter miles south-east of Tyre; but this is too far south for the requirements of the Biblical account (Josh. xix, 28). The antiquities in the vicinity, including the remarkable figures on the rocks, are described in the *Memoirs* accompanying the Ordnance Survey (i, 64). A more probable position is that of *'Ain Kanah*, "twenty miles farther north, on the edge of the hills, ten miles inland, but in sight of Sidon"

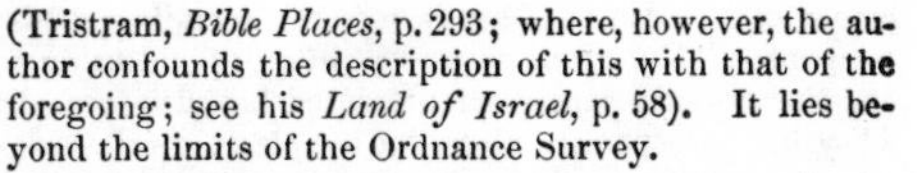

(Tristram, *Bible Places*, p. 293; where, however, the author confounds the description of this with that of the foregoing; see his *Land of Israel*, p. 58). It lies beyond the limits of the Ordnance Survey.

Kancheliyas, a Hindû sect, not uncommon in the south of India, whose worship is that of *Sakti*, the personified energy of the divine nature in action. They insist upon a community of women, and are far gone in bestiality.

Kandele, in the mythology of the Finlanders, is a musical instrument, like a zither; the magicians use it in all their magical cures and conjurations.

Kanon, in Japanese mythology, was the son of Amida. According to Picard (*Cérémonies et Coutumes Religieuses*, vii), this god is half fish, half man, or he crawls out of the throat of a proportionally large fish. The form, almost entirely female, is clothed in a light

Figure of Kanon.

garment, the neck decorated with pearls, and the head with flowers. It has four hands, two of which are lifted up, and two are down. The latter carry a sceptre and a flower, the uplifted right hand is closed to a fist, the left carries a ring. Before this figure there lies a large, open sea-shell, out of which a man projects in the position of worship. This idol stands in the temple of the god at Osaka, where it is worshipped as a fish or sea deity; also as creator of sun and moon.

Kanthai and **Bajusshiak**, in the mythology of the Kamtchatkians. Our figure represents both idols of the north Asiatic nations, especially of the inhabitants of Kamtchatka, just as they stand in the sacred

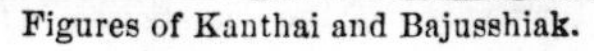

Figures of Kanthai and Bajusshiak.

corner of the common hut where the man keeps his weapons. They grant success in hunting and fishing, and therefore the latter is represented half fish-formed. They had no separate cultus, nor temples, nor priests.

Kapalika, a sect of Hindûs, who formerly sacrificed human victims to Kali and other hideous monster gods. The devotee of this sect is thus described, "His body is smeared with ashes from a funeral pile, around his neck hangs a string of human skulls, his forehead is streaked with a black line, his hair is woven into the matted braid, his loins are clothed with a tiger's skin, a hollow skull is in his left hand for a cup, and in his right he carries a bell, which he rings incessantly, exclaiming aloud, *Ho! Sambhu Bhairava*—Ho! lord of *Kali*."

Kapff, Sixt Carl, a Protestant theologian of Germany, was born at Güglingen, Würtemberg, Oct. 22, 1805. He studied at Tübingen, where he became intimately acquainted with William Hofacker. After filling the positions of vicar at Tuttlingen, teacher at Hofwyl, and *repetent* at Tübingen, he became, in 1833, pastor of the colony of pietists at Kornthal. In 1843 he was dean at Münsingen, and in 1847 at Herrenberg. In 1850 he was made general superintendent and member of the superior consistory, and in 1852 he became the greatly beloved and influential pastor of the "Stiftskirche," at Stuttgart, where he preached twenty-seven years. He died Sept. 1, 1879. Kapff was the most perfect representative of the type of piety prevailing in Würtemberg in the last generation; as a preacher he was not eloquent, but his earnest manner won the heart. His influence as pastor was very great, and yet he found time to write. He published, *Predigten über die alten Evangelien des Kirchenjahres* (3d ed. 1875):—*Predigten über die alten Episteln* (6th ed. 1880):—*Communionbuch* (19th ed. eod.), etc. See Burk, in Plitt-Herzog, *Real-Encyklop.*; Lichtenberger, *Encyclop. des Sciences Religieuses*, s. v.; Carl Kapff, *Lebensbild von Sixt Carl Kapff* (Stuttgart, 1881); Zuchold, *Bibl. Theol.* i, 645 sq. (B. P.)

Kapp, Johann, a Lutheran theologian of Germany, was born Dec. 12, 1739. He studied at Leipsic and Erlangen, was in 1765 teacher at the gymnasium in Hof, in 1774 doctor of philosophy, in 1777 court-preacher and professor of theology at Bayreuth. In 1801 he was made doctor of divinity, and died Aug. 18, 1817, leaving, *Epistola super Dictis Biblicis Quibusdam Novi Testamenti* (Hof, 1767):—*Paralipomena de Magis, Matth. ii*, 1 sq. (1771):—*Progr. Periculum Versionis Psalmi Secundi cum Brevibus Scholiis* (1781):—*Brevis Paraphrastica Explicatio Matth. v*, 33–42 (1783), etc. See Döring, *Die gelehrten Theologen Deutschlands*, s. v. (B. P.)

Kapp, Johann Erhard, a Lutheran theologian of Germany, was born March 23, 1696. He studied at Leipsic, was in 1720 doctor of philosophy, in 1727 professor, and died March 7, 1756. He published, *De Nonnullis Indulgentiarum Quæstoribus* (Leipsic, 1720):—*De Chrysosthomi ad Cæsareum Monachum Epistola*, etc. (ibid. 1723):—*Nachlese einiger grösstentheils noch ungedruckten Urkunden*, etc. (4 parts, 1727–33):—*Historia Concilii Lateranensis*, etc. (1731), etc. See Döring, *Die gelehrten Theologen Deutschlands*, s. v.; Winer, *Handbuch der theol. Lit.* i, 8, 634, 740, 750. (B. P.)

Kapp, Johann Georg, a Lutheran theologian of Germany, was born Nov. 8, 1737. He studied at Jena, Leipsic, and Erlangen. In 1761 he was preacher, and in 1781 subdeacon at Bayreuth, and died Oct. 11, 1814. He published, *Confusio Romanensium circa Potestatem Papæ* (Erlangen, 1758):—*De Meritis Philippi Melanchthonis* (1794). See Döring, *Die gelehrten Theologen Deutschlands*, s. v. (B. P.)

Kara, Joseph *ben-Simeon*, a Jewish writer of the 11th century, is the author of פרוש התורה, or glosses on Rashi's commentary on the Pentateuch; in the same manner he wrote on the Prophets, Job, Ezra, and Chronicles, and the five Megilloth. A collection of glosses from Kara's commentaries is given in נטעי נעמנים (Breslau, 1847); the commentary on Hosea was published from a MS. in the Jewish Theological Seminary at Breslau in 1861. See Zunz, *Gottesdienstliche Vorträge der Juden*, p. 301, 398; *Zur Geschichte und Literatur*, p. 68–70; Geiger, *Beiträge zur jüdischen Literaturgeschichte* (Breslau, 1847), p. 17–29; Fürst, *Bibl. Jud.* ii, 169 sq.; De' Rossi, *Dizionario Storico* (Germ. transl.), p. 157 sq. (B. P.)

Karaite-Tartar (or **Crimean Tartar**) **Version** of the Scriptures. The Karaite-Tartar is vernacular among the Karaite Jews of the Crimea. As to this division among the Jews, see Karaites. They have long been in possession of a Tartar version of the Old Test. When and by whom it was made is unknown. When Dr. Pinkerton was travelling in the Crimea he purchased a complete copy of this version. The two books of Chronicles do not appear to have been inserted in this version, but it comprises the other books of the Old Test. The translation is such, that although the words are mostly of Tartar origin, yet it would not be intelligible to any Tartar nation. The words are ranged in exact order of the Hebrew, and the style, construction, grammatical observances, and idioms are all conformable to the Shemitic type. This version is, in fact, so truly *Hebrew* in its character, that to the Turks and Tartars it is a sealed book. See *Bible of Every Land*, p. 350.

In point of practical utility it is deficient, and for this reason the British and Foreign Bible Society only published a small edition of the book of Genesis in 1819, at the mission press of Astrakhan. A subsequent edition of the entire Old Test. was published by the Jews of South Russia. The imperial library at St. Petersburg is now in possession of some codices which were lately procured, and are described by Strack in the *Catalog der Hebr. Bibelhandschriften der kaiserlichen öffentlichen Bibliothek in St. Petersburg* (Leipsic, 1875), p. 167 sq., which he conjointly published with A. Harkavy. On page 169 we find the first three verses of the book of Leviticus, of which we subjoin the first, together with the Hebrew:

Hebrew. { ויקרא אל־משה וידבר יהוה אליו מאהל מועד לאמר

Karaite. { ויקרא דבקירדי משה גא אהל מועד דן דסוזלדי יוי אגר דמא

It must be observed that the first word does not belong to the translation, but it is the first word of the Hebrew text, which is always placed at the beginning of each verse. Dr. H. Dalton, in his *Das Gebet des Herrn in den Sprachen Russlands* (St. Petersburg, 1870), gives the Lord's Prayer in the Karaite-Tartar which was prepared by the late A. Firkowitsch (q. v.). (B. P.)

Kara Lingis, a sect of Hindû ascetics, found only occasionally among the most ignorant portions of the community. They wander about in a nude state, and profess to worship Siva.

Karass (or **Turkish-Tartar**) **Version** of the Scriptures. The version generally denominated the Karass is so called because a town of that name, on the borders of the Caspian Sea, was the place of its publication. It has also been improperly termed the *Nogay* version, on account of its having been found intelligible to the Nogais, a tribe of Tartars dwelling on the banks of the Kouban and Kouma, in the steppes to the northward of Mount Caucasus. A more correct designation for this version is that of *Turkish-Tartar*, because it consists principally of words that belong in common to the Turks and Tartars. It exhibits the Turkish language in a comparatively pure state, and corresponds in style and language with such books as are circulated among the Tartars in the south of Russia, and is therefore intelligible to all the different Tartar hordes scattered through that extensive region.

The first version of the Scriptures written in this plain, unadorned Turkish style was that published at Oxford in 1666. The translation was made by William Seaman, formerly chaplain to an English ambassador at the Porte. This version, not being free from faults, was used by Mr. Brunton, Scottish missionary at Karass, as the basis for a new translation, for which he was eminently fitted on account of his thorough knowledge of the language. In 1807 he published the gospel of Matthew. He completed the translation of the New Test., and died while it was carried through the press. After his death the sheets were corrected by Mr. Frazer, and the edition was completed in 1813. In 1815 another edition of this translation was published, with a few emendations and an introduction by Mr. Dickson, one of the Scottish missionaries, who also undertook a translation of the Old Test. about the same time. The Psalms were completed and published at Astrakhan in 1815, and a second edition in 1818. The Pentateuch was published in 1878. Other books of the Old Test. were translated, but not printed. From the annual report of the British and Foreign Bible Society for 1883, we learn that Mr. Saleman is examining the text of the New Test. with a view to a new edition, the previous edition having been exhausted. From the report of 1884 we learn that the revision of the New Test. having been completed, the Bible Society's committee have decided to print a new edition, and that the reviser is now engaged in examining certain MS. translations of the Old Test., handed over by the National Bible Society of Scotland to the British Society. See *Bible of Every Land*, p. 347. (B. P.)

Kardoso. See CARDOSO.

Karelian Version. See RUSSIA, VERSIONS OF.

Karen Version OF THE SCRIPTURES. Karen is a language spoken by the Kareens, Karenes, or Careians, a wild and simple people scattered over all parts of the Burmese territories, and of the British provinces of Tenasserim; they are also found in the western portions of Siam, and northward among the Shyans. See *Bible of Every Land*, p. 15.

Till a comparatively recent period, however, Karen, which is remarkably harmonious and well adapted for poetry, was totally unknown to Europeans. About 1835, the missionaries of the American Baptist Missionary Society, Wade and Mason, acquired the language, and for the first time reduced it to writing, by employing the Burmese alphabet, with a few additional characters to express the peculiar sounds of the language. These two missionaries translated the entire New Test. into Karen, which was printed, in 1843, at Tavoy, by the aid of the American and Foreign Bible Society. Besides the translation into the Karen, translations into the different dialects prevalent among the Karens were made. The Karen has four principal dialects, the Bghai, Sgau, Pwo, and Mopgha. Into the latter dialect nothing has as yet been translated. As for the others, there exist in the

Bghai-Karen, parts of the Bible published since 1859, and at present there are published Genesis, and twenty chapters of Exodus, Psalms, St. James and St. John's epistles.

Pwo-Karen, Psalms, Daniel, and Jonah since 1861, added to which was Isaiah.

Sgau-Karen, the Pentateuch since 1864.

The Karen language has been treated by Wade, in *Grammar of the Karen Language* (1861). (B. P.)

Karma, a term used by the Buddhists to denote action, both meritorious and otherwise. When a human being dies, his Karma is transferred to some other being, regulating all the circumstances of his existence.

Karma-visaya, one of the four things which, according to Buddhists, cannot be understood by one who is not of their number. *Karma-visaya* denotes how it is that effects are produced by the instrumentality of Karma (q. v.) The other three things which only a Buddhist can understand are, (1) *Irdhi-visaya*, how it was that Buddha could go, in the snapping of a finger, from the world of men to the *Brahma-lokas*; (2) *Lóka-visaya*, the size of the universe, or how it was first brought into existence; (3) *Buddha-visaya*, the power and wisdom of Buddha.

Karrer, PHILIP JACOB, a Protestant minister of Germany, was born at Memmingen, Oct. 20, 1762. In 1818 he was called as dean and preacher to Kempten, Bavaria, and died in 1834. He is the author of, *Stunden der Andacht* (Kempten, 1825):—*Nachrichten von den protestantischen Pfarrörtern im Königreich Baiern* (ibid. 1825, 1826):—*Feste und Gebräuche in der katholischen und protestantischen Kirche* (Erlangen, 1829):—*Das geänderte und ungeänderte augsburgische Glaubensbekenntniss* (Kempten, 1830):—*Neues vollständig-richtigbiblisches Spruchregister* (ibid. 1833). See Zuchold, *Bibl. Theol.* i, 647; Winer, *Handbuch der theol. Lit.* i, 785, ii, 254, 304, 317. (B. P.)

Karsten, HERMANN RUDOLPH A., a Lutheran theologian of Germany, member of consistory and doctor of theology and philosophy, was born at Rostock, May 20, 1801. In 1825 he was ordained as assistant preacher, and in 1828 was appointed second preacher of St. Mary's, at his native place. In 1848 he was called as pastor to Dobberan, at the same time being appointed superintendent of his diocese. Two years later he was called as pastor primarius to the Schwerin cathedral. In 1876 he retired from the ministry, and died March 20, 1882. He is the author of, *Lehrbuch der christlichen Religion* (Rostock, 1838):—*Die Kirche und das Symbol in ihrem inneren Zusammenhange* (Hamburg, 1842):—*Grundlehren der populären protestantischen Dogmatik* (Rostock, 1847):—*Die protestantische Kirche u. deren zeitgemässe Reorganization* (Leipsic, 1850):—*Die letzten Dinge* (3d ed. Hamburg, 1861):—*Populäre Symbolik* (Nördlingen, 1860, 1863). See Zuchold, *Bibl. Theol.* i, 648. (B. P.)

Kartan. The site which we have proposed for this is marked as *Khan Katanah*, four and a half miles north of Safed, on the *Map* of the Ordnance Survey, but is not described in the accompanying *Memoirs*. Tristram suggests (*Bible Places*, p. 274) a trace of the name in *Wady Kerkerah*, which he vaguely describes as "running down to the sea."

Kashmir Version. See CASHMERIAN VERSION.

Kasi (*the magnificent*) is the ancient name of Benares, and the name by which it is still called among the Brahmins.

Kasina is an ascetic rite among the Buddhists, by the practice of which they hope to acquire supernatural powers. There are ten descriptions of this rite: 1. *Pathawi*, earth; 2. *Apo*, water; 3. *Téjo*, fire; 4. *Wáyo*, wind; 5. *Níla*, blue; 6. *Píta*, golden; 7. *Lóhita*, blood-red; 8. *Odáta*, white; 9. *Alóka*, light; 10. *Akasa*, space.

The priest who performs the *Pathawi-kasina* forms a small circle which he can easily fix his eye upon. The circle must be of clay of a light-red color, placed upon a frame made of four sticks, covered over with a piece of cloth, a skin, or a mat, upon which the clay is to be spread free from foreign substances. After preparing the earth-circle according to these and other directions with the utmost exactness, the priest sits down, and, gazing upon the circle, meditates upon the evils arising from the repetition of existence, and the best modes of overcoming them; on the benefits received by those who practice the *dhyanas* and other modes of asceticism; on the excellences of the three gems; and he must endeavor to secure the same advantages. He must continue to gaze and to meditate until he receive the *nemitta*, or inward illumination, by which all scepticism will be removed, and purity attained.

In performing the *Apo-Kasina* the priest pours water into an alms-bowl or similar vessel, and having chosen a retired place, must sit down and meditate, gazing upon the water, and reflecting that the perspiration and other fluids of his own body are composed of the same material.

The *Téjo-Kasina* is practiced by taking wood, dry and firm, cutting it into small pieces, and placing it at the root of a tree, or in the court of the *wihara*, where it must be ignited. He must then take a mat made of shreds of bamboo, or a skin or a cloth, and making in it an aperture one span and four inches in diameter, he must place it before him, and, looking through the aperture, he must meditate on the fire, and reflect that the fire in his own body is of a similar nature, flickering and inconstant.

The *Wayo-Kasina* is performed by sitting at the root of a tree, or some other convenient place, and thinking of the wind passing through a window or the hole of a wall; the *Nila-Kasina*, by gazing on a tree covered with blue flowers, or a vessel filled with blue flowers, or a blue garment covered with flowers; the *Pita-Kasina* by gazing on a golden-colored object; the *Lohita-Kasina* on a circle made with vermilion; the *Odata-Kasina* on a vessel of lead or silver, or the orb of the moon; the *Aloka-Kasina* by gazing on the light passing through a hole in the wall or the side of a vessel; and the *Akasa-Kasina* by gazing at the sky through a hole in the roof of a hut, or through a hole of the prescribed dimensions in a skin.

From the practice of Kasina in any one of its forms a Buddhist expects to derive many advantages. More especially does he expect the power of working miracles, according to the species practiced. The Kasina is exercised in fourteen different ways. See Hardy, *Eastern Monachism*, p. 252 sq.

Kate, GERHARD TEN, a Dutch theologian, was born in 1699. He studied at Utrecht, was in 1724 professor at the Lingen Gymnasium, in 1728 of philosophy at Deventer, in 1742 of Oriental languages and Church history at Harderwyck, and died Nov. 28, 1749. He wrote, *De Omnipræsentia Dei:—De Regno Dei et Christi:—De Regni Dei et Christi Fatis inter Gentes:—De Rebus Jesu Christi ex Prophetis.* See Jöcher, *Allgemeines Gelehrten-Lexikon*, s. v. (B. P.)

Käuffer, JOHANN ERNST RUDOLF, a Lutheran theologian of Germany, was born in 1793, at Reichenbach, in Upper Lusatia. In 1820 he was con-rector at Bautzen, Saxony, in 1824 professor at Grimma, in 1830 second court-preacher and member of consistory at Dresden, and died Sept. 10, 1865, doctor of theology. He published, besides a number of sermons, *Examinatio Novissima Bretschneideri de loco Rom. v*, 12 (Dresden, 1834):—*De Biblica ζωῆς αἰωνίου Notione* (ibid. 1838):—*Handbuch für den Religionsunterricht höherer Volksschulen* (ibid. 1849):—*Ueberblick der Geschichte der christlichen Kirche* (ibid. 1857):—*Biblische Studien* (1842–46, 4 vols.). See Winer, *Handbuch der theol. Lit.* i, 258; ii, 107, 234; Zuchold, *Bibl. Theol.* i, 654 sq. (B. P.)

Kaufmann, JOHANN, a Lutheran theologian of Germany, was born at Nuremberg in 1566. He studied at different universities, was in 1592 preacher at Wittenberg, in 1597 at Brunswick, and in 1611 at Schweinfurt. He died May 3, 1616, leaving, *Enchiridion Ordinandorum:—De Hamartigenia:—Catechismus Lutheri Minor Notis Illustratus.* See Rethmeyer, *Braunschweigische Kirchen-Historie;* Zeltner, *Diss. de Joh. Kaufmann;* Jöcher, *Allgemeines Gelehrten-Lexikon*, s. v. (B. P.)

Kauta, in the mythology of the Antilles islands, was a mountain of caves in Hayti, called also *Quisqueja.* Two of these caves are the cradle of humanity. The first pair were guarded here by a mighty giant, until the latter was petrified by the sun's light.

Kavanaugh, HUBBARD HINDE, D.D., a bishop of the Methodist Episcopal Church South, was born in Clark County, Ky., Jan. 14, 1802, and was of Irish extraction on his father's side. When young he learned the printing business. He was converted at sixteen, and at twenty-one became an itinerant minister. For some years he was engaged in the work of a circuit preacher, but gradually rose to the highest positions in the Church, and in 1854 was elected bishop. He died March 19, 1884. Before the division of the Church he was a member of the general conferences of 1832, 1836, and 1844, on the last occasion leading the Kentucky delegation. At this time he seems not to have taken any public part in the debates on slavery, though he fully sympathized with the position of the Southern delegates, and his name was signed to all their documents. Bishop Kavanaugh was closely identified with the Southern Church from its origin, and one of the most vigorous men, physically and intellectually, that Methodism has placed in the episcopacy. His presence was commanding, his voice good, his language copious, and his power in the pulpit great. See (N. Y.) *Christian Advocate*, March 27, 1884; Simpson, *Cyclop. of Methodism*, s. v.; *Minutes of the Annual Conferences of the M. E. Church South*, 1884, p. 155.

Kayser, AUGUST, a Protestant theologian, was born at Strasburg, Feb. 14, 1821. For some years assistant librarian at the university of his native place, and private tutor from 1843 to 1855, he accepted, in 1858, a call as preacher to Stossweiler. In 1868 he went to Neuhof, in Alsace, was appointed professor of theology at Strasburg in 1873, and died there, June 17, 1885. Kayser belonged to the so-called liberal Protestants, and contributed largely to the *Revue de Théologie.* He published *De Justini Martyris Doctrina* (Strasburg, 1850), but his main work is *Das vorexilische Buch der Urgeschichte Israels und seine Erweiterungen* (1874). (B. P.)

Kazan-Tartar Version OF THE SCRIPTURES. The Kazan-Tartars number about a million souls. A translation of the gospel of Matthew, in this dialect, was prepared by professor Ilminski, which was printed in 1873. This was tentative. The British and Foreign Bible Society being satisfied with the translator's abilities, agreed, in 1877, to print the gospels in the Arabic and Cyrillic characters, so that they might be read by Mohammedans of Kazan, who would not read them in the Russ character. As professor Ilminski proceeded very slowly in the preparation of the gospels, at the suggestion of Dr. Gottwald, the committee agreed to send Mr. Saleman, of the University Library, for six weeks to Kazan, to arrange with some one for the purpose of bringing out a New Test. in the language of the people, adapted from some of the sister dialects. Mr. Saleman was to edit the work at St. Petersburg, and refer all local peculiarities to the reviser at Kazan. This was agreed upon in 1880. During the year 1882 the gospel of Matthew, translated by Mr. Saleman, was printed at the Kazan University Press, under the care of professor Gottwald, the censor's authorization having been obtained for the entire New Test. In addition to the gospel of Matthew, that of Mark is to be printed during the year 1885. (B. P.)

Ke, one of the entities and essences in the dualistic system of the Chinese philosophers. It consists of matter most ethereal in its texture, and may be styled the ultimate material element of the universe, the primary matter which acts as the substratum on which things endued with form and other qualities rest, or from which they have been gradually evolved. The Ke, when resolved into its constituent elements, gives birth to two opposite essences, *Yang* and *Yin.* See CHINA.

Kedde, JOHANN, a German Jesuit, who died March 27, 1657, is the author of, *Ecclesia Antiqua Romano-Catholica:—Examen Reformatæ Religionis:—Hortulus S. Scripturæ:—Pallium Reformatæ Religionis:—Hortulus Passionis Christi:—Gloria Veræ Ecclesiæ.* See Alegambe, *Bibliotheca Scriptorum Societatis Jesu;* Jöcher, *Allgemeines Gelehrten-Lexikon*, s. v. (B. P.)

Kedesh OF ISSACHAR (or **Kishion**) has of late

Present appearance of Kedesh-Naphtali. (From Thomson's *Central Palestine and Phœnicia.*)

been with great probability identified with *Tell Abu Kudeis*, lying two miles south-east of Lejjûn, and described in the *Memoirs* accompanying the Ordnance Survey (ii, 69) as "An artificial mound, with traces of ruins, scattered pottery, and glass; and on the north are springs."

Kedesh of Naphtali is now represented by *Kades*, four and a quarter miles north-west of the lake of Huleh; its extensive ruins are copiously described in the *Memoirs* (i, 226 sq.) accompanying the Ordnance Survey.

Keene, Samuel, D.D., a Protestant Episcopal clergyman, was born in Baltimore County, Md., May 11, 1734. He graduated from the college in Philadelphia in June, 1759; was ordained deacon by the bishop of Rochester in the palace at Fulham, England, Sept. 21, 1760; and presbyter eight days after. He became incumbent of St. Ann's parish, Md., March 30, 1762; of St. Luke's parish, Queen Anne County, July 27, 1767; and in 1779 he was rector of Chester parish, which he served for two years, and then took charge of St. John's parish, Queen Anne and Caroline counties, probably in connection with St. Luke's, where he remained until 1792, living on his own estate. In 1803 he appears to have resigned St. Luke's, although still residing there, and in 1805 he became rector of St. Michael's Church, Talbot County, where he remained until his death, May 8, 1810, but after 1807 ceased to be its rector. He was one of the committee of examiners appointed in 1783, one of the superintending committee of 1788 and 1789, and one of the standing committee from 1788 to 1795. See Sprague, *Annals of the Amer. Pulpit*, v, 311.

Kehana, a species of divination by arrows, practiced by the ancient Arabians. Seven blunt arrows, called Azlam, each having a particular mark, were placed in a bag, and one was then drawn out and the oracle read by the diviner. It was also a custom used by the Assyrians.

Kehrein, Joseph, a Roman Catholic theologian of Germany, was born Oct. 20, 1808, at Heidesheim, near Mayence. He studied at Giessen, was in 1835 teacher at the gymnasium in Darmstädt, in 1837 at Mayence, in 1855 director of the seminary at Montabaux, and died March 25, 1876. He published, *Geschichte der katholischen Kanzelberedsamkeit* (Ratisbon, 1843, 2 vols.):—*Zur Geschichte der deutschen Bibelübersetzung vor Luther* (Stuttgart, 1851):—*Katholische Kirchenlieder, Hymnen, Psalmen* (1859–65, 3 vols.):—*Lateinische Sequenzen des Mittelalters aus Handschriften* (1873):—*Das deutsche katholische Lied in seiner Entwickelung* (1874). (B. P.)

Keilah. The modern representative of this, *Khurbet Kila*, lies seven miles east of Beit-jibrin, and eight and a quarter north-west of Hebron, and is a ruined village with two wells to the north, and a large terebinth to the south. It is only cursorily mentioned in the *Memoirs* accompanying the Ordnance Survey (iii, 314). In the neighborhood west of it the English engineers "found a sacred place dedicated to *Neby Naaman*, the name now attached to a sacred tree near the ruin called Khurbet Shermeh," which Lieut. Conder explains as a travesty of the native *Nephsa Neemana*, or "Monument of the Faithful," and equivalent to *Barath Satia*, which Sozomen says (*Hist. Eccles.* vii, 29) was the name of a place in his day ten stadia from Keilah, where the tomb of Micah was still found (*Quar. Statement* of "Pal. Explor. Fund," July, 1877, p. 142).

Keim, Carl Theodor, one of the most prominent theologians of Germany, was born at Stuttgart, Dec. 17, 1825. He studied at Maulbronn and Tübingen, where Baur exercised a great influence on him. For some time pastor at Esslingen, he was called, in 1860, as professor of New-Test. exegesis to Zurich, and in 1873 to Giessen, where he died, Nov. 17, 1878. Keim published, *Die Reformation der Reichstadt Ulm* (Stuttgart, 1851):—*Schwäbische Reformationsgeschichte bis zum augsburger Reichstag* (1855):—*Ambrosius Blarer, der schwäbische Reformator* (1860):—*Reformationsblätter der Reichsstadt Esslingen* (eod.). When he went to Zurich he turned his studies to the beginnings of Christianity, and in this department won a lasting reputation by the following works: *Die geschichtliche Würde Jesu Christi* (Zurich, 1860):—*Der geschichtliche Christus* (1865; 3d ed. 1866):—*Die Geschichte Jesu von Nazara* (1867–72, 3 vols.; Engl. transl. *Jesus of Nazareth*, Lond. 1873–82, 6 vols.), a life of Jesus from a rationalistic standpoint, though very learned and instructive. A popular form of this life of Jesus he published under the title, *Die Geschichte Jesu nach den Ergebnissen heutiger Wissenschaft* (Zurich, 1874; 2d ed. 1875). At Giessen he published *Celsus wahres Wort* (1873), and five years later his last work, *Aus dem Urchristenthum.* After his death, H. Zeigler, his literary executor, published from MS. *Rom und das Christenthum* (Berlin, 1881), a work of sterling value. See Lichtenberger, *Encyclop. des Sciences Religieuses*, s. v., and the sketch by Ziegler, prefixed to *Rom und das Christenthum.* (B. P.)

Keimann, CHRISTIAN, a Lutheran hymn-writer of Germany, was born Feb. 27, 1607, in Bohemia. He studied at Wittenberg, was in 1643 con-rector at Zittau, and in 1639 rector. He died Jan. 13, 1662. Of his many hymns some have been translated into English, as: *Meinen Jesum lass ich nicht* ("Jesus will I never leave," in the *Moravian Hymn-book*, No. 392):—*Freuet euch ihr Christen alle* ("O rejoice, ye Christians, loudly," in *Chorale Book for England*, No. 33). See Koch, *Gesch. d. deutschen Kirchenliedes*, iii, 369 sq.; Kämmel, *Chr. Keimann. Ein Beitrag zur Geschichte des Zittauer Gymnasiums* (Zittau, 1856). (B. P.)

Keith, ALEXANDER, D.D., a Presbyterian minister of the Free Church of Scotland, was born in Keith Hall, Aberdeenshire, in 1791. He received his education at Marischal College, Aberdeen. From 1816 to 1843 he was a clergyman of the Established Church of Scotland, at St. Cyrus, Kincardineshire, and subsequently a minister of the Free Church, but for many years, on account of failing health, he was unable to attend to parochial duties. The first edition of *Evidences of the Truth of the Christian Religion, Derived from the Literal Fulfilment of Prophecy*, a work which became a text-book in the colleges of England and Scotland, was published in 1823 (last ed. by his son, with photographic illustrations). Several other works on similar subjects, among which was *Christianity Demonstrated*, were published between 1831 and 1861. As one of the deputation of the Scottish Church to Palestine, he visited many of the scenes of Scripture prophecy, and an account of this mission was published under the title of *A Narrative of the Mission to the Jews*. Dr. Keith died at Buxton, Feb. 8, 1880. See *N. Y. Observer*, Feb. 18, 1880. (W. P. S.)

Kelam (*the science of the Word*), a term used by the Mohammedans to describe their scholastic divinity. The writings on the Kelam are very numerous, and very diverse in their teachings.

Kellach. See CELLACH.

Kellach (1), a Scotch prelate, was bishop of St. Andrews before the year 892 or 893, and held a provincial council under king Constantine III in 906. See Keith, *Scottish Bishops*, p. 6.

Kellach (2), a Scotch prelate, was chosen bishop of St. Andrews about 971, and confirmed by the pope. He ruled this see twenty-five years, and died in 996. See Keith, *Scottish Bishops*, p. 6.

Keller, Andreas, a Swiss theologian, was born at Schaffhausen in 1756. For a time preacher of the Waldensian congregation at Neuhengstrett, Würtemberg, he was called to Illnau, in the Zurich canton, and died in 1834. He is the author of *Kurzer Abriss der Geschichte der Würtemberger Waldenser* (Tübingen, 1796). (B. P.)

Keller, Georg Heinrich, a Lutheran theologian of Germany, was born in 1624. He studied at Tübingen, was in 1653 deacon, in 1659 superintendent, in 1670 doctor and professor of theology at Tübingen, and died Oct. 1, 1702. He wrote, *De Remissione Peccatorum in Veteri Testamento contra Joh. Coccejum*:—*De Reformatione Ecclesiæ*:—*De Convenientia et Disconvenientia Abarbanelis inter Mosen et Jeremiam ad Deut. xviii*, 15-18:—*De Messia Jehovah ad Psa. ii*, 7. See Fischlin, *Memoria Theologorum Virtembergensium*; Jöcher, *Allgemeines Gelehrten-Lexikon*, s. v. (B. P.)

Kelts. See CELTIC RELIGION.

Kemgisel. See CENGILLE.

Kemous, in African mythology, is the only religious festival celebrated by the Abyssinian negroes in the country of Darbanja, to their god Mussa Guzza, by sacrificing a cow.

Kemp (or **Kempe**), JOHN, a distinguished Anglican prelate and statesman, was born at Olanteigh, in the parish of Wye, County Kent. He went to school at Canterbury; became a fellow of Merton College, Oxford, and graduated in laws; but confined his practice to canon law; and in 1418 was employed as a military man, to hold musters at Caen, and to inspect troops. The first dignity to which he was called was the archdeaconry of Durham; it does not appear when he was appointed, but he was in possession of it in 1419. In January of the same year Kemp was elected to the see of Rochester. The following year Henry V made him keeper of his privy seal; and within two years he was nominated chancellor of the duchy of Normandy. He was translated to the see of Chichester, Feb. 28, 1421; was again translated, and sat as bishop of London, Nov. 17 of the same year. On his appointment as a member of the council, which took place immediately after the accession of Henry VI, Kemp resigned the great seal of Normandy. He was sent, in May, 1423, with a letter from the council, in the king's name, to the duke of Bedford, regent of France; and was also commissioned to thank the regent, in the name of the king, for his diligence and service in the government of France and Normandy. In February, 1424, he was sent to the marches of Scotland, to treat for the release of the king of Scots. About a month before his translation to the see of York, which occurred in 1426, Kemp was appointed to succeed Beaufort as lord high chancellor of England, which office he retained six years, and then retired on the plea of ill-health. He resumed this office, however, in 1450. In 1433 he was chosen to represent the Church of England at the Council of Basle; he was also in the year following at the head of an embassy to France, and again in 1439. In the latter year Kemp was created cardinal-priest, with the title of St. Balbina. He established a college at Wye as early as 1431. He enjoyed many important positions up to 1452, when he was appointed archbishop of Canterbury, July 21. Kemp attended to his duties faithfully to the last. He died suddenly, Feb. 24, 1454. See Hook, *Lives of the Archbishops of Canterbury*, v, 188 sq.

Kemper, JOHANN, a convert from Judaism, and professor of Hebrew and archæology at Upsala, where he died in 1714, translated the New Test. into Hebrew, with annotations. Under the title, מקל משה, he wrote an apology of Christianity, based upon the famous cabalistic storehouse, the Zohar. A specimen was published under the title, *Phosphorus Orthodoxæ Fidei . . . ex Pervetusto Libro Sohar Deprompta*, by A. Norrel (Amsterdam, 1720). See Jöcher, *Allgemeines Gelehrten-Lexikon*, s. v.; Fürst, *Bibl. Jud.* s. v. "Krakowia;" Delitzsch, *Wissenschaft, Kunst, Judenthum*, p. 304 sq. (B. P.)

Kendall, JAMES, D.D., a Congregational minister, was born at Sterling, Mass., Nov. 3, 1769. He graduated from Harvard College in 1796, passed two years as assistant teacher in Phillips Academy, Andover, at the same time pursuing his theological studies under the direction of Rev. Dr. Tappen, professor of divinity at Harvard College; was licensed by the Andover Association in 1795; in the same year was chosen tutor of Greek in the college, and removed to Cambridge. He commenced preaching at Plymouth, as a candidate, in 1799, and was ordained there in January, 1800. He was the sole pastor of the Church for thirty-eight years, preaching frequently in other pulpits, and died March 17, 1859. Dr. Kendall published a great many single sermons. In his theological views he is believed to have been an Arian. See Sprague, *Annals of the Amer. Pulpit*, viii, 427.

Kengillus. See CENGILLE.

Kennard, JOSEPH H., D.D., a distinguished Baptist

minister, was born of Quaker parentage near Haddonfield, N. J., April 24, 1798. While residing in Wilmington, Del., he became a Christian, and united with the Baptist Church in that city, where he was licensed to preach, Sept. 5, 1818. In 1819 he was agent for foreign missions in Delaware and New Jersey. He became pastor in Burlington, N. J., Nov. 14, 1819, and in January, 1822, of the Second Hopewell (N. J.) Church, where he remained until called to the Blockley Church, in what was then the suburbs of Philadelphia, Oct. 1, 1823. His labors in this field were abundant and successful. He acted also as a missionary in all the section of country around his home. In January, 1832, he became pastor of what is now the Fourth Baptist Church in Philadelphia, and six years thereafter of the Tenth Baptist Church, where his labors were attended with remarkable success. He died there, June 24, 1866. With all the great benevolent societies of his own denomination he was in hearty sympathy, and with a truly Christian spirit he labored with his brethren of other denominations for the promotion of the cause of God and humanity. See J. Spencer Kennard's *Memoir* (Am. Bapt. Publ. Soc., Phila.). (J. C. S.)

Kennere, *Saint*. See CAINNER.

Kenney, WESLEY, D.D., a Methodist Episcopal minister, was born in Washington County, Pa., May 8, 1808. He was converted in his nineteenth year, licensed to preach in 1831, and in 1832 entered the Pittsburgh Conference. His fields of labor were: Connellsville Circuit; Washington, Pa.; Liberty Street, Pittsburgh; Wheeling, Va.; agent for Allegheny College; Smithfield Street, Pittsburgh; Beaver Street, Allegheny City; Wheeling; presiding elder of Barnesville District, O.; secretary of the Wesleyan Sabbath Union, Washington, Pa.; and Chaplain Street, Wheeling. In 1852 he was transferred to the Newark Conference, wherein he served Central Church and Clinton Street, Newark; in 1855 was transferred to the Philadelphia Conference, wherein he served Trinity Church and Wharton Street, Phila.; Asbury, Wilmington, Del.; Fifth Street, Phila.; St. Stephen's, Germantown; idle one year, 1866; Easton, Md., 1867–69; Odessa, Del., 1870–72; presiding elder of Dover District, Wilmington Conference, from 1873 till his death in Smyrna, Del., June 24, 1875. Dr. Kenney was well educated, though not a college graduate. He excelled as a preacher, a model in pathos, clearness, instructiveness, and spirituality. See *Minutes of Annual Conferences*, 1876, p. 29.

Kenresi, in Thibetan mythology, is the mighty arranger of chaos. Not born of men, but created by the supreme god, he adopted as an ape the name *Prasrinpo*, took the goddess Kadroma as female ape, by the name of Prasrinmo, and populated Thibet, from whence the whole earth became inhabited. We find him in a second incarnation, under the name of *Gnia-thritz-thengo*, in Thibet, where he was teacher of the people, lawgiver, and king. He taught them agriculture, civilized them, and left the kingdom, which he had reigned over for ninety-one years, to his sons, of whom there were twenty-two, who together ruled one thousand one hundred and two years.

Keramians, a Mohammedan sect, deriving their name from their founder, Mohammed ben-Keram, who maintained that God is possessed of a bodily form.

Kerari, a Hindû sect who worshipped Devi in her terrific forms, and were wont to offer up human sacrifices. The only votaries belonging to this sect still remaining in India are those who inflict upon themselves bodily tortures, and pierce their flesh with hooks.

Kerbela, among the Mohammedans, is a place held by the Shiites (q. v.) as peculiarly sacred, because it is the seat of the tomb of Hossein (q. v.), the son of Ali. It is situated in Asiatic Turkey, twenty-eight miles north-west of the ruins of Babylon. It is a favorite place of pilgrimage to the Persian Mohammedans, who carry away small portions of the sacred soil, put it in little bags, which they place before them during their devotions to bow their heads upon, and thus worship on holy ground. The pilgrims resorting annually to Kerbela are estimated at eighty thousand, and they bring with them from Persia eight thousand corpses annually to be interred in the sacred spot.

Kerfoot, JOHN BARRETT, D.D., LL.D., a Protestant Episcopal bishop, was born in Dublin, Ireland, March 1, 1816, and educated at Flushing Institute and St. Paul's College, New York, where he graduated in 1834. He took deacon's orders in 1837, and priest's in 1840; became president of St. James's College, Maryland, in 1842, and continued in that relation till 1864, when he became president of Trinity College. He was consecrated bishop of Pittsburgh, Pa., Jan. 25, 1866, and remained in that office until his death, July 10, 1881.

Kerioth OF SIMEON. Its probable representative, *Khurbet el-Kureitein*, lies twelve miles south of Hebron, and is thus described in the *Memoirs* accompanying the Ordnance Survey (iii, 409):

"Traces of a large ruin and caves; apparently a large town.

"Guérin says that the ruins cover an extent of at least 180 metres in circumference. The direction of many streets can still be distinguished. The houses, whose remains are strewn everywhere over the ground, appear to have been constructed of materials regularly cut; most of them had caves or cellars below them, cut in the rock. He also observed at the western end of the site the ruins of a Christian church, forming a rectangle, lying east and west. Heaps of well-cut stones marked its outline. It was 30 paces long by 17 broad, and was preceded by a square atrium 37 paces on each side."

Kerkaessandi, in Hindû mythology, was the first Buddha, who appeared at the time when men reached the age of forty thousand years, to take their sins upon him. He does not now reign; the present regent is the fourth, and is called Shagkiamuni.

Kern, Friedrich Heinrich, a Lutheran theologian of Germany, was born April 20, 1750, and died at Tübingen, Feb. 3, 1842, doctor and professor of theology. He wrote, *Observationes ad Librum Jobi* (Tübingen, 1826):—*Commentationis de Virtute Christiana* (part i, 1828):—*Der Brief Jakobi untersucht und erklärt* (1838). See Zuchold, *Bibl. Theol.* i, 666; Winer, *Handbuch der theol. Lit.* i, 16, 206, 485. (B. P.)

Kern, Gottlob Christian, a Lutheran hymn-writer of Germany, was born Jan. 13, 1792. He studied at Tübingen, was in 1820 deacon at Besighein, Würtemberg, in 1824 professor at the theological seminary in Schönthal, and died Aug. 5, 1835. Of his many hymns, one has been translated into English: *Wie könnt' ich sein vergessen* ("Oh, how could I forget Him!" by Winkworth, *Lyra Germanica*, ii, 142). Kern's sermons were published by W. Hoffmann and L. Völter, Stuttgart, 1837. See Zuchold, *Bibl. Theol.* i, 666; Koch, *Gesch. d. deutschen Kirchenliedes*, vii, 210 sq. (B. P.)

Kern, Johann, a Lutheran theologian of Germany, was born July 30, 1756. He studied at Tübingen and Göttingen, was in 1781 professor at the gymnasium in Ulm, and after 1790 preacher there besides. He died Jan. 17, 1801, leaving, *Allgemeine Chronologie für die Zeiten nach Christi Geburt* (Leipsic, 1779):—*Der Katholicismus und der Protestantismus in ihren gegenseitigen Verhältnissen* (Ulm, 1792):—*Die Lehre von Gott* (1796):—*Die Lehre von der Freiheit und Unsterblichkeit der menschlichen Seele* (1797). See Döring, *Die gelehrten Theologen Deutschlands*, s. v.; Winer, *Handbuch der theol. Lit.* i, 405, 412. (B. P.)

Kernunos, in Gallic mythology, was a god, represented with horns and deer-ears, on a bas-relief found at Notre-Dame, Paris, in 1702.

Kerr, RICHARD HALL, D.D., an English clergyman, was born in Dublin, Ireland, Feb. 3, 1769. He graduated from Trinity College in 1788, was ordained and appointed domestic chaplain to the bishop of Sodor and Man in 1789, and in the following year went out to

India, where he was appointed principal of the Portuguese College at Mankeim, Bombay. In 1793 he became one of the East India Company's chaplains; in 1796 the superintendent of the Military Male Orphan Asylum at Egmone, Madras; and in the same year junior chaplain of Fort St. George, which office he held in addition to the presidency of the orphanage. In 1804 he was appointed senior chaplain of Madras, in which position he labored earnestly till his death, April 15, 1808. Dr. Kerr was an accomplished scholar, an impressive preacher, and very zealous in all his duties. See *The* (Lond.) *Christian Observer*, Feb. 1812, p. 80, 150.

Keshub Chunder Sen. See Sen.

Kessen, Andrew, LL.D., a Wesleyan preacher, the son of a minister of the Established Church of Scotland, was born in Glasgow in 1814. He was educated at the university of that city, from which he received his degree, early united with the Methodists, began to exhort at the age of fifteen, was received by the British Wesleyan Conference in 1840, and devoted all his attainments to the missionary cause. For fifteen years he was principal of the Government Normal Training Institution in Colombo, Ceylon, for native Christian schoolmasters. He was eminently fitted for such work by his scholarly attainments, his gift of teaching, and his interest in the work. On his return to England he devoted several years to the training of missionary students. His pastoral labors were unwearied; his unassuming kindness made him the true friend of the poor, and his genial disposition won the love of all. His life was pure and upright, and his piety was beautiful in its unaffected meekness, its implicit trustfulness, and its ardent catholicity. He resided in London during the latter part of his life. Kessen died while on a visit to Jersey, July 19, 1879. See *Minutes of the British Conference*, 1879, p. 40.

Kessler, John S., D.D., a learned and pious minister of the German Reformed Church, was born in Switzerland, Aug. 19, 1799. "After graduating at the canton school of Chur, he pursued and completed his theological studies at the University of Basle in 1821, and soon after, at the early age of twenty-two, he was ordained to the gospel ministry at Devos, in the canton Glaris." In this field he labored up to 1840, when he emigrated to America, and became pastor of several congregations in the vicinity of Woodstock, Va. In 1845 he received a call to become assistant pastor to the Rev. J. C. Bucher, in Reading, Pa. He removed to Baltimore in 1847, and took charge of a German congregation lately organized. In this charge he spent seven years of earnest labor, when he was called to assist his son in carrying forward an institution established in Allentown, Pa., to train young men for the profession of teaching. In connection with his duties in the seminary, he also had charge of several country churches. Here he ended his long and useful life, Dec. 22, 1864. Dr. Kessler was a man of superior talents, finished education, amiable disposition, and great humility. He contributed largely to the *Kirchenzeitung*, and also to Dr. Schaff's *Kirchenfreund*, and is the author of an unfinished work, *Biblical Dictionary*. He also aided in getting up a German hymn-book for the use of the Reformed Church. See Harbaugh, *Fathers of the Germ. Ref. Church*, iv, 167–174. (D. Y. H.)

Kestner, Christian August, a Protestant theologian of Germany, was born in 1794, and died at Jena, Oct. 27, 1821, professor of theology. He is the author of, *Ueber den naturhistorischen Kampf unter den beiden ersten Antoninen*, etc. (Jena, 1818):—*Die Agape unter Domitian's Regierung* (1819):—*De Eusebii Auctoritate et Fide* (1815). See Winer, *Handbuch der theol. Lit.* i, 573, 575, 892. (B. P.)

Kethubah (כְּתוּבָה, *written*, i. e. the Jewish marriage contract). See Marriage.

Ketteler, Wilhelm Emanuel, *baron von*, an eminent German ecclesiastic, was born in Münster, Westphalia, Dec. 25, 1811, of a noble race, renowned in German annals in the Church and in the field. From 1824 to 1828 he went to the Jesuit College at Brieg, thence to the universities of Göttingen, Berlin, Heidelberg, and Munich. At Heidelberg he had as fellow-student von Bismarck, afterwards prince-chancellor of the German empire. In 1833 the young baron entered the army, and from 1834 to 1838 he occupied important civic positions in his native town. In the latter year he returned to Munich to study theology; in 1844 he was ordained priest, and was pastor at Beckum, Westphalia, two years, Hopsten, three years, and provost of the Church of St. Hedwige, Berlin. In 1848 he received into the Roman Church the distinguished authoress, Ida, countess of Hahn-Hahn. In 1850 he was appointed to the bishopric of Mayence, where his labors were incessant and fruitful. He reopened the Episcopal Seminary, which had been closed for a quarter of a century, May 1, 1851, and furnished it with a fine staff of professors. After twenty-five years it was closed by order of the German government. Monsignor von Ketteler opened the smaller Seminary of Mayence, Aug. 11, 1864, and May 3, 1869, the one at Dreiburg, both of which disappeared under the new German code. He conducted numerous conferences and retreats, revived the ecclesiastical spirit, introduced severe examinations, and reinvigorated the body ecclesiastic of his diocese. In 1850 bishop von Ketteler recalled to Mayence the order of Capuchins; in 1858 he reinstalled the Jesuits in his diocese; in 1854 he established at Mayence a congregation of Franciscan Sisters, whose duty it was to care for the indigent sick; in 1856 he founded an asylum for unemployed domestics; in 1854 the countess of Hahn-Hahn established at his suggestion a convent of Sisters of the Good Shepherd, wherein the pious foundress remained till her death. Two years after he introduced the Sisters of the Perpetual Adoration. In the same year he founded the orphanage of St. Mary at Neustadt for poor and unprotected girls, and placed it under the direction of the congregation of Finthen (a village near Mayence), a charitable association of religious women, devoted to the free instruction of the poor, which he himself had founded in 1851. For poor orphans he instituted the hospital of St. Joseph at Kleinzimmern, also a school of the Christian Brothers at Mayence. In the last-named year he laid the foundation of the Catholic Working-men's Circle, which has many thousand members in Germany, and, as a companion to it, the Catholic Casino, established at the Hotel Frankfort, Mayence. Baron von Ketteler was at once a patriotic German and a devoted son of the Church. He was equally effective in the national assembly, on the platform, and in the pulpit. He was a man of gigantic frame, princely bearing, tempered by Christian sweetness, a model for his priests, and beloved by his people. When on his fifth visit to Rome, in 1877, to assist in the fiftieth anniversary of the episcopate of Pius IX, he caught the typhoid fever, of which he died, July 13 of the same year. Von Ketteler's literary works were mostly of a polemical character, mainly on questions of present interest, bearing the stamp of his intrepid character, practical mind, and vast knowledge of men and books. See (N. Y.) *Cath. Almanac*, 1878, p. 81.

Kettell, George F., D.D., a Methodist Episcopal divine, was born in Boston, May 18, 1817. He received an exhorter's license in 1840, in 1841 was licensed to preach, and soon took charge of the Church in Haddam, Conn. In 1847 he was received into the New York Conference, and became pastor successively at Haddam, Madison, and Windsor, Conn. In 1847 he was appointed pastor of Vesey Street Church, New York city. Afterwards he had charge of churches in Poughkeepsie, Rhinebeck, Philadelphia, and Brooklyn. He died in the last-named place, March 19, 1883. Dr. Kettell was a most efficient preacher and pastor. He brought the principles of divine revelation to bear upon questions of practical ethics with a subtle power that amounted to genius. Some of these sermons are said to have been attended with remarkable power. See *Minutes of Annual Conferences*, 1884, p. 92.

Keux, John le, an eminent English architectural engraver, was born in London in 1783, and studied with Basire. His works embrace nearly all the choice publications in England, illustrative of Gothic architecture, that appeared in his time, as *Britton's Architectural Antiquities, Cathedrals*, etc.; *Gothic Specimens and Gothic Examples;* the plates of the first volumes of *Neale's Churches*. He died in 1846.

Khakis, one of the Vaishnava (q. v.) sects of the Hindûs, founded by Kil, an indirect disciple of Ramanand. They are few in number, and either reside in certain limited districts or lead wandering lives. They are distinguished from the other Vaishnava sects by the application of clay or ashes to their dress or persons. Those who reside in fixed establishments dress like the other Vaishnavas, but those who lead a wandering life go either naked or nearly so, smearing their bodies with a pale gray mixture of earth and ashes. They worship Siva, Vishnu, Sita, and Hanumar.

Khandas, in Buddhist philosophy, are the elements of sentient existence, of which there are five: 1. The organized body, or the whole of being, apart from the mental processes; 2. Sensation; 3. Perception; 4. Discrimination; 5. Consciousness. The four last Khandas are results or properties of the first, which must be understood as including the soul as well as the body. At death the Khandas are believed to vanish entirely.

Khandoba, in Hindûism, is an incarnation of Siva, which is also called *Bhairav* (q. v.).

Kharejites (or *revolters*), a Mohammedan sect, who originally withdrew from Ali, and maintain that the Imâm need not be of the tribe of Koreish, nor even a freeman, provided he be just and qualified. They maintain, too, that if unfit he may be deposed, and that the office itself is not indispensable.

Kharfester, in Zendic mythology, are a series of wicked beings, who were especially created to punish the crimes of mankind. They were destroyed in the deluge by Tashter, the creative spirit.

Khasi Version of the Scriptures. The Khasi (or Khassee) is the language of the Cossyahs, Cassias, or Khasias, a race of Tartar or Chinese origin, ruled by a number of petty rajahs, who form a sort of confederacy. The first version of Holy Scripture in this language was prepared by a lady. She was the widow of one of the chieftains of the country, and Dr. Carey availed himself of her intelligence in translating the New Test. The preparation of this version occupied ten years; it was printed at Serampore in 1824. For about seven years it remained a sealed book, for no opportunity occurred of distributing it among the people for whom it had been prepared. In 1832 some of the missionaries at Serampore visited Cherrapoonjee, a place in the Khasi country, and their attention was drawn afresh to the spiritual wants of the people. A missionary station was formed there, and Mr. Lish, the first missionary who entered upon the work, turned his attention to a revision of the Khasi version, and in 1834 he produced a new or amended translation of the gospel of Matthew, which was printed at Serampore in Roman characters. In 1841 the Rev. Thomas Jones of the Welsh Calvinistic Methodists occupied this station, and executed a new translation of Matthew's gospel, in Roman characters, which, in 1845, he offered to the British and Foreign Bible Society. A small edition was printed as an experiment. After its value and fidelity was fully attested by competent persons, the translation of the entire New Test. was continued by the missionaries engaged on the above station. In 1871 the British and Foreign Bible Society announced that the translating and printing of the New Test. into this North-east India mountain dialect has been brought to a successful conclusion by the Rev. W. G. Lewis, who was materially aided in his labors by the late Rev. W. T. Meller. The report for 1879 stated that the missionaries of the Calvinistic Methodist Foreign Missionary Society were revising the New Test. The Rev. W. G. Lewis, who read the proofs, is engaged in revising manuscript translations of parts of the Old Test., and is also translating the book of Psalms. Since then the Pentateuch has been published (1884). See *Bible of Every Land*, p. 17. (B. P.)

Khata (or *scarf of blessings*), an article considered indispensable in Thibet, because it bestows upon the individual who possesses it many blessings from above. It is a piece of silk, nearly as fine as gauze, and of so pale a blue as to be nearly white. It is about three times as long as it is broad, and the two ends are usually fringed. They are of all sizes and prices, for a Khata is an article which neither rich nor poor can dispense with, and they are used on all imaginable occasions. See Huc, *Travels in Tartary, Thibet, and China*.

Khatib, an ordinary Mohammedan priest, who conducts the worship of the mosque on Fridays. He recites the prayers, and often preaches a sermon.

Khatmeh, a recitation of the entire Koran, which occupies about nine hours, and is customary at the funerals, weddings, and public festivals of Mohammedans, being regarded as meritorious in those who bear the expense.

Khelfun, a mythical flat-nosed satyr, with crown, leopard's skin, and goat's tail, who, on an Etruscan mirror, is conjoined with the goddess Munthukh.

Khem (or **Horus-Khem**, "The Bull of his Mother"), an ithyphallic deity of the ancient Egyptians, generally represented as standing upright, with his right arm extended in the act of scattering seed, and having behind it the threshing instrument, which is usually called a *flagellum*. His left hand and arm are closely enveloped in a thick robe, which swathes him like a mummy. His phallus is erected; and his head-dress consists of two upright plumes similar to those of the deity Amen-Ra; he wears a large and richly-ornamented collar round his neck. Mythologically, Khem represented the idea of divinity in its double character of father and son. As father he was called the husband of his mother, while as a son he was assimilated to the god Horus. He properly symbolized generative power, surviving death, indeed, but submitting to a state of rigidity and inertion over which he could not triumph till his left arm was freed. In the one hundred and forty-sixth chapter of the Egyptian Ritual of the Dead, the deceased is said to exclaim, when his soul is reunited to his body, "that he has overcome his bandages, and that it is given him to extend his arm." Khem was also the symbolic deity of vegetable life, and it was probably in allusion to this theory that in a vignette to the Book of the Dead, the new birth of the deceased is represented by a tree growing out of his person while he lies upon a bier. The great festival of germination, in the Egyptian husbandry, was held in honor of the god Khem, and it is fully figured on the walls of the palace temple of Rameses III, at Medinet Habu. See Rawlinson, *Hist. of Ancient Egypt*, i, 331 sq.

Khemah, one of the principal female disciples of Buddha (q. v.).

Khirkhah (*a torn robe*), a name given to the dress generally worn by dervishes (q. v.), which Mohammedans claim was the dress worn by the ancient prophets.

Khodum. See Gotama.

Khors, a god worshipped by the ancient Slavonians, an image of whom existed at Kioff before the introduction of Christianity. They were accustomed to offer to this deity the *kororay*, or wedding-cake, and to sacrifice hens in his honor.

Khotbeh, a prayer which Mohammed was accustomed to recite, and in which example he was followed by his successors. It consists of two parts: the first appropriated to the deity, the prophets, the first four caliphs and their contemporaries; the second includes the prayer for the reigning sovereign. Other khotbehs are offered at certain stated seasons.

Khrishna. See KRISHNA.

Khumbandas, an order of beings among the Buddhists, who are believed to be the attendants of *Wirudha*, one of the four guardian Dewas. They are monsters of immense size and disgusting form, have blue garments, hold a sword and a shield of sapphire, and are mounted on blue horses. They form one of the thirteen orders of intelligence exclusive of the supreme Buddhas.

Kiddushin (קידושין, *betrothal*). See MARRIAGE.

Kiel, TOBIAS, a Lutheran theologian of Germany, was born at Ballstädt, near Gotha, Oct. 29, 1584. He studied at Jena, and died as pastor of his native place, in 1627. He is the author of several hymns, one of which, *Herr Gott nun schleuss den Himmel auf*, has been translated into English (*Lyra Germ.* ii, p. 278), "Lord God, now open wide thy heaven." See Koch, *Geschichte des deutschen Kirchenliedes*, ii, 268 sq.; Brückner, *Kirchen und Schulen Staat im Herzogthum Gotha*, vol. iii (Gotha, 1760). (B. P.)

Kienlen, HEINRICH WILHELM, a Protestant theologian of Germany, was born at Berlin in 1816. He studied at Strasburg, was pastor at Colmar in 1842, in 1858 at Strasburg, and died in 1876. He published, *Siebzehn Fest-Homilien über Lehrtexte* (Basle, 1844):—*Encyklopädie der Wissenschaften der protestantischen Theologie* (Darmstädt, 1845):—*Commentaire sur l'Apocalypse* (Paris, 1870). Besides, he contributed to the *Studien und Kritiken*, Herzog's *Real-Encyklopädie*, *Revue de Théologie*, *Revue d'Alsace*, etc. See Lichtenberger, *Encyclop. des Sciences Religieuses*, s. v.; Zuchold, *Bibl. Theol.* i, 668. (B. P.)

Kierkegaard, SÖREN AABY, a Danish philosophical and theological writer, was born May 5, 1813, at Copenhagen. He spent his whole life in his native city, and, being rich and unmarried, became a father to the poor. In 1838 he published pseudonymously *From the Papers of a Living*, and in 1841 a dissertation *On the Idea of Irony*. In the same year he went to Berlin to acquaint himself with Schelling's philosophy. In the following year he returned home, and from 1843 to the time of his death, Nov. 11, 1855, he devoted himself entirely to literary activity. In 1843 he published his *Whether—Or*, in two parts, representing respectively the æsthetical and the ethical type of life, and placing indirectly before the reader the question: Which of these two types ought to be chosen? In the same year he published a small collection of *Sermons*:—*Bits of Philosophy* (1844):—*Stations along the Road of Life* (1845):—*Lilies of the Field* (1849):—*Training for Christianity* (1850):—*How Christ Looks upon Official Christianity* (1855), etc. During twelve years he prepared about thirty volumes for the press, and about as many he left in manuscript. All his writings, as it would seem, were executed according to a preconceived plan; and the subjects chosen were so written that all criticism grew silent. According to Kierkegaard Christianity is no scientific theory, but life and existence. Hence he rejected altogether the ideas of creed, Church, priest, etc. A Christian is, according to him, an insulated individual, alone with God, and in contact with the world only through suffering. Some of his writings were translated into German. As yet we have no biography which gives a satisfactory representation of his philosophical and religious standpoint. See the article "Kierkegaard," in *Nordisk Konversations-Lexikon* (1879); Petersen, *Dr. Sören Kierkegaard's Christendomsforkyndslse* (Christiana, 1877); Martensen, *Christliche Ethik*, § 69, 70, where Kierkegaard is compared with Vinet; Lütke, *Kirchl. Zustände in den skandinavischen Ländern* (Elberfeld, 1864), p. 45-58; Heuche, in *Zeitschrift für luth. Kirche und Theologie*, 1864, p. 295-310; Brandes, *Sören Kierkegaard, ein literarisches Charakterbild* (Leipsic, 1879); Michelsen, in Plitt-Herzog's *Real-Encyklop.* s. v. (B. P.)

Kilconcath, WILLIAM DE, a Scotch prelate, was elected bishop of the see of Brechin about 1260. He died at Rome in 1275. See Keith, *Scottish Bishops*, p. 159.

Killikelly, BRYAN B., D.D., a Protestant Episcopal clergyman, was born on the island of Barbadoes in 1807. He became rector, in 1853, at Kittanning, Pa.; about 1857 of two churches, All-Saints, in Paradise, and Christ Church, in Leacock; and in 1864 returned to Kittanning. In 1866 he was rector of Grace Church, Mount Washington, and in the following year was made a missionary under the ecclesiastical authority of the diocese, residing at Kittanning, and officiating at McKeesport and vicinity, in which service he continued until within a short time of his death, April 11, 1877. See *Prot. Episc. Almanac*, 1878, p. 169.

Kimball, JOSEPH, D.D., a Reformed (Dutch) minister, was born at Newburgh, N. Y., Aug. 17, 1820. He graduated from Union College in 1839, and from Newburgh Theological Seminary in 1843; was licensed by the Associate Reformed Church the same year; was pastor at Hamptonburgh from 1844 to 1852; at Hebron; at Brockport; at Fishkill-on-the-Hudson, from 1863 to 1865; at Brooklyn, from 1865 to 1874, and died Dec. 6 of the latter year. Dr. Kimball was an able theologian, a laborious preacher, and a sympathetic pastor. See Corwin, *Manual of the Reformed Church in America*, 3d ed. p. 328.

Kincaid, EUGENIO, D.D., a distinguished Baptist missionary, was born at Mount Zion, Pa., in 1797, and brought up in southern New York. He was one of five students who formed the first class in what is now Madison University, Hamilton, N. Y. While pursuing his studies, he decided to become a foreign missionary. The war between England and Burmah led to the temporary postponement of his plan. Meanwhile he was pastor, for a time, of the church at Galway, and then, for five years, performed missionary labor in the mountainous districts of central Pennsylvania. In the spring of 1830 he sailed from Boston to Burmah, reaching Maulmain towards the close of that year. He commenced at once the study of the language, giving twelve hours a day for six days to his work, and preaching on the Sabbath to the English soldiers stationed in that section of Burmah. Having acquired a knowledge of the language, he spent a year preaching to the Church in Rangoon, and then went to Ava, the capital, and subsequently spent three months in visiting every town and village along the banks of the Irrawaddy. For nearly two months he lived in his boat, subjected to severe hardships; but he heroically continued his work among the natives, and at the end of fifteen months had baptized eleven converts, and organized them into a church. After many years spent in laborious service for his Master, Dr. Kincaid returned, in 1865, to the United States, broken down in health, and took up his residence in Girard, Kan., where he died, April 3, 1883. See Cathcart, *Baptist Encyclop.* p. 658. (J. C. S.)

King, George Ives, D.D., a Presbyterian minister, was born at Adams, N. Y., June 1, 1815. He studied at Lowville, graduated from Union College in 1838, and from Auburn Theological Seminary in 1841; was licensed by the Presbytery of Columbia, at Hudson, in April, 1840; and for a time was principal of Union Academy, at Belleville, preaching to two feeble churches on alternate Sabbaths. In the fall of 1843 he was ordained pastor of the Westernville Church, by the Presbytery of Utica. In 1846 he contracted throat-disease by overwork, and then spent two years travelling in the Southern States to restore his health; in 1848 was installed pastor of the Church at Hanover, N. J.; in 1856 of the First Church in Quincy, Ill., in 1868 of the First Church in Jerseyville. He died in New Orleans, La., March 12, 1873. See *Hist. of the Presb. Church in Illinois*, vol. i; *Gen. Cat. of Auburn Theol. Sem.* 1883, p. 246.

King, John, D.D., a Presbyterian minister, was born at Chestnut Level, Lancaster Co., Pa., Dec. 5, 1740. He was educated at Philadelphia College; studied theology privately; was licensed by the Second Presbytery of Philadelphia in March, 1767; in 1769 was called to the pastorate of the Presbyterian Church at Conococheague, Pa., where he remained to within a short time of his death, which occurred July 5, 1811. See Sprague, *Annals of the Amer. Pulpit*, iii, 281.

King, Jonas, D.D., an eminent Congregational missionary, was born at Hawley, Franklin Co., Mass., July 29, 1792. He graduated from Williams College in 1816, and from the Theological Seminary at Andover in 1819. At the foundation of the new college at Amherst, in 1821, he was elected professor of Oriental languages and literature, having spent a part of the intervening time in missionary labors in the Southern States, and visited France to better prepare himself for the duties of his professorship. He offered his services to the American Board for three years, and in September, 1822, left Paris for Malta. In January, 1823, he reached Alexandria, in Egypt. There, with others, he spent three months preaching, distributing tracts and copies of the Bible. After passing some time in the Holy Land, he returned to his native country in 1827. Having been invited to proceed to Greece in one of the vessels which was to carry out supplies to the afflicted inhabitants of that country, he resigned his professorship, which he had nominally held six years. In 1830 he again put himself under the direction of the American Board, and in 1831 established a school at Athens, where he remained until his death, May 22, 1869. He wrote numerous works in modern Greek, and, on account of some sentiments thus expressed, he was sentenced to fifteen days' imprisonment and expulsion from the kingdom. The sentence, however, was not executed, on account of an official protest. His principal work is *The Oriental Church and the Latin* (N. Y. 1865). See *Trien. Cat. of Andover Theol. Sem.*, 1870, p. 1819; *Memoirs of Amer. Missionaries*, p. 109; and his *Memoir* (N. Y. 1879).

King, William, D.D., an English Independent minister, was born in Wiltshire, June 9, 1701. He had pious parents, who educated him at the University of Utrecht, Holland, where he began to preach. He returned to England, and was ordained pastor at Chesham, Bucks, in April, 1725. He had offers of preferment in the Church, but being a dissenter from conviction, he refused them. In February, 1740, he settled as pastor at Hare Court, London; in 1748 was appointed one of the merchants' lecturers at Pinner's Hall, and delivered one hundred and ninety-two lectures there, the last in January, 1769. He was also evening lecturer at Silver Street, and a lecturer at Lime Street. He died March 4, 1769, and was interred at Bunhill Field. See Wilson, *Dissenting Churches*, iii, 299.

Kingo, THOMAS, a famous hymn-writer of Denmark, was born Dec. 15, 1634, at Stangerup, in the island of Zealand. He studied theology at Copenhagen, and was appointed pastor of his native parish in 1668, and bishop of Funen in 1677. He died in 1703. Kingo was a poet born, and a powerful Christian character, and he has given the Danish Church some of its very best hymns. He published *Aandelige Sjunge-Chor*, a collection of hymns, 1674; and another collection in 1681. He also compiled, at the instance of the government, a new hymn-book, known as *Kingo's Psalmebog*, 1699, which is still in use. See *Nordish Conversations-lexicon* (1879), s. v.; Brandt og Helweg, *Den Danske Psalmodigtning Historie* (Copenhagen, 1847); Michelsen, in Plitt-Herzog's *Real-Encyklop.* s. v. (B. P.)

Kingsford, EDWARD, D.D., a Baptist minister, was born in Boston, Lincolnshire, England, in 1788. He received a liberal education, and had a high reputation as a scholar. He was for several years an officer in the service of the East India Company. While in this position he was converted, and at once devoted himself to the work of the ministry. For some time he was a pastor in England, and, in 1838, came to America. He labored for a few years in Utica, N. Y., and then removed to Alexandria, D. C. He was highly esteemed and respected wherever he resided, his pulpit efforts being of more than ordinary excellence. He died in Washington, D. C., July 27, 1859. See *Watchman and Reflector*, Aug. 11, 1859. (J. C. S.)

Kingsley, CHARLES, an eminent English clergyman and writer, was born at Holne Vicarage, near Dartmoor, Devonshire, June 12, 1819. He graduated from Magdalen College, Cambridge, in 1842; the same year became curate of Eversley, Hampshire, and rector in 1844, a position which he retained for the rest of his life. In 1859 he was appointed regius professor of history at Cambridge, but resigned in 1869, on being offered a canonry in Chester Cathedral, which four years later was exchanged for one in Westminster Abbey. He was also chaplain in ordinary to the queen, and one of the chaplains to the prince of Wales. He died Jan. 23, 1875. Kingsley belonged to the "Broad Church" party, and was an earnest advocate of social improvement. He wrote a large number of popular works, most of them of a fictitious character, but highly instructive, the most noted of which perhaps was his *Hypatia* (1853):—also *Alexandria and her Schools* (1854). He frequently contributed to *Fraser's Magazine*, the *North British Review*, and wrote some articles for the *Encyclopædia Britannica* (8th ed.). He was also known as a poet. See his *Letters and Memoir*, by his widow (Lond. 1876, 2 vols. 8vo, abridged ed. N. Y. 1877).

Kinika Version OF THE SCRIPTURES. The Kinika is vernacular to the tribes of the Wanika, in eastern Africa. The late Dr. Krapf, who laid the foundation of the grammatical and lexicographical structure of the Kinika language, likewise prepared a Kinika version of the gospels of Luke and John, and of the epistles to the Romans and Ephesians. But only the gospel of Luke was printed in 1848 at Bombay, in the American Mission press. In 1881 the gospel of Matthew was published, the translation having been made by the Rev. Thomas Wakefield, a missionary at Ribe since 1861. See *Bible of Every Land*, p. 438. (B. P.)

Kinninmund, ALEXANDER, a Scotch prelate and doctor of theology, was bishop of Aberdeen, April 1, 1329. While he was in office there, the city of Aberdeen was burned by thirty English ships, in 1333. He died soon after. See Keith, *Scottish Bishops*, p. 110.

Kippurîm (כִּפֻּרִים, *expiations, atonement*), a name given by the Hebrews to the great day of atonement (q. v.), because on that day the sins of the whole people were understood to be expiated or pardoned.

Kirchhofer, JOHANNES, a Protestant theologian, was born Dec. 15, 1800, at Schaffhausen, in Switzerland. He studied at Göttingen and Halle, was in 1827 pastor at Hofwyl, in 1829 professor of theology at the *Collegium Humanitatis*, in his native city; in 1842 he was elected deacon at St. John's, and in 1854 pastor there. He died Feb. 27, 1869. Kirchhofer took a very active part in the ecclesiastical affairs of his country. For a time he was the president of the synod, and as such exercised a great influence upon the younger theologians. Of his writings we mention especially, *Quellensammlung zur Geschichte des neutestamentlichen Canons* (Zurich, 1842-44):—*Leitfaden zur Bibelkunde* (2d ed. Stuttgart, 1860). See *Dr. Johannes Kirchhofer, Dekan*

Church of St. Jeremiah at Kuryet el-Enab. (From Thomson's *Central Palestine and Phœnicia.*)

und Pfarrer in Schaffhausen (Schaffhausen, 1871); Zuchold, *Bibl. Theol.* i, 687. (B. P.)

Kirghese-Tartar Version OF THE SCRIPTURES. The Kirghese-Tartar is a dialect spoken by the Kirghese in Siberia and Turkestan. In 1818 the New Test. was translated by Charles Frazer, a Scottish missionary. Since this mission was abandoned, nothing was done for the circulation of the Word of God among this people, numbering about 1,500,000. In 1879, however, the British and Foreign Bible Society issued an edition of three thousand copies of Mr. Frazer's New Test., it being printed at the Kazan University press, under the care of professor Gottwaldt, who arranged the verses in the new edition as they stand in the Greek and English, besides revising a few passages which were badly translated. See *Bible of Every Land*, p. 349. (B. P.)

Kiriath Shema (*the reading of the Shema*), the recital by the Jews of certain passages of the Old Test., called Shema (q. v.).

Kirin, a fabulous monster, conspicuous in Chinese and Japanese legends. It is supposed to be not only gentle and innocent, but intelligent, virtuous, and holy. It is never seen but at the appearance of a particular constellation, and at the nativity of some worthy benefactor of his race.

Kiritinus, ALBANUS. See BONIFACIUS, QUERETINIUS.

Kirjath-jearim. Lieut. Conder regards this as a different place from the simple KIRJATH, and was inclined at first to locate it at *Soba* (*Tent Work*, i, 22), but finally at *Khurbet Erma*, two and a quarter miles south of Chesalon or Kesla (*Memoirs* accompanying the Ordnance Survey, iii, 46 sq., where he argues the question at length); but most geographers still incline to the position at *Kuryet Enab* (or simply *el-Kuryet*), a full description of the archæology of which is given in the same *Memoirs* (iii, 132 sq.).

Kirk, EDWARD NORRIS, D.D., a Congregational minister, was born in New York, Aug. 14, 1802. He graduated from the College of New Jersey in 1820, studied law eighteen months, and in 1824 graduated from Princeton Theological Seminary. He acted for a

Figures of Kirin.

time as agent for the American Board of Foreign Missions in the Southern States, and in 1828 was settled over a Presbyterian Church in Albany, N. Y. In 1837 he went to Europe, preaching in London, and several months in Paris. In 1839 he returned to the United States, and in 1842 became pastor of the Mount Vernon Congregational Church in Boston, where he labored until 1871, when the failure of his health caused him to transfer the active duties of his office to a colleague. He visited Paris in 1856, in the interests of the American and Foreign Christian Union, to establish American Protestant worship in that city. He afterwards became president of the American Missionary Association. He died in Boston, March 27, 1874. Dr. Kirk was a preacher and writer of rare strength and brilliancy. He published two volumes of *Sermons:—Lectures on the Parables:*—a translation of *Gaussen's Théopneustie*, and other works. See *Cong. Quarterly*, 1878, p. 259.

Kirkham, Robert, a minister of the Church of England, was one of the Oxford Methodists. He, in connection with the Wesleys and Mr. Morgan, were the four young men who began, in November, 1729, to spend evenings together, reading, chiefly, the Greek Test.—the inception of that movement which has so changed the religious life of the world. He was the son of Rev. Lionel Kirkham, of Stanton, in Gloucestershire; was a very intimate friend of Wesley's, and earnest in his desire for higher life, faithfully keeping the rules of the Oxford Methodists. In 1731 he left Oxford and became his uncle's curate. These facts are the limit of our knowledge concerning him. It is to be regretted that no record of his life can be found. See Tyerman, *The Oxford Methodists*, p. 1.

Kislar Aga, the chief of the black eunuchs in Turkey, who is intrusted with the superintendence of all the mosques.

Kist, Nicolaus Christian, a Dutch theologian, was born April 11, 1793. After having completed his studies at Utrecht he was made doctor of theology in 1818, and was called as pastor to Zoelen, in the province of Guelderland. In 1823 he was appointed professor of theology at Leyden, and inaugurated his lectures by a discourse on *De Progressione Ingenii Humani in Dogmatum Historia Christiana Animadvertenda*. In connection with his colleague, Royaards, Kist published *Archief voor Kerkelijke Geschiedenis Inzonderheid von Nederland* (Leyden, 1829–49, 20 vols.; supplement in 2 vols. 1852–54). With W. Moll he published *Archives Historico-Ecclésiastiques* (Amsterdam, 1857–59, 2 vols.). Of his other works we mention, *Oratione iv quæ Ecclesiæ Reique Christianæ Spectant Historiam* (Leyden, 1853):—*De Vrije Wil of de Mensch een Redelijk en Zedelijk Vrijwerkend Wezen* (1859). Kist died Dec. 11, 1859. See Winer, *Handbuch der theol. Lit.* i, 544, 574; ii, 111; Zuchold, *Bibl. Theol.* i, 689 sq.; Lichtenberger, *Encyclop. des Sciences Religieuses*, s. v. (B. P.)

Kiswaheli. See Swahili.

Kitchen. This part of a monastic establishment invariably adjoined the refectory, behind it, in Benedictine houses, and on the side, usually, in Cistercian arrangements. The ordinary shape was square, but there were exceptions: thus, a bottle-form was adopted at Marmoutier, a round at Chartres, Villers, Saumur, and Vendôme, an octagon at Pontlevoy, Caen, Durham, Glastonbury, and with little apses at Fontévrault. At Westminster there was a vaulted way to the hall; at Canterbury a covered alley; but in the smaller orders a hatch or window formed the means of communication. There was also a kitchen for the infirmary, and the abbot had his own kitchen.

Kitchener was the marketer and purveyor who bought the provisions for kitchen use, and was overseer of the cooks, butchery, and fishponds. He visited the sick every morning, and saw that the broken meat was reserved for the poor.

Kitchi Manito, the name by which the Great Spirit was known among the various tribes of American Indians, especially in Canada. He is the chief of their good divinities. See Manito; Indians.

Kito, a god whom the Chinese soldiery honor as their patron.

Kitoo, a particular prayer which is used by the Japanese in all seasons of public distress.

Kitu, homage or reverence paid by one person to another among the natives of Japan. Inferiors being seated on their heels, according to the Japanese fashion, testified their respect for their superiors by laying the palms of their hands on the floor, and bending their bodies so low that their foreheads almost touched the ground. The superior responded by laying the palms of his hands upon his knees, and nodding or bowing, more or less low, according to the rank of the other party.

Kiwasa, a deity among the savages in Virginia. They represented this god with a lighted pipe in his mouth, which a priest, cunningly concealed behind the idol, smoked, thus proving the god to be alive.

Klaproth, Heinrich Julius, a German Orientalist, was born in Berlin, Oct. 11, 1783. In 1802 he published, *Asiatisches Magazin*, and was made adjunct to the academy for Asiatic languages at St. Petersburg:—*Reise in den Kaukasus und Georgien in den Jahren* 1807 *und* 1808 (Halle, 1812–14, 2 vols.; transl. into French, Paris, 1823). In 1812 he left the Russian civil service, went in 1814 to Italy, in 1815 to Paris, where he was made professor of the languages of Asia in 1816. He died Aug. 20, 1835. Besides the above works, he published, *Geogr.-historische Beschreibung des östlichen Kaukasus* (Weimar, 1814):—*Reise nach Georgien und Imirethi* (Berlin, 1815):—*Verzeichniss der chinesischen und mandschuischen Bücher und Manuskripte der königl. Bibliothek in Berlin* (Paris, 1822):—*Asia Polyglotta* (1823):—*Tableaux Historiques de l'Asie* (1834, 4 vols.):—*Mémoires Relatifs à l'Asie* (eod.):—*Collections d'Antiquités Égyptiennes* (1829):—*Examen Critique des Travaux du feu M. Champollion sur les Hiéroglyphes* (1832):—*Aperçu Général des Trois Royaumes, Traduit de l'Original Japonais-Chinois* (1833). (B. P.).

Klausing, Heinrich, a Lutheran theologian of Germany, was born Dec. 28, 1675, in Westphalia. He studied at Wittenberg, commenced his academical career there in 1696, and was doctor of theology in 1710. In 1719 he was called to Leipsic as professor of theology, and died Oct. 2, 1745. His writings are very numerous, and their titles are given by Jöcher, *Allgemeines Gelehrten-Lexikon*, s. v. (B. P.)

Klein, Anton, a Roman Catholic theologian, was born in 1788. In 1811 he received holy orders. He was for some time professor of Church history at Grätz and Vienna, and died at the latter place, April 9, 1867. He is the author of, *Historia Ecclesiæ Christianæ* (Grätz, 1827, 2 vols.):—*Geschichte des Christenthums in Oesterreich und Steiermark* (Vienna, 1840–42, 7 vols.). (B. P.)

Klemm, Johann Conrad, a Lutheran theologian of Germany, was born Nov. 23, 1655. He studied at Tübingen, was in 1687 professor there, and died Feb. 18, 1717. He wrote, *Do voce βάρβαρος ad* 1 *Cor. xiv*, 11:—*Vindiciæ Locorum Pentateuchis Corruptionis Accusatorum:—De κοινωνίᾳ θείας φύσεως ad* 2 *Petr. i*, 3, 4:—*De Concilio Benedicti XIII:—De Papatu Hierarchico:—De Nominibus Hebraicis*, etc. See *Neue Zeitungen von gelehrten Sachen;* Jöcher, *Allgemeines Gelehrten-Lexikon*, s. v. (B. P.)

Kleutgen, Joseph, a Jesuit, was born at Dortmund, Sept. 11, 1811. In 1834 he joined his order, and received holy orders in 1837. For some time he lectured on rhetoric and philosophy at Freiburg and Brieg, Switzerland, went to Rome in 1843, where he became professor at the Collegium Germanicum. He died at St. Anton, in Tyrol, Jan. 14, 1883, leaving, *Die Theologie* *der Vorzeit* (Münster, 1853-65, 2 vols.; 2d ed. 1867-73):—*Die Philosophie der Vorzeit* (1860-63, 2 vols.):—*Institutiones Theologicæ* (1881, vol. i):—*Das Evangelium des Matthäus nach seinem inneren Zusammenhang* (1882). (B. P.)

Knak, Gustav, a Lutheran minister of Germany, was born in Berlin, July 12, 1806. He studied in his native city, was in 1834 pastor at Wusterwitz, in Pomerania, in 1849 Gossner's successor at the Bethlehem Church in Berlin, and died July 27, 1878, at Dünnow, in Pomerania, whither he had gone to restore his feeble health. Knak was famous alike as preacher and hymn-writer. See Zuchold, *Bibl. Theol.* i, 701; Koch, *Gesch. d. deutschen Kirchenliedes*, vii, 194; Wangemann, *Gustav Knak. Ein Prediger der Gerechtigkeit, die vor Gott gilt* (Berlin, 1879). (B. P.)

Knapp, Jacob, a distinguished Baptist evangelist, generally known as "Elder Knapp," was born in Otsego County, N. Y., Dec. 7, 1799. Having pursued his studies at Hamilton, he first settled in Springfield, near his native place, and then in Watertown. After having been in the pastoral office for eight years, he felt that he must henceforth devote himself to the work of an evangelist. At this time he had what he always considered a remarkable religious experience. His early labors as an evangelist in some of the great cities and villages of our land were followed by wonderful results. Thousands of conversions took place. In some of these places "his preaching gathered such crowds and produced such excitement that mobs threatened his meetings, and police force had to be employed to suppress popular violence. By the terrors of the law rather than by tender exhibitions of God's love, he sought to drive men to the Cross for salvation." Many of his sermons were models of reasoning and eloquence, the most gifted men feeling the impression as well as the ignorant. He died at his residence, near Rockford, Ill., March 2, 1874. See Jeffrey, *Memoirs of Jacob Knapp; The Baptist Weekly*, March 12, 1874. (J. C. S.)

Knichin, Charles, a minister of the Church of England, was one of the Oxford Methodists, and a fellow of Corpus Christi College. He left Oxford at about the same time the Wesleys did, and became rector of Dummer, a small village of about four hundred inhabitants. In his parish he kept up the habits of the Oxford Methodists, visited from house to house, catechised the children, and had public prayers twice each day. In 1736 he was chosen dean of Corpus Christi College, but retained his rectory at Dummer. While at Oxford he kept the old Oxford Methodist spirit of work alive, visiting the prisoners and ministering unto them. Mr. Knichin never revived the friendship between him and the Wesleys, but followed them in their struggles after higher life until he himself experienced salvation by faith. At the time when the Established churches refused the Wesleys their pulpit, Mr. Knichin's was one of eight to which they had access. He was intensely religious, "lived it, looked it, breathed it." He died Jan. 4, 1742. See Tyerman, *The Oxford Methodists*, p. 363.

Kniepstro. See Knipstro.

Knife, Eucharistic, was a knife with which to prepare the sacramental bread and for dividing the eulogiæ, anciently found in most sacristies. The holy loaf, out of which they were cut, was ordered to be provided by the parish by the Salisbury constitution of 1254. King Athelstan left his knife on the altar of Beverley, as a pledge for his redemption of a vow of benefaction.

Eucharistic Knife, with a Hard-wood Handle, preserved at St. Andrew's, Vercelli.

Knight, Franklin Lafayette, D.D., a Protestant Episcopal clergyman, was born in Maine, in August, 1824. He graduated from Bowdoin College in 1846; after teaching for several years, was elected professor of Greek and Latin in a Southern university; in 1853 was ordained, and, for some time, exercised his ministry in the state of Maryland; in 1859 he was invited to be chaplain to the bishop of New Jersey. For a few years he was principal of the Diocesan Training and Theological School, in Tennessee. Resigning this position, he removed to Washington, D. C., where, during the remainder of his life, he was assistant minister in the Church of the Epiphany, and also in St. John's. He died there in April, 1876. Dr. Knight was a classical teacher of repute, of blameless life, retiring in disposition, highly esteemed and respected. See *History of Bowdoin College*, p. 622. (J. C. S.)

Knight, Richard, D.D., a Wesleyan Methodist minister, was born in Devon, England, in 1789. He was accepted by the British Conference, and sent to Newfoundland in 1816. He endured persecutions and hardships, escaped perils oft, was appointed to Halifax, N. S., in 1832, labored thenceforth principally in Nova Scotia until his death at Sheffield, N. B., May 23, 1860. Apparently stern and unapproachable at first, a kind heart and large sympathies dwelt in Knight's stalwart frame. Inflexible when right, humble, dignified, zealous, cautious, courageous, yet gentle; he was an excellent preacher, well-read, and one of the ablest and most prominent ministers in the Maritime Provinces. Dr. Knight was a strong friend of temperance, and published an address on the subject. He also published a *Lecture on the Genuineness and Authenticity of Revelations* (St. John's, N. B., 1850). See Huestis, *Memorials of Meth. Ministers in East Brit. America*, p. 56; Morgan, *Bibl. Canadensis*, p. 214.

Knoll, Albert Joseph, a Roman Catholic theologian of Germany, was born in 1796. He received holy orders in 1818 at Trent, and joined in the same year the order of the Capuchins. In 1820 he was teacher of religious philosophy, in 1823 professor of dogmatics, in 1847 custos-general at Rome. He died at Botzen, Tyrol, March 30, 1863. Knoll published, *Institutiones Theologiæ Generalis seu Fundamentalis* (Innsbrück, 1846; 4th ed. 1865):—*Expositio Regulæ F. F. Minorum S. P. Francisci Assisi Congesta* (ibid. 1850):—*Institutiones Theologiæ Theoreticæ seu Dogmatico-Polemicæ Concinnatæ* (Turin, 1862-64, 6 vols.). After his death was published *Institutiones Theologiæ Theoreticæ seu Dogmatico-Polemicæ* (1865, 2 vols.). (B. P.)

Knowlton, Miles Justin, D.D., a distinguished missionary of the American Baptist Missionary Union, was born at West Wardsborough, Vt., Feb. 8, 1825. When quite young he was sent to the academy at West Townsend, and while there determined to enter the Christian ministry. His college and theological studies were pursued at Madison University, Hamilton, N. Y., where he graduated in 1853. He was ordained at West Wardsborough, Oct. 8 of the same year, and, with his wife, Lucy Ann (St. John), embarked for China, and arrived in June, 1854, at Ningpo, where, with singular earnestness and marked success, he labored for nearly twenty years. He died there, Sept. 10, 1874. Among the qualities which made him a model missionary were his remarkable singleness of purpose, his persistency in active labor, and his gentle bearing towards the people. See *Amer. Bapt. Miss. Magazine*, v, p. 91. (J. C. S.)

Knox, Andrew, a Scotch prelate, of the same family with the Scottish reformer, was born at Ranfurly, in Renfrewshire. He was educated at Glasgow, was first minister at Lochwinnoch, and then at Paisley. King James made him bishop of the Isles in April, 1606, where he distinguished himself by his attention to the propagation of religion. In 1622 he was translated to the see of Raphoe, in Ireland, where he remained until his death, Nov. 7, 1632. See Reid, *Hist. of the Presb. Church in Ireland;* Keith, *Scottish Bishops*, p. 308.

Knox, Hugh, D.D., a Presbyterian minister, was born in Ireland, and came to America in 1751. He spent several years in teaching, leading a somewhat dissipated life; but he shook off his follies and entered Nassau Hall, and graduated in 1754. He studied divinity with president Burr. At his ordination, preparatory to his accepting a call to the island of Saba, the New York Presbytery was so much pleased with his trial sermon on the *Dignity and Importance of the Gospel Ministry*, that they unanimously requested it for publication. A sermon preached by him, *On the Sinner's Faultiness and Inability*, was published by bishop Hobart in 1808, and became the subject of much controversy on the distinction between natural and moral inability. The Presbytery corresponded with him yearly through Dr. Rodgers, and expressed regret on hearing after the Revolution of the declining condition of his flock. The celebrated Alexander Hamilton, in early boyhood, was placed under the instruction of Dr. Knox. He published two volumes of sermons on interesting subjects, at Glasgow, in 1772. He spent the closing years of his life at St. Croix, and died there in October, 1790. See Webster, *Hist. of the Presb. Church in America*. (W. P. S.)

Knox, John P., D.D., a Presbyterian minister, was born at Savannah, Ga., July 28, 1811. He graduated from Rutgers College and the Theological Seminary, New Brunswick, N. J., and was ordained pastor of the Reformed Church of Nassau, N. Y. After this he served as pastor of the Reformed Church at Utica, for two years. He then went to St. Thomas, W. I., where he spent ten years of ministerial labor, and then returned to the United States and accepted a call, in 1855, to the Presbyterian Church at Newtown, L. I. In this old church he labored with zeal and success until his death, June 2, 1882. See *N. Y. Observer*, June 8, 1882. (W. P. S.)

Knox, Thomas, a Scotch prelate, and son of Andrew Knox, was made bishop of the Isles upon his father's translation, in 1622. He died in 1626. See Keith, *Scottish Bishops*, p. 308.

Knox, William Eaton, D.D., a Presbyterian minister, was born at Knoxboro, Oneida Co., N. Y., Oct. 16, 1820. He graduated from Hamilton College in 1840, and pursued his theological studies at Auburn Seminary. In 1844 he was ordained pastor of the Presbyterian Church in Watertown, and in 1848 of that in Rome. In 1870 he accepted a call from the First Presbyterian Church at Elmira, where he continued for the rest of his life. He died at Blue Mountain Lake, in the Adirondacks, Sept. 17, 1883. He occupied an elevated position among his clerical brethren. See *N. Y. Observer*, Sept. 28, 1883; *Gen. Cat. of Auburn Theol. Sem.* 1883, p. 70. (W. P. S.)

Knute. See CANUTE.

Koch, August, a Protestant theologian, was born at Helmstädt in 1818. For some time privatdocent at Zurich, he retired from that position, and died, March 4, 1882, at Oberkaufungen, near Cassel. He wrote, *Commentar über den Brief Pauli an Philemon* (Zurich, 1846):—*Commentar über den ersten Brief Pauli an die Thessalonicher* (1849; 2d ed. 1855). See Zuchold, *Bibl. Theol.* i, 706 sq. (B. P.)

Koch, Eduard Emil, a Lutheran theologian, who died April 27, 1871, at Erdmannhausen, near Marbach, is the author of *Geschichte des Kirchenliedes und Kirchengesanges* (Stuttgart, 1866–70, 7 vols.), the best hymnological work now extant. (B. P.)

Koch, Ignatius, D.D., a Protestant Episcopal clergyman, first appears in the record as rector of St. John's Church, Western, Missouri. In 1865 he became rector of St. John's Church, Valparaiso, Ind. The following year he was a teacher in Palmyra College in Missouri. In 1867 he was appointed a missionary to the German population in Maysville, Ky., and served in this relation until about 1870, when he was elected principal of St. John's Academy, Jacksonville, Fla., besides performing missionary work in adjacent places. Here he remained until his death, which occurred Dec. 8, 1872. See *Prot. Episc. Almanac*, 1873, p. 134.

Köcher, Hermann Friedrich, a Lutheran theologian of Germany, was born in 1747 at Osnabrück, and died April 2, 1792. He is the author of, *Nova Bibliotheca Hebraica* (Jena, 1783–84, 2 vols.):—*Versuch einer Erklärung der Geschichte Saul's mit der Betrügerin zu Endor* (Gera, 1780):—*Specimen Observationum Philologicarum in 1 Sam. ii* (Jena, 1772):—*Comm. Sistens Explicationem Vocum* ויאמר *et* ויקרא *Gen. i, 3, 5, de Deo Usurpatorum* (1778):—*Comm. ad Genes. ii*, 18–20, *de Vocatis ab Adamo Animantibus* (1779):—*Stricturarum Antimasorethicarum in Kirjan et Chetib. ad Librum Judicum Specimen* (1780). See Fürst, *Bibl. Jud.* ii, 194; Winer, *Handbuch der theol. Lit.* i, 69. (B. P.)

Kodesh. See KADDISH.

Kodom. See GOTAMA.

Kohen. See COHEN.

Kohen, Jacob Shalom, a Jewish writer of Germany, was born at Meseritsch, Dec. 23, 1771, and died at Hamburg in 1846. He is the author of, סדר העבודה, or *Historisch-kritische Darstellung des jüdischen Gottesdienstes* (Leipsic, 1819):—תורת לשון עברית, a Hebrew grammar (Berlin, 1802, and often):—קורא הדורות, or *History of the Jewish People* (Warsaw, 1838):—מקרא קדש, or *Die ganze heilige Schrift* (Hamburg, 1824, 4 vols.), etc. See Fürst, *Bibl. Jud.* ii, 195 sq. (B. P.)

Kohlbrügge, Herman Friedrich, the founder of the Dutch-Reformed congregation at Elberfeld, was born at Amsterdam, Aug. 15, 1803. He was of Lutheran parentage, and after studying theology became preacher to a Lutheran congregation in Amsterdam. But the rationalism of his colleagues brought him into a conflict which resulted in his deposition. He took the degree of doctor of theology at Utrecht, and after living for several years in retirement joined the Reformed Church. While travelling through the Rhine regions in 1834, where just at that time a kind of revival took place, he preached often, and made a deep impression. After many difficulties, the Reformed congregation at Elberfeld, which had separated from the state establishment, chose Kohlbrügge for its minister (1847), constituting itself as a member of the Church of the Netherlands. At Elberfeld Kohlbrügge labored with great success till his death, March 5, 1875. Besides a considerable number of sermons, he published, *Das siebente Capitel des Briefes Pauli an die Römer* (3d ed. 1855):—*Wozu das Alte Testament* (eod.), etc. See Zuchold, *Bibl. Theol.* i, 709 sq.; Plitt-Herzog, *Real-Encyklop.* s. v.; Lichtenberger, *Encyclop. des Sciences Religieuses*, s. v. (B. P.)

Kohlman, Anthony, an eminent Roman Catholic author, was born at Kaizersberg, near Colmar, July 13, 1771. He was ordained priest in April, 1796, joined the fathers of the Sacred Heart, and in 1799 he served those who were taken with the plague in Hagenbrunn, and was appointed chief chaplain of the Austrian military hospitals in Padua, whose moral and physical state was described as frightful. He exercised the ministry in Upper Germany and in Prussia until, in 1805, he entered the Society of Jesus. In 1807 he was sent to America, a part of the time superior of the Jesuit missions. In 1809 he visited Thomas Paine on his death-bed, in company with father Benedict Fenwick. A faithful account of it is in the *United States Catholic Magazine*, 1842, p. 358. In 1813 the "Catholic Question in America" was discussed in the courts of New York, in which Kohlman took an important part. The case was reported by William Simpson, Esq., one of the counsel, and published in New York by Gillespy. In 1820–21 Kohlman published his *Unitarianism Philosophically and Theologically Examined* (2 vols. 8vo), going through three editions in a short time. He was rector of Washington Seminary in 1824, when the so-called Mathingly Miracle took place, an account of which was published by Wilson (12mo). In 1825 this keen and learned Jesuit was called to Rome to teach moral theology in the Gregorian University, just restored to the Jesuits by Leo XII, who held him in great esteem, and had placed at his service his private library. Kohlman died in Rome, April 10, 1836. See *Cath. Almanac*, 1872, p. 80; De Courcey and Shea, *Hist. of the Cath. Church in the U. S.* p. 356 sq.

Koi Version OF THE SCRIPTURES. The Kois, who are a branch of the Gonds in Central India, number about one hundred thousand souls. At the request of the Church Missionary Society, the British and Foreign Bible Society published, in 1884, a tentative edition of five hundred copies of the gospel of Luke and the 1st epistle of John. The translation was made by general Haig, assisted by three Kois who understood the Telugu Bible. The translator read also the proofs of the edition. (B. P.)

Koitsch, CHRISTIAN JACOB, a Lutheran theologian of Germany, was born in 1671 at Meissen. He studied at Halle, was inspector of the Royal School there from 1700 to 1705, head master of the grammar-school at Elbing, in Prussia, from 1705 to 1725, and died in 1735. Koitsch was a man of eminent piety, and his love to Jesus finds expression in his hymns, of which a few are preserved. The most beautiful of his hymns, *O Ursprung des Lebens, O ewiges Licht*, is found in an English translation in the *Moravian Hymn-Book*, No. 540. See Koch, *Geschichte des deutschen Kirchenliedes*, iv, 370 sq. (B. P.)

Koive, the ancient pagan high-priest of the Prussians. When it thundered they believed that their Koive was conversing with their god Perkun, hence they fell down before that deity, and implored of him to send them more favorable weather.

Kojalowicz, ALBERT WIJUK, a Polish Jesuit, who died at Wilna, Oct. 6, 1677, is the author of, *Colloquia de Sincero et non Adulterato Usu S. Scripturæ ad Probandos Articulos Fidei:—De Electione Unius Veræ Christianæ Religionis.* See Witte, *Diarium Biographicum;* Jöcher, *Allgemeines Gelehrten-Lexikon*, s. v. (B. P.)

Kol Nidrey (כָּל נִדְרֵי, *all the vows of*, being the initial words) is a Jewish prayer which opens the service for the day of atonement. It is repeated three times in the most solemn manner, and runs thus, "All vows, obligations, oaths, or anathemas, whether termed קונם קונס or otherwise, which we shall have vowed, sworn, devoted, or bound ourselves to, from this day of atonement until the next day of atonement (whose arrival we hope for in happiness), we repent, aforehand, of them all; they shall all be deemed absolved, forgiven, annulled, void, and made of no effect; they shall not be binding, nor have any power; the vows shall not be reckoned vows, the obligations shall not be obligatory, nor the oath considered as oaths." This liturgical formula has been turned against the Jews, as if by it they absolved themselves from all obligations, and therefore could not be bound by an oath. But it must be considered that the Kol Nidrey speaks only of vows made voluntarily, and not of oaths made to others, for the latter were regarded as inviolable except by the personal consent of the individual who had received the oath. The Kol Nidrey dates from about the 9th century, and in MS. its form varies. In its general form it might be used by bad men to escape obligations. But hatred of the Jews has turned the possibility into a fact, and against this charge the Jews have protested at all times. See Lehmann, *Die Abschaffung des Kol Nidre* (Mayence, 1863); Aub, *Die Eingangsfeier des Versöhnungstages* (ibid. eod.); Eisenmenger, *Entdecktes Judenthum* (Königsberg, 1711), ii, 489 sq.; Bodenschatz, *Kirchliche Verfassung der heutigen Juden*, ii, chap. 5; Strack, in Plitt-Herzog, *Real-Encyklop.* s. v. (B. P.)

Konkani Version OF THE SCRIPTURES. The Konkani (or Kunkana) is the proper language of the Concan, a long, narrow tract of land, the continuation of Malabar and Canara. It is a dialect of the Marathi, influenced by the Davidian languages of South India. It is spoken by upwards of one hundred thousand inhabitants, chiefly on the western coast. The majority of the people belong to the Hindû faith, but many are Roman Catholics; some of them speak the language with a mixture of Portuguese words. A version of the New Test. into this language was executed at Serampore between the years 1808 and 1819, and was printed in the Devanagari character. In 1821 the Pentateuch left the press. Of late (1883) the gospels of John and Matthew have been published by the Madras Auxiliary Society, in a revised form, so as to be better understood by all classes. See *Bible of Every Land*, p. 129. (B. P.)

Konrad. See CONRAD.

Koopmann, WILHELM HEINRICH, a Protestant theologian of Germany, was born Sept. 4, 1814, at Tönning, in Holstein, and died May 21, 1871, a general superintendent, with the title "bishop" of Holstein. He wrote, *Die Scheidewand zwischen Christenthum und Widerchristenthum* (Heide, 1843):—*Die grundrechtliche Confusion in Staat, Schule, und Kirche* (1850):—*Das evangelische Christenthum in seinem Verhältnisse zu der modernen Kultur* (Hamburg, 1866):—*Die Rechtfertigung allein durch den Glauben an Christum* (Kiel, 1870):—*Phantasie und Offenbarung* (eod.). Besides, he contributed largely to the *Kirchliche Blätter* of Holstein. See Zuchold, *Bibl. Theol.* i, 718 sq.; *Gedenkblätter an Dr. theol. W. H. Koopmann, weiland Bischof für Holstein* (Altona, 1871). (B. P.)

Köpke, RUDOLF ANASTASIUS, a Protestant theologian and historian of Germany, was born at Königsberg, Aug. 23, 1813. He studied theology and history, was teacher at the Joachimsthalsche gymnasium in Berlin from 1838 to 1842; commenced lecturing at the university in 1846, and was made professor in 1856. He died June 21, 1870. Besides his editorial work on the *Monumenta Germaniæ*, he wrote, *De Vita et Scriptis Luidprandi Episcopi Cremonensis* (Berlin, 1842):—*Widukind von Corvei* (1867):—*Hrotsuit von Gandersheim* (1879). (B. P.)

Köpken, DAVID HEINRICH, a Lutheran theologian of Germany, was born Nov. 4, 1677, at Luneburg. He studied at Helmstädt, Jena, and Rostock, and commenced his academical career at the latter place. In 1704 he was doctor of theology, in 1708 professor of philosophy, and died in 1745. He wrote, *De Filio Dei ex Ægypto Divinitus Vocato:—De Donis Ægyptiacis Quibus Abeuntes Israelitæ Donati Fuerunt:—Disp. II de Jesu Christo sub Metu et Tristitia Acerbissime Dolente:—De Via Rationis ad Revelationem:—De Theologia et Religione:—De Revelatione Divina.* See *Bibliotheca Lubecensis;* Jöcher, *Allgemeines Gelehrten-Lexikon*, s. v. (B. P.)

Kordovero, MOSES. See MOSES CORDOVERO.

Koreish, JEHUDA. See IBN-KOREISH.

Korn, SELIG. See NORK.

Korsha, in Slavonic mythology, is a god of physicians and the medical art. Some regard him as the same with *Bacchus*. He is represented naked, with a wreath about his neck. Beer and nectar were offered to him. His idol stood in Kiew, on a large barrel.

Köster, Friedrich Burchard, a Protestant theologian of Germany, was born in 1791 at Loccum, and studied at Göttingen. In 1822 he went to Kiel as professor of theology, was appointed in 1840 general superintendent of the duchies of Bremen and Verden, resigned his position in 1860 on account of feeble health, and died at Stade, Dec. 16, 1878. Of his works we mention, *Das Buch Hiob und der Prediger Salomo's übersetzt* (Schleswig, 1832):—*De Fidei Modestia Nostris Temporibus Maximopere Commendanda* (Kiel, eod.):—*Erläuterungen der heiligen Schrift aus den Klassikern besonders aus Homer* (1833):—*Die Psalmen übersetzt* (Königsberg, 1837):—*Die Propheten des Alten und Neuen Testaments dargestellt* (Leipsic, 1838):—*Die biblische Lehre von der Versuchung* (Gotha, 1859). See Zuchold, *Bibl. Theol.* i, 722; Winer, *Handbuch der theol. Lit.* i, 83, 205, 280, 361, 370, 392, 445, 489, 599; ii, 31; Lichtenberger, *Encyclop. des Sciences Religieuses*, s. v.; Fürst, *Bibl. Jud.* ii, 206. (B. P.)

Köthe, Friedrich August, a Lutheran theologian of Germany, was born July 30, 1781, at Lübben, in Lower Lusatia. He studied at Leipsic, was in 1803 afternoon preacher there, in 1810 professor of Church history and practical theology at Jena, in 1817 doctor of theology, in 1819 first preacher and member of consistory at Allstädt, in Weimar, and died Oct. 23, 1850. He published, *Die symbol. Bücher der evang.-luther. Kirche* (Leipsic, 1830):—*Einfluss des kirchenhistorischen Studiums*, etc. (1810):—*Stimmen der Andacht* (1823):—*Die christliche Volksbildung* (1831):—*Ueber die Kircheneinigung* (1837):—*Die Psalmen* in *Kirchenmelodien übertragen* (1845):—*Geistliche Lieder* (edited by C. B. Meissner, 1851, after the author's death). See Zuchold, *Bibl. Theol.* ii, 723; Winer, *Handbuch der theol. Lit.* i, 16, 26, 322, 530, 862, 866; ii, 19, 323, 325, 333, 343; Koch, *Gesch. des deutschen Kirchenliedes*, vii, 257 sq. (B. P.)

Kottmeier, Adolph Georg, a Protestant theologian of Germany, was born Oct. 31, 1768, at Neuenkirchen, near Osnabrück. In 1789 he was teacher at Halle, in 1790 preacher at Haddenhausen, near Minden, in 1792 at Hartum, in 1810 cathedral-preacher at Bremen, and died Sept. 20, 1842, doctor of theology. He was an ascetical writer of some renown. See Zuchold, *Bibl. Theol.* i, 723; Winer, *Handbuch der theol. Lit.* ii, 67, 99, 185, 233, 294, 375. (B. P.)

Kounboum (*ten thousand images*), a place in the country of Amdo, in Thibet, where grows a wonderful tree, known as the Tree of Ten Thousand Images. The lamasery of Kounboum contains nearly four thousand lamas, and is a great resort for pilgrims from all parts of Tartary and Thibet.

Kouotina, in the mythology of the Caribbeans, is the head of all idols, from whom all the rest flee. Their flight causes the thunder.

Kouren of the Thousand Lamas, a celebrated lamasery in Tartary, which dates from the invasion of China by the Mantchous. The ground and revenues were given by a Chinese emperor, who had recently come into possession of the throne, in token of his gratitude for a favorable prophecy given by a lama before his conquest. It was designed originally to maintain a thousand lamas, but has made such progress that it now contains more than four thousand. The chief officer of the establishment is also governor of the district, and makes laws, administers justice, and appoints magistrates. See Lamaism.

Kousulu. See Hinduwi, Dialects of.

Kouwwonpææelisit, in Finnish mythology, is a lively festival among the nations living in the far north, which was begun with a bear hunt. It is not known in honor of what deity this festival was celebrated.

Koxkox. See Coxcox.

Krabbe, Otto Carsten, a Lutheran theologian of Germany, was born at Hamburg, Dec. 27, 1805. He studied at Bonn, Berlin, and Göttingen, was in 1833 professor at the gymnasium in Hamburg, in 1840 professor of theology and university-preacher at Rostock, in 1851 member of consistory, and died Nov. 14, 1873, doctor of theology. He wrote, *De Codice Canonum qui Apostolorum Nomine Circumferuntur* (Göttingen, 1829):—*Ueber den Ursprung und Inhalt der apostolischen Constitutionen des Clemens Romanus* (Hamburg, eod.):—*Die Lehre von der Sünde und vom Tode* (1836):—*Vorlesungen über das Leben Jesu* (1839):—*Die evangelische Landeskirche Preussens* (Berlin, 1849):—*Das lutherische Bekenntniss* (1859):—*Wider die gegenwärtige Richtung des Staatslebens im Verhältniss zur Kirche* (Rostock, 1873). See Zuchold, *Bibl. Theol.* i, 724. (B. P.)

Kragh, Theodor, a Lutheran theologian and missionary of Denmark, was born in 1795. After having passed his theological examination, he went to Greenland as a missionary. He translated a great part of the Old Test. and many ascetical works into Greenlandish, and published a prayer-book and collection of sermons in that language. He died March 25, 1883, at Oesby, near Hadersleben, in Schleswig. See Fürst, *Bibl. Jud.* ii, 207. (B. P.)

Krakewitz, Barthold von, a German Lutheran divine, was born in the isle of Rügen in 1582. He studied at different universities, was professor of theology at Greifswalde, general superintendent of Pomerania, and died Nov. 7, 1642. He wrote, *Comment. in Hoseam et Jonam*:—*De Bonis Christianorum Operibus*:—*De Jesu Christo θεανθρώπῳ*, etc. See Freher, *Theatrum Eruditorum*; Witte, *Memoriæ Theologorum*; Jöcher, *Allgemeines Gelehrten-Lexikon*, s. v. (B. P.)

Krapf, Johann Ludwig, a famous German missionary, was born Jan. 11, 1810, at Devendingen, near Tübingen. He studied at the latter place, and entered the service of the Church Missionary Society in 1837. He was sent to Africa, where he labored till 1855, when the poor state of his health obliged him to return to Europe. He retired to Kornthal, and spent his time in translating the Scriptures into different dialects of east Africa. He died Nov. 26, 1881, while at prayer on his knees. Of his works we mention, *Reisen in Ostafrika in den Jahren* 1837–55 (Kornthal, 1858, 2 vols.):—his *Dictionary of the Suahili Language* was published after his death (Lond. 1882). (B. P.)

Krause, Heinrich, a Protestant writer of Germany, was born at Weissensee, near Berlin, June 2, 1816. He studied theology under Twesten and Neander at Berlin, and at one time thought of devoting himself to lecturing at the university. With great success he passed the examination as licentiate, in 1843, and published an essay, *Ueber die Wahrhaftigkeit* (Berlin, 1844), which obtained the approval of professor Nitzsch. When about to commence his public lectures at the university, he met with an opposition, the head of which was his former teacher, Twesten. Krause abandoned the theological career, and betook himself to journalism. In 1852 he commenced publishing *Die Protestantische Kirchenzeitung*, to which he devoted all his talents. The *Kirchenzeitung*, as the organ of the so-called *Protestanten-Verein*, became the battle-field against orthodoxy, and Krause's pen was especially directed against men like Hengstenberg, Stahl, and Leo. In his attacks, Krause was supported by such liberal theologians as Sydow, Jonas, Zittel, Karl Hase, Karl Schwarz, and others. Besides his journalistic work, Krause lectured in public on religious subjects. In 1864 the university at Zurich honored him with the doctorate of theology. Krause died at his native place, June 8, 1868. See H. Späth, *Protestantische Bausteine. Leben und Wirken des Dr. Heinrich Krause nebst einer Auswahl aus seinen publicistischen Arbeiten* (Berlin, 1873); Ströhlin, in Lichtenberger, *Encyclop. des Sciences Religieuses*, s. v. (B. P.)

Kraussold, Lorenz, a Lutheran theologian of Germany, who died Oct. 22, 1881, first pastor at Bayreuth, member of consistory, doctor of theology and philosophy, published a number of sermons and ascetical works, for which see Zuchold, *Bibl. Theol.* i, 732 sq.; Winer, *Handbuch der theol. Lit.* ii, 217, 240, 283, 366, 403. (B. P.)

Krauth, Charles Porterfield, D.D., LL.D., an eminent Lutheran divine, eldest son of Dr. Charles Philip Krauth (q. v.), was born at Martinsburg, Va., March 17, 1823. He graduated from Pennsylvania College, Gettysburg, in 1839; studied theology under Drs. Schmucke and Schmidt; was ordained in 1842, and became pastor in Baltimore, Md. He subsequently occupied the same position in Winchester, Va. (1848–55), and Pittsburgh, Pa. In 1859 he was called to the pastorate of St. Mark's Lutheran Church, Philadelphia, and two years afterwards became editor of the *Lutheran and Missionary*. In 1864 he was appointed professor of theology and Church history in the new Lutheran Seminary, in Philadelphia, and in 1868 professor of philosophy in the University of Pennsylvania, of which he became vice-provost five years subsequently, a position which he retained until his death, Jan. 2, 1883. He had continued preaching, having temporary charge of various churches in the same city, and spent some time in the West Indies in 1852, a visit which occasioned his *Sketches of the Danish West Indies*. He is the author of a large number of works, among which we mention, a translation of Tholuck's *Commentary on John* (1859):—*Conservative Reformation* (1872):—Berkeley's *Philosophical Writings* (1874):—and an enlarged edition of Fleming's *Vocabulary of Philosophy* (1877). He was several times president of the Lutheran council, a member of various literary societies, and a member of the American Committee on Bible Revision. His rare attainments, ripe scholarship, genuine catholicity, wise conservatism, and noble spirit made his influence wide and deep, not only in his own denomination, but far beyond it. See *Luth. Church Rev.* July, 1883.

Kreskas. See Crescas.

Krita (or **Satya**), the age of truth, according to the Hindû system, being the earliest in the history of the human race, the one in which man sprang from the hand of his Creator, pure and sinless, not divided into conflicting orders, and with all his faculties working together in harmony.

Kritzler, Heinrich, a Protestant theologian of Germany, was born in 1829. For some time preacher in Fränkisch-Grumbach, Hesse, he was called in 1875 as professor of the theological seminary at Herborn, and died April 11, 1878. He wrote, *Die Heldenzeiten des Christenthums* (Leipsic, 1856):—*Humanität und Christenthum* (Gotha, 1867, 2 vols.):—*Die deutsche evangelische Kirche in der Gegenwart* (1869):—*Civitas Christiana* (Wiesbaden, 1874). (B. P.)

Krodo, in German mythology, was a god represented as a man standing on a large fish, holding a vessel of flowers in his right hand, in his left a wheel. He is said to have a similarity to *Saturn*, but wherein it consists is hard to tell.

Kromayer, Johann Abraham, a German theologian, grandson of Jerome (q. v.), was born in 1665 at Ohrdruf, in Thuringia. He studied theology at Jena, was in 1691 deacon, in 1696 pastor and superintendent at his native place, and died April 19, 1733. He wrote, *De Usu Linguæ Arabicæ in Addiscenda Lingua Ebræa et Explicanda Sacra Scriptura:—Comment. Theol. de Potestate Ecclesiastica:—Dispositiones Memoriales Librorum et Capitum Biblicorum tum Veteris tum Novi Testamenti:—Specimen Fontium Scripturæ Apertorum Editum in Illust. Vaticiniis Hoseæ, Joelis et Amosi.* See Jöcher, *Allgemeines Gelehrten-Lexikon*, s. v. (B. P.)

Kshattrya, the military caste of the Hindûs, sprung from the arm of Brahma, whose office it is to protect their fellows from internal violence and outward assault. Their duties are to defend the people, give alms, and read the Vedas; and at any age up to twenty-two and twenty-four they must be invested with the mark of the caste. It no longer exists, however, as a distinct caste or division of society.

Kualina, in the mythology of the Caribbeans, is the head of the heavenly spirits. He causes thunder by pursuing those who have been guilty of a sin.

Küchler, Carl Gustav, a Protestant theologian of Germany, was born in 1796, and died at Leipsic in 1863, professor of philosophy and licentiate of theology. He wrote, *Præcepta Pauli Apostoli de Tradenda Religionis Doctrina* (Leipsic, 1820):—*De Simplicitate Scriptorum Sacrorum in Commentariis de Vita Jesu Christi Commentatio* (1821, 1827):—*Vita Jesu Christi Græce*, etc. (1835):—*De Locis Aliquot Evangeliorum ab Oratoribus Sacris Perperam haud Raro Usurpatis* (1847). He also published some sermons. See Zuchold, *Bibl. Theol.* i, 748 sq.; Winer, *Handbuch der theol. Lit.* i, 551–568; ii, 265. (B. P.)

Kühn, Andreas, a Lutheran theologian of Germany, was born at Dresden, May 29, 1624. He studied at different universities, and died at Dantzic, Sept. 30, 1702. He wrote, *De Jure Dei in Creaturas:—De Ordine Decretorum Divinorum:—De Puncto et Momento Discrepantiæ Inter Lutheranos et Reformatos:—De Pernicie et Morte Judæ Matt. xxvii, 5:—Aphorismi Practici ex Theologia Morali.* See Jöcher, *Allgemeines Gelehrten-Lexikon*, s. v. (B. P.)

Kulik (or **Kulikétu**), one of the chiefs of the *Nagas*, or serpents, in Hindû mythology, who complained to the Lord of the universe that for no fault of his he was continually tormented by the *Suras*, or inferior gods. In answer to his prayer, Brahma is said to have enjoined that he should receive adoration like the *devas* from each human being, and that mortals who refused to pay such worship to him should be cut off by some unnatural death, and deprived of the power of rising higher in the scale of created beings. See Hardwick, *Christ and Other Masters*.

Kumano-Goo, a species of ordeal in use among the Japanese for the detection of crime. The *goo* is a piece of paper, formally sealed with the signet of the Jammabos (q. v.), on which are drawn several mysterious characters, and the figures of various ill-omened birds. All *goos* are not of equal value; the most powerful, and those most dreaded by the dæmons, come from a place called Kumano. The ordeal above named consists in making the accused party swallow a small piece of *goo* in a certain quantity of water. If he be guilty, the *goo* twinges and gripes him in the most violent manner, till he is obliged to confess his guilt.

Kumaon Version of the Scriptures. The Kumaon dialect is closely allied to the Hinduwee, and is spoken in the province of Kumaon, subject to Great Britain. A version of the New Test. was commenced at Serampore in 1815, and was completed at press about the year 1826. It has never been reprinted since. See *Bible of Every Land*, p. 123. (B. P.)

Kunstmann, Friedrich, a Roman Catholic theologian of Germany, was born at Nuremberg in 1811. In 1847 he was made professor of canon-law at the University of Munich, and died Aug. 15, 1867. He published, *Rhabanus Maurus* (Mayence, 1841):—*Die gemischten Ehen unter den christlichen Confessionen Deutschlands dargestellt* (1839):—*Grundzüge eines vergleichenden Kirchen-Rechtes der christlichen Confessionen* (Munich, 1867). (B. P.)

Kunth, Johann Sigmund, a Lutheran theologian of Germany, was born at Liegnitz, Silesia, Oct. 3, 1700. He studied at different universities, was pastor and superintendent at Baruth, in Upper Lusatia, and died in 1779. Kunth is known as the author of the beautiful hymn, *Es ist noch eine Ruhe vorhanden* (Engl. transl. in

Winkworth, *Lyra Germanica*, i, 195: "Yes, there remaineth yet a rest!"). See Koch, *Geschichte des deutschen Kirchenliedes*, iv, 454 sq. (B. P.)

Kunze, JOHN CHRISTOPHER, D.D., a Lutheran minister, was born in Saxony, and educated at the Orphan House and the University of Halle. Upon a requisition from the St. Michael and Zion churches at Philadelphia, Pa., he was selected by the theological faculty of Halle, and ordained as rector of those churches in 1784. Fourteen years he was connected with the Lutheran congregations in Philadelphia, under various names, and then he accepted a call to a church in New York city, where he labored about twenty-four years. At one time he was professor of Hebrew in Columbia College. By express appointment of the founder of Hartwick Seminary he was made professor of theology in that institution, a position which he continued to hold until his death, July 24, 1807, at the age of sixty-three years. It was said of him that he was the most learned theologian of the Lutheran Church in America. His library was extensive, and he had a large acquaintance with Oriental literature. As a preacher, he was distinguished for eloquence and the instructive character of his discourses. With the assistance of Mr. Streibeck, he published an *English Lutheran Hymn-book* in 1795. See *Quar. Rev. of Evang. Luth. Church*, vii, 277; *Lutheran Observer*, Feb. 15, 1833.

Kupay, in the mythology of the Peruvians, was an evil spirit, whom they did not worship, but at the mention of whose name they spat on the ground, a sign of contempt.

Kurdish Version OF THE SCRIPTURES. The Kurdish is in all probability a remnant of the old Farsi or Parsi language, and bears much resemblance to modern Persian. Like most dialects used merely for oral communication through a large extent of territory, the language of the Kurds, having no literature or written standard of appeal, undergoes very considerable alterations and modifications in different places, by intermixture with the language of neighboring nations. Thus the Kurds dwelling in the Ottoman empire have adopted many Turkish words, while corrupted Syriac words have crept into the dialects of the tribes who live in the vicinity, or have embraced the religion, of the Nestorian Christians. In 1822 the Rev. H. Leeves proposed to the British and Foreign Bible Society to have a version in Kurdish made. The preparation of the version was intrusted to bishop Schevris, at Tabreez. In 1827 Mr. Leeves forwarded to the committee the portions of the New Test. which had been translated. But this translation was not intelligible to the Kurds. In 1856 the above society published in Armeno-Kurdish the gospel of Matthew, which was followed by the other gospels. In the Armeno-Kurdish dialect the entire New Test. is now extant. See *Bible of Every Land*, p. 82. (B. P.)

Kurko was a god of the Lithuanians, or heathen Prussians. His seat was not at Romowe, where the gods of the ancient Prussians presided; but everywhere in the country his idol stood under mighty oak-trees. The first-fruits of the field were sacrificed to him.

Figure of Kurma.

Kurma, in Hindû mythology, is the incarnation of the god Vishnu as a tortoise. When the mountain Mandar was moved into the milky sea, for the purpose of preparing the drink of immortality, it threatened to sink in the waves; but Vishnu, in his second incarnation, supported it as a tortoise, and thus the world now stands.

Kurudu, in Lamaism, is one of the seven holy relics placed on the altars in the temple of the Lamaite deity. It is a drum, in which all the prayers are written on a long strip of parchment, wound around two rolls. If one of these rolls is turned by a crooked handle, the prayers wind themselves around this roll from the other. Thus these prayers all appear in order under the cover of Kurudu. Praying, among the Kalmucks, Tamuls, Mongolians, etc., means to turn this handle and let God read them. Those praying continue their daily occupations during prayer without disturbing the sanctity of the act.

Kusa, the sacred grass of the Hindûs, on which the *Yogi*, or Hindû ascetic, is required to sit motionless and meditate.

Kusaien Version OF THE SCRIPTURES. The Kusaien is a dialect spoken in Strong Island, Micronesia. In 1868 the gospel of John was published in this language by the American Bible Society. (B. P.)

Kusala, *merit*, among the Buddhists, which is included in Karma (q. v.). "There are three principal meanings of the word *kusala*, viz., freedom from sickness, exemption from blame, and reward; but as used by Buddha, its primary idea is that of cutting, or excision. It has a cognate use in the word *kusa*, the sacrificial grass that cuts with both its edges the hand of him who lays hold of it carelessly. That which is cut by kusala is *klésha*, evil desire, or the cleaving to existence. *Akusala* is the opposite of kusala. That which is neither kusala nor akusala is *awrjákrata;* it is not followed by any consequence; it receives no reward, either good or bad." See Hardy, *Eastern Monachism*, pp. 5, 6, 276, 301.

Küster, SAMUEL CHRISTIAN GOTTFRIED, a Lutheran theologian of Germany, was born at Havelberg, Aug. 18, 1762. From 1804 till 1829 he was director of the teachers' seminary; in 1830 he was appointed superintendent and first preacher at the Friedrichs-Werder Church, and died at Neustadt-Eberswalde, Aug. 22, 1838, doctor of theology. Besides sermons and ascetical works, he published *Die Psalmen, mit Einleitungen und Anmerkungen bearbeitet* (Berlin, 1832). See Zuchold, *Bibl. Theol.* i, 754; Winer, *Handbuch der theol. Lit.* ii, 251, 257, 260, 295, 302, 305, 315, 339, 342, 396. (B. P.)

Kutschker, JOHANN BAPTIST, a Roman Catholic prelate, was born April 11, 1810, at Wiese, in Austro-Silesia. He studied at Olmütz, was made priest in 1833, and doctor of theology in 1834. From that time on till 1851 he acted as professor of moral theology at Olmütz, was then appointed court-chaplain at Vienna, and in 1862 cathedral-provost and general-vicar of the Vienna diocese. He was the right hand of cardinal Rauscher (q. v.), and took an active part in all ecclesiastical affairs. At the special request of the latter he was appointed his successor, and his appointment as prince-archbishop of Vienna was made in 1876. In 1877 he was made cardinal, and died Jan. 27, 1881. He was a very moderate prelate, and Austria owes it to him that she was enabled to bring about the present religious legislation, without coming into a bitter conflict with the Roman see. He always went with the government party. He wrote, *Die gemischten Ehen, von dem katholisch-kirchlichen Standpunkte* (3d ed. Vienna, 1842):—*Das Eherecht der katholischen Kirche* (1856–57, 5 vols.). (B. P.)

Kutuchta, the chief priest of the Kalmuck Tartars and Western Mongols. Formerly he was subject to the Dalai-Lama (q. v.) of Thibet, but in course of time he made a schism among the Lamaists, and established himself on an equal footing with the Dalai-Lama himself. He is regarded as a very sacred personage, and there is more or less of mystery always connected with his person in the minds of the common people.

Kuzmany, Carl, a Protestant theologian, who died at Presburg, Hungary, Aug. 14, 1866, and was for some time professor at Vienna, is the author of *Praktische Theologie der evangelischen Kirche augsburgischer und helvetischer Confession* (3 vols.). See Zuchold, *Bibl. Theol.* i, 754 sq. (B. P.)

Kwambak, the first officer at the court of the Dairi (q. v.) in Japan, and who represents that pontiff when the dignity devolves on a woman or a child.

Kwan-shi-in, one of the three divinities unknown to the original Buddhists, but worshipped in China as scarcely inferior to Gotama Buddha himself. He is also known by the name of *Padma-pani*, or lotus bearer. In many districts of Thibet he is incarnate, under the name of *Padma-pani*, in the person of the Dalai-Lama (q. v.). In Thibet and Mongolia he is represented with innumerable eyes and hands, and sometimes with as many as ten heads. In China this deity is exhibited with a female figure and female decorations.

Kyninmund, Alexander de, a Scotch prelate, was elected bishop of Aberdeen in 1357. Here he remained until about 1376, when he was sent on an embassy from king Robert II to renew the ancient league with France, and died at Scone the year after his return, in 1382. See Keith, *Scottish Bishops*, p. 111.

Kyrko-Handbok, the ritual of the Swedish Church, revised and published in 1811. It is divided into fifteen chapters, containing the Psalms, the morning prayer and communion service, the evening prayer and the holy-day service, the Litany, the forms of baptism, confirmation, marriage, and churching of women, the funeral service, the forms of consecration of churches and of bishops, the form of ordination of priests, etc.

Kyrko-Ordningen, a book containing the laws regulating the government and discipline of the Church of Sweden, first published in 1686.

Kyrko-rad (*church council*), a church court in Sweden, inferior to the diocesan consistories, and nearly answering to a presbytery. It is composed of clergymen, and of laymen elected by the parishioners.

L.

Laan, Peter, a Dutch theologian, was born Dec. 24, 1696. He studied at Utrecht and Leyden, and acted as preacher at different places from 1722 to 1739. In the latter year he was called as professor of theology and university preacher to Franeker, and died April 4, 1743. He published, *Disp. ad Inscript. Psalmi xxxi*:—*Ad Job v*, 23:—*De Tolerantia Civili ad Socinianos non Extendenda, Genuinis Mennonitis Minime Iniqua.* See Jöcher, *Allgemeines Gelehrten-Lexikon*, s. v. (B. P.)

Labaree, Benjamin, D.D., LL.D., a Congregational minister and distinguished educator, was born in Charlestown, N. H., June 3, 1801. He graduated at Dartmouth College in 1828, and at Andover Theological Seminary in 1831; was ordained at Bradford, Mass., Sept. 26 of the same year, and for a time was a home missionary in Tennessee. From 1832 to 1837 he was professor of ancient languages, and president of Jackson College; for the next three years secretary of the Central American Educational Society. He was called to the presidency of Middlebury College, Vt., in 1840, and remained in office twenty-six years. From 1867 to 1869 he resided in Hyde Park, Mass., preaching for a part of this time at South Weymouth. His residence thereafter was in West Roxbury (1870-75), Charlestown, N. H., and Walpole from 1880 till his death, Nov. 15, 1883. See *Boston Advertiser*, Nov. 21, 1883; *Trien. Catalogue of Andover Theol. Sem.* 1870, p. 94; *N. Y. Observer*, Nov. 22, 1883; *Cong. Year-book*, 1884, p. 27. (J. C. S.)

Labbé, Martin, a French prelate and missionary, was born at Le Luc, near Caen. He entered the Society of Jesus, and requested to be sent to the foreign missions. He went to Cochin China in 1678, and returned in 1697. Innocent XII made him bishop of Tilopolis. After a short sojourn in Europe the abbot returned to Cochin China, where he lived fifteen years, in the midst of fatigues and perils. He died in 1723, leaving a letter to pope Clement XI, on the worship of the Chinese; also a memoir on the persecutions. See Hoefer, *Nouv. Biog. Générale*, s. v.

Laberenz, Gottfried, a Roman Catholic theologian of Germany, was born at Fulda, May 6, 1802. He received holy orders in 1825, and was appointed at the same time professor of Oriental languages and of Old-Test. exegesis. In 1829 he was cathedral dean, in 1836 doctor of theology, and died March 13, 1875, at his native place. He wrote, *De Vera Jonæ Interpretatione* (Fulda, 1836):—*Katholische Homiletik* (Ratisbon, 1844):—*Grammatik der Hebr. Sprache* (Paderborn, 1867). (B. P.)

Labouchère, Pierre Antoine, a noted French Protestant painter, was born at Nantes, Nov. 26, 1807, and studied in Germany and in England. He had been placed at first in a commercial house at Antwerp, and made, in 1827, a journey to the United States, as secretary of M. Bates, and in 1832 went to China as supercargo of a vessel of Nantes, which belonged to his elder brother. Painting, however, seems to have been his predominating passion, and a visit to Antwerp decided his vocation, and he accordingly became a pupil of Paul Delaroche. He died at Paris in 1873. Labouchère chiefly painted historical subjects, especially those of the Reformation in Germany. He left a set of subjects drawn from the life of Luther, which have been engraved, and are accompanied with a text by Merle d'Aubigné. See Hoefer, *Nouv. Biog. Générale*, s. v.

La Bruyère, Stephen de, a French prelate, was elected bishop of Nantes some time before 1213, and was involved in a contest with Peter Mauclerc, duke of Brittany, on the privileges of the clergy, which resulted in the bishop's forcible expulsion from his diocese in 1219. He withdrew to Rome, but after some months returned to his functions, and died at Nantes, Feb. 8, 1227. See Hoefer, *Nouv. Biog. Générale*, s. v.

Labyrinth. At St. Bertin's, in St. Omer, there was one of those curious floors, representing the Temple of Jerusalem, with stations for pilgrims, and actually visited and traversed by them as a compromise for not going to the Holy Land in fulfilment of a vow. The labyrinth at Sens was destroyed in 1768; those of Arras and Amiens shared the same fate in 1825. There is a round labyrinth in the centre of the nave of Chartres, inlaid with lead; another, of encaustic tiles, in the chapter-house of Bayeux; and a third, of octagonal shape, in the nave of St. Quentin.

La Chartres, Pierre de. See Peter of Chartres.

La Chartres, Renoud de. See Chartres, Renoud de.

Lachish. On the identification of this place, Lieut. Conder remarks (*Tent Work*, ii, 168):

"We visited *Um Lags*, the site proposed by Dr. Robinson, and could not but conclude that no ancient or important city ever stood there, nor has the name any radical similarity to that of Lachish. [This is surely a mistake, for the initial *L* is at least the same, and no more can be said in favor of his own proposal.] Much nearer, indeed, would be the title *el-Hesy*, applying to a large ancient site with springs, near the foot of the hills, about in the proper position for Lachish. The modern site means 'a water-pit,' and, if it is a corruption of Lachish, it would afford a second instance of change which is well known to have taken place in the case of Michmash—the *k* being changed to a guttural *h*. The distance from Beit Jibrin to Tell el-Hesy is not much greater than that given in the *Onomasticon* for Lachish, while the proximity of Eglon

('Ajlân), and the position south of Beit Jibrin, on a principal road, near the hills, and by one of the only springs in the plain, all seem to be points strongly confirming this view."

Tell el-Hesy is laid down on the *Ordnance Map* ten and a half miles south-west of Beit Jibrin, and is described in the accompanying *Memoirs* (iii, 290) as "a truncated cone, with a broad, flat top, and traces of ruins round its base. There are several springs in the neighborhood, but the water is bad." This site was known in the Middle Ages as *Alkassi* (Boheddin, *Vita Salad.* p. 228). But Tristram (*Bible Places*, p. 36) and Trelawney Saunders (*Map of the O. T.*) still adhere to *Um-Lakhis*, which lies three miles north-west of Tell el-Hesy, and twelve and a half miles west by south from Beit Jibrin. Its remains are thus described by Guérin (*Judæa*, ii, 299):

"These ruins cover a space of about a kilometre and a half in circumference. They are situated partly on a hillock, and partly in the midst of fields, either cultivated or bristling with thistles and brambles. A multitude of excavations show that stones, the fragments of ancient buildings, have been taken from the place. There remains, however, a good quantity of materials scattered on the ground. In one of these holes I found a Corinthian capital of grayish white marble, waiting for some one to carry it off. Fifteen ancient *silos* continue to serve the Arabs of the neighborhood."

"Lachrymatory" (from the Roman catacombs). See AMA.

Lachrymatory, a small glass or earthen vessel, formerly supposed to have been used among the ancient heathens to receive the tears of surviving relatives or friends, wept for the dead, but now shown to have been merely pots of ointment or perfume, which, with their contents, were buried with the urns and ashes of the deceased. See TEARS.

Lacroix (*De Chevrières*), **Jean Baptiste de**, a French prelate, belonged at first to the order of the Knights of Malta, was afterwards abbot of Gimont, in the diocese of Auch, and embarked in 1683 for Canada, to preach to the Indians. He was consecrated bishop of Quebec while on a visit to Paris in 1688. He returned soon afterwards to Canada, where he built a hospital, in which he died, Dec. 26, 1727. He left *État Présent de l'Église et de la Colonie dans la Nouvelle-France* (Paris, 1688). See Hoefer, *Nouv. Biog. Générale*, s. v.

Lacroix, John Power, Ph.D., D.D., a Methodist Episcopal minister, was born at Haverhill, O., Feb. 13, 1833. In his boyhood, while at farm work, he displayed an insatiable thirst for book knowledge. He graduated at the Ohio Wesleyan University, Delaware, in 1857; soon after went to New Orleans, where he spent two years in teaching; and then, having cleared himself of college debt, returned north, and in the fall of 1859 entered the Ohio Conference. His fields of labor were Tarlton Circuit, Spencer Chapel, Ironton, and Piketon. He spent sixteen months of close application in the universities of Germany in 1865 and 1866, and in the fall of the latter year was elected to the chair of modern languages and history in the Ohio Wesleyan University, which office he held till his death, Sept. 22, 1879. His translations of De Pressensé's *Religion and the Reign of Terror; or, The Church During the French Revolution*, Naivelle's *Problem of Evil*, Wultke's *Christian Ethics*, together with his own *Life of Rudolph Stier*, will perpetuate his name in scholarly circles. Dr. Lacroix also contributed many able articles to this cyclopædia, as well as writing a valuable *Manual on Ethics* for the Chautauqua Literary Circle, and, in connection with a fellow-professor, an *Introductory Book of Latin*. He was the special friend of young men, and hundreds of students who came under his influence at the university, now scattered all over the land and in other nations, bear cheerful testimony to his great personal worth. As a thinker and writer he was bold, independent, and progressive, fervent in his attachment to truth, ardent in his devotion to the Church, broad in charity, and incapable of bigotry or prejudice. See *Minutes of Annual Conferences*, 1879, p. 47.

Lada (or **Lado**), in Slavonic mythology, was the goddess of beauty and love, worshipped in Kiev. Lel (love), Did (return love), and Polol (marriage) were her sons. There are still traces of an idol worship in the yearly celebrated festival of Lada and Did, which falls on the Thursday before Whitsuntide.

Ladvocat, BILLIARD NICOLAS, a French prelate, was born at Paris in 1620. He entered the ministry, was received in the Sorbonne, Dec. 24, 1652, and became canon of Notre Dame and vicar-general of the coadjutor of Paris, Albert de Conti, cardinal of Retz, whom he assisted for several years in his political intrigues, in the administration of his diocese, and whom he accompanied to Rome in 1675. In 1677 he obtained the episcopal see of Boulogne-sur-Mer. He governed his diocese wisely, where he also founded a seminary and some establishments of instruction and of charity. He died April 14, 1681, leaving *Vindiciæ Parthenicæ* (Paris, 1679), which maintains that the Virgin Mary was taken up into heaven bodily. He also composed the first rules which were observed in the Hôtel Dieu de Paris. See Hoefer, *Nouv. Biog. Générale*, s. v.

Laelius, LAURENTIUS, a Lutheran minister of Germany, was born in Franconia, April 15, 1572. He studied at Jena and Wittenberg, was in 1599 deacon, and attended the colloquy at Ratisbon in 1601; in 1602 he was rector at Heilbronn, in 1605 first preacher at Onolzbach, and died July 26, 1634. He wrote, *Criterium Fidei*:—*Index Hæresium Controversiarum et Schismatum*, etc.:—*Exegesis Articuli de Persona et Officio Christi Bellarmino Opposita*. See Freher, *Theatrum Eruditorum;* Witte, *Diarium Biographicum;* Jöcher, *Allgemeines Gelehrten-Lexikon*, s. v. (B. P.)

Laetus, GEORG, a preacher at Lublin, Poland, who died March 27, 1649, is the author of, *Peregrinatio Pauli Romana*:—*Comment. Pract. in Pauli Conversionem*:—*De Ratione Concionnandi ad Methodum Anglicanam Conformata*. See Winer, *Handbuch der theol. Lit.* i, 569; Jöcher, *Allgemeines Gelehrten-Lexikon*, s. v. (B. P.)

La Ferronnays, JULES BASILE FERRON DE, a French prelate, was born at the castle of St. Mards-lès-Ancenis, Jan. 2, 1735. After he had finished his studies, he entered into orders, and followed cardinal Bernis to Rome, to the conclave which elected Clement XIV, in 1769. On Dec. 24 of the same year he was nominated bishop of St. Brieuc, and was transferred to the bishopric of Bayonne in 1774, and to the episcopal see of Lisieux, where he remained until 1790. He refused to take the oath to the civil constitution of the clergy, and left France in 1791. He was pursued by the French soldiers, and retired to Bavaria, where he died, May 15, 1799. See Hoefer, *Nouv. Biog. Générale*, s. v.

Lafitau, PIERRE FRANÇOIS, a French prelate, was born at Bordeaux in 1685. He studied among the Jesuits, and for some time was very active in the affairs of Jansenism. He was sent to Rome as an ambassador, was consecrated there bishop of Sisteron in 1719, and took possession of his see the following year. He is said to have been immoral early in life, but afterwards a pattern of piety. Lafitau died at Sisteron, April 3, 1764, leaving several works on practical religion, for which see Hoefer, *Nouv. Biog. Générale*, s. v.

Lafo al-jemin (*the thief on the right hand*), a festival observed by the Syrian Christians in commemoration of the penitent thief. It occurs on the octave of Easter.

Laforet, Nicolas Joseph, a Roman Catholic theologian, was born in 1823 at Graide, Namur (Belgium). In 1848 he was called as professor to Louvain, and died Jan. 26, 1872. He wrote, *Histoire de la Théologie Dogmatique:—Vie et Travaux d'Arnold Tits:—Les Dogmes Catholiques:—La Papauté et la Civilisation:—Histoire de la Philosophie.* (B. P.)

Laga, in Norse mythology, was the goddess of the refreshing springs and waters. She lives in Söquabekr, a silver palace, by which the waters of the earth flow. Odin visits her daily to bathe there.

Lagarto, Pedro, a Portuguese prelate and theologian, was born at Setubal about 1524. In 1540 he joined the monks of Arrabida, who lived under the rule of St. Francis; afterwards studied theology at Salamanca, and was elected in 1576 provincial of Arrabida. He died July 28, 1590, leaving *Summa Utilis Omnium Notabilium.* See Hoefer, *Nouv. Biog. Générale*, s. v.

Lagomarsini, Geronimo, a celebrated Italian Humanist, was born Sept. 30, 1698, at Porto-Santo-Maria (Spain). In 1708 he went to Italy, and commenced his studies in the College of the Jesuits at Prato, in Tuscany. In 1721 he began to teach rhetoric at the College of Arezzo. Four years afterwards he went to Rome to complete his theological studies, after which he returned to his duties at Arezzo. In 1732 he was appointed to the chair of rhetoric at Florence, and in 1751 to that of Greek in the Collegium Gregorianum at Rome, which position he occupied until his death, May 18, 1773. He left several works on classical literature, for which see Hoefer, *Nouv. Biog. Générale*, s. v.

Lagrange (*d'Arquien*), Henri de, a French prelate, was born at Calais in 1613, of an ancient family of the 15th century, which had been settled at Berry. He went to Poland about 1674, where he finally devoted himself to the Church, and was consecrated cardinal, in 1695, by Innocent XII. After the death of Sobieski, his son-in-law, the queen retired with her father to Rome, where Lagrange died seven years afterwards, May 24, 1707. See Hoefer, *Nouv. Biog. Générale*, s. v.

Lagrenée, Louis Jean François, an eminent French painter, was born at Paris, Dec. 30, 1724, and studied under Charles Vanloo. He gained the grand prize of the French Academy for his picture of *Joseph Explaining the Dreams*, and at the age of twenty visited England, and was employed by Antonio Verrio upon the large picture of *St. Bartholomew's Hospital.* He was also unanimously chosen by the commissioners to paint the cupola of St. Paul's. He died in Paris, June 17, 1801. See Hoefer, *Nouv. Biog. Générale*, s. v.; Spooner, *Biog. Hist. of the Fine Arts*, s. v.

Lagus, Daniel, a Lutheran theologian of Germany, was born in 1618 at Colberg, Pomerania. He studied at Königsberg and Wittenberg, was in 1653 doctor of theology, and for some time professor of theology at Greifswalde. He died May 30, 1678, leaving, *Comment. Super Epistolas Pauli ad Galatas, Ephesios, Philippenses:—Examen Trium Confessionum Reformatarum, Marchiacæ, Lipsiensis et Thoruniensis:—Vindiciæ Evangeliorum Dominicalium et Festivalium contra Thom. Stapleton.:—De ἐπινικίῳ Jesu Decantato ad Psa. xvi, 10, 11:—De Omnipræsentia Humanæ Christi Naturæ:—De Bonorum Operum Necessitate ad Salutem.* See Witte, *Diarium Biographicum;* Jöcher, *Allgemeines Gelehrten-Lexikon*, s. v. (B. P.)

Laha, a tablet suspended in a Buddhist Wihara (q. v.) in Ceylon, upon which anything might be written which was intended for the information of the priests.

Lahas, in Lamaism, are heavenly spirits who, long before the creation of the world, lived in unspeakable felicity, which was of an earthly nature. Above the earth there were twenty worlds inhabited by these beings, the highest four of which were so purified that their inhabitants lived without food. When the world was created many of these Lahas descended to it, and became so earthly they were subjected to its laws. When they ate of the fruits of this earth they became black, and the sun and moon were therefore created to give light to this otherwise dark world. The human family, as also the sunken animal world, is indebted to the Lahas for their existence.

Lahmam is doubtless the present *Khurbet el-Lahm*, located on the *Ordnance Map* at two and a half miles south of Beit-Jibrin, and described in the accompanying *Memoirs* (iii, 283) as "foundations, heaps of stones, wells, cisterns, and caverns. The masonry seems probably of Byzantine date, but the site to be older."

Lain, *Saint.* See Latuinus.

Laing, John, a Scotch prelate, was first rector of Tannadice, in the shire of Angus, and Linlithgow, and was next preferred to the office of high treasurer in 1465, which office he held until 1468, at which time he was made lord-register, and about the same time enjoyed the rectories of Suthet and Newlands. He was promoted to the episcopal see of Glasgow in 1474; was made lord high chancellor in 1482, and died Jan. 11, 1482–83. See Keith, *Scottish Bishops*, p. 253.

Lairesse, Gérard, an eminent Flemish painter, was born at Liege in 1640. He studied under Bertholet Flemael, and at the age of sixteen had gained considerable reputation from his efforts. He visited Utrecht, and afterwards removed to Amsterdam, where his reputation rose so high that the Dutch esteem him their greatest historical painter. He died at Amsterdam in 1711. The following are some of his best works: *The Fall of our First Parents; Adam and Eve Driven from Paradise; Joseph and his Brethren; The Child Jesus.* See Chalmers, *Biog. Dict.* s. v.; Spooner, *Biog. Hist. of the Fine Arts*, s. v.

Läis, Giuseppe Maria, an Italian prelate, was born March 24, 1775, at Rome, of Bavarian parentage. He was educated at first among the Jesuits, and finished his studies at the University of La Sapienza, where he also took the degree of a doctor *in utroque jure*, and was ordained priest. A short time after he became vicar-general to cardinal Galeffi, and commendatory abbot of Subiaco. In 1817 he was appointed bishop of Hippone *in partibus*, and administrator of the diocese of Anagni. He died at Terentius, July 18, 1836, leaving *De Universa Christi Ecclesia.* See Hoefer, *Nouv. Biog. Générale*, s. v.

Lakshana, a Hindû name for the characteristic beauties or signs of a supreme Buddha. These were divided into three classes: 1. The two hundred and sixteen *Mangalya-lakshana*, of which there were one hundred and eight on each foot; 2. The thirty-two *Mahapurusha-lakshana*, or superior beauties; 3. The eight *Anawyanjana-lakshana*, or inferior beauties.

Figure of Lakshmi.

Lakshmi, in Hindû mythology, was the goddess of beauty and loveliness, the wife of Vishnu, generated from the foam of the sea, similar to Venus Anadyomene of the Greeks. She is also the goddess of plenty, and as such is called *Sri* or *Shiri.* She is also the goddess of felicity, and thus identical with *Mangola Dewta.* She often serves poets as an ideal of womanly beauty.

Lakum. This site Trelawney Saunders (*Map of the O. T.*) confounds with that of Adam, locating it at *Damieh;* perhaps from misunderstanding the ambiguous language of Tristram (*Bible Places*, p. 278), who thinks that "Lakum may be traced in *Kefr Kama*," which is laid down on the *Ordnance Map* at two and a quarter miles south-west of Damieh, and eight miles west from the south end of the Sea of Galilee. The accompanying *Memoirs* (i, 391) say of it: "There are ruins in this village, and portions of fine limestone columns, but no capitals. There is also a circular basalt olive-press and cisterns."

La Lane, Noel de, one of the most famous French theologians of the 17th century, was born of a noble family at Paris, and died in 1673. In 1653 he was sent to Rome to defend the cause of Jansenius, and his famous speech, which he delivered before pope Innocent X, is contained in the twenty-second chapter of the sixth volume of the *Journal de Saint-Amour*. He was a doctor of the Sorbonne, abbot of Notre Dame de Valcroissant, and wrote, *De Initio Piae Voluntatis:—La Grace Victorieuse:—Examen de la Conduite des Religieuses de Port-Royal*, etc. (1664):—*Lettre sur le Livre de M. Chamillard*, etc.:—*Défense de la Foi des Religieuses de Port-Royal* (1667, 2 parts). See Lichtenberger, *Encyclop. des Sciences Religieuses*, s. v. (B. P.)

Lallouette, Ambrose, a French theologian, was born in 1654 at Paris, and died May 9, 1724. He wrote, *Discours sur la Présence Réelle:—Histoire des Traductions Françaises de l'Écriture Sainte:—Extraits sur Differens Points de Morale:—Avis pour Lire Utilement l'Évangile*. See Moreri, *Dictionnaire;* Jöcher, *Allgemeines Gelehrten-Lexikon*, s. v (B. P.)

La Marche, Jean François, a French prelate, was born in the diocese of Quimper in 1729, of a noble family from Brittany. After the peace of Aix-la-Chapelle he left the army to embrace the ecclesiastical calling. He was first canon and grand-vicar of Treguier, then abbot of St. Aubin des Bois, and in 1772 was elected bishop of St. Pol de Leon. At the commencement of the Revolution La Marche refused to obey the civil constitution, and, Jan. 8, 1791, fled to London, where he was befriended by Burke and other Englishmen, who charged him with the distribution of means of relief to the French emigrants. This position he held until his death, Nov. 25, 1806. He wrote, *Mandements*, also a *Lettre Pastorale* and an *Ordonnance*, the last in London, Aug. 20, 1791, to warn his diocesans against schism. See Hoefer, *Nouv. Biog. Générale*, s. v.

Lamasery, a collection of small houses built around one or more Buddhist temples in Tartary and Thibet, as a residence for the Lamas. See Lamaism.

Lamb, Andrew, a Scotch prelate, was bishop of Brechin in 1610, and was translated to the see of Galloway in 1619, which he held until his death in 1634. See Keith, *Scottish Bishops*, p. 167-281.

Lambert, Bernard, a French theologian, the last of the Jansenistic school, was born at Salernes, Provence, in 1738. When made professor of theology, Lambert published some theses, which were at once censured by the Roman see, and he had to leave Limoges in consequence. He then went to Grenoble, where he remained some time. The episcopal see of Lyons was then occupied by the famous Montazet, who gathered about himself all opposed to the Jesuits, including Lambert. When Lambert went to Paris, monsieur de Beaumont, an opponent of the Jansenists, was archbishop there, and refused to receive father Lambert into his diocese; but some bishops interfered in his behalf, and he was admitted on condition that he would write only against philosophers and unbelievers. Lambert died at Paris, Feb. 27, 1813. Of his many writings we mention, *Apologie de l'État Religieux:—Traité sur le Sacrifice de Jésus-Christ* (1778):—*Idée de l'Œuvre des Secours Selon les Sentiments de ses Véritables Défenseurs* (1786):—*Traité Dogmatique et Moral de la Justice Chrétienne* (1788):—*La Verité et la Sainteté du Christianisme* (1796):—*Exposition des Prédictions et des Promesses Faites à l'Église* (1806, 2 vols.), a work in which he admits the doctrine of the Millenarians, and the theory of those who regarded the pope as antichrist. See Lichtenberger, *Encyclop. des Sciences Religieuses*, s. v. (B. P.)

Lamberton, William, a Scotch prelate, was chancellor of the Church of Glasgow in 1292, and elected bishop of St. Andrews in June, 1298. Bishop Lamberton strenuously opposed the encroachments made by king Edward I of England upon the constitution of Scotland, and contributed his hearty endeavors to set and keep king Robert Bruce upon the Scottish throne. He died in 1328. He built a palace for the bishop of St. Andrews, also ten churches belonging to the diocese, and did a great many other good and noble works. See Keith, *Scottish Bishops*, p. 21.

Lami, Bernard. See Lamy.

Lami, François, a French Benedictine, was born at Montireau, near Chartres, in 1636, and died at St. Denis, April 4, 1711. After having served in the army, he embraced a monastic life at the age of twenty-three. In spite of his controversies with Bossuet, Malebranche, Arnauld, Nicole, Duguet, and others, he was highly esteemed by all who knew him for his sincerity and piety. He wrote, *De la Connaissance de Soi-Même* (Paris, 1694-98, 6 vols.; improved ed. 1700):—*Le Nouvel Athéisme Renversé, Contre Spinosa* (1696):—*Vérité Évidente de la Religion Chrétienne* (1694):—*Des Sentiments de Piété sur la Profession Religieuse* (1697):—*Leçons de la Sagesse sur l'Engagement au Service de Dieu* (1703):—*L'Incrédule Amené à la Religion par la Raison* (1710): *Les Gémissements de l'Âme sous la Tyrannie du Corps* (1700):—*Conjectures sur Divers Effets du Tonnerre* (1689). See Lichtenberger, *Encyclop. des Sciences Religieuses*, s. v. (B. P.)

Lamp, The, a ceremony practiced by the Maronites (q. v.), by way of anointing for the sick. They make a cake somewhat larger than the consecrated wafer of the Romanists, and put upon it seven pieces of cotton twisted with little pieces of straw, and place all together in a basin with some oil. Having read a portion of one of the gospels and epistles, with some prayers, they set fire to all the cotton. They now anoint with this oil the forehead, breast, and arms of every one present, and particularly of the sick person, saying at each unction, "May the Almighty, by his sacred unction, pardon all thy sins, and strengthen thy limbs as he did those of the poor man who was troubled with the palsy." Then they let the lamp burn till all the oil is exhausted. This rite is administered to the *sick*, and is not confined to the dying, as in the case of extreme unction in the Roman Catholic Church.

Lampadephoria (from λαμπάς, *a torch*, and φέρω, *to bear*), ancient Grecian games, celebrated in honor of Prometheus, Athena, and Hephæstus, who taught men the use of fire. The game consisted in carrying an unextinguished torch through certain distances by a successive chain of runners, each taking it up at the point where another left it, and the one who permitted it to go out losing the game.

Lampădon Hemĕra (from λαμπάς, *a torch*, and ἡμέρα, *a day*), the name given to the fifth day of the Eleusinian Mysteries (q. v.), because on that day the initiated marched two and two in procession, each with a torch in his hand, into the temple of Ceres at Eleusis.

Lampeter Brethren. See Agapemone.

Lamps, Christian. Many of these of ancient manufacture have been discovered in the catacombs and elsewhere. They were in general of similar form to those used by the Romans at the time, but often with Christian emblems upon them. See Fish.

Lamps, Festival of, a feast celebrated annually in Rajastban, in honor of the Hindû goddess, Lakshmi (q. v.). The festival is called *Dewali*, and every city, village, and encampment exhibits a most brilliant spectacle from the illumination. On this day it is incumbent upon every votary of Lakshmi to try the chance of dice, and from their success in the Dewali the prince, the chief, the merchant, and the artisan foretell the state of their coffers for the ensuing year.

Lampsăcus, Council of (*Concilium Lampsaceum*), held at Lampsaki, on the Hellespont, A.D. 364, as Pagi shows. Orthodox bishops were invited to it; and it is described as a council of Homoöusians by Sozomen (vi, 7) if the reading is correct. But those who directed it must have been really Semi-Arians; for they professed to be partisans of the Homoousian formula, and of the creed published at Antioch, besides siding with Macedonius, by whom the godhead of the Holy Ghost was denied. What made Sozomen think well of them probably was that they were treated with marked favor by Valentinian; while they condemned the extreme party which Valens espoused, and which he ordered them into exile for dissenting from. On this, too, they seem to have despatched a still more orthodox account of themselves to Rome, which contented Liberius (Socinus, iv, 12; comp. Mansi, iii, 378).

Lamson, William, D.D., a Baptist minister, was born at Danvers, Mass, Feb. 22, 1812. He studied at the South Reading (now Wakefield) Academy, graduated from Waterville College (now Colby University) in 1835, and was a tutor there one year. In the autumn of 1837 he was ordained pastor of the Church in Gloucester, Mass., where he remained until 1839, and then went to the Newton Theological Institution and studied two years. He was pastor in Thomaston, Me., about two years (1841 and 1842), and then returned to Gloucester as pastor until 1848. His next settlement was in Portsmouth, N. H., and his last in Brookline, Mass. (1859–75), where he died, Nov. 20, 1882. See Cathcart, *Bapt. Encyclop.* p. 669. (J. C. S.)

Lance (*λόγχη, cultellus*), a liturgical instrument of the Greek Church, in the shape of a small knife formed like a spear, is used in the common Greek rite in the preparatory office of prothesis, to divide the host from the holy loaf previous to consecration. This earlier fraction, the primitive antiquity of which is doubtful, is distinctly symbolical, and has no reference to the subsequent distribution, for which another fraction has always been made. The typical allusion to the circumstances of our Lord's Passion receives greater force and

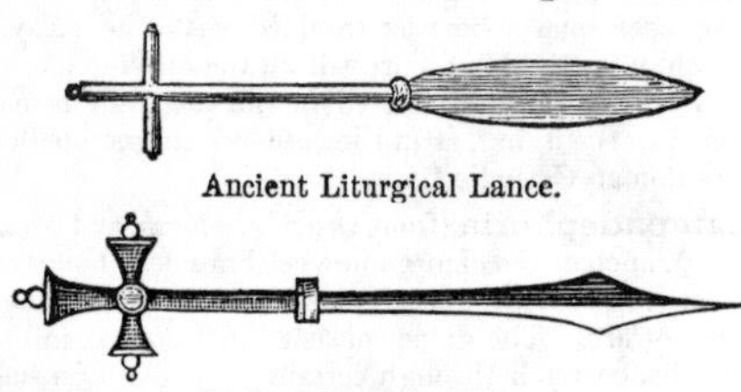

Ancient Liturgical Lance.

Modern Liturgical Lance.

vividness in the Greek Church, from the use of the "holy spear" for the division of the loaf, as commemorative of the piercing of our Lord's body by the Roman soldier. The priest makes four cuts to separate the host from the oblation, and also stabs it more than once, accompanying every cut or stab with appropriate texts of Scripture, e. g. "He was led as a lamb to the slaughter," "One of the soldiers with a spear pierced his side," etc.

The use of the holy spear is not found in the purely Oriental liturgies, e. g. those of the Syrians and Egyptians, a fact which leads Renaudot to question whether the rite is of primitive antiquity, since these churches borrowed their discipline from the Greek Church in the earliest ages. It is entirely unknown in the Western Church.

Läncher, Karl Adolph Ferdinand, a Lutheran theologian of Germany, was born at Schönebeck, near Magdeburg, Jan. 4, 1796. For some time rector of the Lyceum and preacher at Stolberg, in Saxony, he was called as member of consistory and preacher to Neustadt in 1828, and died in 1865, a doctor of philosophy. He published sermons and some ascetical works. See Zuchold, *Bibl. Theol.* ii, 761 sq. (B. P.)

Lanckisch, Friedrich von, a German writer, was born at Leipsic, March 12, 1618. He studied at his native place, was magister of philosophy in 1640, and died Oct. 22, 1669, a bookseller at Leipsic. He published *Concordantiæ Germanico-Hebraico-Græcæ* (Leipsic, 1677, fol. often reprinted; best edition that of Reineccius, 1718). See Winer, *Handbuch der theol. Lit.* i, 175; Jöcher, *Allgemeines Gelehrten-Lexikon*, s. v. (B. P.)

Landaff, Council of (*Concilium Landavense*). Three such are given in Mansi (ix, 763 sq.) dated A.D. 560; but, even if genuine, they were simply meetings of the bishop, his three abbots, and his clergy, for excommunicating or absolving great offenders: in the 1st case Meuric, in the 2d Morgan, kings of Glamorgan; in the 3d Gwaednerth, king of Gwent; all of them under Oudoceus, third bishop of Llandaff, and therefore scarcely before the 7th century. "The book, however, in which these records occur is a compilation of the 12th century" (Haddan and Stubbs, *Councils and Documents*, i, 125, 147).

Landal, William, a Scotch prelate, was early rector of the Church of Kinkell, and was promoted to the see of St. Andrews in 1341. He was still bishop of St. Andrews in 1373, and present at the famous act of Parliament, April 4, that year. He died in the abbey of St. Andrews, on St. Thecla's day, Oct. 15, 1385. See Keith, *Scottish Bishops*, p. 24.

Landauer, Moses H., a Jewish rabbi of Germany, who died Feb. 3, 1841, is the author of, *Jehova und Elohim*, etc. (Stuttgart, 1836):—*Wesen und Form des Pentateuchs* (1838):—*Uebersicht der Geschichte und Literatur der Kabbala* (published in *Literaturblatt des Orients*, vi, 178 sq.). See Fürst, *Bibl. Jud.* ii, 219 sq.; Zuchold, *Bibl. Theol.* ii, 762. (B. P.)

Landerer, Maximilian Albert von, a German theologian, one of the most learned and able, though not one of the best known, representatives of the school of theology occupying an intermediate position between the old supranaturalism and modern rationalism, was born at Maulbronn, Würtemberg, Jan. 14, 1810. He studied at Tübingen, where Dorner (q. v.) was his fellow-student. In 1839 he was deacon at Göppingen, in 1841 professor at Tübingen, and died April 13, 1878. Rejecting the Hegelian principle of absolute knowledge, Landerer emphasized the religious experience in the department of systematic theology. He did not, however, forcibly separate it from the revelation of the Scriptures. The central doctrine in systematic theology he regarded as the perfect union of God and man in Jesus of Nazareth; and he laid special emphasis on the humanity of Christ, insisting, however, upon his supernatural birth and absolute sinlessness. Being not as imposing in presence as Baur or Beck, yet he became one of the most influential of the theologians of his school, and the more intimately the students came in contact with him, the more highly they learned to respect him. Landerer published very little. For the first edition of Herzog he contributed thirteen articles, the most prominent of which was the one on Melanchthon. For the *Jahrbücher für deutsche Theologie* he wrote on "The relation of grace to the freedom of the will in the application of salvation." After his death some of his former pupils published from his manuscripts, *Zur Dogmatik. Zwei akademische Reden*, together with Landerer's *Gedächtnissrede auf F. C. Baur* (ed. by Buder and Weiss, Tübingen, 1879):—*Predigten* (ed. by P. Lang, Heilbronn, 1880):—*Neueste Dogmengeschichte von Semmler bis auf die Gegenwart* (published by Paul Zeller, 1881). See *Worte der Erinnerung an Dr. M. A. Landerer* (Tübingen, 1878); Wagenmann in *Jahrbücher für deutsche Theologie* (1878), part iii; *Würtembergisches Kirchen- und Schulblatt* (eod.), No. 26–28; *Protestantische Kirchenzeitung* (eod.), No. 20; Schmidt, in Plitt-Herzog,

Real-Encyklop. s. v.; Lichtenberger, *Encyclop. des Sciences Religieuses*, s. v. (B. P.)

Landi, Gasparo, an eminent Italian painter, was born at Piacenza in 1756, and studied the grand productions of Correggio and the Caracci. He gained the grand prize at the Academy of Parma for his fine picture of *Tobias and Sarah*, after which he was sent to Rome by the marquis of Landi, and studied under Pompeo Batoni. After gaining a number of prizes at the exhibitions, he was chosen professor of the Academy of St. Luke by pope Pius VI. In 1813 he was commissioned by the French government to execute several works, and was appointed a director of the School of Design established in the convent of Apollinarius. His masterpiece is the picture in the Church of the Dominicans at Piacenza, representing *Christ Ascending Mount Calvary.* He died at Rome, Feb. 24, 1830. See Hoefer, *Nouv. Biog. Générale*, s. v.; Spooner, *Biog. Hist. of the Fine Arts*, s. v.

Landis, Robert Wharton, D.D., an eminent Presbyterian divine, son of Samuel Calvin Landis, a descendant of the old Huguenot family of Calvin, was born at Philadelphia, Pa., Jan. 8, 1809. He was converted at seventeen, joined the Baptist Church, of which his parents were members, and commenced his theological studies in the same year. He remained but fifteen months at an academy, and three months under a private tutor, before entering upon his pastoral labors. At twenty he united with the Presbyterian Church, was licensed in 1831, and ordained in 1832. He continued his studies while carrying forward his work as pastor, and became possessed of rare literary attainments. In 1835 he was pastor at Providence and Norristown; in 1839 at Allentown; in 1842 at Bethlehem, N. J.; in 1849 at Hillsdale, N. Y.; in 1852 at Greenville; in 1853 at Paterson, N. J.; in 1856 at Iona, Mich.; in 1860 at Somerset, Ky.; in 1867 at Wilmington, Del. In all these places his preaching was attended with marked effect upon his hearers, and large numbers were converted. In 1868 he became professor in Danville Theological Seminary, where he remained one year. He died at Danville, Ky., Jan. 24, 1883. Dr. Landis was the author of several valuable works, and contributed largely to the religious and literary journals. See Nevin, *Presb. Encyclop.* s. v.

Landon, Seymour, a veteran Methodist Episcopal minister, was born May 3, 1798, at Grand Island, in Lake Champlain, N. Y. He was converted in 1815, and in 1818 joined the New York Conference. He served the following charges: Charlotte Circuit, Vt.; Ticonderoga Circuit, N. Y. (twice); St. Albans Circuit, Vt.; Chazy Circuit, N. Y.; Whitehall Circuit; Poultney, Vt.; Sandy Hill and Glens Falls, N. Y.; York Street, Brooklyn (twice); Lansingburgh, N. Y.; New York; Rhinebeck; Newburgh; Sugar Loaf; Hudson; Hempstead, L. I.; Sag Harbor; West Winsted, Conn.; Grand Street, Brooklyn, L. I.; Greenpoint; Southport, Conn.; Watertown, N. Y.; Mount Vernon; Astoria, L. I.; Amityville and New Bridge; Springfield; Orient. He was presiding elder of Hartford and Long Island districts. He died at Jamaica, L. I., July 29, 1880. His effective ministry closed at Orient when he was seventy-four years old, after an active ministerial career of fifty-five consecutive years. In 1852 and 1860 he was a delegate to the General Conference, and in 1856 and 1864 he was a reserve delegate. He was a man of excessive diffidence, with a conscientiousness and firmness equally marked. Of majestic figure and handsome face, his amiability of disposition and other personal qualities made him a welcome ornament in every circle of society. See *Minutes of Annual Conferences*, 1881, p. 80.

Landri (Lat. *Landericus*), *Saint*, twenty-eighth bishop of Paris, occupied that see about 650, under Clovis II, between Audebert and Chrodebert. He showed his love for the poor during the famine which desolated Paris in 651, by sacrificing all his own means, and selling even the vessels of the altar to help them. A tradition generally accepted in the diocese of Paris, and admitted by the Bollandists, attributes to St. Landri the founding and endowing of the hospital called Hôtel Dieu. The monk Marculfe dedicated to Landri his *Formules*, which he had probably collected at his instigation. The name of this prelate is found among those of the twenty-four bishops who signed the charter of emancipation which Clovis II accorded, in 653, to the abbey of St. Denis, founded by Dagobert I. The last breviary of Paris places the death of St. Landri in 656, and his festal day on June 3, but he is usually commemorated June 10. He was interred in the Church of St. Germain l'Auxerrois, then called St. Germain le Rond. See Hoefer, *Nouv. Biog. Générale*, s. v.; Smith, *Dict. of Christ. Antiq.* s. v.

Landriot, Jean François Anne Thomas, a distinguished French prelate, was born at Conches-les-Mines in 1816, and died at Rheims in 1874. He was vicar-general of Autun, in 1856 bishop of La Rochelle, and in 1866 archbishop of Rheims. He published, *Discours et Instructions Pastorales* (1856–60, 3 vols.):—*Conférences, Allocutions, Discours et Mandements* (1856–64, 3 vols.):—*La Femme Forte* (1863; 8th ed. 1868):—*La Femme Pieuse* (1863, 2 vols.; 7th ed. 1874):—*La Prière Chrétienne* (1862, 2 vols.; 6th ed. 1874):—*Le Christ de la Tradition* (1865, 2 vols.):—*Les Béatitudes Evangéliques* (1866). See Lichtenberger, *Encyclop. des Sciences Religieuses*, s. v. (B. P.)

Lane, Aaron D., a veteran Presbyterian minister, was born at Lansingburgh, N. Y., Jan. 29, 1797. He studied at the Lenox Academy, Berkshire Co., Mass.; graduated from Union College, N. Y., in 1816, and from Princeton Theological Seminary. He was licensed by the Presbytery of Columbia, Oct. 26, 1819; was ordained pastor of the Presbyterian Church of Waterloo, Seneca Co., N. Y., in 1821, having served as stated supply for nine months. At Waterloo he continued to labor zealously and successfully over fourteen years, until compelled by bronchial affection to cease from preaching. He continued, however, to labor among his former people, loved and appreciated, until his death at Waterloo, Nov. 2, 1880. See *Necrol. Report of Princeton Theol. Sem.* 1881, p. 11. (W. P. S.)

Lane, Edward William, an English Orientalist, was born Sept. 17, 1801, at Hereford. He studied at Cambridge, and spent some years in Egypt (1825–28; 1833–35). He published *An Account of the Manners and Customs of the Modern Egyptians* (Lond. 1836, and often; Germ. transl. Leipsic, 1856):—*Selections of the Kur'ân* (Lond. 1843):—*Arabian Society in the Middle Ages* (1853). In 1842 he went for a third time to Egypt, and after his return, in 1849, began the publication of his main work, *Arabic-English Lexicon*, of which he published five parts (1863–74), and died Aug. 9, 1876. Lane's nephew, Stanley Lane Poole, continues the work of the deceased. (B. P.)

Lanfranco (or **Lanfranchi**), Giovanni, an eminent Italian painter, was born at Parma in 1581, and studied under Agostino Caracci. At the age of sixteen he painted a picture of the *Virgin with Saints*, which was greatly admired, and placed in the Church of San Agostino, at Piacenza. At the age of twenty he visited Rome, becoming the pupil of Annibale Caracci, who employed him in the Farnese palace, and in the Church of San Jago, where he executed a number of works. His fresco paintings in San Agostino, particularly his *Assumption of the Virgin*, were greatly admired. Among his other good works were, *Moses Striking the Rock; Abraham Offering Isaac;* and *The Flight into Egypt.* He procured the commission to paint the cupola of San Andrea della Valle. It was a wonderful work of art, and represented *The Virgin seated in the clouds, surrounded with saints, and contemplating the figure of Christ*, which is in the upper part of the picture. In 1646 he was invited to Naples to paint the cupola of the treasury at that place. He was employed by Urban VIII to paint a picture for the Church of St. Peter, representing that apostle walking on the sea. He died at Rome in 1647. There are a number of excellent plates by him, as follows: *The Messengers of Moses Returning from the Land of Canaan;* also a series of pictures of subjects from the Passion of Christ, for the chapel of the Crucifix. See Hoefer, *Nouv. Biog. Générale*, s. v.; Spooner, *Biog. Hist. of the Fine Arts*, s. v.

Lanfredini, Jacopo, an Italian prelate, was born at Florence, Oct. 26, 1670. He became civil auditor of cardinal Camerlingue in 1722, and the following year was declared domestic prelate, member of the consistorial congregation, and referendary of both signatures. Benedict XIII ordained him priest, March 16, 1727. Clement XIII, his compatriot, appointed him, in 1730, to a canonship in St. Peter's. After having been successively secretary of the congregation of the council, voter of the signature of grace, datary of the penitentiary, he was, in 1735, made cardinal, and bishop of Osimo and Cingoli, in the bounds of Ancona. He died May 16, 1741. See Hoefer, *Nouv. Biog. Générale*, s. v.

Lanfrey, Pierre, a French historian, was born at Chambery, in Savoy, Oct. 26, 1828. He studied at the Collége Bourbon in Paris, and published, in 1857, *L'Église et les Philosophes au XVIIIe Siècle*. In 1858 he issued *Essai sur la Révolution Française. Histoire Politique des Papes* followed in 1860, but his main work is *Histoire de Napoléon I* (1867-75, 5 vols.; Germ. transl. Berlin, 1869-76). He died Nov. 15, 1877. Of his *Œuvres Complètes*, the first volume was published in 1879. (B. P.)

Lang, Heinrich, a Protestant theologian of Germany, was born Nov. 14, 1828, at Frommen, in Würtemberg. He studied at Schönthal and Tübingen, and was in 1848 appointed pastor at Wartau, in Switzerland. Here he commenced, in 1859, the publication of the *Zeitstimmen aus der reformirten Schweiz*, the organ of the liberal reformed Church party. In 1863 he was called to Meilen, and in 1871 he was elected pastor of St. Peter's at Zurich. He died Jan. 13, 1876, leaving, *Predigten* (St. Gall, 1852):—*Versuch einer christlichen Dogmatik* (Berlin, 1858; 2d ed. 1868):—*Ein Gang durch die christliche Welt* (1859):—*Stunden der Andacht* (Winterthur, 1862-65, 2 vols.):—*Religiöse Charaktere* (1862). See Mayer, *Heinrich Lang. Lebensbild eines freisinnigen Theologen* (Basle, 1877); Lichtenberger, *Encyclop. des Sciences Religieuses*, s. v.; Zuchold, *Bibl. Theol.* ii, 763. (B. P.)

Lang, John, an eminent minister of the Society of Friends, was born at Vassalborough, Me., in 1790. He felt a special interest in the North American Indians, and about 1840 was appointed one of a deputation sent out by the New England Yearly Meeting to the Indians west of the Mississippi River, with a view of suggesting and maturing plans for their improvement. President Grant appointed him on the Board of Indian Commissioners, a position which he held till his death. "Both as a commissioner and as a private citizen he served the government several times in missions of great delicacy and difficulty, accomplishing the service to the satisfaction of the government, and securing amicable relations with the tribes visited." He is represented as having been "a man of splendid physique and great vigor, both of body and mind, yet gentle and unassuming in manner, genial and sympathetic, most appreciative of others, and forgetful of self in his efforts for the good of his fellows." He died at his native place, May 25, 1879. See *Friends' Review*, xxxii, 681. (J. C. S.)

Langbecker, Emanuel Christian Gottlieb, a German hymn-writer, was born at Berlin, Aug. 31, 1792, and died Oct. 24, 1843. He published, *Gedichte* (Berlin, 1824, 1828, 2 collections):—*Das deutsche-evangelische Kirchenlied* (1830):—*Gesang-Blätter aus dem 16. Jahrhundert* (1838):—*Leben und Lieder von P. Gerhard* (1841). Some of his spiritual songs are found in the hymn-books of Germany. See Koch, *Geschichte des deutschen Kirchenliedes*, vii, 40 sq.; Zuchold, *Bibl. Theol.* ii, 763. (B. P.)

Langbein, Bernhard Adolph, a Lutheran theologian, was born in 1815 at Wurzen, Saxony. In 1841 he was deacon at Meissen, in 1853 church counsellor at Dresden, in 1866 first court-preacher there, and died July 17, 1873, doctor of theology. Langbein was one of the most prominent preachers of Germany, and the author of many volumes of sermons and ascetical works. Of the latter we mention, *Die Reise aus dem irdischen nach dem himmlischen Vaterhause* (3d ed. Leipsic, 1869):—*Tägliche Erquickung aus dem Heilsbrunnen* (2d ed. 1866):—*Der christliche Glaube nach dem Bekenntniss der lutherischen Kirche* (1873). See Zuchold, *Bibl. Theol.* ii, 763 sq. (B. P.)

Lange, Abraham, a Lutheran theologian of Germany, who died Dec. 20, 1615, at Weimar, doctor of theology, and general superintendent, wrote *Explicatio Catechismi Lutheri:—Explicatio Psalmi lxiv:—Responsum ad iv Quæstiones de Salute:—Responsum Lutheranum ad Anhaltinorum Calvinianorum Defensionem de Imaginibus Abolendis.* See Jöcher, *Allgemeines Gelehrten-Lexikon*, s. v. (B. P.)

Lange, Friedrich Albert, a German philosophical writer, and son of the famous theologian Johann Peter (q. v.), was born Sept. 28, 1828, at Wald, near Solingen. He studied at Zurich and Bonn, was in 1852 professor at the gymnasium in Cologne, and in 1855 privatdocent of philosophy at Bonn. In 1861 he was appointed professor at the Duisburg gymnasium, was called in 1870 to Zurich, in 1873 to Marburg, and died Nov. 21, 1875. His best work is *Geschichte des Materialismus und Kritik seiner Bedeutung in der Gegenwart* (Iserlohn, 1865; 2d ed. 1873-75, 2 vols.; Engl. transl. by E. C. Thomas, Boston, 1877 sq., 3 vols.). See Vaihinger, *Hartmann, Dühring und Lange* (Iserlohn, 1876). (B. P.)

Lange, Friedrich Conrad, a Lutheran theologian of Germany, was born May 12, 1738. He studied at Copenhagen, was in 1771 con-rector at Altona, in 1776 court-preacher at Glückstadt, in 1783 member of consistory, in 1788 doctor of theology, and in the same year provost and first pastor at Altona. He died Jan. 9, 1791, leaving, besides sermons, *De Resurrectione Corporum Nostrorum per Spiritum Sanctum* (Altona, 1787):—*De Jesu Christo, Mortuo quidem quoad Corpus, Spiritu vero Vivente* (ibid. 1789). See Döring, *Die gelehrten Theologen Deutschlands*, s. v.; Winer, *Handbuch der theol. Lit.* ii, 89, 141. (B. P.)

Lange, Johann Christian, a Lutheran theologian of Germany, was born Dec. 25, 1669, at Leipsic. He studied at his native place, and commenced his academical career there in 1694. In 1697 he went to Giessen, was in 1716 member of consistory and superintendent, in the same year doctor of theology, in 1718 general superintendent, and died Dec. 16, 1756. He wrote, *Theologia Christiana in Numeris* (Leipsic, 1702):—*Ordo Salutis sub Ratione Theologici Problematis Delineatus* (Giessen, 1704; 2d ed. 1744):—*Themata Selecta ex Variis Philosophiæ Partibus Deprompta* (1710):—*De Antiquissimo et Novissimo Theologo hoc est*, etc. (1716). See Döring, *Die gelehrten Theologen Deutschlands*, s. v. (B. P.)

Lange, Johann George, a German missionary among the Jews, was born in Silesia, Nov. 30, 1804. In 1824 he was admitted to the mission seminary at Berlin. At the end of 1826 he was engaged by the London Jews' Society, and entered their seminary in 1827. In 1829 he was appointed as missionary, and stationed at Amsterdam. Towards the end of that year he was sent to Warsaw. In 1841 he was stationed at Lublin, and after many years of labor there was again placed at Warsaw in 1853. Towards the end of 1854 he was sent to Breslau, where he died, Aug. 14, 1869. Mr. Lange was not ordained, but had from the

Evangelical Consistory the regular permission to preach in any of the Prussian churches, and to give lectures to the Jews. (B. P.)

Lange, Johann Lobegott Ferdinand, a Protestant theologian of Germany, was born Sept. 26, 1798. He commenced his academical career in 1824, was professor of philosophy in 1828, in 1838 doctor and professor of theology at Jena, and died in 1855. He wrote, *Beiträge zur ältesten Kirchengeschichte* (Leipsic, 1828, 1831, 2 vols.):—*Der Glaube an Jesus Christus den Weltheiland* (1830):—*Die Kindertaufe in der evangelischen Kirche* (Jena, 1834):—*Anleitung zum Studium der christlichen Theologie* (1841):—*Tabellen der Kirchen- und Dogmen-Geschichte* (2d ed. 1848):—*Der Protestantismus in kirchlicher und politischer Hinsicht* (1844):—*Lehrbuch der christlichen Kirchengeschichte* (2d ed. 1845):—*Exercitationes Examinatoriæ ad Theologiam Dogmaticam et Historiam Dogmatum Spectans* (Leipsic, 1846): *Geschichte des Protestantismus* (Elberfeld, 1847). See Winer, *Handbuch der theol. Lit.* i, 301, 367, 434, 451, 548; Zuchold, *Bibl. Theol.* ii, 767. (B. P.)

Lange, Johann Peter, D.D., one of the most prominent German Protestant theologians of the 19th century, was born in Sournborn, near Elberfeld, of Reformed parents, April 10, 1802. He studied at Bonn, was in 1826 pastor of the Reformed Church at Langenberg, and in 1832 at Duisburg. He first attracted public attention by poems and a brilliant series of articles in Hengstenberg's *Evangelical Church Gazette*, at that time the leading orthodox journal in Germany. When Strauss published his famous *Life of Jesus*, Lange wrote in reply an able defense of the historical character of the Gospel-accounts of the infancy of our Saviour. Soon afterwards, in 1841, he received a call as professor of theology to the University of Zurich, a position to which Strauss had been called before, but which he was prevented from occupying by a rebellion of the people against their infidel government. It was there that Lange prepared his great work on the *Life of Jesus* (1844–47, 3 vols.), which is a positive refutation of the infidel work of Strauss, and one of the most original and ingenious among the many biographies of the Son of Man. It has been made known to the English-reading public by a translation published by Clark, in six volumes. In 1854 Lange was called to Bonn, and died July 8, 1884, on the same day on which professor Dorner (q. v.) died. Lange's works are numerous: *Christliche Dogmatik* (Heidelberg, 1849–52, 3 vols.):—*Das apostolische Zeitalter* (1853–54, 2 vols.). But the work by which he is best known and has made himself most useful is his *Theological and Homiletical Bible Work* (1857–68), well known in this country by the English translation in twenty-four volumes. The success of this voluminous commentary has been marked. Lange conceived the plan, wrote the commentary on Genesis, Exodus, Leviticus, Numbers, Matthew, Mark, John, Romans, James, and the Apocalypse. The other books were prepared by a number of German and Dutch divines. Besides the works already mentioned, Lange wrote a number of ascetical and poetical works of high character. He was a poetical theologian, and a theological poet, and though having a theological system of his own, was thoroughly evangelical and in essential harmony with the Reformed type, but adapted to the modern currents of thought. Some of his poems have been translated into English. See Zuchold, *Bibl. Theol.* ii, 764–767; Schaff, *Biographical Sketch of Lange*, in the introduction to the American edition of the *Bible Work;* Koch, *Gesch. des deutschen Kirchenliedes*, vii, 361 sq. (B. P.)

Lange, Samuel Gottlieb, a Lutheran theologian of Germany, was born April 5, 1767, at Ohra, near Dantzic. He studied at Jena, and commenced his theological career there in 1795. In 1798 he was called to Rostock as professor, was in 1799 doctor of theology, and died June 15, 1823. He wrote, *Versuch einer Apologie der Offenbarung* (Jena, 1794):—*Die Schriften Johannis übersetzt und erklärt* (1795):—*Diss. Historico-Critica I et II de Justini Martyris Apologia pro Christianis ad Antoninum Pium* (eod.):—*Ausführliche Geschichte der Dogmen der christl. Kirche* (Leipsic, 1796):—*System der theologischen Moral* (1803):—*Versio Germanica Epistolæ Pauli ad Romanos* (1820–21). See Döring, *Die gelehrten Theologen Deutschlands*, s. v.; Winer, *Handbuch der theol. Lit.* i, 238, 367, 592, 897. (B. P.)

Langeac (or **Langhac**), Jean de, a French prelate, was born at Langeac, in Auvergne, near the close of the 15th century, of a noble Sicilian family. He early embraced the ecclesiastical calling, and received numerous benefices, being preceptor of the Hôtel Dieu of Langeac, rector of Coulange, count of Brionde, dean of the chapter of Langeac, archdeacon of Retz, treasurer of the Church of Puy, count of Lyons, provost of Brionde, abbot of St. Gildas des Bois, of St. Lo, of Charli, of Eu, of Pibrac, then bishop of Avranches, a see which he resigned in favor of Robert Cenalis, after occupying it six months, and took possession of the bishopric of Limoges, June 22, 1533. He was also prothonotary of the sacred see, counsellor of the grand council, grand-almoner of the king in 1516, master of requests in 1518, ambassador to Portugal, Poland, Hungary, Switzerland, Scotland, Venice, Ferrara, England, and finally to Rome. At Limoges he established an episcopal residence, repaired the cathedral, and elaborately ornamented it. His memory is revered at Limoges, where he is still called "the good bishop." Wherever he was sent he firmly defended the rights of the king. At Rome even, he strongly maintained the liberty of the Gallican Church. He was a friend and patron of literature. During his embassy at Venice, he had as secretary Stephen Dolet, who dedicated to him three of his books. He died at Paris, May 22, 1541. Only a collection of synodal statutes in MS. remain of his works. See Hoefer, *Nouv. Biog. Générale*, s. v.; *Biog. Universelle*, s. v.

Langelier, Nicolas, a French prelate, raised to the see of St. Brieuc in 1564, was invested by Pius IV, Aug. 5 of the same year, and took the oath of the king, Feb. 3, 1565. His administration was full of trouble. Having, in effect, taken the part of the League, he became one of the active counsellors of the duke of Mercœur. But the citizens of St. Brieuc and the better part of the diocesan clerks remained faithful to the cause of the king, and struggled with all their might against the encroachments of their bishop. Langelier was nevertheless a distinguished prelate, who well understood canonical questions. He died at Dinan, in September, 1595, leaving *Notæ in Canones*, the manuscript of which formed part of the groundwork of St. Germain, at the Imperial Library, No. 870. See Hoefer, *Nouv. Biog. Générale*, s. v.

Langhans, Friedrich, a Swiss rationalistic theologian, was born in 1829. He studied at Berne, where he became a member of the ministerium in 1853. He died April 17, 1880, at Berne, as professor of systematic theology. He was one of the main movers and promoters of the reform movement, and his writings, as *Pietismus und Christenthum im Spiegel der äusseren Mission* (1849):—*Pietismus und äussere Mission vor dem Richterstuhl ihrer Vertheidiger* (1866):—*Das Christenthum und seine Mission im Lichte der Weltgeschichte* (Zurich, 1875), are the best proofs of his neology. See *Zur Erinnerung an Professor F. Langhans*, in the *Protestantische Kirchenzeitung*, No. 28, 29, for 1880; Lichtenberger, *Encyclop. des Sciences Religieuses*, s. v. (B. P.)

Languet, Hubert, one of the most prominent French writers of the 16th century, was born at Viteaux, near Autun, in 1578. He studied theology, canon law, history, and natural sciences in Poictiers, Padua, and Bologna; visited also Spain, and was, by the reading of Melanchthon's *Loci Theologici*, induced to go to Wittenberg, where he remained from 1549 to 1560, making frequent journeys in Germany and Scandinavia. At what period he definitely embraced the Reformation is not known. In 1560 Languet entered the service of the elector of Saxony, which he left in 1577. The last years of his life he spent in the Netherlands, in intimate connection with William of Orange. Languet died at Antwerp, Sept. 30, 1581. His letters, which are of the greatest interest for the history of his time, were edited by Ludovicus, under the title *Arcana Seculi XVI, Huberti Langueti Epistolæ* (Halle, 1669). But his main work is *Vindiciæ contra Tyrannos* (Edinburgh and Basle, 1579; French transl. by François, Paris, 1581; German by Freitzschke, Leipsic, 1846). In an elaborate manner he treats the question whether subjects (for instance, Protestants) have a right to revolt when oppressed for their religion's sake by their princes. See Philibert de La Mare, *Vie de Languet* (Halle, 1700); Chevreul, *Étude sur le Seizième Siècle, Hubert Languet* (2d ed. Paris, 1856); Haag, *La France Protestante;* Viguié, *Étude sur les Théories Politiques-Libérales au Seizième Siècle;* Hotman, *La Franco-Gallia* (Paris, 1879); Scholz, *Hubert Languet als kursächsischer Berichterstatter und Gesandter in Frankreich* (1560–1572; Halle, 1875); Blasel, *Hubert Languet* (Oppeln, 1872); Plitt-Herzog, *Real-Encyklop.* s. v.; Lichtenberger, *Encyclop. des Sciences Religieuses*, s. v. (B. P.)

Lanigan, JOHN, D.D., an Irish clergyman, was born at Cashel in 1758, and educated in the Irish college at Rome, where he took orders. He was then appointed to the chair of Hebrew, divinity, and the Scriptures, at Pavia, where he remained until the university was deserted in consequence of the war in 1796, when he returned to Ireland, and was elected to a similar position in the College of Maynooth. He declined the appointment, however, and was chosen to a position in the record tower of Dublin castle in 1799, and remained there until 1821, when he was seized with insanity, and died in a lunatic asylum at Finglas, near Dublin, July 7, 1828. He published, *Institutiones Biblicæ* (1794):—*Protestants' Apology for the Roman Catholic Church* (1809):—*Ecclesiastical History of Ireland to the Thirteenth Century* (Dublin, 1822, 4 vols.). See *Appletons' Amer. Cyclop.* s. v.; Allibone, *Dict. of Brit. and Amer. Authors*, s. v.

Lanini (or **Lanino**), BERNARDINO, an eminent Italian painter, was born at Vercelli about 1522, and studied under Gaudenzio Ferrari. He was much employed at Milan and Novara, where he painted the personification of *The Deity* in the dome of the cathedral, also several subjects from the life of the Virgin, and the picture of *Our Saviour after the Flagellation, between two Angels*, in San Ambrogio, at Novara. He died about 1578. See Spooner, *Biog. Hist. of the Fine Arts*, s. v.; Hoefer, *Nouv. Biog. Générale*, s. v.

Lanitho, a dæmon of the air, worshipped by the inhabitants of the Molucca islands.

Lansing, DIRCK CORNELIUS, D.D., an eminent Presbyterian minister, was born of a distinguished family at Lansingburgh, N. Y., March 3, 1785. He graduated from Yale College in 1804. While in college he was converted, and immediately felt impelled to preach the gospel. He studied theology under Rev. Dr. Blatchford of Lansingburgh, and was licensed to preach by the Presbytery of Columbia in 1806. In the autumn of that year he went to an untried field and visited from house to house over a circuit of twenty-five miles, and soon gathered a church where the town of Onondaga now stands, and continued pastor for eight years. Then, on account of failing health, he retired to a farm, preaching as he was able till he became pastor at Stillwater, where he remained two and a half years, and two hundred converts were added to the Church. In 1816 he supplied the Park Street Church in Boston, Mass., and such an interest was awakened in his preaching that in a few weeks more than eighty persons were converted. He next accepted a call from the First Presbyterian Church in Auburn, N. Y. Here he remained twelve years, and his own enthusiasm kindled a corresponding feeling in the hearts of those who heard his preaching and saw his labors, and more than a thousand souls were converted and added to the Church. During a part of the time he occupied the chair of sacred rhetoric in the Theological Seminary. In 1829 he took charge of the Second Presbyterian Church in Utica, and in a short time five hundred persons were converted under his ministry. In 1833 he was installed pastor of a Free Church in New York city, then worshipping in Masonic Hall, but was obliged to retire in 1835 on account of ill-health. For the next ten years he labored chiefly as an evangelist in central and western New York, and one year in Illinois. In 1846 he returned to New York city, and took charge of a feeble church in Chrystie Street. In 1848 he assumed the care of the church on Clinton Avenue, Brooklyn, where his labors were crowned with great success, but, his health giving way, he was obliged to leave in 1855. In the spring of 1856 he removed to Walnut Hills, Cincinnati, O., where he supplied the Vine Street Congregational Church. For fourteen weeks he preached twice each Sunday, until the second Sunday in December, when he suddenly failed. This was his last sermon. He died at Walnut Hills, March 19, 1857. Dr. Lansing projected the Auburn Theological Seminary, and by his personal efforts secured an endowment of $100,000. He was a member of the original board of trustees of Hamilton College. He published *Sermons on Important Subjects* (1825). See Sprague, *Annals of the Amer. Pulpit*, iii, 407; Nevin, *Presb. Encyclop.* s. v.

Lao, ANDRÉ, an Italian Carmelite, and professor of theology at Padua in the 16th century, was one of the most powerful and learned supporters of papacy in his time. After having published a dogmatical treatise of small importance, *Disputationes Theologicæ ad D. Thomam et de Conscientia*, he made himself conspicuous and popular among the clergy by publishing *Brevis de Summo Pontifice Tractatus*, etc. (2d ed. Rome, 1668). See Lichtenberger, *Encyclop. des Sciences Religieuses*, s. v. (B. P.)

Lao Kyun, in Chinese theology, was the originator of a religious sect, whose followers are called "children of immortality." He came two hundred years after Confucius. His priests were magicians and sorcerers.

Laosynactes (λαοσυνάκτης), an officer in the Greek Church, whose duty it is to collect together the deacons and the people.

Lapacci, BARTOLOMMEO, an Italian prelate, was born about 1396 at Florence. He was admitted to the Dominican order, received, in 1427, the diploma of doctor, and was, at the Council of Florence, one of the ten theologians who maintained the articles of union of the Greek with the Latin Church. Pope Eugenius IV recompensed him for this service by appointing him, in 1439, master of the sacred palace in place of Torquemada, who was made cardinal. Being sent to Greece in 1443, in company with F. Condelmerio, he became bishop of Argoli. Two years later he was at Constantinople, where he disputed publicly with Mark of Ephesus. At this time he occupied the see of Caron, and, abandoning it when the Turks became masters of the city, he retired to Florence, where he died, June 21, 1466. He wrote *De Sensibilibus Deliciis Paradisi* (Venice, 1498), and manuscript treatises upon several points of theology, also some sermons, etc. See Hoefer, *Nouv. Biog. Générale*, s. v.

Lapide, CORNELIUS A. See CORNELIUS A LAPIDE.

Lapland MYTHOLOGY. The accounts on this subject are very scant, because the Lapps never had a public divine worship, but conducted their religious services privately in their homes. They had a conception of a supreme being, which the North American Indians call the Great Spirit, the Laplanders, Jamula. The latter see three forces of nature combined in the supreme god. They have the god Tiermes, thunder, the god Storjunkare, the ruler of earth, protector of the woods, and the goddess Baiwe, the sun. These three were united in Jamula. Besides these supreme deities they have numerous others, who are subordinate, but not servants of the former; they have their own smaller circles, as, for instance, the spirits of air, the water deities, mountain deities, and the dreaded evil deities of death, who separate the soul from the body, giving the latter to corruption, and bringing the former into distant regions of good hunting and fishing. They made sacrifices of that which they considered most costly, young male and female reindeer. They offered sacrifices generally in the fall for the whole people. This was the only custom which pointed to a public divine worship. They had no priests nor temples; therefore every father of a household was priest and magician for his family, and taught his own sons. In the autumn, if none of the three gods accepted the offerings, they were sad, because the gods were angry. Although Christianity has entered among them, there are many heathen, who still adhere to their original usages.

Lappish Version OF THE SCRIPTURES. The Lappish is vernacular to the Laplanders. The earliest religious work in the Lapponese is a manual containing the Psalms, the Proverbs, the book of Ecclesiasticus, the dominical gospels and epistles, published at Stockholm in 1648. This work was not generally understood, on account of the peculiarity of the dialect in which it was written, and accordingly another manual was published in 1669. It is not known at what time the New Test. was translated into Lapponese. The first edition of which there is any account was published in 1755, from which a new edition was printed by the British and Foreign Bible Society in 1811. In the same year the Old Test. was published. Of late efforts have been made to give to the Laplanders of Russia, Sweden, and Norway versions in their respective vernacular, and thus there exist now, besides the Lappish version proper, the New Test. and Psalms in Norwegian-Lapp, the gospel of Matthew in Swedish-Lapp, and the same gospel in Russ-Lapp. See *Bible of Every Land*, p. 322; QUÄNIAN VERSION. (B. P.)

La Poype (*de Vertrieu*), JEAN CLAUDE DE, a French prelate, was born in 1655, of an ancient family of Poitou. He became vicar to M. de St. Georges, archbishop of Lyons, and in 1702 was called to the episcopal see of Beziers. This he refused, and the same year became bishop of Poictiers. In 1716 he was one of the prelates who signed the article demanding of the pope an explanation of the bull Unigenitus. He died Feb. 3, 1732, near Poictiers. He was in part author of an estimable work entitled, *Compendiosæ Institutiones Theologicæ* (Poictiers, 1708). The questions are here treated with great precision and method. See Hoefer, *Nouv. Biog. Générale*, s. v.

Lara, DAVID DE, a Jewish writer of Portuguese descent, who died at Hamburg in 1674, is the author of, כתר כהונה, a Talmudico-Rabbinic lexicon (Hamburg, 1667):—עירדויד *de Convenientia Vocabulorum Rabbinicorum* (Amsterdam, 1638). See Fürst, *Bibl. Jud.* ii, 222; De' Rossi, *Dizionario Storico* (Germ. transl. p. 174 sq.; Perles, *David Cohen de Lara's Rabbinisches Lexikon* (Breslau, 1868). (B. P.)

Lararium, that part of an ancient Roman house which was appropriated to the Lares (q. v.), and where the morning devotions were offered up.

Larentalia, a festival among the ancient Romans, which was held in honor of *Acca Larentia* (q. v.). It was also observed in honor of the *Lares* generally.

La Roche (AYMON) **Charles Antoine de**, a French prelate, was born at the chateau of Mainsat, Feb. 17, 1697. He was at first canon of St. Peter's at Macon, and vicar-general of Limoges, before being consecrated bishop of Sarepta, Aug. 5, 1725. He occupied successively the sees of Tarbes, 1729, Toulouse, 1740, Narbonne, 1752, before being appointed grand almoner, July 13, 1760, and archbishop of Rheims, Dec. 5, 1762. He was created cardinal in 1771, invested the following year with the abbey of St. Germain-des-Près, and consecrated Louis XVI on Trinity Sunday, June 11, 1775, having previously baptized him, given to him his first communion, and confirmed his union with Marie Antoinette of Austria. He presided over all the assemblies of the clergy of France from 1760 to 1775, having assisted at all the preceding assemblies from 1735. He was at the time of his death dean of the French episcopacy, having as his coadjutor Alexander Angelique, of Talleyrand Perigord, afterwards archbishop of Paris. He was distinguished for his modest piety and extreme benevolence. He died at Paris, Oct. 27, 1777. See Hoefer, *Nouv. Biog. Générale*, s. v.

La Roche (AYMON), **Ralph de**, a French prelate, was born about 1160. He was a Cistercian monk, was at first abbot of Igny, in the diocese of Rheims, and in 1224 was deemed worthy to succeed St. Bernard at Clairvaux. Having occupied this see for eight years, he was called to govern the Church of Agen, from which Gregory IX transferred him, in 1235, to the metropolitan see of Lyons. Here he died March 5, 1236. His memory is celebrated March 5, and he is called the Happy Ralph de la Roche. See Hoefer, *Nouv. Biog. Générale*, s. v.

La Rochefoucauld, Dominique de, count of St. Elpis, a French prelate, was born in 1713 at St. Elpis, in the diocese of Mende. He was a descendant of a poor and ignorant branch of the house of La Rochefoucauld, which the bishop of Mendes, of Choiseul, discovered in one of his pastoral visits. Frédéric Jérome de la Rochefoucauld, archbishop of Bourges, made known this discovery, and took upon himself the direction of the studies of young Dominique. He placed him at the Seminary of St. Sulpice, and having made him grand-vicar, gave him the archbishopric of Alby in 1747. Being a member of the assemblies of the clergy in 1750 and 1755, he zealously defended the rights of the Gallican Church, and was invested with the abbey of Cluny in 1757. Two years later he was transferred to the see of Rouen, and in 1778 made cardinal. Elected deputy of the clergy of the bailiwick of Rouen to the States-General in 1789, he came out strongly against the principles of the revolution. He was one of the signers of the protest of Sept. 12, 1791, against the innovations made by the national assembly in the matter of religion. In the preceding April he had published a pastoral instruction, which the tribunal of Rouen had torn and burned, as being contrary to the laws of the constituent assembly. After Aug. 10, 1792, the cardinal La Rochefoucauld retired to Germany, and died at Munster, Sept. 2, 1800. See Hoefer, *Nouv. Biog. Générale*, s. v.

La Rochefoucauld, François de, a French prelate, was born at Paris, Dec. 8, 1558, being the son of Charles I, of La Rochefoucauld, count of Randan, and of Fulvie Pic de la Mirandole, lady of honor to the queen. He was destined by his uncles for the priesthood, and completed his studies at the College of Clermont in a very brilliant manner. At the age of fifteen he was invested by the cardinal of Guise with the rich abbey of Tournus, and scarcely had he reached his twenty-seventh year when Henry III appointed him bishop of Clermont. Being a partisan of the Holy League, he sought to excite Auvergne in revolt against the king; but the inhabitants of Clermont revolted against their bishop, and he was obliged to take refuge at his chateau in Mozun. In 1589 the bishop of Clermont called an assembly of the states of his province at Billom. La Rochefoucauld addressed them in a vehement discourse, in which he accused the king of being in harmony with the Protestants. This led the assembly to embrace the side of the sacred union. His father, who governed in the League, was killed in 1590, and Henry IV abjured some years later. The bishop of Clermont yielded, and composed a work upon the spiritual authority of the popes, remaining silent upon the temporal power. Some time after Martha Brossier excited the wonder of the credulous world. François de la Rochefoucauld and his brother, Alexander, travelled from city to city, interrogating the evil spirits concerning the real presence of Jesus Christ in the eucharist. They were at length obliged to desist from this ridiculous business. François de la Rochefoucauld yielded, and in 1607 was made cardinal and bishop of Senlis. In 1618 he became grand almoner of France, and in 1619 of the abbey of St. Genevieve. In 1622 he was made president of the Council of the States, and charged with the reformation of the abbeys of France. This reform occupied the rest of his life. He died at the abbey of St. Genevieve, Feb. 14, 1645, and an elegant tomb was erected for him. Full of zeal for literature, La Rochefoucauld enriched various libraries with Greek and Latin MSS. He wrote, *Statuts Synodaux pour l'Église de Clermont* (1599):—*Statuts Synodaux pour l'Église de Senlis* (Paris, 1621):—*De l'Autorité de l'Église en ce qui Concerne la Foi et la Religion* (ibid. 1603, 1604). His *Life* was written by La Marinière (Paris, 1647). See Hoefer, *Nouv. Biog. Générale*, s. v.

La Rochefoucauld (Bayers), **François Joseph de**, a French prelate, was born at Angoûleme in 1735. He was bishop of Beauvais in 1772, and by this title peer of France, and was sent by the clergy of the bailiwick of Clermont, in Beauvais, to the States-General, which became the constituent assembly. He there defended the privileges of the clergy. Chabot having denounced him before the legislative assembly as taking part in an anti-revolutionary meeting, he fled with his brother, the bishop of Saintes, to the house of their sister, the abbess of Soissons, and then started for Paris. They were arrested at Carmes, and assassinated at Paris, Sept. 2, 1792. See Hoefer, *Nouv. Biog. Générale*, s. v.

La Rochefoucauld, Frédéric Jérome de Roye de, a French prelate, was born July 16, 1701. He was son of François de la Rochefoucauld, of Roye, count of Rouncy. He embraced the ecclesiastical calling, and in 1729 was called to the archbishopric of Bourges. Elected coadjutor of the abbey of Cluny in 1738, he became titular abbot in 1747, by the death of the cardinal of Auvergne. The same year he was made cardinal, and the following year was sent to Rome as ambassador. In 1755 the king appointed him to the abbey of St. Vandrille, and charged him at the same time with the schedule of benefices. He presided over the assemblies of the clergy in 1750 and 1755. In 1756 Louis XV made him grand almoner. He died April 29, 1757. He was a prelate of mild and conciliatory character. See Hoefer, *Nouv. Biog. Générale*, s. v.

La Rochefoucauld (Bayers), **Pierre Louis de**, a French prelate, brother of François Joseph, was born in 1744 in the diocese of Perigueux. In 1770 he was made commendatory prior of Nanteuil by the cardinal La Rochefoucauld, and general agent of the clergy in 1775, which office he held until 1780. In 1782 he was called to the bishopric of Saintes. Being sent to the States-General by the jurisdiction of the seneschal of Saintes, he voted at the national assembly with the minority. Having taken flight with his brother, the bishop of Beauvais, he perished with him at Paris, in the prison of Carmes, Sept. 2, 1792. See Hoefer, *Nouv. Biog. Générale*, s. v.

La Rocheposay, Henri Louis *Chasteignier de*, a French prelate, son of Louis Chasteignier, was born Sept. 6, 1577, at Tivoli, Italy. Having been educated by the celebrated Scaliger, he received at Rome the four minor orders in 1596, and the priesthood at Paris at the hand of Henry de Gondi, who was then cardinal of Retz. Coadjutor of Geoffroi de St. Blin, bishop of Poictiers, he succeeded him in 1611, and bore witness three years later to his fidelity to the king by opposing the entrance of the prince of Conde and his troops. The conduct of this prelate appears little in conformity with the canons, and gave rise, on the part of the celebrated Jean du Vergier de Hauranne, abbot of St. Cyran, to a defence, ingenious as well as paradoxical: *Apologie pour Messire Henri Chasteignier de la Rocheposay*, etc. (1615). La Rocheposay assisted at the assembly which was held at Rouen in 1627, under the presidency of Gaston of France, then at the synod of Bordeaux, and at the general assembly of the clergy in 1628. He occupied himself zealously in trying to purge Poitou of the doctrines of Calvin. He died July 30, 1651, leaving several works, as *Recueil des Axiomes de Philosophie et de Théologie*:—*Rémarques Françaises sur St. Matthieu* (Poictiers, 1619):—*Exercitationes in Marcum, Lucam, Joannem et Acta Apostolorum*, etc. (ibid. 1626):—*In Genesim* (1628):—*In Librum Job* (eod.):—*In Exodum et in Libros Numerorum, Josue et Judicum* (1629):—*In Prophetas Majores et Minores* (1630):—*Dissertationes Ethico-Politicæ*. See Hoefer, *Nouv. Biog. Générale*, s. v.

Laron (or **Loron**), Jourdain de, a French prelate, was at first provost of St. Leonard, which position he occupied until the death of Girard, bishop of Limoges. Several competitors claimed the succession to Girard, but Jourdain de Laron obtained it, and the duke of Aquitania conducted him in triumph to his episcopal city. He was the sub-deacon, but in two years was ordained deacon, priest, bishop, by Islon, bishop of Saintes, assistant of the archbishop of Bordeaux and Boson, Arnauld, Isombert. This ordination was not participated in by the archbishop of Bourges, who had Limoges in his province. The archbishopric of Bourges was at that time occupied by Gauslin, son of Hugh Capet, and therefore brother of king Robert; and he, through jealousy, caused the excommunication of Jourdain and his whole diocese. Jourdain, after a time, made a journey to the Holy Land. On his return, in 1028, he consecrated his cathedral. In 1031, at the Council of Bourges, he discoursed against the armed hordes which devastated the country, which discourse was resented by the bishops. He died in 1052. See Hoefer, *Nouv. Biog. Générale*, s. v.

Larroque, Patrice, a French spiritualistic philosopher, was born in 1801 at Beaume. He had taught with great success at different colleges, and was successively rector at Cahors, Limoges, and Lyons. The last position he held till 1849, when some differences arose between him and archbishop Bonald. In 1851 he took his dismission, and died at Paris in 1879. He published, *Cours de Philosophie*:—*Examen Critique des Doctrines de la Religion Chrétienne* (1859), a kind of manifesto of deism:—*Rénovation Religieuse* (1860), a kind of religious programme of the future, destined to unite all on the ruins of positive religion. See Dumur, in the *Révue Chrétienne*, 1861, p. 581 sq.; Lichtenberger, *Encyclop. des Sciences Religieuses*, s. v. (B. P.)

Larsow, Friedrich, a German Orientalist, who died at Berlin, Oct. 3, 1870, is the author of, *De Dialectorum Linguæ Syriacæ Reliquiis* (Berlin, 1841):—*Des heiligen Athanasius, Bischof von Alexandria, Festbriefe* (Leipsic, 1852):—*Die Genesis übersetzt und schwierige Stellen erläutert* (Berlin, 1843). (B. P.)

Larue, Charles de, a French Benedictine, was born at Corbie, July 12, 1684, and joined his order at Meaux. Being charged by Montfaucon with the edition of the works of Origen, he only succeeded in publishing the first two volumes. While superintending the print of the third volume, he was seized with a paralytic stroke, and died Oct. 5, 1739, at Paris. See Lichtenberger, *Encyclop. des Sciences Religieuses*, s. v. (B. P.)

Larue, Vincent de, a French theologian, nephew of the foregoing, was also born at Corbie. He continued the work commenced by Sabathier, *Bibliorum Sa-*

crorum Latinæ Versionis Antiqua seu Versio Vetus Italica (Rheims, 1743-49, 3 vols.). Larue died at St. Germain-des-Près, March 29, 1762. See Lichtenberger, *Encyclop. des Sciences Religieuses*, s. v. (B. P.)

Lasaulx, Amalie von, a Roman Catholic philanthropist, sister of Ernst (q. v.), was born at Coblentz in 1815. She joined the Sisters of St. Borromeo, and as sister Augustine was made mother superior at Nancy. She was sent, in 1849, to Bonn, and took charge of the hospital of St. John the Baptist. In the German wars against Schleswig and Austria, and during the Franco-German war of 1870, she proved herself a true Samaritan. Her early education, which she received from pupils of Hermes, whose views were condemned at Rome, her connection with the Catholic professors of the University of Bonn, who refused to subscribe to the decisions of the Vatican council, led her to oppose the papal dogmas. She cared not for the menaces of the Ultramontanes, but followed her calling as before. Her self-denying and faithful attention to her onerous duties finally broke down her health. While on her bed of sickness, the general mother superior of Nancy demanded of her that she should recant and accept the Vatican decrees, but she would not yield. At last she was obliged to leave the place of her lifelong activity, and died in 1872. When she was dead, the dress of the order was taken from her corpse. See Reinken, *Amalie von Lasaulx* (Bonn, 1878); Lecoultre, *Courte Notice sur Amélie de Lasaulx* (Paris, 1879); Lichtenberger, *Encyclop. des Sciences Religieuses*, s. v. (B. P.)

Lasaulx, Ernst von, a German antiquarian, was born at Coblentz, March 16, 1805. He studied at Bonn and Munich, spent some time at Vienna, Rome, Athens, Constantinople, and Jerusalem, was in 1835 professor of philology at Würzburg, in 1844 professor at Munich, and was deposed in 1847. In 1848 he was a member of the German National Assembly, and went with the Roman Catholic fraction in all religious questions. In 1849 he was reappointed to his professorship, and died May 10, 1861. He published, *Der Untergang des Hellenismus durch die christlichen Kaiser* (Munich, 1854):—*Die Philosophie der schönen Künste* (1860):—*Ueber die theologische Grundlage aller philosophischen Systeme* (1856):—*Wahrheit der Thatsachen gegründeter Philosophie der Geschichte* (eod.):—*Des Sokrates Leben, Lehre und Tod* (1857):—*Die prophetische Kraft der menschlichen Seele in Dichtern und Denkern* (1858). The last four books were put on the papal index. See Holland, *Erinnerungen an Ernst von Lasaulx* (Munich, 1861). (B. P.)

La Saussaye, Daniel Chantepie de, a Walloon preacher and Dutch publicist, was born at La Haye, Dec. 10, 1818. He studied at Leyden, was preacher at the Walloon Church in Leeuwarde (1842-48), and at Leyden (1848-62). Here he edited a periodical entitled *Ernst en Vrede* (1853-58), in which he defended the ethical principle and supernatural in Christianity against the so-called "modern theology," inaugurated by J. H. Scholten. In 1862 he accepted a call to Rotterdam, where he edited another journal. In 1872 he was called to the chair of dogmatics and Biblical theology, which was formerly occupied by P. Hofstede de Groot, and died shortly afterwards, Feb. 13, 1874, doctor of theology, a distinction conferred on him by the Bonn University in 1858. He published, *L'Existence Permanente du People Juif Expliquée par son Avenir* (Leyden, 1849):—*Témoignages contre l'Esprit du Siècle* (Amsterdam and Leyden, 1852):—*Réflexions sur l'Essence et les Besoins de l'Église* (Leyden, 1855):—*Appréciation de la Doctrine de l'Église Réformée, de J. H. Scholten* (Utrecht, 1859):—*Études Bibliques* (1859-61):—*La Crise Religieuse en Hollande* (Leyden, 1860):—*Sermons* (Leyden and Rotterdam, 1860-66, 5 vols.):—*Leven en Rigting*, i. e. *Life and Tendency* (Rotterdam, 1865):—*Le Surnaturel dans l'Histoire* (Groningen, 1874). See Lichtenberger, *Encyclop. des Sciences Religieuses*, s. v. (B. P.)

Lasharon. Concerning this place Keil remarks (*Commentary*, Josh. xii, 18), "Knobel supposes it to be the place called *Saruneh*, to the west of the lake of Tiberias, and conjectures that the name has been contracted from Lassaron by the aphæresis of the liquid. This is quite possible, *if only we could look for Lasharon so far to the north.* Bachiene and Rosenmüller imagine it to be the village of *Sharon*, in the celebrated plain of that name, between Lydda and Arsof." Nevertheless, Conder (*Tent Work*, ii, 338) and Trelawney Saunders (*Map of the O. T.*) adopt the above position at *Sarona*, which is laid down on the *Ordnance Map* at six miles west of the south end of the sea of Galilee, and described in the accompanying *Memoirs* (i, 414, quoting from Guérin) thus, "The houses are rudely built on two hillocks, which lie round a valley watered by a spring, which is contained in a sort of square chamber, the roof of which is formed of large slabs, and which is preceded by a large vaulted chamber in very regular cut stones, the whole of ancient appearance." Eusebius and Jerome state (*Onomast.* s. v. Sarona) that the region between Tabor and the lake of Tiberias was called *Sharon* in their time.

Lassen, Christian, a famous German Orientalist, was born Oct. 22, 1800, at Bergen, Norway. He studied at Christiana, Heidelberg, and Bonn, spent some years at London and Paris copying and comparing Indian MSS., and published with Burnouf the *Essai sur le Pali* (Paris, 1826). Having returned to Bonn, he commenced his academical career by publishing *Commentatio Geographica atque Historica de Pentapotamia Indica* (Bonn, 1827). In 1830 he was made professor, and died May 8, 1876. He published editions of Jayadeva's *Gitagovinda* (1837):—*Gymnosophista, sive Indicæ Philosophiæ Documenta* (1832):—*Anthologia Sanscritica* (1838; new edition by Gildemeister, 1865, 1868):—*Institutiones Linguæ Pracriticæ* (1837); but his main work is *Indische Alterthumskunde* (1844-62, 4 vols.; 2d ed. vol. i, 1866; vol. ii, 1873). In his *Die altpersischen Keilinschriften* (1836) he deciphered for the first time the cuneiform inscriptions. (B. P.)

Lassenius, Johann, a Lutheran theologian, was born at Waldau, in Pomerania, April 26, 1636. He studied at different universities, and travelled extensively. On account of his writings against the Jesuits he was imprisoned at Vienna. He was taken to the Turkish frontier for the purpose of being sold as a slave to the Turks, but he managed to escape. He took his degree as doctor of theology at Greifswalde, was appointed court-preacher at Copenhagen, and died Aug. 29, 1692. He was a very prolific writer, and wrote a great many ascetical works. See Moller, *Cimbria Litterata;* Jöcher, *Allgemeines Gelehrten-Lexikon*, s. v.; Zuchold, *Bibl. Theol.* ii, 769. (B. P.)

Lathrop, John, D.D., a Unitarian minister, was born in Norwich, Conn., May 17, 1740. He graduated at Princeton College in 1763. For some months after his graduation he was engaged as assistant teacher in Moor's Indian School at Lebanon, Conn., and at the same time studied theology. He was licensed soon after this, labored as a missionary among the Indians, and in 1767 was invited to settle both at Taunton and Reading. In 1768 he accepted a call to become pastor of the Old North Church in Boston, preaching in that city until his death, Jan. 14, 1816. He became a member of the Corporation of Harvard University in 1778. He was also one of the counsellors of the American Academy of Arts and Sciences, vice-president of the Massachusetts Bible Society, and president of the Massachusetts Congregational Charitable Society. His publications consisted of single sermons. See Sprague, *Annals of the Amer. Pulpit*, viii, 68.

Latil, Jean Baptiste Marie Anne Antoine, *duke de*, a French prelate, was born in one of the Isles of Sainte Marguerite, March 6, 1761. Being destined for the ecclesiastical calling, he entered the Seminary of St. Sulpice at Paris, and was ordained priest in 1784. Shortly after he was appointed grand-vicar of the bishop of Vence, who charged him with representing him at the bailiwick assembly of his diocese at the convocation of the States-General. On the breaking-out of the French Revolution Latil refused to take the oath of the civil constitution of the clergy, and withdrew to Coblentz, but in 1792, having returned to France, he was arrested at Montfort l'Amaury, and remained for some time in the prisons of that city. Having recovered his liberty, he retired to Germany, and settled at Düsseldorf, where he devoted himself to preaching. He had determined to set out for America, when the count of Artois sent for him, in 1794, and made him almoner. Latil from this time never left this prince, and at the restoration became his chief almoner. Appointed bishop of Amyclea, *in partibus infidelium*, he was consecrated April 7, 1816; became bishop of Chartres in 1821, and archbishop of Rheims, Aug. 11, 1824. He consecrated Charles X in the metropolis of Rheims, May 29, 1825. He was made a peer of France in 1823, made count by Charles X, and also minister of state. Pope Leo XII made him cardinal, March 12, 1826, and the king gave him the title of duke. The same year he signed the declaration of the clergy of France touching the independence of the temporal power in civil matters. He was accused, however, of being a great partisan of the Jesuits, and of urging Charles X to adopt measures which aided the revolution of July. In view of this Latil fled to England. He soon returned to France and maintained his episcopal see, but refused the oath as peer of France. He died at Geminos in December, 1839. See Hoefer, *Nouv. Biog. Générale*, s. v.

Latimer, James Elijah, D.D., a Methodist Episcopal minister, was born at Hartford, Conn., Oct. 7, 1826. He graduated from Wesleyan University in 1848, and the same year became teacher of languages in Newberry Seminary, Vt., and of Latin and geology in Genesee Wesleyan Seminary, Lima, N. Y.; in 1851 principal of New Hampshire Conference Seminary, Northfield, N. H.; in 1854 principal of Fort Plain Seminary, N. Y.; in 1858 joined East Genesee Conference, and was pastor in Elmira and Rochester, where he made a deep and permanent impression by his learning and devotion. After this he travelled and studied in Europe. In 1869 he became pastor of a Church in Penn Yan, N. Y.; in 1870 professor of historic theology in school of theology of Boston University, and in 1874 dean and professor of systematic theology in the same school. He died at Auburndale, Mass., Nov. 27, 1884. Professor Latimer took high rank as a student of German literature. He possessed a genial temper, and was greatly beloved by all under his instruction. His sermons, essays, and lectures are highly commended. See *Alumni Record of Wesl. Univ.* 1881, p. 91; *Meth. Rev.* March, 1886.

Latinus, Latinius, an Italian critic, was born at Viterbo in 1513. He acted as secretary to cardinals Farnese and Colonna at Rome, and died Jan. 21, 1593. He wrote, *Observationes et Emendationes in Tertullianum:—Bibliotheca Sacra et Profana* (edited by D. Macer, Rome, 1659):—*Epistolæ, Conjecturæ et Observationes Sacra Profanaque Eruditione Omatæ* (2 vols.). See Freher, *Theatrum Eruditorum;* Teissier, *Éloges des Savans;* Jöcher, *Allgemeines Gelehrten-Lexikon*, s. v. (B. P.)

Latonius, Bartholomæus, a German controversial writer, was born at Arlon, Luxemburg, in 1485. He taught Latin at Treves, and rhetoric at Cologne and Freiburg. In 1534 he was called to Paris, and visited Italy in 1539. In 1541 he was appointed counsellor at the electoral court of Treves, with his residence at Coblentz, and died in 1566. Of his controversial writings we mention, *Responsio ad Epistolam Buceri* (1543):—*Adversus Bucerum de Controversiis Quibusdam Altera Defensio:—Responsio ad Convicia et Calumnias Petri Datheni* (concerning the communion and the sacrifice of the mass, Frankfort, 1558):—*De Docta Simplicitate Primæ Ecclesiæ* (1559). At the instance of the emperor Charles V, he also took part in the Ratisbon Colloquy in 1546, and was appointed by him imperial counsellor in 1548. See Du Pin, *Bibl. Eccles.* xxvi, 145 sq.; Jöcher, *Allgemeines Gelehrten-Lexikon*, s. v.; Wagenmann, in Plitt-Herzog, *Real-Encyklop.* s. v. (B. P.)

Latōna, in Greek mythology, was the daughter of Cœus and Phœbe, therefore a Titanide. Being loved by Jupiter, she reaped the hatred of Juno. The latter took an oath from the earth not to grant Latona a place, and persecuted her by the frightful dragon Python. Everywhere the earth refused to receive her. At last an island, Delos, arose from the sea, which had not existed when Juno exacted the oath, where Diana, hardly born, assisted her mother in the birth of her twin brother Apollo. Being one of the oldest goddesses, she was everywhere highly worshipped. Apollo and Diana would not forgive the smallest insult to their mother, as is fully shown by the fate of Niobe, with whom she had stood on intimate friendship. Herodotus relates that she was also worshipped in Egypt.

Latour (*D'Auvergne Lauragais*), Hugues Robert Jean Charles de, a French prelate, was born at the chateau of Auzeville, near Toulouse, Aug. 14, 1768. In the care of his uncle, a canon of Castres, he went to Paris, where he entered the Seminary of St. Sulpice, and pursued a course of theology under Emery. In 1792 and 1793 he was secretly ordained sub-deacon, deacon, and priest by the bishop of Limoges of Argentre. He refused the oath to the civil constitution of the clergy, and withdrew to Picardy, to the house of his aunt, the countess of Vergy, and there performed secretly the offices of his ministry at Amiens. He was finally arrested and thrown into prison. A contractor of the republican army rescued him by taking him into his service. The first consul appointed him bishop of Arras, May 9, 1802. The young bishop reconstructed his diocese, and founded in it all sorts of institutions. On all occasions he manifested his admiration for the chief of the state, who had restored peace to the Church, and advanced the glory of France. The events of 1814 modified his opinions, and on April 8 he sent his approval to the act of forfeiture of the emperor. The restoration brought to him an offer of the bishopric of Rheims, which he refused. The government of July offered still more important archbishoprics. Latour wished to remain in his see, but accepted the Roman purple, Dec. 14, 1840. He died July 20, 1851. He left some catechisms, sermons, etc. See Hoefer, *Nouv. Biog. Générale*, s. v.

Latuinus, *Saint*, traditionary first bishop of Seez, commemorated June 20, is said to have been sent into Gaul by Clement of Rome, and is assigned to some period earlier than A.D. 500. He is believed to be the saint popularly known as *St. Lain*, whom the Bollandists place at the beginning of the second century.

Lau, Johann Theodor, a Lutheran theologian of Germany, was born at Schleswig in 1813. In 1843 he was appointed second pastor at Hettstadt, near Husum, in 1855 pastor at Ottensen, near Altona, and died Dec. 20, 1873. He is the author of, *Gregor I, der Grosse, nach seinem Leben und Lehre geschildert* (Leipsic, 1855):—*Reformationsgeschichte in Schleswig* (Hamburg, 1867). See Zuchold, *Bibl. Theol.* ii, 770. (B. P.)

Laub, Hardenack Otto Konrad, bishop of Viborg, was born in 1805. Having completed his theological studies, he was appointed to a pastorate in the isle of Funen. In 1854 he was made bishop of Viborg, and held this position till 1877, when feeble health obliged him to retire from his ecclesiastical duties. He spent the remainder of his life at Copenhagen, and died May 27, 1882. He was highly honored by the congregations as well as by the ministers of his diocese. (B. P.)

L'Aubespine, Gabriel de. See Aubespine.

L'Aubespine, Sebastien de, a French prelate and diplomatist, was born in Beauce in 1518. His high ability won for him from Francis I the gift of many ecclesiastical benefices, especially that of the abbey of Basse Fontaine, in the diocese of Troyes. Being sent to Switzerland, he there combated the influence of the emperor, in 1543. At the Diet of Worms, he prepared the work of the honorary ambassador, the count of Grignan, a man more distinguished by his ancestry than by his own merit (1545). Henry II afterwards sent him to negotiate with the people of Strasburg in 1548, and to modify the treaty of alliance with the Helvetian cantons. On his return to France he was charged with an embassy to Flanders, but he soon resumed his former functions in Switzerland, and still negotiated with ability and honor. Then he was appointed ambassador to Philip II of Spain. From 1558 he held the bishopric of Limoges, in which city he already held the rich abbey of St. Martial. After rendering various services to the king, and being driven from the court, he withdrew to Limoges, and devoted all his attention to works of piety connected with the episcopacy. Here he died in 1582, and was interred in his cathedral. For mention of his works see Hoefer, *Nouv. Biog. Générale*, s. v.

Lauder, Alexander, a Scotch prelate, was rector of Ratho, promoted to the see of Dunkeld in May, 1440, and died Oct. 11 following. See Keith, *Scottish Bishops*, p. 87.

Lauder, George, a Scotch prelate, was vicar of Crail in 1425, and was afterwards master, or preceptor, of the Hospital of St. Leonard's. He was promoted to the bishopric of Argyle as early as 1427, and was still bishop in 1462. See Keith, *Scottish Bishops*, p. 287.

Lauder, Robert, a Scotch prelate, was probably promoted to the see of Dunblane in 1448, and in 1451 was sent jointly with the bishops of Glasgow and Moray into England. He was probably bishop there in 1465. See Keith, *Scottish Bishops*, p. 177.

Lauder, Thomas, a Scotch prelate, was preferred to the see of Dunkeld in 1452, which see he retained until 1476, when he resigned his charge on account of advanced age. He died Nov. 4, 1481. See Keith, *Scottish Bishops*, p. 89.

Lauder, William, a Scotch prelate, was preferred to the see of Glasgow in 1408. He was bishop there and lord chancellor, April 14, 1424. He died about 1426. See Keith, *Scottish Bishops*, p. 248.

Laudisti, a society which was instituted in Florence, in 1316, for the performance of religious lauds. The society still exists, and is in active operation.

Laue, JOHANN GOTTFRIED, a Lutheran theologian of Germany, was born Dec. 20, 1683. He studied at Leipsic, was in 1708 con-rector at Quedlinburg, in 1710 deacon, in 1715 pastor at Diffurt, and died May 30, 1721. He wrote, *Meditationes Exegetico-practicæ:—Apparatus Exegetico-homileticus:—Historiæ Arcanæ Veteris Testamenti ad Judic. II et 1 Sam. III:—Disput. an Turrium et Campanarum Usus in Ecclesia Deo Displiceat?* See Leporinus, *Germania Literata Vivens;* Jöcher, *Allgemeines Gelehrten-Lexikon*, s. v. (B. P.)

Laufeia, in Norse mythology, was a Jote-woman, the wife of the giant Farbaute, and the mother of Loke, the evil one among the Asas.

Launawater, in the mythology of the Finns, was an evil goddess, whose children were the plagues and sicknesses of men.

Launoy, MATTHIEU DE, a Roman Catholic theologian, was born at Ferté-Alais, but embraced the Reformation at Geneva in 1560, and was admitted to the evangelical ministry. He was pastor at Heidelberg in 1573, afterwards at Sedan, where he had adulterous relations with one of his cousins, and was thus obliged to leave the place. Being excommunicated, he abjured Protestantism, and became one of the most furious preachers of the League. To justify his second apostasy he published, *Défense de Launoy* (Paris, 1578), and *Déclaration et Refutation*, etc. (1579). To secure the favor of the Catholics, he published *Réponse Chrétienne à xxiv Articles*, etc. (1581). In consideration of his return to the Church of Rome, he was made canon of St. Gervais de Soissons, and, with Boucher, was one of the first four pillars of the League. He belonged to the council of sixteen who decreed the assassination of president Brisson. After the capitulation of Paris, Launoy went to Flanders, where he probably died. See Labitte, *De la Démocratie Chez les Prédicateurs de la Ligue et la France Protestante;* Lichtenberger, *Encyklop. des Sciences Religieuses*, s. v. (B. P.)

Laurel, a plant which was sacred to Apollo, the god of prophecy, and much used by those who pretended to inspiration. The heads of ancient seers were usually adorned with laurel wreaths, while they carried in their hands a laurel branch as a magic wand. The heads of victors in the national games were also crowned with laurel wreaths; hence the expression, "winning the laurels."

Laurence (1), a Scotch prelate, was elected bishop of the see of the Isles in 1249, but was drowned the same year. See Keith, *Scottish Bishops*, p. 299.

Laurence (2), a Scotch prelate, was made bishop of the see of Argyle about 1261. About 1269 he ratified to the monks of Paisley the churches of Kilfinan and Kilkeran. He was still bishop in 1299. See Keith, *Scottish Bishops*, p. 286.

Laurent, JOHANN THEODOR, a French prelate, was born July 6, 1804, at Aix-la-Chapelle. He made himself especially conspicuous by his opposition to the Hermesians (q. v.), and in recognition of his merits he was appointed bishop of Cherson, *in partibus infidelium.* As he could not reside in Hamburg, where he intended to live, he went to Rome, and was in 1841 appointed apostolic-vicar at Luxemburg, but was recalled, in 1848, on account of his too rigorous procedure. He retired to Simpelvelde, in the province of Limburg, and died Feb. 20, 1884. (B. P.)

Laurentia. See ACCA.

Laurentie, PIERRE SEBASTIEN, a French Roman Catholic historian and publicist, was born Jan. 21, 1793, at Houg (department of Gers). In 1817 he was professor of rhetoric at the Collège Stanislas in Paris, and in 1818 professor of history at the Polytechnic Institute. In 1823 he was appointed inspector-general of the public schools, but he lost this position in 1826 on account of his opposition to the ministry headed by Villèle, whom he had attacked in his journal, *La Quotidienne.* Laurentie now devoted himself entirely to his journal, which, for a time, was called *L'Union Monarchique*, and after 1848 merely *L'Union.* Laurentie died at Paris, Feb. 9, 1876. Besides his articles, he published, *De la Justice au xix Siècle* (1822):—*De l'Origine et de la Certitude des Connaisances Humaines* (1826):—*Introduction à la Philosophie* (1829):—*Théorie Catholiques des Sciences* (1836; 4th ed. 1846):—*Histoire de France* (1841-43, 8 vols.):—*Les Rois et le Pape* (1860):—*Rome et le Pape* (eod.):—*Histoire de l'Empire Romain* (1861-62, 4 vols.):—*L'Athéisme Scientifique* (1862):—*Le Livre de M. Renan sur la Vie de Jésus* (1863). See Lichtenberger, *Encyclop. des Sciences Religieuses*, s. v. (B. P.)

Laurentii, LAURENTIUS, a German hymn-writer, was born June 8, 1660, at Husum, in Holstein, and died May 29, 1722, at Bremen. He published *Evangelia Melodica*, or spiritual hymns and songs, according to the Christian year, some of which have been translated into English; thus, *Du wesentliches Wort* ("O thou essential Word," in *Lyra Germ.* i, 15):—*Wer im Herzen will erfahren* ("Is thy heart athirst to know," in *Lyra Germ.* ii, 45):—*Jesus was hat dich getrieben* ("Jesus! what was that which drew thee," in *Hymns* *from the Land of Luther*, p. 79):—*Fliesst ihr Augen, fliesst von Thränen* (ibid. p. 92):—*Ermuntert euch ihr Frommen* (ibid. p. 51). (B. P.)

Laurentius, *Saint*. In early Christian art St. Laurence usually carries a copy of the gospels, to denote his office of deacon. In the Church of St. Laurence, in Agro Verano, at Rome, there is a mosaic of the 6th century, representing the martyr with an open book in his hand, on which may be read the words "dispersit, dedit pauperibus" (Ciampini, *Vet. Mon.* tab. lxvi, 2), in allusion to his kindness to the poor.

Early Representation of St. Laurence.

Laurentius, a Scotch prelate, was promoted to the see of Dunblane in 1160, and was witness to a charter to the abbey of Dunfermline. See Keith, *Scottish Bishops*, p. 170.

Laurentius, Jacob, a Dutch theologian, who died at Amsterdam, March 19, 1664, is the author of, *Refutatio Tripartita Fabulæ Papisticæ de Purgatorio, Limbo Patrum et Puerorum:* — *Comment. in Epist. Jacobi ac Utramque Petri:* — *Expositio Septem Epistolarum quas Johannes in Insula Pathmo Scripsit:*—*Apologia Catechesis Heidelbergensis contra Coppensteinium:*—*Explicatio in Loca Difficiliora Epistolarum Pauli:* — *Expositio Historiæ Josephi Gen. xxxvi:*—*De Vera et Legitima S. Scripturæ et Patrum Auctoritate.* See Witte, *Diarium Biographicum;* Jöcher, *Allgemeines Gelehrten-Lexikon*, s. v. (B. P.)

Laurentius, Paulus, a Lutheran theologian of Germany, was born March 30, 1554. He studied at Leipsic, was superintendent at Dresden, and died Jan. 24, 1624, doctor of theology. He wrote, *Erklärung und Auslegung der 2 Bücher Samuelis:*—*Auslegung des Propheten Amos:*—*Predigten über den Propheten Jona:*—*Erklärung des xxii Psalms:*—*Explicatio Symboli Athanasii*, etc. See Witte, *Diarium Eruditorum;* Jöcher, *Allgemeines Gelehrten-Lexikon*, s. v. (B. P.)

Lauretti (or **Laureti**), Tommaso (called *il Siciliano*), an eminent Sicilian painter, was born at Palermo about 1530, studied under Sebastiano del Piombo, and settled early in life at Bologna. He subsequently visited Rome, at the invitation of Gregory XIII, to finish the ceiling of the Sala de Constantino. He was honored with the appointment of president of the Academy of St. Luke. He died about 1610. Among his principal works at Rome are the fresco paintings of the *History of Brutus;* at Bologna are the *Crowning of the Virgin*, in Santa Mattia; the *Resurrection*, in San Giacomo Maggiore. He died about 1592. See Spooner, *Biog. Hist. of the Fine Arts*, s. v.; Hoefer, *Nouv. Biog. Générale*, s. v.

Laurie, Robert, a Scotch prelate, was first minister and then dean of Edinburgh. He was advanced to the see of Brechin about 1670. He was allowed to retain his deanery, and continued to exercise a particular ministry at the Church of the Holy Trinity in Edinburgh until his death in 1677. See Keith, *Scottish Bishops*, p. 168.

Lauterbach, Erhard, a Lutheran theologian of Germany, who died Dec. 16, 1649, at Naumburg, doctor of theology, is the author of, *De Prædestinatione:*—*De Persona Christi:*—*De Officio Christi Regio:*—*De Justificatione Hominis Peccatoris Coram Deo:*—*De Tripudio Solis Paschali:*—*Syntagma de Præcipuis Fidei Articulis.* See Witte, *Diarium Biographicum;* Jöcher, *Allgemeines Gelehrten-Lexikon*, s. v. (B. P.)

Lauterbach, Samuel Friedrich, a Lutheran theologian of Poland, was born at Fraustadt, Oct. 20, 1662. He studied at Breslau and Wittenberg, and died at his native place, June 4, 1728. He is the author of, *Ariano-Socinianismi Olim in Polonia* (Frankfort and Leipsic, 1725):—*Vita, Fama et Fata Valerii Herbergeri.* See Winer, *Handbuch der theol. Lit.* i, 770; Jöcher, *Allgemeines Gelehrten-Lexikon*, s. v. (B. P.)

Lavābo (*I will wash*) is a term expressing the act of washing the priest-celebrant's fingers prior to the celebration of mass. This occurs in the English rite, by custom, after the offertory. The act is performed as a sign of the purity with which he should approach the altar. In the Roman rite, before the priest assumes the sacerdotal vestments, he washes the tips of his fingers. This custom seems to have been almost universal. Whenever sacrifice was about to be offered, the minister of the altar performed special ablutions. Such customs were current among the Jews, having been ex-

Lavabo-dish.

pressly enjoined by the law of Moses (Exod. xxx, 17–21). In the Western Church priests ordinarily recite the last six verses of Psalm xxvi during the act of washing, a practice which is referred to by several fathers, among others St. Clement and St. Cyril, and which became common throughout the whole Church about the 8th century. In St. Cyril's *Catechetical Lectures*, that bishop remarks, "You have seen the deacon provide water for the priest of sacrifice and presbyters around to wash their hands. . . . That washing of hands is a symbol indicating that you ought to be pure from every sin and prevarication."

Lavalette, Louis de Nogaret d'Epernon, a French prelate, was born at Angoûleme in 1593, and was the third and last son of the duke of Epernon. Being destined by his parents for the ecclesiastical calling, he was sent while very young to the abbeys of St. Mesmin of Gard, Bardona, in 1611; of Gimont, St. Victor de Marseille, the Grasse, etc., in 1621. As archbishop of Toulouse he assisted at the States-General held at Paris. Promoted to the Roman purple, Jan. 11, 1621, he took part in the assembly of the clergy the same year, and of that held at Paris in 1625. In 1628 he resigned the archbishopric of Toulouse in favor of Charles de Montchol, his former preceptor, and devoted himself to military service. At his death, which occurred Sept. 28, 1639, the pope refused him the honors customarily rendered to a cardinal, under the pretext that he had commanded the armies of the heretics against the Catholics. See Hoefer, *Nouv. Biog. Générale*, s. v.

Laver OF REGENERATION, a name sometimes given in the early Christian Church to baptism.

Laverna, in Roman mythology, was a protecting goddess of thieves and deceivers at Rome, who had a temple near the Lavernalian gate.

Law, JAMES, a Scotch prelate, was promoted to the see of Orkney in 1606, where he continued until 1615, when he was translated to the bishopric of Glasgow. See Keith, *Scottish Bishops*, p. 227.

Lawa Ailek, in the mythology of the Laplanders, was one of the three deities who are constant companions of the sun.

Lawkapatim, in Slavonic mythology, was worshipped by the Poles as a field-god, and his favor entreated before ploughing.

Lawrence, Francis Effingham, D.D., a Protestant Episcopal clergyman, was a graduate of St. Paul's College, at College Point, N. Y., and in 1852 of the General Theological Seminary; in 1853 he was assistant minister of the Church of the Holy Communion, New York city, and remained such until 1859, when he was chosen rector, and continued in that relation until his death, June 11, 1879, at the age of fifty-three years. See *Prot. Episc. Almanac*, 1880, p. 171.

Lawrence, Samuel, D.D., an English Presbyterian clergyman, was born at Nantwich, Cheshire, in 1693. His father was a Dissenting minister. He was educated at the Glasgow University, became tutor in the family of chief baron Ward, and settled as a minister first at Newcastle, Stafford, in 1714. In 1727 he became pastor at Newcastle-on-Tyne, but his health failing, in 1733, he had to go south, and settled at Monkwell Street, London, where he had a crowded audience for many years, and his ministry was very successful. He was learned, serious, cheerful, modest and polite, zealous and pious. He died, Oct. 1, 1760, and was interred in Bunhill Fields. See Wilson, *Dissenting Churches*, iii, 208.

Lawson, GEORGE, D.D., an eminent Scotch divine, was born March 13, 1749, near West Linton, Peeblesshire. At twenty he had finished his studies, and was licensed to preach. In 1771 he was ordained pastor of the Bergher Secession Church at Selkirk, where he continued during the remainder of his life. For more than thirty years he was also professor of divinity in the school of theology at the same place, and died there Feb. 21, 1820. He was a man of marked ability, extensive scholarship, and earnest piety. Dr. Lawson published many volumes of *Sermons* and *Lectures;* also *Discourses on the Whole Book of Esther*, etc. (Edinb. 1804, 12mo; Lond. 1809, 12mo):—*Lectures on the Whole Book of Ruth*, etc. (Edinb. 1805, 12mo):—*Lectures on the History of Joseph* (1807, 2 vols. 12mo):—*Exposition of the Book of Proverbs* (1821, 2 vols. 12mo; posth. pub. from 80 MS. vols. left by the author). See Macfarlane, *Life* (Edinb. 1861; N. Y. 1881).

Layritz, FRIEDRICH, a famous German hymnologist, was born Jan. 30, 1808, at Nemmersdorf, in Upper Franconia. He studied at Erlangen, was in 1837 preacher in Hirschlach, and died at Schwaningen, near Anspach, in 1859. He is the author of, *Kern des deutschen Kirchengesanges* (3d ed. Nördlingen, 1853-56):—*Liturgische Gemeindegesänge* (1855):—*Geistliche Melodien meist aus dem 16. und 17. Jahrhundert* (3d ed. Erlangen, 1860):—*Die Liturgie eines vollständigen Hauptgottesdienstes* (1849). See Zuchold, *Bibl. Theol.* ii, 772; Koch, *Geschichte des deutschen Kirchenliedes*, vii, 53 sq. (B. P.)

Lazarus, LEVI, a Jewish scholar, was born in 1822 at Filehne, duchy of Posen. He studied philosophy and Oriental languages at Berlin, and for twenty-five years was rabbi at Prenzlau. When Dr. L. Frankel (q. v.), the director of the Jewish rabbinical seminary, died, he was called in 1876 as his successor. Lazarus died April 16, 1879. He was a great Talmudist, and a clever thinker. In 1877 he published a very interesting brochure, *Zur Charakteristik der talmudischen Ethik.* (B. P.)

Lazzari, DONATO. See BRAMANTE.

Le, in the philosophical system of Confucius (q. v.), is the ultimate immaterial element of the universe. It is the absolute, regarded in association with material essences, and manifesting itself in virtue of such association as the cause of organization and order. The spirit of man is strictly of one substance with this principle. The *Le*, therefore, is identical with the *Tai-ki*, the Great Extreme. Beyond it, as the highest pinnacle of heaven, the one ultimate power, the entity without an opposite, no human thought is capable of soaring. "The absolute is like a stem shooting upwards; it is parted into twigs; it puts out leaves and blossoms; forth it springs incessantly until its fruit is fully ripe; yet even then the power of reproduction never ceases to be latent in it. The vital juice is there; and so the absolute still works and works indefinitely. Nothing hinders or can hinder its activity until the fruits have all been duly ripened, and activity gives place to rest."

Leach, BERIAH N., D.D., a Baptist minister, was born at Middletown, Vt., April 28, 1801. He joined the Church in 1815, and was ordained in October, 1826, over the Church at Cornwall. His subsequent pastorates were in Middlebury, Fredonia, Wyoming, Hamilton, and Brooklyn, N. Y., and in Middletown, Conn. His useful life closed Jan. 23, 1869. See Cathcart, *Baptist Encyclop.* p. 676. (J. C. S.)

Leavitt, Jonathan, D.D., a Congregational minister, was born at Cornish, N. H., Oct. 21, 1800. He was educated at Kimball Union Academy, graduated from Amherst College in 1825, and was a member of Andover Theological Seminary for two years. He was ordained an evangelist in 1828, and became a home missionary in Pendleton and Wilmington, S. C., alternately; in 1830 was temporary supply successively in Lincolnton and Macon, Ga., Westbrook, Me., Atworth, N. H., and Waltham, Mass. He was acting-pastor at Bedford in 1835, was installed in 1837, and remained until 1840, when he was next installed pastor of Richmond Street Church, Providence, R. I. He was without charge from 1863 until his death, at Providence, Oct. 7, 1877. See *Trien. Cat. of Andover Theol. Sem.* 1870, p. 80. (W. P. S.)

Leavitt, Joshua, D.D., a Congregational minister, was born at Heath, Franklin Co., Mass., Sept. 8, 1794. He graduated from Yale College in 1814, studied law, and was admitted to the bar in 1819. He soon secured a lucrative practice in his native town, and afterwards in Putney, Vt., but left it to enter Yale Divinity School, where he graduated in 1825. The same year he was ordained pastor of the Congregational Church in Stratford, Conn. After a highly successful pastorate of three years he resigned and became secretary of the Seaman's Friend Society, and editor of the *Sailor's Magazine*, New York city. In 1831 he became editor of the *New York Evangelist;* in 1837 of the *Emancipator;* in 1848 managing editor of the *Independent*, retaining this position till his death, which occurred Jan. 16, 1873, in Brooklyn, N. Y. Dr. Leavitt was a man of great suavity of manner, a graceful writer, and an eloquent speaker. He published, *Easy Lessons in Reading* (1823):—*Christian Lyre* (1831):—and a series of *Readers* (1847).

Leblanc, Guillaume, a French prelate, was born at Alby in 1561. The position of his uncle, a distinguished theologian of the same name, aided his access to ecclesiastical honors. Having been chamberlain to pope Sixtus V, he was appointed, in 1588, to the bishopric of Vence, which a bull of Clement VIII reunited, in 1591, with the episcopal see of Grasse. This reunion, which the chapter of Vence vigorously repelled, became to Leblanc a great source of embarrassment and litigation. He was even the object of an attempted assassination, and sought to destroy the act of union by the parliament of Aix. He died at Aix, Nov. 21, 1601. For mention of his works, see Hoefer, *Nouv. Biog. Générale*, s. v.

Leblanc (*de Beaulieu*), **Jean Claude**, a French prelate, was born in Paris, May 26, 1753. After being canon-regular of St. Genevieve before the Revolution, he became, in 1791, constitutional rector of the parish of St. Genevieve, and subsequently of St. Étienne du Mont. He was chosen archbishop of Rouen on the death of Gratian; consecrated Jan. 18, 1800, at Paris, and held in his metropolitan church a council of the bishops of his diocese the following October. In 1801 he assisted at the national council held at Paris. After the signing of the Concordat, he gave in his resignation, and in 1802 was appointed bishop of Soissons. He established a seminary in his episcopal city. Being invited, in 1815, to be present at a reception of the emperor after his return from the island of Elba, Leblanc wrote to the minister to give assurance of his fidelity to Louis XVIII. This declaration was published, and the bishop of Soissons withdrew to England. The return of the king recalled him to his diocese, and in 1817 he was appointed archbishop of Arles, re-established by the new Concordat. Having resigned in 1822, he withdrew to the Seminary of Foreign Missions at Paris, took charge of the Savoyards, and was appointed member of the chapter of St. Denis. He died July 13, 1825. See Hoefer, *Nouv. Biog. Générale*, s. v.

Lebonah. The modern site, *el-Lubban*, is laid down on the *Ordnance Map* ten miles north of Beitin (Bethel), and is briefly described in the accompanying *Memoirs* (ii, 286, 360) as well as by Guérin (*Samaria*, ii, 112). Five pillars still remain standing, which seem to have been part of an ancient chapel.

Lebrecht, Fürchtegott S., a Jewish scholar, was born at Memmelsdorf, Bavaria, in 1800. He made his Talmudical studies at the rabbinical seminary in Presburg, Hungary, and his philological at Halle, under Gesenius. In 1832 he went to Berlin, where he died, Oct. 13, 1876. Lebrecht contributed largely to the *Literatur-Blatt des Orients* (1841-44), and in connection with Biesenthal edited the dictionary of David Kimchi, called *Liber Radicum*. Besides, he wrote an essay, *Handschriften und erste Ausgaben des babylonischen Talmuds*, published in *Wissenschaftliche Blätter aus der Veitel Ephraimischen Lehranstalt in Berlin* (1862), and *Die Stadt Bether*, in *Magazin für die Wissenschaft des Judenthums* (Berlin, 1876), p. 27-40, 77-93. See Fürst, *Bibl. Jud.* ii, 226 sq. (B. P.)

Lebrun, Charles, an eminent French painter, was born in Paris, March 22, 1619. In 1662 he commenced his great work, *The Battles of Alexander*, which gained him a great reputation. In the Church of Notre Dame are two of his most celebrated pictures, *The Stoning of St. Stephen*, and *The Martyrdom of St. Andrew*. He died in Paris, Feb. 12, 1690. See Hoefer, *Nouv. Biog. Générale*, s. v.; Spooner, *Biog. Hist. of the Fine Arts*, s. v.

Lebrun, Jean Baptiste (surnamed *Desmarets*), a French scholar, was born at Rouen, and partly educated at Port Royal. He labored in different dioceses, and died at Orleans, March 19, 1731, never having been willing to proceed to a higher order than that of acolyth. He left an edition (the second) of the Latin work of John, bishop of Avranches, *De Divinis Officiis* (Rouen, 1679, 12mo):—An edition of *St. Paulinus*, with notes, etc. (Paris, 1685):—*A Concordance of the Books of Kings and Chronicles* (Lat.):—*Le Voyage Liturgique de France*, published under the name of the *Sieur de Moléon* (Paris, 1718, 8vo):—*The Breviaries of Orleans and Nevers*:—*Lactantius*, the edition which passed in MS. to his brother, a bookseller at Rouen, and from him to Langlet du Fresnoy, who published it (2 vols. 4to). He was working at a new edition of the *Martyrology of Usuardus* when he was put into the Bastile, where he remained five years. See Landon, *Eccles. Dict.* s. v.

Le Camus, Étienne, a French prelate and theologian, was born at Paris, Nov. 24, 1632, of an ancient family in the magistracy. He became doctor of the Sorbonne in 1650, and almoner of the king, Louis XIV, while still a minor. He was appointed bishop of Grenoble in 1671, and from that time a great change took place in his life. He was indulgent to the faults of others, and gave an example of charity, modesty, and piety. In 1686 Louis XIV demanded the hat of the cardinal for M. de Harlay, archbishop of Paris. Innocent XI not liking this prelate, sent the Roman purple to Le Camus. This irritated Louis XIV, and he called for the new cardinal, wishing to reproach him, but the bishop of Grenoble disarmed him by his pleasantry. Le Camus left all his goods to the poor of his diocese. He founded two seminaries, one at Grenoble, the other at St. Martin de Misere, and several establishments of charity. He died at Grenoble, Sept. 12, 1707. For mention of his works, see Hoefer, *Nouv. Biog. Générale*, s. v.

Lecanomancy, a species of divination (q. v.), performed by means of a basin, with wedges of gold or silver marked with certain characters. The wedges were suspended over the water, and the dæmon formally invoked, when he gave the response in a low hissing sound passing through the water.

Lecerf de la Vieville, Philippe, a French Benedictine, who died March 11, 1748, is the author of, *Bibliothèque Historique et Critique des Auteurs de la Congregation de Saint-Maur* (Hague, 1726):—*Défense de la Bibliothèque*, etc. (Paris, 1727):—*Histoire de la Constitution Unigenitus, en ce qu' Regarde la Congregation de Saint-Maur* (Utrecht, 1726). See Jöcher, *Allgemeines Gelehrten-Lexikon*, s. v. (B. P.)

Lech, John, an Irish prelate, was elected to the bishopric of Dunkeld, Scotland, in 1309, and was canon of the Church. In 1310 he was promoted to the see of Dublin. In 1312 he was constituted lord treasurer of Ireland. He died Aug. 10, 1313. See D'Alton, *Memoirs of the Archbishops of Dublin*, p. 120.

Le Courrayer, Pierre François, a French theologian, was born at Rouen in 1681. At the age of sixteen he was admitted to the congregation of St. Genevieve, and soon he instructed there in philosophy and theology, was canon in 1701, and librarian in 1711. A dissertation which he published at Brussels in 1723, under the title *Sur la Validité des Ordinations des Anglais*, called forth the opposition of Gervaise, Hardouin, and Lequien, and an assembly of twenty-two bishops who met at St. Germain-des-Près condemned the work, together with Le Courrayer's rejoinder to his opponent. Finally he was excommunicated by the abbot of St. Genevieve and cardinal Noailles; but about the same time the Oxford University made him doctor of theology. He intended to write against the cardinal; but, afraid of being imprisoned, went to England, where he was received by archbishop Wake of Canterbury. Le Courrayer died at London in 1776. He published a French translation of Sarpi's *History of the Council of Trent*, with notes (London, 1736, 2 vols.). See *La France Protestante; Nécrologes des Hommes Célèbres;* Lichtenberger, *Encyclop. des Sciences Religieuses*, s. v. (B. P.)

Le Coz, Claude, a French prelate, was born at Plounevez Parzay, Brittany, Sept. 2, 1740. He pursued his studies at the College of Quimper, and was a professor there at the time of the Revolution. In 1791 he was elected constitutional bishop of the department of Ille-et-Vilaine, and the same year deputy at the legislative assembly. During the Reign of Terror he was imprisoned and sent to Mont Michel, where he remained fourteen months. Obtaining his liberty in 1795, he resumed his episcopal duties, and adhered to the encyclicals published by the synod of the constitutional bishops reunited at Paris. Le Coz presided over the national council of the same bishops, held at the capitol from Aug. 15, 1797, to Nov. 12 of the same year.

In 1799 he assembled a synod at Rennes, but the priests of his diocese did not all recognise his authority. Being called to the presidency of the council of 1801, he opposed the project of a French sacramentarian. At the time of the Concordat of the first consul with the pope, Le Coz resigned, and was appointed archbishop of Besançon. In 1804 he went to Paris to visit the pope, and after some difficulties signed an article of adhesion and submission to the briefs of the holy father. He died at Villevieux, near Lons le Saulnier, May 3, 1815, leaving a number of works, for mention of which see Hoefer, *Nouv. Biog. Générale*, s. v.

Led (or **Leda**), in Slavonic mythology, is the god of war; also among the Russians. He appears armed with sword and shield, a helmet on his head, and a spear in his hand.

Leding, in Norse mythology, is the chain with which the wolf Fenris was chained.

Lee, Henry Washington, D.D., LL.D., a bishop of the Protestant Episcopal Church, was born at Hamden, Conn., July 26, 1815. He was ordained deacon in 1838; became rector at Springfield, Mass., in 1840; and in 1848 of St. Luke's at Rochester, N. Y., where he was consecrated bishop of Iowa, Oct. 18, 1854. His episcopal residence was at Davenport. Griswold College, located in that place, became the object of his special care. He died Sept. 26, 1874. See *Prot. Episc. Almanac*, 1875, p. 144.

Lee, Richard Henry, LL.D., a minister of the Protestant Episcopal Church, rector of Trinity, Washington, Pa., died at that place, Jan. 3, 1865, aged seventy-five years. For many years he was professor in Washington College. See *Amer. Quar. Church Rev.* April, 1865, p. 140.

Lee, Samuel, D.D., a Congregational minister, was born in London, England, in 1625. From his father, Samuel Lee, he inherited a large estate. After remaining some time at St. Paul's school, he went, in 1640, to Oxford, and continued his studies there until 1648, when he received the degree of M.A. Soon after he was appointed to a fellowship in Wadham College, and became proctor of the university in 1656. At that time he was a lecturer in Great St. Helen's Church in London. In 1677 he became associated with the celebrated Theophilus Gale, as minister in a nonconforming congregation in Holborn. In September, 1679, he was preaching at Bignel, in Oxfordshire, where he remained for some time. Afterwards, for several years, he was pastor of an Independent Church at Newington Green. Although strongly advised to enter the Established Church, conscientious scruples forbade it. In 1686 he landed in New England, and was employed to preach in Bristol, R. I. The next year, in May, he was chosen pastor of the newly organized Church there. As religious toleration began to prevail in England, he resolved to return thither. Resigning his pastorate in Bristol, he set sail in 1691, but was captured by a French privateer and carried to St. Malo, where he died in the latter part of the same year. It is said of him that there was scarcely a department of knowledge with which he was not familiar. At one time he devoted a great deal of attention to astrology, but disapproved of it afterwards, and burned a hundred books relating to it. His benevolence was manifested in frequent gifts to the poor. Besides a number of sermons, he published several books. His *Triumph of Mercy* was popular in New England, and was reprinted in Boston in 1718. Another work, *Orbis Miraculum; or, The Temple of Solomon Portrayed by Scripture Light* (1659, fol.), printed at the expense of the University of Oxford, was much admired. Another, *De Excidio Anti-Christi* (eod. fol.), was a study of popery. See Sprague, *Annals of the Amer. Pulpit*, i, 209.

Lee, William, D.D., an Irish prelate, was born in Ireland in 1815. He was educated at Trinity College, Dublin, where he was elected fellow in 1839, in 1857 was appointed professor of ecclesiastical history, and in 1863 lecturer on divinity. In 1874 he was archdeacon of Dublin, and he died May 11, 1883. He is the author especially of, *Introductory Lectures on Ecclesiastical History* (1858):—*Examination of Remarks of Baden Powell* (1861); but is best known by his *Lectures on the Inspiration of the Holy Scriptures* (1852).

Leechman, John, LL.D., a Scotch Baptist minister and missionary, was born at Glasgow, Sept. 2, 1803, and became a Baptist in 1820. He was educated at the Haldane Institution, Grantown, in the north of Scotland, in the Baptist College, Bristol, and the University of Glasgow. He was ordained a missionary to India at Edinburgh, July 3, 1832, and sailed from Liverpool on the 25th for the mission station at Serampore. He began work as tutor in the college, and preacher of the gospel. In 1835 he was ordained co-pastor of the Church at Serampore. In 1837 he sailed for England for the benefit of his wife's health, and to awaken greater interest at home in the mission in India. In 1838 he was induced to settle as pastor of the Church at Irvine, Ayrshire. He removed to London in 1848 as pastor of the Baptist Church in Hammersmith. In 1850 he was sent, with the Rev. Joshua Russell, as a deputation to India and Ceylon, in which they spent some four months. He resigned his pastorate in 1863, and removed to Bath for rest and recuperation. He afterwards engaged in various public labors, and at the close of 1867 accepted the pastorate at Kensington Chapel. He ceased to preach in 1870, and died March 16, 1874. See (Lond.) *Bapt. Hand-Book*, 1875, p. 284.

Leechman, William, D.D., a Scotch divine, was born in 1706, educated at the University of Edinburgh, licensed to preach in 1731, ordained minister of Beith in 1736, elected professor of theology in the University of Glasgow about 1743, principal in 1761, and died Dec. 3, 1785. He was held in high estimation by his brethren in the ministry, having been elected by them, in 1740, to the moderatorship of the Synod of Glasgow and Ayr, and in 1757 of the General Assembly. He was a ripe theologian, a powerful preacher, and a warm advocate of all institutions of a worthy character. A collective edition of his sermons, with a life of the author, by James Wodrow, D.D., was published (Lond. 1789, 2 vols. 8vo; new ed. 1816, 2 vols. 8vo). See *The* (Lond.) *Christian Observer*, Dec. 1812, p. 753; Allibone, *Dict. of Brit. and Amer. Authors*, s. v.

Le Faucheur, Michel, one of the most famous Protestant preachers of the 17th century, was born in the neighborhood of Geneva in 1585. In 1607 he was ordained, and appointed pastor at Annonay. His fame as a pulpit orator was soon made known, and the authorities of Geneva wished him to come there. But Le Faucheur declined, and in 1609 went to Paris. In 1612 he was called to Montpellier, and at different periods represented the churches of Languedoc at the synodical assemblies. He died at Paris in 1657, leaving, *Sermons:—Traité de l'Action de l'Orateur* (Paris, 1657):—*Traité de la Cêne du Seigneur* (Geneva, 1635). See Bayle, *Dict. Historique;* Haag, *La France Protestante*, vi; Lichtenberger, *Encyclop. des Sciences Religieuses*, s. v. (B. P.)

Léger, *Saint*. See Leodegar.

Legge, George, LL.D., a Scotch Congregational minister, was born at Huntley, Aberdeenshire, Oct. 10, 1802. He became a student of King's College, Aberdeen, in 1819, completing his curriculum in 1825, and receiving his degree of M.A.; was converted in 1828; entered Highbury College to prepare for the ministry in 1830, and in 1832 became pastor at Bristol. In 1835 he accepted a call to the pastorate of Gallowtree-gate Chapel, Leicester, and in that capacity continued till his death, Jan. 24, 1861. In 1859 he was chairman of the Congregational Union. Dr. Legge was a man of noble qualities, endowed with a strong intellect, a glowing imagination, a loving heart, and great constancy of purpose. His principal publications were, *Principles of Nonconformity: — Christianity in Harmony with Man's Nature, Present and Progressive: — The Range and Limitations of Human Knowledge*, besides several single sermons. See (Lond.) *Cong. Year-book*, 1862, p. 247.

Legobien, CHARLES, a French Jesuit, was born at St. Malo in 1653; in 1671 he entered the society of Jesus; shortly after taught at Tours; then removed to Paris, where he became first secretary, and afterwards superintendent, of the missions of his order to China. He published, about 1702, a collection of letters from missionaries in China, etc., entitled *Lettres Édifiantes et Curieuses, Écrites des Missions Étrangères.* He died March 5, 1708, at Paris. See Hoefer, *Nouv. Biog. Générale*, s. v.

Le Gouverneur, GUILLAUME, a French prelate, was born at St. Malo. After being canon, then dean of the cathedral of his native place, he became bishop, Jan. 29, 1610. He assisted as deputy of the clergy to the states of Brittany in 1614, founded in his diocese several establishments of charity and religion, and occupied his time in collecting the ecclesiastical regulations laid down by his predecessors. He died at St. Malo, June 25, 1630. See Hoefer, *Nouv. Biog. Générale*, s. v.

Legras, LOUISE DE MARILLAC, *Madame*, foundress of an order of nuns, was born at Paris, Aug. 12, 1591. She was daughter of Louis de Marillac, brother of the celebrated guard of the seals, and of the marshal of this name. In 1613 she married Antoine Legras, secretary of the queen Marie de Medicis. Being eventually left a widow, she devoted herself entirely to religious matters. In connection with Vincent de Paul she bore an important part in the establishment of various charitable institutions. They founded the institution of the sisters of charity called *Sœurs Grises*, on account of the color of their costume. Placed at the head of a community of this order at Paris, madame Legras devoted herself with great self-abnegation to the care of the sick. She aided Vincent de Paul in bestowing large charities in various ways. Her death occurred at Paris in 1662. See Hoefer, *Nouv. Biog. Générale*, s. v.

Le Hennuyer, JEAN, a French prelate, was born in 1497 at St. Quentin. He was successively chief almoner of Henry II, Francis II, Charles IX, and Henry III. Appointed bishop of Lodeve in 1557, and afterwards of Lisieux, he was spiritual director of Catherine de Medicis and of Diane de Poictiers. In this position he always showed a disposition to persecute the Protestants, although some acts to the contrary have been falsely attributed to him. He died in 1578. See Hoefer, *Nouv. Biog. Générale*, s. v.

Lehi. On the identification of this site Lieut. Conder remarks as follows (*Tent Work in Palestine*, i, 276):

"A little way north-west of Zoreah, seven miles from Beit 'Atâb, is a low hill, on the slope of which are springs called 'Ayûn Abu Mehârib, or the 'fountains of the place of battles.' Close by is a little Moslem chapel, dedicated to Sheik Nedhîr, or 'the Nazarite chief;' and, higher up, a ruin with the extraordinary title Ism Allah—'the name of God.' The Nazarite chief is probably Samson, whose memory is so well preserved in this small district, and the place is perhaps connected with a tradition of one of his exploits. The Ism Allah is possibly a corruption of Esm'a Allah—'God heard'—in which case the incident intended might be the battle of Ramath Lehi. Finally, we were informed by a native of the place that the springs were sometimes called 'Ayûn Kâra, in which name we should recognise easily the En hak-Kore, or 'fountain of the crier' (Judges xv, 19). To say that this spot certainly represents Ramath Lehi—'the hill of the jaw-bone'—would be too bold. It seems, however, clear that a tradition of one of Samson's exploits lingers here; the position is appropriate for the scene of the slaughter with the jaw-bone, and we have not succeeded in finding any other likely site."

Lehmann, WILHELM FRIEDRICH, a Lutheran minister, was born Oct. 16, 1820, in Würtemberg. In 1824 he came with his parents to America. He studied at the theological seminaries of Columbus, O., and Philadelphia, Pa., and was for some time preacher at Somerset, O. In 1846 he was appointed professor at the University at Columbus. He died Dec. 1, 1880. For many years he was president of the Lutheran Synod of Ohio. (B. P.)

Lehmus, ADAM THEODOR ALBERT FRANZ, a Lutheran theologian of Germany, was born at Soest, Dec. 2, 1777. He entered the ministry in 1801, was in 1819 dean and pastor at Anspach, and died Aug. 18, 1837, doctor of theology. He wrote, *Die Lehre von der Versöhnung des Menschen mit Gott durch Christum* (Sulzbach, 1821): — *Ueber die Taufe* (Heidelberg, 1807):— *Aufsätze theologischen Inhalts*, etc. (1835):—*Die Rechtfertigungslehre der evangelischen Kirche in ihren Hauptmomenten dargestellt* (1836). See Winer, *Handbuch der theol. Lit.* i, 439, 450; ii, 19, 65, 75, 100, 166; Zuchold, *Bibl. Theol.* ii, 780 sq. (B. P.)

Leib Olmai, in the mythology of the Laplanders, was a deity of the atmosphere, who made the weather favorable to hunting and fishing.

Leiffthus, in Norse mythology, was one of the rivers of hell, which take their origin from the spring Hwergelmer.

Leighton, HENRY DE, a Scotch prelate, was consecrated bishop of Moray, March 8, 1414, where he continued ten years. In 1424 he was translated to the see of Aberdeen. He was one of the commissioners sent to London for negotiating the ransom of king James I, and returned home with him. He died in 1441. See Keith, *Scottish Bishops*, p. 113-142.

Leimburg, JOHANN LEISS VON, a Roman Catholic prelate of Germany, was born in 1821. For some time dean at Bregenz and Innsbrück, he was in 1879 appointed prince-bishop of Brixen, and died April 24, 1884. He was a man of peace, and tolerant against non-Catholics. (B. P.)

Leinbach, THOMAS HARTMAN, an earnest and successful minister of the German Reformed Church, was born in Berks County, Pa., Jan. 18, 1802. He studied privately under the Rev. Dr. F. L. Herman; was licensed and ordained in 1822. After serving for several years a few congregations, located partly in Lancaster and partly in Berks County, he accepted a call from the Tulpehocken charge, where he concluded his long and useful ministry, March 31, 1864. Father Leinbach was celebrated as a "catechist," which eminently fitted him for the particular field to which he was called. He was besides a very able, earnest, and effective preacher, and a most conscientious and successful pastor. See Harbaugh, *Fathers of the Germ. Ref. Church*, iv, 175. (D. Y. H.)

Leiptr, in Norse mythology, was one of the rivers of hell, which have their source in the spring Hwergelmer.

Leire. See LETHRA.

Leiter, SAMUEL B., D.D., a German Reformed minister, was born at Leitersburg, Md., April 19, 1809. His literary and theological training he received at York, Pa. He was licensed and ordained by the Maryland Classis of the Reformed Church in 1835; immediately left for the West, and settled in Ohio, where he successfully exercised his ministry in different sections of the state. Dr. Leiter was a man of good natural parts and extensive requirements, which he conscientiously employed in the service of his Master. He died March 31, 1883. (D. Y. H.)

Lejay (Lat. *Laius*), CLAUDE, one of the fathers of the Jesuit order, was born at Aïse, in Faucigny, in the diocese of Geneva, about 1505. He commenced his studies at the College of La Roche, and completed them at Paris. He allied himself in friendship with Peter

Faure, which, in 1535, led to his becoming a Jesuit, and a great help to his order. In 1545 he assisted at the Council of Trent. He afterwards directed the College of Boulogne, where he received the degree of doctor of theology. He then returned to Germany, taught at Ingolstädt, then at Vienna, in June, 1551, where he died, Aug. 6, 1552. He composed various works, which were only published in the *Speculum Præsulis ex Sacræ Scripturæ, Canonum et Doctorum Verbis* (Ingolstädt, 1625, and in vol. xvii of the *Œuvres* of P. Gretser, Ratisbon, 1741). See Hoefer, *Nouv. Biog. Générale*, s. v.

Le-ke, one of the sacred books of the Chinese. It is the acknowledged guide to rites and manners, prescribing rules for all the relationships of life, and the established orders of society. See CONFUCIUS.

Lekkio, in Finnish mythology, was an evil spirit of the woods, who appeared in various frightful forms.

Lel, in Slavonic mythology, was the god of love, son of Lada, the goddess of beauty, and brother of Did and Polel.

Lelli (*Saint*), CAMILLO DE, founder of an order of Italian friars, was born at Bucchianico, May 25, 1550. An ulcer, resulting from his early vices, led him to enter a convent. The Franciscans rejected him, and he went to Rome, where he was received at the hospital of St. James. He speedily recovered, and was afterwards expelled for misconduct. In 1569 he enrolled himself among the troops of Venice, and after the close of the war, having been dismissed, hired out to the Capuchins of Manfredonio. He wished to become a monk, but was repulsed on all sides on account of his infirmity. He returned to the hospital of St. James, where this time his good conduct obtained for him the position of steward. Thinking that the diseases even then were not well treated at the hospitals, he completed his studies among the Jesuits, was made priest, and founded in 1584 the congregation of Clercs Regulars, especially intended for the care of the sick. This congregation, being approved by Sixtus V, March 8, 1586, was established as a religious order by Gregory XIV, Oct. 15, 1591. St. Camillo de Lelli resigned his supervision in 1607, and was beatified by Benedict XVI in 1742. He died at Rome, July 14, 1614. See Hoefer, *Nouv. Biog. Générale*, s. v.

Le Maire, GUILLAUME, a French prelate, was chosen as successor to Nicolas Gellent, bishop of Angers, having been first chaplain and penitentiary of the cathedral. The newly elected bishop went to Vincennes, May 16, 1291, and took the oath to king Philip. Some years later he excommunicated David de Lesmaisons, bailiwick of Angers, and his sub-bailiwick, Darien Bidoyn. The difficulty was concerning the ecclesiastical immunities. In the unfortunate condition of his treasury the king objected to the subsidies, and his officers levied upon the goods of the Church as well as others. This was opposed by Guillaume Le Maire, together with other bishops. He argued this question against the count of Anjou. The whole administration of Le Maire was laborious and discordant. He died May 13, 1314, leaving a historical work, for mention of which see Hoefer, *Nouv. Biog. Générale*, s. v.

Le Maitre, ANTOINE, a French writer, brother of Isaac Louis le Maitre (better known as *de Sacy*), was born at Paris in 1607. For a time he practised law with great success, but abandoned his profession and joined the recluses of Port Royal. He died Nov. 4, 1658. Le Maitre is the author of, *Vie de Saint Bernard*:—*L'Aumône Chrétienne* (Paris, 1658, 2 vols.):—*Vies de S. Ignace, de S. Jean Climaque, et des Martyrs dé Lyon*, in the *Vies des Saints*, published by Du Fossé (1685); from the Latin he translated Chrysostom's treatise, *De Sacerdotio*. See Clémencet, *Hist. Générale de Port-Royal*, vol. ii and iii; Besoigne, *Histoire de l'Abbaye de Port-Royal*, vol. iii; De Vallée, *Antoine le Maitre et ses Contemporains;* Sapey, *Guillaume du Vair et Antoine le Maitre;* Lichtenberger, *Encyclop. des Sciences Religieuses*, s. v. (B. P.)

Le Mire. See MIRÆUS.

Lemke, HEINRICH, a Lutheran theologian of Germany, was born Dec. 31, 1601, at Lubeck. He studied at different universities, and died at Bergen, Norway, March 7, 1674. He wrote, *Vindicatio Librorum Apocryphorum Veteris et Novi Testamenti*:—*Vindicatio Incarnati Veri Messiæ Promissi ex Thalmud et Rabbinorum Scriptis Desumta*:—*Schola Papistarum Reformata*. See Moller, *Cimbria Litterata;* Jöcher, *Allgemeines Gelehrten-Lexikon*, s. v. (B. P.)

Lemoine, JEAN, a French prelate, was born at Cressy, in the 13th century. Having completed his studies, he took the degree of doctor of theology at the University of Paris, and made a journey to Rome, where he was well received, and appointed auditor of the rota. His commentary upon the sixth book of the *Decretales*, which he wrote at Rome, gained for him the title of cardinal. Boniface VIII appointed him legate to France in 1302, and in this position he strove to re-establish peace between Philip the Fair and the holy see. He acted with so much discretion that he won the esteem of the king without losing his credit with the pope. He assisted, in 1305, at the conclave held at Perugia for the election of Clement V, and accompanied that pontiff to Avignon, where he died, Aug. 22, 1313. His body was borne to Paris, and interred in the church of the college which he had founded in 1303 in that city, on Rue St. Victor, upon the site of the houses, chapel, and cemetery which had belonged to the Augustinian monks.

His brother, ANDRÉ LEMOINE, bishop of Noyon, aided him in the founding of the college which bore the name of the cardinal Lemoine. He died in 1315, and the two brothers were laid in the same tomb. See Hoefer, *Nouv. Biog. Générale*, s. v.

Lenæus, JOHANN CANUTUS, a Lutheran theologian of Germany, was born in 1573, at Lenna, near Upsala. He studied at Wittenberg, Helmstadt, and Rostock, was professor of Greek and Hebrew at Upsala, and died April 25, 1669, doctor of theology, archbishop of Sweden, and pro-chancellor of the Upsala Academy. He wrote, *Comm. in Evangelium Johannis*:—*Comm. in Lucæ Acta Apostolorum*:—*Comm. in Canonicas Epistolas Jacobi, Petri, Johannis et Judæ*:—*Brevis Informatio de Veritate et Excellentia Christianæ Religionis*:—*Judicium de Unione a Calvinianis Petita*. See Witte, *Diarium Biographicum;* Jöcher, *Allgemeines Gelehrten-Lexikon*, s. v.; Winer, *Handbuch der theol. Lit.* i, 185. (B. P.)

Lenet, PHILIBERT BERNARD, a French monk, was born at Dijon, Aug. 24, 1677. Having been received among the canons regular of St. Genevieve, he soon distinguished himself by his piety and learning. For a time professor at Senlis and at Provins, he became director of the seminary at Rheims, and abbot of Grand-Val-des-Écoliers, in the diocese of Langres. Being accused of Jansenism, Lenet was obliged to retire from his position, and died in 1748. He wrote some works, for which see *Nécrologie des Plus Célèbres Défenseurs de la Verité*, vol. iii; Lichtenberger, *Encyclop. des Sciences Religieuses*, s. v. (B. P.)

Le Neve, JOHN, an English clergyman and biographer, was born Dec. 27, 1679, and educated at Trinity College, Cambridge. He became rector of Thornton-le-Moor, Lincolnshire, about 1721, and died about 1741. He was an industrious collector of biographical materials, and has given to the world several important collections. They include, *Lives of the Most Illustrious Persons who Died in* 1711-12 (London, 1713-14, 2 vols. 8vo):—*Fasti Ecclesiæ Anglicanæ* (1716), of which a new edition was published (1854, 3 vols. 8vo) by T. Duffus Hardy, assistant keeper of the public records, with a continuation to the year of publication; the first edition contained eleven thousand entries, while the new edition contains more than thirty thousand names of clergymen:—*Memorials Concerning Dr. Richard Field* (1716):—*Monumenta Anglicana* (1700-19, 9 vols. 8vo): —*Lives of the Protestant Bishops* (1720):—*Lives of the Archbishops* (1723). See *Biographical Notice of Le Neve* in Hardy's edition of the *Fasti.*

Lenfant, David, a French Dominican, who died at Paris, May 31, 1688, is the author of, *Concordantiæ Augustinianæ* (1655-1656, 2 vols. fol.):—*Biblia Augustiniana* (2 vols.):—*St. Bernardi Biblia* (1665):—*St. Thomæ Aquinatis Biblia* (1657-59, 3 vols.):—*Histoire Générale de Tous les Siècles* (1684, 6 vols.). See Lichtenberger, *Encyclop. des Sciences Religieuses,* s. v.; Jöcher, *Allgemeines Gelehrten-Lexikon,* s. v. (B. P.)

Lenglet-Dufresnoy, Nicolas, a French writer, was born at Beauvais, Oct. 5, 1674. He studied theology at Paris, and took holy orders, but soon exchanged his clerical dress for that of a politician and diplomatist. He died Jan. 16, 1755. Of his numerous works we mention the following, bearing upon theology: *Novum Jesu Christi Testamentum Notis Historicis et Criticis Illustratum* (Paris, 1703, 2 vols.; reprinted 1735):—*Imitation de Jésus-Christ, Traduite et Revue* (1771):—*Traité Historique et Dogmatique du Secret Inviolable de la Confession* (1713 and often):—*Réfutation des Erreurs de Spinosa, avec sa Vie à la Tête* (Amsterdam, 1731): —*Traité Historique et Dogmatique des Opérations, des Visions et des Revelations Particulières* (1751, 2 vols.): —*Recueil des Dissertations Anciennes et Modernes sur les Apparitions, les Visions et les Songes* (1752, 4 vols.). He also edited *Lucii Cæcilii Lactantii Opera Omnia* (1748, 2 vols.), the most complete edition of Lactantius's works. See Michault, *Mémoires pour Servir à l'Histoire de la Vie et des Ouvrages de l'Abbé Lenglet;* Lichtenberger, *Encyclop. des Sciences Religieuses,* s. v. (B. P.)

Lengnich, Karl Benjamin, a Lutheran theologian of Germany, was born at Dantzic, Feb. 19, 1743. He studied at Leipsic, was in 1772 second preacher at his native place, and died Nov. 5, 1795, leaving, *Predigten* (Dantzic, 1770):—*Beitrag zur Kenntniss seltener und merkwürdiger Bücher* (ibid. 1776, 2 vols.):—*Nachrichten zur Bücher- und Münzkunde* (ibid. 1780-82, 4 vols.). See Döring, *Die deutschen Kanzelredner,* p. 200. (B. P.)

Lenormant, Charles, a French archæologist and numismatician, was born in Paris, June 1, 1802. In 1828 he travelled in Egypt, was in 1837 conservator at the national library, and after 1835 acted as Guizot's substitute at the Sorbonne, where his lectures, savoring too much of Romish orthodoxy, often caused disturbances, especially in 1846, so that he had finally to give up his lecturing. In 1848 he was called as professor of Egyptian archæology at the Collége de France, and died at Athens, Nov. 24, 1859. Of his works we mention, *Trésor de Numismatique et de Glyptique* (1836-50, 5 vols.): —*Élite des Monuments Céramographiques* (1844-57, 3 vols.). (B. P.)

Lenormant, François, son of Charles, was born in Paris, Jan. 17, 1837. He pursued the same studies which distinguished his father. In 1862 he was sub-librarian of the Institute, in 1874 professor of archæology at the large Paris library, and died Dec. 10, 1883, leaving, *Manuel d'Histoire Ancienne de l'Orient Jusqu' aux Guerres Inédiques* (3d ed. 1869, 3 vols.; transl. into German, Berlin, 1869, 2 vols.; 2d ed. 1871):—*Lettres Assyriologiques et Épigraphiques* (1871-72, 4 vols.):—*Les Premières Civilisations* (1874, 2 vols.; Germ. transl. Jena, 1875):—*Les Sciences Occultes en Asie* (1874-75; Germ. transl. Jena, 1878), two parts; the first treating of *La Magie chez les Chaldéens et les Origines Accadiennes;* the second of *La Divination et la Science des Présages chez les Chaldéens:—Les Origines de l'Histoire d'Apres la Bible et les Traditions des Peuples Orientaux* (1880-82, 2 vols.; Engl. transl. New York, 1882):—*Monnaies et Médailles* (Paris, 1883). (B. P.)

Leo, Gottlob Eduard, a Lutheran theologian of Germany, was born in 1803, and died at Waldenburg, May 7, 1881, member of consistory and doctor of theology. He is the author of, *Geschichte der christlichen Religion und Kirche* (Leipsic, 1831):—*Das Leben Gellert's* (Dresden, 1846):—*Stimmen aus der Kirche* (1845): —*Pauli Epistola i ad Timotheum Græce* (1837):—*Geschichte der Reformation in Dresden und Leipzig* (1839): —*Das Leben August Hermann Francke's* (1848). See Zuchold, *Bibl. Theol.* ii, 786. (B. P.)

Leo, Heinrich, a famous German historian, was born at Rudolstadt, March 19, 1799. He studied at Breslau and Jena, and commenced his academical career at Erlangen in 1820. In 1824 he was at Berlin, accepted a call to Halle in 1830, and died April 24, 1878. Leo was orthodox in religion, and conservative in politics, and from this standpoint wrote his *Lehrbuch der Universalgeschichte* (Halle, 1835-44, 6 vols.; 3d ed. 1849-53). Liberalism found in him a violent opponent, and the liberal tendencies in State and Church he assailed in *Studien und Skizzen zur Naturgeschichte des Staates* (ibid. 1833), *Die Hegelingen* (1838), *Signatura Temporis* (1849), more especially in the *Kreuz-Zeitung,* the organ of the political conservatives, and in *Evangelische Kirchenzeitung,* the organ of orthodoxy. His political tendencies were acknowledged by king Frederick William IV, and in 1863 he was made a member of the Prussian upper house for life. See Lichtenberger, *Encyclop. des Sciences Religieuses,* s. v.; Brockhaus, *Conversations-Lexikon,* s. v. (B. P.)

Leo, Rudolf, a Lutheran theologian of Germany, was born May 6, 1806, at Rudolstadt. He studied at Jena and Göttingen, was tutor of prince Günther of Schwarzburg-Rudolstadt from 1829 to 1839, and professor at the gymnasium of his native place from 1839 to 1844. In the latter year he was appointed second deacon, in 1851 court-preacher and member of consistory, and in 1852 general-superintendent. He retired from the ministry in 1879, and died Jan. 18, 1883. (B. P.)

Leonard, Alexander S., S.T.D., a Protestant Episcopal clergyman, was born in New York city, June 28, 1806. He graduated from Columbia College in 1825; was engaged in mercantile pursuits for twenty years; ordained deacon in 1848; assistant at St. Clement's Church, N. Y.; rector of Emmanuel Church, in the same city, from 1849 to 1865, and died there, May 17, 1878. See *Prot. Episc. Almanac,* 1879, p. 169; *Church Almanac,* 1879, p. 93.

Leonhard, Matthæi d'Udine, a famous Dominican, who died in 1470, provincial of Lombardy, was a doctor of law and divinity. He preached in the principal cities of Italy, especially at Florence, before pope Eugene IV and his court. His *Sermones* have often been printed. See Lichtenberger, *Encyclop. des Sciences Religieuses,* s. v.; Jöcher, *Allgemeines Gelehrten-Lexikon,* s. v. (B. P.)

Leoni, Ottavio (called *il cav. Padovano* and *Padovanino*), an eminent painter and engraver, was born in Rome in 1578. Among his historical works is *The Virgin and Infant,* in Santa Maria della Minerva; *The Annunciation,* in San Eustachio; and *St. Carlo, St. Francesco,* and *St. Niccolo,* in San Urbano. He was chosen director of the Academy of St. Luke, and was appointed knight of the order of Christ, on which occasion he painted the *Martyrdom of St. Martina,* for the Church of the Academy. As an engraver, he did not succeed very well. He, however, executed a number of works. He died in 1630. See Hoefer, *Nouv. Biog. Générale,* s. v.; Spooner, *Biog. Hist. of the Fine Arts,* s. v.

Leopard-worship. The leopard is held in great dread by the natives of different parts of Africa, not only on account of its ferocity, but from the superstitious notion that wicked men metamorphose themselves into these animals, and commit all sorts of depredations without the liability or possibility of being killed. In southern Guinea large villages are sometimes abandoned by their inhabitants, because they are afraid to attack these animals on account of their supposed supernatural powers. In Dahomey, the leopard is accounted so sacred that if any one should kill it he would be convicted of having committed sacrilege, and would be offered in sacrifice to the offended god as a propitiation. The leopard is there looked upon as an impersonation of the supreme god, whom they call *Seh.* If any one is killed by a leopard, his relatives rejoice at the event, and treat the animal with great kindness. See LEOPARD.

Lepcha Version OF THE SCRIPTURES. Lepcha is a dialect spoken by an aboriginal mountain-tribe in north-east India, near Darjeeling. The first attempt at a translation into that dialect was made by the Rev. W. Start, in 1855 or 1856, who printed the gospel of Matthew at his own expense. The Calcutta Auxiliary Bible Society published, in 1871, the gospels of Matthew and John, Genesis, and part of Exodus. (B. P.)

Lepsius, KARL RICHARD, a noted German Egyptologist, was born at Naumburg, Dec. 23, 1810. Well prepared by seven years of classical training at Pforta, he went in 1829 to Leipsic and Göttingen to study philology. When he took his degree, he showed at once by his dissertation that he knew how best to utilize the principles of comparative philology by applying them to the solution of difficult problems of classical scholarship. He took for his subject the Umbrian Inscriptions, and thus laid the foundation of what has proved in the end one of the most successful achievements of the science of language—namely, the decipherment and grammatical analysis of the Eugubian tables. In 1833 he went to Paris to attend lectures, and study in libraries and museums. In 1834 he published *Paläographie als Mittel für die Sprachforschung,* for which was awarded by the French Institute the *Prix Volney.* In 1835 another essay of his, *Ueber die Anordnung und Verwandtschaft des semitischen, indischen, äthiopischen, altpersischen und altägyptischen Alphabets,* was read before the Berlin Academy; and in the same year, while still at Paris, he wrote his paper, *Ueber den Ursprung und die Verwandtschaft der Zahlwörter in der indogermanischen, semitischen, und der koptischen Sprache.* At the time of his residence at Paris, Champollion's star was just rising, but Egyptian studies were only in their infancy. Lepsius felt attracted towards these new studies. Having acquired the first principles of the decipherment of hieroglyphs from Champollion's works, he proceeded from Paris to Italy, which was rich in Egyptian antiquities. He spent some time with Rosellini, at Pisa, and then settled down to steady work at Rome. Here he was attracted by Bunsen, who did everything he could for him. By his *Lettre à M. Rosellini sur l'Alphabet Hiéroglyphique* (1837), Lepsius took his position as one of the leading Egyptologists of the day, and thus entered upon a career which he never left again. But, although Egypt formed the principal object of his studies, his classical tastes, too, found ample food in Italy, as was shown by his edition of the *Inscriptiones Umbricæ et Oscæ* (Leipsic, 1841), and by his papers on *Die Tyrrhenenschen Pelasger in Etrurien* (1842). From Italy he went to England, where he spent two years studying in the British Museum, and shaping plans for future work. In 1842 we find Lepsius established as professor at Berlin. In the meantime he had published some of his best-known works—his *Auswahl der wichtigsten Urkunden des ägyptischen Alterthums* (1842, fol. with 23 tables), and *Das Todtenbuch der Ægypter* (eod. with 79 tables). In the same year followed the great expedition to Egypt, projected by Bunsen, and carried out at the expense of the king of Prussia, Frederick William IV. Lepsius was the leader, and he acquitted himself of this most difficult task with perfect success. Every student of Egyptology knows the fruits of that expedition, as gathered partly in *Denkmäler aus Egypten und Æthiopien* (1849–59, 12 vols. of the largest folio, with 894 tables). In 1849 he published his *Chronologie der Ægypter,* one volume; the second never appeared. Without enumerating the many works which he published after his return from Egypt, we will state that in 1866 he went to the land of the Pharaohs once more, and this second expedition was crowned by the discovery of a new trilingual tablet, a worthy companion of the Rosetta stone. In 1869 he paid his last visit to the land of his lifelong love, being present at the opening of the Suez canal, and afterwards travelled with the crown-prince of Prussia to Upper Egypt and Nubia. The last years of his life were devoted chiefly to the elaboration of his *Nubian Grammar,* a work of enormous labor, full not only of new materials, but of new views on the relationship of the numerous languages of Africa. "Taken all in all," says Max Müller, "Lepsius was the perfect type of the German professor, devoted to his work, full of ideals, and convinced that there is no higher vocation in life than to preserve and to add to the sacred stock of human knowledge, which, though it is seen by the few only, has to be carried, like the Ark of the Covenant, from battle to battle, and kept safe from the hands of the Philistines." Lepsius died July 10, 1884, only one day after Dorner and Lange. Like a Christian, he prepared himself for his last journey, being strengthened before his departure by the Lord's Supper, which he received from the hands of the court-preacher, Dr. Kögel. Besides having received different orders from the hands of kings, he was made doctor of theology by the Leipsic University in 1859. He also introduced the so-called missionary alphabet, or *Standard Alphabet for Reducing Unwritten Languages and Foreign Graphic Systems to a Uniform Orthography in European Letters,* a system which gained support both by scholars and missionaries. See Max Müller, in the *Academy* (Lond. July 19, 1884); Ebers, *Richard Lepsius, ein Lebensbild* (Leipsic, 1885; a list of Lepsius's works is found on p. 376–390); Dillmann, *Gedächtnissrede auf Karl Richard Lepsius,* read before the Berlin Academy of Sciences, July 2, 1885 (Berlin, 1885). (B. P.)

Le Quien, ANTOINE. See ANTHONY LE QUIEN.

Lerad, in Norse mythology, is a mighty tree, standing in Walhalla, in whose boughs the reindeer Eikthyrnir and the goat Hejdrun live and find nourishment. From the drops which fall from the antlers of the former all the rivers of the world are formed.

Lercari, NICOLAS MARIE, an Italian cardinal, was born at Tabia, Genoa, Nov. 19, 1675. He filled various offices at the pontifical court, and afterwards became successively governor of Lodi, of Benevento, of Camerino, of Ancona, of Civita Vecchia, and of Perugia. Being called to Rome in 1724 by Benedict XIII, with whom he had allied himself at Benevento, he was consecrated archbishop *in partibus,* and two years later appointed prime-minister. The foreign ambassadors refusing to treat with him, under the pretext that his position was not sufficiently honorable, he was made cardinal in December, 1726. In his position as secretary of state he showed himself an able negotiator, and several times thwarted the purposes of the imperial court. In 1730, on the death of Benedict XIII, he was despoiled of his honors, and arraigned before a congregation of cardinals to give an account of his administration. His integrity was established, but his influence was gone. He died March 20, 1757. See Hoefer, *Nouv. Biog. Générale,* s. v.

Leschies, in Slavonic mythology, were evil spirits of the woods, whose existence is still believed by the Russians and Lithuanians. They were similar to the Pan or Fauns of the Greeks and Romans, and were brought north probably by the latter.

Lesly. See LESLEY; LESLIE.

L'Espine (Lat. *Spina, or Spinæus*), JEAN DE, a

French theologian, was born about 1506. At first a monk, he renounced Romanism in 1561, and joined the Reformed Church. After the Poissy Colloquy, he was for some time preacher at Fontenay-le-Comte, and afterwards at La Rochelle. In 1564 he published his *Discours du Vray Sacrifice et du Vray Sacrificateur.* In 1568 he was pastor at St. Quentin, in 1572 at Paris, in 1576 at Saumur, in 1578 at Angers, and died in 1594 at Saumur. Besides his *Discours*, he published, *Traité de l'Apostasie* (1583):—*Dialogue de la Cêne* (eod.), etc. See Bayle, *Dict. Hist. et Critique*, s. v. "Spina;" Vincent, *Recherches sur les Commencemens et Premiers Progrès de la Réformation en la Ville de La Rochelle* (Rotterdam, 1693); Lichtenberger, *Encyclop. des Sciences Religieuses*, s. v. (B. P.)

Lestang, Christophe, a French prelate, was born at Brives in 1560. When not more than twenty years of age he was made bishop of Lodeve, in which position he devoted himself to the destruction of Calvinism, then very rife in Languedoc, and for this he received of Henry III a pension of twelve thousand crowns per month. The League counted him among its most fervent advocates. He had a contest with the duke of Montmorency. Lestang lost all the revenues of his bishopric, and the palace which he had built was destroyed. To make amends, Henry III gave to him the episcopal house and the revenues of the bishopric of Carcassonne, which Montmorency had enjoyed. In 1604 he was made bishop of Carcassonne. Louis XIII made him commander of his orders, grand master of his chapel, member of his private council, and director of his finances. Lestang continued to fill important offices until his death, which occurred at Carcassonne, Aug. 11, 1621. See Hoefer, *Nouv. Biog. Générale*, s. v.

Lestonac, Jeanne de, foundress of an order of French nuns, was born at Bordeaux in 1556. She was the daughter of a councillor of the parliament of Bordeaux, and of Jeanne d'Eyquem of Montagne, sister of the celebrated philosopher Michel de Montagne. Although her mother was a Protestant, her father and uncle made her adopt the Catholic religion. In 1573 she married Gaston de Montferrand. After the death of her husband she consecrated herself to the Virgin, and entered, in 1603, the house of the Feuillantines of Toulouse. Shortly after, Jeanne de Lestonac placed herself at the head of a society of young ladies, the greater part taken from Calvinistic families. These new nuns bore the name of Jesuitines. Cardinal de Sourdis opposed the foundation of this order, but the pope favored it and ordered its consecration, which took place, March 25, 1606, and it was confirmed by a brief of Paul V, April 7, 1607. The order grew rapidly in importance. At the time of the death of Jeanne, she had control of twenty-nine houses of Jesuitines. She died at Bordeaux, April 2, 1640. After her death some of her bones were sent to the principal convents of the order, or were used, according to some hagiographers, to perform various miracles. See Hoefer, *Nouv. Biog. Générale*, s. v.

Lestrange, Louis Henri de (*dom Augustine*), the renovator of the order of La Trappe, was born at Viverais in 1754. On his nomination as coadjutor to the archbishop of Vienne in 1780, he retired to La Trappe, in the department of Orne, near Mortaque, the seat of Cistercian monks since 1140, but reformed by the abbé de Rancé in 1662, and which has given its name to all monasteries which have adopted the rigorous rule of Rancé. See Trappists. In 1791 the French government seized the property of the monks of La Trappe, and Lestrange led twenty-four of the religious to Val Sainte, canton of Fribourg, Switzerland, where they were heartily welcomed, constituted an abbey by Pius VI, and Augustine placed at its head. On the invasion of Switzerland, in 1798, by a French army, the Trappists were compelled to flee. They wandered with their leader through various parts of Austria and Bavaria, until Paul I promised them hospitality in his states, and they established themselves in Russian Poland in 1799. In the following year the czar issued a ukase ordering all French emigrants to leave his territories. Augustine then led his brethren to Protestant Prussia, where they found a temporary asylum. Then it was that a party of them, guided by Urban Guillet, embarked at Amsterdam for Baltimore, May 29, 1803. The deliverance of Switzerland, in 1804, soon permitted the monks to return to Val Sainte, and in 1805 Napoleon granted them authority to establish themselves in his empire. Mont Valerian, which rises at the gates of Paris, soon beheld a monastery of this austere order arise, but when the emperor began to persecute the pope, the fervent disciples of Rancé and Lestrange resisted him. In 1810 Dom Augustine accordingly made his monks solemnly retract the oath of fidelity to the constitution of the empire, and Napoleon ordered all houses of La Trappe to be closed, and the abbot Lestrange to be tried by court-martial; but Augustine escaped to Switzerland, and thence traversing Germany, pursued by the imperial police, embarked at Riga for London, and thence for the United States. There (in the city of Boston) he found a second colony of Trappists, under Vincent of Paul, awaiting him. Dom Augustine Lestrange arrived in New York in 1813, to which place he ordered Guillet from Missouri, and Vincent of Paul from Boston, and concentrated at one place the scattered and feeble forces of the brethren. The energetic Lestrange also founded a community of Trappist nuns. Meanwhile the fall of Napoleon opened France to the Trappists, and Dom Augustine returned to restore the black-girdled monks to their home. He embarked for Havre in October, 1814, with twelve monks, the sisters and pupils, when he restored the order to Europe. Lestrange, the indefatigable and heroic successor of Bernard and Rancé, died at Lyons, France, July 16, 1827. See De Courcy and Shea, *Hist. of the Cath. Church in the U. S.* p. 370.

Letfete, in Norse mythology, was one of the twelve famous Asa-horses mentioned in the Edda.

Lethe, in Greek mythology, is the stream of forgetfulness, out of which the souls drank when entering Elysium.

Lethra (now *Leire*), in the island of Zealand, the city of the gods among the ancient Danes. This was the holy place where the nation assembled to offer up their sacrifices, to present their prayers, and to receive the choicest blessings from the gods.

Lettish Version. See Slavonic Versions.

Leuchars, Patrick de, a Scotch prelate, was invested with the see of Brechin in 1354, and some time after was made lord high chancellor of the kingdom. In 1370 he resigned his office of chancellor. He was bishop, and present at Parliament in 1373. See Keith, *Scottish Bishops*, p. 162.

Levi, Giuseppe Emanuelo, a Jewish writer, was born at Vercelli, Italy, in 1814. In 1848 he was appointed "laureatus" (graduate) professor of literature at the University of Turin, and died June 10, 1874, leaving, *Parabole, Legende e Pensieri Raccolti dei Libri Talmudici*:—*Christiani et Ebrei nel Medio Evo* (Germ. transl. by Seligmann, Leipsic, 1863):—*Teocrazia Mosaica*:—*Autobiografia di un Padre di Famigli*:—*Ceremoniale per le Cenna di Pasqua*:—*Dei Pregi della Lingua Ebraica, Discorso Academico.* (B. P.)

Lewis, Isaac, D.D., a Congregational minister, was born at Wilton, Conn., Jan. 1, 1773. He graduated from Yale College in 1794, with his twin-brother, Zechariah Lewis. Remaining at New Haven, he prosecuted the study of theology, and was ordained May 30, 1798. He was installed pastor of the First Presbyterian Church in Cooperstown, N. Y., in 1800; in 1806 of the Presbyterian Church in Goshen; and in 1812 preached in Bristol, R. I.; subsequently served in New Rochelle and

West Farms, N. Y., as a stated supply, and succeeded his father in Greenwich, Conn., in December, 1818. He assumed charge of the Church in Bristol, R. I., Nov. 12, 1828. In September, 1831, the failure of his voice compelled him to resign his charge, though he still preached occasionally until the time of his death, which occurred in New York city, Sept. 23, 1854. See Sprague, *Annals of the Amer. Pulpit*, i, 667.

Lewis, John W., an eminent Baptist minister of Georgia, was born near Spartansburg, S. C., Feb. 1, 1801. He studied medicine, and practiced with success, but was drawn to the ministry, and ordained in 1832. About 1840 he removed to Canton, Ga., where he was pastor for a time, and afterwards of other churches in Cherokee County. In such secular concerns as he undertook he exhibited good judgment and sagacity. During the civil war he was a senator in the Congress of the Confederate States, and had much to do with the establishment of the Supreme Court of Georgia. As a preacher, he was instrumental in the conversion of many souls. His death took place in Cherokee County, Ga., in June, 1865. See Cathcart, *Baptist Encyclop.* p. 691. (J. C. S.)

Lewis, Samuel Seymour, D.D., a minister of the Protestant Episcopal Church, was born in Springfield, Vt., Sept. 4, 1804. His early education was acquired in the district school, but at the age of fiteen he entered the High School at South Berwick, Me., where he prepared for college. After entering Dartmouth, failing sight compelled him to dissolve his connection with it, and he entered into partnership with a friend in Utica, N. Y., and devoted himself to mercantile pursuits. Consulting a distinguished oculist in New York, he was assured that he was simply near-sighted, whereupon he immediately closed up his business, and entered Trinity (then Washington) College, Hartford, Conn. At the end of two years he graduated, Aug. 6, 1829. Shortly after he entered the General Theological Seminary in New York city, but before the end of the year he was elected a tutor in Trinity College, which post he held until he was ordained deacon, June 10, 1832. In the fall of that year he took charge of Christ Church, Tuscaloosa, Ala., and in the following year he was admitted to priest's orders. Accepting an invitation from Mobile, he went there in the latter part of 1835, occupying the only parish in the city, and that a feeble one. Here he remained for ten years. He died there July 9, 1848. His style of preaching was of the evangelical type, and he was especially successful as a pastor. See Sprague, *Annals of the Amer. Pulpit*, v, 714.

Lewis, Tayler, D.D., LL.D., a distinguished Biblical scholar and Congregational divine, was born in Northumberland, Saratoga Co., N. Y., March 27, 1802. He graduated from Union College in 1820, studied law in Albany, and, being admitted to the bar, entered on the practice of his profession at Fort Miller. In 1833 he gave up the practice of law, and opened a classical school at Waterford, and in 1835 removed his school to Ogdensburg. In 1838 he was chosen professor of Greek in the University of New York, which chair he occupied until 1849, when he was appointed professor of the Greek language and literature in his Alma Mater, and occupied that position until his death, May 11, 1877. Through all the years of his professorate he was a thorough, indefatigable student of Oriental and Biblical literature. He employed his attainments to defend and illustrate the truths of divine revelation. Among his first publications were translations and texts of Plato's works, accompanied with valuable notes and critical dissertations. In 1855 he published his *Six Days of Creation*, the work by which he became widely known as one of the ablest defenders of divine revelation. Dr. Lewis contributed largely to magazines, both monthly and quarterly, and his contributions to religious journals were almost without number. To mention only one, the *New York Observer*, that paper contains numerous valuable articles. Among them are, "State Rights," "A Photograph from the Ruins of Ancient Greece," "Heroic Periods in a Nation's History," "A Defence of Capital Punishment," "The People of Africa, their Character, Condition, and Future Prospects." He was one of the authors of the recently published *Life of President Nott*, of Union College, and the translator of Genesis and Ecclesiastes in Lange s *Commentary*. (W. P. S.)

Lewis, William Henry, D.D., a Protestant Episcopal clergyman, was born at Litchfield, Conn., Dec. 22, 1803. He was rector for a number of years of the Church of the Holy Trinity, in Brooklyn, N. Y., until 1861, when he became rector of Christ Church, Watertown, Conn., of which he continued to have charge until 1874. He died at the latter place, Oct. 2, 1877. He published, *Sermons for the Christian Year:—Confession for Christ:—The Early Called:—Position of the Church*, besides several tracts. See *Prot. Episc. Almanac*, 1878, p. 169; Allibone, *Dict. of Brit. and Amer. Authors*, s. v.

Lewis, Zechariah, a Congregational minister and editor, son of Rev. Isaac Lewis, D.D., was born at Wilton, Conn., Jan. 1, 1773. With his twin brother, Isaac, he graduated from Yale College in 1794, and after studying theology at Philadelphia under Ashbel Green, D.D., was licensed to preach in 1796; and in the same year was appointed tutor in Yale College, remaining in that office until 1799. While a theological student he was a private tutor in general Washington's family. Convinced that his health was too much impaired to fulfil the duties of the ministry, he became the editor of the *Commercial Advertiser*, and *New York Spectator*, continuing in that employment until 1820. For six years he was corresponding secretary of the New York Religious Tract Society, out of which sprang the American Tract.Society. Resigning this position in February, 1820, he was elected, in May, a secretary of the United Foreign Missionary Society, which office he held for five years. For several years he was editor of the *American Missionary Register*, which he began to publish in July, 1820. He died in Brooklyn, N. Y., Nov. 14, 1840. See Sprague, *Annals of the Amer. Pulpit*, i, 666.

Lha Ma, in Lamaism, is one of the five upper worlds through which the soul of the departed has to wander.

Lhamoghiuprul, in Lamaian mythology, was the wife of the Thibetanian king, Sazan, one of the most beautiful, pure, and sacred nymphs of the lower heaven. See CIO CONCIOA.

Lha-Ssa-Morou, an annual festival observed by the Lamas of Thibet on the third day of the first moon, at Lha-Ssa. It lasts six days, and is designed to give the devout an opportunity to implore the blessings of the Talé-Lama, and to make a pilgrimage to the celebrated Buddhist monastery called Morou, which occupies the centre of the town. See Huc, *Travels in Tartary and Thibet.*

Libāmen, a name given by the ancient Romans to denote the bunch of hair which was cut from the forehead of the victim about to be sacrificed, and which was thrown into the fire as a kind of first-fruits.

Libanomancy (from λίβανος, *the frankincense tree*, and μαντεία, *divination*), a species of divination (q. v.) which was performed by throwing a quantity of frankincense into the fire, and noting the odor which it emitted. If it burned quickly and gave out an agreeable smell, the omen was favorable; but if the reverse took place, it was unfavorable.

Libelli Pœnitentiāles (*certificates of penitence*), documents frequently issued during and after the 8th century by the Romish priesthood, granting immediate absolution to those who confessed their sins to the priest, and declared themselves ready to fulfil the appointed penance, even though they were not prepared to partake of the communion. Great opposition was made to this practice by the reformers in the time of Charlemagne. See PENITENTIAL.

Liber Albus (*white book*) of the ancient monasteries and guilds contained a personal history of visitors or benefactors, frequently recorded in the handwriting of the persons themselves commemorated.

Liberalia, a festival observed annually by the ancient Romans on March 17, in honor of Liber or Bacchus. A procession of priests and priestesses, wearing ivy garlands, marched through the city, bearing wine, honey, cakes, and sweetmeats, along with a portable altar, having in the middle of it a fire-pan, in which the sacrifices were burned. On this occasion the Roman youths who had reached the age of sixteen were invested with the toga virilis or dress of manhood. The *Liberalia* were much more innocent in their character than the *Bacchanalia* (q. v.), and continued to be celebrated in Rome after that festival was suppressed.

Libĕra nos (*deliver us*) is the amplification of the petition, "Deliver us from evil," in the Lord's Prayer, found in almost all liturgies. For instance, that of the Gallican (which is variable) is on Christmas day—"Libera nos, omnipotens Deus, ab omni malo et custodi nos in omni opere bono, perfecta veritas et vera libertas Deus, qui regnas in sæcula sæculorum." Many liturgies contain supplications for the intercession of saints in the *Libera nos.*

Liberi, PIETRO, an eminent Italian painter, was born at Padua in 1605, and studied under Alessandro Varotari, also the works of the best masters, as Michael Angelo, Raphael, Correggio, and Titian. Among his best productions are the *Murder of the Innocents*, at Venice; *Noah just Landed from the Ark*, in the cathedral at Vicenza; and *The Deluge*, in the Church of Santa Maria Maggiore, at Bergamo. Others of his grand pictures are the *Destruction of Pharaoh's Host*, in the cathedral at Vicenza; *Moses Striking the Rock*, at Bergamo; and the *Sufferings of Job*. He died in 1687. See Spooner, *Biog. Hist. of the Fine Arts*, s. v.; Hoefer, *Nouv. Biog. Générale*, s. v.

Libnah. Some would locate this place at *Beit-Jibrin*, and others at *Ibna*, on the coast road, but Tristram (*Bible Places*, p. 44) and Trelawney Saunders (*Map of the O. T.*) accept the identification with *Arak el-Menshiyeh*, which the *Ordnance Map* lays down at six and a half miles west of Beit-Jibrin, and the accompanying *Memoirs* describe thus (iii, 259): "A mud village on a flat plain, surrounded with arable land, and supplied by three wells. It is of moderate size, with two sacred places. The curious mound north of it is a remarkable feature in the landscape, two hundred and fifty feet high, and consisting of natural rock, but scarped, and appearing to have been artificially made steeper. On the top is a sacred *mukâm*, with a few hedges of prickly pear. This site is evidently ancient and important. The hills near it are of very white chalk, and the name Libnah signifies 'milk white.'"

Libra (*a balance*), the seventh sign of the zodiac. It was supposed that those who were born under this constellation loved equity. There were other kindred superstitions connected with this sign by the ancients.

Libs, in Greek mythology, was the south-west wind. He was represented in Athens, on the tower of winds, as a young man, clothed in a light mantle. In his hands he carries a ship's ornament. See NOTUS.

Figure of Libs.

Lichtenstein, Anton August Heinrich, a Lutheran theologian of Germany, was born Aug. 25, 1753, at Helmstädt, where he also pursued his studies. In 1773 he commenced his academical career in his native place, was in 1777 rector at the Johanneum at Hamburg, and in 1782 professor of Oriental languages there. In 1798 he was called to his native place as professor of theology, general superintendent, and first preacher at St. Stephen's. He died Feb. 17, 1816, leaving, *Doctrinarum Theologicarum Examen ad* 1 *Cor. iii*, 10-17 (Helmstädt, 1771):—*Num Liber Jobi cum Odyssea Homeri Comparari Possit?* (1773):—*Descriptio Duorum Codicum Hebraicorum adhuc Parum Cognitorum* (1776):—*Recensio Codicis Hebr. MS. Helmstadiensis Quinti* (1777), etc. See Döring, *Die gelehrten Theologen Deutschlands*, s. v.; Fürst, *Bibl. Jud.* ii, 245; Winer, *Handbuch der theol. Lit.* i, 96; ii, 167. (B. P.)

Lichtenstein, Friedrich Wilhelm Jacob, a Lutheran minister of Germany, was born of Jewish parentage at Munich, Oct. 8, 1826. In 1842, his mother joining the Church, he was baptized, together with his brother Moritz, at Würzburg. In 1843 he commenced his theological studies at Erlangen, and pursued the same at Halle. In 1848 he was ordained, and appointed assistant pastor at Munich. In 1855 the University of Erlangen bestowed on him the diploma of doctor of philosophy, for a work entitled, *Lebensgeschichte des Herrn Jesu Christi in chronologischer Uebersicht* (Erlangen, 1855). In 1863 he was called to Culmbach, and died March 24, 1875. (B. P.)

Lichtenstein, George Philip, a Lutheran minister of Germany, was born at Frankfort-on-the-Main, March 26, 1606, of Jewish parents. Towards the end of that same year he was baptized, together with his father, who made an open profession of Christ. Lichtenstein made his philosophical studies at Giessen and Marburg, and his theological at Strasburg. He was offered by the Swedish field-marshal, count Horn, who was at that time in Germany, the chaplaincy of the court of Sweden, but he preferred to remain at home, and was ordained to the ministry in 1634. He ministered for several years in the neighborhood of Frankfort, till he was called, in 1657, to the pastorate of St. Catharine's Church. He died Feb. 7, 1682, his funeral sermon being preached by his friend, the famous Dr. Spener. (B. P.)

Lichtenstein, Johannes Leopold, a Presbyterian minister, was born of Jewish parentage, at Hechingen, April 10, 1813. At the age of sixteen he was appointed teacher at Habsheim, in Upper Alsace. When twenty-one years old his way led him to Basle, where a Hebrew Christian prepared himself for missionary work. To bring this lost sheep back to the fold of the synagogue was Lichtenstein's intention, but the would-be victor was soon conquered, and the former teacher became now a disciple of Christ. On Sept. 28, 1834, he was baptized at Strasburg, adding the name Johannes to his Jewish name Leopold. Soon after his baptism he went to Geneva, where he attended the École de Theol. Oratoire, and where Merle d'Aubigne was one of his teachers. From Geneva he went to Strasburg, and attended the upper classes of the Protestant gymnasium. Having passed his examination in 1839, he then went to Erlangen, where Hoffman, Harless, Thiersch, and others were his professors. In 1841 he went to Berlin to complete his theological studies under Hengstenberg, Stahl, Neander, Twesten, and others. In 1842 he was ordained for the ministry at Erlangen, and accepted a call from the Jewish Missionary Society at Strasburg. In 1845 he received a call from New York, to act as superintendent of the Jewish mission there, which he accepted. In 1847 he left his position, and in 1848 was appointed pastor of the German Presbyterian Church at Paterson, N. J. From 1851 to 1854 he labored at New Albany, Ind.; accepted a call of the German Reformed Church at Buffalo, N. Y., where he remained till 1862, when the First German Reformed Church of Cincinnati, O., called him as its pastor. In 1866 he exchanged his position for the pastorate of the First German Presbyterian Church there, and fell asleep in Jesus, Nov. 3, 1882. (B. P.)

Lichtenstein, Moritz, a Lutheran minister of Germany, brother of Jacob, was born Jan. 3, 1824. Like his brother, he studied theology first at Erlangen, and subsequently at Halle. In 1855 he entered actively upon the ministerial career, by being made curate to an aged minister at Bürglen, in Franconia. In 1857 he was appointed to the living of Tann. The place proving injurious, Lichtenstein was transferred to Rittersbach, Central Franconia, in 1860, and died Sept. 3, 1876. (B. P.)

Licnon. See LIKNON.

Lida, DAVID DE, a Jewish writer of the 18th century, is the author of, מגדל דוד, or a cabalistic commentary on Ruth (Amsterdam, 1610):—עיר דוד, homilies on the Pentateuch (ibid. 1719):—עיר מקלט, or a commentary on the 613 precepts (1690). His writings were edited and published under the title of ספר ר״ד כל בו, by his son (Frankfort-on-the-Main, 1727). See Fürst, *Bibl. Jud.* ii, 247. (B. P.)

Liebermann, FRANZ LEOPOLD BRUNO, a Roman Catholic theologian, was born at Molsheim, near Strasburg, in 1759. At the time of the French revolution, to avoid being imprisoned, he fled to Germany, but returned to his parochial work at Ernolsheim in 1795. In 1801 he was called to Strasburg as cathedral-preacher and episcopal secretary, but returned again to Ernolsheim in 1803. In 1804 Liebermann was imprisoned under the pretext of having relations with the Bourbon family. He was released, however, in 1805, and his friend, the bishop of Mayence, appointed him superior of the clerical seminary and canon at the cathedral of Mayence. Liebermann, who died in 1844, is the author of *Institutiones Theologiæ Dogmaticæ* (1819, 5 vols.), a work still used in the seminaries of France, Belgium, Germany, and America. It has also been translated into French in 1856. See Lichtenberger, *Encyclop. des Sciences Religieuses*, s. v.; Winer, *Handbuch der theol. Lit.* i, 307. (B. P.)

Liebetrut, FRIEDRICH, a Protestant theologian of Germany, who died Oct. 17, 1881, at Charlottenburg, near Berlin, doctor of theology, is the author of, *Die Ehe nach ihrer Idee und nach ihrer geschichtlichen Entwickelung* (Berlin, 1834):—*Der Tag des Herrn und seine Feier* (1837):—*Christliche Andachtsstunden für Frauen und Jungfrauen evangelischer Konfession* (1847):—*Ueber die Verehrung der Heiligen, Reliquien und Bilder* (1845):—*Katechismus der christlichen Lehre* (1853):—*Reise nach dem Morgenlande* (1858):—*Dr. Beck und seine Stellung zur Kirche* (1857):—*Ueber die Heuchelei und wider dieselbe* (1859). See Zuchold, *Bibl. Theol.* ii, 793 sq. (B. P.)

Liebner, KARL THEODOR ALBERT, a prominent Protestant theologian of Germany, was born at Schkölen, near Naumburg, March 3, 1806. He studied at Leipsic, Berlin, and Wittemberg, was in 1832 pastor at Kreisfeld, in Saxony, in 1835 professor at Göttingen, in 1851 at Leipsic, and in 1855 general superintendent and court-preacher at Dresden. He died June 24, 1871, at Meran, Switzerland. Liebner is the author of, *Hugo von St. Victor und die theologischen Richtungen seiner Zeit* (Leipsic, 1832):—*Die christliche Dogmatik aus dem christologischen Princip dargestellt* (Göttingen, 1849):—*Introductio in Dogmaticam Christianam* (Leipsic, 1854). Besides, he published *Predigten in der Universitäts-Kirche gehalten* (Göttingen, 1841; 2d ed. 1856):—*Predigt-Beiträge zur Förderung der Erkenntniss Christi in der Gemeinde* (1861), and contributed largely to the *Jahrbucher für deutsche Theologie*. See Zuchold, *Bibl. Theol.* ii, 794; Lichtenberger, *Encyclop. des Sciences Religieuses*, s. v.; Plitt-Herzog, *Real-Encyklop.* s. v. (B. P.)

Liemaeker, NICOLAS (called *the Rose*), an eminent Flemish painter, was born at Ghent in 1575, and first studied under Mark Gerards, and, after the death of that master, with Ottovenius. The name of Rose was given him when a boy on account of his ruddy cheeks. He was one of the most eminent painters of the Flemish school, and his works are in almost every town in the Low Countries. He painted sacred and historical subjects. In the Church of St. Nicholas, at Ghent, are two of his best works, *The Good Samaritan*, and *The Fall of the Rebel Angels*, which last is considered his masterpiece. Also in the Church of St. James are several of his works, one of which is a grand composition, representing *The Last Judgment*. He died at Ghent in 1647. See Hoefer, *Nouv. Biog. Générale*, s. v.; Spooner, *Biog. Hist. of the Fine Arts*, s. v.

Lievens (Livens, or Lywyns), JAN, a Dutch painter and engraver, was born at Leyden, Oct. 24, 1607, and was placed under the direction of George van Schooten, but when ten years of age was placed under Peter Lastman. He painted a number of fine works while quite young, which procured him a favorable reception at the court of England, where he resided three years. At Brussels, in the Church of the Jesuits, is his *Visitation of the Virgin*, and in the Church of St. James, at Antwerp, a fine picture of *The Holy Family*. In 1641 he returned to Leyden, where he executed his celebrated pictures of *David and Bathsheba* and *The Sacrifice of Abraham*. He died probably in 1663. The following is a list of some of his best prints: *The Holy Family; The Virgin Presenting a Pear to the Infant Jesus; St. John the Evangelist; St. Jerome in a Cell, holding a Crucifix; The Raising of Lazarus*. See Hoefer, *Nouv. Biog. Générale*, s. v.; Spooner, *Biog. Hist. of the Fine Arts*, s. v.

Lif and **Lifthrasser**, in Norse mythology, are two human beings who hide themselves with Ragnarokr (destruction of the world), and feed on dew. From them all men are born who will inhabit the rejuvenated earth after the fire of Sutur.

Lifuan Version OF THE SCRIPTURES. Lifu is a language spoken on the Loyalty Islands. In 1869 the book of Psalms, in the Lifu language, was printed in the island of Mare. In 1872 the New Test. was printed in England, under the care of the translator, the Rev. M. Macfarlane, one of the missionaries at Lifu. In 1877 the Pentateuch was issued from the press, under the editorship of the Rev. S. M. Creagh, of the London Missionary Society. From the report of the British and Foreign Bible Society of 1885, we learn that the completion of the revision of the translation of the Bible was made Aug. 29, 1884. The translator, Rev. S. M. Creagh "is now copying the corrections made in the parts already printed, viz. Pentateuch, Psalms, and New Test., and the number of changes in these amount to 52,310. The whole is being prepared for publication." The same translator is also preparing marginal references. (B. P.)

Lifur, in Norse mythology, is a dwarf formed of and living in the earth. He was slain by Thor at Baldur's funeral, and thrown into the burning ship.

Ligature (*ligatura, ligamentum,* δέσις, παρίαμμα, etc.) was a kind of amulet worn by the ancient heathen, either upon their own persons or those of their animals, for the purpose of averting evil. Their use is condemned by early Christian writers (Chrysostom, *Homil. adv. Jud.* viii. 7; *Const. Apostol.* viii, 32, etc.).

Lightenstein, John, D.D., a member of the Cincinnati Presbytery, was born at Hechingen, Hohenzollern, Germany, in 1818. The occasion of his conversion was his zealous efforts to bring back to the Jewish faith a companion who had become a Christian. At different universities he enjoyed the teachings of such men as Merle D'Aubigne, Hengstenberg, Neander, Stahl, and Schelling. He was ordained in 1842, and was for a time a missionary among the Jews of Alsace. He came to New York in 1845, on the invitation of the Society for Ameliorating the Condition of the Jews, and was superintendent of their mission-house. He afterwards became pastor of a German Presbyterian Church in Paterson, N. J., and subsequently of a German Reformed Church in Buffalo, N. Y., where he remained eight years. He removed to Cincinnati in 1866, took charge of the First German Presbyterian Church, and continued there until his death, Nov. 3, 1882. He was a ripe scholar, an able preacher, and a thoroughly evangelical man. See *N. Y. Observer*, Nov. 23, 1882. (W. P. S.)

Lights, Feast of, a name applied by Josephus to the Jewish Feast of Dedication (q. v.).

Lights of Walton, a class of enthusiasts who appeared in the 17th century at Walton-on-Thames, Surrey, England. The story of their origin is related as follows: In the beginning of Lent, 1649, Mr. Fawcet, then minister of Walton, having preached in the afternoon, when he had concluded it was nearly dark, and six soldiers came into the church, one with a lighted candle in a lantern, and four with candles unlighted. The first soldier addressed the people, declaring that he had received in a vision a message from God, which they must listen to and believe on pain of damnation. The message consisted of five lights: 1. The Sabbath is abolished; "and here," said he, "I should put out my first light, but the wind is so high that I cannot light it." 2. Tithes are abolished. 3. Ministers are abolished. 4. Magistrates are abolished, repeating the same words as he had uttered under the first head. Then taking a Bible from his pocket, he declared that it is also abolished, as containing only beggarly elements, which are unnecessary now that Christ is come in his glory, with a full measure of his Spirit. Then taking the lighted candle from his lantern, he set fire to the pages of the Bible, after which, extinguishing the candle, he added, "and here my fifth light is extinguished."

Ligitsch, in Slavonic mythology, was the god of atonement and rest. The wives pray to him after having been angry with their husbands.

Liknon (λίκνον), a long basket, in which the image of Dionysus was carried in the *Dionysia*. The *Liknon* was the winnowing fan into which the corn was received after threshing, and was, very naturally, used in the rites of both Bacchus and Ceres. It was also employed to carry the instruments of sacrifice, and first-fruits or other offerings. See Bacchus.

Lilienthal, Max, a Jewish rabbi, was born at Munich in 1815. He studied at his native place, and graduated in 1837 as doctor of philosophy. In 1839 he received a call as director of the Hebrew school at Riga, Russia. In 1845 he resigned his position and went to New York city, where he was elected rabbi of three congregations, an office which he, however, resigned to open a Jewish boarding-school. In 1855 he accepted a call to the congregation at Cincinnati, and died April 1, 1882. Besides sermons and addresses, he published, *Ueber den Ursprung der jüdisch-alexandrinischen Religionsphilosophie* (Munich, 1839):—*Bibliographische Notizen über die hebräischen Manuscripte der königl. Bibliothek zu München* (printed in the *Beilage der allgemeinen Zeitung des Judenthums*, 1848). See Fürst, *Bibl. Jud.* ii, 249 sq. (B. P.)

Lilith, the name of the first wife of Adam, according to rabbinical tradition. She was made of the earth as was Adam himself, and would not submit to be ruled over by her husband. Seeing no possibility of an agreement between herself and him, she fled away to the sea, where she became the mother of a race of dæmons, and, as a punishment for refusing to return to Adam, one hundred of her children were to die every day. Lilith became noted in Jewish legend as a destroyer of infants, and for this reason they adopted the custom of writing the names of three protecting angels on slips of paper or parchment, and binding them upon the infant, to prevent the evil influence of Lilith. Among modern Jews, when a woman approaches the period of her confinement, the husband inscribes on each of the walls or partitions around the bed, along with the names of Adam and Eve, the words "Begone, Lilith." On the inside of the doors also he writes the names of three angels, which it is believed will defend the child from the injuries which it might otherwise receive from Lilith.

Lillie, Adam, D.D., a Scotch Congregational minister, was born in Glasgow in 1803. He embraced religion very early in life, studied at the university, and becoming animated by a strong missionary desire, offered his services to the London Missionary Society, studied three years at Gosport, and in 1826 sailed to India. His health failing caused his return to Glasgow in the following year. He then settled as teacher, soon after became itinerant minister, in 1833 was chosen copastor at Musselburgh, and in 1834 accepted an invitation to the pastorate at Brantford, Ontario, where he continued during life. In 1840 Dr. Lillie added to his pastorate the tutorship of the Canadian Institute for the training of a local ministry. He died Oct. 19, 1869. Dr. Lillie was an eminent Christian and scholar, and a prodigious worker. See (Lond.) *Cong. Year-Book*, 1870, p. 305.

Limus, an article of dress worn around the loins by the ancient Roman *papa*, or officiating priest, at the sacrifices.

Lincoln, Richard, D.D., an Irish prelate, was promoted to the see of Dublin in 1757. He encouraged his people to a continuance of peaceful and Christian dispositions, and forcibly appealed to those of another communion as to Catholic loyalty and love. He died in 1762. See D'Alton, *Memoirs of the Archbishops of Dublin*, p. 469.

Lincoln, Thomas Oliver, D.D., a Baptist minister, was born in Boston, Mass., May 4, 1809. He graduated from Yale College in 1829, and from Newton Theological Institution in 1834; was ordained pastor of the Baptist Church in Kennebunkport, Me., Dec. 10, 1834, and afterwards served the Free Street Church in Portland; Philadelphia, Pa.; Mount Holly, N. J.; Manchester, N. H.; Utica and Elmira, N. Y.; Williamsport, Pa.; and Roadstown, N. J. He died at Bridgeton, Jan. 20, 1877. (J. C. S.)

Linde, Johann Wilhelm, a Lutheran theologian of Germany, was born Jan. 24, 1760, at Thorn, and died Feb. 16, 1840, at Dantzic, superintendent and member of consistory. He is the author of, *Sententiæ Jesu Siracidæ* (Dantzic, 1795):—*Des Sohnes Sirach Sittenlehre* (Leipsic, 1782, 1795):—*Reinhard und Ammon, oder Predigten-Parallele; als Beitrag zur Homiletik* (Königsberg, 1800). See Winer, *Handbuch der theol. Lit.* i, 233; ii, 48, 64; Fürst, *Bibl. Jud.* ii, 250. (B. P.)

Lindemann, Joachim, a Lutheran theologian of Germany, was born April 7, 1662, at Rostock. He studied at different universities, was in 1684 magister in his native city, in 1688 archdeacon, in 1692 professor, and died Dec. 14, 1698, a doctor of theology. He wrote, *De Obligatione Conscientiæ*:—*De Præjudiciis Philosophicis*:—*De Sanctorum cum Christo Redivivorum Resurrectione, ex Matt. xxvii, 52, 53*:—*De Proto-Canonicis et Deutero-Canonicis S. Scripturæ Libris*:—*De Iis quæ*

Theologia Naturalis Ignorat. See Jöcher, *Allgemeines Gelehrten-Lexikon*, s. v. (B. P.)

Lindesay, David, a Scotch prelate, was preferred to the see of Ross in 1600, and still continued his ministry at Leith until his death, which occurred about 1613. In 1604 he was one of the commissioners for uniting the two kingdoms. See Keith, *Scottish Bishops*, p. 201.

Lindesay, Patrick, a Scotch prelate, was first minister at St. Vigian's, in Angus. In October, 1613, he was preferred to the episcopal see of Ross, and consecrated Dec. 15 of the same year. From this he was translated to the see of Glasgow, April 16, 1633. He died at Newcastle in 1641. See Keith, *Scottish Bishops*, p. 202, 264.

Lindet, Robert Thomas, a French prelate and politician, was born at Bernay (Eure) in 1743. He was pastor of the parish of St. Croix in that town, when he was elected deputy of the clergy of the bailiwick of Evreux to the States-General of 1789. In 1791 he was elected constitutional bishop of Eure. In November, 1792, he married publicly. In 1793 he resigned his episcopate, and all his offices in 1798, and lived thereafter in obscurity, until finally, by the law of amnesty of 1816, he was obliged to leave France. After staying some time in Switzerland and Italy, he was permitted to come home to his native country, where he died in August, 1823. He wrote, *Lettre Circulaire au Clergé de son Diocèse:—Lettres aux Religieuses des Monastères de son Diocèse.* See Hoefer, *Nouv. Biog. Générale*, s. v.

Lindley, Daniel, D.D., a Presbyterian missionary, was born in America in 1800. After receiving his theological education, he was ordained, and went with five others to South Africa in 1834. In 1836 he established a mission on the Allovo river, Port Natal, and commenced his lifelong work of laboring to convert the Zulus to Christ. On account of the numerous wars in that country, his mission was broken up, and for a considerable length of time he was prevented from carrying out his great design. He lived, however, to see a great moral and civil revolution among the inhabitants of that country, and his zeal and perseverance in the great cause in which he was engaged were crowned with success. After toiling for thirty-seven years, he was obliged, on account of his wife's illness, to return to the United States. He travelled extensively throughout the country advocating the cause of missions, until 1877, when he was stricken with paralysis, from which he never recovered. Dr. Lindley died in New York in August, 1880. (W. P. S.)

Lindley, Jacob, D.D., a Cumberland Presbyterian minister, was born June 13, 1774, in western Pennsylvania, and was the fifth in descent from Francis Lindley, one of the passengers in the *Mayflower*. Jacob's father erected a block-house between the Monongahela river and Wheeling, as a defence against prowling Indians, in the winter of 1774 and 1775; and it was long known as Fort Lindley. Young Jacob became a communicant about 1786. For a time he was a student at an academy near his home, and at the age of eighteen entered the institution afterwards known as Jefferson College, at Cannonsburg, Pa. In 1798 he entered Princeton College, from which he graduated in 1800. Having studied theology for a time, he was licensed to preach by the Washington Presbytery, and in 1803 removed to Beverly, O. The first board of trustees of Ohio University selected him to organize and conduct that institution, for which purpose he went to Athens in 1808. For several years he had charge of the infant college, and was the prime mover in securing the erection of the college buildings, and in founding the Presbyterian Church in Athens. During a part of his twenty years' labor there he was the only Presbyterian minister in that section of Ohio. About 1828 he was partially relieved by the appointment to the presidency of Rev. Dr. Wilson, of Chillicothe; although he remained about a year longer in the college as professor of moral philosophy and mathematics. Subsequently he spent one year at Walnut Hills, Cincinnati; then a year or two at the Flats of Grace creek; after which he accepted a call from the Upper Ten Mile congregation, within whose bounds was his birthplace. While here, in western Pennsylvania, he received a mandate from his presbytery forbidding ministerial intercourse with the Cumberland Presbyterians. Refusing obedience to the mandate, charges were brought against him, which he showed to be groundless, and then he demanded from his presbytery a letter of dismission. This was granted, and in this way his connection with the Presbyterian Church was severed. He became a Cumberland Presbyterian, but continued his pastoral relation with the Upper Ten Mile congregation for two or three years. Subsequently he took charge of a Cumberland Presbyterian congregation at Beverly (then Waterford), O. In 1837 he removed to Alabama, still preaching and teaching as opportunity offered. From 1848 Dr. Lindley spent his winters in the South, and his summers in the North. He died at Connellsville, Pa., Jan. 29, 1857. In 1846 he published a small volume, entitled *Infant Philosophy*. See Beard, *Biographical Sketches*, 2d series, p. 45.

Lindner, Friedrich Wilhelm, a Lutheran theologian of Germany, was born in 1779 at Weida. He commenced his academical career at Leipsic in 1806, was in 1825 professor of catechetics, retired in 1860, and died Nov. 1, 1865. He published, *Die wichtigsten Thatsachen und Urtheile für und gegen Missions- und Bibelgesellschaften* (Leipsic, 1825):—*Die Lehre vom Abendmahle* (1831). See Zuchold, *Bibl. Theol.* ii, 800; Winer, *Handbuch der theol. Lit.* i, 454, 587. (B. P.)

Lindner, Wilhelm Bruno, a Lutheran theologian of Germany, who died at Leipsic in 1876, doctor and professor of theology, is the author of, *De Joviniano et Vigilantio* (Leipsic, 1839):—*Lehrbuch der christlichen Kirchengeschichte* (1848–54, 3 vols.):—*Bibliotheca Patrum Ecclesiasticorum Selectissima* (1857):—*Sermons*, delivered in the University Church (1844):—*Christological Sermons* (1855). See Zuchold, *Bibl. Theol.* ii, 800 sq. (B. P.)

Lindo, Elia H., a Jewish writer, who died in London, July 11, 1865, is the author of *History of the Jews of Spain and Portugal* (London, 1849). From the Hebrew he translated a work of Menasseh ben-Israel: *The Conciliator, a Reconcilement of the Apparent Contradictions in Holy Scripture* (1842, 2 vols.). See Fürst, *Bibl. Jud.* ii, 251. (B. P.)

Lindsay (properly **Alexander William Crawford**), *Lord* (known after the death of his father as *Count of Crawford and Balcarres*), an English writer, was born Oct. 16, 1812. He was educated at Eton, and at Trinity College, Cambridge, and graduated in 1833 as master of arts. He then travelled extensively, and published in 1838 his *Letters on Egypt, Edom, and the Holy Land*, in two volumes. In 1844 he published *A Letter to a Friend on the Evidence and Theory of Christianity*, and in 1846 *Progression by Antagonism.* In 1861 he issued his *Scepticism;* in 1870 *Œcumenicity in Relation to the Church of England*, and in 1872 *Etruscan Inscriptions.* He died at Florence, Dec. 13, 1880. A large work on comparative history of the religions of antiquity, which he intended to publish under the title of *The Religion of Noah*, was left incomplete. (B. P.)

Lindsay, Alexander, a Scotch prelate, was preacher at St. Madoes, and bishop of Dunkeld, where he continued until 1638, when he renounced his office, abjured episcopacy, submitted to Presbyterian parity, and accepted from the then rulers his former church of St. Madoes. He acquired the barony of Evelick, in the carse of Gowrie. See Keith, *Scottish Bishops*, p. 98.

Lindsay, David, a Scotch prelate, was minister

at Dundee, made bishop of Brechin, and consecrated at St. Andrews, Nov. 23, 1619. He was translated to the see of Edinburgh, Sept. 17, 1634. He was deposed and excommunicated for reading the liturgy in the High Church of Edinburgh, July 23, 1637. He went to England, and died soon after. See Keith, *Scottish Bishops*, p. 61.

Lindsay, Ingeram, a Scotch prelate, was bishop of Aberdeen in 1442, and also in 1448, 1452, and 1458, when he probably died. See Keith, *Scottish Bishops*, p. 114.

Lindsay, James, D.D., an English Presbyterian clergyman, was born and educated in Scotland, where he began to preach. He came to London, and was ordained pastor at Monkwell Street in May, 1783. In 1787 he was appointed afternoon preacher to the Presbyterians at Stoke-Newington, where he fixed his residence, and opened an academy. In 1803 he removed to Old Ford, and received his diploma from Aberdeen University. He published two funeral sermons, and was minister at Monkwell Street in 1811. See Wilson, *Dissenting Churches*, iii, 215.

Lindsay, John, a Scotch prelate, was promoted to the see of Glasgow about 1325. This prelate was killed in 1335, while returning from Flanders to Scotland. See Keith, *Scottish Bishops*, p. 244.

Lindsay, William, a Scotch prelate, was minister at Perth, and consecrated bishop of the see of Dunkeld, May 7, 1677. He died in 1679. See Keith, *Scottish Bishops*, p. 99.

Linegar, John, D.D., an Irish prelate, was appointed to the see of Dublin in 1734, and held the office until 1739, without being molested in any way. The act of king William, "for disarming the Papists," was enforced, and this caused some disturbance. He died in 1756. See D'Alton, *Memoirs of the Archbishops of Dublin*, p. 466.

Lingam. See Linga.

Lingayets. See Jangamas.

Linn, James, D.D., a Presbyterian minister, was born in Sherman's Valley (now Perry County), Pa., Sept. 4, 1783. He graduated at Dickinson College in 1805, and studied theology with Dr. Williams. He was licensed to preach by the Presbytery of Carlisle, Sept. 27, 1809, visited the congregations of Spruce Creek and Sinking Valley, and was ordained pastor in 1810. He was called to take charge of the churches of Bellefonte and Lick Run, but in 1839 was released from the latter, that he might give his whole time to the former. In 1861 Rev. J. H. Barnard was appointed co-pastor. Dr. Linn died at Bellefonte, Feb. 23, 1868. See *Presbyterian*, March 14, 1868. (W. P. S.)

Linsley, Joel H., D.D., a Congregational minister, was born at Cornwall, Vt., July 16, 1790. Under private tuition, and afterwards at the Addison County Grammar-school, he acquired his preliminary training, and graduated from Middlebury College in 1811. For a year he taught school in Windsor, and in 1812 began the study of law. In 1813 he was appointed tutor in Middlebury College, holding that position for more than two years, still prosecuting his legal studies. He was admitted to the bar in December, 1815, went into a law-partnership, and continued in practice until 1822. Previously, in 1812, he was licensed to preach, and for a time studied at Andover Theological Seminary. After eight months of missionary labor in South Carolina he returned to New England, was ordained, in 1824, pastor of the South Congregational Church in Hartford, Conn., and remained until 1832, in which year he was installed pastor of the Park Street Church, Boston. He resigned to assume the presidency of Marietta College in 1835, and held that position for about ten years. Then for two years he was in the service of the Society for the Promotion of Collegiate and Theological Education at the West. In December, 1847, he became pastor of the Second Congregational Church in Greenwich, Conn., and died there March 22, 1868. He published a volume of lectures on the *Relations and Duties of the Middle-Aged*, besides orations, addresses, reviews, and sermons. See *Cong. Quarterly*, 1868, p. 380.

Lintner, George A., D.D., a Lutheran minister, was born at Minden, Montgomery Co., N. Y., Feb. 15, 1796. At an early age he was admitted to Union College. After graduation he studied theology, and was licensed to preach in September, 1818. The following year he accepted a call to the pastorate of Schoharie and Cobleskill. He was one of the recognised leaders of his synod in opposition to what he called the "Quitman Dynasty of Rationalism." After a time he and others became dissatisfied with the old synod, and at a convention, in 1830, at Schoharie, the Hartwick Synod was organized, of which he was chosen the first president. In 1837 certain members of this synod withdrew, and formed the Franckean Synod, on the widest latitudinarian basis. The movement was revolutionary, and led to controversy and contests in the courts. He was pastor of the Church in Schoharie until 1849, a period of thirty years. From 1827 to 1831 he was editor of the *Lutheran Magazine*. In 1841 and 1843 he was president of the General Synod of the United States. The liturgy of the Lutheran Church of America, published by order of the General Synod of 1832, was prepared by him. During his ministry he organized three new churches as the result of his work—one at Breakabeen, one at Middleburg, and another at Central Bridge. From 1837 until the close of his life he was president of the Schoharie County Bible Society. The last years of his life he visited the Lutheran churches in New York and New Jersey in behalf of the Foreign Missionary Society. He died Dec. 21, 1871. See *Five Years in the Lutheran Ministry*, 1878, p. 206.

Lintrup, Severin, a Lutheran theologian of Denmark, who died March 13, 1731, at Copenhagen, was bishop of Wiburg, in Jütland, in 1720, and in 1725 court-preacher and professor of theology. He wrote, *Specimen Calumniæ Papæo-Calvinianæ in August. Confess. Invariatam:—De θηριομαχίᾳ Paulina* 1 *Cor. xv*, 32*:—De Polymathia Scriptorum Sacrorum, Speciatim Pauli Apostoli:—Meletemata Critica iv ad Selectiora N. T. Loca*, etc. See Moller, *Cimbria Litterata*; Jöcher, *Allgemeines Gelehrten-Lexikon*, s. v. (B. P.)

Lion-worship was particularly prevalent in the city of Leontopolis, Egypt. The lion was the symbol of strength, and therefore typical of the Egyptian Hercules. The lion was also sacred to the Egyptian Minerva. In southern Ethiopia, in the vicinity of the modern town of Shendy, the lion-headed deity seems to have been the chief object of worship. He holds a conspicuous place in the great temple of wady Owáteb, and on the sculptured remains at wady Benat, at the former of which he is the first in a procession of deities, consisting of Rê, Neph, and Ptah, to whom a monarch is making offerings. According to Plutarch, "the lion was worshipped by the Egyptians, who ornamented the doors of their temples with the gaping mouth of that animal, because the Nile began to rise when the sun was in the constellation Leo." Mithras, which is a solar god, was represented with a lion's head. In his mysteries the second degree was that of the lion. Adad, the god of the Syrians, was seated on the back of a lion, which represents his solar nature. In South America the first discoverers found at Tabasco an image of a lion, to which the natives offered human sacrifices. Dr. Livingstone, in his *Travels in Africa*, mentions a tribe who believe that the souls of their chiefs enter into lions, and therefore they never attempt to kill them; they even believe that a chief may metamorphose himself into a lion, kill any one he chooses, and then return to the human form; therefore when they see one they commence clapping their hands, which is their usual mode of salutation. See Lion.

Lipovniczky, STEPHAN VON, a Roman Catholic prelate, who died Aug. 12, 1885, bishop of Gross-Wardein, Hungary, took an active part in the political events of 1849. After the suppression of the Hungarian revolution he was condemned to death. Being pardoned by the emperor of Austria, Lipovniczky resumed clerical duties, and finally became the incumbent of one of the most important episcopal sees of Hungary. (B. P.)

Lippincott, CALEB ATMORE, a veteran Methodist Episcopal minister, was born in Pemberton township, N. J., July 26, 1803. His parents were of Quaker descent, and he was brought up a moral youth, but was full of animal spirits, and fond of all the follies of the age. He was converted among the Methodists in 1825, commenced circuit work in 1829, and in 1830 entered the Philadelphia Conference, wherein he served Tuckerton Circuit, Warren Circuit, Newton, Frankford, Germantown, Philadelphia, and Asbury (West Philadelphia). He then, in 1842, was transferred to the New Jersey Conference, and was sent in turn to Birmingham Mission, Columbus Circuit, Northampton, Flemington, Bordentown, Morristown, Flanders, Rahway District, Stanhope, Hackettstown, Cross Street, Paterson, and Union Street, Newark; then served as tract agent; was then sent to Hurdtown, Hope, Berkshire, Hurdtown and Longwood, and Chester and Denville, at which latter place he died, June 17, 1871. Mr. Lippincott was a man of remarkable powers of mind. He was a natural orator, possessed marvellous powers of description, overflowed with wit and good humor, and was pre-eminently a revivalist. See *Minutes of Annual Conferences,* 1872, p. 34.

Lis (or **Lys**), JAN VAN DER, an eminent Dutch artist, was born at Oldenburg, Germany, in 1570, but studied at Haarlem, under Henry Goltz, and afterwards went to Italy, where he studied the works of Paul Veronese and Domenico Pieti. His subjects are principally taken from sacred history. The chief of them are a picture of *Adam and Eve Mourning over the Body of Abel,* and in San Nicolo, at Venice, is a celebrated painting by him, representing *St. Jerome in the Desert.* He died at Venice in 1629. See Hoefer, *Nouv. Biog. Générale,* s. v.; Spooner, *Biog. Hist. of the Fine Arts,* s. v.

Lisco, FRIEDRICH GUSTAV, a Protestant theologian of Germany, was born Feb. 12, 1791, at Brandenburg. He entered upon his ministerial duties at Berlin in 1814, and died there, July 5, 1866, doctor of theology. Lisco was a prolific writer, and published, *Predigten über die Gleichnisse Jesu* (Berlin, 1828):—*Die Offenbarungen Gottes in Geschichte und Lehre* (2d ed. Hamburg, 1835):—*Die Parabeln Jesu exegetisch-homiletisch bearbeitet* (5th ed. Berlin, 1861):—*Die Bibel mit Erklärungen,* etc. (1852, 2 vols.):—*Das christliche Kirchenjahr* (4th ed. eod. 2 vols.):—*Biblische Betrachtungen über Johannes den Täufer* (1836):—*Die Wunder Jesu, exegetisch-homiletisch bearbeitet* (2d ed. 1844):—*Das christlich-apostolische Glaubensbekenntniss* (4th ed. 1851):—*Die Scheidelehren der protestantischen und römischen Kirche* (1845):—*Dies Iræ, Hymnus auf das Weltgericht* (1840):—*Stabat Mater, Hymnus auf die Schmerzen der Maria* (1843), etc. See Zuchold, *Bibl. Theol.* ii, 802-804; Winer, *Handbuch der Theol. Lit.* ii, 87, 119, 123, 201, 306, 310, 357, 359. (B. P.)

Litaolané. There is a curious tradition among the Bechuanas in South Africa, to the effect that a monster of immense size, at a remote period of time, swallowed up all mankind except a single woman, who conceived miraculously and brought forth a son, to whom she gave the name of Litaolané. This son of the woman attacked the monster and was swallowed up alive, but being armed with a knife he cut open an outlet for himself from the belly of the monster, and thus he obtained deliverance, and all the nations of the earth in him. Thus saved, men sought, without success, to destroy their rescuer.

Litè (λιτή), in the Greek Church, a procession accompanied with prayer, made on various occasions of public calamity and intercession. Forms of service on such occasions are given in the Greek euchology.

Litĕræ Clerĭcæ (*clerical letters*), a name given by Cyprian to letters written by a bishop in ancient times to a foreign Church, and which were sent by the hands of one of the clergy, usually a sub-deacon.

Lithomancy (from λίθος, *a stone,* and μαντεία, *divination*), divination performed by means of stones. The stone used for this purpose was washed in spring water by candle-light, and the person engaged in divining, having purified himself, covered his face, repeated a form of prayer, and placed certain characters in a certain order. Then the stone was said to move of itself, and in a soft, gentle murmur to give the answer. See DIVINATION.

Lithuanian Version OF THE SCRIPTURES. See SLAVONIC VERSIONS.

Litta, LORENZO, a learned Italian prelate, was born at Milan, Feb. 23, 1756. After studying at the Clementine College, in Rome, he was appointed apostolical prothonotary in 1782, in 1793 became archbishop *in partibus* of Thebes, and the year following departed for Poland as nuncio. In 1797 he went in the same capacity to Russia. He died May 1, 1820, leaving *Lettres Diverses,* etc. (Paris, 1809). See Hoefer, *Nouv. Biog. Générale,* s. v.

Little, HENRY, D.D., a Presbyterian minister, was born at Boscawen, N. H., March 30, 1800. He was converted at six years of age, graduated at Dartmouth College in 1826, and from Andover Theological Seminary in 1829. The same year he was ordained as a missionary under the auspices of the American Education Society, for labor in the West. In 1831 he became pastor at Oxford, O., and two years later Western agent of the American Missionary Society; in 1838 pastor at Madison, Ind., a position which he occupied for ten years. The rest of his life was devoted to home missionary work in the Presbyterian Church. He died at Madison, Feb. 25, 1882. He was remarkably successful in pastoral labor, and in organizing missions and raising funds for their support.

Littré, MAXIMILIEN PAUL ÉMILE, the leader of positivism in France, was born in Paris, Feb. 1, 1801. He at first chose medicine as his profession, and, though he did not practice, much of his varied intellectual activity was directed to the scientific and historical side of the subject; indeed, his first work of great importance was his edition and translation of *Hippocrates,* the first volume of which appeared in 1839, while the last came out on the eve of the appearance of his famous *Dictionnaire de la Langue Française.* In the same year, when his *Hippocrates* appeared, he was elected a member of the Academie des Inscriptions et Belles-Lettres, and in 1844 he took Fauriel's place in the company charged by the Academy with the continuation of the *Histoire Littéraire,* in which he did much good work. A great part of his time and energy was also taken up by his connection with Comte and positivism (q. v.). He himself was, by temperament, inclined not to polemics against religion, but to a kind of ignoring of it in favor of science; and he had translated Strauss's *Leben Jesu* within four years of its publication. He adopted positivism, as it at first presented itself, with vigorous partisanship, and produced in 1845 an excellent analysis of the *Philosophie Positive.* His subsequent refusal to follow Comte (q. v.) in his later excursions gave rise to the acrimonious polemic between the party of which he was the real chief, and the thorough-going disciples of the *Politique,* the *Synthèse,* the *Catéchisme,* and the rest. A very few years before his death, Littré, in his "testament," expressed his attitude towards Christianity, in words from which it is evident that he had no hostility, nor even indifference, towards Christianity. He simply could not believe in it. It was an extreme inability, which his intellect could not overcome, as may be learned from his own words:

"Some pious souls have troubled themselves about my conscience. It has seemed to them that, not being an absolute contemner of Christianity, and heartily acknowledging that it possessed grandeur and conferred blessings, there were chords in my heart that it might touch. It was a beginning of faith, they thought, to entertain neither hostility nor contempt for a faith which has reigned for many centuries over men's consciences, and which even now is the consolation of so many faithful souls. As I never experienced nor expressed repulsion or uneasiness in finding myself the subject of the feelings that I have just sketched, and as age and illness warned me of my approaching end—as they have never abandoned the hope that I might experience the sovereign effect of divine grace, nor ceased to appeal from the mature man, too proud of his strength, to the old man, henceforth accessible to the promptings of his weakness—I reply to these solicitations, without wishing to wound their feelings, by saying that I neither share their faith nor experience any misery at being unable to believe. I have questioned myself in vain. It is impossible for me to accept the conception of the world which Catholicism imposes upon its true believers; but I feel no regret at being outside these creeds, and I can feel within me no desire to enter within their pale."

And yet he died, June 2, 1881, within the pale of the Catholic Church, having shortly before his death been baptized. Besides the works already mentioned, Littré also published, *Conservation, Révolution et Positivisme* (Paris, 1852):—*Auguste Comte et la Philosophie Positive* (ibid. 1863):—*Sémites en Compétition avec les Aryens pour l'Hégémonie du Monde* (Leipsic, 1880). Compare Caro, *Littré et le Positivisme* (Paris, 1883). (B. P.)

Lively, Edward, D.D., an English divine of the 16th century, was professor of Hebrew and divinity in the University of Cambridge, a learned Orientalist, and one of the translators of the Authorized Version of the Bible. He died in 1605. He published annotations on several of the *Minor Prophets* (1587):—and *Chronology of the Persian Monarchy* (1597). See McClure, *Translators Revived.*

Liverance, Galfrid, a Scotch prelate, was bishop of Dunkeld in 1236, 1239, 1247, and in 1249. He died at Tippermuir, Nov. 22 of the last-named year. See Keith, *Scottish Bishops*, p. 79.

Livese Version of the Scriptures. The Livese is a dialect spoken by a remnant of the Finnish people in the peninsula of north-west Courland, known by the name of Livs, inhabiting Livonia, a name given to the largest of the Baltic provinces of Russia. The Livs number about five thousand souls. The gospel of Matthew was transcribed for them into the Lettish character by the academician Widemann, at the expense of the British and Foreign Bible Society, and carried through the press in 1879. (B. P.)

Living, a term often used in England to denote a benefice (q. v.).

Living, an English prelate, is first met with as bishop of Wells, to which see he was consecrated in 999. In 1013 he was translated to the see of Canterbury. He continued for seven years, but in that time did very little more than to repair the roof of the cathedral. He did not receive the pallium. He died in 1020. See Hook, *Lives of the Archbishops of Canterbury*, i, 472 sq.

Living Buddha. See Buddha, Living.

Livingstone, David, LL.D., etc., an eminent African traveller and missionary, was born March 19, 1813, at Blantyre, in Lanarkshire, Scotland. At the age of ten he became a "piecer" in a cotton factory, and for many years was engaged in hard work as an operative. An evening-school furnished him with the opportunity of acquiring some knowledge of Greek and Latin, and finally, after attending a course of medicine at Glasgow University, and the theological lectures of the late Dr. Wardlaw, professor of theology to the Scotch Independents, he offered himself to the London Missionary Society, by whom he was ordained as a medical missionary in 1840. In the summer of that year he landed at Port Natal, in South Africa. Circumstances made him acquainted with the Rev. Robert Moffatt, himself a distinguished missionary, whose daughter he subsequently married. For sixteen years Livingstone proved himself a faithful and zealous servant of the London Missionary Society. The two most important results achieved by him in this period were the discovery of Lake Ngami (Aug. 1, 1849), and his crossing the continent of South Africa, from the Zambezi (or Leeambye) to the Congo, and thence to Loando, the capital of Angola, which took him about eighteen months (from January, 1853, to June, 1854). In September of the same year he left Loando on his return across the Continent, reached Linzanti (in lat. 18° 17′ south, and long. 23° 50′ east), the capital of the great Makololo tribe, and from thence proceeded along the banks of the Leeambye to Quilimane, on the Indian Ocean, which he reached May 20, 1856. He then took ship for England, where he arrived Dec. 12 of the same year. The reception accorded him by his countrymen was most enthusiastic. Probably no traveller was ever more affectionately honored. This was owing not merely to the importance of his discoveries, though it would be difficult to overestimate them, but to the thoroughly frank, ingenuous, simple, and manly character of the traveller. In 1857 Livingstone published his *Missionary Travels and Researches in South Africa*, a work of great interest and value. "In all his various journeys," said Sir Roderick Murchison, at a meeting of the Royal Geographical Society, held shortly after Livingstone's return, "he had travelled over no less than eleven thousand miles of African territory. . . . By his astronomical observations he had determined the sites of numerous places, hills, rivers, and lakes, nearly all of which had been hitherto unknown, while he had seized upon every opportunity of describing the physical features, climatology, and geological structure of the countries which he had explored, and had pointed out many new sources of commerce as yet unknown to the scope and the enterprise of the British merchant." In 1858 the British government appointed him consul at Quilimane, whither he returned in the course of the year; it also furnished him with a small steamer, that he might pursue his explorations of the Zambezi River and its tributaries. Livingstone started up this river in January, 1859, but after ascending it for over two hundred miles his farther progress was impeded by the magnificent cataracts of the Murchison. In March, following, he started for a second journey up the Shive, a branch of the Zambezi, and on the 18th of April discovered Lake Shirwa. Then followed the discovery of Lake Nyassa on Sept. 16. In 1864 he was ordered by the British government to abandon the expedition, and, returning to England, he published his second book of travels, entitled *A Narrative of an Expedition to the Zambezi and its Tributaries.* In August, 1865, Mr. Livingstone left England on his third journey to Africa; discovered Lake Liemba in April, 1867, south of Tanganyika, and going westward thence found Lake Maero on the 8th of September. But after eight years of lonely wandering in a previously unknown region, and after achieving discoveries which will permanently benefit mankind, the heroic traveller was overtaken by death. Having made repeated attempts to find the sources of the Nile, and being thwarted every time, in the last instance by severe illness, he requested his followers to take him to Zanzibar, as he was going home. After suffering intensely for several days, he died, May 1, 1873. His body was brought to England and interred in Westminster Abbey. See (Lond.) *Christian Observer*, Jan. 1875, p. 14; *Life*, by Blaikie (Lond. 1874); Waller, *Last Journals* (ibid. eod.).

Livingtoun, James, a Scotch prelate, was first rector of Forteviot and Weems, then dean of Dunkeld, and afterwards, in 1476, bishop of Dunkeld. He was constituted lord chancellor, Feb. 18, 1483, and died at

Edinburgh in the same year. See Keith, *Scottish Bishops*, p. 90.

Livinus, *Saint*, called the apostle of Brabant, was born in Ireland, it is said of noble parents, and received his education there. He was bishop of Dublin in 656. Being actuated by religious zeal, he intrusted his diocese in Ireland to the management of its archdeacon, and went to Ghent with three of his disciples, and, for a month, offered up mass at the tomb of St. Bavo every day, and afterwards went to Esca and preached the gospel, and converted numbers. He was murdered by some of the pagan inhabitants, Nov. 12, 656. See D'Alton, *Memoirs of the Archbishops of Dublin*, p. 16.

Livonian Version OF THE SCRIPTURES. See *Lettish* in the art. SLAVONIC VERSIONS.

Ljada, in Slavonic mythology, was a god of war among the Poles, to whom, before and after battle, human sacrifices were offered.

Llewelyn (or **Llywelyn**), THOMAS, LL.D., a Welsh dissenting minister, was born at Penalltan-isaf, Glamorganshire, about 1724, and having secured a liberal education, became the principal of an academical institution in London. He died in 1783. Although never the pastor of any church, he preached frequently, and was recognised as a minister of the gospel. He was a ripe scholar and a judicious writer. His works are, *Historical Account of the British or Welsh Versions and Editions of the Bible* (Lond. 1768, 8vo):—*Historical and Critical Remarks on the British Tongue*, etc. (1769, 8vo). See *The* (Lond.) *Theological and Biblical Magazine*, Nov. 1806, p. 467; Allibone, *Dict. of Brit. and Amer. Authors*, s. v.

Lloyd, HUMPHREY, D.D., etc., an eminent English divine and scientist, was born in Dublin in 1800. He entered Trinity College in 1815, was elected scholar in 1818, and graduated in 1820. In 1824 he was made fellow and tutor of Trinity College, and was soon ordained a minister of the United Church of England and Ireland. In 1831 he resigned the office of tutor, and was elected to the chair of natural philosophy, and afterwards gave his attention almost wholly to scientific investigations. He died Jan. 17, 1881. Dr. Lloyd was a fellow of the royal societies of London and Edinburgh, and honorary member of the philosophical societies of Cambridge and Manchester, and other scientific societies of Europe and America. In 1846 he was elected president of the Royal Irish Academy; in 1856 he received the degree of D.C.L. from the University of Oxford; and in 1857 was chosen president of the British Association. His works are chiefly scientific. See *Men of the Time*, s. v.

Loanz, ELIAS *ben-Moses* (surnamed *Baal Shem*), who died at Worms in 1636, rabbi, is the author of a cabalistic commentary on the Song of Solomon, entitled רנת דודים (Basle, 1599), and on Koheleth or Ecclesiastes, entitled מכלול יפי. See Fürst, *Bibl. Jud.* ii, 253; Etheridge, *Introduction to Hebrew Literature*, p. 360; Ginsburg, *Commentary on Koheleth*, p. 74. (B. P.)

Löber, CHRISTIAN, a Lutheran theologian of Germany, was born Feb. 2, 1683, at Orlamünde, in Thuringia. He studied at Jena, was in 1705 adjunct of the philosophical faculty, in 1711 superintendent at Ronneburg, in 1717 doctor of theology, in 1731 general superintendent at Altenburg, and died Dec. 26, 1747. He wrote, *Diss. Super* 2 *Tim. iii*, 16:—*De Statu Animarum Credentium Post Mortem*:—*An Judas Proditor Interfuerit Sacræ Cœnæ*: —*De Potestate Ligandi et Secandi ad Matt. xv*, 19; *xviii*, 16:—*De Natura Humana a Filio Dei Demum in Tempore Assumta*:—*De Origine Mali*, etc. See Moser, *Lexikon jetztlebender Gottesgelehrten*; Jöcher, *Allgemeines Gelehrten-Lexikon*, s. v. (B. P.)

Locālēs, a name anciently given to ecclesiastics who were ordained to a ministerial charge in some fixed place. At the Council of Valentia, in Spain, a decree was passed that no priest should be ordained unless he would give a promise that he would be a *localis*. Indeed, ordination at large was not considered valid.

Locherer, JOHANN NEPOMUK, a Roman Catholic theologian of Germany, was born at Freiburg, Aug. 21, 1773, and died at Giessen, Feb. 26, 1837, doctor and professor of theology. He wrote, *Geschichte der christlichen Religion und Kirche* (Ravensberg, 1824–34, 9 vols.):—*Lehrbuch der christlichen Archäologie* (Frankfort, 1832):—*Lehrbuch der Patrologie* (Mayence, 1837). See Winer, *Handbuch der theol. Lit.* i, 14, 543, 608, 854; Zuchold, *Bibl. Theol.* ii, 806. (B. P.)

Lockwood, SAMUEL, D.D., a Congregational minister, was born at Norwalk, Conn., Nov. 30, 1721. After graduating from Yale College in 1745, he studied theology under the direction of his brother, Rev. James Lockwood, of Wethersfield. A society having been formed in Andover, in 1747, embracing Coventry, Lebanon, and Hebron, he was called to preach, as a candidate, in the beginning of the following year. Of this parish he was ordained pastor, Feb. 25, 1749, O. S. He died in New Lebanon, N. Y., June 18, 1791. His manner in the pulpit was marked by gravity rather than vivacity; but he was very popular with his people. See Sprague, *Annals of the Amer. Pulpit*, i, 465.

Locŭlus, a name given to a place for a coffin among the ancient Romans.

Lo-debar, Tristram remarks (*Bible Places*, p. 329), "may be *Dibbin*, near Jerash, where I found a fine ancient fountain and other remains."

Lodrone, PARIS, a German prelate, was born about 1570 at the castle of Lodrone, in the Italian Tyrol. He was the youngest of a nobleman's family, and was destined for the ministry. In 1619 he became prince-archbishop of Salzburg. In the midst of the excitement of the Thirty Year's War, he determined to preserve in that country a complete neutrality, and assured to the adherents of both creeds equal protection, which certainly was a singular example at that time. In 1623 he founded the University of Salzburg, which occupied a very distinguished place among all the older ones. After that he commenced the reconstruction of the cathedral, and founded several establishments for the public benefit. Lodrone died at Salzburg in March, 1653. See Hoefer, *Nouv. Biog. Générale*, s. v.

Loebenstein, ALOIS, D.D., a Methodist Episcopal minister, came to America in 1852, and located at Femme Osage, Mo. He had studied theology at Vienna, and soon was employed as pastor in one of the Evangelical churches. The year succeeding he joined the Methodist Episcopal Church. He was appointed successively to Belleville, Ill.; Newport, Ky.; Buckeye Street, Cincinnati, O.; Indianapolis, Ind.; professor of theology at Wallace College, Berea, O., which position he held for eight years; Lafayette, Ind.; Toledo, O.; Walnut Street, Detroit, Mich.; Beaubien Street, East Saginaw. He died at the last appointment in 1881. He was a member of the Central German Conference. See *Minutes of Annual Conferences*, 1881, p. 312.

Loftus, ADAM, D.D., an Irish prelate, was born at Swinshead, in Yorkshire, and was educated at the University of Cambridge. In 1561 he was rector of Painstown, in the diocese of Meath. In 1562 he was appointed to the see of Armagh, and was consecrated by Hugh, archbishop of Dublin, at the close of that year. In 1564 he was elected dean of St. Patrick's. In August, 1567, he was promoted to the see of Dublin. In 1568 this prelate consecrated Dr. Lancaster as his own successor in Armagh, at Christ Church. In 1573 he was appointed chancellor. In 1582 Loftus was one of the lords justices of Ireland. In 1583 he was the unjust judge that illegally sentenced the Roman Catholic archbishop of Cashel, Dermot Hurley, to the cruelties of death on Osmantown Green. In 1597 Loftus was again one of the lords justices of Ireland, and also in

1599. At the close of that year he was named as one of the assistant councillors to the lord president of Munster, and in 1603 had pardon of intrusion and alienation in reference to the manors, etc. He died April 5, 1605. See D'Alton, *Memoirs of the Archbishops of Dublin*, p. 240.

Lohengrin, in British fable, was the famous guard and protector of the sacred Graal. He saved Elsa, the princess of Brabant, from a magician, by coming to her as a swan. She married the valiant knight, but on condition that she would not inquire as to his ancestry. Finally she asked about this, and Lohengrin fled on his swan back to the sacred Graal.

Lohmann, Bogislav Rudolf, a Lutheran minister of Germany, was born Dec. 28, 1825. He studied at Göttingen and Halle, was in 1853 pastor at Fürstenwalde, in 1865 at Springe, and died Dec. 15, 1879, at Görbersdorf, Hanover. He published, *Kurze Fragstücke zum kleinen Katechismus Luther's* (Berlin, 1858):—*Athanasius, der Vater der Rechtgläubigkeit* (2d ed. 1860):—*Lutherische und unirte Kirche* (1867). See Zuchold, *Bibl. Theol.* ii, 809. (B. P.)

Loll (or **Lull**), in German mythology, was a frightful god of the Franks, who had a sacred grove containing a brazen image in the region of Schweinfurt.

Lollards of Kyle. See Lollards.

Lommatzsch, Karl Heinrich Eduard, a Lutheran theologian of Germany, was born Sept. 22, 1802, at Grosschönau, near Zittau. He commenced his academical career at Berlin in 1829, was in 1832 professor at the theological seminary in Wittenberg, and died Aug. 19, 1882, doctor of theology. Lommatzsch is especially known as the editor of De la Rue's edition of *Origenis Opera Omnia* (Berlin, 1831-48, 25 vols.). (B. P.)

Long, Clement, D.D., LL.D., a Congregational minister, was born in New Hampshire in 1807. He graduated from Dartmouth College in 1828, studied theology for two years in Andover Theological Seminary as a member of the class of 1834, and was ordained. He was a tutor in Western Reserve College, and became professor of intellectual and moral philosophy in that institution in 1834; professor of theology in 1844; professor of theology in the theological seminary at Auburn, N. Y., in 1852; professor of intellectual philosophy and political economy in Dartmouth College in 1854. He died at Hanover, N. H., Oct. 14, 1861. See *Trien. Cat. of Andover Theol. Sem.* 1870, p. 112.

Longstreet, Augustus Baldwin, LL.D., a Methodist minister, was born at Augusta, Ga., Sept. 22, 1790. He studied in the Litchfield (Conn.) Law School, and settled in his native state. In 1823 he represented Greene County in the state legislature, and the following year was made judge of the Superior Court of the state. During the Nullification excitement he established the *Augusta Sentinel*. In 1838 he entered the ministry, and from 1839 to 1848 was president of Emory College, in Oxford. He was then for a short time president of Centenary College, Jackson, La., and from 1849 to 1856 president of the University of Mississippi. Still later he was president of South Carolina College. He died Sept. 9, 1870. He was a frequent contributor to Southern periodicals, and published many separate works, among the best known of which is his humorous collection of *Georgia Scenes*. See *Obituary Record of Yale College*, 1872.

Longueil, Richard Oliver de, a French prelate, was born about 1410, of an illustrious family of Normandy. He was archdeacon of Eu, and became, in 1453, bishop of Coutances. Having been designated among other commissaries, by the pope, in 1455, to revise the proceeding in the case of Joan d'Arc, he exhibited great zeal in rehabilitating the memory of that female hero. King Charles VII sent him as ambassador to the duke of Burgundy, and placed him at the head of his council. He also obtained for Longueil from the pope, Calixtus III, the cardinal's hat, in 1456. In his devotion to the Church that prelate ventured to oppose in the parliament the Pragmatic Sanction, for which he was fined not less than 10,000 livres. Pius II gave him the bishoprics of Oporto and of St. Ruffina, also the legateship of Umbria, and made him archpriest of the basilica of St. Peter. He died at La Pérouse. Aug. 15, 1470. See Hoefer, *Nouv. Biog. Générale*, s. v.

Lonsano, Menachem di, a Jewish writer of the 17th century, is the author of אור תורה, or critical work on the text of the Pentateuch (Amsterdam, 1659 and often). He compared ten MSS., chiefly Spanish ones, with the text of Bomberg's quarto Bible, published in 1544, some of them being five or six hundred years old. See Fürst, *Bibl. Jud.* ii, 255 sq.; De' Rossi, *Dizionario Storico* (Germ. transl.), p. 184 sq. (B. P.)

Loochooan Version of the Scriptures. See Tukudh Version.

Loomis, Harmon, D.D., a Congregational minister, was born at Georgia, Vt., Oct. 26, 1805. He received his preparatory education at St. Albans' Academy, and at a high-school in his native place; graduated from the University of Vermont in 1832, and in the same year entered Andover Theological Seminary, where he spent two years. He was licensed to preach by the North-western Congregational Association of Vermont, Oct. 10, 1834. In 1835 he entered Princeton Seminary, but left in January, 1836, and became stated supply of the Union Presbyterian Church, New York city. He was ordained by a Congregational Council at Vergennes, Vt., Aug. 31, 1836. Soon after he accepted the position of chaplain for the American Seaman's Friend Society of New York, and began preaching to seamen in New Orleans, Jan. 8, 1837. This he did four years, spending his summers in the North and raising funds for the society. From 1841 to 1845 he preached as stated supply to the Presbyterian Church at Mount Joy, Pa. In the last-named year he entered upon the duties of corresponding secretary of the American Seaman's Friend Society, in New York, and continued in that office till 1871. He died in Brooklyn, Jan. 19, 1880. Dr. Loomis published a number of volumes and pamphlets, and did much to promote the temperance cause. He was a man of sincere and earnest piety. See *Necrol. Report of Princeton Theol. Sem.* 1880, p. 25.

Lorck, Josiah, a Lutheran theologian of Copenhagen, was born Jan. 3, 1723, at Flensburg, and died Feb. 8, 1785. He published, *Die Bibelgeschichte in einigen Beiträgen erläutert* (Copenhagen, 1779):—*Beiträge zu der neuesten Kirchengeschichte in den königlichen dänischen Reichen* (1757-62, 2 vols.). See Winer, *Handbuch der theol. Lit.* i, 69, 832. (B. P.)

Lord, Jeremiah Skidmore, D.D., a Reformed Dutch minister, was born at Jamaica, N. Y., May 10, 1812. He graduated from the University of the City of New York in 1836, and from the Union Theological Seminary in 1839; was ordained Aug. 20 of the same year, becoming pastor at Montville, N. J.; went to Grigstown in 1843, to Harlem, New York city, in 1848, and died there, April 2, 1869. See *Gen. Cat. of Union Theol. Sem.* 1876, p. 14; Corwin, *Manual of the Ref. Church in America*, p. 356.

Lord, John Chase, D.D., a Presbyterian minister, was born at Washington, N. H., Aug. 9, 1805. He studied at Plainfield Academy, and Madison and Hamilton colleges, from the last of which he graduated in 1825. After two years' editorial experience in Canada he went to Buffalo, N. Y., began the study of law, and was admitted to the bar in 1828. He united with the First Presbyterian Church of Buffalo in 1830, and soon after entered Auburn Theological Seminary, from which he graduated in 1833, and was called to the Church at Geneseo, where a wonderful revival occurred. In 1835 he became pastor of the Central Church at Buffalo, and remained until he gave up effective work in the ministry in 1873. He died there, Jan. 21, 1877. Dr. Lord was the author of, *Lectures to Young Men* (1838):—*Lectures on Civilization* (1851), besides sermons and pamphlets. See (N. Y.) *Evangelist*, April 26, 1877; *Gen. Cat. of Auburn Theol. Sem.* 1883, p. 263; Nevin, *Presb. Encyclop.* s. v. (W. P. S.)

Lord, William Hayes, D.D., a Congregational minister, son of president Nathan Lord, was born in Amherst, N. H., March 11, 1824. He graduated from Dartmouth College in 1843, and three years after from Andover Theological Seminary; was ordained pastor at Montpelier, Vt., Sept. 20, 1847, and died there, March 18, 1877. He was a trustee of the Washington County Grammar School from 1853, and president from 1865. From 1847 to 1875 he was director of the Vermont Bible Society, and held the same relation to the Domestic Missionary Society from 1853 to 1877. After 1870 he was president of the Vermont Historical Society, of which he had been for some time previously a member. In 1876 he was appointed fish commissioner of Vermont. He was moderator of the General Convention of Vermont in 1861; was corporate member of the American Board of Commissioners for Foreign Missions from 1873; and the following year became editor of the *Vermont Chronicle*. See *Cong. Quarterly*, 1878, p. 446.

Lore, Dallas Dayton, D.D., a Methodist Episcopal minister, was born at Mauricetown, N. J., in 1815. He was converted at the age of fifteen, and at twenty-one entered the Philadelphia Conference, soon receiving the most important charges. In 1847 Mr. Lore sailed for South America as a missionary, and for seven years was the pastor of a large and intelligent congregation in Buenos Ayres, proving himself eminently successful both among the foreign and native population. Upon his return he was sent on a tour of exploration to New Mexico to inspect the condition of the mission field. In 1856 he was transferred to the Newark Conference, and after serving several prominent charges within its bounds, received a transfer to the Genesee Conference, and was appointed to Grace Church, Buffalo. In 1864 he was elected editor of the *Northern Christian Advocate*, in which office he continued till his death, at his residence near Auburn, Jan. 20, 1875. As a theologian, Dr. Lore was diligent and comprehensive in his researches, and careful in his conclusions. As a preacher he was earnest, direct, and practical. As an editor he achieved success by his strong and forcible style, by the boldness and wisdom of his conclusions, and by his devotion to the truth. His zeal in the cause of Christian missions was truly marvellous, and highly exemplary. See *Minutes of Annual Conferences*, 1875, p. 119; Simpson, *Cyclop. of Methodism*, s. v.

Loretz, Andrew, one of the early pioneer ministers of the German Reformed Church in America, a Swiss by birth, was educated in Europe, and emigrated to America towards the close of the last century. "About the year 1789 he commenced preaching and ministering in a wide field, embracing a large part of both the Carolinas, from Orange County, in North Carolina, to beyond the river Saluda, in South Carolina, a distance of two hundred and fifty miles." He died in 1812. Mr. Loretz was a man of superior natural ability, extensive learning, great zeal and energy, and, in his day, "regarded as one of the best pulpit orators in the Carolinas." See Harbaugh, *Fathers of the Germ. Ref. Church*, iii, 15. (D. Y. H.)

Lorimer, Peter, D.D., an eminent English Presbyterian divine, was born in Edinburgh, Scotland, in 1812. He graduated from the university there, was ordained in 1836, and installed pastor of the River Terrace Church, London, which was then in connection with the Church of Scotland. He was at one with those who, in 1843, formed the Free Church of Scotland, and along with his congregation became a constituent part of the Synod of Berwick in 1844, which, until recently, was known as the Synod of the Presbyterian Church of England. From that time forward the first desire of his life was the advancement of that Church to a position worthy of its name. He was connected with the London Theological College from the date of its establishment in 1845, when he was elected to the chair of Hebrew and Biblical criticism. He was made the first principal in 1878, and died suddenly, July 28, 1879. He was the author of several valuable works, among them, *The Life of Patrick Hamilton*:—*The Life of the Scottish Reformer, John Knox*:—and *A History of the Presbyterian Church of England*, a work on which he had spent years of diligent research, but which he was only able to complete in part.

Loriquet, Jean Nicolas, a French Jesuit, famous on account of his historical falsifications, was born Aug. 5, 1760, at Epernay, Champagne. He was professor at the Seminary of Argentière, which was closed by Napoleon in 1807. The events of 1814 made the Jesuits come forward in great numbers, and their colleges were multiplied. Loriquet was intrusted with the direction of the schools at Aix, Provence, and St. Acheul, Picardy, and the pupils who were under his charge were imbued with that spirit which has been detrimental to modern society. In 1830 the people of St. Acheul destroyed the school there, and the reverend fathers had to quit the place. Loriquet went to Switzerland, where he worked in behalf of his order. Under Louis Philippe he returned to France, and died at Paris, April 9, 1845. Loriquet was a prolific writer. For a list of his works, see Lichtenberger, *Encyclop. des Sciences Religieuses*, s. v. (B. P.)

Lorraine (or **Gelée**), Claude, an illustrious French painter, was born in a small town of Champagne, in the diocese of Toul, Lorraine, in 1600, and went to Rome early for instruction, where he made great improvement in his studies, but met with many reverses, and often was almost penniless. Godfrey Waal admitted him into his academy, where he remained probably two years. Agostino Tassi became interested in Claude, took him into the bosom of his family, and made him his familiar companion. Claude, naturally of a religious disposition, feeling profound gratitude for the many benefits he had received, soon after leaving Tassi and quitting Rome, about 1625, performed a pilgrimage to the holy Virgin of Loretto, where he remained some days in devotional meditation. From thence he made a tour through Italy, traversing Romagna, Lombardy, and on to Venice, where he practiced his profession for some time. In 1627 he returned to Rome, and soon found abundant employment. One of his earliest patrons was cardinal Bentivoglio, for whom he painted two pictures which established his reputation. About this time he was employed by cardinal Crescenzi to decorate the rotunda of his palace; he was also similarly engaged in the Muti of the Holy Apostles, and of the Medici alla Trinita de' Monti. These were succeeded by commissions from the duke of Bracciano, the duke de Bouillon, and the prince de Leaucour, for each a picture. The fame of Claude now extended to every part of Europe, and he received commissions from the most distinguished persons. His works were not confined to Rome, Milan, Parma, Lombardy, and Venice, but extended also to Paris, Lyons, Montpellier, Avignon, Antwerp, Amsterdam, and Madrid. He died Nov. 21, 1682. See Spooner, *Biog. Hist. of the Fine Arts*, s. v.

Losing, Herbert, an English prelate, was born probably at Hoxon, Suffolk, his father being an abbot, wives in that age not not being absolutely forbidden the clergy, though his father might have become abbot in his old age. Herbert bought a better preferment for himself, however, giving £1900 to king William Rufus for the bishopric of Thetford. Simony was a fashionable sin at that time. He afterwards went to Rome, returned to England, removed his bishopric from Thetford to Norwich, built the fine cathedral there and five beautiful parish churches, and died July 22, 1119. See Fuller, *Worthies of England* (Nuttall), iii, 13, 166.

Lotto, LORENZO, an eminent Italian painter, was probably born at Bergamo in 1490, and apparently studied at Venice under Giovanni Bellini. His principal works are in the churches at Bergamo, Venice, and Recanati. His picture of the *Virgin and Infant* is considered one of his best performances. In the Church of Santo Spirito is another exquisite picture of the *Virgin and Infant, with St. John Standing at the Foot of the Throne, Embracing a Lamb.* Other masterpieces are to be seen at Bergamo in the churches and private collections, and place him almost upon a level with the first luminaries of art. He died in 1560. See Spooner, *Biog. Hist. of the Fine Arts*, s. v.; Hoefer, *Nouv. Biog. Générale*, s. v.

Lotze, HERMANN RUDOLF, a philosopher of Germany, was born May 21, 1817, at Bautzen, Saxony. He studied medicine and philosophy with such success that, five years after his entrance to Leipsic University, he was able to qualify as a teacher in both faculties. In 1844 he was called to Göttingen as professor of philosophy. Before going there, however, he had published his metaphysics in 1844, and his logic in 1843. In 1881 he was called to Berlin, and died the same year. Lotze was a determined opponent of materialism in philosophy. "It is the glory of Hermann Lotze," says Joseph Cook, "to have broadened, by exact and not mystical methods, the philosophical outlook upon human nature, to have taken the emotions in all their ranges into view, as well as the intellectual faculties; and thus, gradually, through the strictest methods of modern research, to have risen to a philosophy of the soul and of the whole composite nature of man, in harmony with the truths of all the sciences—mental, moral, æsthetic, and physical." Others, however, see in the philosophical system of Lotze a decided tendency to that insidious form of idealistic pantheism which comes near to denying the objectivity of matter, or at least to resolving all phenomena into pure deity. See SCEPTICISM, RECENT PHASES OF. Lotze published, *Metaphysik* (Leipsic, 1841):—*Allgemeine Pathologie und Therapie als mechanische Naturwissenschaften* (1842; 2d ed. 1848):—*System der Philosophie* (2 vols.; vol. i, *Logik*, 1843; new ed. 1874; vol. ii, *Metaphysik*, 1878; 2d ed. 1884; Engl. transl. edited by B. Bosanquet, Oxford, 1883, 2 vols.):—*Ueber den Begriff der Schönheit* (Göttingen, 1845):—*Geschichte der Aesthetik in Deutschland* (Munich, 1868):—*Allgemeine Physiologie des körperlichen Lebens* (Leipsic, 1851):—*Medizinische Psychologie* (1852):—*Mikrokosmus* (1856-64, 3 vols.; 4th ed. 1884):—*Grundzüge der Psychologie* (1881). See Caspari, *Hermann Lotze, eine kritisch-historische Studie* (Breslau, 1883); Pfleiderer, *Lotze's philosophische Weltanschauung* (Berlin, 1882; 2d ed. 1884); Cook, *Spiritual Religion in Lotze's Philosophy* (Boston Monday morning's lecture, published in the [N. Y.] *Independent*, March 20, 1884); Gardiner, *Lotze's Theistic Philosophy* (*Presb. Review*, October, 1885). (B. P.)

Louis, *Saint*, bishop of Toulouse, was born in February, 1274, at the castle of Brignoles, in Provence. He was the second son of Charles II, the hunchbacked king of Naples, and of Mary, the daughter of Stephen V, king of Hungary; was educated by the disciples of St. Francis, took the habit of their order, and was ordained priest in 1296 at Naples, notwithstanding the solicitations of his family, who wished to have him married to the sister of the king of Aragon. From his fourteenth to his twentieth year he served as hostage to his father, and was imprisoned at Barcelona, where he was treated very cruelly. Pope Boniface VIII appointed him to the see of Toulouse, Dec. 27, 1295, although he was not yet of the required age, and charged him with administering the diocese of Parniers. Louis divided his time between the study, works of piety, and the pastoral duties, also making great efforts to destroy the Albigenses. In 1297 he went to Paris with his father. "A princess," says one of his biographers, "sought to test his virtue; in fact, she omitted nothing to seduce him, but the holy prelate disregarded her caresses and her threatenings." He went away from the court as soon as possible, and was invited to visit Aragon and Catalonia. He resolved, however, to go to Rome, in order to surrender into the hands of the pope the burden of the episcopacy; but on arriving at Brignoles he was attacked with fever, and died Aug. 19, 1297. His body was at first taken to Marseilles, and afterwards to Aragon. Pope John XXII, who had been the preceptor of Louis, canonized him, April 7, 1317. See Hoefer, *Nouv. Biog. Générale*, s. v.

Loundres, HENRY DE, an Irish prelate, previously archdeacon of Stafford, succeeded to the see of Dublin in 1213. In July of the same year he was appointed lord-justice of Ireland, where he continued until 1215. He was present, June 15 of that year, in England, when the king executed the Magna Charta at Runnymede. In 1216 king John conferred upon archbishop de Loundres and his successors the manor of Timothan, to which, in 1217 and 1225, various other grants were annexed. During the time this prelate presided over the see of Dublin, he erected the collegiate Church of St. Patrick into a cathedral. He constituted William Fitz-Guy the first dean, and appointed a precentor, chancellor, and treasurer, to whom he allotted lands and rectories. He died in July, 1228. See D'Alton, *Memoirs of the Archbishops of Dublin*, p. 79.

Lounsbury, THOMAS, D.D., a Presbyterian minister, was born at Florida, N. Y., Oct. 4, 1789. He graduated with the highest honors from Union College in 1817; studied theology for more than a year at Princeton, N. J.; then became missionary in Sullivan County, N. Y., from 1821 to 1823; was ordained by the presbytery of Geneva, Sept. 4 of the latter year; preached at Ovid from 1823 to 1849; was afterwards stated supply at Homer, Hector, and Romulus; then went again to Ovid, where he died, Oct. 29, 1867. See Wilson, *Presb. Hist. Almanac*, 1868, p. 217; *Gen. Cat. of Princeton Theol. Sem.* 1881, p. 27.

Loup (Lat. *Lupus*), *Saint*, a French prelate, was born in the neighborhood of Bayeux. There is a legend, according to which St. Ruffinian, bishop of Bayeux, educated the young Loup, who soon became the most learned and most distinguished among all the clerks at Bayeux. Thus, at the death of Ruffinian, he was elected by the whole people his successor, and consecrated by Sylvester, archbishop of Rouen. Saint Loup died about the year 465. To him has often been attributed the *Life of St. Raimbert*, bishop of Bayeux. See Hoefer, *Nouv. Biog. Générale*, s. v.

Loup, *Saint*, bishop OF LYONS, Sept. 25, 542. He began as a monk in the monastery of the Isle of Sainte-Barbe, on the Saône, near Lyons. He became the superior of it, and Saint Virentiol, in the see of Lyons, in 523. He presided at the third council of Orleans, May 7, 538, at which there were passed thirty-three canons to restore discipline in the Church of France. He died Sept. 25, 542, and is said to have been buried in the hermitage of the Isle of Sainte-Barbe. See Hoefer, *Nouv. Biog. Générale*, s. v.

Loup, *Saint*, OF TROYES. See LUPUS.

Low, DAVID, an Anglican bishop, was born in the neighborhood of Brechin, Scotland, in 1768. He received his education at the University of Aberdeen, then studied with bishop Gleig at Stirling, and was settled in charge of the congregation at Pittenweem in 1790, where for more than half a century he fulfilled the duties of the pastoral office without intermission. Dr. Low was consecrated bishop of the united diocese of Argyle, Ross, and Moray, in 1819. Some years subsequently he effected a separation between the diocese of Ross and Moray and that of Argyle, retaining the superintendence of the former. He resigned the see in 1850, and died at Pettenween, Jan. 26, 1855. He was especially intimate with Scottish traditions and historical lore, and was a captivating conversationalist. See *Amer. Quar. Church Rev.* 1855, p. 315.

Löw, Leopold, a Jewish rabbi, was born in 1811 in Moravia. He studied at Prague, and was in 1843 chief rabbi of Great Kanizca, Hungary. He took an active part in the revolution of 1848, and after its suppression was imprisoned and condemned to death. He was, however, pardoned, and in 1851 became chief rabbi at Szegedin, where he died, Oct. 13, 1875. Löw was a voluminous writer, his essays having been published in four volumes, under the title *Gesammelte Schriften* (Szegedin, 1876). Still valuable are his *Beiträge zur jüdischen Alterthumskunde* (Leipsic, 1870):—*Allgemeine Einleitung und Geschichte der Schriftauslegung* (Great Kanizca, 1855). See Fürst, *Bibl. Jud.* ii, 266. (B. P.)

Lowder, Charles Fuge, an Anglican clergyman, of some fame in the history of city missions and of English ritualism, was born at Bath, June 22, 1821, and graduated at King's College School, London, and Exeter College, Oxford. He served his apprenticeship to London church-work under Skinner, at St. Barnabas, Pimlico, from 1851 to 1856. It was a time of vehement anti-Catholic agitation. The ritualism of Skinner and Lowder consisted in (1) Procession of clergy and choristers from and to the vestry; (2) Obeisance towards the altar on entering and retiring from the sanctuary; (3) The eastward position; (4) Colored coverings varied for the season on the altar. Bishop Blomfield allowed some of these, but disapproved of others. These troubles dragged on until the Lushington judgment disheartened the High-Church party, and the first decision of the privy council in December, 1855, was welcomed as a deliverance by hearts which could not foresee the very different treatment which the Rubric on ornaments was to receive from that same body in the Ridsdale judgment. Yet, at the beginning, the ritualism of St. Barnabas "roused such a storm and provoked such outrage that towards the end of 1850 the religious people of the district were so horrified by the blasphemous cries of the mob that they were fain to keep within their houses." In 1856 and 1857 Lowder took charge of mission congregations at Ratcliff Highway and Wellclose Square, where, amid many physical discomforts, and among the rough population of that wild East London district, he left "the record of a very noble life, full of unconscious greatness, to which the term heroic would not be misapplied." He was not a man of brilliant abilities or social attractiveness, by no means eloquent as a preacher, not always a good judge of character, his asceticism impaired his health and his working force, yet one could speak of his calm, unexcited courage, his splendid patience, his unsparing laboriousness, his habitual, far-reaching charity, his burning love of souls, his intense loyalty to Christ as a personal Saviour. In 1858 Lowder welcomed a coadjutor, Alexander Heriot Mackonochie, since so conspicuous in the English Church. In 1859 six clergy were laboring in the parish, with a large staff of lay assistants, fifty-four services were held weekly, and six hundred children were under instruction in the six schools which had been set on foot. This outburst of missionary energy, with services so ritualistic, excited opposition. In September, 1859, Lowder came near being murdered by a mob lashed into fury, and in the beginning of 1860 "the whole service was interrupted by hissing, whistling, and shouting; songs were roared out during the service and lesson; cushions and books were hurled at the altar . . . the clergy were spat upon, hustled, and kicked within the church, and only protected from greater outrages by sixty or eighty gentlemen who, unasked, came to the rescue." The mob gutted St. George's Church of everything savoring of the Roman service, and the bishop (Tait) for the most part gave way to the rioters. After the storm had passed, the patience and Christian spirit of Lowder and his associates began to make itself felt upon the rough zealots. Some of them became choristers in other churches, or assisted priests in mission work. New agencies for good sprang up, one of which was the Working Men's Institute. The Church of St. Peter's, London Docks, was consecrated June 31, 1866, Lowder being its first vicar. Then came the visitation of cholera, which conquered the people and bowed their hearts once for all to the pastor who gave himself up with such absolute devotedness to the work of helping them. Lowder did not set up a system in place of a Person, or his own office as the substitute for an absent, instead of the witness for a present, Lord. The root-idea of confession was the heinousness of sin and the promise of pardon through the blood of Christ, and confession and absolution were freely offered to all those who needed it. He had rituals, because he thought it his duty to put before the eyes of the people the image of the worship of heaven, and the outward appointments of the Church gave an air of comfort and dignity—a lesson for the people to take back to their squalid homes. As the result, not only was open sin swept away from the streets of St. Peter's, where before streets were peopled by houses of ill-fame, but five hundred communicants of St. Peter's were lifted above the suffering life into joy and peace. Lowder's health, undermined for a long time, broke down in 1874 or 1875. In August, 1880, he went abroad, never to return. In the Tyrol, at Zell-am-See, at the age of sixty, among strangers, Sept. 9, 1880, this great and heroic spirit passed away. See *Charles Lowder*, a biography, by the author of the *Life of St. Teresa* (2d ed. Lond. 1882; N. Y. eod.); *Church of England Quar. Rev.* April, 1882, p. 57 sq.; *Twenty-one Years in St. George's Mission*, by Rev. C. F. Lowder, M.A. (Lond. 8vo).

Löwenthal, Isidor, a famous missionary and translator of the Bible, was a native of Poland, and of Jewish parentage. At the age of twenty he had to flee his country, being suspected by the government of conspiracy. He came to America, and at Princeton, N. J., went about as a pedler, hawking jewelry and stationery. In or near Princeton, living a life of retired though literary habits, was a much-respected clergyman, who had more than one conversation with the eloquent pedler. Perceiving in him talent of no common order, he offered to assist him in the prosecution of his studies. An appeal to some princely merchants of New York speedily procured the funds necessary to send the young man to Princeton College. At this time he was a bigoted Jew, but his course of studies, his intercourse with tutors, brought about his conversion, and he received baptism. Having completed his studies, he offered himself as a missionary to the American Presbyterian Board. To India he directed his steps, and fancying from what he had read that among the Afghans might be found traces of the lost tribes, he proposed that he should be sent to Peshawur, as a missionary to the Afghans. There, in 1856, he commenced his work. With rare ability and perseverance, he had so perfected himself in the difficult language of the Afghans as to prepare a translation of the entire New Test.; and although the execution of the work devolved wholly upon himself, it was marked by close adherence to the original texts, and by an idiomatic power of expression which earned the warmest commendation of the Pushtû linguists who were capable of pronouncing a critical opinion on the result of his labors. The question of translating the Old Test. had been discussed, and as the importance of giving the Afghans a complete Bible was deeply felt, Mr. Löwenthal had expressed his willingness to undertake this great and responsible task. But the Divine Master had otherwise appointed, and before he had fairly entered upon the duty, he was assassinated, April 27, 1864. See PUSHTÛ VERSION. (B. P.)

Lubersac, JEAN BAPTISTE JOSEPH DE, a French prelate, was born at Limoges, Jan. 15, 1740. He became first grand-vicar of the archbishop of Arles, in 1768 almoner of the king, and in 1775 bishop of Tréguier. In 1780 he was transferred to Chartres. Having been sent by the clergy to the States-General, he refused to recognise the constitution of the clergy, and March 15, 1791, was forced to emigrate. In 1801 he resigned his bishopric. After his return to France he was appointed canon of the chapter of St. Denis. He died Aug. 30, 1822, leaving, *Journal de l'Émigration du Clergé de France en Angleterre* (Lond. 1802):—*Apologie de la Religion et de la Monarchie Reunies* (ibid. eod.). See Hoefer, *Nouv. Biog. Générale*, s. v.

Luca, ANTONIO DE, cardinal-bishop of Palestrina and vice-chancellor of the Church of Rome, was born Oct. 28, 1805, at Bronte, Sicily. In 1863 he was made cardinal, and died Dec. 29, 1883. He was one of the most prominent members of the college of cardinals, chief of the apostolic chancery, and, with the cardinals Pitra and Hergenröther, had charge of the archives and the Vatican library. (B. P.)

Lucarinos, REGINALDO, an Italian Dominican, who died Oct. 10, 1671, is the author of, *Episcopus Regularis:—Manuale Controversiarum Thomisticarum:—Hermes Biblicus:—Bibliotheca Scriptorum Ordinis Prædicantium*. See Echard, *De Scriptoribus Ordinis Dominicanorum;* Ughelli, *Italia Sacra;* Jöcher, *Allgemeines Gelehrten-Lexikon*, s. v. (B. P.)

Lucatelli (or **Locatelli**), PIETRO, a distinguished Roman painter, was born in 1660, and studied under Ciro Ferri. He was elected a member of the Academy of St. Luke in 1690, and executed some works for the public edifices at Rome. His paintings in the Church of San Agostino, and in the Collegio Fuccioli, are highly commended. He died in 1741. See Spooner, *Biog. Hist. of the Fine Arts*, s. v.

Lucchi, MICHÆL ANGELO, an Italian prelate, was born at Brescia, Aug. 20, 1744. He made his profession at Monte Cassino, where he was appointed to teach philosophy and theology. He visited the principal libraries of Italy, and collected a number of ancient MSS., now in the Vatican. Pius VII called him to Rome, made him cardinal, Feb. 23, 1801, and intrusted him with the censorship of books. He died at Subiaco, Sept. 29, 1802, leaving several works on the Greek and Latin classics. See Hoefer, *Nouv. Biog. Générale*, s. v.

Lucena, LORENZO, a Spanish Roman Catholic theologian, was born in 1807. He was ordained deacon by the bishop of Cordova in 1830, and priest in 1831 by the suffragan bishop of Seville. For eight years he acted as professor of theology at the College of St. Pelagius, in the University of Seville, and for three years held the office of provisional president there. In 1842 he was appointed honorary canon of Gibraltar Cathedral, and reader in the Spanish language and literature in the Taylorian Institution at Oxford, in 1861. He assisted in preparing the new edition of the Spanish Bible, generally known as that of Cipriano de Valera, and published by the British and Foreign Bible Society. He died at Oxford, Aug. 24, 1881. (B. P.)

Luchan, in Mongolian mythology, is a mighty dragon, inhabiting the great sea, constantly growing, and destined finally to devour the universe.

Lucius, *Saint*, of Britain, lived in the 2d century. Bede, in his *Ecclesiastical History*, says that in 154, under the Roman emperors, Marcus Aurelius and Verus, and during the pontificate of Eleutherus, a British king Lucius wrote to the pope, announcing that he wished to become a Christian. Eleutherus favorably received the communication, and sent priests to instruct the Britons in the Christian faith. A similar account may be found in a number of other traditions. See Smith, *Dict. of Christ. Biog.* s. v.

Lucius, Johann Gottlieb, a Lutheran theologian of Germany, was born Sept. 3, 1665, at Dresden. He studied at Leipsic, was in 1687 bachelor of theology, in 1698 licentiate, in 1708 doctor, and in 1712 superintendent at Pirna. Lucius died April 27, 1722. He wrote, *De Lege Æterna:—Vindiciæ Dissertationis Carpzovianæ de Descensu Christi ad Inferos:—De Æternitate Dei:—De Convivificatione Fidelium cum Christo ex Hos. vi*, 2:—*De Cohabitatione et Conglorificatione Fidelium cum Christo ex Joh. xvii*, 24. See Jöcher, *Allgemeines Gelehrten-Lexikon*, s. v. (B. P.)

Lucius, Ludovicus, a German Protestant theologian, was born at Basle, Feb. 9, 1577. For some time professor of Hebrew, in the place of Buxtorf, he was called as deacon and rector to Baden, and died June 10, 1642. He wrote, *Historia Jesuitica:—Notæ in Apocalypsin Johannis:—Dissertatio Amica cum Joa. Piscatore de Causa Meritoria Justificationis Nostræ Coram Deo:—Anti-Christi Occidentalis in Hungaria Persecutio:—Synopsis Anti-Sociniana:—De Fide et Moribus Christianorum:—Dictionarium Novi Testamenti:—Compendium Theologiæ:—Semi-Pelagianismus Remonstrantium:—Historia Augustini ex Operibus Ejus Collecta*. See Winer, *Handbuch der theol. Lit.* i, 531; Jöcher, *Allgemeines Gelehrten-Lexikon*, s. v. (B. P.)

Ludger, *Saint*, a German prelate, was born in Friesland. In his early youth he studied under the discipline of St. Gregory, who governed the school as well as the Church of Utrecht. In 802 he is noticed at Rome, and next at Monte Cassino, where he stayed two years; finally returning to the barbarians, he preached the gospel to the Saxons and the Frieslanders, where, about the same period, he became chief of the Church of Münster. He died March 26, 809, leaving a single work, *The Life of St. Gregory, Abbot of Utrecht* (published in the *Acta Sanctorum*). See Hoefer, *Nouv. Biog. Générale*, s. v.

Ludi Funēbres (*funeral games*) were celebrated at the funeral pyre of distinguished persons among the ancient Greeks and Romans. They were private entertainments, given by survivors in honor of their deceased friends, and were sometimes continued for two or three days.

Ludi Martiāles (*martial games*) were celebrated every year among the ancient Romans in the circus, Aug. 1, in honor of Mars.

Ludki (Polish **Ludschi**) were conceived by the Wends to be earth-spirits. At night they have feasts; they come into houses by way of subterranean passages, do not allow themselves to be disturbed, and avenge every provocation by a knavish trick. German superstitions also admit of such ghost-like beings.

Ludlow, GABRIEL, D.D., a Reformed (Dutch) minister, was born at Acquackanonck, N. J., April 23, 1797. He graduated from Union College in 1817, from New Brunswick Theological Seminary in 1820, and was licensed by the Classis of New Brunswick probably the same year. He was stated supply at Albany for six months thereafter, and at Neshanic, Somerset Co., N. J., from 1821 until his death, Feb. 19, 1878. He was genial and sympathetic, strong in thought, as well as independent. He published several sermons. See Corwin, *Manual of the Ref. Church in America*, 3d ed. p. 358.

Ludovici, CHRISTIAN, a Lutheran theologian of Germany, was born at Landshut, Silesia, in 1663. He studied at Breslau and Leipsic, commenced his academical career in 1687, was professor of Oriental languages in 1699, doctor of theology in 1724, and died at Leipsic, Jan. 15, 1732. He wrote, *Isagoge in Accentuationem Hebraicam:—Hebraismus, Chaldaismus, Targumico-Talmudico-Rabbinicus et Syriasmus ad Harmoniam et Compendium Redacti:—Diss. V in Rabbi Levi ben Gerson Commentarium Rabbinicum in Hiobum:—Schediasma* *de Autoribus, qui de Scriptoribus Ecclesiasticis Egerunt:* —*Historia Concili Nicæni.* See Winer, *Handbuch der theol. Lit.* i, 531, 663; Jöcher, *Allgemeines Gelehrten-Lexikon*, s. v.; *Fürst*, *Bibl. Jud.* s. v. Ludowig, ii, 274. (B. P.)

Ludwig, Edmund A., a German Reformed minister, was born in Switzerland. He received a liberal education, and obtained the degree of doctor of philosophy from a European university. After coming to America he became professor of languages in Washington College, Lexington, Va. Subsequently he went North, engaging as editor and teacher for some years. In 1868 he was licensed to preach, but failing to secure a call, spent the remainder of his life at Erie, Pa., in teaching and as organist. He died in 1880. He was a proficient scholar and devoted Christian. See Harbaugh, *Fathers of the Germ. Ref. Church*, v, 381.

Luigi de Gonzaga, an Italian saint, was born March 9, 1568, at Castiglione, being the son of Ferdinand of Gonzaga, marquis of Castiglione. After being educated at the court of Francis de Medicis, he went to Spain with his father, where Philip II gave him as a page to prince James. In 1585, leaving his worldly goods to his brother Rodolph, he entered upon the novitiate of the Jesuits at Rome. He died June 20, 1591, and was buried in the Church of the Annunciation, but some time later his body was transferred to a chapel which had been built under his invocation by the marquis Scipio Lancelloti. He was beatified in 1621 by Gregory XV, and canonized in 1726 by Benedict XIII. See Hoefer, *Nouv. Biog. Générale*, s. v.

Luini (or **Lovini**), Bernardino, an eminent Italian painter, was probably born at Luino, a small town in the Milanese province, on the Lago Maggiore, in 1480, and is generally considered to have been a pupil of Leonardo da Vinci. His two pictures of *Mary Magdalene* and *St. John Embracing the Lamb*, in the Ambrosian Gallery at Milan, are excellent works. He was no less distinguished for his frescos, of which the most celebrated is *Christ Crowned with Thorns*, in the same gallery. He died in 1530. See Spooner, *Biog. Hist. of the Fine Arts*, s. v.; Hoefer, *Nouv. Biog. Générale*, s. v.

Lukaszewicz, Joseph von, a Polish historian, was born Nov. 30, 1797, at Kromplewo, near Posen, and died Feb. 18, 1872. His works having been translated into German, we give the German titles: *Historische Nachricht über die Dissidenten in der Stadt Posen im* 16. *und* 17. *Jahrhundert* (Posen, 1832; German by Dalitzki, Darmstadt, 1843):—*Ueber die Kirchen der böhmischen Brüder im ehemaligen Grosspolen* (Posen, 1835; German by Fischer, Grätz, 1877):—*Geschichte der Kirchen des helvetischen Bekenntnisses in Litauen* (1842, 2 vols.; German, Leipsic, 1850):—*Geschichte des helvetischen Bekenntnisses in Kleinpolen* (1853):—*Geschichte aller katholischen Kirchen in der ehemaligen posen'schen Diöcese* (1858-63, 3 vols.). (B. P.)

Luke, an Irish prelate, was dean of St. Martin le Grand, London, and treasurer of the king's wardrobe. He was elected to the see of Dublin, and obtained the royal confirmation, Dec. 13, 1228. His election was set aside at Rome as not being canonical, and he was reelected, but not confirmed by the pope until 1230. About 1237 he improved the buildings of Christ's Church, and endowed that of St. John, without the New Gate, with two burgages and six acres of land in St. Kevin's parish. In 1240 he granted to the vicars serving mass at the altar of the Blessed Virgin, in St. Patrick's Cathedral, a certain portion of the revenues of the Church of Alderg. In 1247 archbishop Luke made an act for the purpose of enforcing the residence of the prebendaries of St. Patrick's Cathedral. In the following year he made the Church of Larabrien a prebend of the same cathedral. He died in December, 1255. See D'Alton, *Memoirs of the Archbishops of Dublin*, p. 90.

Lumpkin, John, a distinguished Baptist minister

of Georgia, was born in Pittsylvania County, Va., Nov. 4, 1785, but went, when a child, to Georgia, and was reared in Oglethorpe County, where he spent his whole life. Socially, his relations were of a high character. One of his brothers, Wilson Lumpkin, was governor of the state three years, and another brother, Joseph Henry, chief-justice of the Supreme Court of Georgia. His ordination took place in 1808, and his ministry was exercised in different parts of the county in which he lived. Three new churches were formed during his life, through his personal efforts. He died, greatly lamented, Aug. 1, 1839. See Cathcart, *Baptist Encyclop.* p. 724. (J. C. S.)

Lund, Johann, a Lutheran theologian of Germany, was born Sept. 11, 1638, at Flensburg. He studied at Leipsic, was in 1672 deacon at Tundern, Schleswig, and died Sept. 13, 1686. He is the author of *Beschreibung des Levitischen Gottesdienstes*, which was published by his son under the title, *Jüdische Heiligthümer*. An edition, with notes, was published by Joh. Christ. Wolf (Hamburg, 1738). See Moller, *Cimbria Litterata;* Jöcher, *Allgemeines Gelehrten-Lexikon*, s. v.; Winer, *Handbuch der theol. Lit.* i, 137. (B. P.)

Lundy, Francis J., D.C.L., a Protestant Episcopal clergyman of the diocese of New York, became assistant minister of St. Paul's Church, Newburgh, in 1867, and died April 7, 1868, aged fifty-three years. See *Prot. Episc. Almanac*, 1869, p. 109.

Lupercalia, a noted Roman festival, was celebrated annually on Feb. 15, in honor of *Lupercus*, the god of fertility, or, as is alleged by many, in honor of *Pan*. Plutarch calls it the *feast of wolves*, and declares it to have been of a lustral or ceremonially purifying character. Whatever may have been its origin, it was in some way connected with the legend that Romulus and Remus were suckled by a she-wolf, and accordingly the rites of the Lupercalia were observed in the *Lupercal*, the place where this nursing was supposed to have occurred. On the appointed day the Luperci (q. v.) assembled and offered sacrifices of goats and young dogs. A peculiar ceremony then followed. Two youths of high rank were led forward to the priests, who, having dipped a sword in the blood of one of the victims which had been sacrified, touched their foreheads with it; after which some of the other priests came forward and wiped off the blood with a piece of woollen cloth which had been dipped in milk. The youths now burst into a fit of laughter, and forthwith the general merriment which characterized this festival began. The priests having feasted themselves, and indulged freely in wine, covered their bodies over with the skins of the goats which they had sacrificed. Thus fantastically dressed they ran up and down the streets, brandishing thongs of goat-skin leather, with which they struck all they met, particularly the women, who hailed the infliction of the sacred lash as a species of ceremonial lustration. This festival was long observed in commemoration of the founding of Rome, but having been neglected in the time of Julius Cæsar, it was revived by Augustus, and continued to be celebrated until the reign of the emperor Anastasius.

Luperci, the most ancient order of priests among the Romans. They were sacred to Pan, the god of the country, and particularly of shepherds, whose flocks he guarded. Plutarch derives the name from *lupa*, a she-wolf, and traces their origin to the fabulous she-wolf which suckled Romulus and Remus. They formed originally a college, consisting of two classes: the *Fabii*, or *Fabiani*, and the *Quinctilii*, or *Quinctiliani*. Julius Cæsar instituted a third class, under the name of *Julii* or *Juliani*. At first the Luperci were taken from the higher classes of society, but in course of time the whole order fell into disrepute.

Lupold of Bebenburg (or Eglofstein), a learned German prelate, after having studied jurisprudence at Bologna, under the direction of John Andreæ, became canon successively at Mayence, at Würzburg, and at Bamberg, of which place he had been elected bishop in 1352. He died July 20, 1363, leaving, *De Zelo Veterum Principum Germanorum in Religionem* (Basle, 1497):—*De Juribus et Translatio Imperii* (ibid. eod.). See Hoefer, *Nouv. Biog. Générale*, s. v.

Lupus (originally **Wolf**), Christian, a Roman Catholic theologian, was born June 12, 1612, at Ypern. He joined the order of the Augustinians, was in 1653 doctor of theology and professor primarius at Louvain, and died July 10, 1681. He wrote, *Diss. de Meletii et Arii Personis, Moribus Atque Erroribus:—De Symbolo Apostolico et Nicæo:—De Synodo Nicæna:—De Concilio Sardicensi:—De Concilio Constantinopolitano:—De Synodo Ephesina:—De Latrocinio Ephesino:—De Synodo Sexta:—De Synodo Trullana:—Scholia et Notæ in Canones et Decreta Synodorum Generalium et Provincialium* (5 vols.). After his death was published from his manuscript, *Summum Romanæ Apostolicæ Sedis Privilegium Quoad Evocationes et Appellationes* (Venice, 1729). See Jöcher, *Allgemeines Gelehrten-Lexikon*, s. v.; Winer, *Handbuch der theol. Lit.* i, 659, 664, 913, 920. (B. P.)

Luther's (*Two*) **Catechisms.** By way of supplement to the article Luther (q. v.), we add that both these catechisms, the larger one in the form of a continuous exposition, and the smaller one arranged in questions and answers, appeared in 1529, although the preparatory work dates back to the very beginning of Luther's reformatory activity. In 1518 Johann Schneider collected and published the various expositions of the Lord's Prayer which Luther had given in his sermons and lectures. This induced Luther to publish his exposition in an authentic form. In the same year he published a Latin exposition of the Ten Commandments, and in 1520 these sporadic efforts came to a preliminary consummation in his *Eyn Kurcz form des zehnen Gepoth:—Eyn Kurcz form des Glaubens:—Eyn Kurcz form des Vatter Unsers.* After 1524 Luther's attention was very strongly drawn to the school. His *An die Radherrn aller Stedle deutsches Lands: dass sie christliche Schulen auffrichten und hallten sollen* caused many evangelical schools to be founded, and the necessity arose for a trustworthy handbook in the elements of true Christianity. This necessity was the more felt by Luther himself, when, in his tour of visitation through Saxony in 1528, he saw how sorely both the ministers and congregations stood in need of such a book, and thus, in 1529, both the larger and smaller catechisms appeared. Luther's catechisms, however, are not the first attempts of the kind. There existed such works by Brenz, Althammer, and Lammer, but Luther's catechisms soon took the lead, and were immediately translated into Latin. The smaller catechism, which soon became an almost symbolical book in the Lutheran churches, consists of, I. The Ten Commandments; II. The Creed; III. The Lord's Prayer; IV. The Sacrament of Baptism; V. The Sacrament of the Altar; to which is added, in the editions since 1564, a sixth part, Confession and Absolution, or the Power of the Keys. Considering the smaller catechism as a whole, it is indeed the ripe fruit of many exertions, the full expression after many trials. Wherever Lutherans are found, this catechism too is used. See Plitt-Herzog, *Real-Encyklop.* s. v. (B. P.)

Luther's Hymns. It was a saying among the Roman Catholics in the time of Luther, that "by his songs he has done more harm to the Romanists than by his sermons." And such is the fact. "For," says Mr. Coleridge, "Luther did as much for the Reformation by his hymns as by his translation of the Bible. In Germany the hymns are known by heart by every peasant; they advise, they argue, from the hymns, and every soul in the Church praises God, like a Christian, with words which are natural and yet sacred to his mind." Luther was intensely fond of both music and poetry, and his poetical talent we best perceive in his hymns. Altogether he wrote about thirty-six hymns, which may be divided as follows: (a) Translations of Latin hymns; (b) Amplifications of German hymns from the Latin; (c) Correction and revision of German hymns; (d) Hymns based upon Latin psalms; (e) Hymns based upon passages of the Bible; (f) Original hymns. Spangenberg, in his preface to the *Cithara Lutheri*, in 1545, speaks thus of Luther's hymns, "One must certainly let this be true and remain true, that, among all Meister-singers, from the days of the apostles until now, Luther is, and always will be, the best and most accomplished; in whose hymns and songs one does not find a vain or needless word. All flows and falls in the sweetest and neatest manner, full of spirit and doctrine, so that his every word gives outright a sermon of its own, or, at least, a singular reminiscence. There is nothing forced, nothing foisted in or patched up, nothing fragmentary. The rhymes are easy and good, the words choice and proper, the meaning clear and intelligible, the melodies lovely and hearty, and in *summâ* all is so rare and majestic, so full of pith and power, so cheering and comforting, that, in sooth, you will not find his equal, much less his master." The most famous of Luther's hymns is the Reformation hymn, *Ein' feste Burg ist unser Gott*, which has been translated into very many languages. A collection of the translations of this hymn in nineteen languages has been published by B. Pick (Rochester, 1880); an enlarged edition, comprising twenty-one languages (28 English; 2 Dutch; 1 Danish; 1 Swedish; 5 Latin; 3 French; 1 Spanish; 1 Russian; 1 Polish; 1 Bohemian; 1 Wendish; 1 Lettish; 1 Lithuanian; 1 Finnish; 1 Esthonian; 1 Hebrew; 1 Accra; 1 Tshi; 1 Zulu; 1 Hungarian; 1 Italian), was published by the same author in 1883. But this is not the only hymn which has been translated into English. In fact, all his hymns are translated, as may be seen from Pick's *Luther as a Hymnist* (Philadelphia, 1875). An edition giving the German text, with the English translation and notes, was published by Scribner's Sons (New York, 1883). (B. P.)

Lutherans, Separate. When, in 1817, the union between the Lutheran and the Reformed churches was established in Prussia, the protest of J. G. Scheibel, professor of theology at Breslau, found much sympathy among the Lutherans. For several years, however, the movement was confined within the boundaries of simple literary polemics, especially between Scheibel and David Schultz, also professor at Breslau. But when the breaking of the bread was introduced in the administration of the Lord's Supper by a cabinet order of 1830, Scheibel refused to obey, and asked permission to continue administering the Lord's Supper after the old Wittenberg *agenda*. The permission was not granted, and Scheibel was suspended. Soon he saw himself at the head of about two or three hundred families, who left the State Church and organized themselves into a new Church. They petitioned the minister of public worship to be acknowledged as a Church organization, but this he refused to do. The many vexations which Scheibel had to undergo induced him to leave the country. In the meantime the party had progressed very rapidly under the leadership of professor Huschke. A synod was convened at Breslau in the year 1834, and it was declared that nothing but complete separation from the State Church, and the formation of an independent organization could satisfy the Lutheran conscience. Persecutions then began. Several ministers were kept in prison for many years. A number of well-to-do laymen were reduced to poverty by money fines. Not a few emigrated to America, among others, Grabau (q. v.) and Von Rohr, who formed the so-called Buffalo Synod. With the succession of Friedrich Wilhelm IV, in 1840, a change took place, and July 23, 1845, the concession for the foundation of a free Church was given, and in 1850 the Church numbered fifty pastors and about fifty thousand members. Similar movements took place also outside of Prussia, in Saxony, Hesse, and Baden. Perhaps no separation from the State Church made a deeper impression than that of Theodor Harms (q. v.) at Hermansburg, Hanover. The reason for his separation was neither dogmatical nor constitutional, but a few changes which were introduced by the government in the marriage formularies. Harms refused to accept these changes, and was suspended, Jan. 22, 1878. He immediately formed an independent society, which soon absorbed the majority of the old congregation. Meanwhile the relation between the Separate Lutherans and the State Church Lutherans was often very unpleasant, and bitter controversies arose. Finally, dissensions broke out among the Separate Lutherans themselves, and a party headed by pastor Dietrich, of Jabel, organized the so-called Immanuel Synod in opposition to the party headed by Huschke of Breslau. This was in 1862. A similar split was caused in Saxony by the Missouri Synod. This synod was organized by a certain Stefan, who had emigrated in 1840 to America. Stefan, who was deposed of his office on account of gross immorality, was succeeded by the still living professor Walther of St. Louis, Mo. Some of the Missourians had returned to Saxony, and formed at Dresden a *Lutheranerverein*, which soon occupied a prominent position, under the leadership of pastor Ruhland. The latter soon made war against the Immanuel Synod as being un-Lutheran, and so likewise against the Separate Lutherans of Breslau. The Lutheran churches of the State he condemned altogether, and finally a split was caused among the Missourians themselves. The Separate Lutherans of Germany are now against each other. See Plitt-Herzog, *Real-Encyklop.* s. v. (B. P.)

Lütkens, Franz Julius, a Lutheran theologian of Germany, was born Oct. 21, 1650. He studied at Wittenberg, was in 1676 rector of Brandenburg, in 1679 deacon at Magdeburg, in 1684 pastor primarius and provost at Stargard, Pomerania, in 1704 court-preacher and professor of theology at Copenhagen, and died Aug. 12, 1712. He wrote, *Collegium Biblicum:—Commentarius in Epistolas ad Colossenses et Titum:—Dissertat. de Ideis in Mente Divina:—De Messia Davidis Filio:—De Zohar Antiquo Judæorum Monumento*, etc. See Jöcher, *Allgemeines Gelehrten-Lexikon*, s. v. (B. P.)

Lütolf, Adolf, a Roman Catholic theologian, was born in 1824. He studied under Hirscher and Döllinger, and after having spent some years at St. Gall, Lucerne, and Solothurn, as teacher and as priest, was called, in 1868, to Lucerne as professor of Church history and canon of St. Leodegar. He died April 8, 1879, leaving *Forschungen und Quellen zur Kirchengeschichte der Schweiz* (Lucerne, 1871). (B. P.)

Lutterbeck, Johann Anton Bernhard, a Roman Catholic theologian of Germany, was born at Münster. In 1842 he was professor of Catholic theology at Giessen, but after the determination of bishop Ketteler, in 1851, to ordain no candidate who had pursued his theological studies at Giessen, Lutterbeck became a member of the philosophical faculty. After the Vatican Council he joined the Old Catholics, and died Dec. 30, 1882. He is the author of, *Hermenien aus dem Gebiete der religiösen Spekulation* (2d ed. Mayence, 1851):—*Der neutestamentliche Lehrbegriff* (1852, 2 vols.):—*Die Clementinen und ihr Verhältniss zum Unfehlbarkeitsdogma* (1872):—*Leopold Schmid über die religiöse Aufgabe der Deutschen* (1875). See Zuchold, *Bibl. Theol.* ii, 842 sq. (B. P.)

Luxembourg, Baudoin de, a Franco-German prelate, brother of emperor Henry VII, was born in 1285. While quite young he lost his father, Henry IV, count of Luxembourg, and was educated with care by his mother, Beatrice of Avesnes, at the University of Paris, where he studied belles-lettres, philosophy, theology, and jurisprudence. He was consecrated archbishop of Treves in March, 1308, at Poictiers. In April, 1310, he assembled a provincial council at Treves. From this time Baudoin is no more noticed, except in military expeditions against rebellious chieftains. He died Jan. 21, 1354. See Hoefer, *Nouv. Biog. Générale*, s. v.

Luxembourg, Louis de, a French prelate, was proposed in 1414 for the bishopric of Therouanne. He declared himself for the English party, was made chancellor by Henry VI, in 1425, and attended in 1431 at the crowning of that prince as the king of France, at St. Denis. During several political excitements, and particularly during the time of an insurrection against the English, in April, 1436, this prelate took great interest in the cause of the English in France, thus gathering upon himself the hatred and displeasure of the French. He finally had to take refuge in the Bastile, and on its surrender retreated to Rouen, where he was made archbishop, and would have received the cardinal's hat, but would only accept it on condition of being nominated by the king of England. This prince gave him, some time afterwards, the bishopric of Ely, when he was obliged to take refuge in England. He died at Hartford, England, Sept. 18, 1443. See Hoefer, *Nouv. Biog. Générale*, s. v.

Luxembourg, Philippe de, a French cardinal, was born in 1445. He was the son of Thibauld de Luxembourg, who, after having lost his wife, was received into orders, and became bishop of Mans. The first church which Philippe held in charge was that of Le Mans, which he obtained in 1477, after the death of his father. In 1483 he presided over Tours, and Feb. 3, 1496, was nominated as bishop of Therouanne, but was not appointed till Nov. 12, 1498. In 1516, after Philippe had occupied several more or less important positions in France, he became legate of the pope in that country. He was one of the richest prelates of the kingdom. He founded the College of Mans at Paris, and accomplished also several very extensive missions by order of the king, for which he had no regular allocations. He died at Le Mans, June 2, 1519. See Hoefer, *Nouv. Biog. Générale*, s. v.

Luxembourg, Pierre de, a French prelate, was born at the castle of Ligny-sur-Ornain, July 20, 1369. He began to study theology at Paris in 1377. While still a child, he was made canon of Paris in 1379, and of Cambray in 1382. At the age of fourteen he was provided with the bishopric of Metz by Clement VII. At sixteen the same pontiff appointed him cardinal-deacon at Avignon. He died July 2, 1387, and was buried at the cemetery of St. Michæl, at Avignon. There are a few books which have been erroneously attributed to him, for which see Hoefer, *Nouv. Biog. Générale*, s. v.

Luynes, Paul d'Albert de, a French prelate, was born at Versailles, Jan. 5, 1703. He had at first the name of count of Montfort, and was intended for the military career, but, renouncing it, entered a seminary, was received into orders, appointed abbot of Cerisy in 1727, and bishop of Bayeux in 1729. He held several synods, and organized missions, preaching himself. He became archbishop of Sens, Aug. 18, 1753. De Luynes assisted at the conclaves of 1758, 1769, and 1774. As an abbot of Corbie, he was appointed commander of the order of St. Esprit in 1759. He adhered to the acts of the assembly of the clergy of 1765. He died at Paris, Jan. 21, 1788, leaving several episcopal letters. See Hoefer, *Nouv. Biog. Générale*, s. v.

Luz (Judg. i, 26), Lieut. Conder suggests (*Memoirs to the Ordnance Survey*, i, 95), may be the present *Khurbet el-Lusweiziyeh*, a ruined site four and a half miles north-west of Banias, and consisting of basaltic stones scattered and in rough walls" (ibid. p. 120).

Luzzatto, Philoxene, a Jewish Orientalist, was born at Trieste, July 10, 1829. At a very early age he mastered different languages, and in 1849 published *Le Sanscritisme de la Langue Assyrienne.* In 1850 he wrote, *Études sur les Inscriptions Assyriennes de Persépolis, Hamadan, Van et Khorsabad:—Notice sur*

Present Appearance of Lydda. (From Thomson's *Southern Palestine and Jerusalem.*)

Abou-Jousouf Hasdaï Ibn-Shaprout (1852). While on his travels he was taken sick, but at length arrived at Padua, and died Jan. 25, 1854. The *Mémoire sur les Juifs d'Abyssinie ou Falaschas*, was published after his death in the *Archives Israélites* of Paris. (B. P.)

Lycēa, a festival among the Arcadians, celebrated in honor of Zeus Lycæus. It is said to have been instituted by Lycaon, the son of Pelasgus, who sacrificed a child on the occasion, and sprinkled the altar with its blood. Plutarch says that the Lycea was celebrated in a manner similar to the Roman Lupercalia.

Lydda. *Ludd*, the modern representative of this place, is briefly described in the *Memoirs* accompanying the Ordnance Survey (ii, 252), and its traditional Church of St. George in detail (ibid. p. 267).

Lyell, THOMAS, D.D., a Protestant Episcopal clergyman, was born in Virginia in 1775. While quite a young man he became a minister in the Methodist Episcopal Church; and during that time was one of the chaplains to Congress. In 1804 he was ordained deacon in the Protestant Episcopal Communion, and became rector of Christ Church, New York city, which position he occupied until his death, March 5, 1848. Dr. Lyell was elected secretary of the convention of the diocese of New York in 1811, which office he continued to hold annually until he declined re-election in 1816. Chosen a deputy to the General Convention in 1818, he was elected successively to the position during twenty-six years. He was a powerful extempore speaker, and a preacher of more than ordinary ability. See *Amer. Quar. Church Rev.* 1848, p. 302.

Lynch, PATRICK NIESEN, D.D., a Roman Catholic prelate and scholar, was born at Clones, County Monaghan, Ireland, March 10, 1817. In 1819 his parents came to America, and settled at Cheraw, S. C. At that time there was but one priest in the state, Dr. Gallagher, though Dr. England arrived next year to be the first bishop of Charleston, and opened St. John the Baptist's Seminary, at which Patrick Lynch was one of the earliest pupils. He was sent to the College of the Propaganda, Rome, where he was one of its most brilliant students, and was ordained priest and graduated doctor of divinity. In 1840 he returned to Charleston, and became assistant pastor of the cathedral, of St. Mary's Church, principal of the Collegiate Institute, and vicar-general. On the death of bishop Reynolds, in 1855, Lynch became administrator, and on March 14, 1858, he was consecrated bishop of Charleston. The civil war soon came, and with it the destruction of his cathedral, house, and other Church property in Charleston and throughout the state. The rest of his life was a constant toil with debt, which was too much for his naturally robust constitution and vigorous mind, and brought him prematurely to his end. He died in Charleston, Feb. 26, 1882. Bishop Lynch was noted for his quiet benevolence and literary activity. In 1848 he took charge of a hospital during the yellow fever, and in 1871, on another outbreak of the disease, was never absent from his post. He was a thorough scholar, and a devoted student of applied science. He was a contributor to magazines, author of letters to the *Catholic World* on the Vatican Council, articles on the *Blood of St. Januarius*, in the same, now published anonymously in book form, contributed to the *American Catholic Quarterly Review*, and edited and revised Deharbe's *Series of Catechisms*. He was pleasant and affable in social intercourse, and a fine orator. See (N. Y.) *Catholic Annual*, 1883, p. 57.

Lynd, SAMUEL W., D.D., a Baptist minister, was born at Philadelphia, Pa., Dec. 23, 1796. He was baptized by Rev. Dr. William Staughton in 1820; was well educated, and in 1824 was called to the pastorate of a church in Philadelphia, from which he was soon laid aside by severe illness. For a time, he, with his wife, conducted a female institution in Baltimore. In 1831 he began his labors as pastor of the Sixth Street Church, Cincinnati, O., his ministry being eminently successful. He remained here until 1845, when he removed to St. Louis, Mo., and became pastor of the Second Church in that city. About 1848 he was elected president of the theological institute in Covington, Ky., and remained in this position until 1854, when he took up his residence on a farm near Chicago. His other pastorates were at Lockport, Ill., the North Church, Chicago, and the Mt. Auburn Church, Cincinnati, O. He died at Lockport, Ill., June 17, 1876. See *Minutes of Ill. Anniversaries*, 1876, p. 14. (J. C. S.)

Lyng, GEORG WILHELM, a Lutheran theologian of Norway, was born in 1827. In 1869 he was professor at Christiania, and died May 19, 1884. Lyng is the author of *Hedenskabets Leonetslöb*, i. e. a history of heathenism (1866). (B. P.)

Lyngwe, in Norse mythology, is an island in the

sea Amtswartner, where the wolf Fenris is held by the chain Gleipner.

Lyon, George Armstrong, D.D., a Presbyterian minister, was born at Baltimore, Md., March 1, 1806. He graduated from Dickinson College, Pa., in 1824; spent one year in Princeton Theological Seminary, and was ordained by the Erie Presbytery, Sept. 9, 1829, pastor of the First Church, Erie, Pa., which office he held until his death, at Avon, N. Y., March 24, 1871. See *Gen. Cat. of Princeton Theol. Sem.* 1881, p. 54.

Lyon, James Adair, D.D., a Presbyterian minister, was born near Jonesborough, Tenn., April 19, 1814. He graduated from Washington College in 1832, and afterwards from Princeton Theological Seminary; was ordained as an evangelist by the Holston Presbytery, and after serving, for five years, as a stated supply, the churches of Rogersville and New Providence, became pastor of the Columbus Church, Miss., where he remained six years. He then spent a year in foreign travel, and after his return was installed pastor of the Westminster Church, St. Louis, Mo. In 1850 he established a select high-school for young ladies there, which he taught three years, and returned to his old charge at Columbus. In 1870 he was elected professor of mental and moral science in the University of Mississippi, at Oxford, which position he held for ten years, when failing health compelled him to resign. As a writer, he contributed largely to the *Southern Quarterly Review*. He was moderator of the General Assembly, and repeatedly elected to important positions in connection with literary and theological institutions, among them to the presidency of Washington College, and the chair of didactic theology in Danville Seminary, Ky. He died at Holly Springs, Miss., May 15, 1882. See *Necrol. Report of Princeton Theol. Sem.* 1883, p. 31. (W. P. S.)

Lyser, a name common to a number of eminent Lutheran theologians of Germany, of whom we mention:

1. CHRISTIAN, doctor of theology, pastor and superintendent at Sangerhausen, who died Oct. 5, 1671, is the author of *Dissensus Lutheranorum et Jansenistarum*.

2. FRIEDRICH, who died in 1645, doctor of theology, is the author of *Disp. Inauguralis de Dicto Apostolico Rom. iv*, 22, 23.

3. FRIEDRICH WILHELM, son of Polycarp III, was born at Leipsic, Sept. 4, 1622. He studied at different universities, was in 1650 Saturday-preacher at Leipsic, in 1651 deacon at Halle, in 1662 superintendent at Langensalza, in 1664 cathedral-preacher at Magdeburg, and died Aug. 25, 1691.

4. JOHANNES, brother of Friedrich Wilhelm, was born Sept. 30, 1631. In 1664 he was inspector and pastor at Pforte. Being an advocate of polygamy, he was dismissed. He roamed about through Holland, Denmark, Sweden, Italy, and France. In the latter country he died, in 1684.

5. POLYCARP I (q. v.).

6. POLYCARP II, son of Polycarp I, was born Nov. 20, 1586, at Wittenberg, where he was also promoted as doctor of theology. He wrote, *Centuria Quæstionum Theologicarum de Articulis Christianæ Concordiæ:—An Syncretismus in Rebus Fidei cum Calvinianis coli Possit, et in Politica Conversatione:—Comment. in Augustanam Confessionem et Formulam Concordiæ:—Analysis Scholastica et Theologica in Epistolam ad Galatas:—Dissert. de Sacramentis.* Lyser died Jan. 15, 1633.

7. POLYCARP III, was born at Halle, July 1, 1656. He studied at Jena and Leipsic, and commenced his academical career at the latter place in 1682. In 1685 he was pastor at Magdeburg, in 1687 superintendent, in 1690 doctor of theology, in 1695 general superintendent, and died Oct. 11, 1725.

8. WILHELM, born at Dresden, Oct. 26, 1592, studied at different universities, and died at Wittenberg, Feb. 8, 1649, doctor and professor of theology. He wrote, *Trifolium Veræ Religionis Veteris Testamenti Adamiticæ, Abrahamiticæ et Israeliticæ:—Summarium Locorum Theologicorum:—Systema Thetico-Exegeticum:—Disquisitio de Prædestinatione:—Exercitationes* 21 *in Evangelium Joannis:—Diss. de Genealogia Christi ad Matth. i*, 1–16. See Jöcher, *Allgemeines Gelehrten-Lexikon*, s. v. (B. P.)

Lysius, JOHANN HEINRICH, a Lutheran theologian of Germany, was born June 29, 1704, at Königsberg, Prussia. He studied at Halle, was in 1726 professor of Oriental languages at his native place, in 1730 doctor of theology, and died May 29, 1745. He wrote, *Dissert. II de Historia et Usu Linguæ Syriacæ:—De Silentio Sacræ Scripturæ:—De Commodo Christi Jugo ad Matth. xi*, 30:—*De Christo Homine ἀναμαρτήτῳ ex* 1 *John iii*, 5:—*De Angelo Nativitatis Christi Præcone.* See Arnold, *Historie der königsbergischen Universität;* Götten, *Jetztlebendes gelehrtes Europa;* Jöcher, *Allgemeines Gelehrten-Lexikon*, s. v. (B. P.)

M.

Maarath. For this site Mr. Tyrwhitt Drake proposes (*Quar. Statement* of the "Pal. Explor. Fund," April, 1874, p. 76) the *Mons Mardes* where St. Euthymius found ruins (*Acta Sanctorum*, ii, 306), now *Khirbet Mird*, near Mar Saba, on a round, isolated hill, containing the remains of an aqueduct, wells, and cisterns (*Memoirs* to the Ordnance Survey, iii, 212); but Lieut. Conder suggests (*Quar. Statement*, Jan. 1875, p. 13) an ancient site near Beit Ainûm, where a valley has the corresponding Arabic name, *Wady el-Moghair*. This latter ruin is laid down on the *Ordnance Map*, two miles north-east of Hebron, without any name attached. Later, however, Lieut. Conder suggests (*Tent Work*, ii, 338) *Beit Ummar*, six miles north of Hebron, probably the *Betumair* of Eusebius (*Onomast.* s. v. Baalthamar). It is "a small but conspicuous village, standing on the watershed, and visible from some distance on the north. An ancient road passes through it. Half a mile north-east is a good spring, Ain Kufin. The mosque has a small tower to it. The surrounding neighborhood is covered with brushwood" (*Memoirs* to Ordnance Survey, iii, 303).

Mab, in poetic art, is queen of the fairies (q. v.).

Macarians. See MACARIUS ÆGYPTUS, and MACARIUS OF ALEXANDRIA.

Macariites is the name of a Jewish sect, whose founder is believed to have been Benjamin Nahavendi (q. v.), a Karaite, who flourished about the opening of the 9th century. Their most peculiar doctrine was that God is too elevated to reveal himself directly to man, and that revelation was therefore made by messenger—an angel, a vice-god. If the Bible speaks of God's manifestation to man, it refers, they held, to the manifestation of the divine being in the person of his messenger, who was the first being God created. This angel was the creator of the world, not God himself. (Quite like the evolution theory in our day, advocated by Mivart, who likewise holds that God was only indirectly the creator of the world.) In this and many other respects the Macariites much resemble the Mohammedan sect of *Motazalites*. See Fürst, *Gesch. d. Karäerthums*, i, 26 sq.; Rule, *Karaites*, p. 105, 109; Grätz, *Gesch. d. Juden*, v, 230 sq., 518 sq.

Macassar (and **Bugis**) **Version** OF THE SCRIPTURES. The Bugis and the Macassar dialects are the most prevalent of those spoken among the various native states comprised in the large island of Celebes. They both resemble the Malayan; the Bugis being the most cultured of the two, and possessing a separate alphabet. A translation in each of these dialects was begun by Dr. Leyden about the year 1810, but lived only to complete the version of the gospel of Mark, which has never been printed. In 1849 Dr. Mathes was sent out by the Netherlands Society to Celebes to study these languages, but the result has not transpired. See *Bible of Every Land*, p. 374.

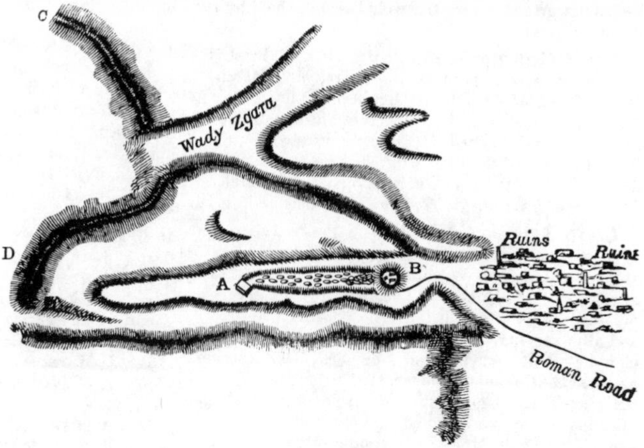

Macbeth, a Scotch prelate, was probably bishop of Ross about 1126. He died in 1128. See Keith, *Scottish Bishops*, p. 184.

Macdonald, JAMES MADISON, D.D., a Congregational minister, was born at Limerick, Me., May 22, 1812. In 1828 he entered Bowdoin College, but at the end of two years removed to Union College, Schenectady, entered the junior class, and was graduated with high honor in 1832. He then spent a year in the theological seminary at Bangor, Me., and thence to Yale Divinity School, graduating in 1835. He was licensed to preach, Aug. 6, 1834, and ordained pastor of the Third Congregational Church of Berlin, Conn., known as the parish of Worthington, April 1, 1835. In 1837 he accepted a call to the recently formed Second Congregational Church in New London; in 1841 to the Presbyterian Church at Jamaica, L. I.; in 1850 to the Fifteenth Street Church in New York city; in 1853 he was installed as pastor of the First Presbyterian Church at Princeton, N. J., and here he continued over twenty-two years. He died April 19, 1876. Dr. Macdonald was a man of untiring industry. In a high degree his ministrations were able, varied, and evangelical. As a preacher he was solid, dignified, instructive, earnest, and tender. He published a number of his sermons at various times, also about six volumes, among which the best known is *My Father's House; or, The Heaven of the Bible*. His greatest and most valuable work appeared since his decease, *The Life and Writings of St. John*. See *Necrol. Report of Princeton Theol. Sem.* 1877, p. 9.

MacCaghwell (Lat. *Cavellus*), HUGH, an Irish Franciscan of the 17th century, studied at Salamanca, and lectured at Louvain. Urban VIII appointed him archbishop of Armagh and primate of Ireland. He died Sept. 22, 1626, in the fifty-fifth year of his age. He wrote, *Scoti Commentaria in Quatuor Libros Sentt.* (Antwerp, 1620, 3 vols.):—*Apologia Apologiæ Scoti contra Nic. Jansenium* (Paris, 1623):—*Duo Tractatus pro Tuenda Observantia* (ibid. 1622). See Chalmers, *Biog. Dict.* s. v.; Jeiler, in Wetzer u. Welte, *Kirchen-Lexikon*, s. v. (B. P.)

Macfarlane, JOHN, LL.D., a Scotch Presbyterian minister, was born at Dunfermline, Fifeshire, in 1807. He was licensed to preach in 1830, and the following year was ordained to the pastorate of the Secession congregation of Kincardine-on-Forth. In 1840 he was called to Glasgow, where he remained till 1861, when he removed to London. Here he labored most faithfully and with much success for twelve years. He died Feb. 7, 1875. As a preacher Dr. Macfarlane was powerful, eloquent, and attractive; as a writer he was able and ready. His works are, *Jubilee of the World:—Christian Missions to the Heathen* (Glasgow, 1842):—*Mountains of the Bible* (2d ed. 1850; 3d ed. 1856):—*The Night Lamp* (1850, 1851, 1853):—*The Hiding-Place* (1852; 3d ed. 1854):—*Why Weepest Thou?* (1854). See *The* (Lond.) *Evangelical Magazine*, June, 1875, p. 343; Allibone, *Dict. of Brit. and Amer. Authors*, s. v.

Plan of Machærus, and the Ravines round it.
A, Square Fort. B, Citadel. C, D, Western Valley of Josephus.

Machærus. This place, represented by the modern *Makaur*, is fully described by Tristram (*Land of Moab*, p. 271 sq.). The fortress stands on a round hill at the eastern end of a narrow and isolated ridge, on which the inhabited city must have been built. It is very different in character from any other ruins in Moab. Nothing remains but a few courses of stones above the foundations. But the whole building material has been collected by the hand of man into one prodigious mass on the crest of the ridge, where it remains in wild desolation, a monument of the vengeance taken by the Roman legions against the last desperate

Castle-mound of Machærus. (From a Photograph by the Editor.)

patriots of the Jewish revolts. The outline of the fortress may still be traced very clearly, and in it two dungeons, one of them deep, and its sides scarcely broken in. One of them must have been the prison-house of the Baptist.

MacHale. See MCHALE.

Machātus, *Saint*, a Scotch prelate, was bishop of the Isles in 498 and 518. To this saint there are many churches dedicated in Scotland. See Keith, *Scottish Bishops*, p. 295.

Machazor. See MACHZOR.

Machir OF TOLEDO, who flourished towards the end of the 14th century, is the author of אבקת רוכל, or an eschatology of Judaism, in three parts—the first treats of the sufferings in the Messianic time, of the advent of the Messiah, resurrection, last judgment, and world to come; the second treats of reward and punishment, paradise and hell; the third of the oral law (Rimini, 1526 and often); a Judaeo-German translation appeared at Fürth in 1691, and the first part was translated into Latin by Hulsius, *Tractatus de Messia* (reprinted in his *Theologia Judaica*, Breda, 1653). See Fürst, *Bibl. Jud.* ii, 285; De' Rossi, *Dizionario Storico* (Germ. transl.), p. 190 sq., and his *Bibliotheca Judaica Antichristiana*, p. 61. (B. P.)

Mack, Martin Joseph, a Roman Catholic theologian of Germany, was born Feb. 17, 1805. In 1832 he was professor of New-Test. exegesis at Tübingen, and in 1839-40 *rector magnificus* of the university. His publication of *Die Einsegnung der gemischten Ehen* (Tübingen, 1840) brought him in conflict with the government. He was deposed from his office, and relegated to the Ziegelbach parish in Würtemberg. He died Sept. 24, 1885, leaving, *Bericht über Strauss' kritische Bearbeitung des Lebens Jesu* (Tübingen, 1837):—*Commentar über die Pastoralbriefe des Apostels Paulus* (2d ed. 1841). See Winer, *Handbuch der theol. Lit.* i, 552. (B. P.)

Mack, William, D.D., a Presbyterian minister, was born at Flushing, L. I., July 29, 1807. He graduated from Union College, Schenectady, in 1831, and from Princeton Theological Seminary in 1834. He was licensed by the Presbytery of New York, Feb. 4 of that year; ordained at Rochester, Feb. 5, 1835; and subsequently was pastor at Knoxville and Columbia, Tenn. In 1858 he became a voluntary evangelist, devoting half his time to the Presbytery of Columbia, and the other half beyond its bounds. From the time of the division of the General Assembly, in 1861, he adhered to the southern portion. He was for some time president of Jackson College at Columbia. He died Jan. 10, 1879. See *Necrol. Report of Princeton Theol. Sem.* 1879, p. 31.

MacKenzie, Murdoch, a Scotch prelate, was born in 1600, received Episcopal ordination, and went as chaplain to a regiment under Gustavus Adolphus. After his return from Germany he became minister at Contin, next at Inverness, and afterwards at Elgin. He was made bishop of the see of Moray, Jan. 18, 1662. From this he was translated to the see of Orkney in 1677, where he continued until his death, in February, 1688. See Keith, *Scottish Bishops*, p. 152-228.

Maclaren, John Finley, D.D., a Presbyterian minister, was born at Manlius, Onondaga Co., N. Y., Feb. 7, 1803. He graduated from Union College in 1825, studied three winters (1825-28) in Princeton Theological Seminary, was licensed in 1828, and ordained pastor of the Church at Geneva in 1830. He edited the *Christian Magazine* at that place, afterwards settled at Hagerstown, Md. (1845), and Pittsburgh, Pa. (1846). He was president for a time (1855-58) of the Western University of Pennsylvania. He died at Princeton, March 14, 1883. See *Necrol. Report of Princeton Theol. Sem.* 1883, p. 18.

Maclean, a Scotch prelate, was early minister at Morevern, Dunoon, and Eastwood, from which last charge he was advanced to the see of Argyle in 1680. He died there in 1687. See Keith, *Scottish Bishops*, p. 292.

Maclean, Robert, a Scotch prelate, was probably bishop of the Isles about 1549. See Keith, *Scottish Bishops*, p. 307.

Macleod, Norman, D.D., a Scotch Presbyterian minister, was born June 3, 1812, at Campbelton, a seaport of Scotland. He was educated at a school in Morven, and at Glasgow University, where he was exceedingly popular. In 1837 he obtained his first ministerial charge, the parish of Loudoun, in Ayrshire, which he served for five years. About this period the disruption of the Scotch Kirk took place, and in the controversy which preceded and followed, Mr. Macleod took an active part. He adhered to the Established Church of Scotland, and in 1843 was appointed to the parish of Dalkeith. In July, 1851, he was inducted minister of the Barony parish, Glasgow, which contained 37,000 souls. At that time he assumed the editorship of *Good Words*, designed as a popular periodical, with a spirit and aim decidedly Christian. Of his journey to the Holy Land in 1867, he gave a full account in his *Eastward*. He was also the author of several other popular works. In 1862 he was chosen by the General Assembly to represent the Church in India; and his reception, when he returned, was very warm. He was unanimously elected by the General Assembly to the office of moderator, in 1869. From 1871 his health gradually declined, and he died June 16, 1872. Dr. Macleod was a genial, large-hearted man, whose untiring energy and Christian philanthrophy placed him in the first rank of public benefactors. See (Lond.) *Christian Observer*, December, 1876, p. 907; *Memoir*, by his brother (Lond. 1876).

MacMahon, Bernard, D.D., a Roman Catholic divine, was born in Ireland in 1816. He studied for the priesthood in France, and about 1842 went to Africa with the first vicar apostolic of Cape Colony, Mgr. Griffith, and he continued until the last to labor among the English-speaking Catholics of the colony. He was soon after made vicar-general, holding that position under bishops Grimley and Leonard, or to his death. He was a hard worker, a close student, and a model priest. Pius I appointed him domestic prelate. He died at Cape Town, Feb. 1, 1882. See (N. Y.) *Cath. Annual*, 1883, p. 117.

Macnaughton, Donald, a Scotch prelate, was elected bishop of Dunkeld in 1436, and died on his way to Rome the same year. See Keith, *Scottish Bishops*, p. 87.

Madagascar Version. See Malagasi.

Madhavis, an order of Hindû mendicants, founded by Madho, an ascetic. They travel up and down the country soliciting alms, and playing on stringed instruments.

Madhwacharis, a division of the Vaishnava sect of the Hindûs, founded by Madhwacharya (q. v.). They have their headquarters at Udipi, where their founder erected a temple, and deposited an image of Krishna. Their appearance is thus described: "The ascetic professors of Madhwacharya's school adopt the external appearance of the *Dondis*, laying aside the Brahmanical cord, carrying a staff and a water-pot, going bare-headed, and wearing a single wrapper stained of an orange color with an ochrey clay; they are usually adopted into the order from their boyhood, and acknowledge no social affinities nor interests. The marks common to them and the lay votaries of the order are the impress of the symbols of Vishnu upon their shoulders and breasts, stamped with a hot iron, and the frontal mark, which consists of two perpendicular lines made with *Gopichandana*, and joined at the root of the nose like that of the *Sri Vaishnavas;* but instead of the red line down the centre, the Madhwacharis make a straight black line, with the charcoal from incense offered to Narayana, terminating in a round mark made with turmeric."

Madmannah. For this site Lieut. Conder suggests (*Tent Work*, ii, 338) *Um Deimneh*, twelve miles north-east of Beersheba, consisting of "heaps of stones, foundations, and two or three caves" (*Memoirs* to Ordnance Survey, iii, 399); but the name has little resemblance.

Madon is perhaps the modern ruin *Khurbet Madin* (Conder, *Tent Work*, ii, 338), a quarter of a mile south of Hattîn, near Lake Tiberias, consisting of "heaps of ruins, some well-dressed stones" (*Memoirs* to Ordnance Survey, i, 403).

Madrasses are colleges in Mohammedan countries, for the training of priests who are to officiate in the mosques.

Madrazo, José Madrazo y Aguda, a Spanish painter, was born at Santander, April 22, 1781. He studied at the Academy of Madrid, under David in Paris, and in Rome. Returning to the former city in 1818, he became director of the Academy, and afterwards of the museum. He died there, May 8, 1859. Among his principal paintings are *Jesus in the House of Ananias; The Sacred Heart of Jesus;* and *The Seizure of Breda*.

Maduwa, the place in which the *Bana*, or sacred books of the Buddhists, are publicly read. It is usually

Present Appearance of Magdala. (From Thomson's *Central Palestine and Phœnicia.*)

a temporary structure, the roof having several breaks or compartments, gradually decreasing in size as they approach the top, in the form of a pagoda, or of a pyramid composed of several platforms. There is one of these structures in the precincts of nearly all the *wiharas* (q. v.). In the centre of the interior area is an elevated platform for the convenience of the priests, and the people sit around it upon mats spread on the ground. The platform is sometimes occupied by several priests at the same time, one of whom reads a portion of the sacred books, in a tone between singing and reading. The Maduwa is also used for other purposes. In it there is a labyrinth made of withs ornamented with the cocoanut leaf; and the people amuse themselves by finding their way through its intricate mazes. In some instances lines are drawn upon the ground in an open space, and these lines are regarded as the limits of the regions assigned to particular dæmons. Dancers approach these lines and defy the dæmons, receiving the applause of the people for their boldness.

Magallianus, COSMAS, a Jesuit and professor of theology at Coimbra, who died Oct. 9, 1624, wrote *Catechismus Japonensis: — Comment. in Moysis Cantica et Benedictiones Patriarcharum: — Comment. in Josuam: —Comment. in Epistolas Pauli ad Timotheum et Titum: —Explanationes Morales in Indicum Historiam:—Opus Hierarchicum seu de Principatu Ecclesiastico Libri III.* See Witte, *Diarium Biographicum;* Jöcher, *Allgemeines Gelehrten-Lexikon*, s. v. (B. P.)

Magaw, SAMUEL, D.D., a Protestant Episcopal clergyman, graduated from the University of Pennsylvania in 1757. Having received ordination, he became a missionary of the Society for the Propagation of the Gospel in Foreign Parts, and served as such in Dover and Duck Creek, Del. In 1779 he was invited to St. Paul's Church, Philadelphia, but did not accept the rectorship until January, 1781. In 1786 the Rev. Joseph Pilmore became his assistant, but Dr. Magaw continued rector until 1804. He was vice-provost of the University of Pennsylvania from 1782 to 1791. About 1800 he aided in founding the Philadelphia Academy, which had a brief existence. He was secretary of several of the early conventions of the Protestant Episcopal Church in Pennsylvania. His death occurred in Philadelphia, Dec. 1, 1812. See Sprague, *Annals of the Amer. Pulpit*, v, 246.

Magdala. The present site, *el-Mejdel*, is merely "a mud and stone village, containing eighty Moslems; situated in the plain; of partly arable soil; no gardens" (*Memoirs* to Ordnance Survey, i, 361, comp. p. 369).

Magians. See MAGI.

Magraw, JAMES, D.D., a Presbyterian minister, was born in Bart Township, Lancaster Co., Pa., Jan. 1, 1775. He graduated from Franklin College, Lancaster, about 1799. After studying theology, he was licensed, Dec. 16, 1801, by the Presbytery of Middletown; preached as a missionary for a year or two; and was ordained April 4, 1804, pastor of the Church in West Nottingham, Cecil Co., Md. Here he remained till 1810, when a church was formed in Upper West Nottingham, which he also served till 1821. In 1822 he organized a church at Charlestown, of which he was pastor till his death, Oct. 20, 1835. Besides preaching, Dr. Magraw was engaged for many years in teaching. (J. C. S.)

Magri (Lat. *Macer*), DOMINICO, a Roman Catholic prelate, was born March 28, 1604, and died March 4, 1672, at Viterbo. He is the author of *Notitia de' Vocaboli Ecclesiastici* (Rome, 1650; Lat. transl. by himself and his brother Carold, *Hierolexicon*, etc., 3d ed. 1677 fol.; latest edition, Venice, 1712). See Winer, *Handbuch der theol. Lit.* i, 608. (B. P.)

Magyar Version. See HUNGARIAN VERSION.

Mahan, MILO, D.D., a Protestant Episcopal clergyman, was born at Suffolk, Va., May 24, 1819. He was educated at St. Paul's College, Flushing, N. Y.; entered the ministry in 1845; in 1851 became professor of ecclesiastical history in the General Theological Seminary, New York city; in 1864 removed to Baltimore, Md., as rector of St. Paul's Church, and in this parish continued to serve until his death, Sept. 3, 1870. He published several religious works, including *Palmoni*, a curious chronological treatise, which were collected, with a memoir, by Rev. J. H. Hopkins, Jr. (N. Y. 1872-75, 3 vols.). See *Prot. Episc. Almanac*, 1871, p. 118.

Mahn, ERNST AUGUST PHILIPP, a Lutheran theologian of Germany, was born Oct. 18, 1787. In 1818 he was professor of Oriental literature at Rostock, and died in 1827. He is the author of, *Berichtigungen zu den vorhandenen Wörterbüchern und Commentaren über die hebräischen Schriften* (Göttingen, 1817):—*Bemerkungen* *und Erklärungen zu schwierigen Stellen des Alten Testaments* (ibid. eod.):—*Ueber die Modalität des orientalischen Studiums* (Sulzbach, 1821):—*Observationes Exegeticæ ad Difficiliora Quædam Vet. Test.* (Göttingen, 1812):—*Darstellung der Lexicographie* (Rudolstadt, 1817):—*Comm. in qua Ducibus Quattuor Evangelistarum Apostolorumque Scriptis Distinguuntur Tempora* (Göttingen, 1811). See Winer, *Handbuch der theol. Lit.* i, 120, 123, 564; Fürst, *Bibl. Jud.* ii, 286. (B. P.)

Mahratta Version. See MARATHI.

Maichel, DANIEL, a Lutheran theologian of Germany, was born Aug. 14, 1693, at Stuttgart. He studied at Tübingen, and travelled through Switzerland, France, England, Holland, and Germany. In 1724 he was appointed professor at Tübingen, and in 1730 was made doctor of divinity. He died Jan. 20, 1752. He wrote, *De Fœdere Legali cum Adamo Inito* (Tübingen, 1719):—*De Præcipuis Bibliothecis Parisiensibus* (Cambridge, 1720; Leipsic, 1721):—*De Recta Theologiam Naturalem Tradendi Ratione* (Tübingen, 1730):—*De Fide Hæreticis Servanda* (ibid. 1741–42):—*In Locum Eccles. iii,* 19–21 (ibid. 1743). See Döring, *Die gelehrten Theologen Deutschlands,* s. v. (B. P.)

Mailly, FRANÇOIS DE, a French prelate, was born at Paris, March 4, 1658. In 1698 he was appointed archbishop of Arles, and in 1710 he succeeded the famous Le Tellier in the archbishopric of Rheims. Mailly distinguished himself by his ardent zeal for the Roman see. When the bull *Unigenitus* was promulgated, he forced it upon his clergy. His pastoral epistles were often suppressed by the parliament. Pope Clement XI, in consideration of his great services, made Mailly cardinal without consulting first the court of France, and the latter forbade the archbishop to wear the insignia of his new dignity. But these prohibitory measures were not always carried out, and Louis XV allowed him to wear the cardinal's hat. Mailly died in the abbey of St. Thierry, Sept. 13, 1721. See Lichtenberger, *Encyclop. des Sciences Religieuses,* s. v. (B. P.)

Main, THOMAS, D.D., moderator of the Free Church General Assembly of Scotland, was ordained pastor of the High Church in Edinburgh in 1839, which position he held until his death, May 23, 1881. In 1880 he was a delegate from the Free Church Assembly to the General Council of the Presbyterian Church held in Philadelphia. He possessed fine talents as a preacher, and proved himself a successful pastor.

Maison, JOHANN GEORG, a Lutheran theologian of Germany, was born at Neustadt-on-the-Aisch, May 24, 1730. He studied at Erlangen and Halle, and acted for some time as teacher at different schools. In 1779 he was appointed to the pastorate at Dottenheim, and died Jan. 28, 1784. He wrote, *Explicatio Psalmi Secundi* (Culmbach, 1771):—*Super Matth. xvi,* 18 (ibid. 1772):—*De Miraculis* (ibid. 1774):—*De Loco Rom. ix,* 18 (ibid. 1776):—*De Immortalitate* (ibid. 1779):—*In Philipp. iv,* 13 (ibid. eod.). See Döring, *Die gelehrten Theologen Deutschlands,* s. v. (B. P.)

Majal, MATHIEU (called *Desuhas,* from his birth-place), a young Huguenot minister, "the martyr of Vernoux," was a pastor at Vivanais, who, having attended the national synod of Bas-Languedoc, Aug. 18, 1744, was arrested for treason Feb. 1 following, and despite the entreaties of his parishioners, was executed Feb. 2, 1746, on the esplanade of Montpellier, at the age of twenty-six years. See Lichtenberger, *Encyclop. des Sciences Religieuses,* s. v.

Major, JOHANN TOBIAS, a Lutheran theologian of Germany, was born at Jena, Feb. 2, 1615. After completing his studies at Leipsic and Jena, he travelled through Holland, France, and Italy, was made in 1645 doctor of theology, and elected professor at Jena in 1646. He died April 25, 1655. Major wrote, *Commentationes in Epistolam ad Hebræos:—De Natura et Cultu Angelorum:—De Oratione pro Defunctis:—Disputationes de Potestate Clavium.* See Witte, *Diarium Biographicum;* Jöcher, *Allgemeines Gelehrten-Lexikon,* s. v.; Winer, *Handbuch der theol. Lit.* i, 427. (B. P.)

Majuma, a little town on the sea-shore of Palestine, seven stadia from Gaza, and considered as its seaport (Strabo, xvi, 759); now represented by the little village *en-Nesleh* (Van de Velde, *Narrative,* ii, 186).

Majus. See MAY.

Makkedah. "*El-Mughâr* ('the Cave'), the site which captain Warren proposes for Makkedah, is a remarkable place, and one of the most conspicuous sites in the plain. A promontory of brown sandy rock juts out southwards, and at the end is the village, climbing up the hillside. The huts are of mud, and stand in many cases in front of caves; there are also small excavations on the north-east, and remains of an old Jewish tomb, with Kokim. From the caves the modern name is derived, and it is worthy of notice that this is the only village in the Philistine plain at which we found such caves. The proximity of Gederoth (Katrah) and Naamah (Na'aneh) to El-Mughâr also increases the probability that captain Warren's identification of El-Mughâr with Makkedah is correct, for those places were near Makkedah (Josh. xv, 41)"—(Conder, *Tent Work,* ii, 174). This position is defended at length by the same writer in the *Quar. Statement* of the "Pal. Explor. Soc." 1875, p. 165. The place is situated nine miles north-east of Ashdod, and is briefly described in the *Memoirs* accompanying the Ordnance Survey, ii, 411, and its antiquities, ibid. p. 427.

Makos, a god of the ancient Slavonians, who was represented partly as a man and partly as a fish. At a later period he presided over rain, and was invoked when the fields were in want of water.

Malagasi Version OF THE SCRIPTURES. Malagasi is the language spoken on the island of Madagascar (q. v.). The gospel was not proclaimed to the people

El-Mughar. (From Thomson's *Southern Palestine and Jerusalem.*)

of this isle till 1818, when the Rev. Messrs. Jones and Beaven were sent to labor among them by the Church Missionary Society. The translation of the Bible occupied the greater part of the time of the missionaries during eleven years. The New Test. was completed in 1825, and, after having been revised twice, was printed in 1830. Parts of the Old Test. was printed in 1832 and 1835, and about the latter year the whole of the Old Test. was printed at Madagascar. The persecution, well known in history, commenced about this time, and lasted till 1851. The Rev. Messrs. Freeman and Jones (formerly missionaries in Madagascar) had, in anticipation of the day when they might be enabled to resume their labors, employed themselves since their return to England in the complete revision of the Malagasi Scriptures. This revision has been accomplished, and, in the immediate prospect of the island becoming again open to the efforts of the Christian ministry, the British and Foreign Bible Society determined to print an edition of five thousand copies of the Malagasi Bible from the revised MS. This work was accordingly commenced, under the editorial care of the Rev. Mr. Griffiths (formerly a missionary on the island), with the aid of the Rev. T. W. Meller; but, after advancing as far as the completion of the New Test., with the Old Test. as far as the 10th chapter of Judges, it had been deemed advisable to suspend further progress. The revision of the text had advanced as far as the end of Job. The work given up in 1858 was again resumed, and the completion of the unfinished parts of the Old Test., left by the late Rev. Mr. Griffiths, together with a profusion of MS. corrections, very difficult to decipher, was happily brought to an end in 1864, through the able assistance of Mr. Sauerwein and the editorial superintendent of the British and Foreign Bible Society. A revised edition of the Malagasi New Test., with marginal references, was printed at London in 1869, under the care of the Rev. R. G. Hartley, of the London Missionary Society, while the Old Test., under the editorship of the Rev. R. Toy, was published in 1871. For a long time the need of a thorough revision of the entire Bible in the Malagasi had been felt. From the report for 1873 we learn that a joint board, representing all the missions on the island, has been formed for the purpose of securing, as far as possible, a thoroughly accurate and idiomatic standard version of the Bible in the Malagasi tongue. This board has ever since been at work, and from the report for 1885 we learn that the preliminary revision of the Bible was completed Sept. 15, 1884. See *Bible of Every Land*, p. 386. For linguistic purposes, see Parker, *A Concise Grammar of the Malagasy Language* (London, 1883). (B. P.)

Malay Version OF THE SCRIPTURES. The Scriptures, either in whole or in part, were translated into Malayan several times. The first translation was made by John Van Hasel, a director of the East India Company, formed in 1602. When he had completed a version of the gospel according to Matthew, he handed over the MS. to Peter de Carpentier, the general of the company, and soon after, in 1612, another version, prepared by Albert Cornelisson Ruyl, was delivered to the same individual, in order that the two versions might be compared. Ruyl's was preferred, and he now devoted himself to the completion of the New Test.; but only lived to translate as far as the close of the gospel of Mark. His MSS. were sent to Holland, and were printed with the Dutch version at Enkhuysen in 1629, and again at Amsterdam in 1638. Van Hasel, far from being discouraged at the preference with which Ruyl's version was regarded, persevered with his translation, and completed a version of the four gospels, of which Luke and John were published at Amsterdam in 1646. Van Hasel also translated the Psalms, in concert with Justus Heurn, who, for fifteen years, presided over the Dutch Church in India. The first portion of this version was printed at Amsterdam in 1648, and the entire Psalter appeared in 1689. Heurn likewise translated the Acts of the Apostles into Malayan, and revised the gospels of Van Hasel and Ruyl, according to the Greek, or rather, perhaps, conformed them to the Low or Belgic version of 1637. This revision, together with the Acts, and the Dutch version in the margin, was printed at Amsterdam in 1651. This was reprinted at Oxford in 1677, at the expense of the Hon. Robert Boyle, and under the superintendence of Dr. Hyde, keeper of the Bodleian Library. A second impression of the same work, in every respect similar to the first, was printed at Oxford in 1704, and the copies were sent to the East for distribution. These, and all the editions above mentioned, were printed in Roman characters. At length, in 1668, the entire New Test. was printed at Amsterdam in Roman letters, translated by Daniel Brower. He lived and died in the East; he also prepared a version of the book of Genesis, which was printed in 1662, and again in 1687, at Amsterdam. A standard Malay version of the Old and New Test. Scriptures was commenced by Dr. M. Leidekker, a Dutch minister of Batavia in 1685. He translated most of the books of the Old Test. twice; and in the New Test. had advanced as far as the 6th verse of the 6th chapter of the epistle to the Ephesians, when he was called away in 1701. After his decease Petrus Van der Vorm was appointed to complete the work, which he did before the close of the year. In 1722 the Dutch government appointed four ministers to examine and correct the work. Besides Van der Vorm, there were Arnaldus Brandts, Cornelius Ninaher, and George Hendrick Werndly. The work was completed in 1728. Two copies appear to have been made, one in Roman, and the other in Arabic characters. The former was printed at Amsterdam (1731–33), under the care of the Rev. G. H. Werndly and Dr. Serruns, aided by two Malay chaplains. The latter was published at Batavia in 1758, under the direction of the Dutch governor, Jacob Mossel. In 1813 George Livett, Esq., a resident at Amboyna, addressed the Calcutta Bible Society in behalf of the Amboynese Christians, who were almost destitute of Bibles. The society had three thousand copies of the Malayan New Test. printed at Serampore in 1814, the text being that of 1731. This edition was in Roman characters. But as there were Malayan districts where the Arabic was still in use, the same society determined upon printing two editions of the Scriptures, one in Roman, the other in Arabic letters. The former was completed in 1817, when the entire Bible from the text of 1731–33 left the press; the latter was not published until 1822, the text of 1758 having been carefully revised and corrected for that purpose by the Rev. Mr. Hutchings and major McInnes. While these editions were published further supplies of the Malayan Scriptures were prepared in London, at the earnest request of the Auxiliary Bible Society at Amboyna. In 1819 the New Test. in the Roman character, from the text of 1733, was printed by the British and Foreign Bible Society, under the care of professor Lee, and in 1822 the entire Bible from the same text was issued. In 1820 the Netherlands Bible Society supplied the Malays with the New Test. which was printed at Haarlem, and in 1824 the whole Bible was published for the Malays by the same society, in an edition of five thousand copies. These editions were printed in Arabic characters from the edition of 1758, under the superintendence of professor Wilmet. In 1822 the same society printed an edition of New Tests. and Bibles in the Roman character from the text of 1733. In 1830 the Calcutta Society printed, at Singapore, an edition of two thousand five hundred copies of Matthew's gospel, in Arabic characters, as the first step towards giving a fresh edition of the entire New Test. This measure was adopted in consequence of the desire manifested among the Western Malays themselves to read the Scriptures—a circumstance never known before, for the Bible had previously been urged upon them rather than freely accepted, and their Mohammedan prejudices had been deemed impregnable. In consequence of their increased demand for the "Englishman's Koran," the Calcutta Society published, in 1833, a revised edition of one thousand copies of the Gospels and the Acts, and one thousand five hundred copies of the entire New Test. from the edition corrected by Mr. Hutchings. The printing was carried on at Singapore, under the care of the Rev. Messrs. Thomson and Burn, of the London Missionary Society. Another version of the New Test., less literal and more idiomatic than former translations, was executed by the agents of the London Missionary Society and of the American Bible Society, at Singapore. Editions in both the Arabic and Roman characters were printed in 1856, under the care of the Rev. B. P. Keasberry. The latter had also undertaken a translation of the Old Test., of which he had already prepared a considerable part, when his death, in 1875, put a stop to the work. Since 1814 the Java Auxiliary Bible Society has contemplated the plan of publishing the New Test. in Low Malay, which is spoken in the lower parts of Java. An edition of the New Test. in the Low Malay, which was commenced by Mr. Robinson, a Baptist missionary, and completed by Dr. Medhurst, left the press at Singapore in 1833. Some Christians at Sourabaya prepared a translation of the Psalms, which was printed at Amsterdam in 1847, under the care of professor Vetti, by the Netherlands Bible Society. In 1877 the British and Foreign Bible Society published the translation of the book of Exodus of Mr. J. L. Marten, which the Rev. E. W. King, who brought it to England from Java, superintended. See *Bible of Every Land*, p. 360.

Linguistic Helps.—Dennys, *A Handbook of Malay Colloquial, as Spoken in Singapore;* Maxwell, *A Manual of the Malay Language* (1882); Swettenham, *Vocabulary of the English and Malay Languages* (Singapore, 1881, 2 vols.); Favre, *Grammaire de la Langue Malaise* (Paris, 1876); *Dictionnaire Malais-Français* (1875, 2 vols.); *Dictionnaire Français-Malais* (1880, 2 vols.). (B. P.)

Malayalim Version OF THE SCRIPTURES. The Malayalim is spoken along the western coast of Peninsular India, from cape Comorin to the borders of Canara, and from the sea to the western Ghauts. This region, sometimes distinguished by the general name of Malayala, comprises the British district of Malabar, under the Madras presidency, and the territories of the several rajahs of Travancore, Cochin, and Coorg. The natives in general are Hindûs. When Dr. Buchanan, at the beginning of the present century, visited the Syrian Christians at Malayala, he found that several attempts had been made by them at different times, though without success, to effect a translation of the Scriptures into Malayalim, their vernacular language. At the suggestion of Dr. Buchanan the design was carried into execution, and the bishop, Mar Dionysius, engaged to superintend the translation. On his second visit to Travancore, in 1807, Dr. Buchanan found that the translation of the four gospels had been completed by Timapah Pillay and Rembar, a catanar or priest of the Syrian Church. The translation had been made from the Tamul version of Fabricius, and an edition of five thousand copies of these gospels was printed at Bombay at the expense of the British and Foreign Bible Society. Timapah Pillay was subsequently placed under the superintendence of the Rev. Mr. Thompson, at Madras, in order to complete the translation of the New Test., which was accomplished in 1813. This version, however, did not prove satisfactory, and Mr. Spring, chaplain at Tellicherry, proposed to enter upon a complete revision of Timapah Pillay's version, so as to render it acceptable to the natives of Malabar; while Mr. Bailey, who was stationed at Cottayam, engaged to execute a new translation for the benefit of the inhabitants of Travancore. Both these translations were completed in 1819, and on examination Mr. Bailey's version was preferred by the Madras Bible Society, at whose expense the New Test. was published at Cottayam, in 1830. The translation of the Old Test. was likewise completed by Mr. Bailey the same year, and this work was submitted to a sub-committee, formed in 1832, in connection with the Madras Society, for the publication of a Malayalim version of the Old Test. In 1834 some parts of the New Test. were printed in London, under the care of Mr. Bailey, who had been compelled to visit England on account of his health. The remainder of the New Test. was printed by him at the mission-press in Cottayam. Complete editions of both the Old and New Tests. in Malayalim have since been issued from the Cottayam press. The version previously in current use was, however, admitted to stand in need of further revision, and a publishing committee was appointed for the purpose. In the report for 1856 we read that the revision of the New Test. has been completed, together with that of the first three books of the Pentateuch. In 1858 the revision had proceeded as far as the end of the second book of Samuel, while in 1863 we are told that the Old Test. had been reprinted, with a few corrections. In 1871 we read that "the New Test., in this southern Indian language, is about to be revised, but the plan of operations has not yet been fully decided upon. The bishops and pastors in the Syrian Church of Malabar have undertaken to aid the English and German missionaries in the work." The meeting of delegates appointed for that purpose took place, according to the report of 1872, July 26, 1871, at Cannanore. The delegates present were the Rev. Messrs. Baker and Justus Joseph, of the Church Missionary Society, and Fritz and Miller, of the German Basle Mission. The work of the delegates progressed very slowly. In the report for 1877 we read that the revision of the New Test. was carried on as far as Heb. v, and, said the Rev. H. Baker, convener of the delegates, "I trust in a few months to see the end of the New Test., and shall hope to praise God for enabling me to do the little I have done towards this edition." His wish, however, has not been fulfilled, for to use the words of the report for 1879, "the Malayalim Revision Committee has lost its senior member, the Rev. H. Baker, of the Church Missionary Society, Cottayam. This, together with the dialectical differences in the language as spoken in North and South Malabar, has made the task very difficult. The revision has been carried on, however, in the New Test. to the end of James, the first two gospels having undergone a second revision." From the report for 1883 we learn that the revision of the New Test. had been brought to a close in 1882, and that an edition of eight thousand copies has been printed. The Old Test. is now in the course of revision. See *Bible of Every Land*, p. 145. For linguistic purposes, see Gundert, *A Malayalim and English Dictionary.* (B. P.)

Malbin, MEIER LEIBISCH, a Jewish author and rabbi, was born in Russia in 1810. In his early youth his intellectual powers roused the utmost admiration; in his sixteenth year his fluency in the Talmud was extraordinary, his memory enabling him to repeat folio after folio. When eighteen years of age he became rabbi at Wreschen, in the province of Posen. From Wreschen he was called to Kempen, and after a long residence there, to Bucharest. Being obliged to leave Roumania on account of his opposition to the Jewish Reform party, he returned to Russia. After a short residence there he went to Königsberg, in Prussia. Malbin died Sept. 8, 1879, at Kiev, on his way to a new position at Esenstockau, in Russia. He wrote commentaries on the Pentateuch, the five Megilloth, and Isaiah, for which see Lippe, *Bibliographisches Lexikon* (Vienna, 1881), s. v. In his expositions he proved himself not only an elegant Hebrew writer, but also a deep thinker. (B. P.)

Malcolm, a Scotch prelate, was bishop of Caithness at the time of the parliament in Scone, April 3, 1373. He died in 1421. See Keith, *Scottish Bishops*, p. 213.

Malcom, Howard, D.D., LL.D., a Baptist minister, was born in Philadelphia, Pa., Jan. 19, 1799. He graduated from Dickinson College in 1813; entered Princeton Theological Seminary in 1818, and remained two years; was licensed to preach by Sampson Street Church, in Philadelphia, June 8 of the same year; became pastor in Hudson, N. Y., May 14, 1819; first general secretary of the American Sunday-school Union, and travelled widely in its service, but resigned this position, July 5, 1827. He soon after became pastor of Federal Street Church, Boston, Mass. In 1835 he went abroad as a deputy of the Baptist Triennial Convention, to visit its foreign mission stations in India, China, Siam, and Burmah, and on his return published, in two volumes, an account of his travels. Next, he was pastor of Sampson Street Baptist Church, Philadelphia, Nov. 25, 1849. He was president respectively of Georgetown College, Ky., and the University of Lewisburg, Pa., which latter position he left, Aug 5, 1857. On account of an affection of the throat the later years of his life were devoted to the Baptist Historical Society. He died March 25, 1879. Dr. Malcom was president of the American Peace Society, and vice-president of the American Foreign Bible Society. Among his published volumes are, *Bible Dictionary* (1828, 1853):—*Travels in South-eastern Asia* (1839):—*Extent of the Atonement* (1830):—*Theological Index* (1870). He also edited many volumes. See *Necrol. Report of Princeton Theol. Sem.* 1879, p. 13.

Maldivian Version of the Scriptures. The Maldivian language is a very mixed one, containing more Cingalese, Hindustani, Sanscrit, and Arabic words than the Malay. The natives have two alphabets of their own, one very peculiar, the other resembling the Persian.

The four gospels were translated into Maldivian by Dr. Leyden, for the Calcutta Bible Society, but for various reasons it had not been printed up to 1860. See *Bible of Every Land*, p. 150.

Malek-taus, a deity adored by the Yezedees (q. v.), in the Lebanon range. He was represented either as a cock, or a man with a cock's head.

Malgrin, John. See Algrin.

Maliseet Version of the Scriptures. The Maliseet is a dialect spoken by the Indians of New Brunswick. The Maliseet Indians are, since 1870, in the possession of the gospel of John, which was translated by the Rev. S. T. Rand, and published by the British and Foreign Bible Society. Before the publication of this gospel they were only acquainted with such fragments and quotations of Scripture as are found in the Roman mass-book. (B. P.)

Mallet, Friedrich Ludwig, a distinguished Reformed theologian of Germany, was born Aug. 4, 1793, at Braunfels, near Wetzlar. He studied at Herborn and Tübingen, and was in 1815 appointed assistant to pastor Buch of St. Michael's, at Bremen, whom he succeeded in 1817. In 1827 he was called to the pastorate of St. Stephen's, and died May 5, 1865. Mallet was a most excellent preacher, and a prolific writer. His publications, however, are mostly polemic, caused by the rationalism and infidelity which he sought to combat. See Zuchold, *Bibl. Theol.* ii, 849 sq.; Hupfeld, *Friedrich Ludwig Mallet* (1865); Meurer, *Zur Erinnerung an Friedr. Ludw. Mallet* (1866); Wilkens, *Friedrich Mallet, der Zeuge der Wahrheit* (1872); Plitt-Herzog, *Real-Encyklop.* s. v. (B. P.)

Mallinckrodt, Pauline von, foundress of the Sisters of Christian Charity, was born at Minden, Westphalia, June 3, 1817. She was the sister of Hermann von Mallinckrodt, the eminent leader of the Catholic party in the Prussian legislature, a speaker and politician of great power, who died suddenly in Berlin, May 26, 1874, aged fifty-three years. When living with her father in Paderborn, Pauline set up a little asylum for blind children. She resolved to secure a permanent organization for carrying out her designs, Aug. 21, 1849. In November, 1850, she took her vows, and soon the sisters of Christian Charity was established. For twenty years the new institution enjoyed the favor of both the civil and ecclesiastical authorities. In May, 1872, the laws against the Catholic Church were passed by the Prussian government, and every house not devoted exclusively to nursing the sick was closed, and its inmates dispersed. In April, 1873, mother Pauline yielded to the wishes of the German Catholics in America, took with her a detachment of sisters, and founded a house in New Orleans. In order to make proper provision for the American undertaking, she established another house at Wilkesbarre, Pa., which is for America what the house at Paderborn had been for Germany. In 1874 she received a request from the Chilian government to make a foundation in their country. In 1876 she went to Rome, and received the pope's approval of her congregation and the erection of two provinces for North and South America. She sailed for America in October, 1879, by way of Cape Horn, and visited every house in the two Americas. She then set out to visit her houses in Belgium, Germany, and Bohemia, returning to Paderborn in March, 1881. There she died, April 30 of that year. There were then (1881) twenty-eight houses of the sisters of Christian Charity in the United States, and forty in North and South America. See (N. Y.) *Catholic Annual*, 1882, p. 94.

Maltese Version of the Scriptures. The Maltese spoken by the natives of Malta is a curious mixture of Arabic and Italian, the grammar being Arabic, but a large number of Italian words have been grafted into the vocabulary. Many years ago the four gospels were translated into Maltese by Mr. Vargalli, and printed at the expense of the Church Missionary Society. Afterwards the Society for Promoting Christian Knowledge had the work revised, and the remainder of the New Test. translated, by Dr. Camilleri, a native of Malta, and a clergyman of the Church of England. The book, however, did not meet with that acceptance which had been hoped for, owing not so much to any defects in the translation as to the awful ignorance of the people, and their benighted adherence to the priests. A deep interest having been taken by a few Englishmen living on the island in the spiritual welfare of this people, the question was again mooted of printing a gospel in the Maltese, as there are about 10,000 Maltese, principally women and children, country people and villagers, who read their own language. In 1870 a translation of Matthew's gospel was made by a native, and sent over to England. After the MS. had been examined and reported on by the editorial superintendent and by the Rev. Dr. Camilleri, it was printed under the editorship of the last-named gentleman, and the orthography was made as simple as possible, so as to present no difficulties to those who were able to read at all in their mother tongue. This was in 1871. In the report for 1872 we read: "The edition of Matthew in this language having proved a great boon to religious inquirers among the Maltese, it was resolved that the Acts of the Apostles should be printed. A third portion, namely the gospel according to John, has now been translated, and is about to be printed. The services of the Rev. Dr. Camilleri have proved exceedingly valuable in aiding the preparation of these works." The two gospels and the Acts are the only parts of the New Test. which the Maltese enjoy at present. See *Bible of Every Land*, p. 53. (B. P.)

Maluk Dasis, a subdivision of the Ramavandi Vaishnavas of Hindustan, founded by Maluk Dás, who lived in the reign of Akbar the Great, in the 16th century. They worship Vishnu, in the character of *Rama*, and accept as their chief authority the *Bhagavat Gita*. The adherents of this sect are said to be numerous, especially among the laboring and trading classes, to the latter of which their founder belonged. The principal establishment of this sect is at Kara Manikpur, the birthplace of the founder, and still occupied by his descendants; and besides this establishment they have six other *Mat'hs* at Allahabad, Benares, Bindraban, Ayudhya, Lucknow, and Jagunnath, which last is of great repute, because rendered sacred by the death of Maluk Dás.

Malumigists, a sect of Mohammedans who teach that God may be known perfectly in this world by the knowledge which men have themselves.

Malvoisin, William, a Scotch prelate, was consecrated bishop of the see of Glasgow in 1200. See Keith, *Scottish Bishops*, p. 236.

Mamakurs, a kind of bracelets worn by the natives of the Moluccas or Spice Islands, particularly Amboyna, and which the women regard as preservatives against all enchantments.

Mamiani (*della Rovere*), Terenzio, *count*, a famous Italian philosopher, was born Sept. 15, 1799, at Pesaro. He studied at Rome, but had to leave his country on account of his participation in the insurrection of 1831. He went to France, but returned to Italy in 1848. In 1857 he was professor of philosophy at Turin, and in 1860 he was made minister of public instruction. In 1870 he took up his abode at Rome, and published the philosophical journal, *La Filosofia delle Scuole Italiane.* Besides, he wrote, *Rinnovamento della Filosofia Antica Italiana* (Paris, 1834; 2d ed. Florence, 1836):—*Dialoghi di Scienza Prima* (Paris, 1846):—*Confessioni d'un Metafisico* (Florence, 1865, 2 vols.):—*Psicologia di Kant* (Rome, 1877):—*La Religione dell' Avvenire* (Milan, 1879):—*Critica della Rivelazione* (ibid. 1880):—*Questioni Sociali* (Rome, 1882). Mamiani died May 20, 1885. (B. P.)

Man, Alexander, a Scotch prelate, was bishop of the see of Caithness in 1389, and was witness to a charter of the earl of Sutherland in 1400. He died in 1409. See Keith, *Scottish Bishops*, p. 213.

Man of Sin. See Sin, Man of.

Manabosho, a deity worshipped by the Chippewa Indians, concerning whom legendary stories are told which closely resemble those related of Litaolané (q. v.).

Manah, the tutelary god of the Hodhail and other tribes of ancient Arabia, occupying the country between Mecca and Medina. The idol was a large stone, the worship of which consisted of the slaughter of camels and other animals. Though the idol was destroyed by order of Mohammed, the rite is still continued.

Manchoo (also Mantchoo, Mandshou) Version of the Scriptures. The Manchoo belongs to Manchooria, an extreme region lying north of Corea and north-east of China proper. It is also the court language of Pekin. An imperfect and very unfaithful translation of part of the Scriptures into Manchoo is said to have been executed by some Jesuit missionaries; and in 1818 an abortive attempt towards the production of a version was made under the sanction of the governor of Irkutsk. The prosecution of this important work ultimately devolved upon Lipoffzoff, a learned member of the Russian Bible Society, who had resided fourteen years at Pekin, by appointment of the Russian government, with the view of studying the Chinese and Manchoo. The translation was carried on under the superintendence of Dr. Pinkerton, and in 1822 an edition of the gospel of Matthew was printed at St. Petersburg, at the expense of the British and Foreign Bible Society. The awful flood which occurred in that city in 1824 destroyed the greater part of this edition. The entire New Test. was published by the same society in 1835, the translation of Mr. Lipoffzoff having been revised by Mr. George Borrow, of Norwich. This edition, which is beautifully printed, was forwarded to London, and there it probably still remains, under the custody of the British and Foreign Bible Society, until a proper time comes for the distribution and circulation of the copies. See *Bible of Every Land*, p. 334. The language has been treated by Gabelentz, *Eléments de la Grammaire Mandchoue* (1833); Adam, *Grammaire de la Langue Mandchoue* (Paris, 1873); Harlez, *Manuel de la Langue Mandchoue* (ibid. 1884); Klaproth, *Chrestomathie Mandchoue* (ibid. 1828). (B. P.)

Manco Capac, the founder of the ancient Peruvian empire, was deified after his death, and altars were erected for his worship. Both he and his wife were regarded as children of the sun, who had been sent from heaven to earth, that they might found a kingdom.

Mandar, in Hindû mythology, is the great mountain which the gods carried into the milky sea, wound the snake Adissesсhen about it, and by churning it produced the food of the gods, Amrita.

Mandingo Version of the Scriptures. The Mandingo is the most important language of modern Negroland, and predominates in many powerful states on both sides of the Gambia. The Rev. Mr. Macbrair, a Wesleyan missionary, was the first to undertake the translation of the Scriptures in this widely extended language. The gospel according to Matthew was printed in London under his superintendence, in 1838, by the British and Foreign Bible Society. The translation of the other three gospels is still in manuscript. See *Bible of Every Land*, p. 406. (B. P.)

Manès is a term by which the ancient Romans used to designate the souls of the departed. Sacrifices were offered in their honor, and a festival called Feralia (q. v.), dedicated specially to the Manes, was celebrated annually on Feb. 19.

Manger, Samuel Heinrich, a Lutheran theologian of Germany, who died at Franeker in 1788, doctor and professor of theology, is the author of, *De Siphra Deque Nomine* דביר (Utrecht, 1751):—*Commentarius in Librum Prophetæ Hoseæ* (Franeker, 1785). See Winer, *Handbuch der theol. Lit.* i, 225; Fürst, *Bibl. Jud.* ii, 320. (B. P.)

Man-ho-pa, the Great Spirit, worshipped by the North American Indians, whom they propitiate by presents, and by fastings and lamentations during the space of from three to five days. Their traditions state that the great waters divide the home of the Great Spirit from the abode of the red man; but there is a very general belief among them that he resides in the extreme west.

Maniple (Lat. *manipulum*). Doubtless this was nothing more than a strip of the finest linen, attached to the left arm of the priest by a loop, with which to wipe the chalice previous to the first oblation, that is, at the offertory. Soon, however, it began to be enriched with embroidery, like the stole, and finally became merely an ornament worn by the priest and his assistants, just above the left wrist, at the celebration of the eucharist. It is now of the same width and color as the stole and the vestment or chasuble, fringed at the ends, and generally about a yard and a quarter in length. It has been kept up in the English Church ever since the alterations in the 16th century, ordinarily in the shape of a napkin folded like a band, for use at the eucharist; and at St. George's Chapel, Windsor, at Durham and Westminster, some of the ancient maniples can still be seen which have been occasionally worn.

Ancient Maniple of the 12th cent. (French).

Manks (or Manx) Version of the Scriptures. This language is spoken to some extent on the Isle of Man, the ancient Mona. It is characterized by the incorporation of many Scandinavian words, which were doubtless introduced during the continued sway of the Danes and of the Norwegians, who succeeded the Saxons in the government of the island. The present version of the Manks Bible was commenced in the jail of Castle Rushen by the excellent bishop Wilson, in concert with Dr. Walker, one of his vicars, in 1722. The gospel of Matthew was translated by Dr. Walker, and printed, under the direction and at the expense of the bishop, in London, in 1748. The other gospels and the Acts were left in a state of readiness for the press by this venerable bishop, who died in 1755. His successor, Dr. Mark Hildesley, entered with the utmost ardor and anxiety on the prosecution of the translation of the New Test., which was finally published in London in 1767, by aid of the Society for Promoting Christian Knowledge. About the time of the completion at press of the New Test., the bishop made arrangements for the translation of the Old Test., dividing it for this purpose among twenty-four different individuals. When the work was completed it was committed for final revision to Dr. Moore and Dr. Kelly. The latter was then only eighteen years of age, but very proficient in the knowledge of Manks, which was his native language. Dr. Kelly transcribed the whole version, from Genesis to Revelation, for the press, and, in conjunction with Dr. Moore, corrected and revised the proof-sheets. In 1772 the Old Test. was completed and published, and in 1775 the Society for Promoting Christian Knowledge published the second edition of the Manks Scriptures; other editions have since been issued by the same society. In 1810 the British and Foreign Bible Society published a stereotyped edition of two thousand copies of the New Test., and in 1819 the entire Bible was published by the same society. Since then no further editions of the Manks Scriptures have appeared, as the Bible in English is now in general circulation on the island. See *Bible of Every Land*, p. 166. (B. P.)

Mann, Carl, a Lutheran theologian of Germany, was born Sept. 22, 1806, at Königsbach, Baden. He studied at Tübingen; was in 1833 preacher at Wilhelmsdorf, Würtemberg; in 1842 at Hochstetten, Baden; in 1852 at Wössingen, near Durlach, and died at Eppingen, Dec. 1, 1861. He published, *Wie und wodurch is Martin Luther der grosse Bibel-Uebersetzer geworden?* (Stuttgart, 1835):—*Jubel-Büchlein der evangelishen Reformation in Würtemberg* (ibid. 1836):—*Die augsburgische Confession erklärt* (Carlsruhe, 1842):—*Evangelischer Confirmations-Unterricht* (1850):—*Was thut unserer Kirche noth?* (1843):—*Die Bibel als das Wort des lebendigen Gottes an die Menschheit* (1855). See Winer, *Handbuch der theol. Lit.* i, 788; ii, 303; Zuchold, *Bibl. Theol.* ii, 851; Koch, *Gesch. des deutschen Kirchenliedes*, vii, 302 sq. (B. P.)

Mannheim, in Norse mythology, was one of the nine worlds of Northern fable, the middle designed as the habitation of men.

Manning, Jacob Merrill, D.D., a Congregational minister, was born at Greenwood, N. Y., Dec. 31, 1824. He studied at Prattsburg, in 1850 graduated from Amherst College, and in 1853 from Andover Theological Seminary; was ordained pastor of the Mystic Church, Medford, Mass., Jan. 5, 1854, and dismissed Feb. 17, 1857. The latter year he was installed as associate pastor of Old South Church, Boston, and so remained until 1872, when he became the sole pastor. He became pastor emeritus, March 15, 1882, and died Nov. 29 of the same year. Among his published addresses and sermons are the following: *The Death of Abraham Lincoln* (1865):—*Peace under Liberty* (eod.):—*Half Truths and The Truth* (1873):—*Helps to a Life of Prayer* (1875), etc. See *Cong. Year-book*, 1883, p. 26.

Manning, John H., D.D., a minister of the Reformed (Dutch) Church, graduated from Rutgers College in 1844, and New Brunswick Seminary in 1847; was licensed by the Classis of New Brunswick the same year; was pastor at Spotswood from 1847 to 1854; South Brooklyn from 1854 to 1873, and thereafter remained without a charge until his death, Oct. 25, 1878. See Corwin, *Manual of the Ref. Church in America*, 3d ed. p. 366.

Manning, Samuel, LL.D., an English Baptist minister, was born at Leicester, Nov. 26, 1821. He was educated at Bristol College, and spent a few terms of study in the Glasgow University. In 1846 he accepted the pastorate of the Church at Sheppard's Barton, Frome, where he remained fifteen years. His labors were eminently successful, and his influence was widely felt. He contributed to the *Eclectic Review*, the *Christian Spectator*, and other periodicals; and in 1857 took the entire editorial management of the *Baptist Magazine*. In 1861 he became book editor of the Religious Tract Society, an office which he was in a high degree qualified to adorn. His talents for the next fifteen years were devoted to the elevation of literature to the Christian standard. In 1876 he became secretary of the same society, and remained an efficient officer until the close of his life, Sept. 13, 1881. Among his publications are several illustrated volumes, viz.: *Italian Pictures*:—*Swiss Pictures*:—*Spanish Pictures*:—*American Pictures*:—*Those Holy Fields*:—and *The Land of the Pharaohs*. See (Lond.) *Baptist Hand-book*, 1882, p. 307.

Manser, George B., D.D., a Protestant Episcopal minister, was born at New Haven, Conn., Aug. 8, 1803. He graduated from Dartmouth College in 1827; studied law; for several years was secretary of civil and military affairs, but afterwards entered the ministry; and for about nine years was rector of the parish in Montpelier, Vt., which he himself had organized. In 1850 he took charge of St. Peter's Church in Bennington, where he remained until death, Nov. 17, 1862. See *Amer. Quar. Church Rev.* April, 1863, p. 151.

Mansfield, Richard, D.D., a minister of the Protestant Episcopal Church, was born at New Haven, Conn., in 1724. In 1741 he graduated from Yale College, and devoted two years to study as a resident-graduate. For three years, from 1744, he was principal of a grammar-school in New Haven. In 1748 he was ordained in London by the archbishop of Canterbury, and received an appointment from the Society for Propagating the Gospel in Foreign Parts. Returning to America in 1749, he began his missionary work in Derby, Conn., in connection with West Haven, Waterbury, and Northbury, a position which he retained until his death, in April, 1820. In 1775 he was compelled to flee for a time from his churches and family to the town of Hempstead, because of his adherence to the English crown. See Sprague, *Annals of the Amer. Pulpit*, v, 131.

Mantchoo Version. See Manchoo.

Mantellētum is a large cape of silk reaching from the neck to below the waist, with open spaces for the arms on each side. It is commonly worn over the rochet, and is no doubt the foreign equivalent to the English *chimere*. Anciently it was of scarlet satin in England. Foreign bishops commonly wear a *mantelletum* of purple silk, lined with silk of the same color, only lighter in shade. Abroad, in some places, monsignori, canons, vicars-general, apostolical prothonotaries, and doctors in canon law wear the *mantelletum*; in which case it is usually of black, though sometimes of scarlet or brown silk. The *mantelletum* is by some affirmed to be the same as the *mozette*.

Mantelletum of Violet Silk (French).

Mantis, The Praying, an insect said to have been worshipped formerly by the Hottentots. It derives its name from the erect position and motion it assumes when alarmed. It was regarded by the Hottentots as a creature of bad omen, and to kill, or even to injure it, was looked upon as in the highest degree unlucky.

Mantra, a secret, the communication of which forms the chief ceremony of initiation in all Hindû sects. It generally consists of the name of some deity, or a short address to him; it is conveyed by the teacher to the disciple in a whisper, and when once known, is carefully concealed from all the uninitiated. The word *mantra* is also employed generally to denote a spell or enchantment, and also a hymn or a prayer.

Manuscripts, HEBREW. That Hebrew MSS. existed at a very early time may be seen from the following passage in the Mishna (*Sopherim*, vi, 4): "R. Simon ben-Lakish says, three codices (of the Pentateuch) were found in the court of the temple, one of which had the reading מְעוֹן, the other זַעֲטוּטֵי, and the third differed in the number of passages wherein היא is read with a *yod*. Thus in the one codex it was written מְעוֹן, *dwelling* (Deut. xxxiii, 27), while the other two codices had מְעוֹנָה; the reading of the two was therefore declared valid, whereas that of the one was invalid. In the second codex, זַעֲטוּטֵי was found (Exod. xxiv, 11), while the other two codices had אֶת־נַעֲרֵי; the reading in which the two codices agreed was declared valid, and that of the one invalid. In the third codex there were only nine passages which had היא written with a *yod* (as it is generally written הוא with a vav), whereas the other two had eleven passages; the readings of the two were declared valid, and those of the one invalid." The minute prescriptions contained in the Talmud concerning the material, color, letters, writing instruments, etc., for the manuscripts, only prove the fact that such manuscripts existed, otherwise St. Jerome could not have written "Veterum librorum fides de Hebraicis voluminibus examinanda est" (*Epist. ad Lucinium*). The greatest care was exhibited in writing of MSS., and three mistakes were sufficient to make a copy worthless (*Menachoth*, fol. 29, col. 2).

When the study of the Talmud was no longer attractive amid the disorder and frequent closing of the Babylonian academies, and ulterior development of the traditions became exhausted, attention was more directed to Scripture. The number of MSS. increased, and to them the various systems of vowel-points and accents, together with the first elements of grammar, were appended. But not all of these MSS. are now extant, some are only known from the quotations made from them by different writers. In treating, therefore, of the different MSS., we shall have to speak of two kinds—of such as are lost, and of such as are extant.

A. LOST MANUSCRIPTS.

1. The *Codex Hillel* (q. v.).
2. The *Codex Sanbuki* (q. v.).
3. The Jericho Pentateuch. Concerning this חומש יריחו Elias Levita writes thus: "The Pentateuch of Jericho is doubtless a correct codex of the Pentateuch derived from Jericho. It discusses the *plene* and *defectives* as הַתּוֹעֵבֹת, 'the abominations' (Lev. xviii, 27), which is in this Pentateuch without the second *vav*. So also יְלִידֵי, which occurs twice in the same chapter (Numb. xiii, 13, 22), of which the first is *plene* (written in the Jericho codex), and the second *defective*."
4. The *Codex Sinai* (q. v.).
5. The *Codex Ben-Naphtali*. Moses ben-David Naphtali, a contemporary of Ben-Asher, flourished about A.D. 900-960. He distinguished himself by his edition of a revised text of the Hebrew Scriptures in opposition to Ben-Asher, in which he had no great success, inasmuch as the different readings he collated and proposed are very insignificant, and are almost entirely confined to the vowel-points and accents. The codex itself is lost, but many of its readings are preserved, e. g. by Kimchi in his *Grammar and Lexicon*, while a complete list of these different readings is appended to Bomberg's and Buxtorf's Rabbinic, and to Walton's Polyglot Bible. Fürst, in his *Concordance*, p. 137, sec. 48, has also given the variations between these two scholars.

The most important difference between Ben-Naphtali and Ben-Asher is the reading of שלהבת יה, Song of Songs, viii, 6, as two words, while Ben-Asher reads it as one word, שלהבתיה, both readings having the same meaning. In a very convenient form these variations are given by Bär and Delitzsch in their edition of the different parts of the Old Test., on *Genesis*, p. 81, *Job*, p. 59, *Psalms*, p. 136, *Proverbs*, p. 55, *Isaiah*, p. 90, *Minor Prophets*, p. 90, *Ezra*, *Nehemiah*, and *Daniel*, p. 91, 126, *Ezekiel*, p. 112.

Our printed editions have for the most part the reading of Ben-Asher; very seldom, however, that of Ben-Naphtali is found, with the exception of such codices as have the Babylonian system of punctuation, and which always follow Ben-Naphtali. The editions in which the reading שלהבת יה (i. e. Ben-Naphtali's) is found are: Bomberg's Rabbinic (1517) and his quarto edition (1518), Stephen's (1543), Münster's (1546), Hutter (1587), Antwerp Polyglot (1571), Bragadin's Hebrew Bible (1614), Simoni's (1767-1828), Jahn's (1806), Bagster's (1839), Basle edition (1827), Hahn-Rosenmüller's (1868).

B. EXTANT MANUSCRIPTS.

I. In order to have a correct opinion of the codices extant, the following points must be observed:

1. *Whether the MS. was written for public or private use.* Those written for public use, commonly called "synagogue rolls" or "sacred copies," were prepared with that care and minuteness of which prescriptions are given in the Talmud, while the others were less carefully made. They are written sometimes in the *square*, at others in the *rabbinical* character. Their size is entirely arbitrary. They are in folio, quarto, octavo, and duodecimo. Of those written in the *square character*, the greater number are on parchment, some on paper. As to the square character employed in the MSS., it has varieties. The Jews themselves distinguish in the synagogue roll (1) the *Tam* letter, with sharp corners and perpendicular coronulæ, used among the German and Polish Jews; (2) the *Velshe* letter, more modern than the *Tam*, and rounder, with coronulæ, particularly found in the sacred copies of the Spanish and Oriental Jews.

2. *Whether the copyist, in writing and correcting the MS., had regard to some version or not.* That such was sometimes the case may be seen from a MS. containing the Psalms, and belonging to the 15th century, known as Scaliger 8 (because Scaliger once had it), and preserved at the Academy of Leyden (comp. Heidenheim, in his *Deutsche Vierteljahrsschrift*, ii, 466-468).

3. *What its date is.* The Jews employed different dates in their MSS. Some used the "Seleucidic" or "Greek" æra (חשבון היונים), called also *Æra Contractuum* (מנין שטרות), which was employed until the 11th century, and ceased entirely in the year A.D. 1511. Another computation was the reckoning from the destruction of Jerusalem (A.M. 3828, A.D. 68). A third computation was the æra of the creation (לבריאה, לבריאת עולם), and was introduced by European transcribers. When it became more general, after the year of the world 4000, the 4000 years were gradually omitted. This system of mentioning only the hundreds and lower numbers was called "the small æra" (לפרט קטן, abbreviated לפ"ק), in contradistinction from the full numbering (פרט גדול).

In order to find out to which year A.D. one of the years of the Seleucidic or Greek æra, or of the Jewish computation, either from the creation or from the destruction, corresponds, it must be borne in mind that the Jewish civil calendar commences with the month of Tishri, תשרי, corresponding to our September or October, and the Seleucidic æra with the first of October, 312 B.C. Thus, e. g. the year 283 of the Seleucidic æra would be the year 30-29 B.C., i. e. 312 — 283 = 29, allowing, however, some months because of the difference in the calendar 30-29.

In Jewish MSS. we frequently find the small æra, or לפרט קטן. Thus cod. 2 of Kennicott has an epigraph which states that it was written in the year 64, that is 5064. By adding to this number the number 240 (i. e. the difference between the Jewish and Christian computation), we get 5304; deducting from this 4000 (i. e. the time from the creation to the birth of Christ), we get the year A.D. 1304; or the same date may be had by adding to the year 64 the number 240=304, combined with the fifth thousand=1304. The date according to the æra of the destruction of Jerusalem is found by adding 68 to the given date; thus the year 900 after the destruction would be 900+68=968, or A.D. 1885 would be the year 1817 after the destruction (i. e. 1885—68=1817).

4. *Where the codices were written*, as there is a difference between the Spanish and the German, the Eastern and Western codices.

(*a*) *As to the Spanish and German codices*, there is a great diversity of opinion. Kennicott and De' Rossi speak of the German very highly, while Jewish authorities prefer the Spanish codices. Thus Elias Levita tells us, "Most of the correct codices I found to be Spanish, and it is upon these that I relied, and it is their method which I followed. . . . The Spanish codices are more correct than all other exemplars."

(*b*) *As to the Eastern and Western codices.* At the beginning of the Christian æra there were two rival academies, one in Palestine and the other in Babylonia. Both had their Talmud (q. v.), respectively known as the Palestinian and Babylonian Talmud, but also their codices, in which they differed from each other. And thus we find in Rabbinical as well as in Biblical codices marginal notes, giving the passages where the Eastern and Western differ from each other. Thus, e. g. cod. Kennic. 516 (Florent. 13, Laur. iii, 3, scr. an. 1291), "The Westerns or Palestinians read עשריה, the Easterns or Babylonians עשיריה." These variations were first collected by Jacob ben-Chayim in the Rabbinic Bible (Venice, 1526), under the title, חלוף המקרא שבין בניארץ ישראל ובן בני בבל. Chayim does not give the source from which he took these variations, but Morinus (*Exercitt. Biblic.* p.409, Paris, 1669 fol.) testifies that he saw a list of these variations in some MSS.

As to the Eastern and Western readings, which were published by Chayim, we must observe (1) *that none occur in the Pentateuch;* (2) *that these readings only refer to letters and words* (with two exceptions, viz. Jer. vi, 6, where the Eastern write עצה מפיק, i. e. עצה with a mappik, and Amos iii, 6, where they note עשה מפיק, i. e. עשה with a mappik); (3) *they seldom change the sense*, as for the most part they concern the omission or addition, or permutation or transposition, of quiescent letters (Lamen. v, 21, יהוה is read by the Occidentals, while the Orientals have אדני); (4) *there are two hundred and sixteen various readings in Chayim's Bible* (and in all Rabbinic Bibles which followed that of Chayim), viz. Joshua, 11; Judges, 8; Sam. 10; Kings, 21; Isa. 18; Jer. 34; Ezek. 22; Minor Prophets, 13; Chron. 11; Psa. 8; Job, 12; Prov. 8; Ruth, 7; Song of Songs, 2; Eccles. 6; Lamen. 6; Esth. 4; Dan. 8; Ezra, 7. (5) The European or Western Jews follow the reading of the Western (מערבאי), and thus it happens that in the one or the other codex we find another reading from that of the Eastern codices. Thus, in 2 Kings xviii, 29, Norzi (q. v.) remarks on the reading להציל אתכם מידו, that those codices which read מידי follow the Babylonian (כבני בבל), but the Palestinian codices, which we follow, give in the list of variations מידו.

II. After these preliminaries, we will speak of the extant codices.

1. The *Codex of Asher.* See *Asher Manuscript.*

2. The *Codex of Cahira.* This codex contains the prophets, and is preserved at Cahira, in the synagogue of the Karaites. It was written in the year 827 after the destruction of the temple, or in the year 4656 of the creation = A.D. 895.

3. *Codex Kennic.* 126. This codex contains the later prophets, and is preserved in the British Museum (*Sloane*, 4708). See *Sloane Codex.*

4. The *Codices of Damascus and Guber.* The former codex the late Dr. Moses Margoliouth saw at Damascus, belonging to the family Farrhi. It is regarded as very sacred, and the Jews themselves are only allowed to look at it once a year, that is on the feast of שמחת תורה, i. e. "the Joy of the Law," which takes place at the termination of the Feast of Tabernacles. Dr. Margoliouth, who saw it, says that this codex "deserves the palm for beauty and execution." According to a notice added later on the title-page, it should belong to the 3d century. Another codex, Dr. Margoliouth states, is at Guber or Juber, near Damascus. "There is a synagogue at that small place which is considered the most ancient in the world; and, moreover, Hebrew writers affirm that it is built over the cave of Elijah. The MS. there is by no means so fine a masterpiece as the Damascus one, but is certainly much older. A most awful anathema is written on the cover, against any one selling or stealing it" (*Pilgrimage to the Land of my Fathers*, i, 257).

5. *Codices Kennicottiani.* Of these we enumerate the following:

(1) Cod. 590—containing the Prophets and Hagiographa, written about 1018 or 1019, now in the Imperial Library at Vienna.

(2) Cod. 536—containing the Pentateuch, Haphtaroth, and Megilloth [i. e. Song of Songs, Ruth, Lamentations, Ecclesiastes, and Esther] (Cæsenæ Bibl. Malatest. Patrum D. Franc. Convent. plut. xxix, cod. 2), of the end of the 11th century. It commences with Gen. ii, 13.

(3) Cod. 162—Joshua, Judges, Samuel (Florentiæ Biblioth. Laurent. plut. i, pars ii, cod. 45), of the beginning of the 12th century.

(4) Cod. 154—Prophets, with both Targums (Carlsruhe, Biblioth. publ.), A.D. 1106. This is the famous Codex Reuchlinianus, which has the epigraph: "In the year 4866 A.M. and 1038 since the destruction of the temple." The Targum, according to this codex, has been published by Lagarde, Leipsic, 1872.

Besides these we may mention:

(5) Cod. 193—Pentateuch, without points (Mediolani Bibl. Ambros. G. 2), A.D. 1287, or somewhat earlier. Of various readings, the following are marked by De' Rossi:

Exod. xii, 31, ויקרא פרעה, so also Sept., Vulg., Syr.

Lev. xii, 7, עליה הכהן, Sam., Sept., Syr.

xxv, 35, וחי אחיך, Sam., Sept.

(6) Cod. 201—Prophets and Hagiographa, of the 12th century (Norimb. Biblioth. Ebner). Jeremiah follows the book of Samuel, and 1 Kings, Ezekiel, and Isaiah follows Jeremiah.

(7) Cod. 210—Bible of the 12th century (Parisiis Biblioth. Reg. 10).

(8) Cod. 224—Prophets and Hagiographa, of the 12th century (Regiomonti Biblioth. Reg.).

(9) Cod. 366—Prophets, in large 4to, of the 12th century (Parisiis San-German. 2). Jer. xxix, 19 to xxxviii, 2 and Hosea iv, 4 to Amos vi, 12 is wanting.

(10) Cod. 293—Pentateuch, with the Megilloth and Masorah in fol., A.D. 1144 (Toleti ap. Bayerum). The epigraph reads, "Written כֹּקֹד, i. e. 4904 A.M." Deut. vii; 13, נשבע יהוה for נשבע, confirming the reading of the Sam. and Sept.

(11) Cod. 531—Prophets and Hagiographa, with the Masorah and Targum, fol., 2 vols., A.D. 1193 (Bononiæ, Biblioth. S. Salvatoris Canon. Reg. 646, 647). The epigraph bears the date 953 (+240) = 1193.

(12) Cod. 326—Hagiographa, Joshua, Judges, Samuel, 4to, A.D. 1198 (Parisiis Bibl. Regian. 48).

6. *De' Rossi's Codices.* Of these we particularize the following:

(1) Cod. 634—fragments of Leviticus and Numbers, 4to, 8th century, containing Lev. xxi, 29 to Numb. i, 50. Lev. xxii, 4, ואיש *a*, so Sept.

(2) Cod. 503—Pentateuch, in 4to, 9th or 10th century, commencing with Gen. xlii, 14 to Deut. xv, 12.

Exod. xxi, 20, בשבט is omitted, as in Sam.

xxii, 9, אוכל הבהמה, Sam., Sept., Syr., Arab.

xxiii, 23, והחתי והגרגשי, Sam., Sept.

xxiv, 12, האבנים, Sam.

13, ויעל משה ויהושע, Sept. ἀνέβησαν.

xxxvii, 5, לשאת את הארן בהם, Sam., Arab.

xxxix, 33, ובריחו, Syr., Arab.

Lev. i, 2, מן הצאן, Sam.

vii, 6, יאכל omitted, Vulg.

(3) Cod. 262—Pentateuch, Megilloth, Haphtaroth, in fol., 11th or 12th century.

Lev. iv, 14, אלפתח אהל, Sept., Vulg.

v, 8, והקריב הכהן, Sept.

xi, 40, יכבס בגדיו ורחץ במים, Sept. (but not in the Complut. and Aldine).

xix, 27, ולא, Sam., Vulg., Arab.

Deut. i, 40, פנו וסעו לכם, Sam.

iii, 14, ויאיר, Sam., Sept., Syr., Arab., Targ., Jonathan.

הארגב, Sam.

vi, 2, ובניך, Sept., Vulg.

xxxiv, 2, כלארץ נפתלי, Sept., Syr.

(4) Cod. 274—Pentateuch, with points, 4to, 11th or 12th century; it ends with Deut. xxxii, 51, and has the Masorah finalis.

Gen. xxxi, 35, ותאמר רחל אל אביה, Syr.

Numb. xxix, 11, ונסכה, Sept.

27, כמשפטם, Sept., Syr.

7. The *Odessa MSS.* In the year 1845 E. M. Primer published his *Prospectus der der Odessaer Gesellschaft für Geschichte und Alterthümer gehörenden ältesten und rabbinischen Manuscripte*, whereby a number of MSS. became known to the literary world. They were bought in 1863, and are now in the Imperial Library at St. Petersburg. A very accurate catalogue of them was published by Harkavy and Strack (Leipsic and St. Petersburg, 1875). Of these codices only two are of great importance, viz., one containing the later prophets, dated A.D. 916, and another containing a complete Old Test. with both Masorahs, on

491 leaves, said to be a copy of Asher's codex (?). It is dated A.D. 1009. Of the latter, Bär and Delitzsch availed themselves in their Hebrew-Latin edition of the Psalms and in the edition of Job, where a fac-simile of that codex is also given. The former has been published by H. L. Strack (*Prophetarum Posteriorum Codex Babylonicus Petropolitanus*, Lipsiae, 1876) in fac-simile, by means of photo-lithography, at the expense of the emperor Alexander II of Russia. The whole work was done in three years, and is a monument to the editor and his imperial patron. The text, surrounded with Masoretic notes, and furnished with the so-called Babylonian system of vocalization, occupies 449 folio pages. The Latin preface gives the history of the codex, and the critical annotations, which follow the text, are intended to help the student in the perusal of the same. The following list of various readings does not affect the vowel points, but merely the consonants. The reading of Van der Hooght is given first:

Isa. i, 7, עריכם—ועריכם, and so many codd., Syr., Arab.

22, לסגים—לסיגים, thus some older and modern editions, as Münster, Hutter, Michaelis, Hahn-Rosenmüller, Letteris, Bär-Delitzsch.

iii, 23, הגלינים—והגלינים, so a great many codd., all versions, Rashi, Kimchi, Ibn-Ezra.

iv, 1, ושמלתנו—ושמלתינו, so some codd., Sept., Syr., Arab., Vulg.

vii, 14, עמנואל—עמנו אל, thus many codd. and editions, as Münster, Hutter, Clodius-Bürkelin, Michaelis, Reineccius, Simonis, Hahn-Rosenmüller, Stier and Theile's Polyglot, the Warsaw Rabbinic Bible.

x, 16, אדני—יהוה, so many codd. and editions.

xv, 2, כל—וכל.

גדועה—גרועה, so many codd., and editions of Athias, Clodius, Opitz, Michaelis, Reineccius, Simonis, Letteris, Bär-Delitzsch.

4, נפשו—ונפשו.

xvi, 7, חרשת—חרשת.

10, לא ירעע—ולא ירעע, the ולא is found in many codd., Sept., Syr., Targ., Vulg., Arab.

xix, 13, והתעו—התעו, many codd., Vulg., Targ., Norzi, and a great many editions.

xx, 2, רגלך—רגליך, codd., Sept., Syr., Vulg., Arab.

xxi, 12, אתא—אתה, so many codd.

xxviii, 2, לאדני—ליהוה, so many codd.

xxix, 19, ואבינו—ואביוני.

23, ומעשה—מעשה.

xxx, 6, עורים, Kethib, עירים, Keri—עירים, Kethib and Keri.

xxxiii, 1, בגדו בך—בגדו בו.

xxxiv, 13, קמוש—קמוש.

xxxv, 9, לא יהיה—ולא יהיה.

xxxvi, 2, רבשקה—רב שקה.

15, לא—ולא.

xxxvii, 9, על—אל.

17, עינך—עיניך, Sept., Syr., Vulg.

38, אסר הדן—אסרהדן.

xxxviii, 11, חדל—חלד.

14, יהוה—אדני.

18, לא ישברו—ולא ישברו.

xxxix, 6, לא יותר—ולא יותר.

xliii, 19, עתה—ועתה.

xliv, 24, מיאתי—מי אתי.

xlv, 21, יועצו—נועצו, but by a later hand יועצו.

xlix, 9, לאשר—ולאשר, many codd., Sept., Vulg., Syr., Targ.

lii, 9, רננו—ורננו.

liv, 9, כי מי—כימי.

lvi, 1, אל יהוה—על יהוה.

lxiii, 11, רעה—רעי, so many codd., Vulg., D. Kimchi, Abarbanel, Solomon ben-Melech.

lxiv, 3, לא האזינו—ולא האזינו, so many codd.

lxv, 20, לא יהיה—ולא יהיה.

22, לא יטעו—ולא יטעו.

lxvi, 2, על דברי—אל דברי.

17, אחד, Kethib, אחת, Keri — אחת, Kethib and Keri.

This very incomplete list from the prophet Isaiah (space prohibits our giving readings from the other prophets) is sufficient to show the great importance of this codex.

8. The *Firkowitsch MSS*. This famous collection of the Karaite Abraham Firkowitsch (q. v.) was bought for the Imperial Library at St. Petersburg in the year 1862, and is also described by Harkavy and Strack in their *Catalogue*. Altogether this collection contains 146 MSS., of which 47 are *synagogue rolls* (1–5 on leather, 6–47 on parchment), three of which contain only the entire Pentateuch (No. 10, dated A.D. 940, 19, dated A.D. 920, and No. 47), and the rest *manuscripts* in book form (viz., No. 48–146; of which 48–123 are without translation, 124–146 with translation, the translations being either Arabic, Tartar, or Persian). In the several parts of the Old Test. edited by Bär and Delitzsch, the prefaces also contain notices concerning manuscripts used by the editors.

Literature.—Tychsen, *Tentamen de Variis Codicum Hebraicorum . . . Generibus* (Rostock, 1772); *Befreytes Tentamen*, etc. (Leipsic, 1774); Eichhorn, *Einleitung in das Alte Testament*, ii, 456–584 (4th ed. Göttingen, 1823); De' Rossi, *Proleg.* i, xix–xxi, § 19; De Wette, *Einleitung*, § 140–146, 8th ed.; § 108–114, 7th ed.; Strack, *Prolegomena Critica*, p. 9–58. For a description of manuscripts, see Le Long, *Biblioth. Sacra*, I, ch. ii, p. 49–61 (ed. Paris, 1723 fol.); Wolf, *Bibl. Hebræa*, ii, 293–324; iv, 79–98; Kennicott, *Dissert. Generalis* (Oxford, 1780 fol.; ed. Bruns, Brunswick, 1783); De' Rossi, I, lix–xciv; xcvii–cxxv; cxxvi–cxxxv; IV, xxii–xxviii; *Manuscripti Codices Hebraici Bibliotheca* (Parma, 1803, 3 vols.); G. B. De' Rossi, *Libri Stampati di Letteratura Sacra Ebraica ed Orientale della Bibliotheca del Dott.* p. 79–82 (ibid. 1812); Köcher, *Nova Bibliotheca Hebraica*, ii, 42–46; Rosenmüller, *Handbuch für die Literatur der bibl. Kritik*, etc., ii, 17 sq.; Winer, *Handbuch der theol. Lit.* i, 96; *Catalogus Universitatis Lipsiensis*, tom. 83 (exeg. appar.), fol. 203–205. Besides these works, compare the different catalogues of public libraries, viz.,

1. *Vatican:* Assemani, *Bibliothecæ Apostolicæ Vaticanæ Codicum Manu Scriptorum Catalogus* (Rome, 1756 fol.).
2. *Bodleian:* Uri, *Catalogus* (Oxford, 1787), and Steinschneider, *Conspectus Codd. MSS. Hebræorum*, etc. (Berlin, 1857).
3. *Cambridge:* Schiller-Szinessy, *Catalogue of the Hebrew MSS. preserved in the University Library* (Cambridge, 1875).
4. *Paris: Catalogue des Manuscrits Hébreux et Samaritans de la Bibliothèque Impériale* (Paris, 1866).
5. *Vienna:* Krafft und Deutsch, *Die handschriftlichen hebräischen Werke der k. Hofbibliothek zu Wien* (Vienna, 1847).
6. *St. Petersburg: Catalog der hebräischen Bibelhandschriften der kaiserlichen öffentlichen Bibliothek in St. Petersburg*, by Harkavy and Strack (1875).
7. *Munich:* Steinschneider, *Die hebräischen Handschriften der k. Hof- und Staats-Bibliothek in München* (1875).
8. *Berlin:* Steinschneider, *Verzeichniss der hebräischen Handschriften der königlichen Bibliothek* (1878).
9. *Leyden:* Steinschneider, *Catalogus Codicum Hebræorum Bibl. Acad. Lugd. Bataviæ* (Leyden, 1858).
10. *Leipsic: Catalogus Librorum Manu Scriptorum. . . . Codices Linguarum Orientalium Descripserunt*, by Fleischer and Delitzsch (Grimma, 1838).
11. *Hamburg:* Steinschneider, *Catalog der Handschriften in der Stadtbibliothek zu Hamburg* (1877).
12. *Turin: Codices Manuscripti Bibliothecæ Regiæ Taurinensis Athenæi*, edd. Pasinus, Rivantella, Berta (Turin, 1749).
13. *Dresden:* Fleischer, *Catalogus Codicum MSS. Orientalium Biblioth. Reg. Dresdensis* (Dresden, 1831).
14. *Florence:* Bisconius, *Bibliothecæ Ebraicæ Græcæ Florentinæ S. Bibliothecæ Medicæo-Laurentianæ Catalogus* (Florence, 1757).
15. *Cesena: Mucciolus, Catalogus Codicum Manuscriptorum Malatestianæ Cæsenatis Bibliothecæ* (1780, 1784, 2 vols. fol.).
16. *Parma.* See above, De' Rossi.
17. *Spain and Portugal:* Neubauer, *Notes sur des Manuscrits Hébreux Existant dans Quelques Bibliothèques de l'Espagne et du Portugal*, in the *Archives des Missions Scientifiques et Littéraires*, II, v, 423–435 (Paris, 1868).

The various readings found in the St. Petersburg manuscripts and in such as have of late come to light, but are enumerated by Bär and Delitzsch in the different parts of their Old-Test. edition, have been made use of by the latter, and are given in a very convenient form in the *Appendices Criticæ et Masoreticæ*, viz. Genesis, p. 74 sq.; Job, p. 33–56; Psalms, p. 83–123; Proverbs, p. 30–54; Isaiah, p. 65–82; Ezekiel, p. 73–107; Minor Prophets, p. 59–85; Daniel, p. 62–85; Ezra-Nehemiah, p. 99–119 (these last three books printed together). Of the St. Petersburg manuscripts, professor Delitzsch has also made use in his commentary on Song of Songs (p. 178–184) and Ecclesiastes (p. 425–435), published at Leipsic in 1875. A comparison of the *Codex Babylonicus* from the year 916, and of the MS. from the year 1009, with Hahn's edition of the Old Test., which in the main is a reprint of Van der Hooght, has been made by Strack with reference to Isaiah, and the result was published in the *Zeitschrift für luth. Theologie*, 1877, p. 17–52. All these various readings do not essentially impair the authority of the Masoretic text, nor materially alter the meaning of any important passage. (B. P.)

Manwantara, a grand period of time in Hindû chronology, including seventy-one *maha-yugs*, or divine ages, being the reign of one Manu (q. v.), with his posterity of sons and grandsons. The reigns of the fourteen Manus who reigned in succession extended to one thousand *maha-yugs*, or one *kalpa*.

Manx Version. See MANKS.

Maori (or New Zealand) Version OF THE SCRIPTURES. The Maori is the most cultivated of all the Polynesian dialects. See NEW ZEALAND. The first copies of portions of the New Test. were printed in 1832, having been translated by the Rev. Mr. Yate, but the first complete edition of the New Test. did not appear till 1840. A second was printed in 1842, and a third in 1844, all at the expense of the British and Foreign Bible Society. A revised edition by bishop Williams and the Rev. T. W. Meller was published more recently. The Old Test. was completed in 1856, the translation being that of the Rev. R. Maunsell. In 1859 a revision of the Bible was undertaken, which was completed in 1867. This revised edition has also been printed since. See *Bible of Every Land*, p. 383. (B. P.)

Maphrida, the second dignitary of the Jacobite Church (q. v.) in the East.

Maracas, idols of the Brazilians. The word is a corruption of *Tamaraca*, which is the name of a certain fruit about the size of an ostrich's egg, and shaped like a gourd. These idols, indeed, were nothing more than the fruit Tamaraca dressed up in beautiful feathers, and fixed on a staff, which the priests stuck in the ground, and ordered the people to bring food and drink before it.

Marae is the name given in the South Sea islands to a heathen temple. All were uncovered, and resembled oratories rather than temples. The form of the interior or area was frequently that of a square or parallelogram, the sides of which extended forty or fifty feet. Two sides of this space were enclosed by a high stone wall; the front was protected by a low fence; and opposite, a solid pyramidal structure was raised, in front of which the images were kept and the altars fixed. These piles were often immense. Within the enclosure, the houses of the priests and keepers of the idols were erected. Ruins of these temples are found in every situation; on the summit of a hill, on the extremity of a point of land extending into the sea, or in the recesses of an extensive and overshadowing grove.

Maramba, an idol of the negroes of Angola, Congo, etc., in Africa. It stands erect over against the temple dedicated to its peculiar service, in a basket formed like a bee-hive. To this divinity the negroes make particular application for success when they go hunting or fishing, and for the relief of such as are sick. Those also charged with crime are obliged to plead their cause before it. In order to do this the accused prostrates himself at the feet of the idol, embraces it with the profoundest veneration, and says, "Behold, Maramba, thy servant is come to justify himself before thee." If the defendant is guilty, he is said to fall dead on the spot. The devotees usually carry little images in small boxes about with them. Maramba always marches at the head of their armies, and he is presented with the first morsel, and the first cup of wine served at the king's table.

Marathi Version OF THE SCRIPTURES. The Marathi, which is spoken by the Marathas or Mahrattas (q. v.), may be regarded as a link between the Sanscrit dialects of northern India and the languages of the Deccan. Some of the words and idioms are obviously of cognate origin with the Bengalee, while in others a notable approximation may be detected to the Tamil, Telinga, and the other languages of the South. Two different characters are used in writing Marathi, the Modior Modhe, a kind of running hand, which is derived from, and still retains a strong resemblance to the Devanagari (or Sanscrit character), and the Balboodh or Balborah, which appears to be almost, if not quite, the Devanagari itself. The former, vulgarly termed Modi, is most generally understood, being employed in all transactions of business; but the latter is preferred for printing, because it possesses several letters in which the Modi is deficient; it is, besides, uniform and regular in appearance, while the Modi varies as much in style as the handwriting of different individuals in Europe.

A version of the Scriptures in Marathi was commenced at Serampore in 1804. The first few copies of the gospel of Matthew were printed in the Devanagari character, but this character was soon replaced by the Modi, as the more generally intelligible to the natives. This latter character was employed in all the subsequent Serampore editions. In 1811 the New Test. was completed, and in 1820 the Old Test. left the press. A second and revised edition of the New Test. appeared about the year 1825.

Another version of the Marathi Scriptures was commenced in 1817 by American missionaries, and in 1826 the entire New Test. was published by them, with the aid of the Bombay Auxiliary and the British and Foreign Bible Society. An improved and carefully revised edition of this Test. was printed in 1830. In 1834 the Bombay Bible Society undertook another revisal of the Marathi New Test. and determined upon issuing an edition in the Balboodh character. The printing of this edition was commenced in 1835, but in the same year it was found necessary to print a separate edition of the gospels in the Modi, or current character, for the use of the lower class of natives.

While these editions of the New Test. were in course of preparation, the American missionaries, together with the Rev. J. Dixon of the Church mission at Nassuck, zealously prosecuted the translation of the Old Test. into Marathi, which was completed at the American mission press in 1855. Mr. Dixon, by whom the greater part of this important version was made, did not live to see the completion of this edition at press. From the report of the British and Foreign Bible Society for 1863 we learn that the entire Bible has been revised, published, and put into circulation. In the report for 1881 it is stated that the revision of the entire Bible has again been inaugurated, with the assistance of Rev. Baba Padmanji. The revision work is still in progress. See *Bible of Every Land*, p. 126.

For linguistic purposes see Ballantyne, *A Grammar of the Mahratta Language;* Bellairs, *A Grammar of the Marathi Language;* Molesworth, *A Dictionary, Marathi and English* (Bombay, 1857); Padmanji, *A Compendium of Molesworth's Marathi and English Dictionary;* Navalkar, *The Student's Marathi Grammar* (new ed. Bombay, 1879). (B. P.)

Marbury, ALEXANDER M., M.D., D.D., a Protestant Episcopal clergyman, was rector in Petersville, Md., for seven years preceding 1858, when he became rector of St. Paul's, Aquasco, in which relation he remained until his death in 1873. See *Prot. Episc. Almanac*, 1874, p. 138.

Marcellius, HENRICUS, a Jesuit, who died at Bamberg, April 25, 1664, wrote, *Canones Explicandæ Sacræ Scripturæ: — De Augustissimo Corporis et Sanguinis Domini Sacramento:—Theologia Divinæ Scripturæ:—De Justificatione Christiana:—Commentarius in Librum Josuæ:—Testimonium Danielis de Regno Christi Inexpugnabili:—Enchiridion Militiæ Christianæ.* See Alegambe, *Bibliotheca Scriptorum Societatis Jesu;* Jöcher, *Allgemeines Gelehrten-Lexikon*, s. v. (B. P.)

Marcello, BENEDETTO, an eminent Italian composer of sacred music, was born at Venice, July 24, 1686. He made a thorough study of music under various masters, and at the same time studied law and became an advocate, holding several offices under the government. He was a member of the Council of Forty, and treasurer at Brescia, where he died, July 17, 1739. His most esteemed work is his music for Giustiniani's version of *Fifty Psalms*, of which a fine edition was published by John Garth, of Durham, in eight volumes folio, with English words. His other works consist of oratorios, masses, cantatas, madrigals, and different parts of the Roman Catholic service. He also left a MS. treatise on music.

Marchant, JACQUES, a Roman Catholic theologian, who died at Couvin, Belgium, in 1648, is the author of *Rationale Evangelizantium* (transl. into French by Ricard, *Le Rational des Prédicateurs de l'Évangile*, Paris, 1876, 4 vols.):—*Hortum Pastorum* (French, *Le Jardin des Pasteurs*), a treatise on faith, hope, and charity:—*Virga Aaronis Florens* (French, *La Verge d'Aaron*), on the sacerdotal life:—*Candelabrum Mysticum*, on the seven sacraments. Marchant's works were published in French by Ricard and Berton, in nine volumes. See Lichtenberger, *Encyclop. des Sciences Religieuses*, s. v.; Jöcher, *Allgemeines Gelehrten-Lexikon*, s. v. (B. P.)

Marcus, a Scotch prelate, was a native of Galloway, in Scotland, and was promoted to the see of the Isles in 1275, and consecrated the same year. He was also lord high-chancellor of Scotland. He held a synod at Kirk-Bradden in March, 1291, where thirty-nine canons were made. He died in 1303. See Keith, *Scottish Bishops*, p. 300.

Mareshah. The ruined site, *Khurbet Merash*, is three quarters of a mile south-west of Beit-Jibrin, and consists merely of "traces of ruins, cisterns, and caves" (*Memoirs* to Ordnance Survey, iii, 284).

Margetson, JAMES, D.D., an Irish prelate, was born in 1600, at Drighlington, in Yorkshire, and received his education in Peterhouse College, Cambridge; was promoted to the parish of Watlas; in 1635 was advanced to the deanery of Waterford; in 1637 to that of Derry, and in 1639 was made dean of Christ Church, Dublin. Throughout the troubled period of 1641 his charity and benevolence to the sufferers were singularly eminent. In July, 1647, he joined in a remonstrance to the commissioners of the English Parliament, praying liberty for the use of the common prayer in their respective churches, and rejecting the directory ordered to be used instead. Soon after, the war obliged him to flee to England, where he was thrown into prison. He finally was released, and sought refuge in London. When Charles II was restored to the throne, Margetson was selected to fill the metropolitan chair of the province of Dublin, and was consecrated Jan. 27, 1660. In 1662 he enforced the principle of jurisdiction and control over the pulpits of his diocese. About this time Margetson was one of the spiritual peers who voted for the third reading of the Act of Settlement. During the time he presided over the see of Dublin he liberally contributed to the repair of both its cathedrals. In 1663 he was translated to the province of Armagh. He was also afterwards chosen vice-chancellor of Trinity College, Dublin. He died in August, 1678. See D'Alton, *Memoirs of the Archbishops of Dublin*, p. 275.

Margoliouth, MOSES, Ph.D., LL.D., a minister of the Church of England, was born of Jewish parentage in 1818, at Suwalki, in Poland. In 1837 he arrived in England, and in the year following openly professed Christianity. In 1840 he entered Trinity College, Dublin, and, after completing his studies, was ordained in 1844. He held various positions in the Episcopal Church, and at the time of his death, Feb. 25, 1881, he was vicar of Little Linford, near Newport Pagnell, Bucks, England. He is the author of many works: *Fundamental Principles of Modern Judaism Investigated* (Lond. 1843): —*The Jews in Great Britain* (ibid. 1846):—*A Pilgrimage to the Land of my Fathers* (ibid. 1850, 2 vols.):—*History of the Jews in Great Britain* (1851, 3 vols.):—*Abyssinia, its Past, Present, and Future* (1866):—*The Spirit of Prophecy* (1864):—*Sacred Minstrelsy: A Lecture on Biblical and Post-Biblical Hebrew Music* (1863): —*The Oracles of God and their Vindication* (1870):—*Vestiges of the Historic Anglo-Hebrews in East Anglia* (eod.):—*The Poetry of the Hebrew Pentateuch* (1871): —*The Lord's Prayer no Adaptation of Existing Jewish Petitions* (1876). Besides, he left a great many works in MS. (B. P.)

Marie (Madeleine) DE LA TRINITÉ, the founder of a religious order, was born June 3, 1616, at Aix, in Provence. She was the daughter of a soldier, and having resolved at the age of fifteen never to marry, placed herself under the direction of a Capuchin, Yvan, who composed for her a book, entitled *Conduite à la Perfection Chrétienne*. With his assistance she founded, in 1632, the order of La Miséricorde. This order, beginning in 1637, at Aix, had considerable difficulties, being much opposed by the archbishop of that place, but approved by the bishop of Avignon, and sustained by the Jesuits. She died at Avignon, Feb. 20, 1678. The order of La Miséricorde was approved, in 1642, by pope Urban VIII, and followed the rule of St. Augustine. See Hoefer, *Nouv. Biog. Générale*, s. v.

Mariette, AUGUSTE FERDINAND FRANÇOIS, a French archæologist, was born at Boulogne-sur-Mer, Feb. 11, 1821. While yet a very young man he was intrusted with the task of arranging the papers of his deceased cousin, Nestor l'Hôte, the companion of Champollion in Egypt from 1827 to 1829. Thenceforth Auguste Mariette became inspired with an eager interest in Egyptian archaeology, and devoted his attention to the study of hieroglyphic and Coptic literature. In 1849 he received a post in the Egyptian department of the Louvre, and was shortly afterwards sent to Egypt for the purpose of seeking and purchasing Coptic MSS. in the monasteries of that country. Soon after his arrival at Cairo he made the great discovery of the long-lost Serapeum, or burial-place of the sacred bulls. This, together with other undertakings, is graphically described in his own narrative, *Le Serapéum de Memphis* (Paris, 1857). He had not long returned to France when he was offered and accepted the appointment of conservator of monuments to the Egyptian government. In this position he undertook a long series of important excavations in various parts of Egypt. The magnificent temples of Denderah and Edfu were completely disinterred, and hundreds of thousands of valuable inscriptions were brought to light. The Sphinx was laid bare; the mysterious building known as the Temple of the Sphinx was discovered; extensive works were proceeded with at Karnak, Deir el-Bahari, Medinet Habu, and Abydos; but we cannot catalogue his archæological achievements. The Bulak Museum, and the many magnificent volumes in which he has recorded the results of his labors, are, after all, the noblest monuments to his memory. His *Denderah* (1873-75, 5 vols.):—his *Monuments Divers* (1872):—his *Abydos* (1870):—his magnificent *Karnak* (1875):—*Deir el-Bahari* (1877):—*Liste Géographique des Pylones de Karnak* (1875), etc., bear witness to his extraordinary industry, and would alone be enough work and honor for any one man. He died at Cairo, Jan. 19, 1881. (B. P.)

Markham, WILLIAM, D.C.L., archbishop of York, was born in Ireland in 1719, but was brought to England in his infancy, and at an early age entered Westminster School. He was afterwards sent to Christ Church College, Oxford, where he obtained the degree of M.A. in 1745. In 1750 he was appointed to the office of high master of Westminster School, the duties of which he discharged with great industry and success for about fourteen years. In 1759 he was made a prebendary of Durham, in 1764 resigned his mastership of Westminster, and in the following year was preferred to the deanery of Rochester, which, in 1767, he vacated for that of Christ Church. In 1771 he was consecrated bishop of Chester, and in 1777 translated to the archiepiscopal see of York, from which he was removed by death, Nov. 3, 1807. The virtues of this distinguished prelate were of a most benevolent and amiable kind. With great learning he was modest; and though raised to the highest station he was meek and humble. See (Lond.) *Annual Register*, 1807, p. 789.

Marlow, MICHAEL, a Church of England divine, was born near London, in November, 1758. He was educated at Merchant Taylor's School, from which he was elected to a scholarship at St. John's College in the eighteenth year of his age. He was admitted actual fellow in 1779; took the degree of B.A. April 5, 1780; that of M.A. Feb. 11, 1784; and became B.D. in April, 1789, being the vicar of St. Giles's, in the suburbs of Oxford, and tutor of the college. In March, 1795, he was unanimously elected president of St. John's, and presented by the society to the rectory at Handborough, near Woodstock. He took the degree of D.D. on March 24 of the same year; served the office of vice-chancellor of the university during four years, viz. from Michaelmas term, 1798, to the same term, 1802; and was preferred to the prebendal stall of Canterbury in 1808. He was nominated one of the select preachers of the university in 1805, and again in 1817; was likewise a delegate of accounts, one of the commissioners of sewers, and curator of the Sheldonian Theatre. He died Feb. 16, 1828. See (Lond.) *Annual Register*, 1828, p. 222.

Marokki, SAMUEL. See MOROCCO, SAMUEL.

Marperger, BERNHARD WALTHER, a Lutheran theologian of Germany, was born at Hamburg, May 14, 1682. He studied at Altdorf and other universities, was in 1705 preacher at Nuremberg, in 1724 court-preacher at Dresden, and died March 29, 1746, a doctor of divinity. He wrote, *Auslegung der ersten Epistel Johannis* (Nuremberg, 1710):—*Diss. Inauguralis de Nexu Veritatis cum Pietate* (Altdorf, 1724; Germ. transl. by Gräff, Leipsic, eod.):—*De Agno ad Aræ Cornua Ligando, ad Illustr. Psa. xcviii*, 8 (Dresden, 1734), etc. See Döring, *Die gelehrten Theologen Deutschlands*, s. v.; Winer, *Handbuch der theol. Lit.* i, 341; Jöcher, *Allgemeines Gelehrten-Lexikon*, s. v. (B. P.)

Marquesan Version OF THE SCRIPTURES. The Marquesan is a dialect spoken in the Marquesas or Washington group of islands, situated about nine degrees south of the equator, at a distance of nine hundred miles north-east of Tahiti. Ever since 1797 various efforts have been made at different intervals to proclaim the glad tidings of the gospel in these islands. For a long period these attempts were rendered abortive, till at length, in 1834, the Rev. Messrs. Rodgerson, Stallworthy, and Darling, agents of the London Missionary Society, met with some encouragement in their endeavors to instruct the people, and reclaim them from idolatry. Mr. Darling devoted himself to the translation of the Scriptures, or, rather, to the adaptation of the Tahitian version to the Marquesan dialect. Single extracts of Scripture were published, but the first complete book of the New Test.—the gospel of John—was not published till 1866. This is up to date the only gospel printed by the British and Foreign Bible Society. See *Bible of Every Land*, p. 380. (B. P.)

Marryat, ZEPHANIAH, D.D., an English Independent minister, was born about 1684. He was first an assistant preacher at Union Street, Southwark, with Mr. Samuel Palmer, who had a controversy with the Rev. John Wesley's father, and succeeded as sole pastor in 1710. He became a master of Greek literature. In 1720 he acquired reputation by a published work, *The Exalted Saviour*, intended to correct prevailing errors on the Trinity. He superintended a large charity-school in Gravel Lane, and preached a Sunday-evening lecture at Lime Street. In 1743 he was chosen divinity tutor at an academy held in Plasterers' Hall, and was very successful. He was also one of the Merchant Lecturers. He died suddenly, Sept. 15, 1754. See Wilson, *Dissenting Churches*, iv, 199.

Marsden, J. B., an English divine, was born about 1803. He graduated from St. John's College, Cambridge, in 1827, and was ordained to the curacy of Burslem, Staffordshire, from whence he removed to the curacy of Harrow, Middlesex. From 1833 to 1844 he held the rectory of Tooting, Surrey, during the minority of his successor. From 1844 to 1852 he was vicar of Great Missenden, Bucks, and from 1852 to his death, in 1870, incumbent of St. Peter's, Birmingham. Mr. Marsden published, *The History of the Early Puritans, from the Reformation to the Opening of the Civil War*:—*The History of the Later Puritans, from the Opening of the Civil War to 1662*:—*The Churchmanship of the New Testament*:—*Discourses for the Festivals of the Church of England*:—*The Law of Fasting, as set forth in Holy Scripture*, a pamphlet:—*Sermons*:—*The Coming of Christ*:—*Sermons from the Old Testament*:—*Christian Churches and Sects*:—*Life of the Rev. Samuel Marsden, of New South Wales*:—*Life of the Rev. Hugh Stowell, of Manchester*:—*Two Sermons on the Life, Ministry, and Death of the Rev. Richard Marks*, author of *The Retrospect*. He was also editor of the *Christian Observer* from 1859 to 1869. Although not gifted as a preacher, he was a ripe scholar, and his writings demonstrate his ability as an author. See (Lond.) *Christian Observer*, August, 1870, p. 633; Allibone, *Dict. of Brit. and Amer. Authors*, s. v.

Marselus, NICHOLAS J., D.D., a minister of the Reformed (Dutch) Church, was born in Mohawk Valley in 1792. He graduated from Union College in 1810, and from New Brunswick Seminary in 1815; was licensed by the Classis of New Brunswick, became pastor at Greenbush and Blooming Grove from 1815 to 1822, New York city from 1822 to 1858, and thereafter was without a charge until his death, May 5, 1876. His publications are, *Translation of Elijah* (1825):—*The Good Old Way* (1830):—*Gospel Ministry* (1842):—*Ministerial Appeal* (1850):—*A Sermon* (eod.). See Corwin, *Manual of the Reformed Church in America*, 3d ed. p. 367.

Marsh, SIDNEY HARPER, D.D., a Congregational minister, son of Rev. Dr. James Marsh, was born at Hampden Sidney, Va., Aug. 29, 1825. He graduated from Vermont University in 1846; from 1846 to 1851 was employed in teaching; and the following year attended Union Theological Seminary. After his ordination as an evangelist, May 1, 1853, he went to Oregon in the service of the Society for Promoting Collegiate Education; became principal of Tualatin Academy, at Forest Grove; was chosen president of Pacific University, when it was incorporated, in 1854, and held that office until his death, Feb. 5, 1879. See *Cong. Yearbook*, 1880, p. 23.

Marshall, Alexander Washington, D.D., an Episcopal minister, was born at Charleston, S. C., Aug. 10, 1798. He graduated from the General Theological Seminary in 1828, and in October of that year was ordained deacon, and took charge of St. David's Church, Cheraw, S. C. Having been ordained to the priesthood, March 14, 1830, he continued there until 1841, when he was called to the organization and care of a city mission, worshipping in St. John's Chapel, Charleston. He died in that city, Nov. 7, 1876. See *Obituary Record of Yale College*, 1877.

Marshall, George, D.D., a Presbyterian minister, was born in Pennsylvania in 1806. He graduated from Jefferson College, and entered upon his ministry at Bethel in 1832, in which relation he continued until his death, April 30, 1872. Dr. Marshall was well known in western Pennsylvania as one of the leaders of the Presbyterian Church. In the councils of the Church he was always heard with respectful attention, and his words were direct and weighty. See *Presbyterian*, May 18, 1872.

Marsollier, JACQUES, a French ecclesiastical writer, was born at Paris in 1647, and died at Uzès in 1724. He is the author of, *Histoire de l'Origine des Dixmes, des Bénéfices et des Autres Biens Temporels de l'Église* (Lyons, 1689):—*Histoire de l'Inquisition et de son Origine* (Cologne, 1693; based upon Limborch's *Historia Inquisitionis*):—*Histoire du Ministère du Cardinal de Ximènez* (Toulouse, 1693; Paris, 1739):—*Histoire de Henri VII, Roi d'Angleterre* (1697):—*La Vie de St. François de Sales* (1700):—*Apologie ou Justification d'Érasme* (1713):—*Entretiens sur les Devoirs de la Vie Civile, et sur Plusieurs Points de la Vie Morale Chrétienne* (1714). See Lichtenberger, *Encyclop. des Sciences Religieuses*, s. v.; Winer, *Handbuch der theol. Lit.* i, 696, 716, 870. (B. P.)

Märtens, KARL ANDREAS AUGUST, a Lutheran theologian of Germany, was born April 18, 1774, and died March 17, 1832, at Halberstadt, doctor of theology and first preacher. He wrote, *Ueber die symbolischen Bücher der evangelisch-lutherischen Kirche*, etc. (Halberstadt, 1830):—*Ueber Pietismus, sein Wesen und seine Gefahren* (ibid. 1826):—*Theophanes oder über die göttliche Offenbarung* (ibid. 1819):—*Eleutheros, oder Untersuchung über die Freiheit des menschlichen Willens* (Magdeburg, 1823):—*Jesus auf dem Gipfel seines irdischen Lebens* (Halberstadt, 1811). See Winer, *Handbuch der theol. Lit.* i, 335, 365, 369, 482, 550; ii, 159; Zuchold, *Bibl. Theol.* ii, 855. (B. P.)

Martensen, HANS LARSEN, one of the most prominent Danish Lutheran theologians, was born Aug. 9, 1808, at Flensburg. He studied at Copenhagen, and in 1832 passed the ecclesiastical examination and received a gold medal. The same year he received from the government a travelling scholarship, and visited Berlin, Munich, Vienna, and Paris, giving particular attention to the study of the philosophy of the Middle Ages. On his return to Denmark, in 1836, he became a licentiate in theology, submitting a thesis on the *Autonomy of the Human Conscience*, which was afterwards translated from the Latin into Danish (1841), and into German (1845). The next year he began to lecture to the younger students in the University of Copenhagen on moral philosophy. The material of these lectures was published in his *Outline of a System of Moral Philosophy*, in 1841. His lectures on *Speculative Dogmatik*, from 1840, when he became professor ordinarius, awakened extraordinary interest. "It was a new and unheard-of gospel, in charming language, that flowed from his inspired, enrapturing lips. Not merely did the students contend with one another for places in his lecture-room, but men advanced in years, of various callings, were found regular hearers." His popularity became greater still when, in 1845, he became court-preacher, and his Hegelianism began to give a coloring to the conscience of his generation. The public was thoroughly prepared to receive his doctrines gladly when, in 1849, he published the most successful and famous of his contributions to theological literature, his *Christian Dogmatics*, which has been translated into most European languages, even into modern Greek, and has exercised as wide an influence on Protestant thought as any volume of our century. In Germany it has enjoyed a popularity even wider than in Scandinavia, and has been honored by a formal refutation from the propaganda at Rome. It was not, however, unchallenged at home, a severe attack upon it having been made by professor Rasmus Nielsen, supported secretly by Kirkegaard (q. v.). In 1854, when bishop Mynster died, Martensen, who had refused the bishopric of Sleswig, accepted the primacy of Denmark, and began his administrative labors in the Church with acts of great vigor and determination. He became in consequence cordially detested, and violently attacked by all those sections of the Danish Lutheran body which wavered to this side or to that from a hierarchical orthodoxy. A great part of Martensen's time and energy henceforth was taken up with polemics against Grundtvig, Nielsen, the Catholics, and the Irvingites. Many of his later writings are of this purely controversial character, his *Exposure of the So-called Grundtvigianism*, which he styled "a leaven, but not a principle," his *Catholicism and Protestantism*, against the claims of the Vatican Council, his *Socialism and Christendom*. The time at his command, after faithful administration of his duties, was, during his earlier years, devoted to the preparation of his *System of Christian Ethics* (1871–78; German, 1878–79; English, 1873–82), and his final scientific work in the line of his early studies of the mystics, on *Jacob Böhme* (1879; German, 1882; English, by T. Rhys Evans, 1885). As a fitting conclusion of his literary activity, he published his *Autobiography* (1883). Dr. Martensen died, Feb. 3, 1884, and was buried with great solemnity in his own cathedral of Our Lady. The king and the Conservative party knew what they owed "to the rigid Tory prelate, whose face was set like a flint against the modern spirit in politics, in literature, in philosophy. He was a great man, a man who did honor to Denmark. It is not the critics of his own country only, it is the more impartial Germans, who have declared Hans Larsen Martensen to be the greatest Protestant theologian of the present century." See Zuchold, *Bibl. Theol.* ii, 856; *Quarterly Review* (Lond. April, 1884); *Lutheran Church Review* (Philadelphia, Pa., July, 1884; *Expositor* (Lond. and N. Y., Jan. 1885). (B. P.)

Martigny, ALEXANDRE, a French archæologist, was born April 22, 1808, at Sauverny, France. He received holy orders in 1832, and died Aug. 19, 1880, at Belley. He is the author of the famous *Dictionnaire des Antiquités Chrétiennes* (Paris, 1864; 2d ed. 1877). In 1865 he published a French translation of De' Rossi's *Bulletino di Archeologia Cristiana*. (B. P.)

Martin (better known as *abbot* **Chaffrey**), a Roman Catholic French writer, was born at Abries in 1813. In 1839 he received holy orders, and was appointed professor at the seminary in Embrun. He was honorary canon of different chapters, and died at Paris in 1872. He published, *Le Panorama des Prédications* (1851–55, 3 vols.; 8th ed. 1864):—*La Bibliothèque des Prédicateurs* (1867–68, 4 vols.):—*Théologie Morale en Tableaux* (1857):—*Répertoire de la Doctrine Chrétienne* (1857; 2d ed. 1859–63, 3 vols.):—*Portraits Littéraires des Plus Célèbres Prédicateurs Contemporains* (1858):—*Mois de Marie des Prédicateurs* (eod. 2 vols.):—*Sermons Nouveaux sur les Mystères de Notre Seigneur Jésus-Christ* (1860, 2 vols.):—*Vies des Saints a l'Usage des Prédicateurs* (1861–68, 4 vols.). See Lichtenberger, *Encyclop. des Sciences Religieuses*, s. v. (B. P.)

Martin, Benjamin N., D.D., a Presbyterian minister and educator, was born at Mt. Holly, N. J., Oct. 20, 1816. He graduated from Yale College in 1837, and from Yale Divinity School in 1840. After serving the Congregational Church in Hadley for five years, he was installed pastor of the Fourth Presbyterian Church in Albany, N. Y. In 1852 he was appointed professor of logic, intellectual and moral philosophy, in the University of New York city, which position he held until his death, Dec. 26, 1883. Among the clergy and literary circles professor Martin enjoyed a large acquaintance. He was very popular among the students, and gave up his whole time to the university. He contributed largely to many religious journals, and was the author of several books. One of his many lectures was delivered before the Yale Theological School, entitled *The Theology of the Doctrine of the Forces*. See *N. Y. Observer*, Jan. 3, 1884; *Cong. Year-book*, 1884, p. 30. (W. P. S.)

Martin, Bon-Louis Henri, a celebrated French historian, was born at St. Quentin, Feb. 20, 1810. He studied at Paris, and like all the other young men of his epoch, fell under the influence of the romantic school, and commenced his literary career with writing verses for periodicals. But he soon betook himself to his life-long study of the history of France. Paul Lacroix suggested that Martin should help him in preparing an immense historical work in forty-eight volumes. It was not to be a history of France, but a collection of extracts from chronicles and histories, extending from the earliest period to 1830. The first volume appeared in 1833, when Martin's colleague deserted him, and he concluded the book in 1836. He then wrote the first volume of a history of Soissons; and believing his studies had fitted him for the task, he commenced the prodigious labor of writing a complete history of France. His interest in the history of the Gauls makes his first volumes the most attractive of all. As successive editions were called for, he spent his time in painstaking revisions of his history, incorporating every new discovery, and keeping his book, up to the fourth edition, in 1878, entirely abreast of the knowledge of the time. In 1878 and 1879 he published a history of France from 1789 to 1830, in four volumes, as a sequel to his great work. In 1878 he was elected a member of the Academie Française, in place of Thiers. Martin died Dec. 14, 1883. With him expired the last of the great historians bred in the school of Thierry. See Hanotaux, *Henri Martin* (Paris, 1885). (B. P.)

Martin, Conrad, a Roman Catholic prelate of Germany, was born May 18, 1812, at Geismar, Prussia, and studied under Allioli and Döllinger, as well as under Gesenius, Tholuck, and Tuch. For some time religious instructor at Cologne, Martin was, in 1844, appointed professor and inspector of the clerical seminary in Bonn. In 1856 he was elected bishop of Paderborn, and from that time was the obedient servant of the papal see. As a member of the Vatican Council, he belonged to those bishops who advocated the infallibility of the pope. He was the first who openly protested against the Prussian May-laws of 1873, and thus he came in conflict with the government. He was fined, and finally imprisoned at Wesel. He escaped into Belgium, and died in exile, July 19, 1879, at St. Guibert. He was buried at Paderborn. He wrote, *Lehrbuch der katholischen Religion für höhere Lehranstalten* (5th ed. Mayence, 1873):—*Lehrbuch der katholischen Moral* (5th ed. ibid. 1865):—*Die Wissenschaft von den göttlichen Dingen* (3d ed. ibid. 1869):—*Die Arbeiten des vatikanischen Konzils* (Paderborn, 1870):—*Vaticani Concilii Documentorum Collectio* (ibid. 1871):—*Drei Jahre aus meinem Leben* (Mayence, 1877), describing his imprisonment and escape:—*Blicke ins Jenseits* (ibid. 1877):—*Zeitbilder* (ibid. 1879, posthumous). (B. P.)

Martin, Jacques, a Protestant theologian of Geneva, was born in 1794. While yet a student, he was obliged to take part in the campaigns against Germany, which the first Napoleon inaugurated. He fought in the battles at Leipsic and Waterloo, and in 1815 went to Geneva. For two years he followed commercial pursuits, and then betook himself to theological study. In 1818 he was enrolled as a student, and in 1822 graduated, presenting for his thesis, *L'Unité de la Foi*. Martin soon distinguished himself, both as an instructor and pulpit orator, and his writings were not only often reprinted, but some of them, as *L'Oraison Dominicale*, were even translated into other languages. He died in 1874. See Bouvier, *Jacques Martin, Prédicateur Patriote*, in the *Étrennes Religieuses* (1877), and the same in Lichtenberger's *Encyclop. des Sciences Religieuses*, s. v. (B. P.)

Martin, James, D.D., an Associate minister, was born at Albany, N. Y., May 12, 1796. He graduated from Union College, Schenectady, in 1819, and after a course in theology in the theological seminary of Philadelphia, was licensed Sept. 2, 1822, and soon after took charge of an Associate Reformed congregation at Albany. He edited the *Religious Monitor* in 1833. In 1842 he was elected professor of didactic theology and Hebrew in the theological seminary at Cannonsburg, Pa. He died June 15, 1846. See Sprague, *Annals of the Amer. Pulpit*, IX, iii, 112.

Martin, Johann, a Reformed theologian, who died at Groningen in 1665, is the author of, *Analysis Popularis in Malachiam Prophetam*:—*Analysis Popularis in Epistolas ad Philippenses et Thessalonicenses*. See Benthem, *Holländischer Kirchen-Staat*; Jöcher, *Allgemeines Gelehrten-Lexikon*, s. v. (B. P.)

Martin (Paschoud), **Joseph**, a Protestant theologian, was born at Nîmes, Oct. 14, 1802. He studied at Geneva, was for some time pastor at Luneray, and in 1828 at Lyons, where he labored with his former classmate, Adolphe Monod. In 1837 he was called to Paris, but after two years of work was obliged to retire from the active ministry for a time on account of an incurable disease. In 1839 he commenced publishing a monthly journal, entitled *Le Disciple de Jésus Christ*. In 1853 he founded *L'Alliance Chrétienne Universelle*, on the following basis: "Love of God, the Creator and Father of all men; love of all men, the immortal creatures and children of God; love of Jesus Christ, the son of God and Saviour of mankind." Adolphe Monod was the first who wrote against the principles of this journal. In 1851 the consistory of Paris appointed the younger Athanase Coquerel as his assistant, and made him retire, under the pretext of heresy, in 1864. In spite of the protests of his medical advisers, Martin resumed his ministerial functions. In 1868 he succeeded Athanase Coquerel, the father, as president of the presbytery, and died May 24, 1873, at Loges, near Versailles. See Lichtenberger, *Encyclop. des Sciences Religieuses*, s. v. (B. P.)

Martin, Samuel, D.D., a Presbyterian minister, was born at Chestnut Level, Lancaster Co., Pa., Jan. 9, 1767. He was converted in his twenty-second year, graduated from the University of Pennsylvania in 1790, was licensed by the Baltimore Presbytery in May, 1793, and soon after was installed pastor of the congregation at Slateridge, York Co., laboring there faithfully for five years, and then accepted a call from the congregation of Chaneford, where he remained until 1812. He died June 28, 1845. Dr. Martin published several sermons: two in which the doctrine of election is proved and illustrated (1806); one on *Regeneration*, printed in the *Spruce Street Lectures*; and one entitled *Children are an Heritage of the Lord*. See Sprague, *Annals of the Amer. Pulpit*, iv, 118.

Martinet, August, a Roman Catholic divine, who died Oct. 11, 1877, at Bamberg, doctor and professor, is the author of, *Hebräische Sprache-Schule für Universitäten* (Bamberg, 1835):—*Chrestomathie aus modernen neuhebräischen Schriften entnommen* (ibid. 1837). See Winer, *Handbuch der theol. Lit.* i, 117; Fürst, *Bibl. Jud.* ii, 232. (B. P.)

Martini, Christian David Anton, a Lutheran theologian of Germany, was born Jan. 22, 1761. He studied at Göttingen, and for some time acted as teacher at his native place. In 1789 he was made professor of theology at Rostock, in 1791 doctor of theology. In

1804 he was called to Würzburg, in 1807 to Altdorf, and in 1809 to Munich. Martin died Sept. 1, 1815. He wrote, *Commentatio Philologico-Critica in Locum Esaiæ lii*, 13; *liii*, 12 (Rostock, 1791):—*Eusebii Cæsareensis de Divinitate Christi Sententia*, etc. (ibid. 1795):—*Persecutionis Christianorum sub Imperatoribus Romanis Causæ et Effectus* (ibid. 1802–1803):—*Ueber die Einführung der christl. Religion als Staatsreligion*, etc. (Munich, 1814). See Döring, *Die gelehrten Theologen Deutschlands*, s. v.; Winer, *Handbuch der theol. Lit.* i, 219, 557, 574, 590, 597, 598. (B. P.)

Martini, Jacob, a Lutheran theologian, was born at Langenstein, near Dresden, Saxony, Oct. 16, 1570, and died at Wittenberg, May 30, 1649, doctor and professor of theology. He wrote, *Disputationum de Messia Decas:—De Causa Peccati:—Libri iii de Elohim:—Vindiciæ Ecclesiæ Lutheranæ contra Valerianum Magnum:—Systema Theologicum:—Collegium Anti-Calvinianum:—Collegium Anti-Photinianum:—Questiones Biblicæ in Genesin:—Partitiones et Questiones Metaphysicæ:—De Theologiæ Constitutione et Verbo Dei Scripto:—Quomodo Sola Fides Justificet.* See Witte, *Memoriæ Theologorum;* Jöcher, *Allgemeines Gelehrten-Lexikon*, s. v. (B. P.)

Maruta (*Saint*), LITURGY OF, one of the twelve liturgies contained in the missal of the Maronites, published at Rome in 1592.

Marx, JACOB, a Roman Catholic theologian of Germany, was born Sept. 8, 1803. In 1829 he received holy orders, was in 1836 professor of Church history and canon law at Treves, in 1861 doctor of theology, in 1869 member of the chapter, and died Feb. 15, 1876. He is the author of, *Ursachen der schnellen Verbreitung der Reformation zunächst in Deutschland* (Mayence, 1834):—*Der Bilderstreit der byzantinischen Kaiser* (Treves, 1839):—*Das Wallfahrten in der katholischen Kirche* (Mayence, 1842):—*Geschichte des heiligen Rockes in der Domkirche zu Trier* (1844):—*Die Ausstellung des heiligen Rockes* (1845):—*Caspar Olevian oder der Calvinismus in Trier im Jahre* 1559 (1846):—*Geschichte des Erzstiftes Trier bis zum Jahre* 1816 (1856–64, 5 vols.). See Zuchold, *Bibl. Theol.* ii, 858. (B. P.)

Masada. The ruins of this stronghold, now called *Sebbeh*, are minutely delineated in the *Memoirs* accompanying the Ordnance Survey (iii, 417 sq.). See also Tristram, *Land of Moab*, p. 46 sq. The following, from Conder's *Tent Work* (ii, 140), embraces the chief points:

"The rock of Masada measures 350 yards east and west, by 690 yards north and south, and its cliffs are 1500 feet in height above the plain on the east. Two paths lead up to the plateau on the top, that on the east being a winding ascent, now almost impassable, but by which captain Warren went up; this is apparently the path called the 'Serpent' by Josephus. The second path, on the west, ascends from a narrow sloping bank of white marl, which is about 1000 feet high, and which Josephus calls the 'White Promontory;' upon this rises the great ramp, about 300 feet high, which the Romans piled up against the rock during the siege, a work so laborious that it seems almost incredible that human efforts could have accomplished it in so short a time. At the top of the ramp is the masonry wall which the besiegers built as a foundation for their engines, before discovering the great tragedy that had been enacted within the fortress, where the garrison had fallen by one another's swords.

"A fatiguing climb brought us to the plateau at the top. Here is a pointed archway, indicative of Crusading masons, and scored with the tribe-marks of the Jâhalîn and Rushâideh Arabs, which were on a former occasion mistaken by a distinguished Frenchman for planetary signs.

"We fell to work at once with tape and compass to plan and describe the ruins. The buildings are principally on the north-west part of the rock, and they are of various dates. The most ancient appear to be the long rude walls, resembling the buildings at Herodium (Jebel Fureidis), but the majority of the masonry is to be ascribed to the Christians of the 5th or 12th centuries. There is a chapel on the plateau, and also a cave, in which I found a curious inscription with crosses, which is, apparently, a new discovery. It is painted in red, and resembles some of the 12th and 13th century inscriptions near Jericho.

"The most extraordinary feature of this wonderful place has yet to be noticed. The Romans in their attack on Masada followed the same method which had reduced Jerusalem. They surrounded the unhappy Jews with a wall of circumvallation. Looking down from the summit, the ruins of this wall—a drystone parapet, running across the plain and up the southern hill-slopes—could be distinctly traced.

"Two large camps, also walled with stone, lay spread out behind this line on the west and east, and six smaller ones, like redoubts, on the low ground; the entire length of the wall was not less than 3000 yards, as measured on our plan, and the whole remains almost as it was left eighteen hundred years ago."

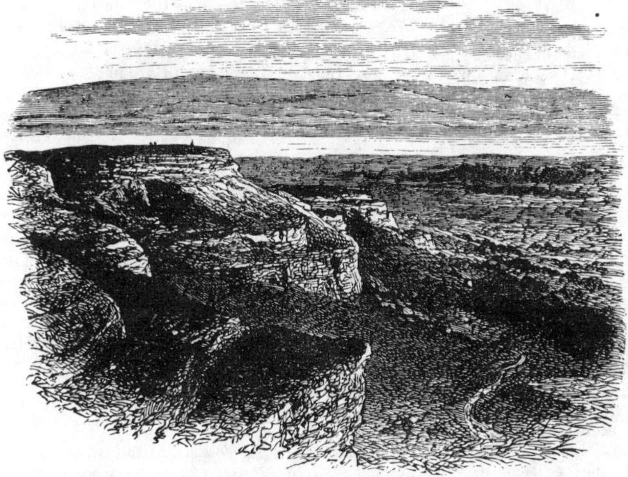

View from the Summit of Sebbeh.

Masbotheans, the disciples of Masbotheus, who is said by some of the ancients to have been a follower of Simon Magus (q. v.).

Masius, HECTOR GOTTFRIED, a Lutheran theologian, was born April 13, 1653. He studied at different universities, went to France in 1682 as chaplain to the Danish embassy, and was made in 1685 doctor and professor of theology at Copenhagen. He died Sept. 20, 1709, leaving, *Défense de la Religion Lutherienne:—Bericht von dem Unterschied der lutherischen und reformirten Lehre:—De Profanatione Hostiæ Consecratæ:—De Pallio Pauli:—Schediasmata Tria Sacra, Scilicet* 1, *De Contemtu Concilii Tridentini;* 2, *De Polymathia Scriptorum Sacrorum;* 3, *De θηριομαχίᾳ Pauli.* See Jöcher, *Allgemeines Gelehrten-Lexikon*, s. v.; Winer, *Handbuch der theol. Lit.* i, 345, 353. (B. P.)

Mason, Charles, D.D., a Protestant Episcopal clergyman, was born July 25, 1812, at Portsmouth, N. H. He graduated with honor from Harvard College in 1832; studied theology at the General Theological Seminary, New York city; was ordained deacon and priest by bishop Griswold; became rector of St. Peter's Church, Salem, Mass., in May, 1837: and of Grace Church, Boston, in 1847, which position he held until his death, March 23, 1862. For a long time he was a member of the standing committee of the diocese, and was prominent in various missionary enterprises. See *Amer. Quar. Church Rev.* 1862, p. 735.

Mason, Cyrus, D.D., a Presbyterian minister, was born at Nassau, N. Y., July 19, 1798. He graduated from Union College in

1824; spent two years in Princeton Theological Seminary; was ordained by the Presbytery of New York, Dec. 7, 1826, pastor of Cedar Street Church, New York city; in 1835 became pastor of the Beneficent Congregational Church, Providence, R. I.; in 1836 professor of political economy and ethics in the University of New York, a position which he retained until 1850. He died in New York city, May 28, 1865. See *Gen. Cat. of Princeton Theol. Sem.* 1881, p. 50.

Mason, Sumner R., D.D., a Baptist minister, was born at Cheshire, Berkshire Co., Mass., June 14, 1819. He was for two years a member of Yale College (1838–40); then became a member of the First Baptist Church in New Haven, and devoted the next seven years to teaching, most of the time in Nashville, Tenn., where he was licensed to preach, Sept. 7, 1844; and studied theology under Rev. Dr. Howell. He was ordained pastor of the First Baptist Church, Lockport, N. Y., Aug. 22, 1849; then became pastor of the First Baptist Church in Cambridge, Mass., March 4, 1855, where he continued an able and successful minister until his death, Aug. 26, 1871. A volume of his sermons and essays, edited by Rev. A. Hovey, D.D., with a sketch of his life and character, by Rev. O. A. Stearns, D.D., was issued by the Riverside (Cambridge) press in 1874. (J. C. S.)

Massaroon, ROBERT, D.D., an Irish Methodist preacher, was born at Londonderry in 1790. He joined the Methodist society in his eighteenth year, and in 1811 entered the ministry of the Irish Conference. He was a pious, prudent, intelligent, and devoted Methodist preacher for nearly fifty years, and, in 1859, from failing health, became a supernumerary, but as a scholar and gentleman he continued to labor as treasurer of the Methodist Annuitant Society and Auxiliary Fund, and closed his useful life in Dublin, March 3, 1871. He filled several official positions in Irish Methodism, was an able advocate of the British and Foreign Bible Society, and a useful guide to young ministers in studying the original text of the Holy Scriptures.

Massoch, STEPHEN C., D.D., a Protestant Episcopal clergyman, first appears in the records as a missionary in St. Louis, Mo., in 1857, and remained there until 1859, when he was appointed to the "Mission of the North-west," which was then under the jurisdiction of Joseph C. Talbot, D.D., missionary bishop. Dr. Massoch was especially to minister to the Germans and Bohemians in Osage, Neb. Shortly after, he removed to Arago, devoting himself to the same work, and remained in this sphere of labor until 1866, when he removed to Baltimore, Md. In 1868 he was a resident of Covington, Ky. He died May 30, 1870. See *Prot. Episc. Almanac*, 1871, p. 118.

Mastricht, PETER VON, a Dutch theologian, was born in 1630. He studied at Duisburg and Utrecht, was for some time professor of Hebrew and of theology at Frankfort, and in 1669 professor at Duisburg. In 1677 he was called to Utrecht, and died Feb. 10, 1706. He wrote, *Theologia Theoretico-Practica* (2 vols.):—*Exercitationes Analyticæ et Exegeticæ ad Esa. liii*:—*Syntagma de Fide Salvifica*:—*Vindiciæ Veritatis et Autoritatis Sacræ Scripturæ in Rebus Philosophicis contra Wittichium*:—*Academiæ Ultrajectinæ Votum Symbolicum.* See Moller, *Cimbria Litterata*; Jöcher, *Allgemeines Gelehrten-Lexikon*, s. v.; Winer, *Handbuch der theol. Lit.* i, 304. (B. P.)

Matahiti (*Maoa Roa*), the ripening or completing of the year, a festival regularly observed in Huahine, Polynesia. Men, women, and children attended this festival, but the females were not allowed to enter the sacred enclosure. They held a sumptuous banquet annually, the time of which was regulated by the blossoming of reeds. When the prayers were finished at the *maræ*, and the banquet ended, each individual returned to his home or family maræ to offer special prayers for the spirits of departed relatives, that they might be liberated from the *po*, or state of night, and ascend to *rohutunoanoa*, the mount Meru of Polynesia, or return to this world, by entering into the body of one of its inhabitants.

Matamoros, MANUEL, a Spanish Protestant, was born Oct. 8, 1835, at Lepe, in the province of Huelva. In 1850 he entered the military school at Toledo, but the life of the soldiers which he witnessed there caused such a dislike for a military career that he left the school and went to Malaga, where his mother was then residing. On a visit to Gibraltar he casually attended a service held by Francisco de Paula Ruet (q. v.), who impressed him so deeply that Matamoros bought a New Test., which convinced him of the errors of Romanism. Through Ruet, Matamoros came into relations with a committee in Edinburgh, and later, with one in Paris, which prosecuted the evangelization of Spain. He went, under commission of the latter, to Granada, Seville, and Barcelona (1860). At Granada he became acquainted with José Alhama, a hat-maker, who had been converted through the instrumentality of an American tract, and was preaching the gospel. When arrested letters were found on his person from Matamoros, Morin, Carrasco, and Gonzalez, all of whom were likewise imprisoned. Two years Matamoros was kept at Granada awaiting his trial. Through the influence of a deputation of the Evangelical Alliance, and the efforts of queen Elizabeth of Prussia, Matamoros was released, May 28, 1863, on condition that he should leave the country. He went on a visit to England, where he was cordially welcomed, and afterwards to Lausanne, where he attended the theological seminary. On a visit to Pau, in southern France, he made the acquaintance of an American lady, whom he induced to establish there a Spanish school. Returning to Lausanne in May, 1866, he died just a few days before the time set for his ordination, July 31, and two years before his country was opened to Protestant missions (1868). His name will not be forgotten beside that of Ruet, Carrasco, Alhama, and other evangelists in Spain. See Lichtenberger, *Encyclop. des Sciences Religieuses*, s. v.; Plitt-Herzog, *Real-Encyklop.* s. v. (B. P.)

Mateer, JOSEPH, D.D., a Presbyterian minister, was born in Hill Head parish, County Down, Ireland. He graduated from Belfast College, and after removing to the United States entered Princeton Theological Seminary, remaining one year, and then went to the Western Theological Seminary, where he graduated in 1854. He was ordained, and installed pastor of the church of Leatherwood, Pa., and also of the Licking Church. After twenty-one years of successful labor he was released, and installed over Sligo Church, from whence he was transferred to New Bethlehem, where he remained till 1881. He died in Bethlehem, Oct. 1, 1883. See *Necrol. Report of Princeton Theol. Sem.* 1884, p. 38.

Mat'h, the residence of a monastic community among the Hindûs. It consists of a number of buildings, including a set of huts or chambers for the *Mahaut* or superior, and his resident *Chêlas* or disciples; a temple sacred to the deity whom they worship, or the Samádh, or shrine of the founder of the sect, or some eminent teacher; and one or more sheds or buildings for the accommodation of the mendicants or travellers who are constantly visiting the Mat'h, both ingress and egress being free to all. The number of permanent pupils in a Mat'h varies from three or four to thirty or forty; besides whom there is also a considerable number of out-door members. Most of the Mat'hs have a small endowment of land, which they either let at a fixed rental, or cultivate on their own account. Besides this they often receive generous contributions from lay votaries, alms gathered by members who go out to seek them, and the profits arising from traffic covertly carried on.

Mathēma (*μάθημα, a lesson*), a name usually given in the ancient Greek writers to the creed, probably because the catechumens were obliged to learn it.

Mather, R. Cotton, LL.D., an English Congregational minister, was born at New Windsor, Manchester, Nov. 8, 1808. He graduated from Glasgow University, studied two years at Homerton Theological College, was ordained June 1, 1833, and the same year proceeded to India in the service of the London Missionary Society, settling in Benares, where he resided till May, 1838, then left for Mirzapore, in order to establish a new mission in that city, laboring there the rest of his missionary life with great success. He wrote tracts, theological treatises, and works of a varied character, both in Hindû and Urdu. He died April 21, 1877. See (Lond.) *Evangelical Magazine*, July, 1877, p. 420; (Lond.) *Cong. Yearbook*, 1878, p. 325.

Mathieu, Jacques Marie Adrien Césaire, a French prelate, was born at Paris, Jan. 26, 1796. He first studied law, but afterwards betook himself to the study of theology, entered the seminary of St. Sulpice, was ordained priest, and became secretary to the bishop of Evreux in 1823. In 1833 he was appointed bishop of Langres, and in the following year he was raised to the archiepiscopal see of Besançon. In 1850 he was made cardinal. As a member of the senate he was a zealous defender of the rights of the Church, and, in spite of the interdict of the government, he published the papal encyclical of Dec. 8, 1864. Mathieu died at Besançon in 1875. Of his brochures we especially mention *Le Pouvoir Temporel des Papes Justifié par l'Histoire* (1863). See Lichtenberger, *Encyclop. des Sciences Religieuses*, s. v. (B. P.)

Matsyavatara, in Hindû mythology, is the incarnation of Vishnu as a fish, the Majafish, with the surname *Cexis.* The fable is told as follows: Brahma had fallen asleep; the giant Hajagriwa stole from the sleeping god the four Vedas, the laws of the world, and the lawless world now sank into the kingdom of evil. Then Vishnu saved the world in the form of a fish, by following the giant, who hid under the sea, and compelling him to surrender the books.

Figure of Vishnu as a Fish.

Matteson, L. J., D.D., a Baptist minister, was born at Laurens, Otsego Co., N. Y. He pursued his studies at Hamilton, graduating from the college there in 1858, and from the theological seminary in 1860. His pastorates were at Watertown and Sing Sing, Brattleboro', Vt., and Troy and Cortland, N. Y., where he died, May 5, 1878. (J. C. S.)

Matthæus (or **Machabæus**), a Scotch prelate, was consecrated bishop of the see of Ross in 1272, and, while attending a council at Lyons, died there in 1274. See Keith, *Scottish Bishops*, p. 186.

Matthäi, Georg Christian Rudolph, a Lutheran theologian of Germany, was born in 1798 at Hameln, and died at Göttingen, Nov. 20, 1872, professor of theology. He published, *Synopse der vier Evangelien nebst Kritik ihrer Wundererzählungen* (Göttingen, 1826):—*Der Religionsglaube der Apostel Jesu* (ibid. 1826–30, 2 vols.):—*Die Lehre vom Geiste wider ihre Gegner* (ibid. 1834):—*Neue Auslegung der Bibel zur Erforschung und Darstellung ihres Glaubens* (ibid. 1831):—*Der Mysticismus nach seinem Begriffe, Ursprunge, und Unwerth* (ibid. 1832):—*Auslegung des Evangeliums Johannes* (ibid. 1837):—*Die Macht und Würde des Fürsten, auf christlichen Standpunkte* (Leipsic, 1841):—*Doctrina Christi de Jurejurando* (1847):—*Das Verhältniss des Christenthums zur Politik* (1850):—*Die Auslegung des Vaterunser nach dem höchsten Grundsatze der Auslegung des Neuen Testaments* (1853). See Zuchold, *Bibl. Theol.* ii, 859; Winer, *Handbuch der theol. Lit.* i, 109, 245, 294, 365, 433. (B. P.)

Matthew, a Scotch prelate, was formerly archdeacon of Lothian, and became bishop of Aberdeen in 1164. See Keith, *Scottish Bishops*, p. 105.

Matthew's (*Saint*) **Liturgy,** one of the twelve liturgies of the Maronites, contained in their missal.

Matthews, John, D.D., a Presbyterian minister, was born in Guilford County, N. C., Jan. 19, 1772. He was licensed to preach in 1801, by the Presbytery of Orange, and crossed the desert country to Natchez, Miss., acting as a missionary there. In April, 1803, he returned to North Carolina, and shortly after received a call to the churches of Nutbush and Grassy Creek, where he continued till 1806, then removed to Martinsburg, Va., and after a year resigned this for the charge at Shepherdstown. Here he continued till 1836, preaching as stated supply of this Church and that of Charlestown, and frequently also at Harper's Ferry. He next took a charge at Martinsburg and Charlestown, and when the theological seminary was established at Hanover, Ind., he was invited to become professor. He died at New Albany, May 19, 1848. His publications are, *Letters on the Divine Purpose*, and *The Influence of the Bible.*

Matthews, John Daniel, D.D., a Presbyterian minister, was born at Shepherdstown, Va., June 9, 1809. He graduated from Jefferson College in 1827, and from Princeton Theological Seminary in 1831. He was ordained an evangelist by the Presbytery of Georgia, became a stated supply of St. Mary's in 1832, and subsequently of the Second Church, Philadelphia. In 1833 he was installed pastor of Opequan and Cedar churches, Va. He became pastor of the Church at Norfolk in 1837, and after five years removed to the McChord Church, Lexington, Ky. After this he supplied the churches of Hopewell, Paducah, and Henderson. For six years he was superintendent of public instruction in Kentucky, after which he supplied the churches of Jackson Street, Mobile; Second Church, Baltimore; New York Avenue Church, Washington City; Portland Avenue Church, Louisville, Ky., and Dennison, Tex. He died at Dallas, March 7, 1884. See *Necrol. Report of Princeton Theol. Sem.* 1884, p. 13.

Matthews, Joseph M'Dowell, D.D., a Methodist Episcopal minister, was born in Augusta County, Va., Dec. 8, 1804. At the age of ten he removed with his parents to Kentucky, and, settling on a farm, was given a thorough private academical education, which he increased by personal effort. He joined the Church at the age of eighteen, was licensed to preach in 1825, in 1827 began a school or academy for boys in Hillsborough, O., which he continued till 1831, when he entered the Ohio Conference. In 1831–32 he served the Church in Chillicothe, and in 1833 in Cincinnati. There his health failed, and he retired to a farm, where he spent nearly six years. In 1839 he opened the Oakland Female Seminary, where he did noble work until 1856, when he took charge of the Hillsborough Female College. In 1860 he became president of Jessamine Female College, Nicholasville, Ky., but in 1863 returned to Hillsborough, and opened a private boarding-school. In 1872 he again accepted a call to the presidency of Hillsborough Female College, where he remained until ill-health led him, in 1877, to resign his office, and retire to his home in the suburbs of Hillsborough, where he died, Aug. 5, 1879. See *Minutes of Annual Fall Conferences*, 1879, p. 15.

Matthews, Robert C., D.D., a Presbyterian minister, was born at Shephardstown, Va., April 2, 1822. He was educated in Illinois, where he practiced law until he was converted, then, after a year or two in the theological seminary, was ordained and installed pastor of the Presbyterian Church in Monmouth, Ill., Dec. 20, 1852. His labors in this Church were attended with great success. He died there, Nov. 15, 1881. See *N. Y. Observer*, Dec. 1, 1881. (W. P. S.)

Matthiä, Christian, a Lutheran theologian of Germany, was born in 1584. He studied at Strasburg and Giessen, was in 1614 rector at the gymnasium in Durlach, in 1618 professor of theology at Altdorf, in 1629 professor at Sora, in Denmark, in 1639 at Leyden, and in 1641 pastor of the Lutheran congregation at the Hague. In 1645 he resigned his position, retired to Utrecht, and died Jan. 22, 1655. He wrote, *Exercitationes Metaphysicæ xii*:—*Methodica Scripturæ Sacræ Loca Vindicandi Ratio*:—*Historia Patriarcharum*:—*Analysis Typica Evangelii Matthæi*:—*Antilogiæ Biblicæ*, etc. See Moller, *Cimbria Litterara*; Jöcher, *Allgemeines Gelehrten-Lexikon*, s. v. (B. P.)

Matthiä, Wolf Christian, a Lutheran theologian of Denmark, was born Jan. 28, 1734. He studied at Kiel, was in 1762 military preacher, in 1770 pastor at Rendsburg, in 1778 member of consistory, and died Jan. 29, 1787. He wrote, *Diss. Historia Samuelis, Sauli et Davidis, ad Annorum Rationes Digesta* (Kiel, 1752):—*Beschreibung der Kirchenverfassung in den Herzogthümern Schleswig und Holstein* (Flensburg, 1778–86, 2 vols.):—*Schriftmässige Betrachtung über das Leiden und Sterben Jesu Christi* (ibid. 1786). See Döring, *Die gelehrten Theologen Deutschlands*, s. v.; Winer, *Handbuch der theol. Lit.* i, 833. (B. P.)

Matūta, in Roman mythology, was originally an ancient Italian goddess of day-dawn, and later confounded with Leucothea (q. v.), and with Albunea (q. v.). Her festival was celebrated June 11, at which mothers took the children of their sisters on their arms, because Ino (Leucothea) had brought up her sister's son, Bacchus.

Mauchart, Immanuel David, a Lutheran theologian of Germany, was born June 2, 1764, at Tübingen, was in 1793 deacon at Nürtingen, in 1803 superintendent at Neuffen, Würtemberg, and died Feb. 6, 1826. He wrote, *Aphorismen über das Erinnerungsvermögen in Beziehung auf den Zustand nach dem Tode* (Tübingen, 1792):—*Kirchliche Statistik des Königreichs Würtemberg evangelisch lutherischen Antheils* (Stuttgart, 1821):—*Andachtsbuch für Confirmanden und Neuconfirmirte* (Tübingen, 1824). See Winer, *Handbuch der theol. Lit.* i, 477, 489,; ii, 374. (B. P.)

Maui fata (*altar-raising*), a religious ceremony in Polynesia. Numbers of figs, with abundance of plantains, were placed upon the altars, which were newly ornamented with branches of the sacred *miro*, and yellow leaves of the cocoanut-tree. These rites extended to every *maræ* in the island, and were designed to secure rain and fertility for the country gained by conquest or recovered from invasion.

Maukisch, Johann, a Lutheran theologian of Germany, was born Aug. 14, 1617. He studied at Leipsic, and died at Dantzic, June 8, 1669, doctor and professor of theology. He wrote, *Notæ Philologico-Theologicæ Notitiam Dei Naturalem ex Selectis Scripturæ Dictis Explicantes*:—*Paulus anti-Calvinianus, Absolutum Decretum per Totam Epistolam ad Romanos Elidens*:—*Scripta anti-Papistica*:—*Exercitationes de Universali Gratia*:—*De Ecclesia in Genere*:—*Programmata de Promissione Messiæ ex Psa. xl, de Adventu Messiæ ex Psa. xiv*, 7, etc. See Witte, *Memoriæ Theologorum*; Jöcher, *Allgemeines Gelehrten-Lexikon*, s. v. (B. P.)

Maulavi, the name usually given to a Mohammedan priest in India.

Maupertuy (or **Maupertuis**), Jean-Baptiste Drouet de, a French ecclesiastical writer, was born at Paris in 1650. He was educated at the Jesuit college of Louis-le-Grand, and for a time dedicated himself to poetry and literature. In spite of his talents he did not achieve anything, owing to the life of dissipation which he led, and which cost him not only his fortune but the best part of his life. At the age of forty he renounced the joys of this world and led a retired life. In 1692 he retired to the abbey of Sept-Fonts, and five years later was made a priest by the archbishop of Vienne. He returned to Paris, and died at St.-Germain-en-Laye, March 10, 1736. He wrote, *Pensées Chrétiennes et Morales* (1703):—*Histoire de la Réforme de l'Abbaye des Sept-Fonts* (1702):—*Les Sentiments d'un Chrétien Touché d'un Véritable Amour de Dieu* (1716):—*L'Histoire de la Sainte Église de Vienne.* Besides, he translated into French the *Institutions of Lactantius*; Salvianus's treatise on *Providence*, etc. See Lichtenberger, *Encyclop. des Sciences Religieuses*, s. v. (B. P.)

Maurer, Franz Joseph Valentin Dominik, a Protestant theologian of Germany, was born at Rottweil, Feb. 14, 1795. In 1820 he received holy orders, but in 1821 joined the Evangelical Church. For some time he was collaborator at the Thomas School in Leipsic, but afterwards retired to Stuttgart, devoting himself entirely to literary work. He died in 1856. He published, *Commentar über das Buch Josua* (Stuttgart, 1831):—*Commentarius Grammaticus Criticus in Vet. Testamentum* (Leipsic, 1832 sq.; vol. i contains all the historical books, Isaiah, Jeremiah, and Lamentations; vol. ii, Ezekiel, Daniel, and the minor prophets; vol. iii, Psalms and Proverbs). There is great disproportion in the mode of treatment. All the historical books from Genesis to Esther are comprised in two hundred and fifty pages, and it is only after Isaiah that the treatment begins to be more ample, and is then really valuable. Maurer's work was continued by August Heiligstedt. Besides, Maurer published, *Praktischer Cursus über die Formenlehre der hebr. Sprache* (Leipsic, 1837):—*Kurzgefasstes hebräisches u. chaldäisches Wörterbuch* (Stuttgart, 1851). See Winer, *Handbuch der theol. Lit.* i, 14, 194, 203; Zuchold, *Bibl. Theol.* ii, 861 sq.; Fürst, *Bibl. Jud.* ii, 335 sq. (B. P.)

Mauritian Creole Version of the Scriptures. This version is intended for the mixed population of Mauritius. A translation of the gospel of Matthew was made by the Rev. S. H. Anderson, who was born in Mauritius, and spent thirty-two years on the island, ten of which he was minister to the Protestant negroes. The same gentlemen also states that the Mauritian Creole is spoken by 350,000 of the 360,000 inhabitants of the island, and that it is the only medium of communication among all the languages and dialects of the island. Mr. Anderson's translation was published during the year 1884 by the British and Foreign Bible Society, and as the report of that society for 1885 states, "the whole consignment was bought up before it was even unpacked, and that half of it was secured by bishop Royston for the inhabitants of Seychelle." (B. P.)

Mauritii, Friedrich Maximilian, a Lutheran theologian of Germany, was born at Basle, Aug. 17, 1724. He studied at Halle, was for some time private tutor, in 1757 rector at Minden, in 1768 professor of theology and member of consistory at Bützow, and died March 5, 1799. He wrote, *Diss. de Perseverantia Credentium Usque ad Finem* (Halle, 1753):—*Versuch einer Erklärung der schweren Stelle Zach. xii*, 11–14 (Rinteln, 1764, 1772):—*Die Göttlichkeit der heiligen Schrift* (Minden, 1765):—*De Incarnatione Filii Dei* (Bützow, 1769–72):—*Quantum Intersit, Jesum Resurrexisse* (ibid. 1770):—*De Inhabitatione Dei* (ibid. 1775). See Döring, *Die gelehrten Theologen Deutschlands*, s. v. (B. P.)

Mauritius, Caspar, a Lutheran theologian of Germany, was born March 2, 1615. He studied at Rostock and Königsberg, was in 1644 professor at Rostock, in 1650 doctor of theology, in 1662 pastor at Hamburg, and died April 14, 1675. He wrote, *Exercitationes anti-Calvinianæ, anti-Socinianæ, Logicæ, Politicæ*:—*In Formulam Concordiæ*:—*Theses de Confessione et Absolutione Privata*:—*Dissertationes de Gratia Irresistibili*:

—*De Nestorianismo:*—*De Ecclesia:*—*De Gentilium in Veteri Testamento ad Regnum Cœlorum Vocatione:*—*De Fato Calvinistico:*—*De Simonia:*—Πρῶτον ψεῦδος *Socinianorum.* See Moller, *Cimbria Litterata;* Jöcher, *Allgemeines Gelehrten-Lexikon*, s. v. (B. P.)

Mauritus, a Scotch prelate, was first abbot of Inchaffray, and became bishop of the see of Dunblane in 1319. He was bishop there in 1333. See Keith, *Scottish Bishops*, p. 175.

Mauro ura (*the red sash*), a very sacred relic, held in the highest estimation by the natives of Tahiti, one of the Society Islands. It "was a piece of network, about seven inches wide and six feet long, upon which the red feathers of the paroquet were neatly fastened. It was used at the inauguration of their greatest kings, just as the crown is with us, and the most honorable appellation which a chief could receive was, *Arii mauro ura*, 'King of the Red Sash.' A new piece, about eighteen inches in length, was attached at the inauguration of every sovereign; to accomplish which several human victims were required. The first was for the *mau raa titi*, or the stretching it upon pegs in order to attach to it the new piece. Another was necessary for the *fatu raa*, or attaching the new portion; and a third for the *piu raa*, or twitching the sacred relic off the pegs. This not only invested the sash itself with a high measure of solemn importance, but also rendered the chiefs who wore it most noble in public estimation." See Williams, *Narrative of Missionary Enterprises in the South Sea Islands.*

Mausolēum, a name originally applied to the magnificent sepulchre erected by Artemisia, at Halicarnassus, B.C. 352, to the memory of her husband, Mausolus, king of Caria. The term has now come to denote any costly tomb.

Maut (or **Mut**), a chief Egyptian goddess, the wife of Amen-Ra, and the second member of the great Theban triad. She was considered as the mother goddess *par excellence*, or the great receptive female principle; and she was generally represented as seated upon a throne, wearing either the Pshent, or sacred double crown, or else the body and plumes of a vulture as her head-dress. She was dressed in a long robe, often richly ornamented, and she held in her right hand the usual Crux-ansata, and in her left the papyrus staff of the goddesses. Her chief titles were, "The Mother," "The Lady of Heaven," and "The Regent of all the Gods." The vulture was both her symbol and her sacred bird. Her analogues were in some of her attributes the *Hera* and *Cybele* and *Thermuthis* of the Greeks, and possibly the *Bona Dea* of the Romans.

Maxwell, John, D.D., a Scotch prelate, was first minister at Murthlack, and then in the city of Edinburgh in 1620. He was advanced to the see of Ross in 1633; deprived in 1638, and fled to England for protection. He died Feb. 14, 1646. See Keith, *Scottish Bishops*, p. 203.

Maxwell, Robert, a Scotch prelate, was rector of Forbolton in 1521, and soon after provost of the collegiate church in Dumbarton. He was bishop of Orkney till after 1536. He built the stalls in his cathedral, and furnished the steeple with a set of bells. See Keith, *Scottish Bishops*, p. 223.

May, Johann Heinrich (1), a Lutheran theologian of Germany, was born Feb. 5, 1653. He studied at Wittenberg, was professor of Oriental languages at Giessen, and died Sept. 3, 1719, doctor of theology. He published, *De Canone Veteris Test.* (Giessen, 1689):—*Animadversiones et Supplementa Cocceji Lexicon* (Frankfort, 1689, fol.; 3d ed. 1714):—*Diss. IV de Sacra Scriptura* (ibid. 1690):—*Selectiora Vet. Testamenti Oracula Explicanta*, etc. (eod.):—*Biblia Hebraica* (ibid. 1692):—*De Lustrationibus et Purificationibus Hebræorum* (ibid. eod.):—*De Salis Usu Symbolico* (ibid. eod.):—*Theologia Davidis* (ibid. 1693):—*Ebraicæ Linguæ Ejusque Accentuationibus Necessitas et Utilitas* (ibid. 1696):—*Theologia Jeremiana* (ibid. 1703):—*Theologia Jesaiana* (ibid. 1704), etc. See Döring, *Die gelehrten Theologen Deutschlands*, s. v. (where 105 titles of his writings are given); Lichtenberger, *Encyclop. des Sciences Religieuses*, s. v. *Maius;* Jöcher, *Allgemeines Gelehrten-Lexikon*, s. v. "Majus." (B. P.)

May, Johann Heinrich (2), a German theologian, son of the foregoing, was born at Durlach, March 11, 1688. He studied at Altdorf and Jena, was professor at Giessen, and died June 13, 1732. He published, *De Jure Anni Septimi* (Giessen, 1707):—*Maimon. Tract. de Jure Anni Septimi et Jubilæi* (1708):—*Jura Fimbriarum* (1710):—*D. Isaaci Abarbanelis* משמיע ישועה (1712):—*Observationes Sacræ* (1713–15; 1716–27):—*Diss. de Schechinah* (1723):—*De Tiara Pontificis Maximi* (1728):—*De Aris et Altaribus Veterum* (1732). See Döring, *Die gelehrten Theologen Deutschlands*, s. v.; Jöcher, *Allgemeines Gelehrten-Lexikon*, s. v. "Majus." (B. P.)

Mayan Version of the Scriptures. Mayan is the vernacular of a tribe of Indians inhabiting Yucatan, a peninsula to the east of Mexico, projecting northward between the gulf of Mexico and the Caribbean sea. In 1864 only a part of the gospel of Luke was published by the British and Foreign Bible Society in this dialect. In 1869 the gospel of John was printed in England, the translation having been made by the Rev. R. Fletcher. See *Bible of Every Land*, p. 468. (B. P.)

Mayer, Georg Karl Wilhelm, a Roman Catholic theologian of Germany, was born in 1807 at Aschbach, Franconia. He received holy orders in 1837, was cathedral chaplain at Bamberg in 1838, in 1842 was appointed professor of theology at the lyceum, in 1862 member of the chapter, and died July 22, 1868. He wrote, *Geist und Natur im speculativen Systeme Günther's* (Bamberg, 1842):—*Der Mensch nach der Glaubenslehre der alten Kirche* (1854, 5 vols.):—*Commentar über die Briefe des Johannes* (Vienna, 1851):—*Aechtheit des Evangeliums nach Johannes* (ibid. 1854):—*Die patriarchalischen Verheissungen und die messianischen Psalmen* (Nördlingen, 1859):—*Messianische Prophezeiungen* (Vienna, 1863–66, 2 vols.). (B. P.)

Mayerhoff, Ernst Theodor, a Lutheran theologian of Germany, was born at Neuruppin, Dec. 5, 1806, and died at Berlin in December, 1837, licentiate and private lecturer in theology. He published, *Die Petrinischen Schriften* (Hamburg, 1835):—*Johann Reuchlin und seine Zeit* (Berlin, 1830):—*Die Waldenser in unsern Tagen* (ibid. 1834):—*Ansgarius oder der Anfangspunkt des Christenthums in Schweden* (ibid. 1837; transl. from the Swedish of H. Reuterdahl):—*Der Brief an die Colosser* (published after the author's death by L. Mayerhoff, ibid. 1838). See Winer, *Handbuch der theol. Lit.* i, 91, 578, 833; Zuchold, *Bibl. Theol.* ii, 863. (B. P.)

Mayitri, a future Buddha, who is destined to appear at the end of five thousand years from the death of Gotama Buddha, and will continue for ages to be the teacher of the human race.

Mayronius, François, a Franciscan, and doctor of the Sorbonne, styled *doctor illuminatus*, who died in 1325, is the author of, *Commentarii in Genesin:*—*De Articulis Fidei:*—*Compendium Librorum S. Augustini de Civitate Dei:*—*Comment. in Augustini Librum Confessionum:*—*Comment. in Dionysium Areopagitam de Mystica Theologia:*—1500 *Quæstiones de Variis Locis Sacræ Scripturæ et Dubiis Theologicis:*—*Comment. in Orationem Dominican*, etc. See Gaddius, *De Scriptoribus Ecclesiasticis;* Jöcher, *Allgemeines Gelehrten-Lexikon*, s. v. (B. P.)

McAll, Robert Stephens, LL.D., an English Congregational minister, was born at Plymouth, Aug. 2, 1792. He was educated at Hoxton Academy and at the University of Edinburgh, studying medicine chiefly. At the age of twenty-one he became pastor at

Macclesfield. In January, 1827, he accepted the charge of the Mosley Street Church, Manchester, where he died, July 27, 1838. He was a preacher of rare eloquence. See (Lond.) *Evang. Magazine*, January, 1839, p. 1.

McAuley, CATHERINE, foundress of the Sisters of Mercy, was born at Stormanstown House, County Dublin, Ireland, Sept. 29, 1787. When of age she formed a regular system for the distribution of food and clothing to the needy, and called in the lame and blind to partake of her bounty. She also erected, in 1824, a large building in a fashionable quarter of Dublin. She made a novitiate in the Presentation Convent in Dublin, professed Dec. 12, 1831, and was appointed by the archbishop superior of her order, the objects of which were, the education of the poor and the protection of good women in distress. When the cholera visited Dublin, in 1832, she and her sisters nursed the hospital patients until they recovered. The women admitted into her houses of refuge were taught various useful employments, and, as soon as possible, provided with good situations. Her order developed rapidly. Many ladies of distinction joined it. Houses were established in London. Ten houses were founded in Ireland during her lifetime, and two in England, and in the course of forty years there were over two hundred convents of the order in Great Britain, United States, Newfoundland, South America, Australia, and New Zealand, with more than three thousand sisters. She died in Dublin, Nov. 11, 1841. Her life has been written by Mother Austin of New Orleans (New York, 1866). See (N. Y.) *Cath. Almanac*, 1882, p. 73.

McBride, JOHN, a very prominent minister of the Presbyterian Church in Ireland during its early history, who suffered persecution from the Established Church because he boldly advocated the rights of Independency, was a native of Ireland, educated at the University of Glasgow, where he was enrolled in 1666. About 1670 he was ordained by the Presbytery of Tyrone to the pastoral charge of the congregation of Clowe, in the county of Armagh, where he officiated nearly twenty years. In 1694 he succeeded Rev. Patrick Adair as minister of the Belfast congregation, where he labored until his death in 1718. He was a popular preacher, and an able and expert disputant. See Reid, *Hist. of the Presb. Church in Ireland.*

McCabe, Edward, a Roman Catholic prelate, was born in Dublin in 1816. In 1856 he was appointed parish priest of St. Nicholas, one of the poorest and most populous localities in Dublin. Archbishop Cullen appointed him one of his vicars-general in 1863, transferring him to the important parish of Kingstown. In 1877 Dr. McCabe, as bishop of Gadara *in partibus*, was appointed bishop-auxiliary. He was confirmed cardinal by the pope, March 24, 1879, and died Feb. 10, 1885.

McCabe, James D., D.D., a Protestant Episcopal clergyman, was rector of a church in Wheeling, Va., in 1853; in 1857 he was serving in Baltimore, being rector of St. Stephen's; in 1861 he was rector of St. James's Parish, Tracy's Landing, Md., where he remained until 1867, when he was chosen rector of Zion Church, in Urbana; to this charge was added the pastorate of St. Peter's, Montgomery County, in 1871. In 1873 he officiated in Baltimore without regular charge. He died Aug. 1, 1875, aged sixty-seven years. See *Prot. Episc. Almanac*, 1876, p. 149.

McCabe, John Collins, D.D., a Protestant Episcopal clergyman, ordained deacon in 1847, was rector for many years in Hampton, Va., until 1855 or 1856; then he became rector of the Church of the Ascension, Baltimore, Md., remaining until 1860, when he accepted the rectorship of St. James's Church, West River, and remained until 1863. Subsequently he went to Virginia, and, immediately after the civil war in the South, became rector of St. Matthew's Church, Bladensburg; in 1868 was rector of St. Ann's, Middletown, Del.; in 1873 rector of Trinity, Chambersburg, Penn. He died Feb. 27, 1875, aged sixty-five years. See *Prot. Episc. Almanac*, 1876, p. 149.

McCaffrey, JOHN, D.D., a Roman Catholic scholar and divine, was born at Emmittsburg, Md., Sept. 6, 1806. He was educated at Mount St. Mary's College and Theological Seminary at that place, was ordained deacon in 1831, priest in 1838, and was almost immediately made president of that college, a position which he resigned in 1871. He was twice offered the mitre, but declined. He died at the college, Sept. 25, 1881. See (N. Y.) *Cath. Annual*, 1883, p. 64.

McCarrell, ALEXANDER, D.D., a Presbyterian minister, was born at Hanover, Washington Co., Pa., Sept. 22, 1817. He graduated from Washington College in 1841, after which he entered upon a course of theological training. He was licensed by the Presbytery of Washington in 1845, and ordained an evangelist; served for a time the churches of Wolf Run and Unity as a stated supply, and afterwards at Claysville, where he was installed, Dec. 6, 1852. He died there, April 18, 1881. See Nevin, *Presb. Encyclop.* s. v. (W. P. S.)

McClintock, JOHN DAVID, D.D., a Presbyterian minister, was born in Nicholas County, Ky., Feb. 24, 1836. He graduated from Hanover College, Ind., in 1858, and from Princeton Theological Seminary in 1862; was licensed by Philadelphia Central Presbytery the same year, and ordained an evangelist, April 11, 1864, by Ebenezer Presbytery, at Augusta, Ky. He first supplied the Church of Flemingsburg in 1862; in November, 1863, went to Cabell County, Va., and supplied the Western (now Huntington) Church, doing evangelistic work until April, 1865, when he took charge as stated supply of Catlettsburg Church, Ky., in connection with Huntingdon Church; was installed pastor of the latter Church, June 7, 1873, by Greenbrier Presbytery, and released May 15, 1876; installed pastor of Columbus Church, Miss., by the Presbytery of Tombeckbee, April 29, 1877, a relation which he held until his death, Dec. 12, 1881. See *Necrol. Report of Princeton Theol. Sem.* 1882, p. 54.

McCloskey, John (1), D.D., a Roman Catholic prelate, was born at Brooklyn, N. Y., March 20, 1810. He studied at Mount St. Mary's College and Seminary, Emmittsburg, Md.; was ordained priest, Jan. 9, 1834; studied two years in Rome, and one in France, and on his return became pastor of St. Joseph's Church, New York. In 1841 he became first president of St. John's College, Fordham; in 1842 resumed the rectorship of St. Joseph's Church; in 1843 was coadjutor of bishop Hughes; in 1847 first bishop of Albany; in 1864 archbishop of New York; in 1875 cardinal-priest, and in 1878 cardinal. He died Oct. 10, 1885. Cardinal McCloskey was a very energetic prelate, establishing religious and charitable houses in his diocese, and actively promoting the interests of his Church.

McCloskey, John (2), D.D., a Roman Catholic divine, was born at Carlow, Ireland, in 1817, soon after which his parents settled in Brooklyn, N. Y. In 1830 he entered Mount St. Mary's College, Emmittsburg, Md., where he was ordained, Dec. 13, 1840, and at the solicitation of the college authorities was allowed to remain as professor. He was made vice-president in 1841, and on the retirement of Dr. McCaffrey, in 1871, was chosen president, which position he held for seven years. On the appointment of Dr. Watterson to the bishopric of Columbus, in 1880, he once more resumed the presidency. He was connected with the college for thirty-five years, devoting heart and soul to his work, and never taking a vacation. He was kind to all, over-indulgent, and beloved by all. He died at Emmittsburg, Dec. 24, 1880. See *Catholic Annual*, 1883, p. 61.

McCluskey, JOHN, D.D., a Presbyterian minister, was born in Lancaster Valley, Chester Co., Pa., June 17, 1795. He received his early education at the common schools in Washington County, and graduated from Jefferson College in 1822. After leaving college he was a year and a half a teacher in the academy at Newtown, Bucks Co. He next taught for a year at New Hope, when, at the invitation of the Rev. Dr. Ezra Styles Ely, he went to Philadelphia, and spent a year studying theology under his guidance. In November, 1825, he entered Princeton Seminary, and remained a year, when he was licensed by the Presbytery of Philadelphia. After supplying for six months the Church of West Alexander, he accepted a call to become its pastor, and was ordained Oct. 8, 1828. In 1854 he became an agent for the Presbyterian Board of Education; in 1855 assistant pastor of the Church at Neshaminy, Bucks Co., and in 1858 pastor elect of the Church at Smyrna, Del. He founded there a church school, in 1864 a female school in West Philadelphia, and in 1870 a school in Hightstown, with the special view to the education of the children of missionaries free of charge. In the same year he returned to West Philadelphia, and for four years was associate principal of the Mantua Academy. He spent several years at Wooster, O., from whence he returned to Philadelphia, where he died, March 31, 1880. See *Necrol. Report of Princeton Theol. Sem.* 1881, p. 24. (W. P. S.)

McCown, Burr Harrison, D.D., a minister of the Methodist Episcopal Church South, was born at Bardstown, Ky., Oct. 29, 1806. He was educated at St. Joseph's College, in his native place, was converted, and joined the Methodists in early life. Before his majority he entered the Kentucky Conference, and in 1830-31 was stationed at Louisville. In 1834 he was professor of ancient languages in Augusta College, and in 1844 occupied a similar position in Transylvania University. He afterwards taught at Goshen Academy, Forest Academy, and Pine Hill, where he died, Aug. 29, 1881. Dr. McCown was an interesting preacher, a diligent student, an impressive instructor, and an earnest Christian. See *Minutes of the M. E. Church South*, 1881, p. 285.

McCron, John, D.D., a Lutheran minister, was born in Manchester, England, Oct. 23, 1807. In 1831 he arrived in America. For some time he and his wife were engaged as teachers in Mechanicsburg, Pa. After a course of study in the Gettysburg Theological Seminary, he was inducted, in 1839, into the Lutheran ministry. Having been sent, the same year, as a missionary to Pittsburgh, he organized the first English Lutheran Church in that city. From that time he continued to serve a number of congregations in Pennsylvania, Ohio, New Jersey, New York, and Maryland, the longest period of service having been given to Baltimore, where he spent twenty years. Leaving Baltimore, he became principal of the female seminary at Hagerstown, where he remained two or three years. In 1846 he was a delegate to the World's Evangelical Alliance in London. While residing in Baltimore he co-operated with Drs. Seiss and Passavant in editing the *Evangelical Psalmist*, a book of tunes adapted to the *Lutheran Hymn-book*, published in Philadelphia in 1860. He died in Philadelphia, April 26, 1881. See *Lutheran Observer*, May 6, 1881.

McCullough, John W., D.D., a Protestant Episcopal clergyman, was employed as a professor in Nashville, Tenn., in 1853 and 1854. In 1858 he was teaching in Baltimore, Md., and the following year was rector of St. Mary's Hall, in that city, a position which he held until 1861. While in Tennessee he was a member of the standing committee of the diocese; was a delegate, in 1855, to the General Convention; served on the missionary and education committees of his own diocese, and held various other important positions. In 1861 he removed to Waverley, N. Y. In 1864 he was rector of St. Paul's Church, Alton, Ill., and remained in that parish until his death, at Waverley, N. Y., Oct. 14, 1867 See *Prot. Episc. Almanac*, 1868, p. 104.

McDaniel, James, D.D., a Baptist minister, was born near Fayetteville, N. C., in 1803. He united with the Church in 1827, and soon after began to preach. Chiefly through his instrumentality the Church in Fayetteville was formed, and he was called to be its pastor, in which relation he continued for thirty-six years, and then was pastor, for six years, of the First Church in Wilmington, during a part of the time acting as editor of a religious journal. For nineteen years he was president of the North Carolina Baptist State Convention, organized in 1830. He died in 1870. "Dr. McDaniel possessed in a rare degree the gifts and graces of the orator, and many are the traditions of the pathos and power of his preaching in his younger days." See Cathcart, *Baptist Encyclop.* s. v. (J. C. S.)

McDonnell, Richard, D.D., LL.D., an Irish clergyman and collegian, was born at Douglas, County Cork, Ireland, in 1787. He graduated from Trinity College in 1805, and became a fellow in 1808. He studied law at first, was called to the Irish bar, then took holy orders; in 1816 was elected professor of oratory by competitive examination; became senior fellow in 1836; bursar for many years, and in 1852 was appointed provost, which office he held till his death, Jan. 24, 1867. Dr. McDonnell's administration of fifteen years was marked by improvements in the undergraduate course, and by a great advance in the status of the college. See *Appleton's Annual Cyclop.* 1867, p. 589.

McElhenny, John, D.D., a Presbyterian minister, was born in Lancaster District, N. C., in March, 1781. He graduated from Washington College, Va.; studied theology there under Dr. Baxter; was licensed in 1808 as an evangelist; became pastor at Lexington the same year, and died in that relation, Jan. 2, 1871. See Nevin, *Presb. Encyclop.* s. v.

McElhiney, George, D.D., a Protestant Episcopal clergyman, was born near Londonderry, Ireland, in 1799. He studied first in London, next at Paris, and then under Rev. E. D. Barry, of Baltimore, Md.; when nineteen years old, he began the study of theology under Rev. Dr. Wyatt, of the same city. In 1820 he was ordained, and began his labors in the parish of St. James, Baltimore County. In 1826 he removed to a parish in Charles County, and shortly after visited Europe. On his return home he resumed charge of his first parish, and in September, 1829, went to Princess Anne parish, Somerset County. In October, 1834, he became rector of St. Anne's Church, Annapolis, and so continued until his death, May 2, 1841. As an agent in behalf of the convention to obtain funds for the support of the episcopate, he secured more than $50,000. See Sprague, *Annals of the Amer. Pulpit*, v, 646.

McElroy, James, D.D., a Protestant Episcopal clergyman, was a native of Ireland, and was educated in Trinity College, Dublin. He was ordained by bishop Chase in 1829, and officiated successively in Ohio, Virginia, and California. During the five years preceding his death he occupied the St. Paul's Mission in San Francisco. He died in Oakland, Cal., June 21, 1880. See Whittaker, *Almanac and Directory*, 1881.

McElroy, Joseph, D.D., a Presbyterian minister, was born near Newville, in the Cumberland valley, Dec. 29, 1792. He graduated from Jefferson College in 1812, and studied theology in New York under Dr. John M. Mason. He was licensed in 1815 by the Presbytery of Monongahela; began preaching in Pittsburgh, and established the First Associate Reformed Presbyterian Church there. After laboring successfully for seven years, he was called to succeed Dr. Mason in the Scotch Presbyterian Church, New York. He was among the most eloquent preachers in that city. For the last five years of his life he was emeritus pastor of the Scotch Church. He died in New York, Sept. 16, 1876. See *Presbyterian*, Sept. 30, 1876. (W. P. S.)

McEwen, Abel, D.D., a distinguished Congregational minister, was born at Winchester, Conn., Feb. 13, 1780. He graduated at Yale College with honors in 1804, and was settled pastor in New London in 1806, which was his only pastorate, as he retired from the active duties in 1854, but preached occasionally afterwards, and died Sept. 7, 1860. Dr. McEwen originated the New London County Home Missionary Society, was a strong advocate of temperance, Sunday-schools, and education. Over four hundred solid and exhaustive essays delivered by him in the New London County Preacher's Meeting are preserved. He published, *Half-century Sermon:—Biographical Sketches of Litchfield County Ministers:—Congregationalists in their Relation to Other Religious Sects.* See *Cong. Quarterly*, 1863, p. 263.

McFarland, Francis, D.D., a Presbyterian minister, was born in County Tyrone, Ireland, Jan. 8, 1788. His parents came to America in 1793. He graduated at Washington College, Pa., in 1818, and spent over one year thereafter at Princeton Theological Seminary. He was ordained evangelist by the Presbytery of New Brunswick, N. J., Aug. 1, 1822; became pastor at Bethel, Va., and died at Staunton, Oct. 10, 1871. He was for six years secretary of the Board of Education of the Old-school Presbyterian Church. See *Presbyterian*, Oct. 28, 1871; *Gen. Cat. of Princeton Theol. Sem.* 1881, p. 24.

McFarland, Francis Patrick, D.D., a Roman Catholic prelate, was born at Franklin, Pa., April 6, 1819. He studied at a private academy in his native town, and then at Mount St. Mary's Seminary, Emmittsburg, Md. He was ordained priest in St. Patrick's Cathedral, New York, by archbishop Hughes, May 18, 1845, and was for one year thereafter professor at St. John's College, Fordham. Thence he went to St. Joseph's Church, New York city, where he remained three months, when he was transferred to the pastorate of the church at Watertown, N. Y. In 1851 he was appointed pastor of St. John's Church, Utica, and remained there until his election to the episcopacy of Hartford, March 14, 1858. This diocese then included Connecticut and Rhode Island, and Providence was the seat; but in 1872 Hendricken was appointed to the see of Providence, and McFarland removed to Hartford, where he died, Oct. 12, 1874. Bishop McFarland was modest, dignified in office, zealous, and studious. See (N. Y.) *Cath. Almanac*, 1875, p. 105.

McGill, John, D.D., a Roman Catholic prelate, was born in Philadelphia, Pa., Nov. 4, 1809. During his childhood his parents moved to Bardstown, Ky., where, at the College of St. Joseph, John was educated. He studied law, was admitted to the bar, and practised his profession there and at New Orleans. He then embraced the sacred calling, studied two years at St. Mary's College, Baltimore, and on his return to Bardstown was ordained priest, June 13, 1830. He subsequently studied at Rome, became missionary in Kentucky, and was the zealous colleague of Dr. Spalding. His *Conferences* on the dogmas of the Church, at Bardstown, made him distinguished as a controversialist. He was editor of the *Catholic Advocate*, pastor at Lexington, Ky., and on the division of Virginia into two dioceses, and the translation of bishop Whelan to Wheeling, Dr. McGill was appointed bishop of Richmond, and consecrated, Nov. 10, 1850. His labors were great. As a learned and convincing preacher he was pre-eminent. His controversial sermons were, it is said, unsurpassed. He took an active part in the councils of Baltimore for twenty years, and was an earnest member of the Council of the Vatican. While attending its sessions his health failed him, he returned home, and died at Richmond, Va., Jan. 14, 1872. See (N. Y.) *Cath. Almanac*, 1873, p. 42.

McGuire, Edward C., D.D., a Protestant Episcopal minister, was born in the borough of Winchester, Va., in 1793. In 1813 he officiated for one year as lay-reader in the Church at Fredericksburg, when he was ordained deacon, and after a rectorate of forty-five years at St. George's Church in that city he died there, Oct. 8, 1858. Dr. McGuire was a very successful minister of the gospel. See *Amer. Quar. Church Rev.* 1859, p. 680.

McHale, John, a Roman Catholic prelate, was born in 1791 at Tubber-navine, County Mayo, Ireland. After completing his education, he became lecturer and professor of dogmatic theology at Maynooth, holding the position about eleven years. He was then named coadjutor-bishop of Killala, "cum jure successionis," and consecrated with the title of bishop of Maroma "in partibus infidelium." On the death of Dr. Kelly he was promoted to the archiepiscopal see of Tuam, which he held until his death, Nov. 7, 1881. He published *Evidences and Doctrines of the Catholic Church*, 1827, which was translated into French and German. He translated sixty of Moore's *Irish Melodies* into the Irish language, retaining the same metre as the originals. In 1861 he produced a large octavo volume, comprising six books of Homer's *Iliad*, with an Irish translation in heroic metre. (B. P.)

McJilton, John N., D.D., a Protestant Episcopal clergyman, was born at Baltimore, Md., in 1805. He was ordained deacon in 1841: was for a long time chaplain of the Maryland Hospital, in that city, and subsequently had the rectorship of Mount Zion Church added to his labors; in 1867 he was rector of that Church and of the Church of the Messiah; in the following year he went to New York city, officiating there until 1874, after which he resided, without special work, in that city until his death, April 13, 1875. See *Prot. Episc. Almanac*, 1876, p. 149.

McKeen, Silas, D.D., a Congregational minister, was born at Corinth, Vt., March 16, 1791. He received his preparatory studies at Haverhill Academy, and his theological studies were conducted by Rev. Stephen Fuller at Berkshire. He was ordained pastor of the Church in Bradford in 1815, where he continued twelve years; the following year he was reinstalled, remaining there twenty-four years. Subsequently he became acting pastor of the Church at Fairlee, and four years thereafter returned to Bradford, where he died, Dec. 10, 1877. He was moderator of the General Convention of Vermont in 1846. Dr. McKeen published several sermons and addresses. (W. P. S.)

McKinley, Daniel, D.D., a Presbyterian minister, was born at Carlisle, Pa., Dec. 7, 1800. He graduated from Dickinson College in 1824; spent more than a year thereafter in Princeton Theological Seminary; was ordained by the presbytery of Carlisle, Oct. 30, 1827; was pastor at Bedford, 1827–31; Carlisle, 1833–38; agent for the Board of Foreign Missions, 1838–41; pastor at Chambersburg, 1841–47; pastor of Sixth Church, Pittsburgh, 1850–52; agent for the Board of Domestic Missions, 1852–55; and died at Chambersburg, Dec. 7 of the latter year. See *Gen. Cat. of Princeton Theol. Sem.* 1881, p. 50.

McKinney, Samuel, D.D., a Presbyterian minister, was born in 1805. Many years before removing to Texas he resided in Tennessee, where the early part of his ministerial life was spent. He became a member of the Presbytery of Brazos, and a leading minister of the Southern Presbyterian Church, indefatigable in advancing all its interests. He was the first president of Austin College, Texas. He died at Huntsville, Nov. 27, 1879. (W. P. S.)

M'Kown, J. Le Grange, D.D., a Methodist Episcopal minister, was born at Guilderland, N. Y., Aug. 13, 1824. He was of Scotch-Irish descent, and reared in the Reformed Church, but at the age of fourteen united with the Methodists. At seventeen he entered Troy Conference Academy, and later graduated from Wesleyan University, Middletown, Conn., in 1849. He was admitted to the Oneida Conference the same year, but ill-health soon obliged him to retire from regular pastoral work, though not from active duty. For eight years he gave his energies to the education of youth, during which time he was professor of Newark Wesleyan Seminary, president of Richmondville Union Seminary, of

Cooperstown Seminary, and of Pittsburgh High School. His health improving, in 1858 he was stationed at Union Chapel, Cincinnati. Thence he was transferred to the New York Conference in 1859, and appointed in turn to Trinity Church, New York city; Washington Street, Poughkeepsie; St. James's Church, Kingston; and St. James's Church, New York city. In 1867 he was stationed in the city of Dubuque, and in 1868 at Union Chapel, Cincinnati, O. His subsequent fields of labor were: president of Albion College, Mich., 1871; pastor of Third Street Church, Rockford, Ill.; Wabash Avenue and Ada Street churches, Chicago; Hedding Church, Jersey City, N. J.; Roseville; and in 1878 he was appointed to Milton-on-the-Hudson, New York Conference, but died before entering upon his work, in Roseville, May 2, 1879. He was refined, amiable, studious, and thorough. He excelled as a pastor. See *Minutes of Annual Conferences*, 1880, p. 45.

McLain, William, D.D., a Presbyterian minister, was born in Ohio, and served several churches as pastor. His last charge was the First Presbyterian Church of Washington city, D. C., which position he resigned to become financial secretary of the Colonization Society, with which he was identified for many years. He died at Washington, Feb. 15, 1873, aged sixty-six years. See (N. Y.) *Presbyterian*, March 1, 1873. (W. P. S.)

McLean, Daniel Veach, D.D., a Presbyterian minister, and member of the Presbytery of Monmouth, N. J., who died at Red Bank, Nov. 23, 1869, was an able preacher, a good scholar, and a friend of temperance, education, the Bible cause, and every Christian and benevolent movement. (W. P. S.)

McLeod, Alexander, D.D., a Protestant Episcopal clergyman, was rector for a number of years at Huntington, Pa.; in 1857 at Clearfield, having charge of St. Andrew's Church, and subsequently serving, in addition, as missionary at Phillipsburg. In 1864 he was chaplain in the United States Hospital, Wilmington, Del., whence he was sent, in 1866, to Fort Delaware, as army chaplain. In 1871 he was removed to Fort Leavenworth, Kan., serving in the same position. He died at Meadeville, Pa., Feb. 9, 1877, in his seventy-seventh year. See *Prot. Episc. Almanac*, 1878, p. 169.

McLeod, John Niel, D.D., a Reformed Presbyterian minister, was born in New York city, Oct. 11, 1806. He graduated at Columbia College in 1826; studied theology under his father, with whom he was associated as pastor in 1828, and whom he succeeded in 1833. He died in New York, April 27, 1874. He had been for many years stated clerk of the synod of his denomination, and professor in the theological seminary then at Philadelphia.

McMaster, Algernon S., D.D., a Presbyterian minister, was born at Mercer, Pa., Nov. 17, 1807. He graduated at Union College, and, after completing his theological studies, was ordained pastor of the Presbyterian Church at Galway in 1833, whence he went in 1838 to Pittsburgh, subsequently to Westfield, and finally to Poland, O., where he labored with zeal and success for twenty-four years, until failing health obliged him to resign. He died at Leetonia, Oct. 2, 1882. See (N. Y.) *Observer*, Oct. 12, 1882. (W. P. S.)

McMasters, Sterling Y., D.D., LL.D., a Protestant Episcopal clergyman, was born at Guilford Court-House, N. C., Dec. 13, 1813. He graduated at the State University, was ordained in 1846, and officiated in 1853 as rector of a church in Alton, Ill. In 1858 he removed to Palmyra, Mo., as president of St. Paul's College in that place, and remained in this position until 1861, when he became chaplain of the 27th regiment of Illinois Volunteers, United States army; in the following year he officiated in St. Paul, Minn., and soon after became rector of Christ Church, in that place, where he remained until his death. He died Nov. 5, 1875. See *Prot. Episc. Almanac*, 1876, p. 150.

McMillan, John (1), D.D., a Presbyterian minister, was born at Fagg's Manor, Chester Co., Pa., Nov. 11, 1752. He graduated from Princeton College in 1770, was licensed by the Newcastle Presbytery in 1774, and spent the two following years preaching in various parts of Virginia and North Carolina. In 1776 he joined the Donegal Presbytery, and was stationed at Chambersburg, where he labored earnestly for several years. He died Nov. 16, 1833. See Sprague, *Annals of the Amer. Pulpit*, iii, 350.

McMillan, John (2), D.D., a Presbyterian minister, was born in South Carolina, but in early life removed to Xenia, O., and afterwards went to Philadelphia, where he received his education. He was ordained pastor of the Scotch Presbyterian Church of Allegheny City, Pa., which position he held for fifteen years with great usefulness and success. He served during the war as chaplain of a Pittsburgh regiment, and afterwards had charge of a church at Mount Pleasant for ten years. He next became pastor of the Fifteenth Street Church, Philadelphia, where he remained until his death at Nantucket, Sept. 1, 1882. See (N. Y.) *Observer*, Sept. 7, 1882. (W. P. S.)

McMullen, Robert Burns, D.D., a Presbyterian minister, was born in Abbeville District, S. C., Feb. 9, 1807. He graduated from the University of Alabama in 1833; spent two years in the Princeton Theological Seminary; was ordained by the Presbytery of Tuscaloosa, April 8, 1837; became pastor at Clinton, Ala., the same year; professor of chemistry in East Tennessee University in 1841; pastor of First Church of Knoxville, Tenn., the same year; president of Stewart College in 1858, and died at Clarkesville, Jan. 14, 1865. See *Gen. Cat. of Princeton Theol. Sem.* 1881, p. 100.

McMurdie, Henry, D.D., a Roman Catholic divine, was born in London, May 21, 1822, and was brought up a member of the Church of England. He entered a commercial house in Liverpool, and during the Tractarian movement joined the Catholic Church. He accompanied bishop O'Connor of Pittsburgh to America, and entered Mount St. Mary's Seminary, where he graduated. He was ordained priest at Loretto, Pa., by bishop O'Connor, Aug. 15, 1854. He returned to Mount St. Mary's, became professor of theology and moral philosophy, afterwards director of the seminary, was vice-president from 1873 to 1875, and was a hard worker to the day of his death, which took place at the seminary, Emmittsburg, Md., Jan. 20, 1880. Dr. McMurdie had a mind which saw through the most abstract questions. He had a marvellous command of English, and was a fine preacher. See (N. Y.) *Catholic Annual*, 1883, p. 63.

McPheeters, Samuel Brown, D.D., a Presbyterian minister, was born at Raleigh, N. C., Sept. 18, 1819. He graduated from the University of North Carolina in 1841; studied law; graduated from Princeton Theological Seminary in 1843; was ordained evangelist in 1848; became pastor of the Pine Street Church, St. Louis, Mo., in 1851, and in 1861 of Mulberry Presbyterian Church, Shelby County, Ky., where he died, March 9, 1870. See *Gen. Cat. of Princeton Theol. Sem.* 1881, p. 141.

McQueen, Donald, D.D., a Presbyterian minister, was born in Chesterfield District, S. C., June 21, 1810, of a Scotch-Irish family. He graduated from South Carolina College in 1832, and from the theological seminary at Columbia in 1836. His sole pastorate was at Sumter, to which was for a time added that of the adjoining town of Concord; he died at the former place, Jan. 22, 1880. See Nevin, *Presb. Encyclop.* s. v.

McRee, James, D.D., a Presbyterian minister, was born in Iredell County, N. C., May 10, 1752, of parents who had emigrated from Ireland in 1730. He was educated in New Jersey College, studied theology privately, was licensed to preach by the Presbytery of Orange in April, 1778, and became pastor in Mecklenburg County, N. C., where he remained twenty years.

He died March 28, 1840. See Sprague, *Annals of the Amer. Pulpit*, iii, 322.

McSparran, James, D.D., an English clergyman, graduated M.A. at the University of Glasgow, Scotland, in 1709, and was selected by the Society for the Propagation of the Gospel in Foreign Parts as a missionary over the Narragansett Parish, R. I. He was ordained Aug. 21, 1720, as deacon, by the bishop of London, and Sept. 25 following, as presbyter, by the archbishop of Canterbury. Besides officiating in Narragansett, he was required to preach at Bristol, Freetown, Swansey, and at Little Compton. In 1725 he assisted in establishing a Church in New London, Conn. In 1736 he visited England, and again in 1754. He died at South Kingstown, R. I., Dec. 1, 1757. He published a work entitled *America Dissected*, etc. (Dublin, 1753). See Sprague, *Annals of the Amer. Pulpit*, v, 44.

McVickar, William Augustus, D.D., a Protestant Episcopal clergyman, was born in the city of New York, April 24, 1827. He graduated from Columbia College in 1846, and from the General Theological Seminary in 1849; became successively rector at Morristown, N. J., and at Dobbs Ferry and Irvington, N. Y.; then of the American Chapel at Nice, France, and for nine years previous to his death was rector of Christ Church, New York city. He died Sept. 24, 1877. See *Prot. Episc. Almanac*, 1878, p. 169.

McWhir, William, D.D., a Presbyterian minister, was born in Ireland, Sept. 9, 1759. He was prepared for college at Belfast, and at nineteen years of age entered the University of Glasgow. He was licensed by the Presbytery of Killyleagh in 1782. In 1783 he sailed for America, and in 1792 settled near Savannah, and took charge of an academy, in connection with his pastoral duties. He died Jan. 31, 1851. See Sprague, *Annals of the Amer. Pulpit*, iii, 439.

McWhorter, Alexander. See Macwhorter.

Mead, Edward N., D.D., a Protestant Episcopal clergyman, graduated from the General Theological Seminary, and resided for some time, without regular charge, first in New York city, and then in Tarrytown, being secretary, in 1859, of the board of trustees of the General Theological Seminary, an office which he held for eighteen years. In 1864 he ministered at St. Mary's Church, Beechwood, N. Y. He died at Sing Sing, Oct. 19, 1877. See *Prot. Episc. Almanac*, 1878, p. 169.

Mead, Hiram, D.D., a Congregational minister, was born at Cornwall, Vt., May 10, 1827. He studied at Burr Seminary, Manchester, and graduated from Middlebury College in 1850. The next two years he was engaged in teaching at Flushing, N. Y. From 1852 to 1854 he was a tutor in Middlebury College. In 1857 he graduated from Andover Theological Seminary. He was ordained pastor of the Church in South Hadley, Mass., Sept. 29, 1858, from which he was dismissed, Nov. 19, 1867. From Dec. 17, following, to Sept. 22, 1869, he was pastor at Nashua, N. H. From 1870 until his death he was professor of sacred rhetoric and pastoral theology in Oberlin College. He died in Oberlin, O., May 18, 1881. Among his publications is the *Manual of Praise, for Sunday and Social Worship* (1880). See *Cong. Year-book*, 1882, p. 34.

Mead, William Cooper, D.D., LL.D., a Protestant Episcopal clergyman, was born at Greenwich, Conn., and ordained deacon in 1824 by bishop Croes. Previous to 1836 he was rector of Christ Church, Reading, Pa., and of Trinity Church, Philadelphia, and from that date of St. Paul's Church, Norwalk, Conn., until his death, July 17, 1879, at the age of eighty years. For more than forty years he served on the standing committee, and in the general convention. See *Prot. Episc. Almanac*, p. 171.

Means, John Oliver, D.D., a Congregational minister, was born at Augusta, Me., Aug. 1, 1822. He graduated from Bowdoin College in 1843, and from Andover Theological Seminary in 1849, having meanwhile served four years as purser in the navy. He was ordained Dec. 3, 1851, pastor at East Medway, Mass., a position which he held for four years, and in 1857 became pastor of the Vine Street Congregational Church, at Roxbury, where he remained for eighteen years. In 1875 he resigned his position to become secretary of the Massachusetts Sunday-school Publication Society, but was soon called into a wider sphere of usefulness, the secretaryship of the American Board of Commissioners for Foreign Missions, which he held at the time of his death, Dec. 8, 1883. Dr. Means also served on the Boston School Board. He was president of the Roxbury Athenæum, and held other trusts. He was also a member of the Royal Geographical Society of England. He visited Europe in the interest of the missionary society, and was highly esteemed by all denominations.

Mears, John William, D.D., a Presbyterian minister and educator, was born at Reading, Pa., Aug. 10, 1825. He graduated from Delaware College at the head of his class in 1844, and from Yale Divinity School in 1851. He was ordained, in 1852, pastor at Camden, N. J.; in 1854 became pastor at Elkton, Md.; in 1857 at Milford, Del.; in 1860 became joint editor of the *American Presbyterian*, at Philadelphia, and later sole editor and proprietor until 1870, when that paper was merged in the *Evangelist*. In 1871 he was elected professor of metaphysics in Hamilton College, a position which he retained until his death, Nov. 10, 1881. Dr. Mears took great interest in the questions of the day, and in 1878 he organized the movement against the Oneida community which gained such force that they were compelled to abolish the objectionable system of complex marriage. He was prominent as a prohibitionist, and was the candidate of that party for governor in one campaign. He was the author of several well-known religious works, among them *The Bible in the Workshop*, and *The Martyrs of France*.

Medeba. The ruins of this site are extensively described by Tristram (*Land of Moab*, p. 321 sq.) and Merrill (*East of the Jordan*, p. 252). They consist especially of two columns, still standing, with their archi-

Columns at Medeba.

trave, the remains of a temple, and a stone reservoir, one hundred and twenty yards square, still perfect, with the usual signs of an ancient town.

Medico, Sixto, a Venetian Dominican, was born about 1501. He was professor of philosophy at Venice, in 1545 professor of theology at Padua, and died Nov. 29, 1561. He is best known as the author of *De Fœnere Judæorum* (Venice, 1551). See Fürst, *Bibl. Jud.* ii, 338; Jöcher, *Allgemeines Gelehrten-Lexikon*, s. v. (B. P.)

Medina, Samuel de, a Jewish writer of the 16th century, was born at Medina del Campo. He was a philosopher, jurist, and teacher of repute, and became the head of the college at Salonica. In 1596 he published his פסקים, a collection of answers to legal decisions, and left a volume of homilies, which were published under the title of בן שמואל, by his grandson, at Mantua, in 1622. See De' Rossi, *Dizionario Storico* (Germ. transl.), p. 215; Lindo, *History of the Jews in Spain and Portugal*, p. 359; Kayserling, *Gesch. d. Juden in Portugal*, p. 89; Fürst, *Bibl. Jud.* ii, 339. (B. P.)

Meelführer, Johann, a Lutheran theologian of Germany, was born at Culmbach, in Franconia, Dec. 25, 1570. He studied at Wittenberg, was preacher and teacher at different places, and died Dec. 3, 1640, at Ansbach. He is the author of, *Manuale Lexici Hebraici* (Leipsic, 1617):—*Clavis Linguæ Hebrææ*, etc. (Nuremberg, 1598, 1628):—*Compendiosa Institutio Grammatica Hebr.* (Ansbach, 1607; Jena, 1623):—*Synopsis Institut. Hebr.* (Leyden, 1642):—*Vindiciæ Evangelicæ*: —*Vindiciæ Apostolicæ*, etc. See Fürst, *Bibl. Jud.* ii, 340; Jöcher, *Allgemeines Gelehrten-Lexikon*, s. v. (B. P.)

Meelführer, Rudolph Martin, a Lutheran theologian of Germany, was born at Ansbach. He studied at different universities, and was made a licentiate of theology. In 1712 he joined the Romish Church, but returned to the Lutheran Church again in 1725. He then went to Gotha and Holland, and while on his way home was imprisoned by the imperial government, and retained at Eger. When Meelführer died is not known. He wrote, *Consensus Veterum Hebræorum cum Ecclesia Christiana* (Frankfort, 1701):—*Causæ Synagogæ Errantis* (Altdorf, 1702):—*Jesus in Talmude* (ibid. 1699):—*De Versionibus Talmudis*:—*De Meritis Hebræorum in rem Literariam*:—*De Impedimentis Conversionis Judæorum*. See Winer, *Handbuch der theol. Lit.* i, 563; Fürst, *Bibl. Jud.* ii, 340 sq.; Jöcher, *Allgemeines Gelehrten-Lexikon*, s. v. (B. P.)

Megas, Joseph ibn. See Migas.

Megiddo. Lieut. Conder (*Tent Work*, i, 128 sq.; and still more extensively in the *Memoirs* to the Ordnance Survey, ii, 90 sq.) impugns the grounds of identity between this place and Legio (now Lejjûn), and prefers *Khurbet el-Mujedda*, a ruin three miles southwest of Beisan; but this is too far from the Kishon.

Meharry, Alexander, D.D., a Methodist Episcopal minister, was born in Adams County, O., Oct. 17, 1831. He was carefully and religiously trained; was converted in his thirteenth year; in 1833 entered into mercantile business; received license to preach in 1841, and in the same year joined the Ohio Conference. His fields of labor were Blendon, Bambridge Circuit, Jacksonville, Deer Creek, Frankfort, and Augusta Circuit, Ky. In 1848 and 1849 he served New Street and East Cincinnati missions. He then acted as agent for the Ohio Wesleyan University, for six years, as well as part of the time as agent for the Springfield High-school. His next appointments were Franklin, Middletown, Finley Chapel, Cincinnati, and Wilmington. In 1866 and 1867 he was agent for the Cincinnati Wesleyan College; from 1868 to 1870 was pastor at Eaton; in 1871 served as presiding elder of Ripley District; in 1872 and 1873 of Springfield District; from 1874 to 1877 held a superannuated relation; and in 1878 was appointed financial agent of the Ohio Wesleyan University. He died in Germantown, Nov. 18 of that year. Dr. Meharry was a plain, practical, bold, and uncompromising preacher; a man of great energy, an indefatigable worker. See *Minutes of Annual Conferences*, 1879, p. 16.

Mehdivis, a Mohammedan sect in India, who take their name from believing their *Wali* or saint to have been the promised *Mehdi* or *Mahadi*. A pretender arose, who claimed to be the twelfth Imam. He was born at Benares, in the year A.D. 1443, and declared himself to be the Mahadi, at the black stone at Mecca, about A.D. 1495. He died at Khorassan, in the year A.D. 1505, after which his followers dispersed, without, however, giving up their belief in the reappearance of their leader as the long-expected Mahadi. They were subjected to a severe persecution by Aurungzebe, but are still found in small communities in various parts of India.

Mehring, Heinrich Johann Friedrich, a Protestant theologian, who died at the age of eighty-one years, May 3, 1879, at Papendorf, near Pasewalk, where he occupied one and the same pastorate over fifty-six years, is the author of, *Das Sündenregister im Römerbrief, oder neue Erklärung der Stelle, Rom. i*, 8-32 (Wriezen-on-the-Oder, 1854):—*Der Brief Pauli an die Römer* (Stettin, 1858, 1 part). See Zuchold, *Bibl. Theol.* ii, 864. (B. P.)

Meier, Christoph Paulus (originally *Solomon ben-Meir*), a rabbi at Frankfort, who embraced Christianity, and was baptized Aug. 5, 1673, at Nordhausen, is the author of, *Jüdischer Narrenspiegel* (Wittenberg, 1685):—*Jewish Ceremonies* (ibid. 1678; Dantzic, 1682): *Tractatus de Brevi et Ridicula Judæorum Expositione Cantici* (Dantzic, 1678), etc. See Wolf, *Bibl. Hebr.* i, 1010, iii, 982; iv, 967; Jöcher, *Allgemeines Gelehrten-Lexikon*, s. v.; Schudt, *Jüd. Denkwürdigkeiten*, ii, 124; Diefenbach, *Judæus Conversus*, p. 169 sq.; Fürst, *Bibl. Jud.* ii, 341. (B. P.)

Meier, Friedrich Christ. (originally *Israel Meier*), a Jew who embraced Christianity, and was baptized with his daughter, at Altona, near Hamburg, Sept. 21, 1701, wrote, *Licht zu erleuchten die Juden* (Leipsic, 1711; Halle, 1713):—*Der güldene Leuchter im A. T.* (Hamburg, 1718):—*Balsam des Lebens*, on Jewish ceremonies (Brunswick, 1719):—*Der 91 Psalm gedeutet* (Rostock, 1704):—*Moses mit Christus verglichen* (Hamburg, 1715):—*Glaubensbekentniss*, etc., or ס׳ מַגִּיד אֱמוּנַת יְשׁוּעַ (Altona, 1701). See Wolf, *Bibl. Hebr.* i, 990; iii, 947; iv, 959; Jöcher, *Allgemeines Gelehrten-Lexikon*, s. v.; Fürst, *Bibl. Jud.* ii, 341. (B. P.)

Meier, Gebhard Theodor, a Lutheran theologian of Germany, was born at Hanover, May 16, 1633. He studied at Helmstädt, was in 1660 professor of theology, and died Dec. 22, 1693. He wrote, *Introductio in Universum Theologiæ Moralis Studium* (1671):—*Politia Ecclesiæ Primitivæ ad Politiam Civilem Formata*:—*Historia Religionum Christianæ, Judaicæ, Gentilis et Muhammedanæ*, etc. See Winer, *Handbuch der theol. Lit.* i, 310, 624, 636, 664, 904; Jöcher, *Allgemeines Gelehrten-Lexikon*, s. v. (B. P.)

Meiner, Johann Werner, a Lutheran theologian, born at Römershofen, Franconia, March 5, 1723, was rector at Langensalza, and died March 23, 1789. He wrote, *Die wahren Eigenschaften der hebräischen Sprache* (Leipsic, 1748):—*Analysis et Versio iii Ecclesiastæ* (ibid. 1751):—*Auflösung der vornehmsten Schwierigkeiten der hebr. Sprache* (Langensalza, 1757):—*Progr. II de Hebræorum Censibus* (1764-66):—*Beitrag zur Verbesserung der Bibelübersetzung* (Ratisbon, 1781). See Fürst, *Bibl. Jud.* ii, 341 sq.; Winer, *Handbuch der theol. Lit.* i, 115. (B. P.)

Meinertzhagen, Gustav, a Protestant theologian, who died at Bremen in 1856, is the author of, *Predigten* (Bremen, 1834):—*Die Hoffnung der Gläubigen* (ibid. 1842):—*Vorlesungen über die Christologie des Alten Testaments* (ibid. 1843):—*Die religiöse Bedeutung der biblischen Wunder* (1845):—*Ueber Werth und Bedeutung* *der biblischen Geschichte* (1849):—*Die Versuchung Christi* (1855). After his death Achelis published *Nachgelassene Predigten* (1857). See Zuchold, *Bibl. Theol.* ii, 865 sq. (B. P.)

Meinhart, Georg Friedrich, a Lutheran theologian of Germany, was born at Ohrdruff, in the county of Hohenlohe, April 5, 1651. He studied at Jena and Wittenberg, was in 1683 superintendent at Arnstadt, and died April 10, 1718, doctor of theology. He wrote, *Meditationes in Zachariæ ix*, 9:—*Disputationes de Propheta Mosi:*—*De Nasiræis Disputationes Tres:*—*De Corban Dissertationes Tres:*—*De Pauli Nasiræatu:*—*De Selenolatria a Jeremia Improbata:*—*De Fabrica Templi Mystici.* See Unschuldige, *Nachrichten;* Jöcher, *Allgemeines Gelehrten-Lexikon*, s. v. (B. P.)

Meintel, Johann Georg, a Protestant theologian of the 18th century, is the author of *Notæ Selectissimorum Commentatorum Judaicorum in Psalmos Davidi* (Schwabach, 1744):—*Monarchie der Hebräer* (Nuremberg, 1751):—*Probe einer kritischen Polyglottenbibel* (ibid. 1764–70):—*Kurze Erklärung des Buches Hiob* (1771):—*Metaphrasis Libri Jobi, sive Jobus Metricus* (1774). See Fürst, *Bibl. Jud.* ii, 342. (B. P.)

Meinwerk, bishop of Paderborn from 1009 to 1036, was of noble descent. He was educated at Halberstadt and Hildesheim, and became royal chaplain under Otto III. Henry II made him bishop, and took him to Italy in 1013. Meinwerk also accompanied Henry's successor, Conrad II, to Italy in 1026, and by the services which Meinwerk thus rendered he greatly advanced the cause of the Church. By the munificence of his royal patrons he was enabled to devote much of his time in the interest of the school and in founding new monasteries. He died June 5, 1036, but was not canonized until 1376. His life is found in Pertz, *Monumenta Germaniæ*, xi, 104–161. See also Wattenbach, *Deutsche Geschichtsquellen* (Berlin, 1878), ii, 29–33, 279; Otto, *De Henrici II in Artes Litterasque Meritis* (Bonn, 1848); Hirsch, *Jahrbücher des deutschen Reichs unter Heinrich II;* Bresslau, *Jahrbücher des deutschen Reichs unter Konrad II;* Plitt-Herzog, *Real-Encyklop.* s. v. (B. P.)

Meis, Friedrich Ernst, a Lutheran theologian of Germany, was born June 26, 1658. He studied at Jena and Leipsic, was in 1688 conrector at Ichleusingen, in 1691 superintendent and pastor primarius, in 1699 doctor of theology, and died Dec. 20, 1744. He wrote, *De Sanguine Vetito ex Genes. ix*, 3, 4:—*De Morte ex Rom. v*, 12:—*De Resurrectione Mortuorum ex Joh. v*, 28, 29:—*De Extremo Judicio ex* 2 *Cor. v*, 10:—*De Inferno ex Matt. xxv*, 41:—*De Deo Unitrino ex Esa. xlviii*, 16:—*De Christo Jesu Nazarens ex Esa. xxviii*, 26:—*De Scriptura Sacra ex* 2 *Tim. iii*, 16, 17:—*De Angelis ex Ebr. i*, 14:—*De Providentia Dei ex* 1 *Pet. v*, 7:—*Explanatio Prioris Hemistichii* 1 *Cor. xv*, 17, *contra Spinozam:*—*Explicatio Jer. xxxii*, 17, *contra Spinozam*, etc. See Ludovici *Notitia Ephororum Schleusingensium;* Neubauer, *Jetztlebende Theologen;* Jöcher, *Allgemeines Gelehrten-Lexikon*, s. v. (B. P.)

Meisner, Johann, a Lutheran theologian of Germany, was born at Torgau, April 4, 1615. He studied at Wittenberg, was rector at his native place, afterwards doctor and professor of theology at Wittenberg, and died in 1681. He wrote, *Theologia Naturalis Tribus Dissertationibus:*—*Compendium Theologiæ Disputationibus xxii:*—*Fasciculi Disputationum Theologicarum ad Genes. i*, 6, 7:—*De Protevangelio Paradisiaco ad Genes. iii*, 15:—*De Confusione Linguarum Babylonica ad Genes. xi*, 1–9:—*De Christo Redemtore Vivo ad Jobi xix*, 25:—*De Plerophoria Hiobi in Gœlem Redivivum ad Jobi xix*, 25 sq.:—*De Origine et Progressu Arianismi:*—*De Persecutionibus et Martyribus Veterum Christianorum:*—*De Vetere Novoque Homine:*—*De Maria Dei Genetrice:*—*De Transsubstantiatione et Missa:*—*De Spiritu Sancto contra Socinianos:*—*Num Christus in Triduo Mortis verus Permanserit Homo?*—*De Peccato in Spiritum Sanctum.* See Witte, *Diarium;* Jöcher, *Allgemeines Gelehrten-Lexikon*, s. v.; Winer, *Handbuch der theol. Lit.* i, 425. (B. P.)

Meisner, Johann Heinrich, a Lutheran theologian, was born at Leipsic, Dec. 11, 1755, and died there, April 10, 1813, doctor and professor of philosophy. He published, *Nova Veteris Testamenti Clavis* (Leipsic, 1800, 2 vols.):—*In Carmine Davidis* 2 *Sam. xxiii*, 1–7 (1783):—*Œconomia Cap. xii Hoseæ* (1788). In connection with Döderlein he published *Biblia Hebraica cum Variis Lectionibus* (1793). See Winer, *Handbuch der theol. Lit.* i, 39, 120; Fürst, *Bibl. Jud.* ii, 347. (B. P.)

Mejarkon. This is held by Lieut. Conder (*Tent Work*, i, 230) to be the *Nahr el-Aujah*, a stream turbid with yellow sand, running into the Mediterranean a few miles north of Jaffa.

Meklenburg, Jacob Hirsch, a Jewish writer, who died at Königsberg, April 6, 1865, is the author of הכתב והקבלה, or *Die Schrift und die Ueberlieferung* (Leipsic, 1839), etc. See Fürst, *Bibl. Jud.* ii, 348; Zuchold, *Bibl. Theol.* ii, 867. (B. P.)

Melcher, Johann Wilhelm, a Protestant theologian of Germany, who died at Freienwalde, Feb. 10, 1880, is the author of, *Verhältniss der vier kanonischen Evangelien unter einander* (Berlin, 1847):—*Beiträge zum Verständniss der Heiligenschrift* (1859). See Zuchold, *Bibl. Theol.* ii, 869. (B. P.)

Melcher, Joseph, a Roman Catholic prelate, studied and took his doctor's degree at Modena, was ordained in 1830, and became chaplain to the court. In 1843 he came to America with bishop Rosati, and was stationed at Little Rock, Ark., whence he was transferred to St. Mary's Church, St. Louis, Mo., of which diocese he became vicar-general. He remained pastor there until he was made the first bishop of Green Bay, Wis., July 12, 1868. He introduced several working orders, such as the Ursulines, Franciscan Tertiaries, Servites, etc. Dr. Melcher died Dec. 20, 1873, at the age of sixty-six, leaving a flock of 60,000 and sixty-nine churches. See De Courcy and Shea, *Hist. of the Cath. Church in the United States*, p. 598.

Melchiades. See Miltiades.

Melchior, Johann, a Reformed theologian of Germany, was born in 1646. He studied at different universities; was in 1667 pastor at Frech, in the duchy of Jülich, in 1672 at Kattekirchen, in 1677 at Düsseldorf, in 1682 doctor of theology, and died at Dillenburg, Oct. 15, 1689. He wrote, *Clavis Prophetica Cantici Canticorum Salomonis:*—*Commentarius in Prophetam Michæam:*—*Parallelismus Locorum Veteris Testamenti in Novo Citatorum:*—*Analysis Epistolæ ad Romanos:*—*Explanatio Epistolæ ad Colossenses:*—*Commentarius in Epistolam ad Hebræos:*—*Quæstiones in Apocalypsin:*—*De Religione ejusque Natura et Principio contra Spinozam:*—*De Œconomia Dei circa Gentes et Judæos ex Parabola Lucæ xv*, 11–32. Melchior's Latin writings were published at Franeker in 1706, with a biography written by Johann Heinrich Florinus. See Jöcher, *Allgemeines Gelehrten-Lexikon*, s. v. (B. P.)

Melech, Salomo Ibn-, a Jewish writer of the 16th century, was a resident at Constantinople, where he published, in 1554, his מִכְלַל יֹפִי, "The Perfection of Beauty," scholia on the Hebrew Bible. It has been repeatedly edited, but the best edition is that of Amsterdam (1685, fol.), with Abendana's additions. It is a very valuable contribution to grammatical exegesis, since it is brief and condensed, giving almost exclusively grammatical and lexical explanations, for the most part from Kimchi's writings. It has been highly valued among Christians, and several parts of it have been translated into Latin; that on *Canticles*, by Chr. Molitor (Altdorf, 1659); on *Joshua* and *Malachi*, by Nik. Köppen (Greifswalde, 1708, 1709); on *Ruth*, by J. B. Carpzov, reprinted in his *Collegium Rabbinico-Biblicum* (Leipsic, 1705); on

Jonah, by G. Chr. Burcklin (Frankfort-on-the-Main, 1697), Joh. Leusden (ibid. 1692), and E. Chr. Fabricius (Göttingen, 1792); on *Obadiah*, by Brodberg (Upsala, 1711), etc. See Fürst, *Bibl. Jud.* ii, 350; Etheridge, *Introduction to Jewish Lit.* p. 417; De' Rossi, *Dizionario Storico Degli Autori* (Germ. transl. by Hamburger), p. 217; Wolf, *Bibl. Hebr.* i, 1075 sq.: iii, 1055 sq. (B. P.)

Mellor, Enoch, D.D., an English Congregational minister, was born at Salendine Nook, near Huddersfield, Nov. 20, 1823. He studied in Huddersfield College, graduated A.M. from the University of Edinburgh in 1845, and afterwards studied theology in the Lancashire Independent College. About the close of the year 1847 he accepted the pastorate of the church at Square Road, Halifax. His fame as a preacher spread rapidly, and he was frequently invited to larger fields of usefulness. In 1861 he became pastor of the church at Great George Street, Liverpool, where he achieved signal success. In 1867 he returned to his former charge in Halifax, where he met with a hearty welcome, and continued to labor until the close of life, Oct. 26, 1881. He was active in the interests of his denomination, and was often called to positions of honor in that connection. He published, *The Atonement; its Relation to Pardon*, etc.:—*Ritualism and its Related Dogmas:—Priesthood in the Light of the New Testament.* See (Lond.) *Cong. Year-book*, 1882, p. 315.

Melo, David Abenatar, a converted Spanish Jew, was born about the middle of the 16th century. Of his early life we know nothing beyond the fact that for several years he was an inmate of the prison of the Inquisition. Whether he was committed there because, as Milman states, he was baptized, and was suspected of not being a true Christian, or in order to crush out of him the betrayal of some of his kindred, or, as Kayserling states, because he translated some of David's Psalms into Spanish, is very difficult to say. He was released in 1611, and found a refuge in Holland, where a great many of his countrymen and co-religionists had settled. He soon became the head of the synagogue at Amsterdam, lecturing at the same time at the Academy of De los Pintos. Melo, whom Barrios calls "traductor harmonioso del Psalterio misterioso," is especially known as the translator of the Psalms into Spanish, which were printed at Frankfort in 1626, under the title, *Los Psalmos de David en Varias Ninas*, and which leads to the supposition that he went thither on his way to Holland, and spent some time there. See Grätz, *Gesch. d. Juden* (Leipsic, 1868), x, 5 sq.; Kayserling, *Sephardim*, p. 169 sq.; De' Rossi, *Dizionario Storico* (Germ. transl. by Hamburger), p. 218; Milman, *History of the Jews* (N.Y. 1870), iii, 454; De los Rios, *Estudios Sobre los Judios de España*, p. 521 sq.; Fürst, *Bibl. Jud.* ii, 351. (B. P.)

Melos, Johann Georg, a Lutheran theologian, was born Aug. 24, 1770, at Grossenmonnra, near Merseburg, and died at Weimar, Feb. 16, 1828, professor at the seminary. He published, *Biblische Geschichten des Alten und Neuen Testaments* (Weimar, 1820):—*Geschichte der Reformation für Bürger- und Landschulen* (5th ed. edited by Rothe, Berlin, 1837):—*Beschreibung des jüdischen Landes zur Zeit Jesu* (Weimar, 1822; 2d ed. 1830):—*Geist des Christenthums* (1824). See Winer, *Handbuch der theol. Lit.* ii, 254, 262, 309, 318; Zuchold, *Bibl. Theol.* ii, 869; Fürst, *Bibl. Jud.* ii, 351. (B. P.)

Figure of Melpomene. From a painting on the walls of Herculaneum.

Melpomĕnē, in Greek mythology, was the muse of tragedy. See Muses.

Melsheimer, Ludwig Friedrich, a Protestant theologian, was born Sept. 18, 1771. He entered upon his ministerial functions in 1795 at Kleinfischlingen, Bavaria, was in 1806 pastor at Böchingen, and died Aug. 8, 1827, doctor of theology. He published, *Das Buch Hiob metrisch übersetzt und erläutert* (Mannheim, 1823):—*Die Sprüche Salomonis übersetzt mit Anmerkungen* (1821). See Winer, *Handbuch der theol. Lit.* i, 206, 212; Fürst, *Bibl. Jud.* ii, 351. (B. P.)

Membership in the Christian Church, Conditions of. We may premise in general that, with the exception of the Quakers or Friends (q. v.), the one essential and universal mode or sign of admission to Church communion is baptism (q. v.), and that all bodies of Christendom, except the so-called Baptists (q. v.), administer the rite to infants as well as to adults, the parents or friends of the former engaging, either formally or presumably, as sponsors (q. v.), the future assumption of the baptismal vows on the part of the children baptized, who meanwhile occupy a subordinate or preparatory stage of membership as catechumens (q. v.).

I. *Basal Principles.*—1. *Of an Ideal Character.*—The Church of God, in its broadest sense, consists of all who, whether on earth or in heaven, have been redeemed by Jesus Christ, and quickened by the Holy Spirit, and have not, by resistance of the Spirit, forfeited God's favor. The visible Church is the whole number of those who, on earth, participate, in some degree, in the common Christian life, faith, and organic fellowship. The conditions of church-membership will vary according as the visible Church, in the form it was designed to assume, be regarded as one, universal, unchangeable, and divine, or otherwise. Again, the Church may be viewed as uniform in its standard of ethical and spiritual life, but diverse in its dogmatic and organic fellowship. The dividing lines of membership must, therefore, depend largely upon the following ideals:

(1) *The Christian Life.*—What is it? When does it begin? Here comes in the question of infant or adult membership. See Pædo-baptism. The term "life," like the term "death," is ambiguous, meaning both the hidden force which renders spontaneous action possible in a favorable environment, in forms of existence above the mineral, and the activity resulting from that force. When a man loves God and his neighbor he is said to be spiritually alive; but this must mean that he exhibits in action a force, the existence of which must have preceded the display of it. Unless we are Pelagians, we must attribute the origin of spiritual life, the capability of spontaneous religious activity, to the influence of God's Spirit on the human mind. Accurately to determine the moment when life begins is as difficult in the spiritual as in the physical realm: all that can be done is to fix a period beyond which it is not reasonable to believe that the life-giving contact is delayed. Put that period of ἄνωθεν γέννησις, or birth from above, at baptism, and the conditions of membership will assume one aspect: put it at the moment of conscious self-surrender and faith, and they will assume another. "Life," however, means not merely capacity for spontaneous action, but, also, action itself—living. He is alive who acts holily. He is dead who lives in sin. On our conceptions of what the divine standard of living is, and of the time when and the means by which the transition from mere capacity for living to actual living, the moral change, renewal, or conversion, occurs, will depend the conditions of membership in our churches. Is there such a divine and unchangeable standard? Does it, if it exists, cover principles only, or overt acts alone, or motives also? How far are motives capable of being tested by Church authorities? Is the beginning of Christian living coincident with such faith as secures reverent obedience to known divine law, or with the faith that gives assurance of acceptance? To what extent is individual liberty in the application of fundamental principles of holy living admissible? If the relation of Christian love to amuse-

ments or business is doubtful, have Church authorities the right to excommunicate him in whom spiritual life may still exist, and whom God may still, in a measure, approve? A just separation from the Church of Christ is separation from Christ. Is it right to enforce, in what professes to be the Church of Christ, rules that would be legitimate only in a voluntary club, organized for special purposes within the Church, but not coterminous with the Church? On the decision given here will greatly depend the conditions of membership in Christian organizations.

(2) *The Ideal of Doctrine.* — One department of church work is, by the application of truth, to lead into action the latent spiritual capability implanted by the Spirit of God. This implies the instruction of those formally enrolled in the organization. What shall they be taught? Has Christianity any one, universal, unchangeable, and divine standard of doctrine? If so, is it confined to facts, or does it embrace theories, also? What are the facts? How much, if any, of this code of doctrine must be demanded of members of the Church? On the answer to these questions will also depend the conditions of membership.

(3) *The Christian Ideal of Organic Fellowship.*—Is there a divinely authoritative standard of organic Church relations? Are divine blessings promised to Christians in their organic capacity, or in their individual capacity only? If a divinely approved standard of life and truth are universally imperative, and if failure to reach that standard is an object of mercy only when circumstances have rendered perfection impossible in him who, nevertheless, sought conformity to that standard, can the preservation, propagation, and enforcement of life and truth in the world be left to purely voluntary religious organizations, guerilla warfare, and free-lances? Or is there one visible organism, superior to all clubs and societies, the heir of special promises, so long as it is faithful to its obligations, and one, a just excision from which is excision from God? Though our Lord did not condemn him who cast out devils, even when he followed not the disciples, were not his preparatory instructions, his special commission, and his peculiar promises given to the disciples whom he was organizing? Let covenant blessings, with corresponding obligations, be attached, even if they are not exclusively so, to a visible organism; and introduction into that organism must bring at once, if they have not been received before, the promised blessings; and these blessings are then to be retained, not sought for, unless, after the reception of them, they have been forfeited. Let covenanted blessings be the inheritance of individuals only, apart from all organic connection, on the occasion of personal acts; then, prior to those acts, it cannot be assumed that such blessings are ever given, even when the individuals concerned are the infant children of believers; while the discredit thrown upon any organic connections possible prior to the personal actions must react on the conditions of membership assumed subsequently to these acts.

2. *Principles of a Practical Character.* — (1) The terms of Church membership further depend upon the source whence we derive our knowledge of the constitution of the Christian Church. The life of one of the original apostles continued beyond the date of the "Acts of the Apostles," and of the Epistles: must the form of the Church which existed prior to the writing of these books be authoritative, and the form which history shows to have probably arisen with his sanction be ignored? Is the constitution of the Church one of cast-iron? When was it cast? At the close of the New-Test. canon? After the first three general councils? After the first seven? Or, is there a living Spirit, ever present with the Church, guiding it by Scripture, by reason and common-sense, by history and the evident necessities of spiritual life in changing circumstances? Is our knowledge of the constitution of the Church gained from the Bible alone, or from the Bible and something else? The conditions of membership will be determined by the answers given to these questions.

(2) These conditions are affected, also, by principles of Scriptural interpretation. What language did the Saviour use? If he speaks of "water and the Spirit," is his word to be interpreted by Hebrew or by Greek analogies? If he uses the term βαπτίζω, or if his reporters use it in rendering the word he may have employed, must the Church limit her conduct by the latest edition of Liddell and Scott? Or are the words of New-Test. Scripture to be regarded as so much the product of the Holy Spirit that all modifying human literary elements are eliminated from them? Is there a development of practice indicated even in the New Test., and must any given passage be interpreted as of perpetual obligation by etymology, apart from the light thrown upon it by this principle of development? Have we any right to say that the governing office of the apostolate was to be changed, but that the introduction of Christian families, as well as adult converts, into the Church was to lead to no change? In a word, must the practices which are legitimate in the Church be limited by a system of interpretation based upon a bald literalism? Or may rites and ceremonies vary when interpretation judges of the obligation of such forms by the light thrown upon the Scriptures from the thousand avenues of a living, perpetually-speaking Providence, so long as the decision is not contrary to the spirit and principles of the New Test.? These questions will suggest the bearing of hermeneutics on membership in the Church.

II. *Illustrations of these Principles in the Practice of Different Denominations.*—1. *Ancient Episcopal Churches.*—These include the Greek or Eastern Church, with its various branches, the Roman Church, the English or British Church, and the National Churches of Denmark, Sweden, and Norway.

(1) *The Greek or Eastern Church.* — "Previous to baptism, the child, though not two months old, must be solemnly initiated into the Church, as a catechumen, through the medium of its sponsors, when exorcism is used." Four prayers, with blowing on the child's mouth, forehead, and breast, and commands to the evil spirit to depart and return no more, precede the trine immersion or affusion of baptism. In Alexandria and the Syrian, or Jacobite, Church affusion exists. Among the Armenians both forms are united. The Copts, in exorcism, make the sign of the cross thirty-seven times. Chrism, or anointing with holy oil, follows immediately after baptism, and answers to confirmation in the Western Church. Within seven days after this another washing occurs, followed by tonsure, or cutting the hair in the form of a cross. Confession four times in the year is prescribed, but is generally practiced but once, as is also communion. In the absence of a priest or a deacon, lay baptism is recognized, if it has been administered in the name of the Trinity. Chrism only is enforced where such baptism has taken place. The Montenegrin Church in South Albania, however, rebaptizes Roman Catholics. The popular impression that the Greek Church recognises the baptism of no other Church is denied by Archbishop Platon, in his supplement to M. Duten's *Œuvres Mêlées*, ii, 170: "Baptismum aliarum ecclesiarum Christianarum non irritum esse putamus, et qui ex iis ad nos veniunt, non iterato baptismate, sed solo sacro chrismate inunctos, recipimus." ("We do not consider the baptism of other Christian churches invalid; and we receive those who come to us from them only by anointing them with the holy chrism, without repeating their baptism.") Submission to the faith of the Church is demanded. The communion is administered in both kinds, even to infants, bread and wine being mixed together, and given in a spoon by the officiating priest. Adult candidates then reverentially salute the clergy by hand-kissing, and are congratulated by their friends as orthodox Christians.

No Russian who has been educated in the Greek Church can lawfully depart from it.

(2) *The Roman Church.*—The leading conditions of membership in this Church are involved in her definition of the term "Church," as "the society of the faithful who are baptized and united, by the profession of the same faith, participation in the same sacraments and the same worship, to each other, and who are under one head in heaven, viz. Christ, and one head on earth, viz. the pope, his vicar." "The Church, though it consists of good and bad members, does not include heretics, schismatics, or (at least in the full sense of membership) persons severed from her unity by the greater excommunication." "Whether 'pure schismatics' (i. e. persons holding the full faith of the Church, but separated by schism) may still be called members of the Church" is a question "agitated in the theological schools." Baptism is believed to be "the origin of spiritual life, and the door of entrance into the Church." The candidate is presented at the door of the church-building, receives catechetical instruction, submits to exorcism, has salt put into his mouth, and the sign of the cross made upon different parts of his body, is touched on ears and nostrils with saliva, renounces Satan, his works and pomps, is anointed with oil, and makes profession of his faith, by sponsors in the case of infants, before baptism. Baptism is by trine affusion. Then follow chrism, robing in white, holding a burning light, and receiving a name of some saint. Confirmation with a chrism of olive-oil and balsam, in the form of a cross, with prayer and imposition of hands, in the name of the Trinity, follows either immediately or, as is usual, at from seven to twelve years of age. Confession at least once a year is imperative. The greater excommunication is reserved only for the most heinous offences.

(3) *The Church of England.*—This Church regards the spirit and principles of the Bible as forever binding; but she refuses not the guidance of subsequent Providential direction. Her terms of membership are founded upon the following principles. The Church's ideal of life, doctrine, and order, as given by Christ and his apostles, is divine and, wherever possible, imperative. Life is most important; and, while order is not indifferent, it may need to yield to the demands of truth and life. Hence she does not exclude from the pale of the Church those who, for the sake of truth and life, have believed themselves compelled to violate even her own historic order, but accepts their acts of baptism, if performed with water in the name of Father, Son, and Holy Spirit, and considers all thus baptized to be members of Christ's Church. Where the obstacles to truth and life which rendered the preservation of order morally impossible have been removed, she regards a return to the primitive apostolic order imperative for the maintenance of unity. Hence, while endeavoring to remove from herself those obstacles, when she sees them to be such, she abstains from such interchanges of membership as would imply that the division of the Church on diverse bases of life, doctrine, or order is normal or ordinarily legitimate. Her first condition of membership is baptism. In this, the sign of the cross is made on the forehead. It may be administered by lay hands, and in any of the various modes. Before baptism, the divinely imparted capacity for spiritual action and enjoyment may, in her opinion, as truly exist as after it; but, inasmuch as the Christian covenant, in Matt. xxviii, 19, 20, is regarded as given to Christians in their collective capacity, and not as individuals only, it is believed that, in baptism, the covenant blessing is surely given. This blessing of the vitalizing Spirit is called "regeneration," not because the moral change now commonly so called is therein wrought, but because the divine capacity for holy living, then, at least, certainly imparted, but impossible by mere human nature, is then, also, first openly manifested or declared, just as natural birth first openly manifests the life which was before concealed. Hence, her second condition of membership, confirmation, is an opportunity given, after instruction, publicly to assume those responsibilities for which candidates are supposed to have been previously prepared by that faith which, working by love, brings the divinely imparted capacity into action, producing the moral change, renewal, or conversion demanded. Church membership is, therefore, a home privilege, with spiritual power believed to be graciously conferred prior to all personal choice, to counteract inherited tendencies of evil, and to enable the child, from the beginning, to see and discharge the duties of Christian faith and love, a privilege to be retained, and not first to be sought after a period of alienation more or less prolonged. Provision is made for the admission of adults by baptism, if this has not been previously given, and by confirmation. She imposes upon candidates no dogmatic theories, but only the facts embodied in the Apostles' Creed. Her moral demands cover no "doubtful disputations," but only the faith and love which are essential to Christianity. Her ceremonial demands enforce no more than attendance upon prayer, the word and the two sacraments of our Lord. Her law of discipline for the punishment and exclusion of lay offenders is, unfortunately, so greatly obstructed by legal considerations as to have become almost obsolete. Believing that she represents, not a voluntary society, but the Church of God, having maintained her historic connection in all essentials with the Church of apostolic times, she considers those baptized by her as hers until they die or are formally excluded or dismissed.

(4) On the principle that the majority of the members of a Church, in their corporate action, are and remain the same Church, the established churches of Denmark, Sweden, and Norway may be classed among ancient episcopal churches, though called Lutheran. In their terms of membership they do not essentially differ from other episcopal churches.

2. *Modern Episcopal Churches, and Quasi-Episcopal Churches, Originating since the Reformation, and Committing the Rights of Ordination and Supervision to One Man, Assisted by Others.*—(1) *The Scottish Episcopal Church.*—The origin of this may be dated from the revival of episcopacy by Charles II, in 1661. Its terms of membership are similar to those of the English Church.

(2) *The Protestant Episcopal Church of the United States.*—This was founded as a separate body in 1784, and has the same conditions of admission as the English Church; but an intention to be confirmed as soon as possible suffices, in certain cases, to secure membership. The use of the sign of the cross in baptism may, on request, be omitted. Letters of transfer to other denominations are sometimes given.

(3) *Moravians* (European, origin, 1727; American, 1800).—In Europe, baptism, with laying on of hands, introduces children into the Church as catechumens, among whom, prior to admission as full members, adult converts take their place. In America, full membership involves a profession of faith in the Bible as the word of God, confidence in the forgiveness of the candidate's sins, determination to follow holiness and to obey the Church, and reception in open congregation by the pastor, after opportunity has been given for the statement of objections to the reception. Retention of membership depends upon obedience to laws, some of which forbid the sale or use of intoxicants, or the renting of property to liquor-dealers, or signing petitions favoring them, and union with secret societies. Exclusion is by a vote of the class, or congregation, after admonition and examination. Transfer to other bodies may take place "by a vote of the charge," and a certificate signed by the pastor.

(4) *The English Wesleyans.*—To be members of the society, persons are required to desire salvation, to meet in class, to avoid evil and do good, according to the de-

nominational standard of evil and good, and attend "the ordinances of God." The communion is not refused to godly persons, though they belong to the congregation only, and not to the society. Baptized children are not members of the Wesleyan organism, and are sometimes sent, for confirmation, to the Church of England.

(5) *The Methodist Episcopal Church of the United States of America.*—The conditions of membership in this Church are less affected than in other Methodist churches by the transition from a voluntary society of adults formed for a special purpose to a self-governing Church. Membership begins by reception as a probationer, on giving evidence of desire for salvation from sin. After six months, on recommendation of the leaders and stewards, baptism having been received, and satisfactory assurances of faith and loyalty having been given to the preacher in charge before the Church, full membership is conferred. Members of other bodies are received, on recommendation from the proper authorities, and on assurance of loyalty to the principles and practices of the M. E. Church. Baptized children of Methodist parents, though regarded as in visible covenant relation with God, and as objects of the Church's care, do not seem to be in any sense members of the Methodist Church until, after having attended class for six months, they are publicly received in regular form. After reception into full membership, attendance upon class-meeting, while strongly recommended, is no more imperative than attendance upon other useful services. For crimes duly proved, members may be expelled; after removal to parts unknown, the name may be dropped; on transference by certificate to another denomination, and on withdrawal while character is unimpeached, membership ceases.

(6) *The Methodist Church of Canada.*—This conforms to the conditions of membership among the English Wesleyans, attendance upon class-meeting being essential, dancing and similar amusements being forbidden, and children, though baptized, not being members of the organization.

(7) *The Wesleyan Methodists of the United States* (dating from 1842).—This adds to the usual Methodist conditions of membership special rules against secret societies, as Freemasons, Odd-Fellows, etc., intoxicants and tobacco.

(8) *Apostolic Catholic Church* (dating from 1832).—In addition to baptism, "the conditions under which any person can become a member of one of the congregations gathered under the restored apostleship" are "that he should fully and heartily recognise the authority of this apostleship, so that he can sincerely work with it, submit to the commandments of the apostles, recognise the grace of Christ in them, and all the ministries authorized by them. Should any, after more or less time, lose their confidence in these restored ministries, and separate themselves from the congregations, they are still remembered and prayed for as negligent or lapsed members, and their names are kept on a separate register."

(9) *Reformed Episcopal Church.*—Baptism and confirmation admit to this Church persons born of parents within its pale. Communicants of other denominations are received by letter or other satisfactory evidence of membership, confirmation being optional with them. As no discrimination between denominations is made, there seems to be no guarantee that even baptism has been duly received. Assent to the principles, doctrine, discipline, and worship of the Church is demanded. Membership may cease during life by presenting a written statement of intention to withdraw, or by exclusion by the Church courts for offence. Some differences of practice exist in different localities.

3. *Presbyterian Churches, in which the Right of Ordination Resides in a Body of Presbyters.*—These churches are governed by principles which do not differ fundamentally, though they differ in details and in verbal expression, from those of episcopal churches. "The basis of Church membership is the covenant of grace which Christ condescends to make with his people, of which covenant faith is the essential condition, and baptism the visible sign; and, as infants cannot in their own person exercise faith, their membership must in the first instance rest upon the faith of their parents, until they come to an age intelligently and voluntarily to embrace and profess Christ themselves." "Every child of believing parents is by his birth a citizen of God's kingdom and an heir of its privileges, subject to the condition of subsequent personal faith." One parent, at least, or one guardian, in the absence of parental custody, if "presumptively believing," must make "an express engagement to train the child to godliness." Children are to be taught the Catechism, the Apostles' Creed, and the Lord's Prayer, to pray and to obey Christ. Baptized children are under the government of the Church. In baptism, there is a grace "conferred by the Holy Ghost;" yet the grace of regeneration is not necessarily connected with baptism, but is so in the case of "such as that grace belongeth unto." "The first element in the process of regeneration is the quickening power of the Holy Spirit exerted directly on the soul." These principles differ not substantially from those of the Church of England, which can be properly understood only when viewed in their relation to Pelagianism. Hooker defines regeneration as "that infused divine virtue of the Holy Ghost which gives to the powers of the soul their first disposition towards future newness of life;" and he says that "grace is not absolutely tied to sacraments," but that, in sacraments, "God imparts the saving grace of Christ to all that are capable thereof." Though differences of opinion may exist as to the appropriateness of words to the representation of facts, yet, on the facts themselves, both Presbyterians and the Church of England seem very nearly to agree. Among Presbyterians, unbaptized adults are received on profession of faith in Christ and on baptism. The enforcing of doctrinal conformity to the theological standards is not necessary or universal. The faith in Christ demanded is not necessarily such as brings assurance of forgiveness. Proper letters from other evangelical churches admit to membership. Censures are given for offences against lawful authority, nature, and Christianity, and excommunication awaits contumacy. These principles generally apply to Presbyterian churches in all lands, the Reformed Presbyterian Church, the Associate Reformed Presbyterian Church, the Cumberland Presbyterian Church, etc. The Dutch Reformed Church makes confirmation the public reception of members after examination in Bible and Church history and doctrines. Presbyterian Lutherans consider confirmation to be the public reception of candidates, with the blessing of the minister, after a doctrinal examination; but variety of practice arises from the large congregational liberty allowed. The United Presbyterians of the United States prescribe rules against the use of hymns, secret societies, and open communion.

4. *Congregational Churches, or those in which each Congregation is Supreme over its own Affairs.*—(1) *Orthodox Pædobaptist Churches.*—Credible personal faith in Christ and consecration to his service are the sole conditions of entrance, the individual Church being the judge of such credibility. Children, prior to personal faith and consecration, are in no sense members, but are to be watched over, that they may become such. Opinions and practice differ as to what children are eligible for baptism, whether those of members only, or others. Absence for a year in parts unknown, transfer to other churches, and, in some instances, resignation without transfer, lead to erasure of the name from the church roll; and contumacious offences lead to exclusion by the Church. The Evangelical Union, or Morisonians, differ from other Congregationalists chiefly in the Arminian doctrines professed, and in making saving

faith, on which members are accepted, to be such that it is not only invariably accompanied by assurance of acceptance, but that it renders prayer before it, and for it, an offence.

(2) *Orthodox Antipædobaptist Churches.* — "The Baptist theory is that the Church should consist of persons in whom the divine life has been begun by regeneration, and who have been baptized on profession of their faith in Christ as their Saviour." Hence, on profession and immersion, if the profession satisfies the local Church, membership is conferred. Excision is similar to that in pædobaptist churches. Some Baptists in England do not regard baptism with water as essential to membership. Free-Will Baptists receive baptized persons of other evangelical churches on testimony of a letter of recommendation by vote of the local Church. Seventh-Day Baptists add to the usual conditions of membership a trine immersion, with laying on of hands and prayer, and the observance of the seventh day of the week, instead of the first. "Disciples of Christ" demand immersion on profession of faith in Christ, and acceptance of the Bible as the rule of faith and morals. Exclusion is the act of the congregation, on conduct judged by them intolerable. Mennonites baptize none before eleven or twelve years of age, and then by pouring water on the head. Strict Mennonites prohibit head-ornaments, fine clothing, and rich furniture, and advocate the separation of the excommunicated from social intercourse.

(3) *Unitarians.*—These are generally Congregationalists, though in Transylvania they are Episcopal, and in Ireland Presbyterian. In the United States the authority that receives into membership is, in many cases, a circle of persons known as the "Church," inside of a larger organization known as the "Society" or parish. Baptism, and the signification to the pastor of a wish to join, with, in some churches, a public recognition by giving "the hand of fellowship," usually admits to membership; but intimation to the pastor of a desire for membership, and consent of his advisers, it is probable, would admit to fellowship, even without baptism or public reception. In many congregations the renting of a sitting, and qualifying for a vote in parish business by accepting the by-laws of the congregation, entitle to all the privileges of membership. There is no form of exclusion. Simple forms of covenant sometimes exist. "An unformulated consensus of opinion, a fidelity in public worship, a reverential support of the Lord's Supper, a deep interest both in piety and ethics, and a readiness in benevolent work," are not always absent from even such loose bonds of union.

(4) *Universalists.*—Persons, whether baptized in Universalist churches or not, of years of discretion, usually sixteen, are received by a majority vote of the congregation, after application has been made one month previously, in open meeting of the Church, in person, by a friend, or by letter. Strangers must present evidences of Christian faith and character. The only profession of faith authorized by the whole body is given in three articles, which recognize (*a*) the Bible, as containing a revelation of God's character, and man's duty, interest, and destiny; (*b*) one God of love, revealed in one Lord, Jesus Christ, by one Holy Spirit of grace, who will finally lead all men through holiness to happiness; and (*c*) the obligation of good works arising from the inseparable connection of holiness and happiness.

5. *Miscellaneous.*—(1) *European Protestant Churches.* i. *National Reformed Churches of France and Switzerland.*—(*a*) Children, after baptism, are first instructed, then examined before the pastor, or the presbyterial assembly (*conseil presbytéral*), or consistory, then received publicly, often after profession of personal faith, and finally admitted to communion at Easter. (*b*) Adults from without, on introduction, declare to the assembly and the pastor adhesion to the general principles of the Church, bear a share in the expenses, and, unless in the case of foreigners, must enjoy civil and political rights. Excommunication is pronounced from the pulpit, in general terms, without a particular application. ii. *Lutheran National Church.*—Nearly the same system exists here. iii. *Free Churches.*—Admission is said to be by public profession of faith. Uniformity of practice does not exist among the Reformed churches. In some cases, in Free churches, rebaptism of converts exists, generally by affusion, but, in the case of Baptists, by immersion.

(2) *New Church*, or *Swedenborgians.*—Baptized infants receive full membership by confirmation on arriving at years of discretion. Members coming from without are usually baptized, though opinions and practice on rebaptism are not uniform. In excluding members, in addition to the directions in Matt. xviii, 17, the following principle prevails: "He who differs in opinion from the minister ought to be left in peace, so long as he makes no disturbance; but he who makes disturbance ought to be separated."

(3) *Friends*, or *Quakers.*—Membership for persons native to the body is a birthright, but it confers rights of work and service on committees only after proved steadfastness. Admission of persons from without is by request, examination by a committee of similar sex with the candidate, and acceptance by the following monthly meeting. Excision is only after contumacious resistance of official efforts for reform, the final one of which is the presentation of a written "testification" before the monthly meeting. This follows a failure of two official interviews between the offender and the committee appointed in the case. Only after a second failure to secure reform is official record made of offences.

(4) *Plymouth Brethren.*—Application must first be made through one of the brethren to a Saturday meeting of the leaders of the various assemblies of the place. The candidate is then visited by leading men, and rigidly examined on doctrines and separation from all other Christian bodies. Satisfactory examination results in recommendation to the Saturday meeting; and, if approved, the person enters next Lord's Day by communing. The mode of baptism is an open question. Fellowship or excision, among "Close Brethren," relates not to one assembly, but to all in the world. From decisions of the Saturday meeting there is no appeal. The chief and most influential Saturday meeting is that of London, England. Among "Open Brethren," individual assemblies are not bound by the excisions of others. "Brethren" avoid the use of the term "members," as of an organization.

(5) *The Reformed Church in America.*—This demands baptism, profession of faith before the consistory, composed of pastor, elders, and deacons, or a letter of recommendation from some other church.

(6) *The Evangelical Association.*—This body holds, in addition to the ordinary rules of admission to Methodist churches, that traffic in liquor is unlawful.

(7) *The "Church of Christ."*—This adopts, as necessary terms of membership, belief that Jesus is the Son of God, repentance and a righteous life, profession of faith by word of mouth, and immersion in the name of Father, Son, and Holy Spirit.

(8) *The "Church of God."*—This body, believing that immortality and incorruptibility arise from the likeness of Christ's resurrection, which, with them, means being immersed, make immersion, with the ordinary demands of Congregational churches, imperative for membership.

(9) "*Christians*" (or the *Christian Connection*).—This demands no more than a profession of Christian faith and a corresponding life, the congregation being the judge of the life, and the person himself of the faith.

This list of organizations, calling themselves, as a whole, or in part, the Church of Christ, is by no means complete; but a sufficient number has been given to show on what comparatively unimportant grounds the majority of sectarian differences are based, and to suggest the question whether, in our reaction from corporate intolerance, we have given due weight to the calm statements of Christ, and the earnest pleadings of St. Paul, on the subject of the unity of Christ's body, the Church. For further particulars, see each religious body in its alphabetical place. (J. R.)

Memmi, SIMONE (called also *Martini*), an eminent Italian painter, was born at Siena in 1285, and was probably a pupil of Giotto. He was invited by the pope to Avignon to do some work for him. His great picture in St. Peter's has perished, but there are several of his works in the churches at Florence, Pisa, and Siena. In the Campo Santo of Pisa are several frescos of the history of St. Ranieri, and the far-famed *Assumption of the Virgin amid a Choir of Angels*. His large pictures may be seen at Florence, among which are several of Christ, of St. Peter the martyr, and St. Domenico. There are some more of this class of pictures in the churches of Siena. Memmi died at Avignon in 1344. See Hoefer, *Nouv. Biog. Générale*, s. v.; Spooner, *Biog. Hist. of the Fine Arts*, s. v.

Memra (*the Word*), a name employed in the Targum of Onkelos, and later Hebrew books, for the expression of the name of the deity in all his relations to man. See WORD.

Menachem DI FANO. See FANO, MENACHEM.

Menachem BEN-JACOB. See SARUK.

Menachem BEN-JEHUDA LONSANO. See LONSANO.

Menachem DA NOLA. See NOLA.

Menachem DI RECANATE. See RECANATI.

Menachem BEN-SALOMO, *of France*, a rabbi who lived in the 12th century, is the author of אֶבֶן בֹּחַן, a dictionary of the Hebrew language, written about 1143. Specimens of this lexicon were published by Dukes in קבץ על יד (Esslingen, 1846). He also wrote a commentary on the Pentateuch, entitled שכל טוב, a specimen of which, under the title תוכחת מגלה, was published at Hamburg in 1784 (in a Latin translation by Delitzsch, in his *Jeshurun sive Isagoge* [Grimma, 1838], p. 184-188). See Fürst, *Bibl. Jud.* ii, 353; De' Rossi, *Dizionario Storico* (Germ. transl.), p. 218; Zunz, *Zur Geschichte und Literatur*, p. 71 sq., 108. (B. P.)

Menageot, FRANÇOIS GUILLAUME, an eminent historical painter, was born in London, July 9, 1744, and was instructed under Deshays, Boucher, and Vien. He carried off the grand prize of painting in 1766, and visited Rome with the royal pension. In 1780 he was chosen an academician, and afterwards appointed professor. In 1800 he returned to Paris, and became professor of the Academy of Painting. He has a fine picture in the sacristy of the Church of St. Denis. He died Oct. 4, 1816. See Hoefer, *Nouv. Biog. Générale*, s. v.; Spooner, *Biog. Hist. of the Fine Arts*, s. v.

Menche, HEINRICH GOTTLIEB, a Lutheran theologian of Germany, was born April 24, 1799. He studied at Marburg, entered the ministry in 1820, was pastor at Röddenau, Hanover, from 1851 to 1882, and died June 21, 1884, at Münden, doctor of theology. (B. P.)

Mende Version OF THE SCRIPTURES. The Mende is spoken by a considerable population to the south and south-east of Sierra Leone. A version of Matthew had been prepared at an early period by American missionaries, who had settled on the border of the Mende country. A translation of the four gospels was made by the Rev. J. F. Schön, of the Church Missionary Society, the standard alphabet of Prof. Lepsius (q. v.) being adopted for the version. Mr. Schön was aided in the work of translation bv Harvey K. Ritchell, of the Mende country. In 1871 the Acts of the Apostles were printed by the British and Foreign Bible Society; the translation having been made by the Rev. H. Johnson, a native African clergyman. In 1872 the Epistle to the Romans was published. The remainder of the New Test. is still in manuscript. (B. P.)

Mengs, ANTONIO RAPHAEL, a distinguished painter, was born at Auszig, in Bohemia, March 12, 1728, and studied the works of Raphael at Rome when but thirteen years of age. In 1744 he was appointed painter at Dresden by the emperor Augustus, with a salary. His first great work was *The Holy Family*, which was exhibited at Rome, and gained him great reputation. In 1754 he received the direction of the new academy at Rome, and in 1757 was employed by the Celestines to paint the ceilings of the church of St. Eusebius. In 1761 he was invited to Madrid by Carlos III, and granted a liberal pension. He executed, among other works, *The Descent from the Cross* and *The Council of the Gods*, for the king's court. He returned to Rome, where he was engaged by Clement XIV to paint in the Vatican a picture of *Janus Dictating to History*, and *The Holy Family*. After an absence of three years he returned to Madrid, where he commenced his celebrated work in the dome of the grand saloon of the royal palace at that place. But his health was failing, and he died at Rome, June 29, 1779. See Hoefer, *Nouv. Biog. Générale*, s. v.; Spooner, *Biog. Hist. of the Fine Arts*, s. v.

Mentzer, JOHANN, a Lutheran theologian of Germany, was born at Jahmen, in Upper Lusatia, July 27, 1658. He studied at Wittenberg, was in 1691 preacher at Merzdorf, in 1693 at Hauswalde, in 1696 at Kemnitz, near Bernstadt, and died Feb. 24, 1734. He wrote about thirty-four hymns, some of which are translated into English, as *Lob sei dir, treuer Gott und Vater* (in *Chorale Book for England*, No. 8, "I praise Thee, O my God and Father"); *O dass ich tausend Zungen hätte* (by Mills, in *Horæ Germanicæ*, p. 189, "Oh that I had a Thousand Voices!"); *Wer das Kleinod will erlangen* (in *Lyra Germanica*, ii, 222, "He who'd make the Prize his Own"). See Otto, *Lexikon der oberlausitzischen Schriftsteller*, ii, 581-584; Koch, *Geschichte des deutschen Kirchenliedes*, v, 220 sq. (B. P.)

Menzel, Karl Adolph, a German historian, was born at Grünberg, Dec. 7, 1784. He studied at Halle, was in 1809 professor and in 1814 pro-rector at St. Elizabeth's, in Breslau. He died Aug. 19, 1855. He is the author of, *Staats- und Religionsgeschichte der Königreiche Israel und Juda* (Breslau, 1853):—*Religion und Staatsidee in der vorchristlichen Zeit* (edited by Wuttke, Leipsic, 1872). (B. P.)

Menzel, Wolfgang, a German historian and critic, was born at Waldenburg, June 21, 1798. He studied at different universities, was for some time teacher at Aarau, went in 1824 to Heidelberg, in 1825 to Stuttgart, and died April 23, 1873. Of his many works we only mention, *Christliche Symbolik* (Mayence, 1854, 2 vols.): —*Kritik des modernen Zeitbewusstseins* (2d ed. 1873):—*Die vorchristliche Unsterblichkeitsfrage* (1869, 2 vols.). His *Denkwürdigkeiten* were published by his son Karl (Bielefeld, 1877). (B. P.)

Mepeham, SIMON, archbishop of Canterbury, was born at Meopham, in Kent, and educated at Merton College. He devoted himself chiefly to the study of the sacred Scriptures, and became a Biblical divine. He was ordained priest at Canterbury on St. Matthew's day, 1297, and became rector of Tunstall, in the diocese of Norwich. He was elected archbishop on Dec. 11, 1327, and received the temporalities from the king at Lynn on Sept. 19, 1329. His attention was chiefly directed to the state of morals and discipline in the Church. We occasionally find him interposing his good offices to effect a reconciliation between parties at variance. His endeavor to compel diocesans to attend to their spiritual duties rendered him anything but popular among his suffragans. Notwithstanding, he was in all things respectable, in nothing great. But the age demanded something more than respectable mediocrity, and Simon Mepeham, by confining himself to his religious duties, was regarded as mean-spirited by those who looked, in his position, for one who could lead them in temporal as well as in spiritual things. He died Oct. 12, 1333. See Hook, *Lives of the Archbishops of Canterbury*, iii, 492 sq.

Merage, LEILAT AL (*the night of the ascension*), a night accounted sacred by the Mohammedans, because in it the prophet made his famous journey to heaven. It is commemorated on the 28th of the month *Regeb*.

Mercado, MOSES *ben-Israel de*, a rabbi of Amsterdam, who flourished in the 17th century, is the author of פ׳ קהלת ותהלים, or a commentary on Ecclesiastes and the Psalms, published after the author's death by Jacob de Mercado (Amsterdam, 1653). See Fürst, *Bibl. Jud.* ii, 368. (B. P.)

Mercersburg Theology. See GERMAN REFORMED CHURCH IN AMERICA.

Meredith, WILLIAM C., D.D., a Protestant Episcopal clergyman, was rector of Tillotson Parish, Curdsville, Va., for many years, until 1861, when he became rector of Christ Church in Winchester, and remained in this pastorate until his death, Nov. 1, 1875. See *Prot. Episc. Almanac*, 1876, p. 150.

Mergilet, ANDREAS, a Lutheran theologian of Germany, was born Dec. 17, 1559, and died March 21, 1606, at Mühlfeld. He is the author of, *Biblidia*, etc.:—*Sententiæ Insignes Patrum Ecclesiæ:—Papa Homo Peccati*, See Fürst, *Bibl. Jud.* ii, 368; Jöcher, *Allgemeines Gelehrten-Lexikon*, s. v. (B. P.)

Meria-pujah, an annual festival among the Khonds in Orissa, in which human sacrifices were offered until the practice was forbidden by the British government. The victims are called *merias*, and consist of Hindûs procured by purchase in the plains by the Panwas, a class of Hindû servitors. The design of this barbarous ceremony was to propitiate Bura-Pennou (q. v.), their earth-god, and thus to secure a favorable harvest.

Mérode, FRANÇOIS XAVIER MARIE FRÉDÉRIC GHISLAIN DE, a Roman Catholic prelate, was born at Brussels in March, 1820. He was descended from a noble Spanish family, and entered the Belgian army in 1841, serving with distinction as a volunteer in Algeria under marshal Bugeaud. He began the study of theology at Rome in 1848, and took priest's orders in 1850. He was then appointed chamberlain to the pope and canon of St. Peter's, and in 1860 was made minister of military affairs. He resigned this office in 1865, in consequence of a disagreement with cardinal Antonelli, but was appointed archbishop of Melitene, June 22, 1866, and private almoner to the pope. He opposed the dogma of papal infallibility in 1869, but in 1870 accepted the decision of the Vatican Council. He died at Rome, July 24, 1874. His wealth was largely devoted to the founding of charitable institutions, to the improvement of the streets and squares in Rome, and to archæological excavations.

Meronoth. It has been suggested (*Memoirs* to the Ordnance Survey, iii, 314) that this may be represented by *Khurbet Marrina*, a ruined site seven miles north of Hebron.

Meroz. Tristram (*Bible Places*, p. 230) identifies this site with that of *Murussas*, about four miles northwest of Bethshan, remarking that "it would command the passage from the plain of Jezreel to the Jordan;" but there do not seem to be any traces of antiquity there (*Memoirs* to the Ordnance Survey, ii, 85).

Merrick, John Austin, D.D., a Protestant Episcopal clergyman, was a missionary in 1853, in Fort Ripley, Minn.; in 1857 he was rector in Paris, Ky., being pastor of St. Peter's Church, and professor of Oriental and Biblical literature in Shelby College. In 1865 he became rector of St. Luke's Church, Hastings, Minn.; in 1866 was president of the Sewanee Mission and Training School, in Winchester, Tenn. The next year he went to San José, Cal., as a missionary. The year following he was a professor in St. Augustine College, Benicia. In 1870 he was officiating in Martinez; in 1872 he removed to West Farms, N. Y., where he resided without charge until his death, July 16, 1877, aged fifty years. See *Prot. Episc. Almanac*, 1878, p. 169.

Merrick (or **Meryek**), **Rowland**, an English prelate of the 16th century, was born at Bodingan, Anglesea, was educated at Oxford, where he became principal of New Inn Hall, and afterwards a dignitary in the Church of St. David's, and here he and others, in the reign of Edward VI, violently prosecuted Robert Farrar, his diocesan, and prevailed so far that the latter was imprisoned (see Fox, *Acts and Monuments*, an. 1555). Dr. Merrick was consecrated bishop of Bangor, Dec. 21, 1559, and died Jan. 24, 1566. See Fuller, *Worthies of England* (ed. Nuttall), iii, 509.

Merseburg, MENAHEM. See MENAHEM OF MERSEBURG.

Merwan IBN-GANACH. See IBN-GANACH.

Mésenguy, FRANÇOIS PHILIPPE, an ascetic writer of France, was born at Beauvais, Aug. 22, 1677. He was educated at Paris, and when the famous Rollin (q. v.) had charge of the college at Beauvais, Mésenguy was tutor there. Under Rollin's successor he became sub-principal of the college, but being opposed to the bull *Unigenitus*, had to resign. At last he retired to St.-Germain-en-Laye, and died Feb. 19, 1763. He published, *Le Nouveau Testament Traduit en Français, Avec des Notes Litterales* (Paris, 1729, 1752, 3 vols.):—*Vies des Saints* (1730, 6 vols.; new ed. 1740, 2 vols.):—*Abrégé de l'Histoire et de la Morale* (1728):—*Abrégé de l'Histoire de l'Ancien Testament*, etc. (1737-38, 3 vols.):—*Missel de Paris* (1738):—*Le Processional de Paris* (1739):—*Expositions de la Doctrine Chrétienne* (1744, 6 vols.):—*Exercises de Piété* (1760):—*La Constitution Unigenitus* (1748), etc. See Lequeux, *Mémoire de Feu M. l'Abbé François-Philippe Mésenguy*, in *Nécrologe des Plus Célèbres Défenseurs et Amis de la Vérité*, vi, 202-218; Picot, *Mémoires du Dix-Huitième Siècle*, vol. iv; *Notice Historique sur les Rites de l'Église de Paris;* Lichtenberger, *Encyclop. des Sciences Religieuses*, s. v. (B. P.)

Meshia and **Meshiana**, ancestors of the human race according to the system of the ancient Persians. Ahriman (q. v.) and Ormuzd (q. v.) were the primary principles of creation, and from the antagonism which the universe thus presented man was the only exception. Ahriman, the evil principle, had no other resource but to slay *Kaiomorts*, the primitive human being, who was at once man and woman. From the blood of the slain Kaiomorts sprang *Meshia* and *Meshiana*, who were soon seduced by Ahriman, and became worshippers of the *Devs*, to whom they offered sacrifices. Evil was thus introduced into the world, and the conflict between the good and evil principles extended also to man.

Messianic Hope. By way of supplement to the article MESSIAH (q. v.), we give in general outlines a *history* of the expectation of the Messiah as developed in the apocalyptic writings.

Of the deepest influence upon the development of the messianic idea were the prophecies of Daniel, the essence of which is the *reign of the pious* (see ii, 44; vii, 14, 27). The apocrypha of the Old Test. contain but few messianic allusions, because, for the most part, they are historical or didactic, and not prophetic. But this does not mean that the messianic idea was not entertained by the authors. Besides the hope of a return of the dispersed of Israel (Baruch, iv, 36, 37; v, 5-9; 2 Macc. ii, 18), of a conversion of the Gentiles (Tobit, xiii, 11-18; xiv, 6, 7), and the perpetual existence of the Jewish nation (Ecclus. xxxvii, 25; xliv, 13), we also find the idea of an everlasting kingdom of the house of David (Eccles. xlvii, 11; 1 Macc. ii, 57).

The richer, however, flows the stream of messianic prophecies in the oldest Jewish *Sibylline Oracles* (q. v.), especially iii, 652-794. Very few messianic comments are found in the groundwork of the Book of

Enoch (q. v.; see xc, 16–38), but more in the Psalter of Solomon (q. v.; see Psa. xvii, 11; xviii, 6–9), and in the Assumption of Moses (q. v.). The messianic time is also depicted in the Book of Jubilees (q. v.). All these documents prove sufficiently that the messianic hope had not been dead in the last centuries before Christ, and this is corroborated by the Targum of Onkelos and Jonathan. Another important witness is *Philo*, who, in *De Execrationibus*, § 8, 9 (ed. Mang. ii, 435 sq.), and *De Præmiis et Pœnis*, § 15–20 (ibid. ii, 421–428), speaks of the messianic hope.

But, aside from these witnesses, we have the New Test., which fully proves that the messianic idea in the time before Christ was by no means extinguished in the consciousness of the people (see Matt. xi, 3; xvi, 13 sq.; xxi; Mark viii, 27; xi; Luke vii, 19, 20; ix, 18 sq.; xix; John xii). For the time after Christ we need no evidence. The many political events prove, beyond the shadow of a doubt, that the people expected the beginning of the kingdom of God on earth. Josephus himself confesses that the messianic hope was one of the most powerful instruments in the insurrection against Rome, although, to please the Romans, he referred the messianic prophecies to Vespasian.

As for the messianic hope after the destruction of Jerusalem, the apocalypses of Baruch and Ezra give ample descriptions. What is expressed there finds its reflection in the Jewish prayer called *Shemoneh Esreh* (q. v.), especially in the 10th, 11th, 14th, 15th, and 17th petitions. Thus far the historical outline. We come now to the *systematic* arrangement of messianic dogmatics.

1. *Signs of the Last Times.*—Almost everywhere, when reference is made to eschatology, we meet with the same thought, that the beginning of the time of salvation is to be ushered in by great tribulations. The basis for these speculations was no doubt Dan. xii, 1, "There shall be a time of trouble, such as never was since there was a nation, even to that same time." Thus originated in the rabbinic dogma the doctrine of the חבלי המשיח, "the birth-pains of the Messiah" (see Matt. xxiv, 8: πάντα δὲ ταῦτα ἀρχὴ ὠδίνων). Glowing descriptions of the signs of the last times are found in *Orac. Sibyll.* iii, 795–807 (comp. 4 Ezra v, 1–13; vi, 18–28; ix, 1–12; xiii, 29–31; Apocalypse of Baruch, lxx, 2–8; Book of Jubilees [see Ewald's *Jahrbüchern*, iii, 23 sq.]; Mishna, *Sota*, ix, 15). See also Matt. xxiv, 7–12, 21; Mark xiii, 19; Luke xxi, 23; 1 Cor. vii, 26; 2 Tim. iii, 1; and comp. Schöttgen, *Horæ Hebraicæ*, ii, 509 sq., 550 sq.; Bertholdt, *Christologia Judæorum*, p. 45–54; Gfrörer, *Das Jahrhundert des Heils*, ii, 225 sq. 300–304; Oehler, in Herzog's *Real-Encyklop.* ix, 436 sq. (2d ed. ix, 666); Hamburger, *Real-Encyklop.* art. "Messianische Leidenszeit," p. 735–738.

2. *Elijah the Forerunner of the Messiah.*—From Mal. iii, 23, 24 (A. V. iv, 5, 6) it was inferred that the prophet Elijah was to return to prepare the way for the Messiah. This idea is already presupposed, Ecclus. xlviii, 10, 11 (see also Matt. xvii, 10; Mark ix, 11; also Matt. xi, 14; xvi, 14; Mark vi, 15; viii, 28; Luke ix, 8, 19; John i, 21). The object of his message is to make peace on earth (see Mishna, *Eduyoth*, viii, 7), and to harmonize differences (*Baba Mezia*, iii, 4, 5; i, 8; ii, 8). Besides these things, he was to anoint the Messiah (Justin, *Dial. cum Tryph.* c. 8, 49), and to raise the dead (*Sota*, ix, 15 s. f.). Besides Elijah, some also expected *the prophet like Moses* (Deut. xviii, 15; comp. John i, 21; vi, 14; vii, 40), while still others thought that *Jeremiah* (Matt. xvi, 16) was to be the forerunner of the Messiah. In Christian writings, *Enoch* is mentioned as one who was to come back (*Ev. Nicodemi*, c. 25; see also Thilo, *Codex Apocryph. Nov. Testamenti*, p. 756–768). On the forerunner of the Messiah, comp. Schöttgen, u. s. p. 533 sq.; Lightfoot, *Horæ Hebr.* on Matt. xvii, 10; Bertholdt, u. s. p. 58–68; Gfrörer, u. s. p. 227–229; Alexandre, *Orac. Sibyll.* 1st ed. ii, 513–516; *Der Prophet Elia in der Legende* (Frankel's *Monatsschrift*, 1863, p. 241–255, 281–296); *Elias who was to Come* (*Journal of Sacred Literature and Biblical Record*, new series, 1867, x, 371–376); Castelli, *Il Messia secondo gli Ebrei*, p. 196–201; Weber, *System der altsynagogalen palästinischen Theologie*, p. 337–339.

3. *Appearance of the Messiah.*—After these preparations, Messiah comes. It is by no means correct to say that pre-Christian Judaism expected the Messiah only *after* the judgment, and that through the influence of Christianity the idea had become prevalent that the Messiah himself was to judge his enemies. For in the books of Baruch and Ezra, Enoch, and in the Targums, in the Psalter of Solomon, and in Philo, Messiah appears everywhere as conquering hostile powers.

As to his names, the common one is *the Anointed, the Messiah* (Enoch xlviii, 10; lii, 4; Baruch xxix, 3; xxx, 1; xxxix, 7; xl, 1; lxx, 9; lxxii, 2; Ezra vii, 28, 29, where the Latin translation is interpolated; xii, 32: "unctus"); Greek, χριστὸς κυρίου (Psalt. of Sol. xvii, 36; xviii, 68), Hebrew, הַמָּשִׁיחַ (Mishna, *Berachoth*, i, 5), Aramaic, מְשִׁיחָא (ibid. *Sota*, ix, 15), or מַלְכָּא מְשִׁיחָא (in the Targums). Peculiar to the Book of Enoch are: "the Son of man" (xlvi, 1–4; xlviii, 2; lxii, 7, 9, 14; lxiii, 11; lxix, 26, 27; lxx, 1), and the "Elect One" (xlv, 3, 4; xlix, 2; li, 3, 5; lii, 6, 9; liii, 6; lv, 4; lxi, 8; lxii, 1). Very seldom is he called the "Son of God" (cv, 2; 4 Ezra vii, 28, 29; xiii, 32, 37, 52; xiv, 9), and only once he is called "Son of the woman" (Enoch lxii, 5). He was to come *from the tribe of David* (Psalt. of Sol. xvii, 5, 23; Matt. xxii, 42; Mark xii, 35; Luke xx, 41; John vii, 42; 4 Ezra xii, 32; Targum on Isa. xi, 1; Jer. xxiii, 5; xxxiii, 15). Hence "Son of David" is the common designation of the Messiah (in the New Test. after υἱὸς Δαυίδ, in the Targum on Hosea iii, 5: בַּר דָּוִד, in the Shemoneh Esreh, 15th petition, צֶמַח דָּוִד). As belonging to the tribe of David he must also be born at *Bethlehem*, in the city of David (Micah v, 1, and the Targum in loco; Matt. ii, 5; John vii, 41, 42).

Whether the pre-Christian Judaism thought of the Messiah as a mere man or as a being imbued with higher power, especially whether it ascribed to him pre-existence, cannot be decided with certainty. In general it can be said that *he was expected as a human king and ruler, but endowed with special gifts and powers by God.* This is especially evident from the Psalter of Solomon (xvii, 23, 47, 35, 41, 46, 42). The same idea we find in *Orac. Sibyll.* iii, 49. But his pre-existence is also described in the Book of Enoch, xlvi, 1, 2; lxii, 7; xlviii, 3, 6; xlvi, 1, 3; xlix, 2–4; comp. also 4 Ezra xii, 32; xiii, 26, 52. And this idea of pre-existence cannot be ascribed to Christian influences, because it fully harmonizes with the Old-Test. idea concerning the Messiah (comp. Micah v, 1; Daniel vii, 13, 14).

4. *The Last Enemies.*—On the appearance of the Messiah the enemies of the Israelites and of God will muster their forces for a last decisive conflict. The picture which Ezekiel drew of the armies of Gog and Magog, and the representation given in Daniel xi, are abundantly reproduced in *Orac. Sibyll.* iii, 663 sq.; 4 Ezra xiii, 33 sq.; Enoch xc, 16, except that the conflict does not concern the Messiah, but the congregation of God. In general, it is supposed that the leader in this conflict is the antichrist, who is called in rabbinic writings *Armilus* (ארמילוס).

5. *Destruction of the Enemies.*—From the dangers which will thus gather round them the Israelites are to be delivered by the signal destruction of their foes. Comp. Assumptio Mosis x; Enoch xc; *Orac. Sibyll.* iii, 652 sq.; Psalt. of Sol. xvii, 27, 39; Apoc. Baruch xxxix, 7–xl, 2; lxx, 9; lxxii, 2–6; 4 Ezra xii, 32, 33; xiii, 27, 28, 35–38.

6. *Renovation of Jerusalem.*—Since the messianic

kingdom is to be founded in the Holy Land, Jerusalem must be renewed. This renovation will take place by purifying the holy city from the Gentiles, who now live in it (Psalt. of Sol. xvii, 25, 33). Besides this view there was another, that there already existed in the pre-messianic time a more glorious Jerusalem than the earthly one, with God in heaven, and that this was to come down on earth at the beginning of the messianic time (Enoch liii, 6; xc, 28, 29; 4 Ezra vii, 26; Apoc. Baruch xxxii, 4). See also Schöttgen, *De Hierosolyma Cœlesti* (*Horæ Hebr.* i, 1205-1248); Meuschen, *Novum Testamentum ex Talmude*, p. 199 sq.; Wetstein, *Novum Test. ad Galatas*, iv, 26; Eisenmenger, *Entdecktes Judenthum*, ii, 839 sq.; Bertholdt, u. s. p. 217-221; Gfrörer, u. s. ii, 245 sq. 308; Weber, u. s. p. 356 sq.

7. *Gathering of the Dispersed.*—That the dispersed of Israel should have part in the messianic kingdom and return to Palestine was a matter of course, even though there were no prophecies of the Old Test. In a poetical manner this is described (Psalt. of Sol. xi, xvii; Baruch iv, 36, 37; v, 5-9; Philo, *De Exsecrationibus*, § 8, 9; 4 Ezra xiii, 39-47). As this hope was so general, it is strange that rabbi Akiba should have doubted the return of the ten tribes (*Sanhedrin*, x, 3 s. f.).

8. *The Kingdom of Glory in Palestine.*—The messianic kingdom has, it is true, the messianic king at its head, but its supreme ruler is God (see *Orac. Sibyll.* iii, 704-706, 717, 756-759; Psalt. of Sol. xvii, 1, 38, 51; *Shemoneh Esreh*, 11th benediction; Joseph. *War*, ii, 8, 1). Hence it is often called *the kingdom of God* (*βασιλεία τοῦ θεοῦ*, so especially in the New Test. by Mark and Luke; *Orac. Sibyll.* iii, 47, 48; *βασιλεία μεγίστη ἀθανάτου βασιλῆος*; see Psalt. of Sol. xvii, 4; Assumptio Mosis x, 1, 3). Besides, we also find "kingdom of heaven," *βασιλεία τῶν οὐρανῶν*. For the latter expression, see Schöttgen, *De Regno Cœlorum* (*Horæ Hebr.* i, 1147-1152); Lightfoot, *Horæ ad Matth.* iii, 2; Wetstein, *in Matth.* iii, 3; Bertholdt, u. s. p. 187-192; De Witte, *Biblische Dogmatik*, p. 175-177; Tholuck, *Bergpredigt*, p. 66 sq.; Fritzsche, *Evang. Matthæi*, p. 109 sq.; Kuinoel, *in Matth.* iii, 3; Wichelhaus, *Commentar. zu der Leidensgeschichte* (1855), p. 284 sq.; Keim, *Geschichte Jesu*, ii, 33 sq.; Schürer, *Der Begriff des Himmelreiches aus jüdischen Quellen erläutert* (*Jahrbücher für prot. Theologie*, 1876, p. 166-187); Cremer, *Bibl. Theolog. Wörterbuch*, s. v. *βασιλεία*.

To the glory of the messianic kingdom belongs, above all things, the *dominion* over the world (see Isa. ii, 2 sq.; xlii, 1-6; xlix, 6; li, 4, 5; Jer. iii, 17; xvi, 19 sq.; Micah iv, 1 sq.; vii, 16 sq.; Zeph. ii, 11; iii, 9; Zech. viii, 20 sq.; and especially Dan. ii, 44; vii, 14, 27). This hope has also been held by later Judaism, but in a different manner; see *Orac. Sibyll.* iii, 698-726, 766-783; Philo, *De Præm. et Pœn.* § 16; Enoch xc, 30, 37; Psalt. of Sol. xvii, 32-35. Otherwise the messianic time, mostly on the basis of Old-Test. passages, is represented as a time of pure *joy and happiness*. There is no war (*Orac. Sibyll.* iii, 371-380, 751-760; Philo, *De Præm. et Pœn.* § 16; Apocal. Baruch, lxxiii, 4, 5). Even the wild beasts serve man (*Orac. Sibyll.* iii, 787-794; Philo, u. s. § 15; Targum on Isa. xi, 6). Earth is very fertile (*Orac. Sibyll.* iii, 620-623, 743-750; Baruch, xxix, 5-8); men are rich and well to do (Philo, § 17, 18); they become nearly one thousand years old, and yet do not feel their age, but are like boys (Ewald, *Jubilees*, iii, 24). All enjoy bodily strength and health; women bear children without pains, etc. (Philo, § 20; Baruch lxxiii, 2, 3, 7; lxxiv, 1). But these external gifts are not the only ones. They are but the consequence of the fact that the messianic congregation represents a holy people, sanctified by God, and led in righteousness by the Messiah. He allows no unrighteousness to dwell among them, nor is any one who knows malice in their midst. Hence they are all holy (Psalt. of Sol. xvii, 28, 29, 36, 48, 49; xviii, 9, 10). The life in the messianic kingdom is a perpetual *λατρεύειν θεῷ ἐν ὁσιότητι καὶ δικαιοσύνῃ ἐνώπιον αὐτοῦ* (Luke i, 74, 75).

With this kingdom of glory in Palestine the eschatological expectation generally closes; indeed, many regard it as without an end. But afterwards the messianic kingdom is described as of a limited period, and in the Talmud the duration of this time is a matter of debate (*Sanhedrin*, fol. 99, col. 1). The same view we find in the Apoc. Baruch xl, 3, and 4 Ezra xii, 34; vii, 28, 29. Wherever, therefore, a temporal duration is ascribed to the messianic kingdom, at the end of the time a renovation of the world and the last judgment is still expected.

9. *Renovation of the World.*—The hope of a renovation of heaven and earth is founded on Isa. lxv, 17; lxvi, 22 (see also Matt. xix, 28; Rev. xxi, 1; 2 Pet. iii, 13). Accordingly, a distinction was made between the present world and the world to come, הָעוֹלָם הַזֶּה and הָעוֹלָם הַבָּא; in the New Test., *ὁ αἰὼν οὗτος* and *ὁ αἰὼν ὁ μέλλων* or *ὁ ἐρχόμενος*. But there was a difference of opinion. Some would make the new world commence with the beginning of the messianic time (Enoch xlv, 4, 5), others with its end (4 Ezra vii, 30, 31). In accordance with these different views, the messianic time is either identified with the world to come, or is still reckoned to the present world. But the older and more original view is the one which identifies the days of the Messiah with the world to come. On the "world to come," see Mishna, *Berachoth*, i, 5; Psa. i, 1; *Kiddushin*, iv, 14; *Baba Mezia*, ii, 11; *Sanhedrin*, x, 1-4; *Aboth*, iv, 1, 16; v, 19; Apoc. Baruth xliv, 15; xlviii, 50; lxxiii, 3; 4 Ezra vi, 9; vii, 12, 13, 42, 43; viii, 8. Comp. also Rhenferdius, *De Sæculo Futuro* (in Meuschen, u. s. p. 1116-1171); Witsius, *De Sæculo hoc et Futuro*, u. s. p. 1171-1183; Schöttgen, u. s. 1153-1158; Lightfoot, *ad Matth.* xii, 32; Wetstein, *ad Matth.* xii, 32; Koppe, *Novum Test.* vi; *Epist. ad Ephes. Exc.* i; Bertholdt, u. s. p. 38-43; Gfrörer, u. s. ii, 212-217; Bleck, *Hebräerbrief*, ii, 1, 20 sq.; Oehler, in Herzog's *Real-Encyklop.* ix, 434 sq.; 2d ed. ix, 664 sq.; Geiger, *Jüdische Zeitschrift*, 1866, p. 124; Weber, u. s. p. 354 sq.

10. *General Resurrection.*—Before the last judgment is held, a general resurrection of the dead occurs. In general, there was a firm belief in the resurrection of the dead, which is for the first time intimated in Dan. xii, 2, and this belief was held by all who were more or less influenced by Pharisaism. Only the Sadducees denied the resurrection (Joseph. *Ant.* xviii, 1, 4; *War*, ii, 8, 14), and the Alexandrian theology substituted for it an immortality of the soul (Wisdom of Sol. iii, 1 sq.; iv, 7; v, 16). The time between death and resurrection is for the righteous a time of preliminary happiness, and for the wicked a preliminary state of misery. The literature on that subject is very rich. See Bertholdt, u. s. p. 176-181, 203-206; Gfrörer, u. s. 275-285, 308 sq.; Herzfeld, *Gesch. d. Volkes Israel*, iii, 307-310, 328-333, 349-351, 504-506; Langen, *Das Judenthum in Palästina*, p. 338 sq.; Rothe, *Dogmatik*, ii, 2, 68-71, 298-308; Oehler, *Theologie des Alten Testaments*, ii, 241 sq.; Hermann Schultz, *Alttestamentliche Theologie*, 2d ed. p. 713 sq. 807 sq.; Hamburger, *Real-Encyklop.* ii, 98 sq. (art. "Belebung der Todten"); Stähelin, *Jahrb. für deutsche Theologie*, 1874, p. 199 sq.; Weber, u. s. p. 371 sq.; Gröbler, *Die Ansichten über Unsterblichkeit und Auferstehung in der jüdischen Literatur der beiden letzten Jahrh. vor Christus*, in *Studien und Kritiken*, 1879, p. 651-700.

11. *Last Judgment. Eternal Blessedness and Damnation.*—A last judgment after the end of the messianic period can only be thought of where the messianic kingdom is of a finite duration (see Baruch i, 4; 4 Ezra vii, 33-35). God himself is the judge of all men (Baruch li, 4, 5; 4 Ezra vi, 2). In general it may be said that all Israel have a part in the future world (*Sanhedrin*, x, 1), with the exception of the wicked in Israel (x, 1-4). They, together with Israel's enemies, go down into the fire of Gehenna (Baruch xliv, 15; li, 1, 2, 4-6; 4 Ezra v, 1-3, 59). As a rule this damnation is regarded as everlasting; but there is also the view which

ascribes a limited duration of hell-punishment (Mishna, *Eduyoth*, ii, 10). The righteous and pious will be received into paradise, and will behold the majesty of God and of his holy angels. Their face shall shine like the sun, and they shall live forever (Baruch li, 3, 7-14; 4 Ezra vi, 1-3, 68-72; Assumptio Mosis x, 9, 10).

Literature.—Besides the works of Schöttgen, Bertholdt, De Wette, Gfrörer, Weber, Hamburger, already mentioned, see Moraht, *De iis, quæ ad Cognoscendam Judæorum Palestinensium, qui Jesu Tempore Vivebant, Christologiam Evangelia Nobis Exhibeant, Deque Locis Messianis in Illis Allegatis* (Göttingen, 1829); Von Cölln, *Biblische Theologie* (1836), i, 479-511; Mack, *Die messianischen Erwartungen und Ansichten der Zeitgenossen Jesu* (in *Tüb. Theol. Quartalschrift*, eod. p. 3-56, 193-226); Bruno Bauer, *Kritik der evangelischen Geschichte der Synoptiker* (1841), i, 391-416; Zeller, *Ueber die Behauptung dass das vorchristliche Judenthum noch keine messianische Dogmatik gehabt habe* (*Theol. Jahrbücher*, 1843, p. 35-52); Hellwag, in *Theol. Jahrbücher von Bauer und Zeller* (1848), p. 151-160; Hilgenfeld, *Die jüdische Apocalyptik in ihrer geschichtlichen Entwickelung* (Jena, 1857); Oehler, art. "Messias," in Herzog, *Real-Encyklop.* ix, 408 sq.; 2d ed. ix, 641 sq.; Colani, *Jesus-Christ et les Croyances Messianiques de son Temps* (2d ed. Strasburg, 1864), p. 1-68; Langen, *Das Judenthum in Palästina zur Zeit Christi* (Freiburg, 1866), p. 391-461; Ewald, *Geschichte des Volkes Israel* (3d ed. 1867), v, 135-160; Keim, *Geschichte Jesu* (eod.), i, 239-250 (Engl. transl. p. 308-321; Lond. 1873); Holtzmann, *Die Messiasidee zur Zeit Jesu* (*Jahrb. für deutsche Theologie*, 1867, p. 389-411); the same, in Weber and Holtzmann's *Geschichte des Volkes Israel* (eod.), ii, 191-211; Hausrath, *Neutestamentliche Zeitgeschichte* (1868), i, 172-184; 2d ed. (1873), p. 165-176; Engl. transl. (Lond. 1878) i, 191-204; Weiffenbach, *Quæ Jesu in Regno Cœlesti Dignitas sit Synopticorum Sententia Exponitur* (Giessen, 1868), p. 47-62; Ebrard, *Wissenschaftliche Kritik der evangelischen Geschichte* (3d ed. eod.), p. 835-849; Wittichen, *Die Idee des Reiches Gottes* (Göttingen, 1872), p. 105-165; Anger, *Vorlesungen über die Geschichte der messianischen Idee* (edited by Krenkel; Berlin, 1873), p. 78-91; Castelli, *Il Messia Secondo gli Ebrei* (Florence, 1874); Vernes, *Histoire des Idées Messianiques depuis Alexandre Jusqu'à l'Empereur Hadrien* (Paris, eod.); Schönefeld, *Ueber die messianische Hoffnung von 200 vor Christo bis gegen 50 nach Christo* (Jena, eod.); Drummond, *The Jewish Messiah* (Lond. 1877); Stapfer, *Les Idées Religieuses en Palestine à l'Époque de Jesus-Christ* (2d ed. 1878), p. 111-132; Reuss, *Geschichte der heiligen Schriften des Alten Testaments* (1881), § 555, 556; Hamburger, *Real-Encyklop. für Bibel und Talmud*, II Abtheilung (1883), articles: "Messianische Leidenszeit," "Messias," "Messiasleiden," "Messias Sohn Joseph," "Messiaszeit" (p. 735-779); also *Armilus, Belebung der Todten, Ewiges Leben, Lohn und Strafe, Paradies, Vergeltung, Zukunftsmahl;* Pick, *Talmudic Notices concerning Messiah* (*Presbyterian Review*, July, 1884); *Old Testament Passages Messianically Applied by the Ancient Synagogue* (*Hebraica*, October, 1884 and seq.); Schürer, *Lehrbuch der Neutestamentlichen Zeitgeschichte* (Leipsic, 1874), p. 563 sq.; 2d ed. with the title *Geschichte des jüdischen Volkes im Zeitalter Jesu Christi* (1886), ii, 417 sq. (B. P.)

Messmer, Joseph Anton, a Roman Catholic theologian of Germany, was born Oct. 17, 1829, and died at Munich, Dec. 23, 1879, doctor and professor of theology. He published, *Ueber den Ursprung, die Entwickelung und Bedeutung der Basilika in der christlichen Baukunst* (Leipsic, 1854):—*Johann Michael Sailer* (Mannheim, 1875):—*Dr. Joseph Hubert Reinkens, katholischer Bischof* (Linz, 1874). (B. P.)

Metatron, an angel frequently mentioned by rabbinical writers, and to whom they ascribe superior prerogatives. He is said to be "the king of angels," and to "ascend to the throne of glory above nine hundred firmaments to carry up the prayers of the Israelites." He is supposed by some to have been the angel who conducted the Israelites through the wilderness, and by others to have been Enoch.

Metawilah, a heretical Mohammedan sect, who maintain that the allegorical and not the literal meaning of the Koran is binding on the faithful. They are found principally in the district lying to the south and east of Tyre, in the regions contiguous to the sources of the Jordan, and in *Cœle-Syria* proper. They are Shiites, and recognise the supreme Imámate of Ali (q. v.).

Metcalf, Kendrick, D.D., a Protestant Episcopal clergyman, devoted nearly the whole of his active life to educational work. For many years he was Hobart professor of the Greek and Latin languages and literature in the Hobart Free College, Geneva, N. Y. For some time he was a member of the standing committee of his diocese. In 1867 he was elected professor of rhetoric, and chaplain of the college. The following year he was Horace White professor of rhetoric and English literature, a position which he retained until his death, Oct. 30, 1872. See *Prot. Episc. Almanac*, 1873, p. 134.

Metonic Cycle. See Cycle.

Meurer, Moritz, a Lutheran theologian of Germany, was born Aug. 3, 1806, at Pretzsch, on the Elbe. He studied at Leipsic, was in 1833 teacher at the seminary in Weissenfels, in 1834 deacon at Waldenburg, in 1835 archdeacon, and in 1841 pastor. He died at Callenberg, May 10, 1877. He is the author of biographical sketches on Luther, Catharine von Bora, Melanchthon, Bugenhagen, Myconius, etc. Besides, he published, *Moses, der Knecht Gottes* (Waldenburg, 1836):—*Der Tag zu Schmalkalden* (Leipsic, 1837); *Der Kirchenbau vom Standpunkte und nach dem Brauche der lutherischen Kirche* (ibid. 1877). See Zuchold, *Bibl. Theol.* ii, 876; Lichtenberger, *Encyclop. des Sciences Religieuses*, s. v. (B. P.)

Mevlevies, an order of rigid Mohammedan monks. The novice receives his preliminary training in the convent kitchen during the period of a thousand and one days, after which he is received into the order. Their doctrines are chiefly those of the Persian *Sûfis* (q. v.). Contrary to the teachings of the prophet they have introduced music and dancing into their worship. They are the best endowed of all the orders of Moslem monks; yet they use only the coarsest fare and the plainest raiment, while they distribute much of their revenue in alms to the poor. They are the *Dancing Dervishes* of Turkey, and consist chiefly of the higher class of Turks. See Dervish; Mohammedanism.

Mexican Religious Beliefs and Fables. The wondrous country lying between North and South America was long inaccessible, and much told of it was fabulous, until A. von Humboldt and some modern travellers lighted up the darkness which hung over the country. The Mexicans accepted four world periods, according thus singularly with the Greeks and the Romans: the first is called *Atonatiuh*, the period of water; it began with the creation of the world, and its destruction by the flood; the second, *Tlaltonatiuh*, the period of earth, closed with an earthquake, which ended the human race, and the sun belonging to this period; the third is called *Ehekatonatiuh*, the period of air, in which men and the sun perished in a frightful storm; the fourth is called *Tletonatiuh*, the period of fire, the period in which we live, and which will end by a universal destruction by fire. At the end of each period all men perished except a few pairs; they did not die, but were changed into fish, apes, and, lastly, into birds. The Noah of the Mexicans was called Coxcox, and his wife Xokiquetzal. They saved themselves in a small ship, and landed on the mountain Colhuäan. Their children learned from wise birds languages so different that they could not understand each other. The protecting goddess of the human race, Omecihuatl, lived in a splendid city of heaven; she gave birth to many children, and lastly to a stone knife, which the children threw to the earth, whereupon sixteen hundred heroes (demi-gods) sprang from it. These had no human beings about them, for all of the latter had perished by the catastrophe of the third period. They, therefore, sent a herald to their mother in heaven, to give them power to produce children. The mother told them to get a bone of a dead human being from the god of the infernal region, and if they would sprinkle it with their blood men would be produced, but they should beware of the god. Xolotl, one of the demi-gods, received a bone from Mietlanteuetli, and, heeding the warning, fled as fast as he could, pursued by the god. They sprinkled the bone with their blood, and a boy and a girl were formed, who propagated the extinguished race. However, from this originated the horrible custom of human sacrifices. The sun was still lacking. The heroes collected about a great fire, and said, whoever should jump in first would become a sun. Nanahuatzin sacrificed himself, and soon appeared as the sun. But he said he would not move until all the heroes had been slain. The hero Xolotl then killed them all, and finally himself. Their dress fell to their servants, men, and the Spaniards found in various temples clothes, divinely worshipped, which were said to belong to these demi-gods. In the same manner the moon originated; because the fire was not so intense it did not receive such splendor. The Mexicans hold the souls of men to be immortal; fallen warriors and mothers dying in child-bed come into the house of the sun, where they live in pleasures. The number of deified heroes, kings, and demi-gods soon reached three thousand. They had also a distinct idea of a supreme being, Teotl (god), sprung from himself, the originator of all things. A being opposed to the latter was Tläatewlolotl, i. e. the sensible owl. The Mexicans believed this dæmon appeared to torture men and frighten them. Besides this good and this evil principle there were three classes of gods; to the first belonged the mother of all gods, the god of providence, the deities of the constellations, of the elements, of war, of hunting, of fishing, of contracts, of punishment, of protection, etc.; to the second class belonged the gods of time; to the third class the family gods. Their idols were placed in their temples, and priests and priestesses placed over them, and sacrifices made. The supreme, or at least the most worshipped of their gods was the bloodthirsty Huitzilopochtli.

Mexican (or **Aztec**) **Version** OF THE SCRIPTURES. At a very early period efforts were made to provide the Mexicans with the Word of God in their own vernacular. Didacus de Santa Maria, a Dominican friar, and vicar of the province of Mexico (1579), is said to have translated the epistles and the gospels into Mexican; and Louis Rodriguez, a Franciscan friar, prepared a translation of the Proverbs and other fragments. But of these translations nothing is known at present. In 1829 Mr. Thomson, agent of the British and Foreign Bible Society, caused a translation of the New Test. to be made—a movement which the bishop of Puebla not only favored, but also consented to superintend. Three persons were appointed by the bishop to execute the translation, but unhappily the bishop died in 1830, and the only portion of Scripture that has hitherto been printed in Mexican consists of the gospel of Luke, which Dr. Pazos Kanki had translated about the year 1829. From the report of the British and Foreign Bible Society for the year 1870, we see that at the request of Mr. J. W. Butler, a native Mexican has been engaged to revise or retranslate the gospel of Luke. The version was made, and after having been committed to an independent person for examination, was printed. This is the only part of the Mexican Scripture now extant. See *Bible of Every Land*, p. 405. (B. P.)

Meyboom, LUDWIG TUSON PETRUS, a Dutch theologian, was born at Emden, April 2, 1817. He studied at Groningen, where he also took his degree as doctor of theology. In 1854 he was called to Amsterdam, in spite of the protest of the orthodox party, and died Nov. 13, 1874. Meyboom belonged to the so-called Groningen school, which believes in a personal God, the historic Christ, the immortality of the soul, and the incessant energy of the Holy Spirit in the Church. He published, *De Ideis et Rebus in Facto Positis, in re Christiana apte Conjunctis* (Groningen, 1840):—*De Francisci Hemsterhusii Meritis* (ibid. eod.):—*History of the Kingdom of God* (1852-54, 3 vols.):—*Life of Jesus* (1854 sq.):—*Principles of the Neo-Christian Tendency* (2d ed. 1874). See Lichtenberger, *Encyclop. des Sciences Religieuses*, s. v.; Zuchold, *Bibl. Theol.* ii, 877. (B. P.)

Meyer, Christian Gottlob, a Lutheran minister of Germany, was a convert from Judaism. From the preface of Prof. Semler, given to the German translation of Levita's *Massoreth ha-Massoreth*, we learn that Meyer, who was a native of Posen, was admitted into the Church by the Rev. Dr. Schultze of Halle. After his baptism Meyer studied theology at Halle, and here it was that he translated Levita's work, at the instance of Semler. After having completed his studies Meyer was admitted into the ministry, and in 1783 was called to the pastorate at Dassensee, in the duchy of Grubenhagen. Besides Levita's work, he also published *Sententiæ Rabbinorum de Successione ab Intestato et Testamentaria* (Halle, 1775). See Fürst, *Bibl. Jud.* ii, 370; Levita, *Massoreth ha-Massoreth* (Germ. transl. 1772). (B. P.)

Meyer, Gottlob Wilhelm, a Lutheran theologian of Germany, was born at Lübeck, Nov. 29, 1768. In 1801 he was university preacher at Göttingen, in 1804 professor and preacher at Altdorf, and in 1813 doctor and professor of theology at Erlangen. He died May 19, 1816, leaving, *De Notione Orci apud Hebræos* (Lübeck, 1793):—*De Fœdere cum Jehova* (Göttingen, 1797):—*Versuch einer Hermeneutik des Alten Testaments* (Lübeck, 1800):—*Grundriss einer Hermeneutik des Alten und Neuen Testaments* (Göttingen, 1801):—*Geschichte der Schrifterklärung seit der Wiederherstellung der Wissenschaften* (1802-1808, 5 vols.):—*Apologie der geschichtlichen Auffassung der historischen Bücher* (Sulzbach, 1811). See Fürst, *Bibl. Jud.* ii, 371; Winer, *Handbuch der theol. Lit.* i, 104, 106-111, 294-335, 588; ii. 96, 177. (B. P.)

Meyer, Heinrich August Wilhelm, a famous German exegete, was born at Gotha, Jan. 10, 1800. He studied at Jena, passed his candidate's examination in 1821, and in 1823 was installed pastor at Osthausen. In 1829 appeared the first part of his work on the New Test., including the Greek text and a German translation. In 1830 followed his *Libri Symbolici Ecclesiæ Lutheranæ*. In the same year, having previously obtained citizenship in the kingdom of Hanover, Meyer was appointed pastor at Harste, near Göttingen. In 1832 appeared the second part of his work on the New Test., containing the commentary on the synoptic gospels. The original design was to embrace the whole commentary in two large volumes, but this he soon found to be impracticable; besides, he discovered that his own strength and time would not be sufficient to complete the work without assistance; accordingly he secured the services of Drs. Lünemann, Huther, and Düsterdieck. In 1837 he was called as superintendent to Hoya, where he remained only four years. In 1841 he was called to Hanover, where he spent the rest of his life as member of consistory, superintendent, and head pastor of St. John's Church. In 1845 Meyer received the degree of doctor of theology from the faculty of the University of Göttingen. In 1848 he gave up his pastorate, retaining only his position in the consistory. In 1861 he was made member of the superior consistory, but in 1865 he retired from public life on a pension, which he received from the government. He died June 21, 1873.

Meyer's reputation beyond Hanover rests upon his commentaries on the New Test., and the excellence of his work was acknowledged not only in his own land, but in England and America, through Clark's translation. Meyer lived to see many editions of his work appear, and continued, down to the time of his death, to work diligently, making improvements. He grew with his work, and in each stage of his growth he expressed himself in his commentaries just as he felt. His study of the New Test. produced in him a more perfect experience of the saving grace and truth of the Gospel. As is the case with most scholars, Meyer became somewhat more dogmatical in his old age. The student who compares the last editions of the commentary with the first will find wide differences: Meyer was constantly correcting himself, and with relentless honesty removing from his work what he had come to regard as defects. Since his death, the continuation of Meyer's commentary in new editions has been intrusted to Prof. Weiss in Berlin, who has associated himself with such scholars as Wendt, Henrici, Sieffert, and others. See a biographical sketch of Meyer by his son, in the fourth edition of the *Commentary on the Philippians;* Düsterdieck in Plitt-Herzog, *Real-Encyklop.* s. v.; Lichtenberger, *Encyclop. des Sciences Religieuses*, s. v.; Zuchold, *Bibl. Theol.* ii, 879. (B. P.)

Meyer, Johann Andreas Georg, a Lutheran theologian of Germany, was born at Hildesheim in 1768, and died March 29, 1841, doctor of theology. He wrote, *Ueber das Verdienst des Christenthums* (Erfurt, 1793):—*De charismate τῶν γλωσσῶν* (Hanover, 1797): —*Versuch einer Vertheidigung und Erläuterung der Geschichte Jesu* (1805):—*Natur-Analogien*, etc. (Hamburg, 1839). See Winer, *Handbuch der theol. Lit.* i, 396, 399, 550; Zuchold, *Bibl. Theol.* ii, 879. (B. P.)

Meyer, Johann Matthias von, a Lutheran theologian of Germany, was born at Ansbach in 1814. In 1839 he was vicar, in 1843 director of the teacher's seminary at Schwabach, in 1844 preacher at Nördlingen, in 1849 at Munich, and in 1855 dean there. In 1872 he was made member of the superior consistory, and became its president at the death of Harless (q. v.). Meyer died Sept. 15, 1882, doctor of theology, and member of the council of the Bavarian empire. He published a few sermons, for which see Zuchold, *Bibl. Theol.* ii, 880. (B. P.)

Meyer, Louis Georg Fréderic, a Lutheran minister of France, was born at Montbeliard, Jan. 1, 1809. He studied at Strasburg, was in 1829 teacher in Switzerland, in 1831 professor of French at Leipsic, and in 1833 he accompanied two young men to Paris, and took up his abode in the house of John Monod. In 1837 he succeeded Mr. Boissart as pastor of the Lutheran Church at Paris, was in 1857 president of consistory and ecclesiastical inspector, and died Oct. 11, 1867. Meyer advanced the cause of home missions within his church, and originated many institutions. After his death were published *Sermons, Lettres et Fragments.* See Lichtenberger, *Encyclop. des Sciences Religieuses*, s. v. (B. P.)

Meyr, Melchior, a philosophical writer of Germany, was born June 28, 1810, at Ehringen, near Nördlingen. He studied at Munich and Heidelberg, and died at Munich, April 22, 1871. Of his many writings we mention, *Die Religion des Geistes* (Leipsic, 1871): —*Gott und Sein Reich* (Stuttgart, 1860):—*Drei Gespräche über Wahrheit, Güte und Schönheit* (1863): *Die Fortdauer nach dem Tode* (2d ed. Leipsic, 1875):—*Die Religion und ihre jetzt gebotene Fortbildung* (1871). After his death Bothmer and Carriere published from his manuscripts *Gedanken über Kunst, Religion und Philosophie* (Leipsic, 1874). (B. P.)

Mezger, Karl Ludwig Friedrich, a Lutheran theologian of Germany, was born at Schonndorf, March 18, 1810. In 1845 he was professor at the seminary in Schönthal, and died Oct. 16, 1885, doctor of theology. He is the author of, *Liber Ruth ex Hebraico in Latinum Versus Perpetuaque Interpretatione Illustratus* (Tübingen, 1856):—*Hülfsbuch zum Verständniss der Bibel* (1879). (B. P.)

Mezzachulians, a Mohammedan sect who believe that those who have any knowledge of God's glory and essence in this world may be saved, and are to be reckoned among the faithful.

Miall, Edward, an English Independent minister and journalist, was born at Portsmouth in 1809. He was educated at the Dissenters' College at Wymondley, Herts, and served for three years an Independent congregation at Ware, and afterwards one at Leicester. In 1841 he went to London, and established the *Nonconformist*, a paper in the interests of religious equality, becoming proprietor and editor, a position which he continued to occupy until his death, April 30, 1881. He was several times a representative in Parliament, and wrote numerous works on political and ecclesiastical subjects.

Mic-Mac Version of the Scriptures. The Mic-Macs, or *Souriquois* of French writers, are a North-American-Indian tribe, inhabiting the peninsula of Nova Scotia, Prince Edward's Island, and the eastern portion of New Brunswick. A version of the Bible into that language is of recent origin. The gospels of Matthew and John were the first portions issued in 1854, by the British and Foreign Bible Society. In 1856 the book of Genesis and the gospel of Luke were also published, the translations being made by the Rev. S. T. Rand, who continued the work. Several portions of the Old Test., and the entire New Test., are at present published. The language has been treated by Maillard, *Grammar of the Mic-Mac Language* (1864). (B. P.)

Michel Angelo. See Caravaggio; Michael Angelo.

Michmash. On this interesting locality, Lieut. Conder remarks as follows (*Tent Work*, ii, 112 sq.):

"The site of the Philistine camp at Michmash, which Jonathan and his armor-bearer attacked, is very minutely described by Josephus. It was, he says, a precipice with three tops, ending in a long, sharp tongue, and protected by surrounding cliffs. Exactly such a natural fortress exists immediately east of the village of Michmash, and it is still called "the fort" by the peasantry. It is a ridge rising in three rounded knolls above a perpendicular crag, ending in a narrow tongue to the east, with cliffs below, and having an open valley behind it, and a saddle towards the west on which Michmash itself is situate. Opposite this fortress, on the south, there is a crag of equal height and seemingly impassable; thus the description of the Old Test. is fully borne out—'a sharp rock on one side, and a sharp rock on the other' (1 Sam. xiv, 4).

"The southern cliff, as we have noticed above, was called Seneh, or 'the acacia,' and the same name still applies to the modern valley, due to the acacia-trees which dot its course. The northern cliff was named Bozez, or 'shining,' and the true explanation of the name only presents itself on the spot. The great valley runs nearly due east, and thus the southern cliff is almost entirely in shade during the day. The contrast is surprising and picturesque, between the dark, cool color of the south side and the ruddy or tawny tints of the northern cliff, crowned with the gleaming white of the upper chalky strata. The picture is unchanged since the days when Jonathan looked over to the white camping-ground of the Philistines, and Bozez must then have shone as brightly as it does now, in the full light of an Eastern sun."

(See illustration on following page.)

Michon, Jean Hippolyte, a French abbot and religious writer, was born at La Roche-Fressange in 1806. He pursued his theological studies at the seminary of St. Sulpice in Paris, accompanied De Saulcy to the East in 1850 and 1860, and was honorary canon of Angoulême and Bordeaux. He died in 1881, leaving, *La Femme et la Famille dans le Catholicisme* (1845):—*Apologie Chrétienne au Dix-Neuvième Siècle*

The Valley of Michmash.

(1863):—*Vie de Jésus* (1865, 2 vols.):—*Solution Nouvelle de la Question des Lieux Saints* (1852):—*Voyage Religieux en Orient* (1854, 2 vols.). See Lichtenberger, *Encyclop. des Sciences Religieuses*, s. v. (B. P.)

Middeldorpf, Heinrich, a Protestant theologian of Germany, was born at Hamburg, Aug. 2, 1788. He commenced his academical career at Frankfort-on-the-Oder, was in 1811 professor of theology at Breslau, in 1814 member of consistory, and died in 1837, doctor of theology. He published, *Nahum übersetzt mit Anmerkungen* (Hamburg, 1808):—*Symbola Exegetico-Critica ad Librum Ecclesiast.* (Frankfort, 1811):—*Commentatio de Institutis Literariis in Hispania* (Göttingen, 1812):—*Curæ Hexaplaris in Jobum* (Breslau, 1817):—*Comm. de Prudentio et Theologia Prudentiana* (1823, 1826):—*Codex Syriaco-Hexaplaris* (1835). See Winer, *Handbuch der theol. Lit.* i, 56, 213, 228, 911; Fürst, *Bibl. Jud.* ii, 377. (B. P.)

Middin. For this site Tristram suggests (*Bible Places*, p. 87) *Khurbet Mird*, two miles north-east of Mar Saba, the *Mons Mardes* of the Middle Ages, a ruin on a strong hill, with an aqueduct, wells, and arches (*Memoirs* to the Ordnance Survey, iii, 212).

Midgard, in Norse mythology, is the earth, the habitation of men, as Asgard is the dwelling of the Asas.

Midrash. By way of supplement, we add here the following works, belonging to the Midrashic literature:

I. *Exegetical.* 1. *Agadath Bereshith*, on Genesis, in eighty-three sections (Venice, 1618). See Zunz, *Gottesdienstliche Vorträge*, p. 256; Steinschneider, *Catalogus Librorum Hebr. in Bibl. Bodl.* 3727–3729.

2. Moses had-Darshan of Narbonne, of the 11th century, wrote annotations on some books of the Bible. Raymund Martini often quotes him in the *Pugio Fidei.* See Zunz, u. s. 287–293; Pusey, in *Introduction to liii. Chapter of Isaiah, according to the Jewish Interpreters*, vol. ii (Oxford, 1877); Neubauer, *The Book of Tobit* (ibid. 1878), p. vii–ix, xx–xxiv.

3. *Midrash Hashkem*, on the Pentateuch, probably of the 10th century (Zunz, p. 281). The part pertaining to Exodus was edited after a Munich MS. by Freimann, also with the Latin title, *Vehishir*, *Opus Continens Midrashim et Halachoth*, etc. (Leipsic, 1873).

4. *Midrash Jonah*, published at Prague in 1595. See Zunz, p. 270, 271.

II. *Halachic Midrash*, viz. *Sheeltoth* (i. e. questions) of Rabbi Acha of Shabcha (about 750), on laws and usages, as contained in the Pentateuch. Best edition is that published at Dyhrerrnfurth in 1786, with the commentary of Jesaiah Berlin or Pik (q. v.). See Zunz, p. 56, 96, 343; Steinschneider, p. 4330.

III. *Historical Haggadoth*, viz. 1. *Seder Olam* (q. v.).

2. *Megillath Taanith*, a calendar containing the non-festive days of the 2d century. Comp. Schmilg, *Ueber Entstehung und historischen Werth des Siegeskalenders Megillath Taanith* (Leipsic, 1874). See Braun, *Entstehung und Werth der Megillath Taanith*, in Grätz, *Monatsschrift*, 1876, p. 375–384, 410–418, 445–460; Wolf, *Bibl. Hebr.* i, 68 sq., 384 sq., ii, 1375 sq., iii, 1195 sq., iv, 1024; Zunz, p. 127, 128; Ewald, *Gesch. d. Volkes Israel*, iv, 497 sq., vii, 402 sq.; Grätz, *Gesch. d. Juden*, iii, 415–428; Fürst, *Bibl. Jud.* i, 9; Derenbourg, *Histoire de la Palestine*, p. 439–446, giving the text and a French translation.

3. *Josippon* (q. v.).

4. *Sepher ha-Jashar*, a history from Adam to the Judges, written, perhaps, in the 12th century (Venice, 1625). See Zunz, p. 154–156; Steinschneider, p. 3581–3586.

5. *Midrash Vayissu*, wars of the sons of Jacob with the Canaanites and Esau, printed in *Beth ham-Midrash* (ed. Jellinek), iii. See Zunz, p. 145.

6. *Pesach-haggada*, for the Easter festival. See Zunz, p. 126; Steinschneider, p. 2671.

7. *Midrash Petirath Aaron*, and 8. *Midrash Petirath Moshe*, on the last days of Moses and Aaron. See Zunz, p. 146; Steinschneider, p. 3996–4000; *Beth ham-Midrash*, i, vi.

9. *Kethib Eldad had-Dani* (i. e. the Book of Eldad the Danite), towards the end of the 9th century, and containing the fable of the Jews beyond the river Sambation. See *Beth ham-Midrash*, ii, iii, iv; Steinschneider, p. 4934; Zunz, p. 139.

10. *Sepher Zerubbabel* (q. v.).

11. *Abba Gorion* treats of the narrative as contained in the Book of Esther, printed in *Beth ham-Midrash*, i. See Zunz, p. 279.

12. *Megillath Antiochos*, on the Wars of the Asmonæans. See Zunz, p. 134. The Hebrew was often printed, see Steinschneider, p. 1382–1388. The Aramaic text was first published by Filipowski at the end of his *Choice of Pearls* (London, 1851); then by Sluzki

(Warsaw, 1863), and by Jellinek in *Beth-ham-Midrash*, vi. A new edition is in the course of preparation by Charles H. H. Wright, *The Megillath Antiochos, a Jewish Apocryphon with the Chaldee Text*, etc.

13. *Midrash Ele Ezkerah*, so called from the first words, "These will I remember," Ps. xlii, 5 (Hebrew text), describes the martyrdom of ten eminent teachers. See Zunz, p. 142[a]; Steinschneider, p. 3730–3732; *Beth ham-Midrash*, ii, vi.

IV. Of a purely *legendary* character are: 1. *Midrash Vayosha*, the tradition about Armilus (the Roman antichrist). See Zunz, p. 282; Steinschneider, p. 3734–3739; *Beth ham-Midrash*, i.

2. *Midrash Esreh had-debaroth*, on the Ten Commandments. See Zunz, p. 142[d]; Steinschneider, p. 3751, 4986[3]; *Beth ham-Midrash*, i.

3. *Chibbur Maasioth* (i. e. story-books). See Zunz, p. 130[b]; Steinschneider, p. 3869 sq.; on the numerous Hebrew and Judæo-German story-books, see ibid. p. 3869–3942.

V. *Ethical Midrashim*, viz. 1. *The Alphabet of Ben-Sira*. See SIRA.

2. *Derech Eretz and Derech Eretz Sutta*. See TALMUD (vol. x, p. 184).

3. *Thanna de Be-Elijahu*, a mélange from the Bible, Talmud, and Prayer-books, thrown into the form of instructions by the prophet Elijah. See Zunz, p. 112–117; Steinschneider, p. 4111, 4112.

4. *Midrash Themura*. See Zunz, p. 118; Steinschneider, p. 3793; *Beth ham-Midrash*, i.

VI. *Cabalistic, Mystic, Metaphysical, etc., Midrashim*, viz. 1. *The Book Jezirah*. See JEZIRAH.

2. *Alphabeth of Rabbi Akiba*. See Zunz, p. 168; Steinschneider, p. 3395–3401; *Beth ham-Midrash*, iii; Lat. transl. by Kircher in his *Œdipus Æg.* (Rome, 1652), ii, 225; Bartolocci, *Bibl. Rabbinica*, iv, 27; Fürst, *Bibl. Jud.* i, 28 sq.

3. *The Great and Small Halachoth*. See Zunz, p. 166, 167; Steinschneider, p. 3457–3459.

4. *Midrash Konen*, a kind of romantic cosmology. See Zunz, p. 169; Steinschneider, p. 3743–3745; *Beth ham-Midrash*, ii.

5. *Sepher Raziel* (which must be distinguished from a later "Sepher Raziel hag-gadol," a kind of commentary on the book Jezirah). See Zunz, p. 187; Steinschneider, p. 4042.

Collections of Midrashim.—Ad. Jellinek, *Beth ham-Midrash* (vol. i-iv, Leipsic, 1853-57; v, vi, Vienna, 1873, 1877); Horowitz, *Sammlung Kleiner Midraschim* (part i, Frankfort and Berlin, 1881).

Translations of Midrashim. — In Latin many are found in Ugolino's Thesaurus *Antiquitatum Sacrarum;* in German, Wünsche's *Bibliotheca Rabbinica* comprises the *Midrash Rabboth* (on the *Pentateuch* and five Megilloth, i. e. *Esther*, *Song of Solomon*, *Lamentations*, *Ecclesiastes*, and *Ruth*), *Proverbs*, and *Pesikta de Rab Kahanah* (Leipsic, 1880 sq.). See Plitt-Herzog, *Real-Encyklop.* s. v. (B. P.)

Mieczyslaw AND THE CHRISTIAN CHURCH IN POLAND. See POLAND, ECCLESIASTICAL HISTORY OF.

Migas, JOSEPH, *Ben-Mëir Ibn-Hal-Levi* (also called *Haram* [הרא״ם], from the initials of הרב אבן מיגש, *Rabbi Ibn-Migas*), one of the greatest Talmudical scholars of his time, was born at Granada in 1077. When twelve years of age he went to Cordova to attend the lectures of Isaac ben-Jacob Alfasi (q. v.), with whom he stayed for fourteen years. The master who gave him the ordination (סמיכה) was very proud of this scholar, of whom he used to say, that even in the age of Moses none could be found like him, and he appointed him as his successor in the presidency of the College of Cordova, which post he held for thirty-eight years (1103–41), until his death. His renown attracted many students, even from Egypt. From all parts his Talmudical decisions were sought for, and the greatest ornament of his school was the celebrated Moses Maimonides (q. v.). He wrote novellas and decisions, which are enumerated by Fürst. See Grätz, *Gesch. d. Juden*, vi, 116 sq.; Braunschweiger, *Gesch. d. Juden in den romanischen Staaten*, p. 61 (Würzburg, 1865); De' Rossi, *Dizionario Storico Degli Autori Ebrei* (Germ. transl. by Hamburger), s. v.; Lindo, *History of the Jews in Spain and Portugal*, p. 55; Fürst, *Bibl. Jud.* ii, 378. (B. P.)

Migdal-el. *Mujeidel*, with which Tristram (*Bible Places*, p. 274) and Conder (*Tent Work*, ii, 338) identify this place, lies three and three quarter miles north-west of Tibnin, and is a considerable village, with ancient wine-presses, sarcophagi, cisterns, etc. (*Memoirs* to the Ordnance Survey, i, 137).

Migdal-gad. The supposed modern representative of this site, *el-Mejdel*, three miles north-east of Ascalon, is an important place of 1500 inhabitants, but without signs of antiquity (*Memoirs* to the Ordnance Survey, ii, 410).

Migne, JACQUES PAUL, a Roman Catholic theologian, was born at St. Flour, Cantal, France, Oct. 25, 1800. He was educated at the theological seminary in Orleans, acted for some time as professor at Châteaudun, and after his ordination served as curate in the diocese of Orleans. In consequence of a controversy with his bishop respecting his (Migne's) book upon the "Liberty of the Priests," he went to Paris, and started *L'Univers Religieux*, later called simply *L'Univers*. In 1833 he sold his interest in the paper, and went to Petit Montrouge, near Paris, where he soon built up an enormous printing establishment, to which he gave the name "Imprimerie Catholique." From this proceeded the famous *Patrologiæ Cursus Completus sive Bibliotheca Universalis, Integra, Uniformis, Commoda, Œconomica Omnium SS. Patrum, Doctorum Scriptorumque Ecclesiasticorum qui ab ævo Apostolico ad Usque Innocentii II Tempora Floruerunt* (Latin series, 221 vols., 1844 sq.; 2d ed. 1878 sq.; 1st Greek series, 104 vols.; 2d ed. 58 vols., both since 1857):—*Collection des Orateurs Sacrés* (100 vols., 1846–48), etc. In 1868 this immense establishment was burned to the ground. Migne died Oct. 25, 1875, at Paris. See Lichtenberger, *Encyclop. des Sciences Religieuses*, s. v.; Vapereau, *Dictionnaire des Contemporains*, ed. 1880, p. 1290. (B. P.)

Mikels, WILLIAM S., D.D., a Baptist minister, was born in Orange County, N. Y., May 18, 1820. He graduated at Madison University in 1843, and from the theological department of the same institution in 1845; soon after became pastor in Rondout, N. Y., remaining there four years; then at Sing Sing six years; next at the Sixteenth Street Church, New York city, and had a successful ministry for seventeen years; and finally of the East Church, in the seventh ward of the same city, where he died, June 20, 1883. See Cathcart, *Baptist Encyclop.* s. v. (J. C. S.)

Miles, Henry, D.D., an English Presbyterian clergyman, was born in 1699, and entered the ministry in early life. He was the minister of a church at Tooting, Surrey, for many years; a learned and ingenious man of considerable ability, and an eminent Christian. His skill in natural science led to his being elected a fellow of the Royal Society. In 1737 he was chosen assistant minister at the Old Jewry Church, where he preached once on the Lord's Day for seven years, but resigned in 1744, and confined himself to Tooting, where he died, much regretted, Feb. 10, 1763. See Wilson, *Dissenting Churches*, ii, 384.

Miles, James Browning, D.D., a Congregational minister, was born at Rutland, Mass., Aug. 18, 1822. He graduated from Yale College in 1849, and from Yale Divinity School in 1854, having one year (1852) attended the Theological Seminary at Andover; also, from 1852 to 1854, acting as tutor in Yale College. He was ordained pastor of the First Church, Charlestown, Mass., Jan. 2, 1855, from which he was dismissed in October, 1871, to become secretary of the American Peace Society. About the same time he became secretary of the International

Code Society. He died at Worcester, Nov. 13, 1875. See *Cong. Quarterly*, 1876, p. 431.

Millan, *Saint*. See EMILIANUS.

Millennial Association, AMERICAN. See ADVENTISTS, EVANGELICAL.

Miller, Ebenezer, D.D., a Protestant Episcopal clergyman, graduated from Harvard College in 1722; obtained ordination in England in 1727; became a missionary of the Society for the Propagation of the Gospel, and as such was made rector of the Church in Braintree, Mass., Dec. 25, 1727. He died Feb. 11, 1763. See Sprague, *Annals of the Amer. Pulpit*, v, 110.

Miller, Josiah, an English minister, who died Dec. 22, 1880, at London, where he had for a long time been secretary to the London City Mission, is best known for his writings on hymnology. His first volume in this branch of religious literature, *Our Hymns, their Authors and Origin*, appeared in 1866; three years later a second edition was published, under the altered title of *Singers and Songs of the Church* (Lond. 1869), which has also been reprinted in New York. (B. P.)

Miller, Samuel, D.D., a Presbyterian minister, was born at Princeton, N. J., Jan. 23, 1816, being the son of professor Samuel Miller of Princeton College. He graduated from the college there in 1833, and the theological seminary in 1844, having been tutor in the college for several years in the meantime. He studied law, and while engaged in its practice prepared a full report of the great suit between the Old and New School branches of the Presbyterian Church at the time of the disruption. He was ordained in 1844, and after serving as stated supply at the Presbyterian Church at Mount Holly, N. J., for many years, became pastor in 1850. He also established a classical school of a high order, which continued there from 1845 to 1857. From 1858 he was stated supply at Columbus for twenty years, and for four years of the churches of Zuckerton and Bass River. He was relieved from the charge of Mount Holly Church in 1873, but continued to supply various pulpits. In 1880 he was installed pastor of the Church of Oceanic, where he labored until failing health obliged him to resign. He died at Hount Holly, Oct. 12, 1883. See *Necrol. Report of Princeton Theol. Sem.* 1884, p. 32. (W. P. S.)

Mills, CYRUS TAGGART, D.D., a Presbyterian minister, was born at Paris, N. Y., May 4, 1819. He graduated from Williams College in 1844, and from Union Theological Seminary in 1847; was ordained in 1848, and in 1849 went out as a missionary to Ceylon, having charge of the Battacotta Seminary. In 1855 failure of health obliged him to return. From 1856 to 1858 he was stated supply at Berkshire, N. Y., and in 1860 was chosen president of the Oahu College, in the Sandwich Islands, where he remained four years, and then resided for a year at Ware, Mass. In 1865 he went as agent of the Board of Commissioners of Foreign Missions to California, where he established in Brooklyn a female seminary. He died in California in 1884.

Minot, THOMAS, an Irish prelate, was consecrated archbishop of Dublin on Palm Sunday in 1363. In 1366, the revenues of the precentor of St. Patrick's having been much reduced by the invasion of the Irish from the mountains, he united to that dignity the Church of Kilmactalway. This addition was for the purpose of enabling the incumbent to live hospitably, give alms, and answer the expenses and charges of his office. About 1370 Minot repaired part of St. Patrick's Church, which had been destroyed by fire. In 1373 he was one of those who advised the customs and assessments imposed, and other arbitrary measures enforced by William de Windsor, lord deputy. In 1374 he erected the Church of Rathsallagh into a prebend, and in 1375 had the royal mandate to attend a council to consider and provide against the hostilities of the O'Briens of Thomond, who invaded Munster. But in June of 1375 he died in London. See D'Alton, *Memoirs of the Archbishops of Dublin*, p. 138.

Mira Bais, a subdivision of the Vallabhacharis (q. v.), originated by Mirá Bai, who flourished in the reign of Akbar, and was celebrated as the authoress of poems addressed to Vishnû. She was the daughter of a petty rajah, the sovereign of a place called Mertá. Further than that her history is enveloped in fable.

Mirus, ADAM ERDMANN, a Lutheran theologian of Germany, was born Nov. 26, 1656. He studied at Wittenberg, was in 1684 conrector at Zittau, and died June 3, 1727. He wrote, *Philologia Sacra* (Leipsic, 1699): —*Philologia Biblica* (1713):—*Isagoge Biblica* (1687): —*Summarium Ebrææ Linguæ xvii Tabulis Inclusum* (1719):—*Onomasticon Biblicum sive Lexicon Nominum Propriorum* (1721):—*De Ebræorum Sectionibus Legalibus et Prophet.* (1683):—*Biblisches Antiquitäten-Lexicon* (1727):—*Kurze Fragen aus der freien Mechanik und Baukunst der Ebräer* (1713):—*Kurze Fragen aus der Heraldica Sacra* (1719):—*Kurze Fragen aus der Musica Sacra* (1707), etc. See Fürst, *Bibl. Jud.* ii, 381; Jöcher, *Allgemeines Gelehrten-Lexikon*, s. v. (B. P.)

Misler, JOHANN NICOLAUS, a Lutheran theologian of Germany, was born in 1615. He was archdeacon at Marburg, was in 1652 professor of theology and Hebrew at Giessen, in 1654 doctor of theology, and died Feb. 20, 1683. He wrote, *Scrutinium Scripturæ Sacræ*:—*Synopsis Theologica Totius Christianæ Religionis*:—*Theognosia sive de Deo Triuno et λόγῳ Incarnato*:—*Speculum anti-Jesuiticum*:—*Diss. V de Sacra Scriptura ex Joh.* v, 39:—*De Dicto Prophetico Esa.* liii, 4:—*De Mysterio Sanctæ Trinitatis*. See Jöcher, *Allgemeines Gelehrten-Lexikon*, s. v. (B. P.)

Mitchell, Jacob Duché, D.D., a Presbyterian minister, was born in Philadelphia, Pa., Nov. 2, 1806. When eighteen years of age he entered the College of New Jersey, where he graduated in 1827, and in the same year went to Princeton Seminary and studied two years there. He was licensed to preach by the Oneida Presbytery, Sept. 18, 1829; first labored in Albany, and was ordained as an evangelist, Nov. 17 of the same year. He afterwards served at Shepherdstown, Martinsburg, and Smithfield, in Jefferson Co., Va. In this early period of his ministry, and for years following, when he labored far and wide in Virginia as a revival preacher, all testimonies agree that he exhibited extraordinary pulpit power. In 1832 he became pastor at Lynchburg, From 1835 to 1837 he served as secretary of the Central Board of Foreign Missions for Virginia and South Carolina. In 1858 he became pastor at Peaks, near Liberty, Va., where he labored for fourteen years, having very great success in winning souls. Next he went to Alexandria and labored as an evangelist in the Chesapeake Presbytery, and in 1873 and 1874 acted as general agent for Hampden Sidney College. He died June 28, 1877. See *Necrol. Report of Princeton Theol. Sem.* 1878, p. 23.

Mitchell, John S., D.D., a Methodist Episcopal minister, was born on Block Island, R. I., in 1800. In his twenty-third year he entered the Genesee Conference; from 1837 to 1842 was agent of the American Bible Society in Maryland; in 1850 was transferred to the New York East Conference, in which he took prominent appointments as pastor and presiding elder; in 1864 was secretary of the Freedmen's Relief Association, and finally superintendent of missions in Virginia and North Carolina. He died at Newburgh, N. Y., Sept. 16, 1882. See *Minutes of Annual Conferences*, 1883, p. 93.

Mithrion, a temple of Mithras, the Persian sun-god.

Mitternacht, JOHANN SEBASTIAN, a Lutheran theologian of Germany, was born at Hardesleben, in Thuringia, March 30, 1613. He studied at Jena and Wittenberg, and was in 1638 pastor at Teutleben, Thu-

View of Neby Samwil. (From Thomson's *Central Palestine and Phœnicia.*)

ringia. In 1642 he was rector at Naumburg, in 1646 at Gera, and died Feb. 25, 1679. He wrote, *Grammatica Ebræa:—De Nativitatis Domini Anno, Mense ac Die:—Notæ Philologicæ, Theologicæ, Chronologicæ et Historicæ in Fabricii Historiam Sacram:—De Abrahami Nomine et Patria Ur:—De Tempore et loco Effusionis Spiritus Sancti ad Actor. ii,* 1:— *Explicatio Philologica Dicti ex Proverb. xxii,* 15:— *Διάσκεψις Philologica Jobi xxiii,* 11, 12:—*Item in Locum ad Hebræos cap. xiii,* 7. See Witte, *Diarium;* Jöcher, *Allgemeines Gelehrten-Lexikon*, s. v. (B. P.)

Mizpeh OF BENJAMIN. Respecting this place Lieut. Conder remarks (*Tent Work*, ii, 117):

"There are plenty of Mizpehs in Palestine, but in positions quite inapplicable, whereas, in the right direction there is no name of the kind (so far as has yet been discovered), for Sh'afât is not apparently derived from Mizpeh, but is a name very like that of Jehosaphat, and the natives of the place say that it was called after a Jewish king. In crusading times the town seems to be also mentioned under the title Jehosaphat.

"The early Christians placed Mizpeh in quite another direction, and Nob at Beit Nûba, which is famous in the history of Richard Lion-Heart. Their site for Mizpeh was near Sôba, west of Jerusalem, and here we found a ruin with the title Shûfa, which in meaning is equivalent to the Hebrew Mizpeh; but this place cannot be described as 'over against Jerusalem,' and its recovery is thus a matter of minor interest.

"There is one other site which has been proposed for Mizpeh, though it is merely a conjecture, and not a name which might lead to the identification: this site is the remarkable hill called Neby Samwîl, north of Jerusalem. The place is conspicuous from the tall minaret which crowns the old crusading church on the summit, and within the church is the cenotaph now revered by the Moslems as the tomb of Samuel—a modern monument covered with a green cloth.

"The crusaders, with their usual contempt for facts, fixed on this hill as the ancient Shiloh; they also called it Ramah, and added besides a title of their own. 'Two miles from Jerusalem,' says Sir John Maundeville, 'is Mount Joy, a very fair and delicious place. There Samuel the prophet lies in a fair tomb, and it is called Mount Joy because it gives joy to pilgrims' hearts, for from that place men first see Jerusalem.'

"The tradition which places Samuel's tomb here seems, however, to be only recent. Rabbi Benjamin of Tudela, who is a tolerably safe guide as regards Jewish sacred sites, discredits the story and speaks of a change of site. 'When the Christians took Ramleh, which is Ramah, from the Mohammedans,' says the rabbi, 'they discovered the sepulchre of Samuel the Ramathi near the Jewish synagogue, and removed his remains to Shiloh, where they erected a large place of worship over them, called St. Samuel of Shiloh to the present day.'"

Neby Samwîl is fully described in the *Memoirs* to the Ordnance Survey, iii, 12, 149.

Moabitic Stone. See MESHA.

Mobah, what may be either done or omitted, according to the law of Mohammed, as being indifferent.

Mobaiedians, a name given to the followers of the famous Mohammedan impostor Borkai or Mokanna (q. v.). They made an insurrection in the province of Khorassan against the caliph Mahadi, who, however, at length defeated them. Their name is derived from an Arabic word signifying white, the color of their dress, by which they were distinguished from the adherents of the caliph, who were clothed in black garments.

Mobeds are the officiating priests among the Parsees of India. They read the holy books in the temples, and superintend all the religious ceremonies, but being themselves unlearned, they seldom understand the meaning of what they read, or the prayers they recite. The *mobeds* are distinct from the *dustûrs*, who are doctors and expounders of the law. There is also an inferior order of clergy among the Parsees, called *hirbeds*, who have immediate charge of the sacred fire, and sweep and take care of the temple. The priests receive their office by inheritance, and have no fixed salary, but are paid for their services. Many of them follow secular employments.

Moberley, GEORGE, D.D., D.C.L., an English prelate, was born in St. Petersburg in 1803. He was educated at Winchester School, and graduated from Balliol College, Oxford, in 1825; was for some years tutor and fellow there; in 1835 was appointed head-master of Winchester School; in 1866 rector of Brixton, in the Isle of Wight; in 1868 a canon of Chester; in 1869 bishop of Salisbury, and died July 7, 1885. Dr. Moberley was the author of numerous sermons and essays, also one of the five clergyman who published revised versions of several parts of the New Test.

Möbius. See MŒBIUS.

Modin. *El-Medieh,* the modern representative of this place, famous in the Maccabæan history, is fully described in the *Memoirs* accompanying the Ordnance Survey, ii, 341 sq. (See illustration on p. 731.)

Moffat, Nicol de, a Scotch prelate, was elected bishop of the see of Glasgow in 1268. He died at Tinningham, in East-Lothian. See Keith, *Scottish Bishops*, p. 241.

Moffat, Robert, D.D., an eminent English missionary, was born at Inverkeithing, Fifeshire, Scotland, Dec. 21, 1795. He was originally a gardener, and was brought up within the fold of the Secession Church, to which his parents belonged. In 1816, having resolved to become a missionary to the heathen, he offered his ser-

Ruined Tomb at Medieh.

vices to the London Missionary Society, and arriving at Cape Town in 1817, immediately proceeded beyond the boundaries of Cape Colony to Namaqualand, where he entered upon his labors at the kraal of Africaner, a chief whose name had long been a terror to the people of the neighboring districts of the colony, but who had lately become a convert to Christianity. Here Moffat labored for three or four years with great success, Christianity and civilization advancing together. But the situation being unsuitable for a principal mission-station, he travelled and labored at several stations in succession in the countries to the north and north-east of Cape Colony. His remarkable personal adventures and hair-breadth escapes in these journeys are graphically described in his work, *Missionary Labors and Scenes in Southern Africa* (Lond. 1842, 8vo), which he wrote and published during a visit of several years to Britain, rendered necessary by the state of his health. In America also Mr. Moffat's book made many friends for the African, and our missionary labors in that field were largely inspired by his appeals. During his stay in England Moffat also carried through the press, at the expense of the British and Foreign Evangelical Society, a version of the New Test. and the Psalms in the Bechuana language. In 1842 he returned to his labors in Africa, and continued his work there, with great success, till 1870, when he returned to Scotland. In 1873 he received a public gratuity of £5800 as a testimonial of his missionary services. He died near London, Aug. 9, 1883. Besides the publication already mentioned, we have from him the *Becuana Hymn-book* (Lond. Relig. Tract Soc. 1843, 18mo). *Moffat's Farewell Services* were edited by Dr. Campbell, and published in 1843 (8vo). Moffat's daughter was the wife of the celebrated missionary and traveller, the late Dr. Livingstone. See Yonge, *Pioneers and Founders* (Lond. 1872, 12mo); Bayard Taylor, *Cyclop. of Mod. Travel* (N. Y. 1856), p. 561 sq.; *Miss. Cyclop.* (ibid. 1873, 8vo), s. v.; *Christian at Work*, Aug. 16, 1883; *Life and Labors* (N. Y. 1883); (Lond.) *Cong. Year-book*, 1884, p. 311.

Mogon, a pagan deity, mentioned by Camden in his *Britannia* as having been worshipped anciently by the Cadeni, who inhabited that part of England now called Northumberland. In the year 1607 two altars were found in that district, bearing inscriptions declaring them to have been dedicated to that god.

Mohawk Version OF THE SCRIPTURES. The Mohawk was spoken by the Indian tribes west of the falls of the Niagara. For the benefit of these peoples the British and Foreign Bible Society published Isaiah and the gospels of Luke and John in the vernacular of the Mohawk Indians, while the Pentateuch and Psalms are translated but not yet published. See *Bible of Every Land*, p. 456. (B. P.)

Mokanna. See ATHA BEN-HAKEM.

Mokissos, an order of deities of the negroes of Congo, Angola, etc., in Africa. They are a kind of genii or spirits, and are in subordination to a superior being, called by the natives Zamban-Pongo. Their idols are composed either of wood or stone; a few are erected in temples or chapels, but the much greater part in the public streets and highways. Some are in the form of four-footed beasts, others are like birds. To these the negroes bow, and offer sacrifices to appease their anger, or to obtain their favor.

Mokludjye, a sect of the Ansarians (q. v.).

Moladah. *Khurbet el-Milh*, the probable representative of this locality, is seven miles and three quarters south-west of Tell Arad, and thirteen and a quarter east of Beersheba. It is briefly described in the *Memoirs* accompanying the Ordnance Survey (iii, 415), and more fully by Tristram, *Bible Places* (p. 19), as follows:

"The two wells are in the shallow valley, very finely built of marble, about seventy feet deep, their sides scored with the ropes of the water-drawers of many centuries. The ground around is strewn with records of the Roman occupation. Fragments of shafts and capitals, probably the support of roofs that covered the wells, and eight large marble water-troughs, lie around the mouths. There are traces of pavement. Just to the south of the wells stands a small isolated 'tell' or hill, covered with ruins, and now used as a burying-ground of the Dhulam tribe. This hill was the fortress of the city below, spoken of by Josephus; and we could clearly trace the circuit of the wall that once surrounded it, nearly square in shape, and still in places three or four feet high. The traces of buildings and fragments of walls cover an extensive area both south and north of the citadel; and near its foot, on the south-east, are the outlines of a building, probably a Byzantine church. The other ruins seem to belong to an earlier and ruder period, and are perhaps the remains of the town of Simeon."

Molhedites, a name sometimes applied to the ASSASSINS (q. v.).

Molitor, WILHELM, a Roman Catholic theologian of Germany, was born Aug. 24, 1819, at Zweibrucken. He first practiced law, but in 1849 betook himself to the study of theology at Bonn, received holy orders in 1851 at Spires, was in 1857 cathedral dean and in 1864 doctor of theology, a distinction conferred on him by pope Pius IX. In 1868 the same pope called him to Rome as consulter to the Vatican council. Molitor died Jan. 1, 1880, at Spires. He published, *Ueber kanonisches Gerichtsverfahren gegen Kleriker* (Mayence, 1856):—*Die Immunität des Domes zu Speyer* (ibid. 1859):—*Fastenpredigten* (1871):—*Predigten auf die Sonn- und Festtage des katholischen Kirchenjahres* (3 vols.); also, in connection with Hülskamp, *Papst Pius IX in seinem Leben und Wirken* (3d ed. 1873). (B. P.)

Moll, Carl Bernhard, a Protestant theologian of Germany, was born at Wolgast, Pomerania, Nov. 20, 1806. He studied at Berlin and Greifswalde, and entered the ministry in 1830 at Naugard. In 1834 he was called to Löknitz, near Stettin, in 1845 to Stettin, in 1850 as professor of theology to Halle, and was made, in 1860, general superintendent of the province of Prussia. He died Aug. 17, 1878, at Königsberg, leaving, *Die gegenwärtige Noth der evangelischen Kirche Preussens* (Pasewalk, 1843):—*Das Heil in Christo in Predigten* (Halle, 1852):—*Das System der praktischen Theologie im Grundrisse dargestellt* (1853):—*Christologia in Epistola ad Hebræos* (1854–55):—*De Justo Attributorum Dei Discrimine* (1855):—*Zeugnisse vom Leben in Christo in Predigten* (1856). For Lange's *Bibelwerk* he wrote the commentary on the Psalms and on the Epistle to the Hebrews. See Zuchold, *Bibl. Theol.* ii, 892 sq. (B. P.)

Moll, Willem, a Dutch theologian, was born Feb. 28, 1812, at Dort. He studied at Leyden, was in 1837 pastor at De Vuursche, in the province of Utrecht, in

1844 at Arnheim, in 1846 professor of theology at Amsterdam, and died Aug. 16, 1879. He is the author of, *Kerk geschiedenis van Nederland voor de Hervorming* (Utrecht, 1864–71, 6 vols.) :—*Geschiedenis van het kerkelijke Leven der Christenen gedurende de zes eerste Eeuwen* (Amsterdam, 1844–46, 2 vols.; 2d ed. Leyden, 1855, 1857) :—*Angelus Merula, De hervormer en Martelaar des Geloofs* (1851) :—*Johannes Brugmann en het godsdienstig Leven onzer Vaderen in de vijftiende Eeuw* (1854). Moll founded the society which from 1856 to 1863 published the *Kalender voor de Protestanten in Nederland.* See Acquoy, *Levensbericht van Willem Moll*, in *Jaarbek van de Koninklijke Akademie van Wetenschappen*, 1879, p. 66–137; Rogge, *Willem Moll*, in *Mannen van Beteekenis in onze Dagen*, 1879; Nippold, *Die römisch-katholische Kirche im Königreich der Niederlande* (Leipsic, 1877), p. 486-489; Plitt-Herzog, *Real-Encyklop.* s. v.; Lichtenberger, *Encyclop. des Sciences Religieuses*, s. v. (B. P.)

Möller, Arnold, a Protestant theologian of Germany, was born Oct. 9, 1791, at Duisburg. In 1817 he was military preacher at Münster, in 1829 pastor at Minden, and died in 1858. He published, *Für christliche Erbauung* (Ratisbon, 1832, 2 vols.) :—*Biblisches Schatzkästlein zur täglichen Erbauung christlicher Pilger* (1831) :—*Tabor und Sinai* (Münster, 1834) :—*Der Tisch des Herrn* (2d ed. 1852) :—*Das Evangelium für Kinder* (1839) :—*Friedrich Adolph Krummacher und seine Freunde* (Bremen, 1849, 2 vols.) :—*Der liturgische Theil des evangelischen Gottesdienstes in den preussischen Landen* (Bielefeld, 1850) :—*Hülfsbuch für den liturgischen Theil* (3 parts, 1851–52). See Zuchold, *Bibl. Theol.* ii, 893 sq.; Winer, *Handbuch der theol. Lit.* i, 544; ii, 255, 270, 287, 310, 333, 337, 368, 392, 396. (B. P.)

Möller, Jens, a Danish theologian, was born in 1779, and died Nov. 25, 1833, doctor and professor of theology at Copenhagen. He published, *Theologisk Bibliothek* (Copenhagen, 1811–21, 20 vols.) :—*Nuie theol. Biblioth.* (1821 sq. 20 vols.) :—*Tidsskrift for Kerke og Theolog.* (1832, 1833, 4 vols.) :—*Compendium theologiæ symbol. eccles. Lutheranæ.* See Winer, *Handbuch der theol. Lit.* i, 12, 338. (B. P.)

Möller, Johann Friedrich, a Lutheran theologian of Germany, was born at Erfurt, Nov. 13, 1789. He studied at Göttingen, was in 1814 professor at the teachers' seminary in his native city, in 1815 deacon, in 1829 pastor, in 1831 senior of the Evangelical ministerium, and in 1832 member of consistory. In 1843 Möller was called as general superintendent to Magdeburg, and died April 20, 1861. He wrote, *Commentatio in verba Christi, Matt. vii*, 12–14 (Erfurt, 1835) :—*Handreichung der Kirche an die Schule* (2d ed. Magdeburg, 1852) :—*Kritisch-evangelische Unterweisung* (ibid. 1855) :—besides he published a number of sermons. See Zuchold, *Bibl. Theol.* ii, 895 sq.; Plitt-Herzog, *Real-Encyklop.* s. v. (B. P.)

Moller, Martin, a Lutheran hymn-writer of Germany, was born Nov. 11, 1547, at Leissnitz, Saxony. In 1572 he was called to the ministry at Kesselsdorf, and in 1575 to Sprottau, Lower Silesia. In 1600 he was appointed pastor primarius at Görlitz, in Upper Lausatia, and died March 2, 1606. Besides his *Praxis Evangeliorum*, a practical exposition on the gospels of the Christian year (1601, 4 vols.), he wrote several hymns, some of which are translated into English, as *Nimm von uns Herr, du treuer Gott* (in Jacobi, *Psalmodia Germanica*, i, 123, "Remove from us, O faithful God"), *O Jesu, süss wer dein gedenkt* (ibid. i, 130 sq., "When thought brings Jesus to my sense"), *Ach Gott, wie manches Herzeleid* (*Chorale Book for England*, No. 136, "Ah God, my days are dark indeed"). See Koch, *Geschichte des deutschen Kirchenliedes*, ii. 211 sq.; Jöcher, *Allgemeines Gelehrten-Lexikon*, s. v. (B. P.)

Molungo, the name given to the Supreme Being by some of the tribes of Central Africa.

Molybdomancy (from μόλυβδος, *lead*, and μαντεία, *divination*), a species of divination among the ancient heathen, in which they drew conjectures concerning future events from the motions and figures presented by melted lead.

Mondari Version of the Scriptures. The Mondari is spoken by the Koles of Chota Nagpore, Bengal Presidency. The Rev. N. Nottrott, of the German Missionary (Gosner's) Society, translated the gospel of Mark into the Mondari in 1875, which was printed in 1876 by the Calcutta Auxiliary. In 1879 the gospel of Luke was printed, and between 1881 and 1882 the gospels of John and Matthew followed. The work of translation was done by the missionary already mentioned and the Rev. L. Beyer. Each translator revised the work of the other by the help of native assistants. (B. P.)

Mone, Franz Joseph, a Roman Catholic writer of Germany, was born May 12, 1796, at Mingolsheim, near Bruchsal. He studied at Heidelberg, commenced his academical career there in 1817, was professor in 1819, and from 1826 also first librarian of the university. In 1827 he accepted a call to Louvain, but returned to Heidelberg in 1831. Mone died at Karlsruhe, March 12, 1871, leaving, *Geschichte des Heidenthums im nördlichen Europa* (Heidelberg, 1822–23, 2 vols.) :—*Lateinische Hymnen des Mittelalters* (Karlsruhe, 1855–57, 3 vols.) .—*Lateinische und griechische Messen aus dem 2. bis 6. Jahrhundert* (1850). See Winer, *Handbuch der theol. Lit.* i, 514. (B. P.)

Mongolian Version of the Scriptures. In the Mongolian there exist different versions:

I. *The Buriat*, or *Northern Mongolian*, for the Buriats about lake Baikal, in Siberia, and for the Kalka tribes of Mongolia. In 1824 the New Test. was printed at St. Petersburg, under the superintendence of Dr. Schmidt, who, with the aid of two learned Buriats, had commenced the translation, but during the work one of the Buriats died. The surviving Buriat was afterwards associated with Messrs. Swan, Stallybrass, and Yuille, missionaries at Selinginsk, in the translation of the Old Test. and the revision of the New Test. The Old Test. was translated from the Hebrew, with constant reference to such critical apparatus as could be obtained. The style of writing adopted in this version holds a middle place between the vulgar colloquial language of the people, which varies in different districts, and the abstruse modes of expression employed in some of their books. It is above the common business dialect, but not so much higher as to place the subject beyond the reach of any one of common understanding. The Old Test. was completed at Khodon, in Siberia, in 1840, and during the same year Messrs. Swan and Stallybrass accomplished a fresh translation of the New Test. from the original Greek, based on the version previously made. An edition of this Testament was completed at press in 1846 at the expense of the British and Foreign Bible Society, while a reprint of it was undertaken in 1878 by the Academy of Sciences at St. Petersburg, under the editorship of Mr. Schiefner, in the Mongolian type instead of the Manchu character, reducing thereby the size of the book by two thirds. This edition was completed at press in 1880, under the editorship of Mr. Pozdnieff, professor of Mongolian in the St. Petersburg University, who had taken the place of superintendent after the death of professor Schiefner.

II. *The Kalmuck*, or *Western Mongolian*, for the Kalmucks of the Don and Volga, in Russia, and Eleuths, Kalmucks, and Soungars, of Mongolia. In this dialect there exist translations of the gospels of Matthew and John and of the Acts of the Apostles, published between 1815 and 1822. Concerning these efforts of translation and the Kalmucks themselves we read the following in the annual report of the British and Foreign Bible Society for the year 1877: "The Kalmucks are a Mongolian tribe, inhabiting the great salt steppe of the province of Astrakhan, about whose mode of life and habits not much is known in Western Europe. While it is not likely that they, at the present time at least, in any way answer to the description given of themselves to the patriarch Nicon by thirty of their chiefs, as recorded by Macarius, and quoted by dean Stanley in his *Eastern Church*—where, being brought into the presence of the patriarch, they are represented as saying to him, 'When we have conquered a man, we cut away his nose, and then carve him into pieces and eat him. Good Lord, whenever you have any men deserving of death, do not trouble yourself about their guilt or punishment, but give them us to eat, and you will do us a great kindness'—they are certainly in a very low state of civilization, even though their chiefs are sometimes educated in Russian schools. Mission work was begun among them early in the present century, and by the preaching of the Gospel and circulation of the Scriptures, parts of which had been translated into Kalmuck by the missionary Conrad Neitz, and others, and subsequently revised by Dr. Schmidt, laboring under the auspices of the emperor Alexander I, and of the British and Foreign Bible Society, a number of conversions took place. But days of trouble and persecution fell upon the mission, and in a recent letter the pastor of the Moravian settlement of Sarepta, founded with the express purpose of evangelizing the Kalmucks, informs your agent that at present no thorough knowledge of Kalmuck is possessed by any of the brethren. A search made in the archives of the village revealed the presence of a few copies of the gospels of Matthew and John, besides a number of Kalmuck tracts. A copy of each of the gospels having been sent by your agent to London, specimen pages of a reduced and convenient size have been printed by the photographic process. These were forwarded to Sarepta, and we now await the result of their critical examination by learned Kalmucks, if there be any, and to know the opinions of the brethren themselves. Should these be deemed satisfactory, and the committee otherwise see fit to proceed with the printing of the Scriptures in the vernacular of this tribe, future reports may contain something more interesting and instructive about the progress of Bible work among its members." From the report for the year 1880 we learn that the agent of the British and Foreign Bible Society at St. Petersburg has been authorized to employ M. Pozdnieff and archpriest Smirnoff to translate the gospel of Matthew. M. Pozdnieff, as an eminent Kalmuck scholar, will make the translation, and archpriest Smirnoff, who lives among the Kalmucks, will see that the words and idioms are suited to the people. On this plan there is reason to hope that an excellent translation will be produced, and the question of proceeding with the other books of the New Test. will depend on the manner in which the gospel of Matthew is received. In the report for 1884 we read the gratifying statement that the committee of the British and Foreign Bible Society have authorized the publication of an edition of two thousand copies of the New Test. prepared by professor Pozdnieff. New type has been cut at the expense of the above society and cast at the expense of the academy.

III. *The Southern*, or *Kalkhas Colloquial.* In this dialect, used in Chinese Mongolia, the gospel of Matthew has been translated by the Rev. J. Edkins and Dr. J. J. Schereschewsky, aided by a native Lama, and was printed in 1872 under the care of the Rev. J. Edkins, of Peking. This is the only part now extant. See *Bible of Every Land*, p. 337.

For the study of the language, see Schmidt, *Grammatik der mongolischen Sprache* (1831); Zwick, *Grammatik der westmongolischen Sprache* (1851); Castren, *Versuch einer bürjalischen Sprachlehre* (1857). (B. P.)

Monod, HORACE, an eminent French Protestant minister, the youngest son of Jean (q. v.), was born in Paris, Jan. 20, 1814. He studied at Lausanne and Strasburg, and in 1838 was deacon at Marseilles. In 1842 he was appointed member of consistory, and died July 13, 1881. For forty years he preached in the same church with great success. He published eight volumes of *Sermons* and a French translation of Hodge's *Commentary on the Epistle to the Romans.* See Lichtenberger, *Encyclop. des Sciences Religieuses*, s. v. (B. P.)

Monoism. See MONADOLOGY.

Monson, ABRAHAM, a Jewish savant who flourished towards the end of the 16th century, was a native of Egypt, and died at Constantinople. He wrote שו״ת, i. e. *Decisiones et Responsa*, which are incorporated in Salomo Cohen's *Decisions* (Salonica, 1596) and in those of Joseph di Trani (Constantinople, 1641). See Fürst, *Bibl. Jud.* ii, 388; Wolf, *Bibl. Hebr.* iii, 52; Jöcher, *Allgemeines Gelehrten-Lexikon*, s. v. (B. P.)

Montandon, AUGUSTE LAURENT, a French Protestant theologian, was born at Clermont-Ferrand in 1803. He studied at Geneva, was for some time pastor at Luneray, and accepted a call in 1832 to Paris as pastor adjunctus. He published *Récits de l'Ancien et du Nouveau Testament*, and took a great interest in the different religious organizations, especially in the work of the Bible Society, to which he rendered great services. Montandon died in 1876. (B. P.)

Montefiore, *Sir* MOSES, a Jewish philanthropist, was born Oct. 24, 1784. He was an opulent merchant of London, and was successively knighted and raised to a baronetcy for his public labors; having served as sheriff of London in 1837, and also high-sheriff of Kent. He went in 1840 on a benevolent mission to the East, and on others in 1840 and 1867, in behalf of his oppressed brethren. In the latter year he founded a Jewish college at Ramsgate. In 1875 he visited Jerusalem the seventh time. He died at Ramsgate, July 28, 1885. See his *Centenary Biography*, by Lucien Wolf (Lond. 1884; N. Y. 1885); *The American Hebrew*, Oct. 9, 1885.

Montet, JOSEPH, a French Protestant theologian, was born at Milhau, Aveyron, in 1790. He studied at Lausanne and Geneva, and was made a licentiate of theology at the latter place, on presenting *Disputatio Theolog. de Authentia Librorum Novi Testamenti*, in 1813. In 1814 he was called as pastor to Réalmont, Tarn; in 1825 he was made professor of Church history at Montauban, and dean of the faculty in 1835. In 1865 he retired from active duty, and died Feb. 24, 1878. See Lichtenberger, *Encyclop. des Sciences Religieuses*, s. v. (B. P.)

Montfort, SECT AT. In the 11th century a mystic Christian sect appeared in the north of Italy, having its headquarters at Montfort, in the neighborhood of Turin. Their presiding officer was one Gerhard, who was called upon by Heribert, archbishop of Milan, to give an account of his doctrines. They were considered heretics, and subjected to great persecution, which they bore with the spirit of martyrs; but the sect made little progress.

Montgomery, ROBERT, a distinguished English missionary, was born at Bangor, Aug. 19, 1811. He studied at Edinburgh, was licensed by his presbytery about the end of 1841, and a few weeks afterwards was set apart for the mission to India. In 1843 he was stationed at Poorbunder, on the western coast, and three years later was transferred to Surat. He early acquired a scholarly knowledge of Gujarati, into which he translated the Epistle to the Romans and the prophecy of Isaiah; likewise two little volumes by Dr. Barth, entitled, *Scripture Stories of the Old and New Testament.* He also prepared a *Dictionary*, English and Gujarati, which stands now as a help to all students of that language. He wrote several hymns, three of which are included in the Gujarati *Book of Praise.* When he returned in broken health in 1876, advantage was taken of his presence to appoint him moderator of the General Assembly. He was one of the delegates at the general missionary conference in London in 1879. Montgomery died in November, 1880. (B. P.)

Moodie, William, D.D., a Scotch Presbyterian minister, who died June 11, 1811, in the fifty-third year of his age, was one of the ministers of St. Andrew's Church, Edinburgh, from 1787, and professor of Hebrew and Oriental languages in the University from 1793. He was a man of considerable literary acquirements, very popular as a preacher, and the author of several works. A volume of his *Sermons* has been published, to which is prefixed a biography of the author (Edinburgh, 1813, 8vo). See *Fasti Eccles. Scoticanæ*, i, 73.

Moody, John, D.D., a Presbyterian minister, was born in Dauphin County, Pa., July 4, 1776. After graduating from Princeton College, in 1796, he studied theology with Rev. James Snodgrass, and was licensed by the Presbytery of Carlisle in 1801. In 1803 he was ordained by the same presbytery pastor of Middle Spring, where he remained until his death, in 1857. During the latter years of his life he was unable to perform his ministerial work. He was a laborious, faithful, and successful pastor. See Alexander, *Princ. Col. 18th Cent.*

Moore, John L., D.D., a pioneer Baptist minister, was born in Lewis County, N. Y., Feb. 17, 1803. He was converted at the age of twenty-two; graduated from the Hamilton Institute in 1831; was ordained the same year at Watertown; visited and preached in several of the larger towns of Ohio, under the direction of the Home Mission Society; and in 1834 settled in Piqua, in that state, spending half his time with a new church at Troy. Next he was pastor at Dayton for two years, and then, for eight years, was in the service of the Ohio Convention, acting a part of the time as an agent of the college at Granville, now Denison University. After a short pastorate in Springfield, he devoted himself to promoting the interests of the theological seminary at Fairmount. In 1855 he became an exploring missionary in Ohio, and finally gave up public life, preaching occasionally. He died in Topeka, Kansas, Jan. 23, 1878. See Cathcart, *Baptist Encyclop.* p. 812. (J. C. S.)

Moore, Smith William, D.D., a minister of the Methodist Episcopal Church South, was born Nov. 1, 1818, in North Carolina. He was converted in 1837, and entered Randolph-Macon College in 1838, but was obliged to leave a few months before graduation. He then taught school in Tennessee for two years, preaching in the meanwhile, and joined the Tennessee Conference in 1844, when he was ordained deacon. From 1849 to 1852 he was professor in the Female Institute at Athens, Ala., when he was elected president, which position he resigned in 1853 to accept the vice-presidency of La Grange College. After a few months he resigned this position, and being transferred to Memphis Conference, became president of Bascom Female Seminary, a position he retained several years. One year he was agent of the Book and Tract Society, and at the same time one of the editors of the conference paper, *Christian Advocate.* In 1866 he was appointed president of Andrew College at Trenton, Tenn., where he continued four years. The remainder of his life was given to the itinerancy, his last appointment being Central Church, Memphis, in 1879. He died at Brownsville, Sept. 2, 1880. Dr. Moore was a polished scholar, skilled theologian, and faithful Christian. His preaching was clear, strong, instructive, and impressive. He was generous, kind, studious, prayerful, laborious, pure in heart, chaste in speech, consistent in life, catholic as well as evangelical, and profoundly earnest as a minister of the gospel. See *Minutes of Annual Conferences of the M. E. Church South*, 1880, p. 167.

Moore, Thomas Verner, D.D., a Presbyterian minister, was born in Newville, Pa., Feb. 1, 1818. He graduated from Dickinson College in 1838; became agent for the Pennsylvania Colonization Society; graduated from Princeton Theological Seminary in 1842; was ordained pastor at Carlisle the same year; was settled at Greencastle in 1845; the First Church, Richmond, Va., in 1847; editor of the *Central Presbyterian*, and pastor of First Church, Nashville, Tenn., in 1869, and died there, Aug. 5, 1871. He was moderator of the General Assembly in 1867. His chief published works are, *Commentary on Haggai, Zechariah, and Malachi* (N. Y. 1856):—*Evidences of Christianity*:—*Occasional Sermons.* His contributions to religious journals were numerous. See *Gen. Cat. of Princeton Theol. Sem.* 1881, p. 124; Nevin, *Presb. Encyclop.* s. v.

Morabites, a Mohammedan sect found chiefly in Africa. They were founded about the 8th century by Mohaidin, the last son of Hossein, who was the grandson of Mohammed. They live in sequestered places, like monks, either separately or in small communities; are very licentious in their habits, and follow many practices utterly opposed to the Koran.

Moraht, Adolph, a Lutheran theologian of Germany, was born Nov. 28, 1805, at Hamburg. He studied at Halle and Göttingen, and for nine years acted as teacher at his native place. In 1838 he was deacon at Mölln, in the duchy of Lauenburg, in 1846 pastor, and died Dec. 6, 1884. He published, *Versuch einer Methodik des Religionsunterrichtes* (2d ed. Merseburg, 1833):—*Harfenklänge, eine Sammlung christlicher Gedichte* (Lüneburg, 1840), besides a number of sermons. See Zuchold, *Bibl. Theol.* ii, 903; Koch, *Geschichte des deutschen Kirchenliedes*, vii, 296. (B. P.)

Moravia, Andrew de, a Scotch prelate, was bishop of Moray from 1224 to 1242, in which year he died. This prelate laid the foundation of that magnificent church which was dedicated to the Holy Trinity, and ordered to be the cathedral church of Moray forever. See Keith, *Scottish Bishops*, p. 138.

Moray, David, a Scotch prelate, was consecrated bishop of the see of Moray in 1299, at Avignon. He died Jan. 20, 1326. This prelate founded the Scots College at Paris in 1325. See Keith, *Scottish Bishops*, p. 140.

Moray, Gilbert, a Scotch prelate, was consecrated bishop of the see of Caithness in 1222. He died at Scrabister in 1245, after having built and consecrated the cathedral church of Caithness, at Dornoch. See Keith, *Scottish Bishops*, p. 207.

Mordvinian Version. See Russia, Versions of.

Morgan, W., D.D., a Welsh Baptist minister, was born in Pembrokeshire in 1801. He studied at Abergavenny, was ordained pastor of a small church in Holyhead, April 19, 1825, and died Sept. 15, 1872. See (Lond.) *Baptist Hand-book*, 1873, p. 267. (J. C. S.)

Mörikofer, Johann Karl, a Swiss theologian, was born at Frauenfeld, Switzerland, in 1799. In 1830 he was rector of the city-school of his birthplace, in 1853 pastor at Gottlieben, in 1870 at Winterthur, and died at Zurich, Oct. 17, 1877. He is the author of, *Die schweizerische Literatur des achtzehnten Jahrhunderts* (Leipsic, 1861):—*Bilder aus dem kirchlichen Leben der Schweiz* (1864):—*Ulrich Zwingli nach den urkundlichen Quellen* (1867-69, 2 vols.):—*Johann Jacob Breitinger* (Zurich, 1874):—*Geschichte der evangelischen Flüchtlinge in der Schweiz* (1876). See Lichtenberger, *Encyclop. des Sciences Religieuses*, s. v. (B. P.)

Morning Hymn. In the *Apostolical Constitutions* mention is made of a hymn for the morning, which is there, however, called the morning prayer. Other writers term it the hymn, the angelical hymn, and the great doxology. It ran in these words: "Glory be to God on high, on earth peace, good will towards men. We praise thee, we laud thee, we bless thee, we glorify thee, we worship thee by the great High Priest, thee the true God, the only begotten, whom no one can approach, for thy great glory. O Lord, heavenly king, God the Father Almighty: Lord God, the Father of Christ, the immaculate Lamb, who taketh away the sin of the world, receive our prayer, thou that sittest upon the cherubims. For thou only art holy, thou only, Lord

Jesus, the Christ of God, the God of every created being, and our King. By whom unto thee be glory, honor, and adoration." This hymn was used daily in the ancient morning service, and is still used in the modern Greek Church.

Morrison, JOHN HUNTER, D.D., a Presbyterian minister, was born in Wallkill Township, Orange Co., N. Y., June 29, 1806. He studied at Bloomfield Academy, N. J.; graduated from Princeton College in 1834; and from the theological seminary there in 1837; and was ordained the same year. Soon after, he sailed for India, and thenceforward his whole ministerial life was spent in the foreign missionary work, in connection with the Presbyterian Board of Foreign Missions, including two brief visits to his native land. During one of these, in 1863, he was elected moderator of the General Assembly. It was at his suggestion, while in India, that the first week of January was set apart for united prayer for the conversion of the world to Christ. He lived and labored successively at Allahabad, Agra, Sabathu, Simla, Ambala, Lahore, Rawal Pindi, Dehra Doon, and died at the last-named place, Sept. 16, 1881. Dr. Morrison was a man of rare devotion to his work. See *Necrol. Report of Princeton Theol. Sem.* 1882, p. 36.

Morse, INTREPID, D.D., a Protestant Episcopal clergyman, was rector of St. Paul's Church, in Steubenville, O., for many years, until 1865, when he removed to Gambier. He died Feb. 15, 1866. See *Prot. Episc. Almanac*, 1867, p. 101.

Morss, JAMES, D.D., a Protestant Episcopal clergyman, was born at Newburyport, Mass., Oct. 25, 1779. After acquiring the rudiments of an education at the public schools of his native town, he commenced to learn the joiner's trade; but in his seventeenth year entered Harvard College, and graduated in 1800. He taught the grammar-school in Brookline after leaving college, and began the study of theology. Soon after, he was employed as lay-reader at Cambridge, and some time later completed his theological course under bishop Bass. He was ordained deacon, July 3, 1803; became assistant to the bishop in St. Paul's Church; in November following rector; and died in that position, April 26, 1842. Among his literary remains are a number of published sermons, addresses, etc. See Sprague, *Annals of the Amer. Pulpit*, v, 492.

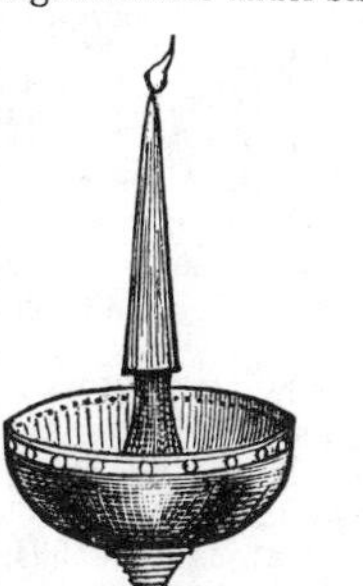

Mortar at St. Mary Magdalen College, Oxford.

Mortar, a broad bowl of brass, latten, or copper, either with a pricket for a thick lighted taper, or else filled with a mixture of perfumed wax and oil, in which a broad wick was kept burning both at festivals and funerals.

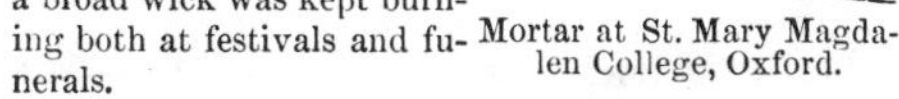

Mosche, GABRIEL CHRISTIAN BENJAMIN, a Lutheran theologian of Germany, was born at Grossen-Erich, in the principality of Schwarzburg-Sondershausen, March 28, 1723. He studied at Jena, and for some time assisted his father in the ministry. In 1748 he was preacher at Erfurt, and lecturer at the university, in 1759 superintendent at Arnstadt, in 1773 preacher at Frankfort-on-the-Main, and died Feb. 8, 1791. He published, *De Anno Sexagesimo Judæis Sacro* (Jena, 1744):—*De Summa Summi Numinis Sapientia in Dilectu Legatorum* (Erfurt, 1750):—*Commentatio de Contemplatione Mortis Atque Resurrectionis Jesu Christi Erga Hominis Amor* (ibid. 1758):—*De Reditu Christi in Vitam* (Arnstadt, 1759):—*Triplex Gloriæ Cœlestis Magnitudo* (ibid. 1768), besides a number of sermons and ascetical works. See Döring, *Die deutschen Kanzelredner des achtzehnten und neunzehnten Jahrhunderts*, s. v.; Winer, *Handbuch der theol. Lit.* i, 192; ii, 196, 291. (B. P.)

Moslems, a name derived from the Arabic verb *salama*, to be devoted to God, and applied to those who believe in the Koran, and who, in the Mohammedan sense, form the body of the faithful.

Motu Version OF THE SCRIPTURES. The Motu is a dialect spoken by the natives round Port Moresby, New Guinea, hence it is also called the *Port Moresby* or *New Guinea* dialect. The Rev. J. Chalmers translated the first three gospels, and of these the gospel of Mark has been carefully revised by the Rev. W. G. Lawes, and an edition of five hundred copies was printed at Sydney during the year 1881 by the New South Wales Auxiliary to the British and Foreign Bible Society. Mr. Lawes, who is preparing other portions for the press, says, concerning the gospel of Mark: "This is the first portion of the Scriptures translated into any language of south-east New Guinea. The Dutch missionaries at Doreby, at the extreme north-west of the island, I think, translated a portion into the language spoken there, but, with that possible exception, this is the beginning of the work of translation on New Guinea." From the report of the British and Foreign Bible Society for 1883, we learn that the gospel of Mark, which has been circulated, is more widely read than was expected. The gospels of Matthew and Luke were also revised by Mr. Lawes, and printed at Sydney in 1882, while the gospel of John, which he translated himself, was published in 1884. (B. P.)

Moulinié, CHARLES ÉTIENNE FRANÇOIS, a Swiss Protestant theologian, was born July 23, 1757. He studied at his birthplace, Geneva, and was ordained in 1781. In 1793 he was pastor at Saconnet, in 1794 at Dardagny, and from 1795 to 1829 at Geneva. He died Aug. 3, 1836. Moulinié was a prolific writer, who left seventeen volumes in manuscript to the library of the ministers' association at Geneva. Of his published works are to be mentioned, *Lait de la Parole* (1789), a catechism:—*Notice sur les Livres Apocryphes de l'Ancien Testament* (1828). See Gautier, *Notice sur la Vie et les Écrits de M. le Pasteur Moulinié*, in the *Chrétien Évangelique* of Lausanne, 1866, p. 535 sq., 648 sq.; Henri de Goltz, *Genève Religieuse au dix-neuvième Siècle*, p. 122; Lichtenberger, *Encyclop. des Sciences Religieuses*, s. v. (B. P.)

Moultan (or **Wuch** or **Ooch**) **Version** OF THE SCRIPTURES. This dialect is spoken north of Sindh, between the Indus, Chenaub, and Gharra rivers. There exists a version of the New Test. in that dialect, which was printed at Serampore in 1819. (B. P.)

Mozah is probably represented by the modern *Khurbet Beit-Mizza*, situated one mile north of Kulonigoh (*Memoirs* to the Ordnance Survey, iii, 17; comp. Conder, *Tent Work*, i, 25).

Mpongwe Version OF THE SCRIPTURES. The Mpongwe is spoken by a West-African tribe, for which various detached portions of the Scriptures have been translated by the missionaries of the American Board of Missions, and several editions of these portions of the Old and New Test. have been issued by the American Bible Society. (B. P.)

Mücke, AUGUST PHILIP, a Reformed theologian of Germany, was born May 29, 1783. In 1805 he was appointed pastor of the Reformed Church in Accum, the only Reformed congregation in Oldenburg, and celebrated his seventy-fifth anniversary in 1880. He died Feb. 13, 1882, being at the time the Nestor of the Protestant clergy of Germany. He published, *Die Dogmatik des 19. Jahrhunderts* (Gotha, 1861):—*Die heutige Unionscontroverse*, etc. (Leipsic, 1872):—*Das apostolische Glaubensbekenntniss* (Berlin, 1873). (B. P.)

Muenscher, JOSEPH, D. D., an Episcopal minister, was born at Providence, R. I., Dec. 21, 1798, of German descent. He graduated from Brown University in

1821, studied one year at Andover Theological Seminary, and was admitted to priest's orders March 13, 1825, his first parish being South Leicester, now Rochdale, Mass., where he remained until 1827, when he became rector of St. John's Church, Northampton. For two years (1831–33) he was rector of Trinity Church, Saco, Me., and then was professor of sacred literature in the Episcopal Seminary at Gambier, Ohio. From 1841 to 1854 he was rector of St. Paul's Church at Mt. Vernon, and remained at that place without parochial charge until his death, Feb. 16, 1884. Dr. Muenscher had a decided musical taste, and in 1839 published *Church Choir*, a collection of sacred music. For several years he was editor of the *Gambier Observer* and the *Western Episcopalian*, and contributed largely to theological reviews and religious periodicals. In 1865 he published a *Manual of Biblical Interpretation*, in 1866 a *Revised Version of the Book of Proverbs*, in 1870, *Orthography and Pronunciation of the English Language*. See *Necrology of Brown University*, 1883–84. (J. C. S.)

Muhlenberg, William Augustus, D.D., LL.D., a distinguished Protestant Episcopal clergyman, great-grandson of Dr. Henry Melchior, was born in Philadelphia, Sept. 16, 1796. He entered the University of Pennsylvania when but fourteen years of age, and graduated in 1814. Having pursued a course of theological study, he became a clergyman in the Episcopal Church in 1817, and for five years was assistant rector of Christ Church, Philadelphia, being associated with bishop White. In 1821 he became rector of St. James' Church in Lancaster; in 1828, principal of St. Paul's College in Flushing, L. I.; in 1846, rector of the Church of the Holy Communion, in the city of New York; in 1858, superintendent and pastor of St. Luke's Hospital, New York (which he was largely instrumental in founding, as also the church village of St. Johnland, on Long Island), holding this office until his death, April 8, 1877. In 1824 there appeared in the *Episcopal Recorder*, of Philadelphia, his admirable hymn, entitled, "I would not live alway," which has been incorporated into nearly every standard church hymn-book. Many years afterwards, when he was the editor of the *Evangelical Catholic*, Dr. Muhlenberg explained the circumstances of its history. He was the author of, *Church Poetry* (1823):—*Music of the Church* (1852):—*The People's Psalter* (1858). His life was devoted to public labors of Christian evangelism and philanthropy. See his *Life and Work*, by Anne Ayres (N. Y. 1880). (J. C. S.)

Mühlhäusser, Carl August, a Protestant theologian of Germany, was born in 1825, at Kleinkems, in Baden. He studied at Heidelberg, was for some time vicar and deacon at Carlsruhe, and in 1852 pastor at Sulzfeld. In 1857 he was called as member of the ecclesiastical council to Heidelberg, but retired in 1864, when the liberal party had obtained its influence upon ecclesiastical affairs. He went as pastor to Wilferdingen, where he died Jan. 20, 1881. Mühlhäusser seemed to have been predestinated to be the leader of the Christian party of his country. Everywhere his counsel was asked for, and his work was appreciated by the Bonn University, which honored him with the doctorate of divinity. He published, *Die christliche Weltanschauung* (Heilbronn, 1876): *Christenthum und die Presse* (ibid. eod.):—he also edited R. Rothe's *Erste Brief Johannis praktisch erklärt* (Wittenberg, 1878). (B. P.)

Muir, James, D.D., a Presbyterian minister, was born at Cumnock, Scotland, April 12, 1757. After the usual course of classical and philosophical studies at the University of Glasgow, at which he graduated in 1776, he prosecuted his theological studies at Edinburgh. In 1781 he was ordained an evangelist and sent to Bermuda, in 1785 joined the New Brunswick Presbytery, and in 1789 became pastor of the Presbyterian Church in Alexandria, Va., where he died, Aug. 8, 1820. See Sprague, *Annals of the Amer. Pulpit*, iii, 516.

Muir, John, a famous Sanscrit scholar, was born at Glasgow in 1810. He studied at his native place, and in 1828 went to Bengal in the service of the East India Company, where he interested himself in the moral and religious welfare of the natives, and for this purpose published, among other works, in 1839, *A Sketch of the Argument for Christianity against Hindûism*, and *Examination of Religions*. In 1853 he returned to his native country. He died March 8, 1882, at Edinburgh. Muir's main work is *Original Sanscrit Texts, on the Origin and History of the People of India, their Religion and Institutions* (Lond. 1868–73, 5 vols.), which is indispensable for the student of ancient Hindû life and thought, dealing principally, as it does, with the Vedic period of Indian literature. The first volume discusses the legendary accounts of the origin of the caste; the second, the primitive home of the Hindûs; the third, the opinions of Hindû writers on the Vedas; the fourth, the contrast between Vedic and later Hindû theology; and the fifth, the cosmological and mythological conceptions of the Indians in the Vedic age. (B. P.)

Muirhead, Andrew, a Scotch prelate, was first rector of Codzow, and next preferred to the see of Glasgow in 1455. He was one of the commissioners who went to England in 1462, in order to negotiate a truce between the two nations. He died Nov. 20, 1473. This prelate founded the vicars of the choir at Glasgow, and beautified the cathedral. He also established a hospital, which he dedicated to St. Nicholas. See Keith, *Scottish Bishops*, p. 252.

Mullens, Joseph, D.D., an English Congregational minister, was born in London, Sept. 2, 1820. He gave his heart to the Saviour at the age of fifteen, and joined the Church a year later. He was educated at Coward College, and in 1841 graduated B.A. from the University of London. In 1842 he was accepted for service by the London Missionary Society. He then studied for a time in Edinburgh University. He was ordained Sept. 5, 1843, and sailed for India on the 9th. On his arrival at Calcutta he entered the institution at Bhowanipore, and in 1846 became pastor of the native church there, in which office he continued for twenty years. He rendered important service to the society by the collection of carefully prepared statistics. In 1866 he returned to England to assist Dr. Tidman in the foreign secretaryship of the society. This office he held till his death. In 1870 he visited America to attend the annual meeting of the American Board of Foreign Missions. In 1873 he visited Madagascar in the interest of the mission there. While making a journey to the heart of Africa to establish the mission at Tanyanyika he died, July 10, 1878. Dr. Mullens is the author of, *Twelve Months in Madagascar* (Lond. 1873):—*Vedantism, Brahmanism, and Christianity*:—*Religious Aspects of Hindûism*:—*Missions in India*, and several other works on missionary subjects. See (Lond.) *Cong. Yearbook*, 1880, p. 342.

Müller, Alexander, a Roman Catholic canonist of Germany, who was born at Zell in 1780, and died at Mayence in 1844, is the author of, *Encyklopädisches Handbuch des gesammten in Deutschland Kirchenrechts* (Erfurt, 1829–32, 2 vols.):—*Ueber die Nothwendigkeit der Reorganisation des Corpus Evangelicum* (Leipsic, 1830):—*Das Christenthum nach seiner Pflanzung und Ausbreitung*, etc. (1831):—*Hauptcharakter und Grundfehler des römischen Katholicismus* (eod.):—*Febronius der Neue* (1838):—*Der Erzbischof von Köln in Opposition mit dem preussischen Staatsoberhaupte*, etc. (eod. 2 vols.). See Zuchold, *Bibl. Theol.* i, 335; ii, 909; Winer, *Handbuch der theol. Lit.* i, 581; ii, 5, 11. (B. P.)

Müller, Christian Gottfried, a Lutheran theologian of Germany, was born Dec. 28, 1747, at Zöblitz, near Marienburg. In 1780 he was rector at Schleitz, in 1786 at Naumburg, in 1788 at Zeitz, and died Aug.

10, 1819, leaving, *De Usu Versionis Vulgatæ* (Schleitz, 1782-85):—*Formula Augustanæ Confess.* (Leipsic, 1808):—*Reformationsgeschichte der Stadt Zeitz* (1817):—*Observatt. in 5 Loca Cypriani* (Gera, 1777). See Winer, *Handbuch der theol. Lit.* i, 109, 320, 802, 906; Fürst, *Bibl. Jud.* ii, 405. (B. P.)

Müller, Johann Georg (1), a Roman Catholic prelate of Germany, was born at Coblentz, Oct. 15, 1798. He studied at different universities, took holy orders in 1821, and received the degree of doctor of theology in 1827. In the same year he was professor of Church history and canon law at the clerical seminary in Treves, in 1847 was elected bishop of Münster, and died in 1870. He published, *Ueber die Aechtheit der zwei ersten Kapitel des Evangeliums nach Matthäus* (Treves, 1830):—*Die bildlichen Darstellungen im Sanctuarium der christlichen Kirchen* (ibid. 1835). See Winer, *Handbuch der theol. Lit.* i, 86, 636; Zuchold, *Bibl. Theol.* ii, 916. (B. P.)

Müller, Johann Georg (2), a Swiss theologian, was born at Basle in 1800, and died there in 1875, doctor and professor of theology. He published, *Blicke in die Bibel*, etc. (Winterthur, 1828-30; new ed. 1840):—*Ueber die Texteskritik der Schriften des Juden Philo* (Basle, 1839):—*Des Juden Philo Buch von der Weltschöpfung* (Berlin, 1841):—the art. *Philo* in the first edition of Herzog's *Real-Encyklop.*:—*Die messianischen Erwartungen des Juden Philo* (Basle, 1870):—*Erklärung des Barnabasbriefes* (Leipsic, 1869). After his death Riggenbach and Orelli published *Des Flavius Josephus Schrift gegen den Apion. Text und Erklärung* (Basle, 1877). See Zuchold, *Bibl. Theol.* ii, 916; Fürst, *Bibl. Jud.* ii, 406. (B. P.)

Müller, Johann Tobias Immanuel, a Lutheran theologian of Germany, was born in 1804, and died Aug. 19, 1884, at Fürth, dean and Church counsellor. He edited *Veit Dietrich's Hauspostille* (Nördlingen, 1845), and is best known by his edition of *Das evangelische Konkordienbuch*, etc. (Stuttgart, 1860 and often). (B. P.)

Müller, Julius, a Protestant theologian of Germany, and brother of Karl Ottfried (q. v.), was born at Brieg, in Silesia, April 10, 1801. He studied jurisprudence at Breslau and Göttingen, according to the wish of his father, and at both universities Müller's dissertations gained prizes, so that in 1871 the faculty at Göttingen made him doctor of laws. But the ideal of a higher life was presenting itself to his mind, and he betook himself to the study of theology at Göttingen. He soon felt that the then Göttingen theology could not satisfy him, and so returned to Breslau, in 1822, to continue his theological studies. While Tholuck was on a visit to Breslau, Müller, at the suggestion of a friend, visited him. He afterwards carried on a correspondence with Tholuck, whose personality, rather than theology, influenced him. In the spring of 1823, Müller, by the urgent advice of Tholuck, went to Berlin, where Strauss, Neander, and Tholuck, but not Schliermacher, met the demands of his heart and mind. In 1825 he was called to the pastorate of Schönbrunn and Rosen, near Strehlen. Here he wrote his *Zur Beurtheilung der Schrift: die katholische Kirche Schlesiens* (Breslau, 1827). A second edition was soon called for. Soon after, he came into conflict with the ecclesiastical authorities, by refusing to introduce the new liturgy, and in May, 1830, announced this as his final decision to the "consistorium." His official relations to the Church were thus endangered; but he was happily delivered from the inconvenience of a removal from his pastorate by a call, in 1831, to Göttingen, as university-preacher, with the promise of a professorship as soon as he should publish a learned book. In 1832 he commenced his academical career by publishing *Lutheri de Prædestinatione et Libero Arbitrio Doctrina*. He soon was made professor. In 1834 an urgent call as professor of systematic theology to Marburg could not be refused, and when Müller

preached his last sermon in Göttingen (March, 1835), Lücke, in behalf of the university, presented him with the degree of doctor of divinity. The contributions which Müller made to the *Studien und Kritiken* after 1833 prepared the way for the work which has immortalized his name, *Die christliche Lehre von der Sünde* (Engl. transl. *The Christian Doctrine of Sin*, Edinburgh, 1877, 2 vols.), of which several editions have been published. In 1839 Müller accepted a call to Halle, where, with Tholuck, he became the chief centre of attraction to the students. In 1850 he founded, in connection with Neander and Nitzsch, the *Deutsche Zeitschrift für christl. Wissenschaft und christliches Leben*, to which he contributed many valuable articles, which, for the most part, have appeared in his *Dogmatische Abhandlungen* (Bremen, 1870). In the summer of 1878 he resigned his professorship, and died Sept. 27 of the same year. A provision of his will stipulated that all his manuscripts should be destroyed. His works, besides those already mentioned, are *De Miraculorum Jesu Christi Natura et Necessitate* (Marburg, 1839):—*Lutheri et Calvini Sententiæ de Sacra Cœna Inter se Comparatæ* (Halle, 1853):—*Die evangelische Union, ihr Wesen und göttliches Recht* (Berlin, 1854), besides several volumes of sermons. See Schulze, *Dr. Julius Müller* (Bremen, 1879); *Zum Gedächtniss an Dr. Julius Müller* (ibid. 1878); Kähler, *Dr. Julius Müller, der hallesche Dogmatiker* (Halle, 1878); Plitt-Herzog, *Real-Encyklop.* s. v.; Schwarz, *Zur Geschichte der neuesten Theologie* (3d ed.), p. 363 sq.; Lichtenberger, *Encyclop. des Sciences Religieuses*, s. v.; Zuchold, *Bibl. Theol.* ii, 917. (B. P.)

Münch, Ernst Hermann Joseph von, a distinguished Roman Catholic historian of Germany, was born at Rheinfelden, Oct. 25, 1798. He studied at Freiburg, was in 1819 teacher at Aarau, in 1824 professor at Freiburg, in 1828 professor of Church history and canon law at Liege. In 1831 he accepted a call to Stuttgart as librarian to the king, and died June 9, 1841. He published, *Die Heerzüge des christlichen Europa wider die Osmanen* (Basle, 1822-26, 5 vols.):—*Franz von Sickingen's Thaten* (Stuttgart, 1827-29, 3 vols.):—*Sammlung aller älteren und neueren Konkordate* (1830-31, 2 vols.):—*Geschichte des Mönchthums* (1828, 2 vols.):—*Allgemeine Geschichte der katholischen Kirche* (1838):—*Römische Zustände und katholische Kirchenfragen* (eod.):—*Denkwürdigkeiten zur politischen Reformations- und Sittengeschichte*, etc. (1839):—*Allgemeine Geschichte der neuesten Zeit* (1833-35, 6 vols.). See Winer, *Handbuch der theol. Lit.* i, 696, 701, 747; Zuchold, *Bibl. Theol.* ii, 920; especially the author's *Erinnerungen und Studien aus den ersten 37 Jahren eines deutschen Gelehrten* (Carlsruhe, 1836-38, 3 vols.). (B. P.)

München, Nicolaus, a Roman Catholic canonist, who died at Cologne, Jan. 29, 1881, doctor of theology and cathedral-provost, is the author of, *Ueber die Bestrafung der Geistlichen nach dem Entwurfe des Strafgesetzbuches für Preussen* (Cologne, 1848):—*Die Amtsentfernung der Geistlichen* (ibid. eod.):—*Das kanonische Gerichtsverfahren und Strafrecht* (2d ed. 1873, 2 vols.). (B. P.)

Münchmeyer, August Friedrich Otto, a Lutheran theologian of Germany, was born in 1807. He studied at Göttingen and Berlin, was pastor at Katlenburg, in Hanover, and finally at Buer, near Osnabrück. He died Nov. 7, 1882. Münchmeyer belonged to the orthodox party in the Lutheran Church, and published, *Gedenkbuch für Konfirmanden* (12th ed. 1882):—*Das Amt des Neuen Testaments nach des Lehre der Schrift und der Bekenntnisse* (Osterode, 1853):—*Das Dogma von der sichtbaren und unsichtbaren Kirche* (Hanover, 1854):—*Zur Kirchenregimentsfrage* (ibid. 1862):—*Huschke und Mejer* (1864):—*Die Offenbarung St. Johannis* (1870):—*Harfenklänge* (1855). See Zuchold, *Bibl. Theol.* ii, 921. (B. P.)

Munier, David, a Protestant theologian of Geneva,

was born in 1798. He studied at his birthplace, and was admitted to the ministry in 1819 on presenting *De Evangelio Primitivo.* In the same year he went to Havre and then to Paris. In the latter place he made the acquaintance of Cousin, and Jean Monod. In 1825 Munier was called to Chêne, in the neighborhood of Geneva, and in 1826 he commenced his lectures on the New Test. at the theological faculty at Geneva, where he was rector from 1832 to 1837. In 1853 he founded *The Société des Protestants*, and took a lively interest in all matters pertaining to the welfare of the Church. His public life has been divided into three periods: from 1825 to 1847 a partisan in the Church and the academy; from 1847 to 1862 a religious conciliator; from 1862 to 1872 a laborious veteran. He died Oct. 9, 1872. His discourses were on *The Parables* (1838):—*The Miracles* (1841):—*The Reading of the Bible* (1850):—*The Divinity of Christianity in History* (1853), etc. See De la Rive, in the *Journal de Genève;* Lichtenberger, *Encyclop. des Sciences Religieuses*, s. v. (B. P.)

Murch, WILLIAM HARRIS, D.D., an English Baptist minister, was born at Honiton, Devon, May 17, 1784. He was baptized in May, 1802, by Rev. Dr. Rippon, and united with the Carter Lane Church, London. Subsequently he became assistant pastor with the celebrated John Foster, and then sole pastor of the Church at Sheppard's Barton, Frome. In 1827 he was appointed president and theological tutor at Stepney College, London. In 1844 he resigned his post on account of ill-health, and a year afterwards became pastor of the Church in Rickmansworth, Herts, where he remained till 1851. After preaching in and around London for a few years he removed, in 1856, to Bath, where he died, July 12, 1859. See (Lond.) *Baptist Hand-book*, 1861, p. 100. (J. C. S.)

Murray, Andrew, a Scotch prelate, was elected bishop of the see of Ross in 1213, but refused to be consecrated. See Keith, *Scottish Bishops*, p. 185.

Murray, George, D.D., a bishop of the Church of England, the second son of lord George Murray, bishop of St. David's, was born in 1784. He was educated at Christ Church, Oxford, graduating B.A. in 1806. In 1814 he was consecrated bishop of Sodor and Man, and in 1827 was transferred to the diocese of Rochester, which was then but a small bishopric, comprising ninety-six benefices; but under the administration of bishop Murray the number was augmented to five hundred and sixty-four. He died Feb. 16, 1860, being at the time the senior of the English bishops. He was a churchman of the old school, and held himself aloof from extremists. See *Amer. Quar. Church Rev.* 1860, p. 184.

Musgrave, GEORGE WASHINGTON, D.D., LL.D., an eminent Presbyterian minister, was born in Philadelphia, Oct. 19, 1804. He studied at the classical academy of the Rev. Dr. Wylie, and although he did not enter college on account of ill-health, he pursued his studies privately under the tuition of Rev. Dr. Archibald Green, and finally entered Princeton Theological Seminary in 1826, and spent nearly two years there. In 1828 he was licensed by the Third Presbytery of Baltimore, and in 1830 was ordained pastor of the Third Presbyterian Church of that city. He continued there twenty-two years, laboring with great success. In 1836 he was chosen a director of Princeton Theological Seminary, and continued in that relation until the time of his death. He was also a trustee of Princeton College. Having received the appointment of corresponding secretary of the Presbyterian Board of Publication, he resigned his pastoral charge and removed to Philadelphia. He was also corresponding secretary of the Board of Domestic Missions. He finally accepted an invitation to the pastorate of the North Tenth Street Church, Philadelphia, where he labored until 1868. Having resigned the post of corresponding secretary of Domestic Missions, he was reappointed, and continued until the board was removed to New York. He was elected moderator of the Old School General Assembly in the same year. Dr. Musgrave took a prominent part in the convention which met in Philadelphia in 1867, composed of delegates from both branches of the Presbyterian Church, the object of which was to promote the reunion of the two. He was a delegate to the First General Council of the Presbyterian Church in Edinburgh in 1879. He was also president of the Presbyterian Historical Society. Dr. Musgrave was a man of warm attachments and strong convictions, honest in his views, and fearless in maintaining them. He died at Philadelphia, Aug. 24, 1882. See *Necrol. Report of Princeton Theol. Sem.* 1883, p. 22. (W. P. S.)

Muskokee (or Creek) Version OF THE SCRIPTURES. The Muskokee is spoken by the Creek Indians, who possess in their vernacular the gospels of Matthew and John, the epistles of John, James, Titus, and Ephesians—all published since 1868 by the American Bible Society. In 1879 the printing of the Acts of the Apostles was commenced at the New York Bible House. (B. P.)

Mussard, PIERRE, a French Protestant theologian, was born at Geneva in 1627, where he also studied theology. In 1654 he was ordained, was in 1656 minister at Lyons, and attended the national synod at Loudun (1659-1660). In 1669 he was president of the provincial synod held at Is-sur-Thil, and in 1675 he accepted a call as pastor of the French Church at London. He died in 1686. Besides two volumes of sermons and other minor works, he published *Les Conformités des Cérémonies Modernes* (Leyden, 1667; new ed. Amsterdam, 1744; a German transl. was published at Leipsic, 1695). See Winer, *Handbuch der theol. Lit.* i, 624; Lichtenberger, *Encyclop. des Sciences Religieuses*, s. v. (B. P.)

Mussulman-Bengali Version. See BENGALI VERSION.

Mutilation OF SELF. See BODY, MUTILATION OF THE.

Muurling, WILLEM, a Dutch theologian, who died at the Hague, Dec. 9, 1882, doctor of theology, was professor of theology at Groningen, and one of the founders of the Groningen school. In later years he became the leader of the so-called liberal theologians. He published, besides, a work on *Practical Theology* (2d ed. 1860, 2 vols.):—*Oratio de Wesseli Ganfortii* (Amsterdam, 1840), and a series of essays in the Groningen periodical *Waarheid en Liefde.* (B. P.)

Muzel, PHILIPP LUDWIG, a Reformed theologian of Germany, was born Nov. 24, 1756, at Prenzlau, and died Dec. 31, 1831, doctor and professor of theology, member of consistory, superintendent and pastor of the Reformed Church at Frankfort-on-the-Oder. He published, *Ueber die Verpflichtung auf die symbolischen Bücher der evangelischen Kirche* (Berlin, 1831):—*Vorlesungen über Christenthum und Deismus* (Dantzic, 1794):—*Christophilos* (Berlin, 1830):—*Ueber den Glauben an die im Neuen Testament erzählten Wunder* (Elberfeld, 1815). See Winer, *Handbuch der theol. Lit.* i, 336, 385, 393, 463; ii, 38; Zuchold, *Bibl. Theol.* ii, 923 sq. (B. P.)

Myrkheim, in Norse mythology, is one of the nine worlds designed as a dwelling-place of the dwarfs.

Myslenta, CŒLESTIN, a Lutheran theologian of Germany, was born March 27, 1588. He studied at different universities, took his degree as doctor of divinity at Giessen in 1619, was professor of theology at Königsberg in the same year, and died April 30, 1653. He wrote, *De Sacrificiis Veteris Testamenti:—De Mysterio Trinitatis:—De Æterna Divinitate Christi:—De Christi ad Inferos Descensu Vero et Reali:—Duæ Quæstiones de Fide:—De Justificatione Hominis Peccatoris Coram Deo:—De Sacramento Baptismi:—De Ecclesia Dei:—De Divina Nostri Prædestinatione ad Vitam Æternam.* See Witte, *Memoriæ Theologorum;* Arnold, *Historie der königsbergischen Universität;* Jöcher, *Allgemeines Gelehrten-Lexikon*, s. v. (B. P.)

N.

Naamah. *Na'aneh*, the latest proposed representative of this place, is merely described in the *Memoirs* accompanying the Ordnance Survey (ii, 408) as "a small mud village on low ground."

Näbe, Friedrich August Adolph, a Lutheran theologian of Germany, was born in 1800 at Döbris, near Zeitz. In 1824 he was catechist at St. Peter's, in Leipsic, and private lecturer there; in 1833 deacon at Königstein, and died in 1855. He published, *Novum Testamentum Græc.* etc. (Leipsic, 1831):—*Compendium Historiæ Ecclesiasticæ* (1832):—*Brevis in Nov. Test. Commentarius* (1837):—*Stimmen der Andacht*, etc. (1844). Zuchold, *Bibl. Theol.* ii, 925; Winer, *Handbuch der theol. Lit.* i, 46, 302, 493, 538. (B. P.)

Nachtigal, Johann Karl Christoph, a Protestant theologian of Germany, was born at Halberstadt, Feb. 25, 1753. He studied at Halle, and in 1773 accepted a call as teacher at the cathedral school of his native place. In 1808 he was made a doctor of theology, in 1812 general superintendent, and died June 21, 1819. He is the author of, *Chrestomathia Hebraica*, etc. (Halle, 1783):—*Die Gesänge David's* (Leipsic, 1796):—*Exegetisches Handbuch des Alten Testaments* (1797-1800, 9 parts):—*Koheleth* (1798-1799, 2 vols.). See Winer, *Handbuch der theol. Lit.* i, 208, 213; Fürst, *Bibl. Jud.* iii, 9; Döring, *Die gelehrten Theologen Deutschlands*, s. v. (B. P.)

Nadab, the ecclesiastical head of the Mohammedans in Persia. His office corresponds to that of the *Mufti* (q. v.) in Turkey, but with this difference, that the *nadab* can divest himself of his spiritual functions, which the mufti cannot do.

Nadhamians, a heretical Mohammedan sect, which maintained that God could do evil, but that he never does it, lest he should appear a wicked and imperfect being.

Nagas, a class of Hindû mendicant monks who travel about in a nude state, but armed with warlike weapons. They are not limited to one sect, there being *Vaishnava* and *Saiva* Nagas. The *Sikh* Nagas, however, differ from those of the other sects by abstaining from the use of arms, and following a retired and religious life.

Nagel, Johann Andreas Michael, a Lutheran theologian of Germany, was born Sept. 29, 1710, at Sulzbach, Bavaria. He studied at Altdorf, Jena, and Leipsic, commenced his academical career at Altdorf in 1737, was in 1740 professor, and died Sept. 29, 1788. He wrote, *De Modo Disputandi Doctorum Judæorum*, etc. (Altdorf, 1737):—*De Lingua Aramæa* (1739):—*Conjugationes Aramææ*, etc. (eod.):—*De Lingua Orbis Babylonici* (1740):—*Observationes in Genes. i*, 1 (1741):—*In Genes. i*, 2 (1742):—*De Ludis Sæcularibus Romanorum*, etc. (1743):—*De Tribus Codicibus Manuscriptis Ebraicis* (1749):—*De Stilo Mosis* (1755):—*Diss. ad Genes. xix*, 26 (eod.):—*Ad Genes. xlix*, 24 (1756):—*Ad Amos iii*, 11 (1757):—*Ad Malach. ii*, 15 sq. (1765):—*Ad 1 Reg. xx*, 14 (1766):—*Ad Nehem. viii*, 8 (1772), etc. See Döring, *Die gelehrten Theologen Deutschlands*, s. v. (where 149 titles of his writings are given); Fürst, *Bibl. Jud.* iii, 13 sq.; Winer, *Handbuch der theol. Lit.* i, 70, 96, 144. (B. P.)

Nagel, Leopold Julius, a Lutheran theologian of Germany, was born in 1809 at Stecklin, Pomerania. He studied at Halle and Berlin, was preacher at Kolzow, and afterwards military preacher at Stargard. In 1848 he resigned his office and joined the separate Lutherans (q. v.). In 1853 he was called to Breslau, the main seat of the independent Lutherans, and died Jan. 17, 1884. He published, *Die Errettung der evangelisch-lutherischen Kirche in Preussen* (2d ed. Erlangen, 1868):—*Die Kämpfe der evangelisch-lutherischen Kirche in Preussen* (Stuttgart, 1869). (B. P.)

Nägelsbach, Carl Wilhelm Eduard, a Lutheran theologian of Germany, who died Feb. 9, 1880, at Gunzenhausen, Bavaria, doctor of theology, is the author of, *Der Prophet Jeremias und Babylon* (Erlangen, 1850):—*Was ist christlich?* (Nuremberg, 1852):—*Der Gottmensch, die Grundidee der Offenbarung* (1853):—*Der Prophet Jeremia* (Bielefeld, 1868):—*Der Prophet Iesaja* (1877), the last two works for Lange's *Bibelwerk*:—*Hebräische Grammatik* (4th ed. 1880):—*Gedanken über die Wiedergeburt* (1871). (B. P.)

Nagle, Nano, foundress of the Presentation order, was born at Ballygriffin, on the banks of the Blackwater, Ireland, in 1728. She was educated in Paris, and while in that city, in 1750, resolved to devote herself to the poor children of her native country. She privately opened schools, first in Dublin and then at Cork. She afterwards assumed the habit of the Ursulines; but since that order undertakes principally the education of the children of the wealthier classes, Miss Nagle left them, and recruited new auxiliaries, who became the root of a new order which was approved after her death by pope Pius VI, in 1791. She also established an asylum for aged females, and the splendid building in the neighborhood of the South Presentation Convent, Cork, is the result of her work. There were in 1873 fifty convents of the Presentation order in Ireland. Miss Nagle died April 26, 1784. See (N. Y.) *Cath. Almanac*, 1874, p. 83; De Courcy and Shea, *Hist. of the Cath. Church in the U. S.* p. 368; *Life of Miss Nano Nagle*, by the late Rev. Dr. Coppinger (Dublin, 1843); *Dublin Review*, 1844, p. 363.

Naglfar, in Norse mythology, is the greatest ship of the world, built out of the nails of the dead, and designed to bring the inhabitants of Muspelheim to combat against the Asas, when Ragnarokr, the destruction of the world, begins.

Nahalal. *Malul*, the site proposed by some for this place, is described in the *Memoirs* accompanying the Ordnance Survey (i, 274) as "a mud village on a hill, with open ground on the west, where stands the prominent ruin Kusr ez-Zîr."

Nain. *Nein*, the present representative of this place, so interesting in New-Test. history, is thus described in the *Memoirs* to the Ordnance Survey (ii, 86):

> "This little village stands on a small plateau at the foot of Jebel ed-Duhy, in a position elevated above the plain. It is of stone and mud, with a little mosque called Mukam Sidna Aisa on the north. There are numerous traces of ruins, extending beyond the boundary of the modern hamlet to the north, showing the place to have been once larger; but these ruins have a modern appearance. There is a small spring north of the village; a second, Aîn el-Baz, exists on the west, and beside it are rock-cut tombs, much defaced, and a tree." (See illustration on following page.)

Nakib, the chief of the Emirs (q. v.) among the Turkish Mohammedans, who is held in great respect as being the head of the descendants of the prophet, and has the power of life and death over the other emirs.

Nama Version of the Scriptures. The Nama is spoken in Namaqualand (q. v.). In 1815 the Rev. C. Albrecht commenced a translation of the gospel of Matthew into the Nama, but it does not appear that he completed the version. Ten years subsequently a translation of the gospels was effected by the Rev. Schmelen, of the London Missionary Society, which was printed at Cape Town at the expense of the British and Foreign Bible Society. In 1846 the gospel of Luke was printed, having been retranslated by Mr. Knudsen, a Rhenish missionary. These two translations differed from each other chiefly in this, that in the former no signs whatever are used to represent the various clicks which occur

Present Appearance of Nain. (From Thomson's *Central Palestine and Phœnicia.*)

so frequently in the language, while in the latter this important omission is supplied. A new effort towards a translation was again made by a missionary of the Rhenish Society, the Rev. G. Krönlein. The British and Foreign Bible Society having consented to meet the expense of printing an edition of the New Test., the translator went to Europe for the purpose of carrying the work through the press, which was completed in 1866. In addition to the New Test., Mr. Krönlein translated the Psalms, which were printed during the year 1872. On Oct. 25, 1881, Mr. Krönlein completed the translation of the Old Test., early portions of the same having been begun on May 23, 1873. The translator is now revising into one harmonious whole the entire books of the Old Test. See *Bible of Every Land*, p. 430.

For the language, see Tindall, *Grammar of Namaque Hottentot;* Wallmann, *Die Formenlehre der Namaqua Sprache* (1857); Hahn, *Die Sprache der Nama* (1870). (B. P.)

Namazi, the five prayers which the Mohammedans repeat regularly every twenty-four hours. Tradition says that the prophet was commanded by God to impose upon his disciples the daily obligation of fifty prayers. By the advice of Moses he solicited and obtained permission to reduce them to five, which are indispensable. The times of prayer are, 1. Daybreak; 2. Noon; 3. Afternoon; 4. Evening; and 5. The first watch of the night. On Friday (their Sabbath) a sixth prayer is added, to be repeated between daybreak and noon. If the prayers are not repeated at the prescribed hours they are useless. The arrival of each of the hours of prayer is publicly announced by the Muezzin (q. v.).

Nasi, the name given by the Jews to the president of the great Sanhedrim, who was held in high respect by the court. Moses is said by the rabbins to have been the first to fill the office. Till the captivity the sovereign or chief ruler acted as *Nasi*, but after that time the two offices became entirely distinct, the right of holding the office of *Nasi* belonging to the descendants of Hillel.

Nasr was one of the five gods of the ancient Arabians, mentioned in the Koran. He was the supreme deity of the Arabs of Yemen, and, as the name signifies an eagle, he may have been the sun-god.

Nassau, Charles William, D.D., a Presbyterian minister, was born in Philadelphia, April 12, 1804. His early education was received in that city and at the academy of Joseph P. Engles. He graduated from the University of Pennsylvania, July 6, 1821, and spent the following year in studying Hebrew under Dr. Banks. In November, 1822, he entered Princeton Seminary, but ill-health caused him to leave in one year. He was licensed by the Presbytery of Philadelphia, April 23, 1824; was stated supply at Norristown, Norriton, and Providence from April 23, 1825, until he was ordained by the same body, Nov. 16 following. He had charge of a school for boys at Montgomery Square, Pa., and was professor of Latin and Greek in Lafayette College. During the eight years spent here he supplied the Durham Church. He was president of Lafayette College for one year, and was proprietor and principal of a female seminary at Lawrenceville, N. J., for twenty-four years. He died Aug. 6, 1878. See *Necrol. Report of Princeton Theol. Sem.* 1879, p. 21.

Nast, Johann, a Lutheran theologian of Germany,

was born Nov. 17, 1722, at Leonberg, Würtemberg. For some time he acted as professor at the gymnasium in Stuttgart, in 1789 he was pastor at Plochingen, and died Dec. 24, 1807. He is the author of, *Historisch-critische Nachricht von den sechs ersten teutschen Bibelausgaben*, etc. (Stuttgart, 1767): — *Litterarische Nachricht von der hochteutschen Bibelübersetzung*, etc. See Winer, *Handbuch der theol. Lit.* i, 172; Zuchold, *Bibl. Theol.* ii, 929. (B. P.)

Natālēs Episcopātus. See NATAL DAYS.

Natigay, a household god of the Mongolian Tartars, is the guardian of families, and presides over the products of the earth. Every house has an image of Natigay, with his wife and children; the former is placed at his left, and the latter in front of him. No one presumes to eat at dinner till Natigay and his family are first served. The entertainment consists in giving the mouths of the images a thorough greasing, after which the fragments are thrown out of doors, for the accommodation of some unknown spirits.

Nativitarians, a name given by Danæus to a heretical sect of the 4th century, who denied the eternal generation of the son of God, maintaining that he was eternal as God, but not as the son of God.

Nativity, CHURCH OF THE, *at Bethlehem*. Of this antique memorial of our Saviour's birth we extract a general account from one of the latest authorities (Conder, *Tent Work*, i, 282 sq.):

"The tradition which indicates the grotto in the old basilica at Bethlehem as the site of the stable where Christ was born, is the most venerable of its kind in existence, the place being noticed by Justin Martyr in the 2d century. It is almost the only site which we can trace earlier than the time of Constantine, and the tradition seems to me credible, because, throughout this part of Palestine, there are innumerable instances of stables cut in rock, resembling the Bethlehem grotto. Such stables I have planned and measured at Tekoa, 'Aziz, and other places south of Bethlehem, and the mangers existing in them leave no doubt as to their use and character.

"The credibility of this tradition thus appears to be far greater than that attaching to the later discoveries, by which the enthusiastic Helena and the politic Constantine settled the scenes of other Christian events; and the rude grotto with its rocky manger may, it seems to me, be accepted even by the most sceptical of modern explorers.

"The Church of the Virgin stands inside a fortress monastery, in which Latin, Greek, and Armenian monks find a common retreat. The basilica was erected, according to contemporary evidence, by order of Constantine, and is thus the oldest church in Palestine, and perhaps in the world. It has escaped destruction on every occasion when other churches in Palestine were overthrown, and the greater part of the work is stated, by competent authority, to be of the original design. In the 11th century, when the mad Caliph Hakim destroyed the Holy Sepulchre churches, the Bethlehem basilica was spared; in 1099 the Crusaders sent a detachment of troops to protect it, and it thus again escaped, nor was it destroyed in the 13th century, although threatened by the Moslems. In this basilica, therefore, we have the only undisputed erection of the time of Constantine in Palestine, and its value cannot be overrated.

"Architectural authorities are of opinion that our information as to the progress of Byzantine art in the East is still very imperfect. M. de Vogüé has done much to elucidate the subject, in his work on the great buildings of northern Syria, many of which are dated with exactitude. In Palestine we have two valuable examples, one of 4th century, and one of 6th century architecture—the basilica at Bethlehem, and Justinian's fortress on Gerizim, with which we may compare ruins of unknown date; and in the first we find M. de Vogüé's opinion confirmed, with respect to the slowness with which Byzantine art developed in style in the East, in comparison with the more rapid progress of the Western Romanesque.

"The basilica is, moreover, interesting because its general plan resembles, very closely, the description given by Eusebius of Constantine's buildings over the Holy Sepulchre at Jerusalem. On the west was an atrium or outer court, parts of the outer walls of which and shafts of its columns still remain. A narrow vestibule or narthex, entered by a door scarcely four feet high, leads into the basilica itself, which consists of a nave and four aisles, with four rows of eleven columns each, a total breadth of about thirty yards, and a length about equal.

"The aisles have flat roofs, above the pillars, which are nineteen feet high, but the nave has a clerestory, with walls some thirty feet high above the capitals, and a pointed roof. A wall has been built across the east end of the basilica, separating off the chancel, which has three apses, north, south, and east, and which forms the Greek church. Beneath the chancel is the grotto of the Nativity. North of the basilica is the more modern Latin chapel of St. Catherine, from which a staircase leads down to vaults communicating with the grotto.

"The pillar shafts are monoliths of red and white marble, painted with figures of saints, now dim with age, and scrawled over with the crests and titles of knightly pilgrims of the Crusading ages. The capitals are of the Corinthian order, debased in style, with the cross carved on the rosettes of each. The wall above was once decorated all over with glass mosaic, fragments of which still remain, representing scenes in our Lord's life, portraits of angels and of Scripture characters, with arabesques and Greek inscriptions. These mosaics, with those on the chancel walls, were executed by order of the Greek emperor, Manuel Comnenos, in the middle of the 12th century. The roof above, once painted and gilded, was put up in 1482, the fine rafters having been given by Philip of Burgundy, the lead (stripped off later by the Moslems to make bullets) by Edward IV of England; and the work was executed in Venice, and brought on camels from Jaffa. Further restorations were made in 1478, and again in 1672 and 1842, but the majority of the work appears to belong to the original structure of the time of Constantine."

The following detailed description of the holy places in the Church is taken from Porter's *Handbook for Palestine*, p. 201 sq.; see also Bädeker, *Palestine*, p. 244 sq.; Wilson, *Lands of the Bible*, i, 390 sq.

"On the south side of the church we first descend a narrow staircase hewn in the rock, lighted by a glimmering lamp placed in a niche on the right hand, before a picture of the Virgin. This staircase leads to a low vault, on entering which we turn suddenly to the right into a long, narrow passage. Proceeding a few steps, we have on the right the altar and tomb of St. Eusebius—not the historian. Passing this, we enter a small oblong chamber, extending north and south at right angles to the passage. Taking first the south end, we have on the east side the altars and tombs of SS. Paula and Eustachia (her daughter), with rude pictures of the two saints over them. Opposite this, on the west, is the tomb of St. Jerome, having over it a portrait of the great father resting on a lion. From the north end of the chamber we ascend by three steps to another square vault, some twenty feet on each side and nine high, surrounded by a stone daïs. This is the study of Jerome—now a chapel, with an altar on its eastern side, and an old painting above it, representing the saint writing and the lion at his feet. 'Here it was,' says Geramb, 'that the illustrious recluse passed a great portion of his life; here it was that he fancied he heard the peals of that awful trump which shall one day summon all mankind to judgment incessantly ringing in his ears; here it was that with a stone he struck his body, bowed by the weight of years and austerities, and, with loud cries, besought

Constantine's Basilica at Bethlehem.

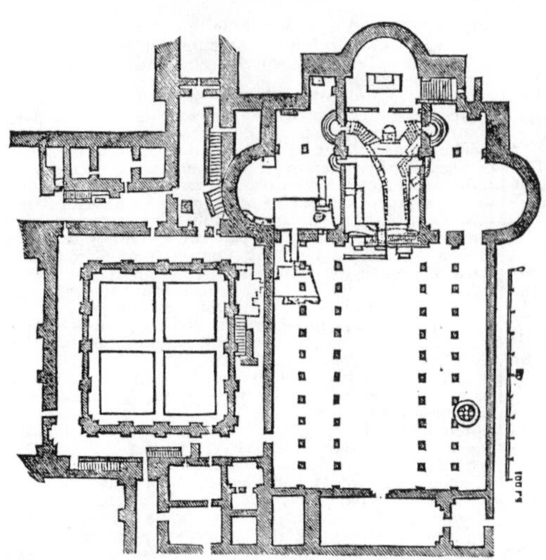

Plan of the Church of the Nativity at Bethlehem. (The dotted lines indicate the grottoes in the crypt below the church.)

mercy of the Lord; and here too it was that he produced those laborious works which have justly earned him the title of the Father of the Church.' This is a spot which the biblical scholar and the ecclesiastical historian will regard with peculiar interest, for there can be no doubt that for many years it formed the home and the study of that remarkable man whose name it bears.

"Returning to the chapel we first entered, we observe on its eastern side, behind a massive column, an altar, said to mark the spot where twenty thousand children murdered by Herod's order were buried, now called, for this reason, the *Altar of the Innocents.* A rude painting over it represents the massacre.

"Adjoining the Chapel of the Innocents on the south is a narrow vault, to which we ascend by five steps; this is called the *Chapel of Joseph*, being the place where the husband of Mary is said to have retired at the moment of the nativity. From this we enter a crooked, narrow passage, some twenty-six feet long, and on reaching the end of it we find a door on the left opening into the west end of

"*The Chapel of the Nativity*, a low vault, apparently hewn in the rock, thirty-eight feet long by eleven wide. At the east end is a small semicircular apse—the *sanctum* of the whole building. On approaching it we find a marble slab fixed in the pavement, with a silver star in the centre, round which are the words, HIC DE VIRGINE MARIA JESUS CHRISTUS NATUS EST, 'Here Jesus Christ was born of the Virgin Mary.' Round the star are suspended sixteen silver lamps, continually kept burning, and behind them, along the sides of the apse, are little gilt pictures of saints. Over the star is a plain altar, without picture or ornament. It is common to all the sects, and each must dress it, when about to celebrate mass, with the requisite trappings.

"In the angles of the grotto beside the apse are two staircases, that on the south leading up to the Greek Chapel, and that on the north to the Armenian; both in the choir of the basilica. Just in the angle between the flight of stairs on the south, and the side of the grotto, is the small chapel of the *Præsepium* or 'Manger.' On its west side is the place of the manger, now represented by a marble trough. The real *Præsepium*, as the Latins tell us, was long ago carried away to Rome, and is deposited in Santa Maria Maggiore. Over the place is a good painting by Maello, of date 1781, representing the *Virgin and Child, with the Shepherds.* On the opposite side of the grotto is the station of the wise men, marked by an altar having a painting, apparently by the same artist.

"These various grottoes are minutely measured off by rule and line, and distributed piecemeal among the rival sects. Many a keen and bitter contest there has been for a few inches of a wall, or the fraction of an altar; and more than once the question of the opening and shutting of one of the doors has well-nigh involved Europe in war!"

Nativity of the Blessed Virgin, a festival observed by the Church of Rome annually on Sept. 8.

Naturalism. See SCEPTICISM, LATEST PHASES OF.

Nazareth. The latest descriptions of this memorable place may be found in Conder's *Tent Work* (i, 138), and the *Memoirs* accompanying the Ordnance Survey (i, 275, 328).

Neale, ROLLIN HEBER, D.D., a distinguished Baptist minister, was born at Southington, Conn., Feb. 13, 1807. He graduated from Columbian College, Washington, in 1830, and from the Newton Theological Seminary in 1833; for a short time was pastor in South Boston and New Haven; and in 1837 of the First Baptist Church in Boston, where he remained, with great usefulness, nearly forty years. He died Sept. 18, 1879. (J. C. S.)

Neander, Conrad, a Lutheran theologian of Germany, who lived at the beginning of the 17th century, belonged to the most excellent Hebraists of his time, and translated into Hebrew *The Epistles of the Christian Year* (Leipsic, 1586):—*Luther's Smaller Catechism* (Wittenberg, 1599):—*The Nicene and Athanasian Confession* (ibid.); besides, he wrote, *De Omnibus Accentibus Hebr. qui in Sacris Biblicis Reperiuntur* (Leipsic, 1598):—*Elementale Ebraicum* (1590):—*Tabulæ Novæ Conjugationum Hebræarum* (1596). See Jöcher, *Allgemeines Gelehrten-Lexikon*, s. v.; Fürst, *Bibl. Jud.* ii, 26. (B. P.)

Neander, John, a Presbyterian minister, was born of Jewish parentage, Nov. 12, 1812, at Neubrück, in the province of Posen. He was educated in accordance with Talmudical Judaism, and in 1835 was called to Bremerlehe, near Bremerhaven, to occupy a rabbinical position there. In 1838, however, he joined the Church at Bremen, and became a missionary to the Jews. In 1845 Neander arrived in New York, and, as in Germany, labored among the Jews. In 1846 he was ordained by the Dutch Reformed Church, and in 1852 settled at Brooklyn, N. Y., where he organized the First German Presbyterian Church, in which he labored for more than thirty years. He died Nov. 6, 1885. (B. P.)

Cave of the Nativity at Bethlehem.

Neballat. Its modern representative, *Beit Nebala*, is "a village of moderate size at the edge of the plain, with a well to the east, and containing cisterns with large cut stones" (*Memoirs* to the Ordnance Survey, ii, 296, 306).

Nebo (Ezra ii, 29; Neh. vii, 33). For this site Lieut. Conder proposes (*Tent Work*, ii, 339) *Nûba*, seven miles north-west of Hebron, described in the *Memoirs* to the Ordnance Survey (iii, 309) as "a small village perched on a low hill, with a well about a mile to the east."

Nebo, MOUNT. This vicinity is included in the reduced *Map* of the Ordnance Survey east of the Jordan, and is described by Lieut. Conder in the *Quar. Statement* of the "Pal. Explor. Fund," Oct. 1881, p. 275 sq. It was also visited by Dr. Merrill, and his investigations (*East of the Jordan*, p. 241 sq.) confirm the views expressed by us under the art. PISGAH. Tristram remarks (*Bible Places*, p. 349), "A recent traveller has endeavored to show that Jebel Shiagha, the spot where these ruins stand, is Pisgah. The arguments adduced would be equally conclusive in behalf of any of the many flat-topped mounds of the neighborhood, one of which must have been Pisgah, although its Arabic equivalent, Fethkhah, seems to have dropped out of the local nomenclature."

Necker, THEODOR, a Protestant minister, was born at Trieste, May 7, 1830. He was a prominent member of the Church at Geneva, where he was the means of founding the Evangelical Society and of promoting the cause of the Young Men's Christian Association. He labored for the cause of the evangelical schools, not only in Geneva, but also in Bohemia and Moravia, where he went for this special purpose. He also visited England and France to promote the kingdom of God, and during the winter of 1870 and 1871 he labored among the Protestant French prisoners in Germany. In fact, there was no branch of home mission work in which he was not engaged, and his sudden death, Jan. 10, 1881, was a heavy loss to the Evangelical Church in Geneva. (B. P.)

Negro Dialect OF SURINAM. See SURINAM.

Neiel. For this place Lieut. Conder suggests (*Tent Work*, ii, 339) *Khurbet Yanin*, a ruined site eight and a half miles east by south from Acre, described in the *Memoirs* accompanying the Ordnance Survey (i, 322) as "a terraced hill, with heaps of stones on the top; the masonry hewn but small; on the north is a well."

Neill, HENRY, D.D., a Presbyterian minister, was born in Philadelphia, Oct. 15, 1815. He entered the University of Pennsylvania in 1829; made a profession of religion in 1832; entered upon a post-graduate course at Amherst; in 1836 became tutor or assistant teacher in Andover Theological Seminary; in 1839 was ordained pastor at Hatfield, Mass.; subsequently was pastor at Lenox, Mass., Detroit, Mich., and New Brunswick, N. J.; in 1873 organized a Presbyterian Church at Bryn Mawr, near Philadelphia, and died there, April 21, 1879.

Nekeb. For this place Lieut. Conder suggests (*Tent Work*, ii, 339) the present *Khurbet Seyadeh*, four miles south-west of Tiberias, described in the *Memoirs* accompanying the Ordnance Survey (i, 405) as "ruined Arab houses, all basaltic and apparently modern." Tristram states (*Bible Places*, p. 278), "But a far more satisfactory identification has been recently discovered in *Nakib*, a site in the Ard el-Hamma, the plain between Tabor and the sea of Galilee." This is precisely the situation of Seyadeh, but the name Nakib does not appear there on the Ordnance *Map*.

Nekir, in Mohammedanism, is one of the two angels who wake up every dead body, and ask for the faith of its former possessor. If he be true, he is refreshed with the dew of paradise, and laid to rest again; but if he is not favorable to Islam, he is whipped with two iron rods until he yells aloud, and then is cast into a snake's nest, where poisonous reptiles gnaw at him until the resurrection.

Nelson, John, D.D., a minister of the Free Church of Scotland, was born in Edinburgh, in October, 1820. After graduating from Edinburgh University, he studied at Berlin, Bonn, and Heidelberg. He became pastor at Greenock in 1851, and exercised there a useful ministry of twenty-six years. In 1855 he visited America, and published, as the result of his observations, an *Essay on National Education in the United States and Canada*. He travelled extensively on the Continent, officiating as pastor of several of the Free churches. He also spent some time in Egypt, Palestine, and Syria, his failing health requiring repeated respite from labor. He was an earnest advocate for the union between the Free and the Reformed Presbyterian churches in Scotland. He died at Abden House, Edinburgh, Jan. 26, 1878. (W. P. S.)

Nelson, Reuben, D.D., a Methodist Episcopal minister, was born at Andes, N. Y., Dec. 13, 1818. He was converted at the age of fifteen, at seventeen was licensed to exhort, at eighteen to preach, studied the next year, and in 1840 entered the Oneida Conference. He preached one year on Otsego Circuit, and one on Westford, serving meantime as principal of the Otsego Academy, at Cooperstown. In 1844 the Oneida Conference founded the Wyoming Seminary, at Kingston, Pa., and Mr. Nelson was chosen its first principal, which office he filled for twenty-eight years, with but one year's exception, during which he was presiding elder of Wyoming District. In 1872 he was elected agent of the Methodist Book Concern, in New York city, which office he held till his death, Feb. 20, 1879. See *Minutes of Annual Conferences*, 1879, p. 67; Simpson, *Cyclop. of Methodism*, s. v.

Nengonese (or **Maré**) **Version** OF THE SCRIPTURES. The Nengone is spoken in the Loyalty Islands. In 1854 a mission was commenced on the island of Maré, under the auspices of the London Missionary Society. The missionaries, the Revs. S. M. Creagh and J. Jones, devoted themselves assiduously to the task of translating portions of the Scriptures into the native language. The Nengonese New Test. was published in 1865 at the Maré mission press. In 1867 a second edition was issued at Sydney under the care of the Rev. J. Jones. In 1869 a revised edition was printed in England, whilst the books of Genesis and Exodus were printed at Maré. In 1874 the Book of Psalms had been added to the translations and editions of Scripture already existing, and was issued from the press in 1877, under the care of the Rev. S. M. Creagh. From the annual report of the British and Foreign Bible Society for 1885 we learn that the translation of the entire Pentateuch is now undergoing revision. See *Bible of Every Land*, p. 394. (B. P.)

Nepaulese (or **Kharpoora**) **Version** OF THE SCRIPTURES. Nepaulese is the principal dialect prevailing in Nepaul (q. v.), and was exclusively used by the higher castes. It is becoming prevalent throughout the whole country, and is rapidly superseding the other dialects. In 1812 a version was commenced at Serampore, and an edition of 1000 copies of the New Test. was issued in 1821. Of late a new translation of portions of the New Test. into this dialect was made by the Rev. W. Stuart. In 1850, 1000 copies of Luke were printed, and in 1852 a revised edition of 1000 was sent to press, together with 1500 of the Acts of the Apostles. From the annual report of the British and Foreign Bible Society for 1885 we learn that the Scotch Mission at Darjeeling has printed Genesis, Exodus, Proverbs, the Gospels, and Acts. See *Bible of Every Land*, p. 121. (B. P.)

Nesselmann, RODERICH, a Lutheran theologian of Germany, was born in 1815, and died June 12, 1881, at Elbing. He is the author of, *Kern der heiligen Schrift* (Elbing, 1845):—*Uebersicht über die Entwickelungsgeschichte der christlichen Predigt* (1862):—*Buch der Predigten* (1862):—*Christliche Predigten* (1865):—*Die augsburgische Confession erläutert* (1876):—*Haus- und Predigtbuch* (Königsberg, 1878). See Zuchold, *Bibl. Theol.* ii, 935. (B. P.)

Netophah. The probable representative of this site appears as *Khurbet Umm Toba* on the Ordnance *Map*, at two and a quarter miles north-east of Bethlehem, but no description is given in the accompanying *Memoirs*.

Neubauer, ERNST FRIEDRICH, a Lutheran theologian of Germany, was born at Magdeburg, July 31, 1705. He studied at Halle and Jena, and commenced his academical career at Halle in 1729, was in 1732 professor at Giessen, in 1736 at Halle, and died March 15, 1748, doctor of theology. He wrote, *De Varia Indole Interpretum Sacræ Scripturæ* (Jena, 1727):—*De Salomonis ad Lætitiam Exhortationibus* (1729):—*De Phrasi: Caro et Sanguis* (1729):—*De Michæle Archangelo* (1732):—*De Corpore Mosis* (eod.):—*De Phrasibus: Videre et Gustare Mortem* (1745), etc. See Fürst, *Bibl. Jud.* iii, 29; Döring, *Die gelehrten Theologen Deutschlands*, s. v.; Winer, *Handbuch der theol. Lit.* i, 105, 851; Jöcher, *Allgemeines Gelehrten-Lexikon*, s. v. (B. P.)

Neubig, Andreas, a Lutheran theologian of Germany, was born at Culmbach, May 6, 1780. For some time rector of the gymnasium at Hof, he was called in 1818 as professor of the gymnasium at Bayreuth, and died in 1855. He is the author of, *Die philosophische und christliche Gotteslehre* (Nuremberg, 1831):—*Philosophie und Christenthum* (Bayreuth, 1832):—*Die philosophische Unsterblichkeitslehre* (1834):—*Das Christenthum als Welt-Religion* (Ratisbon, 1839):—*Ist Jesus Christus mit vollem Rechte den Tod eines Verbrechers gestorben?* (Erlangen, 1836). See Winer, *Handbuch der theol. Lit.* i, 412, 472, 483; Zuchold, *Bibl. Theol.* ii, 936. (B. P.)

Neudecker, Christian Gotthold, a Lutheran theologian of Germany, was born at Gotha in 1807, and died there in 1866. He is the author of, *Allgemeines Lexicon der Religions- und christlichen Kirchengeschichte* (1834-37, 5 vols.):—*Urkunden aus der Reformationsgeschichte* (Cassel, 1836):—*Merkwürdige Aktenstücke aus dem Zeitalter der Reformation* (Nuremberg, 1838):—*Einleitung in das Neue Testament* (Leipsic, 1840):—*Neue Beiträge zur Geschichte der Reformation* (1841, 2 vols.):—*Geschichte der deutschen Reformation* (1842):—*Geschichte des evangelischen Protestantismus in Deutschland* (1844, 2 parts):—*Pacification der evangelisch-protestantischen Kirche Deutschlands* (1846). See Winer, *Handbuch der theol. Lit.* i, 512, 741; Zuchold, *Bibl. Theol.* ii, 936. (B. P.)

Neuffer, Christian Ludwig, a Lutheran theologian of Germany, was born at Stuttgart, Jan. 26, 1769. In 1791 he was preacher at the orphan asylum of his native place, in 1803 deacon at Zell, in 1819 preacher at Ulm, and died July 29, 1839. He is the author of, *Das Gebet des Herrn* (Stuttgart, 1832):—*Vermächtniss für christlich gesinnte Söhne und Töchter* (2d ed. Ulm, 1836):—*Der Christ an den Gräbern der Vollendeten* (1837). See Winer, *Handbuch der theol. Lit.* ii, 342, 376, 389; Zuchold, *Bibl. Theol.* ii, 937; Koch, *Gesch. des deutsch. Kirchenliedes*, vi, 207. (B. P.)

Neufville, Edward, D.D., a Protestant Episcopal minister, was born in Washington, D. C., in 1802. From an early age he was educated by a prominent merchant of Charleston, S. C. For some time he was a member of Columbia College, New York city, but did not graduate. Then he entered the General Theological Seminary. In 1824 he was ordained deacon, and settled in Prince William's Parish, S. C., where he officiated until the winter of 1827, when he was called to the rectorship of Christ Church, Savannah, Ga. He died there, Jan. 1, 1851. His sermons were attractive, without being remarkable for strength. He especially excelled as a reader of the liturgy of his Church. See Sprague, *Annals of the Amer. Pulpit*, v, 661.

Neumann, Wilhelm, a Lutheran theologian of Germany, who died in 1884 at Colombier, in canton Neufchatel, formerly professor of theology at Breslau, afterwards at the academy in Lausanne, is the author of, *Die Wasser des Lebens* (Berlin, 1848):—זבח שלמים *Sacra Veteris Testamenti* (Leipsic, 1854):—*Jeremias ausgelegt* (1856-58, 2 vols.):—*Symbolique du Culte de l'Ancienne Alliance* (Lausanne, 1860):—*Die Weissagungen des Sakharjah* (Stuttgart, eod.):—*Die Stiftshütte in Bild und Wort* (Gotha, 1861):—*Die messianischen Erscheinungen bei den Juden* (1865):—*Geschichte der messianischen Weissagung im Alten Testament* (eod.). See Zuchold, *Bibl. Theol.* ii, 938. (B. P.)

Newell, Samuel, D.D., a Presbyterian minister, was born in Cincinnati, O., April 23, 1811. He graduated from Hanover College in 1834; was ordained pastor in Lebanon in 1836, where he served with great acceptability and usefulness for nine years, and thereafter was pastor at Paris, Ill., where he died, June 22, 1879. (W. P. S.)

New Guinea Version. See Motu.

Newhall, Fales Henry, D.D., a Methodist Episcopal minister, was born in Saugus, Mass., June 19, 1827. He was converted at the age of twelve; graduated from Wesleyan University, Conn., in 1846; taught for several years thereafter; joined the New England Conference in 1851, and occupied several of its most important appointments; in 1863 became professor of rhetoric and English literature in his *alma mater;* in 1867-68 travelled and studied in Europe; in 1871 returned to the itinerant work as a pastor; in 1873 was elected president of the Ohio Wesleyan University, but soon experienced an attack of insanity, from which he never afterwards fully recovered. He died April 6, 1883. Dr. Newhall was an eloquent speaker and writer. He published a number of sermons, essays, etc. See *Alumni Record of Wesl. University*, 1882, p. 77, 610; *Minutes of Annual Conferences*, 1883, p. 91.

Newman, William, D.D., an English Baptist minister, was born in 1772, and early in life became a member of the Church at Waltham Abbey, Essex. For some time he was an associate with the eminent John Ryland, as a teacher. In May, 1794, he was ordained pastor of the Church at Bow, and subsequently, on the establishment of the Baptist College at Stepney, was chosen its president and theological tutor. For the prosperity of this seat of learning he labored most faithfully for many years. He died Dec. 22, 1835. See *Baptist Union*, 1836, p. 19. (J. C. S.)

Newton, Alfred, D.D., a Presbyterian minister, was born at Colchester, Conn., Nov. 11, 1803. He graduated from Yale College in 1828, was tutor there from 1831 to 1834, and in the latter year graduated from the Divinity School. In the spring of 1835 he was invited to supply the pulpit of the Presbyterian Church in Norwalk, O., and was ordained the same year; was installed pastor July 24, 1838, and sustained that relation until Aug. 1, 1870. He remained as pastor emeritus of the Church and a resident of the town till his death, Dec. 31, 1878. See *Obit. Record of Yale College*, 1879.

Newton, Roger, D.D., a Congregational minister, was born at Durham, Conn., May 23, 1737. He graduated from Yale College in 1758; studied theology under Rev. Elizur Goodrich; was constituted pastor of the Church in Greenfield, Nov. 18, 1761; and died Dec. 10, 1816. See Sprague, *Annals of the Amer. Pulpit*, i, 513.

Newton, Thomas Henry, D.D., a Presbyterian minister, was born in Philadelphia, Pa., June 25, 1821. He graduated from Lafayette College in 1846, and from Princeton Theological Seminary in 1849; was licensed by the Presbytery of Philadelphia, and was ordained an evangelist by the same presbytery, Nov. 13, 1850, but was never settled as a pastor. In 1849 he began to labor on the island of St. Thomas as a chaplain, under the appointment of the Seaman's Friend Society; in 1859 as chaplain at St. Louis; in 1863 was missionary in south-western Missouri, where he organized a church at Linn Creek. He afterwards resided, in infirm health, at Carlinville, Ill. The last two years of his life were spent near Richmond, Va. He died at Waverly Station, Nov. 19, 1880. See *Necrol. Report of Princeton Theol. Sem.* 1881, p. 69.

New Zealand Version. See Maori.

Nezib. The modern representative of this site, *Beit-Nusib*, is laid down as a ruin on the Ordnance *Map*, eight miles north-west of Hebron, and described in the accompanying *Memoirs* (iii, 324) as consisting of "cisterns and caves, foundations and ruined walls, with a few pillar shafts. . . . The buildings seem to date back to the Byzantine period, judging from the character of the masonry; but the cisterns and caves are perhaps earlier."

Ngunese Version OF THE SCRIPTURES. Ngunese is a language spoken on the island of Nguna, one of the Sandwich Island group, which lies six miles north of Efate, and has a population of about a thousand souls; but from Nguna fourteen islands are visible, with a population of about seven thousand five hundred souls, who use the same language, or dialects of the same. The islands, with their population, are as follows: Efate, 3000; Lelapa, 100; Mosa, 200; Pele, 200; Nguna, 1000; Emau, 500; Mataso, 100; Emae, 800; Ewose, 80; Valea, 20; Tongariki, 200; Buninga, 150; south end of Epi, 150. On Emae and the Tonga group different languages are spoken on each side of the islands, but the Ngunese is understood throughout them all. In 1881, at the request of the New Hebrides Mission Synod, the British and Foreign Bible Society published an edition of two thousand copies of the gospels of Matthew and John. The translation was made from the Greek by the Rev. Peter Milne, a missionary of the Presbyterian Church of New Zealand, and who for ten years has labored chiefly on Nguna, Pele, and Mataso, each of these islands having a church and a school, with a church attendance of one hundred and fifty, and an attendance at school of one hundred. (B. P.)

Niasian Version OF THE SCRIPTURES. Niasian is spoken on the island of Nias, which lies near Sumatra, and contains a large population, estimated by the Rev. J. Denninger at eighty thousand souls. Up to the year 1871 nothing had been done for the island in the way of printing; but Mr. Denninger, of the Barmen Evangelical Missions, who labored for many years in this and the adjoining island, committed the language to writing, prepared a grammar in it, and translated some parts of the Scripture. In 1873 the British and Foreign Bible Society printed the gospel of Luke, and this is at present the only part of Scripture extant. (B. P.)

Nichols, SAMUEL, D.D., a Protestant Episcopal clergyman, was born Nov. 14, 1787. He graduated from Yale College in 1811; was ordained by bishop Hobart in 1813; from 1815 to 1837 was rector of St. Matthew's Church, Bedford, Conn.; resigning this charge, he retired from the active ministry, and died in Greenfield, July 17, 1880. See Whittaker, *Almanac and Directory*, 1881, p. 174.

Nicholson, Edward G., D.D., a Protestant Episcopal clergyman, appears in the records, in 1864, as having a parish in the city of Mexico; the following year he removed to Kentucky; in 1870 he became a resident of New York city, where he remained until his death, Sept. 1, 1872, at the age of fifty-four years. See *Prot. Episc. Almanac*, 1873, p. 133.

Nicholson, Joseph B., D.D., an English divine, antiquarian, and author, was born in 1795. He graduated at Magdalen Hall, Oxford, in 1820; in 1826 became domestic chaplain to his royal highness the duke of Clarence; in 1835 he was appointed rector, and in 1846 rural dean of St. Albans, where he continued till his death, July 27, 1866. He was also appointed surrogate for the archdeaconry of St. Albans, and in 1862 was nominated an honorable canon of Rochester Cathedral. Dr. Nicholson was a fellow of the Society of Antiquaries, of the Royal Astronomical Society, and a member of the Numismatical Society; was vice-president of the Archæological and Architectural Society; a magistrate for St. Albans and the county of Hertford. In 1851 he published the first edition of a work entitled, *The Abbey of St. Albans*, and soon after an enlarged edition. See *Appleton's Annual Cyclopædia*, 1866, p. 596.

Nickels, CHRISTOPHER MARDENBOROUGH, D.D., a Congregational minister, was born at Pemaquid, Me., Jan. 18, 1805. He graduated from Brown University in 1830, for one year thereafter was principal of an academy in Haverhill, Mass., and in 1835 graduated from the Andover Theological Seminary, spending a year meantime as tutor of Latin and Greek in Brown University. The last-named year he became the minister of the Congregational Church in Gloucester, Mass., where he remained for nearly thirteen years, and was greatly blessed in his work. For the benefit of his wife's health he went to New Orleans, and while there preached at the Bethel, and founded a seamen's home. In the summer of 1850 he came back to the North, and for five years had charge of the Congregational Church at Barre, Mass.; next of the Central Presbyterian Church, Newark, N. J., a position which he resigned on account of ill-health, in 1864, and then spent a year in Europe and the East. In 1867 went abroad the second time, and after seven years he took up his residence in Newark, N. J., whence he removed to Princeton, and finally to New London, Conn., where he died, July 10, 1878. See *Brown University Necrology*, 1879-80. (J. C. S.)

Nicolai, Johann, a Lutheran theologian, who died at Tübingen, Aug. 12, 1708, is the author of, *Libri 4 de Sepulchris Hebræorum* (Leyden, 1706):—*De Juramentis Hebræorum, Græcorum, Romanorum, Aliorumque Populorum* (Frankfort, 1700). See Fürst, *Bibl. Jud.* iii, 32; Winer, *Handbuch der theol. Lit.* i, 145, 515, 634, 844; Jöcher, *Allgemeines Gelehrten-Lexikon*, s. v. (B. P.)

Nicolai, Johann David, a Lutheran theologian of Germany, was born at Hamburg, Feb. 25, 1742. He studied at Göttingen, was in 1770 sub-rector at Stade, in 1778 rector, in 1781 cathedral-preacher at Bremen, and died April 3, 1826. Besides a number of sermons he published *Das Neue Testament*, etc. (Bremen, 1775-76, 2 vols.). See Döring, *Die deutschen Kanzelredner*, p. 264-270; Winer, *Handbuch der theol. Lit.* ii, 159. (B. P.)

Nicolai, Otto Nathanael, a Lutheran theologian of Germany, was born April 5, 1710. He studied at Leipsic, was in 1738 deacon at Naumburg, in 1742 at Magdeburg, and died in 1788, doctor of theology. He wrote, *De Ossibus Regis Edom Combustis* (Leipsic, 1733):—*Schediasma Philologicum de Angelo Israëlitarum per Desertum Duce* (1734):—*Meletema Exegeticum de Prophetarum Veterum Judaicorum Vestitu* (Magdeburg, 1746):—*De Vinea Dei Satis Quidem Culta* (Helmstädt, 1747):—*De Terroribus Hiskiæ in Faucibus Mortis* (1749):—*De Servis Josephi Medicis* (1752):—*De Gratia Dei Privativa* (1760). See Fürst, *Bibl. Jud.* iii, 32; Döring, *Die gelehrten Theologen Deutschlands*, s. v. (B. P.)

Nicolas (1), a Scotch prelate, was made bishop of the Isles in 1203. He went to Ireland to visit the monastery of Benchor. He resigned his bishopric in 1217. See Keith, *Scottish Bishops*, p. 298.

Nicolas (2), a Scotch prelate, was elected to the see of Caithness in 1273, but was never consecrated on account of some objection of the pope. See Keith, *Scottish Bishops*, p. 210.

Nicolas LE GROS, a French theologian, was born at Rheims in 1675. He distinguished himself in philosophy and theology, and was made canon of the cathedral at Rheims by the archbishop Le Tellier. On account of his opposition to the bull Unigenitus (q. v.), Gros was deposed of his office and excommunicated by Tellier's successor, the archbishop Mailli. Gros had to leave the country, and finally settled at Utrecht, and was made professor of theology in the seminary at Amersfoort. He died in 1751. Gros published, *Du Renversement des Libertés de l'Église Gallicane dans l'Affaire de la Constitution Unigenitus* (1716, 2 vols.):—*Manuel du Chrétien*:—*Méditations sur la Concorde des Évangiles* (Paris, 1730, 3 vols.):—*Méditations sur l'Épitre aux Romains* (1735, 2 vols.):—*Méditations sur les Épitres*

Catholiques (1754, 6 vols.): — *Motifs Invincibles d'Attachement à l'Église Romaine pour des Catholiques:— La Sainte Bible Traduite* (Cologne, 1739): — *Dogma Ecclesiæ circa Usuram Expositum et Vindicatum*. See Jöcher, *Allgemeines Gelehrten-Lexikon*, s. v.; *Les Nouvelles Ecclésiastiques* of Jan. 30 and Feb. 6, 1753; *Mémoires pour Servir à l'Histoire Ecclésiastique*, etc., vol. iv; Lichtenberger, *Encyclop. des Sciences Religieuses*, s. v. (B. P.)

Nicolson, James, a Scotch prelate, was minister at Meigle, when he was preferred to the see of Dunkeld in 1606. He died Aug. 17, 1607. See Keith, *Scottish Bishops*, p. 98.

Nieden, Friedrich, a Protestant theologian of Germany, was born Nov. 25, 1812. He studied at Bonn, and was ordained in 1839. In the same year he was called as pastor to Friemersheim, in the county of Moers, in 1866 to Coblentz, was made general superintendent in 1877, and died March 19, 1883, doctor of theology. (B. P.)

Nielsen, Nikolai Johann Ernst, a Lutheran theologian of Germany, was born in 1806 at Rendsburg. He studied at Kiel and Berlin, was in 1832 pastor at Sarau, Holstein, in 1840 provost, in 1848 doctor of theology, in 1851 superintendent at Eutin, in 1853 pastor at Oldenburg, retired in 1879, and died Jan. 26, 1883. He published several volumes of sermons, and some ascetical works, for which see Zuchold, *Bibl. Theol.* ii, 940 sq. (B. P.)

Nielsen, Rasmus, a Lutheran theologian of Denmark, was born in 1809. He studied at Copenhagen, and commenced his academical career there in 1840. For more than forty years he labored as university teacher, and died Sept. 30, 1884. Nielsen was a follower of Kierkegaard, and an opponent of Martensen's speculative system of theology. Of his works which have been translated into German, we mention *Der Brief Pauli an die Römer* (Leipsic, 1843):—*Vorlesungen über philosophische Propädeutik:* — *Die Logik der Grundideen:* — *Religionsphilosophie* and *Allgemeine Wissenschaftslehre in ihren Grundzügen* (1880). (B. P.)

Niemann, Eduard, a Lutheran theologian of Germany, was born Feb. 26, 1804, at Neuenkirchen, in the principality of Osnabrück. After completing his theological studies, he was appointed preacher at his birthplace in 1825, and in 1828 was called to Hanover. Here Niemann's sermons soon attracted all classes of society, and in 1832 he was appointed court-preacher. In 1841 he became a member of consistory, in 1855 general superintendent, and died Aug. 12, 1884, doctor of theology. He published several volumes of sermons, for which see Zuchold, *Bibl. Theol.* ii, 941 sq. (B. P.)

Niemann, Sebastian, a Lutheran theologian of Germany, was born April 2, 1625. He studied at different universities, commenced his academical career at Jena in 1651, was in 1654 professor, in 1657 doctor of theology, in 1666 superintendent and member of consistory, in 1674 general superintendent at Schleswig, and died March 6, 1684. He is the author of, *Disputationes de Miraculis:* — *De anti-Christo:* — *De Visione Diei Christi ab Abrahamo Desiderata*, etc.:—*De Merito Bonorum Operum contra Bellarminum:*—*De Pædobaptismo:*—*De Viribus Liberi Arbitrii in Conversione:*— *De Nikolaitis ex Apocal. ii*, 15:—*De Concilii Nicæni I et Œcumenici Auctoritate et Integritate:* — *De Hæresi Nicolaitarum*, etc. See Moller, *Cimbria Literata;* Jöcher, *Allgemeines Gelehrten-Lexikon*, s. v. (B. P.)

Niemeyer, Hermann Agathon, a German divine, son of August Hermann, was born at Halle, Jan. 5, 1802. He pursued his theological studies at his native place, and commenced his theological career there in 1825. In 1826 he was called to Jena, but returned in 1829 to Halle, and died Dec. 6, 1851. He published, *De Docetis Comment. Hist.-Theolog.* (Halle, 1823):—*De Isidori Pelusiotæ Vita, Scriptis et Doctrina* (ibid. 1825): — *Collectio Confessionum in Ecclesiis Reformatis Publicatarum* (Leipsic, 1840). See Winer, *Handbuch der theol. Lit.* i, 162, 586, 640, 896; Zuchold, *Bibl. Theol.* ii, 943. (B. P.)

Niemeyer, Johann Bartholomæus, a Lutheran theologian of Germany, was born June 24, 1644. He studied at Helmstädt, and died there, May 8, 1708, doctor and professor of theology. He wrote, *De Semine Mulieris Contrituro Caput Serpentis:*—*De Disciplina Ecclesiastica:*—*De Conjugiis Lege Divina Prohibitis:* —*De Existentia Dei nec non Atheismo et Deismo:*—*De Nominibus et Essentia Dei:*—*De Mediocritate Rationis in Virtute Observanda.* See Jöcher, *Allgemeines Gelehrten-Lexikon*, s. v.; Winer, *Handbuch der theol. Lit.* ii, 22. (B. P.)

Nieremberger, Nicolaus, a Lutheran theologian of Germany, was born May 9, 1648. He studied at Wittenberg, was in 1678 teacher at the gymnasium in Ratisbon, in 1681 professor of theology, and died Sept. 29, 1700. He wrote, *De Ritibus Mesusæ* (Wittenberg, 1674; 2d ed. 1714):—*De Deprecatione Calicis Christi* (1677):—*De Angelica de Corpore Christi Disceptatione* (1682):—*De Alphabeto Ebraico* (1691):—*De Scripturæ Sacræ Subjecto* (1694):—*De Notis Numerorum Ebraicis* (eod.):—*De Auctoritate Scripturæ S. Classica* (1699): —*De Nomine* יהוה (1701): — *Diss. Pentagrammata* יהשוה ΙΗΣΟΥΣ, *Jesus*, etc. (1702):—*De Triplici Genere Apocryphorum* (1704). See Döring, *Die gelehrten Theologen Deutschlands*, s. v. (B. P.)

Niermeyer, Antoine, a Dutch theologian, was born Sept. 2, 1814, at Vlaardingen, Holland. He studied at Leyden, and was in 1840 called to the pastorate at S'Heer-Arendskerk, Zealand. His leisure he devoted to the exegesis of the New Test., and in 1846 and 1850 received the golden medal from the Hague Society for the Defence of the Christian Religion, by presenting papers on the authenticity of Paul's epistle to the Ephesians, and on the writings of John. These exegetical labors induced the theological faculty to honor their author with the doctorate of theology, and when his teacher, Van Hengel, died (1853), Niermeyer was appointed his successor. He died April 10, 1855. Niermeyer's principal works are, *Authenticité de l'Épitre aux Ephésiens* (1847-48, 2 vols.):—*État Actuel de la Critique du Nouveau Testament*, a poem (1849):—*Magasin de Critique et d'Exégèse* (Leyden, 1850-52, 3 vols.): —*Authenticité des Écrits Johanniques* (1852-53, 2 vols.). See Lichtenberger, *Encyclop. des Sciences Religieuses*, s. v. (B. P.)

Nina, Lorenzo, a Roman Catholic prelate of Italy, was born at Recanati, near Ancona, May 12, 1812. He was made a priest in 1845, and was appointed by Pius IX assessor inquisitionis and præfectus studii at the lyceum of St. Apollinaris. In 1877 Nina was appointed cardinal-deacon, and in 1879 cardinal-secretary of the state. In his latter capacity he endeavored to bring about a *modus vivendi* with the German government. In 1880, at his own request, he was relieved from the office of secretary and appointed præfect of the congregations of councils. Nina died July 27, 1885. See *Men of the Time* (1879), s. v. (B. P.)

Ningpo Colloquial Version. See Chinese Versions.

Ninian, a Scotch prelate, was promoted to the see of Galloway, April 27, 1459, and was present in Parliament at the forfeiture of the earl of Ross in 1476. See Keith, *Scottish Bishops*, p. 276.

Nisbet, Henry, D.D., a Scotch Congregational minister, was born at Launceston, Glasgow, in 1817, of devout parents. He joined the Church in 1835, graduated at Glasgow University, studied two years (1836-37) at the Theological Hall of Glasgow, offered his services to the London Missionary Society, attended Cheshunt College for two sessions, and, in 1840, in company with his fellow-student and co-worker, Dr.

George Turner, was ordained and appointed to Tanna, an island in the New Hebrides, whither they at once sailed. Here they carried on operations for a short time, but on account of an insurrection among the natives were obliged, under cover of night, to flee for life. They landed at Samoa, set out afresh on their missionary life, and soon met great success. In 1844 they established the Samoan Mission Seminary, which sent forth more than six hundred native agents before Dr. Nisbet's decease, May 9, 1876. He possessed a well-stored mind, and was humble, cultured, and eminently adapted to his work. See *Cong. Year-book*, 1877, p. 402.

Niuean (or **Savage Island**) **Version** OF THE SCRIPTURES. Niue is a lone island four hundred miles from any other land, the nearest groups being the Friendly Islands, in the west, and the Samoan, in the north. In 1849, after long opposition, a Samoan teacher was received in the island. In the course of time, amid his evangelistic labors, he translated the gospel of Mark, which was sent to the missionaries of Samoa, and, after revision, printed by them. When, in 1861, the Rev. W. G. Lawes and his wife went to Niue as the first missionaries, taking with them the printed gospel, they found that the other three gospels and Acts had been translated by the native teachers. The translation was revised by the Rev. G. Pratt, of Samoa, and printed at Sydney, together with the epistle to the Philippians and John's epistles, in 1862, by the New South Wales Auxiliary. The New Test. was completed by Mr. Lawes and printed at Sydney in 1867. The book of Psalms, also translated by Mr. Lawes and revised by the Rev. Mr. Pratt, was printed in 1869 or 1870. The whole has been once more revised, and, together with the books of Genesis and Exodus, was printed in London in 1873, under the superintendence of Mr. Lawes. From the annual report of the British and Foreign Bible Society for the year 1882 we learn that the society has published, not only a new edition of five thousand copies of the New Test. and Psalms, but also three thousand copies of the Pentateuch as prepared by Mr. Lawes, who continues the translation of the other books of the Old Test. (B. P.)

Nob. The probable representative of this place, acquiesced in by Tristram (*Bible Places*, p. 120), and substantially also by Conder (*Tent Work*, ii, 117), is laid down on the Ordnance *Map* as *Khurbet es-Sôma*, at less than half a mile north-east of Shafat, and described in the accompanying *Memoirs* (iii, 125) as "heaps of ruins; a cistern fourteen paces by four, with a rubble roof; and a crumbling building, apparently modern. There is a remarkable knoll of rock in the place, whence the name 'ruin of the heap.' The top of this knoll is surmounted by the remains of a small vaulted chamber. There are also a few rock-cut tombs on the south-east, now closed."

Nobbe, MASON, D.D., a Congregational and afterwards a Presbyterian minister, was born at Williamstown, Mass., March 18, 1809. He studied at Stockbridge Academy; graduated from Williams College in 1827; spent a year in New York city in studying modern languages and in teaching; went to Princeton Theological Seminary in 1828, and spent one year; became a tutor in Williams College, continuing his theological studies; was licensed June 14, 1831, by Berkshire Congregational Association, while a tutor, and was ordained by the same body, Feb. 15, 1832, at Williamstown. His successive fields of labor were as follows: Presbyterian Church in Washington, D. C., from 1832 to 1839; Eleventh Church in New York city, from 1839 to 1850; associate pastor with Rev. Dr. Duncan, of the Independent Presbyterian Church of Baltimore, Md., in 1850 and 1851; principal of a young ladies' seminary in Washington, D. C., from 1851 to 1853, at the same time gathering and organizing the Sixth Street Church; chaplain in the navy, from 1853 to 1861; supply to the First Congregational Church of Williamstown, Mass., in 1865 and 1866. On returning to Washington, in 1870, the Sixth Street Church elected him to be its pastor, and without being installed he thenceforward served until his death, Oct. 24, 1881. See *Necrol. Report of Princeton Theol. Sem.* 1882, p. 24.

Nobilio (or **Nobilis**), FLAMINIO, an Italian theologian, who died at Lucca in 1590, edited, at the instance of pope Sixtus V, *Vetus Testamentum juxta LXX* (Rome, 1587):—and translated the Septuagint into Latin; *Vetus Testamentum Secundum LXX Latine Redditum* (ibid. 1588). He also wrote *Annotationes in Veteris Testamenti LXX Interpretes*, which are found in the London Polyglot. See Winer, *Handbuch der theol. Lit.* i, 47, 48, 886; Jöcher, *Allgemeines Gelehrten-Lexikon*, s. v. (B. P.)

Nodhamians, a heretical Mohammedan sect, who, to avoid falling into the error of making God the author of evil, asserted that neither directly nor indirectly, permissively nor authoritatively, had God any connection whatever with evil. They denied also the miraculous character of the Koran.

Nolasque, ST. PIERRE, a French monk, founder of the order of the *Beata Maria Virgo de Mercede pro Redemptione Captivorum*, was born in 1189 at Le Mas des Saintes Puelles, in Languedoc. In 1228, Nolasque, in company with some other knights and priests, organized the order mentioned above, the special object of which was to redeem Christian captives in Mohammedan countries in extreme cases, when there was danger of a conversion to Islam, even with the sacrifice of liberty and life. At first the order occupied a portion of the royal palace at Barcelona, but in 1232 a splendid monastery was built and dedicated to St. Eulalia, the patroness of Barcelona. The order was confirmed by Gregory IX, in 1230, and soon spread over Spain, Italy, and France. Nolasque died in 1256, and was canonized by Urban VIII in 1628. By Benedict XIII, the order was transformed into a common mendicant order (1725), and a century later it was swept away by the revolution. See *Acta Sanctorum Bolland. ad* 31. *Jan.* ii, 980 sq.; Holstenius-Brockie, *Codex Regularum Monasticarum*, iii, 433 sq.; Helyot, *Histoire des Ordres Monastiques* (Paris, 1714-19); Giucci, *Iconografia Storica Degli Ordini Religiosi*, etc. (Rome, 1844), vii, 88 sq.; Gams, *Kirchengeschichte Spaniens*, iii, 236-239; Plitt-Herzog, *Real-Encyklop.* s. v. (B. P.)

Norse (or **Icelandic**) **Version.** See SCANDINAVIAN VERSIONS.

North, SIMEON, D.D., LL.D., a Congregational divine, was born at Berlin, Conn., in 1802. He graduated from Yale College in 1825; was tutor there the following year, professor of languages in Hamilton College, N. Y., from 1829 to 1839, and thereafter president until 1857. He died Feb. 9, 1884. Dr. North was the author of several sermons, etc.

North American Indians, RELIGIOUS IDEAS OF. It is not necessary to separate all the small tribes according to their religious usages, for they had much in common, and will here be treated accordingly. They do not believe that a dryad was thought to inhabit every tree, but the natives believed in protecting spirits of the woods and trees. These spirits were called, among the northern tribes, *Nantena* (singular *Okki*). Among the Iroquois the whole company of spirits was called *Ayotkon*, or *Hondatkons* (singular *Manitu*). As ruler of all good spirits Tharonhiaonagou was worshipped, who was the grandson of the goddess of all evil, Atahentsik. Both were regarded as living in the land of the blessed. Exalted over these was the great spirit who dispensed grace; he could do as much good as he pleased, but no evil, although he could hinder evil. But only those receive his grace who do good and abandon evil. Sun, moon, and stars, and the natural forces, are objects of nature. In dreams the great spirit sends protecting beings, who are guides all through life. Only in Virginia was there a visible representation of supreme beings—a human figure, with an apron, in a sitting posture. There are many of these, who are called *Kiwasa*, and are considered protectors of the dead. In the southern part of North America the cultus took another form. There idolatry was rife, and there were priests, temples, and bloody sacrifices. In Florida the first male born was brought as a sacrifice to the sun, and this shows the transition to the Mexican cultus. In all acts of worship, politics, or friendship, the tobacco-pipe played a noteworthy part. The natives were also persuaded of a future life; but their ideas concerning it were taken from their present existence. They believed in a continuation of life, but with higher joys and all possible success in hunting, fishing, and war; therefore they buried with the dead his clothes and weapons, nourishment for the journey, and even his pipe and tobacco. They assembled around the dead, and praised his deeds of bravery and valor. All his friends and relatives visited him, and after a meal, which was first handed to the departed, the aboriginal Americans left their village and journeyed away without the dead, who became a prey to the wild animals. Others, who had permanent dwelling-places, buried their dead in various ways. A singular practice, only found among the North American tribes, was the voluntary death of aged people. When they became sick, they awaited their death with the greatest composure. Their physicians informed them that they were unable to heal them. Then the dying made the necessary arrangements, and died jovially and without fear. This was the natural death. But to old people, who could not fish and hunt, life became a burden. The father usually ordered his son to kill him with the club. Then the friends, relatives, and children accompanied him into the woods. Two dogs were killed, that their souls might herald the coming of a warrior into the other world. The old man then smoked a pipe, conversed with his friends, sang his song of death, and gave the sign to his son, whereupon the latter slew him with his club. A small hut was then built over the buried body. The friends of the departed gave away all his goods, even the most costly and precious. Their sorrow was touching. They tortured themselves in the fleshy parts of their body, and sometimes lost so much blood that they died themselves. Often, when a child died, its mother killed herself in the hope of nourishing it beyond death, for they feared that without such nourishment the child would die a second time. The cosmogony of the North American tribes differed from the others in that men were first created and then the world. All human beings originated from woman, and the Turtle tribe, living in the central point of the world, was the first and noblest. See INDIANS, AMERICAN.

Northalis, RICHARD, an Irish prelate, was born in London, and became a Carmelite friar. He obtained a high reputation for his preaching, learning, and acquirements, and attracted the notice of the king, who advanced him to the bishopric of Ossory in 1386. About 1390 he was constituted a commissioner by the king to inquire into the state, losses, abuses, and government of Ireland; in particular, to report how and on what security Nigel O'Neill was enlarged. In 1391 and 1394 he was employed by the same monarch in the quality of an ambassador to pope Boniface IX, and was appointed chancellor of Ireland in 1393. Having spent nine years in the prelacy of Ossory, he was, in 1396, promoted to the archbishopric of Dublin. He died July 20, 1397. See D'Alton, *Memoirs of the Archbishops of Dublin*, p. 149.

Norton, AUGUSTUS THEODORE, D.D., a Presbyterian minister, was born at Cornwall, Conn., March 28, 1808. He graduated from Yale College in 1832; studied theology privately; was licensed as an evangelist; labored first at Windham, N. Y., and afterwards at Griggsfield, Naples, Pittsfield, and Atlas, in southern Illinois. He organized the Second Presbyterian Church in St. Louis, Mo., and in 1839 was called to the pastorate of the First Presbyterian Church in Alton, Ill., where he labored for nineteen years. In 1859 he was appointed district secretary of Church Extension and Home Missions for the West, and was enabled in due time to report every church in his field as supplied with a minister. In 1879 he published a large volume of seven hundred pages, on the *History of the Presbyterian Church in Illinois*. He died at Alton, April 29, 1884.

Norway Lapponese Version. See QUÄNIAN VERSION.

Norwegian Version. See SCANDINAVIAN VERSIONS.

Nott, JOHN, D.D., a Presbyterian minister, was born at Albany, N. Y., Dec. 14, 1801. He graduated from Union College in 1823. In the autumn of the same year he entered Andover Theological Seminary, where he studied until June, 1825. He then entered Princeton Seminary, June 30, and studied there until September, 1826. He was licensed by the Presbytery of Albany, May 3, 1827, and ordained as an evangelist the same month. He was tutor in Union College from 1830 to 1839, and was assistant professor of rhetoric in the same institution for fifteen years. From 1839 to 1841 he was stated supply to the Church at Rotterdam, N. Y. Thence he went to the South as stated supply of the churches of Goldsboro' and Everittsville, in North Carolina. Returning to the North, he became supply of the Dutch Reformed Church at Aurisville, Montgomery Co., N. Y. He died at Fonda, May 13, 1878. See *Necrol. Report of Princeton Theol. Sem.* 1879, p. 23.

Novitiōli is a name applied by Tertullian to catechumens, because they were just entering upon that state which made them candidates for eternal life.

Nubian Version OF THE SCRIPTURES. From the annual report of the British and Foreign Bible Society for 1885 we learn that an edition of five hundred copies of the gospel of Mark has been published for the benefit of the Mohammedans in and around Dongola, East Africa. This version, made in the Fadidja dialect, was prepared by the late professor Lepsius (q. v.), and published as an appendix to his Nubian Grammar. From the latter it was republished, with permission of the translator's son and of the publisher, in Roman characters, under the editorship of professor Reinisch, Vienna. (B. P.)

Nupé Version OF THE SCRIPTURES. Nupé is spoken in a territory of Central Africa situated between Yoruba on the south-west and Haussa on the north, divided into two portions by the river Rowara, which runs through it from a north-westerly direction, till it winds its way southerly after it has cleared the bases of the Rennell mountains. The south-west portion of Nupé is a belt of land not more than twenty-five miles from the river's bank to its boundary with Yoruba land at Saregi, formerly a mutual place of meeting in their hunting expeditions between the two tribes, but now it is an important town, inhabited by both tribes, the Yorubas, however, being the more numerous and influential. The breadth of the northern portion of Nupé is much larger, or some three or four days' journey across, or about sixty or seventy miles broad towards Haussa from the river's bank. The extreme length of the country from Kpatatshi, the last town of Nupé on the boundary of Busa, on the upper parts of the river to the tribes of Is'itakotsi, next to Muye, and Bidon of Kakanda, on the lower parts of the river, is about one hundred and sixty miles. Such is the geographical position of the Nupé country, as described by the Rev. S. Crowther, who, in connection with the Rev. J. F. Schön, translated the first seven chapters of Matthew in the Nupé, which, at the request of the Church Missionary Society, were published in 1860 by the British and Foreign Bible Society as the first instalment of an entirely new translation in a language spoken over a vast extent of country. At present there are extant the gospels of Matthew and Mark in the Nupé. (B. P.)

Nutting, Rufus, D.D., a Presbyterian minister, was born at Old Groton, Middlesex Co., Mass., July 28, 1793. He graduated from Dartmouth College in 1813, and for several years thereafter took charge of a young ladies' seminary at Catskill, N. Y.; in 1821 became principal of Randolph Academy, Vt., which position he held seven years, meantime completing his theological course under the celebrated Dr. John Holt Rice. In 1828 he became professor of languages in the Western Reserve College at Hudson, Ohio; in 1840 resigned his chair, and two years later removed to Romeo, N. Y., taking charge of the branch of the State University then located there. In 1847 he established an academy at Lodi Plains, Washtenaw Co., Mich.; in 1870 removed to the city of Detroit, where he died, July 12, 1878. (W. P. S.)

O.

Oak, Council (or Synod) of the. See Chalcedon, Councils of.

Obi. See Old Man.

O'Brien, John, D.D., a minister of the Protestant Episcopal Church, rector of Zion Parish, Pontiac, Mich., died at that place, Dec. 13, 1864, aged seventy-one years. See *Amer. Quar. Church Rev.* April, 1865, p. 140.

O'Brien, Matthew, D.D., a Roman Catholic clergyman, was a native of Ireland, where he enjoyed a high reputation as a preacher. About 1800 he came to New York, and was attached to St. Peter's Church. He afterwards left New York in consequence of difficulties which arose, and died in Baltimore, Oct. 20, 1816. Dr. O'Brien published *Sermons on the Most Important Subjects of Morality and Religion* (Cork, 1798). See De Courcy and Shea, *Hist. of the Catholic Church in the United States*, p. 351.

O'Bryan, William, the founder of the Bible Christian Societies, was born at Gunwen, in the parish of Luxulion, Cornwall, Eng., Feb. 6, 1778. At the age of seventeen he obtained a clear manifestation of God's pardoning mercy, and almost immediately began to preach. In 1809 he was engaged as a supply in the place of a Wesleyan minister. In 1810 he was formally excluded from the Wesleyan Methodist Society for preaching in an irregular way, and in 1814 he relinquished business in order to devote himself wholly to the work of the ministry. Hearing that there were fourteen parishes in the east of Cornwall and the west of Devon in which there was no evangelical preaching, he visited them. His labors were successful, souls were converted. He organized the first class, or society, which afterwards received the appellation of Bible Christians, at Shebbear, in the county of Devon, Oct. 9, 1815. Twenty-two persons gave their names. At the session of the first conference held at Baddash, Launceston, Aug. 17, 1819, he was elected president. He filled this office each succeeding year until 1828. Unpleasant circumstances arising between himself and the brethren, in 1829 he left the conference. At the conference in 1830 William O'Bryan sought reconciliation with his brethren, and a satisfactory union was effected. Afterwards he left the denomination of his own free will. He came to the United States, crossed the Atlantic between New York and England several times, and died at a good old age, in New York city. His remains are interred in Greenwood Cemetery Brooklyn. See *Jubilee Volume of Bible Christians* (1865); Bible Christians.

Ochiltree, Michael, a Scotch prelate, was dean of the Church of Dunblane in 1425, and was made bishop in 1430. He was bishop at Dunblane in 1439 when he appended his seal to a solemn agreement between the queen-dowager and a committee of parliament, about the keeping of the young king, James II. See Keith, *Scottish Bishops*, p. 177.

O'Connor, Michael, D.D., a Roman Catholic prelate, was born at Cork, Ireland, Sept. 27, 1810. He was educated at Queenstown, and entered the Propaganda at Rome in 1833. He became president of the Roman Catholic Seminary of St. Charles Borromeo, Philadelphia, Pa., in 1838. He was consecrated bishop of Pittsburgh in 1843, translated to the see of Erie, Pa., in 1853, and referred to his former diocese in 1854. He resigned his episcopal office and united with the Jesuits in 1860. He died at Woodstock College, Md., Oct. 18, 1872.

Odenheimer, William Henry, D.D., a bishop of the Protestant Episcopal Church, was born in Philadelphia, Pa., Aug. 11, 1817. He graduated from the University of Pennsylvania in 1835, and from the General Theological Seminary in 1838; was ordained deacon by Bishop Onderdonk, of Pennsylvania, in the same year, and presbyter in 1841. After this he became rector of St. Peter's Church, Philadelphia, of which he remained pastor until his election as bishop of the diocese of New Jersey, April 27, 1859. The consecration to this office occurred Oct. 13 of the same year, in Richmond, Va. In 1874, when the diocese was divided, Bishop Odenheimer selected the "northern" portion. He died at his residence in Burlington, N. J., Aug. 14, 1879. See *Prot. Episc. Almanac*, 1880, p. 170.

Oelreich, Bernhard, a Lutheran theologian of Germany, was born at Itzehoe in 1626. He studied at different universities, was in 1664 court-preacher at Stockholm, in 1665 doctor of theology, and in 1668 pro-chancellor and professor of theology of the academy at Lunden. He then went to Bremen as superintendent and pastor, and died March 30, 1686. He wrote, *De Testamento Christi non Violando*:—*De Angelo*:—*De Sacra Scriptura*:—*De Ecclesia Lutherana.* See Witte, *Diarium Biographicum*; Moller, *Cimbria Literata*; Jöcher, *Allgemeines Gelehrten-Lexikon*, s. v. (B. P.)

Oelrichs, Johann Georg Arnold, a Lutheran theologian of Germany, was born at Hanover, June 8, 1767. He studied at Göttingen, Marburg, and Erlangen, was promoted as doctor of philosophy in 1787, and died at Göttingen, March 7, 1791. He is the author of, *De Ratione sive Relatione Filii cum Patre Sententia* (Göttingen, 1787), a prize essay:—*De Doctrina Platonis de Deo*, etc. (Marburg, 1788):—*Commentarii de Scriptoribus Ecclesiæ Latinæ Priorum VI Sæculorum*, etc. (Leipsic, 1791). See Winer, *Handbuch der theol. Lit.* i, 596, 597, 854; Döring, *Die gelehrten Theologen Deutschlands*, s. v. (B. P.)

Oemler, Christian Wilhelm, a Lutheran theologian of Germany, was born at Dennstädt, near Weimar, Sept. 20, 1728. He studied at Jena, acted for some time as private tutor, and was in 1755 preacher at Dennstädt. In 1764 he was called to Neumark, was in 1766 archdeacon at Jena, in 1776 superintendent and first preacher, and died June 2, 1802. He published, *Der Prediger an dem Krankenbette* (Jena, 1770):—*Repertorium für Pastoraltheologie und Casuistik* (1786–89, 4 parts):—and a number of other ascetical works, for which see Döring, *Die deutschen Kanzelredner*, s. v.; Winer, *Handbuch der theol. Lit.* ii, 33, 40, 49, 50, 54. (B. P.)

Ogden, Joseph Meeker, D.D., a Presbyterian minister, was born at Elizabethtown, N. J., Sept. 21, 1804. He graduated from Princeton College in 1823, and from the Theological Seminary there in 1826; spent two years in evangelistic work in Pennsylvania; was pastor of the Presbyterian Church at Chatham in 1828, of which he became pastor emeritus in 1873, but continued to reside there until his sudden death, Feb.

13, 1884. See *Necrol. Report of Princeton Theol. Sem.* 1884, p. 9.

Ogilby, Frederick, D.D., a Protestant Episcopal clergyman, was born in Ireland, Dec. 27, 1813. He graduated from Rutgers College, New Brunswick, N. J., in 1834, and from the General Theological Seminary in 1837; officiated successively in Grace Church, New York city, and in Burlington, N. J., under bishop Doane; then became rector of the Church of the Ascension, Philadelphia, Pa., from 1842 to 1858; and for the last twenty-three years of his life he was an assistant minister in Trinity Parish, New York city. He died March 25, 1878. See *Prot. Episc. Almanac*, 1879, p. 170.

O'Hanly, Donat, an Irish prelate, was educated in Ireland, and went to England, where he became a Benedictine monk at Canterbury. He returned to Ireland, and was consecrated archbishop of Dublin in 1085. He died Nov. 23, 1095. See D'Alton, *Memoirs of the Archbishops of Dublin*, p. 35.

O'Hanly, Samuel, an Irish prelate, was a nephew of Donat O'Hanly, and became a Benedictine monk. He was a native of Ireland, and succeeded to the archbishopric of Dublin in 1095. He died July 4, 1121. See D'Alton, *Memoirs of the Archbishops of Dublin*, p. 41.

Ojibway Version. See Chippeway.

Old Man of Obi, a remarkable idol of the Ostiac Tartars, who live near the river Obi. It consists of wood, and has a nose resembling the snout of a hog, in which is a hook of iron. The eyes are made of glass, and the head is embellished with a large pair of horns. Its devotees oblige it to change its place of residence every three years, transporting it over the Obi from one station to another with great solemnity, in a vessel made for that purpose. When the ice dissolves, and the river overflows its banks, the Ostiacs flock to this idol in a body and beseech it to prove propitious to their fishery. If the season fails to answer their expectations they load the god with a myriad of reproaches, and insult him as an old, impotent, and despicable deity; but if they prove successful in fishing, the god is allowed part of the booty.

Oliver, George, D.D., an English divine, was born at Papplewick in 1782, and educated at Trinity College, Cambridge, where he graduated in 1803. He took orders, and in 1809 became head-master of King Edward's Grammar-school at Great Grimsby. He became vicar of Scopwick in 1831, incumbent of Wolverhampton in 1834, rector of South Hykeham in 1847, and died at Lincoln, March 3, 1867. He filled the highest offices in the Masonic order, and wrote numerous works on local ecclesiastical history and Freemasonry, for which see Allibone, *Dict. of Brit. and Amer. Authors*, s. v.

Ollier, Pierre, a Protestant theologian of Montauban, was born at that place in 1573. In 1606 he was pastor at Saint-André de Valborgne, in 1610 at Alais, and in 1621 at Montauban, where he died Oct. 5, 1645. He was the successor of Pierre Bérauld in the theological chair, and wrote *La Conférence de St. Antoine entre Pierre Ollier, et Pascal* (Montauban, 1624). See Lichtenberger, *Encyclop. des Sciences Religieuses*, s. v. (B. P.)

Ollivant, Alfred, D.D., an Anglican prelate, was born at Manchester, England, in 1798. He studied at St. Paul's school, London; graduated at Trinity College, Cambridge, in 1821, and became a fellow. In 1820 he was elected Craven University scholar, and in 1822 Tyrwhitt Hebrew scholar. He was vice-principal of St. David's College, Lamfeter, from 1827 to 1843, and from 1843 until 1849 held the regius professorship of divinity at Cambridge. He became bishop of Llandaff in 1849, and died Dec. 16, 1882. He published a number of sermons and some other practical works. He was a member of the Old Test. company of the Bible Revision Committee.

Olmstead, Lemuel Gregory, LL.D., a Presbyterian minister, was born at Maltaville, N. Y., July 5, 1808. He graduated from Union College in 1834, and pursued his studies in the Western Theological Seminary. He was licensed by the Presbytery of Beaver in 1837, and ordained by the Presbytery of Erie, April 20, 1848. He then visited Europe, sojourning in Rome for several years. His principal business was teaching. During the war of the rebellion he acted as chaplain for some three years. He died March 18, 1880. As a scientific scholar and antiquarian Dr. Olmstead has had few equals among his brethren of the Presbytery. See *Necrol. Report of Princeton Theol. Sem.* 1881, p. 54.

Olonetzian Version. See Russia, Versions of.

Olshausen, Detlev Johann Wilhelm, a Lutheran theologian of Germany, was born March 30, 1766, at Nordheim, Hanover. He studied at Göttingen, and after completing his studies acted as private tutor at different places. In 1794 he was deacon at Oldesloe, Holstein; in 1801 first preacher at Glückstadt; in 1815 superintendent at Eutin, and died Jan. 14, 1823. He wrote, *Prolegomena zu einer Kritik aller sogenannten Beweise für und wider Offenbarungen* (Copenhagen, 1791):—*De Immortalitate Hominum Sublata et Doctrina de Animi Simplicitate Certa* (ibid. eod.):—*De Usu Rationis in Religione Revelata* (1792):—*Lehrbuch der Moral und Religion* (2d ed. 1799):—*Predigten über die ganze christliche Pflichtenlehre* (Altona, 1798–1805, 8 vols.). See Winer, *Handbuch der theol. Lit.* ii, 126, 153, 203, 236; Döring, *Die gelehrten Theologen Deutschlands*, s. v. (B. P.)

Olshausen, Justus, a famous German Orientalist, brother of Hermann, was born May 9, 1800, at Hohenfelde, Holstein, and studied at Kiel, Berlin, and Paris. In 1823 he was professor at Kiel, and in 1845 member of the Danish Academy of Sciences. Four years after Holstein was annexed by Denmark, in 1848, Olshausen was deposed of his professorship. He was appointed, in 1853, head-librarian and professor of Oriental languages at Königsberg; in 1858 he was called to a position in the ministry for education at Berlin, from which he retired in 1874. Olshausen died Dec. 28, 1882. Besides his contributions to the monthly reports of the Berlin Academy of Sciences, Olshausen published, *Emendationen zum Alten Testament* (Kiel, 1826):—*Zur Topographie des alten Jerusalem* (1833):—*Erklärung der Psalmen* (Leipsic, 1853):—*Lehrbuch der Hebr. Sprache* (Brunswick, 1861):—*Die Pehlewi-Legenden auf den Münzen der letzten Sassaniden* (Leipsic, 1843):—*Ueber den Charakter der in den assyrischen Keilinschriften erhaltenen semitischen Sprache* (Berlin, 1866). See Winer, *Handbuch der theol. Lit.* i, 98, 151, 520; Fürst, *Bibl. Jud.* iii, 47. (B. P.)

O lux beata trinitas. See Ambrosian Hymns.

O miranda vanitas. See Bernard of Clairvaux's Hymns.

Onachus (or **Onacus**), a Scotch prelate, was probably bishop of the Isles about 1304. See Keith, *Scottish Bishops*, p. 301.

Oncken, John Gerhard, D.D., a German Baptist minister, was born in Varet, in the grand duchy of Oldenburg, Jan. 26, 1800. He went to England in his youth, and was converted. The British Continental Society sent him in 1823 as a missionary to Germany, his labors being principally confined to Hamburg and Bremen, and the province of East Frisia. In 1828 he became the agent of the Edinburgh Bible Society. He and six others were immersed, April 22, 1834, in the river Elbe, near Hamburg, by Rev. Barnas Sears, then of the Hamilton Theological Seminary, pursuing his studies in Germany. At the close of 1879 there were in Germany 16,602 members of Baptist churches, and the gospel was preached in 1173 preaching stations. Later statistics would largely swell these numbers. Mr. Oncken was ordained soon after his baptism, and "his life was one of apostolic toil and blessed success in spreading the gospel through Germany." His pastoral relation with the Church at Hamburg always remained, and that city was made the centre of his evangelistic labors. He frequently visited England to solicit funds to carry on his work in Germany, and in 1853 came to the United States for the same purpose. He died Jan. 2, 1884, in Zurich, where he had resided for two years. See Cathcart, *Baptist Encyclop.* p. 869. (J. C. S.)

Oneirocritica (from ὄνειρος, *a dream*, and κρίνω, *to judge*), the art of interpreting dreams, which among the ancient Egyptians was the duty of the hierogrammateis, or sacred scribes. See DREAMS.

Oneiromancy (from ὄνειρος, *a dream*, and μαντεία, *divination*), divination by means of dreams, or the interpretation of dreams in reference to future events. See DREAMS.

Ono. The probable representative of this place, *Kafr Ana*, is laid down on the Ordnance *Map* at nearly five miles north by west of Ludd (Lydda), and described in the accompanying *Memoirs* (ii, 251) as "a mud village, surrounded with palms and other trees in gardens, and has a well (sebîl) to the north."

Onuphis, one of the sacred bulls of the ancient Egyptians. It was of a black color, had shaggy recurved hair, and is supposed to have been the emblem of the retroceding sun.

Onymus, ADAM JOSEPH, a Roman Catholic theologian of Germany, was born March 29, 1754, at Würzburg, and died there Sept. 9, 1836, doctor of theology, cathedral dean, and vicar-general. He is the author of, *De Usu Interpretationis Allegoricæ in Novi Fœderis Tabulis* (Bamberg, 1803):—*Der* 104. *Psalm übersetzt und mit Anmerkungen* (Würzburg, 1807):—*Die Weisheit Sirach's aus dem Griechischen mit Anmerkungen* (1786–88):—*Die Glaubenslehre der kathol. Kirche praktisch vorgetragen* (Sulzbach, 1820–23, 3 parts):—*Die Sittenlehre der kathol. Kirche in systematischer Form* (1826):—*Das Leben und die Lehre Jesu nach Matthäus, Markus, und Lukas in Homilien vorgetragen* (1831):—*Geschichte des Alten und Neuen Testaments* (1789–97, 5 parts):—*Homilien und Betrachtungen über die Leidensgeschichte Jesu, seine Auferstehung u. Himmelfahrt* (Würzburg, 1827). See Fürst, *Bibl. Jud.* iii, 48 sq.; Winer, *Handbuch der theol. Lit.* i, 109, 233, 307, 317, 596; ii, 118, 258, 402. (B. P.)

Oojein Version. See HINDUWEE, DIALECTS OF.

Oosterzee, JOHANN JACOB VAN, a noted Dutch theologian, was born April 1, 1817, at Rotterdam. He studied at Utrecht, and on leaving the university in 1840 was made doctor of theology for presenting his *Disputatio Theologica de Jesu, e Virgine Maria Nato*. In 1841 he was preacher at Eemnes, in 1843 at Alkmaar, in 1844 at Rotterdam. In 1862 he became professor of theology at Utrecht, and opened his lectures with a Latin oration, *De Scepticismo Hodiernis Theologis Caute Vitando*. Oosterzee lectured upon almost all the branches of theology, and soon became the recognized leader of the evangelical school of Holland. In learning, eloquence, and piety he ranked with the greatest divines of his age. He was also a voluminous writer. Several of his works have been translated, and commend themselves very highly to practical and conservative religious minds in Great Britain and America. Oosterzee died July 29, 1882, at Wiesbaden, Germany, where he had gone to restore his broken health. Besides his opening addresses, as, *Hoe moet het modern Naturalisme bestreden werden?* (1863):—*Zollen wij nog Theologie studeeren of niet?* (1865):—*Welke Theologie is in Staat, de Stormen van dezen Dagen te verduren?* (1866):—*Van welke Theologen is iets goeds voor de Toekomst der Kerk te verwachten?* (1867):—and valuable essays which he published in the *Jaarboeken voor wetenschappelijke Theologie*, edited by himself, and in other reviews, we mention, *Jacques Saurin* (1855):—*Christologie des Oude en Nieuwe Verbonds* (1855–57, 2 parts):—*Het Leven van Jezus* (2d ed. 1863–65):—*Historie of Roman? het Leven van Jezus door Renan vorlooping toegelicht* (1863):—*Het Johannes Evangelie, een viertal apologetische Voorlezingen* (1867):—*De Theologie des Nieuwen Verbonds* (2d ed. 1872; Engl. transl. Lond. 1870; 4th ed. 1882):—*Voor Kerk en Theologie, Mededeelingen en Bijdragen* (1871–75, 2 parts):—*Christelijke Dogmatick* (2d ed. 1876, 2 parts; Engl. transl., Lond. and New York, 1874; 2d ed. 1878):—*Practische Theologie* (Engl. transl. 1878, 2 parts):—*Theopneustie* (1882). For Lange's *Bible Work* Oosterzee wrote the commentary on Luke (1859; Engl. transl. New York, 1866); the Pastoral Epistles and Philemon (1861; transl. 1868); and with Lange he prepared the commentary on James's epistle (1862; Engl. transl. 1867). His *Sermons* comprise twelve volumes. Oosterzee left an autobiography and a work upon apologetics. See Zöckler, in *Beweis des Glaubens*, 1882; Evans, in *Catholic Presbyterian*, October, 1882; Zuchold, *Bibl. Theol.* ii, 959; *Neue evangel. Kirchenzeitung*, 1882, No. 36; Luthardt, *Lutherische Kirchenzeitung*, 1882, col. 810. (B. P.)

Ophni. The modern representative of this place, *Jufna*, is laid down on the Ordnance *Map* at two and three quarter miles north-west of Beitin (Bethel), and thus described in the accompanying *Memoirs* (ii, 294):

"An important Christian village, with a Latin church and convent (Mâr Yûsef), on an ancient road from the north to Jerusalem. The octagonal apse of this church, with colored glass in its east window, and a red-tiled pointed roof, forms a conspicuous feature of the village as seen from the south. The place is situated in a small plain, and on the south, higher up, is a spring called Ain Jelazûm. The road crosses the valley-bed by a small footbridge (now broken), with an inscription in Arabic, and on the south of this is a Greek church of St. George, with a fine walnut-tree and two meiss-trees. There are ruins of a town in the village, and pillar-shafts, as if of a former chapel, east of the Latin monastery. The hills and valleys are cultivated with olives, vines, figs, pears, apricots, and pomegranates. The population is stated by Robinson at two hundred, some Latins, some Greeks."

The Greek church is particularly described, ibid. p. 323.

Ophrah. (1) OF BENJAMIN. The probable modern representative of this place, *et-Tayibeh*, lies four miles north-east of Bethel on the Ordnance *Map*, and is thus described in the accompanying *Memoirs* (ii, 293): "A large village in a conspicuous position, with well-built stone houses. A central tower stands on the top of the hill; on either side are olive and fig gardens in the foreground. The view is extensive on both sides. A ruined church of St. George exists near, and there are remains of a ruined castle in the village. The inhabitants are Greek Christians." The archæological remains are minutely described (ibid. p. 370). (2) OF MANASSEH. For this place Lieut. Conder suggests (*Tent Work*, ii, 339) the modern *Ferata*, south-west of Nablûs; but this is not within Manasseh, and is proposed by Guérin for Pirathon (q. v.). It is more probably (Tristram, *Bible Places*, p. 203) *Arrabeh*, which is laid down on the Ordnance *Map* at two miles south-west of Dothan, and described in the accompanying *Memoirs* (ii, 154) as a very large village on the slope of a bare ridge, with remains of an ancient town.

Opitz, PAUL FRIEDRICH, a German scholar, son of Heinrich, was born at Kiel, March 26, 1684. He studied at different universities, was in 1721 professor of Greek and Oriental languages at his native city, in 1727 professor of philosophy, and died Oct. 5, 1747. He published, *De Custodia Templi Hierosolymitani Nocturna* (Kiel, 1710):—*De Gigantibus* (1715):—*De Amico Israelitarum in Festo Tabernaculorum Consortio* (1717):—*De Christo Apostolo et Pontifice Confessionis Nostræ* (1721):—*De Hadriani Imperatoris Nomine, Indole, Virtutibus ac Vitiis* (1722):—*De Hadriani Imperatoris Moribus, Eruditisque cum Doctoribus Judæorum Controversiis* (1723). See Döring, *Die gelehrten Theologen Deutschlands*, s. v. (B. P.)

Oporin, JOACHIM, a Lutheran theologian of Germany, was born Sept. 12, 1695. He studied at different universities, and commenced his academical career at Kiel in 1719. In 1733 he was professor of theology, in 1735 went to Göttingen, and died Sept. 5, 1753, doctor of theology. He published, *Historiæ Criticæ de Perennitate Animi Humani* (Kiel, 1719):—*Historia Critica Doctrinæ de Immortalitate Mortalium*, etc. (Hamburg, 1735):—*De Messia, cum Infans Esset* (1739):—*De Firmitate ac Inspiratione Divina* (1740):—*Clavis Evangelii Joannis* (Göttingen, 1743):—*Zacharias auf's Neue übersetzt*, etc.:—*Diss. Oracula Esaiæ c.* 40-55 (1750), etc. See Fürst, *Bibl. Jud.* iii, 49; Döring, *Die gelehrten Theologen Deutschlands*, s. v., where a complete list of Oporin's writings is given. (B. P.)

Oppenheim, David, a modern Jewish writer, was born Dec. 18, 1816, at Leipnik, Moravia. He received a thorough rabbinical education, was in 1846 rabbi at Jamnitz, in 1857 at Gross-Beeskerek, Hungary, and died Oct. 21, 1876, at Vienna. Oppenheim contributed to all the leading Jewish journals and reviews, and caused a great stir among Roman Catholics by keenly criticising, in the *Wiener Mitheilungen*, an article on the history of the Jews in Austria, which had appeared in the *Freiberger Kirchenlexikon*. Oppenheim laid bare the falsehoods and misstatements of that article, and elicited the rejoinder of Ritter von Pawlikowski, who, in his book of a hundred sheets, on the relation between Jews and Christians, devoted no less than seventy pages to refute, or rather to insult, Oppenheim. One of his ancestors was David ben-Abraham Oppenheim (q. v.) (B. P.)

Oreads were nymphs who presided over the mountains, daughters of Jupiter. They were very numerous, Diana having a thousand to attend her. These nymphs were accredited with having first reclaimed men from devouring each other, by teaching them to subsist on acorns and chestnuts.

Oreb, The Rock. Tristram (*Bible Places*, p. 230) acquiesces in the identification of this with the remarkable peak two and a half miles north of Riha (Jericho), called *Osh el-Ghurah*, which is the most prominent of all the conical peaks that terminate the terrace running down into the Jordan valley, and is about five hundred feet above the plain (*Memoirs* accompanying the Ordnance Survey, iii, 167).

O'Reilly, Bernard, D.D., a Roman Catholic bishop, was born in Ireland in 1803. He was consecrated bishop of Hartford, Conn., Nov. 10, 1850, and died at sea in January, 1856.

Orenburg-Tartar Version of the Scripture. As the name indicates, this version is intended for the Tartars in the vicinity of Orenburg. The version made into that dialect is not an original translation, but merely an accommodation of Mr. Brunton's Karass Version (q. v.) to the peculiar idioms and orthography of the Kirghisian Tartars, residing in the Russian government of Orenburg. Mr. Charles Frazer, one of the Scottish missionaries at Astrachan, prepared a translation of the New Test., which left the mission-press at Astrachan in 1820, at the expense of the British and Foreign Bible Society. Since 1871 a part of the Old Test. has also been published. (B. P.)

Oriental Literature and Languages is the common designation for the languages and literatures of all the peoples of Asia, as well as of those of Moslem Africa and Europe. Even during the Middle Ages the attention of European savants was turned towards the Oriental languages, especially the Arabic, and this for two main reasons. In the *first* place, it was religious zeal which, by the knowledge of the Arabic, intended to refute the Mohammedans and convert them to Christianity. For this purpose pope Innocent IV ordered that chairs for instruction in Arabic should be founded at Paris, and popes Clement IV and Honorius IV showed also a great interest in the matter. Under Clement V, the synod held at Vienne, in 1311, resolved that professors of Arabic and Chaldee should be appointed at Paris, Rome, Oxford, Bologna, and Salamanca. Pope John XXII especially instructed the bishop of Paris to see that these languages were taught in the Sorbonne. In the *second* place, it was a scientific interest which led to the study of Oriental literature, in order to make the Western nations acquainted with the medical, astronomical, and philosophical writings of the Arabs, and with the works of Aristotle, which were extant only in Arabic translations. Towards the end of the 12th century we meet with Latin translations from the Arabic, which increased during the Middle Ages, and were printed in the 15th century. The Reformation revived the study of Oriental languages by their application to Biblical exegesis. For the Church of Rome the study of Oriental languages became a matter of necessity, because of her missionary stations in the East, and thus pope Urban VIII founded, in 1627, at Rome, the Collegium pro Fide Propaganda, where the Oriental languages were taught. Through the Jesuits in China and Japan, Europe became acquainted with the eastern languages of Asia and their literature. In a more scientific manner the study of the Oriental languages was taken up in the middle of the 18th century. The Englishman, William Jones, while a resident in East India (1780-90), called special attention to the riches of the Indian literature, and founded at Calcutta, in 1784, the Asiatic Society. At Paris, Silvestre de Sacy made the study of Arabic of special interest, and attracted students from all parts of Europe. Till towards the end of the 18th century the study of the Oriental languages had only occupied a subordinate position in the curriculum of sciences; but with the formation of the different Asiatic societies the study of Oriental languages had become a specialty. The societies for promoting this study are as follows, of which the first three are the most important in Europe:

1. The *Asiatic Society of Bengal*, founded in 1784, by Sir William Jones, at Calcutta, published the *Asiatic Researches* (Calcutta, 1788-1832, 17 vols.), which were partly translated into French and German. Since 1832 the *Asiatic Researches* have been superseded by the *Journal of the Asiatic Society of Bengal*, which is published monthly. Under the auspices of this society, but at the expense of the Anglo-Indian government, since 1846 the *Bibliotheca Indica*, a collection of Oriental works in the original, with a translation, of which at the beginning of the year 1880 more than five hundred numbers had already appeared, is published. Besides the Asiatic Society there exist a great many branch societies, which also have their own periodicals.
2. The *Société Asiatique*, at Paris, founded in 1822 by Silvestre de Sacy (q. v.), Klaproth (q. v.), Abel Rémusat, Jomard, Chézy, and others, which, besides editing the *Journal Asiatique*, since 1823, also publishes Oriental works, partly in the original, partly in translations.
3. The *Royal Asiatic Society of Great Britain and Ireland*, which was opened by Colebrooke, March 19, 1823. In the place of the *Transactions* (1824-34, 3 vols.), it now publishes the *Journal of the Royal Asiatic Society*.
4. The *Deutsche morgenländische Gesellschaft*, founded in 1845. Its journal is *Zeitschrift der deutschen Gesellschaft*.
5. The *Société Orientale de France*, at Paris, with the *Revue de l'Orient* as its organ since 1845.
6. The *Syro-Egyptian Society*, at London, with *Original Papers* as the journal since 1850.
7. The *Koninglijke Institüt voor de Taal-, Land- en Volkenkunde van Neederlandsch Indië*, at Amsterdam, which publishes the *Bijdragen* since 1853.
8. The *American Oriental Society*, at Boston, founded in 1842, with the *Journal*, since 1843, for its organ.

See Benfey, *Geschichte der Sprachwissenschaft und orientalischer Philologie in Deutschland* (Munich, 1869); Zenker, *Bibliotheca Orientalis* (Leipsic, 1846-61, 2 vols.); Trübner, *Oriental Literary Record* (Lond. 1865 sq.); Friderici, *Bibliotheca Orientalis* (Leipsic, 1876-83); Klatt u. Kuhn, *Literatur-Blatt für orientalische Philologie* (ibid. 1883 sq.). (B. P.)

Orissa Version. See Uriya Version.

Ornithomancy (from ὄρνις, *a bird*, and μαντεία, *divination*), a species of divination practiced among the ancient Greeks by means of birds. See Augury.

Osbernus, CLAUDIANUS. See OSBERN OF GLOUCESTER.

Osbon, ABIATHAR MANN, D.D., a Methodist Episcopal minister, was born at Pittsfield, Mass., in 1808. He entered the New York Conference in 1829, with which he ever after remained connected, and in which he occupied many of the most important appointments, as pastor and presiding elder, and also as a member of the General Conference. He died Aug. 6, 1882. He often wrote for the periodicals, and published a small volume on the prophecies of Daniel. See *Minutes of Annual Conferences*, 1883, p. 89.

Osgood, Samuel (1), D.D., a Congregational minister, was born at Fryeburg, Me., in February, 1774. He graduated at Dartmouth College in 1805, and in 1809 settled as pastor of the First Congregational Church in Springfield, Me., where he continued till his death, Dec. 8, 1862. Dr. Osgood was an able preacher and an active reformer. He published a number of sermons and addresses. See *Appleton's Annual Cyclop.* 1862, p. 681.

Osgood, Samuel (2), D.D., LL.D., a Protestant Episcopal clergyman, was born at Charlestown, Mass., Aug. 30, 1812. He graduated from Harvard College in 1832, and entered the Unitarian ministry in 1835. In 1837 he was settled over a church in Nashua, N. H. Previous to this he had been the editor, with James Freeman Clarke, of *The Western Messenger*, at Louisville, Ky., a periodical which for a time maintained a high literary rank. In 1841 he became pastor of the Westminster Church. From 1849 to 1869 he was pastor of the Church of the Messiah in New York city. From 1850 to 1854 he was one of the editors of *The Christian Enquirer*, a Unitarian journal published in that city. Having resigned his charge, he travelled abroad for seven months. Returning to New York, he entered the ministry of the Protestant Episcopal Church in 1869. He died in New York city, April 14, 1880. Dr. Osgood's contributions to different magazines, reviews, and newspapers were of a high order; the same is true of the occasional orations, lectures, and addresses which he delivered from time to time. He was a very versatile student, although perhaps his strong point was that of theology and Christian morals; an excellent German scholar, and familiar with all the great German theologians; also fond of historical researches, and a prominent member of the New York Historical Society, of which for a long time he was home corresponding secretary. But although of studious habits, he always took a warm interest in current public events, as a public-spirited citizen, ever ready to co-operate in the advancement of any scheme for promoting literature or art. His last public work was the reading of his paper before the Historical Society on *Channing's Place in American History*. Much of Dr. Osgood's literary work, scattered through periodicals or printed in a pamphlet form, it is impossible here to catalogue. He published, among other works of greater or less importance, translations from Olshausen and De Wette, *The History of Passion* (1839), and *Human Life* (1842). Among his original works are, *Studies in Christian Biography* (1851):—*The Hearthstone* (1854):—*God with Men; or, Footprints of Providential Leaders* (eod.):—*Milestones in our Life Journey* (1855):—*The Holy Gospels*, illustrated by Overbeck (1856):—*Student Life* (1860):—*American Leaves* (1867). Among his principal addresses before the New York Historical Society was one upon *Thomas Crawford and Art in America*, in 1875. He also delivered a discourse before the society on its sixty-second anniversary, Nov. 20, 1866. Many of his essays will be found in *The International Review*, *The North American Review*, *The Bibliotheca Sacra*, *Harper's Monthly Magazine*, and other periodicals. It is stated that he left unfinished a work entitled *The Renaissance of Art in America*, which was to include his papers upon Bryant and Channing.

Osgood, S. M., D.D., a Baptist minister, was born at Henderson, Jefferson Co., N. Y., March 2, 1807. In his early manhood he resided in Cortland, N. Y., and was one of the publishers of the *Cortland Chronicle*. In 1831 he came back to Watertown, and in 1834 received an appointment as missionary printer at Maulmain, Burmah. He returned to the United States in 1846, and performed, for a period of about twenty-nine years, most valuable service as one of the financial agents of the Missionary Union. He received, in 1860, an appointment as district secretary of the Missionary Union for the West, which he held until his death, at his home in Chicago, July 9, 1875. See Cathcart, *Baptist Encyclop.* p. 876. (J. C. S.)

Osiander. By way of supplement we add the following:

1. GOTTLIEB, was born at Stuttgart, March 15, 1786, and died Dec. 6, 1827, dean at Knittlingen. He is the author of different theological essays, for which see Döring, *Die gelehrten Theologen Deutschlands*, iii, 168; Ersch u. Gruber, *Allgemeine Encyclop.* p. 261 sq.

2. JOHANN, a son of Johann Adam (1), was born at Tübingen, April 2, 1657. After completing his studies he travelled through France, and at Paris he made the acquaintance of La Chaise, who in vain endeavored to convert him to the Church of Rome. Having returned, Osiander was in 1686 professor of Hebrew at Tübingen; a few years later professor of Greek and philosophy, and assistant preacher to his father. Osiander died Oct. 18, 1724, having held the highest civic and ecclesiastical positions. See Schmidt, *Leben Johann Osiander's* (1843); Ersch u. Gruber, *Allgemeine Encyclop.* Theil 3, vol. vi, p. 263 sq.

3. JOHANN ERNST, a brother of Gottlieb, was born June 23, 1792, at Stuttgart. In 1820 he was deacon at Metzingen, in 1824 professor at Maulbronn, in 1840 dean at Göppingen, in 1860 doctor of theology, and died April 3, 1870, senior of the Protestant clergy of Würtemberg. He is the author of, *Philipp Melanchthon, eine Rede* (Stuttgart, 1830):—*Zum Andenken Dr. Gottfried Menken's* (Bremen, 1832):—*Apologie des Lebens Jesu gegen Strauss* (Stuttgart, 1837):—*Lehrbuch zum christlichen Religionsunterricht* (1839):—*Commentar über die Briefe Pauli an die Korinthier* (1849, 1858). See Winer, *Handbuch der theol. Lit.* i, 552; Zuchold, *Bibl. Theol.* ii, 963 sq.; *Würtembergisches Kirchenblatt*, 1870, p. 195; Plitt-Herzog, *Real-Encyklop.* s. v.

4. JOHANN RUDOLF, son of Johann, was born May 21, 1689, at Tübingen, and died Oct. 25, 1725, professor of theology. See Gass, *Geschichte der protest. Dogmatik*, iii, 126. (B. P.)

Ossitinian Version. See RUSSIA, VERSIONS OF.

Ostjakian Version. See RUSSIA, VERSIONS OF.

Ostrander, Daniel, a veteran Methodist Episcopal minister, was born at Plattekill, N. Y., Aug. 9, 1772. He was converted at sixteen, entered the New York Conference in 1793, was for fourteen years on circuits, for eight on station (New York, Brooklyn, and Albany), and for twenty-eight years was presiding elder. From 1808 to 1840 inclusive he was elected member of every General Conference. He retired in 1843, and died Dec. 8 of that year. He was firm, faithful, wise in pursuing his course, ever at his post, and always ready to serve. See *Minutes of Annual Conferences*, 1843-44, p. 472; Sprague, *Annals of the Amer. Pulpit*, vii, 221.

Ostrander, Henry, D.D., a Reformed (Dutch) minister, was born at Plattekill, N. Y., March 11, 1781. He graduated from Union College in 1799; studied under Dr. Froeligh; was licensed by the Classis of Paramus in 1800; became pastor at Coxsackie in 1801; at Catskill (or Leeds) in 1810; Caatsban in 1812; also at Saugerties village in 1839; and stated supply at Hurley in 1811. He was without a charge from 1862 until his death, Nov. 22, 1872. Fifteen *Sermons* of his are published in Gordon's *Memoir* of him, with selections from his autobiography, and extracts from his letters. See Corwin, *Manual of Ref. Church in America*, 3d ed. p. 396.

Otey, James Hervey, D.D., a bishop of the Protestant Episcopal Church, was born at Liberty, Bedford Co., Va., Jan. 27, 1800. He graduated at the University of North Carolina in 1820, was ordained deacon in 1825, and presbyter in 1827; afterwards became rector of St. Paul's, in Franklin, Tenn., from which parish he was elected bishop of the diocese, the consecration taking place in Christ Church, Philadelphia, Jan. 14, 1834. He died at Memphis, Tenn., April 23, 1863. From his urbanity and piety he usually went by the name of "the good bishop." He was the author of numerous *Sermons*, etc., and a volume on *The Unity of the Church* (1852). See *Amer. Quar. Church Review*, July, 1863, p. 321.

Otji (Tschi, or Twi) Version of the Scriptures. The language distinguished as "Ashantee Proper, or Otji," is spoken in the south of Asante (Ashantee), in Fantee, Akim, Akwapim, and in Akwam. There are trifling dialectic differences in the language spoken in these several districts, but it may be considered, nevertheless, one and the same with the Akwapim or Otji, the best cultivated of them all. In 1846 the missionaries of the Basle Missionary Society commenced the preparation of a version of the New Test. into Ashantee, and completed the gospels of Matthew and Luke. Since 1855 the Rev. J. G. Christaller, one of the missionaries stationed at Acropong, has prosecuted the task of Scripture translation into the Otji language, and the four gospels, after a careful revision, were printed in 1857 by the British and Foreign Bible Society. In 1861 the book of Genesis, the epistle to the Romans, and the general epistles of John followed, and in 1865 the entire New Test. was in circulation. In 1870 the Old Test. was printed in Europe, under the superintendence of the translator, and since then the entire Bible has been in circulation. (B. P.)

Otji-herero Version of the Scriptures. The Otji-herero is the same as the Damara, and is spoken by a south-western African tribe. The committee of the South African Auxiliary Bible Society printed in 1875 the book of Psalms in that language, the translation having been prepared by the Rev. H. Brincker, of the Rhenish Missionary Society. In 1879 the British and Foreign Bible Society, at the request of Dr. Fabri, of the Rhenish Missionary Society, printed the New Test., which was also translated by Mr. Brincker, and revised by a committee. (B. P.)

Otshirbani, in Kalmuckian worship, was a god of third rank, represented under a singular form. He appears only clothed about the hips. The figure has large eyes, a monstrous open mouth, is contracted, with head turned back, as if in convulsions. This deity was sent to combat the evil dæmons. He was victorious, and decapitated the spirits, from which he made himself a crown, ear-rings, and a long necklace, which extended to the belly. From the mouth through the body there runs a straight channel, which physicians use to give medicine. The idol is placed on the mouth of the sick, a pill is put into the channel, and falls into the mouth of the patient.

Figure of Otshirbani.

Otter, William, D.D., an English prelate, was born at Cuckney, Nottinghamshire, Oct. 23, 1768. He was educated at Jesus College, Cambridge, of which he became fellow and tutor; was presented to the rectory of Colneworth, Bedfordshire, in 1804, with which he held the vicarage of Sturmer, in Essex; appointed to Chetwynd, Shropshire, in 1810; to Kinlet, in 1816; St. Mark's, Kennington, in 1825; was principal of King's College, London, in 1831, and consecrated bishop of Chichester, Oct. 2, 1836. He died Aug. 20, 1840. Bishop Otter was an accomplished scholar, an able preacher, blameless in life, and held in high esteem by all who knew him. He published three *Tracts* respecting the Bible Society against bishop Marsh (1812-13):—*Life and Remains of E. D. Clarke* (1824, 4to; 1825, 2 vols. 8vo):—*Life of T. R. Malthus* (1836). After his death a volume was published of his *Pastoral Addresses* (1841, 8vo). See (Lond.) *Gentlemen's Magazine*, Nov. 1840, p. 539; *London Athenæum*, 1840, p. 364; *The* (Lond.) *Christian Remembrancer*, Jan. 1841, p. 1; Allibone, *Dict. of Brit. and Amer. Authors*, s. v.

Otther, Jacob, the reformer of Esslingen, was born at Lautenburg, in Alsace. He studied at Freiburg, where Wimpheling was his teacher, and while a resident at Strasburg Otther published the sermons of Geiler, of Kaiserberg, in a Latin translation, in 1510. In 1520, while preacher at Wolfenweiler, near Freiburg, he openly declared himself an adherent of Luther. In 1522 he was preacher at Kenzingen, in the Breisgau, but he left that place in 1524 on account of the opposition which he met from the civil and ecclesiastical authorities. Otther went to Neckarsteinach, near Heidelberg, and abolished there the mass and other papistic usages. In 1527 he left that place, and, after a short stay at Strasburg and in Switzerland, finally settled in 1532 at Esslingen, where he brought about the work of reformation, which had been commenced by Ambrosius Blaser. Otther died in the early part of 1547. See Seckendorf, *Ausführliche Historie des Lutherthums* (Leipsic, 1714); Keim, *Reformationsblätter der Reichsstadt Esslingen* (1860) and *Schwäbische Reformationsgeschichte;* Plitt-Herzog, *Real-Encyklop.* s. v. (B. P.)

Otto, Leopold Martin von, a Lutheran theologian, was born at Warsaw, in Poland, Nov. 2, 1819. He studied at Dorpat and Berlin, and acted for some time as vicar at Kalish. In 1844 he was pastor at Petrikau, and in 1849 at Warsaw, where he developed a great activity in founding many Christian institutions. Having taken part in the Polish revolution, he was imprisoned and suspended from his office. From 1866 to 1875 he served as pastor at Teshen, in Austrian Silesia, and when permission was granted for his return to his native town, he resumed his pastorate there again, where he died, Sept. 22, 1885. In acknowledgment of his great efforts for propagating theological literature in the Polish language, the Leipsic University conferred on him in 1864 the degree of doctor of divinity. He published, The Augsburg Confession in the Polish language, in 1852:—*History of the Evangelical Church of the Augsburg Confession of Warsaw, from* 1652 *to* 1781 (1882). He afterwards published an evangelical review, the *Zwiastun Ewangeliczny*. (B. P.)

Ouseel, Philipp, a Lutheran theologian of Germany, was born at Dantzic, Oct. 7, 1671, and studied theology and medicine at different universities. In 1711 he was preacher at Leyden, in 1717 professor at Frankfort, and died April 12, 1724, doctor of theology and medicine. He wrote, *De Lepra Cutis Hebræorum:*—*Introductio in Accentuationem Hebræorum Metricam:*—*De Accentuatione Hebræorum Prosaica:*—*De Auctore Decalogi:*—*De Nominibus Decalogi:*—*De Decalogo soli Israeli Data:*—*De Denario regni Cœlorum:*—*De Natura Decalogi.* See Fürst, *Bibl. Jud.* iii, 60; Jöcher, *Allgemeines Gelehrten-Lexikon*, s. v. (B. P.)

Outrein, Johann d', a Reformed theologian, was born at Middleburg, Oct. 17, 1663. He studied at Franeker, and was preacher there in 1687. In 1688 he was appointed librarian of the academy, in 1691 preacher at Arnheim, in 1703 at Dort, in 1708 at Amsterdam, and died Feb. 20, 1722. He was a voluminous writer. A complete list of his many writings is given in Jöcher, *Allgemeines Gelehrten-Lexikon*, s. v. (B. P.)

Outremont, Hector Albert Chaulet d', a French prelate, was born at Tours, Feb. 27, 1825. He became titular of St. Gatien of Tours in 1862, bishop of Agen in 1871, archbishop of Mans in 1874, and died Sept. 16, 1884.

Ouvrier, Ludwig Benjamin, a Protestant theologian of Germany, was born at Prenzlov, Prussia, May 7, 1735. He studied at Halle, and was for some time private tutor. In 1763 he was made court-preacher at Darmstadt, in 1770 member of consistory, and in 1772 professor of theology at Giessen. Ouvrier died Oct. 1, 1792. He published, *Untersuchung über die Lehrsätze des Christenthums* (Berlin, 1773):—*De Theologia Populari* (Giessen, 1775):—*Annotationes Quædam ad* 2 *Petr. ii*, 2; *Judæ* 6 (1776):—*De Necessitate Satisfactionis a Paulo Rom. viii*, 3 *Asserta* (1777):—*De Theologia Morali* (1779):—*An Actor. iv*, 24 *Spiritus Sanctus Dicatur Universi Creator* (1780):—*De Iisdem in Resurrectione Restituendis Corporibus* (1781):—*Geschichte der Religionen nebst ihren Gründen und Gegengründen* (1781–83, 2 vols.). See Döring, *Die gelehrten Theologen Deutschlands*, s. v. (B. P.)

Overkamp, Georg Wilhelm, a Lutheran theologian of Germany, was born Jan. 9, 1707, at Greifswalde, and died at his birthplace, July 27, 1790, professor and senior of the university. He wrote, *De Significatione Verborum Quibus Induratio Pharaonis in Historia Mosaica Exprimitur* (Jena, 1736):—*De Judæis Primariis Christiani Nominis Hostibus* (eod.):—*De Judæis Frustra a Guilielmo Whistono aliisque Corruptionis Hebræi Codicis Insimulatis* (Greifswalde, 1739):—*De Hebræorum* סגן *Pontificis Maximi in Summo Expiationis de Vicario* (eod.):—*De Peccato ac Pœna Israëlis Typicis* (1743):—*De Divinitus Prædicto ac Definito Tempore Nativitatis Messiæ* (eod.):—*De Philosophia Orientali* (1744):—*De Magis ex Oriente ut Vere Sapientibus* (1749):—*De Salomone, Veræ Sapientiæ Magistro, ex Libro Coheleth Ostenso* (1754):—*Meletema Quadragesimale in Ies. liii*, 7, 8, 9 (1760):—*Commentatio in Ps. xxxii* (1770):—*De Distinctione in Judæos et Græcos, in Græcos et Barbaros* (1782). See Fürst, *Bibl. Jud.* iii, 60 sq.; Döring, *Die gelehrten Theologen Deutschlands*, s. v. (B. P.)

Owen, Isaac, D.D., a Methodist Episcopal minister, was born at Milton, Vt., March 8, 1809. Two years later he removed with his parents to Indiana. He was converted in his sixteenth year, in his twenty-third was licensed to preach, and in 1834 entered the Indiana Conference. For fourteen years he filled without interruption the regular appointments given him by that Conference, and during the last four years of the time served with great efficiency as agent of the Indiana Asbury University. In 1848 he received a transfer to California as a missionary. Upon his arrival in California the interests of the work were mainly placed in his hands. For many years he filled the office of presiding elder; twice he was elected to the General Conference; once, upon the non-arrival of the bishop, he was chosen to fill his place and preside; and he was always among the foremost in Church and literary enterprises. To no one man was California more indebted for her progress in morals and social reform than to Dr. Owen. He died Feb. 9, 1866. Industry, zeal, and faithfulness marked his life. See *Minutes of Annual Conferences*, 1867, p. 233; Simpson, *Cyclop. of Methodism*, s. v.

Owen, Joseph, D.D., a Presbyterian minister, was born in Bedford, N. Y., June 14, 1814. He graduated from Princeton College in 1835, and from the Theological Seminary there in 1838; was ordained in 1839 for the mission-field, in which he did his life-work. Landing in India in 1840, and assigned to the station of Allahabad, he continued to labor there without release or relaxation for four-and-twenty years. After the death of his first wife, in 1864, he obtained a short release, and crossed the Himalaya mountains into Thibet. Five years later he undertook a visit to his native land. In acknowledgment of the value of his translation of the Bible into Hindû, the North India Bible Society presented him money to visit Palestine. He visited Egypt, Jerusalem, Constantinople, Germany, and Scotland on this tour, and was intending to visit America. He died at Edinburgh, Scotland, Dec. 4, 1870.

Owl-headed Minerva. The idea of this goddess is due to the imaginative enthusiasm of Dr. Schliemann, who believed that he saw an owl-headed Athena in the rude attempts at the imitation of the human face on vases and other objects discovered by him at Hissarlik. The faces of certain images of Apollo, found on the coasts of Asia Minor, and now in the British Museum, are ruder than those of the Hissarlik antiquities. Similar faces are also found on the Etruscan blackware from Chinsi, where the spout of the vase serves as a nose, and it is probable that the ornamentation originated in two eyes being set on each side of a vessel's spout or mouth, to ward off the evil eye. Two large eyes are sometimes introduced on Greek vases in the midst of a group of figures. See Minerva.

Oxygrăphus (from ὄξυς, *swift*, and γπάφω, *to write*), a name sometimes given by the Greek fathers to the *Notary* (q. v.) of the ancient Christian Church.

O'zem (Heb. *O'tsem*, אֹצֶם, *strength*; Sept. Ἀσόμ v. r. Ἀσάμ and Ἀσάν; Vulg. *Assom* and *Asom*), the name of two men of the tribe of Judah.

1. The fourth of the sons of Jerahmeel by his first wife (1 Chron. ii, 25). B.C. cir. 1656.

2. The sixth son of Jesse, and brother of David (1 Chron. ii, 15). B.C. cir. 1100.

P.

Pabisch, Francis Joseph, D.D., LL.D., an eminent Roman Catholic scholar and divine, was born at Zlabings, Moravia, March 30, 1825. In his fourteenth year he was sent to the grammar-school of Znaim, and from there to the high-school of Brünn; in 1843 entered the University of Vienna; and in 1847 the archiepiscopal seminary in the same city. In March, 1850, he was ordained priest, and was given a chaplaincy near Vienna. In 1851, on the invitation of Archbishop Purcell, of Cincinnati, he came to America, and was placed in charge of Whiteoak, seven miles from Cincinnati. In 1853 he began to give a few hours a week to teaching ecclesiastical history and German in the Seminary of Mount St. Mary's of the West. Later, he studied theology and canon law at the College of the Propaganda in Rome. He was appointed chaplain to the Church of Santa Maria sopra Minerva, and after four years of arduous study graduated doctor of theology and doctor of civil and canon law. From 1858 to 1860 he practiced as a jurist to the congregation of the Council of Trent. In 1861 Dr. Pabisch returned to the United States, and on his arrival at Cincinnati was given the chair of ecclesiastical history and canon law at the Seminary of Mount St. Mary's, and in 1863 succeeded to the rectorship. On the financial downfall of that institution, his intellect gave way, and he was taken to the Mount Hope Retreat, near Baltimore, where he died, Oct. 2, 1879. In connection with Rev. Thomas S. Byrne, Dr. Pabisch translated Alzog's *Universal Church History* from the German (Cincinnati,

1874, 1876, 1878, 3 vols. 8vo), with additions on the history in England and America. See (N. Y.) *Cath. Annual*, 1881, p. 93.

Pachacamac, the supreme god of the Peruvians. This deity had a magnificent temple in a valley called Pachacama, built by the Incas or emperors of Peru. Such immense treasures had been laid up in this temple that Pizarro found 900,000 ducats in it, though four hundred savages had taken away as much as they could carry. The Peruvians had so great a veneration for this deity that they offered him whatever they esteemed most precious, and so great was their awe of him that they durst not look upon his image. Even their priests and kings entered his temples with their backs towards his altar, and came out again without daring to turn.

Pachmann, THEODOR, a Roman Catholic theologian of Austria, for some time professor of canon law at the university in Vienna, who died Feb. 2, 1881, doctor of theology, is the author of *Lehrbuch des Kirchenrechtes* (Vienna, 1853, 3 vols.; 3d ed. 1863–66). See Zuchold, *Bibl. Theol.* ii, 969. (B. P.)

Packard, ALPHEUS SPRING, D.D., a Congregational minister and educator, was born at Chelmsford, Mass., Dec. 20, 1799, and was the son of Rev. Dr. Hezekiah Packard. He studied at the Phillips Academy of Exeter, and graduated from Bowdoin College in 1816. He was elected tutor of the college in 1819, and, in 1824, professor of languages and classical literature; from 1842 to 1845 filled a vacancy in the chair of rhetoric and oratory; in 1864 was called to the chair of the Collins professorship of natural and revealed religion; and in 1883 and 1884 was acting president. He was chosen a member of the Maine Historical Society in 1828, and was long its secretary and librarian. He died suddenly at Squirrel Island, Boothbay Harbor, Me., July 13, 1884. His sermons, lectures, and contributions of various kinds to the press were numerous. See *Boston Advertiser*, July 14, 1884. (J. C. S.)

Paddock, ZACARIAH, D.D., a Methodist Episcopal minister, was born in Northampton, N. Y., Dec. 20, 1798. He was converted at the age of eighteen, licensed to preach in 1818, and the same year entered the Genesee Conference. His most responsible appointments were: Ridgeway, Clarence, Batavia, French Creek, Westmoreland, Buffalo, Rochester, Auburn, Cazenovia, New York Mills, Sauquoit, Ithica, Binghamton, Oxford, Utica, Wilkesbarre, Honesdale, and Chenango; upon most of which he was eminently successful. He took a superannuated relation in 1870, and died, a member of the Wyoming Conference, at his home in Binghamton, N. Y., July 4, 1879. Dr. Paddock's name in American Methodism in his declining years became a synonym for gentleness, sweetness, and purity. He published several small volumes, and wrote quite extensively for the Church papers and periodicals. See *Minutes of Annual Conferences*, 1880, p. 86.

Padilla, FRANCESCO DE, a Roman Catholic theologian, for some time professor of theology at Seville, who died at Malaga, May 15, 1607, canon and doctor of theology, is the author of *Historia Ecclesiastica de Espanna* (Malaga, 1605, 2 vols, fol.). See Winer, *Handbuch der theol. Lit.* i, 816; Jöcher, *Allgemeines Gelehrten-Lexikon*, s. v. (B. P.)

Page, DAVID COOK, D.D., a Protestant Episcopal clergyman, was, in 1853, rector of a church in Memphis, Tenn.; about 1858 removed to Allegheny, Penn., as rector of Christ Church, and there remained during the greater part of the rest of his life. A short time previous to his death he became rector of Trinity Church, Natchez, Miss. He died in Allegheny City, Penn., May 7, 1878, aged seventy-six years. See *Prot. Episc. Almanac*, 1879, p. 170.

Pagendarm, JOHANN GERHARD, a Lutheran theologian of Germany, was born at Lübeck, Dec. 2, 1681. He studied at Wittenberg, and acted for some time as preacher at different places. In 1730 he commenced his academical career at Jena, and died May 23, 1754. He wrote, *De Codice Judæorum Olsnensium Ebræo* (Jena, 1730):—*De Hebdomatibus Danielis* (1745):—*De* אבי יסכה *et* אבי מלכה *ad Gen. xi*, 29, in the *Bibliotheca Lubecensis*, vi, No. 5. See Döring, *Die gelehrten Theologen Deutschlands*, s. v.; Fürst, *Bibl. Jud.* iii, 62; Jöcher, *Allgemeines Gelehrten-Lexikon*, s. v. (B. P.)

Pahari Version OF THE SCRIPTURE. The Pahari is spoken by the Paharis, a hill tribe in the Rajmahal district, Bengal, who are supposed to be among the earliest settlers in the country. The Rev. E. Droese, of Bhangalpore, who has spent nearly a quarter of a century among the Paharis, and who is the only European that knows much of their language, has translated the gospel of Luke, which was published by the Calcutta Auxiliary Bible Society in 1881. The same scholar also prepared a translation of the gospel of John, which was published in 1883. These are the only parts of the Scripture which are yet printed. (B. P.)

Paine, Robert, D.D., a bishop of the Methodist Episcopal Church South, was born in Person County, N. C., Nov. 12, 1799, of Baptist parents. In early life he removed to Tennessee; was converted Nov. 9, 1817; licensed to preach the same year; the next year was admitted into the Tennessee Conference, and after laboring on several circuits and in important stations, was elected president of La Grange College, Alabama, in 1830, a position which he retained until his elevation to the episcopacy in 1846. He had been a member of every General Conference from 1824, and was active in the discussion that led to the division of the Methodist Church in 1844. His extensive labors as a bishop closed with his death, Oct. 20, 1882. He was a very able preacher, a ready speaker, and a devoted Christian. He wrote *Life and Times of Bishop McKendree*. See *Minutes of Annual Conferences of the M. E. Church South*, 1882, p. 147; Simpson, *Cyclop. of Methodism*, s. v.

Paine, William Pomeroy, D.D., a Congregational minister, was born at Ashfield, Mass., Aug. 1, 1802. He studied at Ashfield Academy; in 1827 graduated from Amherst College, and in 1832 from Andover Theological Seminary; from 1829 to 1831 he was tutor in Amherst College. His only pastorate was of the Church at Holden, Mass., where he was regularly ordained and installed, Oct. 24, 1833. He resigned this charge in February, 1875, but remained pastor emeritus until his death, Nov. 28, 1876. See *Cong. Quarterly*, 1877, p. 421.

Painting, CHRISTIAN. The first law which governed the early Christian sculptors and painters was to present Christ as the source and centre of their life, and so to depict him that other figures in their compositions should appear like rays emanating from him. With respect to the contents and spirit of representation, it may be said that, during the entire period of early Christian art, both sculpture and painting were, for the most part, limited to symbolical expression. In the beginning, symbolical representations were alone permitted. Soon, however, the art impulse partially broke away from these fetters; yet art still remained a sort of *biblia pauperum*, and served chiefly as a mere reminder of the themes of sacred history. Even at a later period, when works of art were employed in multitudes for church decorations, Biblical scenes, especially from the Apocalypse, were still preferred. As early as the 4th century we find a portrait-like representation of sacred personages accompanying these forms of artistic symbolism. It was even believed that veritable portraits of Christ, the Madonna, and the Apostles, existed in paintings from the hand of St. Luke, and in sculpture from that of Nicodemus, in the napkin of St. Veronica, yea, even in the so-called ἀχειροποιήτοις ("likenesses of celestial origin").

In the first third of the early Christian period, from the 3d century to the second half of the 5th century, of which numerous works of art in the so-called cemeteries (catacombs of Rome, Naples, Syracuse, etc.) have been preserved, painting still maintained the ancient plastic method of representation (as may be seen also in the paintings in the cemeteries, in the mosaics of Santa Costanza and Santa Maria Maggiore in Rome, San Giovanni in Fonte, and San Nazario e Celso at Ravenna). In the second third, till the 8th century, painting sought more and more to adapt the antique forms to the idealistic, transcendental spirit of Christianity, as may be seen from the mosaics of Santa Pudentiana and Santi Cosma e Damiano at Rome, of San Appollinare Nuovo, San Appollinare in Classe, and San Vitale at Ravenna, and some miniatures. After the 8th century, painting, and in fact, the entire art of early Christianity, lapsed into a continually deepening decline, till the 11th century, as may be seen in the mosaics of San Prassede, San Marco, and others in Rome, and miniatures of various manuscripts, and the Iconostasis (q. v.) of Greek and Russian churches.

With the new life which the 11th century ushered in in Western Christendom, architecture reached not only the climax of its own development, but also asserted a decided preponderance over sculpture and painting. One spirit and one life prevailed in all three of the sister-arts. The newly awakened art impulse developed itself in the North, especially in Germany, much later in Italy. Here the earliest movement took place in the 12th century, and the following century had been ushered in before the first endeavors were made by single artists of lesser rank to blend the Byzantine style with the ancient Italian, and thus to infuse new life into the old Christian types. The "Romanesque" style of painting first reached completeness in Giovanni Cimabue and in Duccio di Boninsegna of Sienna (fl. about 1282). On this wise there grew up two schools of painting—that of Florence and that of Sienna; the Florentine of a severer type, approaching nearer to the early Christian (Byzantine), the Siennese characterized more by tenderness and sentiment, more independent, and likewise more graceful in the rendering of form. These two masters were followed by Giotto di Bondone of Florence (1276–1336), known under the title of "the father of Italian painting," but in fact only the founder of the Gothic style of painting. He was a bold reformer, and broke through the traditions of art and servile adherence to the early Christian types. The best pupils of Giotto were Taddeo Gaddi, and his son, Angelo Gaddi, Giottino, Orcagna, Spinello, Aretino, Antonio Veneziano, and others.

In Germany, the beginnings of the Romanesque style may be traced back to the 11th century. An improvement is manifest in the 12th century, especially in the famous altar of Verdun (of the year 1180, now in the monastery of Neuburg, near Vienna), in the mural paintings of the grand hall of the monastery of Brauweiler, near Cologne, and the ceiling of the central aisle of St. Michael, at Hildesheim. Far more numerous and important are the works still preserved from the period of the Gothic style, in which the peculiar spirit of mediævalism first attained to complete artistic expression. The development of glass-painting must especially be noted — probably a German invention, dating at the end of the 10th century—examples of which are seen in the windows of St. Cunibert, at Cologne, in the choir of Cologne Cathedral, in the Church of St. Catharine, at Oppenheim, and in Strasburg Cathedral. In easel pictures, which previously appear to have been very little painted, there is manifest no higher artistic endeavor until the middle of the 14th century. After this three separate schools may be distinguished: 1. The Bohemian, or school of Prague, founded by Charles IV; 2. The Nuremberg school, the chief representative monuments of which are several altar-shrines in the Frauenkirche, in St. Laurence, and St. Sebald, at Nuremberg; 3. The school of Cologne, by far the most important, whose chief representatives were master Wilhelm (about 1360) and master Stephan Lochner (about 1430).

With the beginning of the 15th century broke forth, in opposition to the spirit of mediævalism, a decided endeavor after greater truth of expression in art — an endeavor in light, color, drawing, and composition, to bring the spiritual import of representation into harmony with the laws and principles of nature. This naturalistic development first manifested itself in Italy in the Florentine school. Fra Giovanni Angelico da Fiesole (1387–1455), although in other respects wholly dominated by the spirit of mediævalism, was, nevertheless, the first who sought to penetrate into the psychological meaning of the human countenance. Over against him, already decidedly emancipated from mediævalism, stands Tommaso di San Giovanni da Castel, called Masaccio (1401–28), one of the greatest masters of the 15th century. With Fra Angelico are associated the names of Benozzo Gozzoli and Gentile da Fabriano; with Masaccio those of Fra Filippo Lippi, his son Filippino, Domenico Ghirlandajo, and Bastiano Mainardi. Other Florentine artists, as Antonio Pallajuolo and Andrea del Verocchio, who were also sculptors, strove by anatomical studies to transfer plastic forms to painting in a more vigorous modelling of the human figure; while Luca Signorelli of Cortona (1440–1521), by the nobleness and artistic truth of his compositions, presents a strong contrast with the deeper sentiment of the Umbrian school, which, with its chief theatre in the vicinity of Assisi, is an antithesis of the Florentine. Celebrated masters of the Umbrian school were Pietro Perugino (1446–1526), the teacher of Raphael, and the latter's father, Giovanni Santi (died 1494), as well as Raphael's friend, Francesco Francia (died 1517). The remaining schools of Italy, as the Venetian, with its Giovanni Bellini (about 1430–1516), the school of Padua and Mantua, with masters like Francesco Squarcione and Andrea Mantegna (1431–1506), follow the Florentine.

Italian painting reached its climax in the 16th century. The most celebrated masters of that period were Leonardo da Vinci, Cesare da Sesto, Andrea Salaino, Francesco Melzi, and especially Luini. The Venetian school of the 16th century sought to realize by means of color the noble results to which Leonardo had attained. In the quality of color this school achieved a supremacy over all others. Its chief master was Titian. With him labored the distinguished pupils of Giorgione—Fra Sebastiano del Piombo, Giacopo Palma, called *Il Vecchio*, and Pordenone. Among Titian's own pupils the most distinguished was Jacopo Robusti, called Tintoretto. In the renowned Paul Veronese, we have a master of color of the highest rank. The principal seat of the Lombard school in the 16th century was Parma. Its chief master was Correggio. The Florentine school, and, later, almost the entire painting of Italy after the beginning of the 16th century, were ruled by Michael Angelo, and by such lesser lights as Ricciarelli, Venusti, Sarto, and others. The greatest of the five great masters is Raphael. His best pupils were Giulio Romano (1492–1546), Gaudenzio Ferrari, and Giovanni da Udine.

In the Netherlands a new impulse was given to Christian painting by Hubert van Eyck (died 1426), the inventor, or, rather, the improver, of oil painting, and his younger brother and pupil, John van Eyck (died 1441). Their principal pupils were Pieter Christus, Rogier van der Weyden, and particularly Hans Memling. The influence thus begun made itself felt in Holland, where a similar school was founded, whose chief masters were Lucas van Leyden, and his contemporary Jan Mostaert. At the beginning of the 16th century a number of artists followed the style of the Van Eycks. The most distinguished of these was Quintin Massys, the smith of Antwerp (died 1529).

Similar was the career of German art during this period. The Gothic style had a long supremacy; but about the middle of the 15th century all the German schools followed the Italian. The chief masters of this period were, in the school of Cologne, Johann von Mehlem, the painter of the *Death of the Virgin;* in the school of Westphalia, the master of Liesborn monastery; in the school of Ulm and Augsburg, Martin Schön (about 1480), the somewhat younger Bartholomäus Zeitblom, and his successor, Martin Schaffner, of Ulm, and Hans Holbein, father of the renowned Holbein the younger, of Augsburg; in the school of Nuremberg, Michael Wohlgemuth (1434–1519), and more especially his pupil Albrecht Dürer. Mention must also be made of the Saxon school, whose head was the well-known Lucas Cranach (1472–1553), the friend of Luther, whose best pupils were his sons, John and Lucas Cranach the younger. The only artist who can be compared with the great master of Nuremberg is Hans Holbein the younger (1497–1554). His most characteristic works are the Darmstädt *Madonna*, a copy of which is at Dresden, and his well-known *Dance of Death.*

In the second half of the 16th century the painting of Germany and the Netherlands lost its independence by servile imitation of Italian masters. But in Italy, too, we find a sudden decline, which clearly evidences that art had passed its zenith. A second race of pupils became mere imitators, even exaggerating the one-sidedness of Titian, Correggio, and Michael Angelo. The best examples of these so-called "mannerists" were Fr. Salviati, and Giorgio Vasari. In opposition to this confusion, at the end of the century arose the Bolognese school of the Caraccis, whose advent marks for Italy the commencement of the *fourth period* of modern painting. Ludovico Caracci, and his nephews and pupils, Agostino and Annibale Caracci, established a sort of eclectic system, whose purpose it was to imitate the chief distinguishing qualities of the five great masters of painting. Their best pupils were Domenichino (1581–1641), Guercino (1590–1666), Franc. Albani (1578–1660), and especially Guido Reni (1575–1642), the most distinguished of all. A second school of Italian painting arraying itself in opposition to the idealism of the great masters, and developing a one-sided realism and naturalism, was founded in the beginning of the 17th century. Its principal representative was Mic. Angelo Amerighi da Caravaggio, whose pupils, the two Frenchmen, Moyse Valentin and Simon Vonet, and the eminent Spanish master, Gius. Ribero, called *Spagnoletto*, transplanted their influence to France and Spain. Notwithstanding the eminent talents exercised to uphold the fame of Italian painting, yet in the 18th century it reached its lowest level of decadence. It was in Spain that the new revival of catholicism in art found, in the 17th century, its strongest support. The five great masters who represent the completest development of painting in Spain were almost all from the school of Seville. They were: 1. José Ribera; 2. Francesco Zurbaran (1598–1662); 3. Diego Velasquez da Silva (1599–1660), one of the most eminent of portrait-painters; 4. Alonzo Cano; 5. Bartolomé Murillo. The flourishing period of Spanish painting was of short duration; and in the last quarter of the 17th century the schools of Spain degenerated into mere factories of art, such as Luca Giordano of Italy introduced.

In the Netherlands, painting maintained a certain elevation of rank for a somewhat longer period. Here two distinct schools, that of Brabant (Belgium) and that of Holland, developed themselves out of national divisions. The former had its masters in Peter Paul Rubens, and in his pupils, viz. Jac. Jordaens, Caspar de Crayer, and, above all, Anton van Dyck (1599–1641). The latter was represented by Theodor de Keyser, Franz Hals, Barth, Van der Helst, and others, who were almost exclusively portrait-painters. A far higher development was, however, reached in the famous Rembrandt, whose most distinguished pupils and successors were Gerbrandt van der Eeckhout, Solomon Koning, and Ferdinand Bol.

France and Germany can claim no position of importance during this period in a brief review of Christian painting. In Germany, the Thirty Years' War had nearly uprooted all elements of culture, and when, in the 18th century, the country began to recover from these devastations, masters of only subordinate rank, as Balth. Denner, Dietrich, and Raphael Mengs (1728–79), appeared upon the stage. In France, the older and better masters, like Nic. Poussin, Eustache Lesueur, and others, strove in vain to make head against the theatrical style represented by Charles Lebrun, the favorite of Louis XIV. Since the diffusion over Europe of that immoral and irreligious spirit which preceded and followed the French Revolution, Christian painting has naturally experienced a marked decline. But in Germany, France, and Belgium individual schools have again grown up, the excellences of which, in the appreciation of the grand and the beautiful, cannot be denied. In Germany, Munich, Düsseldorf, Berlin, and of late Vienna, must be mentioned as the principal seats of revived painting, in which sacred themes occupy a most significant place, and these treated both in a Catholic and a Protestant spirit, the former by Cornelius, Overbeck, Fürich, H. Hess, Schraudolp, and others; the latter by Lessing, Hübner, Bendemann, Deger, Von Gebhardt, and others. On the whole, however, modern religious painting, corresponding to the religious condition of the present time, seems partly a mere endeavor to revive a greatness and power which has perished, and partly a blind effort to reach a new goal, which is still enshrouded in darkness.

The best modern works on the history of Christian painting are, Kugler, *Handbuch der Geschichte der Malerei seit Constantin dem Grossen* (2d ed. Berlin, 1847; 4th ed. by Lübke, 1872); Ch. Blanc, *Histoire des Peintres de Toutes les Écoles depuis la Renaissance jusqu'à nos Jours* (Paris, 1851 sq.); W. Lübke, *Geschichte der italienischen Malerei vom* 4. *bis* 16. *Jahrhundert* (8th ed. Stuttgart, 1880); A. Woltmann, *Geschichte der Malerei* (Leipsic, 1878; Engl. transl. Lond. and N. Y. 1881); Ruskin, *Modern Painters* (Lond. 1843–60, 5 vols.); Crowe and Cavalcaselle, *Storia della Pittura in Italia dal Secole II al Secolo XVI* (Florence, 1875); the art. *Malerei* in Plitt-Herzog, *Real-Encyklop.;* and *Peinture* in Lichtenberger, *Encyclop. des Sciences Religieuses*, s. v. (B. P.)

Palætyrus. See TYRE.

Palestine, COLONISTS IN. On this subject we present an extract from Lieut. Conder's *Tent Work in Palestine*, ii, 305 sq.:

"The German colonists belong to a religious society known as the 'Temple,' which originated among the Pietists of Würtemburg, who, without leaving the Lutheran Church, separated themselves from the world, and engaged in Sunday meetings for prayer and edification. The Pietists accept as their standard the explanation given by Dr. J. A. Bengel (in his *Gnomon of the New Test.*) of the prophecies in the Revelation. Among the friends and disciples of Bengel was a certain Dr. Hoffmann, who obtained from Frederick, the eccentric king of Würtemburg, a tract of barren land at Kornthal, where his disciples established a Pietist colony, which he intended to transplant later to Palestine. Hoffmann, however, died, and his followers remained contentedly on their lands; but Hoffmann's son was not forgetful of his father's designs, and instituted a new colony at Kirschenhardthof, with a special view to its final removal to the Holy Land. Among his earliest disciples was Herr G. D. Hardegg, who became in time a leader among the Temple Pietists.

"The younger Hoffmann (Christopher) visited Palestine about 1858, and, in 1867, a small trial expedition of twelve men was sent out. They settled in reed huts near Semûnieh, on the edge of the Plain of Esdraelon, west of Nazareth; and in spite of the warning of friends who knew the unhealthy climate of that place, they remained in the malarious atmosphere of the low ground near the springs, until they all died of fever.

"On Aug. 6, 1868, Christopher Hoffmann and G. D. Hardegg left Kirschenhardthof, and in October they reached Palestine; after visiting various places, they resolved on settling at Haifa and Jaffa, and bought land in both places. The Haifa colony was the first founded, that at Jaffa being some six months younger. Hardegg became president of the former, and Hoffmann of the latter.

"The religious views of the colonists are not easily understood, and I believe that most of them have rather vague ideas of their own intentions. Their main motive for establishing colonies in Palestine is the promotion of conditions favorable to the fulfilment (which they expect to occur shortly) of the prophecies of the Revelation and of Zechariah. They suppose it to be a duty to separate themselves from the world, and to set an example of a community living, as closely as possible, on the model of the apostolic age. The spread of infidelity in Germany appears to be the main cause of this separative tendency among the Pietists.

"The tenets of the Temple Society are probably best summarized in the 'Profession of Faith of the Temple,' published by Herr Hoffmann, and including five articles as below:

"'1. To prepare for the great and terrible day of the second coming of Jesus Christ, which, from the signs of the times, is near. This preparation is made by the building of a spiritual temple in all lands, specially in Jerusalem.

"'2. This temple is composed of the gifts of the Spirit (1 Cor. xii, 4), which make the true Church, and every one should strive to possess them.

"'3. The means to obtain these is to seek the kingdom of God, as described by the prophets (Isa. ii, 2; xix, 25; Ezek. xl, 48).

"'4. The temple of Jerusalem is not a building of dead, but of lively stones; of men of every nation (1 Pet. ii, 4–10) united in the worship of God in spirit and truth.

"'5. The Temple service consists of sacrifices such as are described in the New Test. (Rom. xii, 1; Heb. xiii, 15, 16; James i, 27).'

"The writings of Hardegg are far more diffuse and mystic. The main peculiarity which I have been able to extract from them is the belief that it is not to the Jews, but to the true Israel (by which he apparently understands the Temple Society to be intended), that prophecies of a return to Palestine are to be supposed to refer.

"I have stated as far as possible the apparent religious beliefs of the community, but there seem to be many shades of doctrine among them; all, however, agree in an expectancy of some immediate change in the world's affairs, in the arrival of Armageddon and the Millennium, and in the fulfilment of all prophecy.

"In 1875 I had the opportunity of attending one of the Sunday services, in the colony at Haifa. The congregation was devout and earnest; the service was simple and free from extravagance of any kind. The president offered up a long prayer in German, a hymn was sung with the usual musical good taste of Germans, and a chapter of the prophecy of Zechariah read. The president then delivered an exhortation, announcing the immediate advent of the Saviour, who would 'suddenly come to his temple.' Other elders followed, speaking with much earnestness, and another hymn was sung, after which the congregation quietly dispersed from the bare schoolroom in which they had assembled. A discussion of the affairs of the colony often immediately succeeds the religious services.

"Of the history of the Jaffa colony we gathered comparatively little. They have two settlements—one called Sarôna, about two and a half miles north of the town, consisting, in 1872, of ten houses; the second, nearer the walls of Jaffa, was bought from the surviving members of an American colony which came to grief, and this settlement included thirteen houses, with a school and a hotel, the latter kept by Hardegg's son, who also represents the German government in Jaffa.

"In 1872 the Jaffa colony numbered one hundred men, seventy women, and thirty-five children: two of the colonists were doctors, and some twenty were mechanics, the rest being farmers. They employed a few natives, and cultivated four hundred acres of corn-land, paying the ordinary taxes to the Turks. The children are taught Arabic, and European languages, also Latin and Greek. The houses are clean, airy, and well built, and the colony wears an aspect of industry and enterprise, which contrasts with the squalor and decay of the native villages.

"With the Haifa colony we became more intimately acquainted, by living in one of the houses for three months, during the winter of 1872–73, and again in the hotel of the colony, for about two months, during 1875, when we saw a good deal of the working of the community.

"In 1872 the colonists numbered two hundred and fifty-four—forty single and forty-seven married men, thirty-two single and fifty-one married women (four widows), and eighty-four children. There were about fifty mechanics, and the settlement consisted of thirty-one dwelling-houses. The land was four hundred and fifty acres of arable ground, with one hundred and forty olive-trees, and seventeen acres of vineyard.

"In the first three years of its existence only seven deaths occurred in the colony, but the mortality increased later; in 1872 there were eighteen deaths among the two hundred and five colonists at Jaffa, which were due principally to fever, but such a death-rate has never yet occurred at Haifa.

"The little village of well-built stone houses is situated west of the walled town of Haifa, under the shadow of the Carmel range. A broad street runs up from the shore towards the mountain, and the greater number of the buildings stand, in their gardens, on either side. Close to the beach is the Carmel Hotel, kept by a most obliging and moderate landlord, and a little farther up are the school and meeting-house, in one building. Mr. Hardegg's dwelling, farther east, is the largest house in the colony. The total number is stated at eighty-five, including buildings for agricultural purposes.

"In 1875 the colonists numbered three hundred and eleven, having been reinforced principally by new arrivals from Germany; the increase of accommodation since 1872 was thus far greater than that of settlers. The land had also increased, in the same period, to six hundred acres, with one hundred acres of vineyards and gardens; but the soil of the newly-acquired property near Tîreh, in the plain west of Carmel, is of very poor quality, and the Germans have not yet succeeded in their favorite scheme of obtaining grounds on the top of the mountain, where the climate and soil are both good.

"The live-stock consisted of seventy-five head of cattle, two hundred and fifty sheep, goats, and pigs, and eight teams of horses. A superior American threshing-machine had been imported. The trades followed are stone-cutting and masons' work, carpentry and wagon-making. Blacksmiths, coppersmiths, tinsmiths, joiners, shoemakers, tailors, butchers, harness-makers, turners, soap-makers, vintners, and quarrymen are also found among the colonists. There has been an attempt to trade in soap, olive-oil, and olive-wood articles, but, for these undertakings, more capital is required than the Germans at present possess. A good windmill and an olive-press have been brought from England. A tannery was also being put up in 1875, and a general shop exists, which the natives, as well the Germans, frequent.

"The colonists were many of them employed on the English orphanage at Nazareth, which Mr. Shumacher designed and built; and all the masons' and carpenters' work was executed by the Germans. The colonists also have done much to clear the road from Haifa to Nazareth, though they have not *made* it, considering that, from a professional point of view, it is not yet a made road at all. Their wagons are now driven between the two places, and the natives employ them for moving grain.

"The schools in the colony, for the children and younger men, are two in number. In the upper school, Arabic, English, French, and German, arithmetic, drawing, geography, history, mathematics, and music are taught; in the lower, Arabic and German, writing, arithmetic, and singing; in both religious instruction is given; and the girls are taught knitting, sewing, and embroidery.

"The colony has thus been sketched in its religious and practical aspects. Though much talk has been expended on the question of colonizing the Holy Land, there is no other practical attempt which can compare in importance with that of the Temple Society. It remains to be seen what the success of the undertaking will be.

"The colonists belong entirely to the peasant and mechanical classes, and even their leaders are men comparatively uneducated. As a rule they are hard-working, sober, honest, and sturdy; and, however mystic their religious notions may be, they are essentially shrewd and practical in their dealings with the world. They are a pious and God-fearing people, and their natural domesticity renders it highly improbable that they will ever split on the rock which wrecked the former American colony, whose president, it appears, endeavored to follow the example of Brigham Young by introducing polygamy. The German colonists have also a fine field for enterprise, in the introduction into Palestine of European improvements, which are more or less appreciated by the natives; and, as they have no other community to compete with, they might be able to make capital of their civilized education. The wine which they sell is comparatively excellent, and finds a ready market, as do also many of their manufactured articles.

"Such is one side of the picture, but when we turn to the other we find elements of weakness, which seem to threaten the existence of the colony.

"In the first place, there is apparently no man in the community of sufficiently superior talent or education, or with the energy and force of character, which would be required to control and develop the enterprise. The genius of Brigham Young triumphed over the almost insuperable difficulties of his audacious undertaking, despite even the prejudice which the establishment of polygamy naturally raised against his disciples. However superior in piety and purity of motive the leaders of the Haifa colony may be, they cannot compare with the Mormon chief in the qualities to which his success was due.

"In the second place, the colonists are divided among themselves. In 1875 we found that Herr Hardegg had been deposed (temporarily, I understood, till he changed his views) from the leadership of the colony, and he had been succeeded by Herr Shumacher, a master-stonemason and architect, who is, moreover, the representative of the American government at Haifa. This deposition of the original leader had caused dissensions among the Germans, and several of the influential members did not attend the Sunday meetings.

"To internal troubles external ones were added. The colonists are not favorites either with natives or with Europeans, with Moslems or with Christians. The Turkish government is quite incapable of appreciating their real motives in colonization, and cannot see any reason, beyond a political one, for the settlement of Europeans in the country. The colonists, therefore, have never obtained title-deeds to the lands they have bought, and there can be little doubt that should the Turks deem it expedient, they would entirely deny the right of the Germans to hold their property. Not only do they extend no favor to the colony, though its presence has been most beneficial to the neighborhood, but the inferior officials, indignant at the attempts of the Germans to obtain justice in the courts, without any regard to the 'custom of the country' (that is, to bribery), have thrown every obstacle they can devise in the way of the community, both individually and collectively.

"The difficulties of the colonists are also increased by the jealousy of the Carmelite monks. The fathers possess good lands, gradually extending along Carmel round their fortress monastery; they look with disfavor on the encroachments of the Germans, and all the subtlety of Italians is directed against the German interests.

"The peculiar views of the colonists, moreover, cause them to be regarded with disfavor by influential Europeans in the country, who might do much to help them. They are avoided as religious visionaries, whose want of worldly wisdom might, at any time, embroil their protectors in difficulties not easily smoothed over.

"The community has thus to struggle with a positively hostile government, while it receives no very vigorous support from any one. The difficulties are perfectly well known to the native peasantry, who, with the characteristic meanness of the Syrians, take the opportunity to treat with insolence people whom they believe they can insult with impunity. The property of the colonists is disregarded, the native goatherds drive their beasts into the corn, and several riots have occurred, which resulted in trials from which the colonists got no satisfaction.

"The indiscretion of the younger men has brought greater difficulties on the community; they have repaid insolence with summary punishment, and finding no help from the government, have in many instances taken the law into their own hands. Thus the colony finds itself at feud with the surrounding villages, and the hostile feeling is not unlikely to lead to very serious difficulties on some occasion of popular excitement.

"There are other reasons which militate against the idea of the final success of the colony. The Syrian climate is not adapted to Europeans, and year by year it must infallibly tell on the Germans, exposed as they are to sun and miasma. It is true that Haifa is, perhaps, the healthiest place in Palestine, yet even here they suffer from fever and dysentery, and if they should attempt to spread inland they will find their difficulties from climate increase tenfold.

"The children of the present generation will, probably, like those of the Crusading settlers in Palestine, be inferior in physique and power of endurance to their fathers. Cases of intermarriage with natives have, I believe, already occurred; the children of such marriages are not unlikely to combine the bad qualities of both nations, and may be compared to the Pullani of Crusading times. It seems to me that it is only by constant reinforcements from Germany that the original character of the colony can be maintained; and the whole community, in Palestine and in Germany, is said not to number more than five thousand persons.

"The expectation of the immediate fulfilment of prophecy has also resulted in the ruin of many of the poorer members of the community, who, living on their capital, have exhausted it before that fulfilment has occurred. The colony is thus in danger of dissolution, by the gradual absorption of the property into the hands of those who originally possessed the most capital; and in any case it is very likely to lose its original character of apostolic simplicity, some of the members becoming the servants and hired laborers of others.

"The natural desire of those members who find themselves without money is to make a livelihood by any means in their power. Where every man is thus working separately for himself, the progress of the colony, as a whole, is not unlikely to be forgotten, and the members may very probably be dispersed over Palestine, following their various trades where best they can make money."

Pali Version OF THE SCRIPTURES. Pali, though no longer a vernacular language in any country, has for ages been established as the religious and learned language of the Buddhists in the island of Ceylon, in the Burman empire, in Siam, Laos, Pegu, Ava, and throughout almost the whole of the eastern peninsula of India. As a language it is immediately derived from the Sanscrit, and was probably the native language of Magadha, the birthplace of Buddha. A version into the Pali was commenced in 1813, under the auspices of the Colombo Bible Society, by Mr. Tolfrey, assisted by two learned Buddhist priests. The version had advanced as far as the end of the epistle to Philemon, when Mr. Tolfrey died, in 1817. In 1825 the Rev. Benjamin Clough resumed the work, and finally, in 1835, the whole New Test. was printed in Pali. One of the Buddhist priests who assisted Mr. Tolfrey in the translation became a sincere convert to Christianity, and subsequently devoted his whole attention to the completion and revision of this important work. See *Bible of Every Land*, p. 91 sq. (B. P.)

Pallium, a piece of pontifical dress. It is the peculiar mark of primates, metropolitans, and archbishops, and a few privileged bishops, to be worn by them at councils, ordinations, and on certain occasions in church. Its other names were *anophorion*, *superhumerale*, and, in the writings of Theodoret and St. Gregory Nazianzen, *hiera stolè*. It is a circular scarf of plain lambs' wool, worn like a collar about the neck, and having two falling ends fastened over the chasuble by three gold pins fixed on the left shoulder, the breast, and back, the number three signifying charity, or the nails of the cross. Before the 8th century it was ornamented with two or four red or purple, but now with six black, crosses, fastened with gold pins, which superseded an earlier ornament, the Good Shepherd, or one cross, in the 4th century. It has been supposed to be the last relic of an abbreviated toga, reduced to its laticlave by degrees. In the time of Gregory the Great it was made of white linen cloth, without seam or needlework, hanging down from the shoulders. See PALL.

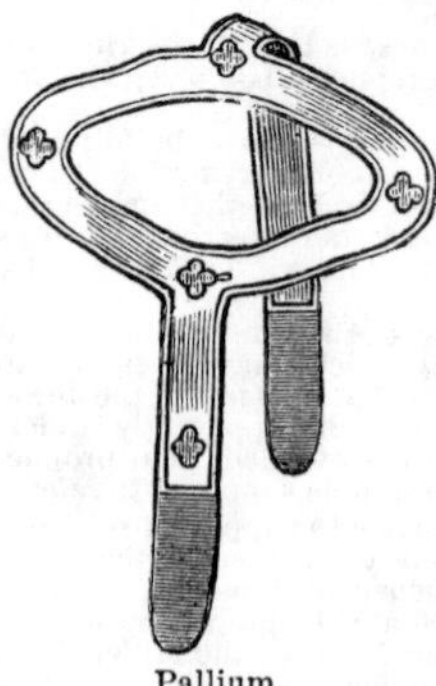
Pallium.

Palm, JOHANN GEORG, a Lutheran theologian of Germany, was born at Hanover, Dec. 7, 1697. He studied at Jena, was for some time court-chaplain at Wolfenbüttel, in 1727 pastor at Hamburg, and died Feb. 17, 1743. He is the author of, *Einleitung in die Geschichte der augsburgischen Confession* (Hamburg, 1730):—*De Codicibus Veteris et Novi Testamenti Quibus Lutherus in Conficienda Interpretatione Germanica usus est* (1735):—*Geschichte der Bibelübersetzung Dr. Martin Luther's* (edited by J. M. Götze, Halle, 1772). See Döring, *Die gelehrten Theologen Deutschlands*, s. v.; Winer, *Handbuch der theol. Lit.* i, 167; Jöcher, *Allgemeines Gelehrten-Lexikon*, s. v. (B. P.)

Palmer, Edward Henry, an English Orientalist, was born at Cambridge, Aug. 7, 1840. In 1868 he took part in the expedition for exploring the Sinai territory, and made an examination of the names of places, traditions, and antiquities of Arabia Petræa. With the same object in view he explored, in connection with Tyrwhitt Drake, the desert Et-Tih and Moab, in 1869 and 1870. Upon his return to England he was made professor of Arabic at Cambridge in 1871. In 1878 he settled at London, and in 1882 went on a secret mission, at the instance of the English government, into the desert east of the Suez canal. On his second trip through the desert he was killed, in October, 1882. Palmer published an Arabic translation of Thomas Moore's *Paradise and the Peri* (1865):—*Oriental Mysticism* (1867):—*Report on the Bedawin of Sinai and their Traditions* (1870):—*The Desert of the Exodus* (1871):—*A History of the Jewish Nation* (1874; Germ. transl. Gotha, 1876):—*A Grammar of the Arabic Language* (London, 1874):—*A Persian-English Dictionary* (1876):—*Life of Haroun Al Raschid* (1878), and for Max Müller's *Sacred Books of the East* he translated the Koran. See Besant, *Life* *and Achievements of Edward Henry Palmer* (London, 1883). (B. P.)

Palmer, Heinrich Julius E., a Lutheran theologian of Germany, was born at Giessen, June 28, 1803. In 1828 he was appointed professor at the gymnasium in Darmstadt, and died in 1865, a doctor of philosophy. He published, *Religiöse Vorträge* (Mayence, 1833; second series, Darmstadt, 1839):—*Lehrbuch der Religion und der Geschichte der christl. Kirche* (1849, 2 vols.):—*Der christliche Glaube und das christliche Leben* (4th ed. 1862):—*Die confessionellen Fragen der Gegenwart vom kirchenrechtlichen und theologischen Standpunkte* (1846). See Winer, *Handbuch der theol. Lit.* ii, 191; Zuchold, *Bibl. Theol.* ii, 971 sq. (B. P.)

Palmer, Karl Christian, father of Heinrich Julius, was born at Delitzsch, May 2, 1759. In 1787 he was professor at Leipsic, and died at Giessen, July 17, 1838, doctor and professor of theology. He wrote, *De Nexu inter Theologiam Moralem et Publicam Religionis Institutio* (Leipsic, 1788):—*Paulus und Gamaliel, ein Beitrag zur ältesten Christengeschichte* (Giessen, 1806):—*Predigten über die Evangelien des ganzen Jahres* (1817). See Winer, *Handbuch der theol. Lit.* i, 495, 569; ii, 134. (B. P.)

Palmer, Walter C., M.D., a devoted Methodist evangelist, was born Feb. 9, 1804. He was converted in 1817, and among the hallowed associations of the "Old Allen Street Church" in New York, grew up to a beautifully developed Christian character. He practiced medicine for many years in that city, and at length, in connection with his saintly wife, gave up his time to labors for the conversion and sanctification of souls, travelling extensively, and holding meetings everywhere in this country as well as in Great Britain. He died at Ocean Grove, July 29, 1883. See (N. Y.) *Christian Advocate*, Jan. 3, 1884; Simpson, *Cyclop. of Methodism*, s. v.

Palpa Version OF THE SCRIPTURES. Palpa is a dialect spoken in the small states north of Oude, below the Himalayas. A version of the New Test. was commenced at Serampore in 1817, and completed at press about 1832. See *Bible of Every Land*, p. 122. (B. P.)

Paniel, KARL FRIEDRICH WILHELM, a Protestant theologian of Germany, was born at Mannheim, April 19, 1802. He studied at Heidelberg, was for some time preacher at Käferthal, near Mannheim, in 1834 at Ziegelhausen, near Heidelberg, in 1839 pastor at Bremen, and died in 1867, doctor of theology. He published, *Allgemeine Uebersicht derjenigen Gegenstände, welche das gegenwärtige Bedürfniss der evangelisch-protestantischen Kirche Badens empfiehlt* (Mannheim, 1832):—*Homiletisches Magazin* (Heidelberg, 1836, 2 vols.):—*Pragmatische Geschichte der christlichen Beredsamkeit und der Homiletik* (Leipsic, 1839-40). See Zuchold, *Bibl. Theol.* ii, 972 sq.; Winer, *Handbuch der theol. Lit.* ii, 129. (B. P.)

Panis Litĕræ ("bread briefs") were letters of recommendation, by which a secular lord ordered a monastery or other institution of charity to receive a certain person for support. The right of issuing such letters was connected with the duty, originally imposed upon such institutions, of showing hospitality to princes and other great lords when they were travelling. During the Middle Ages the emperor of Germany exercised a very extensive right of this kind; but the custom existed also in other countries. Towards the end of the 18th century the princes of the different countries refused to admit such royal briefs in their respective territories, and Frederick the Great openly refused to acknowledge such a brief, and asked to be let alone in future with such imperial orders. See Klüber, *Litteratur des deutschen Staatsrechts* (Erlangen, 1791), p. 540-543, 548; Häberlin, *Pragmatische Geschichte der neuesten kaiserlichen Walkapitulation* (Leipsic, 1792), p. 97; Plitt-Herzog, *Real-Encyklop.* s. v. "Panisbrief." (B. P.)

Paniter, DAVID, a Scotch prelate, was vicar of the Church of Carstairs, in the diocese of Glasgow, prior of St. Mary's Isle in Galloway, and some time commendator of the abbey of Cambuskenneth. In 1543 he was principal secretary of state. He was made bishop of the see of Ross about 1545, and was still there in 1556. He probably died in 1558. See Keith, *Scottish Bishops*, p. 192.

Panjabi Version. See PUNJABI VERSION.

Pape, HEINRICH, a Lutheran theologian of Germany, was born at Bremen in 1745. He studied at Göttingen, was preacher at different places in the duchy of Bremen, and died April 17, 1805. He is the author of, *Das 53. Capitel Iesaiä übersetzt und erklärt* (Bremen, 1777):—*Das Evangelium Lucä umschrieben und erläutert* (1777-81, 2 vols.); besides, he wrote some ascetical works, for which see Döring, *Die gelehrten Theologen Deutschlands*, s. v. (B. P.)

Pappelbaum, GEORG GOTTLIEB, a Lutheran theologian of Germany, was born at Stargard, March 16, 1745, and died at Berlin, March 6, 1826, doctor of theology and archdeacon. He published, *Untersuchung der rauischen Handschrift des Neuen Testaments* (Berlin, 1785):—*Codicis Novi Testamenti Raviani in Bibliotheca Regia Berolinensi Publica Asservati Examen*, etc. (Leipsic, 1796):—*Codicem Græcus Apostolorum Acta et Epistolas Continens Berolini in Bibliotheca Viri Generosissimi*, etc. (Berlin, 1815). See Winer, *Handbuch der theol. Lit.* i, 100, 101; Zuchold, *Bibl. Theol.* ii, 973. (B. P.)

Papst, JOHANN GEORG FRIEDRICH, a Lutheran theologian of Germany, was born at Ludwigstadt, Bayreuth, Oct. 21, 1754. He studied at Leipsic and Erlangen, was in 1783 professor of philosophy at the latter place, in 1794 dean at Zirndorf, near Nuremberg, in 1818 doctor of theology, and died June 7, 1821. He wrote, *De Authentia Capitis XXI Joannis* (Erlangen, 1779):—*De Faustis Christianæ Religionis Initiis* (1786):—*Geschichte der christlichen Kirche* (1787):—*De Ipsorum Christianorum Culpa in Vexationibus Motis a Romanis* (1789-90):—*De Apostolicæ Ecclesiæ Exemplo Caute Adhibendo* (1790):—*Commentar über die Geschichte der christl. Kirche nach dem schröckh'schen Lehrbuch* (1792-1801). See Winer, *Handbuch der theol. Lit.* i, 536, 591; ii, 24; Döring, *Die gelehrten Theologen Deutschlands*, s. v. (B. P.)

Para (du Phanjas), FRANÇOIS, a philosophical writer of France, was born in the castle Phanjas, Dauphiné, in 1724. He joined the Jesuits of Embrun, and soon distinguished himself as a philosopher and mathematician. Para died at Paris in 1797. Of his works we mention, *Elėments de Métaphysiques Sacrée et Profane* (2d ed. Paris, 1779, 3 vols.):—*Les Principes de la Saine Philosophie Conciliés avec Ceux de la Religion* (1774, 2 vols.):—*Institutiones Philosophicæ* (published posthumously, in 1800):—*Tableau Historique et Philosophique de la Religion* (1784). See Lichtenberger, *Encyclop. des Sciences Religieuses*, s. v. (B. P.)

Paradise. There have been at least four notable attempts in very recent times to discover this long-sought locality; two of them by American, and two by German authors. Their theories have been put forth with the greatest assurance, and in most cases supported by a vast array of learning; but they all seem to have failed to satisfy the judgment of the literary world, or to add anything substantial towards a reasonable solution of the question.

1. The view of Friederich Delitzsch, the eminent Assyriologist, son of the well-known commentator, has already been given under the art. EDEN. Brilliant as are the researches of his work, its conclusions have been rejected by the most careful and competent critics. See Halévy, in the *Revue Critique*, 1881, p. 457 sq.; Nöldecke, in the *Zeitschr. d. deutsch. morgenländ. Gesellschaft*, 1882, p. 174; Lenormant, in *Les Origine de l'His-*

toire, vol. ii. We cite (from *The Nation*, N. Y., March 15, 1883) some of the geographical objections:

"Why, if the stream of Eden be the middle Euphrates, is it left unnamed in the narrative, though it is certain that the Hebrews were perfectly familiar both with the middle and the upper course of that river? . . . If the *lower* Tigris be meant by the Hiddekel, why is this river described as flowing in front of Assyria, which lay *above* the central Mesopotamian lowland asserted to be Eden? How should a writer, familiar with the whole course of the Tigris, deem its lower part a branch of the Euphrates? . . . Why is Havilah, if the Arabian border-land so well known to the Hebrews be meant, so fully described by its products? Who tells us that the gold, the bdellium, and the shoham of Babylonia were also characteristic of the adjoining Havilah?"

2. A modern traveller, Rev. J. P. Newman, D.D., had previously indicated a somewhat similar position to the above (*A Thousand Miles on Horseback*, N. Y. 1875, p. 69), namely, at the confluence of the Euphrates and the Tigris; and he was confident that ancient tablets would yet be exhumed fully establishing this location. But the inscriptions recovered by Smith, Rassam, and others in that vicinity do not confirm the theory, and it has thus been brushed aside with the multitude of other conjectures that preceded it.

3. A more startling conclusion is announced by Rev. William F. Warren, D.D., LL.D., president of the Boston University, "that the cradle of the human race, the Eden of primitive tradition, was situated *at the North pole*, in a country submerged at the time of the deluge" (*Paradise Found*, Boston, 1885, 8vo). This is the outcome of his researches in early traditions, noticed under our art. COSMOLOGY. The author brings to the support of this view an amazing amount of reading and investigation, which we have not space to criticise in detail. To such as are prepared to accept the mythologies of antiquity as having a historical basis, and to place the Biblical account on a level of authority with them, and at the same time to extend the origin of the human race to a date contemporary with the thermal æra of geology, this book, which is written in a fascinating style, and illustrated with a copious reference to the literature of the subject, will prove at least an ingenious and plausible, if not a conclusive, argument; but for those who maintain the literal accuracy of the history in Genesis, and the substantial agreement of the topographical conditions there given with the present conditions of the earth's surface, it cannot appear other than a most preposterous and chimerical hypothesis. The great objection which we see in it is the setting aside as an unintelligible narrative the only professed and historic description which we possess of the Garden of Eden, and then resorting to the vague and conflicting testimony of paganism, combined with the scanty and problematical indications of cosmological science, for an identification that is at last claimed as decisive and final. If the Biblical passage (Gen. ii, 10–14), with its explicit items, fails to point out the true spot, we may as well give up the attempt as hopeless. To us that account seems sufficiently clear and consistent; and we believe that explorations in the region thus designated will vindicate the accuracy of the Scripture language beyond any reasonable doubt. It is a question of exegesis and geography, not of mythological comparison.

4. The last formal production in this line is an attempt to show that Paradise was situated about sixty-five miles south-east of Damascus, in a shallow alluvial basin, amid the wild basaltic crags of the desolate volcanic region known as the *Hauran* (*Die Auflösung der Paradies-frage*, by Moritz Engel, Leipsic, 1885, 8vo). An elaborate effort is made to identify the names and circumstances; but the agreement is most fanciful and indistinct. Eden is the present *Ruhbe*, an Arabic term for a rich patch of soil; the four rivers are the wadies which pour down the surrounding slopes in the rainy season; while the most violent processes of rationalism are resorted to for the purpose of disposing of the associated names and features of the narrative: e. g. the cherubim are volcanoes of the Hauran; Cain is only a more specific title for Adam; Cain's sons and Lamech's wives are mountain-peaks adjacent, etc. It would seem as if the *ne plus ultra* of absurdity has now been reached in the vagaries on this subject, and it is time to return to sober examination of the given data, if any success is to be achieved in the exposition.

Parah. The probable site is *Khurbet Farah*, laid down on the Ordnance *Map* at five and a half miles north-east of Jerusalem, and described in the accompanying *Memoirs* (iii, 209) as "heaps of stones only."

Parasurama is the sixth *avatar*, or incarnation of Vishnû, in which he appears as Rama, the son of Jamadagui, armed with a *parasu*, or axe. Arjuna, king of the Haihayas, had obtained, as a reward for his pious deeds, a thousand arms and sovereignty over all the earth. The gods, alarmed at his power, applied to Vishnû, who decided to be born as a son of Jamadagui, in order that he might slay him. Jamadagui was a pious sage, who had married Renuka, a princess, and had obtained by her five sons, the last of whom was Rama, or Vishnû incarnate. On a certain occasion Arjuna came to the hermitage of Jamadagui, and was there hospitably received by the saint, who could treat him and his followers sumptuously, as he possessed a fabulous cow of plenty, that not only supplied him with the milk and butter required for his sacrificial offerings, but with everything else he wished for. Pleased with the precious qualities of this cow, and disregarding the kind treatment he had received, Arjuna carried off with him the cow and her calf. When Rama, who was absent at this time, returned to the hermitage, he took up his axe (or his bow) and slew Arjuna and his army. The sons of Arjuna, to avenge their father's death, attacked the hermitage and succeeded in killing Jamadagui. Thereupon Rama made a vow to extirpate the whole Kshattrîya, or military race, and, not satisfied with destroying the sons of Arjuna, he killed every Kshattrîya whom he met afterwards. It is said that "he cleared thrice seven times the earth" (i. e. slew as many generations) "and filled with their blood the five large lakes of Samautapauchaka, from which he offered libations to the race of Bhrigu." He then performed a solemn sacrifice, and distributed the land and great riches among the ministering priests. There can be little doubt that the legend is in essence historical, recording a great struggle in primeval times between Brahmans and Kshattrîyas, of which we have the parallel in the history of Vasishtha and Viswamitra (q. v.).

Pareau, LOUIS GERLACH, a noted Dutch theologian, son of John Henry, was born at Deventer, Aug. 10, 1800. He studied at Utrecht, and at the age of twenty took the degree of doctor of theology on presenting *Commentatio Critica ad* 1 *Cor. xiii.* On the same day (Sept. 23, 1820) he was also made doctor of philosophy "honoris causa." After ministering for some time at Nederlangbroek and Voorburg, he was made professor of moral theology at Groningen in 1831. He opened his lectures with an address, *De Animo non Minus Theologorum quam Ingenio Academica Institutione Informando.* Pareau was twice rector of the university (in 1843 and 1858), and died Oct. 27, 1866. He is the author of, *Initia Institutionis Christianæ Moralis* (Groningen, 1842):—*Dogmatica et Apologetica Christiana* (1845):—in connection with Hofstede de Groot, *Hermeneutica Codicis Sacri* (1846):—*Encyclopædia Theologi Christiani* (1851), also in connection with Hofstede de Groot. See Lichtenberger, *Encyclop. des Sciences Religieuses*, s. v. (B. P.)

Parizek, ALEXIUS VINCENZ, a Roman Catholic theologian of Austria, was born at Prague, Nov. 10, 1748. In 1765 he joined the Dominicans, and received holy orders in 1771. For a time tutor at the grammar-school in Prague, he went, in 1783, to Klattau, Bohemia, as director of the German grammar-school. In 1786 he was made episcopal notary at Budweis, in 1802 doctor of theology, in 1811 dean of the theological faculty at Prague, and died April 15, 1822. He is the author of a number of ascetical works, for which see Döring, *Die gelehrten Theologen Deutschlands*, s. v.; Winer, *Handbuch der theol. Lit.* ii, 258, 350. (B. P.)

Park, Calvin, D.D., a Congregational minister, was born at Northbridge, Mass., Sept. 11, 1774. He graduated from Brown University in 1797, three years after was appointed tutor in the university, and in 1804 was elected professor of languages. From 1811 to 1825 he was professor of moral philosophy and metaphysics. In 1800 he was licensed to preach, in 1815 ordained an evangelist, and from 1826 to 1840 was pastor of the Evangelical Congregational Church at Stoughton. He died there, Jan. 5, 1847. His literary taste was exquisite, and he instinctively perceived the beauties and defects of a literary performance. See Sprague, *Annals of the Amer. Pulpit*, ii, 460.

Park, Roswell, D.D., an Episcopal minister and educator, was born at Lebanon, Conn., Oct. 1, 1807. He was educated at Union College, and at West Point Military Academy, where he graduated in 1831. He then served as a lieutenant of engineers until September, 1836, when he accepted the chair of natural philosophy and chemistry in the University of Pennsylvania, a position which he held until 1842. He took orders in the Protestant Episcopal Church in 1843, and taught and preached in Pomfret, Conn., from 1846 to 1852. He became president of Racine College in the latter year, and chancellor in 1859. He founded a school in Chicago in 1863, and died there, July 16, 1869. Dr. Park published, *Selections of Poems* (1836):—*A Sketch of the History and Topography of West Point*, etc. (1840):—*Pantology* (1841):—*Hand-book for American Travellers in Europe* (1853). See Allibone, *Dict. of Brit. and Amer. Authors*, s. v.

Parker, Charles Carroll, D.D., a Presbyterian minister, was born at Underhill, Vt., Sept. 26, 1814. He graduated from the University of Vermont in 1841; studied one year at the Union Theological Seminary, N. Y.; taught at Burlington, Vt., one year; was a Congregational pastor at Tinmouth from 1848 to 1854; thereafter served at Waterbury until 1867; at Boston Centre, Me., until 1868; at Goshen until 1871, and finally, as a Presbyterian minister, at Parsippany, N. J., until his death, Feb. 15, 1880.

Parker, Joel, D.D., a Presbyterian divine, was born at Bethel, Vt., Aug. 27, 1799. He graduated from Hamilton College, N. Y., in 1824; was ordained in 1826, and settled at Rochester, where he remained until 1830; was pastor of Dey Street Church, New York city, from 1830 to 1833; at New Orleans from 1833 to 1838, and at the Broadway Tabernacle, New York city, from 1838 to 1840. He was chosen president and professor of sacred rhetoric in the Union Theological Seminary in the latter year, and retained the position two years. During the next ten years he served the Clinton Street Church, Philadelphia. He became pastor of the Bleecker Street Church, New York city, in 1852, and of the Fourth Avenue Presbyterian Church in 1854. He died in New York city, May 2, 1873. Dr. Parker was for some time associate editor of the *Presbyterian Quarterly*, and published, among other works, *Lectures on Universalism* (Rochester, 1829):—*Morsels for a Young Student* (about 1832):—*Reasonings of a Pastor with the Young of his Flock*:—*Sermons on Various Subjects* (1852). See Allibone, *Dict. of Brit. and Amer. Authors*, s. v.

Parker, John, an Irish prelate, was born in Dublin, and was made a petty canon of St. Patrick's in 1642. He was subsequently prebendary of St. Michan's and dean of Killala, whereupon he took his degree of bachelor of divinity in Trinity College, Dublin. He was chaplain to the marquis (afterwards duke) of Ormond. In 1649 he was cast into prison by Cromwell, on suspicion of having been employed as a spy by the marquis, who was then laboring to restore Dublin to the king. On his release he was promoted to the bishopric of Elphin, whence he was translated, in 1667, to Tuam, and in 1678 to the archdiocese of Dublin. With his sees he held in commendam the rectory of Gallowne, the treasurership of St. Patrick's, Dublin, and the prebend of Desertmore, in the church of St. Finbar, in the diocese of Cork. He died Dec. 28, 1681. See D'Alton, *Memoirs of the Archbishops of Dublin*, p. 283.

Parker, Linus, D.D., a bishop of the Methodist Episcopal Church South, was born at Rome, N. Y., April 23, 1829. He went to New Orleans in his sixteenth year, at once joined the Poydras Sunday-school, and became a dry-goods clerk. He volunteered in the Mexican war, and soon after his return received license to preach, and in 1849 entered the Louisiana Conference, in which he filled the most important appointments, including the presiding eldership (1870), the editorship of the *New Orleans Christian Advocate* (in connection with his ministerial labors), and membership in the General Conference, until his election as bishop in 1882. He died in this latter work, March 5, 1885. He was a most faithful pastor, a loving friend, and a graceful writer. See *Minutes of Annual Conferences of the M. E. Church South*, 1885, p. 159; Simpson, *Cyclop. of Methodism*, s. v.

Parmelee, Simeon, D.D., a centenarian Congregational minister, was born at West Stockbridge, Mass., Jan. 16, 1782. He was a student of Middlebury College for a few months; then studied theology with Rev. Lemuel Haynes, of West Rutland, Vt. He was ordained pastor of the Church at Westford, Aug. 31, 1808, and was dismissed, Aug. 8, 1837. From Nov. 9 of that year to April 26, 1843, he was pastor in Williston. He served for a time as acting-pastor at Underhill, and was installed there Sept. 11, 1844, and dismissed Nov. 9, 1854. From 1852 to 1854 he was acting-pastor at Milton; from 1854 to 1857 at Tinmouth; from 1857 to 1863 at Underhill; from 1863 to 1866 at Swanton. With the exception of a short time, during 1868 and 1869, when he again supplied Westford, he resided after 1866, without charge, at Oswego, N. Y. He died there, Feb. 10, 1882. See *Cong. Year-book*, 1883, p. 27.

Parsons, John, D.D., an English prelate, was born at Oxford, July 6, 1761. He graduated from Wadham College; was chosen a fellow of Balliol; and appointed to the college livings of All-Saints' and St. Leonard's, in Colchester. He was recalled to Oxford by his election to the mastership of Balliol, Nov. 14, 1798; received the office of vice-chancellor in 1807; was promoted to the deanery of Bristol in 1810; instituted to the vicarage of Weare, Somersetshire, in 1812; and consecrated bishop of Peterborough in 1813. He died March 12, 1819. Bishop Parsons was an humble Christian, a ripe scholar, an able preacher, and a wise administrator. See *The* (Lond.) *Christian Remembrancer*, June, 1819, p. 384; November, p. 669.

Parsons, Justin Wright, D.D., a Presbyterian minister, was born at Westhampton, Mass., in 1824. He graduated from Williams College in 1845, and from Union Theological Seminary in 1848; was ordained by the New York Presbytery, Dec. 26, 1849, and immediately thereafter sailed for Thessalonica, Greece. After laboring at this post until 1854, he was transferred to Smyrna, Asia Minor, and in 1857 to Baghchijeh, Turkey, thence again in 1861 to Nicomedia, and then, after an absence in the foreign field for twenty years, he returned to his native land on a short visit for the benefit of his health. Having again entered upon his work, in July, 1880, he was making a missionary tour on the mountains east of the sea of Marmora, accompanied by his servant, when they encamped for the night; the next morning they were found by the roadside murdered by a band of Zureks. See *N. Y. Observer*, Aug. 12, 1880. (W. P. S.)

Parsons, Levi, D.D., a Presbyterian minister, was born at Northampton, Mass., Aug. 20, 1779; graduated from Williams College in 1801; subsequently spent two years as tutor, and trained for the ministry under Dr. Hyde of Massachusetts. He was licensed in 1807, and the same year became pastor of the Church in Marcellus, N. Y., where he remained twenty-six years. He then supplied Tully for one year, and Otisco for another; next went to his former charge in Marcellus, held it six years longer, and then spent the remainder of his ministry with the Third Church in Marcellus, and at Borodino. He died Nov. 20, 1864. See Mears, *Presbyterianism in Central New York*, p. 628.

Pasch, Georg, a Lutheran theologian of Germany, was born Sept. 23, 1661, at Dantzic. He studied at Rostock and Wittenberg, was in 1689 professor at Kiel, and died Sept. 30, 1707. He wrote, *Diss. de Rechabitis ex Jerem. xxxv*, an essay prepared while yet at the gymnasium (Dantzic, 1681):—*De Operationibus Dæmonum* (Wittenberg, 1684):—*Diss. Physica de Pluralitate Mundorum contra Cartesianos* (eod.):—*Utrum Pontificii Cogantur Concedere Lutheranos in Religione sua Salvari?* (Kiel, 1689):—*De Philosophia Characteristica et Parænetica* (1705):—*De Variis Modis Moralia Tradendi Liber* (1707). See Döring, *Die gelehrten Theologen Deutschlands*, s. v.; Jöcher, *Allgemeines Gelehrten-Lexikon*, s. v. (B. P.)

Pasch, Johann, a Lutheran theologian of Germany, who died at Hamburg in 1709, is the author of, *De Eclipsi Solis in Die Passionis Christi*:—*De Numero Bestiæ Apocalypticæ*:—*De Tikkun Sopherim*:—*De Angelorum Lingua Sine Lingua*:—*De Signo Caini*:—*De Schemhamphorasch*:—*De Voce Hebraica Selah*:—*De Serpente Seductore*:—*De Morte Immortalium Mortis Christi Testium Judæi et Gentilis*:—*De Johanne Baptista*. See Jöcher, *Allgemeines Gelehrten-Lexikon*, s. v. (B. P.)

Paterson, James, D.D., a Scotch Baptist minister, was born at Dumbarton, on the Clyde, in 1801. His early education was obtained at the burgh school of his native town; and he began life as a school-teacher. He entered the University of Glasgow with the idea of becoming a physician, but never took his degree. During his course there he labored as an evangelist with the Glasgow City Mission. He was invited by Dr. Marshman to become a missionary to Serampore, but declined the invitation. In 1829 he hired a small room in Glasgow, fitted it up with forms, and began preaching to a congregation of very poor persons. Here a Church was organized, and removals were made from time to time to better quarters. In 1850 he undertook the editorship of the *Scottish Temperance Review*, and subsequently of the *Scottish Review*. He was one of the originators (in 1846) of the Glasgow Commercial College, and long one of the instructors. He died Jan. 29, 1880. See (Lond.) *Bapt. Hand-book*, 1881, p. 334.

Paterson, John (1), a Scotch prelate, was first minister at Foveran, and next at Aberdeen. He was advanced to the see of Ross, Jan. 18, 1662, where he remained until his death in 1679. See Keith, *Scottish Bishops*, p. 203.

Paterson, John (2), a Scotch prelate, was first minister at Ellon, Aberdeenshire, and afterwards at the Tron Church, and dean of the city of Edinburgh. He was preferred by the interest of the duke of Lauderdale to the see of Galloway, Oct. 23, 1674, where he continued until March 29, 1679, when he was translated to Edinburgh. In 1687 he was put into the see of Glasgow, where he continued until the revolution in 1688. He died at Edinburgh, Dec. 8, 1708. See Keith, *Scottish Bishops*, p. 64, 270, 282.

Paton, James, a Scotch prelate, was elected bishop of Dunkeld in February, 1571. He was deprived in 1575, and died July 20, 1596. See Keith, *Scottish Bishops*, p. 96.

Patrizi, Francis Xavier, a Jesuit, who died at Rome, April 23, 1881, professor of exegesis at the Collegium Romanum, is the author of, *De Interpretatione Scripturarum Sacrarum* (1844, 2 vols.):—*De Evangeliis* (1853, 2 vols.):—*Commentarius in Evangelium Joannis* (1857):—*Comment. in Evangelium Marci* (1862). (B. P.)

Patten, David, D.D., a Methodist Episcopal minister, was born at Boston, Mass., Oct. 10, 1810. He graduated at the high-school there, went thence to Wilbraham Academy, where he was converted in his eighteenth year, and afterwards to Wesleyan University, Middletown, Conn., where he graduated in 1834. In 1832 he was licensed to preach, and employed as supply at Hartford, and also supplied Power Street Church, Providence, R. I., during his last college year. On completing his course at Wesleyan he was at once called to the principalship of Wilbraham, and in 1835 entered the New England Conference. He served as principal at Wilbraham seven years, then entered the pastoral office, and, receiving a transfer to the Providence Conference, was sent in turn to Chestnut Street, Boston; Nantucket; Elm Street, Bedford; Fall River, and Mathewson Street, Providence, serving two years in each place, and one year to Warren. In 1852 he was appointed presiding elder of Providence District, which office he filled until his election, in 1854, to the professorship of theology in the Biblical Institute at Concord, N. H. By unceasing efforts he secured an enlarged endowment for the institute, its removal to Boston, its establishment on an assured financial basis as a department of Boston University, and retained his position in its chair of homiletics and pastoral theology until 1873. He then, on account of impaired health, relinquished his office and became agent of the university and secretary of the board of trustees, devoting to its interests his unfailing love and unflagging zeal until his death, March 26, 1879. The estimate placed upon Dr. Patten's character and worth by his conference is made manifest by his three elections to the General Conference in 1848, 1852, and 1864. See *Minutes of Annual Conferences*, 1879, p. 80; Simpson, *Cyclop. of Methodism*, s. v.

Patten, William, D.D., a Congregational minister, was born at Halifax, Mass., about 1760, and graduated from Dartmouth College in 1780. He was ordained pastor of the Second Church at Newport, R. I., May 24, 1786, dismissed April 15, 1833, and died in 1839. See Sprague, *Annals of the Amer. Pulpit*, i, 592.

Patterson, Andrew Oliphant, D.D., a Presbyterian minister, was born in Fayette County, Pa., July 1, 1794. He graduated from Washington College in 1814, spent one year in theological study at Princeton, and was ordained by the Presbytery of Redstone, April 18, 1821; preached at Mount Pleasant and Swickley churches until 1834, was agent for the Domestic Board of Missions until 1836, preached at Beaver Church from 1837 to 1839, and at New Lisbon from 1840 to 1851; then became stated supply at Bethel, O., for one year, and settled as pastor from 1853 to 1857. He supplied College Corner for a short time, and died at Oxford, O., Dec. 14, 1868. See *Gen. Cat. of Princeton Theol. Sem.* 1881, p. 28.

Pattison, Dorothy Wyndlow (usually called *Sister Dora*), an English philanthropist, was born at Hauxwell, Yorkshire, Jan. 16, 1832, being the daughter of the rector there. In 1864 she joined the "Sisterhood of Good Samaritans," a religious order recognised by the Church of England, and the next year became a nurse in the Cottage Hospital at Walsale, where she devoted herself in the most exemplary manner and with rare skill to the care of the sick, both in body and soul, until, exhausted in strength, she retired in 1876, and died Dec. 24, 1878. See her *Biography*, by Margaret Lonsdale (London and Boston, 1880).

Pattison, Mark, D.D., an English clergyman,

was born at Hornby, Yorkshire, in 1813, and educated at Oriel College, Oxford. He became a fellow of Lincoln College in 1840 and rector in 1861. He died July 31, 1884, leaving numerous essays and reviews on literary and educational subjects. See *Men of the Time*, s. v.

Patton, William, D.D., a Congregational and subsequently a Presbyterian minister, was born at Philadelphia, Pa., Aug. 23, 1798. He graduated from Middlebury College in 1818, attended Princeton Theological Seminary from 1819 to 1820, and in the latter year (June 8) was ordained an evangelist in Charlotte, Vt. Having gathered a Presbyterian congregation in New York city, named the Central Presbyterian Church, he was installed pastor May 7, 1822, and remained in charge until Sept. 15, 1834. The three years following he was secretary of the Presbyterian Education Society. From October, 1837, to October, 1847, he was pastor of the Spring Street Church, New York city, and from 1848 to 1852 was pastor of the Hammond Street Congregational Church. During the next ten years he resided in New York without charge; then removed to New Haven, Conn., where, in 1863, he was acting-pastor of the College Street Church. Subsequently he resided at New Haven without charge, until his death, Sept. 9, 1879. From 1864 Dr. Patton was one of the vice-presidents of the American Missionary Association. Besides important articles in various periodicals, he published, in 1833, a revised and enlarged edition of *The Cottage Bible*, in two volumes. The same year he published *The Village Testament*, and in 1859 the same work, revised, under the title of *The Cottage Testament*. His other works are, *The Christian Psalmist* (1836):—*The Laws of Fermentation*, etc. (1871):—*The Judgment of Jerusalem* (1877):—*Jesus of Nazareth* (1878):—*Bible Principles Illustrated by Bible Characters* (1879). He also issued editions of *Edwards on Revivals* and *Finney on Revivals*, besides a number of pamphlets. He was an ardent advocate of temperance and a powerful lecturer on that subject. He made fourteen voyages to Europe, at first for health, and afterwards as a delegate to various religious bodies. Dr. Patton was a clear, forcible, and copious writer, a bold and impressive speaker, valiant for the truth, an humble and devout Christian. See *Necrol. Report of Princeton Theol. Sem.* 1880, p. 8; *Cong. Year-book*, 1880, p. 25; *Filial Tribute*, by Dr. William W. Patton (Washington, 1880).

Paul, John de St., an Irish prelate, was prebendary of Donnington, in the cathedral of York, and canon of Dublin, when he was advanced to the archbishopric of Dublin, Sept. 12, 1350. In 1360 he was one of the three whom the king appointed to explore for such mines of gold and silver as were thought to be abundant in various parts of Ireland. In 1361 he had an especial writ of summons to a great council to be held in Dublin, on which occasion he is said to have labored with his usual good sense and judgment to effect a general amnesty and pardon of such of the Irish and English as were then opposed to the government. He died Sept. 9, 1362. See D'Alton, *Memoirs of the Archbishops of Dublin*, p. 134.

Pauli, Carl Wilhelm, a German jurist, was born at Lübeck, Dec. 18, 1792. He studied jurisprudence at Göttingen and Tübingen, and occupied the highest positions in his profession at his native place, where he died, March 18, 1879. For a number of years he belonged to the officers of his Church, which he served everywhere, and for which he undertook the publication of a new hymn-book in 1832. Having thus become interested in hymnology, he continued his studies, and published as their result, *Geschichte der lübeckischen Gesangbücher und Beurtheilung des Gegenwärtigen* (Lübeck, 1875). He was a warm friend of the mission among the heathens, and for a number of years stood at the head of the missionary society at Lübeck. To this period belong his *Der lübeckische Verein zur Beförderung der evangelischen Mission unter den Heiden im Jahre* 1856 (ibid. 1857) and *Nothgedrungene Erklärung in Sachen des lübeckischen Vereins* (ibid. 1857). His essay, *Peter Heyling, der erste deutsche Missionär*, in Warneck's *Allgem. Missions-Zeitschrift* (May, 1876), is a valuable contribution to the history of missions and the Church. (B. P.)

Pauli, Christian William Henry, a minister of the Church of England, was born of Hebrew parentage, at Breslau, Silesia, Aug. 11, 1800. He received a strict Jewish education, and at the age of twenty-four, while yet in the synagogue, published a volume of sermons under the title *Predigten für fromme Israeliten* (Halle, 1824, by *Hirsch Prinz*, as his Jewish name originally was). When twenty-five years of age he embraced Christianity at Minden; on coming to England was for some time a student at Cambridge, and while there was invited to come to Oxford, where he was appointed lecturer in Hebrew. This post he held for thirteen years, and published, in 1839, his *Analecta Hebraica*. In 1840 he was ordained, and sent to Berlin by the Society for Promoting Christianity among the Jews. In 1843 he was stationed at Amsterdam, but resigned his position in 1874. He then retired to Luton, Bedfordshire, England, and died May 4, 1877. He also published, *The Great Mystery; or, How can Three be One?* and *A Translation of the Chaldee Paraphrase of Isaiah* (Lond. 1871). (B. P.)

Pauli, Georg Jacob, a Reformed theologian of Germany, was born at Brunswick, July 24, 1722. He studied at Halle, was in 1746 director of the Reformed gymnasium, in 1750 cathedral preacher, in 1751 preacher at Berlin, in 1774 again at Halle, and died Feb. 23, 1795. He published, *De Occasione Psalmi xxxiv Conscribendi* (Halle, 1747):—*De Conciliando Loca Marc. xv*, 25 *et Joh. xix*, 14 (1748):—*De Auctoribus Classicis in Christianorum Scholis Caute Tractandis* (1749):—*Entwurf einer katechetischen und populären Theologie* (2d ed. 1785):—*Heidelbergischer Katechismus* (1781). See Döring, *Die gelehrten Theologen Deutschlands*, s. v. (B. P.)

Paulinians is a name sometimes applied by the Arians to the ancient Christians, from Paulinus, bishop of Antioch.

Paumier, Louis Daniel, a Protestant theologian of France, was born at Autretot, Feb. 23, 1789. He studied at Lausanne, and in 1813 accepted a call to a parish in the neighborhood of Bolbec. In 1817 he was called to Rouen, where he spent the remainder of his life. Besides his ministerial functions, he instructed in a parochial school, which he had founded in 1820, organized different Christian societies, and succeeded in opening a Protestant hospital. Paumier died Sept. 15, 1865, highly honored by both Protestants and Roman Catholics. See Lichtenberger, *Encyclop. des Sciences Religieuses*, s. v. (B. P.)

Pawson, John, a prominent minister in early Methodism, was born at Thorner, near Leeds, Nov. 12, 1737. He was early convicted under Methodist preaching, and after a long struggle was joyfully brought into the light. He preached his first sermon in 1761, in 1762 Wesley sent him to York, and from that time to Feb. 3, 1806, when he preached his last sermon at Wakefield, he exercised his ministry with marked diligence, ability, and success. He was frequently appointed to the large cities, and in 1785 Wesley ordained him, with Hanby and Taylor, for Scotland, in which country, owing to the Scottish character, creed, and mode of worship, Pawson was convinced Methodism would never make much headway. Triumphantly his busy life was closed at Wakefield, March 19, 1806. Twice Pawson was elected president of the conference (1793 and 1801). "During the trials which followed Wesley's death, he was one of the pillars of the shaken structure of Methodism." He wrote in favor of giving the sacraments to the societies in 1792, commended Kilham's pamphlet on the same subject, proposed the solution of the difficulties at the conference in London in the same year, published a revised and enlarged copy of the *Large Minutes* (1797), and *An Affectionate Address to the Junior Preachers* (1798). He believed Methodist government was not sufficiently articulated, favored the appointment of bishops, and the division of England into four Methodist dioceses, and introduced services in the Established Church hours. He was a man of sound judgment, piety, and zeal, and Adam Clarke published a worthy eulogy of him in the *Methodist Magazine* (Lond. 1807). See Jackson, *Early Meth. Preachers*, iv, 1 sq.; Stevens, *Hist. of Methodism*, iii, 202 (see Index); Smith, *Hist. of Methodism*, ii (see Index); Crowther, *Portraiture of Methodism*, 2d ed. p. 382 sq.

Pay, STEPHEN DE, a Scotch prelate, was prior of the abbey of St. Andrews, and in 1383 was elected bishop of the same. But he was taken prisoner by the English at sea, on his way to Rome, and died in March, 1385. See Keith, *Scottish Bishops*, p. 26.

Payne, George, LL.D., an English Congregational minister, was the son of a Baptist minister at Walgrave, Northamptonshire, and at a very early age gave indications of superior intelligence. He was educated in Hoxton College and the University of Glasgow. In 1807 he became assistant to the Rev. Edwar Parsons, of Leeds, and in the following year to the Rev. George Lambert, of Hull. In 1812 he removed to Edinburgh as pastor of Albany Street Chapel, where he labored eleven years. In 1824 he was called to the theological chair in Lancashire College, Blackburn. After five years in that capacity he became president and theological professor of the Western College, Exeter, where he remained until his death, June 19, 1848, at the age of sixty-seven. He published, *Divine Sovereignty:—Original Sin* (London Congregational Lectures for 1844):—*Elements of Mental and Moral Science:—Elements of Language:*—and a tractate on *Congregationalism.* See (Lond.) *Cong. Year-book*, 1848, p. 234; (Lond.) *Evang. Mag.* 1848, p. 393, 415.

Payne, John, D.D., a missionary bishop of the Protestant Episcopal Church, was consecrated in St. Paul's Church, Alexandria, Va., July 11, 1851, as bishop of Western Africa. He resigned his jurisdiction in October, 1871, and returned to the United States, fixing his residence at Oak Grove, Va., where he continued to reside until his death, Oct. 23, 1874, aged sixty years. See *Prot. Episc. Almanac*, 1875, p. 144.

Payson, CHARLES HENRY, D.D., a Presbyterian minister, was born in Leominster, Mass., Sept. 28, 1831. He graduated at Amherst College in 1852, and from the Union Theological Seminary, N.Y., in 1857; was ordained pastor of the mission chapel connected with the Madison Square Chapel in 1860, where, with the exception of a year and a half spent at Berlin and Heidelberg, he labored uninterruptedly with great zeal and success until his death, Jan. 24, 1877.

Peck, JESSE TRUESDELL, D.D., LL.D., a bishop of the Methodist Episcopal Church, was born at Middlefield, Otsego Co., N.Y., April 4, 1811. He was converted when sixteen years old, immediately united with the Church, and commenced a course of study preparatory to the ministry. After two years he was licensed as a local preacher, and in 1832 was admitted into the Oneida Conference, and sent to Dryden Circuit. The next year he was appointed to Newark, and successively to Skaneateles and Potsdam, when he became principal of Governeur High School, and remained four years. In 1841 he was elected principal of Troy Conference Academy, at Poultney, Vt., a position which he retained till 1848. In 1849 he was chosen president of Dickinson College at Carlisle, Pa.; in 1852 he became senior preacher of the Foundry Church in Washington, D.C.; in 1854 secretary of the Tract Society of the Methodist Episcopal Church; in 1856 he was appointed pastor of Greene Street Church, N.Y. He was next stationed at Powell Street, San Francisco; in 1860 was made presiding elder of San Francisco District. At the close of that year he became pastor in Sacramento City, and after two years was stationed at Santa Clara. From 1864 to 1865 he was pastor of Howard Street Church, San Francisco, and was for several years president of the board of trustees of the University of the Pacific, also president of the California State Bible Society. In 1866 he was appointed to Peekskill, N.Y.; in 1867 to Hudson Street, Albany, where he remained three years, and was then stationed at Centenary Church, Syracuse. In 1872 he was elected bishop, and at once entered upon the duties of that office with great earnestness and intensity of interest, also striving to advance the interests of Christianity, wherever his influence was felt. He was a delegate to the Methodist Œcumenical Conference, held in London in 1881, where he distinguished himself by his able and dignified manner of presiding. He died at Syracuse, May 17, 1883. Bishop Peck's religious experience was especially rich and full, and his life most consistent and irreproachable. He was devoted to Methodism, but his broad, catholic spirit led him to regard Christians of all denominations as brothers in Christ. His sermons were clear and strong; as a pastor he was loving and faithful; and as a bishop, untiring in his energy till attacked by disease, which rendered further labor impossible. He was author of, *The Central Idea of Christianity:—The True Woman:—What must I Do to be Saved?*—and *The History of the Great Republic.* See *Minutes of Annual Conferences*, 1883, p. 76; Simpson, *Cyclop. of Methodism*, s. v.

Pecthelmus, a Scotch prelate, was bishop of the see of Galloway about 730. See Keith, *Scottish Bishops*, p. 271.

Pectoral, a square plate of gold or silver, either jewelled or enamelled, sometimes worn by English and

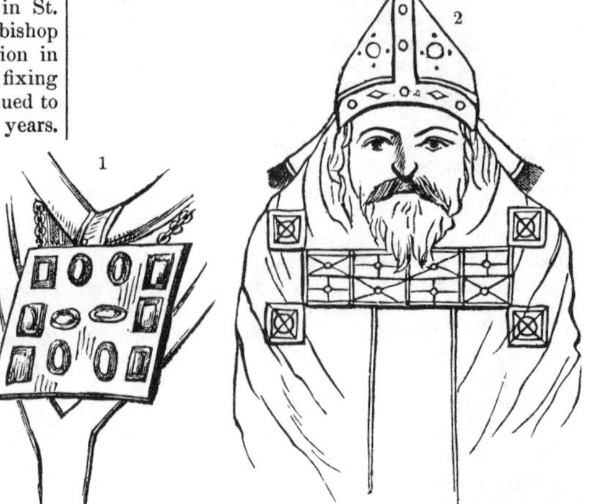

Antique Pectorals: 1. From a Sculpture at Rheims; 2. From an Incised Slab at Freiburg.

other bishops on the breast, over the chasuble, at mass. It is sometimes called a *rationale* or *rational.* Its use appears to have been common during the Middle Ages, for several examples occur on monumental effigies, but since the 14th century it seems to have been disused. It was placed round the neck, and hung on the breast, either by a chain of gold or by three or more silver-gilt pearl-headed pins.

Peebles, JOHN, a Scotch prelate, after enjoying several praiseworthy positions, was preferred to the archdeaconry of St. Andrews, constituted lord chancellor in 1377, and in the same year became bishop of Dunkeld. He died in 1396. See Keith, *Scottish Bishops*, p. 85.

Peguese Version OF THE SCRIPTURES. The Peguese is still spoken in Pegu, a country which formerly included all the sea-coast and the mouths of the rivers of the Burman empire, but the Burmese portion of which, comprising by far the greater part of its extent, is now a province of the British Indian empire. The Peguese language is supposed to be more ancient than the Burmese, although the alphabet is the same, except two additional consonants. A translation of the New Test. was printed at Maulmein in 1847. This is the only part of the Bible now extant. See *Bible of Every Land*, p. 11 sq. (B. P.)

Peip, ALBERT, a Christian philosophical writer of Germany, who was born at Zirke, Posen, in 1830, and died Sept. 29, 1875, professor of philosophy at Göttingen, is the author of, *Christus und die Kunst* (Berlin, 1853):—*Die Wissenschaft und das geschichtliche Christenthum* (eod.):—*Beweis des Christenthums* (1856):—*Christosophie* (1858):—*Philosophie und innere Mission* (Dresden, 1860):—*Jacob Böhme* (Leipsic, eod.):—*Die Kirchen- und Staats-Parteien* (1861):—*Jacob Böhme, in seiner Stellung zur Kirche* (Hamburg, 1862):—*Zum Beweis des Glaubens* (Gütersloh, 1867):—*Das Kreuz und die Weltweisheit* (Hanover, 1869):—*Religionsphilosophie* (published by Theodore Hoppe from Peip's academical lectures, 1879). See Zuchold, *Bibl. Theol.* ii, 981 sq. (B. P.)

Peking-Mandarin Version. See CHINESE VERSIONS, s. v. "Mandarin Dialect."

Pelargus, CHRISTOPH, a Protestant theologian of Germany, was born at Schweidnitz, Silesia, Aug. 3, 1565. He studied at different universities, was in 1586 professor of philosophy at Frankfort, in 1589 doctor, in 1591 professor of theology, and died June 10, 1633. He wrote, *Commentarii in Pentateuchum, Matthæum, Lucam, Johannem et Acta Apostolorum*:—*De Conciliis*:—*Epitome Universæ Theologiæ, seu Explicatio Quattuor Librorum Damasceni de Orthodoxa Fide*:—*De Ascensione Christi in Cœlum*:—*Compendium Theologicum Doctrinæ Christianæ*:—*Josias Imago Piorum Regum ac Principum*. See Jöcher, *Allgemeines Gelehrten-Lexikon*, s. v. (B. P.)

Pelham, GEORGE, D.C.L., an English prelate, youngest son of the earl of Chichester, was born Oct. 13, 1766. He studied at Clare Hall, University of Cambridge; was appointed prebend of Chichester Cathedral in 1790, bishop of Bristol in 1803, translated to Exeter in 1807, and to the bishopric of Lincoln in 1820. He was also clerk of the closet to the king and canon residentiary of Chichester. He died in May, 1827. Bishop Pelham published, *Charge to the Clergy of the Diocese of Bristol* (1804, 4to):—*Sermon* at St. Paul's (1805, 4to). See (Lond.) *Christian Remembrancer*, March, 1827, p. 191; (N. Y.) *Christian Journal*, 1827, p. 160; Allibone, *Dict. of Brit. and Amer. Authors*, s. v.

Pella. For the latest account of this place, see Merrill, *Beyond the Jordan*, p. 442 sq.

Peltanus, THEODOR ANTON, a German Jesuit, born at Pelte, near Liege, was professor of theology at Ingolstadt from 1562 to 1574, and died at Augsburg, May 2, 1584. He wrote, *De Peccato Originali*:—*De Christianorum Sepulturis, Exequiis et Anniversariis*:—*Theologia Naturalis et Mystica*:—*Paraphrasis ac Scholia in Proverbia Salomonis*:—*Catena Græcorum Patrum in Proverbia*. See Jöcher, *Allgemeines Gelehrten-Lexikon*, s. v.; Fürst, *Bibl. Jud.* iii, 70; Winer, *Handbuch der theol. Lit.* i, 880, 883. (B. P.)

Penny, JOSEPH, D.D., a Presbyterian minister, was born in Ireland, was educated at Trinity College, Dublin, and at the University of Glasgow. Two years after he came to America he taught in the academy at Flushing, L. I. In 1821 he took charge of the First Church, Rochester, N. Y.; in 1832 of that at Northampton, Mass., and in 1835 became president of Hamilton College. After leaving that institution, in 1839, he removed to Grand Rapids, Mich., and from there to Pontiac, where his health failed, and he returned to Rochester. He died there, March 20, 1860. Dr. Penny was a man of superior abilities and fine education. In 1829 he visited his native land and organized temperance societies there. See Mears, *Presbyterianism in Central New York*, p. 319, 630.

Pepys, HENRY, D.D., an Anglican prelate, the son of Sir William Weller Pepys, was born April 18, 1783. He was educated at St. John's College, Cambridge, taking the degree of B.A. in 1804 and M.A. in 1807; became rector of Morton, Essex, in 1822, also of Westmill, Hertfordshire, in 1827, and prebendary of Wells in 1836. In 1840 he was consecrated bishop of Sodor and Man, and was translated to the see of Worcester in 1841. He died at Hartleybury Castle, Worcestershire, Nov. 13, 1860. See *Amer. Quar. Church Rev.* 1861, p. 706.

Perché, NAPOLEON JOSEPH, a Roman Catholic prelate, was born at Angers, France, Jan. 10, 1805. He was educated for the Church, and was ordained a priest Sept. 19, 1829. In 1837, when bishop Flaget went to Europe in the interests of his diocese, father Perché offered his services as a missionary, which were accepted, and on his arrival in America he began his labors in Kentucky and founded a church in Portland. In 1842 he was transferred to New Orleans and appointed chaplain of the Ursuline convent, which office he held until April, 1870. Father Perché founded at New Orleans the *Propagateur Catholique*, of which he was principal editor. On May 1, 1870, he was consecrated bishop coadjutor of New Orleans, and on the death of Odin, May 25, 1870, he became the archbishop of the diocese. He died there, Dec. 27, 1883. He was a man of great energy, far-seeing judgment, and great eloquence, and his many charitable acts endeared him to the people, among whom he labored with zeal and fidelity.

Percy, HUGH, D.D., an Anglican prelate, was born in London, Jan. 19, 1784, being a son of the first earl of Beverley. He was consecrated bishop of Rochester in June, 1827, and was transferred to the see of Carlisle in the following September. He was also chancellor of Salisbury and prebendary of St. Paul's. He died suddenly at Rose Castle, near Carlisle, Feb. 12, 1856. See *Amer. Quar. Church Rev.* 1856, p. 145.

Perea. See PERÆA.

Perfect, THE, an appellation frequently applied in the early Christian Church to those who had been baptized, and thereby been admitted to the full privileges of Christians, having a right to partake of the Lord's Supper.

Pericŏpè (περικοπή) is the title of those sections of Holy Scripture which were appointed to be read in the services of the Church. The synagogue, with its parashioth (q. v.) and haphtaras (q. v.), no doubt furnished the pattern which in the different sections of the Church took a different shape. Little of this process has been recorded: it belongs to what Basil calls the ἀγραφατῆς ἐκκλησίας μυστήρια.

The oldest documents which speak of reading the Scriptures in the church belong to the Greek Church, and they are the more important since the Greek Church is the mother of all the Oriental churches, and thus the origin, not only of their liturgies, but also of their lectionaries. The sources at our disposal show the remarkable wealth of the Greek Church in this respect; for not only do the Sundays, the prominent days of Christ's history, and the many saints' days, have their regular gospel and epistolary lessons, but such are also assigned to every day in the week. Thus, for the period between Easter and Pentecost, as Chrysostom already states, the Acts and the gospel of John were read continuously. For the rest of the Church year, three separate and independent series of lessons are employed—one series for the Sundays, beginning with the second after Pentecost; one series for the Sabbaths, beginning in the Pentecost week; and one series for the five weekdays between the Sunday and Sabbath. All three series select both from gospels and epistles, following the order of the books and chapters in the New Test. History explains this strange phenomenon. It is very evident that the Greek Church at first introduced lessons for the Sundays, later for the Sabbaths, and still later for the weekdays.

Next in importance is the Armenian system, which has only become known by professor Petermann's translation from the *Armenian Church Almanac*, published at Venice in 1782, and in German translation found in Alt's *Kirchenjahr*, ii, 136, 225. Scripture-reading is a most important part of the Armenian church-service—more so than in the Greek Church, and lessons from both the Old and New Tests. are employed. Among the Syrians we find for the most part the Greek reading-system, while the Nestorian system of Bible-lessons contains for the first time a series of *lectiones selectæ*, which in some respects deserves to be placed at the side of the Romish pericope system.

The documents with reference to the reading-system of the Jacobite Christians are quite ample; a list of the New-Test. pericopes of the Jacobites is found in the edition of the Syriac New Test. published by Widmanstadt (Vienna, 1855). The Maronites have virtually the same plan of Scripture-reading as the Jacobites. While the lectionary plan adopted by the Alexandrian churches was only a branch of the Greek, that of the Coptic churches was entirely distinct, and is a portion of the Coptic liturgy of St. Basilius. A Latin translation is found in Renaudot's *Collection*, i, 137 sq., from which it is evident that, in every chief service, the Copts read from four different parts of the New Test. Virtually identical with the Coptic is the Ethiopic system. See Renaudot, i, 499, 507 sq.

A proper transition from the eastern to the western systems would be the North-African lectionaries, if we were in possession of such. With the exception of the Mozarabic, prevalent among the African and Spanish Christians in the 13th century, no list has been preserved.

In the Occidental Church we have, in reference to the public reading of Scriptures, a phenomenon similar to that observed in the Church of the East. As, here, the Byzantine system was most predominant, so, in the West, the Roman system gradually supplanted all the rest. A difference between the two consists in this, that the non-Byzantine systems of the East were mostly followed by bodies that stood opposed to the Byzantine Church, while the non-Roman system found a home in bodies on doctrinal and fraternal footing with the Roman Church.

To the reading-systems no more extant belongs the Capuan. Of its existence we have ample proof in the Cod. Fuldensis, corrected in the year 545 by bishop Victor, himself of Capua. That the Christians of Gaul once pursued a peculiar plan in the public reading of the Scriptures is manifest from a letter of the missionary Augustine to Gregory the Great. Besides, there are other scattered evidences from Hilary (354), Sidonius (472), Salvianus (440). See Mabillon, *De Liturg. Gallicana*, p. 29 sq. Then we have a capitular of Charlemagne, abolishing the Gallic liturgy in favor of the Romish. Under the title, *Missa Ambrosiana*, the very ancient liturgy and reading-system of the Milan Church is still preserved. Its original form cannot be definitely determined, as the different printed texts do not agree among themselves. Concerning the Mozarabian liturgy, comp. the art. s. v. Of the Old British and Irish systems not a single trace remains, the Roman having entirely supplanted them. The Roman system of Scriptural reading, like the whole Roman liturgy, has passed through three stages—that of its origin and development, down to the time of the Carlovinians, that of supremacy in the Middle Ages, and that of fixed and formal codification by the Council of Trent.

The oldest traces of it are found in the 5th century, about the time of Jerome, to whom Berno and later writers ascribe its origin. It consists of a double list—one of the epistle, and the other of gospel selections—partly chosen freely, and partly with partiality for certain books.

In the second period, this system made its greatest conquests; in France supplanting the Gallic, in Germany entering with Christianity. It also experienced some internal changes during this time, especially on account of the many saints' days and the introduction of the Corpus Christi festival in 1264.

Finally, the Council of Trent declared the papal system the only legitimate one for the Roman Church, only allowing those churches the use of any other which could prove that the latter had been in constant use there for the past two hundred years.

With the reformation effected by Luther and his German Bible, the traditional character of church services necessarily had to change also. The Bible was read, studied, and explained. The most complete system of Bible-lessons was introduced in England, to some extent, also, in Germany and Switzerland. This whole subject is treated by Ranke, *Fortbestand des herkömmlichen Perikopenkreises* (Gotha, 1859).

The old pericope system has a peculiar history within the section of the Protestant Church that has retained it. In England, Cranmer, in composing the prayer-book, simply took the epistles and gospels as found in the missal of the English bishoprics, omitting only those intended for days not celebrated by Protestants. This latter was also done in Germany; but some other changes were made here, especially at the close of the Epiphany and Trinity Sundays. In the pre-reformatory system there were no lessons for the sixth Sunday after Epiphany, nor for the twenty-sixth and twenty-seventh Sundays after Trinity. This defect was remedied successfully during the 16th century by an unknown master in liturgics, and the present arrangement is the result.

The subordinate services, such as the matins, vespers, as also services during the week, prayer-meetings, and the like, found great favor in the eyes of the Reformers. Luther, in 1526, the Zurich order of worship for 1535, and the Geneva liturgy, gave directions for the use of lessons in such services. The Church of England pursued its own plan in arranging the daily lessons. Not content, as the Continental reformers were, with selecting only certain sections of Scripture to be read, Cranmer arranged for morning and evening services such a course of lessons that in every year the entire Old Test., with the exception of the Psalter and the purely ritual sections of the Pentateuch, was read through once, the New Test. three times, and the Psalter twelve times, i. e. was to be chanted through once a month. In Germany, the services during the week in course of time became almost extinct.

The public Scriptural reading, thus reduced to the regular gospel and epistolary lessons for the different Sundays, could not long satisfy the Church. Already Spener advocated an enlarged pericope system; and since 1769, when the movement was started by the elector George of Hanover, the evangelical authorities in the various provinces of Germany have sought to remedy this defect, especially by the adoption of new series of pericopes. See Suckow, *Die kirchl. Perikopen* (1830); Matthäus, *Die evang. Perikopen des Kirchenjahres* (Anspach, 1844–45, 2 vols.); F. Strauss, *Das evangelische Kirchenjahr* (Berlin, 1850); Piper, *Der verbesserte evangel. Kalender* (1850); Bobertag, *Das evang. Kirchenjahr* (2d ed. Berlin, 1857); Grimmert, *Tabellarische Uebersicht der gewöhnlichen neuen Perikopen reihen* (Zerbst,

1874); Nebe, *Die evang. und epist. Perikopen des Kirchenjahrs* (Wiesbaden, 1875, 8 vols.); Sommer, *Die evang. u. epist. Perikopen* (Erlangen, 1875, 2 vols.); Plitt-Herzog, *Real-Encyklop.* s. v.; Lichtenberger, *Encyclop. des Sciences Religieuses*, s. v. See LESSON. (B. P.)

Peringer, GUSTAV, a Swedish theologian of the 17th century, and professor of Oriental languages at Upsala, is the author of *Historia Linguæ et Eruditionis Arabum;* and translated into Latin the Talmudic treatises *Aboda Sarah* and *Tamid*, both published at Altdorf in 1680. See Jöcher, *Allgemeines Gelehrten-Lexikon*, s. v.; Fürst, *Bibl. Jud.* iii, 78. (B. P.)

Perkins, Aaron, D.D., a Baptist minister, was born at Bridgewater, Mass., May 5, 1792. He was converted in 1811, and ordained June 8, 1813, pastor at Lattentown, N. Y., where he remained twelve years. Twice he was pastor of churches in the city of New York. He died in October, 1881, at Red Bank, N. J. He was remarkably successful in his ministerial labors. See *The Christian at Work*, Oct. 20, 1881. (J. C. S.)

Perkins, Henry, D.D., a Presbyterian minister, was born at Vergennes, Vt., Feb. 9, 1796. He graduated from Union College in 1817, and spent two years thereafter at Princeton Theological Seminary. In 1820 he became pastor of the Presbyterian Church at Allentown, N. J., where he labored faithfully for forty-three years. He retired from active service, and died at Allentown, June 30, 1880. See *Gen. Cat. of Princeton Theol. Sem.* 1880, p. 25.

Permian Version OF THE SCRIPTURES. The Permian is a sister dialect of the Syrjenian and Wotjak, and the three peoples who live in the north-east of European Russia, in the Perm, Wjatka, and Archangel governments, belong to a common race. Mr. Schiefner estimates the number of the Permians at 50,000, the Syrjenians 70,000, and the Wotjaks 200,000. From the annual report of the British and Foreign Bible Society for 1880, we learn that the gospel of Matthew, prepared for prince Louis Lucien Bonaparte by P. A. Popou, has been revised and translated into the Russ character by the academician Wiedemann, and published by the above society. From the report for 1882 we learn that the Holy Synod have sanctioned the publication of the gospel of Matthew, long delayed by the censorial authorities, and that the portion will now be circulated throughout the government of Perm, among the population of about 50,000 souls. (B. P.)

Perreyve, HENRI, a Roman Catholic writer of France, was born at Paris in 1831. At the age of twenty he was made a priest, and in 1861 he was professor of Church history at the Sorbonne. He died in 1865, leaving *La Journée des Malades*, an ascetical work. Father Gratry, the teacher of Perreyve, wrote *Vie de Henri Perreyve* (Paris, 1866). See Lichtenberger, *Encyclop. des Sciences Religieuses*, s. v. (B. P.)

Perrine, Matthew La Rue, D.D., a Presbyterian minister, was born at Freehold, N. J., May 4, 1777. He graduated from Princeton College in 1797, studied theology under Dr. John Woodhull of Freehold, and was licensed by the Presbytery of New Brunswick, Sept. 18, 1799. On the 24th of June, 1800, he was ordained, and for four months acted as a missionary in western New York. On June 15, 1802, he was installed as pastor of the Presbyterian Church at Bottle Hill (now Madison), N. J. In 1809 he made another missionary tour, and on Oct. 31, 1811, was installed as pastor of the Spring Street Church, New York city. Here he continued till the summer of 1820, when, by his own request, the relation was dissolved. In 1821 he was elected to the professorship of ecclesiastical history and Church polity in the Auburn Theological Seminary. He died Feb. 11, 1836. Dr. Perrine had the reputation of being an accurate and thorough scholar. He was of a speculative and metaphysical turn. As a preacher he was always instructive and interesting. He published, *Letters Concerning the Plan of Salvation* (New York, 1816):—*A Sermon Before a French Missionary Society in N. Y.* (1817):—*An Abstract of Biblical Geography* (1835). See Alexander, *Princeton College in the 18th Century; Gen. Cat. of Auburn Theol. Sem.* 1883, p. 193; Aikman, *Historical Discourse* (1876), p. 13.

Perrine, William Henry, D.D., a Methodist Episcopal minister, was born at Lyons, N. Y., Oct. 8, 1827, and moved with his parents to Michigan in 1833. He was converted at the age of thirteen; in 1853 graduated at the Spring Arbor College, having entered the ministry in 1851. The following are his successive appointments: South Albion, Jackson; Lafayette Street, Detroit; Adrian, Ann Arbor; superannuated two years; Flint; professor in Albion College four years; presiding elder of Lansing District; professor again in Albion College; St. Joseph, Albion, Marengo, Parma, Concord. He died in Albion, Mich., Jan. 22, 1881. Dr. Perrine was a fine pulpit orator, and had great versatility of his talent. He took especial interest in Sunday-schools and Bible studies, having visited Palestine in 1857. See *Minutes of Annual Conferences*, 1881, p. 312; Simpson, *Cyclop. of Methodism*, s. v.

Perry, GIDEON BABCOCK, D.D., LL.D., a Protestant Episcopal clergyman, was born at South Kingstown, R. I., Oct. 12, 1800. Among several parishes of which he was rector were St. Paul's, Cleveland, O., and Grace Church, in the same city. He was also the founder of St. James's parish in Cleveland. Subsequently he was rector of Trinity Church, Natchez, Miss., and of Grace Church in Hopkinsville, Ky., where he died, Sept. 30, 1879, having been fifty-seven years in the ministry. See *Providence Journal*, Oct. 13, 1879. (J. C. S.)

Persian Version OF THE SCRIPTURES. By way of supplement we add the following: "As the style in which the gospels of the Polyglots is written has long been antiquated at Ispahan, several efforts were made during the present century to produce a version in the polished dialect now spoken by the Persians. A translation of the gospels was made under the superintendence of colonel Colebrooke, and printed at Calcutta in 1804. In 1812 the Rev. L. Sebastiani had advanced nearly to the end of the Epistles, in a translation of the New Test. from the Greek, and during the same year the gospels of this version were printed at Serampore. In the meantime another translation of the New Test. was progressing at Dinapore, under the superintendence of Henry Martyn. The translators were Sabat and Mirza Firut. This version was completed in 1808, but it was so replete with Arabic and abstruse terms, intelligible only to the learned, that the Rev. H. Martyn determined upon visiting Persia in person for the sake of obtaining a clear and idiomatic version. In 1811 he reached Shiraz, the seat of Persian literature, and remained there nearly a year, in the meantime executing from the original Greek a translation of the New Test. The state of his health compelled him to return to England, but he expired during his journey homeward, at Tokat, Asia Minor, in 1812. Copies of the work were deposited with Sir Gore Ouseley, the English ambassador in Persia, who, on returning to England by way of St. Petersburg, met with prince Galitzin, then at the head of the Russian Bible Society. The suggestion made to the prince to have an edition of Martyn's Test. printed was complied with, and in less than six months the impression was completed.

In 1813 a communication was received by the corresponding committee at Calcutta from Meer Seid Ali, the learned native employed by Mr. Martyn, at Shiraz, in which he informed the committee that the manuscript of the Persian New Test. and of the Psalms (which had likewise been translated at Shiraz) was in his possession, and he waited their orders as to its disposal. He was directed to take four copies of the manuscript, and forward the same to Calcutta, while he was invited himself for the purpose of superintending the publication. The Psalter and the New Test. passed through the press at Calcutta in 1816. The Psalter was reprinted at London, under the superintendence of Dr. Lee, in 1824, and the New Test., edited by the same scholar, in 1827. Other editions followed in 1837 and 1847.

Of all the editions of the Persian New Test., the most incorrect seems to have been that printed at St. Petersburg in 1815, and, at the request of the missionaries, the issue was stopped by the Russian Bible Society. The Rev. W. Glen, of the Scottish mission at Astrakhan, was in consequence led to undertake a version of the Psalms in Persian, for the benefit of the numerous individuals speaking that language who resort to Astrakhan and the south of Russia. In 1826 the British and Foreign Bible Society made arrangements with the Scottish Missionary Society for the services of Mr. Glen in making a translation of the poetical and prophetical books of the Old Test. In the meantime Mirza Jaffier had been engaged by the same society to produce a translation of the historical books of the Old Test. at St. Petersburg, under the eye of Dr. Pinkerton, and according to specific directions given by Dr. Lee. The only portion of Mirza Jaffier's version which was published is the book of Genesis, printed at London in 1827, under the care of Dr. Lee. Mr. Glen's version of the Psalms and Proverbs was published at London in 1830–31, and again in 1836. The entire Old Test., translated by Mr. Glen, left the press in 1847.

In 1824, the Rev. T. Robinson had commenced another translation of the Old Test., which was printed in 1838. A Persian version of the prophecy of Isaiah was purchased by the British and Foreign Bible Society in 1833. This version had been executed by Mirza Ibrahim, of the East India College at Haileybury, and was published in 1834.

Since 1872 a revision of H. Martyn's New Test. has been undertaken by the Rev. R. Bruce, of the Church Missionary Society, stationed at Julfa, near Ispahan, which was completed in 1877. The same translator also commenced the revision of the Old Test. From the report of the British and Foreign Bible Society for 1879, we learn that Mr. Bruce and the Revs. J. Bassett and J. L. Potter, of the American Presbyterian Mission, have formed themselves into a committee for the revision of the Persian Scriptures. The different books of the Old Test. were distributed among the different revisers, and each will carefully examine the work of the others. The revised New Test., too, was to be subjected to a joint revision. From the report for the year 1882, we learn that the latter, after having been thoroughly revised by the translator and professor Palmer of Cambridge, was published by the British and Foreign Bible Society. As for the Old Test., the work of revision is progressing slowly. (B. P.)

Persian-Jewish Version. See JUDÆO-PERSIAN VERSION.

Personality is an attribute of conscious beings only, and thus distinguishes individuals from each other. In the Trinity it is simple and absolute, so that the three persons of the godhead are not three beings, since they have a common consciousness. In man it is compound, consisting of a body and a soul, which are not homogeneous, as are the three divine persons, and yet constitute but a single being, inasmuch as the consciousness essentially resides in the soul, which is therefore *per se* the real person, and remains such after the separation from the body. In Jesus Christ there was a double or complex personality, because he had a complete human soul (as well as body), and was also filled hypostatically with the divine spirit. He consequently may be said to have had a sort of double consciousness; for the divine spirit did not always communicate everything to the human spirit, and the latter could not be commensurate with the former. Yet he was not two persons, inasmuch as the two natures were indissolubly blended, and the twofold personality likewise. The partial lack of homogeneity between the divine and the human spirit in him did not negative this, just as the still greater dissimilarity between human flesh and soul does not negative unity in man.

Perthes, FRIEDRICH MATTHIAS, a Protestant theologian of Germany, son of Friedrich Christoph, was born at Hamburg, Jan. 16, 1800. In 1842 he was pastor at Moorburg, near Hamburg, and died Aug. 29, 1859. He is best known as the author of *Des Bischofs Johannes Chrysostomus Leben* (Hamburg, 1853). See Zuchold, *Bibl. Theol.* ii, 984. (B. P.)

Pertz, GEORG HEINRICH, a famous German historian, was born at Hanover, March 28, 1795. In 1823 he was secretary of the royal archives at Hanover, in 1842 head-librarian at Berlin, and he died at Munich, Oct. 7, 1876. He edited *Leibniz-gesammelte Werke* (Hanover, 1843 sq.), and published *Ueber Leibnizen's kirchliches Glaubensbekenntniss* (Berlin, 1846):—*Ueber die gedruckten Ablassbriefe von* 1454 *und* 1455 (1857). See Zuchold, *Bibl. Theol.* ii, 984. (B. P.)

Peruvian Religion. In the earliest times the inhabitants of the kingdom of Peru, which Manco Capac, the first inca, ruled, seem to have been believers in the coarsest fetichism. They only had one supreme deity, the mother of all, Mama Kocha, in honor of whom wild animals, plants, and prisoners of war were sacrificed. The devouring of fallen or sacrificed enemies was a sacred custom of the Peruvians. A great flood had overflowed the country, and after this Manco Capac, and his wife, Mama Oëllo, children of the sun, came from a foreign country to the shores of the sea Titicaca, where they built the city of Cuzco, collected the remaining people, and gave them laws and sacred teachings, which were carefully preserved until the arrival of the Spaniards. The supreme being of the later Peruvians was called Pachacamac, who was the creator of all beings, also of the sun; the latter was his only visible representative on earth, and was therefore divinely worshipped; but the god himself was exalted above the sacrifices of mortals. The moon and stars also had temples, like the sun, but of less splendor, inasmuch as all that was of gold in the temples of the sun was made of silver in those of the moon and stars. There were male and female priests: of the latter, the maidens of the sun were of two kinds; the higher, from the Inca-family, dedicated their whole lives to the service of the sun, and there were more than fifteen hundred of these in convents. If unfaithful, they and their whole family were to be exterminated, according to the law known as "hard law." But in the entire history of Peru not an instance of this occurs. The second class of servants of the sun did not live in the capital, Cuzco, but in the provinces of the kingdom, and were chosen from all classes. The conditions of reception were beauty and purity. When the cruel Pizarro came to Peru, the immense riches were carried off by the Spaniards, and the beautiful daughters of the Incas, the virtuous sun-maidens, became a prey to the insolent warriors.

Peruvian Version. See QUICHUAN.

Pescheck, CHRISTIAN ADOLPH, a Lutheran theologian of Germany, was born Feb. 1, 1787, at Johnsdorf, Saxony. In 1816 he was pastor at Lückendorf, in 1831 deacon at Zittau, and died in 1859, doctor of philosophy. He is the author of, *Geschichte der Cölestiner des Oybins, urkundlich erforscht und dargestellt* (Zittau, 1840):—*Geschichte der Gegenreformation in Böhmen* (Leipsic, 1843–44, 2 vols.):—*Die böhmischen Exulanten in Sachsen* (1857):—*Die Auswanderung glaubenstreuer Protestanten aus Böhmen und Sachsen im xvii. Jahrhundert* (1858). See Zuchold, *Bibl. Theol.* ii, 984 sq. (B. P.)

Peter (*Saint*), FESTIVALS OF.—I. *Depositio Petri in Catacombas et Pauli in via Ostiensi.* The *Catalogus Liberianus* (354) first mentions the entombment of the bones of Peter and Paul as having taken place in the year of the consuls Tuscus and Bassus (258), and gives the date as *III. Cal. Julii*, that is, June 29. A festival in commemoration of that day is recorded in the

Latin Church by Prudentius in the 4th century, by Augustine (*Serm.* 295-299), Maxim. of Turin (ibid. 66-69), and Leo the Great (ibid. 82-84) in the 5th; after the 6th it is noticed in all martyr chronicles. In the Greek Church it is stated by Theodorus Lector, in his Church history (ii, 16), as having been celebrated in Constantinople towards the close of the reign of Anastasius I (518); after the 7th century it is given in all calendars, even those of Copts, Ethiopians, and Armenians. In 1743 Benedict XIV decreed a celebration of eight days for the city of Rome; and in 1867, the eighteenth centenary, it was renewed with great magnificence by Pius IX.

II. *Festum Cathedræ Petri Antiochenæ*, for Feb. 22, mentioned in the *Calendarium Liberianum*, and celebrated in commemoration of the accession of the apostle Peter to the episcopal chair, without, however, specifying the locality of the chair. The same is the case with the *Calendarium* of Polemius Silvius (448). In the Ambrosian Liturgy, and in the *Sacramentarium* of Gelasius I, the festival is omitted altogether; but is found again in the *Sacramentarium* of Gregory, and after his time always.

III. *Festum Cathedræ Petri Romanæ*, Jan. 18, was generally confounded with II, but became independently established in the 8th century, and formally fixed during the Carlovingian age, to which time, also, belongs the final recognition of the tradition of the double episcopacy of St. Peter.

IV. *Festum Sanctum Petri ad Vincula* or *in Vinculis*, also called *Festum Catenarum Petri*, Aug. 1, is not mentioned until the 9th century, in Wandalbert's *Martyrologium*, and Pseudo-Beda's *Homil. de Vinculis Sancti Petri* (Bedæ, *Opp.* iii, 96). In the Greek Church it is celebrated Jan. 16, in the Armenian Feb. 22. The latter Church also celebrated a festival of "the finger of the apostle Peter" (Assemani, *Euchol. Eccles. Orient.*), and the Abyssinians commemorate on July 31 a festival in honor of St. Peter (Ludolf, *Hist. Æthiop.* p. 424), but the origin and signification of the latter is not known. See Augusti, *Denkwürdigkeiten*, iii, 175 sq.; Sinker, in Smith's *Dict. of Christ. Antiq.* ii, 1623-1628; Nilles, *Kalendarium Manuale Utriusque Ecclesiæ, Orient. et Occident.* vol. ii; Zöckler, in Plitt-Herzog, *Real-Encyklop.* s. v. (B. P.)

Peter of Blois. See Blesen, Peter.

Petermann, Julius Heinrich, D.D., a famous German Orientalist, was born at Glauchau, Aug. 12, 1801. In 1837 he was professor of Oriental literature at Berlin, from 1852 to 1855 he travelled through Asia Minor and Persia, in 1867 and 1868 through Palestine and Syria. He died in June, 1876. Besides his contributions to different periodicals and cyclopædias, he published, *Grammatica Linguæ Armeniacæ* (Berlin, 1837):—*De Ostikanis, Arabicis, Armeniæ Gubernatoribus* (1840):—*Beiträge zu einer Geschichte der neuesten Reformen des Osmanischen Reichs* (1842):—*Pauli Epistola ad Philemonem*, etc. (1844):—*Porta Linguarum Orientalium* (1864-72, 5 vols.):—*Reise in den Orient* (2d ed. Leipsic, 1865, 2 vols.):—*Liber Magnus Vulgo Liber Adami Appellatus* (1867):—*Pentateuchus Samaritanus* (Berlin, 1872 sq., 3 vols.). (B. P.)

Petersen, August, a Protestant theologian of Germany, who died at Gotha, Nov. 1, 1875, doctor of theology and general superintendent, is the author of, *Die Idee der christlichen Kirche* (Leipsic, 1839-46, 3 vols.); *Schleiermacher als Reformator der deutschen Bildung* (Gotha, 1869):—*Die protestantische Lehrfreiheit und ihre Grenzen* (Frankfort, 1865). (B. P.)

Peterson, William, D.D., an English divine, was installed prebendary of the Church at Exeter, Aug. 16, 1619; elected canon residentiary, June 2, 1621; and advanced to the deanery, July 18, 1629. He died Dec. 6, 1661, aged seventy-four years. Dr. Peterson was a man of exemplary life, faithful in preaching the gospel, and charitable to the poor.

Petræus, a name common to several Swedish theologians, of whom we mention the following:

1. Æschilius, who died at Abo in 1657, professor and doctor of theology, is the author of, *Enarrationes in Evangelia Dominicalia et Festivalia*:—*De Veteris et Novi Testamenti Discrimine*:—*De Anti-Christo Magno*, besides a translation of the Bible into Finnish.

2. Laurentius, who died Jan. 7, 1655, is the author of *Canticum Canticorum Salomonis, Paraphrasi tum Ligata Hebræa et Danica, tum Prosa Latina Adornatum* (Hafniæ, 1640).

3. Nicolas (1) was born at Husum, Sept. 10, 1569. He studied at different universities, was in 1600 doctor of theology, and died at Ratzeburg, Jan. 7, 1641, a superintendent.

4. Nicolas (2) was born at Zealand in 1601. He studied at different universities, was professor of Oriental languages at Copenhagen, and died Oct. 4, 1634. He is the author of, *Nomenclator Hebræus* (Hafniæ, 1629):—*Lexicon Hebraicum cum Grammatica Hebraica* (1627, 1633):—*Musæ Hebrææ seu Colloquia Hebræa* (1628).

5. Severin, born in 1609, and died Nov. 25, 1657, professor at Copenhagen, is the author of, *Grammatica Hebræa* (1642):—*Fundamenta Linguæ Sanctæ* (1647):—*Disquisitio de Fundamento Philosophiæ Moralis.*

6. Theodore, who died at Copenhagen in 1673, is the author of, *Prophetia Joelis Æthiop., Interpret. Latina ad Verbum Donata* (Leyden, 1661):—*Prophetia Jonæ Æthiop. et ex Æthiop. in Lat. ad Verbum Versa et Notis atque Adagiis Illustrata* (1660):—*Vaticinium Malachiæ Æthiop. Latino Idiomate ad Verbum Donatum* (1661). See Jöcher, *Allgemeines Gelehrten-Lexikon*, s. v.; Fürst, *Bibl. Jud.* iii, 80; Winer, *Handbuch der theol. Lit.* i, 63, 64. (B. P.)

Petrus, a Scotch prelate, was bishop of Orkney in 1270, and was one of the ambassadors sent by Eric, king of Norway, to negotiate a marriage between that monarch and Margaret, daughter to Alexander III, king of Scotland. He died in 1284. See Keith, *Scottish Bishops*, p. 220.

Peyrat, Napoléon, a Protestant theologian and historian of France, was born at Bordes-sur-Arise, Ariège, Jan. 20, 1809. In 1849 he was appointed pastor at St.-Germain-en-Laye, and he died April 4, 1881. He is the author of *Pasteurs du Desert* (1842), a work which has been styled "un bénédictin romantique." This work was followed by *L'Histoire de Vigilance*:—*Les Reformateurs de la France et de l'Italie au Douzième Siècle* (Pierre de Brueys, Arrigo, Abélard, Arnaud de Brescia, St. Bernard, Bérenger):—*Le Colloque de Poissy*:—*Le Siège du Mas d'Azil*:—*L'Histoire des Albigeois*:—*Béranger et Lamennais, Correspondence et Souvenirs* (Paris, 1861), this last a charming volume. See Mme. Napoléon Peyrat, *Napoléon Peyrat, Poète, Historien, Pasteur* (Paris, 1881); Lichtenberger, *Encyclop. des Sciences Religieuses*, s. v. (B. P.)

Peyron, Amadeo, a famous Italian Orientalist and antiquarian, was born at Turin, Oct. 2, 1785. In 1815 he succeeded his former teacher, the abbot Valperga di Caluso, as professor of Oriental languages at Turin, and he died April 27, 1870. He is especially known by his *Lexicon Linguæ Copticæ* (Turin, 1835) and *Grammatica Linguæ Copticæ* (1841); besides, he wrote a number of essays, published in the *Memorie* of the Turin Academy of Sciences. (B. P.)

Pfannkuche, Heinrich Friedrich, a Lutheran theologian of Germany, was born Nov. 28, 1766. For some time private tutor at Göttingen, he was in 1803 called to Giessen as professor of Oriental languages, and he died Oct. 7, 1833, doctor of theology. He wrote, *Exercitationes in Ecclesiastæ Salomoni Vulgo Tributi Locum Vexatissim. cap. xi, 7-xii, 7* (Göttingen, 1794):—*Observat. Philolog. et Critic. ad quædam Psalmorum Loca, Specimen* (Bremen, 1791):—*De Codicum MSS. Hebr. Veteris Testamenti et Versionum Chaldaicarum in*

Lectionibus Anti-masorethis Consensu (Giessen, 1803). See Winer, *Handbuch der theol. Lit.* i, 213; Fürst, *Bibl. Jud.* iii, 81 sq. (B. P.)

Pfeffinger, DANIEL, a Lutheran theologian of Strasburg, who died Nov. 24, 1724, doctor and professor of theology, is the author of, *De Malo ejusque Causis Intrinsecis:* — *De Cretensium Aritiis ad Tit. i,* 12:—*Duæ Disputt. in Prophetiam Haggai:*—*De Nethinæis ad Jos. ix,* 27 *et Esdr. viii,* 20:—*De Viro Perfecto ad Ephes. iv,* 13, 14: — *De Cultu Angelorum ad Coloss. ii,* 18:—*De Christo pro Nobis Exciso ad Dan. ix,* 26:— *De Pœnitentia Dei ad Genes. vi,* 6, 7:— *De Prophetarum Falsorum Furtis ad Jerem. xxiii,* 30:— *De Michæle Angelorum Auxiliatore*, etc. See Jöcher, *Allgemeines Gelehrten-Lexikon*, s. v. (B. P.)

Pfeiffer, August Friedrich, a Lutheran theologian of Germany, was born at Erlangen, Jan. 13, 1748, where he also commenced his academical career in 1769. In 1776 he was professor of Oriental languages, in 1805 head librarian of the university, and he died July 15, 1817. He wrote, *De Ingenio Oratorio* (Erlangen, 1770):—*De Jobo Patientiam et Christum Prædicante* (1771): — *De Jobæi Libri Scopo* (eod.): — *Progr. in Versionem Syriacam ad i Timoth. Epistolæ* (1776):— *Ueber die Musik der alten Hebräer* (1778):—*Hebräische Grammatik* (3d ed. 1802): — *Neue Uebersetzung des Propheten Hoseas* (1785): — *Philonis Judæi Opera Omnia*, etc. (1785-92, 5 vols.; 2d ed. 1820):—*Progr. super Ps. cx* (1801):—*Progr. super Ps. lxxii* (1803):— *Bibliorum Hebraicorum et Chaldæorum Manuale ad Prima Linguarum Studia Concinnavit* (1809). See Döring, *Die gelehrten Theologen Deutschlands*, s. v.; Fürst, *Bibl. Jud.* iii, 83; Winer, *Handbuch der theol. Lit.* i, 115, 145, 522. (B. P.)

Pfeiffer, Joachim Ehrenfried, a Lutheran theologian of Germany, and father of August Friedrich, was born at Güstrow, Pomerania, Sept. 6, 1709. He studied at Rostock, and commenced there his academical career in 1737. In 1743 he accepted a call to Erlangen as professor of theology, was made doctor of theology in the same year, and died Oct. 18, 1787. He published, *Diss. de Malo Morali*, etc. (Jena, 1737): —*De Lege Interpretandi Prima et Fundamentali* (1740): — *Elementa Hermeneuticæ Universalis* (1743): — *De Calore sub Nube Torrente*, etc. (eod.):—*Trinitas Personarum in Unitate Dei*, etc. (eod.):—*Messias θεάνθρωπος ad Jerem. xxiii*, 5, 6 (eod.):—*Messias Satisfactor Hominum ex Ies. liii*, 4, 5, 6 (1744):—*Processio Spiritus Sancti a Filio Dei ex Ies. xlv*, 3 (1745):—*Messias non Spiritus Sanctus sed Dei Patris Filius ex Ps. ii*, 7 (1751):—*Lux Orta Populo in Tenebris Sedenti ex Ies. viii*, 23 (1754):—*Cognitio Justi Servi Dei Justifica ex Ies. liii*, 11 (1755):—*Spes Resurrectionis apud Jobum xix*, 25, 26, 27 (1760-61), etc. See Döring, *Die gelehrten Theologen Deutschlands*, s. v. (who gives sixty-seven titles of Pfeiffer's works); Fürst, *Bibl. Jud.* ii, 83 sq.; Winer, *Handbuch der theol. Lit.* i, 105, 422, 425, 603. (B. P.)

Pfitzer, JOHANN JACOB, a Lutheran theologian of Germany, was born at Nuremberg, Oct. 29, 1684. He studied at different universities, was in 1713 deacon at his birthplace, in 1717 professor of theology at Altdorf, in 1718 doctor of theology, in 1724 pastor at Nuremberg, and died March 10, 1759. He published, *De Apotheosi Pauli et Barnabæ a Lystrensibus Frustra Tentata* (Altdorf, 1718):—*De Appolline, Doctore Apostolico ex Actor. xviii*, 24-28 (eod.): — *De Beneficiis Typicis* (1723), etc. See Döring, *Die gelehrten Theologen Deutschlands*, s. v.; Fürst, *Bibl. Jud.* iii, 84. (B. P.)

Pharaoh OF THE EXODE. Owing to the deep interest in the history of that event, extraordinary efforts have been made by Biblical scholars to identify this Egyptian king, whose name is not given in the sacred narrative. Most writers have been content to compare the chronologies of Egypt and the Bible together, and rest in the simple synchronism, a result necessarily problematical, from the acknowledged uncertainty of both these chronological schemes. Thus the *Speaker's Commentary* (i, 455, Amer. ed.) concludes that the Egyptian monarch in question was Thothmes III; but this result depends upon a series of chronological calculations and comparisons every step in which is debatable. The most favorite identification, however, of late, has been with Menephthah I, son of Rameses II, or the great Sesostris. This is adopted by Brugsch, Bunsen, Chabas, Ebers, Lenormant, Lepsius, Rawlinson, De Rougé, Vigouroux, and others. We give the reasons *pro et con.*

1. Josephus cites (*Apion*, i, 26 sq.) Manetho as stating that Moses was identical with a certain Osarsiph, or Egyptian priest of Heliopolis, who headed a revolt of a band of lepers in the reign of Amenophis; and this prince appears to be the Menephthah (or Mernephthah) of the monuments, and the Amenophath or Amenephthes of the 19th dynasty of Manetho's lists, by reason of his association, in the above account in Josephus, with Sethos or Rameses as his son, and Rhampses (or Rameses) as his father. But Josephus himself expressly and somewhat passionately contradicts the identification in question, and he alleges, and goes far to prove, numerous inconsistencies and fallacies in it, arguing, in short, that the whole story is a mendacious invention, and especially dwelling upon the fact that the insurgents in that case, so far from succeeding in their escape from Egypt, were ultimately subdued and destroyed by the Egyptians. The statements of Manetho himself, as extant in Syncellus and Eusebius, make no mention of this identification, but variously name Amosis (head of the 18th dynasty) and Achencheroes (ninth king of the same dynasty) as the Pharaoh of the Exode.

In another passage (*Apion*, i, 32, 33) Josephus gives a similar narrative from Chæremon; but, as he justly shows, the contradictions of the story are there still more apparent. In a third account, from Lysimachus (*ibid.* 34) the Egyptian king's name is given as Bocchoris, and so all trace of identity disappears. Josephus himself repeatedly affirms that Manetho's own work gave Tethmosis (or Thummoses, son of Alisphragmuthosis [Misphragmuthosis]) as the name of the Pharaoh of the Exode.

2. The circumstances of Rameses II, father of the Egyptian king under consideration, are supposed to favor his identification with the Pharaoh of the oppression, and so to coincide with the theory in question. Thus he was a great builder of cities, especially (it is alleged) of Pi-Tum and Pi-Ramses, which are held to be the Pithom and Raameses of the Bible. But the last identifications are extremely doubtful, and the name Rameses appears as that of a district as early as Joseph's day (Gen. xlvii, 11). The identification of an oppressed or conquered people in his reign, named *Aperu* on the monuments, with the Hebrews, is equally doubtful, both in the reading and application; it is at all events certain that the people so named were *foreign* serfs, and that they were employed in large numbers at a period considerably later than the Exode (Brugsch, *Hist. of Egypt*, ii, 129). Opposed to this identification is the well-known character of the Rameses in question as a just and humane prince, who cannot have been guilty of the atrocious policy of drowning all the male children of a portion of his subjects.

3. The character and circumstances of Menephthah himself are not given with sufficient detail in the Egyptian chronicles or monuments to enable us to say with definiteness whether they agree or disagree with the Biblical account. There is nothing in them, however, which tallies with the overthrow at the Red Sea. If, as the history in Exodus implies, and as later Scriptural notices expressly affirm (e. g. Psa. cxxxvi, 15), the Egyptian king was himself drowned there, it cannot have been Menephthah, who certainly reigned much longer than the brief interval between Moses' return to

Egypt (Exod. iv, 19; comp. ii, 15) and the Exode. Moreover, Menephthah was one of a large family of sons born to Rameses during his long reign, and this militates decidedly against the adoption of Moses as heir through a daughter. Dr. Schaff adduces (*Through Bible Lands*, p. 102) a circumstance mentioned by Herodotus (ii, 111), that the successor of Sesostris (supposed to be Rameses II) was smitten with blindness for ten years as a punishment for hurling his spear into the Nile during an extraordinary overflow; but this looks to us very little like the catastrophe at the Red Sea; and, besides, the historian calls the king in question Pheron, and he names his successor Proteus, words which have no place in the dynastic lists.

4. Finally and conclusively, the chronology of the period will not allow this identification. The lowest date for the Exode is the Rabbinical, B.C. 1312; Usher's is 1491; Hales's, 1614; our own, 1658; while the dates assigned to the end of Menephthah's reign are as follows: Mariette, cir. B.C. 1288; Lepsius, 1273; Wilkinson, 1200; ours, 1175. The difference, in any case, is from a quarter of a century to four centuries and a half. It is useless to plead the uncertainty of the dates in either line, because it is precisely here that both the Egyptian and the Biblical chronologies begin to be definite; and the tendency of modern criticism is to widen rather than contract the discrepancy at this point. This objection has not escaped Josephus, who expressly remarks (*Apion*, i, 27) that, according to Manetho, "Moses lived many generations earlier" than the king in question, or, more definitely (*ibid.* 26), 518 years, or, according to his own detailed estimate (*ibid.* 15), exactly 327 years. Our calculation, 483 years, is nearly a mean between these. Josephus further states (*Apion*, ii, 2) that "Solomon built the temple 612 years after the Jews came out of Egypt" (he elsewhere makes it variously 592 and 632 years — in our own scheme it was 648 years); and he fortifies this date by a reference to the then well-known contemporaneous Tyrian annals. He adds (*ibid.*) that the date of the Exode, according to the above notice of Lysimachus (i. e. as occurring under king Bocchoris) would make it "1700 years ago," or about B.C. 1630, which again is substantially our date. We conclude therefore that Josephus at least (from whom, be it noted, the whole basis of this proposed identification is derived) was clear and consistent as well as definitely grounded in his chronology, both in its Biblical and its Egyptian relations; and like him we must decidedly reject this synchronism. See MANETHO.

Phasaëlis. The present *Khurbet Fasail* is laid down on the Ordnance *Map* at twelve and a half miles north of Riha (Jericho), and is briefly described in the *Memoirs* accompanying (ii, 392).

Phelps, ELIAKIM, D.D., a Congregational minister, was born at Belchertown, Mass., March 20, 1790. From 1811 to 1813 he was a member of Brown University, but graduated in 1814 from Union College. He was ordained at Brookfield, Oct. 23, 1816, as the colleague of Rev. Ephraim Ward, and continued to minister there until Oct. 25, 1826. During the succeeding three years he was principal of the Ladies' High-school at Pittsfield. In February, 1830, he was installed pastor of the Presbyterian Church at Geneva, N. Y., and held that position until September, 1835. From 1836 he was secretary of the American Education Society in Philadelphia, and of the same in New York to 1845. For one year he was acting-pastor at Kingston, R. I., and served in the same relation at Putnam, Conn., from 1856 to 1858. His residence from 1871 to 1874 was at Andover, Mass., and from 1874 to 1880 at Weehawken, N. J. During 1831–35 he was a commissioner of Auburn Theological Seminary, N. Y., and for the last year of that term was president of the commissioners. He died at Weehawken, N. J., Dec. 29, 1880. Dr. Phelps published a volume of addresses, entitled *The Ministry We Need*, besides pamphlets, etc. See *Cong. Year-book*, 1881, p. 31.

Phenomenalism. See SCEPTICISM, LATEST PHASES OF.

Philaret, archbishop of Tschernigow, who died in 1866, was one of the most learned historians of the Russian Church. He is the author of a work on *Cyril and Methodius, the Apostles of the Slavs* (1846; Germ. transl. Milan, 1848). He also wrote on the *Service of the Russian Church in the Pre-Mongolian Time* (1847):—*History of the Russian Church* (4th ed. 1862, 5 vols.):—*Review of Russian Literature from* 862 *to* 1858 (1859, 2 vols.). (B. P.)

Philip, a Scotch prelate, was in the see of Brechin in 1351. See Keith, *Scottish Bishops*, p. 162.

Philip *the Magnanimous*, landgrave of Hesse, born at Marburg, Nov. 23, 1504, was one of the most prominent characters in the history of the German Reformation. He was only five years old when his father died, and only fourteen when he was declared of age. He was present at the diet of Worms in 1521, but had, at that time, not yet decided with respect to religious matters. He was, however, one of those who insisted that the safe-conduct accorded to Luther should be kept sacred. He visited Luther in his lodgings, and on his return allowed mass to be celebrated in German at Cassel. In February, 1525, he opened his country to the reformation, in May he joined the Torgau Union, and in June he appeared at the Diet of Spires as one of the leaders of the Protestant party, surprising the Roman Catholic bishops by his theological learning, the imperial commissioners by his outspokenness, and king Ferdinand himself by the open threat of leaving the diet immediately if the enforcement of the edicts of Worms was insisted upon. The great task he had on hand was to unite the German and Swiss Protestants into one compact party, and at the Diet of Spires (1529) he succeeded in baffling all the attempts of the Roman Catholics to produce an open breach. The conference of Marburg, in the same year, was also his work, and it had, at all events, the effect of somewhat mitigating the hostility of the theologians. Nevertheless, at the diet of Augsburg (1530), the Lutherans appeared to be willing to buy peace by sacrificing the interests of the Zwinglians. Philip proposed war, open and immediate; but the Lutherans suspected him of being a Zwinglian at heart, and their suspicion made him powerless. He subscribed the *Confessio Augustana*, but reluctantly, and with an express reservation with respect to the doctrine of the Lord's Supper. Finally, when he saw that nothing could be done, while he knew that the emperor could not be trusted, he suddenly left Augsburg. This resoluteness made an impression on the other Protestant princes; and in March, 1531, he was able to form the Smalcaldian League, though he was not able to procure admission to it for the Swiss Reformed. He also opened negotiations with the king of Denmark; in 1532 he compelled the emperor to grant the peace of Nuremberg; in 1534, after the brilliant victory at Laussen, he enforced the restoration of duke Ulrich, of Würtemberg, by which that country was opened to the Reformation; in 1539 he began negotiations with Francis I, and in 1540 he again proposed to wage open war on the emperor. But at this very moment his authority was greatly impaired, and his activity much clogged, by his marriage with Margarethe von der Saal—a clear case of bigamy. The theologians, even Luther and Melanchthon, consented, provided this marriage was kept secret. The duchess of Roonlitz, the sister of Philip, would not keep silent, and the question arose what the emperor would do. The case was so much the worse, as, in 1535, Philip had issued a law which made bigamy one of the greatest crimes in Hesse. The emperor, however, simply used the affair to completely undermine the political position of the landgrave, but the profit he drew from it was, nevertheless, no small one. During the difficult times which followed after the peace of Crespy (1544), the Protestant party had no acknowledged head; during the Smalcaldian war (1546–47), no acknowledged leader. After the war, the emperor treacherously seized the landgrave, and kept him in prison for five years. After his release, in 1552, Philip spent all his energies in ameliorating the condition of his country, which had suffered so much from war. But he still had a lively interest in religious matters, and acted the part of a mediator, especially between the Protestants and Roman Catholics; thus he was very active in promoting the conference of Naumburg in 1544 and that of Worms in 1557. Philip died March 31, 1567. See Rommel, *Philipp der Grossmüthige* (Giessen, 1830, 3 vols.); Lenz, *Briefwechsel Landgraf Philipp's mit Bucer* (vol. i, Leipsic, 1880); Wille, *Philipp der Grossmüthige u. die Restitution Herzog Ulrich's von Würtemberg* (Tübingen, 1882); Plitt-Herzog, *Real-Encyklop.* s. v.; Lichtenberger, *Encyclop. des Sciences Religieuses*, s. v. (B. P.)

Philip, Hermann, a medical missionary, was born of Jewish parentage at Brunswick in 1813. While a student of medicine he joined the Prussian army, which he left after some years' service in order to join a brother of his who was in Java in the Dutch service. Philip embarked at Rotterdam for Batavia, but owing to some accident which happened after the vessel had left the harbor, he came to England. At London, through his employers, he became acquainted with a Presbyterian minister, who spoke to him of Christ and made him think of the Saviour. Philip, with the recommendation from this minister, went to Scotland. At Glasgow he became acquainted with Dr. Duncan, who encouraged him in his inquiries. On Dec. 9, 1839, the Kirk session of St. Luke's Church at Edinburgh admitted him a member of the Church of Christ. Philip now went through a regular course of theological studies, and commenced his missionary labors in 1841, along with the Rev. D. Edward, among the Jews in Moldavia. Being convinced of the great advantage to a missionary of a thorough knowledge of medicine, Philip, after nine years' missionary labor, returned to Edinburgh to complete his medical education. This done, in 1850 he was sent to Algiers, under the auspices of the Scottish Society for the Conversion of Israel, as medical missionary. From Algiers, in 1852, he was sent to Alexandria, in Egypt. In 1860 Philip, who, by this time, had the degree of D.D., in addition to that of M.D., was engaged by the British Society for the Propagation of the Gospel among the Jews, and was sent to labor at Jaffa, the seaport of Palestine, where he remained for six years. When the cholera raged at Jaffa in 1865, and the population was panic-struck, and the civil and military authorities had fled, Dr. Philip was the only practitioner at Jaffa, and acted not only as physician, but also as governor and police. The *Malta Times* of September, 1865, states that "the calls and appeals which Dr. Philip had were constant, insomuch that, when passing through the streets, the crowds thronged upon him to kiss his hands and feet; and while Christians and Jews offered up masses and prayers for him, the Mohammedans forgot their prophet, and the sound was heard in the mosques, 'There is but one God, and the doctor!'" In 1866 Dr. Philip, at his own request, was removed to another field, and sent to Leghorn, where he remained until 1870, when the door was opened to him to preach the gospel to the Jews in Rome. He died Feb. 3, 1882. (B. P.)

Philippi, Friedrich Adolph, a noted Lutheran theologian of Germany, was born of Jewish parentage at Berlin, Oct. 15, 1809. At the age of eighteen he entered the Berlin University to study philosophy. In 1829 he went to Leipsic for the study of philology, and in the same year joined the Lutheran Church. In 1830 he was promoted as doctor of philosophy, and acted for two years as teacher at Dresden. In 1832 he returned to Berlin, passed his examination, and in 1833 received the "facultas docendi." He was appointed professor of ancient languages at the Joachimsthal Gymnasium, a position which he resigned after eighteen months in order to prosecute theological studies. Having passed his examination, he was in 1836 made a licentiate in theology, and commenced to lecture in 1837. In 1841 Philippi was called as professor of theology to Dorpat, in 1851 to Rostock, and died Aug. 29, 1882. He wrote, *De Celsi Adversarii Christianorum, Philosophandi Genere* (Berlin, 1836):—*Der thätige Gehorsam Christi* (1841):—*Commentar über den Brief Pauli an die Römer* (Frankfort, 3d ed. 1866; Engl. transl. Edinburgh, 1878):—but his main work is *Kirchliche Glaubenslehre* (Güterslothe, 1854–82, 6 vols.), a learned and able vindication of strict Lutheran orthodoxy. After Philippi's death there were published from his manuscripts, and edited by his son, *Erklärung des Briefes Pauli an die Galater* (Güterslothe, 1884):—*Symbolik. Akademische Vorlesungen* (1883):—*Predigten und Vorträge* (eod.). See *Mecklenburgisches Kirchen- und Zeitblatt*, 1882, No. 19–21; Plitt-Herzog, *Real-Encyklop.* s. v.; Zuchold, *Bibl. Theol.* ii, 993 sq. (B. P.)

Philippi, Heinrich, a Jesuit who died at Augsburg, Nov. 30, 1636, is the author of, *Introductio Chronologica seu de Computo Ecclesiastico*:—*Quæstiones Chronologicæ in Vetus Testamentum*:—*Chronologiæ Vet. Testamenti Accuratum Examen*:—*Generalis Synopsis Sacrorum Temporum*:—*De Annis Domini, Juliana, Nabonassaris, et Æra Juliana Componendis*:—*Notæ et Quæstiones Chronologicæ in Pentateuchum et Prophetas.* See Jöcher, *Allgemeines Gelehrten-Lexikon*, s. v. (B. P.)

Phillips, Georg, a German professor of canon law, was born Jan. 6, 1804, at Königsberg, Prussia. He studied at Göttingen, and commenced his academical career at Berlin, where he joined the Roman Catholic Church. In 1833 he went to Munich, in 1849 to Innsbruck, in 1851 to Vienna, and died Sept. 6, 1872. His main works are, *Das Kirchenrecht* (Ratisbon, 1845–72, 7 vols.):—*Lehrbuch des Kirchenrechts* (2d ed. 1871):—*Deutsche Reichs- und Rechtsgeschichte* (4th ed. 1859, 2 vols.):—*Vermischte Schriften* (Vienna, 1856–60, 3 vols.). See Zuchold, *Bibl. Theol.* ii, 995; Lichtenberger, *Encyclop. des Sciences Religieuses*, s. v. (B. P.)

Philippus Arabs. See Philip, Emperor.

Phinehas, Hill and Tomb of. According to Lieut. Conder these have been identified. He says (*Tent Work*, i, 77):

"The village of 'Awertah, called Abearthah in the Samaritan dialect, stands in the Plain of the Mŭkhnah, and is sacred to the Samaritans and to the Jews as containing the tombs of Phinehas and Eleazar, Abishua and Ithamar. It is probably to be recognised as the Hill of Phinehas, where Eleazar was buried according to the Bible (Josh. xxiv, 33), and which is described as in Mount Ephraim.

"In 1872 I visited the village and examined the two principal monuments. That of Eleazar, west of the houses, is a rude structure of masonry in a court open to the air. It is eighteen feet long, plastered all over, and shaded by a splendid terebinth. In one corner is a little mosque with a Samaritan inscription bearing the date 1180 of the Moslem æra. The tomb of Phinehas is apparently an older building, and the walls of its court have an arcade of round arches now supporting a trellis covered with a grape-vine; the floor is paved. A Samaritan inscription exists here as well as at the little mosque adjacent. The tombs of Ithamar and of Abishua, the supposed author of the famous roll, are shown by the Samaritans, close by."

(See illustration on following page.)

Piderit, Johann Rudolph Anton, a Lutheran theologian of Germany, was born Aug. 18, 1720, at Pyrmont. He studied at Jena and Marburg, and commenced his academical career at the latter place in 1746. In 1747 he was professor of philosophy, in 1759 doctor of theology, in 1766 professor of Oriental languages at "Collegium Carolinum" in Cassel, and died, after having experienced in a high degree the "odium theologicum," Aug. 2, 1791. He published, *De Voluntate, Decreto et Bonitate Dei* (Jena, 1738):—*Diss. Inauguralis de An-*

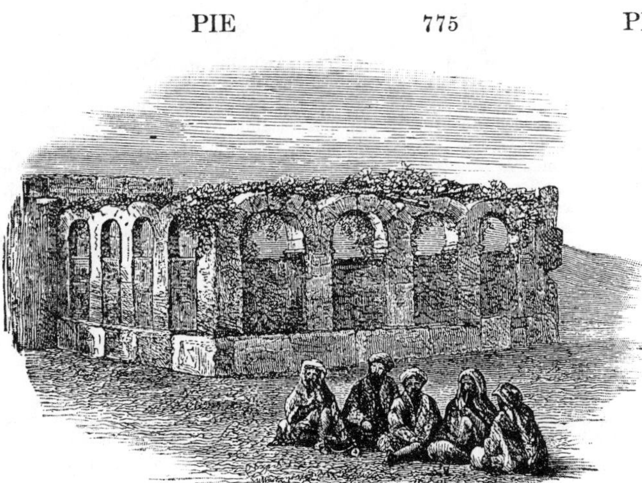

Traditionary Tomb of Phinehas.

ident of the Georgia Female College at Macon in 1840. He was a member of the memorable General Conference of 1844. Having returned to the pastoral work, he was called in 1848 to the presidency of Emory College, and in 1854 to the episcopacy, an office which he filled with eminent ability until his death, Sept. 3, 1884. He was a laborious pastor, an eloquent preacher, and a most upright Christian. See *Minutes of Annual Conferences of the M. E. Church South*, 1885, p. 152; Simpson, *Cyclop. of Methodism*, s. v.

gelis (1746):—*De Characteribus Antichristi* (1750):—*Diss. viii de Erroribus Theologorum Logicis circa Sacram Scripturam* (Marburg, 1752):—*Observationes in Psa. xc* (1758):—*Beiträge zur Vertheidigung und Erläuterung des Kanons der heiligen Schrift* (1775), etc. See Döring, *Die gelehrten Theologen Deutschlands*, s. v.; Fürst, *Bibl. Jud.* iii, 99. (B. P.)

Pie, Louis François Désiré Edouard, a French prelate, was born at Pontgouin (Eure-et-Loir) in 1815. For some time vicar-general of Chartres, he was appointed in 1849 bishop of Poitiers, and made himself conspicuous by his zeal in defending the temporal power of the pope. He opposed the imperial government in a series of pastoral letters, and assembled, in January, 1868, a provincial council at Poitiers to discuss the religious interests of his diocese and of France. From the very beginning of the œcumenical council in 1870 he was one of the most ardent defenders of papal infallibility. Pie was made cardinal in 1879, and died at Angoulême in 1880. He published, *Instruction Synodale sur les Erreurs de la Philosophie Moderne* (1855):—*Instruction sur les Principales Erreurs des Temps Present* (1854):—*Discours Prononcè à l'Occasion du Service Solennel pour les Soldats de l'Armée Pontificale* (1860). See Trolley de Prevaue, *Le Cardinal Pie et ses Œuvres* (Paris, 1882); Lichtenberger, *Encyclop. des Sciences Religieuses*, s. v. (B. P.)

Piedmontese Version of the Scriptures. As early as 1831 a translation of the New Test., faithfully rendered from Martin's French version into modern Piedmontese, was forwarded to the British and Foreign Bible Society by lieutenant-colonel Beckwith. The translation was made by Mr. Berte, pastor of La Tour, and Mr. Gegmet of Lausanne. An edition was completed at press in 1834, but in 1840 the New Test. was put on the index of forbidden books at Rome. In 1837 the British and Foreign Bible Society issued the gospels in parallel columns with the French text, and in 1841 the Piedmontese version of the Psalms, executed from Diodati's Italian version, was published. This edition had also, in parallel columns, the Italian text. Of late, however, things have changed for the better, and the British and Foreign Bible Society now freely circulates the Piedmontese New Test., the Psalms with the Italian text, and the gospels with the French, in parallel columns. See *Bible of Every Land*, p. 286. (B. P.)

Pierce, George Foster, D.D., a bishop of the Methodist Episcopal Church South, son of Dr. Lovick Pierce, was born in Greene County, Ga., Feb. 3, 1811. He graduated from Franklin College, Athens, began to study law, but was soon after converted, and in 1831 was received into the Georgia Conference, in which he filled important appointments until his election as pres-

Pierce, Lovick, D.D., a distinguished minister in the Methodist Episcopal Church South, was born in Halifax County, N. C., March 24, 1785. In early childhood he removed with his parents to South Carolina; in 1803 was converted; in 1804 began to preach; and Jan. 1, 1805, entered the South Carolina Conference. In it he served Pedee Circuit; Apalachee Circuit, Ga.; in 1807 Augusta Station; in 1809 was made presiding elder; in 1812, while stationed at Milledgeville, he was drafted to serve as a soldier, but was soon commissioned as chaplain, in which capacity he acted during the war; about that time he studied medicine, and, retiring from the conference, followed its practice for about six years. In 1823 he re-entered the effective ranks, and was stationed at Augusta. From that time he filled the chief appointments. He was a member of the first General Conference, which met in 1812, and was always elected to represent his conference in the General Conferences. He read much and wrote a great deal; was always ready, clear, cogent, coherent, and powerful. He died at the residence of his son, bishop Pierce, in Sparta, Ga., Nov. 11, 1879. See *Minutes of Annual Conferences of the M. E. Church South*, 1879, p. 88; Simpson, *Cyclop. of Methodism*, s. v.

Pierius, Urban (originally *Birnbaum*), a Protestant theologian of Germany, was born at Schwedt, Pomerania, in 1546. He studied law and theology, was for some time doctor and professor of theology at Frankfort, afterwards pastor at Brandenburg, and superintendent at Cüstrin. In 1589 he was appointed superintendent at Dresden, and in the same year professor of theology and general superintendent at Wittenberg. In 1591 he was dismissed as Crypto-Calvinist, and imprisoned, but was finally released at the intercession of queen Elizabeth of England. Pierius then went to Bremen, and died May 12, 1616, superintendent. He wrote, *Typus Doctrinæ Orthodoxæ de Persona et Officio Christi*:—*Examen und Erläuterung der in der Leichenpredigt Nic. Crell's fürgebrachten neuen Religions-Streitigkeiten*:—*Apologia und Verantwortung des über Nicol. Crell nach gehaltener Leichenpredigt angestellten Examinis.* See Winer, *Handbuch der theol. Lit.* i, 759; Jöcher, *Allgemeines Gelehrten-Lexikon*, s. v. (B. P.)

Pierre, Jean Henri Grand, D.D., a minister of the National Reformed Church of France, was born at Neufchâtel, Switzerland, towards the close of the last century. He was educated at Neufchâtel and at the University of Tübingen, Germany; was called to be an assistant pastor with Vinet at Basle, in 1823, where his piety, zeal, and eloquence were the means of an extensive revival of religion. In 1827 he was called to Paris to take charge of the House of Missions, virtually a theological seminary, in which Dr. Pierre also acted as professor of theology and languages, being a fine classical and Hebrew scholar, as well as an able theologian, ready writer, and eloquent preacher. He was eventually called to L'Oratoire, the great Protestant Church of Paris, where he remained for twenty years. While Vinet was compared to Pascal, and Adolph Monod to Saurin, Dr. Grand Pierre was called the Bourdaloue of the revival. He visited America in 1870 in order to attend the Evangelical Alliance. He died near Basle, Switzerland, July 10, 1874. Dr. Pierre published a considerable number of works, commentaries, sermons, etc., which had a wide circulation. His last production was a volume of sermons dedicated to his former parishioners. For many years he was editor of *L'Esperance*, the principal religious paper of the orthodox Protestants of France. See (N. Y.) *Presbyterian*, Aug. 8, 1874. (W. P. S.)

Pietists, CATHOLIC, a name which was applied to the brethren and sisters of the pious and Christian schools founded by Nicholas Barre in 1678. They devoted themselves to the education of poor children of both sexes.

Pikullos (**Pikollos**, or **Potollos**) was the destroying principle, the third person of the trinity among the Lithuanians, or ancient heathen Prussians, being the opposite of Potrimpos, the preserving principle. An image of this god stood at Romowe, in a hollow of the sacred oak-tree. He was represented as an old bearded man with pale face, the head bound by a white cloth. Three skulls, one of a man, another of a horse, and the third of a bull, were his symbols. Human beings, cattle, horses, and goats, were sacrificed to him, and their blood was poured out at the foot of the great oak-tree to cause its constant growth. Potrimpos was loved, Pikullos feared. He found joy in men's misery. He was not worshipped among other nations, but was compared with Pluto, and with the moon, Loke, Hel, and Odin of the Scandinavians.

Pilet, JEAN ALEXANDRE SAMUEL, a Reformed theologian, was born at Yverdon, Switzerland, Sept. 19, 1797. He studied at Lausanne, and was ordained in 1821. In the same year he was called to Morges as director of the college, and in 1828 succeeded Louis Henri Manuel as pastor of the French Reformed Church at Frankfort-on-the-Main. In 1834 he returned to Switzerland, and was in 1836 appointed professor of Biblical literature at Genoa. He died April 5, 1865. Pilet was one of the Old-Test. translators of the French Bible, called the *Version de Lausanne*. See *Chrétien Évangélique* (1868); A. De Montet, *Diction. Biogr. des Genevois et des Vaudois qui se sont Distingués*, etc. (Lausanne, 1878); Lichtenberger, *Encyclop. des Sciences Religieuses*, s. v. (B. P.)

Pilgrims, POOR, an order of Roman Catholic devotees, which originated about the year 1500. They commenced in Italy, but passed into Germany, where they wandered about as mendicants, barefooted and bareheaded.

Pilmore, JOHN, a Scotch prelate, was consecrated bishop of Moray, April 3, 1325, and continued bishop there for thirty-seven years. He died in the castle of Spynie in 1362. See Keith, *Scottish Bishops*, p. 140, 187.

Pin (*acus*) in ecclesiastical use. Pins made of precious metal, and, in later mediæval times, enriched with jewels, were used for attaching the archiepiscopal (or papal) pallium to the planeta or casula (chasuble). The earliest mention of these is, probably, the description given by Joannes Diaconus of the pallium of Gregory the Great. Their first use, therefore, must probably date between the close of the 6th and the beginning of the 9th century. Innocent assigns to these pins a certain mystical significance.

Pinckney, MILES. See CARR, THOMAS (1).

Pinkerton, ROBERT, D.D., a Scotch Congregational minister, was born in 1780. He left Scotland in 1805 as missionary among the tribes of the Caucasus, under the patronage of the Edinburgh Missionary Society. In 1809 he took up his residence at Moscow, and, in company with Drs. Paterson and Henderson, undertook the visitation of the Russian empire with the view of putting the Bible into universal circulation. When those labors were suspended by imperial authority, Dr. Pinkerton travelled over the entire continent of Europe for the purpose of organizing societies for the dissemination of the Bible, both in Protestant and Catholic countries. He died April 7, 1859. See (Lond.) *Cong. Year-book*, 1860, p. 204.

Pinkham, JOHN, a veteran Free-will Baptist minister, was born at Dover, N. H., Jan. 25, 1808. When he was two years of age his parents moved to Casco, Me., where he was converted at the age of sixteen, and at eighteen became a public exhorter. In 1830 he was ordained pastor of the Church at Sandwich, N. H., where he remained for seven years, and then removed to Gilford, where, for eight years, his labors were greatly blessed. His next settlement, of five years, was at Alton. He was, for the next two years, a resident of Dover, and spent most of the time in assisting pastors in revival work. He then returned to Casco, chiefly occupied as an evangelist. He died there, Jan. 8, 1882. See *Morning Star*, March 1, 1882. (J. C. S.)

Pinkney, WILLIAM, D.D., LL.D., a Protestant Episcopal bishop, was born at Annapolis, Md., April 17, 1810. After graduating from St. John's College, in his native city, he became a rector in Somerset County in 1836, at Bladensburg in 1838, and at Washington in 1855; was consecrated assistant bishop of Maryland Oct. 6, 1870, and became sole bishop Oct. 17, 1879. He died July 4, 1883. Bishop Pinkney was decidedly evangelical.

Pinner, MOSES, a Jewish author, who died at Berlin in 1880, doctor of philosophy, is the author of, *Compendium des babylonischen Talmud* (Berlin, 1832):—*Talmud Babli Tractat Berachot mit interpunctirtem Texte, mit hebr. Commentar nebst deutscher Uebersetzung* (1842):—*Prospectus der alten hebr. und rabbinischen Manuscripte nebst einem Facsimile des Propheten Habakuk* (Odessa, 1845):—*Offenes Sendschreiben an die Nationen Europa's und an die Stände Norwegen's* (1848):—*Aufruf an die orthodoxen Rabbiner Europa's* (1858):—*Geschichte der neuen Reformen der jüd. Gemeinde in Berlin und ihre Bekämpfung* (1857). See Fürst, *Bibl. Jud.* iii, 103; Zuchold, *Bibl. Theol.* ii, 996. (B. P.)

Pinney, JOHN BROOKE, LL.D., a Presbyterian minister, was born at Baltimore, Md., Dec. 25, 1806. He graduated from the University of Georgia in 1828, having studied law while in college; graduated from Princeton Theological Seminary in 1832; was ordained by the Presbytery of Philadelphia the same year, and soon after went to Africa in the service of the American Colonization Society as agent for the colony of Liberia. He returned in 1847, and was installed pastor of the Presbyterian Church at Washington, Pa., where he remained until his appointment as secretary of the New York State Colonization Society, a position which he occupied from 1848 to 1863, and again several years later. He made two visits to Africa to promote the interests of the colony of Liberia. His entire life was devoted to the welfare of the African race, and he engaged in his work with indomitable zeal and energy. He had worn himself out long before his end came, but, though infirm, he labored to the last. He died at his plantation, near Ocala, Fla., Dec. 25, 1882, and was buried under the shade of the oaks near his house, six black men acting as pall-bearers. See *Necrol. Report of Princeton Theol. Sem.* 1883, p. 25. (W. P. S.)

Piquet, FRANÇOIS, an eminent Roman Catholic missionary, was born at Bourg-en-Brasse, France, Dec. 6, 1708. Having been educated at the seminary of St. Sulpice, Paris, he was admitted to that order, and in 1733 was sent to Montreal, of which the Sulpicians were the founders and pastors. In 1740 he was placed in charge of the Iroquois mission at the Lake of the Two Mountains. He accompanied the Iroquois in their ensuing campaign, and tried to found a mission at Oswegatchie, but, protected by count de la Gallissonière and Bigot, he began his work on the site of Ogdensburg, in 1749. The Mohawks burned his mission buildings a few months after, but in two years he received three thousand in Christian instruction. In May, 1752, a bishop conferred the sacraments for the first time within the present limits of New York State. The fall of Canada approaching, Piquet, in 1759, had to abandon Oswegatchie, and retired with his converts to Grande Isle des Galops, where he built a chapel. His register closes July 23, 1760. He then returned to Europe, and the traveller Bossu met him at Corunna in 1762. In France he was occupied in various duties in the Church, and died at Verjon, July 15, 1781. See (N. Y.) *Cath. Almanac*, 1877, p. 60; De Courcy and Shea, *Hist. of the Cath. Church in the U. S.* p. 447.

Pirathon. The modern *Ferata* is laid down on the Ordnance *Map* at five and a half miles south-west of Nablûs, and described in the accompanying *Memoirs* (ii, 162) as "a small village of ancient appearance, standing on a tell or mound, with a rock-cut tomb to the south and a sacred mukâm to the east." It has "a few cisterns and the remains of a sarcophagus" (*ibid.* p. 285). Instead of this identification Lieut. Conder, with less probability, suggests *Ferôn*, lying ten miles west of Sebustieh, and described (*ibid.* p. 164) as "a small village on a slope, at the edge of the plain, with a few trees and a well to the east. The inhabitants are all Greek Christians."

Pirie, William Robinson, D.D., a Scotch divine, son of Rev. George Pirie, D.D., of Slains, Aberdeenshire, was born in that village, July 26, 1804, and educated at the University of Aberdeen. He was appointed minister at Dyce in 1830; professor of divinity in the university of Marischal College, Aberdeen, in December, 1843; minister at Greyfriars, of the same city, in September, 1846; professor of divinity or Church history in united universities, Marischal and King's colleges, in 1860, and in May, 1877, principal and vice-chancellor of the same, a position which he occupied until his death, Nov. 4, 1885. Dr. Pirie was active in every movement which agitated the Scottish Church during the forty years of his public life. He was the author of *Natural Theology* (Edinb. 1868). See *Fasti Eccles. Scoticanæ*, iii, 501.

Pirksoma, in the mythology of the Greenlanders, is the god to whom all other deities are subordinate, and who distributes rewards or punishments according to moral actions.

Pisanski, Georg Christoph, a Lutheran theologian of Germany, was born at Johannisberg, Prussia, Aug. 23, 1725. He studied at Königsberg, and in 1748 was teacher at the cathedral school. In 1773 he was doctor of theology, and died Oct. 11, 1789. He wrote, *Canonica Librorum Omnium Vet. Testamenti*, etc. (Berlin, 1775):—*Λογία τοῦ Θεοῦ Judæorum Fidei Credita*, etc. (Königsberg, 1778):—*Beleuchtung der sogenannten biblischen Dämonologie* (eod.):—*De Errore Irenæi in Determinanda Ætate Christi* (eod.):—*De Miraculosis Spiritus Sancti Donis*, etc. (eod.):—*Vindiciæ Psalmorum*, etc. (1779):—*Adversaria de Accommodationibus Veteris Testamenti*, etc. (1781):—*An Liber Jonas non Historiam sed Fabulam Contineat?* (1789). See Döring, *Die gelehrten Theologen Deutschlands*, s. v.; Fürst, *Bibl. Jud.* iii, 105. (B. P.)

Piscator (i. e. **Fischer**), Peter, a Protestant theologian of Germany, was born at Hanau, April 7, 1571. He studied at different universities, was for some time professor of Hebrew at Jena, in 1605 professor of theology, and died Jan. 10, 1611, doctor of theology. He wrote, *De Baptismo:—De Æterna Prædestinatione Salvandorum:—Problemata Sacra:—Comm. in Formulam Concordiæ:—Dissertationes in Libros Symbolicos:—Quæstiones Miscellaneæ Hebræo-Chaldæo-Syriaco-Græco-Latinæ:—De Peccato e Psalmi li. Enarratione.* See Winer, *Handbuch der theol. Lit.* i, 340; Jöcher, *Allgemeines Gelehrten-Lexikon*, s. v. (B. P.)

Pischon, Johann Karl, a Reformed theologian, was born at Cottbus, in Lower Lusatia, Oct. 12, 1764. He studied at Halle, was in 1790 cathedral-preacher there, in 1799 court-preacher at Potsdam, and died Nov. 18, 1805. He published several volumes of sermons. See Döring, *Die deutschen Kanzelredner*, p. 297 sq.; Winer, *Handbuch der theol. Lit.* ii, 62, 96, 149, 222, 292, 323, 331. (B. P.)

Piscicŭli (*little fishes*), a name which the early Christians sometimes assumed, to denote, as Tertullian alleges, that they were born again into Christianity by water, and could not be saved but by continuing therein. See Ichthus.

Pistōrēs (*bakers*) was a term of reproach applied to the early Christians in consequence of their poverty and simplicity.

Pistorius, Hermann Alexander, a Lutheran theologian of Germany, was born Aug. 27, 1811, at Walbeck. He studied at Halle, was in 1843 preacher at Süpplingen, near Magdeburg, and made himself conspicuous by his opposition against the so-called Friends of Light (q. v.), and by advocating the right of the Lutheran Church in the State Church of Prussia. In 1849 he left the State Church, having the year before published *Aufruf an alle Lutheraner innerhalb der preussischen Landeskirche*, became Lutheran preacher at Wernigerode, afterwards at Wollin, and finally superintendent at Breslau, where he had to pass through many trials. In 1863 he was called to Basedow, Mecklenburg, and died April 27, 1877. He published, *Das christliche Leben in Liedern* (Dresden, 1840):—*Was und wo ist die lutherische Kirche?* (Magdeburg, 1844):—*Richtige Erklärung der Bibelstellen*, etc. (1845):—*Ueber Kraft und Form der Absolution* (Leipsic, 1858). See Zuchold, *Bibl. Theol.* ii, 998 sq. (B. P.)

Pithom. This has recently been identified by Edouard Naville, who has carried on excavations under the auspices of the "Egypt Exploration Fund," with *Tell el-Maskhutah*, or *Abu Kesheid* (usually thought to be the site of Heroöpolis), and he has published the results of his explorations in a volume entitled *The Store-city of Pithom* (Lond. 1885). The identification rests chiefly on the discovery, upon the spot, of a statue of a squatting man, in red granite, the lieutenant of king Osorkon II, "Ank-renp-nefer, the good recorder of Pithom" (p. 4, 5, 13), together with an inscription on a large monument of Rameses at Ismaileh, containing the words "the lord of Theku, of Succoth." This is certainly somewhat slender ground, but it may perhaps be provisionally accepted for the present. Mr. Naville found the remains of what he regards as a large temple with numerous chambers, indicating the existence of a city there in ancient times, but he was unable to make out its plans, or to unearth it to any great extent.

Pitiscus, Martin Friedrich, a Lutheran theologian of Germany, was born at Hamburg in 1721. In 1756 he was preacher at his birthplace, in 1768 professor of Oriental languages, and died Nov. 13, 1794. He wrote, *Versuch von der Religion der Stammeltern des menschlichen Geschlechts* (Hamburg, 1768):—*Eximium Divinæ Sapientiæ Specimen* (1763):—*Ueber den Kanon der Bücher des Alten Testaments* (1776):—*Zur Beurtheilung der von Herrn Hofrath Lessing herausgegebenen Fragmente eines Ungenannten von Duldung der Deisten* (1779). See Döring, *Die gelehrten Theologen Deutschlands*, s. v.; Fürst, *Bibl. Jud.* iii, 106. (B. P.)

Planck, Karl Christian, a philosophical writer of Germany, was born at Stuttgart, Jan. 17, 1819. He studied theology at Tübingen, and commenced his academical career in 1848 as lecturer in philosophy. In

1856 he was professor at the gymnasium in Ulm, in 1869 at the seminary in Blaubeuren, in 1879 ephorus of the seminary at Maulbronn, and died June 7, 1880. He published, *Gesetz und Ziel der neueren Kunstentwickelung* (Stuttgart, 1870):—*Seele und Geist* (1871):—*Wahrheit und Flachheit des Darwinismus* (1872):—*Grundriss der Logik* (1873):—*Anthropologie und Psychologie* (1874):—*Logisches Causalgesetz und natürliche Zweckthätigkeit* (1877):—*Ziel und Entwickelungsgesetz der alten Philosophie* (1877):—*Testament eines Deutschen* (edited after the author's death by K. Köstlin, Tübingen, 1881). (B. P.)

Platt, James McClure, D.D., a Presbyterian minister, was born at Athens, Pa., Dec. 31, 1826. He graduated from the University of the City of New York in 1847, and from Princeton Theological Seminary in 1853; became pastor at Lawesville, O., the same year; at Leetsdale, Pa., in 1867; and at Bath, N. Y., in 1869, where he died, April 14, 1884. See *Necrol. Report of Princeton Theol. Sem.* 1885, p. 47.

Plesken, Meinhard, a Lutheran theologian of Germany, was born at Bremen, June 8, 1696. He studied at Wittenberg. In 1720 he was called as sub-rector to the cathedral school of his birthplace, in 1725 as pastor to Stade, in 1733 he was member of consistory, in 1743 general superintendent, and in 1748 doctor of theology. Plesken died May 30, 1757, leaving, *Judas Iscariotes Sacræ Eucharistiæ Convivus* (Bremen, 1716):—*De Columnis Aeneis Jachin et Boas* (1719):—*De Benjamino Parvo* (1720):—*De Homine, in Cujus Naso est Spiritus* (eod.):—*De Quibusdam pro Existentia Dei Argumentis Sollicitatis* (1725). See Döring, *Die gelehrten Theologen Deutschlands*, s. v.; Fürst, *Bibl. Jud.* iii, 107. (B. P.)

Plessing, Johann Friedrich, a Lutheran theologian of Germany, was born at Conitz, Prussia, Oct. 28, 1720. He studied at Jena and Leipsic, was in 1746 preacher at Cöthen, in 1764 at Wernigerode, and died Dec. 31, 1793. He wrote, *Versuch vom Ursprung der Abgötterei* (Leipsic, 1757–58, 2 vols.):—*Die Auferstehungs-Geschichte Jesu Christi* (1785; 2d ed. 1788):—*Harmonische Geschichte der Auferstehung Jesu Christi* (Wernigerode, 1789):—*Ueber Golgotha und Christi Grab* (Halle, eod.). See Döring, *Die gelehrten Theologen Deutschlands*, s. v.; Winer, *Handbuch der theol. Lit.* i, 560, 561. (B. P.)

Plessner, Solomon, a Jewish rabbi of Germany, was born at Breslau, April 19, 1797. He received a thorough rabbinic education, was in 1822 instructor of religion at Festenberg, Silesia, in 1830 instructor at the teacher's seminary in Berlin, and died at Posen, Aug. 25, 1883, where he had acted as rabbi for nearly forty years. He is the author of, *Die apocryphischen Bücher des Alten Testaments in's Hebräische übersetzt*, etc. (Breslau, 1833):—*Materialien für tiefere Einblicke in das Alte Testament und die rabbinischen Schriften* (Berlin, 1836), also with the title *Belehrungen u. Erbauungen* (ibid. eod.):—*Die kostbare Perle oder das Gebet* (1837–38):—*Jüdisch-Mosaischer Religionsunterricht* (1838–39):—*Religiöse Vorträge* (1840):—*Festreden* (1841). See Fürst, *Bibl. Jud.* iii, 107. (B. P.)

Plitt, Gustav Leopold, a noted Lutheran theologian of Germany, was born March 27, 1836, at Genin, near Lübeck. He studied at Erlangen and Berlin, and commenced his theological career at the former place in 1862. In 1866 he was made professor, and in 1872 doctor of theology. He died Sept. 10, 1880. Plitt, who is best known as the associate editor of the second edition of Herzog's *Real-Encyklopädie für Protestantische Theologie und Kirche*, published the following works: *De Auctoritate Articulorum Smalcaldicorum Symbolica* (Erlangen, 1852):—*Festpredigten des heiligen Bernhard* (1860):—*Melanchthon's Loci Communes in ihrer Urgestalt* (1864):—*Einleitung in die Augustana* (1867–68, 2 vols.):—*Aus Schelling's Leben in Briefen* (1869–70, 3 vols.):—*Die Albrechtsleute oder die Evangelische Gemeinschaft* (1877):—*Die Apologie der Augustana* (1873):—*Grundriss der Symbolik für Vorlesungen* (1875):—*Iodokus Trutfetter von Eisenach, der Lehrer Luther's* (1876):—*Gabriel Biel als Prediger* (1879):—*Dr. Martin Luther's Leben und Wirken* (edited after Plitt's death by Petersen, Leipsic, 1883). See Plitt-Herzog, *Real-Encyklop.* s. v. (B. P.)

Plitt, Johann Jacob, a Lutheran theologian of Germany, was born Feb. 27, 1727, at Wetter, Hesse. He studied at Halle, was in 1749 preacher at Cassel, in 1755 professor at Rinteln, in 1762 preacher at Frankfort-on-the-Main, and died April 7, 1773, doctor of theology. He wrote, *De Gloria Dei in Promulgatione Legis Sinaiticæ* (Göttingen, 1755):—*De Nexu inter Bonitatem Dei Infinitam et Justitiam ejus Punitivam Arctissimo* (1756):—*De Vero Conceptu Ceremoniæ Religionis* (Rinteln, 1759):—*Testimonia Quorundam Ecclesiæ Patrum pro Baptisma Infantum* (1760):—*De Pœnitentia Caini* (1761):—*Theologische Untersuchungen* (1764–71, 3 vols.); besides he published a number of sermons and other ascetical works. See Döring, *Die gelehrten Theologen Deutschlands*, s. v.; Winer, *Handbuch der theol. Lit.* i, 451. (B. P.)

Plum, Friedrich, a Danish Lutheran theologian, who died at Odensee, Jan. 18, 1833, doctor of theology and bishop of Funen, is the author of, *Efteredninger om den udenlandske nyere theologiske og pastorale Litteratur*, etc. (Copenhagen, 1818 sq.):—*Observationes in Textum et Versiones Maxime Græcas Obadiæ et Habacuci* (1796). See Winer, *Handbuch der theol. Lit.* i, 12, 224; Fürst, *Bibl. Jud.* iii, 107. (B. P.)

Plumb, Elijah Whiton, D.D., a Congregational minister, was born at Halifax, Vt., July 28, 1798. He attended Hopkins Academy at Hadley, Mass.; spent one year in Harvard College; graduated from Middlebury College in 1824; taught school the next two years in Brattleboro', Vt.; from 1826 to 1828 was similarly employed in Hampton, N. H.; studied theology with Daniel Dana, D.D., of Newburyport; was ordained pastor, May 18, 1831, at Pawlet, Vt., and dismissed Oct. 29, 1845; from 1846 to 1851 was pastor of the Presbyterian Church in Potsdam, N. Y.; in 1853 became principal of St. Lawrence Academy; and from 1864 to 1867 was acting pastor in Sterling, Ill. The two succeeding years he resided at Potsdam without charge, and then removed to East Bloomfield, which was his residence until his death, July 12, 1879. See *Cong. Year-book*, 1879, p. 26.

Plumer, William Swan, D.D., LL.D., a Presbyterian minister, was born at Greensburg (now Darlington), Beaver Co., Pa., July 26, 1802. He graduated from Washington College, Va., in 1825, and from Princeton Theological Seminary in 1827; having been licensed to preach in 1826, he soon after organized a Presbyterian Church at Danville, subsequently another at Warrenton, N. C., and preached also at Raleigh, Washington, and Newbern, in the same state. In 1834 he became a pastor in Richmond, Va., and in 1837 founded the *Watchman of the South*, a weekly religious journal, which he edited for eight years. The same year he removed as pastor to Baltimore, Md. In 1854 he became professor of didactic and pastoral theology in the Western Theological Seminary at Allegheny City, Pa.; in 1866 was called to the chair of theology in the Theological Seminary at Columbia, S. C., where he remained until it was closed in 1880. He died at the Union Protestant Infirmary, Baltimore, Md., Oct. 22 of the same year. Dr. Plumer was the author of many excellent works, among which are, *Argument Against the Indiscriminate Incorporation of Churches and Religious Societies* (1847, 8vo):—*The Bible True, and Infidelity Wicked* (New York, 18mo):—*Plain Thoughts for Children* (Philadelphia, 18mo):—*Short Sermons to Little Children* (18mo):—*Thoughts Worth Remembering* (New York, 8vo):—*The Saint and the Sinner* (Philadelphia, 18mo):—*The Grace of Christ* (1853, 12mo):—*Rome Against the Bible and the Bible Against Rome* (1854,

18mo):—*Christ our Theme and Glory* (1855, 8vo):—*The Church and her Enemies* (Philadelphia, 1856, 18mo):—*The Law of God as Contained in the Ten Commandments* (ibid. 1864, 12mo):—*Vital Godliness* (New York, 1865, 12mo):—*Jehovah Jireh* (Philadelphia, 1866, 12mo):—*Studies in the Book of Psalms* (1866):—*The Rock of our Salvation* (New York, 1867, 12mo):—*The Words of Truth and Love* (Philadelphia, 1868, 18mo):—also commentaries on the epistles to the Romans and Hebrews, works of great merit:—besides *Memoirs and Select Remains of William Nevins, D.D.* (1836, 12mo):—and an abridgment of Stevenson on the *Offices of Christ* (Philadelphia, 1837, 16mo). He wrote more than fifty religious tracts, issued by six religious societies, several single sermons, and contributed largely to various religious journals and papers. See *Necrol. Report of Princeton Theol. Sem.* 1881, p. 20; Allibone, *Dict. of Brit. and Amer. Authors*, s. v.

Plunket, Thomas Lord, D.D., a bishop of the Church of Ireland, was born in 1799, being the eldest son of William Conyngham Plunket, the Irish chancellor, distinguished as a lawyer, an orator, and a statesman, and whom he succeeded as second baron in 1854. Dr. Plunket was appointed dean of Down in 1831, and promoted to the bishopric of Tuam in 1839. He became ecclesiastical commissioner in 1851, and died at Tourmakready, County Mayo, Oct. 19, 1866, being at the time patron of ninety-five livings in his united diocese of Tuam, Killala, and Achonry. He was an indefatigable laborer in the missionary department of his work, especially in Connaught. See *Amer. Quar. Church Rev.* January, 1867, p. 655.

Pluquet, François André Adrien, an ecclesiastical writer of France, was born at Bayeux in 1716. He was professor of philosophy at the Collège de France, canon of Cambray, and died at Paris in 1790. He published, *Examen du Fatalisme* (Paris, 1757, 2 vols.):—*Dictionnaire des Hérésies, des Erreurs et des Schismes* (1762, 2 vols.):—*Essai Philosophique et Politique sur le Luxe* (1786):—*De la Superstition et de l'Enthousiasme* (published after his death, 1804). See Lichtenberger, *Encyclop. des Sciences Religieuses*, s. v. (B. P.)

Pogatschar, Johannes, prince bishop of Laybach, was born at Brezov, Jan. 22, 1811. From 1838 to 1852 he occupied the theological chair at the Laybach Theological Seminary, was made prince bishop in 1875, and died Jan. 25, 1884. For many years he edited the *Laybach Church Gazette*, and in the ecclesiastico-political affairs he sided with the Austrian government in behalf of the new school-laws. (B. P.)

Pohlman, Henry Newman, D.D., a Lutheran minister, was born at Albany, N. Y., March 8, 1800. In August, 1820, he graduated from Hartwick Seminary —the first student in the first Lutheran theological seminary in the United States. In March following he received license to preach in Rhinebeck, and in May was ordained in New York city. After serving a few months in two small churches at Saddle River and Ramapo, N. J., he took charge of the Lutheran churches in Hunterdon County, which at that time numbered three, many miles apart. For twenty-one years he continued in this work, until each of these congregations was able to support its own pastor. The great event of his ministerial life was a remarkable revival of religion at New Germantown during the winter of 1839–40. In 1843 he became pastor of the Evangelical Lutheran Ebenezer Church in Albany, N. Y., and remained in this pastorate about three years. Of the General Synod he was three times elected president, and was a delegate from 1836 to every meeting of that body. At the time of his admission to the ministry the General Synod had just been formed, and the New York Ministerium, a party to the original convention, had already withdrawn. This led to the creation of two parties in the ministerium, resulting in 1830 in the formation of the Hartwick Synod. Dr. Pohlman, with a few other friends of the General Synod, decided to remain with the ministerium; and in 1836 the ministerium renewed its connection with the General Synod. He took an active part in the work of organizing churches. On Sept. 3, 1867, after the New York Ministerium had decided to withdraw from the General Synod, a new synod was organized, and Dr. Pohlman was elected its first president, and held this position until his death in Albany, Jan. 20, 1874. For many years he was a trustee of the State Idiot Asylum at Syracuse. During thirty years he was a trustee of Hartwick Seminary. For three years he assumed the duties of corresponding secretary of the Lutheran Mission Board in New York, and for some time afterwards was an active member of the executive committee. See *Quar. Rev. of Evang. Luth. Church*, iv, 359.

Poindexter, Abram Maer, D.D., a Baptist divine, was born in Bertie County, N. C., Sept. 22, 1809. He studied at Columbian College, Washington, D. C., but did not graduate. He united with the Church in 1831, was licensed in 1832, and ordained in 1834. Most of his life was spent in Halifax County, Va. For a time he acted as financial agent of Columbian and Richmond Colleges, was secretary of the Southern Baptist Publication Society, and officially connected with the Foreign Mission Board of the Southern Baptist Convention. He died May 7, 1872. Dr. Poindexter ranked high as a preacher, especially on occasions where a large body of the people were assembled. He was also distinguished as a most skilful debater. See Cathcart, *Baptist Encyclop.* p. 924. (J. C. S.)

Polanus, Amandus, a Swiss theologian, was born at Oppeln, Silesia, in 1561, and died at Basle in 1610, professor of theology and Old-Test. exegesis. Polanus was one of the ornaments of the Basle University, and wrote, *Analysis Malachiæ* (Basle, 1597):—*Commentarius in Danielem* (1593):—*Analysis Hoseæ* (1601)—*Commentarius in Ezechielem* (1607):—*Exegesis Aliquot Vaticiniorum Veteris Testamenti de Christi Nativitate, Passione et Morte, Resurrectione et Adscensu in Cælo* (1608):—*De Æterna Dei Prædestinatione* (1600):—*Symphonia Catholica* (1607):—*Theses Bellarminio potissimum Oppositæ* (published after Polanus's death by J. G. Grosse, 1613):—*Institutiones de Concionum Sacrarum Methodo* (1604):—*Syntagma Theologiæ Christianæ* (1612). See Lichtenberger, *Encyclop. des Sciences Religieuses*, s. v.; Jöcher, *Allgemeines Gelehrten-Lexikon*, s. v. (B. P.)

Poles, Ancient Mythology of the. The Poles, a Slavic people, had a religious system agreeing with that of other Slavonic mythologies, and it is an error to call them fire-worshippers, or to say they worshipped Roman gods, as some affirm. Gnesen, the capital of Poland, the seat of prince Primas, contained a row of great temples, of which now only a few traces may be found. There stood the temple of Nija, the god of the soul; of Perun, the god of thunder, etc. There the principal gods of Slavonic heathendom were worshipped with bloody sacrifices. This warlike nation had many gods of war, but some superintended also domestic concerns.

Polish Version of the Scriptures. The revision of the New Test. from the Greek, undertaken for the British and Foreign Bible Society in 1878, by Messrs. Manitius, Diehl, Poplooski, and Fecht, of Warsaw, was completed in 1881, and an edition of five thousand copies was published at Vienna under the care of the Bible society's agent, Mr. E. Millard. See Slavonic Version. (B. P.)

Polyander, Johann, a Reformed theologian, was born at Metz, March 28, 1568. He studied at different universities, was in 1588 pastor at Dort, in 1611 professor of theology at Leyden, and died Feb. 4, 1646. He wrote, *Concertatio anti-Sociniana*:—*Syntagma Exercitationum Theologicarum*:—*Miscellaneæ Tractationes Theologicæ*:—*De Existentia Jesu Christi Es-*

sentiali et Gloria Divina contra Crellium:—Harmonia Locorum Sacræ Scripturæ invicem Discrepantium:—Disputatio adversus Invocationem Sanctorum:—Annotationes in Jonam. See Jöcher, *Allgemeines Gelehrten-Lexikon*, s. v.; Meursius, *Athenæ Batavæ*. (B. P.)

Polychronius, bishop of Apamea, and brother of Theodore of Mopsuestia, was one of the most prominent exegetes of the school of Antioch in the 4th century. Of his life nothing further is known. He wrote commentaries on Job, Daniel, and Ezekiel. Of his commentary on Daniel we have a great many fragments. He explains the book as referring to Antiochus Epiphanes, and not to the anti-Christ; in the fourth monarchy he sees the Macedonian empire, and in the ten heads the diadochai. He everywhere contends for the historical sense and opposes the allegorical interpretation, as well as the theory of a twofold sense. Though he was never formally condemned, yet he was nevertheless considered a heretic. See Plitt-Herzog, *Real-Encyklop.* s. v., but more especially Bardenhewer, *Polychronius* (Freiburg, 1879), and Möller's review, in Schürer, *Theol. Literaturzeitung*, 1879, col. 255 sq. (B. P.)

Polycrătes, bishop of Ephesus, A.D. 196, is known in Church history by his opposition to the Roman bishop, Victor, in the famous Paschal controversy (q. v.). Eusebius has preserved Polycrates' letter of protest, which is given in English by Schaff, *History of the Christian Church* (N. Y. 1883), ii, 216 sq. See also Eusebius, *Hist. Eccles.* v, 24 (ed. Heinichen, i, 250 sq.); Ceillier, *Hist. des Aut. Sacr. et Eccles.* ii, 203 sq.; Lichtenberger, *Encyclop. des Sciences Religieuses*, s. v. (B. P.)

Pontanus, Heinrich, a Protestant theologian, who died at Utrecht, Sept. 5, 1714, doctor and professor of theology, is the author of, *De Sale Sacrificiorum:—De Ritu Mersionis in Baptismate.* See Jöcher, *Allgemeines Gelehrten-Lexikon*, s. v.; Winer, *Handbuch der theol. Lit.* i, 630. (B. P.)

Pontanus, Jacob, a Jesuit, was born at Brück, Bohemia, in 1542, and died at Augsburg, Nov. 25, 1626, professor. He edited *Cyrilli Alex. Comment. in Duodecim Prophetas Minores, Græce et Latine cum Notis* (Ingolstadt, 1607). See Winer, *Handbuch der theol. Lit.* i, 889; Jöcher, *Allgemeines Gelehrten-Lexikon*, s. v. (B. P.)

Poole, George Ayliffe, an English theologian, was born in 1809. He was a scholar of Emmanuel College, Cambridge, and took his degree in 1831. After holding several curacies and a benefice at Leeds, he settled permanently in Northamptonshire, first as vicar of Welford, from 1843 to 1876, and then as rector of Winwick, from 1876 to 1883. Poole, who died Sept. 25 of the latter year, ranked as one of the leading English authorities on ecclesiastical architecture. He published a variety of sermons and theological works, including an account of the *Life and Times of St. Cyprian* (1840). His chief works, however, related to ecclesiology. In 1842 appeared *Appropriate Character of Church Architecture:—Churches, their Structure* (1845):—*History of Ecclesiastical Architecture in England* (1848); in conjunction with Mr. J. W. Hugall, he issued an account of the *Churches of Scarborough, Filey, and Neighborhood*, and *Guide to York Cathedral.* Poole's last work was *History of the Diocese of Peterborough*, for the series of *Diocesan Histories*, in the course of publication by the Society for Promoting Christian Knowledge. (B. P.)

Popo Version of the Scriptures. The Popo or Dahomey is spoken at Dahomey, between the Volta and Lagos. A translation of Matthew and Mark was made by the Rev. T. J. Marshall, a native minister, and printed by the British and Foreign Bible Society at London in 1884. Other parts of the New Test. are now being translated. (B. P.)

Porter, Herschel S., D.D., a Cumberland Presbyterian minister, was born in Butler County, Ky., Feb. 12, 1816. After studying at various academies, he was licensed to preach in May, 1835, and in September, 1837, was ordained at Glasgow, Ky. He spent about four years as an itinerant in Kentucky, travelled also for some time as an agent for Cumberland College; then served a year as pastor at Fayetteville, Tenn.; subsequently made an extensive preaching tour, passing through most of the Southern States, returning to Kentucky in 1843. He spent several months of that year in Western Pennsylvania, then went to Philadelphia to organize a congregation, and remained there until the spring of 1851. In the fall of that year he settled in Memphis, Tenn., and labored there until the latter part of 1855. He died there Oct. 5 of the same year, professor of natural history in the Memphis Medical College. In 1853 he was moderator of the General Assembly. Dr. Porter was devoted to science, and was proficient in astronomy and geology. He published a series of *Astronomical Sermons*, 400 pp.:—*The Atonement:*—and a work on the *Foreknowledge and Decrees of God.* See Beard, *Biographical Sketches*, 1st series, p. 307.

Porter, Noah, D.D., a Congregational minister, was born Dec. 15, 1781, at Farmington, Conn. After his graduation he taught for some time, and then studied theology; was ordained over the Congregational Church in his native town, Nov. 5, 1806, where he had a long and successful ministry. From 1823 to 1862 he was a member of the corporation of Yale College, and was long a member of the prudential committee. He died at Farmington, Sept. 24, 1866. A number of his occasional discourses were published, and among them *A Half-Century Discourse*, preached Nov. 12, 1856. See *Obituary Record of Yale College*, 1867.

Porterfield, John, a Scotch prelate, was bishop of Glasgow in 1571 and 1572. See Keith, *Scottish Bishops*, p. 260.

Portuguese Version of the Scriptures. By way of supplement, we add the following: The first New Test. of Almeida was printed at Amsterdam in 1681; a second or revised edition was published at Batavia in 1693, and another again at Amsterdam in 1712. In 1744 were published at Tranquebar the books of Job, Psalms, Proverbs, Ecclesiastes, and Canticles, and in 1751 followed the four greater prophets; the first three of which were translated by Almeida, and the fourth (Daniel), by C. F. Walther, missionary at Tranquebar. A second edition of the entire Old Test. was published at Batavia in 1748. In this edition a version was given of the books left untranslated by Almeida, by Jacob op den Akker, one of the Dutch missionaries at Batavia. Between 1721 and 1757 two revised editions of the Pentateuch and of the Psalms, two revised editions of the New Test., and one of the four gospels, were printed at Tranquebar and Batavia. Another edition of the Old Test. was printed at the latter place between 1783 and 1804, and no further editions appear to have been given of this version until it was republished by the British and Foreign Bible Society.

A Catholic Portuguese version of the entire Scriptures, from the Vulgate, was published in twenty-three volumes, with annotations, at Lisbon, from 1781 to 1783, by Don Antonio Pereira de Figueiredo, a Portuguese ecclesiastic. An edition containing his latest corrections was commenced at Lisbon in 1794, but was not completed till 1815. On account of the numerous corrections, this edition may be regarded as a new version.

A third translation of the Scriptures was accomplished by the Rev. Thomas Boys, at the expense of the Trinitarian Bible Society. This version, based on Almeida's translation, but faithfully made in accordance with the original, was published in London; the New Test. in 1843 and the Old in 1847.

When the British and Foreign Bible Society undertook the publication of the Portuguese Scriptures, the version of Almeida, the only Protestant one, was selected. But this publication was not received as was anticipated, perhaps, because Almeida was a converted

Protestant, but mostly because it was an antiquated version, many of the words being obsolete, and the style not idiomatic. The complaints against this version were laid before the society, and in 1818 an edition of Pereira's version of the New Test. was printed, which was followed by another edition of both the entire Bible and the New Test. in 1821, Mr. Cavalho correcting the press. Another edition of Pereira's New Test. was printed in 1823, and a revised edition of the whole Bible was given in 1824, under the care of Messrs. Da Costa and Green. In 1857 the American Bible Society published a Portuguese New Test., the version used being a translation made in London from the Greek. Of late the British and Foreign Bible Society has undertaken a revision of Almeida's Bible translation, the version and idiom being modernized. This edition was printed in Lisbon in 1874, the text being accompanied with occasional alternative renderings, and with the most important references from the Old to the New Test. The orthography and style have been modernized, and the translation has been compared with the original throughout by the society's editorial superintendent, who has been assisted by competent natives in completing the edition. The same society published, in 1879, an edition of the Portuguese Bible of Figueiredo, with alternative readings from the Hebrew and Greek, under the care of the Rev. Robert Stewart and the editorial superintendent. From the report of the British and Foreign Bible Society for 1885, we learn that steps have been taken, in connection with the American Bible Society, for the formation of translation committees in Spain and Brazil for the production of a new version of the Scriptures, which will be acceptable on both sides of the Atlantic. (B. P.)

Porubssky, Gustav, a Protestant theologian, was born at Presburg, March 13, 1812. He received his classical and theological training at the lyceum of his native place, which at that time was one of the most prominent Protestant schools of Austro-Hungary. To continue his studies he went, in 1833, to Vienna, and two years later to Berlin. In 1837 he was called as pastor of the Germano-Slavic congregation at Tyrnau, and in 1840 he accepted a call to Vienna. In this important position he developed all his faculties for the benefit of the Church, school, and mission, and his efforts were acknowledged by the Vienna faculty, which honored him in 1871 with the doctorate of theology. He died July 17, 1876. He published, *Evangelische Kanzelvorträge* (Vienna, 1833):—*Festandachten über das Leiden und Sterben Jesu Christi* (1854):—*Jacobus, der Zeuge vom lebendigen Glauben* (1861):—*Die Rechte der Protestanten in Oesterreich* (1867). See Zuchold, *Bibl. Theol.* ii, 1005; Roskoff, *Zur Erinnerung an Dr. Gustav Porubssky* (Vienna, 1876). (B. P.)

Possinus, Pierre, a French Jesuit, was born at Narbonne in 1590. He was an excellent Hebrew and Greek scholar, and died at Rome towards the end of the 17th century. He published, *Thesaurus Asceticus*, etc. (Paris, 1684):—*Collationes Isidorianæ*, etc. (Rome, 1670):—*Nili Opera* (1639):—*Nili Epistolæ* (1657), etc. See Winer, *Handbuch der theol. Lit.* i, 878, 880, 881, 896, 897, 898; Jöcher, *Allgemeines Gelehrten-Lexikon*, s. v. (B. P.)

Postmillenarians. See Premillenarians.

Potrimpos, in Lettish mythology, was a chief deity of the Lithuanians and ancient Prussians before the occupancy of the country by the Germans, being the second person in the Northern trinity, which consisted of Perkunos, Potrimpos, and Pikollos. He was the god of victory in war, and in peace the giver of fruitfulness, of blessing, and of domestic felicity. His image stood at Romowe. It represented a friendly, laughing youth. As Perkunos was a god of the warming and destructive fire, so Potrimpos was a god of the fructifying and destructive water. Ears of corn and wheat were offered to him, and his head was decorated with field products. Many children were also burned as sacrifices to him. In a large brass urn a snake was kept and fed in honor of him; therefore the snake was always a sacred animal among the Prussians. It seems possible that Potrimpos was a female deity, and the wife of Donnerer—at least, some modern writers affirm this. Perhaps this was the mother of the gods, whom Tacitus mentions as worshipped among the Æsthyans.

Potter, Louis Joseph Antoine de, a Belgian writer, was born at Bruges in 1786, and died at Brussels in 1859. He published, *Considerations sur l'Histoire des Principaux Conciles*, etc. (Brussels, 1816; Paris, 1818, 2 vols.):—*Esprit de l'Église*, etc. (Paris, 1821, 6 vols.). These two works were republished under the title *Histoire Philosophique, Politique et Critique du Christianisme et des Églises Chrétiennes* (ibid. 1836-37, 8 vols.), and an abridged edition, entitled *Résumé de l'Histoire du Christianisme* (1856, 2 vols.):—*Vie de Scipion Ricci, Evêque de Pistoie* (Brussels, 1825, 3 vols.; Paris, 1826, 4 vols.):—*Lettres de Pie V, sur les Affaires Religieuses de Son Temps en France* (1827):—*Catéchisme Rationnel* (eod.; reprinted by baron de Pounat in 1862). But all of Potter's works, written in the philosophical spirit of the 18th century, were placed on the "Index" at Rome. See Lichtenberger, *Encyclop. des Sciences Religieuses*, s. v.; Winer, *Handbuch der theol. Lit.* i, 543, 866. (B. P.)

Potton, Richard de, a Scotch prelate, was made bishop of Aberdeen about 1256, and died in 1267. See Keith, *Scottish Bishops*, p. 108.

Pouchen, Levin, a Lutheran theologian of Germany, was born at Königsberg, Oct. 26, 1594. He studied at the theological university of that city, was in 1621 professor, in 1623 second court-preacher, in 1626 professor of Hebrew, in 1640 doctor of theology, in 1645 attended the colloquy at Thoren, and died May 4, 1648. He wrote, *Commentar. in Prophetiam Joel*:—*Explicatio Historiæ Passionis Christi*:—*Disputat. de Usu Philosophiæ in Theologia*:—*De Protevangelio Paradisiaco*:—*De Resurrectione Jesu Christi*:—*De Pia et Vera Philosophandi Ratione*:—*De Ecclesia*:—*De Baptismo*:—*De Resurrectione Mortuorum*:—*De Duabus in Christo Naturis*, etc. See Arnold, *Historie der königsbergischen Universität*; Jöcher, *Allgemeines Gelehrten-Lexikon*, s. v. (B. P.)

Poujoulat, Jean Joseph François, a Roman Catholic writer of France, was born at Fare, Bouches-du-Rhone, in 1800. He studied at Aix, and in 1826 went to Paris, and there published, conjointly with Michaud, the *Bibliothèque des Croisards*, whom he accompanied in 1830 to the East. Poujoulat died at Paris in 1880. He wrote, *Histoire de Jerusalem*, *Tableau Religieux et Philosophique* (1811-42, 2 vols.; 4th ed. 1856):—*Histoire de S. Augustin* (1844, 3 vols.; 3d ed. 1850, 2 vols.):—*Lettres sur Bossuet* (1854):—*Le Cardinal Maury, sa Vie et ses Œuvres* (1855; 2d ed. 1859):—*Vie de Monseigneur Sibour, Archevêque de Paris*:—*Le Père Ravignan, sa Vie, ses Œuvres* (1858):—*Le Pape et la Liberté* (1860):—*Examen de la Vie de Jésus de Mons. Renan* (1863). See Lichtenberger, *Encyclop. des Sciences Religieuses*, s. v. (B. P.)

Poulain, Nicolas, a Reformed theologian, was born at Mesnils, near Luneray, Seine-Inférieure, Jan. 13, 1807. He was pastor of Nanteuil-lès-Meaux in 1832, in 1833 at Havre, in 1857 at Lausanne, and in 1862 at Luneray. Poulain died at Geneva, April 3, 1868. He published, *Qu'est-ce qu'un Christianisme sans Dogmes et sans Miracle?* (1863):—*Réponse a Trois Lettres de M. Albert Reville* (1864):—*L'Œuvre des Missions Évangéliques* (1867), an apologetical work of great value. See Lichtenberger, *Encyclop. des Sciences Religieuses*, s. v. (B. P.)

Power, James, D.D., a Presbyterian minister, was born at Nottingham, Chester Co., Pa., in 1746. He graduated from Princeton College in 1766, was licensed to preach by the Presbytery of Newcastle June 24,

1772, and settled in the western part of Pennsylvania. In 1776 he became pastor of Mt. Pleasant congregation, and retained this position until 1817. He died Aug. 5, 1830. See Sprague, *Annals of the Amer. Pulpit*, iii, 326.

Præbenda, Richard de, a Scotch prelate, was consecrated bishop of the see of Dunkeld, in the Church of St. Andrews, Aug. 9, 1169. He died in 1173. See Keith, *Scottish Bishops*, p. 74.

Præbenda, Robert de, a Scotch prelate, was elected bishop of Dunblane in 1258. In 1268 he, with one other, was sent to protest against the contributions imposed upon the Scotch clergy by Ottobon. He was still bishop here in 1282. See Keith, *Scottish Bishops*, p. 173.

Prætorius, a name common to several Lutheran theologians of Germany, of whom we mention the following:

1. ANDREAS, who died Dec. 20, 1586, at Frankfort-on-the-Oder, doctor of theology, is the author of *Propositiones de Jesu Christo, Dei et Mariæ Filio*. See Jöcher, *Allgemeines Gelehrten-Lexikon*, s. v.

2. CHRISTIAN GOTTLIEB, born Aug. 30, 1693, at Bertzdorf, Upper Lusatia, studied at Wittenberg, and died in 1738 at Bernstadt, in his native province. He wrote *Amœnitates Biblicæ*, comprising only the Pentateuch (1724-29, 6 parts). See Döring, *Die gelehrten Theologen Deutschlands*, s. v.; Jöcher, *Allgemeines Gelehrten-Lexikon*, s. v.

3. EPHRAIM, was born at Dantzic, March 11, 1657. He studied at Wittenberg, was in 1685 preacher at Münsterberg, in 1698 at his native city, in 1705 at Thorn, and died Feb. 14, 1723. He wrote, *Exercitationes theol. de Jona*:—*Atheus Proprio Gladio Jugulatus ex Eccl. iii*, 18-21:—*Bibliotheca Homiletica* (Leipsic, 1691-98, 3 parts; 2d ed. 1711-19). See Döring, *Die gelehrten Theologen Deutschlands*, s. v.; Jöcher, *Allgemeines Gelehrten Lexikon*, s. v. (B. P.)

Prakriti. See PRACRITI.

Prateolus, GABRIEL, a Roman Catholic theologian of France, was born at Marcoussi in 1511, and died at Péronne, April 19, 1588, doctor of theology. His main works are, *De Vitis, Sectis et Dogmatibus Omnium Hæreticorum* (Cologne, 1569):—*Histoire de l'État et Succés de l'Église* (Paris, 1585). See Winer, *Handbuch der theol. Lit.* i, 637; Lichtenberger, *Encyclop. des Sciences Religieuses*, s. v. (B. P.)

Pratje, JOHANN HEINRICH, a Lutheran theologian of Germany, was born Sept. 17, 1710. He studied at Helmstädt, was in 1735 preacher at Horneburg, his native place, in 1743 at Stade, and in 1749 general superintendent of Bremen and Verden. In 1787 his alma mater honored him with the doctorate of theology. He died Feb. 1, 1791. His writings, comprising almost all departments of theology, are given in Döring, *Die gelehrten Kanzelredner*, p. 299-305; Winer, *Handbuch der theol. Lit.* i, 119, 799; ii, 282, 290. (B. P.)

Pratt, James, D.D., a Protestant Episcopal clergyman, was rector in Portland, Me, for several years prior to 1858; then of the Church of the Covenant, in Philadelphia, Pa., where he remained until 1860, when he took charge of Trinity Church, Chicago, Ill. About 1864 he left that parish, and in 1866 was residing in New York city; in 1868 he removed to Philadelphia as the financial secretary of the Evangelical Knowledge Society of the Protestant Episcopal Church. During several years he resided in Philadelphia without assuming the duties of the regular pastorate, until 1873, when he became rector of St. Philip's Church, in that city. He died Jan. 17, 1874, aged sixty-five years. See *Prot. Episc. Almanac*, 1875, p. 144.

Pratt, John, D.D., a Baptist minister and educator, was born in Windham County, Conn., Oct. 12, 1800. After spending a few years in Columbian College, he graduated from Brown University in 1827. For a short time he was a professor in Transylvania University, Ky., and then accepted a call to the pastorate of the First Baptist Church in New Haven, Conn. In 1831, for six months, he had charge of the South Reading, Mass. (now Wakefield), Academy, and then was invited to preside over the Granville, O., Literary and Theological Institution. In 1837 he resigned, and accepted the professorship of ancient languages in that institution, and held this position, with occasional interruptions, for twenty-two years (1837-59), when he retired to private life. He died Jan. 4, 1882. See Cathcart, *Baptist Encyclop.* p. 933. (J. C. S.)

Pratt, Nathaniel Alpheus, D.D., a Presbyterian minister, was born at Centre Brook, Conn., Jan. 29, 1796. He graduated from Yale College in 1820, and from Princeton Theological Seminary in 1823, and was ordained Feb. 25, 1824. From this time till 1826 he labored for the Shrewsbury Church, N. J. From 1827 to 1840 he was pastor of the Church at Darien, Ga. He organized a Church in Roswell, in 1842, where he continued until his death, Aug. 30, 1879. During the time at Roswell he taught, for five years, a boarding-school for boys. See *Necrol. Report of Princeton Theol. Sem.* 1880, p. 11.

Premillenarians is a popular designation of a class of theologians who understand "the first resurrection," spoken of in Rev. xx, 5, as predicting a separate and literal revivification of the saints previous to the millennium, and their personal reign with Christ on earth during that period, in opposition to the usual or *post-millenarian* view, which explains it in a figurative and spiritual sense. Among the advocates of the premillennial scheme have been counted, with more or less reserve, such eminent names as those of Mede, Jurieu, Daubuz, Sir Isaac Newton, archbishop Newcome, bishops Newton, Horsley, and Heber, doctors Gill, Toplady, Bengel, Dorner, Nitzsch, Delitzsch, Van Oosterzee, Hofmann, Aubelen, Ebrard, Rothe, Lange, Christlieb, Luthardt, Gaussen, Godet, Trench, Ellicott, Ryle, Hoare, Tregelles, Elliott, Alford, Bickersteth, Bonar, Tyng, Lord, and many other learned and pious divines, especially among Protestants, while the great majority of scholars and writers of Christendom, in all ages and denominations, have been ranged on the opposite, or post-millennial side, of whom we need mention only, among moderns, Whitby, Faber, Brown, Barnes, Hengstenberg, Stuart, and Wordsworth. The history of the Chiliastic doctrine, both Jewish and Christian, is well summarized in the *Speaker's Commentary*, excursus at the end of Rev. xx. See RESURRECTION, THE FIRST.

Preston, WILLIAM, D.D., a Protestant Episcopal minister, was born at Woodbury, Conn., Aug. 26, 1801. He graduated from Yale College, was first a clerk in New York city, then studied theology in Alexandria, Va., was tutor in Kenyon College for a year, and on Oct. 12, 1828, was admitted to deacon's orders by bishop Chase of Ohio. He began his ministry in the town of Worthington, but soon removed to Trinity Church, Columbus, where he remained for twelve years. In 1841 he accepted a call from the parish of St. Andrew's, in Pittsburgh, Pa., where he continued ten years. He was then called to his former parish in Columbus, but, owing to ill-health, removed some four years later to Christ Church, Bridgeport, Conn., where he labored until 1856, when he went back to his old charge in Pittsburgh. In 1873 he resigned this post, and after a time removed to Bedford, Pa., where he was rector of St. James's Church. He died there, April 25, 1875. See *Obit. Rec. of Yale College*, 1875.

Priapus, in Greek mythology, was the son of Bacchus and Venus. The angry Juno touched the body of the pregnant Venus so that she gave birth to a hideous child with unnaturally large genital organs. The older writers do not know him. He was worshipped as the god of country fruitfulness, and his statues were placed in gardens.

Price, THOMAS, LL.D., an English Baptist minister, was born at Bristol, April 21, 1802. He was converted at fifteen, and baptized in Broadmead Chapel by Dr. Ryland. In 1820 he studied in the Bristol Academy, and afterwards at the Glasgow and the Edinburgh universities; was ordained in 1824 copastor of the Devonshire Square Church, London, and in 1826 became pastor. He delivered popular lectures, which he published in two volumes in 1836, with the title, *A History of Protestant Nonconformity*. He resigned his pastorate the same year, and became one of the founders of the Anti-State-Church Association, now the Liberation Society; he was appointed treasurer, and was one of the society's most zealous advocates. A disease in his throat utterly incapacitated him from public speaking, so he devoted his energies to the founding of the Dissenters and General Fire and Life Assurance Company. He also became proprietor and editor of the *Eclectic Review*, which he conducted for nineteen years. In 1848 he became a confirmed invalid, and died May 29, 1867. See (Lond.) *Baptist Hand-book*, 1868, p. 125.

Prichard, JOHN, D.D., a Welsh Baptist minister, was born near Amlwch, Wales, in March, 1796. He pursued his studies in the College of Abergavenny, and was ordained as pastor of the Church at Llangollen, which was his only settlement. Through his exertions a college was established in the place where he resided, in 1862, for training young men for the ministry, of which he was for a time the president. He died Sept. 7, 1875. See Cathcart, *Baptist Encyclop.* p. 939. (J. C. S.)

Pries, a name common to several Lutheran theologians.

1. JOACHIM HEINRICH (1), was born Nov. 12, 1714, at Rostock, where he began his theological studies, which he continued at Jena. At the university of his birthplace Pries commenced his academical career in 1739. In 1745 he was appointed professor, in 1749 he took the degree of doctor of theology, and died Aug. 1, 1763. He is the author of, *De non Consummatis Patribus Veteris Testamenti ad Dictum Pauli Ebr. xi*, 39, 40 (Rostock, 1749):—*Quo Sensu Æternitas Dei Fixa sit Momentum?* (1752):—*De Jona, Christi Typo* (1753):—*De Præexistentia Dei Ante Abraham* (1755):—*De Prophetis et Apostolis* (1757):—*De Infallibilitate Apostolorum* (1760), etc. See Döring, *Die gelehrten Theologen Deutschlands*, s. v.

2. JOACHIM HEINRICH (2), son of the preceding, was born at Rostock, Sept. 24, 1747. He studied at the universities of his native place and Jena. For some time preacher at Ribnitz, he was appointed professor of theology at Rostock in 1779, took the degree of doctor of theology in 1791, and died Oct. 24, 1796. He wrote, *Progr. in Deut. xviii*, 15 (Rostock, 1779):—*Sapientia Redemptoris in Apparitionibus Post Resurrectionem* (1780):—*Natura Jesu Christi Divina* (1782):—*Mortuorum Resurrectio Veteris Fœdere non Incognita* (1783):—*De Personis quibus Epistola ad Galatas Scripta est* (1786):—*De Morte Christi Vicaria* (1788):—*De Numero Paschatum a Christo Post Baptismum Celebratorum* (1789). See Döring, *Die gelehrten Theologen Deutschlands*, s. v.

3. JOHANN GABRIEL, who died at Güstrow in 1788, rector, wrote, *Progr. in Genes. xli*, 43 (Rostock, 1754):—*De Divina Legum Mosaicarum Præstantia* (1755):—*De Divina Legum Mosaicarum Indole* (1756):—*De Divina Lege, etc., Warburtono Opposita* (1757):—*De Israelitarum Theocratiæ Præstantia* (1759):—*De LXX Interpretibus* (1768). See Fürst, *Bibl. Jud.* iii, 121. (B. P.)

Prime, SAMUEL IRENÆUS, D.D., an eminent Presbyterian divine, son of Dr. N. S. Prime, was born at Ballston, Saratoga Co., N. Y., Nov. 4, 1812. He graduated from Williams College in 1829, and from Princeton Theological Seminary in 1835; was ordained the same year as pastor at Ballston Spa, in 1837 assumed the same relation at Matteawan, but on account of failing health resigned in 1840, and became editor of the New York *Observer;* in 1841 one of the secretaries of the American Bible Society; in 1849 editor of the *Presbyterian*, but the next year resumed the editorship of the *Observer*, with which he remained connected until his death, July 18, 1885. Dr. Prime was a fine scholar, a genial Christian, and a facile writer. Besides numerous anonymous works, he published many popular writings, the chief of which are enumerated in Allibone's *Dict. of Brit. and Amer. Authors*, s. v., the most important being travels and biographies, and several volumes on prayer.

Prindle, CYRUS, D.D., a noted Methodist Episcopal minister, was born at Canaan, Litchfield Co., Conn., April 11, 1800. He was converted in 1816, licensed to preach in 1821, and the same year joined the New York Conference, was appointed to the Plattsburgh Circuit, and thereafter for over half a century continued with but a single month's intermission the active duties of the ministry: twenty-one years in New York, nineteen in Vermont, six in Massachusetts, and ten in Ohio, when he retired in 1877, in the full possession of his bodily and mental powers. In 1843 he was a chief leader in the formation of the Wesleyan Methodist connection in America, which seceded from the Methodist Episcopal Church on account of its alleged connection with slavery; but this being removed by the war of the Rebellion, he returned to his former church in 1867. He died at Cleveland, O., Dec. 1, 1885. Dr. Prindle was a man of great pulpit power and singular purity of character.

Proal, PIERRE ALEXIS, D.D., a Protestant Episcopal minister, was born at Newark, N. J., in 1796. He was ordained deacon in New York, Sept. 18, 1818, his first parish being St. John's Church, Johnstown, where he remained for a short time; then he took charge of St. George's Church, Schenectady; in 1836 he became rector of Trinity Church, Utica, a position which he retained until the spring of 1857, when, on account of impaired health, he resigned. He died in that city Sept. 15 following. Dr. Proal was one of the most prominent clergymen of the diocese of Western New York, from its organization held the post of secretary of the convention, and was deputy to the General Convention. He was an earnest and forcible preacher. See *Amer. Quar. Church Rev.* 1857, p. 465.

Prometheus, in Greek mythology, was the son of the Titan Japetus and the Oceanid Clymene, full of wisdom, art, and might, a friend and companion of the gods, who loved him for his gifts, but in whom he awakened hatred when he doubted their omniscience. He once sought to prove Jupiter's knowledge, and the latter never forgot his audacity, but planned his destruction. Vulcan nailed him to the Caucasus, and the eagle of Jupiter daily came down and devoured his liver, which grew again at night. For a long time he bore these tortures with patience, for he knew a mortal would eventually liberate him. This Hercules did by shooting the eagle. According to others Chiron liberated him. A third myth makes Jupiter himself the

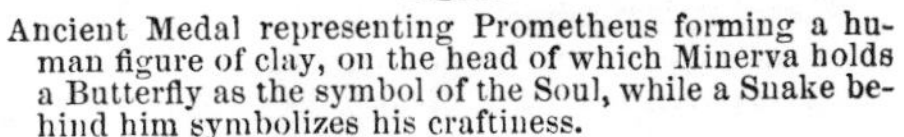

Ancient Medal representing Prometheus forming a human figure of clay, on the head of which Minerva holds a Butterfly as the symbol of the Soul, while a Snake behind him symbolizes his craftiness.

liberator of the great Titan. Prometheus was married to Asia, and was the father of Deucalion. According to the ancient story, he provoked the gods by forming a man, and then stealing fire from heaven to animate the form.

Pronier, CÉSAR LOUIS, a Swiss theologian, was born at Plainpalais, near Geneva, Oct. 19, 1834. He was in early life in business in the United States, but returning in 1853, studied theology at Geneva and Berlin. In 1860 he assisted professor Gaussen in his academical duties at Geneva, and in 1863 became his successor. In 1870 Pronier founded the *Liberté Chrétienne*, a journal designed to plead the separation of the Church from the State. In 1873 he went as a delegate to the Evangelical Alliance, held at New York city, never to return again to Geneva, for the "Ville du Havre," upon which he embarked with two other members of the alliance, Antonio Carrasco of Madrid, and Cook of Paris, collided with the "Loch Earn," and went down, Nov. 22, 1873. Pronier published, *Questions Indiscrètes Adressées à Mme. Armengaud et à M. Ed. Krüger* (Geneva, 1857):—*La Suisse Romande et le Protestantisme Liberal* (Lausanne, 1869):—*La Liberté Religieuse et le Syllabus* (Geneva, 1870). See Ruffet, *Vie de César Pronier* (Geneva, 1875); Lichtenberger, *Encyclop. des Sciences Religieuses*, s. v. (B. P.)

Prosper, a Scotch prelate, was elected bishop of the see of Caithness about 1461, but resigned in favor of John Sinclair. See Keith, *Scottish Bishops*, p. 214.

Prudentius' HYMNS. See SALVETE FLORES MARTYRUM.

Przypcov, SAMUEL, a Socinian of Poland, who died June 19, 1670, had studied at Leyden, and occupied high offices in his country. But being a Socinian, he had to leave Poland, and went to Brandenburg. He wrote, *Cogitationes Sacræ ad Initium Evang. Matth. et Omnes Epistolas Apostolicas* (Amsterdam, 1692 fol.):—*Vita Fausti Socini* (1636), etc., to be found in *Bibliotheca Fratrum Polonorum*. See Winer, *Handbuch der theol Lit.* i, 238, 771; Jöcher, *Allgemeines Gelehrten-Lexikon*, s. v. (B. P.)

Psellus, MICHAEL, one of the most famous Byzantine writers of the 11th century, was born about the year 1020 at Constantinople. He studied at Athens, and held for many years the first chair in philosophy in his native city. The emperor Constantine Ducas appointed Psellus tutor to the imperial princes, and when Michael Ducas, his former pupil, died, in 1078, Psellus retired to a monastery, where he died in 1106. On account of his many writings Psellus was styled πολογραφώτατος. His principal works are, *De Omnifaria Doctrina* 157, διδασκαλία παντοδαπή, a metaphysical exposition of the fundamental ideas of all science:—*De Dæmonum Operatione* περὶ ἐνεργείας δαιμόνων, a dialogue, edited by Boissonade (Paris, 1838), and of special interest for the study of the sect of the Euchites. A comparison between the ancient Christian and Attic orators is contained in *Charakteres SS. Gregorii Theologi, Basilii Magni, Joh. Chrysostomi, Gregorii Nysseni.* All of Psellus's works are found in Migne, *Patrologiæ Græcæ*, vol. cxxii. See Leo Allatius, *Diatriba de Psellis* (Paris, 1864; reprinted in Migne), Dimitracopoulos, *Orthodox Greece* (Leipsic, 1872, Greek), p. 8; Sathas, *Michel Psellus* (Paris, 1874, 2 vols.); Lichtenberger, *Encyclop. des Sciences Religieuses*, s. v.; Plitt-Herzog, *Real-Encyclop.* s. v. (B. P.)

Pseudepigrăpha OF THE OLD TESTAMENT. After a careful examination of the scope of the Biblical canon, the ancient Church divided the mass of Biblical literature, in the widest sense of the word, into three classes: 1, the canonical and inspired; 2, the non-canonical, but on account of their long use, worthy of being read in the churches (ἀντιλεγόμενα and ἀναγιγνωσκόμενα, ἐκκλησιαζόμενα), and, 3, the other books of a Biblical character in circulation (Biblical name in the title, a Biblical form, Biblical contents, but differing greatly in spirit and truth from the canonical books), called apocryphal, or such as should be kept secret (ἀπόκρυφα). Virtually the same books which the ancient Church called apocrypha are embraced under the name Pseudepigrapha by the Protestant Church. Since, after the example of Jerome, the non-canonical books of the Old Test. received the name apocrypha, it became necessary to find a new one for the third class. The name ψευδεπίγραφα is, indeed, taken only from a single and outward mark, namely, the spurious character of the author's name which they bear. It is neither sufficiently comprehensive, nor does it distinguish sufficiently this class of writings from the antilegomena; nor is it applicable to all the writings of the third class. For many reasons, however, it is probably the best term that could be found.

As there is an Old and a New Test., so likewise there are pseudo-epigrapha of each, all writings that claim either to have been written by or to treat of Old-Test. personages, whether these writings are of Jewish or Christian origin, being called pseudepigrapha of the Old Test.; and those writings which pretend to be gospels, acts of the apostles, epistles of apostles, and revelations under a New-Test. name, being termed pseudepigrapha of the New-Test. The latter class might probably be better called *apocrypha* of the New Test. (in the old sense of the word).

In the following the pseudepigrapha of the Old Test., those that are extant as well as those of which only fragments are preserved, or which are only known by name, will be treated. We premise a few remarks on the origin and development of this whole class of literature. The rapid growth and spread of pseudepigraphic literature among the Jews and Christians in the last century before, and the early centuries after, Christ, is a peculiar phenomenon, for which other nations have only distant analogies; and it is all the more remarkable, because such writings are in direct contradiction to the duty of strict truthfulness demanded by both Mosaism and Christianity. That these books were used only in sectarian circles cannot be proved. It is true that heretics in early days of the Church frequently adopted this method of promulgating their errors, but this was in the period of the decay of this literature, and we must remember, on the other hand, that, in the course of the centuries during which it flourished, it generally was employed for honorable and usually noble purposes, and by members of the orthodox Church. There is no doubt that their origin is not to be explained as an imitation of the secret books in possession of the priests of the Gentile temples, but that they are the outgrowth of the peculiarity and life of the Jewish congregation, and were then transferred to the Christian Church. Above all, it must be remembered that it was the custom of Jewish writers not to prefix their names to their productions, as these were written for the benefit of the congregation, not for the author's glorification. Different was the practice with the prophets, who, with their names, guaranteed the truth of the revelation. Thus the names of the authors of nearly all other books have been hidden from posterity. This custom of omitting the author's name explains, to some extent, the origin of writings under a strange name. The other weighty reason lies in the inner rupture in the spiritual life of the Jews, which began before the captivity, but showed itself in great potency in the first centuries of the new Jerusalem. With the ruin of the old political and religious organization, and the sufferings under heathen supremacy, the freedom of the national spirit was also broken, the Holy Spirit of revelation withdrew, the state of affairs and the teachings of former days became decisive for the new period; and as all this led to the formation of a canon in the first centuries after the exile, it also increased the reverence for the old history, the old persons and writings, so much, that these ruled and decided the whole spiritual life of the people. The examination, study, and application of the sacred writings were the fundamental objects of these times. Although, through association with other nations and educational forces (Persians, Greeks, Romans), and through a more systematic and deeper investigation of the old books, new knowledge and aims were born, and although, in extraordinary and dangerous times, prominent men felt themselves called upon to speak to the congregation, yet the lack of personal influence always induced such authors to put their thoughts and words into the mouth of some pious man of antiquity, and conform the shape and style of their writings to those of the Old Test. A thorough acquaintance with these latter facilitated the application of their contents to later circumstances. Such revivification of ancient persons, which makes them the bearers of later thoughts, was common to all literature; and it was but one step further to ascribe a whole book to them. In many respects this kind of literature can be compared with the dramatic works of other nations; but to call it intentionally fraudulent is hardly to be justified, for the multitude of such books shows that the knowledge of their late origin was constantly present to the minds of the readers. Yet the danger of leaving a false impression, at least in the minds of the less cultivated part of the congregation, although for the contemporaries comparatively small, was constantly growing with time, especially when Christianity brought these later spiritual productions of the Jews to nations who did not understand them. The opposition of the early Christian Church against such books can thus be easily understood, but theological science must investigate, and make all possible use of them. The pseudepigraphical form was chiefly adopted for the purpose of instruction, exhortation, and consolation in the great trials and troubles of post-exilic days. What the prophets had been for the past, the later writings were intended to be for the present, by the prophetical character which they assumed. Most of the pseudepigraphical works are prophetical in their nature, some also apocalypses, in imitation of the book of Daniel.

Besides the pseudepigraphical literature, the so-called haggadic midrash, as we find it in the later Targumim, Midrashim, and Talmud, as well as in the Pseudepigrapha, was especially cultivated.

With the rise of Christianity, a new element was introduced into this literature, and contributed to its growth and development, not through the Essenes, as modern Jewish writers would have it, but through the Judaizing sects and the gnosticism arising from them, especially in Asia Minor and Egypt. In the hands of the sects and heretics they later became instruments for dangerous purposes, which resulted in the antagonizing attitude of the Church. The number of Jewish and Christian pseudepigrapha was undoubtedly very large. Even in the apocalypse of Ezra (4 Ezra xiv, 46 Lat., xiv, 51 Ethiop.), seventy apocryphal writings are distinguished from the twenty-four canonical books, which, however, is probably a round number that became authoritative for later times. It is probable that those preserved are the best of their class. Of many we have only the titles, or short extracts in the Church Fathers. The last decades have discovered some that were regarded as lost, and the future may yet furnish us others. They have more than a passing interest, they have historical value, because they were the popular literature of their day. According to their contents, the pseudepigrapha may be divided into different classes, viz.:

I. Lyrical Poetry. To this class belong:

1. *The Psalter of Solomon* (q. v.). By way of supplement to the literature we add Pick, *The Psalter of Solomon* (Greek and English, in the *Presbyterian Review*, October, 1883), and an art. by Dean in the *Expositor* (Lond. December, 1883).

2. A pseudepigraphon of Δαβίδ, mentioned in the *Constit. Apost.* vi, 16. Whether this is Psa. cli of the Greek Bible, or a larger, independent work, cannot now be decided.

II. Prophetic Writings. Under this head we enumerate:

a. The so-called *Apocalypses* or *Revelations*. This is the name assigned to those books of fictitious prophecy which, after the spirit of prophecy had departed from Israel, were written, in the manner of genuine prophetic books, to solve the problems suggested by the fate and sufferings of the people. They seek a solution of the intricacies of the present in predictions of the glory of the future. Accordingly, they do not imitate the old prophets in their chief peculiarity, namely, to counsel and warn the people on account of their sins, but they undertake a subordinate office, that of foreseeing and foretelling the future, their chief object, while they nevertheless endeavor to erect their prophetic building on the foundation of the inspired seers. The chief contents of these revelations are the Messianic times in their relation to the present time and circumstances. Not that the fact that the Messianic time would come, but when and how, was the question for the waiting congregation. The books that seek to answer these questions are called apocalypses. Their contents are most varied and peculiar, their explanation manifold and strange; the topics discussed all referring directly or indirectly to the kingdom of God, and the future of the chosen people; their style enigmatical and highly figurative. A portion of these apocalypses have been treated by Lücke, *Einleitung in die Offenbarung des Johannes* (2d ed. Bonn, 1848); Hilgenfeld, *Die jüdische Apocalyptik* (1857); Langen, *Das Judenthum in Palästina zur Zeit Jesu* (1866); Schürer, *Lehrbuch der N. T. Zeitgeschichte* (1874; 2d ed. with the title, *Gesch. des jüd. Volkes im Zeitalter Jesu Christi*, 1886).

3. *The Enoch and Noah Writings*, combined in the *Book of Enoch* (q. v.). We add, by way of supplement to the literature, Drummond, *The Jewish Messiah* (Lond. 1877), p. 17 sq.; *The Book of Enoch*, in the *British and Foreign Evangelical Review* (Lond. July, 1879); Bissell, *The Apocrypha of the Old Testament* (New York, 1880), p. 665 sq.; Schodde, *The Book of Enoch Translated, with Introduction and Notes* (Andover, 1882); Laurence, *Book of Enoch the Prophet, translated, with Text corrected by his Latest Notes, with an Introduction by the Author of Evolution and Christianity* (Lond. 1883); *Enoch's Gospel*, in the *Expositor*, May, 1884; *Dictionary of Christian Biography* (ed. Smith and Wace), s. v. Enoch, Book of.

4. The Ανάληψις Μωϋσέως, *Assumptio Mosis* (q. v.).

5. *The Fourth Book of Ezra*, see Esdras, Book of, and add Gildemeister, *Esræ Liber IV, Arabice* (Bonn, 1877); Bensley, *The Missing Fragment of the Latin Translation of the Fourth Book of Ezra* (Cambridge, 1875); Drummond, u. s. p. 84–117.

6. The present Jewish *Ezra revelation* found an entrance into the Church, but usually with some modifications. In the editions of the Vulgate it has, besides these, long additions in front and at the close. These, in the MSS., are written as *separate Ezra books*, one of which, at least (chap. i sq.), is of Christian origin, to impress the importance of Christianity upon the stubborn Jews; the other, probably a portion of an independent Jewish work. Both are translations from the Greek.

7. The λόγος καὶ ἀπυκάλυψις τοῦ ἁγίου προφήτου Ἐσδράμ καὶ ἀγαπητοῦ τοῦ θεοῦ, published by Tischendorf, in *Apocal. Apocr.* (Leipsic, 1866), p. 24–33, from a Paris MS., has no value. On other Ezra literature, see Tischendorf, *Studien und Kritiken* (1851), part ii; Lücke, l. c.

8. Closely related to the Ezra prophecies is the apocalypse of Baruch, published in a Latin translation from a Syriac MS. in the Ambrosiana at Milan, by Ceriani (*Monum. Sacra*, I, ii, p. 73 sq.), in 1866, and by Fritzsche (p. 654–699), also in Syriac, by the former, in 1871. It is a revelation to Baruch concerning the destruction of Jerusalem, the ensuing captivity, and the second destruction, to which are added visions of the Messianic future. It is allied in contents and style to 4 Ezra, and called forth by the same historical events, but is a later production. The original language is Greek. See Ewald, *Göttinger Gelehrten Anzeige*, 1867, p. 1706 sq.; Ewald, *Geschichte* (3d ed.), vii, 83 sq.; Langen, *De Apoc. Baruch Comment.* (Freiburg, 1867); Hilgenfeld, *Messias Judæorum*, p. lxiii sq.: Fritzsche, u. s. p. xxx sq.; Schürer, u. s. p. 542 sq.; Renan, *Journal des Savants*, 1877, p. 222 sq.; Drummond, u. s. p. 117–132; Kneucker, *Das Buch Baruch*, p. 190 sq. (Leipsic, 1879).

9. Whether the *Pseudepigraphon Baruchi* mentioned in the *Synopsis Psalmi Athanasii* is the same as the above is uncertain. We still, however, possess a Christian Baruch book, for which see Baruch, Book of, in the supplement of this Cyclopædia.

10. *Eliæ Revelatio et Visio*. See Elias, Apocalypse of.

11. *Ascensio et Visio Isaiæ*. See Ascension of Isaiah.

12. An apocalypse or prophecy of Zephaniah is mentioned in the four catalogues of the Apocrypha, and is also quoted by Clemens Alexand. *Stromata*, v, 11, § 78.

13. An apocryphon of Jeremiah, in Hebrew, used by the Nazarenes, is mentioned by Jerome (see Fabricius, 2d ed. i, 1102 sq.), as the source of the quotation in Matt. xxvii, 9; but this is probably fictitious.

Concerning the apocalypses of, 14. Habakkuk; 15. Ezekiel; 16. Daniel; 17. Zechariah, the father of John the Baptist, we have no further information.

18. An apocalypse of Moses, distinct from the *Book of*

Jubilees (No. 31), and the *Assumptio Mosis* (No. 4), we know only from Syncellus, *Protius Amphil.*, and others (Fabricius, p. 838), who mention it as the source of Gal. vi, 15.

19. A Lamech book is mentioned in the catalogues of Cotelier and Montfaucon; and

20. The Gnostic Sethites possessed an apocalypse of Abraham (q. v.).

b. *Testaments:*

21. A *διαθήκη τῶν πρωτοπλαστῶν*, according to Fabricius, ii, 83, contained the mention that Adam was taken into Paradise when forty days old. It is probably a portion of the *Vita Adami* (No. 35).

22. *The Testaments of the Twelve Patriarchs* (q. v.); to the literature must be added Pick, *The Testaments of the Twelve Patriarchs*, in the *Lutheran Church Review* (Philadelphia, July, 1885); Schnapp, *Die Testamente der zwölf Patriarchen* (Halle, 1884).

23. An apocryphon, *τῶν τριῶν πατριαρχῶν*, is mentioned in the *Const. Apost.* vi, 16.

24. An apocryphal testament of Jacob, mentioned in the *Decretum Gelasii* (Fabricius, i, 437, 799).

25. A *προσευχὴ Ἰωσήφ*, "prayer or blessing of Joseph," is frequently mentioned, and is also counted among those read (*παρ' Ἑβραίοις*) by Origen and others (Fabricius, i, 765–768). It seems to have been strongly cabalistic.

26. A *διαθήκη Μωϋσέως* is mentioned in the four catalogues and in the *Catena* of Nicephorus, i, col. 175.

27. Concerning the *διαθήκη Ἐζεκίου*, *Asc. Jes.* cap. 1–5, see No. 11.

28. The testaments of Adam and Noah are portions of the *Vita Adami* (No. 35).

c. *Other books concerning the Prophets:*

29. In the acts of the Nicene synod (Fabric. i, 845) mention is made of *βίβλος λόγων μυστικῶν Μωϋσέως*. What book is meant is uncertain. The later Jews had a work, *Petirat Moshe*, the death of Moses.

30. *Liber Eldad et Medad* is mentioned in *Pastor Hermæ*, i, vis. 2, 3, and cited as the holy writings generally are; later authorities mention it as an apocryphon of the Old Testament.

III. BOOKS ON HISTORICAL MATTERS AND HAGGADIC WRITINGS. These include:

31. *The Book of Jubilees* (q. v.). To the literature we add Drummond, p. 143–147; Deane, *The Book of Jubilees*, in the *Monthly Expositor*, August and September, 1885; Dillmann, *Beiträge aus dem Buche der Jubiläen zur Kritik des Pentateuch-Textes* (Berlin, 1883, in reports of the Berlin Academy of Sciences); Schodde, *The Book of Jubilees* (translation, etc., in *Bibliotheca Sacra*, October, 1885, etc.).

32. *Jannes et Mambres* treats of the contest between Moses and the Egyptian sorcerers (Exod. vii, 11). Cf. 2 Tim. iii, 8. See Heath, *Quar. Statement* of the "Palest. Exploration Fund," Oct. 1881, p. 311 sq.

33. Manasseh's conversion (2 Chron. xxxiii, 11) early gave rise to an apocryphon of Manasseh, used both by Christian writers and by the Targum on Chronicles (Fabricius, i, 1000 sq.).

34. A novel based on Gen. xli, 45, we have in *Asenath* (q. v.).

35. *Books of Adam*, see ADAM, BOOK OF. To the literature we add, Trumpp, in *Abhandlungen der bayrischen Akademie der Wissenschaften* (Munich, 1880, 1882); Meyer, *Vita Adæ et Evæ*, in the same journal (1879); Malan, *The Book of Adam and Eve* (Lond. 1882).

36. A gnostic writing, called *Noria*, after the wife of Noah, is mentioned by Epiphanius, *Hær.* 26.

37. An Ebionitic book, *ἀναβαθμοὶ Ἰακώβου* (Gen. xxviii), also mentioned by Epiphanius (Fabricius, i, 437).

On the Jewish Midrashim. See MIDRASH, in this Supplement.

Later, this class of literature was used for worldly and evil purposes, and stood in the service of quackery, witchcraft, and sorcery. The name of Solomon was, above all others, connected with this kind of works; sometimes, also, that of Joseph and Abraham (Fabricius, i, 1043, 390, 785). See Plitt-Herzog, *Real-Encyklop.* s. v. (B. P.)

Pseudo-Isidorian Decretals. See DECRETALS, PSEUDO-ISIDORIAN.

Pufendorf, SAMUEL, a German historian, was born at Chemnitz, Saxony, in 1632. He lectured on jurisprudence at Heidelberg and Lund, and finally settled at Berlin as historiographer to the elector of Brandenburg. Pufendorf died in 1694. His principal work is *De Jure Naturæ et Gentium* (Lund, 1672 and often; transl. into German, English, and French). Though essentially only an elaboration and systematization of the ideas of Grotius, it forms the foundation of the modern conception of the doctrine of natural and international rights. Previously that doctrine had been based on the decalogue and developed in accordance with the idea of the justice of God. But Pufendorf emancipated the natural law from theology, without opposing the dogmas of the latter, because he recognised in religion the means of realizing the right and God as its author. Pufendorf's work attracted great attention, but also met with much opposition; indeed, Buddæus and Wolff were the first who fully recognised it. Among his other works, his *De Habitu Religionis Christianæ ad Vitam Civilem* (Bremen, 1687) has also theological interest as a defence of his colleagues' system. In a work published after his death, in 1695, entitled *Jus Feciale Divinum seu de Consensu et Dissensu Protestantium*, he demonstrates the impossibility of uniting the Lutherans and Reformed as long as the latter retain the doctrine of absolute predestination. See Stahl, *Die Philosophie des Rechts* (3d ed. Heidelberg, 1854), i, 182; Hettner, *Literaturgeschichte des XVIII. Jahrhunderts* (Brunswick, 1856–62), iii, 83 sq.; Bluntschli und Brater, *Deutsches Staats-Wörterbuch*, viii, 424–439; Droysen, *Zur Kritik Pufendorf's*, in *Abhandlungen zur neueren Geschichte* (Leipsic, 1876); Franck, *Geschichte der protestantischen Theologie*, ii, 62 sq.; Plitt-Herzog, *Real-Encyklop.* s. v.; Lichtenberger, *Encyclop. des Sciences Religieuses*, s. v. (B. P.)

Pullen (Pulley, Puley, Pulby, or **Bullen),** RICHARD. See PULLEYN.

Pünjer, GEORG CHRISTIAN BERNHARD, a Protestant theologian of Germany, was born at Friedrichsgabekoog, Schleswig-Holstein, June 7, 1850. He studied at different universities, took the degree of doctor of philosophy in 1874, and commenced his academical career at Jena in 1875. In 1880 he was made professor, and in 1883 doctor of theology. Pünjer died May 13, 1885. He is the author of, *Die Religionslehre Kant's* (Jena, 1874):—*De Michælis Serveti Doctrina Commentatio Dogmatico-historica* (1876):—*Geschichte der christlichen Religionsphilosophie seit der Reformation* (Brunswick, 1880, 1883, 2 vols.):—*Die Aufgaben des heutigen Protestantismus* (1885). Besides contributing to different encyclopædic works and literary journals, he started in 1881 the *Theologischer Jahresbericht*, giving an annual review of all theological works published in German, French, English, Dutch, etc., a work indispensable to the student in spite of its many deficiencies. (B. P.)

Punshon, WILLIAM MORLEY, LL.D., an eminent Wesleyan Methodist minister, was born at Doncaster, Yorkshire, England, May 29, 1824. His home influences were decidedly Methodistic, and at the age of seventeen he gave himself to Christ. He at once conscientiously devoted himself to a rigid course of self-culture and energetic usefulness, which he continued until his death. In 1840 he removed to Sunderland, where he became an accredited local preacher. In 1843 he began his preparation for the ministry, under that devoted missionary, Benjamin Clough, at Woolwich. He was accepted as a probationer by the conference in 1844, and went to the theological school at Richmond, but did not complete his course, as he was sent to Maidstone Circuit to supply a vacancy. In 1845 he was appointed to the Whitehaven Circuit. In 1867 he was appointed by the conference as its representative to the Canadian Conference, and also elected to its presidency. He arrived in America in 1868, and met the General Conference of the Methodist Episcopal Church at Chicago the same year, to which he was the representative of the Wesleyan Church. He visited the General Conference of 1872, and his speech before that body at that time was probably by far the best he ever delivered in America. The Wesleyan Church honored him by making him president of the conference in 1874. In 1875 he was appointed one of the secretaries of the Foreign Missionary Society, which position he held until his death, in London, April 14, 1881. Dr. Punshon was undoubtedly the greatest orator which the Wesleyan body of England has produced in this century. He was by nature poetic, and his style was largely controlled by this tendency, highly ornate, with great beauty and variety of illustration. In early life his discourses were rhetorical rather than logical, but during the latter part of his career his efforts "combined, as far as would be possible, the Ciceronian and Demosthenic styles." These qualities, coupled with a wonderful voice and great personal magnetism, gave him a power over an audience which is seldom equalled. His character as a Christian was specially attractive. "A remarkable fact in the history of Mr. Punshon is that he displayed, in the important positions in which he was placed in later years, very great practical sagacity, and proved that a great semi-poetic orator may be a successful man of affairs." He published several volumes of sermons and addresses, also one of poems. See *Minutes of the British Conference*, 1881, p. 36; (N. Y.) *Christian Advocate*, April 21, 1881; also his *Biography* (Lond. 1881).

Purcell, John Baptist, D.D., an eminent Roman Catholic prelate, was born of humble parents at Mallow, County Cork, Ireland, Feb. 26, 1800. In his eighteenth year he left his home for the United States, and in June, 1820, entered Mount St. Mary's College, Emmittsburg, Md. After three years he received minor orders, and the following year was sent to France to complete his theological course at the seminary of St. Sulpice, Paris. On May 21, 1826, he was ordained priest by archbishop Quelen in the Notre Dame cathedral. Immediately on his return to America he was appointed professor of philosophy at Mount St. Mary's College, and in 1828 he became president of it. On Oct. 13, 1833, he was consecrated bishop of Cincinnati. By his unflagging zeal he saw his large diocese flourishing with its churches and charitable and religious foundations. In 1836 he had his great public debate, which lasted a week, with Alexander Campbell. In 1850 Cincinnati was made an archiepiscopal see, and Purcell and Hughes received the pallium together in the pope's private chapel. Bishop Purcell died at St. Martin's, O., July 4, 1883. He was a man of great vigor, devotion, and labor, naturally generous and charitable. His latter years were made unhappy by the memorable financial disaster which overtook him, and which caused him to retire some time before his death to a monastery. He left debts to the amount of one million of dollars. He published several volumes, chiefly sermons and biographies. See *Cath. Annual*, p. 34; Gilmour, *Funeral Oration* (N. Y. 1883).

Purinton, Jesse M., D.D., a Baptist minister, was born at Coleraine, Mass., Aug. 12, 1809. He united with the Church at the age of eleven, studied at Hamilton, N. Y., and was ordained in 1834. His pastorates were in his native place; Arcade, N. Y.; Forestville and Mount Moriah, Pa., and at Morgantown, W. Va. For several years he was a missionary in north-western Virginia, and assisted pastors much in times of revival. He died at Morgantown, June 17, 1869. See Cathcart, *Baptist Encyclop.* p. 950. (J. C. S.)

Purviance, James, D.D., a Presbyterian minister, was born at Baltimore, Md., Feb. 19, 1807. He was educated at St. Mary's College and at the U. S. Academy at West Point, subsequently studied law, and graduated from Princeton Theological Seminary in 1835. He was ordained an evangelist by the Presbytery of Louisiana in 1837; served one year thereafter as stated supply at Baton Rouge; at Carmel, Miss., in 1841, and pastor from 1846 to 1854. He was president of Oakland College from 1855 to 1860; resided at Carrollton, La., from 1861 to 1862; at Natchez, Miss., in infirm health, from 1863 to 1871, and died there, July 14 of the latter year. See *Gen. Cat. of Princeton Theol. Sem.* 1881, p. 90; Nevin, *Presbyterian Encyclop.* s. v.

Pusey, Edward Bouverie, D.D., D.C.L., an eminent Anglican divine, son of the late Hon. Philip Bouverie (half-brother of the first earl of Radnor), who assumed the name of Pusey by royal license, was born in 1800. He was educated at Christ Church College, Oxford, where he graduated with high honor in 1822, and the next year was elected to a fellowship in Oriel College. After studying in Germany for two years, he was appointed in 1828 regius professor of Hebrew at Oxford University, a position to which is attached a canonry in Christ Church, and he retained these offices until his death, Sept. 16, 1882. His connection with the *Tracts for the Times*, and the controversies growing out of them, are detailed under Puseyism (q. v.). Dr. Pusey was a High-churchman of the purest morals and the stanchest orthodoxy, and also a scholar of no ordinary character. Besides his doctrinal writings, he published several exegetical works (on the minor prophets and Daniel), and a number of small volumes on Church-history. See his *Life*, by Bigg (Lond. 1883); *Memorial Sermon*, by Liddon (ibid. 1884).

Puseyites, a term often applied to the High-Church party in the Anglican Church, from their adherence to the views of Dr. Edward Pusey (q. v.), but repudiated both by him and by them.

Pushtu Version of the Scriptures. By way of supplement we add here the following. The first attempt to produce a Pushtu version of Scripture seems to have been made by Dr. Leyden, who in 1811 furnished the corresponding committee of Calcutta with a translation of the gospels of Matthew and Mark. At his death the translation was continued by the Serampore missionaries, with the aid of some learned natives previously in the employ of Dr. Leyden. In 1819 the New Test. was published at Serampore, and in 1832 the Pentateuch and the historical books of the Old Test. were also issued there. Considering the circumstances under which these versions were made, they were very fair productions, in spite of their deficiencies. A need for a new translation was, however, felt more and more, and efforts were made in that direction. Previous to the mutiny in India, the gospel of John, translated by the Rev. R. Clark, and that of Luke, by captain James, had been placed in the hands of the North India Auxiliary Bible Society. But both were destroyed with the press at Agra, in 1857. Copies, however, were soon ready for publication, to which were added the gospels of Matthew and Mark, and the Acts as translated by the Rev. J. Löwenthal (q.v.). In 1864 the entire Pushtu New Test. was printed, the translation having been made by Mr. Löwenthal. He was not allowed to translate the Old Test. into the Pushtu. Before he had fairly entered upon the duty, he was killed, in 1864. The work of translating the Old Test. was taken up by the Rev. T. P. Hughes, of the Church Missionary Society, in 1873. Besides Mr. Hughes, the Rev. T. J. L. Mayer, also of the Church Missionary Society, has been engaged in translating the Old Test., and, assisted by Quazi Abdur Rahman, he translated the Psalms, which were printed in 1881. From the report of the British and Foreign Bible Society for 1885 we learn that considerable progress has been made in translation work, both in the Old and New Tests., and preparations are in progress for a revision of the New Test. The bishop of Lahore has arranged to have meetings of the revision committee in Kohat and at Murri, when it is hoped that the different translations will be harmonized under the guidance of the bishop. (B. P.)

Putnam, Israel Warburton, D.D., a Congregational minister, was born at Danvers, Mass., Nov. 24, 1786. He entered Harvard College in 1805, but left in his sophomore year, and graduated from Dartmouth in 1809. He began the study of law; in 1811 united with the Church in Salem, and not long afterwards began the study of theology, graduating from Andover Theological Seminary in 1814. In October of that year he preached at Brookfield and in various other places, and in January, 1815, accepted a call to the First Church in Portsmouth, N. H. Some time after he engaged in a controversy on Unitarianism with Dr. Nathan Parker, pastor of the South Parish Church in Portsmouth. In October, 1835, he was installed pastor of the Old Pilgrim Church, Middleborough, Mass., and continued in that relation until his death, May 3, 1868. See *Cong. Quarterly*, 1868, p. 317.

Puto (**Pooto, Pouto**, or **Poo-Teon-Shan**) is a small rocky island off the eastern extremity of Chusan, coast of China. It is about seventy miles from the mainland, near Ningpo, in latitude 30° 25′ north, and longitude 122° 40′ east, and is about five miles long and from one to two broad. It is famous in the annals of Chinese Buddhism, as having been devoted to the religious rites and services of that faith for more than a thousand years. It has numerous shrines and temples, and here Chinese Buddhism may be seen in its perfection, its rites being carefully practiced in the great temple.

Pyræum, a fire temple of the ancient Persians. It was simply an enclosure, in the centre of which was placed the sacred fire, and the building was so constructed that the rays of the sun could not fall on this fire. The first pyræum was built by Zoroaster, at Balk, in Persia; and thence the sacred fire was conveyed to other fire-temples both in Persia and India. See PARSEES; ZOROASTER.

Pyre (*πυρά*, from *πῦρ, fire*), the funeral pile of wood on which the ancient Greeks often burned the bodies of their dead. The body was placed upon the top with oils and perfumes, and in the heroic age it was customary to burn animals and even slaves along with the corpse. When the body was consumed and the pyre burned down, the fire was extinguished by throwing wine upon it, and the bones were collected, washed with wine and oil, and placed in urns.

Pyt, HENRI, a Protestant theologian of France, was born April 5, 1796, at Sainte Croix, canton of Vaud, Switzerland. He studied at Geneva, and in 1818 went to Saverdun, France, where he acted as an evangelist. In 1819 he entered the services of the London Continental Society, and was ordained at London in 1821. He was pastor at Bayonne and Béarn, but most of his time he spent in missionary work at Boulogne-sur-Mer, Versailles, and Paris. Pyt died at the latter place, June 24, 1835. Of his literary work we mention the revision of the New Test. into the French Basque, which he undertook at the instance of the British and Foreign Bible Society. See Guers, *Vie de Henri Pyt* (Paris, 1850); A. de Montet, *Dict. Biogr. de Genève et de Vaud*, ii, 344; Lichtenberger, *Encyclop. des Sciences Religieuses*, s. v. (B. P.)

Pythia, the priestess of Apollo at Delphi, who gave forth the oracular responses of the god. At first there was only one Pythia, but afterwards there were always two, who alternately took their seat upon the tripod. See ORACLE.

Pythian Games, one of the four great national festivals of the Greeks. They were celebrated on a plain in the neighborhood of Delphi in honor of Apollo, Artemis, and Leto, and on one occasion they were held at Athens. They are said to have originated in a musical contest, which consisted in singing a hymn in honor of Apollo, with an accompaniment on the cithara. The other exercises customary at the Grecian games were subsequently added. Originally they were celebrated at the end of every eighth year, but in the forty-eighth Olympiad they began to be held at the end of every fourth year, and were regularly observed down to the end of the fourth century. Lesser Pythian games were celebrated in many other places where Apollo was worshipped. See GAMES.

Q.

Quade, MICHAEL FRIEDRICH, a Lutheran theologian of Germany, was born July 28, 1682, at Zachau, Pomerania. He studied at Wittenberg and Greifswalde; was in 1716 rector of the gymnasium at Stettin, and died July 11, 1757. He wrote, *De Dionysio Areopagita Scriptisque eidem Suppositis* (Greifswalde, 1708):—*De Apostasia a Lutheranismo ad Papismum Æternum Exitiosa* (1711):—*De Vita Judæ Apostoli* (eod.):—*De Ritu Veterum Vota Solvendi et Nuncupandi Variisque Votorum Generibus* (1730). See Döring, *Die gelehrten Theologen Deutschlands*, s. v. (B. P.)

Quagutl Version OF THE SCRIPTURES. Quagutl is the vernacular spoken by the Indians of Vancouver's Island. From the report of the British and Foreign Bible Society for 1882 we learn that, at the request of the Church Missionary Society, the gospel of Matthew, translated by the Rev. A. J. Hall, the only European who has studied the Quagutl, has been printed by the British and Foreign Bible Society. The same society also published, in 1884, the gospel of John, prepared likewise by Mr. Hall. (B. P.)

Quarles, FRANCIS, an eminent author and poet, was born at Stewards, near Rumford, Essex, England, in 1592. He was educated at Christ's College, Cambridge, and Lincoln's Inn. He occupied various civil office until the rebellion of 1641 in Ireland, and he died Sept. 8, 1644. Quarles was a man of learning and ability, and the writer of many books in prose and verse, which are admirable for their moral and religious character. The following are a few of his works: *Emblems*, in five books:—*A Feast for Worms, in a Poem on the History of Jonah:—Hadassah, or History of Queen Esther:—The History of Samson:—Job Militant, with Meditations Divine and Moral:—Sion's Sonnets Sung by Solomon the King:—Sion's Elegies Sung by Jeremy the Prophet:—Pantæologia, or the Quintessence of Meditation:—Divine Fancies, Digested into Epigrams, Meditations, and Observations:—Midnight Meditations on Death:—Manual of Devotion:—Hieroglyphics of the Life of Man:—The Enchiridion, containing Institutions Divine and Moral.* See Chalmers, *Biog. Dict.* s. v.; Allibone, *Dict. of Brit. and Amer. Authors*, s. v.

Quetzalcoatl, an idol or god of the Mexicans, particularly worshipped by all persons concerned in traffic. Forty days before the feast of this god, the merchants purchased a well-shaved slave, who during that time represented the deity, spending his time in dancing and rejoicing, and on the day of the festival was sacrificed to the deity at midnight, his heart being first offered to the moon, and then laid before the idol. This deity was worshipped under another name at Cholula, where he was looked upon as the god of the air, the founder of the city, the institutor of penance, and the author of sacrifices. He was represented sitting on a kind of pedestal, habited in a cloak ornamented with red crosses. His devotees drew blood from their tongues and ears to procure his favor; and before going to war sacrificed to him five boys and as many girls of three years of age.

Quichuan Version OF THE SCRIPTURES. Quichua was the predominant language of Peru during the sovereignty of the ancient Incas. It still prevails on the plateau of the Andes, from Quito to Santiago del Estero, and in some districts it is exclusively spoken. Before the year 1880 the Quichuans were entirely without the word of God in their vernacular. At the request of the Rev. F. N. Lett, the British and Foreign Bible Society's agent for Buenos Ayres, the gospel of John was translated by the Rev. J. H. Gibbon-Spilsbury, of the South American Missionary Society, and an edition of one thousand copies was published at the expense of the British and Foreign Bible Society.

This is the first portion of the word of God translated and published in the Quichuan. (B. P.)

Quinby, HOSEA, D.D., a Free-will Baptist minister, was born at Sandwich, N. H., Aug. 25, 1804. He was converted in 1824, and graduated from Waterville College, now Colby University, in 1832. He became principal of the Parsonsfield Seminary, Me., and having been ordained June 2, 1833, preached habitually during his nearly seven years' connection with the institution. He was one of the editors of the *Morning Star*, and began to write a history of the Free Baptist denomination, which was published in part in the *Quarterly Magazine*. For a few years he was pastor and teacher at Meredith village, N. H. Upon the establishment of the Smithville Seminary, afterwards Lapham Institute, in North Scituate, R. I., in 1846, he was appointed its principal, and was very successful in the management of its affairs. Subsequently, as the seminary was greatly embarrassed financially, it was sold to Mr. Quinby, and carried on by him as a private enterprise for several years. For thirty years he did double work as preacher and teacher, and may be said to have been the father of the educational interests of his denomination. In January, 1855, he became, a second time, pastor of the church in Meredith, and resumed his work as a teacher. On Feb. 28, 1857, he entered upon his duties as pastor of the church in Pittsfield, N. H., at the same time having charge of a high-school in the village. His next settlements were at Lebanon, Me., in 1861, and Lake Village, N. H., in 1864. In 1868 he removed to Concord, and devoted himself to literary work, and to his duties as chaplain of the New Hampshire state prison, for several years. His last pastorates were at Nottingham, October, 1872; Pittsfield, January, 1875, and Mellon Mills, in May, 1876, where he died, Oct. 11, 1878. (J. C. S.)

Quinet, EDGAR, a French philosophical writer, was born at Bourg, Bresse, Feb. 17, 1803. He studied at Paris and Heidelberg, was for some time professor at Lyons and Paris, and died at Versailles, March 27, 1875. He published, *De la Grèce Moderne dans ses Rapports avec l'Antiquité* (1830):—*De l'Avenis des Religions*:—*De la Révolution et de la Philosophie*:—*Des la Vie de Jésus par Strauss* (essays written for the *Révue des Deux-Mondes* and *Révue de Paris*. His treatise on the life of Jesus was translated into German by Kleine, 1839):—*Génie des Religions* (1842):—*L'Ultramontanisme ou la Societé Moderne et l'Église* (1843; Germ. transl., Leipsic, 1845):—*Le Christianisme et la Révolution Française* (1846):—*Philosophie de l'Histoire de France* (1855):—*Question Romaine devant l'Histoire* (1867):—*La Création* (1870, 2 vols.). His works were published in 11 vols. (1856-1870). See Chassin, *Edg. Quinet, sa Vie et son Œuvre* (Paris, 1859); Vinet, *Littérature Franç. au Dix-Neuvième Siècle*; Lichtenberger, *Encyclop. des Sciences Religieuses*, s. v. (B. P.)

Quistorp, JOHANN JACOB, a Lutheran theologian of Germany, was born at Rostock, March 19, 1717. He pursued his theological studies at the university of his native place, was in 1743 professor at Kiel, in 1747 court-preacher at Eutin, in 1754 professor at Rostock, and died Dec. 26, 1766. Besides several volumes of sermons, Quistorp published, *De Christo Legem et Prophetas non Solvente, sed Implente* (Rostock, 1759):—*De Sacris Pœnitentiæ Victimis Jansenistarum* (1760):—*De Recentissima Loci de Angelis Bonis ex Theologia Dogmatica Proscriptione Telleriana* (1764). See Döring, *Die gelehrten Theologen Deutschlands*, s. v. (B. P.)

R.

Rabbah (Josh. xv, 60) is conjectured by Lieut. Conder (*Tent Work*, ii, 339) to be the present *Khurbet Rubba*, laid down on the Ordnance *Map* at five miles northeast of Beit-Jibrin, and described in the accompanying *Memoirs* (iii, 360) as consisting of "caves, cisterns, and heaps of stones, ruined walls, bases of pillars and shafts much worn, two lintel stones with crosses, each measuring about seven feet by two and a half feet."

Rabbanism is the name of a school of Jewish doctors in Spain, which flourished for nine generations, covering the period from the beginning of the 11th century to the end of the 15th, after which they succeeded to the *Gaons* (q. v.). The founder of this school was rabbi Samuel Hallevi, surnamed Haragid, or the prince, who lived in 1027. The last of the line was rabbi Isaac Aboab, of Castile, who left that kingdom after the edict of banishment in 1492, and spent the remainder of his life in Portugal. See SCHOOLS, HEBREW.

Rabbath-Ammon. Some additional particulars respecting *Ammân* are given by Merrill, *East of the Jordan*, p. 386 sq.

Rabbith. Tristram (*Bible Places*, p. 237) thinks this may be the modern *Arrabeh*, which, however, does not lie "in the plain" of Esdraelon, but about two miles southwest of Dothan; while Lieut. Conder suggests (*Memoirs* accompanying the Ordnance Survey, ii, 228) *Râba*, a small stone village lying about nine miles southwest of Beisân, and therefore entirely beyond the boundaries of Issachar.

Rabe, JOHANN JACOB, a Lutheran theologian of Germany, was born Jan. 16, 1710, at Lindfluhr, near Würzburg. He studied at Altdorf, was in 1741 deacon at Anspach, in 1764 archdeacon, in 1778 pastor and member of consistory, in 1790 general superintendent. Rabe died Feb. 12, 1798. He is best known by his German translation of the Mishna (Anspach, 1760-63, 6 parts), and by his translation of the treatises Berachoth and Peah, according to the Jerusalem Talmud (1777, 1781). See Fürst, *Bibl. Jud.* iii, 127; Winer, *Handbuch der theol. Lit.* i, 212, 523, 524, 525; Döring, *Die gelehrten Theologen Deutschlands*, s. v. (B. P.)

Racovian Catechism, a Socinian catechism which was published in Poland in the 17th century. It was prepared by Schmalz, a learned German Socinian who had settled in Poland, and by Moskovzewski, a learned and wealthy nobleman. It derived its name from being published at Racow, a little town in southern Poland, the seat of a famous Socinian school. The catechism was published in Polish and Latin, and afterwards translated into German and English. In 1652 the English parliament declared it to contain matters that are blasphemous, erroneous, and scandalous, and ordered "the sheriffs of London and Middlesex to seize all copies wherever they might be found, and cause them to be burned at the Old Exchange, London, and at the New Palace, Westminster." A new English translation was published in 1817 by Abraham Rees, with a historical introduction. There was also a smaller catechism, drawn up by Schmalz in German, and first published in 1605. See CATECHISM; SOCINIANISM.

Radha, in Hindû mythology, was the first wife of the god Krishna. She was afterwards adored as the goddess of love.

Radulfus, a Scotch prelate, was consecrated bishop of the see of Brechin in 1202. He died in 1218. See Keith, *Scottish Bishops*, p. 157.

Radvulf, a Scotch prelate, was ordained bishop of the see of Galloway in 790. See Keith, *Scottish Bishops*, p. 272.

Rae, WILLIAM, a Scotch prelate, was made bishop of Glasgow in 1335, and died in 1367. See Keith, *Scottish Bishops*, p. 244.

Ragnarokr (*Divine twilight*), in Norse mythology, is the final destruction of the world, which threatens the Scandinavian deities, the Asas, their treasures, their creations, and also the earth and its inhabitants. The *Edda* gives the following description of it:

"There will come a winter, called Fimbulweter, in which snow will fall from all sides, with a severe frost and rough winds, whereby the warmth of the sun will be destroyed. Three such winters will succeed each other without a summer intervening. But previous to these there will be three years of bloody war over the whole earth. Brothers will slay each other, and even parents will not spare their children. Then the wolf Skoll will devour the sun, another wolf, Hati, the moon. The stars will disappear from the heavens, the earth will reel, the trees will be torn out by their roots, the mountains fall, and all chains and bands burst asunder. The Fenris-wolf will tear himself loose, the sea boil, because the Midgard-snake will seek the shore. Then also, the ship Naglfar will become loose. It is made out of the nails of human beings. The giant Hrymer is pilot. The wolf Fenris precedes it with open mouth. The Midgard-snake vomits poison, which contaminates the air and the water. In this tumult the heavens will burst, and Muspel's sons come riding, led by Surtur, who is surrounded by fire, and whose sword shines brighter than the sun. When they ride over Bifröst (rainbow bridge) it will collapse. Muspel's sons will come to Fenris and the Midgard-snake. Loke, Hrymer, and all Hrymtusses will join them. Muspel's sons will have their own order of battle. Then Heimdal will blow into the Giallar horn and wake up all the gods. Odin will ride to Mimer's well to get advice for him and his. The ash-tree Ygdrasil will fall, and everything be full of fear in heaven and earth. The Asas will prepare themselves with the Einheriars and proceed to the plain. Before them will ride Odin with a golden helmet, a good armor, and the never-failing spear Gungna. He will battle against Fenris. Thor will fight at his side against the Midgard-snake. Freir will combat against Surtur, and will fall. The cause is the lack of a good sword, which he gave to Skirner. The dog Gramr will tear himself loose, causing much misery. He will combat Tyr, and the two kill each other. Thor will slay the snake, but fall, poisoned by the snake's venom. The wolf will devour Odin, but Vidar will rend open his jaw and pull Odin out. After all this, Surtur will throw fire and burn the whole earth. But then there shall arise out of the sea a beautiful green earth, in which corn will grow. Vidar and Vali will live on the Ida-plain where formerly Asgard lay. There Thor's sons also, Magni and Modi, will appear with the hammer, Miölner. Hödur, Baldur, and Hel will also be there. There will likewise be two human beings, Lif and Lifthrasir, who will become the progenitors of the new race of men."

Rait, John, D.D., a Scotch prelate, was bishop of the see of Aberdeen in 1351. He died in 1355. See Keith, *Scottish Bishops*, p. 111.

Raith, Balthasar, a Lutheran theologian of Germany, was born Oct. 8, 1616. He studied at Tübingen, was there in 1656 professor of theology, and died Dec. 5, 1683, doctor of theology. He wrote, *Quæstionum Anti-Judaicarum Trias de Messia* (Tübingen, 1667):—*Vadum Talmudicum Quoad Priora Capita Testatum* (1658):—*De Proselytismo Judaico-Christiano* (1666). See Fürst, *Bibl. Jud.* s. v.; Jöcher, *Allgemeines Gelehrten-Lexikon*, s. v. (B. P.)

Rajmahali Version of the Scriptures. See Pahari.

Rakkon is thought by Lieut. Conder (*Memoirs* to Ordnance Survey, ii, 263) to be identical with the present *Tell er-Rekkeit*, close to the Aujeh (supposed to represent Mejarkon), and five and a half miles along the shore north of Joppa, where "cisterns and traces of ruins are said to exist under the sand" (ibid. p. 275). Tristram strangely says (*Bible Places*, p. 51), "Mejarkon and Rakkon have recently been identified with *Oyun Kara*, in the plain of Sharon, three miles south-east of Joppa." See Ramath-lehi.

Raleigh, Alexander, D.D., an English Congregational minister, was born at Castle Douglas, Jan. 3, 1817, and removed to Liverpool in his youth. He was educated at the Blackburn Theological Academy, which became, during his course, Lancashire Independent College. In 1844 he went to Greenock as pastor of the Congregational Church, and there labored until compelled by declining health to resign. In 1850 he became pastor at Rotherham, and in 1855 of the Elgin Place Church, Glasgow. In 1859 he accepted an invitation from the Church at Hare Court, for which the new chapel at Canonbury had then just been built. The church was greatly blessed under his labors. From a very small number, it was increased to nearly one thousand members. Other churches were established in the neighborhood, and, for a time, a joint pastorate was arranged with Stamford Hill. His last pastorate was at Kensington, begun in 1875, and continued until his death, April 19, 1880. "The work of Dr. Raleigh was of exceptional quality and power, and entered largely into the religious life of the churches. Few ministries have been more fruitful. His preaching was remarkable for the freshness, vigor, beauty, and felicity of his thought and style, but especially for the unwavering belief and fervid affection with which he held and set forth the great evangelical truths" of the gospel. He published four volumes of sermons, entitled, *Quiet Resting-Places*:—*The Story of Jonah*:—*The Little Sanctuary*:—*The Story of Esther*. His widow has published the posthumous volume, *The Way to the City*. See (Lond.) *Cong. Year-book*, 1881, p. 387.

Ralph of Escures, archbishop of Canterbury, was eminent for his literary attainments and for his surpassing affability. The year of his birth is unknown. He was yet very young when he joined his father at St. Martins and became a monk in 1079. In 1089 he served the offices of sub-prior and prior, and in the same year was elected abbot. He remained abbot of Séez, France, for sixteen years. He became bishop of Rochester in 1108, and was elected to the see of Canterbury April 26, 1114, where he remained until his death, Oct. 20, 1122. See Hook, *Lives of the Archbishops of Canterbury*, ii, 278 sq.

Ralston, James Grier, D.D., LL.D., a Presbyterian minister, was born in Chester County, Pa., Dec. 28, 1815. He graduated from Washington College in 1838, and from Princeton Theological Seminary in 1842, having been licensed meanwhile as a preacher. On account of his weak lungs he was engaged in teaching most of his life, but organized a church at Conshohocken, near Philadelphia, in 1845, and the same year founded the Oakland Female Institute at Norristown, Pa., of which he continued the head, with a period of intermission (1874-77), until his death, Nov. 10, 1880. See *Necrol. Report of Princeton Theol. Sem.* 1881, p. 61; Nevin, *Presb. Encyclop.* s. v.

Ramah of Asher. The Ordnance *Map* exhibits no name corresponding to this in the required locality except *Khurbet Rûmeh*, which lies six miles and a half from the shore, between Ez-Zib (Ecdippa) and Ras en-Nakurah, and is described in the accompanying *Memoirs* (i, 180) as "heaps of scattered stones; a few cisterns."

Ramah of Benjamin. *Er-Ram* lies five miles north of Jerusalem, and is "a small village in a conspicuous position on the top of a high white hill, with olives. It has a well to the south. . . . The houses are of stone, partly built from old materials" (*Memoirs* to Ordnance Survey, iii, 13). The remains in the vicinity are described (ibid. p. 155).

Ramah of Naphtali. *Er-Ramieh* lies seven miles and a quarter south-west of Safed, and is described in the *Memoirs* accompanying the Ordnance Survey (i, 202) as "a small stone village, containing about one hundred and fifty Moslems, situated on a hill-top in a valley, with a few figs, olives, and arable land; the valley to the west turns into a swamp in the winter, owing to its having no drainage; there are cisterns and a large pool for water supply." "There are several large sarcophagi round this village, and one olive-press" (ibid. p. 255). (See illustration on p. 791.)

Ramath-lehi. For this Lieut. Conder suggests (*Tent Work*, i, 277) *Ayûn Kâra*, a name, he says, sometimes given to the springs *Ayun Abu-Meharib*, on the slope of a low hill, seven miles from Beit Atâb, a little way (three miles and a half) north-west of Zoreah; and this he thinks represents the ancient *En hak-Kore*.

Ramath-mizpeh is conjecturally located by Tristram (*Bible Places*, p. 226) at *Tibneh*, a little west of Jebel Ajlûn, the northerly crest of Gilead. "It is the most conspicuous site in the district, a fine natural fortress on an isolated round mamelon-shaped hill, rising above the wide plateau, and commanding a magnificent view of western Palestine." Merrill argues at length (*East of the Jordan*, p. 365 sq.) for its identity with *Kulat er-Rubad*, a few miles south of the above spot.

Ramah of Naphtali. (From Thomson's *Central Palestine and Phœnicia.*)

Ramath-negeb is regarded by Tristram (*Bible Places*, p. 17) as probably the present "*Kurmeh*, south-west of Dhullam, where alone for many miles water is always to be found in plenty, and where the ravine is crossed by a strong dam to retain it. The walls of a fortified town are yet clearly to be traced, with extensive ruins, and it is at the head of the most frequented pass into Palestine from the south-east."

Ramathaim-zophim. Lieut. Conder is inclined (*Tent Work*, ii, 116) to identify this with *Râm Allah*, east of Beth-horon, on the west slope of Mt. Ephraim, overlooking the maritime plain but he admits that the connections are very much disputed.

Rambach, Friedrich Eberhard, a Lutheran theologian of Germany, was born at Pfullendorf, near Gotha, Aug. 24, 1708. He studied at Halle, was in 1730 teacher there, in 1734 deacon, in 1736 preacher at Teupitz, in 1740 deacon at Halle, in 1766 member of the upper consistory at Breslau, and died in 1775. Rambach is best known as translator of the works of Sherlock, Roques, Lenfant, Bentley, Saurin, Chatelain, Serces, Doddridge, Kidder, Stackhouse, Watt, Sarpi, and others. See Döring, *Die gelehrten Theologen Deutschlands*, s. v.; Winer, *Handbuch der theol. Lit.* i, 250, 438, 607, 667, 678, 683; ii, 29; Plitt-Herzog, *Real-Encyklop.* s. v. (B. P.)

Rambach, Johann Jacob, a Lutheran theologian, was born March 7, 1737. He studied at Halle, was in 1760 rector at Magdeburg, in 1765 at Quedlinburg, in 1774 first preacher there, in 1786 pastor at Hamburg, and died Aug. 6, 1818. He wrote, *De Adiaphoris in Utroque Sacramento Obviis* (Halle, 1758):—*De Actionibus Prophetarum Symbolicis* (Magdeburg, 1760), besides a number of sermons. See Döring, *Die deutschen Kanzelredner*, p. 306–315. (B. P.)

Ramoth-Gilead. Dr. Merrill strongly urges the claims of *Jerash* as the site of this place (*East of the Jordan*, p. 284 sq.), but Tristram (*Bible Places*, p. 337) adheres to *es-Salt*.

Ramsay, Edward Bannerman, LL.D., a Scottish clergyman and author, was born at Balmain, Kincardineshire, Jan. 31, 1793, and graduated from St. John's College, Cambridge, in 1815. He took orders in the Church of England, and was a curate in Somersetshire for seven years. In 1830 he became minister of St. John's, Edinburgh, and in 1841 dean of the Reformed Episcopal Church of Scotland. He died at Edinburgh, Dec. 27, 1872. His publications include, a *Manual of Catechetical Instruction* (6th ed. Edinburgh, 1851; 9th ed. 1863):—*Sermons for Advent* (1850):—*Scripture Doctrine of the Eucharist* (1858):—*Reminiscences of Scottish Life and Character* (eod.):—*Diversities of Christian Character Illustrated in the Lives of the Four Great Apostles* (eod.):—*Present State of our Canon Law Considered* (1859):—*Christian Life* (1862):—*Episcopal Church of Scotland* (eod.):—*Two Lectures on Handel* (eod.):—*Christian Responsibility* (1864):—*Thomas Chalmers, D.D.; a Biographical Notice* (1867):—*Pulpit Table-talk* (1868), and other works. See Allibone, *Dict. of Brit. and Amer. Authors*, s. v.

Ramsey, James (1), a Scotch prelate, was rector of Hamilton, and in 1670 was made dean of Glasgow, He was preferred to the see of Dunblane and to the archiepiscopal see of Glasgow. In May, 1684, he was translated from Dunblane to Ross, and here he continued until the abolition of episcopacy in Scotland in 1688. He died at Edinburgh, Oct. 22, 1696. See Keith, *Scottish Bishops*, p. 204.

Ramsey, James (2), D.D., an Associate minister, was born in Lancaster County, Pa., March 22, 1771. It is supposed that he commenced his classical studies under his minister, Dr. Anderson, when twenty-five years of age. He was licensed at Buffalo, N. Y., by the Presbytery of Chartiers, in 1803; ordained and installed pastor of the congregation of Chartiers, Sept. 4, 1805, and in 1821 was chosen professor in the Western Seminary, to which office was added the professorship of Hebrew in Jefferson College. In 1842 he resigned his professorship and continued his duties as pastor. He died March 6, 1855. See Sprague, *Annals of the Amer. Pulpit*, IX, iii, 77.

Ramsey, Peter de, a Scotch prelate, was formerly a monk of Arbroath, but was bishop of Aberdeen in 1250. He died in 1256. See Keith, *Scottish Bishops*, p. 107.

Randall, Benjamin, the founder of the Free-will Baptists, was born in 1749, and converted under the preaching of Whitefield. He joined the Baptists, but in 1779 was silenced for holding Arminian views respecting the atonement and the will. He was nevertheless ordained at Durham, N. H., in 1780, by a party of seceders, and disseminated his opinions so successfully that in 1781 he was joined by a company who, in 1751, had seceded on similar grounds in North Carolina, called "Separate Baptists," and thus the Church now called Free Baptists was formed. Randall died in 1808.

Randall, David Austin, D.D., a Baptist minister, was born at Colchester, Conn., Jan. 14, 1813. He united with the Church in 1827; removed west, and was licensed to preach June 30, 1838; was ordained at Richfield, O., December, 1839, where he was pastor of the Church for five years, during which period he edited a Washingtonian paper, and was an earnest advocate of temperance. He removed to Columbus in 1845, and became one of the editors of the *Journal and Messenger*. From 1850 to 1855 he was pastor of the Church at Columbus, then spent several years abroad, and on his return published a volume entitled *The Handwriting of God in Egypt, Sinai, and the Holy Land*. For six years Dr. Randall was corresponding secretary of the Ohio Baptist Convention. He died at Columbus, July 27, 1884. See Cathcart, *Baptist Encyclop.* p. 955. (J. C. S.)

Randall, George Maxwell, D.D., a Protestant Episcopal minister, was born at Warren, R. I., Nov. 23, 1810. He graduated from Brown University in 1835, and from the General Theological Seminary in New York in 1838. Soon after he became rector of the Church of the Ascension at Fall River, Mass., where he remained six years, and then removed to Boston to take charge of the newly constituted Church of the Messiah, where he continued from 1844 to 1866. During most of this time he was the editor of the *Christian Witness*, the leading organ of the Episcopal Church in New England. He was chosen, in the fall of 1865, missionary bishop of Colorado, Wyoming, and New Mexico, and performed the duties of that office most faithfully for seven years. He died at Denver, Col., Sept. 28, 1873. Bishop Randall published several sermons and tracts.

Randolph, JOHN, D.D., a bishop in the Church of England, was born in 1749. He was the son of Dr. Thomas Randolph, president of Corpus Christi College, Oxford, at which college John was educated. After occupying different academical posts and ecclesiastical preferments, he was, in 1790, raised to the see of Oxford, translated to that of Bangor in 1807, and thence to London in 1811. He performed with zeal and assiduity the duties of his function, and died July 28, 1813. His publications were chiefly occasional sermons and charges, and a Latin prælection on the study of the Greek language. See (Lond.) *Annual Register*, 1813, p. 120.

Ranft, MICHAEL, a Lutheran theologian of Germany, was born Sept. 9, 1700. He studied at Leipsic, was in 1726 assistant preacher to his father at Droysig, in 1729 deacon at Nebra, and succeeded his father in 1743. In 1749 he was preacher at Beerwalde, Altenburg, and died April 18, 1774. He is the author of, *Acta Lipsiensium Academica* (Leipsic, 1723–24, 15 parts):—*Leben und Thaten Pabst Benedict XIV*. (Hamburg, 1743):—*Corpus Doctrinæ Evangelico-Lutheranæ* (Leipsic, 1754-56):—*Commentatio Philologica de Amicis Sponsi ad Joh. iii*, 29 (1758):—*Deutliche Erklärung des ix., x. und xi. Capitels der Epistel Pauli an die Römer* (1760), etc. See Döring, *Die gelehrten Theologen Deutschlands*, s. v.; Winer, *Handbuch der theol. Lit.* i, 694, 857. (B. P.)

Rapheleng, FRANCIS, a famous Dutch Hebraist, was born at Lanoy, near Ryssel, Feb. 27, 1539, and died at Leyden, July 20, 1597, professor. He wrote, *Grammaticæ Hebraicæ Libellus* (printed in the Antwerp Polyglot, 1569–72):—*Compendium Thesauri Santis Pagnini Linguæ Hebraicæ* (1572):—*Variæ Lectiones et Emendationes in Chaldaicam Bibliorum Paraphrasim* (in the Antwerp Polyglot), and published the Syriac New Test. in Hebrew letters (1575). See Fürst, *Bibl. Jud.* iii, 133; Winer, *Handbuch der theol. Lit.* i, 122; Lichtenberger, *Encyclop. des Sciences Religieuses*, s. v. "Ravlenghien." (B. P.)

Rappolt, FRIEDRICH, a Lutheran theologian of Germany, was born Jan. 26, 1615, at Reichenbach, Silesia. He studied at Leipsic, was there professor in 1651, and died Dec. 27, 1676, doctor of theology. He wrote, *Observationes in Epistolas ad Titum et Coloss.:—Theologia Aphoristica Sancti Joannis:—De Inspiratione Divina:—De Peccato Originis:—De Gratia Justificationis ad Mich. vii*, 18–20:—*De Christo Sacerdote Novi Testamenti ad Hebr. ix*, 24–26. J. B. Carpzov published Rappolt's *Scripta Theologica et Exegetica* (1695). See Winer, *Handbuch der theol. Lit.* i, 510; Jöcher, *Allgemeines Gelehrten-Lexikon*, s. v. (B. P.)

Rarotongan Version OF THE SCRIPTURES. By way of supplement, we add that a revised edition of the Rarotongan Bible was printed at London in 1872. The revision was undertaken by the Rev. R. W. E. Krause, who returned to Europe on account of illness. The revisers' chief object was to substitute native words, wherever it was possible, for the foreign words which had been used to a large extent in the version in the first instance. In this labor Mr. Krause was aided by the advice and suggestions of the Rev. G. Gill, who had to complete the latter portion, owing to the alarming and serious illness of the original reviser. From the report of the British and Foreign Bible Society for 1884, we learn that the Rev. W. Wyatt Gill, who has had forty years' experience of the South Sea, is now engaged for the Bible Society Committee on a thorough revision of the Rarotongan Bible, and from the report for 1885 we see that the reviser has reached the close of the New Test. (B. P.)

Rask, ERASMUS, a Danish Orientalist, was born Nov. 22, 1807, and died Nov. 14, 1832, at Copenhagen, professor. He is the author of, *Der aeldeste hebraiske Tidsregning indtil Moses, efter kilderne pa ny bearbejdet og forsynet med et Karl over Paradis* (Copenhagen, 1828; Germ. transl. by Mohnike, Leipsic, 1836):—*Ueber das Alter und die Echtheit der Zend-Sprache* (Germ. transl. by Hagen, Berlin, 1826). See Winer, *Handbuch der theol. Lit.* i, 158, 520; Zuchold, *Bibl. Theol.* s. v.; Fürst, *Bibl. Jud.* s. v. (B. P.)

Rathlef, ERNST LUDWIG, a Lutheran theologian of Germany, was born in 1709, and died April 19, 1768, superintendent at Nienburg, in the county of Hoya. He wrote, *De Simulacro Nebucadnezaris Aureo, ad Dan. iii*, 1 (Helmstadt, 1730):—*De Corpore Mosis ad Epist. Judæ viii* (Hanover, 1733):—*De Maccabæis Sacrorum Antiqui Fœderis Librorum Exulibus* (1739):—*Historia Autographorum Apostolicorum* (1752), etc. See Döring, *Die gelehrten Theologen Deutschlands*, s. v.; Winer, *Handbuch der theol. Lit.* i, 78, 416, 432, 567; Fürst, *Bibl. Jud.* iii, 133 sq. (B. P.)

Ratisbonne, ALFONSO MARIA, head of the Roman

Catholic religious Society of Zion, at Jerusalem, was born at Strasburg, of a respectable Jewish family, his father being the president of the Israelitish Consistory. According to the *Notizia sulla sua Conversione* (Venice, 1842), Ratisbonne owed his conversion to the apparition of the Virgin Mary, which took place at Rome, Jan. 20, 1842, in the Church of San Andrea delle Fratte. He became henceforth the devotee of the Virgin, and desired to bury himself forever in a monastery, and to retain in his own breast the secret of the mysterious vision with which he was favored. But he was led to publish what he had seen, for the good of others, and was for some time subsequently the lion of the day. The general of the Jesuits came to visit him, and he was even presented to the pope. In honor of the auspicious event, a three days' annual festival was appointed to be held in the Church of San Andrea delle Fratte. Ratisbonne died May 6, 1884. (B. P.)

Rattoone, ELIJAH D., D.D., a Protestant Episcopal clergyman, graduated from the College of New Jersey in 1787; was ordained deacon, Jan. 10, 1790; soon after took charge of St. Ann's Church, Brooklyn, N. Y.; in 1792 became professor in Columbia College of Latin and Greek, and in 1794 was made professor of Grecian and Roman antiquities; resigned in 1797 to assume the rectorship of Grace Church, Jamaica, L. I., in which position he remained until April, 1802, when he became associate-rector of St. Paul's Church, Baltimore, Md. A few years after he resigned this charge, and Trinity Church, in the same city, was built for him, where he ministered until the fall of 1809, when he left Baltimore for Charleston, S. C., having been selected president of the Charleston College. His death occurred there in the summer of 1810, of yellow fever. He was an accomplished scholar, and an eloquent preacher. See Sprague, *Annals of the Amer. Pulpit*, v, 265.

Rätze, JOHANN GOTTLIEB, a Lutheran theologian of Germany, who died at Zittau, Sept. 29, 1839, teacher at the gymnasium, was the author of, *Die höchsten Principien der Schrifterklärung* (Leipsic, 1824):—*Betrachtungen über die kantische Religionslehre innerhalb der Grenzen der blossen Vernunft* (Chemnitz, 1794):—*Erläuterung einiger Hauptpunkte in Schleiermacher's Glaubenslehre* (Leipsic, 1823):—*Ansichten von dem Natürlichen und Uebernatürlichen in der christl. Religion* (1803):—*Die Nothwendigkeit den Rationalismus und sein Verhältniss zur christlichen Offenbarung zu prüfen* (Zittau, 1834):—*Das Suchen nach Wahrheit* (1823), etc. See Winer, *Handbuch der theol. Lit.* i, 108, 284, 305, 366, 372, 373, 405, 481, 505; ii, 238; Zuchold, *Bibl. Theol.* s. v. (B. P.)

Rau, SEBALDUS, a Dutch Orientalist, who died in 1810 at Utrecht, professor, was the author of, *Exercitationes Philologicæ ad Hubigantii Prolegomena* (Leyden, 1785):—*Diatribe de Epulo Funebri Gentibus Dando, Ies. xxv,* 6–8 (Utrecht, 1747). See Fürst, *Bibl. Jud.* iii, 134; Winer, *Handbuch der theol. Lit.* i, 94, 218, 227. (B. P.)

Raulston, JOHN, a Scotch prelate, was first rector of Cambuslang and sacrist of Glasgow, next provost of Bothwell, and then dean of Dunkeld. In 1444 he was preferred to be royal secretary, and in 1447 keeper of the privy seal. He was consecrated bishop of the see of Dunkeld, April 4, 1448. In 1449 he was constituted lord high-treasurer. In 1451 he was employed in an embassy to England. He died in 1452. See Keith, *Scottish Bishops*, p. 88.

Rausch, EMIL FRIEDRICH, a Lutheran theologian of Germany, who died Sept. 28, 1884, at Rengshausen, Hesse, was the author of, *Zeugnisse von Christo dem Gekreuzigten* (Cassel, 1837; 2d ed. 1852):—*Christliche Predigten zum Vorlesen in der Kirche, und zur häuslichen Erbauung* (1840):—*Handbuch bei dem Katechismus-Unterricht* (1855):—*Die Herrlichkeit des Herrn* (1866):—*Die ungeänderte augsburger Confession erläutert* (Dresden, 1872). See Winer, *Handbuch der theol. Lit.* ii, 108; Zuchold, *Bibl. Theol.* s. v. (B. P.)

Raymond, JOHN HOWARD, LL.D., an eminent Baptist educator, was born in New York city, March 7, 1814. He entered Columbia College when he was but fourteen years of age, where he remained until nearly the close of the junior year, when he was "suspended," and, as he always admitted, justly. Subsequently he went to Union College, Schenectady, where, in 1832, he graduated with high honors. On leaving college he studied law for two years in New York and New Haven. When he became a Christian, he pursued his theological studies at the Hamilton Theological Seminary, where he graduated in 1838, and was licensed to preach. For ten years (1840–50) he was professor of rhetoric and English literature in Madison University, and filled the same chair in Rochester University from 1851 to 1855, when he was elected president of the Polytechnic Institute of Brooklyn, N. Y., and held that position until his election, in 1864, to the presidency of Vassar College. He died at Poughkeepsie, Aug. 14, 1878. See Dr. Edward Lathrop, in *The Baptist Weekly*, Aug. 22, 1878. (J. C. S.)

Raynald, ODERICH. See RINALD.

Read, THOMAS, D.D., a Presbyterian minister, was born in Maryland in March, 1746. He was educated at the old Academy of Philadelphia; in 1768 received license to preach, and began his ministry at Drawyer's Creek, Del.; in 1772 he was installed as the pastor; and in 1798 accepted a call from the Second Presbyterian Church of Wilmington. He resigned this pastoral charge in 1817, and died July 14, 1823. See Sprague, *Annals of the Amer. Pulpit*, iii, 301.

Reccard, GOTTHELF CHRISTIAN, a Lutheran theologian of Germany, was born at Wernigerode, March 13, 1735, and died at Königsberg, Oct. 3, 1798, doctor and professor of theology. He wrote, *De Neomenia Judæorum Paschali*:—*De Fuga Infantis Jesu in Ægyptum*. See Winer, *Handbuch der theol. Lit.* i, 155; Fürst, *Bibl. Jud.* s. v. (B. P.)

Recchi, IMMANUEL HAYIM, a Jewish author of Ferrara, who died at Leghorn in 1743, is the author of מעשה חושב, a treatise on the structure of the tabernacle, the holy vessels, etc. (Venice, 1716):—חזה ציון, a cabalistic commentary on the Psalms (Leghorn, 1742):—הון עשיר, a commentary on the Mishna (Amsterdam, 1731), etc. See Fürst, *Bibl. Jud.* s. v. (B. P.)

Rechenberg, ADAM, a Lutheran theologian of Germany, was born Sept. 7, 1642, at Leipsdorf, Saxony. He studied at Leipsic, where he began his academical career in 1666. In 1677 he was professor of languages, and in 1678 commenced his theological lectures. In 1699 he was doctor of theology, and died Oct. 22, 1721. He published, *Athenagoræ Apologia pro Christianis* (Leipsic, 1684):—*Athenagoræ Liber de Resurrectione Mortuorum* (eod.):—*Athenagoræ Opera Græce et Latine cum Animadversionibus* (1688):—*Novum Testamentum Græcum cum Præfatione et Libris Parallelis* (1691, 1702, 1709):—*De Justitia Dei Ultrice* (1699):—*Augustini Enchiridion ad Laurentium cum Præfatione de Studio Theologico* (1705):—*Exercitationes in Novum Testamentum, Historiam Ecclesiasticam et Literariam Varii Argumenti* (1707; 2d ed. 1714):—*Hierolexicon Reale, hoc est Biblio-Theologicum et Historico-Ecclesiasticum* (1714):—*De Theologiæ et Philosophiæ Pugna Apparente* (1717). See Winer, *Handbuch der theol. Lit.* i, 321, 446, 533, 884, 903; Döring, *Die gelehrten Theologen Deutschlands*, s. v.; Jöcher, *Allgemeines Gelehrten-Lexikon*, s. v. (B. P.)

Reclam, PETER CHRISTIAN FRIEDRICH, a Protestant theologian, was born at Magdeburg, March 16, 1741. In 1765 he was catechist, and in 1768 preacher of the French congregation at Berlin. He died Jan. 22, 1789. He published, *Mémoires pour Servir à l'Histoire des Refugiés Français dans les États du Roi à Berlin* (1782–94, 8 vols.):—*Mémoire Historique sur la Fondation des Colonies Françaises dans les États du*

Roi (1785):—*Pensées Philosophiques sur la Religion* (eod.):—*Sermons sur Divers Textes de l'Écriture Sainte* (1790, 2 vols.). See Döring, *Die gelehrten Theologen Deutschlands*, s. v. (B. P.)

Rectoral View OF THE ATONEMENT is a phrase expressive of the aspect of the sacrifice of Jesus Christ upon the cross as it bears upon the divine government. While the reconciliation of legal justice with pardoning mercy is indeed thus beautifully exemplified, yet it is a very partial representation of the atonement which would make this the final cause or constraining purpose of it. "That God may be just and yet the justifier of him that believeth on Christ" is truly an important result of the vicarious redemption by the Saviour, but to put it forth as the one grand motive or impulse in the divine mind is to reduce the scheme of salvation to a mere piece of governmental policy, the retrievement of an original blunder, an expedient to remedy a constitutional defect in the divine plan. The atonement would have been equally necessary and equally efficacious had Adam been the sole erring or even the sole intelligent creature in the universe. It was required by the nature of God himself, and is demanded as a full theodicy by the moral sense of the sinner likewise, who is thus "without excuse." Neither the prophylactic nor the curative, the coercive nor the punitive, ends of government are normally involved in it, and except as an exhibition of infinite and sovereign love it is logically abortive. See ATONEMENT, THEORY OF.

Redepenning, ERNST RUDOLF, a Lutheran theologian of Germany, was born at Stettin, May 24, 1810. He studied at Berlin and Bonn, and commenced his academical career at the latter place. In 1836 he was professor there, and in 1839 went to Göttingen, where, in connection with his professorship, he acted as university-preacher. In 1855 he was called as superintendent to Ilfeld, and died March 27, 1883. He is the editor of *Origenis de Principiis* (Leipsic, 1836), and the author of, *Origines. Eine Darstelluug seines Lebens und seiner Lehre* (Bonn, 1841-46, 2 vols.):—*Vorschläge und leitende Gedanken zu einer Kirchenordnung für das protestantische Deutschland* (Göttingen, 1848):—*Umrisse und Bestandtheile einer kirchlichen Lehrordnung* (1849):—*Christliche Wahrheiten für unsere Zeit* (1850). See Zuchold, *Bibl. Theol.* s. v. (B. P.)

Redslob, GUSTAV MORITZ, a Lutheran theologian of Germany, was born May 21, 1804. In 1835 he was professor of philosophy at Leipsic, in 1841 professor of Biblical philology at Hamburg, and died Feb. 28, 1882, doctor of philosophy and theology. He published, *De Particulæ Hebraicæ* כִּי *Origine et Indole* (Leipsic, 1835):—*De Hebræis Obstetricantibus Commentatio* (eod.):—*Die Levirats-Ehe bei den Hebräern* (1836):—*Der Begriff des Nabi bei den Hebräern* (1839):—*Sprachliche Abhandlungen zur Theologie* (1840):—*Die Integrität der Stelle Hosea vii, 4-10 in Frage gestellt* (Hamburg, 1843):—*Die alttestamentlichen Namen der Bevölkerung des wirklichen und idealen Israelitenstaates etymologisch betrachtet* (1846):—*Der Schöpfungs-Apolog Gen. ii, 4-iii, 24 ausführlich erläutert* (eod.), etc. See Fürst, *Bibl. Jud.* s. v.; Zuchold, *Bibl. Theol.* s. v. (B. P.)

Rees, GEORGE, D.D., a Welsh Congregational minister, was born near Brynberian, Pembrokeshire, in 1797, of eminently pious parents. He joined the Church in 1813, and soon began preaching. He received his ministerial education at the Carmarthen Presbyterian College, and, on completing his course, taught and preached for some time in the English portion of Pembrokeshire. Thence he removed to Fishguard, where, with great efficiency, he conducted a grammar-school forty-three years. In 1835 he was ordained pastor at Gideon. His last five years were spent in confinement from paralysis. He died Aug. 31, 1870. Dr. Rees was a thorough Hebrew and Greek scholar. His character was most exemplary. See (Lond.) *Cong. Year-book*, 1871, p. 338.

Reese, DANIEL C., D.D., one of the four brothers who became distinguished ministers in the Methodist Protestant Church, was born at Baltimore, Md., Feb. 17, 1810. He was converted in his fourteenth year, and in 1830 became an itinerant minister in the Maryland Conference of the Methodist Protestant Church, in which he soon took a prominent position. For years he filled the onerous duties of conference steward, was repeatedly elected a representative to the General Conference, and was a member of the convention which met at Montgomery, Ala., in 1867. From 1871 to 1873 he was president of the Maryland Annual Conference, and for forty-four years faithfully served the Church as an itinerant minister. In 1875, on account of feeble health, he was granted a superannuated relation, and died April 23, 1877. See Cobhauer, *Founders of the Meth. Prot. Church*, p. 308.

Reeves, WILLIAMS, D.D., a minister of the Methodist Protestant Church, was born in Kent, England, Dec. 5, 1802. His parents being poor, his early education was limited. He was converted at the age of twenty-three, and united with the Church. Landing in America about the time of the organization of the Methodist Protestant Church, he united with the Ohio Conference at its first session. In 1833, at the formation of the Pittsburgh Conference, he became one of its members, and was frequently its president. At various times he was elected delegate to the general conferences and conventions of the Methodist Protestant Church. He died April 20, 1871. See Cobhauer, *Founders of the Meth. Prot. Church*, p. 437.

Reformers is a term usually applied in a religious sense to those who were most prominent in bringing about the great reformation of the 16th century. The principal of these were Wycliffe, Huss, Luther, Calvin, Zwingli, Melanchthon, Œcolampadius, Bucer, Beza, Cranmer, Latimer, Ridley, and John Knox. There are also many others who are fairly entitled to be called reformers.

Regalia Petri (*the royalties of Peter*) are regarded by Roman Catholics as belonging to the pope in his capacity of sovereign monarch of the universal Church. This claim to royal prerogative is founded on canon law, and has been asserted by the popes with more or less stringency since the 7th century. Among these claims are the following: "To be superior to the whole Church, and to its representative, a general council; to call general councils at his pleasure, all bishops being obliged to attend his summons; to preside in general synods, so as to propose matter for discussion; to promote, obstruct, or overrule the debates; to confirm or invalidate their decisions; to define points of doctrine; to decide controversies authoritatively, so that none may contest or dissent from his judgment; to enact, establish, abrogate, suspend, or dispense with ecclesiastical laws and canons; to relax or do away with ecclesiastical censures by indulgences, pardons, etc.; to dispense with the obligations of promises, vows, oaths, legal obligations, etc.; to be the fountain of all pastoral jurisdiction and dignity; to constitute, confirm, judge, censure, suspend, depose, remove, restore, and reconcile bishops; to exempt colleges and monasteries from the jurisdiction of their bishops and ordinary superiors; to judge all persons in spiritual causes by calling them to his presence, delegating judges, and reserving to himself a final, irrevocable judgment; to receive appeals from all ecclesiastical judicatories, and reverse or confirm their sentences; to be accountable to no one for his acts; to erect, transfer, and abolish episcopal sees; to exact oaths of obedience from the clergy; to found religious orders; to summon and commission soldiers by crusade to fight against infidels or persecute heretics."

Reginald (1), a Scotch prelate, was a Norwegian, and bishop of the Isles about 1181. See Keith, *Scottish Bishops*, p. 298.

Reginald (2), a Scotch prelate, was consecrated bishop of the Isles in 1217. He died about 1225. See Keith, *Scottish Bishops*, p. 299.

Regino, born at Altrip on the Rhine, near Spires, was a monk in the monastery of Prüm, and elected abbot there in 892. In 899 he resigned his position and went to Treves, where archbishop Ratbod made him head of the monastery of St. Martin. Regino died in 915. He is the author of, *Libri duo de Ecclesiasticis Disciplinis et Religione Christiana* (best edition by Wasserschleben, Leipsic, 1840) :—*De Harmonica Institutione* (printed in Coussemaker's *Scriptores de Musica Medii Ævi*, Paris, 1867, ii, 1-73). But his greatest work is the *Chronicon*, the first world's history written in Germany, comprising the time from the birth of Christ to the year 906. The best edition of the *Chronicon* is found in *Monumenta Sacra*, i, 536-612 (Germ. transl. by Dümmler, in *Geschichtschreiber der deutschen Vorzeit*, Berlin, 1857, vol. xiv, part 30). See Wattenbach, *Deutsche Geschichtsquellen* (4th ed. Berlin, 1877), i, 211-214, 297 sq.; Ermisch, *Die Chronik des Regino bis* 813 (Göttingen, 1872); Plitt-Herzog, *Real-Encyclop.* s. v. (B. P.)

Régis, Jean François, a French Jesuit, was born Jan. 31, 1597, at Font-Couverte, Narbonne. In 1616 he joined his order, and intended to go as missionary to Canada. Being, however, denied this by his superiors, he devoted himself entirely to missionary work at home and in churches, chapels, hospitals, prisons, and, in fact, everywhere he preached and exhorted. Régis died Jan. 31, 1640, and was canonized by Clement XII, June 16, 1737. See Daubenton, *Vie de François Régis;* Petit-Didier, *Les Saints Enlevés et Restitués aux Jésuites;* Monlezun, *Histoire de l'Église de Notre-Dame du Puy* (1854); Lichtenberger, *Encyclop. des Sciences Religieuses*, s. v. (B. P.)

Rehhoff, Johann Andreas, a Lutheran theologian of Germany, was born at Tondern, Aug. 24, 1809. He studied at Kiel and Berlin, was for some time archdeacon at his native place, and in 1837 provost and first pastor at Apenrade. In 1851 Rehhoff was called to Hamburg as pastor primarius of St. Michael. In 1870 he was senior of the Hamburg ministerium, resigned in 1879 his pastorate, and died at Kiel, Jan. 9, 1883. Rehhoff published some homiletical works, for which see Zuchold, *Bibl. Theol.* s. v.; also *Zum Gedächtniss an Dr. Johann A. Rehhoff* (Hamburg, 1883). (B. P.)

Rehkopf, Johann Friedrich, a Lutheran theologian of Germany, was born at Leipsic, Jan. 20, 1733. He studied at the university of his native place, was in 1761 deacon at Zwickau, in 1764 archdeacon at Reichenbach, in 1769 doctor and professor of theology at Helmstadt, in 1778 superintendent at Dresden, and died March 15, 1789. He published, *Vitæ Patriarcharum Alexandrinorum* (Leipsic, 1757-59) :—*De Zwickaviensibus Litterarum Orientalium Studio Claris* (1763) :—*Janua Hebrææ Linguæ Veteris Testamenti Olim Adornata a Reineccio* (1769) :—*De Trinitate* (1770) :—*Michæ et Mathæi in Loco Natali Messiæ Consensus* (1772) :—*De Vate Scripturæ Sacræ* (eod.) :—*Legatus Fecialis ad Malach. iii* (1773) :—*De Persona Jesu Christi Scripturarum Novi Testamenti Expositio* (1775), etc. See Döring, *Die gelehrten Theologen Deutschlands*, s. v. (B. P.)

Reichel, Gustav Theodor, a Moravian minister, was born Dec. 15, 1808, at Berthelsdorf, Saxony. In 1852 he was made a presbyter, and labored for some years at Sarepta, when, in 1857, he was made a member of the executive board of the Unitas Fratrum. For nearly twenty-four years he devoted his entire energy to the service of his Church, and his rich experience was of great value to the executive board, whose president he died, Jan. 28, 1882, at Herrnhut. (B. P.)

Reichhelm, Carl August Wilhelm, a Reformed theologian of Germany, was born Jan. 20, 1817, at Bromberg, and studied at Berlin, where he was assistant preacher at the cathedral for some time. In 1842 he was appointed military preacher at Frankfort-on-the-Oder, in 1849 superintendent at Belzig, in 1853 first preacher of the Reformed Church at Frankfort, and died Dec. 6, 1879, member of consistory. He published, *Sinai, Predigten über das Gesetz* (Belzig, 1855) :—*Christus, die rechte Speise und der rechte Frank* (Frankfurt, 1857), sermons on the fourth and fifth chapters of John. See Zuchold, *Bibl. Theol.* s. v. (B. P.)

Reichlin-Meldegg, Carl Alexander von, a Protestant theologian of Germany, was born of Catholic parentage, at Gravenau, Bavaria, Feb. 21, 1804. For some time professor at the gymnasium, and afterwards of the University of Freiburg, he joined the evangelical Church, Feb. 19, 1832, was in 1840 appointed professor at Heidelberg, and died in 1857. He was the author of, *Die Theologie des Magier Manes*, etc. (Frankfort, 1825) :—*Geschichte des Christenthums*, incomplete (Freiburg, 1831) :—*Die mosaische Geschichte vom brennenden Dornbusche* (*Exod. iii.* 1-4) *erklärt* (1831) :—*Heinrich E. G. Paulus und seine Zeit* (Stuttgart, 1853, 2 vols.), the best biography of the famous Heidelberg rationalist. See Zuchold, *Bibl. Theol.* s. v.; Winer, *Handbuch der theol. Lit.* i, 119, 543, 642. (B. P.)

Reid, James Seaton, D.D., an eminent minister of the Presbyterian Church in Ireland, was a native of Lurgan, and the twenty-first child of his parents. He was ordained minister of Donegon, July 20, 1819, from which place he removed to Carrickfergus in 1823. In 1827 he was unanimously chosen moderator of the Synod of Ulster, and in 1830 was appointed its clerk. In 1838 he was chosen professor of ecclesiastical history of the Belfast Institution. In April, 1841, he was nominated for the chair of ecclesiastical and civil history in the University of Glasgow, by the crown, which position he held until his death, March 26, 1851, in the fifty-third year of his age. He is the author of *History of the Presbyterian Church in Ireland* (3 vols. 8vo). Dr. Reid spent about twenty years in collecting materials for the work, and putting it into print. The first two volumes were published during his life. At his death he left, in MS., about seven chapters of the third volume. Dr. W. D. Killen was chosen to finish the work, which he did, and published the third and last volume in 1853. This work is a monument of historical research, and is valued not only for its ecclesiastical history, but also for reclaiming many civil facts which would otherwise have been lost.

Reid, Numa Fletcher, D.D., a minister in the Methodist Episcopal Church South, son of Rev. James Reid, was born in Rockingham County, N. C., July 3, 1825. He was a boy of remarkable and unyielding integrity and filial affection; was educated at Emory and Henry College; began school-teaching in his eighteenth year at Thompsonville; in 1846 opened an academy at Wentworth, where he labored with great success for five years. He was licensed to preach in 1847, and travelled Wentworth Circuit two years as supply, and in 1851 entered the North Carolina Conference. His fields of labor were: 1852-53, Tar River Circuit; 1854, Front Street, Wilmington; 1855-56, Raleigh Station; 1857, Greensboro' Station; 1858-59, presiding elder of Salisbury District; 1860-63, of Greensboro' District; 1864-67, of Raleigh District; 1868-71, of Greensboro' District; and in 1872 was again sent to Raleigh District, but ill-health led him to exchange for work or Greensboro' District, where he died, June 14, 1873. Dr. Reid was four times elected to the General Conference, and three times headed the list of delegates. In all the relations of life he was a model man. He was learned, logical, solicitous, and eminently successful. See *Minutes of Annual Conferences of the M. E. Church South*, 1873, p. 805.

Reid, Robert, a Scotch prelate, was born at Aikenhead, and was educated at St. Salvator's College. He was first sub-dean, in 1526 was nominated abbot of Kinloss, and in 1540 was made bishop of Orkney. He died at Dieppe, Sept. 14, 1558. See Keith, *Scottish Bishops*, p. 223.

Reihing, JACOB, a Roman Catholic divine of Germany, was born in 1579 at Augsburg. He joined the Jesuits at Ingolstadt, taught theology and philosophy there and at Dillingen, and was in 1613 appointed court-preacher to the apostate count-palatine, Wolfgang Wilhelm. In 1615 Reihing published at Cologne, *Muri Civitatis Sanctæ*, etc., a kind of apology for his master's apostasy, which elicited rejoinders from the Lutheran theologians Balthasar Meisner and Matthias Hoë von Hoënegg, and from the Reformed theologian Bassecourt. Reihing, not satisfied with this apology, commenced to Romanize the Palatinate. But the careful study of the Bible, which he found necessary in order to dispute with the Protestants, had its influence. In the beginning of the year 1621 Reihing suddenly fled to Stuttgard, and joined the Evangelical Church Nov. 23 of the same year. In 1622 he was made professor of theology at Tübingen, and died May 5, 1628. His writings are mostly polemical. See Oehler, in Mariott's *Wahren Protestanten*, vol. iii, 1854; Plitt-Herzog, *Real-Encyklop*. s. v. (B. P.)

Reimann, JACOB FRIEDRICH, a Lutheran theologian of Germany, was born Jan. 22, 1668. He studied at different universities, was in 1692 rector at Osterwick, in 1693 at Halberstadt. In 1704 he was appointed pastor primarius at Ermsleben, in the principality of Halberstadt, in 1714 cathedral preacher at Magdeburg, in 1717 superintendent at Hildesheim, and died Feb. 1, 1743. Reimann was a voluminous writer. See Jöcher, *Allgemeines Gelehrten-Lexikon*, s. v.; Fürst, *Bibl. Jud*. s. v. (B. P.)

Reinaldus, a Scotch prelate, was a monk of Melrose when he was made bishop of the see of Ross in 1195. He died in 1213. See Keith, *Scottish Bishops*, p. 185.

Reindl, GEORG KARL VON, a Roman Catholic theologian of Germany, was born at Bamberg, Nov. 3, 1803. For some time tutor of the Bavarian royal family, he was in 1847 appointed dean of the chapter of the episcopal diocese München-Freising, and died at Munich, Dec. 23, 1882. He wrote, *Die Sendung des Propheten Jonas nach Niniveh* (Bamberg, 1826):—*Abriss der christlichen Kirchengeschichte für Katholiken* (1834):—*Tempel der häuslichen Andacht* (Ratisbon, 1841). (B. P.)

Reineccius, JACOB, a Lutheran theologian of Germany, was born at Salzwedel in 1571. He studied at Wittenberg, was for some time pastor at Tangermünde, and in 1601 provost at Berlin. In 1609 he was called to Hamburg, and in 1611 was appointed inspector of the newly-founded gymnasium. Reineccius died in June, 1613. He wrote, *Panoplia sive Armatura Theologica* (Wittenberg, 1609):—*Artificium Disputandi* (eod.) —*Clavis Sanctæ Theologiæ* (Hamburg, 1611, 2 vols.):—*Veteris ac Novi Testamenti Convenientia et Differentia* (1612):—*Calvinianorum Ortus, Cursus et Exitus* (eod.). See Plitt-Herzog, *Real-Encyklop*, s. v. (B. P.)

Reinerding, FRANZ HEINRICH, a Roman Catholic theologian of Germany, was born Sept. 16, 1814, at Damme, Oldenburg. He studied at Münster and at the "Collegium Romanum" in Rome. In 1838 he was a doctor of philosophy, in 1840 he received holy orders, and in 1842 took the degree of a doctor of theology. For some time professor at the gymnasium in Vechta, Oldenburg, Reinerding was in 1851 professor at Fulda, in 1858 at St. Cuthbert's College in Esh, England, in 1863 again at Fulda, and died Feb. 25, 1880. He published, *Der Papst und die Bibel* (Münster, 1855):—*Die Principien des kirchlichen Rechtes in Aufhebung der Mischehen* (1853):—*Clemens XIV. und die Aufhebung der Gesellschaft Jesu* (Augsburg, 1854):—*Der heilige Bonifacius als Apostel der Deutschen* (1855):—*Theologiæ Fundamentalis Tractatus Duo* (Münster, 1864):—*Beiträge zur Liberius- und Honoriusfrage* (1865):—*Gedanken über die philosophischen Studien* (Vienna, 1866). (B. P.)

Reinhard, MICHAEL HEINRICH, a Lutheran theologian of Germany, was born Oct. 18, 1676. He studied at Wittenberg, was in 1699 con-rector at Meissen, in 1700 rector at Hildburghausen, in 1713 preacher at Pretsch, in 1721 superintendent at Sondershausen, in 1730 court-preacher at Weissenfels, and died Jan. 1, 1732. He published, *De Confessione Tripolitana* (Wittenberg, 1694):—*De Cibis Hebræorum Prohibitis* (1697):—*De Sepultura Animalium Hebræis Usitata* (eod.):—*Elementa Linguæ Hebrææ* (2d ed. Hildburghausen, 1719):—*De Sacco et Cinere ex Antiquitate Hebræa* (1698):—*'Οργανοφαλάκιον Musicum Codicis Hebræi* (eod.):—*Pentas Conatuum Sacrorum* (1709):—*De Variantibus Novi Testamenti Lectionibus a Millio Aliisque Collectis ad Matth. i* (1711):—*De Liturgia Ecclesiæ Evangelicæ*, etc. (1721). See Fürst, *Bibl. Jud*. s. v.; Winer, *Handbuch der theol. Lit*. i, 8, 332; Döring, *Die gelehrten Theologen Deutschlands*, s. v.; Jöcher, *Allgemeines Gelehrten-Lexikon*, s. v. (B. P.)

Reinke, LAURENTIUS, a Roman Catholic theologian of Germany, was born Feb. 6, 1797, at Langförden, Oldenburg. He studied at Münster and Bonn, took holy orders in 1822, and commenced his academical career at Münster in 1827. In 1831 he was professor, in 1834 doctor of theology, and in 1847 of philosophy, the latter degree being conferred on him "honoris causa." In 1852 Reinke was made capitular, in 1862 honorary member of the "Société littéraire" of the Louvain University, in 1865 honorary member of the college of doctors of the Vienna theological faculty, and in 1866 "consultor congregationis de propaganda fide pro negotiis ritus orientalis." Reinke died June 4, 1879. He wrote, *Exegesis Critica in Iesaiæ cap. lii*, 13–*liii*, 12 (Münster, 1836):—*Exegesis Critica in Iesaiæ cap. ii*, 2-4 (1838):—*Die Weissagung von der Jungfrau und vom Immanuel* (1848):—*Ueber das zukünftige glückliche Loos des Stammes Juda* (1849):—*Beiträge zur Erklärung des alten Testaments* (1851–72, 8 vols.):—*Der Prophet Malachi* (Giessen, 1856):—*Die messianischen Psalmen* (1857–58, 2 vols.):—*Kurze Zusammenstellung aller Abweichungen vom hebr. Text in der Psalmenübersetzung der LXX. und Vulgata*, etc. (1858):—*Die messianischen Weissagungen bei den grossen und kleinen Propheten des Alten Testaments* (1859–62, 4 vols.):—*Zur Kritik der älteren Versionen des Propheten Nahum* (Münster, 1867):—*Der Prophet Haggai* (1868):—*Der Prophet Zephanja* (eod.):—*Der Prophet Habakuk* (1870):—*Der Prophet Micha* (1874). (B. P.)

Reinmund, J. F., D.D., a Lutheran minister, spent his boyhood and early manhood in Lancaster, O., to which place he removed with his parents when thirteen years of age. His education, classical and theological, was secured at Wittenberg College. Findlay was the scene of his first pastoral labor. From Findlay he went to Lancaster, from which, after a successful pastorate, he removed, in 1868, to Springfield, where he was employed as superintendent of public schools. In 1873 he received and accepted a call to Lebanon, Pa. Dr. Reinmund was a member of the committee of the General Synod that revised the *Hymn and Tune Book*. In the hope of restoring his failing health he went to Jacksonville, Fla., but never returned. He died April 26, 1880. See *Lutheran Observer*, May 7, 1880.

Rekem is thought by Tristram (*Bible Places*, p. 122) to be the present village of *Ain Karim*, about four miles west of Jerusalem.

Remeth is regarded by Tristram and Conder as the present *er-Rameh*, five and a half miles north-west of Sebustieh, "a conspicuous village on a hilly knoll above the small plain, with a high central house. It is of moderate size, with olives below. The sides of the hill are steep" (*Memoirs* to the Ordnance Survey, ii, 154).

Remonstrance, ARMINIAN. This is a document drawn up by Uytenbogaert, and presented, in 1610, to the states of Holland, against the decrees of the Synod of Dort. It specifies the five Calvinistic points of doctrine, and then in five articles states the Arminian positions. On this account it gives rise to what is known as the QUINQUARTICULAR CONTROVERSY (q. v.). The Calvinistic party afterwards presented a *Counter-Remonstrance*. See Schaff, *Creeds of Christendom*, iii, 545.

Rémusat, CHARLES DE, a French statesman and philosopher, was born at Paris in 1797, and died June 6, 1875. Besides *Essais de Philosophie* (Paris, 1834, 2 vols.) and *Philosophie Religieuse* (1864), he wrote biographies of Abelard (1845), Anselm of Canterbury (1853; Germ. transl. by Wurzbach, Ratisbon, 1854), and Bacon (1858). (B. P.)

Remy, FRANZ, a Protestant theologian of Germany, who died at Berlin, May 3, 1882, was a follower of Schleiermacher, and published *Hausandachten aus Schleiermacher's Predigten in täglichen Betrachtungen* (Berlin, 1861–62, 2 vols.). See Zuchold, *Bibl. Theol.* s. v. (B. P.)

Renegger, MICHAEL. See RENNIGER.

Reni, GUIDO, an eminent Italian painter, was born at Bologna in 1575, and first studied under Denys Calvert; afterwards entered the school of the Caracci, and was a brilliant pupil. He soon acquired distinction, and early executed some fine works, particularly his picture of *St. Benedict in the Desert*, for the cloister of San Michele, in Bosco. He afterwards went to Rome, and executed the *Martyrdom of St. Cecilia*, for the church of that saint, and the *Crucifixion of St. Peter* also. He now rose rapidly in public estimation. His most celebrated works in the palaces at Rome are his *Magdalen*, in the Barberini collection, and his fresco of *Aurora*. The paintings of Guido are numerous, and are to be found in all the principal collections in Italy and throughout Europe. He ruined himself by gambling, and died at Bologna, Aug. 18, 1642. To form a fair estimate of his powers, we are to judge by his best pictures, such as *The Magdalen*, at Rome; *The Miracle of the Manna*, at Ravenna; *The Conception*, at Forli; *The Murder of the Innocents*, and *The Repentance of St. Peter*, at Bologna; *The Purification*, at Modena; and *The Assumption*, at Genoa, with many other works at Rome, Bologna, and elsewhere. See Spooner, *Biog. Hist. of the Fine Arts*, s. v.

Rennecke, CHRISTOPH HULDREICH, a Lutheran theologian of Germany, was born in 1797. From 1825 to 1831 he acted as tutor of the duchess Helena of Mecklenburg, afterwards duchess of Orleans. From 1831 to 1871 he was pastor at Dargun, in Mecklenburg, when he retired from the ministry and lived as a patriarch among his people. He died April 27, 1881, at Rostock. Rennecke was a brother-in-law of the well-known professor of Halle, Dr. A. Tholuck, with whom he corresponded on the most important topics of the time. He wrote, *Die Lehre vom Amt der Schlüssel* (Malchin, 1845):—*Begründung der Lehren von der Sünde, von der Person Christi* (Magdeburg, 1848):—*Die Lehre vom Staate*, etc. (Leipsic, 1850). See Zuchold, *Bibl. Theol.* s. v. (B. P.)

Resurrection, THE FIRST, is a phrase occurring in Rev. xx, 4–6:

> "And I saw thrones, and they sat upon them, and judgment was given unto them: and *I saw* the souls of them that were beheaded for the witness of Jesus, and for the word of God, and which had not worshipped the beast, neither his image, neither had received *his* mark upon their foreheads, or in their hands; and they lived and reigned with Christ a thousand years. But the rest of the dead lived not again until the thousand years were finished. This *is* the first resurrection. Blessed and holy *is* he that hath part in the first resurrection: on such the second death hath no power, but they shall be priests of God and of Christ, and shall reign with him a thousand years."

Interpreters have been divided as to the distinction in time here denoted by the two successive resurrections. It was the general opinion of the early Christians (but not universal; see Hengstenberg, *Apocalyp.* ii, 348 note, Carter's ed.) that the thousand years were to be computed from the birth of Christ; and coupled with this reckoning was often expressed a belief in the literal resurrection of saints at that time, prior to the general resurrection; but it is hardly a fair statement that "those who lived next to the apostles and the whole church for three hundred years, understood these words in their literal sense" (Alford, *Comment.* ad loc.). Bishop Wordsworth affirms (*Greek Test. with Notes*, ad loc.) that the spiritual interpretation "is that which has been adopted by the best expositors of the Western and Eastern churches from the days of St. Augustine to those of bishop Andrews." A glance at the conspectus given in such works as Poole's *Synopsis Criticorum*, and Wolff's *Curæ in N. T.*, at this place, will suffice to show the great discrepancy in the earlier interpreters on the subject, and that in Ellicott's *Horæ Apocalypticæ*, ad loc., displays an equal divergence in modern times. Those who hold the literal view maintain (1) that this is the only plain meaning of the text, and (2) that it is sustained by several other passages which speak of a distinction of the righteous as raised first (especially 1 Thess. iv, 16). But these latter passages do not require, nor even admit, so long an interval between the resurrection of the saints and that of others, which, moreover, are elsewhere represented as substantially simultaneous (John v, 28, 29; Rev. xx, 12); indeed, Scripture everywhere (unless in the passage in dispute) knows of but one future advent of our Lord, and that the final and universal one, at least after the figurative one at the destruction of Jerusalem. See ESCHATOLOGY. Moreover, such a temporal and earthly reign of Christ as the literalists here require, is at variance with the whole spirit and economy of the Gospel; and we may add that the anticipations which such a theory engenders have been the bane of Chiliasm (q. v.), and the fosterer of fanaticism in all ages. See MILLENARIANS. Finally and conclusively, the passage in dispute itself explicitly limits the resurrection in this case to the "souls" of the *martyrs* (not all saints), apparently meaning a revival of their devoted spirit, or, at most, their glorification (as in the case of the "two witnesses," Rev. xi, 11, 12); and not a word is said about a *terrestrial* reign, but only one "with Christ," i. e. in the celestial or spiritual sphere. The modern literature of the discussion is very copious, but quite sporadic, and no complete treatise has yet appeared on the subject. The best is that by David Brown, D.D., *Christ's Second Coming* (Lond. 1846, 1847, 1856).

Rettig, HEINRICH CHRISTIAN MICHAEL, a Protestant theologian of Germany, was born at Giessen in 1795, where, after completing his studies, he also established himself as academical teacher. In 1832 he published *Die freie protestantische Kirche oder die kirchlichen Verfassungsgrundsätze des Evangeliums*, in which he advocates separation of State and Church. In 1833 he was called to Zurich as professor of theology, and died March 24, 1836. Of his works we also mention, *Ueber das Zeugniss Justins über die Apokalypse* (Leipsic, 1829):—*Quæstiones Philippenses* (Giessen, 1831). See Zuchold, *Bibl. Theol.* s. v.; Plitt-Herzog, *Real-Encyklop.* s. v.; Winer, *Handbuch der theol. Lit.* i, 92, 263, 555; ii, 18. (B. P.)

Reuchlin, a name common to several Lutheran theologians, of whom we here mention the following:

1. CHRISTOPH, the teacher of the famous Bengel, born in 1660, studied at Tübingen and Wittenberg, and died at the former place, June 11, 1707, doctor and professor of theology. He wrote, *De Artificio Jacobi Magico*, etc.:—*De Diluvio Mosaico*, etc.:—*De Nova Creatione Ephes. ii*, 10:—*De Evangelio ad Rom. i*, 16, 17:—*De Credendis e Scripturæ Sacra Dictis Exegesi Theologica Demonstratis*:—*De Dubitatione Cartesiana*:—*De Arianismo*, etc. See Jöcher, *Allgemeines Gelehrten-Lexikon*, s. v.

2. FRIEDRICH JACOB, born at Gerstheim, near Strasburg, in 1695, and died at the latter place, June 3, 1788, doctor and professor of theology, is the author of *De Doctrina Cypriana* (1751-56, 3 parts). See Winer, *Handbuch der theol. Lit.* i, 906.

3. HERMANN, who died at Stuttgard in 1873, doctor of philosophy, wrote, *Das Christenthum in Frankreich innerhalb und ausserhalb der Kirche* (Hamburg, 1837): —*Geschichte von Port-Royal*, etc. (1839, 2 vols.):—*Pascal's Leben*, etc. (Stuttgard, 1840). See Zuchold, *Bibl. Theol.* s. v. (B. P.)

Reuden, AMBROSIUS, a Lutheran theologian of Germany, was born Feb. 1, 1543, studied at Leipsic and Jena, and died at the latter place, June 1, 1615. He wrote, *Compendium Grammaticæ Ebraicæ* (Wittenberg, 1586):—*Isagoge Grammatica in Linguam Hebraicam* (1604):—*Isagoge Biblica* (Hamburg, 1602):—*Œconomia Veteris et Novi Testamenti, Ostendens quid ibi Observandum sit* (Leipsic, 1603), etc. See Jöcher, *Allgemeines Gelehrten-Lexikon*, s. v.; Fürst, *Bibl. Jud.* s. v. (B. P.)

Reuss, JEREMIAS FRIEDRICH, a Lutheran theologian of Germany, was born Dec. 2, 1700. He studied at Tübingen, travelled extensively, was in 1731 appointed court-preacher and professor at Copenhagen, in 1742 doctor of theology, in 1749 general superintendent of Schleswig and Holstein, in 1757 professor at Tübingen, and died March 6, 1777. He published, *De Usu Experientiæ Spiritualis in Scripturarum Interpretatione* (2d ed. Leipsic, 1735):—*Meletema de Sensu Septem Parabolarum Matth. xiii Prophetico* (1733):—*Meletema de Spiritus Sancti Testimonio* (1734):—*Diss. qua Illustre Oraculum Zachar. vi*, 12, 13 *Explanatur* (1758):—*De Auctore Apocalypseos* (1767), etc. See Döring, *Die gelehrten Theologen Deutschlands*, s. v.; Fürst, *Bibl. Jud.* s. v. (B. P.)

Reuter, Christian, a Lutheran theologian of Germany, was born at Schlawe, Pomerania, June 17, 1675. He studied at Wittenberg, in 1702 was deacon there, in 1708 pastor at Zerbst, in 1711 doctor of theology, and died April 6, 1744. He published, *De Libanio, Nobile Græcorum Rhetore* (Wittenberg, 1699):—*De Cultu Dei Adversus Hobbesium, Cherburg et Spinozam* (1702):—*De Macario Ægyptio* (1703):—*De Fœderibus et Testamentis* (1706):—*De Precibus Beatorum in Cœlis pro Hominibus in Terris* (1714):—*De Lege Morali non Abrogata ex Joh. i*, 18 (eod.):—*Δικαίωμα τοῦ νόμου ex Rom. viii* (1716):—*Typus Doctrinæ et Theologiæ Moralis* (1718):—*Electa Theologica* (1720). See Döring, *Die gelehrten Theologen Deutschlands*, s. v. (B. P.)

Reuter, Quirinus, a German scholar, pupil and successor of Zach. Ursinus, was born at Mosbach, Sept. 27, 1558. He studied at Heidelberg. In 1578 he went to Neustadt, where his former teachers lectured at the newly-founded academy. In 1580 Reuter went to Breslau as private tutor, but returned to Neustadt in 1583. In 1590 he was again at Heidelberg, became in 1601 doctor of theology, in 1602 professor of Old Test. theology, and died March 22, 1613. Of his writings we mention, *Censura Catecheseos Heidelbergensis*:—*Diatriba de Ubiquitate*:—*Tractatus de Ecclesia*:—*Aphorismi Theologici de Vera Religione*:—*Dissertatio de δικαιώματι Legis in Christo et Christianis ad Rom. viii*:—*Commentarius in Obadiam Prophetam una cum Illustriorum Quorundam de Messiæ Persona et Officio Vaticiniorum Explicatione*, etc. See Freher, *Theatrum Vivorum Clariss.*; Jöcher, *Allgemeines Gelehrten-Lexikon*, s. v.; Iselin, *Historisches Universal-Lexikon*, s. v.; Plitt-Herzog, *Real-Encyklop.* s. v. (B. P.)

Révész, EMERII, a Reformed theologian of Hungary, was born in 1826. He studied at Debreczin and Buda, and after spending some time for literary purposes in Belgium, Holland, Switzerland, and Germany, became pastor of two country congregations in succession, but was removed in 1856 to Debreczin, where he labored until his death, Feb. 13, 1881. His learning and character made him the leader in the Reformed Church of Hungary. When, on Sept. 1, 1859, the emperor of Austria issued the famous "Patent," which was followed by the edict issued by the minister of public worship, the Protestants of Hungary felt grieved, for the object of the "Patent" and the edict was nothing less than a complete reorganization of the Reformed Church, involving the destruction of self-government and the transference of ecclesiastical legislation to the civil authority. This attempt to deprive the Reformed Church of her inherent rights aroused the spirit of self-defence against the intrusion of the secular power, and Révész came forward with his *A Protestáns Egyházalkotmány*, etc., i. e. *Fundamental Principles of the Protestant Church Constitution According to the Statements of the Leading Reformers, Confessions, and Church Organizations* (1856), which appeared as a reply to the order issued by the Austrian imperial cabinet. In this work he sets forth the views of the Reformers, especially Calvin, regarding the Church's inherent and indefeasible right of self-government, and delineates the organizations of the German, Swiss, French, and Scottish Reformed churches. His next production was *Opinion Regarding the Chief Points of the Hungarian Protestant Church Constitution* (1857). The Hungarian Reformed Church protested against the intrusion of the secular power, and appealed to a national free synod. All who dared to speak publicly against the edict—and among these was Révész—were summoned before the civil courts, and some were even committed to prison. A great deputation of Protestants was sent (Jan. 25, 1860) to the emperor at Vienna, with a petition for the withdrawal of the "Patent" and the edict. The leading spirit in this movement was Révész. On May 15, 1860, the "Patent" was withdrawn, and amnesty was granted to all who were suffering for their opposition to the decrees. Another struggle began when, under the new constitution, in 1868, the Hungarian parliament hurriedly passed the law for the secularization of the elementary schools. Révész, with his usual deep and wide insight, and true Protestant instincts, stood forth to criticise and assail the law on its dangerous side. With the view of enlightening and directing public opinion, as well as vindicating the right of the Protestant Church to manage her own schools, a right secured by constitutional law, he started a scientific monthly magazine in 1870, called the *Hungarian Protestant Observer* (*Magyar Protestáns Figyelmezö*). A still brighter career was reserved by Providence for the *Observer* in the field of polemics. The views of the German so-called "Protestant Union" found many advocates in Hungary among the professors of divinity and ministers. The "modern," or rationalistic tendency, based on mere negations, and claiming unrestricted freedom in religion and doctrine, began to exercise its terrible influence in the professorial chairs, religious newspapers, and public meetings. After some preparatory skirmishes, the "Liberals" founded the "Hungarian Protestant Union" at Pesth, in October, 1871, declaring its chief aim to be "to renew the religious-moral life in the spirit of Jesus, and to harmonize it with universal culture." This Protestant Union denied revelation, the divinity of Christ, and highly extolled Unitarianism. But when it had reached its height Révész raised the banner of evangelicalism, and every number of his monthly review was eagerly read in both camps. The chief work by him against the negative theology appeared in a separate form, *A Magyar Ooszági Protestáns Egyletröl*, i. e. *Concerning the Hungarian Protestant Union*, reprinted from the pages of the *Observer*. It is an effective and conclusive defence of evangelical Protestantism. So severe was the attack on the so-called "new Reformers" that the rationalistic Unitarian Union soon lost its prestige, evangelical principles were saved, and the famous association silently dissolved. Besides the works already mentioned, Révész published, *Kálvin Élete és a Kálvinizmus*, i. e. *The Life of Calvin and Calvinism* (Pesth, 1864). This is the first classic history of Calvin's life in Hungarian:—*Joannes Sylvester Pannonius, a Hungarian Protestant Reformer* (Debreczin, 1859):—*Mathias Dévay Biro, the First Hungarian Reformer: his Life and Works* (1863). In 1865 Révész filled the chair of Church history, an office which he resigned in 1866, but a volume of general Church history is the fruit of this one year's professorship. In 1871 the Protestant faculty of theology at Vienna conferred on him the degree of doctor of theology. Révész never accepted promotion to any of the higher positions in ecclesiastical government, wishing to remain a simple minister. For Herzog's *Real-Encyklopädie* Révész wrote in German the article on Dévay and the Hungarian reformation. See *Catholic Presbyterian Review*, Dec. 1881. (B. P.)

Revised Version. See AUTHORIZED VERSION.

Reynolds, Ignatius Aloysius, D.D., a Roman Catholic ecclesiastic, was born near Bardstown, Ky., Aug. 22, 1798, and educated at St. Mary's College, Baltimore, Md. He became a priest, and was successively vicar-general of Kentucky, rector of St. Joseph's College, and president of Nazareth Female Institute of Kentucky. He was consecrated bishop of Charleston, S. C., March 18, 1844, and died in that city, March 6, 1855.

Reynolds, Walter, archbishop of Canterbury, was the son of a baker, born in Windsor. Of all the primates who have occupied the see of Canterbury, few seem to have been less qualified to discharge the duties devolving upon a metropolitan than he. He was not equal to the situation as regards his talents, learning, piety, or his virtues. He was elected to the see of Worcester, and was duly consecrated at Canterbury, by archbishop Winchelsey, Oct. 13, 1308. Here he was a failure, but he had some friends, and it is due to them that, Jan. 4, 1314, he was translated to the see of Canterbury, and was also made chancellor. He died a despised old man, Nov. 16, 1327. See Hook, *Lives of the Archbishops of Canterbury*, iii, 455 sq.

Reynolds, William Morton, D.D., an Episcopal clergyman, was born at Little Falls Forge, Pa. He entered the ministry in early manhood, being at first identified with the Lutheran Church; was professor of Latin in Pennsylvania College for several years; afterwards president of Capital University, Columbus, O.; and was also at one time president of Illinois State University, Springfield. He changed his ecclesiastical relations about 1863, entering the Protestant Episcopal Church, and was connected with the diocese of Illinois. During the last five years of his life he was rector successively at Harlem and Oak Park, Ill. He died at Chicago, Sept. 5, 1876, aged sixty-four years. See *Lutheran Observer*, Sept. 15, 1876.

Rhadamanthus, in Greek mythology, son of Jupiter and Europa, and brother of Minos, king of Crete, was a person of such justice that he was fabled to be one of the three judges in the infernal regions.

Rhadegunda, *Saint*. See BRADSOLE.

Rhegius Urbanus. See REGIUS.

Rheinwald, GEORGE FRIEDRICH HEINRICH, a Protestant theologian of Germany, was born May 20, 1802, at Scharnhausen, near Stuttgard, and died at Bonn in 1849, doctor and professor of theology. He is the author of, *Die kirchliche Archäologie* (Berlin, 1830):—*De Pseudodoctoribus Colossensibus Commentatio Exegetico-Historica* (Bonn, 1834):—*Commentar über den Brief Pauli an die Philipper* (Berlin, 1827):—*Abelardi Dialogus inter Philosophum et Christianum* (1831):—*Abelardi Epitome Theologiæ Christianæ* (1835):—and edited *Allgemeines Repertorium für die theologische Literatur und kirchliche Statistik*, vol. i–xlvii (1833–44). See Winer, *Handbuch der theol. Lit.* i, 11, 263, 572, 608, 878, 879; Zuchold, *Bibl. Theol.* s. v. (B. P.)

Rhemoboth. See SARABAITES.

Rhode, JOHANN GOTTLIEB HEINRICH, a Protestant theologian, was born in 1762, and died at Breslau, Aug. 28, 1837. He wrote, *Ueber religiöse Bildung, Mythologie und Philosophie der Hindus* (Leipsic, 1827, 2 vols.):—*Die heilige Sage und das gesammte Religionssystem der alten Bactrer, Meder, Perser und des Zendvolkes* (Frankfort, 1820):—*Gregorii Barhebræi Scholia in Psalmum v et xviii Edita, Translata*, etc. (Breslau, 1832):—*Prolegomenorum ad Quæstionum de Evangelio Apostoloque Marcionis Denuo Instituendam Caput i–iii* (1834). See Winer, *Handbuch der theol. Lit.* i, 519, 521; Zuchold, *Bibl. Theol.* s. v. (B. P.)

Ribbeck, CONRAD GOTTLIEB, a Lutheran theologian of Germany, was born at Stolpe, Pomerania, March 21, 1759. He studied at Halle, was in 1779 teacher at his native place, in 1786 pastor at Magdeburg, in 1805 at Berlin, and died June 28, 1826, doctor of theology and member of the superior consistory. He published ascetical and homiletical works, for which see Döring, *Die deutschen Kanzelredner*, s. v.; Winer, *Handbuch der theol. Lit.* i, 495; ii, 92, 148, 163, 168, 175, 177, 202, 205, 207, 232, 294, 331. (B. P.)

Ribov, GEORG HEINRICH, a Lutheran theologian of Germany, was born Feb. 8, 1703, at Lüchau, Hanover, and studied theology at Halle. In 1722 he went to Bremen as teacher at the gymnasium, and in 1727 to Helmstädt, where he commenced his academical career. In 1732 he accepted the pastorate at Quedlinburg, in 1736 was called to Göttingen, and made doctor of theology in 1737. In 1739 he was appointed professor at the university, but resigned his position in 1759 to accept a call to Hanover. Ribov died Aug. 22, 1774. Of his publications we mention, *De Iis in quibus Christum Imitari nec Possumus nec Par est* (Göttingen, 1737):—*Institutiones Theologiæ Dogmaticæ* (1740):—*De Apostolatu Judaico, Speciatim Paulino* (1745):—*De Termino Vaticiniorum Veteris Testamenti Ultimo* (1748):—*De Antiquitatibus Judaico-Christianis* (1752):—*De Initio Muneris Apostolici Sancti Pauli* (1756):—*De Methodo qua Theologia Moralis est Tradenda* (1759). See Döring, *Die gelehrten Theologen Deutschlands*, s. v. (B. P.)

Rice, Benjamin Holt, D.D., a Presbyterian minister, was born in Bedford County, Va., Nov. 29, 1782. He was licensed by the Orange Presbytery, Sept. 28, 1810; in 1814 was installed pastor of the Presbyterian Church in Petersburg, Va., where he remained for fifteen years; in 1832 was elected secretary of the Home Missionary Society; in 1833 was chosen pastor of the Presbyterian Church in Princeton, N. J., where he remained, discharging his duties faithfully, for fourteen years, and then became pastor of the church near Hampden-Sidney College, Va. He died Jan. 24, 1856. Dr. Rice possessed superior powers as a preacher. See Sprague, *Annals of the Amer. Pulpit*, iv, 625.

Rice, John Holt, D.D., a Presbyterian minister, brother of the foregoing, was born July 23, 1818, at Petersburg, Va. He graduated from the College of New Jersey in 1838, pursued the study of law for three years in Princeton, was admitted to the bar, and practiced for a time at Richmond, Va. He graduated from Princeton Seminary in 1845, and the same year was licensed by the New Brunswick Presbytery. For several months he assisted his father, who was at that time pastor of the First Presbyterian Church of Princeton. Then going south, he labored a year in New Orleans, La., as city missionary. In 1847 he began to preach at Tallahassee, Fla. He next became pastor of the village church at Charlotte Court-House, Va., and was released in 1855. For a time he served as agent of the Presbyterian Board of Publication in Kentucky and Tennessee. In 1856 he was installed pastor of Walnut Street Church in Louisville, Ky., where he remained till 1861. During the civil war he preached in the South, at Lake Providence, La., and Brandon and Vicksburg, Miss. In 1867 he went to Mobile, in 1869 to Franklin, Tenn., and afterwards to Mason, till 1876. After this he labored as an evangelist, preaching to the poor and destitute. He died Sept. 7, 1878. After the division of the Presbyterian Church, in 1861, he adhered to the Southern General Assembly. Dr. Rice had a knowledge wide and varied; his sermons were often of a very high order. See *Necrol. Report of Princeton Theol. Sem.* 1879, p. 49.

Rice, Samuel D., D.D., a general superintendent of the Methodist Church in Canada, was born in Maine in 1815. He studied for some time at Bowdoin College, and was converted in his seventeenth year. In 1837 he entered the itinerant ministry. With the exception of a year at the Sackville Wesleyan College, he spent six years in the city of St. John. From 1853 to 1857 he was treasurer and moral governor of Victoria College; from 1857 to 1860 stationed in the city of Hamilton; from 1863 to 1878 governor of the Wesleyan Ladies' College there; in 1873 and 1874 president of the conference; in 1880 appointed to Winnipeg, where he remained for three years as chairman of that district. In 1882 he was elected president of the Methodist Church of Canada; and at the first session of the General Conference of the United Methodist churches he was elected senior general superintendent. He died Dec. 11, 1884. Dr. Rice was a man of tall and commanding appearance. As a presiding officer he was dignified and firm, as a preacher, earnest and forcible; as a pastor and administrator his principle was "not to mend our rules, but keep them." He was a man of strong faith and lofty courage. See (Canada) *Christian Guardian*, December, 1884.

Richard (1), a Scotch prelate, was elected to the see of St. Andrew's in 1163. He died in 1173. See Keith, *Scottish Bishops*, p. 11.

Richard (2), a Scotch prelate, was made bishop of Moray in 1187. He died at Spynie in 1203. See Keith, *Scottish Bishops*, p. 136.

Richard (3), a Scotch prelate, was probably bishop of Dunkeld in 1249. See Keith, *Scottish Bishops*, p. 80.

Richard (4), a Scotch prelate, was made bishop of the Isles in 1252. He died in 1274. See Keith, *Scottish Bishops*, p. 300.

Richard, archbishop of Canterbury, was by birth a Norman. Very little is known of his early life. When the primary education of Richard was finished he was received into the monastery of Christ Church, Canterbury, and his manner being noticed by archbishop Theobald, he selected him to be one of his chaplains. Richard's first preferment was to the place of prior, in the monastery of St. Martin, Dover, in 1140. He was consecrated to the see of Canterbury, April 7, 1174, at Anagni, and "a more amiable man than archbishop Richard never sat in the chair of Augustine." In 1176 he was sent to Normandy, to arrange a marriage between the princess Joanna and William, king of Sicily. Ten years after he was seized with a violent chill when making a journey to Rochester, and died while there, Feb. 16, 1184. See Hook, *Lives of the Archbishops of Canterbury*, ii, 508 sq.

Richards, John, D.D., a Congregational minister, was born at Farmington, Conn., May 14, 1797. He graduated at Yale College in 1821, at Andover Theological Seminary in 1824; was for a year agent for the American Board of Commissioners for Foreign Missions; pastor at Woodstock, Vt., from 1827 to 1831; associate editor of the *Vermont Chronicle* from 1831 to 1837, and pastor of the Church at Dartmouth College from 1841 until his death, at Hanover, N. H., March 29, 1859. "Dr. Richards was a comprehensive scholar, faithful to Christ, and heartily devoted to the best interests of mankind. No man ever questioned his learning, integrity, and piety." See *Cong. Quarterly*, 1859, p. 316.

Richardson, Elias Huntington, D.D., a Congregational minister, was born at Lebanon, N. H., Aug. 11, 1827. He graduated from Dartmouth College in 1850, and from Andover Theological Seminary in 1853; was ordained at Goffstown, May 18, 1854, and remained there two years, then was pastor at Dover until 1863; next of the Richmond Street Church, Providence, R. I., until 1867; of the First Church, Westfield, Mass., until 1872; of the Center Church, Hartford, Conn., until 1879, and finally of the Center Church, New Britain, until his death, June 27, 1883. See *The Congregationalist*, July 5, 1883. (J. C. S.)

Richardson, Merrill, D.D., a Congregational minister, was born at Holden, Mass., Oct. 4, 1811. He graduated from Middlebury College in 1835, then taught for two years in the Academy of Middlebury, and graduated at Yale Divinity School in 1839. He was ordained pastor at Terryville, Conn., Oct. 27, 1841, remaining there nearly five years. From 1847 to 1849 he was acting pastor at Durham, when he was reinstalled at Terryville. From this charge he was dismissed, Jan. 18, 1858. The same month he was installed pastor of the Salem Street Church, Worcester, Mass., and here he remained until September, 1870. The following November he assumed charge of the New England Church, New York city, from which he was dismissed in May, 1872. From June 12, 1873, he was in charge of the Church at Milford, Mass., until his death, Dec. 12, 1876. During 1847 and 1848 he was secretary of the Connecticut School Board. See *Cong. Quarterly*, 1877, p. 423.

Richmond, Edward, D.D., a Congregational minister, was born at Middleborough, Mass., in 1767. He graduated from Brown University in 1789; studied theology under Rev. Dr. Gurney, of North Middleborough; was ordained pastor of the Church in Stoughton, Dec. 5, 1792; dismissed, Jan. 15, 1817; installed at Dorchester, June 25 following; dismissed in 1833; then resided for several years in Braintree, and died in Boston, April 10, 1842. Dr. Richmond was a candid man, a close and acute reasoner, and was much respected as a minister and a neighbor. See Sprague, *Annals of the Amer. Pulpit*, ii, 417.

Richter, Johann Georg, a Lutheran theologian of Germany, was born in 1727 at Leipsic, where he also pursued his theological studies. In 1750 he commenced his academical career, was in 1751 professor, and in 1756 doctor of theology. He died June 14, 1780, leaving, *De Arte Critica Scripturæ Interprete* (Leipsic, 1750):—*De Vitiis Criticis Luciani et Lexicorum Græcorum* (1752):—*Singulares Quædam Martini Lutheri de Matrimonio Sententiæ* (eod.):—*De Paulo in Vitam Revocati Nuncio ad Act. xii*, 32, 33 (1756):—*De Munere Sacro Johanni Baptistæ Divinitus Delegato* (1757):—*De Theologo Dei Homine ad 2 Tim. iii*, 17 (1765):—*Tabulæ Theologiæ Dogmaticæ ad Usus Lectionum* (1771). See Döring, *Die gelehrten Theologen Deutschlands*, s. v. (B. P.)

Richter, Karl, a Roman Catholic theologian of Germany, was born in 1804 at Warendorf. In 1826 he was director of the gymnasium at Rietberg, in 1828 professor at Paderborn, in 1837 director at Culm, in 1844 canon and professor at Pelplin, in 1849 at Posen, in 1867 at Treves, and died Aug. 24, 1869, doctor of theology. (B. P.)

Riddell, Mortimer S., D.D., a Baptist minister, was born at East Hamilton, N. Y., May 8, 1827. After pursuing secular business for several years, he studied at the Hamilton Institution, graduating in 1858, and was soon after ordained pastor in New Brunswick, N. J., where he took high rank as a preacher, and his eight years' ministry was eminently successful. His labors, during a revival of remarkable power, broke down his health, and he was obliged to suspend his ministerial work. All his efforts to regain his wasted strength proved futile, and he died at Ottawa, Kan., Feb. 1, 1870. See Cathcart, *Baptist Encyclop.* p. 988. (J. C. S.)

Ridley, Joseph James, D.D., a Protestant Episcopal clergyman, was born in North Carolina in 1810. He was confirmed in 1835; made deacon in 1843, and presbyter in 1844; became rector in Oxford, N. C., in 1853, and the following year in Clarksville, Tenn. While in this parish he received the degree of M.D., after having pursued a course of study in medicine. In 1860 he removed to Knoxville, as president of East Tennessee University; the following year returned to Clarksville, as rector of Trinity Church; in 1866 was rector of St. Paul's Church, Louisburg, N. C.; in 1867 of St. Thomas's Church, Somerville, Tenn.; about 1870 of Zion's Church, Brownsville, where he died, March 10, 1878.

Riederer, JOHANN BARTHOLOMÄUS, a Lutheran theologian of Germany, was born at Nuremberg, March 8, 1720. He studied at Altdorf and Halle, was in 1744 afternoon preacher at Nuremberg, in 1745 preacher at Altdorf, in 1752 professor, in 1753 doctor of theology, in 1769 archdeacon, and died Feb. 5, 1771. He wrote, *De Genuino Sensu Jerem. xxxi*, 3 (Altdorf, 1753):—*De Pauli Prædicantis inter Gentes Evangelium Successibus* (1759), etc. See Döring, *Die gelehrten Theologen Deutschlands*, s. v.; Winer, *Handbuch der theol. Lit.* i, 167, 317, 546, 630, 750; Fürst, *Bibl. Jud.* s. v. (B. P.)

Rieger, Georg Conrad, a Lutheran theologian of Germany, was born March 7, 1687, at Cannstadt. In 1715 he was vicar at Stuttgard, in 1718 deacon at Urach, in 1721 professor at the gymnasium in Stuttgard, in 1733 pastor of St. Leonhard, in 1742 dean, and died April 16, 1743. Rieger was an excellent preacher, and his sermons and ascetical writings have been repeatedly reprinted. See Schmidt, *Geschichte der Predigt* (Gotha, 1872), p. 196–198; Zuchold, *Bibl. Theol.* s. v.; Plitt-Herzog, *Real-Encyklop.* s. v.; Döring, *Die gelehrten Theologen Deutschlands*, s. v.; Lichtenberger, *Encyclop. des Sciences Religieuses*, s. v. (B. P.)

Rieger, Karl Heinrich, son of Georg Conrad, was born at Stuttgard, June 16, 1726. In 1753 he was vicar at Stuttgard, in 1754 second deacon at Ludwigsburg, in 1757 court chaplain, and in 1779 court preacher at Stuttgard, and died Jan. 15, 1791. After his death were published, *Ueber die evangelischen Texte an den Sonn-, Fest- und Feiertagen* (Stuttgard, 1794):—*Ueber das Neue Testament* (1828, 4 vols.):—*Ueber die Psalmen und die zwölf kleinen Propheten* (1835, 2 vols.):—*Ueber das Leben Jesu* (1838). See Zuchold, *Bibl. Theol.* s. v.; Plitt-Herzog, *Real-Encyklop.* s. v.; Lichtenberger, *Encyclop. des Sciences Religieuses*, s. v. (B. P.)

Riegler, GEORG, a Roman Catholic theologian of Germany, was born April 21, 1778. In 1806 he received holy orders, and was for some time priest of different congregations, called in 1821 as professor to Bamberg, and died in 1847. He is the author of, *Kritische Geschichte der Vulgata* (Sulzbach, 1820):—*Hebräische Sprachschule* (together with A. Martinet, Bamberg, 1835):—*Das Buch Ruth aus dem Hebräischen mit Erläuterungen* (Würzburg, 1812):—*Der xviii. Psalm erläutert* (1823):—*Die Klagelieder Jeremias erläutert* (1820):—*Christliche Moral* (1823, 3 vols.):—*Der Eid* (2d ed. 1826):—*Biblische Hermeneutik* (1835):—*Die Eucharistie nach Schrift und Tradition* (1845):—*Das heilige Abendmahl mit Controversen* (1845). See Zuchold, *Bibl. Theol.* s. v.; Fürst, *Bibl. Jud.* s. v.; Winer, *Handbuch der theol. Lit.* i, 62, 117, 203, 210, 220, 317, 489, 870; ii, 350, 387. (B. P.)

Ries, FRANZ ULRICH, a Lutheran theologian of Germany, was born Jan. 3, 1695, at Breidenbach, Hesse, and studied at Marburg and Heidelberg. In 1721 he was professor of philosophy at Marburg, in 1725 doctor, and in 1728 professor of theology. Ries died Nov. 6, 1755, and left *De Jesu Nazareno in Vaticiniis Veteris Testamenti Prædicto* (Marburg, 1722):—*De Deo Spiritu ἀσωματῳ* (1724):—*De Morbo Pauli Apostoli ad 2 Corinth. xii*, 7 (eod.):—*De Atheis Eorumque Stultitia* (1725):—*De Sacerdotis Summi in Sanctum Sanctorum Ingressu* (1726):—*De Divinitate Sacræ Scripturæ* (1748):—*De Salute Protoplastorum* (1750):—*De Asylis sive Urbibus Refugii* (1753). See Döring, *Die gelehrten Theologen Deutschlands*, s. v.; Fürst, *Bibl. Jud.* s. v. (B. P.)

Riffel, CASPAR, a Roman Catholic theologian, some time professor of theology at Giessen, who died in 1856, a doctor of theology, is the author of, *Christliche Kirchengeschichte der neuesten Zeit* (Mayence, 1847, 3 vols.):—*Die Aufhebung des Jesuiten-Ordens* (3d ed. 1855):—*Darstellung der Verhältnisse zwischen Kirche und Staat* (1841). (B. P.)

Rifian Version OF THE SCRIPTURES. Rifi is a dialect of Shilha, Morocco. A translation of the gospel of Matthew into this dialect was made by Mr. William Mackintosh, agent of the British and Foreign Bible Society at Morocco, which was printed by the same society in 1855, in Arabic type. (B. P.)

Rigaud, STEPHEN JORDAN, D.D., a colonial bishop of the Church of England, matriculated at Exeter College, Oxford; took the degree of B.A. in 1841; was ordained deacon in 1840 and presbyter in 1842; became fellow, tutor, and examiner of Exeter College in 1845–46; head master of Queen Elizabeth School, Ipswich, in 1850; and was consecrated bishop of Antigua in 1857, his jurisdiction comprising seven hundred and fifty-one square miles. He died of yellow fever at Antigua, West Indies, May 16, 1859. Bishop Rigaud was the author and editor of, *Letters of Scientific Men:—Newton and Contemporaries:—Defence of Halley against the Charge of Religious Infidelity:—Sermons on The Lord's Prayer*, etc. See *Amer. Quar. Church Rev.* 1859, p. 538.

Rigdon, SIDNEY, a prominent Mormon leader, was born in St. Clair, Beaver Co., Pa., Feb. 19, 1793, and received a fair English education. He learned the printer's trade, and was working in an office in Pittsburgh when, about 1812, a manuscript was offered for publication by an eccentric preacher named Solomon Spaulding, which was entitled, *The Manuscript Found, or, The Book of Mormon.* Rigdon was so much interested in the work that he made a copy before it was returned to Spaulding, who died a short time after. About 1817 Rigdon became a Campbellite preacher, with an evident leaning towards Adventism. In 1829 he became acquainted with Joseph Smith, and arranged with him to have the *Book of Mormon* published, as the basis for a new sect. From this time he was closely identified with the Mormon movement, going with the new body, and suffering persecution with them. He was a candidate for the leadership on the death of Smith, and on the election of Brigham Young refused to acknowledge his authority. Accordingly he was excommunicated, and returned to Pittsburgh. He afterwards lived in obscurity, and died at Friendship, N. Y., July 14, 1876. See MORMONS.

Riggs, STEPHEN R., D.D., LL.D., a venerable Presbyterian missionary to the North American Indians, was born at Steubenville, O., March 23, 1812. He graduated from Jefferson College, and pursued his theological studies at Allegheny Seminary. He was ordained and commissioned as a missionary to the Dakota Indians in 1836. He commenced his labors at Laquiparle, where he made encouraging progress in teaching and converting the red men. He reduced the Dakota language to a written form, published text-books for spelling and reading, and translated the Bible. He also published a *Dakota Dictionary*. Upwards of fifty books, consisting of original writings and translations in connection with a history of Dakota, constitute the literary work of his life. In 1880 Dr. Riggs, Hon. W. E. Dodge, and justice Strong of the United States Supreme Court, were appointed a committee by the Presbyterian General Assembly of the United States to present to Congress the need of securing to Indians the rights of white men. Dr. Riggs was the author of the memorial which was read to the Senate committee by justice Strong. More than forty years of his life were spent among the Indians, and he lived to see six of the churches of Dakota transferred to the Board of Foreign Missions. He died at Beloit, Wis., Aug. 24, 1883. See *Presbyterian Home Missionary*, Sept. 1883; Nevin, *Presb. Encyclop.* s. v. (W. P. S.)

Rimmon. On the identification of this *rock* with that of *Rummon*, see the *Quar. Statement* of the "Palest. Explor. Fund," Oct. 1881, p. 247. The village *Rumaneh* is not described in the *Memoirs* accompanying the Ordnance Survey.

Rinck, Friedrich Theodor, a Lutheran theologian of Germany, was born April 8, 1770, at Stave, Pomerania. He commenced his academical career in 1792 at Königsberg, was in 1800 professor of theology, in 1801 first preacher at Dantzic, and died April 27, 1821, doctor of theology. He is the author of, *De Linguarum Orientalium cum Græca Mira Convenientia* (Königsberg, 1788):—*Arabisches, syrisches, und chaldäisches Lesebuch* (eod.):—*Commentarii in Hoseæ Vaticinia Specimen* (1789):—*Neue Sammlung der Reisen nach den Orient* (1807). See Winer, *Handbuch der theol. Lit.* i, 151, 528; Fürst, *Bibl. Jud.* s. v. (B. P.)

Rinck, Heinrich Wilhelm, a Lutheran minister of Germany, was born in 1822 at Bischofingen, Baden. For some time inspector of the "Evangelical Society" at Elberfeld, he was in 1855 elected pastor of the Lutheran congregation, and died in January, 1881. He is the author of, *Die christliche Glaubenslehre, schriftgemäss dargestellt* (Basle, 1854):—*Vom Zustande nach dem Tode* (2d ed. 1866):—*Die Zeichen der letzten Zeit und die Wiederkunft Christi* (1857):—*Bileam und Elisa* (1868):—*Homilien über den Jacobusbrief* (1870):—*Den ersten Johannesbrief* (1872):—*Die drei ersten Kapitel der Offenbarung Johannis* (1875). (B. P.)

Rinck, Wilhelm Friedrich, a Protestant theologian of Germany, was born at Dietlingen, near Pforzheim, Feb. 9, 1793. In 1813 he was pastor of the German evangelical congregation at Venice, in 1821 at Bischoffingen, in 1827 at Eyringen, in 1835 at Grenzach, Baden, and died in 1856. He is the author of, *Lehrbegriff von den heiligen Abendmahl* (Heidelberg, 1818):—*Das Sendschreiben der Korinther an den Apostel Paulus aus dem Armenischen* (1823):—*Lucubratio Critica in Acta Apostolorum, Epistolas Catholicas et Paulinas*, etc. (1833):—*Die angefochtenen Erzählungen in dem Leben Jesu beleuchtet* (1842):—*Apokalyptische Forschungen* (Zurich, 1853). See Zuchold, *Bibl. Theol.* s. v.; Winer, *Handbuch der theol. Lit.* i, 103, 276, 454; ii, 39, 224. (B. P.)

Ripley, George, LL.D., a Unitarian divine and author, was born at Greenfield, Mass., Oct. 3, 1802. He graduated from Harvard College in 1823, and from the Cambridge Divinity School in 1826; the following year became pastor of the Purchase Street Unitarian Church, Boston. After remaining a few years he resigned, and devoted himself exclusively to literary pursuits. In 1847 he became literary editor of the *New York Tribune*, and retained that position until his death, July 4, 1880. He published, *Discourses on the Philosophy of Religion* (1839):—*Letters on the Latest Forms of Infidelity* (1840):—*Specimens of Foreign Standard Literature* (1842). Among his greatest literary labors are, *Appleton's New American Cyclopædia*, which subsequently was revised and greatly enlarged. He was also editor of an *Annual Cyclopædia*, published by the same house. He translated *Philosophical Essays*, by M. Victor Cousin (Edinburgh, 1857). He edited, in connection with R. W. Emerson and S. M. Fuller, *The Dial*, and with C. A. Dana, Parke Godwin, and J. S. Dwight, *The Harbinger*. He contributed numerous articles to the *Christian Examiner*, and Putnam's and Harper's Magazines. See (N. Y.) *Observer*, July 8, 1880; Allibone, *Dict. of Brit. and Amer. Authors*, s. v. (W. P. S.)

Rist, Johann von, a German hymn-writer, was born March 8, 1607, at Pinneburg, Holstein, and died Aug. 31, 1667. He is the author of about six hundred and fifty-eight religious hymns and poems. Some are, indeed, of little value; but very many of them are really good, and some belong to the first rank. They were even read with delight among Roman Catholics, and an empress once lamented "that it were a great pity if the writer of such hymns should be sent to hell." Rist was very much honored, and attained the highest titles in Church and State open to a clergyman, and the emperor honored him in 1654 with the crown of poet-laureate and a patent of nobility. Quite a number of Rist's hymns have been translated into English, as "Auf, auf, ihr Reichsgenossen" (*Lyra Germ.* ii, 23):—"Wach' auf, wach' auf, du sich're Welt" (*ibid.* i, 4):—"Wie wohl hast du gelabet" (*ibid.* ii, 144):—"Folget mir, ruft uns das Leben" (*ibid.* i, 188):—"Werde munter mein Gemüthe" (*ibid.* ii, 112):—"Ehr' und Dank sei dir gesungen" (*ibid.* i, 205):—"O Traurigkeit, O Herzeleid" (*Christian Singers*, p. 191):—"Werde Licht, du Volk der Heiden" (*ibid.* p. 30):—"Gott sei gelobet, der alleine" (*ibid.* p. 192):—"O Ewigkeit du Donnerwort" (Jacobi, *Psalmodia Germ.* i, 97). (B. P.)

Ritter, Heinrich, a philosophical writer of Germany, was born at Zerbst, Nov. 11, 1791. He commenced his academical career at Berlin in 1817, was professor of philosophy in 1824, in 1833 at Kiel, in 1837 at Göttingen, and died Feb. 2, 1869, doctor of theology. He wrote, *Der Pantheismus und die Halb-Kantianer* (Berlin, 1827):—*Ueber die Erkenntniss Gottes in der Welt* (Hamburg, 1836):—*Ueber das Böse* (Kiel, 1839):—*Ueber die Emanationslehre* (Göttingen, 1847):—*Ueber Lessings philosophische und religiöse Grundsätze* (1848):—*Unsterblichkeit* (Leipsic, 1851):—*Die christliche Philosophie nach ihrem Begriff* (1858–59, 2 vols.):—*Encyclopädie der philosophischen Wissenschaften* (1864, 3 vols.):—*Ueber das Böse und seine Folgen* (Gotha, 1869).—*Philosophische Paradoxa* (Leipsic, 1867). (B. P.)

Ritual of the Dead is the name given by Egyptologists to the oldest sacred book of the Egyptian theology. Portions of this book date from the time of king Gagamakhem, a monarch of the third dynasty, the text itself being in many places accompanied by a gloss, which was added at a later period, to render it intelligible. The deities principally mentioned in it are Osiris, Anubis, Horus, and Tum; Amen Ra, as a distinct divinity, being only indirectly referred to. Although the mystical work is now treated as one book, it is really made up of a collection of not less than eighteen separate treatises, including three supplemental chapters and two litanies, which seem to have been added at the time of the new empire. Selections from chapters and illustrations from the ritual abound on the walls of many of the tombs of the eighteenth and nineteenth dynasties, and notably on that of Seti-Menepthah I, in the Biban el-Moluk. Other chapters were used as mystical formulæ to avert diseases, others as a part of the religious worship of the Egyptians, and a few obscure passages as secret mysteries, the meaning of which is now lost. Many hundred of papyri have been found in the mummy-cases, which contain different portions of the ritual, with their accompanying vignette and rubric, but a complete recension and comparison of all the existing texts have not yet been effected. The text of the ritual underwent no less than three different revisions, viz., in the ancient empire, in the period of the nineteenth dynasty, and in the reign of the Saitic kings. This last was the edition which is most commonly met with, but there appears to have been an attempt at a partial re-edition in the Ptolemaic period. The chief divisions or books of which the Ritual of the Dead is composed are as follows:

	CHAPTERS
1. The Manifestation of Light (first book)	i–xvi.
2. The Egyptian Faith	xvii–xx.
3. The Resurrection of the Deceased	xxi–xxvi.
4. The Preservation of the Body in Hades	xxvii–xlii.
5. The Protection in Hades	xliii–li.
6. The Celestial Diet	lii, liii.
7. The Manifestation of Light (second book)	liv–lxxv.
8. The Metamorphoses	lxxvi–xc.
9. The Protection of the Soul; or, Forms for Various Occasions	xci–cxvi.

From these it will be seen that the arrangement of the chapters is inconsecutive so far as their subjects are concerned, and there is every reason to believe that the order in which they now occur, especially in the English translation, is somewhat arbitrary. The ritual is rarely found written in Hieratic, and still more rarely in Demotic. The finest examples are those in the museums of the Louvre and Turin.

River-gods. Deities of streams were worshipped at all times by the Greeks and Romans, each bearing the name of the river over which he ruled.

Rivers, The Four. In ancient art our Lord is frequently represented, either in person or under the figure of a lamb, standing upon a hillock from whence issue four streams of water. These are supposed by many to signify the four rivers of Eden, which went forth to water the earth (Gen. ii, 10); others (Cyprian, *Ep.* 73, § 10, *ad Jubaian.;* Bede, *Expos. in Gen. ii;* Theodoret, *In Psalm. xlv;* Ambrose, *De Paradiso*, c. 3) discern in them the four gospels, flowing from the source of eternal life to spread throughout the world the riches and the life-giving powers of the doctrine of Christ. Ambrose, again (ibid.), is of opinion that the four rivers are emblems of the four cardinal virtues. The first four œcumenical councils, so often by early writers placed on a par with the gospels themselves, are sometimes compared to the four rivers of Paradise. Jesse, bishop of Amiens in the 8th century, in writing to his clergy, thus illustrates the veneration due to these august assemblies (Longueval, *Hist. de l'Égl. Gallicane*, v, 144). In several sarcophagi of ancient Gaul we find two stags quenching their thirst at these streams; these are supposed to represent Christians partaking of the gospels and the eucharist of the "well of water springing up into everlasting life." See Cross. The two stags are occasionally found in mosaics; in that of the ancient Vatican, for example (Ciampini, *De Sacr. Ædif.* tab. xiii).

Antique Representation of the Four Rivers under the Lord's Feet.

Rives, Basile, a Protestant theologian of France, was born at Mazamet in 1815. In 1844 he was called as pastor to Pont-de-Learn, Tarn, and died in 1876. He published, *Le Christianisme Orthodoxe et le Christianisme Liberal:—Le Chrétien, le Vrai Chrétien:—Le Dogme de l'Église:—Opinion d'un Pasteur de Compagne sur la Crise du Protestantisme Français:—Le Grande Foi de Toutes les Orthodoxies*, etc. See Lichtenberger, *Encyclop. des Sciences Religieuses*, s. v. (B. P.)

Robbins, Chandler, D.D., a Unitarian minister, was born at Lynn, Mass., Feb. 14, 1810. He graduated from Harvard College in 1829, and from the Cambridge Divinity School in 1833. He was ordained Dec. 4 of that year pastor of the Second Church, Boston, as the successor of Ralph Waldo Emerson. This was his only pastorate, and continued for forty-one years. He died at Weston, Mass., Sept. 11, 1882. Among his published writings are *A History of the Second Church in Boston, with Lives of Increase and Cotton Mather*, and several sermons. He edited the works of Henry Ware, Jr. (4 vols.), compiled *The Social Hymn-book*, and a *Hymn-book for Christian Worship.* See *Boston Advertiser*, Sept. 12, 1882. (J. C. S.)

Robert (1), a Scotch prelate, was elected bishop of Ross in 1122, but was not consecrated until 1128. He died in 1159. See Keith, *Scottish Bishops*, p. 8.

Robert (2), a Scotch prelate, was an Englishman, and was brought, with five others, into Scotland by Alexander I, to instruct the people and to be good examples to them in the observance of the monastic rules prescribed by St. Augustine. He was made prior of Scone in 1115, and in 1122 became bishop of St. Andrews. He was consecrated in 1126 or 1127. He died in this see in 1159. This prelate founded the priory of Lochleven, to be annexed to his new foundation. See Keith, *Scottish Bishops*, p. 8.

Robert (3), a Scotch prelate, was bishop of the see of Ross in 1214. See Keith, *Scottish Bishops*, p. 185.

Robert (4), a Scotch prelate, was bishop of Brechin in 1456. See Keith, *Scottish Bishops*, p. 163.

Robert (5), a Scotch prelate, was bishop at Dunkeld in 1484, and was witness to a charter of appraisement by king James III of the lands of Bordland of Ketnes, from James, earl of Buchan, to Robert, lord Lisle, May 19, 1485. See Keith, *Scottish Bishops*, p. 91.

Robert (6), a Scotch prelate, was bishop of the Isles in 1492, and received a charter from John, lord of the Isles, of the Church of Kilberry, which was united to the bishopric of a mensal Church. He was in this see in 1492. See Keith, *Scottish Bishops*, p. 305.

Robert, Carl Wilhelm, a Protestant theologian of Germany, was born at Cassel, March 21, 1740. He studied at Marburg and Göttingen, and was ordained in 1762. In 1764 he was second preacher and professor at Marburg, in 1768 doctor of theology, and in 1771 member of consistory. In 1778 Robert resigned his theological position and commenced his career in the faculty of law. In 1779 he took the degree of doctor of law, in 1797 he was called to Cassel, and died April 3, 1803. He published, *De Nomine υἱοῦ Θεοῦ non Regium Christi Munus*, etc. (Marburg, 1768):—*Encyclopædiæ et Methodi Theologici Brevis Ordinatio* (1769):—*Ethicæ Christianæ Compendium* (1770):—*Causa Belli a Isrælitis Adversus Cananæos*, etc. (1778). See Döring, *Die gelehrten Theologen Deutschlands*, s. v. (B. P.)

Robert, Champart, archbishop of Canterbury, was by birth a Norman. He was abbot of Jumiéges, a monastery on the Seine. He had formerly been a monk, and was made bishop of London in 1044. In 1051 he was translated to the see of Canterbury. In 1052 he was deposed, and retired to his monastery at Jumiéges, where he died. See Hook, *Lives of the Archbishops of Canterbury*, i, 494 sq.

Robert, Joseph T., LL.D., a Baptist minister and educator, was born at Robertville, S. C., Nov. 28, 1807. He was baptized in October, 1822, and graduated from Brown University in 1828 with the highest honors of his class. During 1829 and 1830 he was a resident graduate and medical student at Yale College, and in 1831 took his degree at the South Carolina Medical College. In 1832 he was licensed to preach by the Robertville Church, pursued his theological studies at the Furman (S. C.) Seminary, and was ordained pastor of the Robertville Church in 1834, where he remained until 1839, when he accepted a call to the pastorate of the Church at Covington, Ky. In 1841 he took charge of the Church at Lebanon. About 1848 he went to the First Church at Savannah, Ga.; in 1850 he became pastor of the Church at Portsmouth, O.; in 1858 professor of mathematics and natural sciences in Burlington University, Ia.; in 1864 professor of languages in the Iowa State University, and in 1869 president of Burlington University. He returned to

Georgia in October, 1870, and in July, 1871, became principal of the Augusta Institute. Subsequently this institution, established for the education of colored ministers, was removed to Atlanta, and in 1879 was incorporated with the Atlanta Baptist Seminary, under the presidency of Dr. Robert. He died March 5, 1884. See Cathcart, *Baptist Encyclop.* p. 992. (J. C. S.)

Robinson, Stuart, D.D., a Presbyterian minister, was born at Strabane, Ireland, Nov. 26, 1816. He received his preparatory education under Rev. James M. Brown, D.D., in Berkeley County, Va., and Rev. William H. Foote, D.D., at Romney; graduated from Amherst College, Mass., in 1836; went thence to Union Theological Seminary in Virginia, and spent one year; then taught from 1837 to 1839; from 1839 to 1841 studied at Princeton Seminary; was licensed by Greenbrier Presbytery, Va., April 10, 1841; and was ordained by the same presbytery, Oct. 8, 1842, at Lewisburg (now in West Virginia), pastor of the Church at Kanawha Saline, from which he was released May 8, 1847; was installed pastor of the Church at Frankfort, Ky., by the Presbytery of West Lexington, June 18 following, and labored there until Sept. 2, 1852; removed to Baltimore, Md., and supplied the Fayette Street Church in 1852 and 1853; then organized the Central Presbyterian Church in the same city, and was installed its pastor May 10 of the latter year, and released Oct. 27, 1856; was professor of pastoral theology and Church government in Danville Theological Seminary, Ky., in 1856 and 1857; pastor of the Second Church of Louisville from 1858 to 1881, at which time he was released on account of the failure of his health. He died in Louisville, Oct. 5, 1881. Dr. Robinson was a man of rare learning, and one of the finest expository preachers in the country. He wrote much and published much, but his principal productions are the two volumes, *The Church of God*, and *Discourses on Redemption.* See *Necrol. Report of Princeton Theol. Sem.* 1882, p. 42.

Rochat, Auguste Louis Philippe, a Protestant theologian of Switzerland, was born July 17, 1789, at Crassier, Vaud. In 1812 he was ordained, and acted as preacher at different places. In 1825 he founded an independent Church at Rolles, in which he labored till his death, March 7, 1847. Rochat wrote, *Méditations* (1832):—*La Nature, la Constitution et le But de l'Église du Christ* (1837):—*Méditations sur Diverses Portions de la Parole de Dieu* (1838):—*Œuvres Posthumes* (1848). See Burnier, *Notice sur Auguste Rochat* (Lausanne, eod.); A. de Montet, *Dictionnaire des Genev. et des Vaud,* ii, 383, 384; Lichtenberger, *Encyclop. des Sciences Religieuses,* s. v. (B. P.)

Rockwell, Joel Edson, D.D., a Presbyterian minister, was born at Salisbury, Vt., May 4, 1816. In 1837 he graduated from Amherst College, and in 1841 from Union Theological Seminary, N. Y. The same year he became pastor of the Presbyterian Church at Valatie; in 1847 of the Hanover Street Church, Wilmington, Del.; in 1851 of the Central Presbyterian Church, Brooklyn, N. Y. After laboring constantly for eighteen years, he spent five months in Europe for the benefit of his health. During the war of the rebellion he served as a member of the Christian Commission. In 1878 he became pastor of the Edgewater Presbyterian Church, on Staten Island, where he remained until his death, July 29, 1882. Besides fulfilling the duties of an active pastor during all these years, he was a prolific writer, and contributed to a number of religious periodicals. See (N. Y.) *Observer*, Aug. 3, 1882; *Evangelist,* same date. (W. P. S.)

Rockwood, Elisha, D.D., a Congregational minister, was born at Chesterfield, N. H., May 9, 1778. He graduated from Dartmouth College in 1802; taught an academy in Plymouth, Mass., two years; was tutor in Dartmouth College; while there studied theology, and in 1806 was approbated by the Londonderry Presbytery. After preaching as an occasional supply in several places in Vermont and Massachusetts, he was ordained in Westboro', Oct. 28, 1808; was dismissed March 11, 1835; and finally was pastor in Swansey, N. H., from Nov. 16, 1836, until his death, June 19, 1858. See *Hist. of Mendon Association*, p. 164. (J. C. S.)

Rödiger, Moritz, a Lutheran theologian of Germany, was born at Sangerhausen, April 29, 1804, and died at Halle, Oct. 13, 1837, doctor of philosophy. He is the author of *Synopsis Evangeliorum Pericopis Parallelis* (2d ed. Halle, 1839). See Zuchold, *Bibl. Theol.* s. v.; Winer, *Handbuch der theol. Lit.* i, 245. (B. P.)

Roe, Charles Hill, D.D., a Baptist minister, was born in Kings County, Ireland, Jan. 6, 1800, his father being a clergyman of the Established Church. Having become a Baptist, he entered, in 1822, Horton College, Eng., and on the completion of his studies became pastor of the Church in Middleton, Lancashire, not confining his labors to his own church, but preaching extensively in all the neighboring region. He acted as secretary of the Home Mission Society from 1834 to 1842, and then became pastor of the Church in Birmingham, where his labors were greatly blessed. He came to the United States in 1851, accepted a call to Belvidere, Ill., and during a part of the time of the civil war was chaplain of a regiment. He visited England in behalf of the freedmen, and raised funds for educational purposes among them. After a two years' pastorate at Waukesha, Wis., and two years' service for the University of Chicago, he died at Belvidere, June 20, 1872. See Cathcart, *Baptist Encyclop.* p. 1008. (J. C. S.)

Roger (1), a Scotch prelate, was lord high chancellor in Scotland in 1178, and was made bishop of the see of St. Andrews in 1188. See Keith, *Scottish Bishops*, p. 13.

Roger (2), a Scotch prelate, was bishop of Ross in 1340, and is witness to a grant which Duncan, earl of Fife, made to Robert Lauder about that period. See Keith, *Scottish Bishops*, p. 188.

Rogers, Ebenezer Platt, D.D., a Congregational minister, was born in New York city, Dec. 18, 1817. He graduated from Yale College in 1837, studied at Princeton Theological Seminary nearly one year; then, because of weakness of the eyes, two years in private with Rev. L. H. Atwater, D.D., at Fairfield, Conn.; was licensed by the South Association of Litchfield County, June 30, 1840, and ordained by the Hampden Association at Chicopee Falls, Mass., Nov. 4 following. His successive fields of labor were, Chicopee Falls, 1840–43; Northampton, 1843–46; Augusta, Ga., 1847–54; Philadelphia, Pa., 1854–56; Albany, N. Y., 1856–62; New York city, 1862–81. Part of these labors were in the Congregational Church, part in the Presbyterian, and part in the Reformed Dutch Church. He died at Montclair, N. J., Oct. 22, 1881. He published several volumes on religious subjects, besides many sermons. See *Necrol. Report of Princeton Theol. Sem.* 1882, p. 38.

Rogers, Ferdinand, D.D., a Protestant Episcopal clergyman, was born in New York state in 1816. He was ordained to the ministry in 1837, and took charge of his first parish at Brownsville, where he remained till 1846, when he accepted a rectorship in Greene, and continued there till his death, Jan. 17, 1876. See *Appleton's Annual Cyclop.* 1876, p. 623.

Rogers, Richard, an English Puritan minister, was born about 1550, and entered the ministry in 1575. He preached through the eastern counties of England forty-three years, suffering molestation from the officers, but acquiring considerable prominence among the dissenting divines. He died at Weathersfield, Essex, April 21, 1618. His publications include *Seven Treatises* (Lond. 1605, fol. and several other editions), a kind of theological manual, much used by the early divines of New England:—*Certain Sermons* (1612):—*Commentary* *on the Whole Booke of Judges* (1615). Mr. Chester, in his *John Rogers* (1861), p. 238-244, disputes Calamy's oft-repeated assertion that this divine was a descendant of the martyr. See Allibone, *Dict. of Brit. and Amer. Authors*, s. v.

Rogerus, a Scotch prelate, was witness to a charter dated March 4, 1328, at Ross. See Keith, *Scottish Bishops*, p. 187.

Rognon, LOUIS, a Protestant theologian of France, was born at Lyons, Feb. 4, 1826. Having completed his studies, he was successively pastor at Vals (1850), Montpellier (1852), and Paris (1861). He died April 15, 1869, leaving *Mélanges Philosophiques, Religieux et Littéraires*, and *Sermons* (Paris, 1870). See Lichtenberger, *Encyclop. des Sciences Religieuses*, s. v. (B. P.)

Rohrbacher, RENÉ FRANÇOIS, a Roman Catholic theologian of France, was born at Langatte in 1789. For some time professor of theology in the clerical seminary at Nancy, he went in 1849 to Paris, and died in 1856. Rohrbacher is the author of, *Histoire Universelle de l'Église Catholique* (Nancy, 1842-49, 29 vols.; 2d ed. Paris, 1849-53), afterwards translated into German:—*Catéchisme du Sens Commun* (2d ed. 1858):—*La Religion Méditée* (2d ed. 1852, 2 vols.):—*Des Rapports Naturels entre les deux Puissances* (Besançon, 1838, 2 vols.):—*De la Grâce et de la Nature* (eod.):—*Motifs qui ont Ramené à l'Église Catholique un Grand Nombre de Protestants et d'Autres Religionnaires* (Paris, 1841, 2 vols.). See Lichtenberger, *Encyclop. des Sciences Religieuses*, s. v. (B. P.)

Rohrer, FRANZ, one of the best historical scholars of Switzerland, was born at Stanz in 1832, and studied theology at the universities of Freiburg and Tübingen. He was ordained in 1856, and was for some time pastor of Kerns. His chief attention, however, was given to historical research, which his subsequent position as librarian at St. Gall enabled him to prosecute with greater freedom. After the death of Dr. Lütolf he became president of the Historical Society of the Five Cantons and editor of the *Geschichtsfreund*. He was also one of the most active members of the Swiss *Geschichtsforschende Gesellschaft*, and undertook its continuation of the great historical work left incomplete by Kopp, and afterwards by Lütolf, the *Geschichte der eidgenössischen Bünde*, of which a new volume lately appeared, under his care, bringing down the history to the peace of Austria with Lucerne and the Forest Cantons (1330-36). After serving as rector of the gymnasium at Altdorf, he was made a canon of the Stiftskirche at Luzerne in 1873, where he died in September, 1882. He described himself to the last as a theologian of the "Richtung der Lacordaire." (B. P.)

Röhrich, TIMOTHEUS WILHELM, a Protestant theologian of Germany, was born at Alt-Eckendorf in 1802. He studied at Strasburg and Göttingen, and performed the ministerial functions at Fürdenheim, in Alsace. In 1837 he was called as pastor to Strasburg, and died in 1860. Röhrich published, *Geschichte der Reformation in Elsass und besonders in Strassburg* (1830-32, 3 vols.): —*Matthias Zell* (1850):—*Mittheilungen aus der Geschichte der evangelischen Kirche des Elsasses* (1855, 3 vols.):—besides, he contributed largely to the *Zeitschrift für historische Theologie* and the *Strassburger theologische Beiträge*. See Reuss, in *Denkschrift der theologischen Gesellschaft zu Strassburg* (Jena, 1861); Lichtenberger, *Encyclop. des Sciences Religieuses*, s. v. (B. P.)

Rohtlieb, JOHANNES, a Lutheran theologian of Sweden, was born in Germany in 1806. Educated at German universities, he was in 1833 made assistant pastor of the German Church of St. Gertrude, at Stockholm, and in 1839, on the death of the pastor, succeeded to his office, by appointment of the king. In 1853 Rohtlieb became the agent of the British and Foreign Bible Society in Sweden, which he served until his death. In 1875 he retired from the pastoral charge of his congregation, and died April 11, 1881, a doctor of theology. (B. P.)

Rokeby, WILLIAM, an Irish prelate, was a native of Rokeby, in Yorkshire, and a doctor of the canon law. He was a brother to Sir Richard Rokeby, lord treasurer of Ireland. He received his early education at Rotheram and finished at Oxford, when he was presented by the monks of Lewes, in 1487, to the rectory of Sandal, near Doncaster. At the close of the 15th century he was nominated to the vicarage of Halifax, in Yorkshire; in 1498 was constituted lord chancellor of Ireland, and afterwards advanced to the see of Meath, in 1507. On Feb. 5, 1511, he was translated by pope Julius II to the see of Dublin, the temporalities of which were accorded to him in June following. In 1514 this prelate confirmed the establishment of a college of clerks, founded at Maynooth by Gerald, earl of Kildare, which was subsequently remodelled. In 1520 he was despatched by the lord deputy and council to Waterford for the purpose of pacifying such discords and debates as existed between the earl of Desmond and sir Piers Butler. Archbishop Rokeby died Nov. 29, 1521. See D'Alton, *Memoirs of the Archbishops of Dublin*, p. 178.

Roll, REINHARD HEINRICH, a Lutheran theologian of Germany, was born at Unna, Hesse, Nov. 2, 1683, and studied at Rostock. In 1710 he was rector at his native place, in 1712 at Dortmund, in 1730 professor at Giessen, and died Oct. 2, 1768, doctor of theology. He published, *De Nummo Confessionali et Oblatorio* (Rostock, 1707):—*Bibliotheca Nobilium Theologorum Historico-Theologica Selecta* (1708):—*De Sectarum Philosophicarum Scriptoribus Græcis Potioribus* (1709-10): —*De Objecto Psalmi lxix* (1714):—*De Paulo Apostolo Polyhistore* (1715):—*Jobus Scepticismi immerito Accusatus* (1719):—*Lineamenta Theologiæ Naturalis sive Philosophicæ* (1723):—*De Fide Centurionis Capernaitici ad Matth. viii*, 1 sq. (1730). See Döring, *Die gelehrten Theologen Deutschlands*, s. v. (where ninety titles of Roll's works are given). (B. P.)

Rollock, PETER, a Scotch prelate, was made titular bishop of Dunkeld by king James VI. He was one of the lords of session, and accompanied the king to England in 1603. See Keith, *Scottish Bishops*, p. 97.

Rood, HEMAN, D.D., a Congregational minister, was born at Jericho, Vt., Jan. 29, 1795. He graduated from Middlebury College in 1819, was preceptor at Montpelier Academy for two years, and in 1822 tutor at Middlebury College. In 1825 he graduated from Andover Theological Seminary; the next year, July 12, became pastor at Gilmanton, N. H.; in April, 1830, at New Milford, Conn.; in September, 1835, professor of sacred literature at the Gilmanton Theological Seminary, and occupied that position until November, 1843. The next ten years he was employed in teaching at Haverhill. From 1853 to 1858 he was acting-pastor at Quechee, in Hartford, Vt., and from 1858 to 1864 served in the same relation at Hartland. From 1864 to 1878 he resided without charge at Hanover, N. H., and thereafter at Westfield, N. Y., until his death, June 8, 1882. See *Cong. Year-book*, 1883, p. 31.

Roolwer, a Scotch prelate, was bishop of Ross about the year 900, and is buried at St. Mangholds, in the Isle of Man. See Keith, *Scottish Bishops*, p. 296.

Rosecrans, SYLVESTER HORTON, D.D., a Roman Catholic prelate, was born at Homer, O., Feb. 5, 1827. He entered Kenyon College, but on joining the Roman Catholic Church went to St. John's College, Fordham, N. Y., where he graduated with high honors in 1846. He studied five years in the College of the Propaganda at Rome, and was ordained priest in 1852. Returning to the United States, he became an assistant at the cathedral of Cincinnati, a position which he held for seven years, and was at the same time professor of theology at Mt. St. Mary's Seminary and one of the editors of the *Cincinnati Catholic Telegraph*. In 1859 archbishop Purcell established a college in connection with the seminary for the education of Catholics, and Dr.

Rosecrans was appointed president, which position he filled until the college was closed, March 25, 1862. He was made auxiliary bishop of Cincinnati in 1868, and when Columbus was erected into a diocese he was appointed its first bishop, the duties of which office he faithfully discharged until his sudden death, Oct. 21, 1878. See (N. Y.) *Catholic Annual*, 1879, p. 91.

Rosenbaum, Johann Joseph, a Roman Catholic theologian of Germany, was born in 1797. In 1825 he was professor of dogmatics in the clerical seminary at Treves, in 1842 pastor at Andernach, in 1862 member of the chapter at Treves, and died April 13, 1867, doctor of theology. He was one of the founders of the *Zeitschrift für Theologie und Philosophie*, published at Bonn, and printed in defence of Hermes and his philosophical system, *Ueber Glauben* (Treves, 1833). (B. P.)

Rosenkranz, Johann Karl Friedrich, a Protestant theologian and philosopher of Germany, was born April 23, 1805, at Magdeburg. He studied at different universities, and commenced his academical career at Halle in 1828. In 1831 he was appointed professor, and was called to Königsberg in 1833, where he died, June 14, 1879. In his philosophical system he was a follower of Hegel, and published, *Der Zweifel am Glauben, Kritik der Schriften: De Tribus Impostoribus* (Halle, 1830):—*Die Naturreligion* (Iserlohn, 1831):—*Encyclopädie der theologischen Wissenschaften* (Halle, eod.; 2d ed. 1845):—*Kritik der Schleiermacher'schen Glaubenslehre* (Königsberg, 1836):—*Ueber Schelling und Hegel* (1843):—*Kritik der Principien der Strauss'schen Glaubenslehre* (Leipsic, 1845):—*Neue Studien* (1875–77, 3 vols.). See Lichtenberger, *Encyclop. des Sciences Religieuses*, s. v. (B. P.)

Rosenroth. See Knorr von Rosenroth.

Röser, Jacob, a Lutheran theologian of Germany, was born at Sondershausen, Sept. 21, 1641, studied at different universities, and died at Quedlinburg, Nov. 6, 1689, superintendent and court-preacher. He wrote, *De Manifestatione Nominis Jehovah ad Exod. vi*, 2:—*De Fictitia Denominatione Missæ a Papicolis ex Deut. xvi*, 10:—*De Dagone* 1 *Sam. v*, 2-4:—*De Morte Judæ Proditoris Jesu Christi*:—*De Genealogia Christi Secundum Lucam*, etc. See Jöcher, *Allgemeines Gelehrten-Lexikon*, s. v.; Winer, *Handbuch der theol. Lit.* i, 567. (B. P.)

Rosetta Stone. See Hieroglyphics.

Rosmini (*Serbati*), Antonio, an Italian ecclesiastic and philosopher, was born at Roveredo, in the Tyrol, March 24, 1797. He studied at Padua, became a priest at the age of twenty-four, and in 1827 published his first treatise on philosophy, to which he had devoted himself from his early youth. About the same time he formed the acquaintance of Manzoni, and the next year founded a new religious order, the "Instituto del Preti della Carità" (*Brethren of Charity*), visiting Rome in 1830 to obtain the sanction of the pope. In 1834 he returned to Roveredo as archdeacon, and in 1836 became abbot there, and founded a similar female order (*Sisters of Providence*). Meanwhile he continued his philosophical studies and publications, in consequence of the liberality of which he failed to secure the confirmation of his cardinalship (given him in 1848 by Pius IX), and some of his books were even put on the *Index Expurgatorius*. He died at Stresa, July 1, 1855. His writings fill thirty-five volumes. His *Life* has been written by Lockhart (1856) and Garelli (1861). For a notice of his career and philosophy see the *Fortnightly Review*, November, 1881, and July, 1882.

Ross, Arthur, a Scotch prelate, was minister of Birse, in the shire of Aberdeen, and was educated at the University of St. Andrews. In 1665 he was pastor at Glasgow, where he continued until 1675. He was then promoted to the see of Argyle, whence he was transferred to that of Glasgow in 1679, and to that of Galloway the same year. But he was retranslated to the see of Glasgow Oct. 15, the same year, and thence advanced to the see of St. Andrews, Oct. 31, 1684, where he continued until the revolution in 1688, when he was deprived. He died June 13, 1704. See Keith, *Scottish Bishops*, p. 43, 269, 282, 291.

Rossanian Manuscript (*Codex Rossanensis*) is an uncial manuscript designated by the Greek letter Σ, and is so called from Rossano, in Calabria, where it was found. In the spring of 1879 two German scholars, Dr. Oscar von Gebhardt, of Göttingen, and Dr. Adolf Harnack, of Giessen, made a joint expedition into Italy in search of old manuscripts. In his *Hippolyti quæ Feruntur Omnia*, p. 216, Lagarde called attention to a notice from the 16th century, according to which manuscripts of Cyril of Jerusalem, Dionysius Alexandrinus, and of Hippolytus are said to be in the monastery of Santa Maria de lo Patire, near Rossano. This notice induced the two German scholars to search for these writings, of which, however, they could hear nothing, the monastery having long since perished. But they were informed that there was a very old Biblical book in the archiepiscopal palace. They begged to be allowed to look at this. Ushered into the presence of the archbishop, monsignor Pietro Cilento, they beheld, to their astonishment and delight, a quarto volume of the gospels, written in silver, on purple parchment, in old Greek uncial letters, unaccented, the words unseparated, and at the beginning a number of admirably drawn and colored miniatures and historical pictures. It consists of one hundred and eighty-eight leaves of parchment of two columns of twenty lines each. More than half of the original manuscript seems to have perished. What survives contains the whole of Matthew and Mark as far as the middle of the fourteenth verse of the last chapter. The discoverers assign it to the 6th century; the text attaches itself closely to the chief representatives of the amended text of A, Δ, Π, over against the most ancient codices ℵ and B; but where one of these (Δ for example) accords with the older text, Σ also usually follows it, and shows a remarkable agreement with the scattered purple codex of the gospels N. Independent of the new Greek text (a specimen of which is given by Schaff in *A Companion to the Greek Testament*, N. Y. 1883, p. 132), the pictures in the manuscript are believed to be of great value for the early history of painting. While Latin manuscripts with pictures are relatively numerous, only a very few Greek manuscripts prior to the 7th century are thus adorned. Chief among them is the Vienna purple manuscript of Genesis. The newly discovered pictures give a very favorable impression of the art of the 6th century. They are described as being wonderful in distinctness of outline and freshness of coloring. The manuscript is the property of the chapter of the cathedral church of Rossano. See Gebhardt and Harnack, *Evangeliorum Codex Græcus Purpureus Rossanensis*, etc. (Leipsic, 1880); Schürer, in the *Theol. Literaturzeitung*, 1880, No. 19. (B. P.)

Roth, Abraham, a Lutheran theologian of Germany, was born in 1633 at Herwigsdorf, Silesia, studied at Leipsic, and died at Sorau, April 26, 1699, court-preacher and superintendent. He wrote, *De Cerva Auroræ ad Psa. xxii*:—*De Cultu Dei Rejectitio Matt. xv*, 9:—*De Nicolaitis, Apocal. ii*, 15:—*De Essenis*:—*De Molocholatria Judæorum*:—*De Judæorum Ligamentis Precatoriis*. See Grosser, *Lausitzer Merkwürdigkeiten*; Jöcher, *Allgemeines Gelehrten-Lexikon*, s. v. (B. P.)

Rothe, Johann Andreas, a Lutheran theologian of Germany, was born May 12, 1688, at Lissa, Silesia, and studied at Leipsic. Count Zinzendorf selected him to fill the office of pastor at Berthelsdorf, the duties of which Roth discharged to the admiration of all who knew him. He died July 6, 1758. Rothe is the author of several hymns, the best known of which is his *Ich habe nun den Grund gefunden* (Engl. transl. "I now have found, for hope of heaven," in Mills, *Horæ Germanicæ*,

No. 32). See Koch, *Geschichte des deutschen Kirchenliedes*, v, 240 sq. (B. P.)

Rothenburg, Meïr. See Meïr ben-Baruch.

Rougemont, Frédéric de, a Protestant theologian of Switzerland, who died at Neufchatel in 1876, was a very prolific writer, whose works have for the greater part been translated into German. Of his publications we mention, *Du Monde dans ses Rapports avec Dieu* (1841):—*Essai sur le Pietisme* (1842):—*Histoire de la Terre d'Après la Bible et la Géologie* (1856, Germ. transl. by Fabarius, Stuttgard, eod.):—*La Peuple Primitif* (1855-57):—*L'Age de Bronze ou les Sémites en Occident* (1867):—*La Vie Humaine avec et sans la Foi* (1869):—*Théorie de la Redemption* (1876):—*Révélation de Saint Jean Expliquée* (1838):—*Les xii Derniers Livres Prophétiques de l'Ancien Testament* (1841):—*Philosophie de l'Histoire* (1874, 2 vols.):—*Christ et ses Témoins* (1859):—*La Divinité et l'Infirmité de l'Ancien Testament* (1869), etc. See Godet, *Journal Religieux*, 1876, Nos. 16, 17; Lichtenberger, *Encyclop. des Sciences Religieuses*, s. v. (B. P.)

Roumania comprises 4,598,219 inhabitants belonging to the Greek Church, 115,420 to the Church of Rome, 8803 to the Armenian Church, 7790 to the Evangelical Church, 401,051 Jews, 25,033 Mohammedans, and 16,058 who call themselves Lipowanians. The Greek Church is the State Church, organized on strictly hierarchical principles. At the head of the clergy is the archbishop or metropolitan and primate of Roumania, at Bucharest, and the archbishop of Moldavia, at Jassy. The lower clergy are educated at seminaries, and supported by the congregation, whereas the higher clergy, from the archbishops to the protopopes, are paid by the state. What is demanded from the lower clergy is the ability of reading the prescribed formularies and performing the ceremonies. The Roman Catholic Church has two bishops, one at Bucharest and another at Jassy. The Evangelical congregations, with the exception of that at Bucharest, are in connection with the State Church of Prussia, and receive their preachers from the Prussian consistory. These congregations have, however, their own government, but are required to send a very careful report through their ministers to the Prussian ecclesiastical authority. At present there exist eight Evangelical congregations—at Jassy, Bucharest, Galatz, Braila, Pitesti, Crajova, Turnu-Severin, and Atmadscha (Dobrudscha). Each congregation has its own parochial school, with male and female teachers. The latter are from the Kaiserswert house of deaconesses. See Plitt-Herzog, *Real-Encyklop.* s. v. (B. P.)

Rous (**Rouse**, or **Rowse**), Francis, a fanatical supporter of the English commonwealth, was born at Healton, Cornwall, in 1579, and educated at Broadgate Hall (now Pembroke College), Oxford. He afterwards studied law, and was a member of Parliament under Charles I. He was one of the few laymen appointed by the Commons to sit in the Westminster Assembly of Divines, and became provost of Eton in 1643. He died in 1659. His writings were printed in London in 1657, and include a utopian scheme of government modelled after the Jewish, and a metrical version of the Psalms. See Rose, *Biog. Dict.* s. v.

Roussel, Napoléon, a French Protestant theologian, was born at Sauve in 1805. He studied at Geneva, was in 1831 pastor at Saint Étienne, but at the instance of the consistory he had to resign in 1835 because his sermons "bore the stamp of Methodism." In vain did the majority of the Church protest against the intolerance of the consistory. Roussel resigned, and founded an independent chapel. In 1835 he was pastor at Marseilles, in 1838 he went to Paris, where he started a journal called *l'Esperance*, the organ of the orthodox party. He was the means of founding churches at Angoulême, Villefavard, Limoges, Balledant, etc. In 1863 Roussel went to Lyons, but resigned his pastorate in 1867. He then retired to Geneva, and died June 8, 1878. Besides his *Comment il ne faut pas Prêcher*, he published a great many brochures and tracts. See Lichtenberger, *Encyclop. des Sciences Religieuses*, s. v. (B. P.)

Rowden, Philip, D.D., a Baptist minister, was born in England in 1828, and in early life came to New York city. Not long after he was converted, and joined the Church in Newark, N. J. Having subsequently entered the ministry, his pastorates were successively in Newark, Bronson, Mich., and in Chili, Ind. His ministry was attended with powerful revivals. "He was a man of studious habits and deep research." He died in Rochester, Ind., April 4, 1875. See Cathcart, *Baptist Encyclop.* p. 1012. (J. C. S.)

Rowlandson, Michael, D.D., an English divine, was born about 1759, and educated at Queen's College Oxford. At the time of his death, July 8, 1824, he was vicar of Warminster. He was a man whose exemplary life and unceasing fidelity in the work of the ministry won for him the esteem and love of all who knew him. See (Lond.) *Christian Remembrancer*, Aug. 1824, p. 503.

Rowley, George, D.D., an English educator and divine, was born in 1782, and educated at University College, Oxford, of which he became successively fellow, tutor, and public examiner. In 1821 he was elected to the mastership of his college, and in 1832 was appointed to the vice-chancellorship of the University of Oxford, which he held till his death, Oct. 5, 1836. In his official duties he was noted for his punctuality and decision; and in private life he was distinguished for kindness of disposition and unselfishness of character. See (Lond.) *Christian Remembrancer*, Nov. 1836, p. 700.

Roxburgh, Hugo de, a Scotch prelate, was rector of Tullibody, and clerk to Nicoláus, the chancellor of Scotland. He was afterwards archdeacon of St. Andrews. In 1189 he was made chancellor of Glasgow, and in 1199 bishop, but sat only one year. He died in 1200. See Keith, *Scottish Bishops*, p. 236.

Rückert, Friedrich, an Orientalist, and one of the greatest German poets of the 19th century, was born at Schweinfurt, May 16, 1789. He studied at Jena, commenced his academical career in 1811, was professor of Oriental languages at Erlangen in 1826, and in 1841 at Berlin. He retired in 1846 to his country seat at Neusess, and died Jan. 31, 1866. He published, *Hebräische Propheten übersetzt und erläutert* (Leipsic, 1831):—*Leben Jesu, Evangelien-Harmonie in gebundener Rede* (Stuttgard, 1839):—*Heroden der Grosse* (1844). Some of his religious poems have been translated into English, as *Dein König kommt in niederen Hüllen* (in Schaff, *Christ in Song*, p. 33: "He comes, no royal vesture wearing"):—*Er ist in Bethlehem geboren* (ibid. p. 93: "In Bethlehem, the Lord of glory"):—*Das Paradies muss schöner sein* (ibid. p. 657: "Oh Paradise must fairer be"):—*Um Mitternacht bin ich erwacht* (Winkworth, *Christian Singers of Germany*, p. 337: "At dead of night Sleep took her flight"). (B. P.)

Rückert, Leopold Immanuel, a Protestant theologian of Germany, was born in 1797 at Grosshennersdorf, near Herrnhut, Upper Lusatia. He studied theology and philosophy at Leipsic, was for some time deacon at his native place, and published, in 1821, *De Ratione Tractandæ Theologiæ Dogmaticæ*. In 1825 he was appointed teacher at the Gymnasium of Zittau, and while there published, *Kommentar über den Brief Pauli an die Römer* (Leipsic, 1831; 2d ed. 1839):—*Kommentar über den Brief Pauli an die Galater* (1833):—*An die Epheser* (1834):—*An die Korinther* (1836-37). Rückert was made doctor of theology in 1836 by the theological faculty of Copenhagen, and in 1844 he was called to Jena, where he wrote, *Theologie* (Leipsic, 1851, 2 vols.):—*Das Abendmahl. Sein Wesen und seine Geschichte in der alten Kirche* (1856):—*Büchlein von der Kirche* (1857):—*Der Rationalismus* (1859). Rückert died April 9, 1871. See *Protestantische Kirchenzeitung*, 1871, p. 309-311; Zuchold, *Bibl. Theol.* s.v.; Lichtenberger, *Encyclop.*

des Sciences Religieuses, s. v.; Plitt-Herzog, *Real-Encyklop.* s. v. (B. P.)

Rudder, William, D.D., a Protestant Episcopal clergyman, was born in British Guiana; graduated from Trinity College and from the General Theological Seminary; was ordained deacon by bishop Brownell in 1851; officiated successively in St. Paul's Church, Flatbush, L. I.; Calvary Church, New York, as an assistant minister; St. Paul's Church, Albany, as rector; and in St. Stephen's, Philadelphia, Pa., as assistant. On the death of the Rev. Dr. Ducachet, rector of St. Stephen's, in 1865, Dr. Rudder assumed the rectorship, and remained in this pastorate until his death, Jan. 29, 1880, aged fifty-seven years. See Whittaker, *Almanac and Directory*, 1881, p. 174.

Rüdel, Carl Ernst Gottlieb, a Lutheran theologian of Germany, was born in 1769. He commenced his pastoral career at Leipsic in 1801, and died there in 1842, doctor of theology. He published, *Predigten* (1816):—*Festpredigten und Amtsreden* (1828–32, 2 vols.):—*Abendmahls- und Confirmationsreden* (1827–36, 6 vols.), etc. See Winer, *Handbuch der theol. Lit.* ii, 98, 149, 159, 179; Zuchold, *Bibl. Theol.* s. v. (B. P.)

Rüdiger, Johann Bartholomäus, a Lutheran theologian of Germany, was born at Grünberg, Hesse, Oct. 10, 1660. He studied at Giessen, was in 1691 preacher at Wetzlar, in 1697 professor at Giessen, in 1707 doctor of theology, and died July 3, 1729. He wrote, *De Pace inter Lutheranos et Reformatos* (Giessen, 1684):—*De Infinitate Dei* (1700):—*De Præsentia Dei Repletiva* (1701):—*De Natura Dei Perfectissime Simplici* (1706):—*De Angelorum Corpore Subtili et Assumto* (1707):—*De Justificatione Abrahæ ex Genes. xv*, 6 (1707):—*De Conscientia Scrupulosa* (1714):—*De Agno Occiso ab Origine Mundi* (1719):—*De Radicatione Fidelium in Christo* (1722):—*De Christo per Primam et Ultimam Sacra Scripturæ Vocem* (1724). See Döring, *Die gelehrten Theologen Deutschlands*, s. v. (B. P.)

Rüdiger, Franz Joseph, a Roman Catholic prelate of Austria, was born April 6, 1811, at Partheuen. In 1853 he was made bishop of Linz, and died Nov. 24, 1884. Rüdiger was one of those prelates who opposed all measures of the Austrian government which tended towards depriving the Church of any of her prerogatives. Rüdiger only knew one government, the supremacy of the Church. When the dogma of the Immaculate Conception was proclaimed, he celebrated that event by building a splendid cathedral at Linz, and erecting monasteries throughout his diocese. (B. P.)

Rule (Heb. *kav*, קַו, *a line* for measuring, as elsewhere rendered) is mentioned (Isa. xliv, 13) among the tools of the carpenter (חָרַשׁ עֵצִים, *hewer of wood*), the associated implements being the "line" (Heb. *séred*, שֶׂרֶד, probably *a graver*), the "plane" (Heb. *maktsu'âh*, מַקְצֻעָה, probably *a chisel*), and the "compass" (Heb. *mechugâh*, מְחוּגָה, probably *compasses*). See Handicraft.

Rullmann, Georg Wilhelm, a Lutheran theologian of Germany, was born March 16, 1757, and studied at Rinteln and Göttingen. In 1778 he was appointed con-rector at Rinteln, in 1782 professor of theology, in 1788 doctor of theology, and died June 16, 1804. He wrote, *De Insigni Psychologiæ in Theologia Revelata Usu* (Rinteln, 1779):—*Versuch eines Lehrbuchs der römischen Alterthümer* (1782; 2d ed. 1787):—*De Apostolis Primariis Religionis Christianæ Doctoribus* (1788):—*Tabula Harmoniam IV Evangelistorum Exhibens* (1790):—*De Prophetis Novi Testamenti* (eod.):—*Die heiligen Schriften des Neuen Bundes übersetzt und mit Anmerkungen versehen* (1790–91, 3 vols.):—*Observationes Criticæ Exegeticæ in Loca Quædam Epistolorum Pauli*, etc. (1795):—*Die christliche Religionslehre* (1803). See Döring, *Die gelehrten Theologen Deutschlands*, s. v. (B. P.)

Rulman, Merswin, one of the "Friends of God," of the 14th century, was born at Strasburg in 1307. He was a wealthy merchant and banker, when, in 1347, he gave up business, joined the Friends of God, and led a life of severe asceticism, under the guidance of Tauler. In 1366 Rulman acquired the island of Der grüne Wört, in the Ill, near Strasburg, and retired thither. He died July 18, 1382. Rulman's writings are, *Das Bannerbüchlein* (edited by Jundt, *Les Amis de Dieu*, Paris, 1879):—*Das Buch von den neun Felsen* (ed. by Schmidt, Leipsic, 1859), and an old Dutch version of the same, *Dat Boeck van den Oorspronck*, by G. H. van Boossum Waalkes, Leuwarden, 1882). See Schmidt, in *Révue d'Alsace* (1856); in Reuss und Cunitz, *Beiträge zu der theol. Wissenschaft*, vol. v (Jena 1854), and *Nikolaus von Basel* (Vienna, 1866); Jundt, *Les Amis de Dieu*, p. 140 sq.; Plitt-Herzog, *Real-Encyklop.* s. v. (B. P.)

Rumpe, Heinrich, a Lutheran theologian of Germany, was born at Hamburg in 1561, studied at different universities, was in 1592 professor of Hebrew at Helmstädt, in 1597 at Hamburg, and died Aug. 16, 1626. He wrote, *Vaticinia Aliquot de Messia*:—*Isagoge in Linguas Orientales Primarias*, etc. See Moller, *Cimbria Litterata*; Jöcher, *Allgemeines Gelehrten-Lexikon*, s. v.; Fürst, *Bibl. Jud.* s. v. (B. P.)

Runge, David, a Lutheran theologian of Germany, was born in 1564 at Greifswalde, where he was professor of Hebrew in 1589. In 1601 he attended the Colloquy of Ratisbon, and died July 7, 1604. He wrote, *Dissertationes viii de Calvinismo*:—*De Articulo Primo Symboli Apostolici*:—*De Verbis; non Facies Tibi Sculptile, Exod. xx*, 4:—*De Baptismo*, etc. See Jöcher, *Allgemeines Gelehrten-Lexikon*, s. v. (B. P.)

Runge, Johann, a Lutheran theologian of Sweden, was born in 1666, studied at Abo, was preacher there in 1691, in 1697 professor of theology, in 1701 doctor of theology and superintendent at Narva. Runge died Aug. 3, 1704. He wrote, *Comment. in ix, x et xi cap. ad Romanos*:—*De Sede Animæ in Homine*

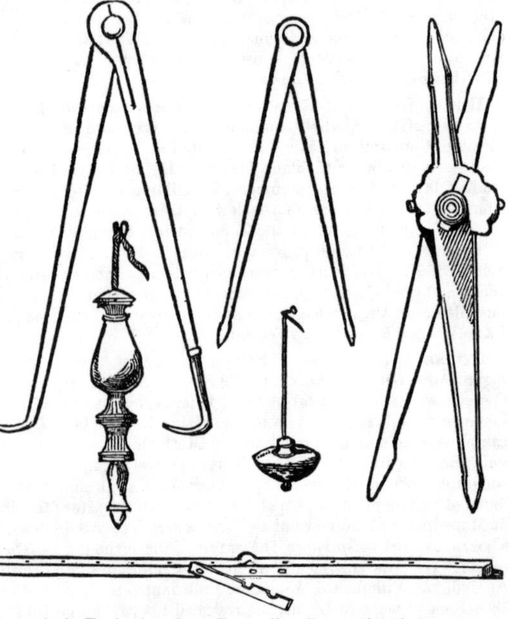

Carpenter's Tools found at Pompeii. (Proportional Compasses, Calipers, Compasses, Rule, and Plumb-lines).

Præcipua. See Stirnmann, *Aboa Literata;* Jöcher, *Allgemeines Gelehrten-Lexikon,* s. v. (B. P.)

Rupp, Julius, a Protestant theologian of Germany, was born in 1809. He belonged to the so-called Friends of Light (q. v.), and founded in 1846 the first free congregation. He died July 11, 1884, doctor of philosophy. Rupp published, *Gregor's, des Bischofs von Nyssa, Leben und Meinungen* (Leipsic, 1834):—*Der Symbolzwang und die protestantische Lehr- und Gewissensfreiheit* (Königsberg, 1843):—*Christliche Predigten* (1843-45):—*Erbauungsbuch für freie evangelische Gemeinden* (1846):—*Von der Freiheit* (1856, 2 vols.):—*Das Sektenwesen und die freie Gemeinde* (1859), etc. See Zuchold, *Bibl. Theol.* s. v. (B. P.)

Rus, Johann Reinhard, a Lutheran theologian of Germany, was born Feb. 24, 1679, and studied at Giessen and Jena. In 1708 he was made adjunct to the philosophical faculty of Jena, in 1712 professor of theology, in 1730 doctor of theology, and died April 18, 1738. He wrote, *De Usu Linguæ Syriacæ in Novo Testamento:—De Usu Accentuationis Hebraicæ Pentade Dictorum Veteris Testamenti Demonstrato:—De Harmonia Vitæ Davidis:—De Zacharia non Summo Pontifice ad Luc. i:—De Serpente non Naturali sed solo Diabolo ad Genes. iii:—De Evocatione Abrahami:—De Sceptro a Juda Ablato ad Genes. xlix:—De LXX Hebdomadibus Danielis:—De Lapidatione Stephani:—De Vario Mosis in Montem Sinai Ascensu:—Bileam Vates Evangelicus ex Num. xxiv, 15-19:—Introductio in Novum Testamentum Generalis:—Harmonia Evangelistarum:—De Magis non Judæis ad Matth. ii,* etc. See Döring, *Die gelehrten Theologen Deutschlands,* s. v.; Winer, *Handbuch der theol. Lit.* i, 244, 590; Jöcher, *Allgemeines Gelehrten-Lexikon,* s. v. (B. P.)

Russel, William, a Scotch prelate, was a native of the Isle of Man and abbot of Rushen. He was consecrated bishop of the Isles in 1248, and held a synod at St. Michael's in 1350, in which five additional canons were made. He died April 4, 1374. See Keith, *Scottish Bishops,* p. 303.

Russell, Andrew, D.D., a Scotch Congregational minister, was born at Winchburgh, Linlithgowshire, Nov. 1, 1807. He was educated in letters at the University of Edinburgh, and in theology at the Glasgow Theological Academy. He was ordained pastor at Haddington in 1833, where he labored some eight years; next at Princes Street Chapel, Dundee, four years. The state of his health at this time requiring a change of climate, he removed to Stirling, where he enjoyed a long and successful pastorate. From Stirling he went to Bradford, Yorkshire, in 1859, and for some years took pastoral charge of the Chapel at Lister Hills. During the last twelve and a half years of his life he was pastor of the Church at Holme Lane, Bradford. He died June 19, 1881, having filled with great honor several denominational offices. See (Lond.) *Cong. Year-book,* 1882, p. 329.

Russell, Charles William, D.D., a Roman Catholic divine, was born at Killough, County Down, Ireland, May 14, 1812. He was educated at Drogheda, at Downpatrick, and at Maynooth College; was elected to the Dunboyne Establishment in 1832, for ten years discharged his duties as professor at Maynooth, and in 1845, when the chair of ecclesiastical history was established, he was appointed thereto. He held this position until the death of Dr. Renehan in 1857, when he became president of the college, which office he filled until his death, on Feb. 26, 1880. Dr. Russell was a regular contributor to the *Dublin Review* and *Edinburgh Review.* He published translations of the *Tales of Canon von Schmid* and Leibnitz's *System of Theology.* His *Life of Cardinal Mezzofanti* (1858) had its origin in an article on that wonderful linguist in the *Edinburgh Review* of 1855, and included notices of the most celebrated linguists of all countries. It was translated into Italian and published at Bologna in 1859. A second edition appeared in 1863. In 1869 Dr. Russell was appointed a member of the royal commission on historical manuscripts, and from 1872 he edited, in conjunction with Mr. Prendergast, several volumes of the *Calendars of State Papers* relating to Ireland, beginning with the reign of James I. Dr. Russell contributed also to the eighth edition of the *Encyclopædia Britannica, North British Review,* the *English Cyclopædia,* the *Academy,* and several other publications. See (N. Y.) *Catholic Almanac,* 1881, p. 106.

Russell, David, D.D., a Scotch Congregational minister, was born in Glasgow, Oct. 10, 1779. He studied literature and the classics privately, and theology at the Edinburgh Theological Academy. In August, 1805, he was sent to Aberdeen, where he supplied the pulpit five months. He then removed to Montrose for nine months, but returned to Aberdeen, where he was ordained pastor in 1807. He went to Dundee in 1809, and became pastor of the Church then assembling in Sailor's Hall. In this charge he continued thirty-nine years, with great honor to all concerned. He died Sept. 23, 1848. Dr. Russell published, among other works, *Letters, chiefly Practical and Consolatory:—On the Old and New Covenants:—The Way of Salvation:—Hints to Inquirers:—Infant Salvation,* etc. See (Lond.) *Cong. Year-book,* 1848, p. 237.

Russell, John, LL.D., a Baptist minister, was born at Cavendish, Vt., July 1, 1793. He graduated from Middlebury College in 1812, was converted just before entering upon his senior year, and soon after his graduation went to Georgia, where he taught school for a time. From 1819 to 1826 he was tutor in a private family in Missouri, and subsequently taught in St. Louis, Vandalia, Alton Seminary, and later in life was principal of Spring Hill Academy, in East Feliciana, La. On Feb. 9, 1833, he was licensed to preach by the Bluffdale Church, Ill. He died Jan. 21, 1863. Dr. Russell wrote, as an advocate of temperance, *Venomous Worm; or, Worm of the Still.* To counteract Universalism he preached a number of discourses, which were afterwards published under the title of *The Serpent Uncoiled.* He was an accomplished linguist and an able scholar. See *Minutes of Illinois Anniversaries,* 1863, p. 13. (J. C. S.)

Russell, Patrick, D.D., an Irish prelate, was promoted to the see of Dublin Aug. 2, 1683. In July, 1685, he held a provincial council at Dublin, in which it was ordained that any priest, celebrating a marriage without license from the ordinary, or the parish priest of the place, should be excommunicated, etc. The council further confirmed the decrees of those held in 1614 by Dr. Eugene Matthews and in 1640 by Dr. Fleming. In 1686 Dr. Russell assisted at a session of the Roman Catholic clergy, held in Dublin. He also presided at a diocesan synod, held there, June 10, 1686, in which it was decreed, in reference to the parochial clergymen having cure of souls, that each should have a schoolmaster in his parish to instruct the little children in "Christian doctrine and good courses." In 1688 he presided at a synod held in Dublin. On the downfall of the Stuart dynasty he fled to Paris. He returned to his native country and died at the close of the year 1692. See D'Alton, *Memoirs of the Archbishops of Dublin,* p. 446.

Rutledge, Francis Huger, D.D., a bishop of the Protestant Episcopal Church, a native of South Carolina, and a son of chancellor Hugh Rutledge, graduated from Yale College in 1820, and was for some time rector of St. John's Parish, Tallahassee, Fla. He was consecrated bishop of Florida, Oct. 15, 1851, in St. Paul's Church, Augusta, Ga., and died at Tallahassee, Nov. 6, 1866, aged sixty-eight years. See *Amer. Quar. Church Rev.* Jan. 1867, p. 646.

Rütz, Franz Georg Christoph, a Lutheran theologian, was born at Ratzeburg, Oct. 22, 1733. He studied at Rostock. In 1762 he was preacher of the

Lutheran Church at Amsterdam, in 1764 was called to Breda, and in 1775 accepted a call to the Hague. Rütz died Dec. 31, 1802, leaving, *Non Placet Nobis Orthodoxia sine Pietate, nec Pietas sine Orthodoxia* (Amsterdam, 1777):—*Exegetische und kritische Briefe* (1779):—*Kleine Bydragen tot de deistische Letterkunde* (Hague, 1782):—*Apologie van het Leeraarampt* (1784), etc. See Döring, *Die gelehrten Theologen Deutschlands*, s. v. (B. P.)

Ryan, George Frederick, D.D., a Welsh Congregational minister, was born at Abergavenny, Monmouthshire, in 1790. He joined the Church at the age of fourteen, began village preaching in his sixteenth year, entered Rotherham College in 1814, and commenced his pastoral life at Bridlington. After four years' labor in that place he removed to Stockport, where he ministered ten years, and then went to Dogley Lane Chapel, near Huddersfield. In 1836 he again returned to Bridlington. He died at Dore, Aug. 19, 1865. His principal publication was entitled *The Dialogist.* He also, at various times, published sermons and pamphlets. See (Lond.) *Cong. Year-book*, 1866, p. 283.

Ryan, Henry, founder of the "Canadian Wesleyan Methodist Church" (so called), or Ryanites, was born of Irish parentage in Connecticut, April 22, 1775. Educated a Roman Catholic, while teaching school he heard the eccentric Methodist preacher, Lorenzo Dow, was converted, united with the Methodists, and was disowned by his parents. He taught school for six years after his conversion, preaching regularly, however, and introducing Methodism into a part of Warren County, N. Y. In 1800 he was received into the New York Conference. His circuits in the United States were Vergennes (large part of Vermont) and Plattsburg, N. Y. In 1805 Asbury sent him and William Case to reinforce the Methodist force in Canada. Firm to obstinacy, of indomitable perseverance and iron will, he had a courage that never quailed. In labors and sacrifices he was abundant. During the war of 1812 the oversight of the societies in Canada devolved upon him, and from 1815 to 1825 he continued to itinerate as a presiding elder, now on the Upper Canada District, then on the Lower Canada District. In 1827 he withdrew from the connection, in consequence of a difference of opinion on Church government. Shortly afterwards some of those who had espoused Ryan's cause organized the Canadian Wesleyan Methodist Church, making lay delegation its distinguishing feature. With this body Ryan united, and with it he continued to be identified during the brief remainder of his earthly existence. He died in September, 1832. See Dr. T. Webster, in the *National Repository*, Sept. 1880; Stevens, *Hist. of the Meth. Episcopal Church* (see Index, vol. iv); Playter, *Hist. of Methodism in Canada* (Toronto, 1862), p. 84, 234, 297–99.

Ryder, John, D.D., an Irish prelate, was created bishop of Killaloe in 1741; transferred to the see of Down and Connor in 1743, and to the archbishopric of Tuam in 1752. He died at Nice, Italy, Feb. 4, 1775, in the seventy-eighth year of his age. See (Lond.) *Annual Register*, 1775, p. 206.

Ryerson, Edgerton, D.D., LL.D., an eminent Canadian Methodist minister, was born in the Province of Ontario, Canada, in 1803. He united with the Methodist Episcopal Church in 1823. He received an early classical education preparatory to the study of law, but entered the itinerant work, preaching his first sermon on Easter Sunday, 1825. In 1829 he became the first editor of the *Christian Guardian;* in 1842 was appointed the first president of Victoria College; and in 1845 was made superintendent of education for the Province of Upper Canada, an office he held for thirty years. On the union of the Wesleyan Methodists, the New Connection, and the Eastern British Conference, he was elected first president of the Methodist Church in Canada. He visited Europe and the United States a number of times in the interests of Methodism and education, and was twice a representative to the British Conference and to the General Conference of the Methodist Episcopal Church of the United States. He died at Toronto, Feb. 19, 1882. Among his writings, aside from editorial work, may be mentioned his *Manual of Agricultural Chemistry:—Compulsory Education:—The Clergy Reserve Question*, etc.

Ryland, John, D.D., a learned English Baptist minister, was born at Warwick, Jan. 29, 1753. His father was a fine scholar and able minister, and taught his son Greek and Hebrew and Scripture history. He was baptized at fourteen, and began to preach in 1778, in and around Northampton, as his father's assistant; then as co-pastor, aiding his father in his academy, in which young men were trained for the ministry. In 1786 he was sole pastor at Northampton. In co-operation with Carey, Fuller, Sutcliffe, and others, he originated the Baptist Missionary Society, Oct. 2, 1792. He became president of the Baptist College, Bristol, and pastor of the Broadmead Chapel in that city in 1794. In 1815 he became secretary of the Baptist Missionary Society. He died May 25, 1825. Dr. Ryland wrote, *Memoirs of Robert Hall, of Drusby:—A Candid Statement of the Reasons which Induce the Baptists to Differ from their Christian Brethren:*—some *Sermons:*—and nearly a hundred *Hymns*, which appeared in magazines, signed "J. R. jun." These have been published in a neat volume by Daniel Sedgwick.

S.

Sabai Version of the Scriptures. Sabai is spoken in several islands in Torres Strait, between Australia and Papua. The gospel of Mark was printed at Sydney in 1883 under the care of the Auxiliary of the British and Foreign Bible Society. The translation was made by a teacher, Elia, who had been fifteen years engaged on the work, and revised by the Rev. S. Macfarlane, of Murray Island. The gospel of Matthew has since then been added. (B. P.)

Sabba, Abraham ibn-, a Jewish writer of the 16th century, who was banished with thousands of Jews from Lisbon in 1499, is the author of a very extensive commentary on the Pentateuch, entitled *The Bundle of Myrrh* צרור המור, in which he largely avails himself of the zohar and other early cabalistic works. The commentary was first published at Constantinople in 1514; then at Venice in 1523, 1546, 1566, and at Cracow in 1595. Pellican has translated this commentary into Latin, and the MS. of this version is in the Zurich library. See Fürst, *Bibl. Jud.* s. v.; Ginsburg, *Kabbalah*, p. 123; Lindo, *History of the Jews in Spain and Portugal*, p. 266; Jöcher, *Allgemeines Gelehrten-Lexikon*, s. v. (B. P.)

Saddler, Isaac P., D.D., a Methodist Episcopal minister, was born in Westmoreland County, Pa., Oct. 5, 1807. He was converted in 1839, licensed to preach in 1840, entered the Pittsburgh Conference in 1853, was superannuated in 1872, and assigned to the East Ohio Conference at its organization in 1876. He died suddenly, March 2, 1882. See *Minutes of Annual Conferences*, 1882, p. 329.

Safed is an important, but comparatively modern town of Palestine, eight miles north-west of the sea of Galilee, famous especially as a mediæval seat of Jewish learning. The following account of it is taken from Murray's *Hand-book for Syria* (p. 418). Further details may be found in the *Memoirs* accompanying the Ordnance Survey (i, 199, 248).

"Safed lies on an isolated peak, which crowns the southern brow of the mountain range. A deep glen sweeps round its northern and western sides, and a shallower one, after skirting the eastern side, falls into the former a few miles to the south. Beyond these, on the north-east, north, and west, are higher hills, but on the south the view is open. The old castle crowns the peak; the Jewish quarter of the town clings to the western side, considerably below the summit, the rows of houses arranged like stairs. There are, besides, two Moslem quarters—one occupying the ridge to the south, and the other nestling in the valley to the east. The population may be estimated at about four thousand, of whom one third are Jews and a very few families Christians.

"The only attraction of Safed is the splendid view it commands. This is best seen from the summit of the castle. The latter is surrounded by a deep, dry ditch, within which was a wall. All is now a mass of ruins. Only a shattered fragment of one of the great round towers has survived the earthquake of 1837. Before that catastrophe it was not in the best repair, still, it afforded accommodation to the governor and his train; but then, in a few minutes, it was utterly ruined, and many of its inmates buried beneath the fallen towers.

"Safed is first mentioned in the Vulgate version of the book of Tobit [rather as *Safat* in the Jerusalem Talmud; perhaps also the *Seph* of Josephus (*War*, ii, 25)]. Tradition has made it the site of *Bethulia* of the book of Judith, but without evidence. The castle seems to have been founded by the crusaders to guard their territory against the inroads of the Saracens. It was garrisoned by the Knights Templars. Its defences, both natural and artificial, were so strong that Saladin besieged it for five weeks before he was able to capture it. After lying in ruins for many years it was rebuilt by Benedict, bishop of Marseilles, in the year 1240. But it only remained twenty years in the hands of the Christians, for, being hard pressed by Sultan Bibars, the garrison capitulated and were murdered to a man, the chief being flayed alive by the barbarous Mohammedans. From that period till the past century it continued to be one of the bulwarks of Palestine.

"We know not when the Jews first settled in Safed, or at what period they raised the town to the rank of a 'holy city.' There were no Jews in the place in the middle of the 12th century, when Benjamin of Tudela visited the country; and it was not, in fact, until four centuries later that the schools of Safed became celebrated. Then a printing-press was set up, synagogues were built, and the rabbis of Safed were acknowledged to be among the chief ornaments of Hebrew literature. The 16th century was their golden age. In the 17th both learning and funds began to decline, and the earthquake of 1837 gave a deathblow to the Jewish cause. Printing-press, synagogues, schools, houses, and people were all involved in one common ruin."

Safford, Jefferson Price, D.D., a Presbyterian minister, was born at Zanesville, O., Sept. 22, 1823. He graduated from the University of Ohio, at Athens, in 1843; taught at Dry Creek Academy, Covington, Ky., and at Indianapolis Academy, Ind., for two years each; was professor of mathematics at Covington, in 1847 and 1848; next entered Princeton Seminary, N. J., where he graduated in 1852; was licensed by the Presbytery of Philadelphia, April 5, 1851; taught mathematics at Richmond Academy, Richmond, Va., three years, supplying also, part of the time, the Church at Bethlehem, and was ordained by the Presbytery of West Lexington, at Frankfort, Ky., Feb. 9, 1855. His fields of labor were the Church at Frankfort, from 1855 to 1857; pastor of First Church, Piqua, O., from 1857 to 1862; First Church, New Albany, Ind., from 1862 to 1867, and district secretary of the Board of Missions for Ohio and Indiana from 1867 to 1870. He served as stated supply to Brownsville (O.) Church from 1870 to 1876, at the same time supplying also Fairmount Church from 1870 to 1877, Rosville Church from 1871 to 1873, acting as president of Zanesville University in 1871 and 1872, supplying Uniontown (O.) Church from 1871 to 1873, Hanover Church in 1873 and 1874, Kirkersville Church from 1874 to 1879, and Claysville and West Carlisle churches until his death, which occurred at Zanesville, July 10, 1881. Dr. Safford was also the accurate and efficient stated clerk of the Presbytery of Zanesville from 1873, and of the synod of Columbus from 1876. See *Necrol. Report of Princeton Theol. Sem.* 1882, p. 48.

Sahm, Peter, D.D., a Lutheran minister, graduated from Gettysburg Theological Seminary in 1831, and entered the ministry in 1832, the period of his service comprising forty-four years. He preached in both German and English, as occasion required. A considerable time he was pastor at Green Castle. At the time of his death he was serving the Church at New Berlin, Pa. He died at Laurelton, March 14, 1876, aged sixty-six years. See *Lutheran Observer*, March 24, 1876.

Saint Aldegonde. See Marnix, Philippe.

Saint Andrews. See Andrew's, St.

Saint Brieuc. See Brieuc, St.

Saint Claude. See Claude, St.

Saint Cyran. See Duvergier.

Saint Denis. See Denis, St.

Saint Edmunds, Alan, a Scotch prelate, was bishop of the see of Caithness in 1290, and in 1291 was made lord chancellor. He died in 1292. See Keith, *Scottish Bishops*, p. 211.

Saint Gall. See Gall, St.

Saint Martin. See Martin (*Saint*), Louis Claude de.

Saint Omer. See Omer, St.

Saker, Alfred, a missionary to the "Dark Continent," was born in England, July 21, 1814. At the age of twenty-nine he was accepted by the Baptist Missionary Society for the mission on the west coast of Africa. In 1845 Saker settled at King Aqua's Town, the seat of a large tribe, on the left bank of the Cameroons River, and about twenty miles from its mouth. With great difficulty he mastered the Dualla language, spoken by the people among whom he lived. Early in November, 1849, he baptized the first convert, and in the afternoon of the day a church was formed, consisting of the missionary and his wife, the native helpers, and the Dualla convert. Mr. Saker translated the Bible into the Dualla language, and died at Victoria, March 13, 1880, having spent thirty-four years in Africa. (B. P.)

Salat, Jacob, a Roman Catholic theologian and philosopher of Germany, was born Aug. 24, 1766. In 1801 he was professor of ethics and pastoral theology at Munich, in 1807 professor of moral philosophy at Landshut, and died in 1851. He published, *Die Religionsphilosophie dargestellt* (Landshut, 1811):—*Grundlinien der Religionsphilosophie* (Sulzbach, 1819):—*Grundlinien der Moralphilosophie* (Munich, 1827):—*Versuche über Supranaturalismus und Mysticismus* (Sulzbach, 1823):—*Sokrates, oder über den neuesten Gegensatz zwischen Christenthum und Philosophie* (1820):—*Ist der Priestercölibat ein Ideal?* (Stuttgart, 1833):—*Die literarische Stellung der Protestanten zu den Katholiken* (1831):—*Aufschluss über den Ultrakatholicismus* (1833):—*Schelling und Hegel* (Heidelberg, 1842). See Zuchold, *Bibl. Theol.* s. v.; Winer, *Handbuch der theol. Lit.* i, 285, 288, 370, 375, 466, 723. (B. P.)

Salim. Lieut. Conder (*Tent Work*, i, 92) advocates the position of this place at *Salîm*, four miles east of Nablûs, urging the abundance of water there, and the presence of a village, Ainûn (Ænon), seven and a half miles to the north-east; and Tristram (*Bible Places*, p. 192) likewise accepts this situation for similar reasons, adding that "it is close to one of the old main lines of road from Jerusalem to Galilee." "The head-springs are found in an open valley surrounded by desolate and shapeless hills. The water gushes out over a stony bed, and flows rapidly down in a fine stream surrounded by bushes of oleander. The supply is perennial, and a continual succession of little springs occurs along the bed of the valley, so that the current becomes the principal western affluent of Jordan south of the Vale of Jezreel. The valley is open in most parts of its course, and we find the two requisites for the scene of baptism of a multitude—an open space and abundance of water" (Conder). Salîm itself is described in the *Memoirs* accompanying the Ordnance Survey (ii, 230) as "a small village, resembling the rest, but evidently ancient, having rock-cut tombs, cisterns, and a tank. Olive-trees surround it; on the north are two springs, three quarters of a mile from the village."

Salkinson, Isaac E., a missionary among the Jews, and an excellent Hebrew scholar, who died June 15, 1883, at Presburg, in the employ of the British Society for Jewish Missions, is the author of a Hebrew translation of *Philosophy of the Plan of Salvation* (Altona, 1858). Besides translating into Hebrew Milton's *Paradise Lost*, Shakespeare's *Romeo and Juliet*, he published *The Epistle of Paul the Apostle to the Romans*, translated from the original Greek (Edinburgh, 1855). At the time of his death he had finished a Hebrew translation of the New Test., which was edited by Dr. Ch. D. Ginsburg of England, and published at the expense of the English Trinitarian Bible Society at the imperial press of K. Fromme, in Vienna. The translation has been made in "classical Hebrew idiom," but "in seeking for elegance of language, exegetical and historical correctness, which are always closely connected with correctness of language, has been lost." See *Theologisches Literaturblatt* (Leipsic, 1885, Nos. 45, 46, 47). (B. P.)

Sall, Andrew, D.D., an English divine, was born near Cashel, Ireland, about 1612, and after having studied for some time at St. Omer's, was transferred to Valladolid, in Spain, that he might become conversant with the rules and institutions of the Jesuits. Having acquired distinction as a theologian, he was appointed successively reader of divinity at Pampeluna, professor at Tudela and Valencia, rector of the Irish College, and lecturer of controversial divinity at the University of Salamanca. It was at this time that many of the influential Roman Catholics in Ireland expressed their willingness to adhere to king Charles II, and renounce the interference of all foreign power, even though the pope should excommunicate them. Under these circumstances it was deemed expedient by the Romish court to send Jesuits to Ireland, and among them was Sall. Some years later, however, a change took place in his religious views, and he joined the Church of England, in connection with which he labored with exemplary diligence till his death, April 6, 1682. His works are, *Recantation*, and a *Sermon on Matt. xxiv, 15–18, in Confutation of the Errors of the Church of Rome* (Lond. 1674, 8vo):—*The Catholick and Apostolick Faith Maintained in the Church of England* (Oxford, 1676, 8vo):—*Votum pro Pace Christiana* (1678, 4to):—*Ethica seu Moralis Philosophia* (1680, 8vo). See (Lond.) *Church of England Magazine*, July, 1841, p. 3; Allibone, *Dict. of Brit. and Amer. Authors*, s. v.

Salle, John Baptist de la, founder of the order of Christian Brothers, was born at Rheims, France, April 30, 1651. At the age of seventeen he was made canon of the Cathedral of his native city, and after studying some time at the Sulpician Seminary in Paris, he took the degree of doctor of divinity, and was ordained priest in 1678. He died in Rouen, April 9, 1719. The order which he established is devoted to teaching, especially among the poorer classes. He introduced the mutual-simultaneous method of instruction, and also composed a treatise on school government. The order was approved by Benedict XIII, and has thousands of schools, and first-class colleges at Passy, near Paris, at Marseilles, Manhattanville, N. Y., St. Louis, Baltimore, etc. Baptist de la Salle was declared venerable by Gregory XVI, May 8, 1840, and beatified by Pius IX in 1873. See (N. Y.) *Cath. Almanac*, 1873, p. 88.

Salthen, Daniel Lorenz, a Lutheran theologian, was born March 16, 1701, at Markin, near Upsala, and died at Königsberg, Jan. 29, 1750, doctor and professor of theology. He wrote, *De Articulis Smalcaldicis* (Königsberg, 1729):—*Introductio in Omnes Libros Sacros* (1736):—*De Auctore Libri Sapientiæ* (1739). See Fürst, *Bibl. Jud.* s. v.; Winer, *Handbuch der theol. Lit.* i, 329; Jöcher, *Allgemeines Gelehrten-Lexikon*, s. v. (B. P.)

Salvation Army, The. This new religious organization is, in some of its agencies and operations, suggestive of the reformation under Luther, and of the religious awakening under the Wesleys. Each of these great movements was so startling in its character that it commanded wide-spread attention, and excited opposition and envy on every hand. Their enemies declared that the work would soon come to naught, and that such inflammable material would soon burn itself out. But these disparaging predictions have not been fulfilled with regard to the former two efforts, nor are they likely to be realized in the case of the Salvation Army. Not designed for any merely human aggrandizement, not antagonistic to any other religious organization, it began with a burning desire in the heart of one Christian minister to "rescue the perishing" in London. It was the privilege of the writer to hear William Booth, the general and founder of the Salvation Army, preach the gospel in a prison when he was only twenty years old, and to be an intimate personal acquaintance of his from that time to the present.

I. *Origin of the Movement*.—1. William Booth was born in the town of Nottingham in the year 1829. His parents belonged to the Church of England, but at the age of fourteen he began to attend the services of the Wesleyan Methodists, then and now a large and influential body in the town. Their services had in them more life and energy than he found in the Established Church, and having experienced a change of heart in these exercises, his affections were naturally centred where he had derived so much good; hence, though young in years, he began to attend mission and open-air services and cottage-meetings among the poor in the neglected parts of the town. He soon became an exhorter, and related at the meetings his own happy experience, persuading others to seek salvation. During the daytime he was employed at the miscellaneous store of a pawnbroker, and there he became practically acquainted with the wants, privations, and sufferings of the poor. His natural quickness of observation and his retentive memory were used by him to advantage. In the evenings and on Sundays, while a mere youth, he began to preach short, earnest sermons, in the open air, in all weathers, inviting sinners to Christ. In 1846, when only seventeen, he was accepted as a local preacher, became zealous and useful, and his labors were much owned of God. He was then a mere stripling, tall, with long, flowing black hair, a piercing eye, and a tongue of fire. Before he was twenty he was urged to enter the Methodist ministry, but in addition to his want of theological training, the doctors told him that one year of the earnest ministerial work, to which he was occasionally called, would probably exhaust the little strength he had; and as he was not physically strong, he waited for a time to see if his health improved. In the meanwhile he was wholly engaged, partly in London and partly in Lincolnshire, as an evangelist, a work in which he took special delight.

At the age of twenty-four he was accepted as a minister on trial in the Methodist New Connection, and placed for a time under the care of the Rev. William Cooke, D.D., for theological training. Shortly afterwards, in 1854, their society at Guernsey invited him to raise their cause, then in a low condition, and at the same time improve his own health in their mild and genial atmosphere. At the first Sunday service he held there thirty persons were converted, and within a month three hundred were added to the church membership. He had to return to London, but the news of his success quickly spread through the Connection, and he soon afterwards had invitations to ten circuits, to hold special services for a week or two in each. The conference that year sent him out as an evangelist, the results of which may be judged by the returns from a few places: at Hanley, Staffordshire, 400 conversions; at Newcastle, in one week, 290; at Sheffield, in four weeks, over 400; at Chester, several hundred. Fifteen of these converts are known to have become ordained ministers of the gospel.

2. Jealousy among a few senior preachers, who could not command such success, obliged him to settle down in a circuit, and he spent three years (1857–59) at Gateshead-on-Tyne, where, by his labors, the membership was trebled. He was next sent to Newcastle, with the same result, having in the meantime married Catharine Mumford, daughter of Mr. J. Mumford, a good London Methodist; and his young wife worked earnestly and lovingly with him. Her piety, zeal, discretion, and ability entitle her to take rank with the late Mrs. Phœbe Palmer, of New York, as one of the specially called and gifted of God to do a great work for him in the world and in the church. Seeing how God was working by Mr. Booth among a class of people seldom reached by the ordinary minister, and feeling the burden of souls pressing upon him, he made a most earnest appeal to the Liverpool Conference of 1861 to again appoint him as an evangelist; and his appeal, worthy of Dr. Coke or George Whitefield, was supported for a while by an equally earnest appeal made by Mrs. Booth from the gallery of the chapel. Some of the older preachers were shocked by a woman addressing the conference, and she was silenced. The conference made a great mistake in not accepting Mr. Booth's services as an evangelist: had they done so, their membership might have been doubled in ten years; instead of which, after the lapse of a quarter of a century, their membership is less to-day than it was then, and does not number thirty thousand after the lapse of nearly ninety years. Mr. Booth resigned his connection with the body, and resolved to await the openings of Providence; without employment, home, or income, he and his devoted wife looked alone to God for guidance, and it soon came.

Visiting Cornwall, he found many earnest Methodists in hearty sympathy with the yearnings of his heart. Mrs. Booth now fully shared his labors, herself preaching and holding revival services both on the Sabbath and on week days. In this way they spent two years as missionaries, in various localities, for three or four weeks each. Fishermen and tin miners came to their services by thousands, whole neighborhoods were stirred all round, the claims of religion became paramount, and men by scores left their work to seek divine mercy. The knowledge of these gracious outpourings of the Holy Spirit spread throughout the country. One chapel was kept open from daylight in the morning till midnight for a whole week. The result of such manifestations awakened general interest in the work, and invitations for the services of Mr. and Mrs. Booth reached them from all parts of England and Wales. These occupied them both for two years more, and in June, 1865, they came to London.

Providentially they were directed to the East End, a locality where, within the limits of half a mile, eighteen thousand persons, men and women, were counted entering drinking-saloons on one Sunday. There, on a heap of refuse, Mr. Booth commenced the work which has developed into the great Christian army known the world over. A small pocket Bible and hymn-book were his only weapons. In 1883 Mrs. Booth, in writing of herself and Mr. Booth in 1865, remarks: "He left a happy and prosperous ministerial career, gave up all that is commonly regarded as valuable in life, came out without any human encouragement or guarantees, and devoted himself to labor among the neglected masses, with no thought beyond that of a local work in the east of London. We surrendered home, income, every friend we had in the world, save my parents [whom they nourished in old age], with four little children under five years old, to trust only in God. During the ten years following, we were groping our way out of the conventionalism in which we had been trained, and often reluctantly following the pillar of cloud by which God was leading us. We tried committees, conferences, and all sorts of governments, showing how far we were wrong till the grand military idea was revealed to us."

Not much consideration was required to convince Mr. Booth that in East London there was labor for a man's life, however earnest and long-lived he might be; and having his sympathies strongly drawn towards the dense mass of godless people in the streets day and night, he gave up invitations to labor in the provinces to devote himself fully to the teeming population of Whitechapel and its surroundings. In ten or fifteen minutes he would gather a congregation of a thousand people, to whom he preached daily the plain gospel in the old-fashioned manner. He was a Methodist to the backbone, and in all his addresses he taught and enforced the necessity of repentance, faith, and holiness. God wonderfully owned the word preached; its effects had been witnessed in Cornwall and other parts, and it was soon found that conversions followed the preaching in London. As there was no place in which to gather the people, Mr. John Eason, an old Methodist, lent Mr. Booth a preaching tent which he had long used on London Fields. Crowds gathered there, many were saved, and these soon began to be useful in their own localities, each one asking himself, after he had found Jesus,

> "What shall I do to make it known
> What Thou for all mankind hast done?"

Mr. Booth prepared a cheap hymn-book, which was sold freely at all the meetings, and thousands were bought and read by the new converts. These, one after another, began to speak of the blessings they had received, and their testimony deepened and intensified the general interest in the services; so that the companions of these poor men, now made rich by faith, began to think there was something in the preaching which had completely changed very bad persons, and made them lovers of home, of God, and of their fellow-creatures. The storms of autumn scattered the tent in which they found shelter, but the work went on in the open air. As winter approached, shelter was required, and one of the lowest of the many drinking-saloons, a very den of infamy, was secured, and converted into a mission hall and book-store, for the sale of hymns, tracts, and such literature as would be suitable to young converts brought up in utter ignorance of religion. Next a large dancing-saloon was taken and used in the same way. Both these places were soon filled by eager listeners, services being held on the ground-floor and the first-floor simultaneously, the stairs and passages crowded at nearly every service by the neglected poor, who saw in these agencies and ministrations the means of rescuing themselves from sin, misery, and poverty. Believing in the advantages of labor, and in the truth of Mr. Wesley's adage, "All at work and always at work," Mr. Booth found employment for many of the converts in extending the mission, and it was soon manifest that they were gradually rising in the moral and social scale. Converts increased, people by thousands attended the exercises, and in less than a year Mr. Booth hired a large theatre for services on Sunday, which proved attractive to the outcast. Crowds gathered there, young and old, most of whom had lived like heathen, with no knowledge of God or regard for his laws. Drunkards became sober, swearers began to pray, those who had lived by stealing stole no more, scores of old and forgotten debts were paid, multitudes of women were rescued from ruin, and appeals now came to Mr. Booth to open new missions at Bethnal Green, Limehouse, Poplar, Canning Town, Croydon, Norwood, and other places; in these localities the applicants were directed to procure a room, and speakers were sent to hold services. It is amusing to survey, at this time, the variety of spots used for the new efforts, many of which the writer personally visited at the time —a club-room, a cellar, a shed, a railway arch, behind a pigeon-shop, an old factory, a schoolroom, a cottage—so eager were the poor people to get the gospel preached to them. They had not been accustomed to churches or chapels; they knew little about the Bible, and parsons they thought their greatest enemies. They belonged to the refuse of mankind—navvies, sailors, gypsies, infidels, scoffers, drunkards, thieves, dog-fanciers, pigeon-keepers; men, women, and children, the roughest, wildest, most ignorant and degraded met together, and on them the full power of the gospel was manifested in their conversion and after-life. Persons from all these classes stood forth and openly declared what the grace of God had done for them, then appealing to their old companions in sin as to the truth of their testimony.

While Mr. Booth was thus evangelizing the masses, his wife was engaged in holding meetings in many of the largest halls and most aristocratic centres in the kingdom. At Hastings, Margate, Brighton, and many other places, crowds of the middle and upper classes attended her services, and numbers, whose interest and sympathy were enlisted, became friends and helpers in the establishment of missions for the working classes on the plans already described. The motto of Mrs. Booth's life seemed to be, "I must be about my Father's business." While thus occupied in public work, her family was not neglected; for she tells us that every hour which was not spent in public work was sacredly devoted to her children, who were mainly educated at home, and trained on the principles laid down in a book entitled *The Training of Children*, recently written by her husband. How completely this task was accomplished is manifest from the fact that all their children were converted early in life, and all who are old enough are doing useful and important labor in the Salvation Army. The work spread faster than Mr. Booth's family could keep pace with it, and their converts carried the holy fire with them into their homes; and thus began fresh missions at Old Ford, Stoke Newington, Shoreditch, Tottenham, Mill Wall, and other parts in and around London, progress being reported monthly in a new periodical which bore the title of *Christian Mission Magazine*.

3. In 1870 a great impulse was given to the movement, when Mr. Booth purchased a pile of rough, strong buildings in Whitechapel, London, which had been used as "a people's market," but having been a commercial failure, was now obtained at a reasonable cost, and fitted up as a hall to hold two thousand people, with numerous

Headquarters of the Salvation Army, 101 Queen Victoria Street, London.

separate rooms, soon occupied as offices, class-rooms, a book-room, and a kitchen. All these were put to active use, and there the new converts found a hearty welcome at the daily services, always fresh and cheery; and in that building many have been saved from every kind of misery, and even from self-destruction, as despair seized upon them. The daily services were well attended, and on Sunday three or four services were regularly held, at which both Mr. and Mrs. Booth labored continuously and earnestly. At length his health gave way, and a long rest was needed; but God raised up ready helpers, much prayer was offered up, and, on his recovery, a fresh campaign was started, in 1873, large additions being made to the membership, and officers sent into new localities to rescue the perishing. In 1874 a new mission was opened at Hammersmith, and others were begun in towns far away from London, operating with the same results as those in the metropolis. In the provinces some remarkable conversions took place of persons who had been notorious sinners, and they soon became as noted in spreading the news of salvation.

These converts were chiefly uneducated people, but were easily led by those who had been helpful to them, and it became necessary to issue suggestions for their guidance. The following five points were accordingly distributed: 1. To hold meetings out of doors, and to march singing through the streets in harmony with law and order; 2. To visit public-houses, gin-palaces, prisons, private houses, and to pray with any who can be got at; 3. To hold meetings in theatres, music-halls, saloons, and other common resorts of those who prefer pleasure to God, and services in any place where hearers can be gathered, especially such as would not enter ordinary places of worship; 4. To use the most popular song-tunes, and the language of every-day life, to convey a knowledge of God to every one in novel and striking forms; 5. To make every convert a witness for Christ, both in public and private. The Whitechapel headquarters soon became a centre of great influence, which reached far beyond London, and the deaths of two of the officers there proved to be a blessing to many, as they verified the truth of the well-known words of the Rev. Charles Wesley, "God buries his workmen, but carries on his work." In six months nine valiant officers came forth to supply the places of those who had died. Quietly, but like a deep and mighty river, the work was spreading through the provinces, and a new departure became necessary, with more efficient organization.

4. After mature consideration, in the spring of 1878, the entire mission was remodelled as a military organization, with the title "The Salvation Army," and the writer was present, by invitation of Mr. Booth, at the first meeting held under the new designation, when the originator was called "General Booth." The reason given by him for the change was that his adherents were really an army of salvation. "The name," said he, "is preferable, because the only reason for which the organization exists being war against sin, common-sense requires that it shall be framed after that pattern which mankind, in all ages, has found to be the most effective, and the only one possible for an army." The novelty of the new designation at once attracted the notice of the press, some to approve, others to oppose; but the object was gained. The mission at once rose from comparative obscurity and weakness to one of strength, and in a few months thirty new stations were opened, most of which have had prosperity. By the end of a year the new openings were increased to eighty, and the number of officers (evangelists) increased from thirty to one hundred and twenty-seven. Thus the leisure-loving Christians saw a spectacle which takes its rank among the marvels of the age, an army "strong in the Lord and in the power of his might." When the army was formed, in 1878, it numbered 29 corps and 31 officers, or evangelists; in 1882 they had increased to 331 corps and 760 officers; in 1885, 1001 corps and 2560 officers, with a total registered membership in June, 1885, of 90,000 in Great Britain and Ireland.

II. *Organization, Characteristics*, etc.—1. As the plan adopted in London is the one in use in all the places where the army has a field of operation, it will be best described by the words of general Booth himself, who says, "Our organization makes every soldier in some degree an officer, charged with the responsibility of so many of his townsfolk, and expected to carry on the war against the locality where he resides. Every corps is mapped to a portion of the country, and every village is placed under the care of a sergeant until a corps be established in it under commissioned officers. England is divided into thirteen districts, each under the command of a major, whose duty it is to direct and inspect the operations of every corps therein; he has to see to the extension of the war, and the calling out of new officers, and to the removal of others unfit for their position. Each corps is under the command of a captain, assisted by one or two lieutenants, who are entirely employed in and supported by the army, their duty being to conduct services out-doors and in-doors, to visit those enlisted, and to plan and work for the salvation of the whole population around. Captains and lieutenants are removed about every six months, to avoid settling into old ruts, and to prevent their forming too strong attachments to either persons or places. We have tens of thousands of soldiers who are ready at a word to leave all and go out to rescue the souls of others, and who glory in submitting to the leadership of either men or women placed over them, for Christ's sake. Experience has taught us that real soldiers care little who leads or how they march, so that there is victory. We have never enjoyed such unbroken peace and harmony as we have had since it was thoroughly understood that the corps is under its captain, the division under its major, and the whole army under its general, with no hope of successful agitation against superior authority. It is a great object with us to avoid using our system of government so as to limit spiritual liberty, or hamper any officer with awkward restrictions, who is seeking the accomplishment of his great mission." In 1883 the army had 509 centres of operation in England, 35 in Scotland, 17 in Ireland, and, at the last account, one each in France, Switzerland, Sweden, United States, Canada, India, South Africa, South Australia, Victoria, New South Wales, Queensland, and New Zealand—a remarkable development as the result of five years' work.

2. Shortly before the army was organized, it was found that property, valued at many thousand pounds, was owned by Mr. Booth's mission, and in order to leave no doubt of its security for the objects for which it had been acquired or built, a deed was drawn up, and enrolled in chancery, Aug. 7, 1875, which declares that the property belongs, first, to William Booth, second, to his son, William Bramwell Booth, and at the death of both these persons the whole is to be vested in trustees for the use of the army so long as it may exist; and the solicitors to the army hold in their possession the deeds, and a complete schedule of all property standing in the name of William Booth, which is increasing rapidly every year.

The finances of the army are derived from various sources. From the first, all who attended the services were taught the duty and privilege of giving in support of the work, and the majority of the corps have long been self-supporting. In 1884 the members of the army contributed among themselves more than $500,000 to carry on the work, and this in addition to subscriptions and donations from the general public, and the sales of their various newspapers and publications. The total revenue for 1884 was $1,350,000, made up as follows: Central, or office funds, $373,325; local funds, $675,000; foreign funds, $315,000. Persons of all religious denominations contribute to this result, and the accounts are under the supervision and yearly audit of regular chartered accountants in London. The net profits on the sale of books, newspapers, medals, and other insignia were, in 1883, $25,000, and in 1884 over $40,000. Out of these results the salaries of the officers were paid, including also general Booth and his family. During the time (about twelve years) previous to the formation of the army, and for several years afterwards, a benevolent Christian gentleman, member of parliament for Nottingham (Mr. Booth's birthplace), afterwards for Bristol, generously provided for the wants of Mr. Booth and his family, and this was continued until the book profits were sufficient for the purpose, without trenching on the general funds. These profits are Mr. Booth's legitimate creation, and as general editor he might claim them, but, instead, he maintains the official staff from that source of revenue.

3. Having to organize mostly by means of uneducated persons, the work has been slow and up-hill. The officers are drawn from the ranks; those who prove the best soldiers are recommended by their captains to headquarters, inspected and reported on by the major, and if then able to answer (to the satisfaction of the general himself) a lengthy series of questions, they are placed in the training-barracks at Clapton. There, a few weeks of East-end London work test their qualities and qualifications severely; meanwhile they are trained in conducting every branch of the service, carefully drilled, and taught the simplest way of conveying the truths of the Bible to the people. Some have to be taught the elements of knowledge, reading, writing, and arithmetic; but the training is not so much scholastic as spiritual, the great necessity pressed upon every one being that of holiness of heart and life. Those who prove unfit for officers are sent back to the ranks: the care in selecting cadets is such that this necessity does not often arise. Few persons are received as officers who do not give up homes or positions more comfortable, from a worldly point of view, than the one they come to, so that self-seeking persons are seldom found in the army. The training lasts from six to twelve weeks; then the cadet is sent as a lieutenant to some captain in the field. Neither captain nor lieutenant has often many shillings in pocket when commencing the work in a new place, whether city or village. Constant dependence on God for the supply of all needs is a lesson often learned amidst hard surroundings. So rapid and complete is success generally that their lot is not often one of much privation. For a few years mob-violence was their chief hardship, but as the army becomes better known and understood by the authorities, and their non-resistant disposition discovered by all classes, the officers are able to give their whole strength to the service. Each officer is expected to conduct from twenty to twenty-five meetings weekly, extending over thirty to thirty-five hours; to spend eighteen hours in visiting from house to house, and to spare no possible effort in seeking the good of souls. The amount of salary to be drawn by a single man-captain is twenty-one shillings weekly, by a woman-captain fifteen shillings, and by a married captain twenty-seven shillings, with one shilling per week per child, so that drones are seldom found in the Salvation Army. A negligent or unsuccessful officer, after sufficient trial, is usually left without an appointment. The frequent removals check all selfish sentiment, and thus the officers, by experience, become examples of self-sacrifice for the salvation of the world.

The uniform worn by the army consists of a plain simple dark-blue dress, trimmed with a neat red braid, and marked with the letter S on the collar: the S on the general's garments is marked in gold. It is found to be useful, attracts attention, gives opportunity for conversation, gathers people at the open-air demonstrations, excites respect in the rougher class of the people, indicates a person's position in the army, and is a safeguard against the fashions of the age. The military form of government, affirms Mr. Booth, in his *Book of Instructions*, contradicts no form of government laid down or practised in the New Test., and is in perfect harmony with the only system described in the Old Test., and cannot therefore be said to be unscriptural.

4. The doctrines taught in the army are Arminian, such as Mr. Booth learned to love and preach when he was a Methodist minister. In describing this matter, he says, "We have not a particle of sympathy with those who desire to let down or adapt the gospel of

Christ to the fancy of the 19th century. The gospel which tells a man that he is thoroughly bad, and under the power of the devil; which drags out the hidden things of iniquity to the light of the judgment throne; which denounces sin without mercy, and warns men of eternal wrath to come unless they repent and believe in the only Saviour; the gospel of a crucified Saviour, who shed real blood to save men from real guilt, real danger, a real hell, and who lives again to give a real pardon to the really penitent—a real deliverance from the guilt, power, pollution, and fact of sin to all who really give up to him a whole heart, and trust him with a perfect faith—such is the gospel of the Salvation Army. We heartily believe the three creeds of the Church, we believe every word of the commination service, and we denounce the wrath of God against sinners as those who believe that all these things are true. We teach men to expect salvation from the guilt of sin the moment they turn from sin to God, and trust him to receive and pardon them. We teach that God is able and willing perfectly to purge the heart from all its evil tendencies and desires, the moment the soul trusts him for it all: we urge the people not to rest until God has thus cleansed the thoughts of their hearts by his Holy Spirit; and we assure them that God will preserve them blameless, and cause them everywhere to triumph, so long as they fully trust and obey him. We teach that sin is sin, whoever commits it, and that there cannot be sin without the divine displeasure; that there is a real, constant, and perfect deliverance from sin provided by Jesus Christ, which all men are responsible either for accepting or rejecting. We teach that all saved men and women ought to lay down their lives for the salvation of others, if required; that being followers of Christ means sacrificing all our own interests, enjoyments, and possessions to save a rebel world, and that whosoever does not so bear the cross has no right to expect the crown."

5. Printing has been a great factor in the progress and success of the army. From the commencement of the mission in East London Mr. Booth has had strong faith in the power of the press. A cheap and good hymn-book was one of his first requisites, and his first collection, sold at one penny, was often enlarged and added to, until it has become one of the best penny hymn-books in use, and hundreds of thousands have been sold of it. He then began a penny monthly magazine, called *The East London Evangelist*, which was followed by another, with the title *Christian Mission Magazine.* Both these were too slow in their operation to satisfy the general of an army. During a few weeks of enforced confinement to his room through an injured foot, Mr. Booth conceived the idea of a weekly newspaper, of four large pages, to sell at one cent; in three days his plans were completed, and within a month appeared No. 1 of *The War-cry*, a startling title for timid people, but it exactly met the wants of the army, and in a few days 7000 of that issue were sold, and of No. 2 fully 20,000 were wanted. In a few months it had a weekly circulation of 100,000, then it became necessary to issue it twice in the week, and it was filled with stirring news of the doings of the army everywhere, illustrated by engravings which strongly appealed to the emotional sensibilities, every column in each issue being filled with intelligence, short, sharp, and fresh. The sales soon ran up to 250,000, and in each issue was printed an account of the number of copies of the paper sold by each corps throughout the country, as a spur to ambition. The *War-cry* is now a valuable property to Mr. Booth, and since January, 1886, it has been enlarged, and issued once a week, at one penny. There are now twenty different papers with that title, four English and sixteen foreign, issued in as many localities, to report the work of the army in those places, and all after the English original. For the children in the army another paper is issued, called *The Little Soldier*, in which are reported the sayings and doings of the juvenile members of the army. People outside the army have frequently complained of articles which have appeared in both papers, but the reply of the officials is, that the soldiers in the army are satisfied, and they are the chief patrons of both papers. Every soldier is expected to take part in selling these papers weekly, and they are sold as freely on Sunday as on any other day, as are also other publications of theirs. Quite a number of books are issued now from the book-room, for which a large publishing-house has been opened in London. One of these is entitled *The Salvation Soldier's Guide*, which contains a Bible chapter for every morning and evening throughout the year, to help the unlearned to a daily increased knowledge of God's word. The army has now a considerable catalogue of its own publications. About twenty tons' weight of printed books is sent out every week from the publishing-house.

Publishing Office of the Salvation Army, 869 Paternoster Square, London.

Printing Works and General Warehouse of the Salvation Army, 96 Southwark Street, London.

6. It has been found that strong prejudice exists among the poor against churches and chapels; to avoid arousing those prejudices in the minds of the outcast class and the ignorant, the terms "Salvation Army," and "barracks," and "stores," and "headquarters" have been adopted as less objectionable than such names as

"Christ Church" or "Jesus College." The carrying of colors, using bands of music, processions, and other sensational methods are justified because other methods have failed to influence the masses. Striking handbills are used as the only means likely to influence drunkards, gamblers, thieves, and neglecters of salvation generally. The terms "Blood and Fire," used on the banners and in their literature, refer to the blood of the Atonement by which men are saved, and fire means the Holy Spirit, who sanctifies, energizes, and comforts all true soldiers of God.

All new converts are taught and encouraged to speak immediately after their conversion, just to tell what the Lord has done for them; it commits them to a life of usefulness in his service before all their old companions, kindred, and friends. God blesses them in so doing, it makes them happy and useful, and has been the means of saving scores from becoming backsliders, by returning to their old ways.

The employment of women to speak and preach has been objected to by some, but it is justified by various passages in the New Test. Beyond these, the fact that they have the gift to preach—and this both Mrs. and Miss Booth have in a very high degree—and preach most effectively, is evidence that the gift should be exercised. Philip the Evangelist had four daughters who were preachers. For ten years and more Mrs. and Miss Booth, and scores of other females in the army, have preached continually to all classes of people, without any evil consequences following; on the contrary, hundreds of people, rich and poor, have been saved under their ministrations. The army does not recruit its ranks by drawing members from any churches, it openly avows its objection to accept members belonging to any existing Church; but churches of most denominations have voluntarily contributed to its funds, especially the Church of England and the Methodists, who best understand its operations and designs. Many of the army converts go to join other churches, and it is known that more than four hundred persons, converted and trained in its ranks, were, in 1885, employed by different religious organizations as ministers, evangelists, missionaries, colporteurs, Bible women, and in other like agencies. Great care is taken of the health of the soldiers in the army, and when unable to attend to the duties of their station they are sent to a House of Rest, which was many years the home of general Booth and his family, and there they remain till recovered strength justifies their return to duty.

III. *Statistics.*—The success of the army, especially in Great Britain and the colonies, has commanded the attention and consideration of persons in all classes of society. On June 30, 1882, queen Victoria intimated her personal disposition towards the army in a letter to Mrs. Booth, from which the following is an extract: "Madam, I am commanded by the queen to acknowledge the receipt of your letter of the 27th inst., and to assure you that her majesty learns with much satisfaction that you have, with other members of your society, been successful in your efforts in winning many thousands to the ways of temperance, virtue, and religion." About the same time the bishops in convocation spoke most favorably of the army, and they unanimously passed a resolution "for a committee of their lordships to inquire into the workings of the army, to see what advice they could give to their presbyters in dealing with them." The archbishop of York and the bishop of Bedford, among others, have gathered large companies of the army and administered the Lord's Supper to them in their churches.*

The great Congress Hall in London is the school for the army. There about one hundred and fifty soldiers are constantly under training in various departments; some have to learn the mere elements of knowledge, and the elements of theology are not forgotten. To many of the cadets the interior of a church or chapel was a place of mystery before their conversion. The army is now so thoroughly before the public, and has met with almost universal endorsement in the minds of unprejudiced persons, that it has become a most important factor in raising fallen and degraded humanity in nearly all lands. As described by general Booth himself, "The end and design of the Salvation Army is to spread throughout the entire world, and to last as long as God has enemies to be fought with and overcome!"

STATE OF THE SALVATION ARMY, DECEMBER, 1885.

	Corps.		*Officers.*	
	1884.	1885.	1884.	1885.
United Kingdom	637	802	1476	1780
France and Switzerland	15	29	55	108
Sweden	4	8	17	36
United States	50	143	120	301
California	5	6	8	12
Canada	71	141	226	418
India and Ceylon	14	16	55	55
Victoria	21	41	35	95
South Australia	35	42	65	71
New South Wales	21	35	33	67
Tasmania	3	6	7	14
Queensland	..	3	..	9
New Zealand	23	33	53	75
South Africa	11	17	14	35
Holland in preparation	..	..	..	..
	910	1322	2164	3076

NUMBER OF SERVICES HELD.

	Weekly.	*Rate per Year.*
During 1884	17,470	877,500
During 1885	25,496	1,362,792
Increase	8026	485,292

(G. J. S.)

Samaria. The archæology of *Sebustieh* is given in detail in the *Memoirs* accompanying the Ordnance Survey (ii, 211 sq.), and the topography somewhat (p. 160). See also Conder, *Tent Work*, i, 88 sq.

Samson, Hermann, a Lutheran theologian of Germany, who died at Riga, Dec. 16, 1642, is the author of, *De Basi Fidei seu de Scriptura Sacra:—De Auctoritate Scripturæ Sacræ:—De Imagine Dei in Primo Homine Statuque Innocentiæ:—De Autore et Causa Peccati:—De Baptismo:—De Sacra Cœna:—De Ecclesia:—Num Sancti sint Invocandi:—De Anti-Christo.* See Jöcher, *Allgemeines Gelehrten-Lexikon*, s. v. (B. P.)

Sanctius, Caspar, a Jesuit, was born in 1554, and died Nov. 16, 1628, professor of theology at Madrid. He is the author of, *In Quatuor Libros Regum et in Duos Paralipomenorum Commentarii* (Antwerp, 1624; Lyons, 1625):—*Commentarii in Libros Ruth, Esdræ, Nehem., Tob., Judith, Estheræ et Machabæorum* (Lyons, 1628):—*Commentarii in Acta Apostolorum. Accessit Disputatio de Jacobi et Pauli in Hispaniam Adventu* (1616; Cologne, 1617). See Winer, *Handbuch der theol. Lit.* i, 203, 204, 250; Fürst, *Bibl. Jud.* s. v.; Jöcher, *Allgemeines Gelehrten-Lexikon*, s. v. (B. P.)

Sandbüchler, Aloys, a Roman Catholic theologian of Germany, was born Feb. 20, 1751. In 1770 he joined the Augustinians at Salzburg, was in 1810 professor of Oriental languages and biblical exegesis at the Lyceum there, and died Feb. 3, 1820, doctor of theology. He published, *Darstellung der Regeln einer allgemeinen Auslegungskunst von den Büchern des Alten und Neuen Testaments nach Jahn* (Salzburg, 1813):—*Kurze Darstellung einer Einleitung in die Bücher des Alten Testaments, nach Jahn* (eod.):—*Abhandlung über die zweckmässigen Mittel, den hebräischen und griechischen Grundtext dem Wortsinne nach richtig zu verstehen* (1791):—*Vertheidigung der Göttlichkeit des mosaischen Gesetzes und des Alten Bundes* (1787–88, 4 parts):—*Ueber die Zuverlässigkeit des Grund-*

* In 1883 the Salvation Army was prohibited by the authorities of the cantons of Geneva, Berne, and Neufchatel, in Switzerland, on an old law, as disturbers of the public peace, and there have been occasional interferences with their Sunday processions in some towns in America by the municipal authorities on similar grounds.—Ed.

textes (1788). See Döring, *Die gelehrten Theologen Deutschlands*, s. v.; Fürst, *Bibl. Jud.* s. v.; Winer, *Handbuch der theol. Lit.* i, 377, 398, 400, 409. (B. P.)

Sandby, George, D.D., a Church of England divine, was born about 1717, and was educated at Merton College, Oxford, where he took the degree of M.A. in 1740, and afterwards was master of Magdalen College, Cambridge, where he took his degree of D.D. in 1760. He was collated to the rectorship of Denton, Norfolk, in 1750, and to the chancellorship of Norwich in 1768. He died at Denton, April 29, 1807. See (Lond.) *Annual Register*, 1807, p. 571.

Sanden, Bernhard von (1), a Lutheran theologian of Germany, was born Oct. 4, 1636, at Insterburg. He studied at different universities, was in 1664 preacher at Königsberg, in 1674 professor, and in 1675 doctor of theology. In 1690 Sanden was made general superintendent, and died April 19, 1703. He published, *Theologia Symbolica Lutherana*:—*Dissertatio ad Gen. xlix, de Propheta Promisso*:—*De Verbis Dei ad Petrum Matt. xvi*, 19:—*Pentas Illustrium Quæstionum Theologicarum*. See Jöcher, *Allgemeines Gelehrten-Lexikon*, s. v. (B. P.)

Sanden, Bernhard von (2), son of the preceding, was born at Königsberg, May 4, 1666. He studied at different universities, was in 1695 professor of theology at the university of his native place, in 1709 first court-preacher, and died Jan. 22, 1721, doctor of theology. He wrote, *De Cive in Republica Hebræorum*:—*De Modis Obtinendi Civitatem Hebræorum*:—*De Proselytismo*:—*In Matt. xvi*, 19:—*In Joh. xxi*, 15:—*In Luc. xxii*, 31, 38:—*In Iesa. lxiv*, 6:—*De Duobis Hircis Festo Expiationis Deo Oblatis*:—*An Concilium Tridentinum sit Œcumenicum*:—*De Prophetis et Prophetiis Veteris Testamenti*:—*De Conjugio Petri et Pauli Apostolorum*:—*De Apparitione Spiritus Sancti in Specie Columbæ*:—*De Sinu Abrahami*:—*De Salute Gentium Infidelium*, etc. See Jöcher, *Allgemeines Gelehrten-Lexikon*, s. v. (B. P.)

Sanford, Miles, D.D., a Baptist minister, a native of Connecticut, was for a time a Methodist, then became a Baptist, and was pastor of the First Baptist Church in Chicago, Ill.; subsequently an editor in Detroit, Mich., from which place he removed to East Boston, Mass., then to Gloucester, and at length to North Adams, whence he went as chaplain of a Western Massachusetts regiment to active service in the late war. Next he was for a short period financial secretary of the American Bible Union, and then became pastor of the First Church in Salem, N. J., where he remained about two years. He died at Salem, Oct. 31, 1874. See Cathcart, *Baptist Encyclop.* p. 1028. (J. C. S.)

Sanford, Peter P., D.D., a Methodist Episcopal minister, was born at Lodi, N. J., Feb. 28, 1781. He was religiously inclined from childhood, converted at the age of eighteen, and in 1807 entered the Philadelphia Conference. In 1810 he was transferred to the New York Conference, and in it continued laborious till his death, Jan. 14, 1857. Dr. Sanford was a thorough divine, an able scholar, and an eminent, honest, and devout man. From 1816 to 1852 he was elected a delegate to every general conference. See *Minutes of Annual Conferences*, 1857, p. 321; Simpson, *Cyclop. of Methodism*, s. v.

Sanger, Ralph, D.D., a Unitarian minister, son of Rev. Zedekiah Sanger, D.D., was born in Duxbury, Mass., June 22, 1786. He graduated from Harvard College in 1808; then, after spending three years in the study of theology under his father, he was appointed tutor at Cambridge; was ordained pastor of the Church at Dover, Mass., Sept. 16, 1812, and continued there until his death, May 6, 1860. See *Necrology of Harvard College*, p. 305. (J. C. S.)

Sanguirese Version of the Scriptures. This language is used in the Sangir Islands, the inhabitants of which, numbering about 80,000 souls, 10,000 of whom have been baptized, have but recently been blessed with a translation of the New Test. From the report of the British and Foreign Bible Society for 1879 we learn that the Rev. Mr. Kelling, who has been laboring twenty years on the island of Tagulandang, where he has formed a church, has completed the New Test., and is giving it a final revision. This translation was published at London, in the Siamo dialect, in 1882, the Rev. E. W. King, of Tilbury, having read the proofs. Encouraged by the good reception which the New Test. had received at the hands of the natives, the committee of the British and Foreign Bible Society agreed, in 1884, to print an edition of the Psalms, the translation having also been made by the Rev. Mr. Kelling. (B. P.)

Sanke, Christopher, a Lutheran theologian of Germany, was born Dec. 12, 1700, at Guben, Lower Lusatia. He studied at Leipsic, and died there, May 4, 1752. He wrote, *Diss. Philol. de Anathemate Pauli Votivo Roman. ix*, 3 (Leipsic, 1729):—*Vollständige Anweisung zu den Accenten der Hebräer* (1740):—*De Differentia Inter Vocationem ac Tentationem circa Munus Ecclesiasticum* (1749). See Döring, *Die gelehrten Theologen Deutschlands*, s. v. (B. P.)

Santes, Pagninus. See Pagninus.

Saphir. The probable representative of this place is thus described in the *Memoirs* accompanying the Ordnance Survey (ii, 413):

"Three mud villages of the name *es-Suâfir* exist close together. It is probably the *Zeophir* in the territory of Ascalon, given as property to the bishop of Bethlehem, A.D. 1100 (William of Tyre). The most ancient of the sites would appear to be Suafir esh-Shemaliyeh (the most northerly of the three), where there are ruined cisterns of rubble masonry. There are small gardens and wells at each village."

Saphir, Jacob, a Jewish traveller, was born in 1830, and died at Jerusalem, June 23, 1885. He visited Egypt, Arabia, India, and Australia; the results of his researches he published in אבן ספיר (1868, 1874, 2 vols.). This work is of great historical and ethnographical value. For the Hebrew codex which Saphir brought from Arabia and sold to the public library at Paris in 1868, see Shapira Manuscript. (B. P.)

Sarchi, Philip, a Jewish writer, who died at Paris in 1830, is the author of, *Grammaire Hebraïque Raisonnée et Comparée* (Paris, 1828):—*An Essay on Hebrew Poetry, Ancient and Modern* (Lond. 1824). See Fürst, *Bibl. Jud.* s. v.; Winer, *Handbuch der theol. Lit.* i, 116. (B. P.)

Sargado. See Ibn-Sargado.

Sarid. Lieut. Conder suggests (*Memoirs* to the Ordnance Survey, ii, 49) that the original name may have been *Sadid* (ר for ד), as in the Sept., and in that case the place may be represented by the modern *Tell Shadûd*, three and a half miles south-west of Nazareth, consisting of "a good-sized artificial mound, with fine springs beneath on the south" (ibid. p. 70).

Sartorius, Christoph Friedrich, a Lutheran theologian of Germany, was born Oct. 22, 1701. He studied at Tübingen, was vicar at Ludwigsburg in 1727, in 1730 at Stuttgart, in 1733 preacher and professor at Bebenhausen. In 1747 he went again to Ludwigsburg, was called to Tübingen in 1755, and took the degree of doctor of theology in 1756. He died Dec. 2, 1785. Sartorius published, *Meditationes ad Psa. liii de Salute ex Zione* (Tübingen, 1735):—*Positiones Generaliores de Libro Geneseos* (1756):—*De Messiæ Filii Dei Generatione Æterna ex Psa. ii, 7 Adserta* (1758):—*De Sacramentis in Genere* (1760):—*De Baptismo* (1761):—*De Sacra Cœna* (eod.):—*De Lege Ceremoniali* (1762):—*Vindiciæ Cantici Canticorum* (1765):—*Diss. Exegetica Super Psa. xix* (1766):—*Theologumena Symbolica* (1769–71):—*De Utilitate Vet. Test.* etc. (1772):—*Diss. ad Dictum Christi Matt. v*, 1–19 (1773). See Döring, *Die gelehrten Theologen Deutschlands*, s. v.; Fürst, *Bibl. Jud.* s. v. (B. P.)

Sartorius, Friedrich Wilhelm, a Lutheran theologian of Germany, was born at Dantzic, Feb. 7, 1715, and died at Lübben in 1784, doctor of theology and general superintendent. He wrote, *De Metempsychosi Pythagorica*, etc. (Lübben, 1760):—*De Scriptura Sacra* (1735):—*De Bello Domini in Amalek* (1736). See Winer, *Handbuch der theol. Lit.* i, 468; Fürst, *Bibl. Jud.* s. v. (B. P.)

Sason, AARON. See AARON BEN-JOSEPH SASON.

Satisfactional View OF THE ATONEMENT. The vicarious sufferings of Jesus Christ upon the cross are often represented by theologians as mainly intended to appease the divine wrath by offering a satisfaction for human guilt. That this, however, is incorrect is evident, not only from the character of God himself, who is no Shylock demanding his "pound of flesh," and is infinitely anxious to be reconciled to the sinner, but it is clear likewise from the fact that no adequate *quid pro quo* was either attempted or achieved in this regard. The virtue and obedience and holiness of Jesus did not in the slightest degree lessen, palliate, or modify the crimes, the sins, and the transgressions of man, nor are they ever represented as any apology or excuse for these. To accept the merit of the pure as a counterpoise of the dereliction of the impure is no reasonable equivalent, much less to condone the fault of the offending by the suffering of the innocent. Such a satisfaction is opposed to the plain teaching of the parable of the prodigal son, in which no reparation, but merely a penitent return, is attempted or spoken of on the part of the wanderer. Nor does this conflict with Paul's doctrine of the release from the claims of the law (Rom. v, 11), for he everywhere represents this from a Judaic or human point of view, and especially insists that these obligations are cancelled for the past and fulfilled for the future simply by a subjective conformity to the will of God (Rom. x, 4, xiii, 10). It is, in fact, the sinner himself who is ultimately and practically called upon to be satisfied with this arrangement, and upon his acceptance of the substitute the whole efficacy of the scheme is finally made to depend. God needs no such inducement, but man does, and this not so much outside parties as the offending individual himself. It is the sinner's conscience that demands a satisfaction, and this he can find only in Christ. See VICARIOUS SUFFERING.

Saubert, JOHANN, a Lutheran theologian of Germany, was born at Nuremberg, Feb. 1, 1638. In 1660 he was professor of Oriental languages, in 1665 professor of theology at Helmstädt, in 1673 professor and pastor at Altdorf, and he died April 29, 1688, doctor of theology. He wrote, *Variæ Lectiones Text. Græci Evangelii Matth.* (Helmstädt, 1672):—*De Templo Hierosolymi* (1665):—*Die heil. Schrift Alten Test.* (pt. i, eod.):—*De Sacrificiis Veterum Collectanea* (ed. Crenius, Leyden, 1699):—*De Studii Hebraicæ Linguæ Multiplici Utilitate et Necessitate* (Helmstädt, 1661, 1678). See Winer, *Handbuch der theol. Lit.* i, 28, 103, 139, 169, 515, Fürst, *Bibl. Jud.* s. v., Jöcher, *Allgemeines Gelehrten-Lexikon*, s. v. (B. P.)

Saul, JOHN, D.D., an Irish Methodist preacher, was born at Dromore, County Down, in July, 1795. He was brought up in the Established Church, converted in his youth, and joined the Methodists to exercise his gift for preaching. He entered the ministry of the Irish Conference in 1826, and for forty-two years employed his talents to the glory of God and the good of man. He was some years treasurer of the Children's Fund, became a supernumerary in 1868, and removed to England. He was for fifty years a diligent student of the Bible in the original languages. He was a happy, pious, and useful minister, and died near Manchester, Oct. 11, 1878. See *Minutes of the British Conference*, 1879, p. 43.

Sauli, ALESSANDRO, an Italian Barnabite, was born at Milan in 1535. He studied at Pavia and Milan with such success that he knew the "Summa" of Aquinas almost by heart. In 1567 Sauli was made superior of his order, in 1570 bishop of Aleria, in 1591 bishop of Pavia, after having refused the archbishopric of Genoa. He died in 1592. Benedict XIV beatified him in 1741. See Argelati, *Bibliotheca Script. Mediol.* (Milan, 1745), vol. ii; *Collezione di Vite dei Piu Distinti Religiosi della Congregazione dei Chierici RR. di S. Paole detti Barnabiti* (ibid. 1861), vol. xiii; *Lettere Inedite del Beat. Alessandro Sauli* (Turin, 1868); *Raccolta di Orazioni in Lode del Beat. Alessandro Sauli* (Lucca, 1743); Lichtenberger, *Encyclop. des Sciences Religieuses*, s. v. (B. P.)

Saunders, EPHRAIM DOD, D.D., a Presbyterian minister, was born near Mendham, N. J., Sept. 30, 1809. After graduating at Yale College in 1831, he remained in New Haven for several months for the purpose of theological study. In the autumn of 1832 he went to Virginia, where he spent a year in teaching and study, He was licensed to preach by the Presbytery of East Hanover, in session at Nottoway, Oct. 18, 1833. After four years of pastoral work, during which time he collected money to build two churches, he opened a school for boys in Cumberland County, which he removed to Goochland County. In 1843 he became principal of the Classical Institute at Petersburg, Va., and held this position for four years. In 1848 he visited Europe, and on his return established a Church in Pottsville, Pa. In 1851 he removed to West Philadelphia, and founded a school for boys, which was afterwards chartered as a college. During the late war a military department was established, the pupils being styled the "Courtland Saunders Cadets," in honor of the founder's only child, who was killed in battle, in September, 1862. Dr. Saunders was made chairman of the Bounty Fund Commission of Philadelphia. In 1871 he offered to give his real estate in West Philadelphia to the Presbyterian Alliance for the purpose of founding a hospital. He also obtained subscriptions to the amount of one hundred thousand dollars towards the endowment of the hospital. He died in West Philadelphia, Sept. 13, 1872. See *Obituary Record of Yale College*, 1873.

Savage Island Version. See NIUEAN VERSION.

Sayres, GILBERT H., D.D., a minister of the Protestant Episcopal Church, a native of New Jersey, died at Jamaica, L. I. (where he had formerly been for many years rector), April 27, 1867, aged eighty years. See *Amer. Quar. Church Rev.* July, 1867, p. 335.

Scambler, EDWARD, D.D., an English Protestant Dissenter and bishop, was born in 1512, and educated at the University of Cambridge. In the reign of queen Mary he was pastor of the first Protestant congregation in London, but went abroad during the Marian persecution, returned in the early days of Elizabeth's reign, and was chaplain to archbishop Parker; consecrated bishop of Peterborough in 1560, translated to Norwich in 1584. He conducted himself with wisdom and moderation, was a learned man, but zealous against the papists. He encouraged religious meetings among the clergy, but the queen suppressed them because Puritans were admitted. He died May 7, 1597, and was interred in Norwich Cathedral. See Wilson, *Dissenting Churches*, i, 4.

Scepticism, RECENT PHASES OF. Scepticism is primarily nothing more than an inquiring state of mind, with provisional suspension of positive conclusions. It soon comes to mean denial, or repudiation of what transcends human observation and inference therefrom, in matters necessarily of faith. See SCEPTICISM in vol. ix. It is in the latter signification that it will now be noticed, and only in its chief recent forms.

Every age has its own philosophical tendencies, recurring under modified fashions, with the change of antecedents and surroundings. Thus, old scepticism reappears with altered face, moving always in a vicious circle. Every philosophy is the imperfect expression of the faintly perceived and feebly understood manifestations of the universe, and of their supposed significance. Each has its own scheme for the interpretation of the mysteries with which "we are girt about," either recognising or excluding the supernatural. Scepticism, therefore, varies with the ages, in degree, in method, and in form. In no period of history has unbelief in revealed or natural religion, which is unbelief in all the foundations of knowledge, assumed so many varying forms and shadows of form as in the present day. Much, very much, of recent thought and speculation is corroded by the burrowing virus of this diseased and morbific tendency. It is difficult to employ familiar phrases and current modes of argument without being involved and entangled, unawares, in some of the ramifications of the pervading infection. All men are creatures of their age and of the intellectual atmosphere encompassing them. The mind is moulded, and its developments and products are shaped or colored, by the influences which it habitually endures. Hence it becomes a difficult task, but urgent in proportion to its difficulty, to examine the modes of aberration, and to detect the fallacies in widely accepted systems of error. Of course it would be impracticable, within any moderate limits, to distinguish the manifold varieties of recent scepticism, to trace the melting hues by which they blend almost insensibly into each other, and to discriminate the multitudinous variations and degrees of diseased perception in the diversities of philosophical sects. No more can be safely or profitably attempted than to note the most accepted types of sceptical speculation in this declining century. All might be included under the single head of RATIONALISM (q. v.), but this term has a more restricted meaning in theological terminology. All proceed from the negation or exclusion of everything in the intelligible universe beyond the grasp of the observing and reasoning faculties.

The species of scepticism which will be estimated here are those which assail, extrude, or undermine religious truth—which reject knowledge or authority, superior to such as may be compressed into the narrow domain of scientific or demonstrative processes. Of these there appear to be six leading classes, the appreciation of which will afford guidance for the criticism of the intermediate or affiliated varieties of incredulity. They are, 1. *Materialism;* 2. *Naturalism;* 3. *Agnosticism;* 4. *Phenomenalism;* 5. *Pessimism;* 6. *Nihilism*, which last approximates to *Neo-Buddhism*. These several schemes have been exhibited in more or less developed proportions since human inquiry gained strength and audacity to propose a systematic answer to the torturing questions, Whence come man and the universe? How are they sustained? What are their meaning, their purpose, and their destiny? What are their relations to the source of their being, of their maintenance, and of their order? The manner in which these enigmas have been answered has continually suffered change with the extension of human knowledge and the consciousness of previous failure. The latest transmutations now attract our regard. Of the six classes, into which the chief recent theories of a sceptical character have been divided, two have been sufficiently considered in the articles specially devoted to them. These are, Materialism and Pessimism (q. v. severally). They require no further notice than may be incident to their relations to other theories.

Before proceeding to the examination of the remaining forms, it may be judicious to indicate the fundamental delusion which underlies and vitiates all schemes of scepticism, using the designation in the restricted sense of unbelief in the transnatural. All knowledge of things included within the observation of physical perception is obviously and necessarily limited by the range of the several senses. The calorific, the actinic, and the chemical rays of light are invisible; yet they are probably more important and more operative in the economy of nature than the color-rays, with their endless service and infinite variety of beauty. There are sounds too loud for the human ear to distinguish, too slight for human hearing; notes that are discord to some races and musical to others; odors too faint or evanescent for man's olfactories to detect; tastes too delicate or too oppressive for the tongue of man to discriminate; things too distant or too small for human discernment. Assuredly there are stars beyond the reach of the telescope, organisms too minute for microscopic vision. These facts are recognised by observation and reflection, aided by artificial contrivances. They prove that the senses cannot attain to the apprehension of a vast variety of unquestionable facts. Intellectual comprehension is limited by its constitution, in like manner, in regard to things intelligible. This is in consonance with the physical or material creation. The conclusion is the same in the one case as in the other. It is only transferred from the senses to the mind, and adapted to a new sphere. It is identical, also, with the irrefragable axiom or postulate that the finite can neither intellectually grasp nor logically deny what lies beyond its comprehension. But it may and must recognise it, or else renounce all validity of thought. Every form of dogmatic scepticism starts out, therefore, with a fatal and utterly irrational assumption.

On any scheme of philosophy the office of the human race on earth is to improve its habitation, its conditions, and itself, through the instrumentalities acquired by the enlargement of its knowledge and the expansion of its capacities. The fulfilment of this destiny or the achievement of this result would be impossible, and, indeed, inconceivable, if the limits of the unknown did not always spread around, and if humanity were not always led on and guided by an imperfect apprehension, a confident intuition, a persistent assurance of further enlargement of its acquisitions. It is the very law of its existence, of the possible sustenance of its increasing numbers, that, as Roger Bacon said, the recognition of the unknown and still unknowable advances more rapidly than the increase of the known. "Quæ scit, pauca sunt et vilia respectu eorum quæ non intelligit sed credit, et longe pauciora respectu eorum quæ ignorat." This is only an illustration of the law which renders fallacious all knowledge dwarfed to the compass of the reasoning faculties of man.

There is another line of procedure—a purely logical argument—which arrives at the same result. Every conclusion must rest on accepted premises. These premises, whether as previous conclusions, or as interpretations of facts, which are also conclusions, must, in their turn, depend upon more remote premises. Ultimately a point must be reached beyond which it is impossible for analysis to go. Yet the first principles repose on surer conviction than any inferences that may be deduced from them. The sphere beyond the utmost range of systematic ratiocination is not the darkness of the unapprehensible, but the realm of the partially unknown, yet inevitably believed. Throughout, the invisible, the incomprehensible, the unattainable, must be received as existent and operative, or all knowledge and all fact must rest upon nothing but pure imagination. This is only the development of the profound and sagacious observation of Aristotle, that whoever demands a reason for ultimate principles takes away all possibility of reasoning. The necessary inference from these truths, which are only diverse aspects of the same truth, is that the whole order of existence, physical and intellectual—the whole procedure of valid reasoning on any subject—requires the constant admission of influences, causes, powers, purposes, and governance beyond the possible limits of formal and systematized knowledge, beyond the grasp of finite intelligence. Hence, any scheme of philosophy which pretends to include all being, and all appreciation of being, within the brief tentacles of human apprehension, is not merely incomplete and fallacious, but absurd.

With this preliminary exposition of the fundamental conditions of thought, the artful sophistry involved in all forms of dogmatic scepticism, and cunningly disguised or ignored in the recent phases of philosophical unbelief, becomes manifest. The countless forms of scepticism lie between the antagonistic extremes of materialism and idealism. These extremes are not necessarily sceptical, but in their development they tend to sceptical issues. Milton and Berkeley were fervent in their religious convictions. Of course, as materialism and idealism are the opposing poles of speculation, every scheme for the exposition of being and its interpretation must approximate more closely to the one or to the other. All may be included in the two. But such absorption of divergent currents of thought tends only to confusion. It will explain, however, the impossibility of separating discordant systems by sharp lines of discrimination. They are variously compounded, and coalesce with each other in various modes and in varying proportions. The failure, then, to maintain sharp distinctions will be due to the nature of the subject divided, not to the error of the division.

I. *Naturalism.*—Materialism, as has been remarked, has already been amply discussed. Naturalism is an extensive species of it, which requires special notice. There is, indeed, one subdivision of naturalism which is the purest idealism, when all nature, concrete and operative, is resolved into the divinity, and this again is dissolved into nature. This occurs in Spinozism, and in all varieties of pantheism. In its current philosophical acceptation, however, naturalism signifies the interpretation of the facts, functions, and developments of existence by the forces and changes of physical realities. It sees nothing beyond. It denies higher causation. It imprisons itself within the domain of the sensible, and affirms that this is the sole and adequate exposition of all things. The voluntary captive, in his self-constructed dungeon, affirms that there is neither sun nor sunlight without. The unreasonableness of the conclusions and of the philosophy erected upon them is shown by the preliminary considerations which have been presented.

It should be remarked that, in these fashions of scepticism, the supposed conclusion is always the starting-point of the doctrine. That which is to be proved is assumed. The philosophy is invented and manipulated for the support of the thesis. Great acuteness and ingenuity, greater self-delusion, and the confidence of wilful ignorance, are shown in the elaborate artifices of the frail but often imposing structure. Every fact of nature, if analyzed—every part of such fact, if further analyzed, and if the analysis be conducted to its utmost limit—inevitably leads "from nature up to nature's God." The same thing is true of every intellectual or emotional experience, which gives facts of another order.

Unquestionably the spontaneous revelation of the transnatural through the forms of the natural does not rest upon the same kind of evidence, or generate the same species of conviction as are characteristic of scientific conclusions. But they come clothed with a firmer and more impressive certainty. This is no novel doctrine, for it is a reply to antiquated error. Thomas Aquinas said, "The dubitation which occurs in regard to articles of faith arises from no uncertainty of the thing, but from the weakness of the human mind. Nevertheless, a minimum of knowledge of the highest things is more to be desired than the most certain knowledge of things little in comparison." Such testimony may be rejected with scorn, as the utterance of a schoolman, a metaphysician, and a theologian. But the Angelic Doctor makes his avowal on the authority of Aristotle, who should be safe from the petty censure of current science. His remark is (*De Part. Animal.* i, 5), "If it be but little of these things that we apprehend, that little, on account of the preciousness of such knowledge, is more acceptable than all within our grasp." Old error should not, on account of its attempted rehabilitation, object to cogent refutation because it, too, is ancient.

II. *Evolutionism* is the most prominent and the most controlling type of naturalism in our age, the credit and the parentage of which are usually assigned to Darwin, though its most elaborate and systematic development is to be sought in the unfinished and interminable treatises of Spencer. The foundations and the main walls of the building are distinctively Darwin's. To him is due the patient, persistent industry by which the materials have been quarried, chiselled into shape, and adapted to their places in the bewildering edifice. But the plan and the purpose of the philosophy may be found in the notes to the prosaic poems and in the prose romances of his grandfather. Nor is the elder Darwin to be considered as the original inventor of the system. Many critics have shown that the whole essence of the speculation and its line of argument were the teachings of Lucretius. The Roman poet proved, in his own case, his maxim, "Ex nihilo nihil fit," and borrowed his dogmas, but not their radiant setting, from Epicurus. In this recurrence to the resuscitated phantasms of long-buried delusion, Darwinism corresponds with all current schemes of sceptical speculation. They return with the revolving cycle. But never before, not even under the Roman republic or the empire, did Epicureanism display so bold a front or arrogate so absolute dominion as Darwinism has presented and received. It claims to be accepted by all scientific and intelligent minds. It has been extensively admitted into nearly all departments of knowledge. These have been remoulded in consonance with it. Now it looks forward to an early sovereignty over the whole realm of thought and action. The eminent naturalist maintained, during his life, that his doctrine was not inconsistent with the Christian faith. His letter to a German student, published after his death, revealed his suppressed conviction that it was so, and that it had proved so in his own case. His declaration may, nevertheless, be so interpreted as to be true. There is no inevitable inconsistency between the creed of Christendom and the hypothesis of a progressive development. Everything depends upon the exposition and the application of the cardinal dogma. To human apprehension there is a more marvellous exhibition of creative intelligence and power in so ordering the world from the beginning, that every force and every creature in the universe should, like the fruit-tree, have "its seed within itself," and exert its characteristic peculiarities in the perpetuation and progressive modification of all developments through endless generations. In this there is a more wondrous exhibition of intelligence and power than in the supposition of constant divine action in maintaining, regulating, combining, and modifying all the successive agencies and results of existence. The immanent operation of divine energy, which Thomas Aquinas considers the most cogent demonstration of the being of God, is imperative in the one case as in the other. The former explanation will not, indeed, satisfy the requirements of either true religious belief or genuine religious appetency; but it is the more difficult of conception. It is not, however, under either aspect that evolution has been promulgated, applauded, and accepted.

One reason of the wide diffusion of evolutionism has, unquestionably, been the plausibility of the doctrine, and the ambiguity of the term. Evolution is true—"sub modo et terminis suis"—as the statement of a fact. Evolutionism is erroneous as a theory. That things change is a commonplace, that organic beings grow is another; that the chicken comes from the egg is undisputed; that plants and animals, including man, will, under suitable circumstances, be modified, improving or retrograding, has never been controverted. But that these mutations can take place only within wider or narrower limits—still, within restricted limits—has never been disproved. It is the baldest assumption and the wildest reverie, to presume that the possible changes are illimitable and uncontrolled, and that one genus can be transmuted into another, even in the imaginary æons of time. This is worse hallucination than alchemy. Evolution is an unfortunate and misleading term. It is wholly arbitrary to employ it as the designation of a philosophical system. Evolution cannot appropriately signify a force, a process, a mode, or a determining rule. It is merely descriptive of a phenomenon—unexplained. Smoke is evolved out of a gun-barrel. Something more than smoke is required to reveal the force, the nature, and the action of the gunpowder. This criticism may appear trivial, but it indicates the frailty and delusiveness of the theory of evolutionism. Certain modes succeed each other, and are noted. This affords no evidence of the fact or character of any philosophical relation between the forms. Nor is there much more to be ascertained from the cabalistic symbols of the school—the differentiation of the homogeneous, and the integration of the heterogeneous. These phrases have meanings, but what their precise meaning may be depends upon the presumptions of the interpreter. Of themselves they are as obscure as "Greek invocations to call fools into a circle."

Abandoning, however, this skirmishing about the outposts, evolutionism, as a heresy, is sufficiently distinct and well understood. It signifies the progressive growth of all existence by successive stages, and through the influence of the surroundings, from primitive and unintelligent germs. There is a recent exposition, elaborated with great skill and acumen, which builds up society in its actual and prospective excellence, from protoplasm; and protoplasm from the diffused, undistinguished, and undistinguishable antecedents of cosmical dust. Where did the dust come from? The elephant may stand on the tortoise, but on what does the tortoise stand?

Into the details and assumptions of evolutionism it is impossible to enter here. A hasty notice of a few salient characteristics is all that should be attempted, notwithstanding the hazard of such brevity. It may be said, however, that there is not a single principle relied upon by the evolutionists that is proved, or that admits of proof, in the latitude required for the theory; that the ingenious multiplication of assimilated details is not argument, and does not authorize the inductions drawn; that the accuracy and propriety of the details is questionable, and has been questioned; and that "the survival of the fittest" is contrary to all known fact, except through such casuistry and quibbling, such limitation and explanation, as constrain the evidence to fit the hypothesis. Throughout the theory there is a latent and unperceived "petitio principii," which conducts, by long, bewildering channels, the original assumption to the conclusion into which it is converted. It is scarcely necessary to repeat the preliminary proposition—that the world of observation reveals and necessitates, at all times, the admission of a higher force, guidance, and wisdom; initiating, sustaining, and directing all that is or can be observed.

The aim of evolutionism is to exclude from the theory of being and of truth everything transcending the manifestations of physical existence. Of course, the virtual effect on the spirit of speculation is the same, whether the supernatural is denied or rigidly ignored. The practical outcome of epicureanism, which relegated the gods to uninterrupted repose, was identical with that of the most absolute atheism. There is a logical and a metaphysical distinction, but little diversity of consequences. Hence Darwinism and evolutionism are on the same plane with positive unbelief, and merge into, even when they are not embodied in, the general procedure of agnosticism. See EVOLUTION.

III. *Agnosticism* is the current designation of the most prevailing type of sceptical philosophism. It rejects all outside of the material and phenomenal. It deems it unnecessary to deny the divine, which it banishes. Indeed, Tyndall, Huxley, Spencer, and other hierophants of the fashionable delusion, have admitted the reality of what they exclude from consideration and from rational inquiry. They do not deny divinity; they do not reject creative energy as a possibility. They are content to say that they know nothing, and can know nothing, about it, and that no one does or can know anything on the subject. They, therefore, refuse to admit it into their contemplation, or to accord it any rational authority over the thoughts and conduct of men. They pass it by with the flippant sneer, "Nihil ad nos." Agnosticism is simply shameless profession of ignorance—*know-nothingism* in all that is essential to philosophy. It is the substitution of human science, or nescience, for human knowledge. It may, accordingly, be extended to all forms of negation, or rejection of what lies beyond the domain of matter, or of physical science. But can physical science, or human reason, in its finite systematizations, fill the whole globe of human thought, feeling, and conduct? of human aspiration and of human duty?

As has already been pointed out, science, observation, experience, reasoning, imperatively require the constant recognition and support of what the agnostics reject as being unknowable. What they repudiate, but what, nevertheless, remains indispensable, is unknowable, in the sense of being irreducible to the forms and precision of scientific knowledge. But there is much knowledge of the highest practical value which is unreduced to such demonstrable form, much which is incapable of being reduced to that form. Scientific knowledge would be vain, a mere phantasm in the clouds, a castle in the air, if it had nothing but propositions reached by induction or deduction to rest upon. In the brilliant developments of modern science the necessary philosophic basis of science is forgotten, and in the pretensions of scientific system-builders it is ignored. The sun shines calmly on, if invisible to the blind, or denied by them. True wisdom is distrustful of itself. It eschews pretension, and avoids the confidence which would restrict the world to the limits of human comprehension. What cannot be scientifically arranged, co-ordinated, and syllogistically or inductively proved, is not absolutely unknown. Were it so, a child could possess no knowledge, and could never learn. In things transcending "the beggarly elements of man," we are and must "be as little children." Here humility is the condition and means of knowledge. The assurance thus gained is accepted in a different form from scientific conclusions; but it is confirmed by a more potent authority, and exercises a more constant and controlling influence over human life. The peaks of the Himalayas are not less lofty or less firmly rooted because they are inaccessible to the foot of man. It is their elevation that renders them inaccessible. Their snow-clad summits, disguised by their white robe, shine in a clearer, purer, more translucent atmosphere than the low hills on which men dwell, which may be measured and traversed amid fogs and exhalations. The extension of precise knowledge widens, or should widen, the vision of an infinitely larger knowledge, which is unprecise. It is equally foolish and unphilosophical to deny the reality of all that cannot be impounded in our own petty preserves. To exclude such knowledge from consideration is the same, in effect, as to deny it, and is even more irrational. But this is what is done by the recent school of agnosticism, which refuses to acknowledge everything which science does not include or hope to embrace.

The attempt of Buckle to affirm, and of Arnold, his Dutch compeers, and many other schemers, in France, Germany, and England, to construct, a system of unspiritual morality, or of immoral morals, is only the adaptation of current agnosticism to ethical doctrine. As in the physical, as in the intellectual, so in the ethical sphere, the characteristic defect is that the building demands a firm foundation, but is deprived of anything to rest upon. Historical and ethical agnosticism are more pernicious than evolutionism. It is possible to investigate physical phenomena apart from their origin or cause, but the essence of morals consists in the acceptance of right, as a rule, extraneously presented, and obligatory in obedience to an authority above and beyond those bound to obey, though they have the power of disobeying. These traditions transcend the reach of rationalistic science.

A more dogmatic, but not more satisfactory, attitude is assumed by that growing sect of physiological psychologists who discern in mind only an exudation from matter, and resolve thought into a cerebral process, stimulated or stimulating, through the telegraphic lines of the nervous cords. Thought is thus, according to Spencer, a complex series of nervous "shocks," like those of an electric battery. If the nature and action of the human intellect are degraded to the level of the electric fluid, or of the currents of sap in vegetative growth, there is neither room nor occupation for any agency higher than organic motions. But how did these motions originate? Whence were their capabilities primarily derived? In all the play of nervous excitation, direct or reflex, where is the intelligence that notes and employs the communications transmitted? In ordinary telegraphing, an operator at each end of the line, or at the completion of the circuit, is indispensable. The apparatus is useless without something diverse from the apparatus, to interpret the messages. The gray matter of the brain, however wonderful its constitution and action, cannot discharge this function. At best, it is only a central office. The mind must be something entirely different from its complicated network of agencies. The spider's web is not the spider. But mind, intangible in its essence and modes, is inconceivable and unmeaning, without a creative mind to form and to inform it, after a fashion far different from any physical changes. Physiology has rendered, and may continue to render, most important services in the interpretation of the physical accompaniments and instrumentalities of mental processes. But Maudsley, and Bain, and Spencer, and the other advocates of human automatism, cannot detect mind or thought under the scalpel, with the aid of any microscope. Their theories are wholly superficial. They deal only with the manifestations on the surface, produced by the underlying forces. They exclude the idea of forces, except as the sequence of changes, and as a substitute for cause. They would exclude the term if they could dispense with it. They fail, however, to see that its indispensability attests the reality of what they would expel. As these speculations confine their attention to the show of things, they might be embraced under the head of phenomenalism.

IV. *Phenomenalism*, however, in its technical signification, is sufficiently distinct to claim separate consideration. It assumes two very divergent positions. It may restrict itself to material semblances. This form has been noticed under *Positivism* (q. v.). It may make matter merely a mental conception. In this case transcendental idealism is the result. The universe is one incessant flux of modifications and convolutions of a single entity, which is all in all, in each, and in everything. This idealistic phenomenalism inevitably runs into pantheism. It has been examined in the article on SPINOZA (q. v.). Notwithstanding the bitter, enduring, and often ill-considered censure bestowed upon Spinozism, it is returning in the speculation of the age, with such alterations of garb as the fashions of the times require. It is a recoil from the innutritious diet proffered by the materialists and naturalists of current science. A noteworthy example of this violent reaction is furnished by the philosophy of Lotze, now rising into favor. Lotze endeavors to unite the results of science with those of transcendental metaphysics, combining, reconciling, and harmonizing them in a more comprehensive scheme. He sees in all things the continuous interaction and reciprocal determination of their mutual relations. These relations constitute all existence and all change—they bear to reality the same analogy that Boscovich's points of force bear to the gravitation and cohesion of matter. These shifting, reciprocally moulding relations constitute at once the circulation and the substance of all being. The universe is one and single; its whole life, and the life of all its parts, are contained in the constant throb and vital activity of these relations. The wheels move incessantly, because there is life in the wheels; but the vitality of each part is the appropriate play in that part of the common, undivided energy which is concentrated in the totality of all the parts combined into one whole. The universe is a web of one piece, weaving itself into changing patterns by interchange of relations through all the phantasmagoria of existence in time and in eternity. This is not Spinozism, but patient discrimination is needed to discriminate them. Lotze would regard his scheme as the negation of pantheism; and the last words of his metaphysics imply his recognition of God as a distinct essence. But the desire to distinguish is not always attended by the ability to do so. If Lotze's philosophy is conceived in opposition to pantheism, its tendency is towards it. The adoption, development, and application of his principles and conclusions could scarcely be prevented from reaching that goal. Pantheism destroys the conception of divine intelligence and government by identifying them with all the phenomena of being, as naturalism repudiates the conception altogether by substituting for the creative energy the blind and unintelligent forces exhibited by matter, and ascribed to matter as their origin.

To this brief notice of the vapory idealism of Lotze may be appended the commemoration of the equally impalpable metaphysics of sir William Hamilton and his acolytes. The inadequacy and baselessness of the *Philosophy of the Conditioned* have been indicated already. See HAMILTON, SIR WILLIAM. The legitimate deduction from it was drawn by Dean Mansel (q. v.), in his *Limits of Religious Thought*, which may be considered as a prelude to Arnold's *Religion without Faith, and Morality without Morals*. The tendency of the metaphysical system of Hamilton is decidedly in the direction of pantheistic idealism, and antagonistic to the safe, but narrow, "common-sense" speculation of the Scotch school. If the admission of a constantly operating first cause must be excluded from the sphere of philosophy, because a first cause cannot be conceived; if the relativity of human knowledge is so interpreted as to render all knowledge a dream or a delusion; if nothing can be accepted as known, except what is precisely known, and known only so far as it is "conditioned," then all the powers, aspirations, and emotions of man are paralyzed, or rendered unsubstantial shadows. All things, so far as man is concerned, would be resolved into the spectral shapes cast on the clouds of the human mind. Even these phantasms must be cast by something, or evoked by something. This primary something is a cause, and a first cause, but its essence is beyond human grasp. There are, therefore, but two existences in the universe, conjoined to each other—the mirror of the mind, and the entity which starts the images from the reflecting surface. Obviously, this reduces the actual, the intelligible, and the active to a single essence, some of whose pulsations manifest themselves as the phantasms of the human mind. This, too, is pantheism.

The fatal defect of the Hamiltonian philosophy, and of its developments, is, apparently, not in the assertion of the relativity and conditionalism of human knowledge, but in the exclusion of all knowledge of the "unconditioned." Knowledge is a very elastic term: "conditioned" is a very ambiguous one. It may be doubted whether incomprehensible technicalities—"absolute," "unconditioned," "infinite," etc.—afford such definite ideas as permit strict reasoning, logical or philosophical, in regard to them. They are shifting phantoms of the mist. Controversies in regard to them are as effective as would be battles of children, fighting with iridescent soap-bubbles. Waiving the discussion of the question, which would be endless, and presumably inconclusive, it must be felt that many paralogisms in philosophy are due to the unperceived diversity of latitude in the meaning of the terms conjured with. Knowledge is of various degrees, kinds, and characters. Some is scientific, some philosophical, some intuitive, some revealed in mode and form apt for human acceptance. If all knowledge be denied, or excluded, but that which is established by logical or scientific reasoning, the human mind must wander "in endless mazes lost." It will stagger helplessly along, led only by the marsh-fires of the night, through forest and bog; mistaking every *ignis fatuus* for eternal sunlight. Science should confine itself to scientific knowledge. The range is wide enough for any ambition. But science must beg its first principles. It must rest on postulates which have a metaphysical basis. Logic observes the processes and sequences of thought, but the mind is, in itself, beyond human observation. All that it receives or produces is derived from impulses within and impulses without, whose existence must be accepted without other testimony than themselves. Thus, in all the grades and species of knowledge, the fundamental and indispensable assurance which renders any knowledge possible is the immutable conviction and the unwavering reception of knowledge, outside of systems of philosophy and provinces of science. Reason demands this. Conscious experience confirms it. Common-sense proceeds at all times from its influence, without a thought of its requirement. The relativity of human knowledge, and its character as "conditioned," should be admitted, but accompanied with the further admission that such knowledge is built upon the "absolute" and the "unconditioned."

Such limited idealism as has shown itself in late years may easily have been provoked by the insufficiency of scientific systems to furnish support or satisfaction to yearning and inquiring spirits. Perplexity, induced by the enigmas presented to the intellect, and despair of their solution, may have suggested another recent phase of scepticism, which differs widely from the forms commented upon. It is the least excusable of all forms, because it runs away from the battle-field, and seeks selfish relief in wilful misrepresentation and morose discontent. This scheme, if it is entitled to be called a scheme, is

V. *Pessimism.*—It might be supposed to be a natural resilience from the optimism of Leibnitz; but the schemes are separated by too wide an interval of time, and exhibit no links of actual connection. It rather grew out of the despair of the disappointed age which witnessed the dissipation of the dreams of the French revolution, and found utterance in the gloomy strains of Byron. Every age presents the results of the preceding philosophy, and moulds the philosophy of the age succeeding. That strange, poetic genius, Leopardi, sang the prelude of pessimism; Schopenhauer gave it form, expansion, and coherence; and Hartmann has endeavored to give it systematic exposition. Pessimism is not so much a negation of creative power and authority as a denigration of creative wisdom and benevolence. It maintains that the order of the universe is so constituted and regulated as to produce only wretchedness and increasing distress. In a period of brilliant industrial and intellectual achievement, but of augmenting disquietude, discontent, and misery, it presents a doctrine disparaging an order of things so often embittering life, and multiplying the myriads of the suffering, the sorrowing, and of those who find no rest. In one respect, pessimism is to be reprobated more severely than agnosticism. It does not merely hide the supernatural behind an impenetrable veil; it calumniates the creator and the creation. It degrades man, and unfits him for the discharge of the duties of humanity. Man's function on earth is not enjoyment; that may be an incident of his life, a result, or a recompense of his conduct. It is not to exult in the possession of pleasures and ease and vanities and gratifications. His office is, through constant trials, recurring sorrows, and "much tribulation," to strengthen and fit himself for the work set before him, and to do it—to make his contemporaries, and posterity, and the world, better and better provided, in consequence of his action —and to serve earnestly and loyally, as private or captain, in promoting the unseen purpose of Providence, and the destinies of humanity. What may be the fortunes or the fate of an individual is of passing moment. Countless bubbles burst every second on the ocean of life; but the movement of the ocean is uninterrupted. Each individual is but one in the army of laborers. When he falls, his place will be taken, usually by one better fitted for the growing task. There would be an impropriety in dwelling on this type of scepticism, as it has been already noticed in this work. See PESSIMISM.

It must suffice to add that the blackening of the unseen, and of its cause, the substitution of a malignant author, or order of creation, for the wise and the beneficent, are as distinctly sceptical procedures as any other mode of repudiating a transcendent authority. These remarks on pessimism have been introduced chiefly for the purpose of noticing an outgrowth, conscious or unconscious. This excrescence has not yet coagulated into a distinct theory, but has an immediate practical effect, and tends to diffuse itself, like a spreading ulcer, through intelligent classes of existing society. Its evangel was Malloch's inquiry: "Is life worth living?" The obvious reply is, "Certainly not, if life is 'propter vitam vivendi perdere causas.'"

VI. *Nihilism* is a convenient designation for the incipient doctrine. Its purpose is to escape from the perplexity of conflicting arguments and the bewilderment of insoluble problems: to make the best, for selfish comfort, of what is presumed to be inevitably bad, as well as uncertain; to seek tranquillity, as far as practicable, in the renunciation of all annoying duties, and of all unselfish aims.

> "How weary, stale, flat, and unprofitable
> Seem to me all the uses of this world!"

Nihilism, and the pessimism from which it descends, display analogies to the rehabilitated Buddhism, which has been recently compared to Christianity, and which is preached as a substitute for it in the midst of the chief centres of modern civilization. There is no folly or delusion, says Cicero, which has not been advocated by some of the schools of the philosophers. If such extravagant reveries meet with acceptance in a cultivated and thoughtful generation, it is a consolation to know that like errors have been welcomed and applauded before—and have been forgotten. They are dreams which vanish with the morning, and belong to "those fashions of the world which soon pass away."

If man be regarded—and the individual perhaps may properly be so regarded—as one ant in the busy ant-hill of humanity, the problem of life and of the universe in respect to him becomes as simple and clear as it is grand. What is needed for earthly necessities he learns by transmission, by observation, by experience, by the advance of science, and the growth of his faculties. Of all that is above him, and that is so strongly felt as to regulate his conduct and his understanding, he knows nothing, of his own knowledge, except imperfectly, for it is "wisdom unsearchable, and past finding out." Can he reject the knowledge, and the author of all his knowledge, because both remain incomprehensible? Whether affirming or denying, he is compelled to accept both. Shall the ant deny the existence of superior beings, which he can neither measure nor comprehend? Shall the clay ignore the hand of the potter? Shall man, walking in obscurity, and seeing only "as through a glass, darkly," reject or exclude all that he cannot fathom with his short plummet line? He has his office upon earth. What that office demands he knows, or may know, so far as is required for its discharge. He works for his family, that others may take his place when his time of labor is over. He works for his countrymen, and for his age; he scarcely knows why, or how. He knows imperfectly what has gone before, made him what he is, and elevated and facilitated his tasks. He thinks he knows the present, in which he lives. He knows nothing certainly of what may come after him. He "struts his hour upon the stage," unconsciously ministering to purposes of which he can hardly dream. When generations have succeeded generations, the retrospect may show a grand result flowing from the purblind activity of himself and his contemporaries. The prospect may reveal a still more glorious advancement to be accomplished. A new earth, if not a new heaven, will proceed from the successive swarms of mankind.

Can it be rationally questioned that there are controlling influences and purposes from the beginning, pressing forward to a determinate end? They necessitate the admission and the governance of a wisdom which man cannot conceive, of a beneficence which man cannot understand, of a plan which man cannot penetrate, and a guidance which man cannot, rationally or logically, ignore or deny.

Inferences.—It is a natural result of the self-confidence of men—an inevitable exorbitancy of that daring thought and speculation which are the handmaids of progress, that, in the hour of intellectual triumph and of material splendor, the bold leaders should undertake the erection, on earthly foundations, of "towers reaching to heaven." In their exultation, they are unmindful that these edifices must totter over, like other Babels, and note their existence by their ruins. The shattered monuments will furnish the quarries for humbler but securer dwellings. The churches and fortalices of mediæval Rome were mainly built with the broken capitals and architraves, columns, statues, and other carvings, of fallen palaces and pagan temples. The strong places of later progress are similarly constructed. We mount on ruins, and on the corpses of those that have preceded us. It would be weak fanaticism to disparage the services to human knowledge and performance rendered by the theories of scepticism which have been surveyed. It would be imbecile ingratitude to refuse admiration to the learning, ingenuity, and perseverance of the high priests of recent aberrations. Their devices may produce a dreary impression—

"We start, for soul is wanting there"—

but there is no reason for consternation or despondency. They have opened new paths through the haunted forest of life. They have made clearings for the daylight, and for cultivation. They have extended our journeyings, noted the dangerous routes, and proved by their failures the limits of human capacity in many directions. They have wrought for ends unseen by themselves. They have erected magnificent abodes for other occupants.

Literature.—The materials for the full appreciation of the recent phases of scepticism must necessarily be sought in the writings of the founders and leaders of the several sects and divisions of sects, and in the criticisms which those writings have provoked. The literature of the subject, accordingly, embraces the works of the prominent philosophers of the last and current generations who have propounded theories of sceptical design or tendency. It equally includes the multitudinous controversies which they have excited, embodied in volumes, pamphlets, and periodicals. The biographies of the authors, as illustrative of their doctrines, constitute a desirable appendage. This literature would form a goodly library, and is too extensive for specification. So vast and so various have been the several schemes, their expositions, their refutations, and their rejoinders, that, instead of multiplying the titles of the embattled hosts of books, it might be appropriate to employ the epitaph of Sir Christopher Wren, in St. Paul's: "Circumspice." Some valuable and accessible treatises may, however, be designated, for the purpose of fuller, but still summary elucidation of the prevalent forms of philosophical incredulity. Such are, Temple, *Bampton Lectures;* Tulloch, *Theism; Modern Theories in Philosophy and Religion;* Flint, *Anti-Theistic Theories;* Martineau, *Types of Ethical Theory.* (G. F. H.)

Schaeffer, Charles Frederick, D.D., an eminent Lutheran divine, was born at Germantown, Pa., Sept. 3, 1807. He graduated from the University of Pennsylvania in 1827, and studied theology with his father and with his father's assistant, the Rev. Charles R. Demme. He was licensed by the Synod of Maryland and Virginia June 17, 1829, and spent some months assisting his brother in New York. His first charge was at Carlisle, Pa., and his ordination took place Oct. 12, 1831. He left Carlisle Dec. 1, 1834, to enter upon the pastorate at Hagerstown, Md., where he remained until 1840, when he received a call to become professor in the Theological Seminary at Columbus, O. His relation to the Ohio synod became unpleasant, and he removed to Lancaster, Nov. 21, 1843. He next removed to Red Hook, Dutchess Co., N. Y., Dec. 23, 1845, where he was much esteemed. In 1851 he became pastor of St. John's Church, Easton, Pa., where he had a prosperous ministry of four years. It was during this period that he translated Kurtz's *Sacred History,* and made a careful revision of the translation of Luther's *Smaller Catechism.* In June, 1855, he was unanimously chosen as German professor in Pennsylvania College and in the Theological Seminary at Gettysburg. The ministerium of Pennsylvania having decided to establish a theological seminary at Philadelphia, in July, 1864, called Dr. Schaeffer to become professor of dogmatic theology, his instruction to be given in German and English equally. In this field he labored until his death, Nov. 23, 1879. Besides the above-named works, he published several single sermons, translated Lange's *Commentary on the Acts* (1866), and contributed numerous articles to the *Evangelical Review* and the *Bibliotheca Sacra.* See a *Memorial* of his life, funeral addresses, etc., in German and English (Phila. 1880).

Schaeffer, David Frederick, D.D., a Lutheran minister, was born at Carlisle, Pa., July 22, 1787. He graduated from the University of Pennsylvania in 1807, and, having finished his theological course, took charge of the evangelical Lutheran congregation at Frederick City, Md., in July, 1808. He was ordained at Philadelphia in 1812, and in 1829 was unanimously elected principal of the Frederick Academy. He died at Frederick City, May 5, 1837. See Sprague, *Annals of the Amer. Pulpit,* i, 123.

Schaeffer, Frederick Christian, D.D., a Lutheran minister, was born at Germantown, Pa., Nov. 12, 1792. He pursued his classical and also his theological studies under his father, was licensed in 1812, and soon after accepted a call from the Harrisburg congregation. He preached two years in New York city. In 1830 he was appointed professor of the German language and literature at Columbia College, but died March 29, 1832. See Sprague, *Annals of the Amer. Pulpit,* IX, i, 145; *Evangelical Review,* viii, 200.

Schaeffer, Frederick David, D.D., a Lutheran minister, was born at Frankfort-on-the-Main, Nov. 15, 1760, and received his education at the gymnasium in Hanau. In 1774 he began a private course in theology. He was licensed in 1786 by the Synod of Pennsylvania, ordained Oct. 1, 1788, and took charge of the Lutheran Church at Carlisle, preaching at different places in other counties. In 1790 he assumed the pastoral charge of Germantown District, and in 1812 removed to Philadelphia, as pastor of St. Michael's and Zion's churches. In 1834, in consequence of declining health, he removed to Maryland, where he died, Jan. 27, 1836. See Sprague, *Annals of the Amer. Pulpit,* IX, i, 79; *Evangelical Review,* vi, 275.

Schaller, Jacob, a Lutheran theologian of Germany, was born at Heilgenstein, near Strasburg, Feb. 25, 1604. He studied at different universities, was in 1633 professor of moral philosophy at Strasburg, in 1634 doctor of theology, and died June 24, 1676. Of his many writings we mention, *De Testamentis Christianis:—De Plantatione Noe ad Libros Philonis Judæi:—De Vanitate Vanitatum ex Eccles. i*, 2:—*De Christo Offensionis Lapide:—De Regno Davidico ad* 1 *Sam. xvi*, 1 sq., etc. See Witte, *Diarium Biographicum;* Jöcher, *Allgemeines Gelehrten-Lexikon*, s. v. (B. P.)

Schamelius, Martin, a Lutheran theologian of Germany, was born at Meuselwitz, Altenburg, June 5, 1668. He studied at Leipsic and Halle, was in 1703 deacon, and in 1708 first pastor at Naumburg. He died in 1742. He is the author of, *Naumburgisches glossirtes Gesangbuch nebst einer kurzgefassten Geschichte der Hymnopolorum* (4th ed. Nuremberg, 1720):—*Evangelischer Liedercommentarius*, etc. (Leipsic, 1724; 2d ed. 1737):—*Vindiciæ Cantionum Sanctæ Ecclesiæ Evangelicæ* (1712-19, 3 parts). See Jöcher, *Allgemeines Gelehrten-Lexikon*, s. v.; Koch, *Geschichte des deutschen Kirchenliedes*, v, 526 sq. (B. P.)

Schappeler, Christoph, a famous theologian and jurist of the reformation period, was born at St. Gall in 1472. In 1513 he was preacher at Memmingen, and in 1520 he joined the reformation by attacking the Church of Rome, not so much in the sense of Luther, but of Zwingli, who wished his countryman to come back to Switzerland. Schappeler, however, remained at Memmingen, where he commenced the work of reformation. He showed to his congregation that the Bible is the centre and source of the Christian belief and of all ecclesiastical institutions. He denounced the mass as of no avail and the priests as unfit persons, who pray without devotion and read mass for the sake of money. The papal power he denounced as a carnal right, and the commandments of the Church as the false papal commandment. Such language had its effect, and the majority of the citizens were brought over to Schappeler's side. The writings of the reformers were circulated and read, especially the New Test. In 1523 Schappeler spent a short time in his native country, where he preached against the abuses of the Church of Rome, and in November of the same year, after his return from Switzerland, he was joined by Christoph Gerung, another preacher of Memmingen, and both now worked together in the interests of reformation. In vain did the bishop ask the town-council to stop Schappeler. When, however, the bishop, on Feb. 27, 1524, pronounced the ban and excommunication over Schappeler, it had only the contrary effect. The citizens openly declared themselves for their preacher, and the council was powerless. In order to bring about a *modus vivendi*, the opponents of Schappeler had to appear at the council hall, on Jan. 2, 1525, for a public disputation. The confession of Schappeler, consisting of seven articles, was read. Five days the deputation lasted, which resulted in favor of the reformation, to introduce which the council now lent its hand. The ministers were allowed to marry, and the monks and nuns to leave the monasteries. Schappeler died at his native place, Aug. 25, 1551. See Bobel, *Memmingen im Reformationszeitalter* (1877); Vogt, in Plitt-Herzog, *Real-Encyklop.* s. v. (B. P.)

Scharbau, Heinrich, a Lutheran theologian of Germany, was born at Lübeck, May 25, 1689. He studied at Jena, Wittenberg, and Leipsic, was in 1715 preacher at his native place, and died Feb. 2, 1759. He wrote, *De Creophagia Ante Diluvium Licita* (Jena, 1709):—*De Fatis Studii Moralis apud Ebræos* (Leipsic, 1712):—*Exercitatio Philol. de Serpentis Ænei Significatione Mystica* (Lübeck, 1713):—*De Caipha ejusque Vaticinio ex Joh. xi*, 49, 50, 51 (1715):—*Judaismus Detectus* (1722):—*Parerga Philologico-theologica* (1719-26, 5 parts):—*Observationes Sacræ*, etc. (1731-37, 3 parts):—besides contributing to the *Bibliotheca Lubecensis*. See Döring, *Die gelehrten Theologen Deutschlands*, s. v.; Fürst, *Bibl. Jud.* s. v. (B. P.)

Schärer, Johann Rudolf, a Swiss theologian, was born at Berne in 1756. In 1793 he was professor of Hebrew, in 1805 professor of Biblical study at the Berne Academy, and he died July 3, 1829, preacher at Bümpflingen. He is the author of, *Das Buch Hiob aus dem Grundtext metrisch übersetzt und erlaütert* (Berne, 1818, 2 parts):—*Die Psalmen metrisch übersetzt mit kurzen Anmerkungen* (1812):—*Religiöses Erbauungsbuch für Gefangene* (1817, 1820). See Winer, *Handbuch der theol. Lit.* i, 206, 209; ii, 320; Fürst, *Bibl. Jud.* s. v. (B. P.)

Scharfenberg, Johann Gottfried, a Lutheran theologian of Germany, was born at Leipsic, Oct. 16, 1743, and died there, March 18, 1786, doctor and professor of philosophy. He is the author of, *Prolusio de Josephi et Versionis Alexandrinæ Consensu* (Leipsic, 1780):—*Fragmenta Versionum Græcarum Veteris Testamenti in Monte-Falconio Collecta* (part i, 1776; ii, 1781):—*Loci Nonnulli Danielis*, etc. (1774). Together with Vogel he edited Lud. Capelli *Critica Sacra* (1778-86, 3 vols.). See Fürst, *Bibl. Theol.* s. v.; Winer, *Handbuch der theol. Lit.* i, 51, 93, 222. (B. P.)

Scharff, Johann, a Lutheran theologian of Germany, was born at Kroppenstadt, near Halberstadt, June 18, 1595. He studied at Wittenberg, was in 1627 professor of philosophy, in 1649 professor of theology, and died Jan. 6, 1660, doctor of theology. He wrote, *De Messia et Jesu Salvatore Mundi:—Collegium Anti-Calvinianum:—Collegium Theologicum Decem Disputationes de Præcipuis Fidei Articulis Continens:—Angelologia Sacra ex Matth. xviii*, 10:—*De Justificatione ex Rom. iii*, 24, 25:—*De Interna Confirmatione Fidelium ex* 2 *Cor. i*, 21, 22:—*De Divinitate Christi ex Veteri et Novo Testamento Asserta*, etc. See Witte, *Diarium Biographicum;* Jöcher, *Allgemeines Gelehrten-Lexikon*, s. v. (B. P.)

Scharling, Karl Emil, a Danish theologian, was born at Copenhagen in 1803, and died in 1877, doctor and professor of theology. In 1828 he published *De Stedingis Commentatio*, and in 1833 *Hvad er Hensigten, Betydningen og Resultaterne af Theologernes videnskabelige Undersogelser om det Nye Testamentes Skrifter?* Upon publishing this treatise he was made professor. For a great many years he edited the *Theologisk Tidsskrift* (1837-55), and published, besides his writings already mentioned, *De Paulo Apostolo ejusque Adversariis Commentatio* (1836):—*Epistola Pauli ad Corinthios Posterior Annotationibus in Usum Studiosorum Illustrata* (1840):—*Jacobi et Judæ Epistolæ Catholicæ Commentariis Illustratæ* (1841):—and some other works which have been translated into German, *Die neuesten Untersuchungen über die sogenannten Pastoralbriefe des Neuen Testaments* (Jena, 1846):—*Michael de Molinos* (Gotha, 1855). See Lichtenberger, *Encyclop. des Sciences Religieuses*, s. v.; Zuchold, *Bibl. Theol.* s. v. (B. P.)

Schartau, Henrik, a Swedish theologian, was born Sept. 27, 1757, at Malmö. He studied at Lund, and at the age of twenty-three was ordained. In 1786 he was called to Lund, where he spent the remainder of his life. Schartau, who died Feb. 2, 1825, was a very eminent preacher and a faithful witness of Jesus. He lifted up his voice, calling to repentance all who were permeated by the leaven of unbelief, which characterized the age. After his death a number of homiletical and ascetical works were published. His followers are known as Schartauans. See Lindeblad, *Schartau's Life and Teaching* (Lund, 1837; Germ. transl. by A. Michelsen, *Schartau's Leben und Lehre*, Leipsic, 1842): Melin, *Henrik Schartau* (Stockholm, 1838); *Biographisk Lexicon öfver namnkundige Svenska Männ*, xiii, 347-367 (Upsala, 1847); Plitt-Herzog, *Real-Encyklop.* s. v. (B. P.)

Schaubach, Konrad Friedrich, a Lutheran

theologian of Germany, was born Jan. 9, 1827, at Meiningen. He studied at Göttingen and Jena, was in 1851 rector at his native place, in 1865 deacon, in 1870 first pastor, in 1882 member of the superior ecclesiastical council, and died Dec. 25, 1884. He published, *Das Leben Philipp Melanchthon's* (2d ed. Meiningen, 1860):—*Ausgewählte Psalmen im Anschlusse an die Evangelien des Kirchenjahres ausgelegt* (Halle, 1863):—*Zur Charakteristik der deutschen Volksliteratur* (a prize essay). See Zuchold, *Bibl. Theol.* s. v. (B. P.)

Schauffler, William Gottlieb, D.D., LL.D., a Congregational minister, was born at Stuttgart, the capital of Würtemberg, Aug. 22, 1798. When he was six years old his father removed to Odessa, Russia, where he held the office of mayor over the German colony. The son early gave much attention to the study of French and Italian. He was converted at the age of twenty-two. With a view of preparing himself for a missionary, under the direction of Joseph Wolf, the Jewish missionary, he went to Constantinople and engaged in the study of the Latin, Turkish, and English languages. To perfect himself in the work of preparation he came to the United States, entered Andover Theological Seminary, and completed the full course in 1830. He was more or less familiar with a score of languages. In 1831 he was ordained, and, after spending five years in America, returned to Constantinople. One of the great works of Dr. Schauffler's life was the translation of the entire Bible into Osmanli Turkish, under the direction of the British and American Bible Societies. This work occupied eighteen years of unremitting labor. His labors for the conversion of the Jews were characterized by zeal and devotion. He translated the Old Test. into Spanish. He was obliged to leave Constantinople on account of the plague in 1836, and travelled in southern Russia preaching the gospel to German residents. He spent three years in Vienna superintending the printing of the Bible. In 1877, in consequence of the infirmities of age, he was obliged to lay aside his active work, and came to the United States to end his days. He died in New York, Jan. 26, 1883. The Tract Society published his *Meditations on the Last Days of Christ.* See *N. Y. Observer*, Feb. 1, 1883. (W. P. S.)

Schaw, Robert, a Scotch prelate, was elected abbot of Paisley, March 1, 1498, and was advanced to the see of Moray in 1524. He died in 1527. See Keith, *Scottish Bishops*, p. 148.

Schäzler, Constantin von, a Roman Catholic theologian, was born of Protestant parentage at Augsburg, in 1827. He studied jurisprudence, and was promoted as doctor of law at Erlangen in 1850. In the same year he joined the Church of Rome at Brussels, studied theology, and was made a priest in 1857 at Liege. In 1859 he was promoted at Munich as doctor of theology, was in 1863 lecturer at Freiburg, in 1866 archiepiscopal counsellor, went to Rome in 1873, and was made chaplain by Pius IX. In 1878 he joined the Jesuits, and died at Interlaken, Sept. 20, 1880. He published, *Die Lehre von der Wirksamkeit der Sacramente* (Munich, 1860):—*Natur und Uebernatur* (1865):—*Gnade und Glaube* (1867):—*Das Dogma von der Menschwerdung Christi* (1870):—*Ueber päpstliche Unfehlbarkeit* (eod.):—*Der heilige Thomas von Aquin als Besieger des Liberalismus* (1874). (B. P.)

Scheffer, Wilhelm, a Reformed theologian of Germany, was born April 15, 1803, at Schrecksbach, Kurhessen, commenced his theological career at Marburg in 1827, was professor of theology there in 1831, member of consistory in 1838, member of superior consistory and superintendent in 1857, and died Feb. 26, 1883, doctor of theology. He published, *Quæstionum Philonianarum Particula I* (Marburg, 1829):—*De Usu Philonis in Interpretatione Novi Testamenti* (1831), besides several sermons. See Zuchold, *Bibl. Theol.* s. v.; Winer, *Handbuch der theol. Lit.* i, 522. (B. P.)

Schegg, Peter, a Roman Catholic theologian of Germany, was born June 6, 1815, at Kaufbeurn. In 1838 he received holy orders, commenced his academical career at the lyceum in Freising in 1843, was professor of exegesis there in 1847, in 1848 at Würzburg, in 1872 at Munich, and died July 9, 1855, doctor of theology. He wrote, *Geschichte der letzten Propheten* (Ratisbon, 1853, 2 parts):—*Uebersetzung und Erklärung der kleinen Propheten* (1854, 2 vols.):—*Uebersetzung und Erklärung der Psalmen* (2d ed. 1857, 3 vols.):—*Die heiligen Evangelien übersetzt und erklärt* (Munich, 1856-70, 7 vols.):—*Sechs Bücher des Lebens Jesu* (Freiburg, 1874-75, 2 vols.):—*Jacobus und sein Brief* (1881):—*Das Todesjahr des Königs Herodes und das Todesjahr Jesu Christi* (Munich, 1882). (B. P.)

Scheibel, Johann Gottfried, a Lutheran theologian of Germany, was born at Breslau, Sept. 16, 1783. In 1811 he was professor of theology at the university of his native place, but was deposed from his office in 1832 on account of his connection with the Separated Lutherans (q. v.), of whom he became a leader. Scheibel retired to Nuremberg, and died in 1842. He wrote, *Observationes Criticæ et Exegeticæ ad Vaticinia Haggaei* (Breslau, 1822):—*Das Abendmahl des Herrn* (1823):—*Actenmässige Geschichte der neuesten Unternehmungen einer Union zwischen der reformirten und lutherischen Kirche* (Leipsic, 1834, 2 vols.):—*Communionbuch* (1827). See Winer, *Handbuch der theol. Lit.* i, 230, 454, 530, 756; ii, 105, 275, 367; Zuchold, *Bibl. Theol.* s. v. (B. P.)

Scheid, Balthasar, a Lutheran theologian of Germany, was born at Strasburg in 1614, and died there Nov. 26, 1670, doctor of theology and professor of Oriental languages. He wrote, *Jonas Propheta Philol. Commentar. Expositus* (Strasburg, 1665):—*Novum Testamentum ex Talmude et Antiquitatibus Hebræorum Illustratum* (ed. by J. Chr. Meuschen, Leipsic, 1736):—*Epistola Pauli ad Titum et Philemon. Syr. Adjuncto Versione* (1668). See Winer, *Handbuch der theol. Lit.* i, 55, 227, 239; Fürst, *Bibl. Jud.* s. v.; Jöcher, *Allgemeines Gelehrten-Lexikon*, s. v. (B. P.)

Schelhorn, father and son, two prominent theologians of the 18th century, whose works are still very valuable to the Church historian.

1. Johann Georg, *Sr.*, was born Dec. 8, 1694, at Memmingen. He studied at Jena, was in 1718 conrector in his native city, in 1734 pastor, in 1753 doctor of theology, in 1754 superintendent, and died March 31, 1773. Of his works, we mention, *De Religionis Evangelicæ in Provincia Salisburgensi Ortu et Fatis* (Leipsic, 1732; also in German and Dutch):—*Amœnitates Historiæ Ecclesiasticæ et Litterariæ* (1737-46, 4 vols.; Germ. translation, Ulm, 1762-64, 3 vols.):—*Acta Historica Ecclesiastica Sæculi XV et XVI* (1738):—*De Vita, Fatis Meritis Ph. Camerarii Commentarius* (Nuremberg, 1740):—*Diatribe de Antiquissima Latinorum Bibliorum Editione* (1760). See Döring, *Die gelehrten Theologen Deutschlands*, s. v.; Meusel, *Lexikon verstorbener deutscher Schriftsteller*, xii, 124 sq.; Lichtenberger, *Encyclop. des Sciences Religieuses*, s. v.; Winer, *Handbuch der theol. Lit.* i, 783, 787; Plitt-Herzog, *Real-Encyclop.* s. v.

2. Johann Georg, *Jr.*, was born at Memmingen, Dec. 4, 1733; studied at Göttingen and Tübingen, was in 1756 preacher at Buxach, near Memmingen, in 1762 at Memmingen, in 1793 superintendent there, and died Nov. 22, 1802. He wrote, *Beiträge zur Erläuterung der Geschichte*, etc. (1772-77, 4 parts):—*Anleitung für Bibliothekare und Archivare* (1788-1791, 2 vols.), etc. See Döring, *Die gelehrten Theologen Deutschlands*, s. v.; Koch, *Geschichte des deutschen Kirchenliedes*, v, 190; vi, 224; Meusel, *Lexikon verstorbener deutscher Schriftsteller*, s. v.; Plitt-Herzog, *Real-Encyclop.* s. v. (B. P.)

Schelwig, Samuel, a Lutheran theologian of Germany, was born March 8, 1643. He studied at Wittenberg, was in 1673 professor of philosophy at Dantzic, in 1675 professor of theology, in 1685 doctor of theology. In 1693 Schelwig inaugurated a controversy with his colleague Constantine Schütze, whom he accused of having spoken in the pulpit in favor of pietism (q. v.) and Spener. The outcome of this controversy was a number of controversial writings published by both parties. In 1694 the town council interfered. But Schelwig would not stop. He now wrote against Spener, who replied. In 1701 Schelwig was joined by Chr. F. Bücher in his polemics against Spener, and he died Jan. 18, 1715. See Prætorius, *Athenæ Gedanenses* (Leipsic, 1713), where a complete list of Schelwig's writings is given; Jöcher, *Allgemeines Gelehrten-Lexikon*, s. v.; Walch, *Religionsstreitigkeiten der evangel.-lutherischen Kirche*, i, 602 sq., 739 sq.; iv, 159; Schmid, *Geschichte des Pietismus*, p. 225 sq., 343; Schnaase, *Geschichte der evangelischen Kirche Danzig's* (Dantzic, 1863); Plitt-Herzog, *Real-Encyclop.* s. v. (B. P.)

Schem, Alexander Jacob, a religious journalist and statistician, was born at Wiedenbrück, Germany, March 16, 1826. After a course of instruction at the gymnasium of Paderborn, he studied theology at Bonn (1843), and Tübingen (1845); became a Roman Catholic priest (1846), but embraced Protestantism, and edited a newspaper in Westphalia (1849). In 1851 he came to America, was professor of languages in Dickinson College (1854-60), and afterwards devoted himself to literary labors, especially in connection with several religious and political newspapers. He died at Hoboken, N. J., May 21, 1881, being at the time assistant superintendent of the public schools in New York city. He was a contributor to Appleton's *Cyclopædia*, M'Clintock and Strong's *Cyclopædia*, editor of the *Deutsch-Amerikanische Conversations-Lexicon* (1869-74), of a *Latin-English Lexicon* (in connection with Dr. Crooks), of a *Cyclopædia of Education* (in connection with Henry Kiddle), and author of several *Year-books*, besides other volumes.

Schenck, Noah Hunt, D.D., a Protestant Episcopal minister, was born near Trenton, N. J., June 30, 1825. He graduated from Princeton College in 1844, studied law, and practiced it for a year in Trenton and three years in Cincinnati, O.; but having decided to enter the ministry, studied theology at the Seminary in Gambier, where he graduated in 1853. His first parish was at Hillsboro'. In 1856-57 he preached at Gambier, and from 1857 to 1859 in Trinity Church, Chicago, Ill. While in that city he founded and edited *The Western Churchman*. In 1859 he accepted a call to Emanuel Church, at Baltimore, where he remained until he went to Brooklyn, in 1867, as rector of St. Ann's Church, where he continued until his death, Jan. 4, 1885. Dr. Schenck travelled several times in Europe, and was the author of several works, mostly letters of travel and sermons. At one time he edited *The Protestant Churchman* of New York, and he was talked of for bishop on several occasions. He was regarded as a preacher of great ability, and always was listened to by large congregations.

Schenkel, Daniel, a Protestant theologian of Germany, was born Dec. 21, 1813, at Dögerlen, Canton Zürich. He studied at Basle and Göttingen, was in 1837 privat-docent at Basle, in 1841 chief pastor at Schaffhausen. In 1846 he began his great work, *Das Wesendes Protestantismus* (1846-51, 3 vols.; 2d ed. 1861), in which he took his stand upon the so-called "Vermittelungstheologie," the *via media* between the old evangelicalism and the new criticism. Upon the death of De Wette, Schenkel was called in 1849 to Basle as professor of theology. In 1851 he was called to Heidelberg. At first evangelical in spirit, in 1857 he sided with the liberal direction in the General Synod, and worked for the reconstruction of the Hessian Church upon the basis of the Congregational principle ("Gemeindeprinzip"). As editor of the *Allgemeine kirchliche Zeitschrift*, he used the press to support the Liberal direction in theology and ecclesiastical constitution. The beginning of his liberalism he showed in the *Christliche Dogmatik vom Standpunkt des Gewissens* (1858-59); but when he published in 1864 *Das Charakterbild Jesu*, one hundred and eighteen parochial clergymen in Baden issued a protest against the book. Schenkel replied in *Die protestantische Freiheit in ihrem gegenwärtigen Kampfe mit der kirchlichen Reaktion* (1865). From 1863 he had labored hard for the foundation of the German "Protestanten Verein." In 1883 he retired from the direction of the homiletical seminary, and in 1884 from academical activity, and died May 19, 1885. Besides the works already mentioned, he published, *Die Grundlehren des Christenthums aus dem Bewusstsein des Glaubens dargestellt* (1877):—*Luther in Worms und Wittenberg* (1870):—*Christenthum und Kirche im Einklang mit der Kulturentwicklung* (1867-72, 2 vols.):—*Das Christusbild der Apostel und der nachapostolischen Zeit* (1879):—in connection with eminent scholars he published *Bibel-lexikon* (1867-72, 5 vols.):—and for Lange's *Bibelwerk* he wrote the commentaries on Ephesians, Philippians, and Colossians, and his volume passed into a second edition; but its place in the series was afterwards occupied by a commentary on the same epistles by Dr. Karl Braune (q. v.). See Zuchold, *Bibl. Theol.* s. v. (B. P.)

Schenkl, Maurus, a Benedictine of Germany, was born at Auerbach, Jan. 4, 1749. In 1768 he joined his order, received holy orders in 1772, was in 1778 professor of theology at Weltenburg, in 1790 at Amberg, and died June 14, 1816. He wrote, *Positiones Theologiæ Dogmaticæ* (Regensburg, 1779-80):—*Positiones ex Theologia Universa* (1781):—*Positiones ex jure Ecclesiastico Universo et Bavarico* (1783):—*Ethica Christiana* (1800-1801, 3 vols.):—*Institutiones Theologiæ Pastoralis* (1802; 2d ed. 1803):—*Compendium sive Institutiones Ethicæ Christianæ* (1807). See Döring, *Die gelehrten Theologen Deutschlands*, s. v.; Winer, *Handbuch der theol. Lit.* i, 316; ii, 9, 35. (B. P.)

Scherer, Johann Ludwig Wilhelm, a Lutheran theologian of Germany, was born at Nidda, Feb. 27, 1777, and died in 1825. He is the author of, *Ausführliche Erklärung der sämmtlichen messianischen Weissagungen*, etc. (Altenburg, 1801):—*Archiv zur Vervollkommnung des Bibelstudiums* (Hamburg, eod.):—*Geschichte der Israeliten vor Jesus* (Zerbst, 1803-1804):—*Der Schriftforscher zur Bildung eines gründlichen Bibelstudiums* (Weimar, 1803-1805, 2 vols.):—*Ausführliche Erklärung der sämmtlichen Weissagungen des Neuen Testaments* (Leipsic, 1803):—*Historische Einleitung zum richtigen Verstehen der Bibel* (Halle, 1802). See Winer, *Handbuch der theol. Lit.* i, 277, 390, 391; ii, 37, 162, 249, 252, 280, 293; Fürst, *Bibl. Jud.* s. v. (B. P.)

Scherzer, Johann Adam, a Lutheran theologian of Germany, born at Eger, Aug. 1, 1628, was in 1657 professor of theology at Leipsic, in 1658 professor of Hebrew, and died Dec. 23, 1683, doctor and professor of theology. He wrote, *Collegium Anti-Calvinianum* (edited by J. Schmid, Leipsic, 1704):—*Collegium Anti-Socinianum* (1672):—*Trifolium Orientale* (containing *Manductio ad Lectionem Talmudico-rabbinicam, Specimen Theologiæ Judæorum Mystice, Abarbanelis Comm. in Haggæum*):—*Nucleus Grammaticorum Ebraicorum* (1660). See Fürst, *Bibl. Theol.* s. v.; Winer, *Handbuch der theol. Lit.* i, 353, 354; Jöcher, *Allgemeines Gelehrten-Lexikon*, s. v. (B. P.)

Schickedanz, Abraham Philipp Gottfried, a Reformed theologian of Germany, was born at Dessau, May 22, 1747. In 1772 he was rector at Frankfort, in 1776 third preacher of the Reformed Church and professor of theology, in 1784 doctor of theology, and died at Zerbst, Nov. 28, 1808. He wrote, *De Caipha Prophetam Simulante ad Joh. xi*, 49-52 (Frankfort, 1773):—*Vestigia Messiæ in Scriptis Josephi atque Philonis* (1774):—*Diss. super Quædam Loca Sabbatariorum Scriptorum Exterorum* (1775-76):—*De Natura Sacrificiorum Veteris Testamenti* (1784), etc. See Döring,

Die gelehrten Theologen Deutschlands, s. v.; Winer, *Handbuch der theol. Lit.* i, 136, 536. (B. P.)

Schiede, JOHANN GEORG, a Reformed theologian of Germany, was born at Cassel, May 15, 1714. He studied at Marburg, was ordained in 1739, and appointed pastor at Carlshafen in 1741. In 1745 he was called to Hanau, was in 1755 member of consistory, and died May 13, 1792. He wrote, *De Velo Tabernaculi*, etc. (Marburg, 1736):—*Biga Observationum Sacrarum de Codice Bibliorum Ebraico MS. Bibliothecæ Casselanæ* (Bremen, 1748). See Döring, *Die gelehrten Theologen Deutschlands*, s. v.; Fürst, *Bibl. Jud.* s. v. (B. P.)

Schirmer, AUGUST GOTTLOB FERDINAND, a Lutheran theologian of Germany, was born in Silesia, May 14, 1791, and died in 1863 at Greifswalde, doctor and professor of theology. He published, *Observationes Exeg.-Criticæ in Librum Esdræ* (Breslau, 1820):—*Die biblische Dogmatik*, etc. (eod.):—*Versuch einer wissenschaftlichen Würdigung des Supernaturalismus und Rationalismus* (1818):—*Die Anbetung Gottes im Geist und in der Wahrheit* (Greifswalde, 1830), etc. See Winer, *Handbuch der theol. Lit.* i, 204, 292, 369; ii, 104, 177; Zuchold, *Bibl. Theol.* s. v. (B. P.)

Schlegel, Gottlieb, a Lutheran theologian of Germany, was born at Königsberg, Feb. 16, 1739, and died at Greifswalde, May 27, 1810, doctor and professor of theology. He published, *De Parallelismo Sermonum Jesu et Scriptorum Apostolicorum* (Greifswalde, 1791):—*Erneuerte Erwägung von der göttl. Dreieinigkeit* (Riga, 1791–92, 2 parts):—*Briefe der Apostel Petrus, Johannes, Jacobus und Judas übersetzt mit einigen Anmerkungen* (Halle, 1783):—*De Principiis Expectationis de Messia in Gente Judaica* (1793), etc. See Döring, *Die gelehrten Theologen Deutschlands*, s. v.; Winer, *Handbuch der theol. Lit.* i, 110, 334, 421, 484, 497, 867; ii, 31, 46, 221, 273. (B. P.)

Schlegel, Johann Carl Fürchtegott, a German theologian, son of Johann Adolf, was born in Hanover, Jan. 2, 1753, and died Nov. 13, 1831, member of consistory. He wrote, *Ueber den Geist der Religiosität aller Zeiten und Völker* (Hanover, 1819, 2 vols.):—*Kirchen- und Reformationsgeschichte von Norddeutschland und den hannover'schen Staaten* (1828–32, 3 vols.):—*Kurhannover'sches Kirchenrecht* (1801–1806, 5 vols.). See Zuchold, *Bibl. Theol.* s. v.; Winer, *Handbuch der theol. Lit.* i, 510, 797; ii, 16, 23. (B. P.)

Schlegel, Karl August Moritz, a German divine, son of Johann Adolf, was born in Hanover, Sept. 26, 1756. He studied at Göttingen, was in 1790 preacher at Harburg, in 1796 at Göttingen, and died Jan. 29, 1826. He published some ascetical works. See Döring, *Die deutschen Kanzelredner*, p. 409–413. (B. P.)

Schleyer, PETER, a Roman Catholic theologian of Germany, who died at Ettenheim, Feb. 28, 1862, doctor and professor of theology, is the author of, *Orakel des Iesaia über den Untergang Babels* (Freiburg, 1839):—*Ueber die neutestamentliche Lehre von der Unauflöslichkeit der Ehe* (1844):—*Der Puseyismus nach seinem Ursprunge und als Lehrsystem dargestellt* (1845). See Zuchold, *Bibl. Theol.* s. v.; Fürst, *Bibl. Jud.* s. v. (B. P.)

Schlichter, CHRISTIAN LUDWIG, a Reformed theologian of Germany, was born at Cothen, Dec. 7, 1705, and died there, April 23, 1765, doctor of theology. He wrote, *De Baptismo ὑπὲρ τῶν νεκρῶν*, etc. (Bremen, 1725):—*De Quatuor Rebus Salomonæis Intellectu Difficillimis ad Prov. xxx*, 18, 19 (Halle, 1730):—*Exercitatio Epistolica*, etc., *ad* האדם *Gen. viii*, 21 sq. (1732):—*Decimæ Sacræ seu Observationum in Utriusque Fœderis Libros Quinque Decades* (eod.):—*Exercitatio Historico-antiquaria de Cruce apud Judæos, Christianos et Gentes* (1733):—*De Panibus Facierum eorumque Mysterio* (1737):—*Libellus Singularis de Suffitu Sacro Hebræorum ejusque Mysterio*, etc. (1754), and other works. See Döring, *Die gelehrten Theologen Deutschlands*, s. v.; Fürst, *Bibl. Jud.* s. v. (B. P.)

Schliemann, ADOLF, a Lutheran theologian of Germany, who died at Schwerin, July 30, 1879, doctor of theology, is the author of, *Die clementinischen Recognitionen* (Kiel, 1843):—*Die Clementinen nebst den verwandten Schriften, und der Ebionitismus* (Hamburg, 1844). See Zuchold, *Bibl. Theol.* s. v. (B. P.)

Schlochow, EMMANUEL MORITZ, a minister of the Episcopal Church, was born of Jewish parentage in 1826, at Winzig, Silesia. In 1848 he joined the Christian Church at Breslau, and in 1851 acted as lay missionary among the Jews in Upper Silesia. In order to make himself more fit for missionary work, Schlochow entered the Hebrew College of the London Society, and in 1853 was appointed to Jassy, where he remained for nearly ten years. In 1863 he was appointed to Mühlhausen, and at the end of the Franco-Prussian war settled at Strasburg, as the most important place in Alsace and Lorraine. At the beginning of the year 1876 he was compelled to retire from the mission-field on account of broken health, and settled at Worthing, England, where he died, Dec. 30, 1876. (B. P.)

Schmid, Christian Ernst, a Lutheran theologian of Germany, was born May 14, 1715, at Rabenau, Saxony, studied at Leipsic, and entered upon his pastoral duties in 1739. He died at Eilenburg, Nov. 27, 1786, superintendent, leaving, *Expositio Ritus Cantandi per Noctes Dierum Festorum apud Hebræos* (Leipsic, 1738):—*De Lege per Peccatum Infirmata* (1739):—*De Veritatis Divinæ Doctoribus Tamquam στύλοις ἐκκλησίας* (eod.):—*De Sacrificio a Perjuris Offerendo* (eod.):—*De Corpore Christi Omnis in Sepulcro Experte Corruptionis contra Anonymi Dubia* (1740). See Döring, *Die gelehrten Theologen Deutschlands*, s. v.; Fürst, *Bibl. Jud.* s. v. (B. P.)

Schmid, Christian Friedrich, a Lutheran theologian of Germany, was born Nov. 20, 1741, at Röglitz, near Merseburg. He studied at Leipsic, and commenced his academical career there in 1764. He was professor in 1767, went to Wittenberg in 1772, took the degree of doctor of theology in the same year, and died May 19, 1778. He wrote, *Versio Alexandrina Optimum Interpretationes Librorum Sacrorum Præsidium* (Leipsic, 1763–64):—*De Herodianis* (1764):—*Super Origine Epistolæ ad Hebræos* (1765):—*Observationes super Epistola ad Hebræos* (1766):—*Observationes super Epistola Judæ* (1768):—*Divina Origo Librorum Canonicorum Veteris Testamenti* (Wittenberg, 1772):—*De Antiqua Forma, Collectione et Conservatione Codicis Sacri Hebraioi* (eod.), etc. See Döring, *Die gelehrten Theologen Deutschlands*, s. v.; Fürst, *Bibl. Jud.* s. v.; Winer, *Handbuch der theol. Lit.* i, 76, 77, 91, 109, 256, 267, 272, 486. (B. P.)

Schmid, Heinrich, a Lutheran theologian of Germany, was born July 31, 1811, at Harburg, near Nördlingen. He studied at Halle and Berlin, commenced his academical career at Erlangen in 1837, was in 1848 professor of theology, and died Nov. 17, 1885. He wrote, *Ueber Schleiermacher's Glaubenslehre* (Leipsic, 1835):—*Die Dogmatik der evangelisch-lutherischen Kirche dargestellt* (6th ed. 1876):—*Geschichte der synkretistischen Streitigkeiten in der Zeit des Georg Calixt* (Erlangen, 1846):—*Lehrbuch der Kirchengeschichte* (2d ed. 1856):—*Handbuch der Kirchengeschichte* (1880–81, 2 vols.):—*Die Theologie Semler's* (1858):—*Lehrbuch der Dogmengeschichte* (1859):—*Geschichte des Pietismus* (1863):—*Kampf der lutherischen Kirche um Luther's Lehre vom Abendmahl* (2d ed. 1873):—*Geschichte der kathol. Kirche Deutschlands*, etc. (1872–74). (B. P.)

Schmid, Johann Andreas, a Lutheran theologian of Germany, was born at Worms, Aug. 28, 1652, was in 1683 professor at Jena, in 1699 at Helmstädt, and died June 12, 1726, doctor and professor of theology. He published, *Compendium Historiæ Ecclesiasticæ*

(Helmstädt, 1701; new ed. 1708):—*De Apostolis Uxoratis* (1704):—*Historia Sæculi Quarti Fabulis Variorum Maculata* (1712):—*De Fatis Calicis Eucharistiæ in Ecclesia Romana* (1708):—*Lexicon Ecclesiasticum Minus* (1712):—*De Cantoribus Ecclesiæ Veteris et Novi Testamenti* (1703):—*De Re Monetali Ebræorum* (1699). See Winer, *Handbuch der theol. Lit.* i, 529, 532, 534, 554, 564, 573, 603, 608, 613, 614, 616, 618, 620, 627, 629, 630–32, 634, 635, 637, 654, 663, 759, 761; Jöcher, *Allgemeines Gelehrten-Lexikon*, s. v. (B. P.)

Schmid, Johann Wilhelm, a Lutheran theologian of Germany, was born at Jena, Aug. 29, 1744, and died there April 1, 1798, doctor and professor of theology. He published, *Immortalitatis Animorum Doctrina* (Jena, 1770):—*De Nexu inter Fidem et Virtutem Christianam* (1784):—*Historia Resurrectionis Christi* (eod.):—*Commentationis, in qua μεσίτου Notio Indagatur, Particulæ Tres* (1785–87):—*De Consensu Principii Moralis Kantiani cum Ethica Christiana* (1788):—*Veræ Nestorii de Unione Naturarum in Christo Sententiæ Explicatio* (1793):—*De Joanne a Jesu Dilecto* (1795), etc. See Döring, *Die gelehrten Theologen Deutschlands*, s. v.; Winer, *Handbuch der theol. Lit.* i, 310, 424, 428, 437, 447, 566, 599; ii, 59, 68. (B. P.)

Schmid, Joseph Anton, a Roman Catholic theologian of Germany, was born in 1827 at Heideck, Upper Palatinate. He received holy orders in 1851, was in 1853 professor of Hebrew and exegesis at the episcopal lyceum in Eichstätt, in 1868 professor of Church history and dogmatics at Bamberg, and died March 9, 1881, at Munich, doctor of theology. He published, *Commentar zum Buch der Weisheit* (Vienna, 1858):—*Kirche und Bibel* (1862). (B. P.)

Schmid, Karl Christian Erhard, a Lutheran theologian of Germany, was born at Heilsberg, Weimar, April 14, 1761, and died at Jena, April 10, 1812, doctor and professor of theology. He published, *Philosophische Dogmatik im Grundrisse* (Jena, 1796):—*Versuch einer Moralphilosophie* (1790–98, 2 vols.; 4th ed. 1802–3):—*De Theologia Biblica* (1788):—*Adiaphora philosophisch, theologisch und historisch untersucht* (1809). See Winer, *Handbuch der theol. Lit.* i, 284, 288, 292, 294, 486, 761; ii, 94. (B. P.)

Schmid, Leopold, a professor of philosophy, who died at Giessen, Dec. 20, 1869, was originally a Roman Catholic divine, and occupied the theological chair at Giessen from 1839 to 1849. In the latter year he was elected bishop by the Mayence chapter, but the papal see did not acknowledge the election. Schmid resigned his position as theological professor, accepted a position in the philosophical faculty, and in 1867 publicly left the Church of Rome, and published *Ultramontan*, etc. Of his writings we also mention, *Erklärung der Genesis* (Giessen, 1835):—*Grundzüge der Einleitung in die Philosophie* (1860). (B. P.)

Schmidt, Johann Ernst Christian, a Lutheran theologian of Germany, was born Jan. 6, 1772, at Busenborn, Hesse. He studied at Giessen, commenced his academical career there in 1793, and died June 4, 1831, doctor and professor of theology. He published, *Genesis xlix neu übersetzt, mit Anmerkungen* (Giessen, 1793):—*Salomo's Prediger, neu übersetzt und erklärt* (1794):—*Philologisch-exegetischer Clavis über das Neue Testament* (1795–1805):—*Bibliothek für Kritik und Exegese des Neuen Testaments* (1796–1802, 2 vols.):—*Lehrbuch der christlichen Dogmatik* (1800):—*Handbuch der christl. Kirchengeschichte* (1801–20, 6 vols.):—*Historisch-kritische Einleitung in das Neue Testament* (1804–5, 2 vols.), *Theologische Encyclopädie* (1811). See Döring, *Die gelehrten Theologen Deutschlands*, s. v.; Fürst, *Bibl. Jud.* s. v.; Winer, *Handbuch der theol. Lit.* i, 10, 15, 75, 201, 213, 236, 299, 474, 537, 577, 604. (B. P.)

Schmidt, Oswald Gottlob, a Lutheran theologian of Germany, was born at Kaditz, Saxony, Jan. 2, 1821. He studied at Leipsic, was in 1845 pastor at Schönfeld, in 1856 at Greifenhain, and in 1866 at Werdau. Schmidt died Dec. 26, 1882, doctor of theology. He published, *Pericula Conjungendorum Ecclesiarum*, etc. (Grimma, 1844):—*Die Lehre von der Rechtfertigung durch den Glauben* (Leipsic, 1859):—*Nicolaus Hausmann, der Freund Luther's* (1860):—*Caspar Cruciger und Georg der Gottselige* (in *Leben der Altväter der lutherischen Kirche*, 1861):—*Petrus Mosellanus* (1866):—*Blicke in die Kirchengeschichte der Stadt Meissen* (1879). He also contributed to the Plitt-Herzog *Real-Encyclop.* s. v. (B. P.)

Schmitt, LEONHARD CLEMENS, a Roman Catholic theologian of Germany, was born in 1810 at Höchstadt-on-the-Aich. He received holy orders in 1834, was doctor of theology at Munich in 1835, and died at Bamberg, Dec. 14, 1869, professor of theology and vicar-general. He published, *Grundriss einer Christologie des Alten Testaments* (1841):—*Praktische Erklärung des ersten Psalms* (1843):—*Die Construction des theolog. Beweises* (1836). (B. P.)

Schmölders, AUGUST, a German Orientalist, was born in 1809 at Bochold, Westphalia, and died at Breslau, Feb. 21, 1880, professor at the university. In 1869 he joined the Old Catholics. Schmölders published, *Documenta Philosophiæ Arabum ex Codice Manuscripto* (Bonn, 1836):—*De Studiis Arabum Grammaticis* (Breslau, 1862). (B. P.)

Schmucker, John George, D.D., a Lutheran minister, was born in Michaelstadt, in the Duchy of Darmstadt, Germany, Aug. 18, 1771. He came to America in 1785, finished his course of study in Philadelphia in 1792, and was admitted as a member of the Synod of Pennsylvania, then at Reading. His first charge consisted of several congregations in York County. In 1809 he became pastor of the congregation at York, where he labored twenty-six years. He died Oct. 7, 1854. See Sprague, *Annals of the Amer. Pulpit*, IX, i, 95; *Evangelical Review*, vi, 412.

Schmucker, Samuel Simon, D.D., an eminent Lutheran minister, son of John George, was born at Hagerstown, Md., Feb. 28, 1799. His preparatory studies were pursued at York (Pa.) Academy. In 1814 he entered the University of Pennsylvania, where he remained until the close of the sophomore year, when he returned to York, and in August, 1816, took charge of the classical department of the York Academy, and held this position until November, 1817. Having studied theology for a time with his father, he entered Princeton Theological Seminary, from which he graduated in 1820. That year he was licensed to preach; for several months assisted his father; then went to Virginia to take charge of congregations in Shenandoah County, which had been under the care of his uncle, Rev. Nicholas Schmucker. He was ordained Sept. 5, 1821, at Frederick, Md. The Shenandoah congregations which he served were, New Market, Solomon's, Reder's, and Armentrout's, and he remained in this charge until 1836. While here he set himself to work to translate, rearrange, and enlarge Storr and Flatt's *Biblical Theology*. In 1822 he began to prepare students for the ministry. In March of the same year he submitted to a committee, appointed for the purpose, a plan which he had drawn up, entitled *The Formula for the Government and Discipline of the Evangelical Lutheran Church in Maryland and Virginia*. It was adopted by the synod in 1822, and approved by the General Synod in 1823. Subsequently it was revised and enlarged in 1827, under his direction, by the Synod of West Pennsylvania; was printed in the *English Hymn-book* in 1829; became the ground-plan of the organization of the congregations within the General Synod, and it has endured until the present time. In 1827 he was directed to prepare the constitution for synods, which was adopted in 1829. When, in 1823, the Ministerium of Pennsylvania withdrew, and the existence of the General Synod was imperilled, he was very active in the measures taken to prolong its life. He edited the *English*

Catechism, and, in company with Rev. C. P. Krauth, prepared the *English Hymn-book.* The work to which he believed himself to be called was the preparation of candidates for the ministry. When the General Synod decided, in 1825, to establish a theological seminary, he was at once elected the first professor. The institution was opened Sept. 5, 1826, at Gettysburg, to which place he removed. For four years he was the sole professor. During his connection with the seminary over four hundred ministers went out from it. After nearly forty years of labor in this office he resigned it in 1864. He was largely instrumental in the establishment of Pennsylvania College, and was one of its trustees from its incorporation until the close of his life, July 26, 1873. In 1838 he published an appeal to the American churches, with a plan for Christian union, and was present, in 1846, when the Evangelical Alliance was organized. His *Popular Theology* passed through eight editions; his *Psychology* reached a third edition. He published forty-four works, most of which were synodical and occasional discourses. It is said that his attempts to produce liturgies were the most unsuccessful of his literary endeavors. As a preacher he was very careful in his preparation, and was always gladly heard. See *Penn. College Year-book*, 1882, p. 154; *Fifty Years in the Lutheran Ministry* (1878), p. 121; (Gettysburg) *Evangelical Review*, Jan. 1874.

Schneck, BENJAMIN S., D.D., a minister of the German Reformed Church, was born near Reading, Pa., March 14, 1806. He studied theology under Rev. Dr. F. S. Herman, was licensed in 1825, and ordained in 1826. His first charge consisted of seven congregations in Centre County, where he labored until 1833. In 1834 he became pastor in Gettysburg and vicinity, but, his health failing, he resigned in 1835. Shortly after he took charge of the *Weekly Messenger*, continuing as editor until 1844. He resumed the editorial management of the *Messenger* from 1847 to 1852. He was also editor of the *Reformirte Kirchenzeitung* from its beginning until 1864, as well as minister at different intervals to congregations in the vicinity of Chambersburg. In 1855 he took charge of St. John's Reformed Church at Chambersburg, of which he continued pastor until his death, April 19, 1874. In 1839 he was president of the synod which met at Philadelphia. For some time before his death he was professor of German in the Wilson Female College, near Chambersburg. He was a man of much general information; a genial, pleasing, and instructive writer. See Harbaugh, *Fathers of the Germ. Ref. Church*, v, 120.

Schneemann, GERHARD, a Jesuit, who died Nov. 20, 1885, at Kirchrath, Holland, is the author of, *Die Irrthümer über die Ehe; Die Freiheit und Unabhängigkeit der Kirche; Die kirchliche Gewalt und ihre Träger; Die kirchliche Lehrgewalt* (published as essays in *Stimmen aus Maria-Laach*, Freiburg, 1866–69):—*Sancti Irenæi de Ecclesiæ Romanæ Principatu Testimonium* (1870):—*Die Kanones und Beschlüsse des vaticanischen Concils* (in German and Latin, 1871):—*Die Entstehung der thomistisch-molinistischen Controverse* (1879):—*Controversiarum de Divinæ Gratiæ Liberique Arbitrii Concordia Initia et Progressus* (1881):—*Weitere Entwickelung der thomistisch-molinistischen Controverse* (1880). (B. P.)

Schneider, LEONHARD, a Roman Catholic theologian of Germany, who died April 25, 1874, at Moorenweis, diocese of Augsburg, is the author of *Die Unsterblichkeitslehre des Aristoteles* (Passau, 1867):—*Studie über Roger Bacon* (Augsburg, 1873):—*Die Unsterblichkeitsidee im Glauben und in der Philosophie der Völker* (Ratisbon, 1870). (B. P.)

Schnorr (*von Carolsfeld*), JULIUS, a famous painter, and, besides Cornelius, Overbeck, and Veit, one of the oldest and most distinguished representatives of Christian painting of modern times, was born in 1794 at Leipsic, and educated at Dresden. In 1817 Schnorr went to Italy, was in 1846 appointed director of the picture-gallery at Dresden, and died May 24, 1872. He published, *Die Bibel in Bildern* (Leipsic, 1860):—*Biblia Sacra Tabulis Illustrata*, etc. (1855–60). (B. P.)

Schöberlein, LUDWIG FRIEDRICH, a Lutheran theologian of Germany, was born at Kolmberg, near Anspach, Sept. 6, 1813. He studied at Munich and Erlangen, and commenced his academical career at the latter place in 1841. In 1850 he was professor at Heidelberg, in 1855 at Göttingen, in 1862 member of consistory, and died July 8, 1881. Schöberlein published, *Die Grundlehren des Heils, entwickelt aus dem Prinzip der Liebe* (Stutgard, 1848):—*Der evangelische Gottesdienst nach den Grundsätzen der Reformation* (Heidelberg, 1854):—*Der evangelische Hauptgottesdienst in Formularen für das ganze Kirchenjahr* (1855; new ed. 1874):—*Das Wesen des christlichen Gottesdienstes* (1860):—*Schatz des liturgischen Chor- und Gemeindegesangs*, etc. (Göttingen, 1863–72, 3 vols.):—*Geheimnisse des Glaubens* (1872):—*Prinzip und System der Dogmatik* (1881). See Lichtenberger, *Encyclop. des Sciences Religieuses*, s. v.; Pünjer, *Theol. Jahresbericht* (1881), i, 374 sq.; Plitt-Herzog, *Real-Encyklop.* s. v. (B. P.)

Schock, JAMES L., D.D., a Lutheran minister, was born in Berks County, Pa., March 16, 1816. He graduated from Pennsylvania College in 1839, after which he was a tutor there, and for a short time studied at the Gettysburg Theological Seminary. In 1841 he was licensed to preach, and that year was pastor in Reading, Pa. For a time he preached in Chambersburg, and in 1852 became pastor of St. James's Church, New York city. He disappeared mysteriously during a mental disturbance, as a result of impaired physical health, Oct. 29, 1865. See *Pennsylvania College Year-book*, 1882, p. 208.

Scholten, JOHANN HEINRICH, a Dutch theologian and leader of the critical theological school in Holland, who died in April, 1885, was in 1840 professor at Franeker, and in 1843 at Leyden. He is the author of, *Disquisitio de Dei Erga Hominem Amore Principe Religionis Christianæ Loco* (Leyden, 1836):—*De Vitando in Jesu Christi Historia Interpretanda Docetismo* (1840):—*De Religione Christiana suæ Ipsa Divinitatis in Animo Humano Vindice* (1844):—*De Pugna inter Theologiam atque Philosophiam Recto Utriusque Studio Tollenda* (1847):—*Dogmatices Christianæ Initia* (2d ed. 1858):—*De Sacris Literis Theologiæ Nostra Ætate Libere Excultæ Fonte* (1857):—*Geschiedenis der godsdienst en wijsbegeerte ten gebruike bij het akademische lessen* (1860):—*Die ältesten Zeugnisse betreffend die Schriften des Neuen Testaments*, from the Dutch, by Manchot (Bremen, 1867):—*Das Evangelium nach Johannes* (transl. by H. Lang, Berlin, 1867):—*Das älteste Evangelium*, etc. (transl. by Redepenning, Elberfeld, 1869):—*Geschichte der Religion und Philosophie* (transl. from the 3d ed. by Redepenning, ibid. 1868; also transl. into French by A. Reville, *Manuel d'Histoire Comparée de la Philosophie et de la Religion*, Paris, 1861):—*Der Apostel Johannes in Kleinasien* (transl. by Spiegel, Berlin, 1872):—*Das Paulinische Evangelium*, etc. (transl. by Redepenning, Elberfeld, 1881):—*Historisch-critische bijetragen naar aanleiding van de nieuwste hypothese aangaande Jezus en den Paulus der vier hoofdrieven* (Leyden, 1882). (B. P.)

Scholz, JOHANN MARTIN AUGUSTIN, a Roman Catholic theologian of Germany, was born Feb. 8, 1794, at Kapsdorf, Silesia, and died at Bonn in 1853, doctor and professor of theology. He published, *Novum Testamentum Græce* (Leipsic, 1830–35, 2 vols.):—*Biblisch-kritische Reise in den Jahren* 1818–21 (1823):—*Curæ Criticæ in Histor. Textus Evangeliorum*, etc. (Heidelberg, 1820):—*Handbuch der bibl. Archäologie* (Bonn, 1834):—*Reise in die Gegend zwischen Alexandrien*, etc. (Leipsic, 1822):—*Die kleinen Propheten übersetzt und erklärt* (1833):—*Einleitung in die heiligen Schriften des Alten und Neuen Testaments* (1845–48, 3 vols.):—*De Vir-*

tutibus et Vitiis Utriusque Codicum Novi Testamenti Familiæ (1845). See Zuchold, *Bibl. Theol.* s. v.; Fürst, *Bibl. Jud.* s. v.; Winer, *Handbuch der theol. Lit.* i, 14, 46, 92, 102, 137, 155, 174, 175, 560, 677. (B. P.)

Schorch, FRANZ EDUARD, a Lutheran theologian of Germany, was born at Hermannsgrün in 1802, and died at Schleiz, Nov. 17, 1881, superintendent and doctor of theology. He published *Das Leben Jesu*, etc. (Leipsic, 1841), and several volumes of *Sermons*, for which see Zuchold, *Bibl. Theol.* s. v. (B. P.)

Schöttgen, CHRISTIAN, a Lutheran theologian and philologist of Germany, was born at Wurzen, Saxony, March 14, 1687. He studied at Leipsic, was in 1716 rector at Frankfort-on-the-Oder, in 1719 at Stargard, Pomerania, in 1728 at Dresden, and died Dec. 15, 1751. He is best known as the author of, *Horæ Hebraicæ et Talmudicæ in Universum Novum Testamentum* (Dresden, 1733):—*Horæ Hebraicæ et Talmudicæ in Theologiam Judæorum Dogmaticam Antiquam et Orthodoxam de Messia Impensæ* (1742):—*Novum Lexicon Græco-Latinum in Novum Testamentum* (Leipsic, 1746; new ed. by Krebs, 1765, and Spohr, 1790). See Döring, *Die gelehrten Theologen Deutschlands*, s. v.; Meusel, *Lexicon der von* 1750-1800 *verstorbenen deutschen Schriftsteller*, xii, 382 sq.; Plitt-Herzog, *Real-Encyklop.* s. v. (B. P.).

Schröder, Johann Joachim, a Lutheran theologian of Germany, was born at Neukirchen, Hesse, July 6, 1680, and died at Marburg, July 19, 1756, professor of theology. He published, *De Historia et Conditione Versionis Armenicæ Sacri Codicis* (Amsterdam, 1711):—*Disputationes de Natura Linguæ Hebraicæ* (Marburg, 1716):—*De Rubo Ardente et non Comburente ad Exod. iii*, i sq. (1714):—*De Annis Achasiæ, Judæorum Regis ad Conciliandi Loca* 2 *Reg. vii*, 26 *et* 2 *Chron. xxii*, 2 (1715):—*De Primæva Lingua Ebraica* (1716):—*De Precibus Ebræorum* (1717):—*De Nethinæis* (1719):—*De Voce* אַבְרֵךְ *ad Gen. xli*, 43 (eod.), etc. See Fürst, *Bibl. Jud.* s. v.; Döring, *Die gelehrten Theologen Deutschlands*, s. v. (B. P.)

Schröder, Johann Wilhelm, a Lutheran theologian of Germany, was born at Marburg, June 15, 1726, and studied at the university in his native place. In 1755 he succeeded his father as professor of Oriental languages and Hebrew antiquities, and died March 8, 1793. He published, *De Sanctitate in Genere et Quibusdam ejus Speciebus, Præcipue de Sanctitate Dei* (Marburg, 1750):—*Commentarius Philologicus in Psalmum x* (Groningen, 1754):—*In Causas Quare Dictio Pure Græca in Novo Testamento Plerumque Prætermissa sit* (1768):—*In Difficiliora Quædam Psalmorum Loca Fasciculus* (1781). See Döring, *Die gelehrten Theologen Deutschlands*, s. v. (B. P.)

Schroeder, JOHN FREDERICK, D.D., a Protestant Episcopal minister, was born in Baltimore, Md., April 8, 1800. He graduated from Princeton College in 1819; studied in the Episcopal Seminary at New Haven, Conn.; was ordained in 1823; had charge of a parish on the eastern shore of Maryland for a few months; was assistant minister of Trinity Church, New York city, from 1824 to 1838; and in the latter year rector of the Church of the Crucifixion, and of St. Thomas's Church, Brooklyn. In 1839 he established a seminary for young ladies, called St. Ann's Hall, at Flushing, L. I. He died in Brooklyn, Feb. 26, 1857. Dr. Schroeder was a fine scholar, a popular preacher, and the author of several volumes; one contains essays on Biblical subjects, and three are on General Washington.

Schröter, ROBERT GUSTAV THEODOR, a Protestant theologian of Germany, who died at Breslau, March 20, 1880, is the author of, *Gregorii Bar-Hebræi Scholia in Psalmum viii, xl, xli, l*, etc. (Breslau, 1857):—*Kritik des Dunasch ben-Labrat über einzelne Stellen aus Saadia*, etc. (1866):—*Die dem Saadia beigelegte arabische Uebersetzung der kleinen Propheten* (in *Merx' Archiv für Erforschung des Alten Testaments*); besides, he contributed to the *Zeitschrift der deutsch. morgenl. Gesellschaft*. (B. P.)

Schubert, JOHANN ERNST, a Lutheran theologian of Germany, was born at Elbing, June 22, 1717, and died at Greifswalde, Aug. 19, 1774, doctor and professor of theology. He published, *Introductio in Theologiam Revelatam* (Jena, 1749):—*Institutiones Theologiæ Polemicæ* (1756-58, 4 vols.):—*Vernünftige und schriftgemässe Gedanken von der göttlichen Dreieinigkeit* (1751):—*Gedanken von der Gnadenwahl* (1754):—*Schriftgemässe Gedanken von der Rechtfertigung eines Sünders vor Gott* (1744):—*Vernünftige und schriftgemässe Gedanken vom Tode* (1743):—*Gedanken vom ewigen Leben und vom Zustande der Seelen nach dem Tode* (1747). See Winer, *Handbuch der theol. Lit.* i, 292, 343, 421, 443, 447, 448, 467, 470; Döring, *Die gelehrten Theologen Deutschlands*, s. v. (B. P.)

Schultze, JOHANN HEINRICH, a Lutheran theologian of Germany, was born Sept. 7, 1810, and died Nov. 21, 1884. He is the author of, *Weihnachtsglocke oder liturgische Vorfeier zum heil. Christtage* (5th ed. Magdeburg, 1858):—*Vesperglocke oder liturgische Andachten zum Sonntag-Nachmittag* (1856):—*Textgemässe Predigt-Entwürfe über die evangelischen und epistolischen Perikopen* (2d ed. Göttingen, 1884, 3 vols.). See Zuchold, *Bibl. Theol.* s. v. (B. P.)

Schwabe, FRANZ, a Lutheran theologian of Germany, who died Aug. 12, 1884, at Friedberg, doctor and professor of theology, is the author of, *Evangelisches Brevier in Lied und Gebet* (2d ed. Friedberg, 1873):—*Geistliches Liederbuch* (4th ed. 1878), and of some homiletical works. (B. P.)

Schwarz, Franz Joseph, a Roman Catholic theologian of Germany, who died at Ellwangen, July 1, 1885, doctor of theology, is the author of, *Neue Untersuchungen über das Verwandtschafts-Verhältniss der synoptischen Evangelien*, etc. (Tübingen, 1841):—*Die katholische Kirche und der Protestantismus auf dem Gebiete der inländischen Mission* (1851):—*Die göttliche Offenbarung von Jesus Christus nach der sogenannten Armenbibel* (2d ed. Freiburg, 1883). (B. P.)

Schwarz, Friedrich Heinrich Christian, a Protestant theologian of Germany, was born May 30, 1766, at Giessen, and studied there. In 1790 he was preacher at Dexbach, near Biedenkopf, Hesse, in 1796 at Echzell, and finally, in 1804, professor of theology at Heidelberg, where he died, April 3, 1837. Schwarz took a great interest in pedagogy, founded prosperous educational institutions, and published *Lehrbuch der Erziehungs- und Unterrichtslehre* (1835, 3 vols.). Of his theological works we mention, *Sciagraphia Dogmatices Christianæ in Usum Prælectorum* (1808):—*Grundriss der kirchlichen protestantischen Dogmatik* (1816):—*Das Christenthum in seiner Wahrheit und Göttlichkeit betrachtet* (1808):—*Handbuch der evangelisch-christlichen Ethik für Theologen und gebildete Christen* (1821; 2d ed. 1830). See Plitt-Herzog, *Real-Encyklop.* s. v. (B. P.)

Schwarz, Friedrich Immanuel, a Lutheran theologian of Germany, was born March 5, 1728, and died at Leipsic, Oct. 25, 1786, doctor and professor of theology. He wrote, *Exercitationes Historico-criticæ in Utrumque Samaritanorum Pentateuchum* (Wittenberg, 1756):—*Jesus Targumicus* (Torgau, 1758-59, 2 parts):—*De Disputatione Vinariensi et Restitutione Cantabrigiensi* (1760):—*De Unctione Pontificis Magni Hebræorum per Crucem* (1756):—*De Scalinis Hebræorum* (1755):—*Martyrium Stephani e Pandectis Hebræorum Illustratum* (1756):—*De Resurrectione Jobi* (1759):—*Vaticinium Iesaiæ de Tumulo Jesu, Commentatio Super Ies. xxi*, 11, 12 (1760):—*Observationes Criticæ de Masora Scripturæ Sacræ Veteris Testamenti Polyglotta* (1754). See Winer, *Handbuch der theol. Lit.* i, 98, 435, 760; Fürst, *Bibl. Jud.* s. v.; Döring, *Die gelehrten Theologen Deutschlands*, s. v. (B. P.)

Schwarz, Gottfried, a Lutheran theologian of Germany, was born at Iglau, Hungary, Nov. 19, 1707. He studied at Jena, was in 1730 conrector at Leutschau, Hungary, in 1742 rector at Osnabrück, in 1749 professor at Rinteln, and died Nov. 13, 1786, doctor of theology. He published, *Trias Observationum Grammaticarum* (Osnabrück, 1744):—*Prolegomena de Præcipuis Nominibus Dei* (1771):—*Annorum Vitæ Tharahhi et Abrahami* (1773), etc. See Döring, *Die gelehrten Theologen Deutschlands*, s. v. (B. P.)

Schwarz, Johann Conrad, a Lutheran theologian of Germany, was born at Coburg in 1676. He studied at Jena and Halle, was in 1706 professor at the academical gymnasium in Coburg, in 1715 doctor of theology, and died June 3, 1747. He published, *De Mohammedis Furto Scripturæ Sacræ Liber Unus* (Leipsic, 1711):—*Commentarii Critici et Philologici Linguæ Græcæ Novi Fœderis Divini* (1736), etc. See Döring, *Die gelehrten Theologen Deutschlands*, s. v.; Winer, *Handbuch der theol. Lit.* i, 125, 128, 530; Fürst, *Bibl. Jud.* s. v.; Jöcher, *Allgemeines Gelehrten-Lexikon*, s. v. (B. P.)

Schwarz, Johann Peter, a Lutheran theologian of Germany, was born at Rudolstadt, July 6, 1721. He studied at Jena and Göttingen, and commenced his academical career in 1739 at the former university. In 1749 he was deacon at his native place, in 1761 court-preacher, and died in 1781. He wrote, *De Pœniculamentis Judæorum* (Göttingen, 1737):—*De Perfectione Linguæ Hebraicæ Quoad Syllabas* (1738):—*De Voto, quo se Invicem Judæi Ineunte Anno Prosequuntur* (Jena, 1736):—*Diss. ad Versionem Jonathanis ben-Usiel Genes. ii*, 1 (1739):—*De Nominibus Veteris Testamenti Propriis, Religionis Ebræorum Monumentis* (1743):—*Paradoxa Theologica de Efficacia Sacræ Scripturæ* (1757), etc. See Döring, *Die gelehrten Theologen Deutschlands*, s. v.; Fürst, *Bibl. Jud.* s. v. (B. P.)

Schwarz, Karl Heinrich Wilhelm, a Protestant theologian of Germany, was born Nov. 19, 1812. He commenced his academical career at Halle in 1842, was professor there in 1849, in 1856 court-preacher and member of consistory at Gotha, and died March 25, 1885, doctor of theology. According to his own request, Schwarz's body was cremated. He published, *De Sancta Trinitate*, etc. (Halle, 1842):—*Das Wesen der Religion* (1847):—*Lessing als Theolog.* (1854):—*Zur Geschichte der neueren Theologie* (4th ed. 1869):—*Predigten aus der Gegenwart* (1859-79, 7 vols.). Schwarz was the leader of the so-called liberal theologians of Germany. See Zuchold, *Bibl. Theol.* s. v. (B. P.)

Schwarzenberg, Friedrich Johann Nepomuk, prince-archbishop of Prague, was born April 6, 1809. In 1836 prince Schwarzenberg was made archbishop of Salzburg, in 1842 cardinal-priest, in 1849 archbishop of Prague, and died at Vienna, March 27, 1885, cardinal-archbishop. At the Vatican council he made an address, May 18, 1870, against the dogma of papal infallibility, which caused a great sensation in all Europe. But the resistance of Schwarzenberg was soon broken; he did not sign the protest of the opposition party, and retired to a monastery to avoid being further pressed by his former adherents. In Rome the papal faction soon proclaimed "Laudabiliter se subjecit." And such was the case, for Schwarzenberg was one of the first who proclaimed the dogma of infallibility in his archdiocese. Otherwise he was one of the most peaceful and tolerant prelates in Austria. (B. P.)

Schwarzhüber, Simpertus, a Benedictine, was born at Augsburg, Dec. 4, 1727, and died at Salzburg, April 30, 1795, doctor of theology. He published, *System der christlichen Sittenlehre* (Salzburg, 1793-94, 2 vols.):—*Gedanken über die bedenklichsten Einwendungen gegen die Untrüglichkeit der Kirche*, etc. (1794):—*Praktisch-katholisches Religionshandbuch für nachdenkende Christen* (1784-86, 4 vols.). See Winer, *Handbuch der theol. Lit.* i, 316, 404; ii, 323; Döring, *Die gelehrten Theologen Deutschlands*, s. v. (B. P.)

Schwarzl, Karl, a Roman Catholic theologian of Germany, was born in Austria, Feb. 19, 1746, and died at Freiburg, March 4, 1809. He wrote, *Elenchus Sanctorum Patrum Ordine Alphabetico* (Innsbruck, 1780):—*Prælectiones Theologiæ Polemicæ* (Vienna, 1781):—*Die Psalmen David's, frei aus dem Hebräischen übersetzt* (Augsburg, 1798):—*Anleitung zu einer vollständigen Pastoraltheologie* (1799, 3 vols.):—*Uebersetzung und Auslegung des Neuen Testaments* (Ulm, 1802-1805, 6 vols.). See Döring, *Die gelehrten Theologen Deutschlands*, s. v.; Winer, *Handbuch der theol. Lit.* i, 342, 670; ii, 35, 70. (B. P.)

Sconce, a movable candlestick of brass, latten, or other metal, sometimes affixed to a wall, placed against a pillar, or let into the rail-moulding of a pew. Sconces were likewise arranged along the top both of the rood-screen and of the side-screens of choirs and lateral chapels, in which, on great festivals, such as Christmas and Candlemas, lighted tapers were placed.—Lee, *Gloss. of Liturg. and Eccles. Terms.*

Scot, John, a Scotch prelate, was archdeacon of St. Andrews, and soon after, in 1200, was made bishop of Dunkeld. He died in 1203. See Keith, *Scottish Bishops*, p. 76.

Scot, Matthew, a Scotch prelate, was archdeacon of St. Andrews and chancellor of the kingdom. He was postulate bishop of the see of Aberdeen in 1228, and about the same time postulate bishop of the see of Dunkeld. He died before he had been consecrated to either see. See Keith, *Scottish Bishops*, p. 79, 106.

Scott, George, D.D., a Reformed Presbyterian minister, was born at Clogher, County Tyrone, Ireland, July 26, 1805, of parents who came of the Covenanter stock, and was well educated. In 1822 he came to America, and, after a short engagement in mercantile pursuits, joined the church of Dr. Samuel B. Wylie, in Philadelphia, by whom he was encouraged to prepare for the ministry. By teaching school, and the most severe economy, he completed his studies privately, and after licensure travelled as an evangelist for some time, but at length was ordained pastor of the Reformed Presbyterian congregations at Little Beaver, Pa., and Austintown, O., April 19, 1831. He afterwards confined his care to the former, until his resignation, Oct. 1, 1880. He died Dec. 16, 1881. Dr. Scott was a most honored, faithful, and successful pastor. See (Pittsburgh) *Presbyterian Banner*, Aug. 9, 1882.

Scott, John Work, D.D., LL.D., a Presbyterian minister, was born in York County, Pa., Nov. 27, 1807. He attended the Lower West Nottingham Academy and Slate Ridge Academy, and graduated from Jefferson College in 1827. He then taught three years at Butler (Pa.), Churchville (Md.), and Chanceford (Pa.). In 1830 he entered the middle class at Princeton Theological Seminary, where he remained two years, at the same time teaching, as an assistant to Prof. Robert B. Pallon, at the Edgehill Seminary at Princeton. He was licensed by the Presbytery of New Castle, Oct. 3, 1832; preached as stated supply at Poland, O., during the winter following, and was also tutor at Jefferson College. In 1836 he became stated supply to the Church at Three Springs, also of the Free Church of Steubenville, O. After this he preached frequently, but had no stated place. Dr. Scott's chief work was as an educator. He was founder and principal of the Grove Academy, at Steubenville, and with this was connected from 1836 to 1847. He was principal of the Lindsley Institute, at Wheeling, Va., until 1853; president of Washington College, Pa., from 1853 to 1865; principal of Woodburn Female Seminary and of the Academy, at Morgantown, W. Va., until 1867; then vice-president of the State University at the same place, and for two years was acting-president. This he was obliged to resign in 1877, because of failing eyesight. His eyes being treated with success, he went, in 1879, to Biddle University, N. C., to fill a vacancy. He died July 25, 1879. Dr. Scott was a man of excellent mental powers, of great vigor of mind. As a teacher he was admirable and rarely surpassed. See *Necrol. Report of Princeton Theol. Sem.* 1880, p. 18.

Scott, Levi, D.D., a bishop of the Methodist Episcopal Church, was born at Cantwell's Bridge (now Odessa), Del., Oct. 11, 1802. He was trained to labor, and began his thorough intellectual discipline after reaching manhood. He grew up in a Christian home, his father being an itinerant minister. Levi was converted in 1822, and entered the Philadelphia Conference in 1825. He served a number of the most important charges in his conference, and soon gained a high reputation as a clear, logical, incisive preacher. In 1840 he became principal of the grammar-school of Dickinson College, where he remained until 1843. The next two years he was pastor of Union Church, Philadelphia; and from 1845 to 1848 presiding elder of the South Philadelphia District. At the General Conference of 1848 he was made assistant book-agent at New York. In 1852 he was elected bishop, and from that time until the close of his active career was most earnest in labors for the Master. Shortly after his election to the episcopal office he visited our mission in Liberia, and for many years suffered from the effects of the climate. In 1880, after twenty-eight years as bishop, and fifty-five in the active ministry, he retired to his childhood's home, where he gradually declined until his death, July 13, 1882. "In his most vigorous days the hearer was first arrested by the searching expression of the preacher's eye; then by the condensed energy of his diction; then by the conciseness and clearness with which point after point of the argument was made out. No time was lost in amplification; the paragraphs of logic were sent home to the conscience with the force of shocks from an electric battery. A torrent of appeal, brief, but intense, followed, and the preacher's work was done." See *Minutes of Annual Conferences*, 1882, p. 301; *Life and Times*, by Dr. Mitchell (N. Y. 1884).

Scott, Thomas Fielding, D.D., a missionary bishop, was for many years a Presbyterian minister in Georgia, but was ordained deacon in 1843 in the Protestant Episcopal Church. His first parish was at Marietta, which was a new field, and where, within six years, a fine church property and a female institute were purchased. In 1851 he became rector of Trinity Church, Columbus, from which he was promoted to missionary bishop in 1853. His jurisdiction extended over Oregon and Washington territories. He died in New York city, July 14, 1867, aged sixty-two years. See *Amer. Quar. Church Rev.* 1867, p. 499.

Scott, Uriah, D.D., a Protestant Episcopal clergyman, was born at Lincoln, England, in 1820. He was first employed as a minister in New Milford, Pa.; but in 1859 was chosen rector of Grace Church, Honesdale, where he remained until 1861. He then went to New York city, where he officiated occasionally, and in 1867 ministered to the Church of the Redemption. In 1870 he was chosen rector of that church, and died in the same city, Dec. 25, 1878. See *Prot. Episc. Almanac*, 1880, p. 172.

Screven, Charles Odingsell, D.D., a Baptist minister, was born at Charleston, S. C., in 1774. He graduated from Brown University in 1795, and was licensed to preach in 1801. His ministerial labors were confined to Liberty and the immediate counties. In 1806 he was elected president of Mt. Enon College, where he remained and taught probably two years. His only publications are two sermons. In 1802 a painful disease began to develop itself in one of his eyes. He continued to prosecute his labors until 1821. The last six years of his life were years of intense and almost uninterrupted pain. He died in New York, July 2, 1830. See Sprague, *Annals of the Amer. Pulpit*, vi, 4391.

Scrogie, William, a Scotch prelate, was minister of Raphan, in Aberdeenshire, and was elected and consecrated bishop of Argyle in 1666, where he continued until his death in 1675. See Keith, *Scottish Bishops*, p. 291.

Seaman, Lazarus, D.D., an English Presbyterian clergyman, was born at Leicester, and educated at Emanuel College, Cambridge, where he took the degree of M.A. in 1631. By diligence and hard study he attained great eminence in literature and in the learned languages. He went to London as chaplain to the earl of Northumberland, and was lecturer at St. Martin's, Ludgate. His ability secured for him the valuable living of Allhallows, Bread Street, given by archbishop Laud in 1642. The next year he was chosen a member of the Westminster Assembly of Divines. He was an able disputant, and defeated two Romish priests in a set controversy. In 1644 he was made master of Peterhouse, Cambridge. He had interviews with king Charles I before his impeachment. Cromwell appointed Dr. Seaman visitor to the University of Cambridge, and vice-chancellor thereof. After the Restoration he lost all his preferments, was ejected from Allhallows in 1662, and gathered a congregation of his former hearers, who formed a new and important church, which met in Silver Street, continued about a century, and had a fine body of ministers. He died in Warwick Court, Newgate Street, Sept. 9, 1695. For more than thirty years his skill as a casuist procured him great fame; as an interpreter of Scripture he was one of a thousand; he was also a model pastor. He published several sermons, and a translation into Turkish, in 1660, of *John Ball's Catechism*. He had a very choice and valuable library, the catalogue of which is preserved in the museum at the Baptist Academy, Bristol. See Wilson, *Dissenting Churches*, iii, 6-12.

Sears, Barnas, D.D., LL.D., an eminent Baptist minister, was born at Sandisfield, Mass., Nov. 19, 1802. In 1825 he graduated from Brown University, and four years later from Newton Theological Seminary. From 1827 to 1829 he was pastor of the First Baptist Church at Hartford, Conn. From 1830 to 1832 he was a professor in the Hamilton Literary and Theological Institution (now Madison University), and from 1833 to 1836 he studied theology at the German universities. During this period he inaugurated the German Baptist Church by immersing Rev. J. G. Oncken and six others in the Elbe, at Hamburg. He was a professor in the Newton Theological Seminary from 1835 to 1847, acting part of the time as president of the institution. He succeeded Horace Mann as secretary and executive agent of the Massachusetts Board of Education in 1848, and served in that position until 1855, when he became president of Brown University. In March, 1867, Dr. Sears was selected as the general agent of the Peabody Educational Fund, and at once went to Virginia to live. In this position he did much towards promoting education in the South. When the fund was established not a single Southern state had a modern system of public schools, but within eight years no state was without such a system. He died at Saratoga Springs, N. Y., July 6, 1880. Dr. Sears succeeded professor James D. Knowles as editor of the *Christian Review* in 1838, and held the position for a number of years. He was also a contributor to the *American Cyclopædia*, and the *Bibliotheca Sacra*. Among the works published by him were the following: Nöhden's *German Grammar with Additions* (1842):—*Classical Studies* (1843):—*The Ciceronian* (1844):—*Select Treatises of Luther* (1846):—*Life of Martin Luther* (1850):—Roget's *Thesaurus* (1854). Dr. Sears also published many addresses, educational reports, and miscellaneous essays, including his discourse at the centennial celebration of Brown University in 1864.

Secacah. For this site Lieut. Conder suggests (*Tent Work*, ii, 339) the modern *Sikkeh*, but he does not indicate the locality. It is thus referred to in the *Quar. Statement* of the "Pal. Explor. Fund," Jan. 1881, p. 55: "In the Judæan desert; possibly the ruin *Sikkeh*, east of Bethany (sheet xvii)." But no such name appears on the *Map* nor in the accompanying *Memoirs*.

Seceders is a term applied in Scotland to those bodies of Christians who have separated from the National Church on grounds not implying a disagreement with its constitution and standards, in which latter case they are termed *Dissenters* (q. v.).

Sechu. Lieut. Conder suggests (*Tent Work*, ii, 116) that this may be represented by *Khurbet Suweikeh*, three and a half miles north-west of er-Ram, consisting of "walls, foundations, and heaps of stones; pieces of tessellated pavement" (*Memoirs* to Ordnance Survey. iii, 126).

Second Adventists. See ADVENTISTS.

Sedulius, an Irish prelate, was called bishop of Dublin in 785 in the martyrologies of Marian Gorman, and those of Tullagh. He died Feb. 12, 785. See D'Alton, *Memoirs of the Archbishops of Dublin*, p. 24.

Segedin, STEPHEN KIS, D.D., a Hungarian divine and educator, was born at Segedin in 1505, and educated at the universities of Cracow and Wittenberg. In the latter place, where he spent three years, he had the privilege of attending on the instructions of Luther and Melanchthon. He commenced his public career at Thasnyadin, where he instructed those who were studious of the best arts, and preached the gospel to the common people. This dual work he prosecuted to the end of his life, laboring successively at the following places: Gyula, Ceglede, Temeswar, Thurin, Bekeny, Tholna, Lascow (where he was ordained pastor by the imposition of hands in 1554), Calmantze, and Kevin. He died May 2, 1572. Dr. Segedin was eminent for piety, distinguished for eloquence, and held in high esteem by the Christian Church of his time for the earnestness and fidelity with which he enforced the doctrines of the Bible. See *The* (Lond.) *Theological Magazine*, Feb. 1802, p. 43.

Segond, LOUIS, a Swiss Protestant theologian, was born in 1810, and died at Geneva, June 18, 1885, professor of Hebrew and doctor of theology. Segond is best known as the latest translator of the Bible into French, whose name will be remembered with that of Le Fevre, Olivetan, De Sacy, Martin, and Osterwald. The Old Test. in Segond's version was first published at Geneva in 1874, then at Nancy in 1877, and lastly at Geneva in 1879. But the entire Bible was issued in 1880 from the Oxford University Press, printed with admirable care and skill. The translation is pronounced an exquisite one. (B. P.)

Ségur, LOUIS GASTON DE, a French prelate, was born at Paris in 1820. In 1856 he was made canon of the chapter of St. Denis, and died in 1881. Ségur was one of the most active and influential members of the clerical party, unjust towards the Protestants, and a promoter of ultramontane ideas. He published, *La Piété et la Vie Intérieure* (1863-64, 4 vols.):—*Instructions Familières et Lectures du Soir sur Toutes les Verités de la Religion* (1865, 2 vols.):—*La Liberté* (1869):—*Le Dogme de l'Infallibilité* (1872):—*Le Jeune Ouvrier Chrétien* (1876), etc. See Lichtenberger, *Encyclop. des Sciences Religieuses*, s. v. (B. P.)

Seidemann, JOHANN KARL, a Lutheran theologian of Germany, was born at Dresden, April 10, 1807. He studied at Leipsic, was for some time private tutor, and in 1834 preacher at Eschdorf, Saxony. In 1871 he retired from the ministry, and died at Dresden, Aug. 5, 1879, doctor of theology. He published, *Thomas Münzer* (Dresden, 1842):—*Die leipziger Disputation im Jahre* 1519 (1843):—*Karl von Miltiz, eine chronologische Untersuchung* (1844):—*Erläuterungen zur Reformationsgeschichte durch bisher unbekannte Urkunden* (eod.):—*Beiträge zur Reformationsgeschichte* (1846):—*Lutherbriefe* (1859):—*Anton Lauterbach's, Diaconi zu Wittenberg Tagebuch* (1872):—*Jacob Schenk* (1875):—*Luther's erste und älteste Vorlesungen über die Psalmen* (1876). See *Neues Archiv für sächsische Geschichte*, 1880, p. 94 sq.; *Zeitschrift des bergischen Geschichtsvereins*, xvi, 257 sq. (Bonn, 1881); Plitt-Herzog, *Real-Encyklop.* s. v. (B. P.)

Selwyn, GEORGE AUGUSTUS, missionary bishop of New Zealand, was born at Hampstead, England, in 1809, and received his earlier education at Eton. He studied at Cambridge, and in 1831 was appointed private tutor to Lord Powis, at Eton, while acting at the same time as a curate at Windsor. In 1841 Selwyn was appointed first bishop of the Anglican Church in New Zealand, and after having been consecrated in October, he sailed in December for his station. He landed at Sydney in April, 1842, and remained some time there to confer with the bishop. In the first year of his arrival Selwyn established a college for the training of candidates for the ministry, and five years after his landing in New Zealand he commenced to work among the isles of the South Sea. In 1854 bishop Selwyn came to England. Twelve years' experience had taught him that his diocese must be divided, and that Melanesia must have some one who could spend all his energies on its many islands and its diverse population. His time in England was not wasted. When he returned to New Zealand he was accompanied by bishop Patteson. For some years he shared and directed Patteson's work among the islands, and in the college at Auckland. Then the diocese was divided, and divided again. In 1866 there were six bishops under Selwyn's direction as primate, and among them Patteson was giving his whole attention to those islands among which he was afterwards to lay down his life. In 1867 Selwyn came again to England, and during his stay the diocese of Lichfield became vacant. It was offered more than once to him, and he refused. At length, on being strongly pressed by archbishop Longley, he yielded. His administration of this new and trying sphere, which comprised the so-called "Black Country," was very vigorous. Selwyn died April 11, 1878. His *Life* has been written by H. W. Tucker (Lond. 1879, 2 vols.). (B. P.)

Seminaries, Theological, IN THE UNITED STATES. Professional schools for the special training of ministers of the gospel are almost peculiar to America. Although most of the universities of Europe were originally instituted chiefly for ecclesiastical education, and clerical studies were for a long time mainly pursued in them, this was only an accident of the time, arising principally from the imperfect views of science then entertained, and the predominance of religious teachers in the world of letters. In some instances, such as the famous Sorbonne (q. v.) of France, the academical studies gradually supplanted the theological; while in but a few cases, such as those of Geneva in Switzerland, Montauban in France, and the Propaganda at Rome, is theology prominently or exclusively taught. To these must be added the training-schools of the English Dissenters, which are comparatively few and uninfluential. As a very general rule, however, the various branches of theology in Europe are included as departments of the great universities, and are therefore taught, almost entirely by lectures, as parts of a *scientific* education.

In America, on the other hand, while nearly all the higher schools were originated and are sustained by various Christian bodies, yet the system of special preparation of candidates for the ministry is very generally carried on in distinct institutions, sometimes included in a so-called university, but nevertheless having each its separate faculty and particular course of study, which is intended and arranged so as to be supplementary to those of the academy and the college. This gives a

THEOLOGICAL SEMINARIES IN THE UNITED STATES AS REPORTED IN 1891.

Name.	Location.	Date of charter.	Date of organization.	Denomination.	President.	Corps of instruction. Resident professors and instructors.	Corps of instruction. Non-resident professors and lecturers.	Present students. Total number.	Present students. College graduates.	Number of volumes in library.	Property, etc. Value of grounds and buildings.	Property, etc. Amount of productive funds.
Theological Department of Talladega College	Talladega, Ala.	1889	1867	Congregational	Rev. H. S. DeForest, D.D.	1	..	16	5	1,500	$5,000	....
Institute for Trained Colored Ministers	Tuscaloosa, Ala.	....	1876	Presbyterian	Rev. C. A. Stillman, D.D.	2	..	26	3	1,200	3,000	....
Pacific Theological Seminary	Oakland, Cal.	....	1869	Congregational	Joseph A. Benton, D.D.	3	..	16	3	4,200	75,000	$120,000
Maclay College of Theology of the University of Southern California	San Fernando, Cal.	....	....	Meth. Episcopal	Rev. R. S. Maclay, D.D., dean	3	1	12	1	300	....	300,000
San Francisco Theological Seminary	San Francisco, Cal.	....	1871	Presbyterian	A. L. Lindsley, D.D., LL.D.	5	..	20	3	16,000	45,000	175,000
Franciscan College	Santa Barbara, Cal.	....	1854	Roman Catholic	Very Rev. Kilian Schloesser, O.S.F.	4	..	1	...	2,600	....	....
Matthews Hall	Denver, Col.	1880	1872	Prot. Episcopal	Rt. Rev. John F. Spaulding, D.D.	1	..	4	1	5,500	50,000	16,000
Hartford Theological Seminary	Hartford, Conn.	1834	1833	Congregational	Rev. Chester D. Hartrauft, D.D.	9	3	47	7	45,000	172,000	399,000
Berkeley Divinity School	Middletown, Conn.	1854	1847	Prot. Episcopal	Rt. Rev. John Williams, D.D., LL.D.	5	1	29	12	20,500	48,500	307,688
Theological Department of Yale University	New Haven, Conn.	1701	1822	Non-sectarian	Rev. George E. Day, D.D., dean	9	5	133	33	8,000	....	....
Theological Department of Howard University	Washington, D. C.	1867	1867	Non-sectarian	Rev. James G. Craighead, D.D.	6	..	38	...	1,230	....	....
Wayland Seminary	Washington, D. C.	....	1865	Baptist	Rev. G. M. P. King, D.D.	8	..	153	22	2,969	80,000	18,000
Gammon School of Theology	Atlanta, Ga.	1883	1883	Meth. Episcopal	Rev. Wilbur P. Thirkield, D.D.	4	..	71	10	7,500	100,000	200,000
Theological Department of Atlanta Baptist Seminary	Atlanta, Ga.	1867	1867	Baptist	Rev. Samuel Graves, D.D.	5	..	147	12	3,000	40,000	....
Theological Department of Mercer University	Macon, Ga.	....	....	Baptist	Rev. James G. Ryals, D.D.	1	..	12	...	....	....	....
Theological Department of St. Viateur's College	Bourbonnais Grove, Ill.	1874	1865	Roman Catholic	Rev. M. J. Marsile, C.S.V.	3	..	20	...	....	....	....
Chicago Theological Seminary	Chicago, Ill.	1854	1858	Congregational	Rev. Franklin W. Fisk, D.D., LL.D.	12	..	145	23	10,000	127,000	460,959
McCormick Theological Seminary of the Presbyterian Church	Chicago, Ill.	1859	1859	Presbyterian	David C. Marquis, D.D.	8	..	134	44	11,000	450,000	350,000
Western Theological Seminary	Chicago, Ill.	....	1885	Prot. Episcopal	Rt. Rev. W. E. McLaren, S.T.D.	2	4	16	3	3,000	250,000	....
Bible Department of Eureka College	Eureka, Ill.	1855	1849	Christian	Carl Johann, A.M., LL.D.	2	1	67	1	4,000	....	....
Garrett Biblical Institute	Evanston, Ill.	1851	1854	Meth. Episcopal	Rev. Henry B. Ridgaway, D.D.	7	..	147	...	....	....	....
Norwegian and Danish Theological School	Evanston, Ill.	....	1886	Meth. Episcopal	Rev. Nels E. Simonsen, A.M., B.D.	1	..	24	...	....	....	....
Swedish Theological Seminary	Evanston, Ill.	....	1870	Meth. Episcopal	Rev. Albert Ericson, A.M.	1	..	24	...	....	8,000	....
Theological Department of German-English College	Galena, Ill.	1880	1868	Meth. Episcopal	Rev. Fr. Schaub, A.M.	6	..	115	...	600	....	....
Theological Department of Lombard University	Galesburgh, Ill.	1869	1881	Universalist	Rev. Nehemiah White, Ph.D.	4	1	10	2	....	....	....
Theological Department of McKendree College	Lebanon, Ill.	1834	1834	Meth. Episcopal	Rev. I. Villars, D.D.	1	..	14	...	....	....	....
Wartburg Seminary	Mendota, Ill.	....	1853	Lutheran	Rev. S. Fritschel, D.D.	3	..	48	17	5,000	10,000	11,064
Baptist Union Theological Seminary	Morgan Park, Ill.	1867	1867	Baptist	Rev. George W. Northrup, D.D., LL.D.	9	1	133	38	30,000	70,465	223,735
Union Biblical Institute	Naperville, Ill.	1874	1876	Evan. Association	Bishop J. J. Esher	2	1	19	3	350	....	28,000
Augustana Theological Seminary	Rock Island, Ill.	1865	1860	Lutheran	Rev. T. N. Hasselquist, D.D.	3	..	41	20	3,000	....	....
Concordia Seminary	Springfield, Ill.	1879	1874	Lutheran	A. Craemer	4	..	156	22	800	25,000	....
Theological Department of Shurtleff College	Upper Alton, Ill.	1835	1827	Baptist	Rev. A. A. Kendrick, D.D.	1	..	...	...	....	....	....
School of Theology of De Pauw University	Greencastle, Ind.	1837	1834	Meth. Episcopal	S. L. Bowman, A.M., S.T.D., dean	5	1	70	4	....	....	....
Berean Department, Union Christian College *	Merom, Ind.	1859	1860	Christian	Rev. L. J. Aldrich, A.M., D.D.	1	2	16	...	275	....	....

St. Meinrad's Ecclesiastical Seminary	St. Meinrad, Ind	....	1857	Roman Catholic	Rt. Rev. Fintan Mundwiler, O.S.B	5	..	56	18	8,000	....	....
Theological Department of Griswold College	Davenport, Iowa	1859	1859	Prot. Episcopal	Rev. W. S. Perry, D.D., LL.D., D.C.L	3	..	3	...	....	....	....
Bible Department of Drake University	Des Moines, Iowa	1881	1881	Christian	David R. Dungan, A.M., dean	2	..	60	...	....	....	....
German Presbyterian Theological School of the Northwest	Dubuque, Iowa	....	1852	Presbyterian	G. Mœry, clerk of the faculty	4	..	30	5	1,750	$25,000	$18,000
German College	Mt. Pleasant, Iowa	1873	1873	Meth. Episcopal	Rev. John Schlagenhauf	1	..	20	...	....	....	....
Bible Department of Oskaloosa College	Oskaloosa, Iowa	1855	1872	Christian	J. A. Beattie, A.M	1	..	12	...	....	....	....
Theological Department of Garfield University	Wichita, Kan	1886	1888	Christian	Alvin I. Hobbs, A.M., LL.D., dean	1	..	12	...	....	....	....
Danville Theological Seminary	Danville, Ky	1854	1853	Presbyterian	Stephen Yerkes, senior professor	6	..	3	2	10,000	8,000	206,000
College of the Bible	Lexington, Ky	1877	1877	Christian	Robert Graham, A.M	3	..	129	10	1,500	....	50,000
Southern Baptist Theological Seminary	Louisville, Ky	1858	1859	Baptist	John A. Broadus	6	..	165	12	16,000	140,000	300,000
Gilbert Haven School of Theology (New Orleans University)	New Orleans, La	1873	1873	Meth. Episcopal	Rev. L. G. Adkinson, D.D	..	..	9	...	....	....	....
Theological Department of Leland University	New Orleans, La	....	....	Baptist	Rev. Edward C. Mitchell, D.D	2	..	30	...	....	....	....
Theological Department of Straight University	New Orleans, La	1869	1870	Non-sectarian	Rev. R. C. Hitchcock, D.D	5	..	20	...	....	....	....
Bangor Theological Seminary	Bangor, Me	1814	1816	Congregational	Rev. Levi L. Paine, D.D	5	..	33	11	16,000	65,000	209,000
Bates College Theological Seminary	Lewiston, Me	....	1870	Free Baptist	Rev. Oren B. Cheney, D.D	4	..	26	...	3,200	....	....
Centenary Biblical Institute	Baltimore, Md	1867	1872	Meth. Episcopal	Rev. Francis J. Wagner, A.M	15	..	195	8	1,600	40,000	17,000
Theological Seminary of St. Sulpice and St. Mary's University	Baltimore, Md	1804	1791	Roman Catholic	Rev. A. Magnien, S.S., D.D	9	..	170	42	26,000	250,000	....
Scholasticate of the Congregation of the Most Holy Redeemer, Mount St. Clement	Ilchester, Md	....	1868	Roman Catholic	Rev. Eugene Grimm, C.S.S.R	6	..	80	...	12,000	....	....
Mount St. Mary's Ecclesiastical Seminary	Mount St. Mary's P. O., Md	1830	1808	Roman Catholic	Very Rev. Edward P. Allen, D.D	8	..	31	6	8,000	150,000	....
Westminster Theological Seminary	Westminster, Md	1884	1882	Meth. Protestant	James Thomas Ward, D.D., F.S.Sc	4	..	24	8	1,400	5,000	....
Andover Theological Seminary	Andover, Mass	1807	1808	Congregational	Rev. Egbert C. Smyth, D.D	9	2	48	8	46,663	225,000	825,000
Boston University School of Theology	Boston, Mass	1869	1847	Meth. Episcopal	William F. Warren, S.T.D	13	..	130	...	7,000	....	....
Divinity School of Harvard University	Cambridge, Mass	1650	1819	Non-sectarian	Charles C. Everett, D.D., dean	10	..	26	3	20,815	....	....
Episcopal Theological School	Cambridge, Mass	1867	1867	Prot. Episcopal	Rev. George Z. Gray, D.D	7	..	37	7	6,000	200,000	120,000
New-Church Theological School	Cambridge, Mass	....	1866	New Church	Rev. John Worcester	2	3	6	3	1,000	....	35,220
Tufts College Divinity School	College Hill, Mass	1852	1869	Universalist	Elmer Hewitt Capen, D.D	5	..	35	...	....	....	....
Newton Theological Institution	Newton Centre, Mass	1826	1825	Baptist	Alvah Hovey, D.D., LL.D	6	1	70	20	18,000	126,303	355,441
School of Theology (Adrian College)	Adrian, Mich	1859	1859	Meth. Protestant	George B. McElroy, acting president	..	..	...	...	....	....	....
Theological Department of Hillsdale College	Hillsdale, Mich	1855	1873	Free Will Baptist	Hon. George F. Mosher, A.M	3	..	36	...	....	....	....
Western Seminary of the Reformed Church of America	Holland, Mich	....	1866	Reformed	Rev. Nicholas M. Steffens, D.D	2	..	8	2	....	....	....
St. John's University, Ecclesiastical Course *	Collegeville, Minn	1857	1857	Roman Catholic	Alexius Edelbrock, O.S.B	3	..	35	...	....	....	....
Seabury Divinity School	Fairibault, Minn	1860	1860	Prot. Episcopal	Rt. Rev. H. B. Whipple, D.D., LL.D	11	..	33	7	7,000	113,000	....
Augsburg Seminary	Minneapolis, Minn	....	1869	Lutheran	Rev. George Sverdrup	2	..	42	9	....	....	....
Red Wing Norwegian Evangelical Lutheran Seminary	Red Wing, Minn	1878	1879	Lutheran	O. S. Meland	6	..	100	4	700	40,000	....
St. Vincent's College and Theological Seminary	Cape Girardeau, Mo	1843	1843	Roman Catholic	Very Rev. Francis V. Nugent, C.M	3	..	11	...	....	....	....
Concordia College (Seminary)	St. Louis, Mo	1853	1839	Lutheran	Francis A. O. Pieper	5	..	115	35	7,000	200,000	....
Eden College	St. Louis, Mo	....	1850	German Evan	Rev. Louis Haeberle	3	..	82	26	1,457	120,000	....
Theological Department of Central Wesleyan College	Warrenton, Mo	1865	1864	German Meth. Epis	Rev. Herman A. Koch, D.D	2	..	42	...	....	....	....
German Congregational Theological Seminary	Crete, Neb	1882	1878	Congregational	Doede Smith	2	..	6	1	500	5,000	7,000
Theological Institute	Santee Agency, Mo	....	1870	Congregational	Alfred L. Riggs	1	..	24	...	50	3,000	....
German Theological School of Newark, N. J	Bloomfield, N. J	....	1869	Presbyterian	Rev. Charles E. Knox, D.D	4	..	35	5	3,800	20,000	33,000
Drew Theological Seminary	Madison, N. J	1868	1867	Meth. Episcopal	Rev. Henry A. Buttz, D.D., LL.D	5	1	120	30	35,000	300,000	270,000
Theological Seminary of the Reformed (Dutch) Church in America	New Brunswick, N. J	1784	1785	Reformed Dutch	Rev. Samuel M. Woodbridge, D.D., LL.D	5	..	32	7	41,000	300,000	350,000
Theological Seminary of the Presbyterian Church	Princeton, N. J	1822	1812	Presbyterian	W. Henry Green, D.D., LL.D	9	..	170	44	50,449	400,000	1,091,771
Diocesan Seminary of the Immaculate Conception	South Orange, N. J	....	1856	Roman Catholic	Rev. William P. Salt, A.M	4	..	5	2	....	....	....
College of the Sacred Heart and Theological Seminary *	Vineland, N. J	....	1885	Roman Catholic	Rev. Eugene H. Porcile, S.P.M	2	..	16	...	....	....	....
St. Bonaventure's Seminary	Allegany, N. Y	1875	1859	Roman Catholic	Fr. Joseph Butler, O.S.F	5	..	58	...	....	....	....

* Statistics of 1887–88.

THEOLOGICAL SEMINARIES IN THE UNITED STATES.—*Continued.*

Name.	Location.	Date of charter.	Date of organization.	Denomination.	President.	Corps of instruction.		Present students.		Number of volumes in library.	Property, etc.	
						Resident professors and instructors.	Non-resident professors and lecturers.	Total number.	College graduates.		Value of grounds and buildings.	Amount of productive funds.
Auburn Theological Seminary	Auburn, N. Y.	1820	1821	Presbyterian.	Rev. S. M. Hopkins, D.D., senior professor.	6	1	60	22	17,313	$200,000	$532,992
Canton Theological Seminary	Canton, N. Y.	1858	1858	Universalist	Isaac Morgan Atwood, D.D.	3	1	26	6	8,000	50,000	113,000
Hamilton Theological Seminary	Hamilton, N. Y.	1819	1819	Baptist	Rev. E. Dodge, D.D., LL.D.	6	3	47	13	15,000	125,000	150,000
Hartwick Seminary Theological Department	Hartwick Seminary, N. Y.	1816	1815	Lutheran	Rev. James Pitcher, A.M., principal	3	2	17	1	....	....	....
General Theological Seminary of the Protestant Episcopal Church	New York, N. Y.	1822	1819	Prot. Episcopal	Rev. Eugene A. Hoffman, D.D., dean	6	1	92	30	19,114	750,000	484,254
Union Theological Seminary	New York, N. Y.	1839	1836	Presbyterian	Thomas S. Hastings, D.D.	10	..	134	36	59,000	685,000	950,000
Theological Department of Niagara University	Niagara University, N. Y.	1883	1856	Roman Catholic	Very Rev. P. V. Kavanagh, C.M.	1	..	63	...	....	....	....
Rochester Theological Seminary	Rochester, N. Y.	1850	1851	Baptist	Rev. Augustus H. Strong, D.D.	12	..	106	34	23,904	102,827	502,037
Christian Biblical Institute	Stanfordville, N. Y.	1868	1869	Christian	Rev. John B. Weston, D.D.	2	3	19	3	2,000	40,000	23,900
St. Joseph's Provincial Seminary	Troy, N. Y.	....	1864	Roman Catholic	Very Rev. Henry Gabriels, D.D.	7	..	144	21	9,000	200,000	....
Theological Department of Biddle University	Charlotte, N. C.	1877	1868	Presbyterian	Rev. W. F. Johnson, D.D.	3	..	13	5	....	....	....
Theological Department of St. Augustine's Normal School	Raleigh, N. C.	1867	1868	Prot. Episcopal	Rev. Robert B. Sutton, D.D.	2	..	12	1	1,500	25,000	....
Theological Department of Shaw University *	Raleigh, N. C.	....	1865	Baptist	Rev. H. M. Tupper, D.D.	2	..	40	...	....	....	....
Theological Department of German Wallace College	Berea, Ohio	1864	1865	Meth. Episcopal	Rev. William Nast, D.D.	2	..	32	2	....	....	....
Hebrew Union College *	Cincinnati, Ohio	1873	1875	Jewish	Isaac M. Wise	7	2	5	1	8,500	30,000	60,000
Lane Theological Seminary	Cincinnati, Ohio	1829	1831	Presbyterian	H. P. Smith, D.D., chairman	7	..	49	13	16,000	200,000	286,000
St. Mary's Theological Seminary	Cleveland, Ohio	....	1849	Roman Catholic	Rev. N. A. Moes, D.D.	4	1	37	8	3,000	75,000	....
German Lutheran Seminary	Columbus, Ohio	1830	1830	Lutheran	Rev. M. Loy, D.D.	3	..	28	8	....	....	....
Union Biblical Seminary	Dayton, Ohio	1873	1871	United Brethren	Rev. G. A. Funkhouser, D.D.	3	..	34	4	1,200	30,000	70,000
Theological Seminary of the Protestant Episcopal Church in the Diocese of Ohio	Gambier, Ohio	1824	1825	Prot. Episcopal	Rt. Rev. G. T. Bedell, D.D.	3	..	8	...	7,000	....	....
Department of Theology (Oberlin College)	Oberlin, Ohio	1833	1835	Congregational	Rev. James H. Fairchild, D.D.	10	..	101	16	....	....	....
Heidelberg Theological Seminary	Tiffin, Ohio	1888	1851	Reformed	Rev. David Van Horne, D.D.	3	..	17	3	....	....	26,009
Theological Seminary of Wilberforce University	Wilberforce, Ohio	1856	1856	Af. Meth. Episcopal	Rev. S. T. Mitchell, A.M.	2	..	8	2	....	....	....
United Presbyterian Theological Seminary of Xenia	Xenia, Ohio	1877	1794	United Presb.	Rev. James Harper, D.D.	3	1	29	10	4,051	15,000	74,000
Theological Seminary of the Reformed Presbyterian Church	Allegheny, Pa.	....	1858	Reformed Presb.	D. B. Wilson	3	..	21	7	3,100	25,000	62,350
Theological Seminary of the United Presbyterian Church	Allegheny, Pa.	1830	1825	United Presb.	Alexander Young, D.D., LL.D.	5	..	52	14	....	80,000	133,000
Western Theological Seminary of the Presbyterian Church	Allegheny, Pa.	1844	1827	Presbyterian	Rev. W. H. Jeffers, D.D., LL.D., acting president	6	..	75	18	20,000	175,000	472,185
Theological Course in St. Vincent's College	Beatty, Pa.	1870	1846	Roman Catholic	Rt. Rev. A. Hintenach, O.S.B.	6	..	46	...	....	....	....
Moravian Theological Seminary	Bethlehem, Pa.	1863	1807	United Brethren	Rev. Augustus Schultze	4	..	29	...	6,000	18,000	75,000
Theological Department of Ursinus College	Collegeville, Pa.	1869	1871	Reformed	Rev. J. H. A. Bomberger, D.D., LL.D.	5	..	11	...	....	....	....

Theological Seminary of the General Synod of the Evangelical Lutheran Church in the United States	Gettysburgh, Pa.	1826	1826	Lutheran	Rev. Milton Valentine, D.D., LL.D.	4	1	50	15	11,500	$75,000	$92,000
Theological Seminary of the Reformed Church in the United States	Lancaster, Pa.	....	1825	Reformed	Rev. Eml. V. Gerhart, D.D., LL.D.	3	..	41	...	10,000	....	....
Meadville Theological School	Meadville, Pa.	1844	1840	Unitarian	Rev. Abiel A. Livermore, A.M.	3	2	37	10	18,000	17,000	175,000
Philadelphia Theological Seminary of St. Charles Borromeo	Overbrook, Pa.	1838	1832	Roman Catholic	Very Rev. John E. Fitzmaurice, D.D.	10	1	140	15	22,000	....	....
St. Vincent's Seminary	Philadelphia, Pa.	....	1868	Roman Catholic	James McGill	7	1	...	...	10,000	....	....
Theological Seminary of the Evangelical Lutheran Church at Philadelphia	Philadelphia, Pa.	1854	1864	Lutheran	Rev. C. W. Schæffer, D.D., LL.D., chairman of faculty	4	..	65	25	17,000	80,000	123,026
Missionary Institute	Selin's Grove, Pa.	1858	1858	Lutheran	Rev. Peter Born, D.D.	2	..	13	5	1,500	15,000	....
Crozier Theological Seminary	Upland, Pa.	1858	1859	Baptist	Henry G. Weston	6	..	64	14	9,600	125,000	350,000
Ecclesiastical Department of Villanova College	Villanova, Pa.	1848	1842	Roman Catholic	Rev. Francis M. Sheeran, S.T.B., O.S.A.	4	..	22	...	....	....	....
Benedict Institute	Columbia, S. C.	....	1871	Baptist	Rev. C. E. Becker	..	..	236	20	1,500	50,000	33,000
Theological Department of Allen University	Columbia, S. C.	1880	1882	Meth. Episcopal	Jos. W. Morris, A.M., LL.B.	3	..	9	...	....	....	....
Theological Seminary of the General Assembly of the Presbyterian Church in the United States	Columbia, S. C.	....	1828	Presbyterian	Rev. James D. Tadlock, D.D., chairman of faculty	4	1	20	3	20,000	40,000	235,000
Associate Reformed Theological Seminary	Due West, S. C.	....	1839	Asso. Ref. Presb.	Dr. James Bryce	4	..	6	3	2,500	....	25,000
Theological Seminary of the South (Newberry College)	Newberry, S. C.	....	1830	Lutheran	Rev. G. W. Holland, Ph.D., D.D.	2	..	4	...	....	....	....
Theological Department of Chattanooga University	Chattanooga, Tenn.	1886	1886	Meth. Episcopal	Rev. E. S. Lewis, D.D.	..	..	16	...	....	....	....
Theological School of Cumberland University	Lebanon, Tenn.	1842	1853	Cumberland Presb.	N. Green, LL.D., chancellor	6	..	37	19	....	....	....
Theological Course in Fisk University	Nashville, Tenn.	1867	1866	Congregational	Rev. Erastus Milo Cravath, D.D.	1	..	9	...	....	....	....
Theological Department of Central Tennessee College	Nashville, Tenn.	1866	1867	Meth. Episcopal	Rev. R. W. Keeler, D.D., dean	2	6	40	...	....	....	....
Theological Department of Roger Williams University	Nashville, Tenn.	1883	1865	Baptist	A. Owen, D.D.	1	..	(a)	...	....	....	....
Theological Department of Vanderbilt University	Nashville, Tenn.	1873	1875	Meth. Epis. South	L. C. Garland, LL.D., chancellor	6	..	52	4	....	....	....
Theological Department of the University of the South	Sewanee, Tenn.	1858	1876	Prot. Episcopal	Rev. Telfair Hodgson, D.D., vice-chancellor	9	..	18	...	....	....	....
Theological Department of Bishop College	Marshall, Tex.	1885	1881	Baptist	S. W. Culver, A.M.	8	..	17	...	700	50,000	....
Union Theological Seminary	Hampden Sidney, Va.	1867	1824	Presbyterian	Thos. E. Peck, D.D., LL.D., chairman of faculty	5	..	67	19	14,500	100,000	287,000
Richmond Theological Seminary	Richmond, Va.	1886	1867	Baptist	Rev. Charles H. Corey, A.M., D.D.	4	..	63	2	4,000	30,000	60,000
Protestant Episcopal Theological Seminary of Virginia	Theological Seminary, Va.	1854	1823	Prot. Episcopal	Rev. Joseph Packard, D.D.	6	..	53	11	14,000	....	....
Mission House	Franklin, Wis.	1868	1862	Reformed	H. A. Muehlmeier, D.D.	3	..	28	7	4,700	35,000	....
Lutheran Theological Seminary of the Synod of Wisconsin	Milwaukee, Wis.	1864	1878	Lutheran	Rev. Ad. Hœnecke	3	..	34	12	1,300	25,000	....
Nashotah House	Nashotah, Wis.	1847	1842	Prot. Episcopal	George G. Carter, S.T.D.	4	2	23	8	9,200	100,000	48,000
Sacred Heart College	Prairie du Chien, Wis.	1881	1880	Roman Catholic	Rev. A. Leiter, S.J.	4	..	16	5	5,000	....	....
Seminary of St. Francis of Sales	St. Francis, Wis.	....	1856	Roman Catholic	Very Rev. Joseph Rainer	5	..	100	...	....	....	....

* Statistics of 1887–88. *a* Included in report of collegiate department.

definiteness and practical character to ministerial training scarcely attainable, or even attempted, by the looser method of European instruction. See MINISTERIAL EDUCATION.

I. *Growth and Character of American Schools of Theology.*—The earliest of these institutions, exclusive of a Roman Catholic one founded in 1791, in Baltimore, Md., which still survives, and a private one established in 1804 by Dr. John M. Mason, in the city of New York, which lasted several years, is the Theological Seminary founded by the Congregationalists at Andover, Mass., in 1808, although a foundation was made somewhat earlier for a similar institution by the Reformed Dutch Church at New Brunswick, N. J., which did not go into operation for a long time. The next great theological seminary was that of the Presbyterians, founded at Princeton, N.J., in 1812, although the College of New Jersey, with which it is connected, was established in 1757. The divinity schools of Harvard and Yale are even more modern, while the universities themselves are much older. After the above dates numerous schools and departments of a strictly theological character sprang up in the more thickly settled states, and in more recent times they have rapidly multiplied throughout the Union. Thus, in the first decade of the present century (1800–1809) there were but two organized, in the second 2, in the third 14, in the fourth 9, in the fifth 8, in the sixth 19, in the seventh 38, in the eighth (1870–79) 30. The Report of the United States Commissioner of Education for 1883 (the latest return) gave the total of theological seminaries and departments as being 145, with an aggregate of 583 resident teachers and 5771 students.

"As to the methods pursued in the theological schools of the United States, it may be remarked that no uniformity, but a general similarity, prevails. In nearly all, primary attention is given to the study of Hebrew and New-Test. Greek, as the foundation of an enlightened Scriptural exegesis. In the departments of ecclesiastical history and systematic and practical theology, instruction is largely given by lectures, with references to text-books and collateral reading. In all the fully-organized seminaries the course of study extends through three years, and is planned in reference to the attainments of graduates of colleges, although partial-course students are admitted on specified conditions." Tuition is free, and arrangements are usually made which reduce the cost of board, etc., to a very low rate.

II. *Statistics.*—The accompanying table, compiled from the above-mentioned report, exhibits a summary account of all the theological institutions in the Union, arranged in the alphabetical order of the several states. For further details, see the annual catalogue of each, which is furnished gratuitously on application to the presiding officer.

Sen, KESHUB CHUNDER, one of the chief priests of the Brahma Somaj (q. v.), was born in India. The sect of which he was a leader was formed in 1830 by Rammohun Roy. In 1859 Keshub Chunder Sen gave a new impulse to the sect by his remarkable ability and enthusiasm. He effected the separation of those who were willing to abolish caste in their communion, as the Brahma Somaj of India. The more conservative remained in the Church at Calcutta, where the first building was opened for worship in 1869. Sen, in his published sermons and tracts, avows his belief in the unity of God, in immediate revelation, in the necessity of a new birth, in the immortality of the soul, and the importance and efficacy of prayer. His morality was pure, and he inculcated a reverence for the character of Jesus Christ, but repudiated the doctrines of his divinity, mediation, and atonement, as taught in the gospels. He believed that Christ was better than Mohammed or Confucius. Sen died in India, Jan. 8, 1884.

Seneca Version OF THE SCRIPTURES. For this branch of the Iroquois the American Bible Society has provided the gospels, published in 1829, while the British and Foreign Bible Society published the gospels of Matthew and Mark. In general the Iroquois version (q. v.) is understood by the Senecas, Mohawks, and Oneidas. See *Bible of Every Land*, p. 458.

Seney, ROBERT, a veteran Methodist Episcopal minister, was born at Queen Anne, Md., Oct. 12, 1799. He lost his father while yet an infant, was educated in New York city, graduated from Columbia College in 1815, studied law, was converted, licensed to exhort, travelled some time with Rev. Nathan Bangs, and in 1820 entered the New York Conference. That year he served Granville Circuit; in 1821, New Rochelle; in 1822, Wethersfield, Conn.; in 1823, Poughkeepsie; in 1824, Middlebury, Vt.; in 1825, Flushing; in 1826 and 1827, New York city; in 1828 and 1829, Newburgh; in 1830 and 1831, Sandy Hill and Glen's Falls; in 1832, White Plains and Greenburg; in 1833, White Plains; in 1834, New Haven; in 1835, Vesey Street and Mulberry Street, New York city; in 1836, Mulberry Street, alone; in 1837 and 1838, Third Street, Brooklyn; in 1839 and 1840, Newburgh; in 1841 and 1842, First Church, Poughkeepsie; in 1843 and 1844, Allen Street Church, New York city; in 1845, Mariner's Methodist Episcopal Chapel; in 1846 and 1847, Washington Street, Brooklyn; in 1848, Danbury, Conn.; in 1849, Carlton Avenue Church, Brooklyn; in 1850, Washington Street Church, as supernumerary; in 1851, South Brooklyn Home Mission, and in 1852 and 1853 supernumerary at Brooklyn, where he continued to reside until the close of his life, July 1, 1854. Mr. Seney was eminently devoted and successful, able and winning. See Sprague, *Annals of the Amer. Pulpit*, vii, 687; Simpson, *Cyclop. of Methodism*, s. v.

Sennara, in Hindûism, is the sacred Brahminical cord, whose use is restricted to the three superior castes as a mark of distinction. It is composed of a definite number of threads of cotton taken from a particular plant. Its length is such as to allow of its being worn diagonally across the body, from the left shoulder to the right side. The stoutest cord is that worn by Brahmins, that of the Kshatriyas being thinner and that of the Vaisyas being very slender, so that the cord serves to distinguish between the castes. (Butler, *Land of the Veda*, says that the Brahmin's cord is made of cotton threads, the Kshatriya's of hemp, and the Vaisya's of wool). Brahminical devotees or saints often wear a snake-skin instead of the cord.

Sepharvaim. Dr. William Hayes Ward, who has recently explored the region in question, and is well versed likewise in Assyriology, finds in the ancient inscriptions *four* cities or districts called *Sippara*, the Greek equivalent of this name. Of these the two principal ones, he thinks, were the "Sippara of the Sun," discovered by Mr. Rassam at Abu-Habba, and the original place, known as the "Sippara of Anuenit," being the one where Sargon I was exposed in his infancy, the town of Xisuthrus, the one captured by Cyrus without fighting, and the seat of the famous Jewish school, which Dr. Ward believes he has found in the large *tell* or mound still bearing the mediæval name of *Anbar*, south of the point of the effluence of the Sokkameh canal from the Euphrates. See *Hebraica*, Jan. 1886, p. 79 sq.

Sepphoris. The modern site *Seffûrieh* is copiously described in the *Memoirs* accompanying the Ordnance Survey (i, 279, 330 sq.). (See illustration on p. 841.)

Serapion. By way of supplement we add the following bearers of that name: (1), eighth bishop of Antioch, successor of Maximus, and opponent of the Montanists; mentioned by Eusebius, *Hist. Eccles.* v, 19, 22; (2), a martyr by the name of Serapion is mentioned by Eusebius, iv, 41, said to have suffered martyrdom under Decius at Alexandria; (3), a third one by the same name is mentioned by Eusebius, iv, 44, as belonging to the *lapsi* (q. v.); (4), another Serapion is mentioned by Cassian in *Collat.* x, 2. See Sozom. viii, 11; Schröckh,

Sepphoris. (From Thomson's *Central Palestine and Phœnicia.*)

viii, 451; Gieseler, i, 2, 244; Plitt-Herzog, *Real-Encyklop.* s. v. (B. P.)

Serpilius, Georg, a Lutheran theologian of Germany, was born at Oedenburg, Hungary, June 11, 1668. He studied at Leipsic, was in 1690 deacon at Wilsdrup, near Dresden, in 1695 pastor at Ratisbon, and died Nov. 23, 1728. He published, *Vollständige Liederconcordanz* (Pirna, 1696):—*Descriptio Synagogæ Serpilianæ Inculenta* (Ratisbon, 1723):—*Personalia Mosis, Josuæ, Samuelis, Esræ, Nehemiæ, Mordechai et Estheri* (Leipsic, 1708):—*Personalia Jobi* (1710):—*Personalia Davidis* (1713):—*Salomo in Continuationem Scriptorum Bibliorum* (1715):—*Personalia Iesaiæ* (1717), etc. See Döring, *Die gelehrten Theologen Deutschlands*, s. v.; Fürst, *Bibl. Jud.* s. v.; Jöcher, *Allgemeines Gelehrten-Lexikon*, s. v. (B. P.)

Servatius, *Saint.* According to Athanasius (*Apol.* ii, 767), a Gallican bishop, by the name of Servatius, was among those who attended the Council of Sardica in 347, and he may probably have been the same whom Sulpicius Severus sent to Rimini in 359 to defend the Athanasian orthodoxy against the Arians. See Rettberg, *Kirchengeschichte Deutschlands*, i, 204 sq.; Friedrich, *Kirchengeschichte Deutschlands*, i, 300 sq.; Hefele, *Conciliengeschichte*, i, 515; Plitt-Herzog, *Real-Encyklop.* s. v.; Lichtenberger, *Encyclop. des Sciences Religieuses*, s. v. Servais. (B. P.)

Session, Church (or **Kirk**). See Presbyterianism.

Set (or **Sutekh**), an ass-headed deity, the national god of the Shemitic Hyksos, who, on their invasion of Egypt in the interval between the thirteenth and eighteenth dynasties, forced his sole worship upon the Egyptians. Set was already one of the cosmical deities of the country, but after the expulsion of the Hyksos his worship was annulled, his statues defaced, and his name everywhere erased. He was represented as an ass-headed man, holding the usual crux ansata, or staff of life, and the *cucufa*, staff of divine power. The Egyptians were accustomed to regard Set as a personification of the evil principle. "The worship of this god passed through two historical phases. At one time he was held in honor, and accounted as one of the greater gods of Abydos. He appears to have had a position analogous to that of the Theban deity Mentu, in which he was the adversary of the serpent Apophis, the symbol of wickedness and darkness. Some time later on, in consequence of political changes, the worship of Set was abolished, and his statues were destroyed. It is difficult to state at what period Set was introduced into the Osirian myths as a personification of evil, and thus became identified with Typhon as the murderer of the great Egyptian god Osiris. The treatise (by Plutarch), *De Iside et Osiride*, makes Nephthys the companion of Set, and she is represented united with him in a group in the Museum of the Louvre, in the Hall of the Gods. The animal symbolical of Set was a carnivorous quadruped, at one time confounded with the ass-god of Josephus and Apion, having a long, curved snout and upright, square-topped ears, which characters are often exaggerated to distinguish him from the jackal of Anubis" (Pierret). After the second restoration of the old mythology, in the period of the nineteenth dynasty, Set was identified with the Hyksos Sutekh, who was properly an Asiatic deity, and whose worship was maintained even by Seti I and Rameses II. Both gods, however, were treated as impious, and their worship as heretical, and it is at the present time impossible to distinguish exactly between them, owing to the complete destruction by the Egyptians of all those parts of the monuments whereon their names occur.

Seventh-day Adventists. See ADVENTISTS, SEVENTH-DAY.

Severus, ALEXANDER. See ALEXANDER SEVERUS.

Seyffarth, GUSTAV, a Lutheran theologian and archæologist of Germany, was born at Ubigau, Saxony, July 13, 1796. He studied at Leipsic, and commenced his academical career there in 1823. In 1857 he came to America, was professor at the Lutheran Concordia College, in St. Louis, Mo., retired in 1871 to New York city, and died Nov. 17, 1885. He published, *Ueber die ursprünglichen Laute der hebr. Buchstaben* (Leipsic, 1824):—*Beiträge zur Kenntniss der Literatur, Kunst, Mythologie und Geschichte der alten Ægypter* (1826-40):—*Chronologia Sacra* (1846):—*Das tausendjährige Reich im Lichte der Offenbarungen des Alten und Neuen Testaments* (N. Y. 1860). See Fürst, *Bibl. Jud.* s. v.; Zuchold, *Bibl. Theol.* s. v. (B. P.)

Sfondrata, CŒLESTINE, prince-abbot of St. Gall, and nephew of Gregory XIV, was born at Milan in 1644. He was educated in the abbey of St. Gall, taught theology, philosophy, and canon law at various places, and was elected prince-abbot of St. Gall in 1689. In 1695 Innocent XII made Sfondrata a cardinal, but he died soon after his promotion, in the same year, at Rome. Sfondrata wrote, *Regale Sacerdotium Romano Pontifici Assertum et Quatuor Propositionibus Explicatum* (1684), which is a defence of the absolute supremacy of the pope over and against the pretensions of the Gallican Church. Five French bishops refuted this work:—*Nodus Prædestinationis . . . Dissolutus* (Rome, 1696; Venice, 1698). This posthumous work was attacked by the Sorbonne, Bossuet, and others, who in vain tried to have the book put on the Index. See Moreri, *Auctores Diarii Italici* (Venice, 1732), vol. vi; *Journal des Savants*, 1698, 1708, and 1709; Lichtenberger, *Encyclop. des Sciences Religieuses*, s. v. (B. P.)

Shaalbim. The probable representative of this place, *Selbît*, lies two miles north of Amwâs. It is a deserted ruin, and "appears to be the *Selebi* of Jerome's *Comment. on Ezek.* xlviii, 22" (*Memoirs* to the Ordnance Survey, iii, 52).

Shaaraim. The probable site is that of *Khurbet Saireh*, three and a half miles north-east of Beit Nettîf, and one a half west of Beit Atab. It consists of "foundations on a hill, with a spring below" (*Memoirs* to the Ordnance Survey, iii, 124).

Shahazimah is conjectured by Lieut. Conder (*Tent Work*, ii, 339) to be the present *Tell esh-Sheikh Kâsim*, "a very large artificial mound near the Jordan" (*Memoirs* to the Ordnance Survey, ii, 128), eight miles south of the Sea of Galilee; but there is no special ground for this identification.

Sharpe, SAMUEL, an Egyptologist and Hebrew scholar, was born in England in 1799. After starting in life as a banker, he soon retired from business, and devoted himself to the studies of Egyptology and Hebrew. The numerous volumes which came from his pen during his long and busy life—he died in August, 1881—were all concerned either with the monuments of ancient Egypt, or with Biblical researches. "A Unitarian and liberal," says the *Academy*, "he occupied himself in popularizing a mode of interpreting the Scriptures which, though it would now be considered at once conservative and narrow, seemed half a century ago startling, if not profane." His chief Egyptological works were the following: *Early History of Egypt from the Old Testament, Herodotus, Manetho, and the Hieroglyphic Inscriptions* (1836):—*Egyptian Inscriptions from the British Museum and other Sources* (first series, 1837; second series, 1855):—*The Rudiments of a Vocabulary of the Egyptian Hieroglyphics* (1837):—*The History of Egypt under the Ptolemies* (1838):—*History of Egypt under the Romans* (1842):—*The History of Egypt from the Earliest Times till the Conquest of the Arabs, A.D. 640* (1846; 5th ed. 1870):—*The Chronology and Geography of Ancient Egypt* (1849):—*Historical Sketch of the Egyptian Buildings and Sculpture* (1854):—*Alexandrian Chronology* (1857):—*Egyptian Hieroglyphics* (1861):—*Egyptian Antiquities in the British Museum* (1862):—*The Decree of Canopus* (1870):—*The Rosetta Stone* (1871). His most important publications on Biblical matters were, *Historic Notes on the Books of the Old and New Testaments* (1854; 3d ed. 1858):—*Critical Notes on the Authorized English Version of the Old Testament* (1856; 2d ed. 1867):—*The Chronology of the Bible* (1868):—*Texts from the Holy Bible Explained by the Help of the Ancient Monuments* (eod.):—*History of the Hebrew Nation and Literature* (1869; 2d ed. 1872):—*On the Journeys and Epistles of the Apostle Paul* (1876):—*A Short Hebrew Grammar without Points* (1877):—*The Book of Isaiah arranged Chronologically in a Revised Translation, and Accompanied with Historical Notes* (eod.). Mr. Sharpe's two lines of study met in his work on *Egyptian Mythology and Egyptian Christianity, with their Influence on the Opinions of Modern Christendom* (1863). In 1875 he brought out a volume on *Hebrew Inscriptions from the Valleys between Egypt and Mount Sinai*, and shortly after his death was published his Βαρναβᾶ Επιστολή, *The Epistle of Barnabas from the Sinaitic Manuscript of the Bible*, with an English translation (1881), in which he seeks to fix its date to the year of the destruction of Jerusalem by Titus. (B. P.)

Sharuhen. The probable representative of this place, *Tell esh-Sheriah*, lies ten miles north-west of Khurbet Bir es-Seba, and is thus described in the *Memoirs* to the Ordnance Survey (iii, 339): "A large mound on the north bank of the valley. Broken pottery and a few small unhewn stones are found on the top. In the valley is a well-cut trough of basalt."

Shaw, WILLIAM, D.D., a Congregational minister, was born at Bridgewater, Mass; ordained pastor of the Church in Marshfield in April, 1769; and died June 1, 1816. See Sprague, *Annals of the Amer. Pulpit*, i, 573.

Shechesh. The archæological remains of the modern *Nablûs* are copiously described in the *Memoirs* to the Ordnance Survey (ii, 203 sq.).

Sheldon, George, D.D., a Presbyterian minister, was born at Northampton, Mass., Oct. 12, 1813. He graduated from Williams College in 1835, and from Andover Theological Seminary in 1838. He was pastor of the Presbyterian Church near Charleston, S. C., from 1840 to 1843, and was afterwards chosen district secretary of the American Bible Society for New Jersey and Delaware, which office he filled for thirty years. It may be said his life was spent in organizing means for the dissemination of the Holy Scriptures, and in the discharge of his duties he displayed great energy, wisdom, and executive ability. He was much esteemed by the citizens of Princeton, where he resided twenty years. He died there, June 16, 1881. See *N. Y. Observer*, June 23, 1881. (W. P. S.)

Sheldon, Luther, D.D., a Congregational minister, was born at Rupert, Vt., Feb. 18, 1786. He graduated from Middlebury College in 1808, and was ordained at Easton, Mass, in 1810, which pastorate he retained until his resignation in 1855. He preached six thousand written sermons, and declined eight calls to larger salaries. He died at Easton, Sept. 16, 1866. See *Cong. Quarterly*, 1867, p. 304.

Shelton, George A., D.D., a clergyman of the Protestant Episcopal Church, rector of St. James's Church, Newtown, L. I.; died Dec. 27, 1863, aged sixty-three years. See *Amer. Quar. Church Rev.* April, 1864, p. 150.

Shelton, William, D.D., a clergyman of the Protestant Episcopal Church, was born at Fairfield,

Conn., in September, 1798, his father being the Rev. Philo Shelton, the first Episcopal clergyman ordained in America. William graduated from the General Theological Seminary of New York in 1823, was ordained deacon the same year, and presbyter in 1826; ministered at Plattsburgh and Red Hook, N. Y., and in his native town, until 1829, when he became rector of St. Paul's Church, Buffalo. In 1879 he was made *pastor emeritus*, and so continued until his death, at the old Fairfield parsonage, Oct. 11, 1883. See (N. Y.) *Church Almanac*, 1884, p. 103.

Shema. The *Sameh* between Tell Milh and Beersheba, proposed for this place, is an error for *Saweh* (i. e. Hazor-Shual); and Tristram suggests (*Bible Places*, p. 18) that Shema (i. e. Sheba) is represented by *Tell es-Seba*, about two miles east of Bir es-Seba. See BEERSHEBA.

Shepard, George, D.D., a Congregational minister, was born in Connecticut in 1802. He graduated from Amherst College in 1824, from Andover Theological Seminary in 1827, and was ordained Feb. 5, 1828, pastor at Hallowell, Me. He became professor of sacred rhetoric in the Theological Seminary at Bangor in 1836, and died there, March 23, 1868. See *Trien. Cat. of Andover Theol. Sem.* 1870, p. 76.

Shepard, Thomas, D.D., a Congregational minister, was born at Norton, Mass., May 7, 1792. After studying at Taunton Academy, he graduated from Brown University in 1813, and in 1816 from Andover Theological Seminary. The two succeeding years he was a home missionary in Georgia. In 1818 and 1819 he was agent for the Connecticut Asylum for the Deaf and Dumb. He was ordained pastor at Ashfield, Mass., June 16, 1819, and remained until May 8, 1833. From 1833 to 1835 Dr. Shepard was agent of the American Bible Society. From April 30, 1835, until his death he was pastor at Bristol, R. I., although he had resigned active service in 1865. In 1846 he was elected a corporate member of the American Board of Commissioners for Foreign Missions. He died Oct. 5, 1879. Among his publications were various sermons and thirty *New Year's Annuals*. See *Cong. Year-book*, 1880, p. 27.

Shepley, DAVID, D.D., a Congregational minister, was born at Solon, Me., in May, 1804. His father dying when David was quite young, he went to Norridgewock, where he resided for a time in the family of Rev. Jonah Peet, and became a Christian. He pursued his preparatory studies at Saco, graduated from Bowdoin College in 1825, and from Andover Theological Seminary in 1828. He was ordained as pastor of the First Church at Yarmouth, Me., in February, 1829, and resigned in April, 1849. He was next pastor at Winslow from September, 1851, until June, 1862; subsequently of the Central Church at Falmouth for a short time, and then provisional secretary of the Maine Missionary Society. His health failing, he removed to Providence, R. I., in 1871, where he remained until his death, Dec. 1, 1881. See *Providence Journal*, Dec. 3, 1881. (J. C. S.)

Sherman, JOSEPH, LL.D., a Congregational minister and educator, was born at Edgecomb, Me., March 3, 1800. He graduated from Bowdoin College in 1826, was principal for six years of the Academy at North Yarmouth, studied two years at Andover, and in 1834 went to Columbia, Tenn., as professor of ancient languages in Jackson College. For fifteen years he was connected with the college, during three of which he was its president. He died in June, 1849. See *Hist. of Bowdoin College*, p. 355. (J. C. S.)

Sherwood, Adiel, D.D., a Baptist minister, was born at Fort Edward, N. Y., Oct. 3, 1791. He studied three years at Middlebury College, graduated from Union College in 1817, studied one year in the Andover Theological Seminary, and then went to Georgia for his health, where he took high rank as a preacher. He was ordained pastor at Bethlehem, near Lexington, in 1820. While at Eatonton, whither he went in 1827, having charge of an academy, as well as preaching, a most remarkable revival began in his church, and for two years it spread through the state. He may be said to have been the originator of what is now Mercer University. In 1837 and 1838 he was a professor in Columbian College, Washington, D. C., and from 1839 to 1841 professor of sacred literature in Mercer University, Ga. For several years he was president of Shurtleff College, Alton, Ill. In 1848 and 1849 he was president of the Masonic College, Lexington, Mo., and from 1849 to 1857 pastor of the Church at Cape Girardeau. Returning to Georgia, he was president of Marshall College for a few years. The closing years of his life were spent in Missouri, his death occurring at St. Louis, Aug. 18, 1879. Among the numerous productions of his pen may be mentioned his *Gazetteer of Georgia*, *Christian and Jewish Churches*, and his *Notes on the New Testament*. In his personal appearance Dr. Sherwood was tall and commanding, with noble and dignified features. See Cathcart, *Baptist Encyclop.* p. 1054. (J. C. S.)

Sherwood, Reuben, D.D., a clergyman of the Protestant Episcopal Church, died at Hyde Park, N. Y., May 11, 1856, aged sixty-six years. He was one of the oldest clergymen of his denomination in Dutchess County, and for the last twenty-two years of his life had been rector of St. James's Church at Hyde Park. He was formerly, for a long time, in charge of the Church at Norwalk, Conn., and was the founder of the parishes at Saugerties and Esopus, N. Y. See *Amer. Quar. Church Rev.* 1856, p. 301.

Shicron is thought by Tristram (*Bible Places*, p. 34) to be the modern *Zernûka*, which lies two and a half miles north-east of Yebnah (Jabneh), and is "a large mud village, with cactus hedges around it, and wells in the gardens" (*Memoirs* to Ordnance Survey, ii, 414). Lieut. Conder suggests (*Quar. Statement* of "Pal. Explor. Fund," Oct. 1876, p. 170, note) that it may be the *Khurbet Sukereir*, a small ruined khan, near the river of the same name, four and a half miles south-west of Yebnah, and exhibiting traces of a cistern, a reservoir, a viaduct, and a canal (*Memoirs*, ii, 425).

Shihon. For this place both Tristram (*Bible Places*, p. 277) and Conder (*Tent Work*, ii, 339) accept *Ayûn esh-Shain*, two miles north-west of Debûrieh, which consists merely of "two springs, built up with masonry, about thirty yards apart; good perennial supply of water; no stream" (*Memoirs* of Ordnance Survey, i, 377). On the other hand, *esh-Shejerah*, four and a half miles north by east of Debûrieh, contains the ruins of an ancient building later used as a mosque (ibid. p. 414).

Shihor-libnath. Both Tristram (*Bible Places*, p. 289) and Conder (*Tent Work*, ii, 339) identify this stream with the *Wady esh-Shagûr*, which comes down the mountains east of Acre, and by its junction with Wady Shuîb forms the Wady el-Halzûn, that runs into the Nahr Numein, or Belus. This, however, is at least fourteen miles north-east of Carmel, and more than twenty from the south-west extremity of Asher.

Shiloh. The archæological remains at *Seilûn* are minutely described in the *Memoirs* accompanying the Ordnance Survey (ii, 367 sq.). The following particulars from Conder's *Tent Work* (i, 81 sq.) are of interest:

"We approached Shiloh from the south, by a mountain-road of evident antiquity, from the little plain. The ruins of a modern village here occupy a sort of tell or mound. On the east and north the site is shut in by bare and lofty hills of gray limestone, dotted over with a few fig-trees; on the south the plateau looks down on the plain just crossed. A deep valley runs behind the town on the north, and in its sides are many rock-cut sepulchres; following its course westward, we again reached the main road, thus avoiding a steep pass, and turning northwards found the village of Lebonah perched on the hillside to the west of the road and north of Shiloh, as described in the Bible.

"Shiloh was for about four hundred years the chosen abode of the tabernacle and ark. It is a question of no little interest whether this was the first spot selected after

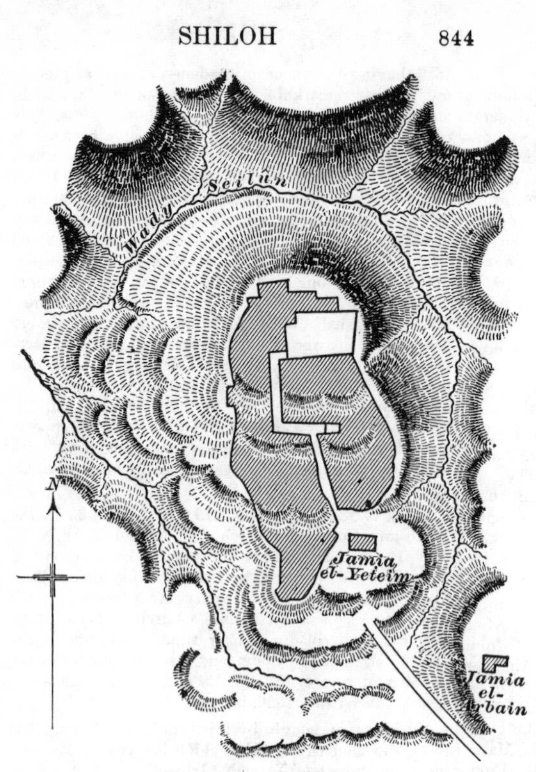

Plan of the Ruins of Shiloh.

the conquest of the hills by Joshua. That Shiloh became the gathering-place after the conquest of Shechem there is abundant proof (Josh. xxii, 12), and it may be inferred that the Tabernacle was placed there early; but, on the other hand, we find 'Sanctuary of the Lord' (or Holy Place of Jehovah) mentioned, by the oak near Shechem (Josh. xxiv, 26), and we may perhaps gather that, though not recognised by the doctors of the Mishna, there was a time when the Tabernacle stood, as is believed by the Samaritans, near Shechem. The date which they give for its transference to Shiloh, in the time of Eli, whom they consider to have been the first schismatical leader of the children of Judah, does not, however, accord with the Biblical account, and the story no doubt originated in consequence of religious hatred.

"The site being so certainly known, it becomes of interest to speculate as to the exact position of the Tabernacle. Below the top of the hill, on the north of the ruins, there is a sort of irregular quadrangle, sloping rather to the west, and perched above terraces made for agricultural purposes. The rock has here been rudely hewn in two parallel scarps for over four hundred feet, with a court between, seventy-seven feet wide, and sunk five feet below the outer surface. Thus there would be sufficient room for the court of the Tabernacle in this area, and it is worthy of notice that the measurement north and south agrees very closely with the width of the court (fifty cubits), which was also measured north and south. From the Mishna we learn that the lower part of the Tabernacle erected at Shiloh was of stone, with a tent above.

"There are, however, two other places which demand attention as possible sites, one being perhaps a synagogue, the other a little building called the 'Mosque of the Servants of God.'

"The building which I have called a synagogue is situate on a slope south of the ruins of Shiloh. It is thirty-seven feet square, and built of good masonry. The door is on the north, and is surmounted by a flat lintel, on which is a design in bold relief, representing vases and wreaths. Inside there are pillars with capitals, seemingly Byzantine. A sloping scarp has been built against the wall on three sides, and a little mosque sacred to El-Arbaîn —'the Forty' Companions of the Prophet—is built on to the east wall. There is a pointed arch on the west wall. Thus we have at least three periods—that of the old synagogue, represented by the lintel, which is similar to the lintels of Galilæan synagogues, that of a later Christian erection, and finally the Moslem mosque, built, probably, where the apse of the chapel would have been placed.

"The Jamia el-Yeteim, or 'Mosque of the Servants of God,' is situated at the southern foot of the tell. It is shaded by a large oak-tree, and is of good masonry, like that of the last; there was nothing very remarkable in the little low chamber within, but the name seems to preserve a tradition of the position of the Tabernacle.

"The only water close to the village was once contained in a little tank with steps, south of the lower mosque. There is, however, a fine spring placed, as is often to be observed in Palestine, at a distance of no less than three quarters of a mile from the town, at the head of the valley which comes down behind the ruins from the east. A good supply of water here issues into a rocky basin, and was once carried by an underground aqueduct to a rock-cut tank, but is now allowed to run waste.

"The vineyards of Shiloh have disappeared, though very possibly once surrounding the spring, and perhaps extending down the valley westwards, where water is also found. With the destruction of the village desolation has spread over the barren hills around.

"A yearly feast was held at Shiloh, when the women came out to dance in the vineyards (Judges xxi, 21). It is possible that a tradition of this festival is retained in the name Merj el-'Aid, 'Meadow of the Feast,' to the south of the present site."

Shimron. The present *Semûnieh* is described in the *Memoirs* accompanying the Ordnance Survey (i, 280) as "a small village on a knoll at the edge of the plain of Esdraelon [five miles west of Nazareth], with three springs . . . and contains probably less than one hundred souls." It has "artificial mounds, traces of ruins, and a sarcophagus" (ibid. p. 339).

Shinn, Asa, an eminent Methodist Protestant minister, was born in New Jersey, May 3, 1781, of poor but honest Quaker parents. He received his education chiefly among the western hills of Virginia, became a Methodist at the age of eighteen, was requested to become an exhorter, and before his twentieth year was employed as a travelling preacher in the Methodist Episcopal Church, in which connection he continued over twenty-seven years. The fact that he never saw an English grammar or a clock until he entered upon his first circuit pictures his illiterate and inexperienced condition; yet such was his progress that in 1809 we find him by appointment in the city of Baltimore. He gave himself wholly to the work, utilized his opportunities as a student, and whether in season or out of season, in town or in country, in the woods or on horseback, his tireless mind was at work, until he became a theologian before whose logic and masterly delivery no foe of the truth could stand. In 1825 Mr. Shinn was transferred to the Pittsburgh Conference, and in 1829 withdrew from the Methodist Episcopal Church, helped to organize the Methodist Protestant Church, and at its first conference, which was held that year, in Ohio, he was elected president. He afterwards was the first president of the Pittsburgh Conference. In 1834 he was elected editor of the *Methodist Protestant*, and served two years. When a young man Mr. Shinn experienced an accidental fracture of his skull, which, because of improper surgical attention, caused his insanity in old age, and he was removed to Brattleboro (Vt.) Lunatic Asylum, where he died, Feb. 11, 1833. Mr. Shinn produced two theological works: *The Plan of Salvation*, and *The Benevolence and Rectitude of the Supreme Being;* they evince great logical power, piety of heart, and loyalty to Christ. See Bassett, *Hist. of the M. P. Church*, p. 325.

Shorsewood, George, a Scotch prelate, was rector of Culter in 1449, and in 1453 was chancellor of the Church of Dunkeld. He was confessor to the king in 1454, in which year he went on an embassy to England. He was made bishop of the see of Brechin, Oct. 22 the same year, was also royal secretary, and afterwards became lord high chancellor. He was bishop there in 1462. See Keith, *Scottish Bishops*, p. 164.

Short, Augustus, D.D., an Anglican prelate, was born near Exeter in 1803. From Westminster School he was sent to Christ Church College, Oxford, where he graduated A.B. in 1824, and A.M. in 1826. He was appointed vicar of Ravensthorpe, Northamptonshire, in 1835; Bampton lecturer at Oxford in 1846, and the first bishop of Adelaide, South Australia, in 1847. He died Oct. 8, 1883.

Short, David Hawkins, D.D., a Protestant Episcopal clergyman, was born in 1806. He graduated from Trinity College in 1833, and from the General Theological Seminary, N. Y., in 1836; was ordained the same year; for a number of years was employed as a teacher in Ridgefield, Conn.; in 1860 became rector of St. James's Church, Waisted; in 1861 of Grace Church, Broadbrook; in 1866 removed to Greenwich as rector of two churches, viz.: Calvary Church, at Round Hill, and Emmanuel Church, in Glenville; in 1867 officiated in St. John's Church, Hartford; the next year in the Memorial Church of the Holy Trinity, Westport. He resided in Portland, in 1870, without charge; but the following year officiated in Trinity Church, in that place; in 1872 he was chosen rector of St. Andrew's Church, Northford, where he remained for several years. He died in Fairfield, Jan. 21, 1877. See *Prot. Episc. Almanac*, 1878, p. 170.

Shoter. See OFFICER.

Shunem. Its modern representative, *Sôlam*, is three and a quarter miles north of Zerîn, and is briefly noted in the *Memoirs* accompanying the Ordnance Survey (ii, 87). The following particulars concerning its situation are given by Conder (*Tent Work*, i, 123):

> "Westward the view includes Fûleh—the crusading Castle of the Bean, with its fosse and marshy pool outside, and extends as far as Carmel, fifteen miles away. Thus the whole extent of the ride of the Shunammite woman (2 Kings iv, 24) under the burning noontide sun of harvest-time is visible. Were the houses of that time no larger than the mud-cabins of the modern village, it was not a great architectural undertaking to build 'a little chamber' for the prophet, and the enumeration of the simple furniture of that chamber—the bed, perhaps only a straw mat, the table, the stool, and the lamp, seems to indicate that it was only such a little hut that was intended. Another point may be noted: how came it that Elisha so constantly passed by Shunem? The answer seems simple; he lived habitually on Carmel, but he was a native of Abel Meholah, 'the Meadow of Circles,' a place now called 'Ain Helweh, in the Jordan valley, to which the direct road led past Shunem down the valley of Jezreel."

Shur. Dr. Trumbull labors at great length (*Kadesh-barnea*, p. 44 sq.) to prove that Shur was the name of a line of fortifications extending from Suez to the Mediterranean; but in that case the word must have taken the article (*the* Wall), which, on the contrary, it never has. His etymologies connecting it in this sense with Etham are very forced. That there may have existed some such defences, in the way of forts, Migdol (q. v.) being the principal one, may very well be granted, without supposing a continuous or wall-like series, of which there is no evidence. Nor is the word itself ever used in any such relation. The phrase דֶּרֶךְ שׁוּר (Gen. xvi, 7), can only mean, in Hebrew idiom, "the way to Shur," like בּוֹאֲךָ שׁוּר (1 Sam. xv, 7), or, more exactly, בּוֹאֲךָ שׁוּרָה (1 Sam. xxvii, 8) not "the Wall-Road."

Shurtleff, ROSWELL, D.D., a Congregational professor, was born at Ellington, Conn., Aug. 29, 1773. He was educated at Chesterfield Academy and Dartmouth College. In 1800 he was appointed tutor, and in 1804 professor of theology and college pastor at Dartmouth. This office he held for twenty-three years, and from 1827 to 1838 he held the professorship of moral philosophy and political economy. His remaining years were spent quietly at home. He died at Hanover, N. H., Feb. 4, 1861. Dr. Shurtleff's mind was clear, farsighted, versatile, and logical; his wit and humor were unfailing; his sympathies were strong, his preaching was powerful, and his learning was ample. In theology he was a Hopkinsian. See *Cong. Quarterly*, 1861, p. 215.

Siber, URBAN GOTTFRIED, a Lutheran theologian of Germany, was born Dec. 12, 1669, at Schandau, Saxony, and studied at Wittenberg. In 1703 he was deacon, and in 1708 archdeacon at Schneeberg. In 1711 he went to Leipsic, was in 1715 professor, in 1734 doctor of theology, and died June 15, 1741. He wrote, *De σκληροκαρδίᾳ e Sententia Græcorum* (Wittenberg, 1697):—*De Gaza, Palæstinæ Oppido ejusque Episcopis ad Actor. viii*, 26 (Schneeberg, 1715):—*Prolegomena ad Historiam Melodorum Ecclesiæ Græcæ* (1714):—*Ecclesiæ Græcæ Martyrologium Metricum* (1727). See Döring, *Die gelehrten Theologen Deutschlands*, s. v.; Winer, *Handbuch der theol. Lit.* i, 590, 614, 621, 685; Jöcher, *Allgemeines Gelehrten-Lexikon*, s. v. (B. P.)

Sieffert, FRIEDRICH LUDWIG, a Lutheran theologian of Germany, was born at Elbing, Prussia, Feb. 1, 1803. In 1826 he commenced his academical career at

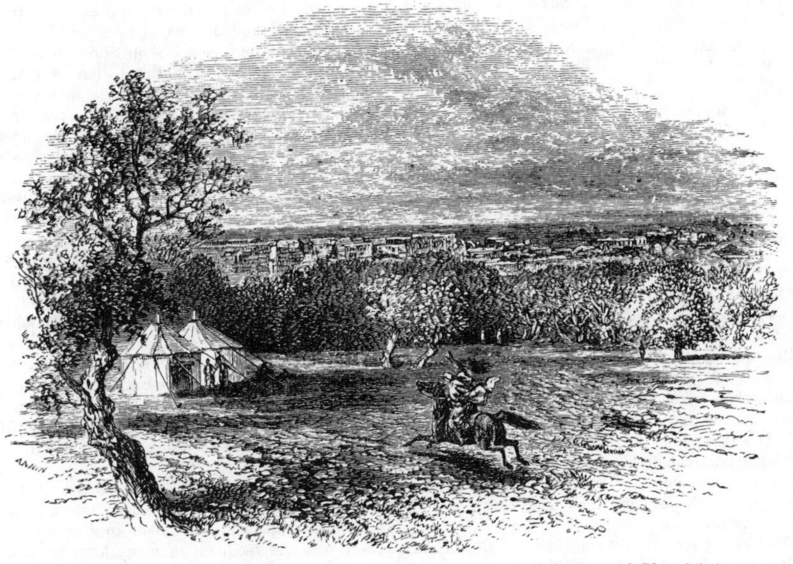

Present Appearance of Shunem. (From Thomson's *Central Palestine and Phœnicia.*)

Königsberg, was in 1828 professor, and died Nov. 2, 1877, doctor and professor of theology. He published, *De Singulorum Librorum Sacrorum Auctoritate Canonica Recte Æstimanda* (Königsberg, 1833):—*Ueber den Ursprung des ersten kanonischen Evangeliums* (1832):—*Theodorus Mopsuest. Veteris Testamenti Sobrie Interpretandi Vindex* (1827):—*Andeutungen über die apologetische Fundamenterung der christlichen Glaubenswissenschaft* (Güterslohe, 1871). (B. P.)

Siegel, Karl Christian Friedrich, a Lutheran theologian of Germany, was born at Marienburg in 1781, and died at Leipsic in 1845, doctor of theology. He published, *Neue Materialien zu Kanzelvorträgen* (Leipsic, 1827-28, 2 vols.):—*Homiletischer Rathgeber* (1832-33, 2 vols.):—*De Artibus Quibus Signum Crucis in Sacris Christianorum materiem Præbuit* (1839):—*Handbuch der christlich-kirchlichen Alterthümer* (1835-39, 4 vols.):—*Die epistolischen Texte in kirchlich-archäologischer exegetischer Hinsicht* (1842-43, 3 vols.). See Zuchold, *Bibl. Theol.* s. v.; Winer, *Handbuch der theol. Lit.* i, 609; ii, 124, 148. (B. P.)

Sigwart, Heinrich Christoph Wilhelm von, professor of philosophy, who died in 1844 at Tübingen, is the author of, *Zusammenhang des Spinozismus mit der cartesianischen Philosophie* (Tübingen, 1816):—*Der Spinozismus, historisch und philosophisch erläutert* (1839):—*Vergleichung der Rechts- und Staatstheorien des Bened. Spinoza und des Th. Hobbes* (1842):—*Das Problem von der Freiheit und der Unfreiheit des menschlichen Willens* (1839):—*Das Problem des Bösen oder die Theodice* (1840). See Fürst, *Bibl. Jud.* s. v.; Zuchold, *Bibl. Theol.* s. v. (B. P.)

Sihler, Wilhelm, a Lutheran minister of Germany, was born in 1801. Having completed his theological studies, he was for a time tutor at the Blochmann Institute at Dresden. In 1843 he came to America, labored for a time in the state of Ohio, and accepted a call as professor at the Lutheran seminary in Fort Wayne, Ind., in 1845, where he died, Oct. 27, 1885. He published, *Lebenslauf als lutherischer Pastor* (1880, 2 vols.):—*Predigten* (1862, 1874, 1883). (B. P.)

Siloam, Pool of. A remarkable Hebrew inscription on an interior passage lately discovered behind the present Fountain of the Virgin, by which the water was reached by the inhabitants of the city, commemorates the cutting of the tunnel leading between these two reservoirs (see Dr. Guthe, in the *Zeitschr. d. deutsch. morgenländ. Geschellschaft*, xxxvi, 3 sq.). The following translation is by professor Sayce (in the *Quar. Statement* of the "Pal. Explor. Fund," Oct. 1883, p. 210):

"1. (Behold) the excavation! Now this had been the history of the excavation. While the workmen were still lifting up

"2. the axe, each towards his neighbor, and while three cubits still remained to (cut through), (each heard) the voice of the other who called

"3. to his neighbor, since there was an excess of the rock on the right hand and on (the left). And on the day of the

"4. excavation the workmen struck, each to meet his neighbor, axe against axe, and there flowed

"5. the waters from the spring to the pool for a thousand two hundred cubits; and . . .

"6. of a cubit was the height of the rock over the heads of the workmen."

Simon, the name of several Scotch prelates:

1. Bishop of Dunblane in the 12th century. See Keith, *Scottish Bishops*, p. 171.

2. Bishop of Ross in the 12th century. See Keith, *Scottish Bishops*, p. 184.

3. Consecrated bishop of the Isles in 1226, and witness to a charter dated Jan. 9, in the seventeenth year of king Alexander II. He held a synod in 1239, where he made thirteen canons, which are to be found in the *Monasticon Anglicanum.* He died at his palace of Kirkmichael, in the isle of Man. See Keith, *Scottish Bishops*, p. 299.

4. Dean of the see of Moray in 1232 and also in 1242, and advanced to the bishopric of Moray in the latter year. He was bishop nine years, and died in 1253. See Keith, *Scottish Bishops*, p. 139.

5. Bishop of Galloway in 1321. See Keith, *Scottish Bishops*, p. 1321.

Simpson, Calovius Abraham, LL.D., an English Congregational minister, was born in 1789. He was educated at the Glasgow University, and left that institution with the highest testimonial of Christian character and scholarly attainment. He essayed to make proof of his ministry first at Fulbourne, and in 1820 removed to Haverhill, where he was ordained, and for eleven years greatly blessed in his work. In 1836 Dr. Simpson settled at Oundle, thence in 1842 he removed to Cardiff, and in 1844 entered upon his final pastorate at Long Sutton, Lincolnshire. He died March 17, 1866. "His literary reading was very wide; he had singular conversational powers and great urbanity of manner; his love of theological and metaphysical questions amounted to a passion, and on them he spoke with decision and authority." See (Lond.) *Cong. Yearbook*, 1867, p. 313.

Simpson, Matthew, D.D., LL.D., a bishop of the Methodist Episcopal Church, was born at Cadiz, Harrison Co., O., June 10, 1810. He graduated from Madison College (afterwards merged into Allegheny University) in 1832. In 1833 he took the degree of doctor of medicine, but before the year was ended had decided to enter the Pittsburgh Conference. The second year thereafter he became pastor of the Liberty Street Church, Pittsburgh, where he soon gave evidence of the eloquence which eventually placed him among the greatest pulpit orators of the age. In 1837 he was called as professor of natural sciences to Allegheny University, and two years afterwards was appointed president of Indiana Asbury University, at Greencastle, Ind. Under his management the college grew in strength and usefulness. In 1848 Dr. Simpson was elected to the editorship of *The Western Christian Advocate*, of Cincinnati. In 1852 he was elected a bishop of the Methodist Episcopal Church. He adorned the episcopal office with gentleness, humility, and devotion. He was indefatigable in the discharge of his duties, and though careful in the maintenance, doctrine, and discipline of his Church, he did so without exciting enmity from those of his own or other sects. He died in Philadelphia, Pa., June 18, 1884. Bishop Simpson will be best remembered by his patriotic labors in aid of the government during the civil war, which gave him a national reputation. He was the trusted friend and adviser of president Lincoln, and it was at his request that bishop Simpson made a series of powerful addresses on the Union in many of the cities of the North. He was the stanch supporter of the colored race, and was urged by the secretary of war to undertake the organization of the freedmen at the establishment of the bureau, and was afterwards invited by president Grant to go as commissioner to San Domingo, both of which offers he declined. Besides the public addresses which the bishop delivered he was employed by the government on many missions of a confidential nature, which aided largely in strengthening the Union cause. In view of these services rendered during the war and under the direction of president Lincoln, it was fitting that he should have been chosen to deliver the nation's eulogy upon her martyred president. In 1870, on the death of bishop Kingsley, bishop Simpson visited Europe to complete the work which had been assigned to him on the Continent, and also as a delegate to the English Conference. In 1874 he visited Mexico, and in 1875 again went to Europe to attend the conferences held in Germany and Switzerland, and also to meet the missionaries on the Continent. In 1881 he attended the Œcumenical Council of the Methodist Church, which was held in London, and while there was the recipient of many kind attentions from the members of his denomination in England. He is the author of *A Hundred Years of Methodism*, a volume of *Yale Lectures on Preaching*, and was the editor of the *Cyclopædia of Methodism*, which contains information on almost every subject of interest to the denomination. Some of his *Sermons* have been edited by Dr. G. R. Crooks (N. Y. 1885); also his *Life* (ibid. 1890).

Sin, MAN OF (ὁ ἄνθρωπος τῆς ἁμαρτίας, 2 Thess. ii, 3). In the admirable essay on this subject appended to Eadie's *Commentary on Thessalonians* (Lond. 1877), the untenableness of the earlier interpretations is clearly shown, and even that the popular application of the phrase by Protestants to the Roman papacy is not conclusive. The only unsatisfactory part of the discussion is the summary dismissal of Elliott's argument for an impersonal antichrist by simply denying the meaning (*successor*) assigned to the participles ὁ κατέχων and τὸ κατέχον, "that withholdeth" or "letteth" (p. 349). The proof that a *person* is meant does not depend upon that signification of these participles, but upon the fact that the personal masculine is thus exchanged for the impersonal neuter, and especially that the principal power is likewise designated by the abstract μυστήριον, "mystery" (ver. 7). In like manner the Johannean term "the antichrist" (ὁ ἀντίχριστος, 1 John ii, 22) is not a proper name, nor even the designation of an individual, for it is used in the plural in the same connection (ἀντίχριστοι, ver. 18; comp. 2 John 7), and also as a neuter or abstract (τὸ τοῦ ἀντιχρίστου). To understand this impersonation of the evil principle (comp. ὁ διάβολος as an embodiment of Satanic influence), we must advert to the conventional use in the New-Test. figures, especially in eschatological passages, of the concrete terms and names of the Old Test., such as especially appears in the adoption of "Gog and Magog" from the prophecies of Ezekiel (xxxviii), where they probably designate a particular people, hostile to Judaism, to express a collective or abstract power of persecution in the future of Christendom (Rev. xx, 8). In like manner the "little horn" of Daniel, which invariably represents Antiochus Epiphanes, has been confounded with the persecuting beast of the Apocalypse. The names of the Old Test. have been typically transferred to the symbolology of the New Test., like *Zion*, *Jerusalem*, *Babylon*, etc., but have never lost their literal, local, and personal meaning. In fact, this very type of Antiochus was evidently in the apostle's mind while employing the masculine in the passage under discussion, and the whole aspect of the persecuting power is evidently borrowed from the description of that blasphemer in the book of Daniel. This explains what has been a puzzle to commentators, the impious arrogance of the future antichrist (2 Thess. ii, 4), which is exactly parallel with the prophet's language (Dan. vii, 8, 20, 25; viii, 10-12; xi, 36). We conclude, therefore, that in the eschatology of the New-Test. writers these expressions are to be interpreted figuratively, and not literally, as in the Old Test.; and that they probably refer to some great onset of infidelity near the close of the present dispensation. See MYSTERY OF INIQUITY.

Sinclair, a Scotch prelate, was dean of Restabrig and Edinburgh, and put into the see of Brechin in the 16th century. He died in 1566. See Keith, *Scottish Bishops*, p. 165.

Sinclair, Henry, a Scotch prelate, was rector of Glasgow in 1539, and in 1541 abbot of the abbey of Kilwinning, which last benefice he exchanged for the deanery of Glasgow in 1550, where he had ministered two years before. He was bishop of Ross in 1561. He died in France, Jan. 2, 1564. See Keith, *Scottish Bishops*, p. 193.

Sinclair, William, a Scotch prelate, was made bishop of Dunkeld in 1312. He probably died in 1337. See Keith, *Scottish Bishops*, p. 82.

Siric, archbishop of Canterbury, was educated at Glastonbury, and, having been a monk there, was removed to St. Augustine's, at Canterbury, where he became abbot. Siric was consecrated archbishop in 990, and went to Rome for his pallium. He was fond of pomp and display. He died in 994. See Hook, *Lives of the Archbishops of Canterbury*, i, 432.

Skillman, ISAAC, D.D., a Baptist minister, was born in New Jersey in 1740, and graduated from the College of New Jersey in 1766. He was sent into the ministry by the First Baptist Church of New York; in 1773 became pastor of the Second Baptist Church at Boston, and in 1787 returned to New Jersey. On Sept. 18, 1790, he was called to the pastoral charge of the Baptist Church at Salem, entered upon his duties the November following, and continued there until his death, June 8, 1799. Dr. Skillman was a man of learning and abilities, but never very popular as a preacher. See Sprague, *Annals of the Amer. Pulpit*, i, 453.

Skinner, John (1), a Scotch Episcopal clergyman, was born at Balfour, Aberdeenshire, in 1721, studied at Marischal College, taught at Kenmay and Moneymusk, and in 1742 became minister at Longside. He died in 1806. In his early years he obtained considerable reputation as a Scotch poet, his poems forming vol. iii of his posthumous works (Edinburgh, 1809). His son edited his theological works, which were published with a memoir (Aberdeen, eod. 2 vols. 8vo). These works contain *Letters to a Candidate for Orders*, *Dissertation on the Shechinah*, *Literal and True Radical Exposition of the Song of Songs*, and *Psalms viii, xxiii, and xlv*, done into Latin verse.

Skinner, John (2), primus of the Scotch Episcopal Church, son of the foregoing, was born May 17, 1744. He was educated at Echt, by his grandfather, and at Marischal College, University of Aberdeen. In 1761 he became private tutor, and in 1763 was ordained by bishop Gerard. He was settled at Ellon, and in 1775 was preacher in a chapel at Aberdeen. In 1782 he was consecrated coadjutor to bishop Kilgour, of that see, and in 1784, on the elevation of Kilgour to the primacy of Scotland, Dr. Skinner was invested with the full honors of the episcopate. In 1788 he succeeded as primus præses of the Episcopal College. He died at Aberdeen, July 13, 1816. Under the fostering hand of this benevolent and untiring bishop, the Scotch Episcopal Church, from obscurity and depression, arose to respectability and distinction. It was bishop John Skinner who, with two other Scottish bishops, in an upper chamber of a mean dwelling-house in a lane in Aberdeen, consecrated the first bishop of the United States, in 1784. He wrote, *A Course of Lectures for the Young* (Aberdeen, 1786):—*An Ecclesiastical History of Scotland* (Lond. 1788, 2 vols. 8vo; a vindication of the Episcopal party):—*A Layman's Account of his Faith and Practice* (Edinburgh, 1801, 12mo):—*Primitive Truth and Order Vindicated* (Aberdeen, 1803, 8vo).

Bishop Skinner's elder son, JOHN, ordained in 1790, was a minister at Forfar, and the author of *Annals of Scottish Episcopacy from* 1788 to 1816, *with a Brief Memoir of Bishop Skinner* (Edinburgh, 1818, 8vo). See the (N. Y.) *Christian Journal*, February and March, 1820, vol. iv; Darling, *Cyclop. Bibl.* s. v.

Skinner, Robert, D.D., an English prelate of the 17th century, was born at Pisford, Northamptonshire, where his father was a clergyman. He became a fellow of Trinity College, Oxford; was rector at Launton, Oxfordshire; bishop of Bristol in 1636, translated to Oxford in 1640 and to Worcester in 1663, and died June 14, 1670. He is said to have been an eminent preacher. See Fuller, *Worthies of England* (ed. Nuttall), ii, 507.

Skinner, William, D.D., a bishop in the Church of Scotland, was born at Aberdeen in 1778, and died there, April 15, 1857. He was educated at Wadham College, Oxford; was ordained priest in 1802, when he became curate to his father at St. Andrew's Church, Aberdeen; in 1816 he was consecrated bishop of Aberdeen, and in 1841 elected primus of the Church in Scotland. See *Amer. Quar. Church Rev.* 1857, p. 314.

Slater, Richard, D.D., a Congregational minister, was born in Boston, Mass., in 1723. He graduated from Harvard College in 1739, studied medicine and became a skilful practitioner; then studied theology, and for some time supplied one of the pulpits in Boston. He was ordained pastor at Mansfield, Conn., June 27, 1744, and died there, April 14, 1789. See Sprague, *Annals of the Amer. Pulpit*, i, 421.

Slaughter, W. B., D.D., a Methodist Episcopal minister, was born in New York city in 1823. He was converted early in life; graduated from Genesee Wesleyan Seminary, Lima, N. Y., and entered the Genesee Conference, in which he served Palmyra, Carlton, and Old Niagara Street Methodist Episcopal Church, Buffalo; then accepted a call to the principalship of the Academy at Condersport, Pa., and later to that of the Genesee Model School, Lima, N. Y. Removing westward, he became pastor of Wabash Avenue Church, Chicago, Ill. He served in one of the Illinois regiments as an officer during the early part of the civil war. His next field of labor was in the Rocky Mountain Conference, he being appointed one of its two presiding elders. The rigor of the climate being too severe for his constitution, he was transferred to the Nebraska Conference, and stationed as pastor at Omaha, then at Lincoln, and three years later was made presiding elder of Omaha District. He died at Omaha, July 26, 1879. He published in 1876 a work of great ability, entitled *Modern Genesis.* He was a patient and thorough student, an affectionate father and friend, and a devoted and successful minister. See *Minutes of Annual Conferences*, 1879, p. 101.

Slavé Version of the Scriptures. The Slavé is spoken by the Indians of Mackenzie River, Canada. A translation of the gospels into Slavé was made by bishop Bompas, and printed by the British and Foreign Bible Society in 1883 in the syllabic character, the proofs having been read by the Rev. W. D. Reeve, archdeacon of Chippewyan Fort. The syllabic character was adopted because, as Mr. Reeve says, "the Roman character is useful for those who have learned English, for 'whites' and others desirous of teaching the Indians, but for the Indians themselves the syllabic edition is the more useful." (B. P.)

Slovakien Version. See Slavonic Versions.

Smallwood, William A., D.D., a Protestant Episcopal clergyman, was born in Washington, D.C., in 1805. He graduated from Columbian College, Washington; studied law at Litchfield, Conn., and theology at Alexandria, Va.; was ordained in 1829, and took charge of St. Matthew's Church, Bladensburg, and of Zion's Church, Prince George County, Md.; in 1836 became rector of St. James's parish, in Zanesville, O., where he remained seventeen years; in 1853 was pastor of Trinity Church, Chicago, Ill.; took charge, in 1857, of Zion and St. Paul's parishes, in Frederick County, Md.; in 1861 became rector of a church in Cincinnati, O., and in 1865 of Holy Trinity parish, St. Anthony's Falls, Minn., where he died, Jan. 2, 1867. See *Amer. Quar. Church Rev.* April, 1867, p. 153.

Smedes, Aldert, D.D., a Protestant Episcopal clergyman, was born in New York city, April 29, 1810. He graduated from Transylvania University in 1826, and from the General Theological Seminary in 1832; from 1836 to 1839 was rector of St. George's Church, in Schenectady, N. Y.; in 1842 opened St. Mary's School, in Raleigh, N. C., of which he was rector until his death, April 25, 1877. See *Prot. Episc. Almanac*, 1878, p. 170.

Smith, Benjamin Bosworth, D.D., a Protestant Episcopal bishop, was born at Bristol, R. I., June 13, 1794. He graduated from Providence College (now Brown University) in 1816, was ordained deacon April 27, 1817, and presbyter June 24, 1818. After having a charge at Marblehead for two years, he became rector of St. George's Church, Accomac, Va.; two years later of Zion's Church, Charlestown, with charge of Trinity Church in Shepherdstown; in 1823 of St. Stephen's Church, Middlebury, Vt. While there he edited *The Episcopal Register.* In 1828 he became rector of Grace Church mission, in Philadelphia, and editor of *The Episcopal Recorder.* In 1832 he was minister of Christ Church, Lexington, Ky. On Oct. 30 of the same year he was consecrated first bishop of the diocese of Kentucky, from which position he retired in 1880, and spent his remaining days in New York city, where he died, June 1, 1884.

Smith, David, D.D., a Congregational minister, was born at Bozrah, Conn., Dec. 13, 1767. He graduated from Yale College in 1795; commenced preaching in Durham, Feb. 15, 1799, and was ordained Aug. 15 following; was dismissed Jan. 11, 1832, and died at Fair Haven, March 5, 1862. When ninety years old he was able to act as chaplain to the Cincinnati Society, in Boston, and preached at Washington, in Congress Hall. See *Chauncy Memorial*, p. 170. (J. C. S.)

Smith, Edward Dunlap, D.D., a Presbyterian minister, was born at Greenwich, N. J., Sept. 17, 1802. He graduated from Princeton College in 1822, and from Princeton Theological Seminary in 1826; was licensed the same year; employed as a home missionary in Georgia in 1828 and 1829, and served as chaplain of the University of Virginia in 1830. In 1831 he was ordained pastor of the Second Presbyterian Church of Washington, D. C., which church he served until 1835. During his pastorate in Washington he was chaplain of the House of Representatives. He next became pastor of the Eighth Street Presbyterian Church, New York city, where he remained until 1842, when he accepted the pastorate of the Chelsea Church, in the same city, and toiled there faithfully until his death, March 28, 1883. Dr. Smith was a fine scholar and an able preacher, but his excessive modesty, amounting to timidity, always kept him in the background. See *Necrol. Report of Princeton Theol. Sem.* 1883, p. 75. (W. P. S.)

Smith, George (1), D.D., an English Wesleyan author, was born about 1800, of humble parentage. He was educated in a Lancasterian school, and although engaged in secular business, acquired a large fund of information, which he used in the preparation of several historico-religious works, especially a series entitled *Sacred Annals*, which were reprinted in New York. He died at Camborne, Cornwall, Aug. 30, 1868.

Smith, George (2), D.D., an English Congregational divine, was born at Poplar, near London, July 31, 1803. After a course of theological instruction, he was sent out to preach under the direction of the "Tent Mission," and in 1827 was ordained pastor of Hanover Chapel, Liverpool. In 1834 he was settled over the New Tabernacle, Plymouth, and in 1842 removed to London as pastor of Trinity Chapel, where for twenty-eight years he preached with great acceptance. He died Feb. 19, 1870. Many large schools, both Sunday and day, were built, and still remain a monument of his labors. Dr. Smith was elected secretary of the Anti-Slavery Society. He was also a director of the London Missionary Society, and secretary of the Irish Evangelical Society and Congregational Union. His published works are, *The Pentateuch:—Prayers for Domestic Use:—The Origin of Language:—The Spiritual Life.* See (Lond.) *Cong. Year-book*, 1871, p. 346.

Smith, George (3), D.D., a bishop of the Church of England, was born in 1815, and graduated from Magdalen Hall, Oxford. When China was opened to the residence of Christian missionaries, Mr. Smith offered himself for service there, and was accepted. After spending several years in the work of a missionary, a bishopric was founded in China, to which he was elected. For sixteen years bishop Smith discharged the duties of the episcopate in the British colony of Hong-Kong, among the British chaplains, and in the missionary fields occupied by the Church Missionary Society in that vast country. As a preacher he exercised a wide influence for good, as a bishop he ruled wisely, and as principal of St. Paul's College, Hong-Kong, he directed the education of many intelligent Chinese youths, who afterwards became influential members of the native community, not a few of them professing Christianity. The bishop twice returned to England to recruit his health, passing on one occasion through India, and on another by Japan and San Francisco through North America. Of his visit to Japan he published a very interesting journal. He died Dec. 14, 1871. See (Lond.) *Christian Observer*, Feb. 1872.

Smith, George (4), an eminent English Assyriologist, was born about 1840. Originally a bank-note engraver, he began, in 1857, the study of the cuneiform inscriptions, and after publishing several interesting discourses in a German periodical, was called in 1867 to a position in the British Museum, where he rendered important aid to Rawlinson in the preparation of volume three of his *Cuneiform Inscriptions of Western Asia*. He made two visits to the ruins in Assyria, one in 1872, and another in 1876, and during the latter died at Aleppo, Aug. 19 of that year. Among his other contributions to antiquarian science are *Chaldæan Account of Genesis* (1876), and many papers in the *Journal* of the Society of Biblical Archæology.

Smith, George Charles, an English Baptist, known for more than half a century all over England as "Boatswain Smith," was born in London in 1782, brought up religiously by a pious mother, and went to sea while a boy. He was forcibly impressed into the king's service in the last century, and transferred into various ships of war, visiting most of the seaports of Europe. He fought in the battle of Camperdown, the battle of Copenhagen, and was engaged in the mutiny at the Nore. The dreadful scenes of immorality he witnessed on board ship and in seaports impelled him after his conversion to devote his life as a missionary to sailors and soldiers; and with a constancy, a persistency, and a self-denial quite heroic, he spent nearly sixty years of his life in that toilsome work, night and day often, and every day. In 1804 he began his labors at Plymouth, in 1807 was ordained to the ministry at Devonport, and in 1809 established the first Sailor's Gospel Mission at Mountbay. The work was blessed by God with the conversion of sailors, and he began to itinerate to all the British seaports, preaching everywhere, and supporting himself by holding his hat for gifts after he had preached. In 1810 Rev. Dr. John Rippon aided Mr. Smith to establish a Sailor's Mission for London, at his chapel, Carter Lane, by the river Thames. He wrote and published a dialogue in the sailor's dialect, and also the immensely popular story of *The Cabin-boy, Bob*. In 1814 he joined the duke of Wellington's army in the Spanish Peninsula as soldiers' missionary. In 1817 he resumed his labors among the sailors, and established the first Floating Chapel and the Bethel Union Society. He also commenced, and edited to the month of his death, *The Soldier's and Sailor's Magazine*, containing for over forty years some of the most remarkable experiences ever put into print, but it was so genuine and honest, though rough and illiterate, that it led the way for the lords of the admiralty to make many changes and improvements in the navy and in the conduct of ships. He established sailor's homes and seamen's friend societies; he benevolently took charge of numerous orphan children of sailors and soldiers; they travelled with him, he preached for them, mostly in the open air, daily—and the boys with their caps collected what was the means of their support for many years. He died at Penzance, Cornwall, Jan. 10, 1862.

Smith, Gervase, D.D., an English Wesleyan minister, was born at Langley, Derbyshire, June 27, 1821. In his youth he received a liberal education, and early began, as a local preacher, to invite sinners to repentance. He was accepted as a candidate for the ministry in 1842, and spent three years in study at Didsbury, receiving his first appointment in 1845. His preaching was eminently evangelical, and very attractive from the beginning of his career. He also had a special adaptability to the presentation of the various benevolent enterprises of the Church. In 1873 he was elected secretary of the conference, and two years later its president. In 1874 he was appointed British representative to the first General Conference of the Methodist Church in Canada; and in 1877 to the Australasian Conference, with instructions to visit the districts in Polynesia formerly under the care of the Wesleyan Missionary Society. For nearly twelve years he was secretary of the Metropolitan Chapel Building Fund; and in 1880 became treasurer of the Auxiliary Fund. He died April 22, 1882. See *Minutes of the British Conference*, 1882, p. 26.

Smith, Henry Augustus, D.D., a Presbyterian minister, was born at Palatine, Montgomery Co., N. Y., May 28, 1828. He graduated from Williams College in 1853 and from Union Theological Seminary in 1856; was ordained pastor of the South Street Church, Philadelphia, in 1858; resigned this charge in 1864 to become pastor of the Northminster Church, West Philadelphia, where he continued eighteen years, until ill-health compelled him to relinquish his work. He died there, March 7, 1883. Dr. Smith was an able, scholarly, eloquent divine, and his labors were attended with success. (W. P. S.)

Smith, James, D.D., a Presbyterian minister, was born in Glasgow, Scotland. He became a deist from reading the works of Volney and Paine, came to America, settled in Tennessee, and edited a paper in Nashville. Soon, however, he was converted, and began to preach. In the winter of 1839, while upon a visit to Columbus, Miss., the home of Olmstead, author of the work, *The Bible its Own Refutation*, he was challenged to a public debate on the evidences of Christianity, and achieved a great victory. He afterwards compiled his argument, and published it in a book entitled *Christian Evidences*. Dr. Smith was connected with the Cumberland Presbyterian Church in Kentucky, but was thoroughly Calvinistic in his theology. The Springfield Church, in Illinois, of which he became pastor, April 11, 1849, prospered under his ministry. He was dismissed Dec. 17, 1856; acted for two or three years as agent for Peoria University, and, on Mr. Lincoln's accession to the presidency, was appointed consul to Glasgow. There he spent the closing years of his life, and died at Dundee, but the date does not appear. See *Hist. of the Presbyterian Church in Illinois*, p. 398.

Smith, J. Brinton, D.D., a Protestant Episcopal clergyman, was rector at Kingsessing, Pa., several years preceding 1856. In 1859 he became rector at Troy, N. Y., whence he removed to Jersey City, N. J., as rector of St. Matthew's Church; in 1866 removed to New York city; in 1867 was elected principal of St. Augustine Normal School and Collegiate Institute, at Raleigh, N. C., and held this position until his sudden death, Oct. 1, 1872. See *Prot. Episc. Almanac*, 1873, p. 134.

Smith, John, an English Wesleyan minister, styled "the revivalist," was born at Cudworth, near Barnsley, Yorkshire, Jan. 12, 1794. Although trained religiously, he became profane, a gambler, and a pugilist. He was converted in 1812, and entered an academy at Leeds, where he enjoyed the instruction of David Stoner. He was received into the ministry in 1816, and labored on the York, Barnard Castle, Brighton, Windsor, Frome, Nottingham, Preston, Lincoln, and Sheffield Circuits. Like William Carvosso and Bramwell, he was a man of intense zeal and mighty faith. On his circuits the whole vicinity was stirred, the worst men were smitten, and hundreds were added to the Church. His chapels were crowded, and his prayer-meetings were like the day of Pentecost. But his work wore him out, and in Sheffield, his last circuit, he died in his prime, Nov. 3, 1831. See Treffrey, *Memoirs of Rev. John Smith* (Lond. 1832, 12mo; 2d ed. with introduction by Dr. Dixon); Stevens, *Hist. of Methodism*, iii, 285 sq., 468; Smith, *Hist. of Wesleyan Methodism*, iii, 33, 153, 154; *Minutes of the British Conference*, 1832; West, *Sketches of Wesleyan Preachers*, p. 33 sq.

Smith, John Cotton, D.D., an eminent Protestant Episcopal clergyman, son of Dr. Thomas M., of Kenyon College, grandson of Dr. Leonard Wood, and a descendant of Cotton Mather, was born at Andover, Mass., Aug. 4, 1826. He studied at Phillips Academy, graduated from Bowdoin College in 1847, and from the Theological Seminary at Gambier, O.; was ordained deacon in 1849, presbyter in 1850, and the latter year became rector of St. John's Church, Bangor, Me.; in 1856 was assistant minister at Trinity Church, Boston, Mass., and in 1860 rector of the Church of the Ascension, New York city, where he died, Jan. 9, 1882. Dr. Smith was a man of great literary acquirements, and of broad and liberal ideas in religion, without, however, overstepping the pale of the orthodoxy of the creed to which he belonged. He was remarkable not only for his pulpit eloquence, but as an after-dinner speaker. He was a prominent member of the University Club, and of other social and religious associations of the day. The Ascension Church Mission was one of his noblest charitable conceptions, to elevate the tenement-house population, and has been very successful. He was the author of a number of works upon theological and social subjects, among which are, *The Charity of Truth:—The Liturgy as a Basis of Union:—The Church's Law of Development:—The Oxford Essays and Reviews:—The Homeric Age:—The Principle of Patriotism:—The United States a Nation:—Evolution and a Personal Creator.* He was also the editor of *Church and State*, an Episcopal journal of high standing. His published works have all been collected in two volumes.

Smith, Thomas Mather, D.D., a Protestant Episcopal clergyman, was born at Stamford, Conn., in 1797. He was a son of Rev. Daniel Smith, who, for fifty years, was pastor of the Congregational Church at Stamford, and a descendant of the Cottons and Mathers of Puritan fame. Thomas graduated from Yale College in 1816, spent the following year in study with his uncle, John Cotton Smith, governor of Connecticut, and graduated from Andover Theological Seminary in 1820. In 1822 he was ordained minister of the Congregational Church at Portland, Me., but, his health failing, he removed to Fall River, Mass.; was next pastor at Catskill, N. Y., and subsequently at New Bedford, Mass. During this period his views of the ministry underwent a change, and he was ordained in the Protestant Episcopal Church. Soon after he was appointed to the Milnor professorship of systematic divinity in the Theological Seminary at Gambier, O. He combined with the duties of his professorship the presidency of Kenyon College during four years. In 1863 he resigned his professorship at Gambier, receiving the appointment of emeritus professor. He died at Portland, Me., Sept. 6, 1864. See *Amer. Quar. Church Rev.* Oct. 1864, p. 484.

Smyth, ARTHUR, D.D., an Irish prelate, was dean of Derry, and in March, 1752, was promoted to the united bishoprics of Clonfert and Kilmacduagh. In 1753 he was translated to the sees of Down and Connor, and in October, 1765, to that of Meath. On April 4, 1766, he was promoted to the archbishopric of Dublin. He died at St. Sepulchre, Dec. 14, 1771. Bishop Smyth amassed property to the amount of £50,000, of which he bequeathed £1000 to augment the funds of Swift's Hospital, £200 to the poor of St. Sepulchre's, and £50 to those of the parish of Tullagh. See D'Alton, *Memoirs of the Archbishops of Dublin*, p. 343.

Society Islands, DEITIES OF. The accompanying figures, colossal busts, from fifteen to twenty feet high and from six to seven feet wide, are representa-

Idols of the Society Islands.

tions of the pagan deities originally found on these islands. They are of stone, and sometimes separate, sometimes grouped, and represent gods or deified progenitors.

Sola, ABRAHAM DE. See DE SOLA.

Solitarius, PHILIP, a Greek monk, who lived in the latter part of the 11th century, in Constantinople, is the author of a mystico-ascetical work, written in the form of a dialogue, and entitled Δίοπτρα, *The Mirror.* It is a representation of the ascetic views of the Greek mysticism of the time. The work found favor, was commentated by Michael Psellus, and translated into Latin prose by the Jesuit Jacob Pontanus (Ingolstadt, 1604). The Latin translation was republished in the *Biblioth. Patr. Colon.* tom. xii, and in the *Biblioth. Patrum Max. Lugdun.* tom. xxi. The Latin translation, however, is, according to Lambecius, very deficient. Of the Greek text only a few fragments have been printed by Oudin, Lambecius, and Cotelerius. See Cave, *De Scriptor. Eccles.* p. 638; Plitt-Herzog, *Real-Encyklop.* s. v. (B. P.)

Somaj. See BRAHMA-SOMAJ.

Sommers, CHARLES G., D.D., a Baptist clergyman and author, was born in London in 1793. His parents removed to America in 1802, and in his early manhood he was employed as the confidential clerk and travelling agent of John Jacob Astor. Having prepared himself for the sacred office, he commenced his labors as preacher at the old almshouse in City Hall Park, New York city. His first regular settlement was with the First Baptist Church of Troy, where he remained several years, and in 1823 received an invitation to become the pastor of the South Baptist Church, New York city. In 1856 he retired to private life. He died in New York, Dec. 19, 1868. Dr. Sommers, at different periods of his life, was called to fill prominent positions in several religious organizations. (J. C. S.)

Sonntag, KARL GOTTLOB, a Lutheran theologian of Germany, was born Aug. 21, 1758. He studied at Leipsic, was in 1787 rector at the cathedral-school at Riga, in 1791 first pastor there, and in 1799 assessor of the Livese consistory. In 1803 he was general superintendent and president of the superior consistory, and died July 17, 1827. He published, *Diss. de Jesu Siracide, Ecclesiastico non Libro, sed Libri Faragine* (Riga, 1792), besides a number of ascetical, liturgical, and homiletical works. See Döring, *Die gelehrten Kanzelredner*, p. 457-462; Winer, *Handbuch der theol. Lit.* i, 835; ii, 92, 164, 167, 173, 177, 296, 328, 370. (B. P.)

Sorek. The village by this name mentioned in the *Onomasticon* is probably represented by the present ruined site *Khurbet Surêk*, lying one and a half miles north of Wady Surar, and the same distance west of Surah (Zorah). It contains "traces of a ruined village, springs, with a rock-cut wine-press and cave to the west, and a sacred tree" (*Memoirs* to the Ordnance Survey, iii, 126).

Sorin, Matthew, D.D., a Methodist Episcopal minister, was born in Philadelphia, Pa., Sept. 7, 1801, of Roman Catholic parents. His father died when Matthew was about nine years of age, and the latter was apprenticed to a paper-maker, whose family, though Protestants, were bitter enemies of the Methodists. He procured a New Test., read it secretly, and began its memorization. He joined the Methodist Episcopal Church in 1817: received license to preach in his early manhood; and in 1823 entered the Philadelphia Conference. He labored on Dauphin Circuit in that year; in Somerset, Md., in 1824; on the shores of the Chesapeake in 1825 and 1826; travelled Snow Hill Circuit in 1827; Salisbury Circuit and Accomac, Va., in 1829 and 1830; became discouraged, and located in 1831 at Drummondtown; started with his wife for the far West in 1832, but was overtaken and induced to return as senior preacher on Snow Hill Circuit, where, early in 1833, he was blessed with a great revival. That year he re-entered the effective ranks of the Philadelphia Conference, and was made presiding elder of the Chesapeake District. In 1836 he was stationed at Asbury, Wilmington, Del., then at Union Church, Philadelphia, Pa.; in 1839 at Ebenezer Church, same city; a failure of his nervous system rendering his supernumeration necessary, he tried book-publishing at Philadelphia between 1842 and 1848; then moved West, within the bounds of the Rock River Conference, and practiced medicine; removed to St. Paul, Minn., in 1852, and to Red Wing in 1853, where he took charge of the mission. His health being somewhat restored, he was transferred to the Missouri and Arkansas Conference in 1865, and appointed presiding elder of St. Louis District; in 1869 of Kansas City District; in 1873 and 1874 was stationed at Austin, Mo.; in 1875 at Rolla; in 1876, at the request of the Philadelphia Conference, he was retransferred to its active ranks, and stationed at Marcus Hook, Pa.; in 1877 was appointed to Bustleton; and in 1878 to Oxford, Chester Co., where he closed his active labors, took a superannuated relation, and spent the remainder of his days travelling in the far West. He died suddenly, in Pueblo, Col., Aug. 11, 1879. By his own energies and perseverance, Dr. Sorin became an able scholar in history, general literature, and theology. He was an intellectual and physical giant, one of the most powerful preachers of his day. See *Minutes of Annual Conferences*, 1880, p. 27; Simpson, *Cyclop. of Methodism*, s. v.

Souché, Pierre, a Protestant theologian of France, was born in 1804. After having finished his studies at Montauban and Strasburg in 1827, he assisted the Rev. Gibaud, at Rouillé, Vienne. In 1829 Souché was elected pastor of the Church at Rouillé, and retired from the ministry in 1871. In acknowledgment of the great services which he rendered to the Church, he was made honorary president of the consistory, and died Jan. 25, 1878, highly respected and honored by both Protestants and Roman Catholics. See Lichtenberger, *Encyclop. des Sciences Religieuses*, s. v. (B. P.)

Spackman, Henry S., D.D., a Protestant Episcopal clergyman, was assistant minister of the Church at Francisville, Pa., in 1853, served in the same relation to St. Clement's Church, Philadelphia, in the following year, and afterwards as its rector until 1864, when he was appointed chaplain in the United States Hospital, Chestnut Hill, same city. In 1866 he became rector of Trinity Church, Williamsport, and continued in this pastorate until 1868, when he was elected chaplain of the Episcopal Hospital, Philadelphia. This situation he retained until his death, Feb. 9, 1875, aged sixty-four years. See *Prot. Episc. Almanac*, 1876, p. 149.

Spalding, Martin John, D.D., an eminent Roman Catholic prelate and author, was born near Lebanon, Ky., May 23, 1810, being descended from the Catholic settlers of Maryland. He graduated from St. Mary's Seminary, Marion County, in 1826, and in theology from St. Joseph's Seminary, Bardstown, after four years' study. In 1830 he went to Rome, and after four years in the Urban College of the Propaganda, publicly defended, for seven hours, in Latin, two hundred and fifty-six propositions in theology, was rewarded with the doctor's diploma, and ordained priest by cardinal Pediana. He was now made pastor of St. Joseph's Church, Bardstown, afterwards president of St. Joseph's College, and again pastor of St. Joseph's. In 1843 he was called to the cathedral of Louisville, where he served five years. He was one of the most zealous missionaries of his time in Kentucky. In 1848 he was consecrated bishop of Lengone *in partibus*, and coadjutor to bishop Flaget, of Louisville. In 1864, on the death of archbishop Kenrick of Baltimore, Dr. Spalding was installed seventh archbishop of Baltimore. He labored assiduously in his office. New churches were erected, schools founded, and noble charities endowed. He convened the Second Plenary Council of Baltimore, over which he presided. He attended the Œcumenical Council of the Vatican at Rome in 1869 and 1870, where he was distinguished by his labors and zeal. With the other American bishops, he favored the dogma of papal infallibility as there defined. His last years were as laborious as his early priesthood. "His amiability, simplicity of character, love of his people, and especially of children, his devotion to the faith and to his duties, have placed his name high among the illustrious prelates" of the American Roman episcopacy. He died in Baltimore, Feb. 7, 1872. Dr. Spalding was a distinguished controversialist and literary reviewer. He was one of the editors of the *United States Catholic Magazine*. His principal works were, *Sketches of the Early Catholic Missions of Kentucky* (1844):—*Hist. of the Prot. Reformation in Europe* (Louisville, 1860, 2 vols.; 4th ed. Baltimore, 1866), being an enlarged ed. of his *Review of D'Aubigne, Ranke*, etc. (1844), which was republished in London and Dublin (1846):—*Lectures on the Evidences of Catholicity* (1847, 4th ed. Baltimore, 1866, 8vo):—*Life and Times of Bishop B. J. Flaget* (Louisville, 1852, 8vo):—*Lectures and Essays: Miscellanea* (Lond., Baltimore, and Louisville, 1855; 4th ed. 1866, 8vo, edited, with introduction and notes, by Abbé and Darras):—*Gen. Hist. of the Catholic Church* (N. Y. 1865-66, 4 vols. 8vo). His works are published in 5 vols. 8vo, by Murphy, Baltimore. See (N. Y.) *Cath. Almanac*, 1873, p. 35, DeCourcey and Shea, *Hist. of the Cath. Church in the United States*, p. 178 sq., Rev. J. L. Spalding, *Life of the Most Rev. M. J. Spalding, D.D.* (N. Y. 1873, 8vo).

Spangenberg, Johann, a Lutheran theologian of Germany, father of Cyriacus (q. v.), was born March 30, 1484, at Hardegsen, near Göttingen. He studied at Erfurt, joined the Lutheran reformation, was in 1521 archdeacon, in 1524 first evangelical preacher at Nordhausen, in 1546 at Eisleben, and died June 13, 1550. He published sermons, hymns, and ascetical writings. See Koch, *Geschichte des deutschen Kirchenliedes*, i, 372 sq.; Beste, *Kanzelredner*, i, 140; Plitt-Herzog, *Real-Encyklop.* s. v. (B. P.)

Sparke, Bowyer Edward, S.T.P., an English prelate, was born about 1759. He was a fellow of Pembroke College, Cambridge, official visitor of Peterhouse, St. John's, and Jesus colleges, and visitor to the master of Trinity College in that university. In 1809 he was consecrated bishop of the diocese of Chester, and in 1812 translated to that of Ely, which he held till his death, April 4, 1836. See *The* (Lond.) *Christian Remembrancer*, May, 1836, p. 314.

Spectacular View of the Atonement is an expression fitly applied to that doctrine of the person of Christ which represents his crucifixion as a mere semblance of suffering intended to impress beholders with his martyr-like sympathy in behalf of mankind, rather than as a veritable death for human sin. The divine nature is thus so far severed from the dying victim as to eliminate its vicarious virtue. The whole scene becomes a human transaction. Jesus is reduced to the level of a moral and religious reformer, who seals his career and attests his sincerity with his blood. The inadequacy of this as a satisfaction to God's law, and an equivalent for man's punishment, is obvious. It is but the old heresy of Docetism revived in a specious Unitarian form. That the sacrifice upon the cross was designed to have a powerful moral influence upon all who should become acquainted with it is certainly true, and, in our opinion, this affords the inner solution of the profound question why that mode of expiation was adopted; but this is a very different position from the above, for it is postulated upon the *bona-fide* union of the two natures in the atoning victim. See ATONEMENT.

Spence, James, D.D., an English Congregational divine, was born at Huntley, Scotland, April 6, 1811. He graduated at King's College, Aberdeen, accepted a call to the Congregational Church, Oxford, in 1848 removed to Preston, and in 1852 settled at Poultry Chapel, London. In 1865 he visited Egypt and the Holy Land. In 1868 Dr. Spence was appointed to the editorship of the *Evangelical Magazine*, and the functions of this office he was able to discharge till his death, Feb. 28, 1876. He published the *Pastor's Prayer for the People's Weal:—Scenes in the Life of St. Peter:—Martha Dryland; or, Strength in Quietness:—Sunday Mornings with my Flock on St. Paul's Letter to the Colossians:—The Martyr Spirit:—The Religion of Mankind: Christianity Adapted to Man in all the Aspects of his Being.* See (Lond.) *Cong. Year-book*, 1877, p. 414.

Spence, Thomas, a Scotch prelate, was bishop of Galloway in 1451, and was employed in several embassies, particularly in the treaty of marriage between the duke of Savoy and Lewis, count de Maurienne, with Arabella, in 1449. In 1451 he was appointed by king James II one of his ambassadors to negotiate a truce with England, and was made keeper of the privy seal in 1458. In 1459 he was translated to the see of Aberdeen. He died April 15, 1480. He erected a hospital at Edinburgh. See Keith, *Scottish Bishops*, p. 114, 275.

Spencer, GEORGE TREVOR, D.D., a missionary of the Church of England, was born in 1800. He graduated at University College, Oxford, in 1822; the same year was nominated incumbent of Buxton, Derbyshire, but resigned this position in 1829, when he was presented to the rectory of Leaden Roding, near Chipping Ongar. In 1837 he was nominated as bishop of Madras, but in 1849 returned to England. In 1860 he became rector of Walton-in-the-Wolds, and the same year chancellor of St. Paul's Cathedral. He died at Edgemoor, Buxton, England, July 18, 1866. See *Amer. Quar. Church Rev.* Oct. 1866, p. 493.

Sperbach, KARL GOTTLIEB, a Lutheran theologian of Germany, was born at Königsbrück, Upper Lusatia, Feb. 26, 1694. He studied at Leipsic, and commenced his academical career there in 1717. In 1734 he accepted a call to Wittenberg, and died July 6, 1772. He published, *Causa Philosophiæ adversus Atheismi Calumnia Defensa* (Leipsic, 1730):—*Diss. qua Versio Syriaca 2 Epist. Johannis cum Textu Græco Confertur* (Wittenberg, 1735):—*Observationes Philologicæ in Nonnulla Pentateuchi Loca* (1756):—*De Vario Accentuum Hebræorum Officio* (1738):—*De Genio Linguæ Hebraicæ* (eod.):—*Academia Jabhnensis atque ejus Rectores* (1740):—*De Judæis* תלואים *ad Hos. xi*, 7 (1747):—*De Voce Jehovah* (1755). See Döring, *Die gelehrten Theologen Deutschlands*, s. v.; Fürst, *Bibl. Jud.* s. v. (B. P.)

Spieker, JOHANNES, a Protestant theologian of Germany, was born March 26, 1756, at Wolfshagen, in Lower Hesse. He studied at Marburg, was in 1776 preacher at Rauschenberg, near Marburg, in 1800 preacher at Hersfeld, and in 1818 director of the theological seminary at Herborn. Spieker died April 18, 1825. He published, besides some catechetical and homiletical works, *Ueber den Mysticismus, dessen Begriff, Ursprung und Werth* (Herborn, 1825). See Döring, *Die deutschen Kanzelredner*, p. 472 sq.; Winer, *Handbuch der theol. Lit.* i, 365, 430; ii, 73, 103, 148. (B. P.)

Spotiswood, JOHN, a Scotch prelate, was born in 1565, became minister of Calder, in Mid-Lothian, in 1586, and in 1602 was chosen to accompany the duke of Lennox, as his grace's chaplain, in his embassy to France; consecrated bishop of Glasgow Oct. 21, 1610; in 1615 translated to the see of St. Andrews, and made chancellor of Scotland, Jan. 14, 1635. He was excommunicated by the rebellious Assembly at Glasgow, and died in London, Nov. 26, 1639. See Keith, *Scottish Bishops*, p. 41, 263.

Sprague, NATHANIEL, D.D., a Protestant Episcopal minister, was born in Cheshire County, N. H., Aug. 20, 1790. At the age of seventeen he entered Dartmouth College, where he remained only two years, but continued his studies privately; spent several years as an instructor in Oneida County, N. Y.; was professor in Royalton Academy, Vt., and began the study of law at that place. He had belonged successively to the Presbyterian and Congregational churches; having joined the Protestant Episcopal communion, he was ordained deacon in 1838, and shortly after became a presbyter, and ministered at Royalton, and afterwards, from 1844, at Drewsville, N. H. An unfortunate habit of stuttering was entirely overcome at the age of thirty-six. He died at Claremont, N. H., Oct. 29, 1853. See *Amer. Quar. Church Rev.* 1854, p. 626.

Sprole, WILLIAM THOMAS, D.D., a Presbyterian minister, was born at Baltimore, Md., March 16, 1809. He studied privately, and spent a year and a half (1827-28) at Princeton Theological Seminary, was licensed in 1829, ordained an evangelist the same year, and became pastor of the First General Reformed Church of Philadelphia in 1832; stated supply of the First Presbyterian Church at Carlisle, Pa., in 1837; pastor of the First Presbyterian Church at Washington, D. C., in 1843, and for five years acted as chaplain of the House of Representatives. In 1847 he received the appointment of chaplain and professor of ethics in the Military Academy at West Point, but resigned in 1856 to accept a call to the First Presbyterian Church at Newburgh, N. Y., from which he was released in 1872. In 1874 he removed to Detroit, Mich., and became pastor of Woodworth Avenue Church, a charge which he resigned in 1877. He died at Detroit, June 9, 1883. See *Necrol. Report of Princeton Theol. Sem.* 1884, p. 12. (W. P. S.)

Spurden, CHARLES, D.D., a Baptist minister, was born in London, England, May 25, 1812. In his twenty-fifth year he entered the Bristol Baptist College. On May 13, 1841, he was ordained pastor of the Baptist Church at Hereford, where he continued until the latter part of 1842, and then, in answer to application from the committee of the Baptist Education Society of New Brunswick, Canada, was sent out to take charge of the Seminary at Fredericton. In 1867 he resigned this position. He was one of the examiners of the University of New Brunswick and of the Provincial Training School until his death, Jan. 13, 1876. Dr. Spurden was a man of literary attainments, prudent, wise, modest, and a devoted Christian. See (Canada) *Baptist Yearbook*, 1876, p. 34; Bill, *Hist. of Baptists in Maritime Provinces* (index).

Stafford, John (1), archbishop of Canterbury, was born at Hook, near Beaminster, England, and educated at Oxford. On Sept. 9, 1419, he became archdeacon of Salisbury, of which diocese he was chancellor in 1421. In 1422 he became dean of St. Martin's, in London, and Sept. 9, 1423, was installed dean of Wells. As a lawyer Stafford soon attracted the attention of archbishop Chicheley, who appointed him his vicar-general, and advanced him to the deanship of the Court of Arches. In May, 1421, he was keeper of the privy seal, and was subsequently appointed lord high-treasurer of England. He was consecrated bishop of Bath and Wells at Blackfriars, London, May 27, 1425. As keeper of the privy seal he accompanied Henry VI to Paris in 1430, to receive the crown of France. On his return he was appointed lord chancellor, an office which he held eighteen years. On May 13, 1443, Stafford was translated to the see of Canterbury. He continued to hold the great seal, and to take an active part in the politics of his party. He was zealous in promoting the marriage of Henry VI with Margaret of Anjou, and officiated at the ceremony, April 22, 1445. John Stafford died at his manor of Maidstone, May 25, 1452. See Hook, *Lives of the Archbishops of Canterbury*, v, 130 sq.

Stafford, John (2), D.D., an English Independent minister, was born at Leicester in August, 1728. He was brought up a wool-comber, but devoting himself to the ministry, studied, first under Dr. Doddridge, at Northampton, then in London, and finally at Mile End, and joined the church of Dr. Guyse, in New Broad Street. He was sent to preach at Royston and St. Neots, but in 1758 accepted a call as pastor in succession to Dr. Guyse, at New Broad Street, and for nearly forty years continued the pastor of that important church. He lived in a constantly prepared state for death, even in full health, and in that spirit died, Feb. 22, 1800. He published, *The Scripture Doctrine of Sin and Grace Considered in Twenty-five Discourses* (1772), which reached a second edition, and a *Funeral Sermon* for his daughter Elizabeth (1774). See Wilson, *Dissenting Churches*, ii, 243.

Stahl, Friedrich Julius, a famous jurist of Germany, was born at Munich, of Jewish parentage, Jan. 16, 1802. At the age of seventeen he embraced Christianity, and though he was entitled at that time to a professorship at the gymnasium, he betook himself to the study of jurisprudence, and was in 1829 made doctor of law. In 1827 Stahl commenced his academical career at Munich, was called in 1832 to Erlangen, and in 1840 to Berlin. Here he gathered crowded audiences, not only of juridical students, but at times, also, of educated people in general, as, for instance, in 1850, when he lectured on *The Present Party Position in Church and State* (which lectures were published after his death, Berlin, 1863). He also held the highest positions in the state government of the Church, and took a very active part in Prussian politics. His brilliant parliamentary talent soon made him one of the most prominent leaders of the conservative party, both in political and ecclesiastical affairs. Democracy and freethinking he understood, and was not afraid of; but he hated liberalism and rationalism. The former is revolution, he said; but the latter is dissolution. Stahl died Aug. 10, 1861. In his *Philosophie des Rechts* (1830-37; 3d ed. 1854) he tried to show that philosophy is not the last end of God, but that God is the last end of philosophy. He called science to "repentance," and thus caused a great stir both among jurists and philosophers. To understand Stahl's greatness and influence one must study his *Kirchenverfassung nach Lehre und Recht der Protestanten* (2d ed. Erlangen, 1862):—*Ueber Kirchenzucht* (Berlin, 1845):—*Der christliche Staat und sein Verhältniss zu Deismus und Judenthum* (1847):—*Was ist Revolution?* (1852):—*Der Protestantismus als politisches Princip* (4th ed. 1853):—*Die katholischen Widerlegungen* (1854):—*Ueber christliche Toleranz* (1855):—*Wider Bunsen* (3d ed. 1856):—*Die lutherische Kirche und die Union* (1860). Stahl was very intimately connected with professor Hengstenberg, and, like the latter, an able advocate of high Lutheran orthodoxy. See Plitt-Herzog, *Real-Encyklop.* s. v.; Lichtenberger, *Encyclop. des Sciences Religieuses*, s. v.; Groen van Prinsterer, *Ter Nagedachtenis van Stahl*, and especially Schwarz, *Zur Geschichte der neuesten Theologie* (4th ed. Leipsic, 1869), p. 240 sq. (B. P.)

Stamp, William Wood, D.D., a Wesleyan Methodist divine, was born at Bradford, Yorkshire, England, May 23, 1801, and educated at Woodhouse Grove School. He was converted in early manhood, during his residence in London as a medical student, entered the ministry in 1823, was governor of Richmond Theological Institution from 1846 to 1848, chairman of important districts, president of the Conference in 1860, became supernumerary in 1873, and died at Waterloo, Liverpool, Jan. 1, 1877. Dr. Stamp had studied the history and polity of Methodism with thoroughness and discrimination, and in its welfare he took persistent interest. During his long tenure of office as chairman he won the confidence, esteem, and admiration of ministers and laymen, by his intelligence, firmness, and urbanity. During the closing years of his life, his experience and judgment made his services in settling questions of discipline in much request. His fidelity as a friend and counsellor was unfailing. He was the author of, *Memoir of Rev. John Crosse, M.A., Vicar of Bradford, Yorkshire* (Lond. 1844, 8vo):—*Domestic Worship: a Sermon* (ibid. 1846, 8vo):—*Historical Notices of Wesleyan Methodism in Bradford and Vicinity* (without date, 12mo):—*The Orphan House of Wesley, with Notices of Early Methodism in Newcastle-upon-Tyne and its Vicinity* (1863, 8vo). For some years, and until the issue for 1878, he was editor of the (Lond.) *Wesleyan Methodist Connectional Record and Year-book*. See *Minutes of the British Conference*, 1877, p. 24; *Wesleyan Methodist Connectional Record and Year-book*, 1878, p. 136; Osborne, *Wesleyan Bibliography*, p. 177.

Stanley, Arthur Penrhyn, D.D., LL.D., an eminent Anglican divine, son of bishop Edward Stanley, and nephew of the first baron Stanley of Alderley, was born at Alderley, Cheshire, Dec. 13, 1815. At the age of fourteen years he entered the Rugby School, and remained there five years. During this time he was a favorite student and enjoyed the especial friendship of Dr. Arnold—a fact which may, without doubt, be assumed to have had close connection with the broadness and liberality of his thought and doctrines as a churchman. In 1834, having won a scholarship in Balliol College, Oxford, young Stanley there entered upon a career that formed a fitting continuation of his brilliant student-life at Rugby. He won, in 1837, the Newdigate prize for his English poem, *The Gypsies*, the Ireland scholarship, gained the first class in classics, and became a fellow of University College. Two years later he received the Latin essay prize, and in 1840 the English essay prize and theological prizes. After his graduation, in 1838, he became for twelve years a tutor in University College. On taking orders in the Church of England he naturally affiliated himself with the "Broad Church" party, although the opposite sentiment prevailed at Oxford. In 1851 and 1852 he was secretary to the University Commission, and in 1858 became regius professor of ecclesiastical history at Oxford and canon of Christ Church College. In 1872 he was a second time chosen select preacher to the University, and on March 31, 1875, was installed lord rector of the University of St. Andrew's. Early attracting attention as a pulpit orator, he was made, in 1854, chaplain to prince Albert; in 1857 to Dr. Tait, bishop of London, and to the queen and prince of Wales in 1862. From 1851 to 1858 he was canon of Canterbury Cathedral. He declined the archbishopric of Dublin in 1863, and early in the following year was made dean of Westminster, a position which he occupied until his death, July 18, 1881. In 1852 and 1853 he made an extensive tour in the East, visiting Egypt, Arabia, and Palestine, and gathering there material for his work on those countries. In 1862 he again visited the East in company with the prince of Wales. In 1878 he visited America in search of health and rest, and was greeted everywhere not only with the respect his genius commanded, but with warm personal friendship. During his stay he addressed the students of the Union Theological Seminary in New York, and preached at Trinity and Grace churches. He also met a number of prominent Baptist preachers, and was given receptions by the Methodist Episcopal clergy and the Century Club. After his college poems and essays dean Stanley's first literary venture was the biography of his former master, Dr. Arnold, in 1846. In the following year he published a volume of *Sermons and Essays on the Apostolic Age*. He edited, in 1851, a volume of his father's addresses and pastoral charges, adding thereto an affectionate memoir. A series of his lectures delivered to the Young Men's Christian Association was published in 1854, and was followed the next year by *The Epistles of St. Paul to the Corinthians, with Notes and Dissertations*:—*Historical Memorials of Canterbury*, and a number of sermons. His well-known work on *Sinai and Palestine* was issued, with some minor volumes, in 1856:—*Lectures on the History of the Eastern Church* (1861):—*Lectures on the Jewish Church* (1862-76):—*Sermons Preached before the Prince of Wales during his Tour in the East, with Descriptions of Places Visited* (1863):—*Historical Memorials of Westminster Abbey* (1867):—*Lectures on the Church of Scotland* (1872). During these years he was the author, also, of numerous other volumes of essays, sermons, lectures, and disputations. He was a voluminous contributor to various reviews and periodicals, and furnished a valuable series of Biblical biographies to Dr. William Smith's *Dictionary of the Bible*. His sermon delivered at the funeral of Sir Charles Lyell in Westminster Abbey, Feb. 27, 1875, and since published, was notable for its hearty recognition of the services of that eminent geologist in having, as he believed, scientifically established the facts in regard to the creation of the earth and the human race. His latest literary work was performed as a member of the association for the revision of the Bible.

Stanley, James, D.D., brother of Thomas, earl of Derby, a native of Lancashire, England, was prebend of London in 1458, of York in 1460, of Durham in 1479, archdeacon of Richmond in 1500, precentor of Salisbury in 1505, and preferred bishop of Ely by Henry VII in 1506. He never resided at his own cathedral, but in the summer with his brother, the earl, and in the winter at his manor at Somersham, Huntingdonshire. He died March 22, 1515. See Fuller, *Worthies of England* (ed. Nuttall), ii, 195.

Stark, Christian Ludwig Wilhelm, a Lutheran theologian of Germany, was born Sept. 28, 1790, at Jena, where he also pursued his theological studies. In 1815 he commenced his academical career there, was in 1817 professor, and was drowned in the Saale, July 1, 1818. He published, *De Notione, quam Jesus Verbo ἔργα Tribuerit* (Jena, 1813):—*Paraphrasis in Evangelii Johannis xiii-xvii* (1814):—*Beiträge zur Vervollkommnung der Hermeneutik, insbesondere der des Neuen Testaments* (1818). See Döring, *Die gelehrten Theologen Deutschlands*, s. v.; Winer, *Handbuch der theol. Lit.* i, 107, 249, 395. (B. P.)

Staudt, Johannes Heinrich, a Lutheran theologian of Germany, who died at Kornthal, Nov. 11, 1884, is the author of, *Predigtsammlungen* (Stutgard, 1852, 1853, 1860):—*Fingerzeige in den Inhalt und Zusammenhang der heiligen Schrift* (2d ed. 1859):—*Erklärung des würtembergischen Konfirmationsbüchleins* (1853). See Zuchold, *Bibl. Theol.* s. v. (B. P.)

Steadman, W., D.D., an English Baptist minister, was born at Eardisland in 1764. He was early converted, and baptized in April, 1784. Three years afterwards he preached his first sermon, and was admitted Aug. 20, 1788, into Bristol Academy. He was ordained, Nov. 2, 1789, pastor in Broughton, Hampshire; in 1804 he became the assistant of Rev. Isaiah Birt, in Devonport; in 1806 pastor of a colony from that Church; and in 1808 removed to Horton, near Bradford, where for more than thirty years he was president and theological tutor in the Baptist College, as well as pastor. He died at his residence, Ashfield Place, near Bradford, April 12, 1837. See (Lond.) *Baptist Magazine*, 1837, p. 229. (J. C. S.)

Steane, Edward, D.D., an English Baptist minister, was born at Oxford, March 23, 1798. He studied privately at Oxford; in 1819 entered the academy at Bristol; and in 1821 went to Edinburgh to prosecute his studies still further. While at Oxford and Edinburgh his services were much in demand as a preacher. In 1823 he entered upon his first and only pastorate at Camberwell. Failing health and the death of his wife induced his retirement from the pastoral office in 1862. He removed to New House Park, near Rickmansworth, where he died, May 8, 1882. Dr. Steane was active and efficient in all the denominational enterprises, and instrumental in the organization of the Evangelical Alliance. He was one of the editors of the *New Baptist Miscellany*, and for some years editor of *Evangelical Christendom*. He published, besides numerous sermons, a volume entitled *The Doctrine of Christ, as Developed by the Apostles*, etc. (1872). See (Lond.) *Baptist Handbook*, 1883, p. 276.

Stearns, Shubael, a noted Baptist minister, was born in Boston, Mass., Jan. 28, 1706. He was converted under the preaching of Whitefield about 1740, and became connected with the Separatists in 1745. In 1751 he embraced the views of the Baptists, was immersed at Tolland, Conn., and on May 20, was ordained for the ministry. He labored in New England for two or three years, and then went South and preached for some time, first in the counties of Berkeley and Hampshire, Va., and then in Guilford County, N. C., where he made his permanent settlement. He died Nov. 20, 1771. His character was indisputably good as a man, as a Christian, and as a preacher. See Sprague, *Annals of the Amer. Pulpit*, vi, 60.

Steck, Daniel, D.D., a Lutheran minister, was born near Hughesville, Lycoming Co., Pa., Nov. 18, 1819. After pursuing a partial course in the college at Gettysburg, he graduated from the theological seminary; in 1846 was licensed; and in 1847 began preaching in English in the German Church at Pottsville, from which grew, in about one year, an English Lutheran Church. In 1858 he was called to St. John's Church, in Lancaster; and in 1862 became pastor of the Main Street Church, Dayton, O., remaining a little more than two years. Subsequently he organized St. John's Church, and became connected with the English Synod of Ohio. The congregation in Pottsville recalled him in 1868, and he served them the second time nearly two years. From 1870 to 1875 he preached in Middletown, Md., and then became pastor of St. James's Church, Gettysburg, Pa. He died there, June 10, 1881. See *Lutheran Observer*, July 1, 1881.

Stedman, James Owen, D.D., a Presbyterian minister, was born at Fayetteville, N. C., Oct. 31, 1811. He graduated from the University of North Carolina in 1832, and from Princeton Theological Seminary in 1836. He was licensed the same year, and became stated supply of the First Church of Baltimore, Md. After this he labored as a missionary in Waynesboro, N. C., for a time, and was ordained pastor of the church in Tuscumbia, Ala., in 1837. In 1845 he became stated supply of the church in Wilmington, N. C., but in 1851, his wife's health failing, he removed to Philadelphia, Pa. During 1852 and 1853 he supplied the First Church of Chester. He was next called to the First Presbyterian Church of Memphis, Tenn., in 1854; and in 1868 organized the Alabama Street Church, in the same city, which he served until 1880, when failing health obliged him to retire from active work. He died in Memphis, April 28, 1882. See *Necrol. Report of Princeton Theol. Sem.* 1883, p. 33.

Steele, John Lawrence, D.D., a Protestant Episcopal clergyman, was residing, in 1872, in Ottawa, Ill., where he became the rector of Christ Church. In 1874 he removed to Key West, Fla., as rector of St. Paul's Church, and continued there until his death, Oct. 13, 1878, at the age of thirty-six years. See *Prot. Episc. Almanac*, 1879, p. 170.

Steele, William, LL.D., a Presbyterian clergyman, was born and educated in Scotland, and began his ministry at Dyserf, in Ayrshire, where he preached for some years. He came to London in 1751, and became pastor at Founder's Hall. His health soon gave way, and he died before he had been a year in the metropolis, yet he was so much esteemed that the Church collected two hundred and fifty pounds for the benefit of his wife and children. See Wilson, *Dissenting Churches*, ii, 497.

Steere, Edward, LL.D., an English missionary prelate, was born in London in 1828. He graduated from the university of that city in 1847; was curate of Kingskerswell, Devonshire, from 1856 to 1858; next of Skegness, Lincolnshire; chaplain to bishop Tozer, in Central Africa, from 1862 to 1868; resigned his rectorship at Little Stepping, Lincolnshire, in 1872; was consecrated bishop of Central Africa at Westminster Abbey in 1874, and died at Zanzibar, Aug. 28, 1883. Besides being lawyer, preacher, and metaphysician, he was printer, master carpenter, and physician. He was the author of *A Sketch of Persecutions under the Roman Emperors*, and prepared an edition of *Bishop Butler's Works*, *A History of the Bible and Prayer-book*, and hymns and stories in the Shambella and Swabili languages.

Steffens, Heinrich, a German philosopher, was born at Stavanger, Norway, May 2, 1773. He was professor of natural sciences at Breslau and Berlin, but in 1831 he renounced his pantheistic errors, and published *Wie ich wieder Lutheraner wurde, und was mir das Lutherthum ist*. In the same year he published *Die falsche Theologie und der wahre, Glaube*, which was directed against the union of the Lutheran and Reformed churches, as inaugurated by king Frederick William III of Prussia. Steffens's main work is *Christliche Religionsphilosophie* (Breslau, 1839, 2 vols.). He died in 1845. See Lichtenberger, *Encyclop. des Sciences Religieuses*, s. v.; Steffens, *Was ich erlebte* (Breslau, 1840, 10 vols.).

Stelè, Sepulchral. These monumental slabs were generally placed at the bottom of the principal chamber of the tombs of the old dynasties of Egypt. They are square, and often of colossal proportions, with large hieroglyphics, sometimes in bas-relief, and spaced out. The representations are the façade of a building or tomb. At the time of the sixth dynasty they still have a degree of archaism. From the earliest period till the twelfth dynasty these tablets are dedicated to Anup, or Anubis, not Osiris, whose name is rarely found. Anubis is invoked as the god who presided over the funereal chapel and the embalming of the dead. The formula of dedication is short and elliptical, the usual expression "to give" is omitted, as also that of the gift; the name of Osiris is not found before that of the deceased, or the expression "justified" after the name. In the formula at this time a kind of abridgment of the calendar is often introduced, as a mention of the festivals of the beginning of the year, the new year, Thoth, that of the greater and lesser heat, the monthly and half-monthly. The numerous titles of the offices held by the deceased are given in detail. The tablets continued rude till the time of the eleventh dynasty, when the mention of the festival of the heliacal rising of Sothis, or the dog-star, is added. Under the twelfth dynasty the tablets change in shape and texts; most of them being rounded at the top, and forming the *hutu* of the texts. The upper part of the tablet has often the winged disk, the *Hut* or *Tebhut*. The dates of the years of the monarchs under whom the deceased was buried appear. The scenes represented are the acts of sepulchral homage or ancestral worship made by the children or other relatives of the dead to himself and his wife, the tables before them being loaded with offerings, among which appear the head and haunch of a calf, and other joints of the same animal, ducks or geese, circular or oval loaves or cakes of bread, gourds, onions, and papyrus or lotus flowers, while jars of wine or beer of conical shape are seen placed under the tables. The name of the god Anubis, which is so prominent in the tablets of Memphis, either disappears or becomes secondary to that of Osiris, and the dedication often contains the names of other deities, as the frog-headed goddess Haka, the ram-headed god Khuum, and others; but no god is represented on the tablets. The texts themselves also differ, as, in addition to the expressions of the fourth dynasty, the verb "to give," omitted at that time, as also the subject of the gift, is introduced into the text, the deceased is called "justified," but the name of Osiris does not precede his. His merits are often told in a verbose style, to which are sometimes added the public works in which he was engaged. The contents of these texts often contain curious historical and other information, throwing much light on the mythology and ethics of the Egyptians. Under the eighteenth dynasty the tablets changed again, and the scenes of ancestral or sepulchral worship became subordinate. The principal scene of the tablet, placed at the upper part, represents the deceased, sometimes attended by his wife, sister, son, or other member of the family, standing or kneeling in adoration to the solar boat, or deities, or Osiris, accompanied by Isis, Nephthys, Anubis, Horus, and other deities who presided over embalming and the future state, before whom is placed a table of altar offerings. A second division generally has the scenes of family worship, while in the accompanying text the adorations to the deities occupy the most important portion; and the merits of the deceased, or his public works, are only slightly mentioned. At the time of the nineteenth dynasty the name of Osiris appears first placed before the name of the deceased, while the title of "justified," or *makhem*, always follows. These tablets were in general use during the eighteenth and nineteenth dynasties, became rarer under the twentieth, exceedingly rare at the period of the twenty-sixth dynasty, and disappear after that time. They reappear, however, again under the Ptolemies, and besides the usual formula of dedication, often contain interesting notices relative to the functions and offices discharged by the deceased, and family details. They are at this period often accompanied by inscriptions in the cursive handwriting, the so-called Demotic, or Enchorial. Under the Romans the art and the inscriptions of the tablets again changed. The subjects are in bas-relief, and the deities represented in the hybrid types prevalent at the epoch. The inscriptions are in Greek, and follow the usual formulas used at that period; the older dedications to the gods being omitted, only the name of the deceased and date of his death being retained, a valedictory address being substituted. The Coptic sepulchral tablets, made after the introduction of Christianity into Egypt and at a late period, and those in Cufic, the tombstones of the Mohammedan conquerors of Egypt, follow also the forms of their respective nationalities, all trace of the old representations and formulas having been obliterated or superseded. See Birch, *Guide to the British Museum* (Vestibule).

Stem, Nathan, D.D., a Protestant Episcopal minister, was born in Chester County, Pa. While young he entered upon a mercantile life in Philadelphia; but, his attention having been called to the ministry, he entered the Alexandria Theological Seminary in 1824. On account of ill-health he left the seminary, and subsequently attended Kenyon College, O.; afterwards removed to Worthington, and pursued his studies under bishop Chase, by whom he was admitted to the diaconate in 1828 and to the eldership in 1829. His first parochial charge was in Delaware, O., where he labored several years; then accepted an invitation to St. Stephen's, Harrisburg, Pa.; in 1838 he was called to St. John's, Norristown, a parish which he served until his death, Nov. 1, 1854, at the age of fifty-four years. See *Amer. Quar. Church Rev.* 1860, p. 179.

Stemler, JOHANN CHRISTIAN, a Lutheran theologian of Germany, was born Oct. 12, 1701. He studied at Leipsic, was in 1728 rector at Sangerhausen, in 1730 at Naumburg, in 1739 superintendent at Torgau, in 1741 doctor of theology, in 1751 professor at Leipsic, and died March 29, 1773. He published, *De Criticæ Profanæ in Sacris Usu* (Leipsic, 1727):—*Conciliatio Pauli et Petri ad Rom. xiii, 2 et Petr. ii,* 13 (eod.):—*De Emphasi Vocis ἀναζωπυρεῖν ad 2 Tim. i,* 6 (1729):—*Nathanælis de Christo Confessio* (1755), etc. See Döring, *Die gelehrten Theologen Deutschlands,* s. v. (B. P.)

Stephen, a Scotch prelate, was bishop of the Isles in 1253, and in the same year confirmed to the monastery of Paisley all the churches and lands they held within his diocese. See Keith, *Scottish Bishops,* p. 300.

Stephen, WILLIAM, a Scotch prelate, was divinity reader in the University of St. Andrews, and was advanced to the see of Dunblane about 1422. He probably died in 1429. See Keith, *Scottish Bishops,* p. 177.

Stern, HENRY AARON, D.D., a minister of the Church of England, was born April 11, 1820, at Unterreichenbach, Hesse-Cassel, of Jewish parentage. In 1840 he embraced Christianity in London, England, and in 1844 the London Jews' Society sent him as a missionary to Bagdad, to labor there among the Jews. At Jerusalem, where he stopped on the journey, he was admitted into deacon's orders by the late bishop Alexander, the first Protestant bishop in the Holy City. In 1849 Stern left his station for England, and was admitted into priest's orders by the bishop of London. In 1850 he returned to Bagdad, a few years afterwards was removed to Constantinople, and from this centre he undertook missionary journeys to Asia Minor, Arabia Felix, and the Crimea. At the request of the London committee, he then proceeded in 1859 to Abyssinia, for the purpose of making known the gospel among the Falasha Jews. For eighteen months he labored there, when he was invited to visit England with a view of setting before his society the importance of laboring in Abyssinia. In 1862 Stern started on his second journey to that country. The events of that journey were eventually to form no unimportant episode in the history of England. The semi-barbarous king of Abyssinia had endeavored in vain to open diplomatic relations with England. The infuriated king imprisoned the helpless missionary who came to pay his respects. The other Europeans, including the British consul, shared in Mr. Stern's sufferings and imprisonment. This happened in October, 1863, and not till April 11, 1868, were the prisoners delivered. Having recovered from his many sufferings, Stern accepted in 1870 the charge of the Home Mission in London. He died May 13, 1885. (B. P.)

Steuber, JOHANN ENGELHARD, a Lutheran theologian of Germany, was born March 16, 1693, at Marburg. In 1716 he commenced his academical career at Jena, was in 1721 professor at Rinteln, and died Dec. 6, 1747. He published, *De Primogenitis,* etc. (Marburg, 1711):—*De Anno Jobelæo* (Rinteln, 1721):—*De Ligatione Festivorum ad Cornua Altaris* (1723):—*De Signo Filii Hominis ad Matt. xxiv,* 30 (eod.):—*De Mutuo Psalmorum Nexu* (1736):—*De Philosophia Platonico-Pythagorea* (1744). See Döring, *Die gelehrten Theologen Deutschlands,* s. v.; Fürst, *Bibl. Jud.* s. v.; Jöcher, *Allgemeines Gelehrten-Lexikon,* s. v. (B. P.)

Stevens, JOHN, D.D., a Baptist minister and educator, was born at Townsend, Mass., June 6, 1798. He graduated from Middlebury College, Vt., in 1821, had charge of the Montpelier Academy for one year, then entered Andover Theological Seminary, was converted, and in 1823 was baptized and united with the First Church in Salem, Mass. From 1825 to 1828 he was a tutor in Middlebury College, and then, for three years, classical teacher in South Reading (now Wakefield) Academy. From 1831 to 1838 he was editor of the Ohio *Baptist Weekly Journal,* and was then chosen professor of moral and intellectual philosophy in Granville College (now Denison University), a position which he occupied till 1843, when he accepted an appointment from the Missionary Union as district secretary for the states of Ohio and Indiana, and held this important office twelve years. In 1844 he was ordained in Cincinnati. In all educational matters affecting the welfare of the denomination he took great interest. For several years he was secretary of the Western Baptist Education Society; and was one of the early and warm friends of the theological institution established at Covington, Ky., and of the institution established at Fairmount, near Cincinnati. He was appointed professor of Greek and Latin in Denison University in 1859, and when a division was made in the two departments, he retained the chair of Latin until 1875; upon his resignation he was continued "emeritus" professor. He died in Granville, O., April 30, 1877. See Cathcart, *Baptist Encyclop.* p. 1103. (J. C. S.)

Stevenson, ANDREW, D.D., a Presbyterian minister, was born at Strabane, Ireland, in 1810. He came to America when a young man, and after passing through a literary and theological course, was ordained pastor of the Second Reformed Presbyterian Church in New York city. He remained pastor of this church until his health failed, and on his resignation was continued senior pastor until his death, June 29, 1881. (W. P. S.)

Stewart, Abel T., D.D., a Reformed (Dutch) minister, was born at Somerville, N. J., Aug. 4, 1822. He graduated from Rutgers College in 1843, from the New Brunswick Seminary in 1846; and in the same year was licensed by the Classis of New Brunswick; was pastor at Greenville from 1846 to 1850, and at Greenville and Bronxville from 1850 to 1852; First Church, Tarrytown, from 1852 to 1866, Holland, Mich., from 1866 to 1878, and died May 24, 1878, at Watkins, N. Y. See Corwin, *Manual of the Ref. Church in America* (3d ed.), p. 468.

Stewart, Alexander, a Scotch prelate, was first prior of Whitern and then abbot of Inchaffray. He was made bishop of Moray in 1527, and remained until 1538. See Keith, *Scottish Bishops,* p. 149.

Stewart, Andrew (1), a Scotch prelate, was subdean of Glasgow in 1456, and soon after rector of Monkland. In 1477 he was provost of Lincluden. He was elected dean of the faculty in the University of Glasgow, and was made bishop of Moray in 1482. He still held that office in 1492, and died in 1501. See Keith, *Scottish Bishops,* p. 146.

Stewart, Andrew (2), a Scotch prelate, was made bishop of Caithness in 1490. He died June 17, 1518. See Keith, *Scottish Bishops,* p. 214.

Stewart, *Hon.* **Charles James**, D.D., a Canadian prelate, was born April 13, 1775. He was educated at All-Souls' College, Oxford, England, of which he became a fellow; ordained, and presented to the rectory of Orton Longueville, Huntingdonshire, and in 1807 proceeded to Canada as a missionary. He first settled at St. Armand, thence removed to Halley, and on Jan. 1, 1826, was consecrated bishop of Quebec. He died July 13, 1837. Bishop Stewart was pre-eminently a good man, and a faithful and successful worker in his adopted field of labor. See *The Church of England Magazine,* July, 1838, p. 35.

Stewart, Charles Samuel, D.D., a Presbyterian minister, was born at Flemington, N. J., Oct. 16, 1798. He graduated from New Jersey College in 1815, and from Princeton Theological Seminary in 1819; was ordained Aug. 14, 1821; served as a missionary to the Sandwich Islands from 1822 to 1825, became chaplain in the United States navy in 1828, made his last cruise in 1862, and died at Cooperstown, N. Y., Dec. 14, 1870. He edited the *United States Naval Magazine* in 1836 and 1837, and published several interesting books of voyages and observations, for which see Allibone, *Dict. of Brit. and Amer. Authors*, s. v.

Stewart, David, a Scotch prelate, was bishop of the see of Moray in 1462, and continued there until his death in 1477. See Keith, *Scottish Bishops*, p. 144.

Stewart, Edward, a Scotch prelate, was bishop of Orkney about 1511. See Keith, *Scottish Bishops*, p. 223.

Stewart, James (1), a Scotch prelate, was dean of the see of Moray and lord-treasurer afterwards, in 1453, and in 1459 was advanced to the bishopric. He died in 1462. See Keith, *Scottish Bishops*, p. 144.

Stewart, James (2), a Scotch prelate, was elected to the bishopric of St. Andrews in 1497, and in 1508 was both bishop and chancellor. This prelate also held the monastery of Arbroath. See Keith, *Scottish Bishops*, p. 32.

Stewart, Robert (1), a Scotch prelate, was elected bishop of the see of Caithness in 1542. He never was in priest's orders. He had the title of bishop in September, 1583, and died at St. Andrews, March 29, 1586. See Keith, *Scottish Bishops*, p. 215.

Stewart, Robert (2), a veteran missionary of the Presbyterian Board, was born in Kentucky in May, 1798. He was licensed to preach and ordained for missionary work in southern Illinois, where he spent a long, laborious, and successful ministry, preaching to the very last of his life. He organized many churches in that destitute region, which he supplied with preaching, and multitudes, through his instrumentality, were brought into the fold of Christ. After an active service of over fifty years, he died, in Troy, Madison Co., Ill., July 11, 1881. See *Presbyterian Monthly Record*, Sept. 1881. (W. P. S.)

Steward, Thomas, a Scotch prelate, was archdeacon of St. Andrews, and was elected bishop of the same in 1401, but declined. He probably died about 1414. See Keith, *Scottish Bishops*, p. 27.

Stewart, William, a Scotch prelate, was born in Glasgow about 1479. He was doctor of laws and afterwards minister of Lochmaben, then rector of Ayr, and a prebendary of Glasgow. In 1527 he was preferred to the deanery of Glasgow, and in 1528 sat in parliament. In 1530 he was made lord-treasurer and provost of Lincluden, and was elected bishop of Aberdeen in 1532. After seven years he resigned the treasury. He died about 1545. See Keith, *Scottish Bishops*, p. 121.

Stichart, Franz Otto, a Lutheran theologian of Germany, was born at Werdan, Saxony, in 1810, and died at Dresden in 1883. He published, *Die Lehre vom Beistande des heiligen Geistes zur Besserung* (Leipsic, 1835):—*Jubelchronik der dritten kirchlichen Säcularfeier der Einführung der Reformation in Sachsen* (1841):—*De Reditu Christi ad Judicium Solenne* (eod.):—*Paulus Odontius aus Werdau* (1843):—*Dr. Martin Luther's Tod* (1846):—*Kirchenpforte oder Belehrung über die heiligen Tage, Orte und Gebräuche der Christen* (2d ed. 1859):—*Die kirchliche Legende über die heiligen Apostel* (1861):—*Erasmus von Rotterdam, seine Stellung zur Kirche und den kirchlichen Bewegungen seiner Zeit* (1870). See Zuchold, *Bibl. Theol.* s. v. (B. P.)

Sticht, Johann Christoph, a Lutheran theologian of Germany, who died at Altona, Jan. 12, 1772, is the author of, *De urbe Hanochia Geneseos iv*, 17, etc. (Jena, 1727):—*Super Dictis Genes. vi*, 6, *Luc. ii*, 12, etc. (1757)—*De Keri et Kethibh* (1760):—*De Œconomo Luc. xvi*, 1-9 (1762):—*De Colloquio Dei cum Caino*, etc. (1766):—*De Colloquio Dei cum Satana Hiobi i*, 5-11 (1767). See Döring, *Die gelehrten Theologen Deutschlands*, s. v.; Fürst, *Bibl. Jud.* s. v. (B. P.)

Stiebritz, Johann Friedrich, a Lutheran theologian of Germany, was born at Halle, Aug. 7, 1707. He studied there and at Jena, commenced his academical career at Giessen in 1731, was professor at Halle in 1738, and died Dec. 12, 1772. Stiebritz published, *De Accommodatione Scripturæ*, etc. (Halle, 1727):—*Nova Loci* 1 *Cor. xv*, 28 *Explicatio* (1731):—*De Propheta a Leone Necato*, 1 *Reg. xiii*, etc. (1733):—*De Deo Medico* (1736):—*De Platonismo, Coloss. ii*, 9 (eod.):—*De Sacerdotibus Vitio Corporis Laborantibus, ad Levit. xxi*, 21-23 (1752):—*De Vero Sensu Hoseæ xi*, 1 *in Matt. ii*, 15 (1753):—*Betrachtungen über Gegenstände der Schrift und der Religion* (1769), etc. See Döring, *Die gelehrten Theologen Deutschlands*, s. v.; Fürst, *Bibl. Jud.* s. v. (B. P.)

Stinson, Joseph, D.D., a Wesleyan minister, was born at Castle Donington, Leicestershire, England. He was converted at Gainsborough when about twenty years of age, received into the ministry in 1823, and appointed to eastern Canada. From 1829 to 1832 he labored on the Gibraltar mission, leaving the Church there in much prosperity. In 1833 he resumed his work in Canada, spending three years in Kingston and five in Toronto, being general superintendent of missions and president of the Canadian Conference in 1838. In 1842 he for the first time received an appointment to a circuit in England (Sevenoaks), and after laboring in Sheffield, Leeds, London, Bradford, and Manchester, he again left for Canada. In 1858 he was again elected president of the Canadian Conference, and he spared no labor to meet the demands upon his time and talents. There was a genial warmth and suavity in his spirit and manners; he had a well-cultivated mind and a fine taste. He died in Toronto, Aug. 26, 1862, in his sixty-first year. See *Minutes of the British Conference*, 1867, p. 18; *Minutes of Canadian Conferences*, 1863; Carroll, *Case and His Contemporaries*, index, vol. v.

Stip, Gerhard Chryno Hermann, a Lutheran theologian of Germany, was born May 4, 1809, at Norden, East Frisia. He studied at Göttingen and Bonn, and was for a time preacher to a country congregation. He then travelled through Switzerland, and settled for a time at Berne, where he became acquainted with Schneckenburger. In 1841 he lived in London, in the house of Bunsen, whose sons he instructed. Having returned to Germany, he settled at Alexandrowka, near Potsdam, and died June 21, 1882. Stip belongs to the most prominent hymnologists of the 19th century, and published, *Beleuchtung der Gesangbuchsbesserung* (Gotha, 1842, 2 vols.):—*Hymnologische Reisebriefe* (1853, 2 vols.):—*Kirchenfried und Kirchenlied* (eod.):—*Das evangelische Kirchenlied und die confessionelle Brandfackel* (1854):—*Unverfälschter Liedersegen* (1851):—*Das Kleinod der evangelischen Religionsfreiheit: Erhalt' uns Herr bei deinem Wort* (1855), etc. See Zuchold, *Bibl. Theol.* s. v. (B. P.)

Stockton, John, D.D., a Presbyterian minister, was born near Washington, Pa., Nov. 18, 1803. He graduated from Washington College in 1820, and was for two years teacher of Latin in that institution; prosecuted his theological studies under Rev. Drs. Wylie and Anderson, and spent one year (1825-26) in Princeton Theological Seminary; was ordained pastor of the Cross Creek Church in 1827, and remained in this charge until 1877, when he was released from responsible duties, with the title of pastor emeritus. During the fifty years of his pastorate, fifteen hundred and forty-five members were added to the Church, more than forty ministers of the Gospel were raised up, and one hundred elders were ordained. One year after his settlement he founded a classical school, which was a means of great usefulness to the surrounding country. He died at Cross Creek, May 5, 1882. See *Necrol. Report of Princeton Theol. Sem.* 1883, p. 20. (W. P. S.)

Stockton, William S, one of the founders of the Methodist Protestant Church, an editor and constant contributor to its press, was born at Burlington, N. J., April 8, 1785. From a youth he developed a taste for good reading that never left him. In 1820 his first book was published, entitled *Truth Versus a Wesleyan Methodist.* In 1821 he published *Seven Nights*, aimed against the use of ardent spirits as a beverage. He became identified with the periodical known as *The Wesleyan Repository*, and was one of the first to agitate with his pen the subject of lay representation. He assisted in the publication of the first American edition of Wesley's works, wrote the article on the "Methodist Protestant Church" in Hay's edition of Buck's *Theological Dictionary*, contributed to the secular press as an editorial writer, and also wrote for Methodist periodicals. One of his most important literary undertakings was the publication of Whitehead's *Lives of John and Charles Wesley.* He was a distinguished philanthropist, and as such was well known in the city of Philadelphia. In 1860 he removed to Burlington, the place of his birth, and died there, Nov. 20 of that year. See Colhouer, *Founders of the M. P. Church*, p. 48.

Stoever, Martin Luther, LL.D., a Lutheran educator, was born at Germantown, Pa., Feb. 17, 1820. In 1833 he entered the preparatory department of Pennsylvania College at Gettysburg, and graduated from that institution in 1838. In the fall of that year he took charge of a school in Jefferson, Md. One year afterwards he became principal of the preparatory department of Pennsylvania College, assisting also in the college proper. During the presidency of Dr. Krauth, professor Stoever lived in the college building, and acted as president pro tem. The last ten years of his life were more especially devoted to instruction in Latin. His literary labors were almost entirely confined to the *Evangelical Quarterly Review*, in every number of which, from its beginning in 1849, with the exception of two issues, one or more of his articles appeared. In 1862 he became sole editor and proprietor of that periodical. During the civil war he was prominently connected with the United States Christian Commission. It was his original purpose to enter the Lutheran ministry, but he was deterred by his hesitancy of speech. In many respects he was one of the most distinguished men in his Church. He died in Philadelphia, July 22, 1870. See *Fifty Years in the Lutheran Ministry*, 1878, p. 252.

Stohlman, Charles F. E., D.D., a Lutheran minister, was born at Klein Bremen, kingdom of Hanover, Germany, Feb. 21, 1810. He studied at the gymnasium of Buckeburg; was a student of theology at the University of Halle, under Dr. Tholuck; after his graduation came to America, in September, 1834, and, with his family, settled in Erie, Pa., taking charge of a small congregation. He began his career in New York city, Sept. 12, 1838, as pastor of St. Matthew's German Lutheran Church, in Walker Street, a position which he held until his death, May 3, 1868. See *Lutheran Observer*, May 15, 1868.

Stolz, Alban, a Roman Catholic theologian of Germany, was born Feb. 3, 1808, at Bühl, Baden. In 1833 he was made a priest, was for some time vicar at Rothenfels, in 1841 teacher at the gymnasium in Bruchsal, in 1848 professor of pastoral theology at Freiburg, and died Oct. 16, 1883. Stolz's writings comprise thirteen volumes (Freiburg, 1877 sq.). (B. P.)

Stone, James R., D.D., a Baptist minister, was born at Westborough, Mass., in 1818. He removed to Providence, R. I., when a child, and united with the First Baptist Church in that city in 1833. After studying two years in Brown University, he became principal of Washington Academy, in Wickford, and, in 1839, was ordained pastor of the church in that place. A few years afterwards he became pastor of the Stewart Street Church, in Providence; subsequently held pastorates in Connecticut, New York, Pennsylvania, and Rhode Island. For two years he had charge of the Worcester (Mass.) Academy. In 1864 he was appointed district secretary of the American Baptist Publication Society for West Virginia, Ohio, Indiana, and Michigan. In 1869 he became pastor of the Church in Fort Wayne, Ind. For several years he was president of the Indiana Baptist State Convention. His last pastorate was in Lansing, Mich. He died Feb. 1, 1884. See Cathcart, *Baptist Encyclop.* p. 1112. (J. C. S.)

Stone, John Seely, D.D., a Protestant Episcopal divine, was born at West Stockbridge, Mass., in 1795. He graduated from Union College in 1823; was ordained deacon in 1826; began his ministry in Maryland; was afterwards (1832–41) settled in New Haven, Conn., Boston, Mass., Brooklyn, N. Y., and Brookline, Mass.; was some years lecturer in the Philadelphia Divinity School; in 1869 became dean of the Theological School at Cambridge, Mass., and died there, Jan. 13, 1882. Besides numerous tracts, etc., he published, *The Mysteries Opened* (1844):—*Life of Bishop Griswold* (eod.):—*The Church Universal* (1846; enlarged under the title *The Living Temple*, 1866):—*The Contrast* (1853):—*Life of James Milnor* (1848):—*Lectures on the Christian Sabbath* (1867):—*The Christian Sacraments* (eod.).

Stork, Theophilus, D.D., a Lutheran minister, son of Rev. Charles A. G. Stork, of Brunswick, Germany, was born near Salisbury, N. C., in August, 1814. He graduated from Pennsylvania College in 1835, and from Gettysburg Theological Seminary in 1837, in which year he was licensed to preach, and was immediately called to Grace Lutheran Church, Winchester, Va. In 1841 he became pastor of St. Matthew's Church, Philadelphia, where he labored nine years. In 1842 he was one of the active promoters of the organization of the East Pennsylvania Synod. The large church, known as St. Mark's, in Philadelphia, was organized by him in 1850. Eight years after he was called to the presidency of the new Lutheran College at Newberry, S. C. In 1860 he became pastor of St. Mark's Church, in Baltimore, Md., where he labored until 1865, and then returned to Philadelphia and organized St. Andrew's Church, which was afterwards merged in the Messiah Mission, since the Church of the Messiah. Impaired health compelled him to resign pastoral labor in 1873. He died in Philadelphia, March 28, 1874. Dr. Stork was a scholar of fine literary taste, an elegant writer, and an eloquent preacher. At various times he was editor of the *Home Journal*, of the *Lutheran Home Monthly*, and joint editor of the *Lutheran Observer;* also author of, *Luther at Home:—Luther and the Bible:—Luther's Christmas Tree:—Children of the New Testament:—Home Scenes of the New Testament:—Jesus in the Temple:—Afternoon.* A volume of his *Sermons* was published after his death. See *Pennsylvania College Year-book*, 1882, p. 201.

Stosch, Eberhard Heinrich Daniel, a Reformed theologian of Germany, was born at Liebenberg, Prussia, March 16, 1716, and studied at Frankfort-on-the-Oder. In 1738 he was assistant preacher at Jerichau, in 1744 at Soldin, in 1748 professor at Duisburg, in 1749 at Frankfort, and died March 27, 1781, doctor of theology. He published, *Commentatio Historico-Critica de Librorum Novi Testamenti Canone* (Frankfort, 1755):—*De Ecclesia Divinam Bibliorum Inspirationem Testante* (1751):—*De Septem Domini Oculis Perlustrantibus Totam Terram ex Zachar. iv*, 10 (1751):—*De Revelatione Divina Ante Mosen Scripto Consignata* (1752):—*Introductio in Theologiam Dogmaticam* (1778):—*Institutio Theologiæ Dogmaticæ* (1779). See Döring, *Die gelehrten Theologen Deutschlands*, s. v.; Fürst, *Bibl. Jud.* s. v.; Winer, *Handbuch der theol. Lit.* i, 77, 292, 305, 394, 535. (B. P.)

Stosch, Ferdinand, a brother of the foregoing, was born Dec. 30, 1717, at Liebenberg. He studied at Frankfort, was in 1743 con-rector at Lingen, in 1761 professor at the Joachimsthal Gymnasium in Berlin, in 1771 member of consistory and general superintendent at Detmold, and died Aug. 17, 1780. He wrote, *De Nominibus Urbis Thyatiræ* (Lingen, 1743):—*De Angelo Ecclesiæ Thyatirenæ* (eod.):—*De Sepultura Jephtæ ad Jud. xii*, 7 (1746):—*De Ecclesia Novi Testamenti Prophetis non Indigente, ad Ephes. iii*, 2, 3 (1748):—*De Septem Epistolarum Apocalypticarum Ordine* (1749):—*De Adamo, Principum Primo ad Psa. lxxxii*, 7 (1754):—*Compendium Archæologiæ Œconomicæ Novi Testamenti* (Leipsic, 1769), etc. See Doring, *Die gelehrten Theologen Deutschlands*, s. v.; Fürst, *Bibl. Jud.* s. v.; Winer, *Handbuch der theol. Lit.* i, 78, 274. (B. P.)

Stowell, William Henry, D.D., an English Congregational minister, was born on the Isle of Man in 1800. He entered secular business at an early age in Liverpool; was there persuaded to enter the ministry; studied theology at Blackburn Academy, and settled as pastor at North Shields in 1821. In 1833 he was invited to the presidency of Rotherham Independent College, and the pastorate at Masborough, which offices he filled until his acceptance of the presidency of Cheshunt College in 1850. He retired from public duty about a year and a half before his death, which took place at his residence at Bransbury, Jan. 2, 1858. Dr. Stowell's scholarship was extensive and varied. He was well acquainted with history and ethics, good in the classics, and able in theology. He published, *History of the Puritans in England* (1837):—*Memoir of Richard Winter Hamilton, D.D., LL.D.* (1850):—*The Work of the Spirit* (1853), and a volume of *Sermons*, as well as several lesser works. See (Lond.) *Cong. Year-book*, 1859, p. 222; Allibone, *Dict. of Brit. and Amer. Authors*, s. v.

Strachan, David, a Scotch prelate, was pastor of Fettercairn, and upon the king's restoration promoted to the see of Brechin, and consecrated June 1, 1662, where he continued until his death in 1671. See *Keith, Scottish Bishops*, p. 167.

Strain, John, D.D., a Scotch Catholic prelate, was born Dec. 8, 1810. He was consecrated bishop of Abila (*in partibus*) by Pius IX, Sept. 25, 1864, and appointed vicar-apostolic of the eastern district of Scotland. On the restoration of the hierarchy by Leo XIII, in March, 1878, he was translated to the archiepiscopal see of St. Andrews and Edinburgh. He died July 2, 1883.

Strathbrock, Robert, a Scotch prelate, was bishop of Caithness about 1444. See Keith, *Scottish Bishops*, p. 214.

Straube, Carl, a Lutheran minister of Germany, was born at Berlin, Oct. 27, 1807. After completing his theological studies, he assisted his father in the ministry at Mittenwalde from 1829 to 1835, was then appointed pastor at Werder, in 1856 at Falkenhagen, and died March 2, 1881. Straube was very active in the work of home and foreign missions, and his *Reisepsalter* has become a household work in the Christian families of Germany. (B. P.)

Strauss, Otto, son of Gerhard Friedrich Abraham (q. v.), who died March 6, 1880, is the author of *Nahum de Nino Vaticinium Explicatum ex Assyriis Monumentis* (Berlin, 1853), the publication of which entitled him to the right of lecturing at the Berlin University. In 1857 he was military preacher at Posen, and in 1865 first preacher of the Sophienkirche, in Berlin, where he labored to his end. Besides the work on *Nahum*, he published, *Ninive und das Wort Gottes* (1855):—*Der Psalter als Gesang- und Gebetbuch* (1859):—and, in connection with his brother, Friedrich Adolph, *Länder und Städte der heiligen Schrift* (1861). See Pank, *Zur Erinnerung an Lic. Otto Strauss* (Berlin, 1880). (B. P.)

Strickland, William Peter, D.D., a Methodist Episcopal, and later a Presbyterian, divine, was born at Pittsburgh, Pa., Aug. 17, 1809. He studied at the Ohio University, entered the Ohio Conference in 1832, labored several years in Cincinnati, and then became agent of the American Bible Society. In 1856 he engaged in literary labor in New York, chiefly in connection with the Methodist press, and as assistant editor of the *Christian Advocate*. In 1862 he was chaplain of the 48th New York regiment at Port Royal, S. C. In 1865 he supplied the pulpit of the Presbyterian Church at Bridgehampton, L. I., and in 1874 was installed its pastor. Three years later he resigned through ill-health, and retired to private literary work. He died at Ocean Grove, N. J., July 15, 1884. Dr. Strickland was a frequent contributor to the religious journals, and also to the cyclopædias, and was the author of numerous volumes, of which we may mention, *Hist. of the Amer. Bible Society* (New York, 1849; new ed. 1856):—*Hist. of Meth. Missions* (1850):—*Genius and Mission of Methodism* (1851):—*Christianity Defended* (1852):—*Memoir of J. B. Finley* (1853):—*Manual of Biblical Literature* (eod.):—*Light of the Temple* (1854):—*Astrologer of Chaldea* (1856):—*Pioneers of the West* (eod.):—*Life of Asbury* (1858):—*Life of Groben* (1859):—*Old Mackinaw* (1860); besides editing the *Literary Casket*, the *Western Review*, and the *Autobiography of Peter Cartwright* (1856).

Strobel, Georg Theodor, a Lutheran theologian of Germany, was born Sept. 12, 1736, and studied at Altdorf. In 1769 he was preacher at Rasch, in the neighborhood of Altdorf, in 1774 at Wörd, and died Dec. 14, 1794. Strobel published, *Melanchthoniana* (Altdorf, 1771):—*Nachrichten von den Verdiensten Melanchthon's um die heilige Schrift* (1773):—*Bibliotheca Melanchthoniana* (Nuremberg, 1775; 3d ed. 1782):—*Literärgeschichte von Ph. Melanchthon's Locis Theologicis* (1776):—*Ph. Melanchthonis Libellus de Scriptoribus Ecclesiasticis* (1780), etc. See Döring, *Die gelehrten Theologen Deutschlands*, s. v.; Winer, *Handbuch der theol. Lit.* i, 295, 745, 746, 767, 851. (B. P.)

Stuart, Andrew, a Scotch prelate, was postulated bishop of the see of Dunkeld in 1515, and was afterwards put into the see of Caithness. See Keith, *Scottish Bishops*, p. 93.

Stuart, John, D.D., an Episcopal minister, was born at Harrisburg, Pa., in 1740. He graduated at the College of Philadelphia, was ordained in 1770, and appointed to the mission at Fort Hunter. He prepared a Mohawk translation of the gospel of Mark, an *Exposition of the Church Catechism*, and a compendious *History of the Bible*. During the revolutionary war he became an object of suspicion, and was subjected to many hardships. At length he removed to Canada, and in 1786 opened an academy at Kingston. About 1799 he was appointed chaplain to the garrison. He died at Kingston in August, 1811. He has been called the "Father of the Upper Canada Church." See Sabine, *Loyalists of the Revolutionary War*, ii, 339. (J. C. S.)

Stuart, Robert L., a philanthropic merchant, was born in the city of New York, July 21, 1806. He inherited a considerable fortune from his father, together with his business, the refining of sugar and the manufacture of candy, by which he amassed a large property, and liberally contributed of it for religious and benevolent purposes, especially to the library and mission enterprises of the Presbyterian Church, of which he was a consistent and devout member. He died in his native city, Dec. 13, 1883. It is estimated that the total gifts of himself and his brother, Alexander (died in December, 1879), amounted to nearly three million dollars.

Stubbs, Alfred, D.D., a Protestant Episcopal minister, was born at Turk's Island, West Indies, May 12, 1815. He passed his school-days at Bloomingdale and in Brooklyn, graduated at Yale College in 1835, and at the General Theological Seminary, New York city, in 1839. In the latter year he was chosen rector of Christ Church, New Brunswick, a position which he continued to hold until his death, Dec. 11, 1882. He was a warm-hearted and generous man, and of untiring energy and earnest devotion to the principles of the Church. In the convention of the diocese he took an active and leading part, and frequently was sent as deputy to the General Convention. He had been for a long time president of the Standing Committee. In 1867 Dr. Stubbs made a charge against the Rev. Stephen H. Tyng, Jr., of violating the canon laws of the Church by preaching in a Methodist meeting-house in New Brunswick. Dr. Stubbs was a prominent person in that trial, which attracted wide attention.

Stutteville, ROBERT DE, a Scotch prelate, was probably bishop of the see of Dunkeld in 1272. He died in 1300. See Keith, *Scottish Bishops*, p. 81.

Stützle, JOHANN NEPOMUK, a Roman Catholic theologian of Germany, born in 1807 at Scheer, Würtemberg, was made a priest in 1832 at Augsburg, called to Balzhausen, Augsburg diocese, in 1849, and died April 17, 1874. He published, *Versuch einer Harmonisirung der Welt- und Kirchengeschichte* (Zurich, 1868):—*Handbuch zum römisch-katholischen Religionsunterrichte* (Augsburg, 1868, 2 vols.):—*Stunden der Andacht für Katholiken* (Troppau, 1869–73). (B. P.)

Styles, JOHN, D.D., an English Congregational minister and author, commenced his ministry in early life at Cowes, Isle of Wight, thence removing to Brighton, where for many years he attracted large audiences. His next charge was Holland Chapel, North Brixton, which he built, and which he left in 1835. From 1836 to 1844 he officiated in Claylands Chapel, at the same place. In the latter year he became pastor at Foleshill, where he remained until his death at Kennington, June 22, 1849. A masculine energy, a noble generosity and benevolence of disposition, were his characteristics. His mind was energetic and powerful, he could write on almost any topic, was an acute critic, had superior colloquial powers, richness of fancy, and his style was polished, vivacious, and luminous. Dr. Styles published, *An Essay on the Stage* (2d ed. Lond. 1807, 12mo):—*Legend of the Velvet Cushion* (exposing in a masterly manner a writer on the Puritans):—*Sermons* (ibid. 1813, 1823, 2 vols. 8vo) [the sermon on *The Spirituality of God* (Isle of Wight, 1806), and that on *Temptations of a Watering-Place* (Brighton, 1815) were published separately]:—*Sermon on Lord Byron's Works* (Lond. 1824): —*Prize Essay on the Prevention of Cruelty to Animals* (elegant and convincing):—*Critical Papers in Ward's Miscellany and in the Evangelical Magazine*. See (Lond.) *Evangelical Magazine*, August, 1849, p. 393.

Summers, THOMAS OSMOND, D.D., LL.D., an eminent divine of the Methodist Episcopal Church South, was born near Corfe Castle, Isle of Purbeck, Dorsetshire, England, Oct. 11, 1812. He was trained by Dissenters, came to America while a youth, joined the Methodists in 1832, was converted the following year, soon began to preach, and entered the Baltimore Conference of the Methodist Episcopal Church in 1835. In 1840 he became a missionary in Texas, and was one of the first members of that conference; was transferred to the Alabama Conference in 1844, with which he ever afterwards remained connected, occupying for several years its most important charges, and afterwards engaged in literary work, as the editor of the *Southern Christian Advocate* (1846), of the *Quarterly Review of the M. E. Church South* (1855), and other periodicals. He acted as secretary of every General Conference of his Church, from its organization in 1845 to his death, which occurred during the session of that body at Nashville, Tenn., May 5, 1882. During the civil war he served as a pastor in Alabama, and for several of his later years he was a professor in the Vanderbilt University. He was a man of encyclopædic information, untiring diligence, and wide liberality of sentiment. He wrote and edited very many works for the press of his Church, and numberless articles of value for its journals. See *Minutes of the Annual Conferences of the M. E. Church South*, 1882, p. 125; Simpson, *Cyclop. of Methodism*, s. v.; *Life* by Fitzgerald (Nashville, 1884).

Sumner, CHARLES RICHARD, D.D., an English prelate, was born at Kenilworth, Warwickshire, in 1790. He was educated at Eton and at Trinity College, Cambridge; became rector of St. Helen's, Abingdon, Bucks, and librarian and historiographer to George IV; prebend of Worcester in 1822; of Canterbury in 1825; dean of St. Paul's, prebend of London, and bishop of Llandaff, all in April, 1826; was translated to Winchester in 1827; and resigned his see, on account of the infirmities of age, in September, 1869. He died Aug. 15, 1874. Bishop Sumner was an earnest, evangelical preacher, and a hearty supporter of the Bible and missionary societies. He published, *Prælectiones Academicæ Oxonii Habita* (Lond. 8vo):—*Ministerial Character of Christ Practically Considered* (ibid. 1824, 8vo; 2d ed. 1835, 8vo), and several *Charges*. See *The* (Lond.) *Christian Observer*, May, 1876, p. 325.

Supper, THE LAST, is a modern phrase often used to designate the Lord's Supper, in view of the fact that it was the last meal of which Jesus partook with his disciples (Matt. xxvi, 29; Mark xiv, 25; Luke xxii, 18). The circumstances of the repast have been so fully discussed in preceding articles, that it remains to consider more particularly only one feature, namely, the relative position of the guests at the table; as this reflects special light upon several incidents and expressions in the narratives of the evangelists.

1. The place of Peter would properly be that of honor among the disciples; and it is agreed upon all hands that such was by custom the uppermost or left-hand one on the highest or left-hand wing of the triclinium or dinner-bed, reckoned according to the fact that the guests reclined upon their left side (so as to leave the right hand free for eating with), each facing the person next below. In this arrangement also he would be the first to whom the Master would come for the foot-washing, as is evident from the account of that incident ("began," John xiii, 5). Moreover, he would thus be opposite John, and sufficiently removed from him to render "beckoning" necessary in order to ascertain through him the person of the traitor (John xiii, 24).

2. The interesting group of which the Lord himself formed the centre consisted, besides him, of Judas and John, who were so situated that the latter, as he lay "in Jesus' bosom," could *lean back* (ἐπιπεσών, John xiii, 25, for which many read ἀναπεσών, both to be carefully distinguished from the ἀνακείμενος of the verse preceding), and whisper to the Master; and the former so located that he could readily receive the sop from the Master's hands. All this renders it plain that Judas occupied the honorable position above, i. e. at the back of Jesus; and John the next favored location below or just in front of him.

According to classical etiquette, the master or host reclined on the middle place of the middle bed; and in that case the arrangement of the whole would be as in the accompanying diagram (see Smith, *Dict. of Class. Antiq.* s. v., triclinium). This meets the ordinary sense of propriety also. But Edersheim maintains (*Life and*

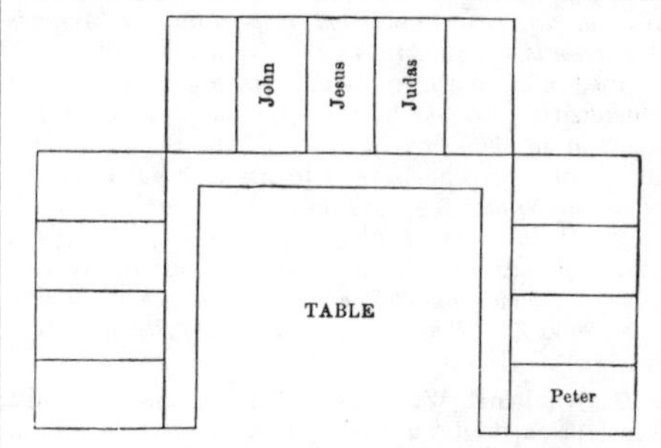

Presumed Classical Order of the Last Supper.

Times of Jesus, ii, 494), from certain rabbinical notices, that the appropriate place for the giver of the feast was at the foot of the table, and in that case John would be exactly opposite Peter, at the other extreme of the entire series, as in the subjoined diagram. In this way, however, these two disciples would seem to be too near each other to suit the need of signs, since they could freely converse across the table; and they would not so fully face one another, since they would be reclining rather back to back. See ACCUBATION.

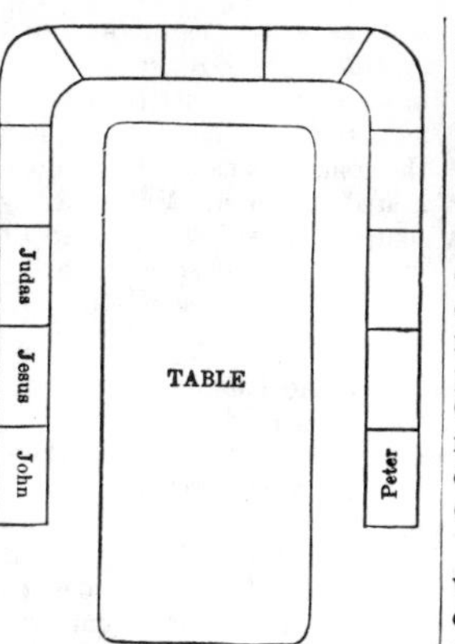

Supposed Rabbinical Order at the Last Supper.

Süsskind, FRIEDRICH GOTTLOB VON, a Protestant theologian of Germany, was born Feb. 17, 1767. He studied at Tübingen, was in 1795 deacon at Urach, in 1798 teacher at Tübingen, in 1805 court-preacher and member of consistory at Stutgard, and died Nov. 12, 1829. He published, *Quonam Sensu suam Jesus Doctrinam Divinam Perhibuerit?* (Tübingen, 1798–1801; in German, ibid. 1802):—*Symbolæ ad Illustranda Quædam Evangeliorum Loca* (1802–1804, 3 parts):—*Magazin für christliche Dogmatik und Moral* (1803–12):—*Prüfung der Schelling'schen Lehre von Gott* (1812). See Döring, *Die deutschen Kanzelredner*, p. 502–505; Winer, *Handbuch der theol. Lit.* i, 21, 284, 400. (B. P.)

Sutcliffe, JOSEPH, M.A., an English Wesleyan minister, was born at Baildon, Yorkshire. He was converted in early life, was appointed by Wesley to Redruth in 1786, introduced Methodism into the Scilly Isles in 1788, spent the last twenty years of his life in retirement in London, and died May 14, 1856. His course was one of "unspotted Christian purity and progressive excellence. In Biblical scholarship he especially excelled." He was an indefatigable writer, publishing in all thirty-two works on religious subjects, the chief being *A Commentary on the Old and New Testament* (Lond. 1834, 2 vols. royal 8vo). See *Minutes of the British Conference*, 1856, p. 211; Stevens, *Hist. of Methodism*, ii, 348; Smith, *Hist. of Wesl. Methodism*, ii, 647; *Wesl. Meth. Magazine*, 1856, p. 503; Osborn, *Meth. Bibliography*, p. 181; *Wesleyan Takings*, i, 303.

Sutton, AMOS, D.D., an English Baptist minister, was born at Sevenoaks, Kent, Jan. 21, 1802. At fifteen he resided in London, at twenty returned home and joined the Baptist Church. He was accepted as a general Baptist missionary, and sailed for Calcutta in 1824, thence to Cuttack, Orissa, India, where he labored till his health failed in 1832, and then returned to England. He returned to Cuttack in 1837, and labored till 1847, when he had again to seek rest in England, and became pastor at Leicester. In 1850 he returned again to India by way of America. He reached his station in India only to die, Aug. 17, 1851.

Swaim, THOMAS, D.D., a Baptist minister, was born at Pemberton, N. J., March 30, 1817. He was for a time a student in Brown University in the class of 1838, and having completed his college course in Madison University, graduated from Hamilton Theological Seminary in 1844. He was ordained in November, 1846, pastor at Washington, Pa. At the end of four years' successful labor, he accepted an agency in the service of the missionary union for six months, and then was pastor in Flemington, N. J., sixteen years. In 1867 he became the financial secretary of the New Jersey Classical and Scientific Institute at Hightstown, and in 1868 district secretary of the American Baptist Home Missionary Society. He died in Philadelphia, Pa., March 24, 1884. See Cathcart, *Baptist Encyclop.* p. 1124. (J. C. S.)

Swain, LEONARD, D.D., a Congregational minister, was born at Concord, N. H., Feb. 26, 1821. He graduated from Dartmouth College in 1841, and from Andover Theological Seminary in 1846; was immediately ordained pastor of the Church in Nashua, establishing from the outset a reputation as an able and eloquent preacher. His next pastorate was over the Central Church of Providence, R. I., from 1852 to 1869. For nearly two years he was laid aside from his work, and died July 14, 1869. See *Rhode Island Biographical Cyclopædia*, s. v. (J. C. S.)

Swan, JABEZ SMITH, a noted Baptist evangelist, was born at Stonington, Conn., Feb. 23, 1800. He had early educational advantages; was converted at the age of twenty-one; licensed the following year; studied at the Hamilton Institute, N. Y.; became pastor at Stonington in 1827; Norwich, N. Y., in 1830; Preston in 1837; Oxford in 1842; New London, Conn., in 1843; Albany, N. Y., in 1848; at New London again in 1849; served as a missionary through the state of New York for several years; became pastor at Waterford, where his health failed in 1862; and died Nov. 19, 1884. He was powerful in prayer and preaching, and great revivals followed his labors. See Cathcart, *Baptist Encyclop.* s. v.

Sycaminum. See HAIFA.

Sydeserf, THOMAS, a Scotch prelate, was translated from Brechin to Galloway in 1638, and was excommunicated. He was the only bishop who survived the troubles, and then was translated to the see of Orkney, Nov. 14, 1662. He died in February, 1676. See Keith, *Scottish Bishops*, p. 228, 281.

Sydow, KARL LEOPOLD ADOLF, a Protestant theologian of Germany, was born Nov. 23, 1800, at Berlin. He studied theology under Schleiermacher; in 1828 was chaplain and tutor in the military school at Berlin, and in 1837 was called as court and military chaplain to Potsdam. In 1841 he was sent by Frederic William IV to England, to study there, in connection with other commissioners, the institutions for the religious care of the population of London and other large cities, and to report of his experience, and at the same time of the newly founded Anglo-Prussian bishopric at Jerusalem. This he did in his *Amtliche Berichte über die in neuerer Zeit in England erwachte Thätigkeit für die Vermehrung und Erweiterung der kirchlichen Anstalten* (1845). As this mission brought him in connection with the queen of England and prince Albert, he was requested to prepare a paper on the movement then pending in Scotland for separating the Church from the State. This he did in his *Beiträge zur Characteristik der kerchlichen Dinge in Grossbritannien* (1844–45, 2 parts), in which he freely advocated the separation. In 1846 he accepted a call as pastor of the Neue Kirche in Berlin, which position he occupied till the year 1876. In connection with Eltester, Thomas, and Pischon, he published the *Monatsschrift*, afterwards *Zeitschrift für die unirte Kirche*, which, in 1854, was replaced by the *Protestantische Kirchenzeitung*. In 1848 he was a member of the Berlin National Assembly, and ten years later the theological faculty of Jena honored him with the doctorate of theology. When, in 1872, he delivered a lecture, in which he declared that Jesus was the natural son of Joseph and Mary, the Brandenburg consistory deposed him from his office. He died Oct. 22, 1882. Besides the writings already mentioned, he published *Sammlung geistlicher Vorträge* (Berlin, 1838), and, in connection with F. A. Schulze, he translated and published fifteen volumes of Channing's works (1850–55). See Zuchold, *Bibl. Theol.* ii, 1301. (B. P.)

Sylburg, FRIEDRICH, a German scholar, was born in 1536 at Wetter, near Marburg, and died Feb. 16, 1596, at Heidelberg. Sylburg is known as the editor of some of the works of the Church fathers, to which he made annotations. Thus he edited the works of Clement of Alexandria, in Greek and Latin (Heidelberg, 1592), an edition which is still highly praised. See Jöcher, *Allgemeines Gelehrten-Lexikon*, s. v.; Winer, *Handbuch der theol. Lit.* i, 331, 883, 888, 898. (B. P.)

Syme, Andrew, D.D., an Episcopal minister, was born in Lanarkshire, Scotland, in September, 1764. He went to Petersburg, Va., before 1800, and remained till his death, Oct. 26, 1845, being at the time the oldest citizen in the town, and the oldest clergyman in the state. See Sturgh, *Amer. Biog. Notes*, p. 386. (J. C. S.)

Symington, W., D.D., a minister in the Reformed Presbyterian Church of Scotland, was born in 1795, and died at Glasgow, professor of theology in the seminary of his mother Church, Jan. 28, 1862, in the forty-third year of his ministry. His works on the *Atonement and Intercession of Christ*, and on the *Mediatorial Dominion of Christ*, were the best known to the public. He was also the author of a volume of *Sermons*. See *Appleton's Annual Cyclop.* 1862, p. 683.

Symmons, Charles, D.D., a Church of England divine, was born in 1749. He was educated at Westminster, at the University of Glasgow, and at Clare Hall, Cambridge, where he took the degree of B.D. in 1776; was presented to the rectory of Narberth by the king in 1778, and died at Bath, April 27, 1826. His first publication was in 1788, an octavo volume of *Sermons*. In 1789 he published in quarto *A Sermon for the Benefit of Decayed Clergymen in the Diocese of St. David's*; and in 1790, *The Consequence of the Character of the Individual, and the Influence of Education in Forming It*; in 1797 he produced *Inez*, a dramatic poem; and in 1800 another called *Constantia*. In 1806 appeared his *Life of Milton*, prefixed to an edition of Milton's prose works, of which he was not the editor. In 1813 he published an octavo volume of poems, partly his own, and partly the compositions of his wondrously gifted, but then deceased, daughter. Subsequently he amused his leisure hours with writing *A Rhymed Translation of the Æneid*, which was published in 1817. His last work was a sketch of Shakespeare's life. See (Lond.) *Annual Register*, 1826, p. 247.

Syriac (*Modern*) **Version** of the Scriptures. The modern Syriac language, written in Nestorian characters, and spoken by the Christians of the latter name, is a very corrupt dialect of the ancient Syriac, abounding in Persian, Turkish, and Kurdish words, and pronounced very harshly. Mr. Perkins, of the American Board of Missions, commenced, in 1836, a translation of the Scriptures from the ancient or ecclesiastical language into the vernacular now in use among the people. The gospels were soon issued from the press at Oroomiah, and later the entire Bible. See *Bible of Every Land*, p. 46.

Syro-Roman Christians are a class of converts to the Romish faith in Malabar and Travancore, in India. They have their own bishops and priests. Their forefathers appear to have belonged to the Christians of St. Thomas, as they were called; and were gained over to the Romish Church by the Portuguese, who compelled the churches nearest the coast to acknowledge the supremacy of the pope. The Syro-Roman Christians, along with the converts from other tribes in the district, are said to amount to upwards of one hundred thousand souls. They are allowed to retain their own language in divine worship, as well as their own liturgy, and they have a Syriac college.

T.

Taanach. The present *Tannuk* lies six miles north-west of Zerîn (Jezreel), and is "a small village on the south-east side of the great tell or mound of the same name, at the [south-west] edge of the great plain [of Esdraelon]. It has olives on the south, and wells on the north, and is surrounded by cactus hedges. There is a white dome in the village. The rock on the sides of the tell is quarried in places, the wells are ancient, and rock-cut tombs occur on the north, near the foot of the mound" (*Memoirs* to Ordnance Survey, ii, 46; comp. p. 63).

Taanath-Shiloh is thought by Tristram (*Bible Places*, p. 195) and Conder (*Tent Work*, ii, 340) to be the present ruin *Tana*, seven miles south-east of Shechem, and two north of Janohoh (Yanûm), containing "foundations, caves, cistern, and rock-cut tombs" (*Memoirs* to Ordnance Survey, ii, 245, comp. p. 232).

Tabaraud, Matthieu Mathurin, a French controversialist, was born at Limoges in 1744. He was educated by the Jesuits, was for some time professor of belles-lettres at Nantes, professor of theology and Hebrew at Arles, in 1783 superior of the college at Pézenas, in 1787 at Rochelle, emigrated in 1791 to England, and died at Limoges, Jan. 9, 1832. He published, *Traité Historique et Critique de l'Élection des Évêques* (Paris, 1792, 2 vols.):—*De la Necessité d'une Religion d'Etat* (1803, 1804):—*Principes sur la Distinction du Contrat et du Sacrement de Mariage* (1802, 1816):—*Histoire de Pierre de Bérulle, Fondateur de la Congregation de l'Oratoire* (1817, 2 vols.). See Winer, *Handbuch der theol. Lit.* i, 726, 820; Lichtenberger, *Encyclop. des Sciences Religieuses*, s. v. (B. P.).

Tables, The Four. During the fierce contest in Scotland between the adherents of the Church of England and the Presbyterians, several outbreaks occurred. On Nov. 15, 1637, there was a meeting of the Privy Council, and large numbers of Presbyterians assembled at the capital. In order to prevent any tumultuous commotion, the nobles were requested to use their influence to induce their friends to return to their homes. This was consented to on condition that a sufficient number should remain to look after their interests. It was arranged that as many of the nobility as pleased, two gentlemen from every county, one minister from every presbytery, and one burgess from every burgh, should form a general commission, representing the whole body of the Presbyterians. Still more to concentrate their efforts, a smaller number was selected, who should reside at Edinburgh, watch the progress of events, and be ready to communicate with the whole body on any emergency. This smaller committee was composed of sixteen persons—four noblemen, four gentlemen, four ministers, and four burgesses; and from the circumstance of their sitting in four separate rooms in the parliament house, they were designated The Four Tables. A member from each of these constituted a chief table of last resort, making a supreme council of four members. See Hetherington, *Hist. of Church of Scotland*, i, 291.

Taboo (or **Tabû**), an institution common to all the Polynesian tribes, which solemnly interdicted whatever was esteemed sacred. Hence the term was used to denote anything devoted. With persons or places that were tabooed, all intercourse was prohibited. There were tabooed or sacred days, when it was a crime to be found in a canoe. Pork, bananas, cocoa-nuts, and certain kinds of fish were tabooed to women, and it was death for them to eat these articles of food. The eating together by man and wife was also tabooed, as was the preparation of their food in the same oven. Anything of which a man made an idol, and articles of food offered to idols, were tabooed to him. There were other instances of taboo, as the ariki, or head chief, of an island, who was so sacred that his house, garments, and everything relating to him were taboo. The taboo arose from the idea that a portion of the spiritual essence of the divinity indwelling in sacred things and persons was more or less transmitted to anything else brought in contact with it.

Tabor, Mount. For the latest description and plan of *Jebel et-Tôr*, see the *Memoirs* to the Ordnance Survey, i, 388 sq.

Tabunisozton, among the Kalmucks, is a deity of the second rank, who has appeared fifty-two times in as many different forms. The principal form is that of a woman, which, in all external appearance, is entirely like that of the Kalmuck women in general. She sits with crossed legs upon an elevation, is in part unclothed, and wherever the flesh appears is painted red. Head-dress and clothing are about tantamount to each other in most Kalmuck deities; the lower part of the body is enveloped in a light robe, while the head is crowned with a towering ornament, and adorned with flowers. Tabunisozton holds in her hands a vessel of fruit, and is regarded as the goddess of earthly fruitfulness, with which her frequent reviviscence agrees.

Tae-Keih is the fundamental unity of the Chinese literati, the absolute, or, literally, the "great extreme." Beyond this, they allege, no human thought can soar. Itself incomprehensible, it girdles the whole frame of nature, animate and inanimate. From it alone, as from the fountain-head of nature, issued everything that is. Creation is the periodic flowing forth of it. Tae-Keih is identical with Le, the immaterial element of the universe.

Tafel, Johann Friedrich Immanuel, a Swedenborgian, who died at Stutgard in 1863, professor, is the author of, *Religionssystem der Neuen Kirche* (Tübingen, 1832):—*Geschichte und Kritik des Skepticismus und Irrationalismus in ihrer Beziehung zur neuern Philosophie* (1834):—*Vergleichende Darstellung und Beurtheilung der Lehrgegensätze der Katholiken und Protestanten* (1835):—*Zur Geschichte der Neuen Kirche* (1841):—*Swedenborg und seine Gegner* (2d ed. eod.):—*Die Hauptwahrheiten der Religion* (1852):—*Die Unsterblichkeit und Wiedererinnerungskraft der Seele* (1853):—*Swedenborg und der Aberglaube* (1856), etc. See Zuchold, *Bibl. Theol*, s. v.; Winer, *Handbuch der theol. Lit.* i, 506, 595. (B. P.)

Tailory, The, a room adjoining the wardrobe in monasteries, where a number of the lay brethren, with a vocation for that useful craft, were continually at work, making and repairing the clothes of the community. These two rooms and the lavatory were in charge of the camerarius or chamberlain. See Hill, *English Monasticism*, p. 20.

Tairi, the principal deity of the Sandwich Islanders.

Tait, Archibald Campbell, D.D., LL.D., an English prelate, was born in Edinburgh, Scotland, Dec. 22, 1811. He graduated from the Edinburgh High School, Edinburgh Academy, Glasgow University, and Oxford University, from the last with the highest honors. He became a public examiner of the university, and in 1842 head master at Rugby, where he remained eight years. He was appointed dean of Carlisle in 1850, where he instituted an extra pulpit service, and gave much time to visiting and instructing the poor. In 1856 he became bishop of London, and successfully originated a scheme for adding to the Church accommodation in the metropolis, by raising in ten years a fund of five million dollars. He was translated to the archiepiscopal see of Canterbury in December, 1868. He presided over the Pan-Anglican Synod in Lambeth in 1867, the Church Congress in Croydon in 1877, and the Congress of Anglican Bishops in Lambeth in 1878. He died in London, Dec. 3, 1882. Archbishop Tait was a churchman of conservative spirit. He wrote, *Dangers and Safeguards of Modern Theology:* — *The Word of God the Ground of Faith:* — *Charge to the Clergy:* — *Some Thoughts on the Duties of the Church of England:*—*Letters on Education and Kindred Topics*, in Scotch and British reviews. (W. P. S.)

Talbot, Richard, an Irish prelate, was collated to the precentorship of Hereford in 1407, and in 1416 was elected to the primacy of Armagh. In 1417 he was consecrated archbishop of the see of Dublin. In 1423 he was lord justice, and subsequently lord chancellor of Ireland, and in 1424 had a grant for all his services of all the estates of Matthew St. John, deceased. He was at the same time constituted justice and guardian of the peace in the county of Dublin. In 1426 he reduced the proxies that were formerly paid by the prior and convent of the Holy Trinity to the archbishops of Dublin, from five marks to two and a half, which concession pope Eugenius afterwards confirmed. He was again constituted lord chancellor in 1428. In 1432 he established a chantry in St. Michael's Church, which, from being a chapel, he constituted parochial, and likewise founded the chantry of St. Anne in St. Audeon's Church, for the maintenance of six priests to pray for the king, the founder, and their successors. In 1443 he was elected archbishop of Armagh, but refused the dignity. In 1445 he was a fourth time lord deputy of Ireland, and in 1447 was appointed deputy to the earl of Ormond, viceroy of Ireland. He died Aug. 15, 1449. See D'Alton, *Memoirs of the Archbishops of Dublin*, p. 153.

Talismans were used by the Chaldæan magicians to prevent the attacks of evil spirits, injury from wicked sorcery, poison, etc. We give the following translation of part of the seventeenth formula on the tablet found in the library of the royal palace at Nineveh:

> "Two double bands of white cloth
> upon the bed on the platform
> as a talisman if he binds on the (right) hand,
> two double bands of black cloth
> if he binds on the left hand."

The possessor of this talisman was assured that all evil spirits and other ills would leave him, never to return. These talismans were of different kinds. First of all there were those which consisted of bands of cloth, covered with certain written formulæ, and were fastened to the furniture or the garments, like the phylacteries of the Jews. There were also Amulets (q. v.). Vessels, containing food and drink for the gods and genii, were placed in the apartments as protecting talismans. The dæmons were represented by figures of such hideous forms that it was believed that they were only to be shown their own image to cause them to flee away. In the museum of the Louvre is a bronze statuette of Assyrian workmanship; a figure of a horrible dæmon in an upright position, with the body of a dog, the feet of an eagle, the claws of a lion, the tail of a scorpion, the head of a skeleton but half decayed, and adorned with goat's horns, the eyes still remaining, and, lastly, four great expanded wings. See Lenormant, *Chaldæan Magic*, p. 850; Volbeding, *Index Programmatum*, p. 160; Thomson, *Land and Book*, i, 140, 217; comp. Charm.

Tall Brothers, an epithet (from their stature) of four Nitrian monks, named Dioscurus, Ammonius, Eusebius, and Euthymius, who were reluctantly induced by Theophilus, the patriarch of Alexandria, to leave the desert and receive ordination. They were so disgusted during the troubles of the time of Chrysostom that they returned once more to their solitude, and although condemned and denounced, A.D. 401, and even personally attacked by Theophilus, they persisted in remaining there.

Tamarisk. See Grove.

Tantălus, a Greek mythological character, was, according to some, a son of Zeus, or, according to others, of Tmolus. All traditions agree in stating that he was a wealthy king, but assign him to different kingdoms, as Lydia, Sipylus, in Phrygia or Paphlagonia, and Argos or Corinth. Tantalus is peculiarly celebrated in ancient story for the severe punishment inflicted upon him after his death. The following are some of the traditions, of which the most common is that Zeus invited him to his table and communicated his divine counsels to him. Tantalus divulged these secrets, and the gods punished him by placing him in the midst of a lake, of which he could never drink, the water always withdrawing when he stooped. Branches laden with fruit hung temptingly near, but withdrew whenever he reached after them. Over his head there was suspended a huge rock ever threatening to crush him. Another tradition relates that, wishing to try the gods, he cut his son Pelops in pieces, boiled them, and set them before the gods as a repast. A third account states that Tantalus stole nectar and ambrosia from the table of the gods, and gave them to his friends; while a fourth relates the following story. Rhea caused the infant Zeus and his nurse to be guarded by a golden dog, whom subsequently Zeus appointed guardian of his temple in Crete. Pandærus stole the dog, and carrying him to Mount Sipylus, in Lydia, gave him to Tantalus to take care of. But when Pandærus demanded the dog back, Tantalus took an oath that he had never received him. The punishment of Tantalus was proverbial in ancient times, and from it the English language has borrowed the verb "to tantalize," that is, to hold out hopes or prospects which can never be realized. See IXION.

Tantras (from *tansu tan, to believe*) are the sacred writings of the Hindûs, which are said to have been composed by Siva, and bear the same relation to the votaries of Siva that the Puranas do to the votaries of Vishnu. The Saiva sect look upon the Tantras as the fifth Veda, and attribute to them equal antiquity and superior authority. The observances they prescribe have, indeed, in Bengal, almost superseded the original ritual. The date of the first composition is involved in considerable obscurity; but professor Wilson thinks that the system originated early in the Christian æra, being founded on the previous worship of the female principle and the practices of the Yoga, with the Mantras or mystical formulæ of the Vedas. The principal Tantras are the *Syamarahasya*, *Rudrayamala*, *Mantramahodadhi*, *Saradatilaka*, and *Kalikatantra*. Rammohun Roy alleges, in his *Apology for Vedantic Theism*, that among the Tantras there are forged works and passages, published as if genuine, "with the view of introducing new doctrines, new rites, or new precepts of secular law." Some of the Tantras appear to have been written chiefly in Bengal, and in the eastern districts of Hindustan, being unknown in the west and south, and the rites they teach having there failed to set aside the ceremonies of the Vedas, although they are not without an important influence upon the belief and practices of the people. The Saktas (q. v.) derive the principles of their sect, and their religious ceremomies, wholly from the Tantras, and hence are often called Tantraists.

Tantum Ergo (*So great therefore*). The concluding part of the hymn for Corpus Christi day, entitled *Pange lingua*, which is sung in the Latin Church when the holy sacrament is exposed for the worship, and elevated for the benediction of the faithful.

"Tantum ergo Sacramentum
Veneremur cernui:
Et antiquum documentum
Novo cedat ritui:
Præstet fides supplementum
Sensuum defectui.

"Genitori, genitoque
Laus et jubilatio,
Salus, honor, virtus quoque,
Sit et benedictio:
Procedenti ab utroque
Compar sit laudatio. Amen."

Tapestry. The Church of the Middle Ages required for various purposes a great number of tapestries —for *dorsalia* at the back of the choir-stalls, for closing the doors and windows, for the protecting enclosures of the altars, for the veiling of the sanctuary during the fast-time (fasting-cloths), and especially for clothing the walls and the floor. At first the tapestry came from the East, until, in the 4th century, a tapestry manufactory was formed at Palermo, which, under the hands of Saracen and Byzantine workmen, imitated the Oriental patterns. These old silk webs, of which we find remains here and there in collections, show a strictly architectonic style, and are covered with figures of animals of a typical character, such as griffins, unicorns, lions, elephants, peacocks, and parrots. In the northern cloisters, tapestry-weaving was learned and soon practiced, even from the beginning of the Romanesque period, and the circle of representations was increased by Biblical and symbolical scenes, to which were added representations out of favorite poets. Tapestry-embroidery was an occupation followed with zeal in the nunneries. From the 14th century, carpets painted with size-colors on linen were also made. With the entrance of Gothic art, there appears in use a frieze-like composition, hand in hand with a naïve naturalistic border, which drives out the severe style of the earlier times. Interesting tapestries of the Romanesque period, partly with antique mythological representations, are to be seen in the treasury of the collegiate church at Quedlinburg; others of the same time, with Christian representations, in the cathedral at Halberstadt, intended for the backs of choir-stalls. A complete selection of tapestries is in the monastery of Wienhausen, near Zell, one of them an embroidery with the history of Tristan and Isolde; others in the St. Elizabeth Church at Marburg, in St. Sebald and St. Lorenz, at Nuremberg, and in many church treasuries.

Tappan, HENRY PHILIP, D.D., LL.D., a distinguished educator, was born at Rhinebeck on the Hudson, April 23, 1805. He graduated from Union College in 1825, and from Auburn Theological Seminary in 1827; became assistant to the Rev. Dr. Van Vechten, in the Reformed Dutch Church at Schenectady; the next year was settled as pastor of the Congregational Church at Pittsfield, Mass.; and in 1831 was compelled by ill-health to resign. In 1832 he was appointed professor of moral and intellectual philosophy in the University of the City of New York, and resigned in 1838. During the next few years he spent most of his time in writing books and conducting a private seminary in New York city. He published, *A Review of Edward's Inquiry into the Freedom of the Will* (1839):—*The Doctrine of the Freedom of the Will Determined by an Appeal to Consciousness* (1840):—*The Doctrine of the Freedom of the Will applied to Moral Agency and Responsibility* (1841):—*Elements of Logic, with an Introductory View of Philosophy in General, and a Preliminary View of the Reason* (1844):—a treatise on *University Education* (1851). In the latter year he went to Europe, and on his return in 1852 published *A Step from the New World to the Old.* He was president of the University of Michigan from 1852 to 1863, and gave it a new life by his administration. After his retirement from this school he lived almost entirely abroad, and died Nov. 15, 1881, at Vevay, Switzerland.

Tappuah. The present *Tuffah*, which probably represents Beth-tappuah (Josh. xv, 53), is briefly described in the *Memoirs* to the Ordnance Survey (iii, 310). *Beit-Atah*, which we have conjectured to be the Tappuah of Josh. xii, 11; xv, 34, is copiously described, ibid. p. 22 sq., 83; but Tristram suggests (*Bible Places*, p. 48) for the latter Biblical site the present *Artuf*, which lies three and a half miles to the north-west of Beit-Atah, and one and a quarter miles south-east of Surah (Zorah). It is described in the above *Memoirs* (iii, 22) as "a small village on a low hill, with an open valley to the west. There is a pool in the valley, where the village obtains its water. Olive-trees occur around the place." There do not seem to be any traces of antiquity. The third Tappuah, or that of Ephraim

(Josh. xvi, 8; xvii, 8), or En-tappuah, is conceded by Tristram (*ut sup.* p. 195) to be the modern *Atûf*, but to this Conder objects (*Memoirs*, ii, 357) that there is no spring and no tombs, and that the names have but one letter in common. The place is "a mud village, built on an older site, and supplied by wells and cisterns" (ibid. p. 227).

Tasso, TORQUATO, a celebrated Italian poet, was born at Sorrento, where his parents were visiting, March 11, 1544. Soon after his parents returned to Naples with him, and committed their son, at the age of three years, to the care of a man of learning. At four he was sent to the college of the Jesuits, where he made such rapid progress that at seven years of age he was pretty well acquainted with the Latin and Greek tongues. Bernardo, the father of the poet, following his patron, the prince of Salerno, into France, committed his son, then nine years old, to Maurice Cataneo, who assiduously cultivated the early disposition of his pupil to polite literature. When Tasso was twelve years of age he went to join his father, who soon afterwards placed him in the University of Padua, where he wrote *Rinaldo*, a poem, being then in his eighteenth year. Invited by the principal persons of the city and college of Bologna, he took up his residence there, but shortly after, upon the invitation of Scipio Gonzaga, prince of the academy at Padua, returned to that city, and became incorporated into the academy, at the age of twenty years. He here formed the design of his celebrated poem, *Jerusalem Delivered*, and being urged by Alphonso II, duke of Ferrara, took up his residence in his palace. He continued to work upon his great poem, which he completed in his thirtieth year, but it was printed, even then, against his will. Not long after, being engaged in a duel, he was arrested by order of the duke, ostensibly to screen him from the designs of his enemies. After about a year's detention, he escaped, and retired to Turin, where he endeavored to remain concealed. He soon became known, and was received by the duke of Savoy, who showed him every mark of esteem. Fearful of being given up to the duke of Ferrara, he left Turin and went to Rome, where he was treated with great honor by all classes. Shortly after he took up his residence with his sister at Sorrento, and then returned to Ferrara, hoping to have his writings restored to him. Failing in this he left that city, and went to Mantua, Padua, and Venice, finally trying his fortune once more with the duke, who, pretending to believe that his mind had become affected, caused him to be confined in the hospital of Santa Anna. After seven years' confinement, his release was procured by Vincentio Gonzaga, prince of Mantua, who brought him to his own city. Wearied with dependence, he resolved to retire to Naples, and from there he went to Bisaccio with his friend Manso. At the approach of winter they returned to Naples, and soon after Tasso went to Rome, where he lived about a year, and, after some wandering, took up his residence at Naples again with the count of Palena. Here he applied himself to the composition of *Jerusalem Conquered.* He abandoned Naples again to go to Rome upon the invitation of cardinal Cynthio Aldobrandini. Disgusted with the life of a courtier, he obtained permission to retire to Naples, where he took up his lodging in the Benedictine convent of San Severino. He was, however, soon recalled to Rome, to be publicly crowned with laurel in the capitol. He arrived in that city in the beginning of 1595, but while the preparations for the ceremony were being made, Tasso fell ill, and died, in the monastery of San Onufrio, April 25, 1595.

Tatwine, archbishop of Canterbury, was a distinguished scholar, poet, and divine. He was appointed to the see of Canterbury in 731, and passed the remainder of his life in the quiet routine of episcopal duty. He died in 734. See Hook, *Lives of the Archbishops of Canterbury*, i, 195 sq.

Tawûs Version. See PERSIAN VERSIONS.

Taylor, Benjamin C., D.D., a Reformed (Dutch) minister, was born in Philadelphia, Pa., Feb. 24, 1801. He graduated from Princeton College in 1819, and from the New Brunswick Theological Seminary in 1822; was licensed the latter year, and immediately became pastor at Greenbush and Blooming Grove, Rensselaer Co., N. Y.; in 1825 at Aquackanock (now Passaic), N. J.; in 1828 at Bergen, where he was made pastor emeritus in 1870, and died, Feb. 2, 1881. He published several sermons and addresses, and a volume entitled *Annals of the Classis and Township of Bergen* (1856).

Taylor, Francis, an English theologian of the 17th century, is the author of a Latin translation of *Aben-Ezra's Commentary on* and *Rashi's Exposition of Lamentations* (Lond. 1645):—*Targum Hierosol. in quinque Libros Legis in Latinum Conversum* (1649):—*Pirke Aboth cum Versione Latina a Phil. Aquino, Additis Notis Marginalibus* (1651):—*Targum Prius et Posterius in Estheram*, etc. (1655). Together with Arnold Boote, he published, *Examen Præfationis Joh. Morini in Biblia Græca de Textus Hebraici Corruptione et Græci Auctoritate* (Leyden, 1636). See Fürst, *Bibl. Jud.* s. v.; Jöcher, *Allgemeines Gelehrten-Lexikon*, s. v. (B. P.)

Taylor, James Barnett, D.D., a Baptist minister, was born at Barton-upon-Humber, England, March 19, 1804. He came to New York with his parents while an infant; removed to Virginia in 1817, having already, at the age of thirteen, made a profession of religion; began to preach at the age of sixteen, and was formally licensed at twenty. He performed, for a year or two, missionary labor in the Meherran District, Va.; was ordained May 2, 1826, at Sandy Creek, and, the same year, was called to the pastorate of the Second Church at Richmond, where he remained thirteen years. He was elected chaplain of the University of Virginia in 1839, and in 1840 became pastor of the Grace Street Church, Richmond, where he remained until 1844, and then entered upon his duties as corresponding secretary of the Southern Baptist Convention, which office he held with distinguished ability for twenty-six years. During thirteen of these years he was pastor of the Taylorsville Church, and was also in the Confederate army as colporteur and post-chaplain. For a short time he was editor of *The Religious Herald.* The *Southern Baptist Missionary Journal* and *Home and Foreign Journal* were established by him. He wrote also a *Life of Lot Carey*, a *Life of Luther Rice*, *Lives of Virginia Baptist Ministers*, and had prepared, in part, a *History of Virginia Baptists.* After the war he took a deep interest in the spiritual welfare of the freedmen. He died Dec. 22, 1871. See Cathcart, *Baptist Encyclop.* p. 1134. (J. C. S.)

Taylor, John Lord, D.D., a Congregational divine, was born at Warren, Conn., May 20, 1811. He graduated from Yale College in 1835 and at the Divinity School in 1839, having been a tutor in the college for two years; was ordained pastor of the South Church, Andover, Mass., the last-mentioned year; became professor of theology and homiletics in Andover Theological Seminary in 1868, resigned in 1879, and died there, Sept. 23, 1884. Besides many contributions to the literary journals, he wrote, a *Memoir of Hon. Samuel Phillips* (1856):—*Memorial of the Semi-Centennial Celebration of Andover Theological Seminary* (1859).

Taylor, Joseph van Sommern, a missionary of India, was born at Bellary, Southern India, in 1820, where his father was a missionary of the London Society. He was educated at the Bishop's College in Calcutta and at Glasgow, graduating at the latter place in 1845. In the same year, having been accepted by the London Missionary Society, he left England for Gujerat, where he labored for thirty-four years, the last twenty-one years in connection with the Presbyterian Church of Ireland. He died in 1881. Mr. Taylor, besides translating the *Confession of Faith* into Gujerati, wrote two of the best grammars in that language. The natives of Gujerat are indebted to him for a *History of the Christian Church*, founded on that of Dr. Barth, as well as for a *Book of Christian Praise* and a *Manual of Devotion.* Several of the best tracts in the list of the Gujerat Tract and Book Society are from his pen. He also translated the *Shorter Catechism*, and was engaged at the time of his death on a translation of the *Philosophy of the Plan of Salvation*, which he left unfinished. (B. P.)

Taytazak. See TAITAZAK.

Tcheremissian Version. See RUSSIA, VERSIONS OF.

Tchuwaschian Version. See RUSSIA, VERSIONS OF.

Teaching of the Twelve Apostles is the title of a newly discovered writing belonging to the Patristic period. In the year 1883 Philotheos Bryennios, metropolitan of Nicomedia, published, from the Jerusalem manuscript of the year 1056, and preserved at Constantinople, a hitherto unknown writing, bearing two titles, *Διδαχὴ τῶν δώδεκα ἀποστόλων* and *Διδαχὴ κυρίου διὰ τῶν δώδεκα ἀποστόλων τοῖς ἔθνεσιν*. An edition with critical emendations was published in 1884 by Hilgenfeld, in his *Novum Testamentum Extra Canonem Receptum* (Leipsic, 1884, iv, 94–103), and from that time the republic of letters has been kept alive by translations, essays, etc.

I. *Contents.*—The "Teaching" comprises sixteen chapters, and may be divided into four parts: ch. i–vi, comprising the doctrinal and catechetical part, setting forth the whole duty of the Christian; ch. vii–x and xiv contains the liturgical and devotional part, giving directions for Christian worship; ch. xi–xiii and xv contains the ecclesiastical and disciplinary part, concerning church officers; and ch. xvi the eschatological part, or the Christian's hope.

II. *Theology of the Teaching.*—God is the Creator (i, 2), who made all things (x, 3), and is our Father in heaven (viii, 2). Nothing can happen without him (iii, 10); he is the giver of all good gifts, the author of our salvation, the object of prayer and praise (ix and x), to whom belongs all glory through Christ Jesus (viii, 2; ix, 4; x, 4). Christ is the Lord and Saviour (x, 2, 3), God's servant and God's son (ix, 2), and David's God (x, 6), the author of the gospel (viii, 2; xv, 4). He is spiritually present in his Church, and will visibly come again to judgment (xvi, 1, 7, 8). Through him knowledge and eternal life have been made known to us (ix, 3; x, 2). The Holy Spirit is associated with the Father and the Son (vii, 1, 3); he prepares man for the call of God (iv, 10), speaks through the prophets, and the sin against the Spirit shall not be forgiven (xi, 7).

The Teaching speaks of the Lord's Day as a day to be kept holy (xiv, 1), and recognises only two sacraments, Baptism and the Eucharist (vii, 1–4; ix, x, xiv).

Man is made in the image of God (v, 2) but sinful, and needs forgiveness (viii, 2); he must confess his transgressions to receive pardon (iv, 14; xiv, 1, 2). There are only two ways, the way of life and the way of death.

III. *Language of the Teaching.*—The "Didache" is written in Hellenistic Greek, like the New Test. It is the common Macedonian or Alexandrian dialect, with "a strong infusion of a Hebrew soul and a Christian spirit." The "Didache" contains 2190 words, 504 are New Test. words, 497 are classical, and 479 occur in the Septuagint, 15 occur for the first time in the "Didache," but are found in later writers.

IV. *Authenticity of the Teaching.*—It is first quoted by Clement of Alexandria (*Stromata*, i, 20), who cites a passage from it as "Scripture." Eusebius (died A.D. 340) mentions it as "the so-called Teachings of the Apostles" (*Hist. Eccl.* iii, 25), and so does Athanasius (died A.D. 373) (*Epist. Fest.* 39, in *Opera*, ed. Bened. i, 2, 963). The last mention of the "Teaching" is by Nicephorus, patriarch of Constantinople (died A.D. 828), who speaks of such a book as among the Apocrypha of the New Test.

V. *Date, Place, and Authorship.*—The most prevailing view as to the time when the Teaching was composed is between A.D. 80 and 120; but this date seems to us rather early. The majority of scholars assign the Teaching to Alexandria in Egypt, a minority to Palestine or Syria. Who the author of the Teaching was is not known. From the work itself, it may safely be stated that he was a Jewish Christian.

VI. *Scripture Quotations and Allusions in the Didache.*—The author of the Teaching quotes not only the Old and New Tests., but also the Apocrypha of the Old Test., as the following table will exhibit:

1. *Quotations from the Old Testament.*

Zech. xiv, 5	Teaching xvi, 7.
Mal. i, 11, 14	xiv, 3.

2. *Allusions to the Old Testament.*

Exod. xviii, 20; Deut. xxxi, 29	i, 1.
xx, 13–17; v, 17–21	ii.
Numb. xviii, 12, 13, 15, 30 Deut. xviii, 3, 4 Ezek. xliv, 30 Neh. x, 35–37	xiii.
Deut. xii, 32	iv, 13.
Job iv, 10	iv, 6.
Isa. lxvi, 2, 5	iii, 8.
Jer. xxi, 8	i, 1.
Dan. iv, 27	iv, 6.

3. *Quotations from, and Allusions to, the Old Testament Apocrypha.*

Tobit iv, 7	iv, 6–8.
15	i, 2.
Ecclus. ii, 4	iii, 10.
iv, 5	iv, 8.
31	iv, 5.

4. *Quotations and Reminiscences from the New Testament.*

Matt. v, 5	iii, 7.
23, 24	xiv, 2.
25, 26	i, 5.
39–41 (Luke vi, 29, 30)	i, 4.
44–46 (Luke vi, 27)	i, 3.
vi, 5	viii, 2.
1, 5	xv, 4.
9–13	viii, 2.
16	viii, 1.
vii, 6	ix, 5.
12	i, 2.
x, 9, 10 (comp. Luke ix, 1–6; x, 4–7)	xiii, 1, 2.
xii, 31	xi, 7.
xviii, 15, 17	xv, 3.
xxi, 9	x, 6.
xxii, 37–39	i, 2.
xxiv, 10–14	xvi, 4, 5.
30, 31	6, 8.
31, 35	1.
42, 44	x, 5.
xxv, 34	"
xxviii, 19, 20	vii, 1.
Luke vi, 27–30	i, 3, 4, 5.
xii, 35	xvi, 1.

5. *Allusions and Parallels to the New Testament.*

Acts iv, 32	iv, 8.
Rom. xv, 27	"
1 Cor. xv, 52	xvi, 6.
" xvi, 22 (Maranatha)	x, 6.
Eph. vi, 5, 9	iv, 10, 11.
1 Thess. iv, 16, 17	xvi, 4–8.
" v, 22	iii, 1.
2 Thess. ii, 8–10	xvi, 4.
Heb. x, 22 (*συνείδησις πονηρά*)	xiv, 1.
25	"
xiii, 7	xv, 1, 2.
1 Pet. ii, 11	i, 4.
Rev. i, 8	x, 2.
10	xiv, 1.
xxii, 15	v, 2.

The absence of any reference to so many books of the New Test. accords with the view that we have before us a very early document; but it does not, of course, prove that the sacred writings were unknown to the writer, and still less does it furnish any argument for the view that they were not then known to the Church in general. The object of the writer was very limited; his intention was to furnish a manual or catechism for catechumens.

VII. *Literature.*—Although so recently discovered, this little tract has already been the subject of very numerous essays and expositions. In addition to the treatise mentioned above and De Romestin, *Teaching of the Twelve Apostles* (Lond. 1884, 8vo), the most complete and exhaustive work, giving, besides the original text, an English translation and literary matter, is the one published by Ph. Schaff, *The Oldest Church Manual, called "The Teaching of the Twelve Apostles"* (New York, 1885). (B. P.)

Tekke Turcoman Version. See JAGHATAI TURKI VERSION.

Tekoa. The present *Khurbet Tekûa* is archæologically described in the *Memoirs* accompanying the Ordnance Survey (iii, 314, 368).

Ten Broeck, ANTHONY, D.D., a Protestant Episcopal clergyman, was born in New York city in 1815. He graduated from Columbia College, and from the General Theological Seminary in 1837; for many years was engaged in teaching; was connected with a school in Orange, N. J., under the supervision of bishop Doane; taught in the Mt. Auburn Institute in Washington; founded the bishop Bowman Institute at Pittsburgh, Pa.; and became rector of Burlington College. He was rector of St. James's Church, Eatontown, N. J., at the time of his death, Sept. 22, 1880. See Whittaker, *Almanac and Directory*, 1881, p. 175.

Tennent, WILLIAM MACKAY, D.D., a Presbyterian minister, graduated from the College of New Jersey in 1763, and in 1772 was ordained pastor at Greenfield, Conn. In 1781 he accepted a call to the Presbyterian Church at Abingdon, near Philadelphia, where he continued until his death, in December, 1810. See Sprague, *Annals of the Amer. Pulpit*, iii, 26.

Tenney, ERDIX, D.D., a Congregational minister, son of Dr. Joshua Tenney, was born at Corinth, Vt., June 11, 1801. He studied at Bradford Academy; in 1826 graduated from Middlebury College; in 1829 from the Andover Theological Seminary; was ordained pastor, Jan. 5, 1831, at Lyme, N. H., and was dismissed Aug. 12, 1867. From 1867 to 1880 he resided at Westborough, Mass., without charge; and from 1880 until death, Nov. 13, 1882, at Norwich, Conn. See *Cong. Year-book*, 1883, p. 33.

Tent. The following description of this Arab domicile, from Conder's *Tent Work*, ii, 275, contains some additional information:

"The tents are arranged in different ways. Among the Sugr a large encampment was set out in parallel lines some fifty yards apart, the tents in each row being close together, end to end. Among the Tâ'amireh and Jâhalîn the usual form is a rectangle. The average length of the tent is from twenty to twenty-five feet, but the small ones will sometimes be only ten feet long, and the larger forty feet. The distance between two tents in a line is about four feet. Thus a camp of twenty tents occupied a space of two hundred feet by seventy feet. In another case the form was a triangle, the reason of this arrangement being that the flocks are driven into the enclosure at night, and thus protected from the attacks of robbers or prevented from straying by themselves.

"The Arab tent is extremely unlike the usual representations, in which it is shown either as a sort of hut, as among the Turkomans, or as a bell-tent, instead of a long black 'house of hair,' with a low, sloping roof and open front. It has, however, been carefully described by Burckhardt, and there is little to add to his account. The canvas of the roof and side walls is of goat's hair, black, with occasionally stripes of white running horizontally (Cant. i, 5). The pieces of stuff are about two feet wide, and thirty to fifty feet long. The tent has generally nine poles ('Awamîd), arranged three and three, those in the centre being the longest; thus the tent has a low ridge both ways in order to run the rain off. The cloths at the side can be easily removed as the sun and wind requires, one side being always left open. The tents are supported by cords and by pegs (Autâd), which are driven with a mallet (Judg. iv, 21). The average height of a tent is about seven feet.

"Frail and cold as these habitations might be thought to prove in winter, they are really far more comfortable than would be expected. Being so low, the wind does not blow them over, and they are, moreover, most skilfully pitched, generally below a steep bank or low swell. Even in heavy storms I have found the interiors dry, and the heavy canvas does not let the rain through. The Arabs, however, suffer very much from rheumatism in winter. In summer they occasionally inhabit reed huts ('Arîsh), which are cooler than the tents."

Ter Haar, BERNARD, a Dutch theologian, was born at Amsterdam, June 13, 1806. He studied at Leyden, and was in 1839 doctor of theology. After having served several congregations with great success, he was in 1843 called to Amsterdam, and was made professor of theology in 1854 at Utrecht. In 1874 he retired to Velp, near Arnheim, and died Nov. 19, 1880. He published, *Jean et Théogène* (Arnheim, 1838):—*Histoire de la Reformation* (1845; 5th ed. 1854):—*De Historiæ Ecclesiasticæ et Theologiæ Moralis Studio* (Utrecht, 1854):—*De Historicæ Religionis Christianæ Indole* (1860):—*L'Historiographie de l'Histoire Ecclésiastique* (1870–71, 2 vols.). See Lichtenberger, *Encyclop. des Sciences Religieuses*, s. v. (B. P.)

Antique Figure of Terpsichore.

Terpsichŏrê, one of the nine Muses (q. v.); she presided over choral song and dancing.

Thalīa, one of the nine Muses (q. v.); regarded in later times as presiding over comedy. She became the mother of the Corybantes, by Apollo.

Antique Figure of Thalia.

Theberath, CHARLES S., D.D., a Presbyterian minister, was born in one of the Rhenish provinces of Prussia in 1807. He came to America in 1840, and settled in New York city, where he founded a Sunday-school in the fifteenth ward, from which sprang the Second German Presbyterian Church. He was the first pastor of this church, where he labored successfully several years. Receiving a call from the German Presbyterian Church of Paterson, N. J., he accepted the same, and remained four years. After this he took charge of a mission-school in Albany, N. Y., where he continued until his health failed, when he resigned and removed to Newark, N. J., where he died, Oct. 8, 1882. (W. P. S.)

Thebez. The modern *Tabûs* is described in the *Memoirs* to the Ordnance Survey (ii, 229, 247).

Theobald, archbishop of Canterbury, was born in Normandy, the year of his birth not being known. He was the third archbishop supplied to the Church of England by the celebrated abbey of Bec. He was appointed prior in 1127, and ten years afterwards was elected abbot. In 1138 he was invited to England by king Stephen and his queen, Matilda. He was consecrated archbishop of Canterbury in 1139. It reflects credit upon the character of Theobald that, in that rude and boisterous age, his residence became the centre of all the learning and ability of the kingdom. "For two generations several of the most distinguished men in the country could refer to the happy hours they had passed at Theobald's court." He appears to have been banished by the king at one time, but he returned to England, and matters were again set right. The last time Theobald appeared in public was at the consecration of Richard Peche, bishop of Lichfield. He was too infirm to officiate, but witnessed the consecration. He died April 18, 1161. See Hook, *Lives of the Archbishops of Canterbury*, ii, 322 sq.

Theological Seminaries. See SEMINARIES, THEOLOGICAL.

Theurer, CARL JOHANN WILHELM, a Protestant minister, was born April 26, 1826, at Waldenbuch, in

Würtemberg. In 1858 he was pastor at Mühlhausen-on-the-Neckar, in 1870 assistant at the hospital church in Stutgard, in 1875 second preacher at the Stiftskirche there, and died July 16, 1882, at Zavelstein. He published, *Das Reich Gottes*, etc. (Ludwigsburg, 1862) :—*Predigten* (ibid. 1874, 2d ed. 1879) :—*Blicke in die Herrlichkeit des Vater-Unsers* (1881, 2d ed. 1882). (B. P.)

Thiersch, Heinrich Wilhelm Josias, a Protestant theologian of Germany, was born at Munich, Nov. 5, 1817. In 1840 he commenced his academical career at Erlangen, and in 1843 was professor at Marburg, but resigned his professorship in 1850 on account of his conversion to the "Catholic Apostolic Church." He spent many years as a private tutor in South Germany, continuing all the time active and fertile in the production of theological works. In 1875 Thiersch retired to Basle, and died Dec. 3, 1885. He published, *Ad Pentateuchi Versionem Alexandrinam Critice Pertractandam Prolegomena* (Erlangen, 1840) :—*De Pentateuchi Versione Alexandrina Libri Tres* (1841) :—*Hebräische Grammatik* (1842; 2d ed. 1858) :—*Versuch zur Herstellung des historischen Standpunkts für die Kritik der neutestamentlichen Schriften* (1845) :—*Einige Worte über die Aechtheit der neutest. Schriften*, etc. (1846) :—*Vorlesungen über Katholicismus und Protestantismus* (eod.; 2d ed. 1848) :—*De Epistola ad Hebræos Commentatio Historica* (Marburg, 1849) :—*De Stephani Protomartyris Oratione Commentatio Exegetica* (eod.) :—*Die Geschichte der christl. Kirche im Alterthum* (2d ed. 1858; 3d ed. 1879) :—*Politik und Philosophie in ihrem Verhältniss zur Religion unter Trajanus, Hadrianus und den beiden Antoninen* (1853) :—*Ueber christliches Familienleben* (1854; often reprinted) :—*Die Bergpredigt Christi und ihre Bedeutung für die Gegenwart* (1867; 2d ed. 1878) :—*Die Gleichnisse Christi nach ihrer moralischen und prophetischen Bedeutung betrachtet* (1867; 2d ed. 1875) :—*Die Genesis nach ihrer moralischen und prophetischen Bedeutung betrachtet* (1870; new ed. 1875) :—*Inbegriff der christlichen Lehre* (published shortly after the author's death, Basle, 1886). See Zuchold, *Bibl. Theol.* s. v.; *Allgemeine evangel. luth. Kirchenzeitung* (Leipsic, 1886), No. 1, 2, 3. (B. P.)

Thomas, the name of several Scotch prelates.

1. Bishop of Galloway, who swore fealty to Edward I of England in 1296, and recognised king Robert Bruce's title to the crown in 1304. He was bishop here before 1309. See Keith, *Scottish Bishops*, p. 273.

2. Bishop of the Isles about 1334. He died in Scotland, Sept. 20, 1338. See Keith, *Scottish Bishops*, p. 303.

3. Bishop of Galloway in 1362. See Keith, *Scottish Bishops*, p. 274.

4. Bishop of Ross in 1481, and founder of the collegiate church of Tain the same year. He was still bishop there in 1487. See Keith, *Scottish Bishops*, p. 189.

Thomas of Wilton, D.D., was made first chancellor and then dean of St. Paul's, London. In his time (during the reign of Edward IV) occurred the contest between the prelates and friars, the latter upbraiding the former for their pomp and plenty. Wilton entered into this contest, and charged upon the monks that, although confessing their poverty, they really, by their influence at the confessional, opened the coffers of all the treasures in the land. He wrote a book, *An Validi Mendicantes sint in Statu Perfectionis*, maintaining that such were rogues by the laws of God and man, and fitter for the house of correction than a state of perfection. Wilton flourished in 1460. See Fuller, *Worthies of England* (ed. Nuttall), iii, 335.

Thomas, Benjamin, D.D., a Baptist minister, was born in South Wales in 1823, and, when quite young, removed to Ohio. He graduated from Denison University, was ordained in 1846, and, for a time, taught in Vermillion College. His pastorates were as follows: Mansfield, Monroeville, First Church in Zanesville, Bradfield, and Newark, all in Ohio. Subsequently he removed to Bloomington, Ill., and became western secretary of the American Bible Union. Having occupied other prominent positions in his denomination in Illinois, he removed to Arkansas in 1864, and became president of the university at Judsonia. During the war he served as a soldier in the Federal army, and became brevet-colonel. He died at Little Rock, Ark., March 5, 1884. See Cathcart, *Baptist Encyclop.* p. 1147. (J. C. S.)

Thomas, John, M.D., the founder of the Christadelphians (q. v.), was born at Hoxton Square, London, April 12, 1805. His father was a Dissenting clergyman while in England and a Baptist clergyman after coming to the United States in 1832. John was educated as a physician, beginning, at the age of sixteen, a medical course under a private physician, and continuing it for three years at St. Thomas's Hospital. He then assisted a London physician a year, and practiced medicine at Hackney three years. Although a member of his father's church from boyhood, his first attention to creeds was in 1830 or 1831, when he began the study of the subject of immortality, upon which he made contributions to *The Lancet*. Purely as a business venture he sailed for New York, May 1, 1832. Shortly after reaching Cincinnati he became acquainted with Walter Scott, the original founder of the "Christians," or Campbellites. Before he was aware of it, he had heard from Scott a full exposition of his doctrines, had assented to them as appearing rational, and had been induced to indicate that assent by immersion at ten o'clock at night in the Miami canal. On a trip east, in 1833, he met and visited Alexander Campbell, was forced reluctantly into assisting him in public addresses, and was so well received by the people that, on reaching Baltimore, he made addresses every evening for a week upon religious topics. During 1834 and 1835 he practiced medicine in Philadelphia, Baltimore, and Richmond, speaking to the Campbellite congregations on Sundays. In May, 1834, he issued the first number of *The Apostolic Advocate*, a monthly magazine, of which five volumes were issued in all. His first opposition to the received views of the sect consisted in publishing, in No. 6 of his magazine, an article on Anabaptism, resulting in controversy between him and Mr. Campbell. The former insisted upon the re-immersion of persons coming to the sect from Baptist churches; the latter denied its necessity. On Dec. 1, 1835, Dr. Thomas made another advance in free-thought by publishing thirty-four questions which hinted at materialism, annihilation of the wicked, a physical kingdom, etc. The chief outcry against him was for his materialistic tendencies. By 1836 Mr. Campbell denounced him openly. About this time Dr. Thomas moved to Amelia County, Va., abandoned the practice of medicine, set up a printing-office on his farm, and devoted himself largely to literary work. In August, 1837, he engaged in a public discussion with a Presbyterian clergyman, Rev. Mr. Watt. In November he was publicly disfellowshipped by Mr. Campbell, while, in response to the demands of the latter, he was called to account by the churches at Painesville and Bethel for his views. They did not, however, see fit to discipline him, contenting themselves with some suggestions concerning the spirit in which he should carry on the discussion. In 1838 he made a preaching tour through the southern counties of Virginia, coming in conflict more or less with Mr. Campbell. In 1839 he removed to Longrove, Ill., took up two hundred and eighty-eight acres of land, and for two years confined his attention to farming. After a brief residence at St. Charles, where his printing-office and physician's office were burned, he opened an office at Hennepin, and was appointed lecturer on chemistry in Franklin Medical College. The *Advocate* having now been suspended for nearly three years, he started, in 1842, a monthly called *The Investigator*, of which he issued twelve numbers. In 1843 he began *The Herald of the Future Age*, at Louisville, Ky., and continued it at Richmond, where, in

1844, he held his first meetings separately from the Campbellites. Collisions with the latter led to further study and to wider divergence of creed. He published his articles of belief at this time, and in October, 1846, delivered a series of ten lectures in New York in defence thereof. Having still further perfected his declaration of belief, he decided, in February or March, 1847, that he ought to be baptized into that belief; accordingly, he requested a friend to immerse him and to say over him, "Upon confession of your faith in the things concerning the kingdom of God and the name of Jesus Christ, I baptize you into the name of the Father, Son, and Holy Spirit." After fourteen years of search he was now satisfied that he had reached the truth. He began to advocate it more earnestly than ever, visiting Baltimore, where he was permitted to speak in the Campbellite meeting-house; Buffalo, where he was furnished with the Millerite place of worship, and New York, where he was received by the Campbellites. With letters from many Campbellites and other friends he sailed from New York in June, 1848, for England. His enemies had communicated his peculiar doctrines to the Campbellites of Nottingham and other places. He was therefore refused audience by them, but he addressed the Millerites of Nottingham, Derby, Birmingham, and Plymouth. The London Campbellites denounced him officially. Those of Lincoln and Newark received him, and the former made him their delegate to the Church convention at Glasgow. An effort to prevent his sitting was unsuccessful, and he addressed large audiences in the City Hall. A call for the publication of his views, while at Glasgow, led to the preparation of *Elpis Israel* (478 pp. royal 8vo). At Edinburgh he delivered a course of ten lectures. Spending the winter of 1848-49 in London, upon his book, he made subsequent tours through England and Scotland lecturing and preaching. In November, 1850, he came again to the United States, resumed *The Herald of the Future Age* in 1851, and published vol. i of *Eureka*. He travelled and advocated his views through the States and Canada until 1862, when the war caused the cessation of his paper, and he sailed for Liverpool. He visited all the places where groups had been organized to advocate his views, and, returning to the United States, issued the second volume of *Eureka*. The third volume was published in 1868. A third trip to Great Britain was made in 1869, when he found that his Birmingham church had grown from twelve to one hundred and twenty-three members. Crossing to the United States for the fourth time, in May, 1870, he began a tour of the country, but was prostrated at Worcester, Mass., and compelled to give up his work. He died in New York, March 5, 1871. In addition to the periodicals and books mentioned above, he issued, *The Apostasy Unveiled* (1838, 148 pp.):—*Anatolia* (1854, 102 pp.):—*Anastasis* (46 pp.):—*Phanerois*, and several tracts and lectures. (C. W. S.)

Thomas, Robert S., D.D., a Baptist minister, was born in Scott County, Ky., June 20, 1805. He united with the Church in 1821, was ordained, in 1830, pastor at Columbia, Mo., and for several years performed much evangelical labor in Missouri, being the first to introduce Sabbath-schools into that state. He was chosen professor of languages and moral science in the State University, and in 1853 president of William Jewell College. He finally removed to Kansas City, where he organized a church, of which he was the pastor until his death, June 12, 1859. See Cathcart, *Baptist Encyclop.* p. 1149. (J. C. S.)

Thomas, Thomas, D.D., a Welsh Baptist minister and educator, was born at Cowbridge, Jan. 12, 1805. He began to preach when fifteen years of age, and labored with much zeal. At the age of seventeen he entered the Baptist College at Abergavenny, and two years later removed to Stepney College, where he spent four years in faithful study. In 1828 he entered upon the pastorate of the Church in Henrietta Street, Brunswick Square, London, where he remained eight years. In 1836, on the removal of Abergavenny College to Pontypool, he became its president, and retained the office until 1877. In the beginning of this work he was energetic in his ministerial labors, and soon formed a Baptist Church, which, in time, became the leading one of the town. He died Dec. 6, 1881. See (Lond.) *Baptist Hand-book*, 1883, p. 278.

Thomas, Thomas E., D.D., a Presbyterian minister, was born in London, England, in 1812, and graduated from Miami University in 1834. His first pastoral charge was at Harrison, near Cincinnati, and his second at Hamilton, for twelve years. He then accepted the presidency of Hanover College, Ind., and passed from that to a professorship in the Theological Seminary at New Albany. In 1859 he became pastor of the First Presbyterian Church at Dayton, O., and in 1871 was elected professor of Biblical literature in Lane Theological Seminary. He died Feb. 2, 1875. Dr. Thomas was a man of strong mind, and one of the leaders of the anti-slavery party in the Presbyterian Church long before the civil war. See *Presbyterian*, Feb. 13, 1875.

Thompson, Thomas Jefferson, D.D., a Methodist Episcopal minister, was born in Dorchester County, Md., March 13, 1803. He was converted in his thirteenth year, began his itinerant career in 1825, and in 1826 entered the Philadelphia Conference. In it he served in turn Milford and Talbot Circuits; St. George's, Philadelphia; Rahway, N. J.; St. John's, Philadelphia; Kent Circuit, Md.; Trenton, N. J.; Newark; East Jersey District; Harrisburg, Pa.; Fifth Street, Philadelphia; St. Paul's; Snow Hill District; Asbury Church, Wilmington; Union Church, Philadelphia; South Philadelphia District; Reading District, as general agent of Wesleyan Female College; Dover, Del.; Easton District, Dover District, and Wilmington District—thus summing twenty-two and a half years on circuits and stations, two years as agent, and twenty-five years as presiding elder. In 1836 the New Jersey Conference was organized and Mr. Thompson became identified therewith, but the next year returned to the Philadelphia Conference. In 1868, on the formation of the Wilmington Conference, he fell within its limits, and therein remained till his death, at Wilmington, Del., Nov. 29, 1874. Dr. Thompson was a member of the General Conferences of 1844, 1852, 1856, 1860, 1868, 1872. He was characterized by promptness and sterling integrity, zeal and solid worth. See *Minutes of Annual Conferences*, 1875, p. 27.

Thorah, Feast of the. See Tabernacles, Feast of.

Thorne, James, an eminent minister of the Bible Christians, was born at Shebbear, Devonshire, England, Sept. 21, 1795. At an early age he was converted, and in 1816 entered the ministry. By nature and grace he was peculiarly fitted to be a leading spirit in the Connection. His gifts were diversified, his piety deep, his devotion to the work thorough, and his spirit catholic, childlike, and forbearing. He was president of the Conference five times, viz., in 1831, 1835, 1842, 1857, and 1865; secretary from 1819 to 1830, from 1832 to 1835, in 1849 and 1850, and in 1853—eighteen times; and for several years editor and book-steward. He died Jan. 28, 1872. See *Minutes of the Conference*, 1872; *Jubilee Volume*, published in 1866.

Thorneborough (or **Thornburgh**), John, B.D., an English divine of the 17th century, was born at Salisbury, Wiltshire, educated at Magdalen College, Oxford, was preferred bishop of Limerick in 1593, dean of York in 1603, bishop of Bristol in 1617, at the same time holding his deanery and his Irish bishopric *in commendam* with it. He was translated to Worcester in the latter year, and died July 19, 1641. His skill in chemistry is spoken of. See Fuller, *Worthies of England* (ed. Nuttall), iii, 326.

Throp, Charles, D.D., F.R.S., an English divine, was born at Gateshead rectory, Oct. 13, 1783. He was educated at the Cathedral School, and at Oxford, where he obtained a fellowship, and subsequently was appointed tutor of University College. In 1807 he was presented with the rectorship of Ryton, where he spent several years in active service; in 1829 was presented with a prebendal stall in the Cathedral of Durham; and about 1831 was promoted to the archdeaconry of Durham. At the same time he was elected one of the lord Crewe trustees, in which capacity he exerted himself to the utmost. On the establishment of the University of Durham, he became its first warden. He died at Ryton rectory, Durham, Oct. 10, 1862. Dr. Throp was proverbial for his love of the fine arts, his gallery of pictures surpassing any other in the north of England. He was a man of rare benevolence, giving £400 per annum to endow the parish of Winlanton, and erecting a house of worship at Greenside, at his own expense, to the memory of his parents. See *Appleton's Annual Cyclop.* 1862, p. 693.

Thube, Christian Gottlob, a Lutheran theologian of Germany, was born in Saxony, March 19, 1742. He studied at Leipsic, was in 1775 rector at Bützow, Mecklenburg, in 1776 preacher at Baumgarten, and died Jan. 25, 1826. He published, *Anleitung zum richtigen Verstande der Offenbarung Johannis* (Minden, 1786; 2d ed. 1799):—*Das Buch des Propheten Daniel, neu übersetzt und erklärt* (1797):—*Das Buch des Propheten Sacharja, neu übersetzt und erklärt* (1801). See Döring, *Die gelehrten Theologen Deutschlands*, s. v.; Fürst, *Bibl. Jud.* s. v. (B. P.)

Thummell, C. B., D.D., a Lutheran minister, was born in Germany in 1802; in 1820 entered the University of Halle, Prussia, and graduated from the University of Tübingen, in Würtemberg. In the spring of 1824 he was licensed to preach, and was ordained in 1826. On his arrival in America, in August of that year, he commenced the study of the English language. The first year he was employed as a missionary. From 1827 to 1838 he was professor of languages in Hartwick Seminary; and then accepted a professorship in the Lutheran Seminary at Lexington, S. C. In 1845 he removed to Prairieville, Ill., where he remained until the close of his life, May 23, 1881. For fifteen years he was secretary and treasurer of the Farmers' Mutual Fire Insurance Company of Palmyra, Ill. See *Lutheran Observer*, July 29, 1881.

Thurston, Eli, D.D., a Congregational minister, was born at Brighton, Mass., June 14, 1808. At the age of seventeen he went to Millbury to learn the gunsmith's trade, but having been converted in his twentieth year, he immediately began to study for the ministry, attending Day's Academy at Wrentham, and graduating from Amherst College in 1834. The year following he spent in Andover Theological Seminary, and the two succeeding studied theology with the Rev. Dr. Jacob Ide, of West Medway. He was ordained pastor in Hallowell, Me., Jan. 3, 1838, and filled this position for ten years. The following twenty years, dating from March 21, 1849, he was pastor of the Central Church in Fall River, Mass. He died there, Dec. 19, 1869. In theology Dr. Thurston was ranked as a Hopkinsian Calvinist, and his sermons were all constructed on the basis of his theology. As a preacher he was remarkable for clearness of statement and directness of argument. See *Cong. Quarterly*, 1871, p. 433.

Tiben (also written **Twin** or **Dwin**), Councils of (*Concilium Thevinense*). Tiben (perhaps the same as Thevis or Divo, supposed by some to be the present Erivan), under Chosroes II, became the capital of Armenia, and the religious centre of the realm. Several councils were held there.

I. The first council, held in 452, declared Tiben the seat of the catholicos.

II. The second council was summoned by the catholicos, Nerses II, in 527, and passed thirty-eight canons, the last of which ordered a fast of one week every month.

III. The third council was held in 551, under Moses II, with a view of regulating the Easter festival. The 11th day of July, 553, was to begin the Armenian æra, and was declared the New Year's day of the first year.

IV. The fourth council, held in 596, was important for bringing about a separation between the Armenians and Georgians. Up to the year 580 the Georgians elected their own catholicos, who was always ordained by the Armenian. About that time, when the Georgian catholicos had died, the Georgians asked Moses II to elect one for them. He appointed Cyrion, a very learned theologian, who decreed the acceptance of the acts of the Council of Chalcedon. Moses' successor, Abraham I, who differed with Cyrion concerning the Council of Chalcedon, urged the Georgian catholicos to reject the decrees of the Council of Chalcedon, but in vain. At the fourth Council of Tiben, Cyrion and his followers were condemned. This act was the occasion of much controversy among the Armenians.

V. The fifth council, held under Nerses III, in 645, condemned all heretics, and especially the Council of Chalcedon and its supporters.

VI. The sixth council was convened by Nerses III, in 648, which again condemned the Council of Chalcedon.

VII. In 719 the seventh council was held, under John IV; thirty-two canons were passed, which provided, among other things, that the altar and baptismal font should be made of stone, unleavened bread and unmixed wine should be used in the communion, the clause "Thou that wast crucified for us," in the Trisagion, should be sung three times, morning and evening, as well as at the mass, etc. The last canon strictly forbade the intercourse with the Paulicians.

VIII. The last or eighth council was held in 726, and condemned Julian Halicarnassensis, his followers, and his writings. Tiben is also celebrated for the martyrdom which some faithful Christians suffered there. See Plitt-Herzog, *Real-Encyklop.* s. v. (B. P.)

Tiberias. The present *Tubariya* is described in the *Memoirs* to the Ordnance Survey, i, 361, 418.

Tibetan Version. See Thibetan Version.

Tidman, Arthur, D.D., an English Congregational minister, was born at Mickelton, Nov. 14, 1792. He was educated for the medical profession, but afterwards studied theology with Rev. George Collison, and in 1813 commenced missionary work in Sidmouth. In 1818 he received a call from Frome, and in 1828 settled at Barbican Chapel, London. During the last years of his pastorate he held the office of foreign secretary of the London Missionary Society. He died March 6, 1868. Dr. Tidman was well versed in all civil and diplomatic questions of the day; cool, far-seeing, and practical in all questions of Church doctrine or government, and especially distinguished by the wisdom, energy, and depth of his spiritual perception. See (Lond.) *Cong. Year-book*, 1869, p. 281.

Tieftrunk, Johann Heinrich, a Lutheran theologian and philosopher of Germany, was born in 1760 at Oeftenhäfen, near Rostock. He studied at Rostock and Halle, was in 1792 professor at Halle, and died Oct. 7, 1837. He published, *Einzig möglicher Zweck Jesu aus dem Grundgesetze der Religion entwickelt* (2d ed. Halle, 1793):—*Versuch einer Kritik der Religion* (1790):—*Censur des christlichen protestantischen Lehrbegriffs nach den Prinzipien der Religionskritik* (Berlin, 1791–95, 3 parts; 2d ed. 1796):—*De Modo Deum Cognoscendi* (1792):—*Dilucidationes ad Theoreticam Religionis Christianæ Partem* (1793, 2 parts):—*Religion der Mündigen* (1800, 2 parts). See Krug, *Philosophisches Wörterbuch*, iv, 173 (2d ed. iv, 197); Baur, *Vorlesungen über Dogmengeschichte*, iii, 336 sq.; Gass, *Gesch. der prot. Dogmatik*, iv, 300 sq.; Pünjer, *Geschichte der Religionsphilosophie*, ii, 52 sq.; Plitt-Herzog, *Real-Encyclop.* s. v. (B. P.)

Timann (or **Tidemann**), JOHANN, the reformer of Bremen, was born at Amsterdam about the year 1500. In 1522 he went to Wittenberg, where he made the acquaintance of Luther and Melanchthon. In 1524 he went to Bremen, and was appointed pastor of St. Martin's. He now introduced those reformatory changes which have immortalized his name. In 1529 count Enno II, of East Frisia, called him to Emden to work there against the Anabaptists. In 1533 the city council adopted a church order, which was, no doubt, prepared by Timann, and was approved by Luther and Bugenhagen. Timan was also present at the colloquy in Worms, and at the meetings held at Ratisbon in 1541. He died Feb. 17, 1557, at Nienburg. See Rotermund, *Lexikon aller Gelehrten in Bremen*, ii, 216 sq. (where a list of Timann's writings is given); Plitt-Herzog, *Real-Encyklop.* s. v. (B. P.)

Timnah (or **Timnath**). There seem to be three localities thus designated.

1. In the mountains of Judah (Gen. xxxviii, 12-14; Josh. xv, 57). For this no modern representative of a corresponding name (Tibneh) has been discovered in the region required, for the ruined site, *Tibna*, two and a half miles east of Beit Nettîf, and nine miles west of Bethlehem, suggested by Conder (*Memoirs* to the Ordnance Survey, iii, 53), and containing only "foundations" (ibid. p. 161), is entirely out of the neighborhood of the associated localities (in Josh.).

2. In the plain of Judah (Josh. xv, 10; Judg. xiv, 1, 2, 5; 2 Chron. xxviii, 18). The present representative, *Tibnah*, lies five and a half miles north-east of Tell es-Safieh (Gath), and eight miles south of Abu Shusheh (Gezer). It is merely described in the *Memoirs* accompanying the Ordnance Survey (ii, 441) as "ruined walls, caves, and wine-presses, with rock-cut cisterns. The water supply is from a spring on the north side."

3. In Mount Ephraim (Josh. xix, 50; xxiv, 30; Judg. ii, 9). The modern ruin, *Tibneh*, which lies ten miles north-west of Beitîn (Bethel), and ten and a half miles north-east of Jimzû, is described at length in the *Memoirs* to the Ordnance Survey, ii, 374 sq. Lieut. Conder remarks (*Tent Work*, ii, 229):

"It seems to me very doubtful how far we can rely on the identity of the site with that of Timnath-Heres. It is certain that this is the place called Timnatha by Jerome, a town of importance, capital of a district in the hills, and on the road from Lydda to Jerusalem, the position of which is fixed by references to surrounding towns. But the Jewish tradition, and also that of the modern Samaritans, points to Kefr Hâris as the burial-place of Joshua. It is remarkable, however, that a village called Kefr Ishw'a, or 'Joshua's hamlet,' exists in the immediate neighborhood of the ruin of Tibneh."

Tiphsah (2 Kings xv, 16) is thought by Lieut. Conder (*Memoirs* to the Ordnance Survey, ii, 169) to be (different from that of 1 Kings iv, 24) the present *Khurbet Tafsah*, six miles south-west of Shechem (Nablûs), and described (ibid. p. 198) as "a small ruined village in gardens, appears to be modern."

Tirzah. The present *Teiasir*, which Tristram assumes (*Bible Places*, p. 196) as the modern representative, lies twelve miles east by north from Sebustieh (Samaria), and is described in the *Memoirs* accompanying the Ordnance Survey (ii, 228, 245). As to the identity of the name, Lieut. Conder remarks (*Tent Work*, ii, 108):

"It contains the exact letters of the Hebrew word, though the last two radicals are interchanged in position, a kind of change not unusual among the peasantry. The beauty of the position and the richness of the plain on the west, the ancient remains, and the old main road to the place from Shechem, seem to agree well with the idea of its having once been a capital; and if I am right in the suggestion, then the old sepulchres are probably, some of them, those of the early kings of Israel before the royal family began to be buried in Samaria."

Titelmann, FRANCIS, a Roman Catholic theologian, was born in 1497 at Hasselt, Belgium, and studied at Liege. Having completed his studies, he joined the Capuchins, went to Rome in 1537, and died the same year. He wrote, *Commentaria in Omnes Psalmos:—Paraphrastica Elucidatio in Librum Job:—Commentaria in Ecclesiasten Salomonis:—Commentaria in Cantica Canticorum:—Collatio pro Editione Vulgata Sacræ Scripturæ:—Elucidatio in Omnes Epistolas Pauli*, etc. See Miraeus, *Elogia Illustrium Belgii Scriptorum;* Andreas, *Bibliotheca Belgica;* Jöcher, *Allgemeines Gelehrten-Lexikon*, s. v. (B. P.)

Titius, GERHARD, a Lutheran theologian of Germany, was born at Quedlinburg, Dec. 17, 1620, and studied at different universities. In 1646 he was professor of Hebrew at Helmstädt, in 1650 doctor of theology, and died June 7, 1681. Titius was a voluminous writer. Of his publications we mention, *De Principio Fidei Christianæ seu Canonica Scriptura:—De Ministris Ecclesiæ:—De Beatitudine et Damnatione Æterna ex Mischnajoth et Commentariis Rabbinorum Considerata:—De Theopaschitarum Hæresi:—De Orthodoxa Fidei Christianæ Doctrina:—De Jesu Christi Officio Prophetico, Sacerdotali et Regio*, etc. See Witte, *Memoriæ Theologorum;* Jöcher, *Allgemeines Gelehrten-Lexikon*, s. v. (B. P.)

Tobenz, DANIEL, an Augustinian, was born at Vienna in 1743. In 1768 he was made a priest, in 1772 doctor of theology, and in 1775 professor of theology at Vienna. In 1811 he retired from his professorship, and died Aug. 20, 1819. He published, *Institutiones, Usus et Doctrinæ Patrum* (Vienna, 1779-83):—*Examen Tractatus Joannis Barbegraci de Doctrina Morali Patrum Ecclesiæ* (1785):—*Commentarius in Novum Testamentum* 1804-6, 2 vols.):—*Paraphrasis Psalmorum ex Hebraico*

Traditional Sepulchre of Joshua at Tibneh. (From Thomson's *Southern Palestine and Jerusalem.*)

Adornata, Notis et Summariis Instructa (2d ed. 1814). His works were published under the title *Opera Omnia* (1822, 15 vols.). See Döring, *Die gelehrten Theologen Deutschlands*, s. v. (B. P.)

Todd, Ambrose S., D.D., a Protestant Episcopal minister, son of Rev. Ambrose Todd, was born at Huntington, Conn., Dec. 6, 1798. His early education was acquired at Cheshire Academy, and Yale College conferred upon him the honorary degree of A.M. in 1824. He was ordained presbyter June 30, 1823, and his first charge comprised the parishes of Reading, Danbury, Greenwich, New Canaan, Darien, and Stamford. For thirty-eight years he was rector of St. John's, in the latter place, and died there, June 23, 1861. He filled many offices of honor and responsibility in the diocese, and was universally respected. See *Amer. Quar. Church Rev.* 1862, p. 557.

Toles, Russell G., D.D., a Baptist minister, was born at Dunham, N. Y., in 1811. He graduated from Madison University at an early age, studied theology, and then took charge of a Baptist Church in Cooperstown, where he was ordained. At the breaking-out of the rebellion he was given control of one branch of the Christian Commission, and stationed at Fortress Monroe. From these duties he was called to the Howard Mission of New York. He founded, with the aid of ten wealthy laymen, the Wanderers' Home, in Baldwin Place, Boston, in 1865. At first it was a mission school as well as a home, and children, and even infants, were carried there in the daytime by their parents, and then taken home at night; but eventually it became a permanent home for children until adopted into families. Dr. Toles died in Boston, July 11, 1884.

Tonei, Simeon de, a Scotch prelate, was bishop of Moray in 1171. He was a monk of Melrose, and before that he had been abbot at Cogshall, in Essex, England. He died in 1184. See Keith, *Scottish Bishops*, p. 136.

Torry, Patrick, D.D., a bishop of the Episcopal Church of Scotland, died at Peterhead, Oct. 3, 1852, aged ninety years. He was consecrated Oct. 12, 1808. At the time of his death he was bishop of Dunkeld, Dumblane, and Fife, Scotland. See *Amer. Quar. Church Rev.* 1853, p. 159.

Tosiphta (תּוֹסֶפְתָּא, *the addition* or *supplement*) is the title of a great halachic work, which originated in the time of the Mishna (q. v.). It is of great importance, because the Tosiphta (or *Tosefta*, as it is also called) contains the decisions of the Jewish teachers in their original form, while the Mishna gives them in an abbreviated manner. Thus many things are contained in the Tosiphta which are not found in the Mishna. The Tosiphta is also richer in quotations from the Old Test. While we have noticed twelve variations in the "textus receptus" of the Mishna—we say "textus receptus," because Lowe's edition, from the Cambridge MS. (*The Mishnah on which the Palestinian Talmud Rests, edited from the unique MS. preserved in the University Library of Cambridge* [Cambridge, 1883]) does not always agree with the common text—and about ninety-five in the Gemara, we have collated two hundred and thirty-three variations from the Tosiphta, that is, more than double the number that the Talmud presents. The best edition is that of M. S. Zuckermandel, *Tosefta nach den Wiener und Erfurter Handschriften herausgegeben* (Pasewalk, 1880), and it is to this edition that our references are made. The following incomplete list of variations will at once show the importance of this work for the Old-Test. scholar.

Exod. xxxix, 43, כל is omitted, p. 521.
Lev. vii, 19, כל is omitted, p. 169.
 vii, 29, the reading is, "the blood of the peace offerings," for "the sacrifice of his peace offerings," p. 47.
 xiv, 57, "and to teach," so Sept., Syr., p. 618.
 xvi, 13, "upon the ark," instead of "upon the testimony," p. 181.
Numb. v, 15, "he shall put no oil upon her nor put frankincense upon her," the reading is עליה for עליו, p. 294.
 xi, 22, the first ומצא לחם omitted, p. 305.
Deut. v, 14, ואבדך ואמתך omitted, p. 355.
 xvii, 9, הכהנים הלוים ואל omitted, p. 211.
 xxiv, 19, בשדך omitted, p. 22.
Josh. i, 1, the last three words omitted, p. 315.
 iii, 16, מאדם, so all versions, p. 310; the Revised Version, "at Adam," with marginal note; another reading, "from Adam."
Josh. iv, 3, the reading is, "hence from under the feet of the priests twelve," p. 310.
 iv, 5, at the end, "and leave them in the place where the feet of the priests stood," p. 310.
 viii, 33, and their officers, ושטריו, p. 311; so also *Targum* (ed. Lagarde), and Mishna, *Sota*, ch. vii, § 5; but Lowe's Cambridge edition reads as the present text of the Bible.
1 Kings x, 27, "for abundance" omitted, p. 71.
2 Kings xviii, 4, "children" omitted, p. 465.
Job xxxvi, 11, "they shall wax old in the good of their days." The Masoretic text reads יכלו, and the mark כן הוא, i. e. it is thus written, viz. with כ, indicates that there already existed a diversity of readings. Indeed, Michaelis (Hebr. Bible, *in loco*) adduces a number of MSS. which read יבלו, with *beth*.
Prov. ix, 1, "wise women build." The plural noun with a singular verb is strange; the Sept., Targ., and Syr. read חכמה.
 xx, 27, "the lamp of God" = נר אלהים, p. 154; so Targ., *Talmud Pesachim*, fol. 7, col. 2; fol. 8, col. 1, and ancient Midrashim.
Ezek. xlvii, 4, "and caused me to pass through the waters, waters that were to the loins." Bär and Delitzsch, in their edition of Ezekiel, remark, *in loco*, "in tractatu *Yoma* 77b, et Tosefta, *Succa* iii, hic locus adducitur, tanquam si scriptum esset כַּמַּיִם מֵי מתנים et revera in Reuchliniano prima manus sic scripserat."
 xlvii, 8, "to Galilee to the Front Sea," אל הג׳ לד׳ הקדמונה, p. 196; the "Front Sea" is explained by זה ימה של סדום, i. e. that is the sea of Sodom. The reading is not, as in the Masoretic text, הַגְּלִילָה, but הַגָּלִילָה, so read Sept., Targ., Syriac. One codex to which Bär and Delitzsch attach great importance, the *codex Jamanensis*, reads, as the two editors note, הַגָּלִילַה, *cum gimel Kamezato.*
 xlvii, 11, לא ירפו, p. 196; so also Bär and Delitzsch, against the ולא of the *textus receptus.*
Zech. viii, 19, "love truth," האמת, p. 241; so also Talmud, *Yebamoth*, fol. 14, col. 2.

A few of these variations have already been noted by De' Rossi in his *Variæ Lectiones*. A complete list is given by Pick in Stade's *Zeitschrift für die alttestamentliche Wissenschaft* (Giessen, 1886). (B. P.)

Totten, Silas, D.D., LL.D., a Protestant Episcopal clergyman, was for a long time engaged in educational work in Williamsburg, Va., until 1859. In that year he was elected president of the Iowa State University, and also ministered in Trinity Church, Iowa City. For a number of years he was one of the standing committee of the diocese of Iowa; was one of the trustees of Griswold College, Davenport, and was identified with the missionary work in his diocese. In 1864 he was rector of St. John's Church, Decatur, Ill.; in 1867 became rector of Christ Church Seminary, Lexington, Ky., in charge of which he remained until his death, Oct. 7, 1873. See *Prot. Episc. Almanac*, 1874, p. 139.

Toussain (Lat. *Thussanus*), Pierre, father of Daniel, was born at St. Laurent, Lorraine, in 1499. He studied theology at Cologne, Paris, and Rome, and was made a canon at the cathedral of Metz. When the persecution against the Protestants began, he fled to Basle, and formally embraced the Reformation. Two attempts which he made to propagate his views in France (at Metz and in Paris) ended with imprisonment; but in 1539 the duke of Würtemberg made him superintendent of Mümpelgard, where he introduced the Reformation, not without great difficulties, however, as he was a Calvinist, and the duke a Lutheran. Toussain died in 1573. See Plitt-Herzog, *Real-Encyklop.* s. v.; Lichtenberger, *Encyclop. des Sciences Religieuses*, s. v. (B. P.)

Townley, Charles Gostling, LL.D., an English Congregational minister, was born in 1780. He devoted himself to the study of law, but with his brother Henry prepared himself for the ministry. After studying divinity at Hoxton Academy he began to preach in Ireland, laboring with self-denying devotedness for the good of both Romanists and Protestants. From 1817 to 1841 he preached in Limerick and vicinity. He then returned to England, where he resided at Brixton, afterwards at Pimlico, and became pastor of a small church at Mortlake, Surrey, where he erected school-houses at his own expense. He died at Pimlico, June 17, 1856. See (Lond.) *Cong. Year-book*, 1857, p. 209.

Townsend, Stephen, M.D., Ph.D., a Methodist Episcopal minister, was born in 1808, and was for forty-six years a member of the Philadelphia Conference, being a supernumerary from 1875 until his death, Aug. 5, 1881. He was a man of extensive scholarship. See *Minutes of Annual Conferences*, 1882, p. 71.

Townson (or Tonson), Robert, D.D., a divine of the 17th century, was born in St. Botolph's Parish, Cambridge, became fellow of Queen's College, being admitted therein when but twelve years of age. He was an excellent preacher, attended king James as chaplain into Scotland, became dean of Westminster in 1617, bishop of Salisbury in 1620, and died May 15, 1621. See Fuller, *Worthies* (Nuttall), i, 231.

Tracy, Samuel Walter, D.D., an English Independent minister, was born at Portsea, in February, 1778. He studied under Rev. Dr. Bogue, preached at Lichfield, next at Hot Wells, near Bristol, then at Yeovil, was secretary of the London Missionary Society, spent several years on the Continent, and afterwards preached at Hounslow, Chelsea, and Brixton Rise. He died Feb. 16, 1853. See (Lond.) *Cong. Year-book*, 1854, p. 256.

Trail, Walter, a Scotch prelate, a canon of St. Andrews, was elected bishop of that diocese in 1385, and was still there in 1400. He died in the castle of St. Andrews in 1401. See Keith, *Scottish Bishops*, p. 26.

Transcaucasian Tartar Version of the Scriptures. A peculiar and rather corrupt dialect of the Turkish is spoken by the greater part of the Moslem population in Georgia, Shusti, Shirwan, Derbend, and North-west Persia. As it is vernacular in numerous tribes in all the Russian provinces beyond the Caucasus, this dialect has been termed, by way of distinction, the Transcaucasian. Parts of the New Test. were prepared in this language many years ago by Mirza Ferookh and the Rev. Dr. Pfander. In 1875 the committee of the British and Foreign Bible Society proposed to reprint the gospels under the superintendence of Mr. Abraham Amirchanjanz, the son of Mirza Ferookh, who has latterly been employed in the service of the Basle missions. From the report of 1877 we learn that the British Bible Society resolved to print the remaining portions of the New Test., and Mr. Amirchanjanz has revised the remainder of his father's manuscript, and translated the Epistle to the Romans. In 1878 the entire New Test. was printed under the superintendence of Messrs. Amirchanjanz and Sauerwein. From the report of 1881 we learn that the British and Foreign Bible Society had secured the entire services of Mr. Amirchanjanz for editorial work, and that he had undertaken a translation of the Old Test. This translation, which was completed in 1883, induced the American missionaries to give up their version, on which they were engaged, and unite with Mr. Amirchanjanz in a final revision of the Old Test., in order to secure but one version of the Bible in the Transcaucasian language. (B. P.)

Trapier, Paul, D.D., a Protestant Episcopal clergyman, a graduate of the General Theological Seminary, was for several years prior to 1856 rector in Charleston, S. C. In 1857 he resided in Lynchburg, Va., and remained there until 1859, when he removed to Camden, S. C., having been appointed professor of ecclesiastical history and the evidences of Christianity in the theological seminary there. When the seminary was removed, in 1866, to Spartansburg, Dr. Trapier removed to that place, holding the same professorship. In 1868 he was assigned to ecclesiastical history and exegesis. In 1870 he removed to Locust Grove, Md., and became rector of Shrewsbury parish, where he remained until his death, July 12, 1872, aged sixty-six years. See *Prot. Episc. Almanac*, 1873, p. 133.

Treat, Selah Burr, D.D., a Congregational minister, was born at Hartland, Conn., Feb. 19, 1804. After studying at Lenox Academy and Hopkins Grammar-school, he graduated from Yale College in 1824; in 1826 was admitted to the bar, and began the practice of his profession at East Windsor Hill, removing, however, in 1831 to Penn Yan, N. Y.; where he became a Christian, and, abandoning the law, graduated from Andover Theological Seminary in 1835. The next year he became pastor of the Third Presbyterian Church, Newark, N. J. In 1840 he was associated with Rev. Dr. Absalom Peters in editing the *Biblical Repository and American Eclectic*, in New York. In 1843 he was appointed editor of the *Missionary Herald*. In 1847 he was elected one of the secretaries of the American Board of Commissioners for Foreign Missions, his special work being the carrying on the correspondence with the missionaries among the North American Indians. In 1859 he was called to take charge of the home department of the board, and continued in this office until a few months before his death, which occurred March 27, 1877. He had continued his editorial labors until 1856, at which time he took a second somewhat extended trip abroad, his first journey having been taken in 1850. See *Cong. Quarterly*, xix, 347, 375. (J. C. S.)

Tregury, Michael, D.D., an Irish prelate, was a native of the village of Tregury, in Cornwall, and for some time fellow of Exeter College, Oxford. He was consecrated in St. Patrick's Church archbishop of Dublin in 1449. In 1450 he had restitution of the temporalities of his see. In 1467 Tregury assigned a moiety of the parish of Lusk for the treasurer of St. Patrick's, and constituted the rectory of St. Andeon in the city. In 1468 he held a visitation in the chapter-house of St. Patrick's Cathedral. He died in 1471. See D'Alton, *Memoirs of the Archbishops of Dublin*, p. 159.

Trench, *Hon.* Power Le Poer, D.D., a prelate of the Irish Episcopal Church, was born June 10, 1770, and educated at Dublin University. His first preferment on being ordained was the union of Creagh, in the diocese of Clonfert. He was consecrated bishop of Waterford, Nov. 21, 1802; in 1810 translated to the see of Elphin; and in 1819 appointed to the archbishopric of Tuam, which he held till his death, March 21, 1839. Archbishop Trench was a fine scholar, a profound theologian, a devout Christian, a brilliant orator, and diligent in the performance of all life's duties. See *The* (Lond.) *Church of England Magazine*, June, 1841, p. 380; *The* (Lond.) *Christian Remembrancer*, May, 1839, p. 315.

Tresenreuter, Johann Ulrich, a Lutheran theologian of Germany, was born Oct. 31, 1710, and studied at Altdorf and Leipsic. In 1733 he commenced his academical career at Altdorf, was preacher at Coburg in 1738, and died March 31, 1744. He published, *De Rababe contra jus Naturæ Juste Agente* (Altdorf, 1733):—*De Paradiso Igne Deleto* (1735):—*De Persona Christi* (1738):—*De Signo, quod Deus Caino Dedit* (eod.):—*De Vaticinatione Henochi in Epistola Judæ*

(1739):—*De Libro, qui Quartus Esræ Vulgo Inscribitur* (1742):—*De Sectis Judæorum in Genere* (1743):—*De Essæorum Nomine* (eod.), etc. See Döring, *Die gelehrten Theologen Deutschlands*, s. v.; Jöcher, *Allgemeines Gelehrten-Lexikon*, s. v. (B. P.)

Trevor, Richard, D.D., a Church of England divine, was born in 1707; became canon of Christ Church, Oxford, in 1735; was consecrated bishop of St. David's in 1744, translated to the see of Durham in 1752, and died at his home in Tenderden Street, Hanover Square, London, June 9, 1771. He published several sermons. See (Lond.) *Annual Register*, 1771, p. 179; *Life* (1776).

Triffechov, Adam, a Lutheran theologian of Germany, was born Aug. 11, 1641, at Lübeck, studied at different universities, was in 1672 ecclesiastical counsellor at Gotha, in 1677 general superintendent, and died Aug. 17, 1687. He published, *Historia Chiliasmi:—De Impositione Manuum in Sacrificiis ex Hebræorum nec non Christianorum Monumentis:—De Emphasibus Scripturæ Sacræ ad Ies. i, 1-6:—De Rechabitis ad Jerem. xxxv:—De Angelis:—De Mose Ægyptiorum Osiride:—De Concursu Dei:—Historia Naturalismi a Prima sua Origine ad Nostra usque Tempora per suas Classes Deducta* (edited and published by his son, Jena, 1700). See Moller, *Cimbria Literata;* Jöcher, *Allgemeines Gelehrten-Lexikon*, s. v. (B. P.)

Trimurti (Sanscrit, *tri*, "three," and *murti*, "form"), the name of the Hindû triad, the gods Brahma (masculine), Vishnû, and Siva, which are considered an inseparable unity, though three in form. Different works assign the chief place to different members, according to the schools from which they emanate. The *Paduca-Purana* of the Vaishnava (q. v.) sect assigns to Vishnû the highest rank in the trimurti, and thus defines its character: "In the beginning of creation the great Vishnû, desirous of creating the whole world, became threefold—creator, preserver, and destroyer. In order to create this world the Supreme Spirit produced from the right side of his body himself, as Brahma; then, in order to preserve the world, he produced from the left side of his body Vishnû; and, in order to destroy the world, he produced from the middle of his body the eternal Siva. Some worship Brahma, others Vishnû, others Siva; but Vishnû, one, yet threefold, creates, preserves, and destroys; therefore let the pious make no difference between the three." The *Matsya-Purana*, speaking of the *Mahat*, or intellectual principle, says, "Mahat becomes distinctly known as *three* gods, through the influence of the three qualities, goodness, passion, and sin; being one person and three gods, viz., Brahma, Vishnû, and Siva." We are thus enabled to see that, aside from sectarian belief, which makes its own god the chief, trimurti implies the unity personified of the three principles of creation (Brahma), preservation (Vishnû), and destruction (Siva). When represented, the trimurti is one body with three heads: in the middle that of Brahma, at its right that of Vishnû, and at its left that of Siva. The symbol of the trimurti is the mystical syllable *om*, in which *o* is equivalent to *a* and *u*, and where *a* means Brahma, *u* means Vishnû, and *m* means Siva.

Figure of the Trimurti.

Trinius, Johann Anton, a Lutheran theologian of Germany, was born Oct. 6, 1722. He studied at Leipsic, Helmstädt, and Halle; was in 1748 assistant minister at Braunroda, in the county of Mansfeld, Saxony, and died at Eisleben, May 3, 1784. He published, *Schediasma Historicum de Conjugiis Proselytorum Judaicorum* (Helmstädt, 1744):—*Diatribe Historico-apologetica de Digamia Clericorum quibusdam Exosa* (1746):—*De Pathopatridalgia Sanctorum* (Rostock, 1752):—*Theologisches Wörterbuch* (Leipsic, 1770), etc. See Döring, *Die gelehrten Theologen Deutschlands*, s. v.; Winer, *Handbuch der theol. Lit.* i, 375, 500, 856. (B. P.)

Triton, in Greek mythology, was primarily a son of Nepture, by Amphitrite, who lived with his father and mother on the bottom of the sea in a golden palace. Hence the name was applied to any dæmon of the Mediterranean Sea, who rode, sometimes upon horses, at other times on monsters of the deep, and occasionally appeared, assisting other deities in riding. Such Tritons are described differently. They are probably of the double nature, half man and half fish. The hair of their head is green, they have fine scales, gills under their ears, a human nose, a broad mouth with animal teeth, green eyes, hands, fingers, and nails rough, and instead of feet they possess the tail of a dolphin. They blow a spiral-formed trumpet.

Antique Representation of a Triton Family.

Trotter, John, D.D., a Scotch Presbyterian clergyman, was born in Edinburgh in 1728, in which city his father was a magistrate. He showed marks of true piety in his youth, and a preference for the ministry. He studied the learned languages, philosophy, and divinity at the City University, passed his trials before the Synod of Edinburgh in 1749, and was soon afterwards presented to the living at Ceres, Fifeshire, where he was very popular for seventeen years. The Swallow Street Church, in London, became vacant in 1769, and Dr. Trotter accepted the pastorate there in December of that year, and with uniform and unwearied diligence performed the duties for nearly forty years. After a short illness he died, Sept. 14, 1808, and was interred in Bunhill Fields Cemetery. He made Calvinistic theology his careful study through his long life of more than fourscore years. He published a short memoir of his first wife in 1771. See Wilson, *Dissenting Churches*, ix, 49.

Trottet, Jean Pierre Philippe, a Protestant theologian of Switzerland, was born at La Tour de Peilz, in the canton of Vaud, Dec. 12, 1818. He studied at Lausanne and at some German universities, and was ordained in 1851. In 1853 he published a volume of *Discours Évangéliques* (Paris), and spent some years at Stockholm as pastor of the French Church. In 1860 he was called to the Hague as pastor of the Walloon Church, where he published, against Groen van Prinsterer, *Le Parti Orthodoxe Pur dans l'Église Wallonne de La Haye:—Le Parti Anti-Revolutionnaire et Confessionnel dans l'Église Réformée des Pays-Bas:—Pourquois je Prends Congé de l'Église Wallonne de La Haye* (1860-61). In 1862 he retired to Geneva, and died Aug. 30 of the same year. He published also, *Grands Jours de l'Église Apostolique, Considérés Relativement à l'Époque Actuelle* (Paris, 1856):—*Génie des Civilisations* (1862, 2 vols.). See Montet, *Dict. Biog. des Genev. et des Vaud*, ii, 583 sq.; *Chrétien Évangélique*, 1859, 1862; Lichtenberger, *Encyclop. des Sciences Religieuses*, s. v. (B. P.)

Trübner, Nicholas, a publisher of London, who died April 3, 1884, deserves an honorable mention for the great interest he took in Oriental research, and more especially in Indian studies. His *Record* has always been a welcome and invaluable visitor to all those who were interested in such pursuits, and the assistance which it has rendered to Oriental learning cannot be overestimated. But Mr. Trübner's interests and sympathies were not confined to these researches. The history of religions, the study of languages, the development of political life in the East, all claimed a share of his time and thoughts. Many struggling scholars have lost in him the best friend they had. (B. P.)

Trudpert is the name of a hermit and founder of a celebrated monastery in the Breisgau, Baden. About the year 640 he came into the region of the upper Rhine, and settled at the river Neumage. Othpert, a German noble, gave to Trudpert the land, besides six servants, who were to assist him in the clearing and making arable the wooded country. Soon a chapel was built in honor of St. Peter. Three years Trudpert led an ascetic life, when two of the servants killed him while resting from his manual labor. Othpert had Trudpert buried in the chapel. During the 8th century the place lay waste, but in 816 Rambert, one of Othpert's descendants, built a splendid basilica in honor of Peter and Paul, and Trudpert's remains were placed there. See Mone, *Quellensammlung zur badischen Landesgeschichte*, i, 17-28; Rettberg, *Kirchengeschichte Deutschlands*, ii, 48-50; Hefele, *Geschichte der Einführung des Christenthums im südwestlichen Deutschland*, p. 314-329; Friedrich, *Kirchengeschichte Deutschlands*, ii, 607-613; Plitt-Herzog, *Real-Encyklop.* s. v. (B. P.)

Trullan Councils, The, were held in a room of the imperial palace at Constantinople, which had a dome (τροῦλλος), whence the name.

I. The first Trullan council was called in 680 by the emperor Constantinus Pogonatus, and held eighteen sittings. The legates of pope Agatho were accorded the highest rank, then followed in order the patriarch George of Constantinople, the legate of the patriarch of Alexandria, Macarius of Antioch, the legate of the patriarch of Jerusalem, three delegates from the Western Church, delegates from Ravenna, and finally the bishops and abbots present. In the very first session the papal legates accused the patriarchs of Constantinople and Antioch of heresy. Macarius defended himself against this accusation, and referred to the canons of the councils of Ephesus and Chalcedon, and of the fifth Constantinopolitan council. In the eighth sitting George of Constantinople went over to the Roman doctrine. In the sixteenth sitting pope Honorius I was anathematized for his monothelitic views, and the anathema was repeated at the eighteenth session. Pope Agatho's confession of two wills in Christ, in his *Epistola ad Imperatores*, was declared the doctrine of the council, and all monothelites were anathematized. The patriarch Macarius was deposed at a later time.

II. The second Trullan council, called together by Justinian in 692, is known as the Concilium Quinisextum, for which see the art. Quinisextum Concilium. See, besides, the Church-histories of Schröckh and Gieseler; Pichler, *Geschichte der kirchlichen Trennung zwischen Orient und Occident* (Munich, 1864), i, 87 sq.; Hergenröther, *Photius, Patriarch von Constantinopel* (Ratisbon, 1867), i, 208-526; Plitt-Herzog, *Real-Encyklop.* s. v. (B. P.)

Truyns, Charles, D.D., a Roman Catholic priest of the Jesuit order, was born in Belgium in 1813. In 1837 he came to the United States, and was an officer of the St. Louis University and of St. Charles College, La. For some time he was engaged in missionary work among the Indians, and, later in life, was pastor of St. Joseph's Church, Bardstown, Ky. He died at St. Louis, Mo., Dec. 14, 1868. See Hough, *Amer. Biog. Notes*, p. 398. (J. C. S.)

Tschi Version. See Otji Version.

Tucker, John, D.D., a Congregational minister, was born at Amesbury, Mass., Sept. 19, 1719. He graduated from Harvard College in 1741, studied theology with Rev. Paine Wingate, of Amesbury, and was ordained at Newbury, Mass., Nov. 20, 1745, as colleague-pastor with the Rev. Christopher Toppan. His death occurred March 22, 1792. He was the author of several published sermons and controversial pamphlets. See Sprague, *Annals of the Amer. Pulpit*, i, 451.

Tucker, Mark, D.D., a Congregational minister, was born at Whitestown, N. Y., June 7, 1795. He studied at Whitestown, graduated from Union College in 1814, and was instructed in theology by president E. Nott, D.D.; ordained pastor at Stillwater, Oct. 8, 1817, and dismissed in 1823; installed colleague with Rev. Solomon Williams, at Northampton, Mass., March 10, 1824, and dismissed Aug. 16, 1827; called to the Second Presbyterian Church, at Troy, N. Y., Oct. 31, 1827; to the Beneficent Church, at Providence, R. I., in June of 1837, and dismissed March 24, 1856; installed at Vernon, Conn., April 15, 1857, and was pastor of this church until 1863. He resided without charge at Ellington and Old Saybrook, and after 1865 at Weathersfield, where he died, March 19, 1875. He was chosen a director of the American Home Missionary Society in 1832, a vice-president in 1844, and was a corporate member of the American Board of Commissioners for Foreign Missions from 1838. See *Cong. Quarterly*, 1876, p. 435.

Tulloch, Thomas de, a Scotch prelate, was bishop at Orkney about 1422. See Keith, *Scottish Bishops*, p. 221.

Tulloch, William, a Scotch prelate, was sent by James III into Denmark in 1468 to negotiate a marriage between him and the princess Margaret of that nation. He was bishop of Orkney in 1470. He was made lord privy seal, March 26, 1473. In 1477 he was translated to the see of Moray. He died about 1482. See Keith, *Scottish Bishops*, p. 222.

Tunisi. See Jacob ben-Chajim.

Tupper, Charles, D.D., a Baptist minister, was born at Cornwallis, N. S., Aug. 6, 1794. He was baptized by Rev. E. Manning, May 14, 1815, taught school in Cornwallis, was ordained July 17, 1817, labored as a home missionary in several parts of the province, became pastor at Amherst in 1819, at St. John, N. B., in 1825, at Tryon and Bedeque, P. E. I., in 1833, at Amherst again in 1834, where he was also in charge of the grammar school, was principal of the Baptist Seminary at Fredericton, N. B., in 1835-36, returned to Amherst in 1840, made several evangelistic tours through the provinces, became pastor at Aylesford, N. S., in 1851, and in this relation he continued until his death, assisted after 1870 by a colleague. He died at Kingston, Aylesford, Jan. 19, 1881. In January, 1827, Tupper became editor of the *Baptist Missionary Magazine of Nova Scotia and New Brunswick*, which he continued until 1833, and followed by the *Christian Messenger* (Halifax, N. S.) in 1837. He published a review of Rev. Dr. G. Burns, of St. John, N. B., on *The Subjects and Modes of Baptism* (1830):—*Baptist Principles Vindicated*, in reply to Rev. J. W. D. Gray, of St. John (1844):—*A Discussion of the Translation of "Baptizo" and a Vindication of the Action of the Baptist Missionaries in Burmah* (1846):—*Expository Notes on the Syriac Version of the Scriptures.* He was a man of vast linguistic learning. He was one of the pioneers of temperance. See Bill, *History of the Baptists in the Maritime Provinces of Canada* (St. John, 1881), p. 680 sq.; *Baptist Year-book of Maritime Provinces*, 1881, p. 71. His autobiography appeared in the *Christian Messenger*, Jan. 2, 1880.

Turkish Version. See Turkey, Versions of.

Turkish-Armenian Version. See Turkey, Versions of.

Turkish-Greek Version. See Turkey, Versions of.

Turkish-Tartar Version. See Karass Version.

Turner, JOHN M., D.D., an Anglican missionary bishop, was born in England about 1786; educated at Christ Church, Oxford; in 1823 presented to the vicarage of Abingdon; in 1824 removed to the rectory of Wilmslow, Cheshire; and in 1829 appointed to the bishopric of Calcutta, India, which he held till his death, July 7, 1831. Bishop Turner was a man of exemplary piety, faithful in the discharge of his duties, and much loved and respected by all with whom he was associated. See appendix to the (Lond.) *Christian Observer* for 1831, p. 815; *The* (Lond.) *Christian Guardian*, Feb. 1832, p. 73.

Turney, EDMUND, D.D., a Baptist minister, was born in Easton, Conn., May 6, 1816. He received his education at the Hamilton Institute, N. Y., and his first pastorate was in the Second Church, Hartford, Conn. Subsequently he was pastor in Granville, O., and Utica, N. Y. He became professor of Biblical criticism in the Hamilton Seminary in 1850, and for five years (1853-58) was professor in Fairmount Theological Seminary, O. After preaching without settlement for a few years, he started, in Washington, in 1865, the first experiment for the education of colored teachers and preachers. With great disinterestedness and self-sacrifice he labored in this department of Christian effort for several years. "He seemed inspired with the conviction that God had specially intrusted this great business to him, and nothing could change his impressions of duty." He died Sept. 28, 1872. See Cathcart, *Baptist Encyclop.* p. 1177. (J. C. S.)

Turpin, a Scotch prelate, was elected to the see of Brechin in 1178. See Keith, *Scottish Bishops*, p. 156.

Tusi. See PERSIAN VERSIONS.

Tustin, SEPTIMUS, D.D., a Presbyterian minister, who died at Washington, D. C., Oct. 28, 1871, was in 1836 chaplain of the University of Virginia, and in 1844 was elected chaplain of the United States Senate. At a later period he was pastor of the Presbyterian Church in Hagerstown, Md., and of the First Presbyterian Church, Germantown, Pa. He was the delegate from the Old-school Assembly to the New-school Assembly, which sat in Philadelphia in 1863. He was warmly interested in the reunion of the Presbyterian Church.

Twi Version. See OBJI VERSION.

Twin, COUNCILS OF. See TIBEN.

Twing, ALIN TABOR, D.D., a Protestant Episcopal clergyman, was born at Topsham, Vt., Feb. 9, 1811. He spent two years at the University of Vermont; studied theology under bishop Hopkins; was ordained deacon Aug. 21, 1836; was rector of St. Paul's, Vergennes; of Trinity, West Troy, N. Y., and of Trinity, Lansingburgh, for twenty-three years; secretary of the domestic committee of the Board of Missions from 1864 till his death, in New York city, Nov. 11, 1882. See *The Church Almanac*, 1883, p. 115.

Tyng, STEPHEN HIGGINSON, D.D., an eminent Protestant Episcopal divine, was born at Newburyport, Mass., March 1, 1800, being the son of Hon. Dudley Atkins, but assumed the name of his relative, James Tyng, whose estate he inherited. He graduated at Harvard College in 1817; engaged for some time in commercial pursuits; afterwards studied theology; was ordained in 1821; and was rector successively in Georgetown, D. C. (1821-23); in St. Anne's Parish, Md. (1823-29); in St. Paul's, Philadelphia, Pa. (1829-33); in the Church of the Epiphany in the same city (1833-45); and thereafter in St. George's, New York city, until 1878, when, on account of failing health, he was made pastor emeritus. He died at Irvington, N. J., Sept. 4, 1885. Dr. Tyng was one of the most evangelical, popular, and useful preachers of his denomination. He was editor at different times of *The Episcopal Recorder*, *The Theological Repository*, and *The Protestant Churchman*, while he was also the author of several religious and homiletical works, including observations made during a visit to Europe.

Tyre. The archæology of *Es-Sûr* is minutely examined in the *Memoirs* accompanying the Ordnance Survey, i, 72 sq.; comp. *Quar. Statement* of the "Pal. Explor. Soc.," July, 1881, p. 178 sq.

U.

Ulff, HERMANN WILHELM, a Swedish theologian, was born June 19, 1830, and studied at Upsala and Erlangen. In 1867 he commenced his academical career at Upsala, in 1872 he was made pastor at Stora Skedwi, in 1877 doctor of theology, and died Dec. 18, 1882, greatly lamented by the Lutheran Church of Sweden. (B. P.)

Ulmann, KARL CHRISTIAN, a German Protestant bishop, who died at Walk, Livonia, Oct. 20, 1871, doctor of theology, is best known as the editor of, *Mittheilungen und Nachrichten für die evangelische Geistlichkeit Russlands* (Dorpat, 1839 sq.); besides he published, *Sermons* (1840):—*Das gegenwärtige Verhältniss der evangel. Brüdergemeinde zur evangelisch-lutherischen Kirche in Lief- und Esthland* (Berlin, 1862):—*Wie die Baptisten der luth. Kirche die Bibel entgegenstellen* (St. Petersburg, 1865). (B. P.)

Ulrich, JEAN, a Protestant theologian, was born Dec. 20, 1622, in Switzerland. He studied at Zurich, and after having travelled through Holland, England, France, and Germany, was appointed pastor at Creutz in 1650; in 1653 became professor of Hebrew, in 1669 pastor at the Frauen-Münster, and died in 1682. He wrote, *Oratio de Duobus Testibus Apocalypseos*:—*Oratio de Anti-Christi Adversus Militantem in Terris Christi Ecclesiam Ultimo Conatu*, etc. See *Allgemeines Historisches Lexikon*, s. v.; Jöcher, *Allgemeines Gelehrten-Lexikon*, s. v. (B. P.)

Ulrici, HERMANN, a philosophical writer of Germany, was born March 23, 1806, at Pförten, Lower Lusatia. He studied law at Halle and Berlin, and commenced to practice in 1827. Upon the death of his father, in 1829, he gave up the practice of law, and began studies which were more congenial to him. In 1833 he commenced his academical career in the philosophical faculty at Berlin, went to Halle in 1834, and died Jan. 11, 1884. Ulrici belonged to the school of speculative philosophy which combated the idealistic pantheism of Hegel by a theistic view of the universe, based upon the facts of natural philosophy and psychology. His principal works are, *Glauben und Wissen, Speculation und exacte Wissenschaft* (Leipsic, 1858):—*Gott und die Natur* (1862; 2d ed. 1866):—*Gott und der Mensch* (1866). (B. P.)

Ummah is probably the present *Alma esh-Shaub*, two and a half miles south-east of en-Nakûrah (near the promontory of the same name), described in the *Memoirs* to the Ordnance Survey, i, 150, as "A large Christian village, containing about five hundred inhabitants. The houses are clean and well built. There are two chapels, and the place seems increasing in size. It is situated on a ridge, with figs, olives, pomegranates, and arable land around. To the east and north the land is covered with brushwood. There is a spring within reach, and about thirty rock-cut cisterns in the village."

Universities. By way of supplement, we give here a list of the European universities that have theological faculties:

A. *In Germany.*

1. *Berlin*, founded in 1810, Protestant (Evangelical).
2. *Bonn*, founded in 1818, mixed, i. e. Protestant and Roman Catholic.
3. *Braunsberg*, Roman Catholic.
4. *Breslau*, founded in 1702, mixed.
5. *Erlangen*, founded in 1743, Lutheran and Reformed.

6. *Freiburg-im-Breisgau*, founded in 1457, Roman Catholic.
7. *Giessen*, founded in 1607, Protestant.
8. *Göttingen*, founded in 1737, Protestant (Lutheran).
9. *Greifswalde*, founded in 1456, Protestant (Evangelical).
10. *Halle*, founded in 1694, Protestant (Evangelical).
11. *Heidelberg*, founded in 1386, Protestant (Evangelical).
12. *Jena*, founded in 1558, Protestant (Lutheran).
13. *Kiel*, founded in 1665, Protestant (Lutheran).
14. *Königsberg*, founded in 1544, Protestant (Evangelical).
15. *Leipsic*, founded in 1409, Protestant (Lutheran).
16. *Marburg*, founded in 1527, Protestant (Evangelical).
17. *Munich*, founded in 1826, Roman Catholic.
18. *Münster*, Roman Catholic.
19. *Rostock*, founded in 1419, Protestant (Lutheran).
20. *Strasburg*, founded in 1538, Protestant.
21. *Tübingen*, founded in 1477, Protestant and Roman Catholic.
22. *Würzburg*, founded in 1582, Roman Catholic.

B. *In Switzerland.*

1. *Basle*, founded in 1459, Reformed.
2. *Berne*, founded in 1834, Protestant and Roman Catholic.
3. *Zurich*, Reformed.

C. *In Russia.*

1. *Dorpat*, founded in 1630, Lutheran.

D. *In Austria.*

1. *Cracow*, founded in 1364, Roman Catholic.
2. *Czernowitz*, founded in 1875, Greek Oriental.
3. *Graz*, founded in 1586, Roman Catholic.
4. *Innsbruck*, founded in 1672, Roman Catholic.
5. *Lemberg*, founded in 1784, Roman Catholic.
6. *Prague*, founded in 1348, Roman Catholic.
7. *Vienna*, founded in 1365, Roman Catholic and Protestant.

Of universities, now no more existing in Germany and Austria, we mention:

1. *Altdorf*, founded in 1578, Protestant, abolished in 1807.
2. *Bamberg*, founded in 1648, Roman Catholic, reduced to a college in 1803.
3. *Cologne*, founded in 1388, Roman Catholic, abolished.
4. *Dillingen*, founded in 1549, Roman Catholic, abolished in 1802.
5. *Duisburg*, founded in 1655, Reformed, abolished in 1804.
6. *Erfurt*, founded in 1392, mixed, abolished in 1816.
7. *Frankfort-on-the-Oder*, founded in 1506, transferred to Breslau in 1811.
8. *Helmstädt*, founded in 1576, Protestant, abolished in 1809.
9. *Herborn*, founded in 1654, Protestant, reduced to a theological seminary.
10. *Ingolstadt*, founded in 1472, Roman Catholic, transferred to Landshut in 1802, and from thence to Munich in 1826.
11. *Linz*, founded in 1636, Roman Catholic, reduced to a college and seminary.
12. *Mayence*, founded in 1477, Roman Catholic, now a theological seminary,
13. *Olmütz*, founded in 1581, Roman Catholic, abolished.
14. *Osnabrück*, founded in 1630, abolished.
15. *Paderborn*, founded in 1615, Roman Catholic, reduced to a seminary.
16. *Rinteln*, founded in 1621, Protestant, abolished in 1809.
17. *Salzburg*, founded in 1623, Roman Catholic.
18. *Wittenberg*, founded in 1502, Lutheran, transferred to Halle in 1817, and now reduced to an Evangelical seminary for candidates for the ministry who have finished their university course. (B. P.)

Uranius, HEINRICH, who lived in the 16th century, is the author of, *Grammaticæ Hebrææ Compendium* (Basle, 1541 and often):—*De Usu et Officiis Literarum Servilium* (Cologne, 1570):—*Puerilis Institutio Literar. Hebr.* etc. (Basle, 1551). See Fürst, *Bibl. Jud.* iii, 461; Jöcher, *Allgemeines Gelehrten-Lexikon*, s. v.; Steinschneider, *Bibliog. Handbuch*, s. v. (B. P.)

Urdu Version. See HINDUSTANI VERSION.

Uzzen-sherah. Tristram (*Bible Places*, p. 177) and Conder (*Tent Work*, ii, 340) identify this with the present *Beit Sîra*, two and a half miles south-west of Beit-ur el-Tahta (Lower Bethhoron), which the recent extension of the border of Ephraim, so as to include Abu-Shusheh (Gezer), allows. The place is described in the *Memoirs* to the Ordnance Survey, iii, 16, as "a small village on a swell in the low hills. A main road passes through it. The water supply is artificial."

V.

Vadian. See WATT, JOACHIM.

Vail, STEPHEN M., D.D., a Methodist Episcopal minister, was born at Union Vale, Dutchess Co., N. Y., Jan. 15, 1816. At fourteen he entered Cazenovia Seminary, where he was converted. In 1838 he graduated from Bowdoin College, and in 1842 from Union Theological Seminary. After completing his studies he joined the New York Conference, and was stationed successively at Fishkill, N. Y.; Sharon, Conn.; and Pine Plains. He was two years principal in Pennington Seminary, N. J., and from 1849 to 1868 was professor of Hebrew in the Biblical Institute at Concord, N. H. His health giving way, he resigned his professorship and returned to his home on Staten Island. In 1869 he was appointed consul to Bavaria, where he remained five years. Returning home, he continued the literary labors in which he had been engaged for years, preaching as he had strength and opportunity, without salary, until his death, which occurred in Jersey City, N. J., Nov. 26, 1880. He wrote numerous articles for the *Quarterly Review* and other periodicals. Among his literary works were, *Ministerial Education*:—*Bible against Slavery*:—and a *Hebrew Grammar*. He lived an earnest, faithful, noble Christian life, characterized by the strictest integrity and honor to the Church. See *Minutes of Annual Conferences*, 1881, p. 85.

Van Doren, WILLIAM H. See DOREN.

Van Ingen, JOHN V., D.D., a Protestant Episcopal clergyman, was rector of a church in Rochester, N. Y., until 1854, and of Christ Church, St. Paul, Minn., until 1862, when he became chaplain in the United States army; in 1864 he returned to Rochester as rector of Trinity Church. While in that city he was appointed chaplain of the Rochester institutions and missionary at Victor. In 1877 he became rector of St. John's, in Clyde. His death occurred Dec. 1 following, at the age of seventy-one years. See *Prot. Episc. Almanac*, 1879, p. 170.

Van Oosterzee. See OOSTERZEE.

Van Pelt, PETER, D.D., a Protestant Episcopal clergyman, served as secretary of the Board of Missions of his Church for several years prior to 1856, residing during that time in Philadelphia. Shortly after he was elected adjunct professor of English literature in the Diocesan College at Burlington, N. J. In 1859 he was professor of Hebrew in that college, and at the same time held the position of secretary to the General Board of Missions in Philadelphia. In 1862, although still holding the secretaryship, he was elected professor of Oriental languages in the Protestant Episcopal Divinity School, in Philadelphia. He retired from this position in 1867, but remained a resident of that city until his death, Aug. 20, 1873, at the age of seventy-five years. See *Prot. Episc. Almanac*, 1874, p. 38.

Van Santvoord, STAATS, D.D., a Reformed (Dutch) minister, grandson of Cornelius, was born at Schenectady, N. Y., in 1790. He graduated from Union College in 1811, and from the New Brunswick Theological Seminary in 1814; was licensed in the latter year, and preached at Belleville, N. J., until 1828, when he became agent for the New Brunswick Seminary for one year, and thereafter successively pastor at Schodack (1829, including Coeymans in 1830), New Baltimore

(1834), Onisquethan (1839, including New Salem in 1843), and Jerusalem (1845-57); in 1864 he engaged in the service of the Christian Commission, at Nashville, Tenn. He died May 31, 1882. Dr. Van Santvoord published several sermons. See Corwin, *Manual of the Ref. Church in America*, 3d ed. p. 521.

Van Zandt, Abraham Brooks, D.D., LL.D., a Presbyterian minister, was born Nov. 16, 1816, in Albany County, N. Y. His preparatory education was acquired under private tutors at Auburn and Schenectady; he graduated from Union College in 1840, teaching the grammar-school at Schenectady during the last half of his senior year, and for the same time after his graduation; studied at Princeton Theological Seminary from 1840 to 1842; was licensed by the Presbytery of Troy, Feb. 18 of the latter year, and ordained by the Presbytery of North River, at Matteawan, Dutchess Co., June 29 following; on the same day he was also installed pastor of the Matteawan Church, from which he was released Oct. 29 following; was pastor of the Reformed Dutch Church of Newburgh from 1842 to 1849; of the Tabb Street Presbyterian Church at Petersburg, Va., from 1849 to 1856; of the Central Reformed Dutch Church on Ninth Street, New York city, from 1856 to 1859; of the Reformed Dutch Church at Montgomery, N. Y., from 1860 to 1872; was inaugurated professor of didactic and polemic theology in the Theological Seminary of the Reformed Dutch Church at New Brunswick, N. J., Sept. 24 of the same year. On account of ill-health he was released from the active duties of this professorship, June 3, 1881, but was continued as professor emeritus until his death, July 21 following. He was a man of marked ability, an eloquent and scriptural preacher, and one of the foremost scholars of his denomination. See *Necrol. Report of Princeton Theol. Sem.* 1882, p. 43.

Vardill, John, D.D., an Episcopal clergyman, was born in 1752. He graduated from King's (now Columbia) College, and, for a time, was tutor in that institution. In 1774 he went to England to take orders, and the same year was elected assistant rector of Trinity Church, New York city, but preferred to remain abroad. The British government employed him in some department of labor. He wrote some satirical poems on the Whigs, and Trumbull alludes to him in his *McFingal*. He became rector of Skirbeck and Fishtoft, Lincolnshire, and died in 1811. See Sabine, *Loyalists of the Revolutionary War*, ii, 381. (J. C. S.)

Vatke, Johann Karl Wilhelm, a Protestant theologian, was born at Behndorf, Saxony, March 14, 1806. He studied theology and philosophy at Halle, Göttingen, and Berlin, and was privat-docent in theology at the latter place in 1830. His publication of *Die Religion des Alten Testaments* (1835) excited the wrath of the late professor Hengstenberg to such a degree that he declared, in Wilhelm Vatke, Peter von Bohlen, and David Friedrich Strauss, the antichrist has appeared, with three heads. Vatke was in 1837 appointed professor in extraordinary, and died April 19, 1882, doctor of theology. Besides the work mentioned already, in which Vatke shows himself to be the forerunner of writers like Wellhausen, Kuenen, Reuss, and others, who regard the prophets as older than the law, and the Psalms as more recent than both, he published *Die menschliche Freiheit in ihrem Verhältniss zur Sünde und zur göttlichen Gnade* (1884). In philosophy Vatke belonged to the left wing of the Hegelian school. See Benecke, *Wilhelm Vatke* (Bonn, 1883). (B. P.)

Vaughan, William, D.D., a Baptist minister, was born in Westmoreland County, Pa., Feb. 22, 1785. In 1810 he was converted, licensed in 1811, and ordained in 1812. He settled in Mason County, Ky., where he preached to several churches, and had charge of a school for about fifteen years. During this period he became an earnest defender of Campbellism. For two and a half years, from 1831, he was in the service of the American Sabbath-school Union, and established in Kentucky not far from one hundred Sunday-schools. He was for a time general agent for Kentucky of the American Bible Society. In 1836 he became pastor of the Bloomfield Church, and resigned in 1868. He died May 31, 1877, universally loved and honored. See Cathcart, *Baptist Encyclop.* p. 119. (J. C. S.)

Vaus, George, a Scotch prelate, was bishop of the see of Galloway in 1489, and was still bishop in 1505. See Keith, *Scottish Bishops*, p. 276.

Veesenmeyer, Georg, a Lutheran theologian of Germany, was born at Ulm, Nov. 20, 1760, and died April 6, 1833, doctor of theology. He published, *Literargeschichte der Briefsammlung und einiger Schriften von Luther* (Berlin, 1821):—*Kleine Beiträge zur Geschichte des Reichstags zu Augsburg* 1530 *und der augsburg. Confession* (Nuremberg, 1830):—*Literarisch-bibliographische Nachrichten von einigen evangelischen catechetischen Schriften*, etc. (Ulm, eod.):—*Denkmal der einheimischen und fremden Theologen*, etc. (1831). See Winer, *Handbuch der theol. Lit.* i, 25, 752; ii, 212; Zuchold, *Bibl. Theol.* s. v. (B. P.)

Vehmic Court (*Fehmgericht*, probably derived from *veme*, i. e. "punishment") was the name of a peculiar judicial institution, which, according to tradition, was founded by Charlemagne and Leo III, and continued to exist, at least nominally, in Westphalia down to the present century, when it was suppressed (in 1811) by Jerome Bonaparte. The tribunal was composed of freemen of spotless character, but not necessarily belonging to any certain social rank or state; both the emperor and the peasant could be members. The presence of seven members was necessary in order to form the court. When duke Heinrich of Bavaria was sentenced, in 1434, over eight hundred members were present. The court took cognizance of all kinds of cases, as heresy, witchcraft, rape, theft, robbery, murder, and summoned all kinds of persons, except ecclesiastics, Jews, and women, to appear before it. Its sittings were partly public—held under open sky—partly secret, and its verdicts were executed by its own members. In the course of time, when the state became able to maintain its laws, the Vehmic Court became superfluous, and in the 16th century it held its last open session. See Wigand, *Geschichte der Vehmgerichte* (Wetzlar, 1847); Walter, *Deutsche Rechtsgeschichte* (Bonn, 1857), ii, 632; Geisberg, *Die Fehme* (Münster, 1858); Kampschulte, *Zur Geschichte des Mittelalters* (Bonn, 1874); Essellen, *Die westfälischen Frei- oder Fehmgerichte* (1877). (B. P.)

Vent, Hans Lorenz Andreas, a Lutheran theologian of Germany, was born at Hademarschen, Holstein, April 10, 1785. In 1811 he was deacon at Tallingstedt, and from 1815 to 1863 pastor in his native city. He resigned the pastorate in 1863, and died April 21, 1879, member of consistory. He published, *Luther's Werke in einer das Bedürfniss der Zeit berücksichtigenden Auswahl* (Hamburg, 1826, 10 vols.):—*Homiletisches Magazin über die evangelischen Texte des ganzen Jahres* (2d ed. ibid. 1839, 2 vols.). See Winer, *Handbuch der theol. Lit.* i, 25, 584; ii, 126, 327; Zuchold, *Bibl. Theol.* s. v. (B. P.)

Vermeil, Antoine, a French Protestant theologian, was born at Nimes, March 19, 1799, and studied at Geneva. In 1824 he was pastor at Bordeaux, where he founded many benevolent institutions. In 1840 he was called to Paris, and died in 1864. Vermeil has immortalized his name by his great monument, The Institute of Deaconnesses, which he founded at a time when Fliedner's name was not yet known in France. A biographical sketch of Vermeil is given in his sermons, *Catéchisme Liturgique*, published after his death (Paris, 1869 sq. 3 vols.). See Lichtenberger, *Encyclop. des Sciences Religieuses*, s. v. (B. P.)

Vernes, Jacob, a Protestant theologian of Geneva, was born in 1728, and died in 1791. He is the author of, *Lettres sur le Christianisme de J. J. Rousseau* (1763)

—*Dialogue sur le Christianisme de J. J. Rousseau* (eod.):—*Confidence Philosophique* (1776, 2 vols.):—*Sermons* (1790, 2 vols.):—*Catéchisme à l'Usage de Toutes les Communions Chrétiennes* (1774; 3d ed. 1778). See Lichtenberger, *Encyclop. des Sciences Religieuses*, s. v. (B. P.)

Verny, Louis Eduard, a Protestant theologian of France, was born at Mayence, March 17, 1803. He studied law at Strasburg, and practiced at Colmar. In 1828 he gave up his profession and betook himself to the study of theology. In 1830 he was appointed principal of the college at Mulhausen, and in 1835 accepted a call to the Lutheran Church at Paris. He died Oct. 19, 1854, in the pulpit of St. Thomas, at Strasburg, where he had made the opening address of the session of the Superior Consistory. After his death a volume of *Sermons*, containing also a biographical sketch, was published (Paris, 1867). See Scherer and Colani, in *Revue Théologique*, of Strasburg, first series, ix, 265 sq.; Lichtenberger, *Encyclop. des Sciences Religieuses*, s. v. (B. P.)

Vialart (*de Herse*), Felix, a French ecclesiastic, was born in Paris, Sept. 4, 1613, of a noble family, and pursued his studies at the Collége de Navarre. In 1638 he was made doctor of theology, and in 1641 coadjutor to the bishop of Châlons, whom he succeeded in the following year. Vialart died June 10, 1680, highly esteemed by all classes. He published, *Rituel ou Manuel de l'Église de Châlons* (Paris, 1649):—*Ordonnances, Mandements et Lettres Pastorales pour le Rétablissement de la Discipline Ecclésiastique* (1660, 1662):—*L'École Chrétienne*, a kind of catechism. See Gouget, *Vie de Messire Vialart de Herse, Évêque et Comte de Châlons* (new ed. Utrecht, 1739). Lichtenberger, *Encyclop. des Sciences Religieuses*, s. v. (B. P.)

Villers, Charles François Dominique de, a distinguished French writer, was born at Belchen, in Lorraine, Nov. 4, 1764. He was educated in the military school at Metz, and entered the army in 1782, but studied at the same time classical literature and philosophy. His *De la Liberté* (1791) proved too moderate for the Jacobins, and in 1792 he was compelled to flee. He settled at Lübeck, and became, in the course of time, thoroughly acquainted with the German language and literature. Having written with great openness against the violence of Napoleon's generals, he was expelled from the Hanse Towns by Davoust in 1806. Villers went to Paris, and obtained from the emperor the repeal of the order. In 1811 he was made professor of philosophy at Göttingen, from which position, however, he was dismissed in 1814 by the returning Hanoverian dynasty. Villers died Feb. 26, 1815. His principal works are, *Essai sur l'Esprit et l'Influence de la Reformation de Luther* (5th ed., published by Maeder, Strasburg, 1851), which received the prize of the French Academy in 1804, and was translated both into German and English:—*Philosophie de Kant* (Metz, 1802, 2 vols.). See Herzog, *Real-Encyklop.* s. v.; Lichtenberger, *Encyclop. des Sciences Religieuses*, s. v.; Winer, *Handbuch der theol. Lit.* i, 325, 326, 742, 743. (B. P.)

Vilmar, Jacob Wilhelm Georg, a Lutheran theologian of Germany, was born in 1804, and died Dec. 7, 1884, at Melsungen. He was the leader of the Separate Lutherans of Hesse, and published, *Die protestantische Lehre der Rechtfertigung durch den Glauben* (Cassel, 1838):—*Was fasst der biblische Begriff der Sünde in sich?* (1840):—*Die kurhessische Kirche* (1845):—*Protestantismus und Christenthum* (1847):—*Der gegenwärtige Kampf der hessischen Kirche um ihre Selbstständigkeit* (1871). (B. P.)

Vincent, Jacques Louis Samuel, a Protestant theologian of France, was born at Nimes, Sept. 8, 1787. After having studied at Geneva, he settled in his native city as pastor. In 1825 he was made president of the consistory. After the revolution, the French Reformed Church gradually sank down into the deism of Rousseau, and its theology became mere conventionalism without any true vitality. Vincent felt the evil, and it is his great merit that he procured the remedy. His first original production was an attack on Lamennais's *Essai sur l'Indifférence en Matière de Religion*, and his *Observations sur l'Unité Religieuse* (1820), and *Observations sur la Voie d'Autorité Appliquée à la Religion*, created quite a sensation. From 1820 to 1824 he published *Mélanges de Religion, de Morale et de Critique Sacrée* (10 vols.), which made the French public acquainted with and interested in German theology. Of still deeper influence were his *Vues sur le Protestantisme* (1829, 2 vols.; republished by Prevost-Paradol, 1860), and *Méditations Religieuses* (most complete edition by Fontanès, 1863). Vincent died July 10, 1837. See Corbière, *Samuel Vincent, sa Conception Religieuse et Chrétienne* (1873); Antonin, *Étude sur Samuel Vincent et sa Théologie* (1863); Plitt-Herzog, *Real-Encyklop.* s.v.; Lichtenberger, *Encyclop. des Sciences Religieuses*, s. v. (B. P.)

Vincent, Philippe, a Reformed theologian of France, was born in 1595. Having completed his theological studies, he was ordained in 1620, was appointed, in 1626, pastor of the Reformed Church at La Rochelle, and died March 12, 1651. He is the author of *Paraphrase sur les Lamentations du Prophète Jérémie* (1646). See Jöcher, *Allgemeines Gelehrten-Lexikon*, s. v.; Lichtenberger, *Encyclop. des Sciences Religieuses*, s.v. (B. P.)

Vinton, Alexander Hamilton, D.D., a Protestant Episcopal clergyman, was born at Providence, R. I., May 2, 1807. He studied medicine at New Haven, Conn., and practiced as a physician from 1828 to 1832. He then studied theology in the Protestant Episcopal Seminary in New York city, and was ordained in 1835. For about a year he was pastor of a church at Portland, Me., and from 1836 to 1842 was stationed at Providence, R. I. From 1842 to 1858 he was a pastor in Boston, Mass. He then went to Philadelphia, Pa., remaining in that city until 1861. He next became rector of St. Mark's Church, New York city, until 1869, when he went to Boston as rector of Emanuel Church, and later was a professor in the Protestant Episcopal Divinity School, Cambridge, Mass. He died there, April 26, 1881. Dr. Vinton published a volume of *Sermons* (1855) and several separate discourses and addresses.

Vinton, Francis, D.D., D.C.L., a Protestant Episcopal clergyman, was born at Providence, R. I., Aug. 29, 1809. He graduated at West Point in 1830; became lieutenant of artillery; was stationed in Boston Harbor; studied law in Harvard College, and acted as civil engineer; left the army in 1836; and after studying in the General Theological Seminary, was rector in Brooklyn, N. Y., several years prior to 1856, and shortly after became assistant minister of Trinity Church, New York city. About 1870, in addition to his pastoral duties, he was elected Ludlow professor of ecclesiastical polity and law in the General Theological Seminary at New York. He died in Brooklyn, Sept. 29, 1872. See *Prot. Episc. Almanac*, 1873, p. 134.

Vormbaum, Reinhold, a Protestant theologian of Germany, who died Oct. 2, 1880, at Kaiserswerth, where he had been laboring for more than thirty years, is the author of, *Evangelische Missionsgeschichte in Biographien* (Elberfeld, 1850-61, 4 vols.):—*Missionssegen. Lebensbilder aus der Geschichte der evang. Heidenmission* (1852):—*Joachim Neander's Leben und Lieder* (1860). See Zuchold, *Bibl. Theol.* ii, 1404 sq. (B. P.)

Vullers, Johann August, a German Orientalist, was born at Bonn, Oct. 23, 1803, and died at Giessen, Jan. 21, 1880, where he had been professor of Oriental languages since 1833. He published, *Fragmente über die Religion des Zoroaster* (Bonn, 1831):—*Institutiones Linguæ Persicæ cum Sanscrita et Zendica Lingua Comparatæ* (Giessen, 1840-50, 2 vols.):—*Lexicon Persico-Latinum Etymologicum* (Bonn, 1855-64, 2 vols.):—*Sup-*

plementum Lexici Persico-Latini, Continens Verborum Linguæ Persicæ Radices (1867):—*Grammatica Linguæ Persicæ* (Giessen, 1870). (B. P.)

Vulliemin, LOUIS, a Protestant theologian, was born at Yverdon, Switzerland, Sept. 7, 1797. He was educated in the institute of the famous Pestalozzi, and pursued his philosophical as well as theological studies at Lausanne. He was ordained in 1821, and acted for several years as vicar in various places. But his delicate health prevented him from assuming a pastorate, and he betook himself to literary work. In 1828 he published an *Essai sur l'Évangile;* in 1829, *Considerations sur les Mœurs des Chrétiens, leur Culte et leur Gouvernement Pendant les Trois Premiers Siècles.* To the same period belongs his translation of *Geschichte der Schweizer Confederation*, by Johannes von Müller. In 1849 Vulliemin was made professor of theology at Lausanne, and took an active part in the ecclesiastical affairs of his country. In 1865 he resigned his professorship, and died Aug. 10, 1879. See Secretan, in the *Gazette de Lausanne*, Oct. 3 and 4, 1879; Pingaud, *Louis Vulliemin* (Besançon, 1881); Marc Debrit, in the *Journal de Genève*, Aug. 12, 1879; Lichtenberger, *Encyclop. des Sciences Religieuses*, s. v. (B. P.)

W.

Wackerhagen, AUGUSTUS, D.D., a Lutheran minister, was born in Hanover, Germany, May 22, 1774. He was educated at the University of Göttingen; employed for a time in a young ladies' seminary, and also as private tutor in a nobleman's family. In 1801 he arrived in America, acted as tutor three years to the son of Mr. Bohlen, a Philadelphia merchant, then visited Europe. Returning to the United States, was shipwrecked, but his life was saved. In 1805 he accepted a call to Schoharie, N.Y.; in 1816 was pastor of various churches in Columbia County; for several years had charge of the academy at Clermont, and died there, Nov. 1, 1865. Dr. Wackerhagen was a diligent student of ancient and modern languages. For twelve years he presided over the New York Ministerium, and was an original trustee of Hartwick Seminary. Except a sermon on the *Lutheran Pulpit*, the only work he published was a German volume, *Faith and Morals* (Philadelphia, 1804). See *Fifty Years in the Lutheran Ministry* (1878), p. 63.

Wadsworth, CHARLES, D.D., a Presbyterian minister, was born at Litchfield, Conn., May 8, 1814. He graduated from Union College in 1837, and after teaching one year at Canajoharie, N. Y., graduated from Princeton Theological Seminary in 1840. He was ordained pastor of the Second Presbyterian Church of Troy, N. Y., Feb. 17, 1842; in 1850 was called to the Arch Street Presbyterian Church, Philadelphia, Pa., which, under his charge, became large, influential, and flourishing; in 1862 he accepted a call to the Calvary Church, San Francisco, Cal.; in 1869 returned to Philadelphia as pastor of the Third Reformed (Dutch) Church, which in 1873 united with the Immanuel Presbyterian Church. He died in Philadelphia, April 1, 1882. Dr. Wadsworth was an earnest, eloquent preacher, and had few equals in the pulpit. See *Necrol. Report of Princeton Theol. Sem.* 1882, p. 39. (W. P. S.)

Wait, SAMUEL, D.D., a Baptist minister, was born in Washington County, N. Y., Dec. 19, 1789. He made a profession of religion March 12, 1809; was ordained at Sharon, Mass., June 3, 1818, and afterwards pursued his studies at Columbian College, Washington, D. C., where for a time he was a tutor. He became pastor at Newbern, N. C., in 1827, and for a number of years travelled through that state. Under his auspices the religious organ of the denomination, the *Recorder*, was established. To him, also, Wake Forest College owes its existence. It was started as a manual-labor institution in 1833, and he was called to preside over it. The school, in 1839, having abandoned the manual-labor feature, was made a college, and Dr. Wait continued at its head until 1846, and then resigned, filling the position of pastor of one or two churches until 1851, when he became principal of a female school in Oxford, N. C., where he remained until 1856. He died July 28, 1867. See Cathcart, *Baptist Encyclop.* p. 1198. (J. C. S.)

Walcott, MACKENZIE E. C., a minister of the Church of England, was born at Bath, Dec. 15, 1821. He was educated at Winchester and Oxford, at a very early period in life entered upon authorship, and for more than thirty years issued a constant succession of works on topographical and ecclesiastical history. As a curate of the churches of St. Margaret and St. James, Westminster, he was naturally drawn to the story of the historical associations connected with those parishes. His three volumes on the narrative of Westminster, and the two most famous parish churches which bear its name, were published before 1851. In that year he published *The English Ordinal: its History, Validity, and Catholicity; with an Introduction, The Three Holy Orders of Ministers in the Church.* In 1863 he was appointed to the precentorship and prebendal stall of Oving, at Chichester, and illustrated the history of the cathedral to which he was attached by numerous volumes on its bishops and episcopal registers. He died at London, Dec. 22, 1880. Besides the writings already mentioned, he published, *Sacred Archæology* (Lond. 1868):—*Traditions and Customs of Cathedrals* (1872):—*The Constitutions and Canons Ecclesiastical of the Church of England* (1874):—*Church-work and Life in English Minsters* (1880). Mr. Walcott was also a frequent contributor to the *Transactions* of the British Archæological Association and the Royal Society of Literature. (B. P.)

Waldby, ROBERT, D.D., an Irish prelate, was born in the city of York, and received the rudiments of his education in the abbey of Tickell, in Yorkshire. He became divinity professor at Toulouse. In 1383 he was sent by Richard II to treat with John, duke of Lancaster, another time to negotiate a neutral league with Charles, king of Navarre, and a third to effect the reduction of John, earl of Armagnac, to true obedience. In 1391 he succeeded to the see of Dublin. In 1392 he was constituted chancellor of Ireland. In 1395 he was summoned to a great council to be held at Kilkenny. He was translated to the see of Chichester, and from that promoted to the archbishopric of York. He died in 1397. See D'Alton, *Memoirs of the Archbishops of Dublin*, p. 146.

Walker, JOSEPH R., D.D., a Protestant Episcopal clergyman, was ordained deacon in 1817. For fifty-five years, that is, from 1823 to 1878, he was rector of St. Helena's Parish, Beaufort, S. C. He died April 2, 1879, aged eighty-three years. See *Prot. Episc. Almanac*, 1880, p. 172.

Walkures. See WALKYRIES.

Wallace, ROBERT, a Scotch prelate, was minister at Barnwell, Ayrshire, and was consecrated bishop of the Isles, at St. Andrews, in January, 1661. He died in 1675. See Keith, *Scottish Bishops*, p. 310.

Waller, WILLIAM J., M.D., S.T.D., a Protestant Episcopal clergyman, was born Jan. 5, 1799. He was ordained deacon in 1844, and presbyter in 1845. From 1847 to 1859 he was president of Shelby College, and then removed to Louisville, Ky. About 1864 he returned to his former position at Shelbyville, and there remained until about 1868, when he went to Lebanon. About 1873 he removed to Louisville. In 1877 he went to Anchorage, where he died, April 21, 1879. See *Prot. Episc. Almanac*, 1880, p. 172.

Walter (1), a Scotch prelate, was probably bishop of St. Andrews in the 12th century. See Keith, *Scottish Bishops*, p. 9.

Walter (2), a Scotch prelate, was bishop of Dunkeld in 1324. See Keith, *Scottish Bishops*, p. 83.

Walters, W. T., D.D., a Baptist minister, was born in Pittsylvania County, Va., in 1825. He made a profession of religion early in life, and graduated from Wake Forest College in 1848, in which he became first a tutor and then professor of mathematics, remaining in that position until the college was closed by the civil war. He was chosen, in 1867, corresponding secretary of the North Carolina State Convention, and for three years was engaged in the duties of that office. He was also for some time occupied in editorial work, being connected for a while with the *Biblical Recorder*, of which for several years he was the agricultural editor. Two churches, those of Littleton and Wilson, N. C., were organized by him. He died Dec. 31, 1877. See Cathcart, *Bapt. Encyclop.* p. 1208. (J. C. S.)

Walton (called *Moustern*), JOHN, an Irish prelate, was the eighteenth abbot of Osney, near Oxford, to the government of which house he was appointed in 1452. From this abbacy he was advanced to the archbishopric of Dublin, consecrated in England, and invested with the pall in 1472. He did not receive formal restitution of the temporalities of his see until 1477. In 1478 this prelate annexed the perpetual vicarage of St. Kevin to his choral vicar of the prebend of Cullen. He resigned in 1484. See D'Alton, *Memoirs of the Archbishops of Dublin*, p. 166.

Warburton, CHARLES MONGAN, D.D., an Irish bishop, was born in 1755, in the north of Ireland. He was intended for the Roman Catholic Church, sent to study in one of the institutions on the Continent endowed for the education of Romish priests, but was thrown by accident into the society of the earl of Moira, who induced him to become a Protestant. He was, after taking orders, appointed chaplain to a regiment in America. Not long afterwards he changed his name from *Mongan* to *Warburton*, became dean of Ardagh, then bishop of Limerick in 1806, and of Cloyne in 1820. He died at Cloyne palace, Aug. 9, 1826. See (Lond.) *Annual Register*, 1826, p. 270.

Ward (prop. מִשְׁמָר or מִשְׁמֶרֶת, φυλακή; occasionally סוּגַר [Ezek. xix, 9], or פְּקֻדָּה [ix, 1, 11], *custody* ["oversight," etc.]), a prison (q. v.) or an apartment thereof (Gen. xl, 3; Acts xii, 10); also a watch-post at the gates of the Temple (Neh. xii, 25; 1 Chron. ix, 23). This term is likewise used to designate a class or detachment of priests or Levites (xxv, 8; Neh. xii, 24; xiii, 30).

Ward, John, LL.D., an English Baptist educator, was born in London in 1679, his father being a Baptist minister. He possessed learning of the highest order, and loved the acquisition of knowledge with an intense affection. He was elected professor of rhetoric in Gresham College in 1720, and died in 1758. Among the productions of his pen were, *The Lives of the Gresham Professors*:—*The Westminster Greek Grammar*. He assisted Horsley in his *Britannia Romana*, and Ainsworth in his *Dictionary*. See Cathcart, *Bapt. Encyclop.* p. 1208. (J. C. S.)

Ward, Seth, D.D., F.R.S., an eminent English divine and mathematician, was born at Buntingford, Hertfordshire, in 1617. He graduated at Sidney Sussex College, Cambridge, about 1637, and became a fellow of the same college in 1640; but was ejected from his fellowship in 1643, for refusing to sign the Solemn League and Covenant. He then became a private tutor, and afterwards went to Oxford, where he was chosen Savilian professor of astronomy in 1649, and remained at that post until 1661. He was elected principal of Jesus College in 1657, but did not receive possession; and president of Trinity College in 1659 but was obliged to resign this position at the Restoration, in 1660. The same year, however, he received the vicarage of St. Lawrence, Jewry, London, and the precentorship of Exeter; and was promoted to the deanery of Exeter in 1661. He became bishop of Exeter in 1662, bishop of Salisbury in 1667, chancellor of the Order of the Garter in 1671, prebendary of Salisbury in 1672, archdeacon of Wilts in 1675, prebendary of Winchester in 1676, chancellor of Salisbury in 1681, and treasurer of Salisbury in 1687. In 1682 he founded at Salisbury a college for the widows of clergymen. About 1687 he lost his mental faculties, and died at Knightsbridge, Jan. 6, 1689. He was a distinguished astronomer, and one of the founders of the Royal Society. He was the author of *An Essay on the Being and Attributes of God; on the Immortality of the Soul*, etc. (Oxford, 1652):—a volume of *Sermons* (Lond. 1674):—*Prœlectio de Cometis*, etc. (1653):—*Astronomia Geometrica* (1656):—and other works.

Warden, a keeper, a guardian; a term sometimes applied to the head of a college, and sometimes to the superior of the chapters in conventual churches.

Wardlaw, WALTER, a Scotch prelate, was archdeacon of Lothian, and secretary to king David II, when he was consecrated bishop of the see of Glasgow in 1368. He was bishop here in 1389. See Keith, *Scottish Bishops*, p. 246.

Wardrobe (בֶּגֶד, 2 Kings xxii, 14; 2 Chron. xxxiv, 22; *clothing* or *garments*, as usually rendered), the vestry of the palace or temple (q. v.).

Warne, JOSEPH ANDREWS, D.D., a Baptist minister, born in London, England, in 1795, was converted in early life, graduated at Stepney College in 1821, in 1822 came to America, settling first in North Carolina, where, after teaching some time, he became pastor of the Church in Newbern, and afterwards principal of the Furman Academy of Edgefield, S. C. Later he came north, and supplied the pulpit successively of the First Baptist Church in Providence, R. I.; South Reading (now Wakefield), Mass.; Brookline (seven years); the Second Baptist Church in Providence, and the Sansom Street Church, Philadelphia. He died at Frankford, March 9, 1881. Dr. Warne was greatly interested in foreign missions. He was editor of a Baptist edition of *The Comprehensive Commentary*. See *The National Baptist*, March 17, 1881. (J. C. S.)

Warneford, SAMUEL WILSON, D.C.L., a clergyman of the English Church, was born at Sevenhampton, near Highworth, in Wiltshire, in 1758. He was educated at University College, Oxford, where he received the degree of A.M. in 1786, and B.C.L. in 1790. He became rector of Liddiard Millicent, Wilts, in 1809; and of Bourton-on-the-Hill, in Gloucestershire, in 1810, where he lived plainly, and bestowed the large fortune of which he was then in possession in gifts of public charity and benevolence. He founded schools and almshouses in his own parish, and contributed largely to schools, colleges, and hospitals throughout the kingdom. To the Clergy Orphan-school he gave thirteen thousand pounds, and to Queen's College, Birmingham, upwards of twenty-five thousand pounds. In 1844 the bishop of Gloucester conferred on him an honorary canonry in Gloucester Cathedral; and in 1849 a statue of him was erected in the Warneford Lunatic Asylum at Oxford, the expense of which was met by public subscription. He died at Bourton, Jan. 11, 1855.

Warnefrid, PAUL. See PAUL THE DEACON.

Warner, John (1), D.D., an English ecclesiastic, was born in the parish of St. Clement Danes, London, in 1585. He was elected demy of Magdalen College, Oxford, in 1599; graduated A.B. in 1602; made perpetual fellow in 1605; dean of Lichfield in 1633; and bishop of Rochester, Jan. 14, 1638. He died in 1666. Being a loyalist, he suffered during the usurpation of Cromwell. He was the author of *Church Lands not to be*

Sold (Lond. 1646):—and *Letter to Dr. Jeremy Taylor concerning the Chapter on Original Sin in the Usum Necessarium* (1656). He also published several sermons. He possessed considerable fortune, and was very liberal with it, giving during his lifetime and bequeathing at his death some twenty thousand pounds for charitable purposes.

Warner, John (2), D.D., an English clergyman, son of Dr. Ferdinando Warner, was born at Ronde, Wiltshire, in 1736. He was educated at Trinity College, Cambridge, from which he graduated in 1758; preached many years at a chapel in Long Acre; became rector of Hockliffe and Chalgrave, Bedfordshire, in 1771, and afterwards of Stourton, Wilts. He died in St. John's Square, Clerkenwell, Jan. 20, 1800. He resided in France during the Revolution, and thus became an ardent republican. He was the author of *Metronariston; or, A New Pleasure Recommended in a Dissertation upon a Part of Greek and Latin Prosody* (Lond. 1797); and *Memoirs of Mekerchus*, in the *Gentleman's Magazine*.

Warpulis, in Slavonic mythology, is the god of the winds; one in the train of followers of Perun, the god of thunder. He causes the roaring of the storm.

Warren, John (1), D.D., an English clergyman, was born in 1670, became prebendary of Exeter in 1709, and died in 1736. He published some single sermons which have been commended. See Allibone, *Dict. of Brit. and Amer. Authors*, s. v.

Warren, John (2), LL.D., an English prelate of the 18th century, became archdeacon of Worcester in 1775, bishop of St. David's in 1779, was translated to Bangor in 1783, and died in 1800. He published six single sermons (1777-92). See Allibone, *Dict. of Brit. and Amer. Authors*, s. v.

Warren, Joseph W., D.D., one of the oldest missionaries of the Presbyterian Board in India, was born at Brunswick, Me., Aug. 30, 1809. After a course of study at the academy at Plymouth, N. H., he learned the art of printing at Concord, and afterwards resumed his studies at Phillips Academy, Exeter, where he was converted, and soon after determined to devote himself to the work of the ministry. At the age of twenty-five he entered Lane Theological Seminary, and was one of the large body of students who left on account of the abolition excitement. He completed his studies at the Allegheny Seminary, where he connected himself with the Presbyterian Church. In October, 1828, in company with Messrs. Freeman and Scott, he left for India, where his knowledge of printing contributed to his great usefulness in superintending the press. He took with him and set up at Allahabad the first mission press ever established in India north of Serampore. He was much engaged in promoting the cause of education in India, and aided in establishing the high-school at Agra for European and Eurasian children. In 1853 he returned to the United States to make provision for the education of his children, and entered for a time upon pastoral work in Indiana. He served also as chaplain during the late civil war. In October, 1872, he returned to India and completed a *Grammar of the Urdu Dialect*, and partially completed a translation of *Gesenius's Hebrew Lexicon*. The Rev. John S. Woodside, of Dehra, Northern India, in communicating the death of Dr. Warren, writes, among other things, "Throughout his illness his constant prayer was for patience, that he might have grace to endure all he had to suffer. He did not desire that his life should be unduly prolonged, but his prayer was, 'Come, Lord Jesus, and come quickly.'" He died at Morar Gualior, March 7, 1879. (W. P. S.)

Warren, Samuel, LL.D., eminent in the history of English Methodism, commenced his career as a Wesleyan minister in 1802. He was a man of large ability, and occupied some of the most important circuits in England. Jealous of the rising influence of Dr. Jabez Bunting, he objected to certain features in the formation of a theological institution in 1834, and not ceasing in his opposition, he was suspended from his ministerial functions at a special district meeting at Manchester, where he was then stationed, in October of that year. Controversial publications were issued by both parties, violent language was indulged in, an extensive agitation followed, and a large defection from the societies was the result, Dr. Warren's case exciting much sympathy. Deeming himself unconstitutionally suspended, Warren appealed to the high court of chancery, but on March 25, 1835, the lord high-chancellor denied the appeal. At the Wesleyan conference at Sheffield, in August following, Dr. Warren was expelled from the connection. Many of his sympathizers amalgamated with the Leeds secessionists, who had adopted the title of the Protestant Methodists in 1828, and assumed the name of the Wesleyan Association Methodists in 1835, and in 1857 both united in the formation of that respectable body, the United Methodist Free Church. Dr. Warren himself, becoming tired of the excitement and extremes connected with an agitation, many features of which could never have been congenial to his sober and deliberate judgment, was received into the Episcopal Church, and became the incumbent of All-Souls' Church, Ancoats, Manchester, which preferment he held until his death, in 1874. Dr. Warren published, besides a number of sermons, *Memoirs and Select Letters of Mrs. A. Warren* (1832, 12mo):—*A Digest of the Laws and Regulations of the Wesleyan Methodists* (2d ed. Lond. 1835). See Stevenson, *Hist. of City Road Chapel*, p. 557; Adeline Waddy, *Life of S. D. Waddy, D.D.*, p. 98; Smith, *Hist. of Wesl. Methodism* (see *supra* and *Appendices H-P*), iii, 575-606; *Minutes of Conference*, 1835, vii, 542-591; Jackson, *Life of Robert Newton, D.D.* (Lond. and N. Y. 1855), p. 142 sq.

Warren, William, D.D., a Congregational minister, was born at Waterford, Me., Oct. 21, 1806. He was a student at Phillips Academy, Andover, Mass.; also in Bowdoin College from 1834 to 1836; graduated from Andover Theological Seminary in 1838; preached in Wells, Me., six months; was ordained at Windham, Feb. 14, 1840; installed at Upton, Mass., Nov. 14, 1849; dismissed April 29, 1856; was district secretary of the American Board of Commissioners for Foreign Missions for northern New England, residing at Gorham, Me., from 1857 to 1878, and died Jan. 28, 1879. He published, *Geography and Atlas* (1843):—*Household Consecration and Baptism* (1846):—*Teacher's Institute Lecture* (1848):—*Spirit's Sword* (1853):—*Funeral Sermon*:—*Religious Progress*:—*A Voice to the Young*, and other sermons. Also a work on, *Theories of the Will*:—*Twelve Years with the Children*:—*Our Indebtedness to Missions*. See *Cong. Year-book*, 1880, p. 31.

Warrener, William, an English Wesleyan minister, was received into the work by Wesley in 1779. After laboring in Great Britain for seven years, he went as a missionary to the West Indies, "being the first of our preachers," say the *Minutes*, "who was regularly appointed to that work." He, with Clarke and Hammet, went over with Dr. Coke, in 1786, on that celebrated voyage intended to terminate in Nova Scotia, but which ended really eighteen hundred miles south, at the island of Antigua. Warrener was stationed on that island, where a most flourishing cause was inaugurated, the society having been, in fact, already formed by Nathaniel Gilbert and John Baxter. In 1797, after a successful career, he returned to his own country and was appointed to a circuit. In 1818 he retired; and on Nov. 27, 1825, in the seventy-fifth year of his age, he passed away, "triumphing gloriously over death." He was the first Methodist missionary who addressed the great annual gatherings of the Wesleyan Missionary Society, doing so at the memorable meeting at Leeds. See Smith, *Hist. of Wesl. Methodism*, iii, 101 sq.; also i, 544; ii, 232,

546; Stevens, *Hist. of Methodism*, ii, 353; iii, 488; *Minutes of the Conference*, 1826; Newcomb, *Cyclopædia of Missions* (revised ed. 1854), p. 763.

Wars OF THE LORD, BOOK OF THE (סֵפֶר מִלְחֲמוֹת יְהוָֹה), a document cited Numb. xxi, 14. It was probably a collection of poems or songs celebrating the victories which had been achieved by the Israelites by the help of God. That it was an Amoritish work, as Michaelis suggested, is disproved by the use of the term יהוה, which Michaelis vainly attempts to show is to be taken as a verb, and the passage translated: "As it is said in the book of the wars, it shall be." There is no reason to doubt that there were minstrels enough in Israel at all times of their history to record the events of that history in song, and those composed before the date of this notice might have been written in a book. What confirms this are the undoubted fragments of ancient songs in ver. 17, 18, and 27-30.

It is not clear what the passage cited means; but it seems to give a geographical notice, and probably was of some importance as indicating the ancient boundaries of the Moabitish territory (Rosenmüller, *ad loc.*; Hävernick, *Einleit.* I, ii, 504, Eng. transl. p. 321; Bleek, *Einleit.* p. 199). Hengstenberg has a peculiar view (*Beiträge*, ii, 223), which Baumgarten (*Theolog. Commentar*, ii, 344) follows. He translates: "And Vaheb (he took—i. e. Jehovah) in the storm, and the brooks, the Arnon and the valley of the brooks which goes down to the dwelling of Ar, and leans on the borders of Moab." This is not very different from the Sept. version: διὰ τοῦτο λέγεται ἐν βιβλίῳ· πόλεμος τοῦ Κυρίου τὴν Ζωὸβ (they probably read זהב for והב) ἐφλόγισε, καὶ τοὺς χειμάῤῥους Ἀρνῶν.—Kitto. It was evidently one of the documents used by Moses in the composition of the Pentateuch. It may have contained, among other matters, the history of the expeditions occasionally made by the Hebrews, while in Egypt, among the surrounding tribes. At any rate, some such document seems to have been used by the writer of Chronicles, and its contents are characterized as "ancient things" (1 Chron. iv, 21-23; vii, 21, 22). See *New-Englander*, Jan. 1862. See PENTATEUCH.

Warton, JOSEPH, D.D., an English clergyman, son of Thomas Warton, Sr., was born at Dunsford, Surrey, in 1722. He was educated at Winchester School, and at Oriel College, Oxford, where he graduated in 1744; took orders in the Church of England, and was curate to his father at Basingstoke from 1744 to 1746; curate at Chelsea from 1746 to 1748; became rector of Winslade, Hampshire, in 1748; travelled in France and elsewhere on the Continent with the duke of Bolton in 1751; became rector of Tunworth in 1754, of Wickham in 1782, and of Upham in 1788. He was second master of Winchester School from 1755 to 1766, and head master from 1766 to 1793. He became chaplain to Sir George Lyttelton in 1756; prebendary of St. Paul's, London, in 1782; and prebendary of Winchester in 1788. He died at Wickham, in Hampshire, Feb. 23, 1800. His principal published works are, *Odes on Various Subjects* (1746):—a poetical translation of the *Eclogues and Georgics of Virgil* (1753):—an *Essay on the Genius and Writings of Pope* (1756-82):—twenty-four critical papers in *The Adventurer*:—and editions of the works of *Pope* (1797, 9 vols.) and *Dryden* (1811, 4 vols.). *A Biographical Memoir of Dr. Joseph Warton*, with a selection from his poetry and literary correspondence, was published in 1806 by Rev. John Wooll, master of the school at Midhurst, in Sussex.

Waser, CASPAR (or GASPAR), a Swiss theologian, was born at Zurich, Sept. 1, 1565. He studied at Altdorf and Heidelberg, travelled extensively through Holland, England, Ireland, and Italy, and after his return, in 1593, was appointed pastor at Witticon, which place he exchanged, in 1596, for the deanery at Zurich, connecting at the same time the professorship of Hebrew. In 1607 he received also the chair of Greek, and in 1611 the theological chair, and died Nov. 9, 1625. He wrote, *Archetypus Gram. Hebraicæ, Duabus præcipue Partibus, Etymologia et Syntaxi Absolutus*, etc. (Basle, 1600, and often):—*Tractatus de Antiquis Nummis Hebræorum, Chaldæorum, et Syrorum* (Zurich, 1605):—*De Antiquis Hebræorum Mensuris*:—*Elementale Chaldaicum*, etc. See Jodoc. a Kuosen, *Oratio de Vita et Obitu C. Waseri*; Witte, *Diarium Biographicum*; König, *Bibliotheca Nova et Vetus*; Jöcher, *Allgemeines Gelehrten-Lexikon*, s. v.; Fürst, *Bibl. Jud.* iii, 494; Steinschneider, *Bibliographisches Handbuch*, s. v.; *Biographie Universelle*, s. v. (B. P.)

Wash (denoted by several Hebrew words of varying import; but in Greek νίπτω, which applies to a part of the person, is clearly distinguished from λούω, which applies to the whole body, in John xiii, 10, where the A. V. unfortunately confounds the two). This act for ordinary purposes of personal cleanliness is considered under BATHE. We here treat it under its ceremonial aspect. See ABLUTION.

The Jews had two sorts of washing for purposes of religious purification: one, of the whole body by immersion, טָבַל, *tabál*, which was used by the priests at their consecration, and by the proselytes at their initiation; the other, of the hands or feet, called dipping, or pouring of water, צָבַע, *tsabá*, which was of daily use, not only for the hands and feet, but also for cups and other vessels used at their meals (Matt. xxv, 2; Mark vii, 3, 4). The six water-pots of stone used at the marriage feast of Cana in Galilee (John ii, 6) were set for this purpose. To these two modes of purification our Lord seems to allude in John xiii, 10, where the being "clean every whit" implies one who had become a disciple of Christ, and consequently had renounced the sins of his former life. He who had so done was supposed to be wholly washed, and not to need any immersion, in imitation of the ceremony of initiation, which was never repeated among the Jews. All that was necessary in such a case was the dipping or rinsing of the hands or feet, agreeably to the customs of the Jews. See WASHING (*the Hands and Feet*). Sometimes the lustration was performed by sprinkling blood or anointing with oil. Sprinkling was performed either with the finger, or with a branch of cedar and hyssop tied together with scarlet wool (Lev. xiv, 4-6; Numb. xix, 18; Psa. li, 7). See BAPTISM.

The practice of frequent ablutions was not peculiar to the Hebrews; we find it rigidly enjoined by the Mohammedan law. We quote the following extract from Taylor, *History of Mohammedanism*:

"The Sonna of the Mohammedans exactly corresponds with the משנה, *Mishnah*, of the Jews, and comprehends all their religious traditions. (*a.*) From it we take the following account of the greater purification, *Ghasl.* It must be remembered that there are seven species of water fit for rightly performing religious ablutions; that is to say, rain, sea, river, fountain, well, snow, and ice water. But the principal requisites for the lustration Ghasl are three: (1) intention; (2) a perfect cleansing; (3) that the water should touch the entire skin and every hair. There are five requisites of the traditional law, or Sonna: (1) the appropriate phrase, Bismillah ('In the name of the most merciful God'), must be pronounced; (2) the palms must be washed before the hands are put into the basin; (3) the lustration Wodú must be performed; (4) the skin must be rubbed with the hand; (5) it must be prolonged. (We omit the cases in which this lustration is required.) (*b.*) The second lustration, *Wodú.* The principal parts, indeed the divine (they are called divine because taken from the Koran) institutions, of the lustration Wodú are six: (1) intention; (2) the washing of the entire face; (3) the washing of the hands and forearms up to the elbows; (4) the rubbing of some parts of the head; (5) the washing of the feet as far as the ankles; (6) observance of the prescribed order.

"The institutes of the traditional law about this lustration are ten: (1) the preparatory formula, Bismillah, must be used; (2) the palms must be washed before the hands are put into the basin; (3) the mouth must be cleansed; (4) water must be drawn through the nostrils; (5) the entire head and ears must be rubbed; (6) if the beard be thick, the fingers must be drawn through it; (7) the toes must be separated; (8) the right hand and foot should be washed before the left; (9) these ceremonies must be thrice repeated; (10) the whole must be performed in uninterrupted succession. (We omit the cases in which this lustration is required.)

"Of purification by sand. The divine institutions respecting purification by sand are four: (1) intention; (2) the rubbing of the face; (3) the rubbing of the hands and forearms up to the elbows; (4) the observance of this order. But the Sonnite ordinances are three: (1) the formula Bismillah; (2) the right hand and foot precede the left; (3) that the ceremony be performed without interruption. The Mohammedans have borrowed the permission to use sand for water, in case of necessity, from the Jews. Indeed, Cedrenus mentions an instance of sand being used for a Christian baptism. Their necessity dictated the permission; we need not therefore have recourse to Reland's strange theory, that sand is really a liquid. Four requisites to its validity are added by the commentators: (1) the person must be on a journey; (2) he must have diligently searched for water; (3) it must be at the stated time of prayer; (4) the sand must be clean."

See LUSTRATION.

Washburn, Alvin H., D.D., a Protestant Episcopal clergyman, was rector of Christ Church, at Hyde Park, Mass., in 1862, and in 1866 removed to Cleveland, O., as rector of Grace Church, where he continued until his death, near Ashtabula, Dec. 30, 1876. See *Prot. Episc. Almanac*, 1878, p. 170.

Washburn, Edward Abiel, D.D., an eminent Protestant Episcopal clergyman, was born in Boston, Mass., April 16, 1819. After receiving a good primary education, he entered the Boston Latin School for preparation for Harvard College, where he was admitted at the age of sixteen. He graduated in 1838 with high honors. After studying a short time at the Theological Seminary at Andover and the Yale Divinity School, he served for about six months as a licentiate under the Worcester Association of Ministers, but in 1843 took orders as a deacon in the Protestant Episcopal Church. In 1845 he was ordained presbyter by bishop Eastburn, of his native state. His first call was to the rectorship of St. Paul's Church at Newburyport. After laboring seven years in this parish, he spent two years in travel in the East and on the continent. Returning home in 1854, he succeeded Dr. Coxe at St. John's Church, Hartford, Conn. His next parish was St. Mark's Church, Philadelphia, Pa. In 1865 he accepted a call to the Calvary Protestant Episcopal Church on East Twenty-first Street, New York city, where he labored until his death, Feb. 2, 1881. Dr. Washburn was a large-minded, warm-hearted theologian, an evangelical preacher, and an admirable pastor. He was also active in the religious enterprises of his day. He was a member of the American committee for the revision of the Bible, aided Dr. Schaff in the preparation of one of the volumes of *Lange's Commentary*, and was the author of a volume of *Sermons on the Ten Commandments*.

Washing THE HANDS AND FEET. The particular attention paid by the Jews to the cleansing of the hands and feet, as compared with other parts of the body, originated in the social usages of the East. As knives and forks were dispensed with in eating, it was absolutely necessary that the hand, which was thrust into the common dish, should be scrupulously clean; and, again, as sandals were ineffectual against the dust and heat of an Eastern climate, washing the feet on entering a house was an act both of respect to the company and of refreshment to the traveller. In the following account of them, we add many particulars not given in previous articles. See WASH.

I. *Washing the Hands* was transformed by the Pharisees of the New-Test. age into a matter of ritual observance (Mark vii, 3), and special rules were laid down as to the times and manner of its performance. The neglect of these rules by our Lord and his disciples drew down upon him the hostility of that sect (Matt. xv, 2; Luke xi, 38). Whether the expression πυγμῇ used by Mark has reference to any special regulation may, perhaps, be doubtful; the senses "oft" (A. V.) and "diligently" (Alford) have been assigned to it; but it may possibly signify "with the fist," as though it were necessary to close the one hand, which had already been cleansed, before it was applied to the unclean one. This sense appears preferable to the other interpretations of a similar character, such as "up to the wrist" (Lightfoot); "up to the elbow" (Theophylact); "having closed the hand" which is undergoing the washing (Grotius; Scaliger). The Pharisaical regulations on this subject are embodied in a treatise of the Mishna entitled *Yadaim*, from which it appears that the ablution was confined to the hand (ii, § 3), and that great care was needed to secure perfect purity in the water used. The ordinary, as distinct from the ceremonial, washing of hands before meals is still universally prevalent in Eastern countries (Lane, i, 190; Burckhardt, *Notes*, i, 63; Thomson, *Land and Book*, i, 184). See HAND.

The Mosaic law directed that in certain cases the Jews should wash their hands, to signify that they were guiltless of the blood of an unknown person found murdered (Deut. xxi, 6). Pilate was probably aware of this custom, for, from Matt. xxvii, 24, we find, "When Pilate saw that he could prevail nothing, he took water and washed his hands before the multitude, saying, I am innocent of the blood of this just person: see ye to it." He knew that this symbolical act was calculated to make an impression, and would be distinctly understood. To himself, also, the adoption of this ceremony was perfectly natural, as the rite was common among the Greeks and Romans as one of expiation for an act of unintentional or unwilling homicide. See the monographs on the subject cited by Volbeding, *Index Program.* p. 55, 59, 121. See RED HEIFER.

II. *Washing the Feet* did not rise to the dignity of a ritual observance except in connection with the services of the sanctuary (Exod. xxx, 19, 21). It held a high place, however, among the rites of hospitality. Immediately after a guest presented himself at the tent-door, it was usual to offer the necessary materials for washing the feet (Gen. xviii, 4; xix, 2; xxiv, 32; xliii, 24; Judg. xix, 21; comp. Hom. *Od.* iv, 49). It was a yet more complimentary act, betokening equally humility and affection, if the host actually performed the office for his guest (1 Sam. xxv, 41; Luke vii, 38, 44; John xiii, 5-14; 1 Tim. v, 10). Such a token of hospitality is still occasionally exhibited in the East, either by the host or by his deputy (Robinson, *Res.* ii, 229; Jowett, *Res.* p. 78, 79). The feet were again washed before retiring to bed (Cant. v, 3). A symbolical significance is attached in John xiii, 10 to washing the feet as compared with bathing the whole body, the former being partial (νίπτω), the latter complete (λούω); the former oft repeated in the course of the day, the latter done once for all; whence they are adduced to illustrate the distinction between occasional sin and a general state of sinfulness. After being washed, the feet were on festive occasions anointed (Luke vii, 38; John xii, 3). The indignity attached to the act of washing another's feet appears to have been extended to the vessel used (Psa. lx, 8). See FOOT-WASHING.

Feet-washing (*pedilavium*) became as might be expected, a part of the observances practiced in the early Christian Church. The real signification, however, was soon forgotten, or overloaded by superstitious feelings and mere outward practices. Traces of the practice abound in ecclesiastical history, and remnants of the abuse are still to be found, at least in the Romish Church. The reader who wishes to see an outline of these may consult Siegel, *Handbuch der christl.-kirchl. Alterthümer*, ii, 156 sq.

Wash-pot (סִיר רַחַץ), a basin or ewer for washing the hands and feet; put figuratively for the meanest vessel (Psa. lx, 10). Respecting the ancient Egyptians, Wilkinson (*Anc. Egypt.* i, 77 sq.) remarks as follows: "To those who arrived from a journey, or who desired it, water was brought for their feet previous to entering the festive chamber. Joseph ordered his servants to fetch water for his brethren that they might wash their feet before they ate (Gen. xliii, 24; comp. also xviii, 4; xxiv, 32; 1 Sam. xxv, 46). It was always a custom of the East, as with the Greeks and Romans (comp. Luke vii, 44, 46). The Egyptians also washed their hands before dinner, the water being brought in the same manner as at the present day; and ewers, not unlike those used by the modern Egyptians, are represented, with the basins belonging to them, in the paintings of a Theban tomb. In the houses of the rich they were of gold or other costly materials. Herodotus mentions the golden

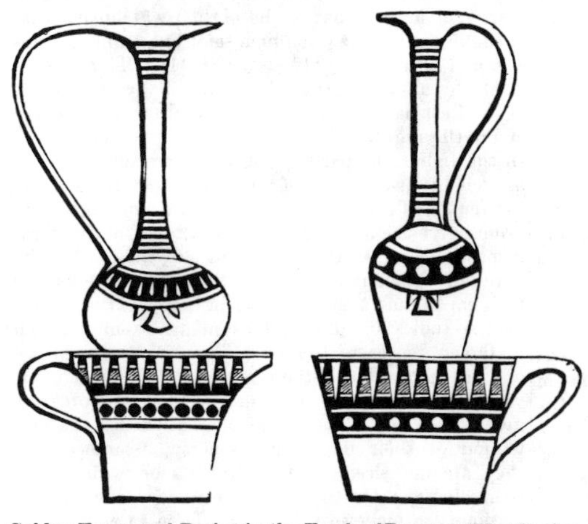

Golden Ewers and Basins in the Tomb of Rameses III at Thebes.

foot-pan in which Amasis and his guests used to wash their feet. The Greeks had the same custom of bringing water to the guests, numerous instances of which we find in Homer—as when Telemachus and the son of Nestor were received at the house of Menelaus, and when Asphalion poured it upon the hands of his master and the same guests on another occasion. Virgil also describes the servants bringing water for this purpose when Æneas was entertained by Dido. Nor was the ceremony thought superfluous, or declined, even though they had previously bathed and been anointed with oil."

Wasmuth, MATTHIAS, a German doctor and professor of theology, was born June 29, 1625. In 1665 he became professor of Oriental languages at Kiel; in 1667, extraordinary professor of theology; and in 1675, professor in ordinary. He died Nov. 18, 1688. He wrote, *Institutio Methodica Accentuationis Hebr.*, etc. (Kiel, 1664, a. o.):—*Smegma Hebræum Defricans Pudendam Barbariem Invectam Nuperis quorundam Falsis, Impiis, et Scandalosis Assertionibus*, etc. (ibid. 1668):—*Hebraismus Facilitati et Integritati suæ Restitutus*, i. e. 1. *Nova Grammatica;* 2. *Accentuationis Hebr. Institutio Methodica;* 3. *Vindiciæ S. S.*, etc. (ibid. 1664, a. o.):—*Defensio Doctrinæ Accentuum Biblicorum* (ibid. 1670):—*Janua Hebraismi Noviter Aperta* (ibid. 1670):—*Pro Sanct. Hebr. Textu Vindiciarum Anti-Cappell-Walton; Pars i, qua Originalis Authentia Divina tam Accentuum et Vocalium quam et Ipsarum Literarum . . . Asseritur; Pars ii, qua Necessarius Accentuum Usus, etc., Demonstratur; Pars iii, Hebrœomastix sive Anti-Conringius Apologet.* etc. (ibid. 1669). See Fürst, *Bibl. Jud.* iii, 495; Steinschneider, *Bibliog. Handbuch*, p. 146; Winer, *Handbuch der theolog. Lit.* p. 93, 114; Hoefer, *Nouv. Biog. Générale*, s. v. (B. P.)

Wasuda (or **Vasuda**) is the earth in India, a sublime goddess whom they worship alike with the preserver Vishnu. She also carries the surname *Surabbi*—cow of plenty; which is not in the least an unbecoming comparison, as it might seem, because the cow in India is worshipped and held sacred to the gods. In poetry she receives still other surnames: the dark border of the ocean, the sea-bordered earth, etc.

Wasuthr, in Norse mythology, is the personification of a condition of the weather. His son was Windloni (ice wind). He made with Swasuthr (warm wind) the season of summer. To this dynasty belong, yet in an unknown degree of kindred, Grimmer and Swalbriostatur.

Watch, in Heb. שָׁמַר, denoting "to cut into," thence "to impress on the mind," "to observe," "to watch," in the sense of keeping or guarding; or צָפָה, the original meaning of which is "to look out," thence "to watch;" as in English, "to keep a lookout," in the sense of spying or noticing. Watching must have been coeval with danger, and danger arose as soon as man became the enemy of man, or had to guard against the attacks of wild animals. Among a primitive and nomadic people this is especially necessary. Accordingly, we find traces of the practice of watching in early portions of the Hebrew annals. Watching must have been carried to some degree of completeness in Egypt, for we learn from Exod. xiv, 24 that the practice had, at the time of the Exode, caused the night to be divided into different watches or portions, mention being made of the "morning watch" (comp. 1 Sam. xi, 11). In the days of the Judges (vii, 19) we find "the middle watch" mentioned (see Luke xii, 38). At a later period Isaiah plainly intimates (xxi, 5, 6) that there was a watch-tower in Jerusalem, and that it was customary on extraordinary occasions to set a watchman. Watchman were, however, even at an earlier day, customarily employed in the metropolis, and their post was at the gates (2 Sam. xviii, 24 sq.; 2 Kings ix, 17 sq.; Psa. cxxvii, 1; cxxx, 6; Prov. viii, 34), where they gave signals and information, either by their voice or with the aid of a trumpet (Jer. vi, 17; Ezek. xxxiii, 6). At night watchmen were accustomed to perambulate the city (Cant. iii, 3; v, 7). In the New Test. we find mention made of the second, the third, and the fourth watch (Luke xii, 38; Matt. xiv, 25). On the watch at Christ's sepulchre (Matt. xxvii, 66), see the monographs cited by Volbeding, *Index Programmatum*, p. 67. See WATCHMAN.

WATCH OF THE NIGHT (אַשְׁמֻרָה; φυλακή). The Jews, like the Greeks and Romans, divided the night into military watches instead of hours, each watch representing the period for which sentinels or pickets remained on duty. The proper Jewish reckoning recognised only three such watches. These would last respectively from sunset to 10 P.M.; from 10 P.M. to 2 A.M.; and from 2 A.M. to sunrise. It has been contended by Lightfoot (*Hor. Heb.* in Matt. xiv, 25) that the Jews really reckoned four watches, three only of which were in the dead of the night, the fourth being in the morning. This, however, is rendered improbable by the use of the term "middle," and is opposed to Rabbinical authority (Mishna, *Berach.* i, 1; Kimchi, *On Psa. lxiii*, 7; Rashi, *On Judg. vii*, 19). We find, however, different opinions on this subject as early as the Talmud (*Berach.* iii, b, etc.). The Old Test. mentions expressly:

1. ראשׁ אַשְׁמוּרוֹת, *head*, first, of the watches (Lam. ii, 19).
2. אַשְׁמֹרֶת הַתִּיכוֹנָה, *middle* watch (Judg. vii, 19), which, according to those who affirm that there were always four, means the middle of those three watches which fell in the time of complete night.
3. אַ׳ הַבֹּקֶר, *morning* watch (Exod. xiv, 24; 1 Sam. xi, 11).

Subsequently to the establishment of the Roman supremacy, the number of watches (*vigiliæ*) was increased to four, which were described either according to their numerical order, as in the case of the "fourth watch" (Matt. xiv, 25; comp. Josephus, *Ant.* v, 6, 5), or by the terms "even, midnight, cock-crowing, and morning" (Mark xiii, 35). These terminated respectively at 9 P.M., midnight, 3 A.M., and 6 A.M. Conformably to this, the guard of soldiers was divided into four relays (Acts xii, 4), showing that the Roman régime was followed in Herod's army. (See Veget. *De Re Milit.* iii, 8, "In quatuor partes ad clepsydram sunt divisæ vigiliæ, ut non amplius quam tribus horis nocturnis, necesse est vigilare;" Censorin, *De Die Natal.* Περὶ φ. τετάρτην; Josephus, *Ant.* xviii, 9, C. Περὶ φ. δευτέραν; Diod. Sic. 18, 40; Xenoph. *Anab.* iv, 1, 5; Buxtorf, *Lex. Talmud.*; Fischerus, *Prolus. de Vitiis Lex. N. Test.*). Accordingly, in the New Test. four night-watches are mentioned (Mark xiii, 35):

1. Ὀψέ, the *late* watch, lasting from sunset to the third hour of the night, including the evening dawn; also called ὀψία ὥρα, even-tide (Mark xi, 11), or simply ὀψία, evening (John xx, 19).
2. Μεσονύκτιον, *midnight*, from the third hour to midnight.
3. Ἀλεκτοροφωνία, *cock-crowing*, from midnight to the third hour after midnight. This ended with the second cock-crowing.
4. Πρωΐ, *early*, from the ninth hour of the night to the twelfth, including the morning dawn or twilight. It is also called πρωΐα, morning-tide or morning (John xviii, 28).

See NIGHT-WATCH; VIGIL.

Watcher (עִיר, *waking*), a class of angelic beings mentioned in the description of Nebuchadnezzar's dream (Dan. iv, 13–17). The Chaldæans appear to have believed that God had delegated the moral government of the earth to celestial spirits, who had the charge of making inquisition into human actions, and punishing the guilty. See ANGEL.

Watchers, a class of monks who are said to have performed divine service without intermission, by dividing themselves into three classes, and taking their turns at the service at stated hours. See ACŒMETÆ. The term is applied to the keepers of the Easter sepulchre. Usually there were two or three who sang psalms and maintained the watch. The term is also used to designate the keepers of the Church who went the rounds at night.

Watching WITH THE DEAD. See WAKE.

Watching Loft is an apartment over the aisle, sacristy, or porch of a Church or cathedral, from which the great shrines were observed by the watchers of the Church. Such lofts remain at Nuremberg, Germany; and at Oxford, Lichfield, St. Albans, Westminster, Exeter, Hereford, and other places in England.

Watchman (נֹצֵר, 2 Kings xvii, 9; xviii, 8; Jer. xxxi, 6; "watcher," Jer. iv, 16; elsewhere "keeper," "preserver," etc.; but usually צֹפֶה or שֹׁמֵר). Even strong walls and double gates would not of themselves secure a city from the enemy. Men were therefore employed to watch day and night on the top of the walls, and especially by the gates. It was thus that the messengers from the army were seen long before they reached the place where David anxiously sat (2 Sam. xviii, 24–27). In like manner the watchman of Jezreel saw in the distance the company of Jehu driving furiously (2 Kings ix, 17–20). So Isaiah, in one of his sublime visions, saw a watchman standing by his tower day and night (Isa. xxi, 5–12). A figurative use of the watchman and his work is beautifully made in Isa. lxii, 6; Ezek. xxxiii, 2, 6, 7; Hab. ii, 1. There were others whose duty it was to patrol the streets of the city and preserve order (see Psa. cxxvii, 1; Song of Solomon iii, 3). There are such in Oriental cities to-day, and they challenge all persons found abroad after certain hours of the night, arresting those that are not able to give a good account of themselves, and sometimes subjecting them to rough treatment. In Persia the watchmen were obliged to indemnify those who were robbed in the streets, and make satisfaction with their own blood for those who were murdered; which accounts for the vigilance and severity which they display in the discharge of their office, and illustrates the character of watchman given to Ezekiel, who lived in that country, and the duties he was required to perform. If the wicked perished in his iniquities without warning, the prophet was to be accountable for his blood; but if he duly pointed out his danger, he delivered his own soul (Ezek. xxxiii, 5). These terms, therefore, were neither harsh nor severe; they were the common appointments of watchmen in Persia. They were also charged to announce the progress of the night to the slumbering city: "The burden of Dumah; he calls to me out of Seir, Watchman, what of the night? watchman, what of the night? The watchman said, The morning cometh, and also the night" (Isa. xxi, 11). This is confirmed by an observation of Chardin, that, as the people of the East have no clocks, the several parts of the day and of the night, which are eight in all, are announced. In the Indies, the parts of the night are made known, as well by instruments of music, in great cities, as by the rounds of the watchmen, who, with cries and small drums, give them notice that a fourth part of the night is past. Now, as these cries awoke those who had slept all that quarter part of the night, it appeared to them but as a moment. There are sixty of these in the Indies by day, and as many by night; that is, fifteen for each division. They are required not only at each watch of the night, but at frequent intervals in the progress of it, to cry aloud, in order to give the people, who depend upon them for the protection of their lives and property, assurance that they are not sleeping at their posts or negligent of their charge. On these latter occasions, their exclamations are made in a form calculated to enliven the tediousness of their duties, as, "God be merciful to you;" while the other responds, "Blessings be on you likewise." This practice of salutation, when they met, in the form of a set dialogue, was observed also by the ancient officers of this description among the Jews, the watchword being then, as we have seen it is still among the watchmen of the caravans, some pious sentiment, in which the name of Jehovah was specially expressed. Two remarkable instances of this occur in Scripture. The one is in the prophecies of Isaiah, where, speaking of the watchmen of the Temple, who were always Levites, and among whom the same regulations subsisted as among other watchmen, he addresses them under the poetical description of "Ye that make mention of the Lord," i. e. Ye whose watchword is the name of Jehovah (Isa. lxii, 6). The other instance is in Psa. cxxxiv, the whole of which, as is justly observed by bishop Lowth, is nothing more than the alternate cry of two different divisions of the watch. The first watch addresses the second, reminding them of their duty; the second answers by a solemn blessing. The address and the answer seem both to be a set form, which each proclaimed aloud at stated intervals to notify the time of night:

> *First band of watchmen*—"Bless ye the Lord, all ye servants of the Lord, who by night stand in the house of the Lord. Lift up your hands in the sanctuary, and bless the Lord."
>
> *Second band of watchmen answer*—"The Lord bless thee out of Zion, the Lord that made heaven and earth."

Watch-night is a Wesleyan custom. Near the beginning of Methodism the members of that body in Bristol began to meet at night, that they might worship without interruption. Mr. Wesley, knowing that such meetings would soon be misinterpreted, made them public, and for a time held them once a month. Afterwards, however, they were observed only on the eve of the new year, which custom prevails to a certain extent to the present time.

Watch-tower (צָפִּית, Isa. xxi, 5; מִצְפֶּה, 2 Chron. xx, 24; Isa. xxi, 8), a structure over or by the side of city gates in the East, in which a watchman was stationed to observe what was going on at a distance, especially in times of danger (2 Sam. xviii, 25). We find that he went up by a staircase from the passage, which, like the roof of the dwelling-houses, was flat, for the purpose of descrying at a distance those that were approaching the place, or repelling the attacks of an enemy. The observations made by the watchman were not communicated by him immediately to the king, but by the intervention of a warder at the outer gate of the tower; and it appears that a private staircase led from the lower room, in which David (in the above passage) was sitting, to the upper room over the gateway; for by that communication he retired to give full vent to his sorrow (see Thomson, *Land and Book*, ii, 411). See CITY; GATE; TOWER.

Waterford, COUNCIL OF (*Synodus Guaterfordia*). Waterford is a city of Ireland, capital of the county of the same name, situated near the southern coast, on the right bank of the Suir, nine miles from the sea. An ecclesiastical council is said to have been held there about 1158, in which it was ordered that all the English slaves throughout Ireland should be liberated to avert the divine wrath. It seems that many of the English had been in the habit of selling their own children to the Irish for slaves, and that not under the pressure of extreme want. See Mansi, *Concil.* x, 1183.

Both the date and place of this council are probably incorrect, as the account of it in Labbe exactly coincides with that of the Council of Armagh in 1171 (q. v.), and in both the council is said to have been convoked *apud Ardmachiam*.—Landon, *Manual of Councils*, s. v.

Waterhouse, EDWARD, an English author who became a clergyman, was born in 1619. He received a learned education, became a member of the Royal Society in 1668, and took holy orders the same year. He died May 30, 1670. He was the author of *Humble Apology for Learning and Learned Men* (1653):—*Two Contemplations* (eod.):—*Discourse of the Piety, Policy, and Charity of Elder Times and Christians* (1655):—*Gentleman's Monitor* (eod.):—*Short Narrative of the Late Dreadful Fire of London* (1667):—and other works. See Allibone, *Dict. of Brit. and Amer. Authors*, s. v.

Waterlanders (or **Waterlandians**), a sect of Anabaptists (q. v.) in Holland, so called to distinguish them from the Flemingians, or Flandrians, and also because they consisted, at first, of the inhabitants of a district in the north of Holland called Waterland. The Flemingians were more rigid in their views and practice than the Waterlandians. Both are governed by presbyters and deacons, and each congregation is independent of all foreign jurisdiction. The Waterlanders are also called *Johannites*, from John de Ries, who was of great service to them in many respects, and who was one of the composers of their *Confession of Faith* in 1580. The Waterlanders of Amsterdam afterwards joined with the Galenists (q. v.). See MENNONITES.

Waterman, HENRY, D.D., an Episcopal clergyman, was born at Centreville, Warwick, R. I., Aug. 17, 1813, and was a graduate of Brown University in the class of 1831. He pursued his theological studies, in part, at Cambridge, at a school taught by Rev. John Henry Hopkins and Rev. George Washington Doane, which, on their appointment as bishops—the one of the diocese of Vermont, and the other of the diocese of New Jersey—was given up. Mr. Waterman completed his course of study at the Episcopal Seminary in New York, and was ordained deacon by bishop Griswold, at Providence, in June, 1835, and presbyter by the same, at Boston, in 1837. He commenced the active duties of the ministry at Woonsocket, R. I., as rector of St. James's Church, where he remained six years (1835-41), and then took charge of the parish of St. Stephen's in Providence, commencing his ministry in November, 1841. Here he continued for four years (1841-45), and then went to Andover, Mass., where he was rector of Christ Church until June, 1849. He spent nearly a year in foreign travel for his health, and, on his return, in the summer of 1850, he again became rector of St. Stephen's Church, occupying that position until October, 1874, a period of twenty-four years, during which a strong and vigorous parish grew up under his administration. Resigning his parish, he continued to reside in Providence, preaching in different parts of Rhode Island and other places as his health allowed him. His death occurred in Providence Oct. 18, 1876. "Dr. Waterman," says Prof. Gammell, "was an instructive and effective preacher, and a careful student of the works of the old English divines, and was thoroughly Anglican in all his ecclesiastical views. Beyond his immediate sphere as a clergyman, he seldom cared to appear in public. In that sphere, however, he exerted a very important influence, and was greatly respected by his brethren." (J. C. S.)

Waters, FRANCIS, D.D., a local deacon and elder, and a noted educator in the Methodist Protestant Church, was born Jan. 16, 1792, in Maryland. He graduated in Pennsylvania University, in 1810, and took charge of Washington Academy in Somerset County, Md. In 1818 he was elected president of Washington College, in Chestertown, Kent Co., and resigned this position in 1823. From this date until 1828 he resided in Somerset County; from 1828 to 1835 he taught private school in Baltimore. In 1840 he became president of the Theological and Literary School for the education of young men for the itinerant ministry of the Methodist Protestant Church; in 1846 he went to reside in Baltimore, and filled several important positions of an educational character until Jan. 30, 1860, when, on account of feeble health, he was obliged to resign. He was president of the General Conference of the Methodist Protestant Church in 1846 and 1862. He died April 23, 1868. See Cothouer, *Founders of the M. P. Church*, p. 182.

Water-spout is the rendering, in the A. V. at Psa. xlii, 7, of צִנּוֹר, *tsinnôr* (from צנר, a root of doubtful import), which Gesenius thinks a *cataract* or water-course ("gutter," 2 Sam. v, 8), and Fürst a pipe or conduit. Water-spouts, it seems, are actually seen on the Mediterranean (see Thomson, *Land and Book*, ii, 256). See GUTTER.

Watson, George, D.D., a Protestant Episcopal clergyman, was rector in Norwalk, O., in 1854, and from that time until 1865 served the parish of St. Paul, in that city. He died Nov. 15, 1870, aged sixty-eight years. See *Prot. Episc. Almanac*, 1871, p. 118.

Watson, James Clemson, D.D., a Presbyterian minister, was born in Donegal township, Lancaster Co., Pa., Jan. 27, 1805. He graduated from the College of New Jersey in 1827; studied at Princeton Theological Seminary between two and three years; was licensed in 1830, and ordained, in 1832, pastor of the united churches of Gettysburg and Great Conewago, Pa., where he labored until 1849; then became pastor at Clinton, N. J.; next at Kingston in 1851, and finally in 1854 at Milton, Pa., where he died, Aug. 31, 1880. See *Necrol. Report of Princeton Theol. Sem.* 1881, p. 31.

Watson, Robert, LL.D., a minister of the Church of Scotland, professor and author, was born at St. Andrew's about 1730. He was educated at the universities of St. Andrew's, Glasgow, and Edinburgh. In 1751 he began to deliver in Edinburgh a course of lectures on rhetoric and belles-lettres, which he repeated for several successive winters. He became a minister of the Church of Scotland in 1758; professor of logic, rhetoric, and belles-lettres in the College of St. Salvator, at St.

Andrew's, soon after; and principal of the United College of St. Leonard and St. Salvator, and minister of the Church and parish of St. Leonard, in 1777. He died at St. Andrew's, March 31, 1781. He was the author of a *History of the Reign of Philip II, King of Spain* (Lond. 1777, 2 vols.); and a *History of the Reign of Philip III* (1783). The latter work was left unfinished at the author's death, and was completed for the benefit of his family by William Thomson, LL.D. The former was translated into French, Dutch, and German. Both works have been republished in the United States (N. Y. 1818), but are of little value, being heavy and inelegant in style, and yielding inevitably to the more philosophical and elegant works of Prescott.

Watson, Thomas (1), D.D., an eminent English prelate, was born about 1520. He was educated at St. John's College, Cambridge, of which he became a fellow and master in 1553. He took orders in the Church of England; was appointed dean of Durham in 1553; bishop of Lincoln in 1557; and was preacher to queen Mary. On the accession of queen Elizabeth, he refused to take the oath of supremacy, was deprived of his bishopric, and from that time until his death adhered firmly to the Roman Church. He was imprisoned near London until 1580, when he was removed to Wisbeck Castle, where he died, Sept. 25, 1582. His published works are *Two Notable Sermons before the Queenes Highnes concerning the Reall Presence* (1554); and *Holesome and Catholyke Doctryne concerninge the Seven Sacramentes* (1558). He was also the author of a Latin tragedy, which was greatly admired, but never published.

Watson, Thomas (2), an eminent Nonconformist divine, was educated at Emmanuel College, Cambridge, and was pastor of St. Stephen's, Walbrook, London, in 1646. Ejected for nonconformity in 1662, he preached in Crosby Hall in 1672, and died in Essex about 1689. Watson was an eminent preacher, and one of his sermons, entitled *Heaven taken by Storm*, was often reprinted. Besides *A Body of Practical Divinity*, consisting of one hundred and seventy-six sermons on the Assembly's Catechism (1692; last ed. N. Y. 1871), he published *The Christian Charter:—The Art of Divine Contentment:—A Discourse of Meditation* (6th ed. Lond. 1660). His *Select Works* were published in London in 1821, and in New York in 1855. See Plitt-Herzog, *Real-Encyklop.* s. v. (B. P.)

Watt (also **Vadianus**), **Joachim von**, the Reformer of St. Gall, was born Dec. 30, 1484, of ancient family in that city. His father was a merchant, his mother a judicious and pious woman. His early education was conducted by his mother and pedagogues of his native town, but he soon went to Vienna in order to avail himself of the superior privileges there afforded. He there became acquainted with Ulric Zwingli and Heinrich Loriti (Glareanus). A period of dissolute behavior ensued in his life, but it was speedily followed by a continuous season of earnest classical study. A Virgil which he was wont to use as a pillow in those days is still preserved in the town library of St. Gall. He also tried his powers in Latin verse, and, in obedience to the customs of his day, changed his name into the Latin *Vadius*, afterwards *Vadianus*. After a tour through Poland, Hungary, and Carinthia, and an essay at teaching in Villach, he returned, by way of Venice, to Vienna, and resumed his studies. He joined the learned society known as the Danube Association, and included jurisprudence, theology, and medicine in his course, obtaining the doctorate in the last-named department. After the death of Cuspinian, Watt filled the chair of the Greek language and literature. In 1514 he was made poet-laureate by the emperor Maximilian. Four years afterwards he returned to St. Gall for a visit, but was given the post of town-physician, by which he was held to that city as long as he lived. In 1519 he married Martha Grebel.

The Church of St. Gall was wholly controlled by the spirit of Middle-Age Catholicism; but Watt, who had become acquainted with the writings of Luther and the ideas of the Reformation while at Vienna, gave himself to the work of improving its spiritual condition. He was assisted in his endeavors by the newly installed minister of St. Laurent, Benedict Burgauer, and his helper, Wolfgang Wetter. He maintained an active correspondence with Zwingli. He presided in the Colloquy of Zurich in 1523, and of Berne in 1526. He became the chief promoter of the Reformation initiated in St. Gall after the Zurich Colloquy, and incurred much hatred in consequence. The Anabaptist movement in St. Gall and Appenzell also gave him trouble; but the continued support accorded him by his fellow-citizens sustained him even when his brother-in-law, Conrad Grebel, of Zurich, was drowned in punishment of his heresies. He was chosen burgomaster of St. Gall repeatedly, and in that capacity gave himself to the work of instructing the populace and increasing their comforts. He also participated in the theological controversies of his time, particularly the Sacramentarian and Schwenkfeldian disputes, and in connection with them wrote several books. He died April 6, 1551, and was mourned by Calvin and others as being lost to the great work of the Reformation in whose promotion he took so influential a part.

The life of Watt was first described by Kessler, the friend whom he had brought under the influence of Luther and Melancthon, and thereby gained for the Reformation. Kessler's MS. is preserved in the Library of St. Gall. Other biographers are, Huber, *Ehrengedächtniss des . . . Joachim v. Watt* (St. Gall, 1683); Fels, *Denkmal schweiz. Reformatoren* (ibid. 1819); Pressel, *Joachim Vadian*, etc. (Elberfeld, 1861), pt. ix.—Herzog, *Real-Encyklop.* s. v.

Watters, Nicholas, a Methodist Episcopal minister, and brother of William Watters, was born in Anne Arundel County, Md., Nov. 20, 1739. He entered the travelling connection about the year 1773, and was appointed as follows: Kent, Md., 1776; Hanover, 1777–78; Union, S. C., 1794; Seleuda, 1799; Harford, Md., 1800; Winchester, Va., 1801; Lancaster, 1802; Broad River, Ga., 1803; Charleston, S. C., 1804, where he died in peace and triumph Aug. 10, 1804. Bennet Kendrick, his colleague in the ministry, reported to the South Carolina Conference that Nicholas Watters was peculiarly attentive in visiting the sick, and would not let a favorable opportunity slip. He exercised a great degree of humanity in his Christian and ministerial duties. His last words were, "I am not afraid to die, thanks be to God!" See *Minutes of Annual Conferences*, 1805, p. 126; Bangs, *Hist. of the M. E. Church*, ii, 174; Stevens, *Hist. of the M. E. Church*, ii, 21; iii, 393; iv, 240–241.

Watters, William, a Methodist Episcopal minister, was born in Baltimore County, Md., Oct. 16, 1751, of Church of England parents. He was naturally vain, self-willed, and passionate, but his devotion to his widowed mother led him to seek religion early in life. He acquired a good education; joined the Methodists at the age of twenty; soon began earnest Christian work by prayer and exhortation; and in 1773 entered the Philadelphia Conference. In 1775 he was appointed to Frederick, in 1776 to Fairfax, in 1777 to Brunswick, and in 1779 to Baltimore Circuit. In 1782 he retired from the regular work to his little farm in Fairfax County. In 1786 he re-entered the active ranks, and was appointed to Berkeley Circuit, Va., but was soon obliged to return home because of sickness. He labored in Alexandria, D. C., in 1801, Georgetown in 1803, Alexandria in 1804, and in 1805 was appointed to Washington city. The remainder of his life was spent on his farm in retirement. He died March 29, 1827. Mr. Watters accomplished a great amount of good under very adverse circumstances, and was universally respected and reverenced. See Sprague, *Annals of the Amer. Pulpit*, vii, 46.

Wave-breast (חֲזֵה הַתְּנוּפָה; Sept. στηθύνιον ἀφωρίσματος or τῆς ἐπιθέματος; A. V. in Exod. xxix, 27, "breast of the wave-offering") was the breast of the victim offered in sacrifice, a ram (Exod. xxix, 27; Numb. vi, 20), at the consecration of a priest or the purification of a Nazarite after his vow; or of any other animal in thank-offerings (Lev. vii, 34; x, 14 sq.); or of the first-born-offering (Numb. xviii, 18). It was so called because waved by the priest (Exod. xxix, 27; Numb. vi, 20), and belonged to him (Exod. xxix, 27; Lev. vii, 34), to be eaten by the members of his family who were in a state of ceremonial purity (x, 14). See WAVING.

Wave-loaf (לֶחֶם הַתְּנוּפָה) was the first-fruit of bread made of fine wheat flour and leavened, which at the Paschal festival was presented to Jehovah in connection with a burnt, sin, or thank offering (Lev. xxiii, 17 sq. See WAVING.

Wave-offering (תְּנוּפָה, "a waving," from נוּף, "to wave," תְּנוּפָה לִפְנֵי יְהוָֹה, "a waving before Jehovah"). This rite, together with that of "heaving" or "raising" the offering, was an inseparable accompaniment of peace-offerings. In such the right shoulder, considered the choicest part of the victim, was to be "heaved," and viewed as holy to the Lord, only eaten therefore by the priest; the breast was to be "waved," and eaten by the worshipper. On the second day of the Passover a sheaf of corn, in the green ear, was to be waved, accompanied by the sacrifice of an unblemished lamb of the first year, from the performance of which ceremony the days till Pentecost were to be counted. When that feast arrived, two loaves, the first-fruits of the ripe corn, were to be offered with a burnt-offering, a sin-offering, and two lambs of the first year for a peace-offering. These likewise were to be waved.

The Scriptural notices of these rites are to be found in Exod. xxix, 24, 28; Lev. vii, 30, 34; viii, 27; ix, 21; x, 14, 15; xxiii, 10, 15, 20; Numb. vi, 20; xviii, 11, 18, 26-29, etc.

We find also the word תְּנוּפָה applied, in Exod. xxxviii, 24, to the gold offered by the people for the furniture of the sanctuary. It is there called זְהַב הַתְּנוּפָה. It may have been waved when presented, but it seems not impossible that תְּנוּפָה had acquired a secondary sense so as to denote "free-will offering." In either case we must suppose the ceremony of waving to have been known to and practiced by the Israelites before the giving of the law.

It seems not quite certain from Exod. xxix, 26, 27, whether the waving was performed by the priest or by the worshipper with the former's assistance. The Rabbinical tradition represents it as done by the worshipper, the priest supporting his hands from below.

In conjecturing the meaning of this rite, regard must be had, in the first instance, to the kind of sacrifice to which it belonged. It was the accompaniment of peace-offerings. These not only, like the other sacrifices, acknowledged God's greatness and his right over the creature, but they witnessed to a ratified covenant, an established communion between God and man. While the sin-offering merely removed defilement, while the burnt-offering gave entirely over to God of his own, the victim being wholly consumed, the peace-offering, as establishing relations between God and the worshipper, was participated in by the latter, who ate, as we have seen, of the breast that was waved. The rabbins explain the heaving of the shoulder as an acknowledgment that God has his throne in the heaven, the waving of the breast that he is present in every quarter of the earth. The one rite testified to his eternal majesty on high, the other to his being among and with his people.

It is not said in Lev. xxiii, 10-14 that a peace-offering accompanied the wave-sheaf of the Passover. On the contrary, the only bloody sacrifice mentioned in connection with it is styled a burnt-offering. When, however, we consider that everywhere else the rite of waving belongs to a peace offering, and that, besides a sin and a burnt offering, there was one in connection with the wave-loaves of Pentecost (Lev. xxiii, 19), we shall be wary of concluding that there was none in the present case. The significance of these rites seems considerable. The name of the month Abib, in which the Passover was kept, means the month of the green ear of corn, the month in which the great produce of the earth has come to the birth. In that month the nation of Israel came to the birth; each succeeding Passover was the keeping of the nation's birthday. Beautifully and naturally, therefore, were the two births—that of the people into national life; that of their needful sustenance into yearly life—combined in the Passover. All first-fruits were holy to God: the first-born of men, the first-produce of the earth. Both principles were recognised in the Passover. When, six weeks after, the harvest had ripened, the first-fruits of its matured produce were similarly to be dedicated to God. Both were waved, the rite which attested the Divine presence and working all around us being surely most appropriate and significant in their case. See WAVING.

Wave-sheaf (עֹמֶר הַתְּנוּפָה, Sept. δράγμα τοῦ ἐπιθέματος, A. V. "sheaf of the wave-offering," Lev. xxiii, 15) was the first-fruit of the harvest, which at the beginning of the harvest or Passover (q. v.) was presented to the Jehovah by the ceremony of waving (Lev. xxiii, 11 sq., 15). See WAVE-OFFERING.

Waving AND HEAVING *as Ceremonial Manipulations of Offerings.* See OFFERING.

I. *Waving before Jehovah* (הֵנִיף לִפְנֵי יְהוָֹה or תְּנוּפָה) occurs as a special ceremony by the priests in the Jewish ritual not only in connection with meat-offerings (Exod. xxix, 24 [Lev. viii, 27]; Numb. v, 25), in the case of the first-fruits and the first-born (Lev. xxiii, 11 sq.; xvii, 25), but also of bloody offerings, whether (especially in thank-offerings) of single pieces only, as the breast or right shoulder or fore-leg (Exod. xxix, 26 sq.; Lev. vii, 30, 34; ix, 21; x, 14; Numb. vi, 20), or of the whole animal (a lamb, Lev. xix, 12, 24; xxiii, 23), which was waved before Jehovah in token of presentation; and this principle extended even to the persons of the Levites as an initiatory rite to their office (Numb. viii, 11, 15). The waving in case of meat-offerings or pieces of animals was performed upon (with) the hands (Exod. xxix, 24; Lev. viii, 27; according to the rabbins, it was held upon the hands of the offerers, beneath which were placed those of the priest [Tosiphta, *Menach.* vii, 17], so as to fulfil the requirement of Exod. xxix, 24; Numb. vi, 19, 20; while whole animals were waved by the hands of the priest alone [Mishna, *Menach.* v, 6]); each having previously been laid upon the altar; in the case of whole animals this was done before slaughtering them (Lev. xiv, 12 sq., 24 sq.). It consisted, according to the rabbins (Mishna, *Menach.* v, 6), like the *porricere* of the Romans (Macrob. *Sat.* iii, 2), also the *obmovere* or *commovere* (Cato, *Res Rust.* 134) in certain respects (Zorn, *Biblioth. Antiq.* i, 74), of a forward and backward motion upward of the articles; while living objects were simply moved to and fro. Whether the motion was ever to the right and left is uncertain, although the import of the word הֵנִיף (see Isa. xxx, 28; Deut. xx, 25) would justify such an opinion, which, moreover, would be highly significant. The act, at all events, indicates a festive surrender to Jehovah as a personal service like the peace-offering; beyond this all is speculation (Bähr, *Symbol.* ii, 376 sq.; see Reland, *Antiq. Sacr.* p. 276). See WAVE-OFFERING.

II. *Heaving* (הֵרִים or תְּרוּמָה) is associated with the tossing (Exod. xxix, 27), as the heave-shoulder (שׁוֹק הַתְּרוּמָה) occurs along with the wave-breast (Exod.

xxix, 27; Lev. vii, 30, 32, 34), and what is called (Exod. xxxviii, 24) wave-gold is also called heave-gold (Numb. xxxi, 52). Indeed, the Jews scarcely distinguish between the two (תְּרוּמָה and תְּנוּפָה) as ritualistic acts, but explain each as an upward and downward motion (Mishna, *Menach.* v, 6), a sort of *elevatio*. Both would thus stand as generally expressive of supreme consecration to God as the universal Owner and Giver (see Gesenius, *Thesaur.* p. 866; Bähr, *Symbolik*, ii, 355 sq., 377). Some moderns incorrectly regard the two acts as identical (Jahn, *Archäol.* iii, 38), or take "heaving" (הֵרִים) in the vague sense of *offerre* or *auferre* (like Gesenius, *Thesaur.* p. 1277), and connect הוּרַם, Exod. xxix, 27, with מֵאֵיל הַמִּלֻּאִים, contrary to the accents and the parallelism; but see Kurtz, *Mos. Opfer*, p. 146 sq. See HEAVE-OFFERING.

Wax (דּוֹנָג or דּוֹנַג, *donág*, supposed to come from a root דנג, significant of *melting* or *yielding*), the soft sticky substance of which bees form their cells, and which is readily separated from the honey by melting in warm water (Psa. xxii, 14; lxviii, 2; xcvii, 5; Mic. i, 4). This is properly called *beeswax*, and is of vegetable origin, although manipulated by the bees from the pollen of flowers. But there are other kinds of wax, made from resins, either vegetable or mineral (the latter originally vegetable likewise), by the addition of proportions of grease, such as shoemaker's wax, grafting-wax, etc. It is doubtful whether the Hebrews were acquainted with any of these artificial sorts.

Waxen Figures. A well-known custom of cursing an enemy in the Middle Ages was that of making a waxen figure, and, as it melted before the fire, the person represented by it was supposed similarly to waste away. This practice is referred to in Horace (*Satires*, i, 8, 30 sq.), and it is worthy of remark that the same custom is described in the incantations of the ancient Accadian sorcerers. See Lenormant, *Chaldæan Magic*, p. 5.

Way. This word has now in ordinary parlance so entirely forsaken its original sense (except in combination, as in "highway," "causeway"), and is so uniformly employed in the secondary or metaphorical sense of a "custom" or "manner," that it is difficult to remember that in the Bible it most frequently signifies an actual road or track. Our translators have employed it as the equivalent of no less than eighteen distinct Hebrew terms. Of these several had the same secondary sense which the word "way" has with us. Two others (אֹרַח and נָתִיב) are employed only by the poets, and are commonly rendered "path" in the A. V. But the term which most frequently occurs, and in the majority of cases signifies (though it also is now and then used metaphorically) an actual road, is דֶּרֶךְ, *dérek*, connected with the German *treten*, and the English "tread." It may be truly said that there is hardly a single passage in which this word occurs which would not be made clearer and more real if "road to" were substituted for "way of." Thus Gen. xvi, 7, "the spring of the road to Shur;" Numb. xiv, 24, "the road to the Red Sea;" 1 Sam. vi, 12, "the road to Bethshemesh;" Judg. ix, 37, "the road to the oak of Meonenim;" 2 Kings xi, 19, "the road to the gate." It turns that which is a mere general expression into a substantial reality. In like manner the word ὁδός in the New Test. is almost invariably translated "way." Mark x, 32, "They were on the road going up to Jerusalem;" Matt. xx, 17, "and Jesus took the twelve disciples apart in the road"—out of the crowd of pilgrims who, like themselves, were bound for the Passover.

There is one use of both *dérek* and ὁδός which must not be passed over, viz. in the sense of a religious course. In the Old Test. this occurs but rarely, perhaps twice: namely in Amos viii, 14, "the manner of Beersheba," where the prophet is probably alluding to some idolatrous rites then practiced there; and again in Psa. cxxxix, 24, "look if there be any evil way," any idolatrous practices, "in me, and lead me in the everlasting way." But in the Acts of the Apostles ὁδός, "the way," "the road," is the received, almost technical, term for the new religion which Paul first resisted and afterwards supported. See Acts ix, 2; xix, 9, 23; xxii, 4; xxiv, 14, 22. In each of these the word "that" is an interpolation of our translators, and should have been put into italics, as it is in xxiv, 22.

The religion of Islâm is spoken of in the Koran as "the path" (*et-tarik*, iv, 66), and "the right path" (i, 5; iv, 174). Gesenius (*Thesaur.* p. 353) has collected examples of the same expression in other languages and religions. See ROAD.

Waynflete, WILLIAM OF, an eminent English prelate of the 15th century, founder of Magdalen College, Oxford, was born of a noble family in Waynflete, Lincolnshire. He was educated at Winchester School and one of the colleges at Oxford. He was ordained deacon in 1420, and presbyter in 1426; became head-master of Winchester School in 1429; rector of Wraxall in 1433; master of St. Mary Magdalen Hospital in 1438; removed to Eton with a part of his school in 1440, by the advice of Henry VI; became bishop of Winchester in 1447, in which position he continued for thirty-nine years. In 1450 he was called upon by king Henry for advice in the matter of the rebellion of Jack Cade, which he tendered with great prudence; and soon after rendered a like service, when Richard, duke of York, took up arms against his majesty. In 1453 he baptized the prince of Wales, afterwards Edward IV. In 1456 he was appointed lord high chancellor, and resigned the office in 1460. He died Aug. 11, 1486, and was buried in Winchester Cathedral, in a magnificent sepulchral chapel, which is kept in the finest preservation by the Society of Magdalen College. He founded Magdalen College, established a free school in his native town, and was a benefactor to Eton College and Winchester Cathedral. He possessed considerable ability as an architect, which he employed in connection with his benefactions.

Wayside Chapel is a small house of worship at some frequented place on a public highway, formerly resorted to on pilgrimage, or as a place of safety by pilgrims. "These buildings were commonly attached to bridges at the entrance of towns—as at Rochester, Stamford, Elvet, Durham, Exeter, Newcastle, and London. Two still exist at Castle Barnard and Wakefield, the latter being of the 14th century. It has a remarkable carving of the Resurrection. In France, Switzerland, and Italy they are still common; there is a good example at Pisa, about 1230. They were frequented sometimes as objects of pilgrimages, but more commonly by pilgrims going and returning from a shrine, and by ordinary travellers when the dangers of the highway and bypaths were considerable. Until recent times the bishop of Chichester was met at St. Roche's Hill by the civic authorities, on his return from Parliament, to congratulate him upon his safe arrival home."

Wayside Cross is a cross erected on the public highway, either to commemorate some remarkable event, to indicate the boundary of an estate, to designate a customary station for a public service, or the temporary resting-place of the corpse on a royal or noble funeral; or to mark the confines of a diocesan, monastic, or parochial boundary. Anciently, in England, wayside crosses were abundant, and reminded the faithful of the duty of prayer. They were often of stone, standing on the steps; though, no doubt, wooden wayside crosses were frequently set up. Stone crosses partook of the distinct architectural features of the age and time in which they were erected. One removed from the site of the abbey is preserved in Langley Park, Norfolk. The Weeping Cross at Shrewsbury was a station on Corpus Christi Day, when the various guilds, religious and corporate bodies visited it; and there offered prayers for an abundant harvest, returning to hear mass in St. Chad's. There was a weeping cross at Caen, erected by queen Matilda in memory of her sorrows at the cruel treatment of her husband, William of Normandy. Sometimes it commemorated a battle, as the Neville's Cross, near Durham, erected in 1346; or a death, like the memorial of Sir Ralph Percy, who was killed on Hedgeley Moor in 1464. There are remains of wayside crosses near Doncaster and at Braithwell, with inscriptions, inviting the prayers of the passing traveller. In Devonshire alone there are one hundred and thirty-five places called by the name of the cross. At Pencran and St. Herbot, Brittany, there are superb specimens; and others, richly carved, at Nevern, Carew, and Newmarket. Valle Crucis Abbey took its name from Eliseg's sepulchral cross of the 7th century. In Spain, Italy, Lubbeck (near Louvain), Willebrock, and on Boonhill, Berwickshire, there are memorials of a violent death. In the life of St. Willebald the English laborers are said to have gathered round a cross in the middle of a field for daily prayer as an ordinary custom.

Webbe, GEORGE, D.D., an English prelate, was born at Bromham, Wiltshire, in 1581. He was educated at Oxford University, took holy orders, and became minister of Steeple Aston, Wiltshire, where he also kept a grammar-school, as he afterwards did at Bath. In 1621 he became rector of St. Peter and St. Paul's in Bath; was made chaplain to Charles I, on his accession to the throne; and was consecrated bishop of Limerick, Ireland, in December, 1634. Some time before his death he was confined in Limerick Castle by the rebels, and died there near the close of 1641. He was the author of *Practice of Quietness* (3d ed. 1631):—*A Brief Exposition of the Principles of the Christian Religion* (1612):—*Arraignment of an Unruly Tongue* (1619):—*Augur's Prayer; or, The Christian Choice* (1621):—*The Protestant's Calendar* (1624):—*Lessons and Exercises out of Cicero ad Atticum*:—some other text-books for schools, and several *Sermons*, which appeared from 1609 to 1619. He was accounted the best preacher in his time in the royal court, and the smoothest writer of sermons that were then published.

Webber, Francis, D.D., an English clergyman of the 18th century, was rector of Exeter College, Oxford; and in 1756 became dean of Hereford. He published five single *Sermons* (1738-58). See Allibone, *Dict. of Brit. and Amer. Authors*, s. v.

Webber, George, D.D., a Methodist Episcopal minister, was born in Shapleigh, Me., March 18, 1801. He embraced religion in early life, and, after spending some time as a student in Maine Wesleyan Seminary, joined the Maine Conference in 1828, and was appointed as junior preacher on Strong Circuit, which embraced nearly the whole valley of Sandy River. His reputation as an able preacher soon spread, and he was sought by all the important charges in the Conference. No preacher in the Maine Conference had ever been so highly honored by his brethren. Sixteen years he served as presiding elder; five times was a delegate to the General Conference; once to the Evangelical Alliance in London; and once to the Methodist Episcopal Church of Canada. At the General Conference of 1852 he was a prominent candidate for the office of bishop. For many years he was a trustee of Maine Wesleyan Seminary, and was prominently connected with all the great interests of the Conference for nearly half a century. As a preacher, Mr. Webber was solid rather than brilliant, profoundly impressive, evincing thorough mastery of his subject, deliberate and exhaustive, and purely extemporaneous. His forty-seven years of ministerial record stand without a blemish. In 1874 he superannuated, and retired to his home at Kent's Hill, and died May 11, 1875. See *Minutes of Annual Conferences*, 1876, p. 86.

Weber, Ananias, a Lutheran theologian of Germany, was born at Lindenhayn, in Saxony, Aug. 14, 1596. He studied at Leipsic, where he also took the different theological degrees. In 1627 he was appointed to the pastorate at Mutschen, in 1634 to the superintendency at Leissnig, having in the same year received the degree of licentiate of theology. In 1638 he went to Leipsic as archdeacon of St. Thomas's, was appointed in 1639 professor of theology, and in 1640 received the doctorate of divinity. In 1645 he was called to Breslau, in Silesia, where he occupied the highest ecclesiastical positions. He died Jan. 26, 1665. He wrote, *Adventus Messianus Dudum Factus et in hunc Mundum Datus*, etc.:—*Problema Theolog. de Auctoritate Divina et Infallibili Verbi Dei Scripti*, etc.:—*Synopsis Doctrinæ Orthodoxæ de Conversione Hominis Irregeniti contra ψευδοδοξίαν Pelagianorum*, etc., *Assertæ; Paulus anti-Calvinianus*, etc. See Kempf, *Memoria Ananiæ Weberi* (Lips. 1739); Freher, *Theatrum Eruditorum; Orationes in Honorem Scriptorum Habitæ;* Jöcher, *Allgemeines Gelehrten-Lexikon*, s. v.; Fürst, *Bibl. Jud.* iii, 496. (B. P.)

Weber, Andreas, a Protestant theologian of Germany, was born March 27, 1718, at Eisleben. From 1738 to 1742 he studied at Jena and Leipsic. In the latter place he publicly spoke on *De Cognitione Spiritus Finiti circa Mysteria* (1742). In 1749 he was called as professor of philosophy to Halle, and in 1750 to Göttingen, where he lectured till 1770, when he accepted a call to Kiel as professor of philosophy and theology. He died May 26, 1781. He wrote, *Die Uebereinstimmung der Natur und Gnade*, etc. (Leips. 1748-50, 3 vols.):—*Commentatio de Prima Melanchthonis Locorum Communium Editione* (Kiloni, 1771):—*Progr. utrum Judæus Mosi ut Legislatori solum, non ob Miracula, quibus Conspicuus erat, Religiosam Obedientiam Debeat*, etc. (ibid. 1771). See Döring, *Die gelehrten Theologen Deutschlands*, iv, 659 sq. (B. P.)

Weber, Beda, a Roman Catholic theologian of Germany, was born Oct. 26, 1798, at Lienz, in the Tyrol. In 1824 he received holy orders, and in 1825 was called as professor to Meran. In 1849 he accepted a call to the pastorate in Frankfort, where he died, Feb. 28, 1858. He wrote, *Tirol und die Reformation* (Innsbruck, 1841):—*Giovanna Maria della Croce und ihre Zeit* (Ratisbon, 1846):—*Predigten an das Tiroler Volk* (Frankfort, 1851):—he also translated six books of Chrysostom on the priesthood (Innsbruck, 1833). See *Theol. Universal-Lexikon*, s. v.; Brühl, *Geschichte der kathol. Lit. Deutschlands* (Vienna, 1861), p. 411 sq. (B. P.)

Weber, Christian Friedrich, a Protestant theologian of Germany, was born March 4, 1764, at Cannstadt, and died as dean at Nurtingen, in Würtemberg, in the year 1832. He wrote, *Beiträge zur Gesch. des neutest. Kanons* (Tübingen, 1791):—*Neue Untersuchungen über das Alter und Ansehen des Evang. der Hebräer* (ibid. 1806):—*Doctrina Ævi Primi ac Prisci præcipue Mosaici de Ente Summo* (Stuttgart, 1828):—*Schnurrer's Leben, Charakter u. Verdienste* (Cannstadt, 1823):—*Hegesippus qui dicitur sive Egesippus de Bello Judaico Ope Codicis Casselani Recognitus* (Marburg, 1858). See Winer, *Handbuch der theol. Lit.* i, 77, 85, 412, 867; Fürst, *Bibl. Jud.* iii, 496. (B. P.)

Weber, Ferdinand Wilhelm, a Lutheran theologian of Germany, was born Oct. 22, 1836, at Schwabach. His preparatory education he received at the gymnasium in Nuremberg, which he left in 1855 for the University of Erlangen. Here he attended the lectures of Hofmann, Delitzsch, Thomasius, Heyder, and Harnack; and, besides theology, he also studied history and Rabbinic literature. After the completion of his academic curriculum, he became vicar of the well-known Löhe, and second teacher at the mission school in Neuendettelsau. On account of a dissertation *Ueber den Begriff des Schönen und Erhabenen bei Kant*, he received the degree of doctor of philosophy. At Neuendettelsau his great talents found a wide scope for usefulness. Here he published his well-known work, *Vom Zorne Gottes* (with an introduction by Delitzsch) in 1862, and his *Introduction to the Writings of the Old and New Testaments* (eod.; 5th ed. 1878). In 1864 he went to Diebach, where he labored until 1872, when he was appointed Löhe's successor. Bodily infirmities, however, soon obliged him to retire to Polsingen, where he died, July 10, 1879. Besides the works already mentioned, he published, *Hermann der Prämonstratenser, oder die Juden und die Kirche des Mittelalters* (Nördlingen, 1861), with a preface by Löhe:—*Kurze Betrachtungen über die Evangelien und Episteln der Sonn- und Festtage des Kirchenjahrs*:—*Der Prophet Jesaja in Bibelstunden ausgelegt* (2 pts. 1875, 1876). He left in manuscript *Grundzüge der palästinisch-jüdischen Theologie aus Targum, Midrasch und Talmud dargelegt*, which will soon be published. See Delitzsch, *Saat auf Hoffnung* (Erlangen, 1879), p. 228 sq. (B. P.)

Weber, Georg Gottlieb, a Protestant theologian of Germany, who was born in 1744, and died Feb. 18, 1801, as court deacon and member of consistory at Weimar, is the author of, *Die Augsburgische Confession nach der Urschrift im Reichsarchiv* (Weimar, 1781):—*Kritische Geschichte der Augsburgischen Confession, aus archivalischen Nachrichten* (Frankf. 1783). See Winer, *Handb. der theol. Lit.* i, 326, 328. (B. P.)

Weber, Johann Georg, a Protestant theologian of Germany, was born at Herwigsdorf, near Zittau, July 10, 1687. He studied at Leipsic, and was appointed there in 1718 preacher in the university church. In 1719 he was called to Weimar, where he was made chief court preacher in 1720. In 1729 he was made general superintendent and chief preacher of St. Paul and St. Peter's, at the same time having the superintendence of the gymnasium there. He died Nov. 24, 1753. Besides a number of ascetical works, he published, *Dissertatio de Sacris Nocturnis* (Lips. 1718):—*Ordo Ecclesiasticus in Augustana Confessione Triumphans* (Vimariæ, 1730):—*Doctrina Tutior de Descensu Christi ad Inferos*, etc. (ibid. 1731):—Ὁ ἈΜΗΝ καὶ τὸ ἈΜΗΝ, *hoc est, Commentatio Exegetico-theologica in Amen Evangelicum, vel Veritatem Doctrinæ Evangelicæ Jurejurando Christi Confirmatam*, etc. (Jenæ, 1734). See Döring, *Die gelehrten Theologen Deutschlands*, iv, 662. (B. P.)

Weber, Joseph, a Roman Catholic theologian of Germany, was born Sept. 23, 1753, at Rhain, in Bavaria. In 1776 he received holy orders; in 1779 he was appointed lecturer on canon law and catechetics at the seminary in Pfaffenhausen; in 1781 he was made professor of philosophical sciences at Dillingen; and in 1800 he was made doctor of divinity. In 1826 he was appointed cathedral dean and general vicar at Augsburg, where he died, Feb. 14, 1831. He wrote, *Leitfaden zu Vorlesungen über die Vernunftlehre* (Dillingen, 1788):—*Institutiones Logicæ* (ibid. 1790):—*Logica in Usum eorum qui eidem Student* (Landshut, 1793):—*Metaphysica in Usum eorum*, etc. (ibid. 1795):—*Charakter des Philosophen und Nichtphilosophen* (Augsburg, 1786):—*Philosophie, Religion und Christenthum im Bunde zur Veredlung und Beseligung des Menschen* (Munich, 1806–11):—*Lichter für Erbauung suchende Christen* (ibid. 1816–20, 3 vols.), etc. See Felder, *Gelehrten-Lexikon*, ii, 482 sq.; Schmid, *Domdecan Joseph v. Weber* (Augsburg, 1831); *Theolog. Universal-Lexikon*, s. v. (B. P.)

Weber, Michael, a German doctor and professor of theology, was born Dec. 8, 1754, at Gröben, near Weissenfeld. In 1784 he was called as professor of theology to Wittenberg, and in 1815 to Halle, where he died, Aug. 1, 1833. He wrote, *Authentia Capitis Ultimi Evangelii Johannis*, etc. (Halle, 1823):—*Eclogæ Exeg.-criticæ ad Nonnullos Libror. N. T. Historicor. Locos* (ibid. 1825–32):—*Interpretatio Nova Novi Præcepti a Christo Dati Joh. xiii, 34, 35* (ibid. 1826):—*Paraphr. Capitis III Epistolæ Pauli ad Galatas* (ibid. 1833):—*De Descensu Christi ad Inferos e Loco 1 Petr. iii, 19 Tollendo*, etc. (Wittenb. 1805):—*Libri Symbol. Ecclesiæ Evang. Lutheranæ, Accur. Editi Variique Generis Animadverss. ac Disputatt. Illustr.* (ibid. 1809):—*Confessio Augustana eaque Invariata ex Editione Melanchthonis principe Accurate Reddita*, etc. (Halis, 1830):—*Confessio Augustana Anno CIƆIƆXL, a Melanchthone Edita, quæ recte quidem Nominata est Variata, temere autem Vitata Accurate Redditur*, etc. (ibid. eod.):—*Doctrina Biblica de Natura Spiritus Sancti* (ibid. 1825):—*Doctrina Biblica de Natura Christi Filii Dei* (ibid. 1826):—*Eclogæ Exegetico-criticæ ad Nonnullos Evangelii Marci Locos* (ibid. 1831). See Winer, *Handb. der theol. Lit.* i, 88, 242, 249, 262, 270, 321, 324, 325, 423, 424, 435, 562; Zuchold, *Bibl. Theol.* ii, 1423. (B. P.)

Webster, Alexander, D.D., a Scotch clergyman, was born in Edinburgh in 1707. He became minister of Culross in 1733, and of Tolbooth Church, Edinburgh, in 1737; drew up for the Scotch government in 1755 the first attempt at a census; published several sermons and poems; and died Jan. 25, 1784. See Allibone, *Dict. of Brit. and Amer. Authors*, s. v.

Webster, Noah, LL.D., the lexicographer, was a learned layman of the Congregational Church, and born in Hartford, Conn., Oct. 16, 1758. Under the guidance of Rev. Nathan Perkins, he was fitted for college, and entered Yale in 1774, at the age of sixteen. The Revolution seriously interrupted the college exercises, and in his junior year he joined the army. Notwithstanding, he graduated with his class in 1778. After graduation he was occupied more or less in teaching, and also in the study of law with Oliver Ellsworth, of Hartford, afterwards Chief-justice of the United States. In 1781 he was admitted to the bar, but still taught school; and for a time was principal of an academy in Goshen, N. Y. In 1782 he conceived the plan of preparing and publishing a series of school-books, and returned from Goshen to Hartford; and in the following year published the *American Spelling-book*. Soon after he issued an *English Grammar* and a *Reader*. The spelling-book attained an unprecedented popularity. Five million copies had been issued up to 1818, and in the year 1847 24,000,000 had been published. After that time the annual demand was about 1,250,000 copies. Since 1861 the sale has been about 500,000 copies annually. Among his publications may be mentioned, *Sketches of American Policy* (1784–85):—*Dissertations on the English Language* (1789):—*Effects of Slavery on Morals and Industry*, etc. In 1788 he began the publication, in New York, of the *American Magazine;* in 1793 he established there a daily paper called the *Minerva;* and afterwards a semi-weekly paper known as the *Herald*. Between 1783 and 1822 his time was passed at Hartford, New Haven, New York, and Amherst. He removed from Amherst to New Haven in 1822, and made that place his residence until his death. His great work is, of course, his *Dictionary of the English Language*, which he began in 1807. Preliminary to this, he had published, in 1806, an octavo dictionary. In 1823 he received the degree of LL.D. from Yale College; and then, having nearly completed his large dictionary, he sailed for France, in June, 1824; spent two months at Paris in consulting rare works in the Royal Library; and then went to England, spending eight months at the University of Cambridge, with free access to the libraries. There he finished the *American Dictionary*. An edition of 2500 copies was printed in the United States at the close of 1828, which was followed by an edition of 3000 in England. In 1840 a second American edition was issued—3000 copies in two volumes. In 1843 he published a volume entitled *A Collection of Papers on Political, Literary, and Moral Subjects*. As a religious man, Dr. Webster was earnest and prayerful, having united with the Church in 1808. The Bible was his daily study, and he prepared a revised edition of the common English version (New Haven, 1833, 8vo). He died at New Haven, May 28, 1843. See *Cong. Quar.* 1865, p. 1.

Webster, Samuel, D.D., a Congregational minister, was born at Bradford, Mass., in 1718. He graduated from Harvard College in 1737; was ordained pastor of the Church at Salisbury, Aug. 12, 1741, and died July 18, 1796. In 1757 he published a pamphlet entitled *A Winter Evening's Conversation upon the Doctrine of Original Sin*, etc., which brought out rejoinders from Rev. Peter Clark and others. Mr. Webster issued a defence of his pamphlet, which led to a general controversy. This was conducted with great spirit and ability on both sides. See Sprague, *Annals of the Amer. Pulpit*, i, 291.

Webster, William, D.D., a learned English divine, was born in 1689. He was educated at Caius College, Cambridge, where he graduated in 1711. He became curate of St. Dunstan in the West, London, in 1715; was removed in 1731; became curate of St. Clement Eastcheap in 1732; rector of Deptden, Suffolk, in 1733; resigned his curacy and rectory for the vicarages of Ware and Thunderidge. He died Dec. 4, 1758. He was the author of, *The Clergy's Right of Maintenance Vindicated:—Two Discourses*, on the nature of error in speculative doctrines and the doctrine of the Trinity (1729):—*A Translation of Simon's New Testament* (1730):—*The Fitness of the Witnesses of the Resurrection of Christ Considered* (1731):—and several other works, chiefly pamphlets of temporary interest. He also edited the *Life of General Monk* (1725); and conducted *The Weekly Miscellany* for a short time, beginning in 1733. See Chalmers, *Biog. Dict.* s. v.

Wechselbalg, in German mythology. The elves or dwarfs sometimes purloin well-formed children from the cradle, and put their own ugly, deformed children, or even themselves, in their stead. These spurious beings are therefore called Wechselbälge. The object for changing seems to be a desire on the part of the elves to improve their race. A protection against such changing, in the popular estimation, is to place a key or a part of the father's clothing, or steel or sewing-needles, in the cradle. An interesting piece of superstition is the manner of freeing one's self from such a Wechselbalg. It is necessary, first, by some strange and unusual act, to bring him to an acknowledgment of his own age, and then of the theft and change, upon which he immediately withdraws and the stolen child returns, as the elves want nothing gratis. For example, if the Wechselbalg should see water boiling in egg-shells over a fire, he calls out, "Now I am as old as Westerwald, and have never yet seen water boil in egg-shells."

Weda, in German mythology, is one of the two gods of war among the Friesians. He was represented and worshipped with his brother god Freda. The head was covered with a feathered helmet, the breast with a shield; and he was also represented as having wings. Because Weda and Freda appeared as twins, it was thought they were Castor and Pollux returned.

Wedag, Friedrich Wilhelm, a Protestant theologian of Germany, was born in 1758 at Neuenrade, in Westphalia. He studied at Halle and Duisburg; and after the completion of his academical curriculum he acted as a private tutor. Having no prospects for obtaining a position in his own country, he thought of going to Amsterdam, and there to obtain from the East India Company a position as preacher in the East or West Indies. Having received a call from the Reformed congregation at Dortmund in 1786, he remained at home. But his position was such that he was often obliged to preach in other congregations in order to keep himself. On one occasion he had to preach at Leipsic, where he proved himself such an excellent pulpit orator that after Zollikofer's death (1788) he was called as his successor. Here he labored until his death, May 18, 1799. He published some works of an ascetical character, for which see Döring, *Deutsche Kanzelredner*, p. 565; Winer, *Handbuch der theol. Lit.* ii, 93, 198, 244. (B. P.)

Wedderburn, James, a Scotch prelate, was born in Dundee, and studied at Oxford. In 1631 he became a prebendary of Whitechurch, in the diocese of Wells, England. He was afterwards professor of divinity at St. Andrews. In February, 1636, he was preferred to the see of Dunblane, and in 1638 deprived and excommunicated by the Assembly at Glasgow. He died in 1639. See Keith, *Scottish Bishops*, p. 182.

Wedding (γάμος, Matt. xxii, 3, 8, 10, 12; Luke xii, 36, xiv, 8, *marriage*, as elsewhere rendered). See the monographs cited in Volbeding, *Index Program.* p. 152, 153. See Marriage; Ring; Wedlock.

Wedge of Gold לָשׁוֹן, *lashôn*, Josh. vii, 21, 24, *a tongue*, as elsewhere rendered; more elliptically, כֶּתֶם, *ke'them*, Isa. xiii, 12, *fine gold*, as elsewhere rendered). See Gold.

Wedlock, a word that occurs but once in the A. V. (in the phrase "break wedlock," נָאַף, Ezek. xvi, 38, to *commit adultery*, as elsewhere rendered); but the relation is very often referred to both in its literal and figurative (spiritual) sense in the Scriptures. The term properly designates the state of lawful matrimony as distinguished from all illicit or irregular connection of the sexes. As this is a subject having extensive social relations, we give here a treatment of the several topics embraced under it, presenting some additional points to those given under previous articles, and supplementing the whole from various sources, especially the prescriptions and regulations of the Talmud.

I. *The Married State.*—This among the Hebrews was contracted by the fathers of the two parties (Gen. xxxiv, 4; xxxviii, 6; 1 Kings ii, 17; comp. Homer, *Iliad*, ix, 394; xix, 291; Arvieux, *Voy.* iii, 254 a), and only in their absence by the mothers (Gen. xxi, 21; by daughters with the consent of their full brothers, xxiv, 50; xxxiv, 10), so that the bride (כַּלָּה) and the bridegroom (חָתָן) often did not even see each other previously (as is still customary, at least with the inhabitants of cities in the East; see Russell, *Aleppo*, i, 414; Burckhardt, *Prov.* p. 178; *Descr. de l'Égypte*, xviii, 84; but comp. Judg. xiv, 1 sq.; Cant. viii, 1 sq.; Tob. vii, 10). Indeed, the parents sought the wife for their son (Gen. xxxiv, 4, 8; xxxviii, 6; Judg. xiv, 1; comp. Rüppell, *Abyss.* ii, 49; yet see Tob. vii, 10), and a formal price (מֹהַר, dowry) had to be stipulated (Gen. xxix, 15 sq.; xxxiv, 12; Exod. xxii, 15 sq.; 1 Sam. xviii, 25; Hos. iii, 2), a rule which prevailed likewise with the ancient Greeks (Homer, *Odyss.* viii, 318 sq.; Aristotle, *Polit.* ii, 8; Pausan. iii, 12, 2), Germans (Tacitus, *Germ.* c. 8; see Strodtmann, *Deutsch. Alterth.* p. 309 sq.), Babylonians (Herod. i, 196), and Assyrians (Ælian, *V. H.* iv, 1; Strabo, xvi, 745), as still among the Arabians (Arvieux, iii, 21, 254; Buckingham, ii, 129; Joliffe, *Trav.* p. 304), Kurds (Niebuhr, *Reis.* ii, 420), Persians (Olear. *Voy.* p. 318), and other Asiatics and Africans (Rüppell, *Abyss.* ii, 49; comp. B. Michaelis in Pott's *Syllog.* ii, 81). This sum was naturally very various (Gen. xxxiv, 12; 1 Sam. xviii, 23; Hos. iii, 2, etc.), but in one case (Deut. xxii, 29) was to be fifty shekels as a minimum (see, on the other hand, Hos. iii, 2). The practice of the modern Egyptians illustrates this; for with them the dowry, though its amount differs according to the wealth of the suitor, is still graduated according to the state of the bride. A certain portion only of the dowry is paid down, the rest being held in reserve (Lane, i, 211). Among the modern Jews also the amount of the dowry varies with the state of the bride, according to a fixed scale (Picart, i, 240). See Dowry. Different from this was the present (מַתָּן) which the wooer bestowed beforehand (Gen. xxiv, 53; xxxiv, 12; Gr. προῖξ). In some cases, where the suitor was poor or a particular task was exacted, the daughter was earned (Gen. xxix, 20, 27; Josh. xv, 16; Judg. i, 13; 1 Sam. xviii, 24 sq.; 2 Sam. iii, 14; comp. Pausan. iii, 12, 2; Herod. vi, 127; Diod. Sic. iv, 42, 64; Burckhardt, i, 465), and sometimes a dowry accompanied the bride (1 Kings ix, 16; comp. Josh. xv, 18 sq.; Tob. viii, 23). But it is a disgrace, according to Oriental ideas, for a maiden to make the match herself (Isa. iv, 1). The Talmudists specify three modes by which marriage might be effected, viz., money, marriage contract, and consummation (*Kiddush.* i, 1). The matrimonial agreement between the parents was verbal in the presence of witnesses, but occasionally ratified by an oath (Mal. ii, 14); it is only after the Exile (Tob. vii, 15) that we meet with a written marriage contract (Talmud, כְּתוּבָּה, lit. *a writing;* see the Mishnic tract entitled *Kethuboth*). The technical term of the Talmudists for the dowry which the wife brought to her husband, answering to the *dos* of the Latins, was נדוניא. The technical term used by the Talmudists for betrothing was *kiddûshin* (קִדּוּשִׁין), derived from קָדַשׁ, "to set apart." There is a treatise in the Mishna so entitled, in which various questions of casuistry of slight interest to us are discussed. As to the age of the parties, nothing is specified in the Mosaic law; but later enactments require full twelve years for the girl and thirteen for the boy (puberty in both sexes being much earlier in warm climates, so that females of ten or eleven years often become mothers, and lads but little older fathers; see Rüppell, *Nub.* p. 42; *Abyss.* i, 201; ii, 50, 57; Harmer, *Obs.* ii, 312), though the usual age was about eighteen (Mishna, *Pirke Aboth*, v, 21; Carpzov in the *Brem. Biblioth.* ii, 907 sq.). See BETROTHAL.

The Mosaic law permitted several wives to one man, as is universally customary in the East; yet before the Exile this practice seems to have been mostly confined to princes and important personages. See POLYGAMY. Second marriages, especially on the woman's part, were held in disesteem (see Rau, *De Odio Secund. Nuptiarum* [Lips. 1803]), at least in later times (Luke ii, 36 sq.; 1 Cor. vii, 8; 1 Tim. i, 9), if we may judge from the priestly (Josephus, *Life*, § 75, 76) and the apostolical regulations (1 Tim. iii, 2; Tit. i, 6), as generally among the Greeks and Romans (Diod. Sic. xiii, 12; Virgil, *Æn.* iv, 23 sq.; Plutarch, *Quæst. Rom.* c. 105; Val. Max. ii, 2, 3; Josephus, *Ant.* xviii, 6, 6). The celibacy of the Essenes (Philo, ii, 482, 633; Josephus, *Ant.* xviii, 1, 5; *War*, ii, 8, 2; Pliny, v, 15) was a disreputable asceticism (1 Tim. iv, 3). See MATRIMONY.

II. *The Wedding Itself.*—In this the most observable point is that there were no definite religious ceremonies connected with it. It is worthy of note that there is no term in the Hebrew language to express the ceremony of marriage. The substantive *chatunnâh* (חֲתֻנָּה) occurs but once, and then in connection with the day (Cant. iii, 11). The word "wedding" does not occur at all in the A. V. of the Old Test. It is probable, however, that some formal ratification of the espousal with an oath took place, as implied in some allusions to marriage (Ezek. xvi, 8; Mal. ii, 14), particularly in the expression "the covenant of her God" (Prov. ii, 17), as applied to the marriage bond, and that a blessing was pronounced (Gen. xxiv, 60; Ruth iv, 11, 12) sometimes by the parents (Tob. vii, 13). But the essence of the marriage ceremony consisted in the removal of the bride from her father's house to that of the bridegroom or his father. There seems, indeed, to be a literal truth in the Hebrew expression "to *take*" a wife (Numb. xii, 1; 1 Chron. ii, 21), for the ceremony appears to have mainly consisted in the taking. Among the modern Arabs the same custom prevails, the capture and removal of the bride being effected with a considerable show of violence (Burckhardt, *Notes*, i, 108). The bridegroom prepared himself for the occasion by putting on a festive dress, and especially by placing on his head the handsome turban described by the term *peër* (Isa. lxi, 10; A. V. "ornaments"), and a nuptial crown or garland (Cant. iii, 11); he was redolent of myrrh and frankincense and "all powders of the merchant" (ver. 6). The bridegroom's crown was made of various materials (gold or silver, roses, myrtle or olive), according to his circumstances (Selden, *Ux. Ebr.* ii, 15). The use of the crown at marriages was familiar both to the Greeks and Romans. The bride prepared herself for the ceremony by taking a bath, generally on the day preceding the wedding. This was probably in ancient, as in modern, times a formal proceeding, accompanied with considerable pomp (Picart, i, 240; Lane, i, 217). The notices of it in the Bible are so few as to have escaped general observation (Ruth iii, 3; Ezek. xxiii, 40; Eph. v, 26, 27); but the passages cited establish the antiquity of the custom, and the expressions in the last ("having purified her by the laver of water," "not having spot") have evident reference to it. A similar custom prevailed among the Greeks (Smith, *Dict. of Class. Ant.* s. v. "Balneæ"). The distinctive feature of the bride's attire was the *tsaiph* (צָעִיף) or "veil"—a light robe of ample dimensions, which covered not only the face, but the whole person (Gen. xxiv, 65; comp. xxxviii, 14, 15). This was regarded as the symbol of her submission to her husband, and hence in 1 Cor. xi, 10 the veil is apparently described under the term ἐξουσία, "authority." The use of the veil was not peculiar to the Hebrews. It was customary among the Greeks and Romans; and among the latter it gave rise to the expression *nubo*, lit. "to veil," and hence to our word "nuptial." It is still used by the Jews (Picart, i, 241). The modern Egyptians envelop the bride in an ample shawl, which perhaps more than anything else resembles the Hebrew *tsaiph* (Lane, i, 220). She also wore a peculiar girdle, named *kishshurîm* (קִשֻּׁרִים; A. V. the "attire"), which no bride could forget (Jer. ii, 32). The girdle was an important article of the bride's dress among the Romans, and gave rise to the expression *solvere zonam.* Her head was crowned with a chaplet, which was again so distinctive of the bride that the Hebrew term *kallâh* (כַּלָּה, "bride") originated from it. The bride's crown was either of gold or gilded. The use of it was interdicted after the destruction of the second Temple, as a token of humiliation (Selden, *Ux. Ebr.* ii, 15). If the bride were a virgin, she wore her hair flowing (*Kethub.* ii, 1). Her robes were white (Rev. xix, 8), and sometimes embroidered with gold-thread (Psa. xlv, 13, 14), and covered with perfumes (ver. 8): she was further decked out with jewels (Isa. xlix, 18; lxi, 10; Rev. xxi, 2). When the fixed hour arrived, which was generally late in the evening, the bridegroom set forth from his house, attended by his groomsmen, termed in Hebrew *mereîm* (מֵרֵעִים; A. V. "companions," Judg. xiv, 11), and in Greek υἱοὶ τοῦ νυμφῶνος (A. V. "children of the bride-chamber," Matt. ix, 15). Winer (*Realw.* s. v. "Hochzeit") identifies the "children of the bride-chamber" with the *shoshbenim* (שׁוֹשְׁבִּנִים) of the Talmudists. But the former were the attendants on the bridegroom alone, while the *shoshbenim* were two persons selected on the day of the marriage to represent the interests of bride and bridegroom, apparently with a special view to any possible litigation that might subsequently arise on the subject noticed in Deut. xxii, 15-21 (Selden, *Ux. Ebr.* ii, 16). These attendants were preceded by a band of musicians or singers (Gen. xxxi, 27; Jer. vii, 34; xvi, 9; 1 Macc. ix, 39), and accompanied by persons bearing flambeaus (2 Esdr. x, 2; Matt. xxv, 7; comp. Jer. xxv, 10; Rev. xviii, 23, "the light of a candle"). With these flambeaus we may compare the δᾷδες νυμφικαί of the Greeks (Aristoph. *Pax*, 1317). The lamps described in Matt. xxv, 7 would be small hand-lamps. Without them none could join the procession (Trench, *Par-*

ables, p. 257, note). See LANTERN. Having reached the house of the bride, who with her maidens anxiously expected his arrival (Matt. xxv, 6), he conducted the whole party back to his own or his father's house. The bride was said to "go to" (בּוֹא אֶל) the house of her husband (Josh. xv, 18; Judg. i, 14)—an expression which is worthy of notice, inasmuch as it has not been rightly understood in Dan. xi, 6, where "they that brought her" is an expression for *husband*. The bringing home of the bride was regarded in the later days of the Roman empire as one of the most important parts of the marriage ceremony (Bingham, *Christ. Ant.* bk. xxii, ch. iv, § 7). This procession was made with every demonstration of gladness (Psa. xlv, 15). From the joyous sounds used on these occasions the term *halál* (הָלַל) is applied in the sense of marrying in Psa. lxxviii, 63 (A. V. "their maidens were not given to marriage," lit. "were not praised," as in the margin). This sense appears preferable to that of the Sept., οὐκ ἐπένθησαν, which is adopted by Gesenius (*Thesaur.* p. 596). The noise in the streets attendant on an Oriental wedding is excessive, and enables us to understand the allusions in Jeremiah to the "voice of the bridegroom and the voice of the bride." On their way back they were joined by a party of maidens, friends of the bride and bridegroom, who were in waiting to catch the procession as it passed (Matt. xxv, 6; comp. Trench, *Parables*, p. 244, note). The inhabitants of the place pressed out into the streets to watch the procession (Cant. iii, 11). At the house a feast was prepared, to which all the friends and neighbors were invited (Gen. xxix, 22; Matt. xxii, 1-10; Luke xiv, 8; John ii, 2), and the festivities were protracted for seven or even fourteen days (Judg. xiv, 12; Tob. viii, 19). The feast was regarded as so essential a part of the marriage ceremony that ποιεῖν γάμον acquired the specific meaning "to celebrate the marriage feast" (Sept. at Gen. xxix, 22; Esth. ii, 18; Tob. viii, 19; 1 Macc. ix, 37; x, 58; Matt. xxii, 4; xxv, 10; Luke xiv, 8), and sometimes to celebrate any feast (Esth. ix, 22). The guests were provided by the host with fitting robes (Matt. xxii, 11; comp. Trench, *Parables*, p. 230), and the feast was enlivened with riddles (Judg. xiv, 12) and other amusements. The bridegroom now entered into direct communication with the bride, and the joy of the friend was "fulfilled" at hearing the voice of the bridegroom (John iii, 29) conversing with her, which he regarded as a satisfactory testimony of the success of his share in the work. In the case of a virgin, parched corn was distributed among the guests (*Kethub.* ii, 1), the significance of which is not apparent; the custom bears some resemblance to the distribution of the *mustaceum* (Juvenal, vi, 202) among the guests at a Roman wedding. The modern Jews have a custom of shattering glasses or vessels by dashing them to the ground (Picart, i, 240). The last act in the ceremonial was the conducting of the bride to the bridal chamber, *chéder* (חֶדֶר, Judg. xv, 1; Joel ii, 16), where a canopy, named *chuppâh* (חֻפָּה), was prepared (Psa. xix, 5; Joel ii, 16). The term occurs in the Mishna (*Kethub.* iv, 5), and is explained by some of the Jewish commentators to have been a bower of roses and myrtles. The term was also applied to the canopy under which the nuptial benediction was pronounced, or to the robe spread over the heads of the bride and bridegroom (Selden, *Ux. Ebr.* ii, 15). The bride was still completely veiled, so that the deception practiced on Jacob (Gen. xxix, 23) was very possible. If proof could be subsequently adduced that the bride had not preserved her maiden purity, the case was investigated; and if she was convicted, she was stoned to death before her father's house (Deut. xxii, 13-21). A newly married man was exempt from military service, or from any public business which might draw him away from his home, for the space of a year (xxiv, 5); a similar privilege was granted to him who was betrothed (xx, 7). See MARRIAGE.

III. *Violation of Marriage Vows.*—Unfaithfulness on the part of the wife was punished with death (Lev. xx, 10; Deut. xxii, 22; Ezek. xvi, 38, 40; Sus. 45; comp. Josephus, *Apion.* ii, 24; *Ant.* iv, 8, 23) by stoning (Deut. xxii, 4; Ezek. xvi, 40), and not by strangulation (as the Talmudists maintain, Mishna, *Sanhedr.* xi, 1, 6). The legislation of other nations was milder (Tacitus, *Germ.* 19; Ælian, *V. H.* xi, 6; xii, 12; xiii, 24; yet see Arnob. iv, 23). The Roman law (*Lex Julia de Adulteris Coercendis*) only prescribed confiscation of part of the culprit's goods, and public infamy, as the extreme penalty. Constantine first made adultery a capital crime (see Dick, in the *Stud. u. Krit.* 1832, vol. iv; Rein, *Röm. Criminalrecht*, p. 839). The ordeal of the bitter waters (Numb. v, 14 sq.) is detailed in the Mishna (*Sota*, ii, 2), and has its parallel in other nations (Ælian, *Anim.* i, 57; Achil. Tat. viii, 3; see Groddeck, in Ugolino, *Thesaur.* xxx; Otho, *Lex. Rabb.* p. 52). See ADULTERY.

IV. *Dissolution of the Marriage Tie.*—Separation of a man from his wife was legitimate (Deut. xxiv, 1), except in two cases (xxii, 19, 29), when he found reason (עֶרְוַת דָּבָר, a phrase that led to much Talmudical casuistry); but must be done by a regular certificate of dismissal (סֵפֶר כְּרִיתוּת, Isa. l, 1; Jer. iii, 8; Talmudic גִּיטָה or גֵּט; βιβλίον ἀποστασίου, Matt. xix, 7; Mark x, 4; or ἀποστάσιον simply, Matt. v, 31; comp. *repudium*, Suet. *Calig.* § 36). The subject is treated at great length in the Talmud (tract *Gittin*), and by Selden (*Ux. Hebr.*) and Buxtorf (*Sponsal. et Divort.*). See DIVORCE.

Wednesday is a day often marked by special religious exercises, being numbered among the Rogation and Ember days in the Church of England. At a very early period in the history of the Christian Church, the custom of meeting for divine worship on Wednesdays and Fridays was adopted. Both days were considered as fasts, on the ground that our Lord was betrayed on a Wednesday and crucified on a Friday. The fasting continued till three in the afternoon; hence they were called *semi-jejuna*, or half-fasts, in opposition to the fast of Lent, which was continued till the evening. Subsequently the Montanists introduced the custom of limiting the kind of food to be taken, which consisted only of bread, salt, and water. These fasts were called *stationes*, from the practice of soldiers keeping guard, which was called *statio* by the Romans. Lent begins on that day (see ASH WEDNESDAY). In the Western Church Saturday at length took the place of Wednesday as a fast. See FAST; LENT.

WEDNESDAY, ASH. See ASH WEDNESDAY.

Wedurhoelner, in Norse mythology, is the hawk, sitting between the eyes of the eagle, that dwells on the top of the ash Ygdrasil.

Weed (סוּף, *sûph*, Jon. ii, 6; elsewhere rendered "flag," Exod. ii, 3; Isa. xix, 6, but usually as an epithet of the Red Sea, lit. the *weed-sea;* Sept. φῦκος; Lat. *alga*, see Pliny, xxxi, 46, 4; ix, 25), the *sea-weed* (*Fucus natans* of Linn.; *Fucus marinus*, Pliny, xxvi, 66 and 79), a sort of sea-grass with lanciform, serrated leaves, and threadlike knotted stalks, which grows in great abundance on the shores of the Mediterranean (Jon. ii, 6; see Hirtius, *Bell. Afric.* 24), but especially of the Hellespont (Ovid, *Heroid.* xviii, 108; Belon, *Observ.* ii, 3), as likewise of the Red Sea (comp. Strabo, xvi, 773; Diod. Sic. iii, 19, μνίον), the last taking its name (יַם סוּף) from that circumstance. See RED SEA. The plant is described by Acosta (in Clusii *Exoticor. Libb.* [Antw. 1605], p. 293), Delile (*Flora Ægypt.* in *Descr. de l'Égypte*, xix, 113), Bochart (*Phaleg*, iv, 29), Celsius (*Hierobot.* ii, 67 sq.). There are several varieties (see Pliny, xxvii, 25; xxxii, 22; Galen, *Med. Simpl.* viii, 21, 9), of which it is uncertain which is the Egyptian species (Pliny, xiii, 44; Theophr. *Plant.* iv, 9; see Gesenius, *Thesaur.* p. 944). See FLAG. Noxious weeds in general seem to be denoted by the phrase "thorns and thistles" (Gen. iii, 18). See THORN.

Weed, Bartholomew, a Methodist Episcopal minister, was born at Ridgefield (now Danbury), Conn., March 6, 1793. He was trained in the Calvinistic faith and became a Baptist in 1809, but joined the Methodist Episcopal Church in the eighteenth year of his age, under the ministry of Rev. Seth Crowell; was licensed to exhort in 1812: obtained local preacher's license in 1815; and joined the Philadelphia Conference in 1817. During his ministry of sixty-four years he filled appointments in Philadelphia, Bridgeton, Trenton, etc., and was four years a presiding elder in the Rock River Conference, from which he was elected delegate to the General Conference of 1844. His last years were spent in the Newark Conference, which, in 1864, gave him a superannuated relation. During the last eleven years of his life he acted as chaplain of Essex County Jail. He died in Newark, N. J., Jan. 5, 1879. Mr. Weed was ardent in his attachment to the doctrines, discipline, and usages of the Methodist Episcopal Church, and bore with cheerfulness a part in the sacrifices and sufferings of her pioneer work. His ministry was characterized by clearness, warmth, and strength. He was a man of simple tastes and manners, of strong convictions and attachments, and of a heroic and magnanimous spirit. Preaching was his loved employment, and it seemed as hard for him to quit it, though in his eighty-sixth year, as it was for him, a few weeks later, to die. See *Minutes of Annual Conferences*, 1879, p. 73. (R. V.)

Weed, Henry Rowland, D.D., a Presbyterian minister, was born at Ballston, N. Y., July 30, 1789. He graduated from Union College in 1812, and with the first class of Princeton Theological Seminary in 1815; was ordained pastor at Jamaica, L. I., in 1816; in 1822 went to Albany, N. Y., as pastor of the First Presbyterian Church; in 1830 became agent for the Board of Education; in 1832 pastor of the First Presbyterian Church at Wheeling, Va., and died at Philadelphia, Pa., Dec. 14, 1870. In the councils of the Church he was greatly respected.

Week (שָׁבוּעַ, or שָׁבֻעַ, *shabûa*, from שֶׁבַע, "seven," lit. a *heptad* of anything, but specifically used for a period of seven days; Sept. ἑβδομάς; Vulg. *septimana*). See SEVEN.

1. The *origin* of this division of time is a matter which has given birth to much speculation. Its antiquity is so great, its observance so wide-spread, and it occupies so important a place in sacred things, that it has been very generally thrown back as far as the creation of man, who, on this supposition, was told from the very first to divide his time on the model of the Creator's order of working and resting. The week and the Sabbath are, if this be so, as old as man himself, and we need not seek for reasons either in the human mind or the facts with which that mind comes in contact, for the adoption of such a division of time, since it is to be referred neither to man's thoughts nor to man's will. A purely theological ground is thus established for the week and for the sacredness of the number seven. They who embrace this view support it by a reference to the six days' creation and the Divine rest on the seventh, which they consider to have been made known to man from the very first, and by an appeal to the exceeding prevalence of the hebdomadal division of time from the earliest age—an argument the force of which is considered to be enhanced by the alleged absence of any natural ground for it. See DAY.

To all this, however, it may be objected that we are quite in the dark as to when the record of the six days' creation was made known; that as human language is used and human apprehensions are addressed in that record, so, the week being already known, the perfection of the Divine work and Sabbath may well have been set forth under this figure, the existing division of time moulding the document, instead of the document giving birth to the division; that, old and wide-spread as is the recognition of that division, it is not universal; that the nations which knew not of it were too important to allow the argument from its prevalency to stand; and that, so far from its being without ground in nature, it is the most obvious and convenient way of dividing the month. Each of these points must now be briefly considered:

(1.) That the week rests on a theological ground may be cheerfully acknowledged by both sides; but nothing is determined by such acknowledgment as to the original cause of adopting this division of time. The records of creation and the fourth commandment give, no doubt, the ultimate and therefore the deepest ground of the weekly division, but it does not therefore follow that it was not adopted for lower reasons before either was known. Whether the week gave its sacredness to the number seven, or whether the ascendency of that number helped to determine the dimensions of the week, it is impossible to say. The latter fact, the ancient ascendency of the number seven, might rest on divers grounds. The planets, according to the astronomy of those times, were seven in number; so are the notes of the diatonic scale; so also many other things naturally attracting observation.

(2.) The prevalence of the weekly division was indeed very great, but a nearer approach to universality is required to render it an argument for the view in aid of which it is appealed to. It was adopted by all the Shemitic races, and, in the later period of their history at least, by the Egyptians. On this side of the Atlantic we find it, or a division all but identical with it, among the Peruvians. It also obtains now with the Hindûs, but its antiquity among them is matter of question. It is possible that it was introduced into India by the Arabs and Mohammedans. So in China we find it, but whether universally or only among the Buddhists admits of doubt. (See, for both, Priaulx's *Quæstiones Mosaicæ*, a work with many of the results of which we may be well expected to quarrel, but which deserves, in respect not only of curious learning, but of the vigorous and valuable thought with which it is impregnated, to be far more known than it is.) On the other hand, there is no reason for thinking the week known till a late period either to Greeks or Romans.

(3.) So far from the week being a division of time without ground in nature, there was much to recommend its adoption. Where the days were named from planetary deities, as among first the Assyrians and Chaldees, and then the Egyptians, there of course each period of seven days would constitute a whole, and that whole might come to be recognised by nations that disregarded or rejected the practice which had shaped and determined it. But, further, the week is a most natural and nearly an exact quadripartition of the month, so that the quarters of the moon may easily have suggested it.

(4.) Even if it were proved that the planetary week of the Egyptians, as sketched by Dion Cassius (*Hist. Rom.* xxxvii, 18), existed at or before the time of the Exode, the children of Israel did not copy that. Their week was simply determined by the Sabbath; and there is no evidence of any other day, with them, having either had a name assigned to it, or any particular associations bound up with it. The days seem to have been distinguished merely by the ordinal numerals, counted from the Sabbath.

2. *History among the Hebrews.*—Whatever controversies exist respecting the origin of the week, there can be none about the great antiquity, on particular occasions at least, among the Shemitic races, of measuring time by a period of seven days. This has been thought to be implied in the phrase respecting the sacrifices of Cain and Abel (Gen. iv, 3), "in process of time," literally "at the end of days." It is to be traced in the narrative of the subsidence of the Flood (viii, 10), "and he stayed yet other seven days;" and we find it recognised

by the Syrian Laban (xxix, 27), "fulfil her week." It is needless to say that this division of time is a marked feature of the Mosaic law, and one into which the whole year was parted, the Sabbath sufficiently showing that. The week of seven days was also made the key to a scale of seven, running through the sabbatical years up to that of jubilee.

We have seen in Gen. xxix, 27 that it was known to the ancient Syrians, and the injunction to Jacob, "fulfil her week," indicates that it was in use as a fixed term for great festive celebrations. The most probable exposition of the passage is that Laban tells Jacob to fulfil Leah's *week*, the proper period of the nuptial festivities in connection with his marriage to her, and then he may have Rachel also (comp. Judg. xiv). So, too, for funeral observance, as in the case of the obsequies of Jacob, Joseph "made a mourning for his father seven days" (Gen. l, 10). But neither of these instances, any more than Noah's procedure in the ark, goes further than showing the custom of observing a term of seven days for any observance of importance. Nor does it prove that the whole year, or the whole month, was thus divided at all times, and without regard to remarkable events.

In Exodus, of course, the week comes into very distinct manifestation. Two of the great feasts—the Passover and the Feast of Tabernacles—are prolonged for seven days after that of their initiation (Exod. xii, 15-20, etc.), a custom which remains in the Christian Church, in the rituals of which the remembrances and topics of the great festivals are prolonged till what is technically called the *octave*. Although the Feast of Pentecost lasted but one day, yet the time for its observance was to be counted by weeks from the Passover, whence one of its titles, "the Feast of Weeks."

The division by seven was, as we have seen, expanded so as to make the seventh month and the seventh year sabbatical. To whatever extent the laws enforcing this may have been neglected before the Captivity, their effect, when studied, must have been to render the words שָׁבוּעַ, ἑβδομάς, *week*, capable of meaning a seven of years almost as naturally as a seven of days. Indeed, the generality of the words would have this effect at any rate. Hence their use to denote the latter in prophecy, more especially in that of Daniel, is not mere arbitrary symbolism, but the employment of a not unfamiliar and easily understood language. This is not the place to discuss schemes of prophetic interpretation, nor do we propose giving our opinion of any such, but it is connected with our subject to remark that, whatever be the merits of that which in Daniel and the Apocalypse understands a year by a *day*, it cannot be set aside as forced and unnatural. Whether days were or were not intended to be thus understood in the places in question, their being so would have been a congruous, and we may say logical, attendant on the scheme which counts weeks of years, and both would have been a natural computation to minds familiar and occupied with the law of the sabbatical year. See DAY.

3. *Christian Observances.*—In the New Test., we of course find such clear recognition of and familiarity with the week as need scarcely be dwelt on. Sacred as the division was, and stamped deep on the minds and customs of God's people, it now received additional solemnity from our Lord's last earthly Passover gathering up his work of life into a week.

Hence the Christian Church, from the very first, was familiar with the week. Paul's language (1 Cor. xvi, 2, κατὰ μίαν σαββάτων) shows this. We cannot conclude from it that such a division of time was observed by the inhabitants of Corinth generally; for they to whom he was writing, though doubtless the majority of them were Gentiles, yet knew the Lord's day, and most probably the Jewish Sabbath. But though we can infer no more than this from the place in question, it is clear that if not by this time, yet very soon after, the whole Roman world had adopted the hebdomadal division. Dion Cassius, who wrote in the 2d century, speaks of it as both universal and recent in his time. He represents it as coming from Egypt, and gives two schemes, by one or other of which he considers that the planetary names of the different days were fixed (Dion Cassius, xxvii, 18). Those names, or corresponding ones, have perpetuated themselves over Christendom, though no associations of any kind are now connected with them, except in so far as the whimsical conscience of some has quarrelled with their Pagan origin, and led to an attempt at their disuse. It would be interesting, though foreign to our present purpose, to inquire into the origin of this planetary week. A deeply learned paper in the *Philological Museum*, by the late archdeacon Hare, gives the credit of its invention to the Chaldees. Dion Cassius was, however, pretty sure to have been right in tracing its adoption by the Roman world to an Egyptian origin. It is very striking to reflect that while Christendom was in its cradle, the law by which she was to divide her time came, without collusion with her, into universal observance, thus making things ready for her to impose on mankind that week on which all Christian life has been shaped—that week grounded on no worship of planetary deities, nor dictated by the mere wish to quadripartite the month, but based on the earliest lesson of revelation, and proposing to man his Maker's model as that whereby to regulate his working and his rest—that week which once indeed in modern times it has been attempted to abolish, because it was attempted to abolish the whole Christian faith, but which has kept, as we are sure it ever will keep, its ground, being bound up with that other, and sharing therefore in that other's invincibility and perpetuity. See TIME.

WEEK, THE GREAT, is the name of the week following Palm Sunday. See LENT.

Weeks, FEAST OF. See PENTECOST.

WEEKS, SEVENTY. See SEVENTY WEEKS.

Weeks, John Willis, D.D., a colonial bishop of the Church of England, died March 25, 1857, having just returned to Sierra Leone, of which he was bishop, on the 17th of that month, after visiting the stations of the Yarriba Mission. His consecration to this see occurred in 1855. See *Amer. Quar. Church Rev.* 1857, p. 471.

Weeks, William Raymond, D.D., a Presbyterian divine, was born at Brooklyn, Conn., Aug. 6, 1783. He graduated at the College of New Jersey in 1809; studied theology at the Andover Theological Seminary; was licensed to preach by the Association in Vermont, and was ordained and installed by the Columbia Presbytery as pastor of the church in Plattsburg, N. Y., in February, 1812. He resigned this charge in 1814, and was occupied in supplying different churches and teaching until 1832, when he became pastor of the Fourth Presbyterian Church in Newark, N. J., where he continued to perform the double duty of preaching and teaching a school until 1846, when, on account of declining health, he had to give up both. He died June 27, 1848. Dr. Weeks had a mind of more than ordinary activity and independence; the classics and the Hebrew language were the studies of his life, and in these departments few have attained to greater accuracy of scholarship. He published, *Nine Sermons on the Decrees and Agency of God* (1813, three editions):—*Scripture Catechism* (1813, two editions):—*Pilgrim's Progress in the Nineteenth Century* (1849, 12mo, posthumous):—also single *Sermons*, *Letters*, and a series of *Short Tracts*. See Sprague, *Annals of the Amer. Pulpit*, iv, 473; Allibone, *Dict. of Brit. and Amer. Authors*, s. v.

Weepers (προσκλαίοντες, *flentes*), the class who lay in the porch weeping and beseeching the prayers of all who entered.—Walcott, *Sacred Archæol.* s. v.

Weeping (בָּכָה, κλαίω). The ancient Hebrews

wept and made their troubles to appear openly, in mourning and affliction; they were not of opinion that courage and greatness of soul consisted in seeming to be insensible in adversity, or in restraining their tears. It was even looked upon as a great disrespect for any one not to be bewailed at his funeral. Job says of the wicked man, "His widow shall not weep" (Job xxvii, 15). The Psalmist, speaking of the death of Hophni and Phinehas, says, "Their priests fell by the sword, and their widows made no lamentation" (Psa. lxxiii, 64). God forbids Ezekiel to weep or to express any sorrow for the death of his wife, to show that the Jews should be reduced to so great calamities that they should not have the liberty even to mourn or bewail themselves (Ezek. xxiv, 16). See MOURNING; TEARS.

Wegelin, Josua, a Lutheran theologian of Germany, was born Jan. 11, 1604, at Augsburg. He studied at Tübingen, and was appointed in 1627 deacon in his native place. In 1629, when, at the command of the emperor Ferdinand III, the evangelical churches were closed and divine service was prohibited, Wegelin had to leave the city with the other evangelical ministers. He returned again in 1632, after Gustavus Adolphus had entered the city, to leave it again in 1635. He went to Presburg, in Hungary, where he died, Sept. 14, 1640. For the benefit of his members in Augsburg, he composed *Augsburger Betbüchlein* (2d ed. Nuremb. 1648), and *Hand-, Land- und Standbüchlein* (ibid. 1637). After his death, his ascetical writings were published under the title *Gebete und Lieder* (ibid. 1660). One of his hymns, *Auf Christi Himmelfahrt allein*, has also been translated into English, "Since Christ has gone to heav'n, his home," in the *Choral Book for England*, No. 64. See Hartmann, *Würtembergisches Magisterbuch*, 15th series; Koch, *Gesch. d. deutschen Kirchenliedes*, iii, 169 sq. (B. P.)

Wegelin, Thomas, a Protestant divine of Germany, was born at Augsburg, Dec. 21, 1577. At the Ratisbon Colloquy he acted as amanuensis of the Protestant theologians. He died as professor of theology and president of the church-convent at Strasburg, March 16, 1629. He wrote, *Dissert. III de Scripturæ Sacræ Auctoritate, Linguis et Versionibus:—Hypomnema Theologicum de Hymno Trisagio:—Prælectiones in Pentateuchum:—De Christo:—De Majestate Christi:—De Indulgentiis:—De Resurrectione Mortuorum*, etc. See Serpilius, *Epitaphia Theologorum;* Witte, *Memoriæ Theologorum;* Jöcher, *Allgemeines Gelehrten-Lex.* s. v. (B. P.)

Weger, LAURENTIUS, a German philologist, was born Dec. 30, 1653, at Königsberg. He prosecuted his studies at his native place and Leipsic, and was appointed, in 1679, professor of Oriental languages in his native city, where he died, May 21, 1715. He wrote, *Dissert. de Verbo Dei Occasione Phraseos Chaldaicæ* מימרא דיי*:—De Osculatione Manus Idololatrica ex Job xxxi*, 26, etc. He also wrote on Psa. xxii; Hos. iii, 4; Ezek. viii, 17. See Arnold, *Hist. der Königsbergischen Universität;* Jöcher, *Allgemeines Gelehrten-Lex.* s. v.; Fürst, *Bibl. Jud.* iii, 497. (B. P.)

Wegleiter, CHRISTOPH, a Lutheran theologian of Germany, was born April 22, 1659, at Nuremberg. He studied at Altdorf and other universities. In 1688 he was appointed professor of theology and preacher at Altdorf, where he died, Aug. 16, 1706. Besides some dissertations, he is also the author of sermons and hymns. See *Programma Funebre in Obitum Dr. Wegleiteri* (Altdorf, 1706); Zeltneri *Vitæ Theol. Altorphin.* (1720), p. 435 sq.; Jöcher, *Allgemeines Gelehrten-Lex.* s. v.; Koch, *Gesch. des deutschen Kirchenliedes*, iii, 502 sq. (B. P.)

Wegner, GOTTFRIED, a Protestant theologian of Germany, was born at Oels, March 18, 1644, and died June 14, 1709, as doctor and professor of theology, and court preacher at Königsberg. He is the author of, *Dissert. Hist.-theol. de Sabbatho Christianorum Judaico* (Königsb. 1702):—*Disput. Histor. Ecclesiast. de Alba Veste Baptizatorum* (ibid. 1700, 1734):—*Horologium Hebræum cum Isagoge* (Frankf. 1678):—*Programma de Computo Ecclesiastico et Accentuatione Hebræa* (ibid. 1680), reprinted in *Syntagma Disputationum Francofurtensium* (ibid. 1700):—*Specimen Analysis Hebr. de Verbo* ברא (ibid. 1670). See Winer, *Handb. der theol. Lit.* i, 617, 631, Fürst, *Bibl. Jud.* iii, 497; Steinschneider, *Bibliog. Handbuch*, No. 2130. (B. P.)

Weimar Hymn-book was a work prepared by Herder at Weimar in 1778. His plan was to restore the old hymns to their original readings, and introduce as many as possible that were already established in the hearts of the people. He thought it subversive of the highest interests of the Church to alter these compositions to meet the peculiar views of theologians of successive generations, yet he would not pursue his own method of restoration without certain restrictions within the bounds of reason. See Hagenbach, *Hist. of the Church in the 18th and 19th Centuries*, ii, 53 sq.

Weinbrenner, FRIEDRICH, an eminent German architect, was born at Carlsruhe in 1766. He was trained as a carpenter and builder, and in 1788 began to travel for improvement, visiting in turn Zurich, Dresden, and Berlin, and in 1792 started for Italy. Here he discovered his own want of training and instruction, and entered upon a thorough course of study and research, supporting himself in part by giving instruction in architecture to numerous persons, some strangers of distinction. He returned to Carlsruhe in 1797, where he became inspector of buildings, and soon after erected a synagogue and some private mansions. He removed to Strasburg two years after, but did not find much employment, and in a short time returned to Carlsruhe in his former capacity. He entertained higher views of his art than his countrymen generally, and did much to diffuse the same sentiment throughout the next generation by his instructions. At Carlsruhe he constructed the Catholic church, Lutheran church, Theatre, Museum, Mint, Hochberg Palace, and other edifices. At Baden he supervised the erection of numerous buildings. He also constructed several churches, mansions, villas, etc., in various parts of Germany. He published a number of works on different branches of architectural study, viz., *Zeichnungslehre* (1810):—*Optik* (1811):—*Perspectivlehre* (1817-24):—*Ueber Form und Schönheit* (1819):—*Ueber architektonische Verzierungen* (1820):—and other works. He died March 1, 1826.

Weinrich, Johann Michael, a Protestant theologian of Germany, was born Oct. 12, 1683, at Dettern, in Franconia, and died as court-deacon at Meiningen, March 18, 1727. He wrote, *Kirchen und Schulenstaat des Fürstenthums Henneberg alter und mittlerer Zeiten* (Leips. 1720):—*Historische und theologische Betrachtungen der merkwürdigen Alterthümer und gelehrten Dinge* (Coburg, 1725):—*Comparatio Poeseos Germanicorum cum illa Hebræorum Veteri* (printed in *Misc. Lips.* x, 76 sq.). See Winer, *Handb. der theol. Lit.* i, 803; Fürst, *Bibl. Jud.* iii, 502. (B. P.)

Weinrich, Thomas, a Protestant theologian of Germany, who died May 4, 1629, at Leipsic, is the author of, *Examen Synodi Dordracenæ de Absoluto Prædestin. Decreto:—Thronum Christi Regalem ex Psa. lx*, 8, *Homiliis Explicatum:—Controversia de Spiritu S. contra Photinianos:*—Ἐξέτασις *Abominationis Pontificiæ*. See Freher, *Theatrum Eruditorum;* Ebert, *Leorinum Eruditum;* Cave, *Hist. Lit. Scriptorum Ecclesiasticorum;* Winer, *Handb. der theol. Lit.* i, 445; Jöcher, *Allgemeines Gelehrten-Lexikon*, s. v. (B. P.)

Weinzierl, FRANZ JOSEPH, a Roman Catholic theologian of Germany, was born Dec. 24, 1777, at Pfaffenberg, in Bavaria. He studied at Munich and Ratisbon, received holy orders in 1801, and acted as chaplain at Penting for a short time. In 1802 he went to Ratisbon as professor of the gymnasium, where he labored until 1806, when he was appointed cathedral preacher. He died Jan. 1, 1829. He published, *Die Klaggesänge des Propheten Jeremias nach der Vulgata, in Versen* (Augsburg, 1805):—*Die sieben Busspsalmen in gereimten Versen* (ibid. 1814):—*Die Psalmen nebst den Klageliedern Jeremiä und den übrigen Gesängen der heiligen Schrift in gereimten Versen* (ibid. 1819; 2d ed. 1823):—*Sprüche der Weisheit, aus den heiligen Büchern in gereimten Versen übersetzt* (ibid. 1821). See Döring, *Die gelehrten Theologen Deutschlands*, iv, 682 sq.; Fürst, *Bibl. Jud.* iii, 502; Winer, *Handb. der theol. Lit.* ii, 113. (B. P.)

Weis, Nicolaus von, a German prelate, was born March 8, 1796, at Schönhof, in the bishopric of Metz. He studied at Mayence, was appointed pastor at Dudenhofen in 1820, and two years later capitulary at Speyer, where he was consecrated as bishop July 10, 1842. He died Dec. 13, 1869. In connection with the bishop of Strasburg, Andreas Räss, he founded the *Catholic*, a very influential paper in Germany, and translated many works into German; thus they translated Butler's *Lives of the Saints* (Mayence, 1821-27, 23 vols.) from the French translation of Godescard; from the latter language they also translated Robelot's work *On the Influence of Luther's Reformation upon Religion, Politics*, etc. (ibid. 1823). See *Literarischer Handweiser für das katholische Deutschland*, 1869, p. 550; Winer, *Handbuch der theol. Lit.* i, 350, 352, 405, 673, 742, 748, 847; ii, 23, 85, 88, 112, 113. (B. P.)

Weise, Georg Andreas, a Lutheran minister of Germany, was born Dec. 11, 1737, at Astrakhan, in Russia. He went to Halle with his father in 1743, and here he received, not only his early education, but also his theological instruction, and Franke, Michaelis, Freylinghausen, Baumgarten, and Knapp were his teachers in the university. From 1761 to 1768 he superintended the schools of the Orphan Asylum; in the latter year he was appointed deacon of St. George's, and in 1774 pastor of that church. In 1783 he was called to Magdeburg, where he died, June 16, 1792. He published, *Ueber die Reden des sterbenden Mittlers* (Halle, 1778):—*Reden über die Weissagung des Jesaias von Christi Leiden und Auferstehung* (ibid. 1780). He also published sermons for the Christian year. See Döring, *Die gelehrten Theologen Deutschlands*, iv, 684 sq. (B. P.)

Weiser, Daniel, D.D., a German Reformed clergyman, was born at Selinsgrove, Pa., Jan. 13, 1799. In his youth he learned the trade of a nailsmith in Lewisburg, and in 1814 served four months in the United States army. He began to study for the ministry at Hagerstown, Md., in 1819, was licensed in 1823, and ordained in 1824. His first charge embraced three congregations in the vicinity of Selinsgrove, which he extended to eleven. After laboring in this field for ten years, he became pastor at New Goshenhoppen and Great Swamp, in Montgomery Co., Pa., to whom he ministered for thirty years. In 1863 he withdrew from the active ministry, but until the close of his life frequently assisted his son, who succeeded him, and supplied neighboring pulpits. He died Dec. 2, 1875. Dr. Weiser was a hard-working pastor, a close student, and a good preacher. See Harbaugh, *Fathers of the German Ref. Church*, v, 146.

Weishaupt, Adam, founder of the sect of the Illuminati (q. v.), was born at Ingolstadt, Feb. 6, 1748. He was educated at the seminary of the Jesuits in his native city, but soon quitted it for the university, where he was made doctor in 1768, and in 1772 professor of jurisprudence. In 1775 he displaced the Jesuits in the chair of canon law, and thenceforth became their opponent, first by means of a powerful secret society, and afterwards by the establishment of the mystical or enthusiastic sect above named, in whose interest his works (for which see Hoefer, *Nouv. Biog. Générale*, s. v.) were written. In 1785 he resigned his professorship, and retired to Gotha, engaged in scientific and social labors, still occupying the honorary position of aulic counsellor. He died there Nov. 18, 1830.

Weismann, Christian Eberhard, a Lutheran theologian of Germany, was born Sept. 2, 1677, at Hirschau. He studied at Tübingen, was appointed in 1701 deacon at Calw, and in 1704 court chaplain at Stuttgart, but in 1707 he exchanged his position for that of professor of church history and philosophy at the gymnasium there. Here he published *Einleitung in die Merkwürdigkeiten der Kirchenhistorie N. Testaments zur Beförderung der Erkenntniss des Reichs Gottes*, etc. (1718, 1719, 2 pts.). In 1721 he was called as professor of theology to Tübingen, was honored in the same year with the degree of D.D., and succeeded G. Hoffmann as provost of St. George's in 1729. He died May 26, 1747. Besides his *Institutiones Theologicæ Exegetico-dogmaticæ* (1739), he wrote some very fine hymns. See Moser, *Beitrag zu einem Lexico der jetzt lebenden luth. und reform. Theologen* (Züllichau, 1740), p. 444-454; Brucker, *Bildersaal heutigen Tages lebender Schriftsteller* (Augsb. 1741); Römer, *Kirchl. Gesch. von Würtemberg* (1848), p. 387-395, 421-423; Koch, *Gesch. des deutschen Kirchenliedes*, v, 50 sq.; Winer, *Handbuch der theol. Lit.* i, 293, 534, 760. (B. P.)

Weiss, Charles, a Protestant theologian, was born at Strasburg, Dec. 10, 1812. On publishing his *Richard de Saint-Victor et la Théologie Mystique*, he was appointed professor of history in the Lycée Bonaparte; and both his *L'Espagne Depuis le Règne de Philippe II*, etc. (Paris, 1844, 2 vols.), and his *Histoire des Réfugiés Protestants de Paris* (1853, 2 vols.) were crowned by the Academy. While preparing a second edition of the last work, Weiss became insane (1864), and spent the rest of his life in an asylum at Vanves, near Paris, where he died in 1881. See Lichtenberger, *Encyclop. des Sciences Religieuses*, s. v. (B. P.)

Weiss (Lat. Weitzius), **George Michael**, a (Dutch) Reformed minister, was a native of the Palatinate of the Rhine, but was licensed and ordained to the Gospel ministry at Heidelberg in 1725. With about four hundred German emigrants, he settled in Pennsylvania in 1726-27, accompanying them by request of his classis as their spiritual teacher. They were aided on their way by the Classis of Amsterdam. In 1731 the colony numbered fifteen thousand souls, who sought here a refuge from oppression. Mr. Weiss settled and founded a Church at Skippach, about twenty-four miles west of Philadelphia. In 1728 he asked help for these scattered sheep in the wilderness from his classis of the Palatinate. But these persecuted "churches under the cross" could only refer them to the Synod of Holland. In 1729-30 he visited Holland with an elder, J. Reif, to solicit money, which was given to a large amount for that day. But Reif stole most of it, only one hundred and thirty-five pounds being recovered. The Classis of Amsterdam sent over ministers and money to sustain these German churches, and thus began that system of missionary labor and supervision out of which the German Reformed Church has grown up, and which formed a strong and early tie between her and the Reformed Church of Holland. When Weiss returned to America in 1731, he settled among the Germans in New York state, in Schoharie and Dutchess and Greene counties, at Catskill (now Leeds), Coxsackie, etc. Indian depredations obliged him about fourteen years afterwards to return to Pennsylvania. He was a member of the first German ecclesiastical assembly, held in Philadelphia in 1746, and was minister of three German congregations west of Philadelphia about fourteen years. He died at the age of sixty-five. He is represented to have been a fine scholar, speaking Latin as well as he did his native German. His ministry was entirely a pioneer work, prosecuted under great difficulties and with manifest blessings attendant upon it. See Corwin, *Manual of the Ref. Church in America*, p. 262, 263. (W. J. R. T.)

Weiss, Michael, a German divine, contemporary with Luther, was born at Neisse, in Silesia. When the Reformation began, the Bohemian Brethren were among the first to hail it; as early as 1522 they sent messengers to Luther to wish him success and confer with him on questions of Church discipline. One of these was Michael Weiss, who afterwards became pastor of the German branch of the Bohemian Brethren at Landskron and Fulneck, in Bohemia, and for their benefit translated into German the finest of the Bohemian hymns, adding some of his own. Weiss died in 1540. Of his own hymns we mention: *Christus ist erstanden* (Eng. transl. in *Chorale Book for England*, No. 58: "Christ the Lord is risen again"):—*Lob sei dem allerhöchsten Gott* (Eng. transl. in *Moravian Hymn-book*, No. 24: "To God we render thanks and praise"). (B. P.)

Weiss, Paul, a Lutheran theologian of Germany, was born in 1543 at Strelen, in Silesia. In 1568 he was appointed professor of Greek at the Königsberg University, and in 1581 professor of theology there. In 1589 he was appointed court preacher, and died Jan. 5, 1612. He wrote, *Disputationes de Peccato Originali ex Jerem. xvii*, 9:—*De Ecclesia ejusque Signis*, etc. See Witte, *Diarium Biographicum;* Arnold, *Historie der königsbergischen Universität;* Jöcher, *Allgemeines Gelehrten-Lexikon*, s. v. (B. P.)

Weisse, Christian Hermann, a Protestant theologian and philosopher of Germany, was born Aug. 10, 1801, at Leipsic. At first he studied law, but betook himself more and more to the study of Hegelian philosophy, and commenced lecturing in his native place in 1823. In 1828 he was appointed professor of philosophy, but in 1837 he retired to spend his time entirely in literary pursuits. Having thus spent a few years, he again commenced lecturing, and in 1845 he was made professor in ordinary of philosophy, lecturing at the same time as *Privatdocent* on theology. He died Sept. 19, 1866, having been honored with the doctorate of divinity in 1838 by the Jena University. At first a follower of Hegel, he soon emancipated himself from that system, as may be seen from his *Ueber den Begriff, die Behandlung und die Quellen der Mythologie* (Leipsic, 1827). Prominent among his works are:—*Die Idee Gottes* (Dresden, 1833):—*Die philosophische Geheimlehre von der Unsterblichkeit* (ibid. 1834):—*Grundzüge der Metaphysik* (Hamburg, 1834):—*Die evangel. Geschichte kritisch und philosophisch bearbeitet* (Leipsic, 1838, 2 vols.):—*Ueber die Zukunft der evang. Kirche* (ibid. 1849):—*Philosophische Dogmatik* (1855–62, 3 vols.):—*Christologie Luthers* (ibid. 1855):—*Die Evangelienfrage in ihrem gegenwärtigen Studium* (ibid. 1856). After his death were published, *Beiträge zur Kritik der paulin. Briefe* (ibid. 1867):—*Psychologie und Unsterblichkeitslehre* (1869). See Seydel, *Chr. H. Weisse* (Leipsic, 1866); *Theolog. Universal-Lexikon*, s. v.; Zuchold, *Bibl. Theol.* ii, 1431; Winer, *Handbuch der theol. Lit.* i, 412, 472. (B. P.)

Weissel, Georg, a Lutheran theologian of Germany, was born in 1590 at Domnau, in Prussia. He was rector at Friedland for three years, and in 1623 became minister of the newly erected Rosengarten Church at Königsberg. He is said to have quickened the poetic powers of others, and especially of Simon Dach, his junior contemporary. He died Aug. 1, 1635. Weissel is the author of some very fine hymns, which are still used in the German Evangelical Church, e. g. *Macht hoch die Thür, das Thor macht weit* (Eng. transl. in *Lyra Germ.* i, 10: "Lift up your heads, ye mighty gates"). See Koch, *Gesch. d. deutschen Kirchenliedes*, iii, 180 sq. (B. P.)

Weissenbach, Joseph Anton, a Roman Catholic divine of Germany, was born Oct. 15, 1734, at Bremgarten, and died April 11, 1801, at Luzerne. He wrote, *Kritisches Verzeichniss der besten Schriften, welche in verschiedenen Sprachen zum Beweis und zur Vertheidigung der Religion herausgekommen* (Basle, 1784):—*De Eloquentia Patrum Libb. XIII* (Augsburg, 1775, 9 vols.). See Winer, *Handbuch der theol. Lit.* i, 380, 882. (B. P.)

Weissenborn, Friedrich Ludwig, a German theologian, was born April 16, 1816, at Parkentin, in Mecklenburg-Schwerin. He occupied the philosophical chair at Halle, and afterwards at Marburg, where he died, June 4, 1874. He published, *Vorlesungen über Schleiermachers Dialektik und Dogmatik* (Leipsic, 1847, 2 pts.):—*Vorlesungen über Pantheismus und Theismus* (Marburg, 1859). (B. P.)

Weissenborn, Jesaias Friedrich, a Lutheran theologian of Germany, was born Nov. 15, 1673, at Smalcald. He studied at Erfurt, in 1700 was appointed pastor of St. Michael's there, was made superintendent in 1722, professor of theology in 1724, and died July 3, 1750. He wrote, *Dissertt. de εὐδαιμονίᾳ:—De Sabbathi Obligatione Naturali:—Jesus Pontificiorum cum Jesu Lutheranorum Collatus:—Detrimentum Fidei et Pietatis e Dogmate Reformatorum de Absoluto Decreto Enatum:—De Negatione Resurrectionis Christi Detestanda e Pauli Verbis* 1 *Cor. xv*, 17, 18:—*De Divinitate Spiritus S. contra Pneumatomachos*, etc. See Moser, *Lexikon jetztlebender Gottesgelehrten;* Neubauer, *Nachricht von jetztlebenden Gottesgelehrten;* Jöcher, *Allgemeines Gelehrten-Lexikon*, s. v. (B. P.)

Weissenborn, Johann, a Lutheran theologian of Germany, was born at Siglitz, in Thuringia, Nov. 21, 1644. He studied at Jena, was appointed rector of the Evangelical Lutheran school at Smalcald in 1672, and in 1683 went to Hildesheim as director of the gymnasium there. In 1691 he received a call as pastor to Erfurt, was made doctor of divinity in 1692, and in 1700 followed a call as professor of theology and superintendent to Jena, where he died, April 20 of the same year. He is the author of *Schmalkaldisches kernhaftes Gebetbuch nebst allerhand geistreichen Lebensregeln* (1706; new ed. 1716). See Pipping, *Memor. Theol. Decas IX* (1707); Zeumeri *Vitæ Prof. Theol. Jenensium*, p. 252; Koch, *Gesch. d. deutschen Kirchenliedes*, v, 418 sq. (B. P.)

Weissensee, Philipp Heinrich, a Lutheran theologian of Germany, was born Feb. 6, 1673, at Vickberg, in Würtemberg. He studied at Tübingen, was appointed in 1703 teacher at the monastery in Maulbronn, and in 1708 he was called for the same position to Blaubeuren. In 1722 he received the prelacy in the same school, and in 1727 that of Hirschau. In 1740 he was appointed provost and general superintendent at Denkendorf, and died Jan. 6, 1767, as senior of the evangelical church of Würtemberg. He is the author of some fine hymns which are still in use in Germany, and published in 1718 an edition of Thomas à Kempis's book, *The Imitation of Christ*, in German rhymes. See Burk, *Der Christenbote*, 1847, No. 3, p. 25–28; No. 11, p. 130 sq.; No. 16, p. 187; No. 25, p. 297; Pregizers, *Gottgeh. Poesie* (Tüb. 1727), p. 280–285; Koch, *Gesch. d. deutschen Kirchenliedes*, v, 79 sq. (B. P.)

Weissmann, Ehrenreich, a Lutheran theologian of Germany, was born July 15, 1641, at Weyerburg, in Lower Austria. Religious intolerance obliged him to leave his country. He went to Würtemberg and studied at Tübingen. In 1662 he was appointed pastor at Hirschau; in 1680 special superintendent and pastor at Waiblingen; in 1693 he was called to Stuttgart; was made general superintendent and abbot at Maulbronn in 1711; and died Feb. 23, 1717. He wrote *Rhetorica Sacra*, besides ten vols. on homiletical subjects. See Winer, *Handbuch der theol. Lit.* ii, 58; Jöcher, *Allgemeines Gelehrten-Lexikon*, s. v. (B. P.)

Weisz, George, a pioneer of the German Reformed Church in Ohio. He was born in Northumberland County, Pa., June 21, 1793. He served as a volunteer in the War of 1812, and was appointed quartermaster. He began his theological studies with Rev. Isaac Gerhart, and finished with Rev. Dr. Samuel Helfenstein in Philadelphia. In 1816 he was appointed by the Synod of the

German Reformed Church as an exploring missionary to Ohio. In 1817 he settled permanently in Lancaster, O., extending his missionary labors over four counties. He laid the foundation of numerous flourishing churches, being in labors abundant to the end of his life. He died in peace, March 10, 1859. He has a son in the ministry.

Weitenauer, Ignatz, a Roman Catholic theologian of Germany who lived in the last century, is the author of, *Trifolium Hebraicum, Chaldaicum, Syriacum, per quod Possis intra Aliquot Horas cum Hierolexico Auctoris Explicare Canonem Biblicum*, etc. (Augsburg, 1759):—*Job, Psalmi, Prov. Salomon. et Siracid., ex Hebraicis Græcisque Fontibus ad Mentem Vulgatæ et Lat. Sermonis Dilucide Explicans* (ibid. 1757):—*Hexaglotton, seu Modus Addiscendi intra Breviss. Tempus Linguam Gall., Ital., Hisp., Græc., Hebraicam et Chaldaicam*, etc. (Frankfort, 1756):—*Novæ Grammaticæ Biblicæ Methodus* (Ulm, 1756):—*Libri Machabæorum cum Commentario Literali, quibus Addita est Diss. de Doctrina Morum e Sacra Scriptura* (ibid. 1773):—*Lexicon Biblicum*, etc. (Augsburg, 1758; Venice, 1860). He also translated into German the Old Testament, to which he added annotations. See Fürst, *Bibl. Jud.* iii, 503; Steinschneider, *Bibliog. Handbuch*, s. v. (B. P.)

Wejones were fortune-tellers of the barbarous Prussians, who foretold future events from the force of the wind and the direction of the clouds.

Weland, Jakob Christoph, a Protestant theologian of Germany, was born July 18, 1752, at Bremen, and died March 10, 1813, as abbot, general superintendent, and first pastor at Holzminden. He wrote, *Ueber Wunder nach den Bedürfnissen unserer Zeit* (Göttingen, 1789):—*Predigten über die Evangelien* (Brunswick, 1813):—*Einleitung in die Bibel, nach den Bedürfnissen unserer Zeit* (Hanover, 1812). See Winer, *Handbuch der theol. Lit.* i, 334, 393; ii, 133, 244, 251, 302, 363. (B. P.)

Welapotren (or **Velapotren**), in Hindû mythology, is that giant who came into existence when Siva, in despair, because of his wife's death, pulled a hair from his head. The giant decapitated the father of this lovely wife, Shakti, as he had been the cause of her death.

Weleda, in German mythology, was one of the most famous fortune-tellers in the 1st century of the Christian æra. A maiden born of princely parents, she is said to have wielded a mighty political influence over her people. Having been brought to Rome as a prisoner, she was carried about in triumph, and received great distinction at the hands of the emperor Vespasian. After her death the Germans honored her as a goddess.

Weles, in Slavonic mythology, was the first of the deities after Perun, the supreme god of the Poles. He was also worshipped in Russia as a god of protection, especially of horses and cattle.

Well, Ecclesiastical. The most ancient examples of Christian baptismal wells are to be found in the Catacombs. Wells occur in crypts, some of which were regarded as possessing waters of miraculous powers, as at Pierrefonds; but very possibly they were made in imitation of the baptismal wells of the Catacombs. There was usually a well or fountain in the centre of a cloister garth. There is one highly enriched in the south nave aisle of Strasburg. Probably these wells, as in cathedrals, served to drain water and supply the baptismal font, as in St. Patrick's, Dublin, and at York, Carlisle, Glasgow, and Winchester. In many of the small Cornish oratories or baptisteries there is a well. St. Keyne's Well, in Cornwall, was an object of frequent visits, as was St. Winifred's, in North Wales, which was built in 1495, and contains a star-shaped basin, formerly surrounded with stone screens and contained within a vaulted ambulatory under an upper chapel. Wells are found also in many of the ancient Cornish churches of the 5th and 7th centuries, at Marden, Kirk Newton, and

Ancient Baptismal Well. (From the Catacomb of St. Domitilla, Rome.)

Durham. Joubert's Well at Poitiers is a good mediæval specimen. At Ratisbon, in the south wing of the transept, there is a well with figures of the Saviour and the woman of Samaria. There is also an ancient well in the cloister of Arles. St. Aldhelm's Well at Shepton Mallet, St. Chad's at Lichfield, St. Julien's at Wellow, Somerset, St. Thomas's at Canterbury, and numerous others in Wales are still regarded as possessing medicinal virtues. Throughout all Christendom such wells exist, and rules concerning them have been made from time to time by canonical decrees, because of abuses which arose in past ages. They were forbidden to be worshipped without the bishop's authority in 960, 1018, and 1102. In 950 they were made sanctuaries. Round them were frithgeards, for sanctuary, which were reputed holy ground. They were determined as holy by the diocesan, by canons passed in 960 and 1102, and abuses were condemned by the Synod of Winchester in 1308. See Lee, *Gloss. of Liturg. and Eccles. Terms*, s. v.; Walcott, *Sacred Archæol.* s. v.

Well-being. See Happiness.

Weller, Hieronymus, a Lutheran theologian of Germany, was born Sept. 5, 1499, at Freyburg. He studied at Wittenberg, where he became intimately acquainted with Luther. In 1535 he took the degree of doctor of divinity, and in 1539 was appointed superintendent at Freyburg, where he died, March 20, 1572. He wrote commentaries on the books of Samuel, Kings, Job; on the epistles to the Ephesians, Philippians, Thessalonians; of Peter and the first of John. He also wrote, *Explicationes in Epistolas et Evangelia Dominicarum et Festorum*:—*De Passione Domini Nostri Jesu Christi*:—besides homiletical, ascetical, and exegetical works in German. See Freher, *Theatrum Eruditorum; Acta Eruditorum Latina*; Jöcher, *Allgemeines Gelehrten-Lexikon*, s. v.; Winer, *Handb. der theol. Lit.* ii, 58. (B. P.)

Weller, Jakob, a Protestant divine of Germany, was born Dec. 5, 1602, at Neukirchen. In 1635 he was appointed professor of Oriental languages at Wittenberg; in 1640 superintendent at Brunswick; and in 1646 first court preacher and church councillor at Dresden, where he died, July 6, 1664. He wrote, *Adnotationes in Epist. Pauli ad Romanos . . . Collectæ a J. Schindlero* (Brunswick, 1654):—לקט הקציר, *Spicilegium Quæstionum Ebræo-Syrarum* (Wittenberg, 1673):—*De Linguæ Hebraicæ Ambiguitate contra Huntleum* (ibid. 1631):—*Disputatio an Puncta Hebr. Literis Coæva?* (ibid.). See Winer, *Handbuch der theol. Lit.* i, 165, 255; Fürst, *Bibl. Jud.* iii, 504; Steinschneider, *Bibliog. Handbuch*, s. v. (B. P.)

Wellesley. See Wesley.

Wellesley, Gerald Valerian, an Anglican prelate, was born in 1809. He graduated from Trinity College, Cambridge, in 1830; held the rectory of Strathfieldsaye, Hants, from 1836 till 1855; became domestic chaplain to the queen in 1849; dean of Windsor in 1854, and died Sept. 18, 1882.

Wellesley, Henry, D.D., an English clergyman, a natural son of Richard Colley Wellesley (marquis Wellesley) and Mlle. H. G. Roland, was born in 1792; graduated at Christ Church, Oxford, in 1816; became rector of Woodmancote, Hurst Monceaux, in Sussex; was appointed principal of New Inn Hall, Oxford, in 1842; became preacher to the University of Oxford; curator of the Bodleian Library, University Galleries, and Taylor Institution; and died Jan. 11, 1866. He was the author of, *Anthologia Polyglotta; or, A Selection of Versions in Various Languages, chiefly from the Greek Anthology* (1849):—and *Stray Notes on Shakespeare* (1865). See Allibone, *Dict. of Brit. and Amer. Authors*, s. v.

Welliamen (or **Velliamen**), in Hindû mythology, was one of the two wives of Kartiavertshunen: the other's name is Devanei, who was the daughter of Indra. Statues of both are erected in the temple of this god.

Well-maids, in Norse mythology, were daughters of Aeger and Ran. They swim upon the stormy sea around their mother, and appear with white veils to assist the unfortunate out of the wild waves, and lay the drowned down in the lap of their mother. Their names are Himingläffe, Dufa, Blödughadda, Heffring, Udur, Raun, Bylgia, Dröbna, and Kolga.

Wells of Pity, "the five wounds of Christ, distilling his sacred blood—for grace, from the right foot; for ghostly comfort, from the left foot; for wisdom, from the right hand; for mercy, from the left hand; and from the heart, for everlasting life—each represented by a drop of blood in rich ruby glass, issuing from a gash which bears a golden crown, as in a pane of Perpendicular glass at Sidmouth."

Wells, Edward Livingston, D.D., a Protestant Episcopal clergyman, began his regular ministry in 1860, as pastor of the Church of Our Saviour, Plainville, Conn.; the following year became rector of Calvary Church, Louisville, Ky.; in 1865 went to Pittsfield, Mass., as rector of St. Stephen's Church, and remained there until 1871, when he became rector of Trinity Church, Southport, Conn., and here he continued to reside until 1879, part of the time without charge, and afterwards as minister of St. John's Church, New Milford, where he died, Aug. 7, 1880, aged forty-six years. See Whittaker, *Almanac and Directory*, 1881, p. 175.

Wells, Eleazer Mather Porter, D.D., a Protestant Episcopal clergyman, was born in 1793, being a descendant of Thomas Wells, who had come to Salem with Winthrop and Wilson in 1629. He entered the ministry in 1823, and preached at Plymouth, Calais, and Bangor, Me. In 1826 he was ordained a deacon by bishop Brownell, of Connecticut, and was professionally engaged for brief periods at more than a dozen places in New England. His special vocation, however, was found when he was placed in charge of the House of Reformation for Juvenile Offenders at Boston, and also became superintendent of St. Stephen's House. He was a most philanthropic city missionary, and up to the time of his death, which occurred in Boston, Dec. 1, 1878, he was "in labors more abundant." (W. P. S.)

Wells, Henry, a distinguished philanthropist, was born in New Hampshire in 1805. He was brought by his parents when a child to Central New York. Without the advantages of an early education, but with a pushing spirit within him, he began his career as an expressman, his first route being from Albany to Buffalo, at which time he carried all the matter in a carpet-bag himself, and gave personal attention to its delivery. His business gradually prospered, and he increased it as circumstances required. Such was its wonderful progress that he organized a company, under the title of "The American Express Company," which subsequently bore the name of "Wells, Fargo & Co." Their business increased to such an extent that it embraced the whole country from the Atlantic to the Pacific, and from Canada to Mexico and across the ocean. The reward of his enterprise and prudence was a princely fortune. With its avails he purchased a beautiful property on the banks of the Cayuga Lake, at Aurora, N. Y., and there erected a palatial residence, which he filled with all the comforts and luxuries of art. In the retirement of his lovely rural home, he conceived the idea of erecting and furnishing at his own expense a seminary or college for the higher education of young women. By the side of his own mansion he laid off a park embracing woodland, hill, and plain, and in the middle of it he erected a splendid brick edifice, with all the appointments that skill, taste, and money could provide for the carrying-out of the great object he had in view. This magnificent edifice, with the entire property, was conveyed by deed as a free gift to a board of trustees, who gave it the name of "Wells College." A board of instruction was soon organized, and the college sprang rapidly into high repute. Its halls were soon filled, and students flocked to it from all parts, many of them the daughters of gentlemen with whom Mr. Wells had been associated in business. Its library and cabinets were made rich by contributions of his friends. The Hon. E. B. Morgan, of Aurora, added the munificent gift of $100,000 to the endowment of the institution, and is about to erect another important building for the college. On Nov. 9, 1878, Mr. Wells sailed for Glasgow, and reached there on the 19th. He was too far enfeebled to proceed farther, and after lingering for a few weeks, his active, eventful, and useful life closed, Dec. 10, 1878. (W. P. S.)

Wells, Horatio T., LL.D., a Protestant Episcopal clergyman, was head master of the English department in Burlington College, N. J., in 1859, and the following year acting rector of the college; in 1862 was principal of a boys' school in Andalusia, Pa., which institution, in 1866, became known as Andalusia College. Mr. Wells was elected president and professor of English literature and commercial law, and remained at the head of the college until his death, in December, 1871. See *Prot. Episc. Almanac*, 1873, p. 133.

Wells, William, D.D., an English Unitarian minister, who afterwards emigrated to America, was born at Biggleswade, Bedfordshire, in 1744. He was educated at the Academy of Daventry; became minister at Bromsgrove, Worcestershire, in 1770; was a friend to the Americans during the Revolution; introduced inoculation for small-pox among his poor neighbors, attending some thirteen hundred cases; removed to America, arriving in Boston with his family, June 12, 1793; settled on a farm at Brattleborough, Vt., in 1794, residing there and preaching to the Society in the town until his death, which occurred Dec. 27, 1827. See Sprague, *Annals of the Amer. Pulpit*, viii, 254 sq.

Wellwood. See Moncreiff.

Welsh Calvinistic Methodists, a considerable body of Methodists, chiefly in Wales, which dates its origin from 1735, sprang from the labors of Mr. Howel Harris, of Trevecca, in Brecknockshire. This young man had gone to Oxford to prepare for the ministry of the Church of England; but, becoming disgusted with the immorality and gross carelessness of that place, he returned home and began to visit from house to house, warning people to flee from the wrath to come. He soon began to preach in public. Crowds flocked to hear him, and many were converted under his preaching. He appointed meetings for religious conversation in several places; hence arose those private societies which form a prominent part of the arrangements of this body. His labors were crowned with extraordinary success, notwithstanding the opposition of the regular clergy and the magistrates; and in 1739, after only four years of effort, he had established as many as three hundred societies in the south of Wales. Mr. Harris was greatly aided in his labors by the Rev. Daniel Rowland, of Llangeitho, Cardiganshire, who attracted large crowds by his eloquence. Several pious ministers of the Establishment seceded and joined the Methodists; a considerable band of itinerant missionaries was formed; a most precious revival spread among the different denominations; and the new sect grew so popular that in seven years from its commencement no fewer than ten ministers of the Church of England had joined it. The first chapel built by the Welsh Calvinistic Methodists was erected at Builth, Brecknockshire, in 1747. In the following year two others were built in Carmarthenshire. The Church made rapid progress in the south of Wales, but was greatly hindered in the north. It was about this time that the Rev. Thomas Charles began his labors. He lived at Bala, Merionethshire, and it is to his exertions and influence that these societies are chiefly indebted for their prosperity. He was converted under the preaching of Mr. Rowland, and, after the usual preparation, entered the ministry of the Church of England. But in 1784 he decided to leave the Established Church and join the Methodists, where he could enjoy greater freedom in evangelical labors. He found the principality in a deplorable condition on account of the ignorance and degradation of the people. A Bible could scarcely be found in any of the cottages of the peasantry, and in some parishes very few were able to read it. He therefore decided to educate the people in the rudiments of learning and religion. He established for this purpose what he called circulating schools, that is, schools which might be removed from one place to another at the end of a definite period, say nine or twelve months. He induced "a few friends to set a subscription on foot to pay the wages of a teacher, who was to be moved circuitously from one place to another, to instruct the poor in reading, and in the first principles of Christianity by catechising them." This work was begun in 1785 with only one teacher. Others were added as the funds increased, until they numbered twenty. At first he instructed the teachers himself, and these in turn instructed others. In this manner many thousands were instructed, and the good seed thus sown produced abundant fruit, religious awakenings occurring in many places where the teachers had labored. In 1799 a religious periodical was started by Mr. Charles, entitled *The Spiritual Treasury*, the design of which was to supply the people thus instructed with religious reading. Hitherto, Bibles in the vernacular had been very scarce, and the want was met by the formation of the British and Foreign Bible Society in 1804. By this organization, Welsh Bibles and Testaments were scattered throughout the principality, and eagerly received.

In the organization of the Welsh Calvinistic Methodist Society Mr. Charles took an active and prominent part. At an association held at Bala in 1790, he drew up a set of Rules for Conducting the Quarterly Meetings of the North Wales Association, consisting of the preachers and leaders; and these Rules form the basis of the present system of Church government of the whole society. In 1801 *Rules of Discipline* were first published, laying down the order and form of Church government and discipline. To these were added, in 1811, several regulations designed to render the organization, in its membership and ministry, permanently independent of the Established Church.

In 1823 they adopted and published a *Confession of Faith*, which was unanimously agreed upon at the associations of Aberystwith and Bala. The doctrines thus avowed are decidedly Calvinistic, and accord with the Thirty-nine Articles and the Westminster Confession in all essential points of doctrine and practice. Their Church government is neither Episcopal, on the one hand, nor Congregational, on the other, but approaches more nearly the Presbyterian form. The private societies are subordinate to the monthly meetings, and these again to the quarterly associations, at which the general business of the body is transacted. Their preachers itinerate from place to place, and, being men of limited education, they are generally dependent on some secular employment for their support. Of late years they have turned their attention towards the importance of an educated ministry. Accordingly, in 1837, a college for the purpose of training theological students was established at Bala, and in 1842 another at Trevecca.

The ministers of the Connection are selected by the private societies, and reported to the monthly meetings, which examine them as to their qualifications, and permit them to begin on trial. After they have preached for five years or more on trial, and are found properly qualified, they are ordained to administer the sacraments, and the ordination takes place at the quarterly associations. The preachers are expected each to itinerate in a particular county; but generally once in a year they undertake a missionary tour to different parts of Wales, when they preach twice every day, each time in a different chapel. Their remuneration is derived from the monthly pence contributed by the members of each congregation; out of which a small sum is given to them after every sermon; but some have a stated stipend.

The Welsh Calvinistic Methodists have about 1000 chapels and about 80,000 communicants, 60,000 of whom are in Wales and 4000 in America, the rest principally in England.

In 1840 they formed an association for sending missionaries to the heathen, and towards the end of the same year a mission was commenced among one of the hill tribes in the northeast part of Bengal. They have also a mission-station in Brittany, France, the language of that country being a sister dialect of the Welsh; and they have, besides, a mission to the Jews. The operations of the home mission of this denomination are carried on among the English population inhabiting the borders between England and Wales. There are several societies in England belonging to the Connection—for example, in London, Liverpool, Manchester, Bristol, Chester, Shrewsbury, etc.—whose worship, public and private, is performed in the Welsh language. There is also a small congregation among the Welsh miners of Lanarkshire, Scotland, who have preaching in their own language. In some parts of Wales, and on the borders of England where the English language is most prevalent, worship is conducted in that tongue.

Welsh Version. The first edition of the New Test. was printed in London in 1567, in consequence of a law enacted by Parliament in 1562. The translation was made by William Salesbury, assisted by a certain Huet, a chanter of St. David's, and Dr. Richard Davies, bishop of the same place. In 1588 the entire Bible was given to the Welsh people, the Old Test. being translated by Dr. W. Morgan, afterwards bishop of St. Asaph, with the aid of several eminent scholars, who also revised Salesbury's version of the New Test. A new and revised edition was prepared by Dr. R. Parry, successor to the see of St. Asaph, and published in 1620. This edition was held in such high estimation that it has been used as the text of all succeeding editions. Being in folio, a small and portable edition was published in 1630, which, besides the Old and New Tests., contained the Apocrypha, the Book of Common Prayer, and a metrical version of the Psalms; the latter, which is still used in the Welsh churches, was prepared by Prŷss, archdeacon of Merioneth. Of the editions of the whole Bible which have appeared from time to time we mention the following:

1654—sometimes called Cromwell's Bible.
1678—with corrections by the Rev. St. Hughes.
1690—published by the Rev. D. Jones.
1690—printed at Oxford for the use of churches, in Roman characters, sometimes called Bishop Lloyd's Bible.
1718—printed at London, often called Moses Williams's Bible.

1727—printed at London; less valuable.
1746—printed at Cambridge; the third edition, published by the Society for Promoting Christian Knowledge, and containing the same as published in the first, in 1718.
1752—reprint of that of 1746.
1769—by the same society.
1770—with notes by the Rev. P. Williams, and reprinted very often.
1789—printed for the use of churches by the same society.
1790—with Mr. John Canne's references.
1799—printed by the Society for Promoting Christian Knowledge.

These editions, with the exception of ten thousand copies of the New Test. printed in the year 1800 at Shrewsbury, were all that appeared before the formation of the British and Foreign Bible Society. The great scarcity of the vernacular Scriptures prevailing in Wales was the cause of finally bringing about the formation of the British and Foreign Bible Society. The first edition of the Scriptures issued by this society was the Welsh Bible, the text adopted being that of 1752. This edition left the press in 1806. Including this, their first edition, the number of copies issued at successive intervals by the British and Foreign Bible Society, from the year 1806 up to March 31, 1879, may be briefly stated as follows:

Bibles	813,466
Testaments	1,038,507
Diglots, Welsh and English	86,686
Total	1,938,659

Besides the British and Foreign Bible Society, the Society for Promoting Christian Knowledge and the American Bible Society have published the Scriptures in Welsh. See *Bible of Every Land*, p. 153 sq. (B. P.)

Welte, BENEDICT VON, a Roman Catholic theologian of Germany, was born in 1805 at Ratzewied, and acted as professor of Old-Test. exegesis at Tübingen from 1838 to 1857. He died May 27, 1885, at Rottenburg, senior of the chapter, and doctor of theology. He published, *Das Buch Job übersetzt und erklärt* (Freiburg, 1849):—*Nachmosaisches im Pentateuch beleuchtet* (Carlsruhe, 1840):—*Historisch-kritische Einleitung in die Schriften Alten Testaments* (eod.); besides he was co-editor of the Freiburg *Kirchenlexikon*, which he published together with Wetzer (q. v.). (B. P.)

Welton, RICHARD, D.D., a Protestant Episcopal clergyman, had been deprived of the rectorship of St. Mary's, Whitechapel, London, on account of his attachment to the non-jurors, and was consecrated in 1722 by Rev. Ralph Taylor. He arrived in America probably in 1723, was invited to take charge of Christ Church, Philadelphia, July 27, 1724, and entered immediately upon his duties. His anomalous relation to the Church as a non-juring bishop occasioned disquietude among the Episcopalians when it became known. Soon after an order came from England to governor Keith of Pennsylvania, enclosing a king's writ addressed to Welton, commanding him to return to England. Accordingly, in January, 1726, after a brief but acceptable ministry, he embarked for Lisbon, where he died shortly after his arrival. See Sprague, *Annals of the Amer. Pulpit*, v, 33.

Weltz, JUSTINIAN ERNST VON, a Hungarian nobleman of the 17th century. He is known on account of his connection with the mystics Breckling, Gichtel, and others. At Ratisbon he met with Gichtel, and both united in forming a fraternity of the pious ("Jesus-Gesellschaft") for the purpose of renewing the inner life of the Church. The members received their names from the society to which they belonged; thus, Weltz received Breckling in Holland under the name of "Der Brechende." Being very rich, Weltz gave $30,000 towards the objects of the fraternity. This was about 1660. The society also had in view a union between the Lutherans and the Calvinists. In 1664 Weltz and Gichtel presented to the *Corpus Evangelicorum* a plan of their tendencies, which Weltz had approved by the most famous theologians. He was also the first who, in two works, reminded the Church of the holy duty of missionary work; but the orthodox superintendent Ursinus, at Ratisbon, dismissed him mockingly. In the same year (1664) Weltz went to Surinam to preach the Gospel there, which he did until his death. This was the beginning of evangelical missions. See Jöcher, *Allgemeines Gelehrten-Lexikon*, s. v.; Plitt, *Gesch. der lutherischen Mission* (Erlangen, 1871), p. 22 sq.; *Theolog. Universal-Lexikon*, s. v. (B. P.)

Wen is the inaccurate rendering in the A.V. of יַבָּל, *yabbâl* (on Lev. xxii, 22), which means *flowing* with a running sore; spoken of a diseased flock.

Wenceslaus (**Wenzel**, or **Venzeslav**), *St.*, a prince of Bohemia, son of Vratislav and Drahomira, was born about the beginning of the 10th century. His education was intrusted to his grandmother Ludmila, a devoted Christian; and he thus received a training which led him to become a pious Christian, and follow the course of a clergyman more than that of a prince. His brother Boleslaus (or Boleslav) was a fierce pagan; and, in conjunction with his mother, also a pagan, secured a visit from him, and slew him at the foot of the altar while engaged in prayer, Sept. 28, 935. Wenceslaus has been the subject of many works of art. See Jameson, *Legends of the Monastic Orders*, p. 175 sq.; Neander, *Hist. of the Church*, iii, 322.

Wendelin (or **Wandelin**), a saint of the 7th century whose day is October 20, and who is said to have been of Scottish family. He established himself as a hermit in a forest in the neighborhood of Treves, and afterwards as a herdsman in the late principality of Lichtenberg. His fidelity in this service led the monks of Tholey on the Saar to elect him their prior. The circumstances of his life and career are to be found recorded solely in the *Acta SS. Boll.* Juli vi, 171, and similar legendary depositories. Comp. Vogt, *Rhein. Gesch. u. Sagen*, i, 283 sq.; Rettberg, *Kirchengesch. Deutschlands*, i, 480; Berlepsch, *Die Alpen in Natur u. Lebensbildern* (Leips. 1861), p. 386 sq.; Herzog, *Real-Encyklop.* s. v.

Wendelin, Marcus Friedrich, a theologian of the Reformed scholastic school in the 17th century, was born near Heidelberg in 1584, and after graduation, presumably at the university of that town, became tutor of the princes of Anhalt-Dessau, and in 1611 rector of the gymnasium of Zerbst. He retained the latter position during a period of forty-one years, and died there Aug. 7, 1652. He composed a number of text-books which bear witness to the breadth of his culture; but his most important works were of a theological character. Among them were, *Compend. Christianæ Theologiæ* (Hanau, 1634):—*Christianæ Theologiæ Systema Majus* (posthumously published, Frankf. 1656 and 1677):—*Exercitationes Theol. contr. Jo. Gerhard. et Danhauer*:—and *Collatio Doctr. Reformatorum et Lutheranorum* (Cassel, 1660). He avoided abstruse discussions, assumed only simple and evident premises, and made only a formal use of dialectics. His method was to discuss the contents of the dogma itself instead of an extraneous addition of Aristotelian tenets to the doctrine. The arrangement of his material and the determination of the problems presented to his mind give evidence of great acuteness. His *Christ. Theol. Systema* was translated into Dutch and Hungarian. See Wendelin's *Works*; Becmann, *Anhaltische Historie*; Jöcher, *Allgemeines Gelehrten-Lexikon*; Herzog, *Real-Encyklop.* s. v.

Wendish Version. See SLAVONIC VERSIONS.

Wends (from *wend*, to "wander"), a Slavic people who as early as the 6th century occupied the north and east of Germany, from the Elbe along the coast of the Baltic to the Vistula, and as far south as Bohemia. They were divided into several tribes, which were successively subdued by the Germans, and either exterminated or Germanized. Charlemagne drove them back towards the Vistula, and by the close of the 13th century his successors in Germany had almost completed the work of extirpation. In the 16th century remnants of this Slavic population were still scattered over the whole region between Berlin and Frankfort-on-the-Oder; and there was a remnant of Wends in Hanover, where they kept up their language until the middle of the 18th century. They are now found in portions of Brandenburg, Silesia, and the kingdom of Saxony, and principally on the banks of the Spree. At present the number of Wends, or those speaking the Wendish language, exclusive of that portion of this people who have been Germanized, is placed at 140,000, of whom 83,000 are in Prussia and 52,000 in Saxony. It is worthy of remark that the Sloventzi of Austria, a Slavic people numbering 1,260,000, are called *Vinds*, and their language the Vindish. To these the name Southern Wends is frequently applied. Most of the Wends are Protestants, though a large portion of those living in Saxony are Catholics. Christianity was introduced among them about the middle of the 11th century by their zealous king Gottschalk, founder of the Wendish kingdom. But they lapsed again into paganism, and were subsequently restored to Christianity by missionaries from the south. The language of the Wends is similar to the other branches of the northwestern stem of the Slavic languages, the Polish and the Bohemian. It has several dialects—the Lower Lusatian, and the Upper Lusatian, which is subdivided into the Evangelical, near Bautzen; the Catholic, near Kamenz and in the northwest; and the Northeastern. The extent of the entire Wendish literature has been estimated at three hundred volumes. The oldest work in the language is a translation of the *Epistle of St. James*, dating from 1548, published at Leipsic (1867). There are grammars of the Wendish language by Ticinus (Prague, 1679), Matthäi (1721), Seiler (Bautzen, 1830), and Jordan (Prague, 1841). There are also some collections of Sorbenian-Wendish songs and ballads. See Giesebrecht, *Wendische Geschichten* (Berlin, 1843); *Das hannöverische Wendland* (Lüchow, 1863); and Obermüller, *Die Urgeschichte Wenden* (Leipsic, 1874).

Wengersk, Andreas, a Protestant minister of the Lublin diocese in Poland, where he died, Jan. 11, 1649, is the author of, *Systema Hist.-chronol. Ecclesiar. Slavonicar., per Provincias Varias præcipue Poloniæ, Bohemiæ, Lituaniæ, Russiæ, Prussiæ, Moraviæ*, etc., *Distinctar. Libris IV Adornatum, Continens Histor. Ecclesiast. a Chr. et Apostolor. Tempore ad A.D.* 1650 (Utrecht, 1652). This work he published under the name of Adr. Regenvolsc; but the new edition which was published at Amsterdam in 1679, with the title *Slavoniæ Reformatæ, Continentes Hist. Ecclesiast. Ecclesiar. Slavonicarum*, etc., gave his original name. See Winer, *Handbuch der theol. Lit.* i, 834. (B. P.)

Wenig, Johann Baptist, a Catholic theologian of Germany, was born in 1826 at Neudorf, in Bohemia. In 1844 he entered the Society of Jesus, studied at Linz and Vals, and received holy orders in 1852. In 1854 he was appointed professor at the Episcopal gymnasium in Linz; and in 1857 professor of archæology and Oriental languages at Innsbruck, where he died, Oct. 25, 1875. He published, *Ueber den Wesensbestand des Menschen* (Innsbruck, 1863):—*Ueber die Freiheit der Wissenschaft* (ibid. 1868):—*Schola Syriaca. Pars Prior: Chrestomathia cum Apparatu Grammatico* (ibid. 1866). See *Literarischer Handweiser*, 1866, p. 154; 1875, p. 433. (B. P.)

Wenigk, Johann Ernst, a Lutheran theologian of Germany, was born in 1701 at Gotha. In 1731 he was appointed pastor at Crobstadt and Grabsleben, and in 1734 he was called to Bischleben, where he died, Feb. 10, 1745. He is the author of *Hilaria Sacra, oder Heilige Sonntagslust der Kinder Gottes* (Arnstadt, 1731), which contains sixty-eight hymns which he wrote. See Brückner, *Kirchen- und Schulenstaat im Herzogthum Gotha* (Gotha, 1758), ii, 29 sq.; Koch, *Gesch. d. deutschen Kirchenliedes*, iv, 536. (B. P.)

Wepler, Johann Heinrich, a Protestant theologian of Germany, was born at Cassel, July 27, 1755. For a number of years he acted as professor of Oriental languages at the Carolinum and Lyceum of his native place. In 1786 was called as professor of theology to Marburg, where he died, Nov. 30, 1792. He is the author of, *Philologische und kritische Fragmente* (Cassel, 1781–86):—*Diss. Inaug. de Cherubis Angelis Tonantibus Hebræorum* (Marburg, 1777):—*Nachrichten von den auf der Cassel'schen Bibliothek befindlichen morgenl. Handschriften* (ibid. 1778):—*Gedanken über die Ursachen, weswegen die Syrer den Hebräern und Arabern in der Dichtkunst so sehr nachstehen*, in the *Mémoires de la Soc. d'Ant. de Cassel*, i, 307 sq. See Winer, *Handbuch der theol. Lit.* i, 280; Fürst, *Bibl. Jud.* iii, 504. (B. P.)

Werdandi (*Present*), in Scandinavian mythology, was one of the three deities of fate. See Urd.

Werder, Peter, a Baptist preacher, was born in 1728, and ordained in May, 1751, at Warwick, R. I. The first nineteen years of his ministry were spent in that vicinity. He removed in 1770 to a Rhode Island settlement, then known as New Providence Grant, within the present limits of Cheshire, Mass., where he labored for thirty-eight years, preaching his last sermon on the Sunday before his death, Feb. 21, 1808. He was an influential and successful preacher, and venerated as a father among the churches of his faith in Western Massachusetts. See *Mass. Bapt. Mag.* ii, 348.

Werembert, a learned Swiss monk of the 9th century, was born at Coira, studied at Fulda under Rabanus Maurus, and became teacher in the Monastery of St. Gall, where he died, May 24 (or 29), 884. He was the author of some musical treatises and commentaries, for which see Hoefer, *Nouv. Biog. Générale*, s. v.

Werenfels, Samuel, a Swiss theologian, was the son of the antistes of Basle, Peter Werenfels, and was born March 1, 1657. He was educated at Basle, Zurich, Berne, Lausanne, and Geneva; became professor of Greek at Basle; and soon afterwards undertook an extended scientific tour through Holland and North Germany. On his return he received the chair of rhetoric at Basle. He was himself an orator, and sought to develop the oratorical faculty in his pupils, encouraging them to cultivate naturalness and simplicity of manner and style, together with elegance of diction. He regarded disputatiousness as a malady having its root in moral conditions, as pride, etc., and for its cure he recommended a universal lexicon containing exact definitions of all scientific conceptions. In 1696 Werenfels became a theological professor, receiving the chair of dogmatics and polemics, and in the same year received the doctor's degree. He interpreted his duty in the new position as having less to do with the antiquated heresies of bygone ages than with the perverse tendencies of the time in which he lived, and as involving the effort of restraining theological zeal within its proper limits. In these opinions he had the sympathy and co-operation of Friedrich Osterwald (q. v.) and Alphonse Turretin (q. v.), with whom he became acquainted at this time, and with whom he formed the so-called theological triumvirate of his day. He also entered into relations with the learned Parisian Benedictine Montfaucon, though by no means indifferent as respects the profound questions at issue between Romanism and Protestantism. In 1703 he was promoted to the chair of Old-Test. exegesis. In this office he devoted himself to an exposition of the Psalms, and introduced a new study into the curriculum of the school—that of hermeneutics. His principles of interpretation were altogether those which were subsequently brought to general recognition and acceptance, viz. the principles of the grammatico-historical method. In 1711 he served for a time as preacher to the French Church, and became very popular, though obliged to speak in an acquired tongue. His sermons were printed and translated into Dutch and German. In the same year he advanced to the foremost theological professorship in the university—that of New-Test. exegesis—and continued to hold that office until his death,

June 1, 1740. He rejected a call to the University of Franeker, secured for him through the intervention of Vitringa, but accepted the honor of membership in the "British Society for the Spread of the Gospel in Foreign Lands" and in the "Berlin Scientific Association."

No striking events occurred in the life of Werenfels by which he might secure a name, nor did he compose any important and epochal theological work. His *Opuscula*, however, contain a collection of treatises on different exegetical and doctrinal subjects which are still deserving of notice. His spirit was irenical, and his labors were put forth in constant endeavors to promote honorable fraternity among Christians. He felt assured that the root of evil is not in the head, but in the heart. As a teacher, he combined practical instruction with theoretical, that he might give a higher fitness to the young men who came under his care. In the evening of his life an effort was made to compel Werenfels to assist in the endeavor to degrade the learned and meritorious Wettstein from the ministry on account of alleged heterodoxy. He consequently absented himself from the sessions of the theological court, and ultimately withdrew from the academical life to privacy.

No suitable biography of Werenfels has yet been prepared, and the many grains of information scattered through his *Opuscula* have not been collected. See the *Athen. Raur.* p. 57 sq.; Hanhart, *Erinnerungen an Sam. Werenfels*, in *Basler wissensch. Zeitschr.* 1824, p. 22; and Hagenbach, *Programme*, 1860.—Herzog, *Real-Encyklop.* s. v.

Werf, Adriaan van der, an eminent Dutch painter, was born at Kralinger-Ambacht, near Rotterdam, in 1659. He studied under Cornelius Picolett for two years, and under Eglon van der Neer during the next four. At the age of eighteen he commenced his career as a painter at Rotterdam, and met with great encouragement. He was commissioned by the elector-palatine to paint a picture of the *Judgment of Solomon* and his own portrait. After finishing these works he went to Düsseldorf, where the elector desired to retain him in his service; but he agreed to paint for him six months of the year, and give the other six to his own engagements. He received a liberal pension from the elector and many valuable presents, and continued in his service until the death of his royal patron, in 1717. Among his pictures in the Düsseldorf Gallery is a life-size *Magdalene*, painted as a companion-piece to the *St. John* of Raphael, but considered, even by his friends and admirers, as inferior to that work. He carried his finishing to a very high pitch, and as a consequence his works are rare and command a high price. He died in 1722.

Werin, in Persian mythology, was an evil dev, placed by Ahriman against Ormuzd, and designed to hinder the falling of rain, and thus also the fruitfulness of the earth.

Werkmeister, Benedict Maria von, a Roman Catholic theologian and representative of the so-called Josephinism or reformatory tendency in his Church, was born at Füssen, in Upper Suabia, Oct. 22, 1745, and became a Benedictine monk in 1765. By direction of his abbot he studied theology at Benedictbeuren, making Oriental languages and exegesis his principal subjects, and finding in father Ægidius Bartscherer a teacher who developed in him the faculty for independent research which he naturally possessed. He soon discovered that ethics, which appeared to him to be of primary importance, was altogether overlooked by theologians in their eagerness to employ their wits upon the mysterious. He could not be satisfied with the schemes of probabilists or probabiliorists, of liberalists or rigorists, among the Romish teachers of ethics, and saw himself obliged to seek for what he wanted in the lectures of the Protestants Gellert and Mosheim, and in the *Life of Jesus* by Hess.

In 1769 Werkmeister became a priest and superintendent of novices at Neresheim, the latter post being associated with that of professor of philosophy. He filled a similar chair at Freysing from 1772 to 1774; then became secretary to the prelate of the empire; archivist and librarian at Neresheim; and afterwards resumed his duties as professor of philosophy at Freysing, and added to them those of a director of the curriculum, of a professor of canon law, and a librarian. Duke Charles of Würtemberg made Werkmeister his court preacher in 1784, and, being a highly enlightened Roman Catholic, permitted him to both preach and administer the ritual of his Church as he might prefer. A fruit of this liberty is presented to view in the *Gesangbuch nebst angehängten Gebeten*, etc., for the ducal chapel (1784–86), which contains a large number of Protestant hymns and tunes, and is wholly in keeping with the general style of hymnology and liturgy in that time.

Physical ailments began to trouble Werkmeister seriously in 1787, and to make it difficult and ultimately impossible for him to preach; and as the presumptive heir to the throne, Louis Eugene, brother of Charles, was known to be a bigot, and likely to dismiss every liberal priest from his service whenever he should have the power, he applied for secularization and the canonry of Spires. The former was granted and the latter denied, and in 1794 Werkmeister and his colleagues were superseded by Franciscans and Capuchins. The duke even requested that Werkmeister should be banished; but the Monastery of Neresheim gave him asylum until another change in the succession of the duchy took place, when he was recalled to his former post at Stuttgart. He now applied for and received the parish of Steinbach (1796). In 1807 he became a member of the ecclesiastical council for the Romish Church in Würtemberg, and in 1810 of the newly erected supervisory council. In 1816 he was appointed to the direction of education, and in 1817 he received the title of high councillor for ecclesiastical affairs and the knight's cross of the Order of the Würtembergian Crown. He died July 16, 1823.

Werkmeister was a rationalist, though of the noble sort, and lacked profoundness of religious thought and feeling. He never penetrated into the spiritual depths of religion, but, on the other hand, he never sought to set aside the authority of Scripture and of the received doctrines of the evangelical faith. He had the boldness to attack various Romish teachings and institutions, e. g. the celibacy of priests, the worship of Mary, the indissolubility of marriage, etc. He did not regard his course in this respect as involving him in conflict with the Church, but only with what was impure and spurious that had fastened itself upon her in the progress of ages. It would seem, nevertheless, that he carried about with him the idea of a German National Church which should be independent of Rome, but none the less Roman Catholic. His works of a literary character possess only historical interest at this distance from his time. The most important is the *Jahresschrift für Theologie und Kirchenrecht der Katholiken* (1806–20, 5 vols., edited by him), in which he opposes many abuses of the Roman Catholic Church. Of his ascetical works, his *Neues Gebetbuch für aufgeklärte katholische Christen* (Heilbronn, 1801; 11th ed. 1818) is especially deserving of mention, as well as his *Sermons* (1812–15, 3 vols.). See Schmidt, *Neuer Nekrolog der Deutschen*, 1823, ii, 578; Herzog, *Real-Encyklop.* s. v.

Wermelskirch, Johann Georg, a Lutheran minister of Germany, was born Feb. 22, 1803, at Bremen. In 1820 he entered the missionary institution of father Jänicke at Berlin, and some time afterwards the seminary of the English missionary society for the Propagation of the Gospel among the Jews at Henstead, near Portsmouth. From 1824 to 1835 he labored among the Jews, when he accepted a pastorate of a Lutheran congregation in Posen. Not being a Prussian, he was obliged to leave the country in 1836, and went to Dresden, where he connected himself with the Lutheran Missionary Society. In 1842 he again returned to Prussia, and in 1844 he became pastor of the Lutheran congregation at Erfurt, and died Dec. 20, 1872. Wermelskirch was very active in behalf of Christian missions, and the Lutheran Missionary Society in Thuringia is the fruit of his labors. (B. P.)

Wernems, Rollwinck de Laer, a Westphalian, and Carthusian monk at Cologne, was born in 1425. He was the author of some works, among them *Fasciculus Temporum*, embracing all the ancient chronicles, coming down to 1480, and continued by John Linturius to 1514. He died in 1502. See Mosheim, *Hist. of the Church*, bk. iii, cent. xv, pt. ii, ch. ii.

Werner, Andreas Konrad, a Protestant theologian of Germany in the first half of the 18th century, is the author of, *Dissertationes Tres de Puritate Fontium Hebræorum Specialim ex Libro Josuæ*, etc. (Stade, 1720–26):—*Diss. de Samaritanis eorumque Templo in Monte Garizim Ædificato* (Jena, 1723):—*De Votis Veterum Israelitarum ex Antiquitate Judaica* (Stade, 1737):—*Diss. de Veritate Doctrinæ Divinæ de Christo, ex Judæorum partim Testimoniis, partim Criminationibus et Calumniis eorum Illustrata et Confirmata* (ibid. 1729):—*Diss. de Bethlehemo apud Hieronymum* (ibid. 1769). See Winer, *Handbuch der theol. Lit.* i, 141; Fürst, *Bibl. Jud.* iii, 505. (B. P.)

Werner, Friedrich, a Lutheran theologian of Germany, was born May 28, 1659, at Flemingen, near Naumburg. He studied at Leipsic, where he died, April 21, 1741, having received the degree of D.D. in his eighty-second year. He wrote, *Præcepta Homiletica:—Tract. Hermeneutico-homileticus in Evangelia Dominicalia et Festivalia:—Dicta Biblica ex V. et N. T. cum Scopo Evangeliorum Annuorum Convenientia:—De Vana Spe Insignis Judæorum Conversionis Simultaneæ ante Diem Extremum adhuc Exspectandæ.* See Ranft, *Leben der chursächsischen Gottesgelehrten;* Fürst, *Bibl. Jud.* iii, 505; Jöcher, *Allgemeines Gelehrten-Lexikon*, s. v. (B. P.)

Wernsdorf, Ernst Friedrich, a Lutheran theologian of Germany, was born Dec. 18, 1718, at Wittenberg. He studied theology and philosophy at Leipsic, was made magister in 1742, and after presenting his dissertation *De Septimia Zenobia, Palmyrenorum Augusta*, was allowed to lecture at the university. In 1746 he was made professor extraordinary of philosophy, and opened his lectures with an oration *De Nexu Historiarum Cognitionis cum Omni Philosophiæ Ambitu.* In 1752 he was appointed to the chair of Christian antiquities, and presented on this occasion a dissertation, *De Quinquagesima Paschali.* Four years later, in 1756, he was called to Wittenberg as professor of theology, where he died, May 7, 1782. Wernsdorf was a very learned man and quite at home in patristic literature, from which, especially from the writings of Ignatius, Eusebius, Tertullian, he explained the Christian antiquities and older ecclesiastical usages which, in the course of time, had either entirely disappeared or received another form. This subject he treated in dissertations like *De Quinquagesima Paschali* (1752):—*De Paschate Annotino* (1760):—*De Sacerdote Latina Lingua ad Altare Cantillante* (1761):—*De Veteris Ecclesiæ Diebus Festis Anniversariis* (1767), etc. See Döring, *Die gelehrten Theologen Deutschlands*, iv, 698 sq.; Winer, *Handbuch der theol. Lit.* i, 557, 617, 618, 619, 631, 638; Fürst, *Bibl. Jud.* iii, 505; Hoefer, *Nouv. Biog. Générale*, s. v. (B. P.)

Wernsdorf, Gottlieb (1), professor of theology in the university, provost in the court church, general superintendent of the diocese of Wittenberg, and ecclesiastical councillor to the duke of Weissenfels, was born Feb. 25, 1668, of a noble but poor family. His theological position was that of strict Saxon orthodoxy, united with Spenerian earnestness as respects the practice of Christianity. His personal piety, and also his irenical disposition, are attested by Zinzendorf, who was at that time a student at Wittenberg (Spangenberg, *Leben Zinzendorfs*, I, iii). The only literary production of Wernsdorf which has come down to us is his *Disputationes Academicæ* (published by Zeiblich, 1736, 2 vols. 4to), whose subjects are the leading questions of his time, e. g. the controversies with Halle and the mystics, and with unbelief and indifferentism. He defends the idea of a *mediate* inspiration of the symbolical books, as well as their soundness throughout, not confining his argument to their doctrinal parts. The witness of the Spirit to our salvation is made by him to consist in a conclusion deduced from the Scriptures by the human mind, and the operation of the Spirit solely in the bringing to mind of all the passages of Scripture which can demonstrate that the judgment of the understanding with respect to our adoption as sons of God is well founded. Wernsdorf's book gives evidence of wide learning, a love of truth, an anxious holding-fast to the traditional views of Wittenbergian orthodoxy, and unfailing moderation. His students admired especially the elegance of his literary style. He died July 1, 1729. See Herzog, *Real-Encyklop.* s. v.; Hoefer, *Nouv. Biog. Générale*, s. v.

Wernsdorf, Gottlieb (2), a Protestant theologian of Germany, son of the preceding, was born Aug. 8, 1717, at Wittenberg, and became doctor of philosophy and teacher of sacred literature, eloquence, and history in the gymnasium at Dantzic, of which he was eventually director. He died Jan. 24, 1774. He is the author of, *Diss. Philologico-critica qua Sententia Jo. Clerici de Arte Poetica Ebræorum Proponitur et Illustratur* (Dantzic, 1744):—*Oratio Auspicatoria de Cognatione Spartanorum et Judæorum ac præcipue de Epistola Arii Regis ad Oniam Pontificem, ad Elucidandum Locum 1 Macc. Cap. xii* (ibid. eod.):—*Diss. de Cultu Astrorum a Deo Gentibus Profanis olim Concesso, ad Deut. iv*, 19, 20 (ibid. 1746):—*Abhandlung von der allgemeiner Bekehrung der Juden zum Christenthum* (ibid. 1748):—*Diss. Fabularis Historia de Baccho ex Mosaica haud Conficta, contra Huetium Aliosque* (ibid. 1753):—*Commentatio de Fide Librorum Maccabæorum qua Frœhlichii Annales Syriæ eorumque Prolegomena ex Instituto Examinantur*, etc. (Breslau, 1747). See Winer, *Handbuch der theol. Lit.* i, 9; Fürst, *Bibl. Jud.* iii, 505, where some works are mentioned which belong to Gottlieb Wernsdorf; Hoefer, *Nouv. Biog. Générale*, s. v. (B. P.)

Wertheim Bible designates a German version of the Pentateuch, which excited great interest at the time of its first appearing (Easter, 1735), but has now lost whatever importance it may have heretofore possessed. It has not even the merit of being rare. It is, as its title indicates, the first volume of an intended issue of the whole Bible, and contains a preface of forty-eight pages, followed by ten hundred and forty pages of subject-matter, in small quarto. The preface sets forth the purpose of the author to show that the questionings of the human mind with respect to the divine authority of the Scriptures are to some extent warranted, and that the current conception of their authority rests largely upon prejudice and unscientific notions; and his further purpose to conform the statements of the Scriptures to the requirements of the human understanding, aided in this work by the light of history and the evidence of sound reason, and also to popularize the language of the Bible more than was done by Luther's version. The work is a simple product of vulgar rationalism, evincing in its features the marks of a half-educated mind and of zealous though private study on the part of its author, who was Johann Lorenz Schmidt, in 1725 and afterwards tutor in the family of Count Löwenstein, and a graduate of Jena. He spent years in the preparation of the book, and submitted it, with varying result, to different scholars. It was printed in secret and published anonymously, and on its appearance excited a controversy which led to the issue of an imperial mandate, Jan. 15, 1737, ordering its confiscation and the apprehension of its author. Schmidt was imprisoned a whole year before the authorities would admit him to bail, and was soon afterwards arrested again. His trial, however, does not appear to have been carried forward to a conclusion. Schmidt disappeared from view, though it was rumored that he had fled to Hamburg, assumed the name of Schroeder, and found employment as a translator from the English (Tindal), Spanish (Spinoza), and French (Cantimir), and afterwards as chamberlain at Wolfenbüttel, where he died in 1750. Schmidt published in 1738 a collection of writings in support of or in opposition to the *Wertheim Bible*, which contains reviews, polemical pamphlets, and his own replies (528 pages, 4to). A similar collection, augmented with documents bearing on the trial, is that of Sinnhold (Erfurt, 1737 sq., 3 pamphlets containing 217 pages, 4to). See also Walch, *Streitigkeiten in d. luth. Kirche*, pt. v; Baumgarten, *Nachrichten von einer Holl. Bibliothek*, pt. viii; Schröckh, *Neuere Kirchengesch.* vii, 598 sq.; Herzog, *Real-Encyklop.* s. v.

Wesalia, JOHN OF. See WESEL.

Wessenburg, IGNATZ HEINRICH, *Baron von*, was a prominent liberal among the prelates in the Romish Church of Germany, and also a theological writer and a participant in civil affairs. He was born at Dresden, Nov. 4, 1774. His education, being largely under the direction of Jesuits, was defective to a degree that impaired his efficiency as a scholar while he lived. He visited the schools at Augsburg, Dillingen, Wurzburg, and Vienna, nowhere finding the assistance which his active, questioning intellect demanded, and eventually confining his efforts to the use of the libraries and the study of art, for which latter employment the society of Vienna afforded opportunity. He had come into the possession of benefices as early as 1792, and to one of them, at Constance, he retired when the unpatriotic policy of the state in the closing years of the century drove him from the capital in disgust. In 1799 he published at Zurich a poetical epistle on the corruption of manners in Germany. In 1800, Dalberg (q. v.) called Wessenburg to be his vicar in the diocese of Constance, and he entered on the duties of the place with enthusiasm. He regulated the secular affairs of the diocese with a skill which elicited the commendation of the pope himself. He sought to help his clergy to a more systematic and thorough culture, and to stimulate it to greater activity, giving to the enterprise his personal efforts and reorganizing the seminary at Meersburg in its behalf. He also sent individual clergymen to Pestalozzi, that they might become more practically acquainted with the work of educating the young, and established teachers' seminaries within his own diocese. By such measures he not only contributed materially to the prosperity of his work, but also arrayed against himself the opposition of Rome, which was yet further intensified by his attempts to introduce the German language into the liturgy, and to place Ess's New Testament and Schmid's *Biblische Geschichte* in the schools as text-books. The nuncio in Luzerne, Testaferrate, succeeded in taking Switzerland from under the jurisdiction of Constance. In 1817 Wessenburg was unanimously chosen to succeed Dalberg as bishop of Constance, having previously been coadjutor to that prelate; but the election was set aside at Rome in the most unqualified manner, and when Wessenburg went to Rome to plead his own cause, he was not granted audience of the pope. The grand-duke Charles of Baden laid the matter before the German Diet, but without effect, and the next duke, Louis (1818), was not favorably disposed towards Wessenburg. On the erection of the archbishopric of Freiburg, the local clergy proposed Wessenburg as its head; but the government this time refused its assent as decidedly as the curia had done in the former instance. The king of Würtemberg next desired him to fill the episcopal chair of Rottenburg, without being able to secure the assent of Rome. In 1819 a new career opened before Wessenburg through his election to the Chambers of Baden, in which he retained a seat during the next fourteen years, and in which he was a most zealous, eloquent, and influential representative of liberalism in its best and purest form. In 1833 he retired to private life, devoting his declining years to literary occupations and to the collection of works of art. His circle of friends was very wide, and his influence over them very strong. Queen Hortense, who resided near Constance, was among his friends, and it was her influence which induced Louis Napoleon in 1838 to voluntarily relieve Switzerland of the embarrassment occasioned by the demand of king Louis Philippe for his banishment by forsaking the country. He died Aug. 6, 1860. His leading ideas as a Churchman had occasioned the erection of a German National Catholic Church, and a revivification of Church councils. His principal work was written with an eye to the latter subject. It is entitled *Die grossen Kirchenversamml. des* 15. *u.* 16. *Jahrhunderts* (Constance, 1840, 4 vols.), and is considered of some value. His other works are of but little importance, because they lack an adequate basis in historical research. See Wessenburg's writings; Beck, *Freiherr I. H. v. Wessenburg* (Wagner, 1862); Baur, *Kirchengesch. d.* 19. *Jahrhunderts*, p. 147 sq.; Herzog, *Real-Encyklop.* s. v.

Wessobrunn Prayer (*Wessobrunner Gebet*). Wessobrunn is a Bavarian village in which, according to documentary evidence, duke Thassilo established a monastery in 760; others say 740. Certain remnants of the studies of the monks there domiciled, upon geography, weights and measures, and also certain important glosses of the 8th century, have been preserved, and particularly this prayer, which exists in a codex now at Munich, and which antiquarians assign to the 8th century. The entire piece, as given in Wackernagel's *Altdeutsches Lesebuch*, 3d ed. p. 61, reads:

Dat gefregin ih mit firahim	This learned I among men
firiuuizzô meistâ,	As the greatest of wisdoms,
dat ero ni uuas	That earth was not
noh ûfhimil,	Neither the heaven above,
noh paum noh pereg	Nor tree nor hill
ni uuas,	Was not,
ni nohheinig,	Neither was any [star],
noh sunna ni scein,	Nor the sun shone not,
noh mâno ni liuhta	Nor the moon gave no light,
noh der mâreo sêo.	Nor the high sea.
Dô dâr niuuiht ni uuas	When there was nothing
enteô nî uunteô	Of ends and bounds
enti dô uuas der eino	And there was the one
almahtîco Cot,	Almighty God,
manno miltisto;	The mildest of men;
enti dâr uuârun auh manakê	And there were also with him
mit inan cootlîhhê geistâ.	Many godlike spirits.
Enti Cot heilac, Cot almahtîco,	And God holy, God Almighty,
dû himil enti erda gauuorahtôs,	Who hast made heaven and earth,
enti dû mannun sô manac coot,	And who hast given to men so many a good;
forgâpi, forgip mir in dînô	Give me true confidence in thy grace
ganâdâ rehta galaupa enti côtan	And good
uuilleon, uuîstôm, enti spâhida,	Will, wisdom, and judgment
enti craft tiuflun za uuidarstantanne	And hope to withstand devils
enti arc za piuuîsanne enti dînan	And throw off the evil and thy
uuilleon za gauurchanne.	Will to perform.

Rettberg argues (ii, 781) from the superscription to the first part of the piece (*De Poeta*) that it was taken from some other source by the author, who appended to it the second part containing his prayer for faith and strength. Part first seems to be designed for a hymn on the creation, which, however, is not carried beyond the stage of God's premundane existence. Part second is almost word for word the same as a prayer in St.

Emmerau's manuscript, with Latin translation, which was closed in 821. Grimm (*Geschichte d. deutschen Sprache*, p. 484 sq.) states that the dialect in which the entire piece is written is genuine old High-German.

See Pertz, *Monum. Germ.* xi, 215 sq.; *Monum. Boica. Mon.* (1766), vii, 327; Mabillon, *Annales Benedict.* ii, 153; Hund, *Metropolis Salisburg. Ratisp.* (1719), iii, 335 sq.; Zedler, *Universal-Lexikon* (Leips. 1748), lv; *Geograph.-Lexikon* (ibid. 1749), xii; Wiltsch, *Handb. d. kirchl. Geogr. u. Statistik* (Berl. 1846), i, 380; Rettberg, *Kirchengesch. Deutschlands*, ii, 166; the brothers Grimm, *Die beiden ältesten deutschen Gedichte* (Cassel, 1812); Massmann, *Erläuterungen zum Wessobr. Gebet;* Wackernagel, *Das Wessobr. Gebet u. d. Wessobr. Glossen* (Berl. 1827):—id. *Auswahl deutsch. Gedichte*, 4th ed. p. 228; Feussner, *Die ältesten alliterirenden Dichtungsreste in hochdeutscher Sprache* (Hanau, 1845); Kehrein, *Proben d. deutsch. Poesie u. Prosa*, i, 18; Pütz, *Altdeutsches Lesebuch* (2d ed. Coblentz, 1863), p. 15, etc. See also Herzog, *Real-Encyklop.* s. v.

Westminster, Councils of (*Concilium Westmonasteriense*). Westminster is a city of England, county of Middlesex, forming the west part of London, having on the south and west Chelsea and Kensington, on the north Marylebone, and on the east the Thames. In 1871 the population was 246,606. It contains numerous magnificent public buildings, and is the seat of many important historic events. Several ecclesiastic councils have been held there.

I. Was held about 1070, by archbishop Lanfranc, in the presence of William I, in which Wulstan, bishop of Worcester, who alone of the Saxon bishops had withstood William, was deprived, upon the plea of want of learning. When he found that he was to be stripped of his episcopal vestments, he boldly exclaimed to William, "These I owe to a better man than thee; to him will I restore them." Whereupon he went to the tomb of Edward the Confessor, who had advanced him to his see, and there taking off his vestments he laid them down, and struck his pastoral staff so deep into the stone that, as the legend states, no human force could draw it out. This miracle, or his deserved reputation for sanctity, produced a revision of the sentence of deprivation, and he retained his bishopric. See Johnson, *Preface to Lanfranc's Canons at Winchester;* Wilkins, *Concil.* i, 367; Wharton, *Anglia Sacra*, ii, 225.

II. Was held in 1102, "in St. Peter's Church, on the west side of London," i. e. at Westminster—Anselm, archbishop of Canterbury, and Gerard of York, being present, with eleven other bishops, and some abbots. In this synod, three great abbots were deposed for simony, three not yet consecrated were turned out of their abbeys, and three others deprived for other crimes. Roger the king's chancellor was consecrated to the see of Salisbury, and Roger the king's larderer to Hereford. Twenty-nine canons were published.

1. Forbids bishops to keep secular courts of pleas, and to apparel themselves like laymen.
2. Forbids to let archdeaconries to farm.
3. Enacts that archdeacons must be deacons.
4. Enacts that no archdeacon, priest, deacon, or canon shall marry, or retain his wife if married. Enacts the same with regard to subdeacons who have married after profession of chastity.
5. Declares that a priest guilty of fornication is not a lawful priest, and forbids him to celebrate mass.
6. Orders that no one be ordained subdeacon, or to any higher order, except he profess chastity.
7. Orders that the sons of priests be not heirs to their fathers' churches.
8. Orders that no clergyman be a judge in a case of blood.
9. Orders that priests go not to drinking-bouts, nor drink "to pegs."
10. Orders that their clothes be all of one color, and their shoes plain.
11. Orders monks or clerks who have forsaken their order to return, or be excommunicated.
12. Orders that the tonsure of clerks be visible.
13. Orders that tithe be paid to the Church only.
14. Forbids to buy churches or prebends.
15. Forbids to build new chapels without the bishop's consent.
16. Forbids to consecrate new churches until all things necessary for it, and the priest, have been provided.
17. Forbids abbots to create knights; orders them to eat and sleep in the same house with their monks.
18. Forbids monks to enjoin penance except in certain cases.
19. Forbids monks to be godfathers, or nuns godmothers.
20. Forbids monks to hire farms.
21. Forbids monks to accept of the impropriations of churches without the bishop's consent, and further forbids them to spoil and reduce to poverty those who minister in their parishes.
22. Declares promises of marriage made without witnesses to be null, if either party deny them.
23. Orders that those who have hair be clipped, so that their ears and eyes shall be visible.
24. Forbids those who are related within the seventh degree to marry.
25. Forbids to defraud the priest of his dues by carrying a corpse for burial to another parish.
26. Forbids to attribute reverence or sanctity to a dead body, or fountain, etc., without the bishop's authority.
27. Forbids to sell men like beasts, as had hitherto been done in England.
28. Anathematizes persons guilty of certain horrible sins of uncleanness.
29. Orders the publication of the above excommunication in all churches every Sunday.

See Johnson, *Eccles. Canons*, A.D. 1102; Wilkins, *Conc.* i, 382.

III. Was held Jan. 13, 1126. Otto, the pope's nuncio, was present, and read a bull of Honorius containing the same proposition which the legate had made to the French clergy assembled at Bourges in November, 1225, viz., that in every cathedral church the pope should nominate to two prebends and in every monastery to two places. The bishops separated without coming to any decision. See Mansi, *Concil.* xi, 303.

IV. Was held Sept. 9, 1126, by William Corbeil, archbishop of Canterbury—John de Cremona, legate from Honorius II, presiding. Thurstan, archbishop of York, and about twenty bishops, forty abbots, and an innumerable assembly of clergy and people, were present. Seventeen canons were published.

1. Forbids simony.
2. Forbids to charge anything for chrism, oil, baptism, visiting and anointing the sick, communion, and burial.
3. Forbids to demand cope, carpet, towel, or basin at the consecration of bishops, or churches, or blessing of abbots.
4. Forbids investiture at the hands of lay persons.
5. Forbids any one to challenge a church or benefice by inheritance, and to appoint a successor. Psa. lxxxiii, 12, 13 is quoted.
6. Deprives beneficed clerks who refused to be ordained (priests or deacons) in order that they might live more at liberty.
7. Orders that none but priests be made deans or priors, nor any but deacons archdeacons.
8. Forbids to ordain any one a priest without a title.
9. Forbids, under pain of excommunication, to eject any one from a church to which he has been instituted without the bishop's sentence.
10. Forbids bishops to ordain or pass sentence upon any one belonging to the jurisdiction of another bishop.
11. Forbids, under pain of excommunication, to receive an excommunicated person to communion.
12. Forbids any one to hold two dignities in the Church.
13. Forbids priests, deacons, subdeacons, and canons to dwell in the same house with any woman, except a mother, sister, aunt, or unsuspected woman. Offenders to lose their order.
14. Forbids the practice of usury among clerks.
15. Excommunicates sorcerers, etc.
16. Forbids marriage within the seventh degree.
17. Declares that no regard is to be paid to husbands who implead their wives as too near akin to them.

See Wilkins, *Conc.* i, 406; Johnson, *Eccles. Canons*, A.D. 1126.

V. Was held in 1127, by William Corbeil, archbishop of Canterbury, the pope's legate; ten English bishops attended, and three Welsh. It is also said that the multitude of clergy and laity of all ranks who flocked to the council was immense, but no mention is made of abbots. The archbishop of York sent excuses, and the bishops of Durham and Worcester were also absent; the sees of London and Coventry were at that time vacant. This synod sat three several days, and ten canons were published.

1. Forbids, "by authority of Peter, prince of the apos-

ties," and that of the archbishop and bishops assembled, the buying and selling of churches and benefices.

2. Forbids any one to be ordained or preferred by means of money.

3. Forbids all demands of money for admitting monks, canons, or nuns.

4. Orders that priests only shall be made deans, and deacons archdeacons.

5. Forbids priests, deacons, subdeacons, and canons to live with women not allowed by law. Those that adhered to their concubines or wives to be deprived of their order, dignity, and benefice; if *parish priests*, to be cast out of the choir and declared infamous.

6. Requires archdeacons and others whom it concerned to use all their endeavors to root out this plague from the Church.

7. Orders the expulsion from the parish of the concubines of priests and canons, unless they are lawfully married there. If they be afterwards found faulty, directs that they shall be brought under ecclesiastical discipline, or servitude, at the discretion of the bishop.

8. Forbids, under anathema, any one to hold several archdeaconries in several bishoprics, and directs him to keep to that he first took; forbids priests, abbots, and monks to take anything to farm.

9. Orders the payment of tithe in full. Forbids churches or tithes or benefices to be given or taken without the consent of the bishop.

10. That no abbess or nun use more costly apparel than such as is made of lambs' or cats' skins.

Matthew of Paris declares that the king (Henry I) eluded all these provisions (to which he had given his consent) by obtaining from the archbishop a promise that he should be intrusted with their execution; whereas, in reality, he executed them only by taking money from the priests as a ransom for their concubines. See Johnson, *Eccles. Canons*, A.D. 1127; Wilkins, *Conc.* i, 410.

VI. Was held in 1138 by Alberic, bishop of Ostia, legate of pope Innocent II, during the vacancy of the see of Canterbury; eighteen bishops and about thirty abbots attended, who proceeded to the election of Theobald to the see of Canterbury. Seventeen canons were published.

1. Forbids to demand any price for chrism, oil, baptism, penance, visitation of the sick, espousals, unction, communion, or burial, under pain of excommunication.

2. Orders that the body of Christ be not reserved above eight days, and that it be ordinarily carried to the sick by a priest or deacon only; in case of extreme necessity by any one, but with the greatest reverence.

3. Forbids to demand a cope, ecclesiastical vestment, or anything else, upon the consecration of bishops and benediction of abbots; also forbids to require a carpet, towel, basin, or anything beyond the canonical procuration, upon the dedication of a church.

4. Forbids to demand any extra fees when a bishop not belonging to the diocese consecrates a church.

5. Forbids lay investitures; orders every one, upon investiture by the bishop, to swear on the gospels that he has not, directly or indirectly, given or promised anything for it, else the donation to be null.

6. Is identical with canon 5, A.D. 1126.

7. Forbids persons ordained by other than their own bishop without letters from him to exercise their office; reserves the restoration of them to their order to the pope, unless they take a religious habit.

8. Deprives concubinary clerks, and forbids any to hear their mass.

9. Deprives usurious clergymen.

10. Anathematizes him that kills, imprisons, or lays hands on a clerk, monk, nun, or other ecclesiastical person. Forbids any but the pope to grant him penance at the last, except in extreme danger of death; denies him burial if he die impenitent.

11. Excommunicates all persons violently taking away the goods of the Church.

12. Forbids any one to build a church or oratory upon his estate without the bishop's license.

13. Forbids the clergy to carry arms and fight in the wars.

14. Forbids monks after receiving orders to recede from their former way of living.

15. Forbids nuns, under anathema, to use parti-colored skins or golden rings, and to wreathe their hair.

16. Commands, under anathema, all persons to pay the tithe of all their fruits.

17. Forbids schoolmasters to hire out their schools to be governed by others.

See Johnson, *Eccles. Canons*, A.D. 1138; Wilkins, *Conc.* i, 413.

VII. Was held in 1176 by cardinal Hugo or Hugezen, who had been sent from Rome to endeavor to settle the dispute between the archbishops of Canterbury and York; the latter of whom claimed the right of having his cross borne before him in the province of Canterbury. Many prelates and clergy attended; but when Roger of York, upon entering the assembly, perceived that the seat on the right hand of the legate had been assigned to the archbishop of Canterbury, and that on the left kept for himself, he thrust himself into the lap of the archbishop of Canterbury; whereupon the servants of the latter and many of the bishops (as Hovenden writes) threw themselves upon the archbishop of York, and forced him down upon the ground, trampled upon him, and rent his cope; upon which the council broke up in confusion. Johnson, *ut sup.*; Wilkins, *Conc.* i, 485.

VIII. Was a national council held in 1200 by Hubert Walter, archbishop of Canterbury, in which fifteen canons were published.

1. Orders the priest to say the canon of the mass distinctly, and to rehearse the hours and all the offices plainly, and without clipping the words. Offenders to be suspended.

2. Forbids to celebrate two masses in one day except in case of necessity. When it is done, it directs that nothing be poured into the chalice after the first celebration, but that the least drop be diligently supped out of the chalice, and the fingers sucked and washed; the washings to be drunk by the priest after the second celebration, except a deacon be present to do so at the time. Orders that the eucharist be kept in a decent pyx, and carried to the sick with cross and candle; care to be taken not to confuse the consecrated and unconsecrated hosts.

3. Orders that baptism and confirmation shall be conferred upon those concerning whom there exists a doubt whether or not they have received them. Forbids fathers, mothers-in-law, and parents to hold the child at the font. Forbids deacons to baptize and give penance, except in case of the priest's absence, or other necessity. Permits even a father or mother to baptize their child in case of necessity, and orders that all that follows after the immersion shall be completed subsequently by the priest.

4. Relates to the administration of penance.

5. Renews the decrees of the Council of Lateran, A.D. 1179, which restrict the expenses and retinue of prelates and other ordinaries when in visitation, and declares the design of visitations to be to see to what concerns the cure of souls, and that every church have a silver chalice, decent vestments, and necessary books, utensils, etc.

6. Orders that bishops ordaining any one without a title shall maintain him till he can make a clerical provision for him.

7. Renews the canon of Lateran, A.D. 1179, which forbids prelates to excommunicate their subjects without canonical warning. Orders the yearly pronunciation of a general excommunication against persons guilty of various specific crimes.

8. Renews canon 7, Lateran, A.D. 1179.

9. Orders the payment of tithe without abatement for wages, etc.; grants to priests the power of excommunicating, before harvest, all withholders of tithe. Orders the tithe of land newly cultivated to be paid to the parish church. Orders detainers of tithe to be anathematized.

10. Forbids to institute any persons to churches not worth more than three marks per annum who will not serve in person. Renews the 11th canon of Lateran, A.D. 1179. Forbids clerks to go to taverns and drinking-booths, and so put themselves in the way of being insulted by laymen. Orders all the clergy to use the canonical tonsure and clerical habit, and archdeacons and dignified clergymen copes with sleeves.

11. Forbids marriage under various circumstances; orders that the banns be thrice published; that marriage be celebrated openly in the face of the Church.

12. Orders those who, being suspected of crimes, deny them, to undergo a purgation.

13. Renews the 23d canon of Lateran, 1179, concerning churches and priests for lepers.

14. Renews canon 9 of Lateran, which forbids the Templars and other fraternities to accept of tithes, churches, etc., without the bishop's consent.

15. Renews canon 10 of Lateran, 1179, and contains various regulations relating to the dress, etc., of the religious.

See Wilkins, *Conc.* i, 505; Johnson, *Eccles. Canons*, ad ann.

IX. Was held about 1229 by Richard Wethershed, archbishop of Canterbury. Twelve constitutions were published, eleven of which are the same with those published in the Council of London, A.D. 1175. The last refers to the duties of physicians. See Johnson, *Eccles. Canons.*

X. Was held in 1229 under master Stephen, chaplain and nuncio of the pope, who, sorely to the discomfort of the assembly, demanded on the part of Rome the tenths of all movables belonging to clergy and laity in England, Ireland, and Wales, in order to enable the Roman pontiff to carry on war against the excommunicated emperor Frederick. The arguments by which, assuming Rome as the head of all churches, it was asserted that her fall would involve the ruin of the members, was met on the part of the laity by a plain refusal; and the clergy, after three or four days' deliberation and no small murmuring, were at length brought to consent from fear of excommunication or an interdict being the consequence of disobedience to the demand. See Wilkins, *Conc.* i, 622.

Whalley, THOMAS SEDGWICK, D.D., a Church of England divine, was born in 1745. He was educated at St. John's College, Cambridge, graduating B.A. in 1767, and M.A. in 1774; was presented to the rectory of Hagworthingham, Lincolnshire, in 1772, and died at La Fleche, Nov. 30, 1828. He published his *Edwy and Edilda*, a tale (1778, 8vo):—*The Fatal Kiss*, a poem, written in the last stage of an atrophy, by a beautiful young lady (1781, 4to):—*Verses addressed to Mrs. Siddons* (1782, 4to):—*Mount Blanc*, a poem (1788, 4to):—*The Castle of Montval*, a tragedy (1781, 8vo):—*Poems and Translations* (8vo):—*Kennet and Finelia*, a legendary tale (1809, 8vo). See (Lond.) *Annual Register*, 1828, p. 267.

Whedon, DANIEL DENISON, D.D., LL.D., an eminent Methodist Episcopal divine, was born at Onondaga, N. Y., March 20, 1808. He graduated from Hamilton College in 1828; studied law in Rochester for a year, and then became teacher in Cazenovia Seminary; in 1831 tutor in his *alma mater;* in 1833 professor of languages in Wesleyan University, Conn.; in 1834 joined the New York Conference; in 1842 was transferred to the Troy Conference, and stationed in 1843 at Pittsfield, Mass.; in 1845 became professor of rhetoric in the University of Michigan; in 1855 pastor at Jamaica, L. I.; in 1856 editor of the *Methodist Quarterly Review*, a position which he retained until 1884. He died at Atlantic Highlands, N. J., June 8, 1885. Dr. Whedon was noted for his incisive, vigorous style, both as preacher and writer, and was remarkably powerful in controversy. He wrote very largely for the denominational press, and prominent among his works are a *Treatise on the Will* (New York, 1864), and a *Commentary on the New Test.* (1860–80, 5 vols. 12mo). See *Alumni Record of Wesleyan University*, 1882, p. xxix, 656.

Wheel. The vision of the wheels demands some remark (Ezek. i, 15, 16, 19–21):—"Now as I beheld the living creatures, behold one wheel upon the earth by the living creatures, with his four faces. The appearance of the wheels and their work was like unto the color of a beryl: and they four had one likeness: and their appearance and their work was as it were a wheel in the middle of a wheel. And when the living creatures went, the wheels went by them: and when the living creatures were lifted up from the earth, the wheels were lifted up. Whithersoever the spirit was to go, they went, thither was their spirit to go; and the wheels were lifted up over against them: for the spirit of the living creature was in the wheels. When those went, these went; and when those stood, these stood; and when those were lifted up from the earth, the wheels were lifted up over against them: for the spirit of the living creature was in the wheels." This vision of Ezekiel has always been regarded both by Jews and Christians as very abstruse and difficult of interpretation, so much so, indeed, that the former anciently forbade it to be read by persons under thirty years of age. Bush observes, "From all that we can gather of the form of these wheels, they appear to have been spherical, or each composed of two of equal size, and inserted the rim of the one into that of the other at right angles, and so consisting of four equal parts or half-circles. They were accordingly adapted to run either forward or backward, to the right hand or to the left, without any lateral turning, and by this means their motion corresponded with that of the four faces of the living creatures to which they were attached. 'When they went upon their four sides, they turned not as they went,' Heb. 'When they went, they went upon the quarter-part of their fourfoldness,' i. e. upon or in the direction of one of the four vertical semicircles into which they were divided, and which looked towards the four points of the compass. When it is said 'they turned not,' it is not to be understood that they had not a revolving or rotary motion, but that they, like the faces, never forsook a straightforward course." A similar *cruciform* position of the wheels is adopted by most commentators. Of verses 19 and 20 the same author observes, "These circumstances are doubtless dwelt upon with peculiar emphasis in order to show the intimacy of relation and harmony of action subsisting between the living creatures and the wheels, or, more properly, between the things symbolically represented by them." Layard observes that the "wheel within wheel" mentioned in connection with the emblematical figures may refer to the winged circle or wheel representing at Nimrûd the supreme deity (*Nineveh*, iii, 352). See CHERUBIM.

Ancient Assyrian Emblems of Deity.

Wheel of Bells, an instrument consisting of a broad wooden wheel to which from eight to twelve silver bells are affixed, rung by a rope at the elevation of the host in certain foreign churches, remarkable examples of which exist at Manresa and Gerona, Spain. The specimen at the former town, placed against the wall of the choir-aisle, is contained in an ornamental eight-sided wooden case with Gothic sound-holes; that at the latter, hung against the north wall, is all of wood, its frame being corbelled out from the wall.

Wheelock, ALONZO, D.D., a Baptist minister, was born in 1801, in Vermont. Although the circumstances of his early life were of a somewhat depressing character, he secured for himself a good classical education, and had almost completed his studies preparatory to entering upon the practice of medicine, when he became a hopeful Christian. He now decided to fit himself for the ministry. He was a graduate of what is now the Theological Seminary of Madison (N. Y.) University, in the class of 1829. He had an honorable and successful ministry. His life as a minister was spent mostly with churches in the State of New York. For several years he had charge of a Church in the city of New York. He was recognised as an able scholar and an attractive preacher, and made hosts of friends wherever he lived. For two or three years before his death he was obliged to retire from the active duties of the ministry. His death occurred at Fredonia, in March, 1873. (J. C. S.)

Whipping was a punishment employed in the ancient Church for the discipline of junior monks and inferior clergy for insubordination. It was also applied to others in certain cases. Bingham (*Christ. Antiq.* bk. vii, ch. iii) quotes from Palladius as follows: "In the Church of Mount Nitria, there were three whips hanged upon three palm-trees—one for the offending monks, another for the correcting of thieves, and a third for the correcting of strangers, whom they entertained in a hospital adjoining." Again, in Bingham's *Antiquities* (bk. xvi, ch. iii), we find these statements: "Cyprian, in the *Life of Cæsarius Avelatensis*, says that bishop observed this method both with slaves and freemen; and that when they were to be scourged for their faults, they should suffer forty stripes save one, according as the law appointed. The Council of Agde orders the same punishment, not only for junior monks, but also for the inferior clergy. And the Council of Mascon particularly insists upon the number of forty stripes save one. . . . The Council of Epone speaks of stripes as the peculiar punishment of the minor clergy for the same crimes that were punished with excommunication for a whole year in the superior clergy." See SCOURGE.

Whirlwind (סוּפָה, *suphâh*, Job xxxvii, 9; Prov. i, 27; x, 25; Isa. v, 28; xvii, 13; xxi, 1; lxvi, 15; Jer. iv, 13; Hos. viii, 7; Amos i, 14; Neh. i, 3; elsewhere "storm," etc., denoting the sweeping force of the wind or *hurricane;* also סַעַר, *sáar* Jer. xxiii, 19; xxv, 32; xxx, 23; elsewhere "tempest," or [fem.] סְעָרָה, 2 Kings ii, 1, 11; Job xxxviii, 1, 6; Isa. xl, 24; xli, 16; Jer. xxiii, 19; xxx, 23; Ezek. i, 4; Zech. ix, 14; elsewhere "storm," etc., which denote rather the violent rain or *tempest*, although accompanied with wind, Psa. cvii, 25; Ezek. xiii, 11, 13). "The two Hebrew terms above noted convey the notion of a violent wind, but with a different radical import—the former, because such a wind *sweeps away* every object it encounters; the latter, because the objects so swept away are *tossed about* and destroyed. In addition to this, Gesenius gives a similar sense to *galgál*, in Psa. lxxvii, 18 (A.V. 'heaven') and Ezek. x, 13 (A.V. 'wheel'). Generally, however, this last term expresses one of the effects of such a storm in *rolling* along chaff, stubble, or such light articles (*Thesaur.* p. 288). It does not appear that any of the above terms express the specific notion of a *whirlwind*, i. e. a gale moving violently round on its own axis, and there is no warrant for the use of the word in the A. V. of 2 Kings ii, 11. The most violent winds in Palestine come from the east; and the passage in Job xxxvii, 9, which in the A. V. reads 'Out of the south cometh the whirlwind,' should rather be rendered 'Out of his chamber,' etc. The whirlwind is frequently used as a metaphor for violent and sweeping destruction. Cyrus's invasion of Babylonia is compared to a southerly gale coming out of the wilderness of Arabia (Isa. xxi, 1; comp. Knobel, *ad loc.*), the effects of which are most prejudicial in that country. Similar allusions occur in Psa. lviii, 9; Prov. i, 27; x, 25; Isa. xl, 24; Dan. xi, 40" (Smith). In a large proportion of the passages the terms in question are employed in a figurative sense with reference to the resistless and sweeping destruction that is sure to overtake the wicked. But this of course implies that tempests of such a character were phenomena not unknown in some parts of Palestine. We have only to look into the accounts of travellers to see how much this is the case, especially in the South Country and the regions bordering on the Dead Sea. Prof. Robinson and party were exposed to a violent sirocco in the desert, in their route from Akabah to Jerusalem, which continued until towards evening.

"The wind had been all the morning N.E., but at eleven o'clock it suddenly changed to the south, and came upon us with violence and intense heat, until it blew a perfect tempest. The atmosphere was filled with fine particles of sand, forming a bluish haze; the sun was scarcely visible, his disk exhibiting only a dun and sickly hue; and the glow of the wind came upon our faces as from a burning oven. Often we could not see ten rods around us, and our eyes, ears, mouths, and clothes were filled with sand. The thermometer at twelve o'clock stood at 88° Fahr., and had apparently been higher; and at two o'clock it had fallen to 76°, although the wind still continued. Our Arabs called it *shurkiyeh*, i. e. an east wind, although it blew from the south. The *simoon*, i. e. *burning* or *poisonous* wind, they said, differs from it only in its greater heat—the haze, and sand, and discoloration of the air being alike in both. Should it overtake a traveller without water, it may, in certain circumstances, prove fatal to him. He needs water, not only to drink, but it is well to wash the skin. The simoon, they said, prevails only during the season when the khamsin blows in Egypt."

Farther on he states, "The tempest had become a tornado. It was with the utmost difficulty that we could pitch our tent, or keep it upright after it was pitched. For a time the prospect was dreadful, and the storm in itself was probably as terrific as most of those which have given rise to the exaggerated accounts of travellers" (*Researches*, i, 287, 289). A similar tempest of hot wind, "the glow of the air being like the mouth of a furnace," and fully charged with dust and sand, overtook him in the Arabah, not very far from the Dead Sea, about the end of May (*ibid.* ii, 504). Lieut. Lynch describes, under April 26, a tempest which assailed him on the Dead Sea. It was with difficulty the boat was rowed ashore. He and his companions were nearly stifled with the wind. They sought relief in a ravine, where they found pools sufficient to bathe in; but the relief was only momentary. The wind increased to a tempest; the sun became red and rayless; the thermometer rose to 104°; and when "some endeavored to make a screen of one of the boat's awnings, the fierce wind swept it over in an instant. It was more like a blast of a furnace than living air" (*Expedition*, p. 314). Kitto remarks (*Pict. Bible*, note on Isa. xxxvii, 36):

"As we have ourselves only felt the mitigated effects of this wind on the skirts of deserts and in the shelter of towns, we cannot from experience speak of the more disastrous effects which it exhibits in the open deserts; but, judging from what we observed under the circumstances indicated, and from such information as we have collected, we have no doubt that the numerous accomplished travellers of the last century and the one before, as Chardin, Shaw, Niebuhr, Volney, Bruce, Ives, and others, are correct in their united testimony, supported as it is by the consenting evidence of natives accustomed to traverse the deserts. It is necessary to mention this, because some more recent travellers, who, on account of the season or direction of their journeys, had no occasion to experience any other than the milder effects of this wind, have seemed to doubt the destructive power which has been attributed to it."

The most complete account of the simoon and its effects is that given by Volney (*Travels*, i, 4). That part which describes its effects in the towns tourists can confirm from their own experience, and the rest is amply corroborated by the testimony of other travellers.

"Travellers have mentioned these winds under the name of *poisonous* winds, or, more correctly, *hot winds of the desert.* Such, in fact, is their quality; and their heat is sometimes so excessive that it is difficult to form an idea of their violence without having experienced it; but it may be compared to the heat of a large oven at the moment of drawing out the bread. When these winds begin to blow, the atmosphere assumes an alarming aspect. The sky, at other times so clear in this climate, becomes dark and heavy, and the sun loses its splendor and appears of a violet color. The air is not cloudy, but gray and thick, and is, in fact, filled with an extremely subtile dust that penetrates everywhere. This wind, always light and rapid, is not at first remarkably hot, but increases in heat in proportion as it continues. All animated bodies soon discover it by the change it produces in them. The lungs, which a too rarefied air no longer expands, are contracted and become painful. Respiration is short and difficult, the skin parched and dry, and the body consumed by an internal heat. In vain is recourse had to large draughts of water; nothing can restore perspiration. In vain is coolness sought for; all bodies in which it is usual to find it deceive the hand that touches them. Marble, iron, water—notwithstanding the sun no longer appears—are hot. The streets are deserted, and the dead silence of night reigns everywhere. The inhabitants of towns and villages shut themselves up in their houses—and those of the desert in their tents, or in pits they dig in the earth—where they wait the termination of the destructive heat. It usually lasts three days; but if it exceeds that time, it becomes insupportable. Woe to the traveller whom this wind surprises remote from shelter! he must suffer all its dreadful consequences, which sometimes are mortal. The danger is most imminent when it blows in squalls, for then the rapidity of the wind increases the heat to such a degree as to cause sudden death. This death is a real suffocation; the lungs, being empty, are convulsed, the circulation disordered, and the whole mass of blood driven by the heat towards the head and breast; whence that hemorrhage at the nose and mouth which happens after death. This wind is especially fatal to persons of a plethoric habit, and those in whom fatigue has destroyed the tone of the muscles and vessels. The corpse remains a long time warm, swells, turns blue, and is easily separated; all of which are signs of that putrid fermentation which takes place when the humors become stagnant. These accidents are to be avoided by stopping the nose and mouth with handkerchiefs. An efficacious method is also that practiced by the camels, who bury their noses in the sand, and keep them there till the squall is over. Another quality of this wind is its extreme aridity, which is such that water sprinkled upon the floor evaporates in a few minutes. By this extreme dryness it withers and strips all the plants; and, by inhaling too suddenly the emanations from animal bodies, crisps the skin, closes the pores, and causes that feverish heat which is the invariable effect of suppressed perspiration."

The ninth plague with which the Lord afflicted the Egyptians was a thick darkness, which is generally identified with the tempest called khamsin, prevalent in Egypt in the months of April and May (Exod. x, 21–23). When the khamsin blows, the sun is pale yellow, its light is obscured, and the darkness is sometimes so great that one seems to be in the blackest night, even in the middle of the day. Sonini says, "The atmosphere was heated, and at the same time obscured by clouds of dust. Men and animals breathed only vapor, and that was mingled with a fine and hot sand. Plants drooped, and all living nature languished. The air was dark on account of a thick mist of fine dust as red as flame." Hartmann says, "The inhabitants of the cities and villages shut themselves up in the lowest apartments of their houses and cellars; but the inhabitants of the desert go into their tents, or into the holes which they have dug in the ground. There they await, full of anxiety, the termination of this kind of tempest, which generally lasts three days." The hot wind of the desert, called by the Italians *sirocco*, and by the Arabs *shurkiyeh*, i. e. an *east wind*, resembles the khamsin of Egypt. The sand-storms occur in the most awful form in deserts, when the fine sand is thrown into hillocks, and these are swept by furious winds, the sand of which they are formed being tossed on high, and whirled rapidly and densely through the air, until the storm has finally subsided. Under this most awful visitation of the sand-storm, it sometimes happens that travellers and their cattle are overwhelmed and suffocated. And even the more common and less dangerous forms of this phenomenon, which occur in regions less absolutely sandy, or where the sands are less extensive than in the great sandy deserts of Asia, are still very formidable and alarming. Mr. Buckingham has given a description of such a storm, of that kind which must have been familiar to the Israelites during their wanderings. It occurred in the desert of Suez, that is, on the western verge of that sandy desert which occupies a considerable portion of the country between Egypt and Palestine.

"The morning was delightful on our setting out, and promised us a fine day; but the light airs from the south soon increased to a gale, the sun became obscure, and as every hour brought us into a looser sand, it flew about us in such whirlwinds, with the sudden gusts that blew, that it was impossible to proceed. We halted, therefore, for an hour, and took shelter under the lee of our beasts, who were themselves so terrified as to need fastening by the knees, and uttered in their wailings but a melancholy symphony. . . . Fifty gales of wind at sea appeared to me more easy to be encountered than one among these sands. It is impossible to imagine desolation more complete. We could see neither sun, earth, nor sky; the plain at ten paces' distance was absolutely imperceptible. Our beasts, as well as ourselves, were so covered as to render breathing difficult; they hid their faces in the ground, and we could only uncover our own for a moment to behold this chaos of mid-day darkness, and wait patiently for its abatement."

Dr. Thomson states (*Land and Book*, ii, 311): "We have two kinds of sirocco—one accompanied by vehement wind, which fills the air with dust and fine sand. I have often seen the whole heavens veiled in gloom with this sort of sand-cloud, through which the sun, shorn of his beams, looked like a globe of dull, smouldering fire." See WIND.

Whirlwind in the Desert.

Whitby (or **Strenechal**), Council of (*Concilium Pharense*). Whitby is a seaport town of England, County of York, North Riding, on the Esk, near its mouth in the North Sea. An ecclesiastical council was held there in 664. This was properly a conference between the English and Scotch bishops on the subject of the celebration of Easter. There were present on the English side Agilbert, a Frenchman, bishop of Dorchester, with his presbyter, Agatho; Wilfred, a young Northumbrian priest, who had studied at Rome; Romanus, who had before contended the point with Finan, late bishop of Lindisfarne; and an old deacon, James, whom Paulinus had left thirty years before. On the Scotch side were Colman, bishop of Lindisfarne; and Cedda, a bishop who acted as interpreter. Oswy, king of Northumbria, was also present, who opened the proceedings, and desired Colman to explain the nature and origin of the rites which his Church had so long practiced. The Scots alleged the example of St. John, Wilfred that of St. Peter, and the latter concluded his address in the following terms: "But for you (Colman) and your adherents, if, after having heard the decrees of the apostolic see, yea, of the whole Church, and these, too, confirmed by Scripture, you refuse to obey them, you certainly are guilty of sin. For, allowing your fathers to have been holy men, is their small handful in a corner of a remote island to be compared to the Church of Christ over the whole earth? And great as that Columba of yours may have been, is he to be preferred to the blessed prince of the apostles, to whom the Lord said, 'Thou art Peter, and upon this rock I will build my Church, and the gates of hell shall not prevail against it; and to thee will I give the keys of the kingdom of heaven?'" This fortunate quotation from Holy Scripture determined the king in favor of the Roman custom; he, as he said, fearing to contradict one who held the keys of heaven, and might peradventure refuse to open to him when he knocked. In this council, moreover, the affair of the tonsure was discussed, the Roman fashion differing from that in use among the Scotch, which the former pretended had been derived from Simon Magus. See Mansi, *Concil.* vi, 491; Wilkins, *Concil.* i, 37.

White (prop. לָבָן, λευκός). In Canaan persons of distinction were anciently dressed in fine linen of Egypt, and, according to some authors, in silk and rich cloth shaded with the choicest colors. The beauty of these clothes consisted in the fineness and color of the stuffs; and it seems the color most in use among the Israelites, as well as among the Greeks and Romans, was white, not improved by the dyer's art, but the native color of the wool, being most suited to the nature of their laws, which enjoined so many washings and purifications. (Indeed, so early as the days of Hesiod the Greeks considered white as the color in which the celestials appeared: men went to heaven in white clothing [*Opera et Dies*, i, 198].) The general use of this color seems to be recognised by Solomon in his direction, "Let thy garments be always white" (Eccles. ix, 8). But garments in the native color of wool were not confined to the lower orders; they were also in great esteem among persons of superior station, and are particularly valued in Scripture as the emblem of knowledge and purity, gladness and victory, grace and glory. The priests of Baal were habited in black, a color which appears to have been peculiar to themselves, and which few others in those countries except mourners would choose to wear. In all countries and all ages white has been regarded as the emblem of purity. See Whitsunday. Isaiah says, "Though your sins be as scarlet, they shall be as white as snow; though they be red like crimson, they shall be as wool" (i, 15). See the monographs cited by Volbeding, *Index Programmatum*, p. 124. See Color.

White of an Egg is the rendering adopted in the A. V. at Job vi, 6 for the Heb. רִיר חַלָּמוּת, *rir challamûth* (Sept. ἐν ῥήμασιν κενοῖς [v. r. καινοῖς], Vulg. *quod gustatum offert mortem*). Most interpreters derive the Hebrew word from חָלַם, *chalám, to dream*, and, guided by the context, explain it to denote *somnolency, fatuity* (comp. Eccles. v, 2, 9), and so *insipidity* (comp. μωρός in Dioscorides, spoken of tasteless roots). The Syriac renders it by *chalamta*, which signifies *portulacca* or *purslain*, an herb formerly eaten as a salad, but proverbial for its insipidity ("portulacca stultior," in Meidan. *Proverb.* No. 344, p. 219, ed. Schultens). The phrase will thus mean *purslain-broth*, i. e. silly discourse. See Mallows. The rabbins, following the Targums, regard it as i. q. Chald. חֶלְמוֹן, the coagulum of an *egg* or *curd;* and so explain the phrase, as the A. V., to mean the slime or *white of an egg*, put as an emblem of insipidity. This in itself is not ill; but the other seems more consonant with Oriental usage. See Gesenius, *Thesaur.* p. 480.

White (or **Whyte**), **John** (1), D.D., an English prelate, was born at Farnham, in Surrey, in 1511. He was educated at Winchester School and at New College, Oxford, of which he became perpetual fellow in 1527; soon after made warden of Winchester College; became rector of Cheyton in 1551; was imprisoned in the Tower for some months during the preceding year for his supposed correspondence with persons abroad who were opposed to Edward VI; was made bishop of Lincoln by queen Mary in 1554; translated to the see of Winchester in 1557; deprived, on the accession of queen Elizabeth, on account of his opposition to Protestantism; and imprisoned for a short time in the Tower in 1559 for his public attacks upon the queen. He died at South Warnborough, Jan. 11, 1560, and was buried in Winchester Cathedral. He was the author of certain Latin poems, and some of his sermons and orations have been published.

White, John (2), D.D., an English clergyman of the latter part of the 16th and the beginning of the 17th century, was vicar of Eccles, and subsequently chaplain in ordinary to James I. He died in 1615. He published *The Way to the True Church*, and other works. See Allibone, *Dict. of Brit. and Amer. Authors*, s. v.

White, John (3), a Puritan divine, known as the *Patriarch of Dorchester*, was born at Stanton, St. John, Oxfordshire, England, in December, 1574. He was educated at Winchester School and New College, Oxford, of which he became perpetual fellow in 1595; here he graduated, took holy orders, and became a frequent preacher at Oxford; became rector of Trinity Church, Dorchester, in 1606; was one of the projectors of the colony of Massachusetts in 1624; had his house plundered and his library carried away by the soldiers of Prince Rupert; escaped to London, and was made minister of the Savoy; was appointed one of the learned divines to assist in a committee of religion selected by the House of Lords in 1640; became a member of the Westminster Assembly in 1643; was chosen rector of Lambeth in 1645; and afterwards returned to Dorchester, where he died, July 21, 1648. He published, *The Planter's Plea; or, The Grounds of Plantations Examined, and the Usual Objections Answered* (1630):—*A Way to the Tree of Life Discovered*, etc. (1647):—*Commentary on the First Three Chapters of Genesis* (1656).

White, Nicholas, a Methodist Episcopal minister, was born at Middletown, Vt., June 8, 1786. He received a careful religious training; experienced religion in 1810; joined the New York Conference in 1813; and from that date to 1854, when he superannuated, he led an active, successful itinerant life. In 1854 he retired to Brooklyn, where he resided until his death, Feb. 14, 1861. Mr. White was earnest and fervent as a speaker, greatly beloved as a pastor, devoted and affectionate as a husband and father. See *Minutes of Annual Conferences*, 1861, p. 76.

White (**Whyte**, or **Vitus**), **Richard**, an English historian, antiquary, and afterwards Catholic priest, was born at Basingstoke, Hampshire. He was educated at Winchester School; admitted fellow of New College, Oxford, in 1557; lost his fellowship on account of his attachment to Romanism in 1564; became regius professor of civil and canon law at Douay, in which relation he remained nearly twenty years; was appointed by that university the chancellor, or *rector magnificus;* was created count palatine by the emperor; after the loss of his second wife, was ordained priest and made a canon of St. Peter's Church in Douay. He died in 1612, and was buried in St. James's Church. Among his publications were, *Ælia Lœlia Crispis; Epitaphium Antiquum quod in Agro Bononiensi adhuc Videtur*, etc. (1618):—*Orationes Quinque* (1596):—*Notœ ad Leges Decemvirorum in Duodecim Tabulis* (1597):—and *Historiœ Britannicœ Insulœ ab Origine Mundi ad Annum Domini Octingentesimum* (1602).

White Brethren, a body of enthusiasts who appeared in Italy about the beginning of the 15th century, and were so called from being all clad in white linen robes reaching to their feet, with hoods of the same material that left only their eyes exposed. They were first collected together by a priest, whose name is unknown, among the villages on the southern side of the Alps. He led them down, a large multitude, into the Italian plains under the pretence that he was the prophet Elias. Bearing a cross at their head, he bade them follow him in a crusade against the Turks for the purpose of regaining the Holy Land; and so great was his influence that not only the peasantry, but some priests and even cardinals, are said to have enrolled themselves among his army of "penitents." They advanced in troops of ten, twenty, and forty thousand, marching from city to city, singing hymns and uttering loud prayers; and wherever they went multitudes were ready to give them alms and join in their pilgrimage. They were met at Viterbo by a body of papal troops, which had been ordered to march against them by Boniface IX under the impression that their leader intended to dethrone him and seize upon the papal dominions. The pilgrims were dispersed by the troops, and their leader taken captive to Rome and burned as a heretic, about the year 1403. Their history is very similar in many respects to that of the Apostolicals, led by Segarelli and Dolcino a century earlier; hence some have supposed that both uprisings were by the same sect. See APOSTOLICI.

Whitefield, James, D.D., a Roman Catholic prelate, was born in Liverpool, England, Nov. 3, 1770. Having received a good education, he engaged for some time in mercantile pursuits, but abandoned this work for the study of divinity, which he prosecuted under Dr. Ambroise Maréchal. He was ordained a priest in 1809, settled in Baltimore, Md., in 1817 as minister of St. Peter's Church, and succeeded Dr. Maréchal as archbishop of Baltimore May 25, 1828. He died at Baltimore, Oct. 19, 1834.

Whitefield, J. G., D.D., a minister of the Methodist Protestant Church, was born in Virginia, Sept. 10, 1810. He was converted when seventeen years of age; in August, 1829, was licensed to preach, and in the following September went to his first appointment. For nearly fifty years he was a faithful minister of the Gospel. He was elected to the General Conferences of 1842, '46, '50, '54, '58, '62, '66, and also of 1870, of which he was president. He was a member of the conventions of 1867 and 1877, when the dissevered Church was reunited. In 1874 he became a member of the North Carolina Conference, and represented that body in the union convention held in Baltimore in May, 1877. He died Aug. 28, 1879. See *Founders of the M. P. Church*, p. 378.

White Garments were worn by the clergy as early as the 4th century, and the use has been continued to the present time in the ritualistic churches. White garments were also worn by persons newly baptized. In the Latin Church this vesture came immediately before confirmation, but in the Greek Church immediately after. This ceremony was to represent the having put off the old man with his deeds, and having put on the new man Christ Jesus. Those who wore the garments were called, in the Greek, λευχειμονοῦντες, and in the Latin, *grex Christi candidus et niveus* (the white flock of Christ). The garments were delivered to them with the following solemn charge: "Receive the white and immaculate garment, which thou mayest bring forth without spot before the tribunal of our Lord Jesus Christ, that thou mayest have eternal life. Amen." These garments were commonly worn eight days, and then laid up in the church. The Sunday after Easter is mentioned as the day appointed for this purpose. That was the conclusion of the Paschal festival, and then the neophytes changed their habit; whence that day is thought to have the name of *Dominica in Albis;* and Whitsunday (q. v.) is said to be so called from this custom of wearing white robes after baptism. These being laid aside, were carefully preserved in the vestries of the church as an evidence against men if they afterwards violated the baptismal covenant. See Bingham, *Christ. Antiq.* bk. xiii, ch. viii; bk. xii, ch. iv; and bk. xx, ch. vi.

Whitehead, David, an eminent English divine of the 16th century, was born at Tuderley, in Hampshire. He was educated at Oxford; became chaplain to Anne Boleyn; retired to Frankfort, in Germany, during the reign of queen Mary, and there became pastor to the English congregation; returned to England on the accession of queen Elizabeth, and was one of the committee appointed to review king Edward's liturgy; was selected as one of the public disputants against the popish bishops in 1559; and declined the archbishopric of Canterbury and the mastership of the Savoy. He died in 1571. The only published works left by him are *Lectures and Homilies on St. Paul's Epistles*, and several of his discourses in *Brief Discourse of the Troubles Begun at Frankfort* (1575). Wood speaks of him as "a great light of learning and a most heavenly professor of divinity." See Chalmers, *Biog. Dict.* s. v.

Whitehead, George, an eminent public preacher of the Quakers, was born at Sunbigg, in the parish of Orton, Westmoreland, England, about 1636. He was educated at the free school of Blencoe, in Cumberland; taught school for a time; began to travel as a Quaker preacher before he was eighteen years old; was several times imprisoned, and sometimes whipped for his preaching; appeared at the bar of the House of Commons in defence of his sect; was very active in behalf of Dissenters, and exercised considerable influence with Charles II. He died in March, 1722. Among his numerous publications the following may be mentioned: *Nature of Christianity in the True Light Asserted* (1671):—*The Christian Quaker*, etc. (1824, 2 pts.), in which he was assisted by William Penn:—*Enthusiasm above Atheism* (1674):—*The Way of Life and Perfection Livingly Demonstrated* (1676):—*An Antidote against the Venom of a Snake in the Grass* (1697):—*Christian Progress of George Whitehead, in Four Parts, with a Supplement, being Memoirs of his Life* (1725). See Chalmers, *Biog. Dict.* s. v.; Smith, *Catalogue of Friends' Books*, ii, 884–908.

Whitehead, John, M.D., a biographer of Wesley, was born in 1740. He studied medicine, and became physician to the old Bethlehem Hospital, Moorfields, London. From 1764 to 1769 he travelled as a Methodist preacher, returning again to his professional duties. He was a Quaker for some years, but afterwards returned to the Methodists. He was chief physician to John and Charles Wesley during their last illnesses. At the request of the executors of John Wesley and the trustees of City Road Chapel, he preached the funeral sermon of Wesley to an audience "still and silent as night," to use Crowther's words, March 9, 1791. This sermon was published, went through several editions, and realized to the Book-room a profit of £200. With Coke and Moore, Wesley appointed him literary executor. A long and unfortunate dispute ensued between Whitehead and his two brethren concerning the papers of Wesley, the former refusing to give them up for examination and a possible cremation. For this he was expelled from membership and from his office as local preacher. Whitehead, having the advantage of the possession of Wesley's papers, at once wrote a plain and valuable account of the *Lives of John and Charles Wesley*, the first volume of which was issued in 1793. In the meantime, however (1792), Coke and Henry Moore published a hastily prepared *Life*, heavy editions of which were at once sold, thus supplanting to a large extent the more authoritative biography by the layman. In 1797, Whitehead restored the papers to his co-executors, and was reinstated in his position in the Church. Having served as physician to the Methodists for many years, he died in London, March 18, 1804.

Dr. Whitehead published the following: *Essay on Liberty and Necessity* (1775, 12mo), in which Mr. Wesley's *Thoughts on Necessity* are examined and defended:—*Materialism Philosophically Examined, or the Immateriality of the Soul Asserted and Proved on Philosophical Principles, in an Answer to Dr. Priestley's Disquisitions on Matter and Spirit* (Lond. 1778, 78 pp.):—a *Discourse* (ibid. 1791, 8vo) delivered at the New Chapel, City Road, March 9, 1791, at the funeral of Rev. John Wesley:—*A True Narrative of the Origin and Progress of the Difference concerning the Publication of the Life of Rev. John Wesley* (1792, 8vo):—a *Defence* (eod. 8vo) of the same:—a *Life of the Rev. John Wesley, M.A.* (Lond. 1793-96, 2 vols. 8vo; reprinted in Dublin in 1806, with an Appendix by the Irish editor, and Whitehead's *Sermon* on Wesley; in Boston, Mass., with Preface by John McLeish, 1844, 8vo; in Auburn and Rochester, N. Y., 1854, 8vo), collected from his private papers and printed works, to which is prefixed some account of his ancestors and relations, with the *Life of Rev. C. Wesley, M.A.*, collected from his private journal and never before published. See Stevenson, *Hist. of City Road Chapel*, p. 87, 377; Crowther, *Delin. of Methodism* (1815, 2d ed.), p. 105; Wesley, *Works* (Lond. 3d ed.), iv, 295, 351; xiii, 15; Tyerman, *Life of John Wesley* (see Index, vol. iii). For the dispute about Wesley's papers, see Myles, *Chron. Hist. of Meth. Ann.* 1792; Smith, *Hist. of Wesley and Methodism* (see Index, iii, 723); Advertisement in Whitehead's *Life of Wesley*, and *Life of Henry Moore* (1791).

Whitelamb, John, one of the Oxford Methodists, was born in 1707, near Wroot, Lincolnshire. He was educated in the charity-school of that place, and while residing with Samuel Wesley at Epworth, was prepared for Lincoln College, Oxford, where he graduated about 1731. In 1733 he became S. Wesley's curate, and afterwards married his daughter. In 1734 he was promoted to the rectory of Wroot, a position which he retained until his death, in July, 1769. In 1742 John Wesley preached once in his pulpit, and friendly but not intimate relations existed between him and Whitelamb ever afterwards. See Tyerman, *Oxford Methodists*, p. 374 sq.

White Stone (ψῆφος λευκή, *a white pebble*), referred to as given to the Christian conqueror (Rev. ii, 17), is supposed by many to refer to the usage among the Greeks of absolving those that were tried on the ground of any accusation, by the use of *white balls* or *stones*, and condemning by *black* ones. The balls were thrown together into an urn, whence they were drawn and counted. But the white stone is given to the victor himself. Hence others think reference is made to the tessera given to the victor at the Olympic games, on which was inscribed the reward to be received from his native city, the value of his prize. But in these cases the white stone is wanting, and the mystic inscription which no one but the recipient could read. The reference is undoubtedly to Hebrew sources. Christians are called kings and priests unto God (Rev. i, 6; v, 10: xx, 6; 1 Pet. ii, 5). On the front of the mitre or turban worn by the Hebrew high-priest was a plate of gold with the inscription "Sacred to Jehovah" (Exod. xxviii, 36). The name Jehovah was the incommunicable and secret name, which could be pronounced only by the high-priest, and was known, as the Jews say, only to him. Victors in the Christian struggle are to be exalted to the dignity of high-priests and kings. Instead of a plate of gold in their mitre they have a white stone, a pellucid or resplendent gem, with an inscription equivalent to "Sacred to Jehovah" (Rev. i, 4), a new name, doubtless some name of the Saviour, perhaps, "Sacred to the Logos or Word," that is, the incarnate Jehovah (John i, 1; xix, 13). The whole probably symbolizes the assurance of the faithful by the indwelling of the Holy Spirit. This is the pellucid gem, the seal of the living God, having the inscription of divine acceptance which no one can read but he who possesses it. See Seal; Stone.

Whitford (Whytford, or Whytforde), Richard, an English monk of the 16th century, was educated at Oxford; subsequently joined the Order of St. Bridget in the monastery called Sion, near Brentford, Middlesex, and styled himself "The Wretche of Syon;" afterwards became domestic chaplain to William Mountjoy. He was the author of several works, among which we note, *The Fruyte of Redempcyon* (1514):—*A Boke Called the Pype or Toune of the Life of Perfection* (1532):—and *Dyvers Instrucyons and Teachynges very Necessarye for the Helthe of Mannes Soule*, etc. (1541).

Whitford, Walter, D.D., a Scotch prelate, was first minister at Monkland and sub-dean of Glasgow, then rector of Moffat. In 1634 he was consecrated bishop of Brechin, in which see he remained until deprived by the assembly in 1638, after which he fled to England, where he died in 1643. See Keith, *Scottish Bishops*, p. 167.

Whitney, Josiah, D.D., a Congregational minister, was born at Plainfield, Conn., Aug. 11, 1731. He graduated at Yale College in 1752, and was ordained at Brooklyn, Conn., in 1756, which charge he retained for sixty-eight years, until his death, Sept. 13, 1824, though two colleagues successively settled with him. To extreme old age Dr. Whitney's mental faculties remained almost as keen as ever; he was social, witty, and yet had the dignity of a Christian old age. In theology Dr. Whitney was a moderate Calvinist. He published seven sermons. See *Cong. Quarterly*, 1859, p. 351.

Whitsunday, a festival of the Christian Church commemorative of the descent of the Holy Ghost upon the apostles, as "they were all assembled together with one accord in one place," on the day of Pentecost (q. v.), from which fact the name Pentecost is sometimes used instead of Whitsunday. Blunt says (*Dict. of Doct. and Hist. Theol.*), "The etymology of the term has been strangely confused. It has been derived (*a*) from White Sunday, in supposed allusion to the white garments of the neophytes, as Whitsuntide was one of the two chief seasons for baptism; and (*b*) from Wytsonday, i. e. Wit, or Wisdom, Sunday, in reference to the outpouring of wisdom upon the apostles. But the real White Sunday is the octave of Easter, or *Dominica in albis*, and both of these derivations must be abandoned when the proper use of the title is considered. It is not Whit Sunday, but Whitsun Day, as Easter is Easter Day; and the week is Whitsun Week, not Whit Week; and the season Whitsuntide, not Whittide. In Yorkshire, and doubtless also in other parts of England, the feast is commonly called Whissun Day, the accent being strongly thrown on the first syllable; and the two days following, Whissun Monday and Whissun Tuesday. The name is thus derived, as Dr. Neale shows (*Essays on

Liturgiology, etc.), directly from Pentecost, passing, by various corruptions, *Pingsten*, *Whingsten*, into the German *Pfingsten* and the English *Whitsun*. The Germans have also their *Pfingsten-Woche*, in exact correspondence to our *Whitsun Week*."

Still other derivations of the term are given, Hamon L'Estrange thinking it is derived from the French *huit*, or eight; because there are eight Sundays between Easter and Pentecost. "Wheatley publishes a letter of the famous Gerard Langbain, written on Whitsuneve, 1650, in reply to a friend who had asked of him the origin of the name, in which it is attempted to be shown that the festival was so called from a custom among our ancestors upon this day to give all the milk of their ewes and kine to the poor for the love of God, in order to qualify themselves to receive the gift of the Holy Ghost; which milk being then (as it is still in some countries) called *white*-meat, therefore the day from that custom took its name." It is also suggested that all persons were required to pay their tithe of young before that day or be liable to the *wite*, or mulct.

Anciently the whole period of fifty days between Easter and Whitsuntide was a sort of festival, and each was observed as a day of joy. We are told that Christians had solemn worship every day, and paid the same respect to these as they did to the Lord's day. All fasting was forbidden, and no one prayed kneeling, the standing posture being considered more in accordance with the joyous spirit of the season, which was the commemoration of our Saviour's resurrection and ascension. At these services the Acts of the Apostles were read, because they contained a history appropriate to the season; alms were freely distributed; slaves were liberated; places of worship were decorated with evergreens; and baptisms were frequently solemnized. At first all persons were baptized as opportunity served; but when the discipline of the Church began to be settled, baptism was confined, except in urgent cases, to Easter and Whitsuntide, including the fifty days' interval.

In countries where Romanism has prevailed, the greatest absurdities have been practiced on this day; fire has been thrown down from elevated places, to represent the cloven tongues of fire; flowers of various hues scattered abroad, in token of the various tongues and gifts of the Spirit; and doves let loose to flutter about the church as an emblem of the Spirit's presence. The following instances are cited from Walcott's *Sacred Archæology* (p. 612-613): "At Lichfield, 1197, 'on Pentecost and the three days ensuing, while the sequence was sung, clouds were by custom scattered.' A circular opening still exists in the centre of the vault of Norwich, and there are similar apertures at Exeter. Through it, on Whitsunday, a man, habited as an angel, was let down to cense the rood. At St. Paul's a white dove was let to fly out of it, and a long censer, reaching almost to the floor, was swung from the west door to the choir steps, 'breathing out over the whole church and company a most pleasant perfume.' At Dunkirk, in 1662, the ceremonial was always performed during the chanting of the *Veni Creator*, as in Spain. Balsamon alludes to the loosing of the dove in the East. At Orleans, on Whitsunday, during the singing of the prose, birds, lighted tow and resin, wildfire, and flowers were thrown into the cathedral. At St. Julien's, Caen, until the end of the 16th century, seven kinds of flowers were showered down. In Sweden churches are on this festival still decorated with the wind flower and Pentecost lily—the daffodil. . . . In most cathedrals the country folk came in procession on this day, and Sir Thomas More mourns over the unwomanly songs of the women who followed the cross; their offerings then made were called Whitsun-farthings or Pentecostals. On Monday, Tuesday, and Wednesday in Whitsun-week the famous Whitsun plays of Chester were acted from the 14th century until 1594 on Whitsun-Wednesday, 'Whitsonday, the making of the Creed,' being performed. Tilts and tourneys amused knights and fair dames; the morris-dancers delighted the common folks; and in many a rural parish the church ale, a sort of parochial picnic, was kept in an arbor, called Robin Hood's Bower, followed by dancing, bowls, and archery. . . . Whitsunday was also called the Easter of Roses.

Whitsun-farthings. See PENTECOSTALS.

Whosoever Psalm, a local term current in parts of England for the Athanasian Creed (q. v.).

Wicelius. See WITZEL.

Wichern, JOHANN HEINRICH, father of the Inner Mission in Germany, and one of the foremost Christian philanthropists of the century, was born at Hamburg, April 21, 1808. He studied theology at Göttingen and Berlin, and reached the degree of "candidate." On his return home, encouraged by his pious mother, he started a Sunday-school for the poorest and most wicked children in the city, and ultimately had five hundred children under his care. It was this school which gave him the idea of the institution which he opened on Nov. 1, 1833, at Horn, a suburb of Hamburg. He called it the "Rauhe Haus" (q. v.). In 1845 Wichern sent out his *Fliegende Blätter aus dem Rauhen Haus*, now the organ of the Inner Mission, in which he urged the duty of laying to heart the misery of our fellow-mortals, and at the same time told the story of his own institutions. In 1848, at the Church diet held at Wittenberg, Wichern presented with such extraordinary eloquence the claims of the sick, the suffering, and sinful, who were their countrymen, that from that hour a new movement on their behalf was begun. This was the so-called "Inner Mission" (q. v.), the very name of which is due to Wichern. Under Friedrich Wilhelm IV, Wichern found favor in court circles, and exerted great influence upon the aristocracy. In acknowledgment of the great services rendered to the cause of the Church, the University of Halle honored Wichern, in 1851, with the doctorate of theology, while Friedrich Wilhelm IV made him a member of the supreme consistory of Berlin. In his official capacity, Wichern was enabled to provide regular religious services in the prisons. In 1858 he founded the "Evangelische Johannisstift" in Berlin, a similar institution to the Rauhe Haus, and organized the Prussian military diaconate. In 1872 he had a stroke of paralysis, from which he never recovered, and died at Hamburg, April 7, 1881. See Oldenberg, *Johann Heinrich Wichern, sein Leben und Wirken* (Hamburg, 1884), vol. i; Krummacher, *J. H. Wichern, ein Lebensbild aus der Gegenwart* (Gotha, 1882); *Monatsschrift für innere Mission* (edited by Schäfer, Güterslohe, 1881), i, 380 sq.; Zöckler, *Handbuch der theol. Wissenschaften* (2d ed. Nördlingen, 1885), iv, 450 sq.; Plitt-Herzog, *Real-Encyklop.* s. v.; Lichtenberger, *Encyclop. des Sciences Religieuses*, s. v. (B. P.)

Wideburg, Christoph Tobias, a Lutheran theologian of Germany, who died at Helmstadt, Dec. 5, 1717, is the author of, *De Inspiratione Divina:—De Peccato in Spiritum Sanctum:—De Persona Christi:—De Unione Personali Duarum Naturarum in Christo:—De Perfectione Hominis Renati:—De Ministerio Ecclesiastico:—De Ministris Ecclesiæ:—De Obscuratione Solis in Passione Dominica ex Matt. xxvii*, 51, etc. See Jöcher, *Allgemeines Gelehrten-Lexikon*, s. v. (B. P.)

Wideburg, Heinrich, a Lutheran theologian of Germany, was born at Gosslar, Feb. 1, 1641. He studied at Helmstadt, was made doctor of theology in 1693, and died May 4, 1696. He wrote, *Systema Theologiæ Positivæ:—De Recta Dubitandi Ratione:—De Operationibus Dei:—De Iis, quæ in Arca Fœderis Fuerunt Servata:—De Scripturarum Sacrarum Divina Inspiratione*, etc. See Pipping, *Memoriæ Theologorum*; Jöcher, *Allgemeines Gelehrten-Lexikon*, s. v. (B. P.)

Widow (אַלְמָנָה, χήρα). The benevolent influence of the Bible is in nothing more apparent than in the superior treatment which woman has experienced among those nations where it has prevailed; especially in that most forlorn and helpless class of females who have been deprived of the support and protection of a husband. Among pagans, on the contrary, and conspicuously in Oriental lands, the condition of widows is most deplorable. They are generally regarded with suspicion and contempt, and, in many countries, with positive abhorrence, as if the cause of their husbands' death. In India this oppression seems to have reached its culmination of misery; and the atrocious custom of widow-burning or *suttee* (q. v.), was for ages the doom of this unfortunate class. See WOMAN.

I. *Widows among the Hebrews.*—Besides the general law against their hard treatment (Exod. xxii, 22-24), there was special legislation respecting them.

1. Their rights should always be respected (Deut. x, 18; xxvii, 19); nor should their clothing or cattle be pledged (xxiv, 17), nor their children be sold for debt (2 Kings iv, 1; Job xxiv, 9). According to Maimonides (*Sanedr.* 21, 6) their cases must be tried next after those of orphans.

2. They must be invited to the feasts accompanying sacrifices and tithe-offerings (Deut. xiv, 29; xvi, 11-14; xxvi, 12 sq.). Childless priest-widows living in their fathers' houses had a right to the priests' meat (Lev. xxii, 13). In later times it was the custom that the rich sent them wine for the passover meal; in the time of the Maccabees widows were also allowed to deposit their property in the temple treasury (2 Macc. iii, 10).

3. Gleanings were left for them (Deut. xxiv, 19-21), and they shared in the battle spoils (2 Macc. viii, 28-30). Their remarriage was contemplated (Lev. xxi, 14, but the high-priest was forbidden to marry one), and only on the childless widow did the Levirate law operate (Deut. xxv, 5; see LEVIRATE). The later Judaism greatly facilitated the remarriage of widows (*Jebamoth*, xv, 1 sq., 4 sq.; xvi, 4 sq.), but this was to be done not less than ninety days after the husband's demise. According to *Kethuboth*, xii, 2 sq.; *Gittin*, iv, 3, if the widow remained in her husband's house the heirs had to provide her with the necessary rooms and means for her support; but if she went to her father's home she forfeited her right to support more than was absolutely necessary, and neither she nor the heirs could lay claim to her dowry until the expiration of twenty-five years, provided she could prove by oath that she had not yet received anything of it. In order to get subsistence, widows were allowed to sell the property of their husbands, both real and personal (*Kethuboth*, viii, 8; ix, 9; Maim. *Ishuth*, xvi, 7 sq.). In case a man left two widows, the first wife had prior claims (ibid. *Conj.* xvii, 1). Betrothed women whose prospective husbands died were considered as widows, and such a one the high-priest was also forbidden to marry. In spite of these laws and regulations, complaints of the unjust treatment of the widows in Israel were heard at different times (Isa. i, 17, 23; x, 2; Jer. vii, 6; xxii, 3; Ezek. xxii, 7; Mal. iii, 3), and even in the New Test. period (Matt. xxiii, 14).

See Selden, *De Succ. ad Leg. Ebr. in bona Defunct.*; Mendelsohn, *Rit. Gesetze*, iv; Gans, *Erbrecht*, i, 152 sq.; Saalschütz, *Mosaisches Recht*, 831 sq., 860 sq.; Fronmüller, *De Vidua Hebræa* (Wittenberg, 1714); Dassovius, *Vidua Hebræa*, in Ugolino's *Thesaurus*, xxx, 1025 sq.; Herzog, *Real-Encyklop.* s. v.; Lichtenberger, *Encyclop. des Sciences Religieuses*, s. v. (B. P.)

II. *Widows among Christians.*—1. In the early Church abundant and careful provision was made for them by special ministration appointed under the apostles themselves (Acts vi, 1-6); and Paul gives particular directions concerning them (1 Tim. v, 3-16) in terms which have been understood by some commentators as ranking them in a special class of Church officials, but which rather seem to indicate their general maintenance at the expense of the body of believers, after a careful discrimination, such as the nature of the times then dictated. The writers who immediately succeeded the apostles often refer to the duty and practice of caring for the poor widows of the Church (Hermas, *Mand.* viii, 10; *Sim.* i, 8; v, 3; Ignatius, *Ad Smyrn.* vi; *Ad Polycarp.* iv; Polycarp, *Ad Philip.* iv, etc.). In still later times the *Apostolical Constitutions* and other authorities speak of a distinct order by this name (τὸ χηρικόν), but these appear to have held an eleemosynary office, rather than to have been themselves beneficiaries. See DEACONESS. They eventually took vows like nuns, and, in fact, devoted themselves to a conventual, or, at least, continent and actively benevolent life. See Smith, *Dict. of Christ. Antiq.* s. v. At the same time this body formed a convenient refuge for the destitute widows of those days, and in the Roman Catholic Church nunneries have largely been recruited from the ranks of bereaved or disappointed women. But, aside from this, Christian churches have in all ages exerted themselves with a praiseworthy diligence and liberality to furnish shelter and maintenance for believing widows whose relatives have been found unable or unwilling to provide for them. In more recent times special retreats, called "Old Ladies' Homes," have been established, where, for a moderate charge or entirely gratuitously, indigent widows are comfortably and pleasantly taken care of, without compelling them to become objects of public charity. See POOR.

Wiedenfeld, KARL WILHELM, a Protestant theologian of Germany, born at Hünshoven, Prussia, April 6, 1801, was in 1824 pastor at Gräfrath, and died in 1856, doctor of theology. He published, *Jeremia's Klagelieder, neu übersetzt und erläutert* (Elberfeld, 1830):—*Kritik des Simonismus* (Barmen, 1832):—*De Homine Sacræ Scripturæ Interprete* (Leipsic, 1835):—*Ueber die Ehescheidung unter den Evangelischen* (1837):—*Parabeln Jesu für Kinder* (1844):—*Christlicher Hausschatz* (1847):—*Geistlicher Rathgeber* (1848), etc. See Zuchold, *Bibl. Theol.* s. v. (B. P.)

Wieseler, KARL GEORG, a Lutheran theologian of Germany, was born at Altenzelle, Hanover, Feb. 28, 1813. He studied at Göttingen, and commenced his academical career there in 1839. In 1851 he was called as professor to Kiel, in 1863 to Greifswalde, was made member of consistory in 1870, and died March 11, 1883, doctor of theology. He published, *De Christiano Capitis Pœnæ* (Göttingen, 1835):—*Num Marc. xvi*, 9-20 *et Joh. xxi Genuini Sint*, etc. (1839):—*Die* 70 *Wochen des Propheten Daniel erörtert*, etc. (eod.):—*Chronologische Synopse* (Hamburg, 1843):—*Chronologie des apostolischen Zeitalters* (Göttingen, 1845):—*Kommentar über den Brief an die Galater* (1859):—*Untersuchung über den Hebräerbrief* (Kiel, 1861):—*Beiträge zur richtigen Würdigung der Evangelien* (Gotha, 1869):—*Geschichte des Bekenntnissstandes der luth. Kirche Pommerns* (Stettin, 1870):—*Die Nationalität der kleinasiatischen Galater* (Güterslohe, 1877):—*Die Christenverfolgungen der Cäsaren* (1878):—*Zur Geschichte der neutestamentlichen Schrift und des Urchristenthums* (1880):—*Untersuchungen zur Geschichte und Religion der alten Germanen in Asien und Europa* (1881), etc. See Plitt-Herzog, *Real-Encyklop.* s. v. (B. P.)

Wieser, JOHANNES, a Jesuit and professor in the university at Innsbruck, who died in 1885 at Botzen, is the author of, *Die Bedeutung der Herz-Jesu-Andacht und des Gebetsapostolates für unsere Zeit* (Innsbruck, 1869):—*Pauli Apostoli Doctrina de Justificatione ex Fide sine Operibus*, etc. (Trient, 1873):—*Die Unfehlbarkeit des Papstes und die münchener Erwägungen* (1870):—*Der jesuitische Krankheitsstoff in der Kirche* (Innsbruck, 1872):—*Die Döllingerische Dreikirchenidee*, etc. (Brixen, 1875):—*Der Spiritismus und das Christenthum* (Ratisbon, 1881). (B. P.)

Wife. See MARRIAGE; WOMAN.

Wigand, JOHANN, a Lutheran theologian of Germany, was born at Mansfeld in 1523. He studied at

Wittenberg, and was appointed pastor of his native city in 1546, superintendent of Magdeburg in 1553, professor of theology at Jena in 1560 (from which position he was discharged the next year), superintendent of Wismar in 1562, and again professor at Jena in 1569. In 1570 he accompanied the duke Johann Wilhelm to the diet at Spires, but after the death of the duke, in 1573, Wigand was expelled from Saxony. At the instance of Martin Chemnitz he was appointed professor at Königsberg, and in 1575 he was made bishop of Pomerania. Wigand died at Liebemühl, Prussia, Oct. 21, 1587. He was an ultra-Lutheran, an ardent champion of Flacius (q. v.), and took part with great vehemence in all controversies of the time, persecuting with blind fanaticism any one who differed from him in opinions. At last he fell out with his own master, with whom he at one time labored for the establishment of a Lutheran popedom, and wrote against him. Wigand's autobiography is found in *Fortgesetzte Sammlung von alten und neuen theologischen Sachen* (Leipsic, 1738), p. 601-620, where a complete list of all his writings is also found; comp. also Zeumer, *Vitæ Professorum Jenensium*, p. 43 sq.; Schlüsselburg, *Oratio Funebris de Vita et Obitu J. Wigandi* (Frankfort, 1591); Salig, *Geschichte der augsburg. Confession*, i, 639 sq.; iii, 279 sq.; Arnold, *Preussische Kirchengeschichte*, p. 346 sq.; Walch, *Hist. und theol. Einleitung in die Religionsstreitigkeiten*, i, 57 sq.; iv, 100 sq.; Planck, *Geschichte des protest. Lehrbegriffs*, iv, 195 sq.; Döllinger, *Reformation*, ii, 476; Preger, *Flacius*, i, 82 sq.; ii, 34 sq.; Frank, *Geschichte der protest. Theologie*, i, 97; Schulte, *Beiträge zur Entstehungsgeschichte der Magdeburger Centurien* (Neisse, 1877); Wegele, *Geschichte der deutschen Historiographie* (1885), p. 328 sq.; Wagenmann, in Plitt-Herzog's *Real-Encyklop.* s. v. (B. P.)

Wigbert, *Saint*, the first abbot of Fritzlar, was a native of England. In 734, when Boniface had become bishop of Mayence, he invited Wigbert to come to Germany, and take charge of the Fritzlar abbey. Under the new abbot the school soon became famous. Wigbert died in 747. See Servatus Lupus, *Vita S. Wigberti, Abbatis Fritzlariensis*, in Mabillon, *Acta Benedict.* iii, 671 sq.; *Miracula Wigberti*, edited by Waitz in Pertz, *Monumenta Hist. German.* vi, 227 sq.; Rettberg, *Kirchengeschichte Deutschlands*, i, 593 sq.; Wattenbach, *Deutschlands Geschichtsquellen im Mittelalter*, 4th ed. i, 195; Ebert, *Geschichte der Literatur des Mittelalters*, ii, 206; Hahn, *Bonifaz und Lul*, p. 141 sq.; Plitt-Herzog, *Real-Encyklop.* s. v.; Lichtenberger, *Encyclop. des Sciences Religieuses*, s. v. (B. P.)

Wighard, an archbishop of Canterbury, was an Englishman by birth. He had been chaplain to Deusdedit, and had been educated in the Church of Canterbury. He was appointed to the see of Canterbury and metropolitan of all England some time between A.D. 664 and 668. He immediately went to Rome to be consecrated, where he died, soon after his arrival, of the plague. See Hook, *Lives of the Archbishops of Canterbury*, i, 142.

Wight, Henry, D.D., a Congregational minister, was born at Medfield, Mass., in 1753, and was a graduate of Harvard College in the class of 1782. His ordination took place at Bristol, R. I., Jan. 5, 1785, in connection with the dedication of a new house of worship. Of this church he continued to be the sole pastor for more than thirty years (from 1785 to 1815). On Nov. 13 of the latter year, the Rev. Joel Mason was ordained as his colleague. Dr. Wight was dismissed at his own request Nov. 11, 1828. His residence during the remainder of his life was among his own people in Bristol. He died Aug. 12, 1837. His ministry in Bristol was a prosperous one, two hundred and thirty-eight persons being received into the membership of the Church during his pastorate. See *Harvard General Catalogue*, p. 37; *Memorials of R. I. Cong. Ministers.* (J. C. S.)

Wightman, William May, D.D., LL.D., a bishop of the Methodist Episcopal Church South, was born at Charleston, S. C., Jan. 8, 1808. He was converted at sixteen, graduated from Charleston College in 1827, entered the South Carolina Conference in 1828, and immediately sprang into position and popularity. After laboring successively on the Pedee, Orangeburg, Sumter, and Abbeville circuits, and in Charleston and Camden stations, he was appointed agent for Randolph-Macon College in 1834; in 1837 was made professor of English literature in that institution; two years later presiding elder of Cokesburg District; in 1840 editor of the *Southern Christian Advocate;* in 1854 president of Wofford College; in 1859 president of the Southern University at Greensboro', Ala.; and in 1866 bishop, an office which he filled with great ability until his death in Charleston, Feb. 15, 1882. He was singularly effective as a preacher, dignified and successful as an administrator, ardent as a friend, and modest and earnest as a Christian. See *Minutes of Annual Conferences of the M. E. Church South*, 1882, p. 151.

Wigram, Joseph Cotton, D.D., a bishop of the Church of England, was born Dec. 26, 1798, being the son of sir Robert Wigram, bart. He graduated at Cambridge in 1820, and was ordained deacon in 1822, and priest the next year; in 1827 he was appointed secretary of the National Society for Promoting the Education of the Poor, and in the same year became assistant minister at St. James's, Westminster; in 1835 he was appointed rector of East Tisted, Hants; in 1847 was made archdeacon of Winchester, holding that position until his appointment as bishop of Rochester, to which he was consecrated in 1860; from 1851 until 1860 he was rector of St. Mary's, Southampton. He died suddenly at London, April 6, 1867. His literary remains consist of a large number of published sermons. See *American Quar. Church Rev.* July, 1867, p. 346.

Wigrdr, in Norse mythology, is the name of the large plain which serves the Asas and the Einheriars, the Muspelheimers, with Hel, Loke, Fenris, and Jörmungand, as a battle-field. It has an area of 10,000 square miles.

Wike, in the mythology of the Finns and Lapps, is a child which the moon with Bil, the daughter of the Asas, exalted to heaven, in order that both might be its constant companions. Some see in this a reference to the different phases of the moon.

Wikeford, Robert de, D.C.L., an Irish prelate, was born in Essex, and was archdeacon of Winchester. For a time he was fellow of Merton College, and was advanced to the see of Dublin, Oct. 12, 1375, before the close of which year he was consecrated. In 1377 he was appointed chancellor of Ireland. In 1378 he had an exemplification and confirmation of the manor of Swords to him and his successors. About 1380 he had a grant to the see of all its possessions. In 1382 De Wikeford was ordered to attend a conference of the prelates, to be held at Naas. In 1385 he was again appointed lord chancellor. In 1390 he visited England, where he died, Aug. 29 of that year. See D'Alton, *Memoirs of the Archbishops of Dublin*, p. 142.

Wila, in Slavonic mythology, is one of the deities worshipped by the Bohemians and Moravians, and was ruler of night and death.

Wilbur, Hervey, D.D., an American minister, was born at Wendell, Mass., in 1787. He was pastor of his native place from 1817 to 1823; subsequently presided over several female seminaries; and died at Newburyport in 1852. He was the author of, *Discourse on the Religious Education of Youth* (1814):—*Reference Bible* (1828):—*Elements of Astronomy* (1829):—*Lexicon of Useful Knowledge* (1830):—and *Reference Testament for Bible Classes* (1831).

Wilbur, John, an American minister of the Society of Friends, was born at Hopkinton, R. I., in 1774. He opposed the introduction into the society of any new doctrines or practices. In 1838 he was accused by several members of the Rhode Island yearly meeting of publishing statements derogatory to the character of Joseph John Gurney, who was then visiting the United States. He was sustained in his course by his own monthly meeting, that of South Kingston; but that body having been superseded by the Greenwich meeting, he was disowned by the latter body, and its action confirmed by the higher powers. His supporters in various parts of New England united in forming a separate yearly meeting, whose members were known as "Wilburites." They maintain the strictest traditions of the sect, and claim that Quakers, as a body, are giving up their principles. Mr. Wilbur died in 1856. He was the author of, *Narrative and Exposition of the Late Proceedings of the New England Yearly Meeting*, etc. (1845):—*A Few Remarks upon the Controversy between Good and Evil in the Society of Friends* (1855):—and his *Journal and Correspondence* have appeared since his death (1859).

Wilburites. See WILBUR, JOHN.

Wilcocks, JOSEPH, D.D., an English clergyman, was born in 1673. He was educated at Magdalen College, Oxford; chosen demy of his college at the same time with Boulter and Addison, from which circumstance this was called "the golden election;" became chaplain to the English Factory at Lisbon; returned to England, where he became chaplain to George I, and preceptor to the children of George II; became prebendary of Westminster in March, 1720; was made bishop of Gloucester in 1721; translated to the see of Rochester in 1731, and at the same time held the deanery of Westminster; and died March 9, 1756. He published some single sermons.

Wild, Friedrich Karl, a Protestant theologian of Germany, who died at Kirchheim, July 3, 1869, is the author of, *Der moderne Jesuitismus* (Nördlingen, 1843):—*Gottes Wort und die Kirche* (Stuttgart, 1845):—*Ein Wort gegen den üblichen Gebrauch und die herkömmliche Stellung der Apokryphen in der evangelischen Kirche* (1854):—*Jacob Heilbrunner. Ein Held unter den Streitern Jesu Christi* (Leipsic, 1859). See Zuchold, *Bibl. Theol.* s. v. (B. P.)

Wild, Johann. See FERUS.

Wild, Johann Christoph Friedrich, a Protestant theologian, was born at Plössberg, June 13, 1803. He studied at Erlangen, was in 1830 preacher at Wassertrüdingen, and in 1839 pastor at Schönberg, where he labored for twenty-nine years. In 1868 he was called to Unterschwaningen, in Bavaria, and died April 5, 1882. He wrote, *Ueber göttliche Strafe und Strafgerichte* (Anspach, 1832):—*Systematische Darstellung der Unterscheidungslehre der katholischen und protestantischen Kirche* (Nördlingen, 1842):—*Der Tod im Lichte der Offenbarung* (Nuremberg, 1847). See Zuchold, *Bibl. Theol.* ii, 1448. (B. P.)

Wild, Robert, D.D., an English Nonconformist divine, poet, and wit, was born at St. Ives, Huntingdonshire, in 1609. He was educated at the University of Cambridge; received his first degree in divinity at Oxford in 1642; was appointed rector at Aynhoe, Northamptonshire, in 1646; ejected at the Restoration; and died at Oundle in 1679. He was the author of, *Tragedy of Christopher Love at Tower Hill* (1660):—*Iter Boreale* (eod.):—*Poem on the Imprisonment of Mr. Edmund Calamy in Newgate* (1662):—*Poems* (1668):—*Rome Rhym'd to Death* (1683), being a collection of choice poems, in two parts, written by the earl of R.[ochester], Dr. Wild, etc.:—*The Benefice; a Comedy* (1689). In 1870 appeared *Poems by Robert Wild, D.D., one of the Ejected Ministers of 1662; with a Historical and Biographical Preface and Notes*, by the Rev. John Hunt.

Wild Ass (פֶּרֶא, *pérè;* once [Job xxxix, 5] עָרוֹד, *arôd;* Chald. [Dan. v, 21] עֲרָד, *arád;* Sept. ὄναγρος [ὄνος ἄγρος]; so the Eastern ὄνος ἄγριος, Photius, *Cod.* xlii, 91; Philostr. *Apoll.* iii, 2; Ælian, *Anim.* v, 52), a species inhabiting the desert (Job xxiv, 5; Isa. xxxii; Jer. ii, 2, 4), roaming free (Job xxxix, 5), living on herbs (vi, 5; Jer. xiv, 6), which is likewise mentioned in profane authors (Aristot. *Anim.* vi, 36; Oppian, *Cyneg.* iii, 184 sq.), and is especially made in Scripture the symbol of a nomadic life (Gen. xvi, 12). The following is a close translation of the poetical description of the wild ass given in the book of Job (xxxix, 5–8):

> Who sent forth [the] wild-ass free;
> Yea, the yoke-bands of the onager who opened?
> Whom I have assigned the desert [as] his house,
> Even his couching-places [the soil sterile as if] salt.
> He will laugh at the crowd of the city;
> The hootings of the driver he cannot hear.
> The quest of the mountains [is] his feed;
> Yea, after every green [thing] will he seek.

From the frequent and familiar allusions to the wild ass in Scripture, we may conclude it was much more numerous in the countries adjacent to Palestine in former times than it is at present. Though well known by name, the wild ass is rarely now found west of the

Wild Ass.

Hauran (Bashan); nor do we find it in the Sinaitic wilderness. The species which is found east of Syria is the *Asinus hemippus*, or Syrian wild ass, which differs from the *Asinus hemione*, the wild ass of Central Asia, in sundry slight particulars of osteology and form. This species was undoubtedly known to the Jews, and is probably the *pére* of Scripture. The *Asinus vulgaris*, or Onager of the ancients, the original of the tame ass, inhabits the Egyptian deserts, and must also have been known. If the species were distinguished from the Syrian one, it may probably be the *arôd* of the Hebrew. Travellers have seen this ass wild in the deserts of North Africa, in small troops of four or five. When riding in the Sahara, they have detected what they took to be antelopes on a slightly elevated mound of sand; then, by their glasses, discovering they had no horns, they suspected they were the horses of Bedawin, who might be concealed behind them, till they allowed an approach sufficiently near to make them out more clearly, when, snuffing up the wind, they dashed off at a speed which the best of horses could not have approached. Tristram saw a wild ass in the oasis of Souf, which had been snared when a colt; but though it had been kept for three years in confinement, it was as untractable as when first caught, biting and kicking furiously at every one who approached it, and never enduring a saddle on its back. In appearance and color it could not have been distinguished from one of the finest specimens of the tame ass. The Syrian wild ass (*Asinus hemippus*) in no way differs from the African in habits. All the species of wild ass are more or less migratory, travelling north and south, according to the season, in large herds. The Asiatic (*Asinus hemippus*) proceed in summer as far north as Armenia, marking their course by grazing the herbage very closely on their march. In winter they descend as far as the shores of the Persian Gulf. In the same manner the African species is only in summer seen on the confines of Egypt, retiring in winter towards the interior. Their habit of congregating at watering-places, and of standing on the watch on any rising ground, are both alluded to in Scripture (Psa. civ, 11; Jer. xiv, 6). See Tristram, *Nat. Hist. of the Bible*, p. 42. See Ass.

Wild Beast is the rendering of the A. V. at Psa. l, 11; lxxx, 13 [elsewhere "abundance," Isa. lxvi, 11], of זִיז, *zîz*, a poetical word for any moving creature of the field. Another Heb. term, *chayâh* (חַיָּה, Sept. θηρίον, ζῶον, θήρ, τετράπους, κτῆνος, ἑρπετόν, θηριάλωτος, βρωτός; Vulg. *fera, animantia, animal*), also rendered "beast," "wild beast," is the feminine of the adjective חַי, "living," used to denote any animal. It is, however, very frequently used specially of "wild beast," when the meaning is often more fully expressed by the addition of the word הַשָּׂדֶה, *has-sadéh* (wild beast) "of the field" (Exod. xxiii, 11; Lev. xxvi, 22; Deut. vii, 22; Hos. ii, 14; xiii, 8; Jer. xii, 9, etc.). Similar is the use of the Chaldee חֵיוָא, *cheyvâh* (Dan. iv, vii). See BEAST.

WILD BEAST OF THE DESERT is the rendering of the A. V. at Isa. xiii, 21; xxxiv, 14; Jer. l, 30 [elsewhere "dwelling in the wilderness," (Psa. lii, 9; lxxiv, 14; Isa. xxiii, 13] of the Heb. word found only in this sense in the plur. צִיִּים, *tsiyîm*, although the sing. צִי, *tsî*, occurs Numb. xxiv, 24; Isa. xxxiii, 21; Ezek. xxx, 9; Dan. xi, 30, in the sense of "ship." It is thought to denote some (or perhaps any) species of animal living in the desert, such as jackals, ostriches, etc. The ancient versions are inconsistent (Sept. θήρια, ἰνδάλματα; Vulg. *bestiæ, dracones*). The Targum understands *apes*, Michaelis (*Suppl.* p. 2086) *serpents*, Aurivillius (*Dissert.* p. 298) *vampyres*, Saadias and Abulwalid *wild bulls*, and others *wild cats*. See Bochart, *Hieroz.* ii, 211.

WILD BEAST OF THE ISLANDS is the rendering of the A. V. at Isa. xiii, 22; xxxiv, 14; Jer. l, 39, of the Heb. word which occurs in this sense only in the plur. אִיִּים, *iyîm*, although it frequently occurs both in the sing. and plur. in the sense of "island." The ancient interpreters variously understand *cats* (Chald. and Kimchi) and *spectres* (Sept. ὀνοκένταυρος); but later writers generally agree that the *jackal* (q. v.) is meant, from its habit of *howling* (Bochart, *Hieroz.* i, 843).

Wild Bull is the rendering of the A. V. at Isa. li, 20, of תּוֹא, *tô* (Sept. σεύτλιον; Vulg. *oryx*), which is now generally thought to denote some of the larger species of *antelope* (q. v.), as the same word in a slightly longer form, תְּאוֹ, *teô*, occurs elsewhere (Deut. xiv, 3, A. V. "wild ox"), where the ancient interpreters (Sept. ὄρυξ; Vulg. *oryx*), as well as the context, agree

Oryx.

in that sense. The particular kind is probably the *oryx*, although no exact species may have been intended. Others, however, are inclined to regard the creature intended as kindred rather with the *reëm*, or "unicorn" of our version. It is a singular fact that various animals of the ox kind are figured on the monuments as tribute to the ancient Assyrians. See BUFFALO.

Wilderness is in the A. V. the most frequent rendering of מִדְבָּר (*midbâr*, ἡ ἔρημος), which primarily denotes a region not regularly tilled or inhabited (Job xxxviii, 26; Isa. xxxii, 15; Jer. ii, 2), but used for pasturage (from דָּבַר, *to track*, referring to the cattle-paths) (Jer. ix, 9; Psa. lxv, 13; Joel ii, 22; Luke xv, 4); mostly treeless and dry, but not entirely destitute of vegetation or fertility, such as are of frequent occurrence in the East (Robinson ii, 656; occasionally cultivated in spots, Josephus, *Ant.* xii, 4, 6). Towers were sometimes erected in them for the protection of flocks (2 Chron. xxvi, 10; 2 Kings xvii, 9; comp. Isa. i, 8). The term is likewise in some instances applied to particular barren tracts of hard arid steppes (Isa. xxxv, 6; xli, 18; xliii, 20; Lam. iv, 3; Mal. i, 3) overrun with wild animals (see Rosenmüller, *Morgenl.* i, 88 sq.); although for such spots the words מִדְבַּר שְׁמָמָה (Joel ii, 3; iv, 19), עֲרָבָה, יְשִׁימוֹן (see Credner, in the *Stud. u. Krit.* 1833, iii, 788 sq.), etc., are usually employed. For a remarkable phenomenon of these dry wastes, see MIRAGE.

Although this kind of region is not particularly characteristic of Palestine, yet the term *midbâr* is applied to the following localities in it or its immediate vicinity [see DESERT]:

1. *The Wilderness of Judah*, also called *Jeshimon* (1 Sam. xxiii, 19; xxvi, 1, 3), is a rocky district in the eastern part of that tribe adjoining the Dead Sea and including the town of Engedi (Josh. xv, 61; Judg. i, 16). It appears to have extended from the vicinity of the Kedron, a few miles east of Jerusalem, to the S.W. shore of the Dead Sea and to the hills of Judah. The convent of Mar Saba (q. v.) is a marked feature of one of its wild and barren dells. See JUDAH, WILDERNESS OF.

Bull, Rhinoceros, and Antelope. (From the Black Obelisk of Nimrûd.)

On the N.W. border of the wilderness of Judah lay *the Wilderness of Tekoa* (2 Chron. xx, 20; 1 Macc.

ix, 33); as in its E. part appears to have lain *the Wilderness of Engedi* (1 Sam. xxiv, 2), and in its S. part *the Wilderness of Ziph* (xxiii, 14 sq.) or *Maon* (q. v.), otherwise called *Jeruel* (2 Chron. xx, 16). The *Wilderness of St. John* (Matt. iii, 1, 3; comp. xi, 7; Luke i, 80) is a part of the desert of Judah; although modern tradition gives that name to the neighborhood of Ain Karim west of Jerusalem. See JOHN THE BAPTIST.

2. *The Wilderness of Beersheba* (Gen. xxi, 14) lay south of that town on the borders of the desert Et-Tih. See BEERSHEBA.

3. *The Wilderness of Jericho* (Josh. xvi, 1), between that city and the Mount of Olives, or rather Bethany, was an extension of the desert of Judah, a rough and stony tract full of precipices (see Josephus, *Ant.* x, 8, 2), which contains the so-called khan of the Samaritans (Luke x, 30). Its N. E. extremity is *the wilderness of Quarantana* (q. v.), and its N. W. extremity *the wilderness of Beth-aven* (Josh. xviii, 12).

4. *The Wilderness of Gibeon*, in the vicinity of that city, north of Jerusalem (2 Sam. ii, 24).

5. *The Wilderness of Reuben* (Deut. iv, 43), denotes the barren tract in the neighborhood of Bezer, on the border of the tribe towards the Arabian desert. See REUBEN.

6. *The Wilderness of Bethsaida* (Luke ix, 10), a pasture-ground adjoining that town, apparently extending on both sides of the mouth of the Upper Jordan. See BETHSAIDA.

For the *Wilderness of Arabia Petræa* or of *Mt. Sinai*, including those of *Etham*, *Paran*, *Shur*, and the *Arabah*, see WILDERNESS OF THE WANDERINGS.

WILDERNESS OF THE WANDERING *of the Children of Israel*. This is a convenient popular designation of the wide region in which the people were led by the divine guidance under Moses, for forty years, from Egypt to Canaan. It was here, amid nature's grandest and wildest architecture, wrapped in nature's profoundest silence and solitude, far removed from the din and distraction of the world of life and action, that the people of Israel met with their God, and witnessed manifestations of his glory and majesty and power such as mortals never witnessed before, and never can witness again. There, as Stanley says, "they were brought into contact with a desolation which was forcibly contrasted with the green valley of the Nile. They were enclosed within a sanctuary of temples and pyramids not made with hands—the more awful from its total dissimilarity to anything which they or their fathers could have remembered in Egypt or Palestine. They were wrapped in a silence which gave full effect to the morning and the evening shout with which the encampment rose and pitched, and still more to the 'thunders, and the voice exceeding loud' on the top of Horeb" (*Sin. and Pal.* p. 20). The appropriateness of these natural features to the scenes recorded in the sacred narrative cannot safely be overlooked by the modern critic and commentator. They tend to demonstrate the perfect consistency of Bible history in its minutest details. In our treatment of it here we give in detail its geographical character and productions. See EXODE.

I. *General Configuration and Features.*—1. *Principal Divisions.*—The country embraced in the "Wilderness of Wandering" extended from the borders of Egypt and the Mediterranean on the west, to the plateau of Arabia on the east. How much of the latter it included cannot be determined, because the eastern boundary of Edom is indefinite; and even were it minutely defined, it would be impossible to ascertain how close to or how far from it the Israelites travelled. There can be little doubt that their march was never conducted, like that of a modern army, in one dense column. It bore a far closer resemblance to the migration of an Arab tribe, whose flocks, herds, shepherds, and guards, with their families, spread over the country for many miles. Travellers in this region often pass through a moving tribe whose outer extremities are twenty miles apart. The southern limits of the wilderness were marked by the Red Sea and its gulfs; and the northern by Canaan, Moab, and Bashan.

This vast tract is divided by the Gulf of Akabah, and the deep valley of the Arabah, into two great sections. The western section is triangular in form, the base being marked by the Mediterranean coast and the hills of Judah, and the apex by Ras Mohammed on the extreme south. The physical geography of this region is very remarkable, and, as it formed the chief scene of the wanderings of the Israelites, it must be described with some minuteness. From the shore of the Mediterranean a great plain extends inland. At first it is very low, and studded with mounds and ridges of drifting sand. It rises gradually, and the sand gives place to a white, flinty soil, which scantily covers the limestone strata. As the elevation increases, long reaches of rolling table-land, and broad ridges with naked crowns and long gravelly slopes, stretch away far as the eye can see, while shallow, naked wadys, and bare, rocky glens, seam its surface and wind away waterless to the sea. Towards the east the table-land becomes still more uneven. The ridges rise higher and are more rugged, and the valleys are deeper and wilder. Here, however, are some smooth expanses of upland plain, and broad beds of wadys, coated with a light but rich soil. Springs and wells also become more frequent, and occasionally a streamlet may be traced for a mile or two along its tamarisk-fringed bed. At length the plateau, having attained an altitude of about two thousand feet, breaks down abruptly, in a series of irregular terraces, or wall-like cliffs, to the great valley of the Arabah. Such are the general features of the desert of et-Tîh. Its name is remarkable. Et-Tîh signifies "The Wandering," and is doubtless derived from the wanderings of the Israelites, the tradition of which has been handed down through a period of three thousand years. It was at the eastern border of the plateau, in the valley of the Arabah, that the camp was pitched so long around the sacred fountain of Kadesh; and it was up the wild passes that lead from the Arabah to the table-land that an infatuated and rebellious people attempted to force their way, against the divine command, into Canaan, when they were driven back with disgrace by the hardy Amalekites (Numb. xiv, 40-45).

On the north the plateau of et-Tîh rises gradually to meet the swelling hills and green vales of Palestine. On the south it also rises in long, bare, gravelly slopes to Jebel et-Tîh, which sweeps round like the arc of a bow, and regular as a colossal wall, from Suez to the head of the gulf of Akabah.

The Arabah is a deep, wide valley, running in a straight line from the gulf of Akabah to the Dead Sea. From the latter it rises in a series of terraces, supported by wall-like cliffs, until it attains an elevation of three or four hundred feet above the level of the ocean; then it declines gently to the shore of the gulf of Akabah. The greater portion of it is a bare and barren desert, covered in part with a light, flinty soil, and in part with loose sand. Low shrubberies of tamarisk appear here and there, and clumps of camel-thorn are met with, but these are its only products. Fountains are almost unknown in it. That of Kadesh is the only one of any note recorded in ancient or modern times. Along its western side runs a range of bare, rugged limestone hills, from two to three thousand feet in height. The range is deeply furrowed by long, dry ravines, like rents in the rocky strata; and these form the only approaches to the plateau of et-Tîh. Most of them are impassable to human feet; and as they cut far into the table-land, they effectually bar all passage along its eastern border. The Israelites, therefore, in their approach to Kadesh from Sinai, must have travelled along the Arabah, or else have treaded the interior of the plateau itself.

On the east side of the valley is a mountain-range of a different character. Its southern section is granite, showing the sharp peaks and deep colors of the Sinaitic group. The granite then gives place to sandstone, whose hues are still more gorgeous. This range formed the country of the Edomites, into which the Israelites never penetrated. They were compelled to turn back from Mount Hor, march down the Arabah, and pass round the southern and eastern sides of Edom. The desert of Arabia thus formed the scene of their last wanderings. It is a vast table-land, extending from the mountain-range of Edom eastward to the horizon, without tree or shrub, stream or fountain. The surface is either bare rock, or white gravel mixed with flints, or drifting sand. The very Bedawin dread the passage of this "great and terrible wilderness." For days together the daring traveller who ventures to cross it must hasten onward, and should the supply of water which he is obliged to carry with him fail, all hope is gone. Wallin, one of the very few who traversed it, says, "It is a tract the most desolate and sterile I ever saw. Its irregular surface is, instead of vegetation, covered with small stones, which, shining sometimes in a dark swarthy, sometimes in a bright, white color, reflect the rays of the sun in a manner most injurious to the eyes" (*Journal of the Roy. Geog. Soc.* xxiv, 135). Mr. Palgrave, who crossed it more recently, almost in the track of Wallin, also gives a frightful account of it (*Travels in Arabia*, i, 8 sq.). It is far more desolate and dreary and terrible than any part of the region west of the Arabah.

2. *The Peninsula of Sinai.*—The twin gulfs of Suez and Akabah, into which the Red Sea separates, embrace this

triangle on its west and east sides respectively. One or other of them is in sight from almost all the summits of the Sinaitic cluster, and from the highest points both branches. The eastern coast of the gulf of Suez is strewn with shells, and with the forests of submarine vegetation, which possibly gave the whole sea its Hebrew appellation of the "Sea of Weeds." The "huge trunks" of its "trees of coral may be seen even on the dry shore," while at Tûr cabins are formed of madrepores gathered from it, and the *débris* of conchylia lie thickly heaped on the beach. Similar "coralline forests" are described (Stanley, *Sinai and Palestine*, p. 83) as marking the coast of the gulf of Akabah. The northern portion of the whole peninsula is a plateau bounded southwards by the range of et-Tîh, which droops across it on the map with a curve somewhat like that of a slack chain, whose points of suspension are, westwards, Suez, and eastward, but farther south, some "sandstone cliffs, which shut off" this region from the gulf of Akabah. The north-western member of this chain converges with the shore of the gulf of Suez, till the two run nearly parallel. Its eastern member throws off several fragments of long and short ridges towards the gulf of Akabah and the northern plateau called from it et-Tîh. The Jebel Dillâl (Burckhardt, *Dhelel*) is the most southerly of the continuations of this eastern member (Seetzen, *Reisen*, III, iii, 413). The greatest elevation in the et-Tîh range is attained a little west of the meridian 34°, near its most southerly point; it is here 4654 feet above the Mediterranean. From this point the watershed of the plateau runs obliquely between north and east towards Hebron; westward of which line, and northward from the westerly member of Jebel et-Tîh, the whole wady-system is drained by the great Wady el-'Arish, along a gradual slope to the Mediterranean. The shorter and much steeper slope eastward partly converges into the large ducts of wadys Fikreh and el-Jeib, entering the Dead Sea's south-western angle through the southern wall of the Ghôr, and partly finds an outlet nearly parallel, but farther to the south, by the Wady Jerafeh into the Arabah. The great depression of the Dead Sea (1300 feet below the Mediterranean) explains the greater steepness of this eastern slope. In crossing this plateau, Seetzen found that rain and wind had worked depressions in parts of its flat, which contained a few shrubs or isolated bushes. This flat rose here and there in heights steep on one side, composed of white chalk with frequent lumps of flint embedded (*ibid.* iii, 48). The plateau has a central point in the station Khan Nûkhl, so named from the date-trees which once adorned its wady, but which have all disappeared. This point is nearly equidistant from Suez westward, Akabah eastward, el-'Arish northward, and the foot of Jebel Mûsa southward. It lies half a mile north of the "Haj-route," between Suez and Akabah, which traverses "a boundless flat, dreary and desolate" (*ibid.* p. 56), and is 1494 feet above the Mediterranean—nearly on the same meridian as the highest point before assigned to et-Tîh. On this meridian also lies um-Shômer, farther south, the highest point of the entire peninsula, having an elevation of 9300 feet, or nearly double that of et-Tîh. A little to the west of the same meridian lies el-'Arish, and the southern cape, Râs Mohammed, is situated about 34° 17′. Thus the parallel 31° and the meridian 34° form important axes of the whole region of the peninsula. A full description of the wilderness of et-Tîh is given by Robinson (*Bibl. Res.* i, 177, 178, 199), together with a memorandum of the travellers who explored it previously to himself.

On the eastern edge of the plateau to the north of the et-Tîh range, which is raised terrace-wise by a step from the level of the Ghôr, rises a singular second, or, reckoning that level itself, a third plateau, superimposed on the general surface of the et-Tîh region. These Russegger (*Map*) distinguishes as three terraces in the chalk ridges. Dr. Kruse, in his *Anmerkungen* on Seetzen's travels (*Reisen*, III, iii, 410), remarks that the Jebel et-Tîh is the *montes nigri*, or μέλανες of Ptolemy, in whose view that range descends to the extreme southern point of the peninsula, thus including, of course, the Sinaitic region. This confusion arose from a want of distinct conception of geographical details. The name seems to have been obtained from the dark, or even black, color which is observable in parts.

The Haj-route from Suez to Akabah, crossing the peninsula in a direction a little south of east, may stand for the chord of the arc of the et-Tîh range, the length of which latter is about one hundred and twenty miles. This slope, descending northwards upon the Mediterranean, is of limestone (Stanley, *Sinai and Palestine*, p. 7), covered with coarse gravel interspersed with black flints and drift (Russegger, *Map*). But its desolation has not always been so extreme, oxen, asses, and sheep having once grazed in parts of it where now only the camel is found. Three passes through the et-Tîh range are mentioned by Robinson (*Bibl. Res.* i, 123; comp. 561–563, App. xxii)—er-Râkineh, the western; el-Mureikhy, the eastern; and el-Wûrsah, between the two. These all meet south of Ruhaibeh (Rehoboth, Gen. xxvi, 22?), in about north latitude 31° 5′, east longitude 34° 42′, and thence diverge towards Hebron and Gaza. The eastern is noted by Russegger as 4853 feet above sea-level. Seetzen took the et-Tîh range for the "Mount Seir," passed on the way from Sinai (Horeb, Deut. i, 2) to Kadesh Barnea by the Israelites (*Reisen*, iii, 28; comp. Kruse, *Anmerkungen*, iii, 417). It would form a conspicuous object on the left to the Israelites, going south-eastwards near the coast of the gulf of Suez. Seetzen, proceeding towards Suez, i. e. in the opposite direction, mentions a high sandy plain (*Reisen*, iii, 111), apparently near Wady Ghŭrŭndel, whence its steep southern face was visible in a white streak stretching westwards and eastwards. Dr. Stanley (*Sinai and Palestine*, p. 7) says, "However much the other mountains of the peninsula vary in form or height, the mountains of the Tîh are always alike—always faithful to their tabular outline and blanched desolation." They appear like "a long limestone wall." This traveller saw them, however, only "from a distance" (*ibid.* and note 2). Seetzen, who crossed them, going from Hebron to Sinai, says of the view from the highest ridge of the lower mountain-line, "What a landscape was that I looked down upon! On all sides the most frightful wilderness extended out of sight in every direction, without tree, shrub, or speck of green. It was an alternation of flats and hills, for the most part black as night, only the naked rock-walls on the hummocks and heights showed patches of dazzling whiteness... a striking image of our globe, when, through Phaeton's carelessness, the sun came too near to it" (*Reisen*, iii, 50). Similarly, describing the scenery of the Wady el-Biâra, by which he passed the et-Tîh range, he says, "On the south side rose a considerable range, desolate, craggy, and naked. All was limestone, chalk, and flint. The chalk cliffs gave the steep offset of the Tîh range on its south side the aspect of *a snow mountain*" (p. 62). The proper entrance to the interior of this line, although not the usual one for travellers, is by Wady Wutah, which lies at the head of Wady Ghŭrŭndel, and is a fair specimen of the passes of this entire region.

The other routes which traverse the peninsula are, that from Hebron to Suez along the maritime plain, at a distance of from ten to thirty miles from the sea, passing el-'Arish; that from Suez to Tûr, along the coast of the gulf of Suez through the Kâa; and that from Akabah, near Ezion-geber, ascending the western wall of the Arabah through the Wady el-Jeib, by several passes, not far from the southern extremity of the Dead Sea, towards Hebron, in a course here nearly north-west, then again north. A modern mountain road has been partially constructed by Abbas Pasha in the pass of the Wady Hebrân, leading from the coast of the gulf of Suez towards the convent commonly called St. Catherine's. The ascent from the

Wady Wutah.

trough of the Arabah (which is steeper-sided at its north-west extremity than elsewhere) towards the general plateau is by the pass el-Khŭrâr, by which the level of that broad surface is attained. The smaller plateau rests obliquely upon the latter, abutting on the Dead Sea at Masada, where its side and that of the lower floor converge, and is reached by ascending through the higher Nukb es-Sŭfa. Its face, corresponding to the southern face of the Tih plateau, looks considerably to the west of south, owing to this obliquity, and is delineated like a well-defined mountain-wall in Kiepert's map, having at the south-east angle a bold buttress in the Jebel Mŭkhrâh, and at the south-west another in the Jebel 'Arâif en-Nakah, which stands out apparently in the wilderness like a promontory at sea. From the former mountain, its most southerly point, at about 30° 20′ north latitude, this plateau extends northward a little east, till it merges in the southern slope of Judæa, but at about 30° 50′ north latitude is cut nearly through by the Wady Fikreh, trenching its area eastward, and not quite meeting the Wady Mŭrrâh, which has its declivity apparently towards the Wady el-'Arish westward. The face of mountain-wall mentioned above may probably be "the mountain of the Amorites," or this whole higher plateau may be so (Deut. i, 7, 19, 20). A line drawn northwards from Râs Mohammed passes a little to the west of 'Arâif en-Nakah.

On the whole, except in the Debbet er-Ramleh, sand is rare in the peninsula. There is little or none on the seashore, and the plain el-Kâa on the south-west coast is gravelly rather than sandy. Of sandstone on the edges of the granitic central mass there is no lack. It is chiefly found between the chalk and limestone of et-Tih and the southern rocky triangle of Sinai. Thus the Jebel Dillâl is of sandstone, in tall vertical cliffs, forming the boundary of er-Ramleh on the east side, and similar steep sandstone cliffs are visible in the same plain, lying on its north and north-west sides (Seetzen, *Reisen*, iii, 66; comp. iii, 413). In the Wady Mokatteb "the soft surface of these sandstone cliffs offered ready tablets" to the unknown wayfarers who wrote the "Sinaitic inscriptions." This stone gives in some parts a strong red hue to the nearer landscape, and softens into shades of the subtlest delicacy in the distance. Where the surface has been broken away, or fretted and eaten by the action of water, these hues are most vivid (*Sinai and Palestine*, p. 10–12). It has been supposed that the Egyptians worked the limestone of et-Tih, and that that material, as found in the pyramids, was there quarried. The hardness of the granite in the Jebel et-Tûr has been emphatically noticed by travellers. Thus, in constructing recently the mountain road for Abbas Pasha, "the rocks" were found "obstinately to resist even the gunpowder's blast," and the sharp, glass-like edges of the granite soon wear away the workmen's shoes and cripple their feet (Hamilton, *Sinai, the Hedjaz, and Soudan*, p. 17). Similarly, Laborde says (*Comm. on Numb.* xxxiii, 36): "In my journey across that country (from Egypt, through Sinai to the Ghôr), I had carried from Cairo two pair of shoes; they were cut, and my feet came through; when I arrived at Akabah, luckily I found in the magazines of that fortress two other pairs to replace them. On my return to Sinai, I was barefoot again. Hussein then procured me sandals half an inch thick, which, on my arrival in Cairo, themselves were reduced to nothing, though they had well preserved my feet." Seetzen noticed on Mt. St. Catherine that the granite was "fine-grained and very firm" (iii, 90). The name Jebel et-Tûr includes the whole cluster of mountains from el-Fureiâ, on the north, to um-Shômer, on the south, and from Mûsa and ed-Deir, on the east, to Hum'r and Serbâl, on the west, including St. Catherine, nearly south-west of Mûsa. By "Sinai" is generally understood the Mûsa plateau, between the Wady Lejâ (Stanley, *Map*) and the Wady Shueib, on its western and north-eastern flanks, and bounded north-westward by the Wady er-Raheh, and south-eastward by the Wady Sebâyeh. The Arabs give the name of Tûr—properly meaning a high mountain (Stanley, *Sinai and Palestine*, p. 8)—to the whole region south of the Haj-route from Suez to Akabah as far as Ras-Mohammed. The name of Tûr is also emphatically given to the cultivable region lying south-west of the Jebel et-Tûr. Its fine and rich date-palm plantation lies a good way southwards, down the gulf of Suez. Here opens on the sea the most fertile wady now to be found in the peninsula (Burckhardt, *Arab.* ii, 362; Wellsted, ii, 9), receiving all the waters which flow down the range of Sinai westward (Stanley, *Sinai and Palestine*, p. 19).

II. *Interior Peaks.*—Nearly in the centre of the peninsula lies a wedge of granite, grünstein, and porphyry rocks, rising to between eight thousand and nine thousand feet above the sea. Its shape resembles a scalene triangle, with a crescent cut from its northern or longer side, on which border Russegger's map gives a broad, skirting tract of old red sandstone, reaching nearly from gulf to gulf, and traversed by a few ridges, chiefly of a tertiary formation, running nearly north-west and south-east. On the south-west side of this triangle a wide alluvial plain—narrowing, however, towards the north—lines the coast of the gulf of Suez, while that on the eastern or Akabah coast is so narrow as almost to disappear. Between these alluvial edges and the granitic mass a strip of the same sandstone is interposed, the two strips converging at Râs Mohammed, the southern promontory of the whole. This nucleus of plutonic rocks is said to bear no trace of volcanic action since the original upheaval of its masses (Stanley, 21, 22). Laborde (*Travels*, p. 105) thought he detected some, but does not affirm it. Its general configuration runs into neither ranges nor peaks, but is that of a plateau cut across with intersecting wadys, whence spring the cliffs and mountain peaks, beginning with a very gradual and terminating in a very steep ascent.

In the present day the name Sinai, as above stated, is given by Christians to the cluster of mountains to which we have referred; but the Arabs have no other name for this group than Jebel et-Tûr, sometimes adding the distinctive epithet *Sina*. In a stricter sense the name Sinai is applied to a very lofty ridge which lies between the two parallel valleys of Sher and el-Leja. Of this ridge the northern end is sometimes termed Horeb, the southern Sinai, now called Jebel Mûsa, or Moses' Mount. The entire district is a heap of lofty granite rocks, with steep gorges and deep valleys. The several mountains in the peninsula seem all to ascend gradually till they reach their highest point in the group of Sinai, which presents a wild aspect of broken, cleft, and irregular masses, with pointed tops and precipitous sides. The entire group is made up of four huge ranges, which run south and north, with an inclination eastward. The ranges are separated from each other by deep valleys or watercourses.

Certain vivid impressions left on the minds of travellers seem to bespeak remarkable features for the rocks of this cluster, and they are generally so replete with interest that a few leading details of the aspect of principal mountains may find place here. Approaching the granitic nucleus from the north side, Seetzen found himself "ever between two high wild and naked cliffs of granite." All possible forms of mountains blended in the view of the group, conical and pointed, truncated, serrated, and rounded (*Reisen*, iii, 67, 69). Immediately previous to this he had been upon the perpendicular sandstone cliffs, which in el-Dillâl bounded the sandy plain er-Ramleh on the eastern side, while similar steep sandstone cliffs lay on the north and north-west. On a nearer view small bright quartz-grit (*Quarz-kiesel*), of whitish-yellow and reddish hue, was observed in the coarse-grained sandstone. Dr. Stanley, approaching from the north-west, from Wady Shellâl, through wadys Sidri and Feirân, found the rocks of various orders more or less interchanged and intermixed. In the first, "red tops resting on dark-green bases closed the prospect in front," doubtless both of granite. Contrast with this the description of Jebel Mûsa, as seen from Mt. St. Catherine (ibid. p. 77), "the *reddish* granite of its *lower* mass, ending in the gray-*green* granite of the *peak* itself." Wady Sidri lies "between red granite mountains descending precipitously on the sands," but just in the midst of it the granite is exchanged for sandstone, which last forms the rock-tablets of the Wady Mokatteb, lying in the way to Wady Feirân. This last is full of "endless windings," and here "began the curious sight of the mountains, streaked from head to foot, as if with boiling streams of dark red matter poured over them, the igneous fluid squirted upwards as they were heaved from the ground. . . . The colors tell their own story, of chalk and limestone and sandstone and granite." Besides these, "huge cones of white clay and sand are at intervals planted along these mighty watercourses (the now dry wadys), apparently the original alluvial deposit of some tremendous antediluvian torrent, left there to stiffen into sandstone" (p. 71). The Wady Feirân is bounded southwards by the Jebel Nediyeh and the Jebel Serbâl, which extend westwards to the maritime plain, and eastwards to the Sinaitic group, and on whose further or southern side lies the widest part of el-Kâa, previously noticed as the "Wilderness of Sin." Seetzen remarks that Jebel Feirân is not an individual mountain, but, like Sinai, a conspicuous group (*Reisen*, iii, 107; comp. iii, 413).

1. Serbâl rises from a lower level than the Sinaitic group, and so stands out more fully. Dr. Stewart's account of its summit confirms that of Burckhardt. The former mounted from the northern side a narrow plateau at the top of the easternmost peak. A block of gray granite crowns it and several contiguous blocks form one or two grottoes, and a circle of loose stones rests in the narrow plateau at the top (*Tent and the Khan*, p. 117, 118). The "five peaks," to which "in most points of view it is reducible, at first sight appear inaccessible, but are divided by steep ravines filled with fragments of fallen granite." Dr. Stanley mounted "over smooth blocks of granite to the top of the third or central peak," amid which "innumerable shrubs, like sage or thyme, grew to the very summit." Here, too, his ascent was assisted by loose stones arranged by human hands. The peak divides into "two eminences," on "the highest of which, as on the back of some petrified tortoise, you stand, and overlook the whole peninsula" (*Sinai and Palestine*, p. 71, 72). Russegger says "the stone of the peak of Serbâl is porphyry" (*Reisen*, iii, 276). Dr. Stewart mentions the extensive view from its summit of the mountains "which arise from the western shore of the gulf of Akabah," seen in

the north-east, and of the Sinaitic range, "closely packed" with the intermediate Jebel Wateiâh, "forming the most confused mass of mountain-tops that can be imagined" (p. 114, 115). His description of the ascent of the eastern peak is formidable. He felt a rarity of the air, and often had to climb or crawl flat on the breast. It was like "the ascent of a glacier, only of smooth granite, instead of ice." At a quarter of an hour from the summit he also "found a stair of blocks of granite, laid one above another on the surface of the smooth, slippery rock" (p. 113). On the northern summit are visible the remains of a building, "granite fragments cemented with lime and mortar," and "close beside it three of those mysterious inscriptions," implying "that this summit was frequented by unknown pilgrims who used those characters" (*Sinai and Palestine*, p. 72).

2. The approach to Jebel Mûsa from the west is only practicable on foot. It lies through Wady Solam and the Nŭkb Hâwy, "Pass of the Wind," whose stair of rock leads to the second or higher stage of the great mountain labyrinth. Elsewhere this pass would be a roaring torrent. It is amid masses of rock, a thread of a stream just visible, and here and there forming clear pools, shrouded in palms, or leaving its clew to be traced only by rushes. From the head of this pass the cliff-front of Sinai comes in sight through "a long-continued plain between two precipitous mountain-ranges of black and yellow granite." This is the often-mentioned plain er-Râheh. Deep gorges enter it on each side, and the convent and its gardens close the view. The ascent of Jebel Mûsa, which contains "high valleys with abundant springs," is by a long flight of rude steps winding through crags of granite. The cave and chapel "of Elias" are passed on the slope of the ascent, and the summit is marked by the ruins of a mosque and of a Christian church. But, Strauss adds, "the 'Mount of Moses' rose in the south higher and higher still," and the point of this, Jebel Mûsa, eighty feet in diameter, is distant two hours and more from the plain below (*Sinai and Golgotha*, p. 116). The Râs Sŭfsâfeh seems a small, steep, and high mountain, which is interposed between the slope of Jebel Mûsa and the plain; and, from its position, surveys both the openings of es-Sheikh north-east and of er-Râheh north-west, which converge at its foot. Opposite to it, across the plain, is the Jebel Fureiâ, whose peak is cloven asunder, and the taller summit is again shattered and rent, and strewn, as by an earthquake, with its own fragments. The aspect of the plain between Jebel Fureiâ, which here forms a salient angle, wedging southwards, and the Râs Sŭfsâfeh, is described as being, in conjunction with these mountains, wonderfully suggestive, both by its grandeur and its suitableness, for the giving and the receiving of the Law. "That such a plain should exist at all in front of such a cliff is so remarkable a coincidence with the sacred narrative, as to furnish a strong internal argument, not merely of its identity with the scene, but of the scene itself having been described by an eye-witness" (*Sinai and Palestine*, p. 42, 43). The character of the Sinaitic granite is described by Seetzen (*Reisen*, iii, 86) as being (1) flesh-red with glass-colored quartz and black mica, and (2) grayish-white with abundance of the same mica. He adds that the first kind is larger-grained and handsomer than the second. Hamilton speaks of "long ridges of arid rock surrounding him in chaotic confusion on every side," and "the sharp broken peaks of granite far and near as all equally desolate" (*Sinai, the Hedjaz, and Soudan*, p. 31). This view of "granite peaks," so thickly and wildly set as to form "a labyrinth" to the eye, was what chiefly impressed Dr. Stanley in the view from the top of Jebel Mûsa (*Sinai and Palestine*, p. 77). There the weather-beaten rocks are full of curious fissures and holes (p. 46), the surface being "a granite mass cloven into deep gullies and basins" (p. 76). Over the whole mountain the imagination of votaries has stamped the rock with tokens of miracle. The dendrites were viewed as memorials of the burning bush. In one part of the mountain is shown the impress of Moses' back, as he hid himself from the presence of God (ibid. p. 30); in another the hoof-print of Mohammed's mule; in the plain below a rude hollow between contiguous blocks of stone passes for the mould of the head of the golden calf; while in the valley of the Leja, which runs, parallel to and overhung by the Jebel Mûsa's greatest length, into er-Râheh, close to Râs Sŭfsâfeh, the famous "Stone of Moses" is shown—"a detached mass from ten to fifteen feet high, intersected with wide slits or cracks . . . . with the stone between them worn away, as if by the dropping of water from the crack immediately above." This distinctness of the mass of the stone lends itself to the belief of the rabbis, that this "rock followed" the Israelites through the wilderness, which would not be the case with the non-detached offset of some larger cliff. The Koran also contains reference to "the rock with the twelve mouths for the twelve tribes of Israel," i. e. the aforesaid cracks in the stone, into which the Bedawin thrust grass as they mutter their prayers before it. Bishop Clayton accepted it as genuine, so did Whiston, the translator of Josephus; but it is a mere *lusus naturæ;* and there is another fragment, "less conspicuous," in the same valley, "with precisely similar marks." In the pass of the Wady es-Sheikh is another stone, called the "Seat of Moses," described by Laborde (*Sinai and Palestine*, p. 45-48, and notes). Seetzen adds, some paces beyond the "Stone of Moses" several springs, copious for a region so poor in water, have their source from under blocks of granite, one of which is as big as this "Stone of Moses." These springs gush into a very small dyke, and thence are conducted by a canal to supply water to a little fruit-garden. . . . Their water is pure and very good. On this canal, several paces below the basin, lies a considerably bigger block of granite than the "Stone of Moses," "and the canal runs round so close to its side as to be half-concealed by it" (*Reisen*, iii, 95). He seems to argue that this appearance and half-concealment may have been made use of by Moses to procure belief in his having produced the water miraculously, which existed before. But this is wholly inconsistent, as indeed is any view of this being the actual "rock in Horeb," with his view of Rephidim as situated at el-Hessueh, the western extremity of the Wady Feirân. Equally at variance with the Scriptural narrative is the claim of a hole in er-Râheh, below Râs Sŭfsâfeh, to be the "Pit of Korah," whose story belongs to another and far later stage of the march.

3. On Mt. St. Catherine the principal interest lies in the panorama of the whole peninsula which it commands, embraced by the converging horns of the Red Sea, and the complete way in which it overlooks the Jebel Mûsa, which, as seen from it, is by no means conspicuous, being about a thousand feet lower. Seetzen mounted by a path strewn with stones and blocks, having nowhere any steps, like those mentioned as existing at Serbâl, and remarks that jasper and porphyry chiefly constitute the mountain. He reached the highest point in three hours, including intervals of rest, by a hard, steep path, with toilsome clambering; but the actual time of ascending was only one hour and three quarters. The date-palm plantation of Tûr is said to be visible from the top; but the haze prevailing at the time prevented this traveller from verifying it (*Reisen*, iii, 89-93). "The rock of the highest point of this mountain swells into the form of a human body, its arms swathed like that of a mummy, but headless—the counterpart, as it is alleged, of the corpse of the beheaded Egyptian saint. . . . Not improbably this grotesque figure furnishes not merely the illustration, but the origin, of the story" of St. Catherine's body being transported to the spot, after martyrdom, from Egypt, by angelic hands (*Sinai and Palestine*, p. 45).

4. The remaining principal mountain of this central cluster is named variously ed-Deir, "the Convent;" "Bestin," from St. Episteme, the first abbess of the nunnery; "Solab," from "the Cross," which stands on its summit; and the "Mount of the Burning Bush," from a legend that a sunbeam shoots down, supposed miraculously, on one day in the year, through the mountain into the chapel "of the Burning Bush" (so called) in the convent (*ibid.* p. 78). In the pass of the convent rocks arise on every side, in long succession, fantastically colored, gray, red, blue, bright yellow, and bronze, sometimes strangely marked with white lines of quartz or black bands of basalt; huge blocks worn into fantastic shapes . . . interrupt the narrow track, which successive ages have worn along the face of the precipice, or, hanging overhead, threaten to overwhelm the traveller in their fall. The wady which contains this pass is called by the name of Shu'eib—a corruption of Hobab, the name of the father-in-law of Moses (*ibid.* p. 32, 33). At the foot of a mountain near the convent Seetzen noticed "a range of rocks of black horn-porphyry, of hornblende, and black jasper, and between their scrolls or volutes white quartz." The gardens, as has been noticed, are in sight from the approach through er-Râheh. Seetzen enlarges on their beauty, enhanced, of course, by the savage wild about them; "indeed, a blooming vegetation appears in this climate wherever there is water" (*Reisen*, iii, 70, 73, 87). These proved capabilities of the soil are of interest in reference to the Mosaic and to every period. As regards the convent, the reader may be referred to Dr. Stanley's animated description of its character, the policy of its founder, and the quality of its inmates (*Sinai and Palestine*, p. 51-56). This traveller took three hours in the ascent. "In the recesses between the peaks was a ruined Bedawin village. On the highest level was a small natural basin, thickly covered with shrubs of myrrh —of all the spots of the kind that I saw, the best suited for the feeding of Jethro's flocks in the seclusion of the mountain" (*ibid.* p. 78). He thought the prospect, however, from its summit inferior in various ways to any of the other views from the neighboring mountains, Serbâl, St. Catherine, Jebel Mûsa, or Râs Sŭfsâfeh.

5. Three or four days' journey south from Jebel Mûsa lies Jebel um-Shômer, which, although not quite so high as Mt. St. Catherine (the summit being 8449 feet high), may yet be said to be the culminating peak of the entire group. It was ascended by an English party in 1862, and still later by captain Palmer, of the exploration engineers. This mountain is connected in Arab legend with a romantic story of a fairy maiden's abode there, in whose honor one of its cliffs has received the name of Hajr el-Bint. The ascent is extremely laborious, but the view from the summit is extremely fine, embracing the Red Sea, the gulfs of Akabah and Suez, and the peaks and ridges be-

Jebel um-Shômer.

tween them, while Mt. St. Catherine bounds the scene on the north (see Palmer's *Desert of the Exodus*, p. 202 sq.).

6. The rocks, on leaving Sinai on the east for Akabah, are curiously intermingled, somewhat as in the opposite margin of the wadys Sidri and Mokatteb. Wady Seyâl contains "hills of a conical shape, curiously slanting across each other, and with an appearance of serpentine and basalt. The wady . . . then mounted a short rocky pass—of hills capped with sandstone—and entered on a plain of deep sand—the first we had encountered—over which were scattered isolated clumps of sandstone, with occasional chalk. . . . At the close of this plain an isolated rock, its high tiers rising out of lower tiers, like a castle." Here "the level ranges of et-Tîh rose in front." Soon after, on striking down, apparently north-eastwards, "a sandy desert, amidst fantastic sandstone rocks, mixed with lilac and dull green, as if of tufa," succeeded. After this came a desert strewn with "fragments of the Tîh," i.e. limestone, but "presently," in the "Wady Ghŭzâleh," which turns at first nearly due northward, and then deflects westward, the "high granite rocks" reappeared; and in the Wady el-'Ain "the rocks rise, red granite or black basalt, occasionally tipped as if with castles of sandstone to the height of about one thousand feet . . . and finally open on the sea. At the mouth of the pass are many traces of flood—trees torn down, and strewed along the sand (*ibid.* p. 80, 81).

III. *Comparative Fertility.*—A most important general question is the extent to which this "wilderness" is capable of supporting animal and human life, especially when taxed by the consumption of such flocks and herds as the Israelites took with them from Egypt, and probably—though we know not to what extent this last was supplied by the manna—by the demand made on its resources by a host of from 2,000,000 to 3,000,000 souls. In answer to this question, "much," it has been observed (*Sinai and Palestine*, p. 24), "may be allowed for the spread of the tribes of Israel far and wide through the whole peninsula, and also for the constant means of support from their own flocks and herds." Something, too, might be elicited from the undoubted fact that a population nearly, if not quite, equal to the whole permanent population of the peninsula does actually pass through the desert, in the caravan of the five thousand African pilgrims, on their way to Mecca. But, among these considerations, it is important to observe what indications there may be of the mountains of Sinai having ever been able to furnish greater resources than at present. These indications are well summed up by Ritter (*Sinai*, p. 926, 927). There is no doubt that the vegetation of the wadys has considerably decreased. In part, this would be an inevitable effect of the violence of the winter torrents. The trunks of palm-trees washed up on the shore of the Dead Sea, from which the living tree has now for many centuries disappeared, show what may have been the devastation produced among those mountains where the floods, especially in earlier times, must have been violent to a degree unknown in Palestine; while the peculiar cause—the impregnation of salt—which has preserved the vestiges of the older vegetation there, has here, of course, no existence. The traces of such a destruction were pointed out to Burckhardt (*Arab.* p. 538) on the eastern side of Mount Sinai, as having occurred within half a century before his visit; also to Wellsted (ii, 15), as having occurred near Tûr, in 1832. In part, the same result has followed from the reckless waste of the Bedawin tribes—reckless in destroying and careless in replenishing. A fire, a pipe, lit under a grove of desert trees, may clear away the vegetation of a whole valley.

"The acacia-trees have been of late years ruthlessly destroyed by the Bedawin for the sake of charcoal," which forms "the chief, perhaps it might be said the only, traffic of the peninsula" (*Sinai and Palestine*, p. 24). Thus, the clearance of this tree in the mountains where it abounded once, and its decrease in the neighbor groups in which it exists still, is accounted for, since the monks appear to have aided the devastation. Vegetation, where maintained, nourishes water and keeps alive its own life, and no attempts to produce vegetation anywhere in this desert seem to have failed. "The gardens at the wells of Moses, under the French and English agents from Suez, and the gardens in the valleys of Jebel Mûsa, under the care of the Greek monks of the Convent of St. Catherine," are conspicuous examples (*ibid.* p. 26). Besides, a traveller in the 16th century calls the Wady er-Raheh, in front of the convent, now entirely bare, "a vast *green* plain" (Monconys). In this wilderness, too, abode Amalek, "the first of the nations," powerful enough seriously to imperil the passage of the Israelites through it, and importantly contributing to subsequent history under the monarchy. Besides them we have "king Arad the Canaanite, who dwelt in the south," i. e. apparently on the terrace of mountain overhanging the Ghôr near Masada, on the Dead Sea, in a region now wholly desolate. If his people were identical with the Amorites or Canaanites of Numb. xiv, 43; Deut. i, 44, then, besides the Amalekites of Exod. xvii, 8, we have *one* other host within the limits of what is now desert who fought with Israel on equal or superior terms; and, if they are not identical, we have *two* such (Numb. xiv, 40-45; xxi, 1; xxxiii, 40; Deut. i, 43, 44). These must have been "something more than a mere handful of Bedawin. The Egyptian copper-mines, monuments, and hieroglyphics in Sŭrâbit el-Khadim and the Wady Mŭghâra imply a degree of intercourse between Egypt and the peninsula" in a period probably older than the Exodus, "of which all other traces have long ceased. The ruined cities of Edom, in the mountains east of the Arabah, and the remains and history of Petra itself, indicate a traffic and a population in these remote regions which now is almost inconceivable" (*Sinai and Palestine*, p. 26). Even the 6th and 7th centuries A.D. showed traces of habitation, some of which still remain in ruined cells and gardens, etc., far exceeding the tale told by present facts. Seetzen, in what is perhaps as arid and desolate a region as any in the whole desert, asked his guide to mention all the neighboring places whose names he knew. He received a list of sixty-three places in the neighborhood of Madŭrah, Petra, and Akabah, and of twelve more in the Ghôr es-Saphia, of which total of seventy-five all save twelve are now abandoned to the desert, and have retained nothing save their names — "a proof," he remarks, "that in very early ages this region was extremely populous, and that the furious rage with which the Arabs, both before and after the age of Mohammed, assailed the Greek emperors, was able to convert into a waste this blooming region, extending from the limit of the Hedjaz to the neighborhood of Damascus" (*Reisen*, iii, 17, 18).

Thus the same traveller in the same journey (from Hebron to Madûrah) entered a wady called el-Jemen, where was no trace of water save moist spots in the sand, but on making a hole with the hand it was quickly full of water, good and drinkable (*ibid.* p. 13). The same, if saved in a cistern, and served out by sluices, might probably have clothed the bare wady with verdure. This is confirmed by his remark (*ibid.* p. 83) that a blooming vegetation shows itself in this climate wherever there is water, as well as by the example of the tank system as practiced in Hindustan. He also notices that there are quicksands in many spots of the Debbet er-Ramleh, which it is difficult to understand, unless as caused by accumulations of water (*ibid.* p. 67). Similarly in the desert Wady el-Kudeis, between Hebron and Sinai, he found a spot of quicksand with sparse shrubs growing in it (*ibid.* p. 48).

Now the question is surely a pertinent one, as compared with that of the subsistence of the flocks and herds of the Israelites during their wanderings, how the sixty-three perished communities named by Seetzen's guide can have supported themselves? It is pretty certain that fish cannot live in the Dead Sea, nor is there any reason for thinking that these extinct towns or villages were in any large proportion near enough to its waters to avail themselves of its resources, even if such existed. To suppose that the country could ever have supported extensive coverts for game is to assume the most difficult of all solutions of the question. The creatures that find shelter about the rocks, as hares, antelopes, gazelles, jerboas, and the lizards that burrow in the sand (el-dsobb), alluded to by this traveller in several places (iii, 67; comp. iii, 415–442, and Laborde, *Comm. on Numb.* xxxiii, 42), are far too few, to judge from appearances, to do more than eke out a subsistence, the staple of which must have been otherwise supplied; and the same remark will apply to such casual windfalls as swarms of edible locusts, or flights of quails. Nor can the memory of these places be probably connected with the distant period when Petra, the commercial metropolis of the Nabathæans, enjoyed the carrying trade between the Levant and Egypt westwards, and the rich communities farther east. There is, least of all, reason for supposing that by the produce of mines, or by asphalt gathered from the Dead Sea, or by any other native commodities, they can ever have enjoyed a commerce of their own. We are thrown back, then, upon the supposition that they must in some way have supported themselves from the produce of the soil. And the produce for which it is most adapted is either that of the date-palm, or that to which earlier parallels point, as those of Jethro and the Kenites, and of the various communities in the southern border of Judah (Numb. xxxiv, 4, 5; Josh. xv, 3, 4; 1 Sam. xxx, 27–31), viz., that of pasturage for flocks and herds, a possibility which seems solely to depend on adequately husbanding the water supplied by the rains. This tallies with the use of the word מִדְבָּר, for "wilderness," i. e. "a wide open space, with or without actual pasture, the country of the nomads, as distinguished from that of the agricultural and settled people" (*Sinai and Palestine*, p. 486, App. § 9). There seems, however, to be implied in the name a capacity for pasturage, whether actually realized or not. This corresponds, too, with the "thin," or rather "transparent coating of vegetation," seen to clothe the greater part of the Sinaitic wilderness in the present day (*ibid.* p. 16, 22), and which furnishes an initial minimum from which human fostering hands might extend the prospect of possible resources up to a point as far in excess of present facts as were the numbers of the Israelitish host above the six thousand Bedawin computed now to form the population of the desert. As regards the date-palm, Hasselquist speaks as though it alone afforded the means of life to some existing Arab communities. Hamilton (*Sinai*, p. 17) says that in his path by the Wady Hebrân, towards the modern Sinai, "small clumps of uncultivated date-trees rise between the granite walls of the pass, wherever the winter torrents have left sufficient detritus for their nourishment." Again, after describing the pass of the Convent, he continues, "beneath lies a veritable chaos, through which now trickles a slender thread of water, where in winter rushes down a boiling torrent" (ibid. p. 19). It is hardly too much to affirm that the resources of the desert, under a careful economy of nature's bounty, might be, to its present means of subsistence, as that winter torrent's volume to that summer streamlet's slender thread. In the Wady Hebrân this traveller found "a natural bath," formed in the granite by the 'Ain Hebrân, called "the Christians' pool" (*ibid.* p. 17). Two thirds of the way up the Jebel Mûsa he came upon "a frozen streamlet" (*ibib.* p. 30); and Seetzen, on April 14, found snow lying about in sheltered clefts of Mt. St. Catherine, where the rays of the sun could not penetrate (iii, 92). Hamilton encountered on the Jebel Mûsa a thunderstorm, with "heavy rain" (*Sinai*, p. 16). There seems on the whole no deficiency of precipitation. Indeed, the geographical situation would rather bespeak a copious supply. Any southerly wind must bring a fair amount of watery vapor from the Red Sea, or from one of its expanding arms, which embrace the peninsula on either side, like the blades of a forfex; while at no greater distance than one hundred and forty miles northward roll the waters of the Mediterranean, supplying, we may suppose, their quota, which the much lower ranges of the Tîh and Ojme cannot effectually intercept. Nor is there any such shelter from rain-clouds on either of the gulfs of Suez and Akabah, as the long line of mountains on the eastern flank of Egypt, which screens the rain supply of the former from reaching the valley of the Nile. On the contrary, the conformation of the peninsula, with the high wedge of granitic mountains at its core, would rather receive and condense the vapors from either gulf, and precipitate their bounty over the lower faces of mountain and troughs of wady, interposed between it and the sea. It is much to be regretted that the low intellectual condition of the monks forbids any reasonable hope of adequate meteorological observations to check these merely probable arguments with trustworthy statements of fact; but in the absence of any such register, it seems only fair to take reasonable probabilities fully into view. Yet some significant facts are not wanting to redeem in some degree these probabilities from the ground of mere hypothesis. "In two of the great wadys" which break the wilderness on the coast of the gulf of Suez, "Ghŭrŭndel, and Useit, with its continuation of the Wady Tayibeh, tracts of vegetation are to be found in considerable luxuriance." The wadys leading down from the Sinai range to the gulf of Akabah "furnish the same testimony, in a still greater degree," as stated by Rüppell, Miss Martineau, Dr. Robinson, and Burckhardt. "In three spots, however, in the desert . . . this vegetation is brought, by the concurrence of the general configuration of the country, to a still higher pitch. By far the most remarkable collection of springs is that which renders the clusters of the Jebel Mûsa the chief resort of the Bedawin tribes during the summer heats. Four abundant sources in the mountains immediately above the convent of St. Catherine must always have made that region one of the most frequented of the desert. . . . Oases (analogous to that of Ammon in the western desert of the Nile) are to be found wherever the waters from the different wadys or hills, whether from winter streams or from such living springs as have just been described, converge to a common reservoir. One such oasis in the Sinaitic desert seems to be the palm-grove of el-Wâdy at Tûr, described by Burckhardt as so thick that he could hardly find his way through it (*Sinai and Palestine*, p. 19, note 1; see Burckhardt, *Arab*, ii, 362). The other and the more important is the wady Feirân, high up in the table-land of Sinai itself" (*ibid.* p. 18, 19). Now, what nature has done in these favored spots might surely be seconded in others by an ample population, familiarized, to some extent, by their sojourn in Egypt with the most advanced agriculturists of the then world, and guided by an able leader who knew the country, and found in his wife's family others who knew it even better than he (Numb. x, 31). It is thus supposable that the language of Psa. cvii, 35–38, is based on no mere pious imagery, but on actual fact: "He turneth the wilderness into a standing water, and dry ground into water-springs. And there he maketh the hungry to dwell, that they may prepare a city for habitation; and sow the fields and plant vineyards, which may yield fruits of increase. He blesseth them so that they are multiplied greatly; and *suffereth not their cattle to decrease.*" Thus we may find an approximate basis of reality for the enhanced poetic images of Isaiah (xli, 19; lv, 13). Palestine itself affords abundant tokens of the resources of nature so husbanded, as in the artificial "terraces of which there are still traces to the very summits" of the mountains, and some of which still, in the Jordan valley, "are occupied by masses of vegetation" (*Sinai and Palestine*, p. 138, 297). In favored spots wild luxuriance testifies to the extent of the natural resources, as in the wadys of the coast, and in the plain of Jericho, where "far and wide extends the green circle of tangled thickets, in the midst of which are the hovels of the modern village, beside which stood, in ancient times, the great city of Jericho" (*ibid.* p. 306). From this plain alone, a correspondent of the British consul at Jaffa asserts that he could feed the whole population of modern Syria (*Cotton Supply Reporter*, June 14, 1862). But a plantation redeemed from the wilderness is ever in the position of a besieged city; when once the defence of the human garrison is withdrawn, the fertility stimulated by its agency must obviously perish by the invasion of the wild. So we may probably suppose that, from numberless tracts, thus temporarily rescued from barrenness, in situations only moderately favorable, the traces of verdure have vanished, and the desert has reclaimed its own; or that there the soil only betrays its latent capacity by an unprofitable dampness of the sand.

Seetzen, on the route from Hebron to Sinai, after describing an "immense flinty plain," the "dreariest and most desolate solitude," observes that, "as soon as the rainy season is over and the warm weather sets in, the pits (of rain-water) dry up, and it becomes uninhabitable," as "there are no brooks or springs here" (iii, 55, 56). Dr. Stewart (*Tent and the Khan*, p. 14, 15) says of the Wady Ahthi, which he would identify with Etham (Exod. xiii, 20; Numb. xxxiii, 6), "sand-hills of considerable height separate it from the sea, and prevent the winter rains from running off rapidly. A considerable deposit of rich alluvial loam is the result, averaging from two to four inches in thickness, by sowing upon which immediately after the rains the Bedawin could certainly reap a rich harvest; but they affect to despise all agricultural labor. . . . Yet," he adds, "the region never could have supplied food by its own natural vegetation for so great a multitude of flocks and herds as followed in the train of the Israelites." This seems rather a precipitate sentence; for one can hardly tell what its improved condition under ancient civilization may have yielded, from merely seeing what it now is, after being overrun for centuries by hordes of contemptuous Bedawin. Still, as regards the general question, we are not informed what numbers of cattle followed the Israelites out of Egypt. We only know that "flocks and herds" went with them, were forbidden to graze "before the mount" (Sinai), and shared the fortunes of the desert with their owners. It further appears that, at the end of the forty years' wandering, two tribes and a half were the chief, perhaps the only, cattle-masters. And, when we consider how greatly the long and sore bondage of Egypt must have interfered with their favorite pursuit during the eighty years of Moses' life before the Exode, it seems reasonable to think that in the other tribes only a few would have possessed cattle on leaving Egypt. The notion of a people "scattered abroad throughout all the land of Egypt" (Exod. v, 12), in pursuit of wholly different and absorbing labor, being able generally to maintain their wealth as sheep-masters is obviously absurd. It is therefore supposable that Reuben, Gad, and a portion of Manasseh had, by remoteness of local position, or other favorable circumstances to us unknown, escaped the oppressive consequences to their flocks and herds which must have generally prevailed. We are not told that the lambs at the first passover were obtained from the flock of each family, but only that they were bidden to "*draw out* and *take* a lamb for an house"—a direction quite consistent in many, perhaps in most cases, with purchase. Hence it is probable that these two tribes and a half may have been the chief cattle-masters first as well as last. If they had enough cattle to find their pursuit in tending them, and the others had not, economy would dictate a transfer; and the whole multitude of cattle would probably fare better by such an arrangement than by one which left a few head scattered up and down in the families of different tribes. Nor is there any reason to think that the whole of the forty years' sojourn was spent in such locomotion as marks the more continuous portion of the narrative. The great gap in the record of events left by the statement of Deut. i, 46, "Ye abode in Kadesh many days," may be filled up by the supposition of quarters established in a favorable site, and the great bulk of the whole time may have been really passed in such stationary encampments. And here, if two tribes and a half only were occupied in tending cattle, some resource of labor, to avoid the embarrassing temptations of idleness in a host so large and so disposed to murmur, would be, in a human sense, necessary. Nor can any so probable an occupation be assigned to the remaining nine and a half tribes, as that of drawing from the wilderness whatever contributions it might be made to afford. From what they had seen in Egypt, the work of irrigation would be familiar to them, and from the prospect before them in Palestine the practice would at some time become necessary: thus there were on the whole the soundest reasons for not allowing their experience, if possible, to lapse. Irrigation being supposed, there is little, if any, difficulty in supposing its results; to the spontaneousness of which ample testimony, from various travellers, has been cited above. At any rate it is unwise to decide the question of the possible resources of the desert from the condition to which the apathy and fastidiousness of the Bedawin have reduced it in modern times. On this view, while the purely pastoral tribes would retain their habits unimpaired, the remainder would acquire some slight probation in those works of the field which were to form the staple industry of their future country. But, if any one still insists that the produce of the desert, however supposably improved, could never have yielded support for *all* "the flocks and herds"—utterly indefinite as their number is—which were carried thither; this need not invalidate the present argument, much less be deemed inconsistent with the Scriptural narrative. There is nothing in the latter to forbid our supposing that the cattle perished in the wilderness by hundreds or by thousands. Even if the words of Psa. cvii, 38, be taken in a sense literally historical, they need mean no more than that, by the time they reached the borders of Palestine, the number so lost had, by a change of favorable circumstances, been replaced, perhaps even by capture from the enemy, over whom God, and not their own sword, had given them the victory. All that is contended for is that the resources of the wilderness were doubtless utilized to the utmost, and that the flocks and herds, so far as they survived, were so kept alive. What those resources might amount to, is perhaps nearly as indefinite an inquiry as what was the number of the cattle. The difficulty would "find its level" by the diminution of the latter till it fell within the limits of the former; and in this balanced state we must be content to leave the question.

Nor ought it to be left out of view, in considering any arguments regarding the possible change in the character of the wilderness, that Egyptian policy certainly lay, on the whole, in favor of extending the desolation to their own frontier on the Suez side; for thus they would gain the surest protection against invasion on their most exposed border; and as Egypt rather aimed at the development of a high internal civilization than an extension of influence by foreign conquest, such a desert frontier would be to Egypt a cheap defence. Thus we may assume that the Pharaohs, at any rate after the rise of the Assyrian empire, would discern their interest and would act upon it, and that the felling of wood and stopping of wells, and the obliteration, wherever possible, of oases, would systematically make the peninsula untenable to a hostile army descending from the north-east or the north.

IV. *Natural History.*—The domestic cattle of the Bedawin will of course be found here, but camels more numerously in the drier tracts of et-Tîh. Schubert (*Reisen*, ii, 354) speaks of Sinai as not being frequented by any of the larger beasts of prey, nor even by jackals. The lion has become very rare, but is not absolutely unknown in the region (*Negeb*, p. 46, 47). Foxes and hyenas, Ritter (xiv, 333) says, are rare, but Mr. Tyrwhitt mentions hyenas as common in the Wady Mughâra; and Ritter (ibid.), on the authority of Burckhardt, ascribes to the region a creature which appears to be a cross between a leopard and a wolf, both of which are rare in the peninsula, but by which probably a hyena is to be understood. A leopard-skin was obtained by Burckhardt on Sinai, and a fine leopard is stated by Mr. Tyrwhitt to have been seen by some of his party in their ascent of um-Shômer in 1862. Schubert continues his list in the *hyrax Syriacus*, the ibex—seen at Tufîleh in flocks of forty or fifty together, and a pair of whose horns, seen by Burckhardt (*Arab.* p. 405, 406) at Kerek, measured three and a half feet in length—the webr, the shrew-mouse, and a creature which he calls the "spring-maus" (*mus jaculus* or jerboa ?), also a *canis famelicus*, or desert-fox, and a lizard known as the *Agama Sinaitica*, which may possibly be identical with one of those described below. Hares and jerboas are found in Wady Feirân. Schubert quotes (ibid. note) Rüppell as having found specimens of *Helix* and of *Coccinella* in this wilderness; for the former, comp. Forskål, *Icones Rerum Natur.* Tab. xvi. Schubert saw a fine eagle in the same region, besides catching specimens of thrush, with stonechat and other song-birds, and speaks of the warbling of the birds as being audible from the *Mimosa* bush. Clouds of birds of passage were visible in the Wady Murrah. Near the same tract of wilderness Dr. Stanley saw "the sky darkened by the flights of innumerable birds, which proved to be large red-legged cranes, three feet in height, with black and white wings measuring seven feet from tip to tip" (*Sinai and Palestine*, p. 82). At Tufîleh crows abound. On Serbâl Dr. Stewart saw the red-legged partridge (*Tent and Khan*, p. 117; comp. Burckhardt, *Syria*, p. 534); and the bird "katta," in some parts of the peninsula, comes in such numbers that boys sometimes knock over three or four at a single throw of a stick. Hasselquist, who saw it here and in Egypt, calls it a partridge, smaller than ours, and of a grayish color (p. 204). Ritter (xiv, 333) adds linnets(?), ducks, prairie-birds, heath-cocks, larks, a specimen of finch, besides another small bird, probably redbreast or chaffinch, the varieties of falcon known as the *Brachydactylus* and the *Niger*, and, of course, on the coast, sea-swallows and mews. Flocks of blue rock pigeons were repeatedly seen by Mr. Tyrwhitt.

Seetzen, going from Hebron to Madura, makes mention of the following animals, whose names were mentioned by his guides, though he does not say that any of them were seen by himself: wolf, porcupine, wild-cat, ounce, mole, wild-ass, and three not easily to be identified, the *Sellek*, dog-shaped, the *Anasch*, which devours the gazelle, and the *Ikkajib*, said to be small and in shape like a hedgehog. Seetzen's list in this locality also includes certain reptiles, of which such as can be identified are explained in the notes: *el-Melledsha*, *Um el-Zleiman*, *el-Lidsha* or *Leja*, *el-Harraba* or *Hirbâ*, *Jerrâr* or *Jarrâreh*, *el-Dâb*, otherwise *Dúde*, *el-Hanne* or *Hanan*, *el-Leffeá*; and among birds the partridge, duck, stork, eagle, vulture (*er-Rakham*), crow (*el-Grâb*), kite (*Hidâyeh*), and an unknown bird called by him *Um-Salêt*. His guides told him of ostriches as seen near *Bteiâha* on the way from Hebron to Sinai, and he saw a nightingale, but it seems at no great distance to the south of Hebron. The same writer also mentions the edible lizard, *el-Dsob*, as frequently found in most parts of the wilderness, and his third volume has an appendix on zoology, particularly describing, and often with illustrations, many reptiles and serpents of Egypt and Arabia, without, however, pointing out such as are peculiar to the wilderness. Among these are thirteen varieties of lizard, twenty-one of serpent, and seven of frog, besides fifteen of Nile-fish. Laborde speaks of serpents, scorpions, and black-scaled lizards, which perforate the sand, as found on the eastern border of Edom near Tufileh (*Comm. on Numb.* xxxiii, 42). The MS. of Mr. Tyrwhitt speaks of starting "a large sand-colored lizard, about three feet long, exactly like a crocodile, with the same bandy look about his fore-legs, the elbows turning out enormously." He is described as covered not only "in scales, but in a regular armor, which rattled quite loudly as he ran." He "got up before the dromedary, and vanished into a hole among some *retem*." This occurred at the head of the Wady Mokatteb. Hasselquist (p. 220) gives a *Lacerta Scincus*, "the Scinc," as found in Arabia Petræa, near the Red Sea, as well as in Upper Egypt, which he says is much used by the inhabitants of the East as an aphrodisiac, the flesh of the animal being given in powder, and in broth. He also mentions the edible locust, *Gryllus Arabicus*, which appears to be common in the wilderness, as in other parts of Arabia, giving an account of the preparation of it for food (p. 230–233). Burckhardt names a cape not far from Akabah, Râs Um Haye, from the number of serpents which abound there, and accordingly applied to this region the description of the "fiery serpents" in Numb. xxi, 4–9. Schubert (ii, 362) remarked the first serpents in going from Suez and Sinai to Petra, near el-Hudherâh; he describes them as speckled. Burckhardt (*Syria*, p. 499, 502) saw tracks of serpents, two inches thick, in the sand. According to Rüppell, serpents elsewhere in the peninsula are rare. He names two poisonous kinds, *Cerastes* and *Scytalis* (Ritter, xiv, 329). The scorpion has given his name to the "Ascent of Scorpions," which was part of the boundary of Judah on the side of the southern desert. Wady es-Zuweirah, in that region, swarmed with them; and De Saulcy says "you cannot turn over a single pebble in the Nejd (a branch wady) without finding one under it" (De Saulcy, i, 529, quoted in *Negeb*, p. 51).

The reader who is curious about the fish, mollusca, etc., of the gulf of Suez should consult Schubert (ii, 263 note; 298 note; and for the plants of the same coast, 294 note). For a description of the coral-banks of the Red Sea, see Ritter (xiv, 476 sq.), who remarks that these formations rise from the coast-edge always in longitudinal extension parallel to its line, bespeaking a fundamental connection with the upheaval of the whole stretch of shore from south-east to north-west. A fish which Seetzen calls the *Alûm* may be mentioned as furnishing to the Bedawin the fish-skin sandals of which they are fond. Ritter (xiv, 327) thinks that fish may have contributed materially to the sustenance of the Israelites in the desert (Numb. xi, 22), as they are now dried and salted for sale in Cairo or at the Convent of St. Catherine. In a brook near the foot of Serbâl, Schubert saw some varieties of *Elaphrus, Dyticus, Colymbetes, Gyrinus*, and other water insects (*Reisen*, ii, 302 note).

As regards the flora of the desert, the most frequently found trees are the date-palm (*Phœnix dactylifera*), the desert acacia, and the tamarisk. The palms are almost always dwarf, as described in *Sinai and Palestine*, p. 20, but sometimes the "dôm" palm is seen, as on the shore of the gulf of Akabah (Schubert, ii, 370; comp. Robinson, i, 161). Hasselquist, speaking of the date-palm's powers of sustenance, says that some of the poorer families in Upper Egypt live on nothing else, the very stones being ground into a provender for the dromedary. This tree is often found in tufts of a dozen or more together, the dead and living boughs interlacing overhead, the dead and living roots intertwining below, and thus forming a canopy in the desert. The date-palms in Wady Tûr are said to be all numbered and registered. The acacia is the *Mimosa Nilotica*, and this forms the most common vegetation of the wilderness. Its Arabic name is *es-Seyâl*, and it is generally supposed to have furnished the "Shittim wood" for the Tabernacle (Forskâl, *Descr. Plant.* Cent. vi, No. 90; Celsius, *Hierobot.* i, 498 sq.; Ritter, xiv, 335 sq.). See SHITTAH-TREE. It is armed with fearful thorns, which sometimes tear the packages on the camels' backs, and of course would severely lacerate man or beast. The gum arabic is gathered from this tree, on which account it is also called the *Acacia gummifera*. Other tamarisks, beside the *mannifera*, mentioned above, are found in the desert. Grass is comparatively rare, but its quantity varies with the season. Robinson, on finding some in Wady Sumghy, north-east from Sinai, near the gulf of Akabah, remarks that it was the first his party had seen since leaving the Nile. The terebinth (*Pistachia terebinthus*, Arab. *Bûtm*) is well known in the wadys about Beersheba, but in the actual wilderness it hardly occurs. For a full description of it see Robinson, ii, 222, 223, and notes, also i, 208, and comp. Celsius, *Hierobot.* i, 34. The "broom," of the variety known as *retem* (Heb. and Arab.), rendered in the authorized version by "juniper," is a genuine desert plant; it is described (Robinson, i, 203 and note) as the largest and most conspicuous shrub therein, having very bitter roots, and yielding a quantity of excellent charcoal, which is the staple, if one may so say, of the desert. The following are mentioned by Schubert (ii, 352–354) as found within the limits of the wilderness: *Mespilus Aaronia, Colutea haleppica, Atraphaxis spinosa, Ephedra alaba, Cytisus uniflorus*, and a *Cynomorium*, a highly interesting variety, compared by Schubert to a well-known Maltese one. To these he adds in a note (ibid.): *Dactylis memphitica, Gagea reticulata, Rumex vesicarius, Artemisia Judaica, Leyssera discoidea, Santolina fragrantissima, Seriola, Lindenbergia Sinaica, Lamium amplexicaule, Stachys affinis, Sisymbrium iris, Anchusa Milleri, Asperugo procumbens, Omphalodes intermedia, Dœmia cordata, Reseda canescens* and *pruinosa, Reaumuria vermiculata, Fumaria parviflora, Hypecoum pendulum, Cleome trinervis, Ærua tomentosa, Malva Honbezey, Fagonia, Zygophyllum coccineum, Astragalus Fresenii, Genista monosperma.* Schubert (ii, 357) also mentions, as found near Abu Suweir, north-east of Sinai, a kind of sage, and of what is probably goat's-rue, also (note, ibid.) a fine variety of *Astragalus*, together with *Linaria, Lotus, Cynosurus echinatus, Bromus tectorum*, and (p. 365) two varieties of *Pergularia*, the *Procera* and the *Tomentosa*.

In the south-west region of the Dead Sea grows the singular tree of the apples of Sodom, the *Asclepias gigantea* of botanists. Dr. Robinson, who gives a full description of it (i, 522, 523), says it might be taken for a gigantic species of the milk-weed or silk-weed found in the northern regions of the United States. He condemns the notion of Hasselquist (p. 285, 287, 288) as an error, that the fruit of the *Solanum melongela*, when punctured by a tenthredo, resulted in the Sodom apple, retaining the skin uninjured, but wholly changed to dust within (ibid. p. 524). It is the *'Osher* of the Arabs. Robinson also mentions willows, hollyhocks, and hawthorns in the Sinaitic region, from the first of which the *Râs Sufsâfeh*, "willow-head," takes its name (i, 106, 109: Stanley, *Sinai and Palestine*, p. 17). He saw hyssop (*Jâdeh*) in abundance, and thyme (*Za'ter*), and in the Wady Feirân the colocynth, the *Kirdhy* or *Kirdi*, a green thorny plant with a yellow flower; and in or near the Arabah, the juniper (*'Arar*), the oleander (*Difleh*), and another shrub like it, the *Zaknûm*, as also the plant *el-Ghŭdah*, resembling the *Retem*, but larger (i, 110, 83; ii, 124, 126, 119 and note). He also describes the *Ghŭrkŭd*, which has been suggested as possibly the "tree" cast by Moses into the waters of Marah (Exod. xv, 25). It grows in saline regions of intense heat, bearing a small red berry, very juicy, and slightly acidulous. Being constantly found among brackish pools, the "bane and antidote" would thus, on the above supposition, be side by side, but as the fruit ripens in June, it could not have been ready for its supposed use in the early days of the Exodus (Robinson, i, 66–69). He adds in a note that Forskâl gives it (*Flor. Egypt. Arab.* p. lxvi), as the *Peganum retusum*, but that it is more correctly the *Nitraria tridentata* of Desfontaines (*Flora Atlant.* i, 372). The mountain Um Shomer takes its name from the fennel found upon it, as perhaps may Serbâl from the *Ser*, myrrh, which "creeps over its ledges up to the very summit"—a plant noticed by Dr. Stanley as "thickly covering" with its "shrubs" the "natural basin" which surmounts ed-Deir, and as seen in the Wady Seyâl, north-east from Sinai (*Sinai and Palestine*, p. 17, 78–80). Dr. Stanley also notices the wild thorn, from which the Wady Sidri takes its name, the fig-tree which entitles another wady the "Father of Fig-trees" (*Abû Hamad*), and in the Wady Seyâl, "a yellow flowering shrub called *Abeithiran*, and a blue, thorny plant called *Silleh*." Again, north-eastwards, in Wady el-'Ain were seen "rushes, the large-leaved plant called *Esher*," and farther down the "*Lasaf*, or caper plant, springing from the clefts." Seetzen's *mesembryanthemum* is noticed by Forskâl, who adds that no herb is more common in sandy desert localities than the second, the *nodiflorum*, called in Arabic the *ghasûl*. Hasselquist speaks of a *mesemb* which he calls the "fig-marigold," as found in the ruins of Alexandria; its agreeable saltish-aromatic flavor, and its use by the Egyptians in salads, accord closely with Seetzen's description. Seetzen gives also Arabic names of two plants, one called *Ickedum* by the guides, described as the size of heath, with blue flowers; the other named *Subbh-el-dich*, found to the north of Wady el-'Ain, which had a club-shaped sappy root, ranged a foot high above the earth, having scales instead of leaves, and covered, when he saw it, with large, golden flowers, clinging close together, till it seemed like a little ninepin (Kegel). Somewhat to the south of this he observed the "rose of Jericho" growing in the dreariest and most desolate solitude, and which appears always to be dead (*Reisen*, iii, 46, 54). In the region about Madura he also found what he calls "Christ's-thorn," Arab. *el-Aussitch*, and an anonymous plant with leaves broader than a tulip, perhaps the *Esher* mentioned above. The following list of plants between Hebron and Madura is also given by Seetzen, having probably been written down by him from hearing them pronounced by his Bedawin guides, and some accordingly it has not been possible to identify with any known names—*el-Khŭrrdy, el-Bureid*, a hyacinth, whose small pear-shaped bulb is eaten raw by the Bedawin, *el-Arta, el-Dschérra, el-Sphára* (or *Zafrà?*), *el-Erbiân, el-Gdime, Schekera* (or *Shakooreeyeh*), *el-Metnân*, described as a small shrub, *el-Hmim, el-Schilllueh*, possibly the same as that called *Silleh*, as above, by Dr. Stanley, *el-Khâla* (or *Khal*), *el-Handegûk* (or *Handakook*), *el-Liddemma, el-Haddâd, Kali, Addan el-Hammár* (or *'Adân el-Himár*). Some more rare plants, precious on account of their products, are the following: *Balsamum Aaronis*, or *nux behen*, called by the Arabs *Festuck el-Ban*, from which an oil is extracted having no perfume of its own, but scented at pleasure with jasmine or other odoriferous leaf, etc., to make a choice unguent. It is found in Mount Sinai and Upper Egypt—*Cucurbita Lágenaria*, Arab. *Charrah*, found in Egypt and the deserts of Arabia, wherever the mountains are covered with rich soil. The tree producing the famous balsam called "of Mecca," is found many days' journey from that place, in Arabia Petræa. Linnæus, after some hesitation, decided that it was a species of *Amyris*. The *olibanum* frankincense is mentioned by Hasselquist as a product of the desert; but the producing tree appears to be the same as that which yields the gum arabic, viz., the *Mimosa nilotica*, mentioned above. The same writer mentions the *Schœnanthus officinalis*, "camel's hay," as growing plentifully in the deserts of both the Arabias, and regards it as undoubtedly one of the precious aromatic and sweet plants which the queen of Sheba gave to Solomon (Hasselquist, p. 255, 288, 296, 297; comp. p. 250, 251, 300). Fuller details on the facts of natural history of the region will be found in the writers referred to, and some additional authorities may be found in Sprengel, *Historia rei Herb.* vol. ii.

Besides these, the cultivation of the ground by the Sinaitic monks has enriched their domain with the choicest fruit-trees, and with a variety of other trees. The produce of the former is famed in the markets of Cairo. The cypresses of the convent are visible far away among the mountains, and there is a single conspicuous one near the "cave of Elias" on Jebel Mûsa. Besides, they have the silver and the common poplar, with other trees, for timber or ornament. The apricot, apple, pear, quince, almond, walnut, pomegranate, olive, vine. citron, orange, cornelian cherry, and two fruits named in the Arabic *Shellûk* and *Bargûk*, have been successfully naturalized there (Robinson, i, 94; Seetzen, iii, 70, etc.; Hasselquist, p. 425; *Sinai and Palestine*, p. 52). Dr. Stanley views these as mostly introduced from Europe; Hasselquist, on the contrary, views them as being the originals whence the finest varieties we have in Europe were first brought. Certainly, nearly all the above trees are common enough in the gardens of Palestine and Damascus. See SINAI.

Wild Goat is the rendering in the A. V. of two Heb. words which seem to refer to cognate species of the caprid tribe. See GOAT.

1. The more frequent term is always found in the plur. יְעֵלִים, *yeëlîm* (Sept. τραγέλαφοι or ἔλαφοι, Vulg. *ibices*), which occurs 1 Sam. xxiv, 2; Job xxxix, 1; Psa. civ, 18; besides the fem. sing. יַעֲלָה, *yaalâh* ("roe," Prov. v, 19), it is not at all improbable, as the Vulg. interprets the word, that some species of *ibex* is denoted, perhaps the *Capra Sinaitica* (Ehrenb.), the *beden* or *jaela* of Egypt and Arabia. This ibex was noticed at Sinai by Ehrenberg and Hemprich (*Sym. Phys.* t. 18), and by Burckhardt (*Trav.* p. 526), who (p. 405) thus speaks of these animals: "In all the valleys south of the Mojeb, and particularly in those of Mojeb and El-Ahsa, large herds of mountain goats, called by the Arabs *beden*, are met with. This is the *steinbock* or *bouquetin* of the Swiss and Tyrol Alps. They pasture in flocks of forty and fifty together. Great numbers of them are killed by the people of Kerek and Tafyle, who hold their flesh in high estimation. They sell the large knotty horns to the Hebrew merchants, who carry them to Jerusalem, where they are worked into handles for knives and daggers. . . . The Arabs told me that it is difficult to get a shot at them, and that the hunters hide themselves among the reeds on the banks of streams where the animals resort in the evening to drink. They also asserted that, when pursued, they will throw themselves from a height of fifty feet and more upon their heads without receiving any injury." Hasselquist (*Trav.* p. 190) speaks of rock goats (*Capra cervicapra*, Linn.) which he saw hunted with falcons near Nazareth. But the *C. cervicapra* of Linnæus is an antelope (*Antilope cervicapra*, Pall.). The *Capra Sinaitica*, however, is not identical with the Swiss ibex or steinbock (*C. ibex*), though it is a closely allied species. The wild goat of Arabia and Palestine differs only from the European in the shape and marking of the horns and in its lighter color. It is still occasionally found in the neighborhood of Engedi, its old resort, which thence took the name (see Tristram, *Nat. Hist. of the Bible*, p. 96). See IBEX.

Wild Goat of Sinai.

Wild Goats.

2. The other word rendered "wild goat" is אַקּוֹ, *akkô*, which occurs only in Deut. xiv, 5, as a clean animal, and

which the Sept. and Vulg. understand to be a kind of deer (τραγέλαφος, *tragelaphus*), and the Targums and Syriac a wild goat (יַעְלָא). Gesenius concludes in favor of the *roebuck;* while others prefer the *chamois*, and others the *gazelle*. Gesenius derives it from Arab. *anak*, while Fürst says it is to be traced to a *radix nominalis*, common to both the Sanscrit and Shemitic tongues. Schultens (*Origines Hebraicæ*) conjectures that the name arose *ob fugacitatem*, from its shyness and consequent readiness to flee; and Dr. Harris points out what he takes to be a confirmation of this conjecture in Shaw's *Travels*, which, from the translations of the Sept. and Vulg., makes it a goat-deer, or Tragelaphus, such as the *lerwî* or *fishtal*, by mistake referred to *Capra mambrica* of Linnæus; whereas that naturalist (*System. Nat.* 13th ed. by Gmelin) places *lerwî* among the synonyms of *Ant. cervicapra*, which does not suit Shaw's notice, and is not known in Western Asia. The *fishtal* is, however, a ruminant of the African desert, possibly one of the larger Antilopidæ, with long mane, but not as yet scientifically described. Some have referred the *akkô* to the *ahu* of the Persians, i. e. the *Capreolus pygargus*, or the "tailless roe" (Shaw, *Zool.* ii, 287), of Central Asia. If we could satisfactorily establish the identity of the Persian word with the Hebrew, the animal in question might represent the *akkô* of the Pentateuch, which might formerly have inhabited the Lebanon, though it is not now found in Palestine. Perhaps the paseng (*Cap. ægagrus*, Cuv.), which some have taken to be the parent stock of the common goat, and which at present inhabits the mountains of Persia and Caucasus, may have in Biblical times been found in Palestine, and may be the *akkô* of Scripture. It is, on the whole, as likely to have been the *beden*, or wild goat of Mt. Sinai, as any other. See DEER; ROE.

Wild Grape is the rendering of the A. V. at Isa. v, 2, 4 of the Heb. word which occurs only in the plur. *beüshîm*, בְּאֻשִׁים, and indicates a noxious species of plant or kind of fruit. In form the word is a pass. participle of בָּאַשׁ, which means to *smell offensively*, as many poisonous vegetables do; and this connects it radically with בָּאְשָׁה, *boshâh* ("cockles," Job xxxi, 40), although the two seem to denote different plants, but both useless. The Sept. gives ἀκάνθας as the Greek equivalent; which is certainly a mistake, unless they had some other reading of the original text. The rendering of Aquila is σαπρίαι, that of Symmachus ἀτελῆ; both of which give rather the etymological meaning or force of the original word than translate it into its Greek equivalent as a significative appellation. The rendering of Jerome is *labruscæ;* and this has been followed by Luther (*Herlinge*) and the A. V. (*wild grapes*). The species of plant intended has been supposed by some to be the *Vitis labrusca*, a plant which produces small berries of a dark-red color when ripe, but sour to the taste; Hasselquist suggests the *Solanum incanum*, or gray nightshade; and Celsius contends for the *Aconitum napellus*, wolfsbane. It seems more probable, however, that no specific plant is referred to in the passage of the prophet; but that the word is simply used as an adjective with its substantive understood, as a designation of bad or worthless grapes. The Lord expected that his vineyard should produce grapes, but it produced only *beüshîm*, vile, uneatable grapes. See Rosenmüller, *Bibl. Bot.* (Eng. transl.), p. 111; and *Comment.* ad loc.; Gesenius, Henderson, Knobel, *ad loc.* See GRAPE.

Wild Ox. See WILD BULL.

Wiley, ISAAC WILLIAM, D.D., LL.D., a bishop of the Methodist Episcopal Church, was born at Lewiston, Pa., March 29, 1825. He was converted when ten years old, at eighteen began to preach, and in 1846 graduated from the medical department of the University of the City of New York. After three years of practice as a physician in Pennsylvania, he joined the Philadelphia Conference, and in 1851 went as a missionary to China. Three years afterwards he returned to America, and was engaged in pastoral work in New Jersey, including an agency for Pennington Seminary. In 1864 he was elected editor of *The Ladies' Repository*, at Cincinnati, and in 1872 bishop, an office which he held until his death, Nov. 22, 1884, at Foo-Chow, China. He was distinguished for a calm but impressive manner, deep cordiality of disposition, and great tact and method in labor. See *Meth. Review*, Jan. 1886; *Minutes of Annual Conferences*, 1884, p. 318.

Wilhelm, LUDWIG WILHELM, a Reformed theologian of Germany, was born at Neuenhain, Nov. 19, 1796. He studied at Marburg and Heidelberg, was in 1816 assistant preacher at Frankfort-on-the-Main, in 1818 third preacher, in 1828 second, and in 1836 first preacher at Wiesbaden. In 1858 he was made bishop of Nassau, and died May 11, 1882, doctor of theology. (B. P.)

Wilhelmina, a fanatical woman of Milan, who died in 1281, pretended to be the daughter of Constantia, queen of Primislaus, king of Bohemia. She spent the last twenty or thirty years of her life in Milan in pious labors, especially in works of active charity. She had organized a band of followers (afterwards known as Wilhelminians), who reverenced her as a saint, and began in her lifetime to make her the object of extravagant and fanatical veneration. This increased after her death to an undue extreme. She had claimed that her birth was announced to her mother by the angel Raphael, just as the birth of Christ was announced to Mary by the angel Gabriel, and that the Holy Spirit became incarnate in her for the purpose of working out the salvation of Jews, Saracens, and false Christians, as that of true Christians had been wrought by Christ. She deluded her followers into the expectation, first, of her repeating in her own person the sufferings of Christ, and, secondly, of her resurrection and return to them after her death. But, with no indications of any fulfilment of such promises, a number of her followers, headed by Andrew Saramita, disinterred the recently buried body, arrayed it in costly robes, erected a magnificent monument over the grave, and proclaimed the worship of the Holy Ghost incarnate in Wilhelmina, as of equal importance with the worship of the incarnate Son of God. She had appointed a nun named Mayfreda, of Tirovano, as her vicegerent under the new dispensation of the Holy Ghost—a female pontiff to represent her as the Roman pontiffs represent St. Peter. The sect was entirely rooted out about the year 1300, the remnant of her followers having perished at the stake, and her tomb and dead body having been destroyed. See Muratori, *Antiq. Ital. Medii Ævi*, v, 95 sq.; Palacky, *Literary Tour to Italy* (Prague, 1838), p. 72 sq.; Mosheim, *Hist. of the Church*, bk. iii, cent. xiii, pt. ii, ch. v.

Wilhelminians. See WILHELMINA.

Wilken, FRIEDRICH, a famous historian, was born May 23, 1777, at Ratzeburg, in the duchy of Lauenburg. He studied at Göttingen, at first theology, but afterwards classic and Oriental philology and history. In 1798 he received the prize for an essay, *De Bellorum Cruciatorum ex Abulfeda Historia;* in 1805 he was appointed professor of history at Heidelberg, and in 1807 director of the university library. In 1817 he was called to Berlin as first librarian and professor in the university, and in 1819 he was made a member of the Academy of Sciences. He undertook a literary journey to Italy in 1826; in 1829 he went in behalf of the government to France and England, and in 1838 to Wiesbaden and Munich. He died Dec. 24, 1840. His main work is the *Gesch. der Kreuzzüge nach morgenländischen und abendländischen Berichten* (Leips. 1807-32, 7 vols.). He also wrote, *Gesch. der Bildung, Beraubung und Vernichtung der alten Heidelberger Büchersammlung* (Heidelb. 1817): — *Gesch. der königlichen Bibliothek zu Berlin* (Berlin, 1828). (B. P.)

Wilkie, *Sir* DAVID, a British painter of great

celebrity, was born at the manse of the parish of Cults, on the banks of Edenwater, in Fifeshire, Scotland, Nov. 18, 1785. He received a limited education at the grammar-school of Kettle, when he was sent to the Trustees' Academy of Edinburgh for the Encouragement of Manufactures. Here, in 1803, he won the prize of ten guineas for painting *Callisto in the Bath of Diana*. In 1804 he returned home, and spent some time in painting portraits and scenes of common life. He then went to London, and entered the Royal Academy as a student. His picture of the *Village Politicians*, exhibited in 1806, gained for the young artist great notoriety, and, indeed, established his fame. He now settled in London, and was busily employed in the execution of his commissions for several years. In 1811 he became a member of the Royal Academy. In 1823 he was appointed limner to the king in Scotland. Two years later he made a tour of the Continent, spending the greater portion of the time in Italy. In 1830 he became painter in ordinary to his majesty. In 1832 he exhibited his celebrated picture of *John Knox Preaching the Reformation in St. Andrew's*, painted for Sir Robert Peel for twelve hundred guineas. It is claimed that his greatest historical work is the picture of *Sir David Baird Discovering the Body of the Sultan Tippo Saib, after Storming Seringapatam*. In 1840 he started for the East, making an extended tour through Holland, Southern Germany, Constantinople, the Holy Land, and Egypt. He died, on his return to England, on board the "Oriental," then off Gibraltar, June 1, 1841. His works have been made known to the world by the engravings of Raimbach, Burnet, Cousins, Doo, and C. Fox.

Wilkins, Ann, an eminent Methodist Episcopal missionary, was born in the state of New York, June 30, 1806. She was converted in 1836, and sailed as a missionary for Africa, June 15, 1837. She labored there until 1841, when she returned to America to recruit her health; went out again in 1842, returned with broken health in 1853; sailed again in 1854, but was once more obliged to return, in 1857. She was preparing for active service in a juvenile asylum, when she suddenly died, Nov. 13 of the last-named year.

Wilkinson, Henry, eldest of those thus named, was born in the vicarage of Halifax, Yorkshire, Oct. 9, 1566. He went to Oxford in 1581, was elected fellow of Merton College, and graduated in 1586, in 1601 became rector at Waddesdon, in Buckinghamshire, and died there, March 19, 1647. He was one of the Puritan divines of the Westminster Assembly, and wrote, *A Catechism:—Debt-book*, etc.

Wilkinson, Jemima, a fanatical Quakeress, was born at Cumberland, R. I., in 1753. In October, 1776, on recovering from an attack of sickness, in which she had fallen into a kind of trance, she announced that she had been raised from the dead, and had received a divine commission as a religious teacher. She gathered around her a few proselytes, who styled themselves "Universal Friends" (q. v.), and formed a settlement between Seneca and Crooked lakes, N. Y., which she called New Jerusalem. Here she secured the belief of her followers in the most absurd pretensions. She claimed to be inspired and to have reached absolute perfection. She pretended to foretell future events, to discern the secrets of the heart, and to have the power of healing diseases. She declared that those who refused to believe in her claims rejected the counsel of God to their own hurt. She even claimed to be Christ in his second coming. On one occasion she declared her intention of walking across Seneca Lake; but when all the preparations were made, she inquired of her followers whether they had faith in her power to do so, and on their replying in the affirmative, said that as they believed in her power it was unnecessary to display it. She claimed to be the one by whom the millennium was to be established, and two of her disciples declared themselves to be the "two witnesses" mentioned in the book of Revelation. She lived in a luxurious style in an elegant house, having amassed a large fortune by the donations made by her followers. She died in 1819. See Hudson, *History of Jemima Wilkinson* (Geneva, N. Y., 1821); and *Memoirs of Bath*.

Wilkinson, John, a Puritan divine, brother of the Henry foregoing, was born in Halifax, and educated at Oxford, where he became fellow of Magdalen College; in 1605 principal of Magdalen Hall, and in 1648 president of Magdalen College. He died Jan. 2, 1649.

Will (*testament*). See Wills.

Will, Georg Andreas, professor at Altdorf, where he died, Sept. 18, 1798, is the author of, *Beiträge zur Geschichte der Anabaptisten in Deutschland* (Nüremberg, 1773):—*Dissertatio de Nethinæis Levitarum Famulis, ex Sacræ Potissimum Scripturæ Fontibus Institutis* (Altdorf, 1785):—*Typus Pronominum Ebraicorum, quæ Suffixa Dicuntur, et Forma Classium Temporumque Verborum Perfectorum in Tabulis* (ibid. 1750). See Winer, *Handbuch der theol. Lit.* i, 767; Fürst, *Bibl. Jud.* iii, 515. (B. P.)

Will Worship (ἐθελοθρησκεία, Col. ii, 23), the invention and practice of such expedients of appeasing or of pleasing God as neither reason nor revelation suggests.

Willard, Samuel, D.D., a Congregational minister, nephew of president Joseph Willard, was born at Petersham, Mass., in 1775. He graduated from Harvard College in 1803, was tutor at Bowdoin College in 1804 and 1805, became pastor of the Church at Deerfield in 1807, and resigned his pastorate, on account of the total loss of sight, in 1829, but preached occasionally until within a month of his death, which occurred Oct. 8, 1859. He was the author of, *The Deerfield Collection of Sacred Music* (1808):—*Original Hymns* (1823):—*An Index of the Bible* (1826):—*An Improved Reader* (1827):—*The General Class-book* (1828):—*Sacred Poetry and Music Reconciled: a Collection of Hymns* (1830):—*An Introduction to the Latin Language* (1835), and other school-books (some anonymous), several sermons, papers in periodicals, and left hymns and other works in MS.

Willelmus, an ecclesiastic of the 11th century, became abbot of Metz in 1073, and was friendly to Gregory VII. Seven of his epistles and an oration have been published in Mabillon's *Analecta*, i, 247. See Mosheim, *Hist. of the Church*, bk. iii, cent. xi, pt. ii, ch. ii.

Willemer, Johann Helvich, a German theologian, who flourished in the latter half of the 17th century, at Wittenberg, is the author of, *Dissert. de Tunica Adami Pellicea* (Wittenberg, 1680):—*Disputatio de Sadducæis* (ibid. eod.):—*Diss. Philolog. de Essenis* (ibid. eod.):—*De Pallio Eliæ ad* 2 *Reg. i*, 8; *ii*, 8, 13, 14 (ibid. 1679):—*De Pronunciatione Nominis* יהוה *per Legem Levit. xxiv*, 16 *Concessa* (ibid. 1677), etc. See Jöcher, *Allgemeines Gelehrten-Lexikon*, s. v.; Fürst, *Bibl. Jud.* iii, 515. (B. P.)

Willes, Edward, D.D., a Church of England divine, was prebend of Westminster in 1724, of Lincoln in 1730, dean the same year, elected bishop of St. David's in 1742, translated to the see of Bath and Wells in 1743, and died Nov. 24, 1773. See (Lond.) *Annual Register*, 1773, p. 176.

Willet, Andrew, a learned English divine, was born at Ely in 1562. He was educated at Peterhouse and at Christ College, Cambridge, where he obtained a fellowship; became prebendary of Ely July 22, 1584; had the rectory of Childerly, in Cambridgeshire, and in 1597 that of Little Grantesden, in the same county; became chaplain to prince Henry, and died at Hoddesden, in Hertfordshire, Dec.

4, 1621. He was the author of, *Synopsis Papismi* (1593):—*Tetrastylon Papisticum* (eod.):—*Sacrorum Emblematum Centuria Una*, etc. (1598):—*A Catholicon* (1602):—*Hexapla on Genesis, Exodus*, etc., and other works.

William, the name of several Scotch prelates.

1. Bishop of Moray some time in the 12th century. He died in February, 1162. See Keith, *Scottish Bishops*, p. 135.

2. Bishop of Dunblane about 1210. See Keith, *Scottish Bishops*, p. 172.

3. Bishop of Argyle in 1240. He was drowned in 1241. See Keith, *Scottish Bishops*, p. 286.

4. Bishop of the see of Dunblane in 1290. On July 12, 1291, he signed a submission to Edward I, king of England. He was bishop here in 1292. See Keith, *Scottish Bishops*, p. 174.

5. Bishop of Dunblane in 1353. See Keith, *Scottish Bishops*, p. 175.

William OF CONCHES, a philosopher of the 12th century, was a native of Conches, Normandy, and instructed at the cathedral-school of Chartres. William was famous as a grammarian, but took part in theological questions. His work, entitled *Philosophia*, in which he espoused Abelard's doctrine of the Trinity, was attacked after his master's condemnation by William of St. Thierry, and the author did not hesitate to recant his errors. William of Conches died in 1154. His *Philosophia* was published three times, with different titles, and under the name of three different authors: 1. *Philosophicarum et Astronomicarum Institutionum Guilielmi, Hirsangiensis Olim Abbatis, Libri Tres* (Basle, 1531); 2. Περὶ *διδάξεων sive Elementorum Philosophiæ Libri IV*, in Beda's *Opera*, ii, 311–343 (Basle 1563); 3. *De Philosophia Mundi*, by Honorius of Autun, in the *Maxima Bibliotheca Patrum*, vol. xx (Lyons, 1667). Another work of William is *Dragmaticon*, in which he rejects the errors expressed in his *Philosophia*. The *Dragmaticon*, too, is extant under at least six different titles. William also wrote a commentary on Boethius's *De Consolatione Philosophiæ*. See Werner, in *Sitzungsberichte der philosophisch-historischen Classe der kaiserlichen Akademie der Wissenschaften in Wien* (1873), lxxv, p. 311 sq.; Hauréau, in *Comptes-Rendus de l'Académie des Inscriptions et des Belles-Lettres* (eod.), 3d series, i, 75 sq.; Prantl, *Geschichte der Logik*, ii, 127; Reginal L. Poole, *Illustrations of the History of Mediæval Thought*, and the same in Plitt-Herzog, *Real-Encyklop.* s. v. (B. P.)

William III OF ENGLAND (*William Henry of Nassau*), prince of Orange, stadtholder of Holland, was born at the Hague, Nov. 4, 1650. He was the son of William II of Orange, by Mary, daughter of Charles I of England, and was born to a large inheritance, though his party was kept in check for some time by the influence of Cromwell. The house of Orange had long sought to obtain supreme power in Holland, a country which its greatest member had freed from the Spanish yoke. The death of William II eight days before the birth of his son put a stop to the projects for the establishment of a despotism over the republic, and threw the power into the hands of the opposite party. For years the Orange party was depressed for want of a representative of sufficient influence to maintain its policy and secure the stadtholdership. The republic was governed by Jan de Witt, the grand pensionary. The attack upon Holland by France and England combined, in 1672, made a great change in the fortunes of the young prince of Orange. He was immediately chosen captain and admiral-general of the United Provinces. The contest was at first unfavorable to the Provinces, but by the wisdom and determination of the young stadtholder, the struggle, which lasted for nearly seven years, was, in 1678, terminated by the treaty of Nimeguen, in a manner highly advantageous and honorable to Holland. This was brought about more especially by the diplomatic abilities of William, who detached England from the alliance and brought her over to the side of the Dutch. A few years before their ruin had seemed inevitable, and the fame of William became great over Europe. In November, 1677, William had married his cousin Mary, eldest daughter of James, duke of York, afterwards James II. This marriage was entered into chiefly for political purposes, and proved very popular in both countries, the prince being regarded as the natural head of the Protestant party, and his wife being expected to succeed to the English throne. James II came to the throne in 1685, and determined to establish the Catholic religion; but William was still the champion of Protestantism, and in 1686 became the head of a league formed among the Protestant princes of Germany, the kings of Spain, Sweden, and others, having for its object the crushing of the power of Louis XIV of France, whose influence was the dread of all Europe, and who was the most dreaded foe of Protestantism. The treaty by which the alliance was constituted was signed at Augsburg in July, 1686. The oppressions of James II drove many of the Protestants into exile, and Holland became the place of refuge for the discontented English. The national dissatisfaction became so great that on June 30, 1688, a number of prominent English statesmen invited the prince of Orange to enter England with an army. William conducted his operations with great secrecy and skill, and on Nov. 15 of the same year he landed at Torbay with an army of fifteen thousand men, composed of English and Dutch. Soon the whole country was at his side, and James was an exile in France. Men of influence of all parties gave him their presence and support; and on Dec. 18 following he entered London triumphantly as a national deliverer. The adherents of James held out for some time in Scotland and Ireland, but the death of Dundee ended the resistance of the Highlanders; while in Ireland it was quelled after a vigorous contest in 1691. In spite of his sterling qualities and of the debt which they owed him, the English nation never really liked William III. In 1695 the death of queen Mary diminished her husband's influence, and leaving factious opposition at home, he had to maintain unequal strife with Louis, until the treaty of Ryswick was brought about by sheer exhaustion on both sides, in September, 1697. During the whole war William had been disturbed by Jacobite plots, some of them against his life. A partition treaty regarding Spain was violated by Louis, who took the throne of that country for his grandson, the duke of Anjou, and the French king, on the death of James II, acknowledged his son as successor. The English, enraged at this, were making preparations for a powerful invasion, when William was thrown from his horse while hunting, and died March 8, 1702. His career was one of incessant and strenuous activity, and he carried himself victoriously amidst immense difficulties and numerous discomfitures. The predominant motive of his foreign policy from the beginning of his career as stadtholder of Holland until the close of it as king of England was resistance to the aggressive and tyrannous policy of Louis XIV. There is little room for doubt that he accepted the English throne for the sole purpose of enhancing his power against French despotism. While it is true that his policy dragged England more thoroughly than before into the circle of European politics, yet it brought to the English a free constitution, with political institutions capable of receiving indefinite improvement without danger of destruction. The sacred principle of toleration, both in civil and ecclesiastical matters, was firmly established, though its full bearings and application were not yet developed or even clearly apprehended. Covenanters, in the North, and high-churchmen, in the South, hated him, but the great mass of moderate and reasonable Protestants felt that he was a thoroughly practical and inflexibly just sovereign. He loved his own countrymen, and advanced them tc positions of trust and honor: but no discredit is to be attached to him on this account, for they were loyal to him and not disloyal to England. While his temper was cold, the nobler passions of man were in him deep and strong, and he possessed that stern love of truth, honor, and right that distinguishes a moral hero. Few greater kings have ever ruled in England, but the massacre of the Macdonalds of Glencoe, and his conduct towards the promoters of the Darien scheme are two blots on his reputation which his most thorough-going apologists have been unable to efface. In addition to the above-mentioned services to the English nation it may be mentioned that during his reign the Bank of England was founded, the modern system of finance introduced, ministerial responsibility recognised, and the liberty of the press secured. His manner was wholly Dutch, and even among his own countrymen he was thought blunt. In his theological opinions he was decided but not illiberal. See Trevor, *Life and Times of William III* (Lond. 1835–36, 2 vols.); Vernon, *Court and Times of William III* (ibid. 1841, 2 vols.); Macaulay, *History of England* (1849–55); Ranke, *Englische Geschichte vornehmlich im* 17. *Jahrhundert* (1859–67, 6 vols.; Engl. transl. 1875).

William OF TYRE, a prominent ecclesiastic and judicious historian, lived in the time of the Crusades. He was born in Syria about A.D. 1130, and reared at Antioch or Jerusalem. About 1160 he visited Italy and France as a student of the liberal arts, and on his return to Jerusalem, after an absence of several years, he became the friend and instructor of king Amalric (reigned 1162–1173). In 1167 he became archdeacon of Tyre, and in the same year was employed by Amalric to negotiate a league with the emperor Manuel I at Constantinople, with a view to the invasion of Egypt. Soon afterwards some unpleasantness arose between his archbishop, Frederic of Tyre, and himself, in consequence of which he visited Rome; and immediately after this Amalric gave him charge of the education and training of his son, the prince Baldwin. In the summer of 1170 a terrible earthquake convulsed the East, destroying many ancient towns and numerous lives, and overthrowing several strong towers in Tyre. King Amalric died July 11, 1173, and his successor, Baldwin, called William to the post of chancellor; about the same time the archbishop Frederic died, and William was given the vacant see, being the sixth incumbent of that diocese since the founding of the kingdom of Jerusalem. In this capacity he was present, in 1178, at the third Lateran synod at Rome, and on his return wrote out the decisions of the synod, together with a list of the names and titles of all participants in its business, in a work which he deposited in the archives of the principal church at Tyre. He spent seven months in Constantinople in the transaction of business for his see, then visited Antioch on a mission from the emperor Manuel, and, after an absence from home of one year and ten months, returned to Tyre. So much may be gathered from his own writings, which form the almost exclusive source for his life. An ancient French writer adds the statement that William was poisoned through the agency of the patriarch of Jerusalem, Heraclius, at Rome, whither he had gone to effect the deposition of that prelate. Another tradition states instead that William acted as a commissioner to the West after the taking of Jerusalem by Saladin in 1188, and was appointed legate in matters pertaining to crusades by pope Gregory VIII, being present as such at a meeting of Philip Augustus of France and Richard of England, which took place between Gisors and Trie.

William of Tyre composed two historical works, one of which contained the history of Eastern princes from Mohammed to his own time, a period of five hundred and seventy years (*Gesta Principium Orientalium*). It was based upon Arabic sources which were placed at his disposal by the liberality of king Amalric. This work is no longer extant. The other work contains the history of the Crusades, from A.D. 1100 to 1184, in twenty-three books, the last of which is unfinished (*Historia Rerum in Partibus Transmarinis Gestarum a Tempore Mahumeth usque ad A.D.* 1184). It was drawn from documentary sources and from his personal observations and carefully managed inquiries among his contemporaries. Its learning is very great as respects natural, political, and ecclesiastical conditions in both the East and West, and the literatures of the Arabic, Syriac, Greek, and Latin languages. Its matter also is very full, and its tone, upon the whole, impartial, and little affected by the credulous belief of his age in wonders. Its style, finally, is that of animated description, such as best harmonizes with the portrayal of events in which the military element plays a principal part. It earned for its author the reputation of being one of the foremost historical writers of the Middle Ages. The oldest edition of this work extant is that of Basle (1549 fol.; 2d ed. 1560). Other editions are by Bongarsius (1564), in *Gesta Dei per Francos*, i, 625 sq.; G. du Préau (in French, Paris, 1573 fol.). The continuation of the work to 1285, by an unknown writer, is given in Martene, *Thesaur.* v, 581. An abridgment is given in Bernhard, *Thesaurus*, with continuation, in French, to 1284; in Latin, by the Dominican Pippin (1320), in Muratori, *Thesaurus*, vii, 657 sq. A German edition was issued in 1844 at Stuttgart, by Kausler, with the title, *Gesch. d. Kreuzzüge u. d. Königreichs Jerusalem.* Comp. Bongarsius, *Præf.;* Vossius, *De Hist. Lat.* p. 53; Fabricius, *Bibl. Lat. Medii Ævi*, h. v.; Wähler, *Handbuch d. Gesch. d. Literatur* (2d ed. Leipsic, 1823), ii, 222; Herzog, *Real-Encyklop.* s. v.

Williamites, an order of monks deriving their name from a hermit, who, after conversion from a licentious life, had made a pilgrimage to Jerusalem by the advice of hermits and pope Eugenius III, and had then, in 1153, established a hermitage in a desert of Tuscany, near Pisa. Disorderly followers destroyed all prospect of retirement here, and he sought a new refuge in the depths of a forest on Monte Pruno. New disciples gathered about him, who, in time, became offended with him and expelled him from their society. He returned to his original retreat on the island of Lupocavia, but found the community unimproved, and therefore journeyed until he discovered a stony vale containing a cave, in the bishopric of Grosseto, in Siena. Here he settled in 1155 and began an ascetical life, whose rigor was somewhat relieved by the lord of Buriano, who built him a cell. In the following year Albert became his associate, and a year later Rainald arrived, though only in time to assist at the burial of William, who had died Feb. 10, 1157. These two men remained at the place, which was at first called Stabulum Rhodis, and afterwards Malavalle, and which became the original of all the congregations of hermits which adopted the name of Williamites. Such congregations extended over the whole of Italy and beyond, to Germany, the Netherlands, and France. The institutions of their founder, together with a description of his life, had been transmitted from Albert. They maintained a perpetual fast. Gregory IX gave them the rule of Benedict, and permitted them to wear shoes. Innocent IV issued a bull in 1248 touching the election of a general prior, and conferring privileges on the order. Alexander IV ordered its incorporation with an order of Augustinian eremites, but recalled his bull of April 13, 1256, in view of the violent protest raised against the scheme, though matters had progressed so far as to occasion serious difficulties in the order, which involved the loss of a number of monasteries in 1266. In 1435 the Council of Basle confirmed the privileges possessed by the order, which then covered the three provinces of Tuscany, Germany, and Flanders and France. At the beginning of the 18th century only twelve convents remained to the order, all of which were in Flanders, and by the end of the century they too were extinct. An order of knights of St. William has been spoken of, but is entirely apocryphal. See Bolland, *Acta Sanctorum*, Feb. 10, with Henschen's *Diss.;* and Helyot, *Hist. d. Ordres Monast. Relig. et Militaires*, i, 250; iii, 13; vi, 142-152; also Herzog, *Real-Encyklop.* s. v.

Williams, Aaron, D.D., a Presbyterian minister, was born at Leetsdale, Pa., Nov. 20, 1807. He graduated from Jefferson College, and in the first class at the Western Theological Seminary at Allegheny. He served with eminent ability as professor of languages in the Ohio University, and subsequently filled the same chair in his alma mater at Cannonsburg, Pa., being at the time a member of the Presbytery of Allegheny. He died at Leetsdale, Dec. 31, 1878. (W. P. S.)

Williams, Alvin P., D.D., a Baptist minister, was born in St. Louis County, Mo., March 13, 1813. At the age of seventeen he was publicly set apart as his father's assistant in the ministry, and afterwards labored as an evangelist. Among his pastorates were Lexington, Miami, Bethel, St. Joseph, and Glasgow, in Missouri. He died at Glasgow, Nov. 9, 1868. He was conspicuous among the most able ministers of his denomination in the South-west. "His sermons, expositions, and essays before the association for twenty-five years mark him as a man of extraordinary ability, a second Andrew Fuller." See Cathcart, *Baptist Encyclop.* p. 1247. (J. C. S.)

Williams, Charles P., D.D., a Protestant Episcopal clergyman, was a teacher for many years in a classical school in Philadelphia, Pa., and died in that city, June 12, 1859, aged sixty-seven years. See *Prot. Episc. Almanac*, 1860, p. 93.

Williams, Isaac, an English clergyman, was born in Wales in 1802. He graduated from Trinity College, Oxford, in 1826, and became a fellow there in 1832; entered into holy orders in 1831, and was curate of Windrush, St. Mary the Virgin's, Oxford, and Bisley, in succession; wrote tracts Nos. 80, 86, and 87 of the Pusey *Tractarian* series; contributed to the *Lyra Apostolica*, and spent his later years in retirement at Stinchcombe, Gloucestershire, where he died, May 1, 1865. He was a voluminous writer, and we name the following among his numerous works: *The Cathedral; or, The Catholic and Apostolic Church of England* (1838):—*Hymns, translated from the Parisian Breviary* (1839):—*Thoughts in Past Years* (1842):—*Harmony and Commentary on the Whole Gospel Narrative* (1842-45; new ed. 1869-70):—*The Baptistery; or, The Way to Eternal Life* (1842-44):—*Christian Scholar* (1849):—*The Altar; or, Meditations in Verse on the Great Christian Sacrifice* (eod.):—*The Seven Days; or, The Old and the New Creation* (1850):—*The Apocalypse, with Notes and Reflections* (1852):—*The Characters of the Old Testament* (1856):—*Female Characters of the Holy Scriptures*, in a series of sermons (1859):—*Beginning of the Book of Genesis* (1861):—*The Psalms Interpreted of Christ* (1864-65).

Williams, John (1), an English missionary, called "the Apostle of Polynesia" and "the Martyr of Erromanga," was born at Tottenham, near London, June 29, 1796. At the age of fourteen he was apprenticed to an ironmonger, and acquired a knowledge of mechanism which was afterwards of great service to him. He was ordained in 1816, and sent by the London Missionary Society to Eimeo, one of the Society Islands, where he learned the language and began to preach to the natives in two months. From Eimeo he soon removed to Huaheine, and afterwards to Raiatea, where he was eminently successful in introducing Christianity and, at the same time, the arts of civilization. In 1823 he removed to Raratonga, the chief of the Hervey Islands, where he established a mission that was remarkably successful, the population of the entire group having embraced Christianity under his influence. He employed native teachers, and prepared the New Test. and other books in the Raratongan language. Being in want of a vessel to journey from island to island, he resolved to build one. He made all the necessary tools, and completed the vessel, which was sixty feet long by eighteen wide, in about fifteen weeks. The sails were of native matting, the cordage of the bark of the hibiscus, the oakum of cocoa-nut husks and banana stumps. With the aid of this vessel he extended his labors during the next four years as far as the Samoa Islands. In 1834 he returned to England, and remained nearly four years, employing himself in the publication of his Raratongan New Test. (by the Bible Society) and in raising £4000 for the purchase and outfit of a missionary ship for the South Sea Islands. In 1838 he returned to the scene of his labors, and in the following year visited the New Hebrides for the purpose of planting a mission, but was killed on the shore of the island of Erromanga, and most of his body eaten by the savage natives, Nov. 20, 1839. Besides his New Test., above mentioned, he was the author of, *A Narrative of Missionary Enterprises in the South Sea Islands* (1837):—*Missionary's Farewell* (1838). See Prout, *Life of the Rev. John Williams, Missionary to Polynesia; Compiled from his Journals, Correspondence, and other Authentic Sources* (1843).

Williams, John (2) (called *Ab Ithel*), a Welsh clergyman, was born at Llangyhafel, Denbighshire, North Wales, in 1811. He graduated from Jesus College, Oxford, in 1834; was ordained in the Established Church, and stationed successively at Llanfor, Nerguis, and Llanymowddwyn; and preferred by the bishop of Bangor to the rectory of Llanenddwyn, Merionethshire, a few months before his death, which occurred Aug. 27, 1861. He published, *The Church of England Independent of the Church of Rome in All Ages:—Ecclesiastical Antiquities of the Cymry* (1844):—*Glossary of Terms Used for Articles of British Dress and Armor* (1851):—*Ancient Welsh Grammar* (1856):—*Brut y Twysogion; or, The Chronicle of the Princes* (1860):—*Barddas, or Bardism: a Collection of Original Documents Illustrative of the Theology, Discipline, and Usages of the Bardo-Druidic System of the Isle of Britain; with Translation and Notes* (1862).

Williams, Samuel, LL.D., a Congregational minister, son of Rev. Warham Williams, of Waltham, Mass., was born there, April 23, 1743. He graduated from Harvard College in 1761; was selected by professor Winthrop to accompany him, the same year, to Newfoundland, to observe the transit of Venus; taught school at Waltham, and pursued his theological studies; was licensed to preach Oct. 11, 1763; preached at Concord and Bradford, Mass., and was ordained in the latter place Nov. 20, 1765. In May, 1780, he was installed in the Hollis professorship of mathematics and natural philosophy in Harvard College. He was a member of the Meteorological Society of Mannheim, Germany, and of the Philosophical Society of Philadelphia; also of the Academy of Arts and Sciences in Massachusetts. In 1786 he went to Penobscot Bay to observe a total eclipse of the sun, in a galley fitted out by the General Court of Massachusetts. The same year the government of Massachusetts appointed him to assist in running the line of jurisdiction between that state and New York. He resigned his professorship in 1788, and removed to Rutland, Vt., preaching there as a stated supply from January, 1789, to October, 1795. Subsequently he preached at Burlington more than two years. He died at Rutland, Jan. 2, 1817. In 1794 he published *The Natural and Civil History of Vermont* (8vo), which was republished in two volumes in 1809. In 1805 governor Tickenor appointed him to ascertain the boundary of the state of Vermont. A course of lectures was delivered by him in the University of Vermont soon after its establishment. Many MSS. on astronomical, philosophical, and mathematical subjects of great value are among his literary remains. See Sprague, *Annals of the Amer. Pulpit*, i, 595.

Williams, Samuel Wells, LL.D., a distinguished Chinese scholar, was born at Utica, N. Y., Sept. 22, 1812. He graduated from the Rensselaer Polytechnic Institute, Troy, learned printing, and in 1833 went to Canton, China, as printer for the American mission, where he assisted in editing *The Chinese Repository*. In 1837 he visited Japan, learned the language, and translated Matthew and Luke into Japanese. Returning to China, he edited many works; became interpreter to commodore Perry's Japan expedition in 1853, and in 1855 to the United States legation. In 1860 he revisited the United States, and in 1875, after various public services in China, permanently settled in New Haven, Conn., where he acted as lecturer on Chinese, until his death, Feb. 16, 1884, at which time he was president of the American Bible Society. He is the author of many works on China, especially *The Middle Kingdom* (N. Y. 1848, 1857).

Williams, William, D.D., LL.D., a Baptist minister, was born at Eatonton, Putnam Co., Ga., March 15, 1821. He united with the Church in 1837; graduated from the University of Georgia in 1840, and from the law-school of Harvard University in 1847; became pastor at Auburn, Ala., in 1851; professor of theology in Mercer University in 1856; professor of ecclesiastical history, etc., in the Southern Baptist Theological Seminary in 1859, and in 1872 of systematic theology, which office he held until his death, at Aiken, S. C., Feb. 20, 1879. See Cathcart, *Baptist Encyclop.* p. 1255. (J. C. S.)

Williams, William Frederick, D.D., a Presbyterian minister, was born at Utica, N. Y., Jan. 7, 1818. For a time he studied at Yale College; graduated in 1847 from Auburn Theological Seminary; in 1848 was licensed, and ordained by the Presbytery of Utica; the same year commissioned by the American Board, and sailed for Syria, his first station being at Beyrout. Thence he was transferred to Mosul, and next was called to Mardin, East Turkey, where he died, Feb. 14, 1871. For some years he was especially engaged in training native helpers and preachers.

Williams, William R., D.D., LL.D., an eminent Baptist divine, was born in New York city, Oct. 14, 1804, being the son of Rev. John Williams (1767–1825), pastor of the Oliver Street Baptist Church for twenty-seven years. He graduated from Columbia College in 1823, studied law and practiced it one year, entered the ministry in 1831, and the ensuing year became pastor of the Amity Street Church, a relation which continued until his death, April 1, 1885. Dr. Williams was an elegant writer, and the author of several valuable works on Baptist history and literature, for which see Allibone, *Dict. of Brit. and Amer. Authors*, s. v.

Willigis, archbishop of Mayence, was a statesman and primate of the German Church in the period of the Saxon emperors. His origin is unknown and was probably obscure. His birthplace was, it may be assumed, the town of Schöningen, in Saxony. He was a canon at Hildesheim, when Volcold, tutor of the young Otto II, whose friendship he had been fortunate enough to gain, recommended him to notice, with the result that he was transferred, about A.D. 970, to the imperial chapel and received into the number of imperial councillors. On Jan. 13, 975, he became archbishop of Mayence and archchancellor and metropolitan of Germany, by the appointment of emperor Otto II and the confirmation of the pope, Benedict VII. The papal bull provided that he should have pre-eminence over all prelates in Germany and Gaul in ecclesiastical matters, and particularly on the occasion of royal coronations and in respect to the holding of synods at places to be chosen by himself. He took part in all the important affairs of the empire until other favorites temporarily usurped his place, but was not a participant in Otto's Italian campaign, A.D. 980. When Otto suffered defeat in Calabria, July 13, 982, Willigis accompanied other German princes to the imperial camp, and at the diet of Verona, where the infant son of Otto was chosen king and successor to his father, he appeared invested in all his former honors. Otto II died Dec. 7, 983, at Aix-la-Chapelle. Willigis officiated at the coronation of the new king as the representative of the transalpine peoples, and in the dispute respecting the guardianship of the young emperor he was the head of the Saxon party and the most terrible opponent of duke Henry of Bavaria, who had seized the prince and had attempted to secure the throne. During this dispute, which closed in 985, Willigis was the constant companion of the empress. When the empress-mother died, June 15, 991, a commission was appointed to assist the grandmother, Adelheid, in exercising care over the prince, and of this commission Willigis was a member. Later authorities even confer upon him a regency of the empire during a period of three years. The education of young Otto was also the peculiar charge of Willigis, and was by him intrusted to his protegé, Bernward, a later bishop of Hildesheim. Willigis prepared the first Roman expedition of his pupil and guided him over the Alps. Easter, 996, was celebrated at Pavia, and a delegation announcing the death of John XV and asking the king to choose a new pope was received in the same place. Willigis, more than any other person, determined Otto to choose his own cousin, Bruno, the son of the duke of Carinthia; and, in connection with Hildibald, chancellor and bishop of Worms, he escorted Bruno to Rome, and was present at his election by the clergy and people, and his enthronement as Gregory V, May 3, 996. Before leaving Rome he induced the pope to convoke a synod, through which he secured the return of Adalbert, bishop of Prague, to the diocese which that prelate had twice abandoned, though the return was not desired by the emperor, the pope, or Adalbert himself.

The next important affair in the life of Willigis was his dispute with bishop Bernward, of Hildesheim, respecting the right to exercise jurisdiction over the nunnery of Gandersheim, where Sophia, the emperor's sister, was about to take the veil. The emperor sided with Bernward, and Sophia with Willigis. The dispute was finally brought before a synod at Rome, which sent a legate to Gandersheim to forward the interests of Bernward. Willigis refused to obey this authority, and was accordingly suspended from his offices by the legate, and cited to appear before the pope. He nevertheless persisted in the exercise of his episcopal functions, and found numerous supporters among the German clergy, as is evident from the large attendance of bishops at a synod convoked by him at Frankfort, Aug. 20, 1002. Bernward's entrance at Gandersheim, on the other hand, was resisted by its inmates with force of arms. The opposition against both pope and emperor was everywhere, whether in Rome or Germany, so strong as to make it possible for Willigis to despise the wrath of either. The emperor's death, followed by the accession of Henry II, occasioned a truce, during which Willigis consecrated Sophia as abbess of Gandersheim; and in 1007 a peace was negotiated, by the renunciation, on the part of Willigis, of jurisdiction in the disputed territory. Otto's idea of establishing a universal empire, in which Bernward and his coadjutors were his principal supporters and Willigis his principal opponent, had, however, been defeated, and papal intervention in the affairs of the German Church had been effectually rebuked, in the course of a quarrel which seemed to concern local matters only, but which, because of the prominence of the persons engaged, involved issues of the gravest importance for the entire Western Church.

On the accession of Henry II, he found in Willigis the most prominent supporter of his claims as against those of margrave Eckard of Meissen and of duke Hermann of Suabia. Willigis, assisted by his suffragans, anointed and crowned the emperor, June 6 or 7, 1002, at Mayence, and the empress Kunigunde, Aug. 10, at Paderborn. He accompanied the emperor to Aix-la-

Chapelle, where the latter was recognised as sovereign by the assembled princes, and to Bruchsal, where the duke of Suabia made a voluntary surrender of his claims. He was present also at a synod held at Theonville, and was the influential personage who caused the punishment of death, denounced upon count Ernest of Austria, for rebellion, to be changed into the imposition of a fine.

Everything in the records thus reveals Willigis as the counsellor and influential friend of the emperor. His power is evidenced in numerous documents, and in many ecclesiastical provisions and arrangements of the time. He was incessantly, energetically active in the affairs of both Church and State. Several churches in the city of Mayence, a number of bridges and other public works, and various works of art, were among the permanent relics of his administration. He died Feb. 23, 1011.

Literature.—Historical works, like Giesebrecht, *Gesch. d. deutschen Kaiserzeit;* Gfrörer, *Allgem. k. Gesch.* iii, 3, 4; and monographs, e. g. *De Willigisi Archicancellarii Regna Germ. et Archiepisc. Mogunt. Vita et Rebus Gestis,* by Ossenbeck (Monasterii, 1859); Euler, *Erzbischof Willigis von Mainz,* etc. (Naumburg, 1860). See also Thietmar, *Chronic.* passim.; Pertz, *Monum. Germ. Script.* ii–vii, etc.; Guden, *Cod. Diplom.; Monum. Boica,* xxxi; *Origg. Guelficæ,* iv; Schunnat, *Hist. Fuldens.* 150, etc.; Böhmer, *Font. Rer. Germ.* iii; Thangmar, *Vita Bernwardi Episc.,* Canaparius, *Vita S. Adalbert;* and Herzog, *Real-Encyklop.* s. v.

Willison (or **Willisone**), JOHN, a divine of the Church of Scotland, was born in 1680; became minister at Brechin in 1703, and in 1716 at Dundee, where he remained until his death, May 3, 1750. He was the author of, *Examples of Plain Catechising* (1737):—*Sacramental Directory; or, a Treatise Concerning the Sanctification of a Communion Sabbath* (1745):—*Afflicted Man's Companion* (1755):—*Sacramental Meditations and Advices* (1769):—*Sacramental Catechism:—Christian Scripture Directory:—Free and Impartial Testimony to the Church of Scotland,* and other works. An edition of his *Works* was published in Aberdeen in 1769, and other editions have since appeared, including his later publications. See *Fasti Eccles. Scoticanæ,* iii, 693, 813; Allibone, *Dict. of Brit. and Amer. Authors,* s. v.

Williston, PAYSON, D.D., a Congregational minister, was born at West Haven, Conn., in 1763; graduated at Yale College in 1783; studied theology at New Haven; became pastor at Easthampton, Mass., in 1789, where he remained until 1833. He died there Jan. 30, 1856. He published a *Sermon* in 1799, a *Half-century Sermon* in 1839, and contributed several articles to Sprague's *Annals of the Amer. Pulpit* (vols. i and ii).

Willm, JOSEPH, a Protestant pedagogue and philosopher, was born at Heiligenstein in 1792. In 1821 he was professor at the gymnasium in Strasburg, in 1826 professor of philosophy at the seminary, and died in 1853. He published, *De l'Éducation du People* (1843):—*Histoire de la Philosophie Allemande Depuis Kant* (1844), which received the prize from the French Academy of Sciences. From 1844 to 1850 he was one of the contributors to the *Dictionnaire des Sciences Philosophiques,* published by Hachette. See Bruch, *Discours Nécrologique* (Strasburg, 1853); Lichtenberger, *Encyclop. des Sciences Religieuses,* s. v. (B. P.)

Willows, BROOK OF (נַחַל הָעֲרָבִים, *Náchal ha-Arabim;* Sept. ἡ φάραγξ Ἄραβας; Vulg. *torrens salicum*), a wady mentioned by Isaiah (xv, 7) in his dirge over Moab. Over this name Jerome takes a singular flight in his *Commentary on Isa.* xv, 7, connecting it with the *Orebim* (A. V. "ravens") who fed Elijah during his seclusion. The prophet's language implies that this brook was one of the boundaries of the country—probably, as Gesenius (*Jesaia,* i, 532) observes, the southern one. It is possibly identical with a wady mentioned by Amos (vi, 14) as the then recognised southern limit of the northern kingdom (Fürst, *Handwb.;* Ewald, *Propheten*). This latter appears in the A. V. as "the river of the wilderness" (נַ׳ הָעֲרָבָה, *Náchal ha-Arabâh;* Sept. ὁ χείμαῤῥος τῶν δυσμῶν; Vulg. *torrens deserti*). Widely as they differ in the A. V., it will be observed that the names are all but identical in the original, the only difference being that it is plural in Isaiah and singular in Amos. In the latter it is *ha-Arabah,* the same name which is elsewhere almost exclusively used either for the valley of the Jordan, the *ghôr* of modern Arabs, or for its continuation, the great Arabah, extending to the gulf of Akabah. If the two are regarded as identical, and the latter as the accurate form of the name, then it is probable that the Wady el-Ahsy is intended, which breaks down through the southern part of the mountains of Moab into the so-called Ghôr es-Safieh, at the lower end of the lake, and appears to form a natural barrier between the districts of Kerak and Jebal (Burckhardt, *Syria,* Aug. 7). This is not improbably also the brook Zered (*nachal-Zered*) of the earlier history. The Targum Pseudojonathan translates the name Zered by "osiers," or "baskets."

Should, however, the *Nachal ha-Arabim* be rendered "the Willow-torrent"—which has the support of Gesenius (*Jesaia*) and Pusey (*Comm. on Amos,* vi, 14)—then it is worthy of remark that the name *Wady Sufsaf,* "Willow Wady," is still attached to a part of the main branch of the ravine which descends from Kerak to the north end of the peninsula of the Dead Sea (Irby, May 9). Burckhardt (*Syria,* p. 644) mentions a fountain called *'Ain Safsâf,* "the Willow Fountain" (Catafago, *Arabic Dictionary,* p. 1051).

The Rev. Mr. Wilton, in his work on *The Negeb, or South Country of Scripture,* endeavors to identify the *Nachal ha-Arabah* of Amos with the Wady el-Jeib, which forms the main drain by which the waters of the present Wady Arabah (the great tract between Jebel Sherah and the mountains of et-Tih) are discharged into the Ghôr es-Safieh at the southern end of the Dead Sea. This is certainly ingenious, but cannot be accepted as more than a mere conjecture, without a single consideration in its favor beyond the magnitude of the Wady el-Jeib, and the consequent probability that it would be mentioned by the prophet.

Willow-Sunday is a local term to designate *Palm-Sunday* in some parts of England; so called because boughs of the willow-tree are used instead of palms.

Wills, John, D.D., a Church of England divine, was born at Seaborough, Somersetshire, in 1740. He graduated M.A. in 1765 at Wadham College, Oxford; succeeded to the wardenship of that college in 1783; served the office of vice-chancellor from 1792 to 1796, and held the rectorships of Seaborough, and of Tydd St. Mary, Lincoln, in the gift of the crown. Dr. Wills died May 16, 1806, very rich, leaving numerous benevolent bequests. See (Lond.) *Annual Register,* 1806, p. 535.

Wills, Samuel, D.D., an English Baptist minister, youngest son of Rev. Alexander Wills, of Ashley, was born at Salisbury in April, 1808. He united with the John Street Church, London, at seventeen. In early manhood he was engaged for several years in preaching in the neighborhood of London; in 1833 opened a boys' boarding-school in Dorking, Surrey, preaching on the Sabbath, chiefly at Mortlake; in 1840 became pastor of a Church in Gosport, remaining till 1846, and then returned to London; in 1847 emigrated to the United States, and in New York established an open-communion church, of which he was the pastor for a time. Besides his ministerial work, he prepared several volumes for the press, which had a large circulation in this country. Among these were, *Daily Meditations* (4 vols.):—*The Seven Churches in Asia:—Christian Ordinances:—A Commentary on the Prophet Daniel.* In 1853 he returned to England, and was pastor at Upper Norwood, then at Vernon Chapel, King's Cross, and of West Row, Suffolk. His last settlements, which was of brief duration, were at Winchester and Milford, Hants. Resigning his pastoral work, he retired to Thornton Heath, Surrey, where he died, April 12, 1873. See (Lond.) *Bapt. Hand-book*, 1874, p. 296. (J. C. S.)

Willstädter, Elias, a Jewish rabbi of Germany, was born in the year 1796, at Carlsruhe. In 1821 he attended the lectures at the Würzburg University, and in 1824, after due examination, was enrolled among the rabbinical candidates of Baden. In 1837 he was appointed to fill the vacancy of the rabbinate at Carlsruhe, and died Nov. 14, 1842. He published, *Abriss der gesammten jüdischen Theologie* (Carlsruhe):—*Predigten bei verschiedenen Gelegenheiten* (ibid. 1829). Together with some other rabbis he edited an edition of the Old Test. for the use of schools (ibid. 1836–38). See Fürst, *Bibl. Jud.* iii, 516; Kayserling, *Bibliothek jüdischer Kanzelredner*, i, 351 sq. (B. P.)

Wilmeid, in Norse mythology, is the progenitor of all the magicians. He is the originator of the sciences of medicine, magic, and fortune-telling.

Wilmer, Joseph Pere Bell, D.D., a bishop of the Protestant Episcopal Church, was for a number of years rector of St. Mark's Church in Philadelphia, Pa., after which, about 1864, he removed to Virginia, residing in Scottsville. In 1866 he was consecrated bishop of Louisiana, in Christ Church, New Orleans, and died Dec. 2, 1878, aged about sixty-five years. See *Prot. Episc. Almanac*, 1879, p. 168.

Wilmsen, Friedrich Eduard, a Protestant theologian of Germany, was born Jan. 29, 1736, at Halle. In 1777 he was called as pastor of the Parochial Church to Berlin, where he died, May 23, 1798. He is the author of, *De Sapientia Christi in Seligendo ad Apost. Gentt. Munus Paullo Conspicua* (Halle, 1756):—*Betrachtungen über Weisheit und Thorheit im gemeinen Leben der Menschen* (Berlin, 1786):—*Moralische Predigten* (ibid. 1798; edited by F. Ph. Wilmsen):—*Predigten für Hausväter und Hausmütter* (Leipsic, 1776). He also translated into German S. Clarke's *Paraphrase of the Four Evangelists* (Berlin, 1763, 3 vols.). See Winer, *Handbuch der theol. Lit.* i, 243, 569; ii, 204, 207. (B. P.)

Wilmsen, Friedrich Philipp, a Protestant theologian of Germany, was born Feb. 23, 1770, at Magdeburg, and died at Berlin, May 4, 1831. He is the author of, *Briefe zur Beförderung des katech. Studiums* (Berlin, 1794–98):—*Die biblischen Geschichten des Alten und Neuen Testaments* (ibid. 1809):—*Das Leben Jesu Christi beschrieben* (ibid. 1816):—*Luther der Reformator* (ibid. 1817):—*Eusebia, Andachtsübungen in Gesängen*, etc. (ibid. 1827):—*Eugenia oder das Leben des Glaubens und der Liebe* (ibid. 1820):—*Herzenserhebungen für stille Abendstunden* (Hanover, 1830). See Winer, *Handbuch der theol. Lit.* i, 862; ii, 62, 71, 130, 253, 257, 262, 266, 333, 370, 393; Zuchold, *Bibl. Theol.* ii, 1453. (B. P.)

Wilson, Harry Bristow, D.D., an English clergyman, was born in London in 1774; educated at Merchant-Taylors' School, and at Lincoln College, Oxford; was appointed third undermaster of Merchant-Taylors' School in 1798, and second undermaster in 1805, in which office he continued until 1824, when he resigned; became curate and lecturer of St. Michael's, Bassishaw, in 1807; and was rector of St. Mary Aldermary and St. Thomas the Apostle from Aug. 2, 1816, until his death, Nov. 21, 1853. He published a volume of *Sermons on Several Subjects* (1807):—*History of Merchant-Taylors' School* (1812–14):—*Index to the Bible* (1818), and other works. See (Lond.) *Gentleman's Magazine*, 1854, i, 536.

Wilson, N. W., D.D., a Baptist minister, was born in Pendleton County, Va., Oct. 20, 1824. He was ordained in 1858, and after having been a pastor of country churches for several years, was invited to the pastorate of the Church at Chapel Hill, N. C., and subsequently to Farmdale, Va., where he remained two years. In 1870 he was called to the Grace Street Church, Richmond; in 1875 he removed to New Orleans, and became pastor of the Colosseum Church. He died of the yellow fever in 1878. He is spoken of as having been "one of the most eloquent ministers in the South." See Cathcart, *Bapt. Encyclop.* p. 1260. (J. C. S.)

Wilson, Thomas (1), an English Puritan divine of the 16th century, preached at St. George's Church in Canterbury thirty-six years, was chaplain to lord Wotton, and died in January, 1621. He was the author of a *Dialogue Concerning Justification by Faith* (1610):—*God's Eternal Purpose* (1611):—*Complete Christian Dictionary* (1612):—*Commentary on the Epistle to the Romans* (1614):—*Receipt against Heresies*:—*Christ's Farewell to Jerusalem* (eod.):—*Theological Rules* (1615), and other works. See Chalmers, *Biog. Dict.* s. v.

Wilson, Thomas (2), an English clergyman and school-master, was born in 1748. He was master of the grammar school at Clitheroe, Lancashire, for about forty years, and died in 1813. He was the author of *An Archæological Dictionary; or, Classical Antiquities of the Jews, Greeks, and Romans, Alphabetically Arranged*, and a volume of *Miscellanies*.

Wimmer, Gabriel, a Lutheran theologian of Germany, was born at Sagan, in Silesia, Oct. 29, 1671, and died at Alten-Mörbitz, in the diocese of Borna, March 14, 1745, in his first and only parish, to which he was appointed in 1697. He is the author of *Ausführliche Liedererklärung* (Altenburg, 1749, 4 parts, published by his son). He also wrote some hymns, which are still in use. See Koch, *Gesch. d. deutschen Kirchenliedes*, v, 497 sq. (B. P.)

Wimpheling, Jakob, a German humanist, was born July 26, 1450. At Freiburg he was the pupil of Geiler von Kaiserberg (q. v.). An epidemic drove him to Erfurt, but he eventually completed his university course at Heidelberg. He became master in philosophy in 1471, and began the study of canon law, exchanging it, however, ere long for that of theology. In 1479 he was made dean of the philosophical faculty, in 1481 superintendent of the Artist College and rector, in 1483 bachelor of theology and licentiate. Soon afterwards he was consecrated to the priesthood, and made preacher and canon at the cathedral of Spires. He was, however, rather suited to be an educator than a preacher, by reason of physical debility and a weak voice, and the natural bias of his mind. He was incessantly busy with his pen, and constantly had charge of a number of young men, whom he inspired with a love of learning and of truth, which made them, as a rule, the ready, and, in some instances, effective supporters of the Reformation, when that movement began. In this period (1497) he wrote the *Isidoneus Germanicus*, one of his most important works, and one of the first to direct the course of education into a new channel. Fourteen years were spent at Spires, when he resolved upon retiring with Christoph von Utenheim (q. v.), Geiler von Kaiserberg, and others, to a hermitage in the depths of the Black Forest, but was hindered from the execution of the plan by a transfer to the faculty of arts at Heidelberg, Sept. 13, 1498. It was characteristic of his spirit that while concerned to introduce a purer Latin, and engaged in the delivery of lectures on rhetoric and poetry, he should confine himself chiefly to the teaching of Christian authors like Jerome and Prudentius, and that he should reject the study of heathen authors as being injurious to youth. From this judgment he excepted Cicero, Virgil, and a few others only; but slight as was this concession, it obliged him to deliver two apologetic discourses to prove, against the assaults of monastic adversaries, the utility of humanistic studies. In 1500 he resigned his professorship on the invitation of Utenheim, to resume the project of a hermit life, but while tarrying at Strasburg, Utenheim was made administrator of the diocese of Basle, and Wimpheling accordingly remained with Kaiserberg, and completed

(1502) the edition of Gerson's works, upon which the latter had been employed since 1488. At this time he came into conflict with the notorious barefoot monk Thomas Murner (q. v.), through the publication of a work intended to promote the loyalty of Strasburg towards Germany, and basing its plea on the false statement that the Gaul of Cæsar's time had never extended to the Rhine, but only to the borders of Austrasia, subsequently a German province; and as he was victorious in the dispute, he retained his erroneous opinion while he lived. In December, 1502, Utenheim succeeded to the see of Basle, and invited Wimpheling to collect and examine existing synodal statutes, with a view to reforming the clergy of the diocese. After completing this work Wimpheling returned to Strasburg to take possession of a summissariat, to which he was appointed, but which was given to another person. He was therefore obliged to resume the training of young men as a means of earning a livelihood, and accepted a tutorship over the sons of his friends, Sturm and Paulus. A tract written at this time for one of these young men, in which he proved that Augustine had never been a monk, and that the boast of monasticism, that all wisdom takes refuge in a cowl, was false, since neither the ancient philosophers nor Moses, nor yet Christ and the apostles, the early fathers of the Church, and later venerable men, such as Gregory the Great, Bede, Alcuin, etc., were in any wise identified with monasticism, brought upon him the full weight of monkish fury, and made him the earliest of humanists to experience its rage. His books enraged many of the secular clergy also, as they contained frequent exposures of the abuses tolerated in the Church, and of vices existing among her ministers, and persisted in demanding a reform of these evils. He was accused at Rome, but pope Julius II commanded the ignorant monks to be silent. Wimpheling now undertook the work of improving the current methods of educating the young, but with indifferent success, as he received no encouragement from persons in authority. He also wrote a history of the diocese of Strasburg, which is still a source of some value. After the death of Geiler von Kaiserberg he wrote an appreciative characterization of the great preacher who had so long been his friend. His next important occupation was the drawing up of the list of complaints laid to the charge of the papacy by the German people, by direction of the emperor Maximilian I. To the list he added a number of recommendations, touching, e. g., the plurality of benefices, and an adaptation of the French *Pragmatic Sanction* to German conditions, which were favorably received, as was a supplementary work entitled *Medulla Sanctionis Pragmaticæ.* A nunnery in the diocese of Basle was placed in his charge by his friend, bishop Utenheim, and in this place he spent several years. In 1512 he wrote a valuable pædagogical work, entitled *De Proba Institutione Puerorum in Trivialibus et Adolescentum in Universalibus Gymnasiis;* but he felt himself to be too old to put his theories into practice at the head of a school, and therefore declined a call to teach theology at Strasburg. The warfare with the monks was continued steadily, and drew forth from him a number of exposures of their conduct, and ultimately a broadside from the authors of the *Epistolæ Obscurorum Virorum.* Towards the close of 1515 he retired to his native town of Schlettstadt, and thenceforward made that place his home. He surrounded himself with a company of ambitious young men, and organized a literary society which included Bucer and Phrygio among its members, and for a time commended the Wittenberg scholars as promoters of improved methods of study. Wimpheling himself greeted the rise of the Reformation, and approved of Luther's course. In 1518 he submitted an opinion to the emperor at the diet of Worms, which, though guarded, was certainly not adverse to Luther's interests. He soon found, however, that the new movement was taking on more extensive proportions, and assuming a more radical character than he had expected, and, with the timidity which characterized the class to which he belonged, he not only withdrew from its support, but even wrote to Luther to persuade him that the canon of the mass contained nothing contrary to the doctrines and usages of the early Church. He saw with pain that the Reformation was the fruitage of a seed which he had himself helped to sow.

Wimpheling's life and character were full of contradictions, growing out of the fact that while he saw clearly the corruption and danger of the Church and the age, he yet failed to understand the methods through which alone a reform could be secured. He trembled at the idea of lay hands attempting an improvement, even though they might be the hands of emperor or king, and shrank in terror from the idea of assailing the pope and existing institutions in the Church. With scholarly bias he thought that the study of theology would alone elevate the clergy and reform the Church. His pædagogical writings contained many ideas which were reduced to practice by Protestant teachers in the next generation, though he was still too much a schoolman to intend more than a reform in grammatical and rhetorical instruction with his proposals. He cared more for a return to the elegant and correct style of classical writers than for the study of the teachings of antiquity as a means of culture for the mind. He studied the hymnology of the Church, and attempted its improvement. He also wrote an *Epitome Rerum Germanicarum,* which is interesting as the first essay towards the writing of German history. Wimpheling's style was easy and perspicuous, precise, often elegant, lively, and witty, though verbose. He wrote poetry which lacked inspiration and fancy, and which may be characterized as mere practice in Latin versification. He was, in brief, rather practical than speculative, and was devoid of originality. His writings were generally brief tractates, filled with citations from other books, and the influence they exerted was largely due to the elevated sentiments they expressed. His personal bearing was amiable, modest, and yet helpful. Reuchlin honored him as a sturdy supporter of religion, and, after his death, Nov. 17, 1528, Erasmus wrote a very beautiful letter in his praise to Vlatten. For material towards his biography, consult Riegger, *Amœnitates Literariæ Friburgenses* (Ulm, 1775; Fasc. 2), and see, generally, Herzog, *Real-Encyklop.* s. v.

Winchell, James Manning, a Baptist minister, was born at North East, Dutchess Co., N.Y., Sept. 8, 1791; was converted about 1807; entered Union College in 1808; graduated from Brown University in 1812; was licensed by the Baptist Church at North East, Oct. 4 of the same year; supplied the Baptist Church at Bristol, R. I., during 1813; was ordained pastor of the First Baptist Church in Boston, Mass., March 30, 1814; and died Feb. 22, 1820. He published an edition of *Watts's Psalms and Hymns, with a Supplement,* and *Two Discourses, Exhibiting an Historical Sketch of the First Baptist Church in Boston from* 1665 *to* 1818 (1819). See Sprague, *Annals of the Amer. Pulpit,* vi, 595.

Winchester, Councils of (*Concilium Wintoniense*). Winchester is a city of England, capital of Hampshire, situated on the right bank of the Itchin, twelve miles north-north-east of Southampton and sixty-two miles west-south-west of London. Several ecclesiastical councils have been held there, as follows:

I. Was held in 856, in the presence of three kings. It was enacted that in future the tenth part of all lands should belong to the Church, free of all burdens, as an indemnification for the losses sustained by the incursion of the Normans who had ravaged England. See Mansi, *Concil.* viii, 243; Wilkins, *Concil.* i, 184.

II. Was held in 975, by St. Dunstan, in consequence of the disturbances raised by certain clerks, whom he had deprived of their churches on account of marriage and scandalous life. The well-known incident of the image of our crucified Saviour having decided in favor of the monks, is said to have occurred in this council. The clerks were condemned, and implored the intercession of the young king Edward, who entreated Dunstan to re-establish them, but in vain. See Mansi, *Concil.* ix, 721; Wilkins, *Concil.* i, 261.

III. Was held in 1021, under king Canute, to confirm the exemption of the abbey of St. Edmund. See Mansi, *Concil.* ix, 843; Wilkins, *Concil.* i, 297.

IV. Was held on the octave of Easter, 1070, in the presence of William the Conqueror. The three legates of Rome, Hermenfride, bishop of Syon, and the cardinals John and Peter, presided. Stigand of Canterbury was deposed, (1) for having retained the bishopric of Winchester together with the archbishopric of Canterbury; (2) for having worn the pall of his predecessor Robert until the pope sent him a new one; and (3) for having received the pall from the anti-pope, Benedict X. Agelmar, bishop of the East Angles, and several abbots were also deposed. Walfred, bishop of Worcester, claimed from William certain lands belonging to his bishopric which the latter had withheld, and the claim was allowed. Thirteen canons were published.

1. Concerning the coming-in of bishops and abbots by simoniacal heresy.
2. Of ordaining men promiscuously, and by means of money.
3. Of the life and conversation of such men.
4. That bishops should celebrate councils twice a year.
5. That bishops ordain archdeacons and other ministers of the sacred order in their own churches.
6. That bishops have free power in their dioceses over the clergy and laity.
7. That bishops and priests invite laymen to penance.
8. Of apostatizing clerks and monks.
9. That bishops have their sees ascertained, and that none conspire against the prince.
10. That laymen pay tithes, as it is written.
11. That none invade the goods of the Church.
12. That no clerk shall bear secular arms.
13. That clerks and monks be duly reverenced, let him that does otherwise be anathema.

See Johnson, *Eccl. Canons*, sub ann.; Mansi, *Concil.* ix, 1202; Wilkins, *Concil.* i, 322.

V. Was held probably in 1071, by archbishop Lanfranc. Sixteen canons were published, the heads only of which remain to us.

1. That no one be allowed to preside over two bishoprics.
2. That no one be ordained by means of simoniacal heresy.
3. That foreign clergymen be not received without letters commendatory.
4. That ordinations be performed at the certain seasons.
5. Of altars, that they be of stone.
6. That the sacrifice be not of beer, or water alone, but of wines mixed with water only.
7. Of baptism, that it be celebrated at Easter or Whitsuntide only, except there be danger of death.
8. That masses be not celebrated in churches before they have been consecrated.
9. That the corpses of the dead be not buried in churches.
10. That the bells be not tolled at celebrating in the time of the Secret (Secretum Missæ).
11. That bishops only give penance for gross sins.
12. That monks who have thrown off their habit be admitted neither into the army, nor into any convent of clerks, but be esteemed excommunicated.
13. That every bishop celebrate a synod once a year.
14. That tithes be paid by all.
15. That clergymen observe continence, or desist from their office.
16. That chalices be not of wax or wood.

It was probably resolved in this council that an institution of penance for the soldiers of William of Normandy, left by the legate Hermenfride, should be executed. It is in thirteen heads. See Johnson, *Eccl. Canons*, 1078; Wilkins, *Concil.* i, 365.

VI. Was convoked by William the Conqueror, and held in 1072; fifteen bishops were present, with Hubert, the Roman legate, and many abbots and barons. The dispute between the archbishops of Canterbury and York was examined with care, and it was established, both from ecclesiastical history and by popular tradition, that, from the time of St. Austin till the last one hundred and forty years, the primacy of the see of Canterbury over the whole of Great Britain had been recognised; that the archbishop of Canterbury had often held ordinations and synods in the very city of York itself. At the following Whitsuntide it was also decided, in a synod held at Windsor, that the see of York was subject to that of Canterbury. See Mansi, *Concil.* ix, 1211; Wilkins, *Concil.* i, 324.

VII. Was held in 1076, by archbishop Lanfranc. Six canons were published.

1. Forbids canons to have wives. Enacts that such priests as live in castles and villages be not forced to dismiss their wives if they have them. Forbids such as have no wives to marry, and bishops to ordain in future any who do not declare that they have no wife.
2. Forbids to receive a clerk or monk without letters from his bishop.
3. Forbids the clergy to pay any service for his benefice but what he paid in the time of king Edward.
4. Laymen accused of any crime to be excommunicated after the third summons to appear before the bishop, if they refuse.
5. Declares a marriage made without the priest's benediction to be a state of fornication.
6. Forbids all supplantation of churches.

See Johnson, *Eccl. Canons;* Mansi, *Concil.* x, 351; Wilkins, *Concil.* i, 367.

VIII. Was held Aug. 29, 1139, under archbishop Theodore, against king Stephen, who had seized upon certain houses belonging to the churches of Salisbury and Lincoln, and thrown the two prelates into prison. Stephen himself was cited to appear before the council. Henry, bishop of Winchester, the pope's legate, complained of the injury done to the cause of religion by those who plundered the property of the Church upon the plea of the ill-conduct of the bishops. He required that the king should begin by re-establishing the injured bishops, who, by the common law, were incapacitated from pleading on account of their seizure. The king sent a warning to the bishops, that none of them should have the boldness to make complaint to Rome against him. Upon this the council broke up without settling anything, for the king refused to submit to the judgment of the prelates, and the latter did not think it advisable to employ ecclesiastical censures against him upon their own responsibility, and surrounded as they were by his power. See Wilkins, *Concil.* i, 419; Mansi, *Concil.* x, 1014.

IX. Was held in 1143, on the Monday after the octave of Easter, by Henry, bishop of Winchester, legate a latere. Two constitutions were published.

1. Declares that none who violated a church or churchyard, or laid violent hands upon a clerk or religious person, should be absolved by any person but the pope.
2. Declares that the plough and husbandman in the field should enjoy the same peace as if they were in the churchyard.

All who opposed these decrees were excommunicated with candles lighted. See Wilkins, *Concil.* i, 421; Johnson, sub ann., Mansi, *Concil.* x, 1024.

Wind (רוּחַ, *rûach;* Sept. πνεῦμα, ἄνεμος; Vulg. *spiritus, ventus*). This Hebrew word signifies *air in motion* generally, as breath, wind, etc. Both the Septuagint words occur in the following definition of wind by Aristotle (*De Mundo*, c. 4): "Wind (ἄνεμος) is nothing else but a large quantity of air flowing, which is called πνεῦμα." So also Plato has μεγάλῳ τινὶ πνεύματι for a high wind (*Phædon*, § 24, edit. Forster). Josephus also uses πνεῦμα βιαῖον for a violent wind (*Ant.* xiv, 2, 2), as Lucian also does, βιαίῳ πνεάματι (*Ver. Hist.* I, i, 714). The Vulgate word *spiritus*, from *spiro*, "to breathe," "blow," is applied in like manner in Latin, as by Virgil (*Æneid*, xii, 365): "Boreæ cum spiritus alto Insonat Ægæo," "When the northern blast roars in the Ægean."

1. The wind as *a natural phenomenon* (Gen. iii, 8; Job xxi, 18; xxx, 15, 22; xxxvii, 21; Psa. i, 4; ciii, 16; Prov. xxx, 4; Eccles. i, 6; xi, 4; Isa. vii, 2; xvii, 13; xl, 7; Jer. x, 13; li, 16; Amos xiv, 13). It is poetically ascribed to the immediate agency of God (Psa. cxxxv,

7; cxlvii, 18; comp. Baruch vi, 61). In the New Test. it occurs in Matt. xi, 7; xiv, 24; Mark iv, 39; John iii, 8; Acts xxvii, 4; Eph. iv, 14; James i, 6; Rev. vi, 13; vii, 1). Throughout the New Test. the word is ἄνεμος, except in our Lord's illustration, John iii, 8. In the Apocrypha ἄνεμος occurs in Wisdom v, 14; xiii, 2, etc.; but πνεῦμα in xvii, 18; Ecclus. v, 9; xxii, 18; Song of the Children, xxvi, 42). We might perhaps attribute the exclusion of the word πνεῦμα, for "the wind," from the New Test., to its having become almost entirely appropriated to "heavenly things." In Acts ii, 2, we have πνοή, translated "wind;" Vulg. *spiritus*. It means the same in Homer (*Iliad*, v, 697), πνοιή for πνοή βορέαο, "the breath or blast of Boreas;" comp. Job xxxvii, 10, Sept. In Gen. iii, 8, "the cool of the day," or rather "*wind* of the day," indicates the evening, since in the East a refreshing breeze arises some hours before sunset; Vulg. *ad auram post meridiem*. Comp. Cant. ii, 17; iv, 6; where the words "until the day break and the shadows flee away" should be rendered "until the day *breathe* or *blow*" (i. e. till evening); Heb. שיפוח; Sept. διαπνεύσῃ; Vulg. *aspiret*. The evening breeze is still called, among the Persians, "the breeze of the day" (Chardin, *Voyage*, iv, 48). In Amos iv, 13, God is said to "create the wind." Although this idea is very conformable to the Hebrew theory of causation, which does not recognise second causes, but attributes every natural phenomenon immediately to the divine agency, yet the passage may perhaps be directed against the *worship* of the winds, which was common among ancient nations. Comp. Wisdom xiii, 2. Herodotus relates the same of the Persians (i, 131). The words of our Saviour, "a reed shaken with the wind" (Matt. xi, 7), are taken by some in the natural, and by others in a metaphorical sense. The former view is adopted by Grotius, Beza, Campbell, Rosenmüller, Schleusner, and Wetstein; and is confirmed, as Rosenmüller observes, by the antithesis of the rich man, whose magnificence all gladly survey. The comparison is adopted to reprove the fickleness of the multitude (comp. ver. 15, and Eph. iv, 14).

2. The wind occurs as the *medium of the divine interposition*, or *agency* (Gen. i, 2; viii, 1; Exod. xv, 10; Numb. xi, 31; 1 Kings xviii, 45; xix, 11; Job i, 19; Isa. xi, 5; Jonah i, 4). In the New Test., the wind was supernaturally employed at the day of Pentecost, like the "sound" and "fire" (Acts ii, 3). Indeed, our Lord's illustration (John iii, 8), and the identity of the Hebrew and Greek words signifying breath, wind, and spirit, lead to the inference that the air in motion bears the nearest resemblance of any created object to divine influence, and is therefore the most appropriate medium of it. See SPIRIT. To this class of instances we refer Gen. i, 2, "And the Spirit of God moved upon the face of the waters." Along with Patrick and Rosenmüller, we construe the phrase, "a wind of God," a wind employed as the medium of divine agency. Rosenmüller compares Psa. civ, 30; cxlvii, 8; Isa. xl, 7. Dr. Lee refers to 1 Kings xviii, 12, 2 Kings ii, 16, and Psa. xxxiii, 6; Isa. xi, 4. In the two latter passages, he observes that the word is equivalent to *power*, etc. The commotions of the elements, etc., through means of which the petulance of Elijah was reproved (1 Kings xix, 11), are best understood as having occurred in vision (comp. Dan. ii, 35; Zech. v, 9).

3. The wind is used *metaphorically* in the following instances: "The wings of the wind" denote the most rapid motion (2 Sam. xxii, 11), where the phrase may be a poetical representation also of the incident recorded (2 Sam. v, 24; Psa. civ, 3). The onomatopœia in the two former passages, in Hebrew, is remarkable. Anything light or trifling is called wind (Job vii, 7; Isa. xli, 29; Psa. lxxviii, 39; comp. Eph. iv, 14; Ecclus. v, 9). Violent yet empty speech is called "a strong wind," or a mere tempest of words (Job viii, 2). "Vain knowledge" is called דעת־רוח, knowledge of wind (Job xv, 2); "vain words," words of wind (xvi, 3). Many expressive *phrases* are formed with this word. "To inherit the wind," denotes extreme disappointment (Prov. xi, 29); "to hide the wind," impossibility (xxvii, 16); to "labor for the wind," to labor in vain (Eccles. v, 16); "to bring forth wind," great patience and pains for no purpose (Isa. xxvi, 18; comp. Hos. viii, 7; xii, 1); "to become wind," to result in nothingness (Jer. v, 13). "The four winds" denote the four quarters of the globe (Ezek. xxxvii, 9); "to scatter to all winds," to disperse completely (v, 10; xii, 11; xvii, 21); "to cause to come from all winds," to restore completely (xxxvii, 9). "The wind hath bound her upon her wings," means deportation into a far country (Hos. iv, 19); "to sow the wind and reap the whirlwind," unwise labor and a fruitless result (viii, 7); "to feed on the wind," to pursue delusory schemes (xii, 1); "to walk in wind," to live and act in vain (Micah ii, 11); "to observe the wind," to be over-cautious (Eccles. xi, 4); to "winnow with every wind," to be credulous, apt to receive impressions (v, 9).

Comparisons.—Disappointment, after high promise or pretension, is "as wind without rain" (Prov. xxv, 14); the desperate speeches of an afflicted person are compared to wind (Job vi, 26).

Symbolically.—Empires are represented as having wings, and "the wind in their wings" denotes the rapidity of their conquests (Zech. v, 9). The wind is often used as the symbol or emblem of calamities (Isa. xxxii, 2; xli, 16; lvii, 13; lxiv, 6); destruction by the Chaldæan army (Jer. iv, 11, 12; comp. Wisd. iv, 4; v, 23; xi, 20). "The windy storm" (Psa. lv, 8) denotes Absalom and his party. The wind is the frequent emblem of the divine chastisements (Isa. xxvii, 8; Jer. xxii, 22; li, 1, etc.

Beautiful expressions occur, as in Isa. xxvii, 2, "He stayeth his rough wind in the day of the east wind;" that is, God doth not aggravate the misfortunes of mankind by his chastisements; to "make a weight for the winds" (Job xxviii, 25).

Mistranslations.—In Psa. lxxviii, 39, "He remembered that they were but flesh, a wind that passeth away and cometh not again," should probably be rendered, "a *spirit* going away and not returning." All the versions make the words relate to the soul of man. Homer has a very similar description of death (*Iliad*, ix, 408). In Eccles. i, 5, 6, the translation is faulty, and the sense further obscured by a wrong division of verses. The passage should be read: "The sun also ariseth and the sun goeth down, and hasteth to his place where he ariseth, going to the south and circulating to the north. The wind is continually whirling about, and the wind returneth upon its whirlings." All the versions give this rendering; our version alone mistakes the meaning. The phrase "brought forth wind," is understood by Michaelis as an allusion to the female disorder called empneumatosis, or windy inflation of the womb (*Syntagma, Comment.* ii, 165). The Syriac translator also understood the passage in this way: "Enixi sumus ut illæ quæ ventos pariunt."

4. The *east wind* (רוח־קדים, ἄνεμος νότος, ἄνεμος καύσων, νότος, *ventus urens, spiritus vehemens, ventus auster*. קדים, καύσων, *ardor, æstus, ventus urens*). Both forms denote the natural phenomenon (Gen. xli, 6, 23; Job xxxviii, 24; Psa. xlviii, 7; lxxviii, 26; Jonah iv, 8). Considerable indefiniteness attends the use of these words. Dr. Shaw remarks that every wind is called by the Orientals קדים, an east wind, which blows from any point of the compass between the east and north, and between the east and south (*Travels*, p. 285). Accordingly, the Sept. often understands this word to mean the south, as in Exod. x, 13; xiv, 21 (see Bochart, *Hierozoicon*, II, i, 15). If the east wind happens to blow a few days in Palestine during the months of May, June, July, and August, it occasions great destruction to the vines and harvests on the land, and also

to the vessels at sea on the Mediterranean (Hos. xiii, 15: Jonah iv, 8; Job xiv, 2; xv, 2; Isa. xl, 7; Gen. xli, 6, 23; Ezek. xvii, 10; xix, 12; xxvii, 26; Psa. xlviii, 7; ciii, 5). In Jonah iv, 8, the phrase occurs, רוח קדים חרישית, a still or sultry east wind. For testimonies to the destructiveness of this wind in Egypt and Arabia, see Niebuhr, *Beschrieb. von Arabien*, p. 8; Thevenot, *Voyages*, I, ii, 34; Hackett, *Illustrations of Scripture*, p. 135.

The east wind crosses the sandy wastes of Arabia Deserta before reaching Palestine, and was hence termed "the wind of the wilderness" (Job i, 19; Jer. xiii, 24). It is remarkably dry and penetrating, and has all the effects of the *sirocco* on vegetation (Ezek. xvii, 10; xix, 12; Hos. xiii, 15; Jonah iv, 8). It also blows with violence, and is hence supposed to be used generally for any violent wind (Job xxvii, 21; xxxviii, 24; Psa. xlviii, 7; Isa. xxvii, 8; Ezek. xxvii, 26). It is probably in this sense that it is used in Exod. xiv, 21, though the east, or at all events the north-east, wind would be the one adapted to effect the phenomenon described, viz. the partition of the waters towards the north and south, so that they stood as a wall on the right hand and on the left (Robinson, *Researches*, i, 57). In this, as in many other passages, the Sept. gives the "south" wind (νότος) as the equivalent for the Greek *kadim*. Nor is this wholly incorrect, for in Egypt, where the Sept. was composed, the south wind has the same characteristics that the east has in Palestine. The Greek translators appear to have felt the difficulty of rendering *kadim* in Gen. xli, 6, 23, 27, because the *parching* effects of the east wind, with which the inhabitants of Palestine are familiar, are not attributable to that wind in Egypt, but either to the south wind, called in that country the *khamsîn*, or to that known as the *samûm*, which comes from the south-east or south-south-east (Lane's *Modern Egypt*, i, 22, 23). It is certainly possible that in Lower Egypt the east wind may be more parching than elsewhere in that country, but there is no more difficulty in assigning to the term *kadim* the secondary sense of *parching*, in this passage, than that of *violent* in the others before quoted. As such, at all events, the Sept. treated the term both here and in several other passages, where it is rendered *kausôn* (καύσων, lit. the *burner*). In James i, 11, the A. V. erroneously understands this expression of the burning heat of the sun. In Palestine the east wind prevails from February to June (Raumer, p. 79).

It is used *metaphorically* for pernicious speech, a storm of words (Job xv, 2); calamities, especially by war (Isa. xxvii, 8; Jer. xviii, 17; Ezek. xvii, 10; xix, 12; xxvii, 26; Hos. xiii, 15). In this latter passage the east wind denotes Shalmaneser, king of Assyria; in Ezek. xxvii, 26, it denotes the Chaldæans. Tyre is there represented under the beautiful allegory of a ship towed into deep waters, and then destroyed by an east wind. A very similar representation is given by Horace (*Carm.* i, 14). The east wind denotes divine judgment (Job xxvii, 21). "To follow the east wind," is to pursue a delusory and fatal course (Hos. xii, 1).

5. *West wind* (רוח ים, ἄνεμος ἀπὸ θαλάσσης, *ventus ab occidente*). The west and south-west winds reach Palestine loaded with moisture gathered from the Mediterranean (Robinson, i, 429), and are hence expressively termed by the Arabs "the fathers of the rain" (Raumer, p. 79). The little cloud "like a man's hand" that rose out of the west, was recognised by Elijah as a presage of the coming downfall (1 Kings xviii, 44), and the same token is adduced by our Lord as one of the ordinary signs of the weather (Luke xii, 54). Westerly winds prevail in Palestine from November to February. See WEST.

6. *North wind* (רוח צפון, Prov. xxv, 23, ἄνεμος βορέας, *ventus Aquilo*). The north wind, or, as it was usually called, "the north," was naturally the coldest of the four (Ecclus. xliii, 20), and its presence is hence invoked as favorable to vegetation, in Cant. iv, 16. It is further described in Prov. xxv, 23, as bringing (A. V. "driveth away" in text; "bringeth forth" in marg.) rain; in this case we must understand the north-west wind, which may bring rain, but was certainly not regarded as decidedly rainy. The difficulty connected with this passage has led to the proposal of a wholly different sense for the term *tzaphôn*, viz. *hidden place*. The north-west wind prevails from the autumnal equinox to the beginning of November, and the north wind from June to the equinox (Raumer, *Paläst.* p. 79). See NORTH.

7. *South wind* (דרום, Job xxxvii, 17; תימן, Psa. lxxviii, 26; λίψ, *ventus Africus*, Luke xii, 55; *νότος* [Sirocco], Acts xxvii, 13). The south wind, which traverses the Arabian peninsula before reaching Palestine, must necessarily be extremely hot (Job xxxvii, 17; Luke xii, 55); but the rarity of the notices leads to the inference that it seldom blew from that quarter (Psa. lxxviii, 26; Cant. iv, 16; Ecclus. xliii, 16); and even when it does blow, it does not carry the *samûm* into Palestine itself, although Robinson experienced the effects of this scourge not far south of Beersheba (*Researches*, i, 196). In Egypt the south wind (*khamsîn*) prevails in the spring, a portion of which, in the months of April and May, is termed *el-khamsîn* from that circumstance (Lane, i, 22). See SOUTH.

8. The *four winds* (ארבע רוחות, *τα τέσσαρα πνεύματα, οἱ τέσσαρες ἄνεμοι, quatuor venti*). The Hebrews speak only of four winds; and so Josephus (*Ant.* viii, 3, 5). This phrase is equivalent to the four quarters of the world (Ezek. xxxvii, 9; 2 Esdras xiii, 5), the several points of the compass, as we should say (Dan. viii, 8). See Tristram, *Nat. Hist. of the Bible*, p. 33.

Phrases.—"Striving of the four winds" is great political commotions (Dan. vii, 2; comp. Jer. iv, 11, 12; li, 1); to "hold the four winds" is by contrary to secure peace (Rev. vii, 1); "to be divided to the four winds" implies utter dispersion (Dan. xi, 4; Jer. xlix, 32; Ezek. v, 10, 12; xvii, 2). So also the phrase ἐκ τῶν τεσσάρων ἀνέμων (Matt. xxiv, 31) means from all parts of the world (Mark xiii, 27).

9. The Hebrews, like other ancient nations, had but few *names of winds*. Homer mentions only βορέας, νότος, ζέφυρος, and εὖρος. Aul. Gellius, indeed, complains of the infrequency of names of winds in ancient writers (*Noct. Att.* ii, 22). The same indefiniteness appears in Herodotus (see Larcher's notes on, i, 188). In the course of time the Greeks and Romans added eight other winds to the original four, but that appearing too minute a division, they reduced the additional ones to four, thus making only eight in all. The names of these may be seen in Larcher (*ut supra*), or Pliny (*Hist. Nat.* xviii, 34). Further information may be found in Coray's *Translation of Hippocrates*, *De Æribus*, *Aquis et Locis* (Paris, 1800); *Discours Préliminaire*, and see index. For a comparative table of the English, Latin, and Greek divisions of the winds, and their names, amounting to more than thirty, see Beloe's Herodotus (*Polymnia*, notes, iii, 293, Lond. 1791).

One Greek name of a wind occurs in Acts xxvii, 14, Εὐροκλύδων, *Euroclydon*, a tempestuous wind in the Mediterranean, now called a *Levanter*. The Alexandrian MS. has Εὐρακύλων; Vulg. *Euroaquilo*; Syriac, אורקלידון. The common reading, Εὐροκλύδων, seems derived from Εὖρος, *Eurus*, "east wind," and κλύδων, "a wave," quasi an eastern tempest. Other MSS. read Εὐρυκλύδων, *Euryclydon*, from εὐρύς, "broad," and κλύδων, "a wave," or rough wavy sea; and then the word would mean the wind which peculiarly excites the waves. Shaw defends the common reading, and describes the wind as blowing in all directions from the north-east round by the north to the south-east (*Travels*, p. 330, 4to; see Bowyer's conjectures, and Doddridge, *in loc.*).

The Hebrews had no single terms indicating the relative velocity of the air in motion, like our words breeze, gale, etc. Such gradations they expressed by some additional word, as "great," רוח־גדולה, "a great wind" (Jonah i, 4), "rough," קשה, etc. Nor have we any single word indicating the destructive effects of the wind, like their verbs סער and שׂער, as ואסערם (Zech. vii, 14, etc.), and answering to the Greek word *ἀνεμόφθορος* (see Sept. of Gen. xli, 6, 23). Our *metaphorical* use of the word *storm* comes nearest. The term *zilaphâh* (זִלְעָפָה), in Psa. xi, 6 (A. V. "horrible"), has been occasionally understood as referring to the *samûm* (Olshausen, *in loc.;* Gesen, *Thesaur.* p. 418); but it may equally well be rendered "wrathful," or "avenging" (Hengstenberg, *in loc.*). The phrase רוח סערה, "stormy wind," *πνεῦμα καταιγίδος*, *spiritus procellæ*, occurs in Psa. cvii, 25, cxlviii, 8. It is metaphorically used for the divine judgments (Ezek. xiii, 11, 13). The word סערה is usually translated "whirlwind;" it means, however, more properly a storm (2 Kings ii, 1, 11; Job xxxviii, 1, xl, 6; Zech. ix, 14; Sept. *συσσεισμός*, *λαῖλαψ*, *νέφος*; Vulg. *turbo;* Ecclus. xliii, 17; *συστροφὴ πνεύματος*, xlviii, 9; *λαίλαπι πυρός*). We have notice in the Bible of the local squalls (λαῖλαψ—Mark iv, 37; Luke viii, 23), to which the sea of Gennesareth was liable in consequence of its proximity to high ground, and which were sufficiently violent to endanger boats (Matt. viii, 24; John vi, 18).

The Hebrew word is used metaphorically for the divine judgments (Isa. xl, 24; xli, 16); and to describe them as sudden and irresistible (Jer. xxiii, 19; xxv, 32; xxx, 23). "A whirlwind out of the north" (Ezek. i, 4) denotes the invasion from Babylon. Another word, סופה, is also translated "whirlwind," and properly so. It occurs in Job xxxvii, 9, Isa. xxi, 1. It is used as a simile for complete and sudden destruction (Prov. i, 27); and for the most rapid motion, "wheels of war-chariots like a whirlwind" (Isa. v, 28; Jer. iv, 13). Total defeat is often compared to "chaff scattered by a whirlwind" (Isa. xvii, 13). It denotes the rapidity and irresistibleness of the divine judgments (Isa. lxvi, 5). The *phrase* "to reap the whirlwind" denotes useless labor (Hos. viii, 7); "the day of the whirlwind," destruction by war (Amos i, 14). "The Lord hath his way in the whirlwind," is probably an allusion to Sinai (Nahum i, 3). A beautiful comparison occurs in Prov. x, 25: "As the whirlwind passeth, so is the wicked no more: but the righteous is an everlasting foundation." See WHIRLWIND.

Windesheim (or **Windesen**), a Dutch monastery of the order of Regular Canons, celebrated as the centre of a somewhat extensive congregation of reformed convents, flourished in the former half of the 15th century. It was intimately connected with the association of *Brethren of the Common Life*, having been established by Radewin, the pupil and successor of Gerhard Groot, to serve as a rallying-point for its members. Berthold ten Have, a citizen of Zwoll, in Zealand, and one of Groot's converts, donated his homestead property of Windesen, worth above three thousand florins, to the prospective monastery on the inception of the plan, and other donations followed, so that the convent became an accomplished fact in 1386. Six brothers constituted its original congregation. The church was dedicated, and the investing of the brothers with the robes of their order was performed Oct. 16, 1387, Henry of Huxaria being made temporary superior, with the title of rector. Vos von Huesden, who succeeded to the government of the convent as prior, four years afterwards, became the real founder of its importance. During thirty-three years he was zealous in the promotion of its internal prosperity, as well as in the erection of its buildings and the extension of its influence. Its riches became immense under his administration, and the number of monasteries, and also of nunneries, connected with it, increased remarkably. Among these the monastery of St. Agnes, near Zwoll, became chiefly famous, through Thomas à Kempis and Johann Wessel, who were its inmates. In 1402 the first convocation of the general chapter was held at Windesheim. In 1435 the Council of Basle directed Windesheim to undertake the reformation of the convents of Regular Canons in Germany. This reformatory work extended in time even to the convents of other orders, and continued until the general reformation of the 16th century brought it to a close. The convent of Windesheim itself continued to exist until the end of the 16th century, and a chapter of Windesheim even until the 18th century. Its members were bound only by the three *substantialia* of monasticism, the vows of poverty, chastity, and obedience, and they employed themselves, particularly during the earlier period, with the copying of manuscripts and industrial pursuits. Their reformatory labors aimed merely at a re-establishment of the earlier monastic discipline by reducing ascetical requirements to a tolerable degree. See Busch, *Chronicon Windesemense* (Antwerp, 1621); *De Ref. Monaster. quorund. Saxoniæ*, in Leibnitz, *Scriptores Brunsvic.* c. ii; Delprat, *Over d. Bröderschap van G. Groote* (2d ed. Arnheim, 1856; Germ. ed. by Mohnike, Leipsic, 1846); Herzog, *Real-Encyklop.* s. v.

Windheim, CHRISTIAN ERNST VON, a Protestant theologian of Germany, was born at Wernigerode, Oct. 29, 1722. He studied at Halle, and after completing his course went to Helmstädt, where he commenced his philosophical lectures. In 1746 he publicly defended a dissertation, *De Intellectu Divino, quo Socianismus Philosophicus Argumentis suis Privatur*, and was appointed adjunct to the philosophical faculty. In 1747 he went to Göttingen as professor of philosophy, and in 1750 to Erlangen, where he also lectured on theology. He died Nov. 5, 1766. He wrote, *Commentatio Philologico-critica de Hebræorum Vav Conversivo Futurorum* (Halle, 1744):—*Diss. de Paulo, Gentium Apostolo* (ibid. 1745):—*Sylloge i–x, Thesium Philosophicarum Miscellanearum* (Helmstädt, 1746–47):—*Conspectus Thesium Philosophicarum* (ibid. 1749):—*Diss. in Danzianam Grammaticam Hebræam* (Erlangen, 1751):—*Diss. Philol. Litteræ Epentheticæ Hebræorum ad Rationem suam Revocatæ, Illæque Voces, quibus Inesse Putantur, Resolutæ, Variaque Loca Scripturæ Sacræ Veteris Testamenti Illustrata* (ibid. 1752), etc. See Döring, *Die gelehrten Theologen Deutschlands*, iv, 728 sq., Fürst, *Bibl. Jud.* iii, 522 sq., Steinschneider, *Bibl. Handbuch*, p. 150; Winer, *Handbuch der theol. Lit.* i, 153, 158, 187, 259, 343, 572, ii, 12, 59. (B. P.)

Winding-sheet, the cloth in which a corpse is wrapped for burial.

Windischmann, FRIEDRICH HEINRICH HUGO, a Roman Catholic theologian of Germany, was born at Aschaffenburg, Dec. 13, 1811. In 1836 he received holy orders, went to Munich in 1838 as professor of canon law and New-Test. exegesis, and was made canon of St. Cajetan in 1839; in 1842 he became a member of the Munich Academy of Sciences, in 1846 general vicar, and died Aug. 24, 1861. He wrote, *Sancara Sacra de Theologumenis Vedanticorum* (Bonn, 1833):—*Ueber den Somacultus der Arier* (Munich, 1846):—*Ursagen der arischen Völker* (ibid. 1853):—*Die persische Anahita* (ibid. 1856):—*Anahita* (ibid. eod.):—*Mithra* (Leipsic, 1857):—*Vindiciæ Petrinæ* (Regensburg, 1836):—*Erklärung des Briefes an die Galater* (Mayence, 1843). His studies on Zoroaster were edited by Spiegel (Berlin, 1863). See *Dr. Friedr. Windischmann. Ein Lebensbild* (Augsburg, 1861); *Theol. Universallexikon*, s. v.; *Literarischer Handweiser*, 1862, p. 18. (B. P.)

Windsor, COUNCILS OF (*Concilium Windoriense*, or *Windleshorense*). Windsor is a town in Berkshire.

England, on the right bank of the Thames, twenty-three miles south-west of London. Its castle is the residence of the queen of England. Old Windsor is a mile and a half east-south-east of this, and was the royal residence during the Saxon dynasty. The present location was chosen by William the Conqueror. Two ecclesiastical councils have been held at Windsor, as follows:

I. Was held on Whit-Sunday, 1070, in which Agelric, bishop of the South Saxons, was deprived, and committed to prison at Marlborough; no crime was imputed to him, and the sole object of the proceeding seems to have been to make room for a Norman. Several abbots were in like manner deposed at the same time. See Johnson, *Eccl. Canons*, sub ann.; Mansi, *Concil.* ix, 1203.

II. Was held April 26, 1114, in which Ralph, bishop of Rochester, was elected to the see of Canterbury, vacant during the five preceding years. See Mansi, *Concil.* x, 793; Landon, *Manual of Councils*, p. 696.

Wine, Ecclesiastical Use of. In the celebration of the Lord's Supper, the common wine was ordinarily used. Such was probably that which our Saviour used at the last supper. The ancients mixed water with the wine; and this practice seems at one period to have been general, and is abundantly authorized by canons of the Church. The proportion of water varied at different times. Sometimes it was one fourth, at others, one third. The Western Church mixed cold water only; the Greek Church first cold, and then warm water. This was said to be emblematical at once of the fire of the Holy Spirit and of the water which flowed from our Saviour's side. Various idle questions respecting the sacred elements were agitated at different times. With some there was a question of what grain the bread should be made. Others mingled salt and oil with the bread. Some substituted water for the wine. Red wine was preferred in order to avoid mistakes by the use of white wine, and also more sensibly to represent the mystery. The Roman Church now uses white wine. In the 17th century claret and in the 18th century sack was employed in England. See Eucharist.

Wine, Sacramental. The Rev. Dunlop Moore, D.D., shows most conclusively, in the *Presbyterian Review* for January, 1882, in opposition to the statements of Dr. Samson (*Divine Law as to Wine*, p. 199 sq.), that the early Christian fathers knew only of fermented wine in this connection; and likewise, by the testimony of the most eminent rabbis of modern times, that the Jews to-day use fermented wine for Passover purposes. The use of steeped raisins is only resorted to where pure wine (i. e. wine free from ceremonial impurity by Gentile contact) cannot be procured; but even in that case the Jews are utterly indifferent as to whether it has fermented or not. They also freely use *vinegar* during the Passover, although this is, of course, the product of fermentation.

Wine-cup (כּוֹס הַיַּיִן, *cup of the wine*). Wine, or the cup in which it is contained, often represents in Scripture the anger of God: "Thou hast made us drink the wine of astonishment" (Psa. lx, 3). "In the hand of the Lord there is a cup, and the wine is red; it is full of mixture, and he poureth out of the same. But the dregs thereof all the wicked shall wring them out and drink them" (lxxv, 8). The Lord says to Jeremiah (Jer. xxv, 15),

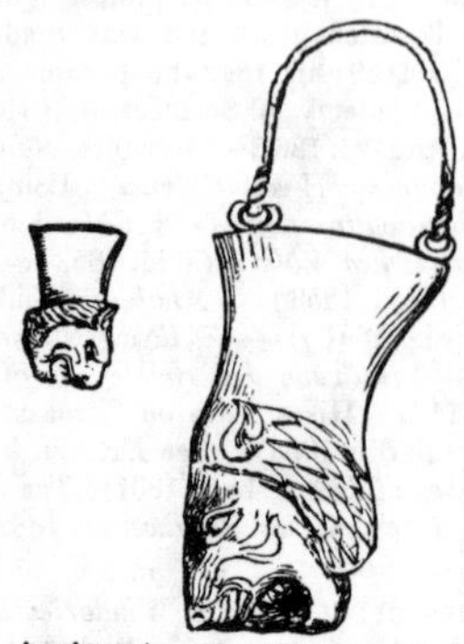

Ancient Assyrian Wine-cups.

Ancient Egyptian Wine-cups.

"Take the wine-cup of this fury at my hand, and cause all the nations to whom I send thee to drink it." Elegant forms of drinking-cups are represented on the Assyrian and Egyptian monuments. See Cup.

Wine-press is the rendering in the A. V. of three Hebrew and one Greek words: גַּת, *gath* ("wine-press," Judg. vi, 11; Neh. xiii, 15; Lam. i, 15; "wine-fat," Isa. lxiii, 2; "press," Joel iii, 13), which denotes the whole apparatus (see Geth-semane), or (as Gesenius prefers) simply the large vat (ληνός) in which the grapes were trodden, the latter being a meaning specifically borne by פּוּרָה, *purâh* ("wine-press," Isa. lxiii, 3; "press," Hagg. ii, 16); while יֶקֶב, *yékeb* ("wine-press," Numb. xviii, 27, 30; Deut. xv, 14; Judg. vii, 25; 2 Kings vi, 27; Job xxiv, 11; Isa. v, 2; Jer. xlviii, 33; Hos. ix, 2, Zech. xiv, 10; "press," Prov. iii, 10; Isa. xvi, 10; "fat," Joel ii, 24; iii, 13; "press-fat," Hagg. ii, 16; "wine," Deut. xvi, 13) is thought to denote the lower trough or receptacle into which the expressed juice flows, the ὑπολήνιον of Mark xii, 1. The last Hebrew word is derived by Gesenius (*Thesaur.* p. 619 b) from a root signifying to hollow or dig out; and in accordance with this is the practice in Palestine, where the "wine-press" and "vats" appear to have been excavated out of the native rock of the hills on which the vineyards lay. From these scanty notices contained in the Bible we gather that the wine-presses of the Jews consisted of two receptacles or vats placed at different elevations, in the upper one of which the grapes were trodden, while the lower one received the expressed juice. The two vats are mentioned together only in Joel iii, 13: "The press (*gath*) is full; the fats (*yekebîm*) overflow"—the upper vat being full of fruit, the lower one overflowing with the must. *Yékeb* is similarly applied in Joel ii, 24, and probably in Prov. iii, 10, where the verb rendered "burst out" in the A. V. may bear the more general sense of "abound" (Gesen. *Thesaur.* p. 1130). *Gath* is also strictly applied to the upper vat in Neh. xiii, 15; Lam. i, 15, and Isa. lxiii, 2, with *purâh* in a parallel sense in the following verse. Elsewhere *yékeb* is not strictly applied; for in Job xxiv, 11, and Jer. xlviii, 33, it refers to the upper vat, just as in Matt. xxi, 33, ὑπολήνιον (properly the vat *under* the press) is substituted for ληνός, as given in Mark xii, 1. It would, moreover, appear natural to describe the whole arrangement by the term *gath*, as denoting the most important portion of it; but, with the exception of proper names in which the word appears, such as Gath, Gath-rimmon, Gath-hepher, and Gittaim, the term *yékeb* is applied to it (Judg. vii, 25; Zech. xiv, 10). The same term is also applied to the produce of the wine-press (Numb. xviii, 27, 30; Deut. xv, 14; 2 Kings vi, 27; Hos. ix, 2). The term *purâh*, as used in Hagg. ii, 16, perhaps refers to the contents of a wine-vat, rather than to the press or vat itself. The two vats were usually dug or hewn out of the solid rock (Isa. v, 2, marg.; Matt. xxi, 33). Ancient wine-presses, so constructed, are still to be seen in Palestine (Robinson, *Bibl. Res.* iii, 137; comp. p. 603). Dr. Tristram examined several of these on Mount Carmel, which he describes as being exactly like others observed in the south of Judah. "In all cases a flat or gently sloping rock is made use of for their construction. At the upper end a trough is cut about three feet deep and four and a half by three and a half feet in length and breadth. Just below this, in the same rock, is hewn a second trough, fourteen inches deep and four feet by three in size. The two are connected by two or three small holes bored through the rock close to the bottom of the upper trough, so that, on the grapes being put in and pressed down, the juice streamed into the lower vat. Every vineyard seems to have had one of these presses" (*Land of Israel*, p. 106). The wine-presses were thus permanent, and were sufficiently well known to serve as indications of certain localities (Judg. vii, 25; Zech. xiv, 10). The upper receptacle (*gath*) was large enough to admit of threshing being carried on in (not "by," as in the A. V.) it, as was done by Gideon for the sake of concealment (Judg. vi, 11). See PRESS; VINEYARD.

Ancient Egyptian Foot-press for Wine.

In Palestine the vintage takes place in September, and is celebrated with great rejoicings (Robinson, *Bibl. Res.* i, 431; ii, 81). The ripe fruit was gathered in baskets (Jer. vi, 9), as represented in Egyptian paintings (Wilkinson, *Anc. Egypt.* i, 41-45), and was carried to the wine-press. It was then placed in the upper one of the two vats or receptacles of which the wine-press was formed, and was subjected to the process of "treading," which has prevailed in all ages in Oriental and South-European countries (Neh. xiii, 15, Job xxiv, 11; Isa. xvi, 10; Jer. xxv, 30; xlviii, 33; Amos ix, 13; Rev. xix, 15). A certain amount of juice exuded from the ripe fruit from its own pressure before the treading commenced. This appears to have been kept separate from the rest of the juice, and to have formed the *gleukos*, or "sweet wine," noticed in Acts ii, 13. The first drops of juice that reached the lower vat were termed the *dema*, or "tear," and formed the first-fruits of the vintage (Sept. ἀπαρχὰς ληνοῦ) which were to be presented to Jehovah (Exod. xxii, 29). The "treading" was effected by one or more men, according to the size of the vat, and, if the Jews adopted the same arrangements as the Egyptians, the treaders were assisted in the operation by ropes fixed to the roof of the wine-press (Wilkinson, *Anc. Egypt.* i, 46). They encouraged one another by shouts and cries (Isa. xvi, 9, 10; Jer. xxv, 30; xlviii, 33). Their legs and garments were dyed red with the juice (Gen. xlix, 11; Isa. lxiii, 2, 3). The expressed juice escaped by an aperture into the lower vat, or was at once collected in vessels. A hand-press was occasionally used in Egypt (Wilkinson, *Anc. Egypt.* i, 45), but we have no notice of such an instrument in the Bible. As to the subsequent treatment of the wine, we have but little information. Sometimes it was drank as must, but more generally it was bottled off after fermentation, and, if it were designed to be kept for some time, a certain amount of lees was added to give it body (Isa. xxv, 6). The wine consequently required to be "refined," or strained, previously to being brought to table (ibid.). For further elucidation of the subject, see Hackett, *Illustr. of Script.* p. 156 sq.; Van Lennep, *Bibl. Lands*, p. 117 sq. See WINE.

Wingate, W. M., D.D., a Baptist minister, was born at Darlington, S. C., July 28, 1828. He graduated from Wake Forest College, N. C., in 1849; for two years was a student of theology at Furman Institute, S. C.; from 1852 to 1854 agent of Wake Forest College, and in the latter year was chosen president, which office he held for twenty-five years. He died Feb. 27, 1879. (J. C. S.)

Winkelers, a sect existing in Strasburg towards the end of the 14th century. Their teachings and usages resembled those of the contemporary Waldenses, though with some divergences; but it is probable that the sect was of native growth, and originated in the increasing sense of need for an improvement in religious teaching, which existed in the consciousness of the people. Its members sustained communication with those of other similar associations in different cities along the Rhine and in Würtemberg and Switzerland. They rejected, on the authority of the Bible, all mariolatry and saints'-worship, the use of images, the priesthood, and the doctrines of meritorious works and purgatory. They wished to restore the worship of God in spirit and truth. They made use of lay teachers, who were required to be unmarried and unencumbered with property, and who itinerated continuously. The teachers were supported by the members of the sect, whose confessions they also received and upon whom they imposed penances. In their assemblies it was customary to offer prayer, read from books, and preach. They attended mass and confessed minor offences to the Ro-

Ancient Egyptian Hand-press for Wine.

mish priests for the sake of peace. In Strasburg laborers and artisans composed the sect, master Johann von Blumstein—later, after he had renounced their errors, syndic of the city—being its most prominent member. A number of Beguins were also among its members. They were not disposed to deal aggressively with the Church, and were content to meet in the secrecy of private houses, but the fear of being discovered sometimes led them into crime. In 1374 a Winkeler, who had returned to the Church, was murdered by direction of the sect, which paid a certain sum for the deed and submitted to undergo the penance imposed by its rulers. At another time the inquisitor, Johann Arnoldi, was so emphatically threatened with death in the confessional that he fled the city. In 1400, however, thirty-two members, both men and women, were arrested and tortured. Twenty-six of them acknowledged their connection with the sect, and were banished from the city and diocese, under the penalty of death by fire if they should return. The documents belonging to the trial are yet in existence, and are given in Röhrich's *Mittheilungen aus der Geschichte der evang. Kirche des Elsasses* (Strasburg, 1855), i, 3 sq. Neither Winkeler nor Waldense was ever found in Strasburg after this trial. See Herzog, *Real-Encyklop.* s. v.

Winkelhofer, Sebastian, a Roman Catholic theologian, was born Jan. 18, 1743, at Munzing, in the Lower-Danube department. When sixteen years of age he joined the order of the Jesuits. Two years later he went to Ingolstadt, where he studied philosophy, Greek, and Hebrew. In 1768 he betook himself to the study of theology, especially of Church history and canon law. In 1772 he received holy orders, and in the year following was made head of the congregation of St. Maria de Victoria. In 1775 he was appointed preacher of St. Maurice, and in 1789 delivered his first sermon as dean in Neuburg, on the Danube. Here he labored till 1794, when he was called as court-preacher to Munich, where he died, Nov. 16, 1806. He wrote, *Reden uber die Bergpredigt unseres Herrn Jesu Christi* (edited by S. M. Sailer, Munich, 1809; 2d ed. 1812); the same editor published his *Vermischte Predigten* (ibid. 1814–17, 4 vols.). See Döring, *Die gelehrten Theologen Deutschlands*, iv, 731 sq. (B. P.)

Winkler, Hermann Erich, a Protestant theologian of Germany, was born April 11, 1738, at Hildesheim. He studied at Göttingen under Walch, Michaelis, and Heilmann. In 1763 he was appointed pastor in his native place; in 1772 accepted a call to Hamburg, where he labored for twenty years; in 1793 was called to Luneburg as superintendent, and while he was delivering his first sermon, on March 13, he was paralyzed, and died a few hours later. Winkler was very well versed in Greek history, philosophy, and literature; Pindar he knew almost by heart. His published writings are of no importance. See Döring, *Die deutschen Kanzelredner*, p. 570 sq. (B. P.)

Winkler, Johann Dietrich, a Protestant theologian of Germany, was born at Hamburg, Dec. 27, 1711. He studied at Leipsic from 1732 to 1736, and in the latter year was made magister, on account of his dissertation, *De Luca, Evangelista Medico.* In the same year he was called as professor to Hamburg, to occupy the chair made vacant by Fabricius. He entered upon his duties by delivering an oration, *De Felici Pariter ac Necessario Nexu Scientiarum Philosophicarum cum Arte Bene et Ornate Dicendi.* In 1744 he accepted a call to Hildesheim as superintendent and member of consistory. The University of Rinteln conferred on him the degree of doctor of divinity on presenting a dissertation, *De Philosophiæ Platonico-Pythagoreæ Fraudibus.* Many professorships offered to him he declined. In 1758 he was called as first pastor of St. Nicolai to his native city, where he died, April 4, 1784. Of his many works we mention, *Disquisitiones Philologicæ*, etc. (1741): —*Hypomnemata Philologica et Critica* (1745): —*Animadversiones Philologicæ et Criticæ* (1750–52, 3 parts). See Döring, *Die gelehrten Theologen Deutschlands*, iv, 735 sq.; Fürst, *Bibl. Jud.* iii, 523; Winer, *Handbuch der theol. Lit.* i, 191, 279, 545, 570, 796, 909. (B. P.)

Winkler, Johann Friedrich (1), father of Johann Dietrich, was born Dec. 13, 1679, at Wertheim, in Franconia. He studied at Greifswalde, and, after completing his course, travelled extensively through Holland and England. With the large material which he had collected in England he went to Frankfort, with the view of preparing a new edition of the Ethiopic grammar, published by Ludolph, his former teacher, in 1702. In 1704 he accepted a call to Hamburg as professor of Oriental languages, and in 1712 was made first pastor of St. Nicolai. He died Oct. 24, 1738. Besides his Ethiopic grammar, which he edited in a second edition, he published a number of sermons, for which see Döring, *Die gelehrten Theologen Deutschlands*, iv, 742. (B. P.)

Winkler, Johann Friedrich (2), a Lutheran theologian, was born Aug. 17, 1809, at Hohen-Priessnitz, in Saxony. He studied theology at Halle, and in 1834 came to America. In 1835 he was called to Newark, N. J., where he labored for seven years. In 1842 he was called as professor to the theological seminary at Columbus, O., where he taught for three years. In 1845 he went to Detroit, Mich., and labored there for twelve years. In the meantime he had become acquainted with pastor Grabau, the head of the Lutheran Buffalo Synod, which he joined, and which appointed him, in 1856, professor of the Martin Luther College. Here he labored until his death, June 9, 1877. (B. P.)

Winkler, Johann Joseph, a Lutheran theologian, was born at Luckau, in Saxony, Dec. 23, 1670. He was at first pastor in Magdeburg, afterwards a chaplain in the army, and accompanied the troops to Holland and Italy. Subsequently he returned to Magdeburg, and became chief minister of the cathedral and member of consistory. He died Aug. 11, 1722. Winkler left some hymns which are still sung in the German Church. Thus, *Sollt' ich aus Furcht vor Menschenkindern* (Engl. transl. in the *Moravian Hymn-Book*, p. 718, "Shall I, thro' fear of feeble man"):—*Ringe recht, wenn Gottes Gnade* (Engl. transl. *Lyra Germ.* i, 46, "Strive, when thou art call'd of God"):—*Meine Seele senket sich* (*ibid.* i, 198, "Yea, my spirit fain would sink"). See Koch, *Gesch. des deutschen Kirchenliedes*, iv, 383 sq. (B. P.)

Winner, Isaac, a Methodist Episcopal minister. Scarcely any data of his life are obtainable. He was admitted into the Philadelphia Conference in 1822, and some time later joined the New Jersey Conference. He died July 4, 1868. He was a remarkable man every way; original, strong in his convictions, peerless in self-respect and self-possession. He was one of the founders and fosterers of Pennington Seminary, and took large interest in all educational matters, except theological schools, which he opposed bitterly, on the ground that they were prolific of theological errors. See *Minutes of Annual Conferences*, 1869, p. 62.

Winnowing (זָרָה, lit. *to scatter*). Among the Hebrews, as still in Palestine, when the grain had been threshed, or, rather, crushed and trodden, in the open threshing-floor, it was thrown out, altogether, into the middle of the floor; it was then tossed up into the wind, which removed the broken straw and the chaff, while the grain, the unthreshed ears, and clods of earth, with grain adhering to them, fell in a separate heap. The earth and other impurities were then removed from the grain by means of a sieve; and the winnowed heap containing many ears that were broken, but not fully crushed out, was exposed again to the threshing operation. This was again thrown across the wind by a shovel (מִזְרֶה, *mizréh*, rendered "fan" in our version of Isa. xxx, 24), when the pure grain fell to the ground

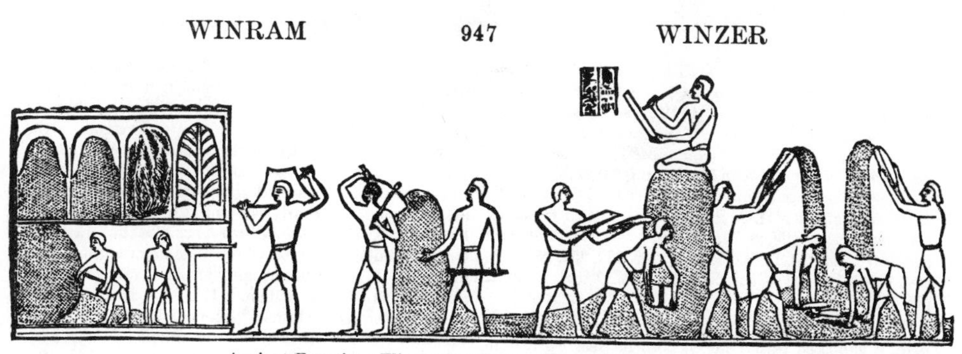

Ancient Egyptians Winnowing Grain. (From the Monuments.)

and the light chaff was borne away by the wind, as the psalmist describes. The scattered *straw*, so far as required for the fodder of cattle and the making of bricks, was collected for use, but the light chaff of the second winnowing was left in the ground entangled with the stubble (the threshing-floor being in the harvest-field), with which it was burned on the ground to help to manure the soil. It therefore furnished a fit symbol of the destruction of the wicked. These winnowing processes are still followed in the East; and, as far as appears by their paintings, are much the same as were practiced by the ancient Egyptians.—Kitto, *Pict. Bible*, note on Psa. i, 4. See AGRICULTURE.

Winram, JOHN, a Scotch reformer of the 16th century, was superintendent of Fife and Stratherne, and died in 1582. He was the author of a *Catechism*, of which all copies are thought to have perished.

Winter, VEIT ANTON, a Roman Catholic theologian, was born May 22, 1754, at Hoheneggelkofen, near Landshut. He studied at Ingolstadt, and in 1778 received holy orders. For two years he continued his studies at Rome, and after his return was appointed pastor at Laichling, near Eggmühl. Some years he spent in travelling with the son of a count, whose tutor he was. After returning home, he was called to Ingolstadt as preacher and professor of Church history. In 1795 he commenced his lectures. When the University of Ingolstadt was removed to Landshut, in 1801, he went there, and died Feb. 27, 1814. He wrote, *Versuch zur Verbesserung der katholischen Liturgie* (Munich, 1804):—*Sammlung kleiner liturgischer Schriften* (ibid. 1811):—*Geschichte der baierischen Wiedertäufer im xvi. Jahrhundert* (ibid. 1808):—*Kirchengeschichte von Altbaiern, Oesterreich und Tyrol* (Landshut, 1814):—*Patrologie* (Munich, eod.). See Döring, *Die gelehrten Theologen Deutschlands*, iv, 746 sq.; Winer, *Handbuch der theol. Lit.* i, 767, 781, 785, 854; ii, 70, 78, 285, 286. (B. P.)

Winterfeld, GEORG AUGUST VIVIGENS CARL VON, a German scholar, was born in 1794, and died at Berlin, Feb. 19, 1852, during the morning prayer. He is well known in the department of Church music, and as editor of the following works: *Der evangelische Kirchengesang und sein Verhältniss zur Kunst des Tonsatzes* (Leipsic, 1843-47, in 3 parts): the first is entitled, *Der evangelische Kirchengesang im* 1. *Jahrhundert der Kirchenverbesserung;* the second, *Das siebenzehnte Jahrhundert;* the third, *Das achtzehnte Jahrhundert:—Dr. Mart. Luther's deutsche geistl. Lieder nebst den während seines Lebens dazu gebrauchten Singweisen* (ibid. 1840):—*Ueber Herstellung des Gemeinde- und Chorgesangs in der evang. Kirche* (ibid. 1848):—*Zur Geschichte heiliger Tonkunst* (ibid. 1850, 1852, 2 parts). It must be remarked that Winterfeld was by profession a jurist. See Zuchold, *Bibl. Theol.* ii, 1456; Koch, *Gesch. d. deutschen Kirchenliedes*, vii, 425, 446, 459, 488. (B. P.)

Winterthur (*Vitoduranus*, or *Ortus de Oppido Wintertur*, "Fratrum Minorum Minimus," as he describes himself), JOHANNES VON, was a Minorite monk of the 14th century, and the author of a chronicle which is preserved in the town library of Zurich, and is a source for the history of South Germany and Switzerland. He was born in the period 1292–1300, at Winterthur, in the present canton of Zurich, and became a Minorite about 1320. He probably died at Zurich after 1348.

The original manuscript of the chronicle was doubtless that owned by Antistes Bullinger of Zurich, a historiographer of the 16th century, and now in the Zurich library. All other manuscripts and editions are derived from that, though an additional codex is mentioned by Montfaucon (*Biblioth. Bibl. Manuscript. Nova*, i, 21, Paris, 1739) as having been transferred from the library of queen Christina of Sweden to that of the Vatican. The period covered by the chronicle extends from the death of the emperor Frederic II to 1348. It is based in part upon more ancient chronicles, in part upon the oral and written statements of contemporary witnesses, and to some extent on personal observations made by the author. The writer was acquainted with the ecclesiastical and profane literature of his time, with the Scriptures, with the works of the masters in his order, Lyra, Occam, etc., and the decretals of the popes. He mentions Aristotle, Æsop, Horace, Isidore, etc. The contents of the book are, however, made up of disconnected notices and illustrations, strung together in chronological order. It is important as a portrayal of the conflicts of the emperor Louis, the Bavarian, with the papacy, and of the consequent disturbances in the life of the Church. It is the earliest report, for Swiss history, of the battle of Morgarten, of the vengeance visited by the dukes of Austria upon the assassin of king Albert, of the history of Zurich, etc. It is also of special importance to the study of the life and conditions of the time in which it originated. See Herzog, *Real-Encyklop.* s. v.

Wintle, THOMAS, a learned English divine, was born at Gloucester, April 28, 1737; received the rudiments of learning in his native city; became scholar, fellow, and tutor of Pembroke College, Oxford, where he graduated M.A. in 1759; was appointed rector of Wittrisham, in Kent, and domestic chaplain to archbishop Secker in 1767, obtained the living of St. Peter's in Wallingford; became rector of Brightwell, in Berkshire, in 1774, where he remained until his death, July 29, 1814. He published, *Daniel, an Improved Version Attempted*, etc. (1792):—*The Expediency, Prediction, and Accomplishment of the Christian Redemption, Illustrated in Eight Sermons* (Bampton lecture, Oxford, 1794):—*Letter to the Lord Bishop of Worcester*.—*Dissertation on the Vision Contained in the Second Chapter of Zechariah* (1797):—*Christian Ethics, or Discourses on the Beatitudes*, etc. (1812).

Winzer, JULIUS FRIEDRICH, a German doctor and professor of theology, was born July 30, 1780, at Chemnitz. In 1802 he was appointed teacher at the famous school in Meissen, in 1809 he was called to Wittenberg as ordinary professor of morals, and in 1812 became ordinary professor of theology. In 1814 he was called to Leipsic, where he died in the year 1845. He wrote, *Adnotationes ad Loca Quædam Epistolæ Pauli ad Romanos* (Leipsic, 1835):—*Commentatio in Locum Pauli* *ad Ephesios Epistolæ Cap. i,* 15 *sq.* (ibid. eod.):—*Commentatio in Locum*, etc., *Cap. iv,* 1 *sq.* (ibid. 1839):—*Annotatio ad Locum Ephes. vi,* 10–17, *Cui Subjunctæ sunt Vitæ Doctorum Theologiæ a Lipsiensium Theologorum Ordine Recens Creatorum* (ibid. 1840):—*Annotationes ad Locum Prioris Epistolæ Petri Cap.i,* 3–12 (ibid. 1843):—*Annotationes*, etc., *Cap. iii,* 18–22 *et iv,* 6 (ibid. 1844). In connection with H. A. Schott he published *Commentarii in Epistolas Novi Testamenti.* See Winer, *Handbuch der theol. Lit.* i, 29, 164, 213, 249, 252, 257, 263, 268, 294, 429, 434, 440, 476; Zuchold, *Bibl. Theol.* ii, 1456. (B. P.)

Winzet (or **Winget**), Ninian, a Scotch clergyman, is supposed to have been born in Renfrewshire in 1518, and to have been educated at the University of Glasgow; was master of the grammar-school of Linlithgow in 1551, and soon afterwards entered into holy orders; was cited before the superintendent of the Lothians in 1561 to answer for his religious opinions, when he gave in his adherence to the Roman Church, in opposition to the Reformation, and was deposed from his office; defended his position, and endeavored to accomplish reform within the Roman Church; was compelled to escape to Flanders in 1563; appointed abbot of the Scottish monastery of St. James at Ratisbon in 1576; and died Sept. 21, 1592. He published, *Certane Tractatis for Reformatoun of Doctryne and Maneris* (1562):—*The Last Blast of the Trumpet of Godis Worde against the Usurpit Auctoritie of Johne Knox and his Calvinian Brether, Intrudit Precheouris* (1592), suppressed by the Protestants in the hands of the printer:—*An Exhortation to Mary Queen of Scottis*, etc. (1562):—*The Buke of Fourescoir and Thre Questions touching Doctrine, Ordour, and Maneris Proponit*, etc. (1563). See Irving, *Lives of Scottish Writers*, i, 98–101.

Wire (פְּתִיל, *pathîl*, Exod. xxxix, 3, a *line* or *thread*, as rendered in Judg. xvi, 9; Ezek. xl, 3).

Wiro, *Saint*, an Irish prelate, was born in the county of Clare, and was at an early period of life elected bishop of Dublin. He went to Rome and was consecrated by the pope. He governed this see some time, and gained a high reputation on account of his sanctity. He finally resigned his bishopric and went to Gaul. He built an oratory at Mons Petri, which he dedicated to the Blessed Virgin, and called it St. Peter's Monastery. He died May 8, on which day his festival is observed. See D'Alton, *Memoirs of the Archbishops of Dublin*, p. 18.

Wirth, Michael, a Roman Catholic theologian of Germany, was born Oct. 1, 1788, at Lauingen, and died as professor of hermeneutics, exegesis, and pædagogics at Dillingen, July 17, 1832. He is the author of *Altes und Neues über den* 1. *Brief an die Korinther* (Ulm, 1825). See Winer, *Handbuch der theol. Lit.* ii, 307. (B. P.)

Wirtz, Johann, a Swiss theologian, who died at Zurich, Sept. 6, 1658, is the author of, *De Munere Ecclesiastico ex* 1 *Cor. iv:*—*De Ecclesia ex* 1 *Tim. iii,* 15:—*Emblema Theologicum ex Apocalypsi:*—*De Communione Sanctorum:*—*De Christo Unico Novi Testamenti Pontifice:*—*De Apostolo Petro:*—*De Bonis Operibus:*—*De Natura Philosophiæ:*—*De Testimonio Divino:*—*De Cœlo*, etc. See Witte, *Diarium Biographicum;* Jöcher, *Allgemeines Gelehrten-Lexikon*, s. v. (B. P.)

Wirz, Ludwig, a Protestant theologian, was born at Zurich in 1756, and died at Mönch-Altdorf, in Switzerland, May 29, 1816. He is the author of, *Helvetische Kirchengeschichte aus Hottinger's älterem Werke und andern Quellen neu bearbeitet* (Zurich, 1808–14, 4 vols.). See Winer, *Handbuch der theol. Lit.* i, 809. (B. P.)

Wisdom of God is that grand attribute of his nature by which he knows and orders all things for the promotion of his glory and the good of his creatures. It is that perfection of God, by virtue of which he realizes the highest designs by the use of best means. The assertion of Spinoza and Strauss, that no design at all can be ascribed to God, is connected with the pantheistic idea of the impersonality of God. Certainly there does not exist for the infinite understanding the opposition, nor even the great disparity, between means and ends, which so frequently hinder us. The exclusion here of the idea of design is the exclusion of the idea that God is a Spirit who thinks and wills. As such he must not only be the All-wise, but also the Only-wise One, in comparison with whom all human wisdom is as nothing. Holy Scripture also presents him to us precisely in this light (1 Tim. i, 17). He is a God who not only possesses in himself wisdom in perfection (Prov. viii, 22), but communicates it to others (James i, 5), and possesses a manifold wisdom manifest for the eye of angels, although for that of man unsearchable (Ephes. iii, 10; Rom. xi, 33).

This wisdom appears in all the works of God's hands (Psa. civ, 24); in the dispensations of his providence (xcvii, 1, 2); in the work of redemption (Eph. iii, 10); in the government and preservation of his Church in all ages (Psa. cvii, 7). This doctrine should teach us admiration (Rev. xv, 3, 4); trust and confidence (Ps. ix, 10); prayer (Prov. iii, 5, 6); submission (Heb. xii, 9); praise (Psa. ciii, 1, 4). See Charnock, *Works*, vol. i; Saurin, *Sermons*, i, 157, Engl. transl.; Gill, *Divinity*, i, 93; Abernethy, *Sermons*, vol. i, ser. 10; Ray, *Wisdom of God in Creation;* Paley, *Natural Theology.*

In Prov. viii, 12–36, we have a beautiful and poetic personification of divine wisdom. Some understand wisdom here to be the same as the *Logos* (q. v.) or *Word*, mentioned in John i, 1, 14. We only need observe here that wisdom, in the passage mentioned, is spoken of as an *attribute* and not a *person;* a virtue, and not a concrete being. See the article following. The term wisdom is used of the divine wisdom as revealed in and by Christ (Matt. xi, 19; Luke vii, 37; xi, 49; Mark vi, 2); also of Christ himself, as the author and source of wisdom (1 Cor. i. 30). See *Bibliotheca Sacra*, April, 1858; July, 1858.

Wisdom Personified. The foundation of this view is to be found in the book of Proverbs, where (viii) wisdom (*Chokmâh*) is represented as present with God before (viii, 22) and during the creation of the world. So far it appears only as a principle regulating the action of the Creator, though even in this way it establishes a close connection between the world, as the outward expression of wisdom, and God. Moreover, by the personification of wisdom, and the relation of wisdom to men (viii, 31), a preparation is made for the extension of the doctrine. This appears, after a long interval, in Ecclesiasticus. In the great description of wisdom given in that book (xxiv), wisdom is represented as a creation of God (xxiv, 9), penetrating the whole universe (4–6), and taking up her special abode with the chosen people (8–12). Her personal existence and providential function are thus distinctly brought out. In the book of Wisdom the conception gains yet further completeness. In this, wisdom is identified with the Spirit of God (ix, 17)—an identification half implied in Ecclus. xxiv, 3—which brooded over the elements of the unformed world (ix, 9), and inspired the prophets (vii, 7, 27). She is the power which unites (i, 7) and directs all things (viii, 1). By her, in especial, men have fellowship with God (xii, 1); and her action is not confined to any period, for "in all ages entering into holy souls, she maketh them friends of God and prophets" (vii, 27). So also her working, in the providential history of God's people, is traced at length (x); and her power is declared to reach beyond the world of man into that of spirits (vii, 23). See Ecclesiasticus.

The conception of wisdom, however boldly personified, yet leaves a wide chasm between the world and the Creator. Wisdom answers to the idea of a spirit vivifying and uniting all things in all time, as distinguished from any special outward revelation of the divine person. Thus, at the same time that the doctrine of wisdom was gradually constructed, the correlative doctrine of the divine utterance was also reduced to a definite shape. The word (*Memra*), the divine expression, as it was understood in Palestine, furnished the exact complement to wisdom, the divine thought; but the ambiguity of the Greek *Logos* (*sermo, ratio*) introduced considerable confusion into the later treatment of the two ideas. Broadly, however, it may be said that the *Word* properly represented the mediative element in the action of God, *Wisdom* the mediative element of his omnipresence. Thus, according to the later distinction of Philo, wisdom corresponds to the *immanent* word (Λόγος ἐνδιάθετος), while the word, strictly speaking, was defined as *enunciative* (Λόγος προφορικός). Both ideas are included in the language of the prophets, and both found a natural development in Palestine and Egypt. The one prepared men for the revelation of the Son of God, the other for the revelation of the Holy Spirit. See LOGOS.

The book of the Pseudo-Solomon, which gives the most complete view of divine wisdom, contains only two passages in which the word is invested with the attributes of personal action (Wisd. of Sol. xvi, 12; xviii, 15; ix, 1 is of different character). These, however, are sufficient to indicate that the two powers were distinguished by the writer; and it has been commonly argued that the superior prominence given in the book to the conception of wisdom is an indication of a date anterior to Philo. Nor is this conclusion unreasonable, if it is probably established on independent grounds that the book is of Alexandrian origin. But it is no less important to observe that the doctrine of wisdom in itself is no proof of this. There is nothing in the direct teaching on this subject which might not have arisen in Palestine, and it is necessary that we should recur to the more special traits of Alexandrian thought in the book which have been noticed before (§ 6) for the primary evidence of its Alexandrian origin; and starting from this there appears to be, so far as can be judged from the imperfect materials at our command, a greater affinity in the *form* of the doctrine on wisdom to the teaching of Alexandria than to that of Palestine (comp. Ewald, *Geschichte*, iv, 548 fol.; Welte, *Einleitung*, p. 161 sq., has some good criticisms on many supposed traces of Alexandrian doctrine in the book, but errs in denying all). See WISDOM OF SOLOMON.

The doctrine of the divine wisdom passes by a transition, often imperceptible, to that of human wisdom, which is derived from it. This embraces not only the whole range of moral and spiritual virtues, but also the various branches of physical knowledge. In this aspect the enumeration of the great forms of natural science in Wisdom of Solomon, vii, 17–20 (viii, 8), offers a most instructive subject of comparison with the corresponding passages in 1 Kings iv, 32–34. In addition to the subjects on which Solomon wrote (Songs, Proverbs: plants, beasts, fowls, creeping things, fishes), cosmology, meteorology, astronomy, psychology, and even the elements of the philosophy of history (Wisd. viii, 8), are included among the gifts of wisdom. So far, then, the thoughtful Jew had already at the Christian æra penetrated into the domain of speculation and inquiry, into each province, it would seem, which was then recognised, without abandoning the simple faith of his nation. The fact itself is most significant; and the whole book may be quoted as furnishing an important corrective to the later Roman descriptions of the Jews, which were drawn from the people when they had been almost uncivilized by the excitement of the last desperate struggle for national existence. See Bruch, *Die Weisheitslehre der Hebräer* (1851). Comp. PHILOSOPHY.

Wise (חָכָם, *chakâm*, σόφος). The Hebrew word, חֲכָמִים, *chakamîm*, rendered "wise men" (Gen. xli, 8; Exod. vii, 11; Eccles. ix, 17; Jer. l, 35; Esth. i, 13) not only signifies men celebrated for wisdom, *magi*, but also *magicians* or enchanters. See MAGIC. The feminine of the same term, חָכְמָה, *chakmâh*, is used for a "wise woman," one noted for *cunning* or *skill* (2 Sam. xiv, 2; xx, 16). See WITCH. The Hebrew word חַרְטֻמִּים, *chartummim*, rendered "magicians" (Gen. xli, 8, 24; Exod. vii, 11, 22; viii, 7, 18, 19; ix, 11; Dan. i, 20; ii, 21), properly signifies *sacred scribes*, skilled in the sacred writing or hieroglyphics; and is applied to a class of Egyptian priests; and also to the *magi* of Babylon and Persia. See MAGI. In Matt. ii, 1–16, the Greek term is μάγος, having the same significance. See STAR IN THE EAST.

Wise, Francis, an English clergyman, was born at Oxford in 1695. He was educated at Trinity College, of which he became a fellow in 1718; was assistant to the Bodleian librarian in 1717; afterwards presented to the living of Ellesfield, near Oxford; custos archivorum in 1726; became rector of Rotherfield Greys in 1745; Radcliffe librarian in 1748; and died Oct. 6, 1767. He published, *Annales Rerum Gestarum Ælfredi Magni* (1722):—*Epistola ad Joannem Masson de Nummo Abgari Regis* (1736):—*A Letter to Dr. Mead Concerning some Antiquities in Berkshire*, etc. (1738):—*History and Chronology of the Fabulous Ages, Considered Particularly with Regard to the Two Ancient Deities, Bacchus and Hercules* (1764), and other works. See Chalmers, *Biog. Dict.* s. v.; Allibone, *Dict. of Brit. and Amer. Authors*, s. v.

Wise, Michael, one of the most eminent of English Church-music composers, was born in Wiltshire about the middle of the 17th century. He was among the first set of children chosen at the Chapel Royal after the Restoration; became organist and master of the choristers in the cathedral of Salisbury in 1668; was appointed gentleman of the Chapel Royal in 1675; and was made almoner of St. Paul's Cathedral in 1686. Quitting his house at night in a state of great irritation, he was stopped by the watchman, with whom he entered into a quarrel, and was killed in the affray, in August, 1687. His anthems, "Awake up, my Glory," "Prepare ye the Way of the Lord," and "The Ways of Zion do Mourn," are still listened to with admiration.

Wiseheart, the family name of several Scotch prelates.

1. GEORGE, was minister at North Leith, and deposed in 1638 for refusing to take the covenant. He went to England in 1660, and soon after had the rectory of Newcastle-upon-Tyne conferred upon him. Upon the restoration of episcopacy in Scotland, he was preferred to the see of Edinburgh, into which he was consecrated, June 1, 1662, at St. Andrews. He died in 1671. See Keith, *Scottish Bishops*, p. 62.

2. JOHN, came into the see of Glasgow in 1319. He was an enemy to the English interest in Scotland. He was taken prisoner and confined in the Tower of London, April 6, 1320, but was probably released in 1322. He died in 1325. See Keith, *Scottish Bishops*, p. 243.

3. ROBERT, was consecrated bishop of Glasgow in 1272. In 1296 he swore fealty to king Edward I of England. He was appointed one of the lords of the regency in 1286, and died Nov. 1, 1316. See Keith, *Scottish Bishops*, p. 241.

4. WILLIAM, was archdeacon of St. Andrews and lord high-chancellor. He was elected to the see of Glasgow in 1270, and afterwards to that of St. Andrews. See Keith, *Scottish Bishops*, p. 241.

Wislicenus, Adolf Timotheus, formerly a leader of the free-religious movement in Germany, and speaker of the society at Berlin, who died at Dresden, March 27, 1883, is the author of, *Beitrag zur Beantwortung der Frage: Ob Schrift? Ob Geist?* (Leipsic, 1845):—*Christus in der Kirche: todt, erstehend und erstanden* (eod.):—*Zur Vertheidigung der freien Gemeinde* (Halberstadt, 1852), etc. See Zuchold, *Bibl. Theol.* s. v. (B. P.)

Wislicenus, Gustav Adolf, a liberal Protestant theologian of Germany, was born Nov. 20, 1803, at Battaune, near Eilenburg. He studied at Halle, and while yet a student was sentenced, in 1824, to prison for twelve years on account of demagogical intrigues. Having been pardoned after five years' imprisonment, he resumed his studies at Berlin in 1829, in 1834 was appointed pastor near Querfurt, and in 1841 was called to Halle. Having become a member of the "friends of light," he lectured in their behalf on May 29, 1844, at Köthen. Professor Guericke, then at Halle, denounced him before the ecclesiastical authorities, in consequence of which Wislicenus published his *Ob Schrift? Ob Geist?* (Leipsic; 4th ed. 1845). In 1846 Wislicenus was deposed of his office, and wrote *Die Amtsentsetzung* (ibid. 1846). He now preached to a congregation of so-called "free members" at Halle, and after the publication of *Die Bibel im Lichte der Bildung unserer Zeit* (Magdeburg and Lübeck, 1853), he left for America, and lectured in New York in 1854. At Hoboken he founded an academy, which he left, in 1856, for Switzerland, where he also founded an academy at Zurich. He soon retired for literary pursuits to Fluntern, where he died, Oct. 14, 1875. Besides the publications mentioned already, he wrote, *Nachrichten über die freie Gemeinde in Halle* (Halle, 1847):—*Beiträge zur Förderung der Religion der Menschlichkeit* (ibid. 1850):—*Aus Amerika* (Leipsic, 1854):—*Die Bibel für denkende Leser* (ibid. 1863-64, 2 vols.; 2d ed. 1866):—*Entweder — Oder* (Zurich, 1868):—*Gegenwart und Zukunft der Religion* (Leipsic, 1873). See Zuchold, *Bibl. Theol.* ii, 1459 sq.; *Theologisches Universallexikon*, s. v.; *Literarischer Handweiser*, 1875, p. 433. (B. P.)

Wissowatius, Andreas, one of the most prominent Socinians, and grandson of F. Socinus, was born in 1608 at Philippovien, in Lithuania. For many years he was pastor of different Socinian congregations in Poland. He died in Holland in 1678. Of his sixty-two writings we mention, *Religio Rationalis* (1685):—*Stimuli Virtutum Freni Peccator* (Amsterdam, 1682). He edited the *Bibliotheca Fratrum Polonorum*, and the *Raccovian Catechism*. Leibnitz wrote against him a treatise on the Trinity. See Winer, *Handbuch der theol. Lit.* i, 308, 374, 485; *Theologisches Universallexikon*, s. v. (B. P.)

Witch of Endor (Heb. אֵשֶׁת בַּעֲלַת־אוֹב בְּעֵין דּוֹר, 1 Sam. xxviii, 7; lit. *a woman, mistress of an Ob in En-Dor;* Sept. γυνὴ ἐγγαστρίμυθος ἐν Ἐνδώρ; Vulg. *mulier pythonem habens in Endor;* A.V. "a woman that hath a familiar spirit in Endor"). The story of "the witch of Endor," as she is commonly but improperly called, is usually referred to magical power. She, however, belongs to another class of pretenders to supernatural powers. See Divination. She was a *necromancer*, or one of those persons who pretended to call up the spirits of the dead to converse with the living (Isa. viii, 19; xxix, 4; lxv, 3). A full account is given of such persons by Lucan (vi, 591, etc.), and by Tibullus (i, 2; v, 45), where the pretensions of the sorceress are thus described—

"Hæc cantu finditque solum, Manesque sepulchris
Elicit, et tepido devocat ossa rogo."

Of much the same character is the sibyl in the sixth book of Virgil's *Æneid*. For the pretended modern instances of such intercourse, see Spiritualism.

It is related as the last and crowning act of Saul's rebellion against God, that he consulted such a person, an act forbidden by the divine law (Lev. xx, 6), which sentenced the pretenders to such a power to death (ver. 27), and which law Saul himself had recently enforced (1 Sam. xxviii, 3, 9), because, it is supposed, they had freely predicted his approaching ruin; although, after the well-known prophecies of Samuel to that effect, the disasters Saul had already encountered, and the growing influence of David, there "needed no ghost to come from the grave to tell them this." Various explanations of this story have been offered. See Necromancer.

1. It has been attempted to resolve the whole into *imposture and collusion.* Saul, who was naturally a weak and excitable man, had become, through a long series of vexations and anxieties, absolutely "delirious," as Patrick observes: "he was afraid and his heart greatly trembled," says the sacred writer. In this state of mind, and upon the very eve of his last battle, he commissions his *own servants* to seek him a woman possessing a familiar spirit, and, attended by two of them, he comes to her "by night," the most favorable time for imposition. He converses with her alone, his two attendants, whether his secret enemies or real friends, being absent, *somewhere*, yet, however, close at hand. Might not one of these, or some one else, have agreed with the woman to personate Samuel in another room? —for it appears that Saul, though he spoke with, did not *see* the ghost (ver. 13, 14): who, it should be observed, told him nothing but what his own attendants could have told him, with the exception of these words, "to-morrow shalt thou and thy sons be with me" (ver. 19); to which, however, it is replied, that Saul's death did not occur upon the morrow, and that the word so translated is sufficiently ambiguous, for though מחר means "to-morrow" in some passages, it means the future, indefinitely, in others (Exod. xiii, 14, and see the margin; Josh. iv, 6, 21; comp. Matt. vi, 34). It is further urged that her "crying with a loud voice," and her telling Saul, at the same time, that she knew him, were the well-timed arts of the sorceress, intended to magnify her pretended skill.

It is, however, objected against this, or any other hypothesis of collusion, that the sacred writer not only represents the pythoness as affirming, but also himself affirms, that she saw Samuel, and that Samuel spoke to Saul, nor does he drop the least hint that it was not the real Samuel of whom he was speaking.

2. The same objections apply equally to the theory of *ventriloquism*, which has been grounded upon the word used by the Sept., ἐγγαστρίμυθος.

3. Others have given a *literal interpretation* of the story, and have maintained that Samuel actually appeared to Saul. Justin Martyr advocates this theory, and, in his dialogue with Trypho the Jew, urges this incident in proof of the immortality of the soul (p. 333). The same view is taken in the additions to the Sept. in 1 Chron. x, 13, καὶ ἀπεκρίνατο ἀυτῷ Σαμουὴλ ὁ προφήτης; and in Ecclus. xlvi, 9, 20, it is said, "and after his death Samuel prophesied, and showed the king his end," etc. Such also is the view Josephus takes (*Antiq.* vi, 14, 3, 4), where he bestows a labored eulogium upon the woman.

It is, however, objected that the actual appearance of Samuel is inconsistent with all we are taught by revelation concerning the state of the dead; involves the possibility of a spirit or soul assuming a corporeal shape, conversing audibly, etc.; and, further, that it is incredible that God would submit the departed souls of his servants to be summoned back to earth, by rites either utterly futile, or else deriving their efficacy from the co-operation of Satan. So Tertullian argues (*De Animâ*, cap. lvii), and many others of the ancients.

4. Others have supposed that the woman induced Satan or some evil spirit to personate Samuel. But this theory, besides other difficulties, attributes nothing less than miraculous power to the devil; for it supposes the apparition of a spiritual and incorporeal being, and that Satan can assume the appearance of any one he pleases. Again, the historian (ver. 14) calls this appearance to Saul, שמואל הוא, "Samuel *himself*" (the latter word is entirely omitted by our translators); which he could not with truth have done if it were no other than the devil; who, besides, is here represented as the severe reprover of Saul's impiety and wickedness. The admission that Satan or an evil spirit could thus personate

an individual at pleasure, would endanger the strongest evidences of Christianity.

5. Others have maintained another interpretation, which appears to us at once tenable, and countenanced by similar narratives in Scripture; namely, that the whole account is the narrative of a miracle, *a divine representation or impression*, partly upon the senses of Saul, and partly upon those of the woman, and intended for the rebuke and punishment of Saul. It is urged, from the air of the narrative in verses 11, 12, that Samuel appeared before the woman had any time for jugglery, fumigations, etc.; for although the word "when" (ver. 12) is speciously printed in Roman characters, it has nothing to answer to it in the original, which reads simply thus, beginning at verse 11: "Then said the woman, Whom shall I bring up unto thee? And he said, Bring me up Samuel. And the woman saw Samuel, and cried with a loud voice." No sooner then had Saul said, "Bring me up Samuel," than Samuel himself was presented to her mind—an event so contrary to her expectation that she cried out with terror. At the same time, and by the same miraculous means, she was made aware of the royal dignity of her visitant. The vision then continues in the mind of Saul, who thereby receives his last reproof from heaven, and hears the sentence of his approaching doom. Thus God interposed with a miracle previously to the use of any magical formulæ, as he did when the king of Moab had recourse to sorceries to overrule the mind of Balaam, so that he was compelled to bless those whom Balak wanted him to curse (Numb. xxiii); and as God also interposed when Ahaziah sent to consult Baal-zebub his god, about his recovery, when by his prophet Elijah he stopped the messengers, reproved their master, and foretold his death (2 Kings i, 2, 16). It may also be observed that Saul was on this occasion simply sentenced to the death he had justly incurred by having recourse to those means which he knew to be unlawful. This theory concerning the narrative of Samuel's appearance to Saul is maintained with much learning and ingenuity by Hugh Farmer (*Dissertation on Miracles*, Lond. 1771, p. 472, etc.). It is adopted by Dr. Waterland (*Sermons*, ii, 267), and Dr. Delaney, in his *Life of David;* but is combated by Dr. Chandler with objections, which are, however, answered or obviated by Farmer. This last-named writer is of opinion that the suppression of the word "himself" (ver. 14), and the introduction of the word "when" (ver. 12), are to be ascribed to the prejudices of our translators. If they do not betray a bias on their minds, these instances support the general remark of Bishop Lowth, upon the English translation, "that in respect of the sense, and accuracy of interpretation, the improvements of which it is capable are great and numberless" (*Preliminary Dissertation to Isaiah*, ad finem). See SAUL.

Witchcraft, BIBLICAL MENTION OF. 1. The word "witchcraft" occurs in the A. V. as a translation of כֶּשֶׁף, *késheph* (but only in the plur.), in 2 Kings ix, 22; Isa. xlvii, 9, 12; Mic. v, 12, Nah. iii, 4 (Sept. φαρμακεία, φάρμακα; Vulg. *veneficium, maleficium*). In the Apocrypha "witchcraft," "sorcery," occur as renderings of φαρμακεία (Wisd. xii, 4; xviii, 13), and in the New Test. (Gal. v, 20; Rev. ix, 21; xviii, 23). As a verb כִּשֵּׁף, *kishshéph*, "he used witchcraft," occurs in 2 Chron. xxxiii, 6 (Sept. ἐφαρμακεύετο; Vulg. *maleficis artibus inserviebat*). This verb, in Arabic, signifies "to reveal" or "discover;" in Syriac *ethpaal*, according to Gesenius, "to pray;" but this word, he observes, like many other sacred terms of the Syrians, as בעל כמרים, etc., is restricted by the Hebrews to idolatrous services; hence כשף means "to practice magic," literally "to pronounce or mutter spells." The word φαρμακός is connected with φαρμακεύω, to administer or apply medicines as remedies or poisons, to use magical herbs, drugs, or substances, supposed to derive their efficacy from magical spells, and thence to use spells, conjurations, or enchantments; hence φαρμακός means, in the classical writers, a preparer of drugs, but generally of poisons, or drugs that operate by the force of magical charms, and thence a magician, an enchanter, *of either sex*. It occurs in the latter sense in Josephus (*Ant.* xvii, 4, 1), and is applied by him to a *female*, τὴν μητέρα αὐτοῦ φαρμακὸν καὶ πόρνην ἀποκαλέσαι (ibid. ix, 6, 3). This word also answers in the Sept. to חרטמים, "magicians" (Exod. ix, 11), φαρμακοί, *malefici*. The received text of Rev. xxi, 8 reads φαρμακεύς; but the Alexandrian, and sixteen later MSS., with several printed editions, have φαρμακός, a reading embraced by Wetstein, and by Griesbach received into the text. Φαρμακεύς occurs in the same sense as φαρμακός in Lucian (*Dial. Deor.* xiii, 1; Joseph. *Life*, § 31). The word φαρμακεία is used of Circe by Aristophanes (*Plut.* p. 302), and in the same sense of enchantment, etc., by Polybius (vi, 13, 4; xl, 3, 7). It corresponds in the Sept. to לטים, להטים, "enchantments" (Exod. vii, 11, 22). The verb φαρμακεύω is employed in the sense of using enchantments by Herodotus (vii, 114), saying that when Xerxes came to the river Strymon, the magi sacrificed white horses to it.

Some other mis-translations occur in reference to this subject. In 1 Sam. xv, 23, "rebellion is as the sin of witchcraft," should be of "divination." In Deut. xviii, 10, the word מְכַשֵּׁף, *mekashshêph*, does not mean "witch," but, being masculine, "a sorcerer." In Acts viii, 9, the translation is exceedingly apt to mislead the mere English reader: "Simon used sorcery, and bewitched the people of Samaria"—Σίμων προϋπῆρχεν ἐν τῇ πόλει μαγεύων καὶ ἐξιστῶν τὸ ἔθνος τῆς Σαμαρείας—i. e. "Simon had been pursuing magic, and perplexing (or astonishing) the people," etc. See also ver. 11, and comp. the use of the word ἐξίστημι, Matt. xii, 23. In Gal. iii, 1, "Foolish Galatians," τίς ὑμᾶς ἐβάσκανε, "who hath *fascinated* you?" (For the use of the words βασκανία and φαρμακεία in magic, among the Greeks, see Potter, *Archæologia Græca* [Lond. 1775], vol. i, ch. xviii, p. 356, etc.). It is considered by some that the word "witchcraft" is used metaphorically, for the allurements of pleasure (Nah. iii, 4; Rev. xviii, 23), and that the "sorcerers" mentioned in xxi, 8 may mean sophisticators of the truth. The kindred word φαρμάσσω is used by metonomy, as signifying "to charm," "to persuade by flattery," etc. (Plato, *Sympos.* § 17), "to give a temper to metals" (*Odyss.* ix, 393).

2. The precise idea, if any, now associated with the word "witch," but, however, devoutly entertained by nearly the whole nation in the time of our translators, is that of a female, who, by the agency of Satan, or, rather, of a familiar spirit or gnome appointed by Satan to attend on her, performs operations beyond the powers of humanity, in consequence of her compact with Satan, written in her own blood, by which she resigns herself to him forever. Among other advantages resulting to her from this engagement is the power of transforming herself into any shape she pleases, which was, however, generally that of a hare, transporting herself through the air on a broomstick, sailing "on the sea in a sieve," gliding through a keyhole, inflicting diseases, etc., upon mankind or cattle. The belief in the existence of such persons cannot be traced higher than the Middle Ages, and was probably derived from the wild and gloomy mythology of the Northern nations, among whom the "Fatal Sisters," and other impersonations of destructive agency in a female form, were prominent articles of the popular creed. This comparatively modern delusion was strengthened and confirmed by the translators of the Bible into the Western languages—a *popular* version of the original text having led people to suppose that there was positive evidence for the existence of such beings in Scripture. Bishop Hutchinson declares that our translators accommodated their version to the

terminology of king James's *Treatise on Demonologie* (*Encyclop. Metropolitana*, art. "Witch," etc.).

3. A very different idea was conveyed by the Hebrew word, which probably denotes a sorceress or magician, who pretended to discover, and even to direct, the effects ascribed to the operation of the elements, conjunctions of the stars, the influence of lucky and unlucky days, the power of invisible spirits, and of the inferior deities (Graves, *Lectures on the Pentateuch* [Dublin, 1829], p. 109, 110). Sir Walter Scott well observes that "the sorcery or witchcraft of the Old Test. resolves itself into a trafficking with idols and asking counsel of false deities, or, in other words, into idolatry" (*Letters on Demonology and Witchcraft* [Lond. 1830], let. 2). Accordingly, sorcery is in Scripture uniformly associated with idolatry (Deut. xviii, 9–14; 2 Kings ix, 22; 2 Chron. xxxiii, 5, 6, etc.; Gal. v, 20; Rev. xxi, 8). The modern idea of witchcraft, as involving the assistance of Satan, is inconsistent with Scripture, where, as in the instance of Job, Satan is represented as powerless till God gave him a limited commission; and when "Satan desired to sift Peter as wheat," no reference is made to the intervention of a witch. Nor do the actual references to magic in Scripture involve its reality. The mischiefs resulting from the *pretension*, under the theocracy, to an art which involved idolatry, justified the statute which denounced it with death; though instead of the unexampled phrase לא תחיה, "thou shalt not suffer to live," Michaelis conjectures לא תהיה, "shall not be" (Exod. xxii, 18), which also better suits the parallel, "There shall not be found among you, etc., a witch" (Deut. xviii, 10). Indeed, as "we know that an idol is nothing in the world, and that there is none other God but one" (1 Cor. viii, 4), we must believe all pretensions to traffic with the one, or ask counsel of the other, to be equally vain. Upon the same principle of suppressing idolatry, however, the prophets of Baal also were destroyed, and not because Baal had any real existence, or because they could avail anything by their invocations.

It is highly probable that the more intelligent portion of the Jewish community, especially in later times, understood the emptiness of pretensions to magic (see Isa. xliv, 25; xlvii, 11–15; Jer. xiv, 14; Jonah ii, 8). Plato evidently considered the mischief of magic to consist in the tendency of the pretension to it, and not in the reality (*De Leg.* lib. 11). Divination of all kinds had fallen into contempt in the time of Cicero: "Dubium non est quin hæc disciplina et ars augurum evanuerit jam et vetustate et *negligentia*" (*De Leg.* ii, 13). Josephus declares that he laughed at the very idea of witchcraft (*Vit.* § 31). For the very early writers who maintained that the wonders of the magicians were not supernatural, see *Universal Hist.* (8vo ed.), iii, 374.

It seems safe to conclude from the Septuagint renderings, and their identity with the terms used by classical writers, that the pretended exercise of this art in ancient times was accompanied with the use of drugs, or fumigations made of them. No doubt the skilful use of certain chemicals, if restricted to the knowledge of a few persons, might, in ages unenlightened by science, along with other resources of natural magic, be made the means of extensive imposture. The natural gases, exhalations, etc., would contribute their share, as appears from the ancient account of the origin of the oracle at Delphi. See PYTHON. The real mischiefs ever effected by the professors of magic on mankind, etc., may be safely ascribed to the actual administration of poison. Josephus states a case of poisoning under the form of a philter or love-potion, and says that the Arabian women were reported to be skilful in making such potions (*Ant.* xvii, 4, 1). Such means doubtless constitute the real perniciousness of the African species of witchcraft called Obi, the similarity of which word to the Hebrew אוב, *inflation*, is remarkable. Among the Sandwich-Islanders, some, who had professed witchcraft, confessed, after their conversion to Christianity, that they had poisoned their victims. The death of sir Thomas Overbury is cited as an instance in England, by sir Walter Scott (ut sup.). There was, indeed, a wide scope for the production of very fantastic effects, short of death, by such means. See MAGIC.

WITCHCRAFT, IN POPULAR ESTIMATION, is the practice and powers of a person supposed to have formed a compact with Satan. The powers deemed to be possessed by the witches, and the rites and incantations by which they acquired those powers, were substantially the same as belonged to the devotees of the Greek Hecate, the Striga and Venefica of the ancient Romans, and the Vala or Wise Woman of the Teutonic pagans. But when, along with the knowledge of the one true God, the idea of a purely wicked spirit, the enemy of God and man, was introduced, it was natural that all supernatural powers not proceeding directly from the true God should be attributed to Satan. This gave an entirely new aspect to such arts; they became associated with heresy; those who practiced them must be in compact with the devil, and have renounced God and the true faith. Previous to the development of this doctrine, if a witch was punished, it was because she had been guilty, or, at least, was believed to have been guilty, of poisoning or some other actual mischief. Now, however, such power was only the power to work evil; and merely to be a witch was in itself a sin and crime that filled the pious mind with horror. This feeling, zealously fostered, first by the Catholic clergy, and then no less by the Protestant, rose to a frenzy that for four centuries filled Europe with the most shocking bloodshed and cruelty.

1. The *creed* of witchcraft, in its full development, involved almost all the notions and practices previously connected with magic and sorcery. What was new and distinctive in the witchcraft of Christendom was the *theory* of magical arts which it involved. The doctrine of Satan, as finally elaborated in the Middle Ages, established in the world a rival dominion to that of the Almighty. The arch-fiend and his legions of subordinate dæmons exercised a sway, doubtless only permitted, but still vast and indefinite, not only over the elements of nature, but over the minds and bodies of men, except those who had been admitted to the number of the faithful, and were guarded by the faith and rites of the Church. But even they were not altogether exempt from diabolical annoyance, for the protection does not seem to have extended to their belongings. All persons in possession of these supernatural powers (and there was no doubt of their existence in all ages) must, therefore, have derived them from the prince of darkness, and be acting under his agency—excepting, of course, those miraculous powers which had been bestowed upon the Church directly by Heaven. But Satan, bestowing these powers, was supposed to demand an equivalent; hence it came to be the established belief that, in order to acquire the powers of witchcraft, the person must formally sell his or her soul to the devil. This, however, was not the early view. Magicians had been diligent students of their art. Alchemists, astronomers, and astrologers had searched into the hidden things of nature as deeply as circumstances would permit. The higher kind of European magic in the Middle Ages was mixed up with what physical science there then was; and the most noted men of the time were addicted to the pursuit, or were, at least, reputed to be so. So far from deriving their power from the kingdom of darkness, the scientific magician, by the mere force of his art, could compel the occasional services of Satan himself, and make inferior dæmons the involuntary slaves of his will. A belief, however, had early existed that individuals in desperate circumstances had been tempted to purchase, at the price of their own souls, the help of the devil to extricate them from their difficulties; and hence the suspicion began to gain adherence that many magicians, instead of seeking to acquire their power by the laborious studies of the regular art, had acquired it

in this illegitimate way. The chief cause of the prominent part in this matter assigned to females, particularly old, wrinkled, and deformed women, is the natural dislike of ugliness. It may also be noted that their more excitable temperament renders them peculiarly liable to those ecstasies which have been associated with the gift of divination from the priestess of the ancient heathen oracle down to the medium of modern spiritualism. And when witchcraft came to be prosecuted for heresy, the part assigned to woman in the Scripture account of the fall led to her being looked upon as specially suited to be the tool of the devil. Upon this circumstance was founded the doctrine in the creed of witchcraft which alleged carnal intercourse between witches and evil spirits.

The bargain by which the soul was sold to the devil was usually in writing, and signed with the witch's own blood. She was rebaptized, receiving a new name, and had to trample on the cross and renounce God and Christ (among the Roman Catholics also the Virgin Mary) in forms parodying the renunciation of the devil in Christian baptism. She received a "witch mark," which remained, and the location of it was known by that part becoming callous and dead—a matter of great interest to witch-finders. The powers conferred by Satan upon these servants were essentially the same as those ascribed to sorcerers, and the mode of exercising them was the same, viz. by charms, incantations, concoctions, etc. The only change was in the theory, that is, that instead of any power inherent in the sorcerer or derived from any other source, the results were all wrought by the devil through the witch as his servant. The power was also exerted exclusively to work evil—to raise storms, blast crops, render men and beasts barren, inflict racking pain on an enemy, or make him pine away in sickness. If a witch attempted to do good, the devil was enraged and punished her, and whatever she did she was powerless to serve her own interests, for witches always remained poor and miserable.

A prominent feature of witchcraft was the belief in stated meetings of witches and devils by night, called Witches' Sabbaths. The places of meeting were always such as had feelings of solemnity and awe connected with them, such as old ruins, neglected churchyards, and places of heathen sacrifices. First anointing her feet and shoulders with a salve made of the fat of murdered and unbaptized children, the witch mounted a broomstick, rake, or similar article, and making her exit through the chimney, rode through the air to the place of rendezvous. If her own particular dæmon-lover came to fetch her, he sat on the staff before, and she behind him; or he came in the shape of a goat, and carried her off on his back. At the place of assembly the arch-dæmon, in the shape of a large goat with a black human countenance, sat on a high chair and received the homage of the witches and dæmons. The feast was lighted up with torches, all kindled at a light burning between the horns of the great goat. Among the viands there was no bread or salt, and they drank out of ox-hoofs and horses' skulls, but the meal neither satisfied the appetite nor nourished. After eating and drinking they danced. In dancing they turned their backs to each other; and in the intervals they related to one another what mischief they had done, and planned more. The revel concluded with obscene debauchery, after which the great goat burned himself to ashes, which he divided among the witches to raise storms. Then they returned as they came. (For a vivid and entertaining description of one of these revels, see the *Tam O'Shanter* of Robert Burns.)

2. The *prosecutions* for witchcraft form a sad episode in human history. Thousands of lives of innocent persons were sacrificed to the silly superstition, and thousands more were tortured in various ways because they were suspected of having some connection with the black art. In the Twelve Tables of Rome there were penal enactments against him who should bewitch the fruits of the earth, or conjure away his neighbor's corn into his own field. A century and a half later one hundred and seventy Roman ladies were convicted of poisoning under the pretence of charms and incantations, and new laws were added. But in these and in all other heathen laws there was no penalty attached, except in the case of positive injury done. Magical or supernatural power was looked upon rather with favor than otherwise, only it was feared that it might be abused by its possessor.

The early Church was severe in its judgments against magic, astrology, augury, charms, and all kinds of divination. The civil law condemned the *Mathematici*, or men that formed calculations for the prediction of fortunes. *Veneficium*, or *Maleficium*, poisoning and mischief-making, was the name given to sorcery. The Church would not, by a law of Constantine, baptize astrologers, nor a special class of them called *Genethliaci*, or those who calculated what stars had been in the ascendant at a man's nativity. The twenty-fourth canon of Ancyra says: "Let those who use soothsaying after the manner of the heathen, or entertain men to teach them pharmacy or lustration, fall under the canon of five years' (penance), viz. three years of prostration, two years of communion in prayer without the oblation." Those who consulted or followed such soothsayers as were supposed to be in compact with Satan were to be cast out of communion. Constantine, however, made such divination a capital crime, as well on the part of those who practiced it as of those who sought information from it. Amulets, or spells to cure disease, were reckoned a species of idolatry, and the makers of such phylacteries shared in the same condemnation. The abraxis or abracadabra (q. v.) of the Basilidians came under similar censure. But the prosecutions against witchcraft as such were of minor importance comparatively until as late as the 11th century, when the prosecutions against heresy were systematically organized. Hitherto magic had been distinguished as *white* or *black;* now no distinction was made, and all magic was reckoned *black*. Almost all heretics were accused of magical practices, and their secret meetings were looked upon as a kind of devil-worship. Fostered by the proceedings against heresy, the popular dread of witchcraft had been on the increase for centuries, and numerous executions had taken place in various parts of Europe. At last Innocent VIII, by his celebrated bull, *Summis Desiderantes,* issued in 1484, gave the full sanction of the Church to these notions concerning sorcery, and charged the inquisitors and others to discover and put to death all guilty of these arts. He appointed two special inquisitors for Germany, Heinrich Institor and Jacob Sprenger, who, with the aid of a clergyman of Constance, Johannes Gremper, drew up the famous *Malleus Maleficarum,* or Hammer for Witches, in which the whole doctrine of witchcraft was elaborated, a form of trial laid down, and a course of examination appointed by which the inquisitors could discover the guilty parties. This was the beginning of the witch-mania proper. The edict of Innocent was reinforced by a bull of Alexander VI in 1494, of Leo X in 1521, and of Adrian VI in 1522, each adding strength to its predecessor, and calculated to increase the popular agitation. The results were deplorable. Armed with the *Malleus Maleficarum,* the judge had no difficulty in convicting the most innocent persons. If the accused did not confess at once, they were ordered to be shaved and examined for "witch-marks." If any strange mark was discovered on the person, no further evidence was required. But failing in this, the accused was put to the torture, which in almost all instances elicited confession. Many, in order to avoid this ordeal, confessed at once, and were forthwith led to execution. Others seem to have become insane because of the prevalent excitement, and fancied themselves witches. The extent of the prosecutions in Germany is appalling to consider. In the bishopric of Bamberg 600 victims fell within four years, and in

Würzburg 900. In the district of Lindheim a twentieth part of the population perished in the same time. And during this inquisition 7000 lives were sacrificed at Trier. Such atrocities were rivalled by 1000 executions in the Italian province of Como within a single year, 400 at Toulouse in one day, and 500 at Geneva in three months. It is said that in France, about the year 1520, fires for the execution of witches blazed in every town. The madness seized upon all nations and all estates of men, alike on Catholics and Protestants, and often on the accused as firmly as on their accusers, so that the trials represented pure and unmingled delusions. Even Luther looked on his earache as "peculiarly diabolical," and exclaimed of witches, "I could burn them all."

England, by its insular position and intense political life, was kept longest from the witch mania; but when it came, it was no less violent than it had been on the Continent. The statute of Elizabeth, in 1562, first made witchcraft in itself a crime of the first magnitude, whether directed to the injury of others or not. The act of James I (VI of Scotland), in the first year of his reign in England, defines the crime still more minutely. It is as follows: "Any one that shall use, practice, or exercise invocation of any evil or wicked spirit, *to or for any purpose*, or take up any dead man, etc., such offenders, duly and lawfully convicted and attainted, shall suffer death." Soon the delusion spread throughout all England, and increased to a frenzy. Witch-finders passed through the country from town to town, professing to rid the community of all witches, and receiving therefor a stipulated sum. Their methods were most inhuman. They stripped the accused, shaved them, and thrust pins into their bodies to discover witches' marks; they wrapped them in sheets with the great toes and thumbs tied together, and dragged them through ponds or rivers, and if they sank they were accounted innocent; but if they floated, which they were sure to do for a time, they were set down as guilty, and executed. Many times the poor creatures were kept fasting and awake, and sometimes walking incessantly, for twenty-four or forty-eight hours. Indeed, such cruelties were practiced as an inducement to confession, that the unhappy victims were glad to confess and end their miseries at once. During the sittings of the Long Parliament, *three thousand* persons are said to have been executed on legal convictions, besides the vast number that perished at the hands of the mob. Even so wise and learned a judge as Sir Matthew Hale condemned two women for witchcraft in 1664. Chief-justices North and Holt were the first to set their faces steadily against the continuance of this delusion. This was in 1694, but summary executions continued as far down as 1716, when the last victim was hanged at Huntington. The English laws against witchcraft were repealed in 1736.

The burning of witches forms a dark chapter in the history of Scotland, and the penal laws are said to have been first inflicted in the reign of James III. In that reign twelve women are said to have suffered, but their witchcraft was associated with treason and murder. James VI was a notorious witch-finder, but his well-known statute was only in accordance with the spirit of the times. The General Assembly of the Church of Scotland and its presbyteries, from convictions of duty, had often taken the matter up, for the Old Test. had expressly said, "Thou shalt not suffer a witch to live." The number of victims in Scotland from first to last is estimated at over four thousand. When the penal laws were at length repealed, the early seceders mourned over the repeal as a sad dereliction of national duty to God. The principal scenes of witchcraft were in the lowlands, the fairies of the highlands being harmless and ingenious sprites, rather than dark, ugly, and impious fiends. Many of the Scottish witches, as appears from their trial, were the victims of miserable hallucination; others seem to have gloried in a fancied power to torment others, and to have profited by it; others, when some sudden calamity happened, or some individual was afflicted with any mysterious malady, malignantly took credit as having had a hand in producing it; and others made the implied compact with Satan a knavish cover for crimes of various kinds, both against families and against the state.

New England was settled at a time when the excitement over witchcraft was very general and intense, and several persons were executed in Massachusetts prior to the extraordinary outburst at Salem. As in Scotland and elsewhere, the clergy were the prime movers. Two clergymen have obtained an unenviable notoriety for the part they had in it. The one was Cotton Mather, a man who was considered a prodigy in learning and piety, but whose writings and proceedings in regard to the trial and punishment of witches display an amount of bigotry almost incredible. The other was Samuel Parris, of Salem Village (now Danvers Centre), who seems to have made use of the delusion to gratify his own personal dislikes. Previous to the outbreak the last instance had been the hanging of an Irish woman in Boston, in 1688, accused of bewitching four children belonging to the family of a Mr. Goodwin. During the winter of 1691 and 1692 a company, consisting mostly of young girls, was accustomed to meet at the house of Mr. Parris for the purpose of practicing magic, necromancy, etc. They soon began to exhibit nervous disorders, contortions, spasms, sometimes dropping insensible to the floor. The children were declared to be bewitched, and, being pressed to reveal the perpetrator of the mischief, they accused an Indian woman, named Tituba, a servant in the family of Mr. Parris; Sarah Good, a woman of ill-repute, and Sarah Osburn, who was bedridden. These were tried before the magistrates March 1, 1692. From this time the excitement became intense. The clergy were zealous in the prosecution, being urged by the belief that Satan was making a special effort to overthrow the kingdom of God in that locality, and all classes were subject, more or less, to the delusion. The special court appointed to try these cases met the first week in June, and continued its sessions until Sept. 9. Nineteen victims were hanged, as a result of the investigation, some of them pious and respectable citizens. An old man, more than eighty years of age, was pressed to death for refusing to plead to a charge of witchcraft. A reaction now set in, and subsequent sentences were not executed. In May following the governor discharged all then in prison, about one hundred and fifty in number.

Witchcraft still remained, in the minds of the people of many countries, a reality for almost a century after the general excitement had abated. The last judicial execution did not occur in Germany until 1756, in Spain until 1780, and in Switzerland until 1782. And from the cessation of executions many think that belief in witchcraft has entirely passed away, but facts are contrary to such a supposition. Some occurrences in England in very recent times point to the fact that the popular mind is still infected with the belief in witchcraft as a thing of the present. In 1865 a poor old paralyzed Frenchman died in consequence of having been dragged through the water as a wizard at Castle Heddingham, in Essex; in 1875 the trial at Warwick Assizes of the murderer of a reputed witch brought out the fact that over one third of the villagers of Long Compton are firm believers in witchcraft; and in April, 1879, at East Dereham, Norfolk, a man was fined for assaulting the daughter of an old woman who was alleged to have charmed him by means of a walking toad. With very rare exceptions educated people do not believe in witchcraft, but among the ignorant and illiterate of all countries the belief still retains a firm hold. To the mass of the adherents of Buddhism, in Central Asia, the *lama*, or priest, is merely a wizard who knows how to protect them from the malignity of evil spirits; and, according to modern travellers, trials and executions for witchcraft are at this day common throughout Africa, as they were in Europe in the 17th century, and under very similar forms.

3. The *literature* of the subject is copious. Among the many works the following may be noted: Wier, *De Præstigiis Dæmonum* (Basle, 1563); Scot, *The Discoverie of Witchcraft* (Lond. 1584); Glanvil, *Sadducismus Triumphatus; or, Full and Plain Evidence concerning Witches and Apparitions* (ibid. 1689); Baxter, *Certainty of the World of Spirits;* Mackenzie, *A History of the Witches of Renfrewshire* (1678); Mather, *Memorable Providences relating to Witchcraft and Possessions, with Discoveries and Appendix* (Lond. and Boston, 1689); Hutchinson, *Historical Essay concerning Witchcraft* (1718); Williams, *Superstitions of Witchcraft* (1865); Mackay, *Extraordinary and Popular Delusions* (1841); Soldan, *Geschichte der Hexenprocesse* (Stuttgart, 1843); Upham, *Salem Witchcraft* (Boston, 1867); Mudge, *Witch Hill: a History of Salem Witchcraft* (N. Y. 1871); Conway, *Demonology and Devil Lore* (Lond. 1879). See SUPERSTITION.

Witenagemot (or **Witan**) (Anglo-Saxon, *witena*, of wise men, from *witan*, to know, and *gemot*, assembly), the great national council of the Saxons, by which the king was guided in all his main acts of government. Each kingdom had its own witan before the union of the heptarchy, in 827, after which there was a general one for the whole country. Its members are all spoken of as men of rank, and most probably included bishops, abbots, ealdormen of shires, and thanes. In 934 there were present at one of these assemblies king Athelstane, four Welsh princes, two archbishops, seventeen bishops, four abbots, twelve dukes, and fifty-two thanes. Every measure of national importance was debated here, the laws received its sanction, and the succession of the crown depended upon its approval. It could make new laws and treaties; it regulated military and ecclesiastical affairs, and levied taxes; without its consent the king had no power to raise forces by sea or land; and it was the supreme court of justice, civil and criminal. The voice of the Church was never absent from its deliberations, so that the right of British prelates to sit and vote in the national assembly was one of the principles of the earliest regular form of government, not derived from Norman laws, but from that time, long before, when the Saxon archbishop, bishop, and abbot took their seats three times a year (at Easter, Whitsuntide, and Christmas) in the Saxon witan. The witenagemot was abolished by William the Conqueror and its powers only in part transmitted to parliament. See Hill, *English Monasticism*, p. 202; Hallam, *Middle Ages*, chap. viii; Palgrave, *Rise and Progress of the English Commonwealth;* Kemble, *Saxons in England.*

With (יֶתֶר, *yéther*, Judg. xvi, 7-9, a *rope;* "cord," Job xxx, 11; "string," Psa. xi, 2). In the passage of Judges cited we read that Delilah bound Samson with "seven green withs which had not been dried." "Green ropes," as distinguished from "dry ropes," is the proper meaning, the peculiarity being in the greenness, not in the material. It may imply any kind of crude vegetable, commonly used for ropes, without restricting it to withs, or tough and pliable rods, twisted into a rope. Such ropes are used in the East, and while they remain green are stronger than any other. In India the legs of wild elephants and buffaloes newly caught are commonly bound with ropes of this sort. Josephus says (*Ant.* v, 9, 11) that the ropes which bound Samson were made with the tendrils of the vine. At the present day ropes in the East are rarely made of hemp or flax. Except some that are made with hair or leather, they are generally formed with the tough fibres of trees (particularly the palm-tree) and roots, with grasses, and with reeds and rushes. These ropes are, in general, tolerably strong, but are in no degree comparable to our hempen ropes. They are very light in comparison, and, wanting compactness, in most cases they are also rough and coarse to the eye. The praises which travellers bestow on ropes of this kind must not be understood as putting them in comparison with those in use among ourselves, but with the bands of hay which our peasants twist, and with reference to the simple and crude materials of which they are composed (Kitto, *Pictorial Bible*, note ad loc.). See CORD.

Withington, LEONARD, D.D., a Congregational minister, was born at Dorchester, Mass., in 1789. He graduated from Yale College in 1814, studied for some time in Andover Theological Seminary, became pastor of the First Church at Newburyport, Mass., in 1816, and died there, April 22, 1885, a colleague having been appointed in 1858. He wrote, *The Puritans* (1836):—*Solomon's Song Explained* (1861), etc.

Witness (עֵד, fem. עֵדָה; Sept. and New Test. μάρτυς; Vulg. *testis*) is used in the English Bible both of persons and things.

I. *Leading Significations.*—This frequent term occurs, 1. In the sense of *a person* who deposes to the occurrence of any fact, a witness of any event. The Hebrew word is from עוּד, *to repeat.* The Greek word is usually derived from μείρω, to "divide," "decide," etc., because a witness decides controversies (Heb. vi, 16); but Damm (*Lex. Hom.* col. 1495) deduces it from the old word μάρη, "the hand," because witnesses anciently held up their hands in giving evidence. This custom, among the ancient Hebrews, is referred to in Gen. xiv, 22; among the heathens, by Homer (*Iliad*, x, 321), and by Virgil (*Æneid*, xii, 196). God himself is represented as swearing in this manner (Deut. xxxii, 40; Ezek. xx, 5, 6, 15; comp. Numb. xiv, 30). So also the heathen gods (Pindar, *Olymp.* vii, 119, 120). These Hebrew and Greek words, with their various derivations, pervade the entire subject. They are applied to *a judicial witness* in Exod. xxiii, 1; Lev. v, 1; Numb. v, 13; xxxv, 30 (comp. Deut. xvii, 6; xix, 15; Matt. xviii, 16; 2 Cor. xiii, 1); Prov. xiv, 5; xxiv, 28; Matt. xxvi, 65; Acts vi, 13; 1 Tim. v, 19; Heb. x, 28. They are applied, *generally*, to a person who certifies, or is able to certify, to any fact which has come under his cognizance (Josh. xxiv, 22; Isa. viii, 2; Luke xxiv, 48; Acts i, 8, 22; 1 Thess. ii, 10; 1 Tim. vi, 12; 2 Tim. ii, 2; 1 Pet. i, 5). So in allusion to those who witness the public games (Heb. xii, 1). They are also applied to any one who testifies to the world what God reveals through him (Rev. xi, 3). In the latter sense the Greek word is applied to our Lord (Rev. i, 5; iii, 14). Both the Hebrew and Greek words are also applied to *God* (Gen. xxxi, 50; 1 Sam. xii, 5; Jer. xlii, 5; Rom. i, 9; Phil. i, 8; 1 Thess. ii, 5); to *inanimate things* (Gen. xxxi, 52; Psa. lxxxix, 37). The supernatural means whereby the deficiency of witnesses was compensated under the theocracy, have been already considered under the articles ADULTERY, TRIAL OF; URIM AND THUMMIM. For the punishment of false witness and the suppression of evidence, see PUNISHMENT. For the forms of adjuration (2 Chron. xviii, 15), see ADJURATION. Opinions differ as to what is meant by "the faithful witness in heaven" (Psa. lxxxix, 37). Some suppose it to mean the moon (comp. Psa. lxxii, 5, 7; Jer. xxxi, 35, 36; xxxiii, 20, 21; Ecclus. xliii, 6); others, the rainbow (Gen. ix, 12-17).

2. The witness or *testimony itself* borne to any fact is expressed by עֵד; μαρτυρία (*testimonium*). They are used of *judicial* testimony (Prov. xxv, 18; Mark xiv, 56, 59). In verse 55, Schleusner takes the word μαρτυρία for μάρτυρ, the abstract for the concrete (Luke xxii, 71; John viii, 17; Josephus, *Ant.* iv, 8, 15). It denotes the testimony to the truth of anything *generally* (John i, 7, 19; xix, 35); that of a poet (Tit. i, 13). It occurs in Josephus (*Cont. Apion*, 1, 21). In John iii, 11, 32, Schleusner understands the *doctrine*, the thing professed; in v, 32, 36, the *proofs* given by God of our Saviour's mission; comp. v, 9. In viii, 13, 14, both he and Bretschneider assign to the word the sense of *praise.*

In Acts xxii, 18, the former translates it *teaching* or *instruction.* In Rev. i, 9, it denotes *the constant profession* of Christianity, or testimony to the truth of the gospel (comp. i, 2; vi, 9). In 1 Tim. iii, 7, μαρτυρία καλή means a *good character* (comp. 3 John 12; Ecclus. xxxi, 34; Josephus, *Ant.* vi, 10, 1). In Psa. xix, 7, "The testimony of the Lord is sure" probably signifies the *ordinances, institutions,* etc. (comp. cxix, 22, 24, etc.). Those ambiguous words, "He that believeth in the Son of God hath the witness in himself" (1 John v, 10), which have given rise to a variety of fanatical meanings, are easily understood, by explaining the word ἔχει, "receives," "retains," etc., i. e. the foregoing testimony which God hath given of his Son, whereas the unbeliever rejects it. The whole passage is obscured in the English translation by neglecting the uniformity of the Greek, and introducing the word "record," contrary to the profession of our translators in their *Preface to the Reader* (ad finem). The Hebrew word, with μαρτύριον, occurs in the sense of *monument, evidence,* etc. (Gen. xxi, 30; xxxi, 44; Deut. iv, 45; xxxi, 26; Josh. xxii, 27; Ruth iv, 7; Matt. viii, 4; Mark vi, 11; Luke xxi, 13; James v, 3). In 2 Cor. i, 12, Schleusner explains μαρτύριον, *commendation.* In Prov. xxix, 14, and Amos i, 11, לעד is pointed to mean *perpetually, forever,* but the Septuagint gives εἰς μαρτύριον; Aquila, εἰς ἔτι; Symmachus, εἰς ἀεί; Vulg. *in æternum.* In Acts vii, 44, and Rev. xv, 5, we find ἡ σκηνὴ τοῦ μαρτυρίου, and this is the Sept. rendering for אהל מועד (which really means "the tabernacle of the *congregation*") in Exod. xxix, 42, 44; xl, 22, 24—deriving מועד from עוד, "to testify," instead of from יעד, "to assemble." On 1 Tim. ii, 6, see Bowyer, *Conjectures.* In Heb. iii, 5, Schleusner interprets εἰς μαρτύριον τῶν λαληθησομένων, "the *promulgation* of those things about to be delivered to the Jews."

3. *To be* or *become a witness,* by testifying the truth of what one knows. Thus the Sept. translates העיד (Gen. xliii, 3), μαρτυρέω, *to bear witness,* and Amos iii, 13: see also 1 Kings xxi, 10, 13. In John i, 7; xv, 26; xviii, 23, Schleusner gives as its meaning, *to teach* or *explain;* in John iv, 44; vii, 7; 1 Tim. vi, 13, *to declare;* in Acts x, 43; Rom. iii, 21, *to declare prophetically.* With a dative case following, the word sometimes means *to approve* (Luke iv, 22). So Schleusner understands Luke xi, 48, "Ye *approve* the deeds of your fathers," and he gives this sense also to Rom. x, 2. In like manner the passive μαρτυρέομαι, "to be approved," "beloved," "have a good character," etc. (Acts vi, 3; 1 Tim. v, 10; comp. 3 John 6, 12). "The witness of the Spirit," alluded to by St. Paul (Rom. viii, 16), is explained by Macknight and all the best commentators, as the extraordinary operation of the Holy Spirit concurring with the filial disposition of converted Gentiles, to prove that they are "the children of God," as well as the Jews. (See below.)

4. "To call or take to witness," "to invoke as witness," μαρτύρομαι (Acts xx, 26; Gal. v, 3; Josephus, *War,* iii, 8, 3). A still stronger word is διαμαρτύρομαι, which corresponds to העיד (Deut. iv, 26). It means "to admonish solemnly," "to charge earnestly," "to urge upon" (Psa. lxxxi, 8; Neh. ix, 26; Luke xvi, 28; Acts ii, 40). In other passages the same words mean to "*teach* earnestly." In Job xxix, 11, a beautiful phrase occurs, "When the eye saw me it gave witness to me." The admiring expression of the eye upon beholding a man of eminent virtue and benevolence, is here admirably illustrated. The description of the mischief occasioned by a false witness, in Prov. xxv, 18, deserves notice: "A man that beareth false witness against his neighbor, is a maul, and a sword, and a sharp arrow." Few words afford more exercise to discrimination, in consequence of the various shades of meaning in which the context requires they should be understood.

II. *Hebrew Usages.*—1. Among people with whom writing is not common, the evidence of a transaction is given by some tangible memorial or significant ceremony. Abraham gave seven ewe-lambs to Abimelech as an evidence of his property in the well of Beersheba. Jacob raised a heap of stones, "the heap of witness," as a boundary-mark between himself and Laban (Gen. xxi, 30; xxxi, 47, 52). The tribes of Reuben and Gad raised an "altar," designed expressly not for sacrifice, but as a witness to the covenant between themselves and the rest of the nation; Joshua set up a stone as an evidence of the allegiance promised by Israel to God; "for," he said, "it hath heard all the words of the Lord" (Josh. xxii, 10, 26, 34; xxiv, 26, 27). So also a pillar is mentioned by Isaiah as "a witness to the Lord of hosts in the land of Egypt" (Isa. xix, 19, 20). Thus also the sacred ark and its contents are called "the testimony" (Exod. xvi, 33, 34; xxv, 16; xxxviii, 21; Numb. i, 50, 53; ix, 15; x, 11; xvii, 7, 8; xviii, 2; Heb. ix, 4).

Thus also symbolical usages, in ratification of contracts or completed arrangements, as the ceremony of shoe-loosing (Deut. xxv, 9, 10; Ruth iv. 7, 8), the ordeal prescribed in the case of a suspected wife (Numb. v, 17-31), with which may be compared the ordeal of the Styx (*Class. Mus.* vi, 386). The Bedawin Arabs practice a fiery ordeal in certain cases by way of compurgation (Burckhardt, *Notes,* i, 121; Layard, *Nin. and Bab.* p. 305). The ceremony also appointed at the oblation of first-fruits (q. v.) may be mentioned as partaking of the same character (Deut. xxvi, 4)

But written evidence was by no means unknown to the Jews. Divorce was to be proved by a written document (Deut. xxiv, 1, 3), whereas among Bedawin and Mussulmans in general a spoken sentence is sufficient (Burckhardt, *Notes,* i, 110; Sale, *Koran,* c. 33, p. 348; Lane, *Mod. Egypt,* i, 136, 236). In civil contracts, at least in later times, documentary evidence was required and carefully preserved (Isa. viii, 16; Jer. xxxii, 10-16).

On the whole Moses was very careful to provide and enforce evidence for all infractions of law and all transactions bearing on it: e. g. the memorial stones of Jordan and of Ebal (Deut. xxvii, 2-4; Josh. iv, 9; viii, 30); the fringes on garments (Numb. xv, 39, 40); the boundary-stones of property (Deut. xix, 14; xxvii, 17; Prov. xxii, 28); the "broad plates" made from the censers of the Korahites (Numb. xvi, 38); above all, the ark of testimony itself—all these are instances of the care taken by the legislator to perpetuate evidence of the facts on which the legislation was founded, and by which it was supported (Deut. vi, 20-25). Appeal to the same principle is also repeatedly made in the case of prophecies as a test of their authenticity (Deut. xviii, 22; Jer. xxviii, 9, 16, 17; John iii, 11; v, 36; x, 38; xiv, 11; Luke xxiv, 48; Acts i, 3; ii, 32; iii, 15, etc.).

2. Among special provisions of the law with respect to evidence are the following:

(1) Two witnesses at least are required to establish any charge (Numb. xxxv, 30; Deut. xvii, 6; xix, 15; 1 Kings xxi, 13; John viii, 17; 2 Cor. xiii, 1; Heb. x, 28); and a like principle is laid down by Paul as a rule of procedure in certain cases in the Christian Church (1 Tim. v, 19).

(2) In the case of the suspected wife, evidence besides the husband's was desired, though not demanded (Numb. v, 13).

(3) The witness who withheld the truth was censured (Lev. v, 1).

(4) False witness was punished with the punishment due to the offence which it sought to establish. See OATH.

(5) Slanderous reports and officious witness are discouraged (Exod. xx, 16; xxiii, 1; Lev. xix, 16, 18; Deut. xix, 16-21; Prov. xxiv, 28).

(6) The witnesses were the first executioners (Deut. xiii, 9; xvi, 7; Acts vii, 58).

(7) In case of an animal left in charge and torn by

wild beasts, the keeper was to bring the carcass in proof of the fact and disproof of his own criminality (Exod. xxii, 13).

(8) According to Josephus, women and slaves were not admitted to bear testimony (*Ant.* iv, 8, 15). To these exceptions the Mishna adds idiots, deaf, blind, and dumb persons, persons of infamous character, and some others, ten in all (Selden, *De Synedr.* ii, 13, 11; Otho, *Lex. Rabb.* p. 653). The high-priest was not bound to give evidence in any case except one affecting the king (ibid.). Various refinements on the quality of evidence and the manner of taking it are given in the Mishna (*Sanhedr.* iv, 5; v, 2, 3; *Maccoth*, i, 1, 9; *Sheb.* iii, 10; iv, 1; v, 1). In criminal cases evidence was required to be oral; in pecuniary, written evidence was allowed (Otho, *Lex. Rabb.* p. 653).

3. In the New Test. the original notion of a witness is exhibited in the special form of one who attests his belief in the gospel by personal suffering. So Stephen is styled by Paul (Acts xxii, 20), and the "faithful Antipas" (Rev. ii, 13). John also speaks of himself and of others as witnesses in this sense (Rev. i, 9; vi, 9; xi, 3; xx, 4). See also Heb. xi and xii, 1, in which passage a number of persons are mentioned, belonging both to Old Test. and New Test., who bore witness to the truth by personal endurance; and to this passage may be added, as bearing on the same view of the term "witness," Dan. iii, 21; vi, 16; 1 Macc. i, 60, 63; 2 Macc. vi, 18, 19. Hence it is that the use of the ecclesiastical term "martyr" has arisen, of which copious illustration may be seen in Suicer, *Thes.* ii, 310, etc. See MARTYR.

WITNESS, FALSE. The early civil and ecclesiastical laws were very severe in their denunciation and punishment of this crime. We learn from Aulus Gellius that the punishment of false witness among the old Romans, by the law of the twelve tables, was to cast the criminal headlong from the top of the Tarpeian rock. Afterwards, by the law called *Lex Remmia*, false witnesses were burned in the face and stigmatized with the letter *k*, denoting that they were calumniators. In opposition to these the law designates honest men as *homines integræ frontis*, or men without such mark. And, though the Christian law abolished it, as it did other laws of undue severity, still false accusation and calumny were corrected with suitable punishments, such as infamy, banishment, and suffering the same evil, by the law of retaliation, which the accuser intended to draw upon others. The substance of the law is as follows: If any one called another man's credit, or fortune, or life, or blood into question in judgment, and could not make out the crime alleged against him, he should suffer the same penalty that he intended to bring upon the other. And no one could formally implead another at law till he had bound himself to this condition, which the law terms *vinculum inscriptionis*, the bond of inscription. While the civil laws were thus severe, the ecclesiastical laws did all that fell within their province to effect the same results. By a canon of the council of Eliberis the false witness in any case was to do penance five years, and in case the false accusation was of murder, the criminal was to be debarred from communion to the very last, as in the case of actual murder. The councils of Agde and Vannes impose a general penance upon such offenders, without naming the term or duration of their penance, which was left to the discretion of the bishop, who was to judge of the sincerity of their repentance. But the first council of Arles obliges them to do penance all their lives, and the second only moderates their punishment so far as to leave it to the bishop to determine of their repentance and satisfaction. See Bingham, *Christ. Antiq.* bk. xvi, ch. x, § ix, and ch. xiii, § i.

WITNESS OF THE SPIRIT is a phrase common with many Christians, especially the Methodists, to denote the inward assurance which every believer has of his filial relation to God, namely, that the Holy Ghost *immediately* and *directly* witnesses to and with (συμμαρτυρεῖ) his spirit that he is a child of God, involving the collateral assurance that through faith in Jesus Christ, who died and rose again for him, all his sins are blotted out, and he is reconciled to God (Rom. viii, 14-17; Gal. iv, 5-7; John i, 12; 1 John v, 9-13). Mr. Wesley observes, "I do not mean hereby that the Spirit of God testifies this by any outward voice; no, nor always by an inward voice, although he may do this sometimes. Neither do I suppose that he always applies to the heart, though he often may, one or more texts of Scripture. But he so works upon the soul by his immediate influence, and by a strong though inexplicable operation, that the stormy wind and troubled waves subside, and there is a sweet calm—the heart resting as in the arms of Jesus, and the sinner being clearly satisfied that all his 'iniquities are forgiven and his sins covered.' The immediate result of this testimony is 'the fruit of the Spirit—love, joy, peace, long-suffering, gentleness, goodness, faith, meekness, temperance' (Gal. v, 22, 23). Without these the testimony itself cannot continue; for it is inevitably destroyed, not only by the commission of any outward sin, or the omission of known duty, but by giving way to any inward sin—in a word, by whatever grieves the Holy Spirit of God." Some claim a similar testimony for special states of grace, and even peculiar experiences or prognostications, but such an extension of the privilege is not authorized by Scripture. See ADOPTION; ASSURANCE.

Witnesses, THE THREE HEAVENLY, is a convenient designation of the famous controversy respecting the genuineness of the clause in the first epistle of John (v, 7), "For there are three that bear record in heaven, the Father, the Word, and the Holy Ghost, and these three are one."

I. *History of its Introduction into the Text.*—In all the first printed Bibles, which were those of the Latin Vulgate, as amended by Jerome, the clause appeared substantially as at present (*Ed. Princeps*, 1462), being found in the great majority of manuscripts of the Vulgate. It may therefore be considered as the generally received form at that period. But when the first edition of the Greek Test. appeared, which was that of Erasmus, published at Basle in 1516, the clause in question ["in heaven, the Father, the Word, and the Holy Spirit, and these three are one; and there are three which bear witness in earth"] was wanting. Erasmus was attacked by Stunica, one of the editors of the Complutensian Polyglot, of which the New Test. in Greek and Latin had been printed in 1514 (and consequently before the appearance of Erasmus's edition), although not published until 1522. Erasmus replied to Stunica by observing that he had faithfully followed the Greek manuscripts from which he had edited his text, but professed his readiness to insert the clause in another edition, provided but a single Greek manuscript was found to contain it. Such a manuscript was found in England, upon which Erasmus, although entertaining strong suspicions respecting this manuscript, yet, faithful to his word, inserted the clause in his third edition, which was published in 1522, as it now stands in the common Greek text.

Nevertheless, the absence of the definite article from the six nouns in the disputed passage in this pretended manuscript is of itself sufficient to excite suspicions of, if not completely to overthrow, its genuineness. What has become of the manuscript is not known, but it is generally believed to have been the same with that now possessed by the library of Trinity College, Dublin, called the *Codex Montfortianus*, or *Dublinensis*, in which the disputed clause appears, but without the conclusion, "and these three are one." Erasmus also speaks of a *Codex Britannicus* as containing the entire clause, with some minute variations (*Annot.* 4th ed. p. 697). See MONTFORT MANUSCRIPTS. The Dublin manuscript is generally ascribed to the 15th or 16th century, and cannot possibly be older than the 13th; it likewise varies from the received Greek text in several lesser particulars. The clause has been also found, although in a form still more corrupt, in a manuscript in the Vatican (*Cod. Ottobon.* 298), of the 15th century, first collated by Dr. Scholz, of Bonn.

The above is the amount of Greek manuscript authority for this celebrated clause, for although all the libraries in existence have been examined (containing above one hundred and eighty Greek MSS., written between the 5th and 15th centuries), no other copy has been found which contains a vestige of it. Nor has it been once cited by a single Greek father, although abundant opportunities presented themselves for introducing it, which they could not have failed to avail themselves of, had it existed in their copies; but they have invariably cited the passage as it has been preserved in all the ancient manuscripts. It found its way, however, into the *received text* of the Greek Test., having been copied from Erasmus's third, fourth, and fifth editions (1522, 1527, and 1535), with more or less of variation, into all Stephens's editions, from the third or folio edition of which it was adopted by Beza in all his editions, the first of which was published in 1565, and again by Elzevir, in his edition of 1624, to which his anonymous editor gave the name of *Textus undique receptus.* The best critical editions since have left out the words as spurious. They are wanting in those of Aldus, Gerbelius, Cephelæus, Colinæus, Mace, Harwood, Matthæi, Griesbach, Scholz, Lachmann, Tischendorf, and others. Bowyer enclosed them in brackets, and Knapp in double brackets, indicating their spuriousness. The clause appears in the principal printed editions of the New Test. before the time of Griesbach. These were the editions of Mill (1707), Bengel (1734), and Wetstein (1751), the two former of whom held it to be genuine.

Luther uniformly rejected this clause from all his translations. It is absent from his last edition (1546), published after his death, and was first inserted in the Frankfort edition of 1574, but again omitted in 1583, and in subsequent editions. Since the beginning of the 17th century, with the exception of the Wittenberg edition of 1607, its insertion has been general. This was, however, in opposition to Luther's injunction.

It is inserted in all the early English printed versions, commencing with Coverdale's in 1536, but is generally printed either in brackets or in smaller letters. It was, however, printed in the editions of 1536, 1552, and in the Geneva Bible (1557), without any marks of doubt. It found its way, perhaps, from Beza's Greek Test. into the then authorized English version.

II. *External Evidence.*—The earliest Greek form in which the disputed clause is found is contained in the Latin translation of the acts of the council of Lateran, held in 1215, and the first Greek writer who absolutely cites any part of it is Manuel Calecas, a Dominican monk of the 14th century, while in the next century it is cited by Joseph Bryennius, a Greek monk.

The clause of the three heavenly witnesses is also absent from all existing manuscripts of the Latin Vulgate, written between the 8th and 10th centuries, anterior to which date there is no manuscript of this version now in existence, containing the Catholic epistles. Nor has any writer of the Western Church cited the passage before Cassiodorus, at the close of the 6th century, although even the fact of his having done so is doubted by Porson. There is, indeed, a preface to the *canonical* epistles, bearing the name of Jerome, in which the omission of this clause is ascribed to "false translators;" but this is a forgery. The clause is also wanting in *all* the manuscripts of the Syriac, Armenian, and other ancient versions.

From the circumstance, however, of the clause in question having been cited by two north-west African writers of the 5th century—Vigilius, bishop of Thapsus (the supposed author of the Athanasian Creed), and Victor Vitensis, the historian of the Vandal persecution —it has been fairly presumed that it existed in their time in some of the African copies of the old Latin version, from whence, or from the citations of these writers, it may have found its way into the later manuscripts of the Vulgate. It is cited by Victor, as contained in the Confession of Faith drawn up by Eugenius, bishop of Carthage. Vigilius, however, cites it in so many various ways, that little reliance can be placed on his authority. After this it is cited by Fulgentius, bishop of Rusopa, in the beginning of the 6th century, but is omitted in the same century by Facundus, bishop of Hermione, from which it is at least evident that the copies in that age and country varied. But, at a much earlier period, the whole clause is cited by Augustine of Hippo. Tertullian and Cyprian have been supposed, indeed, to have referred to the clause, but the proof of this depends on the proof of the previous fact, whether the clause existed or not in their copies.

III. *Internal Evidence.*—Various have been the opinions on this point for and against the genuineness of the passage. The advocates of the clause have generally maintained that the context requires its insertion, while its adversaries maintain that the whole force of the argument is destroyed by it. Lücke, one of the ablest modern commentators on John's writings, maintains that internal evidence alone would be sufficient to reject the passage, inasmuch (besides other reasons) as John never uses ὁ πατήρ and ὁ λόγος as correlatives, but ordinarily, like Paul, and every other writer of the New Test., associates ὁ υἱός with ὁ πατήρ (ii, 22, 23; iv, 14; v, 9, 11, 20, etc.), and always refers the λόγος in Christ to ὁ θεός, and not to ὁ πατήρ. He unites with those critics who look upon the rejected passage as an allegorical gloss, which found its way into the Latin text, where it has, "ever since the 4th century, firmly maintained its place as a welcome and protective passage," etc. He adds, however, that exegetical conscience will, in our age, forbid the most orthodox to apply this passage, even if it were genuine, for such a purpose, as ἓν εἶναι has quite a different sense from that which is required by the doctrine of the trinity. Here Lücke fully coincides with the late bishop Middleton (*Greek Article*). Lücke's conclusion is a strong one. "Either these words are genuine, and the epistle, in this case, a production of the 3d or 4th century, or the epistle is a genuine work of John's, and then these words spurious."

Among the latest attempts to vindicate the genuineness of the passage is that of M. Gaussen, of Geneva, in his *Theopneustia* (1839). But his reasonings are founded on a palpable error—the interpolation of the words ἐν τῇ γῇ (*in the earth*) in the eighth verse, which he absolutely cites upon the authority of Griesbach's text, *where they do not exist!* The corresponding words *in terrâ* are, indeed, found in the *present* text of some MSS. of the Vulgate, and of some ancient writers, although wanting in the seventh verse.

IV. *Literature.*—The following are some of the principal controversies to which this famous clause has given rise, of which a more complete account will be found in Mr. Charles Butler's *Horæ Biblicæ;* and most fully in Orme's *Memoir* (1830) on the subject (under the pseudonym of "Criticus"), especially the American edition by Abbot (N. Y. 1866).

The earliest was the dispute between Erasmus and Lee, afterwards archbishop of York, and between Erasmus and Stunica, one of the Complutensian editors. Erasmus was the first to suspect the genuineness of the preface to the *canonical* epistles above referred to, which ascribes the omission of the clause to false translators or transcribers. The genuineness of this preface, which led Sir Isaac Newton to charge Jerome with being the fabricator of the disputed clause (whereas it is certain that that learned father was totally unacquainted with its existence) of the text, is now given up. It is considered in the Benedictine edition of Jerome's works to be a forgery of the 9th century (Burigni, *Vie d'Erasme*, Paris, 1757, i, 372–381; ii, 163–175; *Crit. Sac.* vii, 1229).

It was afterwards attacked by Sandius the Arian (*Nucleus Hist. Ecclesiast.* Amsterdam, 1669; and *Interpret. Paradox. in Johan.*). It was defended by Selden (*De Synedricis Ebræor.*) and ably attacked by the Roman Catholic father Simon (*Hist. Critique du Texte*, 1680, etc.). It was defended again by Martin (pastor of the Reformed Church in Utrecht, 1717), who was replied to by Thomas Emlyn, the celebrated and much-persecuted English Presbyterian (*A Full Inquiry*, etc., 1715–20), and by Cæsar de Missy, French preacher in the Savoy. There are other able treatises on the same side by Dr. Benson, Sir Isaac Newton, and the learned printer, Mr. Bowyer; and in its favor by Smith (1690), Kettner, Calamy (1722), as well as by Bossuet, and by Calmet (1720) in France, and Semler in Germany (1751). In Germany it was also attacked by Schmidt (*Hist. Antiqua*, 1774), and Michaelis, in his *Introduction;* but found an able defender in the excellent Bengel (*Gnomon*, 1773), who conceived that the passage contained a divine internal evidence, but at the same time maintained that its genuineness depended on the transposition of the two verses so as to make the earthly witnesses precede the heavenly, according to the citation (*supra*) of Vigilius of Thapsus. (See *Christian Remembrancer*, iv, 43, note.)

The third and most important stage of the controversy may be said to commence with the time of Gibbon, and was attacked by archdeacon Travis in three letters (1784–86). This publication gave rise to the most celebrated work which had yet appeared on the subject, professor Porson's *Letters* (1788): "an eternal monument of his uncommon erudition, sagacity, and tact" (*Horæ Biblicæ*). Mr. Butler concludes his enumeration with the *Observations* of Dr. Adam Clarke on the text of the heavenly witnesses (1805).

Griesbach's *Diatribe*, at the close of the second volume of his celebrated critical edition of the Greek Test. (1806), contains a complete and masterly view of the evidence on both sides; but as this eminent critic had completely rejected the passage from the text, he met with an indefatigable adversary in the late bishop Burgess (*Vindication*, 1821, and *Introduction*, 1833). The writings of this prelate drew down many learned replies, but his most able and successful opponent was Dr. Turton, regius professor at Cambridge (*Vindication of the Literary Character of Professor Porson from the Animadversions of the Right Rev. Thomas Burgess, D.D.*, etc., published under the name of Crito-Cantabrigiensis, 1827). A temperate vindication of the genuineness of the passage had been published by the late bishop Middleton (1808), in his work on the Greek article, which was also replied to by Dr. Turton (*ut sup.*).

In the year 1834, Dr. Wiseman renewed the controversy in favor of the clause, in two letters in the *Catholic Magazine*, vol. ii and iii, reprinted at Rome in 1835. Dr. Wiseman's principal arguments are founded on the citations in African writers. Wright's *Appendix* to his *Translation of Seiler's Hermeneutics* contains some account of the state of the controversy respecting this clause to the year 1835, also Horne's *Introduction*, 8th ed. ii, 185, iv, 448–471. Since the time of Griesbach it has been generally omitted in all critical editions, and its spuriousness was especially shown in that of the learned Roman Catholic professor Scholz, of Bonn (1836), who was replied to by bishop Burgess (eod.). The whole ground of the controversy has more lately been reviewed by Dr. Davidson (*Lectures on Biblical Criticism*, 1853, ii, 403–426), who proves conclusively that the clause is indefensible either on its external or internal evidence.

For the exposition of the passage as containing the words in question, see bishop Horsley's *Sermons* (i, 193). For the same passage interpreted without the disputed words, see Sir Isaac Newton's *Hist. of Two Texts* (*Works* [Lond. 1779], v, 528).

Witschel, Johann Heinrich Wilhelm, a Protestant theologian of Germany, was born May 9, 1769, at Hensenfeld, near Nüremberg. In 1801 he was appointed pastor at Igensdorf, in 1811 dean at Gräfenberg, in 1819 pastor and dean at Katzenhochstadt, in Bavaria, and died April 24, 1847. He is the author of an ascetical work entitled, *Morgen- und Abendopfer* (Nüremberg, 1806; 13th ed. 1854):—*Moralische Blätter* (ibid. 1801; 3d ed. with the title, *Stimmen religiöser Erhebung*, 1852):—*Hermolaus* (ibid. 1796):—*Auswahl von Gesängen und Liedern zur häuslichen Erbauung* (Hanover, 1817). See Winer, *Handbuch der theol. Lit.* ii, 334, 383, 395; *Theol. Universallexikon*, s. v.; Zuchold, *Bibl. Theol.* s. v. (B. P.)

Witstack, a citizen of Stettin, Pomerania, of some note, flourished in the early part of the 12th century. He was converted and baptized during the first visit of bishop Otto to Stettin, and endeavored to show his zeal for Christianity by fighting against the pagans. He was taken prisoner on a piratical expedition, and for some time kept in chains. Resorting to prayer for consolation in his confinement, he was, as he thought, providentially released, and made his way back to his home. This deliverance, and some other events of like character, he regarded as the divine call to him to proclaim Christianity to his perishing countrymen. Through his aid Otto was enabled to overcome paganism in Stettin, and place Christianity on a firm footing. See Neander, *Hist. of the Church*, iv, 26.

Witt, Daniel, D.D., a Baptist minister, was born in Bedford County, Va., Nov. 8, 1801. He united with the Church in December, 1821, was licensed April 13, 1822, and itinerated through several counties in his native state for two or three years. About 1825 he became pastor of a Church which he had organized at Sandy River, and for forty-five years occupied that position. During a part of this long ministry he had the pastoral oversight of several churches. He died Nov. 15, 1871. See Cathcart, *Baptist Encyclop.* p. 1267. (J. C. S.)

Wittenberg, The Concord of, signed May 29, 1536, denotes one of the most interesting, as also one of the most important, stages in that series of negotiations which, during the first period of the Reformation, was carried on in order to bring about an agreement between the Swiss and Saxon reformers. Politically, landgrave Philip of Hesse was the motive power of these negotiations; theologically, Bucer; and the personal meeting which the former brought about, in 1534, between the latter and Melanchthon, at Cassel, formed the introduction to the larger assembly at Wittenberg, held in 1536. The hard words which Luther let drop in his letter to Albrecht of Brandenburg, immediately after Zwingli's death, showed the aversion he nourished to him; and it was well known how anxiously he watched that no one inclined to the Zwinglian doctrine of the Lord's Supper should be allowed to keep up community with the Saxon camp, as his letters to Brunswick, Münster, and Augsburg show (De Wette, iv, 472; vi, 143). With Melanchthon, however, a change had taken place. He learned from Œcolampadius's *Dialogus* that many of those passages from the fathers which he had quoted in his *Sententiæ Veterum Aliquot Scriptorum de Cœna Domini* (*Corpus Reformatorum*, vol. xxvi) were mere interpolations, and that Augustine never taught a "manducatio oralis," etc. Thus he wrote to Bucer, in April, 1531: "Aliquando inter nos veram et solidam concordiam coiturum esse, idque ut fiat, deum oro, certe quantum possum ad hoc annitar. *Nunquam placuit mihi hæc violentia et hostilis digladiatio inter Lutherum et Cinglium. Melius illi causæ consultum fuerit, si sinamus paulatim consilescere has tragicas contentiones*" (ibid. ii, 498). Under the influence of Bucer's expositions he gradually lost all interest in Luther's peculiar conception of the Lord's Supper, and became more and more anxious for the elimination of all elements of discord between the two evangelical churches.

In March, 1533, he wrote to Bucer concerning the moderation which both had hitherto shown, and begs of him as instantly as possible "ut det operam, magis ut contentiones istæ sedentur atque consilescant, quam ut excitentur et inflammentur" (ibid. ii, 641); and in a letter written Oct. 10, 1533, Melanchthon even goes so far as to write to Bucer, "Utinam saltem nos aliquando possemus una commentari atque communicare de doctrina" (ibid. ii, 675). The Swiss had also become more susceptible to the idea of concord. Bucer had succeeded in gaining over to the side of reconciliation Myconius in Basel, Bullinger in Zurich, his colleague Capito, etc., and in the summer of 1534 an attempt at practical union was made, and proved successful, in Würtemberg, and on July 31 a colloquy was held at Stuttgart, in the presence of duke Ulrich, between Simon Grynaeus of Basel and Ambrosius Blaurer of Constance, who represented the Swiss, and Erhard Schnepf, the Lutheran representative. In the same year, Dec. 27, Bucer and Melanchthon met at Cassel, and in spite of the very stringent instructions which Luther had given Melanchthon, they succeeded in drawing up a formula of concord which satisfied both. Copies of the formula were sent to Urbanus Rhegius, Brenz, Amsdorf, and Agricola, with the request, "an ita sentientes tolerandi sint, ne damnentur" (ibid. ii, 826). On October 5, 1535, Luther wrote to Strasburg, Augsburg, Ulm, Esslingen, to Gerion Seiler and Huberinus, etc., inviting them to a general discussion of the formula of concord.

Eisenach was decided upon as the place of rendezvous. In April Bucer left Constance, accompanied by nine preachers. As they progressed they were joined by Capito, Musculus, Bonifacius Wolfhard of Augsburg, Gervasius Schuler of Memmingen, and Martin Frecht of Ulm. At Esslingen they were joined by others. Meanwhile Luther had fallen sick, and requested the visitors to come to Grimma; they determined, however, to go directly to Wittenberg. On May 22, at seven o'clock in the morning, Bucer and Capito went to Luther's study. At three o'clock in the afternoon they again went to Luther, accompanied by Bugenhagen, Jonas, Cruciger, Menius, Mecum, Weller, and magister Georg Rovarius. Luther was suffering, irritable, harsh; Bucer became confused. The subject of the debate was the doctrine of the Lord's Supper. Luther demanded that the Swiss should make a formal recantation of what they had hitherto believed and taught; this they refused, on the ground that they could not recant anything which they had never taught or believed. The next day, however, everything was changed. Bucer was clear and adroit, Luther was mild and kind. After some debate the Saxon theologians retired to another room to deliberate in private, and the result was the formula proposed by the Swiss was substantially accepted. May 24 the assembly met in Melanchthon's house. The subjects of the discussion were baptism, absolution, the school, etc., and the agreement which was arrived at was chiefly due to the tact and resolution of Bugenhagen. On Sunday Bucer preached in the forenoon, Luther in the afternoon; and all the members of the assembly took the Lord's Supper together. Lutherans, like Osiander and Amsdorf, were not satisfied with the result; they continued to demand that Bucer should recant. But Luther himself spoke for a long time with great contentment and confidence of the affair. In Switzerland, too, there were some difficulties to overcome; but Bucer succeeded. See Herzog, *Real-Encyklop.* s. v. (B. P.)

Wittesa (or **Vittesa**), in Hindû mythology, is the god of wealth, one of the eight protectors of the world, or of the ten patriarchs, Rishis, masters of created beings. He always appears upon a magnificent wagon, overlaid with precious stones, or on a white feather-covered horse.

Wittich, Christoph, a Reformed theologian of Holland, was born Oct. 7, 1625, at Brieg, in Silesia. He studied at Gröningen and Leyden, was in 1655 appointed professor of theology at Nimeguen, where he lectured for sixteen years. In 1671 he was called to Leyden, where his lectures were received with great favor, and died May 19, 1687. He wrote, *Consensus Veritatis in Scriptura Divina et Infallibili Revelatæ cum Veritate Philosophica a Cartesio Delecta*:—*Comment. in Epist. ad Romanos*:—*Investigatio Epistolæ ad Hebræos*: — *Dissertatio de Natura Dei*. See Bayle, *Dictionnaire Historique Critique*; Benthem, *Holländischer Kirchen-Staat*; Jöcher, *Allgemeines Gelehrten-Lexikon*, s. v.; Winer, *Handbuch der theol. Lit.* i, 303. (B. P.)

Wittichen, Ferdinand Karl, a Protestant theologian, was born April 7, 1832, and died March 30, 1882, at Eschweiler, in Prussia. He is the author of, *Die Lehre Gottes als des Vaters* (Göttingen, 1865): — *Die Idee des Menschen* (ibid. 1868):—*Die Idee des Reiches Gottes* (ibid. 1872):—*Die christliche Lehre, ein Leitfaden für den höheren Religionsunterricht* (ibid. 1874):—*Das Leben Jesu in urkundlicher Darstellung* (ibid. 1876). (B. P.)

Witting, Johann Carl Friedrich, a Protestant theologian of Germany, was born March 30, 1760, at Alfeld, in Hanover. He studied theology and philosophy at Göttingen, and after completing his curriculum he acted for ten years as private tutor in the house of a nobleman. In 1783 he received the pastorate in Ellensen, near Eimbeck. Here he wrote his *Stoff zu Unterhaltungen am Krankenbette* (Göttingen, 1788; 2d ed. 1789):—*Gedanken über Kanzelvorträge und deren zweckmässige Einrichtung* (ibid. 1791). In 1799 he went to Brunswick as second preacher of St. Magnus, and advanced in 1805 to be first preacher. He died Jan. 24, 1824. Belonging to the strict orthodox party, he published, *Ueber Rationalismus und Rationalatrie* (Brunswick, 1822): — *Biblischer Beweiss von der Himmelfahrt Jesu* (ibid. 1820): — *Practisches Handbuch für Prediger* (1791-98, 6 vols.):—*Grundriss der Tugend- und Religionslehre* (1802). See Döring, *Die gelehrten Theologen Deutschlands*, iv, 750 sq.; Winer, *Handbuch der theol. Lit.* i, 369, 400, 491, 562; ii, 40. (B. P.)

Wittmann, Georg Michael, a Roman Catholic prelate of Germany, was born at Finkenhammer, near Pleistein, in the Upper Palatinate, Jan. 23, 1760. He studied at Amberg and Heidelberg, and received holy orders in 1782. In 1803 he became head of the episcopal clerical seminary at Ratisbon, in 1804 was appointed cathedral-preacher, in 1821 made suffragan and general vicar to bishop Sailer, and, at the same time, cathedral-provost there. When Sailer died he was appointed his successor, but before the confirmation reached him from Rome, he died, March 8, 1833. He wrote, *Principia Cathol. de Sacra Scriptura* (Ratisbon, 1793):—*Principia Catholica de Matrimoniis Catholicorum cum Altera Parte Protestantica* (ibid. 1831; Germ. transl. eod.):—*Annotationes in Pentateuchum Moysis* (ibid. 1796):—*Ein Wort über die Denk- und Glaubensfreiheit der Protestanten* (Sulzbach, 1817):—*Confessarius pro Ætate Juvenili* (ibid. 1832; 3d ed. Lat. and Germ. 1852): —*Vollständige Sittenlehre* (Landshut, 1832), and other ascetical works. See *Diepenbrock's Trauerrede* (Stadt-am-hof, 1833); Schenk, *Sailer und Wittmann* (Ratisbon, 1838); Schubert, *Erinnerungen an Overbeck und Wittmann* (Erlangen, 1835); Sintzel, *Erinnerungen an Bischof Wittmann* (Ratisbon, 1841); *Theol. Universal-lexikon*, s. v.; Winer, *Handbuch der theol. Lit.* i, 401, 467; ii, 23. (B. P.)

Witzel (Lat. *Wicelius*), Georg, a German theologian, was born at Vach, Hesse, in 1504. He studied theology at Erfurt, and in 1520 went to Wittenberg to attend the lectures of Luther and Melanchthon, but was nevertheless ordained as priest by bishop Adolph, of Merseburg. Appointed vicar in his native town, he preached the doctrines of the reformation, married, and was expelled in 1525. Driven away by the peasants' war from Lübnitz, in Thuringia, where he had settled, he was, on the recommendation of Luther, appointed pastor of Niemeck, but relapsed into Romanism, began to write with great violence against Luther and Melanchthon, and was expelled in 1530. After some years of uncertain endeavors, he entered the service of abbot John of Fulda, in 1540, published his principal book, *Typus Ecclesiæ Prioris*, and presented his *Querela Pacis* to Charles V at the Diet of Spires (1544), who appointed him to draw up, together with Agricola, the Augsburg Interim. The troubles of the war induced Witzel to leave Fulda in 1554 and to settle at Mayence, where he published, in 1564, *Via Regia seu de Controversiis Religionis Capitibus Reconciliandis Sententia*. He died in 1573. See Strobel, *Beiträge zur Literatur des xvi. Jahrhunderts* (Nuremberg, 1786); Schröckh, *Kirchengeschichte*, i, 570; iv, 242 sq.; Neander, *De Georgio Wicelio* (Berlin, 1839); Holzhausen, in Niedner's *Zeitschrift für histor. Theologie*, 1849, p. 382 sq.; Kampfschulte, *De G. Wicelio ejusque Studiis* (Paderborn, 1856); Schmidt, *Georg Witzel. Ein Altkatholik des xvi. Jahrhunderts* (Vienna, 1876); Herzog, *Real-Encyklop.* s. v.; Lichtenberger, *Encyclop. des Sciences Religieuses*, s. v. (B. P.)

Witzstadt, Hans, an Anabaptist hymn-writer of the 16th century, is known by some hymns which he probably wrote in the first half of that century, because he speaks of the inroad of the sultan, Soleiman II, in 1521, and of the preparations of the emperor Charles V against the Smalkald League, in 1546. One of his hymns, *Kompt her zu mir, spricht Gottes Son*, has been translated into English, "'Come hither,' says the Son of God," by the late Dr. Mills, in his *Horæ Germanicæ*, p. 47. See Schade, in the *Weimars'ches Jahrbuch für deutsche Sprache, Literatur und Kunst* (Hanover, 1856), vol. iv; Koch, *Gesch. d. deutschen Kirchenliedes*, ii, 141 sq. (B. P.)

Wizenmann, Thomas, a German champion of orthodoxy, was born at Ludwigsburg, in Würtemberg, Nov. 2, 1759, of pietistic parents. After having passed through preliminary studies, he was received into the training-school and orphanage of his native town, as *famulus*, Oct. 28, 1775. In the spring of 1777 he resigned that position, however. He received the master's degree in October of that year, and in 1780 passed the theological examination and became vicar at Essingen. He had previously studied deeply the writings of Bengel, Oetinger, and Fricker, and continued to employ his leisure in the examination of standard authors, e. g. Locke, Leibnitz, Wolff, Mendelssohn, Jacob Böhme, Herder. He was also accustomed to commit the results of his thinking to writing, and on many occasions to give them to the public. Pfenninger's *Christliches Magazin* (1780–83) contains an extended series of articles contributed by him; but many papers on theological and psychological subjects were never published, and were found, usually in an unfinished state, among his literary remains after he died. In 1783 Wizenmann exchanged his vicariate for a tutor's place in a private family at Barmen, and, while journeying thither, made the acquaintance of the philosopher Jacobi, which was not without influence over his mental life. Jacobi subsequently made him acquainted with Spinoza's *Ethics* and Kant's *Critique of Pure Reason*. In April, 1784, Wizenmann began a work on the gospel according to Matthew, in which he attempted to make the gospel narrative demonstrate its own genuineness. He died before the work was completed, but it was published as a fragment by Kleuker in 1789. In 1785 he resigned his tutorship and took up his abode in the house of Jacobi. In 1786 he published *Resultate der Jacobischen u. Mendelssohn. Philosophie, kritisch untersucht*, etc., in which he denied the possibility of proving the existence or non-existence of God by the method of demonstration, but asserted the reasonableness of a belief in a revelation whenever trustworthy historical proofs in its support can be adduced. The work excited considerable interest, and was favorably reviewed by many influential scholars, among them Jacobi, but Kant published an unfavorable criticism in the *Berliner Monatsschrift*, alleging that Wizenmann had convicted himself of enthusiasm in the positions assumed in the *Resultate*. Wizenmann felt obliged to reply to the charge of fanaticism emanating from so high a source, and made so masterly an exposure of the weak spots in Kant's argument as gained him friends among those who had not previously approved his book, among them Hamann. The strain upon his delicate constitution had, however, been too severe. His strength gave way, and he lay down to die. The end came Feb. 22, 1787, when he had scarcely begun a course of what promised to be important labors for the cause of truth. A memoir was published by von der Goltz, under the title *Th. Wizenmann, der Freund Jacobi's*, etc. (Gotha, 1859, 2 vols.). See Herzog, *Real-Encyklop.* s. v.

Wjetkærs, a small branch of Russian dissenters, who, about A.D. 1730, during a time of persecution, took refuge in the islands of Wjetka, in a small river between Russia and Poland, from which circumstance they derive their name. Here they formed a separate community and built two monasteries, from which some of them migrated, fifty years later, to Poland, and built a church and convent at Tschernoboltz. They belonged originally to the Popoftschins, and their chief peculiarity is that they will not take oaths nor offer prayer for the emperor.

Wo (usually אוֹי or הוֹי, *οὐαί*, all onomatopoetic) is often used in the English version where a softer expression would be at least equally proper. "Wo to such an one!" is in our language a threat, or imprecation, which comprises a wish for some calamity, natural or judicial, to befall a person; but this is not always the meaning of the word in Scripture. We have the expression "Wo is me," that is, Alas, for my sufferings! and "Wo to the women with child, and those who give suck," etc., that is, Alas, for their redoubled sufferings, in times of distress! It is also more agreeable to the gentle character of the compassionate Jesus to consider him as lamenting the sufferings of any, whether person or city, than as imprecating, or even as denouncing them, since his character of judge formed no part of his mission. If, then, we should read, "Alas, for thee, Chorazin! alas, for thee, Bethsaida!" we should do no injustice to the general sentiments of the place or to the character of the person speaking. This, however, is not the sense in which wo is always to be taken, as when we read, "Wo to those who build houses by unrighteousness, and cities by blood;" wo to those who are "rebellious against God," etc., in numerous passages, especially of the Old Test. The import of this word, then, is in some degree qualified by the application of it; where it is directed against transgression, crime, or any enormity, it may be taken as a threatening, a malediction; but in the words of our Lord, and where the subject is suffering under misfortunes, though not extremely wicked, a kind of lamentatory application of it would seem to be most proper. See Imprecation.

Wodin, the principal deity of the old German nations, to whom, as the god of battles, the captives taken in war were sacrificed. He was the analogue of the great Scandinavian god *Odin* (q. v.).

Wodrow, Robert, a Scotch minister, antiquary, and ecclesiastical historian, was born in Glasgow in 1679. He entered the university in his native city in 1691, and became librarian of the college while studying divinity; was licensed to preach in March, 1703; ordained in the summer of the same year, minister of Eastwood, in Renfrewshire, where he prosecuted his literary labors during the remainder of his life; was active in the interests of a free church, opposing the act of 1712 for re-establishing patronage, and becoming the most prominent member of a committee of five clergymen deputed by the General Assembly to proceed to London, on the accession of George I, to urge its repeal. He died March 21, 1734. He published, *History of the Sufferings of the Church of Scotland, from the Restoration to the Revolution* (1721-22; republished with *Memoir*, etc., 1828-30):—*Life of Professor (James) Wodrow, A.M., Professor of Divinity in the University of Glasgow from* 1692 *to* 1707 (1828):—*Collections upon the Lives of the Reformers and Most Eminent Ministers of the Church of Scotland* (1834-45):—*Analecta; or, Materials for a History of Remarkable Providences*, etc. (1842-43), and other works.

Wodu, one of the sacred lustrations authorized by the Koran. The principal parts of this institution are six: (1) intention, (2) the washing of the entire face, (3) the washing of the hands and forearms up to the elbows, (4) the rubbing of some parts of the head, (5) the washing of the feet as far as the ankles, and (6) observance of the prescribed order. The institutes of the traditional law about this lustration are ten: (1) the preparatory formula, "In the name of the most merciful God," must be used; (2) the palms must be washed before the hands are put into the basin; (3) the mouth must be cleansed; (4) water must be drawn through the nostrils; (5) the entire head and ears must be rubbed; (6) if the beard be thick, the fingers must be drawn through it; (7) the toes must be separated; (8) the right hand and foot should be washed before the left; (9) these ceremonies must be thrice repeated; (10) the whole must be performed in uninterrupted succession. See ABLUTION.

Wohlfarth, JOHANN FRIEDRICH THEODOR, a Protestant theologian of Germany, was born at Teuchel, Dec. 16, 1795, and died at Neustadt-on-the-Orla in 1863, doctor of philosophy. He is the author of, *Ueber die Bedeutung und die Folgen des Streites zwischen Rationalismus, Supernaturalismus und Mysticismus* (Halle, 1833):—*Die Lehre von der heiligen Schrift, von dem Standpunkte der Geschichte und Philosophie* (Neustadt, 1835):—*Ueber den Einfluss der schönen Künste auf die Religion und den Cultus überhaupt* (Leipsic, 1836):—*Triumph des Glaubens an Unsterblichkeit und Wiedersehen über den Zweifel* (2d ed. 1842):—*Tempel der Unsterblichkeit oder neue Anthologie der wichtigsten Aussprüche über Fortdauer und Wiedersehen* (1837):—*Das Leben Jesu* (1842):—*Der Pauperismus nach seinem Wesen, Ursprunge, Folgen und Heilmitteln* (1845):—*Blicke in das Jenseits* (1847):—*Luther im Kreise der Seinigen* (1861), etc. See Zuchold, *Bibl. Theol.* s. v.; Winer, *Handbuch der theol. Lit.* ii, 32, 39, 56, 77, 149, 174, 321, 373. (B. P.)

Wogulian Version. See RUSSIA, VERSIONS OF.

Woken, FRANZ, a German doctor of theology and professor of Oriental languages, born at Ravin, in Pomerania, in 1685, was called to Wittenberg in 1727, where he died, Feb. 18, 1734. He wrote, *Diatribe de Magistris Collectionum* (בעלי אסופות) (Wittenberg, 1727):—*An Moses Genesin e Schedis Patriarcharum Collegerit* (ibid. eod.):—*Dissert. de Utilitate Novæ Pentateuchi Samaritani Editionis* (ibid. 1728):—*Alloquium ad Eruditos de Utilitate Novæ, quam Parat, Editionis Pentateuchi Samaritani* (ibid. 1729):—*Meletemata Antiquaria*, etc. (ibid. 1730):—*Commentatio Exegetico-critica in Canticum* (ibid. 1729):—*Diss. de Usu Fl. Joseph. in V. et N. T.* (ibid. 1720):—*Meditationes Privatæ*, etc. (Leipsic, 1716-18):—*Adnotationes Exegeticæ in Prophetiam Haggæi* (ibid. 1719):—*Samaritani Eusebiani, Quatenus ad Vindicandum Textum Hebræum Præcipue Faciunt* (Wittenberg, 1731):—*Pietas Critica, quæ V. et N. T. Textum Origini*, etc. (ibid. 1718-20, 2 parts):—*Textus V. T. Originalis Ebr. ab Enallagis Liberatus* (ibid. 1726). See Winer, *Handbuch der theol. Lit.* i, 127, 190, 230, 279; Fürst, *Bibl. Jud.* iii, 527. (B. P.)

Wolcott, JOHN, an English satirist, better known as *Peter Pindar*, was born at Dodbroke, Devonshire, in 1738. He was educated as a physician, and in 1767 accompanied sir William Trelawney, governor of Jamaica, to the West Indies as medical attendant. Though an avowed unbeliever, he returned to England, took orders in the Church, and sailed again for Jamaica, where he accepted a small curacy until the death of Trelawney, in 1768, when he returned to England, and spent twelve years in trying to establish himself as a physician at several places in Cornwall. He died Jan. 14, 1819. He published numerous satirical pieces, ridiculing the Royal Academy to such an extent that the government, it is said, thought it worth while to purchase his silence with £300 a year. Collections of his writings appeared between 1789 and 1812.

Wolder, DAVID, a Lutheran theologian of Germany, was born at Hamburg, and studied at Rostock. In 1577 he was appointed deacon of St. Peter's, in his native city, where he died, Dec. 11, 1604. He is the editor of a Polyglot Bible in Hebrew, Greek, Latin, and German, which was issued at Hamburg in 1595. Besides, he published *Neu-Catechismus Gesangbüchlein* (ibid. 1598), in which some of his own hymns are given. See Le Long-Masch, *Bibliotheca Sacra*, i, 387; J. Molleri, *Cimbria Literata* (Havniæ, 1744), i, 740 sq.; Koch, *Gesch. d. deutschen Kirchenliedes*, ii, 296 sq. (B. P.)

Wöldike, MARCUS, a Protestant theologian of Germany, born at Sommersted, in Sleswick, Nov. 25, 1699, was professor of theology at Copenhagen from 1731, and died Sept. 26, 1750. He is the author of, *Caput Secundum ex Tr. Berachot Latine Vertit et cum Annotationibus Nonnullis Adjectis Edidit* (Havniæ, 1738):—*Tractatus Talm. Chagga cum Gemara Hierosol. Latine Versus Notisque Illustratus* (ibid. 1735):—*Explicatio Numini Cujusdam Judæo-cabbalistici* (ibid. 1736):—*Mos. Maimonidis Tract. de Cibis Vetitis*, etc. (ibid. 1722-34):—*Dicta Classica Veteris Testamenti* (ibid. 1735):—*Apologia Concionator. Evangel. adv. Accusation. Episcopor. et Clericorum. Pontificior. Regi et Senatui*, etc. (Copenhagen, 1739). See Winer, *Handbuch der theol. Lit.* i, 327; Fürst, *Bibl. Jud.* iii, 526. (B. P.)

Wolf, Abraham, a Lutheran theologian of Germany, was born at Cabelitz in 1680, studied at Halle, and was appointed professor at Königsberg in 1708. In 1717 he received the chair of Oriental languages, was made doctor of divinity in 1727, received the pastorate of the Altenstadt, together with a seat in consistory, the same year, and died June 20, 1731. He wrote, *Diss. de Animo ad Cohel. iii*, 21:—*De Elihu Amicorum Jobi Optimo:*—*De Loco Cohel. xii*, 11, 12:—*Diss. in Haggai ii*, 5, 6, *de ὀρθοδοξίας et ὀρθοτομιάς Vinculo Necessario*, etc. See Arnold, *Historie der königsbergischen Universität;* Jöcher, *Allgemeines Gelehrten-Lexikon*, s. v. (B. P.)

Wolf (or **Wolff**), **Christian von**, a German philosopher, was born at Breslau, Jan. 24, 1679. He had been dedicated to the ministry from his childhood by his parents, and hence received, as he himself expresses it, an ecclesiastical education. He studied in the gymnasium at home and at the University of Jena, where he developed a special taste for mathematical studies, and applied the principles of the science to theology. He preached a few times with great acceptability, and was noted for the clearness of his explanations. He was a professor at Halle from 1707 to 1723, when he was driven from the country by Frederick William I, and assumed a similar position at Marburg. In 1740 he was recalled to Halle by Frederick II, where he was received with unbounded enthusiasm. Here he remained until his death, April 9, 1754. See Ueberweg, *History of Philosophy*, ii, 116; Hagenbach, *History of the Church in the 18th and 19th Centuries*, i, 117 sq.; *Selbstbiographie* (published by Wuttke, Leipsic, 1841).

Wolf, Friedrich August, a Protestant theologian of Germany, was born July 31, 1784. He was appointed preacher at St. Peter's, in Leipsic, in 1805, and died Aug. 12, 1841. He left in MS. sermons, which were published by Kritz (Leipsic, 1841-44, 6 vols.). See Winer, *Handbuch der theol. Lit.* ii, 171; Zuchold, *Bibl. Theol.* ii, 1466. (B. P.)

Wolf (Lat. *Wolfius*), **Jerome**, a learned German, was born in the principality of Oettingen (Swabia), Aug. 13, 1516. As an envoy to Nordlingen and then to Nüremberg, he made rapid progress in the ancient languages. His misanthropy and morbid asceticism prevented his promotion, but at length, in 1536, the death of his father left him at full liberty to gratify his inclination for study. The fame of Melanchthon attracted him to Wittenberg, where he had opportunities to hear the lectures of Luther and Amerbach. In 1545 he was charged with the direction of a Protestant school at Mülhausen (Thuringia), but he left this position after a very brief trial, and from that time he lived in the homes of his friends at Tübingen and Strasburg, devoting his time to translating the Greek authors into Latin. In 1557 he obtained the position of director of the college of Augsburg, and thus of the library, which position he held until his death, Oct. 8, 1580. He wrote, *De Vero et Licito Usu Astrologiæ* (1558):—*De Expedita Utriusque Linguæ Discendæ Ratione:*—*Judicium de Poetis Legendis:*—*De Christianæ Classis Victoria.* He is better known by his Latin translations, accompanied with notes, of Isocrates (1549, 1570), Demosthenes (1549), Nicetas (1557), Zonaras (eod.), Epictetus (1560), Nicephorus Gregorius (1562), and Suidas (1564). These were published at Basle. See Hoefer, *Nouv. Biog. Générale*, s. v.

Wolf, Martin, a Lutheran theologian of Germany, who died May 31, 1875, at Stulberg, near Homburg, dean and member of consistory, is the author of, *Die Urgeschichte oder Genesis cap. i-vi*, 6 (Homburg, 1860):—*Die Bedeutung der Weltschöpfung nach Natur und Schrift* (1866). (B. P.)

Wolfenbüttel Fragments (or *Fragments of the Wolfenbüttel Anonymous Work*) is the name of a work written from the deistic point of view to contest the truth of the gospel history, of which Lessing (q. v.) began to publish fragments in 1774. As early as 1771, during a visit to Berlin, he tried to find a publisher of the work, in spite of the advice of Ch. F. Nicolai and Moses Mendelssohn to the contrary, but as the royal censor (though he promised not to interfere with the publication) refused to authorize it, he gave up the plan for the time. In 1773, however, he began to issue a kind of periodical publication, *Zur Geschichte und Litteratur aus den Schätzen der herzoglichen Bibliothek zu Wolfenbüttel*, which was exempted from the control of the ducal censor; and in the third number of that publication appeared, in 1774, the first instalment of the work, *Von Duldung der Deisten, Fragment eines Ungenannten*, accompanied with a few cautious remarks by the editor, but very adroitly introduced by the preceding article. The fragment attracted no particular attention; but when, in 1777, the whole fourth number was occupied by fragments, of which some, *Unmöglichkeit einer Offenbarung, Durchgang der Israeliten durch das rothe Meer, Ueber die Auferstehungsgeschichte*, etc., were of a rather pronounced character, quite a sensation was produced; and Lessing did not fail to deepen the impression by publishing, in 1778, in the form of an independent book, a new fragment, *Von dem Zwecke Jesu und seiner Jünger.* He immediately lost his privilege of publishing anything without the permit of the censor, and a violent controversy with the orthodox party began, the most prominent figure of which was the Lutheran pastor, Johann Melchior Götze (q. v.). After the death of Lessing, the seven fragments which he had published appeared in Berlin in 1784 (4th ed. 1835). Some more fragments, which Lessing had had in his possession, but had not published, appeared in 1787, edited by C. A. E. Schmidt, a pseudonym for Andreas Riem, canon of Brunswick. The anonymous author of the fragments, which form one of the most remarkable productions of German deism, was Samuel Reimarus (q. v.). Lessing tried to lead public curiosity on a wrong track by hinting that the author probably was Johann Lorenz Schmidt, editor of the Wertheim Bible (q. v.). But already Hamann mentions Reimarus as the author in a letter to Herder, of Oct. 13, 1777; and the authorship was afterwards established beyond any doubt by the declaration of the son of Reimarus, made in a letter addressed to the managers of the Hamburg town-library, to whom he also presented a complete manuscript of the entire work of his father. The letter, written in 1813, a year before the death of the younger Reimarus, was published by Gurlitt in the Leipsic *Literatur-Zeitschrift*, 1827, No. 55, and by Klose, in Niedner's *Zeitschrift für die historische Theologie* (1850), p. 519 sq. See Röpe, *Johann Melchior Götze* (Hamburg, 1860), p. 152 sq.; Strauss, *Herman Samuel Reimarus und seine Schutzschrift für die vernünftigen Verehrer Gottes* (ibid. 1862); Mönckeberg, *Hermann S. Reimarus und Johann Christian Edelmann* (ibid. 1867); Fischer, *Geschichte der neueren Philosophie* (2d ed. Heidelberg, eod.), ii, 759-772; Plitt-Herzog, *Real-Encyklop.* s. v. "Fragmente." (B. P.)

Wolff, Ludwig, a Lutheran minister of Germany, was born in 1808. He was brought up in rationalism, but the influence of Leo and J. Müller, of Halle, gave him that true foundation on which he afterwards lived and labored. In 1866 he was appointed superintendent of the Ottenstein diocese. He died at Halle, Oct. 15, 1877. (B. P.)

Wölfflin, Christoph, a Lutheran theologian of Germany, was born at Owen, in Würtemberg, Dec. 23, 1625. He studied at Tübingen, was in 1651 deacon at Aurach, in 1657 at Tübingen, in 1659 professor of Greek, and in 1660 was made doctor and professor of theology. In 1669 duke Eberhard III appointed him court-preacher, and provost of Lorch. In 1680 duke Frederic Charles appointed him provost of Stuttgart, a position which has never again been occupied after Wölfflin. He died Oct. 30, 1688. He wrote, *Exercitationes 8 de Lapsu Adami:*—*Exercitt. 7 de Obligatione Credendi in Christum:*—*Exercitt. 5 de Pœnitentia Tyriorum et Sidoniorum:*—*Dissert. de Triduo Mortis Christi:*—*Historia Incestus Lothi*, etc. See Fischlin, *Memoria Theologorum Virtembergensium;* Freheri, *Theatrum Eruditorum;* Jöcher, *Allgemeines Gelehrten-Lexikon*, s. v. (B. P.)

Wolfgang of Anhalt is known from the history of the reformation as one of those German princes who fought for the cause of Luther. Born in 1492, he succeeded his father in 1508. At the Diet of Worms, in 1521, the new doctrine found in him a strong arm and Luther a true friend. In his own country he introduced the reformed doctrine, and was its warmest promoter at home and abroad. He opposed the emperor, signed in 1529 the protest at Spenger, and the Augsburg Confession in 1530; and here (at Augsburg) it was that he, together with George of Brandenburg, told the emperor that they would rather give up their heads than follow the procession on Corpus-Christi day. He belonged to the promoters of the League of Smalkald, and the part which he took in the war brought upon him the ban of the empire and the loss of his estate, which was given to the Spaniard Ladrone. On horseback he left his castle in Bernburg, singing Luther's famous battle-song of the reformation "Ein' feste Burg." In 1552 his estates were returned to him, and he died March 23, 1566. See *Theol. Universallexikon*, s.v. (B. P.)

Wölflein (Lat. *Lupulus*), Heinrich, a Swiss hagiographer, was born about 1470 at Berne. He was director of the gymnasium at his native place, and canon of the chapter. The doctrines of Zwingli, who had been his disciple, he corrupted. He spread with ardor the religious reform, married in 1524, was appointed in 1527 secretary of the consistory, and died in 1532. Wölflein contributed much towards reviving the tone of literature among his compatriots. He wrote, *Vita Nicolai Subsiluani* (1501); it was republished by J. Eichhorn, under the title, *Historia F. Nicolai de Saxo* (Fribourg, 1608; Constance, 1631):—*Officium S. Vincentii Martyris* (Basle, 1517). See Hoefer, *Nouv. Biog. Générale*, s. v.

Wolfrath, Friedrich Wilhelm, a Protestant theologian of Germany, was born Sept. 3, 1757, at Glückstadt. In 1794 he was called as pastor primarius to Husum, in 1798 as court-preacher to Glückstadt, in 1805 as doctor and professor of theology to Rinteln, and died June 26, 1812. He wrote, *Was soll der Candidat der Theologie wissen?* (Altdorf, 1800):—*Versuch eines Lehrbuchs der allgemeinen Katechetik und Didaktik*, etc. (Lemgo, 1807, 1808):—*Fragen über liturgische Gegenstände*, etc. (Hamburg, 1792):—*Predigten* (ibid. 1791–97, 3 vols.):—*Geistliche Reden* (Altona, 1791):—*Menschenleben und Schicksal* (Rinteln, 1808):—*Religionslehrbuch* (Hamburg, 1811):—*Liturgisches Handbuch* (Marburg, 1806). See Winer, *Handbuch der theol. Lit.* ii, 45, 51, 69, 76, 126, 132, 141, 163, 174, 175, 199, 202, 237, 280, 330, 360, 364. (B. P.)

Wolfssohn, Aaron, also called *Aaron Halle*, a German rabbi, was born in 1736, and died at Fürth, March 20, 1835. He was a distinguished disciple of Mendelssohn, and worked in the department of Biblical exegesis and Hebrew literature in conjunction with Joel Löwe, G. Solomon, etc. He published a German translation of Lamentations, with an elaborate Hebrew introduction and commentary by Löwe (Berlin, 1788):—a translation of Esther, with a Hebrew introduction, etc. (ibid. eod.):—a translation of Ruth, with a Hebrew introduction, etc. (ibid. eod.):—a Hebrew commentary on the Song of Solomon, written conjointly with Löwe, accompanying Mendelssohn's translation of this book (ibid. 1789):—the book of Job, with a German translation and Hebrew commentary (Prague, 1791; Vienna, 1806):—the first book of Kings, with a German translation and Hebrew commentary (Breslau, 1809):—critical and exegetical annotations on the vision of Habakkuk (ibid. 1806):—a German translation of the first two chapters of Habakkuk, published in the periodical *Jedidja*, ii, 107 sq.:—a German translation and Hebrew exposition of the Sabbatic and festival lessons (Berlin, 1790):—a Hebrew primer, entitled אבטליון, with an introduction by D. Friedländer (ibid. eod.). See Fürst, *Bibl. Jud.* iii, 533 sq.; Kitto, *Cyclop.* s. v.; Steinschneider, *Catalogus Libr. Hebr. in Bibl. Bodl.* col. 2732–2734; the same, *Bibl. Handbuch*, p. 151; Dessauer, *Gesch. der Israeliten*, p. 508; Delitzsch, *Gesch. d. jüd. Poësie*, p. 100, 107. (B. P.)

Wollaston, George, D.D., an English divine, for some time father of the Royal Society, and sixty-two years member of the Society for the Propagation of the Gospel, was born in 1738. He was educated at the Charterhouse, and afterwards at Sidney College, Cambridge, where he graduated A.B. in 1758. Such was the high character he sustained, that he was chosen mathematical lecturer; and while at Cambridge he was also engaged in editing Newton's *Principia*. He was presented to the rectory of Stratford, Suffolk, in 1754; to the rectory of Dengey, Essex, in December, 1762; and to the rectory of St. Mary Aldermary, London, in 1774. He died Feb. 14, 1826. See (Lond.) *Annual Register*, 1826, p. 226.

Wollaston, William, an English clergyman and author, was born at Coton Clauford, Staffordshire, March 26, 1659; became pensioner at Sidney College, Cambridge, in 1674; took deacon's orders about 1681; became assistant master of Birmingham School; was ordained priest in 1686; inherited a large estate in 1688, and thereafter passed his time in literary leisure in London, where he died, Oct. 29, 1724. He published, *The Design of a Part of the Book of Ecclesiastes; or, the Unreasonableness of Men's Restless Contentions for the Present Enjoyments, Represented in an English Poem* (1691):—and *Religion of Nature Delineated* (1722). He also left a number of works in MS. See Chalmers, *Biog. Dict.* s. v.

Wolle, Christoph, a Protestant theologian of Germany, was born Jan. 24, 1700, at Leipsic, where he also prosecuted his theological, philosophical, and Oriental studies. On presenting and defending his dissertation, *De Facultatibus Intellectualibus in Bonos Habitus Mutandis*, he was allowed to lecture as private docent. In 1746 he was made doctor of divinity, and two years later was appointed to the chair of theology. He opened his lectures with a discourse, *In Anton. Collinum de Christiana Religione ut ab Ipso Christo et Ejus Discipulis Tradita est, Nulli rei Minus quam Piis Fraudibus Favente.* He died July 6, 1761. Of his many writings we mention, *Diss. Philol. Sacra de Regulis xxx Hermeneuticis, ad Circumspectam Scripturæ Sacræ Illustrationem*, etc. (Leipsic, 1722):—*Diss. de Mysteriis Orationis ad Mysteria Revelationis Pædagogicis* (ibid. eod.):—*Diss. Regulæ Hermeneuticæ περί τῆς ἰσοδυναμίας sive συγονυμίας Usu et Abusu* (ibid. 1723):—*Diss. de Dictis Novi Testamenti Quatuor ab Interpunctionibus Novis Vindicatis* (ibid. 1725):—*Die Ruhe der Seelen, das höchste Gut in diesem Leben, oder kurze Auslegung des Predigers Salomo*, etc. (ibid. 1729):—*Diss. de Singulari Facto et Fato Lothi, ad Genes. xxvi*, 26 (ibid. 1730, 1749):—*Diss. de Parallelismo Novi Testamenti Verbali cum lxx Virali Caute Instituendo* (ibid. 1731), etc. See Döring, *Die gelehrten Theologen Deutschlands*, iv, 755 sq.; Fürst, *Bibl. Jud.* iii, 534 sq.; Winer, *Handbuch der theol. Lit.* i, 110, 111, 115, 126, 129, 159, 163, 629. (B. P.)

Wolleb, Johannes, a theologian of the Reformed Church, was born Nov. 30, 1586, at Basle, where his father, Oswald, was a magistrate. At the age of twenty, after preliminary courses in philosophy and theology, in both of which he excelled, he was ordained to the ministry. In 1607 he was made city deacon; in 1611 pastor of St. Elizabeth's; in 1618 pastor at the Cathedral, as successor to Grynaeus, and professor of the Old Test., as successor to Sebastian Beck. He wrote a number of dissertations, and a single theological work, the *Compendium Theologiæ Christianæ* (1626), a volume of only 273 pages, but a masterpiece of compact brevity, clear arrangement, and thorough comprehensiveness as respects all important doctrinal matters. It was made a text-book at Basle and several other reformed universities. A second edition appeared at Basle in 1634, and a third at Amsterdam in 1638. An English edition was prepared by Alexander Ross, and published under the title, *Wollebius' Christian Divinity*. Wolleb did not live to see the success of his book, but died of the plague, Nov. 24, 1629, leaving two sons, Johann Jacob and Theodor, both of whom afterwards became pastors at Basle, and in 1667 died of the same disease. A volume of funeral sermons by Wolleb appeared in print in 1657. See Herzog, *Real-Encyklop.* s. v.

Wollgast, Johann Friedrich, a Protestant theologian of Germany, was born at Schweidnitz, May 16, 1797, and died March 29, 1839. He is the author of *Kirchenagende für Stadt- und Landprediger* (Breslau, 1811, 2 parts). See Winer, *Handbuch der theol. Lit.* ii, 280. (B. P.)

Wöllner, Christoph, the Prussian statesman of the reign of Frederick William II, who originated the famous *religious edict* in which orthodoxy in teaching was commanded, was born in 1732 at Döberitz, and was at first an orthodox, though tolerant, theologian. He became engaged in secular affairs after a time, and resigned his pastorate at Behnitz. During fifteen years (1765–80) he contributed nearly all the reviews on domestic and horticultural matters which appeared in Nicolai's *Allgemeine deutsche Bibliothek*. In 1776 he joined an order of templars founded at Wiesbaden by a certain knight, *Theophilus a Cygna*, which promised to open the way into the most secret mysteries of nature. In 1777 he published in Nicolai's *Bibliothek* a prophecy concerning "the impending destruction of the prevalent rationalistic enlightenment." He became tutor in political economy to the crown-prince in 1782, was ennobled in 1786, and appointed councillor of finance and intendant of royal buildings, etc. On July 3, 1788, he was made minister of the department of justice, which included in its jurisdiction the affairs of the Church, and in that position was employed by the king to place a barrier in the way of the progress of the "enlightenment," which had become powerful in the land. The notorious religious edict, written by Wöllner, was issued in consequence, July 9. It accorded liberty of belief to everybody, but ordered that teachers who could not accept the doctrines of evangelical orthodoxy should either resign their positions or refrain from promulgating their own views, and in public support those of the Church, under penalty of "being dismissed and still more severely punished." The edict, issued in the country of Frederick the Great, and after fifty years of governmental principles of a directly opposite character, produced an immense excitement, and called forth more than a hundred pamphlet reviews, about one third of which were in its favor; and, curiously enough, one by Semler, the father of rationalism, was in this class. Nothing in the way of enforcing the edict was done, however, for about two years; but then a royal order, dated Aug. 13, 1791, compelled Wöllner to proceed against offenders, e. g. Bahrdt (q. v.), who had ridiculed the edict by writing a comedy upon it. A commission, of which pastor Hermes of Breslau was the head, was instituted by the king to give effect to the edict; but as its members were altogether unknown in the learned world, its authority was not great, and its work unimportant. It addressed threatening fulminations to Nösselt, Niemeyer, Kant, the University of Halle, etc., which were followed by no consequences whatever. With the accession of Frederick William III (1797), all the measures taken to advance the cause of orthodoxy were set aside. Wöllner retained his office, and in 1798 attempted to revive the religious edict, but received a cutting rejoinder from the king. He resigned and retired to his estates, where he died, respected for his character and abilities, in the year 1800. See Teller, *Denkschrift auf Herrn Staatsminister v. Wöllner*, etc. 1802; *Das preussische Religionsedikt*, etc. (Leipsic, 1842); Manso, *Gesch. d. preuss. Staats*, i, 165 sq., 201 sq.; Sack, *Gesch. d. geistl. Ministeriums Wöllner*, in Niedner's *Zeitschr. f. hist. Theol.* 1863, No. 3.

Wolters, Albrecht, a Protestant theologian of Germany, who died at Halle, March 30, 1878, doctor and professor, is the author of *Predigten*, published in 1847, 1860, and 1874:—*Reformationsgeschichte der Stadt Wesel bis zur Befestigung ihres reformirten Bekenntnisses durch die weseler Synode* (last ed. Bonn, 1868). (B. P.)

Wolters, Otto Ludwig Siegmund, doctor of theology and pastor of St. Catherine's, at Hamburg, was born there Dec. 17, 1796, and died May 13, 1874. For thirty years he occupied the pulpit of St. Catherine's, in his native place, of which he was one of its truest and most learned sons. His sermons were repeatedly printed. See Zuchold, *Bibl. Theol.* ii, 1469. (B. P.)

Woltersdorf, Ernst Gottlieb, an evangelical hymn-writer, was born at Friedrichsfelde, near Berlin, May 31, 1725. He was a student of Halle, and resided and taught in the orphanage. In 1744 he became a private tutor, and four years afterwards associate pastor at Bunzlau. He evinced great interest in the instruction of the young, and consented to assume the direction of an orphanage founded in his parish by a mason named Zahn. This institution enjoyed his supervision until his death, Dec. 17, 1761. Woltersdorf possessed uncommon readiness in versification, and was continually tempted to spread his thoughts over a great deal of surface. Some of his hymns are largely in the style of Zinzendorf, with whom he shared many doctrinal views, though not otherwise connected with him. Several of them have considerable value, and have found deserved admission, in a revised and abridged form, in the hymn-books of various evangelical churches. He had the ability to seize upon some pregnant word taken from Scripture or other source, and to present it in a different light with every succeeding strophe, and did this in several of his hymns. This power led him to write also a number of parodies. He published a collection of *Psalms* (1750; 2d ed. 1768; a recent ed., by Schneider, accompanied with a biography of the author, Dresden, 1849). A second collection was issued in 1751. This volume contains a list of other writings by Woltersdorf, generally admonitions addressed to the young. After his death a volume of sketches of sermons prepared by him was published. See Herzog, *Real-Encyklop.* s. v.

Wolzogen, Johann Ludwig von, a famous Socinian, was born in 1599, in Austria, of a family belonging to the Calvinistic Church, and died in 1685, at Sohlichtingsheim, near Fraustadt. His exegetical writings are found in the *Bibliotheca Fratrum Polonorum* (Amsterdam, 1656). He also wrote, *Compendium Religionis Christianæ* (ibid. eod.). His *Opera Omnia* were published at Amsterdam in the same year. See Winer, *Handbuch der theol. Lit.* i, 17, 31, 308, 419; Fock, *Der Socinianismus* (Kiel, 1847), *Theol. Universallexikon*, s. v. (B. P.)

Wolzogen, Ludovicus van, a Reformed theologian of Holland, was born in 1632. After completing his studies, he travelled through France and Germany, and was appointed preacher of the French congregation at Gröningen. In 1664 he was appointed professor in Utrecht, and shortly afterwards was called to Amsterdam, where he died, Nov. 13, 1690. He wrote, *Orator Sacer, seu Præceptiones de Ratione Concionandi*:—*Tractatus de Scripturæ Sacræ Interprete*:—*Dissert. Critico-Theologicam de Correctione Scribarum*, etc. After his death there was published, in 1700, *Explication de la Priere*. See Burmann, *Trajectum Eruditum*, *Lettres sur la Vie et sur la Mort de Louis de Wolzogue* (Amsterdam, 1692); *Lud. Wolzogenii Apologia Parentalis, Auctore Pet. Ysarnio* (ibid 1693), Jöcher, *Allgemeines Gelehrten-Lexikon*, s. v. (B. P.)

Woman (Heb. אִשָּׁה, *ishshâh* [plur. נָשִׁים, a masc. form contracted for אֲנָשִׁים, *men*], fem. of אִישׁ, *ish*, as *vira* [in *virago*] from *vir*, and ἀνδρίς from ἀνήρ), like our own term *woman*, is in the Hebrew (and so the Greek, γυνή) used of married and unmarried females. See Man.

I. *Original Position of the Sex.*—The derivation of the word shows that, according to the conception of the ancient Israelites, woman was man in a modified form—one of the same race, the same genus, as man, a kind of female man. How slightly modified that form is, how little in essential structure woman differs from man, physiology has made abundantly clear. Variant, however, in make as man and woman are, they differ still more in character; and yet the great features of their hearts and minds so closely resemble each other, that it requires no depth of vision to see that these twain are one! This most important fact is characteristically set forth in the Bible in the account given of the formation of woman out of one of Adam's ribs: a representation to which currency may have the more easily been given, from the apparent space there is between the lowest rib and the bones on which the trunk is supported. "And Adam said, This is now bone of my bones, and flesh of my flesh: she shall be called Woman, because she was taken out of man." An immediate and natural inference is forthwith made touching the intimacy of the marriage-bond: "Therefore shall a man leave his father and his mother, and shall cleave unto his wife, and they shall be one flesh" (Gen. ii, 21–24). This narrative is hence effectively appealed to as supplying an argument for enforcing the duties of the husband towards the wife (Eph. v, 28–31). Those who have been pleased to make free with this simple narrative may well be required to show how a rude age could more effectually have been taught the essential unity of man and woman—a unity of nature which demands, and is perfected only in, a unity of soul. The conception of the Biblical writer goes beyond even this, but does not extend further than science and experience unite to justify. There was solid reason why it was not good for Adam "to be alone." Without a helpmeet he would have been an imperfect being. The genus homo consists of man and woman. Both are necessary to the idea of man. The one supplements the qualities of the other. They are not two, but one flesh, and as one body so one soul.

The entire aim, then, of the narrative in Genesis was, by setting forth certain great physical facts, to show the essential unity of man and woman, yet the dependence of the latter on the former; and so to encourage and foster the tenderest and most considerate love between the two, founded on the peculiar qualities of each—pre-eminence, strength, intellectual power, and wisdom on the one side; reliance, softness, grace, and beauty on the other—at the same time that the one set of excellences lose all their worth unless as existing in the possession of the other. Many usages of early times interfered with the preservation of this theoretical equality: we may instance the existence of polygamy, the autocratic powers vested in the head of the family under the patriarchal system, and the treatment of captives. Nevertheless a high tone was maintained generally on this subject by the Mosaic law, and, as far as we have the means of judging, by the force of public opinion.

II. *Condition of Ancient Hebrew Females.*—1. *Liberty.*—Women appear to have enjoyed considerably more freedom among the Jews than is now allowed them in western Asia, although in other respects their condition and employments seem to have been not dissimilar. At present, women of all ranks are much confined to their own houses, and never see the men who visit their husbands or fathers, and in towns they never go abroad without their persons and faces being completely shrouded they also take their meals apart from the males, even of their own family. But in the rural districts they enjoy more freedom, and often go about unveiled Among the Jews, women were somewhat less restrained in their intercourse with men, and did not generally conceal their faces when they went abroad. Only one instance occurs in Scripture of women eating with men (Ruth ii, 14), but that was at a simple refection, and only illustrates the greater freedom of rural manners. Instead of being immured in a harem, or appearing in public with the face covered, the wives and maidens of ancient times mingled freely and openly with the other sex in the duties and amenities of ordinary life. Rebekah travelled on a camel with her face unveiled, until she came into the presence of her affianced (Gen. xxiv, 64, 65). Jacob saluted Rachel with a kiss in the presence of the shepherds (Gen. xxix, 11). Each of these maidens was engaged in active employment, the former in fetching water from the well, the latter in tending her flock. Sarah wore no veil in Egypt, and yet this formed no ground for supposing her to be married (Gen. xii, 14–19). An outrage on a maiden in the open field was visited with the severest punishment (Deut. xxii, 25–27), proving that it was not deemed improper for her to go about unprotected. Further than this, women played no inconsiderable part in public celebrations: Miriam headed a band of women who commemorated with song and dance the overthrow of the Egyptians (Exod. xv, 20, 21); Jephthah's daughter gave her father a triumphal reception (Judg. xi, 34); the maidens of Shiloh danced publicly in the vineyards at the yearly feast (Judg. xxi, 21); and the women fêted Saul and David, on their return from the defeat of the Philistines, with singing and dancing (1 Sam. xviii, 6, 7). The odes of Deborah (Judg. v) and of Hannah (1 Sam. ii, 1, etc.) exhibit a degree of intellectual cultivation which is in itself a proof of the position of the sex in that period. Women also occcasionally held public offices, particularly that of prophetess or inspired teacher, as instanced in Miriam (Exod. xv, 20), Huldah (2 Kings xxii, 14), Noadiah (Neh. vi, 14), Anna (Luke ii, 36), and above all Deborah, who applied her prophetical gift to the administration of public affairs, and so was entitled to be styled a "judge" (Judg. iv, 4). The active part taken by Jezebel in the government of Israel (1 Kings xviii, 13; xxi, 25), and the usurpation of the throne of Judah by Athaliah (2 Kings xi, 3), further attest the latitude allowed to women in public life.

2. The *employments* of the women were very various, and sufficiently engrossing. In the earlier or patriarchal state of society, the daughters of men of substance tended their fathers' flocks (Gen. xxix, 9; Exod. ii, 16). In ordinary circumstances, the first labor of the day was to grind corn and bake bread. The other cares of the family occupied the rest of the day. The women of the peasantry and of the poor consumed much time in collecting fuel, and in going to the wells for water. The wells were usually outside the towns, and the labor of drawing water from them was by no means confined to poor women. This was usually, but not always, the labor of the evening; and the water was carried in earthen vessels borne upon the shoulder (Gen. xxiv, 15–20; John iv, 7, 28). Working with the needle also occupied much of their time, as it would seem that not only their own clothes but those of the men were made by the women. Such garments, at all events, were either for the use of the family (1 Sam. ii, 19; Prov. xxxi, 21), for sale (Prov. xxxi, 14, 24), or for charity (Acts ix, 39). Some of the needlework was very fine, and much valued (Exod. xxvi, 36; xxviii, 39; Judg. v, 30; Psa. xlv, 14). The women appear to have spun the yarn for all the cloth that was in use (Exod. xxxv, 25; Prov. xxxi, 19); and much of the weaving seems also to have been executed by them (Judg. xvi, 13, 14; Prov, xxxi, 22). The tapestries for bed-coverings, mentioned in the last-cited text, were probably produced in the loom, and appear to have been much valued (Prov. vii, 16). See HANDICRAFT.

The value of a virtuous and active housewife forms a frequent topic in the book of Proverbs (xi, 16, xii, 4; xiv, 1; xxxi, 10, etc.). Her influence was, of course, proportionably great; and, where there was no second wife, she controlled the arrangements of the house, to the extent of inviting or receiving guests on her own motion (Judg. iv, 18; 1 Sam. xxv, 18, etc.; 2 Kings iv, 8, etc.). The effect of polygamy was to transfer female influence from the wives to the mother, as is incidentally shown in the application of the term *gebîrah* (literally meaning *powerful*) to the queen mother (1 Kings ii, 19; xv, 13; 2 Kings x, 13; xxiv, 12; Jer. xiii, 18; xxix, 2). Polygamy also necessitated a separate establishment for the wives collectively, or for each individually. Thus, in the palace of the Persian monarch there was a "house of the women" (Esth. ii, 9), which was guarded by eunuchs (ii, 3); in Solomon's palace the harem was connected with, but separate from, the rest of the building (1 Kings vii, 8); and on journeys each wife had her separate tent (Gen. xxxi, 33). In such cases it is probable that the females took their meals apart from the males (Esth. 1, 9); but we have no reason to conclude that the separate system prevailed generally among the Jews. The women were present at festivals, either as attendants on the guests (John xii, 2), or as themselves guests (Job i, 4; John ii, 3); and hence there is good ground for concluding that on ordinary occasions also they joined the males at meals, though there is no positive testimony to that effect. See EATING.

3. We have no certain information regarding the *dress* of the women among the poorer classes; but it was

Matron in Full Dress.

probably coarse and simple, and not materially different from that which we now see among the Bedawin women, and the female peasantry of Syria. This consists of drawers, and a long and loose gown of coarse blue linen, with some ornamental bordering wrought with the needle, in another color, about the neck and bosom. The head is covered with a kind of turban, connected with which, behind, is a veil, which covers the neck, back, and bosom. See VEIL. We may presume, with still greater certainty, that women of superior condition wore, over their inner dress, a frock or tunic like that of the men, but more closely fitting the person, with a girdle formed by an unfolded kerchief. Their head-dress was a kind of turban, with different sorts of veils and wrappers used under various circumstances. The hair was worn long, and, as now, was braided into numerous tresses, with trinkets and ribbons (1 Cor. xi, 15; 1 Tim. ii, 9; 1 Pet. iii, 3). With the head-dress the principal ornaments appear to have been connected, such as a jewel for the forehead, and rows of pearls (Sol. Song i, 10; Ezek. xvi, 12). Ear-rings were also worn (Isa. iii, 20; Ezek. xvi, 12), as well as a nose-jewel, consisting, no doubt, as now, either of a ring inserted in the cartilage of the nose, or an ornament like a button attached to it. The nose-jewel was of gold or silver, and sometimes set with gems (Gen. xxiv, 47; Isa. iii, 21). Bracelets were also generally worn (Isa. iii, 19; Ezek. xvi, 11), and anklets, which, as now, were probably more like fetters than ornaments (Isa. iii, 16, 20). The Jewish women possessed the art of staining

Nose-jewel.

their eyelids black, for effect and expression (2 Kings ix, 30; Jer. iv, 30; Ezek. xxiii, 40); and it is more than probable that they had the present practice of staining the nails, and the palms of their hands and soles of their feet, of an iron-rust color, by means of a paste made from the plant called *henna* (*Lawsonia inermis*). This plant appears to be mentioned in Sol. Song i, 14, and its present use is probably referred to in Deut. xxi, 12; 2 Sam. xix, 24. See DRESS.

4. *Family Relations.*—The customs concerning marriage, and the circumstances which the relation of wife and mother involved, have been described in the article MARRIAGE.

The Israelites eagerly desired children, and especially sons. Hence the messenger who first brought to the father the news that a son was born, was well rewarded (Job iii, 3; Jer. xx, 15). The event was celebrated with music; and the father, when the child was presented to him, pressed it to his bosom, by which act he was understood to acknowledge it as his own (Gen. l, 23; Job iii, 12; Psa. xxii, 10). On the eighth day from the birth the child was circumcised (Gen. xvii, 10); at which time also a name was given to it (Luke i, 59). The first-born son was highly esteemed, and had many distinguishing privileges. He had a double portion of the estate (Deut. xxi, 17); he exercised a sort of parental authority over his younger brothers (Gen. xxv, 23, etc., xxvii, 29; Exod. xii, 29; 2 Chron. xxi, 3); and before the institution of the Levitical priesthood he acted as the priest of the family (Numb. iii, 12, 13; viii, 18). The patriarchs exercised the power of taking these privileges from the first-born, and giving them to any other son, or of distributing them among different sons; but this practice was overruled by the Mosaic law (Deut. xxi, 15–17).

The child continued about three years at the breast of the mother, and a great festival was given at the weaning (Gen. xxi, 8; 1 Sam. i, 22–24; 2 Chron. xxxi, 6; Matt. xxi, 16). He remained two years longer in charge of the women, after which he was taken under the especial care of the father, with a view to his proper training (Deut. vi, 20-25; xi, 19). It appears that those who wished for their sons better instruction than they were themselves able or willing to give, employed a private teacher, or else sent them to a priest or Levite, who had perhaps several others under his care. The principal object was that they should be well acquainted with the law of Moses; and reading and writing were taught in subservience to this leading object.

The authority of a father was very great among the Israelites, and extended not only to his sons, but to his grandsons—indeed, to all who were descended from him. His power had no recognised limit, and even if he put his son or grandson to death, there was, at first, no law by which he could be brought to account (Gen. xxi, 14; xxxviii, 24). But Moses circumscribed this power, by ordering that when a father judged his son worthy of death, he should bring him before the public tribunals. If, however, he had struck or cursed his father or mother, or was refractory or disobedient, he was still liable to capital punishment (Exod. xxi, 15, 17; Lev. xx, 9; Deut. xxi, 18–21). See CHILD.

III. *Description of Modern Oriental Females.*—It will at once be seen that under the influence of a religion, at the bottom of which lay those ideas concerning the relations of the sexes one to another, slavery on the part of the woman was impossible. This fact is the more noticeable, and it speaks the more loudly in favor of the divine origin of the religion of the Bible, because the East has in all times, down to the present day, kept women everywhere, save in those places in which Judaism and Christianity have prevailed, in a state of low, even if in some cases gilded, bondage, making her the mere toy, plaything, and instrument of man. Nothing can be more painful to contemplate than the humiliating condition in which Islamism still holds its so-called free women—a condition of perpetual childhood—childhood of mind, while the passions receive constant incense; leaving the fine endowments of woman's soul undeveloped and inert, or crushing them when in any case they may happen to germinate; and converting man into a capricious, haughty idol, for whose will and pleasure the other sex lives and suffers. In those parts of the East where the influence of the Bible has not prevailed, woman has been subjected to degradation, and viewed as little better than the slave of an imperious master. Being mainly immured within the harem, and prohibited from mingling in general society, their minds are left wholly uncultivated; and what time they can spare from their household duties is principally devoted to embroidery, dress, and smoking. This universal want of education, with the influence of polygamy, naturally disqualifies them from being the proper companions of their husbands. The state of morality in the higher circles, in some of the principal Eastern cities, consequent on this condition of society, is just what might be expected. Wherever the influence of Christianity prevails, woman is invariably elevated to her natural position in society—the equal and companion of man.

It will assist the reader in forming a just conception of Hebrew women in the Biblical periods, if we add a few details respecting the actual condition of women in Syria. Mr. Bartlett (*Walks about Jerusalem*, p. 291 sq.) visited the house of a rich Jew in the metropolis of the Holy Land. We give the substance of his observations:

"On entering his dwelling we found him seated on the low divan, fondling his youngest child; and on our expressing a wish to draw the costume of the female members of his family, he commanded their attendance, but it was some time before they would come forward; when, however, they did present themselves, it was with no sort of reserve whatever. Their costume is chastely elegant. The prominent figure in the room was the married daughter, whose husband, a boy of fourteen or fifteen, as he seemed, wanted nearly a head of the stature of his wife, but was already chargeable with the onerous duties of a father. An oval head-dress of peculiar shape, from which was slung a long veil of embroidered muslin, admirably set off her brow and eyes; the neck was ornamented with jewels, and the bosom with a profusion of gold coins, partly concealed by folds of muslin; a graceful robe of striped silk, with long open sleeves, half-laced under the bosom, invested the whole person, over which was worn a jacket of green silk with short sleeves, leaving the white arm and braceleted hand at liberty. An elderly person sat on the sofa, the mother, whose dress was more grave, her turban less oval, and of blue shawl, and the breast covered entirely to the neck with a kind of ornamented gold tissue, and over all was seen a jacket of fur; she was engaged in knitting, while her younger daughter bent over her in conversation; her dress was similar to that of her sister, but with no gold coins or light muslin folds, and, instead of large ear-rings, the vermilion blossom of the pomegranate formed an exquisite pendant, reflecting its glow upon the dazzling whiteness of her skin. We were surprised at the fairness and delicacy of their complexion, and the vivacity of their manner. Unlike the wives of Oriental Christians, who respectfully attend at a distance till invited to approach, these pretty Jewesses seemed on a perfect footing of equality, and chatted and laughed away without intermission."

Many of the daughters of Judah, here and at Hebron,

Syro-Arabian Costume. Indoor Dress.

Garden Dress.

are remarkable for their attractions. Mr. Wolff describes one of them with enthusiasm, and no small unconscious poetry—"the beautiful Sarah," whom his lady met at a "wedding-feast."

"She was scarcely seated when she felt a hand upon hers, and heard a kind greeting. She turned to the voice and saw a most beautiful Jewess, whom I also afterwards saw, and I never beheld a more beautiful and well-behaved lady in my life, except the beautiful girl in the valley of Cashmere; she looked like a queen in Israel. A lovely lady she was; tall, of a fair complexion and blue eyes, and around her forehead and cheeks she wore several roses. No queen had a finer deportment than that Jewess had."

Mr. Bartlett was also admitted into the abode of a Christian family in Jerusalem, of whom he thus speaks (p. 205, 206):

"The interior of their houses is similar to those of the Jews. In our intercourse with them we were received with more ceremony than among the former. The mistress of the family is in attendance with her children and servants, and besides pipes and coffee, the guest is presented with saucers of sweetmeats and small glasses of aniseed; which, when done with, are taken from him by his fair hostess or her servant, who kiss his hand as they receive them. They are more reserved, often standing during the visit. Their dress is more gorgeous than that of the Jewish women, but not so chastely elegant; it suits well with the languor of their air, their dusky complexion, and large black eyes. The head-dress has a fantastic air, like that of a May-day queen in England, and the bust is a little in the style of

'Beauties by sir Peter Lely,
Whose drapery hints we may admire freely.'

A heavy shawl is gracefully wreathed round the figure, and the dress, when open, displays long, loose trousers of muslin and small slippers. The ensemble, it must be admitted, is very fascinating, when its wearer is young and lovely."

We now pass to the peasantry, and take from Lamartine a sketch of the Syrian women, as seen by him at the foot of Lebanon, on a Sunday.

"After having with their families attended divine service, the latter return to their houses to enjoy a repast somewhat more sumptuous than on ordinary days; the women and girls, adorned in their richest clothes, their hair plaited, and all strewn with orange-flowers, scarlet wall-flowers, and carnations, seat themselves on mats before the doors of their dwellings, with their friends and neighbors. It is impossible to describe with the pen the groups so redolent of the picturesque, from the richness of their costume and their beauty, which these females then compose in the landscape. I see among them daily such countenances as Raphael had not beheld, even in his dreams as an artist. It is more than the Italian or Greek beauty; there is the nicety of shape, the delicacy of outline, in a word, all that Greek and Roman art has left us as the most finished model; but it is rendered more bewitching still by a primitive artlessness of expression, by a serene and voluptuous languor, by a heavenly clearness, which the glances from the blue eyes, fringed with black eyelids, cast over the features, and by a smiling archness, a harmony of proportions, a rich whiteness of skin, an indescribable transparency of tint, a metallic gloss upon the hair, a gracefulness of movement, a novelty in the attitudes, and a vibrating silvery tone of voice, which render the young Syrian girl the very houri of the visual paradise. Such admirable and varied beauty is also very common; I never go into the country for an hour without meeting several such females going to the fountains or returning, with their Etruscan urns upon their shoulders, and their naked legs clasped with rings of silver."

The ordinary dress of the women of Palestine is not, perhaps, much fitted to enhance their natural charms, and yet it admits of ease and dignity in the carriage. Dr. Olin thus describes the customary appearance of both male and female:

"The people wear neither hats, bonnets, nor stockings; both sexes appear in loose, flowing dresses, and red or yellow slippers; the men wear red caps with or without turbans, the women are concealed by white veils, with the exception of the eyes" (ii, 437).

The singular beauty of the Hebrew women, and the natural warmth of their affections, have conspired to throw gems of domestic loveliness over the pages of the Bible. In no history can there be found an equal number of charming female portraits. From Hagar down to Mary and Martha, the Bible presents pictures of womanly beauty that are unsurpassed and rarely paralleled. But we should very imperfectly represent in these general remarks the formative influence of the female character as seen in the Bible, did not we refer these amiable traits of character to the original conceptions of which we have spoken, and to the pure and lofty religious ideas which the Biblical books in general present. If woman there appears as the companion and friend of man, if she rises above the condition of being a bearer of children to that noble position which is held by the mother of a family, she owes her elevation in the main to the religion of Moses and to that of Jesus. The first system—as a preparatory one—did not and could not complete the emancipation of woman. The

Young Lady in Full Dress.

Oriental influence modified the religious so materially as to keep women generally in some considerable subjection. Yet the placing of the fondest desires and the glowing hopes of the nation on some child that was to be born, some son that was to be given, as it made every matron's heart beat high with expectation, raised the tone of self-respect among the women of Israel, and caused them to be regarded by the other sex with lively interest, deep regard, and a sentiment which was akin to reverence. There was, however, needed the finishing touch which the Great Teacher put to the Mosaic view of the relations between the sexes. Recognising the fundamental truths which were as old as the creation of man, Jesus proceeded to restrain the much-abused facility of divorce, leaving only one cause why the marriage-bond should be broken, and at the same time teaching that as the origin of wedlock was divine, so its severance ought not to be the work of man. Still further—bringing to bear on the domestic ties his own doctrine of immortality, he made the bond coexistent with the undying soul, only teaching that the connection would be refined with the refinement of our affections and our liberation from these tenements of clay in which we now dwell (Matt. v, 32; xix, 3 sq.; xxii, 23 sq.). With views so elevated as these, and with affections of the tenderest benignity, the Saviour may well have won the warm and gentle hearts of Jewish women. Accordingly, the purest and richest human light that lies on the pages of the New Test. comes from the band of high-minded, faithful, and affectionate women, who are found in connection with Christ from his cradle to his cross, his tomb, and his resurrection. These ennobling influences have operated on society with equal benefit and power. Woman, in the better portions of society, is now a new being. Yet her angelic career is only just begun. She sees what she may, and what under the gospel she ought to be; and ere very long, we trust, a way will be found to employ, in purposes of good, energies of the finest nature, which now waste away from want of scope, in the ease and refinements of affluence, if not in the degradations of luxury —a most precious offering made to the Moloch of fashion, but which ought to be consecrated to the service of that God who gave these endowments, and of that Saviour who has brought to light the rich capabilities, and exhibited the high and holy vocation, of the female sex. See WIFE.

IV. *Literature.*—Atkinson, *Women of Persia* (Lond. n. d. 8vo); Jessup, *Women of the Arabs* (ibid. 1874); Lane, *Modern Egyptians*, pt. i, ch. vi, Thomson, *Land and Book*, i, 174 sq. On special points, see Selden, *Uxor Ebraica* (ibid. 1646, and later); Schröder, *De Vestitu Mulierum Hebr.* (Leyden, 1745, 1776); Spörl, *De Ornamentis Hebr.* (1758); Srach, *De Mulierum Morbis* (Strasburg, 1597); Zipser, *Ueb. d. Wörter* נָשִׁים *und* אֲנָשִׁים (in the *Jewish Chronicle*, vii, 16), and the monographs cited by Volbeding, *Index Programmatum*, p. 105. See WIFE; WOMEN.

Women. The influence of Christianity did much in early times for the female sex. They were freely admitted to the Church, but they sat in upper rooms or galleries set apart for them. In many churches they had a gate of their own by which to enter, and of which the deaconess had charge. See DEACONESS. But women were never allowed to preach, though they might hold the rank of deaconess, and as such might instruct privately catechumens and their own sex generally. The Montanists (q. v.) were an exception to this general rule. As women were not to preach, so they could not baptize; nor were they allowed to keep private vigils. Tertullian thus describes the felicity of domestic life: "How can we find words to express the happiness of that marriage which the Church effects, and the oblation confirms, and the blessing seals, and the angels report, and the Father ratifies! What a union of two believers, with one hope, one discipline, one service, one spirit, and one flesh! Together they pray, together they prostrate themselves, and together keep their fasts, teaching and exhorting one another. They are together at the Church and at the Lord's Supper; they are together in straits and refreshments. . . . Christ rejoices on hearing and beholding such things; to such persons he sends his peace. Where the two are, he is himself; and where he is, there the evil one is not."—Eadie, *Eccles. Cyclop.* p. 662; Bingham, *Christ. Ant.* bk. ii, ch. xxii; see DIVORCE; MARRIAGE; WIDOWS.

The estimate of womanhood in the earliest Christian literature exhibits a remarkable contrast to that of paganism, as both attaching far more importance to female modesty and chastity, and, at the same time, greatly enhancing the dignity of the female character and enlarging the sphere of woman's activities. The epistle of Clement of Rome to the Corinthians speaks of the husbands whom he addresses as exhorting their wives to the discharge of their duties with a blameless, grave, and pure conscientiousness, and in a spirit of conjugal affection, and also teaching them to superintend domestic matters with dignified decorum (σεμνῶς) (c. i, ed. Dressel, p. 48). In the same manner, Polycarp

(*Ad Philipp.* c. 4) exhorts the Christian wives of Philippi to live in the faith, in love and purity, to duly honor their husbands, and to instruct their children in the fear of the Lord. Second marriages being systematically discouraged in the early Church, the advice given by the same writer to the widows seems directed against the faults to which women, when lonely and unemployed, are specially prone—"calumny, speaking against their neighbors, bearing false witness, and avarice" (ed. Dressel, p. 381).

The advice of Tertullian (*Ad Uxorem*, bk. ii, c. 8), that a woman should not refuse to marry one slightly below herself in station, provided he is likely to prove in other respects a good husband, points probably to the existence of a certain social ambition among those to whom his treatise is addressed, which he considered unworthy of the Christian character. As contrasted with the cruelty which too often disgraced the privacy of pagan households, we find Chrysostom observing that it is a shame for a man to beat his female slave, much more his wife (*In Epist.* I, *ad Corinth. Hom.* 26; Migne, *Patrol. Græc.* lxi, 222).

The teaching of the most enlightened of the fathers was undoubtedly to the effect that there was no natural inferiority in the woman to the man. Theodoret (*Græc. Affect. Curat.* bk. v) insists emphatically on their exact equality, and says that God made woman from man in order that the tendencies and action of both might be harmonious. Sometimes, indeed, he observes, woman has been found superior to man in encountering adversity (Migne, lxxxiii, 836). Chrysostom (*Hom.* lxi, 3) says that no one is more fit to instruct and exhort her husband than a pious woman. This conception differed, however, materially from that of Plato (*Repub.* v, 455), in that while the Greek philosopher sought to obliterate the ordinary distinctions between the sexes, the Christian father held that nature assigned to woman her special and distinct province of activity. Chrysostom, in a passage of singular beauty, gives us a comparison between the duties of the wife and those of the husband, the former being represented as in some respects the more dignified; for while the husband is described as engaged in the rougher work of life, in the market or the law-courts, the wife is represented as remaining at home and devoting much of her time to prayer, to reading the Scriptures, *καὶ τῇ ἄλλῃ φιλοσοφίᾳ*. When her husband returns, harassed with his labors, it is her function to cheer and to soothe him, so that he again goes forth into the world purified from the evil influences to which he has there been exposed, and carrying with him the higher influences of his home-life (*In Joann. Hom.* 61; Migne, lix, 340).

The participation of young females in the exercises of the palæstra and in races, commended by pagan theorists (Grote, *Plato*, iii, 217), is condemned by Clemens of Alexandria (*Pæd.* iii, 10) as altogether repugnant to the notions of female modesty (Migne, viii, 626). Chrysostom (*In Matt. Hom.* 1) contrasts the difference in relation to these points between Christian and pagan teaching, and even goes so far as to affirm that true virginity was a notion which paganism was unable to realize (Migne, lvii, 19).

At the same time we have satisfactory evidence that this exalted conception of the female character and female duties did not involve any renunciation of woman's humbler functions. Clemens says that it is right that women should employ themselves in spinning, weaving, and watching the bread-maker (*τῇ πεττούσῃ*), and that it is no disgrace for a wife to grind corn or to superintend the cookery with the view of pleasing her husband (Migne, viii, 626).

The excessive luxury of the 4th century would seem, however, to have been not less fatal to the maintenance of this high ideal than to other features of the Christian character. Amédée Thierry says that, by one of those contradictions which "déroutent la logique des idées," Christianity itself, essentially the religion of the poor, conspired to give to the manners of the Western empire a degree of effeminacy unknown in pagan times (*Saint Jérôme*, p. 2). Chrysostom declares that many of the ladies of Constantinople would not walk across even a single street to attend church, but required to be conveyed for the shortest distance (*In Matt. Hom.* 7; Migne, lvii, 79). When there they were to be seen with their necks, heads, arms, and fingers loaded with golden chains and rings, their persons breathing precious odors, and their dresses of gold stuff and silk (Milman, *Hist. of Christianity*, bk. iv, c. 1). Others, again, affected masculine apparel, and seemed to blush for their womanhood, cutting short their hair, and presenting faces like those of eunuchs (Jerome, *Epist.* 18). According to the same authority, the greater facilities possessed by ecclesiastics for gaining admission to female society was an inducement with some to become priests (ibid.). Elsewhere Jerome strongly dissuades the clergy from accustoming themselves to private interviews with those of the other sex (*Epist.* 52; Migne, xxii, 260).

The exaggerated importance attached by Jerome to the unwedded life, as one of superior sanctity, seems to have led him to dwell somewhat harshly on the weaknesses and worldliness of many of the wealthy matrons of his day. He represents them as given to excessive personal adornment, and bestowing much of their time on preparations for feasts and other household matters. When, however, we find him enumerating such obvious duties as "dispensatio domus, necessitates maríti, liberorum educatio, correctio servulorum," as prejudicial to the higher interests of the soul, we perceive that his tone is that of one to whom the ascetic life alone appeared adequately Christian (*De Perp. Virg.* c. 20; Migne, xxiii, 228). On the other hand, it is evident that the state of Roman society at this time rendered it exceptionally difficult for Christian women to carry the principles of their religion into daily practice. Of this Marcella's retirement to her mansion in the suburbs, as described by the same father, is an indication. He depicts the very different future which her mother, Albina, had designed for her—a splendid marriage and the possession of great wealth, while the daughter rarely issued from her seclusion save to visit the churches of the apostles and martyrs, especially those least frequented by the multitude (*Epist.* 96). The mistresses of large establishments, according to Jerome, were often exposed to exceptional temptations; and he states that young widows would sometimes consent to marry even pagan husbands, in order to avoid being plundered by dishonest stewards, and to escape the anxieties inseparable from the management of a large household, thus bringing home to their children by a former marriage, "not a guardian, but an enemy; not a parent, but a tyrant" (*Epist.* 54; Migne, xxii, 291).

Among other indications of the confusion and demoralization characteristic of that and the following century must be included that laxity of Church discipline which permitted the performance of public religious rites to be sometimes intrusted to women. In the twenty-first canon of the collection ascribed to Gelasius this is spoken of as evidence of the "contempt" into which religion had fallen.

It is generally assumed, though on somewhat scanty and doubtful evidence, that at the period of the conversion of the Teutonic nations the regard for female chastity and the respect paid to the sex were greater among pagan communities than among the Latin races. But however this may have been, it is certain that the views inherited and handed down by the Western Church with regard to "the personal and propriety liberty of women" were greatly superior to those that find expression in any of the barbaric codes. Something of this feeling seems reflected in Jerome when (*Epist.* 130) he censures parents for their too common practice of leaving deformed or otherwise unmarriageable daughters inadequately provided for (Migne, xxii, 981).

"The Church," says sir Henry Maine, "conferred a great benefit on several generations by keeping alive the traditions of the Roman legislation respecting settled property," and he points out that Christianity was really carrying on the tradition of the Roman *dos*. The formula of the marriage service, "With all my worldly goods I thee endow," is one, he says, "which sometimes puzzles the English lawyer from its want of correspondence with anything which he finds among the oldest English law" (*Early Hist. of Institutions*, p. 337; see also De Broglie, *L'Église et l'Empire*, I, ii, 273, and *Éclaircissement* D).

WOMEN, CHURCHING OF (τὸ ἐκκλησιασθῆναι), is alluded to by pope Gregory, in 601, as the thanksgiving, and by the emperor Leo's *Constitutions*, in 460. The Salisbury use calls it the purification after childbirth at the church door, evidently in allusion to the purification of the Virgin Mary. In 1549 the "quire door" was substituted for the original place. A veil, or churching-cloth, of white material, was used in 1560 by the woman and a pew or seat was allotted to her from an earlier date.

Women's Galleries were upper rooms or apartments in ancient churches, set apart for the use of women and catechumens. They were called *κατηχούμενα* and *ὑπερῷα*. The author of the *Constitutions* speaks of it as the custom of the Church in his time, where he gives directions about it that women should sit in a separate place from the men, and thus orders, Let the doorkeepers stand at the gate of the men, and the deaconesses at the gate of the women. Intimations of this custom are frequent in writers on early Church usages. The barrier between the two was usually made by rails, or wooden walls, as they are called by Chrysostom, who has these remarkable words concerning the origin of this custom: "Men ought to be separated from women by an inward wall, meaning that of the heart; but because they would not, our forefathers separated them by these wooden walls. For I have heard from our seniors that it was not so from the beginning. For in Christ Jesus there is neither male nor female. Do we not read that men and women prayed together in their upper room?" (*Homil.* 74 *in Matt.*). In later times, however, as in the Roman and Greek usage, the separation was made by placing the women in galleries directly over the apartments of the men. See Bingham, *Christ. Ant.* bk. viii, ch. v, § 6, 7.

Womock, LAWRENCE, D.D., an English prelate, was born at Lopham, in Norfolk, in 1612. He graduated from Corpus Christi College, Cambridge, in 1632; took deacon's orders, Sept. 21, 1634; is supposed to have succeeded his father in the living of Lopham upon the latter's decease, in 1642, but was ejected by the Norfolk commissioners, and perhaps imprisoned, for his adherence to the cause of Charles I; was made archdeacon of Suffolk and prebendary of Ely at the restoration in 1660; became rector of Horningsheath, in Suffolk; in 1662, and of Boxford, in the same county, in 1663; was made bishop of St. David's, Nov. 11, 1683, and died March 12, 1685. He published, *Beaten Oile for the Lamps of the Sanctuarie; or, The Great Controversie concerning Set Prayers and our Liturgie Examined* (1641):—*The Examination of Tilenus before the Triers* (1685):—*Arcana Dogmatum Anti-Remonstrantium; or, The Calvinists' Cabinet Unlocked* (1659):—*The Result of False Principles* (1661):—*The Solemn League and Covenant Arraigned and Condemned* (eod.):—*Suffragium Protestantium* (1683), and other works.

Wonder (usually פֶּלֶא, τέρας, both generally used in the sense of *prodigy*) is some occurrence, or thing, which so strongly engages our attention by its surprising greatness, rarity, or other properties, that our minds are struck by it into astonishment. Wonder is also nearly synonymous with sign: "If a prophet give thee a sign, or a wonder," says Moses (Deut. xiii, 1), and "if the sign or wonder come to pass," etc. Isaiah says, he and "his children are for signs and wonders" (viii, 18), that is, they were for indications of, allusions to, prefigurations of, things future, that should certainly take place; and they were to excite notice, attention, and consideration in beholders; to cause wonder in them. Wonder also signifies the act of wondering, as resulting from the observation of something extraordinary, or beyond what we are accustomed to behold. See MIRACLES, WONDERS.

Wonderful is the rendering in the A. V. at Isa. ix, 6 of the Heb. פֶּלֶא, *pèlè* (Sept. θαυμαστός; Vulg. *admirabilis*), as an epithet of the Messiah, and designates his incomprehensible character as the God-man.

Wonders, in an ecclesiastical sense, are those remarkable occurrences, whether deceptive or otherwise, which partake of the nature of miracles, and have been regarded as such by those who witnessed them. Miracles were very common in the early Church, and were a powerful weapon in the hands of the clergy, both to convince unbelievers and to secure submission on the part of believers. It is proposed in the present treatment to consider them under the heads of the persons or objects by which they were wrought, and in subdivisions to consider their purpose and the manner of their being wrought.

I. *Wonders Wrought by Living Saints.*—These were performed either by direct means, such as invocation of the name of Christ, prayer, signing of the cross, or the imposition of hands, or by indirect means, such as sending to the sick the garments of saints or others, bread, oil, or water which had been blessed by saints. It is a noticeable fact that in the accounts of miracles which have reached us from the early fathers the writers lay no claim to the performance of the miracles they attest, and do not even mention the authors by name. Under this head we notice,

1. *Miracles of Beneficence.*—These consisted of

(1) *Exorcism and Healing.*—Justin Martyr tells us that Christians, in the name of Jesus, cast out dæmons from those whom pagan enchanters could not cure. Irenæus and Cyprian bear similar testimony to their power, while Tertullian declares, "Devils we not only despise, but both overcome and daily expose and expel from men, as is known to very many." Some of the earliest miracles of this class were wrought by Gregory, bishop of Neo-Cæsarea, in Pontus, in the 3d century, the record of which, however, belongs to the 4th century. Among those recorded may be mentioned the exorcism of a youth by the imposition of hands, and the healing of the plague-stricken of Neo-Cæsarea. Among the miracles of this class wrought by the earlier Eastern monks, those of Antony and Hilarion will serve as examples. As belonging to the former we note the case of a boy in a fishing-boat, whose state of possession was indicated by a foul stench in the boat, but whose spirit yielded to the exorcism of the monk; and also that of a girl from whom he cast out an evil spirit at Alexandria in his old age; while among his cures may be mentioned the case of a man afflicted either with epilepsy or madness, upon whom he employed no means to effect a cure at once, but sent him away into Egypt, declaring that there he would be cured. Hilarion wrought chiefly in Sicily and Palestine. Of his miracles in the former place we have the testimony of a Grecian Jew that "a prophet of the Christians had appeared in Sicily, and was doing so many miracles and signs that men thought him one of the old saints." Jerome, who was his biographer, records among his miracles the restoration of sight to a woman who had been blind for ten years, a cure of paralysis, another of dropsy, and exorcising the possessed, even a camel, which, in its fury, had killed many. In one case a man was dispossessed, and offered a sum of money to the saint for the cure which had been wrought, but was informed that his acceptance of the money would surely bring back the possession. In

another instance he effected the cure of an uneducated Frank, who began at once to speak Syriac and Greek, although having no previous knowledge of those languages. In the West we find, in the 4th century, St. Ambrose curing a woman of palsy, laying his hands on her in prayer while she touched his garment, casting out evil spirits, and, on the other hand, causing a thief to be repossessed on account of his misdeeds; also St. Martin of Tours delivering a slave of a devil, and healing a leper at Paris; while, in the following century, Germanus of Auxerre, at Arles, cures a præfect's wife of a quartan ague, at Alexia bestows power of speech on a girl who had lost it twenty years, at Autun heals a girl of a withered hand, in England a boy of contracted limbs, and at Milan and Ravenna casts out evil spirits.

Thus far the examples have been confined to exorcisms and cures by direct means. Some examples of the same results wrought through *indirect* means will next be presented. The monk Pachomius had been applied to by a man, whose daughter had an evil spirit, to work a cure. The saint bade the man bring him one of his daughter's tunics, warning him at the same time that the blessing he should bestow upon it would be of no avail so long as his daughter continued to live a sinful life. Accordingly, the girl was not cured until she had confessed and forsaken her sin. In another instance the saint had directed that in order to obtain a cure the energumen should, before each meal, take a small piece of a loaf of bread which had been blessed. As, however, he refused to touch the bread, the device was adopted of concealing morsels of it inside dates, but with no better success. The dæmoniac carefully extracted them. At last, having been left some days without food, he took the bread and was cured. By means of consecrated oil Hilarion healed the bites of serpents, and St. Martin of Tours cured a paralytic girl, when at the point of death, by putting into her mouth a few drops of this oil. Threads frayed from St. Martin's garments healed the sick when wound around the neck or fingers, and a letter written by the saint cured a girl of fever when laid upon her chest. Straw upon which Germanus of Auxerre had reposed for a single night cured a dæmoniac when bound upon it, and a barley loaf, which the bishop had blessed and sent to the empress Placidia, possessed and retained for a long time wonder-working properties. St. Geneviève of Paris cast out devils by threads of her garments, and cured the sick by bits of her candle.

With regard to the comparative prevalence of miraculous gifts of healing, as exercised by living saints in different ages, we can form an opinion only from the records which have reached us. It would appear, however, that the power of working cures was in nowise diminished in the 6th, 7th, and 8th centuries. Dæmoniacal possessions, madness, leprosy, paralysis, blindness, deafness, lameness, and many other diseases and infirmities constantly called forth, and found relief through, the thaumaturgic powers with which monks and bishops were endowed, while accidents, such as those to which monks themselves were exposed in the performance of their agricultural labors, were naturally not excluded from the sphere of miraculous treatment. Nor was there any partiality in the distribution of these gifts over the various regions of Christendom, although the accident of the birthplace or dwelling of some of those who undertook to record certain miracles might lead us to a contrary opinion. If, for example, during the 6th century, thaumaturgy, as exercised in the matter of healing and exorcism, shone brightly in the persons of monks and bishops, it shone no less brightly in Palestine in the person of the abbot Theodosius, or in France in the instances of Melanius, bishop of Rennes, and St. Geneviève of Paris.

(2) *Raising from the Dead.*—Irenæus declares that "with much fasting and prayer the spirit of the dead returned;" and again, "before now, as we have said, even the dead have been raised up, and have remained with us many years." We mention a few alleged instances of this wonder occurring at different times. Julian, who suffered martyrdom at Antioch in the Diocletian persecution, raised a dead man to life, and St. James, bishop of Nisibis, in A.D. 325, a man who was brought to him as dead, with a view to obtaining money (presumably to defray the expenses of burial), and who really died while counterfeiting death. St. Martin of Tours restored to life a catechumen, who had died in his monastery unbaptized, by throwing himself upon the dead body and praying earnestly for its restoration, and on another occasion a slave, who had hanged himself. Hilary of Poitiers raised a child to life who had died unbaptized; Marcellus, abbot of a monastery of the Acœmetæ, near Constantinople, in 446, a monk; and Gelasius, abbot of a monastery in Palestine, in 452, a child. Germanus of Auxerre, when at Ravenna, raised a man from the dead; St. Benedict of Nursia, a boy; St. Bavo of Ghent, in 653, a man; St. Walaricus, abbot of a monastery on the Somme, in 662, one who had been unjustly hanged; St. Wulfram, bishop of Sens, in 720, five Frisian youths who had been hanged as a sacrifice to the gods.

(3) *Miracles of Deliverance, Protection, and Succor.*—These afford a series of wonders which range all the way from the deliverance of cities from siege or assault, or of districts from inundation, to the multiplication of corn in a granary, or of wine or beer in a cask. They differ widely from one another in respect of their object and importance, and the sphere they affect, and often degenerate into little else than a display of miraculous power for its own sake, thus losing the character of a true miracle. The raising of the siege of Nisibis will serve as an example of the power ascribed to living saints in this direction. Sapor II was besieging the city. The inhabitants, in their alarm, appealed to their bishop, St. James. In answer to the supplications he offered, swarms of gnats attacked the besiegers, their horses and elephants, irritating them to such a pitch of frenzy that they broke loose. To increase his discomfiture, the Persian king mistook the bishop, when he appeared on the walls in his purple and with his diadem on his head, for the Roman emperor, and thereupon raised the siege. According to Theophanes (*Chronographia*, p. 52, 53), the bishop's prayers had the further result of bringing famine and pestilence upon the besiegers when they returned to their own land. The deliverance of Paris from the Huns by St. Geneviève is a case of like import. The miracle wrought by Gregory Thaumaturgus on the banks of the river Lycus furnishes an instance of the exercise of this power in another direction. The bishop, having been appealed to by the inhabitants of a certain district to deliver them from the calamities to which they were from time to time exposed by the overflowing of this river, made a journey to the place, and, invoking the name of Christ, planted his staff at the particular spot where the stream was wont to burst through the mound which had been erected on its banks to prevent its encroachments. The staff became a tree; the water rose as usual, but henceforth never passed the tree. The miracle had its ethical result in the conversion of the inhabitants, who were at that time heathens. Similar miracles are ascribed to several others in different places.

As a rule, however, such interpositions of miraculous power were in behalf of small communities and frequently of individuals. As illustrations of this fact, we mention the cases in which St. Hilary cleanses the Insula Gallinaria of serpents; St. Martin of Tours, when, in his missionary zeal, he has set fire to a heathen temple, successfully repels the flames from an adjoining building; St. Maur walks on the water to save his friend Placidius; Germanus of Auxerre restores a stolen valise to its owner; St. Benedict of Nursia, and Leutfred, abbot of a monastery near Evreux, in

A.D. 738, cause iron to swim, and others of like import. In marked contrast with the miracles of Christ and his apostles, we find the monks, on their missionary journeys or at home, working miracles in behalf of their own special needs, such as causing water to flow in dry places by the simple expedient of planting a staff in the ground or of striking on the rock with a rod, multiplying wine or beer in the cask, and of quenching the flames when fire had chanced to break out in a monastery or convent.

2. *Miracles of Power.*—In the early Church these assumed the forms of speaking with tongues, prevision of events, and the seeing of visions. Under this head we shall consider,

(1) *Miracles Wrought in Confirmation of Christianity.*—For example, Gregory Thaumaturgus on one occasion was forced, through storm and the approach of nightfall, to take refuge, together with his companions in travel, in a heathen temple which happened to be famous for its oracles. Having invoked the name of Christ and signed the cross, the bishop spent the night in praising God. In the morning the priest of the temple found upon his arrival that the dæmons had forsaken their shrine. Gregory informed him that he could bring them back as well as expel them. Challenged to do so, he wrote upon a piece of paper, "Gregory to Satan — enter," and handed it to the priest, who placed it upon the altar. Forthwith the dæmons gave evidence of their return. To satisfy the priest still further as to the truth of Christianity, Gregory accepted a challenge to move a large stone which lay near, by means of his word alone. He at once moved it, and thus convinced his opponent. Hilarion wrought a remarkable miracle of this class at Gaza. A Christian named Italicus, who bred horses for the chariot-races, applied to Hilarion to help him against a rival who made use of magic to check the speed of his horses, and thus secure the victory for his own steeds. The saint, although at first unwilling to lend his aid in so trivial a matter, acceded to the request, and sent Italicus the vessel he was wont to use in drinking, filled with water, wherewith horses, chariot, and charioteers were to be sprinkled. This done, the Christian's horses, flying like the wind, easily won the race. Whereupon the pagan party, whose god was Marnas, raised a loud shout, "Marnas is conquered by Jesus Christ."

(2) *Miracles Wrought in Confirmation of Orthodoxy.*—St. Arnulph, having received a command from the king of the Visigoths, who wished to test the saint's powers, to rid the land of a serpent whose breath was of so fiery a nature as apparently to dry up water, was conducted to the serpent's lair, where he laid his stole upon the head of the monster, and, bidding him follow, led him to a pond, and forbade him ever to leave it, or thenceforth to injure any living creature. In the same pond lay the body of a man who had died a violent death. Upon the approach of the saint the dead man prayed to be delivered from his miserable resting-place. In answer to the prayer, St. Arnulph raised the body and buried it in a fitting place. These miracles are said to have made such an impression upon the king and his courtiers that they forsook their Arianism and accepted the Catholic faith.

(3) *Miracles Wrought in Punishment of Evil-doers.*—When St. Willibrod, A.D. 739, was on a missionary journey, he, with his company, sought rest one day in a field. The owner of the land proceeded to drive him away, refusing to listen to his remonstrances, or to drink with him in token of amity. "Then drink not," exclaimed the saint, and the man lost the power of drinking, while suffering all the pangs of thirst, nor did he regain it till he had confessed his sin to the saint upon his return in the course of a year.

(4) *Miracles Wrought in Illustration of the Gifts Bestowed upon Men for their Enterprise and Piety.*—St. Benedict of Nursia miraculously detected an infraction of the monastic rules by some of his monks, and a theft on the part of a messenger, and enabled two monks to carry a heavy fragment of a rock. Numerous other examples of miracles performed by living saints might be cited, but the foregoing will suffice.

II. *Wonders Wrought by Relics.*—The relics of a saint perpetuated the benefits which the saint himself, during his lifetime, had conferred upon those who stood in need of healing or succor. They originated in the latter half of the 4th century, and may be divided into

1. *Miracles of Beneficence*, consisting of

(1) *Exorcisms and Miraculous Cures*, wrought

i. *By the Bodies of Saints.* — Many miracles were wrought by St. Stephen's relics. The town of Calama had possessed relics of St. Stephen for about eight years, and that of Hippo for less than two years, when St. Augustine declared that many books would have to be written in order to recount all the miracles of healing alone which had been wrought by means of these relics during this space of time in the two districts of Calama and Hippo, and that of those which had been wrought in the latter district alone nearly seventy accounts had already been written (*De Civitate Dei*, xxii, 8, § 20).

ii. *By Objects brought into Contact with, or Proximity to, the Bodies of Saints, Living or Dead.*—Such miracles, according to Gregory the Great, were likely to make a deeper impression on the popular mind than those wrought by the bodies of the saints themselves, for the reason that in the latter case they might be regarded as wrought in answer to prayer, by the saint himself, whose spirit was supposed to hover about its former tenement. These may be further classified:

(*a*) *The Garments or Possessions of Saints.*—The tunic of St. John the Evangelist, preserved in Rome, worked many miracles; the shoes of St. Gall, A.D. 646, healed a man to whom they were given after the saint's death of contraction of the limbs; while the keys of St. Peter wrought many cures at Rome.

(*b*) *Cloths Laid upon the Bodies of Dead Saints.*—Cloths were laid upon the face of Miletius of Antioch on the occasion of his funeral at Constantinople, in 381, and distributed among the people as prophylactics. Handkerchiefs and garments in use were cast upon relics, in order to invest them with remedial properties, and even threads which had been frayed from a handkerchief that had been used to cover the face of Nicetius, bishop of Lyons, on the day of his death, when laid upon an altar, cured an epileptic who prayed before it.

(*c*) *The Candles or Lamps which Illuminated the Tomb of a Saint.*

(*d*) *The Dust which Gathered upon the Tomb*, e. g. of St. Hilary of Poitiers, was the means of cleansing two lepers, of bestowing sight upon a blind person, and soundness of limb upon two persons with withered hands. Dust from the tomb of martyrs in Lyons, when gathered in a spirit of faith, cured the infirm.

(*e*) *Water with which the Tomb was Washed.*—Several persons at Tours were cured of dysentery by the water with which St. Martin's tomb was washed in preparation for Easter.

(*f*) *The Fabric and Furniture of the Church which Held the Relics.*—A boy suffering from the effects of a poisoned dart was cured upon kissing the threshold of St. Martin's basilica. Sidonius Apollinaris tells a friend that he lost the sense of his debility when prostrate upon the threshold of the Vatican basilica at Rome.

(2) *Raising the Dead.*—A presbyter at Calama, in Africa, laid out as dead, revived when a tunic which had been taken to a memoria containing relics of St. Stephen was placed on his body. A wagon-wheel went over a child and killed him, his mother took him to the same memoria, "and he not only came to life again, but even appeared unhurt" (Augustine, *De Civitate Dei*, xxii, 8, § 12).

(3) *Deliverance, Protection, Succor.*—This belief came into existence along with that in their curative properties, and has been quite as prevalent and deep-seated.

The Romans regarded the relics of St. Peter and St. Paul as safeguards to their city. When a band of rebellious monks, belonging to the monastery of St. Sabas, in Palestine, were on their way to attack the monastery, they were seized with blindness, and unable to reach their destination. This deliverance of the abbot and his party was attributed to the presence of the relics of St. Sabas. In the time of Gregory of Tours, the population of several districts of Gaul were visited with a plague of an infectious character, and among them the province of Prima Germania. The town of Rheims, however, escaped by virtue of the pall or covering of St. Remignis's tomb, which was carried in procession, accompanied by crosses and candles, round the town. The belief in the miraculous virtues of relics led to the practice of carrying them, as the Jews their ark, into battle. The Frankish princes required their army chaplains to carry them at the head of their forces; Chilperic had them carried before him when he entered Paris, and an Eastern king, according to a story repeated by Gregory of Tours, went so far as to insert the thumb of St. Surgius in his own right hand, and was able, by raising his arm, to conquer his enemies. Besides this public use of relics, many individuals were accustomed to carry them about their persons for their own protection, especially when travelling.

2. *Miracles of Power*, consisting of

(1) *Those Wrought in Attestation of the Righteousness of the Innocent and the Guilt of the Wrong-doer.*—Gregory of Tours relates that a priest who had taken refuge in the Church of St. Martin at Tours, and was there put into chains, was proved to be innocent by the fact that his chains fell off him, and could not be made to remain on him when replaced. On the other hand, a priest who had falsely asserted his innocence before the tomb of St. Maximin, in Treves, fell down dead.

(2) *Those Wrought in Punishment of Such as Treated Relics with Contempt.*—For example, when the relics of St. Babylas, bishop of Antioch, had been removed at the emperor Julian's command from Daphne, where their presence was supposed to render dumb the oracles of Apollo, the temple of that god caught fire, and no traces of it were left (A.D. 354).

III. *Wonders Wrought by the Eucharist.*—It is a noteworthy fact that the miracles alleged to have been effected by the eucharist were wrought by it not only as a sacrament, but as that of the Catholic faith, in contradistinction to the rite, and in condemnation of the doctrines, of a heretical creed.

1. *Miracles of Beneficence.*

(1) *Exorcism and Healing.*—A girl possessed of an evil spirit, upon receiving the eucharist from St. Austregisile of Bourges, in 624, at once ceased to shout and rave; and a singer in a church choir, having been exhausted and in a prostrate condition from a conflict with dæmons, revived upon receiving it from Sulpicius, bishop of the same see, in 644.

(2) *Deliverance, Protection, Succor.*—During the reign of Justinian it was customary to distribute among the young children of Christian parents such fragments of the eucharistic bread as remained after communion. By accident a Jewish child, mingling with his Christian companions, received and ate one of these fragments. The father of the boy, a glass-blower by trade, was so enraged that he shut his son into his furnace, in order not only to kill him, but to destroy all traces of him. The child, however, was saved, and the miracle resulted in the conversion of the mother, who was baptized, together with her child.

2. *Miracles of Power*, wrought

(1) *In Condemnation of Immorality.*—Gregory of Tours relates that as a deacon, a man of unholy life, was one day carrying the eucharist into a church, the bread flew out of his hands and placed itself on the altar.

(2) *In Condemnation of Heresy.*—Certain members of the Donatist sect, in token of their contempt for the Catholics, once ordered the eucharistic bread to be given to their dogs. Upon eating it the dogs went mad and bit their masters. A woman receiving some of the eucharistic bread of the Macedonians, to her alarm found that it had turned into stone.

Similar miracles were also wrought by holy baptism. For example, as related by Augustine, the cure of a surgeon afflicted with the gout, and of an actor having paralysis.

IV. *Wonders Wrought by Pictures and Images.*

1. *Miracles of Beneficence.*—A picture of the Virgin Mary at Sozopolis, in Pisidia, was wont to shed, at the point where the hand of the Virgin was represented, a sweet-smelling ointment. The fact has been asserted, it is claimed, by many witnesses. An image of our Lord on the cross, which stood near the great gate of the imperial palace at Constantinople, was supposed to possess miraculous virtues, and, in fact, was believed to have wrought a cure of hemorrhage similar to that mentioned in the gospels.

The victories which Heraclius won over the Persians were attributed to the fact of his carrying at the head of his legions images of our Lord and the Virgin Mary; and the repulse of a Saracen army before the walls of Nicæa, A.D. 718, to the possession by that city of images of the saints.

2. *Miracles of Power.*—A Jew stole a picture of our Lord from a church, and in token of his contempt and hatred for the person it represented transfixed it with a dart. Forthwith blood began to flow from the picture, and in such quantity that the Jew was covered from head to foot. Thereupon he resolved to burn it, but the blood it had shed enabled its rightful owners to trace and bring condign punishment upon the thief.

Images of the cross, as representatives of the true cross, on the same theory, came to be regarded as possessing the same miraculous powers.

V. *Wonders Wrought by Celestial Visitants.*—Whatever miracles were attributed to living saints were also attributed to those beings supposed to possess the holy qualities, the angelic visitants. For example, St. Cuthbert, bishop of Lindisfarne, in 687, was cured of weakness in his knee by an angel who appeared to him on horseback; and a nun in a convent at Pauvilly, in Normandy, of an ulcer in her throat, after the hand of some invisible personage had been placed in support of her head, and a vision had been subsequently accorded to her of one clothed in the white robes of a virgin.

VI. *Wonders Wrought Apart from Human or Angelic Agency.*—Of this class of wonders, those which are best attested are least marvellous, while those which are most miraculous rest on manifestly insufficient testimony. Many of them might be looked upon as special providences, others as extraordinary coincidences; but at the time of their recurrence they were all looked upon as interpositions of Providence, intended to supply the needs or confound the enemies of the faithful. Of these we note

1. *Miraculous Occurrences.*

(1) *Miracles of Beneficence.*—A body of Catholics living in Typasa, in Mauritania, A.D. 484, for the crime of holding assemblies and refusing to communicate with a heretical bishop, had their right hands amputated, and their tongues cut out by the roots, by order of Hunneric, the Arian king of the Vandals. But on the third day after this occurrence they were able to speak as before. At least three of the narrators of this miracle—Æneas of Gaza, a rhetorician and philosopher, the emperor Justinian, and count Marcellinus, his former chancellor—were witnesses of the mutilation inflicted, and of the capacity of some of these martyrs to articulate who were living in their time. Marcellinus adds that one of the confessors having been born dumb, spoke for the first time after the excision of his tongue. Procopius states that two out of their number lost their supernatural power of speech through having lapsed into evil living. No contemporary authority gives the number

of the confessors, but in an old menology it was stated as sixty.

When the emperor Marcus Aurelius was waging war against the Quadri, his troops suffered greatly on one occasion from thirst, owing to the intense heat. Among his soldiers were many Christians. Those who belonged to the Melitene legion fell on their knees in prayer; a shower of rain fell, refreshing and invigorating the Roman army, but terrifying and dispersing the enemy, to whom it had been a storm of thunder and lightning. The account is sometimes given without any mention of the prayers of the Christians, and again the miracle is attributed to the prayers of the emperor.

Individuals are mentioned as having been miraculously protected. We may mention Theotimus, bishop of Tomi, A.D. 400, who became invisible to his pursuers; St. Martin of Tours, the arm of whose assailant fell powerless; Armogastus, a young Catholic in Theodoric's service, whose limbs were freed from their bonds on his signing the cross and invoking Christ.

(2) *Miracles of Power.*—As an example of a primitive miracle, which rests upon ample testimony, we note the fiery eruption on the rebuilding of the Temple of Jerusalem. The emperor Julian had given orders for the rebuilding of the Temple, having intrusted the superintendence of the work to his lieutenant, and himself issued invitations to the Jews of all countries to assemble at Jerusalem and aid him in accomplishing his purpose. Of the marvellous manner in which the work was interrupted and the emperor's designs thwarted, we learn the particulars from several writers. A whirlwind arose, scattering heaps of lime and sand in every direction; a storm of thunder and lightning fell, melting in its violence the implements of the workmen; an earthquake followed, casting up the foundation of the old Temple, filling in the new excavations, and causing the fall of buildings, especially the public porticoes, beneath which the terrified multitude had sought shelter. When the workmen resumed their labors balls of fire burst out beneath their feet, not once only, but as often as they attempted to continue the undertaking. The fiery mass traversed the streets, repelling from the doors of a church, even with the loss of life or limb, those who had fled to it for safety. This miracle has the support of contemporary writers, Gregory Nazianzen (*Orat.* v, 4), and Ammianus Marcellinus (*Hist.* xxiii, 1); and of later historians, Rufinus (*Hist.* i, 37), Socrates (iii, 20), Sozomen (v, 22), Theodoret (*Hist. Eccles.* iii, 20). See also Warburton, *Julian;* Gibbon, *Decline and Fall*, c. xxiii; Newman, *On Miracles*, clxxv; Migne, *Dict. des Mir.* ii, 1115.

2. *Miraculous Appearances.*— Gibbon (c. xv) declares that "it is impossible to overlook the clear traces of visions and inspirations which may be found in the early fathers." The purport of visions was sometimes to allay the fears, to solve the doubts, to direct the steps of those who were in trouble or difficulty, sometimes to forewarn of approaching calamities. They were not restricted in their coming to any particular sort of persons, but appeared to all. We may classify them into

(1) *Apparitions of Beings.*

(*a*) *Angels.*—The appearances of the archangel Michael were numerous, both in the East and the West. An angel appeared to St. Theuderius, directing him where to erect his monastery, two angels to Furseius, A.D. 650, admonishing him, as abbot of a monastery, that monks should pay less attention to the mortification of the body, and more to the cultivation of an humble, contented, and charitable disposition.

(*b*) *Dæmons.*—The evil one appeared to St. Anthony in the guise of a woman, then of a black child; as a monk with loaves in his hands, when the saint was fasting; as a spirit calling himself the power of God, and, lastly, avowing himself to be Satan.

(*c*) *Departed Spirits.*—St. Stephen appeared, A.D. 420, to Pulcheria, sister of Theodosius II, informing her of the safe arrival of his relics (right hand) from Jerusalem. St. Ambrose, on the night, being Easter eve, on which he was laid out for burial, appeared to the newly baptized infants, varying the manner of his appearance, but to the parents of the children remaining invisible, even when pointed out. Again, on the day of his death, he appeared to saints in the East, praying with them and laying his hands on them, while in Florence he was frequently seen after his death, praying before the altar of the church he had built in that city.

(*d*) *Living Saints.*—A child who had fallen into a well was found sitting upon the surface of the water. His account was that St. Julian Sabas, who at the time was entertained by the mother of the child, had appeared to him and borne him up. A similar story is given in the life of Theodosius of Palestine.

(2) *Visions of Purgatory, Hell, and Heaven.*—A vision the martyr Perpetua had of her brother, in whose behalf she had been led to pray, first as suffering and in a place of darkness, and then as comforted and surrounded with light, has been supposed to refer to a state of purgatory. As indicative of the punishment of the wicked, an abbot in Auvergne had a vision of a stream of fire, and of men immersed in it, bitterly bemoaning their sufferings. These had lost their footing when crossing a narrow bridge which spanned the stream, and were men who had been careless in the discharge of their spiritual duties. After this vision the abbot became stricter in the regulation of his monastery. Visions of heaven were accorded among others to St. Furseius and to Salvius, bishop of the Albigenses, as a place paved with gold and silver, and illuminated by a cloud shining beyond the light of sun or moon.

(3) *Apparitions of Crosses.*

(*a*) *In the Air.*—Constantine, when marching against Maxentius, A.D. 311, and in doubt to what deity he should apply for succor against an enemy whose forces outnumbered his own, saw, in company with his whole army, a luminous cross in the sky above the mid-day sun, with this inscription, "In this conquer." The same night our Lord appeared to Constantine in a vision, showed him a cross, and bade him fashion a standard after the pattern of it as a means of victory in his contest against Maxentius. This is the account given by Eusebius in his *Life of Constantine* (i, 28-32), but not till twenty-six years after the occurrence, and which he professes to have heard from the emperor himself, who affirmed his statement with an oath. Socrates, Philostorgius, Gelasius, and Nicephorus speak of the phenomenon as seen in the sky; Sozomen and Rufinus in a dream, although on the authority of Eusebius they also mention the apparition in the sky. On the feast of Pentecost, May 7, 351, a cross appeared in the sky at Jerusalem, stretching from Mount Calvary to Mount Olivet, and shining with a brilliancy equal to that of the sun's rays. The apparition lasted for several hours; the whole city beheld it, and all, residents and visitors, Christians and unbelievers, alike joined in the acknowledgment that "the faith of the Christians did not rest upon the persuasive discourses of human wisdom, but upon the sensible proofs of divine intervention." Of this phenomenon Cyril, then patriarch of Jerusalem, wrote an account to the emperor Constantius, who at the time was fighting against Maxentius in Pannonia, where also, according to Philostorgius (*Hist. Eccles.* iii, 26), it was seen by the contending armies, to the confusion of the pagan and the encouragement of the Christian host. Several other appearances of like character are mentioned.

(*b*) *On the Garments of Men.*—We read that when the emperor Julian was entering Illyricum the vines appeared laden with unripe grapes, although the vintage had taken place, and that dew falling from them on the garments of the emperor and his companions left upon them the imprint of crosses; a phenomenon which by some was supposed to portend that the emperor should perish prematurely, like unripe grapes.

The appearance of the luminous cross in the sky, on the occasion of Julian's attempt to rebuild the Temple, was accompanied by the appearance on the bodies and garments of men of crosses which were luminous at night, in some instances of a dark color, and would not wash out.

(*c*) *On Animals.*—When the emperor Julian was inspecting the entrails of an animal he was offering in sacrifice, he beheld in them the figure of a cross encircled by a crown. St. Placidas, when hunting a stag, beheld amid its horns a luminous cross and the figure of the Crucified, and heard a voice saying, "Why persecutest thou me, Placidas? Behold, I am here on account of thee. I am Christ whom thou, ignorant of, dost worship." St. Minulphus also saw a cross amid a stag's horns.

Besides the foregoing there are many other marvels mentioned in ancient writings, but illustrations of the leading classes have been given. For the credibility of such accounts see MIRACLES, ECCLESIASTICAL.

For additional information see *Acta Sanctorum; Acta SS. Benedict.*; Newman, *On Miracles*; Fleury, *Histoire Eccles.*; Butler, *Lives of the Saints*; Gregory the Great, *Dialogues*; Augustine, *De Civitate Dei*; Gregory of Tours, *De Gloria Martyrum*; Migne, *Dict. des Mir.* and *Patrol. Lat.*; Sulpicius Severus, *Life of St. Martin of Tours*; the various *Apologies* of the fathers, with many of their other writings; and the *Ecclesiastical Histories* of Eusebius, Socrates, Sozomen, Philostorgius, Rufinus, and Theodoret, as well as many of the later writers on the same subject.

Wood, Andrew, a Scotch prelate, was bishop of the Isles, where he continued until 1680, when he was translated to the bishopric of Caithness. See Keith, *Scottish Bishops*, p. 218, 310.

Wood, Jeremiah, D.D., a Presbyterian minister, was born at Greenfield, N. Y., Nov. 11, 1801. He graduated from Union College, Schenectady, in 1824; spent over two years in Princeton Theological Seminary; began his labors at Mayfield, N. Y., Nov. 26, 1826; was ordained as an evangelist, Jan. 10, 1828, and continued his work as stated supply at Mayfield until 1840. He was installed pastor at that place in September, 1841, and continued to labor there until his death, June 6, 1876. Dr. Wood was a man of clear intellect, and of unusual power in the pulpit and in debate; a wise counsellor, deeply pious, consistent in life, and successful as a pastor. See *Necrol. Report of Princeton Theol. Sem.* 1877, p. 20.

Wood, N. N., D.D., a Baptist minister, was born at Fairfax, Vt., May 1, 1808. He graduated from Middlebury College, in 1835; for one year was principal of the Black River Academy; studied theology for a part of the regular course at Madison University; was ordained pastor of the Church at Lebanon Springs, N. Y., in 1838; in 1842 went to Vicksburg, Miss.; resigned his pastorate in 1845, and went to Market Street Church, Zanesville, O., where he remained until 1850, when he was called to the presidency of Shurtleff College, Upper Alton, Ill., holding this office until 1855. For one year after his resignation he was pastor at Palmyra, Mo.; then became a chaplain in the Union army. Near the close of the war he removed to Jacksonville, Ill., where, for several years, he was professor of mental and moral philosophy and logic in the Young Ladies' Athenæum. He died there, Jan. 21, 1874. See *Minutes of Illinois Anniversaries*, 1874, p. 16. (J. C. S.)

Woodbridge, GEORGE, D.D., a Protestant Episcopal divine, was born in Massachusetts. He graduated at West Point, served a short period in the United States army at Old Point, and afterwards at Fort Independence, near Boston; resigned, and went to Maryland, where he edited a political newspaper. He subsequently went to the Theological Seminary at Alexandria, Va., graduating in 1833, was ordained by bishop Moore, and soon after was called to the Monumental Church, Richmond, where he remained until his death, Feb. 14, 1878, at the age of seventy-four years.

Wood-carrying, THE FEAST OF, one of the annual festivals instituted after the Babylonian captivity, although not mentioned in the Bible. See FESTIVAL.

I. *Name of the Festival and its Significance.*—The name קָרְבַּן הָעֵצִים or קָרְבַּן עֵצִים, which literally denotes *the wood-offering*, ξυλοφόρια, *Xylophoria*, or its fuller phrase, יום טוב של קרבן עצים, *the feast of wood-offering*, ἡ τῶν ξυλοφορίων ἑορτή (Josephus, *War*, ii, 17, 6), by which this festival is designated, is derived from Neh. x, 35; xiii, 31. It obtained its name from the fact that on the day in which it was celebrated all the people, without any distinction of tribe or grade, brought wood to the temple, being the last day in the year whereon wood could be felled for the burning of the sacrifices and the perpetual fire on the altar. It is also denominated זמן אעי לכהניא, *the time of wood for the priests* (*Megillath Taanith*, v), because on this festival the priests too, like the rest of the people, offered wood.

II. *The Day, and Manner of its Celebration.*—The day on which this festival was annually celebrated was the 15th of *Ab* (אב=August). This is distinctly attested by the unanimous voice of the most ancient and most trustworthy records (comp. Mishna, *Taanith*, iv, 8; *Babylon Gemara*, ibid. 30 a; *Baba Bathra*, 121 a; *Megillath Taanith*, v; *Midrash Rabba*, on Lamentations, lvii). The remark in Josephus, that this festival was celebrated on the 14th (τῇ δὲ ἑξῆς τῶν ξυλοφορίων ἑορτῆς οὔσης—ἐν ᾗ πᾶσιν ἔθος ὕλην τῷ βωμῷ προσφέρειν, *War*, ii, 17, 6; and τῇ δὲ ἑξῆς, πεντεκαιδεκάτη δὲ ἦν Λώου μηνός, κ.τ.λ., ibid. ii, 17, 7), must therefore be regarded as the error of a copyist (comp. Herzfeld, *Geschichte des Volkes Israel*, i, 144; Grätz, *Geschichte der Juden*, 2d ed. iii, 478). The nine days in the year appointed for the delivery of wood by the respective families were as follows: On the 20th of *Ab*, when the descendants of Pachat Moab b. Jehudah furnished the wood; the 20th of *Elul*, the family of Adeen b. Jehudah; the 1st of *Tebet*, the family of Parosh; the 1st of *Nisan*, the family of Arah b. Jehudah; the 20th of *Tamuz*, the family of David b. Jehudah; the 5th of *Ab*, the family of Parosh b. Jehudah; the 7th of *Ab*, the family of Jondab b. Rechab; the 10th of *Ab*, the family of Senaa b. Benjamin; and on the 15th of *Ab*, the family of Saltu b. Jehudah, with the priests, Levites, and all those who did not know from what they descended, as well as the families of Gonbei Ali and Kozai Kezioth (Mishna, *Taanith*, iv, 3). So general was the delivery of wood on this day (i. e. the 15th of *Ab*) that even proselytes, slaves, Nethinim, and bastards brought fuel (*Megillath Taanith*, v). Hence the remark of Josephus, that on this day all the people brought wood, from which circumstance it derived its name (*War*, ii, 17, 6).

On this day, when all the people were thus congregated together, discarding all distinction of tribe, of rich and poor, of Israelite and proselyte, of master and slave, the maidens of Jerusalem met together for singing joyful and religious songs, and for dancing. Dressed in white garments, which they borrowed in order not to shame those who had none of their own, these damsels assembled together in an open place in the vineyards. They sang strophic songs in the sacred language, and danced in the presence of the congregation. It was on this occasion that the happy choice of partners in life frequently took place, since it was one of the two annual opportunities afforded to the young people of making their attractions known without violating feminine modesty (Mishna, *Megilla*, iv, 8). Cessation from manual labor on this day was, however, not enjoined; but fasting, penitential prayers, and mourning for the dead were forbidden (*Megillath Taanith*, v; Maimonides, *Yad ha-Chezaka Hilchoth Kelei ham-Mikdash*, vi).

III. *Origin and Date of this Festival.*—The origin of this festival is involved in great obscurity, as the ancient Talmudic authorities which describe its celebration differ materially in their opinions about the occasion which gave rise to its institution. From Neh. x, 35; xiii, 31, we learn that this statesman, in order to supply the necessary fuel for the burning of the sacrifices and the keeping up of the perpetual fire on the altar, ordained that each family in rotation was to furnish wood for the temple at a certain period of the year, and that the order and time of delivery were to be settled by casting lots. The result obtained by the casting of lots is not mentioned in the canonical Scriptures; but the post-canonical documents, which describe the temple service, furnish us with a minute account of both the names of the respective families upon whom it devolved to supply the wood, and the periods of the year in which they delivered it. This account is given in the preceding section of this article. It is, therefore, only natural to conclude that the different families who are thus recorded to have offered the wood at appointed times did so in accordance with the results obtained by the casting of lots. Now, the reason why the 15th of *Ab* was kept as a special festival, and why all the nation at large took part in the offering of wood on this day, is, according to some authorities in the Talmud, that on it the people ceased to fell wood for the temple, because, according to R. Eliezer the Great, the heat of the sun begins to diminish on this day, and the wood which was cut after this date did not become sufficiently dry. Hence the 15th of *Ab* was designated "the day on which the axe is broken." As it was also believed that the wood cut down after the 15th of *Ab* is sapless (*Rosh hash-Shana*, 2 a, 14 a), Herzfeld (*Geschichte des Volkes Israel*, i, 145) ingeniously conjectures that the trees were regarded as dead after this date, and the wood of such trees was considered as unfit for the altar. The other ancient opinion about the origin of this festival is, that the furnishing of wood for the temple by the pious, which existed from time immemorial, and which Nehemiah reinstituted after the return from Babylon, was prohibited by some wicked sovereign, and that this interdict was abolished on the 15th of *Ab*. Hence this day was constituted a festival, and the families who jeopardized their lives in stealthily supplying wood for the temple during the time of the prohibition are those named above, who, as a privilege, continued to bring some wood on this festival, whether the fuel was wanted or not. There is, however, a difference of opinion as to who this wicked monarch was. The *Jerusalem Talmud* will have it that it was Jeroboam who placed guards on the roads leading to the temple in order to prevent the people from taking to the sanctuary the first-fruits and the wood, and the families of Gonbei Ali and Kozai Kezioth, mentioned in the Mishna, were those who encountered the danger in clandestinely supplying the wood (*Jerusalem Taanith*, iv, 6). The *Megillath Taanith* (cap. v) again has it that this interdict proceeded from "*the kings of Greece*," who imitated the conduct of Jeroboam; while the *Babylonian Talmud* omits the dynasty altogether, and simply remarks that the prohibition emanated from *some government* (*Taanith*, 28 a). As the reference to Jeroboam on the part of the *Jerusalem Talmud* is simply to make this monarch the author of all the wicked deeds in connection with the Jews, and as, moreover, the ascription of this deed in the *Megillath Taanith* to Greek rulers is unhistorical—since Antiochus Epiphanes, to whom alone it could refer, totally abolished the temple service, which rendered it useless to smuggle the first-fruits and wood—Grätz concludes that this prohibition could only proceed from Alexander Jannæus, who forbade the offering of wood out of hatred to the Pharisees, and that then the above-named pious families clandestinely furnished the fuel. When this interdict ceased with the reign of Alexander, and the ancient custom of wood-offering was resumed, the concluding day for the delivery of it (comp. *Taanith*, 31 a) obtained a higher significance, and was elevated into a national festival (Grätz, iii, 477). It will be seen from the account of the nature of this festival that the custom for all the people to bring large supplies of firewood for the sacrifices of the year could not possibly have been designed to relieve the Nethinim, and that these Nethinim did not bear a conspicuous part in it, as is supposed by many.

IV. *Literature.*—Mishna, *Taanith*, iv, 5, 8; the *Jerusalem* and *Babylon Gemaras* on this Mishna; *Megillath Taanith* (ed. Meyer, Amsterdam, 1724), v, 32–39; Maimonides, *Yad ha-Chezaka Hilchoth Kelei ham-Mikdash*, vi; Herzfeld, *Geschichte des Volkes Israel* (Nordhausen, 1855), i, 67 sq.; 144 sq.; Jost, *Geschichte des Judenthums* (Leipsic, 1857), i, 169; Grätz, *Geschichte der Juden* (2d ed. ibid. 1863), p. 122, 477 ff. See OFFERING.

Wooden Churches. In Walcott's *Sacred Archæology* (p. 614, 615), the principal facts concerning the wooden churches of the Middle Ages and a little later are given in brief.

"Nether Peevor, built in the time of Henry II; a chapel at Bury St. Edmund's until 1303; St. Aldhelm's, Durham, 998; St. Stephen's, Mayence, 1011; a stud Lady-chapel at Tykford, and another at Spalding, in 1059, were all built of wood, as many of the Norwegian churches (like Little Greenstead, 1013; Newtown, Montgomeryshire; and Newland, Worcestershire) are to this day. The latter may have been a grange altered to form a church. Ribbesford has wooden nave-arcades. The excellence of English carpentry is conspicuous in the woodwork preserved to us in roofs, as at Peterborough, Ely, Old Shoreham, Polebrooke, Warmington, and St. Mary's Hospital and the palace kitchen, Chichester; the Gueston-hall, now in a church, at Worcester; and St. Mary's, Reading; doors, as at Beaulieu and Luton; cloisters, like the dean's at Windsor, of the 14th century; lychgates, as at Beckenham; windows, like those of Englefield; stalls, as at Lancaster, and some of early English date at Salisbury; screens, as at St. John's Hospital, Winchester, Roydon, Ewerby, the palace chapel, Chichester, Lavenham, and St. Margaret's, Lynn; or early stall desks, like one preserved at Rochester, of the 12th century. The curious 'fish-scale' ornament of Norman spires is an imitation of the oaken shingle so common in Kent and Sussex, a clear proof that there were earlier spires of wood. Probably the Gothic stone spire was derived from Normandy, where the earliest—the pyramid of Thann—forms a succession of steps, of the end of the 12th century, and was the prototype of Comornes, Basley, and Rosel. But England never produced such a grand example of ornamental carpentry and lead as the flèche of Amiens."

American churches and chapels from the first have been largely of wood; but the present tendency is towards structures built of more substantial material.

Woodford, JAMES RUSSELL, D.D., an English prelate, was born at Henley-on-Thames, April 30, 1820. He graduated from Pembroke College, Cambridge, in 1842; was ordained deacon in 1843, and presbyter in 1845; became incumbent at St. Mark's, Easton, near Bristol, in 1847; vicar at Kempsford, Gloucestershire, in 1855; of Leeds in 1868; bishop of Ely in 1873; and died Oct. 24, 1885. He published several volumes of sermons, lectures, etc.

Woodhead, ABRAHAM, an English clergyman, and subsequently a Roman Catholic controversial writer, was born at Meltham, Yorkshire, in 1608. He was educated in University College, Oxford, of which he became fellow in 1633, and soon after entered into holy orders. In 1641 he was proctor at Oxford, and about this time travelled on the Continent as tutor to some young gentlemen of distinction. While at Rome he became a secret convert to the Catholic religion. In 1648 he was deprived of his fellowship for absence, but was reinstated at the Restoration in 1660. Finding it impossible to conform, however, he obtained leave to travel with an allowance of £20, on which he lived in concealment, teaching Roman Catholic pupils and writing controversial books, at Hoxton, near London, until his death, May 4, 1678. He was considered one of the ablest controversial writers, on the popish side, of his time, and his abilities and candor have been commended by some

Protestant writers. Among his publications we note, *Brief Account of Ancient Church Government* (1662):—*Guide in Controversies, in IV Discourses* (1666):—*Dr. Stillingfleet's Principles* (1671):—*Life of St. Tereza, from the Spanish* (eod.):—*Paraphrase of the Apocalypse* (1682):—*Two Discourses Concerning the Adoration of our Blessed Saviour in the Eucharist* (1687):—*Of Faith Necessary to Salvation*, etc. (1688):—*A Compendious Discourse on the Eucharist*, etc. (eod.):—*Motives to Holy Living* (eod.):—*Catholick Theses* (1689):—and *Concerning Images and Idolatry* (eod.).

Woodland (יְעָרִים, "forests"). The groves of Palestine, inhabited by wild and even rapacious animals (2 Kings ii, 24, Jer. v, 6; xii, 8, Amos iii, 4, etc.), were, especially before the cultivation of the soil by the Israelites, not inconsiderable, but not adequate to supply timber, much less fuel. See WOOD. In the Mosaic law there is reference to forests and their employment (Deut. xix, 5), and conflagrations in them are occasionally noticed (Psa. lxxxiii, 15; Isa. ix, 17, comp. Jer. xxi, 14, James iii, 5). Several tracts of woodland are enumerated in the Bible (Reland, *Palæst.* p. 378 sq.; Hamesveld, i, 436 sq.). See FOREST.

Woodruff, GEORGE W., D.D., a Methodist Episcopal minister, was born in New York city, April 21, 1824. He was educated in the public schools of that city and at Oberlin, O.; joined the New York Conference in 1845, was ordained deacon in 1847, and elder in 1849. His successive appointments were: Greenport, Riverhead, Flatbush, L.I.; New Britain, West Winsted, Conn.; York Street, Brooklyn, N.Y.; Danbury, Conn.; St. John Street, New Haven; Middletown; Waterbury; Hanson Place, Brooklyn; Seventh Street, Alanson Church, New York city; First Church, New Haven; New Rochelle, N.Y.; in 1874 superannuated; St. Paul's, Fall River, Mass.; Allen Street, New York city; Nostrand Avenue, Brooklyn; in 1881 supernumerary. He was secretary of the New York East Conference fourteen consecutive years, and was delegate to the General Conference four times, of which body he was three times secretary. He died March 20, 1882. He was an able and effective preacher, a good pastor, and a zealous counsellor. See *Minutes of Annual Conferences*, 1882, p. 77.

Woodworth, FRANCIS C., a Presbyterian minister and author, was born at Colchester, Conn., Feb. 12, 1813. He served eight years as a printer; was educated at Oneida Institute, N.Y., graduated at Union Theological Seminary in 1840, was licensed by the Third Presbytery of New York, April 26 of that year, and ordained as pastor of the Congregational Church, Fairhaven, Vt., on the 28th of October. Here he labored three years, and then resigned, on the failure of his health, and devoted himself to juvenile literature, in which department he acquired a wide reputation. He died June 5, 1859, on board a steamer, at the wharf in New York, just arrived from Florida. He published, *Uncle Frank's Home Stories* (6 vols. 16mo):—*Uncle Frank's Boys' and Girls' Library* (6 vols. 16mo):—*Uncle Frank's Picture Gallery* (2 vols. 16mo):—*Theodore Thinker's Stories for Little Folks* (12 vols. 18mo). He also published in England, *England as It Is* (18mo):—*Scotland as It Is* (18mo):—*The World as It Is* (2 vols. 18mo):—*Youth's Book of Gems* (8vo):—*Young American's Life of Fremont* (1856, 18mo):—*Uncle Frank's Pleasant Pages for the Fireside* (1857, 12mo):—*A Wheat-sheaf from Our Own Fields* (16mo; republished as *Buds and Blossoms from Our Own Garden*, 16mo):—*String of Pearls for Boys and Girls* (16mo):—*American Miscellany of Entertaining Knowledge* (6 vols. 12mo), which is warmly commended:—*Youth's Cabinet, and Uncle Frank's Dollar Magazine*, of which he edited about fifteen volumes, and which made his name a familiar sound in many households. See Wilson, *Presb. Hist. Almanac*, 1861, p. 168; Allibone, *Dict. of Brit. and Amer. Authors*, s. v.

Woof (עֶרֶב, *éreb, mixture*, as sometimes rendered), the cross-threads inserted into the warp in weaving (Lev. xiii, 48–59). See WEB.

Woog, CARL CHRISTOPH, a German linguist, was born in 1713 at Dresden, and died as professor of Greek and Latin at Leipsic, April 24, 1771. He is the author of, *Presbyteror. et Diaconor. Achaiæ de Martyrio S. Andreæ Epistola Encyclica* (Leipsic, 1749):—*Progr. de Genuinis Antiquitatum Sacrar. in Primitiva Ecclesia Obviar. Fontib.* (ibid. 1745):—*Historiola de Synesio Episc. et Evagrio Philos.* (ibid. 1758):—*Hippolyti Fragmentum ad Prov. ix*, 1–5 (ibid. 1762). See Fürst, *Bibl. Jud.* iii, 536; Winer, *Handbuch der theol. Lit.* i, 566, 606, 900. (B. P.)

Wool (Gr. ἔριον, Heb. ix, 19; Rev. i, 4). The fleece of the sheep, as such, was properly called גֵּז or גִּזָּה, while the material of which it was composed was called צֶמֶר; hence גִּזַּת הַצֶּמֶר, *a fleece of wool* (Judg. vi, 37). Wool was used by the Hebrews from an early period extensively for clothing (Lev. xiii, 47; Deut. xxii, 11; Job xxxi, 20; Prov. xxxi, 13; Ezek. xxxiv, 3; Hos. ii, 5). The importance of wool is incidentally shown by the notice that Mesha's tribute was paid in a certain number of rams "with the wool" (2 Kings iii, 4), as well as by its being specified among the first-fruits to be offered to the priests (Deut. xviii, 4). The wool of Damascus was highly prized in the mart of Tyre (Ezra xxvii, 18), and is compared in the Sept. to the wool of Miletus (ἔρια ἐκ Μιλήτου), the fame of which was widely spread in the ancient world (Pliny viii, 73; Virgil, *Georg.* iii, 306; iv, 334.) Wool is occasionally cited as an image of purity and brilliancy (Isa. i, 18; Dan. vii, 9; Rev. i, 14), and the flakes of snow are appropriately likened to it (Psa. cxlvii, 16). The art of dyeing it was understood by the Jews (Mishna, *Shab.* 1, § 6). See SHEEP; WOOLLEN.

Woollen AND LINEN (i. e. *linsey-woolsey*). Among the Mosaic laws against unnatural mixtures is found one to this effect, "A garment of mixtures (שַׁעַטְנֵז, *shaatnêz*) shall not come upon thee" (Lev. xix, 19); or, as it is expressed in Deut. xxii, 11, "thou shalt not wear *shaatnêz*, wool and flax together." Our version, by the help of the latter passage, has rendered the strange word *shaatnêz* in the former, "of linen and woollen;" while in Deuteronomy it is translated "a garment of divers sorts." In the Vulgate the difficulty is avoided; and κίβδηλος, "spurious" or "counterfeit," the rendering of the Sept., is wanting in precision. In the Targum of Onkelos the same word remains, with a slight modification to adapt it to the Chaldee; but in the Peshito-Syriac of Leviticus it is rendered by an adjective, "motley," and in Deuteronomy a "motley garment," corresponding in some degree to the Samaritan version, which has "spotted like a leopard." Two things only appear to be certain about *shaatnêz*—that it is a foreign word, and that its origin has not at present been traced. Its signification is sufficiently defined in Deut. xxii, 11. The derivation given in the Mishna (*Kilaim*, ix, 8), which makes it a compound of three words, signifying "carded, spun, and twisted," is in keeping with rabbinical etymologies generally. Other etymologies are proposed by Bochart (*Hieroz.* pt. 1, b. 2, c. 45), Simonis (*Lex. Heb.*), and Pfeiffer (*Dub. Vex.* cent. 2, loc. xi). The last-mentioned writer defended the Egyptian origin of the word, but his knowledge of Coptic, according to Jablonski, extended not much beyond the letters, and little value, therefore, is to be attached to the solution which he proposed for the difficulty. Jablonski himself favors the suggestion of Forster, that a garment of linen and woollen was called by the Egyptians *shontnes*, and that this word was borrowed by the Hebrews, and written by them in the form *shaatnêz* (*Opusc.* i, 294). See LINEN.

The reason given by Josephus (*Ant.* iv, 8, 11) for the law which prohibited the wearing a garment woven of linen and woollen is, that such were worn by the priests alone (see Mishna, *Kilaim*, ix, 1). Of this kind were the girdle (of which Josephus says the warp was entirely linen, *Ant.* iii, 7, 2), ephod, and breastplate (Braunius, *De Vest. Sac. Hebr.* p. 110, 111) of the high-priest, and the girdle of the common priests (Maimonides, *Cele ham-Mikdash*, cviii). Spencer conjectured that the use of woollen and linen inwoven in the same garment prevailed among the ancient Zabii, and was associated with their idolatrous ceremonies (*De Leg. Heb.* ii, 33, 3); but that it was permitted to the Hebrew priests, because with them it could give rise to no suspicion of idolatry. Maimonides found in the books of the Zabii that "the priests of the idolaters clothed themselves with robes of linen and woollen mixed together" (Townley, *Reasons of the Laws of Moses*, p. 207). By "wool" the Talmudists understood the wool of sheep (Mishna, *Kilaim*, ix, 1). It is evident from Zeph. i, 8, that the adoption of a particular dress was an indication of idolatrous tendencies, and there may be therefore some truth in the explanation of Maimonides. See DIVERSE.

Woolston, THOMAS, an English divine, who was noted in his day for the boldness of his opinions, was born at Northampton in 1669. He received the proper training in the grammar-school, and entered Sidney College, Cambridge, in 1685, where he subsequently graduated, and became fellow of his college. He was prosecuted before lord chief-justice Raymond for the views advanced in his *Discourses on the Miracles of Our Saviour*, and sentenced to a year's imprisonment and a fine of £100. He purchased the liberty of the rules of the King's Bench, where he continued after the expiration of the year, being unable to pay the fine. Efforts were made for his release, but were unsuccessful, because he refused to desist from offensive writings. He died in the bounds of King's Bench prison, Jan. 27, 1732. Among his principal writings are the following: *The Old Apology for the Truth of the Christian Religion against the Jews and Gentiles Revived* (1705):—*Dissertatio de Pontii Pilati ad Tiberium Epistola* (1720):—*A Free Gift to the Clergy, in Four Parts* (1722–24):—*Moderator Between an Infidel and an Apostate* (1725):—*Six Discourses on the Miracles of Our Saviour* (1727–29):—*Defence of the Six Discourses on the Miracles of Our Saviour* (1729–30).

Worcester, COUNCILS OF (*Concilium Vigorniense*). Worcester is a city of England, capital of the county of the same name, situated on the left bank of the Severn, twenty-five miles south-west of Birmingham. Under the name *Caer Guorangon*, it was one of the principal cities of the ancient Britons. Two ecclesiastical councils have been held there, as follows:

I. Was held about 601, by St. Austin, in which he endeavored, ineffectually, to persuade the bishops of the British Church to observe the festival of Easter, to administer baptism according to the custom of the Latin Church, and to yield obedience to the Church of Rome. See Mansi, *Concil.* v, 1610; Wilkins, *Concil.* i, 24.

II. Was held July 26, 1240, by the bishop Walter of Chanteloup. Fifty-nine constitutions were published, which, among other things, enjoin to baptize conditionally in doubtful cases, but always with trine immersion. Forbids to celebrate mass before having said prime, to plight troth except when fasting, and to observe any particular day or month for marriage. It is also ordered that any person desiring to confess to any other than his own priest, shall first modestly ask permission of the latter. See Mansi. *Concil.* xi, 572; Wilkins, *Concil.* i, 665.

Word is in Hebrew (דָּבָר) often put for *thing* or matter; as Exod. ii, 14, "Surely this thing [Heb. *word*] is known;" "To-morrow the Lord shall do this thing [Heb. *word*] in the land" (ix, 5); "I will do a thing [Heb. *word*] in Israel, at which both the ears of every one that heareth it shall tingle" (1 Sam. iii, 11); "And the rest of the acts [Heb. *words*] of Solomon" (1 Kings xi, 41). So likewise the Gr. ῥῆμα, which properly signifies an *utterance*, came to denote any sensible object or occurrence.

WORD OF GOD, or, OF THE LORD. Sometimes Scripture ascribes to the word of God supernatural effects; or represents it as animated and active. So, "He sent his word, and healed them" (Psa. cvii, 20). Enlarging upon this idea, the apocryphal book of Wisdom ascribes to the word of God the death of the first-born of Egypt (xviii, 15; xvi, 26; ix, 1; xvi, 12); the miraculous effects of the manna; the creation of the world; the healing of those who looked up to the brazen serpent. In a similar sense of omnific power the centurion in the gospel says to our Saviour, "Speak the word only, and my servant shall be healed" (Matt. viii, 8). Referring to the preserving influence of divine truth, Christ says to the devil that tempted him, "Man shall not live by bread alone, but by every word that proceedeth out of the mouth of God" (iv, 4).

From these and other passages we see that the phrase "word of God" or "of the Lord" is taken (1) for that internal word heard by the prophets, when under inspiration from God; (2) for that which they heard externally, when God spoke to them; as when he spoke to Moses, face to face, or as one friend speaks to another (Exod. xxxiii, 11); (3) for that word which the ministers of God, the priests, the apostles, the servants of God, declare in his name to the people; (4) for what is written in the sacred books of the Old and New Tests.; (5) for the only Son of the Father, the uncreated wisdom. For the first four of these, see BIBLE; the last only we propose to discuss here.

I. *The Logos* (ὁ Λόγος) is the name given to the divine or pre-existent nature of Christ, designating him as the great medium of communication between God and man (John i, 1, 14; 1 John i, 1; v, 7; Rev. xix, 13; comp. Heb. iv, 12). This remarkable usage of the term *word*, as designating not a mere *attribute*, but a *hypostasis* in some respects diverse from God, yet at the same time God himself, does not appear to have been derived from the poetical personification of "wisdom," in Prov. viii, 12, 22; nor from the apocryphal books of Wisdom, vii, 22–26; and of Ecclesiasticus, i, 1–10; xxiv, 1–14. Even the Logos of Plato, and that of Philo, is no more than an abstraction or personification of divine power, intelligence, and wisdom. As John has united the idea of proper personality with his designation of the Logos, it is certain that he could not have derived his views from any of those writers. There is an immeasurable discrepancy between the views of John and those of Plato and the Jewish writers. If the Logos of John be the same as theirs, then proper personality and divinity are out of the question. But from the passages cited it is evident that the Logos of the New Test. is a proper and real person, not a mere personification, i. e. a philosophical, speculative, or poetical abstraction, amounting to nothing more than a poetico-rhetorical method of describing either divine attributes or divine operations or energies. In the prologue to the gospel of John, the original state or condition of the Logos, and his essential nature, are first described; and then the developments of himself, which had been made either in the way of creation or redemption. He is eternal; was with God; was God. As such he was the Creator of all things without exception. In particular, he was the source of all life; and as the author of spiritual life, he was the source also of all true spiritual light (1 Cor. viii, 6; Col. i, 15–19; Heb. i, 2, 3). See FULNESS.

How God communed with the first human pair in the innocence of Eden we know not; but after the first transgression his communings were in a different mode, and adapted to man in his altered circumstances. The Logos was *God revealed*—communicating with his creatures, and disclosing to them the way of salvation. The various divine revelations to the patriarchs, and to others under the law, whether as the angel Jehovah, or otherwise in visions, voices, and symbols, were revelations by the Logos. So, in the tabernacle, God of old dwelt, and the *shekinah*, as significant of the abiding divine glory over the mercy-seat, was the symbol of his presence among his people. So also in the theophany described in Isa. iv, 1-13, we learn something of the glory of the Logos before he became incarnate (John i, 14; xii, 41; xvii, 5). Jehovah was indeed revealed in many respects, in the Old Test.; but God as Father, and Christ as Son and Redeemer, and the Holy Spirit as Sanctifier, were, to say the most, only foreshadowed in the Hebrew Scriptures. It is the Logos manifested in the flesh, Christ the Son of God, who hath revealed God, i. e. placed the character and designs of God in the light that the gospel affords. His light shone on the darkness of all the ages which preceded his coming; but this darkness was so gross that little impression was made upon it. In order to save the world from its ruinous state, the Logos became incarnate, i. e. took on him the human form and nature, and thus dwelt among men, and manifested his glory, which was truly that of the Only Begotten of the Father. Neither Moses nor any other prophet ever understood and disclosed the character and designs of God in such a way as was adequate to accomplish the plan of our redemption. But he who is in the bosom of the Father exhibited grace and revealed truth in such a way as fully to satisfy our wants and alleviate our woes. See LOGOS.

II. *The Memrâ* (מֵימְרָא).—The Chaldee paraphrasts, the most ancient Jewish uncanonical writers extant, generally use this name (signifying *word*) where Moses puts *Jehovah*, and it is thought that under this term they allude to the Son of God. Now, their testimony is so much the more considerable, as, having lived before or at the time of Christ, they are irrefragable witnesses of the sentiments of their nation on this article, since their Targum, or explication, has always been, and still is, in universal esteem among them. In the greater part of the passages where the sacred name occurs, these paraphrasts substitute *Memra Jehovah* (מימרא דיי״), *the Word of God*, and as they ascribe to Memra all the attributes of deity, it is concluded that they believed the divinity of the Word. In effect, according to them, Memra created the world; appeared to Abraham in the plain of Mamre, and to Jacob at Bethel. It was to Memra Jacob appealed to witness the covenant between him and Laban: "Let the Word see between thee and me." The same Word appeared to Moses at Sinai, gave the law to Israel, spoke face to face with that lawgiver, marched at the head of that people, enabled them to conquer nations, and was a consuming fire to all who violated the law of the Lord. All these characters, where the paraphrasts use the word Memra, clearly denote Almighty God. This Word, therefore, was God, and the Hebrews were of this opinion at the time when the Targum was composed. See SHEKINAH.

The author of the book of Wisdom, as above observed, expresses himself much in the same manner. He says that God created all things by his Word (Wisd. ix, 1); that it is not what the earth produces that feeds man, but the Word of the Almighty that supports him (xvi, 26). It was this Word that fed the Israelites in the desert, healed them after the biting of the serpents (ver. 12), and who, by his power, destroyed the first-born of the Egyptians (xviii, 15; see Exod. xii, 29, 30), and by which Aaron stopped the fury of the fire that was kindled in the camp, which threatened the destruction of all Israel (Wisd. xviii, 22; see Numb. xvi, 46). See WISDOM PERSONIFIED.

III. *The Bath-Kol* (בַּת קוֹל, *daughter of the voice*).—Under this name the Talmud, the later Targums, and the rabbinical writers make frequent mention of a kind of oracular voice, constituting the fourth grade of revelation, which, although it was an instrument of divine communication throughout the early history of the Israelites, was the most prominent, because the sole, prophetic manifestation which existed during (and even after) the period of the second temple. The *Midrashim* and the *Gemara*, cited in Reland's *Antiq. Sacr.* pt. ii, ch. ix, severally affirm that the Bath-Kol is the voice which spoke to Abraham, Moses, David, Nebuchadnezzar, and others; and the Targums of Jonathan and of Jerusalem make the Bath-Kol appear in Gen. xxxviii, 26; Numb. xxi, 6, and in other places. The treatise *Sanhedrin*, cited in Vitringa's *Obser. Sacr.* ii, 338, uses the words, "From the death of Haggai, Zechariah, and Malachi, the Holy Spirit (רוח הקדש, which, according to the Jewish distinction, is only the second degree of the prophetical gift) was withdrawn from Israel; but they nevertheless enjoyed the use of the Bath-Kol."

The Jewish authorities are not agreed as to what the Bath-Kol was, nor as to the precise reason of its designation. It is disputed whether the persons hearing the Bath-Kol heard the very voice from heaven, or only a daughter of it—an *echo* of it; whether, as thunder is often mentioned as a sign of the divine presence, and as the word *voice* appears to be used for thunder in Exod. ix, 23; Jer. x, 13; Psa. xxix, 3, the Bath-Kol may not signify an articulate voice proceeding out of the thunder; or whether, according to the explanation of Maimonides, "the Bath-Kol is when a man has such a strong imagination that he believes he hears a voice from without himself."

As to the meaning of the name itself, passages are cited in Buxtorf's *Lex. Talm.* s. v. בת, and in Reland's *Antiq. Sacr.* loc. cit., which show that the daughter of the voice sometimes means the echo of a sound, and sometimes merely a primary sound itself. It is certain that the *Peshito* has sometimes rendered the simple Greek φωνή by "daughter of the voice," as in Acts xii, 22; 1 Tim. vi, 20; Heb. iii, 15. It is necessary, however, to remark that, according to a fundamental law of all Syro-Arabian grammar, these two words must either stand to each other in the relation of *apposition* or of the *state construct*. But as apposition can only take place between equivalent and convertible terms, which "daughter" and "voice" are not, accordingly the alternative rendering of *daughter voice* proposed by Prideaux (which Horne also has adopted, *Introduct.* iv, 149) violates that rule, because, in such an English combination, the word "daughter" has the force of an *adjective;* and the Hebrew language, possessing but few adjectives, would have expressed the sense of *daughter voice* (if that had been the sense intended to be conveyed by Bath-Kol) by making Bath the *last* word, depending as a genitive on the former. For instance, what we render the Holy Spirit is literally "the spirit of holiness" in Hebrew. Thus, "*daughter voice*" is not an apposition in English, nor is it the translation of a state construct according to the Hebrew order, but of a state construct in which Prideaux has taken the liberty of transposing the dependent word, i. e. of making "daughter of the voice" become, in effect, "voice of a daughter." Jennings also, in his *Jewish Antiq.* p. 229, when he renders Bath-Kol by "*filiæ vox, seu filia vocis,*" only commits, in the first case, the same error more palpably, and is guilty of quite as great a violation of the first principle of Hebrew grammar as he would be, in the case of Latin, were he to translate *filia vocis* by "voice of the daughter."

The occasions on which it is alleged that the Bath-Kol was heard after the death of Malachi are of very various degrees of solemnity or significance. Supposing the instances mentioned in Josephus (*Ant.* xiii, 10), of the voice which announced to Hyrcanus that his sons had conquered Antiochus, and (*War*, vi, 5) of the awful voice which was heard in the temple, just before the capture of Jerusalem, to exclaim, Μεταβαίνωμεν ἐντεῦθεν! not to belong to the Bath-Kol (as it is to be observed that the pseudo-Josephus ben-Gorion has, in these cases, merely used the Hebrew word for *voice*), most of the other recorded instances fall far short of these in dignity, and some appear irreconcilable with even very credulous notions of the limits of divine interposition. Only a few of them, however, can be classed with quite as trivial a species of divination as the *Sortes Virgilianæ*, which is done in the unfair statement of Prideaux (*Connex.* ii, 354). The fact is, that most Christian writers who have treated of the Bath-Kol have not been able to divest themselves of an undue desire to discredit its pretensions, in consequence of their fearing any comparison which might be instituted between it and the voices from heaven mentioned in the New Test. Indeed, Lightfoot (in his *Hor. Hebr. ad Matt.* iii, 17) considers all cases of Bath-Kol to be either Jewish fables or devices of the devil. Instances of voices from heaven, on occasions outwardly very analogous to some among the Jews, are recorded in the history of the early Christian Church, as the voice which was instrumental in making Alexander bishop of Jerusalem, and that which exhorted Polycarp to be of good courage (Eusebius, *Hist. Eccles.* iv, 15; vi, 11). See BATH-KOL.

Words of Institution are those words which were used by our Saviour when he instituted the sacrament of his body and blood, the essential parts of which are commonly held to be "This is my body" and "This is my blood of the New Testament," words found in all the ancient liturgies.

Wordsworth, CHRISTOPHER, D.D., an English prelate, nephew of the poet, was born in 1807. He graduated from Trinity College, Cambridge, in 1830; was elected a fellow, ordained, and in 1836 appointed public orator at Cambridge and head-master of Harrow School; in 1844 canon in Westminster, and bishop of Lincoln in 1869, a position which he held until his death, March 20, 1885. He was of the Low-church or evangelical type, and the author of numerous critical and historical works, the most important being his *Holy Bible, with Annotations* (Lond. 1856-76, 10 vols.). See COMMENTARY.

Wörger, FRANZ, a Protestant theologian of Germany, was born at Lubeck in 1647. He studied at different universities, became preacher of St. Laurence, in his native place, in 1673, was suspended in 1692 on account of his great zeal, and disobedience against the magistrate, and died, as a private scholar, in 1708. He was a voluminous writer. See Seelen, *Athenæ Lubecenses;* Moller, *Cimbria Litterata;* Jöcher, *Allgemeines Gelehrten-Lexikon*, s. v.; Winer, *Handbuch der theol. Lit.* i, 567. (B. P.)

Works (ἔργα), "works, or deeds, of the law," is equivalent to the works which the law requires, or the entire performance of those works which the *moral* law, whether written or unwritten, i. e. law in general, whether applicable to Gentile or Jew, demands (Rom. ii, 15; iii, 20; ix, 12, 32; x, 6; xi, 3; Gal. ii, 16; iii, 2, 5, 10; Eph. ii, 9). On the ground of works, i. e. of perfect obedience and therefore of merit, none can be justified, because "all have sinned and come short of the glory of God." If, then, any are justified at all, it must be of *grace;* but this grace, although freely bestowed and without any just claims on the part of the sinner, is still *not unconditionally* bestowed. *Faith* in him who died to save sinners is requisite to prepare one for the reception of pardon; and he who is justified in this way, as a consequence of his faith, is still justified in a manner altogether gratuitous.

The reader will mark the difference between the phrase "works of the law," in the above passages, and the expression "work of faith" or "good works" (1 Thess. i, 3; 2 Thess. i, 11; 2 Cor. ix, 8; Ephes. ii, 10; Col. i, 10; 1 Tim. v, 10, 25; vi, 18; 2 Tim. iii, 17; Titus i, 16; ii, 7, 14; iii, 1, 8, 14). In the writings of Paul, *works of the law* always designates the idea of *perfect* obedience, i. e. doing all which the law requires. But *works of faith* or *good works* are the fruits of sanctification by the Spirit of God; the good works which Christians perform, and which are sincere, are therefore acceptable to God under a dispensation of grace, although they do not fulfil all the demands of the law. On the ground of the first, Paul earnestly contends, at length, in his epistles to the Romans and Galatians, that no one can be justified. The latter he everywhere treats as indispensable to the Christian character. So also the apostle James, when disputing with those who make *pretensions* to Christian faith, and mere pretensions, maintains that no man has any good claim to the faith of a Christian who does not at the same time exhibit good works; in other words, he avers that a mere speculative faith is not a real Christian faith (James ii, 14-26). In a word, Paul has taught us that justification is not on the ground of merit, but of grace: James has taught us that a faith which will entitle one to hope for justification must be accompanied with evangelical obedience. Both are true and faithful teachers; the doctrines of both are equally the doctrines of the gospel. *Good works*, in the gospel sense of these words, are an essential condition of our acceptance with God; but on the ground of perfect obedience to the divine law, no one ever was or ever will be accepted. See JUSTIFICATION.

In an evangelical sense, *good works* are those actions which spring from pure principles, and are conformable to truth, justice, and propriety; whether natural, civil, relative, moral, or religious. The phrase is often used of acts of charity. The qualities of a good work, in the Scriptural sense of the term, are, (1) That it be according to the will of God; (2) that it spring from love to God (1 Tim. i, 5); (3) that it be done in faith (Rom. xiv, 23); (4) that it be done to the glory of God (1 Cor. x, 31; Phil. i, 11). The causes of good works are, (1) God himself (Heb. xiii, 21); (2) union with Christ (Ephes. ii, 10); (3) through faith (Heb. xi, 4, 6); (4) by the word and spirit (Isa. iii, 3; Luke viii, 15; 2 Tim. iii, 16). As to the nature and properties of good works in this world, (1) They are imperfect (Eccles. vii, 20; Rev. iii, 2; (2) not meritorious (Luke xvii, 10; Titus iii, 5); (3) yet found only in the regenerate (Matt. vii, 17). The necessary uses of good works, (1) They show our gratitude (Psa. cxvi, 12, 13); (2) are an ornament to our profession (Titus ii, 10); (3) evidence our regeneration (Job xv, 5); (4) are profitable to others (Titus iii, 8). See Gill, *Body of Div.* vol. iii, bk. iv.

World is the English term by which our translators have rendered four Hebrew words (in addition to the general term אֶרֶץ, *érits*, "earth"): 1. חֶדֶל, *chédel*, which is erroneously supposed by some to have arisen by transposition of letters from חלד, comes from a root which signifies "to rest," to "discontinue," and hence "to cease from life," "to be at rest;" and as a noun, "the place of rest," "the grave." The word occurs in the complaint uttered by Hezekiah, when in prospect of dissolution, and when he contemplates his state among the inhabitants, not of the upper, but the lower world (Isa. xxxviii, 11); thus combining with many other passages to show that the Hebrews, probably borrowing the idea from the Egyptian tombs, had a vague conception of some shadowy state where the manes of their departed friends lay at rest in their ashes, retaining only an indefinable personality in a land of darkness and "the shadow of death" (Job x, 21, 22). 2. חֶלֶד, *chéled* (Psa. xlii, 14), means "to conceal," and derivatively "any hidden thing," hence "age," "antiquity," "remote and hidden ages;" also "the world," as the hidden or unknown thing (Psa. xlix, 1). 3. עוֹלָם, *'olâm* (in the New Test. *αἰών*), the root-signification of which is "to hide," denotes a very remote, indefinite, and therefore unknown period in time past or time to come, which metaphysicians call eternity à parte ante, and eternity à parte post (Eccles.

iii, 11). In Psa. lxxiii, 12, it is rendered "world;" but in this and in the previous instance it may be questioned whether the natural creation is really meant, and not rather "the world" in our metaphorical use of the term, as denoting the intelligent world, the rational inhabitants of the earth, and still more specifically that portion of them with which we are immediately concerned. 4. תֵּבֵל, *tebêl* (the usual word so rendered the Greek κόσμος), comes from a root that signifies "to flow," and as water is the unfailing cause of fertility in the East, it denotes "to be productive," "to bear fruit;" and as a noun, "the fruit-bearer," that is, the earth. This word is frequently rendered "world" in the common version, but if more was intended than the earth on which we dwell, it may be doubted if the passages in which it occurs will justify the translators.

In truth, the Hebrews had no word which comprised the entire visible universe. When they wanted to speak comprehensively of God's creation, they joined two words together and used the phrase "heaven and earth" (Gen. i, 1). We have already seen that they had an idea of an under world; the meaning of their ordinary term for earth, אֶרֶץ, which signifies the "lower," shows that they also regarded the earth as beneath the sun; while the term for heaven, שָׁמַיִם, denoting "what is elevated," indicates that their view was that the heavens, or the heights, were above. Above, below, and under—these three relations of space comprehend their conception of the world. See EARTH; HEAVEN.

The following Greek words are also translated "world:" 1. κόσμος, *kosmos*, the world, *universe* (Matt. xiii, 35; xxiv, 21; Luke xi, 50; John xvii, 5, 24; Acts xvii, 24; Rom. i, 20); the inhabitants thereof (1 Cor. iv, 9); also the *earth*, as the abode of man (Matt. xiii, 38; Mark xvi, 15; John i, 9; iii, 19; vi, 14; xvi, 21, 28; xxi, 25; Heb. x, 5; Matt. iv, 8; Rom. i, 8); the *inhabitants* of the earth (Matt. v, 14; John i, 29; iii, 16; xvii, 14, 25; Rom. iii, 6, 19; Heb. xi, 7; 2 Pet. ii, 5; 1 John ii, 2); the *multitude*, as we say "everybody" (John vii, 4; xii, 19; xiv, 22; xviii, 20; 2 Cor. i, 12; 2 Pet. ii, 5); also the *heathen* world (Rom. xi, 12, 15). It likewise designates the *state* of the *world*, as opposed to the kingdom of Christ (Matt. xvi, 26; Mark viii, 36; John xviii, 36; 1 Cor. iii, 22; v, 10; Ephes. ii, 2; Gal. vi, 14; James iv, 4) and men of the world, *worldlings* (John xii, 31; 1 Cor. i, 2; iii, 19; 2 Cor. vii, 10; Phil. ii, 15); also the *Jewish dispensation*, founded on Sinai and ended on Calvary (Ephes. i, 4; 1 Pet. i, 20; Heb. ix, 26). 2. Οἰκουμένη, *Oikouměnè*, the inhabited earth, the *world* as known to the ancients (Matt. iv, 8; xxiv, 14; Luke iv, 5; Rom. x, 18; Heb. i, 6; Rev. xvi, 14); the inhabitants of the earth (Acts xvii, 31; xix, 27; Rev. iii, 10; xii, 9); the Roman empire (Acts xvii, 6; xxiv, 5); Palestine and the adjacent countries (Luke ii, 1; Acts xi, 28). 3. Αἰών, *Aiōn*, the *world*, or *age*, the present *time*, or the future, as implying duration (Matt. xii, 32; Mark x, 50; iii, 28, 29; Luke xviii, 30); the *present world* or *age*, with its cares, temptations, evils, etc. (Matt. xiii, 22; Luke xvi, 8; xx, 34; Rom. xii, 2; 1 Cor. i, 20; ii, 6, 8; 2 Cor. iv, 4; 2 Tim. iv, 10; Tit. i, 12; Gal. i, 4); and men of the world, wicked generation (Ephes. ii, 2; Luke xvi, 8; xx, 34); also the *world itself*, as an object of creation and existence (Matt. xiii, 40; xxiv, 3; Heb. i, 2; xi, 3). This term also denotes the *age* or *world* before the Messiah, i. e. the *Jewish dispensation* (1 Cor. x, 11; Heb. ix, 26); also, after the Messiah, i. e. the *Gospel dispensation* (Heb. ii, 5; vi, 5). See COSMOGONY.

In popular Christian phraseology, *the world* is taken also for a secular life, the present state of existence, and the pleasures and interests which steal away the soul from God. The love of the world does not consist in the use and enjoyment of the comforts God gives us, but in an inordinate attachment to the things of time and sense. We love the world too much (1) when, for the sake of any profit or pleasure, we wilfully, knowingly, and deliberately transgress the commands of God; (2) when we take more pains about the present life than the next; (3) when we cannot be contented, patient, or resigned, under low and inconvenient circumstances; (4) when we cannot part with anything we possess to those who want, deserve, and have a right to it; (5) when we envy those who are more fortunate and more favored by the world than we are; (6) when we honor and esteem and favor persons purely according to their birth, fortunes, and success, measuring our judgment and approbation by their outward appearance and situation in life; (7) when worldly prosperity makes us proud and vain and arrogant; (8) when we omit no opportunity of enjoying the good things of this life; when our great and chief business is to divert ourselves till we contract an indifference for rational and manly occupations, deceiving ourselves, and fancying that we are not in a bad condition because others are worse than we (Jortin, *Sermons*, vol. iii, ser. 9). See Hopkins, *On the Vanity of the World;* Stennet, *Sermon on Conformity to the World;* More, *On Education*, vol. ii, ch. 9; Walker, *Sermons*, vol. iv, ser. 20.

Worm is the rendering, in the A. V., of several Hebrew and one Greek word.

1. *Sâs* (סָס, from its *leaping;* Sept. σής; Vulg. *tinea*) occurs only in Isa. li, 8, "For the *'âsh* (עָשׁ, 'moth') shall eat them up like a garment, and the *sâs* shall eat them like wool." The word probably denotes some particular species of moth, whose larva is injurious to wool, while perhaps the former name is the more general one for any of the destructive *tineæ*, or "clothes-moths." See MOTH.

2. *Rimmâh* (רִמָּה, of uncertain etymology; Sept. σκώληξ, σῆψις, σαπρία; Vulg. *vermis, putredo, tinea*) occurs Exod. xvi, 24; Job vi, 5; xvii, 14; xxi, 26; xxiv, 20; xxv, 6; Isa. xiv, 11, and seems to denote worms in putrid substances, or putridity itself. The Hebrew word points evidently to various kinds of maggots, and the larvæ of insects which feed on putrefying animal matter, rather than to earth-worms. Job, under his heavy affliction, exclaims, "My flesh is clothed with *rimmâh*" (Job vii, 5; see also xvii, 14). There is no reason to doubt that the expression is to be understood literally; a person in Job's condition would very probably suffer from *entozoa* of some kind. In Job xxi, 26; xxiv, 20, there is an allusion to worms (insect larvæ) feeding on the dead bodies of the buried (comp. Ecclus. x, 11; xix, 3; 1 Macc. ii, 62). Our translators, in the well-known passage (Job xix, 26)—"And though after my skin worms destroy this body"—have over-interpreted the words of the original, "My skin shall have been consumed," for there is no mention of worms whatever in the original. These passages, and especially the last, have contributed to the popular impression that the human body, when buried in the grave, is consumed by worms. The Oriental method of burial in wrappers, and of depositing the corpse in caves, etc., would no doubt often afford the spectacle of the human body devoured by the larvæ of different insects; but the allusions in Scripture to such sights do not apply to burial elsewhere, except where the body is buried in a wooden coffin only, in vaults which have communications with the external air, when swarms of a species of fly, of a cimex aspect, insinuate themselves between the lid and lower part of the coffin, and their larvæ batten in the corpse within, while the adult insect sports in the lurid atmosphere of the vault.

3. The distinctive term is *tolâ* (תּוֹלָע, Exod. xvi, 20; Isa. i, 18; Lam. iv, 5), or (fem.) *toleâh*, or *toláath* (תּוֹלֵעָה, or תּוֹלַעַת, Deut. xxviii, 39; Job xxv, 6; Psa. xxii, 6; Isa. xiv, 11; xli, 14; lxvi, 24; Jonah iv, 7; besides the use of the latter in connection with שָׁנִי, together rendered "scarlet" [q. v.]), yet it often stands in parallelism with the preceding term. The manna

that the disobedient Israelites kept till the morning of a week-day "bred worms" (תּוֹלָעִים), and stank (Exod. xvi, 20); while of that kept over the Sabbath and gathered the night before, it is said that "it did not stink, neither was there any worm (רִמָּה) therein." The patriarch uses both terms in Job xxv, 6, where he compares the estate of man to a *rimmâh*, and the son of man to a *toleâh*. Homer also compares a man of inferior consequence to a worm, *ὥστε σκώληξ ἐπὶ γαίῃ κεῖτο ταθείς* (*Iliad*, xiii, 654). תולע is applied to that which preys on human flesh (Job xiv, 11; lxvi, 24); on vegetables, as on the gourd of Jonah (Jonah iv, 7), and on vines (Deut. xxviii, 39). The ancient Hebrews applied such words as indeterminately as the common people now do the words "worm," "fly," etc. Similar indeterminateness attends the Sept. and Vulg. renderings. Aristotle also applies the word *σκώληξ* to the larva of any insect—*τίκτει δὲ πάντα σκώληκα*, "all insects produce a worm" (*Hist. Anim.* v, 19).

The insect which the manna is said to have "bred, when kept till the morning" (Exod. xvi, 20, 24), whatever it was, must be considered as miraculously produced as a punishment for disobedience, since the substance now understood to be the same keeps good for weeks and months, nor did the specimen laid up in the ark breed worms. See MANNA.

An insect is alluded to as injuring vines and grapes (Deut. xxviii, 39; תולע, *σκώληξ*, *vermis*). The Greeks had a distinct name for this insect, and probably as early as the Sept. translation of Exodus was made, *ἴψ* and *ἴξ* (Theophrastus, *De Causis*, iii, 27). It was called by the Latins *involvolus*, *convolvulus*, and *volvox* (Plautus, *Cistell.* act iv, sc. 2; Pliny, *Hist. Nat.* xvii, 28). Rosenmüller thinks it was the *Scarabæus hirtellus*, or the *Scarabæus muticus hirtus testaceo-nigricans* of Linnæus (*Syst. Nat.* I, iv, 1577) Forskål calls it the *Pyralis vitana*, or *Pyralis fasciana*. Various kinds of insects attack the vine, among which one of the most destructive is the *Tortrix vitisana*, the little caterpillar of which eats off the inner parts of the blossoms, the clusters of which it binds together by spinning a web around them. A species of beetle, *Lethrus cephalotes*, is injurious to the vines of Hungary; other species of beetles do similar mischief (*rynchites*, *bacchus*, *eumolpus*). Vine-leaves in France are frequently destroyed by the larva of a moth, *Tortrix vitana*. In Germany another species does great injury to the young branches, preventing their expansion by the webs in which it involves them; and a third species, *Tortrix fasciana*, makes the grapes themselves its food (Kirby and Spence, *Introd. to Entomology* [Lond. 1828], i, 205). It may serve as an illustration of the looseness of popular diction respecting insects to remark that what the farmers call "the fly" in the turnip is in reality a small species of jumping beetle, for which *turnip-flea* would be a more appropriate name.

The "gourd" of Jonah is said to have been destroyed by "a worm" (Jonah iv, 7; תולעת, *σκώληξ*, *vermis*). The identity of the gourd with the *Ricinus communis* has been thought to be well established (see GOURD), and Rumphius (*Herbar. Amboinens.* iv, 95) testifies to the ravages of a species of black caterpillar upon it. These are produced, he says, in great quantities in the summer-time, during a gentle rain, and eat up the leaves of the *Palma Christi*, and gnaw its branches to the pith in a single night (Michaelis, *Suppl. ad Lex. Hebraic.* p. 2187). Allusions to the *worm in wood* occur in the Sept. of Prov. xii, 4, and xxv, 20: *ἐν ξύλῳ σκώληξ*; Vulg. *vermis ligno*, which words have nothing corresponding to them in the present Hebrew text (see Vulg. of 2 Kings xxiii, 8).

It is possible that the word תולע was also given as a proper name; thus "Tola" occurs among the descendants of Issachar (Gen. xlvi, 13), and was also the name of a person of the same tribe (Judg. x, 1). Bochart conjectures that the name was given to these children by their parents because the tribe of Issachar was one of the meanest, and they were themselves in needy circumstances, or that these were very sickly children when born. He remarks, however, that the first Tola became a great man, the head of the Tolaites (Numb. xxvi, 23), who, in the days of David, amounted to 22,600 (1 Chron. vii, 2), and that the latter judged Israel twenty years (Judg. x, 1, 2).

4. In Mic. vii, 17 the words "like worms of the earth" represent the Heb. בְּזֹחֲלֵי אֶרֶץ, lit. "creepers in the dust," "serpents;" Vulg. *Reptilia terræ* (comp. Deut. xxxii, 24).

5. The usual Greek word for worm is *σκώληξ*. In 1 Macc. ii, 62, "Fear not the words of a sinful man, for his glory shall be dung and worms," instead of *κοπρία*, "dung," should be read *σαπρία*, "rottenness," as in the Sept. of Job vii, 5; xxv, 6. So also in Ecclus. xix, 3, "Moths and worms shall have him that cleaveth to harlots," instead of *σῆτες*, "moths," read *σήπη*, "rottenness."

"Worm" occurs in the New Test. in a figurative sense only (Mark ix, 44, 46, 48), "Their worm dieth not, and the fire is not quenched;" words borrowed from Isa. lxvi, 24, which originally relate to a *temporal* state of things, but which had also become, in our Lord's time, the popular representation of future punishment (Jud. xvi, 17; Ecclus. vii, 17). See TOPHET. Origen here understands "worm" in a metaphorical sense, as denoting the accusation of conscience; but Austin, Chrysostom, Cyril of Alexandria, Theophylact, etc., contend that the word should be understood literally.

The death of Herod Agrippa I was caused by worms (*σκωληκόβρωτος*, Acts xii, 23); according to Josephus (*Ant.* xix, 8, 2), his death took place five days after his departure from the theatre. It is curious that the Jewish historian makes no mention of worms in the case of Agrippa, though he expressly notes it in that of Herod the Great (*Ant.* xvii, 6, 5; *War*, i, 33, 5). A similar death was that of Antiochus Epiphanes (2 Macc. ix, 9; see also Eusebius, *Eccles. Hist.* viii, 16; Lucian, *Pseudomant*, i, 904; comp. Wetstein on Acts xii, 23). Whether the worms were the cause or the result of the disease is an immaterial question. The "angel of the Lord struck Herod" with some disease, the issue of which was fatal, and the loathsome spectacle of which could not fail to have had a marked humiliating effect on his proud heart. It has been attempted to explain all these instances as cases of phthiriasis, or the *lousy* disease, but the conjecture is inconsistent with the words employed in the several narratives; and since they are instances of persons being devoured by *worms* while *alive*, contrary to the order of nature, we are compelled to ascribe the phenomenon to divine agency. At all events, the larvæ in Herod's case were internal. On the other hand, the cruel Pheretima, the wife of Battus, whose horrible vengeance is detailed by Herodotus (*Hist.* iv, 202–204), is described by him as dying under a disease which, from the terms he uses, must have been peculiarly terrible. "She died miserably; for even while alive *she swarmed with maggots*. So odious to the gods are the excesses of human vengeance." The word *εὐλαί*, which the father of history employs in this passage, is generally considered as synonymous with *σκώληξ*, inasmuch as it signifies the maggots or larvæ produced by the carrion-eating flies; but the two terms are not equivalent, since the Greek *σκώληξ* has a wider meaning, including all insect larvæ without an exception (Arist. *Hist. Anim.* ii, 1). For the account of insects infesting the human frame, from disease, see Kirby and Spence, *Introd. to Entomology*, i, 84; Bartholin, *Morb. Bibl.* c. 23; Mead, *Bibl. Diseases*, c. 15.

There are several species of earth-worms (*lambricus*) in Palestine similar to our own, but by far the most abundant of the so-called worms there are the *myriapoda*, or mellipedes, especially the *scolopendra*, which appear to perform the functions of the earth-worm in nature, though belonging to a very different order of animal life, and which supply food to many of the birds of the country (Tristram, *Nat. Hist. of the Bible*, p. 301). On the general subject, see Bochart, *Hieroz.* (ed. Rosenmüller, Leipsic, 1793-96), iii, 519 sq.

Worm, CHRISTIAN, a Protestant theologian of Germany, who died in 1737, professor of theology and bishop of Seeland, is the author of, *De Corruptis Antiquitatum Hebraicarum apud Tacitum et Martialem Vestigiis* (Hafniæ, 1693, 1694):—*De Corruptione Antiquitatum Hebr. apud Tacitum* (reprinted in Ugolino's *Thesaurus Antiquitatum Hebr. Sacr.* tom. ii):—*Historia Sabelliana seu de Origine et Incrementis Hæreseos Sabellianæ Usque ad Initium Seculi* 5 *Deductæ ex Antiquitate Ecclesiast. Obserwatt.* (Frankfort, 1696). See Fürst, *Bibl. Jud.* iii, 536; Winer, *Handbuch der Theol. Lit.* i, 137, 642. (B. P.)

Worms, COUNCILS OF (*Concilium Vormatiense*). Worms is a city of Germany, in Hesse, province of Rhein-Hessen, on the Rhine, twenty-six miles south-east of Mentz. It was formerly an imperial city, and is very ancient, having existed before the arrival of the Romans. Three ecclesiastical councils have been held there, as follows:

I. Was held in 829. Several regulations were published, one of which condemns the ordeal by cold water; a treatise written by Agobard against these practices is still extant. See Mansi, *Concil.* vii, 1669.

II. Was held May 16, 868, in the presence of Louis of Germany, to which all the bishops of his kingdom were cited. Having drawn up a confession of faith, in which the procession of the Holy Spirit from the Father and the Son was clearly stated, the council proceeded to publish forty-four canons.

1. Forbids to administer holy baptism except at Easter and Whitsuntide, unless in a case of necessity.
2. Orders that the chrism be consecrated by the bishop only.
3. Forbids bishops to exact any fee or present for the consecration of a church; also forbids them to consecrate any church except there be a writing under the hand of the founder, confirming the foundation, and signifying what endowment he has given.
4. Forbids to offer upon the altar for the eucharist anything save bread, and wine mixed with water. States that wine and water should be used, "quia videmus in aqua populum intelligi, in vino vero ostendi sanguinem Christi," and thus, by the union of the water with the wine, the union of Christ with his Church.
5. Approves the regulations of St. Gregory, upon the subject of single and trine immersion.
6. Gives to the bishop, and not to the founders, the disposal of the revenues of new churches.
7. Orders that all offerings and revenues belonging to a church be divided into four portions—one for the bishop, the second for the clerks serving the church (according to their zeal and diligence), the third for the poor, and the fourth to the fabric.
9. Orders the celibacy of the clergy.
13, 14. Forbid excommunication, without weighty and sufficient cause, and declare that the bishop so excommunicating without sufficient cause shall be deprived of the communion of the neighboring bishops.
15. Enacts that when a robbery shall have been committed in any monastery, the thief being unknown, the abbot or some other priest shall celebrate mass, at which all the inmates shall attend, in order by this to prove severally their innocence.
16. Excommunicates bishops who refuse to attend synods, or who retire before the conclusion of business.
17. Orders bishops keeping sporting dogs, or birds, to be suspended for three months; a priest, two; and a deacon, one.
19. Excommunicates and suspends priests who refuse to obey their bishop.
22. Forbids those who, having been in their infancy offered by their parents to some monastery, for the service of God, and who have accordingly been brought up to the regular life, when they come to the age of puberty, to renounce that life and return into the world.
26. Declares that a man who has murdered a priest shall neither eat meat nor drink wine, but fast on every day, except festivals, till the evening; that he shall never carry arms, never go except on foot, nor enter a church for the space of five years; after which he may enter the church, but shall still not be received to communion. At the expiration of ten years he may be received, but shall fast three times a week to his life's end.
28. Orders that a madman who has killed any one shall be put to a light penance should he ever recover his senses.
31. Orders that the holy eucharist be given to lepers.

See Mansi, *Concil.* viii, 941.

III. Was held Sept. 8, 1122. It was settled that all elections of bishops were to be freely conducted according to the laws of the Church, but under the supervision of the emperor; and that the right of spiritual investiture by ring and staff belonged to the pope, while that of secular infiefment with the sceptre was conceded to the emperor. This agreement was confirmed by the first general council of Lateran in 1123.

WORMS, DIET OF, was held in 1521; for an account of which see LUTHER.

WORMS, EDICT OF, was the edict passed at the diet of Worms, which declared Luther a heretic and schismatic. See LUTHER.

WORMS, (RELIGIOUS) COLLOQUIES OF. This title applies to two conferences held at Worms, in Germany, in the 16th century, for the purpose of effecting a reconciliation between the Romish and Protestant parties in the German states.

I. The first Colloquy of Worms formed a link in the long series of negotiations by which it was hoped to render an appeal to the sword unnecessary. It is certain that the desire for peace was very sincere, whether the situation be regarded in its religious or its political features. The Augsburg Confession, though the ultimatum of the Protestant party at the time, was yet intended to serve as a new basis upon which the entire Church, rather than a separate party, might stand. The Romanists conceded the need of reforms in the Church, and a spirit of improvement seemed disposed to assert itself even in the immediate vicinage of the pope. The emperor, also, though emphatically rejecting the demands of the evangelical party, evinced an intention to make some concessions in important matters. It was natural, therefore, that the Protestants should indulge the hope of ultimate reconciliation, however strongly a few of the more sagacious minds among them might insist that no solid peace could be thus secured. In its political bearings, the Augsburg Confession led to the formation of the Smalkald League (q. v.), an alliance intended to be wholly defensive in its nature, but nevertheless constituting a powerful influence in favor of peace, by reason of the general complication in which the affairs of the empire were involved. The result of these conditions was an alternation of warlike preparation with efforts to preserve the peace, continued through more than a decade of years.

The Reformation had been able, in about twenty years, to extend its rule over regions previously regarded as the strongholds of Romanism, and seemed likely to obtain control of the whole of North Germany. A majority of the electoral college, too, was on its side. These facts, coupled with the pressure brought to bear by the offensive operations of the Turks on the one hand, and the hostile attitude of France on the other, compelled the emperor to give respectful attention to Protestant grievances and demands, and to arrange for a conference which should attempt a reconciliation upon disputed matters of doctrine, such as had been suggested in 1539. The assembly was appointed to meet at Spires, April 2, 1540, but was compelled by an epidemic to convene at Hagenau instead, in June of that year. A preliminary meeting of Romanists, called by king Ferdinand, had been held in May, however, in which Morone, the papal legate, aided by the emperor and king, who imagined the holding of a national council to be contrary to the interests of the empire, was able to start a train of influences which led to the breaking-up of the Hagenau Conference before it had fairly begun. The emperor's necessities, however, compelled its revivification, and a decree recalled its members to Worms to open the renewed conference, Oct. 28. The actual date of its opening was, however, Nov. 25, the imperial chancellor, Granvella, presiding. As at Hagenau, the princes were represented by their political and theological agents. Rome was represented by Campeggio, brother to the cardinal, and bishop of Feltre, whose diplomatic ability was equal to the task of preventing the success of this renewed attempt to secure a national council. He proposed that the discussions should be in writing, and that each party should have but one vote, instead of being permitted to secure victory by a majority of individual voices, both of which measures were rejected. Granvella's proposition, however, that a single theologian from either party should represent his side, but that any member of the conference should be at liberty to add whatever he might deem proper, was rejected by the nuncio, and afterwards admitted only with the proviso that such additions might be made by a majority of either party only, a minority being allowed to submit their objections in writing to the president and the imperial orator. Discussions respecting such matters of form occupied the whole of December. The business of the conference began Jan. 2, 1541. Melanchthon and Calvin were prominent on the Protestant side, and the former was opposed to his familiar antagonist, Eck, the disputation beginning with the charge, advanced by Eck, that the alterations made in the Augsburg Confession marked a departure from the original ground of that instrument, and the response by Melanchthon that the changes made had respect merely to matters of form. The question of original sin was again taken in hand, but with no result, as might have been expected from a disputation to which a man like Eck, whose vanity would permit no retraction even if he were defeated, was a party. The conference was thus fruitlessly occupied from Jan. 14 to 17, and on the following day an imperial rescript brought the Conference of Worms to a close, and transferred its business to Ratisbon, where a diet of the empire had begun to assemble. The result of that congress demonstrated completely the impossibility of a peaceful settlement of existing differences, and left the prospect dark with clouds of strife, which ultimately burst in the Smalkald war.

Documents relating to the first Colloquy of Worms are quite fully given in *Corp. Reform.* iii, 1132–iv, 90. See, in addition, Raynald, ad ann. 1540, 47–59; Seckendorf, *Hist. Luth.* iii, 21, § 79, 80; Salig, *Hist. d. Augsburg Conf.* I, bk. iii, 2, § 3, 4; Ranke, *Deutsch. Gesch. im Zeitalter d. Reformation*, iv, 151 sq.; Herzog, *Real-Encyklop.* s. v.

II. The Colloquy of 1557 was the last in the series of fruitless endeavors to bring together the now completely divided religious parties of the German empire. Its principal importance, however, consists in its bearing upon the internal conditions of the Protestant Church itself. The religious peace of Augsburg had secured the external interests of that Church for a time; but the rise of Flacianism originated most bitter controversy within its own pale, whose subject was the *Augustana*, the confession upon which the Evangelical Church based its right to recognition itself. There was consequently no desire among theologians for a religious congress, particularly such a congress as was called for by the recess of the Diet of Ratisbon in 1557, which directed that a colloquy between the adherents of the Roman Catholic faith and of the Augsburg Confession should be held. Statesmen, for their part, had learned by repeated experiences to regard such measures as wholly unsuited to accomplish the end in view and give the desired rest to Church and country. The wish of king Ferdinand, however, decided the case, and the colloquy was fixed for August, 1557. A previous diet of Protestant princes was convoked at Frankfort, for the purpose of attempting a reconciliation of parties in the evangelical camp, but without result; and the representatives of Ernestinian Saxony went to Worms instructed to labor that a solid front might be presented to the Roman Catholic foe, but to make the utterance of the Flacian *shibboleth* the condition of any unity that might be reached. The arrival of the delegation from electoral Saxony was delayed, and the Flacianists used the opportunity thus afforded to attempt the proselytizing of the representatives of other governments as they arrived; but in this respect their success was very imperfect. An attack directed against Melanchthon in the assembly of Sept. 4 by the theologians of Weimar was equally without satisfactory result, and even led to threats of excluding the troublesome party from the colloquy, the occasion being marked with great violence and passion. A written condemnation of the corrupters of the Augsburg Confession was finally placed in the hands of the Protestant assessors, with the reservation of liberty to publish the paper if it should become necessary. Melanchthon, against whom all those efforts were principally directed, endeavored to harmonize the conflicting elements, and even drew up a formula of consensus, which amounted to a retraction of the points offensive to Flacianists, but was thwarted in his purpose to restore peace by the obstinacy of others, particularly the Würtembergers.

In the absence of the princes king Ferdinand had appointed the bishop of Spires to preside at Worms, and when that prelate became sick he substituted for him the bishop of Naumburg, Julius von Pflug, the only person, perhaps, besides Melanchthon, who cherished a real desire for reconciliation. Pflug was supported by Seldius, the royal vice-chancellor, and each party had its assessors, adjuncts, auditors, and notaries. The principal collocutors were Melanchthon, Brentius, Mörlin, Schnepf, etc., on the Protestant, and the theologian Canisius and the perverts Staphylus and Wicelius (q. v.) on the Romish, side. A preliminary meeting, for agreement on the methods to be observed in the disputation, was held in September, which, however, served only to begin the series of difficulties encountered in the progress of the conference, and to foretell its failure. Melanchthon made a preliminary statement, unequivocally based on the Augsburg Confession, in behalf of the Protestant party; and Sidonius, speaking for the other party, interposed objections, whose effect the president was able to neutralize only by refusing to receive either statement in documentary form. On Sept. 14 the expectation of ultimate failure to realize the ends hoped for from the conference, which the delegates evidently entertained, found expression in the decision to conduct the disputation in writing—a decision which protracted the debate interminably. On the following day a question of fundamental importance was discussed, upon which the parties came to a disagreement so unqualified that no future reconciliation was possible—the question respecting standards of authority by which to test questions of doctrine, etc. The Romanists proposed and insisted on the *Consensus Patrum* as such a standard, but the Protestants interposed a formal protest against the proposition. The attempt to ignore the fundamental character of this difference, made by introducing and proceeding to discuss the doctrine of original sin, met with failure; and as it was now evident that no agreement could be reached where the opposing principles were so surely destructive of each other, the Romish party adopted the tactics of exciting quarrels among their opponents, which should necessitate the adjournment of the conference. Canisius called attention to the many alterations made in the *Augustana*, and Sidonius demanded that the evangelicals should declare whether Zwinglians and Calvinists on the sacraments, Osiandrians on justification, Flacianists with respect to the *De Servo Arbitrio* and good works, and the Picards on many points, were judged to be beyond the pale of the Augsburg Conference. The Weimar theologians now submitted their hitherto unpublished protestation to the president and the Romish councillors, despite the opposition of the Protestant assessors and the threat that they should be excluded from the congress. Duke John Frederic the Intermediate attempted, by personal intervention, to influence Melanchthon to favor the Weimar party, but that theologian could lay the blame for the failure of the colloquy at no other door than that of the Weimar delegation, and was, besides, too closely united with the Würtembergers to become the ally of Weimar. The Flacianists thereupon wrote to Pflug to explain their action, and to protest against their exclusion from the congress; and the Romish assessors, etc., voted against the continuation of the colloquy, on the ground that it was no longer possible to determine the party with which the disputation ought, by the terms of the Ratisbon recess, to be held. Both protestations were officially acknowledged by Pflug, Oct. 6. Duke Christopher of Saxony sent other theologians, but the Romanists persisted in their refusal to dispute. A delegation of French Protestants arrived at this precise juncture to invoke the good offices of their coreligionists with Henry II, who had incarcerated one hundred and thirty-five members of the Evangelical Church in Paris, and their arrival complicated matters by raising the question whether adherents of the Augsburg Confession could properly take action in favor of members of the Reformed churches; and the difficulty was still further aggravated by a violent controversial sermon, with which George Major, at Leipsic, responded to the charges submitted by the Weimarians at Worms. The protest rendered Oct. 21 by the evangelical party, in which they charged the failure of the colloquy upon the Romish opponents, though in some respects authorized, was yet neutralized by the irreconcilable differences which were thus shown to exist among its alleged supporters, and elicited no response. All the papers relating to the colloquy were sent to Ferdinand, and the members of the congress scattered. A royal rescript was received, Nov. 16, ordering, if possible, a renewal of the colloquy, in which the Weimar theologians should be allowed to participate, and in connection with which the Romish party should be satisfied with a general profession of adherence to the Augsburg Confession on the part of its opponents. A long series of protests and responses was the result of this order, whose persistency finally exhausted even the patience of Pflug. He forwarded the whole collection to the king, and reported the impossibility of securing the results desired from a disputation. The last official attempt to unite the two opposing religious parties of Germany was ended.

For documentary sources, see *Corp. Reform.* vol. ix, and Raynald, ad ann. 1557, No. 31-35. The most thorough presentation of the colloquy is that of Salig, *Hist. d. Augsburg Conf.* iii, 9, 1; see also Planck, *Gesch. d. Prot. Lehrbegriffs*, iii, 8, 8; Bucholtz, *Gesch. Ferdinands I*, vii, 5; Herzog, *Real-Encyklop.* s. v.

Wormwood, STAR OF (ἀστὴρ ἄψινθος, Rev. viii, 10, 11), the Apocalyptic appellation for the national dæmon of Egypt, set forth in the vision of Patmos as a luminous *idol* presiding over "the third part of the waters." The vocation of this star was to destroy by *poison*, not by fire, sword, or famine; hence the Talmudic phrase "poison in Egypt" is put in opposition to food or "corn in Ephraim" as the symbol of blasphemy and idolatry (Bab. Talmud, *Menacoth*, fol. 85, 1). Philo also, speaking of Helicon, "the scorpion-like slave," represents him as having cast up τὸν Αἰγυπτιακὸν ἰόν, "the Egyptian venom," against the dwellers in Palestine (*De Legat.* p. 102, ed. Turneb.). Daniel gives a clear intimation of his acquaintance with the prevalent belief that, like Persia, Greece, and Judæa, every nation had a celestial prince or patron, שַׂר, *sar*, or *sir* (Dan. x, 21). This *sar lameala*, "prince on high," of the rabbins had also a representative image in the material firmament (rabbi Salomon on Dan. xi, 1), some (הֵילֵל, *hêlel*) glittering son of the morning (Isa. xiv, 12), or "light of lights" (*morê reô*) among the splendid stars or intercessors above (*Melitim*, Ezek. xxxii, 7, 8), who were "darkened" when Pharaoh was extinguished. Eusebius (*Demons. Evang.* iv, 8, 10) and Iamblichus (*De Ægyptiorum Mysteriis*, § v, c. 25) both mention "the angels who preside over the nations;" and rabbi Solomon, the chief of the Gallican synagogue in his day, affirms that "before God wreaks his vengeance on a people he punishes their *prince*, because it is written, 'The Lord shall punish *the host of the high ones* on high,' and then follows '*and* the kings of the earth upon the earth;' and, moreover, it is written, 'How art thou fallen, O Lucifer, son of the morning!'" (*Comment. on Isa.* xiii, 13). Hence, as the literal fulfilment of Isa. xxiv, 21, the Jews yet anticipate "the extirpation of all the Gentiles, with their princes on high and their (pretended) gods" (*Nizzehon*, p. 255, in Wagenseil's *Tela Ignea*).

John seems to employ this symbol of Egyptian poison and bitterness, as the prototype of a great anti-Christian power, which would poison and embitter the pure waters of Christian life and doctrine, converting them into "wormwood," *mitzraim* being a figure of apostasy and rebellion. See STAR.

Woronicz, JAN PAWEL, an eminent Polish prelate and writer, was born in 1757. He was educated in a Jesuit seminary, entered that order at an early age, and on its abolition, in 1772, entered the Society of Missionaries. In consideration of important literary services rendered bishop Cholm, then vice-chancellor, he was rewarded with the deanship of Lvov. In 1795 he retired to the small town of Kazimierz, and took upon him the duties of a parish priest. When the duchy of Warsaw was formed, in 1808, he was made both a member of the council and dean in the chapter of the cathedral. In 1815 he became bishop of Cracow, and in 1827 archbishop of Warsaw and primate of Poland. Going abroad for medical advice, he died at Vienna, Oct. 16, 1829. He published, among other works, *Sibylla*, a poem:—*Sejm Wislicki*, or the *Diet of Wislica*, also a poem. His sermons were published at Cracow in 1829, under the title of *Kazania, ezyli Nauki Parafjalne.*

Worrell, CHARLES FLAVEL, D.D., a Presbyterian minister, was born in Chester County, Pa., June 30, 1805. He graduated from Lafayette College in 1836, and from Princeton Theological Seminary in 1840. He was licensed by the Presbytery of Newton in 1839. During his last year in the seminary he supplied the churches of Knowlton and Blairstown, N. J., preaching half of his time in Titusville. He was ordained an evangelist by the Newton Presbytery, and supplied the Upper Freehold (now Perrineville) Church for two years, when he was installed pastor. He labored here for twenty-five years, when he was released, in 1868, and supplied the Plumsted Church at New Egypt for one year. His next charge was at Squan Village, where he was installed in 1880. He then retired in very infirm health to his farm in Perrineville, and gradually declined until his death, Jan. 27, 1881. See *Necrol. Report of Princeton Theol. Sem.* 1881, p. 58. (W. P. S.)

Worship (properly some form of שָׁחָה, especially in Hithpael; λατρεία), homage paid to a superior, especially to God (which we consider only), usually expressed by prayer, sacrifice, and ritual. See each term in its place; also ADORATION.

I. *General View.*—The homage of the progenitors of our race was the direct and simple effusion of gratitude (see Schröder, *De Prima Cultus Divini Publici Institutione*, Marburg, 1745). There can be no doubt that the Most High, whose essence no man hath seen, or can see, was pleased to manifest himself in Eden, by an external symbol, to the eyes of his innocent worshippers. This divine manifestation is called the presence of the Lord; and may have been in connection with the tree of life in the midst of the garden (Gen. ii, 9; iii, 8).

After the first transgression the mode of the divine manifestation was altered; and a mediatorial economy was established. Henceforth, the homage paid by man was the service of a creature conscious of crime, approaching God through the medium of sacrifice, pleading for forgiveness, and confiding in mercy. Though the divine manifestation was no longer immediate, yet a visible symbol of Jehovah was still vouchsafed in the *Shekinah* or visible glory, from which Cain was exiled (Gen. iv, 16; comp. 2 Thess. i, 9; Psa. xcvi, 8); which was *seen* by Abraham (Acts vii, 2); by Moses and the people (Exod. iii, 2-6; xiii, 21, 22; xxiv, 16, 18; Numb. xiv, 10; xvi, 19, 42); by the high-priest (Exod. xxv, 22; Lev. xvi, 2); by Solomon in the temple (1 Kings viii, 10-12); and finally in "the WORD made flesh" (John i, 14).

Since this last visible manifestation, the worship of the Most High, which is no longer external and symbolic, has not been confined to any one place. "God is a Spirit, and they that worship him must worship him in spirit and in truth" (John iv, 21-24). God now manifests himself to the spirits of his faithful worshippers, helping their infirmities. Hence the presence of the Lord is in every place where Christ is active in the Spirit, and where through him, the sole mediator, the faithful pay their homage. As the true worship of God is only in the inward heart, and the whole life a spiritual service, every Christian in particular, and every Church in general, now represent a spiritual temple of the Lord. In the assemblies of the faithful, God by his Spirit diffuses his vital and sanctifying influence, and takes his devout worshippers into fellowship with himself, from which they derive strength to do and suffer his will in the various scenes of life, while he there affords them a foretaste of the deep and hallowed pleasures which are reserved for them in his immediate presence forevermore (Matt. v, 8; Heb. xii, 14). See the monographs cited by Volbeding, *Index Programmatum*, p. 107, 127, 130.

II. *Among the Ancient Israelites.*—1. *In General Acts.*—The forefather of the Hebrew nation, Abraham, appears at the outset as a firm monotheist; but in his migrations there are obscure traces of a lingering idolatry, at least in his family (Gen. xxi, 19, 30; xxxv, 2 sq.; comp. Josh. xxiv, 2, 14; Jud. v, 6 sq.; see Jonathan, *Targ.* on Gen. xxxi, 19; also Sonne, *Der Gott Abraham's* [Hanover, 1806]). See TERAPHIM. The worship of the patriarchs (Ben-David, *Ueb. die Relig. der Ebräer vor Moses* [Berlin, 1812], contains strange hypotheses) was exceedingly simple, consisting of offerings and prayer (Gen. xxiv, 63), presented at whatever place of residence, although very early particular spots seem to have been held sacred (i. e. where God had specially manifested himself; see Gen. xii, 7, 8 [comp. xiii, 4]; xlvi, 1 [comp. xxvi, 23]; e. g. anointed pillars, Gen. xxviii, 18; xxxv, 14), heights having the preference to plains (Gen. xxii, 2; xxxi, 54; see Creuzer, *Symbol.* i, 158 sq.; Zachariä, *De More Vett. in Locis Editis Colendi Deum* [Halle, 1704]). See HIGH-PLACE. Subsequently worship was held under (shady) trees and in groves (Gen. xiii, 18; xxi, 33; comp. Tacit. *Germ.* xxxix, 7; Callim. *In Dian.* xxxviii; Soph. *Trach.* 754; Ovid, *Fast.* iii, 295; Apollon. *Rhod.* iv, 1714; see Woken, *De Locis Temporibusque quæ Fideles, Ante Legem Cerimon. Preces Destinerunt* [Rostock, 1720]; Doughtæi *Analect.* i, 24 sq.). See GROVE. In the offerings the ruling idea was that of thanking and propitiating God in general, the proper notion of expiation not yet appearing. See OFFERING. The priests were the heads of the families. See MELCHIZEDEK.

In Egypt the larger part of the Israelites may perhaps have been more or less addicted to nature worship (see Exod. xxxii; Lev. xvii, 7; Josh. xxiv, 14; Ezek. xx, 7), and in the desert traces of Sabaism are evident (Numb. xxv; Amos v, 25 sq.). Moses, however, established the cultus of Jehovah as the exclusive religion, and to him the strict rule of monotheism is due. The ritual of the law is no copy of the Egyptian (Spener) nor of the Phœnician (Vatke) institutions, although particular features may have been derived from the former (Hengstenberg, *Moses*, p. 147 sq.; Bähr, *Symbol.* i, 39 sq.), but recognised Jehovah as the sole national deity, and stood in direct personal as well as public relation to him. See LAW. It contained a multitude of special provisions (such as sacrifices, vows, fasts, etc.), both of a positive and a negative kind, pointing to God as the giver of all good, and the object of all moral obligation, both of blessing and atonement; especially embodying the distinction of *clean and unclean* in all the bodily relations of life. The cardinal sections of this cultus are marked by the regularly recurring festivals (q. v.), and the tabernacle and temple were its central rallying-points as a national system of observance, while the priesthood formed its official conservators and expounders. See PRIEST.

The most marked of its peculiar features were the *invisible* character of the deity adored, in which it stood in bold contrast with all the prevalent idolatries; and the *universality* of its prescriptions, as pertaining not only to the whole nation, but to every individual in it, and to the minutest affairs of social and private economy. See MOSAISM.

In later times, especially after the exile, the national worship was in some degree affected by foreign subjugation, and in process of time abnormal elements gradually crept in, such as Sadduceeism and Essenism. Under Antiochus Epiphanes a violent effort was made to force paganism bodily upon the Jews, but it succeeded only to a small extent. Under the Ptolemies full toleration was allowed, and under Alexander extraordinary privileges were granted even to foreign Jews. During all this period the heathen rulers occasionally contributed to the Mosaic worship (see Ezra vi, 9; 1 Macc. x, 34; 2 Macc. iii, 3; Josephus, *Ant.* xii, 3, 3; xiv, 10-23). It is well known that under the Roman rule, the Jews, even in Rome itself (Dio Cass. xxxvii, 17), were allowed the full exercise of their religion (see Zimmern, *Gesch. d. röm. Privatrechts*, I, ii, 470; Levysohn, *De Judæor. sub Cæsar. Conditione* [L. B. 1828]). See JUDAISM.

2. *In Prayer Particularly.*—This, as constituting the central idea of worship, was always strictly, although not formally, understood in the Mosaic service. There are no directions as to prayer given in the Mosaic law; the duty is rather taken for granted, as an adjunct to sacrifice, than enforced or elaborated. The temple is emphatically designated as "the House of Prayer" (Isa. lvi, 7); it could not be otherwise, if "He who hears prayer" (Psa. lxv, 2) there manifested his special presence; and the prayer of Solomon offered at its consecration (1 Kings viii, 30, 35, 38) implies that in it were offered, both the private prayers of each single man, and the public prayers of all Israel.

It is hardly conceivable that, even from the beginning, public prayer did not follow every public sacrifice, whether propitiatory or eucharistic, as regularly as the incense, which was the symbol of prayer (see Psa. cxli, 2; Rev. viii, 3, 4). Such a practice is alluded to as common in Luke i, 10; and in one instance, at the offering of the first-fruits, it was ordained in a striking form (Deut. xxvi, 12-15). In later times it certainly grew into a regular service, both in the temple and in the synagogue. See SYNAGOGUE.

But, besides this public prayer, it was the custom of all at Jerusalem to go up to the temple, at regular hours if possible, for private prayer (see Luke xviii, 10; Acts iii, 1); and those who were absent were wont to "open their windows towards Jerusalem," and pray "towards" the place of God's presence (1 Kings viii, 46-49; Psa. v, 7; xxviii, 2; cxxxviii, 2; Dan. vi, 10). The desire to do this was possibly one reason, independently of other and more obvious ones, why the house-top or the mountain-top were chosen places of private prayer.

The regular hours of prayer seem to have been three (see Psa. lv, 17; Dan. vi, 10), the "evening," that is, the ninth hour (Acts iii, 1; x, 3), the hour of the evening sacrifice (Dan. ix, 21); the "morning," that is, the third hour (Acts ii, 15), that of the morning sacrifice; and the sixth hour, or "noonday." To these would naturally be added some prayer at rising and lying down to sleep; and thence might easily be developed (by the love of the mystic number seven), the "seven times a day" of Psa. cxix, 164, if this is to be literally understood, and the seven hours of prayer of the ancient Church. Some, at least, of these hours seem to have been generally observed by religious men in private prayer at home, or in the midst of their occupation and in the streets (Matt. vi, 5). Grace before meat would seem to have been an equally common practice (see Matt. xv, 36; Acts xxvii, 35).

The posture of prayer among the Jews seems to have been most often standing (1 Sam. i, 26; Matt. vi, 5; Mark xi, 25; Luke xviii, 11); unless the prayer were offered with especial solemnity and humiliation, which was naturally expressed by kneeling (1 Kings viii, 54; comp. 2 Chron. vi, 13; Ezra ix, 5; Psa. xcv, 6; Dan. vi, 10); or prostration (Josh. vii, 6; 1 Kings xviii, 42; Neh. viii, 6). The hands were "lifted up," or "spread out" before the Lord (Exod. ix, 33; Psa. xxviii, 2; cxxxiv, 2, etc.). In the Christian Church no posture is mentioned in the New Test. excepting that of kneeling; see Acts vii, 60 (St. Stephen); ix, 40 (St. Peter); xx, 36; xxi, 5 (St. Paul); perhaps from imitation of the example of our Lord in Gethsemane (on which occasion alone his posture in prayer is recorded). In after-times, as is well known, this posture was varied by the custom of standing in prayer on the Lord's day, and during the period from Easter to Whitsunday, in order to commemorate his resurrection, and our spiritual resurrection in him. See PRAYER.

II. *Christian Worship.*—This is usually divided into three kinds, according to the extent of the persons engaged in it.

1. *Private Worship*, otherwise called *secret prayer*, is between the individual and his Maker. It is specifically enjoined by our Lord (Matt. vi, 6), and is essential to the maintenance of spiritual life in the soul of the believer. See CLOSET.

The lately discovered *Teaching of the Twelve Apostles* (§ viii) enjoins the use of the Lord's Prayer "three times a day," evidently for private devotion. See LORD'S PRAYER.

Private worship should be conducted with, (1) reverence and veneration; (2) self-abasement and confession; (3) contemplation of the perfections and promises of God; (4) supplication for ourselves and others; (5) earnest desire of the enjoyment of God; (6) frequency and regularity. See DEVOTION.

2. *Family Worship*, i. e. regular domestic prayer. This is obviously called for in order to the proper religious conduct of the Christian household, and its obligation is enforced by nearly every branch of evangelical Christendom. See FAMILY.

3. *Public Worship*, i. e. religious services conducted in the general congregation. Some who have acknowledged the propriety of private worship have objected to that of a public nature, but without any sufficient ground. For Christ attended public worship himself (Luke iv); he prayed with his disciples (Luke ix, 28, 29; xi, 1); he promises his presence to social worshippers (Matt. xviii, 20). It may be argued also from the conduct of the apostles (Acts i, 24; ii; iv, 24; vi, 4; xx, 36; Rom. xv, 30; 1 Cor. xiv; 2 Thess. iii, 1, 2; 1 Cor. xi) and from general principles (Deut. xxxi, 12; Psa. c, 4; 1 Tim. ii, 2, 8; Heb. x, 25).

The obligation of public worship is partly founded upon example, and partly upon precept; so that no person who admits that authority can question this great duty without manifest and criminal inconsistency. The institution of public worship under the law, and the practice of synagogue worship among the Jews, from at least the time of Ezra, cannot be questioned; both of which were sanctioned by the practice of our Lord and his apostles. The preceptive authority for our regular attendance upon public worship is either inferential or direct. The command to publish the gospel includes the obligation of assembling to hear it; the name by which a Christian society is designated in Scripture is a Church, which signifies an assembly for the transaction of business; and, in the case of a Christian assembly, that business must necessarily be spiritual, and include the sacred exercises of prayer, praise, and hearing the Scriptures.

But we have more direct precepts, although the practice was obviously continued from Judaism, and was therefore consuetudinary. Some of the epistles of Paul are commanded to be read in the churches. The singing of psalms, hymns, and spiritual songs is enjoined as an act of solemn worship to the Lord; and Paul cautions the Hebrews that they "forsake not the assembling of themselves together." The practice of the primitive age is also manifest from the epistles of Paul. The Lord's Supper was celebrated by the body of believers collectively; and this apostle prescribes to the Corinthians regulations for the exercises of prayer and prophesyings, "when they came together in the Church"—the assembly. The periodicity and order of these holy offices in the primitive Church, appear also from the apostolic epistle of Clement of Rome: "We ought also, looking into the depths of the divine knowledge, to do all things in order, whatsoever the Lord hath commanded to be done. We ought to make our oblations, and perform our holy offices, at their appointed seasons; for these he hath commanded to be done, not irregularly or by chance, but at determinate times and hours; as he hath likewise ordained by his supreme will where, and by what persons, they shall be performed; that so all things being done according to his pleasure, may be acceptable in his sight." This passage is remarkable for urging a divine authority for the public services of the Church, by which Clement, no doubt, means the authority of the inspired directions of the apostles. See SERVICE.

The ends of the institution of public worship are of such obvious importance that it must ever be considered as one of the most condescending and gracious dispensations of God to man. By this his Church confesses his name before the world; by this the public teaching of his word is associated with acts calculated to affect the mind with that solemnity which is the best preparation for hearing it to edification. It is thus that the ignorant and the vicious are collected together, and instructed and warned; the invitations of mercy are published to the guilty, and the sorrowful and afflicted are comforted. In these assemblies God, by his Holy Spirit, diffuses his vital and sanctifying influence, and takes the devout into a fellowship with himself, from which they derive strength to do and to suffer his will in the various scenes of life, while he there affords them a foretaste of the deep and hallowed pleasures which are reserved for them at his right hand forevermore. Prayers and intercessions are offered for national and public interests, and while the benefit of these exercises descends upon a country, all are kept sensible of the dependence of every public and personal interest upon God. Praise calls forth the grateful emotions, and gives cheerfulness to piety; and that instruction in righteousness, which is so perpetually repeated, diffuses the principles of morality and religion throughout society, enlightens and gives activity to conscience, raises the standard of morals, attaches shame to vice and praise to virtue, and thus exerts a powerfully purifying influence upon mankind. Laws thus receive a force which, in other circumstances, they could not acquire, even were they enacted in as great perfection; and the administration of justice is aided by the strongest possible obligation and sanction being given to legal oaths. The domestic relations are rendered more strong and interesting by the very habit of the attendance of families upon the sacred services of the sanctuary of the Lord; and the meeting of the rich and the poor together, and their standing on the same common ground as sinners before God, equally dependent upon him, and equally suing for his mercy, has a powerful, though often an insensible, influence in humbling the pride which is nourished by superior rank, and in raising the lower classes above abjectness of spirit, without injuring their humility. Piety, benevolence, and patriotism are equally dependent for their purity and vigor upon the regular and devout worship of God in the simplicity of the Christian dispensation.

Public worship therefore is of great utility, as (1) it gives Christians an opportunity of openly professing their faith in and love to Christ; (2) it preserves a sense of religion in the mind, without which society could not well exist; (3) it enlivens devotion and promotes zeal; (4) it is the means of receiving instruction and consolation; (5) it affords an excellent example to others, and excites them to fear God, etc.

Public worship should be (1) solemn, not light and trifling (Psa. lxxxix, 7); (2) simple, not pompous and ceremonial (Isa. lxii, 2); (3) cheerful, and not with forbidding aspect (Psa. c); (4) sincere, and not hypocritical (Isa. i, 12; Matt. xxiii, 13; John iv, 24); (5) pure, and not superstitious (Isa. lvii, 15). See PUBLIC WORSHIP.

WORSHIP OF IMAGES. See IMAGE-WORSHIP.

WORSHIP OF SAINTS. See INVOCATION OF SAINTS.

WORSHIP OF THE VIRGIN MARY. See MARIOLATRY.

Worshipper is a translation of the Greek word *νεωκόρος*, used once only (Acts xix, 35; marg. "temple-keeper"). The *neocoros* was originally an attendant in a temple, probably intrusted with its charge (Eurip. *Ion* [ed. Dindorf], p. 115, 121; Plato, *Leg.* [ed. Bekker], vi, 7; Theodoret, *Hist. Eccles.* iii, 14, 16; Pollux, i, 14; Philo, *De Prov. Sac.* 6, ii, 237; Hesychius explains it by *ὁ τὸν ναὸν κοσμῶν, κορεῖν γὰρ τὸ σαίρειν*; Suidas, *κοσμῶν καὶ εὐτρεπίζων, ἀλλ' οὐχ ὁ σαρῶν* [ed. Gaisf. p. 2579]). The divine honors paid in later Greek times to eminent persons, even in their lifetime, were imitated and exaggerated by the Romans under the empire, especially in Asia (Plut. *Lys.* p. 23; Appian, *Mithr.* p. 76; Dion Cass. xxxi, 6). The term *neocoros* became thus applied to cities or communities which undertook the worship of particular emperors, even in their lifetime, but there is no trace of the special title being applied to any city before the time of Augustus. The first occurrence of the term in connection with Ephesus is on coins of the age of Nero (A.D. 54–68), a time which would sufficiently agree with its use in the account of the riot there, probably in 55 or 56. In later times the title appears with the numerical adjuncts *δίς*, *τρίς*, and even *τετράκις*. A coin of Nero's time bears on one side *'Εφεσίων νεωκόρων*, and on the reverse a figure of the temple of Artemis (Mionnet, *Inscr.* iii, 93; Eckhel, *Doctr. Vet. Num.* ii, 520). The ancient veneration of Artemis and her temple, on the part of the city of Ephesus, which procured for it the title of *νεωκόρος τῆς 'Αρτέμιδος*, is too well known to need illustration; but in later times it seems probable that with the term *νεωκόρος* the practice of neocorism became reserved almost exclusively for the veneration paid to Roman emperors, towards whom many other cities also of Asia Minor are mentioned as neocorists, e. g. Nicomedia, Perinthus, Sardis, Smyrna, Magnesia (see Herod. i, 26; Strabo, xiv, 640; Aristid. *Or.* [ed. Dindorf], xlii, 775; Mionnet, *Inscr.* iii, 97, Nos. 281, 285; Eckhel, *De Num.* ii, 520, 521; Boeckh, *Inscr.* 2617, 2618, 2622, 2954, 2957, 2990, 2992, 2993; Krause, *De Civ. Neocoris;* Hoffmann, *Lex.* s. v. "Neocoros." See EPHESUS.

Worthington, JOHN T., D.D., a Protestant Episcopal clergyman, was rector at Pittsfield, Ill., several years prior to 1856, and then at Prairieville, Mo. In 1859 he became rector at Louisiana, Mo. The following year he served two churches, viz., Calvary Church, in the same place, and St. Mark's Church, in Bowling Green. He served these two parishes until about 1864, when he fixed his residence at Pittsfield, Ill.; but in 1865 again became rector of Calvary Church, in Louisiana, Mo. The following year he was employed as a missionary at Macon City and Shelbina, and in 1867 officiated at Pittsfield, Ill., where he died in 1868, at the age of sixty-six years. See *Prot. Episc. Almanac*, 1869, p. 109.

Wotjakian Version. See RUSSIA, VERSIONS OF.

Wound (usually מַכָּה, *πληγή*, a *stroke;* but prop. פֶּצַע, *τραῦμα*). The Hebrews had but little knowledge of surgery, less than the Egyptians. They seldom used inward remedies, but trusted mainly to outward applications. Isa. i, 6 illustrates the treatment of wounds; they were "closed," that is, the lips of the wound were pressed together and bound, that cohesion of the parts might be effected. "There was, and is, no sewing up of wounds in the East; and hence the edges, healing without being perfectly united, make the scar of a wound more conspicuous and disfiguring than with us. The only attempt to produce cohesion is by 'binding up' the wound, after the edges have been as far as possible 'closed' by simple pressure" (Kitto, *Daily Bible Illustr.* vi, 25). See MEDICINE.

Wrangel, CHARLES MAGNUS, D.D., a Lutheran clergyman, regarded as the ablest of the early Swedish Lutheran ministers, entered upon his labors in America, as provost or chief pastor of the Swedish churches, in 1759. During his brief ministry here two new churches were built at Kingsessing and at Upper Merion, Pa. He preached with facility and acceptance in Swedish, German, and English. The Synod of Pennsylvania recommended the use of his translation into English of Luther's *Catechism.* He preached, not only throughout Pennsylvania, but occasionally in New Jersey, laboring in company with the Rev. Dr. Muhlenberg. He was a man of culture, large and varied acquisitions, and great eloquence. The crowds that attended his preaching compelled him to hold service in the open air. After a residence of nine years in America he was recalled, and returned to Sweden in 1768, where he received from the government an episcopal appointment. He died in 1786. See (Lond.) *Evangelical Review*, ii, 589.

Wrath is great and permanent anger (q. v.). The wrath of God is his indignation at sin and punishment of it. "For the wrath of God is revealed from heaven against all ungodliness and unrighteousness of men who hold the truth in unrighteousness" (Rom. i, 18). The objects of God's anger or wrath are the ungodly, whom he has declared he will punish. His wrath is sometimes manifested in this life, and that in an awful degree, as we see in the case of the old world, of Sodom and Gomorrah, the plagues of Egypt, the punishment and captivity of the Jews, and the many striking judgments on nations and individuals. But a still more awful punishment awaits the impenitent in the world to come, for the wicked, it is said, shall go away into everlasting punishment (Matt. xxv, 46), where the worm dieth not and the fire is not quenched (see Rom. ii, 8, 9). See MEDIATION; PUNISHMENT.

Wreath (שְׂבָכָה, *sebekâh*, a net-work or lattice [as often rendered], i. e. *balustrade*, 2 Kings xxv, 17; 2 Chron. iv, 12, 13; but perhaps really a festoon or checkerwork, as גְּדִל, *gedîl*, 1 Kings vii, 17 ["fringe," i. e. tassel, Deut. xxii, 12] certainly means). Garlands in ancient times were chiefly made of green leaves or twigs (Wisd. ii, 18), which, among the ancient Israelites, likewise were symbols of joy (3 Macc. vii, 16). Accordingly, victorious chieftains and warriors were crowned with such wreaths (Jud. iii, 8; comp. Herod. i, 7, 11), and they were sometimes strewn in their path (Sueton. *Ner.* xxv; Livy, xxxiii, 33; Curtius, ix, 10, 25). Guests were adorned with them (see Heindorf, *Horat. Satir.* [ii, 3], p. 256) at feasts (3 Macc. iv, 8; comp. Athen. xv, 674); and on gala occasions dwellings and sacred objects were decked with them (1 Macc. iv, 57; Let. of Jer. 9 [in the Apocr. Greek]; see Voss, *Virg. Georg.* p. 826; Orelli, *Arnob.* ii, 43), as likewise sacrificial victims (Herod. iv, 11, 8) and altars (Acts xiv, 13; comp. Herod. ii, 45; Strabo, xv, 732; Pliny, xvi, 4; Ovid, *Met.* v, 366; see Tzetzes, *Lycoph.* p. 327; Wetstein, *N. T.* ii, 543; Doughtaei *Anal.* ii, 81; Perezon. *Ælian. V. H.* iii, 3); and finally the worshippers themselves (Herod. i, 132; Athen. xv, 674; Lucian, *De dea Syr.* xlvi; Tibull. i, 10, 28; ii, 2, 16; Apollon. *Rhod.* ii, 159; see Bähr, *Symbol.* ii, 252). See Stuck, *Antiq. Conviv.* p. 368 sq.; Dieteric and Nikolai, in Ugolini *Thesaur.* xxx. See CROWN.

WREATH, ECCLESIASTICAL, is a circular garland of flowers intertwined; a chaplet; that which is interwoven or entwined. Such symbols were made use of to designate certain saints, and are found represented both in old MSS., stained glass, and on the lower panels of rood-screens. A wreath of flowers, sometimes designated a "marriage crown," was often placed on the head of a virgin bride. Wreaths were also carried at funerals. One, of the 17th century, remains suspended in the south aisle of St. Alban's Abbey. And they were anciently, and are now not uncommonly, put upon graves and memorial crosses. See CORONA.

Wren, *Sir* CHRISTOPHER, an eminent English architect and mathematician, son of Dr. Christopher Wren, was born at Knoyle, in Wiltshire, Oct. 20, 1632, and early discovered a special genius for mathematics. He entered Wadham College, Oxford, at the age of fourteen, and graduated A.B. in 1650. He was then chosen fellow of All-Souls' College, and graduated A.M. in 1652. He was made professor of astronomy in Gresham College, London, in August, 1657, and three years later he received the Savilian professorship at Oxford. In 1661 he was appointed by Charles II assistant to sir John Denham, the surveyor-general, and was commissioned, in 1663, to survey and report upon St. Paul's Cathedral, with a view to its restoration in such a form as to harmonize it with the Corinthian colonnade added to it by Jones. The scheme met with such opposition from many quarters that it was indefinitely postponed. Wren was in the meantime employed on some other buildings, as the Sheldonian Theatre at Oxford, from 1664 to 1669, and the library of Trinity College, Cambridge, which, however, was not built until 1772. He visited Paris in 1665, while the works of the Louvre were in progress. After the great fire of 1666 he began at once a plan for the entire reconstruction of the city of London on a magnificent architectural plan, with wide streets and piazzas at intervals. But the immediate necessities of the citizens prevented the accomplishment of so vast a design, so he was obliged to content himself with labors upon individual structures. Among these were the Royal Exchange, Custom-House (both since destroyed by fire and rebuilt), Temple Bar, the Monument, and some churches, including that of St. Stephen's, Walbrook, all of which were built before St. Paul's was begun. He was busy in the meantime with designs for St. Paul's Cathedral, and when it came to the actual construction of the edifice, the plan which he preferred was rejected, and the one chosen he was compelled to modify contrary to his own judgment. The first stone of the present edifice was laid June 21, 1675, and the last stone on the summit of the lantern was laid by the architect's son, Christopher, in 1710. On the decease of sir John Denham, in March, 1688, Wren succeeded him in the office of surveyor-general of his majesty's works, an office which he held until after the death of queen Anne, in 1714. He had resigned the office of Savilian professor in 1673, and accepted that of president of the Royal Society in 1680. He also sat several times in Parliament, but his numerous and important professional engagements left him little leisure for other pursuits or duties. He was found dead in his chair after dinner, Feb. 25, 1723, and received the honor of a splendid funeral in St. Paul's, where his remains were deposited in a crypt, with no other adornment to his tomb than the inscription, "Si monumentum quæris, circumspice." Among his numerous architectural works not already mentioned are, spire and Church of St. Mary-le-Bow (1671–78); St. Lawrence, Jewry (1671–86); Royal Observatory, Greenwich (1675); Chelsea Hospital (1682–90); St. James's, Westminster (1683); Hampton Court (1690), and towers of the west front of Westminster Abbey (1713). See Chalmers, *Biog. Dict.* s. v.; Knight, *Engl. Cyclop.* s. v.

Wrenning-day, a term used in certain parts of England to designate St. Stephen's day, because on that day a wren was stoned to death, in commemoration of the Christian proto-martyr.

Wrest, a screw in a cross or banner-staff.

Wrestling (נַפְתּוּל, Gen. xxx, 8, figuratively; πάλη, Eph. vi, 12, literally; in Gen. xxii, 25, 26, the verb is אָבַק, used in a literal sense). This was one of the principal exercises in all the public games of Greece. The Greeks ascribed the invention of wrestling to mythical personages, and Mercury, the god of all gymnastic exercises, also presided over wrestling. In the Homeric age wrestling was much practiced; during this period wrestlers contended naked, and only the loins were covered with the *perizoma* (περίζωμα), and this custom probably remained throughout Greece until Ol. 15, from which time even this covering was no longer used, and wrestlers fought entirely naked. In the Homeric age the custom of anointing the body for the purpose of wrestling does not appear to have been known, but in the time of Solon it was quite general, and was said to have been adopted by the Cretans and Lacedæmonians at a very early period. After the body was anointed it was strewed over with sand or dust, in order to enable the wrestlers to take a firm hold of each other. The Greeks, in their combats, were generally matched two against two; but sometimes several couples contended at the same time. In case the whole aim and design of the wrestlers was to throw their adversary upon the ground, both strength and art were employed for this purpose; they seized each other by the arms, drew forward, pushed backwards, used many distortions and twistings of the body, locking their limbs in each other's, lifting from the ground, dashing their heads together, and twisting one another's necks. In this manner the athletes wrestled standing, the combat ending with the fall of one of the competitors. See GAMES.

Ancient Greek Wrestlers.

Among the ancient Egyptians likewise, according to Wilkinson, "wrestling was a favorite amusement; and the painting of the grottoes at Beni Hassan presents all the varied attitudes and modes of attack and defence of which it is susceptible. In order to enable the spectator more readily to perceive the position of the limbs of each combatant, the artist has availed himself of a dark and light color, and even ventured to introduce alternately a black and red figure. It is not, however, necessary to give an instance of every position indicated in those varied subjects; and a selection of the principal groups will suffice to convey some idea of their mode of representing the combatants, and of their general system of attack and defence. It is probable that, like the Greeks, they anointed the body with oil when preparing for these exercises, and they were entirely naked, with the exception of a girdle, apparently of leathern thongs. The two combatants generally approached each other holding their arms in an inclined position before the body, and each endeavored to seize his adversary in the manner best suited to his mode of attack. It was allowable to take hold of any part of the body, the head, neck, or legs; and the struggle was frequently

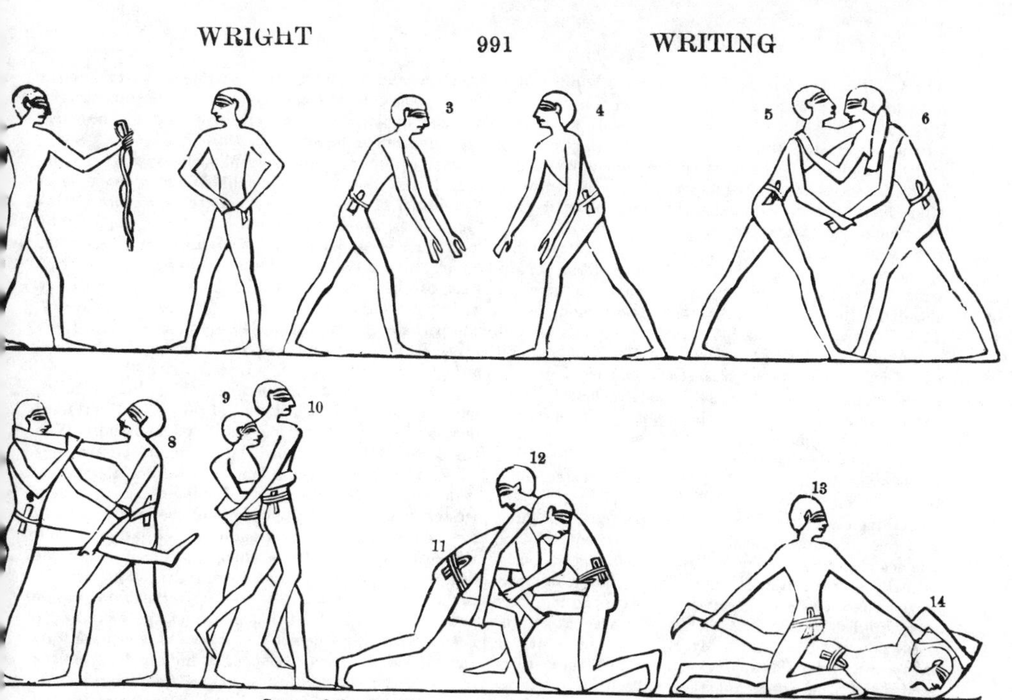

Some of the Positions of Ancient Egyptian Wrestlers.

Fig. 1. A man holding his girdle; 2. Another binding on his girdle; 3, 4. Advancing to the attack; 13, 14. Continuing the attack upon the ground.

continued on the ground, after one or both had fallen, a mode of wrestling common also to the Greeks. I do not find that they had the same sign of acknowledging their defeat in this game as the Greeks, which was by holding up a finger in token of submission; and it was probably done by the Egyptians with a word" (*Anc. Egypt.* i, 204). See SPORT.

Wright, Lyman, D.D., a Baptist minister, was born at Westford, Otsego Co., N. Y., Sept. 28, 1816. He united with the Church Sept. 3, 1831, pursued his studies at Madison University, was ordained as an evangelist Feb. 11, 1838, became pastor at Exeter in 1839, at Cockville in 1841, at Fayetteville in 1845. For one year he was collecting agent of the Missionary Union. In 1854 he became pastor at Norwich, N. Y., in 1858 at Trenton, N. J., returned to Norwich in 1859, where he remained until 1861, when he undertook to raise funds for Madison University. His next pastorate was in Newburgh, from 1864 to 1869, and his next and last in Binghamton, where he died, April 2, 1879. (J. C. S.)

Wright, Robert, D.D., an English prelate, became prebendary of Wells in 1594; bishop of Bristol in January, 1623; of Lichfield and Coventry in 1632, and died in August, 1643. See Allibone, *Dict. of Brit. and Amer. Authors*, s. v.

Wright, William, D.D., an Irish clergyman, was educated at Trinity College, Dublin, and died in 1856. He published, *Doctrine of the Real Presence:—Slavery at the Cape of Good Hope* (1831):—*Biblical Hermeneutics, from the German of G. F. Seiler, D.D.* (1835), etc. See Allibone, *Dict. of Brit. and Amer. Authors*, s. v.

Writing (some form of כָּתַב, *kathâb*, γραφή) is the art of expressing thought by letters or other marks. See LETTER.

I. *Origin and Various Kinds of Writings.*—Language expresses thought, preserves thought, and also suggests or creates thought. But it is obvious that, so long as language is unwritten, it can accomplish these ends only in a very imperfect measure. Hence we may well suppose that, at a very early stage of man's history, attempts were made to present in some way to the eye the thought which spoken language conveyed to the ear, and thus give it visible form and permanence. But we cannot wonder that no record remains of the origin of an art, the beginnings of which must be placed in the political infancy of mankind. Pliny speaks of the "æternus literarum usus" (*N. H.* vii, 56).

The various kinds of writing which have been in use in different ages and in different parts of the world may be classified in two great divisions, according as the object of their inventors was to present the ideas to which they wished to give visible expression directly and immediately to the mind, or indirectly, through the medium of spoken language. Each of these methods—the ideographic and the phonographic or phonetic—has its attendant advantages and disadvantages; but the advantages of the latter method greatly preponderate. The principal recommendation of the former method, in which the depicted idea is caught up immediately by the mind, is that it addresses itself to a much wider circle than the latter, being intelligible, so far as it is intelligible, alike by all classes and in all countries; whereas the latter, in which the *word* is depicted, not the *idea*, is of course intelligible only to those who are acquainted with the language to which the depicted word belongs. On the other hand, the very serious drawbacks attendant upon the direct method are (1) that it is capable of giving distinct expression only to a very limited range of ideas, viz. the ideas of sensible objects and qualities, and if it attempts to go beyond that range at once becomes arbitrary and obscure; and (2) that in its representation even of the limited class of ideas to which it is capable of giving distinct expression, it is cumbrous and altogether unfitted for general use.

The sacred writing of the Egyptians may be regarded as forming a stage of transition between the two sorts of writing just described. Regarding the Mexican writing, see Robertson's *America*, bk. vii, and Prescott's *Mexico*, i, 86. See also Kopp's remarks on the Chinese writing in *Bilder u. Schriften*, ii, 66, 76, 87. Till the present century it was the received opinion that the ancient Egyptian was an exclusively ideographic writing, and to this conclusion the testimonies of those ancient writers who have given any account of it seemed to point (Kenrick, *Anc. Egypt*, i, 285-292). But the labors of Young, Champollion, Wilkinson, Lepsius, and others, during the last half-century, have thrown new light on those ancient and mysterious characters; and it is now agreed that, though very possibly a picture-writing originally, the hieroglyphic, in the form in which it appears on the most ancient monuments, and which it retains unchanged down to the early centuries after Christ, bears a composite character, being in part ideographic, in part phonetic. According to Mr. Kenrick (i, 300, etc.), "the characters are used in three different ways." There is first of all the pictorial use, in which "the character is designed to convey to the mind the idea of the object it represents, and nothing more.... This pictorial representation sometimes stands instead of a phonetic name for the object, but the most common use of it is to make the phonetic group of characters more intelligible by being subjoined to them. Thus, to the names of individuals the figure of a man is subjoined." Such characters Champollion calls *determinatives*. "The second use of the hieroglyphical writing is the symbolical, in which the object delineated is not meant to convey to the mind the idea of itself, but of something associated with it and suggested by it. Thus, a crescent denotes a month, . . . a stretched-out hand the act of giving, etc." "The last class, the phonetic, is really by far the most extensive. The greater part of the characters are as truly letters as if the language were English or Greek; . . . syllabic characters are the exception, not the rule." Mr. Kenrick adds that "in every inscription of any length we find these three modes of writing in use together, but with a great predominance of phonetic." See HIEROGLYPH.

Thus, in the hieroglyphic, we find the point of meeting between the two great classes of written characters, the ideographic and phonetic, and, as it seems, we have some light thrown on their mutual relation, and the manner in which the one arose, or, at least, may have arisen, out of the other. It has been affirmed, indeed, that the two kinds of writing are so entirely distinct that it is impossible to entertain the idea of a historical relationship between them (Kopp, ii, 62). But the fact is, that in the hieroglyphic, and to a certain extent also in the Chinese, such a relationship is already established. No nation which has made any considerable advances towards civilization can remain satisfied with a pictorial or symbolic writing, more particularly if it be disposed to cultivate to any extent intercourse with other nations. To represent by means of such a method of writing foreign words and names is a matter of the utmost difficulty; and it is not improbable that the origin of the phonetic writing may be traced to the intercourse of nations speaking different languages. Thus the Chinese are compelled to employ their ideographic characters phonetically in writing foreign words; and something of the same kind may, it is said, be discovered even in the Mexican writing. In the hieroglyphic the process had advanced much further. In Chinese, the name of the patriarch Shem is represented in writing by the ideograph for "life," *sem* being the Chinese for life (Kopp, ii, 80, 81). Here, consequently, we have an example of the same character used in two ways: (1) ideographically, to represent the idea of life, and (2) phonetically, to represent the sound *sem*.

From this there is but a step to the discovery of an alphabet, viz. the employment of the same sign to represent not the combination of sounds forming the word *sem*, but the initial sound *s*. That this step was actually taken by the Egyptians we appear to have sufficient evidence. "Thus, an eagle stands for A, and its Coptic name is *ahom;* a leaf of an aquatic plant, Coptic *achi*, stands for the same letter; a lion for L, Coptic *labo;* an owl for M, Coptic *moulad*, etc." (Kenrick, i, 305, 306). It is true, as Mr. Kenrick remarks, this correspondence cannot be traced through the whole of the phonetic alphabet. But when we consider how very imperfect is the knowledge which even the most distinguished Egyptologists possess of the ancient Egyptian language, we are fully warranted in putting aside this negative evidence, and receiving the hypothesis just mentioned (which was that of Champollion), as furnishing a very probable explanation of the origin of what may be called the Egyptian alphabet.

Passing now to the purely phonetic system of writing, it is of two sorts, viz. syllabic and alphabetic, in the former of which each character represents a combination of sounds, in the latter a simple sound. The most ancient alphabet is the Hebrew, or Phœnician, which, having its origin in the south-western corner of Asia, the home of the Shemitic nations, was at a very early period introduced by the Phœnicians into Greece, and perhaps at a somewhat later period even into India (Max Müller, *Ancient Sanscrit Literature*, p. 521; *Journal of Asiatic Society*, vi, 461, etc.; *Zeitschrift d. D. M. G.* x, 390, etc.), and thus became the medium through which almost all that is known of the ancient world has been preserved for the instruction of mankind. Who the person was who framed the first alphabet, and thus conferred upon his race a benefit of incalculable value, is unknown. It is the received opinion that in South-western Asia, as in Egypt, the alphabetic writing had for its precursor an ideographic, which, after passing through several stages of change, assumed at last the form in which it has come down to us. This opinion is founded (1) on a comparison with the hieroglyphic and other forms of writing, in which, as has already been observed, we detect the process of transition from the ideographic to the phonographic; and (2) on the names of the letters. These names are all significant; and it is probable that each of the letters in its original form was an ideograph representing the object denoted by the name which the letter still bears. Thus *aleph* (א) in its original form would be the ideograph of ox, *beth* of house, etc. Afterwards, when the ideographic writing gave place to the alphabetic, each of the alphabetic sounds was represented by a character which had formerly been the picture or symbol of an object of whose name that letter was the initial sound. We admit that it is by no means easy in the case of several of the letters to trace the resemblance between the letter form and the object of which, according to this hypothesis, it was originally the picture. But this need not excite our surprise, if we consider how great the change of form which these letters must have undergone as they passed from one country to another, or were transmitted from age to age (see Kopp, ii, 157, 377–399). The ancient Shemitic stone-cutters and engravers were not always careful to preserve an exact uniformity in their delineation of the several characters; they were probably less expert than their Egyptian contemporaries; and, it may be, had no very fixed standard by which to test the accuracy and to correct the errors of their workmanship. Moreover, the wide diffusion of the Shemitic alphabet would naturally occasion still more extensive changes in the forms of the letters. Ewald (*Lehrbuch*, § 77, b) speaks of three main branches from the parent stem, a southern, western, and eastern, viz. (1) the Himyaritic, in Southern Arabia, and the Ethiopic, though the latter is by others brought into closer connection with the Greek form of the Shemitic alphabet; (2) the western, including the Phœnician writing, and the Samaritan, which closely resembles it; and (3) the Babylonian or Assyrian, of which it is generally agreed that the Hebrew square character is an offshoot. Now, it is impossible to say which of these different forms of the Shemitic alphabet approaches nearest to the original. It is probable that all have deviated from it more or less. The original symbolic meaning of the characters having fallen into disuse, there was nothing to be gained by rigid adherence to all the details of the original forms.

Some writers, admitting that a resemblance does exist between the letters and the objects denoted by their names, have attempted to account for it otherwise than by the hypothesis of an earlier ideographic use of the alphabetic forms. They are of opinion that letters were from the first arbitrary signs of sounds, never of objects; and that the names they have so long borne originated, like the names of the constellations, in some fancied resemblance between them and the objects denoted by these names (*Zeitschrift d. D. M. G.* xi, 83). But, not to mention other objections to this view, when we consider that this resemblance in form is not the only point of correspondence, that there is the further correspondence between the sounds expressed by the letters and the initial sounds of the letter-names, it must appear improbable that whoever invented the latter should have been at the pains to search for names bearing to the letters this twofold correspondence, in initial sound and in form, and should not have been satisfied with a single point of correspondence. On the whole, the weight of argument, and also the weight of authority, are in favor of the other hypothesis.

It is impossible with any confidence to decide to which branch of the Shemitic family of nations the invention of the Shemitic alphabet is to be traced. From the names of the letters one might expect to have some light thrown upon this point; but this expectation is not realized. For, though the names are certainly Shemitic, there is no single language of the Shemitic family (so far as these languages are known) in which they all find explanation. But, in truth, of the Shemitic languages in their ancient form, with scarcely the exception of the Hebrew, our knowledge is very imperfect; and it would be extremely rash to say that such and such words did not exist in, for example, the old Phœnician language, because they have not been found in the few fragments of that language which have come down to us. See PHŒNICIA.

It is the opinion of some that the idea of the alphabet was borrowed from Egypt. Hug (*Die Erfindung der Buchstabenschrift*, p. 32, etc.) thinks the Phœnicians resident in Egypt were the inventors of the alphabet, the forms of the letters being Egyptian, the names Phœnician. But if the Shemitic nations did borrow the idea from Egypt, they certainly worked it out much more successfully than those with whom, according to this hypothesis, it originated; and moreover, when we consider that there is no very marked correspondence between the Egyptian and Shemitic alphabets, except in the general idea, it is on the whole safer to conclude, in the absence of all historical evidence, that the two alphabets originated independently of each other, and were alike the offspring of that necessity which is the mother of invention. See ALPHABET.

II. *The Hebrew Alphabet.*—This consists of twenty-two letters. It has been conjectured that several of these letters did not belong to the alphabet in its original form; and there is a traditional statement found in some Greek writers of authority that the Phœnician alphabet (which, there is no question, was identical with the Hebrew) when first introduced into Greece consisted of not more than fifteen letters (see Hug, *Erfindung der Buchstabenschrift*, p. 12, etc). However this may be, it is certain that at a very early period the Hebrew alphabet included the same number of letters as at present. This is ascertained (1) from those Scriptural songs and poems, the several lines or stanzas of which begin with the successive letters of the alphabet (see POETRY); and (2) from the use of the letters as marks of number, particularly when compared with the corresponding use of the Greek letters.

With regard to these twenty-two letters various questions have been started, to some of the more important of which it is necessary briefly to advert.

1. Did these letters originally represent syllables or simple sounds? Some writers, as Lepsius (*Paläographie*, § 19), have maintained that originally one and the same sign stood for both vowel and consonant. They hold that after the ideographic writing comes not the alphabetic but the syllabic, our separation of vowels and consonants being entirely ideal, and never actually possible, inasmuch as consonants cannot find expression without the aid of a vowel sound; and vowels cannot be pronounced except in dependence on a preceding consonantal element more or less distinct. In all this these writers are probably theoretically correct. Of the phonetic writing the syllabic is naturally the earliest stage, and in the Assyrian cuneiform we have the example of such a writing in actual use among the Shemitic nations (Rawlinson, *Ancient Monarchies*, i, 84, 337). But how essentially different in their nature the Assyrian letters are from the Hebrew is evident from the fact that the former, according to Sir H. Rawlinson and M. Oppert, number from three to four hundred, the latter only twenty-two. Indeed, it is impossible that a really syllabic alphabet should have fewer characters, except in the case of such a state of language as Lepsius presupposes, in which all the syllables are open, i. e. end with a vowel, and there is no variety of vowel sounds.

It is to be noted, however, that in the Ethiopic alphabet, in which each letter appears under seven different forms, according to the vowel sound associated with it, the simplest form is not that which the letter takes when no vowel follows, as we might expect, but that which it takes when followed by short *a*. When this sound follows, the original form of the letter is retained unchanged; when no vowel follows, a slight alteration is made in the form of the letter to indicate that it closes the syllable. See ETHIOPIC LANGUAGE.

2. Admitting that the Hebrew writing is alphabetic, is it purely consonantal, or does it contain signs to express vowel sounds as well as consonants? Some have held that the letters א, ו, י, were originally vowels, and that their use as consonants was of later introduction. It has been said that the alphabet of each language must contain a sufficient number of letters to represent all the sounds of the language, and that it is as easy to conceive of a language without vowel sounds as of an alphabet without vowel letters. And further, with regard to the Hebrew alphabet, Kopp (*Bilder u. Schriften*, ii, 112, etc.) thinks it absurd to suppose that it originally contained separate forms for guttural breathings so little differing from one another as א, ה, ח, and not a single sign to represent the vowels, which constitute the life of every language. Now, with regard to the letters ו and י, it is certain they were used as vowels from a very ancient period; but there is no reason whatever to suppose that this use of these letters preceded their use as consonants, but every reason to suppose the contrary. At the beginning of a syllable only ו is ever used as a vowel, and in the few cases in which it is so used it has been softened from an original consonantal sound. In the middle of a word, ו and י appear as vowels much less frequently in the earlier Hebrew books than in the later; and on the surviving monuments of the Phœnician language and writing they have uniformly a consonantal force. Besides, it is known that one of these letters, viz. ו, passed over from the Phœnicians to the Greeks as a consonant, though as a Greek letter it afterwards fell out of use. As for א, it is difficult to conceive how, if it originally stood for A in the Hebrew alphabet, it should, even at the date of the very earliest monuments of the language, have so entirely lost this power, and passed into a simple breathing. With regard to the alleged improbability of so ancient an alphabet distinguishing the closely allied sounds of א, ה, ח, by the use of different characters, we are scarcely in a position to form a sound judgment on such a point, as the languages we speak differ so entirely from the Shemitic tongues, and our organs are consequently incapable of giving distinct expression to the variety of guttural sounds which characterized the ancient Hebrew, as it does the modern Arabic.

3. As to the origin of the Hebrew square characters, which appear in all extant MSS., as well as in our printed Bibles, the most diverse views have been propounded; some, especially among the older scholars, tracing them back to the age of Moses and the tables of the law; and others believing them to be of comparatively recent origin. The latter view is taken by Kopp (*Bilder u. Schriften*, ii, 164), who places their introduction somewhere about the 4th century, chiefly on the ground that the Palmyrene characters, from which, in his opinion, they were derived, were in use, as appears from inscriptions yet extant, as late as the 3d century of our æra. But whatever may be the connection between the square character and the Palmyrene (and there is no doubt it is very intimate), the opinion of Kopp is quite untenable. We have direct testimony to the fact that the square character belongs to a much earlier age than that to which he assigns it. Jerome informs us that in his day the ineffable name Jehovah, יהוה, was sometimes introduced into Greek MSS. in its Hebrew form, and that readers of these MSS. unacquainted with Hebrew often by mistake read the name *Pipi*, IIIIII: from which it is quite certain that, in Jerome's age, the Hebrew Bible must have been written in the square character presently in use, for only on this supposition was such a mistake possible. But, if Kopp's hypothesis be well founded, the square character must then have been quite recently elaborated from the Palmyrene. Was it so? Let us turn to another passage of Jerome, in his celebrated *Prologus Galeatus*, in which he informs us that the Hebrew character in use in his day had been introduced by Ezra, in place of a more ancient character which had passed over to the Samaritans. Is it credible that the square character was invented by the Jewish scholars, and introduced into MSS. for the first time in the 4th century, and yet that before the close of that same century its origin was completely forgotten, and had passed from the region of history to that of tradition or fable?

A similar testimony on the part of Origen carries us back a century earlier. He, too, mentions the Jewish tradition of a change of characters by Ezra, and speaks of MSS. in which the divine name was found even in his day written in the ancient characters (Montfaucon, *Hexapla*, ii, 94). The expression in the sermon on the mount, "not one jot," carries us back a step further still, indeed, almost to the beginning of our æra; for it is evident that the phrase was a proverbial one, and that the alphabet which gave rise to it must have been in use for a considerable time. Now, it is only in the square character (also, though not so decidedly, in the Palmyrene) that the letter *yod* is very much smaller than the others. Kopp, who not unfrequently makes up by strength of assertion for weakness of argument, declares the foregoing argument to be "indescribably weak." He points to the Greek iota (I), in the writing of those days by no means a small letter.

To all this we may now add the still more decisive evidence of monumental inscriptions, from which it appears that even before the period of the Maccabees the square character was in use among the Jews (*Revue Archéol.* 1864; *Zeitschrift d. D. M. G.* xix, 637–641; comp. Chwolson, *Achtzehn Grabschriften aus der Krim*). That another character, more closely allied to the Phœnician and Samaritan, is found on the extant coins of the Maccabees does not militate against this conclusion. Ancient forms and usages often survive in coins and official documents after they have fallen into disuse in common life. Besides, it is not impossible that the Maccabees, vindicating as they did the nationality of Israel against the tyranny of Syria, may have purposely revived the use of the old characters, regarding, it may be, those in common use, which had been introduced under foreign auspices, as a badge of national servitude. However this may be, it is pretty certain that the old Jewish tradition of a change of letters having taken place in the time of Ezra, however erroneous it may be in some of its details, is not without a solid foundation in fact. See HEBREW.

III. *Progressive Diffusion of the Art among the Ancient Hebrews.*—The art of writing is not mentioned in the Hebrew Scriptures previous to the age of Moses. In the book of Genesis there is no allusion to documents of any sort. Abraham buys the field and cave of Machpelah, but there is no bill of purchase as in the case of a similar transaction in the history of Jeremiah (comp. Gen. xxiii with Jer. xxxii). The cave and the field "were made sure unto Abraham for a possession in the presence of the children of Heth, before all that went in at the gate of his city" (Gen. xxiii, 18). There is no hint of any documentary proof of the purchase being given or asked. It does not, however, by any means follow from this absence of allusion to the art of writing in the book of Genesis that that art was altogether unknown in Palestine in the patriarchal age. It may have been unknown, or but rarely practiced, by the nomad and rural population, in the midst of which the scene of the patriarchal story is laid; and yet have been known and practiced in the great centres of population and civilization, as it certainly was in Egypt, and we can scarcely doubt in Mesopotamia also, even at that early period (Kenrick, *Egypt*, ii, 101, 102). In confirmation of this we may refer to the story of Ruth, from which we find that even in a much later age it was not uncommon in Palestine to transact and complete purchases similar to Abraham's without the aid of writing materials, though no one will now maintain that the art of writing was then unknown (Ruth iv, 7–11). Instances of the same sort might be adduced from the history of all nations at a similar stage of social advancement.

When we pass from the age of the patriarchs to that of Moses, from the family life of Palestine to the political life of Egypt, and afterwards of the desert, we first meet with distinct traces of the art of writing. It is probable that the *shoterîm*, or "officers" subordinate to the taskmasters, mentioned in Exod. v, 6–19, whose duty it was to see that the full amount of labor was performed by their enslaved countrymen, were so named from the use they made of writing in the discharge of their degrading functions (Arab. *satara*, to write). But, however this may be, we immediately afterwards read of the two tables of the law, and of the "book of the covenant" which "Moses read in the audience of all the people" (Exod. xxiv, 7, 12); also of a book, in which was entered a record of the victory over Amalek in Rephidim, and which Moses was directed to "rehearse in the ears of Joshua" (Exod. xvii, 14; this *sêpher* or document may afterwards have formed part of the "Book of the Wars of the Lord," mentioned in Numb. xxi, 14); and at a later period mention is made of a written account of the journeyings of the Israelites in the wilderness (Numb. xxxiii, 2). We also read of the high-priest's breastplate with its four rows of stones, on which were engraven, "like the engravings of a signet," the names of the twelve tribes of Israel; and of the mitre with its plate of pure gold, on which was a "writing like to the engravings of a signet," Holiness to the Lord (Exod. xxxix, 14, 30). Of the use of writing in legal transactions and processes mention is made in Numb. v, 23; Deut. xxiv, 1, 3. Specially to be noted is the figurative use which is made of the word *sêpher* in Exod. xxxii, 32, 33: "Blot me out of the book which thou hast written," in which we already meet with the idea of a memorial book kept by God, "for them that feared the Lord and that thought upon his name" (Mal. iii, 16; Psa. lvi, 9 [8]). From all this it is evident that in the age of Moses the art of writing was commonly employed for the purpose of preserving the knowledge of important truths and the memory of important events. The assumption by some writers that the art of writing among the Hebrews is due to and dates from the delivery of the Law on Sinai, is negatived by the fact that it was evidently accepted at that time as a well-known art, and no hint is there given of it as a new invention.

We are not, however, to conclude from this that in that age, or for many ages after, writing was in common use among the body of the people. The knowledge of it was probably confined to the few who occupied an official position; the people being still dependent chiefly on oral instruction for their knowledge of what God had done for them, and what he required of them. Writing was in those days employed rather as a means of preserving than of circulating knowledge. The tables of stone were laid up in the ark. The book of the covenant (mentioned Exod. xxiv) was read to the people. The book of the law (mentioned Deut. xxxi, 24–26) was given to the Levites "to put it in the side of the ark; . . . for a witness against Israel." The song of Moses (ch. xxxii) was not circulated in writing among the people, but "was spoken in their ears" (xxxi, 30); and thus they were taught to repeat it and to transmit it to others (ver. 19, 22). It is only the king who was expressly enjoined to have written out for his special use a copy of the law, and to *read* therein all the days of his life (xvii, 18, 19). Of the people in general it was required that they should learn God's statutes, and have them in their heart, and teach them diligently to their children (vi, 6, 7), plainly by word of mouth; for when it is added (ver. 9), "Thou shalt write them upon the posts of thy house, and on thy gates," the expression is probably to be understood figuratively, like the "binding on the hand, and as frontlets between the eyes" (ver. 8; comp. also Psa. xliv, 2 [1]; lxxviii, 3, with ci, 19 [18]).

Assyrian Scribes making Notes of Prisoners, Heads of Slain, Spoils, etc. (Bas-relief from Kouyunjik, British Museum.)

During the wars under Joshua no advancement in the art of writing is to be looked for. In the book of Joshua, accordingly, there is mention made but of one new document, viz., a geographical description and sevenfold division of the land west of Jordan, drawn up by delegates from the several tribes (Josh. xviii, 9). The *shoterîm* are likewise mentioned among the civil and military officers (i, 10; iii, 2; viii, 23; xxiii, 2; xxiv, 1). In the same connection, also, frequent reference is made to the book of the law, which Joshua, in accordance with the injunction of Moses, wrote upon great stones on Mount Ebal, and afterwards read in the hearing of all the people. The book of Jasher (quoted x, 13) probably belongs to a somewhat later age (2 Sam. i, 18). See BOOK.

Important to our present purpose is the mention in Josh. xv, 15, 16, and Judg. i, 11, 12, of Kirjath-sepher (*book-town*), afterwards named Debir; and with this may be conjoined the allusion in the immortal song of Deborah to the *mechokekîm* (engravers) and *sopherîm* (writers), who led the bands of Machir and Zebulon "to the help of the Lord against the mighty" (Judg. v, 14). As yet the art of writing was not only confined to certain classes, but would seem to have been cultivated chiefly in certain localities (yet comp. viii, 14). The vicinity of Zebulon and Machir to Phœnicia and Damascus is to be noted (Gen. xlix, 13).

Under Samuel the institution of the schools of the prophets must have conduced not less to the literary than to the religious advancement of Israel. The seed which was then sown ripened into an abundant harvest during the glorious reigns of David and Solomon, which were rendered not less illustrious by the literary achievements which distinguished them than by the successful cultivation of the arts of war and peace. During these reigns the art of writing must have been largely employed, not only for literary, but for political purposes. The *sophêr*, or secretary, scribe, was a constant attendant upon the monarch's person (2 Sam. viii, 17; xx, 25); so also the *mazkîr*, or recorder. We also read of David himself writing a letter (*sépher*) to Joab (xi, 14, 15), though the fact that the reply of Joab was by messenger, and not by letter, would seem to indicate that the latter mode of communication was still rare and exceptional.

In the age of Isaiah, in which (or not long before) the strictly prophetic literature may be said to commence, various circumstances contributed to the development of the art of writing, such as the commercial activity of the reign of Uzziah; the closer relations and increased intercourse between Palestine and the great seats of civilization on the banks of the Euphrates and Tigris, on the one side, and of the Nile, on the other; and also the captivity of the ten tribes, and the breaking-up of the local and geographical unity of Israel, which would necessitate a written intercourse between the widely separated branches of the nation. Accordingly, in the book of Isaiah we find various notices illustrative of our present subject, one of which is specially interesting, as it would appear to indicate a wider diffusion than we have had any evidence of previously to this period, of the practice of reading and writing among the people. We refer to Isa. xxix, 11, 12, where the prophet, in describing the blindness of the people, compares the word of God to a sealed book (הַסֵּפֶר הֶחָתוּם), a document of any description, "which men deliver to one that is learned (lit. that knows writing, יֹדֵעַ סֵפֶר), saying, Read this, I pray thee: and he saith, I cannot, for it is sealed; and the book is delivered to him that is not learned (who does not know writing), saying, Read this, I pray thee: and he saith, I am not learned (לֹא יָדַעְתִּי סֵפֶר, I do not know books or writing)." Here we read of two classes of the population, those able to read a written document, and those not able; and though the latter were probably still much the larger class, it would seem from the form of the prophet's language that the knowledge of writing was no longer confined within the limits of an official class, but was diffused somewhat more widely among the people.

This was still more decidedly the case in the age of Jeremiah, as is evident from the frequency with which the art of writing is alluded to in his writings, as compared with those of the earlier prophets. In Jeremiah we read for the first time of a conveyance of property being drawn out in writing, and subscribed not only by the principal parties, but also by witnesses (Jer. xxxii, 10–12). That this was the common practice is evident from ver. 34 of the same chapter. Copies of the sacred writings appear also to have been multiplied (viii, 8). Letters are spoken of more frequently (xxix, 25, 29). The class of *sopherîm*, or scribes, had become numerous (viii, 8; xxxvi, 10, 12, 23, 26; xxxvii, 15, 20; lii, 25; Ezek. ix, 2, 3, 11; 2 Chron. xxxiv, 13). On the whole, the state of matters, with respect to the art of writing at this period in Palestine, was very similar to that which we find delineated on the Egyptian monuments (Kenrick, *Egypt*, i, 283, 284; ii, 52). A still wider diffusion of the art of writing is indicated by the notices in Eccles. xii, 12, and Ecclus. xlii, 7; Luke xvi, 6. See SCRIBE.

IV. *Materials of Writing.*—We have no very definite statement in the Old Test. as to the material which was in most common use for the purposes of writing. In all ages it has been customary to engrave on stone or metal, or other durable material, with the view of securing the permanency of the record; and accordingly, in the very commencement of the national history of Israel, we read of the two tables of the law written in stone, and of a subsequent writing of the law on stone (Deut. xxvii, 3; Josh. viii, 32). In the latter case there is this peculiarity, that plaster (*sîd*, lime or gypsum) was used along with stone, a combination of materials which Hengstenberg, in the valuable dissertation on the art of writing among the Hebrews, contained in his *Genuineness of the Pentateuch*, illustrates by comparison of the practice of the Egyptian engravers, who, having first carefully smoothed the stone, filled up the faulty places with gypsum or cement, in order to obtain a perfectly uniform surface on which to execute their engravings (i, 433, Clarke's transl.; comp. also Wilkinson, *Anc. Egypt.* ii, 111).

The metals also are mentioned as a material of writing; as *lead*, in Job xix, 23, 24 (though whether the reference in that passage is to writing on lead, or filling up the hollow of the letters with lead, is not certain) (comp. Pliny, *Nat. Hist.* xiii, 11; Hengstenberg, i, 433); *brass* (1 Macc. viii, 22; xiv, 18, 27, 48); *gold* (Exod. xxxix, 30). Of stamped coins of the Hebrews there is no trace earlier than the age of the Maccabees (1 Macc. xv, 6).

To the engraving of gems there is frequent reference in the Old Test., as in the account of the high-priest's breastplate (see also Isa. xxix, 11, 12, 18; Jer. xxxii, 14; Dan. xii, 4). In Gen. xxxviii, 18 we read of Judah's signet, and from the recent discoveries in the East we learn that it was the custom of the ancient Chaldæans to carry about with them an engraved cylinder in agate or other hard stone, which was used as a seal or signet, and probably worn round the wrist; but the engraving on these cylinders was not always accompanied with an inscription. (For specimens, see Rawlinson, *Anc. Mon.* i, 87, 117, 118, 134, 211, 331; comp. also Heeren, *Hist. Res.* ii, 203). See SEAL.

The common materials of writing were the tablet (לוּחַ, *lûach*) and the roll (מְגִלָּה, *megillâh*), the former probably having a Chaldæan origin, the latter an Egyptian.

"The tablets of the Chaldæans," says Rawlinson (*Anc. Mon.* i, 85–87), "are among the most remarkable of their remains. . . . They are small pieces of clay, somewhat rudely shaped into a form resembling a pillow, and thickly inscribed with cuneiform characters. . . . What is most curious is that these documents have been in general enveloped, after they were baked, in a cover of moist clay, upon which their contents have been again inscribed, so as to present externally a duplicate of the writing within; and the tablet in its cover has then been baked afresh." The same material was largely used by the Assyrians, and many of their clay tablets still remain. "They are of various sizes, ranging from nine inches long by six and a half wide, to an inch and a half by an inch wide, and even less. . . . Some thousands of these have been recovered; many are historical, some linguistic, some geographical, some astronomical" (comp. Pliny, *Nat. Hist.* vii, 56; Heeren, *Hist. Res.* ii, 185). For the similar use of hollow cylinders, or prisms of six or eight sides, formed of fine terra cotta, sometimes glazed, on which the characters were traced with a small stylus, in some specimens so minutely as to be capable of decipherment only with the aid of a magnifying-glass, see Rawlinson (*Anc. Mon.* i, 330, 478). See BRICK.

In Egypt the principal writing material was quite of a different sort. Wooden tablets are indeed found pictured on the monuments (Wilkinson, *Anc. Egypt.* ii, 100); but the material which was in common use, even from very ancient times, was the papyrus. This reed, found chiefly in Lower Egypt, "had various economic uses; . . . for writing, the pith was taken out, and divided by a pointed instrument into the thin pellicles of which it is composed; it was then flattened by pressure, and the strips glued together, other strips being placed at right angles to them, so that a roll of any length might be manufactured (Pliny's account, *Nat. Hist.* xiii, 23, is partly erroneous)" (Kenrick, *Egypt*, i, 89, 90). That this material was in use in Egypt from a very early period is evidenced by still existing papyrus MSS. of the earliest Theban dynasties (ibid. i, 283, 357, 485, 497; ii, 102, 142; see also Wilkinson, *Anc. Egypt.* ii, 99). As the papyrus, being in great demand, and exported to all parts of the world, became very costly, other materials were often used instead of it, among which Wilkinson mentions leather, a few leather rolls of an early period having been found in the tombs (ibid. p. 152).

Now, as Palestine lay between Babylonia and Assyria on the one hand, and Egypt on the other, and formed the highway of union and commerce between them, we may expect to find the materials of writing very similar to those in common use in the two great centres of civilization, with which it was so intimately connected. Accordingly, we do find mention made in the Old Test. both of the tablet (*lûach*) and of the roll (*megillâh*); but we are not distinctly informed of what substance either tablet or roll was composed. From the character of the soil of Palestine it is pretty certain that the tablet was not, as usually in Assyria and Babylonia, of baked clay, unless we are to suppose an importation of Assyrian tablets, which is scarcely possible, as the writing seems to have been inscribed on these tablets when the clay was fresh, which, of course, it could not be after the lapse of time occupied in in its carriage from Assyria to Palestine. Accordingly, brick is mentioned in Scripture usually in connection with Babylonia or Egypt (Gen. xi, 3; Exod. v, 7–19; Nah. iii, 14; Jer. xliii, 9; Ezek. iv, 1); rarely in connection with Palestine (Isa. ix, 9 [10]); and we read of no tablet of clay, but either of stone (as in the case of the tables of the law), or of metal (1 Kings vii, 36; Isa. viii, 1; comp. iii, 23), or of wood, which was probably the material commonly employed for writing on (Luke i, 63; comp. 2 Esdras xiv, 24), where tablets of box-wood are mentioned.

Egyptian Scribe, with Palette under his Arm, Reading from a Papyrus Roll; Satchel for his Writing Materials in front of him. (Painting from Thebes, in British Museum.)

The roll, מְגִלָּה (or מְגִלַּת סֵפֶר, Psa. xl, 8 [7]; Jer. xxxvi, 2, 4; Ezek. ii, 9), is not mentioned before the time of Jeremiah (unless Psa. xl be earlier), and only in Jer. xxxvi; Ezek. ii and iii, and Zech. v (comp. also Isa. xxxiv, 4, "And the heavens shall be rolled up as a book;" also 1 Esdras vi, 23; Luke iv, 17; Rev. vi, 14). Considering the close connection between Judæa and

Egyptian Scribes.

Egypt, especially in the later period of the kingdom, it is probable that the roll was of papyrus, though we have no actual statement to that effect in the Hebrew Scriptures. All we certainly know is that it was of a substance which might be torn and burned (Jer. xxxvi, 23); that the writing was with ink, דְּיוֹ, *deyô*, and was arranged in columns, דְּלָתוֹת, *delathôth*, lit. *doors* (ibid.); and that both sides of the material were sometimes written on (Ezek. ii, 10). Mention is made of paper in 2 John 12; also 2 Esdras xv, 2; Tobit vii, 14. See PAPER.

That prepared skins were used for writing on by the ancient Hebrews is probable, but we have no direct evidence of the fact. Whether the Hebrew *sêpher*, book or document, was so called from its connection with a root meaning to "scrape," is very doubtful; it is certain that in Hebrew the root *saphár* has no such meaning. The only Scriptural mention of parchment is found in the New Test. (2 Titus iv, 13). See PARCHMENT.

The tablet was inscribed with a stylus, which made an indentation in the substance of which the tablet was

Palette of an Egyptian Scribe. (Brit. Mus.)

composed; the roll was written on with ink (2 Cor. iii, 3; 2 John 12; 3 John 13). In Ezek. ix, 2, 3, 11, the inkstand, קֶסֶת הַסֹּפֵר, is mentioned. As to the stylus or pen, the Hebrew word for it is עֵט, *êt*, the derivation of which is obscure. It is found in four passages, in two of which it has attached to it the epithet "iron" (Job xix, 24; Jer. xvii, 1); in the other two (Psa. xlv, 2 [1]; Jer. viii, 8) it denotes the pen in common use among the *sopherím* or scribes, of whatever sort that may have been. The word חֶרֶט, *chéret*, which is usually conjoined by writers upon this subject with עֵט, is mentioned only in one somewhat obscure passage (Isa. viii, 1) as an instrument of writing; it has probably some connection with *chartummím*, the name of the Egyptian sacred scribes. In Egypt the reed-pen seems to have been in use from the earliest times. It even forms part of one of the ancient alphabetic characters. "The reed-pen and inkstand, and scribes employed in writing, appear among the sculptures in the tombs of Gizeh, which are contemporaneous with the pyramids themselves" (Kenrick, *Egypt*, ii, 102, 142). See PEN.

Wucherer, JOHANN FRIEDRICH, a Lutheran theologian of Germany, was born March 8, 1803, at Nördlingen. He studied at Erlangen, and, after completing his course, acted for some time as assistant minister in his native place. In 1832 he was appointed hospital-preacher of Nördlingen, and pastor at Baldingen. In 1855 he was called to Aha, and died there, Dec. 26, 1881. Wucherer was a faithful follower of his Master, and the many difficulties which he had to overcome in the early period of his ministry proved to be a blessing not only to him but also to his flock. He wrote, *Vom evangelisch-lutherischen Hauptgottesdienst* (Nördlingen, 1846):—*Zu einem Zeugniss* (ibid. eod.):—*Populäre Einleitung in die Schriften des Neuen Testaments* (ibid. 1848–50, 2 parts):—*Ausführlicher Nachweis aus Schrift und Symbolen*, etc. (ibid. 1853). See Zuchold, *Bibl. Theol.* ii, 1475. (B. P.)

Wülfer, JOHANN, a Protestant theologian of Germany, was born at Nuremberg, June 7, 1651, and died there, Sept. 3, 1724. He is the author of, שקלים *Hebraice et Latine cum Amplo et Erudito Commentario Perpetuo* (Altdorf, 1680):—*Theriaca Judaica ad Examen Revocata, etc., Acc. Is. Viva Vindex Sanguinis* (Nuremberg, 1681). See Fürst, *Bibl. Jud.* iii, 537; Winer, *Handbuch der theol. Lit.* i, 525. (B. P.)

Wülffer, DANIEL, a Lutheran theologian of Germany, was born at Nuremberg, July 3, 1617, and died there, May 11, 1685, professor and pastor. He is best known as the author of that fine hymn, *O Ewigkeit, O Ewigkeit*, a favorite with the historian Niebuhr. It has been translated into English in the *Lyra Germ.* i, 26: "Eternity! Eternity! How long art thou, Eternity!" See Will, *Nürnberger Gelehrten-Lexikon*, iii, 1757; *Wülfferische Leichenpredigt* (Nuremberg, 1685); Koch, *Gesch. d. deutschen Kirchenliedes*, iii, 144 sq. (B. P.)

Wulfhelm, archbishop of Canterbury, was consecrated by archbishop Athelm, to whom, both at Wells and at Canterbury, he was the successor. One of the first public acts he was called upon to perform, within two years of his appointment, was to officiate at the coronation of Athelstan, which occurred in 925. In January, soon after the coronation, his services were required at Tamworth, to officiate at a political marriage. Again, at a later period, the good offices of the archbishop of Canterbury were required at the marriage of the daughter of Edward the Elder to Hugh the Great, count of Paris, the son of Robert I. As a ruler he was discreet, and did much to civilize the people and promote Church privileges. He died in 942. See Hook, *Lives of the Archbishops of Canterbury*, i, 339 sq.

Wulflach (or **Wulf**), an ecclesiastic of Longobardian origin, established himself as a stylite, in the latter half of the 6th century, in the district of Triers, France, and gained the admiration of the people for whose conversion he prayed, preaching to the multitudes that thronged around him, and persuading them to destroy their idols. See Neander, *Hist. of the Church*, iii, 28.

Wulfred, an English ecclesiastic of the 10th century, went over as a missionary to Skara, in West Gothland, and very inconsiderately seized an axe and dashed to the ground a much venerated idol, for which act he was attacked by a body of furious pagans and put to death at once. See Neander, *Hist. of the Church*, iii, 292.

Wulfred, archbishop OF CANTERBURY, was nominated by Ethelhard, and was the first occupant of that important office. His consecration took place in August, 805, and it is said that, although he held the archbishopric for more than twenty-eight years, he did nothing worthy of record. He died March 24, 832. See Hook, *Lives of the Archbishops of Canterbury*, i, 270 sq.

Wundemann, JOHANN CHRISTIAN FRIEDRICH, a Protestant theologian, who died doctor of theology and pastor at Wahlendorf, in Schleswig, Dec. 26, 1827, is the author of, *Meletemata de S. Cœna Comm. Exeg. Critic.* (Rostock, 1820):—*Geschichte der christlichen Glaubenslehren vom Zeitalter des Athanasius bis auf Gregor den Grossen* (Leipsic, 1798–99, 2 vols.). See Winer, *Handbuch der theol. Lit.* i, 454, 594. (B. P.)

Wunderbar, REUBEN, a Jewish teacher at Riga, where he died, Aug. 19, 1868, is the author of, חכמת הרפואה לבי, i. e. *Biblisch-talmudische Medicin* (Riga, 1850–60, 2 vols.). Besides, he contributed largely to Fürst's *Orient* and other periodicals. See Fürst, *Bibl. Jud.* iii, 537. (B. P.)

Wundt, DANIEL LUDWIG, a Protestant theologian of Germany, was born Nov. 12, 1741, at Creuznach. He studied at Heidelberg, was appointed in 1765 second preacher at Ladenberg, and in 1770 first preacher at Oppenheim. In 1773 he was called to his native place, where he labored till 1788, when he was appointed second professor of theology at Heidelberg, advancing in 1797 to the first professorship. He died Feb. 19, 1805. Of his writings we mention, *Kurzer Entwurf von Vorlesungen über die Geschichte des jüdischen Volkes* (Heidelberg, 1788):—*Magazin für die Kirchen- und Gelehrtengeschichte des Churfürstenthums Pfalz* (ibid. 1789–90, 2 vols.):—*Magazin für die pfälzische Ge-*

schichte (ibid. 1793). See Döring, *Die gelehrten Theologen Deutschlands*, iv, 758 sq. (B. P.)

Wuorin Väki, in Finnish mythology, were the genii of the rocks and mines, who worked under the guidance of Kämuläinen.

Würdtwein, Stanislaus Alexander, a Roman Catholic prelate of Germany, was born at Amorbach in 1719, and died, as suffragan of Worms, April 12, 1796. He is the author of, *Monasticon Palatinum* (Mannheim, 1793-97, 6 vols.):—*Diœcesis Megunt. in Archidiac. Distr. et Comment. Dipl. Illustr.* (ibid. 1767-77, 3 parts):—*Thuringia et Eichsfeldia Med. Ævi Eccles.* (ibid. 1790):—*Subsidia Diplom. ad Selecta Juris Eccles. Germ. et Historiar. Capita Elucidanda* (Bamberg, 1772-80, 13 parts):—*Nova Subsidia Diplom.* etc. (ibid. 1781-90). See Winer, *Handbuch der theol. Lit.* i, 791, 792, 802, 916; ii, 5. (B. P.)

Würfel, Andreas, a Protestant theologian of Germany, was born at Nuremberg, Feb. 28, 1718, and died at Offenhausen, in Bavaria, Oct. 6, 1769. He is the author of, *Lebensbeschreibungen aller Geistlichen, welche in der Reichsstadt Nürnberg und auf deren Land seit der Reformation gedienet* (Nuremberg, 1756; continued until 1779 by Waldau, ibid. 1779-85):—*Historische Nachricht von der Judengemeinde, welche ehehin in der Reichsstadt Nürnberg angerichtet gewesen, aber anno 1499 ausgeschafft worden* (ibid. 1755):—*Historische Nachricht von der Judengemeinde in der Hofmark Fürth*, etc. (Frankfort and Prague, 1754). See Winer, *Handbuch der theol. Lit.* i, 787; Fürst, *Bibl. Jud.* iii, 538. (B. P.)

Wurskaiti were priests of the third order among pagan Prussians. Griwa takes the lead as supreme head; next in order come the Griwaites, then the Siggones, and lastly the Wurskaiti. They are said to have had in control the management of religious duties. Probably the dedication, cleansing, and sacrificing of the offerings was their main duty.

Würtemberg, The Kingdom of, has, according to the census of 1880, a population of 1,971,255 souls, of whom 1,361,412 are Protestants, 590,405 Roman Catholics, 13,326 Jews, etc. The constitution of the Protestant Church is consistorial. The highest legislative and administrative authority is, so far as regards purely ecclesiastical matters, vested in the consistory, composed of a president, a legal councillor, and seven ordinary councillors (five laymen and two ecclesiastics), who are all appointed by the king. Since 1848, however, there has been established alongside the consistory, and acting in unison with it, a series of parish councils, diocesan synods, and annual synods-general, to which the membership is elective. The territory of the Church is divided into six superintendencies, each with a "prelate" at the head. These prelates superintend 49 deaneries, comprising 906 parishes, with 1021 pastors. Each prelate has to visit his diocese every three years. The general synod meets every four years, and is composed of fifty-six members, viz., of forty-nine members representing the different deaneries, one representing the theological faculty of Tübingen, and six nominated directly by the king. The University of Tübingen has a faculty of Protestant theology, consisting of five ordinary professors, besides professors extraordinary and "Privatdocenten." The Roman Catholics in Würtemberg form the episcopal diocese of Rottenburg, which comprises 672 parishes and 946 priests, paid by the state. The University of Tübingen has also a faculty of Roman Catholic theology, consisting of six professors. The diocese of Rottenburg belongs to the ecclesiastical province of Freiburg, to which its relations have been arranged by the papal bull *Provida solersque*, of Aug. 11, 1821. The present incumbent of the episcopal see at Rottenburg is the famous Church historian Hefele. Besides the Catholic faculty, there is also a clerical seminary at Rottenburg, with three professors. The relations of the Jews are regulated by the law of April 25, 1825. The territory of the synagogue is divided into twelve rabbinates, which are governed by an ecclesiastical council, consisting of the chief rabbi of Stuttgart and five laymen, who are responsible to the ministry for ecclesiastical affairs. See Schmid-Sonneck, *Die evangelische Diaspora Würtemberg's nach Entstehung und gegenwärtigem Bestand* (Stuttgart, 1879); Helfferich, *Chronik der evangelischen Kirche Würtemberg's vom Jahre* 1879 (ibid. 1880); *Hof- und Staats-Handbuch des Königreichs Würtemberg* (1881); Lichtenberger, *Encyclop. des Sciences Religieuses*, s. v.; Herzog, *Real-Encyklop.* s. v. (B. P.)

Würzburg (or **Wurtzburg**), Council of (*Concilium Herbipolense*). Würzburg is a fortified city of Bavaria, capital of the circle of Lower Franconia, one hundred and forty miles north-west of Munich, on the right bank of the Main. An ecclesiastical council was held there March 18, 1287, in the presence of the emperor Rudolph, by the legate, John, bishop of Tusculum, assisted by four archbishops, viz. those of Mayence, Cologne, Salzburg, and Vienna, some of their suffragans, and many abbots. Forty-two canons were published.

The first five relate to the moral conduct and manner of life of clerks, enjoining them not to frequent taverns, nor play with dice, and to dress according to their calling.

7. Forbids to celebrate two masses in one day, except in a case of necessity.

8. Orders that the Body of our Lord shall be carried with proper solemnity to the sick, and to women near the time of their delivery.

10. Forbids to holds two vicarages.

14. Orders those who have received investiture at the hands of laymen to resign their benefices into the bishop's hands, to whom the collation properly belongs.

15. Forbids any fee for the nuptial benediction and for funerals.

28. Forbids to fortify a church without the bishop's consent.

29. Forbids to excommunicate wives or mothers on account of their deceased husband's or children's debts, except they have succeeded to their property.

See Mansi, *Concil.* xi, 1318; Landon, *Manual of Councils*, p. 696, 697.

Wustan. See Wodan.

Wuttke, Karl Friedrich Adolph, a Protestant theologian and philosopher of Germany, was born at Breslau, Nov. 10, 1819. Here he studied theology and philosophy, and lectured from 1843 as a private teacher on philosophy. In 1854 he was called as professor of theology to Berlin, and in 1861 as ordinary professor to Halle, where he died, April 12, 1870. He wrote, *Abhandlung über die Cosmogonie der heidnischen Völker vor der Zeit Jesu u. der Apostel*, a prize essay (Hague, 1850):—*Geschichte des Heidenthums in Bezug auf Religion, Wissen, Kunst, Sittlichkeit und Staatsleben* (Breslau, 1851-53, 2 vols.):—*Der deutsche Volksaberglaube der Gegenwart* (Hamburg, 1850; 2d ed. 1869):—*Handbuch der christlichen Sittenlehre* (Berlin, 1861-62, 2 vols.; Engl. transl. by J. P. Lacroix, *Christian Ethics*, N. Y., 1873, 2 vols.). After his death was published *Zur Vorgeschichte der Bartholomäusnacht von Dr. S. Müller-Frauenstein* (Leipsic, 1879). Besides these works he published some minor writings. See *Literarischer Handweiser*, 1870, p. 489; *Theologisches Universallexikon*, s. v.; Zuchold, *Bibl. Theol.* ii, 1478. (B. P.)

Wyasa, in Hindû philosophy, is probably a generic name of the founders of the Vedanta (q. v.).

Wyatt, Christopher B., D.D., a Protestant Episcopal clergyman, graduated from the General Theological Seminary, N. Y. He was ordained deacon in 1846 and presbyter in 1849; became rector of a church in San Francisco, Cal., which he served until about 1856; in 1858 of St. Thomas's Church, New Windsor, N. Y.; in 1862 of Mount Calvary Church, Baltimore, Md.; in 1864 of Trinity Church, San Francisco, Cal., whence he removed, in 1869 or 1870, to New York city, where he resided until 1872, and then became rector of St. Peter's

Church, Westchester, N. Y., in which office he remained until his death, Nov. 8, 1879, at the age of fifty-four years. See *Prot. Episc. Almanac*, 1880, p. 172.

Wycliffites, the followers of John Wycliffe (q. v.). For their history and doctrines, see LOLLARDS.

Wylie, SAMUEL, D.D., a Reformed Presbyterian minister, was born in Ireland about 1792, and came to the United States when a boy. He was educated under the supervision of his uncle, the Rev. S. B. Wylie, D.D., of Philadelphia. He graduated from the University of Pennsylvania and at the theological seminary of the Reformed Presbyterian Church, and was ordained in 1818. He acted as a home missionary until 1820, when he was settled as pastor of a church at Sparta, Ill., where he remained until his death, March 20, 1872. He exerted a wide influence in his field of labor, above a dozen churches having been formed from the nucleus of his original congregation.

Wymundus, a Scotch prelate, was consecrated bishop of the Isles in the 12th century. He was deprived about 1151. See Keith, *Scottish Bishops*, p. 297.

Wyntown (Wynton, or Winton), ANDREW OF, a Scotch ecclesiastic and poet, was a canon regular of the priory of St. Andrews, and in or before 1395 was elected prior of St. Serf's Inch, Lochleven. He was prior at least as late as 1413, and records the death of Robert, duke of Albany, which occurred in 1420. But the dates of his own birth and death are unknown. He is the third of the early Scotch poets whose works are extant. Of his writings we have *De Orygynale Cronykil of Scotland, be Andrew of Wyntown, Priour of Sanct Serfis Ynche, in Loch Levyn; now first published, with Notes, etc., by David Macpherson* (1795). See Mackenzie, *Scotch Writers;* Irving, *Scotch Poets;* Allibone, *Dict. of Brit. and Amer. Authors*, s. v.

Wyttenbach, DANIEL, one of the most prominent theologians of the Reformed Church of the 18th century, was born at Worb, near Berne, June 26, 1706. He studied in Switzerland, Germany, Holland, and France. In 1746 he was appointed professor at Berne, and in 1756 was called to Marburg, where he also received the degree of doctor of divinity. He died June 29, 1779. He is the author of, *Prælectio de Iis, quæ Observanda sunt circa Theologiam et Dogmaticam et Eleuchticam Docendam* (Berne, 1747):—*De Principiis Statuum Evangelicorum circa Res Ecclesiasticas* (Marburg, 1756):—*Testamen Theologiæ Dogmaticæ Methodo Scientifica Pertractatæ* (Berne, 1741–47, 3 vols.):—*Compendium Theol. Dogmaticæ et Moralis* (Frankfort, 1754), etc. See Curtius, *Memoria D. Wyttenbachii* (Marburg, 1779); Bang, *Elogium in D. Wyttenbachium* (Berne, 1781); Strieder, *Hess. Gell.-Geschichte*, xvii, 322 sq.; Heppe, *Geschichte der theol. Facultät zu Marburg* (Marburg, 1873); *Theol. Universallexikon*, s. v.; Fürst, *Bibl. Jud.* iii, 538. (B. P.)

X.

Xantes Pagninus. See PAGNINUS, SANCTES.

Xan'thicus (Ξανθικός), the name of the sixth month among the Seleucid Syrians (2 Macc. xi, 30, 33 38 [xii, 1]), i. e. in the Macedonian calendar (Ideler, *Handb. d. Chronol.* i, 392 sq.). Josephus makes it parallel with the Jewish *Nisan* (*Ant.* i, 3, 3; iii, 10, 5; comp. *War*, v, 3, 1). See MONTH.

Xanthopulos. See NICEPHORUS CALLISTUS.

Xaverius Society. This is the name of a missionary society founded in 1822 by some laymen at Lyons, in honor of Francis Xavier. This society is found all over the globe. Its income was, in 1869, five millions and a half in francs. See Aloys, *Statist. Jahrbuch der Kirche*, i, 179–182; Marx, *Generalstatistik der Kathol. Vereine* (Trier, 1871). (B. P.)

Xenæans, a Monophysite sect which held a middle line between the *Aphthartodcetæ* (q. v.) and the *Phthartolatræ* (q. v.), maintaining that Christ truly became man, with the same capacities for suffering and the same human sensations as men in general, but that he did so of his own free will and choice, and not by the physical necessity of his human nature. This doctrine originated with Xenaias, of Tabal, in Persia, afterwards known as Philoxenus of Mabug (q. v.). The Xenæan party was strongly opposed, in common with the other Monophysites, by Flavian, the patriarch who succeeded Peter the Fuller.

Xeniădès, a Greek philosopher, was a native of Corinth. The age in which he flourished is uncertain. Our knowledge of him is derived chiefly from Sextus Empiricus, who represents him as the most ultra sceptic, maintaining that all notions are false, and that there is absolutely nothing true in the universe.

Xenaias. See PHILOXENUS OF MABUG.

Xenocrătēs, a Greek philosopher, was born in Chalcedon, 396 B.C. He was originally a pupil of Æschines, the Socratic philosopher, and afterwards of Plato. His intimate connection with Plato is indicated by the account that he accompanied that master to Syracuse. After the death of Plato he betook himself, with Aristotle, to Hermias, tyrant of Atarneus and Assus, and, after his return to Athens, was repeatedly sent on embassies to Philip of Macedonia, and at a later time to Antipater, during the Lamian war. The want of quick apprehension and natural grace he compensated by persevering and thorough-going industry, pure benevolence, purity of morals, unselfishness, and a moral earnestness which compelled esteem and trust even from the Athenians of his own age. Yet even he experienced the fickleness of popular favor, and being too poor to pay the μετοίκιον, or protection money, is said to have been saved only by the courage of the orator Lycurgus, or even to have been bought by Demetrius Phalereus, and then emancipated. He became president of the academy, 339 B.C., even before the death of Spensippus, and occupied the post for twenty-five years. He died in 314 B.C. Xenocrates' doctrines were discussed by Aristotle and Theophrastus, and he was held in high regard by such men as Panætius and Cicero. Diogenes Laertius gives a long list of his writings, but the works themselves have perished. With a more comprehensive work on dialectic there were connected separate treatises on science, on divisions, on genera and species, on ideas, on the opposite, and others, to which probably the work on mediate thought also belonged. Two works on physics are mentioned, as are also books upon the gods, on the existent, on the One, on the indefinite, on the soul, on the affections, on memory, etc. In like manner, with the more general ethical treatises on happiness and on virtue, there were connected separate books on individual virtues, on the voluntary, etc. His four books on royalty he had addressed to Alexander. Besides these, he had written treatises on the state, on the power of law, etc., as well as upon geometry, arithmetic, and astrology. We know little of the doctrines of Xenocrates, but we may infer that he exhibited his opinions in a systematic form, and not in dialogues, like his master, Plato. To him is attributed the division of philosophy into logic, ethic, and physic, or physics. He occupied himself principally with attempting to reduce the ideal doctrines of Plato to mathematical elements. He predicted three forms of being—the sensuous, that which is perceived by the intellect, and that which is compounded and consists in opinion. In his positions we see the tendency of the academy towards the Pythagorean doctrines of number. Unity and duality he considers as the gods which rule the world, and the soul as a self-moving number. Other like conceits are attributed to him. Xenocrates considered that the notion of the deity pervades all things, and is even in the animals which we call irrational. He also admitted an order of dæmons, or something intermediate between the divine and the mortal, which he made to consist in the conditions of the soul. In his ethical teaching he made happiness consist not in the possession of a virtuous mind only, but also of all the powers that minister to it and enable it to effect its purposes. How decidedly he insisted, not only on the recognition of the unconditional nature of moral excellence, but on morality of thought, is shown by the declaration that it comes to the same thing whether one casts longing eyes or sets his feet upon the property of others. His moral earnestness is also expressed in the warning that the ears of children should be guarded against the poison of immoral speeches. See Van de Wynpersee, *Diatribe de Xenocrate Chalcedonio* (1822); Diogenes Laertius, *Xenocrates;* Ritter, *Geschichte der Philosophie*, ii; Ueberweg, *History of Philosophy*, i, 133 sq.; Smith, *Dict. of Greek and Rom. Biog. and Myth.* s. v.

Xenophănès, a Greek philosopher, was born at Colophon, Ionia, probably about 570 B.C. He was the son of Orthomenes, or, according to others, of Dexius. He left his native land as an exile, and betook himself to the Ionian colonies, Sicily, Zancle, and Catana. There can be no doubt that, as the founder of the Eleatic school, he lived for some time at least in Elea (Velia, in Italy, founded by the Phocæans about 536 B.C.), the foundation of which he had sung. His death occurred probably about 480 B.C., though amid the conflicting statements concerning his age it is best to say that he lived between the times of Pythagoras and Heraclitus, for he mentions the one and is mentioned by the other.

Xenophanes was a poet as well as a philosopher. He wrote an epic of two thousand verses on the founding of Elea, and a poem on the foundation of his native city, Colophon. His philosophical doctrines were expressed in poetic form, and from the few fragments of his poetry which remain, and the brief notices of him by other writers, we collect what we know of his doctrines. He attacked Hesiod and Homer, in hexameter verses, elegiacs, and iambic verses, for their representations of the deities, to whom those poets attribute all the vices and weaknesses of men. He taught that God was one, unlike men either in form or mind. He pointed out the fact that men, in their representations of the gods, depict them as having bodies like their own, and declared that if animals could make representations of the deity, they would make them like themselves. Assuming that the deity is the most powerful of beings, he proves that he must of necessity be one, all alike, all endued with equal powers of seeing, comprehending, and hearing. He asserted that the deity is of a spherical form, neither limited nor unlimited, neither moving nor at rest. God rules and directs all, and things as they appear to us are the imperfect manifestations of the One eternal. He maintains that God's true nature cannot be known. He has been charged with being a pantheist, but from this accusation Cousin takes some pains to defend him. In the early history of philosophy the language of the science was not well defined, so that many expressions which have since come to mean certain things did not then have those meanings. Certain expressions of Xenophanes have been quoted by modern writers to prove his pantheism; but other quotations, as, for example, those of Aristotle, show that he speaks of God as a Being eternal, and distinct from the visible universe.

See Diogenes Laertius, *Xenophanes;* Ritter, *Geschichte der Philosophie*, vol. i; Cousin, *Nouveaux Fragmens Philosophiques*, art. *Xenophane;* Simon Karsten, *Xenophanis Colophonii Carminum Reliquæ, de Vita ejus et Studiis Dissernit, Fragmenta Explicavit, Placita Illustravit;* Smith, *Dict. of Greek and Rom. Biog. and Myth.* s. v.

Xenxi, a sect of materialists in Japan, who believe in no other life than the present.

Xeodoxins are a sect among the Japanese who acknowledge a future state, and believe in the immortality of the soul. Amidas is their favorite deity, and the bonzes of this sect go up and down the public streets and roads, summoning devotees by the sound of a bell, and distributing indulgences and dispensations, constantly crying in a chanting tone, "O ever blessed Amidas, have mercy upon us."

Xerophagia (Ξηροφάγια, from ξηρός, *dry*, and φαγεῖν, *to eat*) were fast-days in the early ages of the Christian Church, on which they ate nothing but bread and salt, and drank water; but afterwards pulse, herbs, and fruits were added. Epiphanius says, "throughout the Holy Week people continue to use dry food, viz. bread and salt, using water only in the evening" (*Compend. Doct. Cath.*). This great fast was kept six days of the Holy Week for devotion, and not by obligation; so that the Church condemned the Montanists, who, of their own private authority, would not only oblige all people to observe the xerophagia of the Holy Week, but also other fasts that they had established, as well as several Lents. The Essenes, whether they were Jews or the first Christians of the Church of Alexandria, observed xerophagia on certain days; for Philo says that they put nothing to their bread and water but salt and hyssop. During Lent fish was the only animal food permitted; but, according to some authorities, fowls were afterwards added.

Xerxes (Ξέρξης; Pers. *Kheshwershe*, or *Ks'harsa;* according to Benfey, *K'hshyarshe*), king of Persia, is chiefly known for his gigantic but unsuccessful invasion of Greece (Herod. vii, viii; Diod. Sic. xi). He was the son of Darius Hystaspis, and of Atossa, daughter of Cyrus. He succeeded his father, 485 B.C., having been declared heir to the kingdom of Persia a short time before his father's death, who preferred him before his elder brother Artabazanes, because the latter was born while Darius was a private individual; but Xerxes was born after his elevation to the throne. He was the "fourth" king prophesied of in Dan. xi, 2: "Behold there shall stand up yet three kings in Persia (Cyrus, Cambyses, and Darius, son of Hydaspes), and the fourth (Xerxes) shall be far richer than they all; and by his strength through his riches he shall stir up all against the realm of Greece." Xerxes, on his accession, showed himself very friendly to the Jews of the captivity, and confirmed all the favors granted to them by his father; indeed, Josephus (*Ant.* xi, 5) ascribes to Xerxes the letter in behalf of the returning Jews given in Ezra vii, 11–26. He began his reign by conquering Egypt; and rapidly subdued the Phœnicians, Cilicia, Pamphylia, Pontus, Pisidia, Lycia, Caria, Myria, Troas, Bithynia, the Hellespont, and the Isle of Cyprus. Four years previously the forces of Darius had been defeated by the Greeks under Miltiades at the battle of Marathon, and the interval had been passed in preparing for a second expedition. These preparations Xerxes continued on a scale of magnificence almost incredible, and in the spring of 480 B.C. he commenced his march from Sardis: his army was moved forward with great deliberation, and being numbered on its arrival in Europe was found to muster 1,700,000 foot, and 80,000 horse, besides camels, chariots, and ships of war. These numbers, and the undisciplined crowds who must have attended them, to supply their necessities, are perfectly bewildering to the

Cuneiform and Hieroglyph of Xerxes.

imagination; and they become still more so when their varied costumes, the silken and gilded tents, the standards, the costly armor, and the variety of national weapons are considered. One of the political parties of Greece, it must be borne in mind, was in league with the Persian court, and the terror of the country verged upon despair of maintaining their liberties. Themistocles, however, while the pass of Thermopylæ was defended by Leonidas and his Spartans, succeeded in rallying his countrymen, and, having created a navy, defeated Xerxes at the battle of Salamis. This great event took place in the year of the expedition, 480 B.C. The Persians were allowed to retreat in such order as they could, but Mardonius, one of the principal commanders, reserved a more manageable army, the best he could pick from the flying host, and with these he was defeated by the combined Greeks the year following. After the return of Xerxes from his unsuccessful campaign, he ordered the demolition of all the Grecian temples in Asia; that of Diana at Ephesus alone being spared. He had been instructed in the religion of the magi by Zoroaster, and was inspired with a horror of idolatry; wherefore he also destroyed all the idols in Babylon; thus fulfilling the prophecies of Jeremiah vi, 2, and li, 44-47. See BABYLON. Xerxes was assassinated by Artabanus, one of the great officers of his court, who aspired to found a new dynasty in Persia, 465 B.C. See Smith, *Dict. of Class. Biog.* s. v. See PERSIA.

This prince was, according to most interpreters (see especially Scaliger, *Emend. Temp.* vi, 587, 596), the *Ahasuerus* (אֲחַשְׁוֵרוֹשׁ) of the book of Esther (q. v.), an identification which the whole romantic story of Esther goes to confirm (see Rosenmüller, *Alterth.* I, i, 338 sq.; Hävernick, *Einl. ins A. T.* II, i, 339 sq.; Baumgarten, *De Fide Libri Esth.* p. 123 sq.; Rödiger, in the *Halle Encyclop.* I, xxxviii, 295 sq.). The enumeration of his resources (Esth. i, 2; ii, 16) agrees with the statement of Herodotus (vii, 7 sq.) respecting the rallying of his forces against Egypt; and the date of the great feast, the third year of his reign (Esth. i, 3), tallies with the successful conclusion of that expedition which took place in his second year, the luxurious character of the carousal, moreover, being consistent with Persian customs (Herod. i, 133). Between the dismissal of his sultana Vashti, resulting from that feast, and the reception of Esther into his harem in his seventh year (Esth. ii, 16), falls appropriately the Greek campaign which Xerxes, after several years of preparation, undertook in his fifth year (Herod. vii, 20. The duration of the expedition, from the crossing of the Hellespont by Xerxes [ibid. vii, 33 sq.], to the return to Susa, is disputed by chronologers [see Baumgarten, l. c. p. 142 sq.]; but two years is a most probable interval [see Clinton, *Fasti Hellen.* ii, 28; *L'Art de Vérifier les Dates*, ii, 387 sq.]). Again, the extent of the dominions (Esth. i, 1 sq.) corresponds with the classical description of Xerxes; he occupied Ethiopia, which Cambyses had already attempted (Herod. iii, 20 sq.; moreover, the Ethiopians served in Xerxes' armies, ibid. vii, 69 sq.), as well as India, to which Darius Hystaspis had advanced (ibid. iv, 44 sq.). Moreover, the voluptuousness and imperiousness of women (Esth. v, 3; vii, 3 sq.; viii, 3 sq.; ix, 12) in the time of Xerxes are well known (Herod. ix, 10 sq.). But especially does the vexation which Xerxes experienced from the failure of his expedition to Greece explain why, while living entirely for his own pleasure (Cicero, *Tusc.* v, 7), he should not only abandon the most important affairs of state to an upstart (Esth. iii, 15), but also give his assent to deeds of violence, now on this side, and now on that (iii, 10 sq.; vii, 10; viii, 8); all of which facts characterize, according to our ideas, a senseless (Herod. vii, 35), godless (viii, 109), and cruel despot (vii, 37 sq.). Finally the raising of a large tax (Esth. x, 1) may readily have followed the exhaustion of the royal treasury by the disastrous expedition into Greece. See AHASUERUS.

Xisuthrus (or **Xisithrus**), the Chaldæan *Noah.* See DELUGE.

Xt, Xtian, Xtmas, are abbreviations for *Christ, Christian*, and *Christmas*, respectively. Other abbreviations of a similar character are used: *Xmas*, or *Xm.*, for Christmas; *Xn*, for Christian; *Xnty*, or *Xty*, for Christianity.

Xylolaters (literally, *worshippers of the wood*) was a term of reproach applied by the old iconoclasts to the orthodox Christians, who reverenced both the symbol of their faith and representations of sacred persons and objects.

Xylon (*the wood*), i. e. the *Cross* on which our Lord was crucified.

Xylophoria. See WOOD-CARRYING, FEAST OF.

Xuarez, JUAN, an early Roman Catholic prelate in America, was a native of Valencia, Spain, and entered the Franciscan order in the province of St. Gabriel, established by Martin at a time when, by the zealous reforms of cardinal Cisneros, the Franciscans of Spain were full of fervor and piety. When Cortez applied for Franciscan missionaries to undertake the conversion of the thickly settled towns in the kingdom just reduced by his arms, a Spanish father, Francis de los Angeles, had just been elected general of the order of St. Francis. For the leader of the twelve missionaries chosen, he selected Martin de Valencia, and fourth among their number was Juan Xuarez. With his superior, he embarked at San Lucar, Jan. 15, 1524, and on May 13 they reached the castle of San Juan de Ulloa, before Vera Cruz, and met Cortez at Mexico. Father Xuarez was placed at Huegocongo, and as the result of his labors there the temple, where human sacrifices had often been perpetrated, was destroyed. After laboring here two years he returned to Spain, in 1526, accompanied by some of his Indian pupils, and sent out six more missionaries. In 1527 Xuarez was assigned to the expedition then fitting out by Pamphilo de Narvaez, which was intended to establish in Florida a settlement to rival that of Mexico. Xuarez was not only made commissary of his order, but was nominated bishop of Florida, his diocese to extend from the Atlantic to Rio de las Palmas, Mexico. With four Franciscan fathers and other priests, he sailed from San Lucar, June 17, 1527, and reached Florida in April. Misfortune attended this ill-starred expedition. The people were fierce and hostile, and the force, thinned by disease and constant engagements, crept along the northern coast of the gulf of Mexico. The brave Narvaez was driven out to sea, and never again heard of. The party then scattered, and many perished on an island called Malhado, probably that called Massacre Island by the French. There is no record of the death of bishop Xuarez and his companion, John de Palos. Alvar Nunez Cabeza de Vaca, with three others, reached a Spanish post in Sonora, but has left no details. They either perished of hunger or at the hands of the Indians, about the close of 1528. The portraits of the original twelve Franciscans of Mexico have been preserved, and that of Xuarez appears in the relation of Cabeza de Vaca. See (N. Y.) *Catholic Almanac*, 1872, p. 67.

Y.

Yaalah. See ROE.

Yaanah. See OWL.

Yaçna (literally, *sacrifice*), in Parsee philosophy, is a book of the Zend Avesta (q. v.).

Yadayim. See TALMUD.

Yaël. See WILD GOAT.

Yaën. See OSTRICH.

Yahalom. See DIAMOND.

Yahgan Version OF THE SCRIPTURES. Yahgan is the language spoken by a tribe in the south of Tierra del Fuego. The Rev. T. Bridges, of the South American Missionary Society, who has been laboring among this people for the last eleven years, and has taught them to read and write their own tongue, written according to Ellis's phonetic system, has prepared the gospel of Luke in the above language, spoken by about three thousand people. This is the only part of the Bible which has been published in Yahgan by the British and Foreign Bible Society, and appears for the first time in the seventy-sixth report (1880), in the table of languages. (B. P.)

Yaks are a species of dæmons recognised as remnants of the primitive superstition of the Singhalese in Ceylon. They are supposed to be the authors of diseases and other misfortunes, and the *Yakadura*, or devil-dancer, is almost invariably called upon to overcome their malignity by his chants and charms. In these exorcisms the performers wear horrible masks, which have beaks, and are, in fact, caricatures of birds' heads. These dæmons are believed to marry, and delight in dances, songs, and other amusements. They have great strength, and some of them are represented as possessing splendor and dignity.

Yalden (or **Youlding**), THOMAS, D.D., an English divine and poet, was born at Exeter in 1671. He was educated at Magdalen College, Oxford, and chosen fellow in 1700. He entered into holy orders the following year, became rector of Willoughby, in Warwickshire, and was chosen lecturer of moral philosophy. In 1706 he entered the family of the duke of Beaufort, and soon after became rector of Chalton and of Cleanville, in Hertfordshire. He also had the sinecure prebends of Deans, Hains, and Pendles, in Devonshire. In 1713 he was chosen preacher of Bridewell Hospital, on the resignation of Dr. Atterbury. He was arrested and tried for complicity in what is known as Bishop Atterbury's Plot, in 1722, but was soon released for want of evidence. He died July 16, 1736. He published an *Ode for St. Cecilia's Day* (1693):—*On the Conquest of Namur*, a Pindaric ode (1695):—*The Temple of Fame*, a poem (1700): — *A Hymn to Darkness:* — *A Hymn to Light*, and other works, chiefly poetical. See Johnson, *British Poets;* Dryden, *Miscellanies*, vol. iii, iv; Lintot, *Miscellanies;* Chalmers, *Biog. Dict.*; Allibone, *Dict. of Brit. and Amer. Authors*, s. v.

Yale, ELISHA, D.D., a Presbyterian divine, was born at Lee, Mass., June 15, 1780. He was converted in 1799; pursued his classical and theological studies, under the Rev. Dr. Perkins, at West Hartford, Conn.; was licensed to preach by the North Association of Hartford County in February, 1803, and ordained and installed pastor of the Church at Kingsborough, N. Y., May 23, 1804, where he remained until 1852. He was chosen a corporate member of the American Board of Foreign Missions in 1838. He died Jan. 9, 1853. Dr. Yale was an excellent classical and general scholar. His discourses were always rich in substantial and well-matured thought, and in nothing was he more remarkable than his devotion to the cause of missions and to the preparation of young men for the ministry. He published, *Divine Method for Raising Charitable Contributions* (Boston, 1845):—*Select Verse System, for the Use of Individuals, Families, and Schools* (Rochester, 1853). He also published single sermons and articles in periodicals, and left in MS. *A Review of a Pastorate of Forty-eight Years* and *Helps to Cultivate the Conscience.* See Sprague, *Annals of the Amer. Pulpit*, iv, 348; Allibone, *Dict. of Brit. and Amer. Authors*, s. v.

Yang and **Yin** (or **Yen**) are terms used in Chinese philosophy to indicate the two phases under which the ultimate principle of the universe displays itself in the phenomenal world. They were generated by *Tai-ki*, or the supreme principle — *Yang* being a perfect, subtle, celestial, luminous nature; *Yin* being matter, imperfect, crude, earthly, obscure. From this duality of opposite essences, called the two *Ke*, all created existences have sprung. Gardner (*Faiths of the World*, s. v.) quotes from Hardwick as follows: "According to the different proportions in which Yang and Yin are blended is the character of every created existence. Everything is Yang and Yin together. For the highest actual manifestation in which Yang preponderates we look to heaven itself, which is, accordingly, to be esteemed the aptest image cognizable by the senses of the ultimate and all-embracing principle. Earth is, on the contrary, the highest form of Yin. The same duality, where one or other of the factors operated, either for the purpose of transforming or uniting, issued in the first production of the innate essences, which constitute the five elements of water, fire, wood, metal, and earth. A transcendental union and coagulation now takes place of the ultimate principle, the two essences, and the five elements. The positive essence becomes the masculine power, the negative essence the feminine power, conceived in which character the former constitutes the heavenly mode, or principle; the latter the earthly mode, or principle. By a mutual influencing, the two produce all things in the visible, palpable world, and the double work of evolution and dissolution goes on without end—Yang evincing its peculiar force in every kind of progress, Yin in every kind of retrogression; Yang determining commencement, Yin completion; Yang predominant in spring and summer, and the author of all movement and activity; Yin more visible in the autumn and the winter, passive, drooping, and inert." The same idea pervades their notions of rational as well as irrational beings. In the ethical system of the Chinese, evil is *Yin* of the moral world, and good is *Yang*. See CHINA.

Yanshuph. See OWL.

Yao Version OF THE SCRIPTURES. This language is spoken by the Yaos, occupying the country to the east and south of Lake Nyassa, including the Scotch stations Blantyre and Livingstonia. The Rev. Chauncy Maples, of the Universities' Mission, after working three years at Masasi, in Africa, with bishop Steere, prepared a translation of the gospel of Matthew into that language, which was printed by the British and Foreign Bible Society in London in 1880, at the recommendation of bishop Steere, the translator himself carrying the work through the press. (B. P.)

Yariba (or **Yoruba**) **Version** OF THE SCRIPTURES. Yariba is an African language spoken by the tribes on the right, or west, bank of the Niger. A translation into this dialect is of recent date. The first part printed was the epistle to the Romans, translated by the Rev. S. Crowther, a native of the country. It was published in 1850. In the following year the gospel of Luke, the Acts of the Apostles, together with the epistles of James and Peter, were printed by the British and Foreign Bible Society. Other parts were added from time to time, and at present the

Yorubas enjoy the entire New Test., together with the books of Genesis to Ruth, Psalms, and Daniel, of the Old Test., in their vernacular. (B. P.)

Yarn (מִקְוֵה, *mikvêh*, *a collection;* or מִקְוֵא, *mikvê*). The notice of yarn is contained in an extremely obscure passage in 1 Kings x, 28 (2 Chron. i, 16): "Solomon had horses brought out of Egypt, and linen yarn; the king's merchants received the linen yarn at a price." The Sept. gives ἐκ Θεκουέ, implying an original reading of מִתְּקוֹעַ; the Vulg has *de Coa*, which is merely a Latinized form of the original. The Hebrew received text is questionable, from the circumstance that the second *mikvêh* has its final vowel lengthened as if it were in the *status constructus.* The probability is that the term does refer to some entrepôt of Egyptian commerce, but whether Tekoah, as in the Sept., or Coa, as in the Vulg., is doubtful. Gesenius (*Thesaur.* p. 1202) gives the sense of "number" as applying equally to the merchants and the horses: "A *band* of the king's merchants bought a *drove* (of horses) at a price;" but the verbal arrangement in 2 Chron. is opposed to this rendering. Thenius (*Exeg. Handb.* on 1 Kings x, 28) combines this sense with the former, giving to the first *mikvéh* the sense "from Tekoah," to the second the sense of "drove." Bertheau (*Exeg. Handb.* on 2 Chron. i, 16) and Fürst (*Lex.* s. v.) side with the Vulgate, and suppose the place called *Coa* to have been on the Egyptian frontier: "The king's merchants from Coa (i. e. stationed at Coa) took the horses from Coa at a price." The sense adopted in the A. V. is derived from Jewish interpreters. See LINEN.

Yashpeh. See JASPER.

Yatum, the religion of the Yatus, a name given to the enemies of Zoroaster in the Zend-Avesta. These were overthrown by Darius, the son of Hystaspes, and the religion of Zoroaster re-established. See Lenormant, *Chaldæan Magic*, p. 219.

Year (שָׁנָה, *shanâh*, lit. *repetition*, kindred with שֵׁנִי, *second;* ἔτος), the highest ordinary division of time, marked by the solar revolutions of the seasons. See TIME.

I. *Years, properly so called.*—Two years were known to, and apparently used by, the Hebrews. See CALENDAR.

1. A year of 360 days, containing 12 months of 30 days each, is indicated by certain passages in the prophetical Scriptures. The time, times, and a half, of Daniel (vii, 25; xii, 7), where "time" (Ch. עִדָּן, Heb. מוֹעֵד) means "year," evidently represent the same period as the 42 months (Rev. xi, 2) and 1260 days of the Revelation (xi, 3; xii, 6), for $360 \times 3.5 = 1260$, and $30 \times 42 = 1260$. This year perfectly corresponds to the Egyptian Vague year, without the five intercalary days. It appears to have been in use in Noah's time, or at least in the time of the writer of the narrative of the flood, for in that narrative the interval from the 17th day of the 2d month to the 17th day of the 7th of the same year appears to be stated to be a period of 150 days (Gen. vii, 11, 24; viii, 3, 4; comp. 13), and, as the 1st, 2d, 7th, and 10th months of one year are mentioned (vii, 11; viii, 4, 5, 13, 14), the 1st day of the 10th month of this year being separated from the 1st day of the 1st month of the next year by an interval of at least 54 days (viii, 5, 6, 10, 12, 13), we can only infer a year of 12 months. Ideler disputes the former inference, arguing that as the water first began to sink after 150 days (and then had been fifteen cubits above all high mountains), it must have sunk for some days ere the ark could have rested on Ararat, so that the second date must have been more than 150 days later than the first (*Handbuch*, i, 69, 70, 478, 479). This argument depends upon the meaning of the expression "high mountains," and upon the height of "the mountains of Ararat," upon which the ark rested (Gen. viii, 4), and we are certainly justified by Shemitic usage, if we do not consider the usual inference of the great height attained by the flood to be a necessary one (*Genesis of the Earth and of Man*, 2d ed. p. 97, 98). The exact correspondence of the interval mentioned to 5 months of 30 days each, and the use of a year of 360 days, or 12 such months, by the prophets, the latter fact overlooked by Ideler, favor the idea that such a year is here meant, unless, indeed, one identical with the Egyptian Vague year, of 12 months of 30 days and 5 intercalary days. The settlement of this question depends upon the nature and history of these years, and our information on the latter subject is not sufficiently certain to enable us to do more than hazard a conjecture.

A year of 360 days is the rudest known. It is formed of 12 spurious lunar months, and was probably the parent of the lunar year of 354 days, and the Vague year of 365. That it should have continued any time in use would be surprising were it not for the convenient length of the months. The Hebrew year, from the time of the Exodus, as we shall see, was evidently lunar, though in some manner rendered virtually solar, and we may therefore infer that the lunar year is as old as the date of the Exodus. As the Hebrew year was not an Egyptian year, and as nothing is said of its being new, save in its time of commencement, it was perhaps earlier in use among the Israelites, and either brought into Egypt by them or borrowed from Shemite settlers.

The Vague year was certainly in use in Egypt in as remote an age as the earlier part of the 12th dynasty (cir. 2000 B.C.), and there can be no reasonable doubt that it was there used at the time of the building of the Great Pyramid (cir. 2350 B.C.). The intercalary days seem to be of Egyptian institution, for each of them was dedicated to one of the great gods, as if the innovation had been thus made permanent by the priests, and perhaps rendered popular as a series of days of feasting and rejoicing. The addition would, however, date from a very early period, that of the final settlement of the Egyptian religion.

As the lunar year and the Vague year run up parallel to so early a period as that of the Exodus, and the former seems to have been then Shemitic, the latter then, and for several centuries earlier, Egyptian, and probably of Egyptian origin, we may reasonably conjecture that the former originated from a year of 360 days in Asia, the latter from the same year in Africa, this primitive year having been used by the Noachians before their dispersion.

2. The year used by the Hebrews from the time of the Exodus may be said to have been then instituted, since a current month, Abib, on the 14th day of which the first Passover was kept, was then made the first month of the year. The essential characteristics of this year can be clearly determined, though we cannot fix those of any single year. It was essentially solar, for the offerings of productions of the earth, first-fruits, harvest-produce, and ingathered fruits were fixed to certain days of the year, two of which were in the periods of great feasts, the third itself a feast reckoned from one of the former days. It seems evident that the year was made to depend upon these times, and it may be observed that such a calendar would tend to cause thankfulness for God's good gifts, and would put in the background the great luminaries which the heathen worshipped in Egypt and in Canaan. Though the year was thus essentially solar, it is certain that the months were lunar, each commencing with a new moon. There must, therefore, have been some method of adjustment. The first point to be decided is how the commencement of each year was fixed. On the 16th day of Abib ripe ears of corn were to be offered as first-fruits of the harvest (Lev. ii, 14; xxiii, 10, 11): this was the day on which the sickle was begun to be put to the corn (Deut. xvi, 9), and no doubt Josephus is right in stating that until the offering of first-fruits had been made no harvest-work was to be begun (*Ant.* iii, 10, 5). He also states that ears of barley were offered (ibid.). That this

was the case, and that the ears were the earliest ripe, is evident from the following circumstances. The reaping of barley commenced the harvest (2 Sam. xxi, 9), that of wheat following, apparently without any considerable interval (Ruth ii, 23). On the day of Pentecost thanksgiving was offered for the harvest, and it was therefore called the Feast of Harvest. It was reckoned from the commencement of the harvest, on the 16th day of the 1st month. The 50 days must include the whole time of the harvest of both wheat and barley throughout Palestine. According to the observations of modern travellers, barley is ripe, in the warmest parts of Palestine, in the first days of April. The barley-harvest, therefore, begins about half a month or less after the vernal equinox. Each year, if solar, would thus begin at about that equinox, when the earliest ears of barley must be ripe. As, however, the months were lunar, the commencement of the year must have been fixed by a new moon near this point of time. The new moon must have been that which fell about or next after the equinox, not more than a few days before, on account of the offering of first-fruits. Ideler, whose observations on this matter we have thus far followed, supposes that the new moon was chosen by observation of the forwardness of the barley-crops in the warmer parts of the country (*Handbuch*, i, 490). But such a method would have caused confusion on account of the different times of the harvest in different parts of Palestine; and in the period of the Judges there would often have been two separate commencements of the year in regions divided by hostile tribes, and in each of which the Israelitish population led an existence almost independent of any other branch. It is more likely that the Hebrews would have determined their new-year's day by the observation of heliacal or other star-risings or settings known to mark the right time of the solar year. By such a method the beginning of any year could have been fixed a year before, either to one day, or, supposing the month-commencements were fixed by actual observation, within a day or two. We need not doubt that the Israelites were well acquainted with such means of marking the periods of a solar year. In the ancient Song of Deborah we read how "They fought from heaven; the stars in their courses fought against Sisera. The river of Kishon swept them away, that ancient river, the river Kishon" (Judg. v, 20, 21). The stars that marked the times of rain are thus connected with the swelling of the river in which the fugitive Canaanites perished. So, too, we read how the Lord demanded of Job, "Canst thou bind the sweet influences of Kimah, or loose the bands of Kesil?" (Job xxxviii, 31). "The best and most fertilizing of the rains," in Palestine and the neighboring lands, save Egypt, "fall when the Pleiades set at dawn (not exactly heliacally), at the end of autumn; rain scarcely ever falling at the opposite season, when Scorpio sets at dawn." That Kimah signifies the Pleiades does not admit of reasonable doubt, and Kesil, as opposite to it, would be Scorpio, being identified with Cor Scorpionis by Aben-Ezra. Therefore it cannot be questioned that the Israelites, even during the troubled time of the Judges, were well acquainted with the method of determining the seasons of the solar year by observing the stars. Not alone was this the practice of the civilized Egyptians, but, at all times of which we know their history, of the Arabs, and also of the Greeks in the time of Hesiod, while yet their material civilization and science were rudimentary. It has always been the custom of pastoral and scattered peoples, rather than of the dwellers in cities; and if the Egyptians be thought to form an exception, it must be recollected that they used it at a period not remote from that at which their civilization came from the plain of Shinar.

It follows, from the determination of the proper new moon of the 1st month, whether by observation of a stellar phenomenon, or of the forwardness of the crops, that the method of intercalation can only have been that in use after the captivity, the addition of a 13th month whenever the 12th ended too long before the equinox for the offering of the first-fruits to be made at the time fixed. This method is in accordance with the permission granted to postpone the celebration of the Passover for one month in the case of any one who was legally unclean, or journeying at a distance (Numb. ix, 9-13); and there is a historical instance in the case of Hezekiah of such a postponement, for both reasons, of the national celebration (2 Chron. xxx, 1-3, 15). Such a practice as that of an intercalation varying in occurrence is contrary to Western usage; but the like prevails in all Moslem countries in a far more inconvenient form in the case of the commencement of every month. The day is determined by actual observation of the new moon, and thus a day is frequently unexpectedly added to or deducted from a month at one place, and months commence on different days at different towns in the same country. The Hebrew intercalation, if determined by stellar phenomena, would not be liable to a like uncertainty, though such may have been the case with the actual day of the new moon.

The later Jews had two commencements of the year, whence it is commonly but inaccurately said that they had two years, the sacred year and the civil. We prefer to speak of the sacred and civil reckonings. Ideler admits that these reckonings obtained at the time of the second temple. The sacred reckoning was that instituted at the Exodus, according to which the 1st month was Abib; by the civil reckoning the 1st month was the 7th. The interval between the two commencements was thus exactly half a year. It has been supposed that the institution at the time of the Exodus was a change of commencement, not the introduction of a new year, and that thenceforward the year had two beginnings, respectively at about the vernal and the autumnal equinoxes. The former supposition is a hypothesis, the latter may almost be proved. The strongest point of evidence as to two beginnings of the year from the time of the Exodus, strangely unnoticed in this relation by Ideler, is the circumstance that the sabbatical and jubilee years commenced in the 7th month, and no doubt on the 10th day of the 7th month, the Day of Atonement (Lev. xxv, 9, 10), and as this year immediately followed a sabbatical year, the latter must have begun in the same manner. Both were full years, and therefore must have commenced on the 1st day. The jubilee year was proclaimed on the 1st day of the month, the Day of Atonement standing in the same relation to its beginning, and perhaps to the civil beginning of the year, as did the Passover to the sacred beginning. This would be the most convenient, if not the necessary commencement of a year of total cessation from the labors of agriculture, as a year so commencing would comprise the whole round of such occupations in regular sequence from seed-time to harvest, and from harvest to vintage and gathering of fruit. The command as to both years, apart from the mention of the Day of Atonement, clearly shows this, unless we suppose, but this is surely unwarrantable, that the injunction in the two places in which it occurs follows the regular order of the seasons of agriculture (Exod. xxiii, 10, 11; Lev. xxv, 3, 4, 11), but that this was not intended to apply in the case of the observance. Two expressions, used with reference to the time of the Feast of Ingathering, on the 15th day of the 7th month, must be here noticed. This feast is spoken of as בְּצֵאת הַשָּׁנָה, "in the going out" or "end of the year" (Exod. xxiii, 16), and as תְּקוּפַת הַשָּׁנָה, "[at] the change of the year" (xxxiv, 22), the latter a vague expression, so far as we can understand it, but quite consistent with the other, whether indicating the turning-point of a natural year, or the half of the year by the sacred reckoning. The rabbins use the term תְּקוּפָה to designate the commencement of each of the four seasons into which they divide the year (*Handbuch*, i, 550, 551). Our view is confirmed by the similarity of the

1st and 7th months as to their observances, the one containing the Feast of Unleavened Bread, from the 15th to the 21st inclusive; the other, that of Tabernacles, from the 15th to the 22d. Evidence in the same direction is found in the special sanctification of the 1st day of the 7th month, which in the blowing of trumpets resembles the proclamation of the jubilee year on the Day of Atonement. We therefore hold that from the time of the Exodus there were two beginnings of the year, with the 1st of the 1st and the 1st of the 7th month, the former being the sacred reckoning, the latter, used for the operations of agriculture, the civil reckoning. In Egypt, in the present day, Moslems use the lunar year for their religious observances, and for ordinary affairs, except those of agriculture, which they regulate by the Coptic Julian year.

3. We must here notice the theories of the derivation of the Hebrew year from the Egyptian Vague year, as they are connected with the tropical point or points, and agricultural phenomena, by which the former was regulated. The Vague year was commonly used by the Egyptians; and from it only, if from an Egyptian year, is the Hebrew likely to have been derived. Two theories have been formed connecting the two years at the Exodus.

(1) Some hold that Abib, the 1st month of the Hebrew year by the sacred reckoning, was the Egyptian Epiphi, called in Coptic, Epepi, and in Arabic, by the modern Egyptians, Abîb, or Ebîb, the 11th month of the Vague year. The similarity of sound is remarkable, but it must be remembered that the Egyptian name is derived from that of the goddess of the month, PEP-T or APAP-T (?) whereas the Hebrew name has the sense of "an ear of corn, a green ear," and is derived from the unused root אָבַב, traceable in אֵב, "verdure," Chaldee, אֵב, "fruit," Arabic, *ab*, "green fodder." Moreover, the Egyptian P is rarely, if ever, represented by the Hebrew ב, and the converse is not common. Still stronger evidence is afforded by the fact that we find in Egyptian the root AB, "a nosegay," which is evidently related to Abib and its cognates. Supposing, however, that the Hebrew calendar was formed by fixing the Egyptian Epiphi as the 1st month, what would be the chronological result? The latest date to which the Exodus is assigned is about 1320 B.C. In the Julian year 1320 B.C., the month Epiphi of the Egyptian Vague year commenced May 16, 44 days after the day of the vernal equinox, April 2, very near which the Hebrew year must have begun. Thus, at the latest date of the Exodus, there is an interval of a month and a half between the beginning of the Hebrew year and Epiphi 1. This interval represents about 180 years, through which the Vague year would retrograde in the Julian until the commencement of Epiphi corresponded to the vernal equinox, and no method can reduce it below 100. It is possible to effect thus much by conjecturing that the month Abib began somewhat after this tropical point, though the precise details of the state of the crops at the time of the plagues, as compared with the phenomena of agriculture in Lower Egypt at the present day, make half a month an extreme extension. At the time of the plague of hail, the barley was in the ear and was smitten, with the flax, but the wheat was not sufficiently forward to be destroyed (Exod. ix, 31, 32). In Lower Egypt, at the present day, this would be the case about the end of February and beginning of March. The Exodus cannot have taken place many days after the plague of hail, so that it must have occurred about or a little after the time of the vernal equinox, and thus Abib cannot possibly have begun much after that tropical point; half a month is therefore excessive. We have thus carefully examined the evidence as to the supposed derivation of Abib from Epiphi, because it has been carelessly taken for granted, and more carelessly alleged in support of the latest date of the Exodus.

(2) We have founded an argument for the date of the Exodus upon another comparison of the Hebrew year and the Vague year. We have seen that the sacred commencement of the Hebrew year was at the new moon about or next after, but not much before, the vernal equinox: the civil commencement must usually have been at the new moon nearest the autumnal equinox. At the earliest date of the Exodus computed by modern chronologers, about the middle of the 17th century B.C., the Egyptian Vague year commenced at or about the latter time. The Hebrew year, reckoned from the civil commencement, and the Vague year, therefore, then nearly or exactly coincided. We have already seen that the Hebrews in Egypt, if they used a foreign year, must be supposed to have used the Vague year. It is worth while to inquire whether a Vague year of this time would further suit the characteristics of the first Hebrew year. It would be necessary that the 14th day of Abib, on which fell the full moon of the Passover of the Exodus, should correspond to the 14th of Phamenoth, in a Vague year commencing about the autumnal equinox. A full moon fell on the 14th of Phamenoth, or Thursday, April 21, 1652 B.C., of a Vague year commencing on the day of the autumnal equinox, Oct. 10, 1653 B.C. A full moon would not fall on the same day of the Vague year within a shorter interval than twenty-five years, and the triple near coincidence of new moon, Vague year, and autumnal equinox would not recur in less than fifteen hundred Vague years (*Encyclop. Brit.* 8th ed. "Egypt," p. 458). This date of the Exodus, 1652 B.C., is only four years earlier than Hales's, 1648 B.C., and only six years later than that adopted in this *Cyclopædia*, 1658 B.C. In confirmation of this early date, it must be added that in a list of confederates defeated by Thothmes III at Megiddo, in the twenty-third year of his reign, are certain names that we believe can only refer to Israelitish tribes. The date of this king's accession cannot be later than about 1460 B.C., and his twenty-third year cannot therefore be later than about 1440 B.C. Were the Israelites then settled in Palestine, no date of the Exodus but the longest would be tenable. See CHRONOLOGY.

II. *Divisions of the Year.*—1. *Seasons.*—Two seasons are mentioned in the Bible, קַיִץ, "summer," and חֹרֶף, "winter." The former properly means the time of cutting fruits, the latter, that of gathering fruits; they are therefore, originally, rather summer and autumn than summer and winter. But that they signify ordinarily the two grand divisions of the year, the warm and cold seasons, is evident from their use for the whole year in the expression קַיִץ וָחֹרֶף, "summer and winter" (Psa. lxxiv, 17; Zech. xiv, 8; perhaps Gen. viii, 22), and from the mention of "the winter house" (Jer. xxxvi, 22) and "the summer house" (Amos iii, 15, where both are mentioned together). Probably חֹרֶף, when used without reference to the year (as in Job xxix, 4), retains its original signification. In the promise to Noah, after the flood, the following remarkable passage occurs: "While the earth remaineth, seed-time and harvest, and cold and heat, and summer and winter, and day and night shall not cease" (Gen. viii, 22). Here "seed-time," זֶרַע, and "harvest," קָצִיר, are evidently the agricultural seasons. It seems unreasonable to suppose that they mean winter and summer, as the beginnings of the periods of sowing and of harvest are not separated by six months, and they do not last for six months each, or nearly so long a time. The phrase "cold and heat," קֹר וָחֹם, probably indicates the great alternations of temperature. The whole passage, indeed, speaks of the alternations of nature, whether of productions, temperature, the seasons, or light and darkness. As we have seen, the year was probably then a wandering one, and therefore the passage is not likely to refer to it, but to natural phenomena alone. See SEASON.

2. *Months.*—The Hebrew months, from the time of the Exodus, were lunar. The year appears ordinarily to have contained 12, but, when intercalation was necessary, a 13th. The older year contained 12 months of 30 days each. See MONTH.

3. *Weeks.*—The Hebrews, from the time of the institution of the Sabbath, whether at or before the Exodus, reckoned by weeks, but, as no lunar year could have contained a number of weeks without a fractional excess, this reckoning was virtually independent of the year as with the Moslems. See WEEK.

4. *Festivals, Holy Days, and Fasts.*—The Feast of the Passover was held on the 14th day of the 1st month. The Feast of Unleavened Bread lasted 7 days; from the 15th to the 21st, inclusive, of the same month. Its first and last days were kept as Sabbaths. The Feast of Weeks, or Pentecost, was celebrated on the day which ended 7 weeks, counted from the 16th of the 1st month, that day being excluded. It was called the Feast of Harvest, and Day of First-fruits. The Feast of Trumpets (lit. "of the sound of the trumpet") was kept as a Sabbath on the 1st day of the 7th month. The Day of Atonement (lit. "of Atonements") was a fast, held the 10th day of the 7th month. The Feast of Tabernacles, or Feast of Gathering, was celebrated from the 15th to the 22d day, inclusive, of the 7th month. Additions made long after the giving of the law, and not known to be of higher than priestly authority, are the Feast of Purim, commemorating the defeat of Haman's plot; the Feast of the Dedication, recording the cleansing and re-dedication of the Temple by Judas Maccabæus; and four fasts. See FESTIVAL.

III. *Sacred Years.* — 1. *The Sabbatical year,* שְׁנַת הַשְּׁמִטָּה, "the fallow year," or, possibly, "year of remission," or שְׁמִטָּה alone, kept every seventh year, was commanded to be observed as a year of rest from the labors of agriculture and of remission of debts. Two Sabbatical years are recorded, commencing and current, 164–3 and 136–5 B.C. See SABBATICAL YEAR.

2. *The Jubilee Year,* שְׁנַת הַיּוֹבֵל, "the year of the trumpet," or יוֹבֵל alone, a like year, which immediately followed every seventh Sabbatical year. It has been disputed whether the jubilee year was every forty-ninth or fiftieth. the former is more probable. See JUBILEE.

YEAR, ECCLESIASTICAL. The present arrangement of the ecclesiastical year is one which has grown up and developed during the course of a long time, representing the wisdom of successive ages. It was but natural that the anniversaries of the chief events of our Lord's life, and of the day on which the Holy Ghost came down upon the Church, should be observed by the disciples. Accordingly, it is not surprising that one of the very earliest questions debated in the Church was as to the time of keeping Easter. As early as A.D. 158, Polycarp went to consult Anicetus at Rome on this question, and the controversy, which they could not settle, was brought to a close by the Council of Nicæa. Similar early testimony may be found as to other festivals and solemn days. The anniversary of our Lord's death, Good Friday, must have been kept from the first. So, too, Epiphanius (*Hæres.* lxxv; *Ærian.* vi) speaks of St. Paul as keeping the feast of Pentecost, and quotes Acts xx, 16, in that connection. We find notices of the Epiphany as early as A.D. 200. Augustine observes that it, with other anniversary solemnities, was either instituted by the apostles themselves or by plenary councils.

Next after these "days which the Lord hath made," there arose the commemorations of the saints and martyrs of the Church. These are of very high antiquity. In the epistle of the Church at Smyrna to the Church at Philomelium (Eusebius, *Hist. Eccles.* iv, 15), the Christians of Smyrna tell their brethren where Polycarp's body was entombed, and how they intended to assemble at that place and celebrate his birthday with joy and gladness. The festival of St. Peter is traced back to the 3d century, and no doubt was observed much earlier as a festival of Peter and Paul. Origen names the Commemoration of the Holy Innocents, and Chrysostom the Festival of All Martyrs, which was kept on the octave of Pentecost.

Then, in course of time, other festivals were introduced; such as the Encænia (q. v.). Bishops were also wont to keep the anniversaries of their consecrations, and particular churches had special days of thanksgiving for great mercies and deliverances vouchsafed to them from God. Ordination was gradually limited to the Ember (q. v.) season, that thus there might be a special time of prayer and fasting on behalf of the newly ordained. Marriages were forbidden in certain parts of the year; as from Advent Sunday to Epiphany, from Septuagesima to the octave of Easter, three weeks before the feast of St. John, and from Rogation Sunday to Trinity Sunday. The special times for baptism were Epiphany, Easter, and Whitsuntide, but chiefly the latter two. During certain festal seasons kneeling at prayers was forbidden, as from Easter to Whitsuntide inclusive, as ordered by the twentieth canon of Nicæa. On the Lord's day the standing posture was also adopted, in memory of our Lord's resurrection. Thus gradually were ordered and harmonized the seasons of the Church. Kurtz says:

> "In the East, the symbolical relation between the natural and the ecclesiastical year was ignored, except so far as implied in the attempt to give to the Jewish feasts a Christian adaptation. To some extent, indeed, Western ideas had been imported in reference to the great festivals, such as Christmas, Easter, and Pentecost, but not in connection with the ordinary sun and feast days. At first the ecclesiastical year in the East commenced with Easter, afterwards with Quadragesima or with Epiphany, and ultimately in September, as under the old dispensation. The year was divided into four parts, according to the 'lectio continua' of the gospels, and the Sundays obtained corresponding names. The κυριακὴ πρώτη τοῦ Ματθαίου took place immediately after Pentecost. The Latin ecclesiastical year commenced in Advent, and was divided into a 'Semestre Domini' and a 'Semestre ecclesiæ.' But the idea underlying this arrangement was only carried out in reference to the 'Semestre Domini'—Christmas, Easter, and Pentecost, with the Sundays which they included, indicating the commencement, the development, and the completion of the history of redemption. In reference to the 'Semestre ecclesiæ,' only the commencement of a symbolical arrangement was made. Thus the Feast of Peter and Paul, on June 29, represented the foundation of the Church by the apostles; the Feast of Laurentius, the martyr, on August 10, the contest awaiting the 'Church militant;' and the Feast of Michael, the archangel, on September 29, the complete success of the 'Church triumphant.' That these feasts were intended to form the basis of three cycles of festivals we gather from the circumstance that the Sundays after Pentecost had been arranged as 'Dominicæ post Apostolos, post Laurentii, post Angelos.' But the idea was not developed; the frequency of saints' days not only made this arrangement impossible, but rendered it even necessary to encroach on the 'Semestre Domini.' The principle of attempting to Christianize the worship of the heathen was authoritatively sanctioned by Gregory the Great, who, in 601, instructed the Anglo-Saxon missionaries to transform the heathen temples into churches, and the pagan into saints' festivals or martyr days, 'ut duræ mentes gradibus vel passibus non autem saltibus eleventur.' Saints now took the places of the old gods, and the ecclesiastical was made in every respect to correspond with the natural year, only in a Christianized form."

"Ecclesiastical festivals became seasons of home enjoyment; holy days were turned into holidays; the Church's children learned, in private life, to think and to speak in the Church's way. . . . The governors of the state fell almost unconsciously into the times and seasons of her who is not of this world; sheriffs were pricked on the morrow of St. Martin; lawyers reckoned by Hilary or Trinity term; every class was subject to the same moulding influence. . . . It was the same influence always and everywhere at work; sometimes beautifully, sometimes amusingly, sometimes extravagantly, but always really" (Neale, *Essays*, etc., p. 508). See CALENDAR.

Yebamoth. See TALMUD.

Yedinovertzi, a name signifying co-religionists, was given to some members of the Russian sect of the *Starovertzi* (see RUSSIAN SECTS, I, 4) in the reign of the emperor Alexander (1801–25), when strong hopes were entertained of regaining them to the orthodox communion. They assume for themselves the name of *Blagoslovenni*, or, *The Blessed.*

Yelek. See LOCUST.

Yellow. See COLOR.

Yemim. See MULE.

Yeomans, EDWARD DORR, D.D., a Presbyterian minister, was born at North Adams, Mass., Sept. 27, 1829. He spent one year in Princeton Theological Seminary, N. J., and became stated supply at New Columbia, Pa., from 1847 to 1849; was principal of the academy at Danville, from 1847 to 1850; ordained by the Presbytery of Northumberland, Nov. 29, 1854; pastor at Warrior Run from 1854 to 1858; of the Fourth Church of Trenton, N. J., from 1859 to 1863; at St. Peter's Church, Rochester, N. Y., from 1863 to 1867; of Central Church, Orange, N. J., in 1867 and 1868, and died there, Aug. 25 of the latter year. See *Gen. Cat. of Princeton Theol. Sem.* 1881, p. 160.

Yesterday (prop. אֶמֶשׁ, *e'mesh;* but frequently תְּמוֹל, *aforetime;* χθές) is sometimes used in Heb. to denote all time past, however distant; as to-day denotes time present, but of a larger extent than the very day on which one speaks. "If the ox was wont to push with his horn in time past" (Exod. xxi, 29; Heb. *yesterday*). "And it came to pass, when all that knew him before time (Heb. *yesterday*); whereas thou camest but yesterday" (2 Sam. xv, 20). "Jesus Christ, the same yesterday, to-day, and forever" (Heb. xiii, 8). His doctrine, like his person, admits of no change; his truths are invariable. With him there is neither yesterday nor to-morrow, but one continued to-day. Job says (viii, 9), "We are but of yesterday, and know nothing; because our days upon earth are a shadow."

Yew Sunday is a term used in some parts of England to designate Palm-Sunday (q. v.).

Yew-tree, an evergreen tree of the genus *taxus*, allied to the pines, and valued for its wood or timber, is very commonly found planted in the old English churchyards; and was formerly much used to decorate churches at Christmas, Palm-Sunday, and Easter.

Yezidis, an ancient sect of unknown origin, forming a tribe with a distinct nationality, in the neighborhood of Mosul, in Asiatic Turkey. This obscure race appears to be a relic of the ancient Chaldæans, and their religion seems to be a confused mixture of Gnostic Christianity, grafted upon the Chaldæan superstitions, including Magianism, and then adulterated with Moslemism. They are generally called devil-worshippers, but profess to take their name from Azad, the ancient name for God in the Yezidi dialect. "We are Yezidis," they say, "that is, worshippers of God." The following account is taken from Layard's *Nineveh and its Remains* (New York, 1849), i, 245 sq.:

Common Dress of the Yezidis.

"The Yezidis recognise one Supreme Being, but, as far as I could learn, they do not offer up any direct prayer or sacrifice to him. Sheik Nasr endeavored to evade my questions on this subject, and appeared to shun, with superstitious awe, every topic connected with the existence and attributes of the deity. The common Mohammedan forms of expression—half-oath, half-ejaculation—are nevertheless frequently in the mouths of the people, but probably from mere habit. The name of the evil spirit is, however, never mentioned, and any allusion to it by others so vexes and irritates them that, it is said, they have put to death persons who have wantonly outraged their feelings by its use. So far is their dread of offending the evil principle carried that they carefully avoid every expression which may resemble in sound the name of Satan, or the Arabic word for 'accursed.' . . . When they speak of the devil they do so with reverence, as *Melek Taûs* (king Peacock) or *Melek el-Kût* (the mighty angel). Sheik Nasr distinctly admitted that they possessed a bronze or copper figure of a bird, which, however, he was careful in explaining was only looked upon as a symbol, and not as an idol. It always remains with the great sheik, and is carried with him wherever he may journey. . . . This symbol is called Melek Taûs, and is held in great reverence. . . . They believe Satan to be the chief of the angelic host, now suffering punishment for his rebellion against the divine will, but still all-powerful, and to be restored hereafter to his high estate in the celestial hierarchy. He must be conciliated and reverenced, they say, for as he now has the means of doing evil to mankind, so will he hereafter have the power of rewarding them. Next to Satan, but inferior to him in might and wisdom, are seven archangels, who exercise a great influence over the world: they are Gabrail, Michail, Raphail, Azrail, Dedrail, Azrapheel, and Shemkeel. Christ, according to them, was also a great angel, who had taken the form of a man. He did not die on the Cross, but ascended to heaven.

"They hold the Old Test. in great reverence, and believe in the cosmogony of Genesis, the Deluge, and other events in the Bible. They do not reject the New Test. nor the Koran, but consider them less entitled to their veneration. Still, they always select passages from the latter for their tombs and holy places. Mohammed they look upon as a prophet—as they do Abraham and the patriarchs. They expect the second coming of Christ, as well as the reappearance of Imaum Mehdi, giving credence to the Mussulman fables relating to him. Sheik Adi is their great saint. . . .

"It is difficult to trace their ceremonies to any particular source. They baptize in water, like the Christians; if possible, within seven days after birth. They circumcise at the same age and in the same manner as the Mohammedans; and reverence the sun, and have many customs in common with the Sabæans. . . . They are accustomed to kiss the object on which its beams first fall; and I have frequently, when travelling in their company at sunrise, observed them perform this ceremony. For fire, as symbolic, they have nearly the same reverence: they never spit into it, but frequently pass their hands through the flames, kiss them, and rub them over their right eyebrow, or sometimes over the whole face. The color blue, to them, as to the Sabæans, is an abomination, and never to be worn in dress, or to be used in their houses. Their Kubleh, or the place to which they look while performing their holy ceremonies, is that part of the heavens in which the sun rises, and towards it they turn the faces of their dead. In their fondness for white linen, in their cleanliness of habits, and in their frequent ablutions, they also resemble the Sabæans. . . .

"They have four orders of priesthood, the Pirs, the Sheiks, the Cawals, and the Fakirs; and what is very remarkable, and, I believe, unexampled in the East, these offices are hereditary, and descend to females, who, when enjoying them, are treated with the same respect and consideration as the men.

"The *Pirs*, or saints, are most reverenced after the great sheik, or religious head of the sect. They are believed to have power, not only of interceding for the people, but of curing disease and insanity. They are expected to lead a life of great sanctity and honesty, and are looked up to with great reverence. . . .

"The *Sheiks* are next in rank. They are acquainted with the hymns, and are expected to know something of Arabic, the language in which the hymns are written. Their dress should be entirely white, except the skull-cap beneath their turbans, which is black. As servants of sheik Adi they are the guardians of his tomb, keep up the holy fires, and bring provisions and fuel to those who dwell within its precincts, and to pilgrims of distinction. . . .

"The *Cawals*, or preachers, appear to be the most active members of the priesthood. They are sent by sheik Nasr on missions, going from village to village as teachers of the doctrines of the sect. They alone are the performers on the flute and tambourine, both instruments being looked upon, to a certain extent, as sacred. . . .

"The *Fakirs* are the lowest in the priesthood. They wear coarse dresses of black or dark-brown cloth or canvas, descending to the knee and fitting tightly to the person, and a black turban, across or over which is tied a red handkerchief. They perform all menial offices connected with the tomb, trim and light the votive lamps, and keep clean the sacred buildings."

For many interesting particulars concerning this strange sect, see Layard, *Nineveh and its Remains*, vol. i, chap. ix; *Nineveh and Babylon*, p. 92; Badger, *Nestorians and their Ritual*, i, 105-134.

Ygdrasil, in Norse mythology, is the tree of the world, an enormous ash, whose branches touch the sky and stretch out over the entire surface of the earth. Three roots feed it: one extends to the assembling place of the gods, Asgard; another into the giant country, Jotunheim; and the third reaches down to Niflheim (infernal regions). By the spring, Urdarborn, live the three holy destinies of fate, who daily water the roots with the water from the spring. This fountain is in the country of the Asas. By the other root, in Jotunheim, is the well of Minvers, and in the kingdom of Hel is the spring Hwergelmer, from which the hell-streams flow. The tree is inhabited by different animals. The two harts, Dunair and Duratoor, eat the buds of the tree. In the peak of the tree lives an eagle, who carries the hawk Wedurfölner between his eyes; at the bottom of the tree the reptile Nidhögr lives, and gnaws at the root of the tree; between both there travels up and down a squirrel, Ratatösker, that seeks to cause discord between the eagle and the snake. The harts bite its branches to destroy it, but the tree is preserved by watering, and will be preserved till the destruction of the earth, up to which time the gods will assemble daily in its shade to seek advice — and even at the end of the world it will not be destroyed, but only receive a heavy shock. See NORSE MYTHOLOGY.

Yih-king, "the book of changes," is the oldest of the sacred books of the Chinese. It was written by Fohi, the reputed founder of Chinese civilization, and is described as a very mysterious and almost unintelligible work, treating chiefly of the nature of the universe in general, the harmonious action of the elements, and periodic changes of creation. These ideas were expressed by means of eight peculiar diagrams, which constitute the basis of natural philosophy as well as of religion. Some contend that in Fohi and his family we may recognise Noah and the second parents of our race. Many commentaries have been written on the *Yih-king*, and very varied have been the expositions, so that, from being regarded originally as a cosmological essay, it came to be looked upon as a standard treatise on ethics.

Ymer, in Norse mythology, is the giant from the separate parts of whose body the world was created. The heat at Muspelheim made the ice in Niflheim melt, which caused the creation of the great giant Ymer and the cow Audumbla, from whose milk the former was nourished. The cow satisfied her hunger by licking the salt-stones, by which means the first man, Bure, was created. Ymer himself created the frightful dynasty of the Hrymthussen. But he did not live long, for Bure's nephews, sons of Börs—Odin, Wile, and We — killed Ymer, and of his blood they made the sea, of his flesh the earth, of his bones the rocks and hills, of his skull the firmament, of his brain the clouds, and of his eyelashes the battlements about Asgard.

Yoga (Sanscrit *yug*, "to join;" hence, *junction*, and figuratively, *contemplation*, religious or abstract) is the name of one of the two divisions of the *Sankhya* (q. v.) philosophy of the Hindûs. The main object of the Yoga is to establish the doctrine of a supreme being, and to teach the means by which the human soul may become permanently united with it. The reputed author of the system is Patanjali, who explains the term *Yoga* as meaning "the hindering of the modifications of thinking." These are accomplished either by a repeated effort to keep the mind in its unmodified state, or by dispassion, which is the consciousness of having overcome all desires for objects that are seen or heard of. According to the founder of the system, the practical Yoga by which "concentration" is to be attained comprises mortification, the muttering of certain hymns, and a devoted reliance on the Supreme Being. Through it meditations are established, and afflictions got rid of. By afflictions are understood ignorance, egotism, affection, aversion, and tenacity of life; which terms are then the subject of an especial investigation into the nature of what is to be got rid of, of what is not desired to be got rid of, of what is constituted by the cause, and of what is the constitutive cause.

There are eight means or stages subservient to the attainment of concentration, viz. *yama*, forbearance; *niyama*, religious observance; *asana*, postures; *pranayama*, regulation of the breath; *pratyabara*, restraint of the senses; *dharana*, steadying of the mind; *dhyana*, contemplation; and *samadhi*, profound meditation. The practical part of the Yoga was admitted into the later Vedanta (q. v.). Its ethical part is especially dwelt upon in the Mahabharata (q. v.). But the great power it has at all periods exercised over the Hindû mind is less derived from its philosophical speculations, or its moral injunctions, than from the wonderful effects which the Yoga practices are supposed to produce, and from the countenance they give to the favorite tendency of orthodox Hindûism—the performance of austerities. Frequently these practices were and are merely a cloak for imposture and hypocrisy. Professional Yogins (q. v.), numbers of whom are met with throughout India, are often nothing but lazy mendicants or jugglers, who, by impressing the vulgar with a belief in their supernatural powers, convert it into a source of easy livelihood. Such followers of Yoga pretend, for instance, to foretell future events; they deal in palmistry, and profess to cure diseases. There are instances, too, where, for a handsome consideration, they allow themselves to be buried for a certain time, so as to exhibit the power of the Yoga. Two such cases are related as authentic in the treatise of Navinachandrapala; and it would appear from them that a human being, after having undergone certain preparations, such as the Yoga prescribes, may be shut up in a box, without either food or drink, for the space of a month, or even forty days and nights, and yet remain alive. The author of the treatise endeavors, indeed, to show that the rules laid down by the Yoga regarding the mode of respiration, the postures, and the diet of a Yogin, may have been founded on a careful observation of hibernating animals; and in support of this view he enters into a detailed investigation of the effect of the Yoga practices on animal life. If, as it seems, his statements are correct, much of what otherwise would be incredible in the accounts given of the performances of the Yogins, could be received as true, because admitting of explanation.

The system of Patanjali was taught by him in a little work called *Yogasutra*, which consists of four padas, or chapters, each comprising a number of sutras (q. v.). The oldest commentary on it is ascribed to a *Vyâsa* (q. v.); and this was commented on by Vachaspati Misra. For an elaborate enumeration of works on the Yoga, see *A Contribution towards an Index to the Bibliography of the Indian Philosophical Systems*, by Fitzedward Hall (Calcutta, 1859). The first two chapters of the sutras have been translated, with annotations founded on the commentary of Bhojaveda, by the late J. R. Ballantyne (Allahabad, 1853); and a paraphrase, but somewhat too free, of the same commentary is contained in vol. iv of William Ward's *View of the History, Literature, and Religion of the Hindûs*, etc. (Lond. 1817-20, 4 vols.). For a brief account of the system, see also vol. i of H. T. Colebrooke's *Miscellaneous Essays* (Lond. 1837, 2 vols.); and for the practice of the Yoga, *A Treatise on the Yoga Philosophy*, by N. C. Paul (Benares, 1851).

Yogins are the followers of the Yoga (q. v.) system of Hindû philosophy, but in popular acceptation a term generally denoting a Hindû ascetic or devotee, a man who has entered the fourth stage of religious life as described in the sastras. A large class of such persons forms a division of the votaries of Siva.

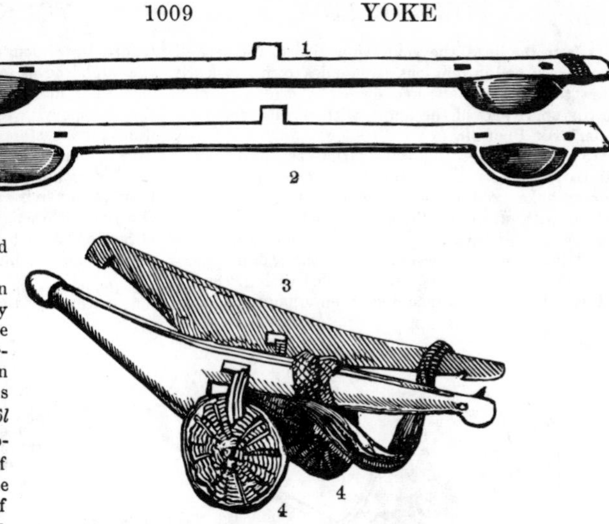

Yoke of an Ancient Egyptian Plough Found in a Tomb.

Figs. 1, 2. The back and front of the yoke. 3. Collar or shoulder-pieces attached to the yoke. 4, 4. The pieces of matting for protecting the two shoulders from friction.

Yoke, an agricultural term used in two senses.

1. The curved piece of wood upon the neck of draught animals, by which they are fastened to the pole or beam. This well-known implement of husbandry is described in the Hebrew language by the terms *môt* (מוֹט), *motâh* (מוֹטָה), and *'ôl* (עֹל), the former two specifically applying to the bows of wood out of which it was constructed, and the last to the application *(binding)* of the article to the neck of the ox. The expressions are combined in Lev. xxvi, 13 and Ezek. xxxiv, 27, with the meaning, "bands of the yoke." The Hebrew word *'ôl* (Numb. xix, 2; Deut. xxi, 3; 1 Sam. vi, 7) is often used as the symbol of servitude or slavery (1 Kings xii, 4–11; Isa. ix, 4; x, 27; xiv, 25; xlvii, 6; Jer. v, 5), and to *break* the yoke is to become free (Gen. xxvii, 40; Jer. ii, 20; v, 5; Nah. i, 13). An *iron yoke* is the symbol of severe bondage (Deut. xxviii, 48; Jer. xxviii, 14). The term "yoke" is also used as the symbol of calamity or suffering (Lam. i, 14; iii, 27). The Hebrew word *motâh* also signifies a yoke as worn chiefly by men; probably such as is still borne by water-carriers, having a vessel suspended by a rope or chain at each end (Jer. xxvii, 2; xxviii, 10, 12). The breaking or removal of the yoke is an emblem of freedom (Isa. lviii, 6, 9; Lev. xxvi, 13; Ezek. xxx, 18; xxxiv, 27; Nah. i, 13). So, likewise, the corresponding Greek term ζυγός is used as the emblem of spiritual *service* (Matt. xi, 29, 36), also of spiritual bondage (Acts xv, 10; Gal. v, 1).

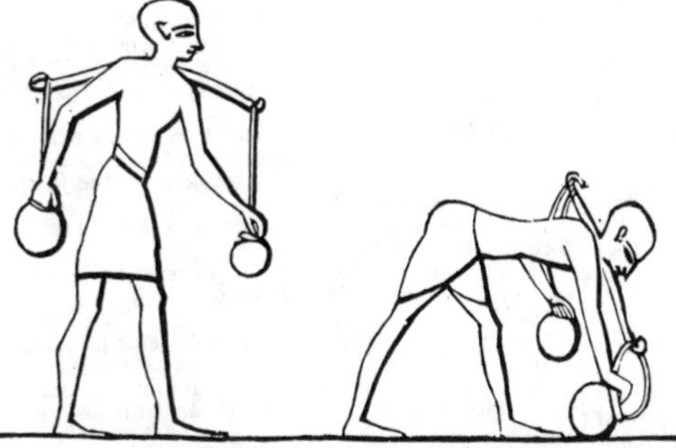

Men Irrigating the Ground with Pots of Water.

Among the ancient Egyptians yokes of different kinds were used for several purposes (see Wilkinson, *Anc. Egypt.* i, 33, 379; ii, 15).

(1) In many instances men were employed to carry the water in pails, suspended by a wooden yoke borne upon their shoulders. The same yoke was employed for carrying other things, as boxes, baskets containing game and poultry, or whatever was taken to market; and every trade seems to have used it for this purpose, from the potter and the brick-maker to the carpenter and the shipwright. The wooden bar or yoke was about three feet seven inches in length; and the straps, which were double, and fastened together at the lower as well as at the upper extremity, were of leather, and between fifteen and sixteen inches long. The small thong at the bottom not only served to connect the ends, but was probably intended to fasten a hook, or an additional strap, if required, to attach the burden; and though most of these yokes had two, some were furnished with four or eight straps; and the form, number, or arrangement of them varied according to the purposes for which they were intended.

(2) For ploughing the mode of yoking the beasts was exceedingly simple. Across the extremity of the pole a wooden yoke or cross-bar, about fifty-five inches or five feet in length, was fastened by a strap lashed backwards and forwards over a prominence projecting from the centre of the yoke, which corresponded to a similar peg, or knob, at the end of the pole; and occasionally, in addition to these, was a ring passing over them as in some Greek chariots. At either end of the yoke was a flat or slightly concave projection, of semicircular form, which rested on a pad placed upon the withers of the animal; and through a hole on either side of it passed a thong for suspending the shoulder-pieces which formed the collar. These were two wooden bars, forked at about half their length, padded so as to protect the shoulder from friction, and connected at the lower end by a strong, broad band passing under the throat.

Sometimes the draught, instead of being from the withers,

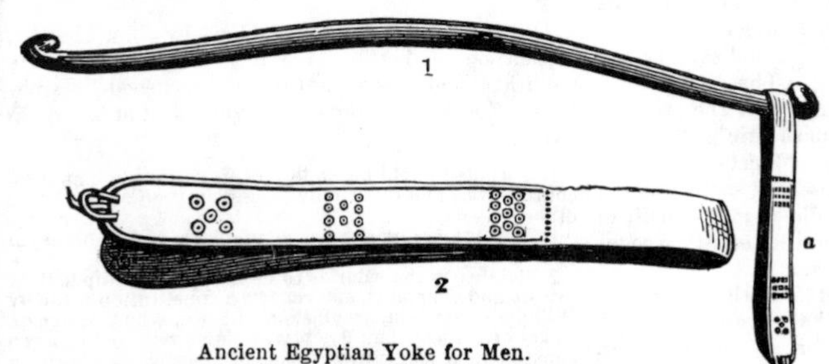

Ancient Egyptian Yoke for Men.

Fig. 1. Wooden yoke and strap found at Thebes. Fig. 2 is the strap *a*, on a larger scale.

was from the head, the yoke being tied to the base of the horns; and in religious ceremonies oxen frequently drew the bier, or the sacred shrine, by a rope fastened to the upper part of the horns, without either yoke or pole. See PLOUGH.

(3) For curricles and war-chariots the harness was similar, and the pole in either case was supported on a curved yoke fixed to its extremity by a strong pin, and bound with straps or thongs of leather. The yoke, resting upon a small, well-padded saddle, was firmly fitted into a groove of metal; and the saddle, placed upon the horses' withers, and furnished with girths and a breast-band, was surmounted by an ornamental knob;

Ancient Egyptian Yoke for a Chariot, with Enlarged View of the Saddle or Pad at either End.

while in front of it a small hook secured the bearing-rein. See CHARIOT.

The word "yoke" also signifies a pair of oxen, so termed as being yoked together (1 Sam. xi, 7; 1 Kings xix, 19, 21). The Hebrew term, *tsémed* (צֶמֶד), is also applied to asses (Judg. xix, 10) and mules (2 Kings v, 17), and even to a couple of riders (Isa. xxi, 7). The term *tsémed* is also applied to a certain amount of land, equivalent to that which a couple of oxen could plough in a day (Isa. v, 10; A. V. "acre"), corresponding to the Latin *jugum* (Varro, *R. R.* i, 10). The term stands in this sense in 1 Sam. xiv, 14 (A. V. "yoke"); but the text is doubtful, and the rendering of the Sept. suggests that the true reading would refer to the instruments (ἐν κόχλαξι) wherewith the slaughter was effected. See OX.

Yoke-fellow (σύζυγος), a *colleague* (Phil. iv, 3). But many interpreters regard the word there as a proper name, *Syzigus* (although the gender is uncertain), as it occurs in connection with other actual names, and the person addressed would not otherwise be specified at all.

Yoma. See TALMUD.

Yonah. See DOVE.

Yonetus. See YVONETUS.

York, COUNCILS OF (*Concilium Eboracense*). York is the second city of England in point of rank, though not in size or in commercial importance, a parliamentary and municipal borough, and county of itself, capital of the county of the same name (Yorkshire), near its centre, at the junction of the Three Ridings on the Ouse, at the influx of the Foss, one hundred and seventy-five miles north-north-west of London. The ecclesiastical authority of the archbishop extends over the province of York, consisting, with the archbishopric, of the bishoprics of Durham, Carlisle, Chester, Manchester, Ripon, and Sodor and Man. It contains York cathedral, the finest structure of the kind in England, mostly built in the 13th and 14th centuries. Several ecclesiastical councils have been held there, as follows:

I. Was held June 14 and 15, 1195, in the Church of St. Peter, at York, by Hubert Walter, archbishop of Canterbury, legate and chancellor of England. No other bishop was present in the council, which was attended by Simon, dean of the Church, the precentor, the archdeacons of Nottingham and Cleveland, the chancellor, Robert, the provost of Beverley, and some of the canons, with almost all the abbots, priors, officials, deans, and pastors of the churches in the diocese of York. Pope Celestine III appears to have suspended Geoffry, archbishop of York (son of the fair Rosamond), from the exercise of all his episcopal functions, and a few years before had cut off from his province the whole of Scotland, which he made immediately subject to the see of Rome. Nineteen constitutions were published.

1. Relates to the administration of the holy communion; directs that the minister shall take care that bread, wine, and water be provided for the sacrifice, that it shall not be celebrated without a lettered minister, that the host be kept in a decent Pyx, and renewed every Lord's day.

2. Directs that the host be carried to the sick with suitable solemnity.

3. Orders archdeacons to take care that the canons of the mass be corrected according to some approved copy.

4. Forbids to impose masses as part of penance, in order to obtain money for saying them. Forbids also priests to make bargains for celebrating masses.

5. Ordains that no more than two or three persons shall take a child out of the sacred font; that a child found exposed shall be baptized, whether it be found with salt or without, for that cannot be said to be iterated which was not known to have been done before.

6. Forbids deacons, except in cases of urgent necessity, to baptize, administer the body of Christ, or enjoin penance at confession. Charges priests, when desired to baptize a child, or administer the communion to the sick, to make no delay.

7. Directs that parsons and vicars shall take care that their churches are kept in proper repair.

8. Directs that in all ministrations the proper ornaments shall be used.

9. Orders that the chalice shall be of silver.

10. Orders all clerks to preserve their crown and tonsure, under pain of losing their benefices, if they have any, and of being forcibly clipped by the archdeacon or dean, if they have not.

11. Forbids priests to go about in copes with sleeves; orders them to wear suitable apparel.

12. Forbids any money to be taken by the judge in ecclesiastical causes.

13. Orders that the tithe be paid to the Church first, before the wages of the harvestmen, etc.

14. Forbids monks to take estates to farm, and to leave their houses without reasonable cause.

15. Forbids nuns to leave the verge of their monastery, unless in the company of their abbess or prioress.

16. Forbids laymen to farm churches or tithes.

17. Orders that every priest shall annually excommunicate, with candles and bells, those who forswear themselves.

18. Requires priests to abstain from drinking-bouts and taverns. Forbids them, under pain of suspension, to keep concubines in their own houses, or in the houses of others.

19. Orders that when any one is suspected of a crime on public report, the dean of the place shall familiarly admonish him thrice; if he do not thereupon reform, the dean shall reprove him in conjunction with two or three more with whom he has lost his reputation; if he cannot be reformed by this means, the dean shall bring the matter before the chapter, in order that the accused may be either punished or canonically purged.

See Wilkins, *Concil.* i, 501; Johnson, *Eccl. Canons*, x, 1791.

II. Was held about the year 1363, by John Thorsby, archbishop of York. Five fresh constitutions were published, and seven constitutions published by archbishop Zouche, in a provincial synod held at Thorp, in 1347.

1. Forbids to hold markets, pleadings, etc., in churches, churchyards, and other holy places, on the Lord's day, or other holy days.

2. Forbids the performance of plays and vanities in churches on vigils.

3. Relates to the salaries to be assigned to stipendiary priests and chaplains, and renews a constitution made by William Greenfield, archbishop of York, which assigns a salary of not less than five marks. Also renews the seven constitutions made by archbishop Zouche, at Thorp, in 1347, viz. i. Relating to the stipends to be assigned to as-

sisting priests, etc. ii. Concerning the overlaying of children. iii. Concerning the obstruction offered by tithe-payers to those who take it, and declares that some hindered the tithe-owner from carrying it by the accustomable way, and compelled him to take it by intricate and roundabout paths; others forbade him to carry it until all their own corn was carried, and maliciously permitted the tithe to be trampled upon and destroyed. iv. Forbids to give away property at death to the injury of the Church's rights, and those of the king's relations, etc. v. Forbids priests to wear ridiculous clothes, and to seek glory from their shoes; declares that many priests did, "out of an affection to show their shapes," in defiance of the canons, wear clothes so short as not to come down to the knees. vi. Relates to the trying of matrimonial causes. vii. Forbids clandestine marriages, and orders that the banns be published on three several solemn days.

4. States how the above statute was in some particulars modified in another provincial council.

5. Specifies for the guidance of rectors, vicars, and other confessors, thirty-seven cases, which were to be reserved, either for the judgment of the archbishop, and his penitentiary, or for that of the pope; and orders that, in each of these cases, the offender shall be sent to the archbishop or his penitentiary, unless he be in danger of death, with letters granted to him free of cost, explaining his case.

See Johnson, *Eccl. Canons*, xi, 2482.

III. Was held in 1444, by John Kemp, archbishop of York, and cardinal of Balbina, in a provincial synod. Two constitutions were published.

1. Is with little variation the same with the fifth constitution of Merton, A.D. 1305.

2. Lays certain restrictions upon the sale of trees, woodlands, etc., and upon the granting of rights, rents, pensions, etc., by abbots, priors, and other administrators of Church goods.

See Johnson, *Eccl. Canons.*

IV. Was held April 26, 1466, in the metropolitan church of York, by George Neville, archbishop. From various causes connected with the state and liberty of the Church, it was assembled without a royal brief. Eleven constitutions were published.

1. Is the same with the ninth constitution of Lambeth, A.D. 1281.

2. Is the same with the fifth constitution of London, A.D. 1343.

3. Is the same with the ninth constitution of London, A.D. 1343.

4 and 5. Are the same with the twelfth constitution of London, A.D. 1343, *mutatis mutandis*, against the obstructors of ecclesiastical process.

6. Is the same with the last constitution of London, A.D. 1343.

7. Declares that some quæstors, in defiance of the decrees of the Council of Lateran, in 1215, had, with extreme impudence, granted indulgences to the people of their own will, had dispensed with vows, absolved for murders; had, for a sum of money, relaxed a third and fourth part of the penance enjoined, had falsely affirmed that they had drawn out of purgatory three or more souls of the parents or friends of those who had given them alms, and conveyed them to the joys of paradise; that they had, moreover, absolved such as had been excommunicated by the ecclesiastical judges, buried suicides in the churchyards, and done all sorts of like abominations. Orders, in consequence, that the decrees of Lateran and Vienne (A.D. 1312), which restricted the operations of the quæstors, be rigidly enforced, and subjects to a fine of forty shillings any rector, vicar, etc., who shall admit any such quæstor to preach contrary to the form prescribed. The fine to be applied to the fabric of the cathedral church of York.

8. Declares parishioners who attend a chapel of ease instead of their parish church, and contribute to the repair of it, shall nevertheless be bound to contribute to the fabric of the mother Church, and to support the other burdens thereof, at the discretion of the ordinary; and orders further, that if they refuse so to contribute, the said chapels shall be interdicted, and no service performed in them.

9. Forbids abbots, priors, and provosts to permit any of the religious belonging to their several houses to dwell alone out of the verge of their monasteries, in their manors, or churches, under penalty of paying forty shillings towards the fabric of York Minster. The religious vagabond himself to be deemed an apostate.

10. Forbids, under pain of excommunication, any ecclesiastical or secular person to arrest, cite, force out, or cause to be arrested, cited, or forced out, any man that is in church, during the celebration of the divine offices.

11. Is the same with the fifth constitution of Merton, A.D. 1305, except that no mention is made of the tithe of wine, whereas it speaks of the tithe of coal where it is dug, and of the tithe of saffron.

After these constitutions follow the constitutions of archbishop Kemp, published in 1444, as given in the preceding council. See Johnson, *Eccl. Canons*, xiii, 1423, Wilkins, *Concil.* iii, 599.

York Use is a term employed to designate that ritual which, taking its name from the cathedral of York, was commonly used in the northern province of England prior to the Reformation. Printed editions of the York Ritual were issued in A.D. 1516, 1518, and 1532. In the main it differs but slightly from that of Salisbury—first, in the manner of making the first oblation; and, secondly, in the words used by the priest in partaking of the sacrament. Other minor differences exist, but they are unimportant. See USE.

Young, John, a Scotch prelate, was professor of divinity in Glasgow, when he was elected bishop of Argyle, but died before he was consecrated, in 1661. See Keith, *Scottish Bishops*, p. 291.

Young, John Freeman, LL.D., a bishop of the Protestant Episcopal Church, was born at Pittston, Me., Oct. 30, 1820. He graduated from the Alexandria Theological Seminary in 1845, was ordained deacon the same year, and became rector of St. John's Church, Jacksonville, Fla.; in 1846 was ordained presbyter, and removed to Texas as a missionary; in 1850 to Mississippi, and in 1852 to Louisiana; subsequently became assistant minister of Trinity Parish, New York city; was consecrated bishop of Florida, July 25, 1867, and died in New York city, Nov. 15, 1885. See *The Church Almanac*, 1886, p. 102.

Young, William McIntosh, D.D., a Baptist minister, was born at Edinburgh, Scotland, about 1820. In early life he went to Providence, R. I., where he was converted, and subsequently graduated from Columbian College, Washington. His first settlement was at Norfolk, Va.; next at Williamsburg, and then at Wilmington, N. C. Afterwards he became pastor at Pittsburgh, Pa.; then successively of churches at Oil City, Woburn (Mass.), Meadville (Pa.), and Cheyenne (Wyoming), where he died suddenly, Feb. 20, 1879. See Cathcart, *Baptist Encyclop.* p. 1288. (J. C. S.)

Younger. Under the Jewish dispensation it was frequently the will of God to prefer the younger sons before the elder, notwithstanding the right of primogenitureship, as Shem before Japheth, Isaac before Ishmael, Jacob before Esau, Joseph, Judah, and Levi, before Reuben, Ephraim before Manasseh, Moses before Aaron, and David before all his brethren. In some of these cases the elder had forfeited his right of primogenitureship by transgression, as Esau and Reuben, but not so the others. The cause of the proceeding of God's providence may be conjectured to have been twofold—first, as a memorial of the sin of Cain, first-born of Adam, by which Seth and his posterity were preferred before them; and, secondly, as a type of the future preference of the Christian, or younger Church, before the Jewish, or elder Church, in consequence of the forfeiture of the latter by unbelief. See AGE.

Younglove, JOHN, D.D., a Presbyterian minister, was a native of Cambridge, N. Y. He graduated from Union College in 1801, was tutor in the college from 1802 to 1805, settled in the ministry at Brunswick, N. Y., and died there in 1833. See Sprague, *Annals of the Amer. Pulpit*, iv, 97.

Youth. The ancients considered youth in a much more extended view than we do. They regarded it relatively with strength, activity, vigor; and while a man retained those attributes he was reckoned a young man, or a youth, without reference to the number of his years. Thus Benjamin is viewed as a mere youth when upwards of thirty years old. So in Numb. xxi, 28, Joshua is called a young man when about forty. The word frequently translated in our version young man is

בָּחוּר, *bachûr*, from בָּחַר, *bachár*, "to choose;" it signifies primarily a choice man—one who may be chosen for some particular qualities. See LAD.

Yuga. See JOGA.

Yule, the old name for *Christmas*, still in provincial popular use in England. It points to heathen times, and to the annual festival held by the Northern nations at the winter solstice as a part of their system of sun-worship. In the *Edda* (q. v.) the sun is styled *fagrahoel* (fair or shining wheel), and a remnant of his worship, under the image of a fire-wheel, survived in Europe as late as 1823. The inhabitants of the village of Konz, on the Moselle, were in the habit, on St. John's Eve, of taking a great wheel wrapped in straw to the top of a neighboring eminence, and making it roll down the hill, flaming all the way: if it reached the Moselle before being extinct, a good vintage was anticipated. A similar usage existed at Trier. The Greenlanders of the present day have a feast at the winter solstice to rejoice at the return of the sun, and Wormius (*Fast. Dan.* lib. i) tells us that in his time the Icelanders dated the beginning of their year from Yule. The old Norse *hoel*, Anglo-Saxon *hveol*, have developed into Iceland *hiol*, Sweden and Danish *hjul*, English *wheel;* but from the same root would seem to have sprung old Norse *jol*, Sweden and Danish *jul*, Anglo-Saxon *geol*, English *yule*, applied as the name of the winter solstice, either in reference to the conception of the sun himself as a wheel, or, more probably, to his wheeling or turning back at that time in his path in the heavens. The general nature of the observances of this festival are noticed under the head of Christmas (q. v.). In the greenery with which we still deck our homes and places of worship, and in the Christmas-trees laden with gifts, we may see a relic of the symbols by which the pagan ancestors of the modern English signified their faith in the power of the returning sun to clothe the earth again with green and hang new fruit on the trees; and the furmety, until lately eaten in many parts of England (in Scotland the preparation of oatmeal called *sowans*) on Christmas eve or morning, seems to be a lingering memory of the offerings paid to Hulda, or Berchta, the divine mother, the Ceres of the North, or personification of fruitfulness, to whom they looked for new stores of grain. The burning of the *Yule-log*, *Yule-clog*, or *Christmas-block*, testifies to the use of fire in the worship of the sun. This custom still survives in the north of England. In 1684 Herrick tells, in his *Hesperides*, how the *Yule-log* of the new Christmas was wont to be lighted "with last year's brand," and already, in the same year, its blazes are condemned by Warmstrey as "foolish and vaine, and not countenanced by the Church." The religious keeping of Yule and Easter had been one of the articles of Perth (q. v.), which had been strongly objected to. On the accession of William and Mary the Scottish discharged what was called the "Yule vacancy" of the Court of Sessions, and compelled the judges to attend court at that period. But in 1712 an act was passed re-enacting the Christmas recess. The act gave great offence to many Presbyterians in Scotland. See Atkinson, *Glossary of the Cleveland Dialect* (1868); Grimm, *Deutsche Mythologie;* Brand, *Popular Antiquities*, s. v.

Yule Boughs are branches of holly, ivy, yew, and mistletoe, used to decorate churches and private houses at Christmas.

Yule Festival is the same as *Yule* (q. v.).

Yule Mass, a name for the three masses of Christmas-day.

Yves (IVES DE RER-MARTIN, known by the name of *Saint*) was born at the manor of Rer-Martin, parish of Menehi, Bretagne, Oct. 17, 1253. Sprung from a noble family of the diocese of Treguier, he was son of Heelor, or Helori, and Azo of Kenquis. Being sent to Paris, he devoted ten years to the study of theology and of civil and canon law (1267–77). Having passed through the University of Orleans, he attended the lectures of William of Blaye, with whom he examined the *Decretals*. Afterwards, at Rennes, under the Franciscans, he studied the *Sentences* of Pierre Lombard and the interpretation of the Scriptures. Having received there the minor orders, he was successively rector of Tredrez (1285) and curate of Lohanec (1293). He was connected with the hospital of the patrimonial estate of Rer-Martin, and appointed *Advocate of the Poor*. The fasts and austerities to which he submitted himself did not hinder him, in the meantime, from actively engaging in preaching, nor from filling his judicial functions with such energy and equity as to make him an object of terror to the evil litigants. The crown found no favor in his eyes in urging fiscal claims against the clergy, and he opposed more than once the levying of royal impositions, which he deemed unjust. He died at Lohanec, May 19, 1303. At the solicitation of duke Jean de Montfort, who made a trip to Avignon for that purpose, the canonization of Ives was declared by a brief of Clement VI on May 19, 1347, and his anniversary has since been held on that day. See Hoefer, *Nouv. Biog. Générale*, s. v. See also IVO.

Yvon, PETER, the friend and successor of Labadie (q. v.), was born at Montauban in 1646. At the age of five he already listened to Labadie's sermons, and his association with him was only severed by the master's death in 1674. He now became the head and leader of the Labadists, settled at Wiewert, in West Frisia, and died in 1687. His writings, mostly in French, but translated into Dutch and German, were once extensively read, and were not without influence upon the formation of Christian life in the Reformed Church. We mention, *L'Impieté Convainone:—Essentia Religionis Christianæ Patefacta:—De Prædestinatione:—Emmanuel, ou la Connoissance du Seigneur Jésus*, etc. See Moller, *Cimbria Litterat.* ii, 1020 sq.; *Theologisches Universallexikon*, s. v.; Jöcher, *Allgemeines Gelehrten-Lexikon*, s. v.; Winer, *Handbuch der theol. Lit.* i, 505. (B. P.)

Yvonetus, a Dominican who was supposed to be the author of a tract of the 13th century, entitled *Tractatus de Hæresi Pauperum de Lugduno*, and given in Marténe and Durand's *Thesaurus Novus Anecdot.* vol. v, p. 1777, of whom nothing else is known. Pfeiffer has proved that the tractate is the production of the Franciscan David of Augsburg early in the 13th century. Two manuscript copies of the piece exist, at Stuttgart and Strasburg. See Pegna, in Eymericus, *Directorium Inquisitorum* (Rome, 1587 fol.), p. 229, 279; D'Argentré, *Collectio Judiciorum de Novis Erroribus*, i, 84, 95; Haupt, *Zeitschr. für Deutsch. Alterthum*, 1853, p. 55; Herzog, *Real-Encyklop.* s. v.

Z.

Zabarella (or **De Zabarellis**), archbishop of Florence and cardinal, the most notable man among the Italians present at the Council of Constance, was born at Padua in 1339. He studied canon law at Bologna, and taught at Padua. During the siege of the city by the Venetians he was deputed to invoke the assistance of France, and, after Padua had surrendered, he was the orator of the fourteen deputies who, in St. Mark's Place in Venice, handed over the Paduan flag. He subsequently migrated to Florence, and engaged in teaching canon law. After a time the town authorities elected him archbishop, but it was found that the pope had already given the place to another. Boniface IX called him to Rome to submit an opinion respecting the best methods for healing the schism in the Church, on which question he wrote the book *De Schismatibus Auctoritate*

Imperatoris Tollendis (Basle, 1565; Strasburg, 1609, 1618), which, together with the preface by Schardius, was placed in the index. He was appointed archipresbyter to the cathedral on his return to Padua, and held a wealthy abbacy for a time, and until the dissolute John XXIII, who favored learned men, called him to Rome and made him archbishop of Florence and cardinal-deacon, with the title of *St. Cosmasand Damianus* (1411). He had previously earned a scholarly reputation by the numerous books which emanated from his pen.

When arrangements were made for the Council of Constance, Zabarella was one of the papal envoys to the court of emperor Sigismund. In the council itself he, as the youngest cardinal, announced the time of the first session and read the bull of John XXIII, intended to regulate the drift of its business. He joined other cardinals in submitting a memorial relating to a reform in the administration of the papal court, and read the offer by which the pope volunteered to abdicate if the antipopes would renounce their pretensions to his office. When John fled from Constance, Zabarella supported the resolutions affirming the superiority of a general council to a pope; but he nevertheless incurred the censure of the council by an unfairness committed in the interest of the pope, in connection with the reading of resolutions which had been agreed upon, affirming the divine right of the council to require the submission of all people, including the pope, in all matters concerning the faith, the removal of the existing schism, and *the reformation of the Church in head and members*, the italicized clause having been omitted by him from the reading. He was eventually sent with a delegation of cardinals to negotiate with John, and obtained from him the unconditional surrender of his pontificate.

Zabarella participated also in the negotiations with Huss, and suggested the drawing up of an exceedingly mild formula of retraction, which the reformer, however, refused to sign. In connection with the schism he delivered a strong argument against pope Benedict, in which he charged the miserable state of the Church upon the obstinacy of its leaders; and when a new pope was to be chosen, he delivered another speech in support of the cardinals' view that the election ought to precede any movement looking towards a reformation of the Church, which was so violent that he predicted it would be the occasion of his death. He soon became dangerously sick, and died Sept. 26, 1417 (others say Nov. 5). It is probable that he would have been chosen pope, instead of Martin V, but for his early death.

Zabarella wrote numerous works of limited extent, e. g. *Comment. in Libros Decretal, et Clementinas* (Venice, 1602):—*Comment. in Clementinas* (ibid. 1481, 1487):—*Consilia Juris* (ibid. 1581):—*Variar. Legum Repetitiones* (ibid. 1587):—*De Schismatibus* (supra), etc. See Von d. Hardt, *Akten d. Const. Concils*, tom. i; Lenfant, *Hist. du Concil. de Constance*, passim; Herzog, *Real-Encyklop.* s. v.

Zabarella, Bartholomew, nephew and heir to the cardinal, a teacher of canon law at Padua, participant in important consultations at the papal court, and ultimately archbishop of Florence. He died in 1445. See Herzog, *Real-Encyklop.* s. v.

Zabarella, Jacob, professor at Padua, A.D. 1564 et seq., and author of the book, *De Inventione Æterni Motoris.* Ideas presented in the book and otherwise, exposed him, before the inquisition, to the charge of doubting the immortality of the soul, from which, however, he was acquitted. He was born at Padua in 1533, and died in 1589. See Herzog, *Real-Encyklop.* s. v.

Zabathaites, the followers of Zabathai Zevi (or Sabatai Sebi), a celebrated Jewish impostor, who appeared at Smyrna about 1666, and, pretending to be the Messiah, promised to deliver the Jews, and re-establish them in more than pristine glory. Multitudes of his nation were deceived by him, and many of his followers pretended to visions and prophetic ecstasies. At length, falling into the hands of the sultan, he ordered him to be placed as a mark for his archers, to prove whether he was vulnerable or not (as he pretended), to avoid which Zevi turned Mohammedan. See MESSIAHS, FALSE. His sect, however, survived, and there is said to be still a remnant of them at Saloniki, who, while they profess to be Mussulmans, observe the Jewish rites in secret, marry among themselves, and all live in the same quarter of the city, without communicating with the Turks, except in commerce, and in the mosques. Zevi, it seems, had also adherents among the Jews of England, Holland, Germany, and Poland, some of which have remained to our own time; and M. Grégoire mentions a musician of this sect who came to Paris so lately as in 1808. See Adams, *Hist. of the Jews*, p. 316, 528; Grégoire, *Hist.* ii, 309-313. See SABBATHAI.

Zabians, an ancient sect, said to be Chaldæans, addicted to astrology and star-worship. The word is derived, according to Pococke, from the Aramaic *tsabâ*, the heavenly host, from which same root the word Sabian is taken, but in the different sense of "to change religion." The Zabians were idolaters, dwelling in the north of Mesopotamia, in the Biblical Haran. An Arabic writer, quoted by Chwolsohn, says that they adopted the name Zabian as being a religion tolerated by the Koran, and so escaped the persecution to which their star-worship would have exposed them. They first gave planetary names to the days of the week; the feast day of each planet being determined by the time of its culmination; hence, also, the alchemists of the Middle Ages, and through them heralds, have borrowed the notion of assigning a particular metal and a particular color to the several planets. In common with other Aramaic races they had a civil year, which began like the Jewish *Rosh Ha-Shanah* in autumn, and an ecclesiastical year commencing at the vernal equinox. Before the time of Mohammed they offered human sacrifices to the deities which they believed were embodied in the planets. See Herzog, *Real-Encyklop.* s. v. See SABIANS.

Zabism, the religion of the Zabians (q. v.), or Haranian idolaters. It was formerly understood that they were a distinct race, and that their religion was composed of Chaldaism, Parsaism, Judaism, Christianity, Neo-Platonism, Gnosticism, and cabalistic speculations. This is not, however, strictly true. They might best be described as Syrians, who, partly descended from Greek colonists, had been subject so long to Syrian influences that they became in a manner Syrianized. Their religion was the old heathenism of their fathers, which had, with incredible obstinacy, resisted not only Christianity, but rendered even Mohammedan ill-will harmless by stratagem. But there were certain non-pagan elements which crept into it during the early centuries, and many other additions of later years. We mention, first of all, a number of legends about Biblical personages, from whom they pretend to be descendants. There are also laws of purity and impurity, and of sacrifices, which are very similar to Judaism. Then again, names of Greek and Roman gods, such as Helios, Ares, and Kronos, occur, a circumstance which may be explained from the prevailing tendency of the period of exchanging the names of native divinities for Greek and Roman names. There are also certain metaphysical and physical views incorporated in their creed, which are distinctly traceable to Aristotle, and finally, the Neo-Platonic philosophy of heathenism, as presented by Porphyry, Proclus, Iamblichus, and others. All these elements, infused into it by the circumstances of the period, do not prevent it from being in reality heathenism.

The sources of information in reference to the creed are written in Arabic, in Hebrew, and in Greek. The Arabic are the most copious; the Hebrew are chiefly represented by Maimonides; and the Greek are ascribed to various pseudonymous writers, among whom are Aristotle and Hermes Trismegistus. From these, though somewhat various and contradictory, the following facts may be gathered in reference to the creed. The Creator is one in essence, primity, originality, and eternity; but manifold in his manifestations in bodily figures. He is chiefly personified by the seven leading planets, and the good, knowing, and excellent of earthly bodies. But his unity, they claim, is not thereby disturbed; and it is "as if the seven planets were his seven limbs, and as if our seven limbs were his seven spheres, in which he manifests himself, so that he speaks with our tongue, sees with our eyes, hears with our ears, touches with our hands, comes and goes with our feet, and acts through our members." Zabism expresses the idea that God is too great and too sublime to occupy himself directly with the affairs of this world; that he therefore has handed over its ruling to the gods, and that he himself only takes the most important things under his special care; and that man is too weak to address himself directly to the highest, and is therefore obliged to direct prayers and sacrifices to the intermediate deities to whom the rule of the world is intrusted. Thus the veneration of the planets, and even the worshipping of idols, is nothing but a symbolical act, the consequence of that original idea. There are many gods and goddesses in Zabism of this intermediate stamp. It is not the planets themselves, but the spirits that direct them, conceived as deities that stand to the spheres in the relation of soul and body. Apart from these there are those gods who cause or represent every action in this world. Every universal natural deed or effect emanates from a universal deity, every partial one from a partial deity that presides over part of nature. These gods know our most secret thoughts, and all our future is open to them. The female deities seem to have been conceived of as the feeling or passive principle. These gods or intelligences emanate directly from God without his will, as rays do from the sun. They are of abstract forms, free of all matter, and neither made of any substance nor material. They consist chiefly of a light in which there is no darkness, which the senses cannot appreciate, by reason of its immense clearness, which the understanding cannot comprehend, by reason of its extreme delicacy, and which fancy and imagination cannot fathom. Their nature is free from all animal desires, and they themselves are created for love and harmony, friendship and unity. Their existence is full of the highest bliss, by reason of their nearness to the Most High; they have a free choice, and always incline to the good; and are the "lords and gods" of the Zabians, their "intermediators and advocates with the Lord of lords and God of gods." All substances and types of the bodily world emanate from the spiritual world, which is one from which everything flows and to which everything returns, and which is full of light, sublime and pure. These two worlds correspond to each other, and are to each other like light and shadow. The way to approach these gods, and through them the highest essence, is by purifying the soul from all passions, by keeping a strict guard over one's words and deeds, by fasting, sincere prayer, invocations, sacrifices, fumigations, and incantations. By steadfastly persevering in these and similar acts of devotion, man may reach so high a step of perfection that he may communicate even directly with the Supreme Power. The planets, as the principal representative and intermediate gods, are to be carefully observed, especially as regards (1) the houses and stations of the planets; (2) their rising and setting; (3) their respective conjunctions and oppositions; (4) the knowledge of their special times and seasons, the hours and days of the ruling of special planets; (5) the divisions of the different figures, forms, climates, and countries, according to their dominant stars—in fact, everything below heaven, according to their belief, was subject in some way to the influence of the stars or the spirits which inhabit them. Every substance and every action, every country and every hour, had its special planetary deity. It is important, therefore, to study carefully the special conjunctions and figures, as well as the special mixtures of incense, which might render the individual numen propitious. Thus, for example, the first hour of Saturday stands under Saturnus, and it is right and advisable at that time to select such prayers, seals, amulets, dresses, and fumigations as might be especially pleasing to that planetary god.

In order to address themselves to *visible* mediators, some of the Zabians are supposed to have directed their devotions to the stars themselves. But they soon found a worship that addressed itself to things that appeared and disappeared in turn very unsatisfactory. Accordingly they manufactured permanent representatives of them in the shape of idols, wrought in as complete accordance as possible with the theurgical rules derived from the nature of the deity to be represented. They were of gold to represent the sun; of silver, to represent the moon. The very temples in which they were placed were of as many corners as were supposed to correspond to the form of certain stars.

Zabism teaches that man is composed of contradictory elements, which make him the vacillating, struggling creature he is. Passions and desires rule him and lower him to the level of the brute creation, and he would utterly lose himself were it not for such religious rites as purifications, sacrifices, and other means of grace, by which he may be enabled to approach the great gods once more and attempt to become like them. The soul of man partakes partly of the nature of the animal soul and partly of that of the angelic soul. The soul never dies, and rewards and punishments will affect only it. These, however, will not be wrought in any future world, but in this, only at different epochs of existence. Thus all our present joys are rewards for good deeds done by us in former epochs, and the sorrows and griefs we endure spring in the same manner from evil actions we committed at former stages. As to the nature of the general world-soul itself, they say it is primitive, for if it were not so it would be material, as every newly-created being partakes of the material nature. Kathibi says, "The soul, which is thus an immaterial thing, and exists from eternity, is the involuntary reason of the first types, as God is the first cause of the intelligences. The soul once beheld matter and loved it. Glowing with the desire of assuming a bodily shape, it would not again separate itself from that matter by means of which the world was created. Since that time the soul forgot itself, its everlasting existence, its original abode, and knew nothing more of what it had known before. But God, who turns all things to the best, united it to matter which it loved, and out of this union the heavens, the elements, and composite things arose. In order that the soul might not wholly perish within matter, he endowed it with intelligence, whereby it conceived its high origin, the spiritual world, and itself. It further conceived through this that it was but a stranger in this world, that it was subject to many sufferings in it, and that even the joys of this world are but the source of new sufferings. As soon as the soul had perceived all this it began to yearn again for its spiritual home, as a man who is away from his birthplace pines for his homestead. It then also learned that, in order to return to its primitive state, it had to free itself from the fetters of sensuous desires, and from all materialistic tendencies. Free from them all, it would regain its heavenly sphere again, and enjoy the bliss of the spiritual world."

The life of the sect holding this creed was but short. After having first been on terms of great friendship with the ruling powers of Mohammedanism, as well as with Christians and Jews, and having filled many of the highest and most responsible posts at the courts of the caliphs, they were, by degrees, made the butt of fanaticism and rapacity. Mulcted, persecuted, banished at different periods, they disappear from history since the middle of the 11th century. Thus obscurely ended a sect which for two hundred years had produced a host of men pre-eminent in every branch of learning and literature, in philosophy, astronomy, history, natural history, poetry, medicine, and the rest. See Chwolsohn, *Die Sabien und die Sabismus* (St. Petersburg, 1856, 2 vols.).

Zaccaria, Antonio Maria, an Italian monk, founder of the congregation of the Barnabites, was born at Cremona in 1500. He studied at first medicine and philosophy at Padua, and afterwards theology also. Having received holy orders, he settled at Milan, where, in 1525, he joined the fraternity of Eternal Wisdom, and where he soon, in connection with several other members, and with the sanction of Clement VII, founded a new congregation, of which he was made superior. From their first church, St. Paul's, in Milan, they were originally called the Regular Clerks of St. Paul's (Paulines), which name they exchanged for Barnabites, when, in 1541, they were presented with the Church of St. Barnabas, in Milan. Zaccaria, who is said to have had the power of prophecy and of working miracles, died, according to his own prediction, July 5, 1539, at Cremona. Of his writings, we mention a compilation from the Church fathers, *Detti Notabili Raccolti da Diversi Autori* (Venice, 1583; printed in French, Lyons, 1625; Latin, by J. A. Gallicus, *Axiomata Sacra*). See Arisius, *Cremona Literata*, ii, 88 sq., Biedenfeld, *Monchsorden*, i, 180; *Theol. Universallexikon*, s. v. (B. P.)

Zacchæans is a local name for the Gnostics, mentioned by Epiphanius (*Hæres.* xxvi, 3), but without adding where they were so called.

Zac′chur (1 Chron. iv, 26). See Zaccur.

Zachalios, an ancient Babylonish writer, is mentioned by Pliny (*Hist. Nat.* xxxvii, 10) as the author of a book on gems and their magical powers, which was dedicated to the king Mithridates. "It was evidently a writing belonging to that Græco-Babylonian literature which was so widely developed during the centuries bordering on the Christian æra, and which had the same connection with the real Chaldæan doctrines as the Grecian literature of the hermetical books had with the doctrine of ancient Egypt" (Lenormont, *Chaldæan Magic*, p. 176).

Zacharia, Just Friedrich, a Protestant theologian, was born at Haina, in Gotha, in 1704. He studied at Jena and Kiel, was appointed at the latter place, in 1735, professor of Oriental languages, in 1742 elected to the chair of Biblical antiquities, and in 1747 to that of theology. He died March 8, 1773. He published, *Dissertatio seu Commentatio Solemnis, Comma Secundam Quinti Hoseæ Capitis Explicans* (Kiloni, 1731):—*Progr. de Usu Linguæ Ebrææ in Philosophia* (ibid. 1736):—*Diss. de Ritibus Scholasticis Judæorum* (ibid. 1745). See Döring, *Die gelehrten Theologen Deutschlands*, iv, 767 sq.; Fürst, *Bibl. Jud.* iii, 540. (B. P.)

Zacharias, bishop of Anagni, Italy, was sent in A.D. 860, as one of the legates of pope Nicholas I, to Constantinople with letters of reply to those of the emperor Michael and the patriarch Photius, making overtures to the Church of Rome for sympathy and co-operation. See Neander, *Hist. of the Church*, iii, 562.

Zacharias Scholasticus, bishop of Mitylene, in the island of Lesbos, was present at the Synod of Constantinople (A.D. 536) which deposed Anthimus, the patriarch of Alexandria. Zacharias had studied philosophy at Alexandria, and for some time practiced as an advocate at Berytus. He is the author of *Ammonius sive de Mundi Opificio*, a dialogue in which he defends the Christian view of creation and government of the world against objections to it raised from the point of view of the Greek philosophy. It was first published at Paris in 1619. The best edition is that by Jean Fr. Boissonade, *Æneas Gazæus et Zacharias Mitylenæus, de Immortalitate Animæ et Mundi Consummatione* (Paris, 1836). He also wrote, *Disputatio contra Ea, quæ de Duobus Principiis a Manichæo quodam Scripta et Projecta in Viam Publicam Reperit Justinianus Imperator* (Latin interpretation by Turriano, in *Bibl. Pat. Max. Lugd.* ix, 794). See Brucker, *Hist. Crit. Philos.* ii, 528; Ritter, *Geschichte der christl. Philosophie*, ii, 495; Herzog, *Real-Encyklop.* s. v. (B. P.)

Zacuto, Abraham. See Sakkuto, Abraham.

Zacynthian Manuscript (designated as Ξ) is a palimpsest uncial fragment in the library of the British and Foreign Bible Society in London, which, under an evangelistary, written on coarse vellum in or about the 13th century, contains large portions of Luke's gospel down to xi, 33, in full, well-formed characters, but surrounded by, and often interwoven with, large extracts from the Lectors, in a hand which cannot be earlier than the 8th century. It was obtained from Zante in 1821. The entire volume must have originally been a large folio (14 inches by 11), of which eighty-six leaves and three half-leaves survive. The readings are very valuable. They were communicated to dean Alford for the fourth edition of his New Test. by Dr. Tregelles, who has since (1861) collated and published it in full. See Scrivener, *Introd. to the New Test.* p. 126; *Christian Remembrancer*, Jan. 1862; *Journ. of Sac. Lit.* Jan. 1862, p. 495. See Manuscript.

Zahab. See Gold.

Zahalon, Abraham ben-Isaac, a Jewish writer of Spain, who flourished in the 16th century, is the author of, מרפא לנפש, or *Healing of the Soul*, an ascetical work, treating on repentance (Venice, 1595):—יד חרוצים, on the Jewish, Christian, and Mohammedan calendar (ibid. 1594–95):—ישע אלהים, a grammatical and pædagogical commentary on the book of Esther (ibid. 1595). See Fürst, *Bibl. Jud.* iii, 541; Jöcher, *Allgemeines Gelehrten-Lexikon*, s. v.; De' Rossi, *Dizionario Storico Degli Autori Ebrei* (Germ. transl.), p. 333. (B. P.)

Zahalon, Jacob ben-Isaac, a Jewish writer of Rome, was born in 1630, and died at Ferrara in 1693. Besides a large medical work, אוצר החיים, he left, in MS., a commentary on Isaiah, entitled ס' ישועות יעקב:—a commentary on Ecclesiastes, קהלת יעקב:—disquisitions on Daniel, דרושים על דניאל:—homiletical expositions on the Pentateuch, חתן אמת ליעקב:—a commentary on the Song of Songs, צהלה ורנה, etc. See Fürst, *Bibl. Jud.* iii, 541, Jöcher, *Allgemeines Gelehrten-Lexikon*, s. v.; De' Rossi, *Dizionario Storico Degli Autori Ebrei* (Germ. transl.), p. 332. (B. P.)

Zahn, a German philanthropist, was a mason of Bunzlau, who wandered about as an orphan in childhood, and learned to read at the age of twenty-four. He carried on a little school in his own house for the benefit of orphans. He made the first movement towards the establishment of an orphan-house in Bunzlau, and went to Berlin to solicit the royal sanction. The corner-stone was laid in 1755. Zahn became the first superintendent, but died of the plague in 1756. The institution was conducted from that time by Ernest Gottlieb Woltersdorf. See Hagenbach, *Hist. of the Church in the 18th and 19th Centuries*, i, 146.

Zair. Conder suggests (*Hand-book to the Bible*, p. 427) that this is "perhaps the ruin *Zueireh* on the south-west shore of the Dead Sea."

Zallwein, Gregorius, a Roman Catholic theologian of Germany, was born at Obervinchtach, in the Palatinate, Oct. 20, 1712. In 1733 he joined the order of the Benedictines, and received holy orders in 1737. In 1744 he was elected prior of the monastery at Wessobrunn, and shortly afterwards was called to Strasburg, in Carinthia, as professor of theology, Church history, and canon law. In 1749 he was called to the Salzburg University, and died Aug. 9, 1766. Of his publications, we mention, *Fontes Originarii Juris Canonici*, etc. (Salzburg, 1754–55):—*Jus Ecclesiasticum Particulare Germaniæ ab Æra Christi usque ad Carolum IX Imp.* (ibid. 1757):—*Collectiones Juris Ecclesiastici Antiqui et Novi*, etc. (ibid. 1760):—*Principia Juris Ecclesiastici Universalis et Particularis Germaniæ* (1763 sq. 4 vols.). See Döring, *Die gelehrten Theologen Deutschlands*, iv, 770; Winer, *Handbuch der theol. Lit.* ii, 8. (B. P.)

Zamora, ALPHONSO. See ALPHONSO DE ZAMORA.

Zampieri, DOMENICO (commonly known as *Domenichino*), an eminent Italian artist, was born at Bologna in 1581, and received his first instructions from Denis Calvart, but, on account of severe treatment by that master, he was removed to the Academy of the Caracci. His great talents did not develop themselves so early as in many other painters, and his studious and thoughtful manner drew from his fellow-students the appellation of the Ox; but Annibale Caracci testified of his abilities by saying to his pupils, "This Ox will in time surpass you all, and be an honor to the art of painting." In the first contest of the students for a prize after he entered the academy, Domenichino was triumphant; but this triumph, instead of rendering him confident and presumptuous, only stimulated him to greater assiduity, and he pursued his studies with such patient and constant application that he made such progress as to win the admiration of some of his contemporaries and to beget the hatred of others. After leaving the school of the Caracci, he visited Parma, Modena, and Reggio, to study the works of Correggio and Parmiggiano; and soon after returning to Bologna he went to Rome, where he commenced his brilliant career. Cardinal Agucchi was the first to patronize him, and he employed him in his palace, and commissioned him to paint three pictures for the Church of St. Onofria, representing subjects from the life of St. Jerome. He was employed about this time to assist Annibale Caracci in his great works in the Farnesian Gallery at Rome, and he executed a part of them from the cartoons of Caracci. He also painted in the loggia, in the garden, from his own designs, the *Death of Adonis*, in which he represented Venus springing from her car to succor her unfortunate lover. He was employed by cardinal Borghese to assist in decorating the Church of San Gregorio, in which his *Flagellation of St. Andrea* is so justly celebrated. Cardinal Farnese next employed him to paint some frescos in a chapel in the abbey of Grotto Farrata, where he executed several subjects from the life of St. Nilo; one of these, representing the cure of a dæmoniac, is considered one of the finest productions at Rome. Soon after this he executed his famous *Communion of St. Jerome*, painted for the principal altar of San Girolamo della Cavitá, a work which has immortalized his name, and which was accounted, next to the *Transfiguration* of Raphael, the finest picture of Rome. This work has experienced some removals, but has been returned to its original place and copied in mosaic to preserve the design, the original having suffered from the effects of time. His next great work was in the Church of San Lodovico, representing the life of St. Cecilia. His great success and increasing fame had by this time so excited the envy and hatred of his contemporaries that he was constrained to leave Rome in disgust. He therefore returned to Bologna, where he resided several years in the quiet practice of his profession, and executed some of his most admired works, particularly the *Martyrdom of St. Agnes*, for the church of that saint, and the *Madonna del Rosario*, both of which were engraved by Gerard Audran for the Louvre at Paris by order of Napoleon. The fame of Domenichino was now so well established that intrigue and malice could not suppress it, and pope Gregory XV invited him back to Rome, and appointed him principal painter and architect to the pontifical palace. Cardinal Montalto employed him to decorate the vault of San Andrea della Valle, where he represented the four evangelists, with angels, in such a masterly manner that they were the admiration of Italy and the study of artists. He also painted in the chapel of cardinal Bandini, in the Church of San Sylvestro, in the Quirinal, four pictures—*Queen Esther before Ahasuerus, Judith with the Head of Holofernes, David Playing on the Harp before the Ark*, and *Solomon and his Mother, Bathsheba, Seated on a Throne*—which were esteemed among his finest works. Soon after he painted the *Four Cardinal Virtues* in the Church of San Carlo Catenari. He was next invited to Naples to paint the chapel of St. Januarius. He executed one of his most admired works in the Palazzo della Torre, representing the dead Christ supported on the knees of the Virgin, together with Mary Magdalene and others. But his life soon became so embittered by the jealousy and hatred of his rivals that he quitted Naples in disgust, and returned once more to Bologna, where he died, in 1641. His work as an architect began with the superintendence of the pontifical palace under Gregory XV, but he executed various other works, particularly two designs for the Church of San Ignazio, at Rome. He was not, however, allowed to complete this edifice, but his designs were combined by the Jesuit Grassi in another edifice. Thereupon Domenichino refused to furnish additional plans, and the building was transferred to Algardi. In Santa Maria Trastevere he designed the rich and ingenious entablature, also the chapel, called Della Madonna di Strada Cupa. He also designed the greater part of the elegant villa Belvidere at Frascati, and designed and erected the picturesque villa Lodoviso at Rome, the gardens of which he laid out with a number of verdant walks, and divided the grove with exquisite taste. No better proof of his great merits as an artist can be desired than the fact that upwards of fifty of his works have been engraved by Gerard Audran, Raphael Morghen, and other famous engravers, and that many of them have been frequently copied. See Spooner, *Biog. Hist. of the Fine Arts*, p. 265, 1119; Milizia, *Lives of Celebrated Architects*, ii, 152.

Zanchi, JEROME, a clergyman and theologian of the German Reformed Church, was born at Alzano, in the territory of Bergamo, Feb. 2, 1516, and was the son of the historian Zanchi. He entered the Augustinian order of regular canons in 1531, engaged in philosophical and theological studies, and, on their completion, came with his friend, count Celso Martinengo of Brescia, to the monastery of Lucca, where Vermigli was teaching, and where they became acquainted with the writings of Luther, Melanchthon, Bullinger, and Calvin. They soon afterwards came into notice as evangelical preachers, and were compelled to flee—Martinengo to Milan and Geneva, where he became pastor of the Italian Church, in 1552, and Zanchi to Switzerland and Geneva, in 1551. In 1553 Zanchi accepted a professorship of the Old Test. at Strasburg, where Marbach and other Lutherans were his colleagues, the association involving him in controversies upon the doctrines of the antichrist, predestination, and the perseverance of the saints, which began in 1561, and were superficially settled by arbitrators, who drew up a formal agreement, which was signed by all the clergy and professors of the city, Zanchi, however, appending a reservation to his signature intended to prevent his being compelled to teach what he did not receive as the truth. Calvin and other reformed theologians, however, censured the yielding temper which Zanchi had exhibited, and thus induced him to speak his sentiments more positively. This naturally renewed the strife and involved disagreeable consequences, from which he was glad to escape by accepting a call to Chiavenna as pastor of the Italian congregation. He had previously declined repeated calls to a similar post at Lyons. False teachers and uneasy Italian agitators troubled him at

Chiavenna, and in 1564 a pestilence interrupted the services of his Church and compelled his retirement to a mountain near Piuri, where he occupied himself with writing a sketch of his controversy with Marbach, which afterwards appeared under the title of *Miscellanea* (1566, 4to). In 1568 he became professor of theology at Heidelberg, and rapidly earned the first place among the scholars of the theological faculty. His advice was sought by persons in every quarter and upon all the debated questions of the day, e. g., the sacraments, the Trinity, the mediation of Christ, and replies in great number were written to inquirers, sometimes in the name of the faculty, and often in his own name, all tending to the confirmation of the teachings of Reformed orthodoxy. He was equally zealous and influential in the work of introducing a strict discipline in the churches of the palatinate. Of larger theological works written by him in this period we mention *De Tribus Elohim*, etc. (1572), which is chiefly important as collocating the grounds upon which the antitrinitarians based their opinions; *De Natura Dei*, etc., a sort of speculative philosophy of religion, in which the doctrine of predestination especially is carried to its logical consequences; and *De Operibus Dei intra Spatium Sex Dierum Creatis*, a cosmology in which dogmatic hypotheses and physical facts are intermingled—interesting as showing the amount of knowledge possessed, or supposed to be possessed, respecting nature and natural forces in that day. A fourth work, *De Primi Hominis Lapsu*, etc., was begun at Heidelberg, but not completed. A Lutheran prince succeeded to the throne of the Palatinate, and Zanchi was dismissed. The newly established University of Neustadt-on-the-Hardt received him, and made him its professor of the New Test. in 1578, and this post he retained until he died, Nov. 19, 1590, though he had been invited to return to Heidelberg when the Palatinate was restored to Calvinism. In 1577 he was required to write a confession by the deputies of the Reformed churches, then assembled at Frankfort, which confession was intended to be opposed to the *Formula of Concord*. This work became the basis of the *Harmonia Conf. Fidei Orthodoxarum* of Beza and Danæus (1581). His children collected his works and published them after his death, though no complete edition appeared prior to that of Geneva (1619, 3 vols. fol. 8 parts). These works rank among the leading sources of the Reformed theology of his time, but are already tainted with the scholastic spirit. See Schmid, in *Stud. u. Krit.* 1859; Herzog, *Real-Encyklop.* s. v.

Zanchius, Basil, a learned Italian monk and writer, was born at Bergamo in 1501. His real name was Peter, which he exchanged for Basil when he became a canon regular. He studied at Rome and various other places, but resided for the greater part of his life at Rome, where he died in 1560. He was the subject of persecution, for some cause not clearly ascertained, and died in prison. He was one of the best Latin poets of his age. His Latin poems were first printed at Rome in 1540, and were often reprinted. He also wrote observations on all the books of Scripture (Rome, 1553). He published *Epithetorum Commentarii* (1542), a second edition of which appeared under the title *Dictionarium Poeticum et Epitheta Veterum Poetarum*, etc. (1612).

Zanoah. (1) In the plain of Judah. The present *Khurbet Zanua* lies one and a half miles north of Beit Nettif and two and a half south-east of Ain Shems (Beth-Shemeh), and is "a large and important ruin on high ground, mainly east of the road; but remains are also found on the hill-top to the west," consisting of chambers with arched entrances, foundations of house-walls, traces of mills, cave-tombs, etc. (*Memoirs* to the Ordnance Survey, iii, 128). (2) In the hills of Judah. The modern *Khurbet Zanuta* lies four and a half miles south-west of Es-Semûa (Eshtemoa), and one and a half north-west of Attû, and consists of "heaps of stones and foundations, fallen pillars, caves and cisterns on a hill" (described in the *Memoirs* to the Ordnance Survey, iii, 410 sq.).

Zanolini, Antonio, a Jewish writer of the 18th century, is the author of, *Quæstiones e Scriptura Sacra* (Padua, 1725):—*Lexicon Hebraicum* (ibid. 1732):—*Lexicon Chaldaico-Rabbinicum* (ibid. 1747):—*Ratio Institutioque Addiscendæ Linguæ Chald.-Rabb.-Talmudicæ cum Singularum Dialectorum Exemplis etiam Latinitate Donatis*, etc. (ibid. 1750). See Fürst, *Bibl. Jud.* iii, 542 sq.; Wolf, *Bibl. Hebr.* iv, 312; Steinschneider, *Bibl. Handbuch*, s. v. (B. P.)

Zanti, Abraham, a Jewish physician, philosopher, and poet, was born in 1670, and died, rabbi of Venice, in 1729. He is the author of כתנת אברהם, or a metrorhythmic paraphrase of the Psalms (Venice, 1719). See Fürst, *Bibl. Jud.* iii, 543; De' Rossi, *Dizionario Storico* (Germ. transl.), p. 335. (B. P.)

Zanzalus, Jacob (called also *Baradæus*), a monk of the 6th century, became conspicuous by reviving the Monophysite (q. v.) sect of the Eutychians (q. v.). They had been reduced to a very small number, but these had ordained Zanzalus bishop of Edessa, and by his zeal and unceasing toil he left the sect, at his death in A.D. 588, in a flourishing condition in Syria, Mesopotamia, Armenia, Egypt, and other countries. These are known as Jacobites (q. v.).

Zaremba, Felician Martin von, a famous missionary, was born at Zaroy, in the Russian government of Grodno, in Lithuania, March 15, 1794. He studied at Dorpat for a political career. In 1816 he was made doctor of philosophy, and in 1817 engaged at St. Petersburg in the college for foreign affairs. In the same year he concluded to give up everything and to work in the service of his Master. He went to Basle in 1818, and having spent there nearly three years, was appointed to commence missionary operations in Grusia. Having received his ordination in 1821, he went to Shuśha, which became the nucleus for his operations. In 1830 he was obliged to leave his post on account of feeble health, and returned to Basle. In 1835 he again returned to his post, but, on his way, an imperial ukase forbade further operations. All representations were in vain, and Zaremba, the first and last missionary of the Basle Society, left Shusha in 1838 for Basle. From 1839 to 1864 he travelled through Europe in behalf of his society, but in 1865 he was struck with apoplexy. He died May 31, 1874. See *Der evangelische Heidenbote*, 1874, No. 7. (B. P.)

Zeal, a passionate ardor for any person or cause. The word in Hebrew is קִנְאָה, *kinâh*, from קָנָא, *kanâh*, "to flush" with passion. The Sept. usually renders it by ζῆλος (the New Test. term), which is derived from ζέω, "to be hot." Thus we say, "a fiery zeal." The psalmist says (Psa. lxix, 9), "The zeal of thine house hath eaten me," or consumed me like fire (see Bauer, *De Messiæ Zelo pro Domo Dei*, Viteb. 1744). Zeal is an earnestness arising either from good or evil motives (2 Sam. xxi, 2; 1 Cor. xiv, 12; Col. iv, 13). Thus Phinehas was commended because he was zealous for Jehovah (Numb. xxv, 11-13); but Jehu, when he slew the priests of Baal and the family of Ahab, was zealous in order to gain public applause (2 Kings x, 16-31). Zeal may be misdirected, or it may be honorable (Phil. iii, 6; Gal. iv, 17, 18; Tit. ii, 14; Psa. lxix, 9; John ii, 17). Zeal is attributed in Scripture to God as well as to man (2 Kings xix, 31; Isa. ix, 7; Ezek. v, 13). There are various kinds of zeal, as (1) an ignorant zeal (Rom. x, 2, 3); (2) a persecuting zeal (Phil. iii, 6); (3) a superstitious zeal (1 Kings xviii; Gal. i, 14); (4) a hypocritical zeal (2 Kings x, 16); (5) a contentious zeal (1 Cor. xi, 16); (6) a partial zeal (Hos. vii, 8); (7) a temporary zeal (2 Kings xii, xiii; Gal. iv, 15); (8) a genuine zeal, which is a sincere and warm concern for the glory of God, and the spiritual welfare of mankind (Gal. iv, 18; Rev. iii, 19). This last is generally compounded of sound knowledge, strong faith, and disinterested regard; and will manifest itself by self-denial, patient endurance, and constant exertion. The motives to true zeal are (1) the divine command (Rev. iii, 19); (2) the example of Christ and the end of his death (John ii, 17; Acts x, 38; Tit. ii, 14); (3) the importance of his service; (4) the advantage and pleasure it brings to the possessor; (5) the instances and honorable commendation of it in the Scriptures: Moses, Phineas, Caleb, David, Paul, etc. (Gal. iv, 18; Rev. iii, 15, etc.); (6) the incalculable good effects it produces on others (James v, 20). See Reynolds and Orton *on Sacred Zeal;* Massillon, *Charges;* Evans, *Christian Temper*, sermon 37; Hughes, Channing, and Chapin, *Sermon on Zeal;* Mason, *Christ. Mor.* sermon 28; *Natural History of Enthusiasm.* See FAITH; FANATICISM; JEALOUSY.

Zealots (ζηλωταί) were, in a technical Jewish sense, the followers of Judas the Gaulonite, or Galilæan (q. v.). Josephus speaks of them as forming the "fourth sect of Jewish philosophy," and as distinguished from the Pharisees chiefly by a quenchless love of liberty and a contempt of death. Their leading tenet was the unlawfulness of paying tribute to the Romans, as being a violation of the theocratic constitution. This principle, which they maintained by force of arms against the Roman government, was soon converted into a pretext for deeds of violence against their own countrymen, and during the last days of the Jewish polity the Zealots were lawless brigands or guerrillas, the pest and terror of the land. After the death of Judas, and of his two sons, Jacob and Simon (who suffered crucifixion), they were headed by Eleazar, one of his descendants, and were often denominated *Sicarii*, from the use of a weapon resembling the Roman sica (Joseph. *Ant.* xviii, 1; *War*, iv, 1-6; vii, 8; see Lardner, *Credibility*, pt. i, bk. i, ch. vi, ix; Kitto, *Palestine*, p. 741, 751). See ZELOTES.

Zedner, JOSEPH, for a long time custodian at the British Museum, in London, was born at Gross-Glosgau in 1804, and died in Berlin, Oct. 10, 1871. He wrote, *Ueber den Wortton in der hebr. Sprache* (Berlin, 1817):—*Auswahl historischer Stücke aus hebr. Schriftstellern vom II. Jahrhunderts bis auf die Gegenwart* (Heb. and Germ. ibid. 1840):—ויוסף אברהם, or *Abraham ben-Ezra's Commentary on the Book of Esther after another Version* (Lond. 1850):—*Catalogue of the Hebrew Books in the Library of the British Museum* (ibid. 1867). He also contributed to the *Ha-Maskir* for 1859 and 1861. See Fürst, *Bibl. Jud.* iii, 546. (B. P.)

Zegedin (or **Szegedin**), STEPHEN DE, an eminent Lutheran divine, was born at Zegedin, a city of Lower Hungary, in 1505. His family name was *Kis.* He studied under Luther and Melanchthon at Wittenberg, taught and preached Lutheranism in several cities in Hungary, and was taken prisoner by the Turks, who treated him with great cruelty. He subsequently officiated as minister at Buda and in many other places. He died at Reven, in Hungary, May 2, 1572. He left the following works, which were afterwards published: *Assertio de Trinitate* (1573):—*Tabulæ Analyticæ in Prophetas, Psalmos, et Novum Testamentum* (1592):—*Speculum Romanum Pontificum Historicum* (1602). See Chalmers, *Biog. Dict.* s. v.

Zeibich, Carl Heinrich, a Protestant theologian of Germany, was born at Eilenburg, June 19, 1717. He studied theology, philosophy, and philology at Wittenberg, was made magister in 1737, on presenting a dissertation, *De Chaldaicorum Veteris Testamenti apud Judæos Auctoritate.* In 1752 he was made professor, and died Aug. 3, 1763. Of his writings we mention, *De Lingua Judæorum Hebraica Temporibus Christi et Apostolorum* (Viteb. 1741):—*De Codicum Veteris Testamenti Orientalium et Occidentalium Dissensionibus* (ibid. eod.):—*De Ritu Baptizandi in Mortem Christi, ab Eunomianis Recentioribus Introducto* (ibid. 1752):—*Σύμμικτα Antiquitatum Tarsicarum ex Scriptorum Veterum Monumentis Collecta* (ibid. 1760). See Döring, *Die gelehrten Theologen Deutschlands*, iv, 772 sq.; Fürst, *Bibl. Jud.* iii, 547. (B. P.)

Zeibich, Heinrich August, a German theologian, was born at Merseburg, June 22, 1729, and died March 30, 1787, at Gera, being professor of elocution there. He is the author of, *Vermischte Betrachtungen aus der Theologie und Philologie* (Leipsic, 1772-74, 3 parts):—*Progr. de Velo Hierosolymitano*, etc. (Gera, 1757):—*Von dem Grabe Mosis* (ibid. 1758):—*Progr. de Vento, Præsentiæ Divinæ Documento* (ibid. eod.):—*Pr. de Thuribulo Aureo* (ibid. 1768):—*Pr. de Radiante Mosis Facie a Cincinorum Cornibus Defensa* (ibid. 1764):—*De Censibus Hebræorum* (ibid. 1764-66):—*De Circumcisionis Origine* (ibid. 1770):—*Progr. duo de Miraculo Manna Israeliticæ* (ibid. 1770-71):—*Pr. Isaaci Ortus in Fabula Orionis Vestigia* (ibid. 1776):—*Pr. de Fl. Josepho Vespasiano Imperium Romanum Vaticinante* (ibid. 1783). See Winer, *Handbuch der theol. Lit.* i, 31; Fürst, *Bibl. Jud.* iii, 547. (B. P.)

Zeisberger, DAVID, a Moravian missionary among the Indians of North America, was born in Moravia, Germany, in 1721, whence his parents emigrated to Herrnhut, in Upper Lusatia, for the sake of religious liberty. He was educated by the Moravians in Saxony, and afterwards lived at their settlement of Nerrendyk, Holland. In 1738 he came to Georgia, where some of his brethren had begun a settlement, that they might preach the gospel to the Creeks. Thence he removed to Pennsylvania, and assisted in the commencement of the settlements of Bethlehem and Nazareth. Soon afterwards he became a missionary to the Indians, and labored among the Delawares at Shamokin, and the Iroquois at Onondaga, N. Y., till after the breaking-out of war in 1754. On the return of peace, after the conspiracy of Pontiac, he led the remnant of the Christian Indians, who had found a refuge in Philadelphia, Pa., to Wyalusing, on the Susquehanna, in Bradford County. In 1767 he established a Church among the Monseys, on the Alleghany. In 1772 he penetrated still farther, exploring the Muskingum region, and laying out the town of Schoenbrunn, on the Tuscarawas, about ten miles from the present Canal Dover, O. Here he was joined by all the Moravian Indians of Pennsylvania, and the mission was greatly enlarged. In 1781, at the instigation of the British commandant at Detroit, a party of Wyandots broke up these settlements, and compelled the Christian Indians to remove to Sandusky. The missionaries were shamefully abused. In the following year a party of ninety-six of those who had been driven to Sandusky returned to their former homes to gather their corn, and were treacherously murdered at Gnadenhütten by a party of the white settlers. After this melancholy incident most of the converts dispersed, and Zeisberger, with a small remnant, went to the Clinton River and formed a settlement in the present state of Michigan. In 1786 he returned to the southern shore of Lake Erie, and soon began another settlement, which he called New Salem. In 1791, however, he was obliged to remove to Canada on account of the hostility of the other Indians. There he founded Fairfield on the Thames. In 1798 the Moravian Indians received a grant from Congress of the tract of land which had been their former home in the valley of the Tuscarawas. To this locality Zeisberger returned with some of his converts, and established a new station, which he called Goshen. Here he remained until his death, Nov. 17, 1808. Perhaps no man ever preached the gospel so long among the Indians, and amid so many trials and hardships. He was a man of small stature, with a cheerful countenance, of a cool, intrepid spirit, with a good understanding and sound judgment. His portrait is prefixed to Heckewelder's *Narrative*. Amid all his privations and dangers he was never known to complain, nor ever regretted that he had engaged in the cause of the Redeemer. He would never consent to receive a salary, although he deemed it proper for some missionaries. He trusted in his Lord for the necessaries of life, and he looked to the future world for his reward. Free from selfishness, a spirit of universal love filled his bosom. A more perfect character has seldom been exhibited on the earth. It is a melancholy fact that he suffered more from white men, called Christians, by reason of their selfishness and depravity and hostility to the gospel, than from the Indians. Had the back settlers of our country participated in the benevolent spirit of the Moravians the benefit to the natives would have been incalculable. Amid all obstacles the brethren, in the days of Mr. Zeisberger, instructed and baptized about fifteen hundred Indians. The calm death of those who were murdered at Muskingum, in 1782, is a striking proof of the influence of the gospel on men, concerning whom it is sometimes said they cannot be made Christians. About 1768 he wrote two grammars of the Onondaga, in English and German, and a dictionary, German and Indian, of more than seventeen hundred pages. In the Lenape, or language of the Delawares, he published a spelling-book, sermons to children, and a hymn-book, containing upwards of five hundred hymns, translated partly from German and partly from English. He left in manuscript a grammar in German of the Delaware language, which has been translated by Mr. Du Ponceau; also a harmony of the four gospels, translated into Delaware. See De Schweinitz, *Life and Times of David Zeisberger* (Philadelphia, 1870); Heckewelder, *Narrative of the Missions among the Delaware and Mohegan Indians* (ibid. 1820); Allen, *Amer. Biog. Dict.* (1857); Allibone, *Dict. of Brit. and Amer. Authors*, s. v.

Zeitmann, Gottfried Thomas, a Lutheran minister, was born of Jewish parentage at Cracow, Poland, in 1696. On account of the war between Poland and Sweden, Zeitmann's father had to leave his country, and settled at Frankfort, where his son Hirschel (this was Zeitmann's name before his baptism) received his early education. In 1707 he was baptized, taking the above-mentioned name. He desired to learn a trade, but his friends advised him to attend the gymnasium of St. Anna, at Augsburg, where he had gone on account of being persecuted by his relatives. In 1717 he commenced his studies at Jena, where he remained till 1721. Having passed some years as a private tutor, he was, in 1728, chosen pastor at Oberode, and in 1736, one of the pastors of Frankfort and Sachsenhausen. He died Feb. 7, 1747. His biographer, Dr. C. H. Martin, says of him, "Zeitmann preferred to speak in Latin, and as oft as we quoted a passage of Scripture, whether of the Old or New Test., he repeated the same in the original, with chapter and verse. He never entered the pulpit without having studied his subject with prayer and meditation. His delivery was distinct, his voice powerful; he could be heard in the largest church in Frankfort." (B. P.)

Zell, Matthew, the earliest Reformed preacher of Strasburg, was born in 1477 at Kaisersberg, in Upper Alsace, and graduated in theology at Freiburg. In 1518 he became pastor to the cathedral of Strasburg, having already been strongly influenced by Luther's *Theses*, and in 1521 he took decided ground as an evangelical preacher, while engaged in the exposition of the epistle to the Romans. Some persons traduced him for his course, but others became his supporters, and even the magistracy of the city pledged themselves in his defence against the chapter. In 1523 his bishop formulated a series of charges against him, to which Zell replied with a refutation, which was at the same time a Scriptural authentication of the evangelical doctrines. In the same year two clergymen publicly renounced their allegiance to the papacy and entered into wedlock, and Zell improved the occasion by publishing a sermon in defence of the marriage of priests. Soon afterwards he was himself married. On Dec. 1, 1523, the magistracy directed all preachers "to proclaim, freely and in public, to the people nothing but the Holy Gospel and the doctrines of God, and whatever may tend to the promotion of love for God and our neighbor." A few months later all the married priests were excommunicated by the bishop, but the measure proved ineffective. Zell replied with an *Appellation*, and the citizens continued in increasing numbers to turn away from Romanism. Zell was as liberal towards all who believed in Christ as he was firm in his own convictions. He gave hospitable entertainment to the fugitive Schwenkfeld, and refused to anathematize the Swiss because of their opinions respecting the sacraments. He attached no great importance to formulated creeds, and took no part in current disputes, nor yet in Bucer's attempt at union. In 1534 he published, in the name of the Strasburg clergy, a catechism (*Kurtze christliche Erbauung für die Kinder u. Angohnden*, etc.) for beginners; which seems suited rather to teachers than to children. He also wrote for the latter class an exposition of the Lord's Prayer. In 1542 he united with his colleagues in sending an opinion respecting images, etc., to the preachers of Frankfort, which decided them to be *adiaphora*, and which asserted the real presence of Christ in the sacrament, but in a heavenly and not bodily manner. Zell died in 1548. His widow, Catharine, was a skilful disputer, and maintained a correspondence with Schwenkfeld during many years, besides issuing a defence of her association with him. She also wrote a brave defence of her husband's memory, in 1557, against an attack made by Louis Rabus. She obtained the reputation of a pious benefactor of the afflicted, and especially of "poor scholars" and such as had fled for refuge to Strasburg on account of their religious convictions, not excluding even Anabaptists. See the biographies of Zell and his wife in Röhrich, *Mittheil. aus d. Gesch. d. Evang. Kirche d. Elsasses* (Strasburg, 1855), iii, 89 sq.; Herzog, *Real-Encyklop.* s. v.

Zella, Council of (*Concilium Zellense* or *Teleptense*), was held in 418, at Zella, or Tella, in the province of Byzacena, in Africa, Donatianus, bishop of Zella, presiding. Various regulations were made.

1. Enacts that no man shall be admitted to holy orders who has served in war after baptism.
2. Enacts that every bishop shall be consecrated by three bishops, with the consent of the metropolitan, and that of the bishops of the provinces, expressed in writing.
3. Declares that one bishop only cannot consecrate another, except in the Roman Church.
4. Exhorts bishops, priests, etc., to observe continence.
8. Directs that the Montanists and Novatianists shall be admitted into the Church by imposition of hands.

See Mansi, *Concil.* ii, 1577.

Zeller, Christian Heinrich, a Protestant pedagogue, was born at Hohen-Entringen, near Tübingen, March 29, 1799. He studied law at Tübingen, which he did not practice, but gave himself entirely to the cause of education. In 1820 he founded his famous institution for children and teachers at Beuggen-on-the-Rhine, where he died, May 18, 1860. He published, *Göttliche Antworten auf menschliche Fragen* (2d ed. Basle, 1852):—*Kurze Seelenlehre* (Stuttgart, 1846):—*Monatsblatt von Beuggen*, which contains a great many essays on various subjects. Zeller also distinguished himself as a hymn-writer; one of his hymns, *Gott bei mir an jedem Ort*, is found in an English translation in *Hymns from the Land of Luther*, p. 27 ("My God with me in every place"). See Zuchold, *Bibl. Theol.* s. v.; Herzog, *Real-Encyklop.* s. v.; Koch, *Geschichte des deutschen Kirchenliedes*, vii, 188 sq. (B. P.)

Zeller, Hermann, a Lutheran theologian of Germany, was born at Neckarweihingen, Aug 26, 1807, and died at Mühlhausen, April 10, 1885. He is best known as the editor of *Biblisches Wörterbuch für das christliche Volk* (3d ed. Leipsic, 1884). (B. P.)

Zeller, Johann, a Protestant theologian, was born at Zurich, June 29, 1807, and died July 6, 1839. He is the author of *Stimmen der deutschen Kirche über das Leben Jesu von Strauss* (Zurich, 1837). His *Predigten* were published after his death (1840). See Zuchold, *Bibl. Theol.* s. v. (B. P.)

Zemzem is the name of a well at Mecca accounted sacred by the Mohammedans. It is said to have been formed from the spring of water which God pointed out to Hagar and Ishmael when they were driven from the house of Abraham and compelled to flee into Arabia. The Mohammedan pilgrims drink of its waters and believe it to be effectual in healing diseases, and even in purifying the soul.

Zend-Avesta is the name commonly given to the sacred books of the Parsees (q. v.), which are ascribed to Zoroaster (q. v.). The word avesta (*avasthâ*) means *text*, or *original text;* zend, or zand, means *translation and paraphrase.* According to the latest researches, it would seem as if only a small portion of the entire collection now extant were formed by avesta, or text, the rest being made up of zend, or commentary, without text. The term *zend* has changed its meaning repeatedly. Originally it indicated an authoritative interpretation coming from the highest source, which was in time embodied in the text itself. Later it came to denote a translation into the *Pehlvi*, or native idiom of Persia, made by the Zoroastrian priests during the Sassanian period. There is also a special zend doctrine which differs considerably from that contained in the avesta. A still further explanation of the zend doctrine is the *pâzend*, a word which often occurs in connection with avesta and zend.

The doctrine of the "Magi," as the Zoroastrian priests were anciently called, as well as those of India and Babylonia, is first alluded to in Jeremiah, where the chief of the Magi is mentioned among Nebuchadnezzar's retinue. In the New Test. (Matt. ii, 1) the Magi came to worship Jesus at Bethlehem. The earliest account among Greek writers is furnished by Herodotus. There are also accounts by Ctesias, the Greek physician of Artaxerxes II, by Denion, Theopomus, and Hermippus. But only fragments from their writings remain, embedded chiefly in Plutarch and Diogenes Laertius. The writings of Pliny, Strabo, Pausanius, Dion Chrysostomus also contain more or less information on the subject. Among the Armenian writers of the 5th century of our æra we find Eznik and Elizæus, from whose records we may gather that the Zoroastrians at their time were split into two parties, the one called Mog, the other Zendik—the former inhabiting chiefly Media and Persia, and acknowledging in the main the avesta; the latter living principally in Bactria, and following the traditional explanations, or zend proper. The nations of modern Europe came into contact with the adherents of Zoroastrianism in the western parts of India, and in the 17th century some MSS. of their sacred books were brought to England. But no one was able to read them; and Hyde himself, the celebrated Oxford scholar, was unable to make any use of them when, in 1700, he wrote his learned work on the Persian religion. The key to this book was first obtained by Anquetil Duperron, a young Frenchman, who went to Bombay in 1754, and there prevailed on some of the dusturs, or learned priests, to introduce him into the mysteries of the holy language and rites, and to sell him some of their most valuable works written in it. In 1759 he commenced a translation of the whole Zend-Avesta. In 1761 he returned to Paris with one hundred and eighty MSS. in different Oriental languages, and in 1771 published in French the first European translation of the Zend-Avesta, to which was added a great deal of supplementary matter. This work produced a profound sensation throughout Europe. In England it was pronounced a forgery by almost all scholars. In France there was but one opinion, viz., that English scholars were trying to run down the work out of sheer spite and jealousy. In Germany, however, opinions were divided; for while some acceded to all the arguments arrayed against it, there arose another renowned German scholar, Kleuker, who, in token of his complete and unreserved trust in the genuineness, set about translating Anquetil's work into German, adding much supplementary matter. After the lapse of more than fifty years, Rash, a Danish scholar, undertook an investigation of the matter. In 1826 he wrote a pamphlet, in which he pointed out (as had been done before) the close affinity between the language of the Zend-Avesta and the Sanscrit, and proved it to be, not a corruption of Sanscrit, but a distinct language. He also proved that modern Persian is derived from Zend, as Italian from Latin, and this gave the key to many of the errors of Anquetil's version. The learned dustur himself, from whom Anquetil derived his information of the language, possessed no grammatical knowledge of it. Rash had pointed out the way, Eugene Burnouf followed it. He, indeed, may be called the father of Zend philology. For more than twenty years this eminent scholar devoted all his energies to elucidating, commenting on, and discussing this language, and the sacred writings couched in it, and in publishing texts and translations. In Germany, Olshausen, Bopp, Müller, Brockhaus, Spiegel, Haug, and in Copenhagen, Westergaard, have been busy ever since in editing and translating the Zend-Avesta or some portions of it.

The Zend-Avesta was originally of very great extent, consisting of vastly more than at present. Pliny says that Zoroaster composed two million verses, and Attavari, an Arabian author, says that his writings covered twelve thousand cow-skins. But from the conquest of Persia by Alexander the Great, in 330 B.C., to the accession of the Sassanidæ, in A.D. 235, the religion of Zoroaster and the wisdom of the Magi were thrown into the background by Greek ideas, and became nearly lost. When, however, the Sassanidæ assumed the rule their principal endeavors were directed to the revival of the ancient faith, and their unceasing efforts after the ancient fragments of the Zoroastrian doctrine have resulted in the small collection which we now possess. The whole Scripture is said to have consisted of twenty-one *nosks*, or parts, each containing avesta and zend, that is, text and commentary. The number, twenty-one, was to correspond to the twenty-one words of which the most sacred prayer of the Zoroastrians (the *Honovar*) was composed. By the unanimous consent of both classical and Persian writers the whole bulk of the sacred literature is ascribed to Zoroaster himself. They are supposed to be the substance, or, as was subsequently held, the very words of divine revelations to the prophet in the form of conversations.

The name Zend-Avesta belongs more particularly to the three collections which are severally called *Vendidad*, *Vispered*, and *Yasna*, while the remaining writings are comprised under the name of *Khorda-Avesta*, or small Avesta. The latter contains short prayers, and especially the *Yashts*, or *Yeshts*, hymns addressed to the different genii, on the days which bear their names and are sacred to them, or on the days of those genii who are considered to be the attendants of the former.

The *Vendidad* consists of twenty-two *fargards*, or sections, which treat of cosmogony, and may be called the religious and civil code of the old Parsees. The first fargard relates how *Ahura-Mazda* (now called Ormuzd), the good spirit, created the several countries and places (of which sixteen are named), excellent and perfect in their kind, but that *Angro-Manyus* (now called Ahriman), the evil or black spirit, created in opposition all the evils which infest these worlds. In the second fargard Zoroaster bids Yima announce to mankind the sacred law which he had taught him, but Yima refuses compliance with this behest. He then bids him enlarge the worlds and make them prosperous. This he obeys, and carries out the orders given him by Ahura-Mazda. The third fargard enumerates the five things which are the most agreeable, then the five things which are the most disagreeable, and afterwards the five things which convey the greatest satisfaction in this world. The fourth fargard may be termed the criminal code of the Avesta. It enumerates, in the first instance, various offences, which are considered to be so grave as to affect, not only the person who commits them, but also his relatives, and then proceeds to define the punishments incurred by the offender. The eight following fargards contain injunctions in reference to impurities caused by dead bodies. The thirteenth fargard begins with the description of two kinds of dogs, the one created by Ahura-Mazda, the other by Angro-Manyus—the killing of the former being a criminal, that of the latter a meritorious, act; and the remaining part of the book is devoted to the proper treatment of dogs in general, while the same subject is continued in the fourteenth fargard, which enumerates also the penalties for injuring dogs. The treatment of young dogs is likewise the subject-matter of the latter part of the fifteenth fargard, which, in its first sections, treats of sexual offences, and the bringing-up of illegitimate children. The great care and attention given to dogs seems to have arisen from the fact that the country was infested with wolves. The sixteenth fargard teaches how to treat women when affected with impurities. The seventeenth fargard treats of impurities caused by the cutting of hair and the trimming of nails. The next fargard is more of a mixed character; it treats of various ceremonies, and gives injunctions on cleanliness, decency, and moral conduct. The nineteenth fargard relates how Angro-Manyus endeavored to kill Zoroaster, but how the latter successfully defended himself with weapons given him by Ahura-Mazda. Then the evil spirit, being aware that it had no material power over Zoroaster, next resorted to temptations; but those, too, were defeated by the prophet, who now resolved to conquer the evil spirit, and for this purpose addressed to Ahura-Mazda various questions on the rites of purification and the condition of souls after death. The twentieth fargard gives some information about the first man who understood curing disease. The twenty-first fargard is devoted to the phenomena of the sky and the luminous bodies, and comprises invocations of the clouds, the sun, the moon, and the stars. The last fargard relates that Angro-Manyus, having engendered diseases, Ahura-Mazda is compelled to devise remedies against them. The book concludes with an account of the creation of various animals and other objects to this end. The form of all these fargards is nearly always that of a dialogue between Ahura-Mazda and Zoroaster, and the same form is occasionally observed in the two other portions of the Avesta, which differ materially from those of the Vendidad.

The *Vispered* contains a collection of prayers, composed of twenty-three chapters, resembling the younger *Yasna*, next to be noticed, and referring to the same ceremonies. The Vispered and the Yasna bear prominently a liturgical character. All that can really be held to emanate from Zoroaster himself are the five *Gathas*, which form part of the Yasna. This Yasna consists principally of prayers to be recited at the sacrificial rites, such as the consecration of Zoöthra, or holy water; of the Baresona, or bundle of twigs of a particular tree; the preparation of the sacred juice of the *homa* (Indian, *soma*, q. v.), taken to be an emblem of immortality; the offering of certain cakes, etc. The whole of the Yasna now comprises seventy-two chapters. It consists apparently of two parts belonging to different periods. The older is written in what has been called the Gatha dialect, and was considered sacred even at the time when the other books of the Zend-Avesta were composed. This "older Yasna" was divided into the Gathas and some minor pieces. The former, five in number, are small collections of sacred prayers, songs, and hymns, arranged in metre, and exhibiting philosophical and abstract thoughts about metaphysical subjects. The name itself signifies *song*. Their metre resembles chiefly that of the Vedic hymns. They are without rhymes, and only the syllables are counted. The first bears the heading (which is implied as to the other four), "The Revealed Thought, the Revealed Word, the Revealed Deed of Zarathustra the Holy; the Archangels first sang the Gathas." They are all more or less devoted to exhortations on the part of the prophet to forsake polytheism, and to bow only before Ahura-Mazda. The difference between monotheism and idolatry is pointed out in the respective sources whence they flow, "existence" and "non-existence." The mission, activity, and teaching of Zoroaster are dwelt upon more or less in all the Gathas, but chiefly in the second. To the other portion belongs the "Yasna of Seven Chapters," which seems to have been composed by early disciples, and which consists of prayers, in prose, addressed to Ahura-Mazda, the angels, the fire, the earth, the waters, and other spiritual beings, genii presiding over the different parts of the good creation. There is also a chapter containing a formula by which the ancient Iranians were received into the new religious community. The so-called younger Yasna, written in the common Zend language, is of more varied contents, such as an invitation to Ahura-Mazda and all the good spirits to be present at the sacrifice, pieces referring to the preparation and drinking of the homa juice, the praises of the genius Serosh, and a commentary on the most sacred prayers.

The *Yashts* are in twenty-four divisions. Yasht (*yesti*) means worship by prayers and sacrifices, and in the Avesta indicates certain laudations of sacred persons and objects, called yazatas (*izad*), or angels; and in so far different in nature from the invocations in the Yasna and Vispered that, while in the latter the divine beings are invited promiscuously, the single yashts are addressed to individual minima. In these songs are also found the primary sources of the legends contained in the Shah-nameh.

There yet remain some smaller pieces. *Khorda-Avesta*, which are now used by the Parsees as common prayers, such as the five *Nijayish*, addressed to the sun, the moon, the water, and the fire; the *Afrigans*, or blessings to be recited over a certain meal prepared for an angel or a deceased person; the five *Gabs*, or prayers to the angels set over the five different times of the day and night; and finally the *Sirozah*, or thirty days, being a calendar, or rather an enumeration, of the thirty divine beings that preside over each of the days. It is chiefly recited on the thirtieth day after the death of a man.

The religious belief taught in the Avesta rests on the dualism of the two great principles—*Ahura-Mazda*, or the good, and *Angro-Manyus*, or the evil principle. The genii subordinate to the former are the *Amesha-spentas*, six of whom are named in the Yasna, viz., Vohumano, who protects living beings; Asha-vahishta, or the genius of fire; Kshathra-vairya, or the genius of metals; Spenta-armaiti, or the genius of earth; Hauroat, or the genius of water; and Ameretat, or the genius of the trees. They are severally opposed by the *Devas*, or dæmons, subordinate to Angro-Manyus, viz., by Akomano, Andar, Saurva, Naonghaithi, Tauru, and Zairicha. Other dæmons are named in the Vendidad. The worshippers of fire belong to Ahura-Mazda, whereas the worshippers of the Devas are possessed by Angro-Manyus. See Zoroaster.

The worship taught by Zoroaster seems to have been of the simplest kind, the adoration of fire by means of hymns and offerings, chiefly, if not exclusively, taken from the vegetable kingdom, an essential concomitant of the sacrifice being the juice of the homa (or soma), which occupies an important part also in the Vedic rites. This worship, however, must not be confounded with the complicated ritual of later periods of the Parsee creed, which assumed a similar development to that based by the Hindûs on the Rigveda text, and is indicated by several portions of the Avesta, which cannot be looked upon as its earliest part. At the present day every Parsee child is taught to repeat long passages in the original Zend; but hardly a single word of that language is intelligible even to the Parsee priests or dusturs.

Literature.—In the Zend language this consists chiefly of its translated text, the accompanying glosses, and a few independent works in the same language, the Huzvaresh, or literary Pehlevi, as the *Bundehesh* and the *Din-karb*, of much later date. It is an important aid to the understanding of the Avesta; yet its interpretation is not to be implicitly trusted. That part of the Zoroastrian literature which is composed in the so-called Parsee dialect is of still more modern date and limited extent. Glosses or interpretations of the Avestan texts, called *Pa-Zend*, versions of certain portions of them and of Pehlevi texts, sundry invocations and ascriptions of praise, and expositions of Parsee doctrine, constitute nearly its whole substance. Several passages of these texts were published in Spiegel's *Parsee Grammar* (Leipsic, 1851). After the settlement of the Parsees in India, a Sanscrit version of the Yasna and some other parts of the Avestan text was made by Nerioseugh. It has been published in a Latin transliteration by Spiegel (Leipsic, 1861). See Spiegel, *Avesta; die heiligen Schriften der Parsen, aus dem Grundtext übersetzt* (Leipsic, 1852–63, 3 vols.; Eng. ed. of the same by Bleek, Lond. 1864); Haug, *Essays* (1st ed. Bombay, 1862); Havelacque, *Grammaire de la Langue Zende* (Paris, 1878); Harlesz, *Avesta, Livre Sacré des Sectateurs de Zoroastre* (Liege, 1875–78, 3 vols.); Burnouf, *Vendidad-Sadé;* Olshausen, *Vendidad Zend-Avestæ;* Rask, *Alter und Æchtheit der Zendsprache;* Spiegel, *Eranische Alterthumskunde* (Leipsic, 1872, 1873, 2 vols.); Müller, *Chips from a German Workshop*, vol. i, lectures v–viii. For the language of the Zend-Avesta, see Pietraszenski, *Abrégé de la Grammaire Zend* (Berlin, 1861, 8vo); Haug, *Outlines of Zend Grammar* (Bombay, 1862, 8vo).

Zend Language. See ZEND-AVESTA.

Zenkel, GEORG PETER, a Protestant theologian of Germany, was born March 20, 1717, at Schwarzenbach, in Bayreuth. He studied theology, Oriental languages, and natural sciences at Jena. In 1740 he was permitted to lecture, and in 1746 was made adjunct to the philosophical faculty. In 1754 he was called as professor of philosophy to Erlangen, and opened his lectures with an address, *De Methodo Docendi apud Veteres Hebræos.* In 1755 he resigned his position, and died Dec. 14, 1760. He wrote, *Commentarii Grammatici Ebrææ Linguæ* (Jena, 1748, 1749):—*Commentarius Evangelico-Homileticus* (ibid. 1747 a. o.):—*Beiträge zur Vertheidigung der Mosaischen Religion*, etc. (Gotha, 1752–56, 2 vols.):—*Diss. Philologica de Sepultura Christi, ad Locum Esaiæ liii, 9* (Jena, 1754). See Döring, *Die gelehrten Theologen Deutschlands*, iv, 782 sq.; Fürst, *Bibl. Jud.* iii, 550; Steinschneider, *Bibl. Handbuch*, p. 152. (B. P.)

Zeno, a reputed bishop OF VERONA, and alleged author of ninety-three sermons, which were published in 1508 by Jacob de Lenco and Albert Castellan under the title, *S. Zenoni Episc. Veronens. Sermones*, after a very ancient manuscript found fifty years before in the episcopal library of Verona by Guarinus. These sermons were previously wholly unknown, and Zeno himself lived only in a few miracle-legends. He was represented with a fish attached to his angle or episcopal staff, because he had, while angling, delivered a drowning man from the clutches of the devil. Eleven of the sermons are certainly not by the author of the general mass. The age of the collection is variously estimated; Vogel, in Herzog (following Dorner), dating them back perhaps to the beginning of the latter half of the 3d century, Baronius to A.D. 200, others to A.D. 450–500. It would seem that they emanated from the mind of a bishop who was endowed with earnestness and dignity of character as well as theological learning, and who presided over an established Church and a regularly organized clergy. See Fessler, *Institut. Patrolog.* (Oenipont, 1851), i, 73 sq.; Wetzer u. Welte, *Kirchen-Lexikon*, s.v.; Jazdzewski, *Zeno, Veronensis Episc.* (Ratisbon, 1862); Dorner, *Entwicklungsgesch d. Lehre von d. Person Christi*, 2d ed. i, 754 sq.; Herzog, *Real-Encyklop.* s. v.

Zenobia. See TADMOR.

Zenonism. See STOIC PHILOSOPHY; STOICS.

Zentgrav, JOHANN JACOB, a Lutheran theologian of Germany, was born at Strasburg, May 21, 1643. He studied at Leipsic and Wittenberg, was in 1676 professor in his native city, in 1678 doctor of theology, and died Nov. 28, 1707. Zentgrav was a voluminous writer. A complete list of his writings, embracing all departments of theology, is given by Jöcher, *Allgemeines Gelehrten-Lexikon*, s. v. (B. P.)

Zephȳrus, in Greek mythology, the representative of the west wind, was a son of Astræus and Eos. He was represented in Athens on the tower of winds, light-

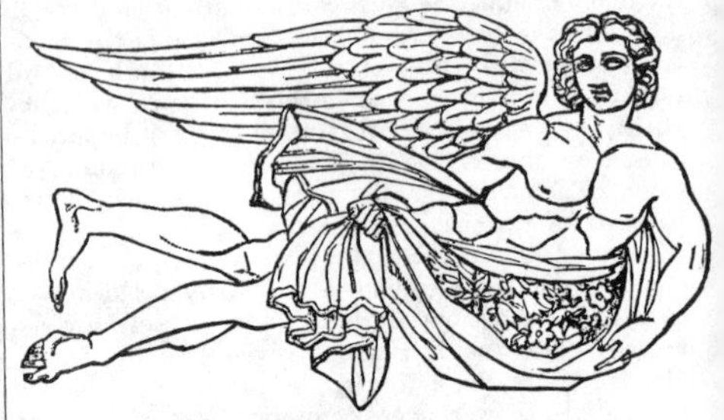

Antique Figure of Zephyrus.

ly draped with a mantle, because he was the warmest wind. In the lap of his mantle he carried a quantity of flowers.

Zer (Heb. *Tsêr*, צֵר, *rock;* Sept. by misapprehension, Τύρος, Vulg. *Ser*), one of the fortified towns of Naphtali (Josh. xix, 35), where it is named between Ziddim and Hamnath; but from the absence of the copulative ("and") between this and the preceding name, as well as from the total ("nineteen cities") in ver. 33, it is evidently a part of the preceding name, Ziddim-zer. See ZIDDIM. Schwarz remarks (*Palest.* p. 182) that Zer is mentioned in the Jerusalem Talmud (*Megillah*, i) as lying near Ziddim.

Zera Abraham (זֶרַע אַבְרָהָם) is the title of a grammatico-historical commentary on the Pentateuch, written by Abraham Seeb, of Brzesc, in the 17th century, and published at Sulzbach in 1685. See De' Rossi, *Dizionario Storico* (Germ. transl.), p. 65; Fürst, *Bibl. Jud.* i, 11. (B. P.)

Zerdust. See ZOROASTER.

Zereda. The present *Surdah* lies twenty-one and a half miles north-west of Beitîn (Bethel), and is "a small village on a hillside, with a garden to the south of it, and the spring Ain Jelazûn on the east" (*Memoirs* to the Ordnance Survey, ii, 295).

Zerremer, HEINRICH GOTTLIEB, a Protestant theologian of Germany, was born at Wernigerode, March 8, 1750. He studied at Halle, and, after completing his studies, accepted a position as teacher of Latin and mathematics at Klosterbergen. In 1775 he was called as pastor to Bayendorf. In 1787 he was appointed first preacher at Derenburg, in the duchy of Halberstadt. In 1810 he was appointed general superintendent at Halberstadt, where he died, Nov. 10, 1811. He was a popular writer, and his publications were greatly esteemed in his day, though of little value for the present. They are given by Döring, in his *Die gelehrten Theologen Deutschlands*, iv, 787; see also Winer, *Handbuch der theol. Lit.* i, 192, 196, 226, 233, 248, 394. (B. P.)

Zestermann, AUGUST CHRISTIAN ADOLF, who died at Leipsic, March 16, 1869, doctor and professor, is the author of, *De Basilicis Libri Tres* (Leipsic, 1847):—*Die antiken und christlichen Basiliken nach ihrer Entstehung, Ausbildung und Beziehung zueinander dargestellt* (1847). See Zuchold, *Bibl. Theol.* s. v. (B. P.)

Zickler, FRIEDRICH SAMUEL, a Protestant theologian of Germany, was born Nov. 14, 1721, at Schwabsdorf, in Weimar. He studied at Jena, where he was made magister in 1744, on presenting a dissertation, *Ad Vaticinium Jacobæum Genes. xlix*, 12. In 1758 he was made professor of philosophy, and at the jubilee of the Jena University was made doctor of theology, presenting a dissertation, *De Glorioso Servatoris in Cœlum Adscensu.* In 1760 he went to Erlangen as third professor of theology and university-preacher. He opened his lectures with a dissertation on *De ὀρθοδοξία et ὀρθοτομία Necessariis in Doctore Ecclesiæ Requisitis.* He returned again to Jena in 1768, advanced rapidly, and died April 25, 1779, having four years before been chosen first professor of theology. He wrote, *Diss. I et II Historico-Exegeticæ, Religionem Bestiarum ab Ægyptiis Consecratarum Exponentes*, etc. (Jena, 1745–46):—*Diss. Exegetica Statum Ecclesiæ Novi Fœderis Primævæ a Jeremiæ iii*, 14 *sq., Prædictum Exponens* (ibid. 1747):—*Chaldaismus Danielis Prophetæ*, etc. (ibid. 1749, etc.). See Döring, *Die gelehrten Theologen Deutschlands*, iv, 789 sq.; Fürst, *Bibl. Jud.* iii, 550. (B. P.)

Ziddim. The modern *Hattîn* lies seven and a quarter miles north-west of Tiberias, and four and three quarters south-west of Mejdel (Magdala); it contains several rock-cut tombs to the west, and the wady of Neby Shuaib (Jethro) on the south (*Memoirs* to the Ordnance Survey, i, 384).

Ziegenbalg, BARTHOLOMÄUS, a well-known Protestant missionary of Germany, was born June 14, 1683, at Pulsnitz, in Lusatia. He studied at Halle, where A. H. Francke enlisted him for missionary service. On Nov. 29, 1705, he left for Tranquebar with his friend Plütschow. For a time his work was opposed by the Danish officers, but finally he succeeded. Having mastered the language, he translated Luther's smaller catechism, the New Test., and commenced the translation of the Old Test. into the Malabar language. He also founded schools and built chapels there. In 1714 he returned to Europe, to return again to Tranquebar in 1716, where he died, Feb. 23, 1719. He published, *Grammatica Damulica* (Halle, 1716):—together with J. E. Gründler, he published *Theologia Thetica in qua Omnia Dogmata ad Salutem Cognoscendam Necessaria Perspicua Methodo Tractantur*, etc. (2d ed. Halle, 1856). See German, *Ziegenbalg und Plütschow* (Erlangen, 1868, 2 vols.); *Theologisches Universallexikon*, s. v.; Zuchold, *Bibl. Theol.* ii, 1491. (B. P.)

Ziegenbein, JOHANN WILHELM HEINRICH, a Protestant theologian of Germany, was born in 1766 at Braunschweig. In 1798 he was appointed pastor of St. Peter's, in his native place, and advanced in 1803 as general superintendent of the duchy of Blankenburg. In 1819 he was appointed abbot of Michaelstein, and died Jan. 12, 1824. Ziegenbein's writings are mostly of a pedagogical nature. He translated from the French Senebrier's lives of Calvin and Beza (Hamburg, 1789); from the English Priestley's *Comparison of the Institutions of Moses with those of the Hindûs and other Ancient Nations; The Life of Gibbon*, etc. See Döring, *Die gelehrten Theologen Deutschlands*, iv, 793 sq.; Winer, *Handbuch der theol. Lit.* i, 142; ii, 73, 95, 228, 237, 239, 245, 248, 260, 339, 354; Fürst, *Bibl. Jud.* iii, 550. (B. P.)

Ziegler, Daniel, D.D., a German Reformed minister, was born at Reading, Pa., July 11, 1804. His parents removing to New Berlin, Union Co., in his infancy, his youth was spent there. He was a saddler by trade, and went to Philadelphia to work; but his mind being turned towards the ministry, he entered the University of Pennsylvania, located at Philadelphia; studied theology in the seminary of the Reformed Church at Carlisle; was licensed in 1830, and became pastor of some congregations in York County; was called to the Kreutzcreek charge, where he spent the whole of his life, with the exception of the last few years, which were devoted to the First Reformed Church in York. He died May 23, 1876. He preached almost exclusively in German, which he spoke with great fluency, accuracy, and elegance. His preaching was calm, clear, and impressive. He was a man of culture, pleasant, open-hearted, kind, and sympathizing. See Harbaugh, *Fathers of the Germ. Ref. Church*, v, 199.

Ziegler, Werner Carl Ludwig, a Protestant theologian of Germany, was born May 15, 1763, at Scharnebeck, in Lüneburg. He studied at Göttingen, some time lectured in the Göttingen University, and was called, in 1792, as professor of theology at Rostock. He died April 24, 1809, leaving, *De Mimis Romanorum Commentatio* (Göttingen, 1788):—*Vollständige Einleitung in den Brief an die Hebräer* (ibid. 1791):—*Progr. Adit. Historia Dogmatis de Redemptione*, etc. (ibid. eod.):—*Beiträge zur Geschichte des Glaubens an das Daseyn Gottes in der Theologie* (ibid. 1792). See Döring, *Die gelehrten Theologen Deutschlands*, iv, 798 sq.; Winer, *Handbuch der theol. Lit.* i, 32, 90, 211, 572, 596, 599, 610; Fürst, *Bibl. Jud.* iii, 551. (B. P.)

Zierold, JOHANN WILHELM, a Lutheran theologian of Germany, was born May 14, 1669, at Neustadt-ober-Wiesenthal, in Meissen. He studied at Leipsic, travelled extensively through Austria, Holland, and England, was appointed, in 1696, pastor and professor of theology at the Gröningen College in Stargard, received the doctorate of theology in 1698, and died Sept. 1, 1731. He wrote, *Analogismus Nominum et Rerum ex Psa. i* (Stargard, 1701):—באר היטב *oder deutliche Erläuterungen der heiligen Schrift* (Leipsic, 1715):—*Der Prediger Salomo aus der Bedeutung der Buchstaben* (ibid. eod.):—*Der Prophet Obadja*, etc. (ibid. eod.):—*Der Prophet Jöel*, etc. (ibid. 1720). See Hildebrand, *Hirten nach dem Herzen Gottes zu Stargard;* Jöcher, *Allgemeines Gelehrten-Lexikon*, s. v.; Fürst, *Bibl. Jud.* iii, 551. (B. P.)

Zigabenus, EUTHYMIUS. See EUTHYMIUS ZIGABENUS.

Ziller, TUISKON, a German philosopher, was born Dec. 22, 1817, and died April 20, 1882, at Leipsic, doctor and professor of philosophy. He was a pupil of Herbart, whose system he followed. Ziller published, *Die Regierung der Kinder* (1859):—*Grundlegung zur Lehre vom erziehenden Unterricht* (1861):—*Vorlesungen über allgemeine Pädagogik* (1876):—*Allgemeine philosophische Ethik* (1880). In 1860 he started with Allihn the *Zeitschrift für exakte Philosophie im Sinne des neueren philosophischen Realismus.* He also organized the society of scientific pedagogics, whose organ, the *Jahrbücher*, he edited for fourteen years. (B. P.)

Zillerthal, a valley of Tyrol, stretching for about five miles along the Ziller, between Salzburg and Innsbrück, and inhabited by about 15,000 souls, has become memorable in Church history on account of the infamous manner in which the Roman Catholic clergy succeeded in suppressing an evangelical rising which took place in our century. As in other countries of Germany, the Reformation found its way into Salzburg and Tyrol, but it was suppressed, in the latter part of the 16th century, in Salzburg, by the archbishops, and in Tyrol by the government, in connection with the nobility and the ecclesiastics. In 1730 archbishop Frinian inaugurated a cruel persecution, with a view of exterminating all adherents to the evangelical faith. Nevertheless it reappeared in the Zillerthal in the beginning of the present century. As soon as the Roman clergy became aware of the danger, the number of priests was doubled in the villages and the strictest watch was kept. When, in 1832, the emperor Francis of Austria visited the valley, the evangelical Zillerthalers petitioned him in behalf of their religion. The emperor promised to do what he could. When the Roman clergy became aware of this, they resorted to violent measures. The toleration edict of Joseph II, and the stipulations of the congress of Vienna, were thrown aside, and, instigated by the fanatical clergy, the provincial estates of Tyrol decreed that no split in the Church of the country should be allowed, that those who would not conform to the Church of Rome should leave the country and settle under an evangelical prince. But before this could be effected the Evangelicals had to suffer many things. Being under the ban of the Church, their neighbors were warned against holding any kind of intercourse with them. The children of the Evangelicals were forced to frequent the Roman Catholic schools, where they were placed on separate seats, as "children of the devil," apart from the "Christian children." When, after eleven years of perpetual chicanery, the Evangelicals were advised from Vienna that they could emigrate, they addressed themselves to Friedrich Wilhelm III of Prussia, in 1837, and by his humane intercession they were allowed to sell their estates and remove to his dominions, where they were settled, four hundred and forty-eight souls, in Hohen-Mittel, and Nieder-Zillerthal, in Silesia. See Rheinwald, *Die Evangelischegesinnten im Zillerthal* (Berlin, 1837); *Evangelische Kirchenzeitung* (1835), p. 813-815, 820-823; (1836), p. 132; (1837), p. 343; Herzog, *Real-Encyklop.* s. v. (B. P.)

Zimmer, PATRIZ BENEDICT, a Roman Catholic theologian of Germany, was born Feb. 22, 1752. He studied theology and philosophy, received holy orders in 1775, was made professor of dogmatics at Ingolstadt in 1789, and died at Steinheim, Oct. 16, 1820. He wrote, *Theologiæ Christianæ Theoreticæ Systema* (Detlingen, 1787):—*Veritas Christianæ Religionis* (Augsburg, 1789-90):—*Theologia Christiana Specialis et Theoretica* (Landshut, 1802-1806):—*Philosophische Religionslehre* (ibid. 1805):—*Untersuchung über den allgemeinen Verfall des menschl. Geschlechts* (ibid. 1809):—*Untersuchung über den Begriff und die Gesetze der Geschichte* (Munich, 1818). See his biography in Widmer's edition of Sailer's works, xxxviii, 117 sq., and appendix to his biography (Uri, 1823); Denzinger, *Religiöse Erkenntniss*, i, 209 sq., 540 sq.; Werner, *Gesch. der kathol. Theologie*, p. 254 sq., 310 sq.; *Theol. Universallexikon*, s. v. (B. P.)

Zimmermann, Ernst, a brother of Karl, was born Sept. 18, 1786. Like his brother, he studied theology and philology at Giessen. In 1805 he was called as assistant preacher and teacher to Auerbach (where he published an edition of Euripides [Frankfort, 1808 sq.], and Suetonius's *History of the Roman Emperors* [Darmstadt, 1810]). In 1809 he was appointed deacon at Grossgerau, in 1814 advanced as court-deacon, and in 1816 made court-preacher, at the same time acting as tutor of prince Ludwig of Anhalt-Köthen. He died June 24, 1832, having been appointed prelate. He was an excellent preacher, and his homiletical works are still of great value. Besides sermons, he published, *Homiletisches Handbuch für denkende Prediger* (Frankfort, 1812-22, 4 vols.):—*Monatsschrift für Predigerwissenschaften* (Darmstadt, 1821-24, 6 vols.):—*Jahrbuch der theol. Literatur* (Essen, 1832-36, 4 vols.):—*Geist aus Luther's Schriften* (Darmstadt, 1828-31, 4 vols.). In 1822 he commenced the *Allgemeine Kirchenzeitung*, which is still published. See Karl Zimmermann, *Ernst Zimmermann nach seinem Leben, Wirken u. Character geschildert* (Darmstadt, 1833); Zuchold, *Bibl. Theol.* ii, 1497 sq.; *Theol. Universallexikon*, s. v. (B. P.)

Zimmermann, Johann Christian, a Lutheran theologian of Germany, was born at Langenwiesen, near Ilmenau, Aug. 12, 1702. He studied at Leipsic, and was appointed court-chaplain at Hanover in 1738. In 1743 he was called as provost and superintendent to Ueltzen, in Hanover, where he died, May 28, 1783. He is the author of several hymns, which are found in *Vermehrtes Hanoverisches Kirchen-Gesangbuch* (edited by Zimmermann, Hanover, 1740). See Koch, *Gesch. d. deutschen Kirchenliedes*, v, 566 sq. (B. P.)

Zimmermann, Johann Jakob (1), an eloquent German preacher, was born in the duchy of Würtemberg in 1644. He was generally regarded as a disciple of Boehman and Brouquelle, whose doctrines he rendered highly popular, making many converts in Germany and the united provinces of the Netherlands. He was for some years professor of mathematics at Heidelberg. He was about to depart for America to escape the persecution to which his preaching had subjected him, when he died at Rotterdam, in 1693. The most noted of his works is entitled a *Revelation of Antichrist*.

Zimmermann, Johann Jakob (2), a Swiss theologian, was born in 1685, became professor at Zurich in 1737, and died in 1756. He introduced more liberal views in his teaching than had been current hitherto, and was often suspected of heresy. See Hagenbach, *Hist. of the Church in the 18th and 19th Centuries*, i, 113; Fritzsche, *Dissertation* (Zurich, 1841); Schweitzer, *Centraldogmen*, ii, 791 sq.

Zimmermann, Karl, a Protestant theologian of Germany, was born at Darmstadt, Aug. 23, 1803. He studied theology and philology at Giessen, and, after having labored for some years in the department of education, was appointed deacon to the court-church at Darmstadt in 1832. From that time he remained in the ministry, advancing rapidly, and was appointed in 1842 first preacher to the court. In 1847 he was made prelate and member of consistory, and filled this high position till 1872, when he retired. He died June 12, 1877. To him the Gustavus Adolphus Society (q. v.) is much indebted for the great interest and activity he showed in its behalf. His publications, mostly sermons, are all specified by Zuchold, *Bibl. Theol.* ii, 1495-97. See also *Theol. Universallexikon*, s. v. (B. P.)

Zimmermann, Mathias, a German theologian, was born at Ypres, Sept. 21, 1625. He began his studies in his native village, and afterwards went to the College of Thun (1639), and thence (1644) to the University of Strasburg, where he studied philosophy. Having decided upon a religious career, he studied at Leipsic, and in 1651 returned home. He was soon nominated rector of the College of Leutsch, in Upper Hungary, but the next year (1652) returned home again. Soon afterwards the elector of Saxony appointed him a colleague of the superintendent of Colditz, and the minister and superintendent of Meissen. He had prepared himself for those positions by a license in theology (Nov. 1661), and in 1666 was made doctor in the university at Leipsic, but died suddenly, Nov. 29, 1689, leaving many religious works, which are enumerated in the *Biog. Universelle*, s. v.

Zimmermann, Wilhelm, historian and controversialist of Neustadt, in the duchy of Würtemberg, was preacher at Wimpfew in 1569, member of consistory and court-preacher at Heidelberg in 1578, and finally (in 1586) inspector of churches and schools at Grotz. He left a *Historia Germanicæ*, and some *Litteræ*, which are inserted by Fecht in his collection of *Epistolæ Theologicæ*.

Zingerle, PIUS, a Roman Catholic Orientalist, was born at Meran, March 17, 1801, and died Jan. 10, 1881, at Mariaberg, Tyrol. He published, *Echte Akten heiliger*

Märtyrer des Morgenlandes, aus dem Syrischen übersetzt (Innsbruck, 1836, 2 vols.):—*Clemens Romanus' zwei Briefe an die Jungfrauen, aus dem Syrischen mit Anmerkungen* (Vienna, 1827):—*Ephraem Syrus' auserwählte Schriften* (Innsbruck, 1830–34, 5 vols.); besides, he contributed largely to the *Zeitschrift* of the German Oriental Society. (B. P.)

Zinzendorf, NICHOLAS LEWIS *Count von*, is entitled to a fuller notice than space allowed in vol. x. The founder of the modern Moravian Church was born at Dresden, May 26, 1700, and died at Herrnhut, Saxony, May 9, 1760. He was descended from an ancient Austrian family. For the sake of the Protestant faith his grandfather relinquished broad domains in Austria, and settled in Franconia. When he was but six weeks old, his father, one of the cabinet ministers of the elector of Saxony, died; while several years later his mother married the field-marshal Von Natzmar, of the Prussian army, and removed to Berlin. Young Zinzendorf did not accompany her, but remained with his grandmother, the baroness Catharine von Gersdorf, one of the most distinguished women of her day, who had organized a Spenerian *ecclesiola* in her castle of Gross Hennersdorf. That he was intrusted to her care proved to be an important event in his life. Amid the influences of that *ecclesiola* he spent his childhood, daily breathing the atmosphere of a transparent piety. His grandmother and aunt Henrietta shaped his religious development. When he was not yet four years old he grasped, with a clear perception and a flood of feeling, Christ's relation to man as a Saviour and divine brother. This consciousness produced a love for Jesus which was the holy and perpetual fire on the altar of his heart; so that in mature years he could truthfully exclaim: "I have but one passion; and it is He—He only!" In 1710 he was sent to the Royal Pædagogium at Halle, at the head of which stood the celebrated Francke; in 1716 he entered the University of Wittenberg; and in 1719, in accordance with the custom of young nobles of that day, began his travels. During all these years he confessed Christ with youthful enthusiasm, and labored for his cause with manly courage. At Halle he organized a fraternity among the students, known as "The Order of the Grain of Mustard Seed;" at Wittenberg he exercised no little influence; in Paris, where he spent an entire winter, neither the blandishments of the royal court nor the flatteries of the highest nobles could seduce him from the path of godliness. His commentary on the French capital, with its hollow gayeties and carnal frivolities, was: "*O Splendida Miseria!*" while the impression which an exquisite *Ecce Homo*—with the inscription, "*Hoc feci pro te, quid facis pro me?*"—in the picture-gallery of Düsseldorf made upon his heart followed him through life. When Zinzendorf returned from his journey, it was his earnest wish to devote himself, in spite of his rank, to the ministry of the gospel. But neither his mother nor grandmother would listen to such a proposition, and insisted upon his adopting, like his father, the career of a statesman. With a heavy heart he yielded, and in 1721 accepted a position as Aulic and Justicial Councillor at Dresden. His purpose to promote the cause of Christ remained, however, unshaken, and soon after attaining his majority he purchased the domain of Berthelsdorf, in Upper Lusatia, with the intention of making that the centre of his Christian activity. In what such activity was to consist he did not as yet know. He was supported in his purpose by his young wife, the countess Erdmuth Dorothy von Reuss, whom he married in 1722, and through whom he became connected with several of the royal houses of Europe. Of the manner in which he was led to grant an asylum on his newly-purchased estate to the remnant of the Moravian Brethren, of the renewal of their Church through his agency, and of the peculiar character which he gave to it, a full account may be found in the article on the MORAVIAN BRETHREN, 2, vi, 585, etc. In all that he undertook in this respect his aim was, not to interfere with the established Church, but rather to make the Moravians a Church within that Church. His course was misunderstood and excited bitter opposition. In 1736 he was banished from Saxony, and, two years later, as he refused to sign a bond acknowledging himself guilty of "offences," banished "forever." The same result which generally grows out of religious persecutions appeared in this case also. His enemies overreached themselves. Instead of putting a stop to his Christian activity, it grew in importance and extended far and wide. A "Church of Pilgrims," as it was called, gathered around Zinzendorf, composed of the members of his family and his chief ministerial coadjutors, and itinerated to various parts of Germany, Switzerland, Holland, and England, everywhere making known the renewal of the *Unitas Fratrum*, and attracting large numbers to its communion. Zinzendorf, with the aid of his fellow-laborers, directed the entire work of the Moravians in Christian and heathen lands. He had long since resigned his civil office at Dresden, and devoted himself to the ministry; and now, May 25, 1737, at the recommendation of the king of Prussia, he was consecrated, at Berlin, a bishop of the *Unitas Fratrum*, by bishops Jablonsky and David Nitschmann. In the following year he set out on a tour of inspection to the mission in St. Thomas, and in 1741 visited America. His course continued to excite opposition, and brought upon him personal defamation of the grossest character. Few servants of the Lord have suffered more in this respect. But he leaned upon the strong arm of his divine Master, and gradually won the victory. The Saxon government recalled him to his native country, and fully acknowledged the Renewed Church of the Brethren; the British parliament recognised the Church, and passed an act encouraging the Moravians to settle in the British colonies; the government of Prussia granted the most favorable concessions. At the time of his death the Church for whose renewal God had appointed him the instrument was everywhere firmly established, and in Germany, over against the State Church, had gained a position even more independent than he had intended to secure. Zinzendorf died full of joy and peace, triumphing in the thought of his "going to the Saviour," blessing his children and fellow-workers, and when speech failed him, looking upon them with a countenance that was irradiated with the brightness of coming glory. Thirty-two presbyters and deacons from Germany, Holland, England, Ireland, North America, and Greenland bore his remains to their last resting-place on the *Hutberg*, at Herrnhut.

Zinzendorf was an extraordinary man, a heroic leader in the Church of Christ, a "disciple whom Jesus loved," a priest of the living God. Like all great men he had his faults, and some of them were of a grave character. He was often impetuous when he ought to have been calm; he allowed himself to be unduly swayed by his feelings; in one period of his career his theological views and utterances, which, however, he subsequently laid aside, were very objectionable; while his efforts to renew the *Unitas Fratrum* and yet make it a part of the established Church of Germany brought him into dilemmas the inevitable outcome of which was offences on the score of insincerity and double-dealing, although nothing was further from his thoughts. On the other hand, his sterling piety, his intense love to the Saviour, his Johannean intercourse with him, his work for the Moravian Church, his labors for the Church universal, the principles which he originated, often misunderstood and ridiculed in his day, but now the common and cherished property of all evangelical Christians, the missions which he inaugurated among the heathen, the lifelong efforts which he made to promote the unity of the children of God of every name, and to bring about the fulfilment of Christ's high-priestly prayer—"that they may be one"—assign to him an exalted place in ecclesiastical history, give him an imperishable name, and justify the epitaph on his tombstone: "He was ordained that he should go and bring forth fruit, and that his fruit should remain." In many respects—and this truth explains to a great degree the opposition with which he met—Zinzendorf was more than a century in advance of his age. His writings number more than one hundred, and consist of sermons, hymnals, offices of worship, controversial works, catechisms, and historical collections. He was a gifted hymnologist. In public service he frequently improvised hymns, which were sung by the congregation as he announced them line by line. Many of his compositions, both in point of the sentiments and the poetry, are worthless; many others are beautiful, and take their place among the standard hymns of the Christian Church. The best collection of them was edited by Albert Knapp, *Geistliche Lieder des Grafen von Zinzendorf* (Stuttgart and Tübingen, 1845).

We append a brief account of Zinzendorf's labors in America. His chief purpose was not to found Moravian churches, but to care for his neglected German countrymen in Pennsylvania. He landed at New York on Dec. 2, 1741, accompanied by his daughter, the countess Benigna, his private secretary, and several others. From New York he proceeded to Philadelphia, and established himself at Germantown, where he rented a house which is still standing. Keeping in view the main object of his visit to America, he opened, in that dwelling, a school for German children; preached the gospel wherever he came, in churches, school-houses, and barns; accepted from the Lutherans of Philadelphia, who were without a minister, an appointment as their temporary pastor, a thing that led, on Muhlenberg's arrival from Europe, to bitter animosities, for which both sides were responsible; and organized the so-called Pennsylvania Synod. This last was his favorite undertaking. He conceived the idea of uniting the German churches and sects of Pennsylvania, upon the basis of experimental religion, into what he called "The Congregation of God in the Spirit." Gaining over to his views Henry Antes, a prominent magistrate of the Reformed persuasion (see McMinn, *Life and Times of Henry Antes*, Moorestown, N. J., 1886), a call was addressed to all German religious bodies within the colony to send representatives to a Union Synod to be held at Germantown. It convened on Jan. 12, 1742, and met again, at various places, seven times during Zinzendorf's stay in America, and eighteen times after his return to Europe. But, however beautiful the ideal, it was premature—no real union was brought about; the interest in the movement gradually waned, and, in the end, it served but to augment the differences among the German religionists of Pennsylvania. Reports of the first seven meetings of this Synod, together with cognate documents, were published by Benjamin Franklin, and form a volume which is as valuable as it is rare. The title of the first report is *Authentische Relation von dem Anlass, Fortgang und Schlusse der in Germantown gehaltenen Versammlung einiger Arbeiter derer meisten Christlichen Religionen und vieler vor sich selbst Gott-dienenden Christen-Menschen in Pennsylvania* (Philadelphia: by Benj. Franklin). Zinzendorf's labors among his own brethren resulted in the organization of several churches, particularly the one at Bethlehem. After he had left the country Moravian enterprises were begun at nearly all the places where he had preached. The Indian mission attracted his earnest attention. He undertook three journeys to the aboriginal domain—the first, in July, 1742, to the Delawares of Pennsylvania; the second, in August, to the Mohicans of New York; and the third, in September, to the Shawnees of the Wyoming Valley. He was probably the first white man who encamped on what is now the site of Wilkesbarre, and he would have been murdered by the savages had it not been for the opportune arrival of Conrad Weisser, the government agent. The rattlesnake story, which has found its way into so many books and is so often quoted as an instance of God's special providence, is a fable. During his stay in America Zinzendorf laid aside his rank as a count, and was known as *Lewis von Thürnstein*, which name formed one of his titles. On Jan. 9, 1743, he set sail for Europe in a chartered vessel commanded by captain Garrison, who afterwards, for many years, was the captain of the Moravian missionary vessel which plied between England and the American colonies.

Literature.—The books in relation to Zinzendorf are very numerous. Besides the works noted in the article on the *Renewed Moravian Brethren*, the most important are the following: Spangenberg, *Leben des Grafen von Zinzendorf* (Barby, 1772–75, 3 vols.; an abridged English translation by Jackson, Lond. 1838); Verbeek, *Leben von Zinzendorf* (Gnadau, 1845); Varnhagen von Ense, *Leben des Grafen Zinzendorf* (Berlin, 1846); Pilgram, *Leben des Grafen Zinzendorf* (Leipsic, 1857), from a Roman Catholic standpoint; Kölbing, *Der Graf von Zinzendorf dargestellt aus seinen Gedichten* (Gnadau, 1850); Braun, *Leben des Grafen von Zinzendorf* (Bielefeld, eod.); Bovet, *Le Comte de Zinzendorf* (Paris, 1865; an English translation under the title of *The Banished Count*, by John Gill, Lond. eod.); *Zinzendorf's Theologie, dargestellt von H. Plitt* (Gotha, 1869–74, 3 vols.); Becker, *Zinzendorf im Verhältniss zu Philosophie und Kirchentum seiner Zeit* (Leipsic, 1886). (E. DE S.)

Zipporis. See SEPPHORIS.

Zipser, MAIER, chief rabbi at Stuhlweissenburg and afterwards at Rechnitz, in Hungary, was born Aug. 14, 1815, and died Dec. 10, 1870. He contributed largely to the *Literaturblatt des Orients* from 1846 to 1850, *Ben-Chananja*, and the *Jewish Chronicle*, published in London. His contributions to the latter periodical, headed "The Talmud and the Gospels," which were called forth by Mr. Newdegate in the British House of Commons, when he opposed the admission of Jews into Parliament, were published separately under the title, *The Sermon on the Mount* (Lond. 1852). After his death, Dr. A. Jellinek published his *Des Flavius Josephus' Werk "Ueber das hohe Alter des jüd. Volkes gegen Apion" nach hebr. Originalquellen erläutert*... (Wien, 1871). See *Maier Zipser, eine Biographie*, in the *Beth el-Ehrentempel verdienter ungarischer Israeliten*, by Ig. Reich (Pesth, 1862, 4 Heft), p. 1–30; Fürst, *Bibl. Jud.* iii, 552 sq. (B. P.)

Zirkel, GREGORIUS, a Roman Catholic theologian of Germany, was born at Silbach, near Hassfurth, July 28, 1762, and died at Würzburg, Dec. 18, 1807, as doctor and professor of theology and regent of the clerical seminary. He is the author of, *Der Prediger Salomon, übersetzt und erklärt* (Würzburg, 1792):—*Untersuchungen über den Prediger nebst kritischen und philologischen Bemerkungen* (ibid. eod.). See Winer, *Handbuch der theol. Lit.* i, 213; ii, 208; Fürst, *Bibl. Theol.* iii, 554. (B. P.)

Zisca (or **Zizka**), JOHN, the military leader of the Hussites, was born at Trocznow, in the circle of Budweis, Bohemia, about 1360. He was of a noble Bohemian family, and in his boyhood lost an eye. At the age of twelve he became a page to king Wenceslas at the court of Prague, but his gloomy and thoughtful temperament unfitted him at this period for the frivolous occupations of the court. Embracing the career of arms, he served as a volunteer in the English army in France, and afterwards joined king Ladislas of Poland, with a body of Bohemian and Moravian auxiliaries, and greatly distinguished himself in the war against the Teutonic knights, deciding the battle of Tannenberg (July 15, 1410), in which the knights suffered a terrible defeat. High honors were heaped upon him by the king; but the war being now over, his restless spirit led him to join the Austrians against the Turks in Hungary, and afterwards to enter the English army, in which he engaged in the battle of Agincourt in 1415. He returned to Bohemia soon after the death of John Huss, and became chamberlain to king Wenceslas. He had early embraced the doctrines of the Hussites, and entered deeply into the feelings of resentment which the execution of Huss and Jerome of Prague excited throughout Bohemia. A powerful party was soon formed, which urged upon the king a policy of resistance to the decisions of the Council of Constance. Zisca was one of the prominent leaders of this party, and his personal influence with the king gained for it the latter's sanction to offer resistance, though the king's vacillating disposition incapacitated him from giving effect to his own honest convictions, and taking open part with his subjects against their oppressors. About the time of the outbreak at Prague (July 30, 1419), Zisca was chosen leader of the Hussite party. On that day, as a procession of Hussite priests was marching to St. Stephen's Church, one of them was struck by a stone which came from the town house, where the magistrates (Roman Catholics) were assembled. Zisca and his followers immediately stormed the building, and threw thirteen of the city council into the yard below, where they were instantly killed by the mob. This was the beginning of the first great religious controversy of Germany, known as the Hussite war. The shock produced by the news of this outbreak was fatal to Wenceslas, and his death gave more of a political character to the contest, for when his brother, the emperor Sigismund, attempted to obtain the throne by advancing an army of 40,000 men into the country, his project was frustrated for a time by the Hussites, who insisted on their religious and political liberties being secured, and totally defeated his army with a force of not more than 4000. In this contest he had captured Prague in the spring of 1420, and he completed the conquest of Bohemia by capturing the castle of Prague in 1421. He secured his hold of the country by the erection of fortresses, the chief of which was that of Tabor, whence his party received the name of Taborites (q. v.). The varied experience acquired by Zisca in foreign warfare was now of immense service to his party; his followers were armed with small firearms, and his almost total deficiency in cavalry was compensated for by the introduction of the *wagenburg*, or "cart-fort," constructed of the baggage-wagons, to protect his little army from the attacks of the mail-clad knights. In 1421 he lost his remaining eye by an arrow shot from the enemy while besieging the castle of Raby; and, though now entirely blind, he continued to lead his armies with the same masterly generalship. He was carried in a car at the head of his troops, and was enabled to give orders for their disposition from the description of the ground given him by his officers, and from his own minute knowledge of the country. About the close of 1421 Sigismund led a second large army into Bohemia, which included a splendid body of 15,000 Hungarian horse. A battle took place at Deutsch-Brod in January, 1422, in which the imperial army was totally routed. Followed closely by Zisca in their retreat to Moravia, the fleeing troops, in crossing the Iglawa on the ice, broke through and 2000 were drowned. He repeatedly vanquished the citizens of Prague who were not disposed to obey his orders, and the uniform success of his arms at last convinced Sigismund that there was no prospect of the reduction of Bohemia. After a short time, therefore, he proposed an arrangement with the Hussites, by which full religious liberty was allowed; and Zisca, who had an interview with the emperor on the footing of an independent chief, was to be appointed governor of Bohemia and her dependencies. But the war-worn old chief did not live long enough to complete the treaty, for while besieging the castle of Przibislaw he was seized with the plague, and died Oct. 12, 1424. He was buried in a church at Czaslaw, and his battle-axe was hung up over his tomb. The story that, in accordance with his express injunction, his skin was flayed off, tanned, and used for the cover of a drum which was afterwards employed in the Hussite army, is a fable. Zisca was victor in more than one hundred engagements, and won thirteen pitched battles. Once only, at Kremsir, in Moravia, he suffered a reverse; and even then the evil consequences were warded off by the skilful manner in which he conducted his retreat. The only accusation which can with justice be made against Zisca is on the ground of excessive cruelty, the victims being the monks who fell into his hands. It would have been strange if Zisca had not laid himself open to such a reproach; for the burning alive of the propagators of the faith to which he adhered, the atrocious cruelties practiced on such Hussite priests as fell into the hands of the imperialists, and the seduction of his own favorite sister by a monk, were events ill calculated to induce him to moderate the hatred entertained by himself and his followers against their opponents. Zisca considered himself the chosen instrument of the Lord to visit his wrath upon the nations, and a fanaticism which asked no mercy for its defenders gave none to its opposers. His line of march could be traced through a country laid waste with fire and sword, and over the ruins of plundered towns. One of the dogmas held by his followers was, "that when all the cities of the earth should be burned down and reduced to the number of five, then would come the new kingdom of the Lord; therefore it was now the time of vengeance, and God was a God of wrath." The cries and groans of the monks and priests whom he sent to the stake he was wont to call the bridal song of his sister. His victories were generally won by the decisive charge of a chosen band of his followers named the invincible brethren. In his great victory at Aussig over the German crusading army, commanded by Frederick the Warlike of Saxony, and the elector of Brandenburg, the furious onset of the Hussites was steadily sustained by the Saxons, and the Bohemians recoiled in astonishment at a successful resistance which they had never before encountered. Zisca, being apprised of the circumstance, approached on his cart, thanked the men for their past services, and added, "If you have now done your utmost, let us retire." Thus stimulated, they made a second charge, still more furious than before, broke the Saxon ranks, and left 9000 of the enemy dead on the field. See Millauer, *Diplomatisch-historische Aufsätze über Johann Ziska von Trocznow* (Prague, 1824). See HUSSITES; TABORITES.

Zith'ri (typographical error in some eds. at Exod. vi. 22). See ZICHRI.

Zittel, KARL, a Protestant theologian and doctor of theology of Germany, was born at Schmieheim, in Baden, June 21, 1802. He studied theology at Jena, was called in 1824 as pastor to Bahlingen, in 1849 to Heidelberg, where he died, Aug, 28, 1871. Zittel is known as leader of the Liberal Church movement in Baden. He published, *Zustände der evangelisch-protestantischen Kirche in Baden* (Carlsruhe, 1843):—*Motion auf Gestaltung einer Religionsfreiheit* (ibid. 1846):—*Begründung der Motion über Religionsfreiheit* (Berlin, eod.):—*Die Sonntagsfeier* (Heidelberg, 1851):—*Der Bekenntnissstreit in der protestantischen Kirche mit besonderer Berücksichtigung der Schrift von Hundeshagen* (Man heim, 1852). He also edited the *Sonntagabend. Blätter für christliche Erbauung und für kirchliches Leben* (Berlin, 1857-63). See Holtzmann, in *Protest. Kirchenzeitung*, 1871; Zuchold, *Bibl. Theol.* ii, 1500; *Theol. Universallexikon*, s. v. (B. P.)

Zizka, JOHN. See ZISCA.

Zoerard, a Polish monk of the 10th century (or early part of the 11th), visited Hungary by invitation of king Stephen for the purpose of instructing the people in the Christian religion which had been recently introduced. See Neander, *Hist. of the Church*, iii, 334.

Zohar (זֹהַר, i. e. *light*) is the name of the standard and code of the cabalistic system, and has been called "the Bible of the cabalists." The titles of the book vary: *Midrash of R. Simon ben-Jochaï*, from its reputed author; *Midrash, Let there be light*, from the words in Gen. i, 4; but more commonly *Sepher haz-Zohar*, from Dan. xii, 3, where the word *Zohar* is used for "the brightness of the firmament." The title in full is, *Sepher haz-Zohar al hat-Torah, me-ish Elohim Kodesh, hu nore meod hat-tana R. Simon ben-Jochai*, etc., i. e. "The book of Splendor on the Law, by the very holy and venerable man of God, the Tanaïte rabbi, Simon ben-Jochai, of blessed memory."

I. *Contents.*—The body of the work takes the form of a commentary, extending over the Pentateuch, of a highly mystic and allegorical character. But the Zohar is not considered complete without the addition of certain appendices, attributed either to the same author, or to some of his personal or successional disciples. These supplementary portions are,

1. *Siphra de Tseniutha* (ספרא ד צניעותא), i. e. "the book of mysteries," given in vol. ii, p. 176b–178b. It contains five chapters, and is chiefly occupied with discussing the questions involved in the creation. It has been translated into Latin by K. v. Rosenroth, in the second volume of his *Kabbala Denudata* (Frankfort-on-the-Main, 1684).

2. *Iddera Rabba* (אדרא רבא), i. e. "the Great Assembly," referring to the community or college of Simon's disciples, in their conferences for cabalistic discussion. It is generally found in vol. iii, p. 127b–145a, and has also been translated into Latin by Rosenroth, l. c. See IDDERA.

3. *Iddera Zuta* (אדרא זוטא), i. e. "the Small Assembly," referring to the few disciples who still assembled for cabalistic discussion towards the end of their master's life, or after his decease. This treatise is given in iii, 287b–296b (ed. Amsterdam, 1805), and is also found in Latin in the *Kabbala Denudata*, l. c. To these three larger appendices are added fifteen other minor fragments, viz.:

4. *Saba* (סבא), "the aged man," also called *Saba demishpatim* (סבא דמשפטים), or *the discourse of the aged in mishpatim*, given in ii, 94a–114a. The aged is the prophet Elias, who holds converse with R. Simon ben-Jochaï about the doctrine of metempsychosis, and the discussion is attached to the Sabbatic section, called משפטים, i. e. Exod. xxi, 1–xxiv, 18.

5. *Midrash Ruth* (מדרש רות), a fragment.

6. *Sepher hab-bahir* (ספר הבהיר), "the book of clear light."

7 and 8. *Tosephta and Mattanitan* (תוספתא and מתניתן), or "small additional pieces," which are found in the three volumes.

9. *Raïa mehemna* (רעיא מהימנא), "the faithful shepherd," found in the second and third volumes.

10. *Hekaloth* (היכלות), i. e. "the palaces," found in the first and second volumes, treats of the topographical structure of paradise and hell.

11. *Sithre Torah* (סתרי תורה), "the secrets of the law."

12. *Midrash han-neelam* (מדרש הנעלם), i. e. "the concealed treatise."

13. *Raze de Razin* (רזי דרזין), i. e. "mysteries of the mysteries," contained in ii, 70a–75a.

14. *Midrash Chazith* (מדרש חזית), on the Song of Songs.

15. *Maamar ta Chazi* (מאמר תא חזי), a discourse, so entitled from the first words "come and see."

16. *Yanuka* (ינוקא), i. e. "the Youth," and is given in iii, 186a–192a.

17. *Pekuda* (פקדא), i. e. "illustrations of the law."

18. *Chibbura kadmaah* (חבורא קדמאה), i. e. "the early work."

The body of the work is sometimes called *Zohar Gadol* (זוהר גדול), and the other portions *Zohar Katon* (זוהר קטון). The *editio princeps* is that of Mantua (1558–1560, 3 vols.), which has often been reprinted. The best edition of the book of *Zohar* is that by Christian Knorr von Rosenroth, with Jewish commentaries (Sulzbach, 1684, fol.), to which his rare *Kabbala Denudata* (1677–1684, 4to) forms an ample introduction. This edition was reprinted with an additional index of matters (Amsterdam, 1714, 1728, 1772, 1805, 3 vols. 8vo). To this last-mentioned issue the references in this article apply. The latest editions are those of Breslau (1866, 3 vols. large 8vo), Brody (1873, 3 vols. 8vo).

II. *Authorship.*—The Zohar pretends to be a revelation from God, communicated through R. Simon ben-Jochaï (q. v.), to his select disciples, according to the *Iddera Zuta* (Zohar, iii, 287b). This declaration and the repeated representation of R. Simon ben-Jochaï, as speaking and teaching throughout this production, made R. Simon the author of it, an opinion maintained not only by Jews for centuries, but even by such distinguished Christian scholars as Lightfoot, Gill (*A Dissertation concerning the Antiquity of the Hebrew Language, Letters, Vowel-points, and Accents*, Lond. 1767), Bartolocci (*Magna Bibl. Rabb.* iv, 230 sq.); Pfeiffer (*Critica Sacra*), Knorr von Rosenroth (*Kabbala Denudata*), Molitor (*Philosophy of History*, vol. iii, Münster, 1839), Franck (*La Kabbale*, Germ. transl. by A. Jellinek, Leipsic, 1844), and Etheridge (*Introduction to Hebrew Literature*, Lond. 1856, p. 314). On the other hand it has been clearly demonstrated by such scholars as Zunz (*Gottesdienstl. Vorträge*, Berlin, 1831, p. 405), Geiger (*Melo Chofnajim*, ibid. 1840, introd. p. xvii), Sachs (*Religiöse Poesie der Juden in Spanien*, ibid. 1845, p. 327), Jellinek (*Moses ben-Shem-Tob de Leon*, Leipsic, 1851), Grätz (*Gesch. d. Juden*, ibid. 1863, vii, 73–87; 442–459; 487–507), Steinschneider (*Jewish Literature*, Lond. 1857, p. 104–122; 249–309), Ginsburg (*The Kabbalah*, p. 85–93), and a host of others, that it is not the production of R. Simon, but of the 13th century, by Moses de Leon (q. v.). For Simon ben-Jochaï was a pupil of R. Akibah; but the earliest mention of the book's existence occurs in the year 1290; and the anachronisms of its style, and of the facts referred to, together with the circumstance that it speaks of the vowel-points and other Masoretic inventions, which are clearly posterior to the Talmud, justify J. Morinus (although too often extravagant in his wilful attempts to depreciate the antiquity of the later Jewish writings) in asserting that the author could not have lived much before the year 1000 of the Christian æra (*Exercitationes Biblicæ*, p. 358–369). This later view of the authorship is sustained by the following reasons:

1. The *Zohar* most fulsomely praises its own author, calls him the *Sacred Light* (בוצניא קדישא), and exalts him above Moses, "the true shepherd" (Zohar, iii, 132b, 144a), while the disciples deify R. Simon (ii, 38a).

2. The *Zohar* quotes and mystically explains the Hebrew vowel-points (i, 16b, 24b; ii, 116a; iii, 65a), which were introduced for the first time by R. Mocha of Palestine (q. v.).

3. The *Zohar* (רעיא מהימנה, "the faithful shepherd") borrowed two verses (sect. קדושים, iii, 82b) from Ibn Gabirol's (q. v.) celebrated hymn, "the royal diadem" (כתר מלכות); comp. Sachs, l. c. p. 229.

4. The *Zohar* (i, 18b, 23a) quotes and explains the interchange, on the outside of the *Mezuza* (q. v.), of the words (יהוה אלהינו יהוה) *Jehovah our God is Jehovah* for (כוזו במוכסז כוזו), *Kuza Bemuchsaz Kuza*, by substituting for each letter its immediate predecessor in the alphabet, which was transplanted from France into Spain in the 13th century (Ginsburg).

5. The *Zohar* (iii, 232b) uses the expression *Esnoga*, which is a Portuguese corruption of synagogue, and explains it in a cabalistic manner as a compound of two Hebrew words, i. e. אש נוגה, *brilliant light.*

6. The *Zohar* (ii, 32a) mentions the Crusades, the momentary taking of Jerusalem by the Crusaders from the Infidels, and the retaking of it by the Saracens.

7. The *Zohar* records events which transpired A.D. 1264.

8. The doctrine of the *En-Soph* and the *Sephiroth* (q. v.), as well as the metempsychosian retribution, were not known before the 13th century.

9. The very existence of the *Zohar*, according to the stanch cabalist Jehudah Chayoth (fl. 1500), was unknown to such distinguished cabalists as Nachmanides (q. v.) and Ben-Adereth (1235–1310); the first who mentions it is Todros Abulafia (1234–1306).

10. Isaac of Akko (fl. 1290) affirms that "the *Zohar* was put into the world from the head of a Spaniard." To the same effect is the testimony of Joseph ibn-Wakkar, who, in speaking of later books which may be relied upon,

recommends only those of Moses Nachmanides and Todros Abulafia, "but," he adds, "the *Zohar* is full of errors, and one must take care not to be misled by them." This, says Dr. Steinschneider, "is an impartial and indirect testimony that the *Zohar* was recognised scarcely fifty years after its appearing as one of the 'latter' works, and not attributed to Simon ben-Jochaï" (*Jewish Literature*, p. 113).

11. That Moses de Leon was the author of the *Zohar*, we have already stated in the art. MOSES DE LEON, and the account given there is confirmed in the most remarkable manner by the fact that—

12. The *Zohar* contains whole passages which Moses de Leon translated into Aramaic, from his works, e. g. ס' הרמון, ס' המשקל, as the erudite Jellinek has demonstrated in his *Moses de Leon*, p. 21 sq.; comp. also Grätz, l. c. p. 498 (2d ed. 1873, p. 477 sq.). It is for these and many other reasons that the *Zohar* is now regarded as a pseudograph of the 13th century, and that Moses de Leon should have palmed the *Zohar* upon Simon ben-Jochaï was nothing remarkable, since this rabbi is regarded by tradition as the embodiment of mysticism.

III. *Diffusion and Influence of the Book.*—The birth of the *Zohar* formed the great landmark in the development of the cabala, and the history of this theosophy divides itself into two periods, the pre-*Zohar* period, and the post-*Zohar* period. During these two periods different schools developed themselves, which Dr. Grätz classifies as follows:

1. *The School of Gerona.*—To this school, which is the cradle of the cabala, belong Isaac the Blind (fl. 1190–1210) (q. v.), Ezra and Azariel his disciples, Jehudah b. Jakar, his pupil Moses Nachmanides (q.v.), and Jacob ben-Sheshet (q.v.). The characteristic feature of this school is that it, for the first time, established and developed the doctrine of the *En Soph* (אין סוף), the *Sephiroth* (ספירות), metempsychosis (סוד העבור), with the doctrine of retribution (סוד הגמול) belonging thereto, and a peculiar christology (סוד משיח). It is the *creative* school; the cabalistic mode of exegesis is still subordinate in it.

2. *The School of Segovia.*—To this school belong Jacob of Segovia, his two sons Isaac and Jacob, jr., Moses ben-Simon of Burgos, Isaac ben-Todros, teacher of Shem-Tob Ibn Gaon (d. 1332), Todros Abulafia (d. 1305), and his son Joseph, the author of מערכת אלהות, and Isaac of Akko (fl. 1290). It is the *exegetical* school, endeavoring to interpret the Bible and the Hagada *per fas et nefas* in accordance with the cabala.

3. *The Quasi-Philosophical School* of Isaac ben-Latif or Allatif (q. v.), which in its doctrines stands isolated.

4. *The School of Abulafia*, so called after Abulafia, the founder (born in 1240, and died about 1292). To this school also belonged Joseph Gikatilla ben-Abraham (fl. 1260). The characteristics of this school are the stress laid on the extensive use of the exegetical rules called *Gematria* (גמטריא), *Notaricon* (נוטריקון) (q. v.), and *Ziruph* (צירוף). In this employment of commutations, permutations, and reduction of each letter in every word to its numerical value, Abulafia and his followers are not original.

5. *The Zohar School*, which is a combination and absorption of the different features and doctrines of all the previous schools, without any plan or method; and we must not be surprised at the wild speculations which we so often find in the writings of the post-*Zohar* period. In Spain especially the study of the *Zohar* took deep root, and found its way to Italy, Palestine, and Poland.

As it penetrated all branches of life and literature, voices were also raised against the *Zohar*. The first among the Jews who opposed its authority was Elia del Medigo, of Candia, who, in his philosophical treatise entitled *An Examination of the Law* (בחינת הדת), which he wrote in 1491, brings forth three arguments against the genuineness of the Zohar, but his voice and those of others had no power to check the rapid progress of the cabala. One of the most daring opponents was *Leon da Modena* (q. v.). In the meantime the *Zohar* had been published; Christians became somewhat acquainted with its contents by the extracts of the *Zohar* translated into Latin by Joseph de Voisin, in his *Disputatio Cabalistica* (Paris, 1635), and afterwards by the celebrated work entitled *The Unveiled Cabalah*, or *Kabbala Denudata* of Knorr v. Rosenroth (Sulzbach, 1677–78, 2 vols.; Frankfort-on-the-Main, 1684). With the 18th century a new æra in the criticism of the *Zohar* commenced, and without quoting the different scholars who made the criticism of the *Zohar* their special study, we can only state, what has already been said above, that almost the unanimous result of criticism is that the *Zohar* was not written, as has hitherto been believed, by R. Simon ben-Jochaï, but by Moses de Leon.

IV. *Literature.* — Besides the authorities already quoted, we will mention Fürst, *Bibl. Jud.* iii, 329–335; Jellinek, *Beiträge zur Geschichte der Kabbala* (Leipsic, 1852); *Ben-Chananja*, vols. i, ii, iii, iv, where a most thorough and instructive analysis of the Zohar is given by Ignatz Stern (Szegedin, 1858–61); Jost, *Gesch. d. Judenthums u. s. Sekten*, iii, 70 sq.; Munk, *Mélanges de Philosophie Juive et Arabe* (Paris, 1859), p. 275 sq.; Pauli, *The Great Mystery*, or *How can Three be One* (London, 1863), an endeavor to prove the doctrine of the Trinity from the Zohar; Wünsche, *Die Leiden des Messias* (Leipsic, 1870), p. 95 sq., gives some passages relating to the atonement and the Messiah. See also the article in the *Theol. Universallexikon.* (B. P.)

V. *Doctrines.*—The treatise of the *Zohar* is difficult and fantastic, embracing, moreover, not merely the origin of the world, but likewise speculating on the essence of God and the properties of man; in other words, covering at once cosmology, theology, and anthropology. It sets out with the conception of divinity as the self-existing, eternal, all-embracing first cause, the active as well as passive principle of all being, for which thought has no adequate measure, or language a fit name, although, while other systems have therefore styled it the great Naught or Void, the *Zohar* terms it the Boundless or Infinite (אֵין סוֹף). Deity at length emerges from this absolutism and reveals itself, i. e. becomes at once active and capable of being known; and thus, through the division of its essence into attributes (which before did not separately exist, because they imply a reduction incompatible with the absolute), is established a connection between the infinite and the finite, or real creator. These attributes are ten, called *Sephiroth* (סְפִירוֹת, *numbers*), constituting so many vessels of the infinite, which contain and are forms of its manifestation, subject always to the contained, like colored glasses that receive the light and irradiate it. The impartation of the contents—in other words, the creation of the Sephiroth, is thus also a beaming or emanation; a fundamental principle of the speculation, as we shall see. The idea is further illustrated by various figurative applications, e. g. the cube, with its three dimensions and six surfaces, making up the perfect decade; and so man, with his limbs (the ten Sephiroth hence being sometimes designated as the *first man*, אָדָם קַדְמוֹן, or ideal form of divinity, in accordance with Ezek. i, 26; Dan. vii, 13), whose shape is represented by the so-called "cabalistic tree" as follows:

1. כֶּתֶר (*Crown*).

3. בִּינָה (*Intelligence*). 2. חָכְמָה (*Wisdom*).

5. דִּין (*Judgment*). 4. חֶסֶד (*Mercy*).

6. תִּפְאֶרֶת (*Beauty*).

8. הוֹד (*Majesty*). 7. נֶצַח (*Splendor*).

9. יְסוֹד (*Foundation*).

10. מַלְכוּת (*Kingdom*).

To each of these Sephiroth correspond certain appellations of the Deity. To the first, which is the concentration and partial development of all the others (called also figuratively the *old* or the *long face*, אֲרִיךְ אַנְפִּין, a title indicative of personality), is assigned the undefined name אֶהְיֶה, "I am." The second and third are the active and passive forms of being growing out of the first, and are considered as the male (father) and female (mother), the knowing and the known, the subject and the object, which with their result, *perception* (דַּעַת, included as a son or product), or else with the unit at the head, make up the metaphysical trinity of the divine essence. To these are attributed the sacred names יָהּ, *Jah*, and יְהוִֹה, *Jehovih;* and they constitute the shoulders of the mystical body. The fourth and fifth (equivalent to Grace and Right, also called Greatness, גְּדוּלָּה, and Power, גְּבוּרָה) represent the arms (still duplicate, or male and female, active and passive, external and internal, soul and body, like all the others), with the sixth as an intermediate principle combining them, like the heart. These correspond to the higher or ethical principles, and are respectively designated by the sacred epithets אֵל, *El*, אֱלֹהִים, *Elohim*, and יְהוָֹה, *Jehovah* (otherwise שַׁדַּי, *Shaddai*). The lower, or physical trinity, consisting of the seventh, eighth, and ninth Sephiroth (equivalent to Radiance [according to another exposition, Triumph], Glory, and Stability), and respectively corresponding to the divine appellations יְהוָֹה צְבָאוֹת, *Jehovah Sabaoth*, אֱלֹהֵי צְבָאוֹת, *Elohe Sabaoth*, and אֵל חַי, *El Chai*, represent the hips and genitals of the body, and are apparently the symbols of motion, quantity, and strength. The last Sephirah, to which the name אֲדֹנָי, *Adonai*, is attached, is a sort of joint conception of all the others, as the feet or basis of the whole.

By further combinations of the different Sephiroth according to the above diagram or chart, the male triad (Nos. 2, 4, 7), or right column, separates from the female triad (3, 5, 8), or left column; but the middle column (Nos. 1, 6, 10), in which No. 9 is omitted, or included in No. 10, gives three fundamental conceptions, namely, absolute existence, ideal existence, and immanent strength, as the three phases of pre-worldly existence; or, if preferred, the three conceptions of Matter, Thought, and Life. In this connection, the sixth Sephirah is sometimes called the *King* or Messiah; and the tenth, the *Queen* or Matron, q. d. inhabitation (שְׁכִינָה). These two are also called the two *persons* (פַּרְצוּפִין, i. e. πρόσωπα). Elsewhere there are five persons counted, the first three Sephiroth being added to these (in both enumerations the residue are included under those named). If we notice that the 6th, as a consequence of the 2d, is called *Son*, and the 10th, as a consequence of the 3d, the *Spirit* (the latter is also considered as female or mother), we will find at once the point of contact of the Gnostic speculation with the Christian, and also the unsolved question of the manner of this connection.

These ten sephiroth or "vessels" (כֵּלִים) of the Infinite, in so far as they are considered at once in their plurality and in their unity, are also called a *world* (עוֹלָם), and, in contradistinction from the other worlds, of which we will speak hereafter, the world of effluence (or *emanation*, אֲצִילוּת). This does not mean to imply that the origin of things outside of that world was in any special manner different from it, which would render the system inconsistent, but rather seeks to establish between the infinite and matter what is the object of every system of emanation—a medium by which, in spite of distance (in every sense of the word, not merely with regard to space) between effect and cause, this working could be understood. Now this medium is established by the two middle worlds, namely, the world of creation (בְּרִיאָה) and the world of formation (יְצִירָה), in which we are not yet led to substantial elements. The first is described as the world of the pure spirit, the latter as that of the angels or heavenly bodies. We can already perceive by this distinction that neither of these names is to be taken in its popular acceptance. In fact, the one treats of ideas, the other of power, physical as well as ethic, but not of actual beings. In both worlds the decade is again found as a representative element. Each is considered as a production of the preceding, which is therein improved, and, at the same time, reflects the original light in a more diffuse and imperfect manner, each also establishing for itself a new unity. Neither must we understand the expressions "creation" and "formation" in their common acceptance. There is no mention made in either of any pre-existing matter, or a creation from nothing as usually understood. The Cabalist generally speaks of such, but mean thereby the original void, the *En-soph*, i. e. the absolute, which is the source of the whole metaphysics. But as by this the pre-existence of all things is implied, we consequently arrive at the principle of the immutability of existing things, while by means of the parallel propositions that these are the same, notwithstanding the mode of their origin, there is established a relative independence, which contains the possibility and cause of the fall and corruption of mind and nature.

This point, however, belongs to the obscure parts of the system, as it does not agree well with the premises, and the modern formula of its explanation has not yet been found (but, on the contrary, a different one, if we are to consider the fall as a materialization itself). Generally it is just in the cosmology we find the greatest obscurity, the least development, so much so that the question as to its being absolutely or only relatively pantheistic is not yet decided. It is also in this part of the system that the poetic garb of personification is the most abundant; for instance, when the stars are represented as the hieroglyphics of the active (speaking divinity). It is often perplexing; as, for instance, when a number of angels' names, virtues, natural forces, etc., become personified as regents of separate spheres of the universe.

We will here remark that the second world is called also the throne of God; the divine, spiritual element of it, which other philosophical systems would perhaps call the soul of the world, is here called *Sandalphon* (συνάδελφος?). It is similar to the third world, that of the natural forces, or the assembling, governing principle, and is then called the angel *Metatron* (מְטַטְרוֹן, i. e. μετὰ θρόνον). The expression "throne" brings us back to Ezekiel, from whose well-known vision the figurative expressions are here employed; so that the first world represents the Glory, and the third the four beasts. These are followed by the four wheels of God's chariot, by the fourth world, or that of action (עֲשִׂיָּה), i. e. the material, the rind of the spiritual, the residuum of the substance of the divine light. As we had just now ten classes of angels, which were leaders of the natural and vital forces, and which were retained in the ethic sense, although not to be considered as endowed with personality, or as angels popularly so called, so are there also ten classes of devils as integuments of existence, i. e. as limits to intelligence and life. These last ten Sephiroth are, first, Wilderness (תֹּהוּ), Void (בֹּהוּ), and Darkness (חֹשֶׁךְ); then the seven houses of corruption (the lapse). Their chief, or principal unity, is Sammaël (poison-god), the angel of death; next to him, as personification of evil, is the harlot, the former representing the active, the other the passive conception of the idea; while both, as a whole, are called the beast (חֵיוָא).

From all these metaphysical ground-ideas spring original views of the nature and destiny of man. From the foregoing scheme itself it follows, in short, that man, in the union of his soul and body, is a representation of the universe, a microcosm, while his body is a raiment of his soul, as the world is of God; and this comparison is sometimes carried out with a greater number of poetical figures. But as more closely united to God himself, according to his divine essence, man in this system attains a higher standing, as was indicated from the first; for the self-manifesting divinity itself was called the original man, because all nature could produce no more noble image for the idea. Thus man is next the image of God, and, like him, a unit and a triad, the latter being spirit (נְשָׁמָה), soul (רוּחַ), and life (נֶפֶשׁ). The first is the principle of thought, the second of feeling, the third of passions and instincts (we think the last can be so understood, although some consider it as a coarser organ of the soul, and some even as the body; at all events, the material substance is not meant thereby). All three are likewise unmistakable consequences of the three middle Sephiroth, from which they at the same time derive their relative dignity. By this, what we may call the pre-existence of the soul is established, and not only it, but also, in one sense, the pre-existence of the body so far as it is a prototype of corporealness—and even of a particular one for each, therefore called in later days יְחִידָה (individual). The entrance into life, and the latter itself, are not considered as an evil or as a state of exile, although the souls would certainly prefer remaining always with God. It is a means of education for the soul, and of redemption for the world: for while the spirit descends even to being mixed up with matter, it still possesses at one point a clear consciousness of itself and of its origin, and is thus the more eager to return to its former position; but, on the other hand, it elevates the matter with which it is combined, enlightening and purifying it. God knows beforehand the destiny of each individual soul, so far at least as it will be affected by this combination with matter, but he does not determine that destiny. In other words, the Cabalist does not speak of predestination, nor, on the other hand, does he solve the problem of the relation between free-will and omniscience; but, in order to afford full scope to this free-will, and yet maintain the apokatastasis, or restoration (a consequence of its fundamental idea), it introduces the wandering (גִּלְגּוּל) of the soul, i. e. an infinite range of probationary life, which is to end only on reaching the aim above mentioned. The souls in their pre-worldly existence are already male and female, and even bound in couples; appearing sometimes to enter into life separately, but they will unite again in matrimony, by which they are completed and merged into one essence: thus they strive jointly towards the great end, which is their junction in heaven, in the temple of love (הֵיכַל אַהֲבָה), with God, who takes them to himself with a kiss (earthly death); and by perfecting themselves in him in thought and in will they become partakers of eternal holiness.

See Herzog, *Real-Encyklop.* s. v. "Kabbalah," and comp. Aharon Selig, עַמּוּדֵי שֶׁבַע (Cracow, 1636), which is a full commentary on the *Zohar*. See also CABALA.

Zoharites, so called from their attachment to the book *Zohar*, are properly to be regarded as a continuation of the sect formed by the famous Sabbathai Zevi (q. v.). Their creed is briefly as follows: 1. They believe in all that God has ever revealed, and consider it their duty constantly to investigate its meaning. 2. They believe the letter of Scripture to be merely the shell, and that it admits of a mystical and spiritual interpretation. 3. They believe in a Trinity of *Parzuphim*, or persons, in *Elohim*. 4. They believe in the incarnation of God; that this incarnation took place in Adam, and that it will again take place in the Messiah. 5. They do not believe that Jerusalem will ever be rebuilt. 6. They believe that it is vain to expect any temporal Messiah; but that God will be manifested in the flesh, and in this state atone, not only for the sins of the Jews, but for the sins of all throughout the world who believe in him.

This sect was revived about the year 1750 by a Polish Jew, of the name of Jacob Frank, who settled in Podolia, and enjoyed the protection of the Polish government, to which he was recommended by the bishop of Kamenetz, in whose presence he held disputes with the orthodox Jews, and who was astonished at the approximation of his creed to the principles of Christianity. On the death of the bishop, he and his adherents were driven into the Turkish dominions; and being also persecuted there by the Rabbinists, they resolved to conform to the rites of the Catholic Church. Frank at last found a place of rest at Offenbach, whither his followers flocked by thousands to visit him, and where he died in 1791. Their numbers do not appear to have increased much of late; but they are to be met with in different parts of Hungary and Poland. See ZOHAR.

Zöllner, JOHANN FRIEDRICH, a Lutheran theologian, was born April 24, 1753. He studied at Frankfort, was in 1779 preacher at Berlin, declined a call as superintendent to Neu-Brandenburg in 1782, and remained at Berlin as pastor of St. Mary's, where he died, Sept. 12, 1804. He published, *Disputatio pro Unicitate Dei* (Frankfort, 1776):—*Ueber Moses Mendelssohn's Jerusalem* (1784), besides a number of sermons. See Döring, *Die gelehrten Kanzelredner*, p. 580–585. (B. P.)

Zonaras, JOHANNES, a Byzantine historian, was born in the last part of the 11th century, and died about 1130. He was secretary to the emperor Alexius Comnenus. After the death of Alexius (1118) he retired to the monastery of St. Elijah, in Mount Athos, and devoted himself to theological and literary studies. His *Chronicle*, from the creation till the death of Alexius, is a mere compilation from Josephus, Eusebius, Xenophon, Herodotus, Plutarch, Dio Cassius, etc., and was edited by Hieronymus Wolf (Basel, 1557), Du Fresne (Paris, 1686, 2 vols.), and Pinder (Bonn, 1841–44, 2 vols.). Of more value is his commentary on the *Syntagma* of Photius: Ἐξήγησις τῶν ἱερῶν καὶ θείων κανόνων τῶν τε ἁγίων καὶ σεπτῶν Ἀποστόλων, καὶ τῶν ἱερῶν οἰκουμενικῶν συνόδων, etc. In Latin and Greek the work was published at Paris in 1619; the best edition, however, is the one published at Oxford in 1672 fol. Zonaras also wrote scholia on the New Test., on which see *Zonaræ Glossiæ Sacræ Novi Testamenti Illustratæ a F. W. Schurz* (Grimma, 1818–20). On the first two works see Schmidt, *Ueber die Quellen des Zonaras*, in *Zimmermann's Zeitschrift für die Alterthumswissenschaft* (Darmstadt, 1839), vol. vi, No. 30–36; Zander, *Quibus e Fontibus Joh. Zonaras Hauserit suos Annales Romanos* (Ratzeburg, 1849); Biener, *De Collectionibus Canonum Ecclesiæ Græcæ* (Berlin, 1827); the same, *Das Kanonische Recht der griechischen Kirche*, in Mittermaier's *Zeitschrift* (Heidelberg, 1855), vol. xxviii, p. 201–203; Mortreuil, *Histoire du Droit Byzantin* (Paris, 1843), iii, 423–428; Herzog, *Real-Encyklop.* s.v.; Lichtenberger, *Encyclop. des Sciences Religieuses*, s. v. (B. P.)

Zoölatry (Greek ζῶον and λατρεία), the worship of animals. See ANIMAL WORSHIP; IDOLATRY.

Zoölogy, BIBLICAL. This, like all other scientific subjects, is practically and incidentally, rather than systematically and designedly, treated in the Scriptures; yet many animals are mentioned, and their characteristics are given with substantial accuracy. In the Talmud a more copious and minute description is given of many animals (see Lewysohn, *Die Zoölogie des Talmuds* [Frankfort-on-the-Main, 1858]). The popular and general classification into beasts, birds, reptiles, etc., is the usual Biblical one, and they are further distinguished as clean and unclean. See each of these designations under its proper head. The following is a full list of all the animals (including certain animal products) mentioned in the Bible, in the alphabetical order of the names in the original, with the ordinary rendering in the A. V., and the real name as nearly as modern research has identified it. See each term in its proper place in the body of this *Cyclopædia*. Comp. NATURAL HISTORY.

Achasteranim' ... mules ... "camels."
Aĕtos ... vulture ... "eagle."
Agur' ... swallow ... "swallow."
Akbar' ... dormouse ... "mouse."
Akkabish' ... spider ... "spider."
Akko' ... goat ... "roebuck."
Akrab' ... scorpion ... "scorpion."
Akris ... locust ... "locust."
Akshub' ... asp ... "adder."
Alektor ... cock ... "cock."
Alōpex ... fox ... "fox."
Alukah' ... vampyre ... "leech."
Anakah' ... lizard ... "ferret."
Anaphah' ... parrot ... "heron."
Arad' ... onager ... "wild ass."
Arbeh' ... locust ... "locust."
Ari' ... lion ... "lion."
Arktos ... bear ... "bear."
Arnĕbeth ... hare ... "hare."
Arob' ... gad-fly ... "swarms."
Arod' ... onager ... "wild ass."
Aryeh' ... lion ... "lion."
Ash ... moth ... "moth."
Aspis ... asp ... "asp."
Atalleph' ... bat ... "bat."
Athon' ... she-ass ... "she-ass."
Attud' ... he-goat ... "he-goat."
Ayah' ... hawk ... "kite," "vulture."
Ayal' ... stag ... "hart."
Ayalah' ... doe ... "hind."
A'yit ... beast ... "bird."
Bakar' ... beef-animal ... "ox."
Barburim' ... goose ... "fatted fowl."
Batrăchos ... frog ... "frog."
Behemah' ... quadruped ... "beast."
Behemoth' ... hippopotamus ... "behemoth."
Bikrah' ... she-camel ... "dromedary."
Chagab' ... locust ... "grasshopper."
Chamor' ... he-ass ... "ass."
Chanamel' ... ant ... "frost."
Chapharpherah' ... rat ... "mole."
Chargol' ... locust ... "beetle."
Chasidah' ... stork ... "stork."
Chasil' ... locust ... "locust."
Chazir' ... swine ... "swine."
Choiors ... swine ... "swine."
Chŏlē ... ?opium ... "gall."
Chôled ... weasel ... "weasel."
Chômet ... lizard ... "snail."
Daah' ... kite ... "glede," "vulture."
Dayah' ... falcon ... "vulture."
Deborah' ... bee ... "bee."
Dôb ... bear ... "bear."
Dishon' ... antelope ... "pygarg."
Drakon ... serpent ... "dragon."
Dukiphath' ... hoopoe ... "lapwing."
Echidna ... viper ... "viper."
Epheh' ... serpent ... "viper."
Eriphion ... kid ... "goat."
Erĭphos ... goat ... "goat."
Ez ... she-goat ... "goat."
Gamal' ... camel ... "camel."
Gazam' ... unwinged locust ... "palmer-worm."
Gêb ... locust ... "locust."
Gedi' ... kid ... "kid."
Gediyah' ... she-kid ... "kid."
Gôb ... locust ... "grasshopper."
Gôr' ... whelp ... "young lion."
Gozal' ... fledgling ... "young bird."
Gûr ... whelp ... "young," "whelp."
Hippos ... horse ... "horse."
Hus ... swine ... "sow."
Iyim' ... jackals ... "wild beasts."
Kaath' ... cormorant ... "pelican."
Kamēlos ... camel ... "camel."
Kéleb ... dog ... "dog."
Kēn ... gnat ... "lice."
Kephir' ... young lion ... "young lion."

Ketos	sea-monster	"whale."
Kinnam'	gnat	"lice."
Kippod'	hedge-hog	"bittern."
Kippoz'	arrow-snake	"great owl."
Kirkaroth'	dromedaries	"swift beasts."
Kôach	lizard	"chameleon."
Kokkos	cochineal	"scarlet."
Kōnōps	gnat	"gnat."
Kôph	ape	"ape."
Kŏrax	crow	"raven."
Kôs	pelican	"owl."
Kuōn	dog	"dog."
Láyish	lion	"lion."
Lebi'	lion	"lion."
Lebiyah'	lioness	"lioness."
Lĕōn	lion	"lion."
Letaah'	lizard	"lizard."
Livyathan'	crocodile	"leviathan."
Lukŏs	wolf	"wolf."
Méshi	thread	"silk."
Namar'	leopard	"leopard."
Nemalah'	ant	"ant."
Nemar'	leopard	"leopard."
Neshar', or *ne'sher*	buzzard	"eagle."
Nêts	hawk	"hawk."
Ochim'	owls	"doleful."
Onariŏn, or *onŏs*	ass	"ass."
Oreb'	raven	"raven."
Ozinyah'	eagle	"osprey."
Parash'	steed	"horse."
Pardălŏs	leopard	"leopard."
Parosh'	flea	"flea."
Perah'	mole	"mole."
Pérè	onager	"wild ass."
Péred	mule	"mule."
Péres	eagle	"ossifrage."
Péthen	serpent	"adder."
Raah'	vulture	"glede."
Racham', or *rachameh'*	vulture	"gier-eagle."
Rëêm	buffalo	"unicorn."
Rékesh	courser	"swift beast."
Rêm	buffalo	"unicorn."
Renanah'	ostrich	"ostrich."
Reym	buffalo	"unicorn."
Rimmah'	worm	"worm."
Saïr'	he-goat	"satyr."
Sâs	moth	"moth."
Schechêleth	purple shell	"onycha."
Selav'	quail	"quail."
Semamith'	lizard	"spider."
Sērĕkōn	silk	"silk."
Sēs	moth	"moth."
Shablul'	snail	"snail."
Sháchal	lion	"lion."
Sháchaph	gull	"cuckoo."
Shalak'	gannet	"cormorant."
Shani'	cochineal	"crimson," "scarlet."
Shaphan'	rabbit	"coney."
Shephiphon'	snake	"adder."
Shual'	jackal	"fox."
Skōlēx	worm	"worm."
Skŏrpiŏs	scorpion	"scorpion."
Solam'	locust	"bald locust."
Spŏngŏs	sponge	"sponge."
Stronthiŏs	sparrow	"sparrow."
Sûs	horse	"horse."
Sûs	swallow	"crane."
Susah'	mare	"mare."
Táchash	seal	"badger."
Tachmas'	? ostrich	"night-hawk."
Tan	jackal	"dragon."
Tannîm'	crocodile	"dragon."
Tannin'	sea-monster	"whale," etc.
Tekêleth	sea-shell	"blue."
Teo'	antelope	"wild ox."
Tinshémeth	lizard	"chameleon."
Tinshémeth	heron	"swan."
Tô	antelope	"wild ox."
Tola'	cochineal	"crimson," etc.
Tôr	dove	"turtle-dove."
Tragŏs	he-goat	"goat."
Trugōn	dove	"turtle-dove."
Tsâb	lizard	"tortoise."
Tsabûă	hyena	"speckled."
Tsebi'	(male) gazelle	"deer."
Tsebiyah'	(female) gazelle	"roe."
Tselatsal'	cricket	"locust."
Tsépha	basilisk	"cockatrice."
Tsephardêă	frog	"frog."
Tsippor'	little bird	"sparrow."
Tsirah'	fly	"hornet."
Tsiyim'	wild beasts	"beasts of the desert."
Tukkiyim'	peacocks	"peacocks."
Yaalah'	(female) ibex	"roe."
Yaanab'	(female) ostrich	"owl."
Yachmur'	oryx	"fallow deer."
Yaēl'	(male) ibex	"wild goat."
Yaēn'	(male) ostrich	"ostrich."
Yanshuph', or *yanshoph'*	bittern	"owl."
Yélek	hairy locust	"cankerworm," etc.
Yonah'	dove	"dove."
Zebub'	fly	"fly."
Zeēb'	wolf	"wolf."
Zémer	gazelle	"chamois."

Zopf, Johann Heinrich, a German theological writer, who lived in the 18th century, is the author of, *Introductio ad Lectionem Veteris Testamenti*, etc. (Leipsic, 1763):—*Josephus' Zeugniss von Jesu Christo* (ibid. 1759):—*Quadriga Dissertt.: 1. De Versione lxx, quos Vocant, Interpretum; 2. De Serpente Protoplastorum Seductore*, etc. (ibid. 1763):—*Introductio in Antiquitates Sacras Veterum Ebræorum* (Halle, 1734):—*Diss. de Jephtæ in Filiam Mitigata Credulitate*, etc. (Essen, 1730):—*Diss. de Pseudo-Samuelis ex 1 Sam. c. xxviii* (ibid. 1747):—*Compendium Grammaticæ Hebrææ Danzianæ* (ibid. 1748). See Fürst, *Bibl. Jud.* iii, 555. (B. P.)

Zorn, Peter, a German theological writer, was born at Hamburg, May 22, 1682. In 1715 he was called as rector to Plön, in Holstein; in 1725 became professor of history, in 1729 that of Church history at the gymnasium in Stettin, and died at Thorn, Jan. 23, 1746. He published, *De Scholis Publicis quas Antiqui Judæi Prope Lacuum, Amn. et Fluviorum Crepidinibus*, etc., *Exstruxerunt* (*Act. xvi*, 13) (Plœnæ, 1716):—*De Epithalamiis sive Carminibus Veterum Hebræorum Nuptialibus* (Hamburg, s. a.):—*De Antiquis Ænigmatibus in Cœnis Nuptialibus Hebræorum, Græcorum et Romanorum* (Leipsic, 1724):—*Historia Bibliorum ex Hebræorum Diebus Festis et Jejuniis Illustrata*, etc. (ibid. 1741):—*Diss. de Baptismo Proselytor. Judaico Sacrament. V. T. juxta Lightfootum* (ibid. 1703):—*Hecatæi Abderitæ Eclogæ* (Altona, 1730):—*Historia Fisci Judaici sub Imperio Veterum Romanorum* (ibid. 1734). See Fürst, *Bibl. Jud.* iii, 555; Winer, *Handbuch der theol. Lit.* i, 32, 140, 632, 899. (B. P.)

Zoroaster (more correctly *Zarathustra*, which in Greek and Latin was corrupted into *Zarastrades* and *Zoroastres*, while the Persians and Parsees changed it into *Zerdusht*) was the founder of the Parsee religion. The original meaning of the word was probably that of "chief," "senior," "high-priest," and it was a common designation of a spiritual guide and head of a district or province. Indeed, the founder of Zoroastrianism is hardly ever mentioned without his family name *Spitima*. He was a native of Bactria. He applied to himself the terms *Manthran* (reciter of "Manthras"), a *messenger* sent by Ahura-Mazda, or a *speaker*, one who listens to the voice of oracles given by the spirit of nature, one who receives sacred words from Ahura-Mazda through the flames. His life is covered with obscurity. The accounts of him are legendary and unhistorical. In the Zend writings he is to a great extent represented, not as a historical, but as a dogmatical personality, vested with superhuman, or even divine, powers, standing next to God. His temptations by the devil, whose empire was threatened by him, form the subject of many traditional stories and legends. He is represented as the fountain of all wisdom and truth, and the master of the whole living creation. One of the prayers of the Fravardin Yasht declares—

> "We worship the rule and the guardian angel of Zarathustra Spitima, who first thought good thoughts, who first spoke good words, who first performed good actions —who was the first priest, the first warrior, the first cultivator of the soil, the first prophet, the first who was inspired, the first who has given to mankind nature, and reality, and word, and hearing of word, and wealth, and all good things created by Mazda, which embellish reality; who first caused the wheel to turn among gods and men, who first praised the purity of the living creation and destroyed idolatry, who confessed the Zarathustrian belief in Ahura-Mazda, the religion of the living God against the devils. . . . Through him the whole true and revealed word was heard, which is the life and guidance of the world. . . . Through his knowledge and speech the waters become desirous of growing; through his knowledge and speech all beings created by the Holy Spirit are uttering words of happiness."

In the older Yasna alone he appears like a living reality, a man acting a great and prominent part, both in the history of his country and that of mankind.

I. *History.* — Zoroaster's father seems to have been called Purusbaspa, and his daughter, the only one of his children mentioned, Puruchista. But the time when he lived remains very obscure. He is usually said to have flourished in the reign of a king Gushtasp, who has, on apparently sufficient grounds, been identified with the Darius Hystaspis of the classical writers (Malcolm, *Hist. of Persia*, i, 234). The dates generally given are as follows: Xanthos of Lydia places him about six hundred years before the Trojan war; Aristotle and Eudoxus place him six thousand years before Plato; others, again, five thousand years before the Trojan war. Berosus, a Babylonian historian, makes him a Babylonian king, and the founder of a dynasty which reigned over Babylon between 2200 and 2000 B.C. The Parsees place him at the time of Hystaspes, the father of Darius, whom they identify with a king mentioned in the Shah-Nameh, from whom, however, Hystaspes is wholly distinct. This account would place Zoroaster at about 550 B.C. Yet there is scarcely a doubt that he must be considered as belonging to a much earlier age, not later than 1000 B.C. It is almost certain that Zoroaster was one of the Sosbyantos, or five priests, with whom the religious reform first arose, which he boldly carried out. The Aryans seem to have originally led a nomad life, until some of them, reaching, in the course of their migrations, lands fit for permanent settlements, settled down into agriculturists. Bactria and the parts between the Oxus and the Jaxartes seem to have attracted them most. The Iranians became gradually estranged from their brother-tribes, who adhered to their ancient nomad life, and by degrees came to consider those peaceful settlements a fit prey for their depredations and inroads. The hatred thus engendered and nourished soon came to include all and everything belonging to those devastators—even their religion, originally identical with that of their own. The Deva religion became, in their estimation, the source of all evil. Moulded into a new form, styled the Ahura religion, the old elements were much more changed than was the case when Judaism became Christianity. Generation after generation further added and took away, until Zarathustra, with the energy and the clear eye that belongs to exalted leaders and founders of religions, gave to that which had originally been a mere reaction and spite against the primitive Brahminic faith a new and independent life, and forever fixed its dogmas, not a few of which sprang from his own brain.

II. *Doctrines.*—Zoroaster is commonly spoken of as the great reformer of the Magian system after it had suffered corruption; but it would be more correct to say that on the primitive dualistic worship of the Persians he superinduced some notions borrowed from the element-worship, with which Magism at a later period coalesced. His doctrines, as far as they can be gathered from the extant fragments of the Zend-Avesta, especially the Vendidád Sade, and from the *Ulemai Islam* (a treatise on the Parsee doctrine by an Arabic writer, supposed to belong to the 6th or 7th century of our æra), relate principally to theology and ethics, with occasional references to questions of a cosmological and physiological character.

The problem of the world in relation to God he answers by reference to the antithesis of light and darkness, good and evil; all things, according to him, consist in the mingling of antitheses. His primary physical principle is the *Zerwane Akerene*, the Endless Time (with which may be compared the τὸ ἄπειρον of Anaximander; see Arist. *Physic.* i, 4, 5; iii, 4-7). Everything else save time has been made. The original spiritual power was Ormuzd, the luminous, the pure, the fragrant, devoted to good and capable of all good. Gazing into the abyss, he beheld, afar off, Ahriman, black, unclean, unsavory, the evil-doer. He was startled at the sight, and thought within himself, I must put this enemy out of the way; and set himself to use the fit means for this end. All that Ormuzd accomplished was by the help of Time. After the lapse of twelve hundred years the heavens and paradise were made, and the twelve signs which mark the heavens were fixed there. Each sign was formed in one thousand years. After the first three were formed, Ahriman arose to make war on Ormuzd, but failing of success he returned to his gloomy abode, and remained there for other three thousand years, during which the work of creation advanced, and three other signs were made. During this period the earth and the sea were also formed, man was created, and plants and animals produced. Again Ahriman assailed heaven with all his might, but failing in this, he attacked the world. He afflicted Kajumert, the first man, with a thousand plagues till he was destroyed; but was himself taken and driven into hell through the same opening by which he had come into the world. In man there is much of Ormuzd and much of Ahriman: in his body are fire, water, earth, and air; he has also soul, understanding, judgment, a *ferver* ("principe des sensations," Anquetil), and five senses. By the soul are moved all the members we possess, and without the soul we are nothing. All these he has from Ormuzd. From Ahriman he has desire, need, envy, hatred, impurity, falsehood, and wrath. When a man dies, the four elements of which his body is composed mingle with the four primitive elements; his soul, understanding, and judgment unite with the ferver, and all become one. In this state man goes to judgment, and according as his good works or his bad works have preponderated during life, he is rewarded with immortality in paradise, or punished by being cast into hell. During life he is in constant conflict with the Dews or Divas, a class of beings possessing a body formed of the four elements—beings essentially evil, and who tempt men to sin, but at the resurrection they shall be annihilated, and all men at last shall be received into paradise. Even Ahriman himself shall be accepted and blessed; for the Dews are gradually abstracting from him the evil and darkness that are in him, so that at last he shall be left pure and bright (see Hyde, *Hist. Rel. Vet. Pers.* [Oxon. 1700]; Anquetil du Perron, *Zend-Avesta* [Par. 1771, 3 vols. 4to]; Vullers, *Fragmente über die Rel. des Zoroaster* [Bonn, 1831]).

It is chiefly from the Gathas, however, that Zarathustra's real theology, unmutilated by later ages, can be learned. His leading idea was monotheism. While the five priests before him, the Sosbyantos, worshipped a plurality of good spirits called Ahuras, as opposed to the Indian Devas, he reduced this plurality to unity. This one supreme being he called Ahuru-Mazda, or the creator of the universe — the Auramazda of the cuneiform inscriptions of the Achemenidian kings, the Ahurmazd of Sassanian times, and the Hormazd, or Ormuzd, of the modern Parsees. This supreme god is, by Zoroaster, conceived to be "the creator of the earthly and spiritual life, the lord of the whole universe, at whose hands are all the creatures." Ahura-Mazda is to Zoroaster the light and the source of light. He is wisdom and intellect; he possesses all good things, temporal and spiritual, among them the good mind, immortality, wholesomenesss, the best truth, devotion, piety, and abundance of all earthly good. All these gifts he grants to the pious man who is pure in thought, word, and deed. He rewards the good and punishes the wicked; and all that is created, good or evil, fortune or misfortune, is his work alone.

Nothing was further from Zoroaster's mind than to assume anything but one supreme being, one and indivisible. But the great problem of the ages, the origin of evil and its incompatibility with God's goodness, holiness, and justice, he attempted to solve by assuming two primeval causes, which, though different, were united, and produced the world of the material things as well as that of the spirit. The one who produced the *reality* is called Vohu-Mano, the good mind; the other, through whom the *non-reality* originated, is the Akem-Mano, the evil mind. To the former belong all good, true, and perfect things; to the second, all that is delusive, bad, wicked. These two aboriginal moving causes of the universe are called twins. They are spread everywhere, in God as in man. When united in Ahura-Mazda they are called Spento-Manyus and Angro-Manyus, i. e. white or holy, and dark or evil, spirit. It is only in later writings that these two are supposed to stand opposed to each other in the relation of God and devil. The inscriptions of Darius know but one God, without any adversary whatsoever. But while the one side within him produced all that is bright and shining, all that is good and useful in nature, the other side produced all that is dark and apparently noxious. Both are as inseparable as day and night, and, though opposed to each other, are indispensable for the preservation of creation. The bright spirit appears in the blazing flame, the presence of the dark is marked by the wood converted into charcoal. The one has created the light of the day, the other the darkness of the night; the former awakens men to their duty, the other lulls them to sleep. Life is produced by the one and extinguished by the other, who also, by releasing the soul from the fetters of the body, enables her to go up to immortality. See DUALISM.

Thus the original monotheism of Zoroaster did not last long. False interpretations, misunderstandings, changes, and corruptions crept in, and dualism was established in theology. The two principles then, for the first time, became two powers, hostile to each other, each ruling over a realm of his own, and constantly endeavoring to overthrow the other. Hence monotheism was, in later times, broken up and superseded by dualism. But a small party, represented by the Magi, remained steadfast to the old doctrine, as opposed to that of the followers of the false interpretation, or Zend, the Zendiks. In order to prove their own interpretation of Zoroaster's doctrines they had recourse to a false and ungrammatical explanation of the term Zervana Akarana, which, merely meaning time without bounds, was by them pressed into an identity with the Supreme Being; while the passages on which the present Parsee priests still rest their faulty interpretation, simply indicate that God created in the boundless time, or that he is from eternity, self-existing, neither born nor created.

The following is a brief summary of the principal doctrines of Zoroaster, drawn from certain passages from the Gathas, which probably emanated from Zoroaster himself.

1. Everywhere in the world a duality is to be perceived, such as the good and the evil, light and darkness; this life and that life, human wisdom and divine wisdom.
2. Only this life becomes a prey to death, but not that hereafter, over which the destructive spirit has no power.
3. In the universe there are, from the beginning, two spirits at work, the one making life, the other destroying it.
4. Both these spirits are accompanied by intellectual powers, representing the ideas of the Platonic system on which the whole moral world rests. They cause the struggle between good and evil, and all the conflicts of the world, which end in the final victory of the good principle.
5. The principal duty of man in this life is to obey the word and commandments of God.
6. Disobedience is punished with the death of the sinner.
7. Ahura-Mazda created the idea of the good, but is not identical with it. This idea produced the good mind, the Divine Spirit, working in man and nature, and devotion—the obedient heart.
8. The Divine Spirit cannot be resisted.
9. Those who obey the word of God will be free from all defects and immortal.
10. God exercises his rule in the world through the works prompted by the Divine Spirit, who is working in man and nature.
11. Men should pray to God and worship him. He hears the prayers of the good.
12. All men live solely through the bounty of God.
13. The soul of the pure will hereafter enjoy everlasting life; that of the wicked will have to undergo everlasting punishment, or as modern Parsee theologians explain, to the day of the resurrection.
14. All creatures are Ahura-Mazda's.
15. He is the reality of the good mind, word, and deed.

III. *Literature.*—Haug, *Essays on the Sacred Language, Writings, and Religion of the Parsees* (Bombay, 1862); Spiegel, *Evanische Alterthumskunde* (Leipsic, 1871–78, 3 vols.); Darmsteter, *Ormazd et Ahriman* (Paris, 1877); Ursinus, *De Zoroastre* (Nuremberg, 1661); Mulert, *De Nomine et Vita Zoroastris* (Wittenberg, 1707); Clarke, *Ten Great Religions* (Boston, 1871); Hardwick, *Christ and Other Masters* (London, 1855–57; 2d ed. 1863); Müller, *Chips from a German Workshop* (Index). See also the following with the references under them: AHRIMAN; GUEBERS; MAGI; ORMUZD; PARSEES; ZEND-AVESTA.

Zorab'abel (Ζοροβάβελ), the Greek form (1 Esd. iv, 13; v, 5–70; vi, 2–29; Ecclus. xlix, 11; Matt. i, 12, 13; Luke iii, 27) of the name of Zerubbabel (q. v.)

Zor'phi (Heb. with the art. *hats-Tsorephi'*, הַצֹּרְפִי; Sept. τοῦ Σαρεφί; Vulg. *aurificis;* A. V. "the goldsmith") is a marginal suggestion in Neh. iii, 31, for the name of the father of Malchiah, as if a proper name, but probably without good reason.

Zubly, JOHN JOACHIM, D.D., a Presbyterian minister, was born about the year 1730. In 1775 he took an active part in political matters, and was selected as one of the Georgia delegates to the Continental Congress at Philadelphia. The Georgia divine did not prove loyal to the Whig side, and a correspondence of his with the royal governor of the state having been discovered, he was compelled to resign his position in Congress, and subsequently his property was forfeited under the Confiscation Act. He died at Savannah, before the war ended, in July, 1781. He is said to have been "a man of great learning, of vigorous and penetrating mind." See Sabine, *Royalists in the Rev. War*, ii, 467. (J. C. S.)

Zuckrigl, JAKOB, a Roman Catholic theologian of Austria, was born July 26, 1807, at Grossolkowitz, in Moravia. In 1831 he received holy orders, in 1837 was appointed professor of Christian religious philosophy and university-preacher in Vienna, and in 1847 the Freiburg University honored him with the doctorate of divinity. In 1848 he was called to the chair of apologetics, theological encyclopædia, and philosophy at Tübingen, where he died, June 9, 1876. He wrote, *Wissenschaftliche Rechtfertigung der christl. Trinitätslehre*, etc. (Vienna, 1846):—*Die Nothwendigkeit der christl. Offenbarungsmoral* (Tübingen, 1850). Besides, he contributed largely to the *Tübingen Theological Quarterly*, the *Freiburger Kirchenlexikon*, and the *Bonner theologische Literaturblatt.* See *Literarischer Handweiser*, 1867, p. 1; 1876, p. 288; Zuchold, *Bibl. Theol.* ii, 1503. (B. P.)

Zulu Version OF THE SCRIPTURES. In this language, which is vernacular to the Kaffres, a translation of the New Test. has existed since 1869. It was published by the aid of the American Bible Society. It was formerly supposed that the analogies and general principles subsisting between the Kaffre and Zulu dialects were so proximate that one translation would meet the wants of the two tribes. This idea has been relinquished, and a translation was prepared by American missionaries to provide the Word of God for a million of benighted heathen. From the annual report of the British and Foreign Bible Society for 1879 we see that an edition of the New Test., slightly revised, but conforming to the society's rule, has been issued by the American Zulu Mission, and that this society has shared largely, as on former occasions, in the work. (B. P.)

Zunz, LEOPOLD, a famous Jewish writer, was born at Detmold, Germany, Aug. 10, 1794. He studied at Berlin, was in 1820 preacher at the new synagogue there, in 1835 at Prague, and in 1839 director of the Teacher's Seminary at Berlin. When that institution was closed, in 1850, Zunz retired to private life, devoting all his energies to the production of works which have made him famous in the republic of letters. Zunz died at Berlin, March 18, 1886. He was a voluminous writer, and of his many works we especially mention *Lebensgeschichte des Salomo Jizchaki, genannt Raschi* (Lemberg, 1840):—*Die gottesdienstlichen Vorträge der Juden, historisch entwickelt* (Berlin, 1832):—*Zur Geschichte und Literatur* (1845):—*Die Synagogale Poësie des Mittelalters* (1855):—*Die Ritus des synagogalen Gottesdienstes* (1859):—*Literaturgeschichte der synagogalen Poësie* (1865). His minor writings were issued under the title of *Gesammelte Schriften* (1875, 1876, 3 vols.). See Fürst, *Bibl. Jud.* iii, 555-558; Morais, *Eminent Israelites of the 19th Century* (Philadelphia, 1880), p. 360 sq. (B. P.)

Zurich Letters is the name of an English publication of the Parker Society. On the accession of queen Mary, more than a thousand of the Reformers sought refuge on the Continent, and many of them settled in Zurich. On the return of the Zurich exiles to England, at the accession of Elizabeth, in 1558, they naturally maintained a correspondence with the minister and magistrates of Zurich, who had so kindly welcomed them and given them shelter. A portion of these letters have been published, and show the opinion of that time on subjects which afterwards produced such agitation. To these letters is added a letter of later date, written in 1590, by queen Elizabeth to the thirteen Swiss cantons; also a few letters from Peter Martyr, Bullinger, and Gualter, in reply to some of the English Reformers before mentioned.

Zurich Refugees. See ZURICH LETTERS.

Zwickau Prophets, a local sect of fanatic Lutherans (A.D. 1521), who believed themselves to be the subjects of immediate inspiration. The leaders of the party were Nicholas Storch (q. v.), a weaver of Zwickau, Mark Thomas, of the same trade and place, Mark Stübner, a former student at Wittenberg, and Thomas Münzer, Lutheran pastor of Zwickau, subsequently the rebel chief of the Anabaptist rebellion. These fanatics rejected the Bible, considered human learning a hinderance to religion, and predicted the overthrow of the existing governments to make way for the millennial reign of the saints (themselves). Storch declared that the angel Gabriel had appeared to him in a vision, saying to him, "Thou shalt sit on my throne;" and in anticipation of the new kingdom the prophets chose from the number of their followers twelve apostles and seventy evangelists. They drew after them a great many of the laboring classes and tradespeople; but when open sedition broke out, the magistrates drove the leaders out of Zwickau. See ABECEDARIANS; ANABAPTISTS.

Zwinger, Johann, a son of Theodor, and grandson of the younger Buxtorf, was born Aug. 26, 1634, became professor of the Old Test. at Basle in 1675, and of the New Test. in 1685. He died of apoplexy, while engaged in lecturing to his students, in 1696. He was a rigid predestinarian, a correspondent of Megarius, the pupil of Gomarus, and an opponent of Copernicus, concerning whose system he waged a literary war with the Basle mathematician, Peter Mezerlin.

Zwinger, Johann Rudolf, a son of Johann, was born Sept. 12, 1660, and died Nov. 18, 1708, and was antistes to the Basle Church and theological professor. He wrote dissertations and sermons, and also a book on the conversion of the Jews, entitled *Der Trost Israel's* (1706).

Zwinger, Theodor, a Swiss theologian, was born Nov. 21, 1597, at Basle. He was a strict Calvinist, and defended the doctrine of predestination in a disputation at Heidelberg. In 1630 he was made antistes to the Church of Basle, to which position was attached a professorship of theology. The breaking of bread instead of the use of the host in the sacrament was introduced at Basle under his administration, respecting which event he published a report in his work on the Lord's Supper (1655). Of other works by his pen we mention a *Commentary on Romans* (1655). Both these works were published soon after his death, which occurred Dec. 27, 1654. See Herzog, *Real-Encyklop.* s. v.

Zwinglianism. See ZWINGLI; ZWINGLIANS.

Zwinglians, a name given to the early Swiss Protestants from their leader Zwingli (q. v.). It is also used as a controversial designation of those who hold Zwingli's view respecting the mere memorial character of the eucharist. The theology of Zwingli is of interest as having influenced the English Puritans to a considerable extent, until Zwingli was overshadowed by Calvin during the reign of queen Elizabeth. Zwingli's innovations respecting the ministerial office began, like those of Luther, with the principle that every one, in virtue of the priesthood common to all Christians, is at liberty to preach, preaching being the chief function of the ministry. The irregularities of the Anabaptists, however, compelled him to have recourse to some form of mission from the Church. He lays down the necessity of a call to the ministry, notices three modes of election named in the Scripture, and states that it is proper for the election to rest with the body of the faithful, advised by learned men (*Eccles.* ii, 52-54). But he rejected all notion of priesthood or holy orders. The Basle Confession places the election in the ministers and church deputies, and mentions imposition of hands. The Helvetic Confession decrees that ministers be called by an ecclesiastical and lawful election, either by the Church or its deputies. It adheres strictly to the Zwinglian principle that all ministers have one and the same power and function; but it departs from this principle in assigning them some power of governing, and in vesting in them some power of excommunication. Zwingli considered the exercise of the power of the keys to be nothing more than the general preaching of the gospel. His magisterial excommunication was only an external, not a spiritual sentence. The Helvetic Confession gives the same account of the power of the keys, and the excommunication which it restores to the ministers still belongs, therefore, only to the *forum externum*, not to the *forum conscientiæ*.

Zwingli's doctrine of the sacraments is peculiar. He holds that they are mere signs of initiation or of pledging of continuance. They confer no grace; they do not free the conscience; they are not even pledges of grace. Every spiritual efficacy which has been attributed to them is denied. Baptism does not make sons of God, but those who are sons already receive a token of their sonship. It does not take away sin. The baptism of Christ and his apostles was the same as the baptism of John. The eucharist is regarded in the same way.

The liturgical forms of Zwingli and his followers were constructed on the basis of the doctrines held. The form of baptism in Zwingli's *Works* (ii, 98) has a prayer for the infant that God would give him the light of faith, that he may be incorporated into Christ, buried with him, etc. This refers all to a faith to be given to the child as he grows up to a capacity of faith. The form carefully avoids, either in prayer or declaration, any mention of remission of sins or of regeneration. The *Liturgia Tigurina* has the same prayer, and reads the same gospel from St. Mark. It adds the Creed, recited to the sureties as the belief in which the child is to be brought up, and the minister addresses the sureties: "We will bring unto the Saviour this child as far as it lieth in our power; that is, through baptism we will receive him in his Church, and give him the earnest of the covenant and of the people of God." The form of administration of the eucharist in the liturgy is the same as that in Zwingli's *Works* (ii, 563), and is adapted to the doctrine of sacraments already stated.

Theoretically, Zwingli did not view the community in its two capacities, civil and ecclesiastical, and recognise as belonging to it two independent jurisdictions, temporal and spiritual; the community to him was a Church, and nothing else. His magistrates were Church officers, deriving their authority equally with the ministry from the body of the faithful, and distinguished from them only by the character of the work which a division of labor assigned to each. Practically, however, the result was that the sovereignty in spiritual as well as in temporal matters was vested in the civic authorities of each community.

The system of Zwingli was in some measure modified by Bullinger, who introduced something approaching to a recognition of a clergy and of efficacy in sacraments; and, again, the influence of the Geneva ministers added to the Zurich doctrine of the Lord's Supper something of that Calvinistic teaching regarding receiving the body and blood of Christ, which corresponds to the present accepted belief. It was Swiss theology, so modified by Bullinger, that found advocates in England. Hooper was a faithful follower of Bullinger. Peter Martyr, à Lasco, Dryander, and Ochino were on the same side, and with them acted most of the party of the Marian exiles (see ZURICH LETTERS), who had been received with great hospitality at Zurich. Hoadley's doctrine of the Lord's Supper is not distinguishable from Zwingli's. See Zwingli's *Works*, by Gualter (1544–45), especially the treatises *Expositio Fidei Christianæ*, *De Vera et Falso Religione*, *Ecclesiastes*, *Archeteles;* also *Basle Confession* (1536), *Helvetic Confession* (1566), *In Sylloge Confessio* (Oxford, 1827), and *Liturgia Tigurina* (Engl. transl. Lond. 1693). See also EUCHARIST; REAL PRESENCE; SACRAMENT; TRANSUBSTANTIATION.

Zyro, FERDINAND FRIEDRICH, a Protestant theologian, and formerly professor of theology at Berne, who died May 10, 1874, at Rheinfeldern, is the author of, *Ein freies Wort über die gegenwärtigen Verhältnisse der evangelisch-reformirten Kirche und ihrer Diener im Kanton Bern* (Berne, 1831):—*Des praktischen Theologen Gesinnung in dieser Zeit* (ibid. 1834):—*Die evangelisch-reformirte Kirche u. ihre Fortbildung im XIX. Jahrhundert* (ibid. 1837):—*De Optima Theologos, qui Dicuntur, Practicos Formandi via ac Ratione* (ibid. 1845):—*Des Apostels Paulus Sendschreiben an die Galater, Epheser, Philipper, Kolosser u. Thessalonicher. Neu übersetzt* (Aarau, 1860):—*Handbuch zum Heidelberger Katechismus* (Berne, 1848). See Zuchold, *Bibl. Theol.* ii, 1509. (B. P.)

ADDENDA.

A.

Abbot, Ezra, D.D., LL.D., a distinguished Unitarian scholar, was born at Jackson, Me., April 18, 1819. He studied at Phillips Academy, Exeter, N. H.; graduated from Bowdoin College in 1840, taught for about five years at East Machias, Me.; removed to Cambridge, Mass., in 1847; in 1856 became assistant librarian of Harvard University, and in 1872 professor of New-Test. criticism, a position which he retained until his death, March 21, 1884. In 1855 Dr. Abbot edited Andrew Norton's posthumous *Translation of the Gospels*, and in 1856 Norton's *Statement of the Reasons for not Believing the Doctrines of Trinitarians*. In 1864 he published his *Literature of the Doctrine of Future Life*, in which he gave a list of more than five thousand works on that subject. In 1865 he edited Lawson's *Church of the First Three Centuries*, and in 1866 Orme's *Memoir of the Controversy on the Three Heavenly Witnesses*. In 1860 he edited and revised Hudson's *Critical Greek and English Concordance of the New Testament*. He was one of the writers for the American edition of Smith's *Dictionary of the Bible*, and his additions to the bibliography of that work are exceedingly valuable. He gave substantial aid to the Rev. Dr. Noyes in his *Translation of the New Testament*, which was published in 1869. His work on *The Authorship of the Fourth Gospel: External Evidences*, brought out in 1880, is well-known to European and American scholars. Among his last labors was the assistance which he gave to Dr. C. R. Gregory, of Leipsic, in the preparation of his *Prolegomena* to Tischendorf's last critical edition of the Greek Test. Dr. Abbot was also a voluminous contributor to the periodical literature of the day, in Europe and America. He was a member of the American Bible Revision Committee. In the special department of Biblical literature he stood among the foremost scholars of the present day, and in textual criticism he was probably superior to any other in America. He was a man of singular modesty and disinterestedness, and was endowed with an almost unlimited capacity for work, possessing withal the qualities of thoroughness and accuracy, and in all his studies was more anxious to learn the truth than to establish any foregone conclusion.

Abeken, Heinrich, a Protestant theologian of Germany, was born at Osnabrück, Aug. 19, 1809. He studied at Berlin, was appointed in 1834 chaplain to the Prussian ambassador at Rome, and in 1841 at London, where he was also actively engaged in the founding of the bishopric at Jerusalem. In 1842 he accompanied professor Lepsius to Egypt and Ethiopia, and in 1848 was appointed member of the Prussian ministry for foreign affairs. During the Franco-Prussian war, in 1870–71, he accompanied prince (then count) Bismarck to France, and died Aug. 8, 1872. He is known by his biography of Bunsen in *Unsere Zeit*, vol. v (Leipsic, 1861), and by his *Babylon und Jerusalem* (Berlin, 1853), written against the countess Ida Hahn-Hahn, who had embraced Roman Catholicism. (B. P.)

Abercrombie, Richard Mason, D.D., a Protestant Episcopal minister, was born in Philadelphia in 1822, being the son of the Rev. James Abercrombie. After a liberal education in his native city, he graduated from the General Theological Seminary in New York city in 1843, was ordained the same year, and took charge of a church at Rahway, N. J. He was successively rector of the Church of the Intercession, in New York city (1843–50); St. John's, Clifton, S. I.; Christ Church, Hartford, Conn.; St. Paul's, Rahway, N. J.; and St. Matthew's, Jersey City, where he died, Dec. 7, 1884. He was practically the founder of Christ Church Hospital in that city, and of the Clergymen's Retiring Fund Society. See *The Church Almanac*, 1886, p. 102.

Abernethy (or **Abernethie**), John, D.D., a Scotch prelate, studied at the University of Edinburgh, was laureated in 1587, and became reader in 1588. He was a member of the Assemblies in 1601, 1602, 1608, and 1616; signed a protest against introducing episcopacy in 1606; was chosen constant moderator of the Presbytery; solicited the appointment to the archbishopric of Glasgow in 1615; was a member of the Court of High Commission in 1616; made bishop of Caithness the same year, and demitted Sept. 15, 1635; deposed in 1638, but was permitted to minister in any place. He died April 24, 1639, aged about seventy-two years. He published, *Christian and Heavenly Treatise concerning Physick for the Soul* (1615):—*Two Letters to King James VI* (1620):—*The Duty and Dignity of a Christian* (Lond. eod.). See *Fasti Eccles. Scoticanæ*, i, 480.

Ablon, a little village on the Seine, about thirteen miles from Paris, is noted in the history of French Protestantism as the place where the reformed worship was first held after the concession by the edict of Nantes, May 2, 1598, in consequence of the opposition to that liberty in Paris by the Romanists. See Lichtenberger, *Encyclop. des Sciences Religieuses*, s. v.

Acworth, James, LL.D., an English Baptist minister, was born at Chatham, Aug. 1, 1798. He studied in the Baptist College at Bristol, graduated from the University of Glasgow, settled as co-pastor at Leeds in 1823, and the next year became sole pastor. In 1835 he was chosen president of Horton College, Bradford, a position which he held with great efficiency until 1863. He died Oct. 13 of the same year. Dr. Acworth was active in all the public religious associations of his day, and was the author of several addresses, sermons, etc. See (Lond.) *Baptist Hand-book*, 1884, p. 279.

Adam, a Scotch bishop, was witness to a charter by William Bisset to William de Newbigging. He was bishop of Galloway in 1359. See Keith, *Scottish Bishops*, p. 274.

Adam, Johannes, a Jesuit, was born at Limoges in 1608. He made himself known by his controversial writings against the Huguenots and Jansenists. For forty years he preached at Paris, Poitiers, Sedan, Bordeaux, and other cities, making proselytes wherever he could. His work, *Calvin Défait par Soy-mesme et par les Armes de St. Augustin* (1650), elicited a rejoinder from the famous Jansenist, cardinal Noris. Against the un-Catholic *Heures de Port-Royal* of Maistre de Sacy,

Adam published, in 1651, the *Heures Catholiques.* When Innocent X condemned Jansenism, Adam published *Le Tombeau du Jansénisme* (1654):—*La Conduite des Fidèles par les Règles de la Foi* (1656). During the session of the Reformed synod held at Laudun in 1659, he converted the Calvinist Cottibi, who, in the year following, joined the Church of Rome. When the Jesuits erected a college at Sedan, he became its rector, and published, in 1671, *Le Triomphe de la Ste. Eucharistie ou la Présence Réelle contre le Ministre Claude.* He died at Bordeaux, May 12, 1684. See R. Bauer in Wetzer u. Welte's *Kirchenlexikon*, s. v. (B. P.)

Adam, Scotus (also called Adamus Anglicus), a Præmonstratensian of the 12th century, was born in Scotland. About the year 1150 he entered the monastery of St. Andrew in Scotland, and in order to become better fitted for asceticism he spent some time at the monastery in Premontré, in the diocese of Laon. Having returned to Scotland, he was made abbot and bishop of Casa Candida (Witherne), in Galloway. The time of his death cannot exactly be given. He wrote, *Liber de Ordine, Habitu et Professione Præmonstratensium* (14 sermons):—*De Tripartito Tabernaculo* (part 3):—*De Triplici Genere Contemplationis.* These works were printed in 1578. An enlarged edition, containing besides forty-seven sermons and two books, entitled *Soliloquia de Instructione Animæ*, was published by Godefr. Ghiselbertus, at Antwerp, in 1659. A complete edition of his works is given by Migne, in *Patrol. Lat.* cxviii. See Schenid, in Wetzer u. Welte's *Kirchenlexikon*, s. v. (B. P.)

Adams, Elisha, D.D., a Methodist Episcopal minister, was born at Williamstown, Vt., July 29, 1815. He studied at Newbury Seminary for some time, and spent three years at Norwich University; was licensed to preach in 1835; in 1838 was ordained deacon, and elder in 1840. Of the forty years spent in the ministry in the New Hampshire Conference, eleven were given to district work, eighteen to stations, and three to the agency of the conference seminary, of which he was a trustee from the beginning. His labors were everywhere acceptable and successful, and three times he was a member of general conferences. He was a man of one work, and as a preacher was strictly evangelical. He died in Concord, N. H., Aug. 15, 1880. See *Minutes of Annual Conferences*, 1881, p. 91.

Adams, George F., D.D., a Baptist minister, was born at Dorchester, Mass., Oct. 3, 1802. He removed to Ohio with his father's family in 1805, was baptized at the age of ten, and licensed to preach at twenty. He graduated from Columbian College, Washington, D. C., in 1829, having been ordained at the Navy-Yard Baptist Church of that place, April 22, 1827. After teaching for several years, he became the pastor of a church at Fredericksburg, Va.; in 1835 removed to Baltimore, and, in January, 1836, became pastor of the Calvert Street Church. After serving as general missionary of his denomination in Maryland, he took charge of the Second Church, Baltimore, in 1848; in 1860 went to Hampton, Va., as pastor, and on the breaking-out of the civil war was, for a short time, a chaplain in the Confederate army. For about three years (1862–65) he acted a second time as state missionary in Maryland. After teaching a year or two, he returned to Hampton, and was pastor nine years (1867–76), and then returned to Baltimore, where he was city missionary for a few months, and died there, April 16, 1877. See Cathcart, *Baptist Encyclop.* p. 10. (J. C. S.)

Adams, Jasper, D.D., a Protestant Episcopal clergyman, was born in Massachusetts. He graduated from Brown University in 1815; spent two years in Andover Theological Seminary; was tutor in Brown University in 1818 and 1819; was ordained deacon Sept. 2, 1819, and presbyter Aug. 4, 1820. He was professor of mathematics in Brown University from 1819 to 1824; president of Charleston College, S. C., from 1824 to 1826; of Geneva College, N. Y., from 1826 to 1828; of Charleston College again from 1828 to 1836; chaplain and professor of ethics at U. S. Military Academy, West Point, N. Y., from 1838 to 1840, and died at Pendleton, S. C., Oct. 25, 1841. See *Gen. Cat. of Andover Theol. Sem.* 1870, p. 39.

Adams, *Mrs.* **Sarah Flower**, an English poetess, daughter of Benjamin Flower, a Liberal editor and author, was born at Harlow, Essex, Feb. 22, 1805, and in 1834 married William B. Adams, an engineer and writer. She died Aug. 13, 1849. Mrs. Adams published a dramatic poem, entitled *Vivia Perpetua* (1841), and a catechism with hymns, entitled *The Flock at the Fountain* (1845). She was a member of the Unitarian congregation of William Johnson Fox, to whose volume of *Hymns and Anthems* (1840) she contributed thirteen pieces, the most noted of which is "Nearer my God to thee." In later years she is said to have become a Baptist. Her sister, Eliza Flower, set some of Sarah's songs to music, and herself wrote a number of poems.

Adams, Seymour Webster, D.D., a Baptist minister, was born at Vernon, Oneida Co., N. Y., Aug. 1, 1815. He was converted at seventeen years of age; graduated from Hamilton College and Theological Seminary; was ordained in 1843, and served as pastor in his native place for two years, and thereafter in Cleveland, O., until his death, Sept. 27, 1864. He wrote a memoir of his father-in-law, Dr. N. Kendrick, and his own *Life* was edited by J. P. Bishop (1866). See Cathcart, *Baptist Encyclop.* s. v.

Adams, Thomas, D.D., a Congregational minister, was born at West Brookfield, Mass., Feb. 7, 1792. He studied at Leicester Academy, graduated from Dartmouth College in 1814, and then studied theology with Rev. Dr. Thomas Snell, of West Brookfield. He was ordained pastor in Vassalborough, Me., Aug. 26, 1818, and remained there until April 1, 1834. In 1835 he was agent for a temperance society. The following year he was installed pastor at Waterville, and remained nearly two years. The five subsequent years he was editor of the *Temperance Gazette;* and from 1843 to 1846 was agent of the Tract Society. The next year he was acting-pastor at Hampden, O.; and until 1856 he sustained the same relation to the Church at Thompson. From 1856 to 1860 he was the Ohio agent of the Congregational Board of Publication; in 1863 acting-pastor in Pittston, Me.; and from 1864 to 1870 filled the same position in Vassalborough. After this he resided, without charge, at Winslow, where he died, Feb. 4, 1881. Several of his sermons have been published. See *Cong. Year-book*, 1882, p. 17.

Adeloga, saint, virgin, and abbess of the 8th century, was the daughter of Charles Martel, by Kunehilda. She was of singular beauty, so that she was greatly sought in marriage, but she constantly refused, having given her heart to a heavenly spouse. Her father, exasperated, treated her with studied brutality and public insult. She sought comfort in the advice of her director, his chaplain, and they were both expelled from the palace. Adeloga and the priest journeyed till they came to a wild and desert place, Kitzingen, in the present margrave of Anspach, and there they built a convent. To her came virgins, the priest gave her the veil, made her abbess, enjoining her to adopt the rule of St. Benedict and St. Scholastica. He attended to the temporal affairs of the convent till he died. In after-years Charles Martel was reconciled to his daughter, endowed her monastery with lands, and visited her. St. Adeloga has a place in the Benedictine martyrology, and those of Ferrarius, Menardus, etc. There is an ancient, apparently authentic, life, by an anonymous writer, published by Bollandus. See Baring-Gould, *Lives of the Saints*, Feb. 4, ii, 42.

Adhem, one of the most ancient Mohammedan Quietists, who is said to have obtained in one of his visions the high privilege of having his name written by an angel among those who love God. Among his extravagant expressions are the following: "Hell is preferable with the will of God to heaven without it." "I would rather go to hell doing the will of God than go to heaven disobeying him." Mohammedan mystics often resort to such statements to show their high regard for the deity.

Ægidius A LESSINIA (also DE LESSINIS), a Dominican, who flourished about 1278, was a contemporary with Albertus Magnus and Thomas Aquinas. He took an active part in the controversies against Averroism, and wrote many philosophical, theological, and chronological works, of which only a few fragments are extant. He also wrote *De Usuris*, which is generally quoted in the editions of the works of Thomas Aquinas as *Opusculum* 73. B. Haréau, in his *La Philosophie Scolastique* (Paris, 1850), i, 248, quotes a few passages from his *De Unitate Formæ*, in which he defends the Thomistic doctrine of the unity of the *forma substantialis*. See Bach, in Wetzer u. Welte's *Kirchenlexikon*, s. v. (B. P.)

Ægidius DE PRÆSENTATIONE, a Portuguese scholastic, was born at Castel Branco in 1539, and died in 1626, professor of theology at Coimbra and provincial of the Portuguese Augustinian-Eremites. Besides the writings in praise of his order (*Primas Augustinianæus* [Cologne, 1627] and *Apologia seu Defensorium Ordinis S. Aug.*), he wrote, *Disputationes ad Priores V Quæstiones* 1, 2 *S. Thomæ* (Coimbra, 1609, 1615, 3 vols.)—*De Voluntario et Involuntario* (2 vols.):—*Philosophia Naturalis et Supernaturalis:—De Immac. Concept. B. M. V.* (ibid. 1617, book 4). See Ossinger, *Bibl. August.* 356; Streber, in Wetzer u. Welte's *Kirchenlexikon*, s. v. (B. P.)

Æthelwold. See ETHELWOLD.

Agathias, a Byzantine historian, was born at Myrina, in Æolis, about 536 or 537 A.D. He resided at Alexandria, and after 554 at Constantinople, where he practiced law, but whether he was a Christian or a heathen is uncertain. He died between 582 and 594. He wrote a valuable history of the eastern Roman empire, from 553 to 559, which was published in Greek by Vulcanus at Leyden (1594). The best edition is that of Niebuhr, in the *Corpus Script. Byzant.*

Agricola, IGNATIUS, a Jesuit, was born at Zusamaltheim, in the bishopric of Augsburg, July 31, 1661. In 1677 he entered the Society of Jesus, was for a long time professor at the Jesuit gymnasium at Munich, and died Jan. 23, 1729. He wrote *Historia Provincial Societatis Jesu Germaniæ Superioris* (Augsburg, 1727–29, 2 vols.), reaching down to 1600, and continued to 1640 by Flott and Khopf. See Baader, *Gelehrtes Bayern;* Sattler, *Geschichte der marianischen Congregation in Bayern*, 1864, p. 279; Schlösser, in Welte u. Welte's *Kirchenlexikon*, s. v. (B. P.)

Aiton, JOHN, D.D., a Scotch clergyman, studied at the Edinburgh University, was licensed in 1819, presented to the living at Dolphinton in 1824, and died at Essex, May 15, 1863. He was the author of, *Owen's Objections to Christianity Refuted* (1824):—*Life and Times of Alexander Henderson* (1836):—*Clerical Ethics* (1842):—*Letter on Imprisonments in Naples* (1851):—*Lands of the Messiah, Mohammed, and the Pope* (1852):—*The Drying up of the Euphrates*, etc. (1853):—*Appeal in Behalf of Jerusalem and the Holy Land* (1854):—*St. Paul and his Localities* (1856):—*Manual of Domestic Economy* (1857), and other works. See *Fasti Eccles. Scoticanæ*, i, 221.

Akers, PETER, D.D., a veteran Methodist Episcopal minister, was born in Campbell County, Va., Sept 1, 1790. He was reared in the Presbyterian Church, studied at the high-schools in Virginia and North Carolina, taught school and practiced law a few years, editing likewise a weekly journal; was converted in 1821, and the same year joined the Methodist Church; began to preach, and was admitted to the Kentucky Conference, in which and in the Illinois (1832) and the Minnesota conferences (1857) he occupied prominent appointments, with great efficiency, until 1858, when he became superannuated, and retained that relation until his death, at Jacksonville, Ill., Feb. 21, 1886. He twice (1833 and 1851) served as president of M'Kendree College, and was often a member of the General Conference. He was a powerful preacher and a genial Christian. He published an elaborate work on *Biblical Chronology* (Cincinnati, O., 1855, 8vo). See (N. Y.) *Christian Advocate*, Aug. 5, 1886.

Alaric. See GOTHS.

Albert OF RIGA. See ALBERT OF LIVONIA.

Alberti, ALOYSIUS. See ALBERTI, LUIGI.

Albrecht, son of Casimir, margrave of Culmbach, was born March 28, 1522. He entered into the confederacy formed by Maurice, elector of Saxony, and other princes, against the emperor Charles V, and committed many excesses in the war, burning towns and levying heavy contributions wherever he marched. Subsequently a league headed by Maurice himself was formed against him, and in 1553 a great battle was fought at Sivershausen, in which Maurice was slain and Albrecht wounded. He was afterwards put under the ban of the empire, and deprived of his possession. While suffering exile he composed the hymn *Was mein Gott will, gescheh' allzeit* (Engl. transl. in the *Monthly Religious Magazine* [1864], xxxi, p. 80, "Whate'er God will, let that be done"), and died as a penitent and believing Christian, Jan. 8, 1557, at Pforzheim, in the house of his brother-in-law, the margrave Charles II, of Baden. See Koch, *Geschichte des deutschen Kirchenliedes*, i, 339 sq. (B. P.)

Albright, JACOB, the founder of the Evangelical Association, was born near Pottstown, Pa., May 1, 1759. His parents were members of the Evangelical Lutheran Church, and in youth he was received as a member into its communion. About 1790 he was converted, and joined the Methodist Episcopal Church. In October, 1796, he commenced his work as an itinerant minister, preaching to the Germans in Pennsylvania and Virginia in a stirring, practical manner. In 1800 he organized the persons who had been intrusted to his care into classes or societies. The first three of these were formed in the counties of Bucks, Berks, and Northampton, in the state of Pennsylvania. Soon afterwards other classes were formed. His first colleague after this organization was John Walter, his second was Abraham Liesser. A council was held Nov. 3, 1803, at which these three and fourteen others of the society were present. Albright was recognised as their spiritual father, and his two associates, with the assent of the others, solemnly ordained him an elder, adopting the Holy Scriptures as their articles of faith and practice. At the first conference, held in November, 1807, in Lebanon County, Pa., Jacob Albright was elected bishop. From the time of this conference session his health failed rapidly. On his way home from Singlestown he became so weak that he was compelled to stop at the house of Mr. George Becker, in Lebanon County. He died May 18, 1808. The immediate fruit of his labors was the conversion of three hundred souls. His public prayers and sermons were powerful, penetrating, and convincing. See Yearkel, *Albright and his Co-laborers* (Cleveland, O., 1883).

Albro, JOHN ADAMS, D.D., a Congregational minister, was born in Connecticut in 1800. He graduated from Andover Theological Seminary in 1827, and was ordained Nov. 21 of the same year pastor at Chelmsford, Mass.; in 1833 he became pastor at Fitchburg; in 1835 of First Church, Cambridge. He was without charge at Cambridge from 1865 until his death at West Roxbury, Dec. 20, 1866. See *Trien. Cat. of Andover Theol. Sem.* 1870, p. 73.

Alden, Joseph, D.D., LL.D., a noted educator and author, was born at Cairo, N. Y., Jan. 4, 1807. He graduated from Union College in 1828, and from Princeton Theological Seminary in 1830; was tutor two years in the College of New Jersey; ordained over the Congregational Church in Williamstown, Mass., July 3, 1834; professor in the college there from 1835 to 1852; and in Lafayette College, Pa., thereafter until 1857, when he was elected its president; from 1863 to 1865 preached as stated supply at Boiling Spring, N. J.; from 1867 to 1880 was principal of the New York State Normal School at Albany, and died in the city of New York, Aug. 30, 1885. He wrote chiefly for the young, especially in the department of Sunday-school literature, and in the religious journals.

Alexander, Robert, D.D., a minister of the Methodist Episcopal Church South, was born in Tennessee, Aug. 7, 1811. He was converted at the age of seventeen; the next year was licensed to exhort, and the following year joined the Tennessee Conference; in 1833 was transferred to the Mississippi Conference; in 1836 was appointed missionary to Texas, and labored zealously and successfully in that field in various capacities until near the time of his death, which occurred in 1882. See *Minutes of Annual Conferences of the M. E. Church South*, 1882, p. 119.

Alexander, Stephen, LL.D., a Presbyterian minister, was born at Schenectady, N. Y., Sept. 1, 1806. He graduated from Union College in 1824, and from Princeton Theological Seminary in 1832, when he became a tutor in Princeton College, and, in 1834, professor of mathematics, astronomy, and mechanical philosophy, and was connected with the college for upwards of fifty years. Professor Alexander, in 1860, went to the coast of Labrador, at the head of a government astronomical expedition, to observe the eclipse of July 18. In 1869 he was at the head of an expedition to the Rocky Mountains to observe the solar eclipse of that year. He was the author of numerous papers on astronomy and mathematics, which attracted much attention in this country and in Europe. He was one of the founders of the National Academy of Science, a member of the American Philosophical Association, of the Academy of Arts and Sciences, and of the American Association for the Advancement of Science, of which he was president. He was a devout Christian, and an elder in the Presbyterian Church. His old age passed away in the quiet study of the stars, his favorite pursuit. He died at Princeton, N. J., June 26, 1883. See *Necrol. Report of Princeton Alumni*, 1884, p. 16; Nevin, *Presb. Encyclop.* s. v. (W. P. S.)

Alexander, William Lindsay, D.D., an eminent English Independent minister, was born at Leith, near Edinburgh, Aug. 24, 1808. He graduated while young from the High School of Edinburgh and the University of St. Andrews, and in 1828 was appointed classical tutor in the Lancashire College, then located at Blackburn, but subsequently removed to Manchester. He had expected to study medicine, but having been religiously educated, he officiated in a small chapel in Wales, whither he had retired for his health, and subsequently in Newington Chapel, Liverpool. After a course of study at the German universities, he accepted the pastorate of the North-College Church, Edinburgh, in 1835. In 1854 he was appointed professor of theology in the Scottish Theological Hall, in 1861 examiner in philosophy at St. Andrew's University, but resigned these positions at the close of 1882. He died Dec. 20, 1883. Dr. Alexander was noted no less as a preacher than as a scholar. He was a member of the Old-Test. company of the Bible Revision Committee, and the author of numerous Biblical and theological works, the principal of which are the *Congregational Lectures* for 1840 (new ed. 1853):—*Anglo-Catholicism not Apostolical* (1843):—*Christ and Christianity* (1854):—*Life of Dr. Wardlaw* (1856):—*Christian Thought and Work* (1862):—*St. Paul at Athens*, and many articles in the reviews and cyclopædias, besides editing the third edition of Kitto's *Cyclopædia*. See (Lond.) *Cong. Year-book*, 1886, p. 146; Allibone, *Dict. of Brit. and Amer. Authors*, s. v.

Alfonso, PEDRO, formerly *rabbi Moses of Huesca*, in Aragon, was born in 1062. At the age of forty-four he was baptized in the cathedral of his native city, on St. Peter's day, and in honor of the saint and his godfather, the king Alfonso, he took the name of *Pedro Alfonso*. He was, besides being physician to the king, Alfonso VI, a very learned and fine writer of the mediæval Church, highly praised by all Spanish writers. He wrote a defence of Christianity, and a refutation of Jewish incredulities, in the form of a dialogue between Moses and Pedro Alfonso, under the title of, *Dialogi in quibus Impiæ Judæorum Opiniones Credentissimis tam Naturalis quam Cœlestis Philosophiæ Argumentis Confutantur*, etc. (Cologne, 1536), a work spoken of in high terms, and which has since been in great use in Spain. He also wrote a *Disciplina Clericalis*, a very popular book, which was translated into French in the 13th century. The date of Alfonso's death is not known. The *Disciplina Clericalis* was edited by F. W. V. Schmidt (Berlin, 1827). See Fürst, *Bibl. Jud.* i, 36; Kalkar, *Israel und die Kirche*, p. 22; Bartolocci, *Bibl. Rabb.* iv, 69; Antonii *Bibl. Hisp.* ii, 7; Wolf, *Bibl. Hebr.* iii, No. 1824; Lindo, *History of the Jews of Spain and Portugal* (London, 1848), p. 55; Fürst, in Delitzsch's *Saat auf Hoffnung* (1876), xiii, 142 sq. (B. P.)

Alison, FRANCIS, D.D., a Presbyterian minister, was born at Lac, County Donegal, Ireland, in 1705. He came to America when about thirty years of age, and engaged in teaching. In May, 1737, he was ordained pastor at New London, Pa., and in 1749 took charge of the Philadelphia Academy, afterwards the University of Pennsylvania, of which he was vice-provost and professor of moral philosophy, at the same time serving as assistant minister of the First Presbyterian Church. He died Nov. 28, 1779. Dr. Alison was a prominent actor in the public enterprises of his time. See Nevin, *Presb. Encyclop.* s. v.

Allen, A. C., D.D., a minister of the Methodist Episcopal Church South, was born in Iredale County, N. C., March 18, 1818. He was converted in early life; was educated at Emory and Henry College; joined the North Carolina Conference in 1842; was ordained deacon in 1844, and elder in 1846. He filled some of the best appointments in the conference. In 1852 he located and moved to Mississippi, where he accepted the presidency of a female college at Okolona, remaining there until the war, when he entered the Confederate army as chaplain. In 1864 he joined the Memphis Conference, wherein he served one term as presiding elder. In 1870 he was transferred to the North Mississippi Conference, in which he served in a like capacity. He was transferred to the North Texas Conference in 1874, where he served three charges. The year 1877-78 he was president of a college in the city of Dallas. He was a delegate to the general conferences of 1870 and 1874. His death occurred at Fort Worth, Jan. 17, 1880. See *Minutes of Annual Conferences of the M. E. Church South*, 1880, p. 203.

Allen, Robert Welch, D.D., a Presbyterian minister, was born in Shelby County, Ky., March 25, 1817. He graduated from Wabash College, Ind., in 1839. From thence he entered Princeton Seminary, where he remained two years, when failing health compelled him to leave. He was ordained by the Crawfordsville Presbytery, and served three years as stated supply of several churches, when he was installed pastor of Jefferson and Frankford churches, and remained in that charge for nine years. He next became pastor of the Pisgah Church, near Lexington, Ky., which he served with great acceptance until 1857, when he accepted a call to the Church of Jacksonville, Ill. This pastorate he held for over eleven years, afterwards he served as missionary, and supplied the Church of St. Charles, Mo. At the end of two years he returned to Jacksonville, and supplied the churches of Union and Murrayville until a new church was organized called Unity, over which he was installed pastor, and which relation he continued during life. He died at Jacksonville, Ill., July 29, 1882. See *Necrol. Report of Princeton Theol. Sem.* 1883, p. 39. (W. P. S.)

Alline, Henry, a remarkable character in the religious history of the last century, was born in Rhode Island in 1748. In 1760 he went to Nova Scotia and settled at Newport. Six years after he commenced preaching without ordination, although, in 1779, he received the imposition of hands at Cornwallis as an itinerant preacher. He preached in Nova Scotia from 1776 to 1784, then went to the United States, where he died at the residence of Rev. David M'Clure, Northampton, N. H., Feb. 2 of the latter year. He travelled throughout the provinces, preaching with remarkable fervor and power, assailing all denominations, causing divisions in the churches, and making many converts. Alline rejected the doctrine of creation, denied that man possessed a material body before the fall, and affirmed that all souls were actually created at the beginning of the world and sinned in Eden. He also denied the resurrection of the elemental body. He had a keenly metaphysical mind and a love of speculation. Some of his writings were published, now very rare, viz., *Mites on Some of the most Important and Disputed Points of Divinity Cast into the Treasury* (Halifax, N. S., 1781):—*Sermons* (1782–83):—*The Anti-Traditionists* (1783):—*Life and Journals* (Boston, 1806, 12mo). Of the first-mentioned work it has been said, "In its statement of doctrine it is a confused medley, almost resembling a sick man's dreams, and yet it is varied with the most impassioned and eloquent appeals, when he touches upon some of the grander or more tender topics of religion." His autobiography is a book of thrilling interest. Alline had an agreeable manner and a natural eloquence. He never left the Congregational ranks, in which he was brought up. He was indifferent as to the mode of baptism, and cared little for the ordinance at all. Some of his followers joined the Baptists, but the majority united with the Free-will or Free Christian Baptists. See his *Life and Journals;* Morgan, *Biblioth. Canad.* s. v.; Smith, *Hist. of Methodism in East British America*, vol. i; Bill, *Hist. of the Baptists of the Maritime Provinces* (St. Johns, 1881), p. 13–18.

Altenburg, a Benedictine abbey, in Lower Austria, was founded by Hildeburg, countess of Buige. In 1144 a number of monks settled there from St. Lambrecht, in Styria. Till 1878 this abbey had forty-five abbots, the first of whom was Gottfried. Altenburg was several times destroyed by fire, twice by the Hussites, and suffered greatly from the peasants' war, and from the Swedes, Russians, and French. The famous abbot was the thirty-eighth, Maurus Boxler, who greatly promoted the spiritual as well as material interests of the abbey. His clergy were educated at the universities of Vienna and Salzburg. Under the forty-fifth abbot, Honorius Burger, who died in 1878, the seventh centenary of this institution was celebrated in 1844. Burger also wrote the history of his abbey, and published the documents concerning the same in *Fontes Rerum Austriacarum, Diplom. et Acta, xxi* (Vindob. 1865). Besides Marian, *Gesch. der österr. Klerisei* (Vienna, 1787), see Burger's *History* (ibid. 1862); Wolfsgruber, in Wetzer u. Welte's *Kirchenlexikon*, s. v. (B. P.)

Altieri, Luigi, a Roman Catholic prelate, was born in Rome, July 17, 1805, of a noble family. He began his career under the immediate eye of Gregory XVI, and lodged in the Vatican as private chamberlain to the pope. His next step was to the secretaryship of the Congregation of Studies, whence he was promoted to the nunciature at Vienna, and consecrated by Gregory himself archbishop of Ephesus, July 17, 1836. He was created cardinal Dec. 14, 1840, and published April 23, 1845. During the twenty years of his cardinal's life he occupied some of the most laborious and important posts, as chamberlain of the holy Roman Church, archpriest of the patriarchal basilica of St. John Lateran, lord chancellor of the Roman University, and bishop of the suburbicarian see of Albano, about fourteen miles from Rome. While (1867) receiving the oaths and distributing the diplomas to the students of the university, a hasty messenger arrived announcing the scourge of cholera desolating his diocese. Without a moment's hesitation he broke up the meeting, summoned a notary, made his will, and rode hastily to the stricken town of Albano. He at once assumed control of the municipal as well as religious government of his see, seconded by the Papal Zouaves, and the cholera was at length brought under control. But Altieri was seized himself with the disease, and died Aug. 11, 1867. See (N. Y.) *Catholic Almanac*, 1876, p. 103.

Amalie of Lasaula. See Lisaula.

Ambrose Podobjedow, a Russian ecclesiastic, was born Nov. 30, 1742, in the government of Vladimir. He was educated at the Troiz monastery and took holy orders in 1768. Having been elevated to the bishopric of Sjewsk, he took charge, in 1785, of the Kasan eparchy; was in 1794 elected member of the Holy Synod, and in 1799 made archbishop of St. Petersburg, Esthonia, and Finland. In the year following he received the archepiscopal see of Novgorod, with the appointment as metropolitan, and died May 21 (June 2), 1818. He wrote an ascetical work, in three vols. (Moscow, 1810), and *A Guide to the Reading of the Holy Scriptures* (new ed. ibid. 1840). His most important work, however, is his Russian Church history, *Istoria Rossijskoi Ierarchij* (ibid. 1807–15, 6 vols.; 2d ed. 1827). (B. P.)

American Colleges. See Colleges.

American Wesleyan Methodists. See Wesleyan Methodist Connection of America.

Ammon, Friedrich Wilhelm Philip von, a German theologian, son of Christoph (q. v.), was born Feb. 7, 1791, at Erlangen, where he also studied theology, as well as at Jena. In 1813 he was appointed pastor at Buttenheim, near Bamberg, and in 1820 became archdeacon at Erlangen, where he finally died pastor, doctor, and professor of theology, Sept. 19, 1855. He wrote, *Geiler von Kaisersberg's Leben, Lehren und Predigten* (Erlangen, 1826):—*Denkmal zur dritten Säcularfeier der augsburger Confession* (ibid. 1829):—*Evangelisches Jubelfestbuch zur dritten Säcularfeier der augsburger Confession* (ibid. 1831):—*Gallerie der denkwürdigsten Personen, welche im XVI., XVII. und XVIII. Jahrhunderte von der evangelischen zur katholischen Kirche übergetreten sind* (ibid. 1833). See Zuchold, *Bibl. Theol.* i, 24; Winer, *Handbuch der theol. Lit.* i, 578, 755, 909, 916; ii, 333. (B. P.)

Ammonian Sections are those numerical divisions of the text of the Greek Testament which were introduced by Ammonius of Alexandria into his *Diatessaron*, or harmony of the four gospels, and were retained in the margin of many of the early copies of the gospels as being useful for comparing the parallel accounts. See New Testament.

Anastasy, Bratanowsky, one of the most famous pulpit orators of Russia, was born in 1761, in the neighborhood of Kiev. He studied at the theological school in Perejaslav, became in 1790 a monk, was appointed in 1797 bishop of White Russia, in 1801 archbishop, and in 1805 member of the Holy Synod. He died in 1816, archbishop of Astrachan. He published a collection of religious discourses, in four vols. (St. Petersburg, 1796; Moscow, 1799–1807):—*Tractatus de Concionum Dispositionibus Formandis* (Moscow, 1806). (B. P.)

Ancellon, CHARLES, a French Protestant lawyer, and writer in behalf of political liberty, son of David, was born at Metz, Jan. 28 or 29, 1659. He began his studies there, but prosecuted them at Hanau, and afterwards at Marburg, Geneva, and Paris. After the revocation of the edict of Nantes he represented his co-religionists in their efforts to obtain redress from the government. He retired to Berlin, where he was treated with marked favor, and died there, July 5, 1715. He is the author of a number of historical and political works, for which see Hoefer, *Nouv. Biog. Générale*, s. v.

Anderson, Alexander, LL.D., a Scotch Baptist minister and educator, was born at Peterhead, Aberdeen County, in September, 1808. He studied at St. Andrew's University, was ordained pastor at Boyndie in 1830, joined the Free Church party in 1843, in 1845 was settled over a church in Old Aberdeen, but in 1847 resigned his charge on account of a change of views on the subject of baptism, and took charge of the Chanonry House School, in Aberdeen, to which he joined the pastoral care of a Baptist congregation in George Street Hall, which eventually united with that in Crown Terrace. He died at Aboyne, Oct. 25, 1884. See (Lond.) *Baptist Hand-book*, 1886, p. 101.

Anderson, David, D.D., an English prelate, was born in London, Feb. 10, 1814. He studied at Edinburgh Academy, and graduated from Exeter Hall, Oxford, in 1836. In 1841 he was made vice-principal of St. Bee's College, Cumberland; in 1848 incumbent of All-Saints' Church, Derby; in 1849 was consecrated the first bishop of St. Rupert's Land, but resigned that see on being appointed vicar of Clifton in 1864; in 1866 he was made chancellor of St. Paul's Cathedral, and died in London, Nov. 5, 1885. He was the author of, *Notes on the Flood: — Net in the Bay:* — five *Charges*, and some *Ordination Sermons*.

Anderson, Thomas D., D.D., a Baptist minister, was born in Philadelphia, Pa., June 30, 1819. He removed in early life to Washington, his father holding an office under the government. In 1838 he graduated from the University of Pennsylvania, and in 1841 from the Newton Theological Institution. In 1842 he was ordained pastor of the First Baptist Church at Salem, Mass., in 1848 he became pastor of the First Baptist Church at Roxbury, and in 1862 of the First Baptist Church in New York city. He achieved distinction and success in the difficult field in which he was called to labor. During nearly all his ministry he was officially connected with the American Baptist Missionary Society, the American Baptist Home Missionary Society, and, while in New York, with the American Tract Society. For four years he acted as president of the Rutgers Female College, in New York city. Other important positions in benevolent and educational institutions he also filled. In the summer of 1878 he resigned his charge in New York, and not long after became pastor of the South Church, in Boston, where he died, Dec. 19, 1883. Dr. Anderson published only a few occasional discourses. See Cathcart, *Baptist Encyclop.* s. v. (J. C. S.)

Andreas, ANTONIO, a Spanish Minorite of the 14th century, was one of the most prominent pupils of Duns Scotus, whose method he also adopted. The skill with which he made the more difficult principles of Duns Scotus more simple and intelligible acquired for him, by his students, the surname of *Doctor Dulcifluus*. He died about 1320. See Antonio, *Biblioth. Hispan.* ii, 97; Cave, *Hist. Lit.* append. 12; Stöckl, *Geschichte der Philosophie des Mittelalters*, ii, 875; Grammer, in Wetzer u. Welte's *Kirchenlexikon*, s. v. (B. P.)

Angelis, FILIPPO DE, an Italian canonist, was born at Canterano, near Subiaco, Feb. 10, 1824. He studied philosophy and theology at Rome, and after having received holy orders in 1846, practiced law. When quite young he was made professor of canon law at Rome. In 1871 he resigned his position, and died March 5, 1881. Pope Leo XIII, who appreciated his great talents as a teacher and expounder of canon law, made him canon of Maria Maggiore. He wrote *Prælectiones Juris Canonici ad Methodum Decretalium Gregorii Exactæ* (Rome, 1877–80, 3 vols.). See Streber, in Wetzer u. Welte's *Kirchenlexikon*, s. v. (B. P.)

Angerville (or **Angarvill**, alias **Bury**), RICHARD DE, an English prelate of the 14th century, son of sir Richard Angerville, was born at Bury, Suffolk, and educated at Oxford, where he attained to great eminence in learning; was governor to king Edward III while a prince, and the latter afterwards advanced him to be his cofferer, treasurer of his wardrobe, dean of Wells, bishop of Durham (1333), chancellor, and lord treasurer of England (1334). He was noted for his charities, bestowing on the poor every week eight quarters of wheat baked, and other benefactions. He was a great lover of books, confessing himself "extatico quodam librorum amore potenter abreptum," and he had more books than all the bishops of England in that age put together, which library he bequeathed to the University of Oxford. The most eminent foreigners were his friends, and the most learned Englishmen were his chaplains until his death, April 14, 1345. He wrote *Philobiblos*. See Fuller, *Worthies of England* (ed. Nuttall), iii, 166.

Anglo-Saxon Church. See ENGLAND, CHURCH OF.

Anquetil (*Duperron*), ABRAHAM HYACINTHE, a French Orientalist, brother of Louis, was born at Paris, Dec. 7, 1731. He studied theology at his native place, Auxerre, and Amersfoort, and with the subvention of his government he went, in 1755, to India, to study Sanskrit and Zend there. At Surat he succeeded in obtaining the help of some Parsee priests, who dictated to him in the neo-Persian language the contents of their books written in Zend and Pehlevi. Having returned, in 1762, to Paris, he was appointed interpreter of Oriental languages at the royal library, and published a translation of the Zend-Avesta (Paris, 1771). In 1778 he published, at Amsterdam, the *Legislation Orientale*, which was followed by the publication of *Recherches Historiques et Géographiques sur l'Inde* (Berlin and Paris, 1787, 2 vols.). He also published a Latin translation of a Persian extract from the *Upanishads*, or the theologico-philosophical treatises of the Vedas. He died at Paris, Jan. 17, 1805. (B. P.)

Anselm, a name common to several archbishops OF MILAN, of whom we name the following:

1. ANSELM BILIUS (814–822), who was exiled with other bishops on account of the part he took in the conspiracy of Bernard. He was, however, restored again, and crowned, in 821, king Lothar, at Monza.

2. ANSELM CAPRA (823–897), who crowned, in 888, Berengarius, at Pavia, as king of Italy.

3. ANSELM OF RAUDE (1086–1093), was a faithful adherent of the pope and opponent of Henry IV, and crowned his rebellious son Conrad in 1093.

4. ANSELM VALVASOR (1097–1101), second successor to the former, and also a papal adherent. In 1098 he held a large synod, went to the Holy Land, but returned in 1099. The second time he took the cross to join the crusades, but died at Constantinople.

5. ANSELM OF PUSTERLA (1123–1135), refused to accept the pallium from the hands of Honorius II. He crowned, in 1128, Conrad, the rival of Lothair, in consequence of which he was put under the ban by the pope, together with Conrad. When Anacletus II was elected antipope, Anselm sided with him, and accepted the pallium from the hands of his legate. The legitimate pope replied with an interdict, which only increased the confusion, since Anselm inflicted ecclesiastical punishment upon faithful adherents of the pope. At last the people of Milan expelled Anselm, in 1133, and the council held at Pisa in 1135 confirmed the act of the people of Milan. While on his way to the antipope, Anselm was taken prisoner, and died at Rome, Aug. 24,

1136. See Ughelli, *Italia Sacra*, vol. iv; Scherer, in Wetzer u. Welte's *Kirchenlexikon*, s. v. (B. P.)

Anspach, Frederick Reinhardt, D.D., a Lutheran minister, was born in January, 1815, in Potter Township, Centre Co., Pa. He studied at Mifflinburg Academy, graduating from Pennsylvania College in 1839; subsequently pursued the theological course at Gettysburg, and was licensed to preach in 1841, when he became pastor of the Barren Hill and Whitemarsh charge, Montgomery County; from 1850 to 1854 he was pastor in Hagerstown, Md., and remained there until 1857. He was interested in the founding of the Hagerstown Female Seminary. About this time he became co-editor and proprietor of *The Lutheran Observer*. From 1857 to 1861 his residence was in Baltimore; and subsequently, owing to failing health, he retired from active work and resided principally in Anne Arundel County. He died in Baltimore, Sept. 16, 1867. Among his published works are the following: translations from the German of *Heavenly Balm*, etc., by Caspar Schwenkfeld (1853):—*The Sepulchres of our Departed* (1854):—*The Sons of the Sires* (1855):—a lecture on *Spiritualism* (eod.):—*The Two Pilgrims: The Israelite and the Christian* (1857), etc. See *Pennsylvania College Book*, 1882, p. 204; *Lutheran Observer*, Sept. 27, 1867.

Anstice, Joseph, an English poet, was born at Madeley Wood, Shropshire, in 1808; educated at Westminster and Oxford; in 1830 became professor of classical literature in King's College, London, and died at Torquay, Feb. 29, 1836. Among his productions were a select number of *Hymns* (anonymously published in 1836), several of which are quite popular.

Antioch, Councils of. In addition to those noticed in vol. i, councils were also held at this place in 340, at which the Arian Gregory of Cappadocia was elected to the see of Alexandria; in 360, at which the Arian Miletius of Sebastia was elected patriarch of Antioch; in 391, at which Flavianus anathematized the Massalians; and in 417, at which Pelagius was again condemned.

Antliff, William, D.D., a prominent minister of the English Primitive Methodist Conference, was born in 1813. In his seventeenth year he began to preach. He held nearly all the positions of honor it was in the power of his denomination to bestow. From 1862 to 1867 he was Connectional Editor, and at the request of the conference he wrote an excellent biography of *Hugh Bourne*. He was twice president of the conference. For some time he was principal of the Sunderland Institute. He died in December, 1884. See *Christian Guardian*, Dec. 17, 1884.

Antonius, a Christian poet of the 3d century, is the author of *Carmen Adversus Gentes*, which consists of two parts, the first treating of the vanity of heathenism, the second of the truth of Christianity. The first edition of this poem was published by Muratori, in his *Anecdota*, vol. i (Milan, 1697), and in *Opera S. Paulini* (Verona, 1736), where it is erroneously ascribed to Paulinus of Nola. Other editions are given in Gallandi, *Biblioth.* vol. iii; Migne, *Patrol. Lat.* vol. v. See Schmid, in Wetzer u. Welte's *Kirchenlexikon*, s. v. (B. P.)

Antonius a matre Dei, a name common to two Carmelites.

1. The first lived about the beginning of the 16th century at Alcala, and is the author of *Collegii Complutensis Discalceatorum Fratrum Ordinis B. Mariæ de Monte Carmeli Disputationes, I. In Octo Libros Physicorum Aristotelis; II. In Duos Libros de Generatione et Conceptione seu de Ortu et Interitu; III. In Tres Libros Aristotelis de Anima.* See Hurter, *Nomenclator.* i, 697; Peters, in Wetzer u. Welte's *Kirchenlexikon*, s. v.

2. He lived in the second half of the 17th century, and was professor of theology in the college of his order at Salamanca. He is the author of *Præludia Isagogica ad Sacrorum Bibliorum Intelligentiam*, etc. (Leyden, 1669). See Kaulen, in Wetzer u. Welte's *Kirchenlexikon*, s. v. (B. P.)

Apelt, Ernst Friedrich, a German philosopher, was born March 3, 1812, at Reichenau, near Zittau. He studied at Jena and Leipsic; commenced his lectures at Jena in 1839; was, in 1840, professor of philosophy, and died Oct. 27, 1859. He published, *Metaphysik* (Leipsic, 1857):—*Die Religionsphilosophie* (ibid. 1860):—*Die Epochen der Geschichte der Menschheit* (Jena, 1845–46, 2 vols.; 2d ed. 1852):—*Wie muss das Glaubensbekenntniss beschaffen sein, das zur Vereinigung aller Konfessionen führen soll?* (ibid. 1846). See Zuchold, *Bibl. Theol.* i, 36. (B. P.)

Appearances of our Lord *to his Disciples after the Resurrection.* Professor Gardiner has given a "synopsis of the events, so far as the points of difficulty extend," that relate to Mary Magdalene and the other women, with a view to accommodating the statement in Mark xvi, 9 (that he appeared first to her); and his scheme, if practicable, would be a desirable solution. It is as follows (*Harmony of the Gospels in Greek*, p. 253):

"The resurrection itself occurred at or before the earliest dawn of the first day of the week. The women, coming to the sepulchre, find the stone rolled away and the body gone. They are amazed and perplexed. Mary Magdalene alone runs to tell Peter and John. The other women remain, enter the tomb, see the angels, are charged by them to announce the resurrection to the disciples, and depart on their errand. Meantime Peter and John run very rapidly to the sepulchre. They enter the tomb and are astonished at the orderly arrangement of the grave-clothes, and then return to the city. Mary follows to the tomb, unable quite to keep pace with them, and so falling behind. She remains standing at the entrance after they have gone, and, looking in, sees the angels. Then, turning about, she sees Jesus himself, and receives his charge for the disciples. This was our Lord's first appearance after his resurrection (Mark xvi, 9).

"To return to the women who were on their way from the sepulchre to the disciples. They went in haste, yet more slowly than Peter and John. There were many of them, and, being in a state of great agitation and alarm, they appear to have become separated and to have entered the city by different gates. One party of them, in their astonishment and fear, say nothing to any one; the others run to the disciples and announce all that they had seen, viz. the vision of the angels.

"At this time, before any report had come in of the appearance of our Lord himself, the two disciples set out for Emmaus.

"Soon after, Mary Magdalene comes in, announcing that she had actually seen the risen Lord.

"While these things are happening, the first-mentioned party of the women are stopped on the way by the appearance of the Lord himself, and they also receive a charge to his disciples."

The proper test of this scheme is to tabulate it, allowing a reasonable interval for each incident. It must be borne in mind that all the parties were more or less in haste; and as the entire breadth of the city is but little more than a mile, and the sepulchre was very near the city, fifteen or twenty minutes is sufficient time for any person, under the circumstances, to have passed from any probable point within the city to the sepulchre. Reckoning, therefore, from any fixed point, say four o'clock, the record, on that theory, would stand about as follows:

	A.M.
Resurrection	4:00
The women set out together	4:10
They arrive at the sepulchre	4:30
Mary sets out to return	4:35
The other women set out to return	4:45
Peter and John set out for the sepulchre, on the return of Mary	4:50
They reach the sepulchre	5:00
Some of the other women reach the city, and report	5:00
Peter and John leave after inspecting the tomb	5:10
Mary arrives the second time	5:15
She sees Jesus	5:20
The other party of women see Jesus, but do not report	5:30
Mary arrives and announces her news	5:40

If we can believe that it took any of the women three quarters of an hour to go part of the way back to the city, when it is especially said that "they fled in haste," "departed quickly," under an urgent message, which "they ran" to deliver, we may accept the above scheme, but not otherwise. It should, moreover, be observed that the supposition of a division of their company, and a delay in consequence, are unwarranted by the sacred narratives, which invariably speak of them all together, except Mary. The statement in Mark xvi, 8, that "they said nothing to any man," evidently means "no person whom they met on the way." We are not at liberty to refer the report alluded to by the disciples on the way to Emmaus (Luke xxiv, 22–24) to a single division of the women, for the same evangelist (ver. 10) distinctly includes Mary among those who made it.

The true solution of this problem lies not in any forced harmony of the events, but in a just apprehension of the language of the several evangelists. Matthew mentions in general terms the appearance to the women, including Mary; Mark speaks only of the appearance to Mary as the representative of the whole company of women; Luke (as Paul in 1 Cor. xv, 4–8) does not recognise any appearance to the women at all; John gives the details of the appearance to Mary, but makes no allusion to the other women.

Appelbe, WILLIAM PARKER, LL.D., an Irish Wesleyan minister, was born at Bandon, Nov. 19, 1807. He was educated at Trinity College, Dublin, with a view to the established Episcopal ministry, but on the completion of his course decided to enter the Methodist itinerancy. He was received by the Conference in 1834, and appointed to the Londonderry Circuit. He labored on the most important circuits in the Conference, and was chosen to nearly all the principal offices in the connection, having been twice elected president of the Conference. During the last nine years of his life, in addition to his circuit work, he filled the important office of theological tutor in the college at Belfast, a position for which his learning, culture, and sympathies eminently qualified him. He died at Belfast, June 22, 1882. See *Minutes of the British Conference*, 1882, p. 39.

Appuhn, AUGUST WILHELM, a Lutheran theologian of Germany, was born Oct. 4, 1804. In 1834 he was appointed pastor at Attenhausen, and in 1852 cathedral-preacher and member of consistory at Magdeburg. He retired from the ministry in 1871, and died at Wernigerode, June 6, 1882. He published, *Mose, der Knecht Gottes* (Magdeburg, 1845):—*Festpredigten* (ibid. 1857): *Entwürfe zu Predigten an den Festen und Festzeiten* (ibid. 1876). See Zuchold, *Bibl. Theol.* i, 37. (B. P.)

Araujo, a name common to some theologians of the Society of Jesus:

1. ALPHONSO (or ILDEFONSO DE PEÑAFIEL), was born at Riobambo, in Peru (now Ecuador), in 1594. He joined his order in 1610, was professor of theology and philosophy at Cusco and Lima, and died at Guanca-Velica, Nov. 18, 1657. He wrote, *Cursus Integri Philosophici* (Leyden, 1653–70, 4 vols.):—*Theologia Scholastica Naturalis*, etc. (ibid. 1666, 2 vols.).

2. JOSEPH, was born at Oporto, in Portugal, Oct. 10, 1696. In 1712 he joined his order, was professor at Coimbra, Oporto, and Lisbon, and died in 1759. He wrote *Cursus Theologicus* (Lisbon, 1734–37, 2 vols.). See Bauer, in Wetzer u. Welte's *Kirchenlexikon*, s. v. (B. P.)

Arbues, PEDRO, a Spanish inquisitor, was born at Epila, in Aragon, in 1442. He studied at Huesca and Bologna, and was, in 1471, professor of moral philosophy at the latter place. In 1473 he was made doctor of theology and in 1474 canon of Saragossa. After having returned to his native place, he joined, in 1476, the order of the Augustinians, and in the following year received holy orders. As a preacher he attracted large crowds, and as an instructor of the young clergy was very successful. In 1484 he was appointed, together with the Dominican, Caspar Juglar, inquisitor of Aragon. This appointment was made by the grand-inquisitor Torquemada. With cruel fanaticism Arbues executed the orders of his chief, and many Jews and Moors were delivered to the stake. Among the relatives of his many sacrifices a conspiracy was effected and murderers were hired to kill all members of the inquisition. In the night of Sept. 14th, 1485, Arbues, while kneeling at the altar, received a deadly blow, and died on the 17th of that month. His murderers, together with many of the conspirators, had to pay the penalty of their deed. In the Romish Church Arbues is celebrated as a martyr. Pope Alexander VII pronounced him blessed in 1661, while Pius IX canonized him in 1867. The famous Kaulbach painted, in 1871, a picture, on which Arbues is represented as condemning heretics to death. See Zirngiebl, *Peter Arbues und die spanische Inquisition* (3d ed. Munich, 1872). (B. P.)

Arevalo, RODRIGUES SANCHEZ DE, a Spanish bishop, was born at St. Maria de Nieva, in the diocese of Segovia, in 1404. He studied law at Salamanca, and the kings, John II and Henry IV of Castile, whose secretary he was, made use of his talents on several occasions. When, in 1455, he was sent to Rome to bring to pope Calixtus III the congratulations of his monarch, he was made bishop of Oviedo. Under Paul II he occupied the episcopal see of Zamora, next of Calahorra, and finally that of Palencia. He died Oct. 4, 1470. Most of his works are still in MS. in the Vatican Library; only three have been published, *Speculum Vitæ Humanæ* (Rome, 1468):—*Historia Hispanica*, giving the history from the earliest times to the year 1469 (ibid. 1470):—*De Monarchia Orbis et de Origine et Differentia Principatus Imperialis et Regalis* (ibid. 1521). See *Biog. Générale*, xliii, 249 sq.; Hamberger, *Zuverlässige Nachrichten*, iv, 800 sq.; Stansnik, in Wetzer u. Welte's *Kirchenlexikon*, s. v. (B. P.)

Arius (usually pronounced *A'rius*, but strictly *Arīus*, Ἄρειος, meaning *martial*), the famous heresiarch, was born about A.D. 256 in North Africa (Cyrenaica, Lybia, or Egypt), but nothing is known of his early life or circumstances. He is said to have been educated by Lucian, a presbyter in Antioch, and ordained deacon by Peter of Alexandria and elder by Achillas, Peter's successor, who placed him (A.D. 313) in charge of Baucalis, one of the great churches of Alexandria. On the death of this bishop he came near being elected to the see, such was his popularity, but was defeated by Alexander, through envy of whom (as Theodoret asserts, *Hist. Eccles.* i, 2) he began, about A.D. 318, a controversy respecting the nature of Christ, which ultimately involved the whole of Christendom. See ARIANISM. Arius had previously fallen under censure for connection with the schism of Meletius, but in some way had been restored to favor. He was now excommunicated for heresy by a council held at Alexandria in 321, and his views formally condemned by the Council of Nicæa in 325. Constantine banished him to Illyria, but in 331 he recalled him through the intercession of his sister, Constantia, and Eusebius of Nicomedia. Athanasius, however, refused to recognise the heretic. In 336 Athanasius himself was banished to Treves, and Arius, after a personal interview with the emperor, was about to be received in full honor at Alexandria, when he suddenly died of a disease of the bowels, apparently a violent attack of dysentery, which his enemies attributed to the visitation of God and his friends to the effect of poison. His views are but the outcropping of the earlier errors of Cerinthus and the Gnostics, now put into a definite shape by the virtual denial of the divinity of our Lord. Arius was evidently a man of much acuteness, but little depth of intellect, and of a controversial turn. No charge of immorality was ever alleged against him. He is said to have been tall in person, easy and eloquent in manner, but austere in habits. The representation of him in the recent romance, entitled *Arius the Lybian* (New York, 1883), is lively but somewhat too favorable.

Armistead, JESSE H., D.D., a Presbyterian minister, was educated at Hampden-Sidney College and the Union Theological Seminary of Virginia. He was licensed to preach in 1826, when he is thought to have been twenty-eight years of age. His first fields of labor were at Cartersville and the Brick Church at Fluvianna; in 1828 he became pastor at Buckingham Courthouse, and in 1842 at Cumberland. He died at Woodville, Va., May 30, 1869. He was eminently useful, and his ministry was blessed with powerful revivals. See Nevin, *Presbyterian Encyclop.* s. v.

Arms, HIRAM PHELPS, D.D., a Congregational minister, was born at Windsor, Conn., June 1, 1799. He studied at Phillips Academy, Andover; graduated from Yale College in 1824, and from Yale Divinity School in 1828; was ordained June 30, 1830, pastor at Hebron, where he remained until Oct. 10, 1832; in February, 1833, became pastor at Walcotville; in 1836 of the First Church, Norwich, of which he remained pastor emeritus from the time of his resignation, Feb. 20, 1873. He died at Norwich, April 6, 1882. From 1866 he was a member of the corporation of Yale College. Besides several published sermons, he was the author of a pamphlet, *Notes of the Congregational Churches in New London County, Conn., from* 1836 *to* 1869. See *Cong. Year-book*, 1883, p. 17.

Arnold OF BONNEVAL, a Benedictine writer of the 12th century, was, in 1144, appointed abbot of Bonneval, in the diocese of Chartres. Like his predecessors he had to undergo many trials. His appeal to pope Lucius II was of no avail, and he went to Rome a second time, where he succeeded, in 1154, in receiving the permission of pope Hadrian IV to resign. He died at Marmoutiers, where he had retired. Arnold enjoyed the friendship of St. Bernard, who, on his death-bed, sent a letter full of expressions of love for Arnold. After St. Bernard's death the monks of Clairvaux requested Arnold to continue the life of the saint, which William of Thierry had commenced to write. Thus the *Vita Secunda S. Bernardi* (Migne, *Pat. Lat.* clxxxv, 267 sq.), which is erroneously ascribed to a Cistercian Arnold (comp. Oudin, *Script. Eccles.* ii, 1293), originated. Arnold also wrote a speculative treatise on the *Hexæmeron:—Homilies on the* 132*d Psalm:*—a book entitled *De Donis Spiritus S.:—De Septem Verbis Domini in Cruce:—Meditationes*, and *De Cardinalibus Operibus Christi.* It is remarkable that the latter work, which was dedicated to pope Hadrian IV, was regarded for a long time as a work of St. Cyprian, and was published by Pamelius in his edition of Cyprian (Amsterdam, 1568). Arnold's works are published by Migne, *Pat. Lat.* clxxxix (1513). See Streber, in Wetzer u. Welte's *Kirchenlexikon*, s. v. (B. P.)

Arnold, Albert Nicholas, D.D., a Baptist minister, was born at Cranston, R. I., Feb. 12, 1814. He graduated from Brown University in 1838, and from the Newton Theological Institution in 1841; was ordained pastor at Newburyport, Mass., Sept. 14, 1841; in 1843 appointed a missionary to Greece, and stationed successively at Athens and in the island of Corfu. For eleven years he was engaged in his missionary work, and then returned to the United States. For two years he was a professor at Newton, for seven years pastor of the Church at Westborough, Mass., for five years professor in the Hamilton Theological Institution, and for four years professor in the Chicago Theological Seminary. In 1878 he returned to his early home, near Providence, R. I., where he died, Oct. 11, 1883. See *Rhode Island Biog. Encyclop.* s. v. (J. C. S.)

Arnold, John Motte, D.D., a Methodist Episcopal minister, was born at Acra, Greene Co., N. Y., Oct. 15, 1824. He was converted early in life, and in 1848 joined the Michigan Conference, in which he was successively pastor at Port Huron, St. Clair, Flint, Coruna, presiding elder of Owasso District, pastor at Dexter, Woodward Avenue, in Detroit, and Walnut Street, in the same city. In 1863 he was placed in charge of the Detroit Methodist Book Depository, and later of the *Michigan Christian Advocate.* He died suddenly in Detroit, Dec. 5, 1884. See *Minutes of Annual Conferences*, 1885, p. 331.

Arnot, ROBERT, D.D., a Scotch clergyman, was licensed to preach in 1769; presented to the living of Ceres in 1770; elected presbytery clerk in 1777; resigned in 1792; was appointed professor of divinity in the new college of St. Andrews in 1799; minister of Kingsbarns in 1800, but opposed on account of already holding one important office; the General Assembly of 1800 approved of the double appointment. He died July 2, 1808, aged sixty-three years. See *Fasti Eccles. Scoticanæ*, ii, 444, 478.

Arnpeck, VEIT, a Bavarian historian, was born about the year 1440 at Landshut. He studied at Amberg and Vienna, was for some time pastor of St. Martin's, in his native city, and died about the year 1505. He is the author of, *Chronicon Austriacum* to the year 1488 (reprinted by Pez, *Script. rer. Austr.* i, 1165):—*Liber de Gestis Episcoporum Frisingens.* (reprinted by Deutinger, in *Beiträge zur Geschichte des Erzbisthums München-Freisingen*, vol. iii):—*Chronicon Baivariæ*, 539–1495 (reprinted by Pez, *Thesaurus*, iii, 2, 19 sq.). See Aretin, *Literarisches Handbuch für die bayer'sche Geschichte*, i, 154; Pertz, *Archiv.* i, 487; iv, 553; *Deutsche Biographie*, i, 596; Wetzer u. Welte's *Kirchenlexikon*, s. v. (B. P.)

Arras (in France), COUNCIL OF (*Concilium Attrebatense*, from the Atrebati, who were the original inhabitants of that region), was held in the year 1025, chiefly upon the subject of the holy communion, against certain heretics who had come from Italy. Seventeen chapters were published.—Landon, *Manual of Councils*, s. v.

Arthur, WILLIAM, D.D., a Baptist minister, father of the recent president of the United States, was born in County Antrim, Ireland, being by descent Scotch-Irish, and was a graduate of Belfast College. In his eighteenth year he came to America, and subsequently entered the Baptist ministry. For about eight years he was pastor of the Calvary Church, New York city; afterwards of several churches in Vermont, and then of churches in the state of New York, among them those in Schenectady, Lansingburg, West Troy, and Newtonville. In the last-named place he died, in October, 1875. He is spoken of as "an author of extensive learning, and a minister of great usefulness and piety." See Cathcart, *Baptist Encyclop.* p. 1291. (J. C. S.)

Articles, IRISH. The articles of religion of the Protestant Church of Ireland, numbering one hundred and four, were probably drawn up by archbishop Usher, and adopted by the Irish Episcopal Church in 1615. They are in striking agreement with the Westminster Confession, and may be found in Schaff, *Creeds of Christendom*, i, 662; comp. iii, 526. They were ignored, however, by the Irish convocation of 1635, and the thirty-nine articles of the English Church have ever since been the standard of the Irish Church also.

Aschbach, JOSEPH, a Roman Catholic historian of Germany, was born in 1801 at Höchst. He studied at Heidelberg, was in 1823 professor of the gymnasium in Frankfort-on-the-Main, in 1842 professor of history at Bonn, and in 1854 at Vienna. He died, April 25, 1882. He is best known as the editor of *Allgemeines Kirchenlexikon* (1846–50, 4 vols.), to which he contributed largely. (B. P.)

Assamese Version. Assam is a British province, now forming part of the eastern frontier of India. The original language of the Assamese nation was the Ahom, a branch of the Siamese family of languages. When the people adopted the religion of Bengal in the middle of the 17th century, they also gradually habituated themselves to the use of its language, till at length the ancient Ahom tongue became extinct. During the lapse of years the language now spoken in Assam has contracted several peculiarities of its own, distinguishing it from the Bengalee, so that in printing the Scriptures it was found impracticable to use the Bengalee characters, and a new font of type had to be cast for that purpose. In 1815 the first two gospels were printed at Serampore, while the whole New Test. was finished at press in 1819, with the title *The New Testament Translated from the Original into the Assam Language by the Serampore Missionaries.* In 1822 the Pentateuch left the press, and the printing of the entire Old Test. was subsequently completed. The annual report of the British and Foreign Bible Society for 1863 stated that "preparations are being made for revision;" but how far the work has progressed we are unable to state. For the study of the language, see Brown, *Grammatical Notices on the Assamese Language* (Sibsagor, 1848). (B. P.)

Asseburg, ROSAMUNDE JULIANE VON, a German visionary, was born in November, 1672, at Eigenstedt, near Magdeburg. According to her own statement, she had visions at different times. When seven years of age she saw the Saviour, who told her of his sufferings and the future of his kingdom. The news concerning the visionary soon reached Magdeburg, and Pfeiffer, a young theologian of Lauenburg, sought the opportunity of becoming acquainted with Fräulein Asseburg. Pfeiffer wrote to Petersen concerning the visionary, and the latter, after some correspondence, in company with his wife paid a visit to her. As the result of his visit he published *Species facti von dem adeligen Fräulein Rosamunda Juliana von Asseburg*, with an appendix (1691). This was intended as an address to the most prominent theologians, in order to ascertain whether they accepted the revelations of Rosamunde as divine inspirations or not. Some assented, others violently opposed. Spener, whose opinion was asked, was too cautious to commit himself in any way. Meanwhile Fräulein Asseburg's name became known in France, England, and Denmark. The consistory, however, at the instance of the preachers of Lüneburg, who accused Petersen because he allowed the visionary to stay at his house, took the matter into consideration, and in accordance with a decision of the theological faculty at Helmstädt, deposed Petersen, in 1692, from his office, and banished him from the country. With this verdict, an opinion was publicly pronounced upon Fräulein Asseburg, who accompanied her friend first to Wolfenbüttel, then to Magdeburg. From Magdeburg she went to Berlin, where she lived in the house of a countess. In 1708 she saw once more her friend Petersen at Berlin, but after this she rapidly lost her prestige, and sank into oblivion. Not even the date of her death is known. The famous Leibnitz defended her moral and religious character, and as to her visions he compared her to Brigitta, Hildegard, and Melchthildis, who were regarded as saints among the more faithful of the Middle Ages. See Petersen, *Autobiography* (2d ed. 1719); Bertram, *Reformations- und Kirchenhistorie Lüneburgs* (Braunschweig, eod.); Planck, *Geschichte der protest. Theologie von der Konkordienformel an bis in die Mitte des* 18. *Jahrhunderts* (Göttingen, 1831), p. 248 sq.; Barthold, *Die Erweckten im protestantischen Deutschland*, in Raumer's *Histor. Taschenbuch* (1852); Dibelius, in Herzog-Plitt's *Real-Encyklop.* s. v. (B. P.)

Assemani, is the Italian form of the name of a learned Maronite family; namely, GIUSEPPE SIMONE, the head of it, STEFANO EVODIO, and GIUSEPPE LUIGI (in Lat. *Aloysius*, born about 1710), two of his nephews, and his grandnephew SIMONE, who was born March 14, 1749, at Tripoli. He was educated in the Maronite College at Rome, and after completing his studies spent twelve years as a missionary in his native country, and then went to Padua as teacher of Oriental languages, where he died, April 7, 1821. He wrote a famous work *On the Civilization, Literature, and Manners of the Arabs* (Padua, 1787). See Wetzer u. Welte's *Kirchenlexikon*, s. v. (B. P.)

Athune, JAMES, D.D., a Scotch clergyman, son of a commissary of Orkney, was born at Kirkwall in 1613; took his degree of M.A. at the Edinburgh University in 1636; studied divinity at Oxford in 1637; was chaplain to the marquis of Hamilton in 1638; presented by the king to the living of Birsay in 1642; deposed in 1649, and for taking part with the marquis of Montrose in 1650 he was excommunicated. He fled to Holland in 1653, afterwards returned to Edinburgh, and lived privately till 1660. Parliament granted him £100 for his sufferings. On visiting London he was collated by Brian Walton, bishop of Winchester, to the living of Winnifrith; was appointed minister at Elgin in 1677; elected bishop of Moray the same year; consecrated in 1679; transferred to the see of Galloway in 1680, and died Nov. 15, 1687. He made a bold stand in Parliament, in 1686, against rescinding the penal statutes respecting popery. See *Fasti Eccles. Scoticanæ*, iii, 392–452, 778.

Atkinson, JOHN MAYO PLEASANT, D.D., a Presbyterian minister, was born at Mansfield, Va., Jan. 10, 1817. He graduated from Hampden-Sidney College in 1835, and from the Virginia Union Theological Seminary; was ordained as an evangelist, and became a stated supply of the Church in Houston, Texas; was afterwards installed pastor at Warrenton and Salem, Va. In 1850 he was installed pastor of Bridge Street Church, Georgetown, D. C. In 1857 he was elected president of Hampden-Sidney College, and continued in that position until near the date of his death, Aug. 25, 1883. His life was full of good deeds, generous impulses, and Christian sacrifice. See *Necrol. Report of Princeton Alumni*, 1884, p. 26. (W. P. S.)

Attigny, COUNCIL OF (*additional*), held in May, 870, at which Charles the Bold brought his son Carloman to judgment, and Hincmar of Laon was compelled to submit to royal and ecclesiastical authority. See Landon, *Manual of Councils*, s. v.

Atwater, LYMAN HOTCHKISS, D.D., LL.D., an eminent Presbyterian divine, was born at Cedar Hill (now in New Haven), Conn., Feb. 23, 1813. He graduated from Yale College in 1831, spent the ensuing year at the head of the classical department of Mount Hope Institute, Baltimore, Md., and then entered Yale Divinity School. At the end of the first year he was appointed tutor of mathematics in Yale College, where he remained two years, continuing his theological studies. He was licensed to preach in 1834, and became pastor of the First Church in Fairfield, Conn., where he remained twenty years. In 1854 he was appointed professor of intellectual and moral philosophy in Princeton College, which position he substantially held until the close of his life, Feb. 17, 1883. In 1861 he was appointed to the lectureship extraordinary in Princeton Theological Seminary, which office he held for five years. He was a member of the joint committee on the subject of the reunion of the old and new school branches of the Presbyterian Church. He was acting president of Princeton College from the retirement of Dr. McLean to the inauguration of Dr. McCosh. He was a voluminous writer, especially for the reviews, and became editor of the *Princeton Review*, which position he held until it was united with the *Presbyterian Review*. His contributions greatly exceeded those of any other man, beginning, in 1840, with his well-known essay on *The Power of Contrary Choice.* Many of his articles have been republished in this country and in Europe. He was held in the highest esteem by his colleagues, and was very popular with the students. See *Necrol. Report of Princeton Alumni*, 1883, p. 8; Nevin, *Presb. Encyclop.* s. v. (W. P. S.)

Auber, *Miss* Harriet, an English poetess, was born in London, Jan. 20, 1773. She lived a long but retired life, and died at Hoddesdon, Hertshire, Jan. 20, 1862. Of her poetry only a single volume was published, entitled *The Spirit of the Psalms* (anonymously, 1829), containing some selected pieces, but much original matter of great value, which has been largely adopted in modern hymnals.

Auburn Declaration, a popular designation of the "Exscinding Act," passed in that city (N. Y.) against the churches in the western part of the state as non-Presbyterian, for failing to come up to the higher Calvinistic theology assumed in the document. It has been practically a dead-letter. For its text, see Schaff, *Creeds of Christendom*, ii, 777.

Aufsess, Jobst Bernhard von, dean of Bamberg and Würzburg, was born March 28, 1671, at Mengersdorf, in Franconia. He was baptized in the Lutheran Church, but through the influence of his uncle, Carl Sigismund, dean of Bamberg and Würzburg, he was brought up in the Roman Catholic faith. From 1683 to 1690 he was educated at the seminary in Würzburg, was in 1695 dean of Bamberg, and in 1714 he received besides the deanery of Würzburg. In 1723 he was also appointed provost of St. Stephen at Bamberg. He died April 2, 1738. He founded the famous seminary at Bamberg. See *Archiv für Geschichte von Oberfranken*, vol. i in 1838; vol. x in 1866; *Refutation in Sachen der katholischen Barone von Aufsess* (Bamberg, 1739); Gutenäcker, *Gesch. des Freiherrn v. aufsessischen Studienseminars* (ibid. 1866); Weber, *Das Aufsessische Seminar* (ibid. 1880); Wittmann, in Wetzer u. Welte's *Kirchenlexikon*, s. v. (B. P.)

Augustine, *Sister*. See Lisaulx.

Aurelian (fully Lucius Domitius Valerianus Aurelianus), Roman emperor, was born about A.D. 212, at Sirmium, in Pannonia, or, according to some, in Dacia or Mœsia, of very humble parentage. He gradually rose as a soldier under Claudius, whom he succeeded in August, 270, by the proclamation of the legions. He reigned until March, 275, with great military vigor, subduing Zenobia and the other Oriental powers. His civil administration, however, was harsh, and he is said to have been a persecutor of the Christians. See Smith, *Dict. of Class. Biog.* s. v.

Austin, Thomas Ralph, LL.D., a Protestant Episcopal minister, was born in London, June 16, 1810. He graduated from Oxford, was ordained in England, and then came to America, but in 1833 returned and studied medicine. Once more coming to America, he settled in Indiana. During the late civil war he was commissioned as a surgeon in the army. At its close he preached at Terre Haute and Jeffersonville, and was fifteen years rector of St. James's Church, Vincennes, where he died, Feb. 6, 1884.

Autun Inscription. One of the most remarkable Christian epigraphs was found in 1839 in the cemetery St. Pierre l'Estrier, near Autun, where the Christians, during the persecutions, used to hold divine service. The plate, consisting of eight pieces, contains a metric inscription in Greek. It originally was attached to a wall or a tomb. According to Garucci (with additions and corrections placed within brackets) the inscription reads thus:

'Ιχθύος ο[ὐρανίου θε]ῖον γένος, ἤτορι σεμνῷ
  Χρῆσε, λαβὼ[ν πηγὴ]ν ἄμβροτον ἐν βροτέοις.
Θεσπεσίων ὑδάτ[ω]ν. τήν σήν, φίλε, θάλπεο ψυχ[ην]
  Ὕδασιν ἀενάοις πλουτοδότου σοφίης.
Σωτῆρος ἁγίων μελιηδέα λάμβαν[ε βρῶσιν],
  Ἔσθιε πινάων, ἰχθὺν ἔχων παλάμαις.
'Ιχθύϊ χό[ρταζ'] ἄρα, λιλάιω, δέσποτα σῶτ[ερ],
Εὖ εὕδοι μ[ή]τηρ, σε λιτάζομε, φῶς τὸ θανόντων.
'Ασχάνδιε [πάτ]ερ, τώμῳ κε[χα]ρισμένε θυμῷ,
Σὺν μ[ητρὶ γλυκερῇ καὶ ἀδελφει]οῖσιν ἐμοῖσιν,
'Ι[χθύος εἰρίγνῃ σέο] μνήσεο Πεκτορίουο.

"The heavenly Ichthys' divine race, a pure heart
Keep, having received among mortals the immortal fount
Of divine waters. Refresh, O friend, thy soul
With the ever-flowing water of riches-giving wisdom.
The honey-sweet meat of the saints' Saviour receive,
Eat with hunger, the Ichthys holding in the hands.
With the Ichthys satisfy then, I long, my Lord Saviour.
Sweet rest to the mother, I entreat thee, light of the dead!
Aschandios, O dearest father to my heart,
With the best mother and my brethren,
In the peace of Ichthys remember thy Pectorios!"

It is not improbable that the first part, containing six verses, belongs to another author, as may be seen from the language of that part in opposition to that of the other. According to the character of the writing, the epigraph belongs to the 4th, if not to the 5th, century. For the meaning of *Ichthys*, see that article. The first two lines are a clear testimony of the divinity of Christ. Pohl suggests that the first six lines contain an ancient liturgical formula from the time of Irenæus, which perhaps was used at the celebration of the eucharist. The rest contains a prayer of Pectorios for the soul of his deceased mother, and a petition that she, in connection with the father and brethren, may remember the living son. See Le Blant, *Inscr. Chrét. de la Gaule*, vol. i, p. 9, pl. 1, n. 1; Rossignol, *Revue Archéol.* (1856), xiii, 65, 491; Garucci, *Mél. d'Épigr. Anc.* p. 32; Kirchhoff, *Corp. Inscr. Gr.* iv, 9890; Becker, *Die Darstellung Jesu Christi unter dem Bilde des Fisches* (Breslau, 1866); Marriot, *The Testimony of the Catacombs* (Lond. 1870), p. 114, 214; Pohl, *Das Ichthys-Monument von Autun* (Berlin, 1880); Heuser, in Kraus's *Real-Encyklop. der christl. Alterthümer*, p. 524; Klein, in Wetzer u. Welte's *Kirchenlexikon*, s. v. (B. P.)

Avancinus, Nicholas, a Jesuit, was born at Tyrol in 1612. At the age of fifteen he joined the order at Graz. For about ten years he lectured on ethics and scholastic theology at Vienna, was then appointed rector of the colleges of Passau, Vienna, and Graz, and in 1676 he was made provincial of the order in Austria and visitor of Bohemia. He died Dec. 6, 1686. His main work is *Vita et Doctrina Jesu Christi ex Quatuor Evangelistis Collecta* (Vienna, 1665), which has repeatedly been reprinted (best edition by Westhoff, 1844), and translated into German by Feichtenleine (Augsburg, 1820), Wittmann (ibid. 1822; 2d ed. 1834), by a Catholic priest (Munich, 1850; 3d ed. 1860), by Zollner (Regensburg, 1867), Dötsch (ibid. 1871), Ecker (Freiburg, 1877), also into Polish. See Sotwell, *Bibl. Script. S. J.*; Stöger, *Scriptores Provinciæ Austriacæ S. J.*; Backer, i, 329–334; iii, 1932; Cornely, in Wetzer u. Welte's *Kirchenlexikon*, s. v.; Zuchold, *Bibl. Theol.* i, 58. (B. P.)

Aveling, Thomas William Baxter, D.D., an English Dissenting minister, was born at Castletown, Isle of Man, May 11, 1815. He was educated by a kind guardian, joined the Independent Church at Wisbeck when sixteen years of age, at nineteen began to preach in the neighborhood, graduated from Highbury College in 1838, entered upon his ministry the same year at Kingsland, near London, and continued there until his death, July 3, 1884. Dr. Aveling was for many years the honorable secretary of the Asylum for Fatherless Children at Reedham, travelled in Italy, Egypt, and Syria, visited America more than once, was chairman of the Congregational Board in 1873, and in 1874 of the Congregational Union. He published, *Naaman:—The New Year's Party:—The Irish Scholar:—Voices on Many Waters:—Memorials of the Clayton Family:*—besides addresses and poems, and for five years edited the *Jewish Herald*. See (Lond.) *Cong. Year-book*, 1885, p. 176.

Avery, Benjamin, LL.D., an English Presbyterian, and an accomplished scholar, was educated for the ministry in England and Holland. He was chosen assistant pastor at the Bartholomew Close Church, under Thomas Freke, afterwards under John Munckley. He died at an advanced age, July 23, 1764. In 1713 he published a *Sermon on Mic. vi*, 5, preached on Nov. 4 of that year. He took part in the Dissenting Synod at Salter's Hall in 1719, and took sides with the non-subscribing ministers. He was a warm friend to religious liberty and to the advancement of learning. He resigned the ministry in 1720, was chosen secretary of deputies from the three denominations in 1732, began to practice medicine, was one of the physicians of Guy's Hospital, and one of the writers in the *Occasional Paper* published in 1716. See Wilson, *Dissenting Churches*, iii, 381–383.

Ayrault, WALTER, D.D., a Protestant Episcopal clergyman, was born at Geneva, N. Y., Nov. 28, 1822. He graduated from Hobart College in 1840, was ordained deacon in 1846, and presbyter in 1847; settled at Hagerstown, Md., in 1853; at Canandaigua, N. Y., in 1856; at Genesee in 1862, at Oxford in 1865, and in 1875 became chaplain in Hobart College, where he died, Oct. 19, 1882.

Azaria, ARISTACES, an Armenian Catholic general-abbot and archbishop, was born at Constantinople, July 18, 1782. At the age of fifteen he went to Rome to be educated there at the College of the Propaganda. When the French entered Rome, in 1798, he had to leave the city. At Venice and Trieste he was kindly received by the Mechitarists, whom he joined March 25, 1801, exchanging his name Joseph for Aristaces. In 1802 he made his vows, and in 1803 he received holy orders. The peace of Presburg connected Trieste with the kingdom of Illyria, and the new government persecuted the Mechitarists as Austrian subjects and confiscated their property. At last, in 1810, the congregation was permitted to settle in Vienna with the injunction to take care entirely of itself. In 1816 Azaria was made vartabed, i. e. doctor, by the general-abbot Adeodat. He then went to Rome, and from thence to Constantinople, where he labored in behalf of his Church. In 1821 he returned home again. In 1822 he went again to Rome, was appointed assistant to Adeodat, and succeeded him after his death, in 1825, as general-vicar and superior, and in 1826 as general-abbot. In 1827 Leo XII appointed him archbishop of Cæsarea. Under his guidance his congregation was soon in a flourishing state. He founded schools and propagated Armenian literature, to which he also contributed. He died at Vienna, May 6, 1854. See Hurter, *Aus dem Leben des hochw. Herrn Aristaces Azaria* (Vienna, 1855); Brunner, *Wiener Kirchenzeitung*, 1855, No. 91; Hergenroether, in Wetzer u. Welte's *Kirchenlexikon*, s. v. (B. P.)

Azpilcueta, MARTIN, a canonist of the 16th century, was born Dec. 13, 1493. He studied at Alcala and Toulouse, and commenced his lectures in 1520 at Cahors. For fourteen years he lectured at Salamanca with such success that king John III de Portugal called him, in 1544, to the newly founded university at Coimbra, where he remained sixteen years. He defended the Toledan archbishop Bartholomeo de Carranga-Miranda before the tribunal of the inquisition at Valladolid, and afterwards at Rome, in 1557, where he also died, June 21, 1586. His *Consilia et Responsa* were published (Lugd. 1594, 2 vols.); his other works (ibid. 1595, 3 vols.). See Scherer, in Wetzer u. Welte's *Kirchenlexikon*, s. v. (B. P.)

B.

Bachmann, PAUL, a German controversialist, was born at Chemnitz about 1466. He joined the Cistercians, and was abbot of Altenzelle from 1522 to 1535. In connection with Cochlæus, Emser, Peter Forst, and Augustin von Alveldt, he opposed the Lutheran Reformation in Saxony. He tried to reform monastic life, but could not prevent many of his co-religionists from going over to the Church of the Reformation. He wrote against Luther, but was answered in a satire, written after the manner of the *Epistol. Obscur. Virorum*, entitled *Mors et Sepultura Doctrinæ Lutheranæ*, reprinted in Strobel, *Opuscula Quædam Satirica et Ludicra Tempore Reform. Scripta* (1784), Fasc. i, 49 sq. See Streber, in Wetzer u. Welte's *Kirchenlexikon*, s. v. (B. P.)

Backus, JOHN CHESTER, D.D., LL.D., a Presbyterian minister, was born at Wethersfield, Conn., Sept. 5, 1810. He studied at Albany Academy, spent two years at Columbia College, and graduated from Yale College in 1830; studied law one year, and theology one year at New Haven, joining the Congregational Church there in the meantime; spent part of a year at Andover Theological Seminary; graduated from Princeton Theological Seminary in 1835; was licensed to preach the same year, and ordained the next, serving meanwhile as assistant secretary of the Board of Domestic Missions. On Sept. 16, 1836, he became pastor of the First Presbyterian Church at Baltimore, Md., and remained there until his death, April 9, 1884, having been pastor emeritus from October, 1875. His talents were of a high order, and few had greater influence in the Church. See *Necrol. Report of Princeton Theol. Sem.* 1885, p. 21.

Bacon (de Baccone, or Bachone), FRANCISCO, a Spanish theologian, was born at Gerona, or at Peralada, in Catalonia. He joined the Carmelites of his native country, studied at Paris, where he also lectured on theology. He is known by the name of *doctor sublimis*. He also became provincial of his order in Catalonia, and died at the monastery of Camprodon, Aug. 8, 1372. He wrote, *Commentarius super Sentent. I*, 4:—*Repertorium Prædicantium*. See Schmidt, in Wetzer u. Welte's *Kirchenlexikon*, s. v. (B. P.)

Baird, GEORGE, D.D., a Scotch clergyman, was born at Inveravon in 1762; licensed to preach in 1786; presented to the living of Dunkeld in 1787, and took his M.A. degree the same year; was transferred to the New Greyfriar's Church, Edinburgh, in 1792; transferred to the New North Church in 1798; held in conjunction the principalship of the university in 1799; was transferred to the High Church in 1801, and died Jan. 14, 1840. At his suggestion the General Assembly, in 1824, formed a committee for extending education and religious instruction, especially in the Highlands and islands of Scotland. He devoted much time and money to this work, and travelled seven thousand miles in furtherance of the benevolent scheme. See *Fasti Eccles. Scoticanæ*, i, 30, 69, 71; ii, 785, 786.

Baker, *Sir* **Henry Williams**, an English clergyman and poet, was born in London, May 21, 1821, being the son of a baronet. He graduated from Trinity College, Cambridge, in 1844; was ordained deacon the same year, presbyter in 1846, became vicar of Monkland, Herefordshire, in 1851, and died there, Feb. 11, 1877. Besides writing some essays, he was one of the editors of *Hymns Ancient and Modern* (Lond. 1861, 1868, 1874), which contains several of his own composition.

Baker, William Mumford, D.D., a Presbyterian minister, was born in Washington, D. C., June 5, 1825. He joined the Church at sixteen, graduated from the College of New Jersey in 1846, and after studying theology with his father one year, and in Princeton Seminary another year, he was licensed to preach in 1848; became stated supply at Batesville, Ark., in 1849; evangelist at Little Rock in 1850; served as pastor at Austin, Tex., for fifteen years, with some interruption during the war; at Zanesville, O., from 1866 to 1872, afterwards in Boston, Mass., and finally in Philadelphia, Pa., from November, 1881, to February, 1883. He died at South Boston, Mass., Aug. 20 of the last-named year. Dr. Baker was well known by his numerous publications, among which were, *Inside, a Chronicle of Secession*:—*The New Timothy*:—*The Virginians in Texas*:—*His Majesty Myself*. His last pulpit labors were in the Presbyterian Church, South Boston. Although, in addition to his numerous books, he contributed largely to journals and magazines, he always made his literary labors incidental and subordinate to his pastoral duties. He was a man of brilliant mind and untiring energy. See *Necrol. Report of Princeton Theol. Sem.* 1884, p. 35.

Ballandre, Pierre Simon, a French mystical philosopher, was born at Lyons, Aug. 4, 1776; became a printer and proprietor of the *Bulletin*, in that city, and died in Paris, Aug. 7, 1847. He wrote a number of religious and other works, for which see Hoefer, *Nouv. Biog. Générale*, s. v.; Lichtenberger, *Encyclop. des Sciences Religieuses*, s. v.

Bambridge, Christopher. See Bainbridge.

Bannister, Henry, D.D., a Methodist Episcopal minister and educator, was born at Conway, Mass., Oct. 5, 1812. He united with the Church at the age of sixteen, studied at Cazenovia Seminary, N. Y., graduated from Wesleyan University, Conn., in 1836, taught one year at Lowville, N. Y., studied two years at Auburn Theological Seminary, teaching one year meanwhile at Cazenovia; in 1840 became principal of Fairfield Academy; in 1843 of Cazenovia Seminary; in 1856 professor of exegetical theology at Garret Biblical Institute, Evanston, Ill., and died there, April 15, 1883. In 1869 he took a trip abroad. He was a delegate to the General Conference in 1864, 1868, and 1872. He was licensed to preach in 1838, in 1842 joined the Oneida Conference, and in 1857 was transferred to the Wisconsin Conference. He was an able divine, a fine scholar, and an excellent teacher. Besides numerous contributions to the periodical press, he prepared the part on Isaiah for Whedon's *Commentary*. See *Minutes of Annual Conferences*, 1883, p. 322; *Alumni Record of Wesl. Univ.* 1882, p. 10, 544.

Baptism, Heretical, i. e. when administered by heretics, has been generally held, at least in the Roman Church, ever since the Donatist schism, to be valid; so likewise if performed by women, heathen, or even in sport, but not if self-administered (Smith, *Dict. of Christ. Antiq.* s. v.). See Baptism, Lay.

Bär (Lat. *Berus*, i. q. *Baeher*), Ludwig, a Swiss humanist and theologian, was born at Basle towards the end of the 15th century. He studied at his native place and at Paris. In the latter city he was promoted to the doctorate of theology. In 1513 he was appointed professor of theology at his native place, and soon attracted many students. At the beginning of the Reformation, he sided, in connection with Erasmus, with that movement. But when the intentions of the leaders became more and more known, he stood up for his Church, and, as one of the leaders of the theological faculty, opposed Œcolampadius and Pellican. When, however, in 1529 the evangelical party had gained the victory and the Church of Rome was declared to be abolished at Basle, Bär, in connection with Erasmus, Glarean, and other professors and canons, left Basle and settled at Breisgau. He died at the last-named place, April 14, 1554. He wrote, *De Christiana ad Mortem Præparatione Liber:—Psalmorum Expositio:—Quæstio, an Tempore Pestis Fugere Liceat.* See Herzog, *Athenæ Rauricæ* (Basle, 1778); Vischer, *Geschichte der Universität Basel von der Gründung* 1460 *bis zur Reformation* 1529 (ibid. 1860); Fiala, in Wetzer u. Welte's *Kirchenlexikon*, s. v. (B. P.)

Barbier, Josué, a French pervert, was born at Die about 1578. He was pastor of the Protestant congregations at Quint, St. Marcellin, and Livron (1603–1615), but was bribed by the bishop of Valence to turn Romanist, and after entering the royal service as advocate at Grenoble, wrote several abusive books against his former co-religionists, for which see Lichtenberger, *Encyclop. des Sciences Religieuses*, s. v.

Barrows, Comfort E., D.D., a Baptist minister, was born at Attleborough, Mass., Dec. 11, 1831. He graduated from Brown University in 1858, and from the Newton Theological Institution in 1861; was ordained Dec. 25 of the same year pastor at South Danvers (now Peabody), Mass., and in 1865 became pastor of the First Church at Newport, R. I. He died there, Dec. 26, 1883. Besides articles for reviews and papers, Dr. Barrows published several sermons and addresses. See *R. I. Biog. Encyclop.* p. 531. (J. C. S.)

Barry, John, a Roman Catholic prelate, was made administrator of the diocese of Savannah, and on Aug. 2, 1857, consecrated bishop. Florida was at this time made a vicariate, and the diocese of Savannah embraced only Georgia. He labored earnestly and zealously in his capacity of bishop, as he had in that of a priest, but his health was broken down. Going to Europe to recruit, he was prostrated in Paris, and died there, Nov. 19, 1859, aged fifty. See De Courcy and Shea, *Hist. of the Catholic Church in the U. S.* p. 533.

Basil of Jerusalem, a Jacobite patriarch in the 9th century, is the author of *Epistola Synodica de SS. Imaginibus ad Theophilum. Ed. Gr. Lat. Combefisii Manipulus Origg. Rerumque Constantinopolitan* (Paris, 1664), an epistle addressed to the emperor Theophilus, on account of his severe edict against the image-worshippers. See Milman, *Hist. of Latin Christianity*, ii, 363; Peters, in Wetzer u. Welte's *Kirchenlexikon*, s. v. (B. P.)

Bastida, Fernando, a Spanish Jesuit, was born at Salamanca in 1572. He joined his order in 1588, and went to Rome as procurator of Molina. Here he defended the doctrine of predestination as held by his order. Having returned to Spain, he was obliged to leave his order on account of some defect which debarred a candidate from becoming a member, but which was not known at the time of his entrance. Up to his death he was canon and professor primarius at the University of Valladolid. See Meyer, *Historia Congreg. de Auxiliis;* Schneemann, in Wetzer u. Welte's *Kirchenlexikon*, s. v. (B. P.)

Bathurst, William Hiley, an English clergyman and poet, was born near Bristol, Aug. 28, 1796. He graduated from Christ Church College, Oxford; was ordained in 1819; in 1820 became rector of Barwick-in-Elsnet, Yorkshire, resigned in 1852, and in 1863 retired to his estate at Sydney Park, Gloucestershire, where he died in 1877. Besides *An Essay on Human Knowledge* (1827) and a *Translation of Virgil's Georgics* (1849), he published two volumes of poems, entitled respectively *Psalms and Hymns for Public and Private Use* (Lond. 1831, 1842) and *Metrical Thoughts in Verse* (1849), from the former of which several pieces have been quite popular, especially the hymns beginning "Oh for a faith that will not shrink," and "Oh for that flame of living fire."

Bayle, Marc Antoine, a French religious author, was born at Marseilles in 1825, and died in 1877. He wrote, *Vie de Saint Vincent Ferrier* (Marseilles, 1856):—*Vie de Saint Philippe de Néri* (ibid. 1859):—*Massillon* (1867):—*Oraison Funèbre du R. P. Lacordaire* (1862):—*Homélies sur les Évangiles* (Tournay, 1865, 2 vols.). He also translated Döllinger's work, *Christenthum und Kirche in der Zeit der Grundlegung*, and took an active part in the publication of the *Conseiller Catholique* and *L'Ami de la Religion.* See Lichtenberger, *Encyclop. des Sciences Religieuses*, s. v. (B. P.)

Bayley, James Roosevelt, D.D., a distinguished Roman Catholic prelate, was born in New York city, Aug. 23, 1814. He graduated from Washington (now Trinity) College, Hartford, Conn., in 1835, and studied theology under Dr. Samuel Jarvis at Middletown; was ordained a minister of the Protestant Episcopal Church; preached at Harlem, N. Y., and afterwards at Hagerstown, Md. He went to Rome, entered the Roman Catholic Church in 1842, studied theology in the Sulpitian Seminary at Paris, and was raised to the priesthood in New York by archbishop Hughes, March 2, 1844. He was engaged thereafter in teaching and pastoral duties in New York city, and in filling the position of secretary to archbishop Hughes. On Oct. 30, 1853, he was consecrated first bishop of Newark, N. J., and on Oct. 12, 1872, he received the pallium of the archbishopric of Baltimore. He took part in the three provincial councils of New York, in the second plenary council of Baltimore, and in the œcumenical council of the Vatican. He also visited Rome in 1862 for the canonization of the Japanese martyrs, and in 1867 for the centenary of the apostles. In 1877 he went to Europe for the Vichy waters, but, receiving no benefit, returned to America, and got as far as Newark, where he died, Oct. 3, 1877. Archbishop Bayley wrote, *Sketch of the History of the Catholic Church on the Island of New York* (N. Y. 1853; new ed. 1869):—*Memoirs of Simon G. Bruté, First Bishop of Vincennes* (1860):—*Pastorals for the People.* See (N. Y.) *Catholic Almanac*, 1878, p. 38.

Beatty, Charles Clinton, D.D., LL.D., a venerable Presbyterian minister, was born near Princeton, N. J., Jan. 4, 1800. He joined the Church there in 1817, graduated from the College of New Jersey in 1818, and from the Theological Seminary at the same place in 1822. After serving as an evangelist in Indiana, Illinois, and Kentucky, he was ordained pastor of the First Presbyterian Church at Steubenville, O., in 1823. In 1829 he founded a female seminary in that town, to which he devoted his chief attention thereafter until 1879. In 1837 he resigned his position as pastor, but continued to act as stated supply in adjacent churches for several years thereafter. He died at Steubenville, Oct. 30, 1882. He possessed rare executive ability, and was enabled to amass a large fortune, of which he gave liberally to various causes of benevolence. See *Necrol. Report of Princeton Theol. Sem.* 1883, p. 10.

Beatty, William Trimble, D.D., a Presbyterian divine, was born of Scotch-Irish parentage, in Fairfield County, O., June 1, 1833. He joined the Church at the age of seventeen, graduated from Miami University in 1857, spent one year at the Danville Seminary, Ky., and finished his theological studies at the Western Seminary, Alleghany City, Pa. He was licensed to preach in 1859, and ordained pastor at Greencastle in 1861. Two years afterwards he became pastor at New Brunswick, N. J., and in 1867 at Shady Side, Pittsburgh, Pa., where he continued until 1880, and then resigned on account of ill-health. He died at Minneapolis, Minn., April 10, 1882. He was an excellent preacher, and active as secretary of his presbytery and of several literary institutions. See Nevin, *Presb. Encyclop.* s. v.

Bebenburg, Lupold von, a German prelate, who died in 1363, descended from a noble family in Franconia. He studied canon law at Bologna. In the controversy between Ludwig the Bavarian and the popes John XXII, Benedict XII, and Clement VI, Bebenburg sided with the emperor. In 1338 he was canon of Mayence, Würzburg, and Bamberg, and from 1352 to 1363 bishop of the latter place. He wrote, *De Zelo Religionis Antiquorum Principum Germanorum* (Basle, 1497; reprinted in the *Bibliotheca Patrum*, xv, Cologne, 1622):—*Tractatus de Juribus Regni et Imperii Romanorum* (Strasburg, 1508, etc.):—*Dictamen Rhymaticum Querulosum de Modernis Cursibus et Defectibus Regni ac Imperii Romani* (ed. by Peter, Würzburg, 1841, and by Böhmer, *Geschichtsquellen des 14. Jahrhunderts*, Stuttgart, 1843, 497 sq.). See Schreiber, *Die politischen und religiösen Ideen unter Ludwig den Bayern* (Munich, 1858); Riezler, *Die litterarischen Widersächer der Päpste zur Zeit Ludwig des Bayern* (Leipsic, 1874); Mejer, in Herzog's *Real-Encyklop.* (2d. ed), s. v.; Wittmann, in Wetzer u. Welte's *Kirchenlexikon*, s. v. (B. P.)

Bec, Abbey of, a celebrated French Benedictine monastery, belonging to the congregation of St. Maur, situated at the confluence of the Bec and the Rille, nine leagues from Rouen, was founded about 1034, by St. Herluin, its first abbot, near the present site. It became famous as a seat of learning under Lanfranc, then prior, afterwards archbishop, of Canterbury, and was eventually exempted from episcopal jurisdiction, but is now in ruins. See Landon, *Eccles. Dict.* s. v.

Beccarelli, Giuseppe, a Milanese spiritualist, a follower of Molinos (q. v.), and an active promoter of the education of youth, was seized by the Inquisition in 1708, and after recantation in 1710, at Venice, was condemned to the galleys.

Beckedorff, Georg Philipp Ludolf von, a pedagogue, statesman, and author, of Germany, was born April 14, 1778, at Hanover. At first he studied theology at Jena, and afterwards medicine at Göttingen, where he was also promoted in 1799 as M.D. In 1810 he accepted a call as tutor of the electoral prince of Hesse, and in 1811 he went to Ballenstedt as tutor of the prince of Anhalt-Bernburg. When, in 1818, the union between the Reformed and Lutheran Church was decreed, his mind was greatly occupied with questions concerning the Church, and at that time he already regarded the Catholic Church as the historical development of the Apostolic Church. To this time belongs his *Zur Kirchenvereinigung* (Halle, 1814), and *Briefwechsel zwischen zwei Geistlichen bei Gelegenheit der Versuche zur Kirchenvereinigung* (Leipsic, 1818). In 1819 he was called into the Prussian ministry for worship and instruction, but his joining the Church of Rome, in 1827, resulted in his discharge from office. When Frederick William IV ascended the throne in 1840, he did justice to Beckedorff by appointing him to some high position, on which occasion he published his *An gottesfürchtige protestantische Christen. Worte den Friedens und der Wiederversöhnung* (Weissenburg, 1840). Besides, he wrote, *Das Verhältniss von Haus und Staat und Kirche zu einander*, etc. (Berlin, 1849):—*Offenbarung und Vernunft* (Ratisbon, 1853). He also founded some charitable institutions, and died Feb. 27, 1858, at Grünhof, in Pomerania. See Rosenthal, *Convertitenbilder*, i, 466–475; Clarus, *Simeon oder Heimkehr und Wanderungen eines christlichen Forschers* (Schaffhausen, 1862), ii, 371–380; Zuchold, *Bibl. Theol.* i, 88; Binder, in Wetzer u. Welte's *Kirchenlexikon*, s. v. (B. P.)

Beckmann, Otto, canon and "professor eloquentiæ" at Wittenberg, was a friend of Luther and Melanchthon, although he did not join them in the work of Reformation. "Alitur nescio quid monstri," he writes to Spalatin, Feb. 24, 1519, speaking at the same time of the exciting sermon in which Luther had openly attacked the power of the pope (Löscher, *Vollständige Reform. Acta* (Leipsic, 1729), iii, 90 sq. In 1525 he was pastor at Warburg, his native place, where he wrote his *Precatio Dominica contra Impios et Seditiosos Lutheranorum Errores* (Cologne, 1528):—*Comment. super Orationem Dominicam et Symbolum Apostolorum* (ibid. eod.). In the year 1528 he held an open colloquy with a certain Hecker, at Münster, defending the primacy of the pope. He died provost of St. Ægidius, at Münster. See Driver, *Bibl. Monast.* p. 6; Hamelmann, *Opp. Geneal. Hist.* (Lemogov, 1711), p. 338, 1130, 1191, 1422; Panzer, *Annales Typogr.* vi, 392; ix, 68; Streber, in Wetzer u. Welte's *Kirchenlexikon*, s. v. (B. P.)

Begg, James, D.D., a Scotch clergyman (son of Dr. Begg, of Monkland), graduated from Glasgow University; was licensed to preach in 1829; appointed assistant minister at North Leith in 1830; elected minister of lady Glenoreby's Chapel, Edinburgh, in 1831; promoted to Paisley the same year; joined the Free Secession in 1843; was elected moderator of the Free General Assembly in May, 1865, and died Sept. 29, 1883, aged seventy-four years. Dr. Begg was one of the foremost men in the Free Church of Scotland since the death of Dr. Chalmers. Among many other smaller works, he published, *Are You Prepared to Die?* (1845):—*How to Promote and Preserve the Beauty of Edinburgh* (1849):—*Pauperism and the Poor Laws* (eod.):

National Education for Scotland Practically Considered (1850):—*Reform in the Free Church* (eod.):—*Scotland's Demands for Electoral Justice* (1857):—*A Hand-book of Popery* (1863):—*The Art of Preaching* (eod.):—*Account of the Parish*, etc. See *Fasti Eccles. Scoticanæ*, i, 81, 117, 606.

Begundelli, Basso Antonio, a canonist of the 17th century, who died Oct. 9, 1713, general vicar at Freising, is the author of *Bibliotheca Juris Canonico-Civilis Practica.* See Hurter, *Nomenclator Literarius*, ii, 857; *Historisch-politische Blätter*, lxxii, 585 sq.; Kreutzwald, in Wetzer u. Welte's *Kirchenlexikon*, s. v. (B. P.)

Belfast Society is noted in the history of the Presbyterian Church in Ireland for its having intensely agitated the Church for many years upon the question of subscription to the Westminster Confession of Faith. It had its origin with Rev. John Abernethy, jr., who became minister at Antrim in 1703. He was a diligent student, and soon drew around him as associates Rev. William Taylor, of Randalstown, Rev. Alexander Brown, of Donegore, and Rev. James Kirkpatrick, of Templepatrick—all young men of much promise. They were soon joined by Rev. Thomas Orr, of Comber, Rev. Alexander Colville, of Dromore, licentiates and theological students, and a few laymen of Belfast. The object of the organization was theological improvement. They first gave their organization the name of Belfast Society in 1705. "At their meetings, generally held monthly, each member preached in succession; chapters out of the Old and New Tests., previously agreed upon, were read in the original languages, and their difficulties discussed; reviews and analyses of books read by the members since the previous meeting were given; and dissertations were read on important theological topics, specially on those questions which were then attracting the attention of divines elsewhere, and becoming the subjects of controversy." Their sermons treated of "the nature and Scriptural terms of the unity of the Christian Church, the nature and mischief of schism, the rights of conscience and of private judgment, the sole dominion of Christ in his own kingdom, the nature, power, and effects of excommunication, and other subjects of that kind." Through Mr. Abernethy the latitudinarian notions on the inferiority of dogmatic belief and the nature of religious liberty, which had obtained currency on the Continent and in England, were introduced into the Belfast Society, and thus into Ireland. This society held and diligently promulgated their ideas, principal of which are the following: error is innocent when not wilful; that every man's persuasion of what is true and right is the sole rule of his faith and conduct; "that the Church has no right to require candidates for the ministry to subscribe to a confession of faith prepared by any man or body of men, and that such a required subscription is a violation of the right of private judgment, and inconsistent with Christian liberty and true Protestantism." There is much evidence which leads one to believe that this society was guilty of the heresy of Arianism; such was the prevalent impression at that time. Such views, held by some of the most learned of the Church, soon caused widespread alarm. The question of subscription became the topic of the day. The controversy was taken to the press, and over fifty pamphlets were published by the members of the society and their opponents. In 1721 the General Synod met at Belfast, when the orthodox Calvinists attempted to enforce subscription. A law to that effect was passed by the synod, to which all conformed except the members of the Belfast Society; after which time the Belfast Society was principally known by the appellation of non-subscribers. The synod, however, did not now expel, but passed pacific resolutions. The controversy still continued with unabated fury. The non-subscribers formed a presbytery (the Presbytery of Antrim). The subscribers refused communion with the non-subscribers. Finally, in 1726, the synod expelled the non-subscribers, some of whom established independent churches, others lost their following, and ceased from the ministry; thus a most unfortunate quarrel was settled, and the Belfast Society passed out of existence. In August, 1727, the Belfast Society published a very valuable work; though partial and one-sided, it contains an elaborate defence of their peculiar views. It contains compilations from original documents, and reports of the synod's debates, which are nowhere else preserved: *A Narrative of the Proceedings of Seven General Synods of the Northern Presbyterians in Ireland, with Relation to their Differences in Judgment and Practice, from the Year* 1720 *to* 1726, *in which they Issued in a Synodical Breach.* See Reid, *Hist. of the Presb. Church in Ireland.*

Bell, George, a Calvinistic Methodist, who was the first of John Wesley's followers to make a division in the Methodist societies, was a local preacher in Southwark, a man of heated imagination, who said he possessed a miraculous discernment of spirits. His doctrinal sentiments were high Antinomianism, mixed with enthusiasm. He first separated from the Foundery Society, with the Rev. Thomas Maxfield, in February, 1763, and was a member of his church in Princes Street, Moorfields, but soon afterwards set up as preacher himself, and took one of Mr. Wesley's preaching places, situated in Baker's Court, near Gray's Inn Lane, London. There he had many followers, and preached there many years. Bell's fanaticism obliged Mr. Wesley to expel him from the Foundery Society. He afterwards prophesied the destruction of the world on a certain day, against which Mr. Wesley preached, as great fear was created by the prophecy. The failure did not disconcert Bell, who continued his wild enthusiasm. See Wilson, *Dissenting Churches*, iii, 418–419.

Bell, L. G., a pioneer Presbyterian minister, was born in Augusta County, Va., in 1788. He served in the war of 1812, and entered the ministry in 1827 in Tennessee, but afterwards devoted himself to missionary work in the West, especially in Iowa, where he raised up numerous churches. He died May 20, 1868. See Nevin, *Presbyterian Encyclop.* s. v.

Benkert, Franz Georg, a Roman Catholic theologian of Germany, was born at Nordheim, Sept. 25, 1790, studied at Würzburg, and received holy orders in 1816. In 1823 he took the degree as doctor of theology by presenting his dissertation, *De Duplici Missa Catechumenorum et Fidelium.* In 1832 he was appointed regent of the clerical seminary, and in 1838 succeeded the famous Möhler as cathedral-dean of Würzburg. He died May 20, 1859. In 1822 he commenced the publication of the *Religionsfreund*, a periodical for systematic theology, literature, and contemporaneous history. For practical theology he founded *Athanasia* in 1827. In 1840 he resigned his connection with these two periodicals to devote himself entirely to the history of Franconia, and published as the result of his studies several interesting treatises in the *Archiv des historischen Vereins von Unterfranken.* See Stamminger, in Wetzer u. Welte's *Kirchenlexikon*, s. v. (B. P.)

Bennie, Archibald, D.D., a Scotch clergyman, was born Nov. 1, 1797. He graduated from the Glasgow University, where he obtained three prizes; was licensed to preach in 1820, and appointed assistant and successor at the Free Chapel of Ease, Glasgow, in 1823; promoted to the third charge at Stirling in 1824; presented to the living at Lady Yester's Chapel, Edinburgh, in 1835; appointed a chaplain in ordinary to the queen of England and a dean of the Chapel Royal in 1841, and died at Dunoon, Sept. 21, 1846. He published five sermons from 1825 to 1839:—*A Letter to Patrick Arkley, Advocate, Edinburgh* (1846):—*Discourses, with a Memoir* (1847); and he edited, for two years (1836–37), *The Edinburgh Christian Instructor.* See *Fasti Eccles. Scoticanæ*, i, 64; ii, 34.

Bentivoglio, Cornelio, an Italian prelate, was born at Ferrara in 1668. Pope Clement XI made him chaplain, afterwards titular archbishop of Carthage, and legate at the French court. His zeal against the Jansenists gained for him the favor of Louis XIV, but when the latter died he was recalled. In 1719 he was made cardinal, and in 1720 *legatus a latere* for Ravenna and the Romagna. Under Benedict XIII he was appointed by the king of Spain, in 1726, as his representative at the papal curia. He died in 1732. See Kaulen, in Wetzer u. Welte's *Kirchenlexikon*, s. v. (B. P.)

Beresford, Marcus Gervais, D.D., an Irish Protestant prelate, was born in 1801. He was educated at Richmond School, Yorkshire, and Trinity College, Cambridge, where he was made bachelor of arts in 1824; appointed rector of Kildallen in 1825, afterwards vicar of Drung and Lara, also vicar-general of Kilmore, and archdeacon of Armagh. In 1854 he was consecrated bishop of Kilmore, Elpin, and Ardagh, and in 1863 translated to the see of Armagh, and made primate of Ireland. He died Dec. 26, 1885.

Bernard de Botono. See Bernard of Bologna (1).

Bernard of Constance, who died March 15, 1088, was teacher at the cathedral-school of Constance. He wrote *De Damnatione Schismaticorum*. See Ussermann, *Prodrom.* ii, 188 sq.; Giesebrecht, *Geschichte der deutschen Kaiserzeit* (4th ed.), iii, 1034 sq.; Lütolf, in Wetzer u. Welte's *Kirchenlexikon*, s. v. (B. P.)

Bernard of Pavia, a canonist, and bishop of Pavia about 1198, is the author of *Breviarium Extravagantium*, i. e. *Decretorum et Canonum Extra Decretorum Corpus Vagantium*. (B. P.)

Bernard of Pomerania was a Spanish monk, whom pope Paschal II had appointed bishop of that country. In 1122 he undertook, accompanied by his chaplain and an interpreter, to preach the gospel to the Pomeranians. But the Pomeranians would not recognise him because he was dressed like a hermit. When, however, Bernard was about to cut down the jul-tree, the tutelar deity of the inhabitants of the city of Julin, the Pomeranians drove him out of their country. In company with his chaplain and interpreter, Bernard retired to Bamberg and induced bishop Otto to undertake the conversion of the Pomeranians, but in a more pompous manner. See Andreæ, *Abbat. S. Michæl prope Bamberg, Vita S. Ottonis, Episc. Bamberg*, in Ludwig, *Scriptor. Rerum Episc. Bamberg*, i, 464; Alzog, in Wetzer u. Welte's *Kirchenlexikon*, s. v. (B. P.)

Bernard of Waging, a Benedictine, was born about 1400, studied at Salzburg and Vienna, and joined the Benedictines at Tegernsee in 1446. On account of his piety and learning he was appointed prior of the convent at Tegernsee; hence he is generally called *prior Tegernseensis*. He now labored for the benefit of his monastery, and for his clergy he wrote, *Confessionale: — Speculum Mortis: — Consolatorium Tribulatorum:—Remediarius Pusillanimium:—De Cognoscendo Deum:—De Sentimentis Spiritualibus*, etc. For the monks at Wiblingen he wrote, in 1456, *Contra Esum Carnium;* for those at St. Ulrich, in Augsburg, *De Materia Eucharistica* and *Contra Vitium Propriet.* In 1461 he assisted bishop John of Aich in the reformation of the Pergen monastery, and prepared for the clergy, *Præparat. ad Missam; Formula Communis;* and *Speculum Pastorum*. With the cardinal Nicolaus of Cusa, with whom he was intimately connected, he also assisted in reforming the monasteries at Georgenberg and Sonnenburg in 1554, and whose work, *De Docta Ignorantia*, he defended against the attacks of the Carthusian prior, Vincent of Axbach. He died Aug. 2, 1472. See Pez, *Bibl. Ascet.* tom. vii, præf. n. 10; Braunmüller, in Wetzer u. Welte's *Kirchenlexikon*, s. v. (B. P.)

Beyer, Hartmann, a Lutheran theologian of Germany, was born at Frankfort-on-the-Main, Sept. 30, 1516. He studied at Wittenberg under Luther and Melanchthon. In 1545 he was called to his native place as preacher. At that time Calvinism flourished at Frankfort, and yet Beyer at last succeeded in founding a Lutheran Church in 1554. Not only against the Calvinists, but also against the Roman Catholics, Beyer showed his dislike. His sermons, comprising forty-nine volumes, are still preserved in the city library at Frankfort. He died Aug. 11, 1577. See Steiss, in Herzog's *Real-Encyklop.* s. v. (B. P.)

Bialobrzeski, Martin, bishop of Kamieniec, was born in 1522, and died in 1586 at his episcopal see, which he had occupied since 1577. He was one of the most talented pulpit orators and writers of Poland. The rights of his Church he defended everywhere, especially against heretics. Thus he opposed, in behalf of his chapter, at the Diet of Proszowice, the confederation of 1575 *de pace inter dissidentes in religione tenenda*, and pointed out its danger for Church and State. Against "the errors of his time" he wrote a catechism (Cracow, 1567). He also wrote against the Socinians *Orthodoxa Confessio de Uno Deo* (ibid. 1579), and likewise published *Postilla Orthodoxa* (ibid. 1581, 1838). See Hotowinski, *Homiletyka*, p. 395 sq.; Letowski, *Katalog Biskupów*, etc., ii, 23; Mecherzynski, *Hist. Wymowy*, p. 82; Nowodworski, *Encyklop. Kościelna*, s. v.; Lüdtke, in Wetzer u. Welte's *Kirchenlexikon*, s. v. (B. P.)

Bickersteth, Robert, D.D., an English prelate, was born at Acton, Suffolk, Aug. 24, 1816. He graduated from Queen's College, Cambridge, in 1841; became curate of Sapcote the same year; of St. Giles's, Reading, in 1843; at the parish church of Clapham in 1845; incumbent of St. John's, in the same place, the same year; rector of St. Giles-in-the-Fields in 1851, canon residentiary of Salisbury in 1854, and bishop of Ripon in 1856, in which office he died, April 15, 1884. He published, *Bible Landmarks* (1850): — *Lent Lectures* (1851), besides sermons and charges.

Bigelow, Andrew, D.D., a Congregational minister, was born at Boylston, Mass., Dec. 13, 1809. He graduated from Amherst College in 1838; studied theology with his half-brother, Rev. Jonathan Bigelow, of Rochester; was ordained pastor at South Dartmouth, Mass., in 1841; in 1847 became pastor at West Needham (now Wellesley); in 1853 at Westhampton; in 1855 at Medfield; in 1866 acting-pastor at Boylston; in 1874 at Southboro'; after 1875 he was without charge, and died Sept. 23, 1882. See *Cong. Year-book*, 1882, p. 19.

Bigelow, John F., D.D., a Baptist minister, was born at Paxton, Mass., April 25, 1818. He studied two years at Brown University, and graduated from Columbia College, N. Y.; studied theology first in New York, and completed his education in Berlin, Germany. Soon after his return he became pastor at Bristol, R. I.; subsequently at Middleborough, Mass.; Keesville, N. Y.; and established a church at St. Albans, Vt. In 1872 he became associated with his brother in conducting the Athenæum Seminary, Brooklyn, N. Y. He died June 20, 1884. Dr. Bigelow was an eloquent preacher, and a man of scholarly attainments. See *The Christian at Work*, June 26, 1884. (J. C. S.)

Billick, Eberhard, one of the most famous Roman Catholic theologians of the 16th century, was born at Bilk, near Düsseldorf, and died in the year 1557. He belonged to the Carmelite order, and was professor at Cologne. When it was intended to call Butzer to Cologne, he opposed this movement by publishing his *Judicium Deputatorum Universitatis et Secundarii Cleri Coloniensis* (1543). In 1545 he published another polemical work against Protestantism, which was propagated at Cologne, under the title, *Judicii Universitatis et Cleri Coloniensis Adversus Calumnias Philippi Melanchthonis, Martini Buceri*, etc. In 1546 he was present at the Ratisbon colloquy. Pope Paul IV honored him with the title of bishop of Cyrene. See Hartzheim,

Bibl. Col. p. 174 sq.; Hagen, *Geschichte Aachens*, ii, 139; Ennen, *Geschichte der Stadt Köln*, iv, 1875; Varrentrapp, *Hermann von Wied* (Leipsic, 1878); Pastor, in Wetzer u. Welte's *Kirchenlexikon*, s. v. (B. P.)

Bird, Milton, D.D., a Cumberland Presbyterian minister, was born Oct. 23, 1807, in Barren County, Ky. In 1830 he was ordained an evangelist, and the next year visited Western Pennsylvania as a missionary; for some time was pastor of the Waynesburg congregation, and for several years at Pleasant Hill, Washington Co. In 1840 he became professor of moral and intellectual philosophy and natural theology in Madison College, but resigned in 1842. Meanwhile he assumed control of the *Union Evangelist*. For a time he also served as pastor at Uniontown, where he began, in 1845, the publication of the *Theological Medium*, afterwards the *Medium and Quarterly*. Besides he preached extensively in Pennsylvania, and his influence became very great. In 1847 he removed to Jeffersonville, Ind., and while residing there took charge of the Book Concern in Louisville, where, in July, 1850, he commenced the publication of the *Watchman and Evangelist*. In 1855 he became pastor at Princeton, Ky. For some time, also, he was nominally president of the old Cumberland College. In 1858 he became editor of the *St. Louis Observer*. When the Civil War began he removed to Jeffersonville, Ind. He was several times moderator of the General Assembly. In 1864 he returned as pastor to Caldwell County, Ky. He died July 26, 1871. He published *Doctrines of Grace* (1856). See Dr. Beard's *Biographical Sketches*, 2d series, p. 339.

Blake, Mortimer, D.D., a Congregational minister, was born at Pittston, Me., Jan. 10, 1813. He graduated from Amherst College in 1835; was principal of Franklin Academy, Mass., for three years, while studying theology with Rev. Elam Smally, D.D.; taught in Hopkins Academy, Hadley, one year; was ordained pastor at Mansfield in 1839; installed over Winslow Church, Taunton, in 1855, and died there, Dec. 22, 1884. He published several sermons and addresses. See *Cong. Year-book*, 1886, p. 20.

Blakeney, Richard Paul, D.D., LL.D., an Anglican divine, was born at Roscommon, Ireland, June 2, 1820. He was educated at Trinity College, Dublin, taking a first-class place in theology in 1843; became curate of St. Paul's, Nottingham, the same year; vicar at Ison-Green, Nottinghamshire, in 1844; at Christ Church, Claughton, Birkenhead, in 1852; at Bridlington, Yorkshire, in 1874; canon of Fenton, in York Cathedral, in 1882; and died Jan. 1, 1885. He wrote largely on the Catholic controversy, and was the author of, *Manual of the Romish Controversy* (1851 and often): —*Hist. and Interpretation of Common Prayer* (1865 and since):—besides two very popular *Catechisms*.

Blakesley, Joseph William, an English divine, was born in London in 1808. He graduated in 1831 at Trinity College, Cambridge, of which he was afterwards fellow and tutor; in 1845 became vicar of Ware; in 1863 canon in Canterbury Cathedral; in 1872 dean of Lincoln; and died April 18, 1885. Besides several ecclesiastical honorary positions, he was a member of the Bible Revision Committee, and author of, *A Life of Aristotle* (1839):—*Herodotus*, in the *Bibliotheca Classica* (1854): —*Four Months in Algeria* (1859), and other works.

Blanchard, Amos, D.D., a Congregational minister, was born in Massachusetts in 1807. He graduated from Yale College in 1826, studied theology for one year in Andover Seminary, and was ordained Dec. 25, 1829. He was tutor in Yale College in 1828 and 1829, studying in the theological department there at the same time. He became pastor of the First Church, Lowell, Mass., in 1829; of Kirk Street Church, in the same city, in 1845, and died there, Jan. 14, 1870. See *Trien. Cat. of Andover Theol. Sem.* 1870, p. 85.

Blanckart, Nikolaus, a Carmelite, was a native of Utrecht, and joined his order at Cologne. In 1546 he held a public disputation on the doctrine of purgatory, and was made licentiate of theology; in 1551 he was appointed professor of theology and dean of the theological faculty at Cologne. In the same year he also went to Trent to attend the council there. He died in 1555 at Cologne. He wrote against Calvin, *Judicium Johannis Calvini de Sanctorum Reliquiis Collatum cum Orthodoxorum S. Ecclesiæ Catholicæ Patrum Sententia*, etc. (Cologne, 1551). He also prepared a translation of the Bible in Low German, which was published in 1548. See Streber, in Wetzer u. Welte's *Kirchenlexikon*, s. v. (B. P.)

Blarer (*von Wartensee*), Jacob Christoph, a Swiss prelate, was born May 11, 1542. He studied at Freiburg, in Breisgau, and was in 1575 elected prince-bishop of Basle. When Blarer entered upon his duties, he found that Protestantism had greatly advanced in his diocese. But by his perseverance and energy he at last succeeded in restoring the bishopric of Basle. He died April 18, 1608. See Vautrey, *Jacques-Christophe Blarer de Wartensee*, in the *Revue de la Suisse Catholique*, x, 65–82; Burckhardt, *Die Gegenreformation in den ehemaligen Vogteien Zwingen, Pfeffingen und Birseck des Bisthums Basel* (Basle, 1855); Vautrey, *Histoire du Collège de Porrentruy* (Porrentruy, 1866); Fiala, in Wetzer u. Welte's *Kirchenlexikon*, s. v. (B. P.)

Böckhn, Placidus, a German Benedictine, was born in 1690 at Munich, joined his order in 1706, and took holy orders in 1713. Having received, in 1715, the degree of doctor utriusque juris, he went to Rome. In 1721 he returned, and was appointed professor of canon law at Salzburg. In 1733 he took the chair of Biblical exegesis. He died Feb. 9, 1752. His main work is *Commentarius in Jus Canonicum Universum* (Paris, 1776). See Sedelmayer, *Hist. Univ. Salisburg.* p. 405; Ziegelbauer, *Hist. Rei Litt. O. S. B.* iii, 484, 485; Mittermüller, in Wetzer u. Welte's *Kirchenlexikon*, s. v. (B. P.)

Böhm, Johann, a German religious fanatic, known under the name "der Pauker von Niklashausen," came before the public in the name of the mother of God, at whose direction he commenced preaching. He was especially severe against the clergy, whom he charged with avarice and other vices. The people, poor as well as rich, flocked from all parts, till at last bishop Rudolf of Würzburg made him a prisoner, and ordered him to be burned, July 19, 1476. See *Archiv des historischen Vereins von Unterfranken und Aschaffenburg* (Würzburg, 1858), xiv, No. 3, 1–108; Liliencron, *Histor. Volkslieder*, ii, No. 148; Ludewig, *Geschichtsschr. von dem Bischofthum Würzburg*, p. 852–855; Langhorst, in Wetzer u. Welte's *Kirchenlexikon*, s. v. (B. P.)

Bolten, Johann Adrian, a Protestant theologian of Germany, was born at Süderstapel, in Sleswig, Sept. 11, 1742. In 1772 he was appointed deacon, and in 1782 third pastor, at Altona, and died Aug. 11, 1807. He was well acquainted with the languages of the East, and published *Diss. de Keri et Kethibh Vocabulis Compositis ac Divinæ Dignitatis* (Altona, 1760):—*Die Bergpredigt Jesu in einer neuen Uebersetzung mit Anmerkungen* (Hamburg, 1768):—*Der Bericht des Matthäus von Jesus dem Messias, übersetzt u. mit Anmerkungen* (Altona, 1795):—*Der Bericht des Johannes*, etc. (ibid. 1797): —*Die Geschichte der Apostel von Lukas*, etc. (ibid. 1799): —*Die neutestamentlichen Briefe*, etc. (ibid. 1800–5). See Winer, *Handbuch der theol. Lit.* i, 172, 833; Döring, *Die gelehrten Theologen Deutschlands*, i, 145 sq. (B. P.)

Book of the Dead. See Ritual of the Dead.

Bosco, Johannes, a famous Scotist, was born at Antwerp in 1613. For some time he occupied the *cathedra Scoti* at the University of Louvain. His main work is *Theologia Sacramentalis, Scholastica et Moralis ad Mentem Doctoris Subtilis* (Louvain and Antwerp, 1665–85, 6 vols. fol.). After his death some smaller treatises of his were published at Antwerp, with the title, *Theologia Spiritualis* (1686, 2 vols. fol.). See

Scheeben, in Wetzer u. Welte's *Kirchenlexikon*, s. v. (B. P.)

Boström, Christoffer Jakob, a Swedish philosopher, was born at Pitea, Jan. 1, 1797. He studied at Upsala, where he also commenced his lectures in 1827, which he continued till 1863, when he retired from his professorship. He died March 22, 1866. Boström was the most independent thinker of Sweden, and founded a philosophical school, the influence of which has essentially prevented the propagation of materialistic and pessimistic teachings in Sweden. (B. P.)

Botzheim, Johann von, a Swiss theologian, was born in 1480 at Botzheim, near Schlettstadt. He studied at Heidelberg, and having completed his studies in Italy, where he was made doctor of canon law, he was appointed after his return, in 1512, dean of Constance. In 1518 he became acquainted with some of Luther's writings, and became greatly attached to Luther and his cause. In 1520 he wrote to Luther, encouraging him in his work; but he soon turned his back upon him. In 1527 he was obliged to leave the place, and went to Freiburg, where he died in 1535. He was on very good terms with Erasmus, and it was mainly his influence which led Erasmus to write the *Catalogus Elucubrationum*. See Döllinger, *Reformation*, i, 519; Walchner, *Johann von Botzheim und seine Freunde* (Schaffhausen, 1836); Hartmann, in *Allgemeine deutsche Biographie*, iii, 208; Göpfert, in Wetzer u. Welte's *Kirchenlexikon*, s. v. (B. P.)

Bouelle, Stephen, D.D., a Presbyterian minister of Huguenot descent, was born in Cumberland County, Pa., in 1770. He was educated at Dickinson College, and studied theology under Dr. David Rice, of Kentucky. He was licensed in 1796; in 1798 went to Abingdon, Va.; from 1804 he was pastor at Sinking Springs and Green Springs, also teaching and occasionally making missionary tours into Indiana. In 1837 he removed to Missouri, and died at Paris, Ill., in December, 1840. He was widely influential. See Nevin, *Presbyterian Encyclop.* s. v.

Bouhours, Dominique, a learned French Jesuit, was born at Paris in 1628. At the age of sixteen he joined his order, studied under the care of the Jesuits, and died May 27, 1702. Besides a number of works pertaining to belles-lettres, he wrote, *Vie de S. Ignace* (Paris, 1679):—*Vie de S. François Xavier* (ibid. 1682): —*Pensées Chrétiennes pour les Jour du Mois:—Maximes Chrétiennes.* In connection with the Jesuits Tellier and Bernier he translated the New Test. from the Latin into French, which was published in 1697; latest edition in 1859. See *Biog. Universelle*, v, 211; Ersch u. Gruber, *Encyklop.* xii, 115; Fritz, in Wetzer u. Welte's *Kirchenlexikon*, s. v. (B. P.)

Boulainvilliers, Henri, *count of*, a French philosopher, was born at St. Saire, in Normandy, Oct. 11, 1658, and died Jan. 23, 1722. He was an enthusiastic admirer of Mohammed, and a fierce opponent of Christianity. He wrote *Réfutation des Erreurs de B. de Spinosa* (Brussels, 1731). See Tennemann, *Geschichte der Philosophie*, x, 486; Ersch u. Gruber, *Encyklop.* s. v.; Hefele, in Wetzer u. Welte's *Kirchenlexikon*, s. v. (B. P.)

Boulanger, Nicolas Antoine, who belonged to the French encyclopædists, was born in 1722, and died in 1759. He was an opponent of Christianity and of all revelation, and wrote, *L'Antiquité Dévoilée par ses Usages* (Amsterdam, 1766; Germ. transl. Greifswald, 1769):—*Dissertation sur Élie et Énoch* (1765). To him is also ascribed the authorship of *Examen Critique de la Vie et des Œuvrages de St. Paul* (London, 1770), as well as of *Le Christianisme Dévoilé* and *L'Histoire Critique de la Vie de Jésus Christ, ou Analyse Raisonnée des Évangiles* (eod.), which were probably written by his friend Holbach. His works were collected (Paris, 1791, 10 vols.; 1792, 8 vols.; Amsterdam, 1794, 6 vols.). See Hefele, in Wetzer u. Welte's *Kirchenlexikon*, s. v. (B. P.)

Bower, Edwin Rea, D.D., a Presbyterian minister, was born in Lancaster County, Pa., Sept. 5, 1826. He joined the Church when eighteen years of age, graduated from the College of New Jersey in 1851, spent one year in teaching, graduated from Princeton Theological Seminary in 1855, acting one year also as tutor in his *alma mater;* was ordained pastor at Wappinger's Falls, N. Y., in 1855; installed over the Second Church, Springfield, O., in 1861; elected professor of theology in Lincoln University, Pa., in 1867, and died in that office, April 7, 1883. See *Necrol. Report of Princeton Theol. Sem.* 1884, p. 40.

Boyd, Archibald, D.D., an Anglican divine, was born at Londonderry, Ireland, in 1803. After passing through the diocesan college of that city, he graduated from Trinity College, Dublin, in 1823; became curate of the cathedral at Derry in 1827; of Christ Church, Cheltenham, in 1842; canon of Gloucester cathedral in 1857, vicar of Paddington in 1859, and dean of Exeter in 1867, a position in which he died, July 11, 1883. He was the author of several works on ecclesiastical and religious topics.

Boynton, Charles Brandon, D.D., a Congregational minister, was born at West Stockbridge, Mass., June 12, 1806. After spending one year (1827) at Williams College, and some years in business and legal practice, he studied theology with Rev. Dr. Woodbridge, of Spencertown, N. Y.; was ordained associate pastor at Housatonic, Mass., in 1840, and installed there in 1842; acting pastor at Lansingburg, N. Y., in 1845; at Vine Street, Cincinnati, O., in 1846; pastor at South Church, Pittsfield, Mass., in 1856; again at Cincinnati in 1857; at Washington, D. C., in 1865, at the same time acting as chaplain of the House of Representatives; a third term in Cincinnati, from 1873 to 1877, and finally without charge there until his death, April 27, 1883. He published several books of travel and history. See *Cong. Year-book*, 1884, p. 20.

Braman, Milton Palmer, D.D., a Congregational minister, was born at New Rowley (now Georgetown), Mass., Aug. 6, 1799. He graduated from Harvard College in 1819, and from Andover Theological Seminary in 1824; was pastor at Danvers from 1826 until 1863, and thereafter resided successively at Brighton and Auburndale until his death, April 10, 1882. He published several sermons and addresses. See *Cong. Year-book*, 1883, p. 20.

Brassicanus, Johann Alexander, an opponent of the reformation, belonged to a family of Constance, originally named *Kohlor Köl*, which, however, took the Latin name of Brassicanus in the 15th century. In 1493 a certain *Johannes Köl*, called Brassicanus, was promoted at Tübingen; he was Melanchthon's teacher, and is probably the father of Johann Alexander, who was professor at Ingolstadt in 1523. At first Alexander belonged to the secret adherents of Luther, but his patristic studies made him soon a decided opponent of the Reformation. In 1524 he was called to Vienna, where he died, Nov. 27, 1539. See Döllinger, *Reformation*, i, 525 sq.; Hefele, in Wetzer u. Welte's *Kirchenlexikon*, s. v. (B. P.)

Braun, Placidus, a Benedictine, was born in 1756 at Peuting, in Upper Bavaria. In 1775 he entered the monastery of St. Ulric, at Augsburg, and, having charge of the library, published *Notitia Hist. Litt. de Libris ab Artis Typogr. Inventione*, etc. (Aug.-Vind. 1788–89), and *Notitia Hist. Litt. de Codicibus MSS. in Bibl. Monasterii Exstantibus* (1791–96, 6 vols.). In 1808 he was made member of the Bavarian Academy of Sciences, and edited *Codex Diplom. Monasterii S. Udalrici* (in the *Mon. Boica*, tom. xxii, xxiii), and collected the *Codex Episcopatus Augustani.* He also published a history of the bishops of Augsburg, in four volumes

(Augsburg, 1813-15). He died Oct. 23, 1829. See Lindner, *Schriftsteller des Bened. Ordens in Bayern seit* 1750 (Regensburg, 1880), ii, 124; Streber, in Wetzer u. Welte's *Kirchenlexikon*, s. v. (B. P.)

Bremer, Friedrich, a Roman Catholic theologian of Bavaria, was born at Bamberg, Jan. 10, 1784. In 1807 he took holy orders, and in 1808 received the degree of doctor of theology. In 1813 he was appointed subdirector of the clerical seminary at Bamberg, and in 1820 its director, at the same time occupying the chair of dogmatics at the lyceum there. In 1821 he became a member of the newly founded chapter, in 1844 its dean, and died Aug. 20, 1846. He wrote, *Versuch einer historisch-philosophischen Darstellung der Offenbarung* (1810):—*Katholische Dogmatik* (1815-17, and often, 3 vols.):—*Geschichtliche Darstellung der Verrichtung und Ausspendung der Sacramente* (1818-24, 3 vols.):—*Das Gericht*, etc. (1829). See Thiem, in the *Twelfth Annual Report of the Historical Society at Bamberg*, 1849, p. 14, 21; Jäck, *Zweites Pantheon* (Bamberg, 1843), p. 12, 13; Wittmann, in Wetzer u. Welte's *Kirchenlexikon*, s. v. (B. P.)

Brillmacher, Peter Michael, a Jesuit, was born at Cologne in 1542, and studied at Paris under Maldonatus. For six years he was rector at Speyer, and in 1588 went to Münster, where he founded the college of the Jesuits, whose rector he was for eight years. He died Aug. 25, 1595, leaving, *De Communione sub Altera Tantum Specie* (Cologne, 1582):—*De Eucharistiæ Sacramento Dialogi V* (1580-84):—*Christiana et Solida Detectio Errorum Joannis a Münster* (1591). See Hartzheim, *Bibl. Colonsensis;* Reiffenberg, *Historia Soc. Jes. ad Rhen. Inf.* p. 319; Strunck, *Annal. Paderborn*, iii, 539, 566; Bauer, in Wetzer u. Welte's *Kirchenlexikon*, s. v. (B. P.)

Bristol, Daniel Wheelock, D.D., a Methodist Episcopal minister, was born at Adams, Jefferson Co., N. Y., Dec. 15, 1812. He joined the Church in 1833, was licensed the following year, and entered the Oneida (afterwards Central) Conference, in which he continued until his death, at Syracuse, Nov. 2, 1883, having filled the most important positions and been several times a delegate to the General Conference. See *Minutes of Annual Conferences*, 1883, p. 320.

Bronson, Miles, D.D., a Baptist missionary, was born at Norway, N. Y., July 20, 1812. He studied at the Hamilton (N. Y.) Literary and Theological Institution, was ordained at Whitesborough, and appointed missionary April 29, 1836. He reached Sadiya, Assam, in July, 1837, where he remained until his removal to Jaipur in the spring of 1838. He did good service also at Nowgong. In 1857 he visited his native land, but in 1860 went back to the East, where he again carried on his work at Nowgong for nine years, and then made another short visit to the United States. In July, 1874, he removed to Gowahiti, and was at that station for several years. Returning once more to his native land, he died, Nov. 10, 1883. See Cathcart, *Baptist Encyclop.* p. 141. (J. C. S.)

Brooke, Benjamin Franklin, D.D., a Methodist Episcopal minister, was born and reared within the bounds of the old Baltimore Conference. He was educated at Dickinson College, and entered the Baltimore Conference while yet in his youth. In 1873 he was transferred to the Pittsburgh Conference, and in 1876 to the East Ohio. His last work was that of presiding elder of the Canton District. He died at Winchester, Va., Sept. 25, 1882. See *Minutes of Annual Conferences*, 1882, p. 329.

Brown, Andrew, D.D., a Scotch clergyman, was born at Biggar, Aug. 22, 1763. He became tutor in the Cranston family; was licensed to preach in 1786; ordained in 1787 minister to the Presbyterian congregation at Halifax, Nova Scotia; admitted minister at Lochmaben, Scotland, in 1795; transferred to New Greyfriars, Edinburgh, in 1799; promoted to the Old Church in 1800; appointed professor of rhetoric and belles-lettres in the university in 1801, which he held in conjunction; elected moderator of the General Assembly in 1813, and died Feb. 19, 1834. He was characterized by eloquent composition, unobtrusive manners, and kindly feelings. He published a series of sermons, and the *Life of Alexander Christison*. See *Fasti Eccles. Scoticanæ*, i, 12, 71, 360, 642.

Brown, John, D.D., a Protestant Episcopal clergyman, was born in New York city, May 19, 1791. He graduated from Columbia College in 1811, was ordained deacon in 1812, and was rector of St. George's Church, Newburgh, from 1815 until his death, Aug. 15, 1884.

Brown, *Mrs.* **Phœbe Hinsdale** (her maiden name), a poetess, was born at Canaan, N. Y., May 1, 1773. She had no early education; married a painter of Ellington, Conn.; lived a humble and painful, but Christian life, and died at Marshall, Ill., Oct. 10, 1861. Among her hymns the most noted is "I love to steal awhile away," written in 1818, and included with others in Nettleton's *Village Hymns* (1824). She also wrote for the newspapers, and was the author of several tracts and a series of tales, entitled *The Tree and its Fruits* (N. Y. 1836). See (N. Y.) *Independent*, Jan. 6, 1881.

Brown, Samuel Gilman, D.D., LL.D., a Congregational divine, was born at North Yarmouth, Me., Jan. 4, 1813. He graduated from Dartmouth College in 1831, and from Andover Theological Seminary in 1837; was principal of Ellington (Conn.) High-school in 1832 and 1833, and of Abbot Academy, Andover, from 1835 to 1838; spent two years thereafter in Europe; became professor at Dartmouth College in 1840, president of Hamilton College in 1867, instructor at Dartmouth College in 1881, at Bowdoin College in 1883, and died, Nov. 4, 1885, at Utica, N. Y. He had been ordained in 1852, but was without charge. He was the author of numerous works of a popular character, chiefly biographies and addresses. See *Cong. Year-book*, 1886, p. 20.

Brown, William Lawrence, D.D., a Scotch clergyman (son of the professor of divinity and Church history at St. Andrews), was born at Utrecht, where his father was then minister, Jan. 7, 1755. He graduated from the University of St. Andrews in 1772; was licensed to preach in 1777, ordained for the English congregation at Utrecht, and appointed professor of moral philosophy at the Utrecht University in 1788. Being threatened by the revolutionary army of France, he fled to England; was elected minister at Greyfriar's Church, Aberdeen, in 1795, and promoted to be principal of Marischal College, which he held in conjunction; was appointed one of the chaplains in ordinary to the king in 1800, dean of the Order of the Thistle in 1803, resigned the living at Greyfriar's in 1828, and died May 11, 1830. He was a man of great talents and gifts; with warmth of temper, he was open, sincere, and generous, exercising unbounded liberality. He published, *An Essay on the Folly of Scepticism* (Lond. 1788):—*Oratio de Religionis et Philosophia Societate et Concordia Maxime Salutari* (Utrecht, eod.):—*Oratione Imaginatione in Vitæ Institutione Regenda* (ibid. 1790):—*Essay on the Natural Equality of Man* (Edinburgh, 1793):—seven single sermons (Lond. eod.):—*Speech in the General Assembly on the Settlement at Kingsbairns of the Rev. Dr. Arnot* (Edinburgh, 1800):—*Letters to the Rev. Principal Hill* (Aberdeen, 1801):—*Sermons* (Edinburgh, 1803):—*A Letter to Principal Hill* (1807):—*Philemon; or, The Progress of Virtue*, a poem (1809, 2 vols.):—*An Attempt towards a New Historical and Political Explanation of the Revelation* (1812):—*An Essay on the Existence of a Supreme Creator* (Aberdeen, 1816, 2 vols., for which was adjuged Bennett's prize of £1250):—*A Comparative View of Christianity* (Edinburgh, 1826, 2 vols.). See *Fasti Eccles. Scoticanæ*, iii, 475-476.

Brunner, Karl, a Swiss theologian and architect, was born at Hemberg, in the Toggenburg, in 1831.

He studied at Zurich and Tübingen. At the latter university he became a zealous disciple of the then prevailing "Tübingen school," to which he remained faithful until his death, although throughout his life he maintained friendly intercourse with men of all parties. His first ministerial duty was at Kappel, where he served as vicar. In 1856 he was elected pastor of Henau, and in 1858 of Bühler, in Appenzell. His zeal for the schools drew him away from his clerical work, and in 1864 he was called to the cantonal school of Appenzell, at Trogen, and in 1867 invited to become rector of the gymnasium at Biel. In 1873 the government of Aargau invited him to take charge of its rich archives, a task to which he devoted the remainder of his life, without, however, attaining the great object—the complete organization of the archives of the illustrious "gau" of the Aar. He died Jan. 26, 1881. (B. P.)

Brunson, Alfred, D.D., a Methodist Episcopal minister, was born at Danbury, Conn., Feb. 9, 1793. He was educated in the common-schools and trained as a shoemaker; converted July 3, 1809, while living with an uncle at Carlisle, Pa., and licensed to exhort. Returning to Connecticut the same year, he settled at Bridgeport and began to hold religious services. In 1812 he removed to Ohio, and entered the army under general Harrison. He was licensed to preach in 1815, and in 1818 formed a large circuit in Huron County, O. In 1820 he became connected with the Pittsburgh Conference, formed that year. Here he labored and studied law until 1836. In July, 1836, he removed to Prairie du Chien, Wis., to labor in behalf of the Indians. In 1839 he relinquished his ministerial labors on account of ill-health, was admitted to the bar, and practiced for ten years, during which period he filled several secular offices. He resumed pastoral work in 1850, and served several important charges, including Prairie du Chien district. In 1862 he was commissioned chaplain of the Thirty-first Wisconsin Volunteer Infantry, but resigned on account of failing health one year later. He remained on the superannuated list until 1869, when he again became effective. He travelled until the fall of 1872, when he was superannuated for the last time. He was four times elected a member of the General Conference, and closed his remarkable career at Prairie du Chien, Aug. 3, 1882. He was a frequent contributor to the secular and religious journals, and especially to the *Methodist Quarterly Review*. He published his autobiography, in two volumes, entitled *The Western Pioneer*, and also a *Key to the Apocalypse*. See *Minutes of Annual Conferences*, 1882, p. 308.

Brus, Anton, a Bohemian prelate, was born at Müglitz, in Moravia, Feb. 13, 1518. He studied at Prague, where he also received holy orders. In the war against the Turks, 1542–45, he was Austrian chaplain. In 1558 the emperor, Ferdinand I, made him bishop of Vienna, and in 1562 he was raised to the archepiscopal see of Prague. He also attended the council at Trent. He died Aug. 28, 1580. See *Oesterreichische Vierteljahrsschrift für Katholische Theologie* (Vienna, 1874), where his biography is given; Borowy, in Wetzer u. Welte's *Kirchenlexikon*, s. v. (B. P.)

Büchsenschütz, Ludwig Jacob Theodor, a Lutheran minister of Germany, was born March 20, 1814. In 1846 he entered upon his first ministerial duties, and in 1853 was appointed superintendent of the Lützelstein diocese in Alsace. In 1859 he was removed to Weyer, the centre of his diocese, where he labored for twenty-three years, zealously defending the sacred rights of evangelical faith. He died July 6, 1882. (B. P.)

Bugbee, Lucius H., D.D., a Methodist Episcopal minister, was born in Gowanda, N. Y., Nov. 25, 1830. He was converted in boyhood, licensed as an exhorter at eighteen, graduated from Genesee College in 1853 and Amherst College in 1854, became teacher in Cooperstown Academy in 1855, joined the Upper Iowa Conference in 1857, and was appointed president of its university; in 1860 was transferred to the Rock River Conference, and served several important stations; in 1865 became president of the Female College, Evanston, Ill.; in 1868 of that in Cincinnati; in 1875 of Allegheny College; being then transferred to the Pittsburgh Conference, in which, in 1882, he was appointed to Monongahela city, but his health failed, and he died at Geneva, N. Y., July 28, 1883. See *Minutes of Annual Conferences*, 1884, p. 323; Simpson, *Cyclop. of Methodism*, s. v.

Bulfinch, Stephen Greenleaf, D.D., a Unitarian minister and poet, was born in Boston, Mass., June 18, 1809. He graduated from Columbia College, Washington, D.C., in 1826, and from the Harvard Divinity School in 1830; served chiefly as pastor at Augusta, Me., for the next seven years; afterwards preached and taught at Pittsburgh, Pa., and in Washington, D. C.; in 1845 became pastor at Nashua, N. H.; in 1852 at Dorchester, Mass.; and died at Cambridge, Oct. 12, 1870. He published several prose works, as well as *Poems* (Charleston, S. C., 1804). See Duyckinck, *Cyclop. of Amer. Lit.* ii, 345.

Burigny, Jean Lévesque, a French historian, was born at Rheims in 1692, and died at Paris, Oct. 8, 1785. He wrote, *Traité de l'Autorité du Pape* (1720, 4 vols.): —*Histoire de la Philosophie Païenne* (1724, 1754, 2 vols.): —*Vie de Grotius* (Amsterdam, 1750, 1754, 2 vols.):—*Vie d'Érasme* (1757, 2 vols.):—*Vie du Cardinal Duperron* (1768). See Quérard, *La France Littéraire*, s.v.; Dacier, *Éloge de Burigny* (Paris, 1788); Walkenaer, *Recueil de Notices Historiques* (ibid. 1850), p. 286; *Biog. Général.* vii, 840; Gams, in Wetzer u. Welte's *Kirchenlexikon*, s. v. (B. P.)

Burleigh, William Henry, a reformer and poet, was born at Woodstock, Conn., Feb. 2, 1812. He early became a temperance and anti-slavery lecturer; removed to Pittsburgh, Pa., in 1837, where he published the *Christian Witness*, and afterwards the *Temperance Banner;* in 1843 to Hartford, Conn., as editor of the *Christian Freeman*, soon known as the *Charter Oak;* in 1849 to Albany, N. Y., as editor of the *Prohibitionist;* in 1855 to New York city as harbor-master, and subsequently as one of the port-wardens. He died at Brooklyn, March 18, 1871. He was the author of *Poems* (Philadelphia, 1841; enlarged, with biography by his wife, New York, 1871). See Duyckinck, *Cyclop. of Amer. Lit.* ii, 859.

Burns, John, D.D., a minister of the Methodist Protestant Church, was born in 1807. He was an honored member of the Muskingum Conference, and was one of the best known of his denomination in Ohio; a strong preacher, had good executive ability, and wherever he was stationed the Church prospered. For some years he was chaplain of the Ohio Penitentiary. He died at Cadiz, Sept. 12, 1883. See *The Methodist Recorder*, Sept. 22, 1883.

Busæus. See Busee.

Byrom, John, an English poet, was born at Kersall, near Manchester, in 1691. After studying at Merchant-Taylors School in London, he graduated from Trinity College, Cambridge, in 1711, became a fellow there, travelled in France, next gave lessons in stenography in London, and at length settled upon his native estate, and died there, Sept. 28, 1763. He was of a mystical turn, and besides various miscellaneous essays and pieces, he published *Hymns and Sacred Poems* (1739; reprinted 1773, 1814, and in his collected poems, 1857), some of which are quite popular.

C.

Caldwell, James, D.D., a Congregational minister, was born at Kilmarnock, Scotland, in the spring of 1809. He was educated at Glasgow University; ordained in 1837; preached at Biggar, Greenock, and Stockton-on-the-Tees (Eng.); came to America in 1851; was acting pastor successively at Kent, Conn., Sheffield, Mass., Beardstown, Ill., Post Mills, in Thetford, Vt., and without charge at Barnard and Post Mills until his death, April 9, 1885. See *Cong. Year-book,* 1886, p. 21.

Calinich, HERMANN JULIUS ROBERT, a Lutheran theologian of Germany, doctor of philosophy and theology, was born in 1834, at Niederfriedersdorf, Saxony. In 1860 he was teacher at the gymnasium in Dresden, in 1863 deacon, afterwards pastor of St. Jacobus, at Chemnitz, and since 1872 pastor primarius of St. Jacobus at Hamburg. He died at Wiesbaden, Jan. 13, 1883. He wrote, *Luther und die Augsburgische Confession* (Leipsic, 1861):—*Kampf und Untergang des Melanchthonismus,* etc. (ibid. 1866):—*Wie Sachsen orthodoxlutherisch wurde* (ibid. eod.):—*Zwei sächsische Kanzler* (ibid. 1868):—*Der Papst und das ökumenische Concil* (ibid. eod.):—*Der Naumburger Fürstentag* (ibid. 1870): —*De Conventu Anno MDLXXIV. Torgæ Habito* (ibid. 1873):—*Dr. M. Luther's kleiner Katechismus. Beitrag zur Textrevision desselben* (ibid. 1882). (B. P.)

Calvinus, JUSTUS, a Roman Catholic controversialist, was born about the year 1570, at Xanten, in Cleve. He was the son of a Calvinistic preacher. He studied at Heidelberg under the famous Junius, went to Rome, where he made the acquaintance of Bellamin and Baronius, whose works he now studied. After his return to Germany, he joined the Church of Rome. When or where he died is not known. He published at Mayence in 1601, *Pro Sacrosancta Catholica Romana Ecclesia Apologia:—Epistolarum Catholicarum Liber Unus:—De Latitudine Ecclesiæ Dei, et Moderata Coërcitione Hæreticorum.* The first two works were also published in a second edition at Heidelberg in 1756. His main work is *Præscriptionum Adversus Hæreticos Perpetuarum ex SS. Orthodoxis Potissimum Patribus Tractatus IV* (Mayence, 1602; 2d ed. 1756). See Räss, *Convertitenbilder,* iii, 537-620; Kobler, in Wetzer u. Welte's *Kirchenlexikon,* s. v. (B. P.)

Cambuslang, WALTER, a Scotch prelate, was bishop of the see of Dunblane in 1362, and signed as witness the fourteen years' truce between Scotland and England, executed at Edinburgh, July 20, 1369. See Keith, *Scottish Bishops,* p. 176.

Cameron, ANDREW, D.D., a Scotch divine and editor, was born at Edinburgh in 1822, and educated in the university there. He early became connected with the press, first as a reporter, and, in 1845, as the projector of the *Christian Treasurer,* later of the *Free Church Magazine,* and other periodicals. He eventually became pastor at Maryton, Fifeshire, and in 1870 at St. Kilda, Melbourne, where he died in 1877.

Campbell, John M'Leod, D.D., a Scotch clergyman, son of the minister at Kilninver, born May 4, 1800, was presented to the living at Row in 1825, and ordained; deposed in May, 1831, for teaching universal atonement and pardon, also that assurance is necessary to salvation. He continued teaching these doctrines to his followers, first at Kilninver, and afterwards in a chapel at Glasgow until 1859. He died at Roseneath, Feb. 27, 1872. His publications were, *Sermons* (1831, 2 vols.):—*Notes of Sermons:—Speech at the Bar of the Synod* (eod.):—*Letters on Keeping a Conscience Void of Offence* (1834):—*Christ the Bread of Life* (Edinburgh, 1851):—*Atonement* (1854):—*Nature of the Atonement* (1856):—*Thoughts on Revelation* (1862). See *Fasti Eccles. Scoticanæ,* ii, 371; Campbell, *Memorials* (Lond. 1877).

Campbell, William Graham, D.D., an Irish Wesleyan preacher, was born near Sligo in 1805. He was converted in 1822, and soon began preaching, his first regular appointment being the Killeshandren Circuit in 1831, and he spent twenty-five years of great power in the general work. He died Feb. 24, 1885. See *Minutes of the British Conference,* 1885, p. 35.

Campeggio. We notice two other members of this family.

1. ALESSANDRO, son of Lorenzo, was born at Bologna in 1504. He was educated by the most learned men of Italy, and appointed, in 1526, by pope Clement VII, as his father's successor in the bishopric of Bologna. The ninth and tenth sessions of the Tridentine Council were held at his palace. Pope Julius III made him cardinal in 1551. He died Sept. 20, 1554.

2. CAMILLO, inquisitor of Ferrara, and bishop of Nepi-Sutri, who died in 1569, is the author of *De Primatu Romani Pontificis contra M. Flacium Illyricum* (reprinted by Rocaberti, in *Bibl. Magn. Pontif.* vol. vii). See Gams-Kreutzwald, in Wetzer u. Welte's *Kirchenlexikon,* s. v.; Jöcher, *Allegemeines Gelehrten-Lexikon,* s. v. (B. P.)

Camus, ÉTIENNE, a French Jansenist and prelate, was born Nov. 16, 1632. In 1660 he was already a doctor of the Sorbonne, but his unchristian walk brought on him the disfavor of Mazarin, and he was banished. Prince Conti, governor of Languedoc, however, received him, and brought him under the influence of the Jansenistic bishop, Pavillon of Alet. Louis XIV made him, in 1671, archbishop of Grenoble. In 1686 pope Innocent XI made him cardinal, and he was present, in 1700, at the conclave held at Rome for the election of Clement XI. He died in 1707. He founded a clerical seminary at Grenoble. See *Gallia Christ.* xv, 255; Guarnacci, *Hist. Pont. Rom. et Card.* i, 237; Loyson, *L'Assemblée de* 1682, p. 188-235; Arnauld, *Œuvres,* i, 689 sq.; Bauer, in Wetzer u. Welte's *Kirchenlexikon,* s. v. (B. P.)

Caribbean MYTHOLOGY. Like all uncivilized nations, this people had but superficial conceptions of the creation of the world, the population of the earth, and of a life beyond. They believed that heaven was from eternity; it encircled an earth more beautiful and better than the present one. The latter was originally soft and at rest. A stranger, Louguo, gave it form and motion, and put fishes into the sea. The origin of terrestrial animals was not known, but human beings sprang from the navel of Louguo, who first inhabited the earth, then died, was raised to life again, and withdrew to that better heavenly world. Men became worse and worse, and because they did not make any sacrifices to the gods the latter sent a great flood, by which all men save a few were destroyed. The first men lived very long, some of them being changed into stars and made immortal for their good works. After the flood they lived in poverty and want. The Caribs, however, expected a happier existence in that upper world—better houses, more food, more women, no work, no sickness, but an unbroken life of pleasure. They worshipped the sun and moon, and on the occurrence of earthquakes they fasted for a number of days. Very seldom did they make sacrifices, for they took it for granted that the gods have no need of human service.

Carrasco, ANTONIO, a leading Spanish Protestant preacher, was born in Malaga, Jan. 19, 1843. He was converted in youth, and was imprisoned for Bible reading, but released in 1863 at the remonstrance of the Evangelical Alliance. After studying at Geneva, Switzerland, he returned to Spain in 1868, and zealously engaged in the publication of the true gospel there, becoming pastor of the Free Church in Madrid. On his way home from a visit to America he was drowned by the sinking of the steamer *Ville du Havre,* Nov. 22, 1873. See *Report of the Evangelical Alliance,* 1874, p. 764.

Carroll, JOHN, D.D., a minister of the Methodist Church in Canada, was born on the Bay of Fundy, Aug. 8, 1809. In 1818 his parents went to Toronto, where he was converted. In 1827 he entered the itinerant ranks, in which he occupied prominent stations in Canada, London, Toronto, Kingston, Ottawa, and elsewhere. He died in Toronto, Canada, Dec. 13, 1884. For nearly thirty years he was chairman of the districts in which his appointments were located. He was a most faithful and laborious pastor. Besides the history of his early years, called *My Boy Life*, he published several small volumes, a number of pamphlets and magazine articles, especially *Case and his Contemporaries* (Toronto, 1867, 5 vols.). See *Christian Guardian*, Dec. 17, 1884.

Cashmerian Version OF THE SCRIPTURES. Of late the work of translation into this dialect has again been resumed, for the annual report of the British and Foreign Bible Society for 1884 states that the Rev. T. R. Wade, formerly of Trinagar, now of Amritsar, has completed the translation of the New Test., on which he has been engaged for six years, and in the annual report of the same society for 1885 we read that the New Test. has been published. (B. P.)

Caswell, EDWARD, an English clergyman and poet, was born at Yateby, in Hampshire, July 15, 1814. He was educated at Brasennose College, Oxford, ordained presbyter in 1839, in 1840 became curate of Stratford-under-Castle, in 1847 joined the Roman Catholic Church, and died Jan. 2, 1878. Besides several prose works, he published metrical translations of many mediæval hymns, entitled *Lyra Catholica* (1848), and other poetical effusions, collected in *Hymns and Poems* (1873).

Catholic Emancipation, an enactment to relieve Roman Catholics of the civil and religious disabilities imposed by the laws passed in the time, chiefly, of Elizabeth. These forbade a Catholic priest receiving a neophyte into the Church in England under penalty of death; Jesuits forfeited life by appearing in the country; no man could plead at law or become a schoolmaster, or hold any office, especially in Ireland, without taking the oaths of supremacy and against transubstantiation. All this was abolished by the act of parliament of April 23, 1829, since which time Catholics and Protestants have enjoyed equal protection and liberty before the law.

Cawood, JOHN, an English clergyman and poet, was born at Matlock, Derbyshire, March 18, 1775. He graduated from St. Edmund's Hall, Oxford, in 1801; became curate at Ribbesford, Dowles, and Bewdley, and died Nov. 7, 1872. Besides several prose works, he published occasional hymns, a number of which were inserted in Cotterill's collection, and the one beginning "Hark, what mean those holy voices," has become especially popular.

Chandler, George Clinton, D.D., a Baptist minister, was born at Chester, Vt., March 19, 1807. He was baptized in 1825, and licensed to preach in 1831; graduated from Madison University in 1835, and from Newton Theological Institution in 1838; preached as a missionary among the Indians, and at Terre Haute, Ind.; became pastor at Indianapolis in 1839, president of Franklin College in 1843, in 1850 of the new Baptist college in Oregon, but soon resumed missionary work; became pastor at Dalles in 1874, and died there in November of the same year. See Cathcart, *Baptist Encyclop.* s. v.

Chandler, John, an English clergyman and poet, was born at Witley, in Surrey, June 16, 1806. He graduated from Corpus Christi College, Oxford, in 1827; became vicar of Witley in 1837, afterwards rural dean, and died at Putney, July 1, 1876. Besides some prose productions, he published translations called *Hymns of the Primitive Church* (1837), of which several have been inserted in most hymnals.

Channing, WILLIAM HENRY, a Unitarian divine, nephew of Dr. William E. Channing, was born in Boston, May 25, 1810. He graduated from Harvard College in 1829, and from Cambridge Divinity School in 1833; was ordained in 1839; successively served independent congregations at Meadville (Pa.), New York city, Cincinnati, O., Nashua, N. H., Boston, Mass., Rochester, N. Y., and Liverpool, Eng., and finally resided without charge in London until his death, Dec. 24, 1884. He edited various journals, wrote frequently for the reviews, and was the author of several sermons and memoirs, particularly of his uncle (1848, 3 vols.).

Chaplin, CHARLES CRAWFORD, D.D., a Baptist minister, was born at Danville, Va., Sept. 22, 1831. He was converted in 1853, spent two years in Richmond College, became pastor at Danville in 1856, at Owensborough, Ky., in 1870, at Paducah in 1873, and died at Brentana, Texas, Nov. 2, 1884. See Cathcart, *Baptist Encyclop.* s. v.

Chapman, ROBERT MARTIN, D.D., a Protestant Episcopal clergyman, was born at Petersburg, Va., April 20, 1810. He was ten years president of the State University, Vincennes, Ind.; rector successively at Jeffersonville, Ind., Pewee Valley, Ky., Sacramento and Oakland, Cal., and died at Los Gatos, April 8, 1883.

Chase, BENJAMIN, D.D., a Presbyterian minister, was born at Litchfield, N. H., Nov. 20, 1789. He graduated from Middlebury College in 1814, and labored as a missionary in Louisiana; in 1828 took charge of "Carmel Church," ten miles south of Natchez, Miss.; in 1830 became Bible-agent in the South-western states; in 1840 declined in health, and died Oct. 11, 1870. See Nevin, *Presbyterian Encyclop.* s. v.

Christian, JAMES W., D.D., a minister of the Methodist Episcopal Church, South, was born in Merriweather County, Ga., in 1844. He was converted in early manhood, licensed to preach in 1868, admitted into the Alabama Conference in 1872, labored on the Fredonia Circuit, at Monticello, and at Birmingham; was appointed editor of the *Alabama Christian Advocate* in 1881, and died Oct. 7, 1882. See *Minutes of Annual Conferences of the M. E. Church, South*, 1882, p. 79.

Clarke, Dorus, D.D., a Congregational minister, was born at Westhampton, Mass., Jan. 2, 1797. He graduated from Williams College in 1817, and from Andover Theological Seminary in 1820; was pastor at Blandford, Mass., from 1823 to 1825; at Chicopee Falls, from 1835 to 1840; editor thereafter of various religious journals, and died March 8, 1884. He was the author of numerous popular works. See *Cong. Year-book*, 1885, p. 20.

Clarke, Henry Steele, D.D., a Presbyterian minister, was born at Somers, Conn., in 1818. He graduated from Yale College in 1841; became pastor first at Willoughby, O.; in 1849 at Manchester, N. H.; in 1852 of the Central Church, Philadelphia, and died Jan. 17, 1864. See Wilson, *Presb. Hist. Almanac*, 1865, p. 83.

Clarkson, ROBERT HARPER, D.D., LL.D., a bishop of the Protestant Episcopal Church, was born at Gettysburg, Pa., Nov. 19, 1826. He graduated from Pennsylvania College in 1844, and studied theology at St. James's College; was ordained deacon in 1848; became rector of St. James's Church, Chicago, in 1849; was consecrated bishop of Nebraska, Nov. 15, 1865, and died March 10, 1884.

Cleptomania. See KLEPTOMANIA.

Clinch, JOSEPH H., D.D., a Protestant Episcopal clergyman, was born Jan. 30, 1806. He served as rector of St. Matthew's Church, South Boston, was secretary of the Diocesan Convention, and died July 5, 1884.

Close, FRANCIS, D.D., an Anglican divine, was born near Alton, Hampshire, in 1797. He graduated from St. John's College, Cambridge, in 1820; became curate of the Lawford Church, near Rugby; in 1822 of Wellesden and Kingsbury, Middlesex; in 1824 at Cheltenham, in 1856 dean of Carlisle, and died Dec. 18, 1882.

Closs, WILLIAM, D.D., a minister of the Methodist

Episcopal Church South, was born in Botetourt County, Va., in 1809. He entered the Virginia Conference in 1833, and was identified with the North Carolina Conference from its organization. He spent nearly fifty years in the itinerant ministry, twenty-eight of them as presiding elder; and was many times a delegate to the General Conference. His ability as a debater was unsurpassed. He died in Enfield, N. C., July 8, 1882. See *Minutes of Annual Conferences of the M. E. Church South*, 1882, p. 109.

Coan, TITUS, D.D., a Congregational minister, was born at Killingworth, Conn., Feb. 1, 1801. He joined the Presbyterian Church at Riga, N. Y., in 1828; studied privately, graduated from Auburn Theological Seminary in 1833, was ordained the same year a missionary to Patagonia, in 1835 went to Hawaii, where he labored with great success at Hilo until his death, Dec. 1, 1882. Besides some tracts, essays, etc., he published *Adventures in Patagonia* (1880):—*Life in Hawaii* (1882). See *Cong. Year-book*, 1884, p. 21.

Cochran, WILLIAM PORTER, D.D., a Presbyterian minister, was born at Millerstown, Pa., Nov. 10, 1803. He graduated from Dickinson College in 1824, and from Princeton Theological Seminary in 1827; was ordained an evangelist in 1829, became stated supply at Columbus, Mo., the same year, at Palmyra in 1834, at Big Creek in 1841, pastor there in 1857, preached in various churches in 1861, was pastor at Millerstown in 1867, and evangelist from 1869 until his death near West Ely, Mo., Dec. 25, 1884. See *Necrol. Report of Princeton Theol. Sem.* 1885, p. 14.

Cocker, BENJAMIN FRANKLIN, D.D., LL.D., a Methodist Episcopal divine, was born in Yorkshire, England, in 1821. He was brought up as a Wesleyan, converted in early life, and at eighteen became a local preacher. He was educated at King James's Grammar-school for one of the learned professions, but after spending several years in business in England, and from 1850 several more in Australia, he came to America in 1856, settled at Adrian, Mich., and the next year joined the Detroit Conference, being sent to Palmyra; the following year was stationed at Adrian, afterwards at Ypsilanti, Ann Arbor, and Adrian; and in 1869 was appointed professor of philosophy in Michigan University, a position which he retained until his death, April 8, 1883. He was a fine scholar and a brilliant writer. He was the author of, *Christianity and Greek Philosophy*:—*Theistic Conception of the World*:—*Student's Hand-book of Philosophy*. See *Minutes of Annual Conferences*, 1883, p. 315.

Coggeshall, SAMUEL D., D.D., a Methodist Episcopal minister, was born at Lynn, Mass., Feb. 18, 1811. He was converted in early life, and immediately began to preach; was admitted in 1832 into the New England Conference, in which and (after 1840) in the Providence (now the New England Southern) Conference he occupied important positions until his death, Oct. 30, 1885. By private studies he acquired a good degree of scholarship, and was well known as a writer, especially on historical subjects, in the periodicals of his denomination. See *Minutes of Annual Conferences*, 1886, p. 90.

Coit, THOMAS WINTHROP, D.D., LL.D., a Protestant Episcopal divine, was born at New London, Conn., June 28, 1803. He graduated from Yale College in 1821; became rector of St. Peter's, Salem, Mass., in 1827; of Christ Church, Cambridge, in 1829; of Trinity Church, New Rochelle, N. Y., in 1839; afterwards of St. Paul's Church, Troy; president of Transylvania University, Lexington, Ky.; professor of Trinity College, Hartford, in 1849; in Berkeley Divinity School, Middletown, Conn., in 1872, and remained in that position until his death, June 21, 1885. He was the author of, *Theological Commonplace Book* (1832, 1857):—*Remarks on Norton's Statement of Reasons*, etc. (1833):—*Bible in Paragraphs* (1834; an abridgment of Townsend's *Chronological Bible*, which he also edited in full, 1837):—*Puritanism* (1844), besides frequent contributions to the journals of his denomination.

Colleges, AMERICAN. The methods of organization and instruction adopted in these institutions naturally grew out of those pursued in the educational establishments of the mother country, especially the great universities of Oxford and Cambridge, in which the colleges proper are subordinate or detailed schools. See UNIVERSITIES, EUROPEAN. In a few, chiefly the older and better-endowed colleges of the Eastern and Middle States, the original academic foundation has gradually expanded into a fully-developed university, and in many of the newer institutions the entire curriculum has been laid out for future completion; hence the use of the title "university" has been not altogether inappropriate, although few American educational incorporations cover the entire field of liberal arts and learned professions. In one instance, the University of the State of New York, the European idea has been substantially adopted, but without any local apparatus of buildings, teachers, or personal instruction. Special schools of technical training are generally relied upon to supplement the literary course in the departments of law, medicine, theology, engineering, etc. See THEOLOGICAL SEMINARIES. In many of the newer colleges of America, and in a few of the older ones, ladies are now admitted to the full privileges and honors of study and graduation, and there are numerous institutions, often styled "Female Colleges," in which women exclusively have nearly equal literary advantages, besides the ornamental branches more appropriate to their sphere. The honorary degrees (A.B., etc.) are in America sometimes conferred by schools which in reality are little above the rank of ordinary "academies." See EDUCATION.

The following tables are compiled from the *Report of the (U. S.) Commissioner of Education* for 1883-84 (the latest return). Detailed information on nearly all the colleges may be found in Kiddle and Schem's *Cyclopædia of Education*, under the title of each.

CLASSIFICATION OF AMERICAN COLLEGES.

According to States.		*Avowed Denominationalism.*	
Alabama	4	African Meth. Episc.	2
Arkansas	5	Assoc. Ref. Presb.	1
California	11	Baptist	35
Colorado	3	Christian	16
Connecticut	3	Congregational	15
Dakota	2	Cong. and Presb.	3
Delaware	1	Cumb. Presb.	5
District of Columbia	5	Disciples	1
Georgia	6	Evangelical	1
Illinois	29	Evangelical Associate.	1
Indiana	15	Evangelical Lutheran	11
Iowa	19	Friends	4
Kansas	8	Free-will Baptist	4
Kentucky	15	German Baptist	2
Louisiana	10	German Meth. Episc.	3
Maine	3	Hebrew	1
Maryland	9	Lutheran	3
Massachusetts	7	Methodist Episcopal	36
Michigan	9	Meth. Episc. South	16
Minnesota	4	Meth. Protestant	2
Mississippi	3	New Church	1
Missouri	19	Non-sectarian	82
Nebraska	5	Presbyterian	29
New Hampshire	1	Presb. Old Style	1
New Jersey	4	Protestant Episcopal	10
New York	29	Reformed	2
North Carolina	9	Reformed Dutch	1
Ohio	33	Reformed German	1
Oregon	6	Roman Catholic	56
Pennsylvania	26	Seventh-day Adventist	2
Rhode Island	1	Southern Presbyterian	1
South Carolina	9	United Brethren	7
Tennessee	20	United Presbyterian	3
Texas	11	Universalist	4
Utah	1	Total	365
Vermont	2		
Virginia	9		
Washington Territory	2		
Wisconsin	7		

AMERICAN COLLEGES ESTABLISHED DURING THE LAST CENTURY.

Organized.	Name.	Location.	Prevailing Denomination.	Teachers.	Students.
1639	Harvard College	Cambridge, Mass	Unitarian	58	1040
1701	Yale College	New Haven, Conn	Congregational	41	691
1746	College of New Jersey	Princeton, N. J	Presbyterian	38	434
1748	University of Pennsylvania	Philadelphia, Pa			143
1754	Columbia College	New York city, N. Y	Prot. Episcopal	14	285
1765	Brown University	Providence, R. I	Baptist	17	270
1770	Dartmouth College	Hanover, N. H	Congregational	15	232
1771	Rutgers College	New Brunswick, N. J	Dutch Reformed	18	68
1776	Hampden-Sidney College	Hampden-Sidney College, Va.	Presbyterian	6	72
1782	Washington College	Chestertown, Md		3	38
1783	Dickinson College	Carlisle, Pa	Meth. Episcopal	7	90
1785	College of Charleston	Charleston, S. C		5	17
1789	St. John's College	Annapolis, Md		8	49
1789	Georgetown College	West Washington, D. C	Roman Catholic	28	216
1793	Williams College	Williamstown, Mass	Congregational	17	275
1794	Greeneville College	Tusculum, Tenn	Presbyterian	4	19
1795	University of North Carolina.	Chapel Hill, N. C		13	188
1795	Union College	Schenectady, N. Y		19	119

Collier, William, D.D., a minister of the Methodist Protestant Church, was born at Hagerstown, Md., March 11, 1803. He was converted at the age of fourteen, joined the Methodist Episcopal Church, and became a local preacher. In 1828 he united with the Methodist Protestant Church, in 1829 was admitted into the Maryland Conference, in 1851 transferred to the Pittsburgh Conference, and in 1853 to the Muskingum Conference, in all which he took prominent positions, being several times president. He held a superannuated relation from 1863 to 1869, and again from 1874 until his death, July 12, 1884. He was a powerful preacher. See *Methodist Recorder*, Sept. 20, 1884.

Conceptualism, a term used to designate that form of speculative philosophy which does not deny the reality of objective existences, but still holds them to be certain only as results of subjective perception or cognition. It was substantially that of Abelard, Peter the Lombard, and Albert the Great. See Nominalism and Realism. It has recently been revived in a modified form by Kant, Lotze, and others.

Concursus Divīnus, a term used in scholastic philosophy to designate the coincidence between the divine agency, as a *final cause*, and natural agencies, as the *efficient cause* of events and processes. It was elaborated by Thomas Aquinas, and a similar distinction may be traced in the discussions on the human will and scientific evolution.

Condit, Robert Woodruff, D.D., a Presbyterian minister, was born at Stillwater, N. Y., Sept. 17, 1795. He graduated from the College of New Jersey in 1814, was licensed in 1818, and after preaching in various parts of Virginia, settled as pastor at Montgomery, N. Y., from December, 1820, to April, 1830, and at Oswego, from April, 1831, until his death, Feb. 11, 1871. He was an excellent preacher, and active in all ecclesiastical work. See *Gen. Cat. of Auburn Theol. Sem.* 1883, p. 241; Nevin, *Presbyterian Encyclop.* s. v.

Coombe, Pennel, a noted Methodist Episcopal minister, was born at Smyrna, Del., Aug. 5, 1811. He was converted in 1829; received a good English education; filled a vacancy as preacher at Elkington, Md., in 1834, and the next year was admitted into the Philadelphia Conference, in which he occupied important positions, as preacher, presiding elder, and agent for various Church enterprises, and especially in the temperance cause, until his death, near Philadelphia, Jan. 31, 1884. See *Minutes of Annual Conferences*, 1884, p. 81.

Cooper, J. T., D.D., a Methodist Episcopal minister, was born at Dover, Del., March 16, 1806. He was converted when about twenty-three years old, entered the Philadelphia Conference in 1834, and in it occupied important stations until the failure of his health, in 1851, after which he labored occasionally, chiefly in the Wilmington Conference, until his death, April 12, 1884. See *Minutes of Annual Conferences*, 1885, p. 84.

Coppin (**Copyn**, or **Copping**), John, a layman (some say a minister) of Bury St. Edmunds, Eng., was imprisoned in 1570 for holding public religious services, and hanged, June 5, 1583, as a disseminator of heretical books. See Dexter, *Congregationalism*, p. 210.

Cotterill, Thomas, an English clergyman and poet, was born at Cannock, Staffordshire, Dec. 4, 1779. He was educated at St. John's College, Cambridge; ordained in 1806; labored in the ministry successively at Tutbury, Lane End, in the Staffordshire potteries, and at St. Paul's, Sheffield (1817), until his death, Dec. 29, 1823. Besides a book of family prayers, he published (aided by James Montgomery) a *Selection of Psalms and Hymns* (1819), among which the version of Psa. ciii, beginning "O bless the Lord, my soul," has become especially popular. Mrs. M. J. Cotterill's hymn, "O thou who hast at thy command, The hearts of all men in thy hand," is from the same collection.

Cotton, Nathaniel, an English physician and poet, was born in 1707. He studied medicine at Leyden under Boerhave; established an asylum for lunatics first at Dunstable, Bedfordshire, and afterwards at St. Albans, and died Aug. 2, 1788. Besides two medical books, he published *Visions in Verse* (1751, and since). His works, both in verse and prose, were edited by his son (1791, 2 vols.).

Cowley, Abraham, an English poet, was born in London in 1618, and educated at Westminster School, and Trinity College, Cambridge. In 1643 he was compelled to retire to Oxford on account of his royalistic sentiments, and afterwards left England for ten years, and spent the rest of his life in studious retirement. He died at Chertsey, July 28, 1667. Besides some scientific and philosophical treatises, he published many poems, which, however, are now little valued.

Craik, James, D.D., LL.D., a Protestant Episcopal clergyman, was born at Alexandria, Va., in 1806. He graduated from the Transylvania University; practiced law at Kanawha, W. Va.; was ordained in 1839; was rector five years at Weston, and thereafter of Christ Church, Louisville, Ky., until his death, June 9, 1882. He was president of the General Convention in 1865, 1868, 1871, and 1874, and for many years a member of the standing committee of the diocese of Kentucky.

Crane, William Carey, D.D., LL.D., a Baptist minister and educator, was born at Richmond, Va., March 17, 1816. He graduated from Columbian College, D. C.; was converted in 1832, and ordained in 1838; was pastor successively at Montgomery, Ala., Columbus, Vicksburg, and Yazoo City, Miss., from 1839 to 1851; in 1863 president of Baylor University, Texas, and died Feb. 26, 1885. See Cathcart, *Baptist Encyclop.* s. v.

Cretenet, Jacques, a noted French ecclesiastic, was born at Champlitte (Franche Comté) in 1604. He studied surgery at Lyons, and devoted himself to the relief of the victims of the memorable plague in that city. After the death of his wife, who had brought him a large property, he entered the clerical state, and founded the order of Josephists, devoted to missions and education, which met with much opposition, the head himself being excommunicated by the archbishop of Lyons. Cretenet died at Montheel, Sept. 1, 1666. See Hoefer, *Nouv. Biog. Générale*, s. v.

Crossman, Samuel, an English clergyman and poet, was born at Bradley, Suffolk, in 1824; became prebendary of the first stall at Bristol in 1667, dean in 1683, and died Feb. 4, 1684. Besides *Sermons*, he published *The Young Man's Meditations* (1664, 1863), which contains several popular hymns.

Cruelty to Animals is a subject which has lately attracted much public attention from moralists and legislators. The principle upon which owners are restrained from exercising unnecessary severity in the treatment of their beasts is not, as often imagined, because brutes have any moral rights in themselves, but because society requires to be protected from exhibitions of cruelty, inasmuch as these not only outrage the feelings of humane spectators, but also tend to generate ferocity in the individuals who practice such excess, and thus render them dangerous to their fellow-beings. On this ground Christianity, as soon as it succeeded in gaining control of public sentiment in the Roman empire, abolished the atrocious customs of the amphitheatre, not even allowing beasts to contend with each other in mortal combat for the amusement of the populace; and the same benign influence has nearly banished the bull-fight, the cock-pit, and pigeon-shooting, as sports, from Christendom. Wanton infliction of suffering is at variance with the fundamental law of the Gospel, and invariably reacts with injury upon its perpetrator. Even criminals are not to be executed with needless severity, nor with prolonged or aggravated misery. Pain may be, often must be, inflicted, and that of intense character, but never unnecessarily nor for the gratification of revenge, malice, or barbarity. The heavenly Father himself, like the wise surgeon, cuts keenly and cauterizes sorely, but only for the good of the sufferer. So the human lord of creation has a right to take the life of inferior creatures when this is subservient to his own or others' important advantage, but he is not authorized to superadd torture. The modern laws passed in most Christian countries to prevent cruelty to animals have this principle for their only legitimate foundation. Hence they should be judiciously administered, so as not rashly to interfere with the proper rights of ownership, nor subject parties to vexatious interference. The practice of *vivisection* for scientific and medical purposes has especially been, in our judgment, unduly restrained by some of the enactments in certain states as well as in Great Britain. The valuable information to be acquired by this means alone should not be lost for squeamish regard to nervous individuals, who are not compelled nor expected to witness such operations. Provided no unnecessary amount of pain is caused the animal, nor any aggravating circumstances introduced into the operation, these experiments should be fostered by the statute law, rather than repressed. They ought doubtless to be placed under regulation, but not prohibited. They should, of course, be performed in private, and by scientific practitioners. When carried on properly they are a means of mercy and not an act of inhumanity.

Curran, Richard Augustus, D.D., a Presbyterian minister, was born at Mifflintown, Pa., July 15, 1808. He graduated from Washington College in 1834, and from Princeton Theological Seminary in 1837; was licensed the same year, and became stated supply at various churches in New Jersey, Ohio, and Georgia until 1842, after which he was pastor of several churches successively, in Pennsylvania chiefly, teaching occasionally at the same time until 1875, when he retired to Indiana. He died there, March 26, 1883. See *Necrol. Report of Princeton Theol. Sem.* 1884, p. 22.

Currey, George, D.D., an English divine, was born in London, April 7, 1816, and educated at Charterhouse School and St. John's College, Cambridge, graduating in 1838. He became a fellow of the latter in 1839, in 1840 a lecturer, in 1844 a tutor, in 1845 Whitehall preacher, in 1849 preacher at the Charterhouse, and in 1871 its master. He died Feb. 7, 1882.

D.

Dabentonne. See Daubentonne.

Damon, Samuel Chenery, D.D., a Congregational minister, was born at Holden, Mass., Feb. 15, 1815. He graduated from Amherst College in 1836, attended Princeton Theological Seminary for two years, graduating from Andover Theological Seminary in 1841; was ordained seaman's chaplain and editor of *The Friend*, at Honolulu, Hawaii, from 1842 until his death, Feb. 7, 1885. He published numerous sermons and addresses. See *Cong. Year-book*, 1886, p. 22; *Necrol. Report of Princeton Theol. Sem.* 1885, p. 38.

Davies, Benjamin, Ph.D., LL.D., a Baptist scholar, was born at Wern, near St. Clear's, in Carmarthenshire, Wales, Feb. 26, 1814. He began to preach before he was sixteen years old, entered Bristol College in 1830, studied at the universities of Dublin and Glasgow, and finally at Leipsic; in 1838 took charge of the Baptist Theological Institution at Montreal, Canada; in 1844 of Stepney College, England; in 1847 became professor in McGill College, Montreal; in 1857 in Stepney College; then removed to Regent's Park, London, and died July 19, 1875. He was active in philological and Biblical labors, and published numerous works in that line. He was a member of the Bible Revision Committee. See (Lond.) *Baptist Hand-book*, 1876, p. 341.

Davies, *Sir* **John**, an English writer, was born at Tisbury, Wiltshire, in 1570. He graduated from Queen's College, Oxford, in 1590, studied law, became a member of Parliament in 1601, in 1603 solicitor-general of Ireland, in 1608 chief-justice in England, in 1616 returned to Ireland, and died Dec. 7, 1626. Besides several political essays he published a somewhat noted poem, entitled *Nosce Teipsum* (Lond. 1594, and often). See Chalmers, *Biog. Dict.* s. v.

Dead, Book of the. See Ritual of the Dead.

Dean, James Alexander, D.D., a Methodist Episcopal minister, was born at Hubbardton, Vt., April 3, 1823. He graduated from Wesleyan University, Conn., in 1847; studied one year in Andover Theological Seminary; taught for several years in Virginia, North Carolina, Ohio, and Indiana, joining meanwhile (1852) the North Carolina Conference of the Methodist Episcopal Church South, and later (1860) the Providence Conference of the Methodist Episcopal Church, in which he occupied important stations until 1872, after which he was engaged by turns as teacher, preacher, and author until his death, March 30, 1885. See *Alumni Record of Wesleyan University*, 1883, p. 81, 564; *Minutes of Annual Conferences*, 1886, p. 81.

De Koven, Henry, D.D., a Protestant Episcopal clergyman, was born Jan. 24, 1819, at Middletown, Conn. He studied some time at the Wesleyan University there, then travelled in Europe, studied theology under Dr. Jarvis at Middletown, in 1842 became instructor of modern languages in the university there, in 1844 rector at East Haddam, in 1845 assistant minister of Christ Church, New York city, in 1848 rector at Red Hook, N. Y., in 1862 professor in the Berkeley Divinity School, Middletown, Conn., and died at Engelburg, Switzerland, July 10, 1884.

Deshon, Giles Henry, D.D., a Protestant Episcopal clergyman, was born at New London, Conn., March

31, 1820. He graduated from Yale College in 1840, and from the General Theological Seminary (N. Y.) in 1843; ministered thereafter at Windham, Conn., until 1844, at South Glastonbury until 1848, and at Meriden from 1850 until his death, Jan. 1, 1883.

Dickinson, John, LL.D., an English Independent minister, was born near Whitby, Oct. 27, 1797. He was received as a preacher among the Wesleyans, but left them to study under Dr. Wardlaw at Glasgow, and at the Edinburgh University. In 1838 he became pastor at Kilmarnock, in 1846 at Hounslow, in 1852 at Bury, Lancashire, and in 1857 at Bridlington, where he died, Oct. 5, 1884. See (Lond.) *Cong. Year-book*, 1885, p. 190.

Diefendorf, Sanders, D.D., a Presbyterian minister, was born at Minden, N. Y., April 24, 1816. He graduated from Yale College in 1836; became pastor of Nashville and Hopewell churches, in Ohio, in 1845; in 1849 professor in Vermilion Institute, where he remained, with some pastoral and educational changes in the interim, until his death, Feb. 14, 1884. See Nevin, *Presb. Encyclop.* s. v.

Dirck, Cornelius Lansing, D.D., a Presbyterian minister, was born at Lansingburgh, N. Y., March 3, 1785. He became pastor at Onondaga in 1807, at Stillwater in 1814, at Park Street, Boston, Mass., in 1816, at Auburn, N. Y. (First Church), in 1817, at Utica (Second Church) in 1829, at Houston Street, New York city, in 1833, resided in Auburn from 1835 to 1838, in Illinois in 1839, was pastor successively at Utica, Syracuse, and Auburn until 1846, of churches in New York city and Brooklyn until 1855, and died March 19, 1857. He was also a professor in Auburn Theological Seminary from 1821 to 1826. See Nevin, *Presb. Encyclop.* s. v.

Disembodied State of the Soul after Death. In our almost total ignorance of the essential nature, whether of matter or spirit, and of the bond of union between them in the human constitution, we are able to predicate very little with certainty respecting the condition of the soul after its separation from the body. Neither science nor revelation affords us much positive information on the subject. After all the long and earnest inquiries of Christian as well as pagan philosophers a few general points only have been definitely ascertained. They may, in fact, be summed up in the two following propositions. See Psychology.

1. *The Soul Preserves its Consciousness after Death.*—The continuity of its intellectual and emotional powers is indeed essential to its identity, if not to its very existence, for we can form no conception of a disembodied spirit where these are absent. The so-called "soul-sleep" is a contradiction in terms, for literal sleep is a state of the *body* rather than of the mind, or, at least, a status of the latter superinduced by a certain condition of the former. In like manner all the analogies based upon temporary unconsciousness by reason of accidents or disease *during life* are false and self-confuted, since the very relation of corporeity upon which they are hypothecated is absent in the premises. It is scientifically certain that all such comatose or insensible states are merely the result of injury or inaction on the part of the brain and other nervous centres, and are produced by purely physical causes; hence, if they prove anything at all in the case, they would argue a total and final cessation of all consciousness at death—in other words, the mortality of the soul equally with that of the body. If the spirit really survives the dissolution of the flesh —and this is conceded by those who maintain the theory in question—then it must continue to possess and exercise its faculties, or else drop into a state which is tantamount to non-existence. A disembodied soul is difficult enough for us to apprehend in any supposition without this superadded notion of inanition of thought. It is as nearly as possible analogous to a mere *point*, but this, if devoid of properties or functions, is a sheer nonentity. Moreover, a restoration to consciousness by means and in consequence of a reunion with the body would be a *recreation* and a total destruction of the idea of identity. See Resurrection.

Accordingly, the uniform testimony of Scripture is clear as to the continued exercise of all its essential powers by the soul after death. Whatever else the parable of Lazarus and Dives may or may not mean, it certainly includes this, and the frequent, nay customary, use of such expressions as "being with Christ," etc., must imply, at least, as much as this. That the penitent thief and the apostle Paul expected to fall into absolute unconsciousness is abhorrent to common-sense and opposed to the plain tenor of their language. There could be no joy in such an anticipation, and there can be no comfort in it to modern believers. It is as unscriptural as it is irrational. See Soul-sleep.

2. *The Disembodied Soul Ceases to Hold its Present Relations to Earth and Sense.*—This follows necessarily from the absence of the body, through which alone it maintains these relations. The supposition of the development or continuance of spiritual senses, or some occult faculty by which it discerns outward objects, is a sheer fancy destitute of logical or scientific support. A great deal of vague phraseology and equally indefinite imaginings is often indulged in by Christians on this point. Swedenborg carried his speculations so far as to invent a whole new world of post-mundane wonders, and to people it with the creations of his fertile fancy. Sober theology should be wary of such extravagance. The figurative expressions of Scripture must not be pressed into the service of visionary conceptions. Nothing can be more certain than the total suspension of all communication with the external or physical universe by the disruption of the tie between the body and the spirit at death, and prior to its resumption at the resurrection. How far a disembodied spirit may be able to hold intercourse with another is a pure matter of conjecture, upon which experience affords no information. That God, and perhaps angelic beings, have direct access to the mind in that state is a reasonable supposition, but it must be purely by internal and spiritual influences, which leave no trace of means or method upon the consciousness—as, in fact, they do not in the embodied state (John iii, 8). They can be detected only by their character and tendency (1 John iv, 1). The joys of the righteous and the misery of the wicked will doubtless be intensified by the absence of all distracting influences in the disembodied state, and will result chiefly, perhaps wholly, from the recollections and combinations of their former habits and associations of thought and feeling, just as in the state of final beatification or perdition they will be mainly due to similar causes. The soul will continue its usual state fixed by the absence of probation and external influences. Nor will it pursue the hallucinations of *dreams*, which are the effect of a suspension of the rational and perceptive faculties during sleep in a corporeal state, but will have the full consciousness of its position as to guilt or innocence, and the clear apprehension of its final award. A practical lesson, this, of the importance of cultivating those moral faculties and spiritual aspirations upon which the happiness of a rational and accountable creature must everlastingly depend! See Intermediate State.

Dobell, John, an English hymnist, born in 1757, was a pious layman of moderate education, who died at Poole, Dorsetshire, in May, 1840, leaving, besides two volumes on *Baptism* (1807) and *Humanity* (1812), a *New Selection of Hymns* (Lond. 1812, 8vo, and later), containing several of his own.

Dodge, Richard Varick, D.D., a Presbyterian minister, was born at Kaskaskia, Ill., Aug. 4, 1821. He graduated from Yale College in 1840, spent one year studying law, graduated from Princeton Theological Seminary in 1844, served as pastor or stated supply at various places in Indiana, Illinois, Virginia, Pennsylvania, Wisconsin, and California, spent several years in foreign travel, became pastor at San Diego, Cal., in 1879, and died there, Feb. 26, 1885. See *Necrol. Report of Princeton Theol. Sem.* 1885, p. 43.

Dorrien, PATRICK, D.D., an Irish Roman Catholic prelate, was born at Downpatrick, County Down, March 29, 1814. He entered Maynooth College in 1833, was ordained in 1837, was curate at Belfast until 1847, parish priest of Loughlin Island until 1860, when he became bishop of Gabala *in partibus*, coadjutor of the see of Down and Connor in 1865, sole bishop in the same year, and died Nov. 3, 1885. He published some sermons and charges. See Brady, *Episc. Succession*, i, 275; ii, 363.

Drummond, WILLIAM, the first Scottish poet who wrote well in English, was born at Hawthornden, Dec. 13, 1585. He graduated from Edinburgh University in 1605, studied law at Bruges, in France, settled upon his native estate in 1609, spent several years (1625–30) abroad, but was so affected by the execution of Charles I that he died, Dec. 4, 1649. Besides some political productions, he published numerous poems (a few religious), which have been issued collectively (1711, 1832, 1833, 1857). See *Life*, by Masson (Lond. 1873).

Du Bois, JOHN CLARKSON, D.D., a Protestant Episcopal minister, born Dec. 13. 1829, was rector of St. John's Church, Fredericksted, Santa Cruz, and died at Antigua, Nov. 27, 1884.

Duff, ARCHIBALD, D.D., a Congregational minister, was born in the Gallowgate, Aberdeen, in 1810, and educated in Marischal College, then one of the two universities of that city. Visiting Canada on a commercial commission, he earnestly engaged in religious labor, and on his return to Scotland, in 1836, entered Glasgow Theological Academy. In 1841 he was ordained pastor at Fraserburg; in 1845 joined the seceding Scotch Church, accepting the pastorship of the newly-formed Ebenezer Chapel; in 1848 became pastor at Hawick; in 1856 entered the service of the Colonial Missionary Society, laboring first at Comansville, Canada, and after 1862 at Sherbrooke. In 1880 he resigned his charge, and, returning to England, died at Putney, Nov. 19, 1883. See (Lond.) *Cong. Year-book*, 1884, p. 288.

Dunwody, JAMES, a veteran minister of the Methodist Episcopal Church South, was born in Screven County, Ga., May 4, 1790. He joined the Methodist Episcopal Church in 1810, was licensed to preach in 1816, was admitted to the Carolina Conference in 1818, and labored earnestly in hard fields until 1870, when he took a superannuated relation, which he sustained until his death, July 31, 1884. See *Minutes of Annual Conferences of the M. E. Church South*, 1884, p. 129.

Dutton, WARREN BACKUS, D.D., a Presbyterian minister, graduated from Yale College in 1829, studied at the Union Theological Seminary of Virginia, became assistant pastor in Farmville, Va., in 1838, pastor at Charlestown in 1841, devoted 1866–67 to recruiting his health, labored from 1868 to 1870 at Harper's Ferry, and afterwards resided at Charlestown until his death, Sept. 5, 1874, at the age of seventy years. See Nevin, *Presb. Encyclop.* s. v.

E.

Edmeston, JAMES, an English architect and poet, was born in London, Sept. 10, 1791, and died at Homerton, Jan. 7, 1867. He published, besides some prose works, several volumes of religious lyrical compositions, from which a few pieces have been inserted in most modern hymnals.

Elliott, *Miss* CHARLOTTE, an English poetess, sister of the author of *Horæ Apocalypticæ*, was born in 1789, and died at Brighton, Sept. 22, 1871. She wrote several volumes of religious poems, of which a number may be found in recent hymnals, especially "Just as I am, without one plea," which was composed after she had become a permanent invalid. Her sister-in-law, Mrs. Julia Anne Elliott, who died in 1841, also contributed several hymns to one of her earliest publications.

Emerson, DANIEL HOPKINS, D.D., a Presbyterian minister, was born at Salem, Mass., Jan. 23, 1810. He graduated from Dartmouth College in 1830, studied two years at Andover Theological Seminary, graduated from Yale Divinity School in 1833, taught school in Richmond, Va., was ordained pastor at Northborough, Mass., in 1836, in 1840 became pastor in East Whiteland, Pa., in 1845 at York, in 1855 at St. George's, Del., in 1869 of the Eastern Mariners' Church, Philadelphia, Pa., in 1873 general secretary of the Young Mens' Christian Association of Oswego, N. Y., in 1878 missionary of the First Presbyterian Church in Philadelphia, and died July 6, 1883.

Espy, T. B., D.D., a Baptist minister, was born in Cass County, Ga., in 1837. He was educated at Howard College, Ala., served three years as chaplain in the Confederate army, two years as pastor at Athens, Ga., two at Little Rock, Ark., in 1873 became editor of the *Western Baptist*, in 1879 of the *Baptist Reflector*, and later of the *American Baptist Flag*, St. Louis, Mo. He died at Little Rock, Feb. 7, 1881. See Cathcart, *Baptist Encyclop.* s. v.

European Universities. See UNIVERSITIES.

Ewer, FERDINAND CARTWRIGHT, D.D., a Protestant Episcopal minister, was born at Nantucket, Mass., May 22, 1826. He graduated from Harvard College in 1846, became rector of Grace Church, San Francisco, Cal., in 1857, in 1858 assistant minister of St. Ann's, New York city, in 1860 of Christ Church in the same city, later of the parish of St. Ignatius, and died in Montreal, Oct. 10, 1883.

F.

Field, JULIUS, a veteran Methodist Episcopal minister, was born April 2, 1799. In 1821 he entered the New York Conference (which then extended into Vermont), in which he continued to labor with earnestness and success as pastor and evangelist until 1839; then in the Wisconsin Conference as presiding elder, Sunday-school and Bible agent, and pastor until 1846; then again as pastor in his former conference until his superannuation in 1866. He died Sept. 22, 1884. See *Minutes of Annual Conferences*, 1885, p. 99.

Fitch, ELEAZAR THOMPSON, D.D., a Congregational divine, was born at New Haven, Conn., Jan. 1, 1791. He graduated from Yale College in 1810, and from Andover Theological Seminary in 1815; was ordained in 1817, became professor in the Yale Divinity School the same year, lecturer on homiletics in 1853, professor emeritus in 1863, and died there, Jan. 31, 1871. He often wrote for the religious reviews, published several sermons, and aided in compiling Congregational hymnals.

Follen, *Mrs.* ELIZA LEE (*née* **Cabot**), a poetess, wife of Dr. Charles T. C. Follen (q. v.), was born in Boston, Aug. 15, 1787. She was married in 1828, and died at Brookline, Mass., Jan. 26, 1860. Besides several works in prose, she published *Poems* (1839), some of which became quite popular. See Duyckinck, *Cyclop. of Amer. Literature*, i, 989.

Fontaine, EDWARD, LL.D., a Protestant Episcopal clergyman, was born at Greenwood, Va., Aug. 5, 1814. He was educated in the military academy at West Point, N. Y.; became a Methodist minister in Texas in 1840; held various parishes in Mississippi, Texas, and Louisiana from 1847 until 1855, when he was admitted to the bar. He served as captain in the battle of Manassas. He died at Belvidere, Miss., Jan. 19, 1884.

Forbes, JOHN MURRAY, D.D., a Protestant Episcopal clergyman, was born in 1807. He served as rector of St. Luke's Church, New York city, and dean of the General Theological Seminary there, and died at Elizabeth, N. J., Oct. 11, 1885.

Fraser, JAMES, D.D., an Anglican prelate, was born at Prestbury, near Cheltenham, in 1818. He graduated from Lincoln College, Oxford, in 1839; in 1840 became a fellow of Oriel College, and acted as tutor there for five years; in 1847 became rector at Cholderton, Wiltshire; in 1860 at Upton Nervet, near Reading; in 1870 bishop of Manchester, and died Oct. 22, 1885. He was the author of several reports, charges, and addresses on politico-religious subjects.

French, EDWARD WARNER, D.D., a Presbyterian minister, was born at Barre, Vt., Aug. 23, 1829. He graduated from Williams College in 1852; studied two years in the Union Theological Seminary, N. Y.; became pastor at Bergen, N. J., in 1856, and died Feb. 4, 1885.

Frothingham, NATHANIEL LANGDON, D.D., a Unitarian divine, was born in Boston, July 23, 1793. He graduated from Harvard College in 1811, and the next year was appointed professor of rhetoric in his *alma mater;* in 1815 became pastor of the First Church, Boston; resigned in 1850, but continued to reside there, chiefly thereafter engaged in literary labors, until his death, April 3, 1870. Besides contributions to the periodical press, he published *Sermons* (1852) and *Metrical Pieces* (1855–70), including hymns from the German. See Duyckinck, *Cyclop. of Amer. Literature*, ii, 33.

Fuller, Erasmus Q., D.D., a Methodist Episcopal minister, was born at Carlton, N. Y., April 15, 1828. He was converted at fourteen years of age; studied at Adrian, Mich.; entered the Rock River Conference in 1856, in which, and in the Georgia Conference (1868), he served very efficiently as preacher, presiding elder, and editor (of the *Methodist Advocate*, at Atlanta), until his sudden death, Oct. 16, 1883. He was a member of the General Conference in 1868 and thereafter. He published a volume on Sunday-schools, and another in defence of missions in the South (Cincinnati, O., 1876). See *Minutes of Annual Conferences*, 1883, p. 314; Simpson, *Cyclop. of Methodism*, s. v.

Fuller, R. W., D.D., a Baptist minister, was born at Beaufort, S. C., Nov. 27, 1829; studied theology with his uncle, Dr. Richard Fuller; was pastor at Atlanta, Ga., afterwards agent for the Georgia Baptist Orphan's Home, and for Mercer University. He died June 10, 1880. See Cathcart, *Baptist Encyclop.* s. v.

G.

Gadsby, WILLIAM, a noted English Baptist minister, was born at Attleborough in January, 1773. He was early converted among the Congregationalists, baptized in 1793, ordained in 1800, was pastor at Hinckley until 1805, and thereafter at Manchester until his death, Jan. 27, 1844. He was very eccentric in preaching. See Cathcart, *Baptist Encyclop.* s. v.

Geer, GEORGE JARVIS, D.D., a Protestant Episcopal clergyman, graduated from Trinity College, Hartford, in 1842, and from the General Theological Seminary, N. Y., in 1843; was rector of Christ Church, Ballston Spa, from 1845 to 1852, then associate rector of the Church of the Holy Apostles, New York city, and finally of St. Timothy, in the same city, until his death, March 16, 1885.

George, AUGUSTUS C., D.D., a Methodist Episcopal minister, was born at Avon Springs, N. Y., April 22, 1824. He was educated at the Wesleyan Seminary, Lima, joined the Genesee Conference in 1847, in which, and in the East Genesee, Missouri, Central New York, West Virginia, and Rock River conferences, he occupied important positions until his death, at Englewood, near Chicago, Ill., Aug. 7, 1885. Dr. George was often a member of the General Conference, and distinguished as a man of patriotic and ecclesiastical influence. See *Minutes of Annual Conferences*, 1885, p. 337; Simpson, *Cyclop. of Methodism*, s. v.

Gibson, WILLIAM J., D.D., a Presbyterian minister, was born at Ryegate, Vt., Aug. 22, 1810. He graduated from Jefferson College, Pa., in 1826, studied theology privately, was licensed to preach in 1831, became pastor of the Ninth Presbyterian Church, Philadelphia, in 1832, at Hollidaysburg in 1838, subsequently of various other churches in Pennsylvania until 1861, and died Oct. 5, 1883. See Nevin, *Presb. Encyclop.* s. v.

Gilbert, LYMAN, D.D., a Congregational divine, was a native of Vermont. He graduated from Middlebury College in 1824, and from Andover Theological Seminary in 1827; was pastor of the Second Church, Newton, Mass., from 1828 to 1858, thereafter at Malden, N. Y., and finally resided without charge at Brooklyn, until his death, March 28, 1885.

Gilder, JOHN LEONARD, a noted Methodist Episcopal minister, was born Aug. 8, 1816. He was early converted, licensed to preach in 1829, and in the same year joined the Philadelphia Conference, in which and in the New York East Conference he occupied important positions, including several years occupied in teaching, until his sudden death, July 3, 1883. See *Minutes of Annual Conferences*, 1884, p. 92.

Gleason, ANSON, a noted Congregational minister, often designated as "father Gleason," was born at Manchester, Conn., May 2, 1797. He was a missionary to various tribes of Indians from 1823 to 1835, in which latter year he was ordained, general missionary from 1848 to 1851, then again to the Indians until 1861, and thereafter city missionary successively in Rochester, Utica, and Brooklyn, until his death, Feb. 24, 1885. *Cong. Year-book*, 1886, p. 25.

Goode, WILLIAM, M.A., an English writer, was born at Buckingham, April 2, 1762. He entered Magdalen Hall, Oxford, in 1780, became curate of Abbots-Langley, Hertfordshire, in 1784, curate of St. Ann's, Blackfriars, London, in 1786, rector in 1795, and died April 15, 1816. He was the author of a *New Version of the Psalms in Metre* (1811, 1816):—*The Scripture Names of Christ* (1822, 6 vols.). See *Memoir*, by his son (Lond. 1828).

Gordon, SAMUEL R., D.D., a Protestant Episcopal clergyman, was born in Somerset County, Md. He graduated from the General Theological Seminary (N. Y.) in 1843, served as assistant at St. Paul's, Baltimore, rector of St. Luke's, Queen Anne's County, of St. Paul's, Kent County, of St. Thomas's, Prince George County, in 1853, and died there, Aug. 19, 1883, aged seventy years.

Gowan, ANTHONY T., D.D., a Scotch Independent minister, was born in 1811 at Whitehaven, Cumberland. He was educated at the Glasgow University, became pastor at Blackhills, near Aberdeen, afterwards at Dalkeith, and finally colleague of Dr. Alexander in the Theological Hall at Edinburgh. He died Dec. 16, 1884. See (Lond.) *Cong. Year-book*, 1886, p. 169.

Grahame, JAMES, a Scottish poet, was born April 22, 1765, at Glasgow. He graduated from the university there in 1784, was bred to the law, but took orders in the English Church, and became curate first at Shipton, Gloucestershire, and then at Sedgefield, near Durham, and died Sept. 14, 1811. His poetry, all in blank verse, is religious; the principal pieces are, *The Sabbath:* — *The Bards of Scotland:* — *British Georgics.* See *English Cyclop.* s. v.

Grant, *Sir* ROBERT, an English poet, was born in 1795, graduated from Cambridge in 1806, studied law, entered Parliament in 1826, became governor of Bombay in 1834, and died at Dapoorie, India, July 9, 1838. Besides some volumes on India, he wrote twelve sacred lyrics, which were published by his brother, lord Glenelg, under the title of *Sacred Poems* (1839), and are so excellent that several of them appear in most modern hymnals.

Grier, Isaac, D.D., a Presbyterian minister, was born at Jersey Shore, Pa., Jan. 7, 1806. He graduated from Dickinson College in 1828, and from Princeton Theological Seminary in 1833, became stated supply at Shamokin and Washington, Pa., the same year; the next year pastor at the latter place until 1852, at Buffalo in 1854, and so continued until his death at Mifflinburg, June 24, 1884. See *Necrol. Report of Princeton Theol. Sem.* 1885, p. 19.

Griggs, Leverett, D.D., a Congregational minister, was born at Tolland, Conn., Nov. 17, 1808. He graduated from Yale College in 1829, studied at Andover Theological Seminary, and graduated from Yale Divinity School in 1834; became pastor successively at North Haven, in 1833; Chapel Street, New Haven, in 1845; Milbury, Mass., in 1847; Bristol, Conn., in 1856; agent of several educational societies from 1870 to 1881, and died at Bristol, Jan. 28, 1883. He published numerous sermons and addresses. See *Cong. Year-book*, 1884, p. 24.

H.

Habington, William, an English poet, was born at Hindlip, Worcestershire, Nov. 5, 1605. He was educated at St. Omer's Jesuit College, and afterwards at Paris; spent his life in literary and rural leisure, and died on his native estate, Nov. 13, 1645. Besides some historical works, he published occasional poems of a serious vein, which were collected in a volume entitled *Castara* (1635, 1640). See Chalmers, *Biog. Dict.* s. v.

Hall, James, a veteran Methodist Episcopal minister, was born at Rutland, Vt., March 4, 1790. He entered the Genesee Conference in 1813, in which he labored faithfully until his superannuation in 1852. He died at Mayville, N.Y., Oct. 6, 1882. See *Minutes of Annual Conferences*, 1883, p. 224.

Halliday, David Moffat, D.D., a Presbyterian minister, was born at Morristown, N. J., Feb. 9, 1807. He graduated from the College of New Jersey in 1829, studied (1835-36) in the Princeton Theological Seminary, was licensed to preach in 1837, became pastor at Danville, Va., in 1838, Peekskill, N. Y., in 1843, without charge after 1867, residing during his latter years at Princeton, N. J. He died at Brooklyn, N. Y., Dec. 8, 1884. See *Necrol. Report of Princeton Theol. Sem.* 1885, p. 34.

Hammond, J. Pinkney, D.D., a Protestant Episcopal minister, was born at Annapolis, Md., May 20, 1826. He graduated from St. John's College in 1845, was settled successively at Upper Marlborough, Md., Bangor, Me., Morrisania, N. Y., Reading, Pa., Omaha, Neb., Annapolis, Md., and finally at Whittingham Church, Baltimore. He died Aug. 9, 1884.

Harper, James, D.D., a Presbyterian minister, was born in Glasgow, Scotland, July 28, 1802. He graduated from Glasgow University in 1823, studied divinity under Dr. Dick, was ordained by the United Secession Presbytery of Glasgow, came to New York in 1833, became pastor at Galway, then at Ellicott city, Md. (1838), and finally at Shippensburg, Pa. (1840), until his resignation in 1870. He died May 9, 1876. See Nevin, *Presb. Encyclop.* s. v.

Harrington, Calvin Sears, D.D., a Methodist Episcopal educator, was born at St. Johnsbury, Vt., May 17, 1826. He graduated from Wesleyan University, Conn., in 1852, and immediately engaged in teaching; in 1854 joined the New Hampshire Conference, in 1861 became professor of languages in his *alma mater*, and retained that position until his death, Feb. 16, 1886. See *Alumni Record of Wesleyan University*, 1883, p. 116, 577; *Minutes of Annual Conferences*, 1886, p. 91.

Harvard, John, the founder of Harvard University, was born in England about 1608. He graduated from Emmanuel College, Cambridge, in 1631, came to New England in 1637, officiated as clergyman in the Massachusetts colony in 1638, and died at Charlestown, Sept. 14 of the same year. He gave about £800 and his library to the establishment of the college on a strictly orthodox basis. See Drake, *Dict. of Amer. Biog.* s. v.

Hastings, Thomas, D.M., was born at Washington, Conn., in 1784, and at twelve years removed with his father to Clinton, N.Y. From 1824 to 1832 he conducted a religious journal in Utica, and thereafter resided in New York city, engaged in musical instruction, until his death, May 15, 1872. He published many of the most popular books of sacred music used in the country.

Heginbotham, Ottiwell, an English poet, was born in 1744. He was ordained as a Congregational minister at Sudbury in 1765, and died there in 1768. His hymns, about twenty-five in all, were printed in 1794, and again in 1799 as a *Supplement to Watts.* Several of them are found in modern hymnals.

Hemans, *Mrs.* Felicia Dorothea (*née* **Browne**), an English poetess, was born at Liverpool, Sept. 25, 1794. She married a military man in 1812, separated from him in 1818, and died May 16, 1835. She published numerous volumes of poems, largely religious, which have been widely popular. They have been published collectively as her *Works* (with a *Memoir*, Lond. 1839, 7 vols., and often since).

Henry, Caleb Sprague, D.D., LL.D., a Protestant Episcopal minister, was born at Rutland, Mass., Aug. 2, 1804. He graduated from Dartmouth College in 1825, studied one year at Andover Theological Seminary, served as Congregational minister at Greenfield, Mass. (1829-31), and at West Hartford, Conn. (1833-35); was ordained deacon in the Episcopal ranks the last-named year, and presbyter in 1836; was professor in Bristol College, Pa. (1835-38), and in New York University (1838-52); rector of St. Clement's, N. Y. (1847-50), of St. Michael's, Litchfield, Conn. (1870-73), and died at Newburgh, N. Y., March 9, 1884. He published several historical and religious works.

Herron, Robert, D.D., a Presbyterian minister, was born in Washington County, Pa., April 10, 1817. He graduated from Muskingum College, O., in 1845, and from Allegheny Theological Seminary in 1847; became assistant at Beech Spring Church, O., in 1848 pastor at Ridge Church, resigned in 1876, and died at Scio, June 17, 1884. See Nevin, *Presb. Encyclop.* s. v.

Hill, John Henry, D.D., LL.D., a Protestant Episcopal minister, was born in New York city, Sept. 11, 1791. He graduated from Columbia College in 1807, in 1830 was appointed missionary to Greece, also (1845-51) chaplain to the British Legation in Athens. He died there, July 1, 1882. He translated several works into modern Greek.

Hill, Stephen P., D.D., a Baptist minister, was born at Salem, Mass., April 17, 1806. He was converted at the age of fourteen, began to preach at seventeen, studied at Waterville College, graduated from Brown University in 1829, and from the Newton Theological Institution in 1832, became pastor at Haverhill, Mass., preached one winter (1833-34) near Charleston, S. C., was pastor thereafter in Baltimore, Md., and Washington, D. C., until 1861, and died in the latter city, Sept. 15, 1884. He published several sermons and addresses, likewise some works on hymnology and for the young. See Cathcart, *Baptist Encyclop.* s. v.

Hines, Richard, D.D., a Protestant Episcopal minister, was born in North Carolina, and educated at the university of that state. He became rector of St. Mary's, Memphis, Tenn. (1857-71), then of Meridian and Enterprise parishes, Miss., and died March 30, 1883.

Hoes, Cantine Farrell, D.D., a Reformed (Dutch) minister, was born at Middleburgh, N. Y., July 13, 1811. He graduated from Amherst College in 1832, studied two years in Princeton Theological Seminary, was licensed to preach in 1834, became pastor at Chittenango, N. Y., in 1836, at Ithaca in 1837, at Kingston in 1845, resigned in 1867, and died at the last named place, Feb. 9, 1883. See *Necrol. Report of Princeton Theol. Sem.* 1883, p. 29.

Hoff, JOHN FRANCIS, D.D., a Protestant Episcopal minister, was born at Lancaster, Pa., Jan. 10, 1814. He graduated from the University of Pennsylvania in 1833, and from the General Theological Seminary, N. Y., in 1836; was ordained deacon in 1837, became rector of Trinity Church, Georgetown, D. C., in 1838, of Christ Church, Millwood, Va., in 1847, of Trinity Church, Towsonton, Md., in 1858, and died in Baltimore, Dec. 18, 1881. He served twelve years on the standing committee of his diocese.

Holman, RUSSELL, D.D., a Baptist minister, was born at Warwick, Mass., Aug. 14, 1812. He graduated from Brown University, became a pastor in Greene County, Ky., in 1839, in 1842 of the Coliseum Church at New Orleans, in 1845 secretary of the Southern Baptist Home Mission, an office which he retained (with a pastoral interval from 1851 to 1856) until 1862, after which he labored occasionally as health would permit in Louisiana, Illinois, Kentucky, and Missouri, until disabled by paralysis in 1876. He died Dec. 2, 1879. See Cathcart, *Baptist Encyclop.* s. v.

Hood, EDWIN PAXTON, an English Independent minister and author, was born in London, Oct. 24, 1820. He was early trained in religious work, especially as a speaker in the temperance cause; in 1857 became pastor at Islington, in 1862 at Brighton, in 1873 at Islington again, in 1877 at Manchester, in 1881 at Falcon Square, Lond., and died June 12, 1885. He visited America in 1880. He was an eloquent speaker, and wrote over sixty volumes of a popular character. See (Lond.) *Cong. Year-book*, 1886, p. 178.

Hornberger, LEWIS P., D.D., a Baptist minister, was born in Philadelphia, Pa., Oct. 25, 1841. He was converted at the age of fifteen, graduated from Madison University in 1865, became pastor of Spring Garden Church, Philadelphia, the same year, in 1872 of Gethsemane Church, and died in that city, March 27, 1884. He was a very successful pastor. See Cathcart, *Baptist Encyclop.* s. v.

Horne, JAMES WESLEY, LL.D., a Methodist Episcopal minister, was born on the island of Jamaica, W. I., March 24, 1823. He graduated from Wesleyan University, Conn., in 1852, and in 1853 became the first principal of Monrovian Academy, Liberia, Africa. Returning in broken health to America, he joined the New York East Conference in 1858, and from that time (with the exception of a visit to Europe and the East in 1870) continued to fill important pastoral positions until his sudden death, Sept. 6, 1884. See *Minutes of Annual Conferences*, 1885, p. 98; *Alumni Record of Wesleyan University*, 1883, p. 116, 586.

Howson, JOHN SAUL, D.D., an Anglican divine, was born in 1816. He graduated with honor from Trinity College, Cambridge, in 1837; was ordained in 1845, becoming the same year senior classical master, and in 1849 principal of the Liverpool College; in 1866 vicar of Wisbech, afterwards chaplain to the bishop of Ely; in 1867 dean of Chester, and died Dec. 15, 1885. Besides contributions to the religious periodical press and to Smith's *Dict. of the Bible*, he wrote various lectures and sermons, and was the joint author, with Dr. Conybeare, of the well-known work on the *Life and Epistles of St. Paul.*

Hurlburt, RUSSELL HIGLEY, M.D., D.D., a Methodist Episcopal minister, was born at Winchester, Conn., April 21, 1826. He was converted in 1845, joined the Erie Conference in 1850, and filled important stations in it until his death, at Marion, Ia., April 14, 1883. See *Minutes of Annual Conferences*, 1883, p. 319.

Hyde, *Mrs.* ABBY BRADLEY (her maiden name), a poetess, was born at Stockbridge, Mass., Sept. 28, 1789; married Lavius Hyde (q. v.), a Congregational minister, in 1818, and died at Andover, Conn., April 7, 1872. Some of her pieces were inserted in Nettleton's *Village Hymns* (1824), and a few have been incorporated into some later hymnals.

I.

Ingersoll, EDWARD, D.D., a Protestant Episcopal clergyman, was born at New Haven, Conn., Nov. 26, 1810. He graduated from Yale College in 1831; became minister at Westport, also at Troy and Genesee, N. Y.; rector of Trinity Church, Buffalo, in 1834, a position which he retained for thirty years, and died there, Feb. 6, 1883.

Inskip, JOHN S., a noted Methodist Episcopal minister, was born at Huntingdon, England, in 1816, and came to America in 1820. He was converted at fourteen years of age, in 1836 joined the Philadelphia Conference, in 1845 was transferred to the Ohio Conference, in 1852 to the New York East Conference, later to the New York Conference, the Baltimore Conference, and, finally, again to the New York East Conference, in all of which he occupied important stations until his superannuation in 1873, after which he was editor of the *Christian Standard*, in Philadelphia, until his death, at Ocean Grove, N. J., March 7, 1884. He was a pleasing and successful evangelist, and in his later years a powerful advocate of entire sanctification. He made a memorable defence of himself before the General Conference of 1852 from the charge of innovation in his pastoral rulings at Springfield, O., concerning family sittings in the congregations. See *Minutes of Annual Conferences*, 1884, p. 94.

Irons, WILLIAM JOSIAH, D.D., an English clergyman, was born at Hoddesdon, Hertshire, Sept. 12, 1812. He graduated from Queen's College, Oxford, in 1833; became curate at Newington in 1835, rector at Walworth in 1837, of Barkway in 1838, of Brompton in 1842; prebendary of St. Paul's, London, in 1860; rector at Wadingham, Lincolnshire, in 1870; of St. Mary's, Woolnoth, London, in 1872, and died June 19, 1883. Besides numerous lectures, sermons, and ecclesiastical essays, Dr. Irons published several poetical works, especially *Hymns for the Church* (1875), from which a number of pieces have been adopted in many modern hymnals, notably his version of the *Dies Iræ* (q. v.).

J.

Johnson, EDWIN A., D.D., a Methodist Episcopal minister, was born at Gowanda, N. Y., Oct. 30, 1829. He joined the Church when eleven years of age, and in 1852 entered the Erie Conference, in which he labored with efficiency as a pastor until his appointment (1868–72) as assistant editor of the *Pittsburgh Christian Advocate.* He died at Allegheny, Pa., June 30, 1885. He wrote several popular volumes. See *Minutes of Annual Conferences*, 1885, p. 330; Simpson, *Cyclop. of Methodism*, s. v.

Johnston, CYRUS, D.D., a Presbyterian minister, was born in Mecklenburg County, N. C., Dec. 23, 1797. He graduated from Hampden-Sidney College in 1821; became pastor of Bethesda and adjoining churches, S. C., in 1824; at Providence and Sharon in 1839; principal of a female academy at Charlotte, N. C., in 1845, pastor there in 1846, and died Jan. 25, 1855. See Nevin, *Presbyterian Encyclop.* s. v.

Jones, HUGH, D.D., a Welsh Baptist minister, was born at Bodedeyrn, Anglesea, July 10, 1831. At the age of seventeen he was baptized, soon after began to preach, in 1857 graduated from the college at Haverfordwest, became pastor at Llandudno, in 1859 at Llangollen, in 1862 assistant at the new college there, in 1866 its president, and died there, May 28, 1883. See (Lond.) *Baptist Hand-book*, 1884, p. 292.

K.

Kelley, SAMUEL, a veteran Methodist Episcopal minister, was born at Salem, N. H., Feb. 1, 1802. He joined the Church in 1820, and in 1822 entered the New England Conference, in which and in its later subdivisions he labored faithfully, for the last thirteen years as chaplain to the Sailor's Home in Quincy, Mass., until his death, Sept. 6, 1883. See *Minutes of Annual Conferences*, 1884, p. 85.

Kepler, SAMUEL, a veteran minister of the Methodist Episcopal Church South, was born at Baltimore, Md., Nov. 15, 1804. He was converted when a boy, early established a mission-school near his native city, studied at Dickinson College, entered the Baltimore Conference in 1827, from 1863 to 1865 preached for an independent Methodist Church at Williamsport, Pa., in 1867 joined the Baltimore Conference of the Methodist Episcopal Church South, in 1871 became supernumerary, and died at Baltimore, Aug. 1, 1884. See *Minutes of Ann. Conferences of the M. E. Church South*, 1884, p. 145.

Keshub Chunder Sen. See SEN.

Kohlor Köl. See BRASSICANUS.

Kreutziger. See CREUTZIGER; CRUCIGER.

L.

Laird, FRANCIS, D.D., a Presbyterian minister, graduated from Dickinson College under Dr. Nisbet, became pastor at Plumb Creek and Pike Run, Pa., in 1800, at Murrayville in 1831, resigned in 1850, and died April 6, 1851. See Nevin, *Presb. Encyclop.* s. v.

Lance, LUCIEN CHARLES, D.D., a Protestant Episcopal clergyman, was born at Bordentown, N. J., Sept. 7, 1832. He graduated from Charleston College, and in 1854 from the General Theological Seminary, N. Y.; became pastor of All-Saints', Waccamaw, N. C.; after the war in Wye and Queenstown, Md., rector of Ascension Church, Frankfort, Ky., two years; at Kenosha, Wis., from 1872; in 1879 chaplain in Kemper Hall; and died Jan. 12, 1883.

Lawrence, EDWARD ALEXANDER, D.D., a Congregational minister, was born at St. Johnsbury, Vt., Oct. 7, 1808. He graduated from Dartmouth College in 1834, and from Andover Theological Seminary in 1838; became pastor of Centre Church, Haverhill, Mass., in 1839, at Marblehead in 1845, professor in Hartford Theological Seminary in 1854, pastor at Oxford, N. H., in 1865, South Church, Marblehead, in 1868, and remained there without charge from 1873 till his death, Sept. 4, 1883. He published a number of religious essays. See *Cong. Year-book*, 1884, p. 28.

Latta, WILLIAM, D.D., a Presbyterian minister, was born in Bucks County, Pa., in May, 1769. He graduated from the University of Pennsylvania, studied theology with his father, Dr. James Latta, was ordained over the Church in Great Valley, Pa., in 1798, and continued there until his death in February, 1847. See Nevin, *Presb. Encyclop.* s. v.

Lay, HENRY CHAMPLIN, D.D., LL.D., a Protestant Episcopal bishop, was born at Richmond, Va., Dec. 6, 1823. He graduated from the University of Virginia in 1842, and from the theological seminary at Alexandria in 1846, became rector of the Church of the Nativity, Huntsville, Ala., in 1847, and bishop of Arkansas in 1859, bishop of Easton in 1869, and died Sept. 17, 1885.

Leacock, WILLIAM T., D.D., a Protestant Episcopal clergyman, was born on the island of Barbadoes in 1796, ordained in 1824, was rector of Christ Church, New Orleans, from 1852 to 1878, and died at Beauvoir, Miss., Dec. 28, 1884.

Lee, Leroy Madison, D.D., a minister of the Methodist Episcopal Church South, was born at Petersburg, Va., April 30, 1808. He was converted in 1827, soon began to preach, was admitted into the Virginia Conference the next year, occupied important stations, in 1832 was appointed editor of the *Christian Sentinel*, Richmond, Va., in 1839 became the editor of the *Richmond Christian Advocate*, in 1858 returned to pastoral work, in 1881 became superannuated, and died April 20, 1882. He was an able preacher, a powerful controversialist, and the author of several books, of which the *Life and Times of Jesse Lee* (1847) is the most important. See *Minutes of Annual Conferences of the M. E. Church South*, 1882, p. 60.

Lee, Nathanael H., D.D., a minister of the Methodist Episcopal Church South, was born in Campbell County, Va., April 29, 1816. He studied at Urania College, Ky., was converted in his twentieth year, in 1838 was admitted into the Kentucky Conference, in which he soon attained eminence, and continued to preach, with a few intermissions in other religious work, until his superannuation in 1880. He died June 14, 1881. See *Minutes of Annual Conferences of the M. E. Church South*, 1881, p. 300.

Leeds, GEORGE, D.D., a Protestant Episcopal clergyman, was born at Newburyport, Mass., in 1816. He graduated from Amherst College in 1835, and from Andover Theological Seminary in 1839, served successively at Utica, N. Y., Salem, Mass. (1853-60), St. Peter's, Philadelphia, Pa., Grace Church, Baltimore, Md., and died in Philadelphia, April 15, 1885.

Lenox, JAMES, a philanthropic layman, was born in New York city in August, 1800. He graduated from Princeton College, studied law, and spent his life in literary pursuits and charity. Possessed of ample wealth, he founded the Lenox library in 1870, which is particularly rich in rare Bibles and other specialties, and gave large sums to public institutions of the Presbyterian Church, of which he was a member. He died in New York city, Feb. 17, 1880.

Lewis, John J., LL.D., a Baptist minister and educator, was born at Utica, N. Y., Dec. 25, 1843. He graduated from Hamilton College in 1864, became professor in the Brooklyn Polytechnic Institute the same year, in 1867 pastor at Syracuse, in 1868 professor in Madison University, and died at Hamilton, N. Y., Dec. 5, 1884.

Lewis, Josiah, D.D., a minister of the Methodist Episcopal Church South, graduated with honors from Emory College in 1859, began the study of law, entered the ministry in 1861, joined the Georgia Conference in 1866, served as professor in Emory College, in 1871 engaged in pastoral work, in 1876 was transferred to the Alabama Conference, and appointed president of the university at Greensborough, in 1882 was transferred to pastoral work in the North Georgia Conference, and died at Sparta, Feb. 13, 1885. See *Minutes of Annual Conferences of the M. E. Church South*, 1885, p. 98.

Linfield, WILLIAM F. M., D.D., a minister of the Methodist Episcopal Church South, was born at Charleston, S. C., Aug. 25, 1824. He was converted in 1849, in 1851 entered the Alabama Conference, in which and adjoining conferences he labored, with but one year's intermission, until his death, March 16, 1882. See *Minutes of Annual Conferences of the M. E. Church South*, 1882, p. 115.

Little, JACOB, D.D., a Presbyterian minister, was born in New Hampshire, May 1, 1795. He graduated from Dartmouth College in 1822, and from Andover Theological Seminary in 1825, preached at Hoosick, N. Y., and at Belpre, O., in 1827 became Congregational pastor in Granville, in 1867 stated supply of the Presbyterian Church in Warsaw, Ind., in 1874 removed to Wabash, and died there, Dec. 17, 1876. See Nevin, *Presb. Encyclop.* s. v.

Lloyd, WILLIAM FREEMAN, an English poet, was born at Uley, Gloucestershire, Dec. 22, 1791. He was for many years secretary of the Religious Tract Society of London, and died April 22, 1853. He wrote several hymns, of which some are found in most modern hymnals.

Lynch, Thomas Toke, an English poet, was born at Dunmore, Essex, July 5, 1818, served as pastor in various chapels near London, and died May 9, 1871. Besides several prose works, he published a book in verse, called *The Revealed* (1855). See his *Memoirs*, by White (Lond. 1874).

M.

Maclean, John, D.D., LL.D., an eminent Presbyterian divine, was born at Princeton, N. J., March 3, 1800. He graduated from the college of his native place in 1816, and its theological seminary in 1819; became teacher in his alma mater in 1822, and in 1823 professor, a position which he retained, with a transfer of chairs, until his election as president in 1854. He resigned in 1857, but continued to reside at Princeton, loved and honored, until his death, Aug. 10, 1886. He often wrote for the religious press, and published several sermons, essays, etc. See Nevin, *Presb. Encyclop.* s. v.

Magill, Seagrove William, D.D., a Congregational minister, was born at St. Mary's, Ga., Sept. 27, 1810. He graduated from Yale College in 1831, and from Princeton Theological Seminary in 1834; preached in various Presbyterian and Congregational churches of Virginia, Georgia, Ohio, Vermont, and Connecticut, with several intermissions as agent of educational institutions, and died at Amherst, Mass., Jan. 20, 1884. See *Cong. Year-book*, 1885, p. 26; *Necrol. Report of Princeton Theol. Sem.* 1885, p. 28.

Manly, Robert Woolf, D.D., a Methodist Episcopal minister, was born in Muskingum County, O., Aug. 5, 1830. He studied three years (1847-50) in the Ohio Wesleyan University, joined the Ohio Conference in 1859, was transferred to the Colorado Conference in 1881, and died at Denver, July 15, 1883. See *Minutes of Annual Conferences*, 1883, p. 310; Simpson, *Cyclop. of Methodism*, s. v.

Marshall, Abraham, a pioneer Baptist minister, was born at Windsor, Conn., April 23, 1748. He was converted in South Carolina at the age of twenty-two; soon began to preach in Georgia; was licensed in 1771, and ordained in 1775. In 1784 he became pastor at Kiokee, Ga., and labored there and in all the adjoining region as a flaming evangelist until his death, Aug. 15, 1819. See Cathcart, *Baptist Encyclop.* s. v.

Marshall, Matthew Morton, D.D., a Presbyterian minister, was born at Fredericksburg, Va., Feb. 19, 1804. He began to preach at the age of twenty, and continued, chiefly at Trenton, Tenn., until his death, at Chattanooga, Aug. 23, 1874. See Nevin, *Presbyterian Encyclop.* s. v.

Martin, John Wynne, D.D., a Presbyterian minister, was born in Ireland, and entered the ministry there. In 1837 he became principal of the Deaf and Dumb Asylum at Belfast, in 1840 of that at Dublin, and in 1846 returned to that at Belfast. In 1853 he sailed for America; in 1857 became rector at Doe Run, Pa.; in 1880 professor in Lincoln University, and afterwards labored in the City Mission, N. Y., and as principal of the Beaver Academy, Pa. He died at Norristown, June 11, 1883. See Nevin, *Presbyterian Encyclop.* s. v.

Mason, J. O., D.D., a Baptist minister, was born at Fort Ann, N. J., Dec. 25, 1813. He was converted in his eighteenth year; graduated from the Literary and Theological Institute at Hamilton, N. Y., in 1836; labored as a missionary among the Creek Indians; in 1840 became pastor at Fort Ann, and in 1844 at Greenwich, N. Y., where he died, Dec. 16, 1881. See Cathcart, *Baptist Encyclop.* s. v.

Matlack, Lucius C., D.D., a Methodist Episcopal minister, was born at Baltimore, Md., April 28, 1816. He was converted when sixteen years of age; licensed to preach in 1837, but refused admittance the same year and also the one following into the Philadelphia Conference, on account of his anti-slavery sentiments; in 1840 was admitted into the New England Conference; in 1842 withdrew from the Methodist Episcopal Church and joined in the organization of the Wesleyan Methodist Connection; was admitted into the Philadelphia Conference in 1867, and labored successfully until his death, at Cambridge, Md., June 24, 1883. See *Minutes of Annual Conferences*, 1884, p. 79; Simpson, *Cyclop. of Methodism*, s. v.

McEwen, Robert, D.D., a Congregational minister, was born at New London, Conn., June 22, 1808. He graduated from Yale College in 1827, and from Yale Divinity School in 1833; was home missionary for one year at Pontiac, Mich.; pastor at Middletown, Conn., from 1835 to 1838; at Enfield, Mass., from 1842 to 1861, and died at New London, Aug. 29, 1883. See *Cong. Year-book*, 1884, p. 30.

McGinley, Amos A., D.D., a Presbyterian minister, was born near Fairfield, Pa., in 1778. He graduated from Dickinson College in 1798, studied theology privately, and was pastor at Upper and Lower Path Valley from 1803 until his death, May 1, 1856. See Nevin, *Presbyterian Encyclop.* s. v.

McInnis, Richmond, D.D., a Presbyterian minister, was born in Greene County, Miss., March 17, 1817. He graduated from the literary department of Oakland College in 1839, and studied theology there likewise; became pastor at Yazoo City in 1840, in 1841 at Jackson, and editor of the *True Witness*, which, in 1857, he removed to New Orleans; afterwards preached as an evangelist, and died Jan. 13, 1881. See Nevin, *Presbyterian Encyclop.* s. v.

McKenzie, J. W. P., D.D., a minister of the Methodist Episcopal Church South, was born in Burke County, N. C., April 26, 1806. He graduated from the University of Georgia in 1824; taught ancient languages for a few years there and at Gainesville; in 1831 went to Tennessee, where he was converted; in 1836 joined the Arkansas Conference, and labored as a missionary among the Choctaws; in 1841 opened a school near Clarksville, Texas; in 1871 became president of Marvin College, resigned the next year, and died June 20, 1881. See *Minutes of Annual Conferences of the M. E. Church South*, 1881, p. 348.

McKnight, John, D.D., a Presbyterian minister, was born near Carlisle, Pa., Oct. 1, 1754. He graduated from Princeton College in 1773, and studied theology privately; was pastor at Lower Marsh Creek, Pa., from 1775 to 1783; colleague of Dr. Rodgers, in New York, from 1789 to 1809; in 1815 president of Dickinson College, but resigned the next year, and died Oct. 21, 1823. See Nevin, *Presbyterian Encyclop.* s. v.

McLaren. See Maclaren.

Means, Alexander, D.D., LL.D., a minister of the Methodist Episcopal Church South, was born at Statesville, N. C., Feb. 6, 1801. He studied four years at the academy in his native place; taught school one year at Mocksville; studied medicine, and practiced it six years at Covington, Ga.; became a local preacher in 1829; and from 1833 devoted himself to the cause of education, as principal of the Georgia Conference Manual Labor School (1834), professor in Emory College (1838), in the Medical College of Georgia (1840), president of Masonic Female College (1853), analytical chemist of Georgia (1869). He entered the Georgia Conference in 1839, and died in 1883. See *Minutes of Annual Conferences of the M. E. Church South*, 1883, p. 78.

Medley, Samuel, an English poet, was born at Cheshunt, Hertfordshire, June 23, 1733. After various adventures on land and sea, he was converted in 1759, became pastor of a Baptist Church at Waterford in 1768, of one at Liverpool in 1772, and died there, July 17, 1799. He published numerous hymns in sheets, which were collected (1789-1800), and several of them (especially "Oh, could I speak the matchless worth") have found their way into most modern hymnals.

Mercer, Alexander Gardiner, D.D., a Protestant Episcopal clergyman, was born at Philadelphia, Pa., Jan. 4, 1817. He graduated from the College of New Jersey in 1837, and studied one year in Princeton Theological Seminary; became rector of St. John's Church, Clifton, N. Y., in 1847; in 1853 professor in the University of Pennsylvania; in 1855 rector of Trinity Church, Newport, R. I.; in 1860 assistant at Trinity Church, Boston; in 1862 rector of All-Saints' Chapel, Newport, where he remained until his death, Nov. 3, 1882. See *Necrol. Report of Princeton Theol. Sem.* 1883, p. 43.

Miller, Charles W., D.D., a minister of the Methodist Episcopal Church South, was born in Mercer County, Ky., June 22, 1837. In 1857 he entered the Kentucky Conference, in which, with the exception of a short time as chaplain in the Southern army, he continued to preach efficiently until attacked by disease, in 1882. He died Jan. 10, 1885. See *Minutes of Annual Conferences of the M. E. Church South*, 1885, p. 14.

Moncrief, *Sir* Henry Wellwood, D.D., a Scotch minister, grandson of his namesake, the Rev. "Sir Harry," was born at Edinburgh in 1809. He graduated from Balliol College, Oxford, was ordained minister at Baldernock in 1836, transferred to East Kilbride in 1837, joined the Free Church in 1843, was transferred to Free St. Cuthbert's in 1852, appointed principal clerk to the Free General Assembly in 1855, and died at Edinburgh, Nov. 4, 1883. He published several letters and addresses. See *Fasti Eccles. Scoticanæ*, ii, 291, 344.

Morgan, Abel, an early Baptist minister, was born at Welsh Tract, Del., April 18, 1713. He was baptized at twenty years of age, and began to preach soon after; became pastor at Middletown, N. J., in 1739, and continued there until his death, Nov. 24, 1785. He was an eminent revivalist. See Cathcart, *Baptist Encyclop.* s. v.

Morgan, John, D.D., a Congregational divine, was born at Cork, Ireland, in November, 1802. He graduated from Williams College in 1826; taught some years in New York, while studying theology; was afterwards instructor in Lane Seminary, professor in Oberlin Theological Seminary (1835-80, *emeritus* thereafter), ordained in 1837, and died Sept. 27, 1884. He published a few essays and sermons. See *Cong. Year-book*, 1885, p. 28.

Morgan, Richard U., D.D., a Protestant Episcopal clergyman, was born in Delaware County, Pa., Jan. 9, 1800. He was ordained deacon in 1822, presbyter in 1823, was rector for twenty-three years of Trinity Church, New Rochelle, N. Y., and died at Stamford, Conn., Oct. 9, 1882.

Morris, Francis A., D.D., a minister of the Methodist Episcopal Church South, son of bishop Morris, was born at Marietta, O., Sept. 3, 1817. He graduated from the old Augusta College in 1836; studied law, was admitted to the bar in 1838, and practiced successfully in Texas; was converted in 1842; taught languages two years in St. Charles College, Mo.; in 1845 joined the Missouri Conference, in which and in the Louisville Conference (1851-60) he filled important stations until his death, in 1882. See *Minutes of Annual Conferences of the M. E. Church South*, 1882, p. 143.

Morris, Robert Desha, D.D., a Presbyterian minister, was born at Washington, Ky., Aug. 22, 1814. He graduated from Augusta College in 1834, and from Princeton Theological Seminary in 1838; was ordained pastor at Newtown, Pa., in the latter year; removed to Ohio in 1856; in 1859 became president of the Female College at Oxford, and died there, Nov. 3, 1882. See *Necrol. Report of Princeton Theol. Sem.* 1883, p. 35.

Morrow, Thomas, D.D., a Presbyterian minister, was born in Greenville District, S. C., July 31, 1805. He graduated from Centre College, Ky., in 1830; studied one year each in Princeton Theological Seminary and Union Seminary, Va.; was engaged in the Creek Indian mission from 1833 to 1837, and thereafter as an evangelist, organizing churches in Alabama and Mississippi, and at times (1860-61, 1867-74) as superintendent of public-schools in Morgan County. He died at Hartsells, Ala., March 12, 1885. See *Necrol. Report of Princeton Theol. Sem.* 1885, p. 22.

Morsell, Joshua, D.D., a Protestant Episcopal clergyman, was born in 1815. He graduated from the Alexandria Theological Seminary in 1843, was rector of Grace Church, City Island, N. Y., and died there, Dec. 16, 1883.

O.

Owen, Francis A., D.D., a minister of the Methodist Episcopal Church South, was born in Brunswick County, Va., Feb. 8, 1804. In 1822 he entered the Tennessee Conference, in which and in the St. Louis Conference (after 1874) he served efficiently as preacher, missionary to the Indians, and editor of the *Memphis Christian Advocate* (1854), until compelled to take a supernumerary and finally a superannuate relation. He died March 16, 1883. See *Minutes of Annual Conferences of the M. E. Church South*, 1883, p. 75.

P.

Page, Joseph Rusling, D.D., a Presbyterian minister, was born in New Brunswick, N. J., Aug. 1, 1817. He united with the Methodists at sixteen years of age, studied in Auburn Theological Seminary two years (1841-43); was preacher at Plymouth, N. Y., in 1838, pastor at Perry, from 1839 to 1841, from 1843 to 1857, and from 1859 to 1868; in the interim at Stratford, Conn. (1857-59), thereafter financial agent of Ingham University; resident at East Avon, N. Y., five years, and pastor at Brighton from 1875 until his death at Rochester, Dec. 17, 1884. See *Gen. Cat. of Auburn Theol. Sem.* 1883, p. 75.

Pan-Presbyterian Council. See Presbyterian Alliance.

Parker, H. J., D.D., a Baptist minister, was born at Cavendish, Vt., Nov. 12, 1812. He was converted at eighteen, graduated from Harvard College in 1840, studied theology at Newton, was ordained in 1842, became pastor at Burlington, Vt., in 1844; in 1854 removed to Beaver Dam, Wis., in 1856 became pastor there; in 1861 removed to Austin, Minn., in 1872 to California, and died at Riverside, Jan. 30, 1885. See Cathcart, *Baptist Encyclop.* s. v.

Parry, Richard, D.D., an English divine, was born at Ruthin, Flintshire. He was educated at Oxford, whence he was preferred dean of Bangor (1599), and finally bishop of St. Asaph (1604). He died Sept. 26, 1623. He possessed eminent episcopal qualities. See Fuller, *Worthies of England* (ed. Nuttall), p. 539.

Partridge, Alfred H., D.D., a Protestant Episcopal minister, was born Dec. 11, 1811. He graduated from the General Theological Seminary, N. Y., in 1838, was rector of St. Matthew's, Bedford, seventeen years, then of Christ Church, Brooklyn, until his death, April 8, 1883.

Patterson, Robert, D.D., a Reformed Presbyterian minister, was born at Littlekenny, County Donegal, Ireland. He studied there and at Londonderry, attended the Theological Seminary of the Reformed Presbyterian Church in Philadelphia, Pa., was licensed to preach in 1851 and ordained in 1852; became pastor at Cincinnati,

O., in 1854, at Chicago, Ill., in 1857, of the Jefferson Presbyterian Church in the same city in 1867; removed to California in 1873, became pastor at San Francisco the same year, at Cincinnati, O., in 1878, in 1880 minister at Brooklyn, Cal., and died at San Francisco, Jan. 17, 1885. See Nevin, *Presb. Encyclop.* s. v.

Paulinier, PIERRE ANTOINE JUSTIN, a French prelate, was born at Pézanas (Hérault), Jan. 19, 1815. He was at first curé of St. Roch, Montpellier, made bishop of Grenoble in 1870, archbishop of Besançon in 1875, and died Nov. 14, 1881, leaving some pastoral letters and essays.

Pendleton, WILLIAM N., D.D., a Protestant Episcopal minister, was born in Hanover County, Va., Dec. 26, 1809. He graduated from West Point Military Academy in 1830, was ordained in 1837; was successively professor in Newark College, Del., principal of a high-school in Virginia, rector of All-Saints', Frederick, Md., and from 1855 of Grace Church, Lexington, Va., until his death, Jan. 15, 1883.

Pennell, GEORGE CASPAR, D.D., a Protestant Episcopal minister, was born in New York city, July 11, 1832. He graduated from Columbia College in 1852, and from the General Theological Seminary in 1855; was successively assistant rector of St. Paul's, Troy; rector of Grace Church, and afterwards of St. James', Buffalo; of St. Mary's, Mott Haven; of Christ Church, Rouse's Point; of St. John's, Newark, N. J.; and finally of St. John's Mission, Deadwood, Neb., where he died, May 20, 1882.

Pictorial Bibles. The value and interest added to books of almost all sorts by graphic illustrations has not escaped the attention of editors of the Holy Scriptures. In the Middle Ages this was effected by *illuminating* copies by hand. See ILLUMINATION, ART OF. Since the invention of printing and the discovery of engraving, a similar effect has been more cheaply produced by designs on wood, metal, or stone, either etched or in relief. The romantic scenes of Bible history have been so often reproduced in paint and pencil, and the remains and scenes of Bible lands are so rich in apt and important elucidations of ancient customs and institutions, that a just idea of Oriental life and manners can hardly be conveyed without some such aid to the eye. Accordingly both fancy and fact have been put into requisition for this purpose, and multitudes of volumes have appeared expressly aimed at this result. One of the earliest is the *Poor Man's Bible*. See BIBLIA PAUPERUM. The most noted is that of Hans Holbein (q. v.). In modern times artists and authors have vied with each other, and publishers have been lavish in their endeavors to enrich and beautify the sacred pages with pictorial additions, representing not only the realities of antiquarian research, but also the conceptions of creative genius. Much of this is of little real help to the student, and some of it has really misled readers by imaginary notions and false analogies. But a real gain has been effected by most of the delineations borrowed from books of travel and exploration. These have been also incorporated in a compact and convenient form in the best Bible dictionaries now so widely circulated. One of the most popular and really serviceable of all the pictorial Bibles is that edited by the late Dr. John Kitto (q. v.). More expensive and elaborate ones have been issued by several English and American houses, which are an ornament to the household and an heirloom to the family.

Pike, GUSTAVE DORMAN, D.D., a Congregational minister, was born at Topsfield, Mass., Aug. 6, 1831. He graduated from Dartmouth College in 1858, and from Andover Theological Seminary in 1861, became co-pastor at Nashua, N. H., in 1862, pastor at East Haddam, Conn., in 1865, agent of the American Missionary Association at Rochester, N. Y., in 1867, and was its secretary from 1870 until his death, Jan. 29, 1885. He published a few missionary works. See *Cong. Year-book*, 1886, p. 30.

Plurality of Worlds. See WORLDS, PLURALITY OF.

Poisal, JOHN, D.D., a minister of the Methodist Episcopal Church South, was born at Martinsburg, W. Va., May 13, 1807. He was converted when a youth, and in his nineteenth year was admitted into the Baltimore Conference of the Methodist Episcopal Church, in which, and in the corresponding Conference of the Methodist Episcopal Church South, after its separation, he continued, with the exception of a few years in the New York and the Philadelphia conferences, to labor with great efficiency and success until his death, June 25, 1882. See *Minutes of Annual Conferences of the M. E. Church South*, 1883, p. 14.

Porter, ABNER, D.D., a Presbyterian minister, was born at Ashville, N. C., in 1817. He graduated from Princeton College in 1836 or 1837, studied at the Theological Seminary in Columbus, S. C., in 1842 became pastor in Greene County, Ala., in 1846 at Charleston, S. C., in 1851 at Selma, Ala., and finally became a missionary agent in Texas until his death, Dec. 8, 1872. See Nevin, *Presb. Encyclop.* s. v.

Presbyterian Alliance is the popular name of "The Alliance of the Reformed Churches throughout the World Holding the Presbyterian System," which was formed in London, England, in July, 1875, on the plan of voluntary association, by those bodies that chose to send delegates, and which held its first general council, so composed, at Edinburgh, Scotland, July 3 to 10, 1877, and its second in Philadelphia, Pa., Sept. 23 to Oct. 2, 1880. At these meetings topics of general fraternal interest were discussed in papers formally prepared by divines appointed for this purpose, and the proceedings of each were published in full.

Purdy, JAMES SOUVERAINE, D.D., a Protestant Episcopal minister, was born at Rye, N. Y., Sept. 1, 1825. He graduated from Trinity College, Hartford, Conn., in 1849, and from the General Theological Seminary, N. Y., in 1852; became rector at Southport, Conn., in 1853, of Calvary Chapel, N. Y., in 1860, and died at Saratoga, March 21, 1883.

Purefoy, GEORGE W., D.D., a Baptist minister, was born in 1809. He was baptized in 1830, began to preach at once, labored in North Carolina, and died in 1880. He wrote some controversial tracts. See Cathcart, *Baptist Encyclop.* s. v.

R.

Ramsey, JAMES BEVERLIN, D.D., a Presbyterian minister, was born near Elkton, Md., May 20, 1814. He graduated from Lafayette College in 1836, and from Princeton Theological Seminary in 1840; became pastor at West Farms, N. Y., in 1841, after 1846 a missionary to the Choctaw Indians, teacher and stated supply in various places, until his death, July 23, 1871. See *Gen. Cat. of Princeton Theol. Sem.* 1881, p. 112; Nevin, *Presb. Encyclop.* s. v.

Reading OF THE BIBLE. The regular and constant perusal of the Holy Scriptures is so delightful a privilege of Christians that it is spontaneously adopted by the converted heart, and the book has such a charm both for the young and the old, the scholar and the unlearned, as to be a perpetual theme of study for every intelligent mind. It is also enjoined as a religious duty, as well in the volume itself (Deut. vi, 7; John v, 39), as in the prescriptive rules of most ecclesiastical bodies. The public use of the Bible was practiced by the Jews and by the early Christians, and has been continued among all Protestant bodies. See LESSONS. Especial officers were detailed in the early Church for the more general diffusion of this work. See READER. In the Roman Catholic Church, however, and to some extent in the Greek, the promiscuous perusal of the Scriptures, in the vernacular, has been prohibited. See BIBLE, USE OF, BY THE LAITY. Much of the modern so-called

"Bible-reading" is rather a mode of sermonizing, or a casual stringing together of disconnected texts on some fanciful principle.

Reding, Joseph, a pioneer Baptist minister, was born in Fauquier County, Va., about 1750. He was baptized in 1771; began to preach immediately; labored successfully in South Carolina and Kentucky, and died in December, 1815. See Cathcart, *Baptist Encyclop.* s. v.

Rees, Thomas Swansea, D.D., a Welsh Congregational minister, was born in Carmarthenshire, Dec. 13, 1815. He was converted at thirteen, began to preach in 1832, was ordained in 1836, labored with great success in various pastorates in Wales, and died April 29, 1885. See (Lond.) *Cong. Year-book*, 1886, p. 204.

Richards, Austin, D.D., a Congregational minister, was born at Plainfield, Mass., Feb. 9, 1800. He graduated from Amherst College in 1824, and from Andover Theological Seminary in 1827, was pastor at Francestown, N. H., and at Nashua thereafter until 1870, and died at Boston, Mass., May 9, 1883. See *Cong. Year-book*, 1884, p. 33.

Richardson, Nathan Smith, D.D., a Protestant Episcopal clergyman, was born at Middlebury, Vt., Jan. 8, 1810. He graduated from Yale College in 1834, studied at the General Theological Seminary, N. Y., became minister at Watertown, Conn., in 1838, at Ansonia in 1844, editor of the *American Church Review* in 1848, rector at Bridgeport in 1868, editor of *The Guardian* in 1879, and died Aug. 7, 1883. He published *Reasons Why I am a Christian*, and other works.

Riggs, Cyrus C., D.D., a Presbyterian minister, was born at Fairfield, Pa., April 10, 1810. He graduated from Jefferson College in 1836, studied at the Western Theological Seminary, was licensed to preach in 1839, ordained in 1840, pastor in Illinois until 1845, then in Maryland and Pennsylvania, and teacher in Beaver, Pa., in 1869. He died Aug. 29, 1883. See Nevin, *Presb. Encyclop.* s. v.

Ross, Frederick A., D.D., a Presbyterian minister, was born in 1796. His long life was devoted to the service of Christ. He was remarkable for the vigor of his intellect, boldness and zeal in the pulpit, and the contributions of his pen to the literature of the Church. He died at Huntsville, Ala., April 18, 1883. See (N. Y.) *Observer*, April 26, 1883. (W. P. S.)

Roszell, Stephen Samuel, D.D., a minister of the Methodist Episcopal Church South, was born at Philadelphia, Oct. 29, 1812. He graduated early from Augusta College, Ky., taught in Baltimore, Md., became professor in Dickinson College, joined the Baltimore Conference in 1838, and continued one of its distinguished preachers until laid aside by infirmity. He died April 27, 1882. See *Minutes of Annual Conferences of the M. E. Church South*, 1883, p. 13.

S.

Sanford, David Platt, D.D., a Protestant Episcopal clergyman, was born at Redding, Conn., Jan. 29, 1819. He graduated from Trinity College, Hartford, in 1844; became minister at Woodbury in 1846, at Oxford and Quaker's Farms in 1847; Walcottville in 1849; St. Louis, Mo., in 1850; New Milford, Conn., in 1851; Brooklyn, N. Y., in 1853; Faribault, Minn., in 1858; Long Hill, Conn., in 1859; chaplain in the army in 1862; rector at Wolcottville in 1864; Rochester, Minn., in 1869; Winsted, Conn., in 1870; Hazardville in 1874, and died at Thompsonville, April 3, 1883.

Santa Sophia. See Sophia (*Saint*), Church of.

Sawtell, Eli Newton, D.D., a Congregational minister, was born at Milford, N. H., Sept. 8, 1799. He graduated from Greeneville College, Tenn., in 1823, from Marysville Theological Seminary in 1825, and studied at Andover in 1826; was Presbyterian minister at several places in Tennessee and Kentucky until 1836; then went as chaplain to Havre, and filled other ecclesiastical offices until 1864; Congregational minister at Saratoga Springs, N. Y., from 1865 to 1867; thereafter served in ecclesiastical commissions until 1878, and died on Staten Island, April 6, 1885. See *Cong. Year-book*, 1886, p. 32.

Sawtelle, Henry Allen, D.D., a Baptist minister, was born at Sidney, Me., Dec. 11, 1832. He graduated from Colby University in 1854, and from the Newton Theological Institution in 1858; was pastor at Limerick, Me., one year; missionary to China from 1859 to 1861; pastor at San Francisco, Cal., in 1862; at Chelsea from 1877 until his death, Nov. 22, 1885. He wrote frequently for the religious journals, also a volume entitled *Things to Think of.* See Cathcart, *Baptist Encyclop.* s.v.

Scott, Robinson, D.D., LL.D., an English Methodist minister, was born at Bainbridge, Sept. 17, 1814. In 1835 he entered the Wesleyan ministry, in 1845 was appointed governor of the connectional school at Dublin, and subsequently of that at Belfast. He was foremost in the work of Methodist education in Ireland. He died Dec. 22, 1883. See *Minutes of the British Conference*, 1884, p. 33.

Scott, William Anderson, D.D., LL.D., a Presbyterian minister, was born at Rock Creek, Bedford Co., Tenn., Jan. 31, 1813. He was converted at fifteen, licensed to preach at seventeen, and immediately began his itinerant ministry. He graduated from Cumberland College, Ky., in 1833, studied one year at Princeton Theological Seminary, was ordained in 1835, labored several years as missionary and teacher in Louisiana, Arkansas, and Tennessee; pastor at Nashville in 1838; at Tuscaloosa, Ala., in 1840; New Orleans, La., in 1843; San Francisco, Cal., from 1855 to 1861; travelled in Europe, and served as pastor at Birmingham, England; at New York city in 1863; and at San Francisco from 1870 until his death, Jan. 14, 1885. See *Necrol. Report of Princeton Theol. Sem.* 1885, p. 30.

Scovel, Sylvester, D.D., a Presbyterian minister, was born at Peru, Mass., March 3, 1796. He graduated from Williams College in 1822, and studied two years at Princeton Theological Seminary; labored as a missionary on the Delaware River; was pastor at Woodbury, N. J., in 1825; supply at Norristown, Pa., in 1828; in Ohio from 1833 to 1836; agent of domestic missions until 1846; and president of Hanover College, Ind., until his death, July 4, 1849. See Nevin, *Presb. Encyclop.* s. v.

Seely, Raymond Hoyt, D.D., a Congregational minister, was born at Norwalk, Conn., Feb. 19, 1812. He graduated from New York University in 1839, and from Union Theological Seminary in 1842; became pastor at Bristol, Conn., in 1843; Springfield, Mass., in 1849; at the American Chapel, Paris, in 1858; Haverhill, Mass., in 1860, and died there, Sept. 7, 1885. He published several sermons and addresses. See *Cong. Year-book*, 1886, p. 32.

Sessions, John, D.D., a Presbyterian minister, was born at Putney, Vt., Sept. 29, 1795. He graduated from Dartmouth College in 1822, studied one year at Princeton Theological Seminary, ministered at various Presbyterian and Congregational churches in New York, Ohio, and Connecticut, teaching several years meanwhile until 1863, when he removed to California, and in 1879 to Honolulu, where he died, April 6, 1884. See *Necrol. Report of Princeton Theol. Sem.* 1885, p. 10.

Shafer, Joseph L., D.D., a Presbyterian minister, was born at Stillwater, N. J., May 9, 1787. He graduated from Princeton College in 1808, studied theology under Rev. Dr. Woodhull, was licensed to preach in 1810, served two years as a missionary, and thereafter as pastor at Newton (with the exception of three years at Middletown Point), until his death, Nov. 12, 1853. See Nevin, *Presbyterian Encyclop.* s. v.

Shailer, William H., D.D., a Baptist minister, was born at Haddam, Conn., Nov. 20, 1807. He graduated from Madison University in 1835; studied at the Newton Theological Institution, teaching meanwhile; became pastor at Deep River, Conn., in 1836; at Brookline, Mass., in 1837; at Portland, Me., in 1854, and without charge from 1877 until his death, Feb. 20, 1881. See Cathcart, *Baptist Encyclop.* s. v.

Siegmund, George F., D.D., a Protestant Episcopal clergyman, was born in Prussia in 1838. He studied at the University of Halle; came to America in 1872; became assistant at the Church of the Annunciation, New York city, in 1874, and afterwards at Grace Church; founded the German Church Society, and died in New York city, Feb. 23, 1884.

Smiley, George W., D.D., a Presbyterian minister, was born in Perry County, Pa., in 1818. He studied two years in Dickinson College; removed to Lexington, Ky., where he was converted; joined the Methodist Church, and for twenty years served as an itinerant preacher, then as a Reformed Dutch minister at Philadelphia, and finally, for fourteen years, as a Presbyterian minister at Pottsville. He died June 19, 1883. See Nevin, *Presbyterian Encyclop.* s. v.

Smith, Albert Patterson, D.D., a Protestant Episcopal clergyman, was born in New Hampshire in 1809. He graduated from the General Theological Seminary, N. Y., in 1842, served at Camden, N. J., then as rector of St. Peter's Church, Cazenovia, for thirty-three years, until his death, March 14, 1882.

Society for Promoting Christian Knowledge, an important religious association of the Church of England, founded in 1698, designed to support charity-schools in England and Wales, and to circulate annotated Bibles, tracts, and books, chiefly in the British dominions. It has published many valuable works of a popular religious character. It is distinct from, but somewhat akin with, the Religious Tract Society, which was instituted in 1799, and which has a wider field. It is supported by endowment, contributions, and sales, and has an annual income of about half a million dollars.

Sophia (*Saint*), Church (or Mosque) of, the most notable edifice in Constantinople, built by the emperor Constantine, A.D. 330, and so named in honor of the divine wisdom (Σοφία). It was one of the first Christian churches permitted after the persecution by Diocletian. Thirteen years afterwards it was enlarged by Constantius, son of Constantine; was burned in 404, rebuilt in 415 by Theodosius II; burned a second time in 532, and in 538 was reconstructed from the foundation by Justinian, and dedicated on Christmas eve, 549. In 1453, when the Turks entered the city, the people gathered together in this church, but they were seized and massacred, the building being saved from destruction by Mohammed II, who conceived the idea of transforming it into a mosque. The whole aspect, both internally and externally, was entirely changed to accommodate the new worship; the pictures and mosaics were covered over, the altar rebuilt in the corner towards Mecca, a minaret was added at one corner, and the form of the church was changed to that of a crescent. Since then other buildings have been added to the original, a sacristy and baptistery being the most prominent. Among the sacred curiosities found in the crypt are, according to tradition, the block of red marble used as the cradle of our Saviour, the cup used by Mary in washing Jesus, both from Bethlehem; also the "sweating column," "shining stone," and "cold window," visited by Moslem pilgrims as miraculous. The original form of the church was that of a cross enclosed in a square, whose sides measure two hundred and forty-five feet; including the portico, two hundred and sixty-nine feet. Having been enlarged and rebuilt several times, the original form has been lost, and now the exterior of this edifice is singularly heavy. Uncouth and disproportionate in appearance, even the effect of its unusual dimensions is

Exterior of the Church of St. Sophia.

Interior of the Church of St. Sophia.

destroyed by its lack of symmetry, it presenting an irregular mass of cupolas, half-domes, shelving roofs, and stunted minarets. Even the great dome, rising in the centre, so celebrated for its architectural beauty, looks low and flat, and from the outside produces nothing of the effect which was its purpose. The west side forms the entrance. The first vestibule was called in ancient times the narthex. The gallery for the women runs around three sides, supported by many magnificent columns borrowed from ancient buildings. The chief object of beauty is the dome, called the "ærial dome," on account of its exceeding light weight, consisting of pumice-stone bricks from Rhodes. It rises to the height of one hundred and eighty feet, resting on four massive arches. In the corners of this dome are four seraphim in mosaic, and on the arches can still be traced the sketches of madonnas and saints. Most of the ornamentation has been replaced by gigantic specimens of Turkish caligraphy, quotations from the Koran, on circular tablets. On the top of the cupola the verse "God is the light of the heavens and the earth" is illuminated during the festivals. Like all mosques

Ground-plan of the Church of St. Sophia.

Street leading to the Balbî Humayûn, Sublime Porte, and westward to the At-Meldan and the Mosque of Ahmed. A, Officers' court; B, Aldash house; D, E, First and second porch, or narthex; F, Formerly the emperor's and patriarch's seats; G, Formerly the altar; H, Mihrab, where the Koran is kept; I. The four minarets; K, Circumference of dome; L. Outer doors; M, Side galleries; N. Front gallery.

this is closed to Christian visitors except upon special firman, which may be easily obtained, at a small expense, through the interposition of the masters of the principal hotels.

Spotswood, JOHN BOSWELL, D.D., a Presbyterian minister, was born in Dinwiddie County, Va., Feb. 8, 1808. He graduated from Amherst College in 1828, and from Princeton Theological Seminary in 1832; became pastor in Sussex County, Va., in 1833; at Ellicott's Mills in 1840; at New Castle, Del., in 1842; resigned in 1884, and died there, Feb. 10, 1885. See *Necrol. Report of Princeton Theol. Sem.* 1885, p. 23.

St. Sophia. See SOPHIA.

Sterling, JOHN WHELEN, D.D., a Presbyterian minister, was born at Black Walnut, Pa., July 17, 1816. He graduated from the College of New Jersey in 1840, and from Princeton Theological Seminary in 1844; became pastor at Tunkhannock, Pa., in 1845; professor in Carroll College, Wis., in 1846; teacher at Waukesha in 1847; professor in the University of Wisconsin in 1848, and died in office, March 8, 1885. See *Necrol. Report of Princeton Theol. Sem.* 1885, p. 44.

Stiles, JOSEPH CLAY, D.D., LL.D., a Presbyterian minister, was born in Savannah, Ga., Dec. 6, 1795. He graduated from Yale College in 1814, studied and practiced law, spent one year (1825) in Andover Theological Seminary, became an evangelist in Georgia and Florida (1829), and afterwards (1835) in Kentucky; pastor in Richmond, Va. (1844), at Mercer Street, New York city (1848), agent of the American Bible Society (1850), pastor in New Haven, Conn. (1853), and finally an evangelist in several of the Southern states. He died March 27, 1875. See Nevin, *Presb. Encyclop.* s. v.

Stock, JOHN, LL.D., an English Baptist minister, was born in London, Dec. 7, 1817. He began to preach at the age of sixteen, studied two years at University College, London, became pastor at Chatham in 1842, at Devonport in 1857, and died May 3, 1884. In 1867 he visited the United States, and was most cordially received. He published a large number of religious volumes and tracts. See (Lond.) *Baptist Hand-book*, 1885, p. 157.

Suddards, WILLIAM, D.D., a Protestant Episcopal clergyman, was born in 1800. He was originally a Methodist preacher, was ordained by bishop M'Ilvaine, was rector of Grace Church, Philadelphia, Pa., over forty years, and died there, Feb. 20, 1883.

Sumner, M. T., D.D., a Baptist minister, was born in Massachusetts, Sept. 6, 1815. He graduated from Brown University in 1838, engaged in teaching and preaching in Richmond, Va., in 1840, became agent of the American Tract Society in 1854, secretary of the Baptist Mission Board in 1858, subsequently held several other agencies, became pastor at Athens, Ala., in 1880, and died Aug. 23, 1883. See Cathcart, *Baptist Encyclop.* s. v.

Sunderland, LA ROY, a brilliant but erratic character, was born at Exeter, R. I., May 18, 1802. He became a Methodist preacher in 1823, and soon was known as a prominent orator on temperance, antislavery, and eventually on physiology and psychology. He died a professed infidel, May 15, 1885. He was the editor of various journals, and the author of several volumes on the above subjects.

T.

Talbot, JOSEPH CRUIKSHANK, D.D., LL.D., a Protestant Episcopal bishop, was born at Alexandria, Va., Sept. 5, 1816. He studied at the Alexandria Academy; in 1835 removed to Kentucky, and engaged in mercantile pursuits; in 1843 became a candidate for clerical orders, in 1846 was ordained deacon, and in 1848 presbyter; was in charge of St. John's Church, Louisville, seven years, and in 1853 became rector of Christ Church, Indianapolis; in 1859 was elected assistant bishop of Indiana, and in 1872 became bishop of the diocese. He died Jan. 16, 1883.

Taylor, ELISHA E. L., D.D., a Baptist minister, was born at Delphi, N. Y., Sept. 25, 1815. He graduated from Madison University, and from the theological seminary at Hamilton, became pastor in Pierrepont Street, Brooklyn, in 1865 secretary of the Baptist Church Edifice Fund, and died Aug. 20, 1874. See Cathcart, *Baptist Encyclop.* s. v.

Tefft, BENJAMIN FRANKLIN, D.D., LL.D., a Methodist Episcopal divine, was born near Utica, N. Y., Aug. 20, 1813. He graduated from Wesleyan University, Conn., in 1835, became successively teacher and preacher in New England until 1843, thereafter professor in Indiana Asbury University, in 1846 editor of *The Ladies' Repository*, from 1852 to 1862 teacher and pastor in New York and Maine, from 1862 to 1865 engaged in United States commissions abroad and at home, in 1866 pastor at Portland, Me., in 1873 editor of the *Northern Border*, having assumed the position of a local preacher, and died at Bangor, Me., Sept. 17, 1885. He published several works, the latest of which was an elaborate volume on *Evolution*. See *Alumni Record of Wesleyan University*, 1883, p. 9, 645.

Thurston, STEPHEN, D.D., a Congregational minister, was born at Sedgewick, Me., Dec. 22, 1797. He graduated from Bangor Theological Seminary in 1825, became pastor at Searsport (then Prospect), Me., in 1826, was secretary of the Maine Missionary Society from 1864 to 1876, and died May 27, 1884. He published several sermons. See *Cong. Year-book*, 1885, p. 35.

Toby, THOMAS W., D.D., a Baptist minister, was for several years a missionary to China, afterwards pastor in North Carolina, professor in various literary institutions, pastor at Union Springs, then at Camden, Ala., and finally principal of the Collegiate Institute at Eufala, among the Creek nation. He died at Lake Weir, Fla., in February, 1885, aged sixty-five years.

Trench, RICHARD CHENEVIX, D.D., a prelate of the Irish Church, was born in Ireland, Sept. 9, 1807. He was educated at Harrow and at Trinity College, Cambridge, and took his degree in 1829. He was shortly afterwards ordained as curate to Hugh James Rose of Hadleigh. At this time Trench joined the High-Church party, without having the smallest leaning Romewards. He had a tolerance for, though not intellectual sympathy with, the broad school. While holding a small incumbency in Hampshire, Trench became acquainted with the Rev. Dr. (afterwards bishop) Wilberforce, whose curate he became. In 1845 Wilberforce was made dean of Westminster, and Trench became rector of Itchenstoke, a small village near Winchester, joining to his work there, as soon as Wilberforce became bishop, that of examining chaplain, and soon after that of theological professor at King's College. In 1856 Trench was made dean of Westminster, a position which he held to the end of 1863. On Jan. 1, 1864, he was consecrated archbishop of Dublin. He resigned his office in 1885, and died March 28, 1886. As a writer, Trench is known beyond the confines of his own country. He was poet, philologist, and theologian. Of his many writings the best known are, *On the Authorized Version of the New Testament* (N. Y. 1858):—*Synonyms of the New Testament* (8th ed. revised, Lond. 1876):—*Exposition of the Sermon on the Mount*, etc. (3d ed. 1869):—*Studies in the Gospels* (1870):—*The Star of the Wise Men* (1850):—*Commentary on the Epistles to the Seven Churches in Asia, Rev. ii, iii* (1864):—*Notes on the Parables of Our Lord* (1871):—*Notes on the Miracles of Our Lord* (eod.):—*On the Lessons in Proverbs* (1865):—*Lectures on Mediæval Church History* (1878):—*Sermons Preached before the University of Cambridge* (1866):—*Sermons Preached in Westminster Abbey* (1861):—*The Hulsean Lectures* *for* 1845 *and* 1846 (1860):—*Sermons Preached for the Most Part in Ireland* (1873):—*Sacred Latin Poetry* (1864):—*English, Past and Present* (7th ed. 1871):—*A Select Glossary of English Words* (1872):—*On the Study of Words* (1868):—*Brief Thoughts and Meditations on Passages of Holy Scripture* (1884). Trench was also a member of the English Company for the Revision of the New Test. (B. P.)

Trimble, ROBERT W., LL.D., a Protestant Episcopal clergyman, was born at Wheeling, W. Va., Feb. 2, 1829, ordained deacon in 1858, and presbyter in 1860, was rector at Pine Bluff, Ark., for twenty-one years, and died April 18, 1882.

Tucker, SILAS, D.D., one of five brothers, all Baptist ministers, was born May 16, 1813, baptized in 1833, licensed the next year, studied in the seminary at Hamilton, N. Y., in 1837 became pastor in Cleveland, O., subsequently of other churches in Ohio, Indiana, and Illinois, and died at Aurora, Ill., Nov. 7, 1872. See Cathcart, *Baptist Encyclop.* s. v.

Turnbull, ROBERT, D.D., a Baptist minister, was born at Whiteburn, Linlithgowshire, Scotland, Sept. 10, 1809. He was religiously trained, graduated from Glasgow University, studied with Dr. Chalmers, preached a year and a half at Westmancotte, Worcestershire, England; came to America in 1833, became pastor at Danbury, Conn., for two years, afterwards at Hartford; in 1839 at Boston, Mass., in 1845 again at Hartford, in 1869 preached in various places with much success, in 1872 became secretary of the Connecticut Baptist Association, and died Nov. 20, 1877. He published a number of popular religious works. See Cathcart, *Baptist Encyclop.* s. v.

W.

Wadsworth, EDWARD, D.D., a minister of the Methodist Episcopal Church South, was born at New Berne, N. C., Aug. 28, 1811. He was converted in 1829, entered the Virginia Conference in 1831, in which, and subsequently (1855) in the Alabama Conference, he filled important stations until 1859, when he became a professor in the Southern University, and in 1871 he returned to pastoral work, in which he continued until his death, in the spring of 1883. See *Minutes of Annual Conferences of the M. E. Church South*, 1883, p. 97.

Wallace, ROBERT HOWARD, D.D., a Presbyterian minister, was born at Montgomery, N. Y., Nov. 12, 1796. He studied with Rev. Dr. McJimpsey of his native place, was licensed to preach in 1824, served in the domestic missions of the Associate Reformed Church, became pastor at Little Britain and Caledonia, N. Y., in 1825, and died in that relation, Feb. 9, 1868. See Nevin, *Presb. Encyclop.* s. v.

Walsh, JOHN JOHNSTON, D.D., a Presbyterian minister, was born at Newburgh, N. Y., April 4, 1820. He joined the Church at the age of eighteen, graduated from Union College in 1839, and from Princeton Theological Seminary in 1843, went as a missionary to India, returned after thirty years of labor, was pastor at Millerstown, N. Y., from 1874 to 1876, and died Feb. 7, 1884. See *Necrol. Report of Princeton Theol. Sem.* 1884, p. 31.

Warren, JONAH G., D.D., a Baptist minister, was born at Ward, Mass., Sept. 12, 1812. He graduated from Brown University in 1835, and from the Newton Theological Institution in 1838, became pastor at Chicopee the same year, at North Troy, N. Y., in 1849, secretary of the American Baptist Mission Union in 1855, resigned in 1872, and died at Newton Centre, Mass., Feb. 27, 1884. See Cathcart, *Baptist Encyclop.* s. v.

Watkins, WILLIAM H., D.D., a minister of the Methodist Episcopal Church South, was born in Jefferson County, Miss., April 11, 1815. He was converted early in life, entered the Mississippi Conference in 1835, and labored earnestly and successfully until his death, Feb. 5, 1881. See *Minutes of Annual Conferences of the M. E. Church South*, 1881, p. 311.

Watson, JOHN LEE, D.D., a Protestant Episcopal clergyman, was born at Boston, Mass., Aug. 27, 1797. He graduated from Harvard College in 1815, became rector at Fishkill, N. Y., in 1835, assistant at Trinity Church, Boston, in 1836, rector of Grace Church, Newark, N. J., in 1846, of Burlington College in 1853, chaplain of the United States Navy in 1855, was placed on the retired list in 1861, and died at Orange, N. J., Aug. 12, 1884.

Webster, JOHN CALVIN, D.D., a Congregational minister, was born at Hampton, N. H., Jan. 19, 1810. He graduated from Dartmouth College in 1832, and from Andover Theological Seminary in 1835; preached at Wells, Me., two years thereafter; was seamen-chaplain at Cronstadt, Russia, in 1838; pastor at Hopkinton, Mass., until 1864; professor in Wheaton College, Ill., until 1876; acting-pastor at Lisbon, in the same state, from 1878 to 1882, and died at Wheaton, Aug. 12, 1884. He published several sermons. See *Cong. Yearbook*, 1885, p. 37.

Wellwood. See MONCRIEF.

Wentworth, ERASTUS, D.D., a Methodist Episcopal minister, was born at Stonington, Conn., Aug. 5, 1813. He was converted in 1831; studied at Cazenovia, N. Y.; graduated from Wesleyan University, Conn., in 1837; became a teacher in Gouverneur Seminary in 1838, and in 1841 in Troy Conference Academy, joining the Troy Conference the same year; in 1846 was elected president of M'Kendrie College, Ill.; in 1850 professor in Dickinson College, Pa.; in 1854 went as a missionary to Foochow, China; in 1862 became pastor of North-second Street Church, Troy, N. Y.; in 1865 of State Street Church, in the same city; in 1868 at Pittsfield, Mass.; in 1871 at Amsterdam, N. Y.; in 1872 editor of *The Ladies' Repository*, at Cincinnati, O.; in 1877 became superannuated, and died at Sandy Hill, N. Y., May 25, 1886. He was possessed of remarkable and varied talents, wrote much and brilliantly, especially for the journals, and several times was a member of the General Conference. See *Alumni Record of Wesleyan University*, 1882, p. 17, 654.

Wesleyan Methodist Connection OF AMERICA. This society grew out of a separation from the Methodist Episcopal Church, on account of the connection of that body with slavery, and the arbitrary character of its government. The withdrawal of Revs. O. Scott, J. Horton, L. R. Sunderland, Luther Lee, and Lucius C. Matlack, in the latter part of 1842, and the establishment of a religious paper known as the *True Wesleyan*, are regarded as the commencement of the movement which led to the Wesleyan organization. A call, signed by all of the above-named persons except L. C. Matlack, was issued in the *True Wesleyan*, and otherwise circulated, for a Wesleyan anti-slavery convention, to be held at Andover, Mass., commencing Feb. 1, 1843; and fifty-two delegates from Massachusetts, Rhode Island, Connecticut, and New Hampshire, responded to the call. In this convention a large number of resolutions were presented and adopted, setting forth the principles which had guided them in their separation from the mother church. Provisions were also made in this convention for another general convention to be held in Utica, N. Y., May 31 following, for the purpose of effecting the permanent organization of the Wesleyan Methodist Connection. One hundred and fifty-three delegates responded to the last-named call, representing New York, Michigan, Connecticut, Vermont, Rhode Island, New Hampshire, Ohio, Pennsylvania, and Massachusetts.

At this latter convention a discipline was formulated, and among the principles set forth for the government of the Church the following were some of the most prominent:

1. Opposition to slavery.
2. No affiliation with secret, oath-bound societies.
3. Plainness in apparel and manner of living.
4. Equal representation of ministers and laymen in the government of the Church.

Six annual conferences were established, viz.; New England, Champlain, New York, Miami, Alleghany, and Michigan, and the youthful denomination started upon its heaven-appointed mission. The first general conference was held in Cleveland, O., commencing Oct. 2, 1844.

Like all other reformatory bodies, this society was born in the midst of the most bitter persecution; and, viewed from a human standpoint, under the most unfavorable circumstances. Their opposition to the institution of American slavery at a time when the masses of the people either believed it to be right, or as a matter of policy apologized for it, made them a target for all kinds of abuse, and the opportunity was not neglected by the people. A single illustration in this connection will be sufficient. On one occasion, while Rev. Luther Lee was speaking against slavery, he was treated to a solution of whiskey and lampblack, which was thrown over him, and not only marred his personal appearance, but ruined his suit of clothes. He continued his address, however, and that meeting proved to be one of the best for the cause that was ever held.

The growth of the denomination was very encouraging notwithstanding these unfavorable surroundings; and within ten years the membership in the various conferences aggregated more than ten thousand. They were not of the popular and aristocratic class, neither were they altogether poor and unlearned. Among the membership were men and women of remarkable intellectual ability, who were instrumental in the hands of God in building up and establishing the educational interests of the Connection, until they were not behind other denominations of equal size in this particular.

Early in the history of the society the propriety of establishing an institution of learning was urged upon the people, and efforts were made in this direction at Leoni, Jackson Co., Mich., and also at Wheaton, Ill., but the matter finally took a more definite form in the location of a denominational college at Adrian, Mich. The citizens of Adrian donated largely towards the enterprise with the understanding and agreement that, if within five years the Wesleyans should erect buildings and secure property, free from debt, amounting to $100,000, the school should become the property of the denomination. Much more than the required sum was raised in the given time, and the terms having been complied with, an unquestionable title was secured. A competent faculty was placed in charge of the college, and astonishing success attended the enterprise from the beginning. Students flocked in from all parts of the country, and many were compelled to find rooms in private residences near the college, all of the desirable rooms in the two large buildings erected for that purpose being occupied.

After the war of the rebellion had closed and peace had been declared, leaving the nation free from the curse of human bondage, some of the leading men in the Connection, believing that the mission of the denomination was ended, conceived the idea of uniting all non-Episcopal Methodist churches into one body, and combined their efforts with others in effecting the proposed combination. A convention was held in the city of Cleveland, O., June 21, 1865, where committees were appointed and steps taken looking towards such a union of churches. Provisions were also made for another convention, which met in Cincinnati, May 9, 1866, and at this convention the basis of the union was decided upon and the foundation laid. The expectations of the Wesleyan leaders were not met, however, from the fact that the denomination, as a whole, were not satisfied with the terms of the union, and also from their general disagreement with the proposition that the mission of their Church was ended. When the reformatory principles adopted by the Wesleyans were presented for the consideration of the convention, they were entirely ignored, and secret societies were eulogized instead of being reproved. Finding that the union was not a success, most of the Wesleyan leaders in the movement withdrew and united with other religious communions, and a number of local churches followed their example. These may be properly termed the "dark days" of the Connection, and when the "smoke of battle" had cleared away, it was found that somewhat serious injuries had been sustained. Not the least of these was the transfer of Adrian College to the control of another denomination. In the midst of the exciting scenes connected with the union movement a majority of the trustees were prevailed upon to make the transfer, though not in harmony with the wishes, and without the consent, of the denomination. Committees have been appointed by the General Conference to look after the legality of the transfer, and to consider the feasibility of taking legal steps for the recovery of the college. Notwithstanding the tidal wave of adversity that had swept over the Connection, those who remained true and stood by their "colors" were not disheartened. Other men as noble as the first—and of greater value to the Connection, because of the fact that they remained true to principles through the struggle that tried men's souls—took the helm, and succeeded in steering the vessel through the breakers to the calm sea of renewed prosperity. The troubles of the conflict only intensified the zeal of the tried and true, and the result was a general revival all through the Connection, and a healthful growth has been realized since that time both in membership and finances.

A large and commodious publishing house has been erected in the city of Syracuse, N. Y., which is the headquarters of the denomination, where the principal part of the business of the Connection is transacted. Rev. D. S. Kinney is connectional agent, and not only has charge of the business transacted at the office, but visits the various annual conferences, and looks after the denominational interests in connection therewith. Rev. N. Wardner is editor of the *Wesleyan Methodist*, the official organ of the denomination, and of the *Bible Standard*, a monthly magazine devoted to the doctrine and experience of Scriptural holiness, both of which are published at the publishing house in Syracuse, and receive a liberal patronage from the people. He is also editor of *The Children's Banner*, and *Good Words*, papers devoted to Sunday-school interests. The publishing interests of the Connection, including building, printing machinery, etc., are valued at about $50,000, to which additions are constantly made, and all is free from debt.

Two seminaries are now the property of the Connection, one located at Wasioja, Dodge Co., Minn., with professor E. G. Paine as principal, and the other at Houghton, Alleghany Co., N. Y., with professor A. R. Dodd as principal. Both of these schools are in a prosperous condition, and an honor to the Connection. Added to these is a theological seminary, in connection with Whearton College, Ill., under the care of Rev. L. N. Stratton, D.D., as president, where a goodly number of young men are in course of education each year for the Christian ministry.

There are at this date (September, 1886), twenty-one conferences in the denomination, aggregating about five hundred ministers and twenty thousand members. Officers of the General Conference are, president, Rev. N. Wardner, Syracuse, N. Y., and secretary, Rev. E. W. Bruce, of the same place, who are the joint authors of this article.

Westgate, George Lewis, a Methodist Episcopal minister, was born at Fall River, Mass., April 12, 1844. He graduated from Wesleyan University, Conn., in 1865; studied two years in Union Theological Seminary, N. Y., and in 1867 joined the Providence Conference, in which and afterwards (1874) in the New York

East Conference he occupied important stations until his election, in 1880, as professor of social science in his *alma mater*, a position which he retained until his death, June 28, 1885. See *Alumni Record of Wesleyan University*, 1883, p. 212; *Minutes of Annual Conferences*, 1886, p. 83.

White, WILLIAM SPOTTSWOOD, D.D., a Presbyterian minister, was born in Hanover County, Va., July 30, 1800. He attended Hampden-Sidney College, studied theology under Dr. John H. Rice, and was licensed to preach in 1827; labored in Nottoway, Amelia, Lunenberg, and Dinwiddie counties, Va.; in 1832 became pastor at Scottsville, in 1834 agent of the American Tract Society, in 1836 principal of a female school, in 1848 pastor at Lexington, Va., and died there, Nov. 29, 1873. See Nevin, *Presbyterian Encyclop.* s. v.

Williams, JAMES ALFRED, D.D., a Protestant Episcopal clergyman, was born at Orange, N. J., Sept. 6, 1809. He graduated from Columbia College in 1831, and from the General Theological Seminary in 1836; became rector of St. Mark's Church, Orange, in 1837, and continued there until his death, Sept. 2, 1883. He was president of the standing committee of his diocese for many years.

Williamson, SAMUEL, D.D., a Presbyterian minister, was born in York District, S. C., June 12, 1795. He graduated from South Carolina College in 1818, and studied theology under Rev. James Adams; became pastor at Providence in 1822, professor in Davidson College in 1840, its president from 1841 to 1854, and pastor at Washington and Columbus, Ark., from 1857 to 1876. He died March 12, 1882. See Nevin, *Presbyterian Encyclop.* s. v.

Wilson, John A., D.D., a Protestant Episcopal clergyman, was born at Washington, D. C., in 1810. He graduated from Kenyon College and Gambier Theological Seminary; was rector of Zion Church, Pontiac, Mich., from 1840 to 1847, and thereafter of St. Luke's Church, Ypsilanti, until 1882. He died May 7, 1885.

Wilson, John Glasgow, D.D., a minister of the Methodist Episcopal Church South, was born in Maury County, Tenn., in 1826. He was piously reared in the Presbyterian Church, graduated from Nashville University at the age of sixteen, and licensed to preach at twenty-four; served for twenty years as president of Huntsville Female College and Warren College, Ky.; in 1876 became pastor of St. John's Church, St. Louis; in 1880 presiding elder, and died Aug. 5, 1884. See *Minutes of Annual Conferences of the M. E. Church South*, 1884, p. 142.

Wilson, Samuel B., D.D., a Presbyterian divine, was born in South Carolina about 1782, studied in the usual schools of the day, was pastor for thirty-seven years, and subsequently professor in the Union Theological Seminary of Virginia, at length *emeritus* until his death, in August, 1869. See Nevin, *Presbyterian Encyclop.* s. v.

Wilson, Samuel Jennings, D.D., LL.D., an eminent Presbyterian minister and educator, was born near Washington, Pa., July 19, 1828. He graduated from Washington College in 1852, and from the Western Theological Seminary in 1855, was licensed to preach the same year, served two years as teacher in the seminary, in 1857 became professor there, and continued in office until his death, Aug. 17, 1883. See Nevin, *Presbyterian Encyclop.* s. v.

Winkler, EDWARD THEODORE, D.D., a Baptist minister, was born at Savannah, Ga., Nov. 13, 1823. He graduated from Brown University in 1843, and studied in the Newton Theological Institution; in 1845 was assistant editor of the *Christian Quarterly*, and supplied the pulpit at Columbus, Ga., for six months; in 1846 became pastor at Albany, and subsequently at Gallisonville; in 1852 secretary of the Southern Baptist Publication Society; in 1854 pastor at Charleston, S. C.; in 1872 at Marion, in 1874 editor of the *Alabama Baptist*, and died Nov. 10, 1883. He wrote several denominational works. See Cathcart, *Baptist Encyclop.* s. v.

Witherspoon, ANDREW, D.D., a Methodist Episcopal minister, was born at Leith, Scotland, May 16, 1808, and emigrated to America with his parents when nine years old. He was converted at sixteen, licensed to preach in 1832, and next year admitted into the Troy Conference, in which he held prominent appointments until his superannuation, in 1877, when he removed to Kansas, and died there, Feb. 9, 1885. He was a member of six general conferences. See *Minutes of Annual Conferences*, 1885, p. 95.

Worlds, PLURALITY OF. The question whether other globes besides the earth are inhabited is one of great interest both to the student of nature and to the theologian. There are two classes of arguments that may be brought to bear upon its solution.

1. *Probabilities from Analogy.*—From the fact that our own globe is populated, it has naturally been inferred that the stellar bodies are so likewise. Else why do they exist? Surely, it is contended, they cannot have been formed merely for the delectation of the comparatively few denizens of this relatively insignificant orb. But are we sure of that? If man be the only intelligent creature, it is inconsistent neither with reason nor with Scripture to suppose that the whole visible creation was intended for his express benefit and behoof. Moreover, the presumption from analogy almost wholly breaks down if extended to its legitimate results in this question. If the other celestial spheres are inhabited, it is doubtless with rational and moral beings like ourselves, for mere unaccountable animals would be a sorry outcome of so vast creative power and skill. In that case they are free of will, and some of them, at least, have probably fallen, like men and angels. Has a Redeemer been provided for them also? It would seem not, from the silence of revelation on the subject, or rather from the implications of soteriology. It is hazardous to aver that Christ has died for other worlds than our own, or that he will ever do so. Here is apparently an incongruity which clogs the hypothesis of other planetary bodies being inhabited.

2. *Evidence of Science.*—This is really a problem within the domain of physics, and should be decided by an appeal to known facts. These are neither few nor indistinct. The moon, which is our nearest and most familiar neighbor, is pronounced by the latest observers to be utterly uninhabitable. She has neither atmosphere nor water, at least not on the hemisphere which is constantly presented towards us. But she has enormously deep craters, which speak of fearful convulsions upon her surface, and her face appears to be entirely destitute of all possibilities even of vegetation. In fact, an ordinary-sized farm, or even a considerable dwelling, had it existed there, would probably have been detected by the powerful telescopes which have scanned and even photographed the lunar landscape.

Turning now to Venus, our nearest fellow-planet, we find her not much more favorably situated. She has so wide a variation of temperature at different seasons of the year, owing to the great obliquity of her ecliptic, as must be fatal to all animal or vegetable existence. Mercury, the sole other planet within our orbit, is even worse off, being so near the sun that no life could possibly endure the terrific heat. Mars, our first outside neighbor, is circumstanced most like ourselves; but the close observation, for which he affords peculiar facilities, have failed to discover any positive indications of habitability. Of the remaining members of our own planetary system, Jupiter and Saturn may perhaps have a temperature capable of supporting life, but the different colored moons of the former and the singular electric zone of the latter, besides their exceedingly low density, imply a difference of constitution incompatible with the conditions known upon our own globe. The improbability of their being inhabited is increased by the revelations of the *spectrum*, which discloses a composition of each materially different from the other and from the earth's. As for the asteroids, which occupy the place of a lost intermediate sphere, they seem to have consisted of terribly explosive materials, fragments of which frequently fall to us in the form of meteorolites, and furnish compounds not found in terrestrial bodies. The more distant planets are too intensely cold to admit of life in any form.

The only remaining member of our planetary family is the central orb, the sun itself. If its body is coequal with its luminous disk, the surface must be too rare to sustain beings of anything more than ethereal weight; and whether this be the real body of the sun, or whether the interior sphere, glimpses of which are obtained through the so-called "spots," and which only appear dark by contrast with the vivid incandescence of the atmosphere, still the fiery ardor of the surface must be such as to preclude all life of which we can form any conception.

The fixed stars are but the central suns of other systems, and are evidently of a like nature with our own. Their planets, if they have any, are a matter of pure conjecture. Comets and nebulæ are too flimsy in their structure to form a habitable abode for creatures of any sort; they seem, indeed, to be but fire-mist or electric vapor. We have thus exhausted the range of space, and find no home except earth at all suitable or possible for a creature having the least resemblance to man. To suppose a being capable of existing under the abnormal and intolerable conditions of vitality such as we have ascertained is as gratuitous as it is preposterous. We cannot, it is true, limit the power and resources of the Almighty, but we are forced by the facts in the case, and by the invariable analogies of all life with which we are acquainted, to deny its existence upon the other celestial bodies. Nor is there the slightest evidence that any of the globes except our own has ever been inhabited, or is likely to be so in the future. See Proctor, *Other Worlds than Ours* (Lond. 1870).

Wylie, William, D.D., a Presbyterian minister, was born in Washington County, Pa., July 10, 1776. He studied at various schools; became pastor of Upper and Lower Sandy and Fairfield Church, Ky., in 1802; in 1805 of Rehoboth and Round Hill; in 1810 preached at Uniontown, Pa.; in 1823 became pastor at Wheeling, Va.; in 1830 at Newark, O., where he continued twenty years, and died at Wheeling, May 9, 1853. See Nevin, *Presbyterian Encyclop.* s. v.

Y.

Yale, Elihu, F.R.S., was born at New Haven, Conn., April 5, 1648, but removed to England with his parents at ten years of age, and never returned to America. In 1678 he went to the East Indies, became governor of Madras, amassed a fortune, and returned to England, where he died (in London), July 22, 1721. He gave above $2000 in books and money to found a college at his birthplace, which therefore took his name.

Yantis, John Lapsley, D.D., a Presbyterian minister, was born at Lancaster, Ky., Sept. 14, 1804. He studied privately, was licensed to preach in 1829, became pastor at Stanford and Lancaster in 1830, removed to Saline County, Mo., in 1833, and thereafter labored alternately as teacher and pastor in various places, especially Danville, Ky., where he died, May 28, 1882. See Nevin, *Presbyterian Encyclop.* s. v.

Yong (or **Younge**), John, D.D., an English prelate, born at Cheapside, London, England, became master in Pembroke Hall, Cambridge, rector of St. Giles's Church, Cripplegate, prebend of Westminster (1572), and at last bishop of Rochester (1578). He was a faithful preacher, and queen Elizabeth deferred much to his judgment in Church matters. Better bishoprics were offered to him, but as often declined. He died April 10, 1605. See Fuller, *Worthies of England* (ed. Nuttall), ii, 357.

Young, Nicholas Dominic, a Roman Catholic missionary, was born near Washington, Md., June 11, 1793. He studied with the English Dominicans at Bornhem, Belgium, and became a member of their order in 1810. In December, 1817, he was ordained priest by bishop Flaget, at Bardstown, Ky., and in 1822 became superior of the Convent of St. Joseph, Perry County, O. He was provincial of his order from September, 1832, to May, 1857. In 1851 he established a house of his order at Washington. He died in that city, Nov. 28, 1878. See (N. Y.) *Catholic Annual*, 1882, p. 55.

Z.

Zschokke, Johann Heinrich Daniel, a German writer, was born at Magdeburg, March 22, 1771. He was erratic in his early youth, but studied at the University of Frankfort-on-the-Oder, and although proficient in philosophy, history, and mathematics, was refused a position as professor on account of his opposition to the government. Leaving Prussia, therefore, he travelled through Germany and France, and settled in Switzerland as a teacher, but the French revolution compelled him to take refuge in Aarau, where he played an active part in those times. He died there, Jan. 22, 1848. His later productions were chiefly poetical and historical, many of them novels. His best known is *Stunden der Andacht* (1806; twice transl. in English, *Meditations on Death*); but, as might be expected from his career, it is neither profound nor inspiring. His collected works were published at Aarau (1825, 40 vols. 8vo). See Hoefer, *Nouv. Biog. Générale*, s. v.

FURTHER ADDENDA.

A.

Abbott, Amos, a Congregational minister, was born in Wilton, N. H., June 2, 1812. He was educated at Phillips Academy and Andover; was a missionary of the A. B. C. F. M. in Western India, 1834-47; city missionary at Manchester, N. H., 1850-51; Portsmouth, 1851-56; resident licentiate at Andover, 1856-57; again became a missionary to India in 1857-69; was without a charge at Nashua, N. H., in 1869-74; but graduated from the Philadelphia Homœopathic College in 1871; was resident at Steele City, Neb., 1874, but practiced his profession and was also home missionary at Alexandria in 1876-77; at Fairfield, 1877-78, and the Otoe Reservation, 1878-79; and without charge at Ryde, on the Isle of Wight, from 1887 until his death, April 24, 1889. He was the author of an arithmetic that was used in the mission schools for forty years. He also wrote, *Pilgrimages:—Cholera:—Index to the New Testament:—Logic:—Vicarious Punishment:—Diseases of Women:*—and translated several works, among them a *Natural Philosophy*.

Aiken, Charles Augustus, a Presbyterian minister and educator, was born at Manchester, Vt., Oct. 30, 1827. After graduating from Dartmouth College in 1846, and Andover Theological Seminary in 1853, having spent some time in Germany studying, he was pastor of the Congregational Church at Yarmouth, Me., 1854-59; professor of Latin in Dartmouth College, 1859-66; in Princeton, 1866-69; president of Union College, 1869-71; professor of ethics and apologetics in Princeton Theological Seminary, 1871-82; professor of Oriental and Old-Testament literature at the same place, from 1882 until his death, Feb. 14, 1892. He translated Zöckler's *Commentary on Proverbs* (in Schaff's ed. of Lange), and has contributed to various periodicals. He was one of the American revisers of the Old Testament.

Allibone, Samuel Austin, a bibliographical author, was born in Philadelphia, Pa., April 17, 1816. In early life he engaged in mercantile pursuits. He was book editor and corresponding secretary of the American Sunday-School Union, 1867-73, and again in 1877-79. In 1879 he became librarian of the Lenox Library, New York city. He died at Luzerne, Switzerland, Sept. 23, 1889. He was the author of *A Critical Dictionary of English Literature and British and American Authors*, 3 vols., containing 46,499 authors. See *Appletons' Cyclopædia of American Biography*.

Allon, Henry, D.D., an English Congregational minister, was born at Welton, near Hull, Oct. 13, 1818, and entered Cheshunt College as a student in 1839, where his course was abbreviated by his accepting the assistant pastorship of Union Chapel, Islington, in 1843; at the end of the year he became pastor, his principal having died, and he served this church in that capacity until his death, April 16, 1892. From 1866 to 1886 he was editor of the *British Quarterly Review*. He was also the author of *The Life of Rev. James Shearman:—The Congregational Psalmist Hymnal:*—two volumes of sermons, besides other works. See (Lond.) *Cong. Year-book*, 1893.

Andrews, Israel Ward, D.D., LL.D., a Congregational minister, was born in Danbury, Conn., Jan. 3, 1815; attended Amherst College in 1833-34; was teacher at Danbury, Conn., 1834-35; graduated from Williams College in 1837; was teacher in Lee, Mass., 1837-38; tutor and professor of mathematics and natural philosophy in Marietta College, Ohio, 1839-55; ordained in May, 1868; was a corporate member of the A. B. C. F. M. from 1867, and director of the A. H. M. S. from 1864 to 1879. He died at Hartford, April 18, 1888. Dr. Andrews wrote quite a number of pamphlets, and a *Manual of the Constitution* (1874, p. 374; revised edition, 1887).

Andrus, Reuben, D.D., a Methodist Episcopal minister and educator, was born in Rutland, N. Y., Jan. 29, 1824. In 1850 he became principal of the preparatory department of Illinois Wesleyan University, and in 1851 professor of mathematics in the same institution. He had joined the Illinois Conference in 1850, and in 1852 began his active pastorate; in 1854 became president of the Illinois Conference Female College, but in 1856 he returned to the pastorate. From 1872 to 1875 he was president of Indiana Asbury University, serving in the pastorate until his death, Jan. 17, 1887. See *Minutes of Annual Conferences* (Fall), 1887, p. 362.

Arms, William, a Congregational minister, was born in Fairfield, Vt., May 18, 1802; graduated from Amherst College in 1830, and from Andover Theological Seminary in 1833; was missionary of the A. B. C. F. M. to Patagonia in 1833-34; Borneo, Batavia, and Singapore, 1835-38; graduated M.D. from Dartmouth College in 1839, and practiced medicine until his death, June 21, 1889.

Atkinson, George Henry, D.D., a Congregational minister, was born at Newburyport, Mass, May 10, 1819; graduated from Dartmouth College in 1843, and from Andover Theological Seminary in 1846; was pastor at Oregon City in 1848-62; at Portland, 1863-72; general missionary of the American Home Missionary Society, 1872-80; and superintendent of the same for Oregon and Washington from 1880 until his death, Feb. 25, 1889.

Atwater, Edward Elias, a Congregational minister, was born in New Haven, Conn., May 28, 1816; graduated from Yale College in 1836, and from the Theological Seminary in 1840; was a pastor until 1870; and thereafter engaged in literary pursuits until his death at Hawthorne, Fla., Dec. 2, 1887. His published works are, *Genealogical Register* (1851):—*The Sacred Tabernacle of the Hebrews* (1875):—*History of the Colony of New Haven* (1881):—*History of the City of New Haven* (1887).

Atwood, Edward Sumner, D.D., a Congregational minister, was born in Taunton, Mass., June 4, 1833. He graduated from Brown University in 1852; from Andover Theological Seminary in 1856; the same year was ordained pastor at Grantville, Mass.; in 1864 became the colleague of Brown Emerson, D.D., in the South Church, Salem, and after his death its sole pastor. He was a corporate member of the A. B. C. F. M. from 1873, and member of its prudential committee from

1886. He was the first president of the Essex Congregational Club. He died May 13, 1888.

Ayres, Rowland, D.D., a Congregational minister, was born in Granby, Mass., May 1, 1817. He graduated from Amherst College in 1841; studied one year at Andover and one at Princeton; became pastor of the Church at Hadley, Mass., in 1848, where he served until 1883, and remained pastor emeritus until his death, Jan. 31, 1891. He was a member of the Hadley School Committee twenty-three years; representative to the General Court in 1882; a trustee of Hopkins Academy and president of the board. He was the author of *The History of the Hopkins Fund*, and several pamphlets. See (Am.) *Cong. Year-book*, 1892.

B.

Barnard, Frederick Augustus Porter, S.T.D., LL.D., L.H.D., an Episcopalian educator, was born in Sheffield, Mass., May 5, 1809. Graduating from Yale College in 1828, he became tutor there in 1830; a teacher in asylums for the deaf and dumb, 1831–37; professor in the University of Alabama, 1837–54; professor in the University of Mississippi, 1854–56; president of the same, 1856–58; chancellor, 1858–61. He was in charge of the chart printing of the U. S. Coast Survey, 1863–64. In May, 1864, he became president of Columbia College, which position he held until his death, April 27, 1889. He belonged to many scientific societies, and published many technical and educational works. See *Appletons' Cyclop. of Amer. Biography*.

Barnum, Samuel Weed, a Congregational minister and author, was born at North Salem, N. Y., June 4, 1820. He graduated at Yale College in 1841, and the Theological Seminary in 1844; served as pastor at Granby, Conn.; Feeding Hills, Chesterfield, and Phillipston, Mass.; Bethany, Conn.; retired in 1863 for the purpose of devoting himself to authorship, and died Nov. 18, 1891. He was the author of *Romanism as It Is*, a book which had a very large sale:—*A Vocabulary of English Rhymes*:—and also had charge of the pronunciation marking of *Webster's International Dictionary*. See (Am.) *Cong. Year-book*, 1892.

Barrows, Elijah Porter, D.D., a Presbyterian minister, was born in Mansfield, Conn., Jan. 5, 1805; graduated from Yale College in 1826; was principal of the Hartford Grammar School, 1826–31; ordained evangelist at Simsbury, Conn., in 1832; pastor of the Dey Street Presbyterian Church, New York, 1835–37; professor of sacred literature in Western Reserve College, Hudson, O., 1837–52; professor of sacred literature in Andover Theological Seminary, 1852–66; without charge at Middletown, Conn., 1867–69; instructor in Union Theological Seminary, 1869–70; at Oberlin, 1871; professor of Old Testament literature and Biblical theology, Oberlin Theological Seminary, 1872–80, and without charge there until his death, Oct. 29, 1888. He wrote, *View of Slavery* (1836):—*The Thornton Family* (1837):—*Memoir of David H. Clark* (eod.):—*Life of E. Judson* (1852):—*Companion to the Bible* (1867):—*Sacred Geography*.

Barrows, William, D.D., a Congregational minister, was born at New Braintree, Mass., Sept. 19, 1815; graduated from Amherst College in 1840, and spent one year in Union Theological Seminary; served as pastor at Norton, Mass.; Grantville; Old South Church, Reading; in 1869 became secretary of the Congregational Sunday-school and Publishing Society; in 1873 of the Massachusetts Home Missionary Society; in 1887 financial agent of Whitman College, and died Sept. 9, 1891. He was the author of *The Church and Her Children*:—*Purgatory; Doctrinally, Practically, and Historically Opened*:—*Oregon; the Struggle for Possession*:—*The United States of Yesterday and To-morrow*, and several pamphlets. See (Am.) *Cong. Year-book*, 1892.

Bayliss, Jeremiah H., D.D., LL.D., a Methodist Episcopal minister, was born at Wednesbury, England, Dec. 20, 1835. In 1857 he joined the Genesee Conference. He was a pastor in various conferences until 1884, when he was elected editor of the *Western Christian Advocate*, which office he held until his death, Aug. 14, 1889. See *Minutes of Annual Conferences* (Fall), 1889, p. 383.

Beaudry, Louis N., a Methodist Episcopal minister, was born at Highgate, Vt., in 1834, of Roman Catholic parents. Largely through the influence of Joseph Cook he was led to embrace Protestantism, and devoted his life to the service of his French Canadian countrymen, serving as missionary among them at Albany (N. Y.), Montreal, Quebec, Worcester (Mass.), and Chicago (Ill.). During the civil war he served as chaplain in the United States Army. He died at Chicago, Jan. 3, 1892. He was author of *The Spiritual Struggles of a Roman Catholic*, an autobiography. See *Minutes of the Annual Conferences* (Fall), 1892.

Beecher, Henry Ward, an eminent Congregational minister, was born in Litchfield, Conn., June 24, 1813. Graduating from Amherst College in 1834, he then studied theology at Lane Seminary, of which his father was president. He married in 1837, and settled as a Presbyterian minister in Lawrenceburg, Ind. In 1839 he removed to Indianapolis, and in 1847 accepted the call to become pastor of Plymouth Church, Brooklyn, where he remained until his death, March 8, 1887. After 1859 his sermons were published weekly. During his theological course in 1831 he was editor of the *Cincinnati Journal*, a religious weekly. While pastor at Indianapolis he edited the *Farmer and Gardener*. He was one of the founders, and for twenty years an editorial contributor, of the N. Y. *Independent*. In the summer of 1874 Theodore Tilton, formerly his associate in the editorship of that journal, charged him with criminal commerce with Mrs. Tilton. A committee of the Plymouth Church reported the charges to be without foundation; but Mr. Tilton brought a suit against Mr. Beecher, placing his damages at $100,000. The trial lasted six months. The jury failed to agree—three standing for the plaintiff and nine for the defendant. Mr. Beecher was prominent as a public speaker. In April, 1865, he delivered an address at Fort Sumter on the anniversary of its fall. In 1878 he was elected chaplain of the Thirteenth Regiment, N. G. S. N. Y. He delivered the first three annual courses of lectures in the Yale Divinity School, "Lyman Beecher Lectureship." He was very prolific as a writer, and a list of his works will be found in *Appletons' Cyclopædia of American Biography*. See also the *Congregational Year-book*, 1888, p. 19.

Bennett, Charles Wesley, D.D., an educator, was born at East Bethany, N. Y., July 18, 1828. Graduating from Wesleyan University in 1852, he taught until 1862, when he entered the Methodist ministry. In 1864 he became principal of Genesee Wesleyan Seminary at Lima, N. Y.; in 1866–69 studied at the University of Berlin; in 1871 became professor of history and logic in Syracuse University, and in 1885 professor of historical theology in Garrett Biblical Institute. He died April 17, 1891. He was for a time art editor of the *Ladies' Repository*, and was the author of *Christian Archæology*.

Bennett, William Wallace, D.D., a minister of the Methodist Episcopal Church, South, was admitted to the Virginia Conference in 1842, and graduated from the University of Virginia in 1850. In 1862 he became a chaplain in the Confederate army, and in 1866 editor of the *Richmond Christian Advocate*. In 1877 he was elected president of Randolph Macon College, which position he held until 1886. He died July 6, 1887. He was a member of every General Conference of his church since 1858, and delegate to the Œcumenical Conference of 1881. See *Minutes of Annual Conferences of the M. E. Church, South*, 1887, p. 105.

Bird, Frederic Meyer, D.D., a Presbyterian and eventually an Episcopalian minister, was born in Philadelphia, June 28, 1838; graduated at the University of Pennsylvania in 1857, and Union Theological Seminary in 1860; became a Lutheran minister in the same year; an army chaplain in 1862-63; and entered the Episcopal ministry in 1868. He became professor at Lehigh University in 1881, teaching psychology, Christian evidences, and rhetoric. He died in 1890. He gave special attention to the study of hymnology, and his library on the subject, numbering about 4000 volumes, is now in Union Theological Seminary. He edited, *Charles Wesley as Seen in his Finer and Less Familiar Hymns* (1867):—with Dr. B. M. Smucker, the Lutheran Pennsylvania ministerium *Hymns* (1865), now used as the Lutheran General Council *Church-book*:—and with bishop Odenheimer, *Songs of the Spirit* (1871). He also wrote most of the hymnological articles in the *Schaff-Herzog Encyclopædia*, and most of the American matter in Julian's *Dictionary of Hymnology*.

Blackwell, John Davenport, D.D., a minister of the Methodist Episcopal Church, South, was born in Fauquier County, Va., June 17, 1822. He graduated from Dickinson College, and joined the Virginia Conference in 1846, in which he served as pastor or presiding elder until his death, June 26, 1887. He was a member of four General conferences, and delegate to the Centennial Conference of Methodism held in Baltimore in 1884, before which he read a paper entitled *An Essay on the Mission of Methodism*. See *Minutes of Annual Conferences of the M. E. Church, South*, 1887, p. 108.

Bledsoe, Albert Taylor, D.D., a minister and educator, was born in Frankfort, Ky., Nov. 9, 1809. He graduated from the U. S. Military Academy at West Point in 1830, and served in the army until August, 1832. In 1833-34 he was adjunct professor of mathematics and teacher of French at Kenyon, and in 1835-36 professor of mathematics at Miami. Having studied theology, he was ordained a clergyman in the Protestant Episcopal Church, and preached until 1838. In that year he began the practice of law at Springfield, Ill., and continued to practice there and at Washington, D. C., until 1848. From 1848 to 1854 he was professor of mathematics and astronomy in the University of Mississippi; from 1854 to 1861 professor of mathematics in the University of Virginia. In 1861 he entered the Confederate service as colonel, but was soon made chief of the War Bureau and acting assistant secretary of war. In 1863 he went to England to collect material for his work on the Constitution. He next settled in Baltimore, and became editor of the *Southern Review*. In 1868 he became principal of the Louisa School, Baltimore, and in 1871 was ordained a minister of the Methodist Episcopal Church, South. He died at Alexandria, Va., Dec. 8, 1877. He published, *An Examination of Edwards on the Will* (1845):—*A Theodicy, or Vindication of the Divine Glory* (1853):—*Is Davis a Traitor? or, Was Secession a Constitutional Right Previous to the War of* 1861 (1866):—*Philosophy of Mathematics* (1866). See *Appletons' Cyclop. of Amer. Biography*.

Bliss, Isaac Grout, an American missionary, was born in West Springfield, Mass., July 5, 1822. He graduated from Amherst College in 1844; studied at Andover and Yale Theological seminaries, and was ordained as a missionary of the A. B. C. F. M. in 1847. He was married and sailed for Turkey in September of that year, and was stationed at Erzrûm. Unintermitting labor broke his health, and in 1852 he returned to this country. He occupied the pastorate first at Southbridge, Mass., and afterwards at Boylston, having severed his connection with the Board. In 1858 he went to Constantinople as agent of the American Bible Society in the Levant, and in 1866 returned to America to raise funds for the erection of the Bible House. He came to New York again in 1870 for consultation in regard to the publication of the Arabic Bible. He made visits to this country also in 1883 and in 1886. He died at Assiût, Egypt, Feb. 16, 1889. See *Congregational Yearbook*, 1890, p. 19, *Missionary Herald*, April, 1889; *Missionary Review of the World*, April, 1889, p. 318.

Bobbett, William Hilliard, a minister of the Methodist Episcopal Church, South, was born in Halifax County, N. C., March 11, 1826. Joining the North Carolina Conference in 1846, he served as pastor or presiding elder nearly all his life. He also served one year as agent of the American Bible Society. He died Nov. 22, 1890. See *Minutes of Annual Conferences of the M. E. Church, South*, 1890, p. 116.

Bonar, Horatius, D.D., a minister of the Free Church of Scotland, was born in Edinburgh, Dec. 19, 1808. He studied at the University of Edinburgh; was pastor at Kelso from 1838 to 1866, and died July 13, 1889. In 1849 he founded the *Quarterly Journal of Prophecy*. He was the author of *Prophetical Landmarks* (1847):—*The Night of Weeping* (1850):—*The Morning of Joy* (1852):—*The Desert of Sinai* (1857):—*Hymns of Faith and Hope* (1857-71, 3 vols.):—*The Land of Promise* (1858):—*Light and Truth* (1868-72, 6 vols.):—*The White Fields of France* (1879):—*The Song of the New Creation* (1872):—*Hymns of the Nativity* (1878):—*Life of G. T. Dodds* (1884):—*Songs of Love and Joy* (1888).

Brace, Charles Loring, a philanthropist, was born in Litchfield, Conn., in 1826. He graduated from Yale College in 1846, and studied theology at Union Theological Seminary. In 1850 he went to Europe. While in Hungary, in 1851, he was arrested as the secret agent of the American Hungarian revolutionists. He was court-martialled and imprisoned, but was soon set at liberty, and an apology was made to him. On his return to this country in 1852, he became a worker at the Five-Points Mission. In 1853 he, with others, organized the Children's Aid Society (q. v.). In 1854 he founded, outside of the society, the first newsboys' lodging-house in this country. In 1856 he was a delegate to the International Convention for Children's Charities in London. In 1865 he carried out a special sanitary investigation in the cities of Great Britain. He was a delegate to the International Prison Convention in London, 1872. He died Aug. 12, 1890. His works are, *Hungary in* 1851 (New York, 1852):—*Home Life in Germany* (1853):—*The Norse Folk* (1857):—*Short Sermons to Newsboys* (1861):—*Races of the Old World* (1863):—*The New West* (1868):—*The Dangerous Classes of New York, and Twenty Years' Work Among Them* (1872; 3d ed. enlarged, 1880):—*Free Trade as Promoting Peace and Good-will among Men* (1879):—*Gesta Christi; or, a History of Humane Progress under Christianity* (1883; 3d ed. 1885). See *Appletons' Cyclop. of Amer. Biography*, s. v.

Bright, Edward, D.D., a Baptist minister and editor, was born in 1808, at Kington, Herefordshire, England, but removed with his father to this country at an early age, and settling in Utica, N. Y., learned the printer's trade, eventually forming a publishing firm known as Bennett & Bright. A few years afterwards he became pastor of the Baptist Church at Homer, N. Y., and two or three years thereafter foreign secretary of the American Baptist Union, having its headquarters in Boston. In 1855 he removed to New York city, purchased the *Register*, a Baptist weekly religious newspaper, which he continued to own and edit, under the names of the *Chronicle* and the *Examiner*, until his death, May 17, 1894. He was for years a trustee of many Baptist public institutions.

Brown, James Baldwin, B.A., an English Congregational minister, was born in the Inner Temple, London, Aug. 19, 1820. After graduating at University College in 1839, he studied law for two years, and then theology at Highbury College. He became an Independent minister, serving two churches, London Road Chapel, Derby, and Claylands Chapel, Clapham Road, London. Afterwards the latter congregation moved to a new church in Brixton, and he was pastor there until his death, June 23, 1884. He published, *Studies of First Principles* (1849):—*The Divine Life in Man* (1859):—*The Doctrine of the Divine Fatherhood in Relation to the Atonement* (1860):—*The Soul's Exodus and Pilgrimage* (1862):—*Aids to the Development of the Divine Life* (eod.):—*Divine Mystery of Peace* (1863):—*Divine Treatment of Sin* (1864):—*The Home Life in the Light of its Divine Idea* (1866; 5th ed. 1870):—*Idolatries, Old and New: their Cause and Cure* (1867):—*Misread Passages of Scripture* (1869; 2d series, 1871):—*The Christian Policy of Life* (1870):—*The First Principles of Ecclesiastical Truth: Essays on the Church and Society* (1871):—*The Sunday Afternoon* (eod.):—*Buying and Selling and Getting Gain* (eod.):—*Young Men and Maidens* (eod.):—*The Higher Life* (1874; 5th ed. 1878):—*The Battle and the Burden of Life* (1875):—*The Doctrine of Annihilation in the Light of the Gospel of Love* (eod.):—*Church and State* (1876):—*Home: Its Relation to Man and Society* (1883; 3d ed. 1884). See *In Memoriam: James Baldwin Brown*, by his wife (Lond. 1884).

Bullock, Joseph James, D.D., a prominent Presbyterian minister, was born near Lexington, Ky., Dec. 23, 1812. Graduating from Center College in 1832, he next took up the study of theology, spending part of a year in Princeton Theological Seminary. After being ordained in 1837, he was made pastor of the Church at Frankfort, and with his Church went with the Southern Presbyterians the same year. After continuing here for ten years, serving as superintendent of public education in Kentucky in 1838, and visitor to West Point in 1839, he was corresponding secretary of the Board of Domestic Missions; acting as pastor of the Church at Walnut Hill, Ky., 1849-53, and at the same time principal of the Walnut Hill Female Seminary, and later a second term of five years given at the same institution. His next twenty years were spent as pastor. From 1879 to 1884 he was chaplain of the United States Senate. He died at Lexington, Ky., Nov. 9, 1892. See *Necrological Report of Princeton Theol. Sem.* 1893.

Burgon, John William, B.D., a clergyman of the Church of England, was born at Smyrna, in Asia Minor, Aug. 21, 1813. He graduated from Worcester College, Oxford, in 1845. In 1846 he became fellow of Oriel College, and Gresham lecturer in divinity in 1868. He was made vicar of St. Mary the Virgin, Oxford, in 1863, and dean of Chichester in 1876. He died Aug. 4, 1889. Among his works are, *Petra: a Poem* (1846):—*Oxford Reformers* (1854):—*Plain Commentary on the Book of Psalms* (1857, 2 vols.):—*The Last Twelve Verses of the Gospel according to St. Mark Vindicated against Recent Critical Objectors and Established* (1871):—*Poems* (1885).

Burkhead, Lingurn Skidmore, a minister of the Methodist Episcopal Church, South, was born in Davidson County, S. C. In 1849 he was admitted into the North Carolina Conference, and served as pastor and presiding elder until his death, Dec. 2, 1887. Five times he was a member of the General Conference of his church, and a delegate to the Œcumenical Conference of 1881. See *Minutes of Annual Conferences of the M. E. Church, South*, 1887, p. 133.

Burton, Nathaniel Judson, D.D., a Congregational minister, was born in Trumbull, Conn., Dec. 17, 1824; graduated from Wesleyan University in 1850, and from Yale Theological Seminary in 1854; and until his death, Oct. 13, 1887, served successively as pastor of the church at Fair Haven, Conn., the Fourth and Park churches, Hartford. He was Lyman Beecher lecturer in Yale Theological Seminary in 1884.

Byington, Theodore L., a missionary, was born at Johnsbury, N. J., March 15, 1831. He graduated from Princeton College in 1849; spent four years in the study and practice of law; graduated from Union Theological Seminary in 1857; was ordained, and sailed for the East under the auspices of the American Board in 1858. He established a station at Eski Zaghra, European Turkey, in 1859, and returned to the United States in 1867, being released from connection with the Board; for the next seven years was pastor at Newton, N. J. The Board reappointed him in 1874, and he resided at Constantinople till 1885, when he returned to the United States disabled. He died in Philadelphia, Pa., June 18, 1888. He wrote a work on *Christian Evidences*, which was published in the Bulgarian language, and afterwards translated into Armenian. For twelve years he was editor of the weekly and monthly *Zornitza*, which did much to shape the nascent national Bulgarian movement.

C.

Campbell, William Henry, D.D., a Dutch Reformed minister and educator, was born at Baltimore, Md., Sept. 14, 1808. He graduated from Dickinson College in 1828, and studied in Princeton Seminary. He entered the pastorate in 1831, but in 1833 he became principal of Erasmus Hall, Flatbush, L. I. He was pastor again from 1839 to 1848, and principal of Albany Academy from 1848 to 1851. Then he was called by the General Synod of the Reformed Church to the chair of Oriental literature in the Theological Seminary at New Brunswick, N. J. In connection with his professorship in the seminary he also filled the professorship of belles-lettres in Rutgers College until 1863, when he was elected president of the college. This he resigned in 1882, but was a pastor the rest of his life. He died Dec. 7, 1890. See *Appletons' Cyclop. of Amer. Biography*, s. v.; Corwin, *Manual of the Ref. Church in America*, 3d ed., p. 206.

Caughey, James, an American evangelist, was born in Ireland about 1810. Coming to this country, he was converted, and joined the Troy Conference in 1832. In 1840 he went on a visit to friends in Europe, spending some time in Canada on his way to Halifax, whence he sailed. For six years he labored in England, over twenty thousand conversions resulting from his work. Returning to America, he engaged in revival work wherever his services were demanded. He died at Highland Park, N. J., Jan. 30, 1891. Among those converted under his ministry was general Booth of the Salvation Army. He was unable to work much the last twenty years of his life, owing to feeble health. He was the author of *Methodism in Earnest:—Revival Miscellanies:—Earnest Christianity:*—and *Glimpses of Soul-Saving.* See *Methodism in Earnest: The Christian Advocate*, Feb. 26, 1891.

Channing, William Henry, a Unitarian minister, nephew of William Ellery, was born in Boston, May 25, 1810. He graduated from Harvard University in 1829, and the divinity school in 1833; became pastor at Cincinnati in 1839; at Boston in 1847; afterwards at Rochester and New York. During a visit to England in 1854 he was much admired as a preacher, and in 1857 was established as the successor of Rev. James Martineau, of Hope Street Chapel, Liverpool. In 1862 he returned to America, and became pastor in Washington, D. C., and served as chaplain of the House for two years. After the war his life was chiefly spent in England, and he died in London, Dec. 23, 1889. He edited his uncle's *Life and Correspondence* (1848):—also published a translation of Jouffroy's *Ethics:—A Memoir of James H. Perkins:*—and was chief editor of the *Memoirs of Margaret Fuller d'Ossoli.* See his *Life*, by O. B. Frothingham (1886).

Cheever, George Barrell, D.D., a Congregational and Presbyterian minister, was born in Hallowell, Me., April 17, 1807. He was educated at Hallowell Academy and Bowdoin College, graduating in 1825; also from Andover Theological Seminary in 1830, and was ordained pastor of the Howard Street Congregational Church, Boston, in 1832. In 1835 he published, in a Salem newspaper, an allegory entitled *Inquire at Deacon Giles's Distillery*, for which he was tried for libel and imprisoned thirty days. He then resigned his pastorate and went to Europe. On his return, in 1839, he took charge of the Allen Street Presbyterian Church, New York city. In 1843 he held three public debates with J. L. O'Sullivan on capital punishment. He was in Europe in 1844. In 1845 he was principal editor of the New York *Evangelist*. From 1846 to 1870 he was pastor of the Church of the Puritans, New York city, which was organized for him. He retired from the ministry in 1870, and died Oct. 1, 1890. He was the writer of many volumes and articles, but is especially known as the composer of hymns. He delivered lectures on *Pilgrim's Progress*, also on *Hierarchical Despotism*, the latter being a reply to archbishop Hughes. See *Appletons' Cyclop. of Amer. Biog.* s. v.; *The Magazine of Christian Literature*, Nov., 1890, p. 136.

Childs, George W., an American philanthropist, was born in Baltimore, May 12, 1829. He left school at an early age, and drifted into the United States navy, in which service he remained fifteen months at Norfolk, Va. When about fourteen he went to Philadelphia, entering the employ of P. Thomson, a bookseller. At eighteen he set up a small bookstore for himself, and three years later with his father-in-law began as a book publisher under the firm name of R. E. Peterson & Co., which later became Childs & Peterson. In 1864 he purchased the *Public Ledger*, with which he was connected until his death, Feb. 3, 1894. Among his many charitable works were the founding of the home for aged printers at Colorado Springs, supplying memorial windows to George Herbert and William Cowper in Westminster Abbey, a monument to Edgar Allan Poe, and other work of like character. His greatest work was in aiding the young to secure an education, many owing their knowledge and position to his open purse.

Christlieb, Theodor, Ph.D., D.D., a German theologian, was born at Birkenfeld, Würtemburg, March 7, 1833. He studied at Tübingen from 1851 to 1855, and in 1863 became pastor of a German congregation in London. In 1865 he became pastor at Friedrichshafen, on the lake of Constance, and in 1868 professor of practical theology and university preacher at Bonn. He died Aug. 15, 1889. He was a member of the Evangelical Alliance Conference of 1873, and read a paper before that body. He was a Knight of the Red Eagle. Among his works the chief ones are, *Modern Doubt and Christian Belief* (1874):—*Protestant Missions to the Heathen; a General Survey* (1882). See *The Homiletic Review*, Oct., 1889, p. 366; *The Missionary Review of the World*, Nov., 1889, p. 872.

Christophers, Samuel W., an English Wesleyan minister, was born at Falmouth in 1810. The public baptism of a young Jewess, and her confession of faith in Christ, led him to earnestly seek for pardon. He entered the ministry in 1835, and in several circuits in Devon and Cornwall his ministry brought many to Christ. He spent the last years of his life at Formby, near Liverpool, and died Aug. 14, 1889. He is widely known as the author of *Hymn Writers and their Hymns*:—*The Poets of Methodism*:—*The Homes of Old English Writers*:—*The Methodist Hymn-book and its Writers*:—and smaller works. See *Minutes of the British Conference*, 1890, p. 13.

Church, Richard William, born at Cintra, April 25, 1815. He graduated from Wadham College, Oxford, in 1836; was fellow of Oriel College, 1838-53; junior proctor, 1844-45; ordained deacon in 1838; priest in 1850; rector of Whatley, 1853-71; select preacher at Oxford in 1869, 1875, 1881; appointed dean of St. Paul's, Sept. 6, 1871; elected honorary fellow of Oriel College in 1873; and died in 1890. He wrote several works, the principal ones being, *Life of St. Anselm*:—*Civilization Before and After Christianity*:—*Discipline of the Christian Character*.

Clark, William, D.D., a Congregational minister, was born in Hancock, N. H., Sept. 28, 1798; graduated from Dartmouth College in 1822, and from Andover Theological Seminary in 1827; was pastor, 1828-37; agent of the American Tract Society, 1835-36; district secretary of the A. B. C. F. M. for northern New England, 1840-56; secretary of the N. H. M. Society, 1856-74; member of the legislature, 1867-68; chaplain of the House of Representatives in 1869, and resided at Amherst, Mass., from 1856 until his death, Jan. 26, 1887.

Clarke, James Freeman, D.D., a Unitarian minister, was born at Hanover, N. H., April 4, 1810. He graduated from Harvard College in 1829, and from Cambridge Divinity School in 1833. Thenceforth he was pastor until his death, June 8, 1888. He was the author of many works, among which are, *Orthodoxy: its Truths and its Errors* (1866):—*Ten Great Religions* (1870, 2 vols.):—*Manual of Unitarian Belief* (1884). See *Appletons' Cyclop. of Amer. Biography*.

Coles, Joseph Benjamin, an English Congregational missionary, was born in London in 1819, and was educated at Spring Hill College, Birmingham. In 1843 he sailed for India, being appointed to the city of Mysore; and in 1849 removed to Bellary, where he labored until 1886. In 1887 he was appointed senior tutor in the society's Training Seminary for Native Evangelists, where he served until his death, Jan. 2, 1891. As a missionary he was eminently successful. See (Lond.) *Cong. Year-book*, 1892.

Conant, Thomas Jefferson, D.D., a Biblical scholar, was born at Brandon, Vt., Dec. 13, 1802. Graduating from Middlebury College in 1823, he became tutor in Columbian College, Washington, D.C., 1825-27, and in 1827 professor of Greek, Latin, and German in Waterville College, Maine. In 1835-50 he was professor of languages and Biblical literature at Hamilton, N. Y.; and in 1851-57 professor of Hebrew and Biblical exegesis at Rochester. He then went to Brooklyn, and became reviser of the Scriptures for the American Bible Union, which position he occupied until 1875. He was a member of the American Old Testament committee of Bible revision. He died April 30, 1891. His works are principally revisions of books of the Bible, with notes on the same. See *Appletons' Cyclop. of Amer. Biography*.

Conder, Eustace Rogers, D.D., an English Congregational minister, was born at St. Michaels, near St. Albans, Herts, April 5, 1820; graduated with honors at London in 1844; in the same year being appointed pastor at Poole, Dorsetshire; next at Leeds, where the remainder of his life was spent. In 1873 he was chairman of the Congregational Union of England and Wales; in 1879 of the Yorkshire Congregational Union; and in 1887 the Congregational lecturer. He died July 6, 1892. He was the author of *Why are We Dissenters?* and a contributor to the *Leeds Tracts*. See (Lond.) *Cong. Year-book*, 1893.

Constantine, George, a Congregational minister, was born at Athens, Greece, Jan. 1, 1833; came to America in 1850; graduated from Amherst College in 1859, and Andover Theological Seminary in 1862; was immediately ordained and sent as missionary of the American and Foreign Christian Union to Athens; from 1880 until his death, Oct. 6, 1891, he was a missionary of the American Board of Commissioners for Foreign Missions at Smyrna. He served as United States vice-consul and acting consul at Athens several years, and revisited America in 1872, 1880, and 1889. He was the author of *A Commentary on the Gospels* (2 vols.):—*A Treatise on the Character of Christ*:—*The Greek Church*:—*A Bible Dictionary*:—and several pamphlets. See (Am.) *Cong. Year-book*, 1892.

Cook, Frederic Charles, a clergyman of the Church of England, was born at Millbrook, Dec. 1, 1804. He was educated at St. John's College, graduating in 1828. He then became one of her majesty's inspectors of schools; prebendary of St. Paul's Cathedral, 1856-65; preacher at Lincoln's Inn, 1860-80; prebendary of Lincoln Cathedral, 1861-64; chaplain in ordinary to the queen, 1857; canon of Exeter, 1864; chaplain to the bishop of London, 1869; precentor of Exeter, 1872. He died June 22, 1889. He was the author of *Acts of the Apostles, with Commentary* (1849):—*Sermons at Lincoln's Inn* (1863):—*Church Doctrine and Spiritual Life* (1879):—*The Revised Version of the First Three Gospels Considered in its Bearings upon the Record of Our Lord's Words and of Incidents in His Life* (1882):—*Deliver us from Evil* (1883):—*The Origin of Religion and Language* (1884):—*Letters Addressed to Rev. H. Wace and J. Earle* (1885). He also edited the *Bible* (Speaker's) *Commentary* (1871-82, 10 vols.), contributing the introductions to *Exodus, Psalms*, and *Acts*, and the comments on *Job, Habakkuk, Mark, Luke*, and *First Peter*; also the comments on *Exodus, Psalms*, and *Matthew*.

Cox, Samuel, D.D., a Baptist minister and editor, was born in London, England, April 19, 1826. Graduating from Stepney (now Regent's) College in 1851, he was ordained pastor of a Baptist church; but owing to failure of his voice, he devoted his attention to journalism from 1860 to 1863. For twenty-five years following he was pastor of the Mansfield Road Church, Nottingham. He died March 27, 1892. He was the first editor of the *Expositor*, from 1875-84. He also wrote quite a number of volumes, chiefly expository and exegetical. His most famous book was *Salvator Mundi*. See *The* (Lond.) *Baptist Hand-book*, 1894.

Crawford, Robert Blakely, D.D., a minister of the Methodist Episcopal Church, South, was born in Russell County, Ala., Nov. 15, 1840. He joined the Alabama Conference in 1860. During the war he served as a private in the Confederate army. In 1872 he was elected secretary of his conference, which he continued to be until his death, May 18, 1889. He was a member of the General Conference of his church in 1882 and 1886. See *Minutes of Annual Conferences of the M. E. Church, South*, 1889, p. 114.

Crosby, Howard, D.D., LL.D., an eminent Presbyterian minister and reformer, was born in New York city, Feb. 27, 1826. At the age of fourteen he entered the University of the City of New York; after a time became professor of Greek in his alma mater, and in 1859 occupied the same chair at Rutgers College. From 1863 he was pastor of the Fourth Avenue Presbyterian Church until his death, March 29, 1891. During part of this time he was also chancellor of the University of the City of New York. He was one of the founders and the president from the first of the Society for the Prevention of Crime. In 1873 he was moderator of the General Assembly. He was also a member of the Bible Revision Committee. His principal writings are, *Jesus: His Life and Work as Narrated by the Four Evangelists*:—*True Humanity of Christ*:—and several *Commentaries*.

Cullen, George Downie, an English Congregational minister, was born at Doune, in October, 1799. Receiving his education at Glasgow College and Theological Academy, in 1822 he accepted a call to Leith, which church he served until his retirement in 1869. He served as secretary of the Widows' Fund of the Scottish Churches, and chairman of the fund until his death. He also carried on the Yardheads Mission and Leith Sailors' School in connection with his pastorate, and was one of the founders of the Edinburgh Medical Missionary Society, and of the National Bible Society of Scotland, and was also connected with several other societies of like character. He died Oct. 1, 1891. See (Lond.) *Cong. Year-book*, 1892.

Cummings, Joseph, D.D., LL.D., a Methodist educator, was born in Falmouth County, Me., March 3, 1817. Graduating from Wesleyan University in 1840, he taught at Amenia (N. Y.) Seminary, becoming principal in 1843; in 1846 he joined the New England Conference; in 1853-54 he was professor of theology in the Concord Biblical Institute; in 1854-57 was president of Genesee College; in 1857-75 president of Wesleyan University, remaining there as professor for two years thereafter. The following four years he was in the pastorate. In 1881 he became president of Northwestern University at Evanston, Ill. He died May 7, 1890. He left numerous addresses and sermons, and an edition of Butler's *Analogy of Religion*.

Curry, Daniel, D.D., LL.D., a Methodist Episcopal minister, was born near Peekskill, N. Y., Nov. 26, 1809. He graduated from Wesleyan University in 1837, and immediately afterwards became principal of Troy Conference Academy; then professor in the female college at Macon, Ga., in 1839, and in 1841 joined the Georgia Conference. When the Church separated into Northern and Southern, he came North and joined the New York Conference, in which he served as pastor until 1854. For three years thereafter he was president of Asbury University, Greencastle, Ind. He next served various churches as pastor until 1864, when he became editor of the *Christian Advocate*, continuing in that position until 1876. He edited the *National Repository* from 1876 to 1880, and then resumed pastoral work until 1884, when he was elected editor of the *Methodist Review*, of which he had been assistant editor since 1881, and continued in that position until his death, Aug. 17, 1887. He published, besides many articles in periodicals, *New York: a Historical Sketch* (1853):—*Life Story of Bishop D. W. Clark* (1873):—*Fragments, Religious and Theological* (1880):—*Platform Papers* (eod.). He also superintended an American edition of Southey's *Life of John Wesley* (1847):—a condensed edition of *Clarke's Commentary*, and a work on *The Book of Job* (1887). See Simpson, *Cyclop. of Methodism*, s. v.; *Minutes of Annual Conferences* (Spring), 1887, p. 100.

D.

Day, Henry Noble, LL.D., an American educator, was born at New Preston, Conn., Aug. 4, 1808; graduated from Yale in 1828, and the Divinity School there in 1834. After preaching four years, he became professor of rhetoric in the Western Reserve College, in 1844 succeeding to the chair of practical theology. From 1858 to 1864 he served as president of the Ohio Female College, Cincinnati. The rest of his life was spent in literary pursuits at New Haven, Conn. He died Jan. 12, 1890. He was the author of nineteen works, the best known of which are, *The Art of English Composition* (1867):—*Elements of Psychology* (1876):—*Elements of Mental Science* (1886). See (Am.) *Cong. Year-book*, 1891.

Deane, George, B.A., D.Sc.. an English Congregational minister, was born at Wells, Somerset, in 1838. After receiving his education in Cheshunt College and London University, in 1862 he took charge of a church at Harrold, in Bedfordshire, at the same time continuing his course in London University. In 1869 he was appointed professor of mathematics in Spring Hill College, and the following year professor of Hebrew and Old-Testament exegesis. In 1877 he became resident tutor. For four years he served as teacher of the geological class in the Midland Institute. He died July 7, 1891. He was a fellow of the Geological Society, a member and at one time president of the Natural History and Microscopical Society, and also a member of the British Association for the Advancement of Science. See (Lond.) *Cong. Year-book*, 1892.

Deems, Charles Force, D.D., LL.D., an eminent Methodist minister and writer, was born in Baltimore, Md., Dec. 4, 1820. After graduating from Dickinson College in 1839, he entered the ministry of the Methodist Episcopal Church, going with the southern section in 1844. He served as general agent of the American Bible Society for North Carolina, 1840-41; professor of logic and rhetoric in the University of North Carolina, 1842-45; of chemistry in Randolph-Macon College, 1845-46; president of Greensborough Female College, 1850-55; and from 1866 until his death, Nov. 18, 1893, was pastor of the Church of the Strangers, New York city. He was editor of the *Southern Methodist Pulpit* (1846-51); *The Annals of Southern Methodism* (1849-52); *The Sunday Magazine* (1876-79), and *Christian Thought* (1883-93). He was the founder and president of the American Institute of Philosophy from 1881 until his death. He published about twenty volumes, among which were *Poems* and *Sermons*:—also *Jesus; the Gospel of Spiritual Insight*:—*Weights and Wings*:—*My Septuagint*:—*The Gospel of Common-Sense*, etc. Dr. Deems was a beautiful character as a Christian, a preacher, a friend, and an author.

Delitzsch, Franz, D.D., a German Lutheran theologian, was born at Leipzig, Feb. 23, 1813. He studied at his birthplace, and became professor at Rostock in 1846; at Erlangen in 1850; at Leipzig in 1867, and from that time until his death, March 4, 1890. He is the author of many volumes, chiefly commentaries; also of *A System of Biblical Psychology*:—*Jewish Artisan Life in the Time of Our Lord*:—and in connection with S. Baer he issued revised Hebrew texts of *Genesis*, *Ezra*, *Nehemiah*, *Job*, *the Psalms*, *Proverbs*, *Isaiah*, *Ezekiel*, and the *Minor Prophets*. He also translated the New Testament into Hebrew. See the *Hebraica* for April, 1890.

Dexter, Henry Martyn, D.D., an eminent Congregational minister, was born at Plympton, Mass., Aug. 13, 1821. He graduated from Yale College in 1840, and from Andover Theological Seminary in 1844. He then became pastor of a church in Manchester, N. H., and in 1849 of what is now Berkeley Street Church, Boston. In 1851 he became connected with the *Congregationalist*, and in 1867 its editor. He died at New Bedford, Nov. 13, 1890. A complete list of his writings will be found in *Appletons' Cyclop. of Amer. Biography*, s. v. His chief work is *Congregationalism as Seen in its Literature* (1880), which has a bibliography of 7500 titles. At the time of his death he had nearly completed a *History of the Pilgrims*, in the preparation of which he visited England seventeen times.

Döllinger, Johann Joseph Ignaz, Ph.D., D.D., LL.D., an Old Catholic, was born in Bamburg, Bavaria, Feb. 28, 1799. Since 1826 he was professor of church history in the University of Munich, except in 1847-49. In 1871 he was excommunicated by the pope for refusing to accept the dogma of infallibility, but, notwithstanding this, was elected rector of the university, in 1873, by a vote of fifty-four to six. He presided over the Old Catholic Congress of 1871, and was at that of 1872, but took no other part in the movement. He was president of the Bonn Conferences in 1875 and 1876. He died Jan. 11, 1890. His chief works translated into English are, *History of the Church* (4 vols.):—*Hippolytus and Calistus*:—*The Gentile and the Jew in the Courts of the Temple of Christ*.

Duffield, George, D.D., a Presbyterian minister, was born in Carlisle, Pa., Sept. 12, 1818. He graduated from Yale College in 1837, and from Union Theological Seminary in 1840; was a pastor in New York city and vicinity, and in Michigan. He died July 6, 1888. He was one of the regents of Michigan University. He was the author of many hymns, the best known of them being, *Stand up, Stand up for Jesus*. See *Appletons' Cyclop. of Amer. Biography*.

E.

Eddy, Zachary, D.D., a Congregational minister, was born at Stockbridge, Vt., Dec. 19, 1815; received his education in the Jamestown (N. Y.) Academy, and studied theology with Rev. James D'onnell. He served several churches, retired in 1888, and died Nov. 15, 1891. He was a corporate member of the American Board of Commissioners for Foreign Missions. He was the author of *Immanuel; or, the Life of Jesus Christ Our Lord*:—*Hymns of the Church*:—*Hymns and Songs of the Church*:—and many pamphlets. See (Am.) *Cong. Year-book*, 1892.

Edersheim, Alfred, D.D., an English clergyman, was born of Jewish parents at Vienna, March 7, 1825. He was a student at Vienna University, and entered New College, Edinburgh, in 1843. In 1849 he became minister of the Free Church, Old Aberdeen. On account of ill-health he went, in 1861, to Torquay, in England, where a congregation gathered about him and built a church for him. In 1875 he was ordained deacon and priest of the Church of England. In 1876 he became vicar of Loders, Dorsetshire, but resigned in 1883, and removed to Oxford, where he remained until his death, March 16, 1889. In 1880-84 he was Warburtonian lecturer at Lincoln's Inn, London; in 1884-86 was select preacher of Oxford University. He also lectured in its "Honors School of Theology." He wrote many works, the principal ones being, *The Temple: its Ministry and Services as they were in the Time of Christ* (1874):—*Life and Times of Jesus the Messiah* (1883, 2 vols.), on which he labored for seven years. At the time of his death he was at work on a *Life of St. Paul*, and had just completed a series of lectures on the Septuagint.

Edwards, John, a Wesleyan Methodist preacher, was born at Bridford, Devonshire, in 1804. In 1830 he joined the Conference, and in 1832 was sent as a missionary to South Africa. For seven years he worked in the interior; in 1876 became a supernumerary; and died at Grahamstown, Nov. 11, 1887. He wrote *Reminiscences; or, Fifty Years of Mission Life*.

Elliott, Charles, D.D., a Presbyterian educator, was born at Castleton, Scotland, March 18, 1815. After graduating from Lafayette College in 1840, he spent one year in Princeton Theological Seminary, and then taught two years in an academy at Xenia, O. From 1847-49 he was professor of belles-lettres in the Western University of Pennsylvania at Pittsburg; 1849-63 professor of Greek in Miami University, Oxford, O.; 1863-82 professor of biblical literature and exegesis in the Presbyterian Seminary at Chicago, Ill.; thereafter professor of Hebrew in Lafayette College. He died Feb. 14, 1892. He was the author of *The Sabbath* (1866):—*A Treatise on the Inspiration of the Scriptures* (1877):—*Mosaic Authorship of the Pentateuch*:—and translated Cellérier's *Biblical Hermeneutics*.

Evans, Llewellyn Joan, D.D., LL.D., a Presbyterian minister and professor, was born at Trenddyn, near Mold, North Wales, June 27, 1833; graduated in the scientific and classical courses of the college at Racine, Wis.; next entered Lane Theological Seminary, graduating in 1860. He was made pastor of the Seminary Church the same year, and was successively the occupant of the chair of church history (1863), biblical literature and exegesis (1867), and New Testament Greek and exegesis (1875). In 1856-57 he served as a member of the Wisconsin Legislature. He died at Bala, Wales, July 25, 1892. He translated Zöchler's *Commentary on Job*, in Schaff's edition of Lange; also publishing many sermons and pamphlets.

Evans, Thomas Saunders, D.D., a clergyman of the Church of England, was born at Belper, Derbyshire, March 8, 1816. He graduated from St. John's College, Cambridge, in 1839, and immediately became assistant master of Rugby School. In 1862 he became canon residentiary of Durham, and professor of Greek and classical literature in the University of Durham, occupying these positions until his death in May, 1888. He was the author of the *Commentary on First Corinthians*, in the *Speaker's Commentary:—The Nihilist in the Hay-field*, a Latin poem (1882).

F.

Fairchild, Edward Henry, D.D., a Congregational minister, was born in Stockbridge, Mass., Nov. 29, 1815; graduated from Oberlin College in 1838, and from the Theological Seminary in 1841. He became acting pastor at Cleveland, O., 1841-42; Birmingham, Mich., 1842-49; Elmira, N. Y., 1849-50; Hartford, O., 1850-53; principal of the preparatory department of Oberlin College, 1853-69; president of Berea College, Ky., from 1869 until his death, Oct. 2, 1889.

Finlayson, Thomas Campbell, D.D., an English Congregational minister, was born in 1836; was first a member of the United Presbyterian Church; in 1859 became pastor at Cambridge, and in 1865 at Manchester, where he served until his death, Feb. 7, 1893. He was a frequent contributor to various magazines, and author of *Biological Religion*, a reply to Prof. Drummond's *Natural Law in the Spiritual World:*—also *Koheleth:—The Divine Gentleness:*—a volume of sermons, and a posthumous volume of essays, addresses, etc. See (Lond.) *Cong. Year-book*, 1894.

Flack, Alonzo, Ph.D., a Methodist Episcopal educator, was born at Argyle, N. Y., Sept. 19, 1823. He graduated from Union College in 1849, and began a course at the Concord Biblical Institute, but before completing it was elected the principal of a school at Charlotteville. He became the president of the Hudson River Institute in 1855. In 1869 the board of regents of the state of New York granted it a college charter. He died in March, 1885. See *Minutes of Annual Conferences* (Spring), 1885, p. 97.

Folsom, Nathaniel Smith, D.D., a Congregational minister and educator, was born at Portsmouth, N. H., March 12, 1806; graduated from Dartmouth College in 1828, and Andover Theological Seminary in 1831; in 1833 became professor of languages in Lane Theological Seminary; the next three years professor of biblical literature in the Western Reserve College; and resumed the pastorate in 1836, serving various churches. In 1847-49 the *Christian Register* was under his editorial care; 1849-61 he occupied the chair of Biblical literature in the Theological Seminary at Meadville, Pa. The rest of his life was spent in retirement. He died at Asheville, N. C., Nov. 10, 1890. See (Am.) *Cong. Year-book*, 1891.

G.

Gardiner, Frederic, a Protestant Episcopal minister, was born at Gardiner, Me., Sept. 11, 1822. He graduated from Bowdoin College in 1842; became rector of Trinity Church, Saco, Me., in 1845; of St. Luke's, Philadelphia, Pa., in 1847; of Grace Church, Bath, Me., from 1848 to 1853; of Trinity Church, Lewiston, in 1855-56; in 1865 professor of the literature and interpretation of Scripture in the Protestant Episcopal Seminary, Gambier, O.; in 1867 assistant rector at Middletown, Conn.; in 1869 professor in Berkeley Divinity School at the same place, and continued to be such until his death, July 17, 1889. He wrote, *The Island of Life, an Allegory* (1851):—*Commentary on the Epistle of St. Jude* (1856):—*Harmony of the Gospels in Greek* (1871):—*Harmony of the Gospels in English* (eod.):—*Diatessaron: The Life of Our Lord in the Words of the Gospels* (eod.):—*Principles of Textual Criticism* (1876):—*The Old and New Testaments in their Mutual Relations* (1885). He also wrote *Leviticus*, in the American edition of Lange, and *Second Samuel* and *Ezekiel* in bishop Ellicott's *Commentary for English Readers*. See *Appletons' Cyclop. of Amer. Biography.*

Gilmour, Richard, D.D., a Roman Catholic bishop, was born in Scotland, Sept. 28, 1824. In 1829 his people came to Nova Scotia, and later settled at Latrobe, Pa. At eighteen he went to study in Philadelphia, where he made the acquaintance of a priest who led him to embrace the Romish faith. He wished to enter the priesthood, and with that end in view he began his studies at Mount St. Mary's, Emmittsburg, Md. He was ordained in 1852, and appointed first to Portsmouth, O., next to St. Patrick's, Cincinnati, and later to Dayton, in the mean time having served a year as professor in Mount St. Mary's of the West. In 1872 he was appointed bishop of Cleveland. He died April 13, 1891. He was a vigorous defender of parochial schools, and compiled a series of readers for their use. He also founded the *Catholic Universe* in 1874. See Sadlier, *Catholic Directory*, 1892.

Godwin, John Hensley, an English Congregational minister, was born June 18, 1809, at Bristol. He studied at Highbury College and the University of Edinburgh. In 1839 he became resident and philosophical tutor at Highbury. When the union of Homerton, Coward, and Highbury colleges was completed in 1850 he received the chairs of New Testament exegesis, mental and moral philosophy, and English in New College, London, which he held until 1872, when he retired; but he remained honorary professor in the college until his death, Feb. 26, 1889. His literary activity was great. He wrote a work on *Christian Baptism*, and delivered the Congregational lecture entitled *Christian Faith.* Two or three of his works have to do with mental and moral philosophy. Volumes on the apocalypse, the gospels of Matthew and Mark, the epistles to the Romans and Galatians, bear witness to his diligence in this department of study. See (Lond.) *Cong. Yearbook*, 1890, p. 143.

Gotch, Frederic William, D.D., LL.D., an English Baptist minister, was born at Kettering, Northamptonshire, in 1807. He studied at Bristol College in 1832, and graduated from Trinity College, Dublin, in 1838. He immediately became pastor at Boxmore, going from thence to Stepney College, where he remained until 1845. In the same year he became classical and mathematical tutor at Bristol; resident tutor in 1861, and president in 1868, holding that position until 1882, when he became honorary president, retaining that relation until his death, May 17, 1890. In 1846 he was appointed one of the examiners of Scripture by the senate of the London University. He also served as a member of the Old Testament Revision Committee, and was chairman of the Baptist Union in 1868. He was the editor of the Revised English Bible Version of the Pentateuch, and also of the Old Testament issued by the Religious Tract Society. He was a frequent contributor to Kitto's *Journal of Sacred Literature.* See (English) *Baptist Hand-book*, 1891, p. 140.

Green, William Mercer, D.D., LL.D., a Protestant Episcopal bishop, was born in Wilmington, N. C., May 2, 1798. He graduated from the University of North Carolina in 1818, and then studied theology. He entered the ministry of his Church, and was rector until 1837, when he became chaplain and professor of belles-lettres in the University of North Carolina. In 1850 he was ordained bishop of Mississippi. He was one of the founders of the University of the South at Sewanee, Tenn., and in 1867 became its chancellor. He died Feb. 13, 1887. He was the author of *Memoirs of Bishops Ravenscroft and Otey*, and of *Sermons on Baptismal Regeneration* and *Apostolic Succession.* See *Appletons' Cyclop. of Amer. Biography.*

Gulick, Luther Halsey, M.D., D.D., an American missionary, was born in Honolulu, June 10, 1828. He graduated in medicine from the University of the City of New York in 1850, and was sent as missionary to

Micronesia. From 1863–70 he served as secretary of the Hawaiian Evangelical Association; 1870–71 as district secretary of the American Board of Commissioners for Foreign Missions; 1871–73 as missionary to Spain; 1873–75 as missionary to Italy; as agent of the American Bible Society at Yokohama, 1876–81, and at Shanghai, 1881–89. He died April 8, 1891. He was the founder of the *Medical Missionary Journal*, and editor of the *Chinese Recorder*. See (Am.) *Cong. Year-book*, 1892.

H.

Hague, William, D.D., a Baptist minister, was born at Pelham, N. Y., Jan. 4, 1808. Graduating from Hamilton College in 1826, and from Newton Theological Institute in 1829, he entered the ministry of his Church, serving as pastor until 1869, when he became professor of homiletics at the Chicago Baptist Theological Seminary. He died Aug. 1, 1887. He was the author of *The Authority and Perpetuity of the Christian Sabbath*, and other volumes. See *Appletons' Cyclop. of Amer. Biography*.

Hannay, Alexander, D.D., an English Congregational minister, was born at Kirkcudbright, East Galloway, Feb. 27, 1822. In 1846 he left college to take charge of a church in Dundee. About the year 1866 he became secretary of the Colonial Missionary Society, and in 1870 secretary of the Congregational Union of England and Wales. He died Nov. 12, 1890. He was one of the founders of the London Congregational Union, and occupied its chair in 1888. "There was scarcely a society among English Congregationalists in which he was not an active and valued counsellor." See (English) *Cong. Year-book*, 1891, pp. 176–180.

Harris, Samuel Smith, D.D., LL.D., a bishop of the Protestant Episcopal Church, was born in Autauga County, Ala., Sept. 14, 1841. Graduating from the University of Alabama in 1859, he was admitted to the bar in 1860. After practicing for some time, he entered the ministry of his Church, and was successively rector at Montgomery, Ala.; Columbus, Ga.; New Orleans, La., and Chicago, Ill. He was consecrated bishop of Michigan in 1879. He died Aug. 21, 1888. He was the author of *The Relation of Christianity to Civil Society* (1882). See *Appletons' Cyclop. of Amer. Biography*.

Harris, William Logan, D.D., LL.D., a Methodist Episcopal bishop, was born near Mansfield, O., Nov. 14, 1817. He was converted in 1834; afterwards studied in Norwalk Seminary; was licensed to preach in 1837, and entered the Michigan Conference the same year. In 1845 he became tutor in Ohio Wesleyan University; in 1848 principal of Baldwin Institute; in 1851 principal of the preparatory department of Ohio Wesleyan University; in 1852 professor of chemistry and natural history in the same school; was elected assistant missionary secretary in 1860; served as member and secretary of the General Conference in 1858, 1860, 1864, 1868, and 1872; and was elected bishop in 1872, continuing in that office until his death, Sept. 2, 1887. In 1873 he made a missionary tour around the world; in 1880 visited the missions in Mexico, and again in 1884 and 1885; in 1881 those in South America, returning by the way of Europe in 1882. He also organised the Japanese mission. He wrote a work on *The Powers of the General Conference* (1859), and, conjointly with judge William J. Henry of Illinois, a treatise on *Ecclesiastical Law* (1870). See Simpson, *Cyclop. of Methodism*, s. v.; *Minutes of Annual Conferences* (Fall), 1887, p. 347.

Hart, Ichabod Andrus, a Congregational minister, was born at Marshall, N. Y., Feb. 16, 1803; graduated from Hamilton College in 1826, and from Andover Theological Seminary in 1830; was agent of the American Educational Society, Central N. Y., 1831–33; pastor, 1833–56; agent of the Walworth County Institute, Illinois, 1856–60; without a charge, 1860–65; agent of the Western Tract and Book Society, 1865–67; treasurer of Wheaton College and editor of the *Cynosure*, 1867–73; resident at Wheaton, Ill., from 1865 until his death, Aug. 20, 1887.

Hatfield, Robert Miller, D.D., an eminent Methodist Episcopal minister, was born Feb. 19, 1819, at Mount Pleasant, Westchester Co., N. Y. Joining the Providence Conference in 1841, he served as pastor in the East and West until within a few years of his death, when failing health compelled him to cease. He was a trustee of Northwestern University, and a member of the General Missionary Committee. He was a member of the General Conferences of 1860, 1864, 1876, 1880, and 1884. He died March 31, 1891. He was distinguished as an eloquent public speaker. See the *Northwestern Christian Advocate*, April 8, 1891.

Hecker, Isaac Thomas, a Roman Catholic priest, was born Dec. 18, 1819. He was brought up a Protestant. At first he was engaged in business, but in 1843 joined the community at Brook Farm. In 1849, having entered the Catholic Church, he was ordained by cardinal Wiseman. At first he joined the Redemptorist Fathers, but soon planned, and in 1859 founded, the Congregation of St. Paul, the members of the order being converts from Protestantism. He has been chief of the order from the start. In 1865 he founded the *Catholic World*. He died Dec. 21, 1888. See *Appletons' Cyclop. of Amer. Biography*.

Hellier, Benjamin, an English Methodist preacher, was born at Wick, St. Lawrence, near Bristol, in 1825; in 1844 entered Richmond College; in 1847 was appointed assistant tutor at Dedsbury, and from that time, with the exception of six years spent in the ministry, he was employed in the various departments of the Theological Institution. In 1884 he delivered the Fernly lecture on *The Universal Mission of the Church of Christ*. He died March 8, 1888.

Hickok, Laurens Perseus, D.D., LL.D., a Presbyterian minister, was born at Bethel, Conn., Dec. 29, 1798. He graduated from Union College in 1820, and studied theology with Rev. William Andrews and Bennet Tyler, D.D.; was pastor at Kent, Conn., 1824–29; Litchfield, 1829–36; professor of theology, Western Reserve College, 1836–44; Auburn Theological Seminary, 1844–52; professor of mental and moral philosophy, and vice-president of Union College, 1852–66; president of the same, 1866–68; and thereafter without charge at Amherst, Mass., until his death, May 6, 1888. He was moderator of the Presbyterian General Assembly in 1856, and corporate member of the A. B. C. F. M. from 1848. He wrote *Rational Psychology* (1848):—*System of Moral Science* (1853):—*Empirical Psychology* (1854): – *Creator and Creation* (1872):—*Humanity Immortal* (eod.):—*Logic of Reason* (1875).

Higbie, Elnathan Elisha, a German Reformed minister and educator, was born at St. George, Vt., March 27, 1830. He graduated from the University of Vermont in 1849, and completed his theological course at Mercersburg, Pa. In 1864, while Dr. Philip Schaff was in Europe, he occupied the chair of church history and exegesis, and in 1866 was elected to succeed him. In 1871 he was made president of Mercersburg College, and in 1881 appointed superintendent of public instruction for Pennsylvania, which position he held until his death, Dec. 13, 1888. He was a frequent contributor to the *Mercersburg Review*.

Hight, John J., D.D., a Methodist Episcopal minister, was born at Bloomington, Ind., Dec. 4, 1834. In 1854 he joined the Indiana Conference, and spent two years in circuits, eleven in stations, three in the army as chaplain, one as agent for the centenary fund, four as presiding elder, and eleven as assistant editor of the *Western Christian Advocate*. He died Dec. 18, 1886. See *Minutes of Annual Conferences* (Fall), 1887, p. 350.

Hilary, THOMAS HUDSON, D.D., a minister of the Methodist Episcopal Church, South, was born near Mocksville, N. C., Nov. 15, 1823. He entered Randolph-Macon College, but did not finish his course. Joining the North Carolina Conference, he served several churches, laboring in the pastorate until his death, June 20, 1892. In 1872 he was associate editor of the *Raleigh Christian Advocate*. He served twice as presiding elder, and was a member of two general conferences of his Church. He was the author of *Methodist Armor:—Shield of the Young Methodist:*—and other works. See *Minutes of Annual Conferences of the M. E. Church, South*, 1892.

Hodge, CASPAR WISTAR, D.D., a Presbyterian minister and educator, was born at Princeton, N. J., Feb. 21, 1830, being a son of the late Charles Hodge. Graduating from Princeton College in 1848, and from the Seminary in 1853, he entered the pastorate and served until 1860, when he became professor of New Testament literature and Biblical Greek in Princeton Theological Seminary, serving until his death, Sept. 28, 1891. He was the author of *Apostolic History and Literature* (1887):—and *A Gospel History* (1889).

Holdich, JOSEPH, D.D., a Methodist Episcopal minister, was born at Thorney, near Peterborough, England, April 20, 1804. At the age of fourteen he came to the United States; in 1822 joined the Philadelphia Conference, but was transferred to the New York Conference in 1834; in 1836 was elected professor of moral science and belles-lettres at Wesleyan University, which position he held until 1849, when he became corresponding secretary of the American Bible Society, serving until 1878, when the state of his health forced him to retire. He died April 10, 1893. He was the author of a *Life of Wilbur Fisk:*—a *Treatise on Political Economy:*—and a *Bible History*. See *Minutes of the Annual Conferences* (Spring), 1893.

Hopkins, MARK, D.D., LL.D., an eminent Congregational educator, was born in Stockbridge, Mass., Feb. 4, 1802. He graduated from Williams College in 1824; was a tutor there from 1825 to 1827; graduated from the Berkshire Medical College in 1829; was professor of rhetoric and moral philosophy in Williams College, 1830–36; of moral and intellectual philosophy and president from 1836 to 1872; professor of theology, 1858–72, and died June 17, 1887. He was a fellow of the American Academy, corporate member of the American Board from 1838, and president from 1857. Dr. Hopkins was the author of seventy-five different publications, including pamphlets and addresses. A complete list is to be found in the *Cong. Year-book*, 1888, p. 28.

Howson, JOHN SAUL, D.D., an English prelate, was born at Giggleswick, May 5, 1816. He graduated from Trinity College, Cambridge, in 1837; obtained the members' prize in 1837 and 1838, and the Norrisian prize in 1840. In 1845 he became senior classical master, and in 1849 principal of the Liverpool College, which post he held till the close of 1865. He was appointed vicar of Wisbeck in 1866; from 1867 to 1873 was examining chaplain to the bishop of Ely; in 1867 became dean of Chester, in which position he died, Dec. 15, 1885. He was the author of various works: the Hulsean lectures on the *Character of St. Paul:*—and, in connection with the Rev. W. J. Conybeare, the *Life and Epistles of St. Paul.*

Humes, THOMAS WILLIAM, D.D., a Protestant Episcopal clergyman and educator, was born at Knoxville, Tenn., Nov. 22, 1815. After graduating from the East Tennessee College in 1830, and studying theology for two years with Rev. Stephen Foster of Knoxville, he entered Princeton Seminary in 1832. In 1837 he joined the Protestant Episcopal Church, and was ordained in 1845. With the exception of two years, he preached until 1869. From 1865–83 he was president and professor of moral philosophy and Christian evidences; 1884–86 engaged in home mission work; 1886–92 librarian of the Lawson McGhee Library of Knoxville. He died Jan. 16, 1892. See *Necrological Report of Princeton Theol. Sem.* 1893.

Humphrey, EDWARD PORTER, D.D., a Presbyterian minister and educator, was born at Fairfield, Conn., Jan. 28, 1809. He graduated from Amherst College in 1828, and from Andover Theological Seminary in 1833. He was a pastor until 1853, when he became professor of church history in the Presbyterian Theological Seminary at Danville, Ky., remaining there until 1866, when he became pastor at Louisville. He was made pastor emeritus in 1879. He died Dec. 9, 1887. In 1861 he was associate editor of the *Danville Review*. See *Appletons' Cyclop. of Amer. Biography*.

I.

Ireland, WILLIAM, a missionary, was born near Oswestry, Shropshire, England. He graduated from Illinois College in 1845, from Andover Theological Seminary in 1848, and the same year left for Zululand. During the first thirteen years he was stationed at Ifumi. In 1855 he was appointed to take charge of the boys' seminary at Adams, and for seventeen years continued his work there. He died in Boston, Mass., Oct. 12, 1888.

J.

Jones, JOHN, an English Wesleyan minister, was born at Llandwrog, Carnarvonshire, in 1825, entered the ministry in 1854, and died Dec. 17, 1889. He published a work on the *Atonement:—Expository Sermons:—Poem on the Bible:—Logic:*—besides contributing to many periodicals. See *Minutes of the British Conference*, 1890, p. 24.

K.

Kalisch, MARCUS, Ph.D., M.A., a Jewish scholar, was born at Trepton, Pomerania, Prussia, May 16, 1828. He was educated at Berlin University, and subsequently studied at Halle. In 1849 he left Prussia and settled in England, filling the post of secretary to the chief rabbi. In 1852, through the kindness of the Rothschilds, leisure was secured him for his work in the preparation of a commentary on the Old Testament. Genesis, Exodus, Leviticus, and Jonah were all that he could finish. He also wrote on the *Prophecies of Baalam*, and a *Hebrew Grammar*. He died Aug. 23, 1885.

Kalkar, CHRISTIAN ANDREAS HERMAN, Ph.D., D.D., a Lutheran minister, was born at Stockholm, Sweden, Nov. 26, 1802, of Jewish parentage. He studied law and theology at the University of Copenhagen. In 1827 he became adjunct in the cathedral school at Odense, and in the same year head master; in 1842 he visited most of Western Europe, and in 1843 became pastor at Gladsaxe, near Copenhagen, which position he resigned in 1868. He received the medal of the Haager Society; was Knight of the Danish Order; member of the Leyden Society of Literature, and of the Danish Bible Society; president of the Danish Missionary Society, 1860–73; member of the royal commission to revise the Danish Bible, 1866–74; president of the Danish branch of the Evangelical Alliance, and presided over the Copenhagen Conference in 1884. He is the author of a *Commentary on the Old Testament*, and of several works on missions. He died Feb. 2, 1886.

Karr, WILLIAM STEVENS, D.D., a Presbyterian minister, was born at Newark, N. J., Jan. 9, 1829. He studied at Rutgers College in 1847–48; graduated from Amherst in 1851, and from Union Theological Seminary in 1854; was pastor of the Third Presbyterian Church, Brooklyn, N. Y., 1854–67; at Chicopee, Mass., 1867–68; Keene, N.H., 1868–72; Cambridgeport, Mass., 1873–75; and Riley professor of theology in Hartford Theological Seminary thereafter until his death, March 4, 1888. He edited two volumes of Prof. H. B. Smith.

Keil, Johann Carl Friedrich, Ph.D., D.D., a Lutheran theologian, was born at Oelnitz, Saxony, Feb. 26, 1807. He studied at Dorpat, 1827-30; at Berlin, 1831-33; became privat-docent at Dorpat in 1833; professor extraordinary in 1838; ordinary professor in 1839; and from 1859 was professor emeritus, residing at Leipzig, and engaged in literary work until his death, in 1889. His principal works are, *Der Tempel Salomo's* (1839):—*Commentaries* on nearly all of the Old Testament, and on Matthew, Mark, Luke, John, Peter, and Jude.

Kennedy, Benjamin Hall, D.D., a clergyman of the Church of England, was born at Summer Hill, near Birmingham, Nov. 6, 1804. He graduated with honors from St. John's College, Cambridge, in 1827; was fellow of his college and classical lecturer, 1828-36; assistant master at Harrow, 1830-36; head master of Shrewsbury School, 1836-66; prebendary of Gaia Major in Lichfield Cathedral, 1843-67; select preacher to the University, 1860; rector of West Felton, 1865-67; became regius professor of Greek in the University of Cambridge, and canon of Ely in 1867, where he continued until his death, April 8, 1889. He was elected a member of the University Council in 1870, and lady Margaret preacher for 1873. He was elected honorary fellow of St. John's College in 1880. He was also a member of the New Testament Revision Committee. His works are largely school-books, or translations, but he also published, *Between Whiles* (1877):—*Occasional Sermons* (eod.):—and Ely lectures on *The Revised Translation of the New Testament* (1882).

L.

Latimer, James Elijah, D.D., a Methodist Episcopal minister, was born at Hartford, Conn., Oct. 7, 1826. He graduated from Wesleyan University in 1848; taught in various schools until he joined the Genesee Conference, and held several pastorates until 1870, when he became professor of historical theology in Boston Theological Seminary. In 1874 he became dean and professor of systematic theology, which position he held until his death, Nov. 26, 1884. See Simpson, *Cyclop. of Methodism*, s. v.; *Minutes of Annual Conferences* (Fall), 1885, p. 343.

Lee, Alfred, D.D., LL.D., a bishop of the Protestant Episcopal Church, was born at Cambridge, Mass., Sept. 9, 1807. Graduating from Harvard College in 1827, he studied law and was admitted to the bar, but in 1837 graduated from the General Theological Seminary, entered the ministry, and in 1841 was ordained bishop of Delaware. In 1884 he became presiding bishop of the Protestant Episcopal Church. He died April 12, 1887. He was a member of the American Committee for the Revision of the New Testament, and the author of several volumes. See *Appletons' Cyclop. of Amer. Biography*.

Lee, James, M.A., an English Congregational minister, was born at Newmarket, March 4, 1823. After graduating from London University in 1848, he took charge of a church at Broseley, Salop, serving also churches at Churchtown, Portishead, and Crick in 1858, and the ten years following he conducted a school at Broughton, Manchester. The remainder of his life, with the exception of three years in the pastorate, was spent in literary work. He died July 22, 1893. He was the author of *Bible Illustrations* (6 vols.), and several pamphlets. See (Lond.) *Cong. Year-book*, 1894.

Liddon, Henry Parry, an English clergyman, was born at Stoneham, Hants, Aug. 20, 1829. He was educated at Eton and at Christ Church, Oxford, graduating in 1850. The following year he was Johnson theological scholar. He was ordained deacon in 1852, and priest in 1853. From 1854 to 1859 he was vice-principal of the Theological College of Cuddesdon, and at the same time examining chaplain to the bishop of Salisbury. In 1864 he was appointed prebendary in Salisbury Cathedral; in 1863-65, 1870-72, 1877-79, and 1884, he was select preacher at Oxford; in 1870 he was promoted to be canon residentiary of St. Paul's, London, and the same year was appointed Ireland professor of exegesis in the University of Oxford, which latter position he held until 1882. He died Sept. 10, 1890. In 1866 he was Bampton lecturer, and in 1884 select preacher at Cambridge. He has written, *Lenten Sermons* (1858):—*Divinity of Our Lord and Saviour Jesus Christ* (Bampton lect., 1866):—*Sermons Preached before the University of Oxford* (1st series, 1869; 2d series, 1880):—*Walter Kew Hamilton, Bishop of Salisbury: a Sketch* (1869):—*Some Elements of Religion* (1871):—*Sermons on Various Subjects* (1872, 1876, 1879):—*Report of Proceedings at the Bonn Reunion Conference in* 1875:—*Thoughts on Present Church Troubles* (1881):—*Easter in St. Paul's*:—*Sermons on the Resurrection* (1885, 2 vols.). See *Contemporary Review*, Oct. 1890.

Lightfoot, Joseph Barber, D.D., an English prelate, was born at Liverpool, April 13, 1828. He graduated from Trinity College, Cambridge, in 1851, and was made fellow in 1852. In 1853 he was Norrisian university prizeman; in 1854 he was ordained deacon, and in 1855 priest. Dr. Lightfoot's appointments were: tutor at Trinity College, 1857; select preacher at Cambridge, 1858; chaplain to the late prince consort, 1861; honorary chaplain in ordinary to her majesty, 1862; Hulsean professor of divinity in the University of Cambridge, 1861; Whitehall preacher, 1866; examining chaplain to Dr. Tait, archbishop of Canterbury, 1868; canon residentiary of St. Paul's Cathedral, 1871; honorary fellow of Trinity College, Cambridge, 1872; one of the deputy clerks of the closet to her majesty, 1875; Margaret professor of divinity at Cambridge, 1875. In 1879 he was consecrated bishop of Durham, and died in that office, Dec. 23, 1890. He was one of the original members of the New Testament Revision Committee. Dr. Lightfoot wrote, commentaries on *Galatians* (1865):—*Philippians* (1868):—*Colossians* and *Philemon* (1875):—*The Apostolic Fathers* (1885, 3 vols.):—*On a Fresh Revision of the English New Testament* (1871).

Locke, John, an English Wesleyan minister, was born at Lyme, Dorset, in 1814, entered the Wesleyan ministry in 1841, and died Jan. 2, 1890. He was a diligent student, and published a *System of Theology* in 1862, which had a large circulation in England, America, and Australia. See *Minutes of the British Conference*, 1890, p. 24.

Logan, Robert William, a missionary, was born at York, O., May 4, 1843. He served as a soldier in the Union army in 1862; studied at Oberlin College, and graduated from the Theological Seminary there in 1870. After supplying a congregation at Rio, Wis., for a year, he sailed for Micronesia in June, 1874, and was stationed at Ponape; in 1879 he volunteered to go to the Mortlock islands to take charge of the work there; in 1884 took up his residence within the Ruk archipelago, and died at Anapano, Dec. 27, 1887.

Loomis, Augustus Ward, D.D., a Presbyterian minister, was born at Andover, Conn., Sept. 4, 1816. After graduating from Hamilton College in 1841, and Princeton Theological Seminary in 1844, he became missionary to China, 1844-50; missionary to the Creek Indians, 1852-53; in regular pastoral work, 1853-59; and in 1859-91 missionary to the Chinese in San Francisco, where he died, July 26, 1891. He was the author of *Learn to Say No* (1856):—*Scenes in Chusan* (1857):—*How to Die Happy* (1858):—*Scenes in the Indian Country* (1859):—*A Child a Hundred Years Old* (ibid.):—*Profits of Godliness* (ibid.):—*Confucius and the Chinese Classics* (1867):—*Chinese and English Lessons* (1872).

Lyman, Chester Smith, an American educator, was born at Manchester, Conn., Jan. 13, 1814. Graduating from Yale College in 1837, and the Theological Seminary in 1842, he preached for two years, but his health prevented his continuance in the ministry. In 1859 he became professor of mechanics and physics in the Scientific School at New Haven; in 1871 of astronomy and physics; in 1884 of astronomy; in 1889 emeritus professor. He died Jan. 29, 1890. See (Am.) *Cong. Year-book*, 1891.

M.

Machebœuf, Joseph Projectus, a Roman Catholic bishop, was born in the diocese of Clermont, France, Aug. 11, 1812. He was educated by the Sulpicians at Montferran. After three years' labor in his own country, he came to America to preside over the diocese of Cleveland, and was located at Sandusky. He went to New Mexico in 1851; from thence to Colorado, where he erected the first Catholic church at Denver. When Colorado became a vicariate, he was consecrated bishop of Epiphania and vicar apostolic. In 1887 he was made bishop of Denver. He died July 9, 1889.

Magoon, Elias Lyman, D.D., a Baptist minister, was born at Lebanon, N. H., Oct. 20, 1810. He graduated from Waterville College, Me., in 1836, and from Newton Theological Seminary in 1839; was settled over a church at Richmond, Va., for six years, until the division of his church on the question of slavery led him to resign. He next served a church in Cincinnati, O., until 1849, when he took charge of a church in New York city. In 1857-67 he was pastor of a church in Albany; in 1867-84 pastor of the Broad Street Church, Philadelphia, Pa. He retired from the pulpit in 1884, and died Nov. 25, 1886. Dr. Magoon published, *Eloquence of the Colonial Times* (1847):—*Orators of the American Revolution* (1848):—*Proverbs for the People* (eod.):—*Living Orators in America* (1849):—*Republican Christianity* (eod.):—*Westward Empire* (1856).

Mahan, Asa, D.D., LL.D., a Congregational minister, was born in Vernon, N.Y., Nov. 9, 1799; graduated from Hamilton College in 1824, and from Andover Theological Seminary in 1827; was a pastor until 1835, when he became president of Oberlin College (1835-50); president and professor of mental and moral philosophy in Cleveland University, 1850-54; was pastor again in 1855-61; thereafter president and professor of mental and moral philosophy in Adrian College until 1871; after that date without charge; and after the year 1874 resided in England until his death, April 4, 1889. Dr. Mahan edited, for many years, a monthly entitled the *Divine Life*. He published several works on *Philosophy*:—*Doctrine of the Will*:—*Lectures on Romans ix*:—*A Critical History of the Late American War*:—and several works on the higher life.

Mangum, Adolphus Williamson, D.D., a minister and educator of the Methodist Episcopal Church, South, was born April 1, 1834. At the age of twenty-one he graduated from Randolph-Macon College, and, joining the North Carolina Conference in 1856, he served as pastor and chaplain until 1875, when he was elected professor of mental and moral science in the University of North Carolina, which post he occupied until his death, May 12, 1890. See *Minutes of Annual Conferences of the M. E. Church, South*, 1890, p. 114.

Manley, Basil, D.D., LL.D., a Baptist minister, was born in Edgefield County, S. C., Dec. 19, 1825. After graduating from the University of Alabama in 1843, and from Princeton Theological Seminary in 1847, he became pastor until 1854; from 1854 to 1859 president of Richmond Female Institute; 1859-71 professor of Biblical introduction and Old Testament interpretation in the Southern Baptist Theological Seminary; 1871-79 president of Georgetown College, Ky.; thereafter professor in the Southern Baptist Theological Seminary, and died Jan. 31, 1892. He was the author of *A Call to the Ministry* (1867):—and *The Bible Doctrine of Inspiration Explained and Vindicated* (1888).

Manning, Henry Edward, D.D., a Roman Catholic prelate, was born at Potteredge, Hertfordshire, July 15, 1808. He graduated from Baliol College, Oxford, in 1830, and was elected fellow of Merton College. In 1834 he became rector at Lavington, and in 1840 archdeacon of Chichester. He was a leader in the "Oxford movement," and in 1851 gave up his preferments and went to Rome, studying there until 1854. Returning to England in 1857, he organised, at Bayswater, "The Oblates of St. Charles Borromeo," and became their first superior, founding a university at Kensington in 1874. He became successively provost of the archdiocese of Westminster, 1857, prothonotary apostolic, 1860, archbishop of Westminster, 1865, cardinal priest, 1875. He occupied a seat in the Vatican council of 1869-70. He died in 1890. He was the author of a large number of volumes. See W. S. Lilly, *Cardinal Manning's Characteristics, Political, Philosophical, and Religious* (1885).

Martin, John Satchell, D.D., a minister of the Methodist Episcopal Church, South, was born at Alexandria, Va., Sept. 7, 1815. He joined the Baltimore Conference of the Methodist Episcopal Church in 1835, and in 1866 entered the ministry of the Methodist Episcopal Church, South. He was secretary of his conference from 1853 until his death, July 8, 1888. In 1856 and again in 1860 he was a member of the General Conference of the Methodist Episcopal Church, South, and subsequently a member of every General Conference of the same Church, and secretary of that body in 1882 and 1886. He was secretary of the great Methodist Centenary also. See *Minutes of Annual Conferences of the M. E. Church, South*, 1888, p. 157.

Masson, John, an English Congregational minister, was born at Aberdeen, Scotland, Oct. 29, 1806. His education was received in King's College, Aberdeen, and Homerton College, London. In 1834 he began his labors as a minister of the Gospel, and served successively Harray in Orkney, Brechin, Letham, and Dundee, retiring in 1878. In 1876 he was chairman of the Congregational Union of Scotland, and from 1868 to 1870 one of the secretaries of the Ministers' Provident Fund. He was also, for a time, editor of the *Scottish Congregational Magazine*, and also of the publications of the Scottish Temperance League. He died Feb. 20, 1893. See (Lond.) *Cong. Year-book*, 1894.

McAll, Robert Whitaker, D.D., F.L.S., a Congregational minister, was born at Macclesfield, Cheshire, England, Dec. 17, 1821. He first studied architecture, but afterwards turned his attention to theology, and became a pastor in 1847, in which relation he continued until 1871, when he went to Paris with his wife for the purpose of viewing the scenes of the Franco-Prussian war. While he was standing on a street corner and distributing tracts to the passers-by, a man stepped from the throng and said: "Sir, I perceive you are a clergyman; if any one like you is ready to come over here and teach us a gospel, not of superstition, priestcraft, and bondage, but of simplicity, liberty, and charity, there are many of us ready to hear; but we have done with priests." Mr. McAll and his wife considered this a divine call, and accordingly rented a room in Belleville, and on Jan. 17, 1872, held the first meeting; twenty-eight were present. Mr. McAll could not speak French readily, but he could say, "God loves you," and "I love you;" and that won them. The work has grown from this humble beginning until, in 1889, there were 126 stations and 27 missionaries, employed not only in Paris, but in the provinces. The income of the mission is from private donations and legacies, and has amounted to £17,408 12*s.* 3½*d.* The mission is administered on a very economical plan, spending for the year £16,480 16*s.* 10½*d.* Meetings to the number of 14,083 were held for adults, and 5320 for children. The aggregate attendance of adults was 919,925; of children, 235,927; 26,131 visits were made, and 500,307 Bibles, Testaments, tracts, etc., circulated. There is also a medical mission and two dispensaries. Each station has a small free lending library. Dr. McAll died May 11, 1893. The work is now carried on by his widow. There is an office of the mission at Room 21, No. 1710 Chestnut Street, Philadelphia. See Bonar, *White Fields of France* (N. Y. 1879); *Missionary Review of the World*, Aug., Dec., 1889; July, 1890; (Lond.) *Cong. Year-book*, 1890, 1894.

McAuley, "Jerry," an evangelist, was born in Ireland in 1839. His father came to this country to escape arrest. Jerry never received any schooling, and when nineteen years old was committed to Sing Sing state-prison for fifteen years on the charge of robbery. While there he was religiously impressed, but, after his pardon in 1864, he returned to his old pursuits. In 1872 he found friends who stood by him, and in October of that year he opened his "Helping Hand for Men" on Water Street, New York city, which resulted in the conversion of many. In 1876 the old building was replaced by a new one, called "The McAuley Water Street Mission." In 1882, feeling that his work was done in that quarter of the city, he began a new mission in West Thirty-second Street, called the "Cremorne Mission." In June, 1883, he began the publication of *Jerry McAuley's Newspaper*, which is still published every other week. He died Sept. 18, 1884. See *Jerry McAuley: His Life and Work*, by R. M. Offord (N. Y. 1885).

McClosky, John, D.D., a Roman Catholic prelate, was born in Brooklyn, N. Y., March 20, 1810. After completing a seminary course of five years, he was ordained priest in 1834. In 1835-37 he was at Rome and travelling; in 1837-41 was over St. Joseph's Church, New York city; in 1841 was president of St. John's College, Fordham, but the next year resumed his parish work; in 1844 was consecrated bishop of Axieren *in partibus;* in 1847 bishop of Albany; in 1864 archbishop of New York; in 1875 was made cardinal, and died Oct. 10, 1885. He completed the cathedral in New York, and founded the Theological Seminary at Troy.

McFerrin, John Berry, D.D., a minister of the Methodist Episcopal Church, South, was born in Rutherford County, Tenn., June 15, 1807. In 1825 he was admitted to the Tennessee Conference, and served his Church for eighteen years as editor of the *Southern Christian Advocate;* seventeen years as book agent; four years as secretary of Domestic Missions, and eight as secretary of Foreign Missions. He died May 10, 1887. He was the author of *Methodism in Tennessee* (3 vols.). See *Minutes of Annual Conferences of the M. E. Church, South*, 1887, p. 25.

McGill, Alexander Taggart, D.D., a Presbyterian minister and educator, was born at Cannonsburg, Pa., Feb. 24, 1807. He graduated from Jefferson College in 1826; was admitted to the bar in Georgia, and appointed by the legislature as state surveyor to trace interstate lines, after having served one year as clerk of the House. In 1831 he turned his attention to theology, and graduated from the Associate Presbyterian Seminary at Cannonsburg in 1835. He was a pastor until 1842, when he became professor of church history in Western Theological Seminary, Allegheny, Pa.; in 1848 he was moderator of the General Assembly; in 1852 he became professor in the Presbyterian Seminary at Columbia, S. C., but in 1853 returned to his former chair in Allegheny. In 1854 he became professor of ecclesiastical, homiletic, and pastoral theology at Princeton Seminary, and in 1883 was retired as emeritus professor. He died Jan. 13, 1889. See *Appletons' Cyclop. of Amer. Biography.*

McTyeire, Holland Nimmons, D.D., a bishop of the Methodist Episcopal Church, South, was born in Barnwell County, S. C., July 28, 1824; graduated from Randolph-Macon College, Va., in 1844; joined the Virginia Conference in 1845; in 1851 became editor of the *New Orleans Christian Advocate*, and in 1858 of the *Nashville Christian Advocate;* in 1866 was elected bishop; in 1873 was made president of the board of Vanderbilt University, and died Feb. 15, 1889. He was the author of *Duties of Christian Masters* (1851):—*Catechism on Church Government* (1869):—*Catechism on Bible History* (eod.):—*Manual of Discipline* (1870):—*History of Methodism* (1884).

Mendenhall, James William, D.D., a Methodist Episcopal minister, was born at Centreville, O., Nov. 8, 1844. Graduating from Ohio Wesleyan University in 1864, he joined the Cincinnati Conference. With the exception of two years spent as president of the Fremont Collegiate Institute at Sidney, Iowa, he was in the pastorate until 1888, when he was elected editor of the *Methodist Review;* and re-elected in 1892. He died June 18, 1892. He was the author of *Plato and Paul:*—and *Echoes from Palestine.* See *Minutes of the Annual Conferences* (Fall), 1892.

Moberly, George, D.C.L., a prelate of the Church of England, was born in St. Petersburg, Russia, Oct. 10, 1803. He was educated at Baliol College, Oxford, graduating in 1825; was fellow and tutor in his college; public examiner in the University in 1830, 1833-35; select preacher, 1833, 1858, 1863; head master of Winchester College, 1835-66; rector of Brightstone, Isle of Wight, 1866-69; fellow of Winchester College, 1866-70; Bampton lecturer, 1868; canon of Chester, 1868-69; consecrated bishop in 1869, and died July 6, 1885. He was the author of a number of volumes of sermons, and a member of the New Testament Revision Committee.

Molesworth, William Nassau, a clergyman of the Church of England, was born at Millbrook, Nov. 8, 1816. Graduating from Cambridge University in 1839, he took orders and was a rector the rest of his life. He died Dec. 19, 1890. Among his works are, *Religious Importance of Secular Instruction* (1857):—*Plain Lectures on Astronomy, England and France* (1860):—*History of the Reform Bill* (1864):—*System of Moral Philosophy* (1867):—*History of England* (1871-73):—*History of the Church of England* (1882).

Moody, Granville, D.D., a Methodist Episcopal minister, was born at Portland, Me., Jan. 2, 1812. In 1833 he joined the Ohio Conference, and served as a pastor until 1860, when he became colonel of the Seventy-fourth Ohio regiment. He served until May, 1863, when illness forced him to resign. He again entered the pastorate, and served as pastor and presiding elder until 1882, when he took a supernumerary relation, which he held until his death, June 4, 1887. See *Minutes of Annual Conferences* (Fall), 1887, p. 366; *Appletons' Cyclop. of Amer. Biography.*

Morgan, William Ferdinand, D.D., a clergyman of the Protestant Episcopal Church, was born at Hartford, Conn., Dec. 21, 1817. He graduated from Union College in 1837, and from the General Theological Seminary in 1840. He was a rector in Norwich, Conn., and New York city until his death, May 18, 1888. In 1864 he was sent to Paris to preach the sermon at the dedication of Holy Trinity, the first Protestant Episcopal church on the Continent. See *Appletons' Cyclop. of Amer. Biography.*

N.

Neeshima, Joseph Hardy, LL.D., a Japanese educator and missionary, was born at Yeddo, Japan, Feb. 15, 1844. He found his way as a boy to America, and adopted the name of his benefactor, the captain of the ship in which he came. After studying in the Phillips Andover Academy, and graduating from the scientific department of Amherst College in 1870, he graduated from Andover Theological Seminary in the special course of 1874, and in the same year was sent to his own country by the American Board of Commissioners for Foreign Missions. In 1875 he became the founder and president of the training-school which afterwards became Doshisha College. He died Jan. 23, 1890. See (Am.) *Cong. Year-book*, 1891.

Nelles, SAMUEL SOBIESKI, D.D., LL.D., a Canadian educator, was born at Mount Pleasant, Ontario, Oct. 17, 1823. Graduating from Wesleyan University in 1846, he entered the ministry of the Methodist Church in 1847, serving as pastor until 1850, when he was appointed president of Victoria College. He died Oct. 17, 1887. He was the author of a work on *Logic*.

Nevin, ALFRED, D.D., LL.D., a Presbyterian minister, was born at Shippensburg, Pa., March 14, 1816. He graduated from Jefferson College in 1834, and was admitted to the bar in 1837. In 1840 he graduated from the Western Theological Seminary. He was a pastor until 1861, when he became editor of the *Standard*, which was subsequently merged into the *Northwestern Presbyterian*. In 1872–74 he was editor of the *Presbyterian Weekly*, and in 1875–80 of the *Presbyterian Journal*. He edited the *Presbyterian Cyclopædia*. He died Sept. 4, 1890. For a list of his works, see *Appletons' Cyclop. of Amer. Literature*.

Newman, JOHN HENRY, D.D., a Roman Catholic prelate, was born in London, Feb. 21, 1801. He was educated at Trinity College, Oxford, graduating in 1820. In 1822 he was made fellow of Oriel College; in 1825 vice-principal of St. Alban's Hall; in 1826 tutor of his college, which post he held until 1831; in 1828 he became incumbent of St. Mary's, Oxford, with the chaplaincy of Littlemore, but resigned St. Mary's in 1843. In 1842 he established at Littlemore an ascetic community modelled after those of mediæval times, over which he presided for three years. He joined Dr. Pusey as the recognised leader of the High-Church party, and took a prominent part in the Tractarian controversy, contributing the final tract, No. 90. In October, 1845, he seceded from the Established Church, and was received into the Roman Catholic communion. After being ordained priest, he was appointed head of the Oratory of St. Philip Neri at Birmingham. In 1854 he was appointed rector of the newly founded University of Dublin, but resigned in 1858, and established a school for the sons of Roman Catholic gentry at Edgebaston, near Birmingham. Dr. Newman was elected an honorary fellow of Trinity College, Oxford, Dec. 18, 1877. On May 12, 1879, pope Leo XIII. created him a cardinal deacon of the Holy Roman Church. He died Aug. 10, 1890. A collected edition of his writings was published in London (1870–79, 36 vols., eleven of which are sermons). As a hymn writer he will be especially remembered as the author of "Lead, kindly Light!" See *Contemporary Review*, Sept., 1890; *Annals of the Tractarian Movement*, by E. G. K. Brown (London, 1861); *William George Ward and the Oxford Movement*, by Wilfrid Ward (ibid. 1890).

Norton, WILLIAM, LL.D., an English Baptist minister, was born Dec. 25, 1812, at Woodhouse, Norfolk. He studied at a private school in Norwich and at Stepney College. In 1835 he offered himself as a missionary for India, but was refused on account of his health. From 1836 to 1840 he was a pastor; in 1839 became joint editor of the *Primitive Communionist*, and in 1841 of the *Primitive Church Magazine*; in the same year he was, with others, the founder of the Baptist Tract Society, and its editor until 1870. He died Aug. 12, 1890. He translated the New Testament into the Spanish language, compiled a selection of 1113 hymns, and was the author of *Responsibility*. See (English) *Baptist Year-book*, 1891, pp. 149, 150.

P.

Palmer, RAY, a Congregational minister, was born at Little Compton, R. I., Nov. 12, 1808; graduated from Yale College in 1830; taught, 1830–34; was pastor, 1835–66; secretary of the American Congregational Union, 1866–78; associate pastor in Newark, N. J., 1881–84, and died March 29, 1887. He was a corporate member of the A. B. C. F. M. from 1854; visitor of Andover Theological Seminary, 1865–78; director of the A. H. M. Society, 1862–83. He was the author of *Hymns and Sacred Pieces* (1865):—*Home; or, The Unlost Paradise* (1868). His *Complete Poetical Works* were published in 1876.

Patterson, WILLIAM MCKENDREE, D.D., a minister of the Methodist Episcopal Church, South, was born near St. Louis, Mo., Sept. 19, 1838. He graduated from St. Charles College, Mo., in 1860; in 1861 he joined the St. Louis Conference; next he became a chaplain in the Confederate army; in 1865 an agent for the American Bible Society; in 1868 he again entered the ministry, joining the Memphis Conference; in 1872 he became agent for Vanderbilt University; in 1878 a missionary to Mexico, and met with phenomenal success. He was elected to the General Conference of 1886, and edited the *Mexican Evangelista*. In April, 1888, he became agent for the American Bible Society in Venezuela, South America. He died at Caracas, of yellow fever, April 19, 1888. See *Minutes of Annual Conferences of the M. E. Church, South*, 1889, p. 35.

Patton, WILLIAM WESTON, D.D., LL.D., a Congregational minister, was born in New York city, Oct. 19, 1821; graduated from the University of New York in 1839, and from Union Theological Seminary in 1842; was a pastor until 1867; until 1872 editor of the *Advance;* western secretary of the American Missionary Association, 1873–74; lecturer at Chicago and Oberlin Theological seminaries, 1874–77; president of Howard University, Washington, D. C., 1877–89; and died Dec. 31, 1889. Dr. Patton was a corporate member of the A. B. C. F. M. from 1869; one of the founders of the American Missionary Association; vice-president of the Sanitary Commission of the North-west; member of the Society of the Cincinnati; honorary member of the Society of Science, Literature, and Art (London, 1885). For a list of his published works, see the *Congregational Year-book*, 1890, p. 34.

Peck, JONAS ORAMEL, D.D., a Methodist Episcopal minister, was born at Groton, Vt., Sept. 4, 1836. Of hardy robustness and active habits from youth, he was converted in early years, graduated from Amherst College in 1862, and immediately entered the New England Conference, in which he held important charges; in 1873 was transferred to Chicago, thence successively to Baltimore, Brooklyn, New Haven, and again to Brooklyn, with increasing usefulness both as a preacher and a pastor. In 1888 he was elected one of the corresponding secretaries of the missionary society of his denomination, re-elected in 1893, and rendered efficient service in that capacity until his death in New York city, May 17, 1894. He left ready for the press the MS. of a work on *Revivals*.

Peirce, BRADFORD KINNEY, D.D., a Methodist Episcopal minister, was born at Royalton, Vt., Feb. 3, 1819. He graduated from Wesleyan University in 1841, and joined the New England Conference in 1846. He was editor of the *Sunday-School Messenger* and *Sunday-School Teacher*, 1844–45, and agent of the Sunday-School Union, 1854–56; superintendent and chaplain of the State Industrial School at Lancaster, Mass., 1856–62; chaplain of the House of Refuge on Randall's Island, N. Y., 1862–72; editor of *Zion's Herald* for sixteen years, and finally financial agent for Boston University. He died April 19, 1889. See *Minutes of Annual Conferences* (Spring), 1890, p. 104.

Pettingell, JOHN HANCOCK, a Congregational minister, was born in Manchester, Vt., May 11, 1815; graduated from Yale College in 1837; was professor in the Deaf and Dumb Institute, New York, 1838–43; studied in Union Theological Seminary in 1841; was pastor, 1843–52; district secretary of the A. B. C. F. M., 1853–60; pastor, 1860–66; seamen's chaplain, in Antwerp, Belgium, 1866–72; and thereafter without a charge until his death, Feb. 27, 1887. He was the author of *Language: Its Nature and Functions* (1876):—*Homiletical Index* (eod.):—*The Theological Trilemma* (1878):—*Platonism vs. Christianity* (1881):—*Bible Terminology* (eod.):—*Life Everlasting* (1882):—*The Unspeakable Gift* (1884):—*Views and Reviews* (1887).

Phelps, Austin, D.D., a Congregational minister and professor, was born at West Brookfield, Mass., Jan. 7, 1820. He graduated from the University of Pennsylvania in 1837; and was pastor of Pine Street Church, Boston, 1842–48; and professor of sacred rhetoric in Andover Theological Seminary, 1848–79. He died at Bar Harbor, Me., Oct. 13, 1890. He was the author of *The Still Hour* (1859):—*Hymns and Choirs* (1860):—*The New Birth* (1867):—*Sabbath Hours* (1870):—*Studies of the Old Testament* (1879):—*The Theory of Preaching* (1881):—*Men and Books* (1882):—*My Portfolio* (eod.):—*English Style* (1883):—*My Study* (1885):—*My Note Book* (1890). See *Appletons' Cyclop. of Amer. Biography*.

Phillips, Zebulon, a Methodist Episcopal minister, was born at Amsterdam, N. Y., in 1808. He joined the Troy Conference in 1834, and served as pastor until 1848, when he became presiding elder of the Troy district. During this period he was also a member of the book committee, and in 1852 was appointed assistant agent of the Methodist Book Concern in New York city. In 1856 he became agent of the Troy University, and in 1860 entered into business. He died Feb. 8, 1885. See *Minutes of Annual Conferences* (Spring), 1886, p. 100.

Pillsbury, Benjamin, D.D., a minister of the Methodist Episcopal Church, was born at Boscawen, N. H., Oct. 25, 1824. He graduated in 1847 from Wesleyan University, and in 1850 from Yale Theological Seminary. He entered the New York East Conference in 1848, and served as pastor and presiding elder until his death, Feb. 28, 1887. See *Minutes of Annual Conferences* (Spring), 1887, p. 93.

Plumptre, Edward Hayes, D.D., a clergyman of the Church of England, was born in London, Aug. 6, 1821. Graduating from University College, Oxford, in 1844, he became fellow of Brasenose College 1844–47. In 1851–58 he was assistant preacher at Lincoln's Inn, and select preacher at Oxford, 1851–53, 1864–66, 1872–73. He was also chaplain of King's College, London, 1847–68, and professor of pastoral theology there, 1853–63, and dean of Queen's College, London, 1855–75; prebendary of Portpool, in St. Paul's Cathedral, 1863–81, and professor of exegesis in King's College, London, at the same time. In 1869–73 he was rector of Pluckley, Kent. He was Grinfield lecturer on the Septuagint at Oxford in 1872–74, and vicar of Bickley, Kent, in 1873–81; principal of Queen's College, London, 1875–77. In 1881 he was installed as Dean of Wells. He died in January, 1891. He was the Boyle lecturer for 1866–67, and a member of the Old Testament Committee of Revision. He was the author of several *Commentaries*:—*Introduction to the New Testament*:—*Life and Letters of Thomas Kerr*:—and other volumes.

Porter, James, D.D., a minister of the Methodist Episcopal Church, was born in Middleborough, Mass., March 21, 1808. In 1830 he joined the New England Conference, and served as pastor until 1856, when he was elected one of the agents of the Methodist Book Concern. From 1852–55 he was a member of the Board of Overseers of Harvard College; from 1855–71, a trustee of Wesleyan University; and from 1868–82, secretary of the National Temperance Society. He died April 16, 1888. He was a member of every General Conference from 1844 to 1872. He published, *Camp Meetings Considered*:—*Chart of Life*:—*True Evangelist*:—*The Winning Worker*:—*Compendium of Methodism*:—*Revivals of Religion*:—*Hints to Self-Educated Preachers*:—*Christianity Demonstrated by Experience*:—*Self-Reliance Encouraged*:—*Commonplace Book*. See *Simpson's Cyclopædia of Methodism; Appletons' Cyclop. of Amer. Biography; Minutes of Annual Conferences* (Spring), 1889, p. 108.

Porter, John S., D.D., a Methodist Episcopal minister, was born at Snow Hill, Md., Aug. 23, 1805. He was trained as a Presbyterian, but became a Methodist, and joined the Philadelphia Conference in 1829, continuing to serve the church as pastor and presiding elder until 1873, when he was obliged to retire from the active ministry. He died Oct. 2, 1890. He was a member of several General Conferences, and a charter member of the Board of Trustees of Drew Theological Seminary. See the *Christian Advocate*, Oct. 9, 1890.

Post, Truman Marcellus, D.D., a Congregational minister, was born in Middlebury, Vt., June 3, 1810; graduated from Middlebury College in 1829; was tutor there, 1829–32; student at Andover, 1832; professor of languages and history at Illinois College, 1833–47; pastor, 1840–82; corporate member of the American Board from 1857, and its preacher at Salem, 1871; director A. H. M. Society, 1863–83. He was also lecturer on history at Washington University, St. Louis; on ecclesiastical history in Chicago Theological Seminary; and on congregationalism in Andover Theological Seminary. He died Dec. 31, 1886. He published, *The Skeptical Era in Modern History* (1856), and several pamphlets.

Potter, Horatio, D.D., LL.D., D.C.L., a Protestant Episcopal bishop, was born at Beekmans, N. Y., Feb. 9, 1802. He graduated from Union College in 1826; was rector at Saco, Me., 1828–33; rector of St. Peter's, Albany, 1833–54; provisional bishop of New York, 1854–61; bishop of New York in 1861; and died Jan. 2, 1887. He took an active part in the Lambeth Conferences of 1867 and 1878. He was also influential in movements relating to city mission work. See *Appletons' Cyclop. of Amer. Biography*.

Powell, James, D.D., a Congregational minister, was born in Newtown, England, Dec. 25, 1843; graduated from Dartmouth College in 1866, and from Andover Theological Seminary in 1869; was pastor at Newburyport, Mass., 1869–73; district secretary of A. M. A., Chicago, 1873–83; assistant and associate corresponding secretary from 1883 until his death, Dec. 27, 1887.

Prentice, William S., D.D., a Methodist Episcopal minister, was born in Saint Clair County, Ill., May 21, 1819. In 1849 he was admitted into the Illinois Conference. He served as a presiding elder and pastor until 1884, when he took a supernumerary relation, which he held until his death, June 28, 1887. He was a delegate to the General Conferences of 1860, 1872, 1876, 1880, 1884. See *Minutes of Annual Conferences* (Fall), 1887, p. 366.

Pressensé, Edmond de, D.D., an eminent French Protestant minister, was born in Paris, Jan. 24, 1824. He studied at the University of Paris, and theology with Vinet, Tholuck, and Neander. He was pastor of the Free Evangelical Congregation of the Taitbout at Paris, 1847–70; deputy to the National Assembly from the Department of the Seine, 1871–76; elected life senator of Paris in 1883. After 1854 he was editor of the *Revue Chrétienne*, which he founded. He was president of the Synodical Commission of the Free Church of France, also a chevalier of the Legion of Honor. He died April 7, 1891. As an author he was very voluminous, having written many books relating to the Reformation and the life of Christ.

Prime, Edward Dorr Griffin, D.D., an eminent Presbyterian minister, was born at Cambridge, N. Y., Nov. 2, 1814. Graduating from Union College in 1832, he spent some time in teaching, then studied medicine for a time, but finally studied for the ministry, graduating from Princeton Seminary in 1838, serving as pastor for some time. From 1856 he was associated with his brother in editorial labor on the New York *Observer*. He died April 7, 1891. Besides contributing much to periodical literature, he was the author of several works on missions.

Prime, Samuel Irenæus, D.D., a noted Presbyterian minister, was born in Ballston, N.Y., Nov. 4, 1812. He graduated from Williams College in 1829; taught for three years, and then entered Princeton Theological Seminary, but before the first year was completed he was attacked by a severe illness, and was never able to resume his studies. He was pastor at Ballston Spa, 1833–35; at Matteawan, 1837–40. Thereafter he was editor of the New York *Observer*, except in 1849, when he acted as secretary of the American Bible Society, and a few months in 1850, when he edited the *Presbyterian*. In 1853 he visited Europe, and again in 1866–67, and 1876–77. In 1867 he attended the fifth General Conference of the Evangelical Alliance at Amsterdam. On his return he was elected a corresponding secretary of the American Evangelical Alliance, which position he held until 1884. He was vice-president and director of the American Tract Society, and of the American and Foreign Christian Union; president of the New York Association for the Advancement of Science and Art; a trustee of Williams College, and president and trustee of Wells College for Women; also a member of a large number of religious, benevolent, and literary societies. He died July 18, 1885. Dr. Prime was the author of over forty volumes, besides pamphlets, addresses, and scattered articles.

R.

Ranke, LEOPOLD VON, D.D., a German historian, was born at Wiehe, Thuringia, Dec. 21, 1795. He embraced the profession of teacher, and in 1818 became head master of the Gymnasium at Frankfort-on-the-Oder. In 1825 he was invited to Berlin as professor extraordinary of history in the university, and was sent in 1827 by the Prussian government to Vienna, Rome, and Venice, to examine the historical materials there. In 1841 he was appointed historiographer of Prussia, and in 1848 he was elected a member of the National Assembly at Frankfort. He was ennobled in 1866. He collected a large and valuable library pertaining to historical matters, which after his death, May 23, 1886, was purchased and presented to Syracuse University, N. Y. He was the author of many volumes, chief of which are his *History of the Popes*, and *German History in the Time of the Reformation*.

Robbins, ELIJAH, was born in Thompson, Conn., March 12, 1828. He graduated from Yale College in 1856, and from East Windsor Theological Seminary in 1859, and in the latter year sailed for the Zulu Mission. Here he labored for nearly thirty years. For the first few years he was stationed at Umzumbe, but later in connection with the mission training-school at Adams. He died June 30, 1889.

Rooke, THOMAS GEORGE, an English Baptist minister, was born in 1838 in London. After four years devoted to legal studies, the state of his health compelled him to travel in the East. On his return he determined to enter the ministry, and was accordingly received and educated in Regent's Park College. In 1862 he again travelled in the East, and on his return became pastor at Sheppard's Barton, Frome, serving until 1876, when he became president of the college at Rawdon. He acquired an exceptional knowledge of the Oriental languages. He died Dec. 8, 1890. See (Lond.) *Baptist Hand-book*, 1892.

Rush, WILLIAM MARION, a minister of the Methodist Episcopal Church, South, was born in Marion County, Mo., about the year 1821. He joined the Missouri Conference in 1841, preaching until 1884. He died June 12, 1886. He was a member of every General Conference of his Church from 1866 to 1886. See *Minutes of Annual Conferences of the M. E. Church, South*, 1886, p. 13.

Russell, DAVID, D.D., a Scotch Congregational minister, was born at Dundee, Oct. 7, 1811. Graduating from the Glasgow Theological Academy in 1839, he was immediately ordained pastor of the Brown Street Chapel, Glasgow, which he served until 1889, then retiring from the pastorate. From 1861 to 1877 he was secretary of the Congregational Union of Scotland, and in 1874 chairman; he was also first president of the Total Abstinence Society; in 1874 chairman of the Conference, serving as secretary from 1869 to 1876. He was one of the founders of the Supplementary Stipend Fund, and its secretary from 1872 to 1876. He also served as president of the Scottish Bible Society. He died May 15, 1892. For some years he was editor of the *Congregational Magazine*. See (Lond.) *Cong. Year-book*, 1894.

S.

Schaff, PHILIP, D.D., LL.D., a prominent Presbyterian minister, author, and professor, was born at Coire, Switzerland, Jan. 1, 1819. He received his education in his native place, and at Stuttgart, Tübingen, Halle, and Berlin. Lecturing in Berlin University, 1842–44, on exegesis and Church history, he next received and accepted a call to a professorship in Mercersburg Theological Seminary, where he remained until 1863; from 1864–69 was secretary of the New York Sabbath Committee; 1870–72 professor of theological encyclopædia and methodology in Union Theological Seminary; 1872–74 of Hebrew; and thereafter of sacred literature until his death, Oct. 20, 1893. Dr. Schaff was a most genial Christian gentleman, and a scholar of wide and accurate attainments. He was a very voluminous writer and editor, principally in the line of Church history, especially *The Creeds of Christendom* (3 vols.):—and *History of the Christian Church* (7 vols.), upon which his reputation will most permanently rest. He also edited several commentaries, such as that of Lange; also *The Popular Commentary*, and *The International Revision Commentary*, besides many works of reference, most important of which is the *Schaff-Herzog Religious Encyclopædia*. In 1886 he became the editor of *A Select Library of the Nicene and Post-Nicene Fathers;* he was also the editor of *The Philosophical and Theological Library*. He was chairman of the American Committee of Revisers of the English Bible, and labored ardently on the N. T. portion of that work.

Service, JOHN, D.D., a minister of the Church of Scotland, was born at Campsie, Feb. 26, 1833. He studied at the University of Glasgow in 1858–62, but did not graduate. He was sub-editor of Mackenzie's *Imperial Dictionary of Universal Biography*. For ten months in 1862 he was minister at Hamilton, but was compelled by ill-health to resign. He next went to Melbourne, Australia, for two years, leaving it for Hobart Town, Tasmania, where he remained for four years, 1866–70. He then returned home, and in 1872 was appointed to the parish of Inch, which he left in 1879 for Hyndland Established Church, Glasgow, where he remained until his death, March 15, 1884. He wrote a novel, *Lady Hetty* (3 vols., 1875):—*Salvation Here and Hereafter:—Sermons and Essays* (1876).

Sherwood, JAMES MANNING, a Presbyterian minister, was born at Fishkill, N. Y., Sept. 29, 1814. After an education mainly through private tutors, he served various churches as pastor from 1835 to 1858, and then owing to ill-health took up literary work, until his death, Oct. 22, 1890. He was editor of the *National Preacher*, *Biblical Repository*, New York *Evangelist*, *Eclectic Magazine*, *Princeton Review*, *Hours at Home*,

Homiletic Review, and *Missionary Review of the World.* He also wrote *A History of the Cross*, and superintended an edition of the *Life of David Brainerd.* See the *Missionary Review of the World*, Jan., 1891, pp. 1–3.

Shipp, ALBERT MICAJAH, D.D., a minister and educator of the Methodist Episcopal Church, South, was born in Stokes County, N. C., June 15, 1819. He graduated from the University of North Carolina, and entered the South Carolina Conference in 1841. He served six years as a pastor; one as a presiding elder; two and a half as president of a female college at Greensboro, N. C.; nine years as professor of history in his alma mater; sixteen years president of Wofford College, S. C.; ten years professor of exegetical theology at Vanderbilt University, serving three years of that time as dean of the theological faculty and three as vice-chancellor of the university. He retired to private life in 1885, and died June 27, 1887. He was author of a *History of Methodism in South Carolina.* See *Minutes of Annual Conferences of the M. E. Church, South*, 1887, p. 121.

Shorter, JAMES ALEXANDER, a bishop of the African M. E. Church, was born in Washington, D. C., Feb. 4, 1817. Entering the ministry in 1846, he served as pastor until his election to the episcopacy in 1868. He was a delegate to the Œcumenical Conference in 1881. He died July 1, 1887. See *Appletons' Cyclop. of Amer. Biography.*

Sibley, JAMES W., a missionary, was born in Litchfield, O., in 1847. After a course of study at Oberlin College, he sailed for India in 1877. He went out independently, but in 1886 was received by the American Board and stationed at Satara, where he died Aug. 13, 1888.

Skinner, THOMAS HARVEY, D.D., LL.D., a Presbyterian minister, was born in Philadelphia, Pa., Oct. 6, 1820. After graduating from the University of the City of New York in 1840, and Union Theological Seminary in 1843, he entered the pastorate and served various churches until 1881, when he became professor of Didactic and Polemic Theology in McCormick Theological Seminary, where he remained until his death, Jan. 4, 1892.

Smith, James William, a Congregational minister, was born in Stamford, Conn., July 8, 1810; graduated from the N. Y. Medical College, and joined the mission of the American Board at Hawaii in 1842; was stationed at Koloa, or Kawai, in 1844, and there remained until his death, Dec. 1, 1887. He was ordained pastor of the Koloa Church in 1854.

Smith, William Augustus, D.D., a minister of the Methodist Episcopal Church, was born at Brockville, Canada, May 27, 1834. In 1863 he was admitted into the Rock River Conference, and served as a pastor until his death, Sept. 30, 1887. For sixteen years he was the secretary of his conference, and was a member of the General Conference of 1876, and reserve delegate to that of 1880. See *Minutes of Annual Conferences*, (Fall), 1887, p. 354.

Smith, William Robertson, LL.D., a Scotch Hebraist and author, was born at Keig, Aberdeenshire, Nov. 8, 1846. His education was received at Aberdeen University, New College, Edinburgh, Bonn, and Göttingen. From 1868 to 1870 he was assistant in physics at Edinburgh; 1870–81 professor of Hebrew in the Free Church College, Aberdeen, from which position he was removed for alleged heretical teaching. He next was associate editor of the ninth edition of the *Encyclopædia Britannica;* 1883–86, lord almoners' professor of Arabic at Cambridge University; and from 1886 until his death, March 31, 1894, librarian of the university. He was the author of *The Old Testament in the Jewish Church:—The Prophets of Israel and their Place in History to the Close of the 8th Century:—Kinship and Marriage in Early Arabia.*

Spurgeon, CHARLES HADDON, an eminent English Baptist minister, was born at Kelvedon, Essex, June 19, 1834. He began preaching at the age of seventeen at Waterbeach, near Cambridge, where he remained for two years, thence going to New-Park-Street Chapel, London. In 1856 and the three years following services were held in the Surrey Gardens Music Hall. In 1859 the Metropolitan Tabernacle, costing nearly £32,000, was opened. During Mr. Spurgeon's pastorate 14,691 members were added to the church. There he acquired his world-wide reputation as a preacher. His Pastors' College was first planned in 1854. As the head of the Stockwell Orphanage his work was very severe. As an author his work was voluminous and variform. His greatest work, *The Treasury of David*, 7 vols., reached a large sale on both sides of the Atlantic. He was also author of *Commenting and Commentaries:—John Ploughman's Talk:—The Clue of the Maze:—My Sermon Notes:*—and others. His works, including all but *The Treasury of David*, have been published in twenty volumes. He died at Mentone, France, Jan. 31, 1892. See Shindler, *From the Usher's Desk to the Tabernacle Pulpit.* Several other lives have also appeared.

Stevens, WILLIAM BACON, D.D., LL.D., a bishop of the Protestant Episcopal Church, was born in Bath, Me., July 13, 1815. He studied medicine and practiced for several years in the earlier part of his life. In 1841 he received the appointment of state historian of Georgia, and published several volumes. In 1843 he entered the ministry of his Church, and served as rector until 1865, when he was ordained bishop of Pennsylvania. He died June 11, 1887. See *Appletons' Cyclop. of Amer. Biography.*

Stevenson, JOHN FREDERICK, B.A., LL.B., D.D., an English Congregational minister, was born at Loughborough in 1833. Graduating from London University in 1853, he entered the ministry and served at Long Sutton, Lincolnshire; Mansfield Road Chapel, Nottingham; Trinity Congregational Church, Reading. In 1874 he went to Montreal to assume the pastoral work of Zion Church; returning to England and becoming pastor of the church at Brixton, then returning to Canada for his health in 1890. He died Feb. 1, 1891. In addition to his work as pastor in Montreal, he was principal of the Congregational College of Canada from 1882 to 1886. See (Lond.) *Cong. Year-book*, 1892.

Stolz, ALBAN, a Roman Catholic priest, was born at Bühl, Baden, Feb. 8, 1808; ordained in 1833; professor of pastoral theology and pedagogic at Freiburg, 1848–80; and died Oct. 16, 1883. He was a very prolific writer, his collected works making 13 volumes.

T.

Tarbox, INCREASE NILES, D.D., a Congregational minister, was born at East Windsor, Conn., Feb. 11, 1815. He graduated from Yale College in 1839, and from the Theological Seminary in 1844; was a teacher at East Hartford in 1839–41, and tutor at Yale College in 1842–44; pastor at Framingham, Mass., in 1844–51; from 1851 till 1874 secretary of the American Education Society, and from 1874 to 1884 secretary of the American College and Education Society; thereafter without charge until his death, May 3, 1888. Dr. Tarbox was a member of the New England Historical and Genealogical Society, and its historiographer from 1881; one of the editors of the *Congregationalist*, 1849–51, and of the *Congregational Quarterly*, 1875–78. He published, *Nineveh, a Buried City* (1864):—*Tyre and Alexandria* (1866):—*Missionary Patriots: Memoirs of James H. and Edward M. Schneider* (1867):—*Uncle George's Stories* (1868, 4 vols.):—*Winnie and Walter Stories* (1869, 4 vols.):—*Life of Israel Putnam* (1876):—*Songs and Hymns for Common Life* (1885):—*Diary of Thomas Robbins, D.D.*, with annotations (2 vols).

He also edited, with a *Memoir*, Sir Walter Raleigh's *Colony in America* (1884).

Taylor, Marshall William, D.D., a Methodist Episcopal minister, was born at Lexington, Ky., July 1, 1847. In 1872 he entered the Lexington Conference. He was a delegate to the General Conference of 1884, which elected him editor of the *South-western Christian Advocate*, and held that position until his death, Sept. 11, 1887. See *Minutes of Annual Conferences* (Spring), 1888, p. 93.

Thiersch, Heinrich Wilhelm Josias, D.D., an Irvingite minister, was born in Munich, Bavaria, Nov. 5, 1817, studied philology at Munich, and theology at Erlangen and Tübingen; became *privat-docent* at Erlangen in 1839; professor of theology at Marburg in 1843; resigned in 1850 in order to labor in the interest of the Catholic Apostolic Church; had charge of a small congregation at Augsburg, and subsequently at Basel, and died at the latter place, Dec. 3, 1885. He is the author of many works, among which are *Commentaries on Genesis* (translated), and on *Daniel*.

Thomas, John, D.D., a Welsh Congregational minister, was born at Holyhead, Feb. 3, 1821. After being educated at Martin School and Frevdyval Seminary he entered the ministry, serving several churches, the Tabernacle at Liverpool enjoying his ministry from 1854 until his death, July 14, 1892. In 1865 he visited the Welsh churches of the United States, and again in 1876. He was chairman of the Welsh Congregational Union in 1878, and of the Congregational Union of England and Wales in 1885. He was widely known as a lecturer, and was a frequent contributor to the Welsh magazines, and was always in demand as a preacher at county associations and the like. See (Lond.) *Cong. Year-book*, 1893.

Thompson, William, D.D., a Congregational minister, was born at Goshen, Conn., Feb. 18, 1806; graduated from Union College in 1827, and from Andover Theological Seminary in 1832; was pastor for one year, at the end of which he became Nettleton professor of the Hebrew language and literature in East Windsor (now Hartford) Theological Seminary, 1834–81; and thereafter emeritus professor and dean of the faculty until his death, Feb. 27, 1889. Dr. Thompson was also chaplain of the Retreat for the Insane seventeen years.

Thomson, William, D.D., a prelate of the Church of England, was born at Whitehaven, Feb. 11, 1819. He graduated from Queen's College, Oxford, in 1840, and became successively fellow, tutor, dean, bursar, and provost of Queen's College. In 1842 he was rector of St. Nicholas, Guilford. In 1848 and again in 1856 he was select preacher of the University; and in 1853 he was Bampton lecturer. He was rector of All-Saints, Marylebone, in 1855, and from 1858 to 1861 was preacher at Lincoln's Inn. In 1860 he became chaplain to the queen, and the following year bishop of the sees of Gloucester and Bristol, and in 1863 archbishop of York and primate of England. He died Dec. 25, 1890. He wrote, *An Outline of Necessary Laws of Thought* (1848):—*Sermons Preached at Lincoln's Inn Chapel* (1861):—*Life in the Light of God's Word* (1868):—*The Limits of Philosophical Inquiry* (1868):—*Word, Work, and Will* (1879).

Tiffany, Otis Henry, D.D., a prominent Methodist Episcopal minister, was born in Baltimore, Md., July 3, 1825. After graduating from Dickinson College in 1844, he entered the Baltimore Conference; and with the exception of ten years spent at Dickinson as assistant professor of Greek and mathematics, he was in the pastoral work to the end of his life, serving successively some of the most prominent churches in his denomination. He died in Minneapolis, Oct. 24, 1891. See *Minutes of the Annual Conferences* (Fall), 1892.

Torsey, Henry P., LL.D., a Methodist Episcopal educator, was born at Monmouth, Me., Aug. 7, 1819. His education was acquired at Monmouth and in the Maine Wesleyan Seminary. In 1841 he taught at East Greenwich, R. I.; two years later at Kent's Hill, and in 1844 was elected principal of Maine Wesleyan Seminary, which position he held for thirty-eight years. One year after the war he was United States Treasury agent in the South, and was offered the governorship of one of the territories by President Lincoln. He was a member of the Maine Conference and of three General Conferences of his Church. He died Sept. 16, 1892. See *Minutes of the Annual Conferences* (Spring), 1893.

Trechsel, Friedrich, D.D., a German scholar, was born at Berne, Switzerland, Nov. 30, 1805; studied at Berne, Paris, Göttingen, Halle, and Berlin; in 1829 became chaplain of the city hospital at Berne and *privat-docent* in the academy; pastor at Vechigen in 1837; of the minster at Berne in 1859; retired on a pension in 1876; and died Jan. 30, 1885. He was the author of several works, and of several articles in Herzog's *Real-Encyklopädie*.

Trestrail, Frederick, D.D., an English Baptist minister, was born July 1, 1803, at Falmouth, Cornwall. He studied at the Academy at Stoke's Croft, Bristol. He became pastor, serving various places until 1844, when he became secretary of the Irish Mission, and in 1849 one of the secretaries of the Baptist Missionary Society, acting in that capacity for twenty-one years. He was again in the pastorate for the next twelve years. In 1880 he became president of the Baptist Union of Great Britain and Ireland. He died Nov. 4, 1890. See (English) *Baptist Hand-book*, 1891, p. 160 A–D.

Trimble, Joseph McDowell, D.D., a Methodist Episcopal minister, was born in the year 1807. After graduating at the University of Ohio in 1829, he joined the Ohio Conference. From 1836 to 1840 he was professor of mathematics in Augusta College. For thirty-one years he was secretary of his conference, and represented it in thirteen General Conferences. For thirty-nine years he was a trustee, and for twenty years agent of Ohio Wesleyan University. For thirty-two years he was a member of the General Missionary Committee, and for four years one of the missionary secretaries. He died May 6, 1891. See *Cyclop. of Methodism; Christianity in Earnest*, May–June, 1891.

Trowbridge, Tillman Conklin, LL.D., a missionary, was born in Troy County, Mich., Jan. 28, 1831. He graduated from the University of Michigan in 1852, and Union Theological Seminary in 1855. Taking appointment under the American Board, he reached Constantinople early in 1856. The first year of service was in Constantinople; from there he was sent through Northern Armenia, returning in 1861. The six years following he had charge of the city mission work in Constantinople. In 1868 he removed to Marash to take part in the theological instruction there. In 1872 he was appointed to raise funds for the college then decided upon at Aintab. In 1876 he returned and was appointed president of the college, which position he held until his death, July 20, 1888.

Trumbull, David, D.D., a Congregational minister, was born at Elizabeth, N. J., Nov. 1, 1819; graduated from Yale College in 1842, and from Princeton Theological Seminary in 1845; was ordained and went to Valparaiso, Chili; first as missionary of the Foreign Evangelical Society, and then of the American Seaman's Friend Society; next became pastor of the Independent Church there until his death, Feb. 1, 1889.

Tuigg, John, a Roman Catholic bishop, was born in Cork, Ireland, Feb. 19, 1820. He was educated at All-Hallows College and St. Michael's Seminary, Pittsburgh; ordained in 1850, and appointed to St. Bridget's Church, Pittsburgh, but in 1853 became pastor of Altoona. His success here led to his appointment as bishop of Pittsburgh. He was consecrated March 19, 1876, and was soon after charged with the administration of the diocese of Allegheny. He was stricken with paralysis in 1863, and subsequently lived in retirement at Altoona, where he died, Dec. 6, 1889.

Tulloch, JOHN, D.D., LL.D., a minister of the Church of Scotland, was born in Perthshire, June 1, 1823. He was educated at St. Andrews and Edinburgh; became parish minister of Dundee in 1845; of Kettins, in Forfarshire, in 1849; and on the death of principal Haldane, in 1854, became principal of St. Mary's College, University of St. Andrews. In 1855 he received the Burnett prize of £600 for an essay on *The Being and Attributes of God*, which was published under the title *Theism*. In 1856 he was appointed one of the examiners of the Dick bequest. In 1858 he formally opened the Scotch Presbyterian Church in Paris; in 1859 he was appointed one of her majesty's chaplains for Scotland; in 1862 became deputy clerk of the General Assembly, and in 1875 clerk; in 1878 was elected moderator. He died Feb. 13, 1885. Besides the prize essay, Dr. Tulloch was author of *Leaders of the Reformation* (1859):—*English Puritanism and its Leaders* (1861):—*Beginning Life* (1862):—*The Christ of the Gospels and the Christ of Modern Criticism* (1864):—*Rational Theology and Christian Philosophy* (1872, 2 vols.):—*Facts of Religion and Life* (1876):—*Pascal* (1876):—*The Christian Doctrine of Sin* (1877):—*Modern Theories in Philosophy and Religion* (1884):—*Movements of Religious Thought in Britain during the Nineteenth Century* (1885).

Tyerman, LUKE, an English Wesleyan minister, was born at Osmotherly, Feb. 6, 1820; in 1842 entered the ministry, continuing to preach until 1864, when he became supernumerary, and devoted his attention to literary work. He died March 20, 1889. He was author of *The Life and Times of the Rev. Samuel Wesley*:—*The Life and Times of the Rev. John Wesley* (3 vols.):—*The Oxford Methodists*:—*Wesley's Designated Successor*:—*The Life of the Rev. John Fletcher*:—*The Life of the Rev. Geo. Whitefield.*

Tyng, STEPHEN HIGGINSON, D.D., an eminent Protestant Episcopal minister, was born at Newburyport, Mass., March 1, 1800; graduated from Harvard College in 1817, and for two years was engaged in a mercantile life; in 1819-21 he studied theology at Bristol, R. I.; was rector at Georgetown, D. C., 1821-23; at Queen Anne Parish, Md., 1823-29; at St. Paul's Church, Phila., 1829-33; Church of the Epiphany, 1833-45; St. George's Church, N. Y., 1845-78; in 1878 he was retired as pastor emeritus, and died Sept. 4, 1885. For several years he was editor of the *Episcopal Recorder* and the *Protestant Churchman*. He is the author of numerous volumes.

U.

Upham, FREDERIC, D.D., a Methodist Episcopal minister, was born at North Malden, Mass., Oct. 4, 1799. Joining the New England Conference in 1821, he served as pastor until 1883, when the infirmities of age compelled him to desist. He was a member of the General Conferences of 1832, 1840, 1844, and 1872, and a member of the General Missionary Committee in 1860-64. He died March 20, 1891.

V.

Van Dyke, HENRY JACKSON, D.D., a Presbyterian minister, was born in Abington, Pa., March 2, 1822. He graduated from the University of Pennsylvania in 1843, and from Princeton Theological Seminary in 1845. Though always a pastor, he was chosen four times as a theological professor by the seminaries at Columbia, S. C., Allegheny, Pa., Oakland, Cal., and New York city. He died May 25, 1891. He was moderator of the General Assembly of 1876.

Vermilye, THOMAS EDWARD, D.D., LL.D., a prominent Presbyterian minister, was born in New York city, Feb. 27, 1803. Entering Yale in 1818, and pursuing his course with distinction, he was not given a diploma with his class in 1822 for having married during his senior year, but this was awarded in 1867. After studying theology at Princeton, he was ordained and became pastor of the Vandewater Street Presbyterian Church, N. Y., in 1826; in 1830 pastor of the Congregational Church of West Springfield, Mass.; 1835 to 1839 of the North Dutch Reformed Church of Albany; this charge he left to assume one of the pastorates of the Collegiate Dutch Reformed Church in New York, celebrating in 1889 the fiftieth anniversary of his pastorate. He died March 17, 1893. See *Necrological Report of Princeton Theol. Sem.*, 1893.

W.

Walker, JAMES BARR, a Congregational minister, was born in Philadelphia, Pa., July 29, 1805; studied at the Western Reserve College, and in its theological department; was editor and evangelist, 1839-42; pastor, 1842-72, but president of Grand Traverse College part of that time; professor of intellectual and moral philosophy in Wheaton College, 1871-76; and resident at Wheaton, Ill., until his death, March 6, 1887. He published, *The Philosophy of the Plan of Salvation* (1855; revised ed. 1868):—*God Revealed in Creation and in Christ* (1855):—*Living Questions of the Age* (1869):—*Doctrine of the Holy Spirit* (1869):—*The Immortality and Worth of the Soul* (1871)—*Pioneer Life in the West: an Autobiography* (1881).

Webster, ALONZO, D.D., a Methodist Episcopal minister, was born at Weston, Vt., Jan. 27, 1818. In 1837 he joined the Vermont Conference. He was presiding elder four years, and for four years agent of the American Bible Society. During the war he was chaplain. In 1865 he was sent to South Carolina to extend the work among the colored people. He was the founder and first president of Claflin University, and served seventeen years in this field as presiding elder, and was such at the time of his death, Aug. 1. 1887. He was a member of six General Conferences, editor and proprietor of the *Charleston Advocate*, the *Southeastern Advocate*, and the *Methodist Messenger* successively. See *Minutes of Annual Conferences* (Spring), 1888, p. 99.

Welch, RANSOM BETHUNE, D.D., LL.D., a Presbyterian educator, was born at Greenville about 1825. He graduated from Union College in 1846, and from Auburn Theological Seminary in 1852. In 1854-59 he was in the pastorate. In 1866-76 he was professor of rhetoric, logic, and English literature in Union College, and since 1876 professor of theology in Auburn Theological Seminary. He died June 29, 1890. He was the author of *Faith and Modern Thought* (1876):—and *Outlines of Christian Theology* (1881). See *Appletons' Cyclop. of Amer. Biography.*

Wentworth, JOHN BROADHEAD, D.D., a Methodist Episcopal minister, was born at Bristol, N. H., Aug. 29, 1823. After graduating from the University of Vermont in 1848, he joined the Genesee Conference in 1851, serving two years as principal of Coudersport Academy, three times as presiding elder, and six times as a member of the General Conference of his Church. He died Aug. 6, 1893. He was author of *The Logic of Introspection*. See *Minutes of the Annual Conferences* (Fall), 1893.

Whedon, DANIEL DENISON, D.D., LL.D., a Methodist Episcopal minister, was born at Onondaga, N. Y., March 20, 1808. He graduated from Hamilton College in 1828, and then studied law; taught at Cazenovia, N. Y., 1830-31; was tutor at Hamilton, 1831-32; and 1833-43 professor of ancient languages and literature in Wesleyan University. In 1836 he was ordained, and became pastor in Pittsfield, Mass., in 1843–45; in 1845–52 he was professor of logic, rhetoric, and history in the University of Michigan, where he served as president of the faculty in 1847–48; in 1855 was pastor at Jamaica, L. I.; in 1856–84 editor of the *Methodist Quarterly Review*, and general editor of the publications of the Book Concern. He died June 8, 1885. Besides many articles contributed to various periodicals, Dr. Whedon published, *Public Addresses, Collegiate and Popular* (1856):—*Commentary on Matthew and Mark* (1860):—*Freedom of the Will* (1864):—*Commentary on the New Testament* (5 vols.):—*On the Old Testament* (7 vols.). Two volumes of his collected papers appeared in 1886.

Wheeler, Alfred, D.D., a Methodist Episcopal minister, was born in Huron Co., O., Sept. 14, 1824. He was educated in the Ohio Wesleyan University, and in 1852 graduated from the Jefferson Medical College; but soon after joined the North Ohio Conference. In 1862 he entered the army as chaplain, part of the time serving as surgeon. From 1876 to 1884 he was editor of the *Pittsburg Christian Advocate*. He served his church as presiding elder of three districts, was a member of six General Conferences, of the Œcumenical Conference at London in 1884, and of the Centenary Conference at Baltimore in 1884. He died July 7, 1892. See *Minutes of the Annual Conferences* (Fall), 1892.

Williams, John Aetheruld, D.D., a Canadian Methodist minister, was born at Carmarthen, Wales, Dec. 19, 1817. In 1833 he removed to Canada, and in 1850 entered the ministry of the Methodist Church. In 1874 he was elected president of the London Conference, and fraternal delegate to the Methodist Episcopal Church in 1876. In 1883 he was president of the United General Conference for the Union of the Methodist Churches in Canada. In 1884 he was the representative of the Methodist Church of Canada at the Centennial Conference in Baltimore. In the following year he was appointed general superintendent of his church. He died Dec. 17, 1890. See Simpson's *Cyclopædia of Methodism*, p. 950.

Williams, Samuel Wells, LL.D., a missionary, was born in Utica, N. Y., Sept. 22, 1812. While attending the Rensselaer Polytechnic Institute at Troy, he accepted a proposal to go to China and take charge of a printing-office recently established there by the American Board of Missions. He arrived at Canton, Oct. 25, 1833, and joined with E. C. Bridgman as editor of the *Chinese Repository*, which he both printed and edited until it ceased in 1851. He contributed about one hundred and thirty articles to this magazine. In 1835 he removed his office to Macao, in order to complete the printing of Dr. Medhurst's *Hokkeën Dictionary*. During the winter of 1837–38 he began to print the *Chinese Chrestomathy*, to which he contributed one half, and he also devoted his attention to learning Japanese. In 1844 he returned to the United States, but went to China again in the same year. In 1853–54 he accompanied Commodore M. C. Perry in two expeditions to Japan, and gave material aid in concluding the treaty. In 1855 he was appointed secretary and interpreter to the United States legation in China. He resigned his connection with the American Board in 1857. In 1862 he went to Pekin and resided there for several years, completing here, besides his official duties, *A Syllabic Dictionary of the Chinese Language*. In order to superintend the printing personally, he spent the year 1873 at Shanghai, where it was stereotyped and published. His health being broken, he returned to the United States in 1875, but went back to China in 1876 to close up his affairs there. During his service he had acted as chargé-d'affaires nine times, which amounted to about five years of service as acting minister. In 1877 he was appointed professor of Chinese in Yale College. In 1881 he was elected president of the American Bible Society, and in the same year president of the American Oriental Society. He died Feb. 16, 1884. Outside of his philological work, he published the *Middle Kingdom* (2 vols. 1883). See his *Life and Letters*, by his son (N. Y. 1888).

Wood, Aaron, D.D., a Methodist Episcopal minister, was born in Pendleton, Va., Oct. 15, 1802. He joined the Ohio Conference in 1827. He was fourteen years presiding elder, twelve years agent for benevolent institutions and societies, and chaplain six years. He died Aug. 20, 1887. He was a member of the General Conferences of 1840, 1844, 1864, 1868, 1876, and reserve delegate five times. See *Minutes of Annual Conferences* (Fall), 1887, p. 356.

Wood, Francis Asbury, D.D., a minister of the Methodist Episcopal Church, South, was born in Charleston, S. C., June 23, 1830. He graduated from Charleston College in 1850, and was admitted into the South Carolina Conference in the same year. During the war he was commissioned as chaplain, and served in the Charleston hospitals. In 1869 he became president of Soulé University, and in 1873 of the Southwestern University, Georgetown, Tex., remaining there until his death, Nov. 11, 1884. See *Minutes of Annual Conferences of the M. E. Church, South*, 1885, p. 63.

Woolsey, Theodore Dwight, D.D., LL.D., an eminent educator, was born in New York city, Oct. 31, 1801; graduated from Yale College in 1820, and attended Princeton Theological Seminary in 1821–23; was tutor at Yale College, 1823–25; student in Europe, 1827–30; was professor of Greek language and literature in Yale College, 1831–51; president in 1846–71; and thereafter resided at New Haven until his death, July 1, 1889. Dr. Woolsey was a fellow of the American Academy, and a corporate member of the A. B. C. F. M., 1859–68. He published, among other works, an *Introduction to the Study of International Law*, which has so far had five editions:—*Political Science* (2 vols.):—and *Communism and Socialism*.

Wordsworth, Christopher, D.D., a prelate of the Church of England, was born at Bocking, Oct. 30, 1807. He was a nephew of the poet and son of the master of Trinity College, Cambridge. He graduated there in 1830, and was elected fellow of his college; in 1836 was appointed public orator at Cambridge and head master of the Harrow School, which post he held until 1844, when he became a canon of Westminster Abbey. He was Hulsean lecturer at Cambridge in 1847–48, and in 1869 was appointed bishop of Lincoln. He took part in the "Old Catholic" Congress at Cologne in 1872. He died March 21, 1885. Bishop Wordsworth is the author of many works, numbering over forty volumes, the chief of which is his *Commentary on the Bible* (10 vols.).

Wray, James Jackson, an English Congregational minister, was born at Sancton, Yorkshire, Aug. 12, 1832. After receiving an education in Westminster Normal College he took charge first of the school at Madeley Wood, and later at Oldham. In 1858 he was received into the Wesleyan Methodist Conference, and sent to Freetown, Sierra Leone. At the end of a year he returned and served several churches, but soon left the Wesleyans and became pastor of the church in Tottenham Court Road, and later in Market Weighton. He died Oct. 26, 1892. He was editor of *Good Company*, and a contributor to other magazines, besides being the author of several books. He was also widely known as a lecturer. See (Lond.) *Cong. Year-book*, 1893.

Wylie, William Howie, an English Baptist minister and journalist, was born at Kilmarnock, Scotland, in 1833. He early became connected with journalistic work, serving on the *Kilmarnock Journal*, the *Ayr Advertiser*, the *North British Mail*, *Pall-Mall Gazette*, and many others. In 1855 he was a student in Edinburgh University, and in 1857 in Regents Park College. He served Ramsey Hunts, Blackburn Road, Acrington, and Blackpool as pastor. His health giving way, he returned to journalism in 1876. In 1882 he became editor and later sole proprietor of the *Christian Leader*. He was the author of *Thomas Carlyle: The Man and His Books*. He died Aug. 5, 1891. See (Lond.) *Baptist Hand-book*, 1892.

Y.

Young, WILLIAM, D.D., a Methodist Episcopal minister, was born at Staunton, Va., June 20, 1807. He entered the Ohio Conference in 1830, and served as a pastor, with the exception of a few years spent as agent for Ohio Wesleyan University, Cincinnati Female College, the American Tract Society, and the Preachers' Relief Society. He died Aug. 25, 1887. He was a member of the General Conferences of 1856, 1860, 1864, and 1868. See *Minutes of Annual Conferences* (Fall), 1887, p. 365.

Z.

Zabriskie, FRANCIS NICHOLLS, D.D., a minister of the Reformed (Dutch) Church, was born at Hackensack, N. J., in April, 1832. He graduated from the University of the City of New York in 1850, and from the New Brunswick Seminary in 1855. For three years he was editor of the *Intelligencer*. He died May 13, 1891. He wrote a *Life of Horace Greeley*, and several other volumes. See Corwin, *Manual of the Reformed* (Dutch) *Church in America*, 3d ed. p. 568.

Zilliox, JACOB, D.D., a Roman Catholic monk, was born Oct. 14, 1849, in Newark, N. J. He was educated at St. Mary's Academy and St. Vincent's College, in Pennsylvania, then went to the American College at Rome, and from there to the Jesuit University at Innspruck. He returned to America in 1875, and became professor of theology in St. Vincent's College, and in 1880 prefect. In 1885 he was elected abbot of the Order of St. Benedict, with headquarters at Newark. He died Dec. 31, 1890.

Zunz, LEOPOLD PHEINKARD, a Hebrew scholar, was born at Detmold, Germany, Aug. 10, 1794. He was educated at the University of Berlin, and became rabbi of a synagogue there in 1820. After two years he organized a society for Jewish culture. One of its members was Heine. The society, however, soon broke up. In 1824–32 Zunz was director of the new Jewish Congregational School; in 1825–35 he edited the *Spener'sche Zeitung;* in 1835–39 was rabbi again at Prague; in 1839–50 director of the Normal Seminary in Berlin. He died March 21, 1886. His life was one of literary activity, and his works were many.